CAR SECTION CONTENTS

Section	Manufacturer	Models	Page
13	GENERAL MOTORS Rear Wheel Drive Buick	Regal, Regal Limited, Regal Sport Coupe, Le Sabre, Le Sabre Custom, Le Sabre Limited, Electra, Estate Wagon	13-2
14	GENERAL MOTORS Rear WHeel Drive Cadillac	DeVille, Fleetwood	14-2
15	GENERAL MOTORS Rear Wheel Drive Chevrolet	Caprice Classic, Corvette, Malibu, Monte Carlo, Impala	15-2
16	GENERAL MOTORS Rear Wheel Drive F Body	Chevrolet — Camaro, Camaro Berlinetta Pontiac — Firebird, Firebird Trans AM, SE	16-2
17	GENERAL MOTORS Rear Wheel Drive P Body	Pontiac — Fiero, Fireo SE	17-2
18	GENERAL MOTORS Rear Wheel Drive T Body	Chevrolet — Chevette, Chevette Scooter Pontiac — T1000, 1000	18-2
19	GENERAL MOTORS Oldsmobile	Cutlass Supreme, Cutlass Salon, Cutlass Supreme Brougham, Cutlass Calais, Delta 88 Royale, Delta 88 Royale Brougham, Custom Cruiser, Olds 98, Olds 98 regency, Olds 98 Regency Brougham, Hurst Olds	19-2
20	GENERAL MOTORS Rear Wheel Drive Pontiac	Bonneville, Bonneville LE, Bonneville Brougham, Grand Prix, Grand Prix LE, Grand Prix Brougham Safari SW, Parisienne, Parisienne Brougham, Parisienne Brougham Wagon	20-2

UNIT REPAIR SECTIONS CONTENTS

Section	Unit	Page
21	Alternators/Regulators	21-2
22	Air Conditioning (Minor Service)	22-2
23	Automatic Transmissions Trouble Diagnosis On Car Services	 23-2 23-2
24	Brakes Anti-Lock System Disc Brake Service Drum Brake Service	 24-2 24-2 24-2
25	Carburetors Adjustments & Specifications	 25-2
26	Clutch Service	26-2
27	Diesel Engines Minor Services	 27-2
28	Drive Axles Specifications Overhaul Procedures	 28-2 28-2

Section	Unit	Page
29	Electronic Engine Controls	29-2
30	Electronic Ignition Systems	30-2
31	Fuel Injection	31-2
32	Manual Transmissions/Transaxles Overhaul Procedures	 32-2
33	Starters/Switches/Solenoids	33-2
34	Steering Gears Manual Power	 34-2 34-2
35	Suspensions Front & Rear	 35-2
36	Transfer Cases AMC Overhaul Procedures	 36-1
	Mechanics' Data	36-6

MODEL IDENTIFICATION

Car Sections

Car Name	Section No.	Car Name	Section No.	Car Name	Section No.	Car Name	Section No.
Aries	2-2	DeVille (FWD)	7-2	Impala	15-2	Phoenix (FWD)	6-2
		Diplomat	3-2	Imperial	3-2	Pontiac T1000	18-2
Berlinetta	16-2	Dodge 400	2-2	J2000	10-2	Pontiac J2000	10-2
Bonneville	20-2	Dodge 600	2-2	Lancer	2-2	Pontiac 6000	6-2
Calais	11-2	E-Class	2-2	Laser	2-2	Regal	13-2
Camaro	16-2	Eagle	1-4	LeBaron (RWD)	3-2	Regency (RWD)	19-2
Capri	5-2	Eagle SX-4	1-4	LeBaron (FWD)	2-2	Reliant	2-2
Caprice	15-2	Eldorado	8-2	LeBaron GTS	2-2	Riviera (FWD)	8-2
Caravelle	3-2	Electra (RWD)	13-2	LeSabre (RWD)	13-2		
Cavalier	10-2	Electra (FWD)	7-2	LeSabre (FWD)	9-2	Sable	4-2
Celebrity	6-2	Escort	4-2	Lincoln	5-2	Seville (FWD)	8-2
Century (FWD)	6-2	Executive Sedan	2-2	LN7	4-2	Shadow	2-2
Charger	2-2	Estate Wagon	13-2	LTD	5-2	Shelby Charger	2-2
Chevette	18-2	EXP	4-2	LTD Crown Victoria	5-2	Skyhawk (RWD)	10-2
Chevette Scooter	18-2			Lynx	4-2	Skyhawk (FWD)	10-2
Chrysler E-Class	2-2	Fairmont	5-2			Skylark (FWD)	11-2
Ciera	6-2	Fiero	17-2	Malibu Classic	15-2	Somerset Regal	11-2
Cimarron	10-2	Firebird	16-2	Mark VI, VII	5-2	Spirit	1-4
Citation	6-2	Firenza	10-2	Marquis	5-2	St. Regis	3-2
Cobra (Mustang)	5-2	Fifth Avenue (RWD)	3-2	Mirada	3-2	Sunbird	10-2
Colony Park	5-2	Fleetwood (RWD)	14-2	Monte Carlo	15-2	Sundance	2-2
Concord	1-4	Fleetwood (FWD)	7-2	Mustang	5-2		
Continental	5-2	Futura	5-2	Mustang Ghia	5-2	Taurus	4-2
Cordoba	3-2					TC3	2-2
Corvette	15-2	GTS	2-2	Newport	3-2	Tempo	4-2
Cougar	5-2	Grande (98)	9-2	New Yorker (RWD)	3-2	Thunderbird	5-2
Country Squire	5-2	Gran Fury	3-2	New Yorker (FWD)	2-2	Topaz	4-2
Crown Victoria	5-2	Gran Fury Salon	3-2	Ninety-Eight	19-2	Toronado	8-2
Custom Cruiser	19-2	Gran Marquis	5-2	Nova (FWD)	12-2	Town & Country	3-2
Cutlass (RWD)	19-2	Grand Am	11-2			Town Car	5-2
Cutlass	19-2	Grand Prix	20-2	Omega (FWD)	6-2	T Type (Buick)	6-2
		Grand Safari	20-2	Omni	2-2	T1000	18-2
Daytona	2-2			Omni Miser	2-2	Turismo	2-2
Delta 88 (RWD)	19-2	Horizon	2-2	024	2-2		
Delta 88 (FWD)	9-2	Horizon Miser	2-2			XR-7	5-2
DeVille (RWD)	14-2	Hurst Olds	19-2	Parisienne	20-2	Zephyr	5-2
				Park Avenue (FWD)	7-2		

CHILTON'S 1987 AUTOMOTIVE SERVICE MANUAL

Managing Editor John H. Weise, S.A.E. ☐ **Assistant Managing Editor** David H. Lee, A.S.E., S.A.E.

Service Editors Lawrence C. Braun, S.A.E., A.S.C., Dennis Carroll, Nick D'Andrea, Jack T. Kaufmann, Robert McAnally, Ron Webb
Editorial Consultants Edward K. Shea, S.A.E., Stan Stephenson

Production Manager John J. Cantwell
Manager Editing & Design Dean F. Morgantini
Art & Production Coordinator Robin S. Miller
Supervisor Mechanical Paste-up Margaret A. Stoner
Mechanical Artists Cynthia Fiore, William Gaskins

National Sales Manager Albert M. Kushnerick ☐ **Assistant** Jacquelyn T. Powers
Regional Sales Managers Joseph Andrews, David Flaherty, James O. Callahan

OFFICERS
President Lawrence A. Fornasieri
Vice President & General Manager John P. Kushnerick

CHILTON BOOK COMPANY Chilton Way, Radnor, Pa. 19089
Manufactured in USA ©1986 Chilton Book Company ISBN 0-8019-7690-1
ISSN 0736-1793 Library of Congress Catalog Card No. 82-72944
1234567890 5432109876

SAFETY NOTICE

Proper service and repair procedures are vital to the safe, reliable operation of all motor vehicles, as well as the personal safety of those performing repairs. This manual outlines procedures for servicing and repairing vehicles using safe, effective methods. The procedures contain many NOTES, CAUTIONS and WARNINGS which should be followed along with standard safety procedures to eliminate the possibilty of personal injury or improper service which could damage the vehicle or compromise its safety.

It is important to note that the repair procedures and techniques, tools and parts for servicng motor vehicles, as well as the skill and experience of the individual performing the work vary widely. It is not possible to anticipate all of the conceivable ways or conditions under which vehicles may be serviced, or to provide cautions as to all of the possible hazards that may result. Standard and accepted safety precautions and equipment should be used when handling toxic or flammable fluids, and safety goggles or other protection should be used during cutting, grinding, chiseling, prying, or any other process that can cause material removal or projectiles.

Some procedures require the use of tools specially designed for a specific purpose. Before substituting another tool or procedure, you must be completely satisfied that neither your personal safety, nor the performance of the vehicle will be endangered

PART NUMBERS

Part numbers listed in this reference are not recomendations by Chilton for any product by brand name. They are references that can be used with interchange manuals and aftermarket supplier catalogs to locate each brand supplier's discrete part number.

Although information in this manual is based on industry sources and is complete as possible at the time of publication, the possibilty exists that some car manufacturers made later changes which could not be included here. While striving for total accuracy, Chilton Book Company cannot assume responsibility for any errors, changes or omissions that may occur in the compilation of this data.

No part of this publication may be reproduced, transmitted or stored in any form or by any means, electronic or mechanical, including photocopy, recording, or by information storage or retrieval system withiout prior written permission from the publisher.

QUICK LOCATOR INDEX

American Motors
Section 1

Chrysler Corporation
Sections 2–3

Ford Motor Company
Sections 4–5

General Motors Company
Sections 6–20

Unit Repair
Sections 21–36

American Motors
CONCORD • EAGLE • EAGLE SX4 • SPIRIT

SPECIFICATIONS

Brakes	24-2	Serial Number Identification	1-5
Camshaft	1-7	Torque	1-8
Capacities	1-8	Torque Sequence (Cylinder Heads)	1-38
Crankshaft & Connecting Rod	1-7	Tune-Up	1-6
Firing Order	1-6	Valve	1-7
General Engine	1-6	Wheel Alignment	1-8
Piston & Ring	1-8		

INDEX

A
- Alternator R&R 1-9
- Automatic Transmission 1-66
  - Adjustment 1-66
  - On car Service 23-1
  - Assembly R&R 1-66
- Axle Assembly R&R 1-66
- Axle Shaft R&R 1-68
- Axle Half Shaft R&R 1-73

B
- Ball Joints 35-1
- Belt Tension 1-9
- Brake System 1-63
- Brake Booster 1-63
- Brake Caliper Overhaul 24-2
- Brake Caliper R&R 24-4
- Drake Drum, rear 24-2
- Brake Master Cylinder 1-63
- Brake Pad
  - Front 24-2
- Brake Shoe
  - Rear 24-2

C
- Camshaft R&R 1-43
- Carburetor R&R 1-27
- CHassis Electrical 1-9
- Clutch 1-64
  - Adjustment 1-64
  - R&R 1-64
- Component Locations 1-17
- Control Arm R&R 35-2
- Cooling System 1-24
- Cruise Control 1-19
- Cylinder Head 1-37
  - R&R 1-37

D
- Differential 28-2
  - Inspection 28-2
- Dimmer Switch R&R 1-13
- Disc Brakes 24-2
- Distributor R&R 1-10
- Drive Axle 1-69
- Drive Belt Tension 1-9
- Driveshaft R&R 1-69

E
- Electronic Ignition 30-2
- Emission Controls 1-31
- Engine 1-32
  - Identification 1-5
  - R&R 1-32
- Engine Electrical 1-10
- Engine Lubrication 1-47
- Engine Mechanical 1-32
- Engine Mounts R&R 1-35
- Exhasut Manifold R&R 1-30

F
- Front Suspension 35-2
  - Alignment 1-8
- Fuel Pump R&R 1-27
- Fuel Mixture Adjust m
- Fuses 1-18
- Fusible Links 1-18

H
- Headlight Switch 1-13
- Heater Blower R&R 1-24
- Heater Core R&R 1-26
- Heater Unit R&R 1-26
- Horn Switch 1-13

I
- Idle Speed Adjust 1-27
- Ignition Switch 1-12
- Ignition Timing 1-10
- Insturment Cluster R&R 1-14
- Intake Manifold R&R 1-29

L, M
- Lower Control Arm R&R 35-2
- Master Cylinder R&R 1-63
- Manual Steering Gear 1-53
  - R&R 1-53
- Manual Transmission
  - Overhaul 32-1
- Manual Tranmission R&R 1-65

N, O
- Neutral Safety Switch R&R 1-12
- Oil Pan R&R 1-47
- Oil Pump 1-50
  - R&R 1-50
- Oil Seal R&R
  - Rear Main 1-52

P
- Parking Brake 1-63
  - Adjustment 1-63
- Piston & Connecting Rod 1-47
- Power Brake Unit R&R 1-63
- Power Steering Pump R&R 1-53

R
- Rear Main Oil Seal R&R 1-52
- Rear Suspension 35-2
- Regulator 1-9

- Rocker Assemblies 1-35
- Ride Control, Adjust 1-70

S
- Select Drive (4WD) 1-60
- Serial Number 1-5
  - Engine 1-5
  - Vehicle 1-5
- Shock Absorber R&R
  - Front 35-2
  - Rear 1-66
- Springs
  - Front 35-2
  - Rear 1-71
- Starter R&R 1-10
- Starter Drive Replacement 1-10
- Steering Column R&R 1-55
- Steering Gear R&R 1-53
  - Manual 1-53
  - Power 1-53
- Steering wheel R&R 1-54
- Stoplight Switch R&R 1-12
- Speedometer R&R 1-17
- Suspension R&R 35-2
  - Service 35-2

T
- Throttle Linkage, Adjust 1-66
- Timing Chain 1-42
- Timing Gear Cover 1-41
  - Oil Seal Replacement 1-41
- Transfer Case R&R 1-68
- Tune-Up 1-6
- Turn Signal Switch R&R 1-13

U, V
- U-Joint Overhaul 28-2
- Valve Tappetts R&R 1-36
- Valve Timing, adjust 1-37
- Valve System 1-35
- Voltage Regulator 1-9

W, Y
- Water Pump R&R 1-24
- Wheel Alignment
  - Front 1-8
- Wheel Bearings 1-56
- Wheel Cylinders
  - Rear 24-2
- Windshield Wiper 1-14
  - Linkage R&R 1-14
  - Motor R&R 1-14
  - Switch R&R 1-14
- Year Identification 1-5

BEFORE SERVICING BE CERTAIN TO READ THE SAFETY NOTICE

American Motors 1983–87

CONCORD • EAGLE • EAGLE SX4 • SPIRIT

YEAR IDENTIFICATION

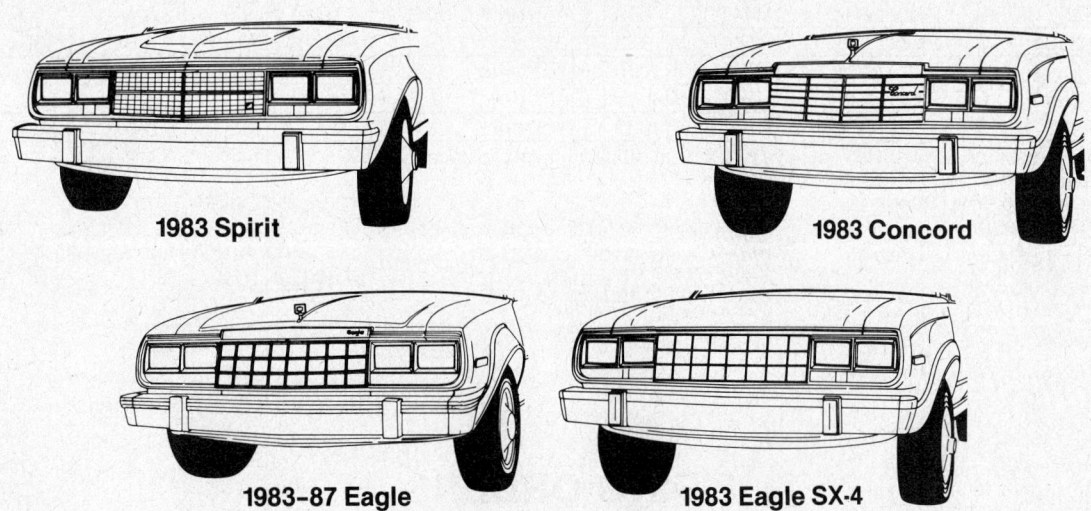

1983 Spirit   1983 Concord

1983–87 Eagle   1983 Eagle SX-4

VEHICLE IDENTIFICATION NUMBER (VIN)

It is important for servicing and ordering parts to be certain of the vehicle and engine identification. The VIN (vehicle identification number) is a 13 or 17 digit number visible through the windshield on the driver's side of the dash and contains the vehicle and engine identification codes. It can be interpreted as follows:

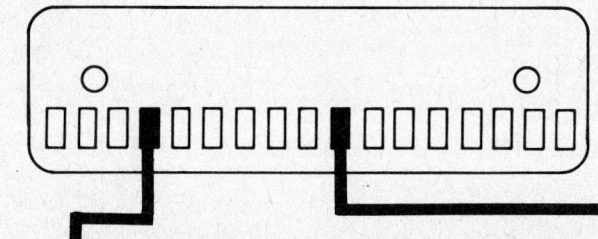

Engine Code					
Code	Cu. In.	Liters	Cyl.	Carb.	Eng. Mfg.
B	151	2.5	4	2V	Pontiac
U	150	2.46	4	2V	AMC
C	258	4.2	6	2V	AMC

Model Year Code	
Code	Year
D	1983
E	1984
F	1985
G	1986
H	1987

The seventeen digit Vehicle Identification Number can be used to determine engine identification and model year. The tenth digit indicates model year, and the fourth digit indicates engine code.

American Motors
CONCORD • EAGLE • EAGLE SX4 • SPIRIT

GENERAL ENGINE SPECIFICATIONS

Year	Eng. VIN Code	Engine No. Cyl. Displacement (cu. in.)	Eng. Mfg.	Carburetor Type	Horsepower @ rpm■	Torque @ rpm (ft lbs)■	Bore × Stroke (in.)	Compression Ratio	Oil Pressure @ 2000 rpm
'83	B	4-151	Pontiac	2 bbl	99 @ 4000	132 @ 2400	4.000 × 3.000	8.3:1	36-41
	C	6-258	AMC	2 bbl	110 @ 3200	210 @ 1800	3.750 × 3.900	8.3:1	46
'84–'87	U	4-150	AMC	1 bbl	83 @ 4200	116 @ 2600	3.876 × 3.188	9.2:1	40
	C	6-258	AMC	2 bbl	110 @ 3200	210 @ 1800	3.750 × 3.900	8.3:1	46

■ Horsepower and torque are SAE net figures. They are measured at the rear of the transmission with all accessories installed and operating. Since the figures vary when a given engine is installed in different models, some are representative rather than exact.

TUNE-UP SPECIFICATIONS

(When analyzing compression test results, look for uniformity among cylinders rather than specific pressures.)

Year	Engine No. Cyl. Displacement (cu. in.)	Eng. VIN Code	HP	Eng. Mfg.	Spark Plugs Orig. Type	Gap (in.)	Distributor Point Dwell (deg.)	Point Gap (in.)	Ignition Timing (deg.)▲ Man. Trans.	Auto. Trans.	Valves Intake Opens ■(deg.)	Fuel Pump Pressure (psi)	Idle Speed (rpm)▲ Man Trans.	Auto Trans.*
'83	4-151	B	2 bbl	Pontiac	R44TSX	.060	Electronic		10B ②	12B ①	25	6½-8	900	700
	6-258	C	2 bbl	AMC	RFN14LY	.033	Electronic		③	④	9	5-6½	680	600
'84	4-150	U	1 bbl	AMC	RFN14LY	.035	Electronic		12B ⑤	12B ⑤	27B	6½-8	750 ⑥	700 ⑥
	6-258	C	2 bbl	AMC	RFN14LY	.033	Electronic		③	④	9	5-6½	680	600
'85–'87	6-258	C	2 bbl	AMC	RFN14LY	.033	Electronic		③	④	9	5-6½	680	600

▲ If underhood emissions decal differs, always use the specifications on the decal.
* With transmission in Drive.
■ All figures before Top Dead Center
B Before Top Dead Center
TDC Top Dead Center (zero degrees)
① 8B—Eagle for Calif.
   Not used
② Eagle except for Calif.—11B
③ Concord, Spirit—6B
   Eagle except Calif.—8B
   Eagle Calif.—4B High Alt.—15B
④ Concord, Spirit—6B
   Eagle except Calif.—8B
   Eagle Calif.—6B High Alt.—15B
⑤ High Alt.—19° ± 1°
⑥ ± 50 RPM

FIRING ORDERS

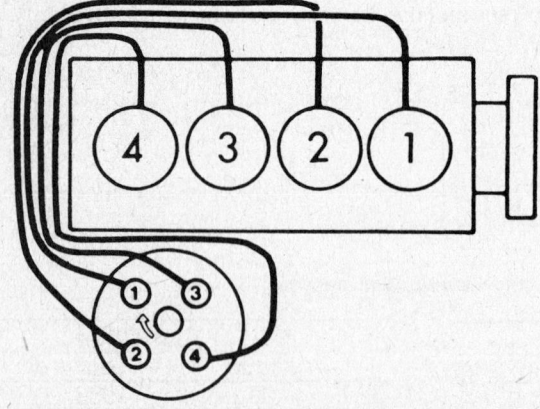

AMC 151 4-cyl
Engine firing order: 1–3–4–2
Distributor rotation: clockwise

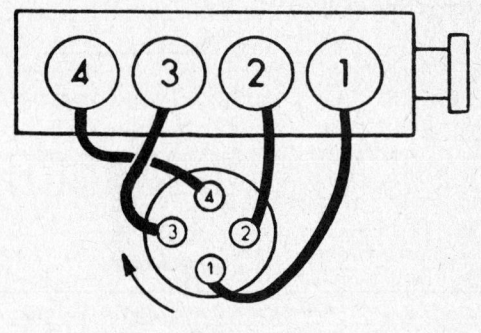

AMC 150 4-cyl
Engine firing order: 1–3–4–2
Distributor rotation: clockwise

AMERICAN MOTORS
CONCORD, EAGLE • EAGLE SX4 • SPIRIT

FIRING ORDER

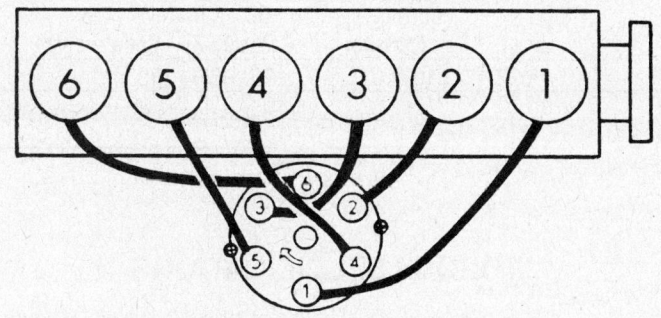

AMC 258 6-cyl
Engine firing order: 1–5–3–6–2–4
Distributor rotation: clockwise

VALVE SPECIFICATIONS

Year	Engine No. Cyl. Displacement (cu. in.)	Seat Angle (deg.) ①	Face Angle (deg.) ②	Outer Spring Test Pressure (lbs. @ in.)	Spring Installed Height (in.)	Stem-to-Guide Clearance (in.) Intake	Stem-to-Guide Clearance (in.) Exhaust	Stem Diameter (in.) Intake	Stem Diameter (in.) Exhaust
'83	4-151	46	45	176 @ 1.254	1.660	0.0010-0.0027	0.0010-0.0027	0.3423	0.3423
	6-258	44.5	44	195 @ 1.411	1.786	0.0010-0.0030	0.0010-0.0030	0.3720	0.3720
'84-'87	4-150	45	44	212 @ 1.203	1.625	0.0010-0.0030	0.0010-0.0030	0.3115	0.3115
	6-258	44.5	44	195 @ 1.411	1.786	0.0010-0.0030	0.0010-0.0030	0.3720	0.3720

① Exhaust valve seat angles are shown. Intake valve seat angles are 30°, except 150 and 151 cu. in. engines, which are 46°.
② Exhaust valve face angles are shown. Intake valve face angles are 29°, except 150 and 151 cu. in. engines, which are 45°.

CAMSHAFT SPECIFICATIONS
(All measurements in inches.)

Engine	Journal Diameter 1	Journal Diameter 2	Journal Diameter 3	Journal Diameter 4	Bearing Clearance	Lobe Lift Intake	Lobe Lift Exhaust	Camshaft End Play
4-151	1.8690	1.8690	1.8690	—	0.0007-0.0027	0.398	0.398	.0015-.0050
6-258	2.0290-2.0300	2.0190-2.0200	2.0090-2.0100	1.9990-2.0000	0.001-0.003	0.253	0.253	0
4-150	2.0290-2.0300	2.0190-2.0200	2.0009-2.0100	1.9990-2.0000	0.001-0.003	0.265	0.265	0

CRANKSHAFT AND CONNECTING ROD SPECIFICATIONS
All measurements are given in inches

Year	Engine	Crankshaft Main Brg. Journal Dia	Crankshaft Main Brg. Oil Clearance	Shaft End-Play	Thrust on No.	Connecting Rod Journal Diameter	Connecting Rod Oil Clearance	Side Clearance
'83	4-151	2.2988	0.0005-0.0022	0.0035-0.0085	5	2.000	0.0005-0.0026	0.017
'84	4-150	2.4996-2.5001	0.0010-0.0025	0.0015-0.0060	2	2.0934-2.0955	0.0010-0.0030	0.010-0.019
'83-'87	6-258	2.4986-2.5001	0.0010-0.0030	0.0015-0.0065	3	2.0934-2.0955	0.0010-0.0030	0.005-0.014

American Motors
CONCORD • EAGLE • EAGLE SX4 • SPIRIT

PISTON AND RING SPECIFICATIONS
All measurements are given in inches

Year	Engine Type/ Disp.	Piston-to-Bore Clearance	Ring Gap			Ring Side Clearance		
			Top Compression	Bottom Compression	Oil Control	Top Compression	Bottom Compression	Oil Control
'83	4-151	0.0025-0.0033	0.010-0.022	0.010-0.028	0.015-0.055	.0030	.0030	.0000
'84	4-150	0.0009-0.0017	0.010-0.020	0.010-0.020	0.010-0.025	0.0017-0.0032	0.0017-0.0032	0.0010-0.0080
'83-'87	6-258	0.0009-0.0017	0.010-0.020	0.010-0.020	0.010-0.025	0.0017-0.0032	0.0017-0.0032	0.0010-0.0080

TORQUE SPECIFICATIONS
(All specifications in ft. lbs.)

Year	Engine	Cylinder Head Bolts	Connecting Rod Bearing Bolts	Main Bearing Bolts	Crank Pulley Bolt	Flywheel Bolts	Manifold	
							Intake	Exhaust
'83	6-258	80-90	30-35	75-85	70-90	95-115	18-28	18-28
'84	4-150	80-90	30-35	75-85	75-85	50-65	20-25	20-25
'83-'87	4-151	80-103	27-33	62-68	157-163	65-71	34-40	36-42

CAPACITIES

Year	Engine No. Cyl. Displacement (cu. in.)	Model	Engine Crankcase Add 1 qt. for New Filter	Transmission (Pts. to Refill After Draining)			Drive Axle (pts.)	Cooling System (qts.)	
				3-Speed	4-Speed	Automatic		With Heater	With A/C
'83	4-151	Spirit, Concord	3.0	—	3.5②	14.2	3	6.5	6.5
	4-151	Eagle	3.0	—	3.5②	14.2	3①	6.5	6.5
'84	4-150	Eagle	4.0	—	7.4	15.8	2.5	10.0	10.0
'83-'87	6-258	Spirit, Concord	4.0	—	3.5②	17.0	3	11	14
	6-258	Eagle	4.0	—	3.5②	17.0	3①	14	14

① 2.5—front axle
② 83 and later:
  T4 Spirit-Concord; 4.0 pts.
  T4 Eagle; 3.5 pts.
  T5 Spirit-Concord; 4.5 pts.
  T5 Eagle; 4.0 pts.
—Not applicable

WHEEL ALIGNMENT SPECIFICATIONS

Year	Model	Caster		Camber		Toe-in (in.)	Steering Axis Inclin. (deg.)	Wheel Pivot Ratio	
		Range (deg.)	Pref. Setting (deg.)	Range (deg.)	Pref. Setting (deg.)			Inner Wheel (deg.)	Outer Wheel (deg.)
'83	Spirit, Concord	3½P-5P	4½P	①	②	1/16 to 3/16	7¾	38	N.A.
'83-'87	Eagle	3P-5P	4P	1/8N-5/8P	3/8P	1/16 to 3/16	11½	38	N.A.

N Negative
P Positive
N.A. Not Available
① Left: ¾P to 1/8P; Right: ½P to 1/8N
② Left: 3/8P; Right: 1/8P

American Motors
CONCORD • EAGLE • EAGLE SX4 • SPIRIT

ELECTRICAL SECTION

Charging System

A Delco 10-SI series, negative grounded charging system is used on all vehicles. The standard alternator used with the four cylinder engines is rated at 42 amperes. The optional heavy duty alternators are rated at 56 amperes. The standard alternator used with the six cylinder engines is rated at 56 amperes. The optional heavy duty alternators are rated at 66 and 78 amperes.

ALTERNATOR

Removal and Installation

FOUR AND SIX CYLINDER ENGINES

1. Disconnect the negative battery cable.
2. Disconnect the terminal wire connector and the output wire from the rear of the alternator.
3. If required, remove the power steering and/or air conditioning compressor drive belts.
4. Remove the mounting and adjustment bolts, washers and nuts from the six cylinder engine models and remove the alternator.
5. Remove the top mounting and adjusting bolts, washers and nuts from the four cylinder engine models.

NOTE: All bolts and screw threads on both engine models are in the metric dimensions.

6. Raise the four cylinder vehicle models and support safely.
7. Remove the lower alternator bracket and lower the alternator through the opening at the underside of the vehicle.
8. The installation of the alternators on both the four and six cylinder engine models is accomplished in the reverse of the removal procedure.

DRIVE BELT TENSIONING

Procedure

The drive belts are tensioned to a specific rating with the use of an appropriate belt tension gauge, placed midway between the pulleys.

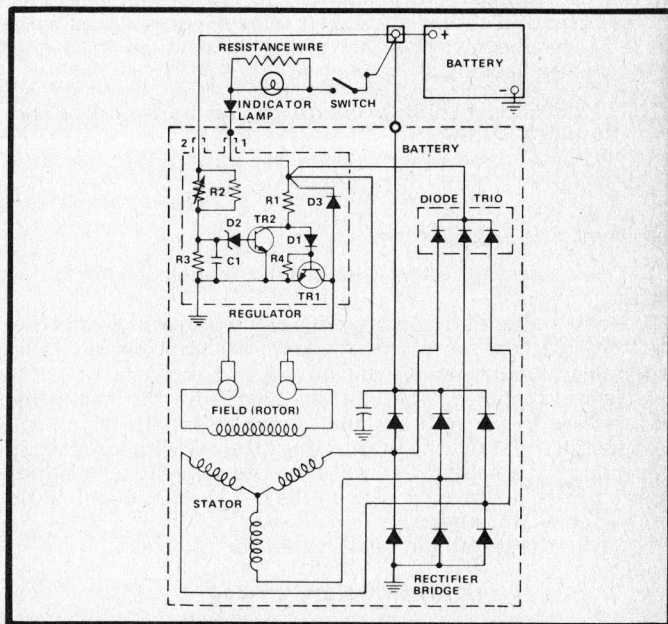

Delco S-10 charging system schematic
(© American Motors Corp.)

VOLTAGE REGULATOR

The voltage regulators are an integral part of the alternator assemblies.

Removal and Installation

INTEGRAL REGULATOR

The alternator must be either partially or completely disassembled to remove or install the regulator assembly.

NOTE: Information on alternator and regulator troubleshooting and repairs can be found in the Unit Repair Section.

DRIVE BELT ADJUSTMENT TENSIONS

	New Belt		Used Belt	
	Ft. Lbs.	Newtons	Ft. Lbs.	Newtons
Serpentine Drive Belt				
Four and Six Cylinder Engines	180-200	800-890	140-160	616-704
Alternator Drive Vee Belt				
Four and Six Cylinder Engines	125-155	556-689	90-115	400-512
Air Condition Compressor Vee Belt				
Four and Six Cylinder Engines	125-155	556-689	90-115	400-512
Air Pump Vee Belt				
Four Cylinder Engine	125-155	556-689	90-115	400-512
Six Cylinder Engine W/O P.S.	125-155	556-689	90-115	400-512
Six Cylinder Engine W/P.S.	65-75	289-334	60-70	267-311
Power Steering Vee Belt				
All Engines	125-155	556-689	90-115	400-512

1-9

AMERICAN MOTORS
CONCORD • EAGLE • EAGLE SX4 • SPIRIT

Starting System

American Motors cars, except when equipped with the 4–151 engine, are equipped with an integral positive engagement drive starter and a separate starter relay. Cars equipped with the 4–151 engine have the starter solenoid mounted on the top of the starter housing.

NOTE: *Starter repair procedures can be found in the Unit Repair Section.*

STARTER

Removal and Installation

1. Disconnect the battery lead and the solenoid lead from the starter, if used.
2. From underneath the car, remove the bolts which hold the starter to the bell housing (and starter-to-engine brace on the 4–151 engine) and remove the starter.
3. Before installing the starter, make sure the mounting surfaces are free from burrs and foreign material.
4. Install the starter to the housing together with any shims, and tighten the bolts to 18 ft. lbs. on the six cylinder engine. Tighten the bolts to 17 ft. lbs. on the 4–151 engine and 33 ft. lbs. on the 4–150 engine.
5. Clean the terminal(s) and install the cable(s).

IGNITION SYSTEM

The 4–150 and the six cylinder engines are equipped with the Solid State Ignition (SSI) system. The 4–151 CID engine is equipped with the Delco-Remy High Energy Ignition (HEI) system. For testing and repair procedures, refer to the Electronic Ignition System of the Unit Repair Section.

DISTRIBUTOR

Removal

1. Remove the distributor cap, mark the position of the rotor relative to the distributor body and mark the body relative to the block. Remove the carburetor air cleaner if necessary, the distributor primary wire and the distributor vacuum lines. Tag any disconnected wires or hoses for installation as required.
2. Remove the hold-down bolt and pull the distributor up and out of the block.
3. The rotor and body are marked so that they can be returned to the position from which they were removed. Do not turn the engine after distributor removal.

Installation
ENGINE NOT DISTURBED – TIMING RETAINED

1. Install the distributor in the reverse order of removal.
2. Be sure that the rotor and distributor are installed with the marks, which were made during removal, in alignment.
3. Adjust the timing as required.

ENGINE DISTURBED – TIMING LOST

NOTE: *If the rotor position was not noted during distributor removal, or if the engine was cranked with the distributor out, install the distributor in the following manner.*

1. Remove the spark plug from the No. 1 cylinder and position a compression gauge or a thumb over the spark plug hole.
2. Slowly crank the engine until compression pressure starts to build up.
3. Continue cranking the engine so that the timing mark or pointer aligns with the TDC mark.
4. Install the distributor with its drive meshed, so that the rotor points to the No. 1 terminal on the distributor cap with No. 1 cylinder piston at TDC.
5. Complete installation in the reverse order of removal and adjust the timing as required.

NOTE: *Some engines may be sensitive to the routing of the distributor sensor wires. If routed near the high-voltage coil wire or spark plug wires, the electromagnetic field surrounding the high-voltage wires could generate an occasional disruption of the ignition system operation.*

IGNITION TIMING

Adjustment

1. A scale located on the timing chain cover and a notch milled into the vibration damper are used as references to set ignition timing.
2. A Magnetic timing probe socket is provided integral with the timing degree scale for use with a special magnetic timing probe.
3. The probe socket is located at 9.5° ATDC and the equipment used is calibrated to compensate for the location.

CAUTION
Do not use the timing probe socket as a reference point to check the ignition timing when using a conventional timing light.

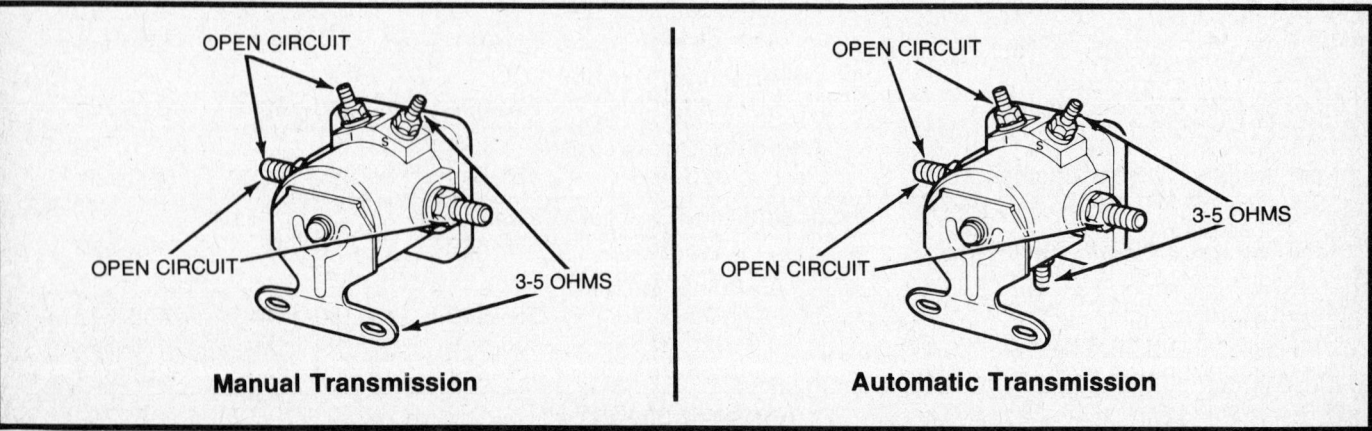

Starter solenoid ohmmeter check (© American Motors Corp.)

NOTE: Connect a tachometer to the SSI ignition system in the conventional way; to the negative (distributor) side of the coil and to a ground. HEI distributor caps have a "Tach" terminal. Some tachometers may not work with a SSI, or HEI ignition system and there is a possibility that some could be damaged. Check with the manufacturer of the tachometer to make sure it can be used.

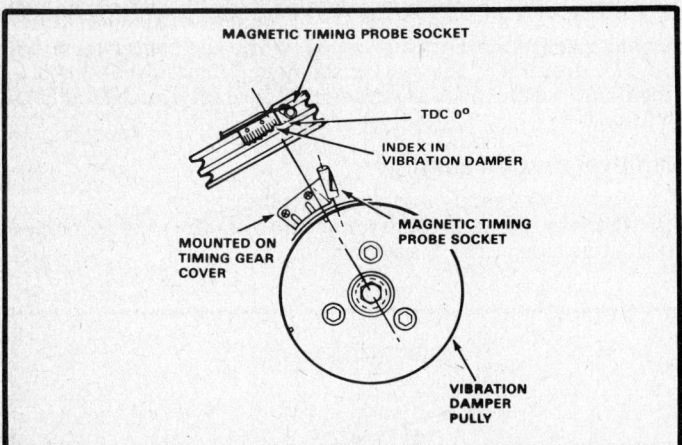

Magnetic timing probe socket and timing degree scale (© American Motors Corp.)

4–151 CID ENGINES

1. Disconnect the vacuum hose, at the distributor vacuum unit. Plug the vacuum line to prevent leakage.
2. Connect a timing light and a tachometer in accordance with the manufacturer's instructions. If the timing light has an advance control, be sure that it is off.
3. Start the engine. Adjust the carburetor curb idle screw so that the engine idles at the specified curb idle speed at operating temperature. If there is a throttle stop solenoid, disconnect it electrically. Aim the timing light at the pointer marks.
4. Adjust the timing by loosening the distributor clamp nut and rotating the distributor. Set the timing to the proper specification.

NOTE: On some models, a white paint mark is applied to the scale for the specified, initial timing setting. Do not mistake this mark for TDC.

5. Check the timing again after tightening the distributor clamp.
6. Connect the vacuum hose and set the idle speed to specifications.

4–150 AND 6–258 CID ENGINES WITH SSI SYSTEMS

1. Have the engine at normal operating temperature.
2. 4–150 CID engines—Disconnect the three wire connector to the vacuum input switch.
3. Disconnect and plug the distributor vacuum advance hose.
4. Attach a timing light and a tachometer to the electrical system of the engine.
5. Start the engine and increase the speed to 1600 rpm while observing the initial timing with the timing light.

NOTE: If a timing light incorporating an advance control feature is used, have the control in the OFF position.

6. If necessary, adjust the ignition timing to specifications as listed in the specifications tables or on the emission control information label, located under the hood. Adjust the ignition timing by moving the distributor body.

AMERICAN MOTORS
CONCORD • EAGLE • EAGLE SX4 • SPIRIT

CAUTION

If the specifications listed in the charts differ from the specifications on the emission control label, use the specifications as listed on the label.

---

7. Connect the distributor vacuum advance hose, the vacuum switch electrical connector on the 4–150 CID engines.
8. Remove the timing light and the tachometer from the engine wiring.

Electrical Controls

IGNITION LOCK

Removal and Installation

1. Remove steering wheel and lock plate, and pull turn signal switch assembly up out of the way.

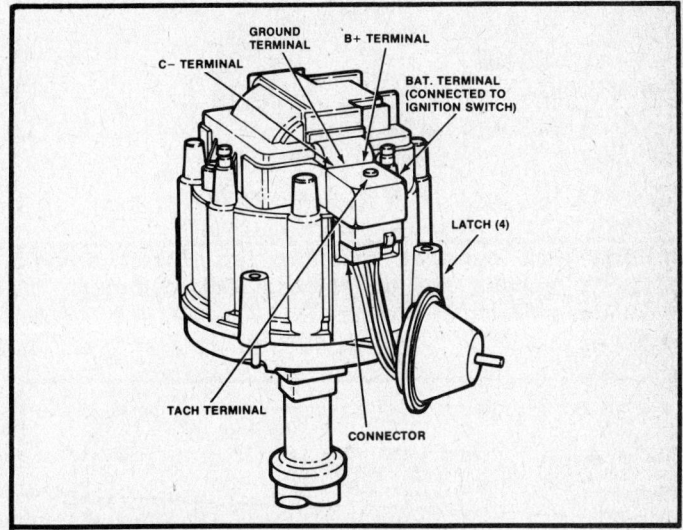

HEI distributor terminal locations (© American Motors Corp.)

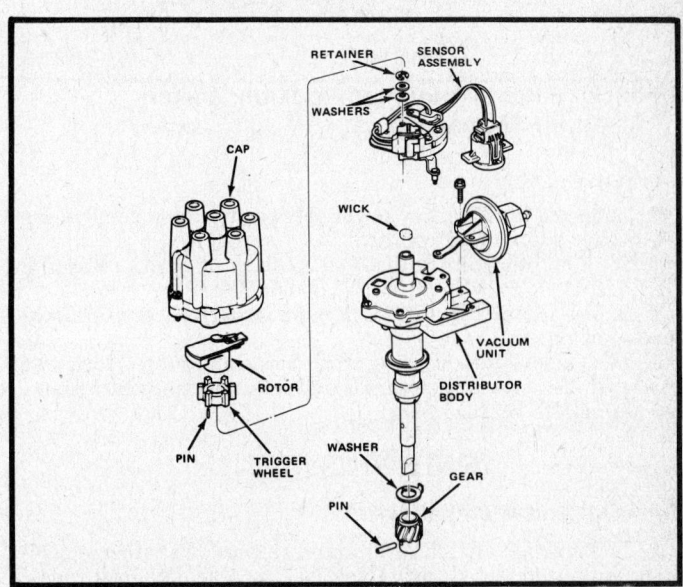

Exploded view of SSI distributor (© American Motors Corp.)

1–11

AMERICAN MOTORS
CONCORD • EAGLE • EAGLE SX4 • SPIRIT

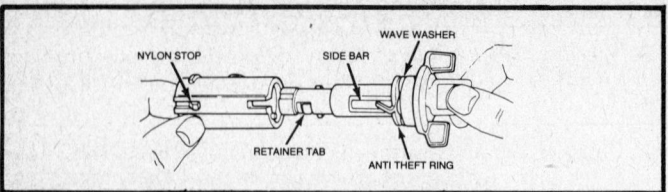
Lock cylinder and sleeve assembly
(© American Motors Corp.)

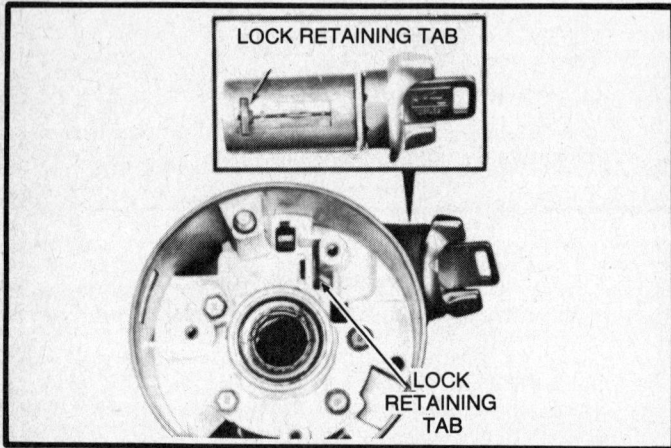
Ignition lock cylinder retaining tab. Insert small probe in access slot to release lock cylinder
(© American Motors Corp.)

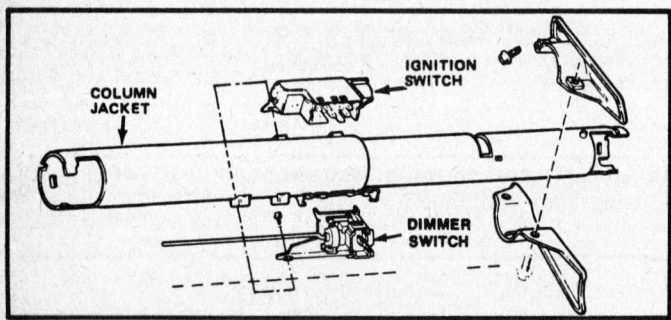
Steering column mounted ignition switch
(© American Motors Corp.)

2. Turn the ignition key to the ON position and remove the key buzzer switch and contacts.
3. With cylinder in the "LOCK" position, depress retaining tab and pull lock cylinder out of housing.
4. Before installing, turn lock cylinder to full counterclockwise position.
5. Push sleeve into housing while rotating counterclockwise until cylinder mates with sector and retainer snaps into place.
6. Complete reassembly.

IGNITION SWITCH

Removal and Installation

1. The ignition switch is mounted on the lower steering column and is connected to the key lock by a remote lock rod.
2. With key in "OFF LOCK" position, remove mounting screws, rod and wiring.

3. When installing, move slider to extreme left of switch pointing inward toward steering column. Put actuator rod in slider hole and install switch.
4. On tilt wheel columns, remove lash by pushing downward on switch before tightening mounting screws.

NEUTRAL SAFETY SWITCH

The neutral safety switch is a three-connector plunger switch mounted to the automatic transmission case. The outside terminals operate the back-up lamps, while the center terminal provides ground for the starter solenoid circuit. Ground is provided only when the transmission is in PARK or NEUTRAL positions.

Removal and Installation

1. Raise the vehicle and support safely.
2. Remove the three wire connector from the switch, located on the left side of the transmission.

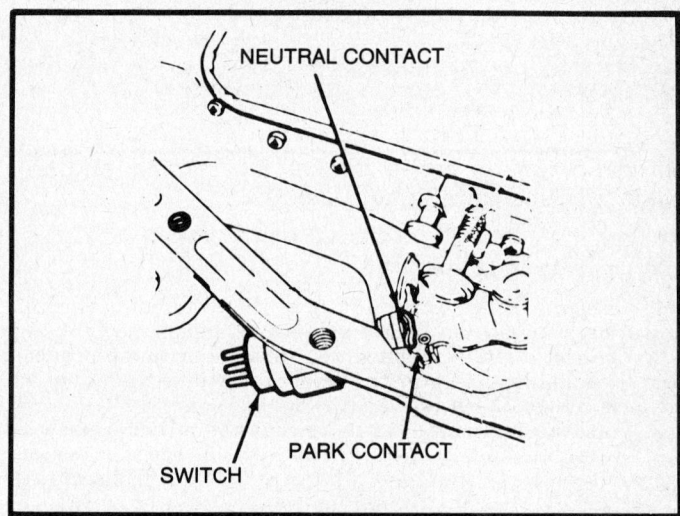
Neutral start switch installed in automatic transmission (© American Motors Corp.)

3. Unscrew the switch from the case. Transmission fluid will drain from the case with the switch out.
4. Install the new switch and switch seal in the transmission case and torque to 24 ft. lbs.
5. Lower vehicle, test switch and correct the transmission fluid level.

STOP LIGHT SWITCH

The stop light switch is mounted on the brake pedal and is not adjustable.

Removal and Installation

1. To remove the switch, the package tray must be removed, if equipped.
2. Each time the brake pedal bolt, holding the stop light switch is removed, a new locknut and new stamped nut MUST be used upon installation.
3. The brake lamps should illuminate at the first 1/2 in. travel of the brake pedal.
4. The brake pedal has two mounting bolt holes. On vehicles equipped with power brakes, install the bolt in the lower hole. On vehicles with standard brakes, install the bolt in the upper hole.

AMERICAN MOTORS
CONCORD • EAGLE • EAGLE SX4 • SPIRIT

HEAD LIGHT SWITCH

Removal and Installation

1. Disconnect battery cables.
2. Relocate anything preventing full access to switch such as instrument cluster bezel, package tray, speedometer cable or switch overlay assembly.
3. Remove screws and tilt cluster assembly away from instrument panel.
4. Place switch in full "ON" position. Pull on knob and press shaft release button to release shaft and knob assembly.
5. Remove mounting sleeve nut, wiring connector, ground wire and remove switch.
6. Install in reverse order.

DIMMER SWITCH

Removal
COLUMN MOUNTED

1. Disconnect the negative battery cable.
2. Remove the lower finish panel, tube cover and the package tray, if equipped.
3. Remove the wiring connector from the switch.
4. Tape the actuator rod to the column, remove the switch retaining screws and remove the switch by pulling it from the actuator rod.

Installation and Adjustment

1. Position the switch by pushing in onto the acutator rod and install the retaining screws.
2. Remove the tape holding the actuator rod to the column.
3. Adjust the switch by depressing it slightly and inserting a ³⁄₃₂ in. drill bit into the hole on the outer face of the switch (hole A on the illustration). This prevents horizontal switch movement.
4. Move the switch towards the steering wheel to remove the lash from the actuator rod.
5. Tighten the switch retaining screws to 35 inch lbs. (4 Nm) torque.
6. Remove the drill bit and install the wiring connector.
7. Check the operation of the switch.
8. Install the finish panel, the tube cover and the package tray, if equipped.
9. Connect the negative battery cable.

TURN SIGNAL SWITCH

Removal and Installation

1. Disconnect battery.
2. Remove steering wheel, anti-theft cover, lock plate and turn signal cancelling cam.
3. Place turn signal lever in right turn position and remove the lever.
4. Depress hazard warning light switch and remove button by turning counterclockwise.
5. Remove wire harness connector block. On column shift automatic transmission vehicles, use a stiff wire to depress the lock tab holding the shift quadrant light wire in the connector block.
6. Remove switch screws and pull the switch and wire harness out of the column.
7. Install in reverse order.

HORN SWITCH

Removal and Installation

1. Disconnect battery.

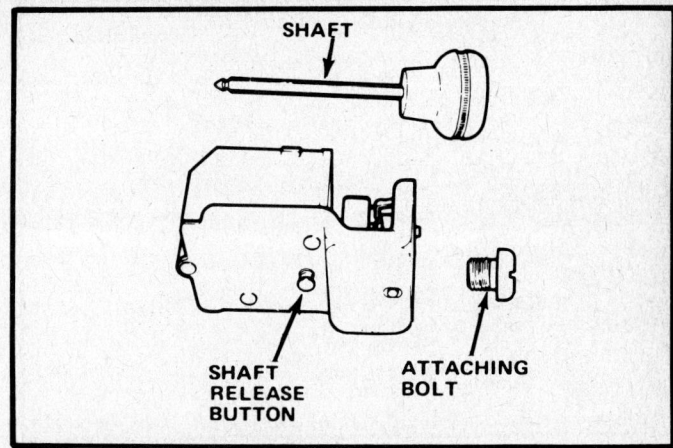

Light switch components—typical
(© American Motors Corp.)

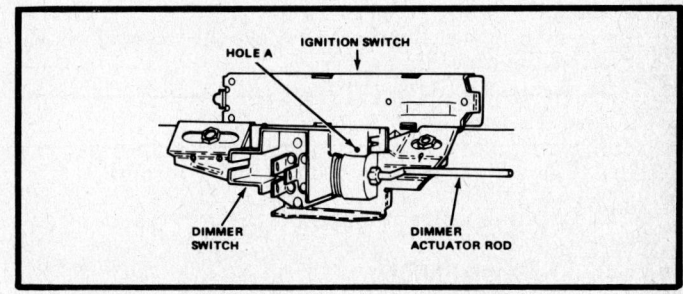

Adjustment of dimmer switch assembly
(© American Motors Corp.)

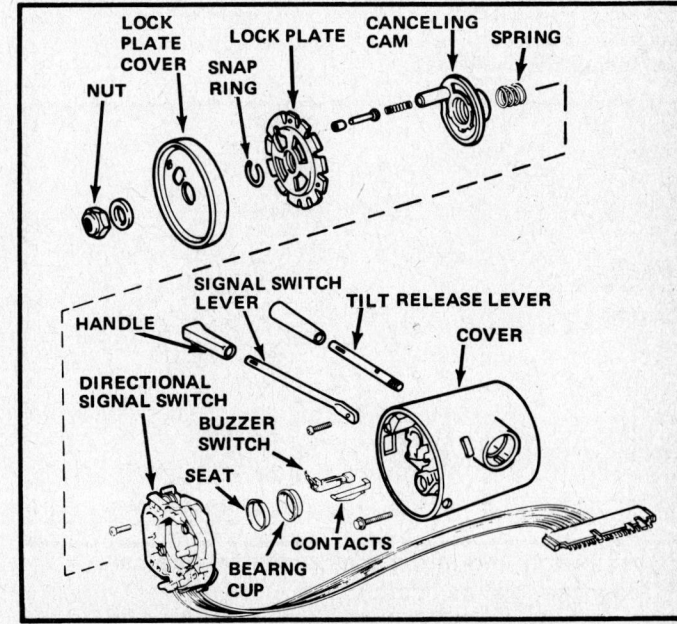

Turnsignal switch and component parts
(© American Motors Corp.)

2. On steering wheels with center horn buttons, remove the button by first lifting it up and then pulling it out. On other types, remove the mounting screws at the back of the wheel and pull the horn wire plastic retainer out of the turn signal cancelling cam and remove the button.

AMERICAN MOTORS
CONCORD • EAGLE • EAGLE SX4 • SPIRIT

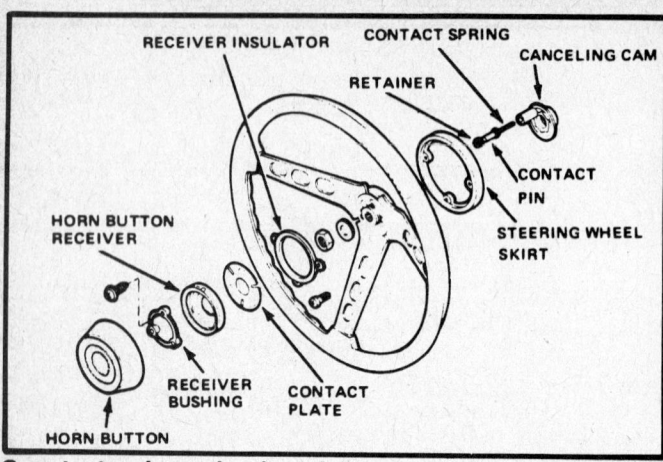

Sport steering wheel and horn switch components (© American Motors Corp.)

3. Use a steering wheel puller to remove the steering wheel.
4. Remove the cancelling cam.

CAUTION
Do not hammer on the end of shaft.

5. Install in reverse order of the removal procedure.

WINDSHIELD WIPER SWITCH

Removal and Installation

1. On all models, remove the control knob. A small screwdriver can be used to overcome the spring tension which holds the knob in place.
2. Separate switch from instrument panel and wiring. Remove the switch.
3. Install in reverse order.

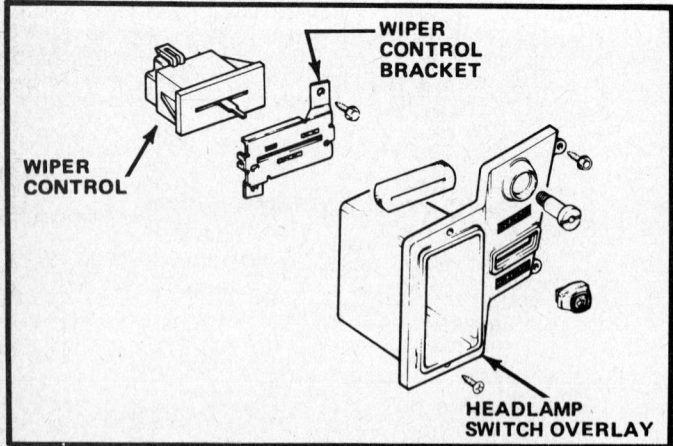

Wiper switch mounting components—typical (© American Motors Corp.)

WINDSHIELD WIPER MOTOR

Removal and Installation

1. Remove the wiper arms and blades.

2. Remove the attaching screws, the wiring connector and pull the motor and linkage out of the dash panel opening.
3. Raise up the lock tab of the drive link-to-crank stud retaining clip and slide the clip from the stud. Remove the wiper motor.
4. The installation is the reverse of the removal procedure. Check for positive retention of the retaining clip on the crank stud.
5. Tighten the attaching screws to 25 inch lbs. (3 Nm).
6. After locating the park position of the motor, install the arms and blades.

WINDSHIELD WIPER LINKAGE

Removal and Installation

1. Remove the wiper arms and blades.
2. Remove the pivot shaft to cowl top attaching nuts and washers.
3. Remove the wiper motor.

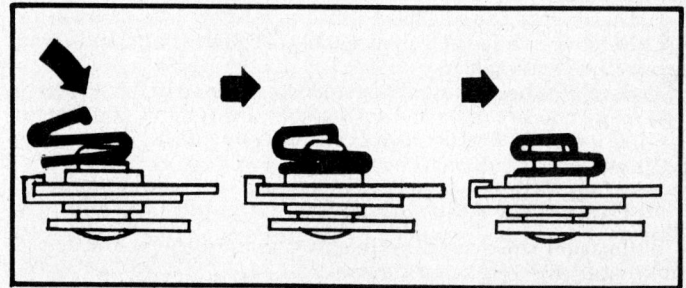

Correct positioning of windshield wiper linkage retaining clip (© American Motors Corp.)

4. Slide the pivot shaft body and the linkage assembly to the left to clear the right pivot shaft from the opening and move the assembly to the right side of the vehicle to remove.
5. The installation is the reverse of the removal procedure.
6. Position the flat side of the pivot shafts to index with the flat side of the cowl openings. Tighten the pivot shaft nuts to 120 inch lbs. (14 Nm).

Instrument Cluster Components

INSTRUMENT CLUSTER

Removal and Installation

1. Disconnect the battery cable.
2. On certain models, the lower steering column cover must be removed, while on other models, the gear selector cable must be disconnected from the steering column shift shroud. Remove the package tray, if equipped.
3. Remove the bezel retaining screws across top, over radio and behind the glove box door. Disconnect wire to box light. Tip bezel outward at top and disengage bottom tabs.
4. Disconnect the speedometer cable and push down on the three illumination lamp housings above the bezel to clear the instrument panel.
5. Disconnect the headlamp switch, the wiper control connectors and the switch lamp.
6. Remove the cluster illumination sockets and the instrument cluster wire connectors.
7. If equipped with clock or tachometer, remove their attaching screws. Disconnect the wiring harness from the printed circuit board.

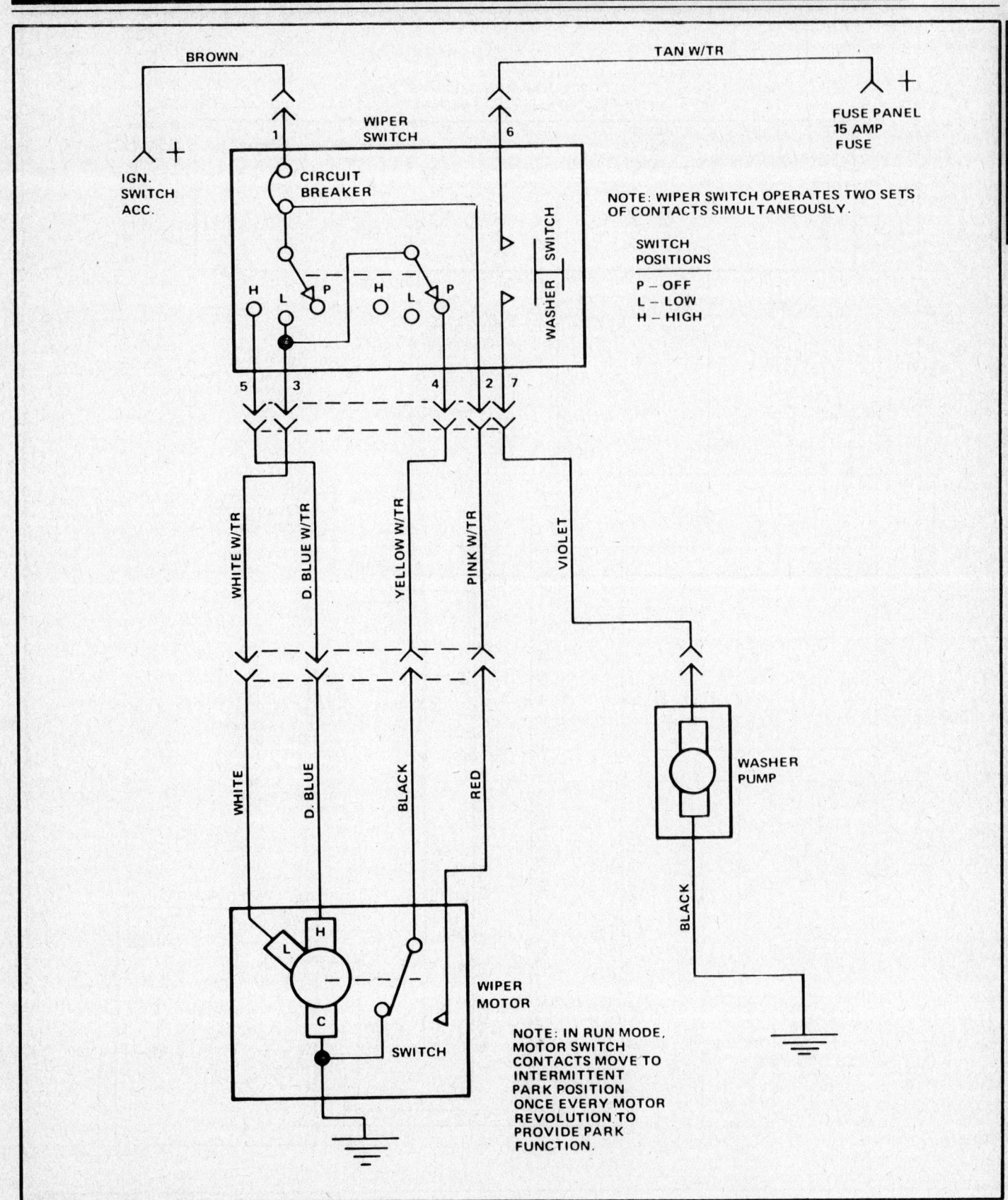

Wiper system electrical schematic
(© American Motors Corp.)

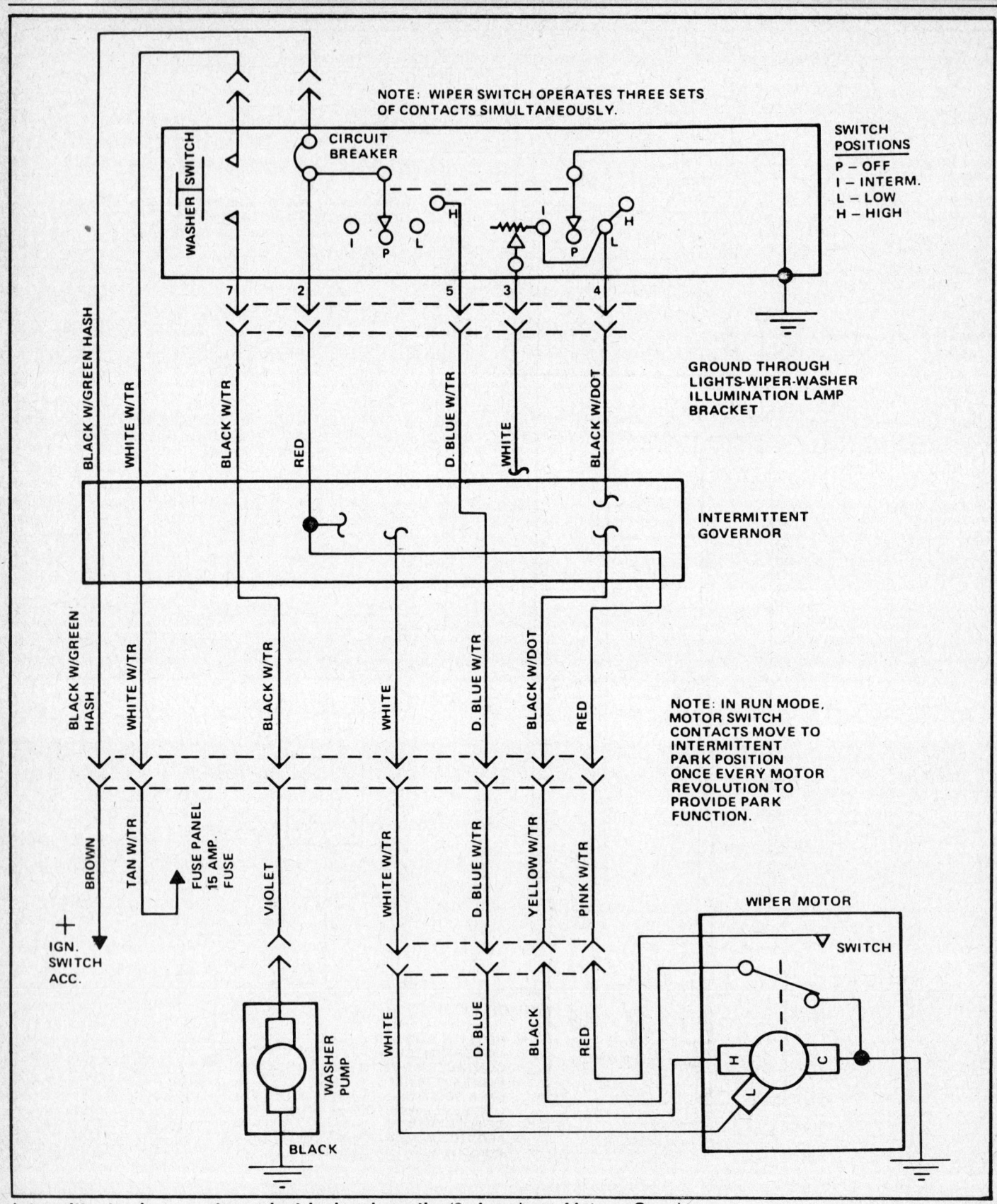

Intermittent wiper system electrical schematic (© American Motors Corp.)

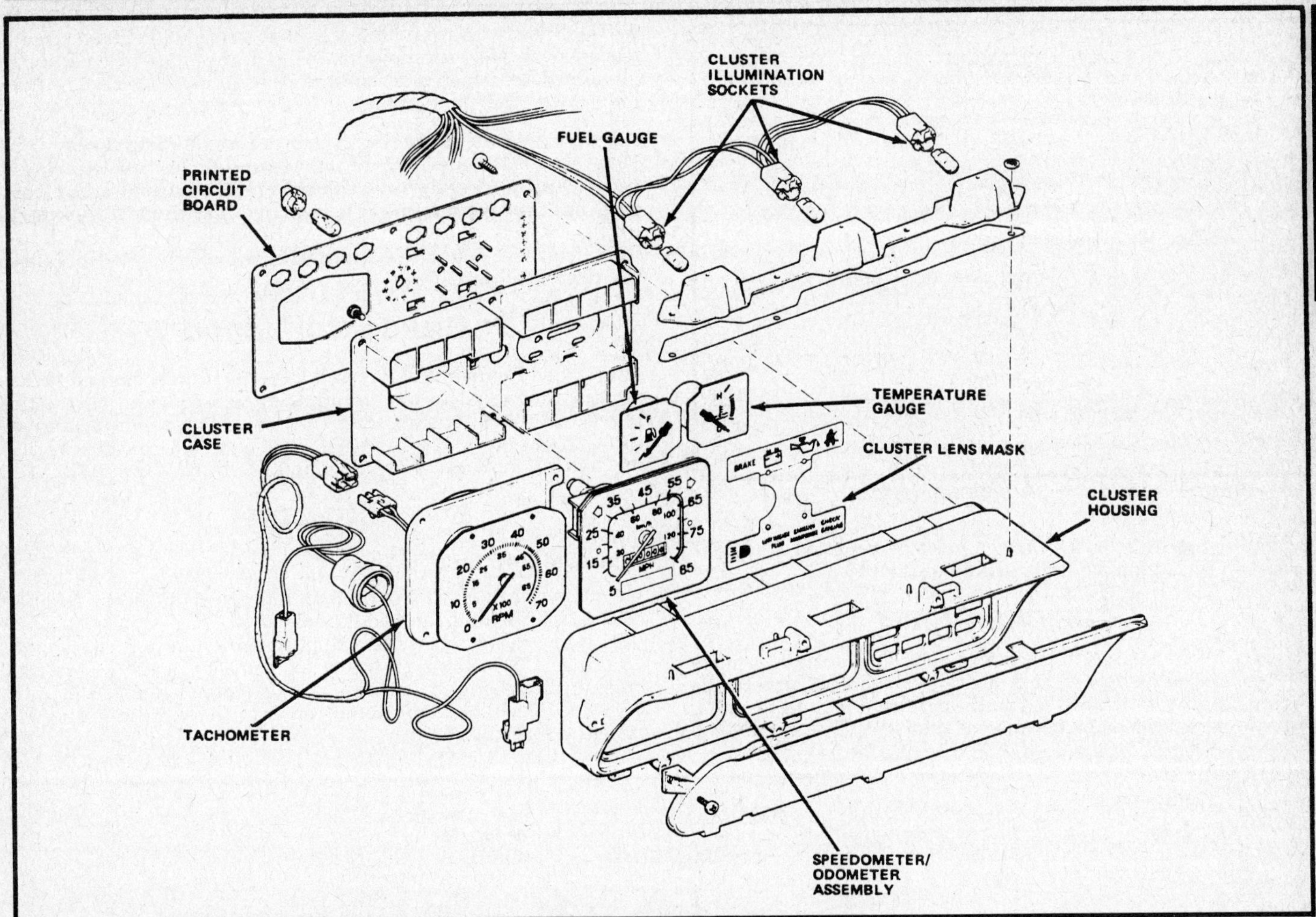

AMERICAN MOTORS
CONCORD • EAGLE • EAGLE SX4 • SPIRIT

Exploded view of instrument cluster (© American Motors Corp.)

8. Remove the cluster housing and circuit board to bezel attaching screws and remove the assembly from the bezel.
9. The installation is the reverse of the removal procedure.

SPEEDOMETER AND GAUGES

Removal and Installation

1. Remove the instrument cluster as previously outlined.
2. Remove the cluster housing and the printed circuit board, exposing the speedometer and the gauges, mounted to the cluster case.
3. Remove the speedometer and/or gauges as required.
4. The installation is the reverse of the removal procedure.

SPEEDOMETER CABLE

The cable is attached to the rear of the speedometer with a threaded knurled nut. A bolt retains the cable end at the transmission.

ELECTRICAL COMPONENT LOCATIONS

1. The turnsignal flasher—located on the instrument panel behind the headlamp switch.
2. The hazard warning flasher—is plugged into the fuse panel.
3. The fuse panel—located on the left side of the passenger compartment, adjacent to the parking brake mechanism.
4. Circuit breakers are an integral part of the headlamp switch and the wiper switch to protect each circuit.
5. 1000 Hour Emission Maintenance E-Cell Timer—located in the passenger compartment within the wire harness leading

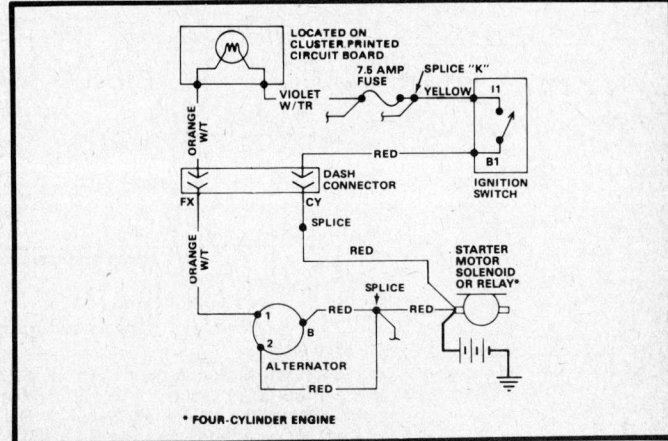

Alternator warning lamp circuit
(© American Motors Corp.)

SECTION 1

AMERICAN MOTORS
CONCORD • EAGLE • EAGLE SX4 • SPIRIT

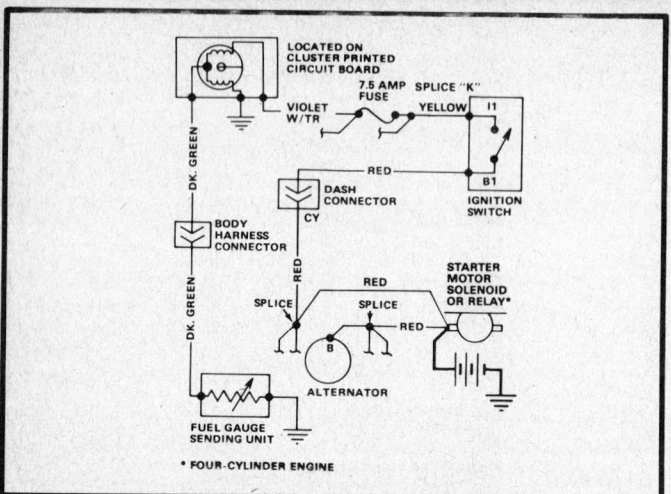

Fuel gauge circuit (© American Motors Corp.)

to the microprocessor. The timer must be replaced when the Emission Maintenance light illuminates.

FUSIBLE LINKS

Fusible links are used to prevent major wire harness damage in the event of a short circuit or an overload condition in the wiring circuits which are normally not fused, due to carrying high amperage loads or because of their locations within the wiring harness. Each fusible link is of a fixed value for a specific electrical load and should a link fail, the cause of the failure must be determined and repaired prior to installing a new fusible link of the same value.

NOTE: When replacing a protective electrical relay on 1984 and later models, be very sure to install the same type of relay. Verify that the schematic imprinted on the original and replacement relays are identical. Relay part numbers may change. Do not rely on them for identification. Instead, use the schematic imprinted on the relay for positive identification.

Cruise Command

The Cruise Command is a closed loop electro-mechanical servo system that consists of the following components; electronic regulator, speed sensor, servo, control switch, vacuum storage can and check valve. The release mechanism consists of the mechanical vacuum vent valve and the brake lamp switch.

REGULATOR

Removal and Installation

1. The regulator is mounted on a bracket under the instrument panel behind the headlamp switch.
2. Remove the screws and unplug the connector.
3. Insert a suitable thin tool to depress the tab inside the hole on the regulator identified by "Terminal Release."
4. To install, plug the connector into the regulator and install the screws.

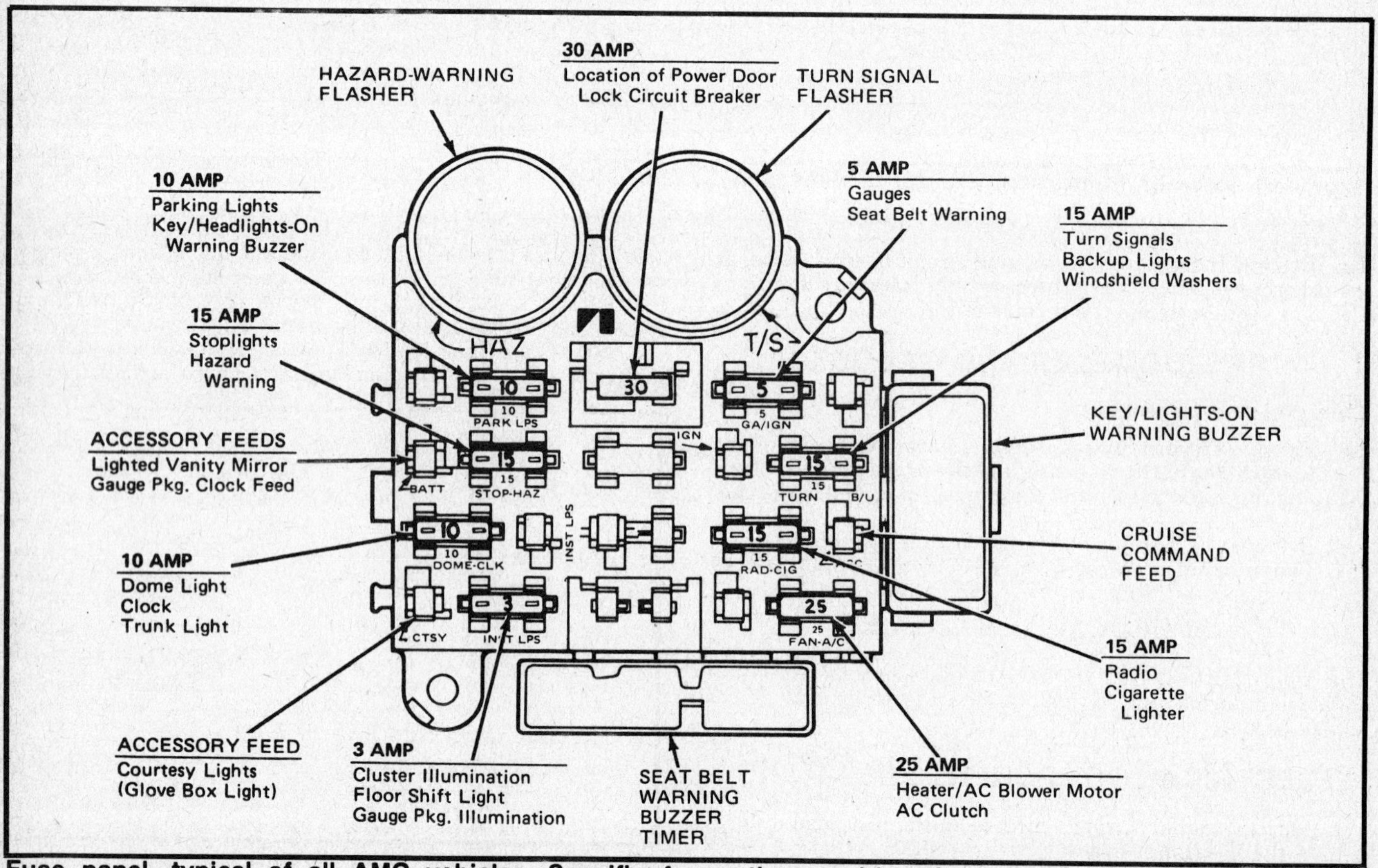

Fuse panel, typical of all AMC vehicles. Specific fuse ratings and locations vary from model to model and year to year (© American Motors Corp.)

1-18

Adjustment

Regulator adjustments are pre-set by the manufacturer but if all other components of the system appear to be functioning normally and the cruise command remains inoperative, perform the following adjustments to determine if the regulator is functional.

CAUTION

The adjustment potentiometers are extremely delicate. Insert the screwdriver into the slots very carefully and do not push hard or turn hard against the wiper arm stops. The potentiometer wiper arms have a maximum turning angle of 270 degrees (three-quarter turn).

---

1. Turn the centering adjustment (1) to the 10 o'clock position.
2. Turn the low speed adjustment (2) to the 10 o'clock position.
3. Turn the sensitivity adjustment (3) full clockwise.

NOTE: The adjustments may not be precisely correct for the automobile, but will be acceptable to determine if the regulator is functioning. The need for more precise adjustments can be determined by a road test.

4. If the adjustments have no effect on the cruise command operation, replace the regulator.

NOTE: The regulator is the only component of the system that cannot be isolated and tested separately. It must be tested while connected to the components of the system.

Testing

1. To adjust the regulator for engagement speed complaints, drive the vehicle on a level road surface and check operation.
2. If the actual engagement speed is 3.2 km/h (2 mph) or more above the selected engagement speed, stop the vehicle, turn the regulator centering screw approximately $\frac{1}{16}$ of a turn counterclockwise and check the engagement speed again. Readjust the speed as needed.
3. If the actual engagement speed is 3.2 km/h (2 mph) or more below the selected engagement speed, stop the vehicle, turn the regulator centering screw $\frac{1}{16}$ of a turn clockwise and check the engagement speed again.

VACUUM (MECHANICAL) VENT VALVE

Adjustment

1. Depress the brake pedal and hold in the depressed position.
2. Move the vacuum vent valve toward the bracket on the pedal as far as possible.
3. Release the brake pedal.

CONTROL SWITCH

The cruise command control switch assembly is integral with the turn signal switch and headlamp high/low beam switch lever. The switch is not repairable. The switch and harness assembly can be replaced only as a complete unit.

Removal

1. Remove the lower steering column cover.
2. Disconnect the four-wire harness connector located under the instrument panel.
3. If equipped with a tilt steering column, remove the wires from the connector.
4. Fold back and tape two of the four wires to the wire harness.
5. Tie or tape string to the wire harness.

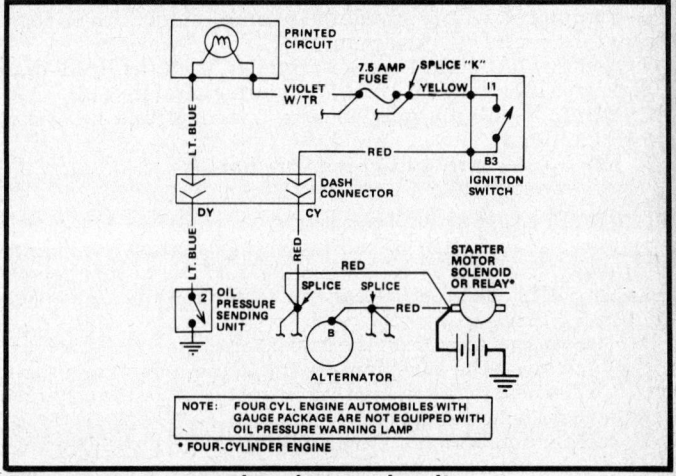

Oil pressure warning lamp circuit
(© American Motors Corp.)

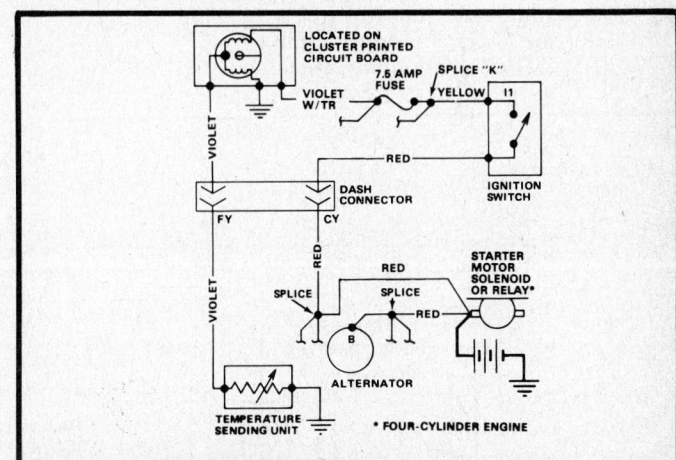

Coolant temperature gauge circuit
(© American Motors Corp.)

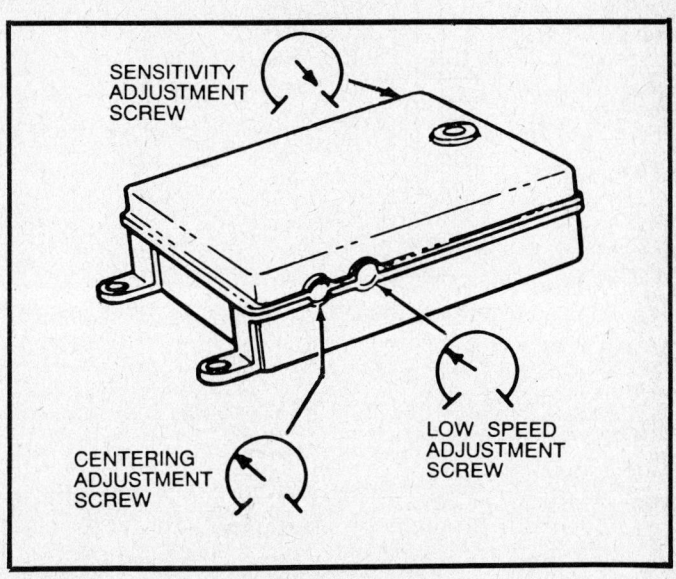

Location of speed control regulator adjusting screws (© American Motors Corp.)

1-19

American Motors
CONCORD • EAGLE • EAGLE SX4 • SPIRIT

6. If equipped with a standard steering column, tie or tape string to the wire harness connector.

7. Remove the control switch assembly from the headlamp high/low beam (dimmer) switch by pulling straight out.

8. Carefully pull the wire harness up through and out of the steering column.

9. Remove the string from the wire harness.

Installation

1. Test the operation of the replacement cruise command control switch assembly by connecting it to the system before installing it in the steering column (Refer to Control Switch Continuity Test).

2. Remove the wires from the connector. Tape two of the four wires back along the wire harness (tilt column only) and tape or tie the harness to the string that was attached to the original wire harness before removal.

3. Pull the replacement harness down through the steering column. On tilt steering columns, the harness must pass through the hole on the left side of the steering shaft.

4. Install the control switch assembly.

5. Install the harness wires in the connector (tilt column only) and connect the connector to the system.

6. Install the lower steering column cover.

7. Test the Cruise Command operation.

SERVO

Removal

1. Remove the retaining nuts and cable housing from the servo.

2. Spread the clip that connects the cable to the servo and remove.

3. Disconnect the vacuum hoses from the servo.

4. Remove the retaining nut and servo from the bracket. Note the position of the ground cable.

5. Disconnect the wire harness connector under the instrument panel. Carefully maneuver the wire harness through the dash panel and remove the servo.

Installation

1. Install the servo and nut on the bracket. Tighten with 60 inch lbs. (7 Nm) torque. Ensure the ground cable is positioned on the stud.

2. Maneuver the wire harness through the dash panel and connect the connector.

3. Attach the cable to the servo and squeeze the clip to retain the cable.

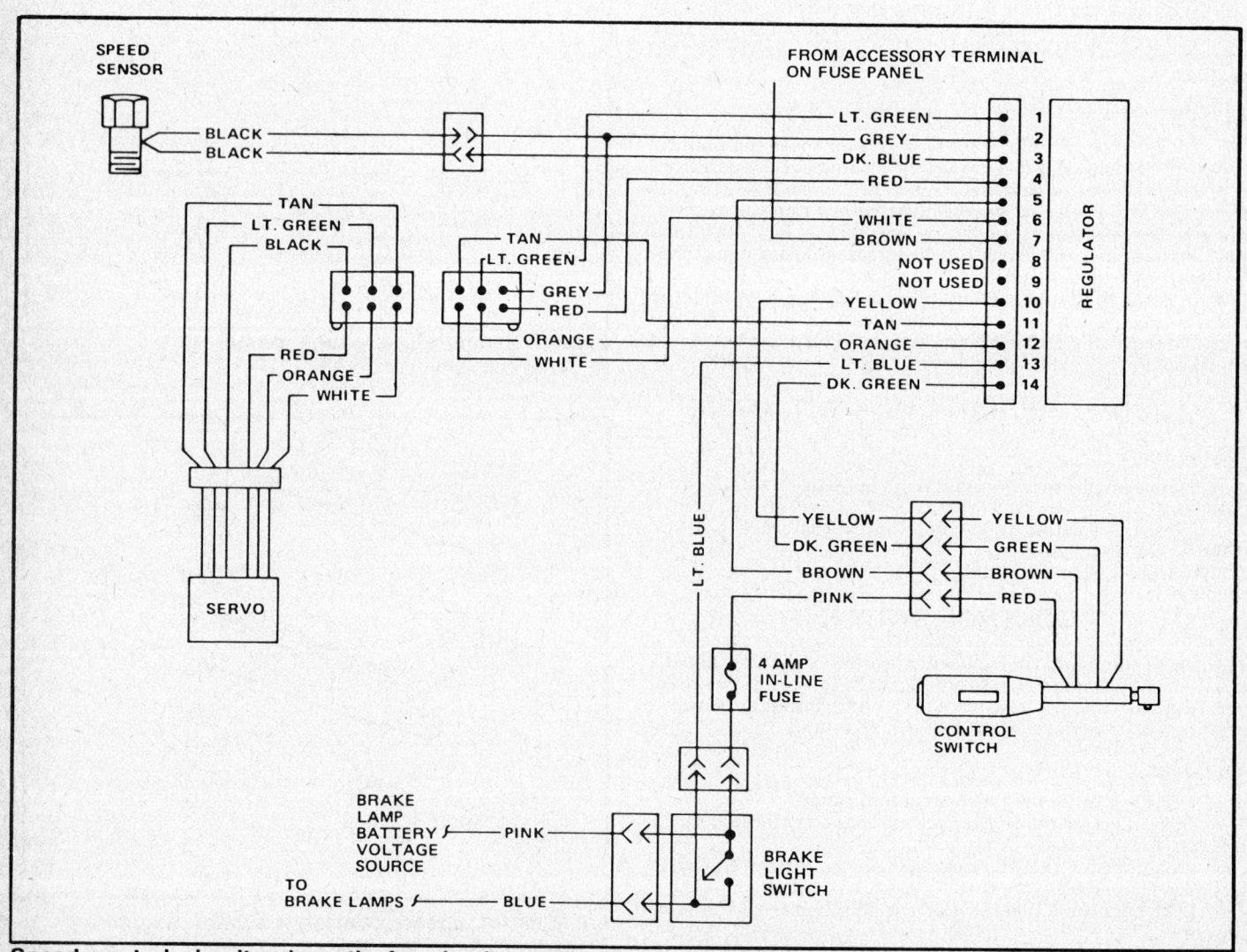

Speed control circuit schematic for circuitry tests (© American Motors Corp.)

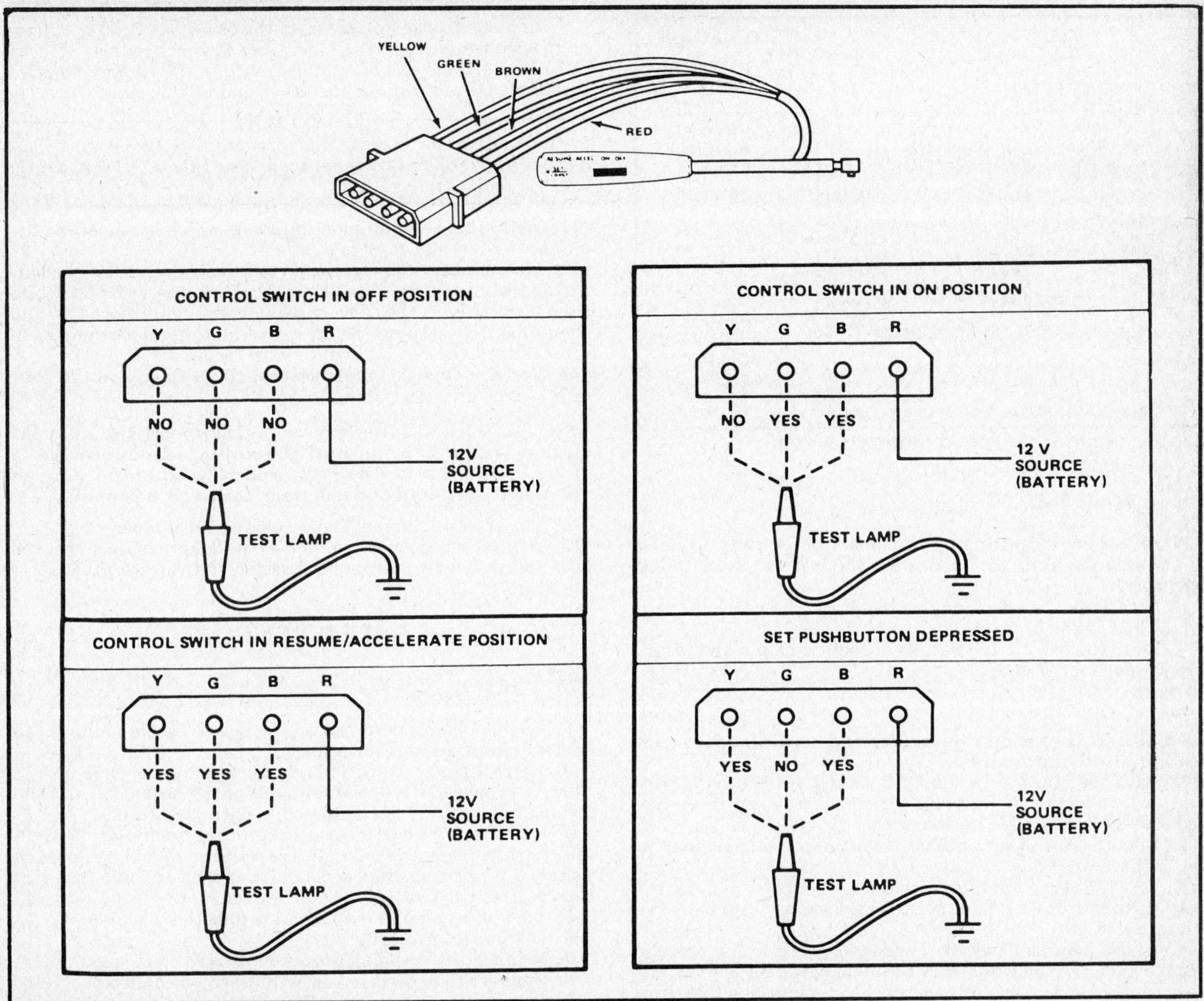

American Motors
CONCORD • EAGLE • EAGLE SX4 • SPIRIT

Speed control switch continuity test (© American Motors Corp.)

NOTE: Mounting studs are not equally spaced from the hole in the servo. Ensure the housing is installed correctly.

4. Connect the vacuum hoses.

SERVO CABLE

Removal

1. Remove the clip and washer from the pin on the bellcrank and remove the lost motion link.
2. Squeeze the tabs that retain the cable housing in the bracket and remove the cable from the bracket.
3. Remove the retaining nuts and the cable housing from the servo.
4. Spread the clip that connects the cable to the servo and remove.

Installation

1. Attach the cable to the servo and squeeze the clip to retain the cable.

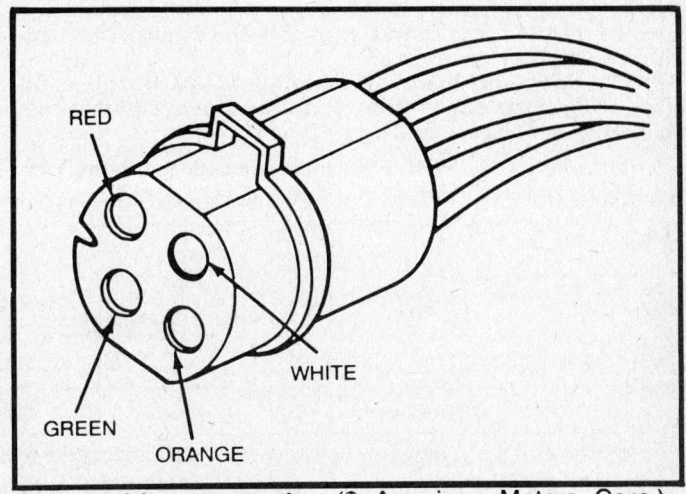

Servo wiring connector (© American Motors Corp.)

1-21

American Motors
CONCORD • EAGLE • EAGLE SX4 • SPIRIT

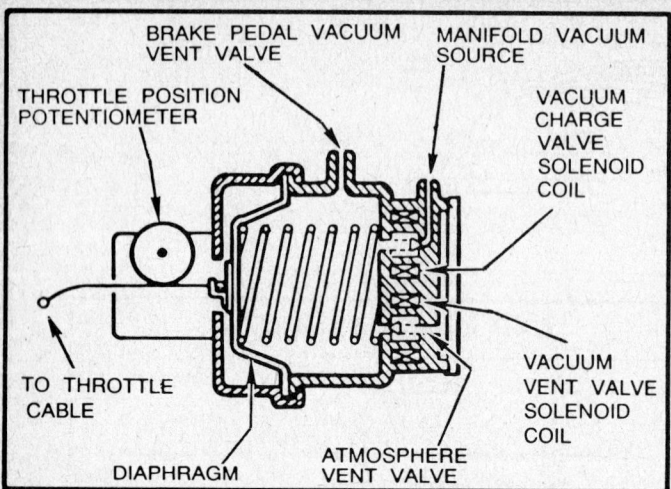

Cross section of speed control servo
(© American Motors Corp.)

2. Install the cable housing on the servo.

NOTE: The mounting studs are not equally spaced from the hole in the servo. Ensure the housing is installed correctly.

3. Attach the cable housing on the bracket. Ensure the tabs are locked in the bracket.
4. Place the lost motion link on the bellcrank pin and install the washer and lock clip.

Test

NOTE: This test can be performed with the servo installed in the automobile.

1. With the ignition switch OFF, disconnect the servo wire harness connector. Remove the vacuum hose from the brake pedal vent valve nipple on the servo.
2. Disconnect the servo cable from the throttle linkage at the carburetor.
3. Test the servo for short circuits to ground.
4. Connect the ohmmeter negative (black) probe to the servo mounting stud.
5. Touch the ohmmeter positive (red) probe to the red, the orange and then the white wire terminal of the servo wire harness connector. Observe the ohmmeter during each test. Infinite resistance should be indicated for each wire terminal.
6. If the ohmmeter indicates less than infinite resistance on any wire terminal, the servo has a short circuit to ground and must be replaced. The short circuit will also damage the regulator and it must be replaced.

NOTE: With no load (or insufficient load), the solid state circuitry in the regulator will be damaged by excessive current flow.

7. If the servo does not have a short circuit(s) to ground, continue with the test.
8. Connect a vacuum gauge to the brake pedal vent valve nipple.
9. Connect a jumper wire from the chassis ground to the orange wire terminal in the servo wire harness connector.
10. Connect one end of a jumper wire to the battery positive terminal. Do not connect the other end at this time.

--- **CAUTION** ---
Use extreme caution when the engine is operating. Do not stand in direct line with the fan. Do not put hands near pulleys, belts or fan. Do not wear loose clothing.

11. With the transmission in Park or Neutral, start the engine.
12. Momentarily connect the jumper wire attached to the battery positive terminal simultaneously to the red and white wire terminals in the servo wire harness connector. Vacuum should be indicated on the gauge while the jumper wire is in contact with the red and white wire terminals.
13. Perform this same test several times to ensure the solenoid valves are functioning normally.

NOTE: With 12V (battery voltage) applied, the solenoid charge valve is open and the solenoid vent valve is closed. With no voltage applied, the solenoid charge valve is closed and the solenoid vent valve is open.

14. Turn the engine OFF and remove the jumper wires.
15. If the servo is defective, replace it. Otherwise, connect the vacuum hose, wire harness connector and throttle linkage to the servo.

SPEED SENSOR

Test

1. Disconnect the speed sensor wire harness connector.
2. Connect a voltmeter set on the low AC scale to the speed sensor wire connector terminals.
3. Raise the rear (front and rear for Eagle automobiles if not in the two-wheel drive mode) wheels of the automobile off the ground and support the automobile with jack stands.
4. Operate the engine (wheels spinning freely) at 48 km/h (30 mph) and note the voltage. The voltage should be approximately 0.9 volt. Increases of 0.1 volt per each 16 km/h (10 mph) increase in speed should also be indicated.
5. Turn off the engine and slowly halt the wheels.
6. Disconnect the voltmeter.
7. Replace the speed sensor, if defective.
8. Connect the speed sensor wire harness connector.
9. Remove the safety stands and lower the automobile.

SERVO CHAIN OR CABLE

Adjustment
FOUR CYLINDER ENGINES

1. Allow seven beads of the chain outside the tabs.
2. Squeeze the tabs and attach the chain to the bell crank.

SIX CYLINDER ENGINES

1. A cable with an integral "lost motion link" at the throttle end connects the servo to the throttle linkage.

CRUISE COMMAND
Service Diagnosis

Condition	Cause	Correction
System does not engage in "on" position	1. Restricted vacuum hose or no vacuum. 2. Control switch defective.	1. Locate restriction or air leak and repair. 2. Replace switch.

American Motors
CONCORD • EAGLE • EAGLE SX4 • SPIRIT

CRUISE COMMAND (continued)
Service Diagnosis

Condition	Cause	Correction
System does not engage in "on" position	3. Regulator defective. 4. Speed sensor defective. 5. Brake lamps defective. 6. Brake light switch defective. 7. Brake light switch wire disconnected. 8. Open circuit between brake light switch and brake lamps. 9. Mechanical vent valve position improperly adjusted.	3. Replace regulator. 4. Replace sensor. 5. Replace brake lamp bulbs. 6. Replace switch. 7. Connect wire to switch. 8. Repair open circuit. 9. Adjust vent valve position.
Resume feature inoperative	1. Defective servo ground connection. 2. Control switch defective.	1. Check servo ground wire connection and repair as necessary. 2. Replace switch.
Accelerate function inoperative	1. Accelerate circuit in regulator inoperative. 2. Control switch defective.	1. Replace regulator. 2. Replace switch.
System re-engages when brake pedal is released	1. Regulator defective. 2. Mechanical vent valve not opening. 3. Kink in mechanical vent valve hose. 4. Brake light switch defective.	1. Replace regulator. 2. Adjust position or replace valve. 3. Reroute hose to remove kink. 4. Adjust or replace switch.
Carburetor throttle does not return to idle position	1. Improper linkage adjustment. 2. Improper chain adjustment. 3. No slack in lost motion link.	1. Adjust properly (four-cyl. engine only). 2. Adjust chain (four-cyl. engine only). 3. Adjust servo cable (six-cylinder engine only).
Road speed changes more than 2 mph (3.2 km/h) when setting speed	1. Centering adjustment set wrong.	1. Adjust centering screw.
Engine accelerates when started	1. No slack in bead chain. 2. Vacuum hose connections reversed at servo. 3. Servo defective.	1. Adjust chain. 2. Check connection and correct. 3. Replace servo.
Automobile continues to accelerate when set button is released	1. Servo defective. 2. Regulator defective.	1. Replace servo. 2. Replace regulator.
System engages but slowly loses set speed	1. Air leak at vacuum hose connections or in hoses. 2. Air leak at vent valve on brake pedal.	1. Check hoses and connections. Repair as necessary. 2. Replace vent valve.
System disengages on level road without applying brake	1. Loose wire connection. 2. Loose vacuum hose connection. 3. Servo linkage broken. 4. Defective brake light switch.	1. Repair connection. 2. Check vacuum hose connection and repair as necessary. 3. Repair linkage. 4. Replace switch.
Erratic operation	1. Reverse polarity. 2. Servo defective. 3. Regulator defective.	1. Check position of speed sensor wires at connector. 2. Replace servo. 3. Replace regulator.

COOLING AND HEATER SYSTEM

WATER PUMP

Removal and Installation

The water pump is a centrifugal unit having a non-adjustable packless seal. It is nonserviceable and must be replaced if defective. No maintenance is required.

4-CYLINDER

1. Drain the cooling system.
2. Remove all drive belts.
3. Remove the fan and pump pulley.
4. Unbolt and remove the pump from the engine.
5. Clean the gasket surfaces, coat the new gasket with non-hardening type sealer and position the gasket on the block.
6. Coat the threaded areas of the bolts with waterproof sealer and install the pump. Torque the bolts to 25 ft. lbs.
7. Install the pulley and fan.
8. Install the drive belts. The belts should be adjusted as specified in the Alternator Removal and Installation procedure.

6-CYLINDER

1. Drain the cooling system. Disconnect the negative cable from the battery.
2. Unfasten the radiator and the heater hoses at the pump.
3. Loosen the adjustment bolts from the alternator and the power steering pump (if so equipped). Remove the V-belts.
4. Unfasten the fan ring. Remove the fan and pump pulley assembly. Withdraw the fan ring (or shroud).
5. Remove the securing bolts from the water pump. Withdraw the pump along with its gasket.
6. Installation is the reverse order of removal. Always use a new pump gasket.
7. Bleed the radiator by running the engine and opening the heater control valve. Run the engine long enough so that the thermostat opens. Check the coolant level.
8. The water pump securing bolts should be tightened to 10-15 ft. lbs. Adjust the belts as specified in the Alternator Removal and Installation procedure.

HEATER/AIR CONDITIONING BLOWER MOTORS

Removal

1. Disconnect the wiring to the blower motor.
2. Remove the blower motor retaining bolts or nuts. Remove the blower motor from the housing.
3. Remove the blower fan from the motor shaft.

Installation

1. Install the blower fan onto the motor shaft. Position the fan so that a 0.350 in. clearance exists between the mounting plate of the motor and the end of the blower fan.
2. Position the ears of the spring clip retainer over the flat surface of the motor shaft. The edge of the clip must be flush with the edge of the fan hub.
3. Install the blower motor into the housing and install the retaining bolts or nuts.
4. Connect the wiring to the motor and check operation of the motor and fan assembly.

CONTROL PANEL

Removal

HEATER EQUIPPED

1. Disconnect the negative battery cable.
2. Open the glove box and remove all screws holding the center housing to the instrument panel.
3. Remove the dash receiver and retainer screws.
4. Remove the radio knobs and attaching nuts, if equipped.
5. Remove the center housing and disconnect the electrical wiring and connections.
6. Remove the control panel attaching screws.
7. Disconnect the cables from the control levers.
8. Disconnect the electrical connectors at the switch.
9. Remove the control panel.
10. The switch can be replaced with the control panel out of the dash assembly.

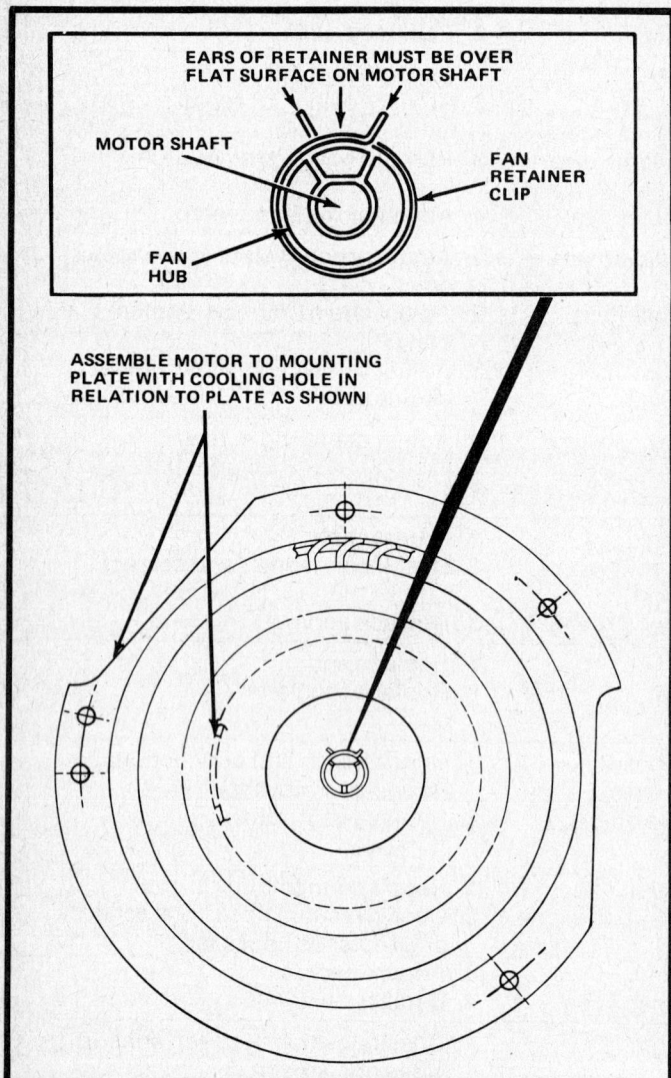

Blower fan retainer specifications
(© American Motors Corp.)

American Motors
CONCORD • EAGLE • EAGLE SX4 • SPIRIT

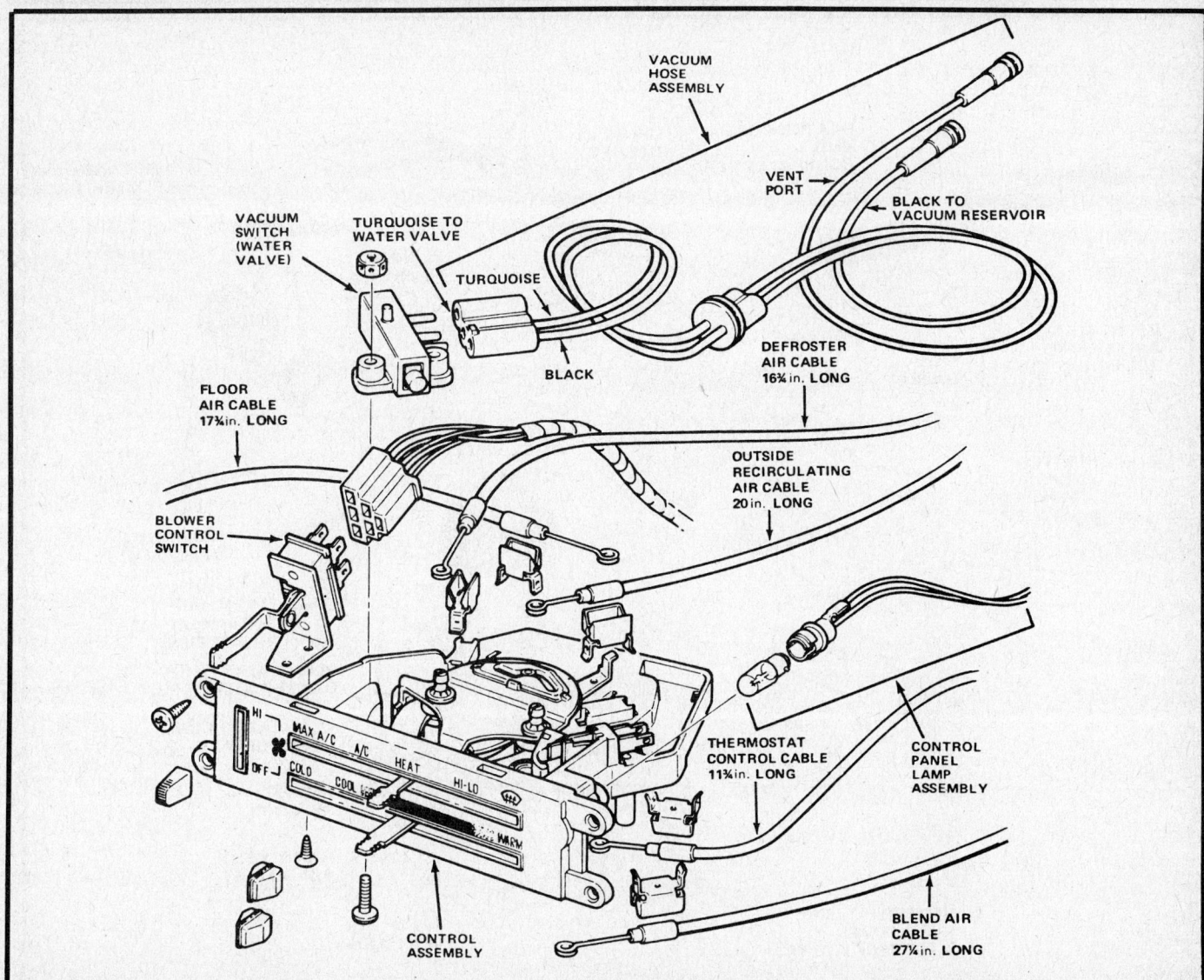

Exploded view of AC/heater control assembly (© American Motors Corp.)

Installation

1. Position the control panel in place.
2. Install the electrical wiring connectors to the switch.
3. Connect the cables to the control levers.

NOTE: The control cables must be installed with the colored tape in the center of the clips attached to the control panel.

4. Install the control panel retaining screws.
5. Install the instrument panel center housing in the reverse order of its removal.
6. Connect the negative battery cable.

CONTROL PANEL

Removal
HEATER/AIR CONDITIONING EQUIPPED

1. Disconnect the negative battery cable.
2. Refer to the procedure in the removal of the heater equipped control panel for removal of the instrument panel center housing.
3. Remove the control panel attaching screws.
4. Remove the center upper discharge duct.
5. Remove the radio, if equipped.
6. Remove the attaching screws and the lower control panel from the instrument panel and disconnect the cables from the control levers.
7. Disconnect the vacuum hose assembly from the vacuum switch.
8. Disconnect the electrical connectors.
9. Remove the control panel from the instrument panel.
10. The blower motor control switch attaching screw is accessible from the bottom of the control assembly after the panel removal.

Installation

1. Install the control panel in the reverse of the removal procedure.
2. Adjust the cables as required and check for proper system operation.

1-25

AMERICAN MOTORS
CONCORD • EAGLE • EAGLE SX4 • SPIRIT

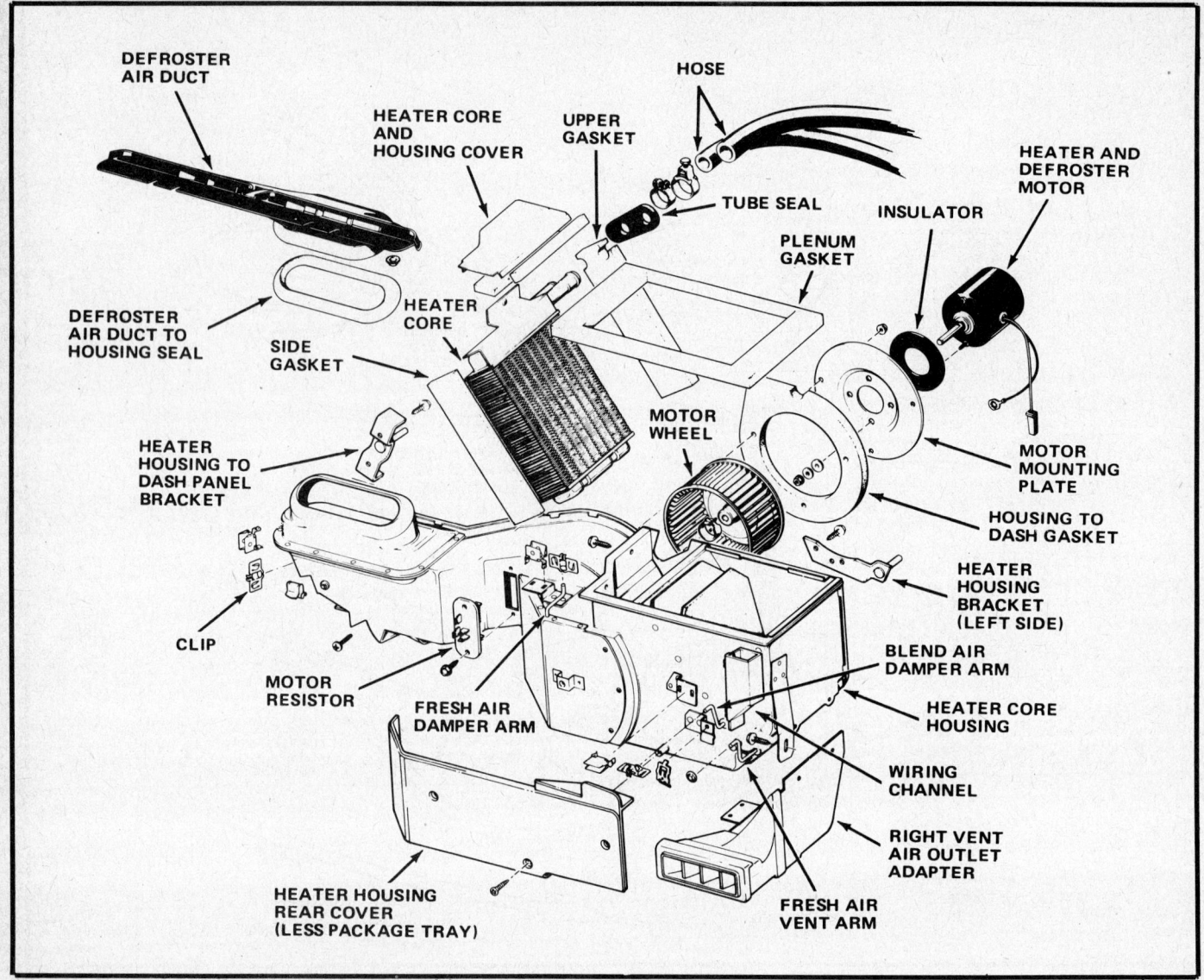

Exploded view of heater core assembly (© American Motors Corp.)

HEATER CORE, DEFROSTER AND BLOWER MOTOR HOUSINGS

Removal

LESS AIR CONDITIONING

1. Disconnect the negative battery cable.
2. Drain the radiator to remove approximately two quarts of coolant from the cooling system.
3. Disconnect the heater hoses from the heater core tubes and plug the tubes to prevent coolant from draining during the removal.
4. Disconnect the blower motor wires and remove the blower motor and fan assembly.
5. Remove the housing retaining nuts in the engine compartment near the blower motor position.
6. Remove the package tray, if equipped.
7. Disconnect the wiring connector at the blower motor resistor.
8. Snap the wiring harness cover open on the right side of the plenum chamber and remove the harness.

NOTE: Tape the harness to the plenum chamber.

9. Disconnect the heater, defroster and blend-air door cables at the housing.
10. Remove the right door sill plate and remove the right cowl trim kick panel.
11. Remove the right windshield pillar moulding, the instrument panel upper attaching screws and the screw attaching the instrument panel to the right door hinge post.
12. Remove the housing retaining screws.
13. Pull the right side of the instrument panel slightly rearward and remove the housing.
14. Remove the cover and screws retaining the heater core to the housing and remove the heater core from the housing.

Installation

1. The installation of the heater core, the defroster and blower housings is the reverse of the removal procedure.
2. Ensure the heater core seals are properly installed to prevent air leakage around the perimeter of the heater core.
3. Properly adjust the control cables during the installation.
4. Be sure air is expelled from the cooling system during the engine operation.

AMERICAN MOTORS
CONCORD • EAGLE • EAGLE SX4 • SPIRIT

FUEL SYSTEM

FUEL PUMP

Removal
4-151, 4-150 ENGINES, EXCEPT IN EAGLES

1. Disconnect the negative battery cable.
2. Loosen the fuel line at the carburetor. Remove the fuel line at the fuel pump outlet pump.
3. Raise the vehicle and support safely. Disconnect the inlet fuel line from the fuel pump.
4. Remove the two retaining bolts and remove the fuel pump.

Installation

1. Position the fuel pump at its opening on the block and engage the pump actuating lever to the cam surface of the camshaft.
2. Install the two fuel pump retaining bolts and tighten alternately and evenly.
3. Install the inlet and outlet pipes or hoses. Lower the vehicle.
4. Connect the negative battery cable.
5. Start the engine and inspect for leakage.

Removal
4-151, 4-150 ENGINE EQUIPPED EAGLES

1. Disconnect the negative battery cable.
2. Remove the alternator with the wiring attached and lay aside. Disconnect the mounting bracket from the cylinder block and the intake manifold.
3. Loosen the bottom bolt of the intake manifold-to-right side engine mount bracket and move the bracket towards the fender panel.
4. Disconnect the carburetor vent hose and re-route the heater hoses to gain clearance.
5. Tag to identify the vacuum hoses and disconnect.
6. Disconnect the inlet and outlet lines at the fuel pump.
7. Install an engine holding fixture and attach to the engine.
8. Remove the right engine mount through-bolt and raise the engine slightly.
9. Raise the vehicle and support safely.
10. Disconnect the right side engine cushion bracket from the block and axle bracket.
11. Lower the vehicle and raise the engine to maneuver the bracket for access clearance to the fuel pump bolts.
12. Remove the two retaining bolts and remove the fuel pump.

Installation

1. Clean the block mounting surface of gasket material. Install new gasket and the fuel pump. Tighten the mounting bolts 15 ft. lbs. torque.

NOTE: Raise and lower the vehicle as required to install the fuel pump and during the installation of the engine mount.

2. Connect the fuel lines to the fuel pump.
3. Connect the engine mount bracket to the cylinder block and to the axle bracket.
4. Lower the engine onto the mount. Install the mount through-bolt and nut.
5. Remove the engine holding fixture.
6. Connect the vacuum lines and re-route the heater hoses to their original positions.
7. Install the intake manifold-to-mount bracket.
8. Install the alternator mounting bracket and mount the alternator to the holding bracket.

CAUTION
Be sure the wiring is not pinched during the installation.

---

9. Install and adjust the belts as required.
10. Connect the negative battery cable.

Removal
SIX CYLINDER ENGINES

1. Disconnect the negative battery cable.
2. Disconnect the fuel lines from the fuel pump.
3. Remove the attaching bolts and the pump from the engine block.

Installation

1. Install the pump and the new gasket on the engine block. Retain with the two retaining bolts.

NOTE: Be sure the actuating arm of the pump is positioned on the top of the camshaft eccentric.

2. Install the fuel inlet and outlet lines to the fuel pump.
3. Install the negative battery cable.
4. Start the engine and check for leakage.

CARBURETOR
Removal and Installation

1. Disconnect the negative battery cable to avoid a fire hazard when the fuel line is disconnected from the carburetor.
2. Remove the vacuum hoses, the air cleaner assembly and flange gasket. Mark the hoses to aid in assembly.
3. Disconnect the fuel line and vacuum hoses from the carburetor. Mark the hoses to aid in assembly.
4. Disconnect the throttle linkage and electrical wire connectors.
5. Remove the carburetor attaching bolts and nuts. Remove the carburetor from the intake manifold.
6. Clean the gasket from the carburetor base and from the intake manifold.
7. The carburetor installation is the reverse of the removal procedure.

Idle Speed and Mixture Adjustment
IDLE SPEED

Adjustment

NOTE: Follow instructions on the Emission Control label as to the position of the A/T control lever.

MODEL 2SE CARBURETOR

1. Connect a tachometer to the ignition coil or the pigtail wire connector above the heater blower motor.
2. Disconnect and plug the vacuum hose at the distributor vacuum advance.
3. If necessary, adjust the ignition timing with the engine speed at or below the specified engine idle speed.
4. Re-connect the vacuum hose to the distributor vacuum advance unit.
5. Disconnect the deceleration valve hose and canister urge hose. Plug the hoses and remove the air cleaner assembly.
6. If equipped with A/C, turn the A/C control switch to the

AMERICAN MOTORS
CONCORD • EAGLE • EAGLE SX4 • SPIRIT

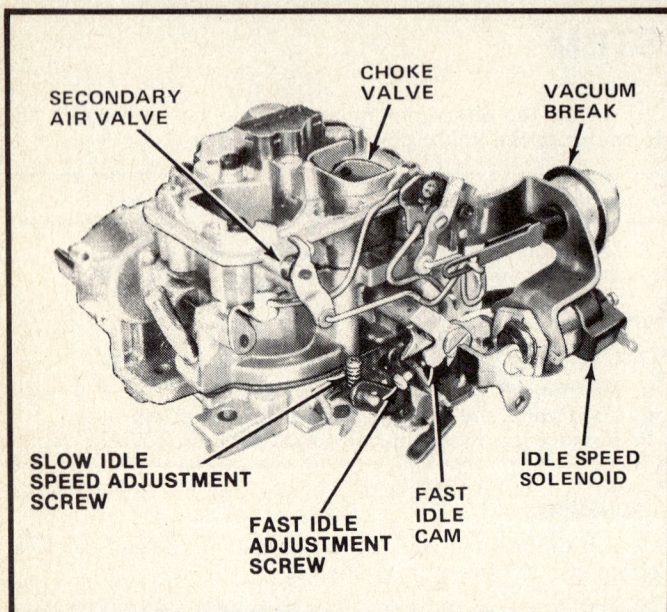

Idle speed adjustment locations, Models E2SE and 2SE carburetors (© American Motors Corp.)

ON position and open the throttle momentarily to insure the solenoid armature is fully extended. Adjust the solenoid idle speed screw to obtain the specified engine curb idle speed rpm. Turn the A/C control switch off.

7. If not equipped with A/C, energize the solenoid and adjust the engine idle speed with the solenoid idle speed screw. Disconnect the solenoid wire and adjust the curb idle speed rpm.

8. Install the carburetor air cleaner assembly and connect all hoses and connectors.

MODEL E2SE CARBURETOR

1. Connect a tachometer to the ignition coil or pigtail wire connector above the heater blower motor.
2. Disconnect and plug the vacuum hose to the distributor vacuum advance.
3. Adjust if necessary, the ignition timing with the engine at or below the specified idle speed.
4. Connect the vacuum hose to the distributor vacuum advance unit.
5. Disconnect the deceleration valve and purge hose from the vapor canister and plug the hoses. Remove the air cleaner assembly.

NOTE: The electronic fuel control system must be operated in the closed-loop mode during the idle speed adjustment. The system must be operated in the closed-loop mode when the engine heats to normal operating temperature. However, to ensure the engine is in the closed-loop mode, the use of a dwell meter is recommended.

6. Insert the dwell meter probes into terminal 6 (+) and terminal 13 (-) of the diagnosis connector. Turn the meter selector switch to the six cylinder scale.

NOTE: Step 6 is not applicable to vehicles equipped with the C-4 system.

7. The dwell meter needle should be oscillating with a 15 degree maximum sweep and the pointer should be located between the 10-50 degree range.

NOTE: If the dwell meter indicates the system is in the closed loop mode of operation, continue with the adjustment procedure. If not, the engine may not be sufficiently heated and is in the open-mode of operation.

8. If equipped with A/C, adjust the idle speed screw to obtain the specified engine rpm. Turn the A/C control switch to the ON position. Open the throttle momentarily to ensure the solenoid armature is fully extended. Adjust the solenoid idle speed screw to obtain the specified engine rpm. Turn the A/C control switch to the OFF position.

9. If not equipped with A/C, adjust the solenoid idle speed screw with the solenoid energized to obtain the correct engine idle speed. Disconnect the solenoid wire and adjust the idle speed screw to obtain the specified idle speed. Connect the solenoid wire.

MODEL YF, BBD CARBURETORS

1. Have the engine at normal operating temperature.
2. Adjust the Sol-Vac Vacuum Actuator by removing the vacuum hose to the unit. Plug the hose.
3. Adjust the idle speed by using the vacuum actuator adjustment screw on the throttle lever. This adjustment is made with all accessories off.
4. Refer to the specifications or Emission Information Label for the correct engine rpm.
5. After the vacuum actuator adjustment is completed, leave the vacuum hose plugged and disconnected.
6. Adjust the curb idle using the $\frac{1}{4}$ in. hex-headed adjustment screw on the end of the Sol-Vac unit. Adjust to specifications.

NOTE: The engine speed will vary 10-30 rpm during this mode due to being in the closed loop fuel control.

FUEL MIXTURE

Adjustment
MODEL 2SE CARBURETOR

— CAUTION —
The mixture adjustment should only be performed if the idle mixture screw was removed or replaced because of carburetor overhaul.

1. Connect a tachometer and operate the engine until normal operating temperature is reached.
2. Chock the wheels, apply the parking brake and place the A/T equipped vehicles in the D position. Place the gear selector in the N position when equipped with manual transmission.
3. Adjust the idle speed as previously outlined.
4. With an appropriate tool, turn the mixture screw clockwise (lean) until a loss of engine rpm is noted.
5. Turn the mixture screw counterclockwise (rich) until the highest engine rpm is attained.

NOTE: Do not turn the screw any further than the point at which the highest engine rpm is attained. This is referred to as the 'best lean idle'. Engine speed will increase above curb idle speed an amount that corresponds approximately to the lean drop specifications.

6. As the final adjustment, turn the idle mixture screw clockwise in increments until the specified speed drop is reached as noted on the Emission Information Label for the vehicle being serviced.

NOTE: If the final engine rpm differs more than 30 rpm plus or minus, from the original set curb idle speed, adjust the curb idle speed to the specified engine rpm and readjust as required.

MODEL E2SE CARBURETOR

— CAUTION —
The idle mixture adjustment should only be performed if the adjustment screws were removed during a carburetor overhaul procedure.

AMERICAN MOTORS
CONCORD • EAGLE • EAGLE SX4 • SPIRIT

1. Connect a tachometer and warm the engine to normal operating temperature.
2. Set the parking brake firmly and chock the wheels. Position the gear selector in neutral for standard transmission equipped vehicles and in the D position for A/T equipped vehicles.
3. Adjust the idle speed as previously outlined.
4. Adjust the idle mixture screws clockwise (lean) until a loss of engine rpm is noted.
5. Turn the mixture screws counterclockwise (rich) until the highest engine rpm indication is obtained.

NOTE: Do not turn the screws any further than the point at which the highest engine rpm is first obtained. This is referred to as 'best lean mixture'. The engine idle speed will increase above curb idle speed an amount that corresponds approximately to the idle drop specifications listed on the Emission Information Label.

6. As the final adjustment, turn the mixture screws clockwise (lean) to obtain the specified drop in engine idle rpm. Turn both idle mixture screws in small, equal amounts until the specified idle drop is achieved.

NOTE: If the final engine rpm differs more than 30 rpm plus or minus, from the original curb idle rpm, adjust the curb idle speed to specifications and repeat the adjustment procedure.

7. Install the dowel pins after completing the idle mixture adjustment. Use care to prevent disturbing the mixture screw positions.

NOTE: It is necessary to remove the carburetor to gain access to the dowel pin locations. After the carburetor has been reinstalled, again check the idle speed specifications. Correct as required.

MODEL YF, BBD CARBURETORS

1. Set the idle mixture screw to the same number of turns as noted during the disassembly.

--- CAUTION ---
The idle mixture screw must be set to the exact number of turns as noted during the disassembly.

2. Install a new tamper proof plug.

INTAKE MANIFOLD
Removal and Installation

4–150 ENGINE

1. Remove the air cleaner assembly, fuel and vacuum lines, the carburetor and the electrical connections. Remove the heat tube from the heat stove on the exhaust manifold.
2. Remove the exhaust pipe retaining bolts, supporting the pipe as it is removed. Remove the EGR tube and coolant hoses, if equipped.
3. Remove the exhaust and intake manifold retaining bolts and remove the manifold assembly.

NOTE: The exhaust and intake manifolds are two separate pieces with a gasket for the intake manifold only.

4. Install the exhaust manifold and finger tighten the center retaining bolt.
5. Position the intake gasket and install the intake manifold.
6. Tighten the intake and exhaust manifold bolts in the proper sequence to 23 ft. lbs. (31 Nm) torque.
7. Install the EGR tube, the heat tube, electrical connectors, the carburetor, the fuel and vacuum lines and remaining components.

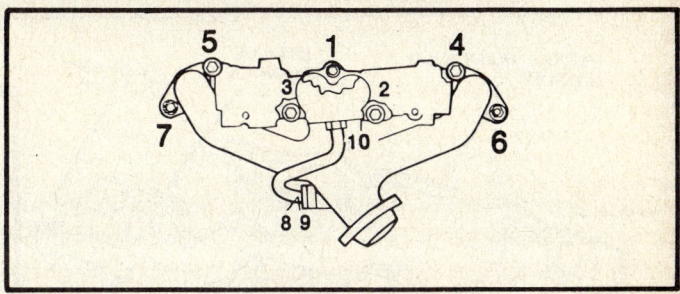

4–150 engine intake/exhaust manifold bolt tightening sequence (© American Motors Corp.)

8. Start the engine and bring to normal operating temperature. Recheck torque on manifold retaining bolts.
9. Install the air cleaner assembly.

4–151 ENGINE

1. Remove the air cleaner. Drain the cooling system. Disconnect the heater hose from the intake manifold.
2. Disconnect and label the fuel line, all vacuum lines and electrical connectors from the carburetor, insulator and the intake manifold.
3. Disconnect the throttle linkage.
4. Remove the carburetor and insulator.
5. Remove the alternator rear support bracket from the manifold.
6. Remove the A/C compressor, if so equipped.
7. Remove the intake manifold bolts and remove the manifold.
8. To install, place a new gasket against the cylinder head, then install the manifold in place by starting all bolts finger tight.
9. Torque the intake manifold bolts to 25 ft. lbs. in two stages, using the torque sequence shown. The rest of installation is the reverse of removal.

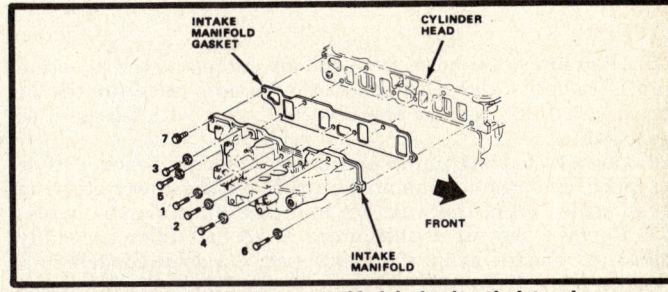

4–151 engine intake manifold bolt tightening sequence (© American Motors Corp.)

6–258 ENGINE

The intake manifold is mounted on the left-hand side of the engine and bolted to the cylinder head. A gasket is used between the intake manifold and the head; none is required for the exhaust manifold.

1. Remove the air cleaner. Disconnect the fuel line, vent hose, and solenoid wire, if equipped.
2. Disconnect the accelerator cable from the accelerator bellcrank.
3. Disconnect the PCV vacuum hose from the intake manifold and the TCS solenoid and bracket, if so equipped.
4. Remove the spark CTO switch and EGR valve (or exhaust back-pressure sensor) vacuum lines from each of these components.

1–29

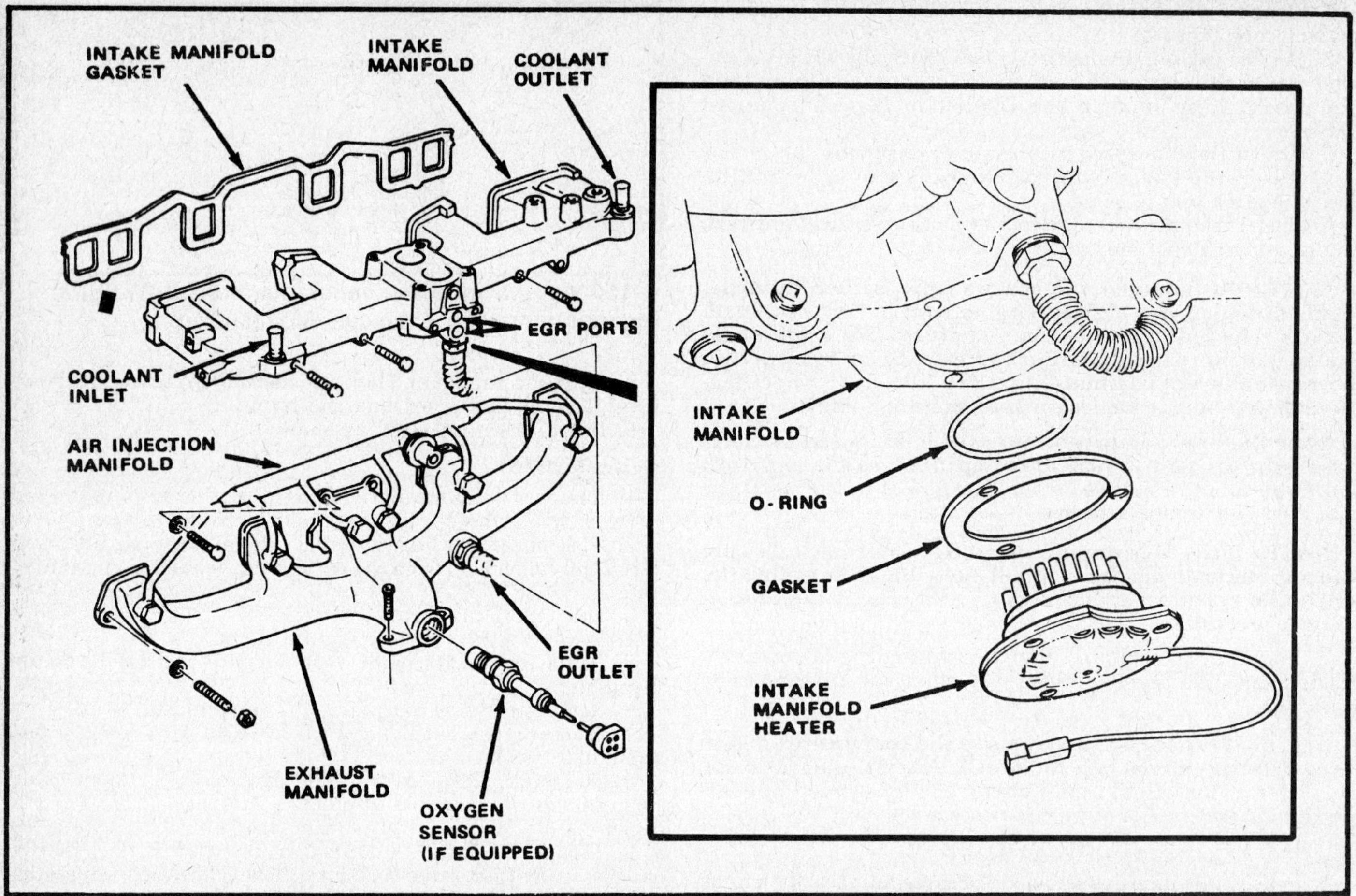

AMERICAN MOTORS
CONCORD • EAGLE • EAGLE SX4 • SPIRIT

Exploded view of 6-258 engine intake/exhaust manifold assembly with intake manifold heater (© American Motors Corp.)

5. Disconnect the hoses from the air pump and the injection manifold check valve. Disconnect the vacuum line from the diverter valve and remove the diverter valve with hoses, if so equipped.

6. Remove the air pump and power steering bracket (if so equipped) and remove the air pump. Move the power steering pump aside, out of the way, without disconnecting the hoses.

7. Remove the air conditioning drive belt idler assembly from the cylinder head, if so equipped. On some models it is necessary to remove the A/C compressor. Do not discharge the A/C system; just lay the compressor aside.

8. Disconnect the throttle valve linkage if equipped with automatic transmission.

9. Disconnect the exhaust pipe from the manifold.

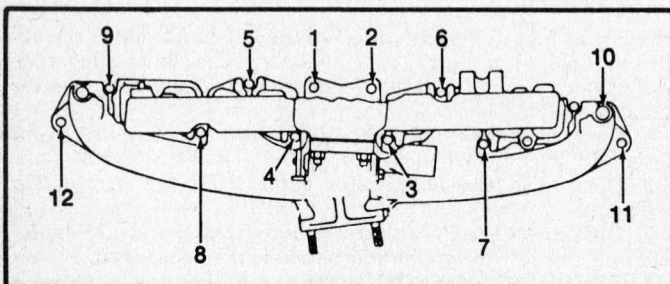

6-258 intake/exhaust manifold bolt tightening sequence (© American Motors Corp.)

10. On some models, an oxygen sensor is screwed in the exhaust manifold just above the exhaust pipe connection. Disconnect the wire and remove the sensor, if so equipped.

11. Remove the manifold attaching bolts, nuts, and clamps and remove the intake and exhaust manifolds as an assembly. Discard the gasket. The two manifolds are separated at the heat riser.

12. To install the intake and exhaust manifolds:
   a. Clean all the mating surfaces on the cylinder head and the manifolds.
   b. Assemble the two manifolds together and tighten the heat riser retaining nuts to 5 ft. lbs.
   c. Position the manifold to the engine together with a new intake manifold gasket and tighten the manifold attaching bolts and nuts in the proper sequence to the specified torque.
   d. Install the remaining components in the reverse order of removal. Adjust the automatic transmission throttle linkage, if so equipped. Adjust the drive belt(s) tension.

EXHAUST MANIFOLD
Removal and Installation

4-150 ENGINE
The exhaust manifold is removed along with the intake manifold, although both are separate pieces. Refer to the Intake Manifold Removal and Installation outline.

AMERICAN MOTORS
CONCORD • EAGLE • EAGLE SX4 • SPIRIT

4-151 ENGINE

1. Remove the air cleaner and the hot air tube.
2. Remove the Pulsair system from the exhaust manifold.
3. Disconnect the exhaust pipe from the manifold at the flange. Spray the bolts first with penetrating sealer, if necessary.
4. Remove the engine oil dipstick bracket bolt.
5. Remove the exhaust manifold bolts and remove the manifold from the head.
6. To install, place a new gasket against the cylinder head, then install the exhaust manifold over it. Start all the bolts into the head finger tight.
7. Torque the exhaust manifold bolts to 37 ft. lbs. in two stages, using the torque sequence illustrated.
8. The remainder of installation is the reverse of removal.

6-258 ENGINE

The exhaust manifold is removed along with the intake manifold; see previous instructions in the removal and installation of the Intake Manifold outline.

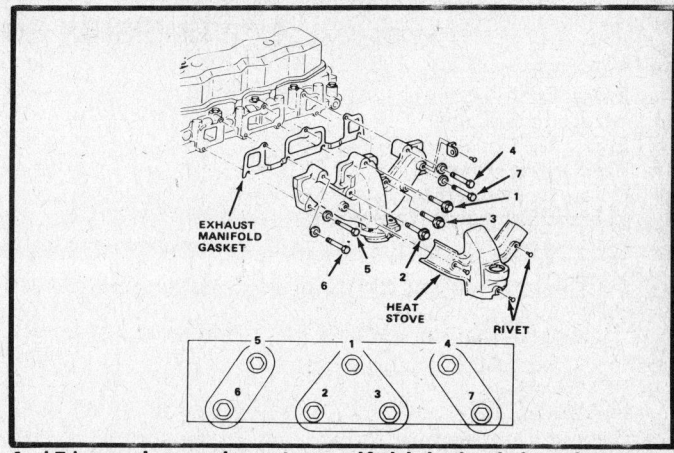

4-151 engine exhaust manifold bolt tightening sequence (© American Motors Corp.)

EMISSION CONTROL SYSTEMS

EMISSION EQUIPMENT USED

1983
Pulse Air Injection (6-258)
Air Control Valve (6-258)
Pulse Air Check Valve (6-258)
Air Switch Solenoid (6-258)
Catalytic Converter
Coolant Temperature Switch (6-258)
EGR Valve
EGR TVS Switch
Canister Purge/EGR CTO Valve
TAC System
TAC TVS (Calif. 4-151)
TAC Delay Valve and Check Valve
Ignition CTO Valve
Ignition Electronic Spark Retard (6-258)
Ignition Control Solenoid (4-151)
Ignition Delay Valve (4-151)
Carburetor Vent to Canister
Electric Choke
Sol-Vac Idle Control (6-258)
Thermal Electric Switch (6-258, Calif. 4-151)
Oxygen Sensor (6-258, Cali. 4-151)
Microprocessor (6-258, Calif. 4-151)
Vacuum Switch Assembly
Trap Door, Air Cleaner (6-258)
PCV System
PCV Solenoid (6-258)
Coolant Temperature Switch (6-258)
Knock Sensor (6-258)
Decel Valve (Calif. 6-258 w/MT, 4-151)
E-Cell Timer (Calif. 4-151)

1983½ (4-140)
Pulse Air Injection
Air Control Valve
Pulse Air Check Valve
Air Switch Solenoid
Catalytic Converter
Coolant Temperature Switch
EGR Valve
EGR TVS Switch
Canister Purge/EGR CTO Valve
TAC System
TAC TVS (Calif. 4-151)
TAC Delay Valve and Check Valve
Ignition CTO Valve
Ignition Electronic Spark Retard
Carburetor Vent to Canister
Electric Choke
Sol-Vac Idle Control
Thermal Electric Switch
Oxygen Sensor
Microprocessor
Vacuum Switch Assembly
PCV
Control Valve
Coolant Temperature Switch
Knock Sensor

1984 (4-150)
Pulse Air Injection
Air Control Valve
Pulse Air Check Valve
Air Switch Solenoid
Catalytic Converter
Coolant Temperature Switch
EGR Valve
EGR TVS Switch
Canister Purge/EGR CTO Valve
TAC System
TAC TVS (Calif. 4-151)
TAC Delay Valve and Check Valve
Ignition CTO Valve
Ignition Electronic Spark Retard
Carburetor Vent to Canister
Electric Choke
Sol-Vac Idle Control
Thermal Electric Switch
Oxygen Sensor
Microprocessor
Vacuum Switch Assembly
PCV
Control Valve
Coolant Temperature Switch
Knock Sensor

SECTION 1

AMERICAN MOTORS
CONCORD • EAGLE • EAGLE SX4 • SPIRIT

EMISSION EQUIPMENT USED

1984 (6-258)
- Pulse Air Injection
- Air Control Valve
- Pulse Air Check Valve
- Air Switch Solenoid
- Catalytic Converter
- Coolant Temperature Switch
- EGR Valve
- EGR TVS Switch
- Canister Purge/EGR CTO Valve
- TAC System
- Vacuum Switch
- Trap Door, Air Cleaner
- PCV System
- PCV Solenoid
- Coolant Temperature Switch
- Knock Sensor
- Decel Valve (Calif. w/MT)
- Oxygen Sensor
- Microprocessor
- Carburetor Vent to Canister
- Electric Choke

1985-87 (6-258)
- Pulse Air Injection
- Air Control Valve
- Pulse Air Check Valve
- Air Switch Solenoid
- Catalytic Converter
- Coolant Temperature Switch
- EGR Valve
- EGR TVS Switch
- Canister Purge/EGR CTO Valve
- TAC System
- Vacuum Switch
- Trap Door, Air Cleaner
- PCV System
- PCV Solenoid
- Coolant Temperature Switch
- Knock Sensor
- Decel Valve (Calif. w/MT)
- Oxygen Sensor
- Microprocessor
- Carburetor Vent to Canister
- Electric Choke
- Sol-Vac Idle Control Valve
- Thermal Electric Switch
- TAC Delay Valve and Check Valve
- Ignition CTO Valve
- Ignition Electronic Spark Retard

MAJOR CHANGES AFFECTING 1985 AND LATER EMISSION CONTROL SYSTEMS

ENGINE
The 4-150 CID engine has been deleted from the engine availability list for the 1985 and later Eagle models. The 6-258 CID engine is the only available power plant for the 1985 and later Eagle models.

AUTOMATIC TRANSMISSION
The lock-up torque converter has been eliminated from the model 998 automatic transmission, beginning with the 1985 model year.

FRONT DRIVE AXLE
American Motors Corporation has discontinued the use of its Disconnect-type front axle assembly, beginning with the 1985 model year.

Resetting Emission Maintenance Indicators

1983
4-151 CALIFORNIA W/ST
4-151 49 STATES W/AT

The Emission Maintenance lamp illuminates after 1,000 hours of engine operation to indicate the required replacement service of the oxygen sensor. An E-Cell timer printed circuit board must be replaced with a replacement timer. The timer is located in the passenger compartment within the wiring harness leading to the feedback system microprocessor.

NOTE: Refer to Engine section in Unit Repair for service information on the C-4 and CEC systems.

GASOLINE ENGINE SECTION

Engine Assembly

Removal and Installation

4-150 ENGINES

NOTE: The engine is removed separately from the vehicle.

1. Disconnect the battery cables and remove the battery from the engine compartment.
2. Drain the cooling system from both the engine and the radiator.
3. Match mark the hood hinges and remove the hood.
4. Disconnect the electrical wires from the alternator, the coil, distributor, oil pressure sending unit and the starter. Carefully remove the wiring harness for the CEC system.
5. Disconnect the fuel line from the front fuel pipe and plug the openings.
6. Disconnect the right front engine support cushion to bracket screw and disconnect the engine ground strap.

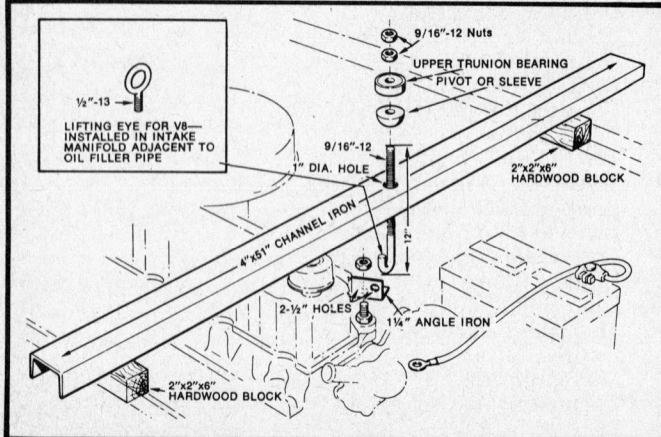

Lifting fixture can be fabricated as illustrated to facilitate oil pan and motor mount removal
(© American Motors Corp.)

AMERICAN MOTORS
CONCORD • EAGLE • EAGLE SX4 • SPIRIT

7. If equipped with air conditioning, front seat the valves and remove the compressor charge by loosening the low pressure service valve to the compressor head.
8. Remove the service valves and lay the hoses aside. Cap or plug all openings.
9. Remove the air cleaner assembly. Mark the vacuum hoses as necessary.
10. Disconnect the vacuum purge hose at the canister and disconnect the TAC vacuum hose at the intake manifold.
11. Disconnect the idle speed control solenoid wire connector and disconnect the fuel return line from the fuel filter.
12. Disconnect the carburetor bowl vent hose from the canister. Disconnect the throttle cable and remove it from the bracket.
13. If equipped, disconnect the throttle valve rod at the bellcrank.
14. Disconnect the carburetor mixture control solenoid wire connector.
15. Disconnect the oxygen sensor wire connector and remove the heater control vacuum hose from the intake manifold, if equipped.
16. Disconnect the coolant temperature sender wire connector and remove the upper and lower radiator hoses at the radiator.
17. Remove the fan shroud screws, disconnect the A/T fluid cooling pipes from the radiator and remove the radiator and shroud.
18. Remove the fan and spacer or the Tempatrol fan assembly.
19. Remove the power brake vacuum check valve from the unit, if equipped.
20. If equipped with power steering disconnect the hoses at the steering gear and drain the system.
21. Raise the vehicle and support safely. Remove the starter motor.
22. If equipped with automatic transmission, remove the converter access cover, matchmark the converter to drive plate and remove the retaining bolts.
23. If equipped with manual transmission, remove the flywheel access cover and disconnect the back-up lamp switch wiring harness at the firewall to gain access to the flywheel housing bolts.
24. Remove the engine mount cushion to bracket screws.

---- **CAUTION** ----

Both half shafts must be disconnected and the front axle assembly removed to allow engine removal. Otherwise, damage to the axle halfshafts may occur.

25. Support the axle assembly and remove the half shaft to axle flange bolts. Compress the half shafts inward towards the wheels to prevent the shafts from separating. Secure the half shafts to the frame side rail with wire.
26. Remove the bolts from the axle bracket at the axle tube and the right engine support cushion. Remove the axle bracket.
27. Remove the bolts from the axle bracket at the pinion end of the axle. Remove the bolts at the left engine support cushion to front axle bracket.
28. Disconnect the axle vent hose, lower the axle assembly and remove from under the vehicle.
29. Disconnect the exhaust pipe from the manifold. Remove the upper converter or flywheel housing bolts and loosen the bottom bolts.
30. Lower the vehicle and attach a lifting device to the engine. Raise the engine off the front supports.
31. Place a support stand under the converter or flywheel housing, remove the remaining bolts and lift the engine from the engine compartment.
32. The installation of the engine is the reverse of the removal procedure.

33. Observe the following torque specifications:
   a. Half shafts to axle bolts—45 ft. lbs.
   b. Drive plate to converter bolts—40 ft. lbs.
   c. Transmission to engine bolts—54 ft. lbs.
   d. Clutch housing to engine bolts—55 ft. lbs.

NOTE: Flywheel drive plate bolts must not be reused on four and six cylinder engines.

4-151 ENGINE
SPIRIT, CONCORD AND EAGLE

NOTE: The engine/transmission is removed as an assembly from the Spirit and Concord vehicles. The engine is removed separately from the Eagle models.

1. Disconnect the battery and remove from the engine compartment to avoid damage during the engine/transmission removal and installation.
2. Drain the cooling system, both at the radiator and the drain plug on the left rear of the engine block. Remove the air cleaner assembly.

---- **CAUTION** ----

Do not drain the cooling system if the system has not had time to cool and the pressure has not been released.

3. Remove the top and bottom radiator hoses. Disconnect the oil cooler lines, if equipped. Remove the fan and shroud. Remove the radiator.
4. If equipped with power steering, loosen the pump and remove the belt.
5. If not equipped with air conditioning, remove the alternator wiring.
6. If equipped with air conditioning, discharge the A/C system carefully and disconnect the hoses from the compressor.

NOTE: Cap the hose ends to prevent the entrance of moisture and foreign material.

7. Remove the coolant hose from the rear of the manifold and water pump.
8. Remove the throttle clip and remove the cable from the bracket.
9. On A/C equipped vehicles, disconnect the wiring harness from the alternator and pull the wiring through the tube.
10. Remove the power steering hoses from the steering gear.
11. Remove the vacuum hoses and identify for easier installation.
12. Disconnect the carburetor MC solenoid, if equipped, the choke heater, idle speed solenoid, coolant temperature sending unit and if equipped, the oxygen sensor wire connectors.
13. Disconnect the dipstick tube assembly from the exhaust manifold and pull it from the engine block.
14. Eagle Models only:
   a. Remove the left front axle to engine mount bracket attaching bolts.
   b. Raise the vehicle and support safely. Remove the splash shield.
   c. Disconnect the left and right half shafts from the front axle. Compress the half shafts inward (towards the wheels) and secure with wire to the side frame rails.
   d. Matchmark and disconnect the front drive shaft.
   e. Support the front axle with a jacking device. Disconnect the axle at the right tube support and at the pinion end of the axle. Disconnect the vent hose and remove the axle.
   f. Remove the axle support bracket from the engine block. Remove the starter and its shims from the engine.
   g. Disconnect the wires from the distributor, oil pressure sending unit and the neutral start/back-up light switch, if equipped with A/T.
   h. Disconnect the rubber fuel hose from the fuel pipe on the right frame rail.

1-33

AMERICAN MOTORS
CONCORD • EAGLE • EAGLE SX4 • SPIRIT

15. Eagle models equipped with manual transmission:
    a. Disconnect the clutch slave cylinder from the flywheel housing.
    b. Position a wood block between the transfer case and the skid plate.
    c. Remove the transmission to flywheel housing bolts.
16. Eagle models equipped with automatic transmission:
    a. Disconnect the transmission linkage pivot at the converter housing.
    b. Remove the access cover and remove the bolts to disconnect the torque converter from the drive plate after matchmarking the converter-drive plate position.
    c. Remove the converter housing to engine bolts.
    d. Disconnect the exhaust pipe at the manifold. Lower the vehicle.
    e. Connect a lifting device to the engine assembly and remove the engine mount bolts.
    f. Raise the engine slightly and remove the left engine mount bracket.
    g. Remove the engine from the vehicle.
17. Spirit and Concord models—Raise the vehicle and support safely.
18. Remove the engine mount cushion nuts at the crossmember and ground cable from the left engine cushion bracket at the cylinder block.
19. Remove the rubber fuel line at the steel line on the right frame rail.
20. Disconnect the wires from the starter assembly.
21. Disconnect the wires from the distributor and oil pressure sending unit.
22. Loosen the crossmember, lower it slightly and remove the following:
    a. ATF cooler pipes, if equipped, and the speedometer cable at the transmission.
    b. Transmission linkage and neutral start/back-up lamp switch wiring.
    c. Remove the transmission rear mount.
23. Remove the crossmember.
24. Remove the exhaust pipe to manifold retaining nuts. Secure the exhaust pipe to the strut rod bushing with wire. Disconnect the catalytic converter support bracket from the transmission.
25. Matchmark the drive shaft rear universal joint caps and remove the shaft.
26. Lower the vehicle and attach a lifting device to the engine.
27. Raise and remove the engine/transmission assembly from the vehicle. Separate the engine from the transmission after the assembly has been secured of the shop floor or holding tool.
28. The installation of the engine (Eagle) or engine/transmission assembly (Spirit and Concord) is in the reverse of the removal procedure.
29. The following torques must be observed:
    a. Converter to drive plate 40 ft. lbs.
    b. A/T converter housing to engine bolts 28 ft. lbs.
    c. M/T flywheel housing to engine bolts 54 ft. lbs.

NOTE: Flywheel drive plate bolts must not be reused on four and six cylinder engines.

30. Evacuate and charge the air conditioning system.
31. Be sure the fluid levels are correct before starting the engine. Recheck after the engine has reached normal operating temperature.

ENGINE REMOVAL
6-258—ALL MODELS

NOTE: The engine is removed separately from the transmission.

1. Drain the coolant from the engine and radiator.

— **CAUTION** —
Do not drain the cooling system until the coolant has cooled and the system pressure has been released.

2. Scribe the hood hinge locations and remove the hood.
3. Disconnect the battery cables and remove the battery to avoid damage during the engine removal and installation.
4. Disconnect the wiring from the distributor, coil, distributor and the oil pressure sending switch.
5. Remove the vacuum switch assembly bracket from the cylinder head cover.
6. Disconnect the front fuel pipe from the fuel pump and insert a plug into the pipe.
7. Disconnect the right engine ground strap and remove the right front engine support cushion to bracket bolt.
8. If the vehicle is equipped with air conditioning, release the compressor charge after front seating the valves. Cap all openings. Disconnect the compressor clutch wire.
9. Remove the cable from the starter motor.
10. Remove the air cleaner assembly. Tag hoses as necessary.
11. Disconnect the idle speed control solenoid wire connector, the fuel return hose from the fuel filter and the carburetor bowl vent hose from the canister.
12. Disconnect the throttle cable and remove from the bracket. Disconnect the throttle rod, if equipped. Disconnect the throttle rod at the bellcrank. Disconnect the stepper motor wire connector and oxygen sensor wire connector, if equipped.
13. If equipped, disconnect the heater control vacuum hose from the manifold and disconnect the temperature sending gauge wire connector.
14. Disconnect the upper and lower radiator hoses, the coolant hoses from the rear of the manifold and the thermostat housing.
15. Remove the fan shroud screws, disconnect the A/T oil cooler pipe fittings from the radiator, if equipped. Remove the radiator and the shroud.
16. Remove the fan assembly from the hub.
17. Remove the power brake vacuum check valve, if equipped.
18. If the vehicle is equipped with power steering, disconnect the hoses from the steering gear fittings and drain the system.
19. Remove the A/T filler tube, if equipped.
20. Raise the vehicle and support safely. Remove the starter motor.
21. If equipped with automatic transmission, remove the converter access plate, matchmark the converter to the drive plate and remove the converter to drive plate bolts. Remove the exhaust pipe support brace from the converter housing.

NOTE: This brace also supports the inner end of the transmission linkage.

22. If equipped with manual transmission, remove the flywheel access cover and the clutch release bellcrank inner support screws. Disconnect the springs and remove the clutch release bellcrank. Remove the outer bellcrank to throw-out lever rod bracket retainer. Disconnect the back-up lamp switch wire harness under the hood at the firewall for access to the flywheel housing bolts.
23. Remove the engine mount cushion to bracket screws.
24. Eagle models only:

— **CAUTION** —
Both half shafts must be disconnected and the front axle assembly removed to allow engine removal. Otherwise the half shafts could be damaged during the engine removal and installation procedures.

   a. Support the axle assembly.
   b. Remove the half shaft to axle flange bolts and compress

American Motors
CONCORD • EAGLE • EAGLE SX4 • SPIRIT

the half shafts inward (towards the wheels) to prevent the shafts from separating. Wire the shafts to the frame rails.

  c. Remove the bolts from the axle bracket at the axle tube and the right engine support cushion. Remove the axle bracket.

  d. Remove the bolts from the axle bracket at the pinion end of the axle.

  e. Remove the bolts at the left engine support cushion to front axle bracket.

  f. Remove the axle vent hose and lower the axle assembly and remove to allow oil pan clearance.

25. Disconnect the exhaust pipe from the manifold, loosen the upper converter or flywheel housing to engine bolts and loosen the bottom bolts. Lower the vehicle.

26. Remove the A/C compressor idler pulley and the mounting bracket, if equipped.

27. Attach a lifting device to the engine and raise the engine off the front supports. Place a support stand under the converter or flywheel housing and remove the remaining bolts.

28. Remove the engine assembly from the engine compartment.

29. The installation of the engine assembly is the reverse of the removal procedure.

30. The following torques must be observed:
  a. Drive plate to converter bolts 22 ft. lbs.
  b. Converter housing to engine bolts 54 ft. lbs.
  c. Half shafts to axle 45 ft. lbs.

NOTE: Flywheel drive plate bolts must not be reused on four and six cylinder engines.

ENGINE MOUNTS

Removal and Installation

To remove either the front or rear engine/transmission mounts, the weight of the engine must be removed from mount and bracket. It may be necessary to remove other components to expose the retaining bolts of the particular mount being changed. The use of wooden blocks to insulate the engine from direct contact with the lifting tool, is advised.

--- CAUTION ---
Block the engine to mount bracket or crossmember while the engine mount is loose or out to avoid accidental dropping of the engine side.

Valve System

HYDRAULIC VALVE TAPPETS

The 4-150, 4-151 and 6-258 engines use hydraulic valve tappets, eliminating the need for valve lash adjustment. The tappet plunger is positioned to a pre-set dimension when the valve train is bolted into place, allowing for noiseless operation of the valve system.

VALVE ROCKER ASSEMBLIES

Removal and Installation

4-150, 6-258 ENGINES

1. Remove the engine top cover, marking the vacuum hoses and electrical connections as required.

2. Remove the bolts at each bridge and pivot assembly. Alternately loosen each bolt one turn at a time to avoid damaging the bridges.

3. Remove the bridges, pivots and corresponding pairs of rocker arms and keep them in the order of removal.

4. The installation is the reverse of the removal procedure, with special emphasis on installing the components into their original positions.

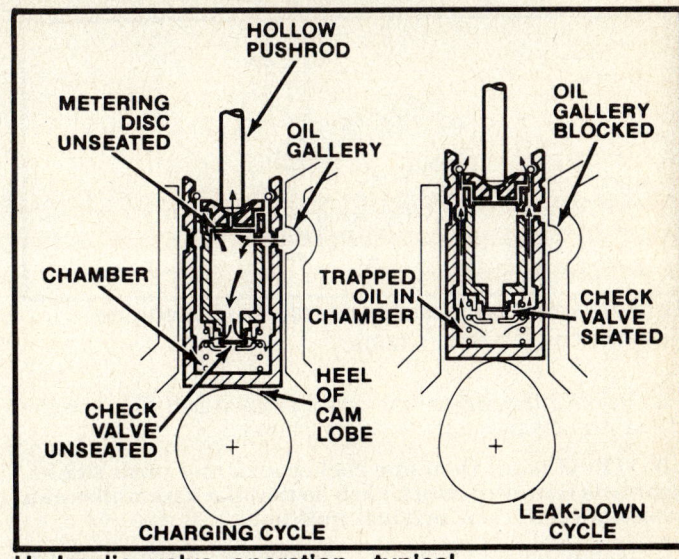

Hydraulic valve operation—typical
(© American Motors Corp.)

5. At each bridge, tighten the bolts alternately one turn at a time, to avoid damage to the bridge. Tighten the bolts to 19 ft. lbs. with a re-torque of 16-26 ft. lbs.

Removal and Installation

4-151 ENGINE

1. Remove the cylinder head cover, marking the vacuum hoses and electrical connections as required.

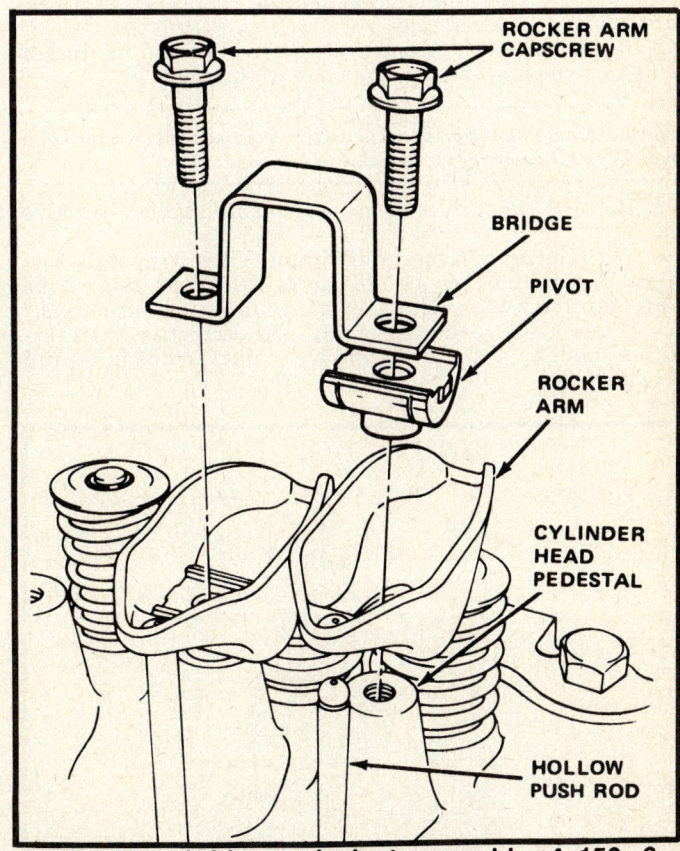

Rocker arm, bridge and pivot assembly, 4-150, 6-258 engine models (© American Motors Corp.)

1-35

American Motors
CONCORD • EAGLE • EAGLE SX4 • SPIRIT

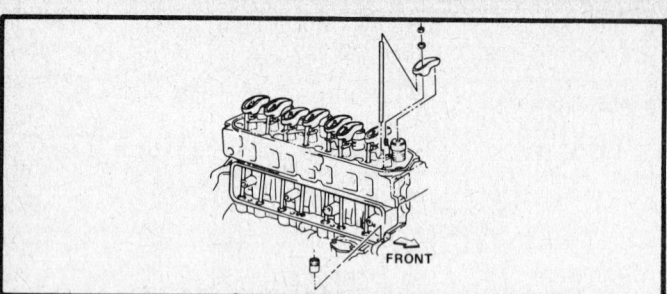

Rocker arms and components, 4-151 engine
(© American Motors Corp.)

2. Remove the rocker arm bolt and pivot ball. Remove the rocker arm, push rod guide and push rod.

NOTE: If more than one rocker arm and push rod assembly is removed, mark each so that the assemblies can be installed in their original positions.

3. Install the assemblies in the reverse of their removal procedure.
4. Tighten the rocker arm bolt to 20 ft. lbs. of torque.
5. Complete the assembly of the cylinder head cover and components.

VALVE TAPPETS
Removal and Installation
4-150 MODEL

1. Remove the cylinder head cover and related components. Tag vacuum hoses and electrical wiring connectors as necessary for easier installation.
2. Remove the bridge and pivot assemblies and the rocker arms by removing the two bolts at each bridge.

----- CAUTION -----
To avoid damaging the bridge, alternately loosen each bolt a turn at a time. Keep all components in order as removed.

3. Remove the push rods, keeping them in their respective order.
4. With the use of a special Hydraulic Valve Tappet Removal and Installation tool, J-1884 or its equivalent, remove the tappets through the push rod openings in the cylinder head.
5. While keeping the tappets in their respective order, examine each to determine the wear pattern of bore and camshaft.

Removing tappets with special tappet remover tool, typical (© American Motors Corp.)

6. To install, dip each tappet in AMC Engine Oil Supplement or its equivalent.

NOTE: It is not necessary to charge each tappet assembly with engine oil, as they will charge themselves within a short period of engine operating.

7. Install the pushrods, the rocker arms and bridges in their respective locations.
8. Tighten the bolts in the bridges alternately, one turn at a time, to avoid damaging the bridge. The service set-to torque is 19 ft. lbs. with a recheck torque of 16 to 26 ft. lbs.
9. Complete the assembly with the installation of the top engine cover.
10. Pour the remaining EOS over the entire valve actuating assembly.

NOTE: The EOS must remain with the engine oil for at least 1000 miles before draining.

Removal and Installation
4-151, 6-258 ENGINES

1. Remove the cylinder head cover, the intake manifold and pushrod cover. Refer to the appropriate outline for the removal and installation procedure.
2. Loosen the rocker arm capscrew and rotate the rocker arm for access clearance to the push rod.
3. Remove the push rod, keeping in its respective order. Remove the tappet, using Hydraulic Valve Tappet Removal tool, J-3049 or its equivalent.
4. Dip each tappet in Engine Oil Supplement and install into the engine block.
5. Install the push rods, the push rod guides, rocker arms and pivot balls.
6. With each tappet on the heel of the cam lobe, tighten the rocker arm bolts to 20 ft. lbs.
7. Install the push rod cover, the intake manifold and the cylinder head cover.

Removal and Installation
6-258 ENGINE

1. Remove the cylinder head cover, the bridge and pivot assemblies, and rocker arms.

NOTE: To avoid damaging the bridges, alternately loosen each bridge bolt one turn at a time.

2. Remove the push rods, keeping them in their respective order.
3. Remove the cylinder head assembly and manifolds.

NOTE: Refer to the appropriate outline for the removal and installation procedure.

4. Remove the tappets from the engine block, through the push rod openings, with Hydraulic Valve Tappet Removal and Installation Tool, J-21884 or its equivalent. Retain the tappets in their respective removed order.
5. To install the tappets, dip each into AMC Engine Oil Supplement or its equivalent. Using the Tappet Removal and Installation Tool, install the tappets into the bores.

NOTE: Install the used tappets into their original bores.

6. Install the cylinder head assembly onto the engine block, using a new head gasket. Install the manifolds, if removed separately. Refer to the Cylinder Head Removal and Installation Procedure for head bolt tightening torque and sequence.
7. Install the push rods into their original positions and install the rocker arms and bridges and the pivot assemblies. Tighten the bridge bolts one turn at a time, alternately, to avoid damaging the bridges.

8. Pour the remaining EOS over the valve train.

NOTE: The EOS must remain with the engine oil for at least 1000 miles before draining.

9. Install the cylinder head cover and complete the assembly as required.

ENGINE VALVE TIMING

4-150, 6-258 ENGINES

1. Remove the spark plugs from the cylinders.
2. Remove the cylinder head cover, marking the vacuum hoses and electrical connections for ease of installation.
3. Remove the bridge and pivot assembly from the number one cylinder, along with the rocker arms.
4. Rotate the crankshaft in the direction of normal rotation, until the number four (4) cylinder piston (4-150 engine) or the number six (6) cylinder piston (6-258 engine) is at top dead center (TDC), on its compression stroke.
5. As viewed from the front of the engine, rotate the crankshaft 90 degrees counterclockwise.
6. Install a dial indicator stem on the end of the number one cylinder intake push rod, using a piece of rubber tubing to secure it to the push rod.
7. Set the dial indicator pointer to the ZERO position. Rotate the crankshaft clockwise until the dial indicator pointer indicates 0.012 in. travel or push rod lift.
8. The timing notch on the crankshaft pulley should be aligned with the TDC indicator mark on the timing degree scale.
9. If the timing notch is more than ½ in. away from the TDC mark, in either direction, the valve timing is incorrect.

NOTE: If the valve timing is incorrect, the cause may be a broken camshaft pin. It is not necessary to replace the camshaft due to this failure, since new spring pins are available for service replacement.

4-151

The manufacturer's recommended procedure for valve timing has not been established.

Cylinder Head

CYLINDER HEAD COVER

Removal and Installation

4-150 ENGINE

1. Remove the air cleaner assembly and the PCV moulded hose.
2. Disconnect the fuel pipe at the fuel pump to allow clearance for cover removal.
3. Disconnect the PCV valve from the cover grommet. Disconnect the PCV valve shut-off valve vacuum hose.
4. Mark and remove all the necessary vacuum and electrical components, wires or hoses to allow removal of the cover.
5. Remove the retaining bolts from the cover. Pry the cover from the cylinder head at the pry ramps that are identified by the words "PRY HERE".
6. Install the cover with either a standard gasket or a bead of RTV sealant. Torque the retaining bolts to 55 inch lbs.
7. Complete the assembly in the reverse of the removal procedure.

Removal and Installation

4-151 ENGINE

1. Remove the air cleaner assembly, the PCV valve and hose.

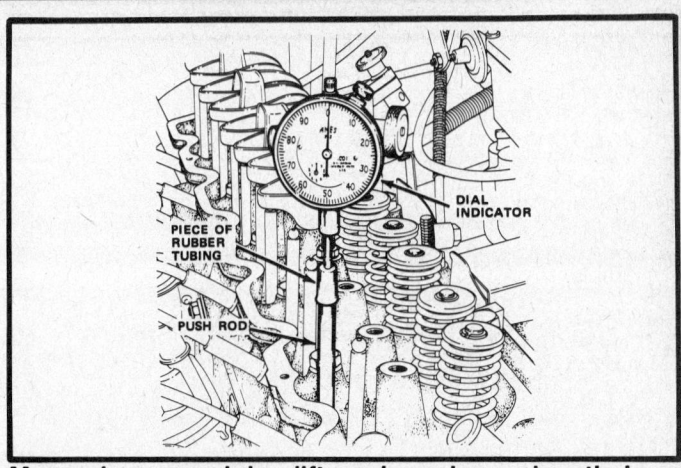

Measuring cam lobe lift and engine valve timing with dial indicator, 4-150 and 6-258 engines (© American Motors Corp.)

2. Remove the cover retaining bolts, the spark plug wires and retainers.
3. Remove the cover assembly by tapping it with a rubber hammer to loosen the RTV sealant.

——————— **CAUTION** ———————

Do not pry on the cover.

4. To install the cover, install a bead of RTV sealant on the cover to form the gasket.
5. Install the cover in the reverse of its removal procedure. Torque the bolts to 80 inch lbs.

Removal and Installation

6-258 ENGINE

1. Remove the air cleaner and the PCV valve moulded hose.
2. Disconnect the distributor vacuum advance hose from the CTO valve. Disconnect the fuel line at the fuel pump.
3. Disconnect the PCV valve from the cover rubber grommet and disconnect the PCV shutoff valve vacuum hose.
4. Remove the vacuum switch and bracket assembly, the diverter valve and bracket and the necessary vacuum hoses and electrical connections to provide clearance for cover removal.
5. Remove the cover retaining bolts and detach the cover from the cylinder head with the use of a putty knife or a razor blade.

——————— **CAUTION** ———————

Do not pry the cover upward until the seal has been completely broken. Cover distortion can occur.

6. If the cover cannot be removed due to dash panel (firewall) interference, remove the fan shroud retaining bolts and allow the shroud to rest on the fan.
7. Raise the vehicle and support safely. Support the crossmember and loosen the front crossmember bolts and nuts approximately five turns.

——————— **CAUTION** ———————

Do not remove the nuts and bolts.

8. Lower the crossmember and rotate the cover to the left and remove it from the engine compartment.
9. To install the cover, RTV sealant must be used. The cover and sealant must be installed on the cylinder head before the sealant begins to set up.
10. Install the cover retaining bolts and torque to 28 inch lbs.

SECTION 1

AMERICAN MOTORS
CONCORD • EAGLE • EAGLE SX4 • SPIRIT

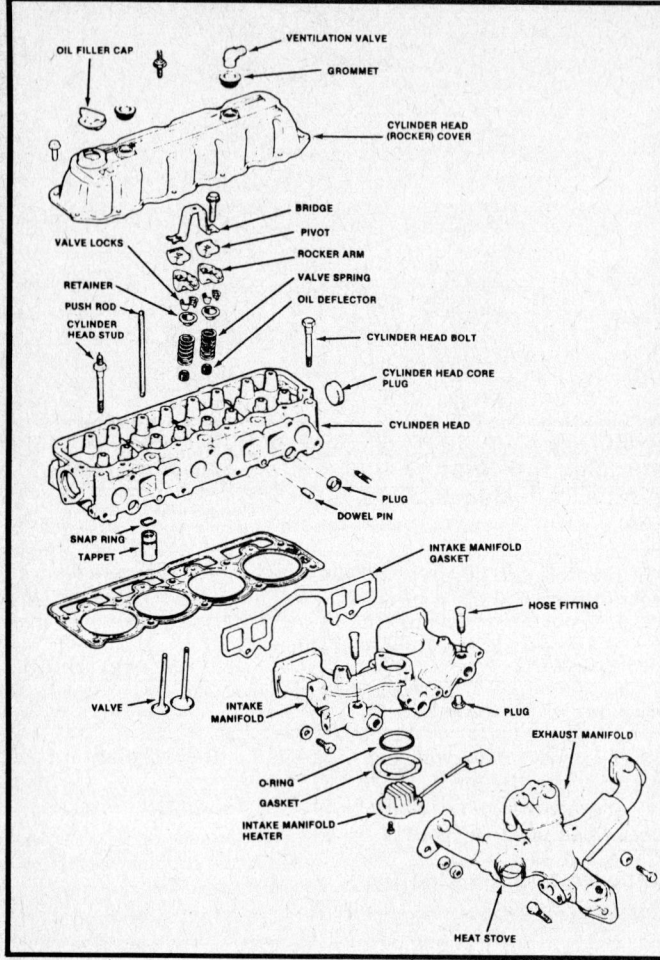

Exploded view of 4-150 engine cylinder head
(© American Motors Corp.)

11. Complete the installation of the cover in the reverse of the removal procedure.

CYLINDER HEAD

Removal and Installation

4-150, 6-258 ENGINES

1. Disconnect the negative battery cable.
2. After the cooling system has cooled, drain the engine block and the radiator. Disconnect the hoses at the thermostat housing.

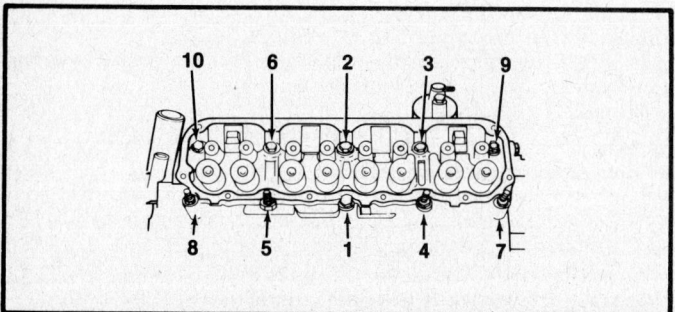

4-150 engine cylinder head bolt tightening sequence (© American Motors Corp.)

3. Remove the air cleaner and its components.
4. Remove the cylinder head cover. Refer to the cover removal and installation procedure as previously outlined.
5. Alternately loosen the bridge and rocker arm pivot bolts, one turn at a time, to prevent damage to the bridges. Remove the push rods.

NOTE: Keep the push rods, bridges, pivots and rocker arms in their order of removal for ease of installation.

6. Without disconnecting the hoses, disconnect the power steering pump bracket and set the assembly aside.
7. Remove the intake and exhaust manifolds from the cylinder head.
8. If equipped with Air Conditioning, complete the following:
   a. Remove the A/C compressor drive belt.
   b. Loosen the alternator belt and remove the A/C compressor/alternator bracket-to-head mounting bolt.
   c. 6-258 engines, remove the bolts from the air compressor and set the compressor aside.

NOTE: The 6-258 engine serpentine drive belt tension is released by loosening the alternator.

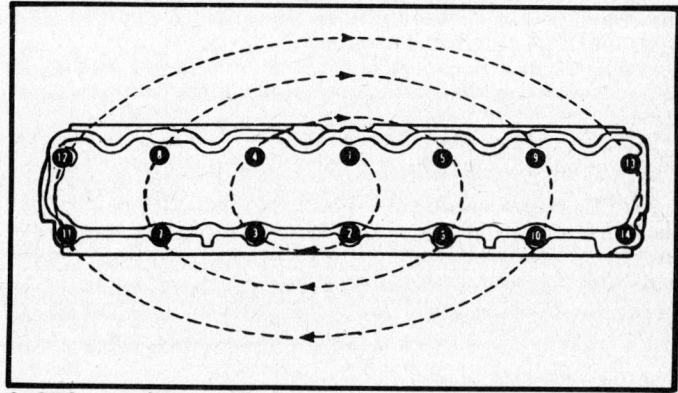

6-258 engine cylinder head bolt tightening sequence (© American Motors Corp.)

9. Remove the spark plugs, disconnect the temperature sending wire connector and the negative battery cable. Remove the ignition coil and bracket.
10. Remove the cylinder head bolts and remove the cylinder head from the engine block.
11. After cleaning, inspection and overhaul, the cylinder head can be installed in the reverse order of its removal.
12. Apply an even coat of Perfect Seal sealing compound, or its equivalent, to both sides of the replacement head gasket. Position the gasket on the cylinder block with the work 'TOP' facing upward.

CAUTION

Do not apply sealing compound on the cylinder head or engine block gasket surfaces. Do not allow sealer to enter the cylinder bores.

13. 4-150 engines—coat the threads of the left front (number 8 in the tightening sequence) with Loctite 592 sealant, or its equivalent. Tighten this bolt to 75 ft. lbs. torque.
14. Tighten the remaining 4-150 engine cylinder head bolts and all the cylinder head bolts of the 6-258 engine to 85 ft. lbs. torque.

NOTE: The cylinder head gasket is made of an aluminum coated embossed steel and does not require retorquing of the cylinder head bolts.

15. During the completion of the cylinder head installation, torque the bridge bolts to 19 ft. lbs., turning each, alternately,

American Motors
CONCORD • EAGLE • EAGLE SX4 • SPIRIT

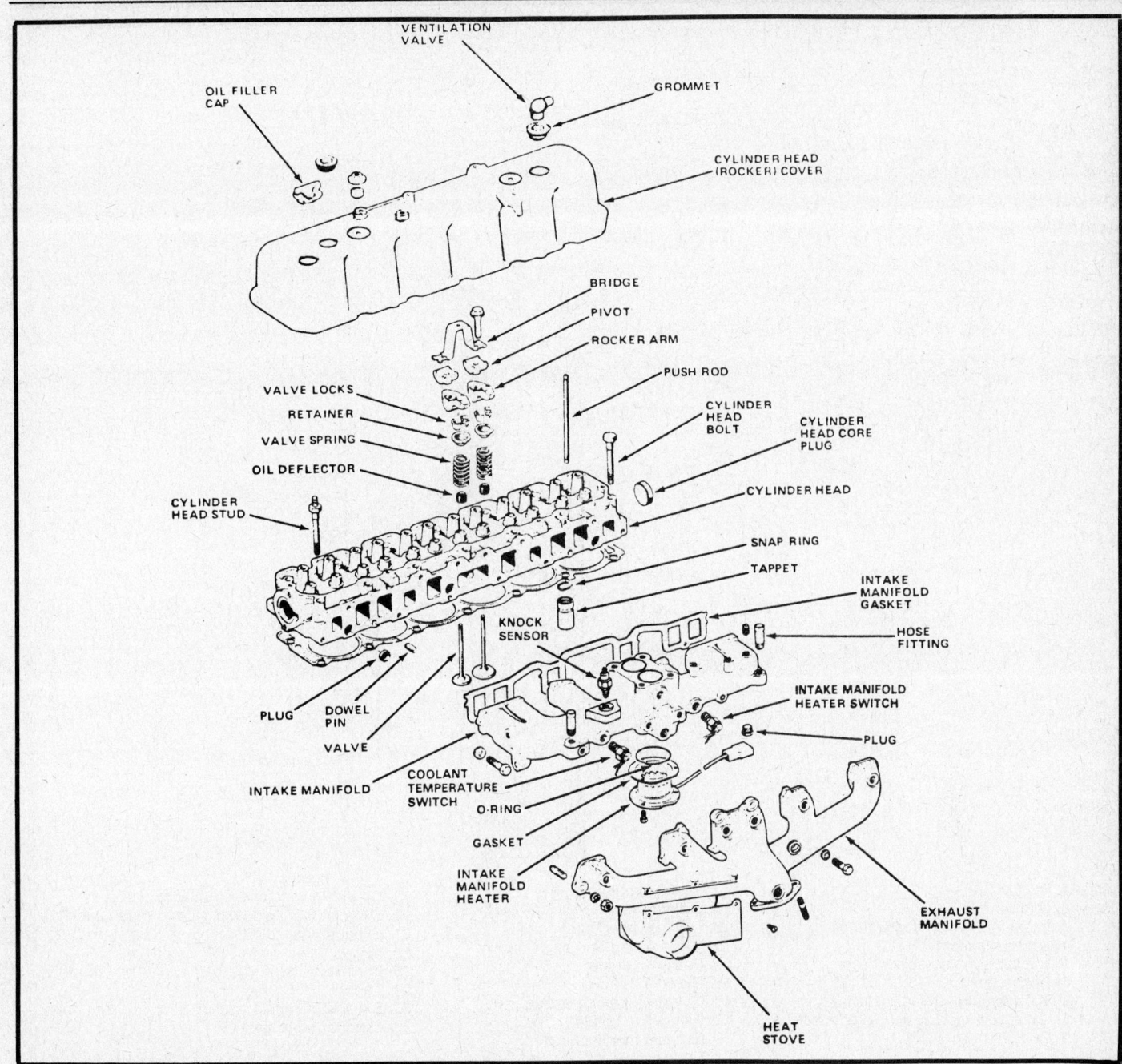

Exploded veiw of 6-258 engine cylinder head (© American Motors Corp.)

one turn at a time until the specified torque has been reached. Torque the cylinder head cover retaining bolts to 55 inch lbs. on the 4-150 engines and 28 inch lbs. on the 6-258 engines.

Removal and Installation

4-151 ENGINE

1. Disconnect the negative battery cable.
2. Remove the cylinder head cover. Refer to the previously outlined procedure.
3. After the engine cooling system has cooled, drain both the radiator and the engine block.
4. Disconnect the exhaust pipe from the exhaust manifold.
5. Remove the vacuum hoses and tag each for easier instal-

lation. Remove the air pump and/or A/C compressor, if equipped, and set aside. Note the position of spacers and brackets for installation ease.

NOTE: Do not disconnect the A/C hoses.

6. Disconnect the fuel line at the carburetor. Position pipe to allow cylinder head removal and installation.
7. Remove the upper radiator hose. Remove the rear coolant hose from the intake manifold.
8. Loosen the alternator belt on A/C equipped vehicles and swing the alternator to allow clearance for the power steering pump removal.
9. Remove the power steering pump and bracket assembly.

1-39

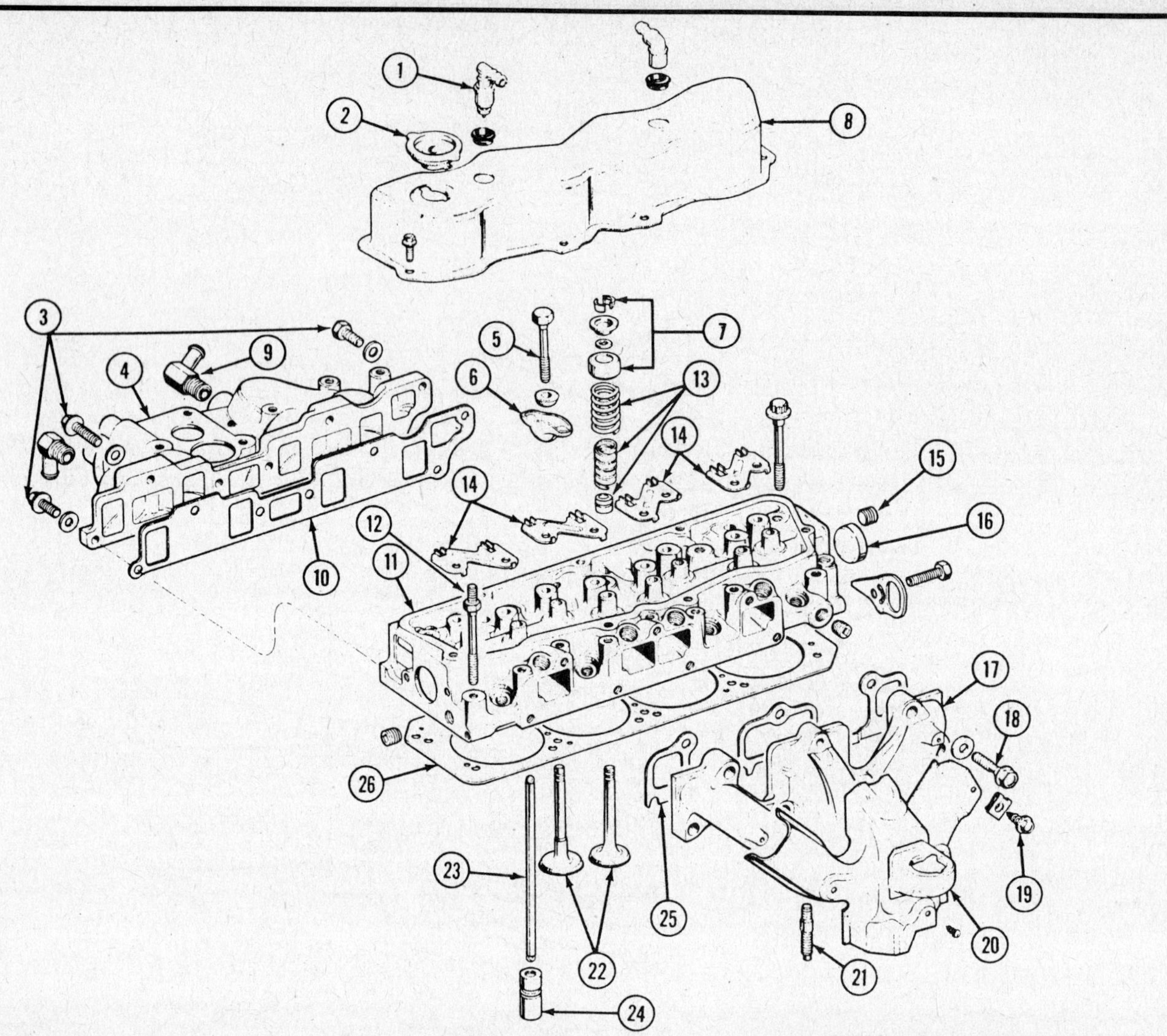

AMERICAN MOTORS
CONCORD • EAGLE • EAGLE SX4 • SPIRIT

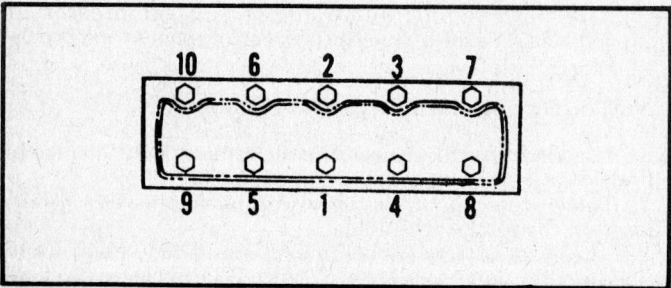

1. PCV Valve
2. Oil filler cap
3. Intake manifold attaching bolts
4. Intake manifold
5. Rocker arm cap screw
6. Rocker arm
7. Valve spring retainer assembly
8. Cylinder head cover (rocker cover)
9. Coolant hose fitting
10. Intake manifold gasket
11. Cylinder head
12. Cylinder head stud bolt
13. Valve spring and oil deflector
14. Push rod guide
15. Cylinder head plug
16. Cylinder head core plug
17. Exhaust manifold
18. Exhaust manifold bolt
19. Oil level indicator tube attaching screw
20. Exhaust manifold heat shroud (heat shield)
21. Exhaust manifold to exhaust pipe stud
22. Valves
23. Push rod
24. Tappet
25. Exhaust manifold gasket
26. Cylinder head gasket

Exploded view of 4–151 engine cylinder head (© American Motors Corp.)

4–151 engine cylinder head bolt tightening sequence (© American Motors Corp.)

NOTE: Do not disconnect the hoses from the power steering pump.

10. Remove the dipstick, the rocker arm assemblies and the push rods. If the rocker arms and push rods are to be used again, keep them in their respective order.
11. Remove the metric cylinder head bolts. Remove the cylinder head by inserting a pry bar into the A/C compressor, if equipped, or the alternator bracket and prying upward.
12. During the installation of the cylinder head, dowel pins should be used to guide the head into place, avoiding damage to the cylinder head gasket.
13. Tighten the cylinder head bolts to a final torque of 92 ft. lbs.

AMERICAN MOTORS
CONCORD • EAGLE • EAGLE SX4 • SPIRIT

14. Tighten the rocker arm capscrews to a torque of 20 ft. lbs.
15. Tighten the cylinder head cover to 80 inch lbs. torque.

CRANKSHAFT VIBRATION DAMPER PULLEY HUB

Removal
ALL ENGINES

1. Remove the drive belts.
2. 4-151 Engine—Remove the metric center bolt and slide the damper pulley and hub from the crankshaft.
3. 4-150, 6-258 Engines—Remove the retaining bolts and remove the vibration damper pulley from the vibration damper. Remove the vibration damper retaining bolt and washer (metric on 4-150 engine). Using a special puller tool, remove the damper from the crankshaft.

NOTE: Due to different lengths of puller tool bolts, it may be necessary to loosen and raise the radiator to gain working area. Avoid damage to the radiator core, if any way possible.

Installation

1. Align the key slot of the vibration damper hub with the crankshaft key and tap the damper onto the crankshaft.
2. 4-151 Engine—Install and tighten the retaining bolt to a torque of 160 ft. lbs.
3. 4-150, 6-258 Engines—Install and tighten the retaining bolt to a torque of 90 ft. lbs. Install the damper pulley and retaining bolts. Tighten the bolts to 20 ft. lbs. torque.
4. Install the belts and tighten to specified tensions.

TIMING CASE COVER OIL SEAL

Removal and Installation

1. Remove the vibration damper assembly as previously outlined.
2. The oil seal can be pryed from the timing gear cover on the 4-151 engines, being careful not to distort the sheet metal of the cover.
3. A seal removing tool is available to remove the seal from the timing gear cover on the 4-150 and 6-258 engines.
4. 4-151 Engine—To install the seal, place the helical lip towards the rear of the engine and drive the seal into place with a seal installer tool.
5. 4-150, 6-258 Engines—To install the seal, apply a light coat of perfect seal sealant, or its equivalent, on the outside diameter of the seal. Position a seal installer tool and the seal over the end of the crankshaft and, using the threads on the crankshaft end, draw the seal into its bore in the cover.

NOTE: If the above type of seal installer is not available, the seal can be carefully driven into place with the driver type seal installer.

6. Complete the assembly by installing the vibration damper and adjusting the belts.

TIMING GEAR COVER

Removal
4-151 ENGINE

1. Remove the battery negative cable.
2. Remove the vibration damper as previously outlined.
3. Remove the fan assembly and shroud retaining bolts. Loosen the belts, remove the fan and shroud.
4. If equipped with A/C, loosen the compressor idler pulley and position it to allow working space.

NOTE: Considering the radiator's vulnerability to damage, it is a good practice to either cover the core area, raise the assembly or remove it from the vehicle completely.

5. Remove the oil pan-to-timing gear cover retaining screws. Pull the cover forward just enough to permit cutting of the oil pan front oil seal flush with the engine block at both sides of the cover.
6. Remove the cover and the attached part of the oil pan front oil seal.
7. Remove and clean the gasket surfaces.

Installation

1. Install new oil seal into the timing cover seal bore.
2. Cut the tabs from the replacement oil pan front seal. Install the front oil seal on the timing gear cover and press the tips of the seal into the holes provided in the cover.
3. Coat the cover gasket with gasket sealant and place in position. Apply a bead of RTV sealant to the joint formed at the oil pan and the engine block.
4. Install a timing cover alignment tool into the cover oil seal and install the cover onto the oil pan and engine block. Install and partially tighten two oil pan to timing cover bolts. Install the remaining bolts and tighten the cover-to-engine bolts to 80 inch lbs. Tighten the front oil pan bolts to 45 inch lbs. Remove the cover aligning tool.
5. Complete the assembly of the components and tighten the belts to their specified tensions.

Removal
4-150, 6-258 ENGINES

1. Remove the drive belts, engine fan and hub assembly, vibration damper, pulley and woodruff key.

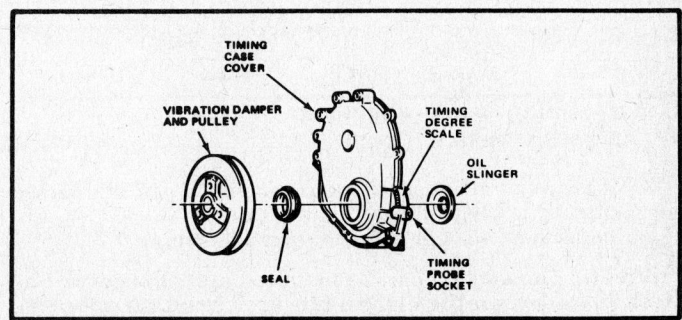

Typical timing case assembly—6-258 engine
(© American Motors Corp.)

NOTE: Considering the radiator's vulnerability to damage, it is a good practice to either cover the core area, raise the assembly or remove it from the vehicle completely.

2. 4-150 Engines—Remove the A/C compressor and alternator bracket, if equipped.
3. Remove the oil pan-to-cover bolts and the cover-to-engine block bolts.
4. Remove the front cover assembly from the engine.
5. Cut off the oil pan side gasket end tabs flush with the front face of the cylinder block and remove the gasket tabs.
6. Remove the oil seal from the timing cover and clean all gasket material from the sealing surface.

Installation

1. Apply sealant to both sides of the gasket and install on the cover sealing surface.

1-41

AMERICAN MOTORS
CONCORD • EAGLE • EAGLE SX4 • SPIRIT

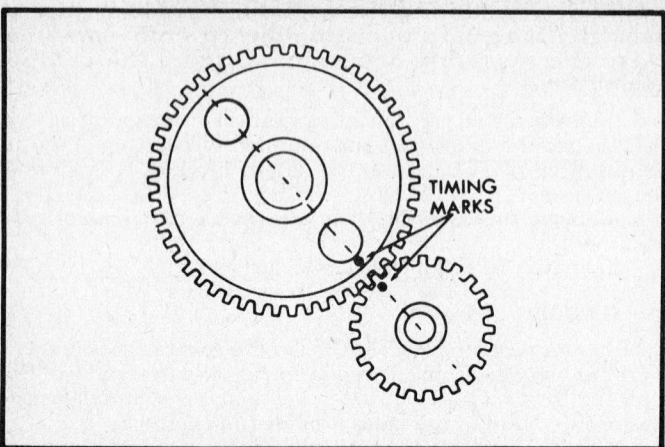

4-151 engine timing mark alignment
(© American Motors Corp.)

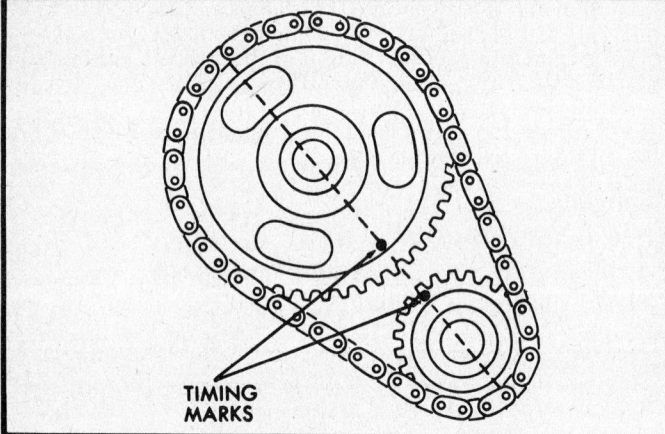

6 cyl – timing mark alignment
(© American Motors Corp.)

2. Cut the end tabs from the replacement eagle oil pan side gasket and cement the tabs on the oil pan.
3. Install new oil seal into the cover assembly.

NOTE: The oil seal can be installed after the cover has been installed on the engine block, depending upon the cover aligning tools available.

4. Coat the front cover seal end tab recesses with RTV sealant and position the seal on the cover bottom.
5. Position the cover on the engine block and position an alignment tool into the crankshaft opening.

NOTE: Two types of alignment tools are available, without seal in housing or with seal in housing.

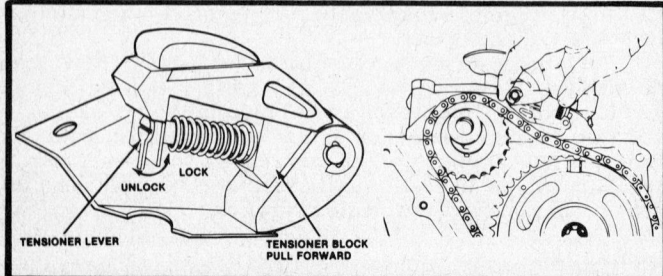

4-150 engine timing chain tensioner assembly
(© American Motors Corp.)

6. Install the cover-to-engine block bolts and the oil pan-to-cover bolts. Tighten the cover-to-engine block bolts to 5 ft. lbs. torque and the oil pan-to-cover bolts to 11 ft. lbs. torque.
7. Install the seal, if not done previously.
8. Complete the assembly of the vibration damper with key, fan and hub assembly, belts and properly adjust, and remaining components.

TIMING GEARS

Removal and Installation

4-151 ENGINE

Two gears are used to facilitate the timing between the crankshaft and the cam shaft components. To replace the camshaft gear, the camshaft must be removed from the engine. Refer to the Camshaft Removal and Installation for this procedure.

1. The camshaft gear is pressed onto the camshaft. A press is needed to remove the old gear and to install the new gear.
2. With the old gear pressed off the camshaft, place the gear spacer ring and the thrust plate over the end of the camshaft. Install the woodruff key and position the cam gear onto the camshaft. Press in place.
3. End clearance of the thrust plate must be 0.0015-0.0050 in. If less than 0.0015 in., the spacer ring should be replaced. If more than 0.0050 in., the thrust plate should be replaced.
4. Refer to the Camshaft Removal and Installation for the installation of the gear/camshaft assembly.

TIMING CHAIN

Removal

4-150, 6-258 ENGINES

NOTE: A timing chain tensioner is used with the timing chain on the 4-150 engine and not with the 6-258 engine.

1. Disconnect the negative battery cable.
2. Remove the vibration damper assembly and the timing chain cover. Refer to the vibration damper and timing chain cover removal and installation procedures, previously outlined.

NOTE: Considering the radiator's vulnerability to damage, it is a good practice to either cover the core area, raise the assembly or remove it from the vehicle completely.

3. Rotate the crankshaft until the zero timing mark on the crankshaft sprocket is closest to and on the centerline with the timing mark of the camshaft sprocket.
4. 4-150 Engine – Pull the tensioner block towards the tensioner lever to compress the spring. Hold the block and turn the tensioner lever to the LOCK (up) position.
5. Remove the camshaft sprocket retaining bolt. Remove the crankshaft sprocket, camshaft sprocket and chain as an assembly.

NOTE: If the timing chain deflects more than 1/2 in. when mounted on the gears and in place on the engine, replace it.

Installation

1. Assemble the crankshaft sprocket, the camshaft sprocket and the timing chain, with the timing marks properly aligned.
2. With the crankshaft and the camshaft in the same position as when the gears and chain were removed, install the gears on the camshaft and the crankshaft.

NOTE: Be sure the woodruff key is in its position on the crankshaft and the locating pin/dowel is in place on the camshaft.

AMERICAN MOTORS
CONCORD • EAGLE • EAGLE SX4 • SPIRIT

3. Verify the timing marks are closest to and on a centerline through both the crankshaft and the camshaft.

4. Install the camshaft retaining bolt and torque to 50 ft. lbs.

5. To verify the correct installation of the timing chain, turn the crankshaft to locate the camshaft sprocket timing mark at approximately the one o'clock position. This positions the crankshaft sprocket timing mark where the adjacent tooth meshes with the chain at the three o'clock position. Count the number of chain pins between the timing marks of both sprockets. There must be 20 pins on the 4-150 engine and 15 pins on the 6-258 engine.

6. 4-150 engine—Turn the tensioner lever to the unlock (down) position and be sure the tensioner is released and mated with the chain.

7. Install the timing chain cover as outlined previously. Install the vibration damper and remaining components.

CAMSHAFT PIN

Replacement

When the valve timing is incorrect and the timing chain is considered to be within specifications for slack, the cause may be a broken camshaft gear locating pin. When replacing the pin, this procedure must be followed to prevent damage to the camshaft plug during the pin installation.

1. Remove the fuel pump. Install a suitable tool into the fuel pump opening on the engine block and wedge the tool against the side of the opening and the camshaft to prevent the camshaft from moving.

2. If the pin is a spring type, remove the pin by installing a self-tapping screw into the pin and carefully pulling the pin from the camshaft.

3. If the pin is a dowel type, center punch the exact center of the dowel and drill into the pin with a $\frac{5}{32}$ drill bit. Insert a self-

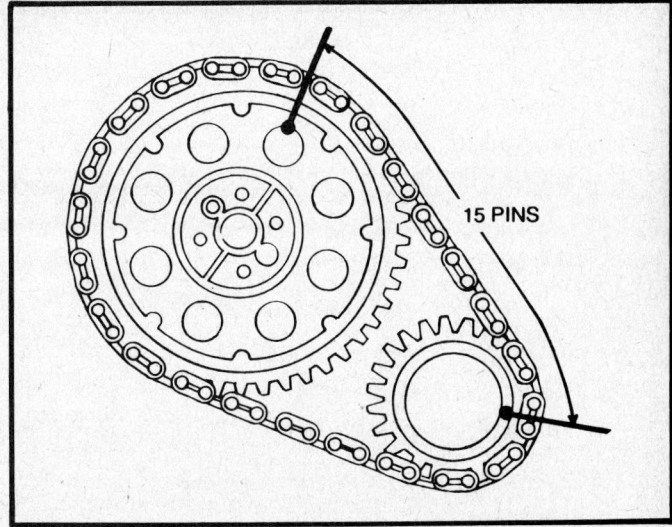

To verify correct installation, rotate crankshaft until camshaft sprocket timing mark is at about a one o'clock position. There must be 15 pins between the timing marks.

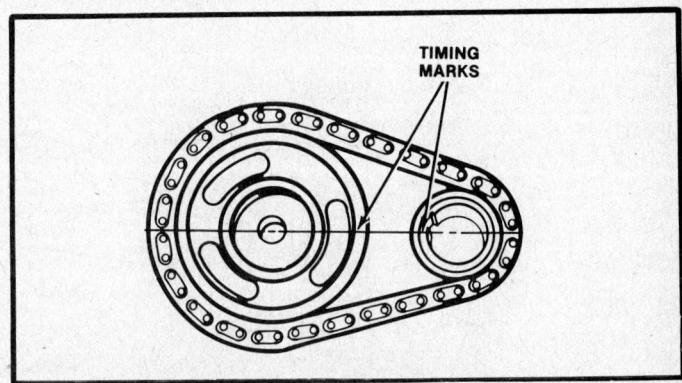

4-150 engine timing mark alignment
(© American Motors Corp.)

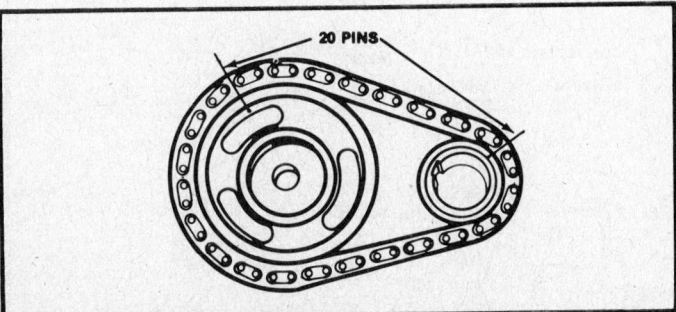

To verify correct installation, rotate the crank shaft until camshaft sprocket timing mark is approximately at one o'clock position. There must be 20 pins between the marks (© American Motors Corp.)

tapping screw into the drilled hole and carefully pull the dowel from the camshaft.

4. Compress the center of the replacement spring pin with a vise grip type tool. Carefully drive the pin into the camshaft until it is seated.

5. Complete the assembly as previously outlined.

CAMSHAFT

Removal

4-150 ENGINE

1. After the coolant has cooled, drain both the radiator and the engine block. Remove the fan and shroud.

2. Remove the radiator. Remove the A/C condensor and receiver assembly as a charged unit, if equipped.

3. Remove the fuel pump, the distributor and the ignition wires.

4. Remove the cylinder head cover as outlined previously. Remove the bridges and pivot assemblies and the rocker arms.

NOTE: Alternately loosen each bolt one turn at a time to avoid damage to the bridges.

5. Remove the push rods and the hydraulic tappets. Keep the components in their respective order for installation.

6. Remove the timing chain cover, the timing gears and chain as previously outlined.

7. Carefully remove the camshaft from the engine block. Do not scuff the camshaft bearings as the shaft is removed.

Installation

1. Lubricate the camshaft with AMC Engine Oil Supplement, or its equivalent.

2. Install the camshaft carefully into the engine block to avoid damage to the camshaft bearings.

3. Install the timing chain and sprockets, aligning the timing marks as previously outlined. Install the camshaft sprocket retaining bolt and tighten to 50 ft. lbs. torque.

1-43

SECTION 1
AMERICAN MOTORS
CONCORD • EAGLE • EAGLE SX4 • SPIRIT

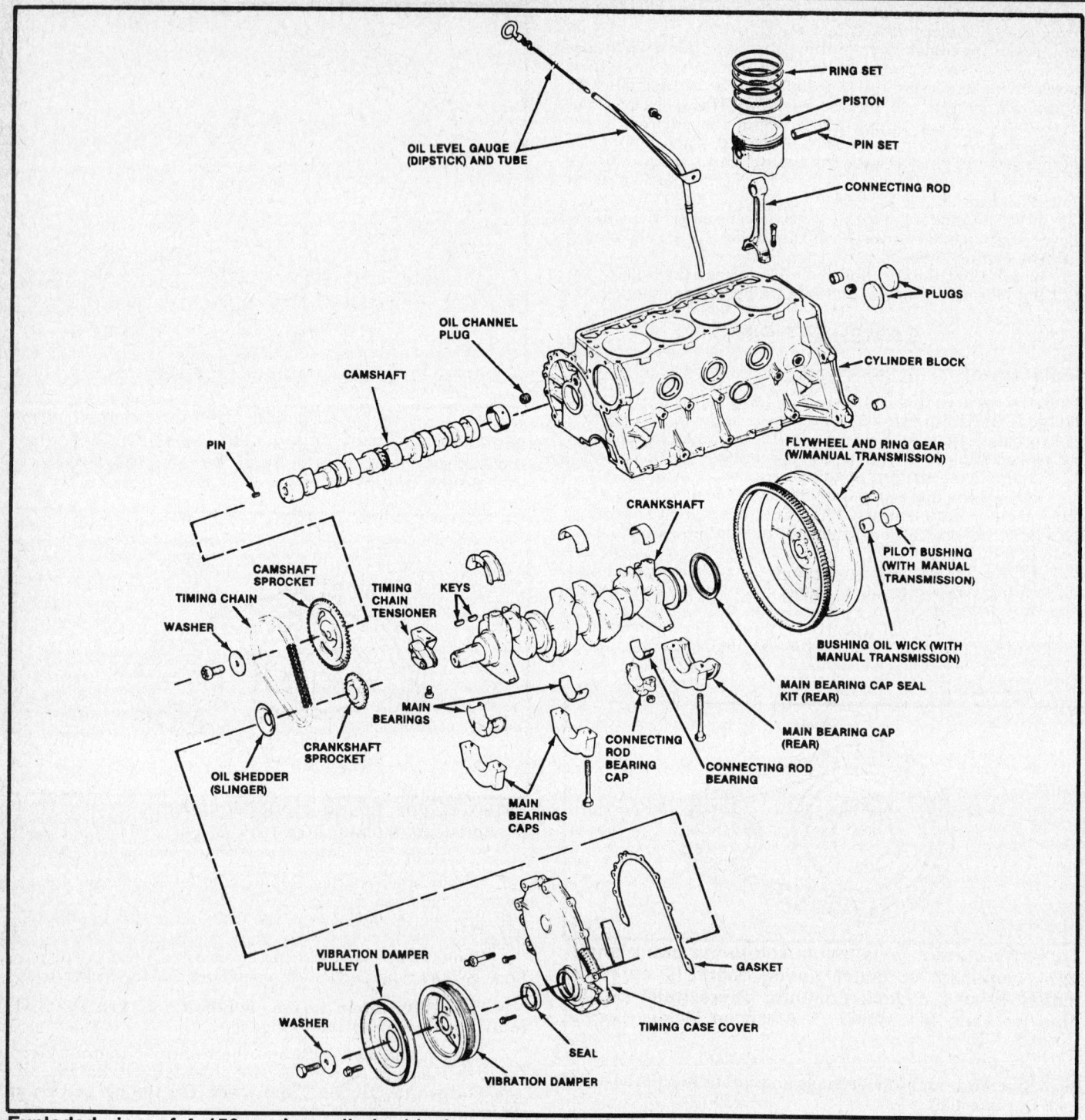

Exploded view of 4-150 engine cylinder block components (© American Motors Corp.)

4. Install the timing chain cover, the vibration damper, the fan and shroud. Install the drive belts and tighten to specifications. Install the fuel pump.

5. Rotate the crankshaft to place the number one cylinder piston at TDC, on its compression stroke. Install the distributor and align the rotor to the number one cylinder spark plug wire terminal in the distributor cap.

NOTE: If the crankshaft/camshaft remain in position with the timing marks aligned, the number four cylinder piston will be on its compression stroke.

6. Install the tappets, the push rods, the rocker arms, bridges and pivots. Install the top engine cover.

7. If equipped, install the condensor and receiver assembly.

AMERICAN MOTORS
CONCORD • EAGLE • EAGLE SX4 • SPIRIT

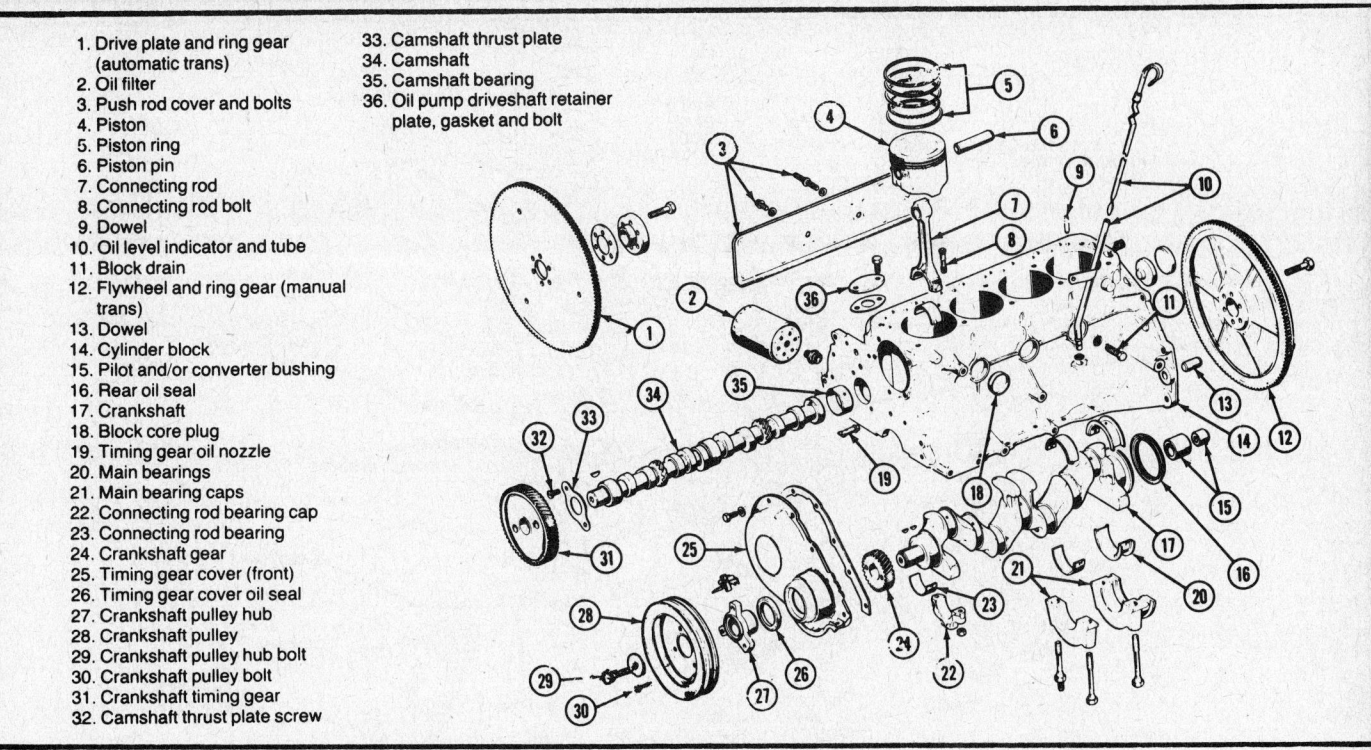

1. Drive plate and ring gear (automatic trans)
2. Oil filter
3. Push rod cover and bolts
4. Piston
5. Piston ring
6. Piston pin
7. Connecting rod
8. Connecting rod bolt
9. Dowel
10. Oil level indicator and tube
11. Block drain
12. Flywheel and ring gear (manual trans)
13. Dowel
14. Cylinder block
15. Pilot and/or converter bushing
16. Rear oil seal
17. Crankshaft
18. Block core plug
19. Timing gear oil nozzle
20. Main bearings
21. Main bearing caps
22. Connecting rod bearing cap
23. Connecting rod bearing
24. Crankshaft gear
25. Timing gear cover (front)
26. Timing gear cover oil seal
27. Crankshaft pulley hub
28. Crankshaft pulley
29. Crankshaft pulley hub bolt
30. Crankshaft pulley bolt
31. Crankshaft timing gear
32. Camshaft thrust plate screw
33. Camshaft thrust plate
34. Camshaft
35. Camshaft bearing
36. Oil pump driveshaft retainer plate, gasket and bolt

Exploded view of 4-151 engine cylinder block components (© American Motors Corp.)

Open service valves as required. Install the radiator, fan and shroud. Fill the system with coolant.

NOTE: Lubricate the hydraulic valve train with the Engine Oil Supplement and allow it to remain with the engine oil for at least 1000 miles.

8. Make necessary adjustments to the engine idle and ignition timing as required.

Removal
4-151 ENGINE

1. Remove the air cleaner assembly. After the coolant has cooled, drain the engine block and the radiator.
2. Remove the timing gear cover, the intake manifold and the tappet cover, referring to the appropriate outline.
3. Remove the radiator assembly. If equipped with A/C, move the condensor to a protected fender panel. Relocate the evaporator-to-dryer hose as required.
4. Remove the two thrust plate bolts, accessible through holes in the camshaft gear.
5. Remove the valve tappets, the distributor, oil pump drive and fuel pump.
6. If necessary, remove the front bumper and remove the camshaft from the front of the engine. Do not scuff the camshaft bearings as the shaft is removed.

Installation

1. Coat the camshaft with AMC Engine Oil Supplement, or its equivalent. Carefully install the camshaft into the engine block so as not to damage the camshaft bearings.
2. Turn the crankshaft and camshaft gears until the timing marks on the gear teeth are aligned. This positions the number four cylinder piston on its compression stroke. To position the number one cylinder piston on its compression stroke, the crankshaft must be rotated one revolution.

3. Install the bolts in the thrust plate and torque to 80 inch lbs.
4. Install the timing gear cover, vibration damper pulley, tightening the bolt to 160 ft. lbs. torque.
5. Install the valve tappets, push rods, oil pump shaft/gear assembly and the fuel pump.

NOTE: Lubricate the hydraulic valve train with Engine Oil Supplement and allow it to remain with the engine oil for at least 1000 miles.

6. Install the distributor and position the rotor, if the crankshaft is not rotated, pointing to the number four cylinder distributor cap segment, or rotate the crankshaft one full revolution so that the number one cylinder exhaust and intake valve tappets are both on the heel of the cam lobes and the vibration damper timing index mark is aligned with the TDC mark on the timing degree scale, which positions the number one cylinder piston on TDC. Then align the rotor to the number one cylinder distributor cap segment.
7. Place each tappet, in turn, on the heel of the cam lobe and tighten the rocker arm bolt to 20 ft. lbs. torque.
8. Complete the assembly of the push rod cover, the intake manifold, condensor (if equipped), radiator, fan and shroud.
9. Complete the assembly of the components, verify correct fluid levels and adjust the engine timing and idle as required.

Removal
6-258 ENGINE

1. Allow the coolant to cool and drain the radiator and engine block. Remove the radiator assembly, and if equipped, remove the A/C condenser and receiver assembly as a charged unit and set aside.
2. Remove the fuel pump, the distributor and wiring and the cylinder head cover.
3. Remove the bridge and pivot assemblies, the rocker arms and push rods.

AMERICAN MOTORS
CONCORD • EAGLE • EAGLE SX4 • SPIRIT

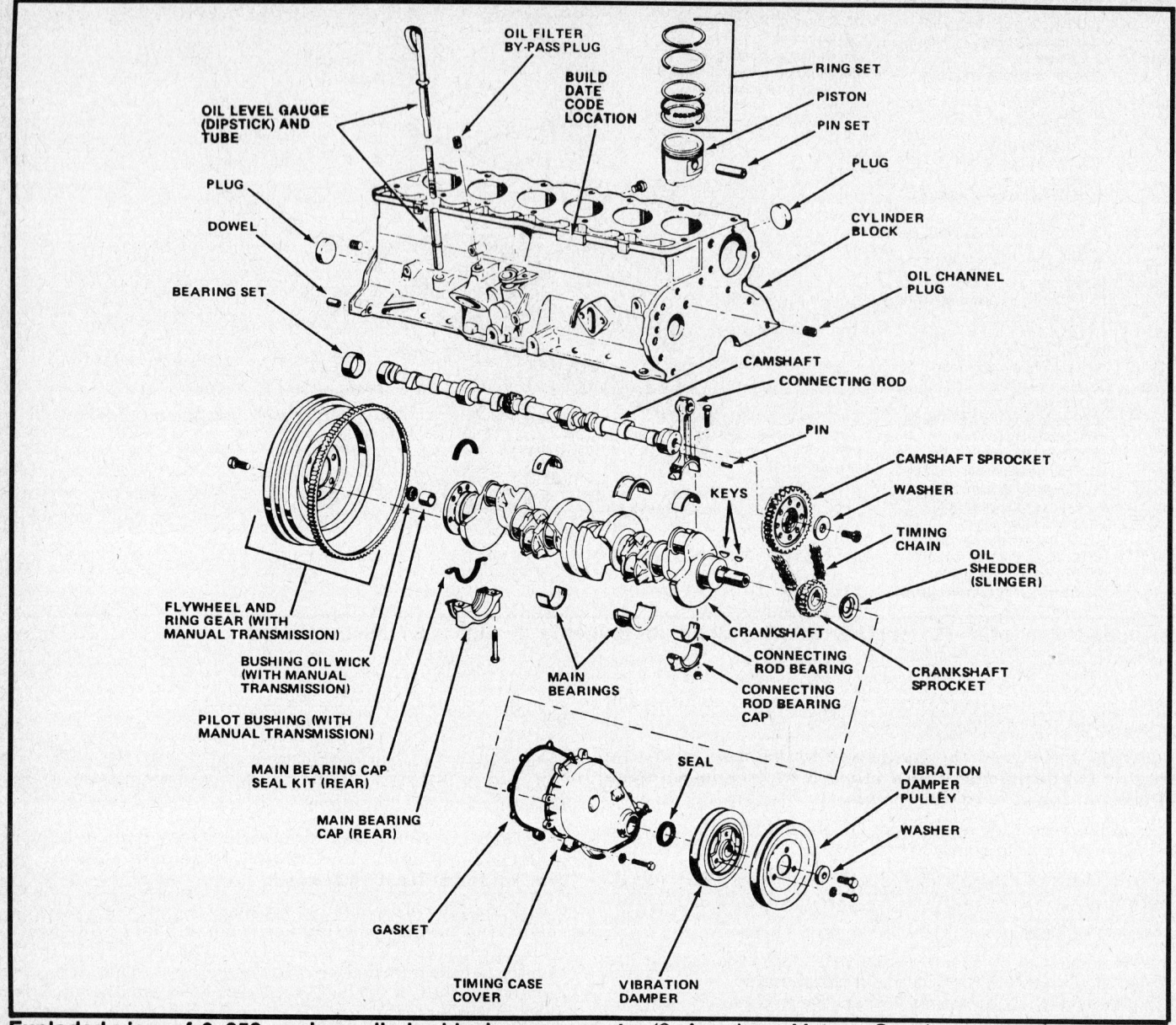

Exploded view of 6-258 engine cylinder block components (© American Motors Corp.)

NOTE: **Alternately loosen each bolt one turn at a time to avoid damaging the bridges. Keep all components in order for installation purposes.**

4. Remove the cylinder head assembly, the hydraulic valve tappets and the timing chain cover. Refer to the appropriate outline.
5. Remove the timing chain and sprockets.
6. Remove the front bumper and/or grille as required.
7. Carefully remove the camshaft from the engine block so as not to damage the camshaft bearings.

Installation

1. Lubricate the camshaft with AMC Engine Oil Supplement, or its equivalent. Carefully install the camshaft into the engine to avoid damage to the camshaft bearings.
2. Install the timing chain and sprockets, with the timing marks aligned. Install the camshaft sprocket retaining bolt and torque to 50 ft. lbs.
3. Install the timing chain cover with the new seal and gasket. Install the vibration damper and pulley, the fan assembly and shroud and install the drive belts and tighten to specifications. Install the fuel pump.
4. Rotate the crankshaft one full revolution to place the number one cylinder piston on its compression stroke. Install the distributor so that the rotor is aligned with the number one spark plug terminal of the distributor cap.

NOTE: **If the crankshaft/camshaft remains in position with the timing marks aligned, the number six cylinder piston will be on its compression stroke.**

5. Install the tappets, the cylinder head and gasket, the push rods, the rocker arms, the bridges and pivots. Tighten each of the two bolts for each bridge alternately, one turn at a time, to avoid damage to the bridges. Refer to the appropriate outline for installation procedures.

AMERICAN MOTORS
CONCORD • EAGLE • EAGLE SX4 • SPIRIT

NOTE: Lubricate the hydraulic valve train with Engine Oil Supplement and allow it to remain with the engine oil for at least 1000 miles.

6. Install the cylinder head cover, if equipped, the A/C condenser and receiver assembly, the radiator and shroud and fill with coolant.
7. Install the front bumper/grille, if required.
8. Adjust the ignition timing and idle as required.

Pistons and Connecting Rod Positioning

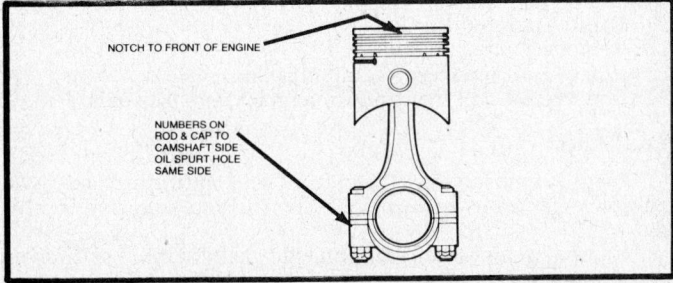

Direction of piston installation, 6-258 engine, typical of 4-150 engine (© American Motors Corp.)

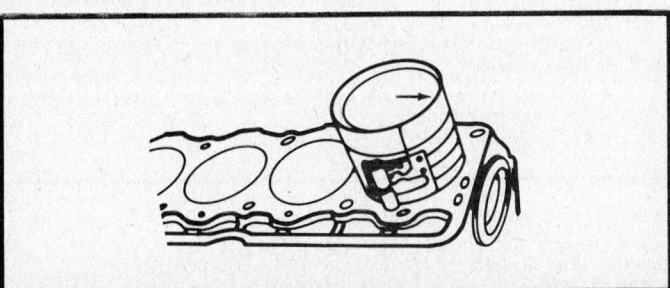

Connecting rod oil squirt holes should face the camshaft and arrows on the piston top should face the front of the engine (© American Motors Corp.)

Lubrication

OIL PAN

Removal

4-151 ENGINE, EXCEPT EAGLE

1. Remove fan shroud screws and slide shroud toward engine.
2. Raise automobile and support at side sills.
3. Drain engine oil.
4. Remove starter and flywheel inspection plate.
5. Remove engine cushion nuts at crossmember.
6. Raise engine with jack positioned beneath front damper.
7. Lower front crossmember by loosening nut on left side and removing right nut and screws.
8. Remove oil pan screws.
9. Pry crossmember down on right side and remove oil pan.

— CAUTION —
Do not raise more than 1 to 2 in. because the bellhousing may contact the floor panel.

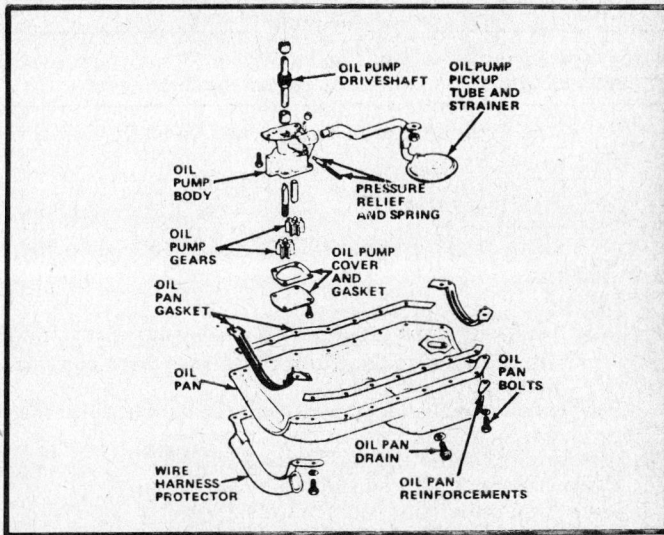

Oil pump and pan, 4-151 engine (© American Motors Corp.)

Installation

1. Install rear oil pan gasket in rear main bearing cap and apply small quantity of RTV in depressions where pan gasket engages block.
2. Position oil pan gasket on pan. Apply $1/8 \times 1/4$ in. (3 x 6 mm) bead of silicon adhesive at split lines of front and side gasket.
3. Install pan and tighten side screws with 75 inch lbs. (6Nm) torque. Install oil pan-to-timing cover bolts last and torque with 90 inch lbs. (10 Nm).
4. Raise crossmember and tighten nuts with 65 ft. lbs. (88 Nm) torque.
5. Install engine cushion nuts and tighten with 35 ft. lbs. (45 Nm) torque.
6. Install starter bolts and tighten with 27 ft. lbs. (37 Nm) torque.
7. Install starter bracket and tighten:
   a. Bracket-to-block bolt with 20 ft. lbs. (27 Nm) torque.
   b. Bracket-to-starter nut with 40 inch lbs. (5 Nm) torque.
8. Install shroud.
9. Refill with oil, start engine and check for leaks.

Removal

4-151 ENGINE, EAGLE

1. Remove battery negative cable.
2. Remove fan shroud screws and slide shroud toward engine.
3. Raise car and support safely.
   a. Support front axle with jack.
   b. Scribe mark location of front drive shaft for assembly reference.
   c. Disconnect front drive shaft.
   d. Disconnect both half shafts at axle. Compress shafts inward (toward wheels) and secure to frame sills (in compressed position) with wire.
   e. Disconnect axle assembly at right axle tube, at left engine mount and at pinion mount. Lower axle assembly slightly to remove vent hose.
   f. Remove axle assembly.
4. Drain engine oil.
5. Remove starter motor.
6. Remove engine mount cushion nuts at crossmember.

American Motors
CONCORD • EAGLE • EAGLE SX4 • SPIRIT

CAUTION

Do not raise engine more than 1 to 2 in. (25 to 51 mm) because the flywheel (or converter) housing may contact the floor panel.

---

7. Raise the engine with jack positioned beneath vibration damper.
8. Lower right side of front crossmember.
9. Remove oil pan screws.
10. Pry crossmember down on right side and remove oil pan.

Installation

1. Clean oil pan and gasket surface.
2. Install rear oil pan gasket in rear main bearing cap and apply small quantity of sealant in depressions where pan gasket mates with cylinder block.
3. Position oil pan gasket on pan. Apply sealant at split lines of front and side gasket.
4. Install oil pan and tighten screws.
5. Raise crossmember and tighten nuts.
6. Install engine mount cushion nuts.
7. Install starter motor.
8. Raise and support axle assembly in installation position.
9. Attach vent hose and connect axle assembly at left engine mount, at pinion end and at right axle tube. Tighten axle assembly connections with 45 ft. lbs. (61 Nm) torque.
10. Connect half shafts to axle and tighten with 45 ft. lbs. (61 Nm) torque.
11. Connect front drive shaft to axle and tighten with 15 ft. lbs. (20 Nm) torque. Ensure installation reference marks are aligned. Remove axle support.
12. Install fan shroud.

Removal
6–258 ENGINE, SPIRIT AND CONCORD

1. Turn steering wheel to full left lock position.
2. Support engine with holding fixture.
3. Raise car and support with support stands at side sills.
4. Disconnect steering idler arm at side sill and disconnect steering linkage center cross link from pitman arm. Lower linkage.
5. Disconnect engine front support cushions at engine brackets.
6. Loosen sway bar link nuts to end of bolt threads. Remove bolts attaching sway bar clamps to side sills. Lower sway bar, if equipped.
7. Remove front crossmember-to-side sill bolts and nuts and pull crossmember down.
8. Remove engine right support bracket from engine.
9. Loosen strut rods at lower control arm. Do not remove screws.
10. Drain engine oil.
11. Remove starter motor.
12. Remove oil pan screws and oil pan.
13. Remove oil pan front and rear neoprene oil seals.

Installation

1. Install replacement oil pan front seal on timing case cover and apply generous amount of RTV silicone adhesive to end tabs.
2. Cement replacement oil pan side gaskets into position on engine block.
3. Coast inside curved surface of replacement oil pan rear seal with soap. Apply RTV silicone adhesive to gasket contacting surface of seal end tabs.
4. Install seal in recess of rear main bearing cap. Ensure it is fully seated.
5. Apply engine oil to oil pan contacting surface of front and rear oil pan seals.
6. Install oil pan. Tighten screws and drain plug securely.
7. Install starter motor.
8. Install engine right support bracket.

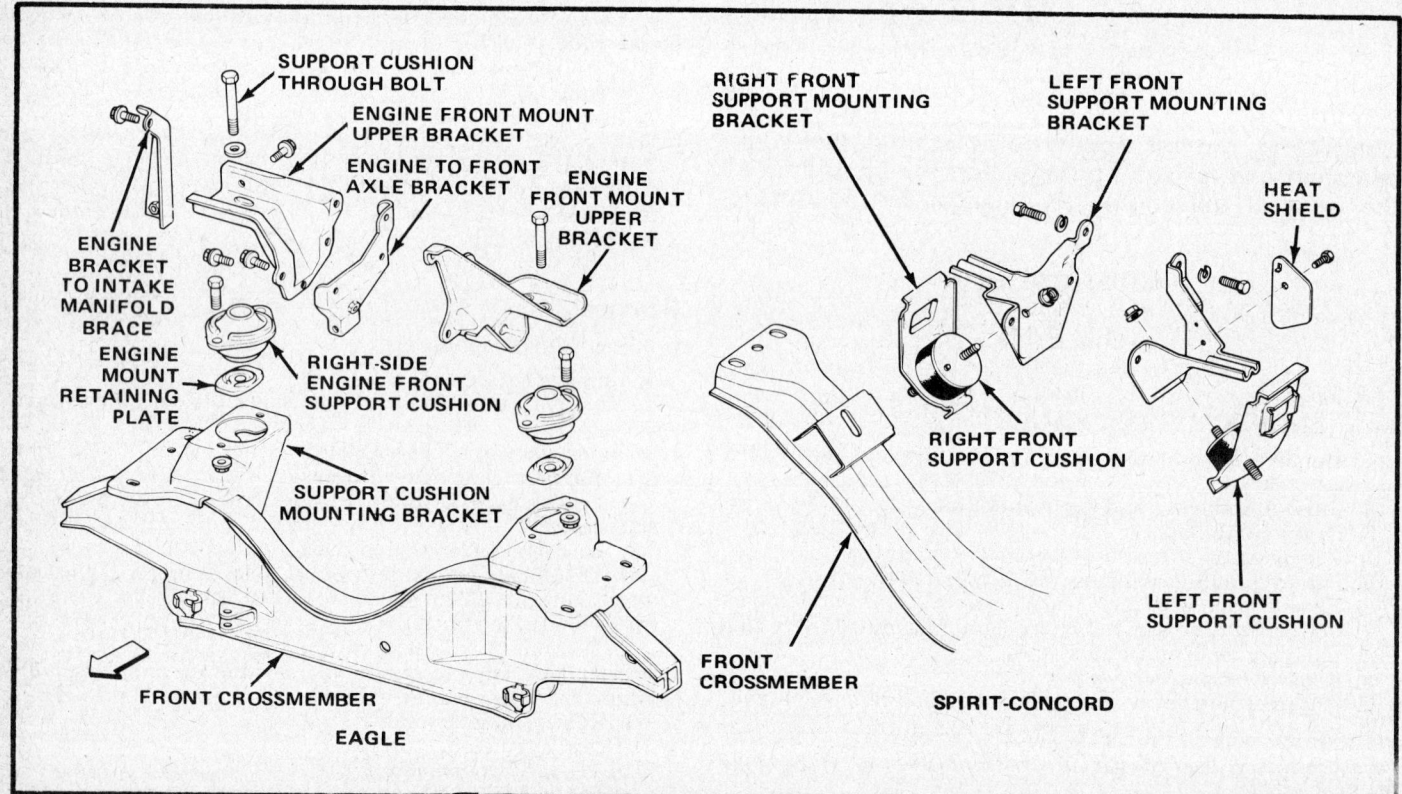

Engine mounting brackets (© American Motors Corp.)

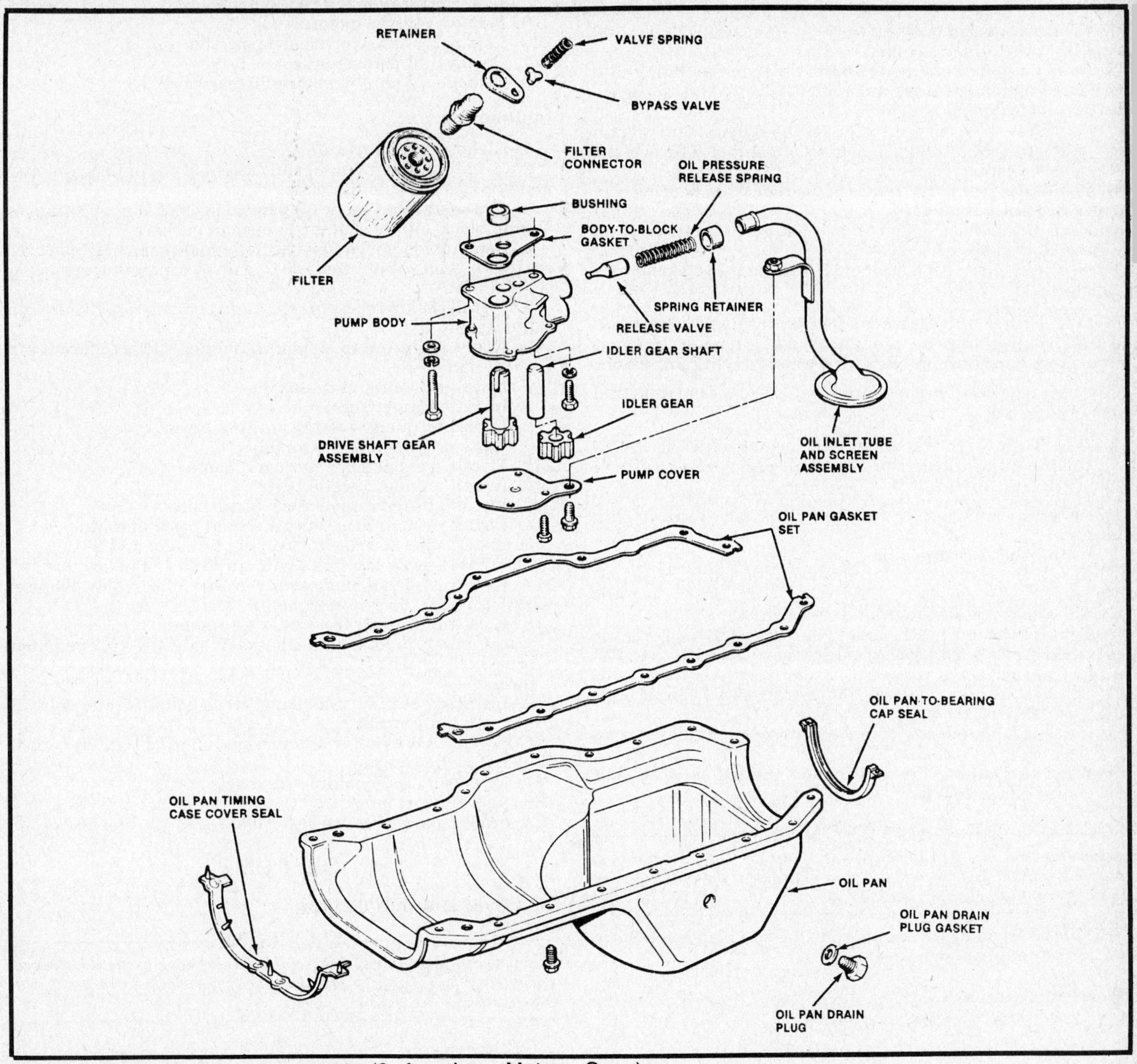

American Motors
CONCORD • EAGLE • EAGLE SX4 • SPIRIT

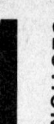

Oil pan and related components (© American Motors Corp.)

9. Install crossmember-to-side sill screws and nuts.
10. Tighten strut rod screws.
11. Install engine front support cushion-to-bracket screws.
12. Tighten sway bar link nuts.
13. Install steering idler arm to side sill and tighten attaching nuts.
14. Fill crankcase with oil and operate engine and check for leaks.

Removal

4-150 ENGINE

1. Drain the engine oil.
2. Mark the front drive shaft for assembly reference and disconnect the shaft.
3. Support the axle assembly with a jack.
4. Disconnect the half shafts from the axle. Compress the half shafts inward (toward the wheels) and secure them in a compressed position with wire attached to the frame sills.
5. Remove the through bolt from the bracket at the right axle tube.
6. Remove the bolts from the left upper axle bracket at the upper end.
7. Remove the bolts from the pinion end bracket at the pinion.
8. Remove the vent hose and remove the axle assembly.
9. Remove the starter motor.
10. Remove the torque converter housing access cover.
11. Remove the oil pan screws.
12. Remove the oil pan by sliding it to the rear.

AMERICAN MOTORS
CONCORD • EAGLE • EAGLE SX4 • SPIRIT

Installation

1. Clean the gasket and seal surfaces. Remove all sludge and grime from the oil pan sump.
2. Install a replacement oil pan front seal on the timing case cover and apply a generous amount of RTV sealant to the recesses in the tab ends.
3. Coat the inside curved surface of the replacement oil pan rear seal with soap. Apply a generous amount of RTV sealant to the gasket contacting surface of the seal end tabs.
4. Install the seal in the recess of the rear main bearing cap. Ensure it is fully seated.
5. Cement the replacement oil pan side gaskets into position on the cylinder block.
6. Apply a generous amount of RTV sealant to the end tabs of the gaskets.

NOTE: Either one of two sealing methods may be used. An RTV sealant may be used instead of a gasket. If a gasket is used, coat both sides with a quick drying adhesive.

7. Apply engine oil to the contacting surface of the front and rear oil pan seals.

NOTE: Tighten the $\frac{1}{4}$–20 oil pan screws with 7 ft. lbs. (9 Nm) torque and tighten the $\frac{5}{16}$–18 oil pan screws with 11 ft. lbs. (15 Nm) torque.

8. Install the oil pan. Tighten the screws and the drain plug securely.
9. Install the starter motor.
10. Install the torque converter housing (if equipped) access cover.
11. Raise and install the front axle assembly.
12. Connect the axle at the axle tube, upper left axle bracket and pinion bracket. Tighten all axle connections with 45 ft. lbs. (61 Nm) torque.
13. Install the front universal clamp strap bolts. Tighten with 14 ft. lbs. (19 Nm) torque.
14. Connect both half shafts to the front axle and tighten with 45 ft. lbs. (61 Nm) torque.
15. Raise the automobile and remove the sill supports and jack. Lower the automobile.

---- **CAUTION** ----

Use extreme caution when the engine is operating. Do not stand in a direct line with the fan. Do not put your hands near the pulleys, belts or fan. Do not wear loose clothing.

16. Fill the oil pan with engine oil to the specified level. Start the engine and inspect for leaks.

Removal

6-258 ENGINE, EAGLE

1. Drain engine oil.
2. Lock steering wheel.
3. Remove air cleaner.
4. Support engine with holding fixture.
5. Raise automobile and support at side sills.
6. Remove front axle universal joint clamp strap bolts.
7. Remove bolts at engine cushions.
8. Remove bolts from sill-to-crossmember brace bar at crossmember, and rotate bar out of way.
9. Loosen pitman arm at gear.
10. Loosen idler arm at steering linkage.
11. Remove bolt from steering damper at crossmember.
12. Loosen sway bar bolts and lower sway bar.
13. Support axle and crossmember assembly.
14. Remove bolt from right bracket at axle tube bolt bars.
15. Remove bolts from left upper axle bracket at upper end.
16. Remove bolts from pinion end bracket at pinion.
17. Remove crossmember nuts and bolts.
18. Lower crossmember and axle assembly.
19. Remove starter motor.
20. Remove torque converter inspection shield.
21. Remove oil pan screws.
22. Remove oil pan by sliding it rearward.

Installation

1. Clean gasket surface.
2. Install replacement oil pan front seal on timing case cover and apply sealant to tab ends.
3. Cement replacement oil pan side gaskets into position on engine block. Apply sealant to ends of gaskets.
4. Coat inside curved surface of replacement oil pan rear seal with soap. Apply sealant to gasket contacting surface of seal end tabs.
5. Install seal in recess of rear main bearing cap. Ensure it is fully seated.
6. Apply engine oil to oil pan contacting surface of front and rear oil pan seals.
7. Install oil pan and drain plug.
8. Install starter motor.
9. Install torque converter housing access cover.
10. Raise crossmember assembly.
11. Install crossmember nuts and bolts.
12. Install engine cushion bolts.
13. Install sill-to-crossmember brace bolts.
14. Install pitman arm (onto steering gear) and nut.
15. Install idler arm (onto steering linkage) and nut.
16. Tighten sway bar bolts with 25 ft. lbs. (34 Nm) torque.
17. Install steering damper on crossmember bolt. Tighten with 50 ft. lbs. (68 Nm) torque.
18. Raise and install front axle assembly.
   a. Connect at axle tube, upper left axle bracket and pinion bracket. Tighten all axle connections with 45 ft. lbs. (61 Nm) torque.
19. Install front universal clamp strap bolts. Tighten with 14 ft. lbs. (19 Nm) torque.
20. Connect both half shafts to front axle and tighten with 45 ft. lbs. (61 Nm) torque.
21. Remove engine holding fixture.
22. Install air cleaner.
23. Start engine and check for leaks.

OIL PUMP

Removal and Installation

---- **CAUTION** ----

Whenever the oil pump is disassembled or the cover removed, the gear cavity must be filled with petroleum jelly (vaseline) for priming purposes. Do not use grease.

4-150 ENGINE

1. Raise the vehicle and support safely. Drain the engine oil and remove the oil pan assembly. Refer to procedures outlined previously.
2. Remove the oil pump retaining bolts, oil pump and gasket.

NOTE: The oil pump removal or installation will not affect the distributor timing. The distributor gear remains in mesh with the camshaft.

---- **CAUTION** ----

Do not disturb the position of the oil inlet tube and strainer assembly in the pump body. Should the tube be moved in the body, a replacement tube must be installed to assure an airtight seal.

3. To insure self priming of the oil pump, fill the gear cavity with petroleum jelly before installation.

AMERICAN MOTORS
CONCORD • EAGLE • EAGLE SX4 • SPIRIT

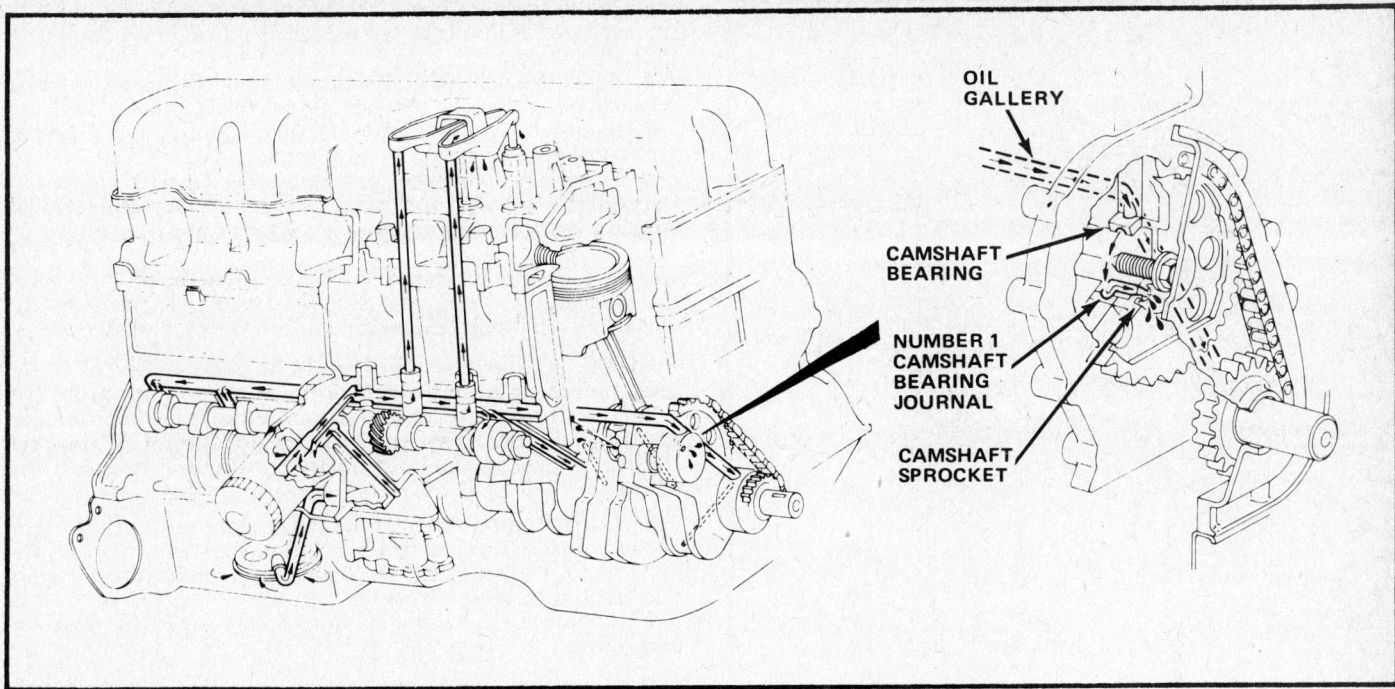

6-258 engine oil circuit, typical of 4-150 engine (© American Motors Corp.)

4. Install the oil pump and tighten the short bolts to 10 ft. lbs. and the long bolts to 17 ft. lbs.

5. Complete the installation and assembly in the reverse of the removal procedure.

Removal and Installation

4-151 ENGINE

1. Raise the vehicle and support safely. Drain the engine oil and remove the oil pan. Refer to the Oil Pan Removal and Installation Procedure as outlined previously.

2. Remove the two flange mounting bolts and nuts from the main bearing cap bolt and remove the oil pump, pick up tube and strainer as an assembly.

CAUTION

Do not disturb the oil pick up tube position at the strainer or the pump body. If disturbed, the complete pump assembly must be replaced.

3. Align the oil pump shaft slot to mate with the oil pump drive shaft and tang. Install the oil pump, positioning the flange over the oil pump drive shaft lower bushing. Do not use a gasket. Tighten the bolts to 18 ft. lbs.

4. Install the oil pan and complete the assembly in the reverse order of removal.

Removal and Installation

6-258 ENGINE

1. Raise the vehicle and support safely. Drain the engine oil and remove the oil pan. Refer to the Oil Pan Removal and Installation Procedure.

2. Remove the oil pump retaining bolts, the oil pump and gasket.

NOTE: *The oil pump removal and installation will not affect the distributor timing because the distributor drive gear remains meshed with the camshaft.*

CAUTION

Do not disturb the position of the oil inlet tube and strainer assembly in the pump body. If the tube is moved in the body, a replacement tube and strainer must be installed to assure an airtight seal.

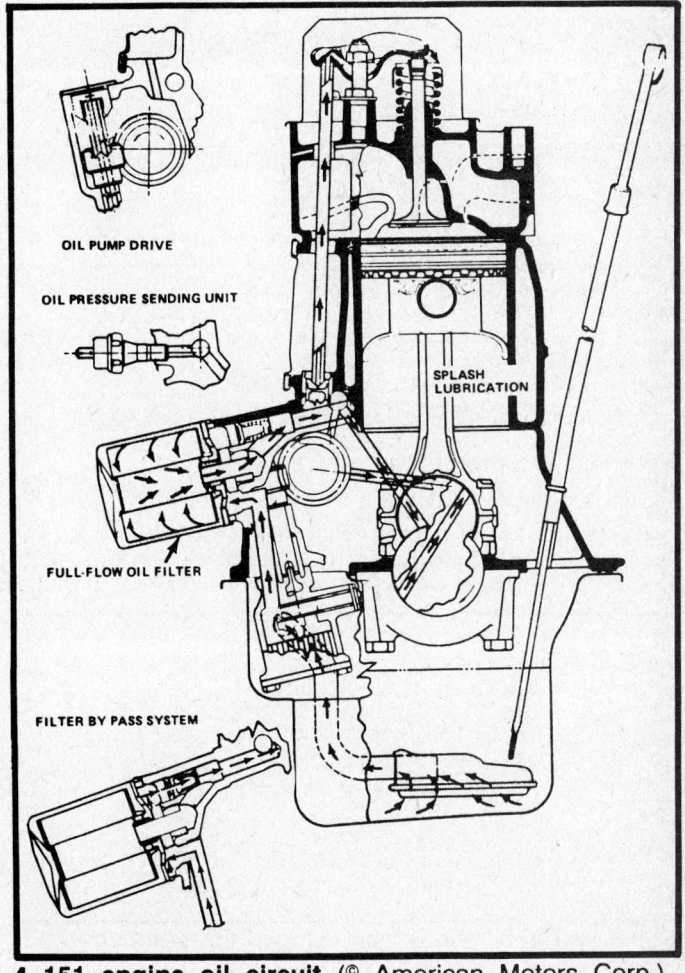

4-151 engine oil circuit (© American Motors Corp.)

1-51

AMERICAN MOTORS
CONCORD • EAGLE • EAGLE SX4 • SPIRIT

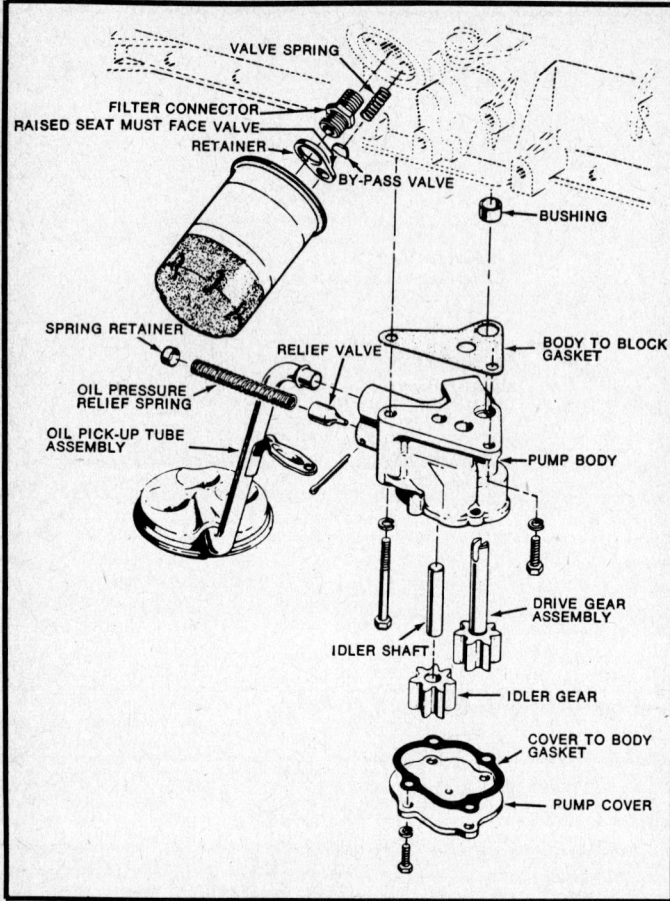

Exploded view of oil pump assembly — 6-258 engine (© American Motors Corp.)

3. To insure self priming, fill the gear cavity with petroleum jelly before installing the cover.
4. Install the pump with a new gasket. Tighten the short bolts to 10 ft. lbs. and the long bolts to 17 ft. lbs.
5. Install the oil pan using new gaskets and seals. Complete the assembly as required.

REAR MAIN BEARING OIL SEAL

Removal and Installation

4-150, 4-151 ENGINES

1. The crankshaft rear oil seal is a one-piece, single lip seal that fits securely between the cylinder block and the crankshaft. The oil pan or crankshaft do not have to be removed to replace the seal, however, the transmission assembly must be removed. Refer to the Transmission Removal and Installation Procedure Outline.
2. Raise the vehicle and support safely. Remove the transmission assembly, the flywheel or converter drive plate.
3. Remove the oil seal from the crankshaft flange by prying around the flange area.
4. To install a new seal, coat the inner lip with engine oil. Carefully fit the seal into place and gently tap the seal flush with the cylinder block, using a rubber or plastic mallet.
5. 4-150 Engine — Install the converter drive plate or flywheel. Tighten the converter drive plate bolts (automatic transmission) to 40 ft. lbs. plus 60 degrees. Tighten the flywheel bolts (manual transmission) to 50 ft. lbs. plus 60 degrees.

NOTE: A metric socket should be pre-marked at 60 degree increments and a reference mark made on the flywheel or drive plate after the correct torque specification has been made. Turn the bolt an additional 60 degrees tighter by using the pre-marked indicator lines on the socket.

6. 4-151 Engine — Install the drive plate and spacer (automatic transmission) at their original locations. Torque the bolts to 45 ft. lbs. Install the flywheel (manual transmission) and tighten the bolts to 68 ft. lbs.
7. Complete the assembly in the reverse of the removal procedure.

Removal and Installation

6-258 ENGINE

1. The crankshaft rear main bearing seal consists of two pieces, an upper and a lower seal, each with a single lip.
2. Raise the vehicle and support safely. Drain the engine oil and remove the oil pan. Refer to the Oil Pan Removal and Installation procedure.
3. Remove the lower rear main bearing cap and discard the oil seal.
4. Loosen all the main bearing caps. Tap the upper seal with a brass drift and hammer, or other suitable tool, until the seal protrudes enough to grasp it and pull it from the engine block.
5. To install the seal, coat the lip of the seal with engine oil and position the seal with the lip towards the front of the engine. Install the seal into the engine block.
6. Position the lower half of the seal into the rear main bearing cap, after coating both sides of the lower seal tabs with RTV sealant and the lip of the seal with engine oil. Coat the outer curved surface of the seal with soap. Seat the seal firmly into the rear main bearing cap.
7. Install the rear main bearing cap and torque the bolts to 80 ft. lbs.
8. Install the oil pan and its components. Complete the assembly in the reverse of the removal procedure.

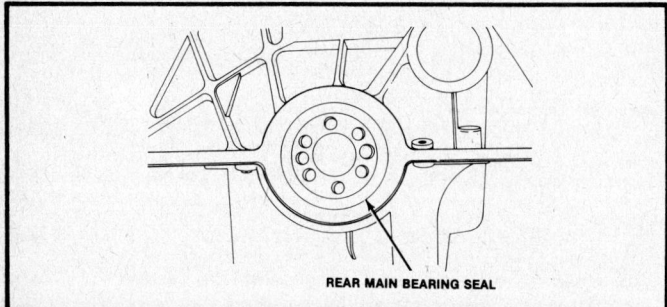

Four cylinder, one piece, single lip crankshaft rear seal (© American Motors Corp.)

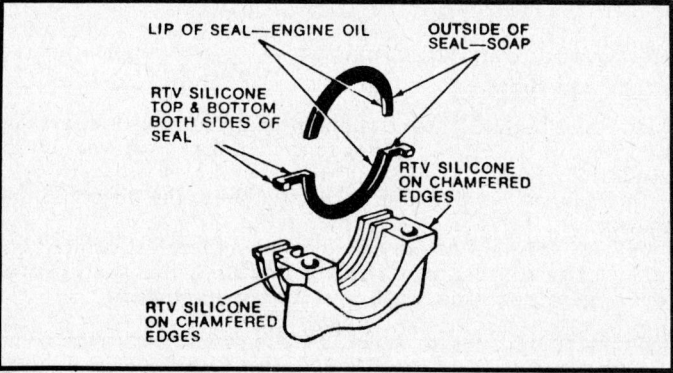

Rear main bearing seal components, 6-258 engine (© American Motors Corp.)

AMERICAN MOTORS
CONCORD • EAGLE • EAGLE SX4 • SPIRIT

STEERING

NOTE: For Front Suspension Services, refer to the Unit Repair Section. For Steering Gear Overhaul, refer to the Unit Repair Section.

STEERING GEAR

Removal and Installation

1. Have the wheels in a straight-ahead position. Place a drain pan under the steering gear assembly, if power steering.
2. Disconnect the power steering hoses, if equipped with power steering.
3. Remove the flexible coupling to intermediate shaft attaching nuts.
4. Raise and support the vehicle safely.
5. On Eagle models, remove the following:
   a. Skid plate, if equipped.
   b. Left side crossmember-to-sill support brace.
   c. Stabilizer bar brackets from the frame.
6. Mark the pitman arm for alignment and remove using special puller.
7. Remove the steering gear mounting bolts and remove the steering gear assembly.
8. The installation is the reverse of the removal procedure.

POWER STEERING PUMP

Removal and Installation

NOTE: The power steering pump on 1983 6–258 CID engine equipped vehicles sold in California, is driven by a single Serpentine belt. Do not attempt to move the pump to adjust the belt. Use the adjusting hole in the alternator bracket and adjust the tension to 140 pounds force.

1. Remove the fan belt.

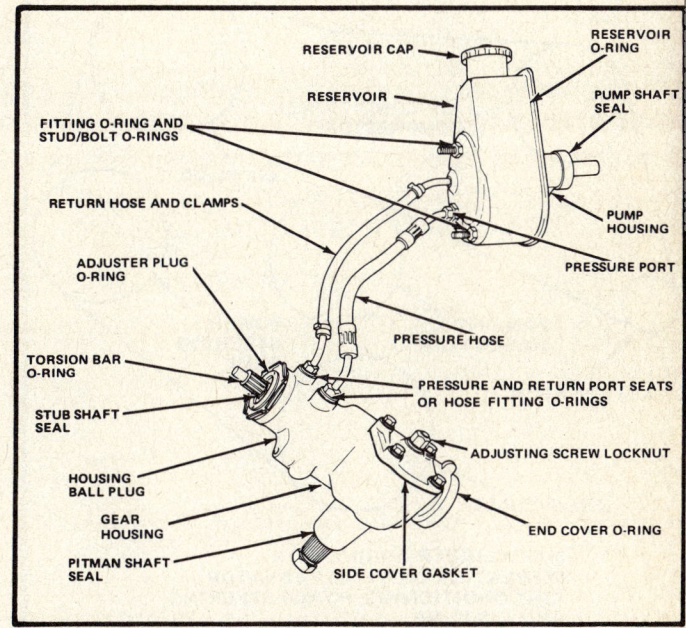

Power Steering system—typical (© American Motors Corp.)

2. Place a container under the pump to catch fluid. Remove the fuel vapor storage canister and six cylinder air cleaner if necessary.
3. Disconnect the hoses and cap the outlets, so that the power steering unit does not lose fluid. Remove the air pump belt.

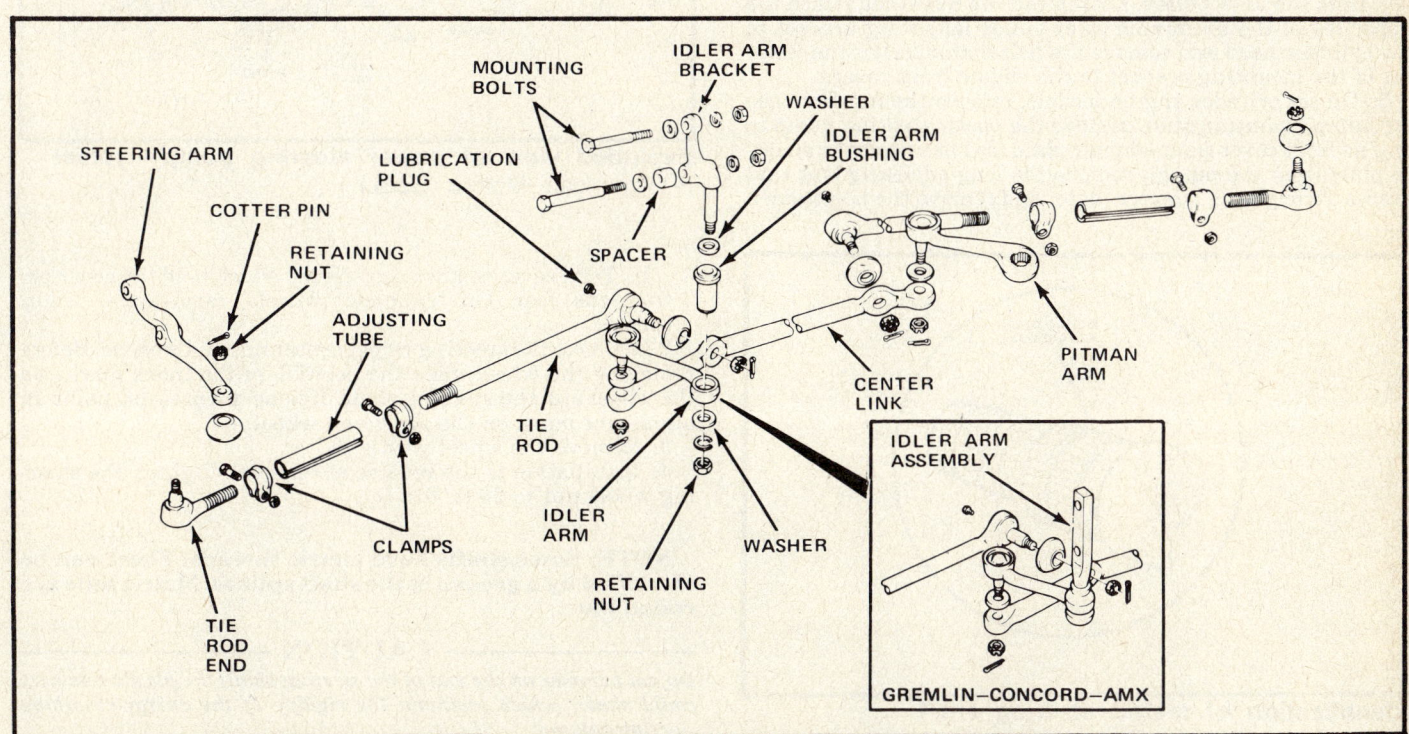

Exploded view of steering linkage components (© American Motors Corp.)

American Motors
CONCORD • EAGLE • EAGLE SX4 • SPIRIT

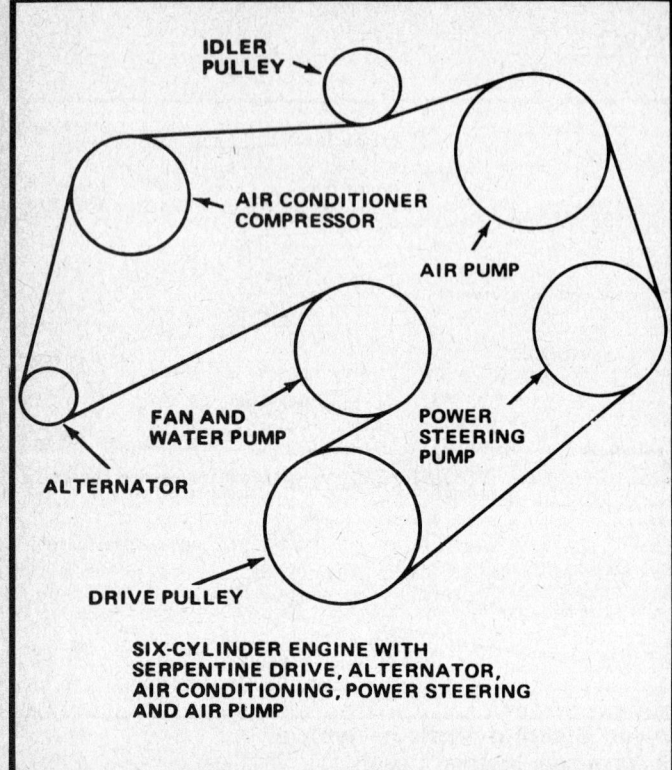

Typical serpentine drive belt arrangement, 6–258 engine (© American Motors Corp.)

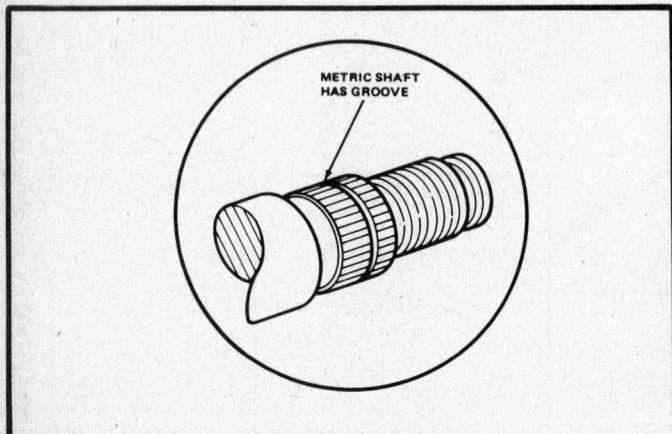

Identification of metric steering shaft (© American Motors Corp.)

behind the flange in the rear adapter plate. Remove the pump, adapter plate and mounting bracket together.

6. On four cylinder engine models, remove the adjuster locknuts and washers which retain the pump and pivot bracket to the mounting bracket. All of the pump mounting bolts are metric except for the $9/16$ in. adjuster locknuts. Move the pump and remove the belt. Remove the bolts which connect the front bracket to the rear bracket and engine block, and remove the pump complete with the pivot and front brackets.

7. After installation, fill the system with DEXRON or AMC power steering fluid. Bleed the system of air by raising the front of the car and turning the wheels from side to side without hitting the stops several times. Check the level frequently.

STEERING WHEEL

Removal and Installation

1. Disconnect the battery and remove the horn button by one of the following methods:
   a. Center button lift upward.

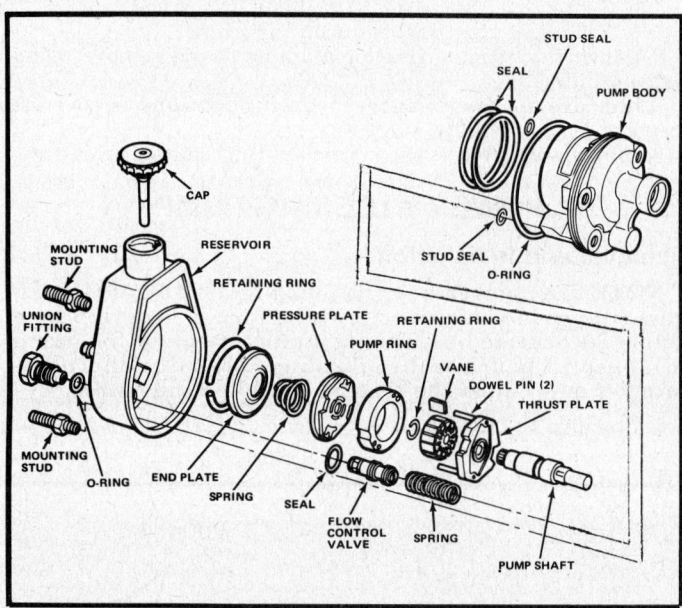

Exploded view of power steering pump—typical (© American Motors Corp.)

b. Trim cover remove the screws, which hold the cover on, from the rear. On "rimblow" wheels, remove the center contact.

2. Remove the steering wheel center nut and washer. Before removing the wheel, note the position of the index marks on the wheel and the steering shaft. If none are present, paint an alignment mark on the shaft and wheel.

3. Remove the wheel with a puller.

4. Installation is the reverse of removal. Tighten the steering wheel nut to 20 ft. lbs.

NOTE: Some shafts have metric threads. These can be identified by a groove in the shaft splines. Metric nuts are coded blue.

CAUTION
Do not hammer on the end of the steering shaft; the plastic retainers could shear, which maintain the rigidity of the energy-absorbing steering column.

4. On six cylinder engine models with air conditioning, loosen the idler pulley adjusting bolt and idler pulley, air pump adjusting strap mounting bolt and remove the compressor drive belt from the idler pulley. Loosen the two nuts that attach the upper leg of the aluminum idler pulley mounting bracket to the cylinder head and remove the bolt that attaches the lower leg of the mounting bracket to the engine front cover.

5. On six cylinder engine models, remove the nut from the air pump mounting stud, remove the power steering pump to engine front cover front adapter plate (do not unbolt the adapter plate from the pump), remove the long adjusting bolt that passes through the adapter plate, and remove the bolt hidden

AMERICAN MOTORS
CONCORD • EAGLE • EAGLE SX4 • SPIRIT

STEERING COLUMN

Removal

1. Disconnect battery negative cable.
2. Paint identifying marks on intermediate shaft and gear to aid assembly.
3. Remove flexible coupling nuts and disengage intermediate shaft from coupling.
4. On column shift cars, disconnect shift rod from steering column shift lever.
5. Move seat to rear as far as possible.
6. Remove lower finish panel or tube cover.

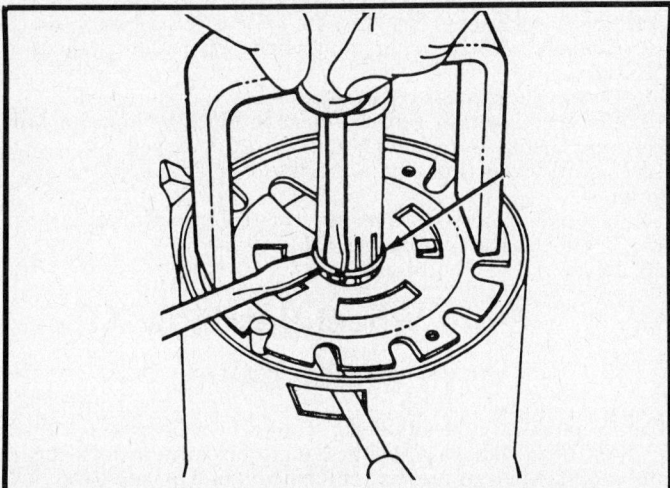

Removing lock plate retainer and snap ring
(© American Motors Corp.)

7. Remove package tray, if equipped.
8. Lift locking tab on steering column harness connector and separate column harness from instrument panel harness connector.
9. Press locking tabs on ignition switch harness connectors and disconnect harness from switch (remove black connector first).
10. Disconnect Cruise Command harness connector, if equipped.
11. Unhook shift quadrant pointer control cable from shift bowl.
12. Remove toeplate bolts from dash panel.
13. Remove bolts attaching steering column mounting bracket to column.

— CAUTION —
The column mounting bracket bolts are metric and are color-coded blue for identification. Keep these bolts with the bracket for assembly.

14. Support column assembly and remove nuts attaching column mounting bracket to instrument panel. Remove bracket and store in safe place to protect break-away capsules.
15. Remove column assembly from car.

Installation

— CAUTION —
Use only the specified screws, bolts, and nuts during assembly, and tighten them to the specified torque to maintain proper energy-absorbing action of the assembly. Over-length bolts must not be used as they may prevent a portion of the assembly from compressing under impact. The bolts or nuts attaching the column mounting bracket to the instrument panel must be tightened to the specified torque so the column mounting bracket will break away under impact.

1. Remove column holding fixture and install mounting bracket on column. Tighten bracket attaching bolts to 20 ft. lbs. torque.
2. If intermediate steering shaft was removed, install shaft on column using alignment marks made during removal.
3. Install column in car.

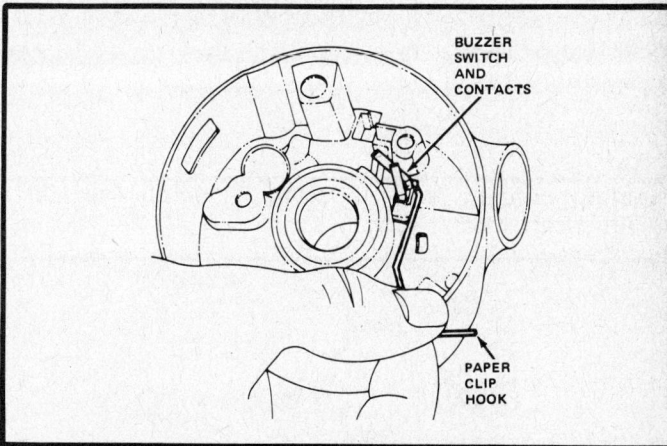

Removing buzzer switch and contacts
(© American Motors Corp.)

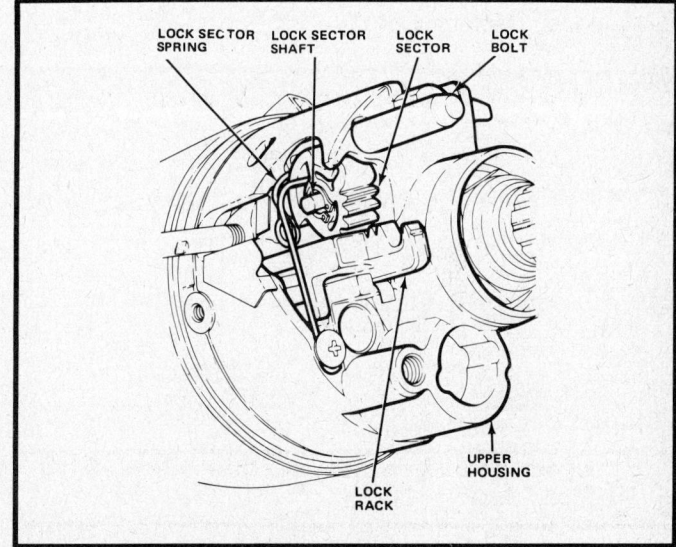

Position of lock sector tension spring
(© American Motors Corp.)

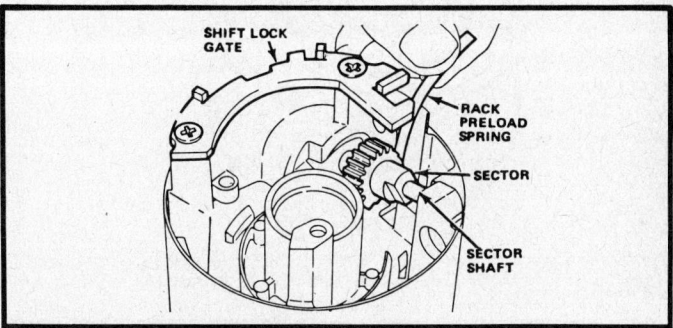

Removing rack preload spring
(© American Motors Corp.)

American Motors
CONCORD • EAGLE • EAGLE SX4 • SPIRIT

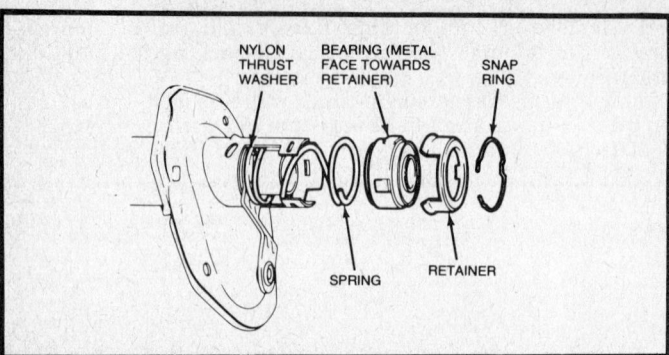

Steering column lower bearing assembly—typical (© American Motors Corp.)

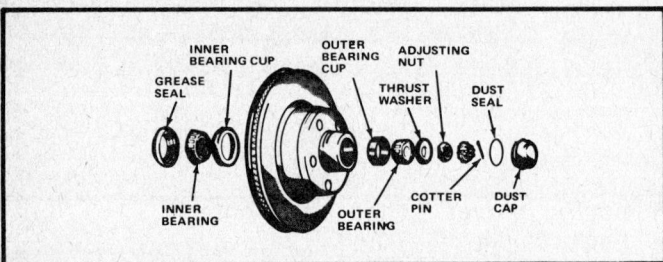

Front wheel bearing assembly, two wheel drive (© American Motors Corp.)

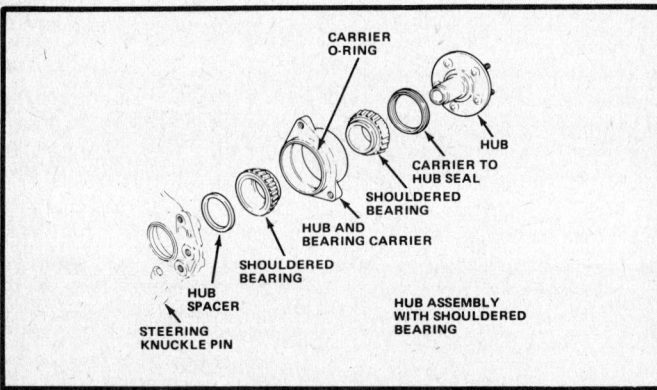

Front wheel bearing assembly, four wheel drive (© American Motors Corp.)

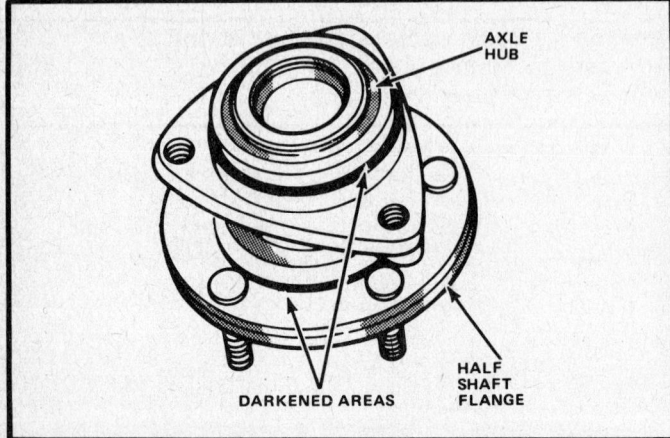

Darkened area locations on four wheel drive front wheel bearing (© American Motors Corp.)

4. Engage intermediate shaft flange with steering gear flexible coupling, and loosely install two column mounting bracket-to-instrument panel attaching nuts. Finger-tighten nuts only.
5. Install toeplate gasket, toeplate, and toeplate attaching bolts. Finger-tighten bolts only.
6. Install flexible coupling nuts and tighten to 30 ft. lbs. torque.
7. Install remaining column mounting bracket-to-instrument panel attaching nuts. Finger-tighten nuts only.
8. Position column so flexible coupling is flat and not distorted, and tighten column mounting bracket-to-instrument panel attaching nuts to 10 ft. lbs. torque.
9. Align toeplate and clamp and tighten attaching bolts to 10 ft. lbs. torque.
10. Connect shift linkage and check operation. Adjust if necessary.
11. Connect quadrant cable to shift-bowl, if equipped.
12. Connect ignition switch harness, steering column harness, and Cruise Command connector, if equipped.
13. Install lower finish panel, tube cover, or package tray, if equipped.
14. Remove protective covering from column painted areas.
15. Connect battery negative cable.
16. Reset clock, if equipped.

Front Wheel Bearings

TWO WHEEL DRIVE

When repacking and adjusting front wheel bearings, use an EP-type, lithium base wheel bearing lubricant. Pack the bearings with a generous amount of lubricant and place extra lubricant in the rotor hub cavity between the bearings. Always use a new grease seal during assembly.

When inspecting, replacing, or repacking bearings, be sure the inner cones of the bearings are free to creep on the spindle. The bearings are designed to creep to allow a constantly changing load contact between the cones and the rollers. Polishing and applying lubricant to the spindle will permit this movement and prevent rust formation.

Adjustment

1. Raise and support front of automobile.
2. Remove hub cap, grease cap and O-ring, cotter pin and nutlock.
3. On automobiles with styled wheels, remove wheel and hub cap. Install wheel.
4. Tighten spindle nut to 25 ft. lbs. (34 Nm) torque while rotating wheel to seat bearings.
5. Loosen spindle nut 1/3 turn. While rotating wheel, tighten spindle nut to 6 inch lbs. (0.7 Nm) torque.
6. Install nutlock on spindle nut so cotter pin holes in nutlock and spindle are aligned.
7. Install replacement cotter pin, grease cap and hub cap.
8. On automobiles with styled wheels, remove wheel, install hub cap and install wheel.

FOUR WHEEL DRIVE

Adjustment

Four wheel drive models have a unique front axle hub and bearing assembly. The assembly is sealed and does not require lubrication, periodic maintenance, or adjustment. The hub has ball bearings which seat in races machined directly into the hub. There are darkened areas surrounding the bearing race areas of the hub. These darkened areas are from a heat treat-

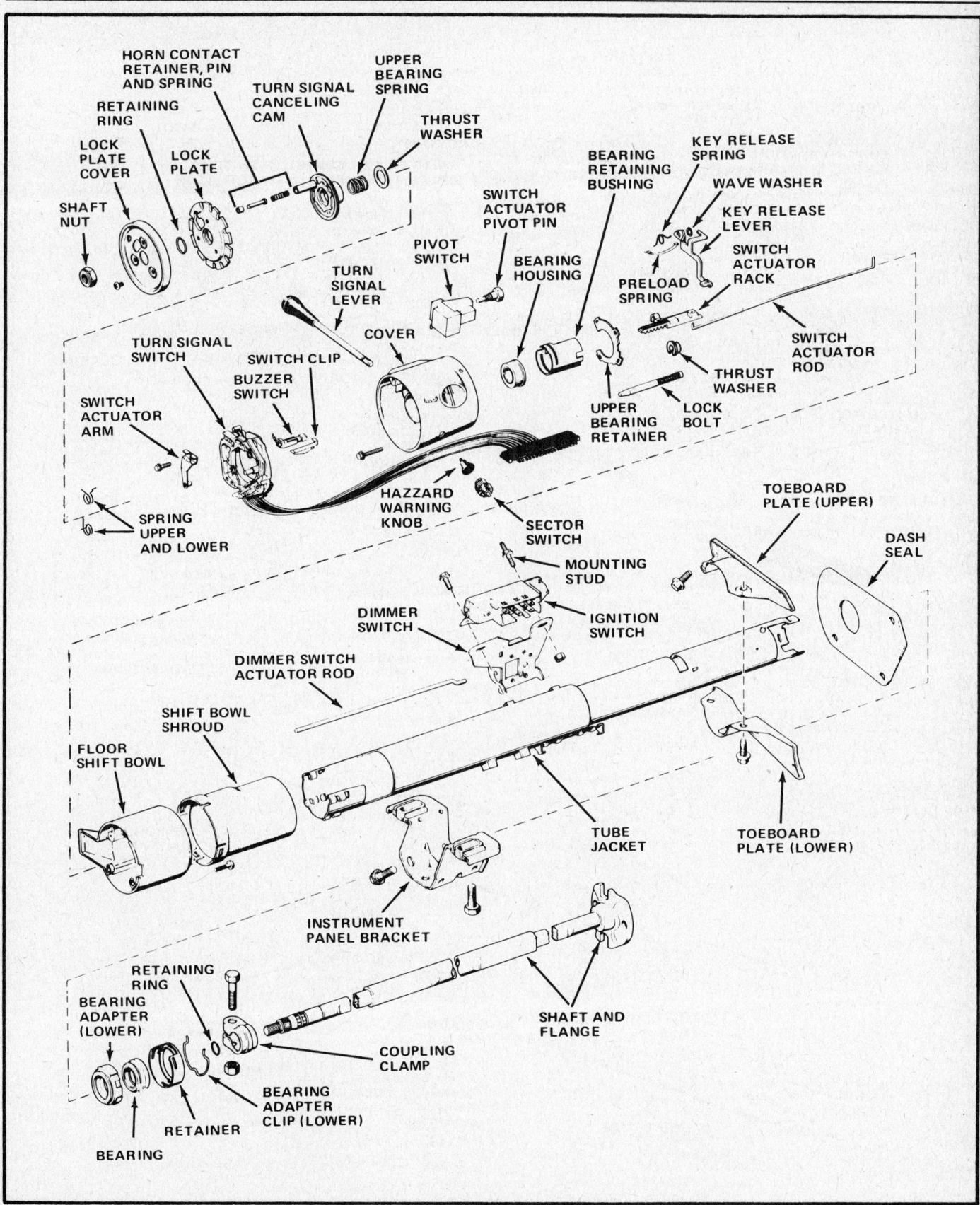

Exploded view of standard type column (© American Motors Corp.)

SECTION 1

AMERICAN MOTORS
CONCORD • EAGLE • EAGLE SX4 • SPIRIT

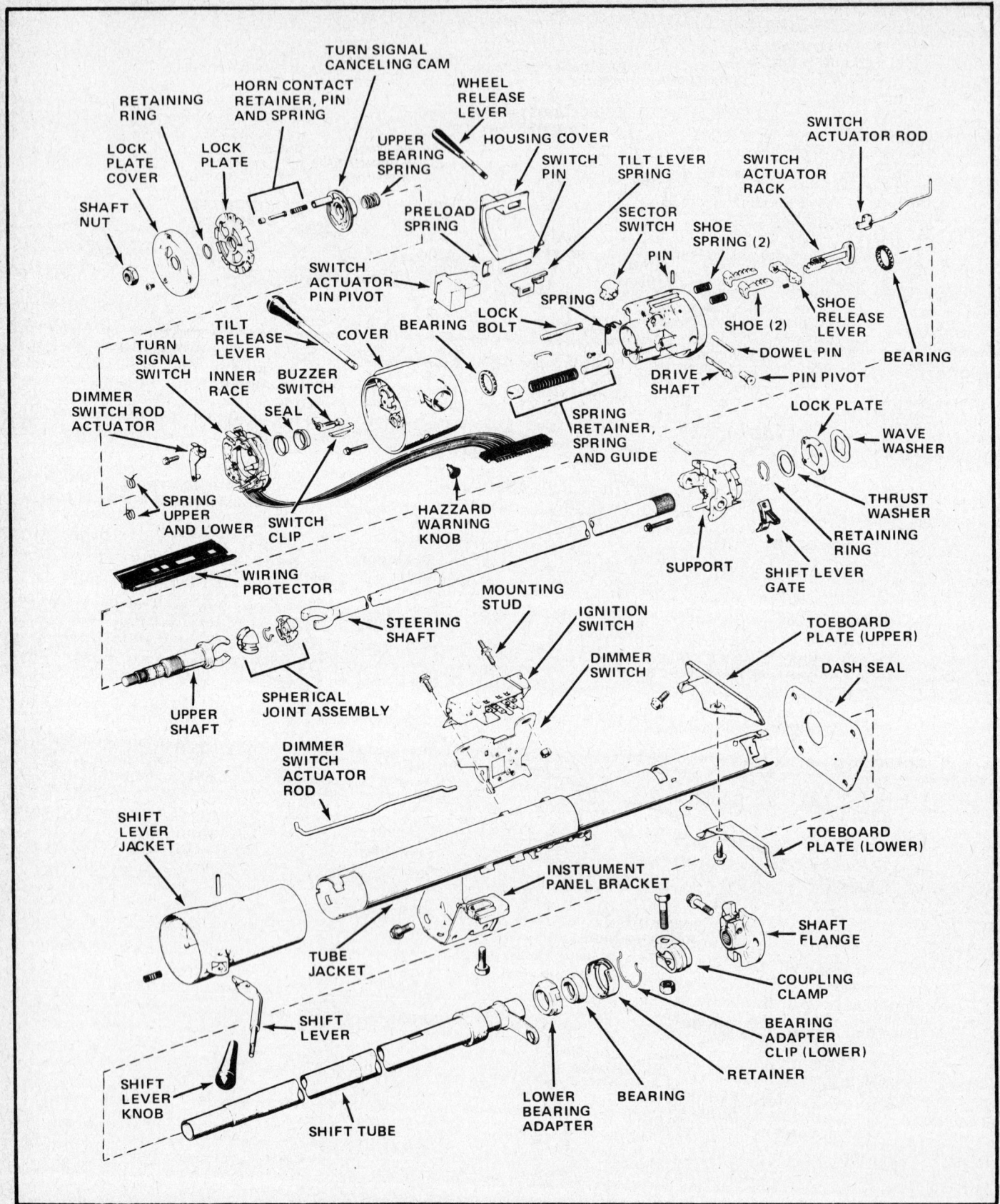

Exploded view of tilt steering column (© American Motors Corp.)

American Motors
CONCORD • EAGLE • EAGLE SX4 • SPIRIT

ment process, are normal, and should not be mistaken for a problem condition.

Removal

1. Remove wheel, caliper and rotor.
2. Remove bolts attaching axle shaft flange to halfshaft.
3. Remove cotter pin, nut lock and axle hub nut.
4. Remove halfshaft.
5. Remove steering arm from steering knuckle.
6. Remove caliper anchor plate from steering knuckle.
7. Remove three Torx head bolts retaining hub assembly using tool set J–25359 or equivalent.
8. Remove hub assembly from steering knuckle.
9. Clean grease from steering knuckle cavity.

Installation

1. Partially fill hub cavity of steering knuckle with chassis lubricant and install hub assembly.
2. Tighten hub Torx head bolts to 75 ft. lbs. (102 Nm) torque.
3. Install caliper anchor plate and plate retaining bolts.
4. Tighten caliper anchor plate retaining bolts to 100 ft. lbs. (136 Nm) torque.
5. Install halfshaft. Install axle flange-to-shaft bolts and install hub nut.
6. Tighten halfshaft-to-flange bolts to 45 ft. lbs. (61 Nm) torque.
7. Tighten hub nut to 175 ft. lbs. (237 Nm) torque.
8. Install nut lock and cotter pin.
9. Install rotor, caliper and wheel.

FRONT SUSPENSION

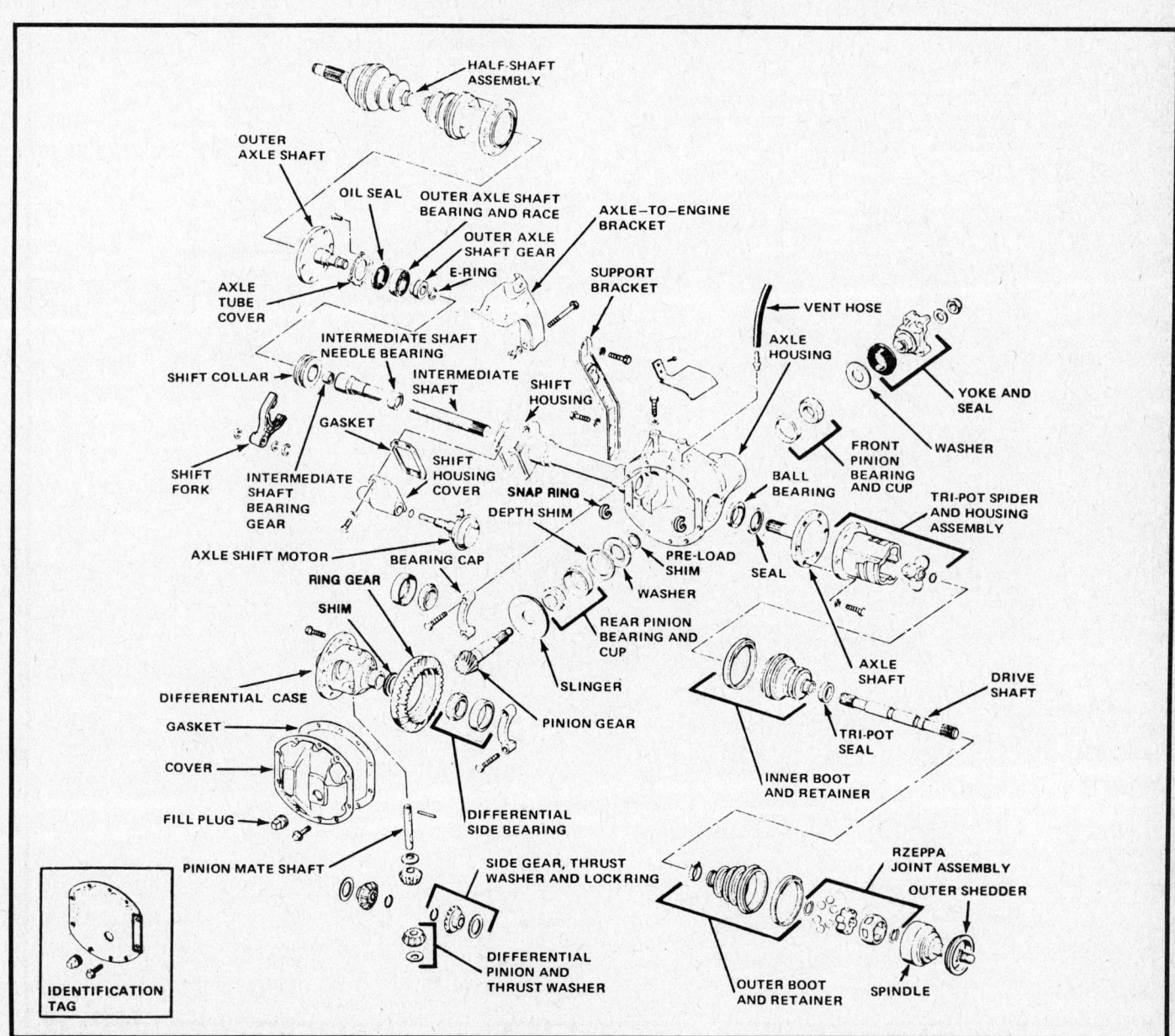

Exploded view of front axle assembly—Select Drive System (© American Motors Corp.)

American Motors
CONCORD • EAGLE • EAGLE SX4 • SPIRIT

NOTE: Refer to the Suspension Section for repair procedures.

Four Wheel Drive
SELECT DRIVE

EAGLE

The Select Drive gives the operator the option of driving in the two wheel or four wheel driving modes, merely by changing a switch, located on the dash. The model 30 front axle is used with the Select Drive system, having the two wheel drive disconnect mechanism located on the right hand axle tube.

A second disconnect mechanism is located on the transfer case. Both the axle and transfer case disconnect mechanisms are operated by vacuum controlled servo type motors. The vacuum shift motors are not interchangeable. The axle shift motor is vented to prevent lubrication from being drawn out of the axle by vacuum, should the shift motor seals become worn or damaged. The transfer case shift motor is not vented.

During the changes in the drive mode, the axle and the transfer case are shifted into the selected mode in sequence,

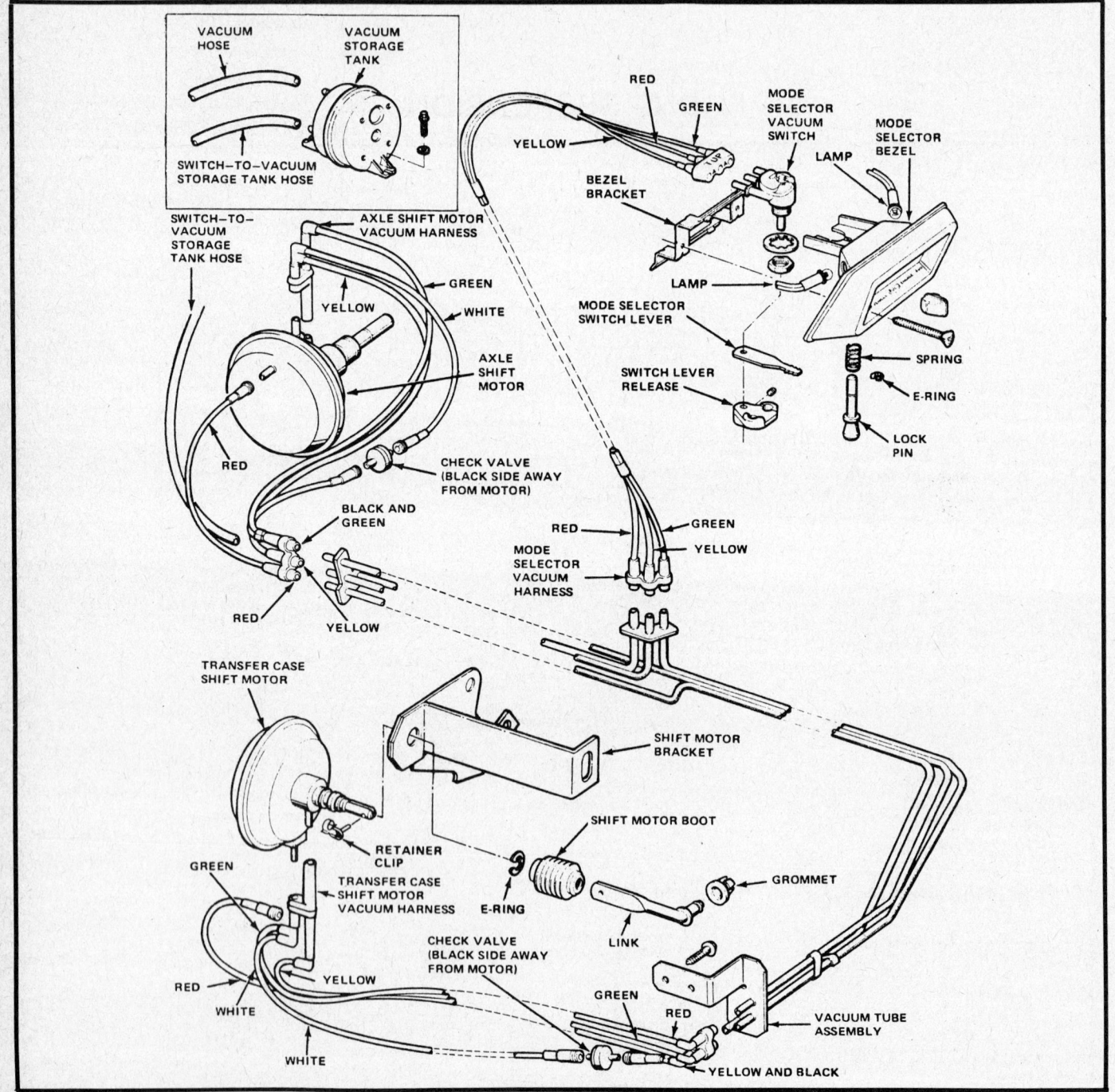

Vacuum control components—Select Drive System (© American Motors Corp.)

AMERICAN MOTORS
CONCORD • EAGLE • EAGLE SX4 • SPIRIT

NOT simultaneously. When the four wheel driving mode is selected, the axle is shifted first. When the two wheel drive mode is selected, the transfer case is shifted first.

OPERATION

NOTE: It may be necessary to move the vehicle forward or backward slightly, to fully engage or disengage the axle and transfer case.

When shifted to the four wheel drive mode, the axle shift motor is operated first. As complete axle engagement occurs, vacuum is directed from the axle shift motor to the transfer case motor, activating the motor and cause the transfer case to shift into the four wheel driving mode.

When shifted into the two wheel drive mode, vacuum is routed to the transfer case shift motor, opposite of the apply, which is vented, and the transfer case is disengaged. As the transfer case shift motor disengages the transfer case, a vacuum port is opened to the axle shift motor, causing it also to disengage in the same manner as the shift motor of the transfer case. Each shift motor is dependent upon the other to engage or disengage, depending upon the drive mode selected by the operator. One-way check valves incorporated in the system ensure that the axle and transfer case shift in the correct sequence and are vented properly. The check valves are located in the vacuum lines.

CAUTION
The vehicle must be at a complete stop when changing driving modes and may require a backward or forward motion of the vehicle to engage the axle and/or transfer case.

Testing

TRANSFER CASE SHIFT MOTOR

1. Disconnect the vacuum harness from the transfer case shift motor. Connect a controlled vacuum source to the shift motor from port.
2. Apply 15 in. Hg. of vacuum to the shift motor while rotating the rear propeller shaft to fully engage the transfer case in the four wheel drive mode.
3. The shift motor should maintain the applied vacuum for a minimum of 30 seconds. If the vacuum is not held, replace the motor.
4. If the motor holds the vacuum, connect the controlled vacuum source to the rear port of the shift motor and plug the front axle connecting port. Apply 15 in. Hg to the rear port.
5. If vehicle is equipped with automatic transmission, shift into the PARK position. If equipped with manual transmission, shift into first gear. The shift motor should maintain vacuum applied for a minimum of 30 seconds. If vacuum is not held, replace the motor.

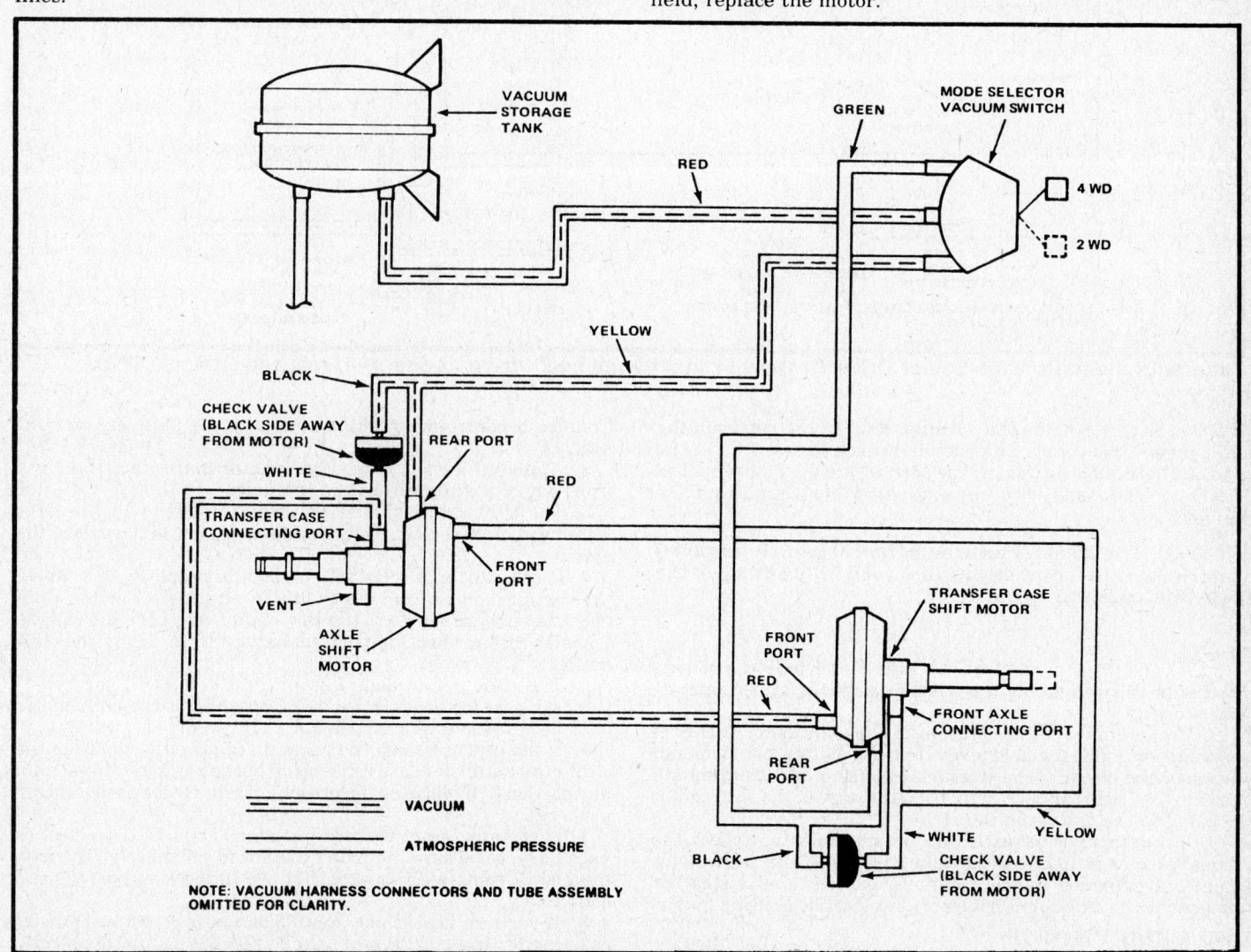

Vacuum schematic with Select Drive System in the four wheel drive mode (© American Motors Corp.)

1-61

AMERICAN MOTORS
CONCORD • EAGLE • EAGLE SX4 • SPIRIT

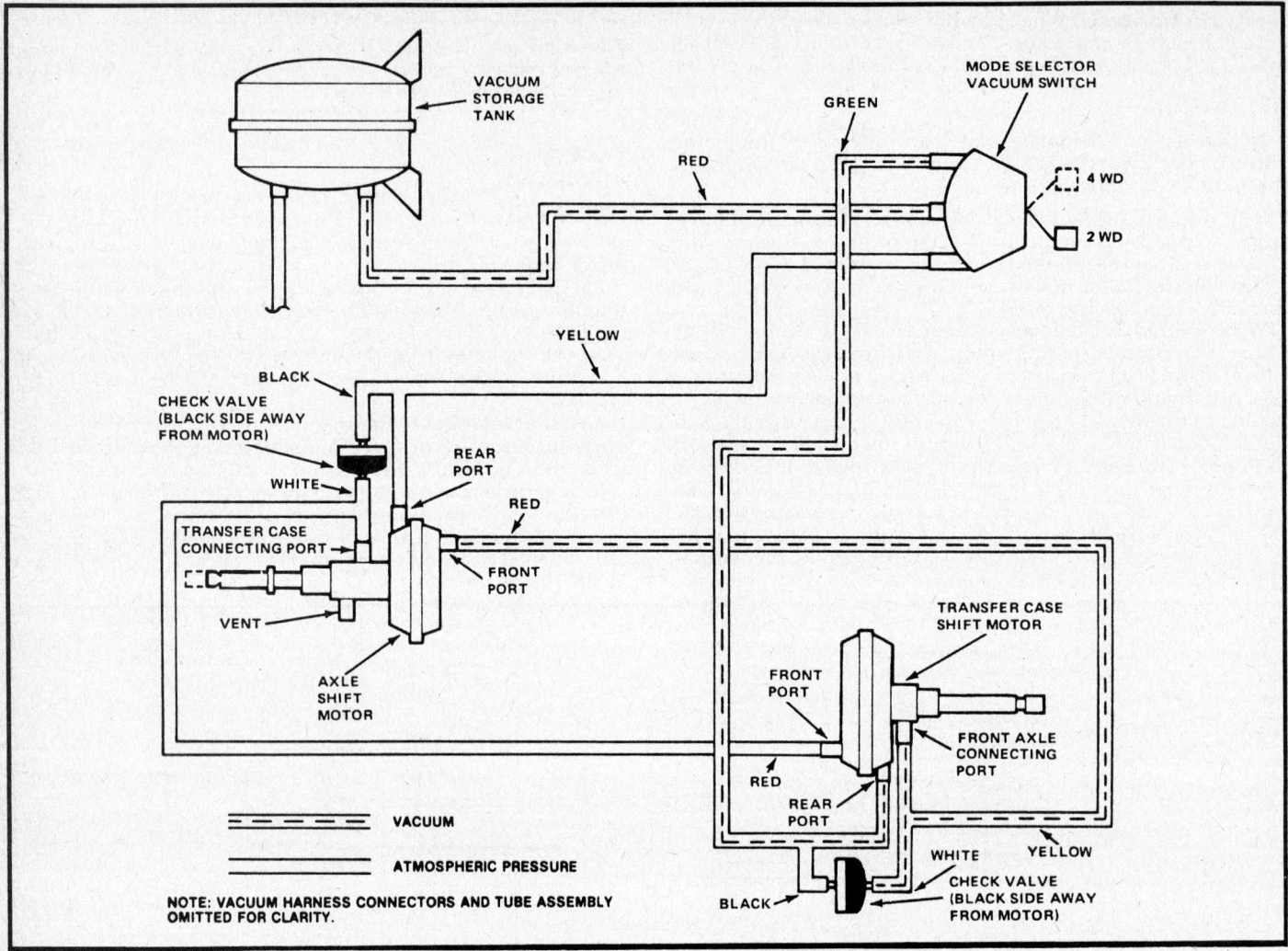

Vacuum schematic with Select Drive System in the two wheel drive mode (© American Motors Corp.)

6. If the motor holds the vacuum, remove the cap from the shift motor axle connecting port and check for vacuum at the port. If there is no vacuum at the port, rotate the rear propeller shaft as necessary, to ensure complete transfer case engagement.

NOTE: *The transfer case must be completely engaged before the shift motor stem will extend fully and open the axle interconnecting port.*

7. If vacuum is present at the shift motor axle connecting port after fully engaging the transfer case, the unit is operating properly.

8. If vacuum is still not present at the shift motor axle connecting port, slide the boot away from the shift motor stem and measure the distance the stem has extended. The stem should be extended a distance of $5/8$ in. from the edge of the shift motor housing to the E-ring on the stem.

9. If the stem has not extended to its specification, check the mode selector switch and vacuum harness. If the shift motor stem has extended to specifications, but vacuum is still not present at the axle connecting port, replace the shifting motor.

AXLE SHIFT MOTOR

1. Disconnect the vacuum harness from the axle shift motor. Connect a controlled vacuum source to the shift motor front port.

2. Apply 15 in. Hg to the shift motor and rotate the right front wheel to fully disengage the axle.

3. The shift motor should retain the applied vacuum for a minimum of 30 seconds. If the vacuum is not held, replace the motor.

4. If the shift motor holds the vacuum properly, disconnect the vacuum source from the front port on the shift motor. Connect the vacuum source to the shift motor rear port and cap the transfer case connecting port, and apply 15 in. Hg to the shift motor.

5. The shift motor should maintain the applied vacuum to the rear port for a minimum of 30 seconds. If the shift motor does not hold the vacuum, replace the motor.

6. If the motor retains the vacuum, remove the cap from the shift motor transfer case connecting port and check for vacuum at this port. If vacuum is present, shift motor is operating properly.

7. If vacuum is not present, rotate the right front wheel as necessary, to be sure the axle has shifted completely. The axle must shift completely in order for the connecting port to open completely.

8. If vacuum is still not present at the shift motor transfer case connecting port, replace the motor. If vacuum is present, the unit is operating properly.

American Motors
CONCORD • EAGLE • EAGLE SX4 • SPIRIT

BRAKES

All American Motors cars are equipped with tandem (dual reservoir) master cylinders. This allows one set of brakes to operate, should the other set fail. A switch in the system, connected to a warning light on the instrument panel, indicates a difference in pressure between the front and rear brake lines, thus indicating the failure of one brake system. Repair procedures for both the master cylinder and the switch are found in the Unit Repair Section.

All drum brakes have automatic brake adjusters. These compensate for lining wear, by operating when the brakes are applied while the car is backing up. The automatic mechanism is attached to the star wheel adjuster, which it works through.

Information on brake adjustments, lining replacement, bleeding procedure, master and wheel cylinder overhaul can be found in the Unit Repair Section.

MASTER CYLINDER
Removal and Installation

1. Disconnect the front and rear brake lines from the master cylinder. On cars equipped with drum brakes, the check valves will keep the fluid from draining out of the cylinder. If the car is equipped with disc brakes, one or both of the outlets must be plugged, to prevent fluid loss.
2. Remove the nuts which attach the master cylinder to the firewall or the power brake booster (if so equipped).
3. On cars that have non-power brakes, disconnect the pedal push rod at the brake pedal.
4. Remove the master cylinder from the car.
5. Installation is the reverse of removal. Remember to bleed the brake system after the master cylinder has been installed.

POWER BRAKE UNIT
Removal and Installation

1. Disconnect the power brake clevis pin from the power unit operating rod at the linkage under the hood, or from the brake pedal inside the car, depending on which type is being serviced.
2. Remove the vacuum hose from the check valve.
3. Separate the master cylinder from the power unit.
4. Do not disconnect the hydraulic lines from the master cylinder.
5. Remove the power unit mounting bolts and lift the unit from the car.
6. Installation is the reverse of removal.

PARKING BRAKE
Adjustment

1. Apply the brakes several times while backing up to adjust the drum brakes. Make one forward application for each reverse application to equalize the adjustment. Fully apply the parking brake about 10 times. Set the pedal on the first notch from the released position.
2. Block the front wheels and raise the rear wheels.
3. Tighten the cable at the equalizer so that the wheels can just barely be turned forward. Be sure to hold the end of the cable screw to prevent the cable from turning.
4. Release the parking brake and check for rear brake drag. The wheels should rotate freely with the parking brake off.

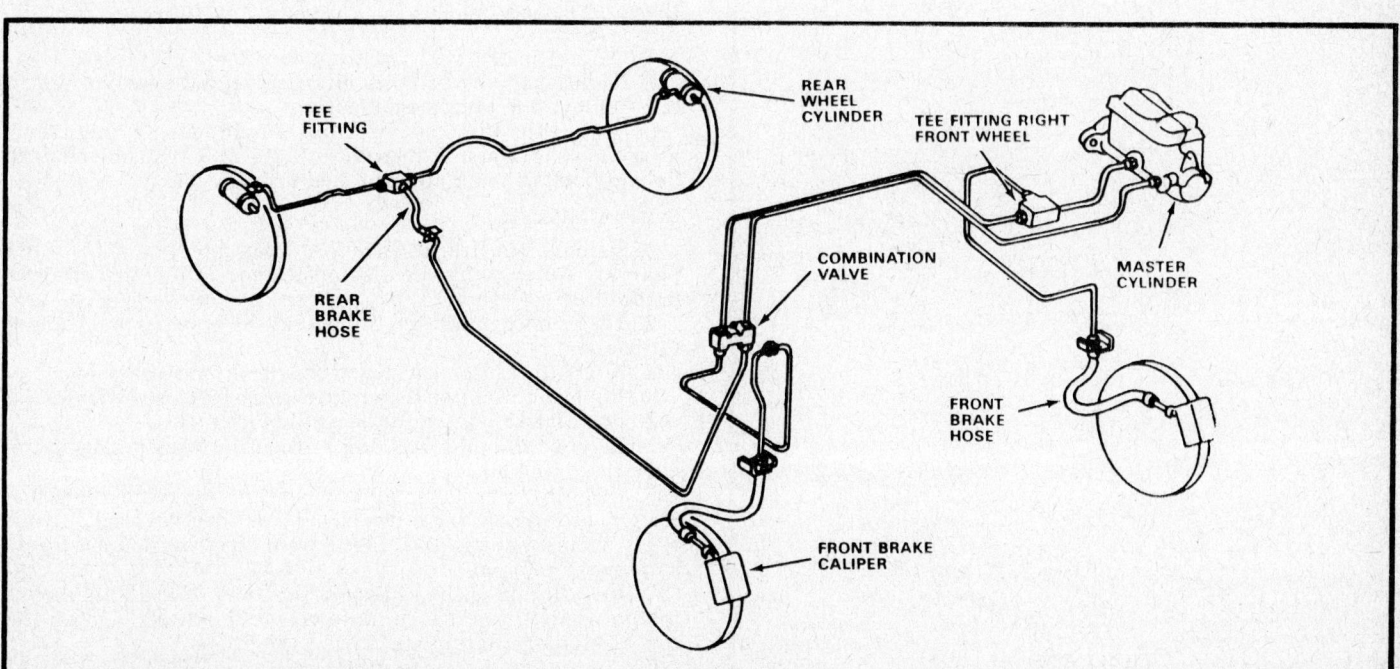

Typical dual brake system routing (© American Motors Corp.)

American Motors
CONCORD • EAGLE • EAGLE SX4 • SPIRIT

CLUTCH TRANSMISSION, TRANSFER CASE

Clutch

All models use a single, dry disc driven plate and a diaphragm type clutch cover. On all four cylinder models and Eagles equipped with six cylinder engines, the clutch is operated by a hydraulic mechanism. On the Spirit and Concord models with six cylinder engines, the clutch is operated by mechanical linkage.

PEDAL FREE PLAY

Adjustment

MECHANICAL LINKAGE

Adjust the free play of the clutch pedal to $7/8 - 1\ 1/8$ in. This is done by changing the length of the link between the throwout lever rod and the bellcrank assembly.

HYDRAULIC LINKAGE

No adjustment is required on the hydraulically actuated clutch mechanism.

CLUTCH REPLACEMENT

NOTE: Flywheel bolts must not be reused on four and six cylinder engines.

4-150, 4-151 ENGINES

1. Remove the starter, disconnect the slave cylinder spring at the throwout lever, and remove the transmission. Refer to Transmission Removal and Installation procedure.

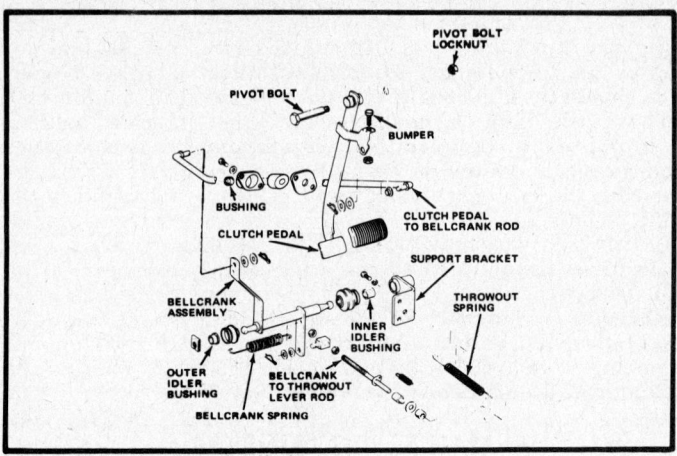

Mechanical clutch linkage
(© American Motors Corp.)

2. Remove the clutch housing-to-engine bolts. Remove the housing.
3. Remove the throwout bearing.
4. Matchmark the clutch cover and flywheel for installation. Loosen the clutch cover bolts alternately and evenly, to avoid distortion, and remove the clutch cover and disc.
5. Inspect the parts for signs of overheating (blue color), scoring, or abnormal wear. Overheated parts should be replaced. Deep scoring or wear may require replacement of the disc and cover, and refacing or replacement of the flywheel.
6. Place the disc and cover on the flywheel, aligning the marks made previously if the same cover is being used. Be sure the cover is engaged with the dowel pins. Install the cover bolts finger tight.
7. Align the disc with an alignment tool.
8. Tighten the cover bolts alternately and evenly to 23 ft. lbs. Remove the alignment tool.
9. Install the throwout bearing, clutch housing, and transmission. The housing-to-engine bolts and transmission-to-housing bolts should be tightened to 54 ft. lbs.

6-258 ENGINE

1. Remove the transmission, starter motor and throwout bearing. Refer to Transmission Removal and Installation procedure.
2. Disconnect the clutch linkage at the housing and remove the housing.
3. Mark the clutch cover and flywheel for reassembly.
4. Remove the clutch cover and the driven plate by loosening the bolts alternately and in several stages.
5. Remove the pilot bushing lubricating wick and soak the wick in engine oil.
6. Inspect the parts for signs of overheating (blue color), distortion, scoring, or wear. Overheated or deeply scored or worn parts should be replaced. Light wear may be cleaned up by sanding or refacing.
7. Installation is the reverse of removal. Use an alignment tool to position the driven plate on the flywheel. Tighten the cover bolts alternately and in several stages.

HYDRAULIC CLUTCH SYSTEM BLEEDING

Procedure

1. Fill the reservoir with brake fluid.

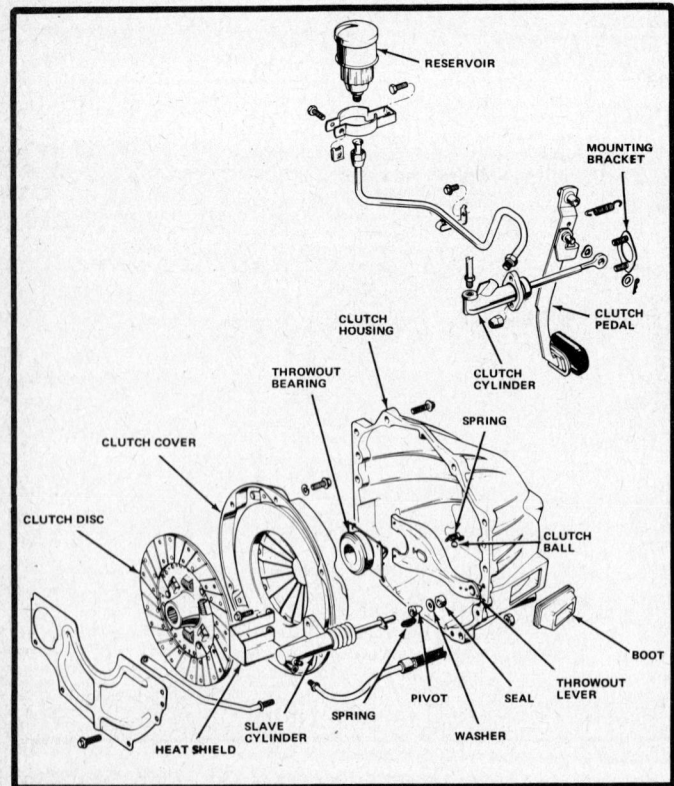

Hydraulic control clutch assembly
(© American Motors Corp.)

AMERICAN MOTORS
CONCORD • EAGLE • EAGLE SX4 • SPIRIT
SECTION 1

NOTE: On 1984 and later Eagle models with the four cylinder engines, remove the slave cylinder from the clutch cover housing and remove the push rod. Compress the slave cylinder plunger using tool J–24420–A, or its equivalent. Re-install when the bleeding operation is completed.

2. Loosen the bleed screw, have the clutch pedal pressed to the floor.
3. Tighten the bleed screw and release the clutch pedal.
4. Repeat the bleeding operation until the fluid is free of air bubbles.

CAUTION
Do not allow the reservoir to run out of fluid during the bleeding operation.

NOTE: It is suggested to attach a hose to the bleeder and place the other end into a container at least one-half full of brake fluid during the bleeding operation.

Manual Transmission
LINKAGE

Adjustment
COLUMN SHIFT

1. Disconnect shift rods from steering column levers, and put a 3/16 in. diameter rod through alignment holes in steering column shift levers. Put column gearshift lever in reverse, lock column, and put transmission first/reverse rod in reverse.
2. Adjust column shift rod trunnion for free pin fit in transmission shifter lever and tighten trunnion locknuts.
3. Unlock column and put gearshift lever in neutral with both transmission shift rods in neutral.
4. Adjust second/third shift rod trunnion to obtain free pin fit in column levers. Tighten trunnion locknuts.
5. Check that column will lock in reverse without binding.

Removal
EXCEPT EAGLE

1. On floor shift operated transmissions, remove the shift lever mechanism as follows, after placing the transmission in the neutral position.
   a. SR-4 Remove the knob, bezel, boot and bolts attaching the gear shift lever to the lever mounting flange on the extension housing. Lift the lever from the transmission.
   b. T-4, T-5 Remove the bezel, slide the boot and bezel upward on the lever. Remove the attaching bolts and lift the lever from the transmission.
2. Raise the engine hood to allow movement of the engine, avoiding damage to the hood or air cleaner.
3. Raise the vehicle and support safely.
4. Match mark the drive shaft and the rear axle yokes for reference during assembly. Remove the drive shaft.
5. Disconnect the speedometer cable, backup light switch wires. Disengage the wire harness from the retaining clips on the transmission, if used.
6. Install a support stand under the engine or clutch housing.
7. Remove converter support bracket.
8. If a ground strap is used, disconnect at the support cushion bolt.
9. Remove the bolts retaining the crossmember at the side sills.

CAUTION
Using the support stand, relieve the weight of the engine/transmission assembly from the crossmember before bolt removal.

---

10. On Spirit and Concord models, remove the crossmember. Maneuver the crossmember as necessary to clear the exhaust pipe.
11. Remove the two lower transmission-to-clutch housing bolts and install guide bolts, if available.
12. Lower the engine/transmission assembly far enough to remove the transmission from under the body.
13. Remove the two upper transmission-to-clutch housing bolts and slide the transmission from the guide pins, if used. Remove the transmission from the clutch housing.
14. During the removal of the transmissions, care must be exercised to prevent damage to the clutch shaft, pilot bushing and driven clutch plate.

Installation

1. If the pilot bushing has a lubricating wick, soak the wick in engine oil and re-install.
2. Shift the transmission in first gear and carefully slide the clutch shaft into the driven clutch plate.
3. If guide pins are used, slide the transmission over the pins, using the two lower transmission-to-clutch housing holes.
4. As the transmission clutch shaft is pushed into the clutch disc splines, rotate the transmission output shaft to align splines. Do not disturb the throwout bearing alignment during the transmission installation.
5. Raise the engine/transmission assembly and complete the assembly in the reverse order of the removal procedure.
6. Lower the vehicle and complete the assembly of the shifting lever.

NOTE: The internal shift linkage will have to be returned to the neutral position before the gearshift lever is installed.

Removal
EAGLE MODELS

1. Shift the transmission in the neutral position.
2. Remove the shift lever from the transmission adapter housing.
3. Remove the bolts attaching the gearshift lever mounting cover to the transmission adapter and remove the mounting cover to provide access to the transfer case upper mounting stud nut in the transmission adapter housing.
4. Remove the nut from the transfer case upper mounting stud.
5. Raise the vehicle and support safely.
6. Remove the skid plate, the speedometer adapter and cable.

NOTE: Mark the speedometer adapter before removing it from the transmission for ease in assembly.

7. Match mark the drive shafts and rear axle yokes. Remove the drive shafts.
8. Disconnect the back-up lamp switch wire.
9. Place a support stand under the engine and support the transmission and transfer case with a transmission jack. Remove the rear cross member.
10. Remove the catalytic converter bracket from the transmission and the brace rod from the bracket.
11. Remove the bolts retaining the transmission to the clutch housing and remove the transmission and transfer case as a unit.
12. The transmission can then be separated from the transfer case.

Installation

1. Lubricate the pilot bushing wick by soaking in engine oil. Install the wick in place.

1–65

American Motors
CONCORD • EAGLE • EAGLE SX4 • SPIRIT

2. Shift the transmission in first gear and install the transmission/transfer case assembly into position.
3. Install the retaining bolts through the transmission and into the clutch housing.
4. Complete the assembly in the reverse order of the removal procedure.
5. Lower the vehicle and shift the internal shift linkage to the neutral position. Install the gearshift lever.

Automatic Transmission

Removal

4 AND 6 CYLINDER MODELS

1. Open the engine hood and disconnect the fan shroud. Remove the fill tube attaching bolt.
2. Raise the vehicle and support safely.
3. Remove the skid plate on the Eagle models.
4. Match mark and remove the drive shaft(s).
5. Remove or loosen necessary exhaust system components and bracing brackets.
6. Remove the starter assembly. Remove stiffening braces on Eagle models.
7. Match mark and remove speedometer adapter and cable assembly.
8. Disconnect the shift and throttle linkage. On column shift vehicles, remove the bellcrank bracket bolt at the converter housing.
9. Disconnect the neutral start and back-up light switch connector. Remove the TCS switch oil line, if equipped.
10. Remove cover in front of the converter, if equipped and match mark converter to the converter drive plate.
11. Remove the converter to drive plate bolts.
12. Support the transmission assembly with a lifting and lowering device. Safety chain the transmission assembly to the device.

NOTE: On Eagle models, the transfer case will be removed with the transmission as a unit.

13. Remove bolt(s) at the rear support cushion.
14. Remove the rear cross member and groundstrap, if equipped with strap.
15. Move the transmission as necessary and remove the oil cooler lines.
16. Place a support stand under the engine as required.
17. Remove transmission fill tube, as required.

NOTE: Transmission fluid will drain out. Plug fill tube hole.

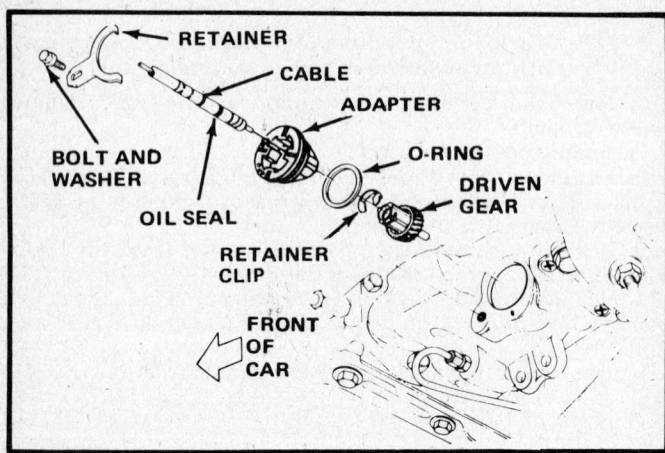

Speedometer cable adapter—typical
(© American Motors Corp.)

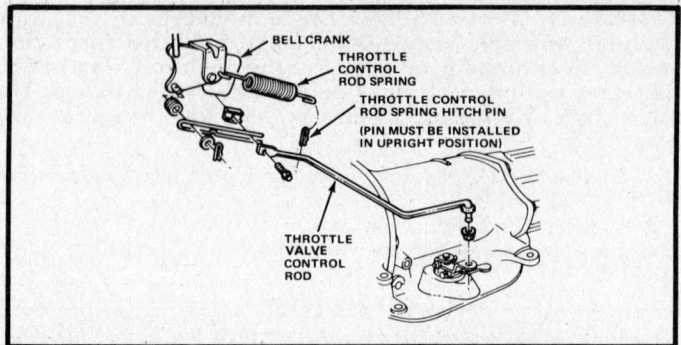

Throttle valve control mechanism—typical
(© American Motors Corp.)

18. Remove bolts attaching transmission to the engine.
19. Move the transmission assembly rearward and while holding the converter in position, lower the assembly from under the vehicle.

Installation

1. The installation of the transmission is the reverse of the removal procedure. However, varied steps must be accomplished or checked before and during the installation of the unit.
    a. If the torque converter was removed or inadvertently separated from the transmission, a new pump seal should be installed and the pump rotor drive lugs re-aligned with an aligning tool, before the converter is re-installed.
    b. With a lifting device, raise the transmission assembly and align the converter housing with the engine attaching flange dowel pins. Match the marks between the converter and the drive plate. Install the attaching bolts, eat the converter housing flush with the engine flange before tightening the bolts.

NOTE: Drive plate bolts must not be reused on four and six cylinder engines.

    c. Install the oil cooler lines, the rear engine crossmember and the mount bolt(s).
    d. Complete the assembly and check the fluid level of the transfer case lubricant on the Eagle models.
    e. Lower the vehicle and complete the assembly topside.
    f. Fill the transmission with fluid and correct the level as necessary.
    g. Road test the vehicle and check the transmission operation.

THROTTLE LINKAGE

Adjustment

4-150, 6-258 ENGINE MODELS

1. Disconnect the throttle control rod spring.
2. Use the throttle control rod spring to hold the adjusting link in the forward position against the nylon washer.
3. Block the choke open and set the carburetor throttle off the fast idle cam.
4. Raise the vehicle and loosen the retaining bolt on the throttle control adjusting link.

NOTE: Certain late models use two retaining bolts. Loosen both. On four cylinder engines, do not remove spring clip and nylon washer.

5. Connect one end of a spare throttle return spring on the throttle lever and the other end in the cast boss on the side of the torque converter housing or to the bellcrank bracket.

American Motors
CONCORD • EAGLE • EAGLE SX4 • SPIRIT

6. Push on the end of the link to eliminate the lash and pull the clamp rearward so the bolt bottom sin the rear slot of the rod. Tighten the forward clamp bolt.
7. Pull the throttle control rod rearward so the bolt in the rod bottoms in the front slot of the rod. Tighten the rearward retaining bolt.
8. Remove the spare throttle return spring from the throttle lever and lower the vehicle.
9. Remove the throttle control rod spring from the adjusting link and install the spring on the control rod.

THROTTLE CABLE

Adjustment

4–151 ENGINE MODELS

1. Remove the air cleaner assembly, remove the spark plug wire separator from the throttle cable bracket and set aside.
2. Raise the vehicle and support safely.
3. Remove the strut rod bushing heat shield to gain access to the throttle control lever.
4. With a spare throttle control rod spring, attach to hold the throttle control lever rearward against its stop.
5. Lower the vehicle and block the choke valve open. Set the carburetor throttle off the fast idle cam.
6. On models without air conditioning, energize the throttle stop solenoid throughout the adjustment.
7. Unlock the throttle cable by releasing the "T" shaped cable adjuster clamp by lifting upward with a small pry tool.
8. Grasp the cable outer sheath and move the cable and sheath forward to remove any cable load on the throttle bellcrank (part of carburetor throttle linkage).
9. Adjust the cable by moving cable and sheath rearward until there is zero lash between the plastic end and the bellcrank ball.
10. Lock the cable by depressing the "T" shaped cable adjusting clamp until the clamp snaps into place.
11. De-energize the throttle stop solenoid. Install the spark plug wires and separator and any other component that was removed or disconnected.
12. Install the air cleaner assembly.
13. Raise the vehicle and support safely. Remove the holding spring from the throttle control lever and install the strut rod bushing heat shield.
14. Lower the vehicle and road test to check transmission operation. Readjust the throttle cable, if necessary.

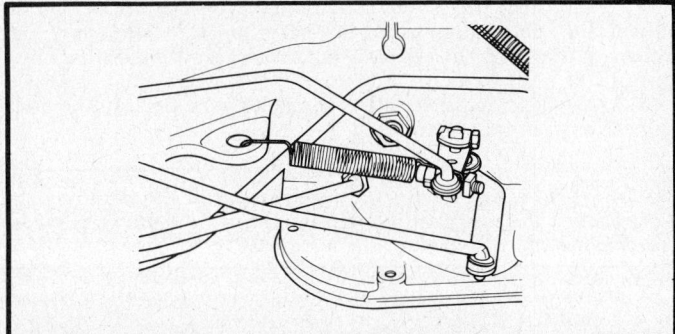

Installing throttle control lever spring
(© American Motors Corp.)

MANUAL LINKAGE

Adjustment

1. Place the shift lever in the Park position and lock the steering column.
2. Raise the vehicle and loosen the shift rod trunnion and move the transmission lever into the park detent.

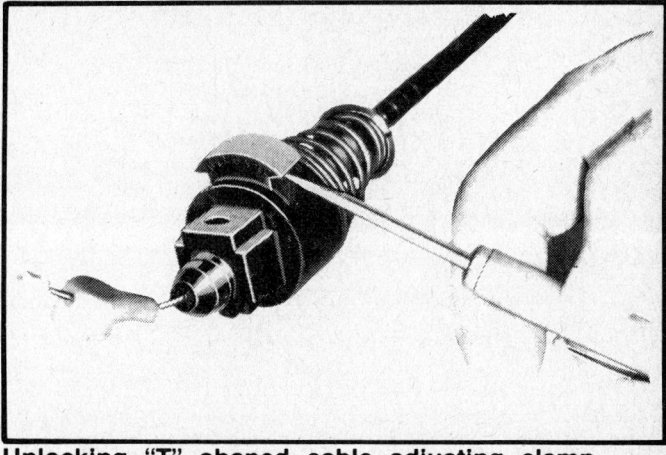

Unlocking "T" shaped cable adjusting clamp
(© American Motors Corp.)

3. Check the park lock operation by attempting to rotate the drive shaft. If operation is satisfactory, shaft will not turn.
4. Tighten the shift rod trunnion and lower the vehicle.
5. Check the engine for proper starting in the Park and Neutral positions only.

SHIFT QUADRANT POINTER

Adjustment

1. Remove the steering column tube cover and place the shift lever in the Neutral position.
2. Loosen the adjusting clip retaining screw and move the clip up or down as required to center the quadrant needle at the Neutral position.
3. Tighten the retaining screw and re-check the needle positioning.
4. Install the steering column tube cover.

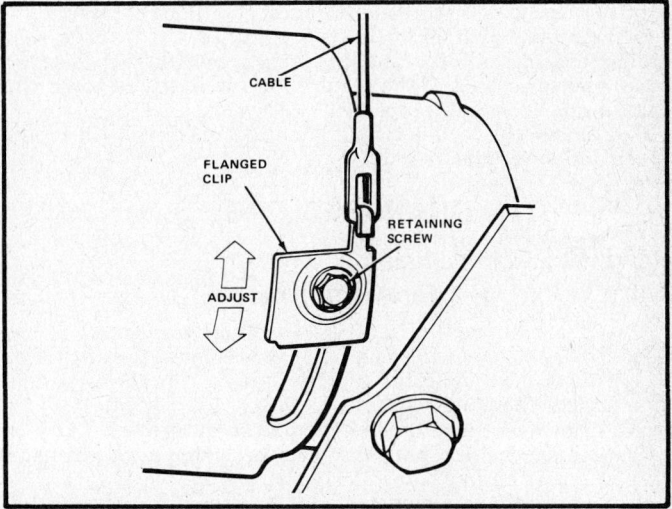

Shift quadrant indicator cable adjustment
(© American Motors Corp.)

Transfer Case Model 129

TORQUE BIAS TEST

This test may be performed to determine the condition of the viscous coupling, which is the "heart" of the AMC transfer case. Note that if a malfunction in the coupling is observed, the

AMERICAN MOTORS
CONCORD • EAGLE • EAGLE SX4 • SPIRIT

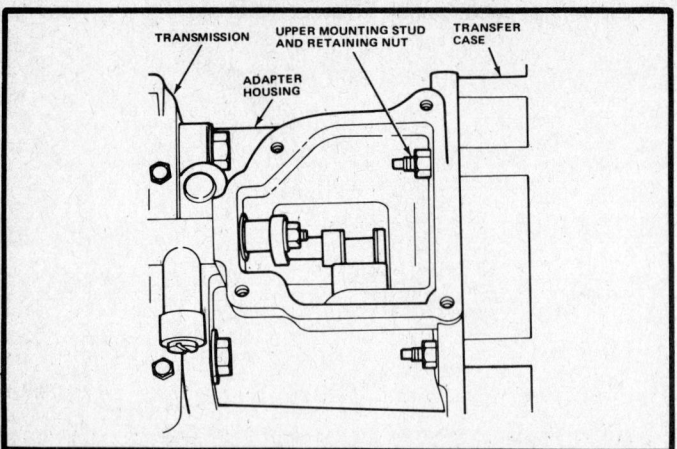

Transfer case mounting stud location when the engine is equipped with SR-4 transmission
(© American Motors Corp.)

coupling cannot be repaired in any way, but must be replaced if defective. The following procedure is an in-vehicle test. If the transfer case is to be disassembled, test the coupling as outlined within the overhaul procedure (bench test) in the Unit Repair Section.

1. Drive the vehicle onto a level surface, turn the engine OFF, and place the transmission shift lever in Neutral. On 1983 and later models, place the Select Drive lever in the 4WD position.
2. Raise one of the front wheels off of the floor, then remove the wheel cover from the raised wheel.
3. Attach a socket (of the same size as the lug nuts) to a torque wrench. Install the socket and torque wrench to any one of the lug nuts of the raised wheel.
4. Rotate the wheel with the torque wrench and note the amount of torque required to turn the wheel.
5. A reading of 45 ft. lbs. minimum should be obtained. If a reading of less than 45 ft. lbs. was obtained, the transfer case must be disassembled, and the bench test of the coupling should be performed. If the reading was 45 ft. lbs. or more, the coupling is operating properly.
6. Remove the torque wrench and socket, install the wheel cover and lower the vehicle.

TRANSFER CASE

Removal and Installation
WITH MANUAL TRANSMISSION

1. When equipped with a SR-4 manual transmission, the gearshift lever mounting cover must be removed to gain access to the upper mounting stud and retaining nut in the transmission adapter housing.
2. All models Raise the vehicle and support safely.
3. Remove the skid plate and rear brace rod at the transfer case. Support engine/transmission assembly.
4. Remove the speedometer adapter and cable, after match marking the adapter to the housing.
5. Match mark the drive shafts and remove from the transfer case yokes.
6. Remove the vacuum shift motor harness.
7. Support the transfer case and remove the retaining nuts from the studs and remove the transfer case.
8. The installation of the transfer case assembly is the reverse of the removal procedure.
9. Make all connections and check the fluid level in the transfer case and re-install shift lever mounting cover on the SR-4 transmission.

WITH AUTOMATIC TRANSMISSION

1. Raise the vehicle and support safely.
2. Support the engine/transmission assembly.
3. Disconnect catalytic converter support bracket at the adapter housing, if equipped.
4. Remove the skid plate and rear brace rod at the transfer case.
5. Match mark the speedometer adapter and remove it and the speedometer cable.
6. Match mark the drive shafts and disconnect from the transfer case yokes.
7. Disconnect the gearshift and throttle linkage at the transmission. Support the transfer case.
8. Lower the rear cross member.
9. Remove the retaining case to adapter housing stud nuts and remove the transfer case.
10. The installation is the reverse of the removal procedure.
11. Install new speedometer adapter O ring and correct the fluid levels of the transmission and transfer case.

NOTE: 1983 and later Eagle Models -- If the transfer case has been disassembled and repaired, fill the transfer case to the bottom edge of the filler hole with appropriate lubricant and install the plug. Drive the vehicle approximately 8-10 miles and recheck the lubricant level. Refill as necessary. This method results in a more accurate lubricant fill.

Rear Axle, Axle Shaft, Bearing and Seal

Removal and Installation

1. The hub and drum are separate units and are removed after the wheel is removed. The hub and axle shaft are serrated together on the taper. An axle shaft key assures proper alignment during assembly.
2. With the wheel on the ground and the parking brake applied, remove and discard the axle shaft nut cotter pin and remove the nut. Raise the car and remove the wheel. Release the parking brakes and remove the drum.
3. Attach a puller to the rear hub and remove the hub. The use of a "Knock-out" puller should be discouraged, since it may result in damage to the axle shaft, wheel bearings or differential thrust block.
4. Disconnect the parking brake cable at the equalizer.
5. Disconnect the brake tube at the wheel cylinder and remove the brake support plate assembly, oil seal, and axle shims. Note that the axle shims are located on the left side only.
6. Using a screw type puller, remove the axle shaft and bearings from the axle housing.

CAUTION

On Twin-Grip axles, rotating the differential with one shaft removed will misalign the side gear splines, preventing installation of the replacement shaft.

---

7. Remove the axle shaft inner oil seal and install new seals at assembly.
8. The bearing is a press fit and should be removed with an arbor press.
9. The axle shaft bearings have no provision for lubrication after assembly. Before installing the bearings, they should be packed with a good quality wheel bearing lubricant.
10. Press the axle shaft bearings onto the axle shaft with the small diameter of the cone toward the outer (tapered) end of the shaft.
11. Soak the inner axle shaft seal in light lubricating oil. Coat the outer surface of the seal retainer with sealant.
12. Install the inner oil seal.

13. Install the axle shafts, indexing the splined end with the differential side gears.
14. Install the outer bearing cup.
15. Install the brake support plate. Sealant should be applied to the axle housing flange and brake support mounting plate.
16. Install the original shims, oil seal and brake support plate. Torque the nuts to 30-35 ft. lbs.

NOTE: The oil seal and retainer go between the axle housing flange and the brake support plate.

17. To adjust the axle shaft end-play, strike the axle shafts with a lead mallet to seat the bearings. Install a dial indicator on the brake support plate and check the play while pushing and pulling the axle shaft. End-play should be 0.004-0.008 in., with 0.006 in. desirable. Add shims to the left side only to decrease the play and remove shims to increase the play.
18. Slide the hub onto the axle shafts aligning the serrations and the keyway on the hub with the axle shaft key.
19. Replace the hub and drum, install the wheel, lower the car onto the floor and tighten the axle shaft nut to 250 ft. lbs. If the cotter pin hole is not aligned with a castellation on the nut, tighten the nut to the next castellation.

NOTE: A new hub must be installed whenever a new axle shaft is installed. Install two thrust washers on the shaft. Tighten the new hub onto the shaft until the hub is 1 $^3/_{16}$ in. (30.14 mm) from the end of the shaft. Remove the nut; remove one thrust washer. Install the nut and torque to 250 ft. lbs. New hubs do not have serrations on the axle shaft mating surface. The serrations are cut when the hub is installed to the axle shaft.

20. Connect the parking brake cable at the equalizer.
21. Connect the brake tube at the wheel cylinder and bleed the brakes.

AXLE ASSEMBLY

Removal and Installation

1. Apply the parking brake to lock the rear wheels. Remove the axle shaft nuts.
2. Raise the vehicle and support safely. Remove the rear wheels.

NOTE: The brake drums and axle shafts can be removed at this time, or can be removed after the axle assembly has been removed from the vehicle.

3. Disconnect the flexible brake line at the body floorpan bracket. Release and disconnect the parking brake cables at the equalizer.
4. Mark the propeller shaft and yokes for assembly reference.
5. Remove the stabilizer bar, if equipped.
6. Disconnect the axle vent hose and support the rear axle with a lifting device.
7. Disconnect the shock absorbers at the spring tie plates.
8. Remove the spring U-bolts, spring plates and spring clip plate if equipped with the stabilizer bar.
9. Lower the axle assembly and remove from under the vehicle.
10. The installation of the rear axle is in the reverse of the removal procedure.
11. Tighten the U-bolt nuts to 55 ft. lbs. torque.

NOTE: The driveshaft is a balanced unit; care must be used in handling. Do not bend or distort the tube or yokes, or vibration will result.

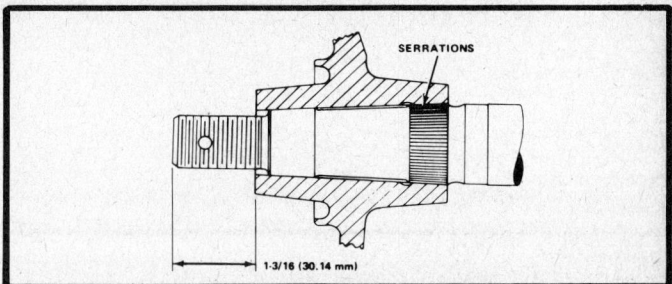

Measurement for replacement hub installation onto axle shaft (© American Motors Corp.)

DRIVESHAFT

Removal and Installation

CONCORD AND SPIRIT

1. Matchmark and disassemble rear U-joint by removing nuts. Retention is by U-bolts or straps, depending on model.
2. Drop rear of driveshaft and slide front yoke out of transmission.
3. To install, reverse removal procedure, tightening U-joint nuts to 15 ft. lbs.

EAGLE

Both driveshafts are secured at the transfer case end and the axle yoke end by straps. The straps are retained by Torx head bolts.

1. Shift into Neutral. Raise and support the car.
2. Matchmark the driveshaft(s) at the transfer case and axle yoke for alignment reference.
3. Remove the retaining straps with a Torx bit tool of the proper size. Remove the driveshaft(s).
4. To install, align the matchmarks made during removal to assure proper balance. Seat the universal joints in the yokes and install the straps, tightening to 17 ft. lbs.

UNIVERSAL JOINT

Overhaul

NOTE: Overhaul procedures can be found in the Drive Axles and U-Joints Unit Repair Section.

REAR SUSPENSION

NOTE: Refer to the Suspension Section the Unit Repair section for Removal and Installation Procedures.

All Spirit, Concord and Eagle models use a four or five-leaf semi-elliptic spring, and live axle rear suspension. Shock absorbers are mounted at their lower ends to studs and are bayonet or stud type at their upper ends.

SHOCK ABSORBER

Replacement

NOTE: When installing new shocks purge them of air by repeatedly extending them in their normal position and compressing them while inverted. It is normal for there to be more resistance to extension than to compression.

1. Support the rear axle with jacks or a lift; this allow the weight of the car to compress the rear spring.
2. Remove the lower shock attachment.

AMERICAN MOTORS
CONCORD • EAGLE • EAGLE SX4 • SPIRIT

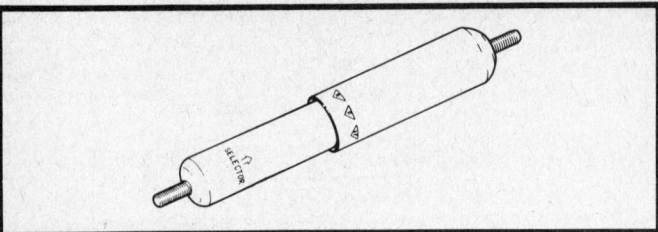

Adjustable shock absorber
(© American Motors Corp.)

3. Remove the shock absorber from the upper mounting bracket to the underbody panel.
4. Remove the shock from under the car.
5. Installation is the reverse of removal.

RIDE CONTROL

Adjustment
WITH ADJUSTABLE SHOCK ABSORBERS

1. Raise and safely support the vehicle.
2. Remove the slower shock absorber attaching nut assembly.
3. Locate the adjustment setting indicators on the upper part of the shock absorber and the selector arrow on the lower part of the shock body.
4. Compress the shock absorber completely.
5. Hold the upper part of the shock and turn the lower part until the selector arrow aligns with the desired setting of R (Regular), F (Firm) or XF (Extra Firm).
6. A noticeable click will be heard as the shock position is adjusted to the desired setting.
7. Re-assemble the lower shock to spring clip plate.

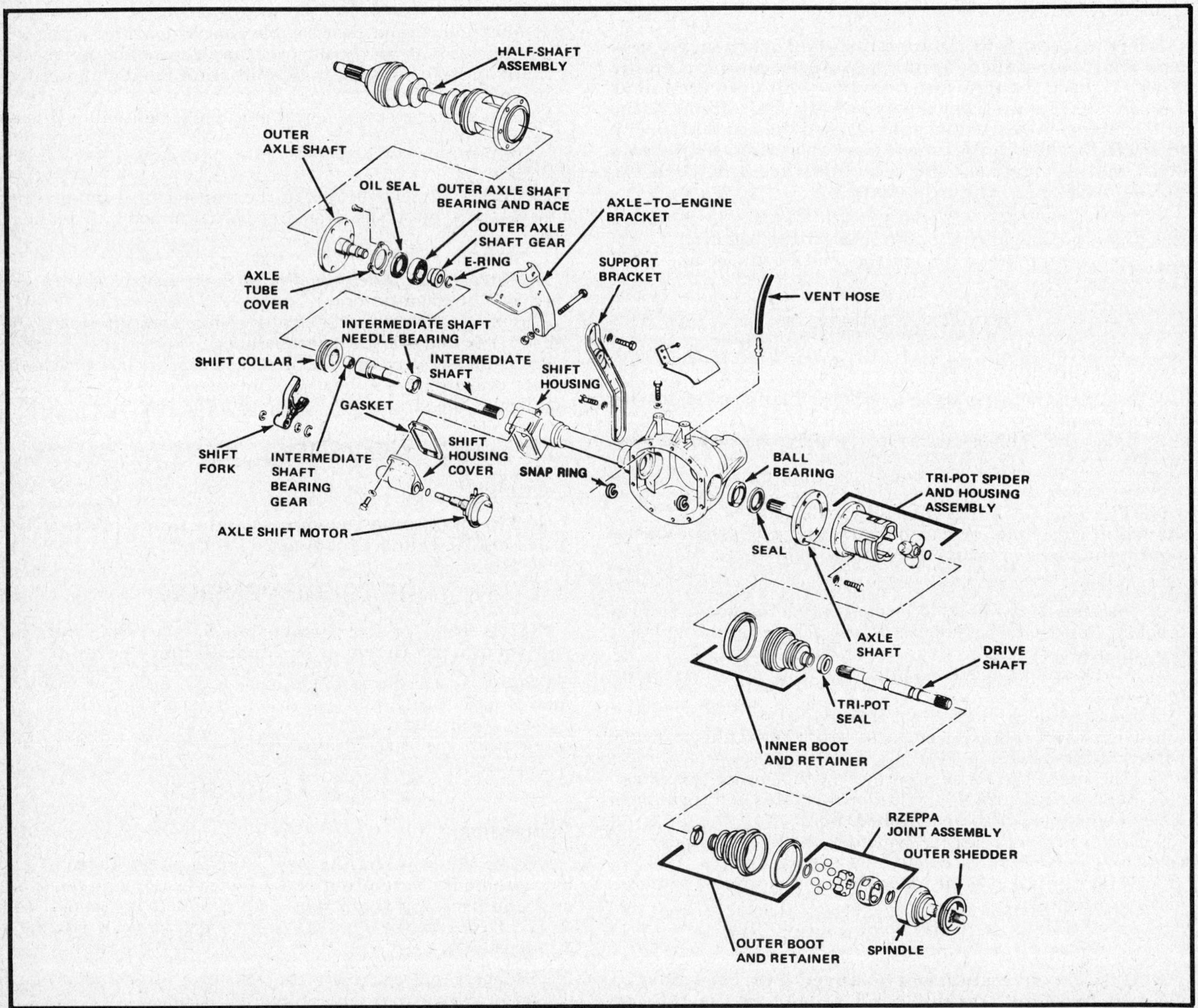

Exploded view of left and right axle assemblies—Eagle Select Drive System (© American Motors Corp.)

American Motors
CONCORD • EAGLE • EAGLE SX4 • SPIRIT

SECTION 1

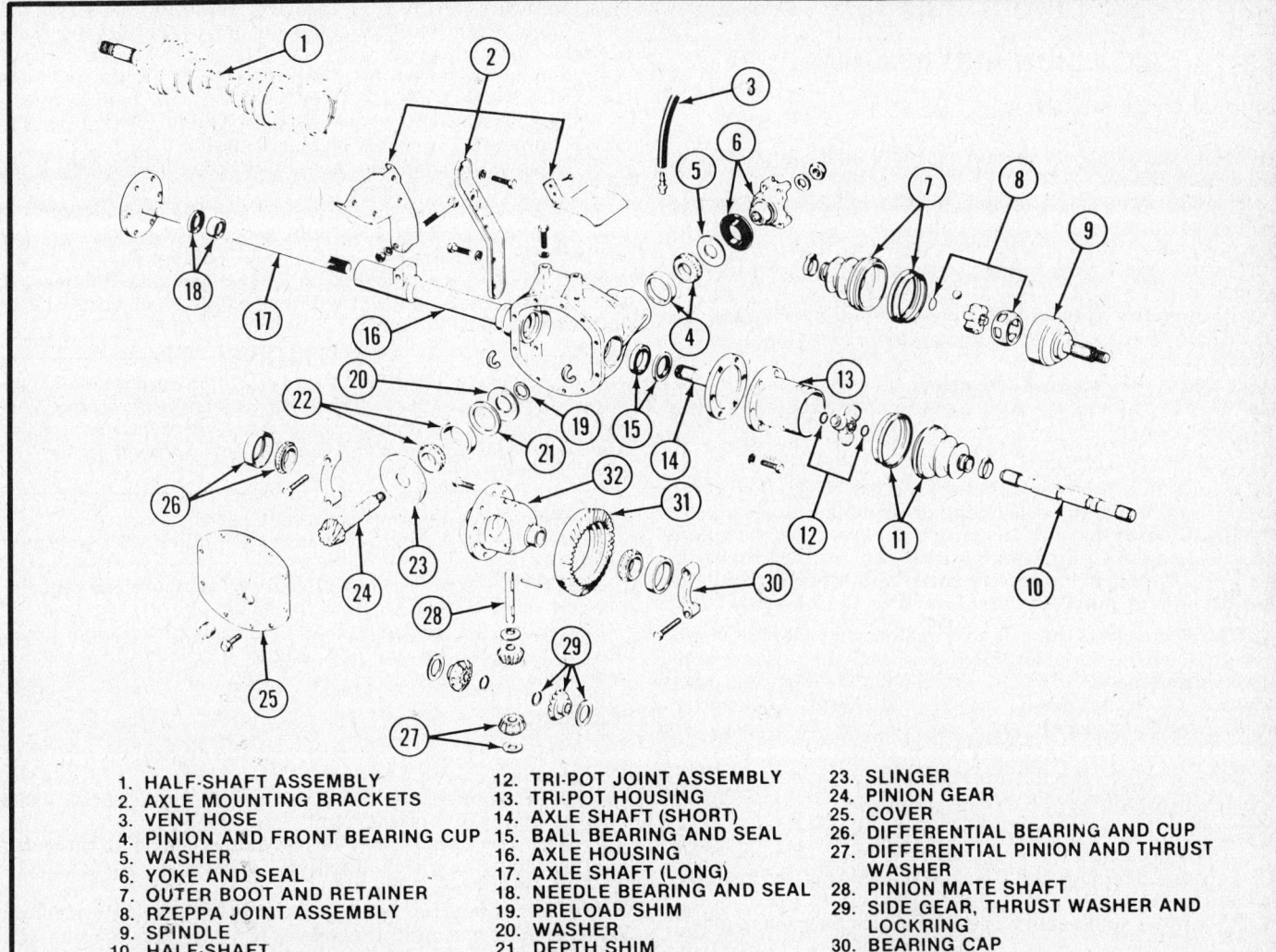

1. HALF-SHAFT ASSEMBLY
2. AXLE MOUNTING BRACKETS
3. VENT HOSE
4. PINION AND FRONT BEARING CUP
5. WASHER
6. YOKE AND SEAL
7. OUTER BOOT AND RETAINER
8. RZEPPA JOINT ASSEMBLY
9. SPINDLE
10. HALF-SHAFT
11. INNER BOOT AND RETAINER
12. TRI-POT JOINT ASSEMBLY
13. TRI-POT HOUSING
14. AXLE SHAFT (SHORT)
15. BALL BEARING AND SEAL
16. AXLE HOUSING
17. AXLE SHAFT (LONG)
18. NEEDLE BEARING AND SEAL
19. PRELOAD SHIM
20. WASHER
21. DEPTH SHIM
22. PINION REAR BEARING AND CUP
23. SLINGER
24. PINION GEAR
25. COVER
26. DIFFERENTIAL BEARING AND CUP
27. DIFFERENTIAL PINION AND THRUST WASHER
28. PINION MATE SHAFT
29. SIDE GEAR, THRUST WASHER AND LOCKRING
30. BEARING CAP
31. RING GEAR
32. DIFFERENTIAL CASE

Front Axle assembly—1985 and later Eagle models (© American Motors Corp.)

REAR SPRING

Removal and Installation
ALL MODELS

1. Raise the car. Support the rear axle with jacks or a lift to take the load off the rear springs.
2. Disconnect the rear shock from the lower mounting stud.
3. Disconnect the axle U-bolts.
4. Remove the nut from the bolt which attaches the eye of the spring to the front mount. Remove the bolt.
5. Remove the nuts from the rear shackle. Remove the shackle.
6. Installation is the reverse of the removal procedure.

FRONT AND REAR DRIVE AXLE AND SUSPENSION

NOTE: For axle overhaul procedures and suspension services, refer to the Unit Repair Section.

Front/Rear Propeller Shaft

Removal and Installation

1. Have the transmission in Neutral, raise the vehicle and support safely.
2. Mark the axle and propeller shaft yokes for assembly references at both ends when on a four wheel drive vehicle and the one end when on a two wheel drive vehicle.
3. Remove the universal joint retaining clamps at both ends of the shaft on the four wheel drive vehicles and remove the shaft.
4. Remove the universal joint retaining clamp at the yoke end of the shaft and pull the shaft assembly from the transmission extension housing and off the output shaft.
5. The installation of the drive shafts are in the reverse of the removal procedure. It is most important the shafts are properly aligned to maintain the propeller shaft balance.

1-71

American Motors
CONCORD • EAGLE • EAGLE SX4 • SPIRIT

Front Axle

AXLE HUB AND BEARING

Removal and Installation

1. Raise and support the vehicle safely. Remove the wheel, caliper and rotor.
2. Remove the bolts attaching the axle flange to the halfshaft. Compress the halfshaft and wire to prevent the shaft from separating.
3. Remove the axle hub nut assembly and remove the halfshaft.
4. Remove the steering arm from the steering knuckle.
5. Remove the caliper anchor plate from the steering knuckle.
6. Remove the three Torx headed bolts and remove the hub assembly. The hub must be pressed from the hub and bearing carrier.

NOTE: **If the hub contains tapered bearings, the internal components may be serviced or replaced as required. If the hub contains ball bearings, it cannot be serviced and if damaged, the assembly must be replaced with a new hub assembly. If a replacement hub is to be installed, the hub spacer must be transferred to the new hub.**

7. The assembly of the axle hub and bearing assembly is in the reverse of the removal procedure. The halfshaft-to-flange bolts are tightened to 45 ft. lbs. torque and the hub nut is tightened to 175 ft. lbs. torque. Be sure the nut lock and a new cotter pin is installed on the hub nut.

AXLE HOUSING

Removal

1. Raise and safely support the vehicle. Remove the halfshaft-to-axle flange bolts. Secure the axle halfshafts to the vehicle's underbody.
2. Compress and secure the halfshafts to prevent shaft separation.
3. Mark the propeller shaft and axle yoke for ease of installation.
4. Support the axle assembly on a lifting device, remove the brace rod at the axle and the shift motor shield.
5. Remove the axle mounting bolts, five on the left side and one on the right side.
6. Disconnect the vacuum harness from the axle shift motor (Pre 1985 vehicles), and partially lower the axle assembly to allow access to the vent hose.
7. Remove the vent hose, lower the axle assembly and remove from under the vehicle.

Installation

1. The installation of the axle assembly is in the reverse of the removal procedure.
2. Tighten the mounting bolts to 50 ft. lbs. of torque. Tighten the halfshaft-to-flange bolts to 45 ft. lbs. torque.

SHIFT HOUSING, INTERMEDIATE SHAFT, SEAL AND BEARINGS, AND OUTER AXLE SHAFT -- RIGHT SIDE

Removal

1. Remove the front axle assembly from the vehicle.
2. Remove the axle cover and drain the lubricant.
3. Remove the shift housing cover retaining bolts and the cover. Remove the shift fork, housing and the shift motor as an assembly.
4. Remove the axle tube retaining bolts. The bolts are accessible through the access hole in the outer axle shaft flange.
5. Remove the outer axle shaft assembly by tapping the shaft flange with a rubber or plastic mallet.
6. Remove the snapring that retains the intermediate shaft in the differential housing.
7. Remove the intermediate shaft and the shift collar.
8. Remove the outer axle shaft bearing race with a special puller and slide hammer tools or their equivalents.
9. With the use of a special puller tool and slide hammer, or their equivalents, remove the intermediate shaft needle bearing from the axle tube end.

--- CAUTION ---
The intermediate shaft gear is retained on the intermediate shaft by an internal-type, expandable snapring. When removing the bearing from the gear, support the gear face on vise jaws or their equivalent, to avoid pulling the gear from the shaft. The gear and shaft are serviced as an assembly only.

10. Remove the intermediate shaft gear bearing.
11. Remove the E-ring that retains the outer axle shaft gear on the shaft.
12. Mark the outer axle shaft gear position for easier assembly and remove the gear from the shaft.
13. Remove the outer axle shaft bearing using an arbor press.
14. Remove the oil seal and axle tube cover from the outer axle shaft.

Installation

1. Install the axle tube cover and the oil seal on the outer axle shaft.
2. With the use of an arbor press, install the outer axle shaft bearing and race on the shaft.
3. With the gear splines facing outward, install the outer axle shaft gear on the shaft with the arbor press. Install the E-ring on the outer axle shaft.
4. Using a bearing installer tool, install the intermediate shaft needle bearing in the axle tube.
5. Install the intermediate shaft gear needle bearing in the gear bore, using an arbor press.
6. Install the intermediate shaft in the axle tube. Install the shift collar on the intermediate shaft and seat the shaft in the differential.
7. Install the lock ring that retains the intermediate shaft in the differential. Install the outer axle shaft assembly and install the axle tube cover bolts evenly and in a cross pattern to seat the bearing race and seal. Torque the bolts to 144 inch lbs.
8. Install the gasket on the shift housing cover and install the gasket and axle shift housing. Tighten the housing bolts to 108 inch lbs.
9. Install the axle housing cover and gasket. Tighten the bolts to 20 ft. lbs. torque. Fill the shift housing cavity and the gear housing with specified gear lubricant. Install the fill plugs and tighten securely.

AXLE SHAFT SEAL, LEFT SIDE, ALL MODELS, AND RIGHT SIDE, 1985 AND LATER EAGLE MODELS

Removal and Installation

1. Remove the axle assembly from the vehicle. Refer to the Axle Removal and Installation Procedure.
2. Remove the axle housing cover and drain the lubricant.
3. Remove the C clips retaining the axles in the differential and remove the axles.

AMERICAN MOTORS
CONCORD • EAGLE • EAGLE SX4 • SPIRIT

4. Remove the axle seals using a pry bar. Install the replacement seal with a seal installer tool.
5. Install the axle shaft and the retaining C clip.
6. Install the housing cover with a new gasket. Torque the bolts to 20 ft. lbs. Fill the differential housing and the shift housing with the same specified lubricant.
7. Install the axle assembly into the vehicle in the reverse of the removal procedure.

AXLE SHAFT BEARING, LEFT SIDE, ALL MODELS AND RIGHT SIDE, 1985 AND LATER EAGLE MODELS

Removal and Installation

NOTE: Two different style axle shaft bearings are used on the front axle assembly. The left side axle shaft uses a ball bearing, while the right side axle shaft uses a needle bearing.

1. Remove the axle assembly from the vehicle. Refer to the Front Axle Assembly Removal and Installation Procedure.
2. Remove the axle housing cover and drain the lubricant. Remove the C clips from the axle shaft ends. Remove the axle shafts. Refer to the Intermediate Shaft, Outer Axle Shaft and Shift Housing Assembly, Right Side Removal and Installation Procedure.
3. Remove the axle shaft seal, using a pry bar. Remove the axle shaft bearings with appropriate special tools.

NOTE: If needle bearing removal tools are not available, a 15/16 in. socket and a three foot extension can be used to drive the needle bearing from the tube after the differential assembly is removed from the housing.

4. Install the axle shaft bearings with the appropriate special tools. Install the axle seals with seal installer tools.
5. Install the axle shafts and the C-clips. Install the housing cover with a new gasket. Torque the retaining bolts to 20 ft. lbs.
6. Fill the axle housing and the axle shift housing with the specified lubricant.
7. Install the axle housing in the reverse of its removal procedure.

FRONT AXLE HALF-SHAFTS

Three types of axle half-shafts are used on the Eagle models. They are designated Type A, Type B and Type C. Each are identified by its configuration of the tripot housing and its inner boot. Although the three types of half-shafts are similar in overall design, the service procedures vary. Identify the type of half-shaft used and refer to the appropriate procedure.

Disassembly

TYPE A HALF-SHAFT

1. Cut and remove the small clamp from the outer boot.
2. Separate the outer boot from the metal retainer, using a brass punch. Slide the boot away from the constant velocity (CV) joint assembly.
3. Open the exposed snapring and remove the constant velocity (CV) joint from the shaft. Remove the boot and retainer.
4. Tap the CV joint cage until it is tilted out far enough to remove the first ball. Remove the remaining balls in the same manner.
5. Rotate the CV joint cage outward until it is at a 90 degree angle to the installed position, and remove the cage and inner race. Rotate the inner race upward and out of the cage.

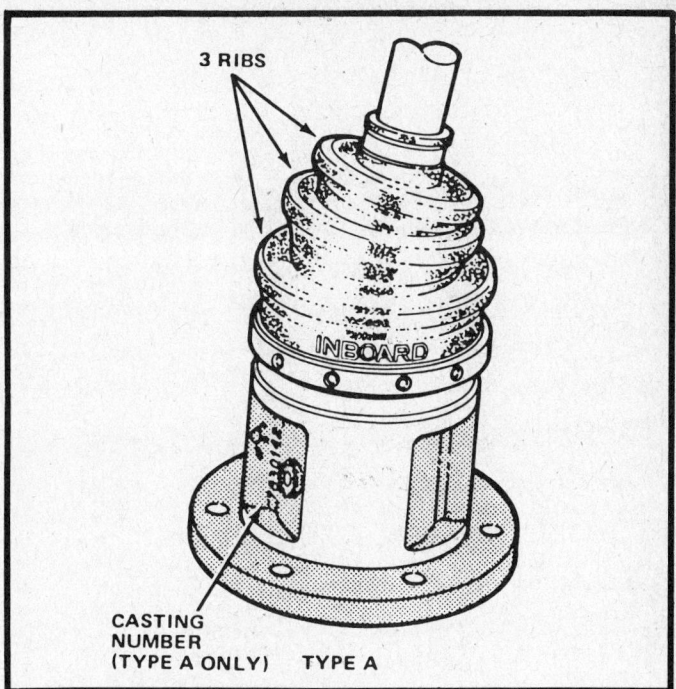

Type a front axle halfshaft
(© American Motors Corp.)

6. Remove the small clamp from the inner boot. Separate inner boot from the metal retainer. Slide the boot and retainer away from the tripot joint.
7. Remove the tripot joint and shaft from the housing. Remove the inner snapring from its groove and slide the tripot joint on the shaft to expose the outer snapring. Remove the outer snapring and remove the tripot joint.
8. If the boot is to be replaced, remove the inner snapring from the shaft and remove the boot.

NOTE: The outer constant velocity and inner tripot joint are serviced as assemblies only.

Assembly

1. Pack the spindle hub with the lubricant provided in the service packet.
2. Install the outer CV joint inner race into the cage. Tilt the cage at a 90 degree angle from the installed position and insert the cage and race into the spindle hub. Be sure the large diameter of the bearing cage faces out.
3. Tilt the cage outward and install the first ball into the spindle hub. Install the remaining balls in the same manner. Pack the assembly with the lubricant supplied.
4. Install the outer boot and retainer on the shaft. Install the inner race retaining snapring into the inner race snapring groove of the shaft.
5. Install the joint onto the shaft, until the race retaining snapring seats in the groove.
6. Seat the metal boot retainer onto the spindle, using a brass punch.
7. Install the boot in the metal retainer.

NOTE: If the boot is difficult to install, press the retainer into the boot with an arbor press.

8. Install the small outer boot clamp, using special tools or their equivalent.
9. Pack the tripot housing with the lubricant provided. Install the inner boot and the retainer ring onto the shaft. If re-

SECTION 1
AMERICAN MOTORS
CONCORD • EAGLE • EAGLE SX4 • SPIRIT

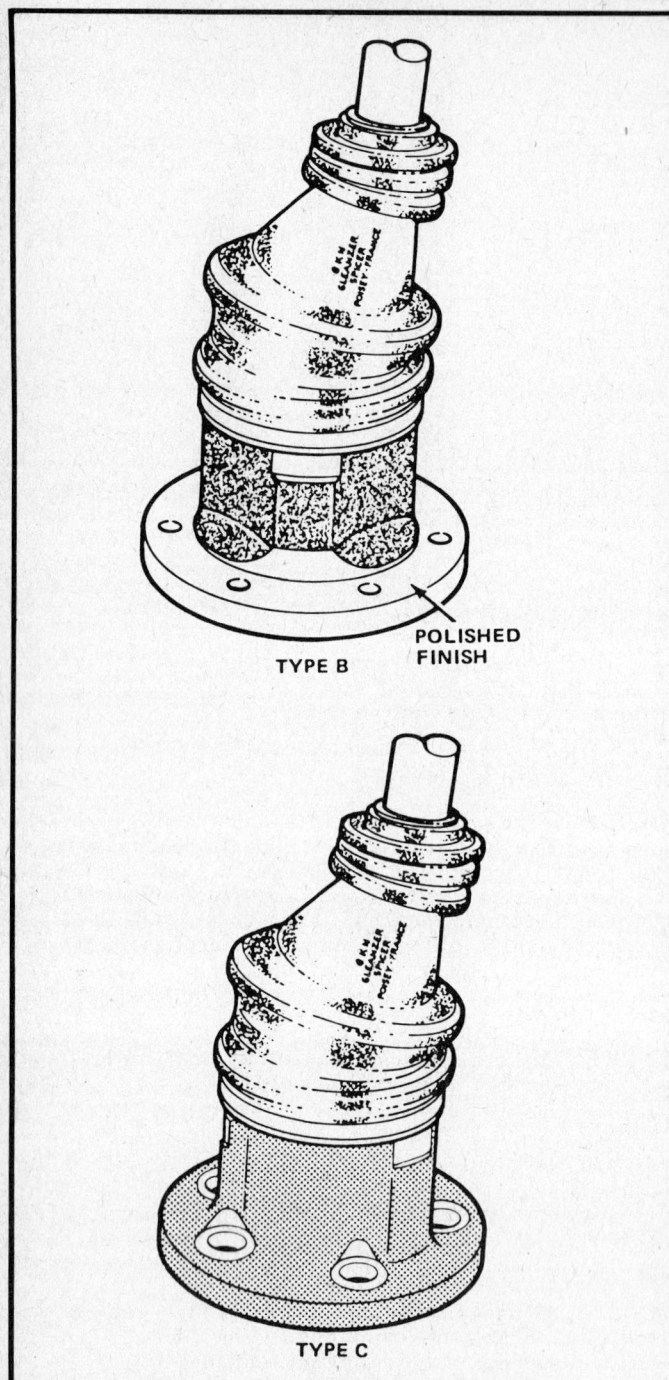

Type B and Type C front axle halfshaft
(© American Motors Corp.)

moved, install the inner snapring and slide it onto the shaft past the snapring groove.

10. Install the tripot joint onto the shaft and install the outer snapring into its groove.

11. Position the tripot joint towards the outer snapring and slide the inner snapring into its groove.

12. Install the tripot joint and shaft into the tripot housing. Seat the inner boot metal retainer on the tripot housing. Install the boot in the metal retainer. Install the small inner boot clamp.

Disassembly
TYPE B AND C HALF-SHAFTS

1. Cut and remove both outer boot clamps. Roll the outer boot away from the outer constant velocity (CV) joint.
2. Drive the CV joint from the shaft with a block of wood seated on the inner race. Remove and discard the shaft circlips.
3. Tap the outer CV joint cage with a brass punch, until the cage is tilted outward far enough to remove the first ball. Remove the remaining balls in the same manner.
4. Rotate the outer CV joint cage with the brass punch until the cage is at a 90 degree position from its installed position. Align the two oblong holes in the outer joint cage with the slots in the interior wall of the spindle housing and remove the cage and inner race.
5. Remove the inner race from the cage by aligning the shoulder between the race grooves with the inside of the oblong cage holes. Rotate the inner race out of the cage by using the larger of the two openings in the cage.
6. Remove both snaprings from the shaft and remove the outer boot. Remove the rubber retaining ring from the small end of the inner boot.
7. Separate the inner boot from the metal retainer ring and slide the boot and retainer away from the tripot housing.
8. Remove the tripot joint and shaft from the housing.
9. Remove the snapring that retains the tripot joint on the shaft and remove the joint.
10. Remove the inner boot, if it is to be replaced. Remove any remaining snaprings from the shaft, if necessary.

Assembly.

1. Pack the spindle hub with the special lubricant as supplied with the service package.
2. Install the outer joint inner race into the cage. Install the cage and race assembly into the spindle hub. The small diameter of the cage and stopping groove in the race must face outward.
3. With the aid of the brass punch, tilt the cage outward until the first ball can be installed in the cage. Install the remaining balls in the same manner.
4. Pack the assembly with the special lubrication provided in the service packet. Install the outer boot on the shaft and install the inner and outer snaprings.
5. Install the CV joint onto the shaft until the inner race contacts the inner snapring.
6. Slide the outer boot onto the CV joint. With the special clamping tool or its equivalent, install both boot clamps.
7. Pack the tripot housing with lubricant provided in the service packet.
8. Install the inner small rubber retainer ring, boot and large end boot retainer ring onto the shaft.
9. Install the tripot joint and the snapring onto the shaft. Install the tripot joint and shaft into the housing.
10. Install the boot and metal retainer onto the tripot housing. Carefully seat the boot and retainer, using a brass punch. Install the rubber retainer ring over the small end of the boot.

--- **CAUTION** ---
Do not exceed the specified installed length. This could reduce flexibility and shorten boot life.

---

11. Check and adjust the installed length of the boot. Total installed length must be 4.134 in. (105 mm). Move the small end of the boot in or out on the shaft to obtain the specified length. On 4 cylinder models, there should be a gap of about $1\frac{1}{8}$ in. (28 mm) between the inner and outer boots. On 6 cylinder models, the boot should touch (no gap).

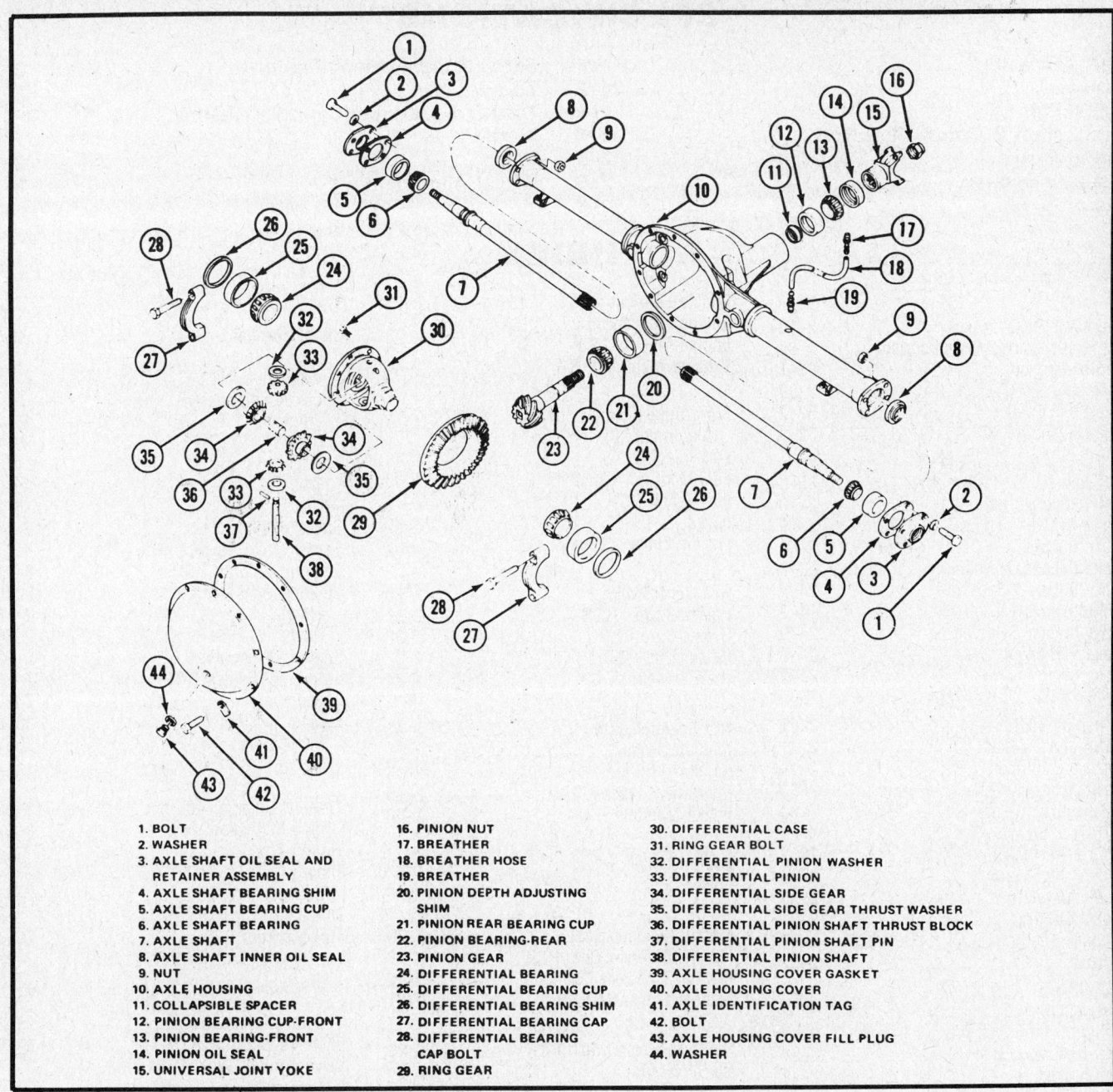

Rear axle with standard differential—7 9/16 axle (© American Motors Corporation)

SECTION 2

CHRYSLER CORPORATION
FRONT WHEEL DRIVE CARS

SPECIFICATIONS

Belt Tension	2–15
Brakes	24–2
Capacities	2–8
Crankshaft & Connecting Rod	2–7
Firing Order	2–6
General Engine	2–6
Piston & Ring	2–8
Serial Number Identification	2–5
Torque	2–8
Torque Sequence (Cylinder Heads)	2–58
Tune-Up	2–6
Valve	2–7
Wheel Alignment	2–8

INDEX

A
- Alternator R&R ... 2–10
- Automatic Transaxle Adjustment ... 2–82
- On Car Service ... 23–2
- Assembly R&R ... 2–83
- Axle Shaft R&R ... 23–2, 32–2
- Axle Halfshaft R&R ... 23–2, 32–2

B
- Ball Joints ... 35–2
- Belt Tension ... 2–10
- Brake System ... 2–79
- Brake Booster ... 2–80
- Brake Caliper Overhaul ... 24–2
- Brake Caliper R&R Front ... 24–2
- Brake Drum Rear ... 24–2
- Brake Master Cylinder ... 2–79
- Brake Pad Front ... 24–2
- Brake Shoe Rear ... 24–2

C
- Camshaft R&R ... 2–61
- Carburetor R&R ... 2–41
- Chassis Electrical ... 2–18
- Clutch ... 2–80
  - Adjustment ... 2–80
  - R&R 2–80
- Control Arm R&R ... 35–2
- Cooling Fan Motor ... 2–36
- Cooling System ... 2–35
- Cruise Control ... 2–31
- Cylinder Head ... 2–57
  - R&R ... 2–57

D
- Differential ... 23–2, 32–2
  - Inspection ... 23–2, 32–2
- Dimmer Switch R&R ... 2–21
- Disc Brakes ... 24–2
  - Front ... 24–2
- Distributor R&R ... 2–14
- Drive Axle ... 23–2, 32–2
- Drive Belt Tension ... 2–15
- Driveshaft R&R ... 2–85

E
- Electric Fuel Pump R&R ... 2–40
- Electronic Ignition ... 30–2
- Electronic Monitor ... 2–34
- Electronic Fuel Injection ... 2–49
- Emission Controls ... 2–52
- Engine ... 2–52
  - Identification ... 2–5
  - R&R ... 2–52
- Engine Electrical ... 2–14

- Engine Lubrication ... 2–74
- Engine Mechanical ... 2–52
- Engine Mounts R&R ... 2–54
- Exhaust Manifold R&R ... 2–46

F
- Front Suspension ... 2–76
  - Alignment ... 2–8
- Fuel Injection ... 2–49
- Fuel Mixture, Adjust ... 2–45
- Fuel Pump R&R ... 2–40
- Fuses ... 2–30
- Fusible Links ... 2–28

H
- Headlight Switch ... 2–20
- Heater Blower R&R ... 2–37
- Heater Core R&R ... 2–38
- Heater Unit R&R ... 2–37
- Horn Switch ... 2–24

I
- Idle Speed Adjust ... 2–41
- Ignition Switch ... 2–20
- Ignition Timing ... 2–15
- Instrument Cluster R&R ... 2–25
- Intake Manifold R&R ... 2–46

L
- Lock Cylinder ... 2–18
- Lower Control Arm R&R ... 35–2

M
- Master Cylinder R&R ... 2–79
- Manual Steering Gear R&R ... 2–76
- Manual Transaxle Overhaul ... 32–2
- Manual Transaxle R&R ... 2–81

N, O
- Neutral Safety Switch R&R ... 2–23
- Oil Pan R&R ... 2–74
- Oil Pump ... 2–74
  - R&R ... 2–74
- Oil Seal R&R
  - Rear Main ... 2–74

P
- Parking Brake ... 2–80
  - Adjustment ... 2–80
- Piston & Connecting Rod ... 2–63
- Power Brake Unit R&R ... 2–80
- Power Steering Pump R&R ... 2–76

R
- Rear Main Oil Seal R&R ... 2–74
- Rear Suspension ... 2–89
- Regulator ... 2–10
- Rocker Shaft/Assy R&R ... 2–56

S
- Serial Number ... 2–5
  - Engine ... 2–5
  - Vehicle ... 2–5
- Shock Absorber R&R
  - Front ... 35–2
  - Rear ... 35–2
- Springs
  - Front ... 35–2
  - Rear ... 35–2
- Starter R&R ... 2–14
- Starter Drive Replacement 2–14
- Steering Column R&R ... 2–77
- Steering Gear R&R ... 2–76
  - Manual ... 2–76
  - Power ... 2–76
- Steering Wheel R&R ... 2–77
- Stop Light Switch R&R ... 2–23
- Speedometer ... 2–28
- Suspension R&R ... 35–2
  - Service ... 35–2

T
- Throttle Linkage, Adjust ... 2–82
- Timing Belt R&R ... 2–67
- Timing Chain ... 2–64
- Timing Gear Cover ... 2–64
  - Oil Replacement ... 2–64
- Tune-Up ... 2–6
- Turbocharger R&R ... 2–50
- Turn Signal Switch R&R ... 2–23

U, V
- U-Joint Overhaul ... 28–2
- Valve Tappette R&R ... 2–55
- Valve Timing, Adjust ... 2–57
- Valve System ... 2–54
- Voltage Regulator ... 2–10
- Voice Alert ... 2–31

W, Y
- Water Pump R&R ... 2–35
- Wheel Alignment ... 2–8
  - Front ... 2–8
- Wheel Bearings Front ... 2–78
- Wheel Cylinder
  - Rear ... 24–2
- Windshield Wiper ... 2–25
  - Linkage R&R ... 2–25
  - Motor R&R ... 2–25
  - Switch R&R ... 2–24
- Year Identification ... 2–3

BEFORE SERVICING BE CERTAIN TO READ THE SAFETY NOTICE

Chrysler Corp.
1983–87 Front Wheel Drive Cars

CHRYSLER—E CLASS • EXECUTIVE SEDAN • LE BARON
NEW YORKER • TOWN & COUNTRY • LE BARON GTS
DODGE—ARIES • ARIES CUSTOM • ARIES SE
CHARGER • SHELBY CHARGER • DAYTONA
DODGE 400, 400 LS • DODGE 600, 600 ES
LASER • TC3 • OMNI • OMNI MISER • 024
TURISMO • LANCER
PLYMOUTH—HORIZON • HORIZON MISER • TC3 • LASER
RELIANT • RELIANT CUSTOM • RELIANT SE
• SUNDANCE • SHADOW

YEAR IDENTIFICATION

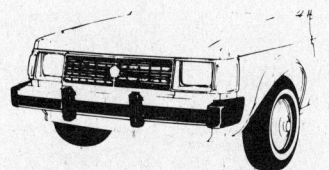
1983 Omni

1984 Omni

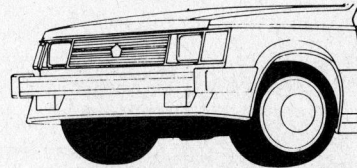
1985 and later Omni GLH

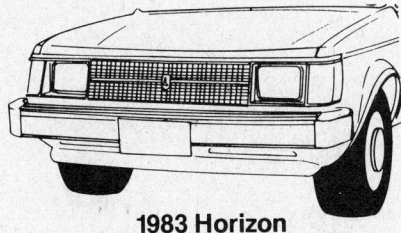
1983 Horizon

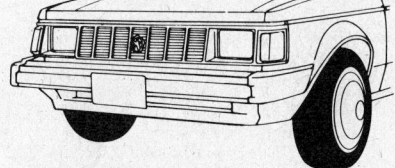
1984–87 Horizon

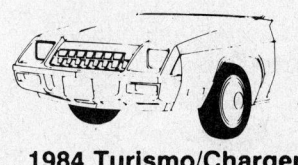
1984 Turismo/Charger

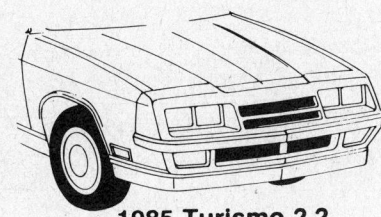
1985 Turismo 2.2

1985–86 Turismo Duster

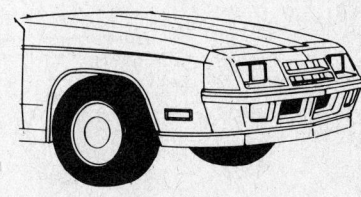
1985–87 Charger 2.2L

SECTION 2

CHRYSLER CORPORATION
FRONT WHEEL DRIVE CARS

YEAR IDENTIFICATION

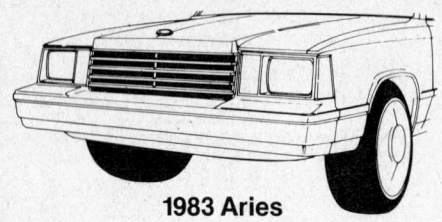
1983 Aries

1984 Aries

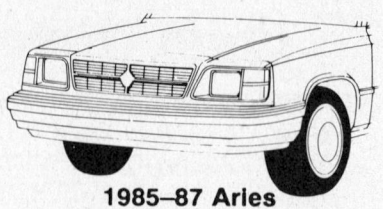
1985–87 Aries

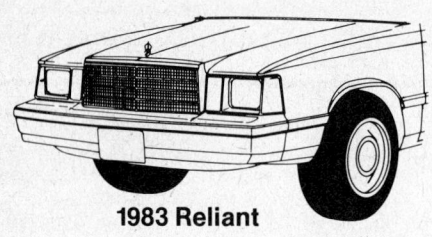
1983 Reliant

1984 Reliant

1985–87 Reliant

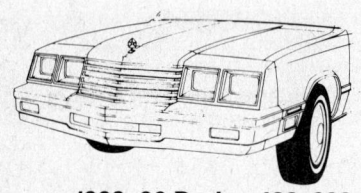
1983–86 Dodge 400, 600

1985–87 Lancer

1984–86 Daytona Turbo

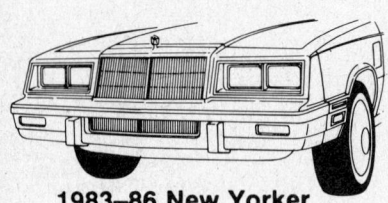
1983–86 New Yorker

1984–86 Shelby Charger

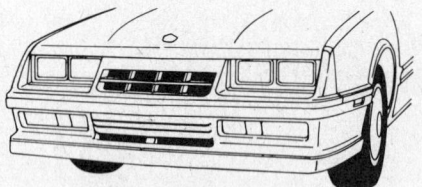
1984–86 Daytona

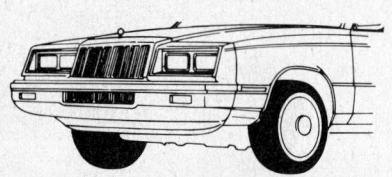
1985–86 LeBaron

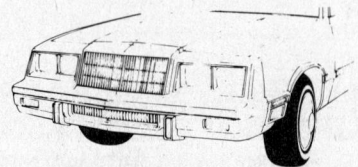
1984–86 LeBaron, E Class

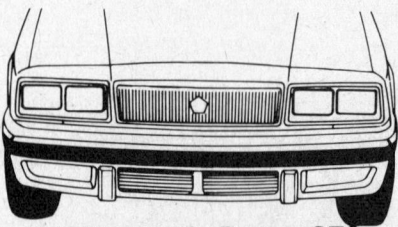
1984–1987 LeBaron, GTS

2–4

CHRYSLER CORPORATION
FRONT WHEEL DRIVE CARS
SECTION 2

YEAR IDENTIFICATION

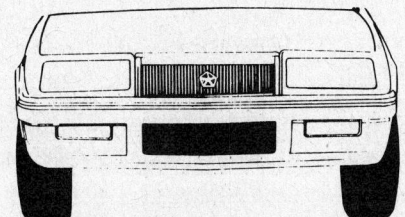
1984–1987 LeBaron, E-Class

1984–86 Laser

1984–86 Laser XE

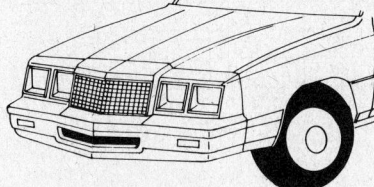
1985–86 Caravelle

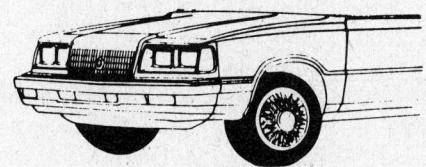
1987 Caravelle SE

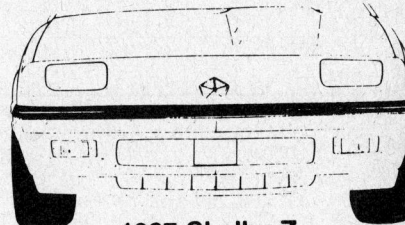
1987 Shelby Z

1987 Shadow

1987 Shadow D.C.

1987 Sundance

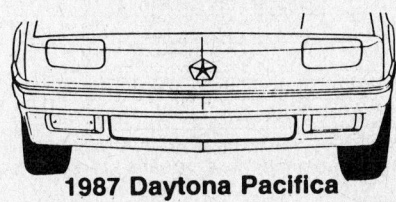
1987 Daytona Pacifica

VEHICLE IDENTIFICATION NUMBER (VIN)

It is important for servicing and ordering parts to be certain of the vehicle and engine identification. The VIN (vehicle identification number) is a 13 or 17 digit number visible through the windshield on the driver's side of the dash, and contains the vehicle and engine identification codes. It can be interpreted as follows:

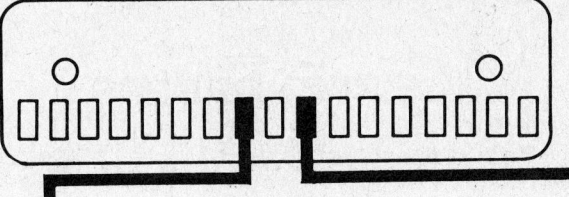

ENGINE CODE

Code	Cu. In.	Liters	Cyl	Carb. bbl	Eng. Mfg.
A (84-85)	98	1.6	4	2	Peugeot
B (83)	105	1.7	4	2	VW
C (83-87)	135	2.2	4	2	Chrysler
D (83-87)	135	2.2	4	EFI	Chrysler
E (84-87)	135	2.2	4	Turbo	Chrysler
G (83-85)	156	2.6	4	2	Mitsubishi
K (86-87)	153	2.5	4	EFI	Chrysler

MODEL YEAR CODE

Code	Year
C	82
D	83
E	84
F	85
G	86
H	87

The seventeen digit Vehicle Identification Number can be used to determine engine application and model year. The tenth indicates the model year, and the eighth digit identifies engine displacement.

2–5

CHRYSLER CORPORATION
FRONT WHEEL DRIVE CARS

GENERAL ENGINE SPECIFICATIONS

Year	Eng. V.I.N. Code	Engine No. Cyl Displ. Cu. In.	Eng. Mfg.	Carb. Type	Horsepower at rpm ■	Torque (ftlb.) at rpm ■	Bore X Stroke (in.)	Compression Ratio	Oil Pressure (psi)
'83	A	4-98	Peugeot	2 bbl.	64 @ 4800	83 @ 3200	3.07 × 3.46	8.8:1	40-90 ①
'84-'86	A	4-98	Peugeot	2 bbl.	64 @ 4800	87 @ 2800	3.07 × 3.46	8.8:1	40-90 ①
'83	B	4-105	VW	2 bbl.	63 @ 4800	83 @ 2400	3.13 × 3.40	8.2:1	28 ②
'83	C	4-135	Chrysler	2 bbl.	94 @ 5200	117 @ 3200	3.44 × 3.62	9.0:1	50 ②
'84-'87	C	4-135	Chrysler	2 bbl.	96 @ 5200	119 @ 3200	3.44 × 3.62	9.5:1	40 ②
'83-'87	D	4-135	Chrysler	EFI	99 @ 5600	121 @ 3200	3.44 × 3.62	10.0:1	40 ②③
'84-'87	E	4-135	Chrysler	Turbo	146 @ 5200	168 @ 3600	3.44 × 3.62	8.5:1	40 ②③
'83	G	4-156	Mitsubishi	2bbl.	93 @ 5600	132 @ 2800	3.59 × 3.86	8.2:1	45-90 ①
'84-'85	G	4-156	Mitsubishi	2bbl.	101 @ 5600	140 @ 2800	3.59 × 3.86	8.7:1	45-90 ①
'86-'87	K	4-153	Chrysler	EFI	100 @ 4800	136 @ 2800	3.44 × 4.09	9.0:1	25-80 ①

■ Horsepower and torque are SAE net, with all accessories installed and operating. Figure may vary from model-to-model and is intended to be representative rather than exact.
① @ 3000 rpm
② @ 2000 rpm
③ @ 1985-86, 25-90 psi @ 3000 rpm

TUNE-UP SPECIFICATIONS

Year	Eng. V.I.N. Code	No. Cyl Displ. Cu. In.	Eng. Mfg.	h.p.	Spark Plugs Orig. Type	Gap (in.)	Ignition Timing (deg.) ▲ Man. Trans.	Ignition Timing (deg.) ▲ Auto Trans.	Intake Valve Opens (deg.) ■	Fuel Pump Pressure (psi)	Idle Speed (rpm) ▲ Man. Trans.	Idle Speed (rpm) ▲ Auto Trans.	Valve Lash (in.) ▲ Intake	Valve Lash (in.) ▲ Exhaust
'84-'86	A	4-98	Peugeot	64	RN12YC	.035	12B	12B	16.5	4.5-6.0	850	1000	.012H	.014H
'83	A	4-105	VW	63	65PR	.035	20B	12B	14	4.4-5.8	900	900	.008-.012H	.016-.020H
'83-'86	C	4-135	Chrysler	All	RN12YC	.035	10B	10B	16 ⑤	4.5-6.0	900	900	Hyd.	Hyd.
'84-'85	D ⑦	4-135	Chrysler	99	RN12YC	.035	12B	12B	10.5	36	850	750	Hyd.	Hyd.
'84-'85	E ⑥	4-135	Chrysler	146	RN12YC	.035	12B	12B	10	53	950	950	Hyd.	Hyd.
'83-'85	G	4-156	Mitsubishi	92	RN11YC4 ③		7B	7B	25	4.5-6.0	800 ①	800 ①	.006H ⑧	.010H
'86-'87	K	4-153	Chrysler	100	RN12YC	.035	⑨	⑨	12	14.5 ⑩	⑨	⑨	Hyd.	Hyd.

NOTE: The underhood specifications sticker often reflects tune-up specification changes made in production. Sticker figures must be used if they disagree with those in this chart. Part numbers in this chart are not recommendations by Chilton for any product by brand name.

▲ See text for procedure
■ Before top dead center
Hyd.—Hydraulic
H—Hot
C—Cold
① 750 rpm-Canada
③ .035-.040 RN11Y—.030 in For Canada
⑤ Shelby and Hi Performance—10.5° BTDC
  Turbocharged—10° BTDC
⑥ Turbo with multipoint fuel injection
⑦ EFI with single point fuel injection
⑧ Jet valve clearance—.010 in.
⑨ Refer to underhood emission control information label
⑩ '86-'87 with multipoint fuel injection—55 lbs

FIRING ORDERS

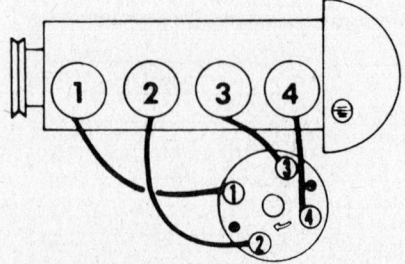

Chrysler Corp. 1.7L
Engine Firing Order: 1-3-4-2
Distributor Rotation: Clockwise

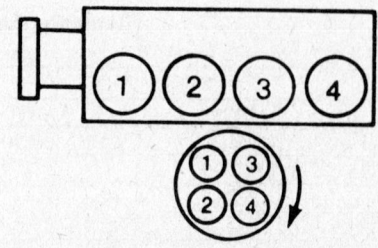

Chrysler Corp. 2.2L/2.5L
Engine Firing Order: 1-3-4-2
Distributor Rotation: Clockwise

CHRYSLER CORPORATION
FRONT WHEEL DRIVE CARS

FIRING ORDERS

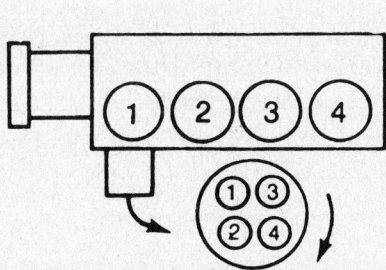

Chrysler Corp. (Mitsubishi) 2.6L
Engine firing order: 1-3-4-2
Distributor rotation: clockwise

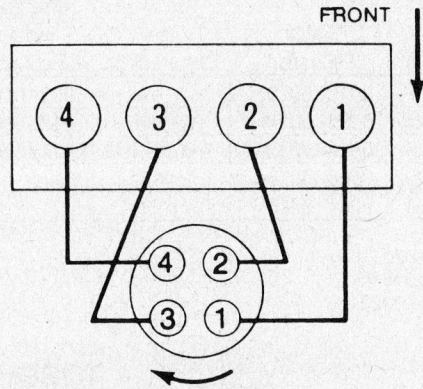

Chrysler Corp. 1.6L
Engine firing order: 1-3-4-2
Distributor rotation: clockwise

VALVE SPECIFICATIONS

Year	Engine	Seat Angle (deg.)	Face Angle (deg.)	Spring Test Pressure (lb in.)	Spring Installed Height (in.)	Stem-To-Guide Clearance (in.) Intake	Stem-To-Guide Clearance (in.) Exhaust	Stem Diameter (in.) Intake	Stem Diameter (in.) Exhaust
'84-'86	4-98	45	45	③	③	.0005-.0018	.0013-.0026	.3140-.3146	.3132-.3138
'83	4-105	45	45	①	②	.0028 max.	.0035 max.	.314	.313
'83-'87	4-135	45	45	175 @ 1.22 ⑥	1.65	.0009-.0026	.0030-.0047	.3124	.3103
'83-'85	4-156	45 ④	45 ⑤	61 @ 1.59	1.59	.0012-.0024	.0020-.0035	.315	.315
'86-'87	4-153	45	45	175 @ 1.22	1.65	.0009-.0026	.0030-.0047	.3124	.3103

① outer: 101 @ .878
   inner: 49 @ .720
② outer: 1.28
   inner: 1.13
③ Spring Free Length, All—1.905 inch
④ Jet Valve Seat Angle—45°
⑤ Jet Valve Face Angle—45°
⑥ '84 VIN C&D: 129-141 @ 1.22
   '85 VIN C&D: 144-156 @ 1.22

CRANKSHAFT AND CONNECTING ROD SPECIFICATIONS

All specifications in inches.

Year	Engine	Main Brg. Journal Dia.	Main Brg. Oil Clearance	Crankshaft End Play	Thrust on No.	Connecting Rod Journal Dia.	Rod Bearing Oil Clearance	Rod Bearing Side Clearance
'84-'86	4-98	2.046	.0009-.0031	.0035-.011	3	1.612	.001-.0025	.006-.009
'83	4-105	2.1236-2.1244	.0008-.0030	.003-.007	3	1.809-1.813	.0011-.0034	.014
'83-'87	4-135	2.362-2.363 ③	.0003-.0031 ①	.002-.007	3	1.968-1.969	.0008-.0034 ②	.005-.013
'83-'85	4-156	2.3622	.0008-.0028	.002-.007	3	2.0866	.0008-.0028	.004-.010
'86-'87	4-153	2.362-2.363	.0003-.0031	.002-.007	3	1.968-1.969	.0008-.0034	.005-.013

① Turbo: .0004-.0023 in.
② Turbo: .0008-.0031 in.
③ Turbo: 2.3622-2.3627

SECTION 2
CHRYSLER CORPORATION
FRONT WHEEL DRIVE CARS

PISTON, RING AND PIN SPECIFICATIONS
All specifications in inches.

Year	Engine	Piston Clearance	Ring Gap			Ring Side Clearance			Pin Clearance In Piston
			Top Compression	Bottom Compression	Oil Control	Top Compression	Bottom Compression	Oil Control	
'84–'86	4-98	.0016–.0020	.012–.018	.012–.018	.010–.016	.0018–.0028	.0018–.0020	.010–.016	①
'83	4-105	.0005–.0015	.012–.018	.012–.018	.016–.055	.0016–.0028	.008–.0020	.008–.0020	.00004–.00035
'83–'87	4-135	.0005–.0015 ④	.011–.021 ②	.011–.021 ③	.015–.055	.0015–.0031	.0015–.0037	—	①
'83–'85	4-156	.0008–.0016	.01–.018	.01–.018	.0078–.035	.0024–.0039	.0008–.0024	—	.00020–.00035
'86–'87	4-153	.0005–.0015	.011–.021	.011–.021	.015–.055	.0015–.0031	.0015–.0037	—	①

① Press Fit
② Turbo: .010–.020 in.
③ Turbo: .009–.018 in.
④ Turbo: .0015–.0025 in.

TORQUE SPECIFICATIONS
ft. lbs.

Year	Engine	Cylinder Head Bolts	Connecting Rod Bearing Bolts	Main Bearing Bolts	Crankshaft Bolt	Flywheel-to-Crankshaft Bolts	Camshaft Cap Bolts
'84–'86	4-98	52	28	48	110	55 ⑥	—
'83–'84	4-105	60 ①	35	47	58	55 ②	168 ④
'83–'87	4-135	③⑦	40 ①	30 ①	58	55 ②	168 ④
'83–'85	4-156	69 ⑤	34	58	87	65	165 ④
'86–'87	4-153	⑦	40 ①	30 ①	50	55 ⑧	165 ④

① plus 1/4 turn more
② 50 with auto trans.
③ For torque sequence—30, 45, 45 + 1/4 turn more
④ Inch lbs.
⑤ Cold
⑥ Manual transaxle
⑦ 1986 and later 4-135 (2.2L) and 4-153 (2.5L) engines
   1st—45 ft. lbs.
   2nd—65 ft. lbs.
   3rd—65 ft. lbs.
   4th— + 1/4 turn
⑧ Manual flywheel bolts—70 ft. lbs.

CAPACITIES

Year	Engine	Crankcase Incl. Filter	Pints To Refill After Draining		Fuel Tank (gal.)	Cooling System (qts.)	
			Manual	Automatic		With Heater	With A/C
'84–'85	4-98	3.5	⑤	16 ①	13	7.0	—
'83	4-105	4	②③	16.75 ①	13	6.0	6.0
'83–'87	4-135	4 ④	②③	17.75 ①	13	9	9
'83–'85	4-156	5	②③	17.75 ①	13	9	9

NOTE: 1983 models, determine identity of the transaxle by the selector shaft housing on the top of the transaxle case. The A-460, A-525 and A-465 have removable selector shaft housing. Use only Dexron® II in the A-460, A-465, A-525 Transaxles.
① Includes torque converter. Approx. 6 pts without draining converter.
② 4 speed: 3.75—use Dexron® II lubricant
③ 5 speed: 4.55—use Dexron® II lubricant
④ '84–'86 2.2 Turbo engines: 5 qts.
⑤ 1.9 w/A-460 Transaxle

WHEEL ALIGNMENT SPECIFICATIONS
Caster is not adjustable

Year and Model	Caster	Front Camber		Rear Camber		Toe-In (inches)	
		Range (deg.)	Preferred	Range (deg.)	Preferred	Front	Rear
CHRYSLER '83–'85 LeBaron, GTS, E. Class, New Yorker, Laser	1 3/16 P ①	1/4N–3/4P	5/16P	1N–0	1/2N	1/16	0

CHRYSLER CORPORATION
FRONT WHEEL DRIVE CARS
SECTION 2

WHEEL ALIGNMENT SPECIFICATIONS
Caster is not adjustable

Year and Model	Caster	Front Camber Range (deg.)	Front Camber Preferred	Rear Camber Range (deg.)	Rear Camber Preferred	Toe-In (inches) Front	Toe-In (inches) Rear
'86–'87 LeBaron GTS, New Yorker Laser	1 3/16P ①	1/4N–3/4P	5/16P	1 1/4N–1/4P	1/2P	1/16	0
DODGE							
'83–'85 Aries, 400, 600, 600 ES Daytona, Lancer	1 3/16P ①	1/4N–3/4P	5/16P	1N–0	1/2N	1/16	0
'86–'87 Aries, 400, 600, Daytona, Lancer, Shadow	1 3/16P ①	1/4N–3/4P	5/16P	1 1/4N–1/4P	1/2P	1/16	0
'83–'85 Omni, 024, Rampage, Charger	1 7/8P ②	1/4N–3/4P	5/16P	1 1/4N–1/4N	3/4P ③	1/16	3/32
'86–'87 Omni, Charger	1 7/8P	1/4N–3/4P	5/16P	1 1/4N–1/4N	3/4N	1/16	3/32
PLYMOUTH							
'83–'85 Reliant, Caravelle	1 3/16P	1/4N–3/4P	5/16P	1N–0	1/2N	1/16	0
'86–'87 Reliant, Caravelle, Sundance	1 3/16P	1/4N–3/4P	5/16P	1 1/4N–1/4P	1/2P	1/16	0
'83–'85 Horizon, TC3, Turismo, Scamp	1 7/8P	1/4N–3/4P	5/16P	1 1/4N–1/4N	3/4N ③	1/16	3/32
'86–'87 Horizon, Turismo	1 7/8P	1/4N–3/4P	5/16P	1 1/4N–1/4N	3/4N	1/16	3/32

① Wagon—7/8P°
② 4 door—1 3/8P°
③ Rampage, Scamp—Rear Camber
   Min.—1 1/8N°
   Max.—1/8N°
   Pref—5/8N°

ELECTRICAL SECTION

For Overhaul Procedures, Refer to Unit Repair Section

Charging System

Conventional alternators are used. See the Unit Repair Section for testing and overhaul procedures.

An electronic voltage regulator regulates the vehicle electrical system voltage by limiting the output voltage that is generated by the alternator. The regulator has no moving parts and requires no adjustment. The regulator may be mounted separately, as an integral part of the alternator, or with-in the engine control electronic systems of the power and logic modules.

The following alternators may be found on the various vehicle models;
1. Chrysler 60/70 amp alternator with external electronic voltage regulator.
2. Chrysler 40/90 amp alternator with voltage regulator in the engine electronics.

2–9

3. Chrysler 60 and 78 amp alternator with voltage regulator in the engine electronics.
4. Bosch 65 amp alternator and Chrysler electronic voltage regulator.
5. Bosch 40/90 and 40/100 amp alternators with voltage regulators in the engine electronics.
6. Bosch alternator and internal (integral) electronic voltage regulator.
7. Mitsubishi Alternator and internal (integral) electric voltage regulator

With the removal of the plastic cover on the rear of the Chrysler 40/90 alternator, the brushes and the diode assemblies can be replaced without the removal of the alternator assembly.

The voltage regulators located in the engine electronics are located in the power module (by the battery) and controlled by the logic module, (inside the vehicle). A combination of electronic controls are needed for this type of regulator operation and could require the replacement of both electronic units, should the regulator be found defective.

VOLTAGE REGULATOR TEST USING ON-BOARD DIAGNOSTIC SYSTEM FAULT CODES

Testing

WITH DIAGNOSTIC READOUT BOX

A diagnostic readout box is available through Chrysler Corporation or Test Equipment suppliers to diagnose the on-board diagnostic system in three different modes of testing. Only one mode is used to diagnose the charging circuit. To test the charging system, follow the tester manufacturer's recommended procedures.

WITH POWER LOSS OR POWER LIMIT LAMP FOR CODES

To activate this function, turn the ignition key ON–OFF–ON OFF–ON within five seconds. The power loss lamp will then come on for two seconds as a bulb check. Immediately following this, it will display a fault code, if one is present in the system, by flashing on and off. There is a short pause between flashes and a longer pause between digits. All codes displayed are two digit numbers with a four second pause between codes.

An example of a code is as follows;
1. The lamp flashes on for two seconds, then turns off.
2. The lamp flashes four times, pauses and then flashes once.
3. The lamp pauses for four seconds, flashes four times, pauses and then flashes seven times.
4. The two codes are 41 and 47. Any number of codes can be displayed as long as they are in the memory. The lamp will flash until all of them are displayed.
5. To exit the diagnostic mode, simply turn the ignition key to the OFF position.

NOTE: The fault codes identifies which circuit (but not a specific component in the circuit) that may be defective. Refer to the Unit Repair Section.

ALTERNATOR

Removal and Installation

1.6L, 1.7L AND 2.2L/2.5L ENGINES

1. Disconnect the battery ground cable.
2. Remove the wires from the alternator.
3. Support the alternator, remove the mounting bolts and lift out the unit.
4. Reverse the procedure for installation. Proper belt tension on the alternator should be set with special belt tightening scale or torque wrench.

2.6L ENGINES

1. Disconnect the battery ground cable.
2. Remove and tag the wires from the alternator.
3. Remove the alternator brace bolt and support bolt nut. Disconnect the belt.
4. Remove the support bolt and the alternator.
5. To install, reverse the removal procedure. Clearance between the alternator leg and front case should be less than 0.008 in. Shims are available to adjust the clearance.

BELT TENSION

Satisfactory performance of the belt driven accessories depends on proper belt tension. Three tensioning methods are given in order of preference:
1. Belt tension gauge method
2. Torque equivalent method
3. Belt deflection method

Because of space limitations in the engine compartment of front wheel drive vehicles, the belt tension gauge method is usually restricted to use after the vehicle has been raised on a hoist and the splash shield has been removed.

Belt Tension Gauge Method (Except on 2.2L Engine Air Pump and 2.6L Engine Water Pump)

1. For conventional belts, affix the Burroughs gauge to the belt.
2. For poly-V belt (1.6L engine, alternator/water pump belt and 2.2L engine, alternator/water pump belt when equipped with Bosch alternator) use a Poly-V Burroughs gauge.

Torque Equivalent Method

Each adjustable accessory bracket is provided with a ½ in. (13mm) square hole for torque wrench use. Equivalent torque values for adjusting each accessory drive belt are specified.

Belt Deflection Method

Place a straight edge across two adjacent pulleys and adjust belt tension with a force (push-pull) of 10 lbs. (44 N) applied at the mid point to produce a belt deflection. A small spring scale can be used to establish the 10 lbs. (44 N load).

REGULATOR

Removal and Installation

1.6L, 1.7L AND 2.2L/2.5L ENGINES

1. Disconnect the battery ground cable.
2. Remove the wires from the regulator.
3. Remove the two sheet metal screws securing the regulator to the right side fender skirt.
4. Installation is the reverse of removal.

2.6 ENGINES

NOTE: Some 2.6L engines may use a Chrysler external regulator with the Bosch alternator. If so, refer to the procedures under "1.6L, 1.7L and 2.2L/2.5L Engines" for regulator removal. Others may use a Bosch alternator with an internal electronic voltage regulator.

Most 2.6L engines are equipped with a Mitsubishi-built alternator that contains a built-in regulator. See the alternator replacement procedures for removal and installation. Refer to the Unit Repair Section for overhaul.

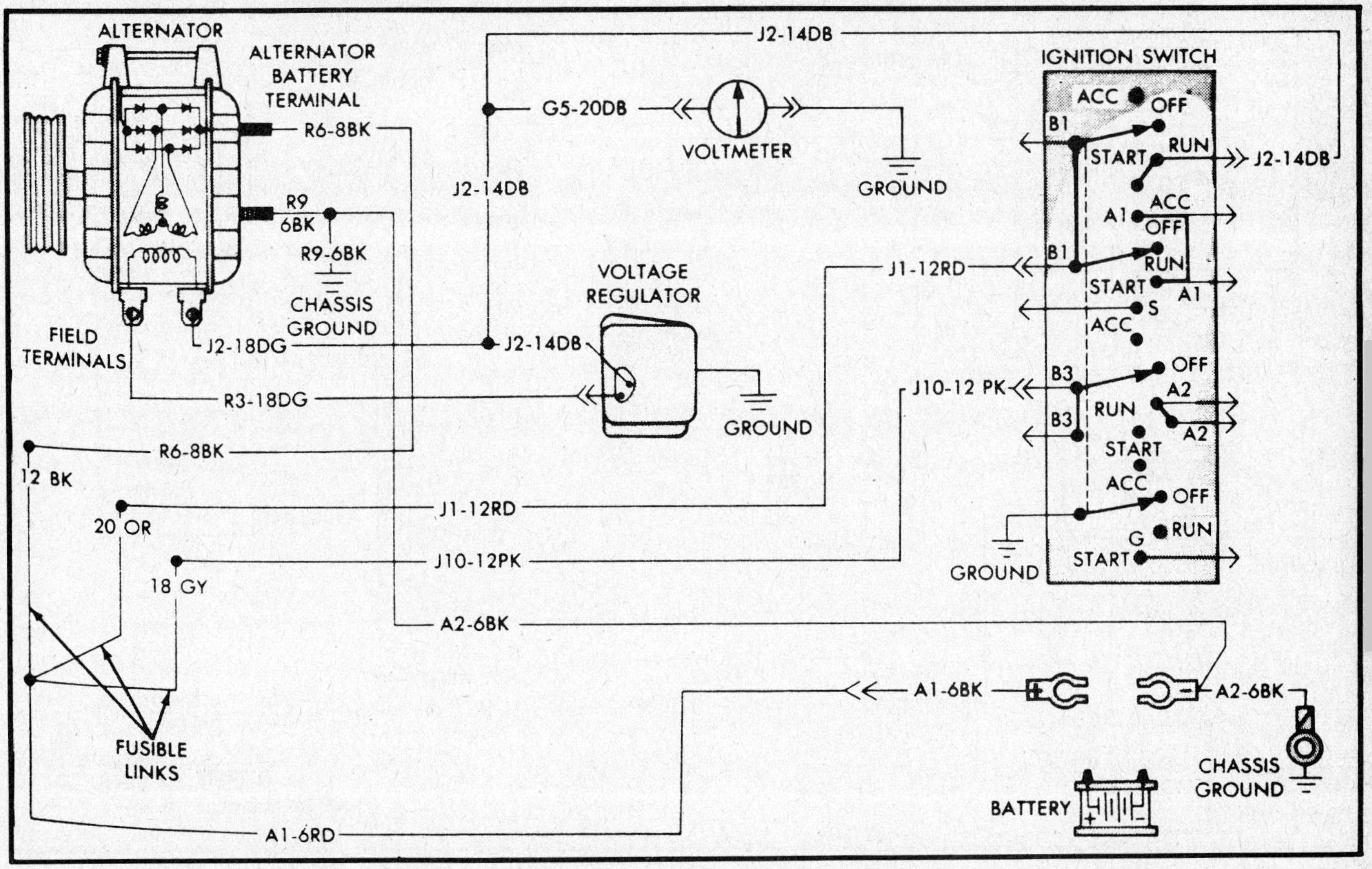

CHRYSLER CORPORATION
FRONT WHEEL DRIVE CARS

SECTION 2

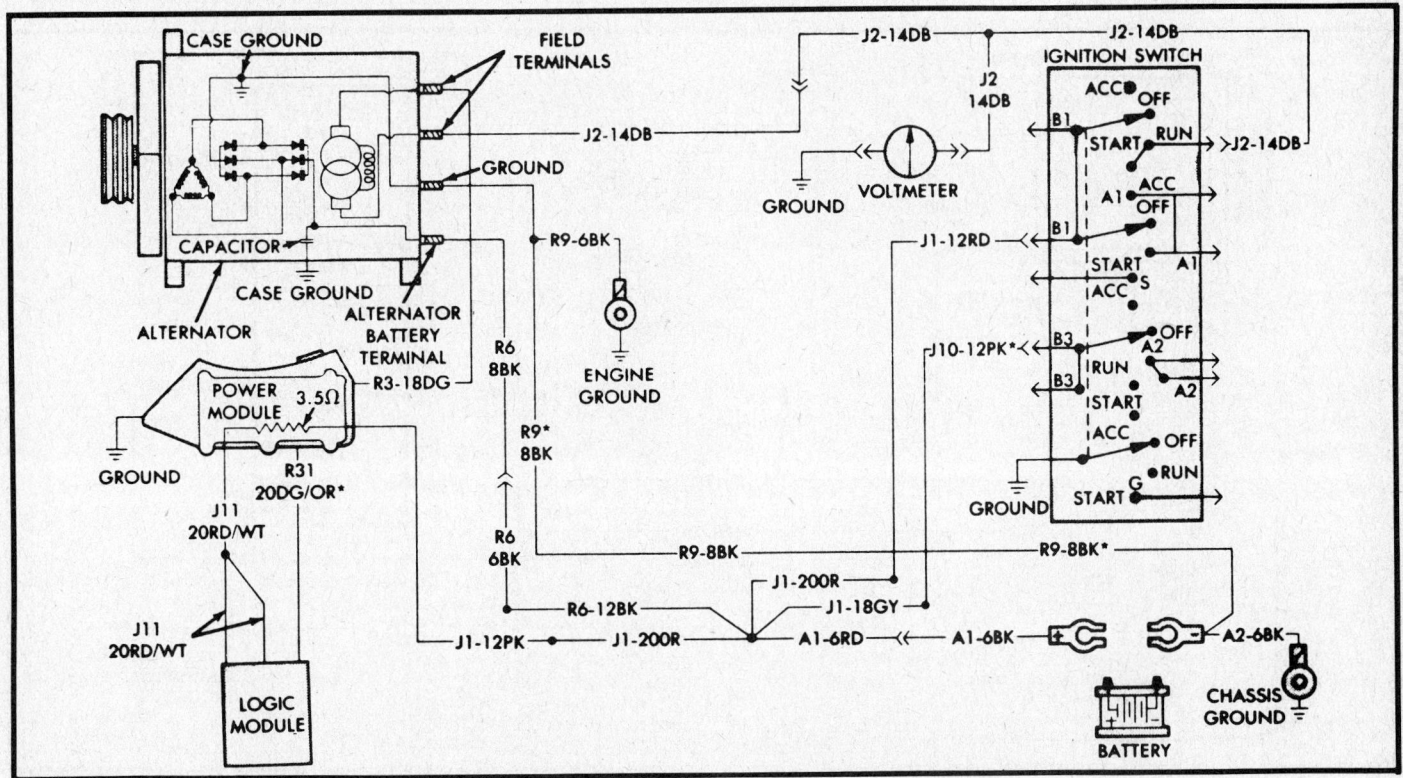

Chrysler standard alternator schematic with external voltage regulator—typical

Chrysler 40/90 Amp alternator schematic with voltage regulator in engine electronics

2-11

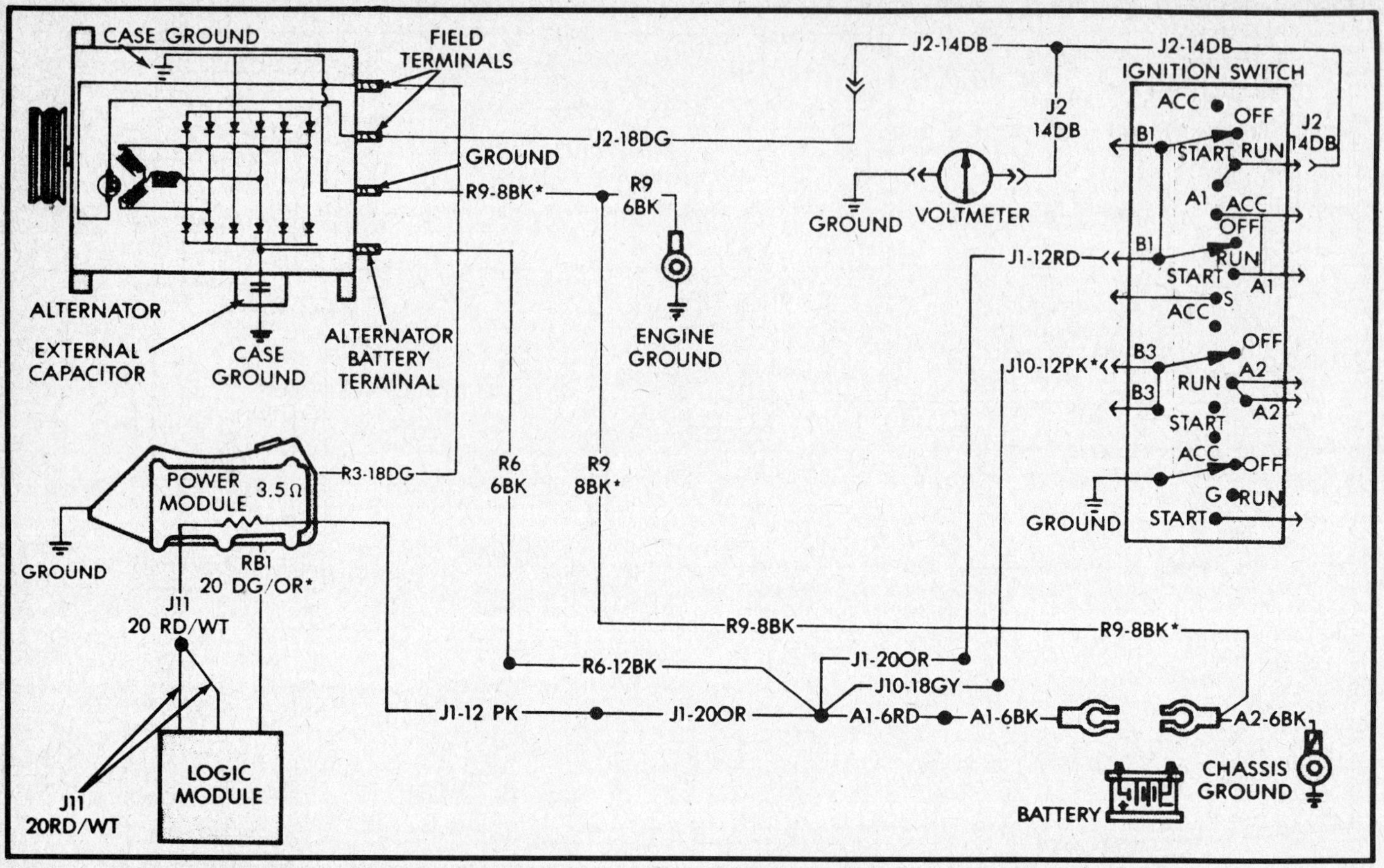

Section 2: CHRYSLER CORPORATION
FRONT WHEEL DRIVE CARS

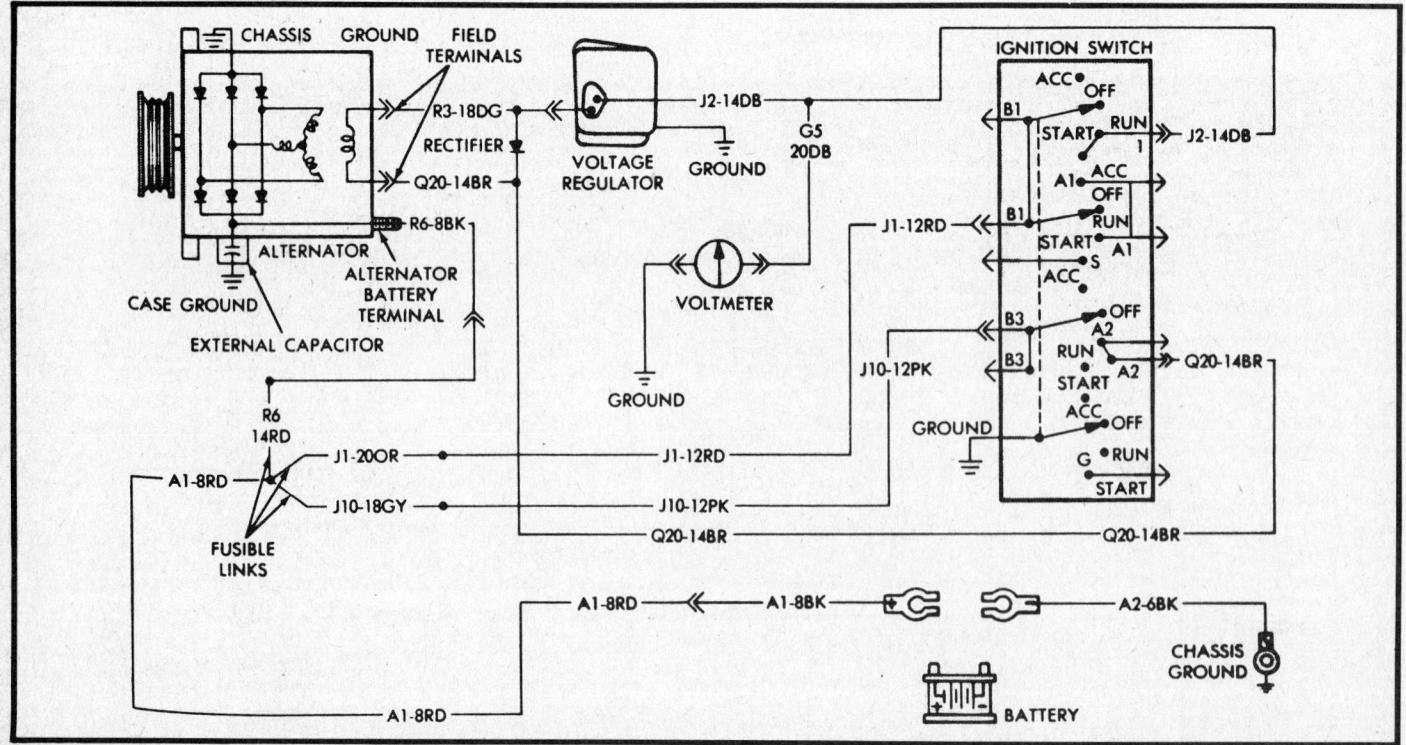

Bosch 40/90 Amp alternator schematic with voltage regulator in engine electronics. Bosch 40/100 Amp alternator schematic similar

Bosch 65 Amp alternator schematic with external voltage regulator

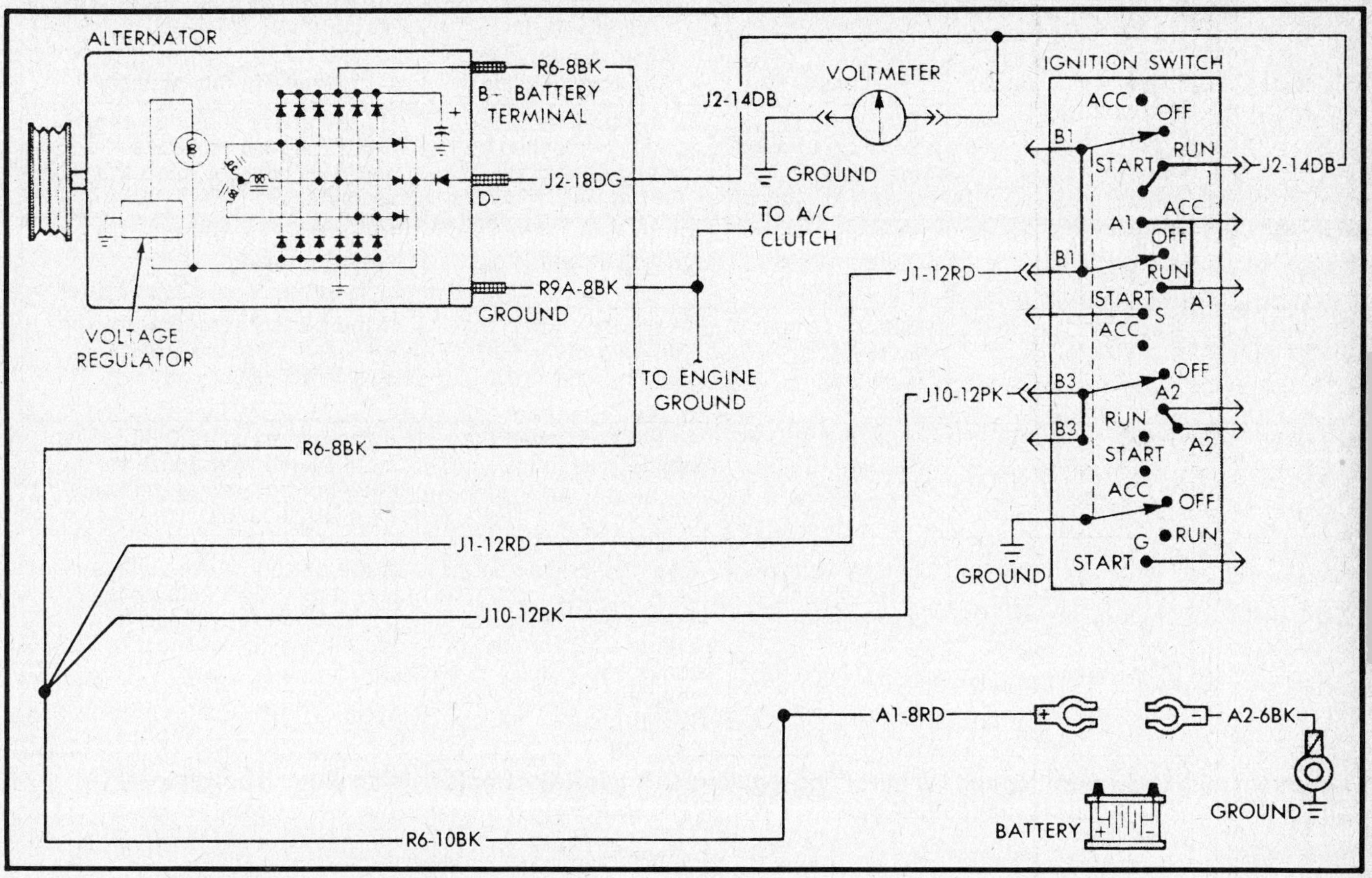

CHRYSLER CORPORATION
FRONT WHEEL DRIVE CARS

SECTION 2

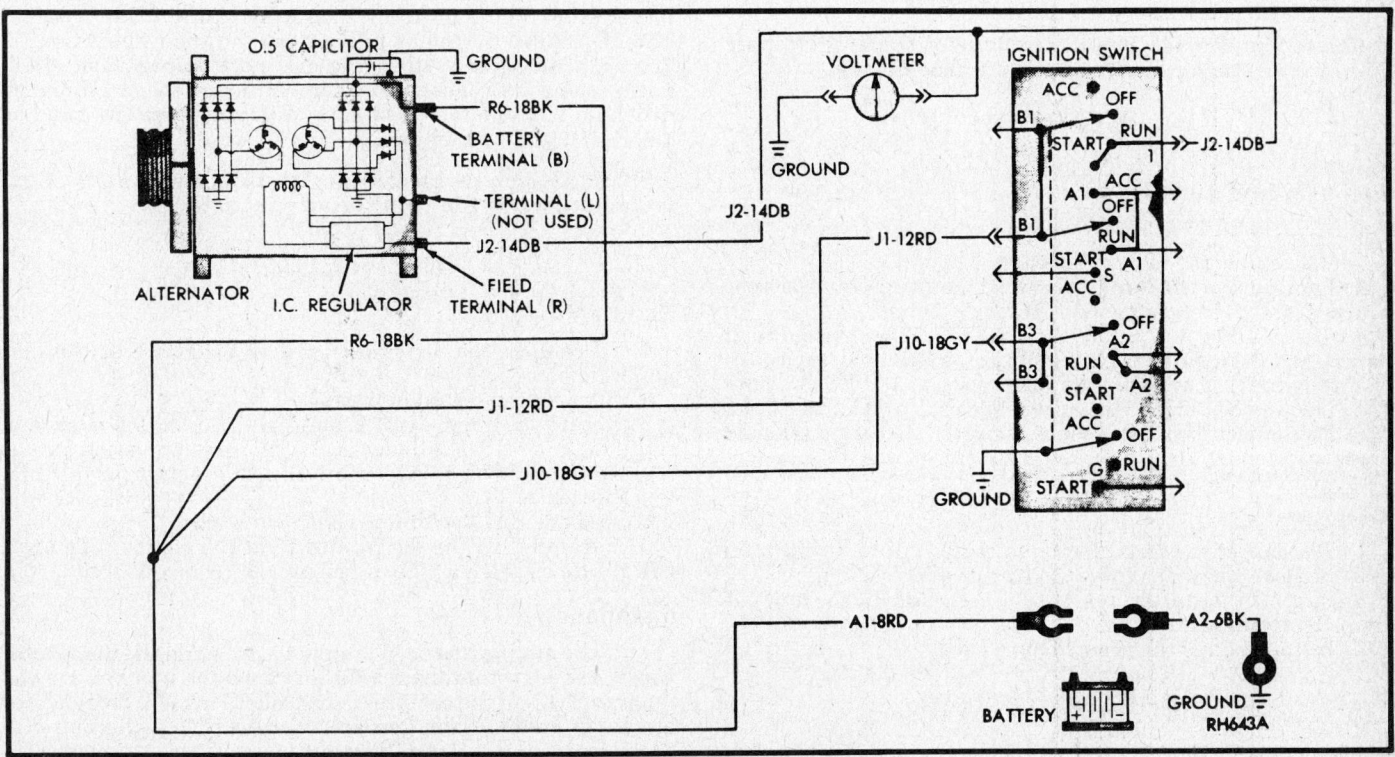

Bosch alternator schematic with internal regulator

Mitsubishi alternator schematic with internal electronic voltage regulator

2-13

SECTION 2

CHRYSLER CORPORATION
FRONT WHEEL DRIVE CARS

Code	Type	Power Loss Lamp	Circuit	When Monitored By The Logic Module	When Put Into Memory
16	Fault	Yes	Battery Voltage Sensing (Charging System)	All the time after one minute from when the engine starts.	If the battery sensing voltage drops below 4 or between 7½ and 8½ volts for more than 20 seconds.
41	Fault	No	Alternator Field Control (Charging System)	All the time when the ignition switch is on.	If the field control fails to switch properly.
44	Fault	No	Battery Temperature Sensor (Charging System)	All the time when the ignition switch is on.	If the battery temperature sensor signal is below .04 or above 4.9 volts.
46	Fault	Yes	Battery Voltage Sensing (Charging System)	All the time when the engine is running.	If the battery sense voltage is more than 1 volt above the desired control voltage for more than 20 seconds.
47	Fault	No	Battery Voltage Sensing (Charging System)	When the engine has been running for more than 6 minutes, engine temperature above 160°F and engine rpm above 1,500 rpm.	If the battery sense voltage is less than 1 volt below the desired control voltage for more than 20 seconds.

Alternator fault code chart for units with voltage regulator in engine electronics, using either a power loss/power limit lamp or a diagnostic readout box

Starting System

Refer to the Starter Motor segment of the Unit Repair Section for starter motor overhaul procedures.

STARTER

Removal and Installation

1.6L, 1.7L, 2.2L/2.5L ENGINES

1. Disconnect the negative battery cable.
2. Remove the starter to flywheel housing and the rear bracket to engine or transaxle attaching bolts.
3. On models equipped with 2.2L/2.5L engine and if equipped, loosen air pump tube at exhaust manifold, then position tube bracket away from starter motor.
4. If equipped, remove the heat shield clamp and heat shield.
5. Disconnect the starter cable at starter motor and solenoid leads at solenoid, then remove the starter motor.
6. Installation is the reverse of removal.

2.6L ENGINE

1. Disconnect the battery ground cable.
2. Remove the wires from the starter and solenoid.
3. Support the starter, remove the bolts and lift the unit out from the flywheel housing.
4. Installation is the reverse of removal.

Ignition System

Models using 1.6L, 1.7L and 2.2L/2.5L engines are equipped with a Lean Burn/Electronic Spark Control system. This consists of a spark control "computer", various engine sensors and a specially calibrated carburetor. The function of the system is to help the engine burn an unusually lean fuel/air mixture. The Lean Burn System is fully covered in the Engine Control Section, Unit Repair. All engines use electronic ignition, eliminating the point/condenser system, although the electronic ignition on 2.6L engines is slightly different from that used on 1.6L, 1.7L and 2.2L engines.

NOTE: Refer to Electronic Ignition and Engine Control chapters in the Unit Repair Section.

DISTRIBUTOR

Removal

1. Disconnect the distributor pickup lead wire at the harness connector.
2. Remove the distributor cap.
3. Rotate the engine crankshaft (in the direction of normal rotation) until No. 1 cylinder is at TDC on compression stroke. Make a mark on the block where the rotor points for installation reference.
4. Remove the distributor holddown screw.
5. Carefully lift the distributor from the engine. The shaft will rotate slightly as the distributor is removed.

Installation

1. If the engine has been cranked over while the distributor was removed, rotate the crankshaft until the number one piston is at TDC on the compression stroke. This will be indicated by the "O" mark on the flywheel or crank pulley aligning with the pointer on the clutch housing or engine front cover. Position the rotor just ahead of the No. 1 terminal of the cap and

CHRYSLER CORPORATION
FRONT WHEEL DRIVE CARS

BELT TENSION CHART

Accessory Drive Belt	Gauge		Deflection	Torque
1.6L ENGINE				
Air Pump	New	95 lb.	7/32 in. (5.558mm)	37 ft. lbs. (50 Nm)
	Used	70 lb.	5/16 in. (7.938mm)	28 ft. lbs. (39 Nm)
Alternator-Water Pump	New	95 lb.	1/4 in. (6.35mm)	—
	Used	60 lb.	5/16 in. (7.398mm)	—
Power Steering	New	95 lb.	3/8 in. (9.525mm)	—
	Used	70 lb.	7/16 in. (11.113mm)	—
1.7L ENGINE				
Air Conditioning Compressor	New Belt	—	5/18 in. (8mm)	90 ft. lbs. (122 Nm)
	Used Belt	—	7/16 in. (9mm)	45 ft. lbs. (61 Nm)
Air Pump/Water Pump	New Belt	—	3/16 in. (4mm)	70 ft. lbs. (95 Nm)
	Used Belt	—	3/16 in. (5mm)	40 ft. lbs. (54 Nm)
Alternator/Water Pump	New Belt	—	1/8 in. (3mm)	65 ft. lbs. (88 Nm)
	Used Belt	—	1/4 in. (6mm)	40 ft. lbs. (54 Nm)
Power Steering Pump	New Belt	—	1/4 in. (6mm)	80 ft. lbs. (108 Nm)
	Used Belt	—	5/16 in. (8mm)	50 ft. lbs. (68 Nm)
2.2 L/2.5L ENGINE				
Air Conditioning Compressor	New	95 lb. ①	5/16 in. (8mm)	40 ft. lbs. (54 Nm)
	Used	80 lb.	7/16 in. (9mm)	30 ft. lbs. (41 Nm)
Air Pump	New	—	3/16 in. (5mm)	45 ft. lbs. (61 Nm)
	Used	—	1/4 in. (6mm)	35 ft. lbs. (47 Nm)
Alternator/Water Pump "V" Belt and Poly "V"	New	115 lb.	1/8 in. (3mm)	110 ft. lbs. (149 Nm)
	Used	80 lb.	1/4 in. (6mm)	80 ft. lbs. (108 Nm)
Power Steering Pump	New	95 lb.	1/4 in. (6mm)	75 ft. lbs. (102 Nm)
	Used	80 lb.	7/16 in. (11mm)	55 ft. lbs. (75 Nm)
2.6L ENGINE				
Power Steering Pump	New	95 lb.	1/4 in. (6mm)	110 ft. lbs. (194 Nm)
	Used	80 lb.	3/8 in. (9mm)	75 ft. lbs. (102 Nm)
Alternator	New	115 lb.	3/16 in. (4mm)	—
	Used	80 lb.	1/4 in. (6mm)	—
Alternator/Air Conditioning Compressor	New	115 lb.	1/4 in. (6mm)	—
	Used	80 lb.	5/16 in. (8mm)	—
Water Pump	New	—	5/16 in. (8mm)	—
	Used	—	3/8 in. (9mm)	—

① 1985 and later—105 lb

lower the distributor into the engine. With the distributor fully seated, the rotor should be directly under the No. 1 terminal.

2. If the engine was not disturbed while the distributor was out, lower the distributor into the engine, engaging the gears and making sure that the gasket is properly seated in the block. The rotor should line up with the mark made before removal.

3. Tighten the holddown screw and connect the wires.
4. Check and, if necessary, adjust the ignition timing.

NOTE: 1.6L, 1.7L and 2.2L/2.5L engines use distributor cap with positive locking secondary wires. These wire locks can be released from inside the distributor cap if the wires need to be replaced. The 2.6L engines use conventional type caps, with push/pull wire terminal ends. All caps have a vent tower.

IGNITION TIMING

1.6L, 1.7L, 2.2L/2.5L AND 2.6L ENGINES WITH CARBURETORS

NOTE: Disconnect and plug the vacuum line at the spark control computer.

The ignition is timed on No. 1 cylinder (left-hand side) facing the car.

NOTE: 2.6L engine No. 1 cylinder is located on right side, when facing the car.

1. Connect a timing light according to the manufacturer's instructions.
2. Run the engine to normal operating temperature.
3. Make sure the idle speed is correct.
4. Loosen the distributor holddown screw just enough so that the distributor can be rotated.
5. Ground the carburetor switch, if equipped. Disconnect and plug the vacuum line at the Spark Control Computer.
6. Remove the timing hole access cover, if equipped, and aim the timing light at the hole in the clutch housing.

NOTE: The 2.6L engine timing marks are on the crankshaft pulley and front cover.

7. Carefully rotate the distributor until the timing marks are aligned.
8. Tighten the distributor and recheck the timing.
9. Check, and if necessary adjust, the idle speed, but do not change the timing setting.
10. Reconnect the vacuum hose to the Spark Control Computer assembly. Disconnect the ground wire from the carburetor switch.

CHRYSLER CORPORATION
FRONT WHEEL DRIVE CARS

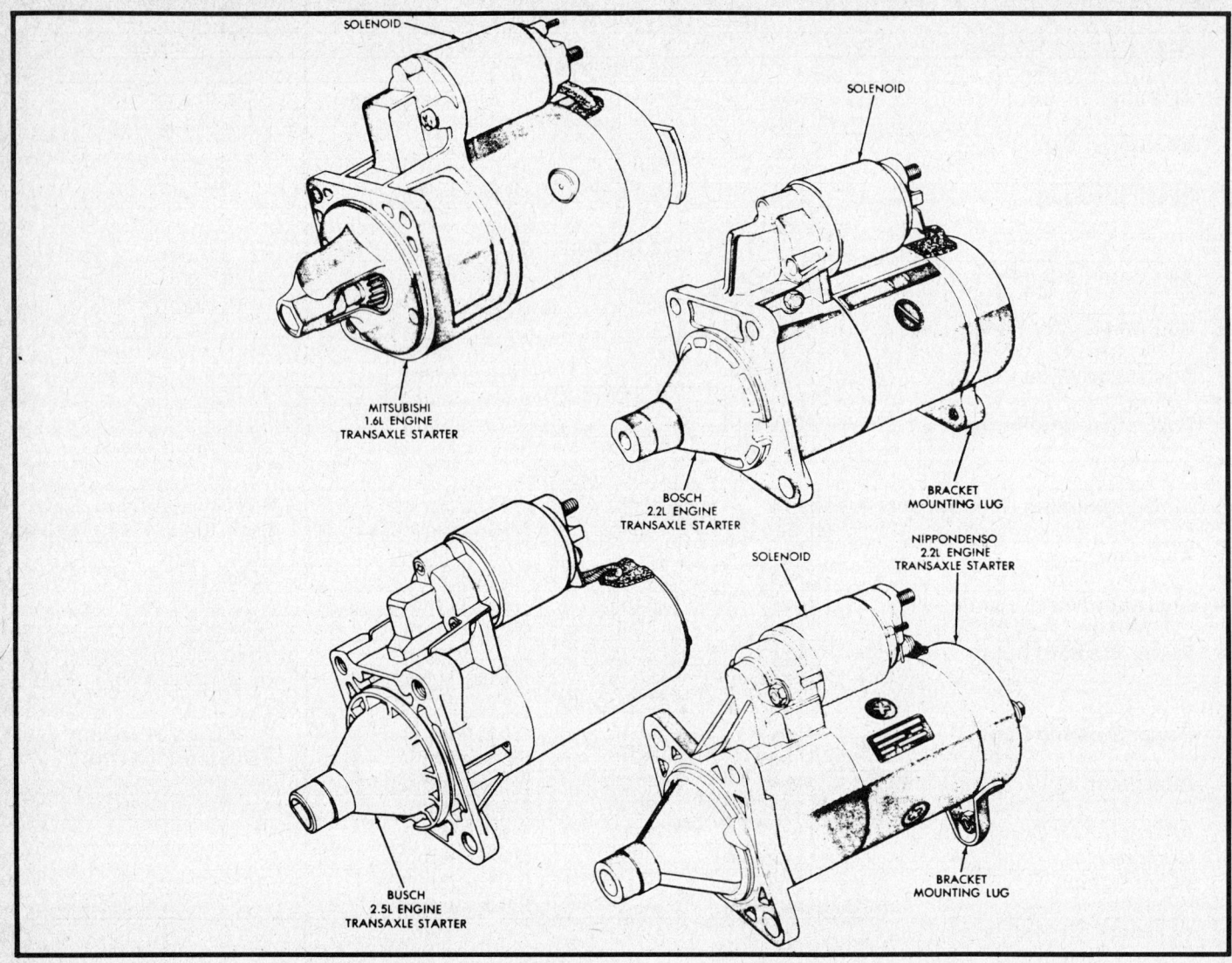

Typical starters used with varied engine applications

2.2L/2.5L ENGINES WITH ELECTRONIC FUEL INJECTION (EFI)

1. Connect a power timing light to the number one cylinder spark plug wire, or a magnetic timing unit to the engine.

NOTE: Always check the timing light instructions for any special connection combinations.

2. Connect a tachometer to the engine and turn selector to the proper cylinder position.
3. Start engine and run until operating temperature is reached.
4. Disconnect and reconnect the water temperature sensor connector on the thermostat housing. The Power Loss Lamp on the dash must come on and stay on. Engine RPM should be within emission label specification.

NOTE: Limp-In Mode is the attempt by the Logic Module to compensate for the failure of certain components by substituting information from other sources. If the Logic Module senses incorrect data or no data at all from the MAP Sensor, Throttle Position Sensor or Coolant Temperature Sensor, the system is placed into Limp-In Mode and the Power Loss lamp on the instrument panel is activated.

5. Aim power timing light at timing hole in bell housing or read the magnetic timing unit.
6. Loosen distributor and adjust timing to emission label specifications if necessary.
7. Shut engine off, disconnect and reconnect positive battery quick disconnect. Start vehicle, the Power Loss Lamp should be off.
8. Shut engine off, then turn ignition on, off, on, off, on within 5 seconds. Fault codes should be clear with 88−51−55 shown on the Power Loss Lamp.

NOTE: Code 88 means start of message and 55 means end of message. Code 51 means a problem is recorded in standby memory. This code appears if direct battery feed to the logic module is interrupted. The code will clear from memory after about 30 ignition on/off cycles, with battery current reconnected to the logic module.

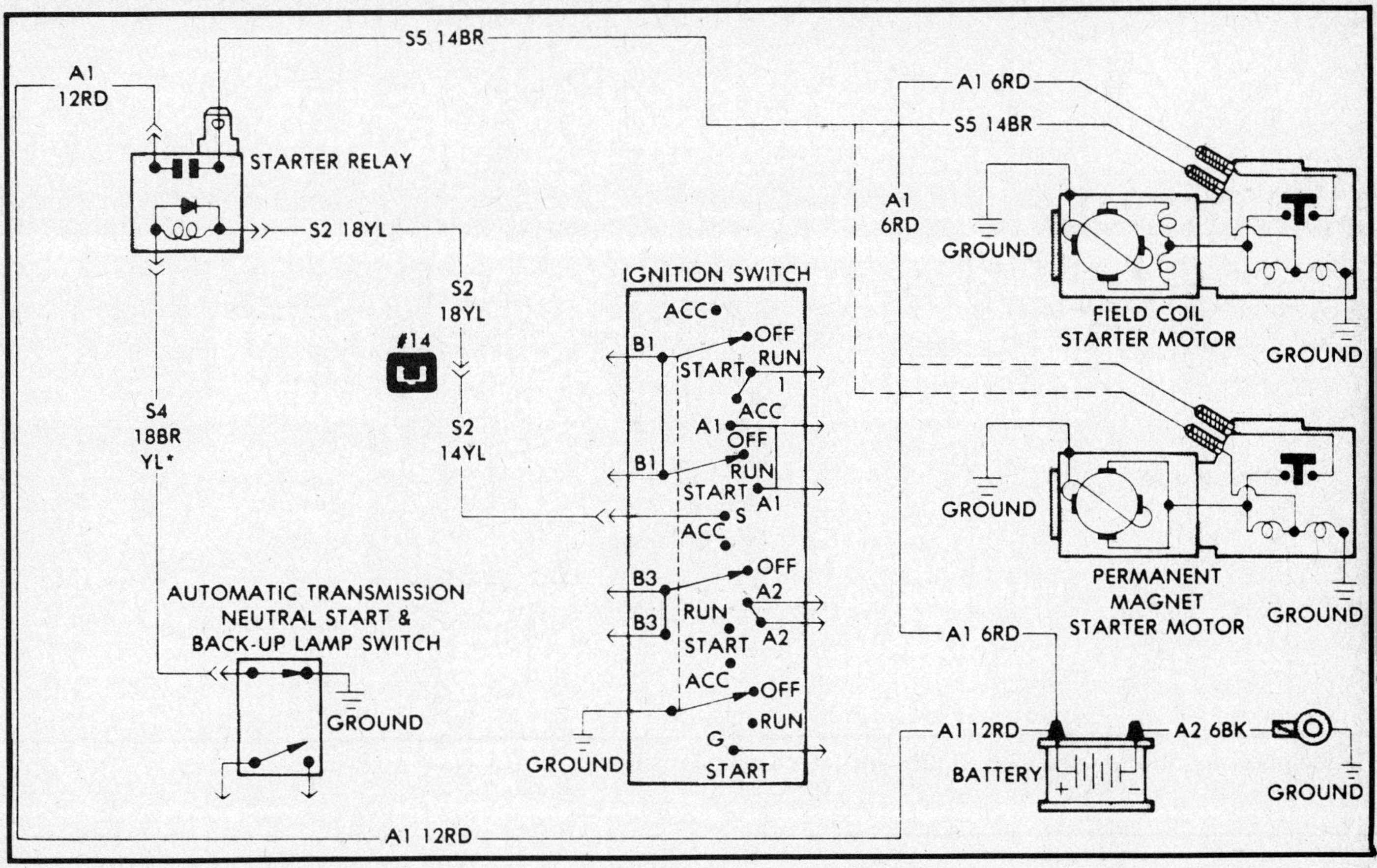

CHRYSLER CORPORATION
FRONT WHEEL DRIVE CARS

Section 2

Typical starting system circuit

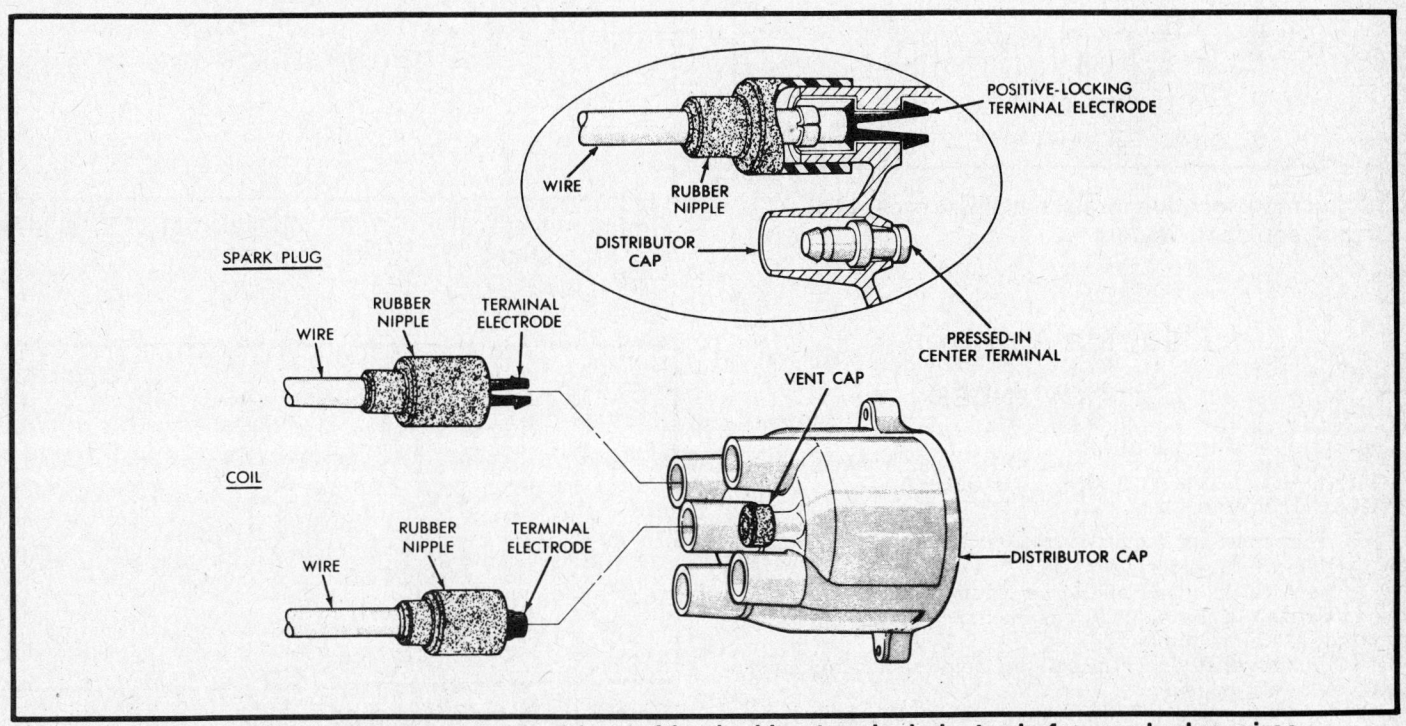

Coil and spark plug terminals. Note removable positive locking terminal electrode for spark plug wires
(© Chrysler Corporation)

2-17

SECTION 2
CHRYSLER CORPORATION
FRONT WHEEL DRIVE CARS

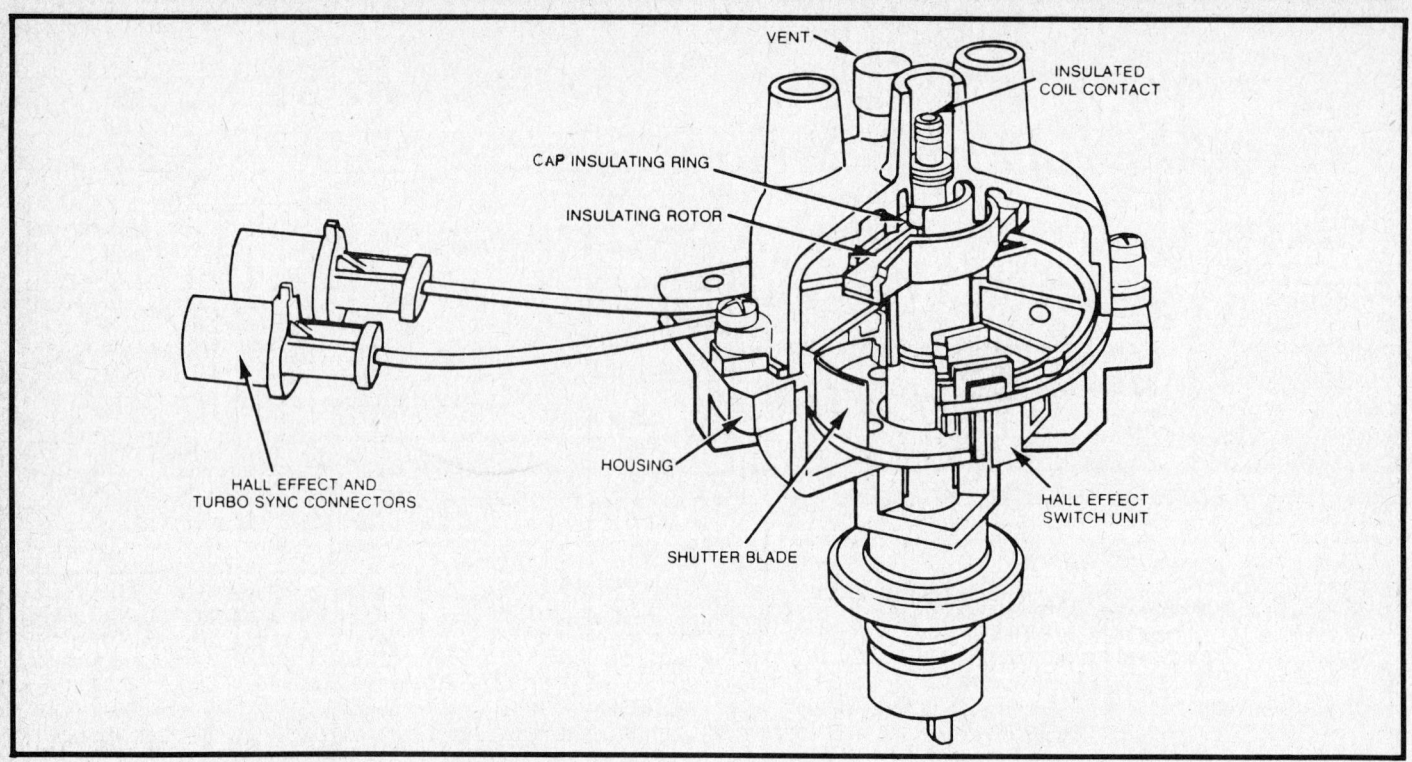

Redesigned distributor used with all 1986 and later 4 cylinder engines

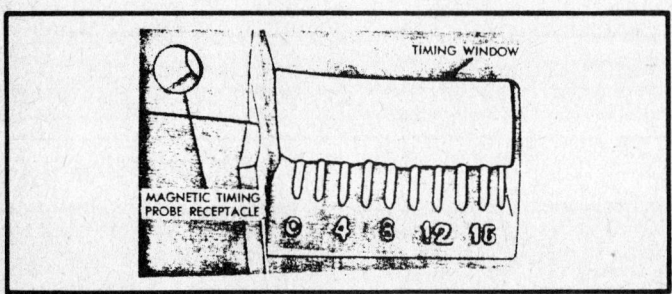

Timing mark location for 1983 engines, except 1.6L engine equipped models

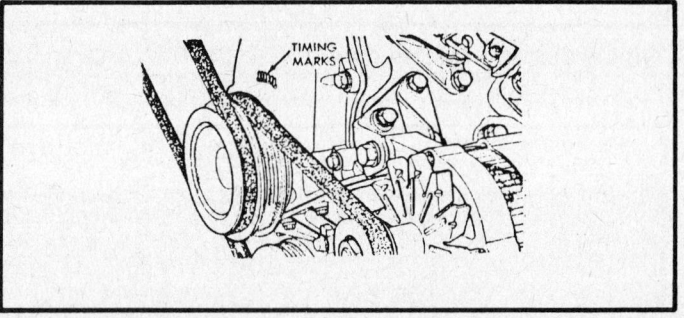

Timing mark location—1983 and later 1.6L, 1984 and later 2.2L engines (© Chrysler Corporation)

Electrical Controls

LOCK CYLINDER

Removal and Installation

OMNI, HORIZON, TC3, 024, TURISMO AND CHARGER MODELS

1. Disconnect the negative battery cable.
2. Remove the steering wheel.
3. Remove the upper and lower column covers.
4. Using a hacksaw blade, cut the upper ¼ in. from the key cylinder retainer pin boss.
5. Using a drift, drive the roll pin from the housing and remove the key housing.
6. Insert the new cylinder into the housing, making sure that it engages the lug on the ignition switch driver.
7. Install the roll pin and complete the reassembly.

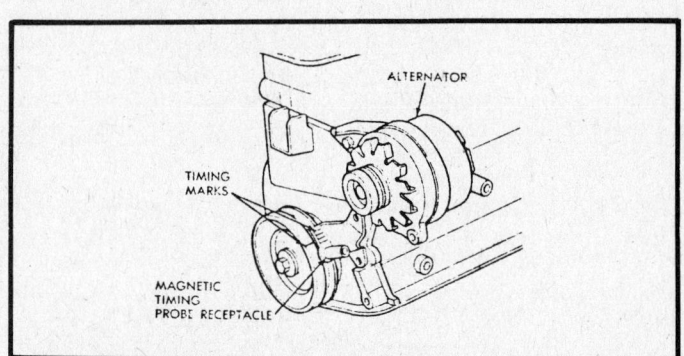

Timing mark location—2.6L engine (© Chrysler Corporation)

2–18

CHRYSLER CORPORATION
FRONT WHEEL DRIVE CARS

NOTE: The removal and installation of the key cylinder must be done with the key removed.

ARIES, RELIANT, DODGE 400, 600, E CLASS/NEW YORKER, DAYTONA, LASER, LEBARON, CARAVELLE, LANCER, LEBARON GTS, SHADOW AND SUNDANCE MODELS— —WITHOUT TILT COLUMN

1. Disconnect the negative battery cable.
2. Remove the steering wheel.
3. Remove the wash/wipe switch assembly and necessary covers.
4. Remove the turn signal switch and upper bearing retainer screws. Remove the retainer and lift the switch up out of the way.
6. Remove the bearing housing retaining screws. Remove the snap ring from the upper end of the steering shaft. Remove the bearing housing from the steering shaft.
7. Remove the lock plate spring and lock plate from the steering shaft.
8. Remove the ignition key from the cylinder. Remove the buzzer/chime switch.
9. With the lock cylinder in the "LOCK" position, insert a small diameter probe or similar tool into the lock cylinder release holes and push in to release the spring loaded lock retainers.
10. Grasp the lock cylinder and pull from the lock cylinder bore of the housing.
11. To install the lock cylinder, turn the key to the "LOCK" position and remove the key. Insert the cylinder into the housing to contact the switch actuator, insert the key, press inward and rotate the cylinder. As the parts align, the cylinder will lock into place.
12. Continue the assembly in the reverse of the removal procedure.

WITH FLOOR SHIFT COLUMN

1. Remove the upper and lower steering column covers.
2. From underneath the lock cylinder, remove the lock cylinder plunger spring and screw.
3. Using a suitable tool, depress the release plunger through the small access hole in the top of the lock cylinder housing.
4. With the release plunger depressed, pull the lock cylinder (without key) from the lock cylinder housing.
5. To install the lock cylinder, install the assembly into the housing until the plunger engages the lock cylinder and retains it in the lock cylinder bore.
6. Complete the assembly in the reverse of the removal procedure.

WITH TILT COLUMN

1. Remove the negative battery cable.
2. Remove the steering wheel.
3. Remove the tilt lever, push the hazard warning light knob in and unscrew to remove. Remove the ignition key lamp assembly.
4. Pull the knob off the wash/wipe switch assembly, pull the hider up the stalk, remove the two retaining screws that attach the sleeve to the wash/wipe switch and remove the sleeve.
5. Rotate the shaft in the wiper switch to the full clockwise position and remove the shaft by pulling straight out of the switch.
6. Remove the plastic cover from the lock plate and using a special tool, depress the lock plate to gain access to the retaining snap ring. Remove the ring from its groove and remove the lock plate, canceling cam and upper bearing spring.
7. Remove the switch actuator screw and arm. Remove the switch and wiring to gain access to the key lamp. Remove the key lamp.
8. Position the lock cylinder in the "LOCK" position and remove the key.

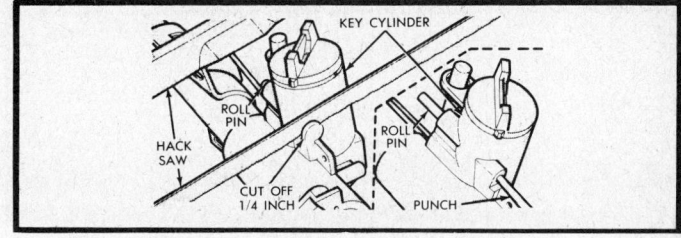

Cutting retainer pin boss to remove key cylinder
(© Chrysler Corporation)

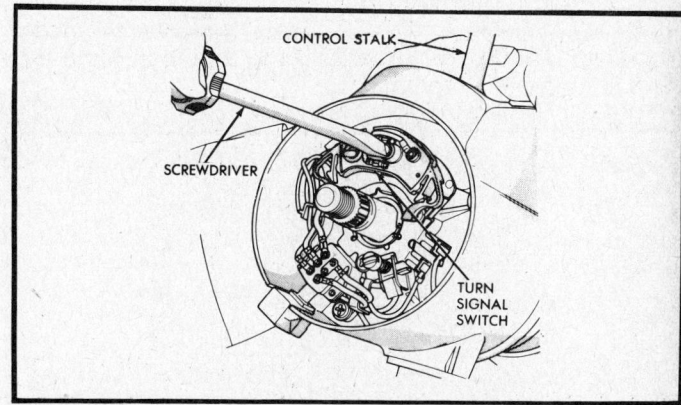

Wash/wipe switch removal and installation, all models except Omni and Horizon (© Chrysler Corporation)

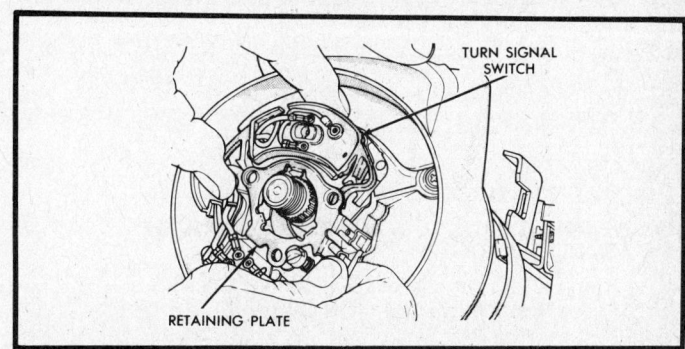

Removing or installing switch and retainer
(© Chrysler Corporation)

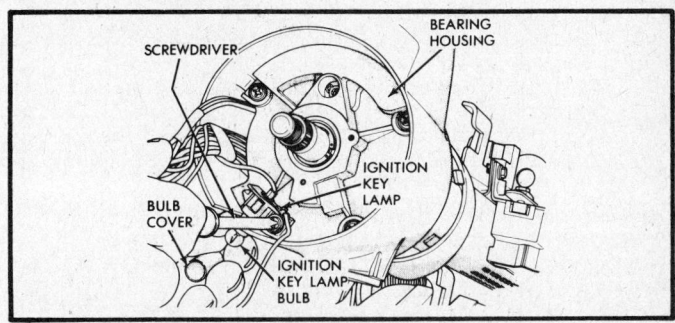

Ignition key lamp removal (© Chrysler Corporation)

9. Insert a small probe into the slot next to the switch mounting screw boss (right hand slot) and depress the spring latch at the bottom of the slot, releasing the lock cylinder. Pull the cylinder from the housing bore.
10. Install the lock cylinder in the reverse of the removal procedure and complete the assembly of the column components.

CHRYSLER CORPORATION
FRONT WHEEL DRIVE CARS

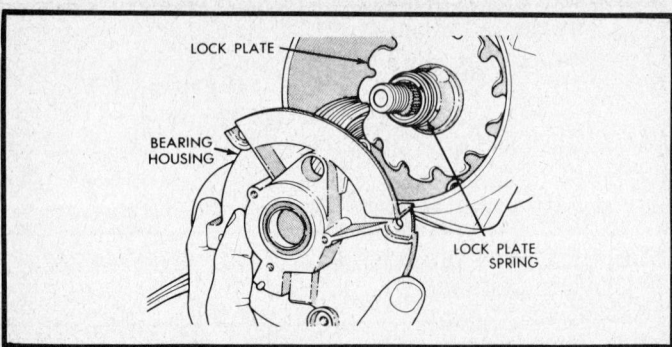

Bearing housing, lock plate spring and lock plate location (© Chrysler Corporation)

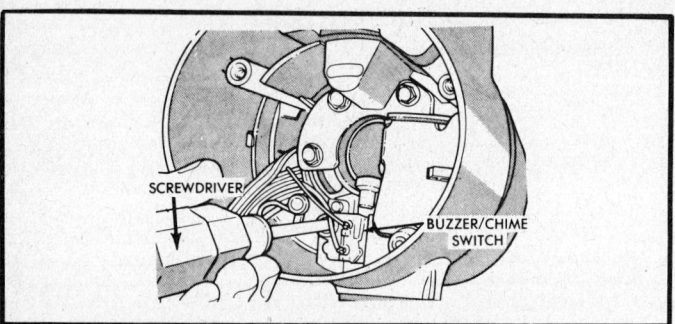

Removing ignition key buzzer/chime switch (© Chrysler Corporation)

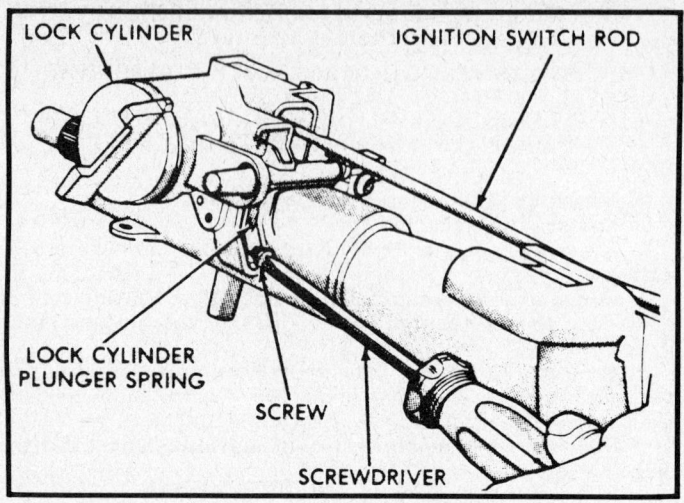

Removing lock cylinder plunger spring

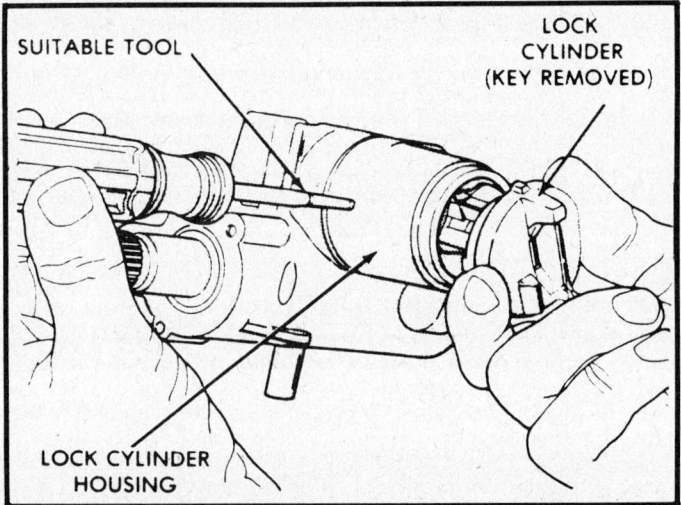

Depressing retainer to allow lock cylinder removal

IGNITION SWITCH

Removal and Installation

OMNI, HORIZON, TC3, 024, TURISMO AND CHARGER MODELS

1. Remove the connector from the switch.
2. Place the key in the LOCK position.
3. Remove the key.
4. Remove the two mounting screws from the switch and allow the switch and pushrod to drop below the jacket.
5. Rotate the switch 90 degrees to permit removal of the switch from the pushrod.
6. To install the switch, position the switch in LOCK (second detent from the top).
7. Place the switch at right angles to the column and insert the pushrod.
8. Align the switch on the bracket and install the screws.
9. With a light rearward load on the switch, tighten the screws. Check for proper operation.

ARIES, RELIANT, DODGE 400, 600, E CLASS/NEW YORKER, DAYTONA, CARAVELLE, LANCER, LEBARON GTS, LASER, LEBARON, SHADOW AND SUNDANCE MODELS

1. Remove steering column cover.
2. Remove under panel sound deadener.
3. Loosen two screws on ignition switch mounting plate to adjust switch by pushing up gently on the switch to take up rod system slack.
4. Remove speed control switch and/or wires, as required.
5. Drop steering column from dash, if necessary, for switch replacement.
6. Remove two screws attaching switch to the column.
7. Rotate switch to 90 degrees and pull up to disengage from ignition switch rod.
8. Rotate switch to 90 degrees and push up to engage to ignition switch rod.
9. Install two screws on ignition switch mounting plate, but do not tighten.
10. Adjust switch by pushing up gently on the switch to take up rod system slack. Tighten two screws attaching switch to the column.
11. Install steering column to dash, if removed.
12. Install speed control switch and/or wires.
13. Install steering column cover.
14. Install under panel sound deadener.

HEADLIGHT SWITCH

Removal and Installation

OMNI, HORIZON, TC3, 024, TURISMO AND CHARGER MODELS

1. Disconnect the battery ground.
2. Pull the headlight knob from the switch.
3. Unscrew the collar from the instrument panel side of the switch.

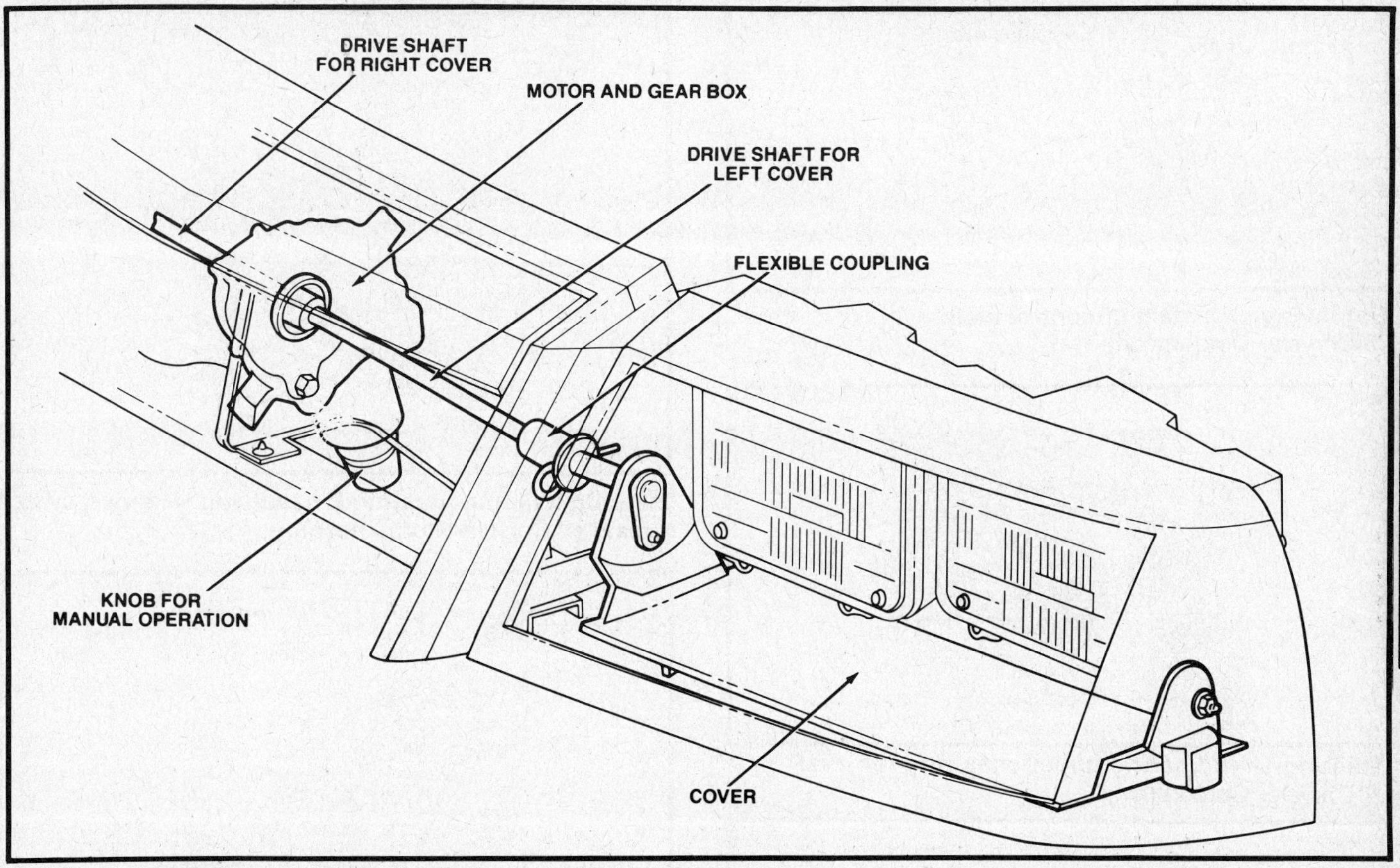

CHRYSLER CORPORATION
FRONT WHEEL DRIVE CARS

Concealed headlamps—1987 Le Baron models (©Chrysler Corporation)

4. Push the switch through the panel and let it drop; disconnect the wires.
5. Installation is the reverse of removal.

ARIES AND RELIANT, DODGE 400, 600, E CLASS/ NEW YORKER, CARAVELLE, LANCER, LEBARON GTS, DAYTONA, LASER, LEBARON, SHADOW AND SUNDANCE MODELS (WITH CLUSTER BEZEL REMOVED)

1. Remove the three screws securing the headlamp switch mounting plate to the base panel.
2. Pull the switch and plate reward and disconnect the wiring connector.
3. Depress the button on the switch and remove the knob and stem.
4. Snap out the escutcheon, then remove the nut that attaches the switch to the mounting plate.
5. Installation is the reverse of removal.

NOTE: The 1987 Lebaron is equipped with covered headlamps, which are controlled by the headlamp switch. Should the covers become inoperative, a rotating mechanical means of raising the covers is incorporated next to the cover operating mechanism and is accessible through the hood opening.

DIMMER SWITCH

Removal and Installation

ALL MODELS
1. Remove steering column cover.
2. Remove upper panel sound deadener.

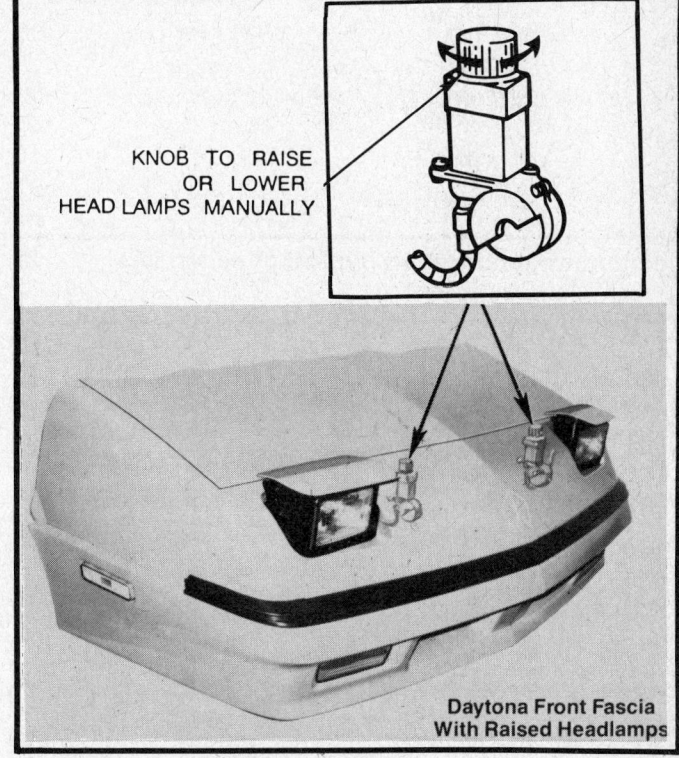

Concealed headlamps—1987
(©Chrysler Corporation)

2-21

SECTION 2
CHRYSLER CORPORATION
FRONT WHEEL DRIVE CARS

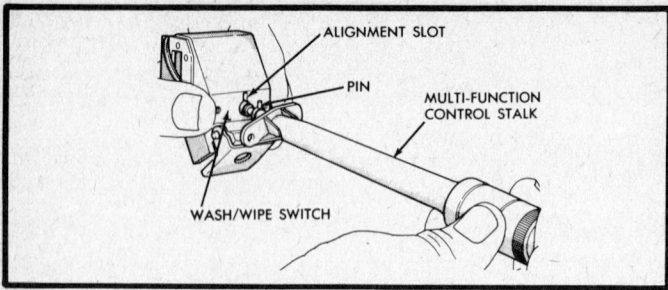

Removing or installing control stalk
(© Chrysler Corporation)

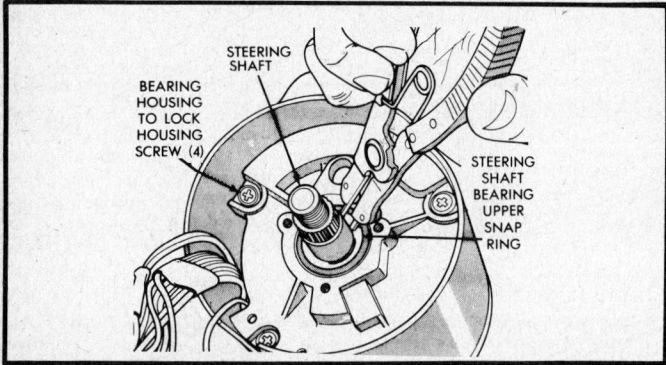

Steering shaft bearing upper snap ring removal
(© Chrysler Corporation)

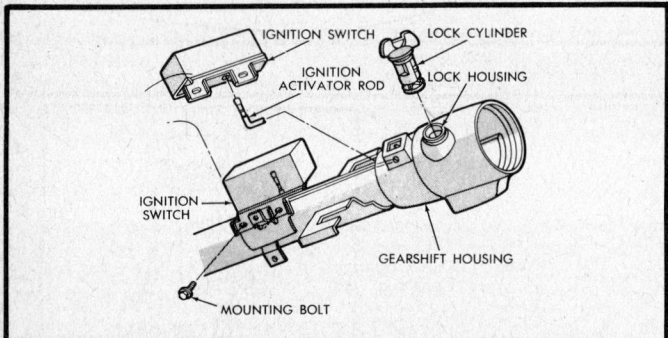

Ignition switch location, typical of all models
(© Chrysler Corporation)

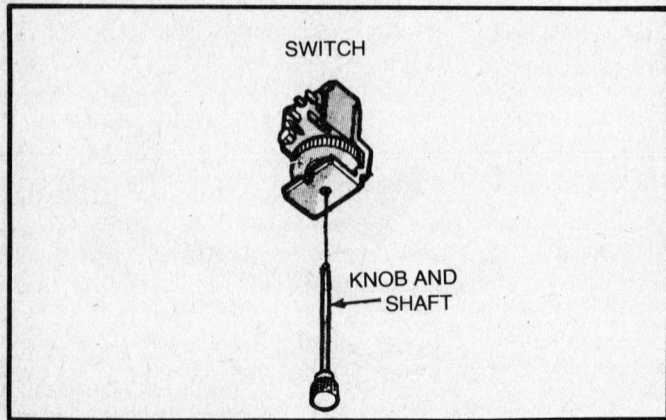

Head lamp switch with shaft and knob
(© Chrysler Corporation)

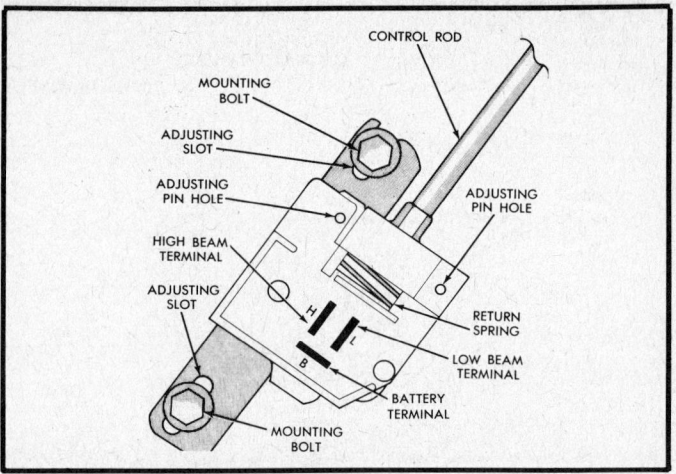

Steering column mounted headlamp dimmer switch, typical (© Chrysler Corporation)

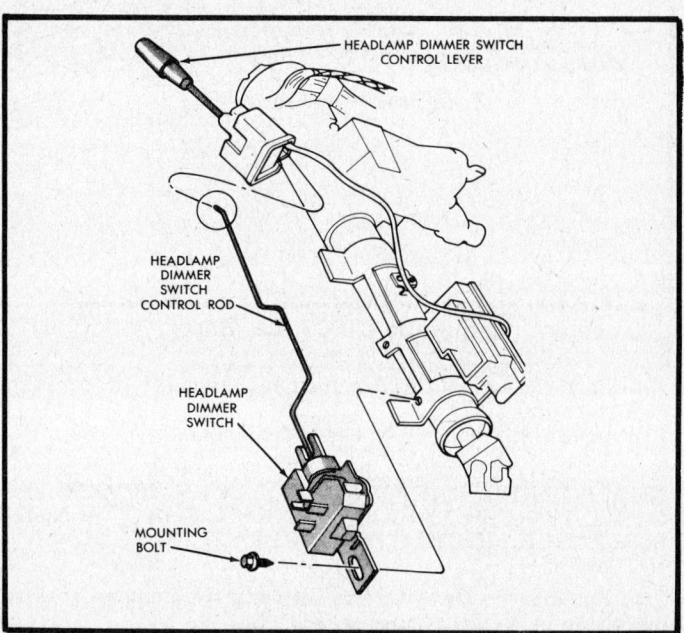

Steering column mounted dimmer switch controls
(© Chrysler Corporation)

3. Disconnect electrical connector.
4. Loosen two screws on dimmer switch mounting plate to adjust or remove switch.
5. Insert pin in switch hole to lock switch in adjustment position.
6. Adjust switch, tighten screws and remove pin.
7. Remove two screws on dimmer switch mounting plate to replace switch.
8. Position new switch. Install two screws, do not tighten.
9. Insert pin in switch hole to lock switch in adjustment position.
10. Adjust switch by pushing gently up on switch to take up the rod slack.
11. Tighten screws and remove pin.
12. Connect electrical connector.
13. Install upper panel sound deadener.
14. Install steering column cover.

CHRYSLER CORPORATION
FRONT WHEEL DRIVE CARS

Use of a drill bit to adjust the dimmer switch
(© Chrysler Corporation)

NEUTRAL SAFETY/BACKUP LIGHT SWITCH

Removal and Installation
AUTOMATIC TRANSAXLE EQUIPPED VEHICLES

The neutral safety switch is mounted in the transmission case. When the shift lever is placed in either the Park or Neutral position, a cam, which is attached to the transmission lever inside the transmission, contacts the neutral safety switch and provides a ground to complete the starter solenoid circuit.

The back-up lamp switch is incorporated into the neutral safety switch. The center terminal is for the neutral safety switch and the two outer terminals are for the back-up lamps.

There is no adjustment for the switch. If a malfunction occurs, first check to make sure that the transmission gearshift linkage is properly adjusted. If the malfunction continues, the switch must be removed and replaced.

To remove the switch, proceed as follows:
1. Place a container under the switch to catch transmission fluid. Unscrew the switch.
2. Select Park and then Neutral while checking to see that the operating fingers for the switch are centered in the case opening.
3. Screw a new switch and a new seal into the transmission. Tighten the switch to 24 ft. lbs.
4. Retest continuity. Replenish the transmission fluid, as required.

STANDARD TRANSAXLE EQUIPPED VEHICLES

The back-up lamp switch is located on the selector shaft housing and is operated by the reverse shift rail and components. The switch is removed and installed by unscrewing it from the housing and replacing the switch with a new unit and gasket. The use of Anti-Seize on the threads is suggested. Tighten the switch snugly.

STOP LAMP SWITCH

Removal and Installation
1. Lower the steering column.
2. Remove the nut located on the inboard side of the brake support bracket which fastens the switch to the bracket.
3. Remove the wiring from the dash and disconnect the wiring connector.
4. Remove the switch.
5. The installation is the reverse procedure of the removal.

Adjustment
OMNI, HORIZON, TURISMO, TC3, 024 AND CHARGER

1. Loosen the switch to pedal bracket attaching screw and slide the assembly away from the pedal blade.
2. Push the brake pedal down and allow to return on its own. Do not pull the pedal back.
3. Place a 0.130 in. spacer gauge on the pedal blade and slide the switch toward the pedal blade until the switch plunger is fully depressed against the spacer gauge.
4. Tighten the switch bracket screw to 75 inch lbs. torque and remove the spacer.
5. Operate the brake pedal and be sure the brake stop light switch does not prevent full pedal return.

ARIES, RELIANT, DODGE 400, 600, E CLASS/NEW YORKER, DAYTONA, CARAVELLE, LANCER, LEBARON GTS, LASER, LEBARON, SHADOW AND SUNDANCE MODELS

The stop lamp switch is self-adjusting during the installation.
1. Install the switch in the retaining bracket and push the switch forward as far as it will go.
2. The brake pedal will move forward slightly. Pull the pedal back, bringing the striker back towards the switch until the pedal will go no further.
3. This movement of the pedal will cause the switch to ratchet backwards to the correct position. Very little movement is required and no further adjustment is necessary.

TURN SIGNAL SWITCH

Removal and Installation
OMNI, HORIZON, TURISMO, TC3, 024 AND CHARGER

1. Disconnect the electrical connector at column.

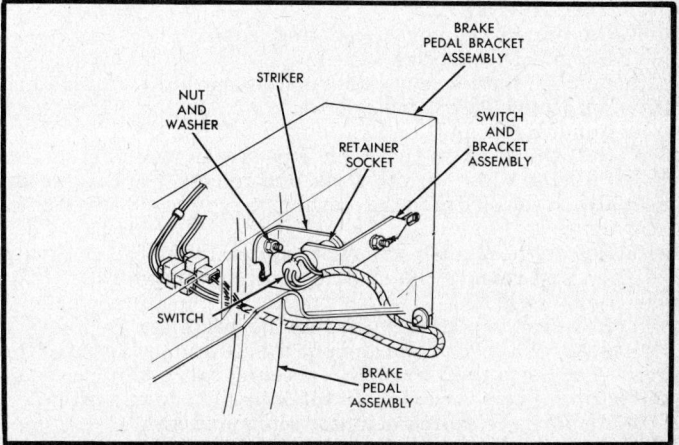

Stoplight switch assembly, typical of Aries, Reliant, Dodge 400, 600 and LeBaron models
(© Chrysler Corporation)

Turn signal switch, Omni and Horizon
(© Chrysler Corporation)

2-23

CHRYSLER CORPORATION
FRONT WHEEL DRIVE CARS

2. Remove the steering wheel.
3. Remove the lower column cover.
4. Remove the wash/wipe switch.
5. Remove the wiring clip and the three screws securing the turn signal switch.
6. Installation is the reverse of removal.

ARIES AND RELIANT, DODGE 400, 600, E CLASS/ NEW YORKER, CARAVELLE, LANCER, LEBARON GTS, DAYTONA, LASER, LEBARON, SHADOW AND SUNDANCE MODELS – WITHOUT TILT WHEEL

1. Disconnect the negative battery cable.
2. Remove the steering wheel. Remove lower instrument panel bezel. Remove wire trough.
3. On vehicles equipped with intermittent wipe or intermittent wipe with speed control, remove the two screws that attach the turn signal lever cover to the lock housing and remove the turn signal lever cover.
4. Remove the wash/wipe switch assembly.
5. Pull the hider up the control stalk and remove the two screws that attach the control stalk sleeve to the wash/wipe switch.
6. Rotate the control shaft to the full clockwise position and remove the shaft from the switch by pulling straight out of the switch.
7. Remove the turn signal switch and upper bearing retainer screws. Remove the retainer and lift the switch up and out.
8. Installation is the reverse of removal.

WITH TILT WHEEL

1. Disconnect the negative battery cable.
2. Remove the steering wheel.
3. Remove the tilt lever and push the hazard warning knob in and unscrew it to remove it.
4. Remove the ignition key lamp assembly.
5. Pull the knob off the wash/wipe switch assembly.
6. Pull the hider up the stalk and remove the two screws that attach the sleeve to the wash/wipe switch and remove the sleeve.
7. Rotate the shaft in the wiper switch to the full clockwise position and remove the shaft by pulling straight out of the wash/wipe switch.
8. Remove the plastic cover from the lock plate. Depress the lock plate with special tool and pry the retaining ring out of the groove. Remove the lock plate, canceling cam and upper bearing spring. Place turn signal switch in right turn position.
9. Remove the switch actuator screw and arm.
10. Remove the three turn signal switch attaching screws and place the shift bowl in low position. Wrap a piece of tape around the connector and wires to prevent snagging, then remove the switch and wires.
11. Installation is the reverse of removal.

HORN SWITCH
Removal and Installation

1. Disconnect the turn signal switch electrical connector.
2. Remove the horn button by lifting it with the fingers.
3. Remove the steering wheel nut and the horn switch.

NOTE: On four spoke steering wheels, remove the two screws from the rear of the steering wheel in order to remove the horn pad.

4. Installation is the reverse of removal.

WINDSHIELD WIPER SWITCH
Removal and Installation

OMNI, HORIZON, TURISMO, TC3, 024 AND CHARGER

1. Disconnect the electrical switch connector from both the

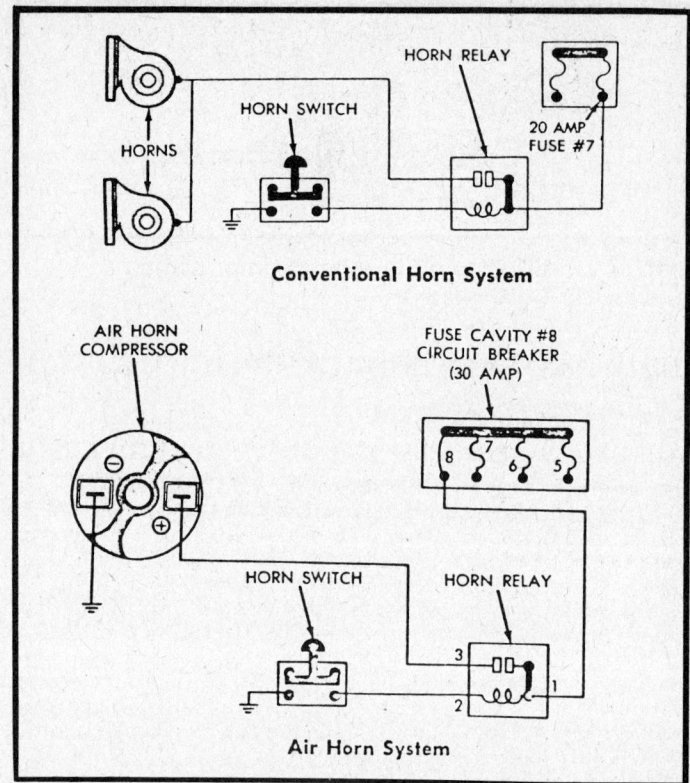

Conventional and air horn system electrical schematics
(© Chrysler Corporation)

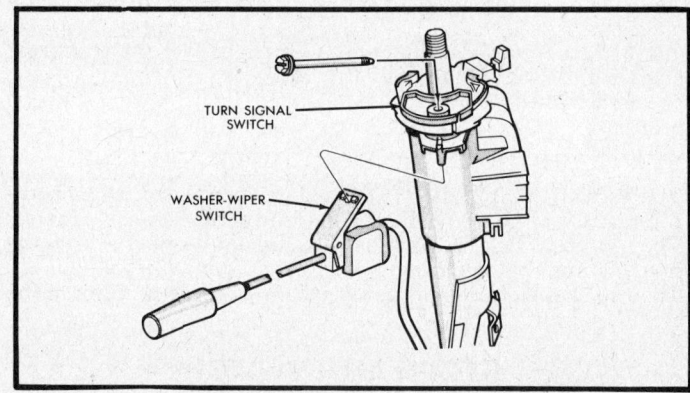

Steering column windshield wiper switch, typical
(© Chrysler Corporation)

wash/wiper switch and the turn signal switch.
2. Remove the lower column cover.
3. Remove the horn button and the wash/wiper switch hider disc.
4. Rotate the ignition switch to the OFF position and turn the steering wheel so that the access hole in the hub area is at the 9 o'clock position.
5. With the appropriate tool, loosen the turn signal lever screw through this access hole.
6. Disengage the dimmer push rod from the wash/wipe switch.
7. Unsnap the wiring clip and remove the switch.
8. The installation is in the reverse of the removal procedure. Properly position the dimmer push rod in the wash/wipe switch and secure the wiring clip. Complete the installation.

Removal and Installation

ARIES, RELIANT, CARAVELLE, 600, 400, E CLASS/NEW YORKER, CARAVELLE, LANCER, LEBARON GTS, LEBARON, DAYTONA, LASER, SHADOW AND SUNDANCE

1. Disconnect the battery negative cable.
2. Remove the steering wheel assembly.
3. Remove the wiring trough retainers and lift the wiring trough.
4. Remove the two screws retaining the turn signal lever cover to the lock housing and remove the turn signal cover.
5. Remove the wash/wiper switch assembly.
6. Pull the hider up the control stalk and remove the two retaining screws holding the control stalk to the wash/wiper switch.
7. Rotate the control stalk shaft to the full clockwise position and remove the shaft from the switch by pulling the shaft straight out of the switch.
8. The installation is the revere of the removal procedure.

Removal and Installation

FIFTH AVENUE, DIPLOMAT AND GRAN FURY

1. Remove the negative battery cable.
2. Remove the steering wheel assembly.
3. Remove the lower instrument panel bezel.
4. If equipped with tilt steering column;
   a. Remove the gear shift indicator.
   b. Remove the two nuts mounting the column to the lower panel reinforcement.
   c. Remove the mounting bracket from the steering column by removing the four attaching bolts.
5. Remove the wiring trough from the column.
6. Remove the turn signal switch.
7. Remove the retaining screws for the lock housing cover and remove the lock housing cover.
8. Gently pull the wiper switch up from the column while straightening and guiding the wires up through the column opening.
9. The installation is in the reverse of the removal procedure.

WIPER MOTOR, CRANKS AND LINKAGE ASSEMBLY

Removal

OMNI, HORIZON, TURISMO, TC3, 024 AND CHARGER

1. Remove wiper arm assemblies.
2. Remove the tie down nuts and washers from left and right pivots.
3. Open the hood assembly.
4. Remove the wiper motor plastic cover and washer hose attaching clip.
5. Disconnect the wiper motor wiring harness.
6. Remove three (3) bolts that fasten motor mounting bracket to body sheet metal.
7. Disengage the pivots from the cowl top mounting positions.
8. Remove wiper motor, mounting bracket, cranks, pivots and drive links assembly from cowl plenum chamber. Make certain pivot marked "L" is positioned to drivers side of vehicle.
9. On bench, remove the motor from the drive crank.

Installation

1. Put the assembly together after the service has been performed.
2. Install wiper motor, mounting bracket, cranks, pivots and linkage into cowl plenum chamber.
3. Engage the pivots through cowl top mounting holes and loosely install pivot shaft nuts and washers.
4. Install three (3) bolts to motor mounting bracket.
5. Connect the wiper motor wiring harness.
6. Install the wiper motor plastic cover and attach washer hose clip.
7. Close the hood assembly.
8. Tighten tie down nuts on left and right pivot shafts.
9. Install and adjust wiper arm assembly.

Removal

ARIES, RELIANT, DODGE 400, 600, E CLASS/NEW YORKER, DAYTONA, CARAVELLE, LANCER, LEBARON GTS, LASER, LEBARON, SHADOW AND SUNDANCE

1. Park the wiper motor system.
2. Open the hood assembly.
3. Remove wiper arms and blades, disconnect hoses from tee connector.
4. Remove the cowl top plastic screen. Remove reservoir hose from T-connector, if equipped.
5. Remove pivot screws.
6. Remove wiper motor cover and disconnect wiring harness.
7. Remove three (3) motor mounting nuts.
8. Push pivots down into plenum chamber, pull motor out until it clears the mounting studs and then as far to the drivers side (outboard) as it will go, then pull right pivot and link out through opening, then shift motor to opposite side (inboard) of opening and remove motor, left link and pivot.
9. Clamp motor crank in a vise and remove nut from end of motor shaft. Do not rotate motor output shaft from park position.

Installation

1. Assemble linkage to motor; make sure crank fits over "D" slot on motor shaft. Torque mounting nut to 95 inch lbs. (11Nm). Be sure motor is still in park position before assembling to linkage, if not temporarily connect motor to wiring and operate switch to position motor in park before assembling linkage.
2. Place left pivot and link into plenum chamber and slide all the way to the left (outboard) until motor clears studs and crank is behind sheetmetal, then push right pivot and link through opening. Move assembly right and position motor on studs.
3. Install three (3) motor mounting nuts and torque to 55 inch lbs. (6 Nm).
5. Connect wiring to motor.
6. Install motor cover. Torque screws to 35 inch lbs. (4 Nm).
7. Attach reservoir hose to T-connector, if equipped, through hole provided in cowl screen.
8. Use plastic fasteners to install cowl screen, if equipped.
9. Install arm and blade assemblies. Connect arm washer hoses to T-connector.

Instrument Cluster

CLUSTER ASSEMBLY

Removal and Installation

NOTE: On certain models, after the bezel, mask/lens assemblies have been removed, the gauges are accessible for replacement as required. Extreme care must be exercised to avoid damage to the instrument panel components.

CHRYSLER CORPORATION
FRONT WHEEL DRIVE CARS

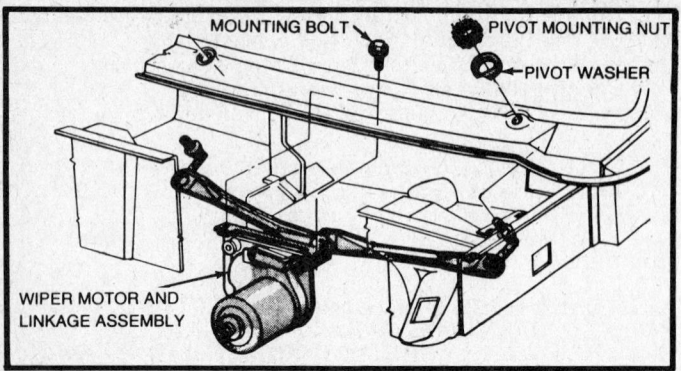

Wiper motor and linkage—typical
(© Chrysler Corporation)

1983 OMNI, HORIZON, TC3 MODELS, E–TYPE, 024 MODELS, CHARGER, TURISMO

1. Disconnect the negative battery cable.
2. Remove the two mask/lens assembly lower attachment retaining spring pins by pulling rearward with pliers.

NOTE: *Rearward direction is toward the rear of the vehicle.*

--- **CAUTION** ---
Prevent contact with the mask/lens to avoid breakage.

3. Allow the mask/lens to drop slightly as it is moved rearward and remove it from the cluster.
4. The standard or ralley clusters are now accessible for service or for removal from the instrument panel as an assembly.
5. To remove the cluster assembly, remove the speedometer assembly two retaining screws.
6. Disengage two wiring harness connectors. Remove the four cluster retaining screws.
7. Pull the cluster away from the instrument panel and disconnect the clock and tachometer wires, if equipped.
8. Disconnect the speedometer cable and remove the cluster assembly from the panel.
9. The installation is the reverse of the removal procedure.

Removal and Installation

1984 AND LATER OMNI, HORIZON, TC3, 024, TURISMO, CHARGER

1. Disconnect the negative battery cable.
2. Remove the cluster bezel. Remove the two mask/lens lower attaching screws, allow the mask/lens to drop slightly and remove, as required.
3. If the cluster is to be removed, the mask/lens would be removed with the cluster, as outlined in the following Steps.
4. Remove the four screws retaining the cluster to the instrument panel.
5. Pull cluster away from the panel, disconnect the speedometer and the wiring connector.
6. Remove the cluster assembly from the instrument panel.
7. The installation is the reverse of the removal procedure.

1983 ARIES AND RELIANT, DODGE 400, 600 AND LEBARON MODELS

1. Place the gearshift lever in position "1" and disconnect negative battery cable.
2. Remove the instrument panel trim strip, if equipped.
3. Remove the left upper and lower cluster bezel screws.
4. Remove the right lower cluster bezel screw and retaining clip.
5. Remove the instrument cluster bezel by snapping the bezel off of the five retaining clips.
6. Remove the retaining screws and remove the upper right bezel.
7. Remove the rear instrument panel top cover mounting screws.
8. Lift the rear edge of the panel top cover and remove the two screws attaching the upper trim strip retainer and cluster housing to the base panel.
9. Remove the trim strip retainer.
10. Remove the two screws attaching the cluster housing to the base panel of the lower cluster.
11. Lift the rearward edge of the panel top cover and slide the cluster housing rearward.
12. Disconnect the right printed circuit board connector from behind the cluster housing.
13. Disconnect the speedometer cable connector.
14. Disconnect the left printed circuit connector.
15. Remove the cluster assembly.
16. Installation is the reverse of removal.

Removal and Installation

1984 AND LATER ARIES, RELIANT, DODGE 400, LEBARON

1. Remove the negative battery cable.
2. Place the shift lever in the position "1".
3. Remove the upper left and lower cluster bezel screws.
4. Remove the instrument cluster bezel by snapping the bezel off the five retaining clips.
5. Remove the instrument panel cluster mask by snapping the mask off the four retaining clips.
6. Remove the instrument panel top cover mounting screws and lift the edge of the top panel to remove the two screws attaching the cluster housing to the base panel.
7. Lift the rearward edge of the top panel and slide the cluster housing rearward.

NOTE: *Rearward direction is toward the rear of the vehicle.*

8. Reach behind the cluster assembly and disconnect the right and left printed circuit board connector.
9. Disconnect the speedometer cable and remove the cluster assembly.

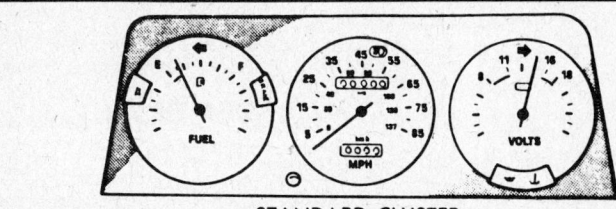
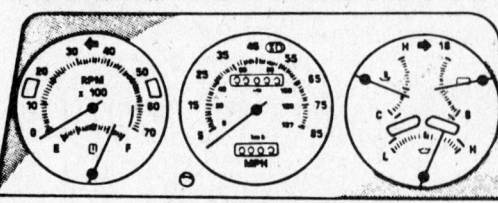

Two types of instrument panel clusters for Omni, Horizon, Turismo, Charger, TC3 and 024 models—typical (© Chrysler Corporation)

STANDARD CLUSTER | RALLYE CLUSTER

CHRYSLER CORPORATION
FRONT WHEEL DRIVE CARS

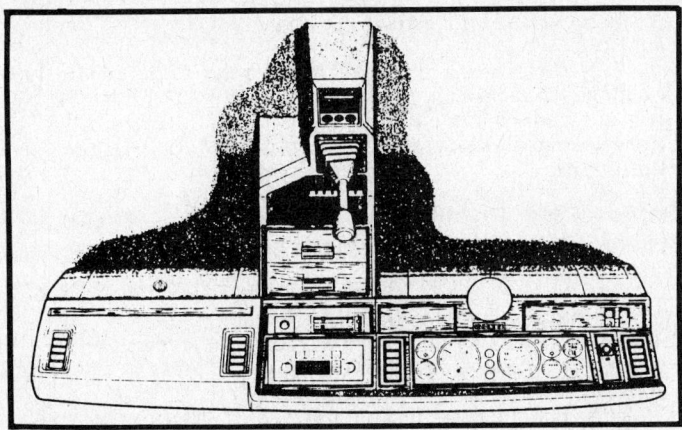

Instrument panel and console—1985 Aries/Reliant models (© Chrysler Corporation)

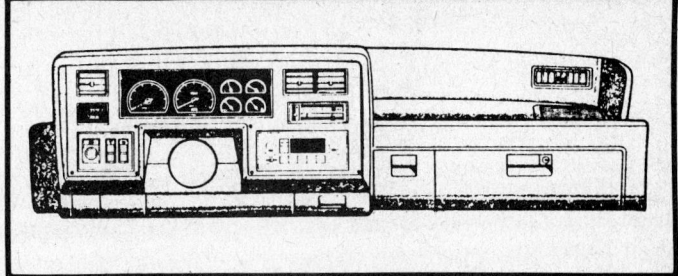

Instrument panel assembly—1985 Lancer/LeBaron GTS models (© Chrysler Corporation)

10. The installation is the reverse of the removal procedure.

Removal and Installation

1984 AND LATER CARAVELLE, LANCER, LEBARON GTS, LEBARON, 600, E CLASS/NEW YORKER

NOTE: The electronic cluster is serviced as an assembly. The individual gauges cannot be serviced separately.

1. Disconnect the negative battery cable.
2. Place the shift lever in the position "1".
3. Remove the radio knobs and the six screws from the cluster bezel.
4. Remove the bezel by snapping the bezel off of the five retaining clips.
5. Remove the cluster mask by snapping the mask off the four retaining clips.

NOTE: The electronic cluster is removed and installed in the same manner as the conventional cluster, except for the speedometer cable. When replacing the electronic cluster, the odometer memory chip can be installed into another electronic cluster.

6. Remove the rearward screws from the instrument panel upper pad assembly.

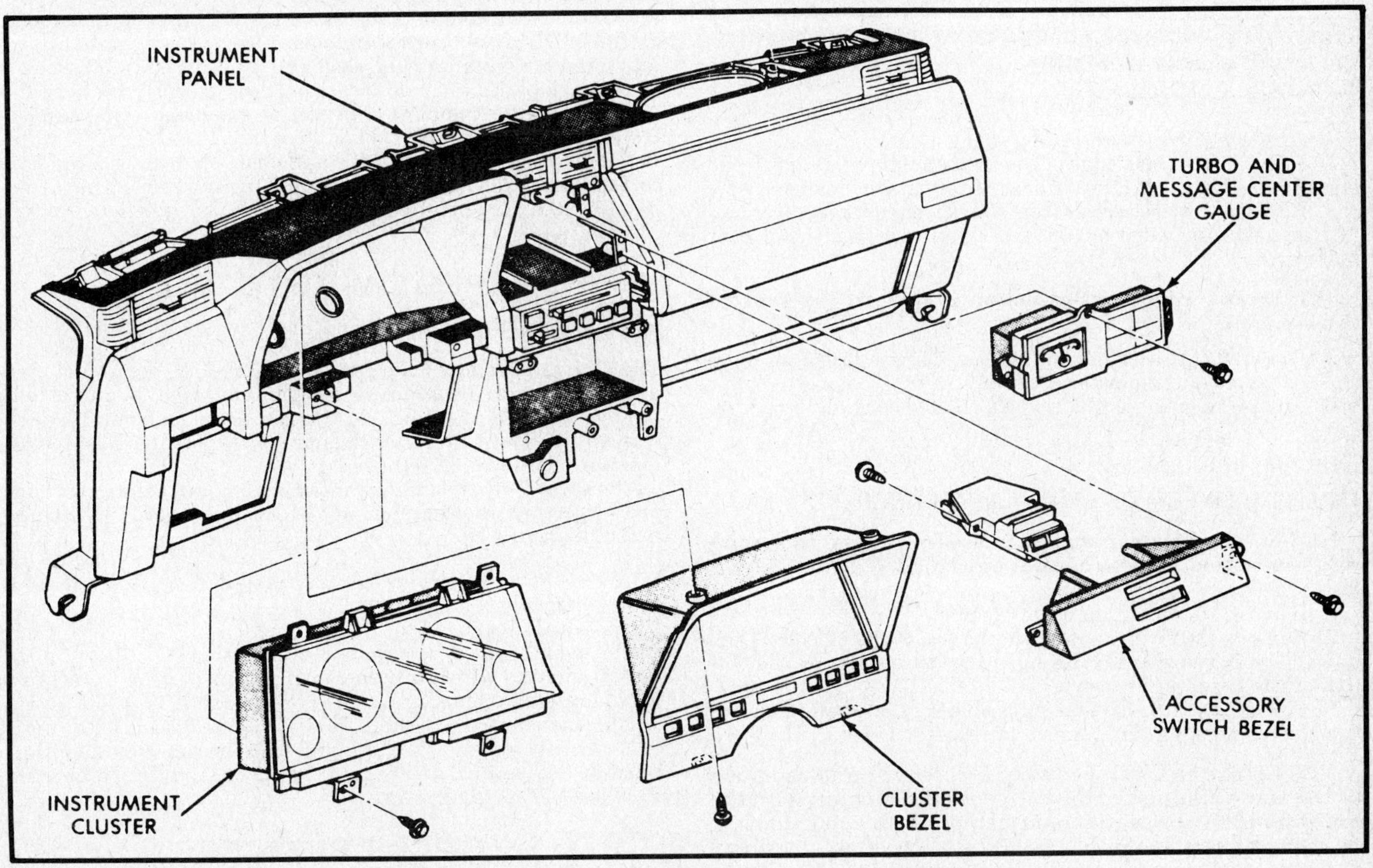

Shadow and Sundance upper instrument panel components

CHRYSLER CORPORATION
FRONT WHEEL DRIVE CARS

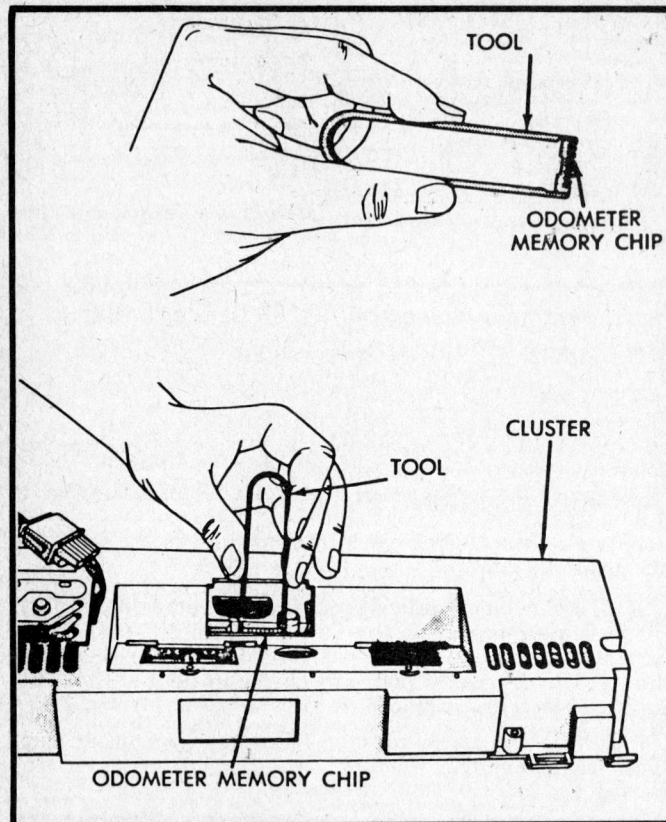

Removal or installation of odometer memory chip in the electronic cluster assembly
(© Chrysler Corporation)

7. Lift the rearward edge of the instrument panel upper pad and remove the two screws from the top of the cluster.

8. Remove the two screws from the bottom of the cluster and lift the rearward edge of the upper pad and pull the cluster rearward.

NOTE: The rearward direction is toward the rear of the vehicle.

9. Disconnect the wiring and the speedometer cable from the cluster. Remove the cluster assembly.

10. The installation is the reverse of the removal procedure.

Removal and Installation
1984 AND LATER DAYTONA AND LASER

NOTE: The electronic cluster is serviced as an assembly. Individual gauges cannot be replaced separately.

1. Remove the negative battery cable.
2. Remove the five screws from the top of the cluster bezel, pull the bezel rearward to disengage the three clips on the bottom of the bezel and remove.
3. Remove the five bayonet clips holding the cluster mask to the cluster housing and remove the cluster mask.

NOTE: The electronic cluster is removed and replaced in the same manner as the conventional cluster, with the exception of the speedometer cable. The electronic cluster must be serviced as an assembly. The odometer memory chip can be replaced from the original cluster to the new cluster.

4. Remove the four screws retaining the cluster to the base panel.
5. Pull the cluster rearward, reach behind the cluster and disconnect the speedometer cable and the wiring harness. Remove the cluster assembly.
6. The installation of the cluster is the reverse of the removal procedure.

Removal and Installation
1987 SHADOW AND SUNDANCE

Remove the instrument cluster bezel.
2. Remove the instrument cluster retaining screws
3. Move the cluster assembly rearward for access to the speedometer cable and cluster wiring connectors.
4. Pull the cluster rearward and towards the center of the vehicle to remove it from the dash.

NOTE: It is not necessary to remove the instrument cluster from the vehicle for gauge removal. The cluster bezel, mask and lens must be removed to expose the gauges. The gauges must be pulled straight out from the cluster to avoid damage to the gauge pins.

5. The installation of the cluster is the reverse of its removal procedure.

SPEEDOMETER

Removal and Installation

The speedometer assembly is removed from the cluster after the mask/lens have been removed. The speedometer can be removed without complete cluster removal on certain models. However, because of working clearance, it is suggested to remove the complete cluster assembly and disassemble it on a clean work bench to avoid loss of parts or dropped components.

The odometer memory chip can be removed from the electronic cluster assembly and installed into a new cluster, retaining the vehicle's accumulated mileage. Special tweezer type tool must be used for the removal and installation of the memory chip and its installed position must be noted for proper installation.

SPEEDOMETER CABLE

Removal and Installation

The Omni, Turismo, Charger, TCC3,024 and Horizon models use a plastic ferrule which is attached to the panel and is held in place by a metal spring clip. The remaining models use a ferrule on the speedometer cable end which must be released before the cable can be removed.

The speedometer assembly must be removed before servicing of the core or replacement of the housing assembly can be accomplished.

FUSIBLE LINKS

Fusible links are used to prevent major wire harness damage in the event of a short circuit or an overload condition in the wiring circuits which are normally not fused, due to carrying high amperage loads or because of their locations within the wiring harness. Each fusible link is of a fixed value for a specific electrical load and should a link fail, the cause of the failure must be determined and repaired prior to installing a new fusible link of the same value.

CIRCUIT BREAKERS

Circuit breakers are used along with the fusible links to pro-

CHRYSLER CORPORATION
FRONT WHEEL DRIVE CARS

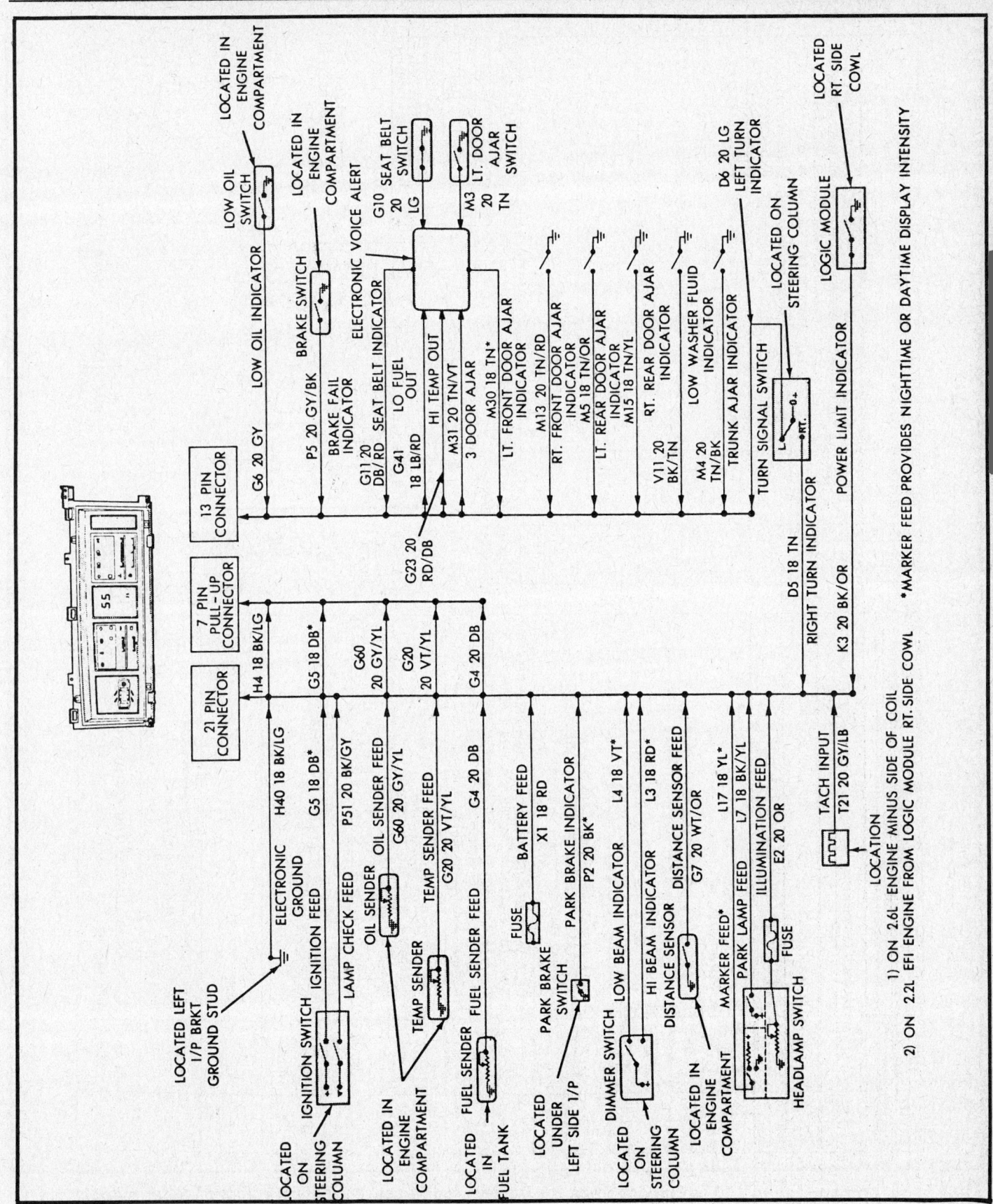

Electronic cluster wiring diagram—typical (© Chrysler Corporation)

SECTION 2
CHRYSLER CORPORATION
FRONT WHEEL DRIVE CARS

CAVITY	FUSE/COLOR	ITEMS FUSED
1	20 AMP YL	HAZARD FLASHER
2	20 AMP YL	BACK-UP LAMPS, TRIP NAVIGATOR, ELAPSED TIMER FAN RELAY COIL ELECTRONIC VOICE ALERT (11 FUNCTION) TRANSMISSION PRESSURE SWITCH (24 FUNCTION)
3	30 AMP C/BRKR SILVER CAN	POWER WINDOW MOTORS
4	30 AMP LG	A/C, ATC OR HEATER BLOWER MOTOR
5	20 AMP YL	CAVITY 12 (CLUSTER), PARK, TAIL, SIDE MARKER & LICENSE LAMPS; ELECTRONIC DISPLAY INTENSITY & TAIL LAMP OUTAGE
6	20 AMP YL	STOP, DOME, MAP AND CARGO LAMPS; TIME DELAY RELAY, ATC MEMORY ELECTRONIC MONITOR (C-P-24) ELECTRONIC VOICE ALERT (24 FUNCTION), STOP LAMP OUTAGE TOROIDS, BRAKE SENSE, POWER MIRROR MOTORS AND ILLUMINATED ENTRY COIL AND LAMP AND TBI OR TURBO LOGIC MODULE
7	20 AMP YL	GLOVE BOX LAMP, CIGAR LIGHTER, MEMORY FOR RADIO AND ELAPSED TIMER-TRIP NAVIGATOR, ELECTRONIC VOICE ALERT (11 OR 24 FUNCTION), CHIMES, ELECTRONIC CLUSTER, HORN AND RELAY
8	30 AMP C/BRKR SILVER CAN	AIR HORNS & RELAY, POWER SEAT MOTOR & POWER DOOR LOCKS
9	10 AMP TN	RADIO
10	20 AMP YL	TURN SLIGNAL LAMPS; HEATED REAR WINDOW REALY ATC CONTROL AND IN CAR SENSOR
11	20 AMP YL	FRONT WINDSHIELD WIPER AND WASHER AND INTERMITTENT WIPE MODULE
12	5 AMP TN	CLUSTER ILLUMINATION LAMPS MECHANICAL OR ELECTRONIC CLUSTER HEATED REAR WINDOW, REAR WASH AND WIPE, A/C AND HEATER CONTROL, RADIO, ASH RECEIVER, CIGAR LIGHTER, ELAPSED TIMER, NAVIGATOR, MESSAGE CENTER, CONSOLE GEAR SELECTOR AND ELECTRONIC DIMMING
13	5 AMP TN	CLUSTER PRINTED CIRCUIT BOARD GAUGES AND WARNING LAMPS, CHIMES, SPEED CONTROL SERVO, INCANDESCENT MESSAGE CENTER, ELECTRONIC VOICE ALERT (11 OR 24 FUNCTION) ELECTRONIC MONITOR ILLUMINATED ENTRY SEAT BELT LAMP ELECTRONIC CLUSTER
14	6 AMP C/BRKR GOLD CAN	REAR WASH WIPE & LIFTGATE RELEASE SOLENOID
15		
16		

AMPS	FUSE	COLOR CODE
3	VT	VILOET
4	PK	PINK
5	TN	TAN
10	RD	RED
20	YL	YELLOW
25	NAT	NATURAL
30	LG	LIGHT GREEN

Fuse panel and corresponding circuit coverage for Daytona and Laser models. Typical of other models
(© Chrysler Corporation)

CHRYSLER CORPORATION
FRONT WHEEL DRIVE CARS
SECTION 2

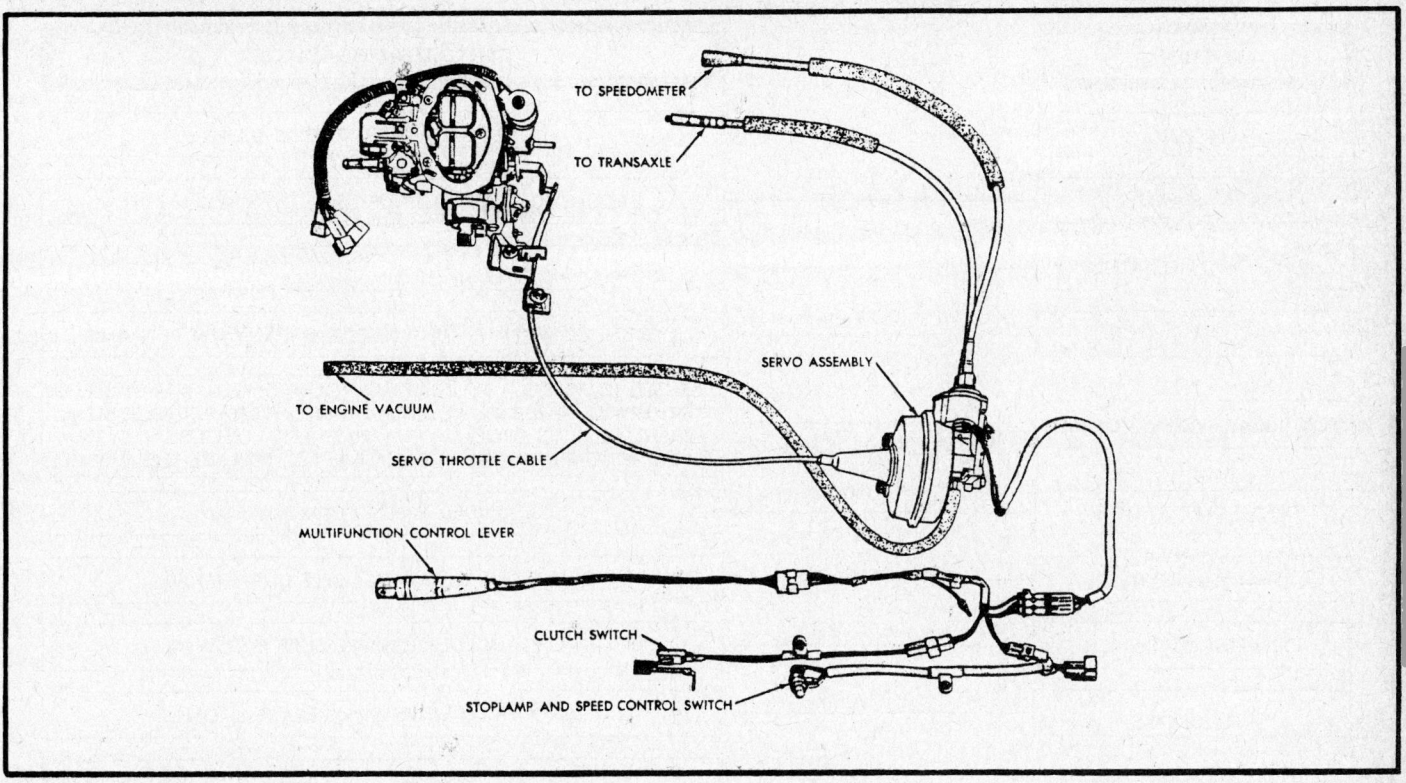

Speed control components—typical of all models (© Chrysler Corporation)

tect the various components of the electrical system, such as the headlamps, the windshield wipers, electric windows, tailgate front switch and tailgate rear switch. The circuit breakers are located either in the switch or mounted on or near the lower lip of the instrument panel, to the right or left of the steering column.

FUSE PANELS

The fuse panel is used to house the fuses that protect the individual or combined electrical circuits within the vehicle. The turn signal flasher, the hazard warning flasher and the seat belt warning buzzer/timer are located on the fuse panel for quick identification and replacement.

The fuses are usually identified by abbreviated circuit names or number, with the number of the rated fuse needed to protect the circuit printed below the fuse holder.

Speed Control

SPEED CONTROL CABLE

Adjustment

1. Start the engine and bring to normal operating temperature.
2. Remove the snapring from the cable clevis to throttle lever stud.
3. The clearance between the throttle lever stud and the cable clevis should be $1/16$ in. (1.66 mm).
4. To adjust, loosen the cable retaining clamp nut, located approximately seven inches from the throttle lever stud.
5. Pull all slack out of the cable, using the head of the throttle stud as a gauge.

CAUTION

Do not pull the cable so tight that it moves the throttle away from the curb idle position.

---

6. Tighten the retaining clamp nut to 45 ft. lbs. torque and move the cable clevis back on the round portion of the throttle lever stud.
7. Install the snapring.

SERVO LOCK–IN SCREW

Adjustment

1. If the speed drops more than 2–3 mph when the speed control is activated, turn the lock-in screw, located on the servo, counterclockwise approximately $1/4$ turn per one mph correction required.
2. If the speed increases 2–3 mph when the speed control is activated, the lock-in screw should be turned clockwise approximately turn per one mph correction required.

CAUTION

This adjustment must not exceed two turns in either direction or damage to the unit may occur.

Electronic Voice Alert (11 Functions)

DESCRIPTION OF FUNCTIONS

"YOUR HEADLIGHTS ARE ON"

Will occur after drivers door is closed, the headlamps are in the on position, the ignition key is turned on and off, the key removed from the ignition and the drivers door opened.

2–31

CHRYSLER CORPORATION
FRONT WHEEL DRIVE CARS

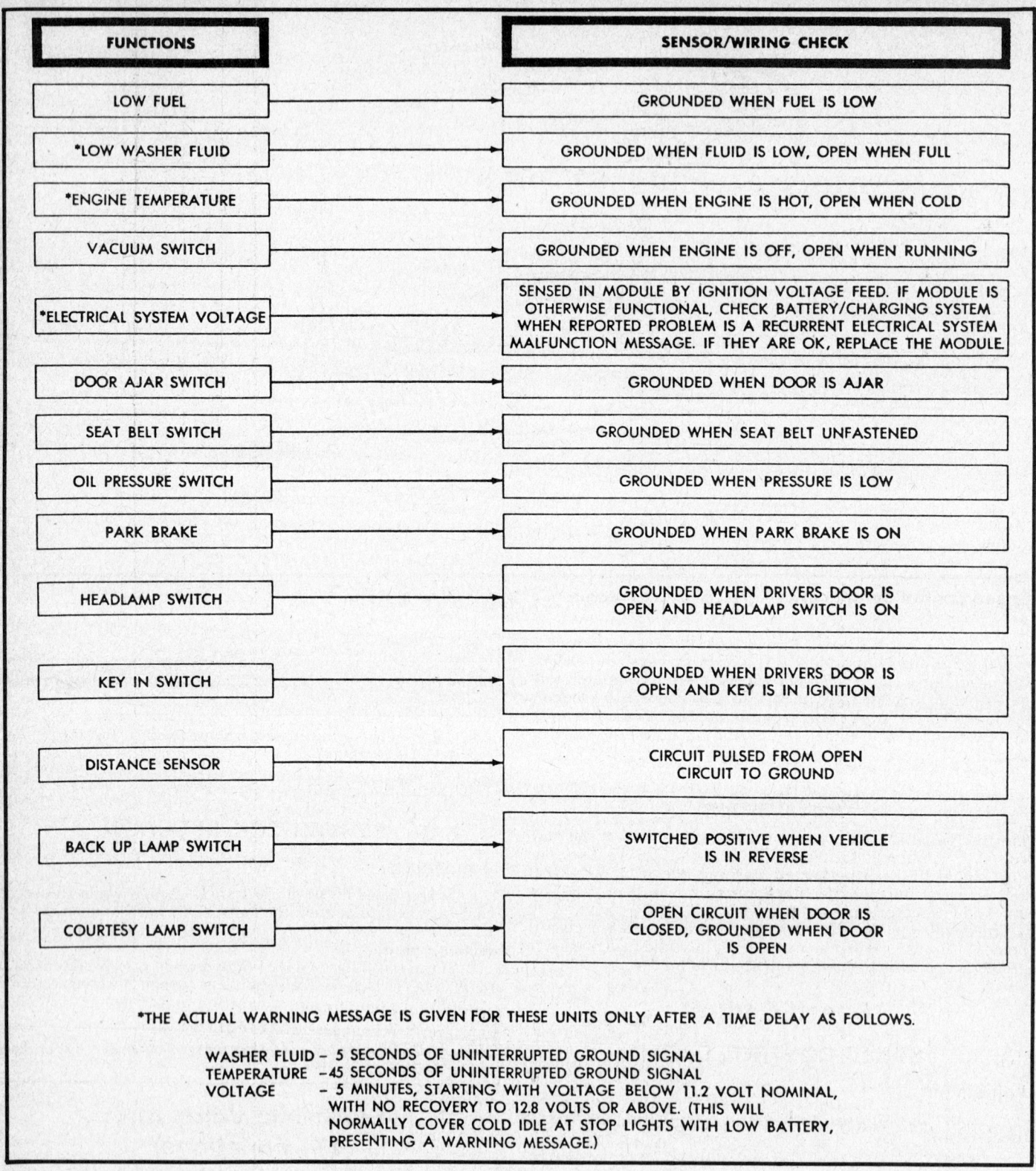

FUNCTIONS	SENSOR/WIRING CHECK
LOW FUEL	GROUNDED WHEN FUEL IS LOW
*LOW WASHER FLUID	GROUNDED WHEN FLUID IS LOW, OPEN WHEN FULL
*ENGINE TEMPERATURE	GROUNDED WHEN ENGINE IS HOT, OPEN WHEN COLD
VACUUM SWITCH	GROUNDED WHEN ENGINE IS OFF, OPEN WHEN RUNNING
*ELECTRICAL SYSTEM VOLTAGE	SENSED IN MODULE BY IGNITION VOLTAGE FEED. IF MODULE IS OTHERWISE FUNCTIONAL, CHECK BATTERY/CHARGING SYSTEM WHEN REPORTED PROBLEM IS A RECURRENT ELECTRICAL SYSTEM MALFUNCTION MESSAGE. IF THEY ARE OK, REPLACE THE MODULE.
DOOR AJAR SWITCH	GROUNDED WHEN DOOR IS AJAR
SEAT BELT SWITCH	GROUNDED WHEN SEAT BELT UNFASTENED
OIL PRESSURE SWITCH	GROUNDED WHEN PRESSURE IS LOW
PARK BRAKE	GROUNDED WHEN PARK BRAKE IS ON
HEADLAMP SWITCH	GROUNDED WHEN DRIVERS DOOR IS OPEN AND HEADLAMP SWITCH IS ON
KEY IN SWITCH	GROUNDED WHEN DRIVERS DOOR IS OPEN AND KEY IS IN IGNITION
DISTANCE SENSOR	CIRCUIT PULSED FROM OPEN CIRCUIT TO GROUND
BACK UP LAMP SWITCH	SWITCHED POSITIVE WHEN VEHICLE IS IN REVERSE
COURTESY LAMP SWITCH	OPEN CIRCUIT WHEN DOOR IS CLOSED, GROUNDED WHEN DOOR IS OPEN

*THE ACTUAL WARNING MESSAGE IS GIVEN FOR THESE UNITS ONLY AFTER A TIME DELAY AS FOLLOWS.

WASHER FLUID – 5 SECONDS OF UNINTERRUPTED GROUND SIGNAL
TEMPERATURE – 45 SECONDS OF UNINTERRUPTED GROUND SIGNAL
VOLTAGE – 5 MINUTES, STARTING WITH VOLTAGE BELOW 11.2 VOLT NOMINAL, WITH NO RECOVERY TO 12.8 VOLTS OR ABOVE. (THIS WILL NORMALLY COVER COLD IDLE AT STOP LIGHTS WITH LOW BATTERY, PRESENTING A WARNING MESSAGE.)

Electronic voice alert diagnosis (© Chrysler Corporation)

"DON'T FORGET YOUR KEYS"

Will occur if the ignition is turned on and then off, the key left in the ignition and the drivers door is open.

"YOUR WASHER FLUID IS LOW"

This message will be heard, when the windshield washer fluid is low for a period longer than five seconds and the engine is running.

"YOUR FUEL IS LOW"

Will be heard when the fuel level sensor indicates low fuel level and the engine is running.

"YOUR ELECTRICAL SYSTEM IS MALFUNCTIONING" – "PROMPT SERVICE IS REQUIRED"

Will occur only if the charging voltage falls below 11.3 volts and subsequently remains below 12.7 volts while the engine is above idle speeds for 5 minutes.

"YOUR PARKING BRAKE IS ON"

Will occur when the parking brake is applied and the vehicle has moved several feet.

"A DOOR IS AJAR"

Occurs if a door is open or not fully latched and the vehicle is in motion.

"PLEASE FASTEN YOUR SEAT BELTS"

This will occur if the drivers seat belt is not fastened and the vehicle is in a forward motion.

"YOUR ENGINE IS OVERHEATING" – "PROMPT SERVICE IS REQUIRED"

Will occur when the engine temperature remains above normal for a period of 50 seconds while the engine is running.

"YOUR ENGINE OIL PRESSURE IS LOW" – "PROMPT SERVICE IS REQUIRED"

Occurs when the engine oil pressure is low for a minimum of two seconds and the engine is running.

"ALL MONITORED SYSTEMS ARE FUNCTIONING"

The all systems message shall be generated if a low oil pressure, high temperature, or electrical system warning message has been delivered and the unsatisfactory condition ceases to exist for at least 5 seconds and that unsatisfactory door ajar, brake, and low fuel conditions do not exist.

"THANK YOU"

Will occur whenever an unsatisfactory seatbelt, door ajar, parking brake, key in and headlamp on condition has been corrected.

All messages are proceeded by a group of beeps and followed by a tone. Warning messages are repeated with each key on until the unsatisfactory condition is corrected.

Some messages are not heard unless the vehicle is in a forward motion. These are controlled by a distance sensor and the backup lamp switch. The distance sensor delays selected messages until the vehicle is in motion. The backup lamp switch locks out selected messages when the transmission selector lever is in the reverse position. A volume control is located in the underside of the module and can be adjusted for desired volume. An on/off switch is located on the module and is accessible through an opening on the top right inside of the glove box. This switch, when moved toward the rear of the vehicle, will cancel only the voice signal (if so desired).

All warning lamps and tones will still continue to function normally even if the voice alert muting switch is off.

System Test

1. Condition: Drivers door closed and keys out of ignition for at least 15 minutes.
   a. Open driver's door and turn on headlamps. A low frequency tone with brief periods of silence should be heard.
   b. Insert key. A higher frequency pulsating tone should be heard.
2. Condition: Drivers door closed and keys out of ignition for less than 15 minutes.
   a. Open drivers door and turn on headlamps. A verbal headlamps on reminder followed by a lower frequency tone should be heard.
3. Condition: Key in ignition.
   a. Turn ignition on. Fasten seat belt warning tones should be heard and the seat belt warning lamp should light for about 6 seconds.
4. Condition: Drivers door closed and key in run position.
   a. Fasten drivers seat belt. A "thank you" should be heard.
5. Condition: Engine running.
   a. Depress parking brake and move vehicle. A verbal "Parking brake on" message should be heard followed by a "Thank you" when the door is closed.
   b. Open each door and move vehicle forward (5 mph) and then close door. Upon opening each door, a verbal warning "Door ajar" should be heard, followed by a "Thank you" when the door is closed.
   c. Test low fuel warning with a known good sending unit. When the sending unit is in the empty position the low fuel lamp should light and the "Low fuel warning" should be heard.
   d. Depress the float in the windshield washer bottle. A verbal low washer fluid message should be heard.
6. Condition: Engine turned off. The following "Engine running warnings" are tested with the engine turned off and vacuum switch disconnected; low oil pressure, engine over heating, and low system voltage.
   a. With the engine turned off, disconnect the Electronic Voice Alert vacuum switch. Turn the ignition on without starting engine. The engine warning lamp should light and the verbal "Low oil pressure" warning should be heard.
   b. Turn ignition on without starting engine. Disconnect wire from engine temperature switch. Connect a jumper wire from disconnected wire to a good ground. After 45 seconds, verbal warning "Engine over heating" should be heard. Reconnect temperature switch wire after test.
   c. Turn ignition on without starting engine. Turn on electrical items such as: blower motor, headlamps, heated backlight. The charging system lamp should light. After 5 minutes, the verbal warning "Electrical system" should be heard.

NOTE: Reconnect vacuum switch after test.

FUNCTIONS TEST PROCEDURES

Demonstration Mode

The demonstration or test mode is activated, by first removing the key from the ignition switch, turning off the headlamp switch, and closing all doors, wait one minute, open the drivers door, then press and hold the door ajar button located on left "B" post. Be sure to hold the door ajar button in to hear all messages.

This demonstration or test mode checks the module only, it cannot detect a problem in the wiring or sensors.

If the voice alert module does not announce any messages, conduct the following tests:

1. Make sure the connectors at rear of module are tightly installed with no terminal pushouts.
2. Test the battery feed and ground circuit of the module.
3. Test left door ajar switch and wiring.
4. Test left door courtesy lamp switch (located on the left "A" post).

CHRYSLER CORPORATION
FRONT WHEEL DRIVE CARS

After each circuit is tested good or repaired activate the demonstration mode to verify repair. If all circuits test good, replace the electronic voice alert module.

NOTE: If the system announces all messages upon each left door opening and closing, a ground exists in the left courtesy lamp switch or wiring.

"YOUR HEADLIGHTS ARE ON"

Turn ignition switch on and then off, remove ignition key from ignition switch, pull headlamp switch to the on position and open drivers door.

"Your headlights are on" should be the response. If no response is heard, connect a known good chime module in the module connector. Perform the above test procedure (i.e., headlights on, left door open). If chimes are heard, headlamp circuit to module is okay. Replace voice alert module. If chimes are not heard, repair headlamp circuit to module.

"DON'T FORGET YOUR KEYS"

Turn ignition key on and off (leave off) open the drivers door. "Do not forget your keys" should be heard. If no message is heard, connect a known good chime module into voice alert module circuit. Repeat the test procedure (i.e. ignition on/off, door opened, etc.). If chimes are heard, replace voice alert module. If chimes are not heard, repair key-in circuit.

"YOUR WASHER FLUID IS LOW"

Turn the ignition on. Disconnect vacuum switch wire located on left inner fender. Remove windshield washer reservoir float from reservoir (or use a known good washer float assembly). Extend the float to the lowest position. Within 10 seconds, a message should be heard as follows;"Your washer fluid is low." If no message is heard, check washer fluid sensor wiring. If sensor wiring is okay, replace voice alert module.

"YOUR ELECTRICAL SYSTEM IS MALFUNCTIONING" – "PROMPT SERVICE IS REQUIRED"

Turn the ignition key on. (Do not start the engine.) Turn on all accessories (which cause a high battery load. Disconnect the vacuum switch located inside left fender. After a five minute period, the electronic voice alert should announce the warning message. If response is heard, turn all accessories off. Reconnect vacuum switch. Start the engine, operate the engine above idle speeds for approximately five minutes. No response or message should be heard from voice alert.

If a warning message is heard "Your electrical system is malfunctioning," the charging system needs repairing. If charging system is functioning properly, check battery and ignition feeds to the voice alert module for low voltage (it must not be lower than 1 volt of battery voltage). Check ground circuit for high resistance to the voice alert module. If battery, ignition and ground circuits are okay, replace electronic voice alert module.

"YOUR PARKING BRAKE IS ON"

Start the engine. Set the parking brake to the first or second click or notch or until brake warning light is on. Place the transmission selector lever in drive and move the vehicle forward a few feet.

If no response is heard, test the brake lamp switch and wiring, the distance sensor and wiring to the voice alert module. Repair as necessary and repeat the parking brake on mode test. If no response is heard, replace the voice alert module.

"A DOOR IS AJAR"

Start the engine, place transmission selector lever in drive, open the drivers door, release the parking brake and move the vehicle forward several feet. The response should be "A door is ajar." Closing the door the voice alert will respond with "Thank you."

If no response is heard, test the door ajar switch and wiring, test the speed sensor and wiring, test the back up light switch and wiring. If all of the circuits test okay, replace the voice alert module.

"PLEASE FASTEN YOUR SEAT BELTS"

Start the engine. Close the drivers door, place transmission selector lever in drive. Do not fasten seat belt. Release parking brake and move the vehicle forward several feet. The voice alert should respond with "Please fasten your seat belts." Fastening the seat belt will cause the voice alert module to announce "Thank you." If no response is heard, test the engine vacuum switch and wiring. Test the seat belt switch and wiring. Test the speed sensor and wiring. Test the back up light switch and wiring. If all circuits test okay, replace the voice alert module.

"YOUR ENGINE IS OVER HEATING" – "PROMPT SERVICE IS REQUIRED"

Using a jumper wire, ground the temperature sending unit wire. Start the engine, wait 50 seconds. The voice alert module should respond with "Your engine is overheating," etc. If this response is not heard, perform demonstration or test mode. Test the temperature sensor wiring. Test the engine vacuum sensor and wiring. If all above circuits test okay, replace the voice alert module.

"YOUR OIL PRESSURE IS LOW" – "PROMPT SERVICE IS REQUIRED"

Using a jumper wire, ground the oil pressure warning lamp switch (not the oil pressure gauge sending unit). Start the engine, wait approximately 2 seconds. The voice alert module should announce "Your engine oil pressure is low" etc. If no response is heard, test the oil pressure warning lamp switch and wiring. Test the engine vacuum sensor and wiring. If all circuits test okay, replace the voice alert module.

"THANK YOU"

The electronic voice alert module will respond with this message only after any of the following unsatisfactory conditions are corrected (i.e., close doors, fasten seat belts, turn headlamps off, release parking brake, remove key from ignition).

"ALL MONITORED SYSTEMS ARE FUNCTIONING"

This message should be heard if two conditions are met:
1. Low oil pressure, high temperature, or electrical system warning message has been delivered and the unsatisfactory condition ceases to exist for at least 5 seconds.
2. Unsatisfactory door ajar, brake, and low fuel conditions do not exist.

ELECTRONIC VOICE ALERT MODULE

The Electronic Voice Alert Module is located above the glove box and attached to the instrument panel. To gain access to the module, remove the glove box from the vehicle.

VOICE ALERT VACUUM SWITCH

The Voice Alert Vacuum Switch is mounted on the left front inner fender panel, near the radiator fan and starter relays.

Electronic Monitor – Twenty Four Functions

1984 AND LATER DAYTONA AND LASER

The twenty four function monitor system operates basically as does the eleven function Electronic Monitor system, with the

CHRYSLER CORPORATION
FRONT WHEEL DRIVE CARS
SECTION 2

exception that thirteen more functions are monitored by the system.

This system give the operator twenty four different audible and visual warnings and messages. This monitor system includes the electronic monitor module, an electronic voice alert module and various sensors which supply signals to the monitor module.

The electronic monitor scans the different sensor inputs for warning conditions. When a warning condition is detected, the electronic monitor will display the warning message, send the voice alert module a tone and talk signal. This causes the voice alert module to speak the appropriate audible message. When more than one warning condition exists, the above sequence will be followed for each message. The monitor will then alternately display each message at a four second rate. When warning conditions that are operator correctable, are corrected, the monitor will send the voice alert a tone signal. This tone signal is called a "Thank you" tone, which indicates the warning condition has been corrected.

The system check button, located on the front of the message center, will put the system into a demonstration mode. By pressing this button, the system will sound a tone and visually and audibly cycle through some messages. If this button is pressed twice within one-half second, the system will automatically shut off until the unit is powered down. The system will automatically return to normal operation after the complete demonstration sequence or when the check button is pressed during the demonstration sequence.

A mute switch is located on the electronic voice alert module, which selects the voice alert of the audible tone system desired.

ELECTRONIC MONITOR SIGNALS

Car Graphic
Exterior lamps on
Key-in ignition
Monitored systems OK
Washer fluid low
Rear washer fluid low
Fuel level low
Voltage low
Park brake engaged
Brake fluid low
Disc brake pads worn
Headlamp out
Tail lamp out
Brake lamp out
Passenger door ajar
Driver door ajar
Fasten seat belts
Engine temperature high (two levels)
Low oil pressure
Hatch ajar
Coolant level low
Low transmission pressure
Mute engaged

NOTE: Information concerning the diagnosis and repair of the twenty-four Electronic Monitor system can be related to the eleven monitor system. However, more detailed diagnostics and service procedures can be found in Chilton's Chassis Electronics Manual.

COOLING AND HEATER SECTION

Cooling System

The cooling system consists of a radiator, overflow tank, water pump, thermostat, coolant temperature switch, electric fan and radiator fan switch. The use of an electric fan is necessitated by the transversely mounted engine. A radiator bypass system is used for faster warmup.

WATER PUMP

Removal and Installation

1.6L ENGINE

1. Remove the radiator cap and drain the cooling system through water pump drain plug.
2. Disconnect pump to block coolant hose at pump.
3. Loosen the alternator/water pump drive belt and remove the pump pulley.
4. Remove four pump to crankcase extension screws and remove assembly.
5. Position water pump on crankcase extension with new gasket.
6. Install and tighten four pump to extension screws to 9 ft. lbs. (12.5 Nm).
7. Install pump to block hose, tighten clamp to 35 inch lbs. (4.1 Nm).
8. Install pump drain plug and torque to 13 ft. lbs. (17 Nm).
9. Install the pump pulley and adjust the belt tension.
10. Refill the cooling system.

1.7L ENGINE

1. Drain the cooling system. Disconnect the negative battery cable.

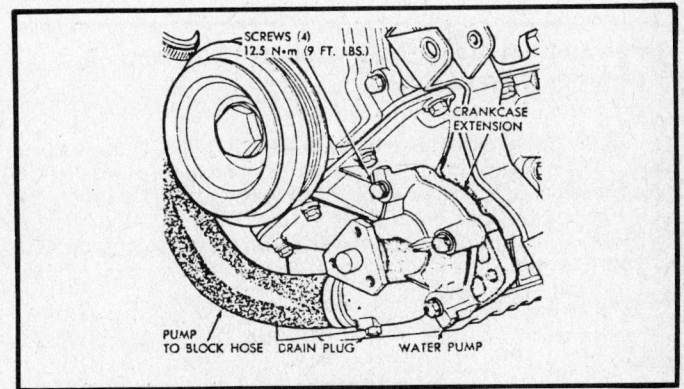

Water pump location—1.6L engine
(© Chrysler Corporation)

2. Without discharging the system, remove the compressor from the engine brackets and set aside.
3. Completely remove the alternator.
4. Remove the water pump pulley.
5. If so equipped, disconnect the diverter valve hose at the diverter valve, remove the front and rear pump bracket.
6. Remove the alternator bracket attached to the water pump.
7. Disconnect the lower radiator hose and the by-pass hose.
8. Unbolt the timing belt cover bolt and the two top water pump bolts and remove the water pump.
9. Installation is the reverse of removal. It is important that the following torque sequence be followed. Tighten the two up-

SECTION 2

CHRYSLER CORPORATION
FRONT WHEEL DRIVE CARS

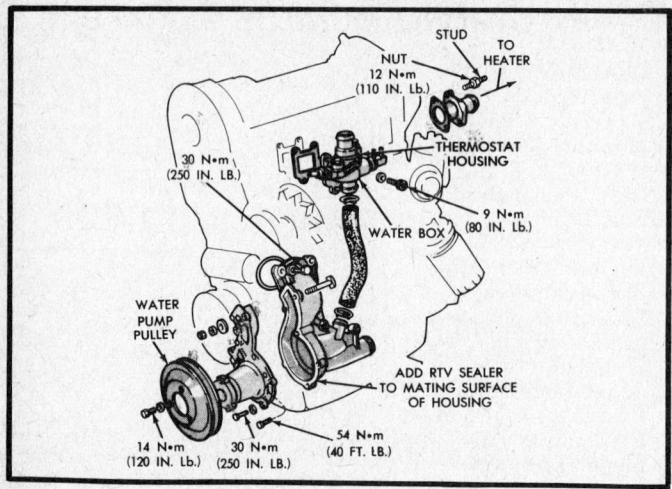

Water pump assemby and thermostat housing, 1.7L engine (© Chrysler Corporation)

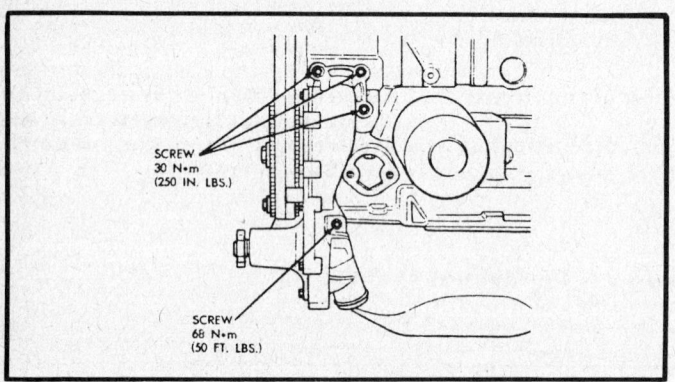

Water pump/housing bolt location—2.2L engine (© Chrysler Corporation)

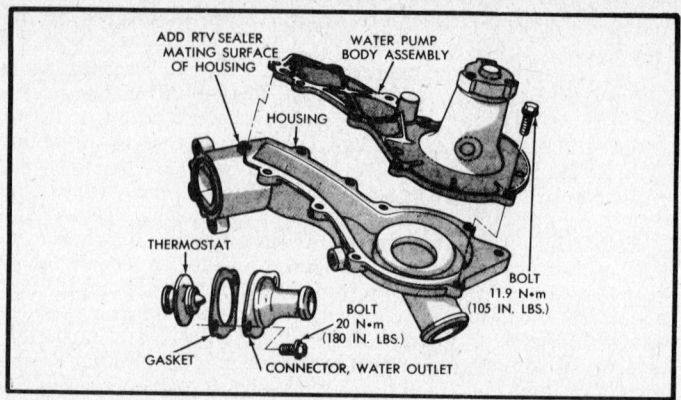

Water pump assembly and thermostat housing, 2.2L engine (© Chrysler Corporation)

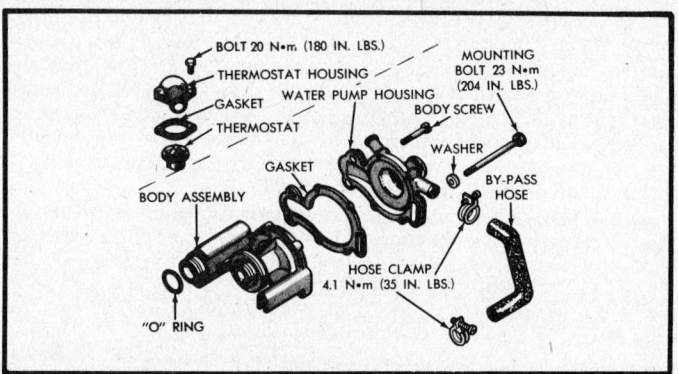

Water pump assembly and thermostat housing, 2.6L engine (© Chrysler Corporation)

per water pump attaching bolts to 250 inch lbs. Next, tighten the two front air pump brackets to the water pump bolts, one to 250 inch lbs. and one to 40 ft. lbs. Next, install the air pump and tighten the two bolts to 24 ft. lbs. Next, tighten the two rear air pump brackets and lower water pump to engine bolts to 250 inch lbs.

2.2L/2.5L ENGINES

1. Drain the cooling system. Remove the negative battery cable.
2. Remove the upper radiator hose.
3. Without discharging the system, remove the air conditioning compressor from the engine brackets and set to one side.
4. Remove the alternator and move to one side.
5. Disconnect the lower radiator hose and the bypass hose and remove the water pump by removing the pump housing to engine retaining screws. Separate the water pump from the housing, after removal.
6. Installation is the reverse of removal. Tighten the top three retaining screws to 250 inch lbs. and the lower screw to 50 ft. lbs.

2.6L ENGINE

1. Drain the cooling system.
2. Remove the radiator hose, by-pass hose and heater hose from the water pump.
3. Remove the drive pulley shield.
4. Remove the locking screw and pivot screws.
5. Remove the drive belt and water pump from the engine.
6. Installation is the reverse of removal. After adjusting the belt tension tighten the locking screw and pivot screws to 204 inch lbs. Tighten the drive pulley shield to 105 inch lbs.

ELECTRIC COOLING FANS

ALL MODELS

The electrically driven fan is actuated by the radiator fan switch on the 1.6L engine equipped vehicles and by the on-board computer on the 2.2L/2.5L engines. Either control automatically shuts off the fan motor when it is not needed on non-air conditioned vehicles, or air conditioned vehicles when the air conditioning is turned off.

NOTE: When the air conditioning compressor clutch is engaged, the radiator fan motor is also on.

The 1.6L, 1.7L and 2.6L engine equipped vehicles have a thermostatically-controlled motor that runs only when the coolant temperature at the radiator fan switch reaches 193–207° F. or when the air conditioning compressor is running and will turn off when the temperature drops to 175° F.

The 2.2L/2.5L engine equipped vehicles on-board computer controlled fan motor will operate on the non-air conditioned vehicles or on air conditioned equipped vehicles with the air conditioning off, at vehicle speeds above 40 mph, only if the coolant temperature reaches 230° F. and will turn off when the temperature drops to 220° F. At speeds below 40 mph, the fan switches on at 210° F and off at 200° F.

NOTE: With certain parts kits available through the Chrysler/Dodge/Plymouth dealer body to aid in driveability related modifications, the electric fans may operate AFTER the engine has been turned off. Caution must be exercised to prevent personal injury, should repairs be required after the engine has been turned off and the fan begins to operate.

RADIATOR FAN SWITCH

Calibration Test

1.6L AND 2.6L ENGINES

The radiator fan switch is located in the left hand radiator tank and is internally isolated from the radiator. The switch is normally open and contains a bi-metal contact arm to close the switch when the coolant temperature reaches a temperature of approximately 200° F.

NOTE: **If the fan motor turns off and on, the fan switch does not have to be tested.**

To check the fan motor switch, refer to the following procedure;
 1. Disconnect the wiring connector to the fan switch and install a jumper wire in the female connector, simulating a closed fan switch at any temperature.
 2. If the fan does not operate with the ignition switch on, the problem is elsewhere.
 3. Check for current supply to the connector and/or refer to Chilton's Wiring Diagram Manual for wire routing information.

Check Switch Calibration

 1. Remove the switch from the radiator and immerse the conductor portion of the switch (not the electrical terminals) into a circulation oil bath, heated to 212° F.
 2. Use a continuity light to determine if the switch is closed.
 3. Using the continuity light, lower the temperature to at least 170° F. to assure that the switch opens.

RADIATOR FAN SWITCHING

2.2L/2.5L ENGINES

1985 and later 2.2L engine models no longer use a temperature sensing switch in the radiator. For both the 2.2L and the 2.5L engines, fan control is accomplished by the on-board computer as the coolant temperature is sensed by the computer's temperature sensor. This sensor is the same for turbocharged and TBI, but with carbureted engines, two thermister sensors are used, one of which is for the cooling system fan.

Switching through the on-board computer provides fan control for the following conditions;
 1. The fan will not operate during cranking until the engine starts, no matter what the coolant temperature is.
 2. The fan will always run when the air conditioning clutch is engaged as on the previous models.
 3. On non-air conditioned vehicles or with air conditioning off, the fan will run at vehicle speeds above approximately 40 mph, only if the coolant temperature reaches 230° F. and will turn off when the temperature drops to approximately 220° F.
 4. Models with turbochargers or TBI engines also include a method to help prevent "Steaming" (water evaporated by hot water circulating through the radiator, evaporating moisture on the outside of the radiator and then when there is no ram air to blow it under the vehicle) the fan will operate only between 100–195° F. coolant temperature and only at idle, below 60° F. ambient temperature and at zero car speed for only three minutes.
 5. On turbocharged or TBI engines equipped with on-board diagnostic indicators, the circuitry and temperature sensors are diagnosed by the diagnostic indicator.

ELECTRIC FAN MOTOR

To check out the electric fan motor, disconnect the fan motor wiring connector and using a jumper wires from the battery posts, connect the jumper wires to the connector, observing proper polarity (positive to the male end and negative to the female end) and observe the fan. If the fan functons, problems may lie in the wiring or connectors. If the fan motor does not operate, the fan motor is probably defective.

ELECTRIC FAN MOTOR RELAY

1.6L AND 2.6L ENGINES WITH AIR CONDITIONING

The relay is mounted on the left shock housing. If the fan is not operating and the relay is suspected, replace it with a good relay. Remove the connector from the radiator fan switch and insert jumper wires into both connector terminals. This operation eliminates the need to raise the coolant temperature to 200° ± 7° F., in order to close the radiator fan switch. Turn the ignition key to the accessory position. If the fan operates correctly, the replaced relay is at fault. It must be understood that the fan also operates whenever the A/C compressor operates, regardless of the engine coolant temperature.

THERMOSTAT

Removal and Installation

The thermostat is located in the bottom radiator hose neck in the water pump on 1.7L and 2.2L/2.5L engines or under the upper radiator hose on the 1.6L and 2.6L engines.
 1. Drain the cooling system to a level below the thermostat.
 2. Remove the hoses from the thermostat housing.
 3. Remove the thermostat housing.
 4. Remove the thermostat and discard the gasket. Clean the gasket surfaces thoroughly.
 5. Using a new gasket, position the thermostat and install the housing and bolts. Make sure that the thermostat is seated properly.
 6. Refill the cooling system.

Heater System

HEATER OR HEATER/AC CONTROL WITH BLOWER SWITCH

Removal and Installation

OMNI, HORIZON, TURISMO, 024 AND CHARGER

 1. Remove the light switch and left bezel.
 2. Remove the two control mounting screws and remove the control, after disconnecting the electrical leads, vacuum lines and control cable.
 3. Reverse the removal procedure to install the control unit.

ARIES, RELIANT, DODGE 400, 600, E CLASS/NEW YORKER, DAYTONA, CARAVELLE, LANCER, LEBARON GTS, LASER, LEBARON, SHADOW AND SUNDANCE MODELS

Left Side of Instrument Panel

 1. Remove the headlamp switch knob.
 2. Remove the bezel screws, roll the bezel out and lift up to free the bezel locking lugs.
 3. Remove the control mounting screws and remove the control from the dash.
 4. Disconnect the cables, vacuum hose and electrical wiring.

SECTION 2: CHRYSLER CORPORATION
FRONT WHEEL DRIVE CARS

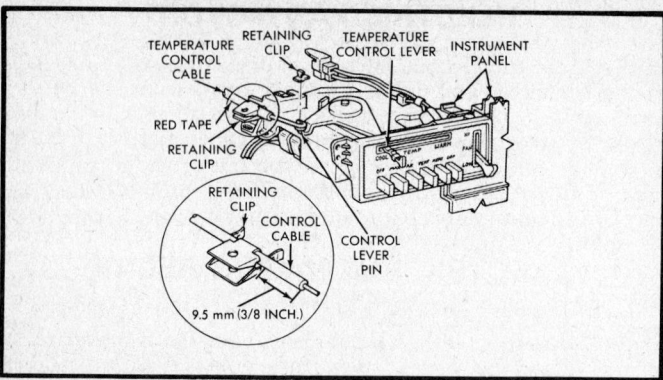

Temperature control unit, typical
(© Chrysler Corporation)

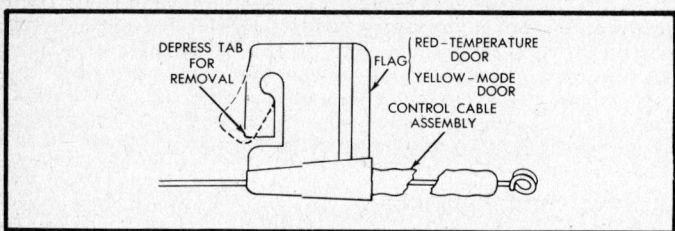

Control cable flag tab location (© Chrysler Corporation)

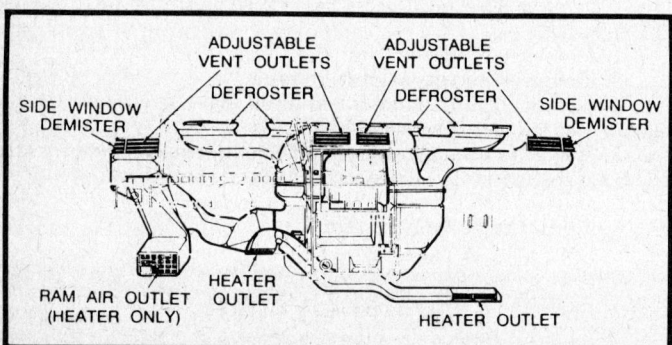

Heating and ventalating system—Sundance and Shadow (©Chrysler Corporation)

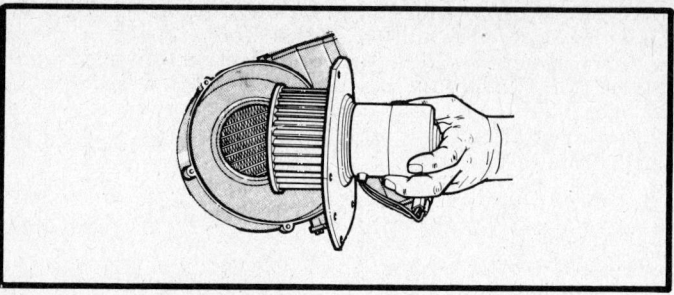

Blower motor removal or installation
(© Chrysler Corporation)

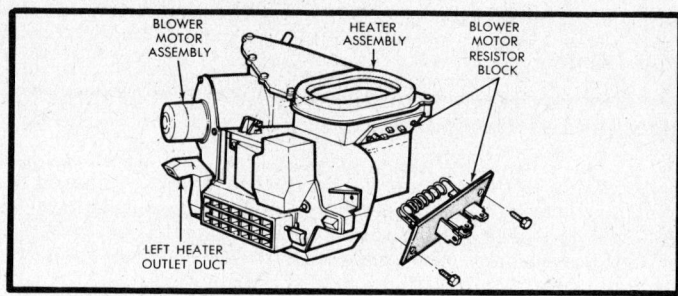

Heater/blower assembly, typical
(© Chrysler Corporation)

5. Installation is the reverse.

Center of Instrument Panel
1. Remove bezel attaching screws.
2. Remove bezel by rolling out and lifting up to free bezel locking feet.
3. Remove the control retaining screws and slide the control outward.
4. Disconnect the cables, vacuum hose and wiring.
5. The installation is the reverse of the removal.

BLOWER MOTOR

Removal and Installation

ALL MODELS WITH AIR CONDITIONING

NOTE: The blower motor on the front wheel drive vehicles must be serviced from behind the glove box in the passenger compartment.

1. Disconnect the battery ground cable.
2. Remove the blower motor feed wire and ground wire. The ground is attached to the air conditioning unit support brace screw.
3. Remove the wires from the retaining clip on the recirculating housing.
4. Remove the blower motor vent tube from the air conditioning unit, if equipped. The vent tube will remain attached to the blower motor.
5. Remove the three to five blower motor mounting nuts and washers. Remove the blower motor assembly from the recirculating housing unit.
6. Remove the spring tension clip from the blower motor shaft and lift off the fan.
7. The installation is the reverse of the removal procedure.

HEATER CORE—WITHOUT AIR CONDITIONING

Removal and Installation

OMNI, HORIZON, TURISMO, 024 AND CHARGER

1. Disconnect battery ground cable.
2. Drain radiator coolant.
3. Remove ash tray.
4. Depress tab on temperature control cable flag and pull cable out of receiver on heater assembly.
5. Disconnect blower motor wiring connector.
6. Disconnect heater hoses at core connections and seal core openings.
7. Remove two nuts securing unit to dash.
8. Remove glove box and its door.
9. Remove screw securing heater brace bracket to instrument panel.
10. Remove unit support strap nut. Remove strap from plenum stud and lower heater unit from under dash panel.
11. Disconnect mode control cable and remove unit from car.
12. Remove heater core cover.
13. Reverse procedure for installation.

CHRYSLER CORPORATION
FRONT WHEEL DRIVE CARS

ARIES, RELIANT, DODGE 400, 600, E CLASS/NEW YORKER, DAYTONA, CARAVELLE, LANCER, LEBARON GTS, LASER, LEBARON SHADOW AND SUNDANCE MODELS

NOTE: Minor sequence differences may be encountered during the removal procedure of the Heater Core, from the varied models.

1. Disconnect the negative battery cable. Drain cooling system.
2. Disconnect the blower motor electrical wiring.
3. From under the heater assembly, depress the tab on the mode door and temperature control cables, pull the flags from the receivers and remove the self-adjusting clip from the crank arm.
4. Remove the glove box assembly.
5. Remove the heater hoses at the unit on the engine side and seal the hoses and core outlets.
6. Remove the screw attaching the hanger strap to the heater assembly through the glove box opening. Remove hanger strap.
7. Remove demister adapter to top of heater assembly, if equipped.
8. Remove the retaining nuts on the engine side of the heater assembly to dash panel.
9. Slide the heater assembly from under the instrument panel. It may be necessary to flex the bottom of the instrument panel outward.
10. The installation is the reverse of the removal procedure.

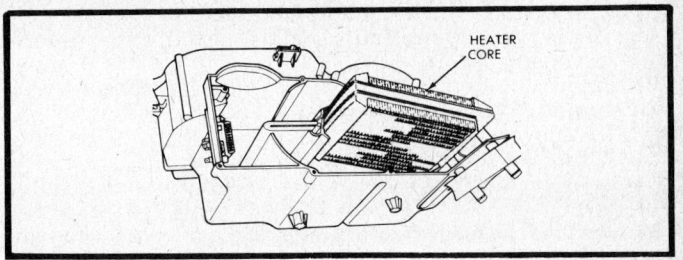

Heater core removal—typical (© Chrysler Corporation)

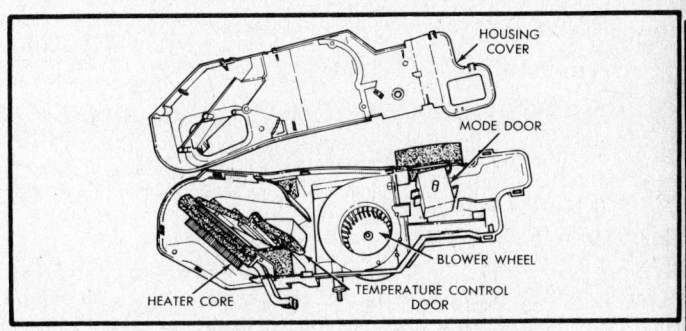

Heater core location—typical of all models
(© Chrysler Corporation)

HEATER CORE/EVAPORATOR—WITH AIR CONDITIONING

Removal and Installation

OMNI, HORIZON, TURISMO, 024 AND CHARGER

1. Discharge refrigerant system.
2. Drain radiator coolant.
3. Disconnect battery ground cable.
4. Disconnect temperature door cable from evaporator heater assembly.
5. Remove glove box and door.
6. Disconnect blower motor feed wire and anti-diesel relay wires.
7. Remove central air duct cover from central air distribution duct.
8. Remove three screws securing central A/C air distribution duct, remove duct from under dash panel.
9. Remove defroster duct adaptor.
10. Disconnect heater hoses. Remove condensate drain tube from unit.
11. Disconnect vacuum lines at engine intake manifold and water valve.
12. Remove unit to dash retaining nuts.
13. Remove panel support bracket.
14. Remove right side cowl lower panel. Remove top cover of instrument panel. Remove all but left panel-to-fenceline screws.
15. Remove instrument panel pivot bracket screw from right side.
16. Remove screws securing lower instrument panel and steering column, as required.
17. Pull carpet rearward as far as possible.
18. Remove nut from A/C to plenum mounting brace and blower motor ground cable.
19. Support unit and remove brace from its stud.
20. Lift unit and pull rearward as far as possible to clear dash panel and liner. At this time also pull rearward on the lower instrument panel to gain enough clearance for unit removal.

NOTE: This operation may require two people.

21. Slowly lower unit to floor and then slide rearward out from under dash panel.
22. Remove unit from car.
23. Remove nut from mode door actuator arm on top cover and two retaining clips from front edge of cover.
24. Remove two screws securing mode door actuator to cover and remove actuator.
25. Remove screws securing cover to heater evaporator assembly and remove cover.
26. Lift mode door out of unit.
27. Remove heater core tube retaining bracket and screw and lift core out of unit.
28. Reverse the removal procedure for installation.

ARIES, RELIANT, DODGE 400, 600, E CLASS/NEW YORKER, DAYTONA, CARAVELLE, LANCER, LEBARON GTS, LASER, LEBARON, SHADOW AND SUNDANCE MODELS

1. Remove the negative battery cable, discharge the air conditioning system and drain the cooling system.
2. Disconnect the heater hoses at the heater core. Plug the tube and hose openings.
3. Disconnect the vacuum lines at the intake manifold and at the water valve.
4. Remove the right side scuff plate and the cowl side trim panel.
5. Remove the glove box assembly, the A/C control, the console, if equipped and the forward console mounting bracket, if equipped.
6. Remove the center distribution tube and pull the defroster adapter from under the panel.
7. Remove the Corbin clamp (spring clamp) and the condensation drain tube.
8. Disconnect the unit from the wiring harness.
9. Remove the control cables by depressing the tab on the flag and then pulling the flag out of the receiver on the evaporator/heater assembly.
10. Remove the right side-cowl-to-plenum brace.
11. Pull the carpet back from the underside of the unit.

CHRYSLER CORPORATION
FRONT WHEEL DRIVE CARS
SECTION 2

12. Remove the screw retaining the hanger strap to the unit. Remove the four retaining nuts holding the unit to the firewall from the engine side.
13. Pull the unit rearward until the studs clear the dash liner and allow the unit to drop vertically, until it comes in contact with the converter tunnel.
14. Rotate the unit around the instrument panel lower reinforcement, making sure not to allow the unit to slide in either direction.
15. Remove the mode door actuator arm nut from the top cover and the two retaining clips from the front edge of the cover.
16. Remove the retaining screws attaching the cover to the assembly and lift off the cover. The mode door can be removed also.
17. Remove the screw from the heater core tube retaining bracket and lift the core from the housing.
18. The assembly of the unit is the reverse of the removal procedure.

--- **CAUTION** ---
During the assembly, be careful of the vacuum lines to prevent their hanging up on the accelerator or becoming trapped between the assembly and the dash.

FUEL SYSTEM

FUEL PUMP
Removal and Installation
MECHANICAL TYPE

A mechanical fuel pump is located on the left side of the engine. To remove the pump, disconnect the fuel and vapor lines and remove the attaching bolts. Installation is the reverse of removal. Always use a new gasket when installing the pump and make certain the gasket surfaces are clean. On 2.6L engines, coat both sides of the insulator and gasket with sealer.

EFI FUEL SYSTEM PRESSURE RELEASE
2.5L/2.5L EFI AND OPTIONAL 2.2L TURBO MODELS

The early EFI fuel systems, ('84–'85 with single point fuel injection) were under a constant pressure of approximately 36 psi. The '84–'85 Turbo models with multipoint fuel injection were under a constant pressure of 53 psi. Beginning with the 1986 and later single point fuel injection models, the pressure was reduce to 14.5 psi. The '86 and later turbo multipoint models fuel pressure was raised to 55 psi. However, on both the early and the later versions, before servicing the fuel tank, fuel pump, fuel lines, fuel filter, or fuel components of the throttle body, the fuel pressure must be released as follows.

1. Loosen gas cap to release any in-tank pressure.
2. Remove wiring harness connector from injector.
3. Ground one injector terminal with a jumper.
4. Connect a jumper wire to second terminal and touch battery positive post for no longer than 10 seconds.
5. Remove jumper wires.
6. Continue fuel system service.

ELECTRIC FUEL PUMP
Removal and Installation
2.2L/2.5L EFI AND OPTIONAL 2.2L TURBO

The fuel pump is located within the fuel tank, which must be removed to gain access to the fuel pump.

1. Perform the fuel system pressure release procedure.
2. Disconnect the negative battery cable.
3. Remove the fuel tank filler cap, if not previously done. Remove fuel, using an outside pump. Store the fuel in an approved safety container.
4. Remove the screws retaining the fuel filler tube to the quarter panel.
5. Raise the vehicle and support safely.
6. Remove the draft tube cap on the tank sending unit.
7. Disconnect the pump wiring and fuel hose.

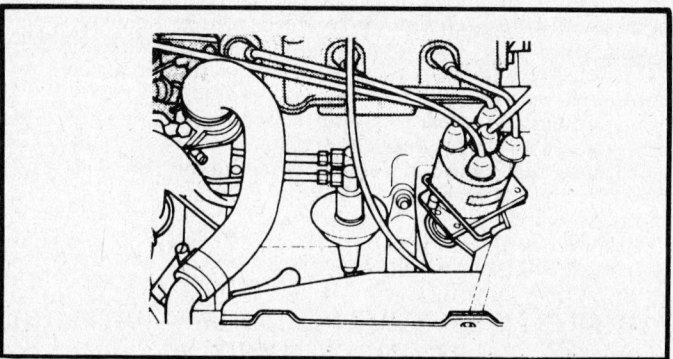
Fuel pump location – typical (© Chrysler Corporation)

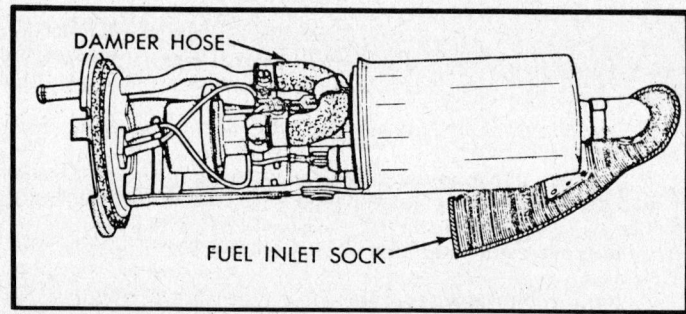
In-tank electric fuel pump – EFI fuel system
(© Chrysler Corporation)

8. Remove the retaining nuts from the fuel tank straps and lower the fuel tank from the vehicle.
9. Remove the lock ring from the pump in a counterclockwise direction and remove the pump from the fuel tank.
10. The installation of the fuel pump is the reverse of the removal procedure. 11.
Use a new O-ring seal between the fuel pump and the tank during the installation.

CARBURETOR APPLICATION

1983
Holley 5220 – – 2.2L, 1.6L (Canada) Engines
Holley 6520 EFB – – 1.6L, 1.7L, 2.2L Engines
Mikuni – – 2.6L Engine

1984
Holley 5220 – – 1.6L, 2.2L Engines

CHRYSLER CORPORATION
FRONT WHEEL DRIVE CARS
SECTION 2

HMolley 6520 EFB——2.2L Engine
Mikuni EFB——2.6L Engine

1985
Holley 5220——1.6L, 2.2L Engines
Holley 6520 EFB——2.2L Engine
Mikuni EFB——2.6L Engine

1986–87
Holley 5220—1.6L, 2.2L Engines
Holley 6520——2.2L Engine
E.F.I.——2.2L, 2.5L Engines
(Single point, Multi Point–Turbo)

EFB = Electronic Feedback Carburetor
EFI = Electronic Fuel Injection

Removal and Installation

---- CAUTION ----
Do not attempt to remove the carburetor from the engine of a vehicle that has just been road tested. Allow the engine to cool sufficiently to prevent accidental fuel ignition or personal injury.

1.6L, 1.7L and 2.2L/2.5L ENGINES

1. Disconnect battery ground cable.
2. Remove air cleaner.
3. Remove fuel tank pressure vacuum filler cap (fuel tank could be under a small pressure).
4. Place a container under fuel inlet fitting to catch any fuel that may be trapped in fuel line.
5. Disconnect fuel inlet line and all wiring.
6. Disconnect throttle linkage and all hoses.
7. Remove carburetor mounting nuts and carefully remove carburetor from engine compartment. Hold carburetor level to avoid spilling fuel from fuel bowl.
8. Installation is the reverse of the removal procedure.

2.6L ENGINE

1. Disconnect battery ground cable.
2. Remove air intake housing from carburetor air horn.
3. Remove fuel tank pressure vacuum filler cap (fuel tank could be under a small pressure). Drain radiator.
4. Remove carburetor protector.
5. Disconnect vacuum and coolant hoses at carburetor.
6. Disconnect wiring at connector.
7. Place a container under fuel inlet fitting to catch any fuel that may be trapped in fuel line and disconnect fuel hose from the carburetor inlet nipple.
8. Disconnect throttle linkage.
9. Remove carburetor mounting bolts and nut, and carefully remove carburetor from engine compartment. Hold carburetor level to avoid spilling fuel from fuel bowl.
10. Install the carburetor in the reverse order of the removal procedure.

IDLE SPEED ADJUSTMENT

1983 HOLLEY 5220 CARBURETOR

1. Disconnect and plug the vacuum connector at the CCEGR/CVSCC.

NOTE: CCEGR/CVSCC = Coolant Controlled Exhaust Gas Recirculation/Coolant Vacuum Switch Cold Closed.

2. Unplug the connector at the radiator fan and install a jumper wire so that the fan will run continuously.
3. Unplug the PCV valve from the engine and allow it to draw underhood air.
4. Connect a tachometer to the engine.
5. Ground the carburetor switch with a jumper wire.

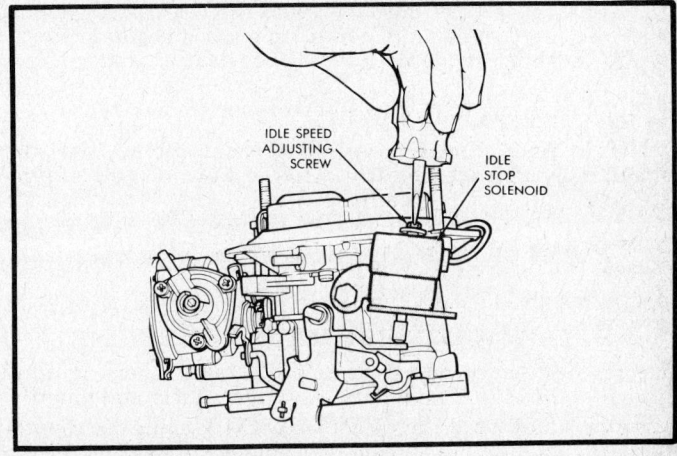
Idle RPM adjustment, typical of 1.7L and 2.2L engines (© Chrysler Corporation)

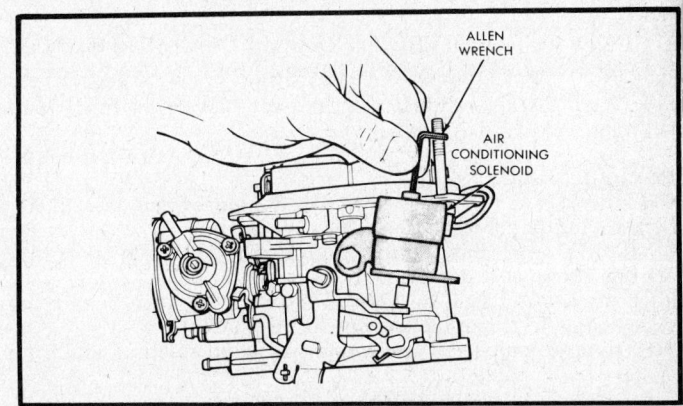
Air conditioning idle speed adjustment—typical of 2.6L engine (© Chrysler Corporation)

6. Start and run the engine until normal operating temperature is reached.
7. If the engine rpm is not to specifications, turn the idle speed screw until the correct idle set rpm is reached.
8. Reinstall vacuum connector and PCV valve.
9. Remove jumper wire and reinstall radiator fan connector.

NOTE: After Steps 8 and 9 are completed, the curb idle speed may be different than the idle set RPM. This is normal and engine speed should not be readjusted.

10. Turn engine off. Remove tachometer and carburetor ground switch.

1984 AND LATER HOLLEY 5220/6520 CARBURETORS

Before checking or adjusting any idle speed, check ignition timing and adjust, if necessary.

1. Disconnect and plug vacuum connector at the CVSCC (Coolant Vacuum Switch Cold Closed).
2. Unplug connector at radiator fan and install jumper wire so fan will run continuously.
3. Remove PCV valve and allow valve to draw underhood air.
4. Connect tachometer to engine.
5. Ground carburetor switch with jumper wire.
6. Disconnect O_2 system test connector located on left fender shield on 6520 equipped vehicles.
7. Start and run engine until normal operating temperature is reached.

2-41

SECTION 2
CHRYSLER CORPORATION
FRONT WHEEL DRIVE CARS

8. If tachometer indicates rpm is not to specifications, turn idle speed screw until correct idle speed is obtained.

9. Reconnect PCV valve O_2 connector and vacuum connector.

10. Remove jumper wire and reconnect radiator fan.

NOTE: After Steps 9 and 10 are completed, the idle speed may change slightly. This is normal and engine speed should not be readjusted.

AIR CONDITIONING IDLE SPEED

Adjustment

1983 HOLLEY 6520 CARBURETOR, 1.7L ENGINE

Before checking or adjusting any idle speed, check ignition timing and adjust if necessary. Also, disconnect and plug the vacuum connector at the CCEGR/CVSCC. Unplug the connector at the radiator fan and install a jumper wire so that the fan will run continuously. Remove the PCV valve from the moulded rubber connector. Allow PCV valve to draw underhood air. Connect a tachometer and start engine. Do NOT Remove air cleaner.

NOTE: CCEGR/CVSCC = Coolant Controlled Exhaust Gas Recirculation/Coolant Vacuum Switch Cold Closed.

1. Turn on air conditioning and set blower on low. Open throttle slightly to energize solenoid.
2. Remove adjusting screw and spring from top of air conditioning solenoid.
3. Insert a $1/8$ in. Allen wrench into solenoid and adjust solenoid to obtain correct idle speed.
4. Make sure that the air conditioning clutch is operating during the speed adjustments. Air conditioning compressor head pressure should be 1725 kPa (250 PSI) since head pressure does affect the loading on the engine.
5. Replace adjusting screw and spring on solenoid and turn off air conditioner.
6. Proceed to idle set RPM adjustment.

1983 AND LATER HOLLEY 5220/6520 CARBURETORS, 2.2L ENGINES

2.2L air conditioned vehicles are equipped with either a vacuum kicker or a solenoid kicker.

It is not necessary to set the air conditioning idle speed, but the kicker operation should be checked.

1. Start and run engine until normal operating temperature is reached.
2. Set temperature control lever to coldest position and turn on air conditioning.
3. As the air conditioning compressor clutch cycles off and on, the kicker plunger should move in and out. If so, proceed to Step 5. If not proceed to Step 4. The air cleaner may be removed to allow the kicker to be more visible.
4. Check the kicker system for vacuum leaks in the hoses. Check the operation of the vacuum solenoid. If no problems are found replace the kicker and repeat Steps 1–3.
5. Turn off air conditioning.
6. Turn off engine and install air cleaner if removed.

IDLE SPEED

Adjustment

1983 HOLLEY 6520 CARBURETOR

1. Disconnect and plug the vacuum connector at the CCEGR/CVSCC.

NOTE: CCEGR/CVSCC = Coolant Controlled Exhaust Gas Recirculation/Coolant Vacuum Switch Cold Closed.

2. Unplug the connector at the radiator fan and install a jumper wire so that the fan will run continuously.
3. Remove the PCV valve from the molded rubber connector. Allow the PCV valve to draw underhood air.
4. Install a tachometer.
5. Ground the carburetor switch with a jumper wire.
6. Start the engine and run until normal operating temperature is obtained.
7. If the tachometer indicates the RPM is not to the specifications, turn the idle speed screw until the correct idle set RPM is reached.
8. Reinstall vacuum connector and PCV valve.
9. Remove jumper wire and reconnect radiator fan connector.

NOTE: After Steps 8 and 9 are completed, the curb idle speed may be different than the idle set RPM; this is normal and engine speed should not be readjusted.

10. Turn engine off, remove tachometer and carburetor ground switch wire.

1983 AND LATER 2.2L EFI ENGINE

Before adjusting idle speed check the operation of the Automatic Idle Speed motor (AIS), engine vacuum, EGR leaks, engine timing and coolant temperature sensor operation.

1. Bring the engine up to operating temperature.
2. Turn all accessories off and install a tachometer.
3. Turn the engine off and install a jumper wire to make the radiator fan run continuously.
4. Remove the throttle body 6–way connector. Remove the brown with white tracer AIS wire from the connector and re-install the connector.
5. Apply 12 volts to the brown and white wire (1984 models, apply 12 volts to the AIS wire for only 5 seconds). This will drive the AIS fully closed the idle rpm should drop.
6. Apply the parking brake and block the drive wheels.
7. Place the transmission selector in drive.
8. Record the engine rpm, it should be 650–675 rpm (1983).
9. If rpm does not meet specifications, adjust the idle stop on the throttle body with Chrysler special tool C–4804 or equivalent. Adjust w/tool to obtain 800 ± 10 rpm (manual) or 725 ± 10 rpm (automatic–in neutral) on 1984 models.

NOTE: Loosen the lock ring on the idle stop before adjusting it and re-tighten the lock ring after making the adjustment.

10. If the idle rpm will not adjust to specification, inspect the AIS for vacuum leaks, or check for throttle body damage.
11. Turn off the engine and reconnect the AIS wire into the 6–way connector. Remove the radiator fan jumper wire.
12. Start the engine and allow the rpm to stabilize. Check for 600–800 rpm.

IDLE SPEED

Adjustment

1983 MIKUNI CARBURETOR

1. Set the parking brake and place the transmission in neutral.
2. Turn off all the lights and accessories and disconnect the cooling fan.
3. Connect a tachometer to the engine following the manufacturer's instructions.
4. Start the engine and allow it to reach normal operating temperature.
5. Check the timing and adjust if necessary.
6. Remove the timing light and read the rpm indicated on the tachometer. If it is not the same as the curb idle specified on the emission label, adjust the idle speed adjusting screw. The

2–42

CHRYSLER CORPORATION
FRONT WHEEL DRIVE CARS

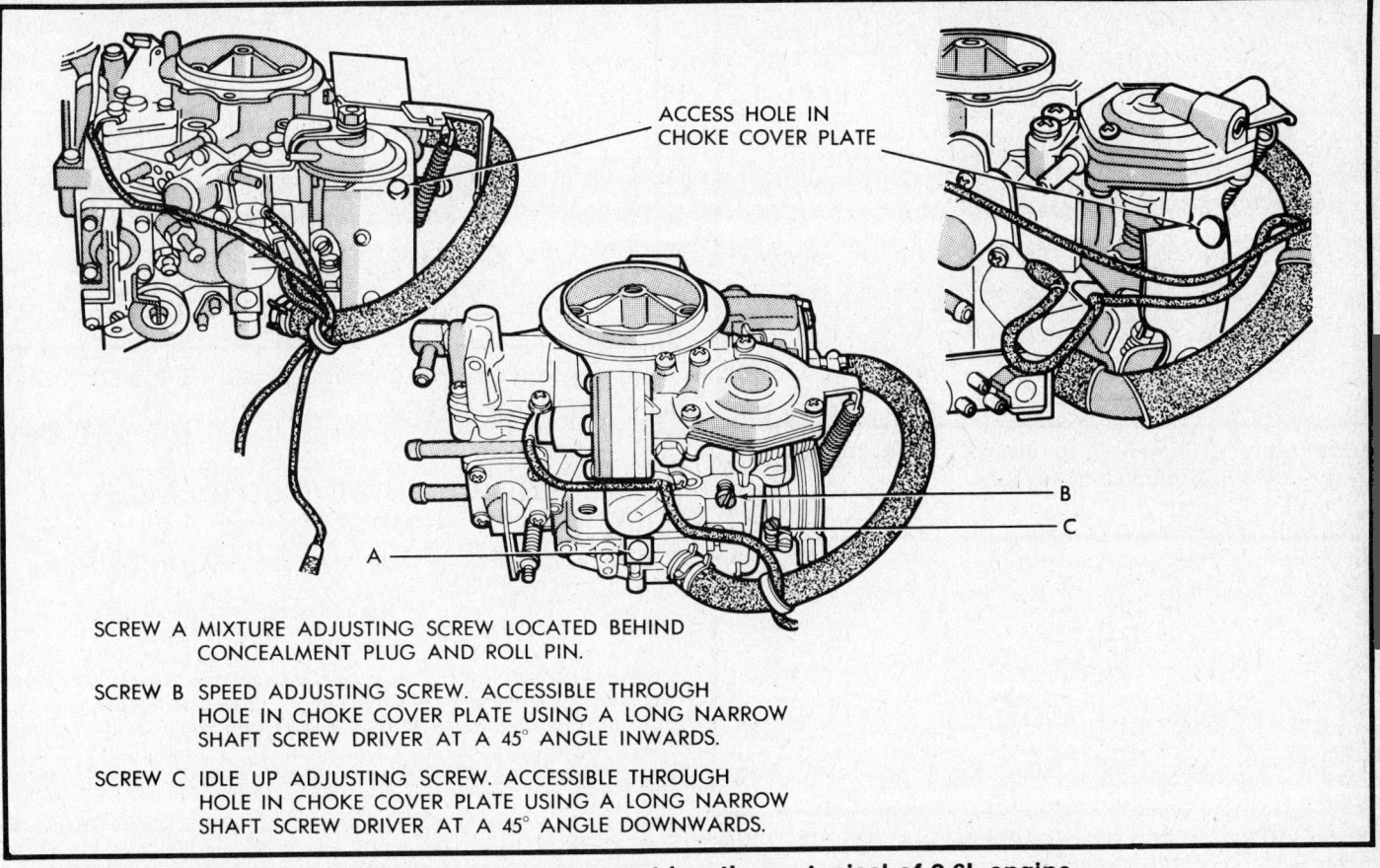

SCREW A MIXTURE ADJUSTING SCREW LOCATED BEHIND CONCEALMENT PLUG AND ROLL PIN.

SCREW B SPEED ADJUSTING SCREW. ACCESSIBLE THROUGH HOLE IN CHOKE COVER PLATE USING A LONG NARROW SHAFT SCREW DRIVER AT A 45° ANGLE INWARDS.

SCREW C IDLE UP ADJUSTING SCREW. ACCESSIBLE THROUGH HOLE IN CHOKE COVER PLATE USING A LONG NARROW SHAFT SCREW DRIVER AT A 45° ANGLE DOWNWARDS.

Adjustment of idle speed and carburetor component locations—typical of 2.6L engine
(© Chrysler Corporation)

screw is accessible through the hole in the choke cover plate using a long narrow screwdriver at a 45° angle inwards.

7. After adjusting the curb idle speed, press the A/C button on. With the compressor running, set the engine speed to 900 rpm by turning the idle up adjusting screw. The idle up adjusting screw is accessible through a hole in the choke cover plate using a long narrow screwdriver at a 45° angle downwards.

8. Turn the engine off, disconnect the tachometer and reconnect the cooling fan.

1984 AND LATER MIKUNI CARBURETOR

Before checking or adjusting any idle speed, check ignition timing and adjust, if necessary.

1. Set parking brake and place transaxle in neutral. Turn off all lights and accessories. Disconnect radiator fan. Connect tachometer to engine.
2. Start and run engine until normal operating temperature is reached.
3. On O₂ feedback equipped vehicles, turn off engine. Disconnect cable from negative battery terminal for 3 seconds then reconnect cable. Disconnect engine harness lead from O₂ sensor. Restart engine. Open throttle and allow engine run at 2500 RPM for 10 seconds. Return engine to idle.

CAUTION
Care should be exercised so that no pulling force is placed on sensor wire. The bullet connector to be disconnected is 4 in. from sensor. Use care in working around sensor as exhaust manifold is extremely hot.

---

4. Wait 2 minutes and read rpm indicated on tachometer. If rpm is not the same as that specified on VECI label, turn adjusting screw until correct rpm is obtained. Remove idle switch connector on O₂ feedback models.

5. On O₂ feedback models, turn off engine and reconnect wiring to sensor. On air conditioned models, restart engine and wait two minutes.

6. On air conditioned models, set temperature control lever to coldest position and turn on air conditioning. With air compressor running, set engine speed to 900 rpm by turning idle up screw.

7. Turn off engine, reconnect fan, disconnect tachometer and reconnect idle switch connector.

CONCEALMENT PLUGS

Removal

1983 HOLLEY 5220/6520 CARBURETORS

1. Remove carburetor from engine.
2. Clamp carburetor in a vise with idle mixture screw facing up. Protect gasket surface from vise jaws.
3. Drill a 5/64 in. pilot hole in the casting surrounding the idle mixture screw then redrill the hole to 1/8 in.
4. Insert a blunt punch into the hole and drive out plug.
5. Reinstall carburetor on engine.

1984 AND LATER HOLLEY 5220/6520 CARBURETORS

1. Remove air cleaner crossover assembly.
2. Remove canister purge and diverter valve vacuum hoses.
2. Remove canister purge and diverter valve vacuum hoses.
3. Center punch at a point 1/4 in. from end of mixture screw housing.

2-43

CHRYSLER CORPORATION
FRONT WHEEL DRIVE CARS

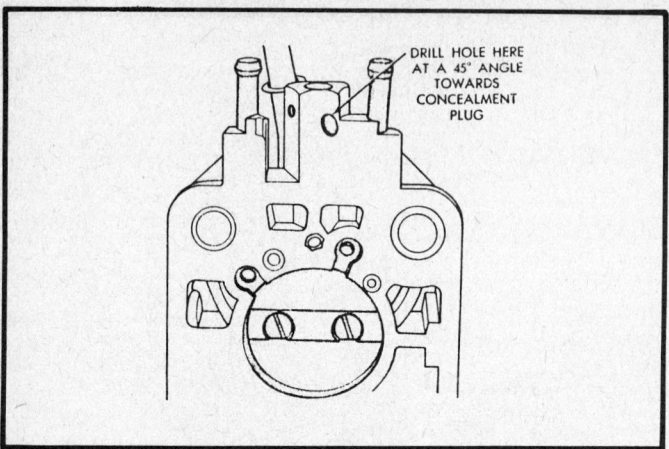

Location for drilling hole to remove concealment plug—1983 5220/6520 carburetors

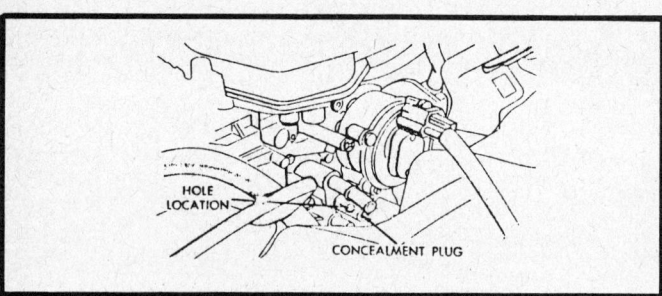

Location for drilling hole to remove concealment plug—1984 and later 5220/6520 carburetors
(© Chrysler Corporation)

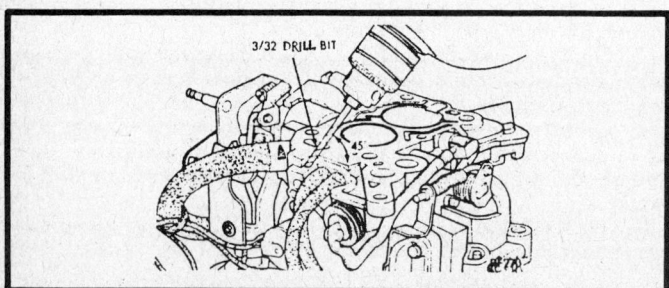

Drilling access hole—Mikuni carburetor
(© Chrysler Corporation)

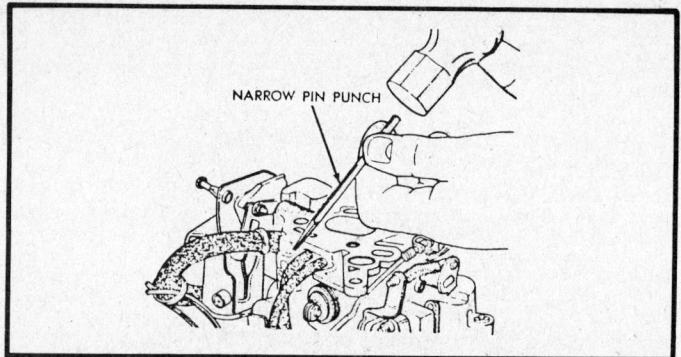

Driving concealment plug from base—Mikuni carburetor
(© Chrysler Corporation)

PROPANE ASSISTED IDLE SET PROCEDURE

HOLLEY MODELS 5220 AND 6520 CARBURETORS, 1982 AND LATER

--- CAUTION ---

Tampering with the carburetor is a violation of Federal law. Adjustment of the carburetor idle air-fuel mixture can only be done under certain circumstances and should only be used if an idle defect still exists after normal diagnosis has revealed no other faulty condition, such as incorrect idle speed, incorrect basic timing, faulty hose or wire connections, etc. It is also important to make sure the combustion computer systems are operating properly. Adjustment of the air-fuel mixture should also be performed after a major carburetor overhaul.

Adjustment

1. Set the parking brake and place transaxle in neutral. Turn off all lights and accessories. Connect a tachometer to the engine. Start the engine and allow it to warm up on the second highest step on the fast idle cam until normal operating temperature is reached. Return engine to curb idle.
2. Disconnect and plug the vacuum hose at the EGR valve, 1983 and later, disconnect and plug vacuum connection at the CCEGR/CVSCC. Disconnect the vacuum hose to the headed air door sensor at the three way connector, and in its place, install the supply hose from the propane bottle. Make sure that both valves are fully closed and that the bottle is upright and in a safe location.
3. Unplug the connector at the radiator fan and install a jumper wire so that the fan will run continuously. Remove the PCV valve from the moulded rubber connector and allow the valve to draw underhood air. Disconnect and plug the 3/16 in. diameter control hose at canister. Connect a jumper wire between carburetor switch and ground. 1984 and later Holley 6520 models, disconnect the O_2 test connector located on the left fender shield.
4. Open the propane main valve. With the air cleaner in place, slowly open the propane metering valve until maximum engine rpm is reached. When too much propane is added, engine speed will decrease. "Fine tune" the metering valve for the highest engine rpm.
5. With the propane still flowing, adjust the idle speed screw on top of the solenoid to get the specified propane rpm. "Fine tine" the propane metering valve to get the highest engine rpm. If there has been a change in the maximum rpm, re-adjust the idle speed screw to the specified propane rpm.
6. Turn off the propane main valve and allow engine speed to stabilize. With air cleaner in place, slowly adjust the mix-

4. Drill through outer housing with a 3/16 in. drill bit.
5. Pry out concealment plug and save for reinstallation.

MIKUNI CARBURETOR

1. Remove carburetor from engine.
2. Place carburetor in a vise. Protect carburetor from vise jaws.
3. Drill a 3/32 in. pilot hole at a 45° angle behind the plug. Redrill the hole to 1/8 in.
4. Drive out the concealment plug with a narrow pin punch. Blow away all metal chips with compressed air.
5. Remove impact plate and reinstall carburetor using a new flange gasket.

ture screw to achieve the specified idle set rpm. Pause between adjustments to allow the engine speed to stabilize.

NOTE: An Allen wrench is used to turn the idle mixture screws.

7. Turn on the propane main valve. "Fine tune" the metering valve to get the highest engine rpm. If the maximum engine speed is more than 25 rpm different than the specified propane rpm repeat Steps 4–7.

8. Turn off both valves on the propane bottle. Remove the propane supply hose and reinstall the vacuum hose. Connect fan.

9. On non-air conditioned vehicles, perform the fast idle speed adjustment and reinstall the concealment plug. The plug can be installed with the carburetor on the engine from 1982 and later.

10. On air conditioned vehicles, perform the air conditioning idle speed, idle set rpm, and fast idle speed adjustments. Replace the concealment plug. The plug can be installed with the carburetor on the engine.

IDLE MIXTURE

Adjustment

1983 2.6L ENGINE WITH MIKUNI CARBURETOR

NOTE: Upon completion of the carburetor adjustment, it is important to restore the roll pin and plug as described in the following detailed procedure.

This procedure should only be used if an idle defect still exists after normal diagnosis has revealed no other faulty conditions such as incorrect idle speed, faulty hose or wire connection, etc. Adjustment of the carburetor air-fuel mixture should also be performed after a major carburetor overhaul.

1. Set the parking brake and place transaxle in neutral. Turn off all lights and accessories. Disconnect cooling fan. Connect a tachometer to the engine. Start the engine and allow it to warm up on fast idle until normal operating temperature of 170°–190°F. (80°–90°C.) is reached and the choke is fully open. Return engine to idle. Connect timing light to engine. Check and adjust, if necessary, perform idle adjustment and remove timing light.

2. Disconnect the air hose running between the pulse air feeder and the air cleaner and plug the air hose to stop any secondary air flow into the pulse air feeder.

3. Insert probe from infrared exhaust gas analyzer into tailpipe per equipment manufacturers' instructions.

4. Set the idle CO and the engine speed to their specified values by simultaneously turning the speed adjusting and the mixture screw "A". Idle CO: 0.5% at specified curb idle speed as shown on the Emission Information label.

5. Remove the plug from the air hose and reconnect to the air cleaner.

6. If necessary, reset the engine speed to the specified curb idle speed by adjusting the speed adjusting screw.

7. Install new roll pin and concealment plug into their respective holes to seal the idle mixture adjusting screw.

PROPANE ASSISTED IDLE CHECK

Checking Procedure

1984 AND LATER MIKUNI CARBURETOR

Before checking or adjusting any idle speed, check ignition timing and adjust, if necessary.

1. Set parking brake and place transaxle in neutral. Turn off all lights and accessories. Connect a tachometer to the engine. Start and run engine until normal operating temperature is reached.

2. On Feedback equipped vehicles, turn engine off. Disconnect negative battery cable for 3 seconds, then reconnect cable. Disconnect engine harness lead from Oxygen sensor. Restart engine. Open throttle and allow engine to run at 2500 rpm for 10 seconds. Return engine to idle.

CAUTION
Care should be exercised so that no pulling force is put on the wire attached to the Oxygen sensor. The "bullet" connector to be disconnected is approximately 4 in. from the sensor. Use care in working around the sensor as the exhaust manifold is extremely hot.

---

3. Disconnect radiator fan and allow engine to idle for two minutes. Remove fresh air duct from air cleaner. Insert propane supply hose into air cleaner approximately 4 in. Make sure that both valves are fully closed and the bottle is upright and in a safe location.

4. Open propane main valve. Slowly open propane metering valve until maximum engine rpm is reached. If too much propane is added, engine rpm will decrease. The metering valve must be "fine tuned" for the highest engine rpm.

5. Check engine rpm increase. Engine rpm increases should be as follows:
   Federal – 40 to 90 rpm
   California – 25 to 75 rpm
   Canada – 50 to 100 rpm

If engine rpm increase is not within the above specifications proceed to Propane Assisted Idle Set Procedure. If the increase is within specifications proceed to next Step.

6. Turn off both propane valves. Remove propane supply hose and reinstall fresh air duct. Reconnect wire to oxygen sensor. Reconnect radiator fan and remove tachometer.

PROPANE ASSISTED IDLE SET

Setting Procedure

1984 AND LATER MIKUNI CARBURETO

This adjustment is to be performed only after the Propane Assisted Idle Check Procedure.

1. Remove concealment plug. Reconnect cooling fan. Start the engine and allow it to warm up until normal operating temperature is reached.

2. On vehicles equipped with O_2 system, turn engine off. Disconnect the cable from the negative terminal of the battery for 3 seconds. Reconnect the cable to its terminal. Restart the engine. Open the throttle and allow engine to run at 2500 rpm for 10 seconds. Return engine to idle. Remove boot from idle speed adjustment screw.

3. Allow engine to idle for two minutes. Insert the propane supply hose from the propane bottle into the air cleaner snorkel 4 in. Make sure that both valves are fully closed and that the bottle is upright and in a safe location.

4. Open the propane main valve. Slowly open the propane metering valve until maximum engine rpm is reached. When too much propane is added, engine speed will decrease. "Fine Tune" the metering valve for the highest engine rpm.

5. With the propane still flowing, adjust the idle speed screw to get the propane rpm specified. "Fine Tune" the propane metering valve to get the highest engine rpm. If there has been a change in the maximum rpm, readjust the engine speed to the specified propane rpm.

6. Turn off the propane main valve and allow engine speed to stabilize. Slowly adjust the mixture screw to achieve the specified idle rpm. Pause between adjustments to allow engine speed to stabilize.

7. Turn on the main propane valve. "Fine Tune" the metering valve to get the highest engine rpm. If the maximum engine speed is more than 25 rpm different than the specified propane rpm, repeat Steps 4–7.

8. Turn off both valves on propane bottle. Remove propane

supply hose and reinstall the fresh air duct to the air cleaner. If disconnected, reconnect the engine harness lead to the O₂ sensor. Reinstall the concealment plug and, if removed, the impact plate. On O₂ system vehicles, reconnect the boot removed to get at the idle speed screw.

9. If equipped with air conditioning, set the temperature control lever to the coldest position and turn on air conditioning. With the compressor running, set the engine speed to 900 rpm by turning the idle up adjusting screw.

ANTI-DIESELING CONTROL

Adjustment

1983 1.7L ENGINE EQUIPPED WITH HOLLEY 6520 MODEL

NOTE: Anti-dieseling is controlled by the engagement of the compressor clutch on air conditioned equipped vehicles. When the engine is turned off, an anti dieseling relay energizes the compressor clutch from 4—20 seconds, thus preventing engine overrun. The anti diesel relay is located on the evaporator housing on Omni/Horizon models and on the left side of the engine compartment on the remaining models.

1. With engine fully warmed up, place transaxle in neutral and set parking brake. Headlights off.
2. Ground the idle stop carburetor switch with a jumper wire.
3. Disconnect idle stop solenoid wire at connector.
4. Adjust the throttle stop screw to 700 rpm.
5. Reconnect idle stop solenoid wire at connector and remove jumper wire from idle stop carburetor switch.

1983 AND LATER HOLLEY 5220/6520 MODELS

NOTE: Anti-dieseling is controlled on the following 1983 carburetors by either an idle stop solenoid or solenoid kicker, while anti dieseling is controlled on the remaining models by high run ignition timing.

CHRYSLER NO.	VENDOR NO.
4227382	R-40023A
4227383	R-40024A
4227384	R-40025A
4227385	R-40026A

1. With engine fully warmed up, place transaxle in neutral and set parking brake. Headlights off.
2. Ground the idle stop carburetor switch with a jumper wire.
3. Remove the red wire terminal from the 6-way connector on the carburetor side of connector.
4. Adjust the throttle stop screw to 700 rpm.
5. Reconnect wire at connector and remove jumper wire from idle stop carburetor switch.

INTAKE MANIFOLD

Removal

1.6L ENGINE

1. Disconnect battery.
2. Remove air cleaner and disconnect all vacuum lines, electrical wiring and fuel line from carburetor.
3. Drain cooling system. Disconnect inlet hose.
4. Disconnect EGR tube at manifold.
5. Remove eight mounting nuts and washers attaching intake manifold and remove from engine.
6. Remove carburetor from intake manifold.

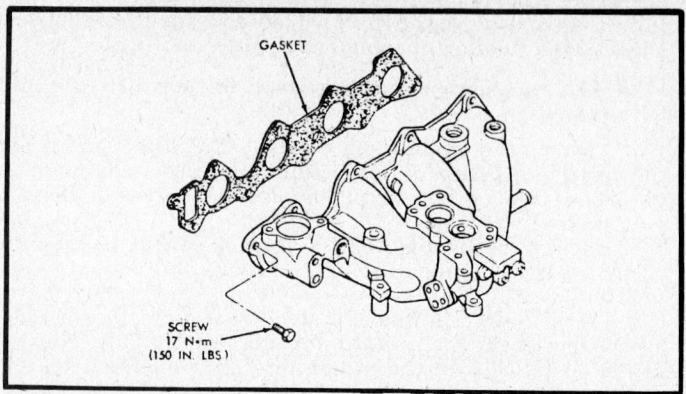

Intake manifold—2.6L engine (© Chrysler Corporation)

Installation

1. Assemble carburetor to intake manifold.
2. Install new gasket on cylinder head and install intake manifold to cylinder head.
3. Install washers and nuts to intake manifold mounting studs. Torque to 133 inch lbs. (15 Nm).
4. Reverse removal procedures to complete installation.

Removal

2.6L ENGINE

1. Disconnect battery.
2. Drain cooling system. Disconnect cooling hose from water pump to intake manifold.
3. Disconnect carburetor air horn and move to one side.
4. Disconnect vacuum hoses attached to carburetor and intake manifold.
5. Disconnect throttle control linkage.
6. Disconnect fuel inlet line at fuel filter.
7. Remove fuel filter and fuel pump and move to one side.
8. Remove mounting nuts and washers attaching intake manifold and remove manifold from engine.
9. Remove carburetor from intake manifold.

Installation

1. Assemble carburetor to intake manifold.
2. Install new gasket on cylinder head and install intake manifold to cylinder head.
3. Install washers and nuts to intake manifold mounting studs. Torque to 150 inch lbs. (17 Nm).
4. Install fuel pump and fuel filter.
5. Reverse removal procedures for installation.

EXHAUST MANIFOLD

Removal

1.6L ENGINE

1. Disconnect battery.
2. Separate carburetor air heater tube from manifold stove.
3. Remove oxygen sensor.
4. Disconnect air injection pipe from manifold.
5. Separate EGR assembly from manifold.
6. Raise vehicle and remove exhaust pipe from manifold.
7. Remove exhaust retaining nuts and remove assembly.
8. Remove carburetor air heater from manifold.

Installation

1. Install carburetor air heater assembly on exhaust manifold.

CHRYSLER CORPORATION
FRONT WHEEL DRIVE CARS

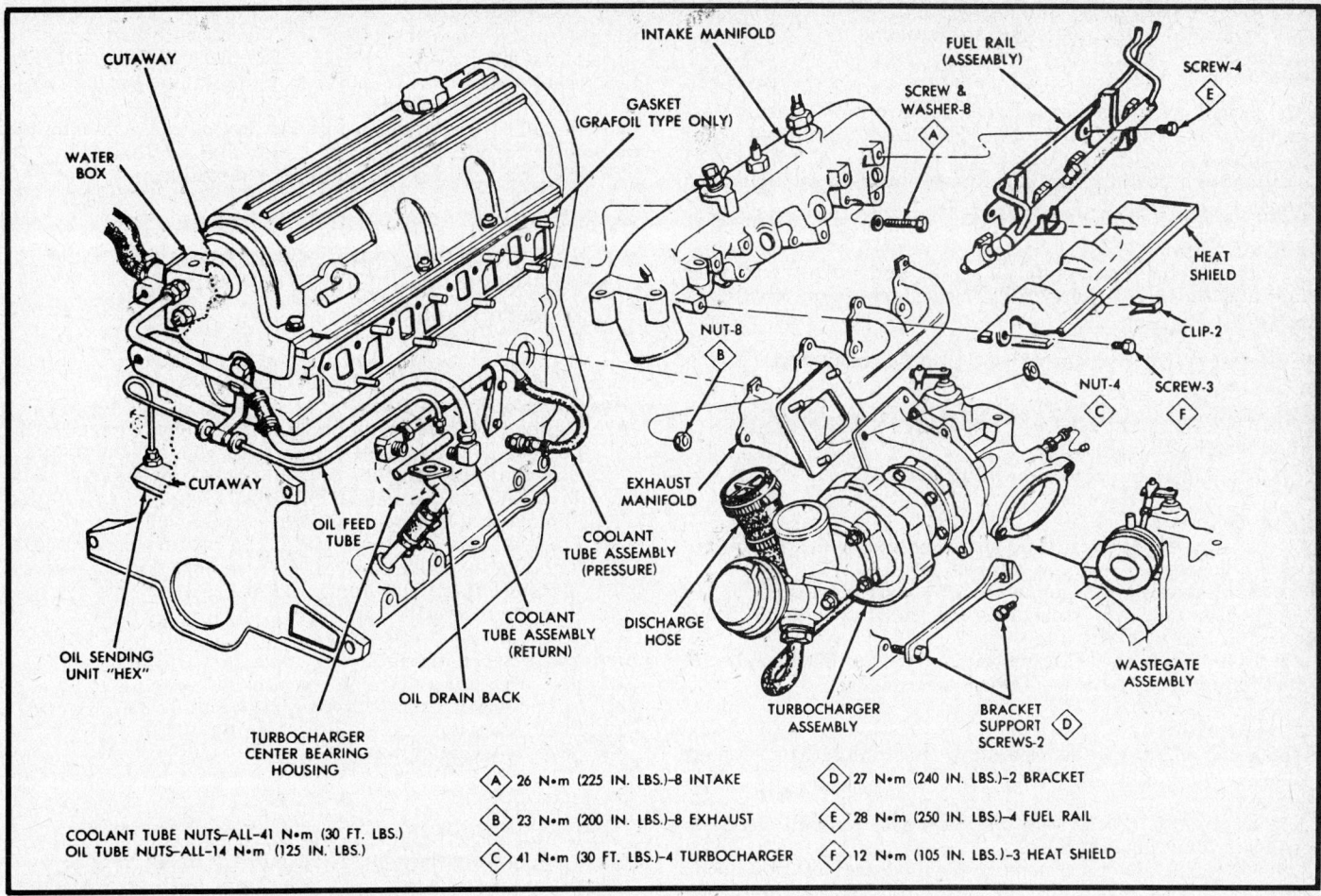

Intake/exhaust/turbocharger assembly—2.2L engine (© Chrysler Corporation)

2. Install new manifold gasket on cylinder head.
3. Install manifold assembly and torque nut and washer assemblies to 15 ft. lbs. (20 Nm).
4. Reverse removal procedures for installation.

Removal
2.6L ENGINE

1. Disconnect battery.
2. Drain cooling system.
3. Remove air cleaner.
4. Loosen power steering pump and remove belt.
5. Raise vehicle and remove exhaust pipe from manifold.
6. Disconnect air injection tube assembly from exhaust manifold and lower vehicle.
7. Disconnect air injection tube assembly from air pump and move tube assembly to one side.
8. Remove power steering pump assembly and set aside.
9. Remove heat cowl from exhaust manifold.
10. Remove exhaust manifold retaining nuts and remove assembly from vehicle.
11. Remove carburetor air heater from manifold assembly.
12. Remove retaining screws holding exhaust manifold and front catalytic converter together.

Installation

1. Install a new intake and exhaust manifold gasket coated lightly with sealer on manifold side.

2. Set exhaust manifold in place. Torque retaining nuts starting at center and progressing outward in both directions to 200 inch lbs. (23 Nm). Repeat this procedure until all nuts are at specified torque.
3. Set intake manifold in place.
4. Raise vehicle and torque retaining screws starting at center and progressing outward in both directions to 250 inch lbs. (28 Nm). Repeat this procedure until all screws are at specified torque.
5. Reverse removal procedures for installation.

INTAKE/EXHAUST MANIFOLD COMBINATIONS

Removal
1.7L ENGINE

1. Disconnect battery.
2. Remove air cleaner and disconnect all vacuum lines, electrical wiring and fuel line from carburetor.
3. Remove throttle linkage.
4. Loosen power steering pump and remove belt.
5. Remove power brake hose from intake manifold.
6. Raise vehicle and remove exhaust pipe from manifold.
7. Remove power steering pump assembly and set aside.
8. Remove intake and exhaust manifold retaining nuts and screws.
9. Lower vehicle and remove carburetor, intake and exhaust manifold assembly.

CHRYSLER CORPORATION
FRONT WHEEL DRIVE CARS

10. Remove carburetor and gasket.
11. Separate intake and exhaust manifolds.

Installation

1. Install a new gasket between the two manifolds and assemble intake and exhaust manifolds. Do not tighten screws at this time.
2. Install a new intake and exhaust manifold gasket coated lightly with Sealer on cylinder head.
3. Install carburetor to manifold assembly and set assembly in place.
4. Raise vehicle and snug all intake and exhaust manifold nuts and screws to the cylinder head (approximately 10–15 inch lb.).

Removal (With Cylinder Head and Turbocharger Assembly)

2.2L STANDARD/SHELBY ENGINE INTAKE AND EXHAUST MANIFOLDS

1. Disconnect battery and drain cooling system.

From Below

2. Disconnect exhaust pipe at articulated joint and disconnect O₂ sensor at electrical connections.
3. Remove turbocharger to block support bracket.
4. Loosen oil drain back tube connector hose clamps. Move tube down on block fitting.
5. Disconnect turbocharger coolant inlet tube at cylinder block and disconnect tube support bracket.

From Above

6. Remove air cleaner assembly including throttle body adaptor, hose and air cleaner box with support (to block) bracket.
7. Disconnect accelerator linkage, throttle body electrical connector and vacuum hoses.
8. Relocate fuel rail assembly. Remove four bracket to intake manifold screws and two bracket to heat shield retaining clips to lift and secure fuel rail (with injectors, wiring harness, and fuel lines intact) up out of the way.
9. Disconnect turbocharger oil feed line at oil sending unit tee.
10. Disconnect upper radiator hose from thermostat housing.
11. Remove cylinder head with manifolds and turbocharger attached as an assembly.
12. With assembly on the bench, loosen upper turbocharger discharge hose end clamp. DO NOT DISTURB CENTER DESWIRLER RETAINING CLAMP. Remove 3 throttle body to intake manifold screws and remove throttle body assembly.
13. Disconnect turbocharger coolant return tube at water box and retaining bracket on cylinder head.
14. Remove 3 heat shield to intake manifold screws and remove heat shield.
15. Remove 4 nuts attaching turbocharger to exhaust manifold and remove turbocharger assembly.
16. Remove intake manifold retaining screws and washer assemblies and remove intake manifold.
17. Remove exhaust manifold retaining nuts and remove exhaust manifold.

Installation

1. Install new gasket between exhaust manifold and front catalytic converter. Torque the mounting screws (6) to 24 ft. lbs. (32 Nm).
2. Install carburetor air heater on exhaust manifold assembly. Torque screws (3) to 80 inch lbs. (9 Nm).
3. Install new manifold gasket coated lightly with sealer on cylinder head side.
4. Install manifold assembly and torque CENTER Mounting nuts (4) to 150 inch lbs. (17 Nm). Torque outboard mounting nuts (4) to 150 inch lbs. (17 Nm). Torque outboard mounting nuts (4) to 150 inch lbs. (17 Nm). DO NOT OVERTIGHTEN.
5. Install heat cowl to exhaust manifold and torque screws (3) to 80 inch lbs. (9 Nm).
6. Install air cleaner support bracket on exhaust manifold assembly. Torque screws (2) to 200 inch lbs. (23 Nm).
7. Reverse removal procedures for installation.

Removal

2.2L/2.5L ENGINE INTAKE AND EXHAUST MANIFOLDS (EXCEPT TURBOCHARGED)

1. Disconnect battery.
2. Drain cooling system.
3. Remove air cleaner and disconnect all vacuum lines, electrical wiring and fuel lines from carburetor.
4. Remove throttle linkage.
5. Loosen power steering pump and remove belt.
6. Remove power brake vacuum hose from intake manifold.
7. Canadian cars—remove coupling hose from diverter valve to exhaust manifold air injection tube assembly.
8. Remove water hoses from water crossover.
9. Raise vehicle and remove exhaust pipe from manifold.
10. Remove power steering pump assembly and set aside.
11. Remove intake manifold support bracket.
12. Remove EGR tube.
13. Canadian cars—remove four air injection tube bolts and air injection tube assembly.
14. Remove intake manifold retaining screws.
15. Lower vehicle and remove intake manifold.
16. Remove exhaust manifold retaining nuts.
17. Remove exhaust manifold.

Installation

1. Install new two-sided Grafoil, or equivalent, intake/exhaust manifold gasket. DO NOT APPLY SEALER.
2. Set exhaust manifold in place. Apply anti-seize compound to threads, install and torque retaining nuts starting at center and progressing outward in both directions to 200 inch lbs. (23 Nm). Repeat this procedure until all nuts are at specified torque.
3. Position intake manifold, install and torque retaining screw and washer assemblies starting at center and progressing outward in both directions to 225 inch lbs. (26 Nm). Repeat this procedure until all screws are at specified torque.
4. Connect turbocharger outlet to intake manifold inlet tube and position turbocharger in place on exhaust manifold, apply anti-seize compound to threads and torque retaining nuts to 30 ft. lbs. (41 Nm). Tighten connector tube clamps to 30 inch lbs. (41 Nm) torque. Install tube support bracket to cylinder head.
6. Install heat shield to intake manifold and tighten 3 attaching screws to 105 inch lbs. (12 Nm).
7. Install throttle body air horn into turbocharger inlet tube and install 3 throttle body to intake manifold screws to 250 inch lbs. (28 Nm). Tighten tube clamp to 30 inch lbs. (3 Nm).
8. Install cylinder head assembly.
9. Reconnect turbocharger oil feed line to oil sending unit tee (and bearing housing, if disconnected). Tighten tube nut(s) to 125 inch lbs. (14 Nm).
10. Install air cleaner assembly and reconnect vacuum lines and accelerator cables.
11. Reposition fuel rail, install and tighten 4 bracket screws to 250 inch lbs. (28 Nm) and install 2 air shield to bracket retaining clips.
12. Connect turbocharger inlet coolant tube to cylinder block. Tighten tube nut to 30 ft. lbs. (41 Nm). Install tube support bracket.
13. Install turbocharger housing to block support bracket, and install screws finger tight. Tighten block screw FIRST to

CHRYSLER CORPORATION
FRONT WHEEL DRIVE CARS

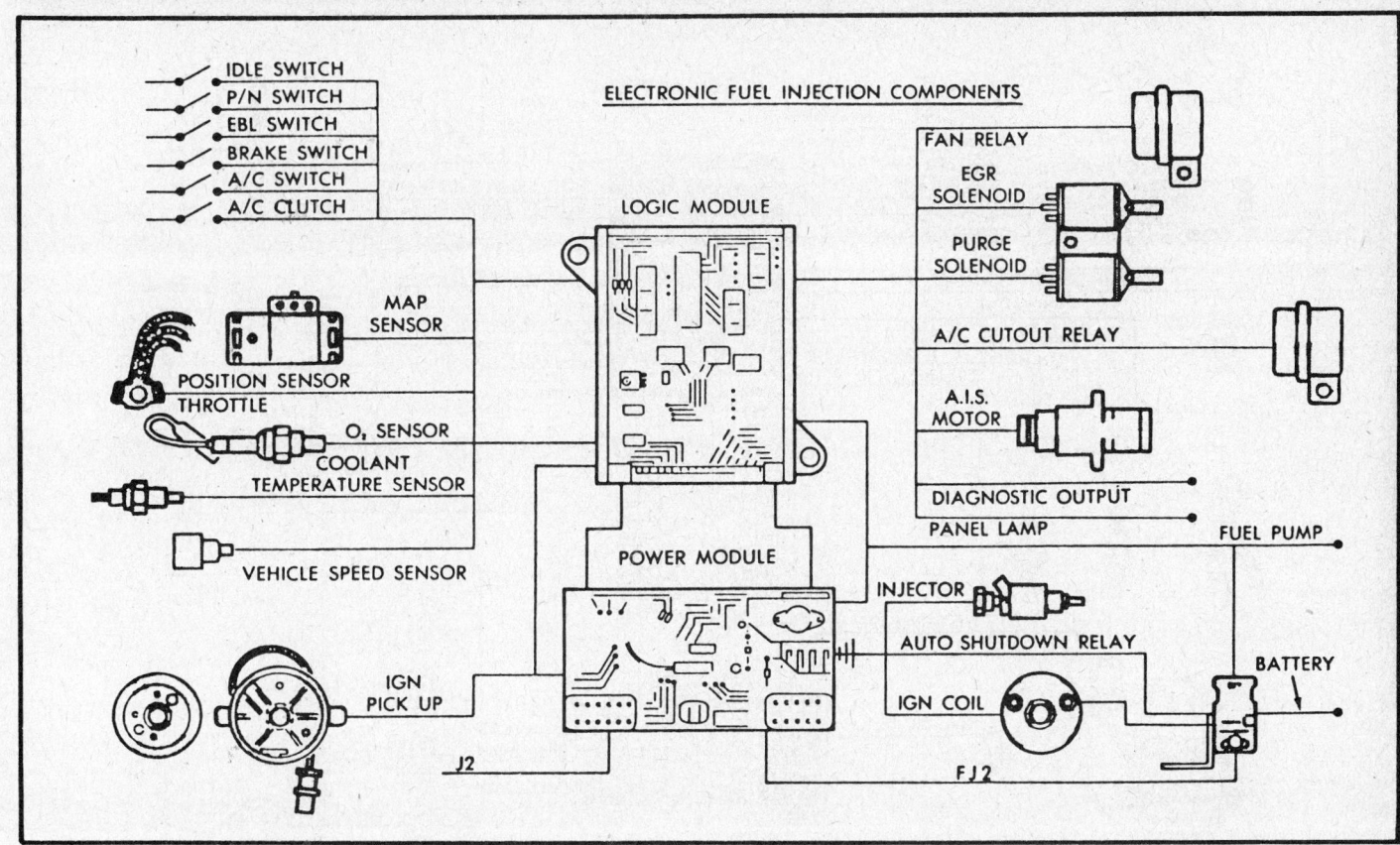

Single point EFI fuel system components (© Chrysler Corporation)

40 ft. lbs. (54 Nm) then, tighten screw to turbocharger housing to 20 ft. lbs. (27 Nm).

14. Reposition drain back tube (hose) connector and tighten hose clamps. Reconnect exhaust pipe.

15. Connect upper radiator hose to thermostat housing. Tighten hose clamp to 35 inch lbs. (4.1 Nm).

16. Fill cooling system.

Electronic Fuel Injection

SINGLE POINT FUEL INJECTION

1983 AND LATER 2.2L ENGINES

The Electronic Fuel Injection System is a computer regulated single point fuel injection system that provides precise air/fuel ratio for all driving conditions. At the center of this system is a digital pre-programmed computer known as a Logic Module that regulates ignition timing, air-fuel ratio, emission control devices and idle speed. This component has the ability to update and revise its programming to meet changing operating conditions.

Various sensors provide the input necessary for the Logic Module to correctly regulate the fuel flow at the fuel injector. These include the Manifold Absolute Pressure, Throttle Position, Oxygen Feedback, Coolant Temperature, and Vehicle Speed sensors. In addition to the sensors, various switches also provide important information. These include the Neutral-safety, Heated Back Lite, Air Conditioning, Air Conditioning Clutch switches, and an Electronic Idle switch.

All inputs to the Logic Module are converted into signals sent to the Power Module. These signals cause the Power Module to change either the fuel flow at the injector or ignition timing or both.

The Logic Module tests many of its own input and output circuits. If a fault is found in a major system, this information is stored in the Logic Module. Information on this fault can be displayed to a technician by means of the instrument panel power loss lamp or by connecting a diagnostic read out and reading a numbered display code which directly relates to a general fault.

NOTE: Refer to Electronic Fuel Injection Section in the Unit Repair for Checks, Inspection and Repair.

MULTI-POINT FUEL INJECTION (TURBO)

1984 AND LATER 2.2L ENGINES

The turbocharged multi-point Electronic Fuel Injection system combines an electronic fuel and spark advance control system with a turbocharged intake system.

At the center of this system is a digital pre-programmed computer known as a Logic Module that regulates ignition timing, air-fuel ratio, emission control devices and idle speed. This component has the ability to update and revise its programming to meet changing operating conditions.

Various sensors provide the input necessary for the Logic Module to correctly regulate fuel flow at the fuel injectors. These include the Manifold Absolute Pressure, Throttle Position, Oxygen Feedback, Coolant Temperature, Charge Temperature, and Vehicle Speed Sensors. In addition to the sensors, various switches also provide important information. These include the Transmission Neutral-Safety, Heated Backlite, Air Conditioning, and the Air Conditioning Clutch Switches.

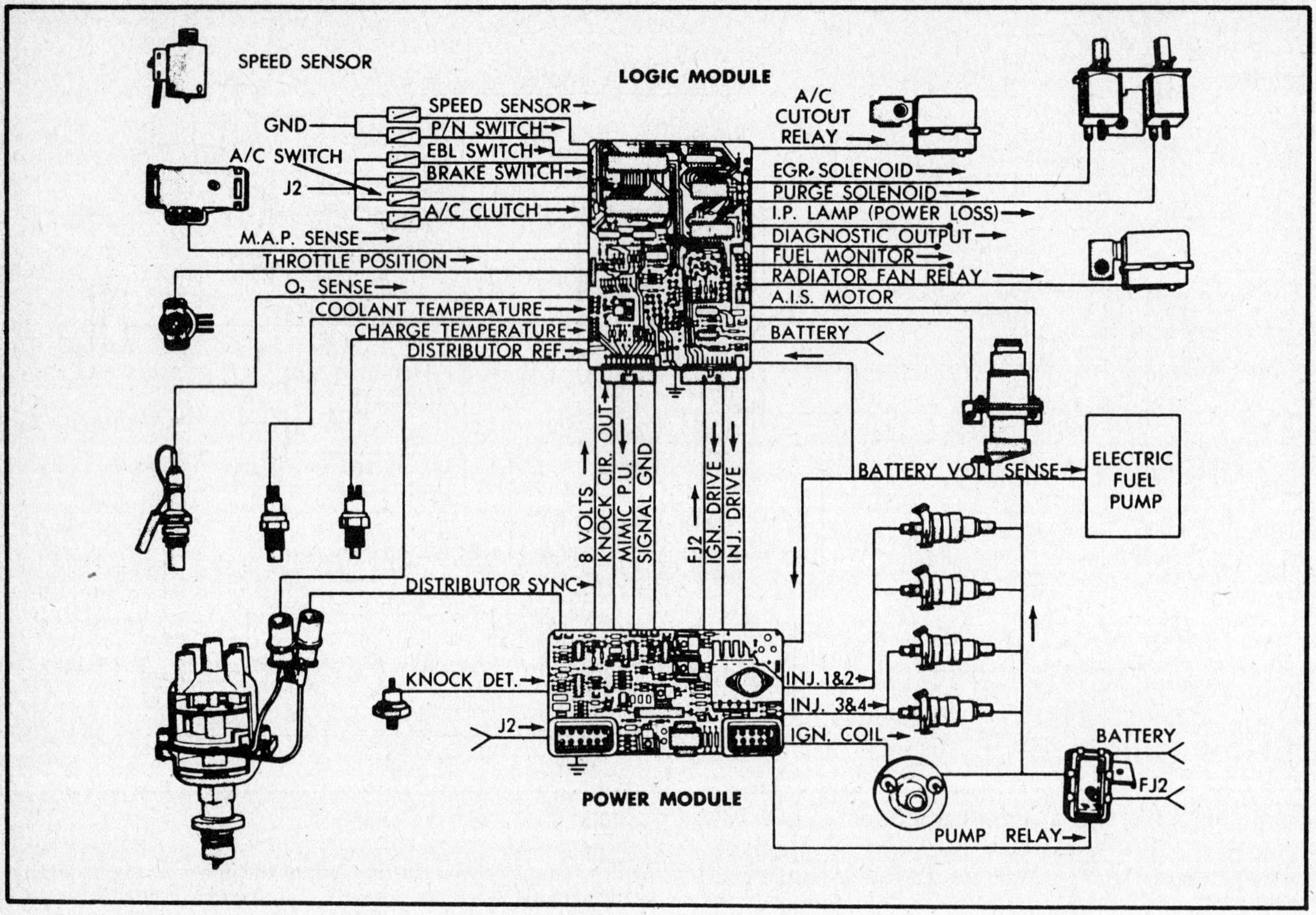

CHRYSLER CORPORATION
FRONT WHEEL DRIVE CARS

Multi-point EFI fuel system (turbo) components (© Chrysler Corporation)

Inputs to the Logic Module are converted into signals sent to the Power Module. These signals cause the Power Module to change either the fuel flow at the injector or ignition timing or both.

The Logic Module tests many of its own input and output circuits. If a fault is found in a major circuit, this information is stored in the Logic Module. Information on this fault can be displayed to a technician by means of the instrument panel power loss lamp or by connecting a diagnostic readout and observing a numbered display code which directly relates to a general fault.

NOTE: Refer to Electronic Fuel Injection Section in Unit Repair for Checks, Inspection and Repairs.

Turbocharger System

TURBOCHARGER

NOTE: The turbo boost pressure is 9 psi for manual transmission vehicles and 10 psi for automatic transmission vehicles.

Remove

2.2L ENGINE
1. Disconnect battery and drain cooling system.

From Below
2. Disconnect exhaust pipe at articulated joint and O_2 sensor at electrical connector.
3. Remove turbocharger housing-to-block support bracket.
4. Loosen oil drain back tube connector hose clamps and move tube (hose) down on block nipple.
5. Disconnect turbocharger coolant tube nut at block outlet (below steering pump bracket) and tube support bracket.

From Above
6. Remove air cleaner assembly, including throttle body adaptor, hose and air cleaner box with support (to block) bracket.
7. Disconnect accelerator linkage, throttle body electrical connector and vacuum hoses.
8. Loosen throttle body (to turbocharger) inlet hose clamps.
9. Remove 3 throttle body to intake manifold attaching screws and remove throttle body.
10. Loosen turbocharger discharge hose end clamps ONLY. (Center band retains).
11. Relocate fuel rail. Remove 4 bracket screws from intake manifold and 2 bracket to heat shield retaining clips. This will lift and secure fuel rail (with injectors, wiring harness and fuel lines intact) up out of the way.
12. Remove 3 screws attaching heat shield to intake manifold and remove shield.
13. Disconnect coolant return tube/hose assembly from turbo-

CHRYSLER CORPORATION
FRONT WHEEL DRIVE CARS

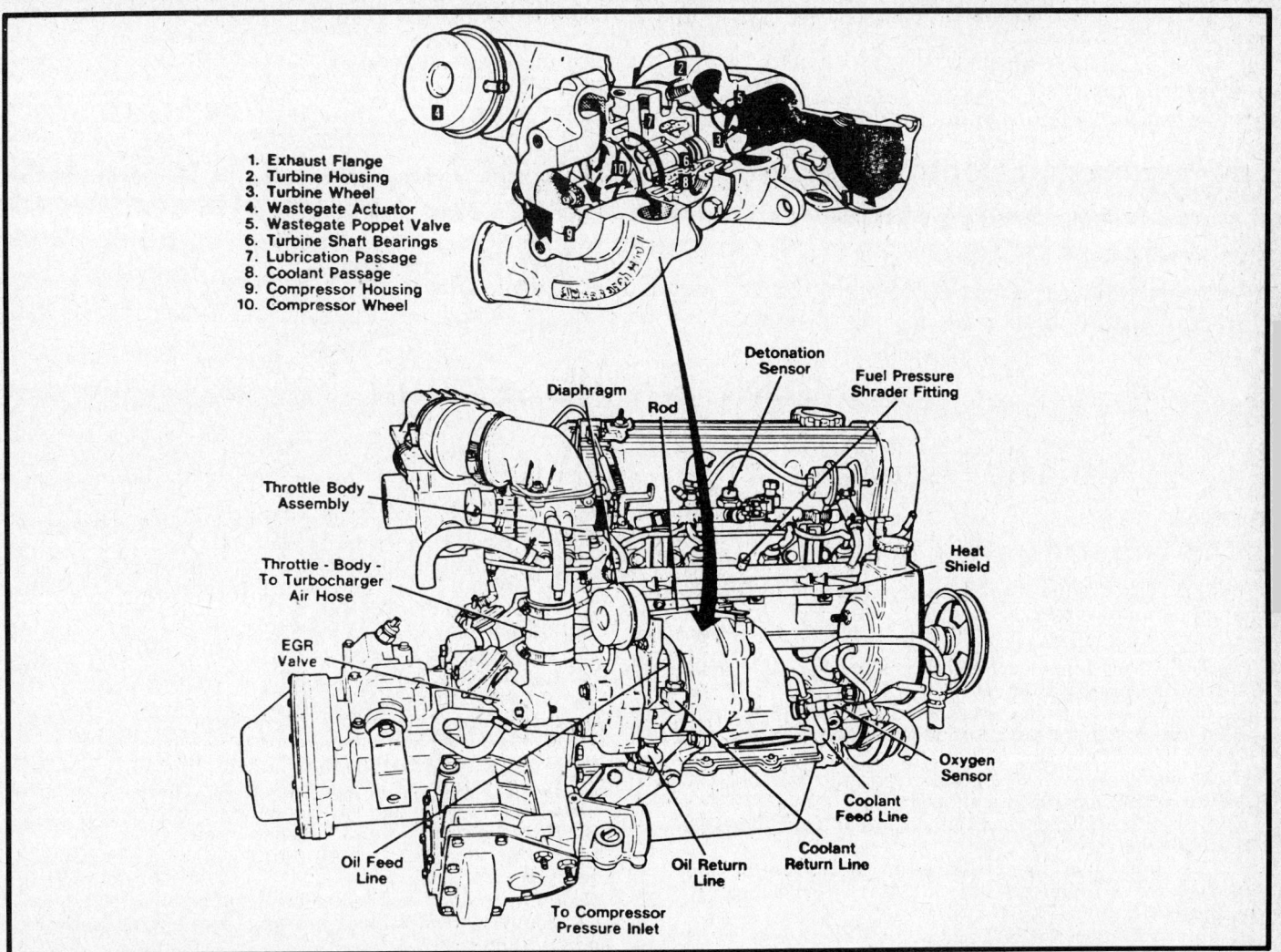

1. Exhaust Flange
2. Turbine Housing
3. Turbine Wheel
4. Wastegate Actuator
5. Wastegate Poppet Valve
6. Turbine Shaft Bearings
7. Lubrication Passage
8. Coolant Passage
9. Compressor Housing
10. Compressor Wheel

Key features of 2.2L turbo engine (© Chrysler Corporation)

charger housing to water box. Remove tube support bracket from cylinder head and remove assembly.

14. Disconnect oil feed line from oil sending unit hex tee and turbocharger bearing housing. Remove support bracket and remove assembly.
15. Remove 4 nuts attaching turbocharger to exhaust manifold.
16. Remove turbocharger assembly by lifting off exhaust manifold studs, push downward toward passenger side (of unit) up and out of engine compartment.

Install

Reverse removal procedure Steps, paying particular attention to fastener torque values and/or special instructions as follows:

1. Reposition turbocharger assembly on exhaust manifold studs. Making sure that the turbocharger discharge tube is in position between the intake manifold and turbocharger.
2. Apply anti-seize compound to threads and torque 4 nuts to 30 ft. lbs. (41 Nm).
3. Torque oil feed line tube nuts (to sending unit hex tee and turbocharger center housing) to 125 inch lbs. (14 Nm). Install and tighten support bracket screw.
4. Tighten 3 heat shield to intake manifold screws to 105 inch lbs. (12 Nm).
5. Tighten coolant tube nuts to 30 ft. lbs. (41 Nm) and install bracket screw.
6. Tighten 4 fuel rail bracket to intake manifold retaining screws to 250 inch lbs. (28 Nm) torque. Reinstall shield to bracket clips.
7. Tighten discharge tube (hose) clamp to 35 inch lbs. (4.1 Nm) torque.
8. Tighten 3 throttle body to intake manifold screws to 250 inch lbs. (28 Nm) torque.
9. Tighten throttle body hose clamps to 35 inch lbs. (4.1 Nm) torque.
10. Reconnect accelerator linkage, electrical connector and vacuum hoses.
11. Tighten 2 hose adaptor to throttle body screws to 55 inch lbs. (6 Nm) and air cleaner box support bracket screws to 40 ft. lbs. (54 Nm) torque.
12. Tighten coolant tube nut to block connector to 30 ft. lbs. (41 Nm) torque.
13. Reposition oil drain back hose and tighten clamps to 30 inch lbs. (3 Nm) torque.
14. Install turbocharger-to-block support bracket and install screws finger tight. Tighten block screw FIRST to 40 ft. lbs. (54 Nm), then tighten screw to turbocharger housing to 20 ft. lbs. (27 Nm).

SECTION 2

CHRYSLER CORPORATION
FRONT WHEEL DRIVE CARS

15. Tighten articulated (ball) joint shoulder bolts to 250 inch lbs. (28 Nm) torque.
16. Fill cooling system, and reconnect battery.

NOTE: Inspection and Service Information on the turbocharger can be found in the Unit Repair Section.

Emission Control System

EMISSION EQUIPMENT

1983–87 Models

Heated Inlet Air
Positive Crankcase Ventilation System
Carburetor Calibration
Distributor Calibration
Initial Timing
Air Pumps
Exhaust Gas Recirculation System
Electric Choke
Evaporation Control System with canister
Catalytic Converter, Mini and Regular
Electronic Feedback Carburetor
Jet Air Control Valve
Pulse Air Feeder System
Aspirator Air System

GASOLINE ENGINE SECTION

ENGINE ASSEMBLY

Removal

1.7L ENGINE WITH MANUAL TRANSAXLE

NOTE: The engine and manual transaxle must be removed as an assembly.

1. Disconnect battery.
2. Scribe hood hinge outline on hood and remove hood.
3. Drain cooling system.
4. Remove hoses from radiator and engine.
5. Remove radiator (and shroud assembly, if so equipped).
6. Remove air cleaner with hoses.
7. Remove air conditioning compressor mounting bolts and set compressor aside (if so equipped).
8. Disconnect all electrical connections at alternator, carburetor and engine.
9. Disconnect fuel line, heater hose and accelerator cable.
10. Remove air diverter valve and lines from air pump. (If equipped).
11. Remove alternator belt and alternator.
12. Raise vehicle on hoist.
14. Disconnect driveshafts from transmission and secure with wire to vehicle.

NOTE: The inboard stub axle shafts are retained by constant spring tension. With the outer shaft removed from the hub, the drive shaft can be removed by pulling the assembly from the transaxle, except with the right shaft, which must first have the speedometer gear removed.

15. Disconnect exhaust pipe from manifold.
16. Remove air pump hoses and lines. (If equipped.)
17. Remove air pump belt and air pump. (If equipped.)
18. Remove transmission linkage.
19. Lower vehicle from hoist.
20. Attach lifting fixture to engine/transmission assembly.
21. Raise engine assembly slightly and remove front engine mounting bolt.
22. Remove right engine mounting bolt.
23. Remove left engine mounting bolt.
24. Lift engine and transmission assembly from vehicle.
25. Align dimple on flywheel to indicator before removing transmission from engine.
26. Remove transmission to engine bolts and remove transmission from engine.

Installation

1. Install transmission to engine. Be sure the flywheel recess is lined up. Only in this position can the transmission be installed to the engine.
2. Install engine lifting fixture to the engine and lower engine into the engine compartment.
3. Align engine mounts and install mounting bolts. Do not tighten until all 3 mounting bolts have been loosely installed. Tighten to 40 ft. lbs. (54 Nm).
4. Remove engine lifting fixture.
5. Raise vehicle on hoist.
6. Install driveshafts.
7. Connect transmission linkage.
8. Install air pump and air pump belt.
9. Connect air pump hoses and lines. (if equipped)
10. Connect exhaust pipe to manifold.
11. Lower vehicle from hoist.
12. Connect clutch and speedometer cable.
13. Install alternator and alternator belt.
14. Connect diverter valve and lines to air pump. (if equipped.)
15. Connect fuel line, heater hose and accelerator cable.
16. Connect all electrical connections to engine, carburetor and alternator.
17. Install air conditioning compressor (if equipped).
18. Install air cleaner with hoses.
19. Install radiator (and shroud assembly, if so equipped).
20. Fill cooling system.
21. Install oil filter, refill crankcase with proper oil to correct level.
22. Install hood.
23. Connect battery.
24. Start engine and run until operating temperature is reached.
25. Check timing and adjust carburetor and transmission linkage if necessary.

Removal

1.7L ENGINE WITH AUTOMATIC TRANSAXLE

NOTE: The engine can be removed without removing the automatic transaxle.

1. Disconnect battery.
2. Scribe hood hinge outline on hood and remove hood.
3. Drain cooling system.
4. Remove hoses from radiator and engine.
5. Remove transmission cooler lines.
6. Remove radiator (and shroud assembly, if so equipped).
7. Remove air cleaner with hoses.
8. Remove air conditioning compressor mounting bolts and set compressor aside (if so equipped).

CHRYSLER CORPORATION
FRONT WHEEL DRIVE CARS

Typical engine lifting fixture (© Chrysler Corporation)

9. Disconnect all electrical connections at alternator, carburetor and engine.
10. Disconnect fuel line, heater hose and accelerator cable.
11. Remove air diverter valve and lines from air pump. (if equipped.)
12. Remove alternator belt and alternator.
13. Remove upper bell housing bolts.
14. Raise vehicle and remove wheel assembly.
15. Remove left splash shield.
16. Remove wheel assembly.
17. Remove right splash shield.
18. Remove power steering pump and belt, set pump aside.
19. Remove lower radiator hose from water pump.
20. Remove water pump pulley and crankshaft pulley.
21. Remove front engine mounting bolt.
22. Remove inspection cover from transmission and remove flex plate bolts.
23. Remove starter.
24. Remove remaining lower bell housing bolts.
25. Lower vehicle and place floor jack under transmission.
26. Attach lifting fixture to engine.
27. Remove oil filter.
28. Remove right engine mount.
29. Lift engine from vehicle.

Installation

1. Lower engine into engine compartment.
2. Install upper bell housing bolts.
3. Install right engine mount.
4. Remove engine lifting fixture.
5. Remove floor jack from under transmission.
6. Raise vehicle and install center engine mount.
7. Install flex-plate bolts and inspection cover.
8. Install starter.
9. Install oil filter. Refill engine crankcase with proper oil to correct level.
10. Install crankshaft pulley and water pump pulley.
11. Install power steering pump and belt.
12. Lower vehicle.
13. Connect alternator and install belt.
14. Install lower radiator hose.
15. Install compressor and belt (if so equipped).
16. Install upper radiator hose.
17. Connect fuel line, heater hose and accelerator cable.
18. Connect hoses to thermostat housing. Fill cooling system.
19. Connect booster hose to intake manifold.
20. Connect carburetor linkage and all electrical connections to carburetor and engine.
21. Raise vehicle and connect exhaust pipe to manifold.
22. Lower vehicle and install air cleaner.
23. Connect PCV valve to air cleaner.
24. Connect battery.

25. Install hood.
26. Start engine and run until operating temperature is reached.
27. Check timing and adjust carburetor if necessary.

ENGINE ASSEMBLY

Removal

1.6L, 2.2L/2.5L AND 2.6L ENGINES

NOTE: The engines are removed separately from either the automatic or manual transaxles. With different accessories and added brackets mounted to the varied engines, it may be necessary to modify the removal and installation procedures of each engine.

1. Disconnect battery.
2. Scribe hood hinge outline on hood and remove hood.
3. Drain cooling system.
4. Remove hoses from radiator and engine.
5. Remove radiator and shroud assembly.
6. Remove air cleaner and hoses.
7. Remove air conditioning compressor mounting bolts and set compressor aside (if so equipped).
8. Remove power steering pump mounting bolts and set pump aside (if so equipped).
9. Remove oil filter.
10. Disconnect the electrical connects for alternator, carburetor and engine.
11. Disconnect fuel line, heater hose and accelerator cable connections.
12. Remove alternator mounting bolts and set alternator aside.
13. Disconnect clutch cable (manual).
14. Remove transmission case lower cover.
15. Disconnect exhaust pipe at manifold.
16. Disconnect starter and lay aside.
17. Remove transmission case lower cover.
18. Mark flex plate to torque converter.
19. Remove screws holding torque converter to flex plate.
20. Attach C-clamp on front bottom of torque converter housing to prevent torque converter from coming out.
21. Install transmission holding fixture.
22. Attach lifting hoist to engine.
23. Remove right inner splash shield.
24. Remove ground strap.
25. Remove right engine mount screw.
26. Mark insulator position on side rail. Reinstall to exact position if removed.
27. Remove transmission case to cylinder block mounting screws.
28. Remove front engine mount screw and nut.
29. Remove manual transmission anti-roll strut or damper.
30. Lift engine from the vehicle.
31. Remove insulator through bolt (from inside wheelhouse) or insulator bracket to transmission screws.
32. Remove engine from vehicle.

Installation

1. Install hoist to the engine and lower engine into the engine compartment.
2. Align engine mounts and install bolts, but do not tighten until all of the mounting bolts have been installed. Tighten to 40 ft. lbs. (54 Nm).
3. Install transmission case to cylinder block mounting screws. Tighten to 70 ft. lbs. (95 Nm).
4. Remove engine hoist and transmission holding fixture.
5. Secure ground strap.
6. Install right engine splash shield.
7. Connect starter.

CHRYSLER CORPORATION
FRONT WHEEL DRIVE CARS

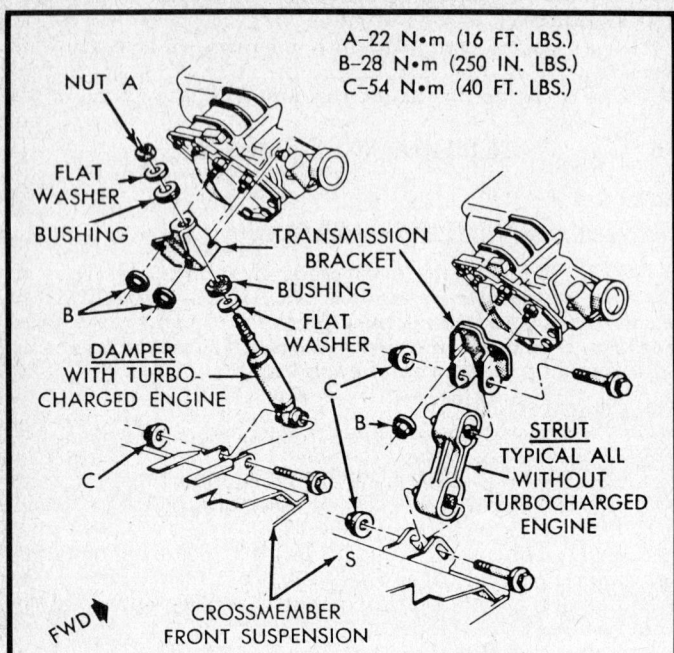

Engine anti-roll strut/damper components
(© Chrysler Corporation)

8. Connect exhaust system. If equipped with manual transaxle, connect the clutch cable. Install transmission case lower cover.
9. Remove C-clamp from torque converter housing. Align flex plate to torque converter and install mounting screws. Tighten to 40 ft. lbs. (54 Nm). Install transmission case lower cover.
10. Install alternator.
11. Connect fuel line, heater hose, and accelerator cable.
12. Connect all electrical connectors for alternator, carburetor and engine.
13. Install oil filter. Refill engine crankcase with proper oil to correct level.
14. Install power steering pump (if so equipped).
15. Install air conditioning compressor (if so equipped).
16. Install air cleaner and hoses.
17. Install radiator and shroud assembly. Install radiator hoses. Fill cooling system.
18. Install hood.
19. Connect battery.
20. Start engine and run until operating temperature is reached.
21. Adjust carburetor if necessary.

ENGINE MOUNTS

Removal and Installation
The engine mounts can be removed and installed by first supporting the engine/transaxle assembly with a floor jack type tool.

RUBBER MOUNT INSULATORS

1.6L, 2.2L/2.5L and 2.6L ENGINES
Insulator location on frame rail (right side) and transmission bracket (left side) are adjustable to allow "right/left" drive train adjustment in relation to driveshaft assembly length.

Check and reposition right engine mount insulator (left engine mount insulator centers itself with engine weight removed). Adjust drive train position, if required, for the following conditions:
a. Driveshaft distress.
b. Any front end structural damage (after repair).
c. Insulator replacement.

Adjustment
1. Remove the load on the engine motor mounts by carefully supporting the engine and transmission assembly with a floor jack.
2. Loosen the right engine mount insulator vertical fasteners and the front engine mount bracket to front crossmember fasteners.

NOTE: Left engine mount insulator is sleeved over shaft and long support bolt to provide lateral movement adjustment with engine weight removed.

3. Pry the engine right or left as required to achieve the proper driveshaft assembly length. Refer to front drive axle chapter within this section.
4. Tighten right engine mount insulator vertical bolts to 250 inch lbs. (28 Nm), tighten front engine mount fasteners to 40 ft. lbs. (54 Nm) and "center" left engine mount insulator.
5. Recheck driveshaft length.

ENGINE VALVES

Checking/Adjusting Valve Clearance
1.6L ENGINE

NOTE: Valve clearance must be set with the piston at TDC on the compression stroke with the engine COLD.

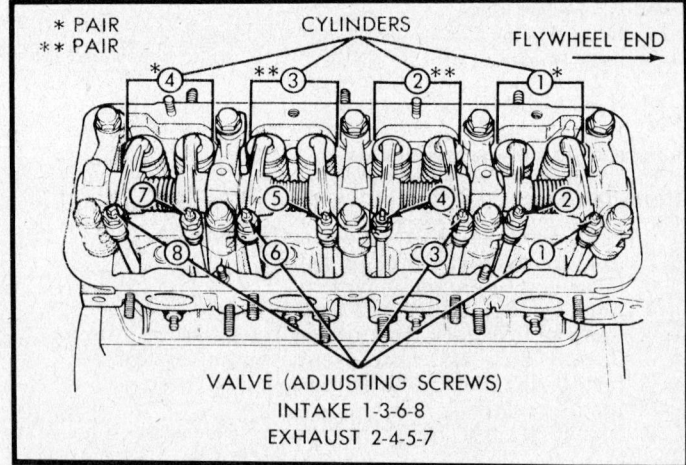

Adjusting valve clearance—1.6L engine
(© Chrysler Corporation)

1. Turn crankshaft and watch movement of exhaust valves. When one is closing—moving upward—continue turning slowly until the inlet valve on the same cylinder just starts to open. This is the "valve rocking" position. The piston in the opposite cylinder is then at TDC on compression and its valve clearance can be checked and adjusted.
2. Example, to check valve clearances on No. 1 cylinder, position valves on the companion cylinder number four in rocking position, as follows:
 a. Observe rockers on companion cylinder number four. Turn crankshaft until exhaust valve rocker is moving upward (valve closing)—keep turning slowly until intake valve

CHRYSLER CORPORATION
FRONT WHEEL DRIVE CARS

Valves 'Rocking' on Cylinder Number	Adjust Valves on Cylinder Number
4	1
2	3
1	4
3	2

rocker just starts to move down (valve opening)—stop.

   b. Check both valve clearances on No. 1 cylinder.

  3. After checking both valve clearances, rotate the crankshaft one half turn, the next cylinder in the firing order should have its valves "rocking" and the companion cylinder can be adjusted.

  4. Adjust valves as needed.
    Intake .010 in.
    Exhaust .012 in.

Valve Adjustment

1.7L ENGINE

Valve adjustment is not required as a matter of routine maintenance. It is, however, necessary to check the valve clearance after head repairs. Adjusting clearance is a matter of substituting discs located in the top of the cam follower. The discs are available in 0.05mm increments from 3.0mm to 4.24mm. One disc is located in each follower. A special tool is required for disc removal and installation. Cold clearance should be 0.15–0.25mm (0.006–0.010in.) intake and 0.35–0.45mm (0.014–0.018in.) exhaust; warm clearance is 0.20–0.30mm (0.008–0.012in.) intake and 0.40–0.50mm (0.016–0.020in.) exhaust.

Procedure

The valves should be checked and adjusted with the engine at normal operating temperature and in the firing order rotation of 1–3–4–2.

  1. Run the engine to normal operating temperature.
  2. Remove the valve cover.
  3. Use a socket wrench on the crankshaft pulley or bump the engine around until the camshaft lobes of No. 1 cylinder are positioned properly. Due to the design of the camshaft lobes, it is not necessary that the lobes be pointing directly away (perpendicular) to the adjusting disc.

━━━━━━ CAUTION ━━━━━━
Do not turn the engine using the camshaft pulley and only turn the engine in the direction of normal rotation.

  4. Using a feeler gauge, check the valve clearance between the camshaft lobe and the valve adjusting disc.

  5. If the measured clearance is not as specified, the valve adjusting disc can be removed and replaced with another of the proper size to give the correct valve clearance.

  6. To remove the disc:
    a. Depress the cam follower with Tool L–4417 or equivalent. This tool is necessary to remove the disc without damaging the camshaft or cylinder head.
    b. Remove the valve adjusting disc with a magnet.
    c. Calculate the thickness of a new disc and install one of the proper size. Be sure the number indicating the thickness (measured in mm) of the disc faces down when installed.
    d. Recheck the valve clearance.

  7. Recheck or adjust all other valves in the same manner.

NOTE: When the camshaft is in position to check the valves of No. 1 cylinder, cylinders No. 3 and 4 can also be checked or adjusted. It is only necessary to turn the engine one time to position the camshaft to check No. 2 cylinder.

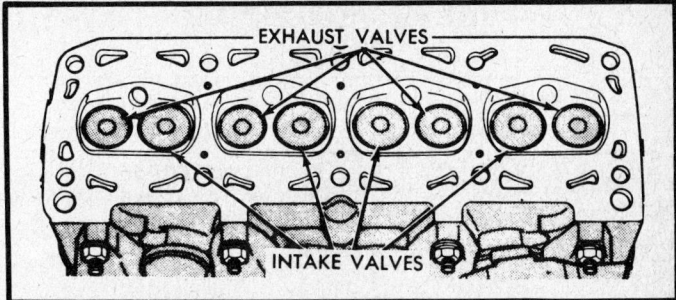

Valve arrangement—1.7L engine
(© Chrysler Corporation)

Meaasuring valve clearance—1.7L engine
(© Chrysler Corporation)

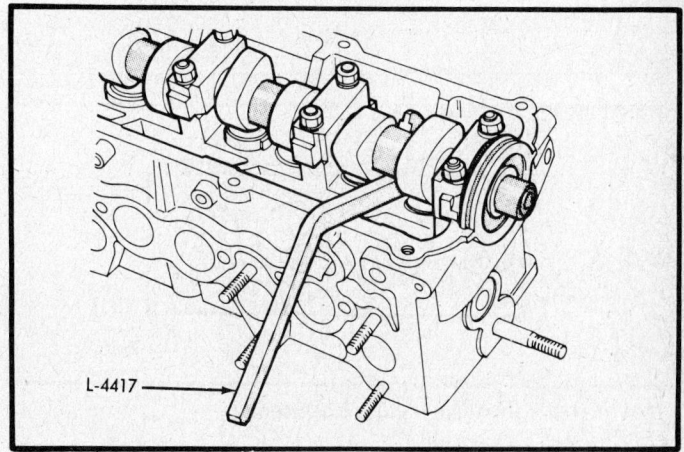

Clearance disc replacement—1.7L engine
(© Chrysler Corporation)

  8. Reinstall the valve cover.

2.2L/2.5L ENGINES

The 2.2L/2.5L engines use hydraulic lash adjusters. No periodic adjustment or checking is necessary, unless valves are refaced and cylinder head serviced. Refer to cylinder head removal and installation procedures.

2.6L ENGINE

The 2.6 engine has a jet valve located beside the intake valve of each cylinder.

NOTE: When adjusting valve clearances, the jet valve must be adjusted before the intake valve.

CHRYSLER CORPORATION
FRONT WHEEL DRIVE CARS

VALVE ADJUSTING DISCS

Thickness (mm)	Part Number
3.00	5240946
3.05	5240945
3.10	5240944
3.15	5240943
3.20	5240942
3.25	5240941
3.30	5240573
3.35	5240574
3.40	5240575
3.45	5240576
3.50	5240577
3.55	5240578
3.60	5240579
3.65	5240580
3.70	5240581
3.75	5240582
3.80	5240583
3.85	5240584
3.90	5240585
3.95	5240586
4.00	5240587
4.05	5240588
4.10	5240589
4.15	5240590
4.20	5240591
4.25	5240592

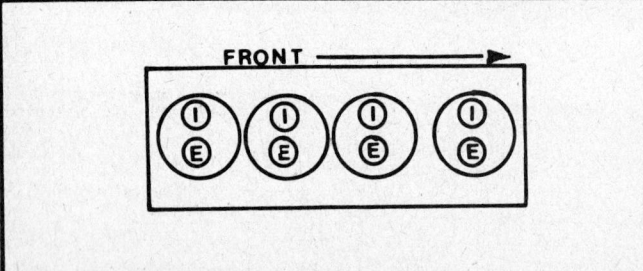

Valve arrangement—2.6L engine
(© Chrysler Corporation)

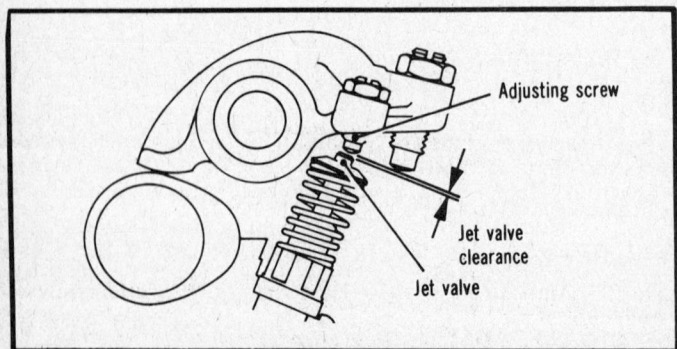

Adjusting jet valve clearance (© Chrysler Corporation)

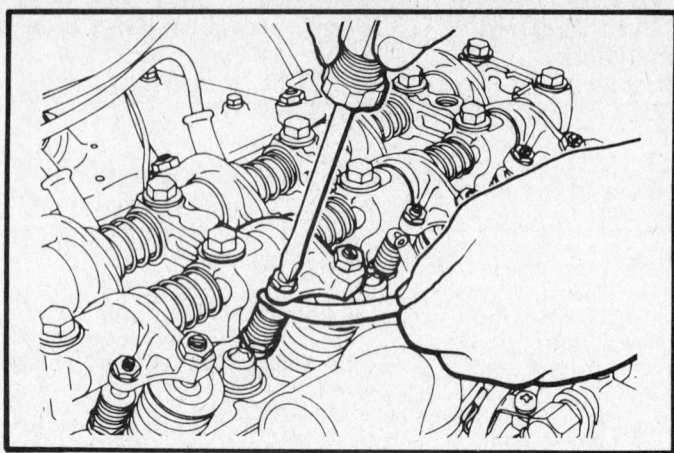

Adjusting intake and exhaust valves
(© Chrysler Corporation)

1. Start the engine and allow it to reach normal operating temperature.
2. Stop the engine and remove the air cleaner and its hoses. Remove any other cables, hoses, wires, etc., which are attached to the valve cover, and remove the valve cover.
3. Disconnect the high tension coil-to-distributor wire at the coil.
4. Watch the rocker arms for No. 1 cylinder and rotate the crankshaft until the exhaust valve is closing and the intake valve has just started to open. AT this point, No. 4 cylinder will be at Top Dead Center (TDC) commencing its firing stroke.
5. Loosen the locknut on cylinder No. 4 intake valve and back off the intake valve adjusting screw 2 or more turns.
6. Loosen the locknut on the jet valve adjusting screw.
7. Turn the jet valve adjusting screw counterclockwise and insert a 0.006 in. feeler gauge between the jet valve stem and the adjusting screw.
8. Tighten the adjusting screw until it touches the feeler gauge.
Take care not to press on the valve while adjusting because the jet valve spring is very weak.

NOTE: If the adjusting screw is tight, special care must be taken to avoid pressing down on the jet valve when adjusting the clearance or a false reading will result.

9. Tighten the locknut securely while holding the rocker arm adjusting screw with a screwdriver to prevent it from turning.
10. Make sure that a 0.006 in. feeler gauge can be easily inserted between the jet valve and the rocker arm.
11. Adjust No. 4 cylinder's intake valve to 0.006 in. and its exhaust valve to 0.010 in. Tighten the adjusting screw locknuts and recheck each clearance.
12. Perform Step 4 in conjunction with the chart below to set up the remaining three cylinders for valve adjustments.
13. Replace the valve cover and all other components. Run the engine and check for oil leaks at the valve cover.

CYLINDER COVER AND ROCKER ARM ASSEMBLY

Removal
1.6L ENGINE
1. Separate the crankcase ventilator system from the cover and disconnect the diverter hose from the bracket.

CHRYSLER CORPORATION
FRONT WHEEL DRIVE CARS

Exhaust Valve Closing	Adjust
No. 1 Cylinder	No. 4 Cylinder Valves
No. 2 Cylinder	No. 3 Cylinder Valves
No. 3 Cylinder	No. 2 Cylinder Valves
No. 4 Cylinder	No. 1 Cylinder Valves

Removing rocker arm assembly—1.6L engine
(© Chrysler Corporation)

2. Remove the retaining screws holding the cover to the cylinder head.
3. With the cylinder head cold, release the headbolts evenly, beginning at the ends and working towards the center.

NOTE: Brackets supporting the rocker assembly are located on dowels and retained by the cylinder head bolts. Only brackets number 2 and 4 are pinned to the rocker arm shafts. Roll pins must be removed to replace shafts.

4. Tie the end brackets and remove the rocker arm assembly.
5. The rocker arm assembly can then be disassembled for service or replacement.
6. The installation is the reverse of the removal procedure. The head bolts must be tightened progressively to 52 ft. lbs. (70 Nm) in sequence. The cylinder head cover screws must be tightened to 60 inch lbs. (5 Nm) torque.

1.7L AND 2.2L/2.5L ENGINES

The 1.7L and 2.2L engines use no rocker arm shaft, since both are overhead cam (OHC) engines, with the camshaft lobes making direct contact with the valve mechanism. Refer to cylinder head removal and installation section.

Removal and Installation
2.6L ENGINE

1. Remove the air cleaner and duct assembly.
2. Remove the crankcase ventilation hose.
3. Remove the water pump pulley cover and remove the water pump drive belt.
4. Remove the cylinder head cover.

NOTE: The rocker arm shafts are interconnected with the camshaft bearing caps. It is suggested that removal of the rocker arm assembly be accomplished with the weight of the timing chain removed from the camshaft gear. Refer to the timing chain removal and installation procedures within this section.

5. When removing the camshaft bearing caps, do not remove the bolts from the bearing caps. Remove the rocker arms, rocker shafts and bearing caps as an assembly.
6. Upon installation of the rocker arm shaft assemblies, tighten the camshaft bearings in the following order to 85 inch lbs. (10 Nm).
   a. Number 3 cap
   b. Number 2 cap
   c. Number 4 cap
   d. Front cap
   e. Rear cap
7. Repeat the tightening sequence and increase the torque to 175 inch lbs. (18 Nm).
8. Install the cylinder head cover and tighten the screws to 55 inch lbs. (6 Nm) torque.

VALVE TIMING

NOTE: Refer to the timing chain/belt removal and installation procedures within this section.

CYLINDER HEAD

Removal and Installation
1.6L ENGINE

NOTE: The cylinder head must be cold before removal to avoid distortion.

1. Remove the valve cover and any necessary vacuum lines. Drain cooling system.
2. Release cylinder head bolts evenly, beginning at ends and working toward center. Brackets supporting rocker assembly are located on dowels and retained by the head bolts. Only brackets 2 and 4 are pinned to the rocker arm shafts.
3. Tie end brackets and remove rockers as an assembly.
4. Remove push rods and identify so that they can be installed in the same position.
5. Remove cylinder head.
6. Installation is the reverse of removal. When reinstalling the head, tighten the bolts progressively to 52 ft. lbs. Run the engine to operating temperature. Allow it to cool to normal air temperatures. Retorque the head bolts as needed.

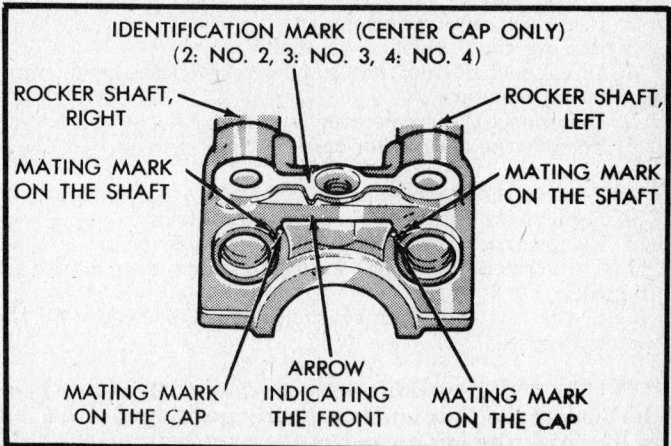

Camshaft bearing cap identification—2.6L engine
(© Chrysler Corporation)

CHRYSLER CORPORATION
FRONT WHEEL DRIVE CARS

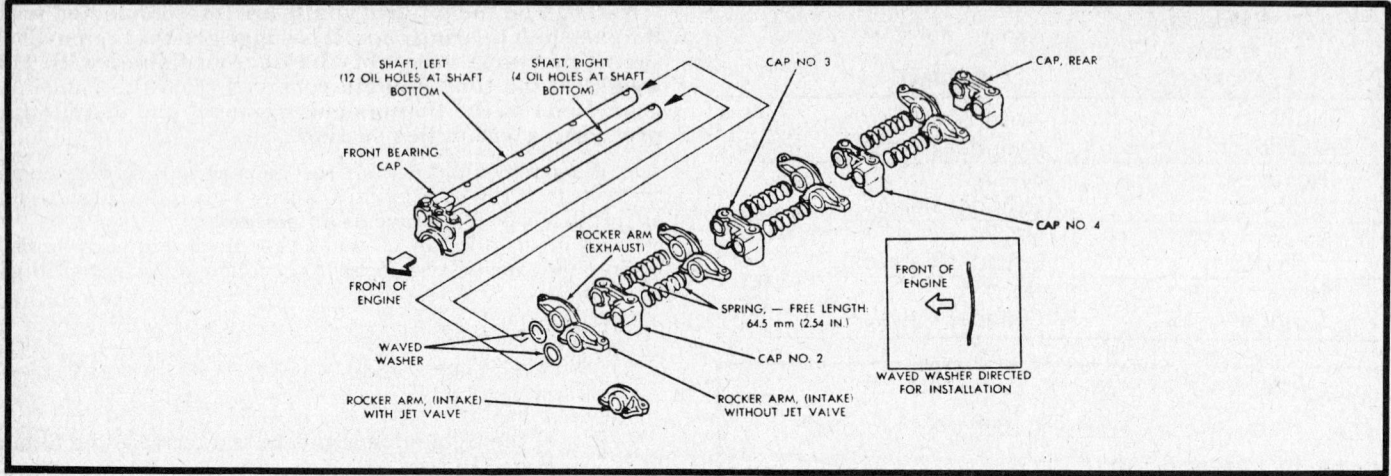

Exploded view of rocker arm shaft—2.6L engine (© Chrysler Corporation)

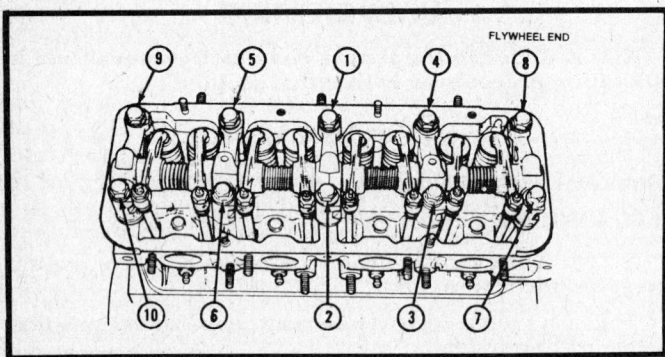

Head bolt tightening sequence—1.6L engine
(© Chrysler Corporation)

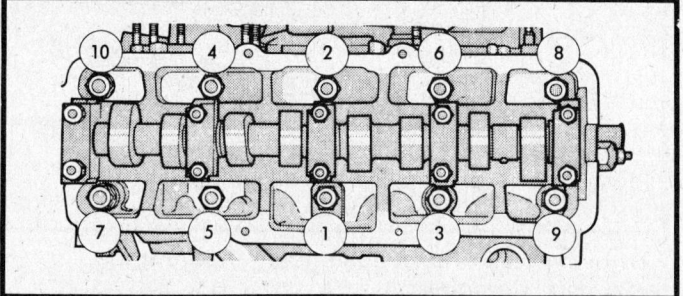

Cylinder head bolt tightening sequence—1.7L engine
(© Chrysler Corporation)

NOTE: Always use a new head gasket upon reinstallation.

1.7L ENGINE

NOTE: The cylinder head should be cold before removal.

1. Disconnect the battery.
2. Drain the cooling system.
3. Remove the air cleaner assembly.
4. Disconnect all lines, hoses and wires from the head, manifold and carburetor.
5. Disconnect the accelerator linkage.
6. Remove the distributor cap.
7. Disconnect the exhaust pipe.
8. Remove the carburetor.
9. Remove the intake and exhaust manifolds.
10. Remove the upper portion of the front cover.
11. Turn the engine by hand until all gear timing marks are aligned.
12. Loosen the drive belt tensioner and slip the belt off the camshaft gear.

NOTE: The camshaft timing mark on 1.7L engine is on the back of the gear and is properly positioned when it is in line with the left corner of the camshaft cover at the head.

13. If equipped with air conditioning, remove the compressor from the mounting brackets and support it out of the way with tie wires. Remove the mounting brackets from the head.
14. Remove the valve cover, gaskets and seals.
15. Remove head bolts in reverse order of the tightening sequence.
16. Lift off the head and discard the gasket.
17. Installation is the reverse of removal. Make certain all gasket surfaces are thoroughly cleaned and are free of deep nicks or scratches. Always use new gaskets and seals.
18. The word "OBEN" (top) on the 1.7L engine head gasket faces up. Never reuse a gasket or seal, even if it looks good.
19. When positioning the head on the block, insert bolts 8 and 10 to align the head. Tighten bolts in sequence to 30 ft. lbs., tighten again to 60 ft. lbs. Retighten all bolts in proper sequence another $\frac{1}{4}$ (90°) turn.
20. Make sure all timing marks are aligned before installing the drive belt. The drive belt is correctly tensioned when it can be twisted 90° with the thumb and index finger midway between the camshaft and the intermediate shaft.

2.2L/2.5L ENGINES

—————— **CAUTION** ——————
Do not perform this operation on a warm engine. Remove the head bolts in reverse of installation sequence shown. Loosen evenly in several steps. Do not attempt to slide the cylinder head off of the block. Lift the head straight up and off of the engine block.

1. Disconnect the negative battery cable. Drain the cooling system.

CHRYSLER CORPORATION
FRONT WHEEL DRIVE CARS

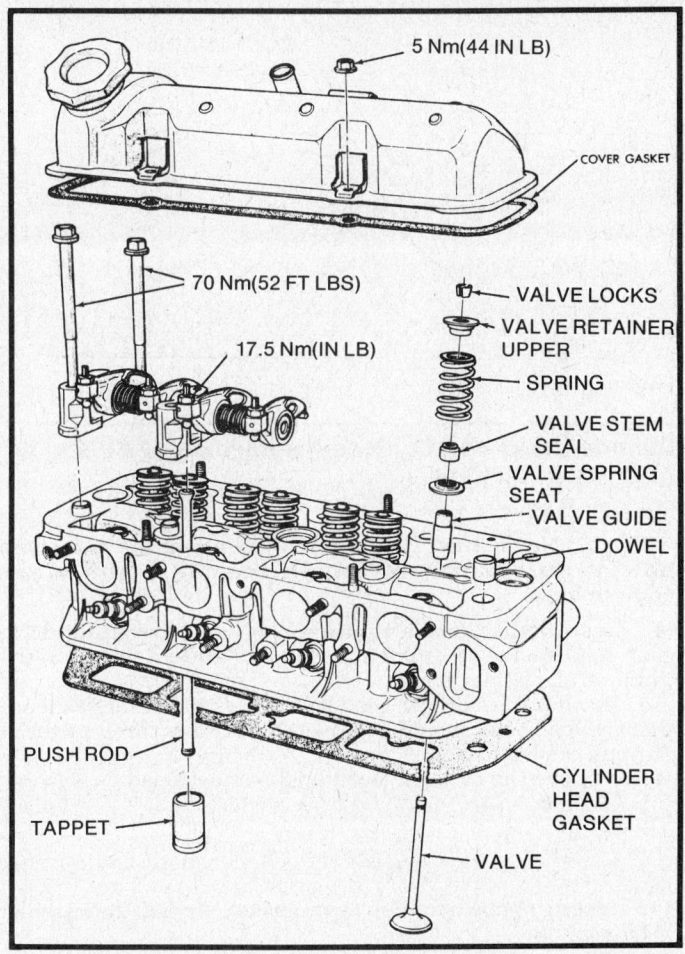

Exploded view of cylinder head assemby—1.6L engine
(© Chrysler Corporation)

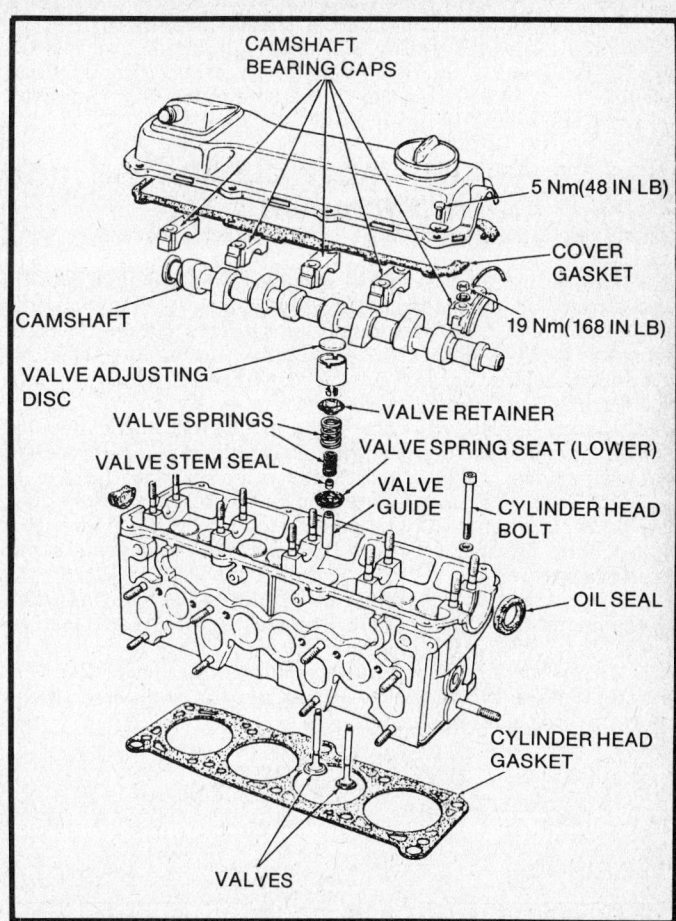

Exploded view cylinder head assembly—1.7L engine
(© Chrysler Corporation)

2. Remove the air cleaner assembly. Mark the various hoses for installation identification.
3. Disconnect all lines, hoses, wiring harnesses, etc. from the manifold, carburetor and cylinder head.
4. Disconnect the accelerator linkage. Remove the carburetor. Disconnect the converter and exhaust pipe. Remove the intake and exhaust manifolds.
5. Remove the upper part of the timing case (front cover).
6. Turn the engine by hand until all gear timing marks line up (engine at TDC, No. 1 piston).
7. Loosen the drive belt tensioner and slip the timing belt off of the camshaft gear.
8. If the car is equipped with air conditioning, remove the compressor and mounting brackets, place out of the way. Do not disconnect any of the compressor lines unless the system is safely bled of freon.
9. Remove the valve cover, gaskets and seals. Remove the head bolts in the reverse order of the tightening sequence.
10. Lift off the cylinder head, clean all gasket surfaces.

NOTE: The cylinder head bolt size has been increased in 1986 and later 2.2L/2.5L engines from 10mm to 11mm, which allows a greater bolt torque and better gasket sealing. This change may be found on certain 1985 2.2L models as a running production change. The new 11mm bolt has a number "11" on the bolt head. DO NOT MIX THE TWO BOLTS IN THE SAME CYLINDER HEAD. Use the size cylinder head bolts that are required with the engine.

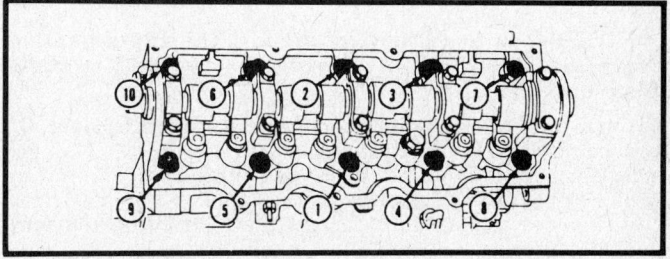

Head bolt tightening sequence—2.2L engine
(© Chrysler Corporation)

Undersized bolts can cause the cylinder block bolt holes to strip out.

11. Installation is in the reverse order of removal. Refer to the timing belt replacement section to check camshaft timing. Make sure all gasket surfaces are cleaned and free of deep nicks or scratches. Always install new gaskets and seals. Tighten bolts in sequence, following 4 Step torque procedure:

   a. 30 ft. lbs. (41 Nm) 10mm bolts, 45 ft. lbs. (61 Nm) 11mm bolts

   b. 45 ft. lbs. (61 Nm) 10mm bolts, 65 ft. lbs. (88 Nm) 11mm bolts

   c. 45 ft. lbs. (61 Nm) 10mm bolts, 65 ft. lbs. (88 Nm) 11mm bolts

d. Both 10mm and 11mm bolts, additional ¼ turn

12. Make sure all timing marks are aligned before installing the drive belt. The drive belt is correctly tensioned when possible to twist 90° with the thumb and index finger midway between the cam and intermediate shafts.

SPRING HEIGHT, VALVE CLEARANCE AND DRY LASH

2.2L/2.5L ENGINE

1. Check installed height of springs. Measurement is to be taken from the lower edge of the valve spring to its upper edge. Do not include the spring seat or retainer flange. Correct height is 1.62–1.68 in. (41.2–42.7mm). If seats have been reground, an additional spring seat may be required to maintain correct installed spring height.

2. Install adjusters, rocker arms (in order) and camshaft. Check for clearance between the projecting ears (either side of valve tip) of the rocker arms and the valve spring retainers. At least 0.020 in. (0.5mm) clearance must be present. if necessary, the rocker arm ears may be ground to obtain this clearance.

3. Check dry lash. Dry lash is the amount of clearance that exists between
the base circle of an installed cam and the rocker arm pad when the adjuster is completely collapsed. Specified dry lash is 0.024–0.060 in. (0.62–1.52mm).

4. Drain the adjuster of oil to perform this check. Refill before final assembly and allow 10 minutes for adjusters to bleed down before rotating cam.

CYLINDER HEAD

Removal

2.6L ENGINE

--- **CAUTION** ---

Do not perform this operation on a warm engine. Remove the head bolts in sequence, in several Steps. Loosen the head bolts evenly, not one at a time. Do not attempt to slide the cylinder head off the block, as it is located with dowel pins. Lift the head straight up and off the block.

NOTE: It is necessary to support the engine and remove the motor mount in order to remove the engine front cover.

1. Disconnect the battery and drain the cooling system. Disconnect the upper radiator hose.
2. Remove the breather hoses and purge hose.
3. Remove the air cleaner and fuel line.
4. Remove the vacuum hose at the distributor and purge control valve.
5. Disconnect the spark plug wires after marking them for reinstallation.
6. Remove the distributor cap and distributor by removing the retainer nut and pulling the unit out.
7. Disconnect the heater hose at the intake manifold.
8. Disconnect the water temperature gauge unit wire.
9. Place No. 1 piston on the TDC position to take pressure off the fuel pump rocker arm. Disconnect the fuel hoses and plug the line leading to the gas tank to prevent fuel leakage.
10. Remove the fuel pump mounting nuts or bolts and remove the pump assembly. Remove the insulator and gaskets.
11. Disconnect the exhaust pipe at the exhaust manifold flange.
12. Remove the rocker cover.
13. Remove its breather and semi-circular seal.
14. After slightly loosening the camshaft sprocket bolt, turn the crankshaft until No. 1 piston is at TDC on compression stroke (both valves closed).

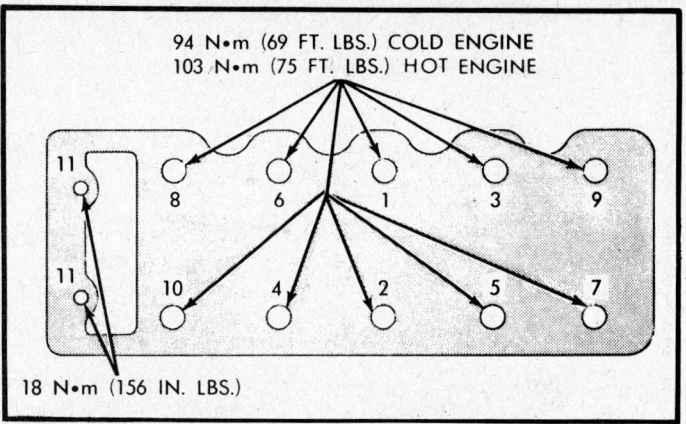

Cylinder head bolt tightening sequence—2.6L engine
(© Chrysler Corporation)

NOTE: Never turn the engine over using the camshaft bolt; it puts undue strain on the chain and other components.

15. Remove the camshaft sprocket bolt and distributor drive gear. Remove the camshaft sprocket and allow it to rest in the chain on the holder below.
16. Remove the cylinder head bolts in reverse of the sequence shown. Head bolts should be loosened in two or three stages to prevent head warpage.
17. Remove the cylinder head and cylinder head gasket.

Installation

1. Clean all gasket surfaces of cylinder block and cylinder head.
2. Install a new cylinder head gasket. Install the cylinder head assembly.

NOTE: Do not apply sealant to the head gasket and do not reuse an old head gasket. The head gasket has the number "54" stamped at the front of the upper surface.

3. Install the ten cylinder head bolts. Starting at top center, tighten all cylinder head bolts to specifications.
4. Tighten the two front bolts to 11–15 ft.lb.
5. Verify that No. 1 cylinder is at TDC. Align the dowel pin in the end of the camshaft sprocket with the groove in the top of the front camshaft bearing cap and install the camshaft sprocket and chain while pulling up on the sprocket.
6. Install the distributor drive gear and the sprocket bolt.
7. Turn the crankshaft about 90° back, and tighten the camshaft sprocket bolt back to 37–43 ft.lb. Very slowly turn the engine over two times to make sure the valve timing is correct. If the engine locks at a certain point in these two revolutions, the valve timing is not correct. Repeat timing Steps.

--- **CAUTION** ---

At this point, do not turn the engine over using the starter. If the valve timing is off, several of the valves could be bent.

8. Install the breather and semicircular seal to the cylinder head after applying sealant to surface contact points. Install the rocker cover with a new gasket.
9. Connect the exhaust pipe to the exhaust manifold flange. Tighten the bolts to 11–18 ft.lb.
10. Put No. 1 cylinder at TDC and install the fuel pump with a new gasket and insulator. Connect all hoses.
11. Connect the water temperature gauge unit wire. Connect the heater hose to the intake manifold.
12. Install the distributor and spark plug cables.

CHRYSLER CORPORATION
FRONT WHEEL DRIVE CARS

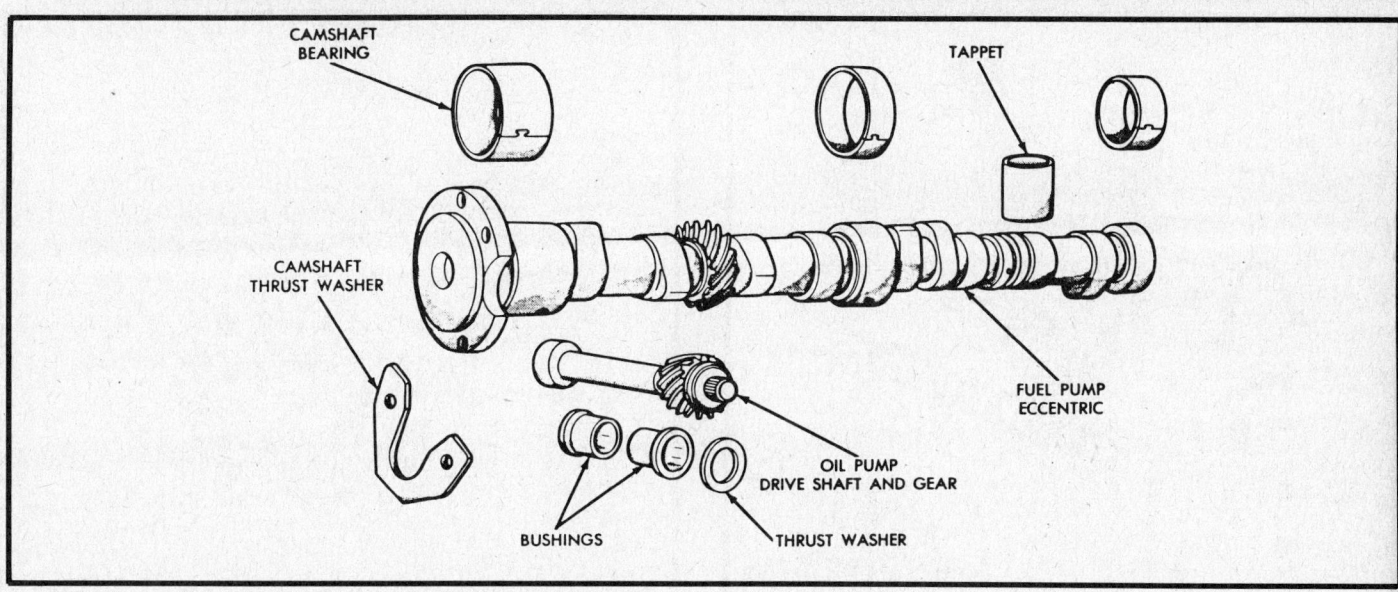

Camshaft and components—1.6L engine (© Chrysler Corporation)

13. Connect the vacuum hose to the distributor and purge control valve.
14. Connect the upper radiator hose and fill the cooling system with coolant.

CAMSHAFT

Removal and Installation
1.6L ENGINE
1. Remove the oil pump.
2. Remove distributor and drive housing. Mark crankcase in relation to drive slot.
3. Remove distributor drive from driveshaft spindle with magnet.
4. Remove shaft drive gear circlip.

NOTE: A shop towel inserted in the cavity around the gear will help insure that the circlip does not fall into the crankcase during removal or installation.

5. Tap driveshaft toward pump side of crankcase until gear is free from the spline. Remove the gear.
6. Remove driveshaft from the pump side of the crankcase.
7. Remove fuel pump and tappets. Identify tappets to ensure installation in original position.
8. Remove camshaft thrust plate.
9. Carefully remove camshaft.
10. Installation is the reverse of removal. Tighten thrust plate bolts to 132 inch lbs. Check camshaft end play (0.004–0.008 in.).

NOTE: When installing new camshaft or tappets, add one pint of Chrysler Crankcase Conditioner, Part Number 3419130 or equivalent, to engine oil. Retain the oil mixture for a minimum of 500 miles. When replacing camshaft, all of the tappets should be replaced. However, should the original tappets be used, the bottom face of the tappets must be inspected for negative crowning, using a straight edge. If any negative crown (dishing) is observed, the tappet in question must be replaced.

Removal and Installation
1.7L ENGINE
1. Remove the timing belt cover.

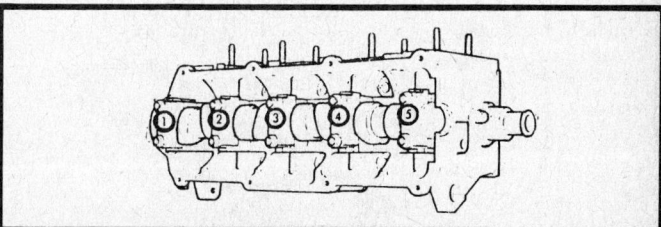

Camshaft bearing caps—1.7L engine
(© Chrysler Corporation)

2. Remove the timing belt.
3. Remove the air cleaner assembly.
4. Remove the valve cover.
5. Remove the Nos. 1, 3, and 5 camshaft bearing caps.
6. Loosen caps 2 and 4 diagonally and in increments.
7. Lift the camshaft out.
8. Lubricate the camshaft journals and lobes with engine assembly lubricant and position it in the head.
9. Install a new oil seal.
10. Install the Nos. 1, 3, 5 bearing caps and torque the nuts to 14 ft. lbs.
11. Install the Nos. 2 and 4 caps and diagonally torque the nuts to 14 ft. lbs.

--- CAUTION ---
All bearing caps are slightly offset. They should be installed so the numbers on the cap read right side up from the drivers seat.

12. Position a dial indicator so that the feeler touches the front end of the camshaft. Check for end play. Play should not exceed 0.006 in.
13. Place a new seal on the No. 1 bearing cap. If necessary, replace the end plug in the head.
14. Follow the procedures under Timing Belt Removal and Installation for belt installation and timing.
15. Check the valve clearance and ignition timing.

Removal and Installation
2.2L/2.5L ENGINE
1. Remove the timing belt.

2-61

CHRYSLER CORPORATION
FRONT WHEEL DRIVE CARS

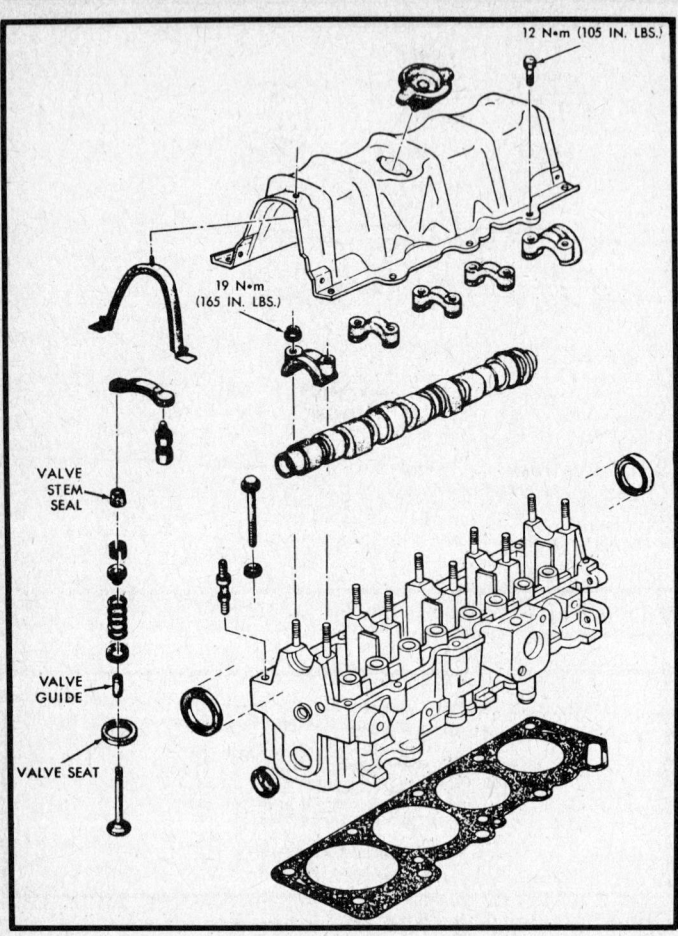

Exploded view of cylinder head assembly—2.2L engine
(© Chrysler Corporation)

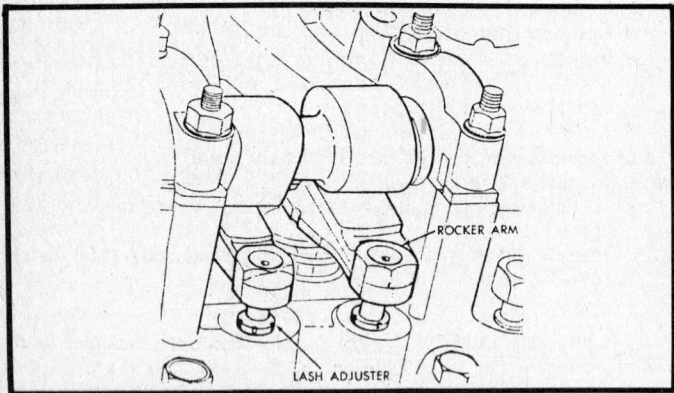

Rocker arm and lash adjuster—2.2L engine
(© Chrysler Corporation)

2. Mark the rocker arms for installation identification.
3. Loosen the camshaft bearing capnuts several turns each.
4. Using a wooden or rubber mallet, rap the rear of the camshaft a few times to break it loose.
5. Remove the capnuts and caps being very careful that the camshaft does not cock. Cocking the camshaft could cause irreparable damage to the bearings.
6. Check all oil holes for blocking.
7. Install the bearing caps with No. 1 at the timing belt end

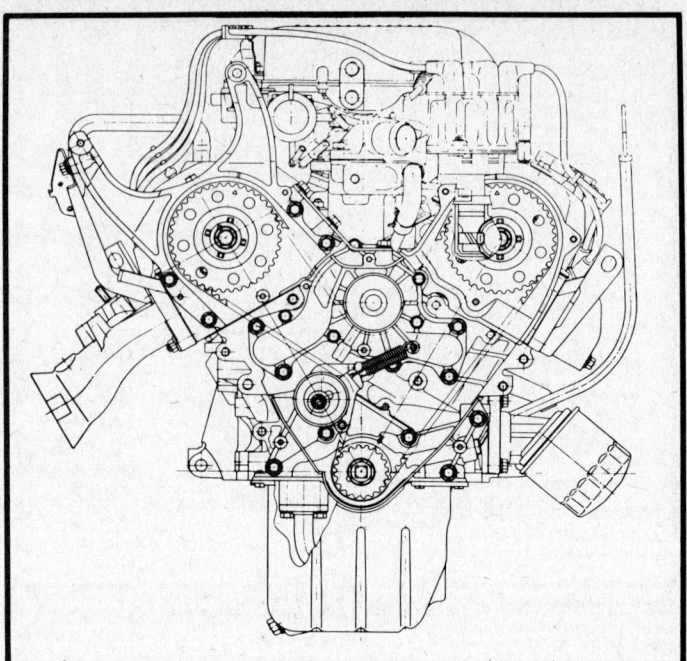

3.0L V6 engine showing camshaft and water pump drive (©Chrysler Corporation)

and No. 5 at the transmission end. Caps are numbered and have arrows facing forward. Cap nut torque is 14 ft. lb.
8. Apply RTV silicone gasket material to numbers one and five bearing caps.
9. Install the bearing caps BEFORE the seals are installed.
10. The rest of the procedure is the reverse of disassembly.

Camshaft Endplay Check

2.2L/2.5L ENGINES
1. Move the camshaft as far forward as possible.
2. Install a dial indicator.
3. Zero the indicator, push the camshaft backward, then forward as far as possible and record the play. Maximum end play should be 0.006 in. for 2.2L engines up to and including 1985 models and 0.005–0.013 in. end play for 1986 and later 2.2L/2.5L engines.

Removal and Installation

2.6L ENGINES
1. Remove the breather hoses and purge hose.
2. Remove the air cleaner and fuel line.
3. Remove the fuel pump. Remove the distributor.
4. Disconnect the spark plug cables.
5. Remove the rocker cover.
6. Remove the breather and semi-circular seal.
7. After slightly loosening the camshaft sprocket bolt, turn the crankshaft until No. 1 piston is at TDC on compression stroke (both valves closed).
8. Remove the camshaft sprocket bolt and distributor drive gear.
9. Remove the camshaft sprocket with chain and allow it to rest on the camshaft sprocket holder.
10. Remove the camshaft bearing cap tightening bolts. Do not remove the front and rear bearing cap bolts altogether, but keep them inserted in the bearing caps so that the rocker assembly can be removed as a unit.
11. Remove the rocker arms, rocker shafts and bearing caps as an assembly.

CHRYSLER CORPORATION
FRONT WHEEL DRIVE CARS

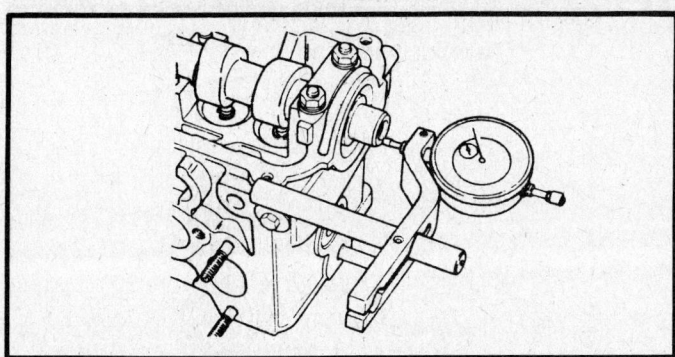

Checking camshaft end play—2.2L engine
(© Chrysler Corporation)

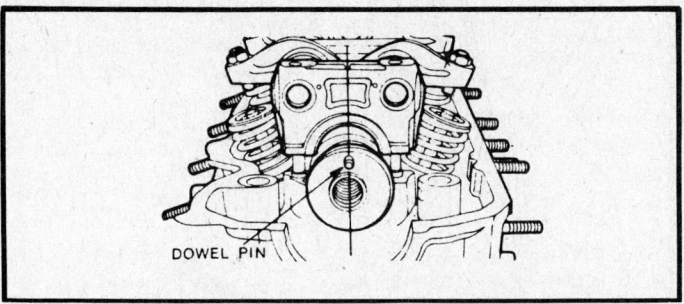

Install the camshaft on 2.6 engines by aligning the dowel pin with the notch in the top of the front bearing cap
(© Chrysler Corporation)

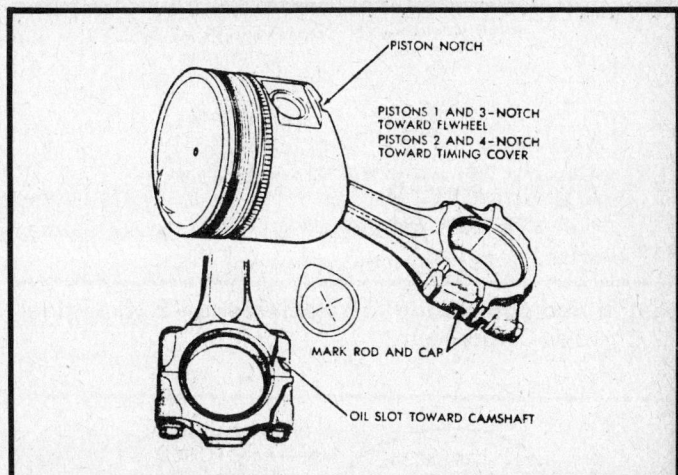

Piston and connecting rod positioning—1.6L engine
(© Chrysler Corporation)

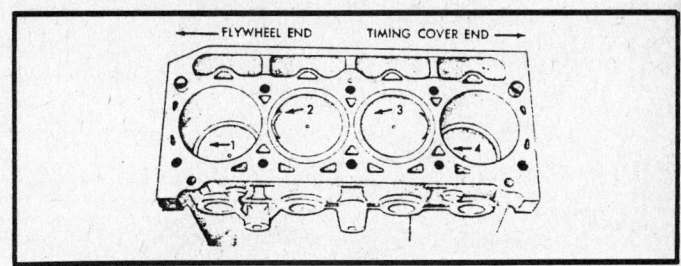

Cylinder and piston identification—1.6L engine
(© Chrysler Corporation)

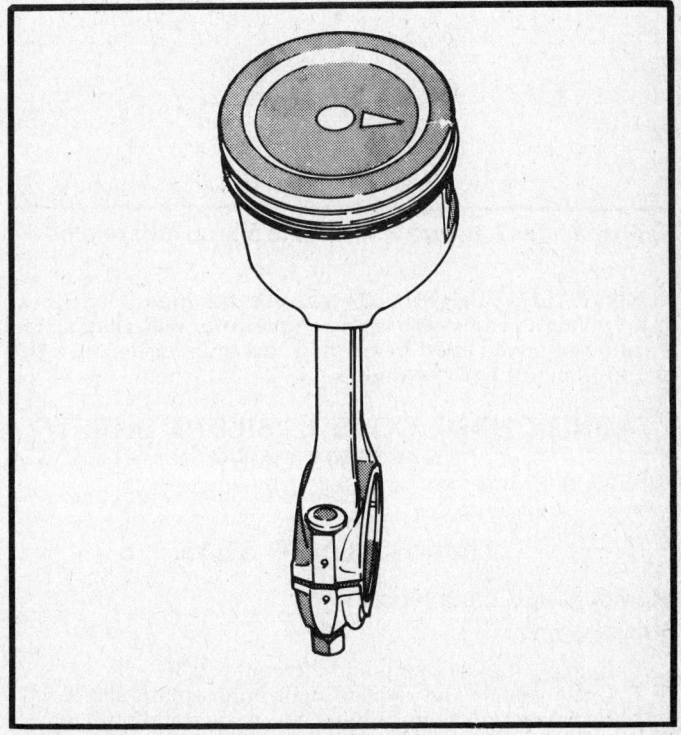

Piston positioning with mark towards timing chain—2.6L engine (© Chrysler Corporation)

12. Remove the camshaft.
13. Installation is the reverse of removal. Lubricate the camshaft lobes and bearings and fit camshaft into head. Install the assembled rocker arm shaft assembly. The camshaft should be positioned so that the dowel pin on the front end of the cam is in the 12 o'clock position and in line with the notch in the top of the front bearing cap.
14. Tightens the camshaft bearing cap bolts in the following order to 85 inch lbs.
    a. No. 3 cap
    b. No. 2 cap
    c. No. 4 cap
    d. Front cap
    e. Rear cap
15. Repeat Step 14 and increase the torque to 175 inch lbs.

PISTONS AND CONNECTING RODS

ALL ENGINES

The piston crown is marked with an arrow which must point toward the timing belt or chain end of the engine when installed. On 1.7L and 2.2L engines, the connecting rod and cap are marked with rectangular forge marks which must be mated when assembled and which must be on the intermediate shaft side of the engine when installed.

In the 1.6L engine, the No. 1 and No. 3 pistons are installed with the piston skirt notch facing the flywheel, while No. 2 and No. 4 piston skirt notches are toward the timing cover.

Lighter connecting rods was a production change during the 1985 model year on the 2.2L engine. Consequently, some 1985 2.2L engines may not have the lighter connecting rods while others will. The engines that have the lighter connecting rods will have the letters "LW" ink-stamped on the engine block core plug, nearest the distributor. The lightweight rods will have the letters "LW" cast in the shank of the rod.

CHRYSLER CORPORATION
FRONT WHEEL DRIVE CARS

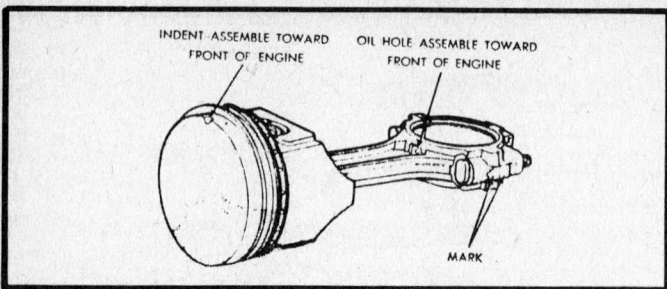

Piston and connecting rod positioning—2.2L engine
(© Chrysler Corporation)

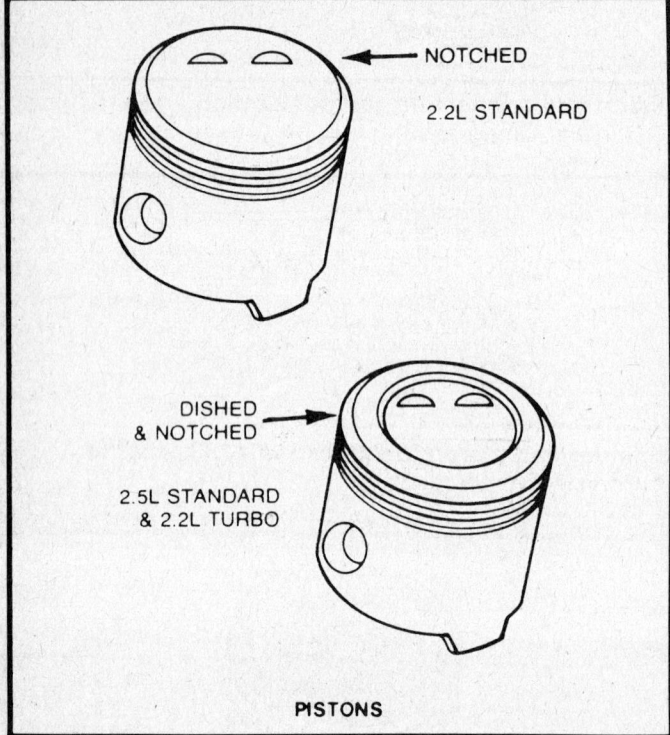

1986 and later 2.2L and 2.5L engine piston differences

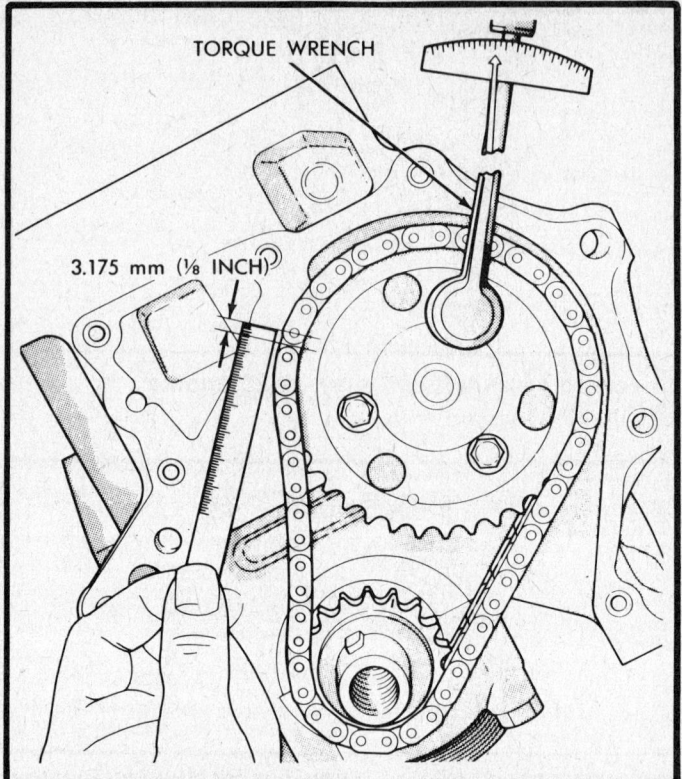

Measuring timing chain stretch—1.6L engine
(© Chrysler Corporation)

NOTE: Lightweight rods cannot be mixed with the heavyweight rods, as engine vibrations will result. The connecting rods must be used in sets only, either all lightweights or all heavyweights.

TIMING CHAIN, COVER, "SILENT SHAFTS" AND TENSIONER

TIMING COVER SEAL

Removal and Installation

1.6L ENGINE

1. Remove the air pump and alternator belts.
2. Raise vehicle and remove right inner splash shield.
3. Remove crankshaft pulley bolt, washer and pulley.
4. Install seal remover Tool C–4762–1 over crankshaft nose and turn tightly into seal.
5. Tighten thrust screw to remove seal.

6. Installation is the reverse of removal. Use seal installation tool C–4761 when installing the new seal. Tighten crankshaft pulley bolt 110 ft. lbs.

TIMING COVER/CHAIN

Removal and Installation

1.6L ENGINE

1. Remove the air pump and alternator belts.
2. Raise vehicle and remove right inner splash shield.
3. Remove crankshaft pulley bolt, washer and pulley.
4. Drain the cooling system through water pump drain plug. Remove water pump to timing cover hose.
5. Raise slightly and carefully support engine (timing cover end).
6. Remove bolts securing engine mount bracket to timing cover and block.
7. Remove crankcase extension to cover and cover to block screws. Two cover block screws pass through tubular locating dowels. Make sure dowels do not fall into crankcase extension during cover removal. Remove timing cover.
8. Rotate camshaft sprocket so that one (of three) bolt heads is located at the top of a centerline drawn through the camshaft and crankshaft sprockets.
9. With torque wrench and socket installed on the top bolt head, apply torque in the direction of crankshaft rotation to take up slack; 30 ft lbs. cylinder head installed or 15 ft. lbs. cylinder head removed. Do not allow crankshaft to rotate during this procedure.
10. Holding a ruler even with the edge of a chain link, apply the same torque, described above, in the reverse direction and note amount of chain movement. If chain movement exceeds ($\frac{1}{8}$ in.), install new chain.

CHRYSLER CORPORATION
FRONT WHEEL DRIVE CARS

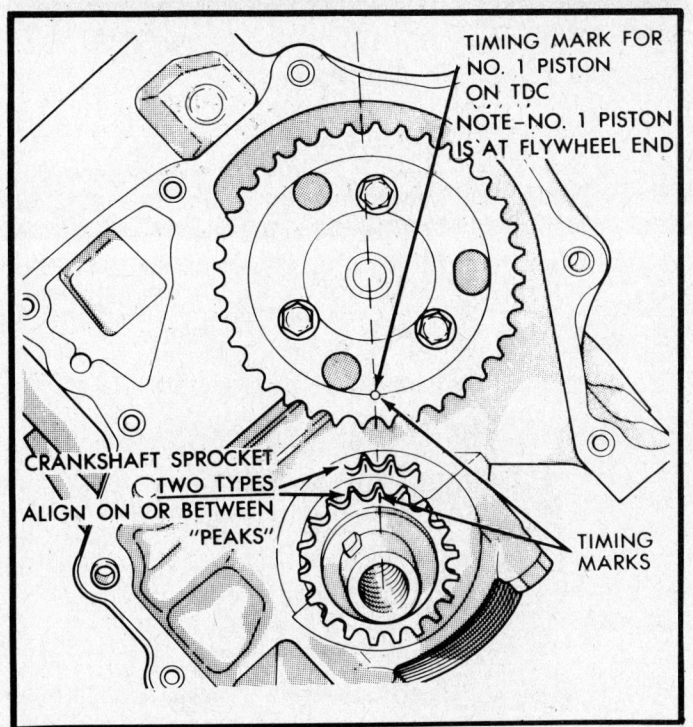

Timing mark alignment, 1.6L engine. Note two different types of sprockets used and their markings
(© Chrysler Corporation)

11. Remove the timing gear bolts, timing gear, and chain.
12. Installation is the reverse of removal. Align the timing marks. Torque the camshaft sprocket bolts 113 inch lbs.

2.6L ENGINES

NOTE: All 2.6L engines are equipped with two "Silent Shafts" which cancel the vertical vibrating force of the engine and the secondary vibrating forces, which include the sideways rocking of the engine due to the turning direction of the crankshaft and other rolling parts. The shafts are driven by a duplex chain and are turned by the crankshaft. The silent shaft chain assembly is mounted in front of the timing chain assembly and must be removed to service the timing chain.

1. Remove the battery cables.
2. Drain the radiator and remove it from the vehicle.
3. Remove the cylinder head.
4. Remove the cooling fan, spacer, water pump pulley and belt.
5. Remove the alternator and water pump.
6. Raise the front of the vehicle and support it on jack stands.
7. Remove the oil pan and screen. Remove the crankshaft pulley.
8. Remove the timing case cover.
9. Remove the chain guides, side (A), top (B), bottom (C), from the "B" chain (outer).
10. Remove the locking bolts from the "B" chain sprockets.
11. Remove the crankshaft sprocket, silent shaft sprocket and the outer chain.
12. Remove the crankshaft and camshaft sprockets and the timing chain.
13. Remove the camshaft sprocket holder and the chain guides, both left and right.

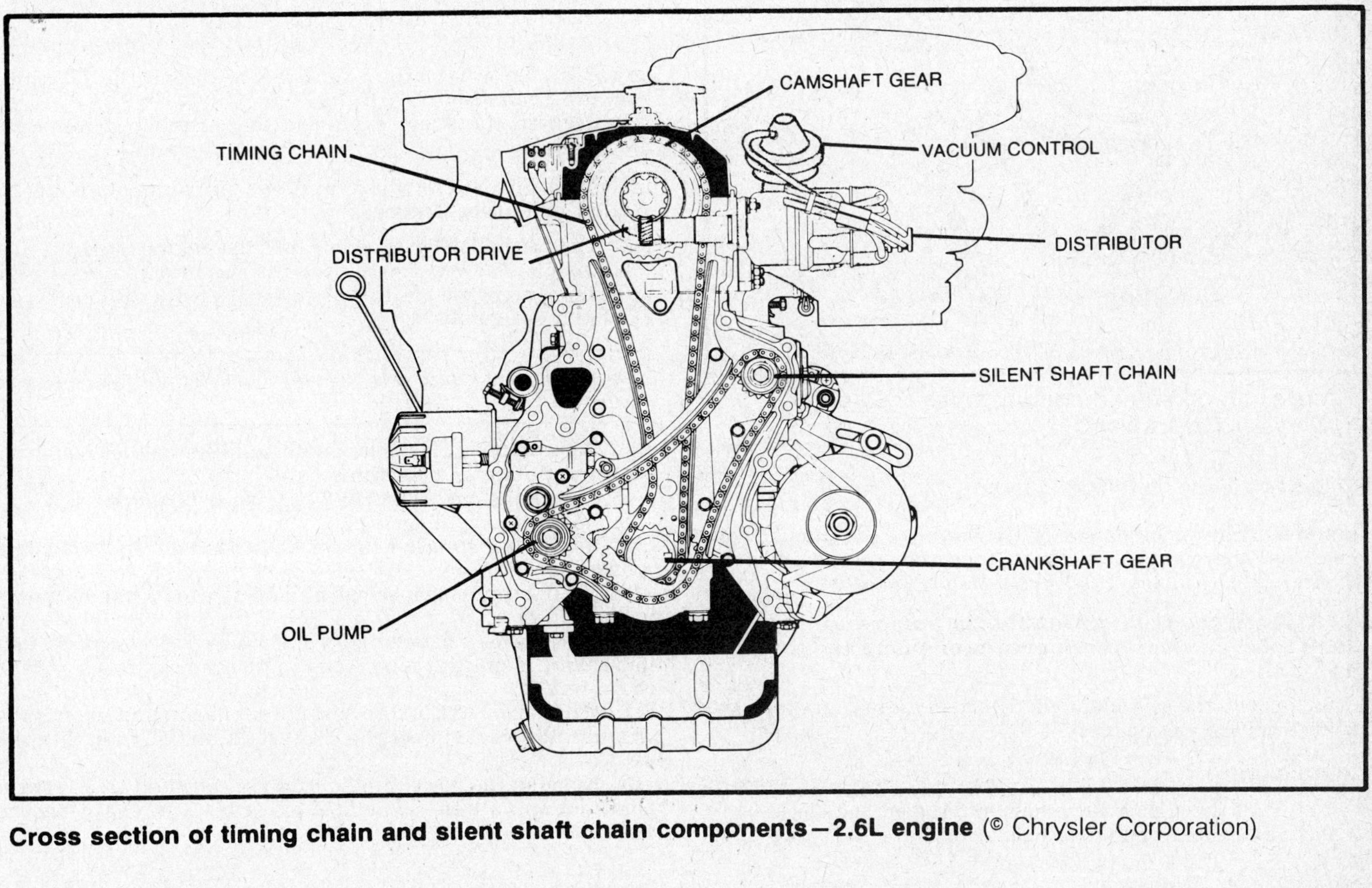

Cross section of timing chain and silent shaft chain components—2.6L engine (© Chrysler Corporation)

2-65

SECTION 2
CHRYSLER CORPORATION
FRONT WHEEL DRIVE CARS

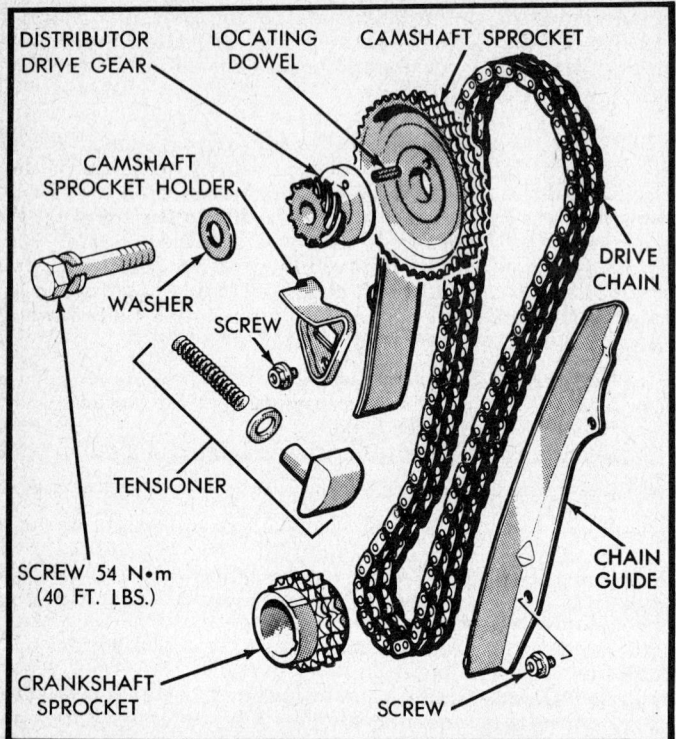

Camshaft drive chain (© Chrysler Corporation)

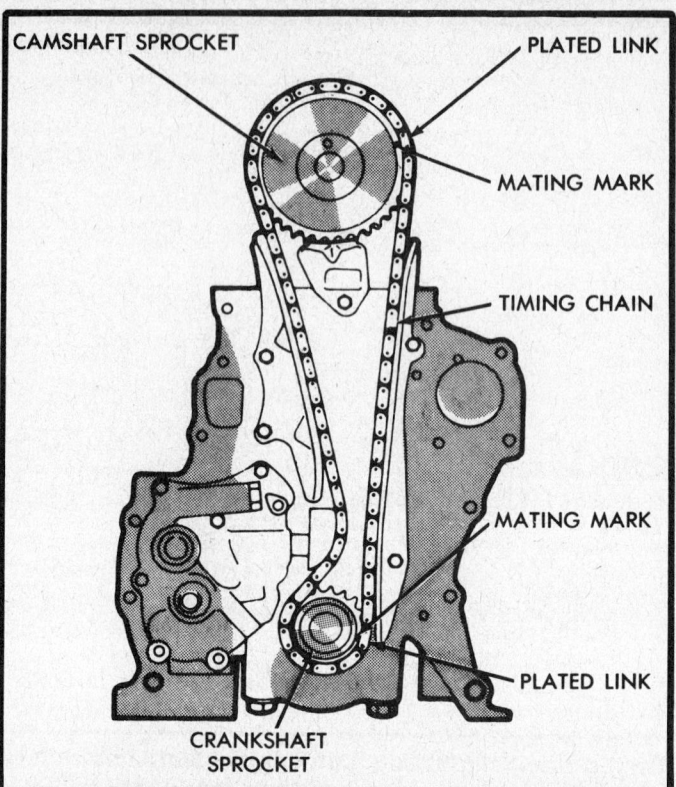

Installing and adjusting timing chain—2.6L engine (© Chrysler Corporation)

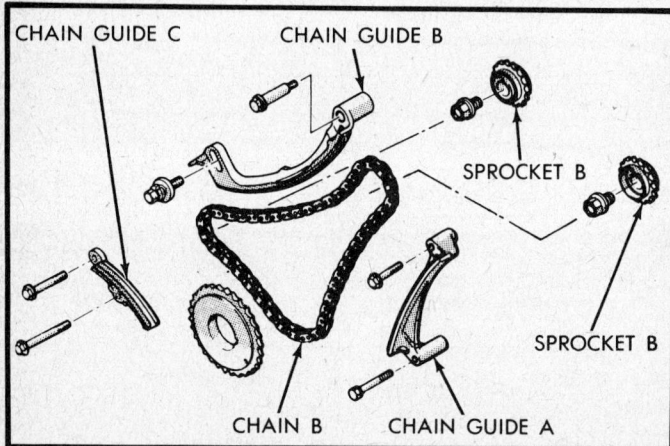

Silent shaft chain and components—2.6L engine (© Chrysler Corporation)

14. Remove the tensioner.
15. Remove the sleeve from the oil pump. Remove the oil pump by first removing the bolt locking the oil pump driven gear and the right silent shaft, then remove the oil pump mounting bolts. Remove the silent shaft from the engine block.

NOTE: If the bolt locking the oil pump and the silent shaft is hard to loosen, remove the oil pump and the shaft as a unit.

16. Remove the left silent shaft thrust washer and take the shaft from the engine block.

Installation

1. Install the right silent shaft into the engine block.
2. Install the oil pump assembly. Do not lose the woodruff key from the end of the silent shaft. Torque the oil pump mounting bolts from 6–7 ft. lbs.
3. Tighten the silent shaft and the oil pump driven gear mounting bolt.

NOTE: The silent shaft and the oil pump can be installed as a unit, if necessary.

4. Install the left silent shaft into the engine block.
5. Install a new O-ring on the thrust plate and install the unit into the engine block, using a pair of bolts without heads, as alignment guides.

— **CAUTION** —
If the thrust plate is turned to align the bolt holes, the O-ring may be damaged.

6. Remove the guide bolts and install the regular bolts into the thrust plate and tighten securely.
7. Rotate the crankshaft to bring No. 1 piston to TDC.
8. Install the cylinder head.
9. Install the sprocket holder and the right and left chain guides.
10. Install the tensioner spring and sleeve on the oil pump body.
11. Install the camshaft and crankshaft sprockets on the timing chain, aligning the sprocket punch marks to the plated chain links.
12. While holding the sprocket and chain as a unit, install the crankshaft sprocket over the crankshaft and align it with the keyway.
13. Keeping the dowel pin hole on the camshaft in a vertical position, install the camshaft sprocket and chain on the camshaft.

CHRYSLER CORPORATION
FRONT WHEEL DRIVE CARS

NOTE: The sprocket timing mark and the plated chain link should be at 2 to 3 o'clock position when correctly installed.

CAUTION
The chain must be aligned in the right and left chain guides with the tensioner pushing against the chain. The tension for the inner chain is determined by spring tension.

14. Install the crankshaft sprocket for the outer or "B" chain.
15. Install the two silent shaft sprockets and align the punched mating marks with the plated links of the chain.
16. Holding the two shaft sprockets and chain, install the outer chain in alignment with the mark on the crankshaft sprocket. Install the shaft sprockets on the silent shaft and the oil pump driver gear. Install the lock bolts and recheck the alignment of the punch marks and the plated links.
17. Temporarily install the chain guides, Side (A), Top (B) and Bottom (C).

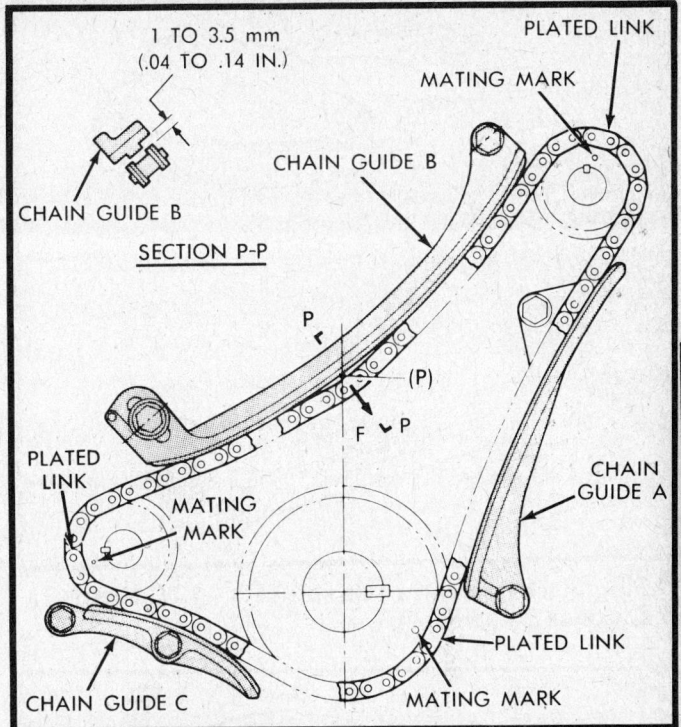

Silent chain timing marks (© Chrysler Corporation)

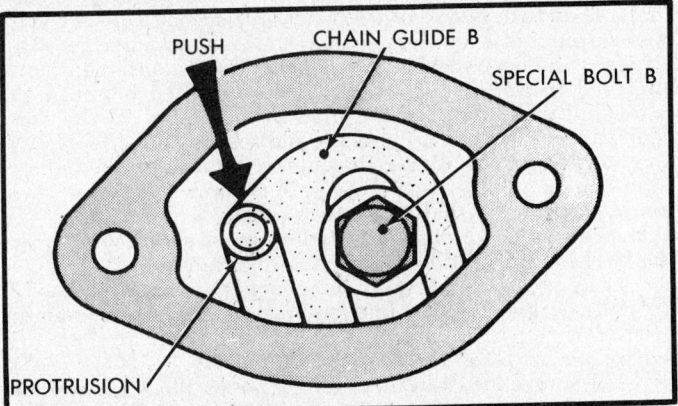

Timing chain adjustment (© Chrysler Corporation)

18. Tighten Side (A) chain guide securely.
19. Tighten Bottom (B) chain guide securely.
20. Adjust the position of the Top (B) chain guide, after shaking the right and left sprockets to collect any chain slack, so that when the chain is moved toward the center, the clearance between the chain guide and the chain links will be approximately 9/64 in. Tighten the Top (B) chain guide bolts.
21. Install the timing chain cover using a new gasket, being careful not to damage the front seal.
22. Install the oil screen and the oil pan, using a new gasket. Torque the bolts to 4.5–5.5 ft. lbs.
23. Install the crankshaft pulley, alternator and accessory belts, and the distributor.
24. Install the oil pressure switch, if removed, and install the battery ground cable.
25. Install the fan blades, radiator, fill the system with coolant and start the engine.

TIMING COVER AND BELT
Removal and Installation
1.7L ENGINE
1. Disconnect the battery.
2. Remove the air compressor, alternator, power steering pump and drive belts and set to one side.
3. Raise the vehicle and remove the splash fender shield.
4. Remove the idler pulley assembly.
5. Remove the crankshaft pulley.
6. Remove the lower timing belt cover.
7. Lower the vehicle and place a jack under the engine.

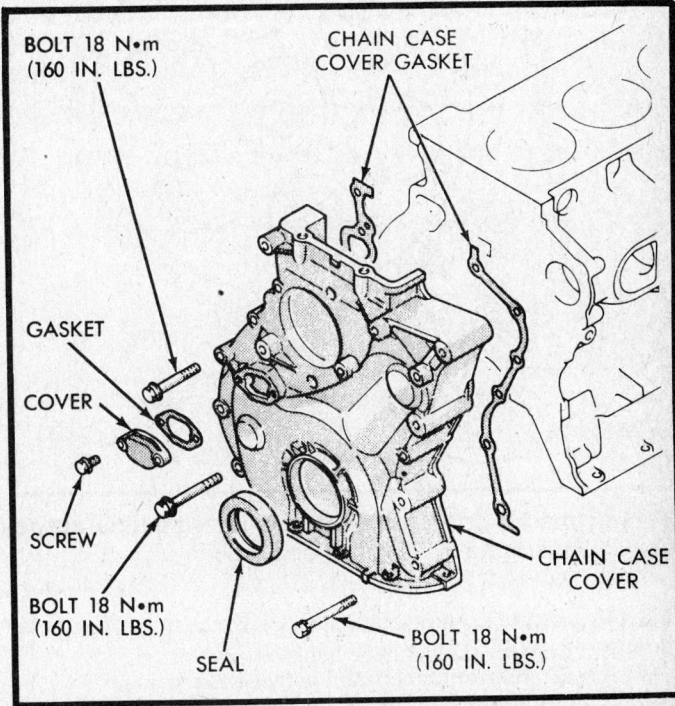

Chain case cover—2.6L engine (© Chrysler Corporation)

8. Remove the right engine mounting bolt and raise the engine slightly.
9. Loosen the timing belt tensioner and remove the timing belt.
10. To install, turn the crankshaft and intermediate sprockets until both markings on the sprockets are aligned.

2-67

CHRYSLER CORPORATION
FRONT WHEEL DRIVE CARS

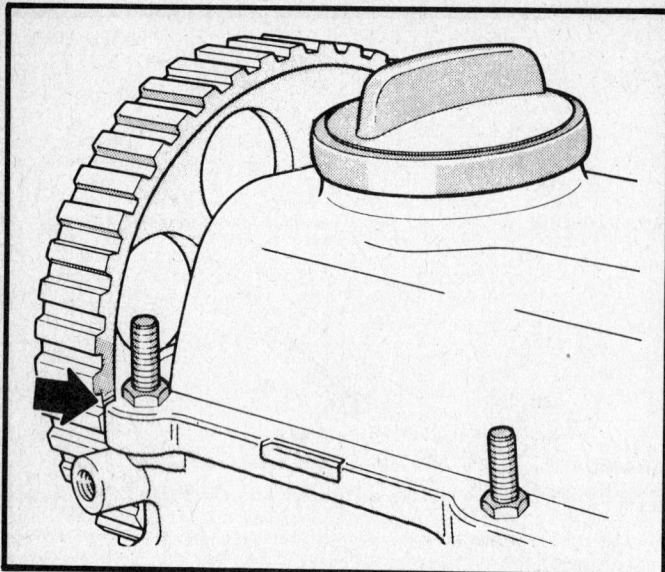

Timing marks on camshaft sprokets—1.7L engine
(© Chrysler Corporation)

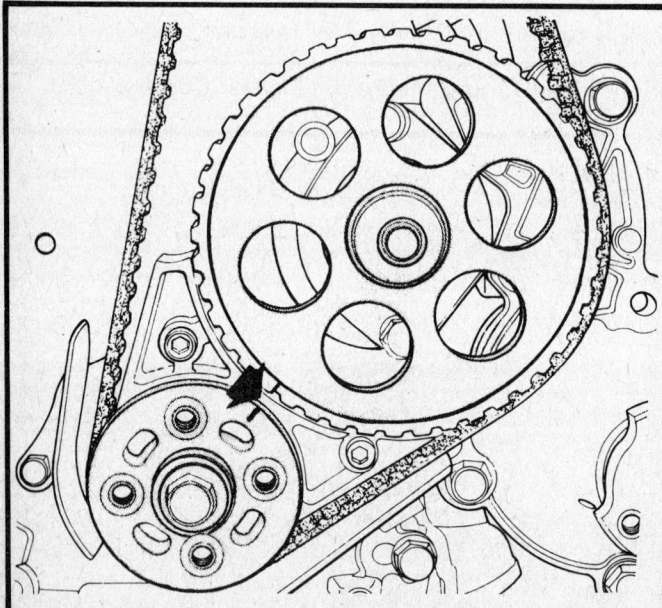

Timing marks on crankshaft and intermediate sprockets—1.7L engine (© Chrysler Corporation)

11. Turn the camshaft sprocket until the mark on the sprocket is in line with the cylinder head cover.
12. Install the timing belt and adjust the tension.
13. Remove the spark plugs and rotate the crank to TDC position.
14. Place a belt tension tool No. L-4502 horizontally on the large hex of the timing belt tensioner pulley and loosen the tensioner lock nut.
15. Reset the belt tension tool L-4502 index if necessary to have axis within 15° of horizontal.
16. Turn the engine clockwise from TDC two crank revolutions to TDC.
17. Tighten the locknut to 32 ft. lbs.

NOTE: If a whirring noise is heard from the timing belt with the engine running the belt is too tight.

18. The rest of the installation is the reverse of removal.

2.2L/2.5L ENGINE

With the engine in the vehicle, it is necessary to remove the right front wheel while supporting the body safely. Remove the special bolts (inverted Torx) from the belt pulley mounted to the crankshaft pulley. Remove the belt cover, the A/C compressor and set aside, without discharging the system. Remove the A/C bracket from the engine. Support the engine and remove the bolts from the top engine mount on the right side. The belt can then be removed and installed following the procedures outlined.

The 2.5L engine is equipped with a pair of dual counter-rotating balance shafts, below and on both sides of the crankshaft, at almost a center position.

The two counter-rotating eccentric balance shafts, interconnected by gears, are driven by a short chain from the crankshaft. They turn at two times the engine speed to offset the reciprocating mass of the pistons and connecting rods. This achieves the desired balancing effect. The balance shafts are enclosed in an aluminum housing, mounted beneath the crankshaft. The housing is bolted to the bottom of the main bearing webs of the engine block and rests in the oil supply of an enlarged oil pan. When the engine is running, the balance shafts pump oil out of the housing to minimize the drag which would occur if the shafts spun in the oil.

The timing belt removal procedure must be followed before the twin balance shaft assembly can be removed.

1. Remove the necessary components, such as the alternator and the air conditioning compressor. Remove the timing belt cover retaining bolts in both timing cover sections. Remove both halves of the cover and lay aside.
2. Remove the right inner fender panel. Place a jack under the engine and raise the engine slightly. Remove the right engine mounting bolt.
3. While holding the large hex on the tension pulley, loos-

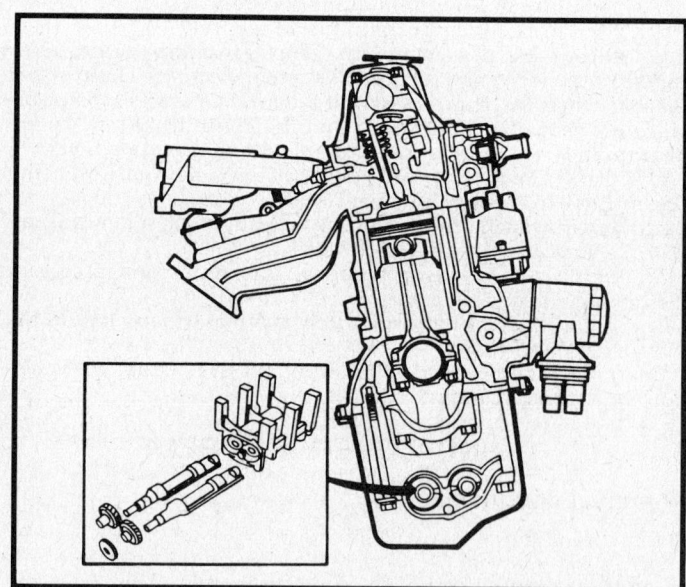

Front cross section of 1986 and later 2.5 liter engine with balance shaft assembly location and exploded view of balance shaft assembly
(© Chrysler Corporation)

CHRYSLER CORPORATION
FRONT WHEEL DRIVE CARS

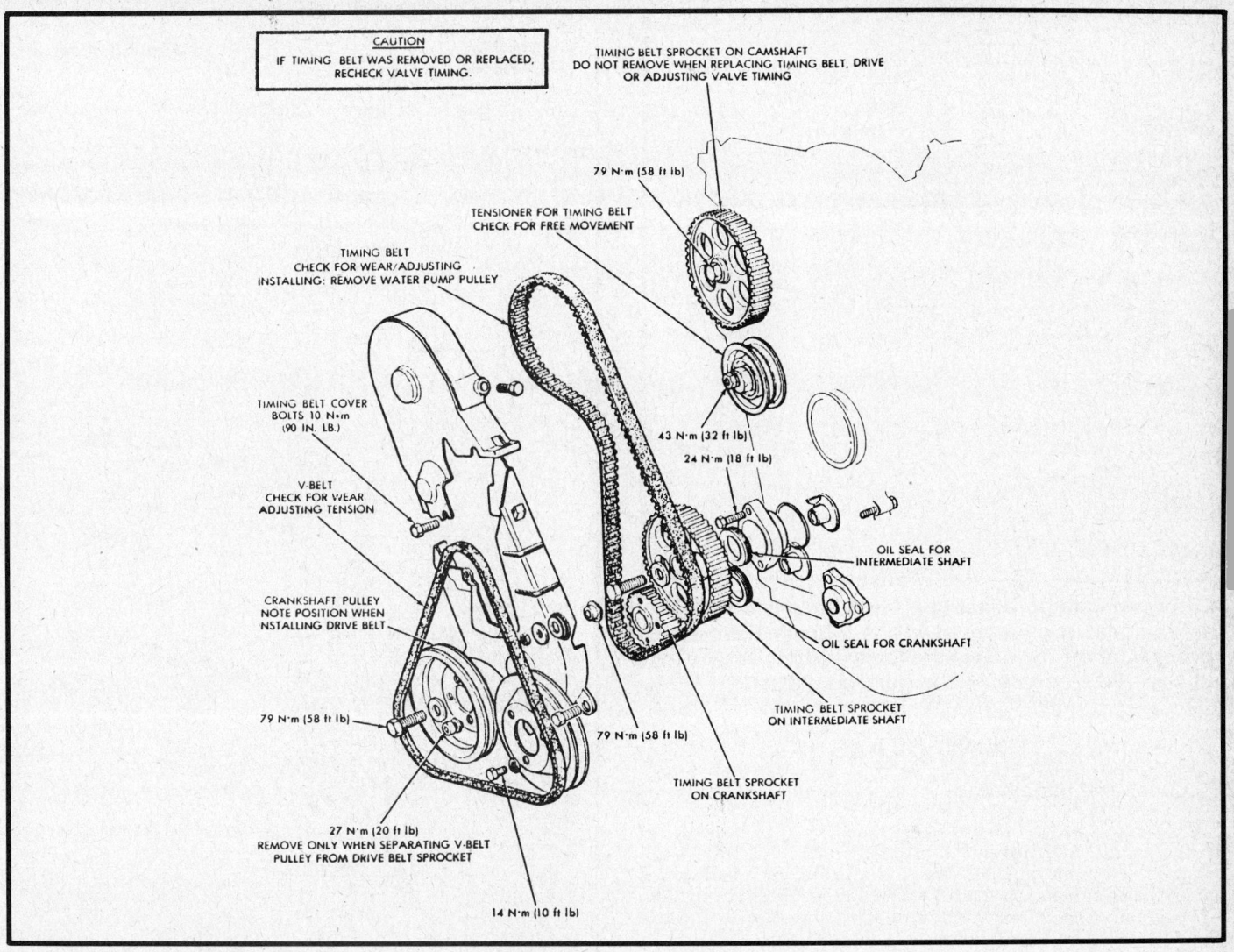

Timing belt, sprockets and oil seals—1.7L engine (© Chrysler Corporation)

en the pulley nut. Remove the belt from the tensioner.

4. Slide the belt off the three toothed pulleys.

NOTE: The crankshaft sprocket gear may be removed at this time with special puller tools. The crankshaft intermediate shaft and camshaft oil seals may also be removed at this time.

5. With the crankshaft pulley back on the crankshaft, turn the crankshaft and the intermediate shaft until the markings on the sprockets are in line. (bisecting an imaginary line between the bolt head of the crankshaft gear and the bolt head of the intermediate shaft gear).

---- CAUTION ----

If the timing marks are not perfectly aligned, poor engine performance and engine damage will result.

6. Turn the camshaft until the arrows on the hub are in line with No. 1 camshaft cap to the cylinder head line. The small hole must be in the center line of the engine.

NOTE: The center line of the engine will be canted to the left of vertical, when looking at the crankshaft/camshaft gear end of the engine.

7. Install the belt on the pulleys. If a weighted wrench is available, its axis must be within 15° of horizontal during the adjustment of the timing belt.

8. If a weighted wrench is not available, adjust the tensioner by turning the large tensioner hex to the right. Tension is correct when the belt can be twisted 90° with the thumb and forefinger, midway between the camshaft and intermediate pulleys.

9. Tighten the tensioner locknut.

10. Rotate the crankshaft two full revolutions and recheck the timing.

11. Install the timing belt cover.

NOTE: To check the timing with the timing belt cover installed, have the number one cylinder at the TDC position. Remove the cover timing hole plug. The small hole in the sprocket must be centered in the timing belt cover hole.

12. Install the remaining components and check the ignition timing.

CHRYSLER CORPORATION
FRONT WHEEL DRIVE CARS

Arrows on cam sprocket hub must be in line with No. 1 camshaft cap to cylinder head line, with small hole in the sprocket, at the top and in the top to bottom engine vertical line—2.2L engine (© Chrysler Corporation)

TIMING GEARS

Removal and Installation

1.7L ENGINE

The camshaft, intermediate shaft, and crankshaft pulleys are located by keys on their respective shafts and each is retained by a bolt. To remove any or all of the pulleys, first remove the timing belt cover and belt and then use the following procedure.

NOTE: When removing the crankshaft pulley, don't remove the four socket head bolts which retain the outer belt pulley to the timing belt pulley.

1. Remove the center bolt.
2. Either carefully pry off the pulley or use a gear puller tool to remove the pulley from the shaft.
3. Remove the pulley and key. The oil seal may now be carefully pried out. Install the new seal.
4. Install the pulley in the reverse order of removal.
5. Tighten the center bolt to 58 ft. lbs.
6. Install the timing belt, check valve timing, tension belt, and install the cover.

2.2L/2.5L ENGINE

1. Raise and support the car on jackstands.
2. Remove the right inner splash shield.
3. Remove the crankshaft pulley.
4. Unbolt and remove both halves of the timing belt cover.
5. Take up the weight of the engine with a jack.
6. Remove the right engine mount bolt and raise the engine slightly.
7. Remove the timing belt tensioner and remove the belt.
8. Remove the crankshaft sprocket bolt, and with a puller, remove the sprocket.
9. Using special tool C-4679 or its equivalent, remove the crankshaft seal.

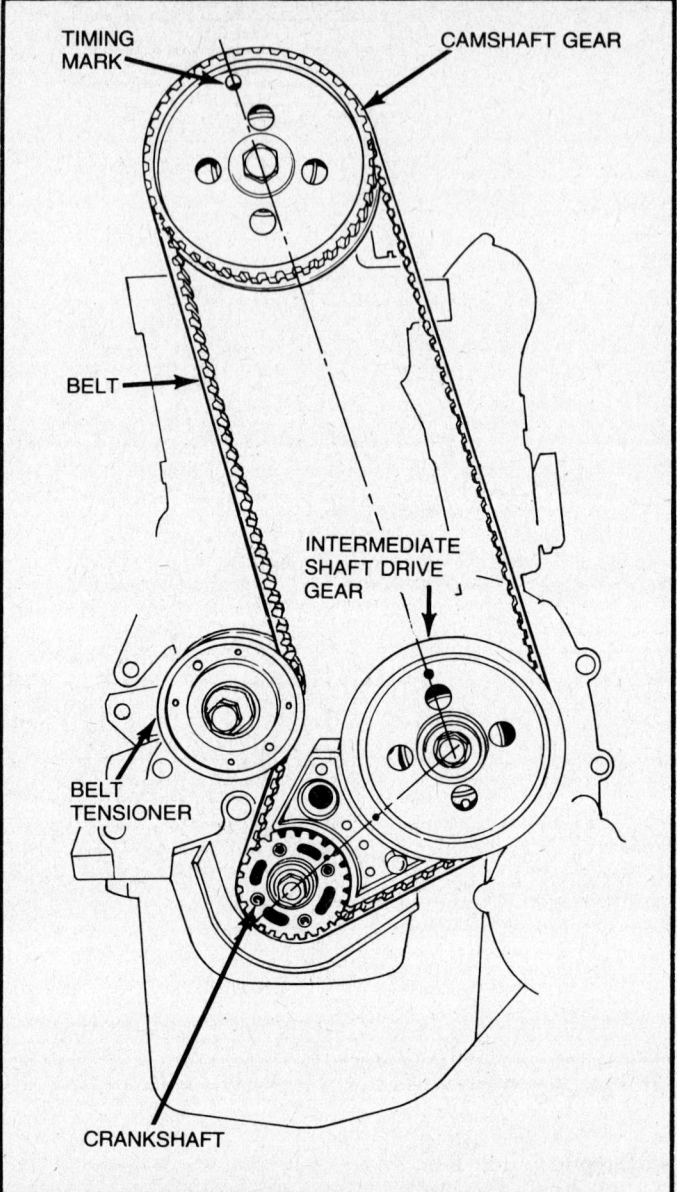

2.2L engine valve timing and sprocket alignment
(© Chrysler Corporation)

10. Unbolt and remove the camshaft and intermediate shaft sprockets.
11. To install the crankshaft seal, first polish the shaft with 400 grit emery paper. If the seal has a steel case, lightly coat the OD of the seal with Loctite Stud N'Bearing Mount® or its equivalent. If the seal case is rubber coated, generously apply a soap and water solution to facilitate installation. Install the seal with a seal driver.
12. Install the sprockets making sure that the timing marks are aligned. When installing the camshaft sprocket, make certain that the arrows on the sprocket are in line with the No. 1 camshaft bearing cap-to-cylinder headline.
13. The small hole in the camshaft sprocket must be at the top and be in line with the center line of the engine, top to bottom.
14. Install the belt.
15. Rotate the engine to the No. 1 piston TDC position.

CHRYSLER CORPORATION
FRONT WHEEL DRIVE CARS

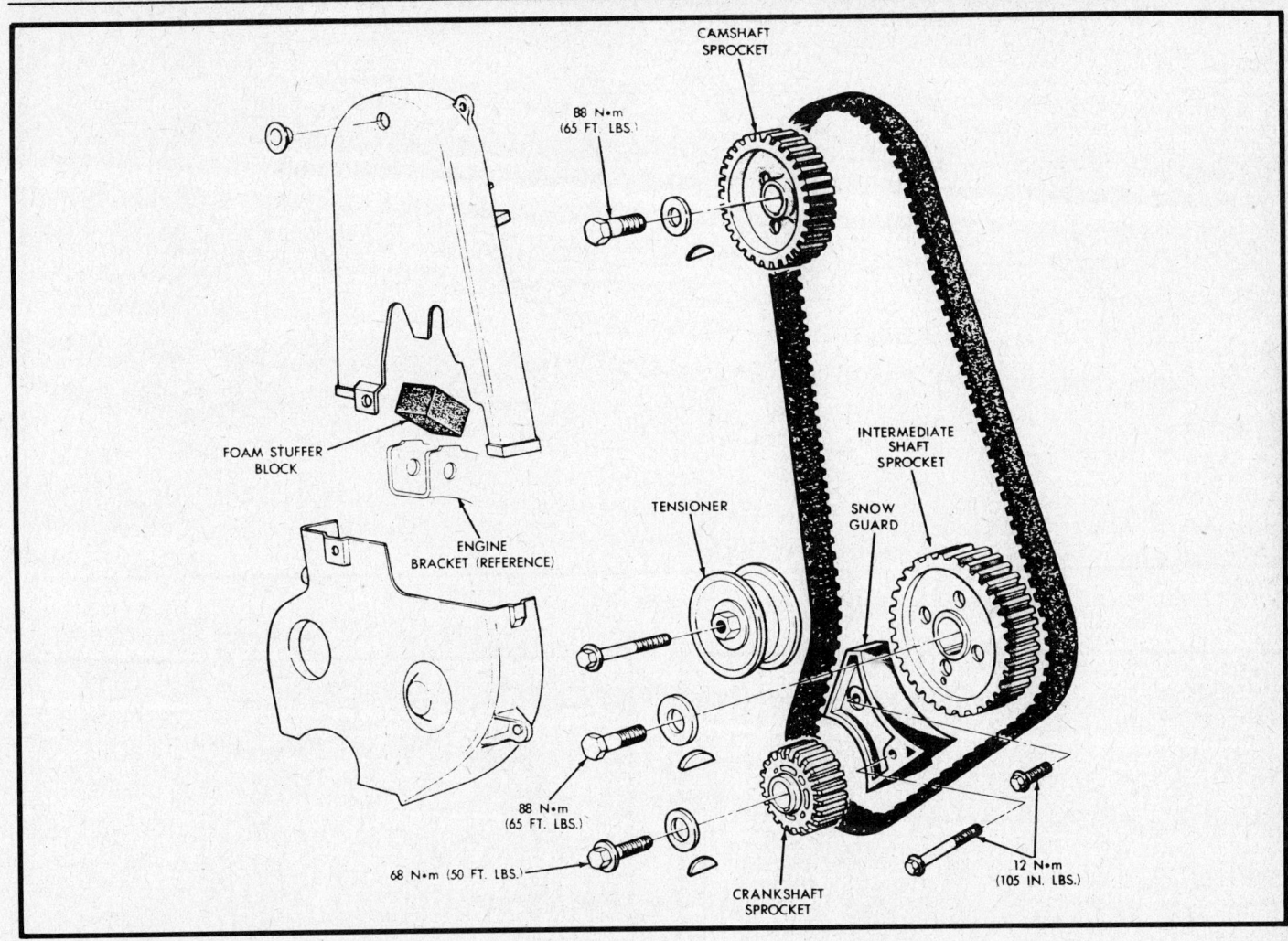

Timing belt sprockets and components—2.2L engine (© Chrysler Corporation)

16. Install the belt tensioner and place tool C-4703 on the large hex nut.
17. Reset the belt tension so that the axis of the tool is about 15° off of horizontal.
18. Turn the engine clockwise two full revolutions to No. 1 TDC.
19. Tighten the tensioner locknut using a weighted wrench. Torques:
  Timing belt cover bolts, 105 inch lb.
  Camshaft sprocket bolt, 65 ft. lb.
  Crankshaft sprocket bolt, 50 ft. lb.
  Intermediate shaft sprocket bolt, 65 ft. lb.

BALANCE SHAFTS

Removal and Installation

2.5L ENGINES

Note: The oil pan, oil pickup, timing cover, belt, crankshaft belt sprocket and front crankshaft oil seal retainer must be first removed to gain access to the drive chain and sprockets.

1. Remove the chain cover, guide and tensioner.
2. Remove the balance shaft gear and chain sprocket retaining screws and the crankshaft chain sprocket Torx screws.
3. Remove the chain and sprocket assembly.
4. Remove the gear cover retaining stud (double ended to also retain the chain guide). Remove the cover and the balance shaft gears.
5. Remove the carrier rear cover and balance shafts.
6. Remove the six carrier to crankcase attaching bolts to separate the carrier.

NOTE: The carrier assembly can be removed as an assembly, consisting of the gear cover, gears balance shafts and the rear cover.

7. To remove the carrier assembly, remove the chain cover and driven balance shaft chain sprocket screw.
8. Loosen the tensioner pivot and adjusting screws, move the driven balance shaft inboard (through) the driven chain sprocket. The sprocket will hang in the lower chain loop.
9. Remove the carrier to crankcase attaching bolts to remove the carrier.

Timing and Installation

1. With the balance shafts installed in the carrier, position the carrier on the crankcase and install the six retaining bolts. Tighten to 40 ft. lbs.
2. Turn the balance shafts until both shaft keyways are in the "UP" position (parallel to vertical centerline of the engine).

2-71

CHRYSLER CORPORATION
FRONT WHEEL DRIVE CARS

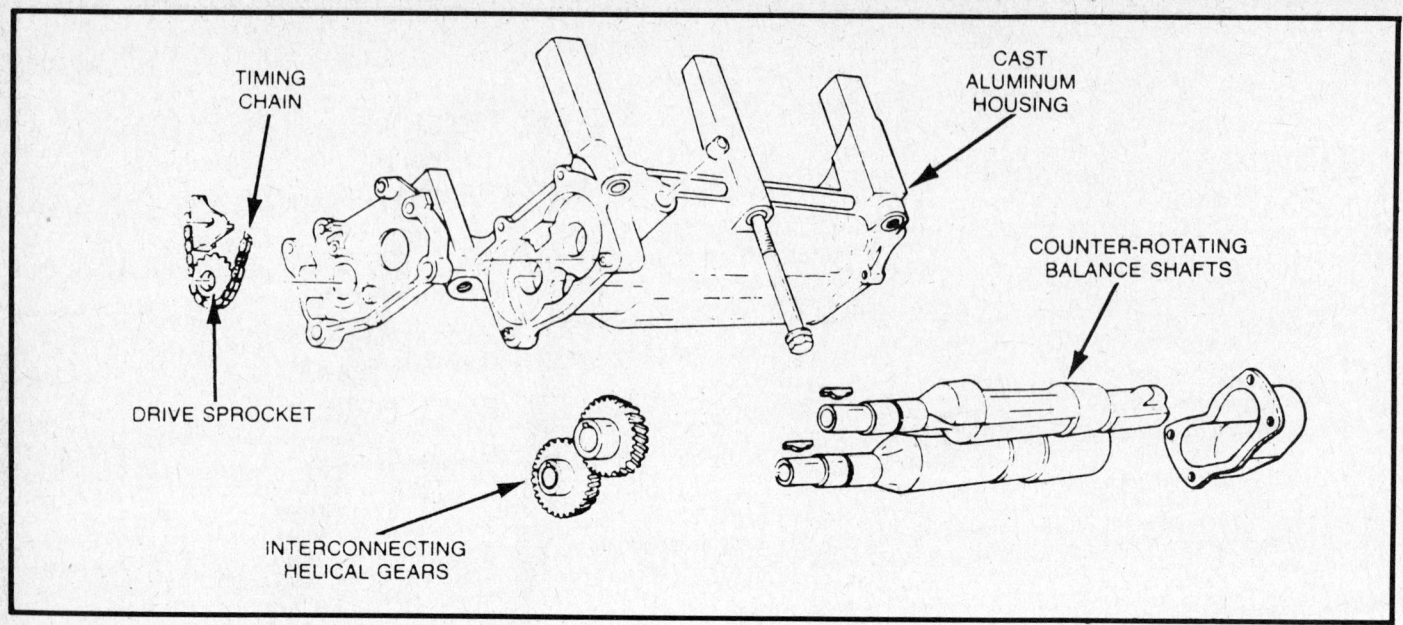

Balance shafts and housings—2.5L engine

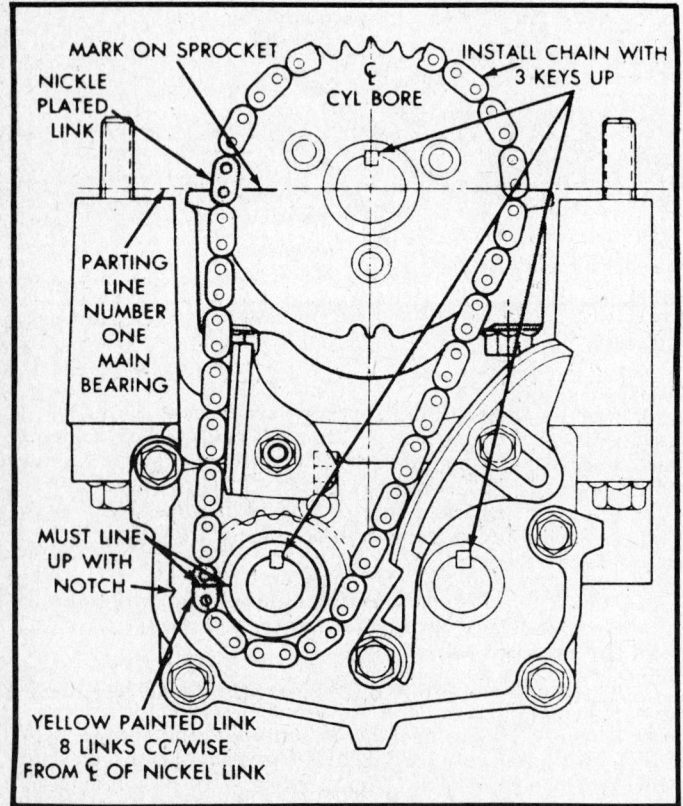

Balance shaft sprocket timing to crankshaft sprocket—2.5L engine

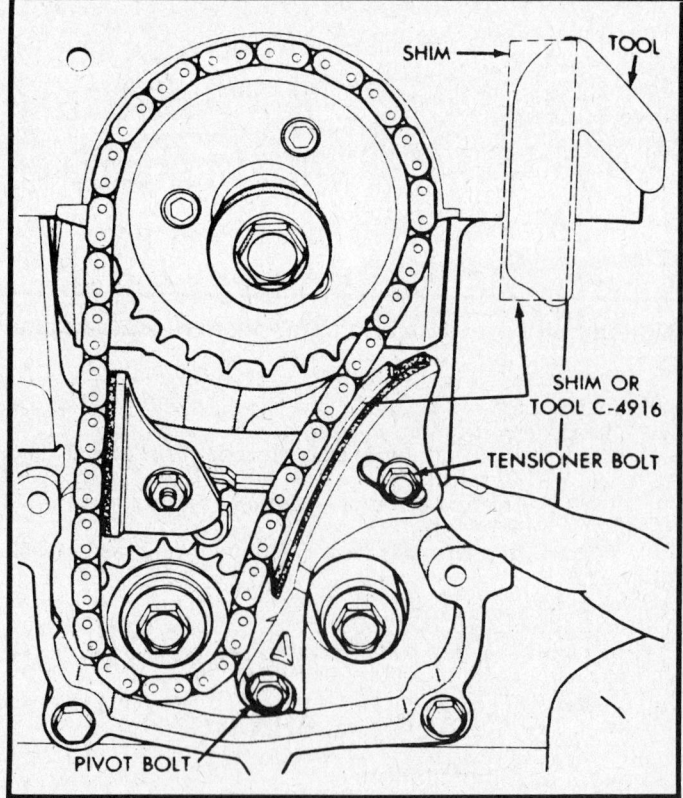

Adjustment of chain tensioner—2.5L engine

3. Install the short hub drive gear on the sprocket driven shaft and the long hub gear on the gear driven shaft.

4. After installation, the gear and the balance shaft keyways must be in the "UP" position with the gear timing marks meshed together (3 and 9 O'clock positions).

5. Install the gear cover and tighten the double ended stud/washer fastener to 105 inch lbs.

6. Install the crankshaft sprocket and tighten the socket headed Torx screws to 130 inch lbs.

7. Turn the crankshaft until No. 1 cylinder is at TDC. The

CHRYSLER CORPORATION
FRONT WHEEL DRIVE CARS

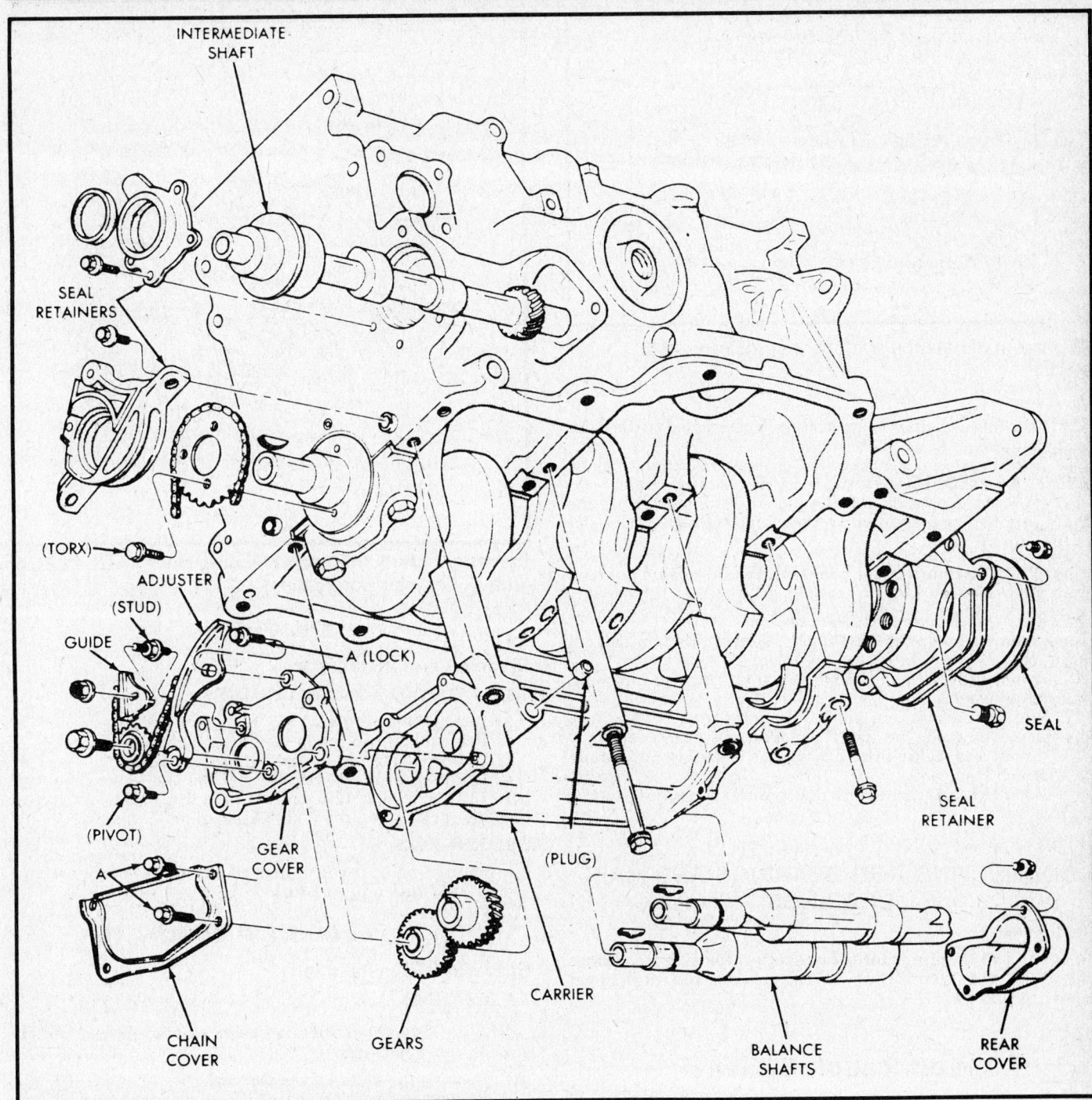

Balance shafts and intermediate shaft locations—2.5L engine

timing marks on the chain sprocket should line up with the parting line on the left side of No. 1 main bearing cap.

8. Place the chain over the crankshaft sprocket so that the nickel plated link of the chain is over the timing mark on the crankshaft sprocket.

9. Place the balance shaft sprocket into the timing chain so that the timing mark on the sprocket (yellow dot) mates with the yellow painted link on the chain.

10. With the balance shaft keyways pointing "upwards" or at the 12 O'clock position, slide the balance shaft sprocket onto the nose of the balance shaft. The balance shaft may have to be pushed in slightly to allow for clearance.

NOTE: The timing mark on the sprocket, the painted link and the arrow on the side of the gear cover should line up if the balance shafts are timed properly.

11. If the sprockets are timed correctly, install the balance shafts bolts and tighten to 250 inch lbs. The crankshaft can be held by a wooden block to prevent its rotating.

SECTION 2
CHRYSLER CORPORATION
FRONT WHEEL DRIVE CARS

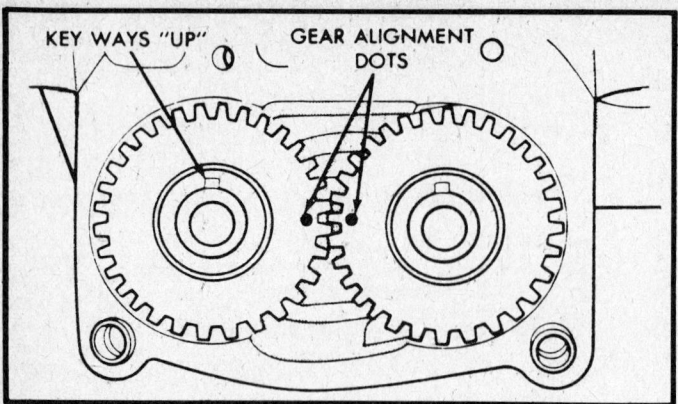

Alignment of balance shaft gear sprockets—2.5L engine

12. Install the chain tensioner, loosely assembled to the front of the engine.
13. Install a special clearance tool or place a 0.039 in. thick by 2.75 in. long shim between the tensioner and the chain.
14. Push the tensioner and the tool or shim up against the chain. Apply firm pressure directly behind the adjustment slot to take up all slack.

NOTE: The chain must have total shoe radius contact with the adjuster.

15. With the firm pressure load applied, tighten the top tensioner bolt first, then the bottom pivot bolt. Tighten the bolts at 105 inch lbs.
16. Remove the shim or special tool from between the chain and the adjuster.
17. Position the guide on the double ended stud, making sure the tab on the guide fits into the slot on the gear cover.
18. Install and tighten the nut/washer assembly and torque to 105 inch lbs.
19. Install the carrier covers and tighten the screws to 105 inch lbs.

CONNECTING ROD BEARINGS AND MAIN BEARINGS

Refer to the engine rebuilding section for service procedures on the installation of connecting rod and main bearing inserts.

Lubrication System

OIL PAN

Removal and Installation

1. Drain the oil pan.
2. Support the pan and remove the attaching bolts.
3. Lower the pan and discard the gaskets.
4. Clean all gasket surfaces thoroughly and install the pan using gasket sealer and a new gasket.
5. Torque the pan bolts to 111 inch lbs. 1.6L engine, 7 ft. lbs. on the 1.7L engine, M8 screws to 200 inch lbs. and M6 screws to 105 inch lbs. on the 2.2L/2.5L engines and 60 inch lbs. on the 2.6L engine.
6. Refill the pan, start the engine, and check for leaks.

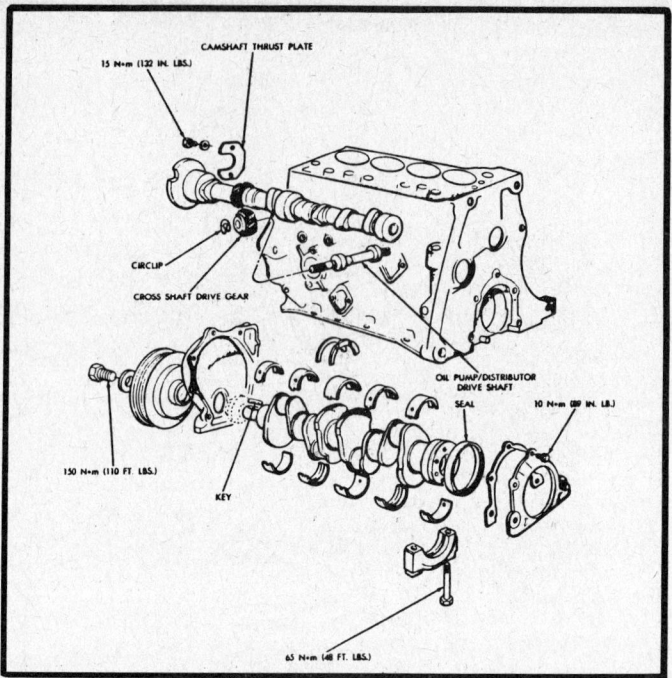

Camshaft, crankshaft and oil pump drive shaft—1.6L engine (© Chrysler Corporation)

OIL PUMP

Removal and Installation

1.6L, 1.7L AND 2.2L/2.5L ENGINES

1. Remove the oil pan.
2. Remove the two pump mounting bolts.
3. Pull the pump down and out of the engine.
4. Installation is the reverse. Torque the pump mounting bolts to 111 inch lbs. 1.6L engine, 14 ft. lbs. on the 1.7L engine and 200 inch lbs. on the 2.2L/2.5L engines.

2.6L ENGINES

See Timing Chain, Cover, "Silent Shaft" and Tensioner removal and installation procedure.

REAR MAIN SEAL

Removal and Installation

1.6L ENGINE

NOTE: This procedure is easier to complete if the engine is removed first.

1. Remove the engine from the car.
2. Remove the rear oil seal and housing.
3. Place the housing inner surface on two blocks of wood, allowing clearance for seal removal.
4. Remove the seal.
5. Installation is the reverse of removal. Torque housing bolts to 111 inch lbs.

NOTE: Special tool C-4759 or its equal is needed for this procedure. This tool can be used for removing or installing the seal.

1.7L AND 2.2L/2.5L ENGINES

The rear main seal is located in a housing on the rear of the block. To replace the seal, it is necessary to remove the engine.
1. Remove the transaxle and flywheel.

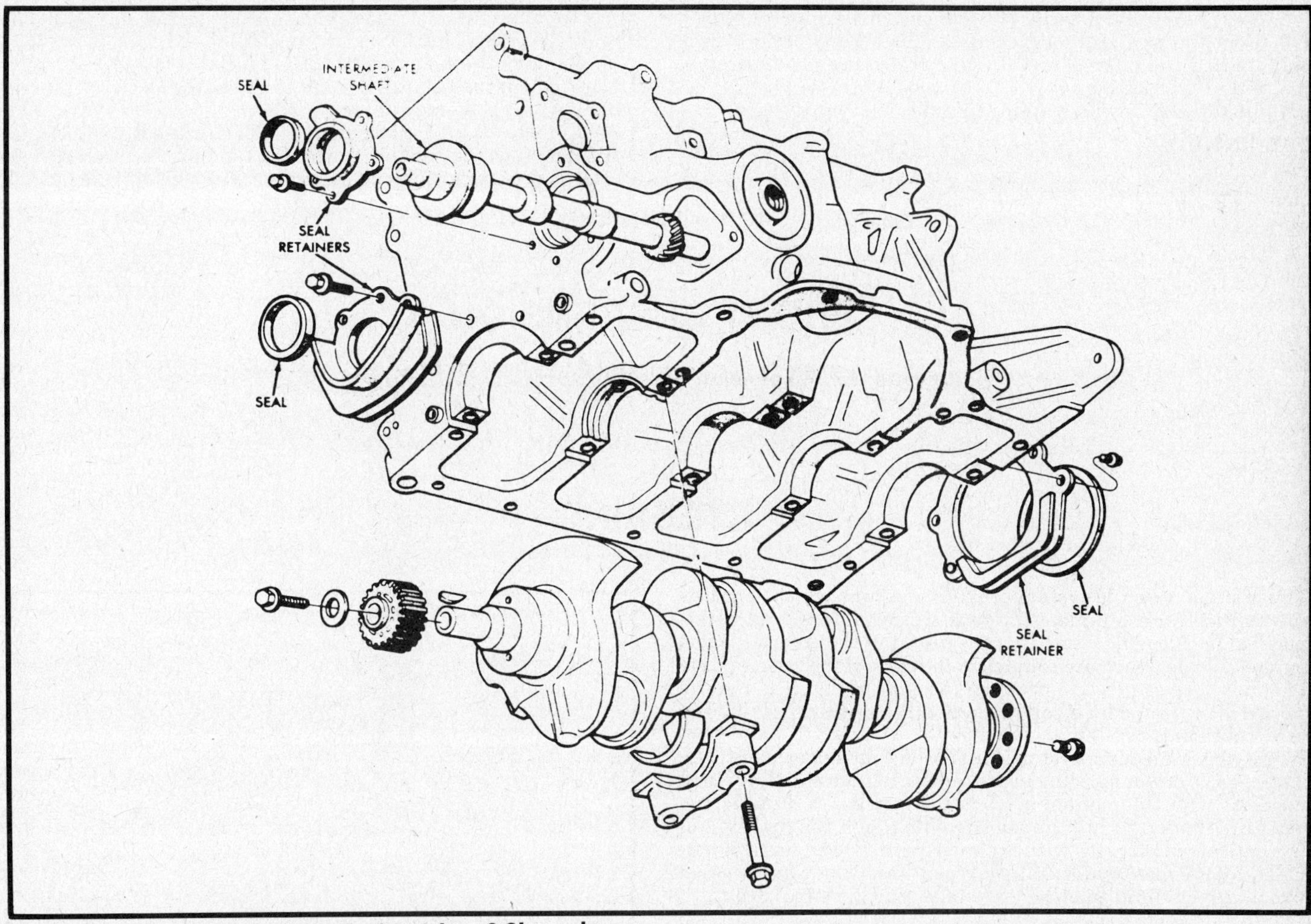

CHRYSLER CORPORATION
FRONT WHEEL DRIVE CARS

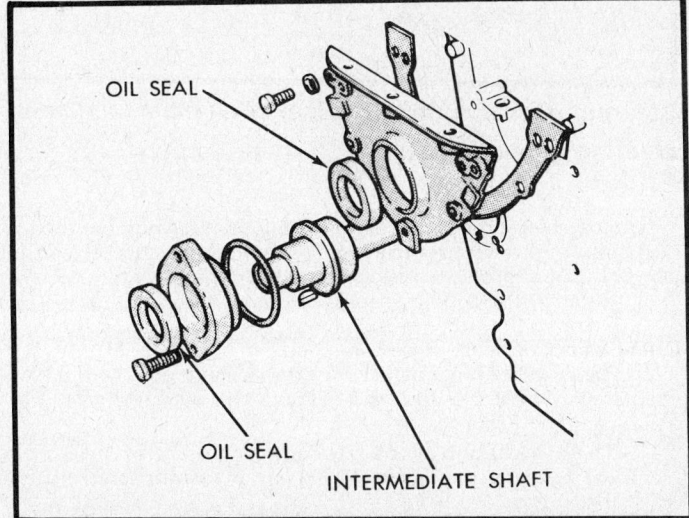

Crankshaft and intermediate shaft seals—2.2L engine

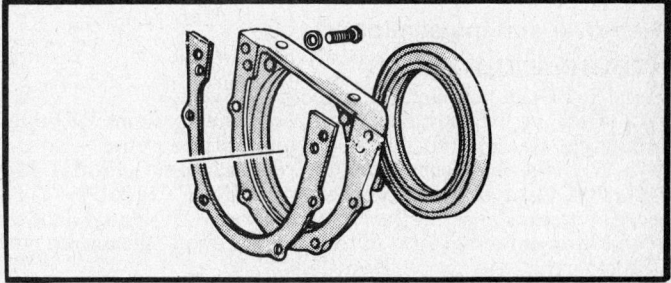

Front oil seal 1.7L engine (© Chrysler Corporation)

Rear main bearing oil seal—1.7L engine, typical of 2.2L engine (© Chrysler Corporation)

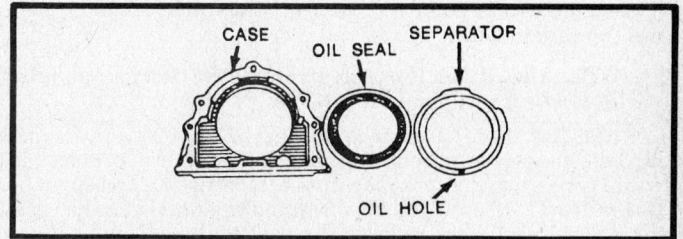

Rear main oil seal on 2.6 engines (© Chrysler Corporation)

CAUTION
Before removing the transaxle, align the dimple on the flywheel with the pointer on the flywheel housing. The transaxle will not mate with the engine during installation unless this alignment is observed.

2. Very carefully, pry the old seal out of the support ring.
3. Coat the new seal with clean engine oil and press it into place with a flat piece of metal. Take great care not to scratch the seal or crankshaft.
4. Install the flywheel and transaxle.

2.6L ENGINES

The rear main oil seal is located in a housing on the rear of the block. To replace the seal, remove the transaxle and do the work from underneath the vehicle or remove the engine and do the work on the bench.
1. Remove the housing from the block.
2. Remove the separator from the housing.
3. Pry out the old seal.
4. Lightly oil the replacement seal. The oil seal should be installed so that the seal plate fits into the inner contact surface of the seal case. Install the separator with the oil holes facing down.

FRONT SUSPENSION

Refer to the Suspension Section for repair procedures.

STEERING

The manual steering system consists of a tube which contains the toothed rack, a pinion, the rack slipper, and the rack slipper spring. Steering effort is transmitted to the steering arms by the tie rods which are coupled to the ends of the rack, and tie rod ends. The connection between the ends of the rack and the tie rod is protected by a bellows type oil seal which retains the gear lubricant.

The power steering system consists of four major parts: the power gear, power steering pump, pressure hose and the return hose. As with the manual system, the turning of the steering wheel is converted into linear travel through the meshing of the helical pinion teeth with the rack teeth. Power assist is provided by an open center, rotary type, three-way control valve which directs fluid to either side of the rack control piston.

STEERING GEAR

Removal and Installation
POWER AND MANUAL
1. Raise the vehicle and support safely.
2. Remove both left and right road wheels. Remove the left and right tie rod ends, using the appropriate puller.
3. Remove the steering column on the Aries, Reliant, Dodge 400, 600, Caravelle, Lancer, LeBaron GTS, E Class/New Yorker, LeBaron, Daytona, Laser, LeBaron, Shadow and Sundance models. The lower universal joint of the steering shaft is removed with the steering gear on these models.
4. Remove the anti-rotational link from the crossmember, if equipped, and the air diverter valve bracket, if equipped from the left side of the crossmember.
5. On the Omni, Turismo, Charger, TC3, 024 and Horizon models, drive the lower roll pin from the universal joint, holding the pinion shaft.

NOTE: Use a back-up to protect the universal joint, while driving out the roll pin.

6. On the Omni, Turismo, Charger, TC3, 024 and Horizon models, support the front crossmember with a hydraulic jack while removing the two rear nuts attaching the crossmember to the frame. Loosen the two front bolts and lower the crossmember slightly for access to the boot seal shields.
7. On the Aries, Reliant, Dodge 400, 600, Caravelle, Lancer, LeBaron GTS, E Class/New Yorker, Daytona, Laser, LeBaron, Shadow and Sundance models, support the crossmember with

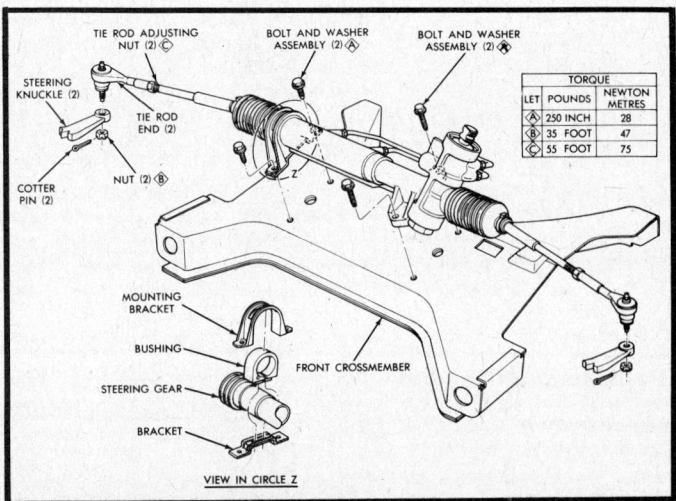

Steering gear mounting, typical of all models. Power steering gear illustrated (© Chrysler Corporation)

a transmission type jack, remove the four crossmember attaching bolts and lower the front suspension crossmember so that the roll pin can be driven from the universal joint.
8. Remove the splash shields and boot seals shields.
9. Remove the tubes to the power steering pump, if the vehicle is equipped with power steering.
10. Remove the bolts attaching the steering gear to the front suspension crossmember and remove the steering gear from the left side of the vehicle.
11. The installation of the steering gear is the reverse of the removal procedure. Tighten the gear attaching bolts to 250 inch lbs. torque.
12. Adjust the toe and check for oil leaks.

POWER STEERING PUMP

Removal and Installation

NOTE: All power steering pump mounting nuts and bolts are metric.

CHRYSLER CORPORATION
FRONT WHEEL DRIVE CARS
SECTION 2

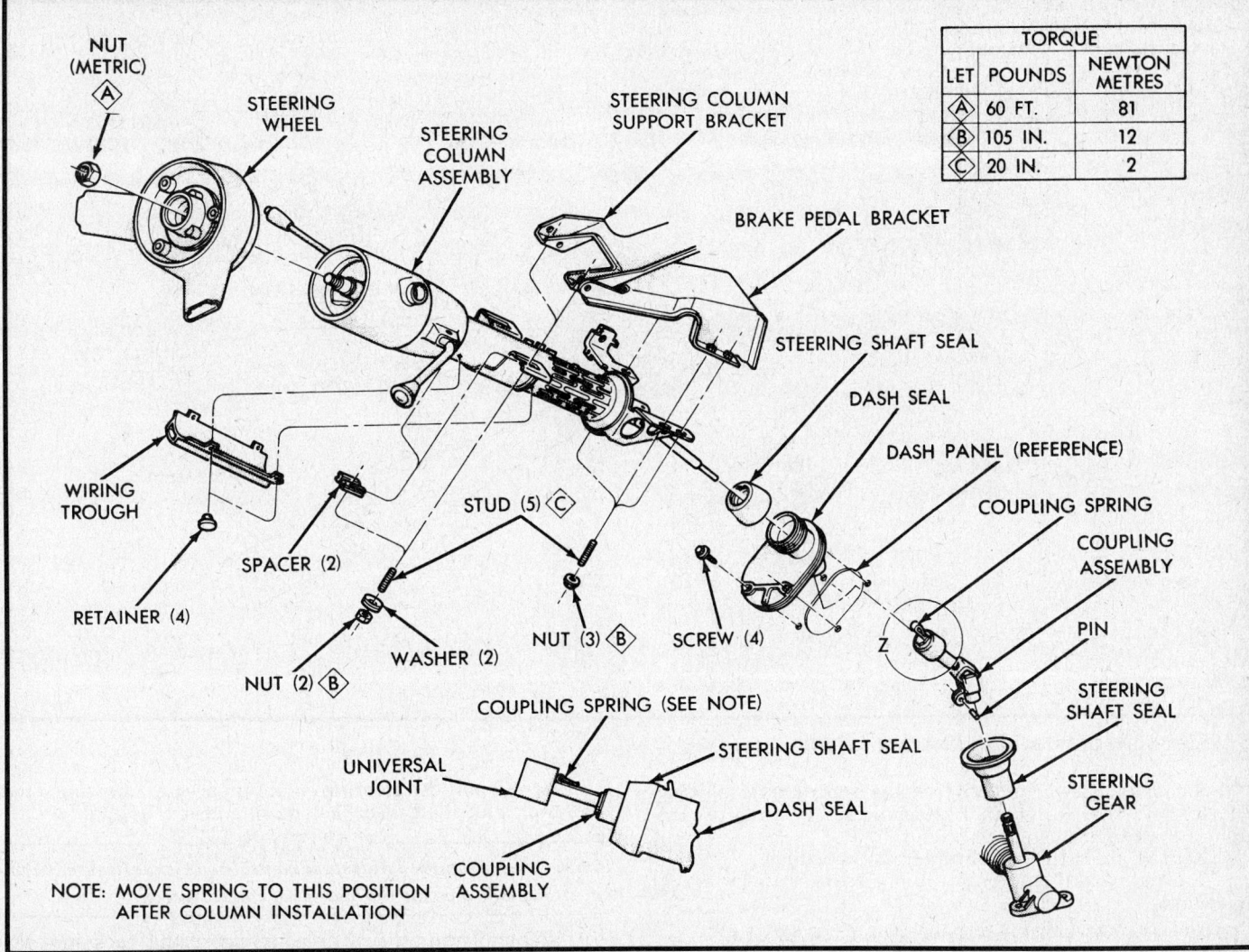

Steering column assembly—typical (© Chrysler Corporation)

1. Disconnect the vapor separator hose from the carburetor and the two wires from the air conditioning clutch cycling switch (if so equipped).
2. Loosen the two drive belt adjustment bolts and nut at the rear of the pump and remove the belt from the pump pulley.
3. Raise the car on a hoist and remove the pressure hose locating bracket bolt at the crossmember.
4. Disconnect the pressure hose from the gear and drain the oil from the pump through the end of the hose.
5. Remove the right side splash shield that protects the drive belts.
6. Disconnect both hoses from the pump.
7. Remove the two rear most bolts and loosen the one bolt that attaches the bracket.
8. Lower the car and remove the adjustment bolts and bracket from the front of the pump and the nut at the rear of the pump.
9. Move the bracket and carefully remove the pump.
10. To install reverse the removal procedure. Adjust the belt to the correct tension and fill the pump reservoir to the top of the filler neck with the proper power steering fluid.

STEERING WHEEL
Removal and Installation

1. Remove the horn button and horn switch.
2. Remove the steering wheel nut.
3. Using a steering wheel puller, remove the steering wheel.
4. Align the master serration in the wheel hub with the missing tooth on the shaft. Torque the shaft nut to 60 ft. lbs.

— **CAUTION** —
Do not torque the nut against the steering column lock or damage will occur.

5. Replace the horn switch and button.

STEERING COLUMN
Removal and Installation
OMNI, TURISMO, CHARGER, TC3, 024 AND HORIZON

1. Disconnect all column wiring connectors.

2-77

CHRYSLER CORPORATION
FRONT WHEEL DRIVE CARS

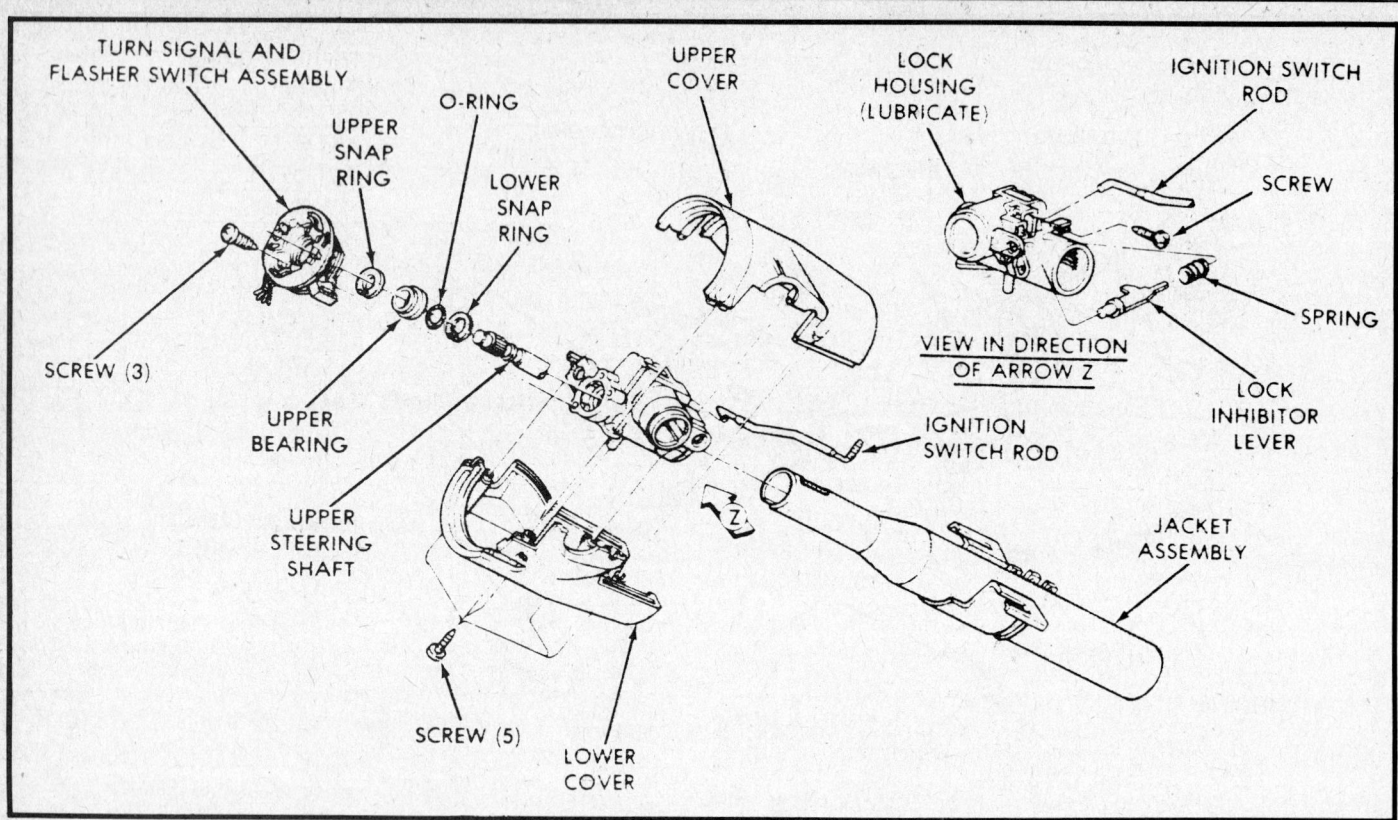

Exploded view of floor shift steering column

2. Remove the lower roll pin from the upper universal joint.
3. Remove the four column attaching screws from the column to instrument panel.
4. Remove the steering column from the vehicle.
5. To install the steering column, reverse the removal procedure.

ARIES, RELIANT, DODGE 400, 600, CARAVELLE, LANCER, LEBARON GTS, E CLASS/NEW YORKER, DAYTONA, LASER, LEBARON, SHADOW AND SUNDANCE MODELS

1. Disconnect the negative battery cable from the battery.
2. On vehicles equipped with column shift, disconnect the cable rod, remove the cable clip and remove the cable from the lower bracket.
3. Disconnect all the wiring connectors at the steering column.
4. Remove the steering wheel and components.
5. Remove the instrument panel steering column cover and lower dash reinforcement. Disconnect the bezel, exposing the steering column brackets.
6. Remove the indicator set screw and remove the shaft indicator pointer from the shift housing, if equipped.
7. Remove the nuts attaching the steering column bracket to the instrument panel support and lower the bracket support.

— CAUTION —
Do not remove the roll pin to remove the steering column assembly.

8. Firmly pull the steering column rearward, disconnecting the lower stub shaft from the steering gear coupling.

— CAUTION —
If the vehicle is equipped with speed control and manual transmission, do not damage the clutch pedal speed control switch.

9. Reinstall the anti-rattle coupling spring back into the lower coupling tube. Be sure that the anti-rattling spring snaps into the slot in the coupling.
10. Remove the column assembly out through the passenger compartment.

— CAUTION —
Do not damage the paint or trim.

11. Install a new grommet from the rod side of the shift lever whenever the rod is disconnected from the lever.
12. To install the steering column, reverse the removal procedure.

FRONT WHEEL BEARINGS

No Adjustment is required on front wheel bearings. Refer to Unit Repair, Suspension Section, for bearing service information.

CHRYSLER CORPORATION
FRONT WHEEL DRIVE CARS
SECTION 2

BRAKES

A convention front disc/rear drum setup is used. The front discs are single piston caliper types; the rear drums are activated by a conventional top mounted wheel cylinder. Disc brakes require no adjustments, the drum brakes are self-adjusting by means of the parking brake cable. The system is diagonally balanced, that is, the front left and right rear are on one system and the front right and left rear on the other. No proportioning valve is used. Power brakes are optional.

NOTE: For Brake Service, refer to the Unit Repair Section.

MASTER CYLINDER

Removal and Installation

WITH POWER BRAKES

1. Disconnect the primary and secondary brake lines from the master cylinder. Plug the openings.
2. Remove the nuts attaching the cylinder to the power brake booster.
3. Slide the master cylinder straight out, away from the booster.
4. Position the master cylinder over the studs on the booster, align the pushrod with the master cylinder piston and tighten the nuts to 16 ft. lbs.
5. Connect the brake lines.
6. Bleed the brakes.

WITH NON-POWER BRAKES

1. Disconnect the primary and secondary brake lines and install plugs in the master cylinder openings.
2. Disconnect the toplight switch mounting bracket from under the instrument panel.
3. Pull the brake pedal backward to disengage the pushrod from the master cylinder piston.

NOTE: This will destroy the grommet.

4. Remove the master cylinder-to-firewall nuts.
5. Slide the master cylinder out and away from the firewall. Be sure to remove all pieces of the broken grommet.
6. Install the boot on the pushrod.
7. Install a new grommet on the pushrod.
8. Apply a soap and water solution to the grommet and slide it firmly into position in the primary piston socket. Move the pushrod from side to side to make sure it's seated.
9. From the engine side, press the pushrod through the master cylinder mounting plate and align the mounting studs with the holes in the cylinder.
10. Install the nuts and torque them to 16 ft. lbs.
11. From under the instrument panel, place the pushrod on the pin on the pedal and install a new retaining clip.

--- **CAUTION** ---
Be sure to lubricate the pin.

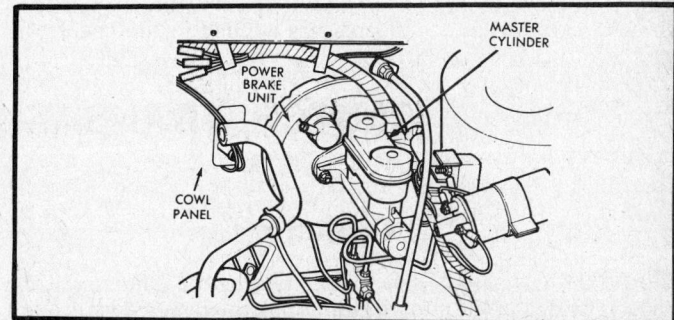

Master cylinder and power brake unit location, typical
(© Chrysler Corporation)

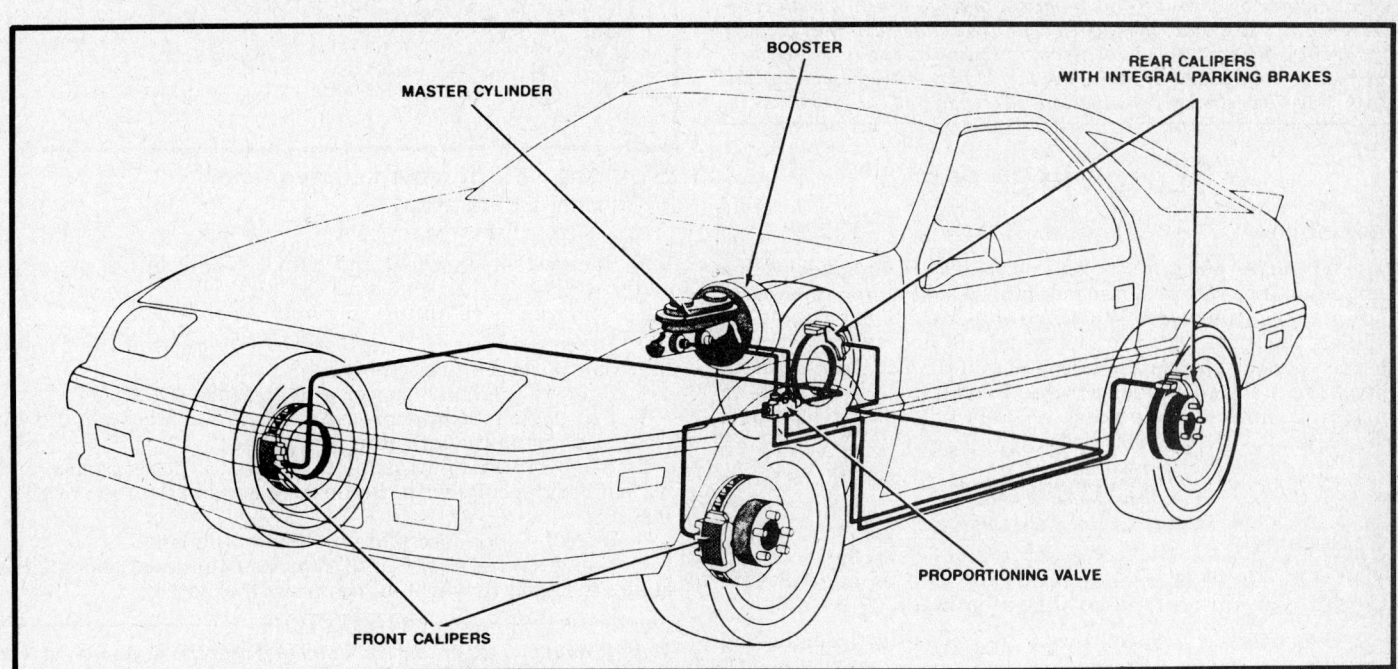

FOUR WHEEL DISC BRAKES DODGE DAYTONA SHELBY

CHRYSLER CORPORATION
FRONT WHEEL DRIVE CARS

12. Install the brake lines on the master cylinder.
13. Bleed the system.

POWER BOOSTER

Removal and Installation

1. Remove the master cylinder; it can be pulled far enough out of the way to allow booster removal without disconnecting the brake lines.
2. Disconnect the vacuum hose from the booster.
3. Under the instrument panel, pry the retainer clip center tang over the end of the brake pedal pin and pull the retainer clip from the pin. Discard the clip.
4. Remove the four booster attaching nuts.
5. Remove the booster from the vehicle.
6. Position the booster on the firewall.
7. Torque the nuts to 20 ft. lbs.
8. Carefully position the master cylinder on the booster.
9. Install the mounting nuts and torque them to 18 ft. lbs.
10. Connect the vacuum hose to the booster.
11. Coat the baring surface of the pedal pin with chassis lube.
12. Connect the pushrod to the pedal pin and install a new clip.
13. Check the stoplight operation. With vacuum applied to the power brake unit and pressure applied to the pedal, the master cylinder should vent (force a jet of fluid through the front chamber vent port).

---- CAUTION ----
Do not attempt to disassemble the power brake unit, since the booster is serviced as a complete assembly only.

PARKING BRAKE

Adjustment

1. Fully release the parking brake.
2. Locate the cable connector at the rear suspension crossmember and thoroughly clean the assembly.
3. Loosen the adjusting nut until there is slack in the cable.
4. Insert a thin screwdriver through the slot in the brake backing plate and rotate the starwheel so there is light shoe-to-drum contact.
5. Back off the starwheel to allow free drum rotation.
6. Tighten the cable adjusting nut until a slight drag is felt at the wheels.
7. Loosen the cable adjusting nut until both rear wheels turn freely.
8. Back off the cable adjusting nut two full turns.
9. Apply and release the parking brake several times to make sure that free rotation exists at the wheels.

CLUTCH, TRANSAXLE, DRIVE AXLE SECTION

Clutch

The clutch is a simple dry disc unit, with no adjustment for wear provided in the clutch itself. Adjustment is made through an adjustable sleeve in the pedal linkage.

---- CAUTION ----
When servicing clutch assemblies or components, do not create dust by sanding or by cleaning clutch parts with a dry brush or with compressed air. Use a water dampened cloth. The clutch disc may contain "Asbestos Fibers" which could become airborne as dust is created during the service operation. Breathing this airborne dust containing the "Asbestos Fibers" may cause serious personal medical problems.

CLUTCH FREE PLAY

Adjustment

The A-460, A-465 and A-525 Transaxles are equipped with a self-adjusting clutch release mechanism. The clutch release cable cannot be adjusted. When the clutch cable is properly installed, the spring in the clutch pedal will hold the cable in the proper position, regardless of clutch disc wear. The adjuster pivot grabs the positioner adjuster to hold the release cable in place to assure complete clutch release when the clutch pedal is depressed.

CLUTCH DISC

Replacement

NOTE: Chrysler recommends the use of special tool C-4676, or equivalent for disc alignment.

1. Remove the transmission as described in the following section.
2. Loosen the flywheel-to-pressure plate bolts diagonally, one or two turns at a time to avoid warpage.

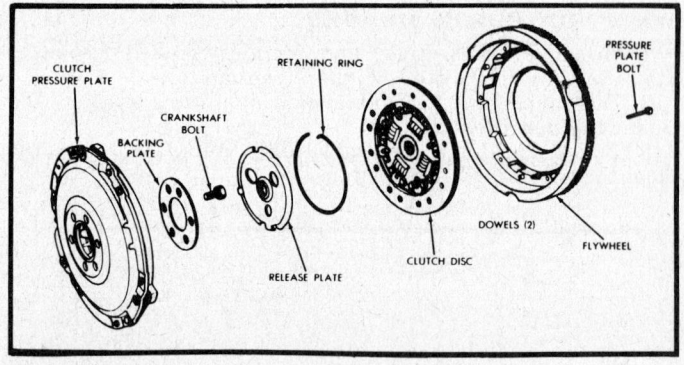

Exploded view of clutch components
(© Chrysler Corporation)

3. Remove the flywheel and clutch disc from the pressure plate.
4. Remove the retaining ring and release plate.
5. Diagonally loosen the pressure plate-to-crankshaft bolts. Mark all parts for reassembly.
6. Remove the bolts, spacer and pressure plate.
7. The flywheel and pressure plate surfaces should be cleaned thoroughly with fine sandpaper.
8. Align marks and install the pressure plate, spacer and bolts. Coat the bolts with thread compound and torque to 55 ft. lbs.
9. Install the release plate and retaining ring.
10. Using special tool C-4676 or its equivalent, install the clutch disc and flywheel on the pressure plate.

---- CAUTION ----
Make certain that the drilled mark on the flywheel is at the top, so that the two dowels on the flywheel align with the proper holes in the pressure plate.

CHRYSLER CORPORATION
FRONT WHEEL DRIVE CARS

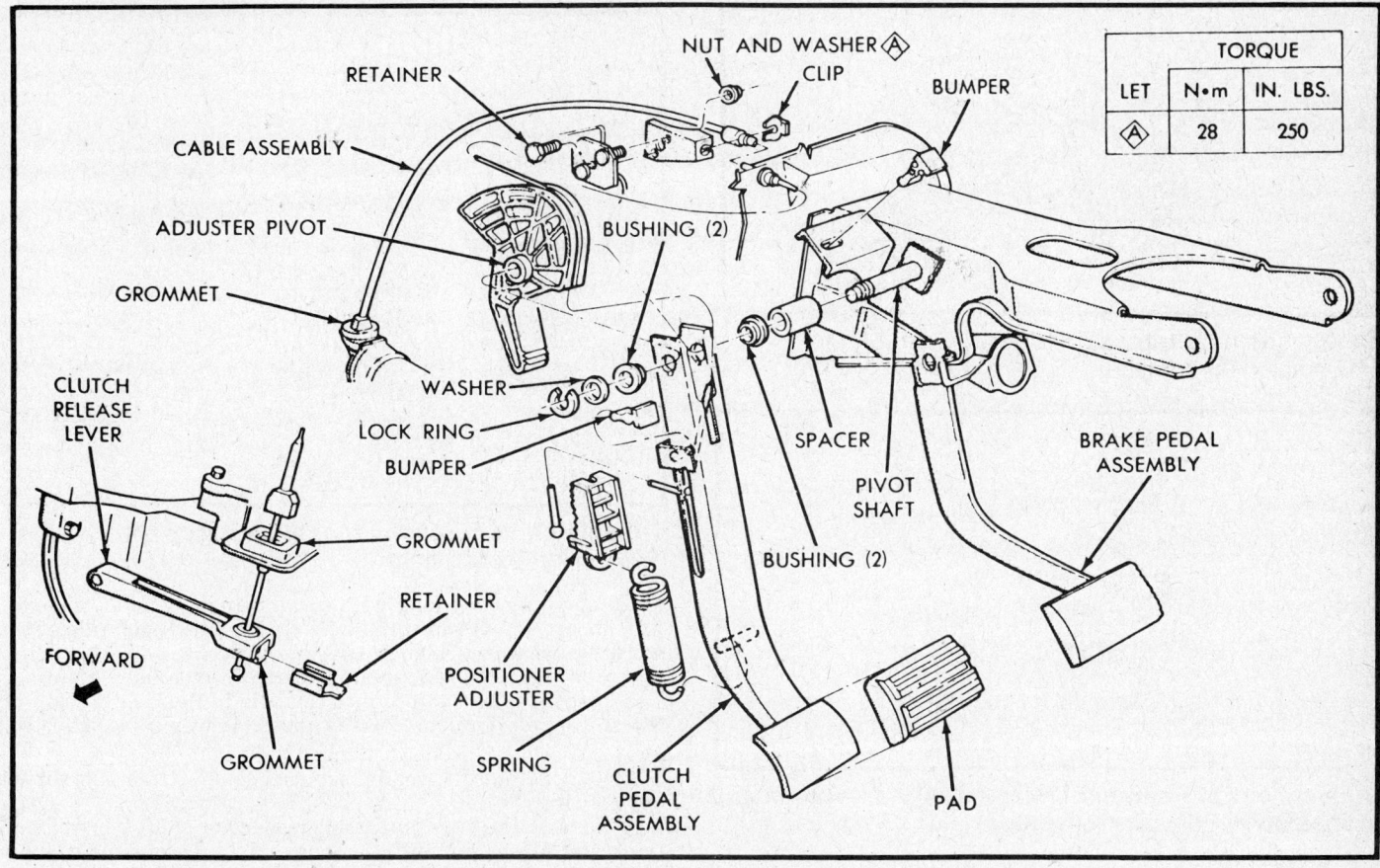

Exploded view of automatic of self—adjusting clutch linkage (© Chrysler Corporation)

11. Install the six flywheel bolts and tighten to 14.5 ft. lbs.
12. Remove the aligning tool.
13. Install the transmission.
14. Properly install the clutch release cable and components.

Manual Transaxle

Removal and Installation

NOTE: Whenever the differential cover is removed, a new gasket should be formed using RTV sealant.

1. Remove the engine timing mark access plug.
2. Rotate the engine to align the drilled mark on the flywheel with the pointer on the engine.
3. Disconnect the battery ground.
4. Disconnect the shift linkage rods.
5. Disconnect the starter and ground wires.
6. Disconnect the backup light switch wire.
7. Remove the starter.
8. Disconnect the clutch cable.
9. Disconnect the speedometer cable.
10. Support the weight of the engine from above, preferably with a shop hoist or the fabricated holding fixture.
11. Raise and support the vehicle.
12. Disconnect the driveshafts and support them out of the way.
13. Remove the left splash shield.
14. Drain the transaxle.
15. Unbolt the left engine mount.
16. Remove the transaxle-to-engine bolts.
17. Slide the transaxle to the left until the mainshaft clears, then, carefully lower it from the car.
18. Installation is the reverse of removal.
19. Adjust the clutch cable.
20. Adjust the shift linkage.
21. Fill the transaxle.

SHIFT LINKAGE

Adjustment

A-460, A-465, A-525 MODELS WITH ROD OPERATED SHIFT LINKAGE

The transaxle uses a double ended pin that is used to lock the linkage in place prior to adjustment.

1. Remove the screw from the top and reinsert the other end, locking the linkage in place.
2. The linkage is locked in the Neutral detent between 1st and 2nd gears.
3. Align the marks on the linkage.
4. Remove the pin and replace it in its original location. Check the operation of the shift linkage.

A-460, A-465, A-525 MODELS WITH CABLE OPERATED SHIFT LINKAGE

1. Working over the driver's side front fender, remove the lock pin from the transaxle selector shaft housing.
2. Reverse the lock pin (so long end is down) and insert lock pin into same threaded hole while pushing the selector shaft into the selector housing. A hole in the selector shaft will align with the lock pin, allowing the lock pin to be screwed into the housing. This operation locks the selector shaft in the 1-2 neutral position.

CHRYSLER CORPORATION
FRONT WHEEL DRIVE CARS

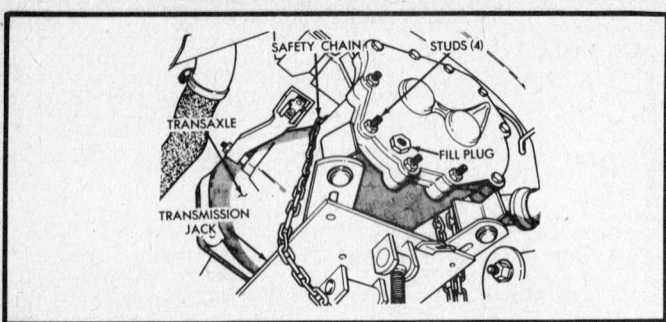

Safety chaining transaxle to jack assembly
(© Chrysler Corporation)

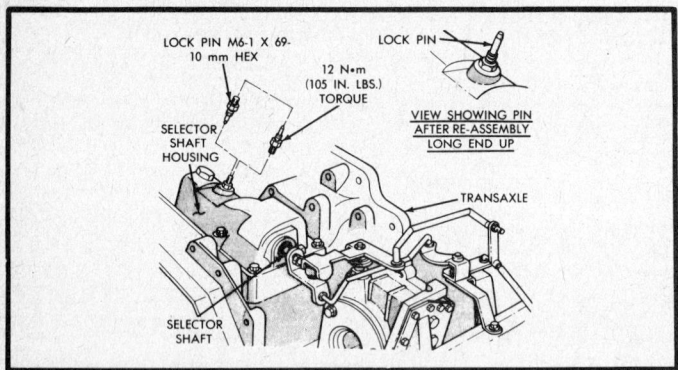

Adjustment of gearshift linkage on the A–460 manual transaxle (© Chrysler Corporation)

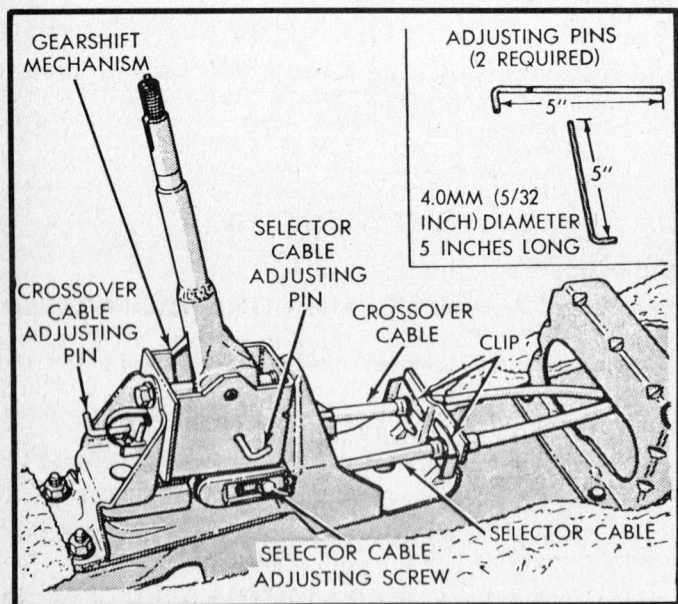

Fabricating transmission cable adjusting pins and adjusting the selector cable on console shifter
(© Chrysler Corporation)

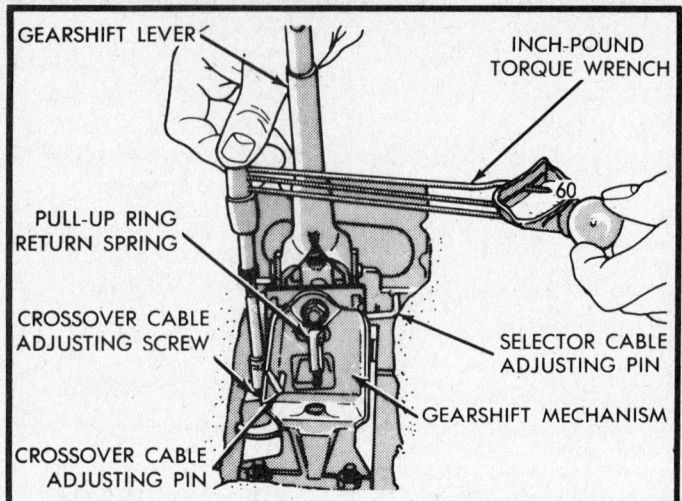

Console shifter crossover cable adjustment
(© Chrysler Corporation)

3. Remove the gearshift knob, retaining nut and pull-up ring from the console shift lever.
4. Remove the console cover.
5. Fabricate two (2) adjusting pins from 5/32 in. wire stock. Make the pins 5 in. long with a right angle bend at one end.
6. Insert one pin into the hole on the passenger side of the shifter mechanism. Loosen the selector cable adjusting screw and then tighten the screw to exactly 60 inch lbs. (7 Nm).
7. Insert the second pin into the hole in the rear bracket on the shifter mechanism. Loosen the crossover cable adjusting screw and then tighten it to exactly 60 inch lbs. (7 Nm).
8. Remove the fabricated adjusting pins from the shifter mechanism.
9. Remove the lock pin from the selector shaft housing and reinstall the lock pin with the long end up. Torque the lock pin to 105 inch lbs. (12 Nm).
10. Check for shifting into first and reverse and blockout into reverse. Install the console cover and shift lever parts.

Automatic Transmission

The automatic transaxle combines a torque converter, fully automatic 3–speed transmission, final drive gearing and differential into a compact front wheel drive system. Officially, they are designated the A–404, A–413, A–415 and A–470 Torqueflite Automatic Transaxle.

All automatic transmission on-car service procedures are contained in the Automatic Transmission Unit Repair Section.

THROTTLE CABLE

Adjustment

1. Perform transaxle kickdown cable adjustment while engine is at normal operating temperature, or make sure carburetor is not on fast idle cam by disconnecting choke.
2. Loosen adjustment bracket lock screw. Bracket must slide freely on its slot. The bracket should be positioned with both bracket alignment tabs touching the transaxle cast surface.
3. Slide bracket to the left (toward engine) to the limit of its travel.
4. Release bracket and move throttle lever fully right to its internal stop. This will pull the bracket back to its correct position. Tighten adjustment screw to 105 inch lbs. (12 Nm).
5. When correctly adjusted, the transmission throttle lever will move with the slightest carburetor throttle opening and will come to within 0.080 in. (2mm) of full travel at wide open throttle.

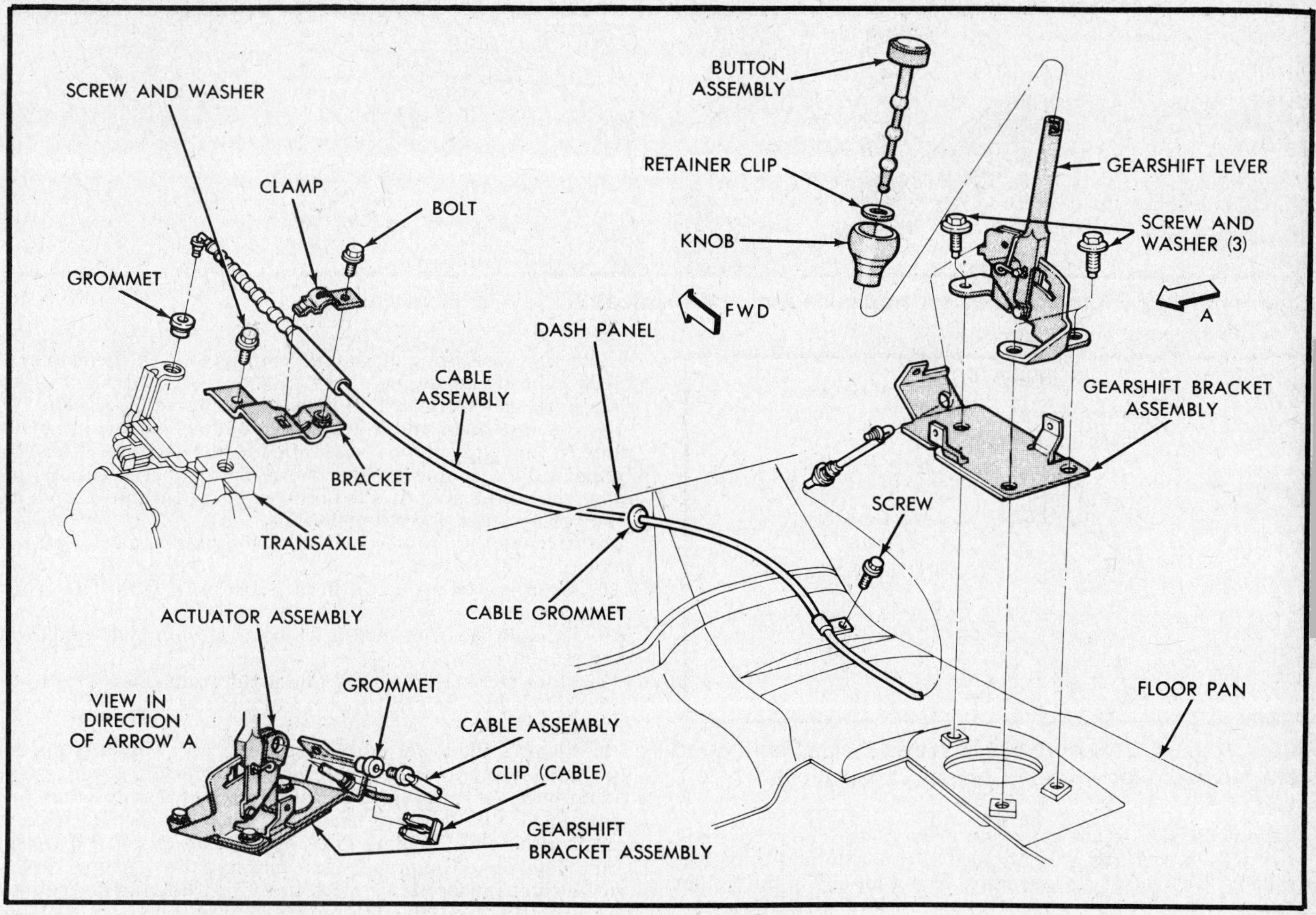

CHRYSLER CORPORATION
FRONT WHEEL DRIVE CARS
SECTION 2

Automatic transaxle shift detent control linkage (© Chrysler Corporation)

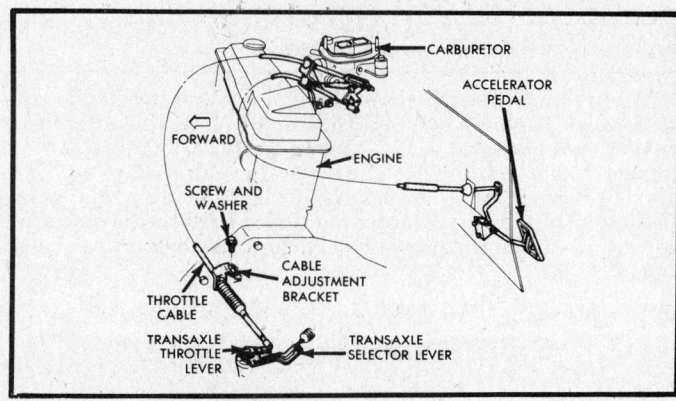

Throttle control cable components
(© Chrysler Corporation)

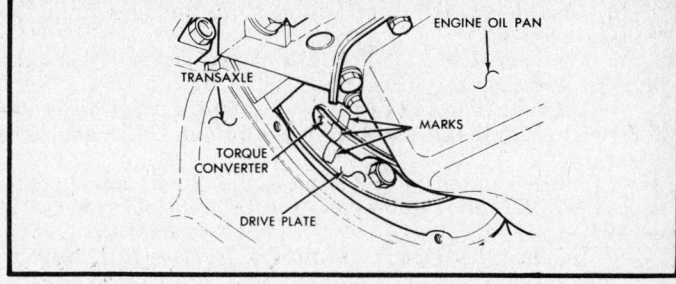

Marking torque converter and drive plate before removal
(© Chrysler Corporation)

SHIFT LINKAGE

Adjustment
A-404, A-413, A-415, A-470

NOTE: When it is necessary to disconnect the linkage cable from the lever, which uses plastic grommets as retainers, the grommets should be replaced.

1. Make sure that the adjustable swivel block is free to slide on the shift cable.
2. Place the shift lever in Park.
3. With the linkage assembled, and the swivel lock bolt loose, move the shift on the transaxle all the way to the rear detent.
4. Tighten the adjuster swivel lock bolt to 8 ft. lb.
5. Check the linkage action.

Removal and Installation
While the removal of the transaxle does not require the removal of the engine, it should be noted that care must be used to

2-83

SECTION 2

CHRYSLER CORPORATION
FRONT WHEEL DRIVE CARS

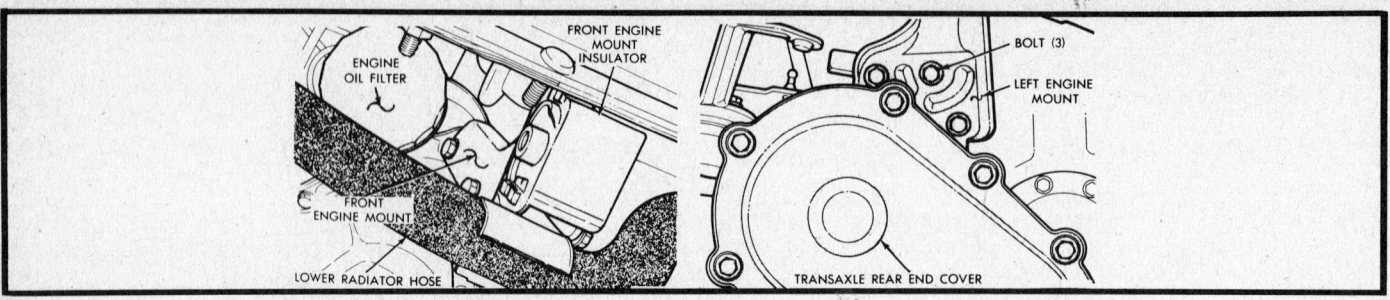

Disconnecting engine mounts for transaxle removal—typical (© Chrysler Corporation)

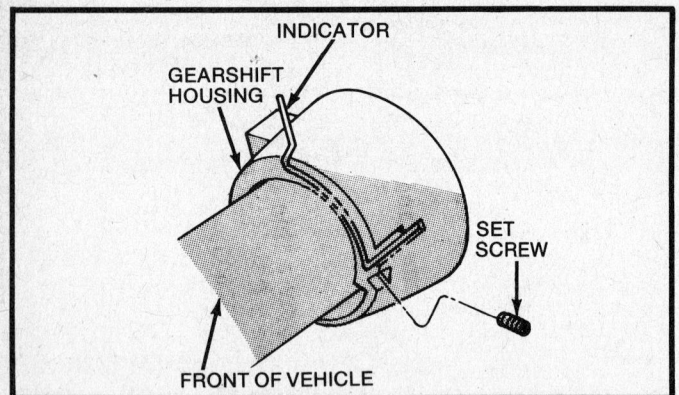

Aries, Reliant, LeBaron, 400, 600 and E class shift quadrant indicator location (© Chrysler Corporation)

prevent damage to the converter drive plate. The drive plate will not support any weight, so the transaxle and converter must be removed as an assembly. Do not let any of the weight of the transaxle or converter rest on the drive plate during removal. Also, after installing the transaxle, fill the differential with Dexron® before lowering vehicle.

1. Disconnect the negative battery cable.
2. Disconnect the throttle and shift linkages from the transaxle levers.
3. While vehicle is still on floor (apply brakes), loosen the hub nut and then the wheel nuts.
4. Raise vehicle and remove the hub nuts, the washer under the nut and the wheel nuts. Remove the wheel/tire assembly.
5. Inside the left fender, remove the splash shield. Then drain the differential and remove the differential cover, (early models).
6. Remove the upper coolant tube. Remove the speedometer adapter and pinion assembly from right drive shaft.
7. Remove the sway bar and the lower ball joint to steering knuckle bolts. Pry the ball joint from the steering knuckle.
8. Push the hub outward and pull drive shaft splined end from hub.
9. (Early models)—Turn the drive shafts to expose the ends of the circlips. These are squeezed together with needle nose pliers while prying them out. The circlips are removed and installed with the shaft.
10. Remove the drive shafts, being careful of the boots and supporting the joints at each end. (Early models)—Take note that the circlips are aligned with the flattened end of the shaft. Always install new clips on the inner shaft when reassembling and align carefully. Failure to do so will cause jamming or component damage.
11. Lower vehicle and install a suitable fixture to hold the engine weight. This is very important for the engine mounts will be removed. Snug up the bolt connected to the head to hold the weight of the engine.
12. Remove the upper bell housing-to-engine block bolts.
13. Raise vehicle and mark the torque converter and drive plate so that they can be reinstalled in the same relationship. Remove the torque converter bolts. To rotate the engine, remove the access plug that is in the right splash shield, and use a suitable socket and extension.
14. Remove the lower cooler tube and pull connector off the neutral safety switch.
15. Remove the engine mount bracket from the front crossmember.
16. Remove the front mount insulator through bolt and front engine mount bolts.
17. Place transmission jack under the transaxle.
18. Remove the left engine mount, and the long bolt through the mount.
19. Remove the lower bell housing bolts. Pry against the engine and lower transaxle, being careful of the torque converter. Installation of the transaxle is a reversal of the procedure but remember to fill the differential with Dexron® automatic transmission fluid before lowering the car. Also pay particular attention to the proper positioning of the "circlips" on the drive shaft inboard ends, with the "tangs" laying on the flattened end of the shaft. Holding the joint housing, a quick, firm push will complete the lock-up of the "circlips" on the axle side gear.

--- **CAUTION** ---
Make sure the clips are positioned correctly.

When reinstalling the lower ball joint to the steering knuckle, torque the clamp bolt to 50 ft. lbs. (68 Nm). The differential cover is not installed with a gasket, but with TRV sealant in a ribbon about 1/8 in. wide. The screws are torqued to 165 inch lbs. (19 Nm). If the inner drive shaft boots appear collapsed or deformed, slip a small round rod under the boot to vent some air into it since a vacuum may have formed when it was pushed home.

SHIFT QUADRANT POINTER

Adjustment

NOTE: Always check for proper automatic transmission linkage adjustment before changing the adjustment of the shift quadrant indicator.

1. Remove the instrument panel steering column cover. Set the shift lever in park position.
2. Loosen the set screw holding the indicator wire and adjust the wire to align with "P" park.
3. Re-tighten the set screw and install the steering column cover.
4. Check for indicator alignment from low position through park and readjust if necessary.

CHRYSLER CORPORATION
FRONT WHEEL DRIVE CARS
SECTION 2

DRIVESHAFT AND U–JOINTS

CONSTANT VELOCITY JOINTS

The driveshaft assemblies are three piece units. Each driveshaft has an inner sliding constant velocity (Tripode) joint bolted to the transaxle and an outer constant velocity (Rzeppa) joint with a stub shaft splined into the hub. The connecting shafts for the CV–joints are unequal in length and construction. The left side is a short solid shaft and the right is longer and tubular.

NOTE: All 2.2L turbocharged vehicles use equal length shafts.

DRIVESHAFT

Removal and Installation

A–460, A–465, A–525 MANUAL TRANSAXLE

The inboard CV–joints have stub shafts splined into two differential side gears. The drive shafts are retained in the side gears by a constant spring force provided by spring contained within the inboard CV–joints. These shafts have no circlips and their removal does not require differential cover removal.

1. For removal of right driveshaft, the speedometer pinion must be removed before shaft removal.
2. Remove the clamp bolt securing the ball joint stud into steering knuckle.
3. Separate the ball joint stud from the steering knuckle by prying against knuckle leg and control arm.

— CAUTION —
Do not damage ball joint or CV–joint boots.

4. Separate the outer CV–joint splined shaft from the hub by holding CV–housing while moving knuckle (hub) assembly away.

— CAUTION —
Do not pry on or otherwise damage wear sleeve on outer CV–joint.

5. Support assembly at CV–joint housings. Remove by pulling outward on the inner joint housing.

— CAUTION —
Do not pull on the drive shaft.

6. Installation is the reverse of removal. Fill the differential with Dexron® automatic transmission fluid. Torque the hub nut to 180 ft. lbs. (245 Nm).

NOTE: The 1984 and later 024, Daytona/Laser Models have equal length half shafts. The half shafts are fastened by bolts to a flange at the transaxle end. The steering knuckle end of the shafts is removed in the same manner as previous models.

1983 AND LATER MODELS

The drive axles are removed and replaced following the procedure for the A–460/A–465/A–525 manual transaxles.

DRIVESHAFT IDENTIFICATION

Driveshafts are identified as "A.C.I.", "G.K.N.", "S.S.G." or "CITROEN" assemblies. Vehicles can be equipped with any of these four assemblies, however, they should not be intermixed.

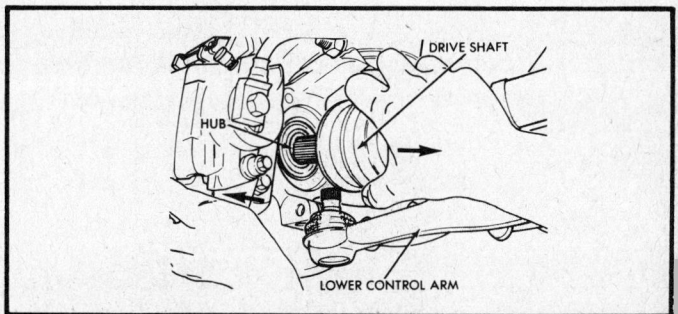

Pulling drive shaft from transaxle, A460, A465 and A525 manual transaxle models (© Chrysler Corporation)

DRIVESHAFT POSITIONING SPECIFICATIONS

Front wheel drive vehicles have engine mounts with slotted holes allowing for side to side positioning of the engine. If the vertical bolts on the right or left upper engine mount have been loosened (e.g., engine removal and installation) for any reason, or if the vehicle has experienced front structural damage, driveshaft lengths must be checked and corrected, if required. A shorter than required driveshaft length can result in objectionable noise. A longer than required driveshaft length may result in potential damage.

Use of the following procedure will insure satisfactory driveshaft engagement under all normal vehicle operating conditions.

1. The vehicle must be completely assembled. Front wheels must be properly aligned and in the straight ahead position. The vehicle must be in a position so that the full weight of the body is distributed to all four tires. A platform hoist, or front end alignment rack, is recommended.
2. Using a tape measure or other suitable measuring device, measure the direct distance from the inner edge of the outboard boot to the inner edge of the inboard boot on both driveshafts. This measurement must be taken at the bottom (six o'clock position) of the driveshafts. Note the required dimension varies with car-line, engine, transaxle, and driveshaft manufacturer.
3. If the lengths of both shafts are within the range specified, no further action is required.
4. If either the left or right shaft length is not within the specified range, position the engine according to the driveshaft lengths specified.
5. If proper driveshaft lengths cannot be achieved within the travel limits available in the slotted engine mounts, check for any condition that could effect the side to side position of the measurement locations (e.g., engine support brackets, siderail alignments, etc.).
6. After insuring proper driveshaft lengths, the transmission shift linkage must be readjusted to insure proper operation.

C/V JOINT BOOTS

Handling and Cleaning

It is vitally important during any service procedures requiring boot handling that care be taken not to puncture or tear by overtightening clamps or misuse of tool(s) or pinching the boot.

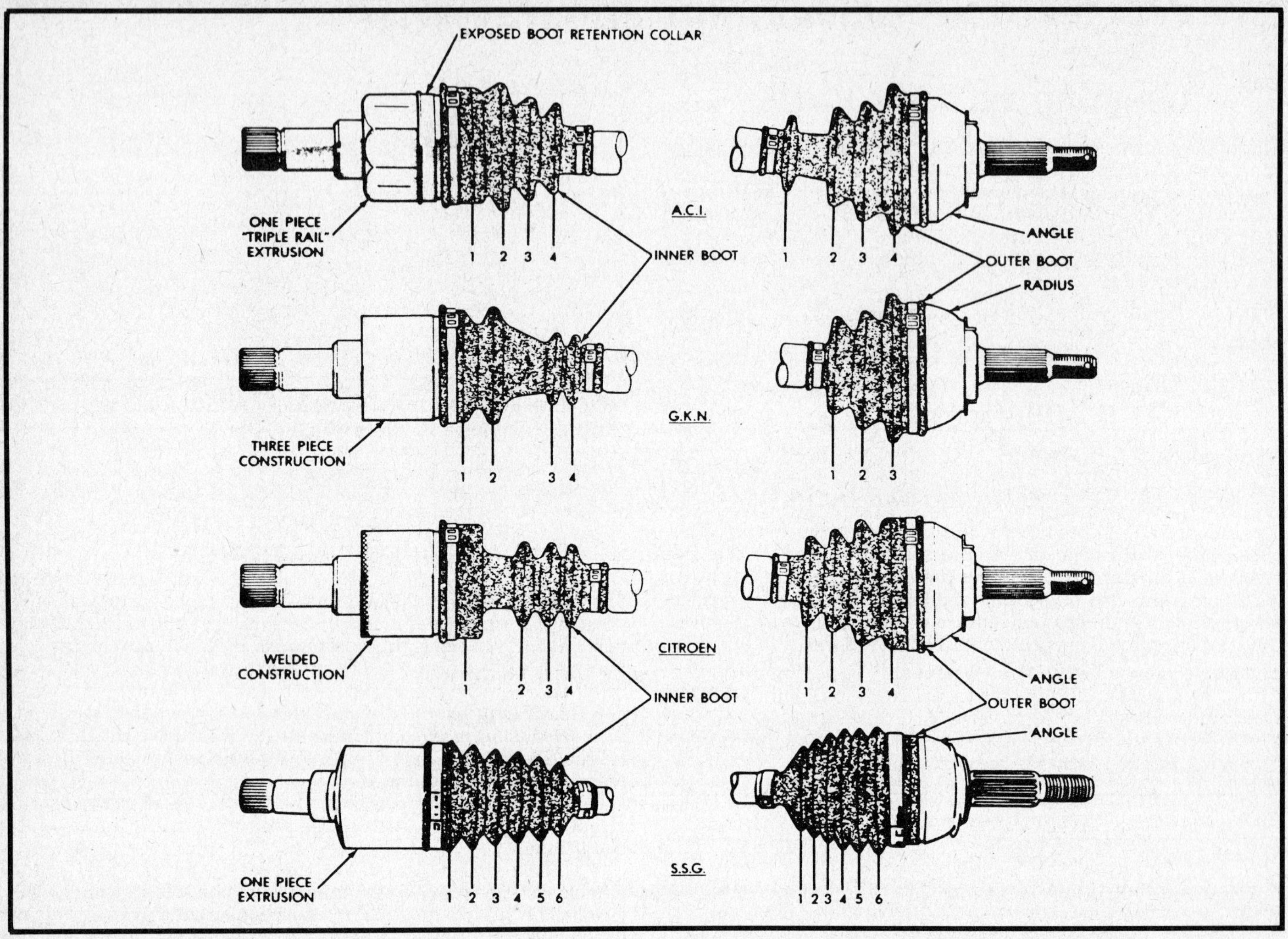

CHRYSLER CORPORATION
FRONT WHEEL DRIVE CARS

Drive shaft identification

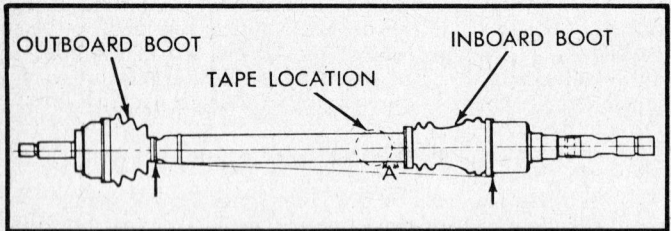

Drive shaft positioning measurement location
(© Chrysler Corporation)

Pinching can occur by rotating the CV–joints (especially the tripod) beyond normal working angles.

The rubber material in driveshaft boots is not compatible with oil, gasoline, or cleaning solvents. Care must be taken that boots never come in contact with any of these.

NOTE: The only acceptable cleaning agent for driveshaft boots is soap and water. After washing, boot must be thoroughly rinsed and dried before reusing.

Inspect

Noticeable amounts of grease on areas adjacent and on the exterior of the CV–joint boot is the first indication that a boot is punctured, torn or that a clamp has loosened. When a CV–joint is removed for service, the boot should be properly cleaned and inspected for cracks, tears and scuffed areas on interior surfaces. If any of these conditions exist, boot replacement is recommended.

Installation

Different boot clamping methods are used on the various driveshaft assemblies. A.C.I. and G.K.N. units generally use metal "ladder" type clamps. However, two alternate clamps are also used. A small rubber clamp for the housing Citroen units use a two piece clamp consisting of a strap and buckle. This clamp is used at all boot attachment points and can also be used for A.C.I. and A.K.N. applications.

S.S.G. C/V joints use two different types of boots, one made of plastic and the other of rubber. The plastic boot requires a heavy duty clamp and installer No. C–4975. The soft boot requires a clamp with a rounded edge to prevent the clamp from cutting the boot.

A.C.I. and G.K.N. boot installations require the use of a clamp installer, Tool C–4124 or equivalent, to compress the clamp bridge. Proceed with boot installation as follows:

1. If so equipped, slide small rubber clamp onto the shaft.
2. Slide the small end of the boot over the shaft, position as follows:
   a. Right Inner CV–Joint – Position the small end of the

CHRYSLER CORPORATION
FRONT WHEEL DRIVE CARS

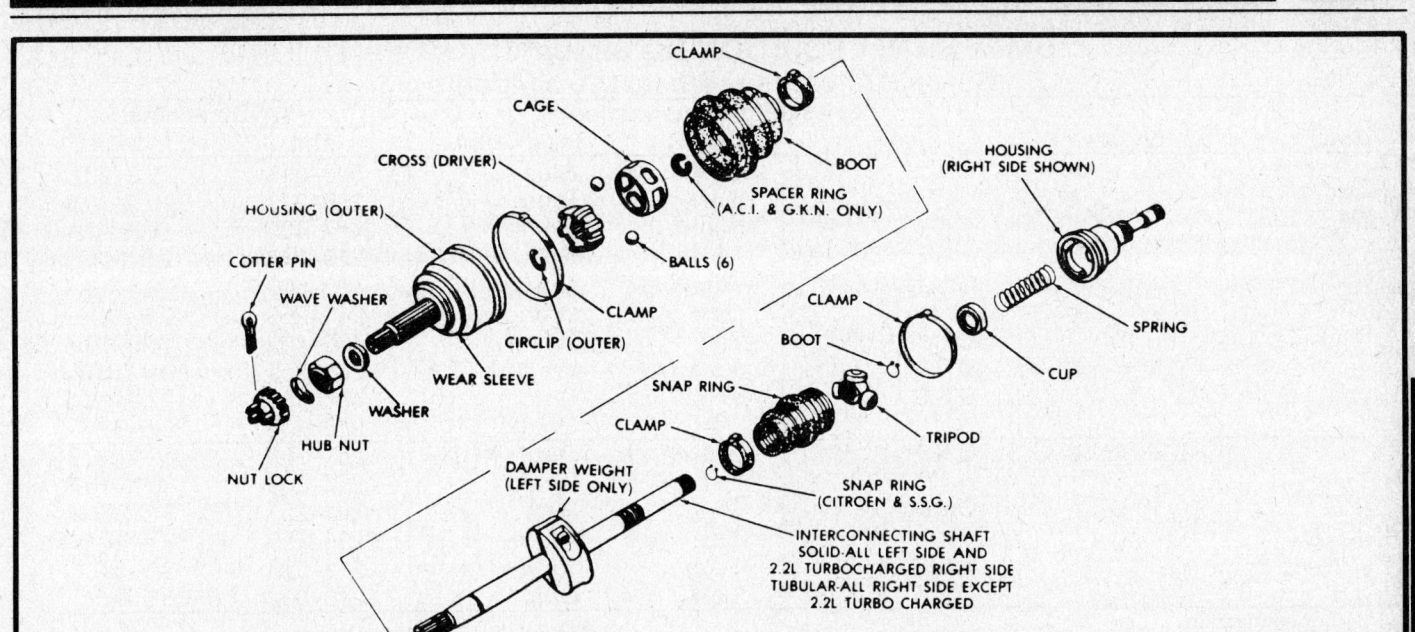

Exploded view of drive shaft components—typical

DRIVE SHAFT POSITIONING SPECIFICATIONS
1984 and later Front Wheel Drive Models

Body	Engine	Driveshaft Identification			"A" Dimension	
		Type	Side	Tape Color	mm	Inch
L	1.6L/2.2L	G.K.N.	Right	Yellow	498–509	19.6–20.0
			Left	Yellow	240–253	9.5–10.0
		A.C.I.	Right	Red	469–478	18.5–19.0
			Left	Red	208–218	8.2–8.6
	2.2L Turbo	Citroen	Right	Orange	211–220	8.3–8.7
			Left	Orange	211–220	8.3–8.7
L-GLH	2.2L	Citroen	Right	Green	465–477	18.3–18.8
			Left	Green	211–220	8.3–8.7
		A.C.I.	Right	Blue	463–472	18.2–18.6
			Left	Blue	204–213	8.0–8l.4
K,E,G,H	2.2L/2.5L	G.K.N.	Right	Blue	505–515	19.9–20.3
			Left	Blue	259–277	10.2–10.9
		A.C.I.	Right	Green	477–485	18.8–19.1
			Left	Green	229–244	9.0–9.6
		G.K.N./A.C.I.	Right	Orange	492–500	19.4–19.7
			Left	Orange	243–258	9.6–10.2
		Citroen	Right	White	480–492	18.9–19.4
			Left	White	238–255	9.4–10.0
		S.S.G.	Right	Gold	457–469	17.9–18.5
			Left	Gold	216–232	8.5–9.1
	2.6L	G.K.N.	Right	Silver	501–510	19.7–20.1
			Left	Silver	254–269	10.0–10.6
		Citroen	Right	Yellow	480–492	18.9–19.4
			Left	Yellow	238–255	9.4–10.0
K,E,G,H	2.2L Turbo	G.K.N.	Right	Tan	257–265	10.1–10.4
			Left	Silver	254–269	10.0–10.6
		Citroen	Right	Red	241–251	9.5–9.9
			Left	Yellow	238–255	9.4–10.0

CHRYSLER CORPORATION
FRONT WHEEL DRIVE CARS

DRIVE SHAFT POSITIONING SPECIFICATIONS
1984 and later Front Wheel Drive Models

Body	Engine	Driveshaft Identification			"A" Dimension	
		Type	Side	Tape Color	mm	Inch
P	2.2L	G.K.N.	Right	Blue	505-515	19.9-20.3
			Left	Blue	259-277	10.2-10.9
		A.C.I.	Right	Green	477-485	18.8-19.1
			Left	Green	229-244	9.0-9.6
		G.K.N./A.C.I.	Right	Orange	492-500	19.4-19.7
			Left	Orange	243-258	9.6-10.2
		Citroen	Right	White	480-492	18.9-19.4
			Left	White	238-255	9.4-10.0
		S.S.G.	Right	Gold	457-469	17.9-18.5
			Left	Gold	216-232	8.5-9.1
P	2.2L Turbo	G.K.N.	Right	Tan	257-265	10.1-10.4
			Left	Silver	254-269	10.1-10.6
		Citroen	Right	Red	241-251	9.5-9.9
			Left	Yellow	238-255	9.4-10.0
		S.S.G.	Right	Turquoise	219-228	8.6-9.0
			Left	Gold	216-232	8.5-9.1

Body Identification
L—Horizon, Turismo, Omni, Charger, Shelby Charger
G—Daytona, (and Turbo), Laser
H—Lancer, LeBaron GTS
K—Aries, Reliant, Caravelle (Canada), 600 ① LeBaron, Executive Sedan
E—Caravelle (U.S.), 600 ② New Yorker
P—Shadow, Sundance
① 100.3 inch wheel base
② 103.3 inch wheel base

boot lip face in line with the mark on the shaft.

b. Left Inner and Outer CV–Joint Boots—Position the small end of the boot in the groove provided.

3. Fasten the small boot end by placing the rubber clamp over the boot groove or fit the metal clamp in the boot groove. Make sure the boot is properly located on the shaft. Locate the clamp tangs in the slots making the clamp as tight as possible by hand.

4. Clamp bridge with Tool C–4124 and squeeze to complete tightening.

NOTE: During this operation care must be taken not to cut through the clamp bridge or damage boot.

5. After attaching the boot to the shaft, install the inner or outer CV–joint.

6. Locate the large end of the boot in the housing groove, or over the retaining shoulder, making sure the boot is not twisted. Install the metal spring clamp or fit the metal ladder clamp in the boot groove and locate the clamp tangs in the slots. Make the ladder clamp as tight as possible by hand.

7. Clamp bridge with Tool C–4124 or equivalent and squeeze to complete tightening.

NOTE: During this operation care must be taken not to cut through clamp bridge or damage boot.

---- CAUTION ----

Seal/Wear Sleeve Lubrication–During any service procedures where knuckle and driveshaft are separated, throughly clean seal and wear sleeve with suitable solvent (solvent must not touch boot) and relubricate both components prior to reinstalling driveshaft Lubricate wear sleeve and seal with MOPAR Multi-Purpose Lubricant, Part Number 2932524 or equivalent.

8. Apply on the full circumference of the Wear Sleeve a bead of lubricant that is ¼ in. (6mm) wide to seal contact area. Fill lip to housing cavity on Seal, complete circumference, and "wet" seal lip with lubricant.

CITROEN BOOT
Citroen boot installation requires use of clamp installer Tool C–4653 or equivalent, to tighten and cut the strap type clamp. Proceed with boot installation as follows:

1. Slide the small end of the boot over the shaft. If Installing an outer CV–joint boot, position the vent sleeve under the boot clamp groove. Position as follows:

a. Right Inner CV–Joint Boot—Align the boot lip face with the inboard edge of the part number label. If the label is no longer attached, align the edge of the boot lip with the mark remaining on the shaft where the previous boot was attached.

b. Left Inner and Outer CV–Joint Boots—Position the boot between the locating shoulders and align the edge of the boot lip with the mark remaining on the shaft where the previous boot was attached.

NOTE: Boot clamping procedures are the same for attachment to the shafts or CV–joints.

2. Wrap binding strap around boot twice, PLUS 2 ½ in. (63mm).

3. Pass the strap through the buckle and fold it back about 1 ⅛ in. (29mm) on the inside of the buckle.

4. Put the strip around the boot with the eye of the buckle toward you. Wrap the strip around the boot once and pass it through the buckle, then wrap it around a second time also passing it through the buckle.

5. Fold the strip back slightly to prevent it from slipping backwards.

6. Open the Tool all the way and place strip in narrow slot approximately ½ in. (13mm) from buckle.

7. Hold the binding strip with the left hand and push the Tool forward and slightly upward, and then fit the hook of the Tool into the eye of the buckle.

8. Tighten the strip by closing the tool handles. Then rotate the tool (handles) downward while slowly releasing the pressure on the tool handles. Allow the tool (handles) to open progressively. Then open the tool entirely and remove them sideways.

9. If the strap is not tight enough, re-engage the tool a second or even a third time, always about ½ in. (13mm) from the buckle. When tightening always be careful to see that the strap slides in a straight line and without resistance in the buckle, that is without making a fold. An effective grip will be ob-

tained only by following the above instructions.
10. If the strip is tight enough, remove the tool sideways and cut off the strap 1/8 in. (3mm), so that it does not overlap the edge of the buckle. Complete job by folding the strip back neatly.

---- **CAUTION** ----

During any service procedures where knuckle and driveshaft are separated, thoroughly clean seal and wear sleeve with suitable solvent and relubricate BOTH components at reassembly. Do not allow solvent to contact boot.

---

11. Lubricate wear sleeve (and seal) with MOPAR Multi-Purpose lubricant, or equivalent, as follows:
  a. Wear sleeve: Apply a full circumference 1/4 in. (6mm) bead of lubricant to seal contact area.
  b. Seal: Fill lip to housing cavity (full circumference) and "wet" seal lip with lubricant.
12. Complete installation of inner or outer CV–joint and remaining end of boot by following installation procedures for clamping.

TYPE S.S.G. WITH PLASTIC BOOT (LEFT INNER, LEFT AND RIGHT OUTER C/V JOINT)

1. With the axle assembly removed from the vehicle and disassembled, remove the plastic and rubber boots from the shaft assembly. Prepare the assembly before installing the boot.
2. To install the plastic boot, slide the small clamp onto the shaft.
3. Position the small end of the boot over the shaft with the lip of the boot in the third groove, towards the center of the shaft.
4. Position the clamp evenly over the boot, place the clamp installer tool No. C–4975 or equivalent, over the bridge of the clamp and tighten the nut until the jaws of the tool are completely closed, face to face.
5. After attaching the boot to the shaft, assemble and install the C/V joint.
6. Position the large end of the boot on the housing and install the clamp. Crimp the bridge of the clamp with the tool.

---- **CAUTION** ----

Use only the clamps provided in the boot package for this application, otherwise damage to the boot or C/V joint may occur.

TYPE S.S.G. WITH RUBBER BOOT (RIGHT INNER C/V JOINT)

1. With the axle assembly removed from the vehicle and disassembled as required, remove the rubber boot. Prepare the assembly before installing the boot.
2. Slide the small clamp onto the shaft assembly.
3. Install the boot onto the shaft, positioning the the flat between the locating shoulders.
4. Position the clamp on the boot and crimp the bridge of the clamp with tool No. C–3250 or its equivalent.
5. Install the C/V joint assembly. Position the large end of the boot on the housing and install the clamp and crimp the bridge of the clamp with the tool.

---- **CAUTION** ----

During any service procedures where the knuckle and the driveshaft are separated, thoroughly clean the seal and wear sleeve with a suitable solvent. Relubricate both components at time of reassembly.

---

6. Apply a full circumference bead (1/4 in.) of lubricant to the seal contact area of the wear sleeve.
7. Fill the seal lip to housing cavity and "WET" seal lip with lubricant.

DAMPER WEIGHTS

1984 AND LATER

Damper weights are used on the left driveshaft assemblies of all front wheel drive vehicles. These weights are attached to the interconnecting shaft and are not available as a separate service part. However, they can be removed from the driveshaft assembly during driveshaft positioning specifications procedures. When the weights are reattached between the locating shoulders, tighten the fasteners to the following specifications:
A.C.I.–8 ft. lbs. (11 Nm)
CITROEN and S.S.G.–21 ft. lbs. (28 Nm).
G.K.N.–23 ft. lbs. (30 Nm)

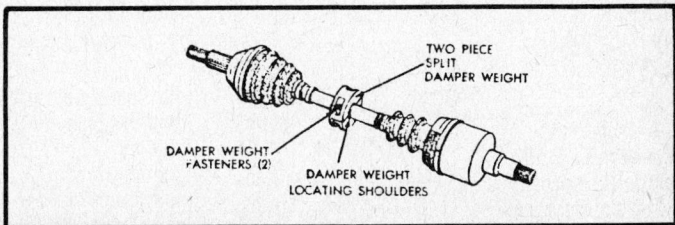

Installation of damper weight on drive shaft
(© Chrysler Corporation)

REAR SUSPENSION

OMNI, HORIZON, TURISMO, TC3, 024 AND CHARGER

A trailing, independent arm assembly, with integral sway bar is used. The wheel spindles are attached to two trailing arms which extend rearward from mounting points on the body where they are attached with shock absorbing, oval bushings. A crossmember is welded to the trailing arms, just to the rear of the bushings. A coil spring over shock absorber strut assembly, similar to the front suspension, is used.

ARIES AND RELIANT, DODGE 400, 600, CARAVELLE, LANCER, LEBARON GTS, E CLASS/ NEW YORKER, DAYTONA, LASER, LEBARON SHADOW AND SUNDANCE MODELS

These cars use a flexible beam axle with trailing links and coil springs. One shock absorber on each side is mounted outside the coil spring and attached to the body and the beam axle. Wheel spindles are bolted to the outer ends of the axle.

NOTE: For service information on the rear suspension, refer to the Unit Repair Section.

SECTION 3

CHRYSLER CORPORATION
REAR WHEEL DRIVE CARS

SPECIFICATIONS

Belt Tension	3–7	Serial Number Identification	3–4
Brakes	24–2	Torque	3–6
Capacities	3–6	Torque Sequence (Cylinder Heads)	3–36
Crankshaft & Connecting Rod	3–5	Tune-Up	3–5
Firing Order	3–5	Valve	3–5
General Engine	3–4	Wheel Alignment	3–6
Piston & Ring	3–6		

INDEX

A
Alternator R&R 3–7
Automatic Transmission
   Adjustment 3–49
   On Car Service 23–2
   Assembly R&R 3–48
Axle Assembly R&R 3–51
Axle Shaft R&R 3–51

B
Ball Joints 35–2
Belt Tension 3–7
Brake System 3–47
Brake Booster 3–47
Brake Caliper Overhaul 24–2
Brake Caliper R&R
   Front 24–2
Brake Drum
   Rear 24–2
Brake Master Cylinder 3–47
Brake Pad
   Front 24–2
Brake Shoe
   Rear 24–2

C
Camshaft R&R 3–39
Carburetor R&R 3–22
Circuit Breakers 3–19
Chassis Electrical 3–8
Component Locations 3–16
Control Arm R&R 35–2
Cooling System 3–19
Cruise Control 3–16
Cylinder Head 3–35
   R&R 3–35

D
Differential 28–2
   Inspection 28–2
Dimmer Switch R&R 3–12
Disc Brakes 24–2
   Front 24–2
Distributor R&R 3–7
Drive Axle 28–2
Drive Belt Tension 3–7
Driveshaft R&R 3–50

E
Electrical Component
   Location 3–16
Electronic Ignition 30–2
Emission Controls 3–31

Engine 3–31
   Identification 3–4
   R&R 3–31
Engine Electrical 3–7
Engine Lubrication 3–40
Engine Mechanical 3–31
Engine Mounts R&R 3–32
Exhaust Manifold R&R 3–28

F
Front Suspension 3–43
   Alignment 3–6
Fuel Injection 3–30
Fuel Mixture, Adjust 3–23
Fuel Pump R&R 3–22
Fuses 3–17
Fusible Links 3–19

H
Headlight Switch 3–11
Heater Blower R&R 3–20
Heater Core R&R 3–20
Heater Unit R&R 3–20
Horn Siwtch 3–13

I
Idle Speed Adjust 3–23
Ignition Lock 3–8
Ignition Switch 3–11
Ignition Timing 3–8
Instrument Cluster R&R 3–13
Intake Manifold R&R 3–28

L, M, N
Lower Control Arm R&R 35–2
Master Cylinder R&R 3–47
Neutral Safety Switch
   R&R 3–11

O
Oil Pan R&R 3–40
Oil Pump 3–41
   R&R 3–41
Oil Seal R&R
   Rear Main 3–41

P
Parking Brake 3–47
   Adjustment 3–47
   Cable R&R 3–47
Piston & Connecting Rod 3–33
Power Brake Unit R&R 3–47
Power Steering Pump R&R 3–45

R
Rear Main Oil Sear R&R 3–41

Rear Suspension 35–2
Regulator 3–7
Rocker Shaft/Assembly R&R 3–32

S
Serial Number 3–4
   Engine 3–4
   Vehicle 3–4
Shock Absorber R&R
   Front 35–2
   Rear 35–2
Springs
   Front 35–2
   Rear 35–2
Starter R&R 3–7
Starter Drive Replacement 3–7
Steering Column R&R 3–45
Steering Gear R&R 3–45
   Manual 3–43
   Power 3–43
Steering Wheel R&R 3–13
Stop Light Switch R&R 3–11
Speedometer R&R 3–14
Spindle R&R 35–2
Spindle R&R 35–2

T
Throttle Linkage, Adjust 3–49
Timing Chain 3–38
Timing Gear Cover 3–37
   Oil Seal Replacement 3–38
Tune-Up 3–5
Turn Signal Switch R&R 3–12

U, V
U–Joint Overhaul 28–2
Valve Tappette R&R 3–32
Valve Timing, Adjust 3–35
Valve System 3–32
Voltage Regulator 3–7

W, Y
Water Pump R&R 3–19
Wheel Alignment 3–6
   Front 3–6
Wheel Bearings
   Front 3–45
   Rear 35–1
Wheel Cylinders Rear 24–2
Windshield Wiper 3–13
   Linkage R&R 3–13
   Motor R&R 3–13
   Switch R&R 3–13
Year Identification 3–3

BEFORE SERVICING BE CERTAIN TO READ THE SAFETY NOTICE

Chrysler Corp.
1983–87 Rear Wheel Drive Cars

CHRYSLER—CORDOBA • IMPERIAL • TOWN & COUNTRY
NEW YORKER • 5TH AVENUE
DODGE—DIPLOMAT • DIPLOMAT SALON • MIRADA
PLYMOUTH—CARAVELLE • GRAN FURY •
GRAN FURY SALON

YEAR IDENTIFICATION

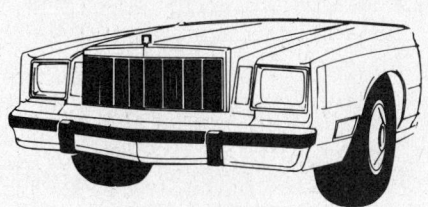

1983 Cordoba

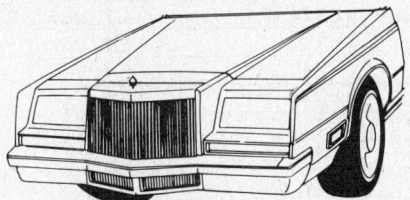

1983 Imperial

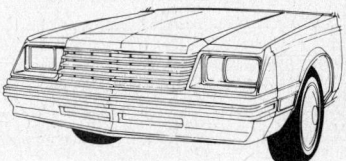

1983 Mirada

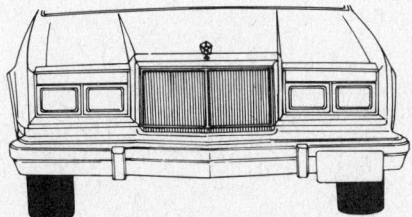

1983 New Yorker, Fifth Avenue

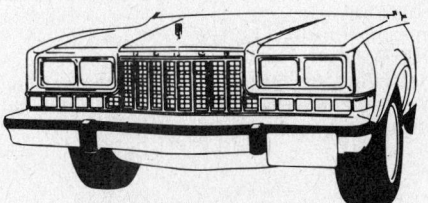

1983–84 Diplomat

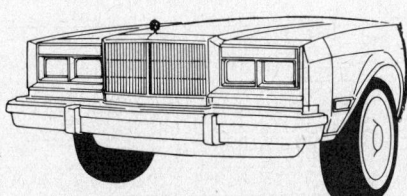

1984–87 Fifth Avenue

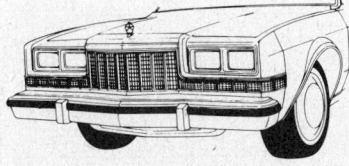

1983–87 Gran Fury

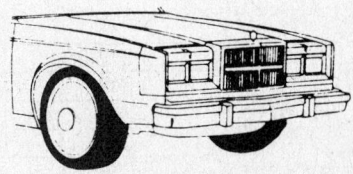

1985–87 Diplomat SE

SECTION 3
CHRYSLER CORPORATION
REAR WHEEL DRIVE CARS

VEHICLE IDENTIFICATION NUMBER (VIN)

It is important for servicing and ordering parts to be certain of the vehicle and engine identification. The VIN (vehicle identification number) is a 17 digit number visible through the windshield on the driver's side of the dash and contains the vehicle and engine identification codes. It can be interpreted as follows:

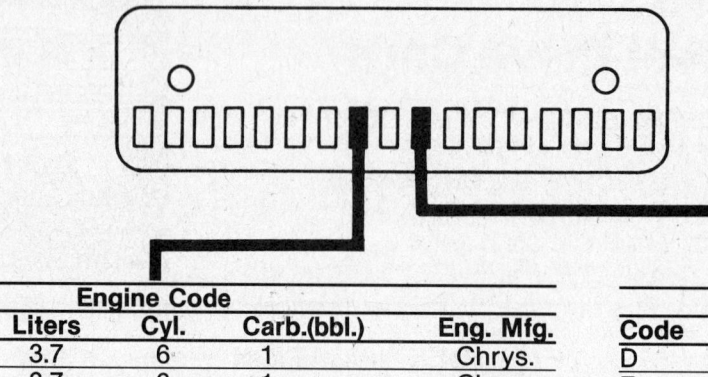

Engine Code

Code	Cu. In.	Liters	Cyl.	Carb.(bbl.)	Eng. Mfg.
E	225	3.7	6	1	Chrys.
H	225	3.7	6	1	Chrys.
F	225	3.7	6	1 H.D.	Chrys.
J	225	3.7	6	1 H.D.	Chrys.
G	225	3.7	6	2 ①	Chrys.
K	225	3.7	6	2 ①	Chrys.
H	225	3.7	6	2 H.D. ①	Chrys.
L	225	3.7	6	2 H.D. ①	Chrys.
K	318	5.2	8	2	Chrys.
P	318	5.2	8	2	Chrys.
L	318	5.2	8	2 H.D.	Chrys.
J	318	5.2	8	EFI	Chrys.
N	318	5.2	8	EFI	Chrys.
R	318	5.2	8	4	Chrys.
M	318	5.2	8	4	Chrys.
N	318	5.2	8	4 H.D.	Chrys.
S	318	5.2	8	4 H.D.	Chrys.

Model Year Code

Code	Year
D	1983
E	1984
F	1985
G	1986
H	1987

H.D. = Heavy Duty
EFI = Electronic Fuel Injection
① = Canada Only

The seventeen digit Vehicle Identification Number can be used to determine engine application and model year.
The 10th digit indicates the model year, and the 8th digit identifies the factory installed engine.
EFI Electronic Fuel Injection

GENERAL ENGINE SPECIFICATIONS

Year	Eng. VIN Code	Engine No. Cyl. Displacement (cu. in.)	Mfg. Mfg.	Carburetor Type	Horsepower @ rpm ■	Torque @ rpm (ft. lbs.) ■	Bore × Stroke (in.)	Compression Ratio	Oil Pressure @ 2000 rpm
'83	E	6-225	Chrys.	1 bbl	85 @ 3600	165 @ 1600	3.406 × 4.125	8.4:1	55
	E	6-225 Calif.	Chrys.	1 bbl	90 @ 3600	165 @ 1200	3.406 × 4.125	8.4:1	55
	K	8-318	Chrys.	2 bbl	130 @ 4000	235 @ 1600	3.910 × 3.310	8.6:1	55
	M	8-318 Calif.	Chrys.	4 bbl	165 @ 4000	240 @ 2000	3.910 × 3.310	8.5:1	55
	J	8-318	Chrys.	EFI	140 @ 4000	245 @ 2000	3.910 × 3.310	8.5:1	55
'84–'87	P	8-318	Chrys.	2 bbl	130 @ 4000	235 @ 1600	3.910 × 3.310	8.6:1 ①	55
	R	8-318	Chrys.	4 bbl	165 @ 4000	240 @ 2000	3.910 × 3.310	8.5:1 ①	55
	S	8-318 HD	Chrys.	4 bbl	165 @ 4000	240 @ 2000	3.910 × 3.310	8.5:1 ①	55

■Horsepower and torque are SAE net figures. They are measured at the rear of the transmission with all accessories installed and operating. Since the figures vary when a given engine is installed in different models, some figures are representative rather than exact.
HP High Performance
HD Heavy Duty
ESC Electronic Spark Control
EFI Electronic Fuel Injection
① 1985-86-9.0:1

CHRYSLER CORPORATION
REAR WHEEL DRIVE CARS
SECTION 3

TUNE-UP SPECIFICATIONS

When analyzing compression test results, look for uniformity among cylinders rather than specific pressures

Year	Eng. V.I.N. Code	Engine No. Cyl. Displacement (cu. in.)	Carb. (bbl.)	Spark Plugs Orig. Type	Spark Plugs Gap (in.)	Distributor Point Dwell (deg)	Distributor Point Gap (in.)	Ignition Timing (deg.)	Valves Intake Opens ■(deg.)	Fuel Pump Pressure (psi)	Idle Speed (rpm)
'83	H,J,K,L	6-225	1 & 2	RBL-16Y	.035	Electronic		⑤	6	4.0–5.5	750
	N,P,R,S	8-318	2 & 4	RN-12Y	.035	Electronic		⑤	10	5.75–7.25	700
'84–'87	P,R,S	8-318	2 & 4	RN-12Y	.035	Electronic		⑤	10	5.75–7.25	700

NOTE: The underhood specifications sticker often reflects tune-up specification changes made in production. Sticker figures must be used if they disagree with those in this chart.
Part numbers in this chart are not recommended by Chilton for any product by brand name.
■ All figures Before Top Dead Center
EFI Electronic Fuel Injection
⑤ See underhood sticker

FIRING ORDERS

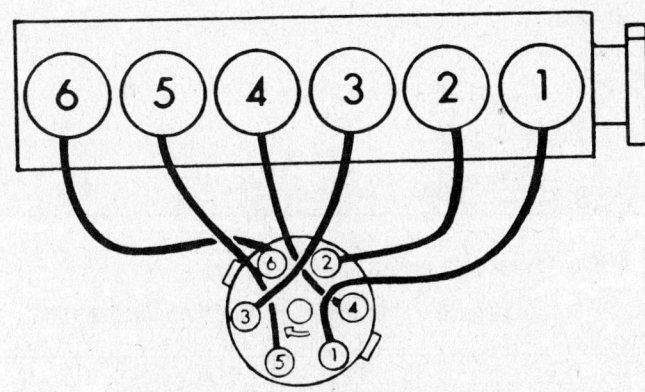

Chrysler Corp. 6-cyl.
Engine firing order: 1–5–3–6–2–4
Distributor rotation: clockwise

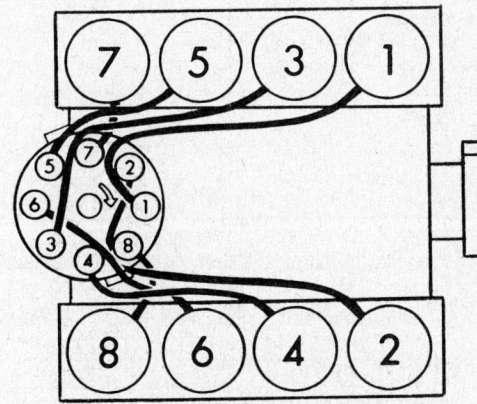

Chrysler Corp. 318, V8
Engine firing order: 1–8–4–3–6–5–7–2
Distributor rotation: clockwise

VALVE SPECIFICATIONS

Year	Engine No. Cyl. Displacement (cu. in.)	Seat Angle (deg.)	Face Angle (deg.)	Spring Test Pressure (lbs @ in.)	Spring Installed Height (in.)	Stem-to-Guide Clearance (in.) Intake	Stem-to-Guide Clearance (in.) Exhaust	Stem Diameter (in.) Intake	Stem Diameter (in.) Exhaust
'83–'87	6-225	45	①	143 @ 1.31	1 21/32	.0010–.0030	.0020–.0040	.3725	.3715
	8-318	45	45	177 @ 1.31 ②	1 11/16 ⑦	.0010–.0030 ③	.0020–.0040 ④	.3725 ⑤	.3715 ⑥

① Intake 45°, Exhaust 43° ③ 318 EFM—.0015–.0035 ⑤ 318 EFM—.3720 ⑦ 318 HP—1 21/32
② 318 EFM—193 @ 1.25 ④ 318 EFM—.0025–.0045 ⑥ 318 EFM—.3710

CRANKSHAFT AND CONNECTING ROD SPECIFICATIONS

All measurements are given in inches

Year	Engine No. Cyl. Displacement (cu in.)	Crankshaft Main Brg. Journal Dia	Crankshaft Main Brg. Oil Clearance	Crankshaft Shaft End-Play	Thrust on No.	Connecting Rod Journal Diameter	Connecting Rod Oil Clearance	Connecting Rod Side* Clearance
'83	6-225	2.7495–2.7505	.0010–.0025	.0035–.0095	3	2.1865–2.1875	.0010–.0025	.007–.013
'83–'87	8-318	2.4995–2.5005	.0005–.0020	.002–.010	3	2.1240–2.1250	.0005–.0025	.006–.014

*total for two rods on V8s

3–5

SECTION 3
CHRYSLER CORPORATION
REAR WHEEL DRIVE CARS

PISTON AND RING SPECIFICATIONS
All measurements are given in inches

Year	Engine No. Cyl. Displacement (cu in.)	Ring Gap			Ring Side Clearance			Piston Clearance ③ Piston-to-Bore Clearance
		Top Compression	Bottom Compression	Oil Control	Top Compression	Bottom Compression	Oil Control	
'83–'87	6-225, 8-318,	.010–.020	.010–.020	.015–.055	.0015–.0030 ①	.0015–.0030 ①	.0002–.0050	0.0005–0.0015

① .0015–.0040 in. on 1983–'84 318
③ At top of skirt

TORQUE SPECIFICATIONS
All readings in ft. lbs.

Year	Engine No. Cyl. Displacement (cu. in.)	Cylinder Head Bolts	Rod Bearing Bolts	Main Bearing Bolts	Crankshaft Damper Bolt	Flywheel-to-Crankshaft Bolts	Manifold	
							Intake	Exhaust
'83	6-225	70	45	85	Press fit	55	①	10
'83–'87	8-318	95 ④	45	85	100	55	45 ⑤	15/20 ②

① Intake to exhaust manifold bolts—17 ft. lbs., studs—20 ft. lbs.
② Nuts/screws
④ For '83 318 engines, see step #15 under "Cylinder Head Removal, V8" in text
⑤ 40—1983

CAPACITIES

Year	Engine No. Cyl. Displacement (Cu. In.)	Engine Crankcase Add 1 Qt For New Filter	Transmission pts to Refill After Draining			Drive Axle (pts)	Gasoline Tank (gals)	Cooling System (qts.)	
			Manual		Automatic			With Heater	With A/C
			3-Speed	4-Speed					
'83–'87	6-225	4	4.75	7.0 ④	17 ⑧	③	18	11.5	14.5 ②
	8-318	4	—	—	17 ⑧	③	18.0	15.0 ⑦	16.5 ⑨
	8-360	4	—	—	17 ⑧	③	18.0	16.0	16.0

② 15 qts on Cordoba, Mirada
③ 7¼" axle—2.1 pts., 8¼" axle—4.4 pts., 9¼" axle—4.5 pts.
⑦ 15.5 qts. on Imperial
⑧ A904 trans.; 15.9 pts.—A727 trans.
⑨ 17.5 on Imperial and heavy duty cooling systems.

WHEEL ALIGNMENT SPECIFICATIONS

Year	Model	Caster		Camber		Toe-in (in.)	Steering Axis Inclin. (deg.)	Wheel Pivot Ratio	
		Range (deg.)	Pref. Setting (deg.)	Range (deg.)	Pref. Setting (deg.)			Inner Wheel	Outer Wheel
'83–'87	Diplomat, Gran Fury, Newport, 5th Avenue	1¼P to 3¾P	2½ ± 1	1.4N–1¼P	½P ± ½	1/8 + 1/16	8	20	18

FRONT END HEIGHT

Year	Model	Front End Height (± 1/8 in.)
'83–'87	5th Avenue	12½ ①②

① ± ¼ in.
② Measured from the head of the suspension crossmember front isolater bolt to ground

3-6

CHRYSLER CORPORATION
REAR WHEEL DRIVE CARS
SECTION 3

BELT TENSION SPECIFICATIONS
Gauge Method

New Belt (All)	Used Belt (All)
120 Lbs. (530N) Gauge Reading	70 Lbs. (310N) Gauge Reading

BELT TENSION SPECIFICATIONS
Torque Method
All Measurements in ft. lbs.

Engine Displacement (cu. in.)	New Belt 225	New Belt 318	Used Belt 225	Used Belt 318
Alternator				
With A/C	60 (81 Nm)	75 (101 Nm)	40 (54 Nm)	50 (68 Nm)
Without A/C	60 (81 Nm)	75 (101 Nm)	40 (54 Nm)	40 (54 Nm)
Air Pump				
With A/C	40 (54 Nm)	—	25 (34 Nm)	—
Without A/C	75 (101 Nm)	—	50 (68 Nm)	—
Power Steering				
With A/P ①	—	120 (163 Nm)	—	60 (81 Nm)
Without A/P	—	50 (68 Nm)	—	40 (54 Nm)
Air Conditioning				
Without A/P ②	35 (48 Nm)	—	20 (27 Nm)	—

① Initial orientation of torque wrench is approximately horizontal.
② Adjusted at idler pulley bracket.

ELECTRICAL SECTION

For Overhaul Procedures, refer to the Unit Repair Section.

Charging System

ALTERNATOR

Removal and Installation

1. Disconnect the negative battery terminal.
2. Disconnect the Battery and Field leads from the alternator.
3. Remove the alternator by removing two mounting bolts; the belt tensioner bracket bolt and the drive belt.
4. Installation is the reverse of removal. Tighten the belt so that it can be depressed about ½ in. by moderate thumb pressure in the center of the longest span between pulleys. Some alternator brackets have a square hole into which a ½ in. square socket drive can be inserted to adjust the belt.

NOTE: Never attempt to polarize an alternator, or short the regulator.

REGULATOR

Removal and Installation

1. Disconnect the negative battery cable. Release the spring clips and pull off the regulator wiring plug.
2. Unbolt and remove the regulator.
3. Installation is the reverse of removal. Be sure that the spring clips engage the wiring plug and the unit has a good ground.

Starting System

STARTER

Removal and Installation

1. Disconnect the ground cable at the battery.
2. Remove the cable from the starter and heat shield.
3. Disconnect the solenoid leads at the solenoid terminals.
4. Remove the starter securing bolts and remove the starter from the engine flywheel housing. On some models with automatic transmissions, the fluid cooler tube bracket will interfere with starter removal. In this case, remove the starter securing bolts, slide the cooler tube bracket off the stud and then remove the starter.
5. Installation is the reverse of the above. Be sure that the starter and flywheel housing mating surfaces are free of dirt and oil. When tightening the bolt and nut, hold the starter away from the engine to ensure proper alignment during its seating as the bolt is tightened. Do not damage the flywheel housing seal, if so equipped.

Ignition System

DISTRIBUTOR

Removal

1. Remove the cap and wire assembly.
2. Disconnect the vacuum line at the distributor. Disconnect the lead wire at the harness connector.
3. Mark the relative positions of the distributor and rotor on the engine block or distributor housing edge.

SECTION 3

CHRYSLER CORPORATION
REAR WHEEL DRIVE CARS

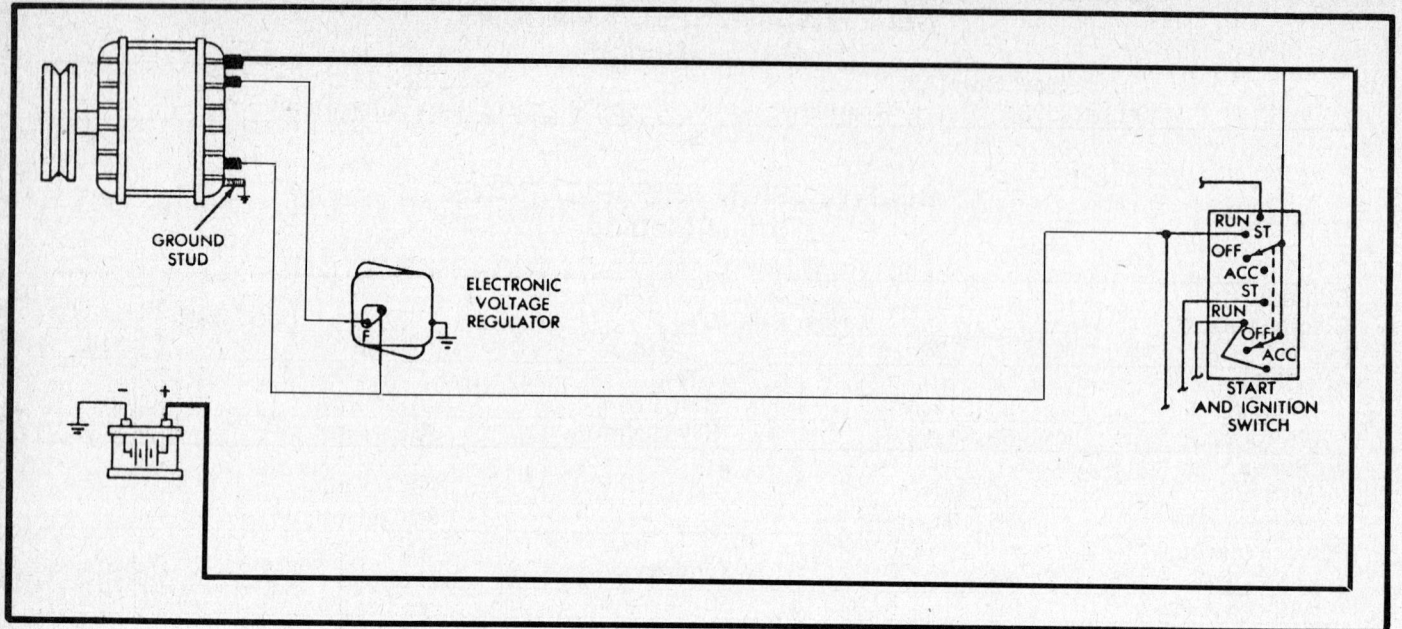

Schematic of typical charging circuit (© Chrysler Corp.)

4. Loosen the distributor mounting and lift out the distributor. Should the distributor shaft rotate slightly during the removal, make a second match-mark to indicated rotor positioning for installation.

NOTE: To simplify reinstallation, do not disturb the engine while the distributor is out.

5. Reinstall by reversing the above procedure, aligning the distributor rotor and the mark on the block when installing the distributor.

Replacement (When Engine Has Been Disturbed)

6 CYLINDER ENGINE
1. Rotate the engine until No. 1 piston is up on the compression stroke at top dead center. This is determined by the compression pressure and the 0 mark on the crankshaft pulley hub being aligned with the timing pointer, as the engine is rotated.
2. Rotate the rotor to a position just ahead of the No. 1 distributor cap terminal.
3. Lower the distributor into the opening, engaging the distributor gear with the drive gear on the camshaft. With the distributor fully seated on the engine, the rotor should be under the cap No. 1 tower.
4. Install the cap, tighten the hold-down arm bolt and check the timing with a timing light.

V8 ENGINE
1. Rotate the crankshaft until No. 1 cylinder is at top dead center.
2. The pointer on the chain case cover should be over the 0 mark on the crankshaft pulley.
3. The slot in the intermediate shaft which carries the gear that drives the oil pump and the distributor should be parallel (or nearly so) to the crankshaft.
4. Hold the distributor over the mounting pad on the cylinder block so that the distributor body flange coincides with the mounting pad and the rotor points to the No. 1 cylinder firing position.
5. Install the distributor while holding the rotor in position, allowing it to move only enough to engage the slot in the drive gear.

6. Install the cap, snug down the hold-down bolt and check the ignition timing with a timing light.

IGNITION TIMING
The ignition timing test indicates correct timing of the engine only at idle and with the engine hot. Check timing as follows:
1. Disconnect the vacuum hose at the distributor and plug the line, if not equipped with spark control computer.
2. Connect a timing light to No. 1 spark plug and to the battery terminals. Connect tachometer to engine.
3. Start the engine and set it to the specified idle speed with the transmission in Neutral.
4. If equipped with carburetor ground switch, connect jumper wire between switch and ground. If the engine is not equipped with a Spark Control Computer, disconnect and plug the vacuum line at the distributor.
5. If timing is out of allowed specifications, loosen and rotate distributor housing.
6. Turn the distributor housing in the direction of rotor-rotation to retard the timing. Rotate the distributor housing against its directions of rotation to advance the timing.
7. Tighten distributor locking bolt securely.
8. Recheck engine idle and remove test equipment. Complete connections and assemble component previously removed.

NOTE: A magnetic timing probe receptacle is mounted to timing indicator, should this type of tool be available. Follow the tool manufacturer's recommended timing procedure.

Electrical Controls

NOTE: Before removal of electrical components or switches, remove the battery negative cable.

IGNITION LOCK
Removal and Installation
STANDARD COLUMN
1. Remove the steering wheel and turn signal lever. Pull the

CHRYSLER CORPORATION
REAR WHEEL DRIVE CARS
SECTION 3

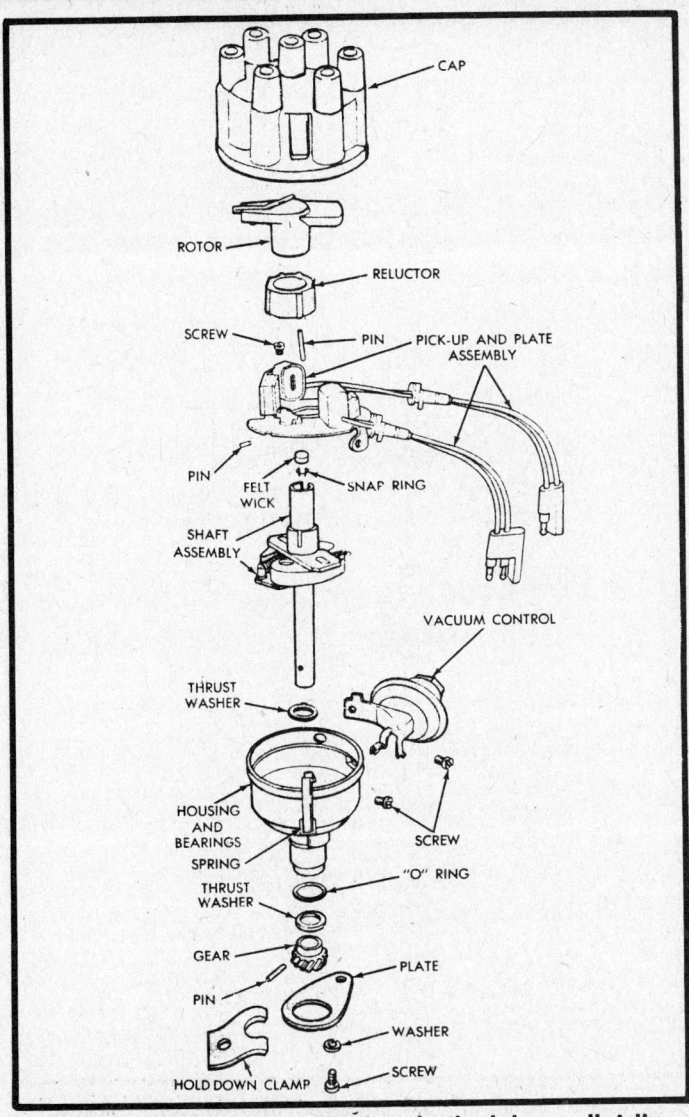

Exploded view of six cylinder dual pick-up distributor with governor and vacuum control (© Chrysler Corp.)

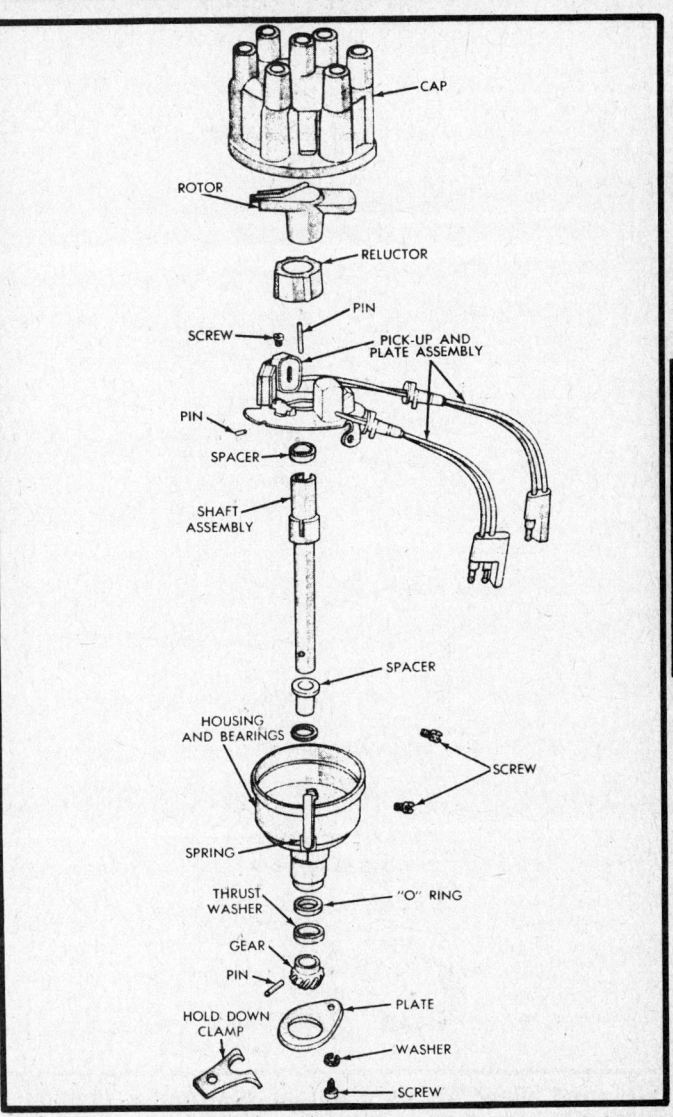

Exploded view of six cylinder ESA dual pick-up distributor (© Chrysler Corp.)

turn signal switch up out of the way.
2. Remove the retaining snap ring and pry the upper bearing housing off the steering shaft.
3. Press out the pin that attaches the lockplate to the steering shaft and remove the lockplate. Remove the lock lever guide plate. Remove the buzz/chime switch.
4. With the ignition lock cylinder in the "LOCK" position and the ignition key removed, insert two thin suitable tools into the lock cylinder release openings to release the spring-loaded lock retainer. Pull the lock cylinder out of its housing.
5. To install, place the lock cylinder into the housing, positioning it in the "LOCK" position and remove the key. Insert the lock cylinder far enough into the housing to contact the switch actuator. Insert the key, press and turn until the retainer snaps into place.
6. Complete the reassembly in the reverse order of disassembly.

TILT COLUMN
1. Remove the steering wheel, shaft lock cover, turn signal lever, tilt control lever and hazard warning knob.

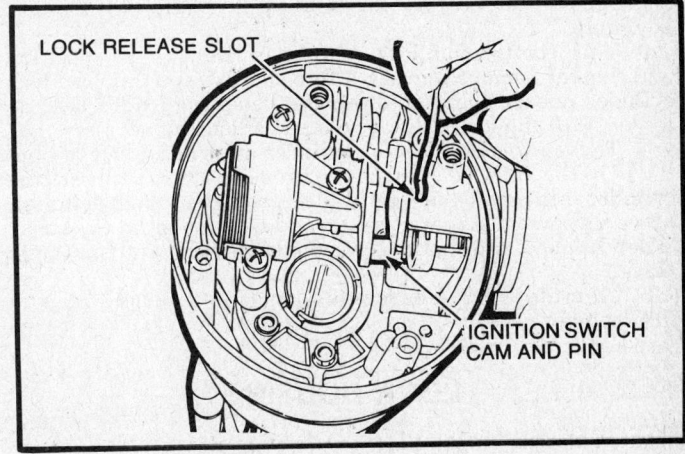

Using a wire probe to release the ignition lock, standard steering column (© Chrysler Corp.)

3-9

CHRYSLER CORPORATION
REAR WHEEL DRIVE CARS

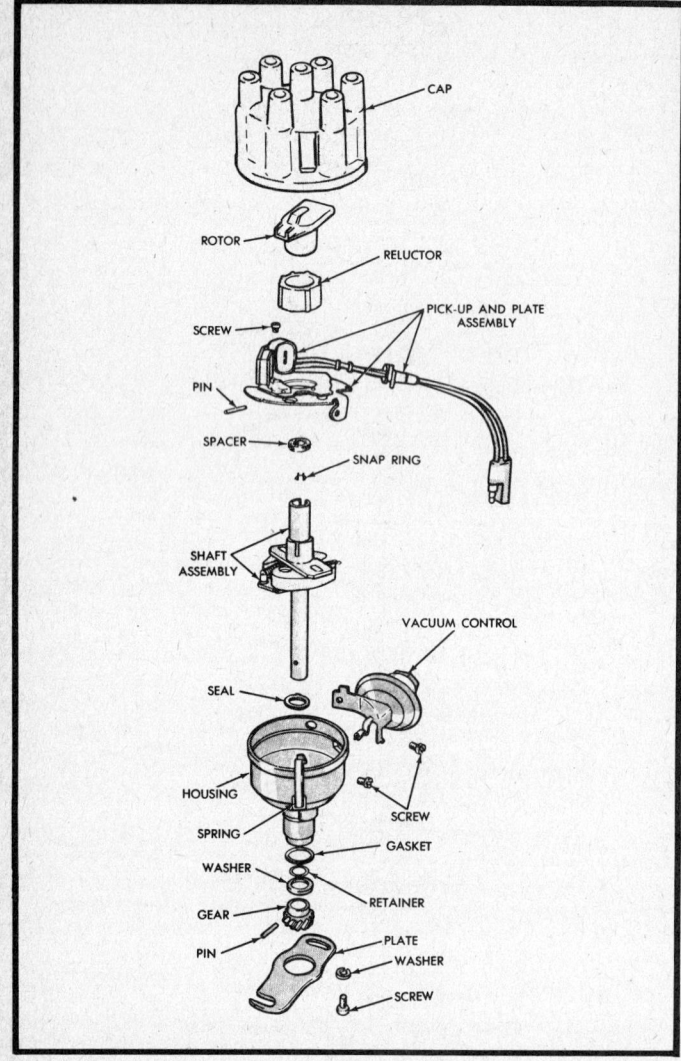

Exploded view of six cylinder distributor—typical
(© Chrysler Corp.)

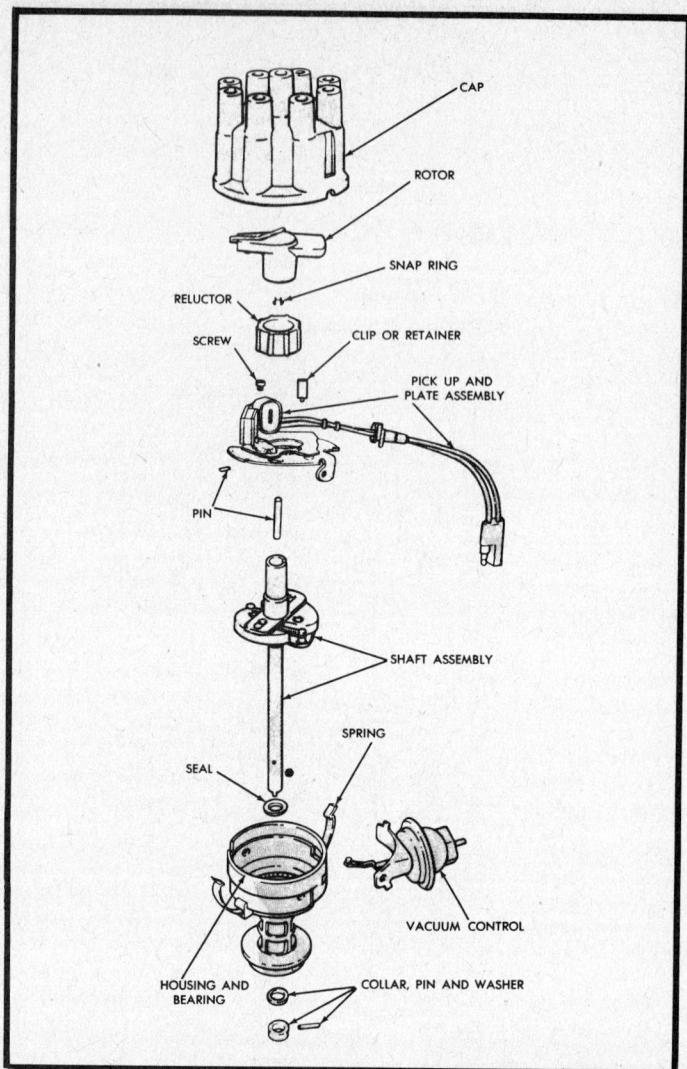

Exploded view of V8 engine distributor—typical
(© Chrysler Corp.)

2. Remove the lockplate, canceling cam and spring, disconnect and pull the turn signal switch up out of the way. Remove key lamp.
3. With the ignition lock cylinder in the "LOCK" position and the key removed, insert a thin suitable tool into the lock cylinder release opening to release the spring-loaded lock retainer. Pull the lock cylinder out of its housing.
4. To install, place the lock cylinder in its housing, positioning it in the "LOCK" position and remove the key. Insert the cylinder into the housing until it contacts the switch actuator. Move the switch actuator rod up and down to align the parts. When aligned, move the lock cylinder inward and snap into place.
5. Complete the reassembly in the reverse order of disassembly.

LOCK HOUSING

Removal and Installation
STANDARD COLUMN
1. Remove steering wheel, the turn signal switch and lockplate. Remove the ignition key. Remove the screw and lift out buzzer/chime switch.
2. Remove the two screws attaching the ignition switch.
3. Remove the ignition switch by rotating the switch 90° on the rod and sliding off the rod.
4. Remove the two mounting screws from the dimmer switch. Disengage the switch from the actuator rod.
5. Remove the two screws that mount the bellcrank. Slide the bellcrank up in the lock housing until it can be disconnected from the ignition switch actuator rod.
6. Place the cylinder in the "LOCK" position and remove the key. Insert two small-diameter suitable tools into the lock cylinder release holes and push in to release the spring-loaded lock retainers. At the same time, pull the lock cylinder out of the housing bore.
7. Grasp the lock lever and spring assembly and pull straight out of the housing.
8. Remove the four lock housing to column jacket hex head retaining screws and remove the lock housing plate and housing from the jacket.
9. When removing the lock housing, turn the lock housing 90° to disengage it from the ignition switch actuator rod.
10. Installation is the reverse of removal.

CHRYSLER CORPORATION
REAR WHEEL DRIVE CARS
SECTION 3

TILT COLUMN

1. Remove the steering wheel, shaft lock cover, turn signal lever, tilt control lever and hazard warning knob.
2. Remove the lockplate, canceling cam and spring, disconnect and pull the turn signal switch up out of the way. Remove the key lamp.
3. With the ignition lock cylinder in the "LOCK" position and the key removed, insert a thin suitable tool into the lock cylinder release opening to release the spring-loaded lock retainer. Pull the lock cylinder out of the housing.
4. Carefully remove the buzzer/chime switch straight out of the housing.

NOTE: *If the lock cylinder is not removed first, the lock must be in the "ON" position.*

---- **CAUTION** ----
If the wedge spring is dropped during its removal, it could fall into the column, requiring complete disassembly to retrieve the spring.

5. Remove the three housing retaining screws and remove the cover.
6. The installation of the cover is in the reverse of the removal procedure.

IGNITION SWITCH

Removal and Installation

1. On a standard column, remove the steering wheel, wash/wipe switch, turn signal switch, bearing housing, lock plate, the ignition lock cylinder; then remove the ignition switch. Rotate switch 90° to remove from actuator rod.
2. On a tilt column, the ignition switch is mounted externally on the lower section of the steering column. To install, place both the switch and lock in "ACCESSORY" position.

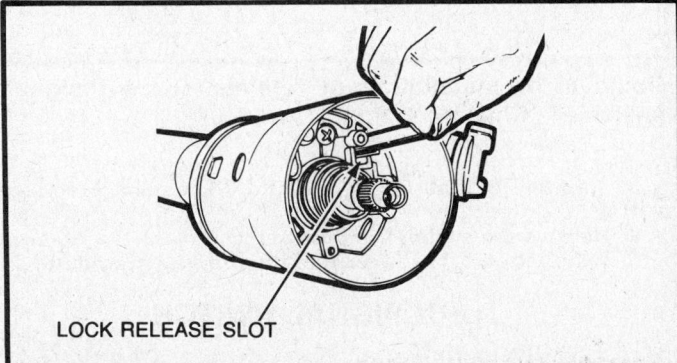
Slide a thin probe into the lock release and depress latch to remove ignition lock from tilt column (© Chrysler Corp.)

NEUTRAL START SWITCH

Removal and Installation

1. The neutral start switch is located on the left side of the automatic transmission. Fluid will drain from the transmission when the switch is unscrewed and removed.
2. Use a new seal when installing and replenish lost fluid. Torque to 25 ft. lbs.

STOPLIGHT SWITCH

The stoplight switch and its mounting bracket are attached to

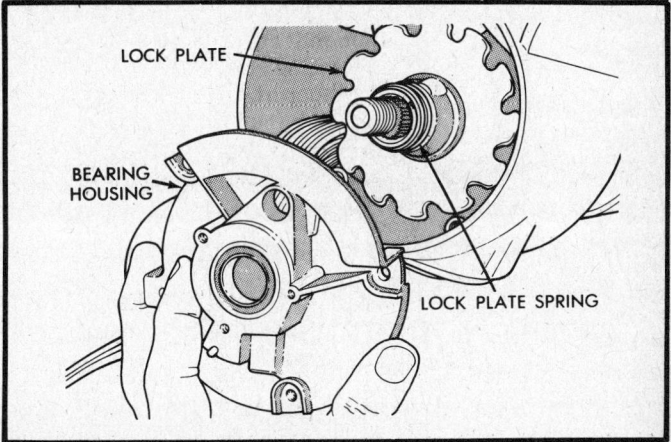
Removal of bearing housing, lock plate spring and lock plate (© Chrysler Corp.)

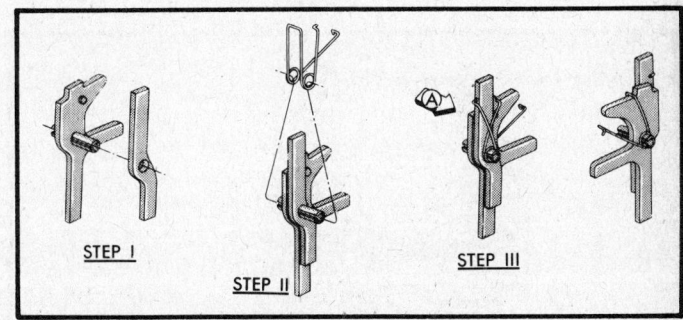
Assembling lock levers and spring (© Chrysler Corp.)

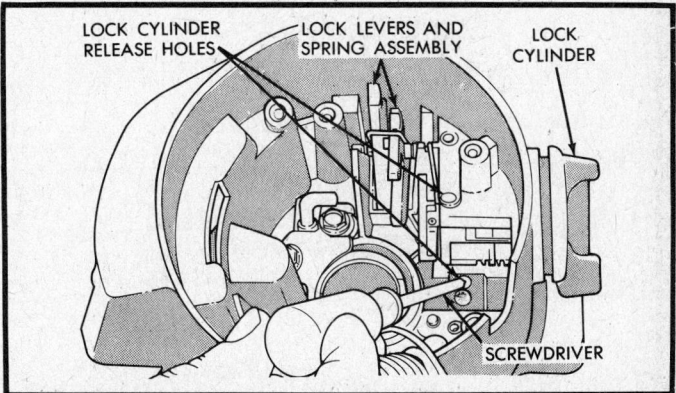
Removal of lock cylinder and lock levers (© Chrysler Corp.)

the brake pedal bracket. Adjustment is correct when stoplights illuminate after 1/2 in. brake pedal travel.

HEADLIGHT SWITCH

Removal and Installation

1. Disconnect negative battery cable. Relocate anything preventing full access to switch, such as instrument cluster bezel or air conditioner ducting.
2. Place switch in full "ON" position. Pull on knob and press shaft release button to release shaft and knob assembly.

3-11

CHRYSLER CORPORATION
REAR WHEEL DRIVE CARS

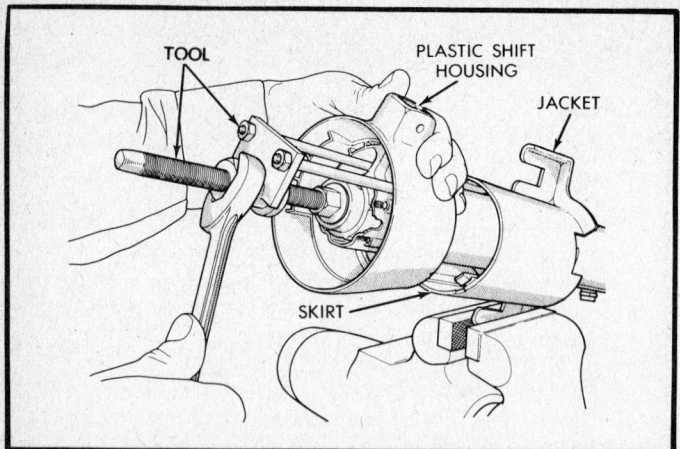

Removal of plastic shift housing (© Chrysler Corp.)

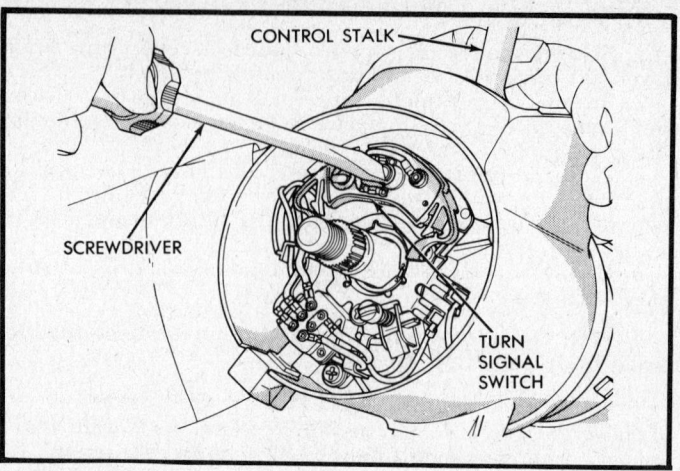

Turnsignal switch removal or installation (© Chrysler Corp.)

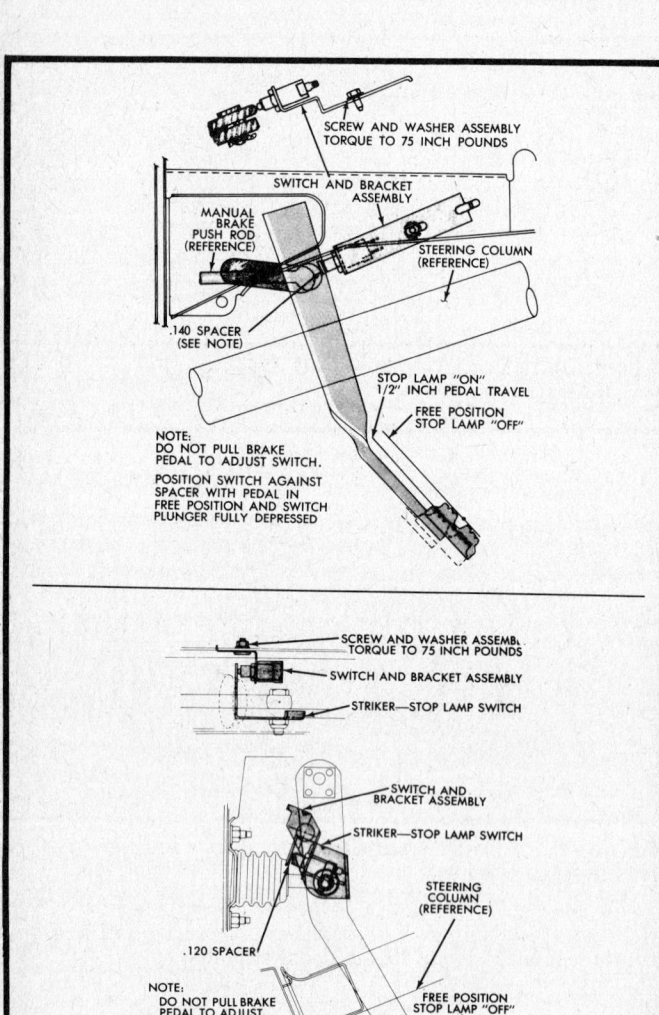

Stoplight switch adjustment, typical (© Chrysler Corp.)

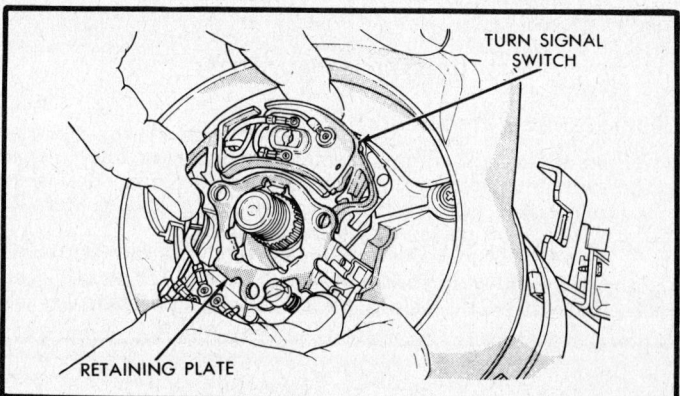

Removal or installation of retainer and turnsignal switch (© Chrysler Corp.)

3. Remove mounting device and disconnect electrical wiring.
4. Remove the switch from the vehicle.
5. Installation is the reverse of the removal procedure.

TURN SIGNAL SWITCH

Removal and Installation

1. Remove the steering wheel and the steering column cover.
2. On a tilt column, remove the gearshift indicator, the nuts retaining the column to the lower panel reinforcement, the mounting bracket and the wiring trough.
3. Position gearshift lever to full clockwise position on a standard column and midpoint on a tilt column.
4. Remove the turn signal lever.
5. Remove the turn signal switch retaining screws. Pull the switch and wiring up through the column.
6. Installation is the reverse of the removal procedure.

DIMMER SWITCH

Removal and Installation

1. Disconnect the negative battery cable.
2. Remove the steering column lower cover.
3. Disconnect all the electrical connections from the switch.

CHRYSLER CORPORATION
REAR WHEEL DRIVE CARS
SECTION 3

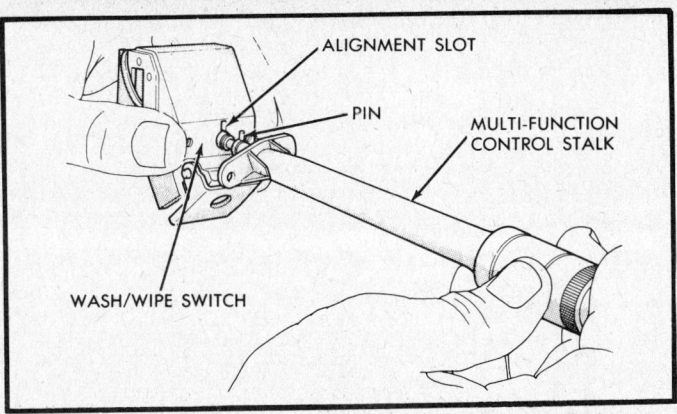

Multi-function control stalk removal or installation
(© Chrysler Corp.)

4. Remove the dimmer switch retaining nuts. Disengage the switch from the push rod. Remove the switch from the vehicle.
5. Install the switch to its proper mounting. Insert two $^{3}/_{32}$ in. drill shanks through the alignment holes.
6. Install the push rod into the washer/wiper switch pocket. Once the switch is installed, remove the two drill shanks.

HORN SWITCH AND STEERING WHEEL

Removal and Installation

1. Remove steering wheel center pad assembly. Disconnect wires and remove horn switch.
2. Remove steering wheel retaining nut and use a puller to remove the steering wheel.

NOTE: Do not hammer on the end of the shaft.

3. Installation is the reverse of the removal procedure. Tighten the steering wheel nut to 45 ft. lb.

WINDSHIELD WIPER SWITCH

Removal and Installation

1. Disconnect the negative battery cable.
2. Remove the steering wheel.
3. With tilt wheel only, remove the lock plate cover and the lock plate.
4. Remove the lower instrument panel bezel.
5. With tilt wheel only:
   a. Remove the gear shift indicator.
   b. Remove the two nuts retaining the column to the lower panel reinforcement.
   c. Remove the mounting bracket from the steering column after removing the retaining bolts.
6. Remove the wire trough from the steering column by un-snapping the four plastic retainers.
7. Remove the turn signal switch.
8. Remove the two retaining screws and remove the lock housing cover.
9. Gently pull the wiper switch up from the column while guiding the wires through the column opening.
10. The installation is in the reverse order of the removal procedure.

WINDSHIELD WIPER MOTOR

Removal and Installation

1. Disconnect the battery negative cable.
2. Remove the cowl screen.
3. Remove the crank-nut while holding the drive crank with a wrench or suitable tool to prevent overloading the gears.
4. Remove the drive crank from the motor and disconnect the electrical wiring connector.
5. Remove the three nuts retaining the motor to the dash panel. Remove the motor carefully, so as not to lose the spacers and rubber grommet.
6. The installation is in the reverse order of the removal procedure. Be sure the wiper motor is correctly grounded by having the ground strap under one of the retaining nuts.
7. Tighten the crank nut to 95 inch lbs. torque.

WINDSHIELD WIPER LINKAGE

Removal and Installation

1. Remove the drive crank from the wiper motor and the drive link.
2. Remove the pivot assembly mounts and remove the linkage assembly.
3. The installation is in the reverse of the removal procedure.

INSTRUMENT CLUSTER

Removal and Installation

NEW YORKER, DIPLOMAT, GRAN FURY, FIFTH AVENUE AND NEWPORT

1. Disconnect the negative battery cable.
2. Remove the instrument cluster bezel.
3. Loosen the shift pointer set screw and remove the pointer.
4. From under the dash, disconnect the speedometer cable.

NOTE: The speedometer cables are attached to the speedometer by two different methods. One method uses a snap-on plastic ferrule, which attaches directly to the speedometer head and must be disconnected before the speedometer or cluster can be removed. The second method is uses a plastic ferrule which is attached to the cluster or panel and held in place by a metal spring clip. This type allows minor movement or service work to be done on the cluster or speedometer without having to disconnect the speedometer.

5. Remove the cluster retaining screws and pull the cluster away from the carrier. Disconnect the electrical wiring.
6. Remove the cluster assembly from the dash.
7. To install the cluster assembly, reverse the removal procedure.

CORDOBA AND MIRADA

NOTE: Remove headlamp switch knob. Place selector level in the "L" position.

1. Remove the negative battery cable.
2. Remove the cluster bezel.
3. Remove the left and right lower trim panels.
4. Remove the accessory switch bezel.
5. Pull the gear shift pointer cable from the steering column.
6. Lower the steering column.
7. From under the dash, disconnect the speedometer cable.

NOTE: The speedometer cables are attached to the speedometer by two different methods. One method uses a snap-on plastic ferrule, which attaches directly to the speedometer head and must be disconnected before the speedometer or cluster can be removed. The second method is uses a plastic ferrule which is attached to the cluster or panel and held in place by a metal spring clip. This type allows minor movement or service work to be done on the cluster or speedometer without having to disconnect the speedometer.

CHRYSLER CORPORATION
REAR WHEEL DRIVE CARS

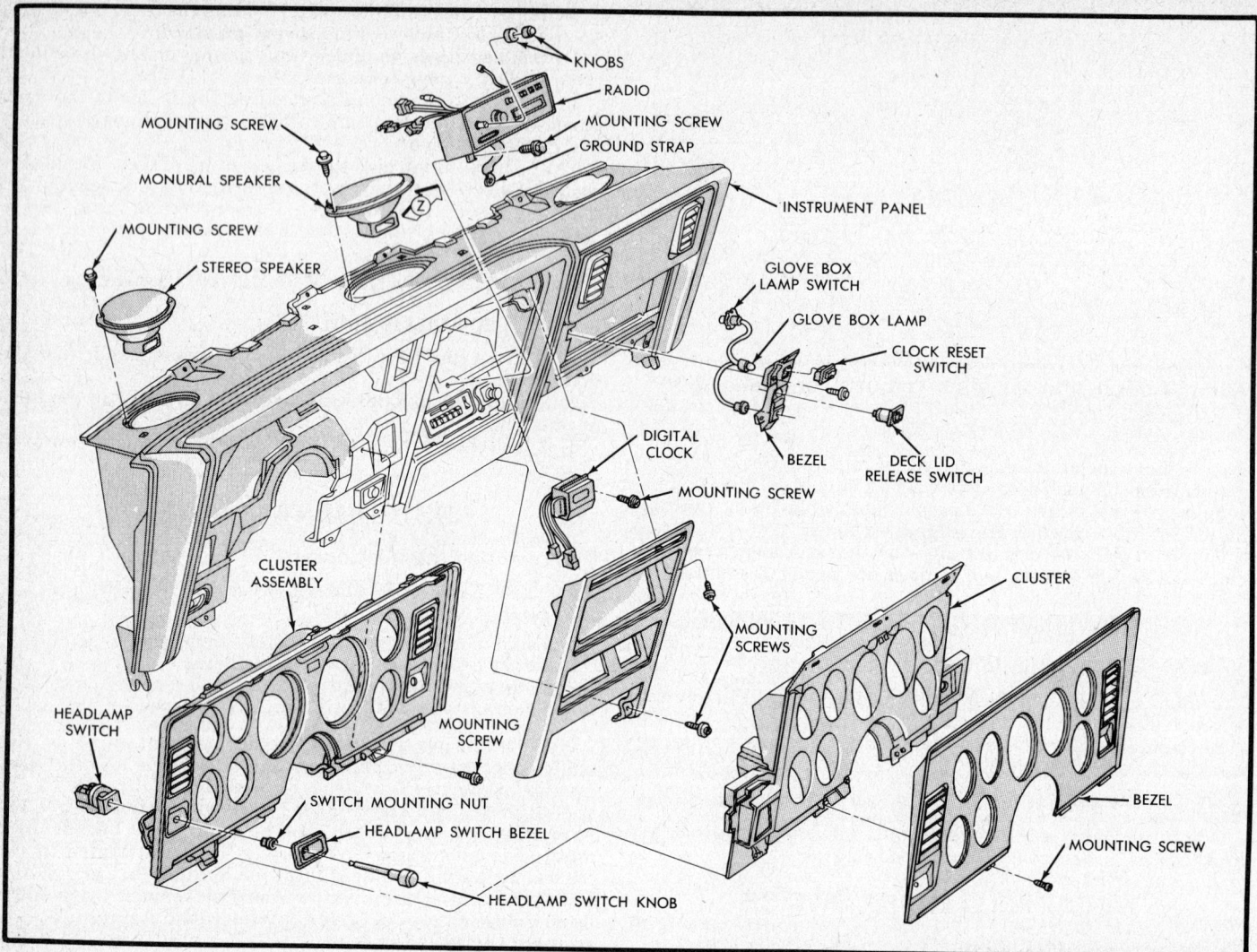

Instrument panel, Cordoba/Mirada (© Chrysler Corp.)

8. Disconnect the right remote mirror control assembly.
9. Remove the cluster retaining screws and "roll" the cluster downward to disconnect the headlamp switch and the cluster wiring.
10. Remove the cluster assembly from the dash.
11. To install the cluster, reverse the removal procedure.

IMPERIAL (ELECTRONIC CLUSTER)
1. Disconnect the negative battery cable.
2. Remove the center cluster bezel, ash tray and cigar lighter.
3. Remove the lower bezel and the cluster bezel from the instrument panel.
4. Remove the six plastic push-pull pins and remove the mask assembly.
5. Remove the cluster retaining screws, pull the cluster rearward to remove wiring connectors and remove the cluster.

NOTE: If the electronic cluster or switch module is defective, there is no repair procedure; the assembly must be replaced as a unit.

6. To install the cluster assembly, reverse the removal procedure.

Speedometer

The speedometer is removed from the instrument cluster assembly after the cluster is removed from the vehicle. The disassembly of the clusters will vary to a small degree from each car line to another. It is most important to mask surfaces that may become scratched or damaged during the disassembly or assembly procedures. Extreme care should be exercised when handling the internal components of the speedometer/cluster assembly. The electronic units cannot be repaired, but must be replaced. A memory chip for the accumulated mileage must be removed from the old unit and installed into the new unit to preserve the vehicle's mileage record. Again, care must be exercised to prevent damage to the memory chip or the cluster during the changeover procedure.

SPEEDOMETER CABLE

The speedometer cables are attached to the speedometer by two different methods. One method uses a snap-on plastic ferrule, which attaches directly to the speedometer head and must be disconnected before the speedometer or cluster can be removed. The second method is uses a plastic ferrule which is attached to

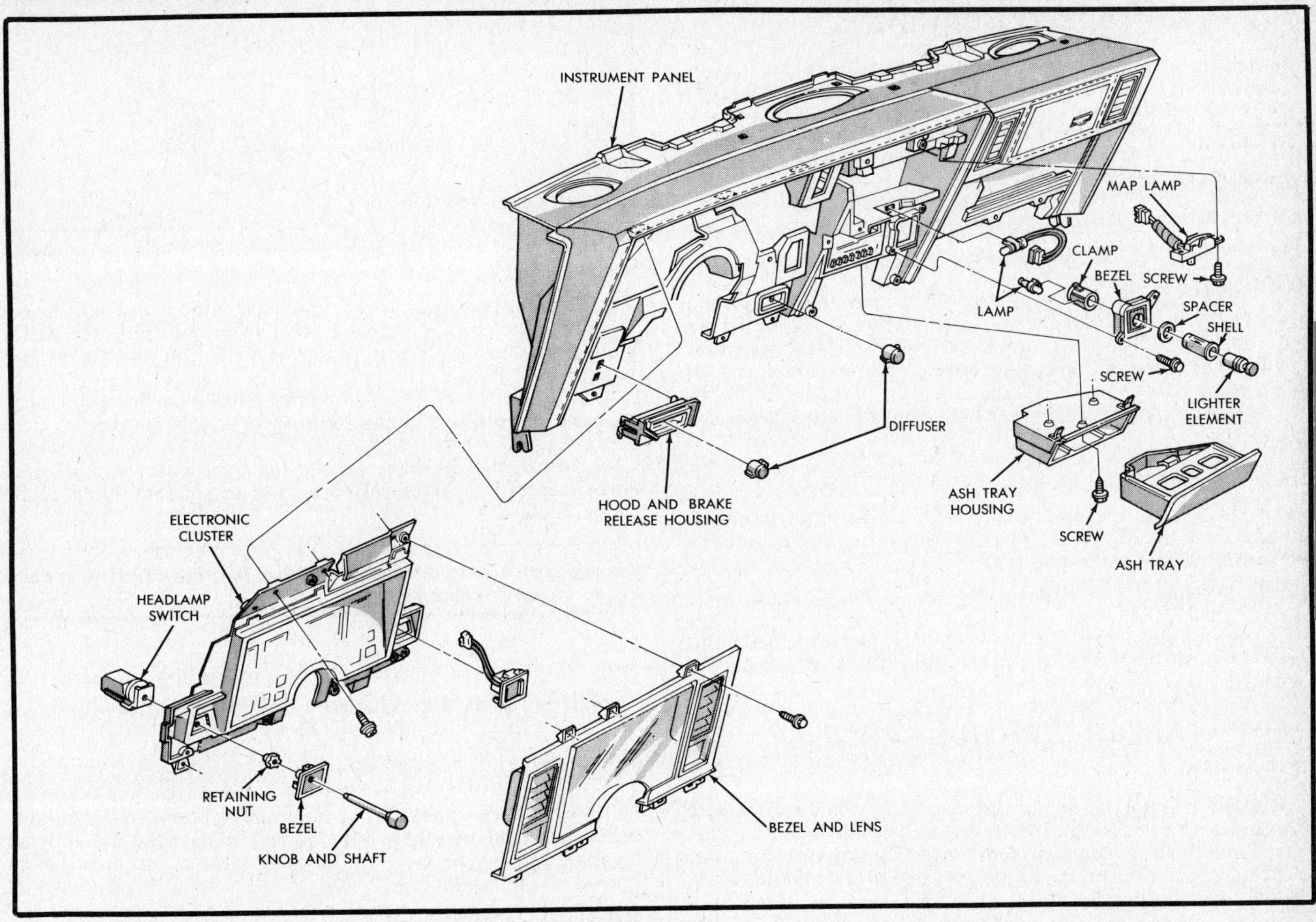

CHRYSLER CORPORATION
REAR WHEEL DRIVE CARS
SECTION 3

Electronic instrument cluster, Imperial (© Chrysler Corp.)

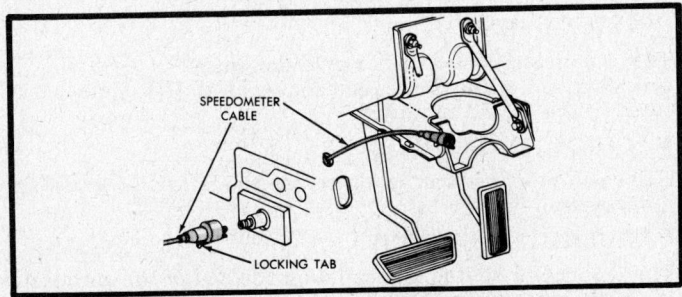

Speedometer cable with locking tab
(© Chrysler Corp.)

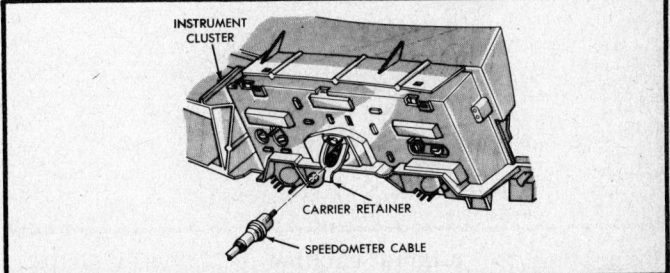

Speedometer cable and cluster with cable carrier retainer (© Chrysler Corp.)

the cluster or panel and held in place by a metal spring clip. This type allows minor movement or service work to be done on the cluster or speedometer without having to disconnect the speedometer.

On most models, the lower steering column cover must be removed before reaching under the instrument panel to depress the tab on the ferrule and pulling the cable away from the speedometer head. On vehicles equipped with speed control, it is advisable to first disconnect the cable from the speed control in order to provide additional working cable length at the speedometer head.

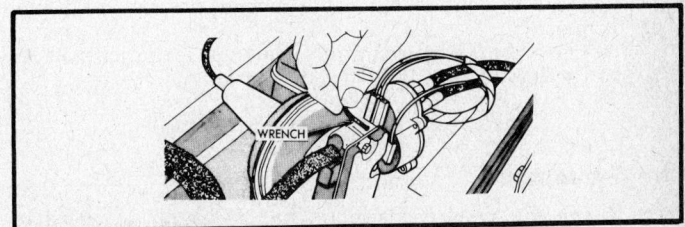

Adjusting lock-in screw (© Chrysler Corp.)

Speed Controls

The speed control unit is electrically activated and vacuum operated. The control switch is located on the multipurpose control handle on the steering column and consists of three positions for the speed control operation, "OFF", "ON" and "RESUME". The "SET" speed button is located in the end of the multipurpose control handle.

TEST PROCEDURES

Road Test

A road test should be made to determine what malfunctions are occurring to the speed control system. Particular attention should be directed to the speedometer operation, which should be smooth and without flutter at all speeds. Speedometer problems must be corrected before other repairs to the system are made.

Electrical Test

The electrical input should be checked at the servo with the use of a test lamp tool. Typical electrical schematics are included to aid in the electrical diagnosis.

Vacuum Test

With the engine operating and a vacuum gauge attached to the servo vacuum feed hose, a minimum of 10 in. Hg. must be present.

SPEED CONTROL CABLE

Adjustment

1. Have the engine at normal operating temperature with the choke off and the engine speed at curb idle.
2. Remove the spring clip from the lost motion link stud. The clearance between the stud and the cable clevis should be $1/16$ in.

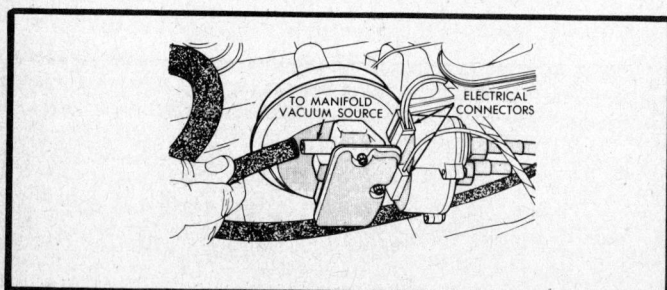

Inspecting for engine vacuum (© Chrysler Corp.)

3. Insert a gauge pin ($1/16$ in.) between the cable clevis and the stud. Loosen the clip at the cable support bracket.
4. Pull all the slack from the cable, but do not pull the throttle away from the curb idle position.
5. Tighten the clip at the cable support bracket to 45 inch lbs. torque.
6. Remove the gauge pin and install the spring clip on the stud of the lost motion link.

SERVO LOCK-IN SCREW

Adjustment

1. If the set speed drops more than 2–3 mph, or speed increase of more than 2–3 mph when the speed control is activated, the lock-in adjusting screw can be adjusted.

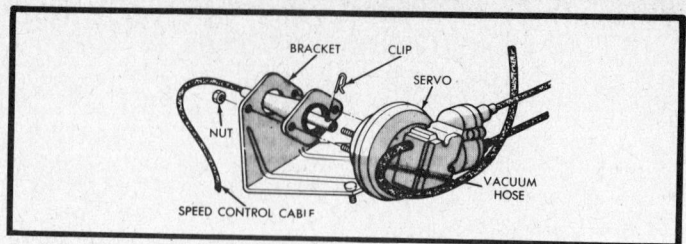

Removal of throttle cable cover (© Chrysler Corp.)

2. It must be remembered that lock-in accuracy will be affected by poor engine performance, power to weight ratio (loaded or empty vehicle), or improper slack in the throttle control cable.
3. Adjust the lock-in screw counterclockwise for an increase in speed correction of approximately one mph per quarter turn of the lock-in screw.
4. Adjust the lock-in screw clockwise for a decrease in speed correction of approximately one mph per quarter turn of the lock-in screw.

--- CAUTION ---

This adjustment must not exceed two turns in either direction, or damage to the servo unit may occur.

ELECTRICAL COMPONENT LOCATION

Computer

The computer is located on the carburetor air cleaner. Should it become necessary to replace the computer, remove the mounting screws from inside the air cleaner. Do not take the computer apart for any reason. It is not serviceable and must be replaced as an assembly.

PICK-UP ASSEMBLIES

Both magnetic pick-up assemblies (start and run) are located within the distributor housing.

COOLANT SENSOR

The coolant sensor for the six cylinder engine is located in the cylinder head, while the coolant sensor for the V8 engines is located in the intake manifold.

VACUUM TRANSDUCER

The vacuum transducer is located on the Spark Control Computer assembly.

CARBURETOR SWITCH

The carburetor switch is located on the end of the carburetor idle stop, when the vehicle is equipped.

DETONATION SUPPRESSOR

When equipped with the detonation suppressor system, the V8 engine detonation sensor is located on the number two branch of the intake manifold. This systemn is not used on the six cylinder engines.

OXYGEN SENSOR

The oxygen sensor is located in the exhaust manifold and is used with the Feedback carburetor only.

CHARGE TEMPERATURE SWITCH

The charge temperature sensor is located in the number eight intake manifold branch runner on the V8 engines and on the number six intake manifold branch runner on the six cylinder engines.

CHRYSLER CORPORATION
REAR WHEEL DRIVE CARS
SECTION 3

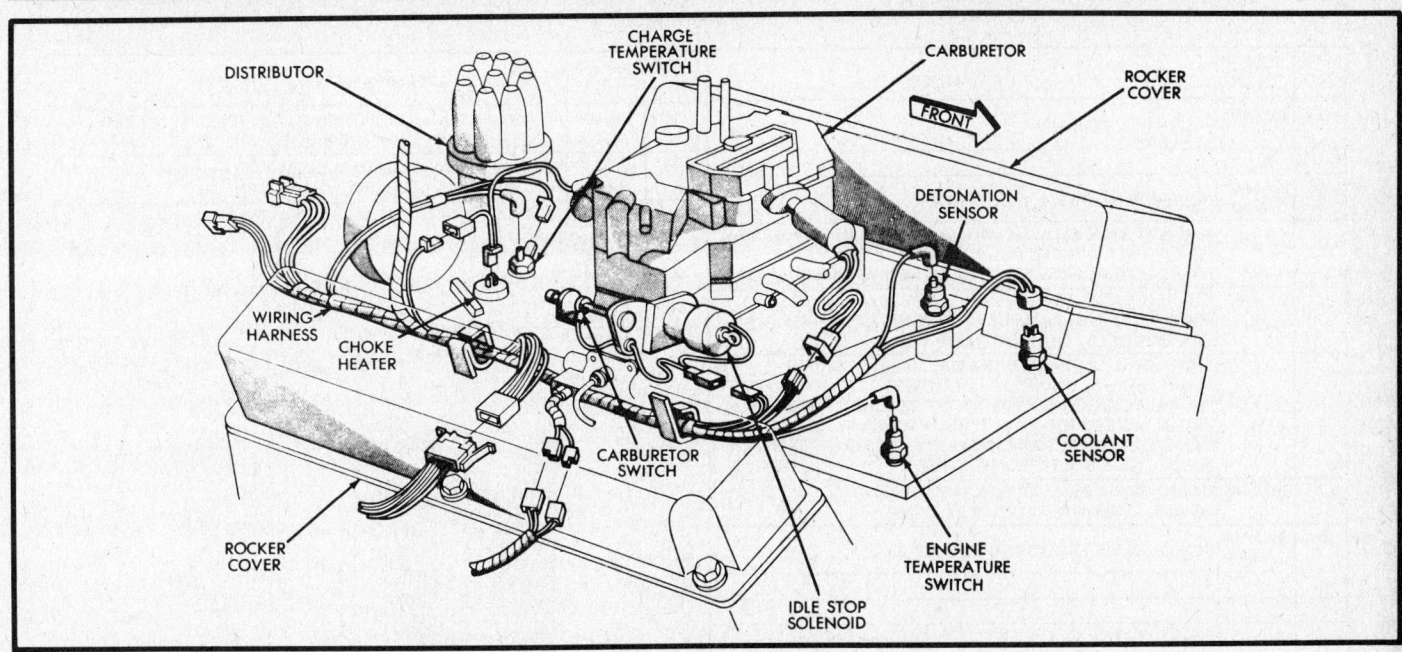

Location of switches and sensors, V8 engines typical (© Chrysler Corp.)

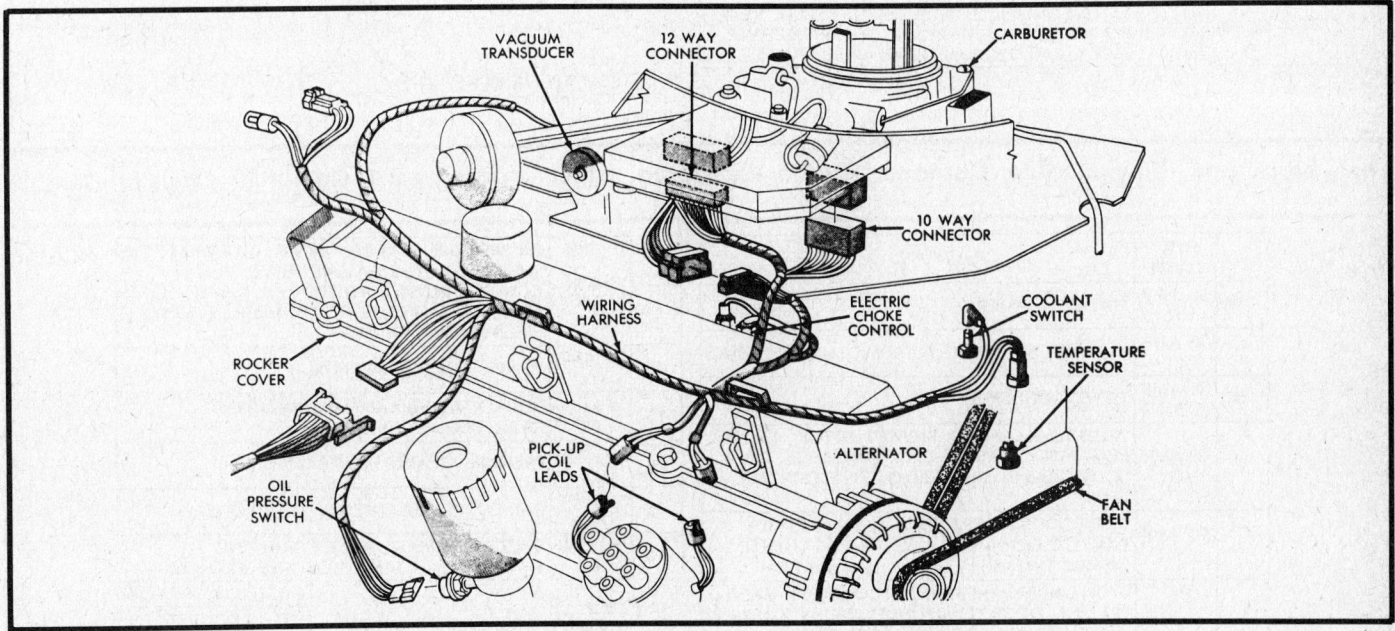

Location of switches and sensors, 6-cyl engines typical (© Chrysler Corp.)

MICROPROCESSOR ELECTRONIC SPARK CONTROL

The microprocessor is an electric module located within the computer assembly.

Relays/Fuse Panel/Circuit Breaker Locations

The relays and circuit breakers are located on the fuse panel and, if necessary, can be changed quickly by pulling the assembly from the fuse panel and inserting a new one in its place.

The fuse panel is located on the left side of the passenger compartment, either mounted to the underside of the dash panel or to the inner side of the firewall panel.

TURN SIGNAL FLASHER/HAZARD WARNING FLASHER LOCATIONS

Both the turn signal and hazard warning system flashers are mounted to the fuse panel. Both can be removed and replaced by simply pulling the flasher from the fuse panel and installing a new one in its place.

3–17

SECTION 3
CHRYSLER CORPORATION
REAR WHEEL DRIVE CARS

CAV	FUSE/COLOR	ITEMS FUSED
1	20 AMP YL	HAZARD WARNING
2		
3	30 AMP C/BRKR	POWER WINDOWS & MOON ROOF
4	30 AMP LG	A/C & HEATER BLOWER MOTOR, HEATED REAR WINDOW RELAY, DECK LID RELEASE SOLENOID, ILLUMINATED ENTRY ELECTRONICS SENSE & CORNERING LAMPS
5	20 AMP YL	CLUSTER, PARK, TURN SIGNAL, TAIL, LICENSE, SIDE MARKER, OPERA LAMPS & ELECTRONIC RADIO DISPLAY & CASSETTE DOLBY LIGHT INTENSITY
6	20 AMP YL	STOP, IGNITION SWITCH, TRUNK, VANITY MIRROR MAP/READING, UNDERPANEL COURTESY, DOOR COURTESY, "B" PILLAR, DOOR LOCK & FRONT HEADER LAMPS, KEY-IN BUZZER, IGNITION SWITCH TO RELAY, CLOCK MEMORY, DIGITAL RADIO MEMORY, ILLUMINATED ENTRY ELECTRONICS & ELECTRONIC CHIMES.
7	20 AMP YL	HORN, HORN RELAY, CIGAR LIGHTER & AUTO POWER ANTENNA, GLOVE BOX LAMP
8	30 AMP C/BRKR	POWER SEATS & DOOR LOCK SOLENOIDS
9		
10		
11	5 AMP TN	BRAKE WARNING, OIL PRESSURE, DOOR AJAR, SEAT BELT & LOW FUEL WARNING LAMPS, VOLTAGE LIMITER, TEMPERATURE & FUEL GAUGE, RADIO CAPACITOR, SEAT BELT BUZZER (CHIMES) & SPEED CONTROL.
12		
13	4 AMP PK	A/C & HEATER CONTROL, CLUSTER, HOOD & PARK BRAKE, HEATED REAR WINDOW, CIGAR LIGHTER, ASH RECEIVER, DIGITAL CLOCK, RADIO & CONSOLE GEAR SEL LAMPS
14	20 AMP YL	PREMIUM SPEAKER RELAY & REAR AMPLIFIER
15	5 AMP TN	POWER ANTENNA CONTROL, RADIO (DIGITAL SEARCH TUNE & STEREO INDICATOR) & DIGITAL CLOCK (DISPLAY)
16	20 AMP YL	BACK-UP, TURN SIGNAL & CORNERING LAMPS A/C CLUTCH & SLOW IDLE SOLENOID

FUSE	COLOR CODE
LG	LIGHT GREEN
YL	YELLOW
TN	TAN
PK	PINK

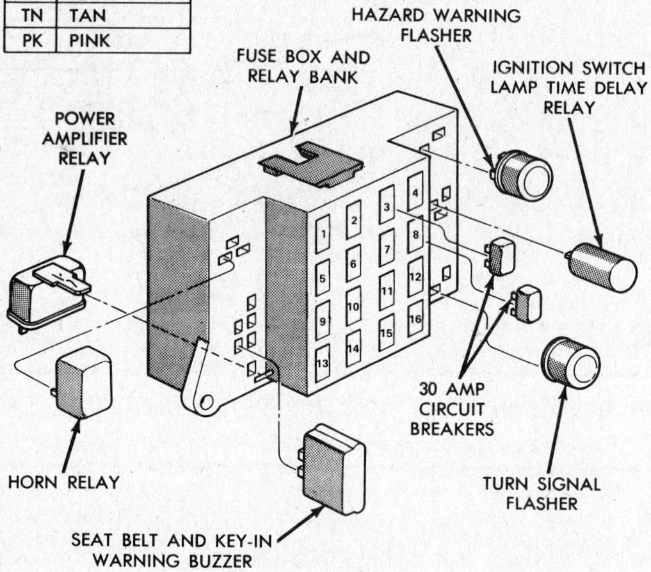

Fuse block and relay module, Cordoba, Mirada illustrated, other model years similar (© Chrysler Corp.)

CAV	FUSE/COLOR	ITEMS FUSED
1	20 AMP YL	HAZARD FLASHER
2	20 AMP YL	IN TANK FUEL PUMP (ELECTRONIC FUEL METERING)
3	30 AMP C/BRKR	POWER WINDOWS
4	30 AMP LGY	AUTO TEMP CONTROL BLOWER MOTOR, HEATED REAR WINDOW RELAY, DECK LID RELEASE SOLENOID & ILLUMINATED ENTRY ELECTRONIC SENSE
5	20 AMP YL	PARK, SIDE MARKER, OPERA, LICENSE & TAIL LAMPS; CLOCK, RADIO & ELECTRONIC CLUSTER DISPLAY INTENSITY CLUSTER ILLUMINATION
6	25 AMP YL	STOP, UNDER PANEL & DOOR COURTESY, MAP/READING, DOOR KEY CYLINDER, TRUNK, IGNITION SWITCH, UNDER HOOD & VANITY MIRROR LAMPS; ELECTRIC MIRROR MOTORS, IGNITION SWITCH TIME DELAY RELAY, ELECTRONIC CHIMES, ELECTRONIC SEARCH TUNE MEMORY, ILLUMINATED ENTRY ELECTRONICS, ELECTRONIC CLUSTER MEMORY & SECURITY ALARM, ELECTRONIC CLUSTER SEAT SWITCH
7	25 AMP NAT	HORN, HORN RELAY, CIGAR LIGHTER & AUTO POWER ANTENNA; GLOVE BOX
8	30 AMP C/BRKR	POWER SEATS & POWER DOOR LOCK SOLENOIDS
9		
10		
11	5 AMP TN	OIL PRESSURE, SEAT BELT, DOOR AJAR, BRAKE WARNING & TEMPERATURE LAMPS; SPEED CONTROL, CLUSTER ELECTRONICS; FUEL LEVEL SENSOR, CHANGE LIGHT, LOW VOLTAGE LIGHT, SPEED SENSOR, CHIMES
12	20 AMP YL	HEATED SIDE VIEW MIRROR
13	4 AMP PK	CLUSTER, TITLE & RADIO ILLUMINATION; RADIO DISPLAY DIMMING
14	20 AMP YL	PREMIUM SPEAKER POWER BOOSTER
15	5 AMP TN	RADIO & POWER ANTENNA CONTROLLER
16	20 AMP YL	BACK-UP, TURN SIGNAL & CORNERING LAMPS; A/C CLUTCH & SLOW IDLE SOLENOID

FUSE	COLOR CODE
LG	LIGHT GREEN
TN	TAN
PK	PINK
YL	YELLOW
NAT	NATURAL

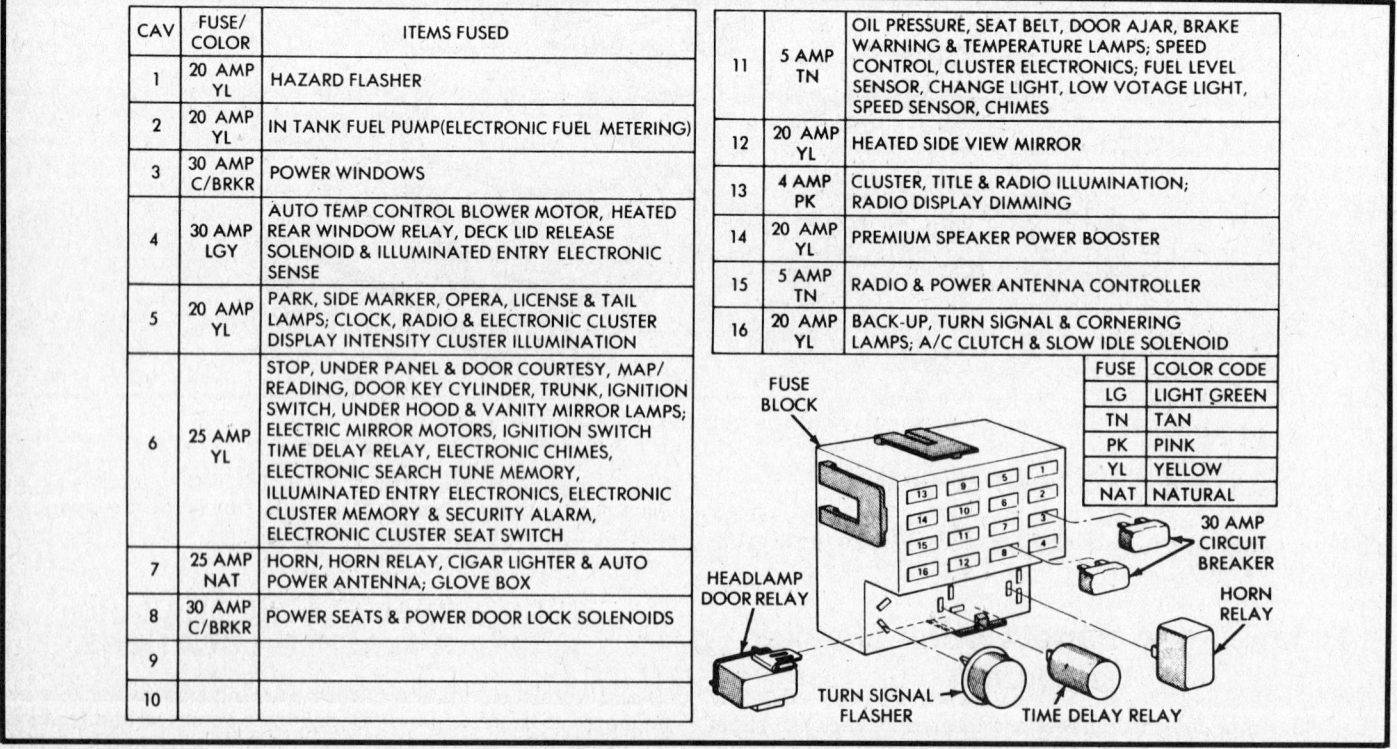

Fuse block and relay module, Imperial illustrated, other model years similar (© Chrysler Corp.)

CHRYSLER CORPORATION
REAR WHEEL DRIVE CARS
SECTION 3

CAV	FUSE/COLOR	ITEMS FUSED
1	20 AMP YL	HAZARD FLASHER
2	20 AMP YL	SPEED CONTROL, HEATER REAR WINDOW CORNERING LAMPS
3	30 AMP C/BRKR	POWER WINDOWS AND MOON ROOF
4	20 AMP YL / 30 AMP LG	HEATER BLOWER MOTOR A/C, ATC & HEATER WITH HI-LO (B) BLOWER MOTOR
5	20 AMP YL	DOME, TRUNK, CLUSTER, TAIL, LICENSE, SIDE MARKER, OPERA PARKING & MAP/DOME LAMPS ELECTRONIC SEARCH TUNE CB & DOLBY DISPLAY INTENSITY
6	20 AMP YL	MAP, GLOVE BOX & OPEN DOOR (HN), COURTESY, VANITY, READING & STOP LAMPS, SEAT BELT/KEY-IN/HEADLAMP BUZZER, IGNITION TIME DELAY RELAY & POWER DOOR LOCK RELAY, BUZZER/CHIMES & ILLUMINATED ENTRY
7	20 AMP YL	HORN & HORN RELAY, STOP & GLOVE BOX LAMPS, CIGAR LIGHTER, CLOCK FEED POWER ANTENNA CONTROLLER & SEARCH TUNE RADIO MEMORY
8	30 AMP C/BRKR	POWER SEATS & DOOR LOCK SOLENOIDS
9		
10		
11	5 AMP TN	BRAKE, T/GATE, OIL PRESSURE, DOOR AJAR, LOW WASHER & SEAT BELT LAMPS, VOLTAGE LIMITER & FUEL, OIL TEMPERATURE GAUGE, & SEAT BELT BUZZER
12		
13	3 AMP VI	CLUSTER, PARK BRAKE, RADIO, DIGITAL CLOCK, HEATED REAR WINDOW, A/C/ATC/HEATER CONTROL, CIGAR LIGHTER ASH RECEIVER LAMPS & SEARCH TONE AND C-B RADIO DISPLAY DIMMING
14	6 AMP C/BRKR	REAR WIPE/WASH MOTOR LIFTGATE RELAY AND DECK LID RELEASE SOLENOID
15	5 AMP TN	RADIO, DIGITAL CLOCK DISPLAY POWER ANTENNA CONTROLLER
16	20 AMP YL	BACK-UP & T/SIGNAL LAMPS, A/C CLUTCH AND SOLENOID IDLE STOP

FUSE	COLOR CODE
LG	LIGHT GREEN
TN	TAN
YL	YELLOW
VI	VIOLET

Fuse block and relay module, Gran Fury, Newport, New Yorker illustrated, other model years similar
(© Chrysler Corp.)

HORN RELAY

The horn relay is mounted in the fuse block. It can be removed and replaced by simply pulling the old one out and inserting the new horn relay in its place.

CIRCUIT BREAKERS

Circuit breakers are used in varied circuits to control amperage surges and if the circuit is opened, to re-set themselves as the heat from the current flow load has diminshed. Should a continual interuption of power be experienced when operation of a controlled electrical component is attempted, repairs to the circuits/components or replacement of the component must be accomplished.

FUSIBLE LINKS

The fusible links are used to prevent major damage to wire harnesses in the event of a short circuit or an overload condition in the wiring circuits which normally are not fused, due to carrying high amperage loads or because of their locations within the wiring harness. Each fusible link is of a fixed value for a specific electrical load and should the link fail, the cause of the failure must be determined and repaired prior to installing a new fusible link of the same value.

When replacing fusible links that are connected to the battery terminal or starter relay, they should be serviced with the same type of prefabricated fusible link. All other fusible links can be replaced with fusible link wire cut from bulk rolls.

― CAUTION ―
When replacing fusible links, use only rosin core solder. Do not use acid core solder.

COOLING AND HEATER SYSTEM

WATER PUMP

Removal and Installation
SIX AND V8 ENGINES

1. Drain the cooling system.
2. Remove the fan shroud securing screws and move the shroud out of the way.
3. It may be necessary to remove the radiator on some models to obtain the working clearance necessary to remove the water pump.
4. Loosen the alternator mounting bolts. Loosen the mounting bolts for the power steering pump. idler pulley, air conditioning compressor, and air pump (if so equipped). Remove all the accessory belts.
5. Remove the fan, spacer or fluid drive, and the pulley.

3-19

Section 3: CHRYSLER CORPORATION
REAR WHEEL DRIVE CARS

CAUTION

For fluid-coupled fan drives, do not set the drive unit down with its shaft pointing downward. Keep the unit in a vertical position as fitted on the engine. This will prevent the silicone fluid from leaking out.

---

6. On some models, it may be necessary to remove the alternator or compressor mounting bracket bolts from the water pump to swing the alternator or compressor out of the way. Keep the compressor in an upright position.

7. On some vehicles it may be necessary to unbolt the power steering pump and set it aside, leaving the hoses connected. Also remove the air pump and brackets, if so equipped.

8. Detach the hoses from the water pump. Remove the bolts which secure the water pump body to its engine block housing. Remove the water pump and discard the gasket.

9. Install the bypass hose to the pump with the second clamp temporarily in the center of the hose. Install the water pump with a new gasket, using sealer, on its housing. Torque its securing bolts to 30 ft.lbs.

10. Rotate the pump shaft by hand to be sure that it rotates freely. Refit the alternator or compressor mounting bracket to the pump if either was removed. Install the pulley, spacer or fluid drive and the fan. Torque their retaining nuts to 15 ft.lbs.

11. Refit all the accessory drive belts. Adjust them to get about ½ in. of play under moderate thumb pressure on the longest run of belt between pulleys.

12. Install the radiator if it was removed.

13. Install the fan shroud. Fill the cooling system to 1 ¼ in. below the filler neck with correct water and antifreeze mixture, without a coolant reserve tank. With a reserve tank, fill the radiator and fill the tank to the indicated level. Warm up the engine with the heater on and inspect the water pump for any leaks. Check the coolant level and add as required.

BLOWER MOTOR WITH OR WITHOUT AIR CONDITIONING

NOTE: All service to the blower motor is made from inside the vehicle, under the right side of the instrument panel.

Removal
IMPERIAL, NEW YORKER, DIPLOMAT, GRAN FURY, FIFTH AVENUE

1. Disconnect the battery ground cable.
2. Remove the blower motor feed and ground wires at the connector.
3. Remove the blower motor mounting nuts from the bottom of the recirculation housing or separate lower blower housing from upper housing.
4. Remove the blower motor assembly from the recirculation housing.
5. Remove the blower motor mounting plate screws.
6. Separate the blower motor housing from the blower motor and fan assembly.

Installation
1. Position the grommet on the feed wire into place on the blower motor housing.
2. Set the blower motor and fan assembly into the blower motor housing and install the housing to mounting plate screws.
3. Position the blower assembly up into the recirculation housing and install the retaining nuts.
4. Install the blower motor feed and ground wire connector.
5. Install the battery ground cable.
6. Test the blower motor operation on all fan speeds.

Removal
NOTE: All service to the blower motor and blower fan must be done inside of the vehicle at the passenger side of the instrument panel.

CORDOBA, MIRADA, NEWPORT
1. Disconnect the negative battery cable.
2. Remove the glove box assembly.
3. Disconnect the blower motor feed and ground wires at the resistor block.
4. Remove the heater assembly to plenum mounting brace.
5. Remove the screws fastening the blower motor assembly to the heater housing.
6. Remove the blower motor assembly.

Installation
1. Before installing the blower motor assembly, be certain that the blower fan bottoms on the motor shaft is fastened securely.
2. Position and fasten the blower motor assembly to the heater housing.
3. Install the brace from the heater assembly to plenum.
4. Install the blower motor feed and ground wires on the resistor block.
5. Install the glove box assembly.
6. Install the negative battery cable and check the operation of the blower motor.

HEATER/AIR CONDITIONING CONTROL UNIT

Removal and Installation
ALL MODELS
1. Disconnect the negative battery cable.
2. Remove the necessary cluster bezels, radio, if necessary, accessory switch bezel, lower, right or left trim panels and necessary air ducts to expose the heater/air conditioning control unit.
3. Remove the retaining screws and separate the control linkage, vacuum and electrical leads from the control unit. Remove the unit from the dash.
4. To install the control unit, install the control linkage, vacuum and electrical leads to the control unit, install it on the dash and complete the installation in the reverse of the removal order.

HEATER CORE WITH A/C

Removal
GRAN FURY, DIPLOMAT, IMPERIAL, NEW YORKER, MIRADA, CORDOBA, FIFTH AVENUE

1. Discharge the A/C system, disconnect the battery ground cable, drain the coolant, remove the air cleaner, and disconnect the heater hoses. Plug the core tubes to prevent spillage.
2. Remove the H-type expansion valve.
3. Slide the front seat all the way back.
4. Remove the instrument cluster bezel assembly by removing the four screws along the lower edge, placing the automatic transmission selector in 1, and pulling out to detach the upper edge clips.
5. Remove the instrument panel upper cover by removing the mounting screws at the top inner surface of the glove box, above the instrument cluster, at the left end cap mounting, at the right side of the pad brow and in the defroster outlets.
6. Remove the steering column cover (the instrument panel piece under the column).

CHRYSLER CORPORATION
REAR WHEEL DRIVE CARS

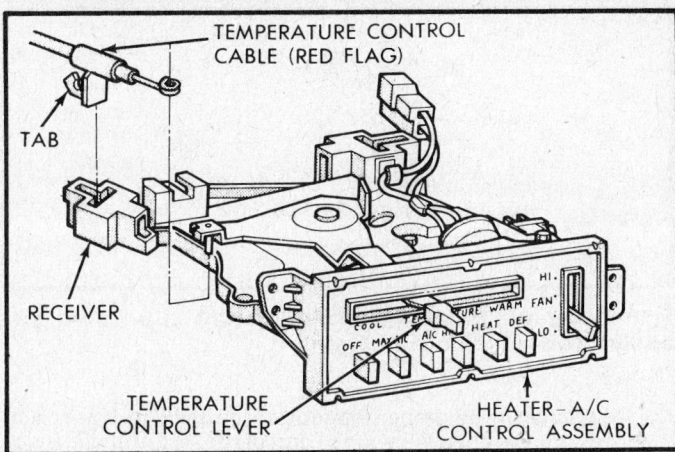

Temperature control, pushbutton type
(© Chrysler Corp.)

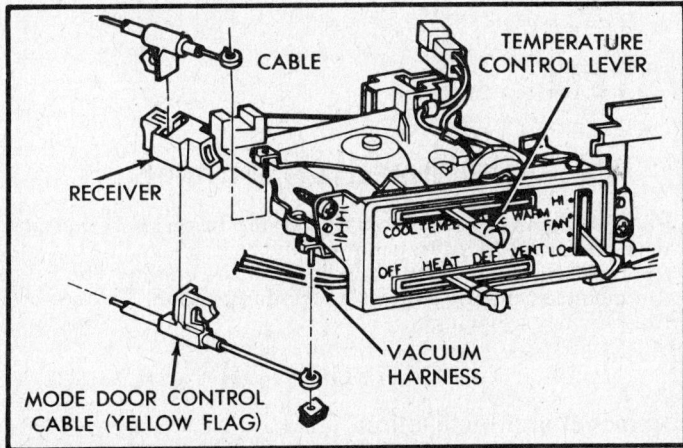

Temperature control, lever type (© Chrysler Corp.)

7. Remove the right intermediate side cowl trim panel. Remove the lower instrument panel (the part with the glove box). Remove the instrument panel center to lower reinforcement.
8. Remove the floor console, if any.
9. Remove the right center air distribution duct. Detach the locking tab on the defroster duct.
10. Disconnect the temperature control cable from the housing. Disconnect the blower motor resistor block wiring.
11. Detach the vacuum lines from the water valve and tee in the engine compartment. Detach the wiring from the evaporator housing. Remove the vacuum lines from the inlet air housing and disconnect the vacuum harness coupling.
12. Remove the drain tube in the engine compartment. Remove the mounting nuts from the firewall.
13. Remove the hanger strap from the rear of the evaporator and plenum stud.
14. Roll the unit back so that the pipes clear and remove it.
15. Remove the blend air door lever from the shaft. Remove the screws and lift off the top cover. Lift the heater core out.

Installation
1. Position evaporator housing on front floor of vehicle under instrument panel.
2. Tip evaporator housing up under instrument panel and press mounting studs through dash panel, making sure defroster duct and A/C distribution duct is properly seated on unit and gasket is installed properly. Connect locking tab on defroster duct.
3. While holding housing in position, install nut on mounting bracket, top of unit and plenum stud.
4. In engine compartment, install retaining nuts and tighten securely. Install condensate drain tube.
5. Connect electrical connectors to resistor block and connect control cable.
6. Connect vacuum lines in engine compartment, making sure grommet is seated. Connect vacuum lines to inlet air housing and vacuum harness coupling.
7. Install right center air distribution duct.
8. Install instrument panel center to lower reinforcement.
9. Install lower instrument panel.
10. Install right intermediate side cowl trim panel.
11. Install steering column cover.
12. Install instrument panel upper cover.
13. Install cluster bezel assembly.
14. From engine compartment, remove plugs from core tubes and connect hoses to heater. Install condensate tube and Corbin clamp.
15. Install H-valve and install refrigerant lines to valve. Replace gaskets.
16. Fill cooling system and inspect for leaks.
17. Install air cleaner and connect battery negative cable.

After the evaporator heater housing assembly is installed in the vehicle, it will be necessary to evacuate and then recharge

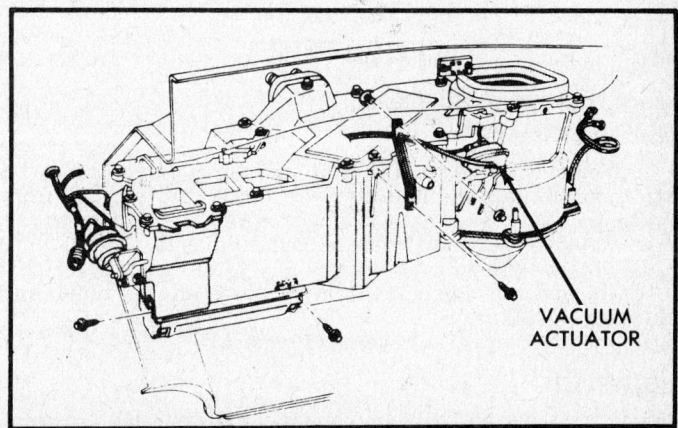

Rear view of the heater and A/C system—Fury/New Yorker/Diplomat models (© Chrysler Corp.)

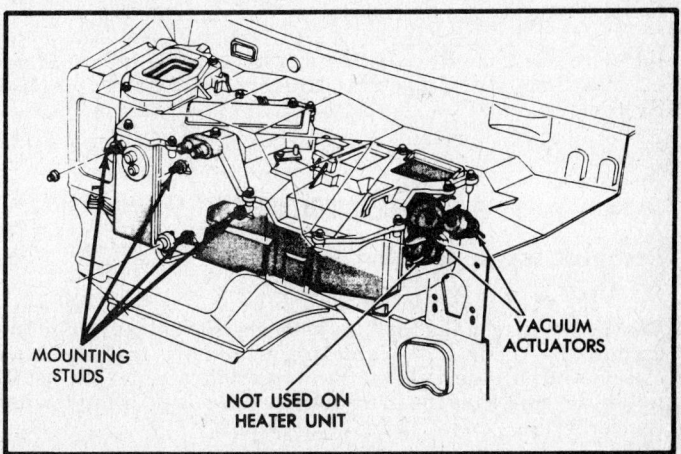

Front view of the heater and A/C system—Fury/New Yorker/Diplomat models (© Chrysler Corp.)

SECTION 3
CHRYSLER CORPORATION
REAR WHEEL DRIVE CARS

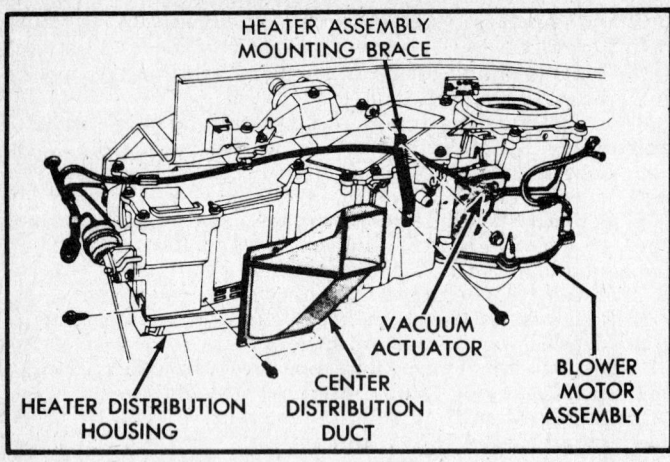

Rear view of the heater and A/C system—Cordoba/Mirada/Imperial models (© Chrysler Corp.)

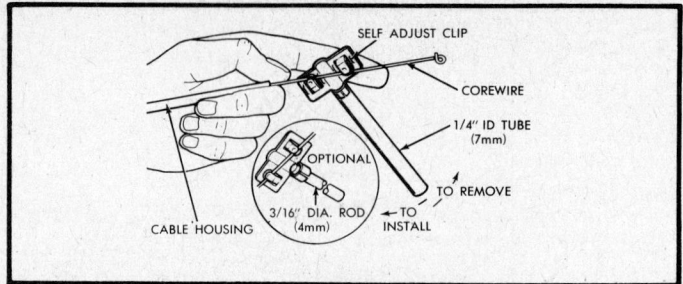

Removing or installing self-adjusting clip using an assist rod (© Chrysler Corp.)

the system with the proper amount of refrigerant. It is recommended that the operation of all controls be tested and an overall performance test be made after the repair or replacement of the evaporator assembly.

FUEL SYSTEM

FUEL PUMP

Removal and installation

MECHANICAL

1. Remove the two fuel lines from the fuel pump. It may be necessary to plug the line from the tank to prevent fuel from leaking out.
2. Remove the pump to block mounting bolts.
3. Remove the pump.
4. Remove the old gasket from the pump and use a new one during reinstallation.
5. Installation is the reverse of removal.

ELECTRIC

An electric in-tank fuel pump and fuel indicator gauge assembly is used with the Electronic Fuel Injection system used on Chrysler Imperial Models. The fuel tank must be removed and the fuel pump/fuel indicator gauge assembly removed from the tank in the same mannner as the removal of the conventional fuel indicator gauge assembly.

Refer to the Unit Repair Section for service information on the Chrysler Imperial Electronic Fuel Injection System.

FUEL FILTER

Removal and Installation

CARBURETED ENGINES

Locate the filter in the fuel line between the fuel pump and the carburetor. Using hose-clamp pliers, remove the attaching clamps and pull the filter off. Reverse this procedure for installation. Be sure that the arrow on the filter is pointing toward the carburetor (direction of fuel flow).

NOTE: Some filters have a third line, the purpose of which is to prevent vapor lock by allowing fuel vapors to return to the tank.

FUEL INJECTED ENGINES

The Electronic Fuel Injected Chrysler Imperial is equipped with parallel fuel filters mounted in the delivery line between the fuel tank and the throttle body on the engine. The filters are mounted side by side on a common bracket. Replace both filters when servicing.

CARBURETOR

Removal and Installation

--- CAUTION ---

Do not attempt to remove the carburetor from the engine of a vehicle that has just been road tested. Allow the engine to cool sufficiently to prevent accidental fuel ignition or personal injury.

1. Disconnect battery ground cable.
2. Remove air cleaner.
3. Remove fuel tank pressure vacuum filler cap.
4. Place a container under fuel inlet fitting to catch any fuel that may be trapped in fuel line.
5. Disconnect fuel inlet line using two fitting wrenches to avoid twisting the line.
6. Disconnect throttle linkage, choke linkage and all vacuum hoses.
7. Remove carburetor mounting bolts or nuts and carefully remove carburetor from engine compartment. Hold carburetor level to avoid spilling fuel from fuel bowl.

Adjustments

Tampering with the carburetor is a violation of Federal law. Adjustment of the carburetor idle air fuel mixture can only be done under certain circumstances, as explained below. Upon completion of the carburetor adjustment, it is important to restore plugs and roll pins that may have been removed during the servicing of the carburetor.

This procedure should only be used if an idle defect still exists after normal diagnosis has revealed no other faulty condition, such as incorrect basic timing, incorrect idle speed, faulty wire or hose connections, etc. It is also important to make sure the combustion computer system is operating properly. Adjustment of the carburetor air fuel mixture should be performed, if necessary, after a major carburetor overhaul.

Make all adjustments with engine fully warmed up, transmission in neutral, headlights off, air conditioning compressor not operating, idle stop carburetor switch (if so equipped) grounded with a jumper wire, and the vacuum hose at EGR valve (if so equipped) and distributor or spark control unit disconnect and plugged. On ESC equipped vehicles, wait one minute after returning to idle before checking timing.

NOTE: Refer to the underhood Emission Control Specification label for any further requirements or late changes in specifications before making carburetor or engine adjustments. On a new vehicle (under 300 miles/500km), reduce rpm settings by 75 rpm.

Idle Check And Set Procedure

CONCEALED PLUG — 1983

Removal and Installation

HOLLEY 1945, HOLLEY 6145 ELECTRONIC FEEDBACK CARBURETOR

1. Remove carburetor from engine.
2. Remove throttle body from the carburetor.
3. Clamp the throttle body in a vise with the gasket surfaces protected from the vise jaws.
4. Drill a $5/64$ in. hole in the casting surrounding the idle mixture screw, then redrill the hole to $1/8$ in.
5. Insert a blunt punch into the hole and drive out the plug.
6. Reassemble the carburetor and reinstall it on the engine.
7. Proceed to propane assisted idle set procedure.

CARTER BBD CARBURETOR

1. Remove carburetor from engine.
2. Remove throttle body from carburetor.
3. Place the throttle body in a vise with the concealment plugs facing up and the gasket surfaces protected from the vise jaws.
4. Drill a $5/64$ in. pilot hole at a 45° angle toward concealment plugs.
5. Redrill hole to $1/8$ in.
6. Install a blunt punch into the hole and drive out the plug. Repeat procedure on the opposite side.
7. Reinstall the carburetor on the engine. The carburetor does not have to be removed to install new concealment plugs.
8. Proceed to propane assisted idle set procedure.

THERMO-QUAD CARBURETOR

1. Remove carburetor from engine.
2. Place the carburetor in a vise with the concealment plugs facing up and the gasket surfaces protected from the vise jaws.
3. Drill a $5/64$ in. pilot hole at a 45° angle towards concealment plugs.
4. Redrill hole to $1/8$ in.
5. Install a blunt punch into the hole and drive out the plug. Repeat procedure on the opposite side.
6. Reinstall the carburetor on the engine. The carburetor does not have to be removed to install new concealment plugs.
7. Proceed to propane assisted idle set procedure.

PROPANE ASSISTED IDLE SET RPM

HOLLEY 1945 CARBURETOR
Idle Set–RPM
625 rpm R-9627A
730 rpm R-9628A

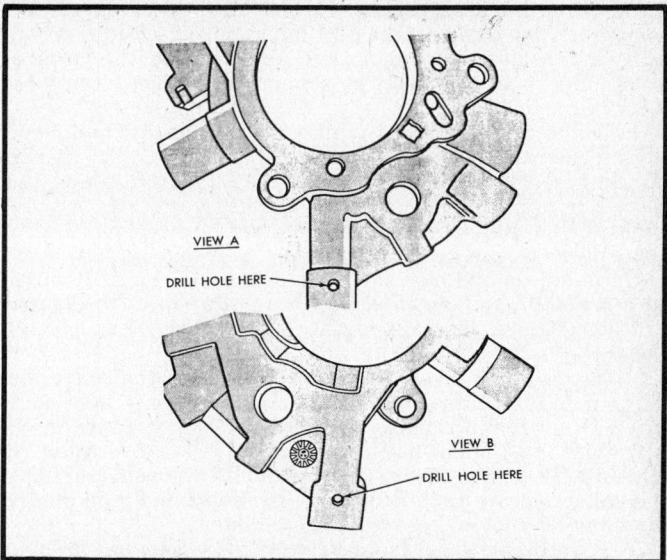

Location for drilling access holes at idle mixture screws—1983 Holley 1945 and 6145 carburetors (© Chrysler Corp.)

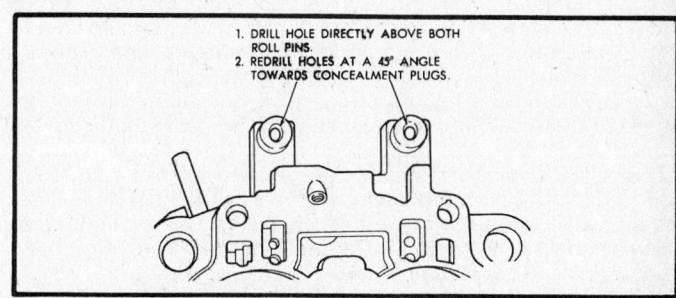

Location for drilling access hole at idle mixture screws—1983 Carter BBD carburetor (© Chrysler Corp.)

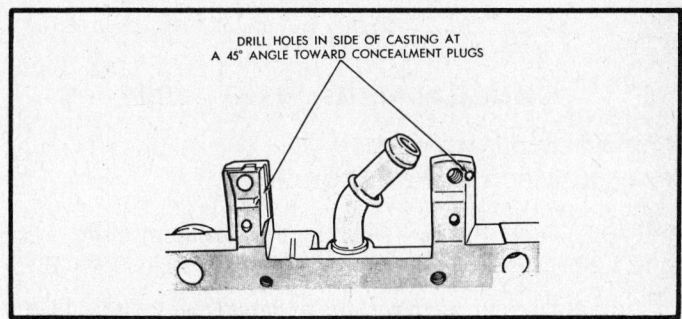

Location for drilling access holes at idle mixture screws—1983 ThermoQuad carburetor (© Chrysler Corp.)

With Propane–RPM
725 rpm R-9627A
855 rpm R-9628A

NOTE: On a new vehicle (under 300 miles/500 km) reduce rpm settings by 75 rpm.

This procedure should only be used if an idle defect still exists after normal diagnosis has revealed no other faulty conditions, such as incorrect basic timing, incorrect idle speed, faulty wire or hose connections, etc. Adjustment of the carburetor air fuel mixture should be done after a major carburetor overhaul.

1. Remove the concealment plug. Set the parking brake and place transmission in neutral. Turn all lights and accessories off. Connect a tachometer to the engine. Start the engine and allow it to warm up on the second highest step of the fast idle cam until normal operating temperature is reached, then return engine to idle.

2. Disconnect and plug the vacuum hoses at the EGR valve, the distributor, and the hoses from the carburetor to the heated air temperature sensor and the OSAC valve. Remove air cleaner.

3. Disconnect the vacuum supply hose from the choke diaphragm at the tee and install the propane supply hose in its place. Other connections at the tee must remain in place.

4. With the propane bottle upright and in a safe location, remove the PCV valve from the cylinder head cover and allow the valve to draw underhood air. Disconnect and plug the 3/16 in. diameter control hose from the canister.

5. Open the propane main valve. Slowly open the propane metering valve until maximum engine rpm is reached. When too much propane is added, engine rpm will decrease. "FINE TUNE" the metering valve to obtain the highest engine rpm.

6. With the propane still flowing, adjust the idle speed screw on the solenoid to obtain the correct propane rpm. "FINE TUNE" the metering valve again to obtain the highest engine rpm. If there has been a change in the maximum rpm, readjust the idle speed screw to the correct propane rpm.

7. Turn off the propane main valve and allow the engine speed to stabilize. Slowly adjust the mixture screw, pausing between adjustments to allow the engine speed to stabilize, to achieve the smoothest idle at the specified idle set rpm.

8. Turn on the propane main valve. "FINE TUNE" the metering valve to obtain the highest engine rpm. If the maximum speed is more than 25 rpm different than the specified propane rpm, repeat Steps 5–7.

9. Turn off the propane main valve and metering valve. Remove the propane supply hose and reinstall the choke vacuum hose. Install a new concealment plug. Perform the Solenoid Idle Stop, Idle Set rpm, and Fast Idle Speed adjustment.

CONCEALMENT PLUG—1984

Removal and Installation

CARTER BBD CARBURETOR

1. Remove air cleaner.
2. Disconnect all hoses from front of carburetor base.
3. Center punch at a point ¼ in. from end of mixture screw housing.
4. Drill through outer housing at punch mark with a 3/16 in. drill bit.
5. Pry out and save concealment plug for reinstallation.
6. Reinstall hoses and air cleaner.

THERMO-QUAD CARBURETOR

1. Remove air cleaner.
2. Disconnect PCV hose from carburetor base.
3. Center punch at a point ¼ in. from end of mixture screw housing.
4. Drill through outer housing at punch mark with a 3/16 in. drill bit.
5. Pry out and save concealment plug for reinstallation.
6. Reinstall air cleaner and PCV hose.

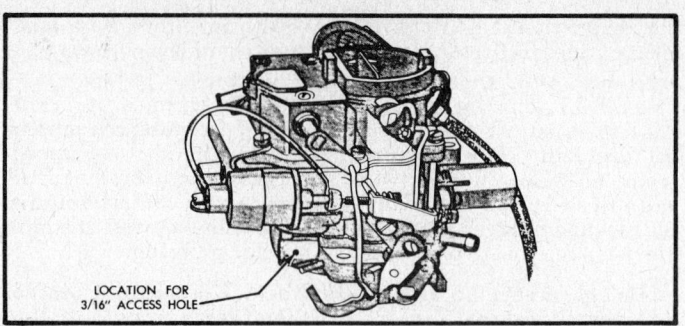

Location for drilling access holes at idle mixture screws—1984 and later Carter BBD carburetor
(© Chrysler Corp.)

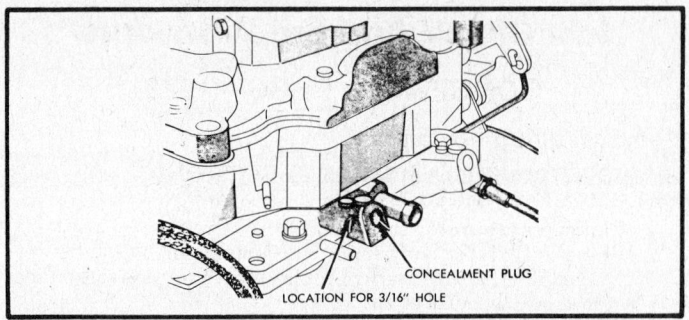

Location for drilling access holes at idle mixture screws—1984 and later Thermo-Quad carburetor
(© Chrysler Corp.)

PROPANE ASSISTED IDLE SET RPM

BBD CARBURETOR
Idle Set—RPM
 600 rpm BBD 8291S
 730 rpm BBD 8292S & 8369S
 750 rpm BBD 8290S
 675 rpm BBD 8385S
 730 rpm BBD 8369S

With Propane—RPM
 760 rpm BBD 8291S
 830 rpm BBD 8292S & 8369S
 885 rpm BBD 8290S
 775 rpm BBD 8385S
 830 rpm BBD 8369S

NOTE: On new vehicles (under 300 miles/500km) reduce rpm settings by 75 rpm.

This procedure should only be used if an idle defect still exists after normal diagnosis has revealed no other faulty conditions, such as incorrect basic timing, incorrect idle speed, faulty hose or wire connections, etc. Also, it is important to make sure the combustion computer systems are operating properly. Adjustment of the carburetor air fuel mixture should be performed after a major carburetor overhaul.

1. Remove the concealment plug. Set the parking brake and place the transmission in neutral. Turn all lights and accessories off. Connect a tachometer to the engine. Start the engine and allow it to warm up on the second highest step of the fast idle cam until normal operating temperature is reached. Return engine to idle.

2. Disconnect and plug the vacuum hose at the EGR valve. On vehicles equipped with a carburetor ground switch, connect

a jumper wire between the switch and a good ground. On vehicles not equipped with a Spark Control Computer (SCC), disconnect and plug the vacuum hoses at the heated air temperature sensor and at the OSAC valve. Remove the air cleaner except on vehicles equipped with SCC where the air cleaner cannot be removed but may be propped up.

3. Disconnect the hose from the heated air door sensor at the carburetor and install the propane supply hose in its place.

4. With the propane bottle upright and in a safe location, remove the PCV valve from the cylinder head cover and allow the valve to draw underhood air. Disconnect and plug the 3/16 in. diameter control hose from the canister.

5. On vehicles equipped with the O_2 feedback system, proceed to Step 6. On vehicles without the O_2 feedback system, proceed to Step 8.

6. Disconnect engine harness lead from the O_2 sensor and ground the engine harness lead. Remove and plug the vacuum line at the vacuum transducer at the SCC. Connect an auxiliary vacuum supply to the vacuum transducer and apply 16 in. Hg.

--- **CAUTION** ---
Care should be exercised so that no pulling force is put on the wire attached to the O_2 sensor. The "bullet" connector to be disconnected is approximately 4 in. from the sensor. Use care in working around the sensor as the exhaust manifold is extremely hot.

7. Allow the engine to run for two minutes to allow the effect of disconnecting the O_2 sensor to take place. Proceed to Step 9.

8. Allow the engine to run for one minute.

9. Open the propane main valve. Slowly open the propane metering valve until the maximum engine rpm is reached. When too much propane is added, engine rpm will decrease. "FINE TUNE" the metering valve to obtain the highest engine rpm.

10. With the propane still flowing, adjust the idle speed screw on the solenoid to obtain the correct propane rpm. Again, "FINE TUNE" the metering valve to obtain the highest engine rpm. If there has been a change in the maximum rpm, readjust the idle speed screw to the specified propane rpm.

11. Turn off the propane main valve and allow the engine speed top stabilize. Slowly adjust the mixture screws by equal amounts, causing between adjustments to allow engine speed to stabilize, to obtain the smoothest idle at the correct idle set rpm.

12. Turn on the propane main valve and "FINE TUNE" the metering valve to obtain the highest rpm. If the maximum engine speed is more than 25 rpm different than the specified propane rpm, repeat Steps 8–12.

13. Turn off propane main end metering valves. Remove the propane supply hose and reinstall the heated air sensor hose. Reinstall new concealment plug. If installed, remove O_2 sensor ground wire and reconnect O_2 sensor. If disconnected, reconnect vacuum line on SCC. Perform the solenoid idle stop, idle set rpm and fast idle speed adjustment procedures.

PROPANE ASSISTED IDLE SET RPM

1983 HOLLEY 6145 ELECTRONIC FEEDBACK, 1983–84 THERMO-QUAD CARBURETORS

Idle Set–RPM
- 675 rpm R-9936A
- 650 rpm TQ-9372S
- 725 rpm R-40042A
- 650 rpm TQ-9385S
- 650 rpm TQ-9374S
- 650 rpm TQ-9389S

With Propane–RPM
- 820 rpm R-9936A
- 775 rpm TQ-9372S
- 775 rpm TQ-9385S
- 775 rpm TQ-9374S
- 800 rpm TQ-9389S
- 835 rpm R-40042A

This procedure should only be used if an idle defect still exists after normal diagnosis has revealed no other faulty condition such as incorrect basic timing, incorrect idle speed, faulty wire or hose connections, etc. It is also important to make sure that the combustion computer systems are operating properly. Adjustment of the carburetor idle air fuel mixture should be performed after a major carburetor overhaul.

Adjustment

1. Remove concealment plug. Set the parking brake and place transmission in neutral. Turn all lights and accessories off. Connect a tachometer to the engine. Remove exhaust manifold heat shield for access to the O_2 sensor. Start engine and allow it to warm up on the second highest step of the fast idle cam until normal operating temperature is reached. Return engine to idle.

2. Disconnect and plug the vacuum hose at the EGR valve. Connect a jumper wire between the carburetor switch and a good ground. Do not remove the air cleaner. The air cleaner may be propped up to provide access to the carburetor.

3. Disconnect vacuum supply hose from the choke diaphragm at the tee and install propane supply hose in its place. Other connections at the tee must remain in place.

NOTE: Thermo-Quad Carburetor—Remove the bowl vent vacuum hose from the carburetor nipple. Install a "T" fitting between the nipple and the vacuum hose. Install the propane supply hose to the "T".

4. With the propane bottle upright and in a safe location, remove the PCV valve from the valve cover and allow the valve to draw underhood air. Disconnect and plug the 3/16 in. diameter control hose from the canister.

5. Disconnect the engine harness lead from the O_2 sensor and ground the engine harness lead. Remove and plug the vacuum line at the vacuum transducer on SCC. Connect an auxiliary vacuum supply to vacuum transducer and set at 16 in. Hg.

--- **CAUTION** ---
Care should be exercised so that no pulling force is put on the wire attached to the O_2 sensor. The "bullet" connector to be disconnected is approximately 4 in. from the sensor. Use care in working around the sensor as the exhaust manifold is extremely hot.

6. Allow engine to run for two minutes to allow the effect of disconnecting the O_2 sensor to take place.

7. Open propane main valve. Slowly open propane metering valve until maximum engine rpm is reached. When too much propane is added, engine rpm will decrease. "FINE TUNE" the metering valve to obtain the highest engine rpm.

8. With the propane still flowing, adjust the idle speed screw on solenoid to obtain the specified propane rpm. Again, "FINE TUNE" the metering valve to obtain the highest engine rpm. If there has been a change in the maximum rpm, readjust the idle speed screw to the specified propane rpm.

9. Turn off propane main valve and allow engine to run for one minute to stabilize. Slowly adjust the mixture screw, pausing between adjustments to allow the engine to stabilize, to achieve the smoothest idle at the specified idle set rpm.

10. Turn on propane main valve. "FINE TUNE" metering valve to obtain the highest engine rpm. If the maximum engine speed is more than 25 rpm different than the specified propane rpm, repeat Steps 7–9.

11. Turn off propane main valve and metering valve.

12. Remove the propane supply hose and reinstall the vacu-

CHRYSLER CORPORATION
REAR WHEEL DRIVE CARS

um supply hose from the choke. Remove O_2 sensor ground wire and reconnect O_2 sensor. Reconnect vacuum line on SCC.

NOTE: Thermo-Quad carburetor—Turn off propane main and metering valves. Remove the propane supply hose and "T".

13. Reinstall the PCV valve. Reinstall new concealment plugs. Reconnect vacuum line on SCC.
14. Install concealment plug and perform solenoid idle stop, idle set rpm and fast idle speed adjustments.

IDLE RPM ADJUSTMENT RPM
1985 AND LATER HOLLEY 2280 CARBURETOR

NOTE: Before checking or adjusting any idle speed, check ignition timing and adjust if necessary. Disconnect and plug the vacuum hose at the EGR valve. Also disconnect and plug the vacuum hose from the carburetor at the heated air temperature sensor. Remove the air cleaner and disconnect and plug the control hose at the canister. Remove the PCV valve from the cylinder head cover and allow the valve to draw underhood air. Disconnect and plug vacuum hose at distributor. Install tachometer. Start and run engine until normal operating temperature is reached.

1. Run the engine for about one minute in order for the engine to stabilize.
2. The correct idle rpm is 730. On a new vehicle with under 300 miles the specification is 75 rpm less.
3. If the engine rpm is not correct, turn the idle speed screw to obtain the correct idle rpm.
4. Turn off engine. Unplug and reconnect vacuum hoses at EGR valve, canister, and distributor.
5. Reinstall air cleaner and unplug and reconnect vacuum hose from carburetor to heated air temperature sensor on air cleaner. Remove tachometer and reinstall PCV valve.
6. Idle speeds with the engine in normal operating condition, all hoses and wires connected, may vary from set speeds. Do not readjust.

SOLENOID IDLE SPEED AND IDLE RPM ADJUSTMENT
1985 AND LATER HOLLEY 6280 CARBURETOR

NOTE: Before checking or adjusting any idle speed, check ignition timing and adjust if necessary. Disconnect and plug the vacuum hose at the EGR valve. Disconnect and plug the hose from the carburetor at the heated air temperature sensor. Remove air cleaner and disconnect and plug the canister purge hose at the canister. Remove the PCV valve from the valve cover and allow the valve to draw underhood air. Install tachometer and start and run engine until normal operating temperature is reached. Turn off engine. Disconnect, then reconnect, fusible link at battery.

Adjustment

1. Ground the carburetor switch. Disconnect the engine harness lead from the oxygen sensor and ground the engine harness lead.

NOTE: Care should be used so that force is not put on the wire that is attaching the oxygen sensor; the connector is to be disconnected about four inches from the sensor.

2. Start the engine and allow it to run for about four minutes.
3. Connect a jumper wire between the positive battery terminal and the solenoid idle stop lead wire. Be sure to attach the wire to the right solenoid or damage to the wiring harness will occur.
4. Open throttle slightly to allow solenoid plunger to extend. Remove solenoid outer screw and spring. Insert a 1/8 in. Allen wrench into solenoid and adjust solenoid idle speed to specification.
5. Install screw and spring and turn in screw until it lightly bottoms out. Remove jumper wire. Set idle speed to specification by turning out solenoid screw.
6. The solenoid rpm is 900 and the idle rpm is 680. If the vehicle is new with less than 300 miles, deduct 75 rpm from the above specification.
7. Remove the tachometer. Unplug and reconnect all hoses. Reinstall the PCV valve and the air cleaner.

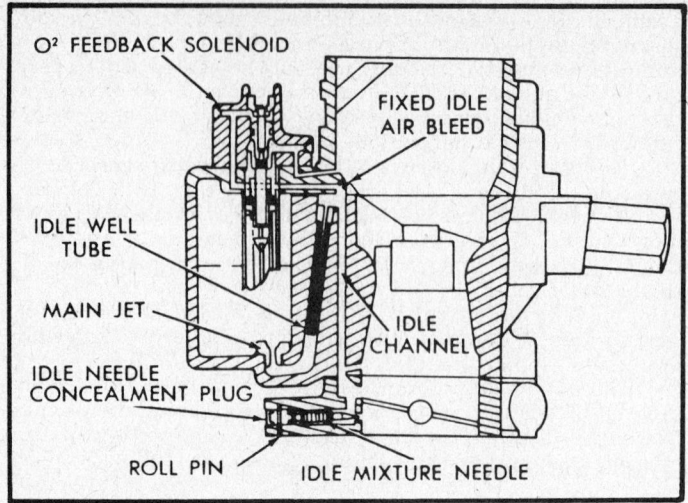

Idle system (© Chrysler Corp.)

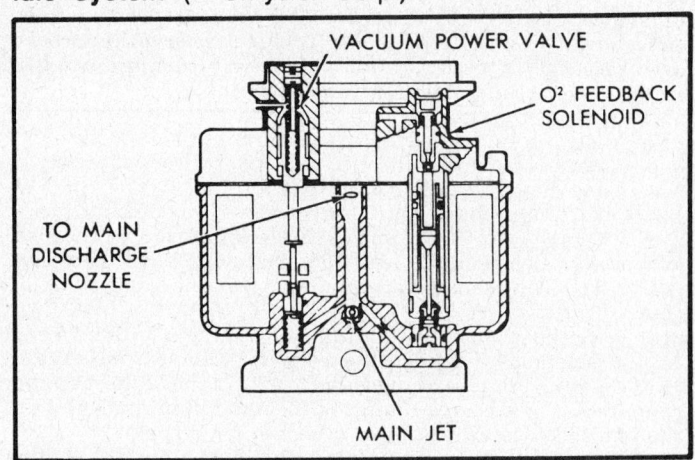

Main metering system (© Chrysler Corp.)

FAST IDLE SPEED
ADJUSTMENT
1985 AND LATER HOLLEY 2280 AND 6280 CARBURETORS

NOTE: Before checking or adjusting any idle speed, check ignition timing and adjust if necessary.

1. Disconnect and plug the vacuum hose at the EGR valve. Also disconnect and plug the vacuum hose from the carburetor at the heated air temperature sensor.

CHRYSLER CORPORATION
REAR WHEEL DRIVE CARS
SECTION 3

2. Remove the air cleaner and disconnect and plug the 3/16 in. diameter control hose at the canister. Remove the PCV valve from the cylinder head cover and allow the valve to draw underhood air.

3. Disconnect and plug the vacuum hose at the distributor. Install tachometer.

4. Start and run engine until normal operating temperature is reached.

5. Open the throttle and place the fast idle adjusting screw on the second highest step of the fast idle cam.

6. With the choke fully open, turn the fast idle adjusting screw until the correct fast idle speed is obtained.

7. For carburetor number 6280, the rpm setting should be 1700. For carburetor number 2280, the rpm setting should be 1600. If the vehicle has less than 300 miles on it, reduce the setting by 75 rpm.

8. Return to idle, then reposition the adjusting screw onto the second highest step of the fast idle cam to verify fast idle speed. Readjust if necessary.

9. Return to idle and turn the engine off. Unplug and reconnect the vacuum hoses at the EGR valve and canister.

10. Reinstall the air cleaner and unplug and reconnect the vacuum hose from the carburetor to the heated air temperature sensor on the air cleaner. Remove the tachometer and reinstall the PCV valve.

11. Idle speeds with the engine in normal operating condition and everything connected may vary from set speeds. Do not readjust.

PROPANE ASSISTED IDLE SET

Adjustment

1985 AND LATER HOLLEY 2280 CARBURETOR

1. Remove the concealment plug. Set the parking brake and place the transmission in neutral. Turn all lights and accessories off. Connect a tachometer to the engine.

2. Start the engine and allow it to warm up on the second highest step of the fast idle cam until normal operating temperature is reached. Return the engine to idle.

3. Disconnect and plug the vacuum hoses at the EGR valve, the distributor, and the hoses from the carburetor heated air temperature sensor. Remove the air cleaner.

4. Disconnect the vacuum supply hose from the choke diaphragm at the carburetor and install the propane supply hose in its place. Other connections at the tee must remain in place.

5. With the propane bottle upright and in a safe location, remove the PCV valve from the cylinder head cover and allow the valve to draw underhood air. Disconnect and plug the 3/16 inch diameter control hose from the canister.

6. Open the propane main valve. Slowly open the propane metering valve until maximum engine rpm is reached. When too much propane is added, engine rpm will decrease. "FINE TUNE" the metering valve to obtain the highest engine rpm.

7. With the propane still flowing, adjust the idle speed screw to obtain the specified propane rpm. "FINE TUNE" the metering valve again to obtain the highest engine rpm. If there has been a change in the maximum rpm, readjust the idle speed screw to obtain the specified propane rpm.

8. Turn off the propane main valve and allow the engine speed to stabilize. Adjust the idle mixture screws 1/16 turn at a time, waiting 30 seconds between adjustments, until the smoothest idle at the specified idle rpm is obtained.

9. The idle rpm specification is 730. The propane rpm specification is 850. If the vehicle has less than 300 miles on it, reduce the settings by 75 rpm.

10. Turn on the propane main valve. "FINE TUNE" the metering valve to obtain the highest engine rpm. If the maximum speed is more than 25 rpm different than the specified propane rpm, repeat Steps 5–7.

11. Turn off the propane main and metering valves. Remove the propane supply hose and reinstall the choke vacuum hose. Install new concealment plugs.

12. Perform the idle rpm and fast idle speed adjustment.

PROPANE ASSISTED IDLE SET

Adjustment

1985 AND LATER HOLLEY 6280 CARBURETOR

1. Remove the concealment plug. Set the parking brake and place the transmission in neutral. Turn all lights and accessories off. Connect a tachometer to the engine.

2. Start the engine and allow it to warm up on the second highest step of the fast idle cam until normal operating temperature is reached. Return the engine to idle and turn off engine.

3. Disconnect and plug the vacuum hoses at the EGR valve and ESA computer. No vacuum is to be applied to the computer. Disconnect and plug canister purge hose at canister.

4. Ground carburetor switch. Disconnect, then reconnect, battery fusible link.

5. Disconnect engine harness lead from sensor and ground engine harness lead. Care should be used so that no pulling force is put on the wire attached to the sensor. The bullet connector to be disconnect is approximately 4 inches from the sensor. Use care in working around the sensor, as the exhaust manifold is extremely hot.

6. Start and run engine for at least 4 minutes.

7. Disconnect the vacuum supply hose from the choke diaphragm at the carburetor and install the propane supply hose in its place. Other connections at the tee must remain in place.

8. With the propane bottle upright and in a safe location, remove the PCV valve from the cylinder head cover and allow the valve to draw underhood air.

9. Open the propane main valve. Slowly open the propane metering valve until the maximum engine rpm is reached. When too much propane is added, engine rpm will decrease. "FINE TUNE" the metering valve to obtain the highest engine rpm.

10. With the propane still flowing, adjust the idle speed screw on the solenoid to obtain the correct propane rpm. Again, "FINE TUNE" the metering valve to obtain the highest engine rpm. If there has been a change in the maximum rpm, readjust the idle speed screw to the specified propane rpm.

11. Turn off the propane main valve and allow the engine speed to stabilize. Slowly adjust the mixture screws by equal amounts, pausing between adjustments to allow engine speed to stabilize, to obtain the smoothest idle at the correct idle rpm.

12. The idle rpm specification is 680. The propane rpm is 740. If the vehicle has less than 300 miles on it, reduce the settings by 75 rpm.

13. Turn on the propane main valve and "FINE TUNE" the metering valve to obtain the highest engine rpm. If the maximum engine speed is more than 25 rpm different than the specified propane rpm, repeat Steps 8–12.

14. Turn off propane main and metering valves. Remove the propane supply hose and reinstall the heated air sensor hose. Reinstall new concealment plugs. If installed, remove sensor ground wire and reconnect oxygen sensor. Reconnect vacuum line on ESA.

15. Perform the solenoid idle stop, idle rpm and the fast idle speed adjustment procedures.

SOLENOID IDLE SPEED AND IDLE RPM

Adjustment

1985 AND LATER ROCHESTER QUADRAJET CARBURETOR

NOTE: Before checking or adjusting any idle speed, check ignition timing and adjust if necessary.

3-27

CHRYSLER CORPORATION
REAR WHEEL DRIVE CARS

1. Disconnect and plug the vacuum hose at the EGR valve.
2. Disconnect and plug the hose from the carburetor at the heated air temperature sensor.
3. Remove air cleaner and disconnect and plug the canister purge hose at the canister.
4. Remove the PCV valve from the cylinder head cover and allow the valve to draw underhood air.
5. Install tachometer and start and run engine until normal operating temperature is reached.
6. Disconnect carburetor electrical connector. Attach a jumper wire between the ground switch terminal of the wiring harness connector (violet wire) and a good ground.
7. Attach a jumper wire between solenoid coil terminal of the carburetor connector (red wire) and battery positive post. Open throttle slightly to allow solenoid plunger to extend.
8. Remove outer screw and spring from solenoid. Insert a $1/8$ in. Allen wrench into solenoid and adjust solenoid idle speed to specifications.
9. The solenoid rpm specification is 800. The idle rpm specification is 750. If the vehicle has less than 300 miles on it, reduce the settings by 75 rpm.
10. Install screw and spring and turn in outer screw until it lightly bottoms out. Remove jumper wire from carburetor connector and battery. Turn outer solenoid screw until correct idle rpm is obtained.
11. Remove remaining jumper wire and reconnect carburetor connector. Remove tachometer, unplug and reconnect all hoses, reinstall PCV valve and air cleaner.

FAST IDLE SPEED

Adjustment

1985 AND LATER ROCHESTER QUADRAJET CARBURETOR

NOTE: Before checking or adjusting any idle speed, check the ignition timing and adjust if necessary.

1. Disconnect and plug the vacuum hose at the EGR valve. Connect a jumper wire between the carburetor switch and a good ground.
2. Disconnect and plug the $3/16$ in. diameter hose at the canister.
3. Remove the PCV valve from the cylinder head cover and allow the valve to draw underhood air.
4. Connect a tachometer to the engine. Start and run engine until normal operating temperature is reached.
5. Disconnect the engine harness lead from the oxygen sensor and ground the engine harness lead. Use care when removing the oxygen sensor so that no pulling force is put on the wire attached to the sensor.
6. Allow the engine to run for 4 minutes to allow the effect of disconnecting the oxygen sensor to take place.
7. Open the throttle slightly and place the fast idle adjusting screw on the second highest step of the fast idle cam.
8. With the choke fully open, turn the fast idle adjusting screw until the correct fast idle rpm is obtained.
9. The rpm specification is 1450. If the vehicle has less than 300 miles on it, reduce the specification by 75 rpm.
10. Return to idle, then reposition the fast idle adjusting screw on the second highest step of the fast idle cam to verify fast idle speed. Readjust if necessary.
11. Return to idle and turn engine off. Unplug and reconnect the vacuum hose at the EGR valve and canister and remove all ground and jumper wires. Reconnect oxygen sensor wire.
12. Idle speed with the engine in normal operating condition (all hoses and wire connected) may vary with idle set speeds. Do not readjust.

PROPANE ASSISTED IDLE SET

Adjustment

1985 AND LATER ROCHESTER QUADRAJET CARBURETOR

1. Remove concealment plugs. Set parking brake and place transmission in neutral. Turn off all lights and accessories, connect a tachometer to engine.
2. Start engine and allow it to warm up on second highest step of fast idle cam until normal operating temperature is reached. Return engine to idle. Turn off engine.
3. Disconnect and plug vacuum hose at EGR valve and canister purge hose at canister. Disconnect idle solenoid connector. Ground carburetor switch (black wire).
4. Remove choke vacuum hose from carburetor nipple and install propane supply hose in its place.
5. With the bottle upright and in a safe location, remove the PCV valve from the valve cover, and allow the valve to draw underhood air.
6. Disconnect the engine harness lead from the oxygen sensor and ground the engine harness lead. Care should be used so that no pulling force is put on the wire attached to the oxygen sensor. The bullet connector to be disconnected is approximately 4 in. from the sensor. Use care in working around the sensor, as the exhaust manifold is extremely hot.
7. Start and run engine for at least 2 minutes to allow effect of disconnecting the sensor to take place. Open propane main valve.
8. Slowly open propane metering valve until maximum engine rpm is reached. When too much propane is added, engine rpm will decrease. "FINE TUNE" the metering valve to obtain the highest rpm.
9. With propane still flowing, adjust the idle speed screw on the solenoid to achieve the specified propane rpm. Again, "FINE TUNE" the metering valve to obtain the highest engine rpm. If there has been a change in the maximum rpm, readjust the idle speed screw on the solenoid to the specified propane rpm.
10. The rpm specification for propane is 800. The rpm specification for idle is 750. If the vehicle is new and has less than 300 miles on it, reduce the settings by 75 rpm.
11. Turn off propane main valve and allow engine speed to stabilize. Slowly adjust the idle mixture screws using tool C-4895 or equivalent by equal amounts, pausing between adjustments to allow engine speed to stabilize, to achieve the smoothest idle at the specified rpm.
12. Turn on propane main valve. "FINE TUNE" the metering valve to obtain the highest engine rpm. If the maximum speed is more than 25 rpm different than the specified rpm, repeat Steps 7–9.
13. Turn off propane main and metering valves. Remove the propane supply hose. Reinstall PCV valve. Unplug and reconnect all hoses. Remove jumper wire and reconnect the oxygen sensor.
14. After adjustments are complete, seal the mixture screws in the throttle body using silicone sealant, RTV rubber, or equivalent. The sealer is required to discourage unnecessary adjustments of the setting and to prevent fuel vapor loss in that area.
15. Perform the solenoid idle stop, idle rpm and fast idle adjustments.

INTAKE AND EXHAUST MANIFOLD ASSEMBLY

Removal

6 CYLINDER

1. Disconnect air cleaner vacuum line from carburetor and

flexible connector between air cleaner and carburetor air heater.

2. Disconnect breather cap to air cleaner line and remove air cleaner.
3. Disconnect distributor vacuum control line, crankcase ventilator valve hose and carburetor bowl vent line, if so equipped.
4. Remove carburetor air heater.
5. Disconnect fuel line, automatic choke rod and throttle linkage from carburetor and remove carburetor.
6. Disconnect exhaust pipe at exhaust manifold.
7. Remove nuts and washers attaching manifold assembly to cylinder head and remove manifold.
8. Remove three screws securing intake manifold to exhaust manifold and separate manifolds.

Installation

1. Install a new gasket between the two manifolds and install the stud nut and two long screws securing the manifolds. Do not tighten screws at this time.
2. Position manifold assembly on cylinder head, using a new gasket (of steel and composition construction). Install triangular washers and nuts on upper studs and on the four lower studs opposite Nos. 2 and 5 cylinders. The eight triangular washers should be positioned squarely on the machined surfaces of both intake and exhaust manifold retaining pads. These washers must be installed with cup side against manifold. Install nuts and washers only when engine is cold.
3. Install steel conical washers with cup side facing manifold, one on center upper stud and two on center lower studs. Install brass washers at each end with flat side to manifold. There must be at least $1/16$ in. (1.6mm) clearance at the minimum point between the exhaust manifold and the two end brass washers. Install nuts with flat side away from washer. Snug all nuts.
4. Tighten three intake to exhaust screws, starting with inner stud. Torque to 240 inch lb. (27 Nm). Torque $5/16$ (7.9mm) screws to 200 inch lb. (23 Nm).
5. Tighten all nuts in sequence to 120 inch lb. (14 Nm).
6. Attach exhaust pipe to manifold flange, using a new gasket and tighten stud nuts to 35 ft. lb. (47 Nm).
7. Install carburetor air heater.
8. Install air injection tube with a new gasket. Tighten to 200 inch lb. (23 Nm).
9. Install carburetor and connect fuel line, automatic choke rod and throttle linkage.
10. Install distributor vacuum control line and carburetor bowl vent line if so equipped.
11. Install air cleaner and connect breather cap to air cleaner line.
12. Install air cleaner vacuum line to carburetor and flexible connector between air cleaner and carburetor air heater.

INTAKE MANIFOLD

Removal and Installation

V8 ENGINES

1. Drain the cooling system. Disconnect the negative battery cable.
2. Remove the alternator, the air cleaner and disconnect the fuel line(s) from the carburetor or throttle body.
3. Disconnect all vacuum lines and throttle linkage that attach to the carburetor or throttle body, and intake manifold.
4. Disconnect the spark plug wires from the plugs and remove the distributor cap and wires as an assembly.
5. Disconnect the wires from the coil and the temperature sending unit.
6. Disconnect the heater hose and by-pass hose from the intake manifold.

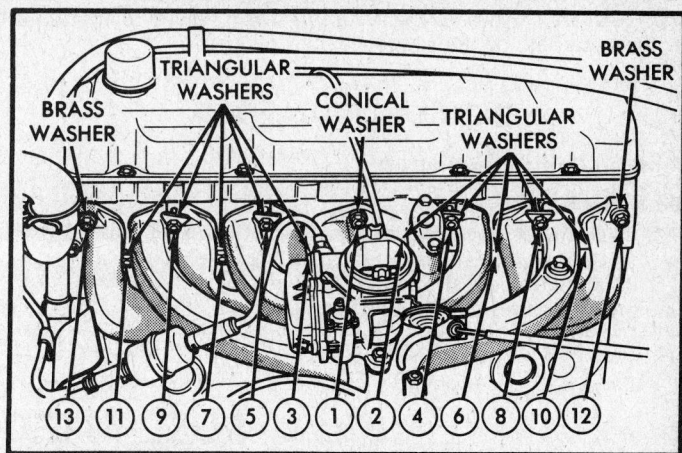

Manifold assembly bolt tightening sequence — 6 cylinder engine (© Chrysler Corp.)

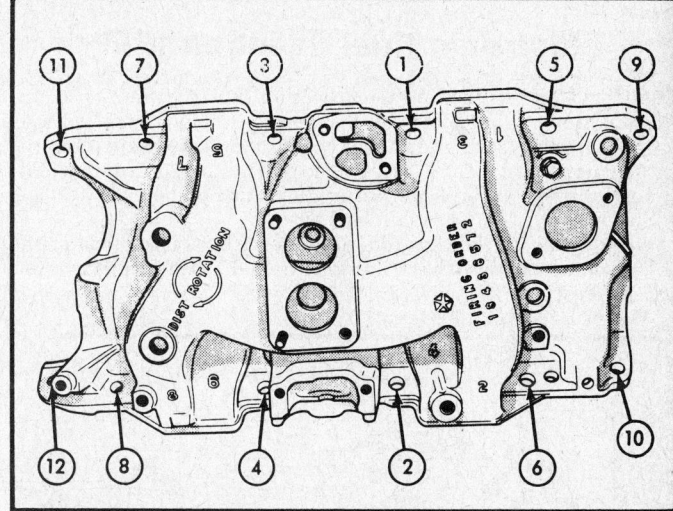

Intake manifold bolt tightening sequence — V8 engine (© Chrysler Corp.)

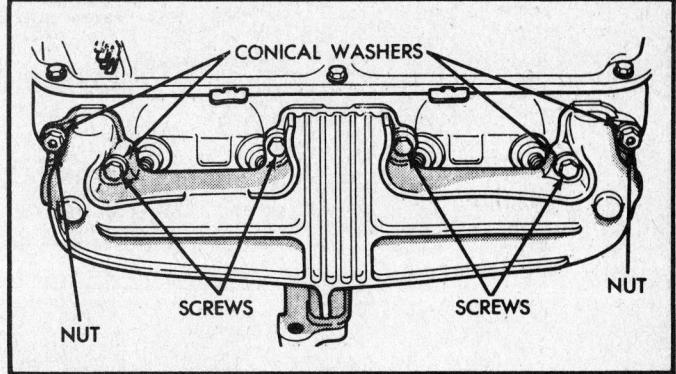

V8 engine exhaust manifold bolt tightening sequence (© Chrysler Corp.)

7. Remove the intake manifold attaching bolts and remove the manifold, carburetor, or throttle body, and coil from the engine as an assembly.
8. Clean all gasket mounting surfaces and firmly cement new gaskets to the engine.

CHRYSLER CORPORATION
REAR WHEEL DRIVE CARS

9. Reverse the procedure to install. Torque bolts to 45 ft. lbs. in three passes, in the sequence shown.

EXHAUST MANIFOLD

Removal and Installation

V8 ENGINES

1. Disconnect the exhaust manifold at the pipe flange. Access to these bolts is from underneath the vehicle.
2. If so equipped, disconnect the air injection nozzles and carburetor heated air stove.
3. Disconnect any components of the EGR system which are in the way. Remove the exhaust manifold by removing the securing bolts and washers. To reach these bolts, it may be necessary to jack the engine slightly off its front mounts.4. When the exhaust manifold is removed, sometimes the securing studs will come out with the nuts. If this occurs, studs must be replaced with the aid of sealing compound on the coarse thread ends. If this is not done, water leaks may develop at the studs.
5. To install the exhaust manifold, reverse the removal procedure.

NOTE: On the center branch of the manifold, no conical washers are used.

FUEL INJECTION SYSTEM

For more information on Fuel Injection System, refer to Unit Repair Section.

Electronic Fuel Injection (EFI)

The Chrysler Electronic Fuel Injection (EFI) System is a continuous flow, single point, fully electronically controlled system. A single system monitors the ratio of air to fuel electronically, comparing it to an ideal ratio and adjusts it automatically to changing environmental and engine conditions.

Specifically, the Chrysler EFI system:
1. Provides an integrated and pre-programmed computer that commands ignition timing, air-fuel ratio and emission control systems.
2. Employs an unusually wide variety of sensor inputs on which to base its command decisions and insure more precise control.
3. Has the ability to update and revise its programming to better suit current ambient and engine operating conditions.
4. Can function with a high degree of precision, even when certain sensor inputs are inoperative or misleading.

Since EFI's fuel metering is electronically commanded, it is not subjected to low airflow errors of venturi-controlled metering used by carburetors. Also, since fuel is delivered under positive pressure through injection nozzles, excellent fuel atomization is assured, even at low airflow rates. This improves air-fuel mixing and minimizes variations in the air-fuel ratio delivered to each cylinder.

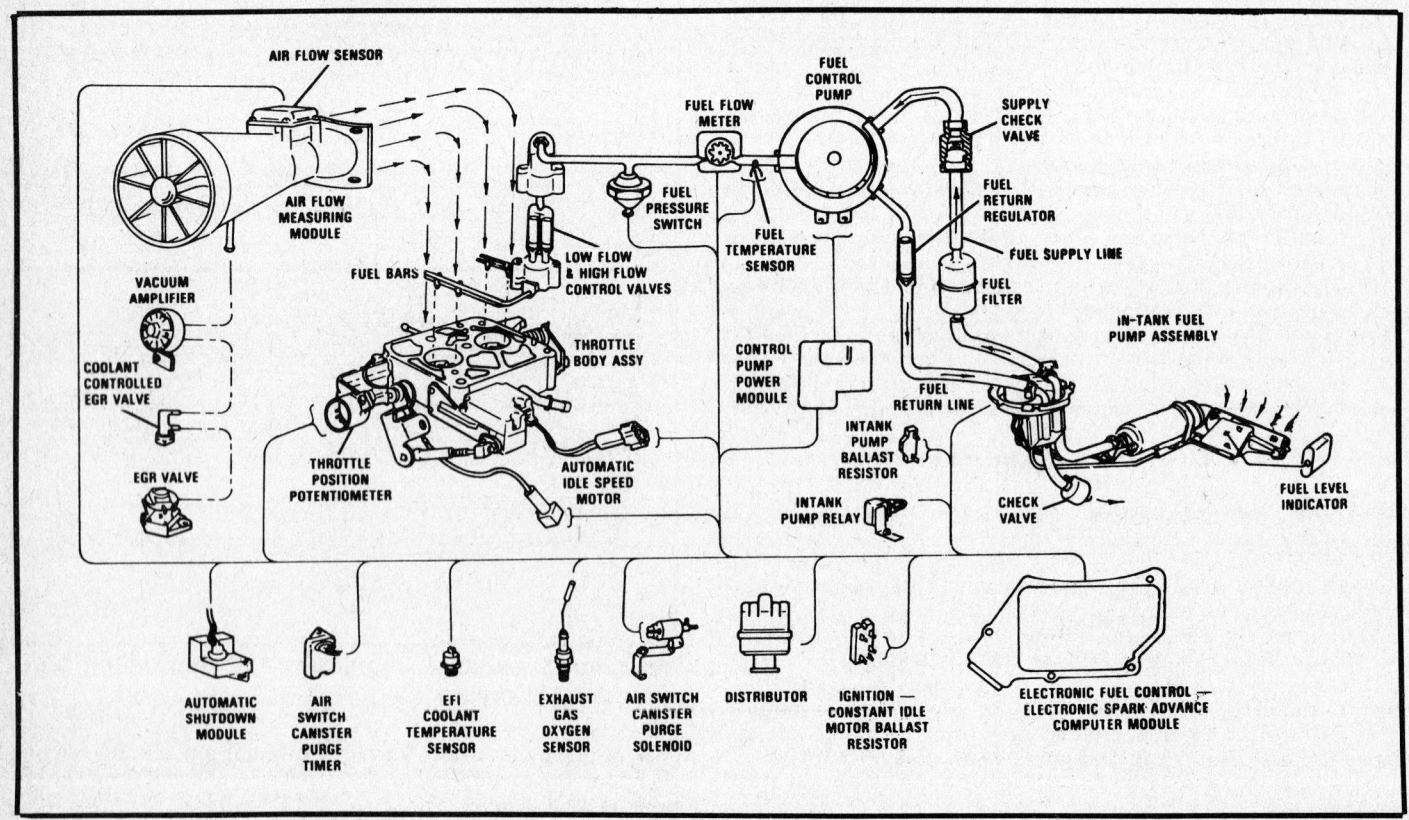

Electronic Fuel Injection System schematic (© Chrysler Corp.)

CHRYSLER CORPORATION
REAR WHEEL DRIVE CARS
SECTION 3

EMISSION CONTROL SYSTEMS

EQUIPMENT USED

1983

- Air injection system
- Catalytic converter
- Electronic spark control
- Evaporation control system
- Emission calibrated carburetor
- Emission calibrated distributor
- Electric choke
- Exhaust gas recirculation system
- Heated inlet air
- Orifice spark advance control
- Closed positive crankcase ventilation system

Three-way catalytic converter system
Air switching valve

1984 AND LATER

- Closed crankcase ventilation valve
- Heated air cleaner
- Evaporation control system with canister storage
- Exhaust gas recirculation system
- Emission calibrated carburetor
- Emission calibrated distributor
- Catalytic converter
- Fresh air intake
- Electric choke
- Orifice spark advance system
- Air injection system
- Air aspirator system

ENGINE SECTION

ENGINE ASSEMBLY

Removal

6 CYLINDER ENGINE

1. Scribe hood hinge outlines on hood and remove hood.
2. Drain cooling system and remove carburetor air cleaner.
3. Remove radiator/heater hoses and remove radiator. Set fan shroud aside.
4. Remove air conditioning compressor and set aside without disconnecting hoses.
5. Remove vacuum lines, distributor cap and wiring.
6. Remove carburetor, linkage, starter wires and oil pressure wire.
7. Remove power steering hoses, if so equipped.
8. Remove starter motor, alternator, charcoal canister and horns.
9. Remove exhaust pipe at manifold.
10. Remove bell housing bolts and inspection plate.
11. Remove torque converter drive plate bolts from torque converter drive plate. Mark converter and drive plate to aid in reassembly.
12. Support transmission with transmission stand tool. Attach a C-clamp on front bottom of transmission torque converter housing. This will assure that the torque converter will be retained in proper position in the transmission housing.
13. Disconnect the engine from the torque converter drive plate.
14. Install engine lifting fixture. Attach a chain hoist to fixture eyebolt.
15. Remove engine front mount bolts.
16. Remove engine from engine compartment and install in engine repair stand.

Installation

1. Remove engine from repair stand and install in engine compartment.
2. Install bell housing bolts and front engine mounts.
3. Install torque converter drive plate bolts and inspection plate. Remove stand from transmission.
4. Remove engine lifting fixture and install carburetor and lines.
5. Install starter motor, alternator, charcoal canister and lines.
6. Install vacuum lines, distributor cap and wiring.
7. Connect exhaust pipe at manifold using new gasket and torque to 35 ft. lbs. (47 Nm).
8. Connect carburetor linkage and wiring to engine.
9. Install radiator, radiator hoses and heater hoses.
10. Set fan shroud in position. Fill the cooling system.
11. Install carburetor air cleaner. Connect vacuum hoses and power steering hoses, if so equipped.
12. Install emission control components.
13. Install air conditioning equipment, if so equipped.
14. Start the engine, bring to normal operating temperature and adjust as required.
15. Install hood.
16. Road test vehicle.

Removal

V8 ENGINE

1. Scribe hood hinge positions and remove hood.
2. Drain cooling system, remove battery and carburetor air cleaner.
3. Remove radiator/heater hoses and remove radiator. Set fan shroud aside.
4. Remove air conditioning compressor and set aside without removing lines.
5. Remove vacuum lines, distributor cap and wiring.
6. Remove carburetor, linkage, starter wires and oil pressure wire.
7. Remove power steering hoses, if so equipped.
8. Remove starter motor, alternator, charcoal canister and horns.
9. Remove exhaust pipe at manifold.
10. Remove bell housing bolts and inspection plate.
11. Remove torque converter drive plate bolts from torque converter drive plate. Mark converter and drive plate to aid in re-assembly.
12. Support transmission with transmission stand tool. Attach C-clamp on front bottom of transmission torque converter housing. This will assure that the torque converter will be retained in proper position in the transmission housing.

3-31

13. Disconnect the engine from the torque converter drive plate.
14. Install engine lifting fixture. Attach a chain hoist to fixture eyebolt.
15. Remove engine front mount bolts.
16. Remove engine from engine compartment and install in engine repair stand.

Installation

1. Remove engine from repair stand and install in engine compartment.
2. Install bell housing bolts and inspection plate. Remove stand from transmission.
3. Install torque converter drive plate bolts and front end mounts. Remove C-clamp. Install inspection plate.
4. Remove engine lifting fixture and install carburetor and lines.
5. Install starter motor, alternator, charcoal canister and lines.
6. Install vacuum lines, distributor cap and wiring.
7. Install exhaust pipe. Torque to 24 ft. lbs. (33 Nm). Tighten nuts alternately so space between manifold flange and exhaust pipe flange is approximately equal.
8. Connect carburetor linkage and wiring to engine.
9. Install radiator, radiator hoses and heater hoses.
10. Install fan shroud. Fill cooling system.
11. Install battery and carburetor air cleaner. Connect vacuum hose and power steering hoses, if so equipped.
12. Install air conditioning equipment, if so equipped.
13. Warm engine and adjust.
14. Install hood.
15. Road test vehicle.

ENGINE MOUNTS

Removal

ENGINE FRONT MOUNTS

1. Raise hood and position fan to clear radiator hose and radiator top tank.
2. Disconnect throttle linkage at transmission and at carburetor.
3. Remove torque nuts from insulator studs.
4. Raise engine just enough to remove engine front mount assembly.

Installation

1. Install insulator to engine bracket and tighten as specified.
2. Lower engine and install washers and prevailing torque nuts to insulator studs; tighten nuts as specified.
3. Connect throttle linkage at transmission and carburetor.

Removal

ENGINE REAR MOUNTS

1. Raise vehicle, support safely with enough under-vehicle working clearance.
2. Install transmission jack or equivalent under transmission.
3. Remove engine rear crossmember from frame and rear mount from transmission.

Installation

1. Install rear crossmember to frame. Tighten to specifications.
2. Install rear mount to crossmember and transmission. Tighten to specifications.
3. Remove transmission jack or equivalent.
4. Lower vehicle.

Valve System

VALVE ADJUSTMENT

All V8s and 6 cylinders use hydraulic lifters and non-adjustable rocker arms. The lifters take up lash automatically and no adjustment is possible. After engine re-assembly, these lifters adjust themselves shortly after oil pressure builds up.

VALVE LIFTERS

Removal and Installation

6 CYLINDER AND V8 ENGINES—EXCEPT 1985 AND LATER WITH ROLLER TAPPETS

1. Remove valve cover, rocker assembly and push rods and identify push rods to insure installation in original location.
2. Slide Tool (C-4129 or equivalent), through opening in cylinder head and seat tool firmly in the head of tappet.

NOTE: Although it is possible to remove the valve lifters without removing the intake manifold on the V8 engine, it is recommended that the manifold be removed.

3. Pull the tappet out of the bore with a twisting motion. If all tappets are to be removed, identify tappets to insure installation in original locations.

CAUTION

The plunger and tappet bodies are not interchangeable. The plunger and valve must always be fitted to the original body. It is advisable to work on one tappet at a time to avoid mixing of parts. Mixed parts are not compatible. Do not disassemble a tappet on a dirty work bench.

4. To install the tappets, lubricate tappets completely with engine oil.
5. Install tappets and push rods in their original positions.
6. Install rocker arm and shaft assembly.
7. Install valve cover.
8. Start and operate engine. Warm up to normal operating temperature.

CAUTION

To prevent damage to valve mechanism, engine must not be run above fast idle until all hydraulic tappets have filled with oil and have become quiet.

V8 ENGINE—1985 AND LATER WITH ROLLER TAPPETS

1. Disconnect the negative battery cable.
2. Remove the valve cover. Remove the rocker assembly and push rods. Identify the push rods to insure proper installation.
3. Remove the intake manifold. Remove the valve lifter yoke retainer and aligning yokes.
4. Remove the valve lifters using a valve lifter removal tool. Identify the lifters to insure proper installation.
5. Repair or replace the valve lifters as required.
6. Installation is the reverse of the removal procedure.
7. When installing the aligning yokes, make sure that the arrow points toward the camshaft. Torque the retaining bolt to 200 inch lbs.

ROCKER ARMS AND SHAFT ASSEMBLY

Removal

6 CYLINDER ENGINES

1. Disconnect vacuum hoses and wires. Mark as required.
2. Disconnect fender support bracket.
3. Remove valve cover mounting bolts.

CHRYSLER CORPORATION
REAR WHEEL DRIVE CARS
SECTION 3

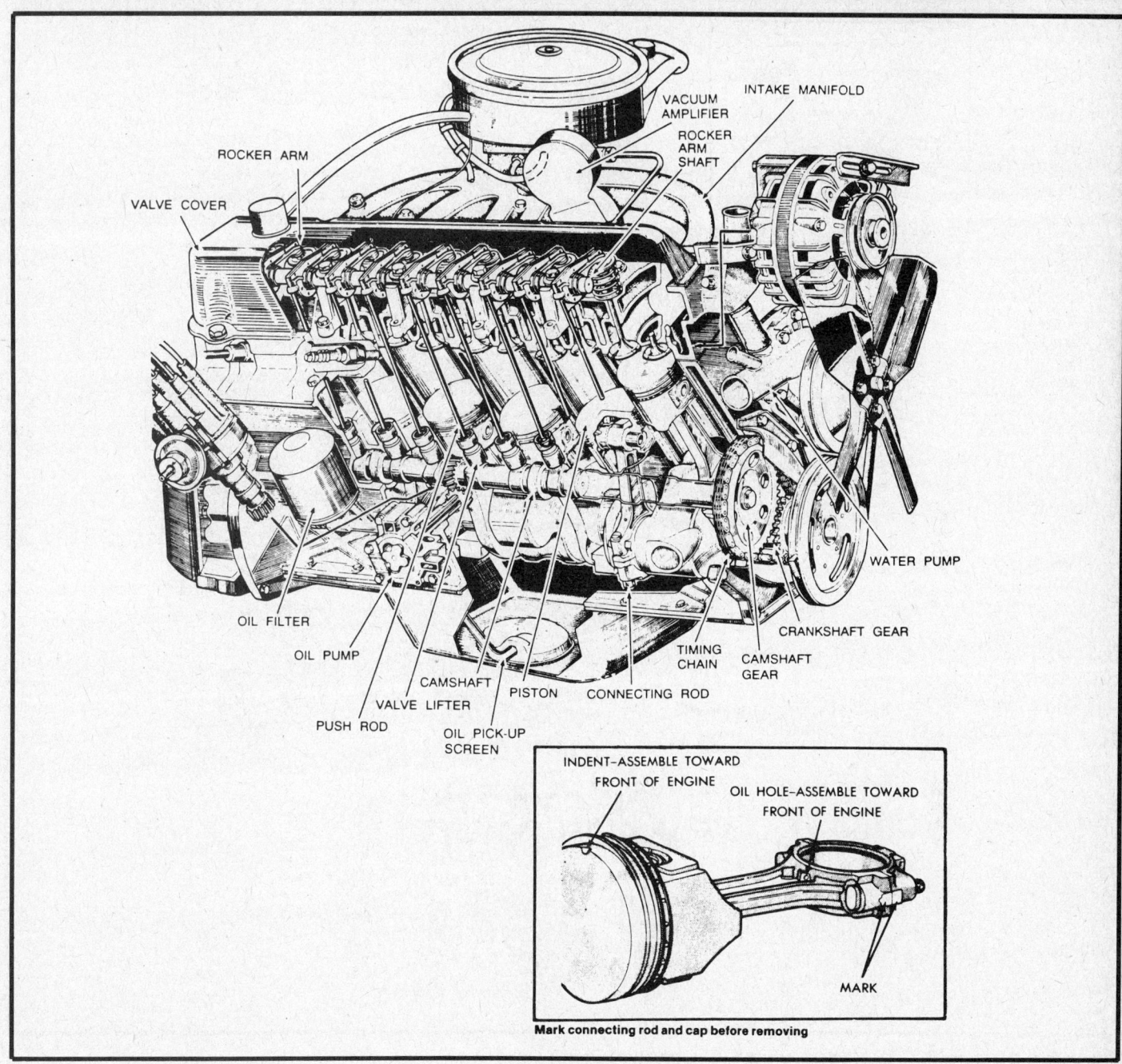

Chrysler 6 cyl 225 cu. in. 3.7L engine (© Chrysler Corp.)

4. If equipped with air conditioning, hold the A/C hoses up out of the way when removing valve cover and gasket.
5. Remove rocker shaft bolts and retainers.
6. Remove rocker arms and shaft assembly.

Installation

1. Rocker arms and shaft assembly must be installed so the oil holes are on the bottom of the shaft. The shaft requires the special bolt be installed properly. This is necessary to provide proper lubrication to rocker assemblies.
2. Install rocker shaft retainers between rocker arms so they seat on rocker shaft and not on the extended bushing of rocker arm. Be sure to install long retainer in center position only.
3. Install rocker shaft bolts. Install special bolt at the rear of the engine. Tighten all bolts to 25 ft. lbs. (34 Nm).

─── **CAUTION** ───
Tighten all bolts uniformly and slowly to allow tappets to leak down. If bolts are run down quickly, bent pushrods may result.

4. Inspect cylinder head cover gasket flange for distortion. Straighten if necessary.
5. Place new service gasket in position and install cylinder head cover with load spreader fasteners. Tighten to 80 inch lbs. (9 Nm).
6. Install closed ventilation system and evaporation control system.

3-33

CHRYSLER CORPORATION
REAR WHEEL DRIVE CARS

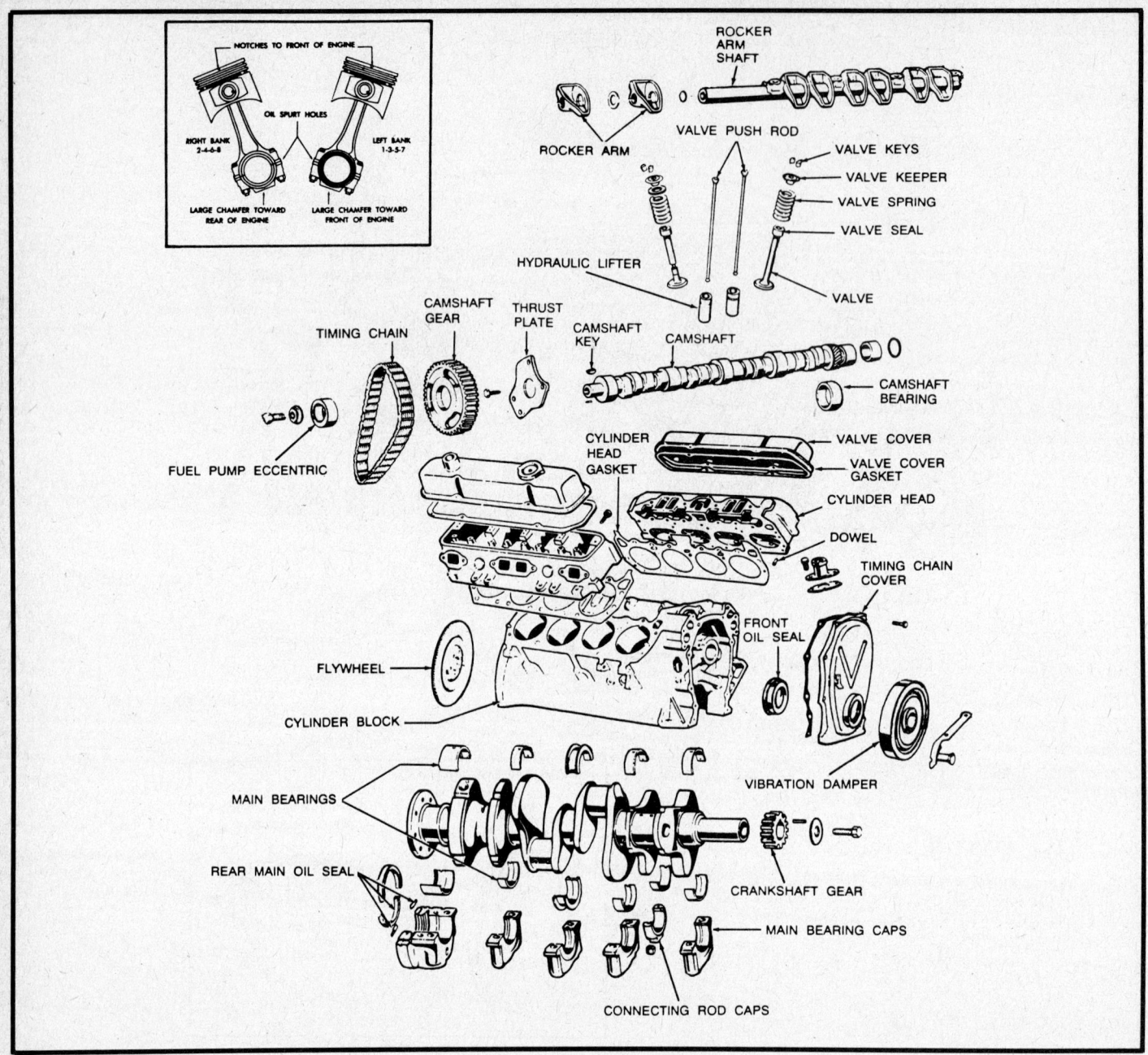

Chrysler V8 engine—exploded view (© Chrysler Corp.)

7. Reconnect all vacuum hoses and wires removed.

Removal

V8 ENGINES

1. Disconnect spark plug wires by pulling on the boot straight out in line with plug.
2. Disconnect closed crankcase ventilation system and evaporation control system from cylinder head cover.
3. Remove cylinder head cover and gasket.
4. Remove five rocker shaft bolts and retainers.
5. Remove rocker arms and shaft assembly.

Installation

1. Install rocker arm and shaft assemblies with "NOTCH" on end of rocker shaft pointing to centerline of engine and toward front of engine on the left bank and to the rear on right bank, making sure to install the long stamped steel retainers in the number two and four positions. Tighten bolts to 200 inch lbs. (23 Nm).
2. Clean cylinder head cover gasket surface. Inspect cover for distortion and flatten if necessary.
3. Clean head rail if necessary. Install cylinder head cover and tighten bolts to 80 inch lbs. (9 Nm).
4. Install closed crankcase ventilation system and evaporation control system.

CHRYSLER CORPORATION
REAR WHEEL DRIVE CARS

SECTION 3

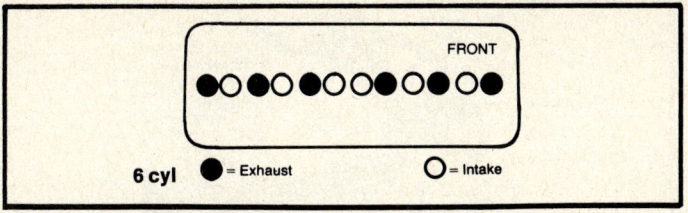

Valve arrangement (© Chrysler Corp.)

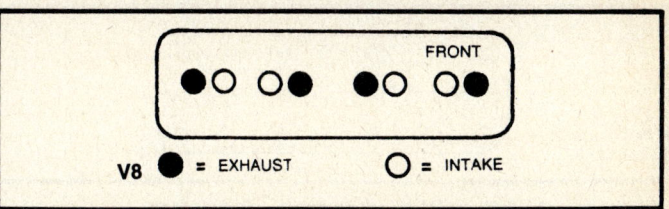

Valve arrangement (© Chrysler Corp.)

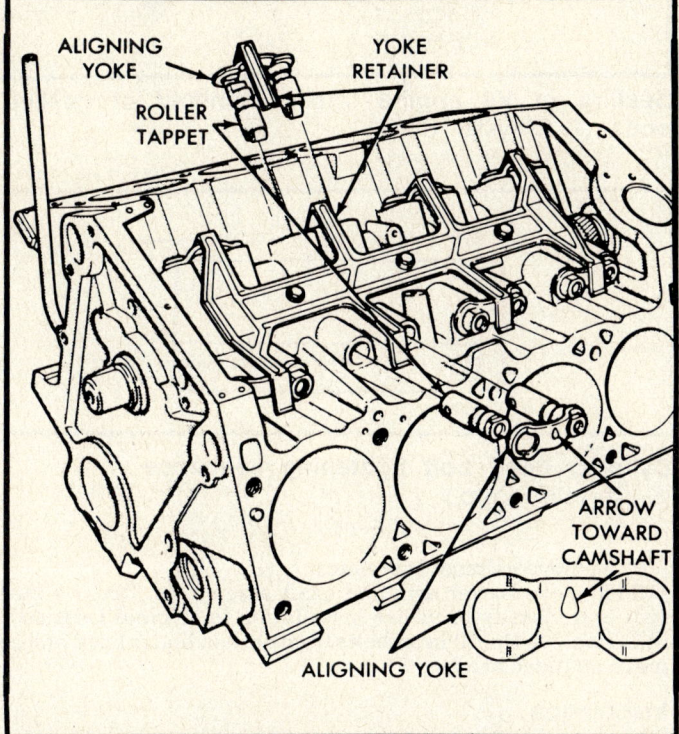

Valve lifter installation (© Chrysler Corp.)

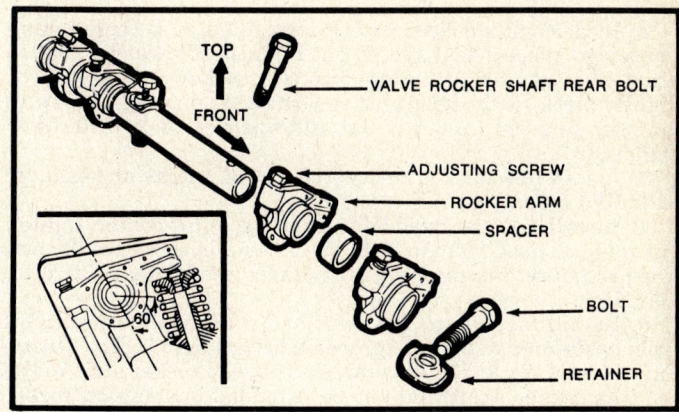

Six cylinder rocker arm and shaft assembly
(© Chrysler Corp.)

V8 Engine
The timing of the crankshaft pulley should now read from 10° before top dead center to 2° after top dead center. Remove spacer.
    5. If reading is not within specified limits:
       a. Check sprocket index marks.
       b. Inspect timing chain for wear.
       c. Check accuracy of DC mark on timing indicator.

CYLINDER HEAD

Removal
6 CYLINDER ENGINES
    1. Drain cooling system.
    2. Remove carburetor air cleaner and fuel line.
    3. Disconnect accelerator linkage.
    4. Remove vacuum control tube at carburetor and distributor.
    5. Disconnect spark plug wires by pulling straight out in line with the plug.
    6. Disconnect heater hose and clamp holding by-pass hose.
    7. Disconnect heat indicator sending unit wire.
    8. Disconnect exhaust pipe at exhaust manifold flange.
    9. Disconnect diverter valve vacuum line from intake manifold and remove air tube assembly from cylinder head, if so equipped.
    10. Remove closed ventilation system, evaporation control system and cylinder head cover.
    11. Remove rocker arm and shaft assembly.
    12. Remove push rods and tappets and identify to insure installation in original location.
    13. Remove 14 head bolts and, with the aid of an assistant, remove cylinder head, intake and exhaust manifold as an assembly.

Installation
    1. Clean all gasket surfaces of cylinder block and cylinder head.

VALVE TIMING

Procedure
6 AND V8 ENGINES
    1. Turn crankshaft until the No. 6 exhaust valve is closing and No. 6 intake valve is opening.
    2. Insert a ¼ in. (6.35mm) spacer between rocker arm pad and stem tip of No.1 intake valve. Allow spring load to bleed tappet down, giving in effect a solid tappet.
    3. Install a dial indicator so plunger contacts valve spring retainer as nearly perpendicular as possible. Zero the indicator.
    4. Rotate the crankshaft clockwise (normal running direction) until the valve has lifted 0.010 in. (0.254mm).

CAUTION

Do not turn crankshaft any further clockwise, as valve spring might bottom and result in serious damage.

6 Cylinder Engine
The timing of the crankshaft pulley should now read from 12° before top dead center to top dead center. Remove spacer.

3-35

CHRYSLER CORPORATION
REAR WHEEL DRIVE CARS

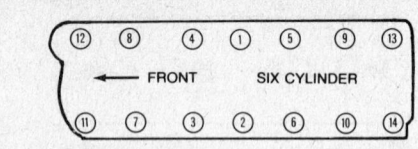

Cylinder head bolt tightening sequence
(© Chrysler Corp.)

2. Inspect all surfaces with a straightedge, if there is any reason to suspect leakage. If out of flatness exceeds 0.00075 times the span length in any direction, either replace head or lightly machine the head gasket surface. As an example, if a 12 in. span is 0.004 in. out of flat, allowable is 12 × 0.00075 = 0.009 in.
3. Install new gasket and cylinder head, intake and exhaust manifold assembly.
4. Install cylinder head bolts. Starting at top center, tighten all cylinder head bolts to 35 ft. lb. (47 Nm) in sequence. Repeat the procedure, retightening all cylinder head bolts to 70 ft. lb. (95 Nm).
5. Install tappets, rocker arms and shaft assembly with oil hole positioned to provide proper lubrication to rocker assemblies. Install rocker shaft retainers between rocker arms to the seat on rocker shaft and not on extended bushing on rocker arms. Be sure to install long retainer in center position only. Install rocker shaft bolts ($5/16$ screw at rear of engine) and tighten to 25 ft. lb. (34 Nm).
6. Install the spark plugs.
7. Connect heater hose and by-pass hose clamps.
8. Connect heat indicator sending unit wire, accelerator linkage and spark plug cables.
9. Install vacuum control tube at carburetor and distributor.
10. Install air tube assembly with a new gasket to cylinder head. Tighten to 100 inch lb. (12 Nm). Install diverter valve vacuum line, if so equipped.
11. Connect exhaust pipe to exhaust manifold flange.
12. Install fuel line and carburetor air cleaner.
13. Fill cooling system.
14. Inspect cylinder head cover gasket flange. Check flange for distortion. Straighten if necessary.
15. Follow "Form-In-Place Gasket" instructions closely, except be certain to apply RTV to cylinder head, not the cylinder head cover.
16. Use two piloting dowels, one in diagonally opposite corners to prevent smearing.
17. Install cover and tighten screws to 80 inch lbs. (9 Nm) withing 10 minutes of RTV application.
18. Install closed ventilation system and evaporation control system.

Removal
V8 ENGINES

1. Drain cooling system and disconnect battery ground cable.
2. Remove alternator, carburetor air cleaner and fuel line.
3. Disconnect accelerator linkage.
4. Remove vacuum control hose between carburetor and distributor.
5. Remove distributor cap and wires.
6. Disconnect coil wires, heat indicator sending unit wire, heater hoses and by-pass hose.
7. Remove closed ventilation system, evaporation control system and cylinder head covers.
8. Remove intake manifold, ignition coil and carburetor as an assembly.

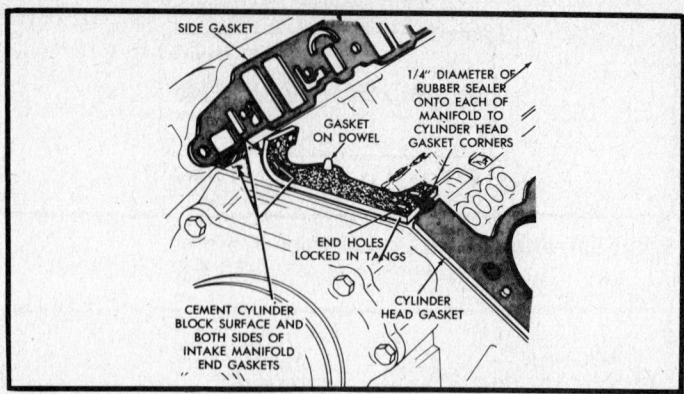

Sealing of V8 engine intake manifold at gasket ends (© Chrysler Corp.)

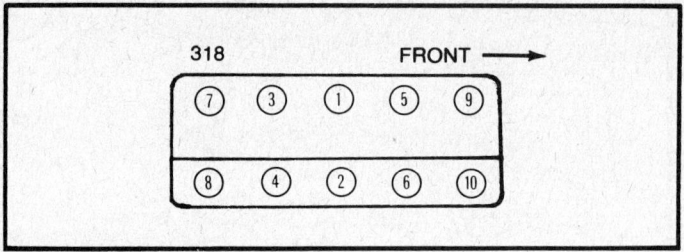

Cylinder head bolt tightening sequence
(© Chrysler Corp.)

9. Remove exhaust manifolds.
10. Remove rocker arm and shaft assemblies. Remove push rods and identify to insure installation in original location.
11. Remove the 10 head bolts from each cylinder head and remove cylinder heads.

Installation

1. Clean all gasket surfaces of cylinder block and cylinder heads.
2. Inspect all surfaces with a straightedge if there is any reason to suspect leakage. If out of flatness exceeds 0.00075 inch times the span length in any direction, either replace head or lightly machine the head gasket surface. As an example, if a 12 in. span is 0.004 in. out of flat, allowable is 12 × .00075 equals 0.009 in.
3. Remove cylinder heads from holding fixtures, install gaskets and place heads on engine.
4. Clean pipe sealant from bolt threads and bolt holes. Apply Mopar Lock N' Seal or equivalent to bolt threads. Install cylinder head bolts. Starting at top center, tighten all cylinder head bolts to 50 ft. lb (68 Nm) in sequence. Repeat procedure, retighten all cylinder head bolts to 95 ft. lb. (129 Nm).
5. Inspect push rods and replace worn or bent rods.
6. Install push rods, rocker arm and shaft assemblies with the "NOTCH" on the end of rockershaft pointing to centerline of engine and toward front of engine on the left bank and to the rear on right bank, making sure to install the long stamped steel retainers in the number two and four positions, tighten to 200 inch lb. (23 Nm).
7. On 318-2bbl engines, coat intake manifold side gaskets lightly with sealer. On 318-4bbl engines, do not use any sealer on side composition gaskets.
8. Install side gaskets to cylinder head.
9. Clean cylinder block front and rear gasket surfaces using a suitable solvent.

10. Apply a thin, uniform coating of a quick dry cement to the intake manifold front and rear gaskets and cylinder block gasket surface. Allow to dry 4 to 5 minutes or until tack free.

NOTE: When installing gaskets, the center hole in the gasket MUST engage dowels in block. End holes in seals MUST be locked into tangs of head gasket.

11. Carefully install the front and rear intake manifold gaskets.
12. Place a drop (approximately 1/4 in. diameter) of rubber sealer onto each of the four manifold to cylinder head gasket corners.
13. Carefully lower intake manifold into position on the cylinder block and cylinder heads. After intake manifold is in place, inspect to make sure end seals are in place.
14. Install the twelve attaching cap screws "FINGER TIGHT". Tighten cap screws 25 ft. lb. (34 Nm), using the tightening sequence. Tighten the cap screws to 40 ft. lb. (54 Nm) and follow by retightening the cap screws to 45 ft. lb (61 Nm) in sequence.
15. Install exhaust manifolds and tighten screws to 20 ft. lb. (27 Nm) and nuts to 15 ft. lbs. (20 Nm).
16. Adjust spark plugs and install the plugs, tightening to 30 ft. lb. (41 Nm).
17. Install coil wires, heat indicator sending unit wire, heater hoses and by-pass hose.
18. Install vacuum control hoses between carburetor and distributor.
19. Install throttle linkage and adjust as necessary.
20. Install distributor cap and wires.
21. Install fuel line, alternator and drive belt. Tighten alternator mounting bolt to 30 ft. lb (41 Nm) and adjusting strap bolt to 200 inch lb. (23 Nm).
22. Be certain cylinder head covers are not distorted at screw holes—flatten if necessary.
23. Place new cylinder head cover gaskets in position and install cylinder head covers. Tighten to 80 inch lb. (9 Nm) using load spreader fasteners.
24. Install closed crankcase ventilation system and evaporation control system.
25. Fill cooling system and install battery ground cable.

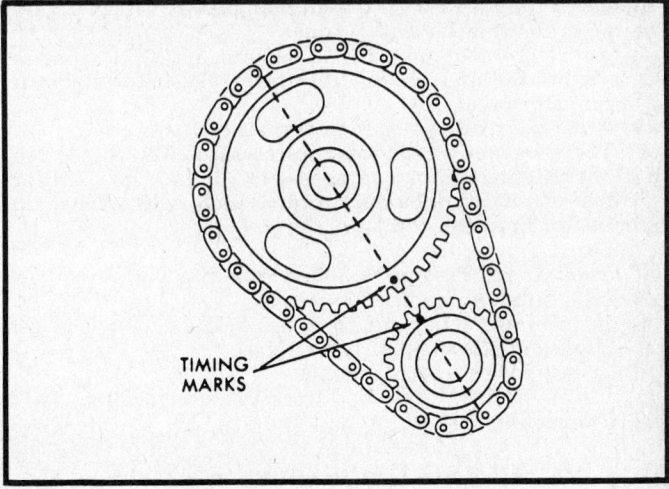
Timing mark alignment—6 cyl

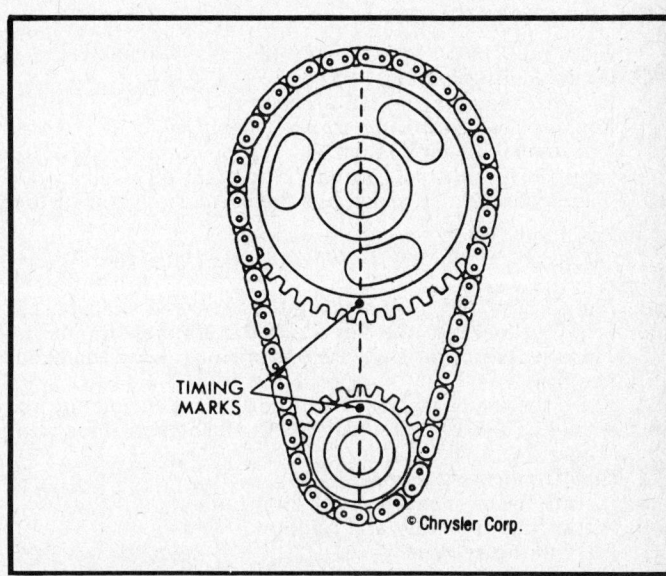
V8 engine timing marks

TIMING CHAIN COVER

Removal
6 CYLINDER ENGINES

1. Drain cooling system.
2. Remove radiator and fan.
3. Pull vibration damper assembly off end of crankshaft.
4. Loosen oil pan bolts to allow clearance and remove chain case cover and gasket.

Installation

1. Be sure mating surfaces of chain case cover and cylinder block are clean and free from burrs.
2. Add 1/8 in. dia. bead of sealer at junction of rubber pan seals and cork oil pan gaskets.
3. Using a new gasket, slide chain case cover over locating dowels and tighten bolts to 200 inch lb. (23 Nm). Be sure all oil pan gaskets are in place and tighten oil pan bolts to 200 inch lb. (23 Nm).
4. Place damper pulley assembly hub key in the slot in crankshaft, lubricate seal lip with Lubriplate and slide hub on the crankshaft.
5. Place installing tool in position and press damper pulley assembly on the crankshaft.

Removal
V8 ENGINES

1. Drain cooling system.
2. Remove water pump.
3. Remove power steering pump.
4. Remove pulley from vibration damper and bolt and washer securing vibration damper on crankshaft.
5. Using proper pulling tool, remove the vibration damper from end of crankshaft.
6. Remove fuel lines and fuel pump.
7. Loosen oil pan bolts and remove the front bolt at each side.
8. Remove chain case cover and gasket using extreme caution to avoid damaging oil pan gasket.

Installation

1. Be sure mating surfaces of chain case cover and cylinder block are clean and free from burrs.
2. Using a new cover gasket, carefully install chain case cover to avoid damaging oil pan gasket. A 1/8 inch diameter bead of

sealer is recommended on the oil pan gasket. Do not tighten chain case cover bolts at this time.

3. Lubricate seal lip with lubriplate, position vibration damper hub slot on crankshaft. Damper will act as a pilot for the crankshaft seal.

4. Press vibration damper on crankshaft.

5. Tighten chain case cover capscrews to 30 ft. lb. (41 Nm) first, then tighten oil pan capscrews to 200 inch lbs. (23 Nm).

6. Install vibration damper retainer bolt with washer and tighten to 135 ft. lb. (183 Nm).

7. Position pulley on vibration damper and attach with bolts and lockwashers. Tighten to 200 inch lb. (23 Nm).

8. Install fuel pump and fuel lines.

9. Install water pump and housing assembly, using new gaskets. Tighten bolts to 30 ft. lb. (41 Nm).

10. Install power steering pump.

11. Install fan/belt assembly, hoses and close drains.

12. Fill cooling system.

TIMING COVER OIL SEAL

Removal
6 CYLINDER ENGINES

1. Disconnect battery negative cable.
2. Drain cooling system.
3. Remove radiator and fan assembly.
4. Remove power steering crankshaft pulley.
5. Remove vibration damper.
6. Using a suitable tool behind the lip of the oil seal, pry outward, being careful not to damage the crankshaft seal surface of cover.

Installation

1. Install new seal by installing the threaded shaft part of the installing tool into the threads of the crankshaft.
2. Place seal into opening with seal spring toward the inside of the engine.
3. Place the installing tool with the thrust bearing and nut on the shaft. Tighten nut until tool is flush with the timing chain cover.
4. Install vibration damper.
5. Install power steering crankshaft pulley.
6. Install fan assembly and radiator.
7. Fill cooling system.
8. Connect battery negative cable.

Removal
V8 ENGINES

1. Disconnect battery.
2. Loosen and remove belts from crankshaft pulley.
3. Remove radiator shroud retainer screws and set shroud back over engine.
4. Remove fan and shroud from engine.
5. Remove crankshaft pulley and vibration damper bolt and washer from end of crankshaft.
6. Pull vibration damper from end of crankshaft.
7. Using a suitable tool behind the lips of the oil seal, pry outward, being careful not to damage the crankshaft seal surface of cover.

Installation

1. Install new seal by installing the threaded shaft part of the installing tool into the threads of the crankshaft.
2. Place seal into opening with seal spring toward the inside of the engine.
3. Place the installing tool with the thrust bearing and nut on the shaft. Tighten nut until tool is flush with the timing chain cover.

4. Lubricate damper hub and install vibration damper.

5. Install retainer bolts and washer and torque to 135 ft. lb (183 Nm).

6. Install pulley on vibration damper and torque to 200 inch lb. (23 Nm).

7. Set radiator shroud back over engine and install fan and belts.

8. Install radiator shroud to radiator.

9. Connect battery negative battery cable.

TIMING CHAIN

Measuring Timing Chain for Stretch (Cover Off)
6 CYLINDER AND V8 ENGINES

1. Place a scale next to the timing chain so that any movement of the chain may be measured.

2. Place a torque wrench and socket over the camshaft sprocket lock bolt and apply torque in the direction of crankshaft rotation to take up slack; 30 ft. lb (40.6 Nm) (cylinder head installed) or 15 ft. lb. (20 Nm) (cylinder head removed). With torque applied to the camshaft sprocket bolt, crankshaft should not be permitted to move. It may be necessary to block the crankshaft to prevent rotation.

3. Holding a scale with dimensional reading even with the edge of a chain link, apply torque in the reverse direction 30 ft. lb (40.6 Nm) (cylinder head installed) or 15 ft. lb (20 Nm) (cylinder head removed) and note the amount of chain movement.

4. If chain movement exceeds 1/8 in. (3.175mm), install a new timing chain.

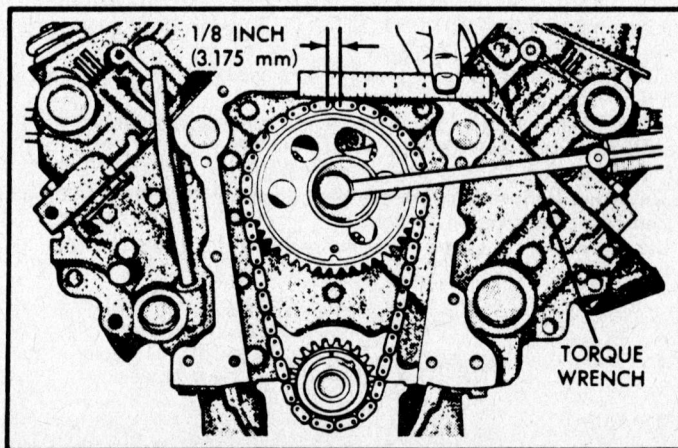

Measuring timing chain wear and stretch
(© Chrysler Corp.)

Alternate Method of Timing Chain Slack Inspection
V8 ENGINE IN VEHICLE

NOTE: The in-vehicle timing chain check will require a measuring tool fabricated from a 1/4 in. diameter round stock to the accompanying illustration specifications.

1. Remove the fuel pump and gasket from the chain case cover.

2. Rotate the crankshaft to position number six piston at TDC on its compression stroke.

3. With the number six piston positioned as described in Step 2, a 1/4 in. hole, adjacent to the timing index mark in the camshaft chain sprocket, should be at the six o'clock position and the vibration damper mark should be at 0°.

4. Insert the fabricated tool through the fuel pump opening and engage the tool hook into the camshaft sprocket 1/4 in. hole.

5. With the tool engaged and held horizontally, read the tool

CHRYSLER CORPORATION
REAR WHEEL DRIVE CARS — SECTION 3

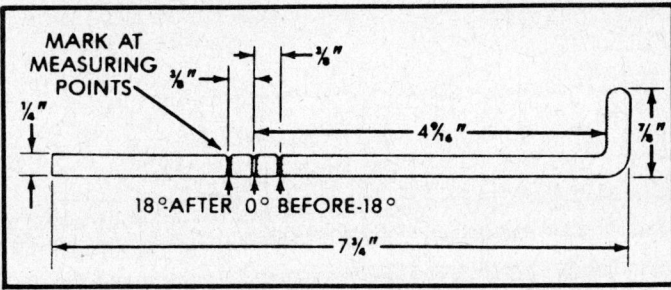

Fabricated valve timing checking tool (© Chrysler Corp.)

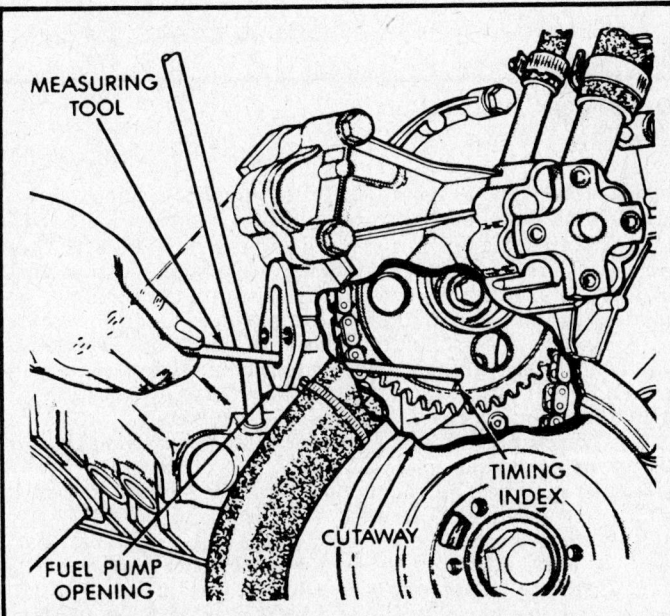

Using fabricated valve timing checking tool (© Chrysler Corp.)

gauge ("Before"-"O"-"After") marks at the edge of the fuel pump mounting surface.

6. If the tool indicator is at "O", the valve timing is correct.
7. If the tool indicator is "Before" or "After" the "O" mark, the valve timing is incorrect, indicating the camshaft to crankshaft relationship is off approximately 18°.

NOTE: 18° would indicate the chain installation is off by one camshaft sprocket tooth.

Removal and Installation
6 CYLINDER ENGINES

1. If chain slack is not satisfactory, remove camshaft sprocket attaching bolt and remove timing chain with camshaft sprocket.
2. Turn crankshaft to line up the centerline of camshaft and crankshaft with the timing mark on crankshaft sprocket.
3. Install camshaft sprocket and timing chain.
4. Line up timing marks on the sprockets with the centerline of crankshaft and camshaft.
5. Tighten camshaft sprocket lock bolt to 35 ft. lb (47 Nm).

Removal and Installation
V8 ENGINES

1. If chain is not satisfactory, remove camshaft sprocket attaching cup washer, fuel pump eccentric and remove timing chain with crankshaft and camshaft sprockets.
2. Place both camshaft sprocket and crankshaft sprocket on the bench with timing marks on exact imaginary center line through both camshaft and crankshaft bores.
3. Place timing chain around both sprockets.
4. Turn crankshaft and camshaft to line up with keyway location in crankshaft sprocket and in camshaft sprocket.
5. Lift sprockets and chain (keep sprockets tight against the chain in position as described).
6. Slide both sprockets evenly over their respective shafts and use a straight edge to check alignment of timing marks.
7. Install the fuel pump eccentric, cup washer and camshaft bolt. Tighten bolt to 35 ft. lb (47 Nm).
8. Check camshaft for 0.002–0.006 in. (0.051–0.0152mm) end play with a new thrust plate and up to 0.010 in. (0.254mm) end play with a used thrust plate. If not within these limits, install a new thrust plate.

CAMSHAFT

Removal
(Engine Removed from Vehicle)
6 CYLINDER ENGINES

1. Remove tappets and push rods.
2. Identify tappets to insure installation in original location.
3. Remove timing sprockets, distributor and oil pump.
4. Remove fuel pump.
5. Install a long bolt into the front of camshaft to facilitate removal of the camshaft; remove camshaft, being careful not to damage cam bearings with the cam lobes.

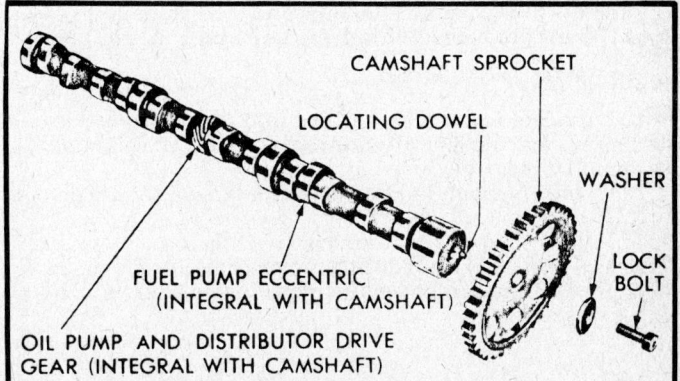

Camshaft and sprocket assembly — six cylinder engine (© Chrysler Corp.)

Installation

NOTE: When replacing camshaft, all of the tappet faces must be inspected for crown using a straight edge. If any negative crown (dishing) is observed, tappet must be replaced. The tappet must have a definite crown.

1. Lubricate camshaft lobes and camshaft bearing journals and insert the camshaft in cylinder block.

NOTE: Whenever an engine has been rebuilt and/or a new camshaft and/or new tappets have been installed, add one pint of Chrysler Crankcase Conditioner, Part Number 3419130 or equivalent, to engine oil to aid in break-in. The oil mixture should be left in engine for a minimum of 500 miles (805km) and drained at the next normal oil change.

2. Install the timing sprockets and chain, cover, fuel pump,

CHRYSLER CORPORATION
REAR WHEEL DRIVE CARS
SECTION 3

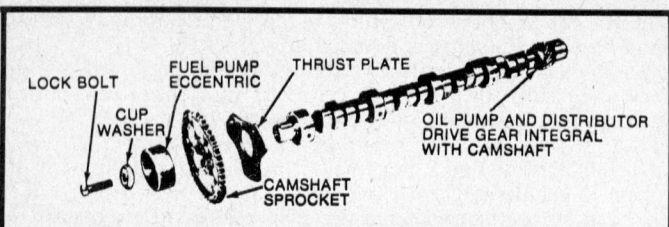

Camshaft and sprocket assembly—V8 engine
(© Chrysler Corp.)

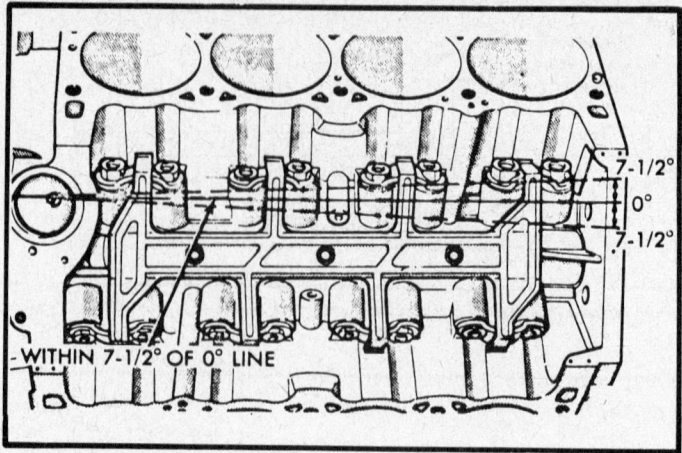

Drive gear installation

distributor and oil pump. Install the tappets and pushrods in their original locations.
3. Complete the assembly as required.

Removal
(Engine Removed from Vehicle)

V8 ENGINES

1. Remove rocker arm and shaft assemblies.
2. Remove pushrods and tappets; identify so each part will be replaced in its original location.
3. Remove distributor and lift out the oil pump and distributor drive shaft.
4. Remove camshaft thrust plate; note location of oil tab.
5. Install a long bolt into front of camshaft to facilitate removal of the camshaft; remove camshaft, being careful not to damage cam bearings with the cam lobes.

NOTE: To reduce internal leakage and help maintain higher oil pressure at idle, cup plugs have been pressed into the oil galleries behind the camshaft thrust plate.

Installation

1. Lubricate camshaft lobes and camshaft bearing journals and insert the camshaft to within 2 in. (50.8mm) of its final position in cylinder block.
2. Install camshaft holding tool with tongue back of distributor drive gear.
3. Hold tool in position with distributor lock plate screw. This tool will restrict camshaft from being pushed in too far and prevent knocking out the cup plug in rear of cylinder block. Tool should remain installed until the camshaft and crankshaft sprockets and timing chain have been installed.
4. Install camshaft thrust plate and chain oil tab with three screws. Make sure tang enters lower right hole in thrust plate. Tighten to 210 inch lbs. (24 Nm). Top edge of tab should be flat against thrust plate in order to catch oil for chain lubrication.
5. Place both camshaft sprocket and crankshaft sprocket on the bench with timing marks on exact imaginary center line through both camshaft and crankshaft bores.
6. Place timing chain around both sprockets.
7. Turn crankshaft and camshaft to line up with keyway location in crankshaft sprocket and in camshaft sprocket.
8. Lift sprockets and chain (keep sprockets tight against the chain in position as described).
9. Slide both sprockets evenly over their respective shafts and use a straight edge to check alignment of timing marks.
10. Install the fuel pump eccentric, cup washer, and camshaft screw and washer assembly and tighten to 35 ft. lb. (47 Nm).
11. Measure camshaft end play. If not within limits, install a new thrust plate.
12. With damper timing indicator on "O", coat the distributor drive shaft and gear with engine oil. Install the shaft so that after gear spirals into place, it will index with oil pump shaft.

Lubrication

OIL PAN

Removal
6 CYLINDER ENGINES

1. Disconnect battery negative cable and remove oil dipstick.
2. Remove shroud attaching screws, separate shroud from radiator and position rearward on engine.
3. Raise vehicle, support safely and drain oil pan.
4. Remove engine-to-transmission support bracket.
5. Remove exhaust pipe.
6. Remove torque converter inspection shield.
7. Remove center link from steering arm and idler arm ball joints.
8. Support front of engine with a jackstand placed under the right front corner of engine. (Do not support the engine at the crankshaft pulley or vibration damper.)
9. Remove front mount bolts. Raise engine approximately 1½–2 in. (3.81–5.08cm).
10. Remove oil pan. Rotate engine crankshaft as required for oil pan to clear counterweights.

Installation

1. Using a new pan gasket set (California engines require a high temperature left side gasket), add ⅛ in. (3.175mm) diameter drops of sealer to four corners of rubber seal and slide gasket. Install oil pan and tighten screws to 75 inch lb. (4 Nm). Then retighten to 200 inch lb. (23 Nm).
2. Lower engine to its original position and install engine front mount bolts.

3–40

CHRYSLER CORPORATION
REAR WHEEL DRIVE CARS

3. Install engine-to-transmission support bracket.
4. Install exhaust pipe.
5. Install torque converter inspection shield.
6. Connect steering and idler arm ball joints to center link. Tighten retainer nuts to 40 ft. lb (54 Nm) and secure with cotter pins.
7. Lower vehicle and install fan shroud.
8. Connect battery cables.

Removal
V8 ENGINES
1. Disconnect battery ground cable and remove dipstick.
2. Raise vehicle, support safely and drain the oil from the pan.
3. Remove exhaust crossover pipe. Disconnect and lower center steering link.
4. Remove starter and starter mounting stud.
5. Remove torque converter inspection plate.
6. Remove the engine oil pan assembly.

Installation
1. Inspect alignment of oil strainer. Bottom of strainer must be parallel with the machined surface of the cylinder block. Bottom of strainer must touch bottom of oil pan with 1/16–1/8 in. (1.587–3.175mm) interference desirable.
2. Using a new pan gasket set, add drop of sealer at corners of rubber and cork.
3. Install oil pan and torque screws to 200 inch lb. (23 Nm).
4. Install torque converter inspection plate.
5. Install starter mounting stud and starter.
6. Install crossover pipe. Torque to 24 ft. lb (33 Nm).
7. Connect center steering link.
8. Lower vehicle, install dipstick and fill engine with motor oil, connect battery ground cable, start engine and check for leaks.

OIL PUMP

Removal and Installation
6 CYLINDER ENGINES
1. Disconnect the negative battery cable.
2. Remove the fan shroud from the radiator, if equipped.
3. Raise the vehicle and support the front of the engine under the right front corner of the oil pan. Do not support the engine at the crankshaft pulley or the vibration damper.
4. Raise the engine about 2 inches in order to gain clearance to the oil pump retaining bolts.
5. Remove the oil filter. Remove the oil pump retaining bolts. Remove the oil pump from the engine block, along with the pump body gasket.
6. Installation is the reverse of the removal procedure. Torque the oil pump retaining bolts to 200 inch lbs. Be sure to use a new pump gasket.

Removal and Installation
V8 ENGINES
1. It is necessary to remove the oil pan and remove the oil pump from the rear main bearing cap.
2. Prime the oil pump before installation by filling the rotor cavity with engine oil and rotating the shaft.
3. Install the oil pump on the rear main bearing cap and tighten the retaining bolts to 30 ft. lb. (41 Nm).

REAR MAIN BEARING OIL SEAL

Service seals are of split rubber type composition. The seals make it possible to replace the upper rear seal without removing the crankshaft. The seal must be used as an upper and lower set.

Oil pan gasket, typical of V8 engine
(© Chrysler Corp.)

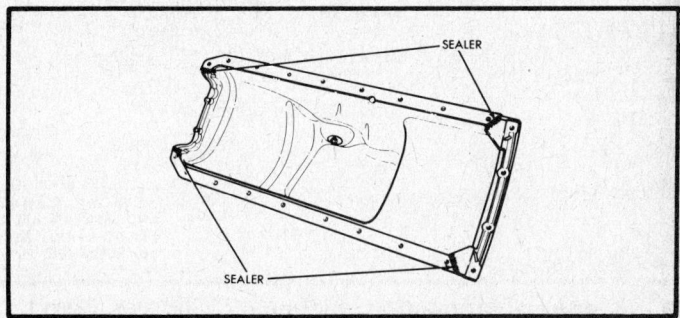

Oil pan gasket, typical of six cylinder engine
(© Chrysler Corp.)

Removal
6 CYLINDER ENGINES
1. With oil pan removed, remove rear seal retainer and rear main bearing cap.
2. Remove lower oil seal by pushing the end with a small suitable tool.
3. Remove upper seal by pressing with a small suitable tool on the end of the seal, being careful not to damage the crankshaft.

— CAUTION —
Always wipe crankshaft surface clean, then oil lightly before installing a new seal.

4. Oil seal lip lightly with engine oil.
5. Hold seal (with paint stripe to the rear) tightly against crankshaft with thumb to make sure that the sharp edge of the groove in the block does not shave or nick the back of the seal, install seal in the block groove. Rotate the crankshaft, if necessary, while sliding seal into groove. Care must be exercised not to damage the sealing lip.
6. Install other half of the seal into the lower seal retainer with paint stripe to rear.
7. Install rear main bearing cap, tighten to 85 ft. lb (115 Nm).
8. Install two side seals into grooves in seal retainer.
9. Lightly grease retainer side seals for ease of assembly into block.
10. Install lower seal retainer, tighten to 30 ft. lb. (40.6 Nm). Do not use sealer or cement on crankshaft seal ends of lip. Apply small amount of gasket sealer to bottom of seal retainer, both sides.

CHRYSLER CORPORATION
REAR WHEEL DRIVE CARS

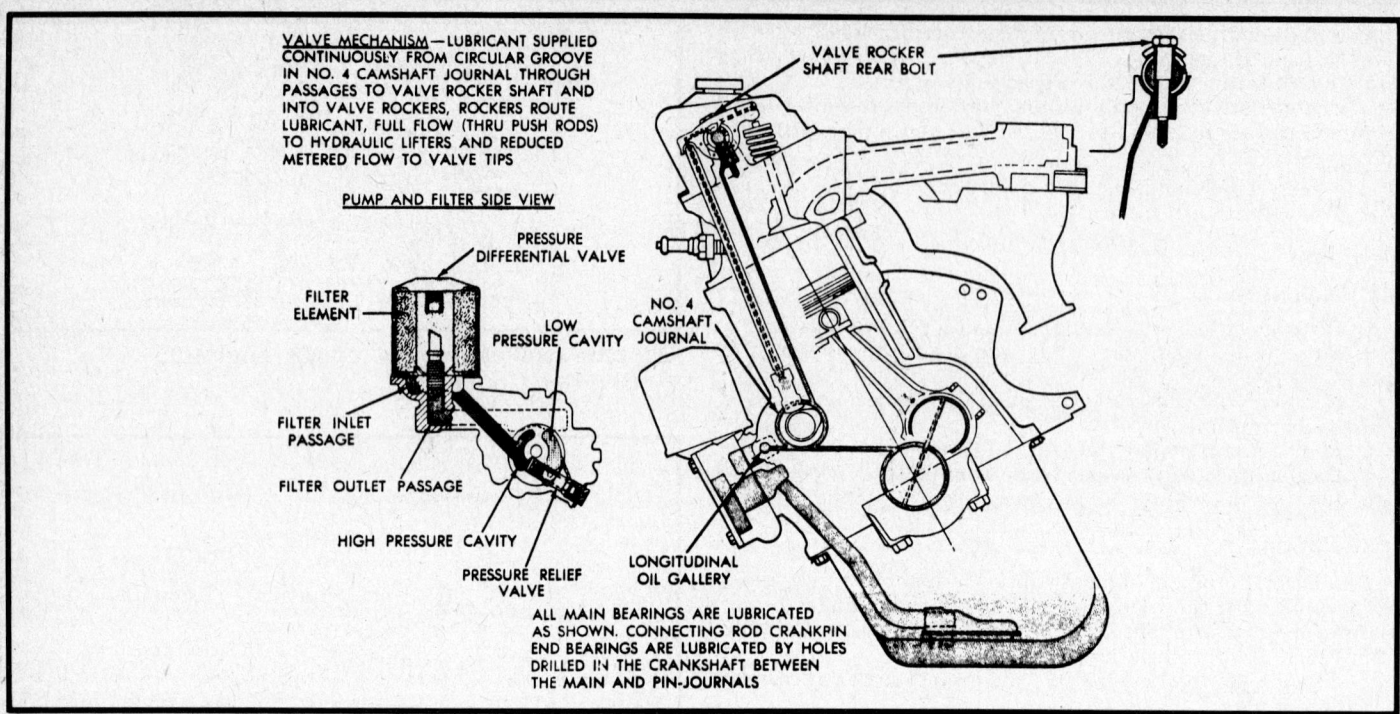

6 cyl engine lubrication system (© Chrysler Corp.)

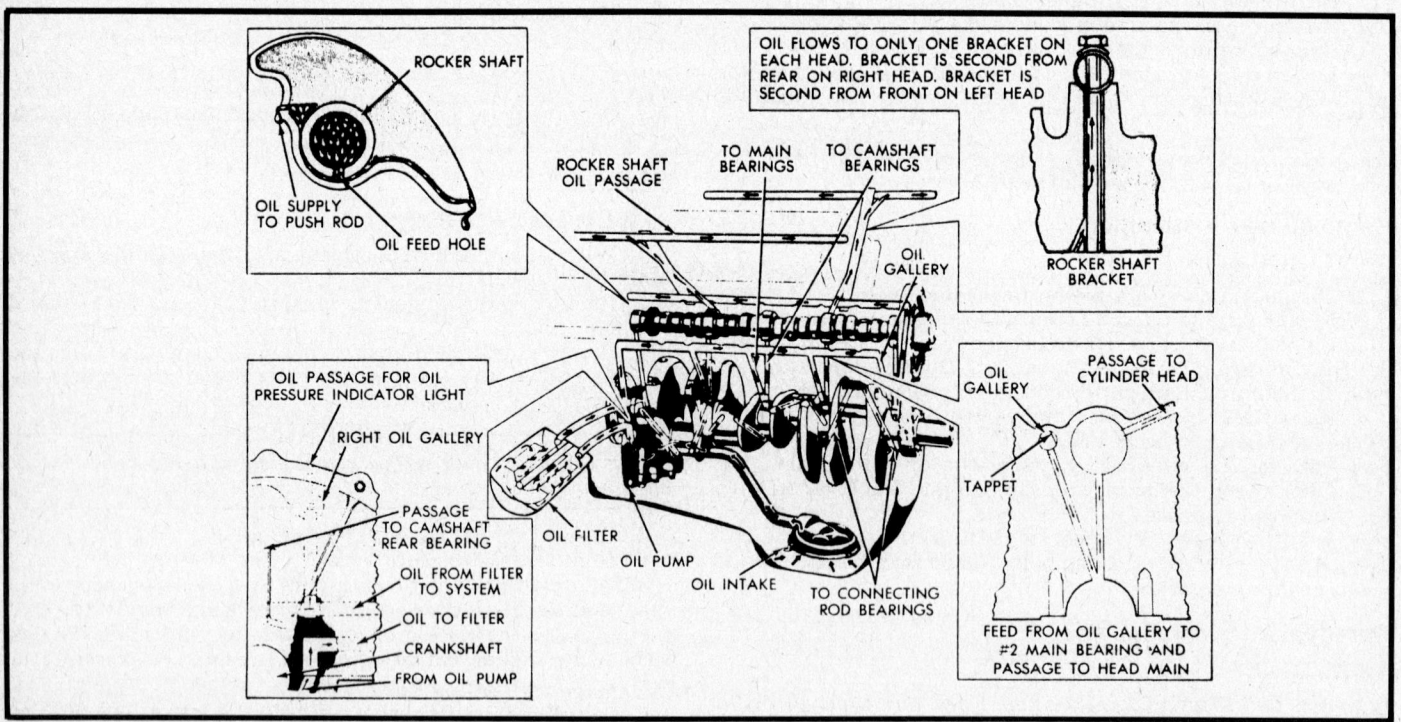

V8 engine oiling system (© Chrysler Corp.)

Removal

V8 ENGINES WITH RUBBER TYPE OIL SEALS

1. With the oil pan and oil pump removed, remove the rear main bearing cap.

2. Remove lower oil seal by pushing the end with a small suitable tool.

3. Remove upper oil seal by pressing with a small suitable tool on the end of the seal, being careful not to damage the crankshaft.

CHRYSLER CORPORATION
REAR WHEEL DRIVE CARS

Installation

CAUTION

Always wipe crankshaft surface clean, then oil lightly before installing a new seal.

1. Insert cap seals into slots in bearing cap.
2. If this is not done, oil leakage will occur. Install seal edge toward inside of shoulder.
3. Lightly oil lips of crankshaft seals.
4. Rotate half seal into cylinder block with paint stripe toward rear. Be careful not to shave or cut outer surface of seal.
5. Place the other half seal in bearing cap with paint stripe toward rear.
6. Assemble bearing cap to cylinder block. Install cleaned and oiled cap bolts and torque to 85 ft. lbs. (115 Nm).

Removal and Installation
1985 AND LATER V8 ENGINES WITH ROPE TYPE SEALS

NOTE: Do not remove the upper seal half. Leave it in the engine block and modify a new lower seal in the following manner. Should the crankshaft be removed, then install a new upper rope seal.

1. Remove the lower rope oil seal by prying from the side of the bearing cap with a small pry tool.
2. Install a new lower seal half in the cap. Tap the seal down into position with a rope seal installing tool.
3. Cut the right bank seal end flush with the cap.
4. Remove the rope seal, rotate it end for end and re-install the seal back into the bearing cap with the cut end protruding above the surface so as to tightly fill the block half seal end compressed above the block/cap parting line.
5. Re-press the seal into the cap with the rope seal installing tool and cut the left bank side flush with the cap surface.

NOTE: This modification procedure insures that the protruding end is properly formed without a frayed end.

6. Lightly oil the lower rope seal half with engine oil. Install the side seals in the bearing cap. Be sure the side seal identified with yellow paint is installed on the right side.
7. Install the rear main bearing cap, being careful not to

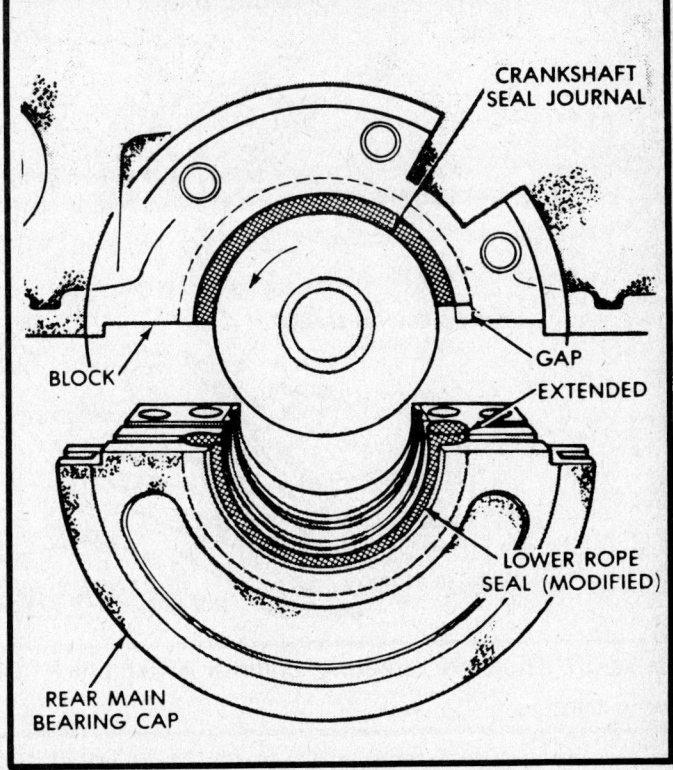

Modifying lower rear main bearing cap rope seal
(© Chrysler Corp.)

crimp the extended side of the oil seal between the cap and the block.

8. Install the main bearing bolts and torque to 85 ft. lbs. (115 Nm).
9. Complete the assembly of the oil pump and oil pan assembly. Add sealer at the bearing cap to block joint to provide oil pan end sealing.

FRONT SUSPENSION AND STEERING SECTION

For Front Suspension Services, Refer to Unit Repair Section. For Steering Gear Overhaul, Refer to Unit Repair Section.

STEERING WHEEL

Removal and Installation

CAUTION

All models are equipped with collapsible steering columns. A sharp blow or excessive pressure on the column will cause it to collapse. Do not hammer on the steering wheel.

1. Disconnect the ground cable from the battery.
2. Remove the padded center assembly. This center assembly is often held on only by spring clips. There are usually holes in the back of the wheel so the pad can be pushed off. However, on some deluxe interiors it is held on by screws behind the arms of the wheel. Remove the horn wire, if necessary.
3. On the tilt and telescoping steering column, remove the locking lever knob by releasing the clip on its underside. Remove the locking lever screws and the lever.
4. Remove the large center nut. Mark the steering wheel and steering shaft so that the wheel may be replaced in its original position. In most cases, the wheel can only go on one way.
5. Using a puller, pull the steering wheel from the steering shaft.
6. Reverse the procedure to install the wheel. When placing the wheel on the shaft, make sure the front tires are in the straight ahead position and the steering wheel and shaft are properly aligned. Tighten the retaining nut to 45 ft. lbs.

STEERING GEAR

Removal and Installation

1. Separate from the steering gear input shaft and remove the steering column.

NOTE: Chrysler Corporation recommends complete detachment from the floor and instrument panel of the

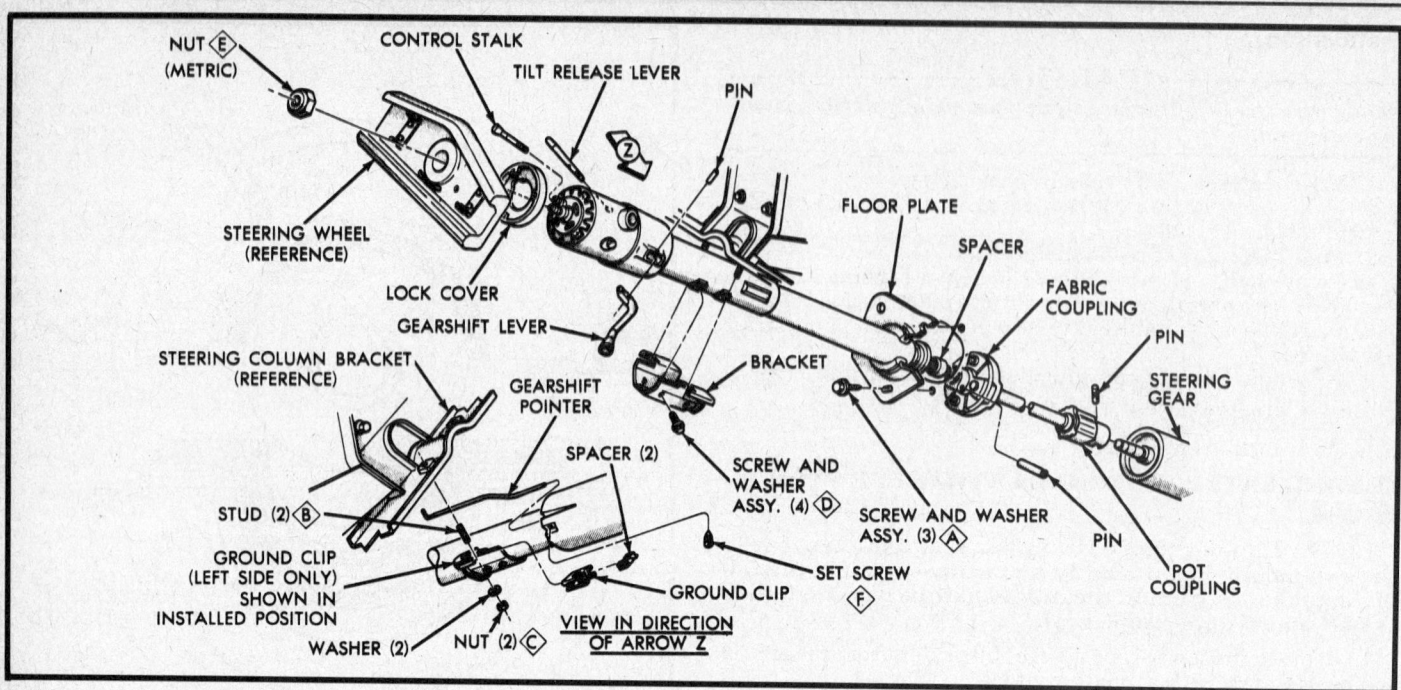

LeBaron, Diplomat steering column assembly (© Chrysler Corp.)

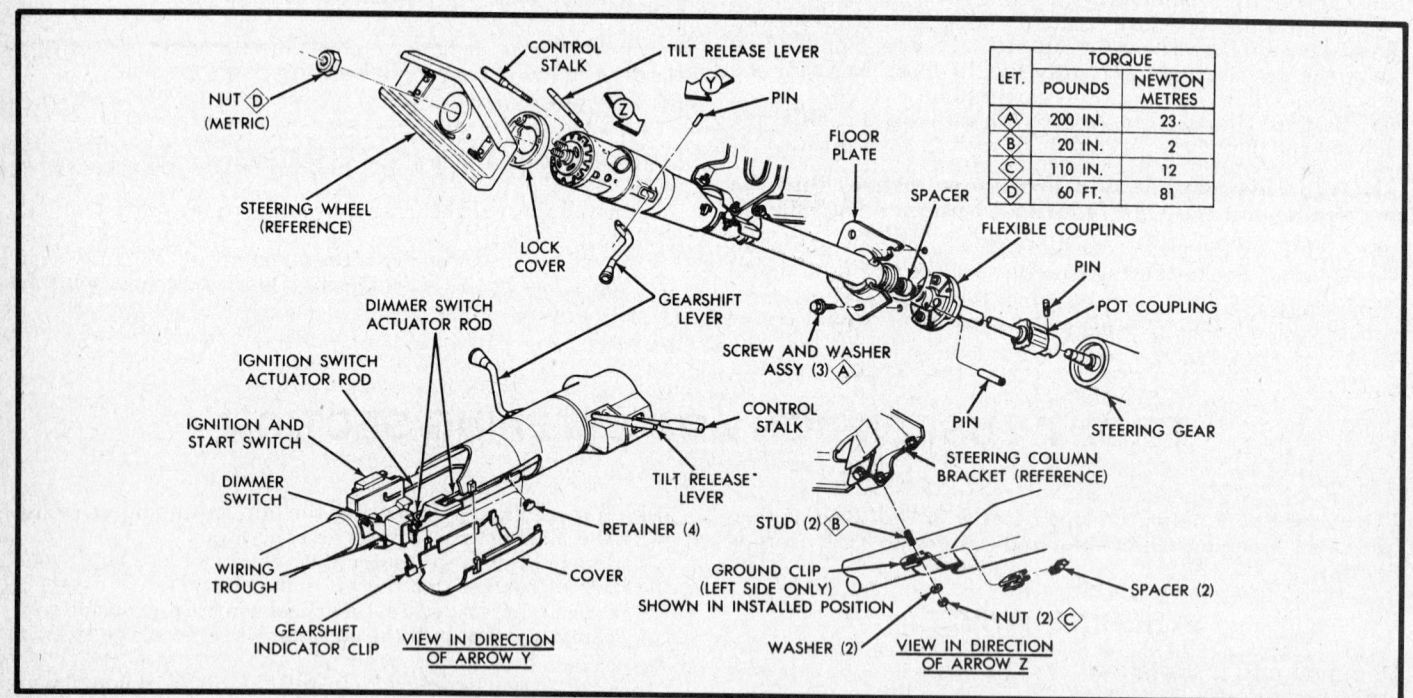

Standard steering column assembly components (© Chrysler Corp.)

steering column to avoid damage to the energy absorbing steering column components.

2. Remove the pressure and return fluid lines.
3. Raise the vehicle and support safely. Remove the retaining nut and washer from the steering gear arm (sector shaft). With a puller tool, remove the steering gear arm.

NOTE: On some vehicles it may be necessary to remove the starter heat shield and drop the exhaust system.

4. Remove the steering gear assembly to frame retaining bolts or nuts and remove the steering gear.
5. To install, center the sector shaft to its mid point of travel.
6. Position the gear assembly on the frame and tighten the bolts or nuts.
7. Align the master serrations on the sector shaft to the splines in the steering arm, install and tighten the nut and washer.
8. Lower the vehicle and install the pressure and return fluid lines.

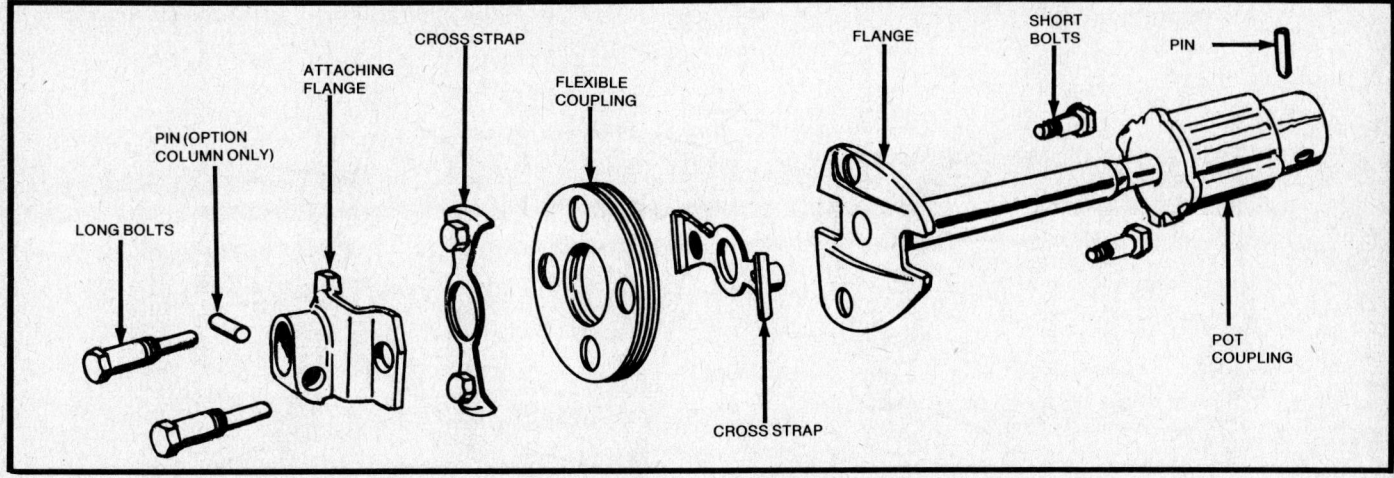

Flex coupling assembly for steering shaft—typical (© Chrysler Corp.)

9. Install the steering column, fill the reservoir with fluid, start the engine and turn the steering wheel several times from stop to stop to bleed the system of air.

FRONT WHEEL BEARINGS

Adjustment

1. Raise the vehicle and support it safely.
2. Remove the grease cup, cotter pin and locknut.
3. Back off on the adjusting nut.
4. Check for free wheel rotation.
5. While rotating the wheel, tighten the wheel bearing adjustment nut to 240–300 inch lbs.
6. Loosen the nut, then retighten the nut so that it is finger tight.
7. Position the nut lock so that one pair of slots is in line with the cotter pin hole and install the cotter pin. This adjustment should give 0.001–0.003 in. end play.
8. Install the rest of the components removed.

POWER STEERING PUMP

Removal and Installation

1. Back off the pump mounting and locking bolts. Remove the pump drive belt.
2. Disconnect all hoses at the pump.
3. Remove the pump bolts and pump with the bracket.
4. To install the pump, place the pump in position and install the mounting bolts.
5. Install the pump drive belt and adjust. There should be no more than $\frac{1}{2}$ in. of play, under moderate thumb pressure, on the longest run of belt. Some pump brackets have a $\frac{1}{2}$ in. square hole for use in tensioning the belt. Torque the mounting bolts to 30 ft. lbs.
6. Connect the pressure and return hoses. Replace the pressure hose O-ring, if there is one.
7. Fill the pump with power steering fluid.
8. Start the engine and rotate the steering wheel from stop to stop several times. This will bleed the system. Check the pump fluid level and fill as required.
9. Be certain the hoses are away from the exhaust manifolds and are not kinked or twisted.

STEERING COLUMN

Removal and Installation

NOTE: Due to variations in the vehicle models, this removal and installation procedure is to be used as a guide. Certain procedures may be accomplished in another sequence than listed.

1. Remove the negative battery cable.
2. On vehicles equipped with column shift, disconnect the link by prying the shift rod out of the grommet in the shift lever.
3. Remove the steering shaft lower coupling to worm shaft roll pin.
4. Disconnect the wiring connectors at the steering column jacket.
5. Remove the steering wheel center pad assembly and disconnect the horn switch, if applicable.
6. Remove the steering wheel assembly from the steering shaft.

CAUTION

Do not bump or hammer on the steering shaft to remove the steering wheel.

7. Remove the floor plate to floor pan attaching screws.
8. To expose the steering column bracket retaining screws, the following procedures must be done to the listed car lines.
   a. Diplomat, LeBaron – Remove instrument panel steering column cover and lower reinforcements.
   b. Mirada, Cordoba, Imperial – Remove the lower bezels and disconnect automatic shift indicator pointer from shift housing.
9. Remove the nuts holding the steering column bracket to the instrument panel supports.
10. Carefully remove the lower coupler from the steering gear wormshaft, then remove the column assembly out through the passenger compartment.

CAUTION

Do not damage the paint or trim during the removal procedure.

11. Should a new grommet be needed in the shift rod, install from the rod side of the lever.
12. The installation of the steering column is the reverse procedure of the removal.

SECTION 3
CHRYSLER CORPORATION
REAR WHEEL DRIVE CARS

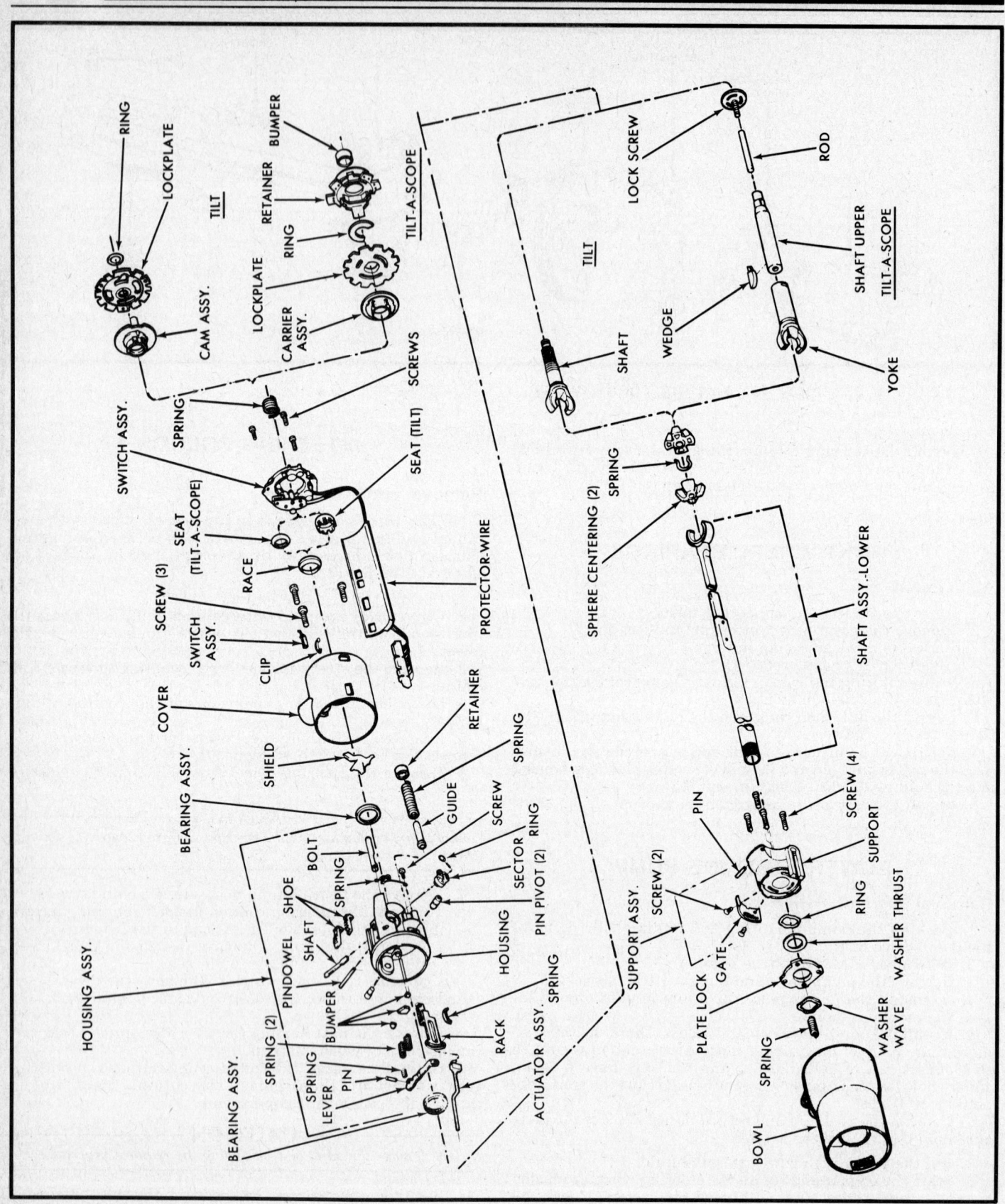

Exploded view of tilt steering column—typical
(© Chrysler Corp.)

CHRYSLER CORPORATION
REAL WHEEL DRIVE CARS
SECTION 3

BRAKE SECTION

For Brake Service, refer to Unit Repair Section

MASTER CYLINDER

Removal and Installation

1. Disconnect the brake lines from the master cylinder. Plug the brake line outlets to prevent fluid loss.
2. Remove the nuts that attach the master cylinder to the brake booster.
3. Slide the master cylinder straight out and off the brake booster.
4. Reverse above procedure to install and bleed brake system.

POWER BRAKE BOOSTER

Removal and Installation

1. Remove the nuts that attach the master cylinder to the brake booster and position the master cylinder out of the way without disconnecting the lines. Use care not to kink the brake lines.
2. Disconnect the vacuum hose from the brake booster.
3. Working under the dash, remove the nut and bolt or retainer clip that attaches the brake booster pushrod to the brake pedal.
4. Remove the brake booster attaching nuts and washers.
5. Remove booster assembly from the vehicle.
6. Reverse above procedure to install. Torque mounting nuts to 200–250 inch lbs. and pushrod nut/bolt to 30 ft. lbs.

PARKING BRAKE

Adjustment

1. Raise the rear of the vehicle and support it safely.
2. Insert an adjusting tool through the brake adjusting hole and rotate the star wheel until a slight drag is felt while rotating the wheels. Back off the star wheel until no drag is felt with the aid of a welding rod type probe, to move the adjusting lever out of engagement with the star wheel.
3. Tighten the cable adjusting nut until a slight drag is felt in the rear wheels when the rear wheels are rotated. Loosen the cable adjusting nut until the rear wheels can be rotated freely. Back off the cable adjusting nut two additional turns.
4. Apply and release the parking brake several times and check to verify that the rear wheels rotate freely, without any brake drag.

PARKING BRAKE CABLE

Removal
FRONT CABLE

1. Disengage front parking brake cable from left connector.
2. Using a suitable tool, force cable housing and attaching clip forward out of body crossmember.
3. Fold back left front edge of floor covering and remove rubber cable cover from floor pan.
4. Engage parking brake and work brake cable up and out of clevis linkage.
5. Using a suitable tool, force upper end of cable housing and clip down out of pedal assembly bracket.
6. Work cable and housing assembly up through floor pan.

Installation

1. Insert parking brake cable through floor pan.
2. Insert retainer into hole in the bottom of the parking brake pedal assembly bracket. Insert cable through hole and insert cable end fitting into linkage clevis. Force upper cable housing into retainer until firmly seated against pedal assembly bracket.
3. Insert retainer into hole in crossmember. Insert cable through hole in crossmember and force cable housing into retainer until firmly seated.
4. Install rubber cable cover and floor pan clip.
5. Attach cable to connector.

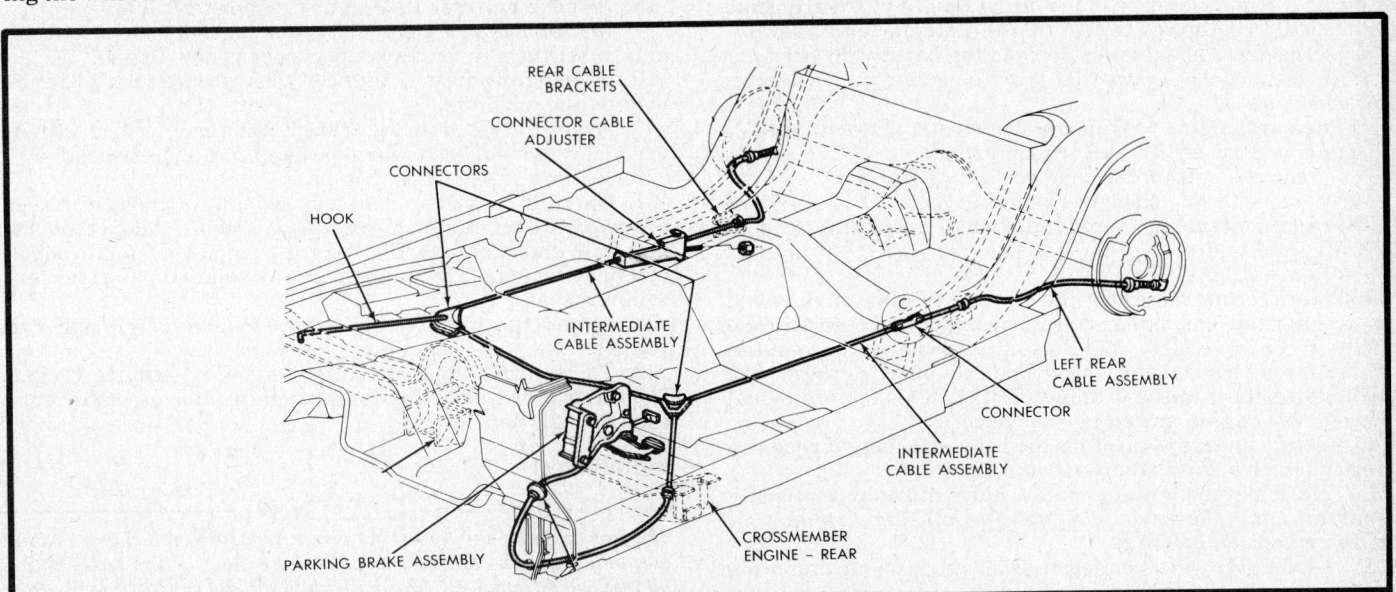

Typical parking brake cable assemblies (© Chrysler Corp.)

SECTION 3
CHRYSLER CORPORATION
REAR WHEEL DRIVE CARS

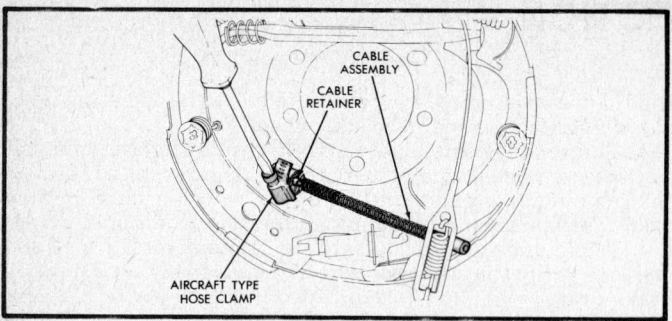

Use of aircraft type hose clamp to compress cable legs during the removal procedure
(© Chrysler Corp.)

6. Adjust service brakes and parking brake system.
7. Apply brakes several times and test for free wheel rotation.

Removal
REAR CABLE
1. With vehicle jacked up or on a suitable hoist, remove rear wheels.
2. Disconnect brake cable from connector.
3. Remove retaining clip from brake cable bracket.
4. Remove brake drum from rear axle.
5. Remove brake shoe return springs and adjuster mechanism.
6. Remove brake shoe retaining springs.
7. Remove brake shoe strut and spring and disconnect brake cable from operating arm.
8. Compress retainers on end of brake cable housing and remove cable from support place.

Installation
1. Insert brake cable and housing into brake support plate making certain that housing retainers lock the housing firmly into place.
2. Holding brake shoes in place on support plate, engage brake cable into brake shoe operating lever. Install parking brake strut and spring.
3. Install brake shoe retaining springs, adjuster mechanism and brake shoe return springs.
4. Install brake drum and wheel.
5. Insert brake cable and housing into cable bracket and install retaining clip.
6. Insert brake cable into equalizer.
7. Adjust service brakes and then parking brake cable.

AUTOMATIC TRANSMISSION AND DRIVESHAFT SECTION

For Overhaul Procedures, Refer to Unit Repair Section.

AUTOMATIC TRANSMISSION
Removal
1. The transmission and torque converter must be removed as an assembly; otherwise, the converter drive plate, pump bushing, or oil seal may be damaged. The drive plate will not support a load; therefore, none of the weight of the transmission should be allowed to rest on the plate during removal.
2. Disconnect negative cable from the battery for safety.
3. Some models require that the exhaust system be dropped for clearance.
4. Remove engine to transmission struts, if so equipped.
5. Remove cooler lines at transmission.
6. Remove starter motor and cooler line bracket.
7. Remove torque converter access cover.
8. Loosen oil pan bolts and tap the pan to break it loose, allowing fluid to drain.
9. Reinstall pan.
10. Mark torque converter and drive plate to aid in re-assembly. The crankshaft flange bolt circle, inner and outer circle of holes in the drive plate, and the four tapped holes in front face of the torque converter all have one hole offset so these parts will be installed in the original position. This maintains balance of the engine and torque converter.
11. Rotate engine to position the bolts attaching torque converter to drive plate, and remove bolts.
12. Mark parts for re-assembly, then disconnect propeller shaft at rear universal joint. Carefully pull shaft assembly out of the extension housing.
13. Disconnect wire connector from the back-up lamp and neutral starting switch.
14. Disconnect gearshift rod and torque shaft assembly from transmission.

NOTE: When it is necessary to disassemble linkage rods from levers that use plastic grommets as retainers, the grommets should be replaced with new grommets. Use a prying tool to force rod from grommet in lever, then remove the old grommet. Use pliers to snap new grommet into lever and rod into grommet.

15. Disconnect throttle rod from lever at the left side of transmission. Remove linkage bellcrank from transmission, if so equipped.
16. Remove oil filler tube and speedometer cable.
17. Install engine support fixture with frame hooks or a suitable substitute, that will support rear of the engine.
18. Raise transmission slightly with service jack to relieve load on the supports.
19. Remove bolts securing transmission mount to crossmember and crossmember to frame, then remove crossmember.
20. Remove all bell housing bolts.
21. Carefully work transmission and torque converter assembly rearward off engine block dowels and disengage converter hub from end of crankshaft. Attach a small C-clamp to edge of bell housing to hold torque converter in place during transmission removal.
22. Lower transmission and remove assembly from under the vehicle.
23. To remove torque converter assembly, remove C-clamp from edge of bell housing, then carefully slide assembly out of the transmission.

Installation

—————— **CAUTION** ——————
The transmission and torque converter must be installed as an assembly; otherwise, the torque converter drive plate, pump bushing, and oil seal will be damaged. The drive plate will not support a load; therefore, none of the weight of transmission should be allowed to rest on the plate during installation.

3-48

CHRYSLER CORPORATION
REAR WHEEL DRIVE CARS
SECTION 3

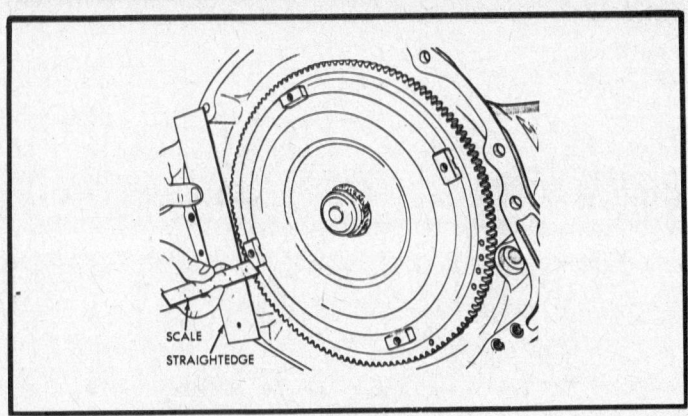

Measuring converter face for full engagement in front pump gears (© Chrysler Corp.)

1. Rotate pump gears with alignment tool until the two small holes in handle are vertical.
2. Carefully slide torque converter assembly over input shaft and reaction shaft. Make sure torque converter hub slots are also vertical and fully engage pump inner gear lugs.

NOTE: Test for full engagement by placing a straightedge on face of the case. The surface of torque converter front cover lug should be at least $\frac{1}{2}$ in. to rear of straightedge when torque converter is pushed all the way into transmission.

3. Attach a small C-clamp to edge of torque converter housing to hold torque converter in place during transmission installation.
4. Inspect torque converter drive plate for distortion or cracks and replace if necessary. Torque the drive plate to crankshaft bolts to 55 ft. lbs. (75 Nm). When drive plate replacement has been necesssary, make sure both transmission dowel pins are in engine block and they are protruding far enough to hold transmission in alignment.
5. Coat converter hub hole in crankshaft with multipurpose grease. Place transmission and torque converter assembly on a service jack and position assembly under vehicle for installation. Raise or tilt as necessary until transmission is aligned with engine.
6. Rotate torque converter so mark on torque converter (made during removal) will align with mark on drive plate. The offset holes in plate are located next to $\frac{1}{8}$ in. hole in the inner circle of plate. Carefully work transmission assembly forward over engine block dowels with torque converter hub entering the crankshaft opening.
7. After transmission is in position, install converter housing bolts and tighten to 30 ft. lbs (41 Nm). If so equipped, re-install vibration damper weight on rear of extension housing.
8. Install crossmember to frame and lower transmission to install mount on extension to the crossmember. Tighten bolts.
9. The engine support fixture may now be removed.
10. Install oil filler tube and speedometer cable.
11. Connect throttle rod to transmission lever.
12. Connect gearshift rod and torque shaft assembly to transmission lever and frame.
13. Place wire connector on the combination back-up lamp and neutral/park starter switch.
14. Carefully guide sliding yoke into extension housing and on the output shaft splines. Align marks made at removal, then connect propeller shaft to rear axle pinion shaft yoke.
15. Rotate engine clockwise with socket wrench on vibration dampener bolt, as needed to install torque converter to drive plate bolts, matching marks made at removal. Tighten to 270 inch lbs. (31 Nm).
16. Install torque converter access cover.
17. Install starter motor and cooler line bracket.
18. Tighten cooler lines to transmission fittings.
19. Install engine to transmission struts, if so equipped. Tighten bolts holding strut to transmission before strut to engine bolts.
20. Replace exhaust system, if it was disturbed and adjust for clearance.
21. Adjust shift and throttle linkage.
22. Refill transmission with Dexron® II type automatic transmission fluid.

CONTROL LINKAGE
Adjustment

NOTE: Chrysler Corporation recommends that when it is necessary to disassemble linkage rods from their levers which use plastic grommets for retainers, the grommets should be replaced with new ones.

COLUMN SHIFT

1. Make sure all linkage is free, especially the adjustable slide on the shift rod, so that the pre-load spring action is not reduced by friction. Disassemble, clean and lube if necessary.
2. Put the shift lever in Park.
3. With the adjustable swivel loose, move the shift lever all the way to the rear-most detent position, which is Park.
4. Tighten swivel lock bolts to 90 inch lbs.
5. Verify that the vehicle will only start in Park or Neutral.

CONSOLE SHIFT

1. Adjustment is similar to above, but no pre-load spring is used. Make sure that with the shift handle in Park, the transmission lever is in the rear-most detent position, which is Park.
2. Tighten swivel lock bolt with no load applied in either direction on the linkage to 90 inch lbs.
3. Verify that the vehicle will only start in Park or Neutral.

THROTTLE LINKAGE
Adjustment

1. Perform transmission throttle rod adjustment while engine is at normal operating temperature. Otherwise, make sure carburetor is not on fast idle cam.
2. Raise the vehicle on hoist to make adjustment at transmission throttle lever.
3. Loosen adjustment swivel lock screw.
4. To insure proper adjustment, swivel must be free to slide along flat end of throttle rod so that preload spring action is not restricted. Disassemble and clean or repair parts to assure free action, if necessary.
5. Hold transmission lever firmly forward against its internal stop and tighten swivel lock screw to 100 inch lbs. (11 Nm).
6. The adjustment is finished and linkage backlash was automatically removed by the preload spring.
7. Lower vehicle, reconnect choke if disconnected, and test linkage freedom of operation by moving throttle rod rearward, slowly releasing it to confirm it will return fully forward.

SHIFT QUADRANT POINTER
Adjustment
WIRE TYPE

NOTE: Always check for proper automatic transmission linkage adjustment before changing the adjustment of the shift quadrant indictor.

3-49

CHRYSLER CORPORATION
REAR WHEEL DRIVE CARS

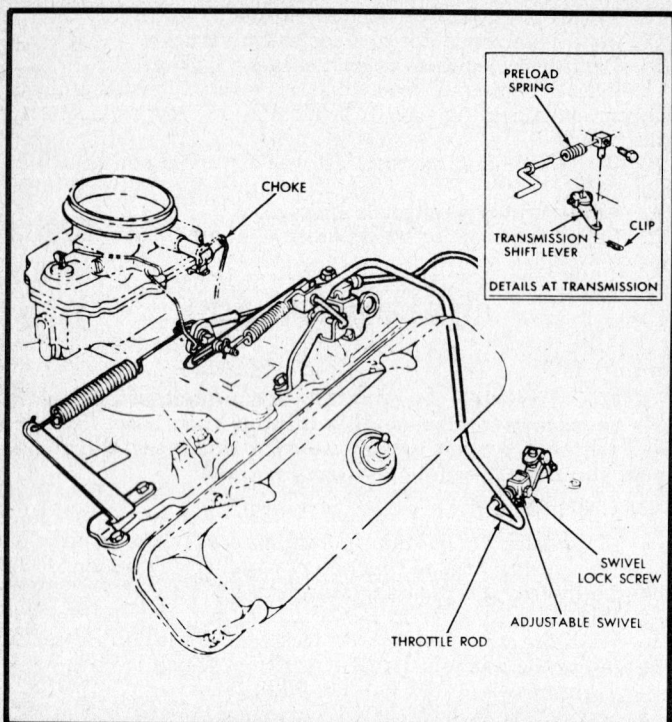

Throttle rod adjustment, typical for V8 engines equipped with rod type linkage (© Chrysler Corp.)

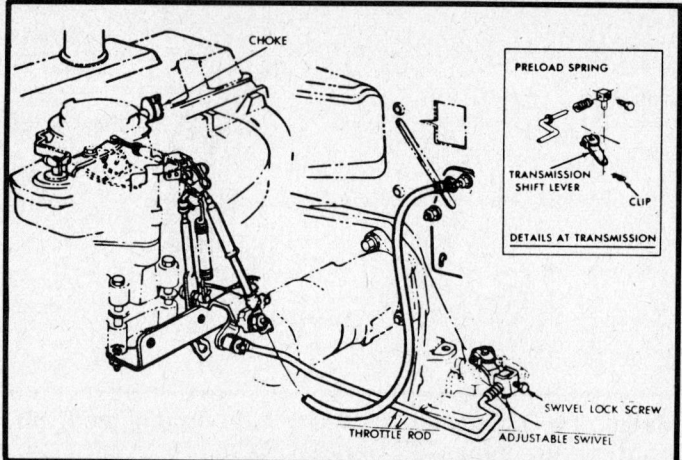

Throttle rod adjustment—typical of six cylinder engines equipped with cable type linkage (© Chrysler Corp.)

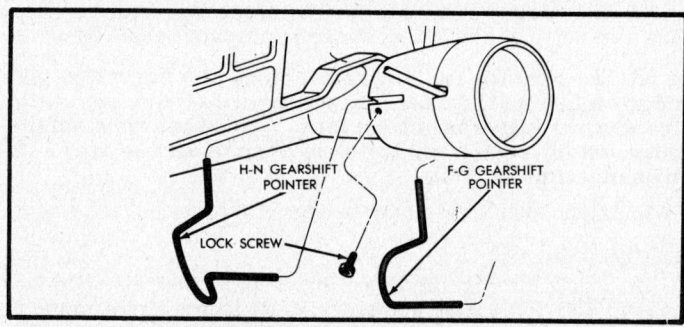

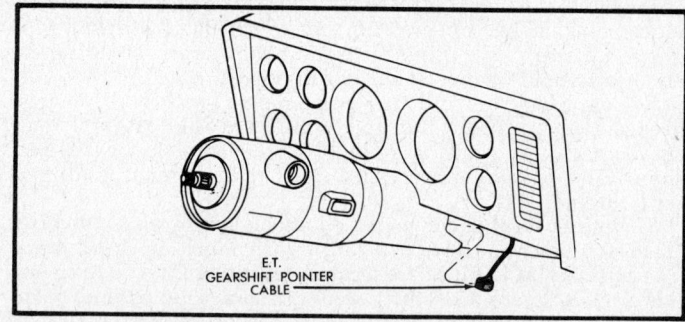

Gearshift pointer wire (© Chrysler Corp.)

1. Remove the instrument panel steering column cover. Set the shift lever in park position.
2. Loosen the set screw holding the indicator wire and adjust the wire to align with Park.
3. Re-tighten the set screw and install the steering column cover.
4. Check for indicator alignment from low position through park and readjust if necessary.

CABLE TYPE

1. Set the shift lever in Park position. Adjust the clip on the steering column to insure that the indicator is centered on the "P". Check the position of the indicator in all models.

ELECTRONIC TYPE

The Imperial electronic instrument includes an electronic gearshift quadrant indicator. There is adjustment for the electronic indicator through a self-positioning switch on the steering column held by two retaining screws.

Driveshaft and U-Joints

The driveshaft is a one-piece tubular shaft with two universal joints, one at each end. The front joint yoke serves as a slip yoke on the transmission output shaft. The rear universal joint is the type that must be disassembled to be removed.

DRIVESHAFT

Removal and Installation

1. Match-mark the driveshaft, U-joint and pinion flange before disassembly. These marks must be realigned during reassembly to maintain the balance of the driveline. Failure to align them may result in excessive vibration.
2. Remove both of the clamps from the differential pinion yoke and slide the driveshaft forward slightly to disengage the U-joint from the pinion yoke. Tape the two loose U-joint bearings together to prevent them from falling off.

CAUTION
Do not disturb the bearing assembly retaining strap. Never allow the driveshaft to hang from either of the U-joints. Always support the unattached end of the shaft to prevent damage to the joints.
---

3. Lower the rear end of the driveshaft and gently slide the front yoke/driveshaft assembly rearward disengaging the assembly from the transmission output shaft. Be careful not to damage the splines or the surface with the output shaft seal rides on.
4. Check the transmission output shaft seal for sign of leakage.
5. Installation is the reverse of removal. Be sure to align the match marks. The torque for the clamp bolts is 14 ft. lbs.

U-JOINT OVERHAUL

See the Drive Axles and U-Joints Unit Repair Section for overhaul procedures.

REAR AXLE AND SUSPENSION

For Axle Overhaul Procedures and Suspension Service Refer to Unit Repair Section.

REAR AXLE ASSEMBLY

Removal and Installation

1. Raise the vehicle and support it safely. Install suitable stands at the front of the rear springs.
2. Block the brake pedal in the up position, using a wooden block or equivalent.
3. Drain the lubricant from differential housing.
4. Loosen and remove rear wheels. Do not removed drum retaining spring clips or brake drums.
5. Disconnect hydraulic brake lines at wheel cylinders and cap fittings to prevent loss of brake fluid.
6. Disconnect parking brake cables.
7. Disconnect propeller shaft at differential pinion flange and secure in a near horizontal position to prevent damage to front universal joint.
8. Remove shock absorbers from spring plate studs and loosen rear spring U-bolt nuts and remove U-bolts.
9. Remove axle assembly from vehicle.
10. Installation is the reverse of the removal procedure.

Axle Shafts and Bearings

AXLE SHAFT COLLAR (7-$\frac{1}{4}$ INCH AXLE)

Removal

7-$\frac{1}{4}$ INCH, 8-$\frac{1}{4}$ INCH AND 9-$\frac{1}{4}$ INCH AXLES

---- CAUTION ----
Under no circumstances should rear axle bearing cones, cups, bores or journals be subjected to heating with a torch, beating with a hammer or any other abnormal abuse, permanent damage may result.

Removal

1. Remove wheel cover and wheel and tire assembly. Remove brake drum.
2. Loosen housing cover and drain lubricant from rear axle. Remove cover.
3. Turn differential case to make differential pinion shaft lock screw accessible and remove lock screw and pinion shaft.
4. Push axle shafts toward center of vehicle and remove the C-washers from recessed groove of axle shaft.
5. Remove axle shaft from housing being careful not to damage the straight roller-type axle shaft bearing which will remain in the rear axle housing.
6. Inspect the axle shaft bearing surfaces for signs of brinnelling, spalling or pitting. If any of these conditions are present both the shaft and the bearing should be replaced. The normal bearing contact on the shaft will be a dull gray and may appear lightly dented.
7. Remove axle shaft seal from housing bore. Using a slide hammer motion, remove axle shaft bearing. If axle shaft and bearing show no signs of distress, they can be reinstalled along with a new axle shaft seal. Never reuse an axle shaft seal.

---- CAUTION ----
Inspect housing bearing shoulder for burrs, and remove any if present

Installation

1. Wipe axle shaft bearing cavity of axle housing clean. The axle shaft oil seal bores at both ends of housing should be smooth and free of rust and corrosion. This also applies to brake support plate and housing flange face surface.
2. Insert axle shaft bearing into cavity making sure it bottoms against the shoulder and it is not cocked in bore.

---- CAUTION ----
Under no circumstances should the seal be used to position or bottom the bearing in its bore as this would damage the seal.

3. Install axle shaft bearing seal using special tool, until the outer flange of tool bottoms against housing flange face. This positions the seal to the proper depth beyond the end of the flange face.
4. Lubricate bearing and seal area of axle shaft, slide axle shaft into place being careful that splines of shaft do not damage oil seal and properly engage with splines of differential side gears.
5. With axle shaft in place, install the C-washers in recessed grooves of axle shaft, and pull outward on shaft so the C-washers seat in the counterbore of differential side gear.
6. Install differential pinion shaft through case and pinions, aligning hole in shaft with lock screw hole. Install lock screw and tighten to 100 inch lbs. (11 Nm).
7. Clean up mating surfaces, and apply a $\frac{1}{16}$-$\frac{3}{32}$ in. bead of silicone rubber sealant along the bolt circle of the cover. Allow sealant to cure.

SECTION 4

FORD MERCURY
FRONT WHEEL DRIVE CARS — ESCORT • EXP • LYNX • TEMPO • TOPAZ • TAURUS • SABLE

SPECIFICATIONS

Belt Tension	4–8	Piston & Ring	4–7
Brakes	24–2	Serial Number Identification	4–5
Camshaft	4–6	Torque	4–7
Capacities	4–7	Torque Sequence (Cylinder Heads)	4–55
Crankshaft & Connecting Rod	4–6	Tune–Up	4–5
Firing Order	4–5	Valve	4–6
General Engine	4–5	Wheel Alignment	4–8

INDEX

A
Alternator R&R	4–9
Automatic Transmission	4–84
Adjustment	4–86
On car service	23–2
Assembly R&R	4–84
Axle Shaft R&R	4–90
Axle Half Shaft R&R	4–90

B
Ball Joints	35–2
Belt Tension	4–8
Brake System	4–78
Brake Booster	4–79
Brake Caliper Overhaul	24–2
Brake Caliper R&R	24–2
Brake Drum, Rear	24–2
Brake Master Cylinder	4–78
Brake Pad Front	24–2
Brake Shoe Rear	24–2

C
Camshaft R&R	4–58
Carburetor R&R	4–42
Chassis Electrical	4–9
Clutch	4–81
Adjustment	4–81
R&R	4–81
Combination Switch	4–19
Control Arm R&R	35–2
Cooling Fan Motor	4–33
Cooling System	4–31
Cruse Control	4–27
Cylinder Head	4–54
R&R	4–54
CV Joint R&R	4–95

D
Differential	23–2, 32–2
Inspection	23–2, 32–2
Dimmer Switch R&R	4–19
Disc Brakes	24–2
Distributor R&R	4–10
Drive Axle	32–2, 23–2
Drive Belt Tension	4–8
Driveshaft R&R	4–90

E
Electronic Ignition	30–2
Emission Controls	4–50
Engine	4–51
Identification	4–4
R&R	4–51
Engine Electrical	4–10
Engine Lubrication	4–65

Engine Mechanical	4–52
Engine Mounts R&R	4–52
Exhaust Manifold R&R	4–44

F
Front Suspension	35–2
Alignment	4–8
Fuel Pump R&R	4–37
Fuel Mixture, Adjust	4–39
Fuses/Circuit Breakers	4–26
Fuisble Links	4–27

H
Half Shaft R&R	4–90
Headlight Switch	4–18
Heater Blower R&R	4–35
Heater Core R&R	4–36
Heater Switch	4–34
Horn Switch	4–21

I
Idle Speed Adjust	4–39
Ignitoin Switch	4–14
Ignition Timing	4–12
Instrument Cluster R&R	4–24
Intake Manifold R&R	4–44

L, M, N
Lower Control Arm R&R	35–2
Master Cylinder R&R	4–78
Manual Steering Bear R&R	4–68
Manual Transmission Overhaul	32–2
Manual Transmission R&R	4–81
Neutral Safety Switch R&R	4–16

O
Oil Pan R&R	4–65
Oil Pump R&R	4–66
Oil Seal R&R	
Rear Main	4–67

P
Parking Brake	4–79
Adjustment	4–79
Cable R&R	4–80
Piston & Connecting Rod	4–60
Power Brake Unit R&R	4–79
Power Steering Pump R&R	4–73

R
Rear Main Oil Sear R&R	4–67
Rear Suspension	35–2
Regulator	4–9
Rocker	4–53

S
Serial Number	4–4
Engine	4–4
Vehicle	4–4
Shock Absorber R&R	
Front	35–2
Rear	35–2
Springs	
Front	35–2
Rear	35–2
Starter R&R	4–10
Starter Drive Replacement	4–10
Steering Column R&R	4–74
Steering Gear R&R	4–68
Manual	4–68
Power	4–69
Steering Wheel R&R	4–68
Stop Light Switch R&R	4–17
Speedometer R&R	4–26
Spindle R&R	4–99
Suspension R&R	35–2
Service	35–2

T
Throttle Linkge, Adjust	4–86
Timing Belt Air	4–62
Timing Chain	4–63
Timing Gear Cover	4–62
Oil Seal Replacement	4–61
Tune-Up	4–5
Turbocharger R&R	4–43
Turn Signal Switch R&R	4–19

U, V
U-Joint Overhaul	28–2
Valve Tappette R&R	4–54
Valve Timing, Adjust	4–53
Valve System	4–52
Voltage Regulator	4–9

W, Y
Water Pump R&R	4–31
Wheel Alignment	
Front	4–8
Rear	4–102
Wheel Bearings	
Front	4–73
Rear	4–102
Wheel Cylinders	
Rear	24–2
Windshield Wiper	4–22
Linkage R&R	4–23
Motor R&R	4–22
Switch R&R	4–21
Year Identification	4–3

BEFORE SERVICING BE CERTAIN TO READ THE SAFETY NOTICE

Ford • Mercury
1983–87 Front Wheel Drive Cars

ESCORT • EXP • LYNX • LN7 • TEMPO • TOPAZ
TAURUS • SABLE

YEAR IDENTIFICATION

1983–85 Escort

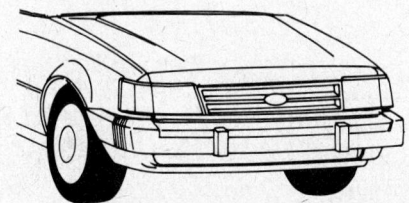

1985½–87 Escort

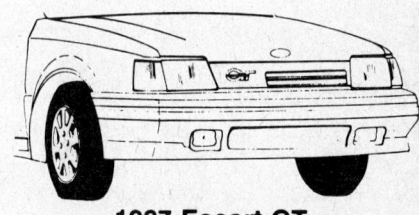

1987 Escort GT

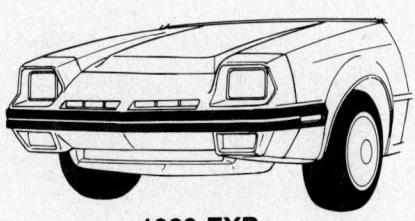

1983 EXP

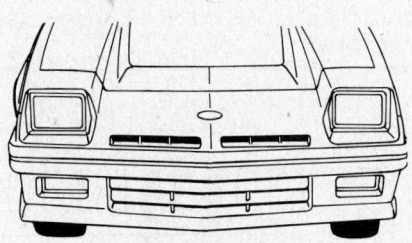

1984–85 EXP

1987 EXP

1983–84 Lynx

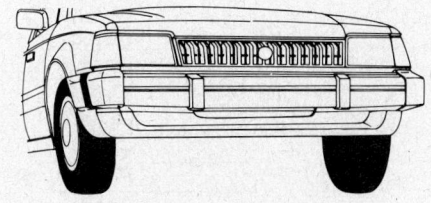

1985½–87 Lynx

1986–87 Lynx XR3

SECTION 4

FORD MERCURY
FRONT WHEEL DRIVE CARS—ESCORT • EXP • LYNX • TEMPO • TOPAZ • TAURUS • SABLE

YEAR IDENTIFICATION

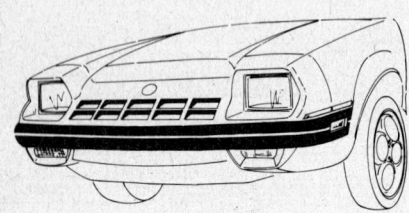
1983 LN7

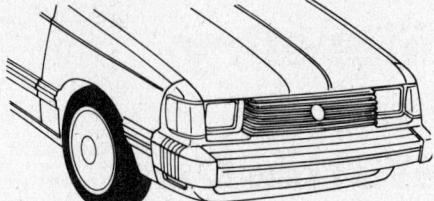
1984–85 Topaz

1986–87 Topaz

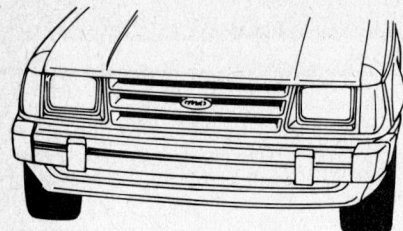
1984 Tempo

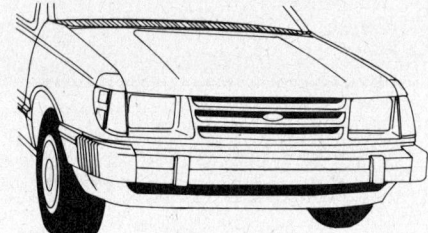
1985 Tempo

1986–87 Tempo

1987 Taurus

1987 Sable

VEHICLE IDENTIFICATION NUMBER (VIN)

It is important for servicing and ordering parts to be certain of the vehicle and engine identification. The VIN (vehicle identification number) is a 13 or 17 digit number visible through the windshield on the driver's side of the dash and contains the vehicle and engine identification codes. It can be interpreted as follows:

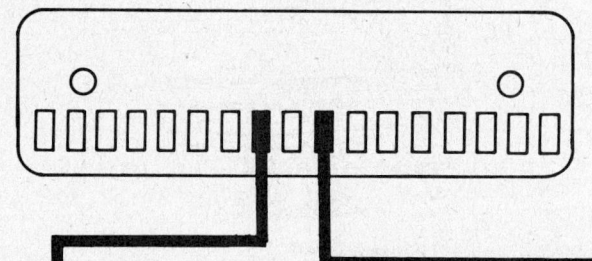

Engine Code						Model Year Code	
Code	Cu. In.	Liters	Cyl.	Carb.	Eng. Mfg.	Code	Year
2	98	1.6	4	2	Ford	D	'83
5	98	1.6	4	EFI	Ford	E	'84
4	98	1.6 HO	4	2	Ford	F	'85
H	121	2.0	4	Diesel	Mazda	G	'86
R	140	2.3 (HSC)	4	1/EFI	Ford	H	'87
9	116	1.9	4	2	Ford		
D	153	2.5 (HSC)	4	CFI	Ford		
U	182	3.0	6	EFI	Ford		

The seventeen digit Vehicle Identification Number can be used to determine engine application and model year. The tenth digit indicates the model year, and the eighth digit identifies engine code.

Ford Mercury

FRONT WHEEL DRIVE CARS—ESCORT • EXP • LYNX • TEMPO • TOPAZ • TAURUS • SABLE

GENERAL ENGINE SPECIFICATIONS

Year	Eng. VIN Code	Engine No. Cyl. Displacement (cc)	Eng. Mfg.	Carburetor Type	Horsepower @ rpm ■	Torque @ rpm (ft. lbs.) ■	Bore × Stroke (mm)	Compression Ratio	Oil Pressure @ 2000 rpm
'83–'87	2	4-1597	Ford	2bbl	70@4600	89@3000	80.0 × 79.5 ①	8.8:1	40
	4	4-1597	Ford	2bbl	80@5800	88@3400	80.0 × 79.5 ①	9.0:1	40
	5	4-1597	Ford	EFI	90@5800	89@3000	80.0 × 79.5 ①	9.0:1	40
	—	4-1597	Ford	Turbo	120@5200	120@3400	80.0 × 79.5 ①	8.0:1	35–65
	H	4-2000	Mazda	Diesel	52@4000	82@2400	86.0 × 86.0 ②	22.5:1	③
	R	4-2300	Ford	1bbl	84@4600	118@2600	93.5 × 84 ④	9.0:1	55–70
'85–'87	9	4-1901	Ford	2bbl	108@5200	114@4000	82.0 × 88.0 ⑤	9.0:1	35–65
'86–'87	D	4-2508	Ford	CFI	88@4600	130@2800	93.5 × 91 ⑥	9.7:1	55–70
'86–'87	U	6-2983	Ford	EFI	140@4800	160@3000	89.0 × 80 ⑦	9.3:1	40–60

■ Horsepower and torque are SAE net figures. They are measured at the rear of the transmission with all accessories installed and operating.
① 3.15 × 3.13 in.
② 3.39 × 3.39
③ Greater than 0.7 KG/CM² @ 700 RPM Oil Temp. 80°C
④ 3.70 × 3.30
⑤ 3.23 × 3.46
⑥ 3.70 × 3.60
⑦ 3.50 × 3.10

TUNE-UP SPECIFICATIONS

When analyzing compression test results, look for uniformity among cylinders rather than specific pressures.

Year	Eng. VIN Code	Engine No. Cyl. Displacement cu. in. (cc)	Eng. Mfg.	Spark Plugs Orig. Type •	Spark Plugs Gap (in.)	Distributor Point Dwell (deg.)	Distributor Point Gap (in.)	Ignition Timing (deg.) ▲ Man. Trans •	Ignition Timing (deg.) ▲ Auto Trans	Valves Intake Opens ■ (deg.)	Fuel Pump Pressure (psi)	Idle Speed (rpm) ▲ Man Trans	Idle Speed (rpm) ▲ Auto Trans
'83–'87	—	4-97.6 (1597)	Ford	AWSF-34 ②	0.042–0.046	Electronic		①	①	—	4–6 ③	①	①
'84–'87	R	4-140 (2300)	Ford	AWSF-62	.044	Electronic		10B	15B	—	5	①	①
'85–'87	9	4-116 (1901)	Ford	AWSF-34C ②	0.042–0.046	Electronic		①	①	—	5–6	①	①
'86–'87	0	4-153 (2508)	Ford	AWSF-32C	0.042–0.046	Electronic		①	①	—	35–45	①	①
'86–'87	U	6-182 (2983)	Ford	AWSF-32C	0.042–0.046	Electronic		①	①	—	35–45	①	①

NOTE: The underhood specifications sticker often reflects tune-up specification changes made in production. Sticker figures must be used if they disagree with those in this chart. Part numbers in this chart are not recommended by Chilton for any product by brand name.

▲ See text for procedure
■ All figures Before Top Dead Center
• Figure in parenthesis is for California
B Before Top Dead Center
— Not applicable

① Calibration levels vary from model to model. Always refer to the underhood sticker for your car requirements.
② EFI Models: AWSF24
③ EFI pressure: 35–45 psi

FIRING ORDERS

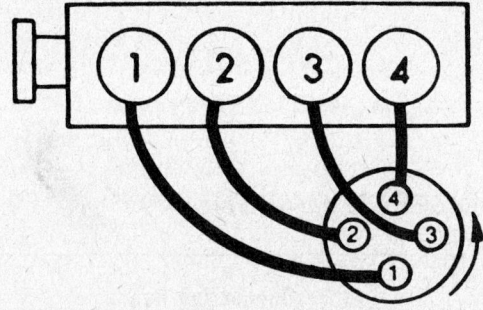

Ford Motor Co. 1600cc 4 cyl engine
Firing order: 1–3–4–2
Distributor rotation: counterclockwise

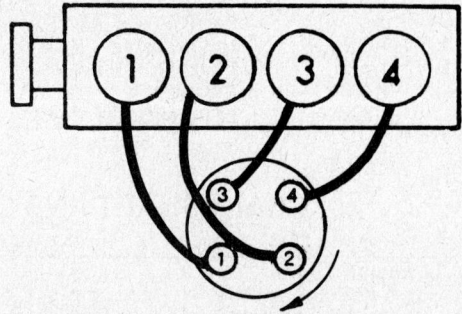

Tempo/Topaz 2300 HSC engine
Firing order: 1–3–4–2
Distributor rotation: clockwise

Ford Mercury
FRONT WHEEL DRIVE CARS—ESCORT • EXP • LYNX • TEMPO • TOPAZ • TAURUS • SABLE

FIRING ORDERS

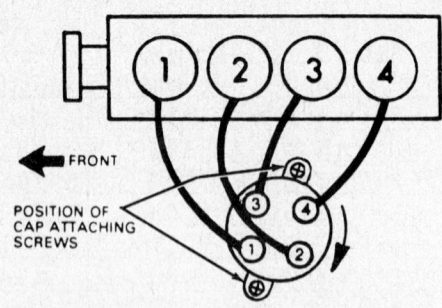

Ford 2500 cc 4 cyl (2.5L)
Firing order: 1–3–4–2
Distributor rotation: clockwise

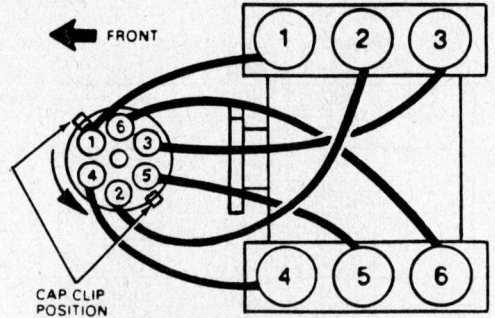

Ford 3000 cc 6 cyl (3.0L)
Firing order: 1–4–2–5–3–6
Distributor rotation: counterclockwise

VALVE SPECIFICATIONS

Year	Engine No. Cyl. Displacement (cc)	Seat Angle (deg)	Face Angle (deg)	Spring Test Pressure (lbs @ in.)	Spring Installed Height (in.)	Stem-to-Guide Clearance (in.)		Stem Diameter (in.)	
						Intake	Exhaust	Intake	Exhaust
'83–'87	4-1597	45	45½	200 @ 1.09 ①	1.480 ②	.0008–.0027	.0018–.0037	.316	.315
'84–'87	4-2000	45	45	—	1.7760	.0016–.0029	.0018–.0031	.3138	.3138
'84–'87	4-2300	45	45½	182 @ 1.10	1.49	.0018	.0023	.3415	.3411
'85–'87	4-1901	45	45	200 @ 1.09 ①	1.48–1.44	.0008–.0027	.0018–.0037	.316	.315
'86–'87	4-2508	90	45	182 @ 1.13	1.49	.0018	.0023	.3422	.3418
'86–'87	6-2983	45	44	185 @ 1.11	1.85	.0001–.0027	.0015–.0032	.3126	.3121

① HO and EFI Engines: 216 @ 1.016
② HO and EFI Engines: 1.450–1.480

CAMSHAFT SPECIFICATIONS
All measurements are given in inches.

Year	Engine No. Cyl. Displacement (cc)	Lobe Lift	Valve Lift @ Zero Lash		Camshaft End Play	Journal-to-Bearing Clearance	Journal Diameter	Journal Out-of-Round Limit
			Intake	Exhaust				
'83–'87	4-1597	.229 ①	.377 ②	.377 ②	.0018–.006	.0008–.0028	③	.008
'84–'87	4-2000	—	—	—	.008–.0059	.001–.0026	1.2582–1.2589	—
'84–'87	4-2300	④	.392 ⑥	.377 ⑥	.009	.001–.003	⑤	.005
'85–'87	4-1901	0.240	0.468 ⑦	0.468 ⑦	0.006–0.0018	0.0013–0.0033	1.8017–1.8007	0.0003
'86–'87	4-2508	④	0.392	0.377	0.009	0.001–0.003	⑤	0.005
'86–'87	6-2983	0.260	0.419	0.419	⑧	0.001–0.003	2.0074–2.0084	0.001

① HO and EFI: .240
② HO and EFI: .396
③ No. 1: 1.761–1.762
　No. 2: 1.771–1.772
　No. 3: 1.781–1.782
　No. 4: 1.791–1.792
　No. 5: 1.801–1.802
④ IN: .249
　EX: .239
⑤ Not Available
⑥ IN: 0.413
　EX: 0.413
⑦ EFI—IN: 0.396
　　　EX: 0.396
⑧ The camshaft is restrained by a spring, there is no end play.

CRANKSHAFT AND CONNECTING ROD SPECIFICATIONS
All measurements are given in inches.

Year	Engine No. Cyl. Displacement (cc)	Crankshaft				Connecting Rod		
		Main Brg. Journal Dia.	Main Brg. Oil Clearance	Shaft End-Play	Thrust on No.	Journal Diameter	Oil Clearance	Side Clearance
'83–'87	4-1597	2.2826–2.2834	0.0008–0.0015	0.004–0.008	3	1.885–1.886	0.0002–0.0003	0.004–0.011
'84–'87	4-2000	2.3598–2.3605	0.0012–0.0020	0.0016	3	2.0055–2.0061	0.0031	0.0043–0.0103

Ford Mercury
FRONT WHEEL DRIVE CARS — ESCORT • EXP • LYNX • TEMPO • TOPAZ • TAURUS • SABLE
SECTION 4

CRANKSHAFT AND CONNECTING ROD SPECIFICATIONS
All measurements are given in inches.

Year	Eng. VIN Code	Engine No. Cyl Displacement (cu. in.)	Liters	Eng. Mfg.	Crankshaft Main Brg. Journal Diameter	Main Brg. Oil Clearance	Shaft End-Play	Thrust on No.	Connecting Rod Journal Diameter	Oil Clearance	Side Clearance
'84–'87	4-2300	2.2489–2.2490			0.0008–0.0024	0.004–0.008		3	2.1232–2.1240	0.0008–0.0015	0.0035–0.0105
'85–'87	4-1901	2.2835–2.2827			0.0008–0.0015	.004–.008		4	1.8862–1.8854	0.0008–0.0015	00.004–00.011
'86–'87	4-2508	2.2489–2.2490			0.0008–0.0015	.004–.008		3	2.1232–2.1240	0.0008–0.0015	0.0035–0.0105
'86–'87	6-2983	2.5190–2.5198			0.001–0.0014	.004–.008		3	2.1253–2.1261	00.001–0.0014	00.006–00.014

PISTON AND RING SPECIFICATIONS
All measurements are given in inches

Year	Engine Displacement (cc)	Piston Clearance	Ring Gap Top Compression	Ring Gap Bottom Compression	Ring Gap Oil Control	Ring Side Clearance Top Compression	Ring Side Clearance Bottom Compression	Ring Side Clearance Oil Control
'83–'87	1597	0.0018–0.0026	0.012–0.020	0.012–0.020	0.016–0.055	0.001–0.003	0.002–0.003	Snug
'84–'87	2000	0.0013–0.0020	0.0079–0.0157	0.0079–0.0157	0.0079–0.0157	0.0020–0.0035	0.0016–0.0031	Snug
'84–'87	2300	0.0013–0.0021	0.008–0.016	0.008–0.016	0.015–0.055	0.002–0.004	0.002–0.004	Snug
'85–'87	1901	0.0016–0.0024	0.010–0.020	0.010–0.020	0.016–0.055	0.0015–0.0032	0.0015–0.0035	Snug
'86–'87	2508	0.0012–0.0022	0.008–0.016	0.008–0.016	0.015–0.055	0.002–0.004	0.002–0.004	Snug
'86–'87	2983	0.0012–0.0023	0.01–0.02	0.01–0.02	0.010–0.049	0.0016–0.0037	0.0016–0.0037	Snug

CAPACITIES

Year	Engine No. Cyl. Displacement (cc)	Engine Crankcase Capacity Including Filter (qts.)	Transmission Pts. to Refill After Draining Manual	Transmission Pts. to Refill After Draining Automatic (Total Capacity)	Drive Axle (pts.)	Gasoline Tank (gals.)	Cooling System (qts.) With Heater	Cooling System (qts.) With A/C
'83–'87	4-1597	4.0	5.0 ①	②	③	④	6.7	8.1
'84–'87	4-2000	7.2 ⑤	①	—	③	⑥	8.1	8.1
'84–'87	4-2300	4.5 ⑦	6.1	②	③	⑥	8.1	8.1
'85–'87	4-1901	5.0	5.0 ①	⑧	1.9	⑨	8.3	7.8
'86–'87	4-2508	5.0	5.0 ①	⑩	③	⑪	8.3	8.3
'86–'87	4-2983	4.5	5.0 ①	⑩	③	⑪	11.0 ⑫	11.0 ⑫

① 5 speed: 6.1
② Total dry capacity—converter, cooler and sump drained. 1983-86: 16.6 pts. Partial fluid change (pan sump only), add 8 pts, start engine and check level. Add necessary fluid until correct level is reached.
③ Included in transmission capacity
④ 1983: 10 gal. Standard
11.3 gal. Extended range
1983-'86: 10 gal. FE models
13 gal. Standard
13 gal. EXP/LN7
⑤ Capacity for complete system-pan capacity is 5.3 qts.
⑥ 1984: 14 gal; 1986: 15.2 gal.
⑦ After filter replacement, add 4 qts of oil and run engine. Shut engine off and check oil level. Add ½ qt if necessary.
⑧ All automatic transaxle models except the all-wheel drive models are: 8.3
The all-wheel drive models are: 10.0
⑨ Standard Fuel Tank: 15.4
All-wheel drive model fuel tank: 13.2
⑩ Automatic transaxle with overdrive (AXOD): 10.9
Standard automatic transaxle: 8.3
⑪ Standard fuel tank: 16.0
Optional Extended range fuel tank: 18.6
⑫ Station wagon equipped with A/C and the 3.0 liter engine: 11.8

TORQUE SPECIFICATIONS
All readings in ft. lbs.

Year	Engine No. Cyl. Displacement (cc)	Cylinder Head Bolts	Rod Bearing Bolts	Main Bearing Bolts	Crankshaft Bolt	Flywheel-to-Crankshaft Bolts	Manifold Intake	Manifold Exhaust
'83–'87	4-1597	①	19–25	67–80	74–90	59–69	12–15 ②	15–20
'84–'87	4-2000	①	51–54	61–65	115–123	130–137	12–16	16–19 ③

4–7

SECTION 4

FORD MERCURY
FRONT WHEEL DRIVE CARS—ESCORT • EXP • LYNX • TEMPO • TOPAZ • TAURUS • SABLE

TORQUE SPECIFICATIONS
All readings in ft. lbs.

Year	Eng. VIN Code	Engine No. Cyl Displacement (cu. in.)	Liters	Eng. Mfg.	Cylinder Head Bolts	Rod Bearing Bolt	Main Bearing Bolt	Crankshaft Pully Bolt	Flywheel to Crankshaft Bolts	Manifold Intake	Manifold Exhaust
'84–'87	4-2300		81	③	21–26	60–74	82–103	54–64	15–23	20–30	③
'85–'87	4-1901		①		19–25	67–80	74–90	54–64	12–15	15–20	
'86–'87	4-2508		④		21–26	51–66	140–170	54–64	15–23	20–30	③
'86–'87	6-2983		⑦	⑥	65–81	141–169	54–64	⑤	20–30	③	

CAUTION: Verify the correct original equipment engine is in the vehicle by referring to the VIN engine code before torquing any bolts.
① See head removal procedure for instructions
② Manifold stud nuts: 12–13 ft. lbs.
③ Tighten in two stages
④ Tighten in two steps: 52–59 ft. lbs. and then the final torque of 70–76 ft. lbs.
⑤ Tighten in three steps: 11, 18 and the final torque of 24 ft. lbs.
⑥ Tighten to 20–28 ft. lbs. and then back off the nuts a minimum of two revolutions, then apply the final torque of 20–25 ft. lbs.
⑦ Tighten in two steps: 48–54 ft. lbs. and then the final torque of 63–80 ft. lbs.

WHEEL ALIGNMENT SPECIFICATIONS

Year	Model	Caster Range (deg)■▲	Caster Pref. Setting (deg)	Camber Range (deg)■	Camber Pref. Setting (deg)	Toe-in (in.)	Steering Axis Inclin. (deg)
'83	Escort, Lynx, EXP/LN7	9/16P to 2 1/16P	1 5/16P	(Left) 1 13/32P to 2 29/32P (Right) 31/32P to 2 15/32P	2 5/32P 1 23/32P	1/32 to 7/32	14 21/32 15 3/32
'84–'87	Escort, Lynx, EXP	5/8P to 2 1/8P	1 2/3P	(Left) 1 3/8P to 2 7/8P (Right) 15/16P to 2 7/16P	2 1/8P 1 11/16P	1/64 (in) to 7/32 (out)	14 21/32 15 3/32
'84–'87	Tempo, Topaz	9/16P to 2 1/16P	1 5/16P	(Left) 1 1/8P to 2 5/8P (Right) 11/16P to 2 3/16P	1 7/8P 1 1/2P	1/32 (in) to 7/32 (out)	14 5/8 15 1/8
'86–'87	Taurus/Sable Front	3P to 6P	4P	1 3/32N to 3/32P	1/2N	7/32 (out) to 1/64 (in)	15 3/8
'86–'87	Taurus/Sable Rear	■	■	■	■	1/16 (out) to 3/16 (in)	N/A

■ Caster and chamber are pre-set at the factory and cannot be adjusted
▲ Caster measurements must be made on the left side by turning left wheel through the prescribed angle of sweep and on the right side by turning right wheel through prescribed angle of sweep for the equipment being used. When using alignment equipment designed to measure caster on both the right and left side, turning only one wheel will result in a significant error in caster angle for the opposite side.

BELT TENSION CHART

Year	Model	Belt Type		
1983	Excort/Lynx EXP/LN7	6 Rib Type	New	110–140 lbs.
			Used Reset	110–130 lbs.
			Used Min.	75 lbs.
		5 Rib Type	New	110–140 lbs.
			Used Reset	110–130 lbs.
			Used Min.	75 lbs.

Ford Mercury
FRONT WHEEL DRIVE CARS—ESCORT • EXP • LYNX • TEMPO • TOPAZ • TAURUS • SABLE

BELT TENSION CHART

Year	Model	Belt Type		
1984	Tempo/Topaz Escort/Lynx/EXP	6 Rip Type	New Used Reset Used Min.	110–140 lbs. 110–130 lbs. 75 lbs.
1985	Tempo/Topaz Escort/Lynx/EXP	6 Rib Type	New Used Reset Used Min.	110–140 lbs. 110–130 lbs. 75 lbs.
1986	Tempo/Topaz Escort/Lynx/EXP Taurus/Sable	6 Rib Type	New Used Reset Used Min.	110–140 lbs. 110–130 lbs. 75 lbs.
1987	Tempo/Topaz Escort/Lynx/EXP Taurus/Sable	6 Rib Type	New Used Reset Used Min.	110–140 lbs. 110–130 lbs. 75 lbs.

ELECTRICAL SECTION

NOTE: To perform overhaul procedures, refer to the unit repair section.

Charging System

ALTERNATOR

Removal and Installation

ALL MODELS

1. Disconnect the negative battery cable and remove the pulley cover shield, if so equipped.
2. Loosen the alternator pivot bolt and remove the adjustment bracket to alternator bolt. Slide the alternator downward and remove the drive belt.
3. Disconnect and label the alternator wiring (this will aid in correct installation).

NOTE: Some models use a push-on wiring connector on the field and stator connections. Pull or push straight when removing or installing and be careful not to damage the connector.

4. Remove the pivot bolt and the alternator.
5. Installation is the reverse order of the removal procedure. Adjust the drive belt tension so that there are approximately ¼–½ in. deflection on the longest belt span between the pulleys.

VOLTAGE REGULATOR

Removal and Installation

NOTE: There are three different types of regulators being used, depending on the model, engine, alternator output and type of dash mounted charging indicator used (light or ammeter). The regulators are 100% solid state and are calibrated and preset by the manufacturer. No re-adjustments are required or possible on these regulators.

1. Remove the battery ground cable.
2. Disconnect the regulator from the wiring harness.
3. Remove the regulator mounting screws and remove the regulator.
4. Install the new regulator in the reverse of the removal procedure.
5. Test the system for proper voltage regulation.

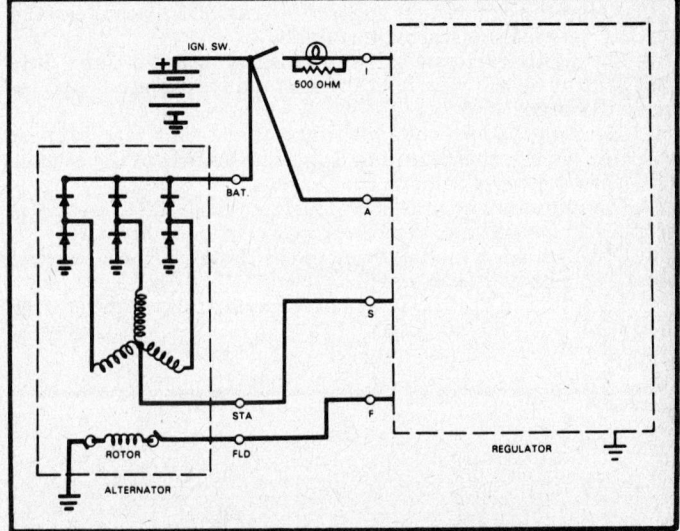

Charging system schematic with electronic regulator and indicator lamp (© Ford Motor Co.)

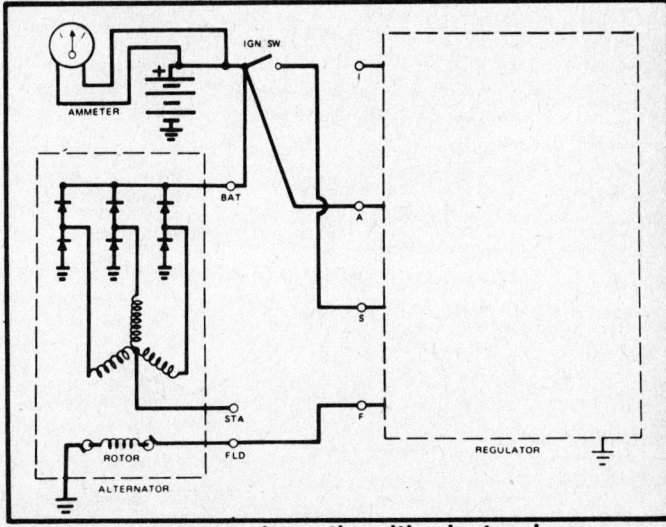

Charging system schematic with electronic regulator and ammeter (© Ford Motor Co.)

SECTION 4 — FORD MERCURY
FRONT WHEEL DRIVE CARS—ESCORT • EXP • LYNX • TEMPO • TOPAZ • TAURUS • SABLE

Schematic of starter circuit (© Ford Motor Co.)

Starting System

STARTER

Removal and Installation

ALL MODELS EXCEPT THE TAURUS/SABLE

1. Disconnect the negative battery cable.
2. Raise the vehicle on support stands and disconnect the starter cable at the starter terminal.
3. On manual transmission models, remove the three nuts that attach the roll restricter brace to the starter studs and remove the brace.
4. Remove the two bolts attaching the starter rear support bracket, remove the retaining nut from the rear of the starter stud thru bolt, and remove the bracket.
5. On manual transmission models, remove the three starter mounting studs and remove the starter assembly. On automatic transmission models, remove the three starter mounting bolts and remove the starter.
6. Installation is the reverse of removal. Torque the starter mounting bolts 30–40 ft. lbs.

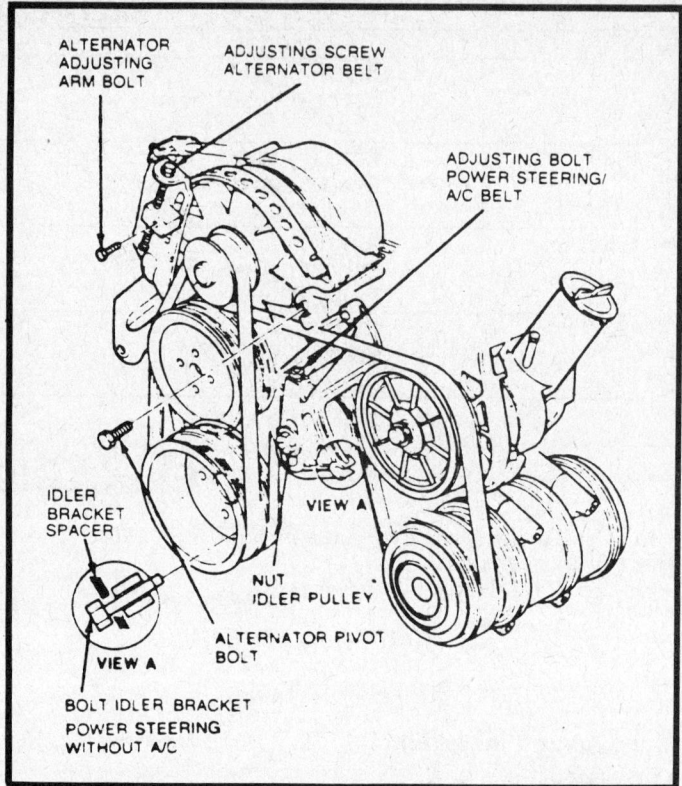

Belt, installation and tension adjustment—3.0L engine

TAURUS/SABLE

1. Disconnect the negative battery cable and the cable at the battery.
2. Raise and support the front of the vehicle safely and block the rear wheels.
3. Remove the cable support and ground cable connection from the upper starter stud bolt.
4. Remove the starter brace from the cylinder block and the starter.
5. On the 2.5L engine, remove the three starter to bell housing bolts. On the 3.0L engine, remove the two starter to bell housing bolts.
6. Remove the starter between the sub-frame and radiator on the automatic transaxle models. Remove the starter between the sub-frame and the engine on the manual transaxle models.
7. Installation is the reverse order of the removal procedure. torque the starter bolts to 30 ft. lbs.

Ignition System

DISTRIBUTOR

Removal and Installation

1.6L AND 1.9L ENGINES

The camshaft-driven distributor is located at the top left end of the cylinder head. It is retained by two hold-down bolts at the base of the distributor shaft housing.

1. Turn the engine over until No. 1 cylinder is a TDC of the compression stroke. disconnect the vacuum hose from the advance unit. Disconnect the primary wire at the coil.
2. Remove the capscrews and remove the distributor cap.
3. Scribe a mark on the distributor body, showing the position of the ignition rotor. Scribe another mark on the distribu-

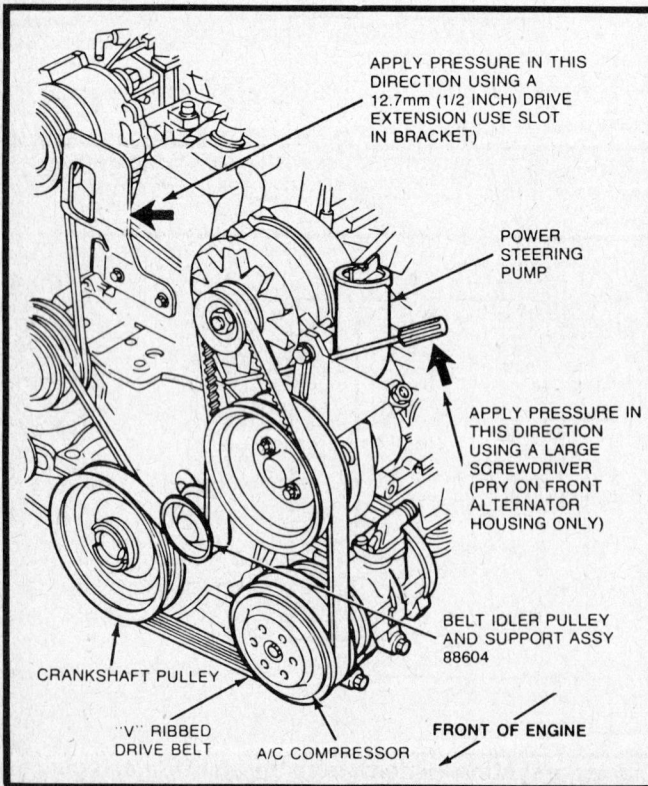

Belt, installation and tension adjustment—2.3L engine

tor body and cylinder head, showing the position of the body in relation to the head. These marks can be used for reference when installing the distributor, as long as the engine remains undisturbed.

4. Remove the two distributor hold-down bolts. Pull the distributor out of the head.

NOTE: **Some engines are equipped with a security type distributor hold-down bolt and special tool No. T82L-12270-A or equivalent must be used to remove this hold down bolt. The 1.9L engine uses two hold-down bolts.**

5. To install the distributor with the engine undisturbed, place the distributor in the cylinder head, seating the off-set tang of the drive coupling into the groove on the end of the camshaft. Install the two distributor hold-down screws and tighten them so that the distributor can just barely be moved. Install the rotor (if removed), the distributor cap and all wiring, then set the ignition timing.

6. If the crankshaft was rotated while the distributor was removed, the engine must be brought to TDC (Top Dead Center) on the compression stroke of the No. 1 cylinder. Remove the No. 1 spark plug. Place your finger over the hole and rotate the crankshaft slowly (use a wrench on the crankshaft pulley bolt) in the direction of normal engine rotation, until engine compression is felt.

—— CAUTION ——

Turn the engine only in the direction of normal rotation. Backward rotation will cause the cam belt to slip or lose teeth, altering engine timing.

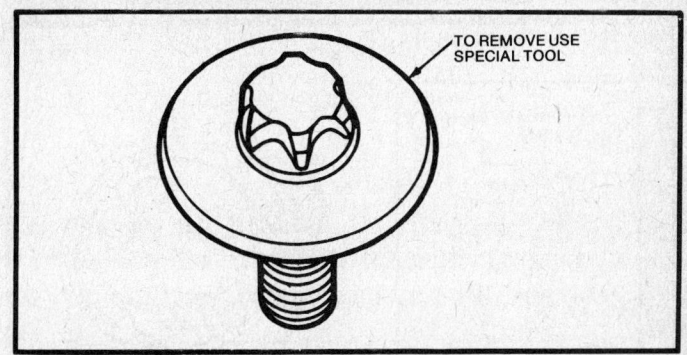

Security distributor hold down bolt used on some Tempo/Topaz models (© Ford Motor Co.)

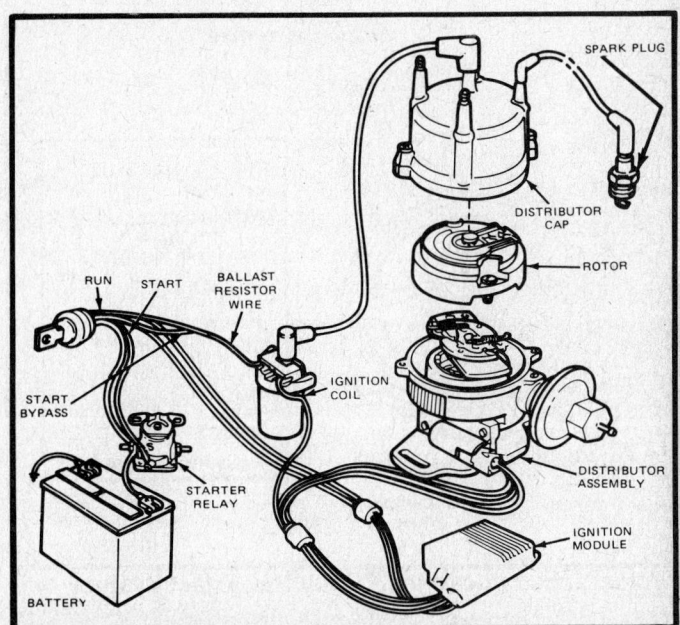

Escort/Lynx, EXP/LN7 ignition system (© Ford Motor Co.)

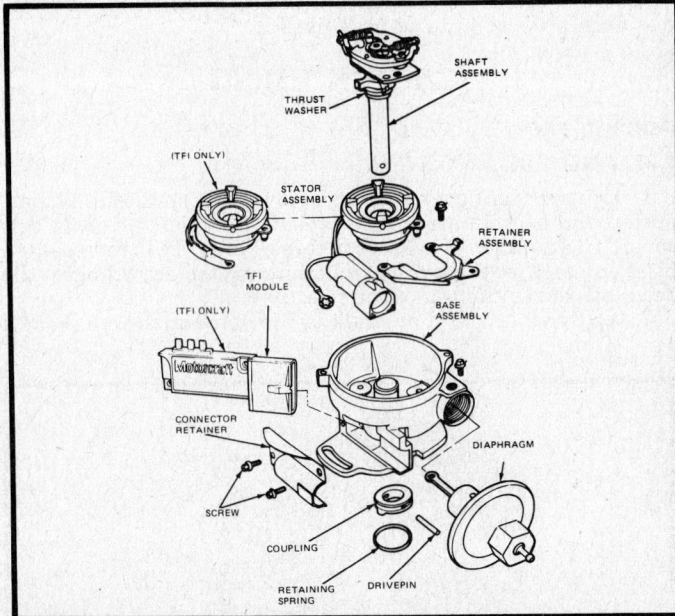

Exploded view of distributor used with 1982 and later 1.6 liter engine, T.F.I. components illustrated (© Ford Motor Co.)

When engine compression is felt at the spark plug hole, indication that the piston is approaching TDC, continue to turn the crankshaft until the timing mark on the pulley is aligned with the "O" mark (timing mark) on the engine front cover. Turn the distributor shaft until the ignition rotor is at the No.1 firing position. Install the distributor into the cylinder head.

2.3L, 2.5L and the 3.0L ENGINES

The distributor is a new universal design which is gear driven and has a die cast base that incorporates in integrally mounted

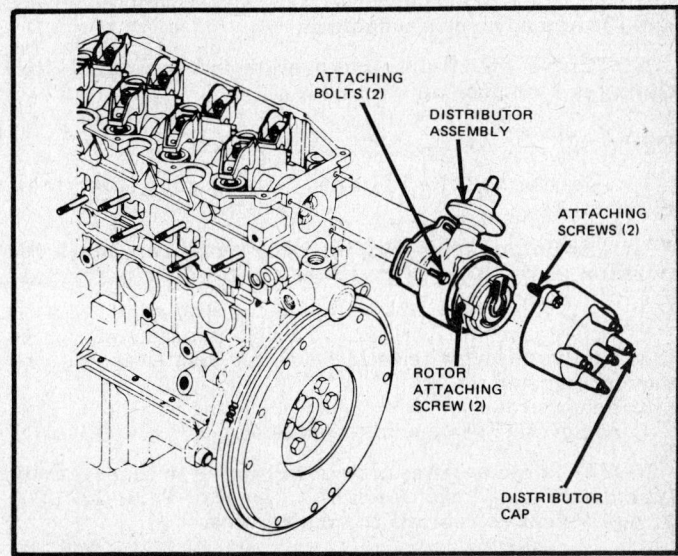

Distributor location—Escort/Lynx, EXP/LN7 (© Ford Motor Co.)

4-11

FORD MERCURY
FRONT WHEEL DRIVE CARS—ESCORT • EXP • LYNX • TEMPO • TOPAZ • TAURUS • SABLE

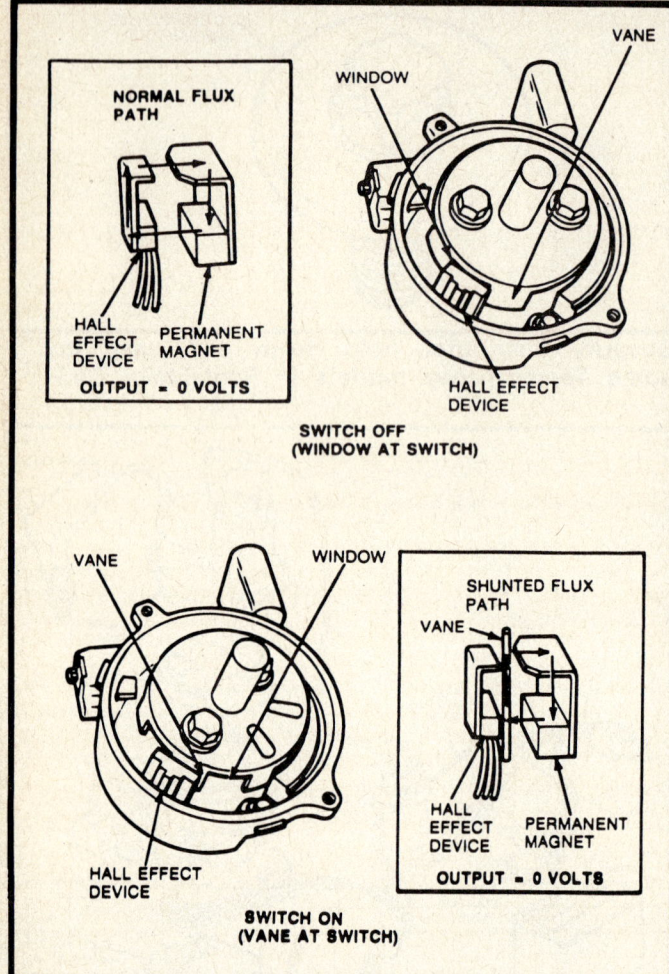

Typical schematic of the EEC-IV Hall Effect System

TFI-IV (Thick Film Ignition) ignition module, a "Hall Effect" vane switch stator assembly, and provision for fixed octane adjustment. The new design deletes the conventional centrifugal and vacuum advance mechanisms.

NOTE: No distributor calibration is required. Initial timing is a normal adjustment.

Removal

1. Disconnect the primary wiring connector from distributor.

NOTE: Before removing the distributor cap, mark the position of the No. 1 wire tower on the distributor base for future use.

2. Using a screwdriver, remove distributor cap and position it and the attached wires aside so as not to interfere with removing distributor.
3. Remove rotor.
4. Remover TFI-IV harness connector.

NOTE: Some engines may be equipped with a security type distributor hold down bolt. Use tool T82L-12270-A or equivalent to remove the distributor.

5. Remove distributor hold down bolt and clamp. Remove the distributor Be careful not to disturb the intermediate driveshaft.

Installation

1. Rotate the engine until No.1 position is on compression stroke.
   a. Align timing marks for correct initial timing.
   b. Rotate distributor shaft so that center rod on multi-point rotor is pointing toward mark previously made on distributor base.
   c. Continue rotating slightly so that leading edge of vane is centered in the vane switch stator assembly.
   d. Rotate distributor in block to align leading edge and the vane switch stator assembly and verify that the rotor is pointing at No.1 cap terminal.
   e. Install distributor hold down bolt and clamp. Do not tighten at this time.
2. If the vane and vane switch stator cannot be aligned by rotating the distributor in the block, pull distributor out of block enough to disengage distributor gear and rotate distributor shaft to engage a different distributor gear tooth. Repeat Step 1 as necessary.
3. Connect distributor to wiring harness.
4. Install distributor cap, rotor and ignition wires. Check that ignition wires are securely connected to the distributor cap and spark plugs. Tighten distributor cap screws to 18–35 in.lb. (2.8–3.9 Nm).
5. Set initial timing with a timing light. Refer to the Vehicle Emission Control Information Decal.
6. Tighten distributor hold down bolt to 17–25 ft.lbs. (23–34 Nm).
7. Recheck initial timing. Readjust if necessary.

NOTE: Technical information on 2.5L and 3.0L engines not available at time of publication.

IGNITION TIMING

Adjustment
1.6L AND 1.9L ENGINES

1. Ignition timing marks consist of a notch on the crankshaft pulley and a graduated scale molded into the camshaft belt cover. The number of degrees before or after TDC represented by each mark in the scale can be interpreted according to the decal affixed to the top of the belt cover.
2. Apply white paint or chalk to the notch in the crankshaft

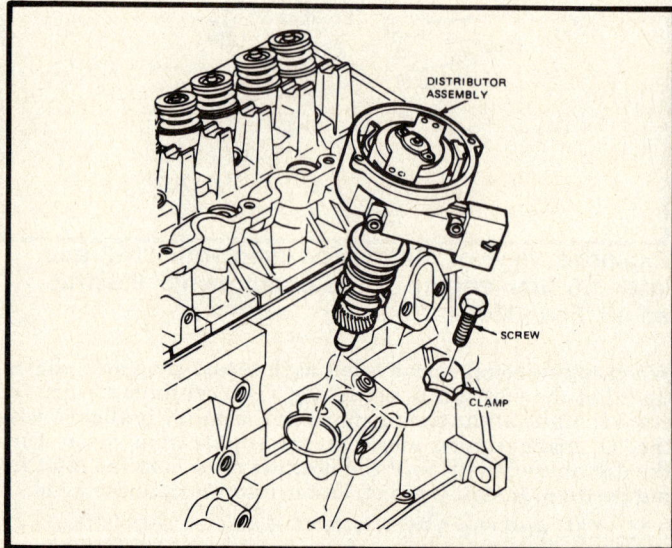

Tempo/Topaz distributor mounting
(© Ford Motor Co.)

pulley and the appropriate mark in the degree scale. See the underhood emission control decal for timing specifications.

3. Warm the engine until it reaches normal operating temperature.

4. Shut off the engine. Disconnect and plug the vacuum hose from the distributor advance diaphragm. Make sure the transmission is in Park or Neutral, apply the parking brake and block the wheels.

5. Connect a timing light and a tachometer to the engine.

6. Start the engine and allow it to idle at 700 rpm or less. Aim the light at the marks. If they are not aligned, loosen the distributor clamp bolts slightly and rotate the distributor body until the marks are aligned under timing light illumination.

7. Tighten the distributor clamp bolts and recheck the ignition timing. Shut off the engine and connect the vacuum hose. Adjust idle speed.

2.3L, 2.5L and The 3.0L ENGINES

On engines with a manual transaxle the timing marks are located on the flywheel and visible through a hole in the transmission case. The timing cover plate must be removed in order to adjust the timing.

On engines with an automatic transaxle the timing marks are visible through a hole in the transmission case. There in no cover plate. To adjust the timing, align the pointer in the transmission case with the mark on the flywheel. The 3.0L engine employs timing degree numbers on the crankshaft pulley and a timing pointer near the pulley.

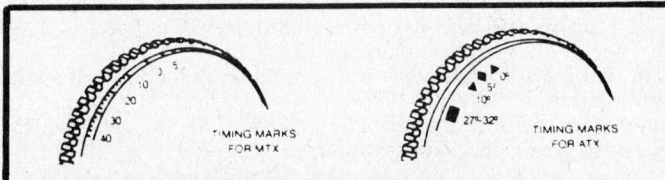

Timing mark locations for the 3.0L engine

NOTE: Some distributor hold down bolts have a security type head and can not be loosened, to adjust timing, unless Ford special tool T82L-12270-A or equivalent is available.

Adjustment

1. Place the transaxle in the Park or Neutral position depending on what type of transaxle the vehicle is supplied with.

2. Open the hood and clean the timing marks with a stiff brush or solvent. On the manual transaxle models, it will be necessary to remove the cover plate which allows access to to the timing marks.

3. Using a white chalk or paint mark the specified timing mark and pointer.

4. Remove the in-line spout connector. The spout connector is the center wire between the electronic control assembly (ECA) connector and the thick film ignition (TFI) module.

5. Connect a suitable inductive type timing light to the No. 1 spark plug wire. Do not, puncture and ignition wire with any type of probing device.

NOTE: The high ignition coil charging currents generated in the EEC-IV ignition system may falsely trigger timing lights with capacitive or direct connect pick-ups. It is necessary that an inductive type timing light be used in this procedure.

6. Connect a suitable tachometer to the engine. The ignition coil connector allows a test lead with an alligator clip to be connected to the Distributor Electronic Control (DEC) terminal without removing the connector.

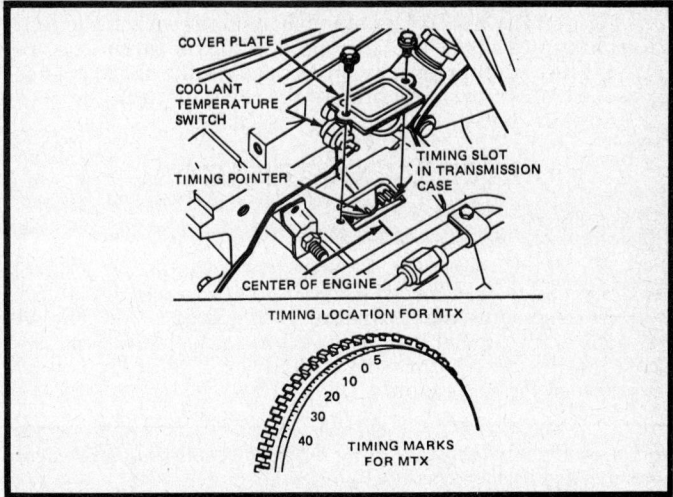

Tempo/Topaz manual transaxle timing marks
(© Ford Motor Co.)

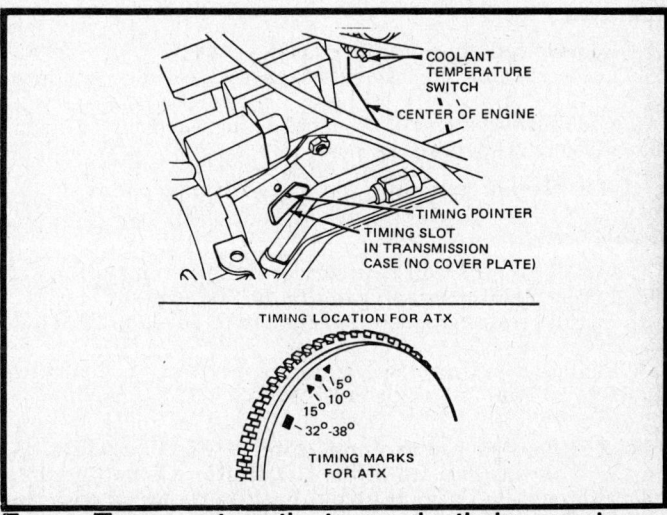

Tempo/Topaz automatic transaxle timing marks
(© Ford Motor Co.)

7. Start the engine and let it run until it reaches normal operating temperature.

8. Check the engine idle rpm if it is not within specifications, adjust as necessary. After the rpm has been adjusted or checked, aim the timing light at the timing marks. If they are not aligned, loosen the distributor clamp bolts slightly and rotate the distributor body until the marks are aligned under timing light illumination.

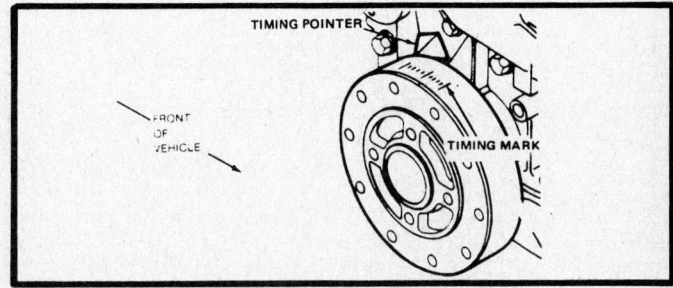

Timing mark locations for the 2.5L engine

SECTION 4

FORD MERCURY
FRONT WHEEL DRIVE CARS—ESCORT • EXP • LYNX • TEMPO • TOPAZ • TAURUS • SABLE

7. Tighten the distributor clamp bolts and recheck the ignition timing. Re-adjust the idle speed. Shut the engine off, remove all test equippment, reconnect the in-line spout connector to the distributor and reinstall the cover plate on the manual transaxle models.

UNIVERSAL DISTRIBUTORS

Adjustments

ALL MODELS

Provisions have been incorporated in the universal distributor to allow fixed adjustment capability for octane needs. The adjustment is the accomplished by replacing the standard 0° rod located in the distributor bowl with a 3° or 6° retard rod which are released for service only.

CAUTION
Do not change the timing by using different octane rods, as Federal Emission Requirements will be affected.

OCTANE ROD

Removal

1. Remove cap and rotor for visual access.
2. Locate octane adjustments boss and remove retaining screw.
3. Slide Rod/grommet out to a point where rod can be disengaged from stator retaining post.

NOTE: Retain grommet for use with new rod.

Installation

1. Install grommet on new service rod and reinstall in the distributor, making sure to capture the stator post.
2. Install retaining screw and tighten to 15–35 in.lbs. (1.8–4.3 Nm).
3. Replace cap and rotor. Tighten caps screws to 33–43 inch lbs. (2.0–2.6 Nm) and rotor to 25–35 in.lbs. (2.8–3.9 Nm).

NOTE: Except for the cap, rotor, TFI-IV module, O-ring and octane rod, no other distributor assembly parts are replaceable. There is no calibration required with the universal distributor.

Electrical Controls

IGNITION LOCK

Removal

ALL MODELS

1. Disconnect the negative (ground) battery cable from the battery.

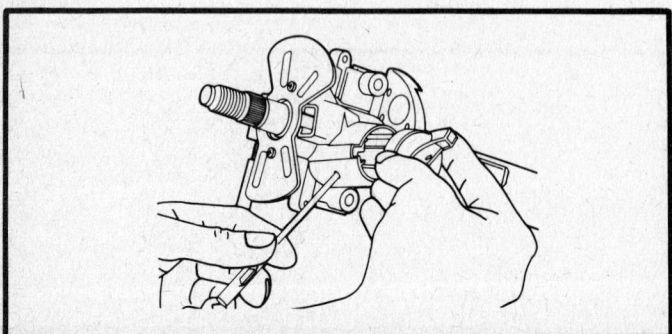

Removing lock cylinder (© Ford Motor Co.)

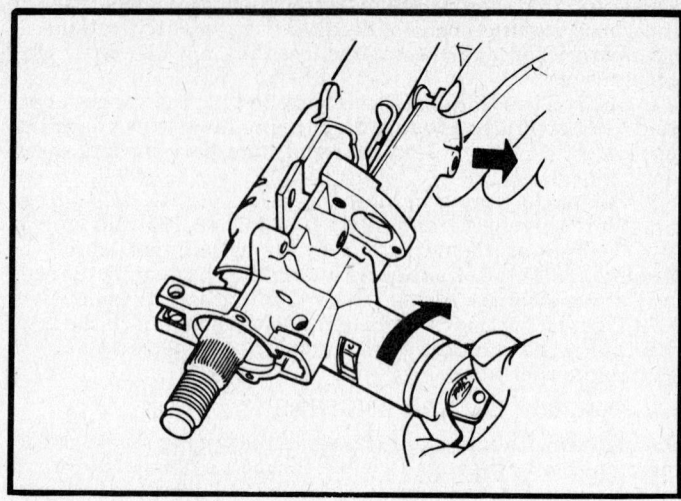

Removing casting from steering shaft
(© Ford Motor Co.)

2. Remove the steering column lower shroud on Escort/Lynx/ EXP. On Tempo/Topaz models, remove the two trim halves by removing the five attaching screw. On models with tilt wheel, Remove the upper extension shroud by un-snapping from a retaining clip that is located at the nine o'clock position.
3. Disconnect the warning buzzer electrical connector. Turn the key cylinder to the Run position.
4. Take a ⅛ in. diameter pin or small punch and push on the cylinder retaining pin. The pin is visible through a hole in the mounting surrounding the key cylinder. As you push on the pin pull out on the lock cylinder.

Installation

1. Install the lock cylinder by turning it to the Run position and depressing the retaining pin. Insert the lock cylinder is fully seated and aligned in the interlocking washer before turning the key to the Off position. This action will permit the cylinder retaining pin to extend into the cylinder housing hole.
2. Rotate the lock cylinder, using the lock cylinder key, to ensure correct mechanical operation in all positions.
3. Install the electrical connector for the key warning buzzer.
4. Install the lower steering column shroud.
5. Connect the negative (ground) battery cable to battery terminal.
6. Check for proper start in Park or Neutral. Also, make certain that that the start circuit cannot be actuated in the Drive and Reverse positions and that the column is locked in the Lock position.

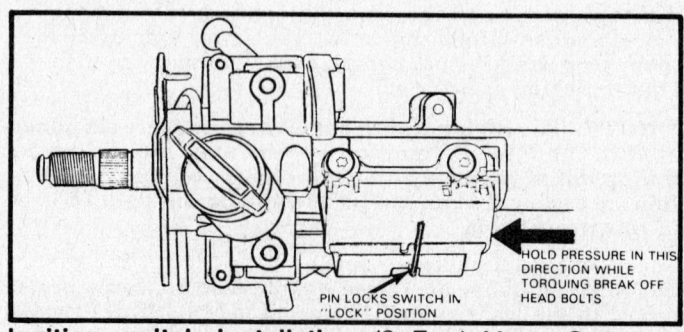

Ignition switch installation (© Ford Motor Co.)

Ford Mercury
FRONT WHEEL DRIVE CARS—ESCORT • EXP • LYNX • TEMPO • TOPAZ • TAURUS • SABLE

IGNITION SWITCH

ALL MODELS EXCEPT THE TAURUS/SABLE

The ignition switch has blade type terminals with one multiple connector. The switch is attached to the steering column with break-off head bolts. The bolts must be removed with an easy-out tool or other means.

Removal

1. Disconnect the negative (ground) battery cable from the battery terminal.
2. Remove the steering column upper and lower trim shroud by removing five self-tapping screws. The four steering column attaching nuts may have to be loosened enough to allow removal of the upper shroud.
3. Disconnect the ignition switch electrical connector.
4. Rotate ignition key lock cylinder to On position.
5. Drill out the break-off head bolts that connect the switch to the lock cylinder housing using an 1/8 in. drill.
6. Remove the two bolts using an suitable easy-out tool.
7. Disengage the ignition switch from the actuator pin.

Installation

NOTE: If reinstalling the old switch, it must be adjusted to the Lock or Run (depending on year and model) position. Slide the carrier of the switch to the required position and insert a 1/16 in. drill bit or pin through the switch housing into the carrier. This keeps the carrier from moving when the switch in connected to the actuator. It may be necessary to wiggle the carrier back and forth to line up the holes when installing the drill or pin. New switches come with a pin in place.

1. Adjust the ignition switch by sliding the carrier to the switch on position. Insert a 1/16 in. Drill bit or smaller tool through he switch housing and into the carrier, thereby preventing movement of the carrier with respect to the switch housing. It may be necessary to move the carrier slightly back and forth to align the carrier and housing adjustment holes.

NOTE: A new replacement switch assembly includes an adjusting pin already installed.

2. Rotate the lock cylinder to the On position.
3. Install the ignition switch on the actuator pin.
4. Install the new break-off head bolts and hand tighten.
5. Move the ignition switch up the steering column until all the travel in the screw slots in used. Hold the switch in this position and tighten the break-off head bolts until the heads break off.
6. Remove the adjustment drill bit or pin.
7. Connect the electrical connector to the ignition switch.
8. Position the upper shroud and tighten the steering column attaching nuts to 17–25 ft. lbs. (23–33 Nm) if they were loosened. Mate the lower shroud to the upper shroud and tighten the five attaching screws.
9. Connect the negative (ground) battery cable to the battery terminal.
10. Check the ignition switch for proper starting in Park or Neutral. Also make certain that the start circuit can not be actuated in the Drive or Reverse position and that the column is locked in the Lock position.

TAURUS/SABLE

1. Disconnect the negative battery cable.
2. Rotate the ignition lock cylinder to the Run position and depress the lock cylinder retaining pin through the access hole in the shroud with a 1/8 in. punch. As you push on the pin pull out on the lock cylinder.
3. On models equipped with tilt sreering columns, remove the tilt release lever by removing the allen head cap screw that holds the tilt lever to the steering column.
4. On all models, remove the lower steering column/instrument panel cover by removing the four retaining screws.
5. Remove the steering column shroud by removing the three self tapping screws.
6. Remove the two bolts and nuts that attach the steering column to support bracket and lower column. Disconnect the ignition switch electrical connector.
7. Remove the lock actuator cover plate by removing the one tamper resistant Torx® head bolt.

NOTE: The lock actuator assembly will slide freely out of the lock cylinder housing when the ignition switch is removed.

8. Remove the ignition switch and cover by removing the two tamper-resisant Torx® head bolts.

Installation

1. Ensure ignition switch is in the Run position by rotating the steering column shaft fully clockwise to the Start position and releasing it.
2. Install the lock actuator assembly into the ignition switch

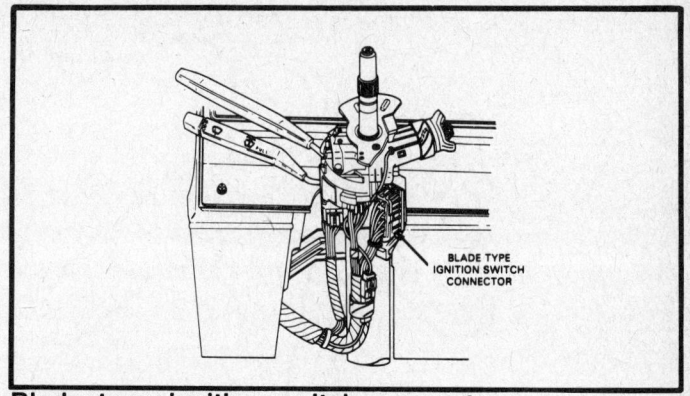

Blade type ignition switch connector
(© Ford Motor Co.)

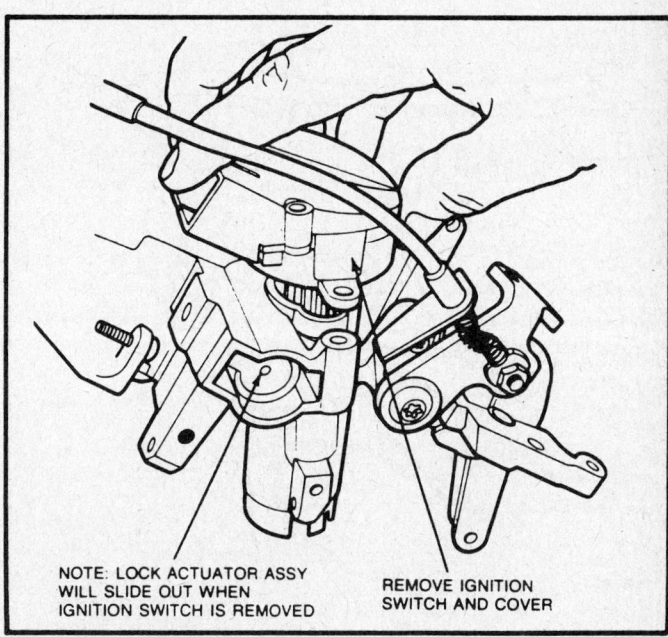

Removing the ignition switch and cover—Taurus/Sable

Ford Mercury
FRONT WHEEL DRIVE CARS—ESCORT • EXP • LYNX • TEMPO • TOPAZ • TAURUS • SABLE

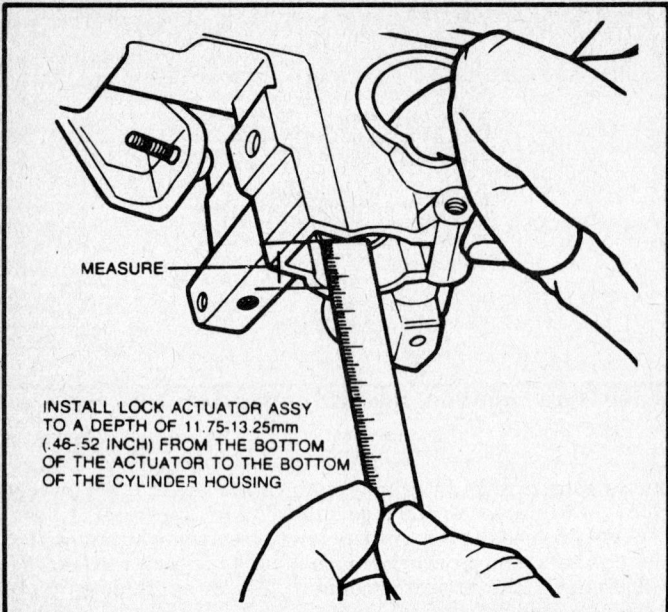

Making the lock cylinder depth measurement—Taurus/Sable

housing to a depth of 0.46–0.54 in. (11.75–13.25mm) from the bottom of the actuator assembly top the bottom of the lock cylinder housing.

3. While holding the actuator assembly at the proper depth, install the ignition switch.
4. Install the ignition switch and cover along with the two torx head screws. Torque the screws to 30–48 in.lbs.
5. Install the lock cylinder. Rotate the ignition switch to the Lock position and measure the depth of the actuator assembly. The actuator must be 0.92–1.00 in. (23.5–25.5mm) inside the lock cylinder housing. If the actuator depth does not meet specifications, it must be removed and reinstalled.
6. Install the lock actuator cover plate with the torx head screw and torque the screw to 30–48 in.lbs. Install the ignition switch electrical connector.

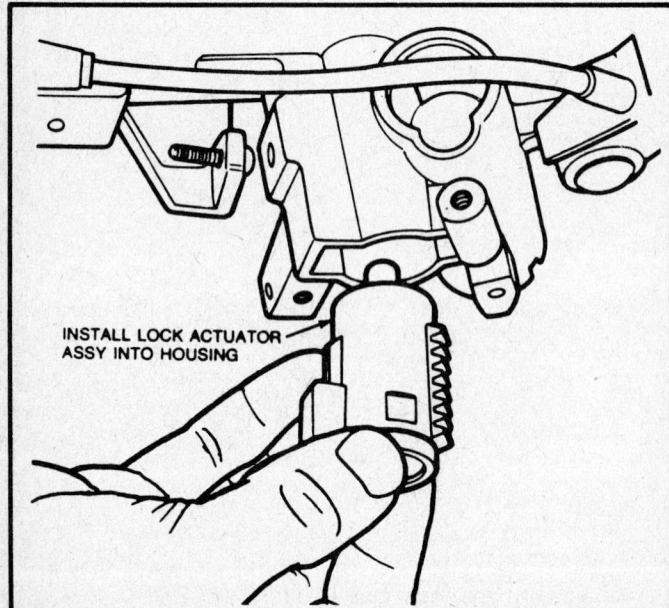

Installing the lock cylinder—Taurus/Sable

7. Connect the negative (ground) battery cable to the battery terminal.
8. Check the ignition switch for proper starting in PARK or Neutral. Also make certain that the start circuit can not be actuated in the Drive or Reverse position and that the column is locked in the Lock position. Re-install all the steering column trim panels, brackets and levers.

NEUTRAL START SWITCH

Removal and Installation

AUTOMATIC TRANSAXLE (ALL MODELS)

1. Disconnect the battery negative cable.
2. Remove the two valve supply rear hoses and all the vacuum hoses from the managed air valve.
3. Remove the managed air valve supply hose band to intermediate shift control bracket attaching screw.
4. Remove the air cleaner assembly.
5. Disconnect the wire connector from the neutral start switch.
6. Remove the retaining screws from the neutral start switch and remove the switch.
7. To install the switch, place the switch on the manual shift shaft and loosely install the two retaining bolts. Have the transaxle in neutral.
8. Use a No. 43 drill (0.089 in.) and insert it into the switch to set the contacts.
9. Tighten the retaining screws of the switch, remove the drill and complete the assembly.

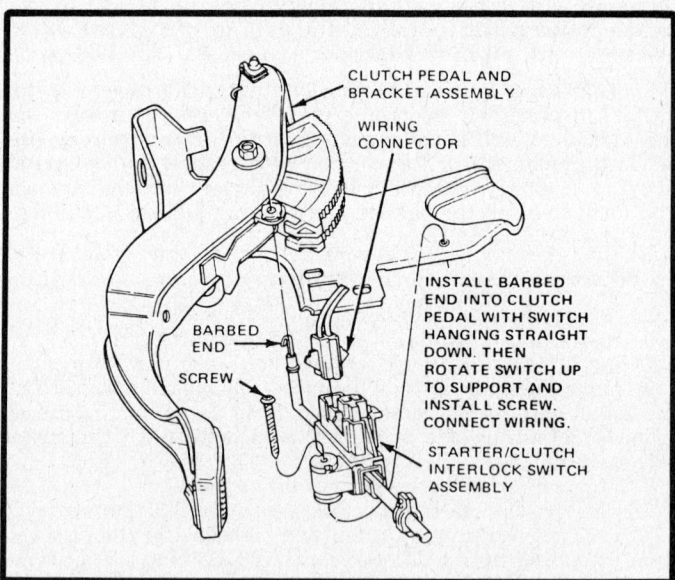

Starter/clutch interlock switch installation
(© Ford Motor Co.)

STARTER/CLUTCH INTERLOCK SWITCH

Removal

ALL MODELS

1. Remove panel above clutch pedal on the Tempo/Topaz and Taurus/Sable models.
2. Disconnect wiring connector.
3. Remove lower speed control/EFI/diesel switch attachment to bracket, if so equipped.
4. Remove clutch interlock attaching screw (and hairpin clip, if so equipped) and allow switch to rotate down.

5. Depress barb at end of rod and withdraw rod from clutch pedal.

Installation

NOTE: Always install the switch with the self-adjusting clip about 1 in. (25.4mm) from the end of the rod. The clutch pedal must be fully up (clutch engaged). Otherwise, the switch may be maladjusted.

1. Insert barbed end of rod into bushing on clutch pedal.
2. Swing switch around to line up hole in mounting boss with corresponding hole in bracket. Attach with screw.
3. Install speed control/EFI/diesel switch, if so equipped and adjust.
4. Reset clutch interlock switch by pressing clutch pedal to floor.
5. Connect wiring connector.
6. Install the panel above the clutch on the Tempo/Topaz and Taurus/Sable models.

STOPLIGHT SWITCH WITHOUT POWER BRAKES

Removal

1. Disconnect the wire harness at the connector from the switch.

NOTE: The locking tab must be lifted before the connector can be removed.

2. Remove the hairpin retainer. Slide the stop lamp switch, the push rod and the white nylon washer and black busing away from the pedal. Remove the switch by sliding the switch up/down.

NOTE: Since the switch side plate nearest the brake pedal is slotted, it is not necessary to remove the brake master cylinder push rod black busing and one white spacer washer nearest the pedal arm from the brake pedal pin.

Installation

1. Position the switch so that the U-shaped side is nearest the pedal and directly over/under the pin. The black bushing must be in position in the push rod eyelet with the washer face on the side closest to the retaining pin.
2. Then slide the switch up/down, trapping the master cylinder push rod and black bushing between the switch side plates. Push the switch and push rod assembly firmly towards the brake pedal arm. Assembly outside the white plastic washer to pin and install the hairpin retainer to trap the whole assembly.

--- CAUTION ---
Do not substitute other types of pin retainer. Replace only with production hairpin retainer.

3. Assembly the wire harness connector to the switch.
4. Check the stop lamp switch for proper operation. stoplights should illuminate with less than 6 lbs. applied to the brake pedal at the pad.

NOTE: The stoplamp switch wire harness must have sufficient length to travel with the switch during full stroke at the pedal.

STOPLIGHT SWITCH WITH POWER BRAKES

Removal

1. Disconnect the negative battery cable.

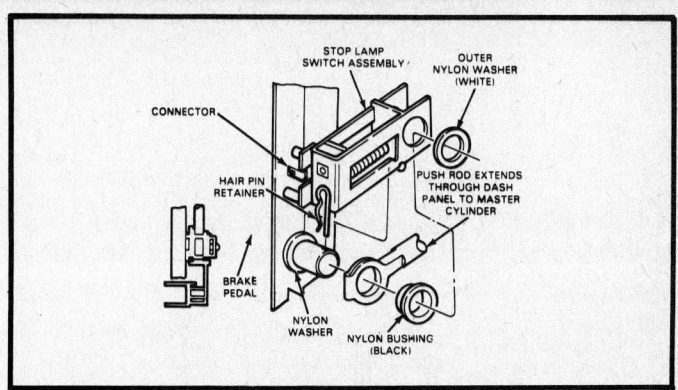

Stoplamp switch components (© Ford Motor Co.)

2. Disconnect the stoplamp switch wire connector from the switch.
3. Remove the hairpin retainer and outer white nylon washer from the pedal pin. Slide the stoplamp switch off the brake pedal pin just far enough for the outer side plate of the switch to clear the pin. Then remove the switch.

Installation

1. Position the new stoplamp switch so that it straddles the push rod, with the slot on the pedal pin and the switch outer frame hole just clearing the pin. Slide the switch downward onto the pin and push rod. Slide the assembly inboard toward the brake pedal arm.
2. Install the outer white nylon washer and the hairpin retainer.
3. Connect the stoplamp switch wire connector to the switch. Connect the negative battery cable.
4. Check the stoplights for proper operation with the engine running. stoplights should illuminate with less than 6 pounds applied to the brake pedal at the pad.

HIGH MOUNT STOP LIGHT

Removal and Installation

ESCORT/EXP, LYNX 2 and 4 DOOR HATCHBACK

1. Remove the two lens screws and lens. Drill out the two rivets holding the lamp body to the sheet metal.
2. With the lamp assembly detached from the vehicle, disconnect the lamp wire assembly from the wiring harness.
3. Installation is the reverse order of the removal procedure.

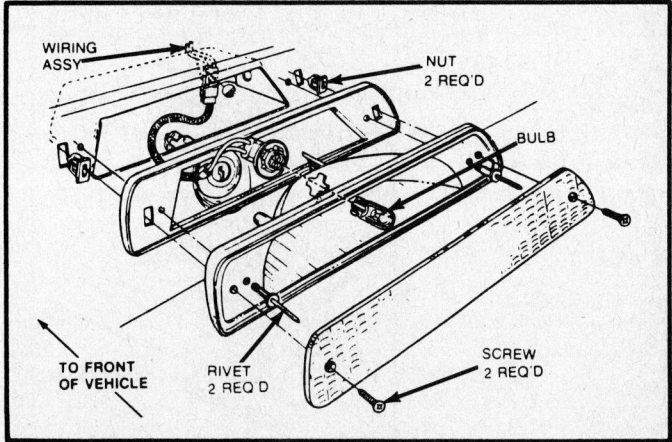

Removal and installation of the high mount stop light— Escort/Lynx wagon

SECTION 4

FORD MERCURY
FRONT WHEEL DRIVE CARS—ESCORT • EXP • LYNX • TEMPO • TOPAZ • TAURUS • SABLE

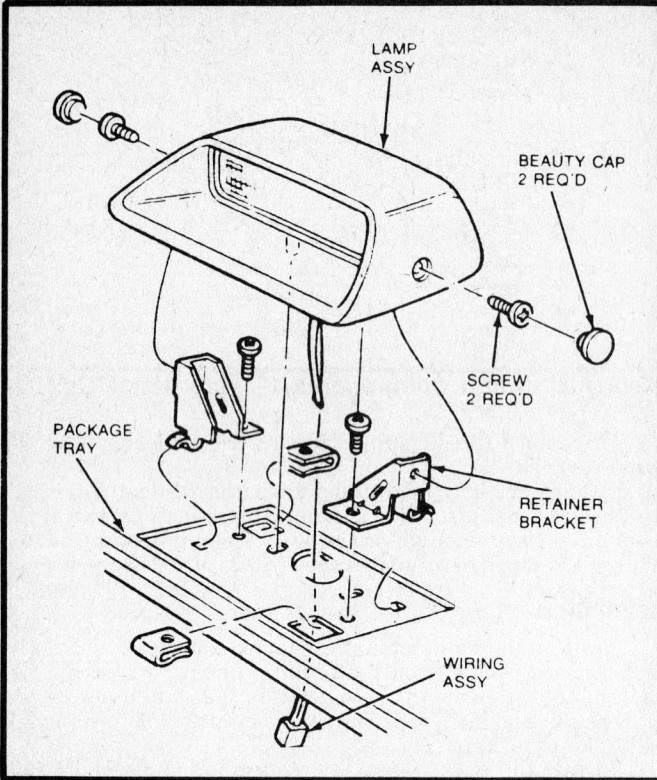

Removal and installation of the high mount stop light—Tempo/Topaz

ESCORT/LYNX WAGON

1. Remove the two screws from the lens face. With the lamp assembly detached from the bezel housing, disconnect the lamp wire assembly from the wire harness.
2. The bezel housing can be removed if necessary, by removing the two screws which secure the bezel housing to the vehicle.

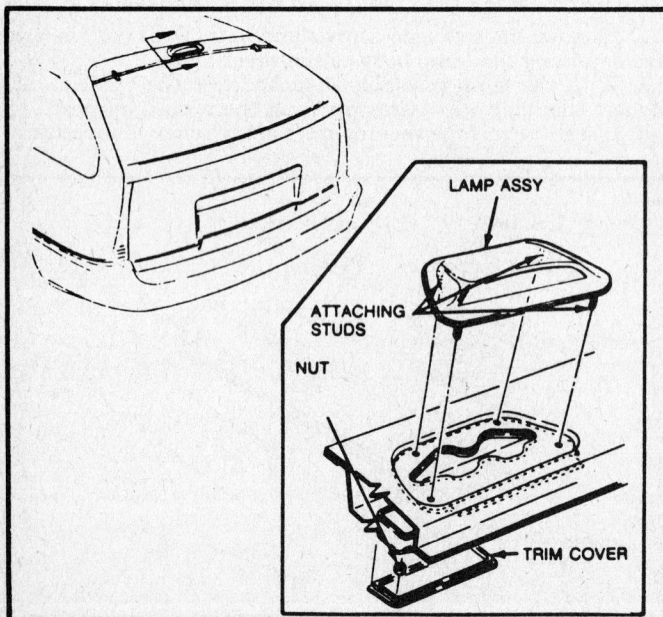

Removal and installation of the high mount stop light—Taurus/Sable wagon

3. Installation is the reverse order of the removal procedure.

TEMPO/TOPAZ

1. Locate the wire to the high mount stop light under the package tray, from inside ther luggage compartment. Pull the wire losse from the platic clip. Remove the two beauty caps from the lamp cover.
2. Remove the two screws which can be accessed from the side of the lamp. Pull the lamp assembly toward the front of the vehicle. The bulb sockets cab now be removed by turning them counterclockwise.
3. Installation is the reverse order of the removal procedure.

TAURUS/SABLE SEDAN MODELS

1. Remove the two screws which retain the lamp assembly to the retainer and remove the lamp assembly.
2. Installation is the reverse order of the removal procedure.

TAURUS/SABLE STATION WAGON MODELS

1. Remove the lamp assembly trim cover, located at the top of the liftgate frame. Remove the four nuts attached to the lamp mounting studs and remove the lamp assembly.
2. Installation is the reverse order of the removal procedure.

HEADLIGHT SWITCH

Removal and Installation
ALL MODELS EXCEPT TAURUS/SABLE

1. Disconnect batttery ground cable.
2. Insert a thin flat blade under flange at side of switch, to depress spring retaining clip. Twist blade to remove switch on one side.

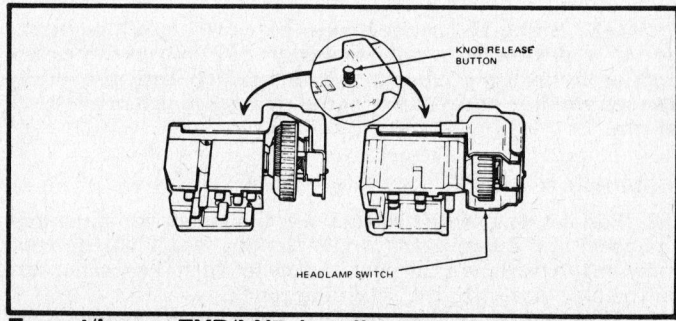

Escort/Lynx, EXP/LN7 headlamp switch knob release button (© Ford Motor Co.)

3. Repeat Step 2 on other side of switch.
4. Pull switch and connector out from instrument panel.
5. Disconnect electrical connector.

Installation

1. Install connector on switch.
2. Insert headlamp switch into instrument panel. Push on front face of switch until switch is retained by the spring clips.
3. Connect battery ground cable and test headlamp switch operation.

Removal and Installation
TAURUS/SABLE

1. Disconnect the negative battery cable. On the Taurus models, remove the headlight switch knob.
2. On the Taurus models, remove the bezel retaining nut and remove the bezel. On the Sable models, remove the lower left finish panel from the instrument panel.

Ford Mercury
FRONT WHEEL DRIVE CARS—ESCORT • EXP • LYNX • TEMPO • TOPAZ • TAURUS • SABLE
SECTION 4

3. On the Taurus models, remove the instrumnet cluster finish panel and remove the two screws retaining the headlamp switch to the instrument panel. Pull the switch out of the instrument panel and disconnect the electrical connector. Remove the switch from the vehicel.

4. On the Sable models, remove the two screws retaining the headlight switch to the finish panel, disconnect the electrical connector and remove the switch from the vehicle.

5. Installation is the reverse order of the removal procedure.

COMBINATION SWITCH

Removal
ALL MODELS EXCEPT THE TAURUS/SABLE

1. Disconnect the negative (ground) battery cable from the battery terminal.
2. Remove the five shroud screws and remove the lower shroud.
3. Loosen the four steering column attaching nuts enough to allow the removal of the upper trim shroud.
4. Remove the upper shroud.
5. Remove the turn signal switch lever by pulling the lever straight out from the switch. To make removal easier, work the outer end of the lever around with a slight rotary movement before pulling it out.
6. Peel back the foam sight shield from the turn signal switch.
7. Disconnect the two turn signal switch electrical connectors.
8. Remove the two self-tapping screws that attach the turn signal switch to the lock cylinder housing and disengage the switch from the housing.
9. Transfer the ground brush located in the turn signal switch cancelling cam to the new switch assembly on vehicles equipped with speed control.

Installation

1. Align the turn signal switch mounting holes with the corresponding holes in the lock cylinder housing and install two self-tapping screws until tight.
2. Stick the foam sight shield to the turn signal switch.
3. Install the turn signal switch lever into the switch by aligning the key on the lever with the keyway in the switch and pushing the lever toward the switch to full engagement.
4. Install two turn signal switch electrical connectors to full engagement.
5. Install the steering column trim shrouds.
6. Torque the steering column attaching nuts to 17–25 ft. lbs. (23–33 Nm).
7. Connect the negative (ground) battery cable to the battery terminal.
8. Check the steering column for proper operation.

Removal
TAURUS/SABLE

1. Disconnect the negative battery cable and if equipped with a tilt steering column, set the tilt column to its lowest position and remove the tilt lever by removing the allen head retaining screw.
2. Remove the ignition lock cylinder as previously outlined. Remove the three steering column shroud screws and remove the upper and lower shroud.
3. Remove the wiring harness retainer and disconnect the three electrical connectors.
4. Remove the two self tapping screws attaching the switch to the steering column and disengage the switch from the steering column.

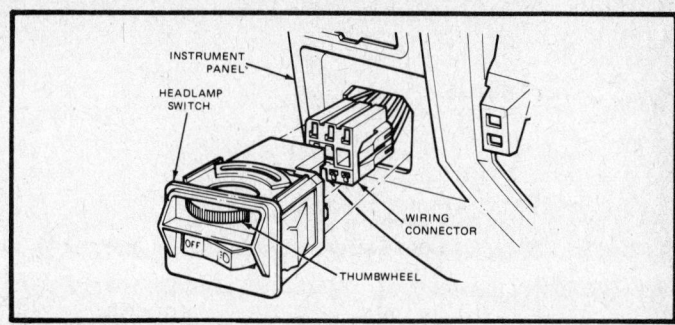
Headlamp switch mounting on Tempo/Topaz
(© Ford Motor Co.)

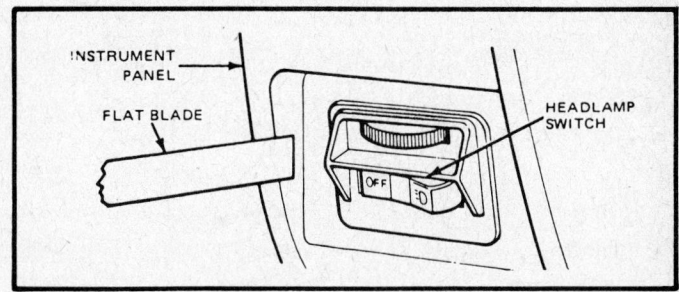
Headlamp switch removal (© Ford Motor Co.)

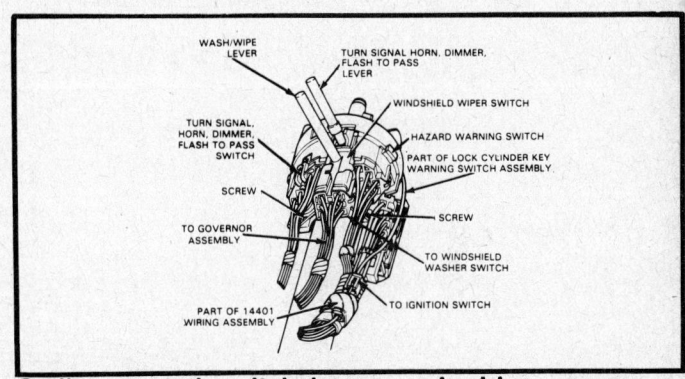
Stalk mounted switch levers and wiring assembly (© Ford Motor Co.)

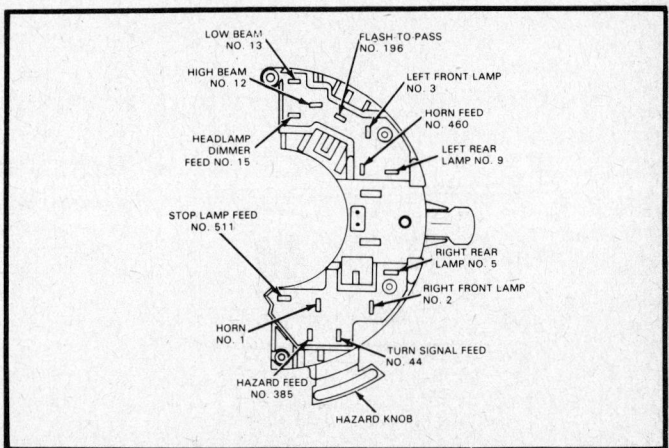
Electrical test circuits for the turnsignal switch
(© Ford Motor Co.)

4-19

SECTION 4

FORD MERCURY
FRONT WHEEL DRIVE CARS—ESCORT • EXP • LYNX • TEMPO • TOPAZ • TAURUS • SABLE

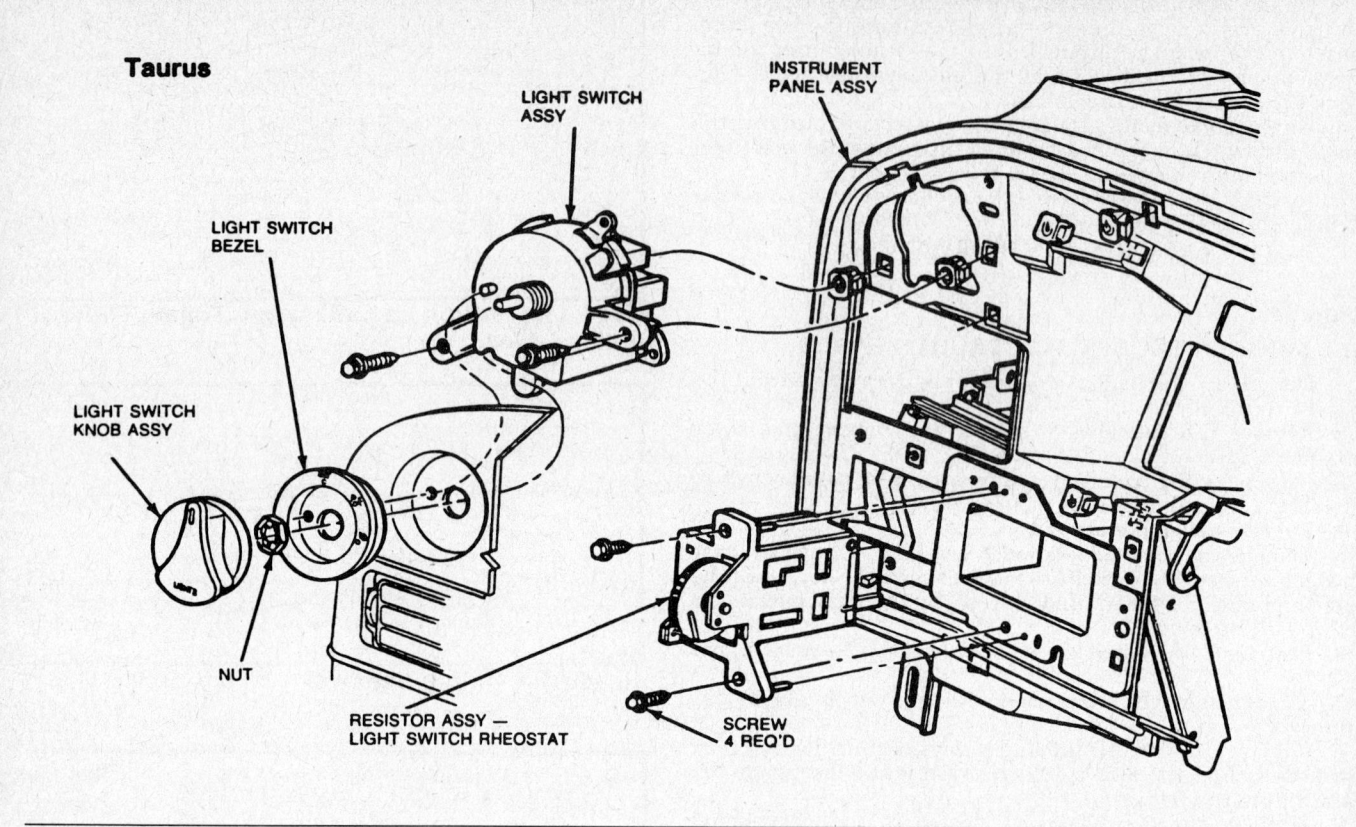

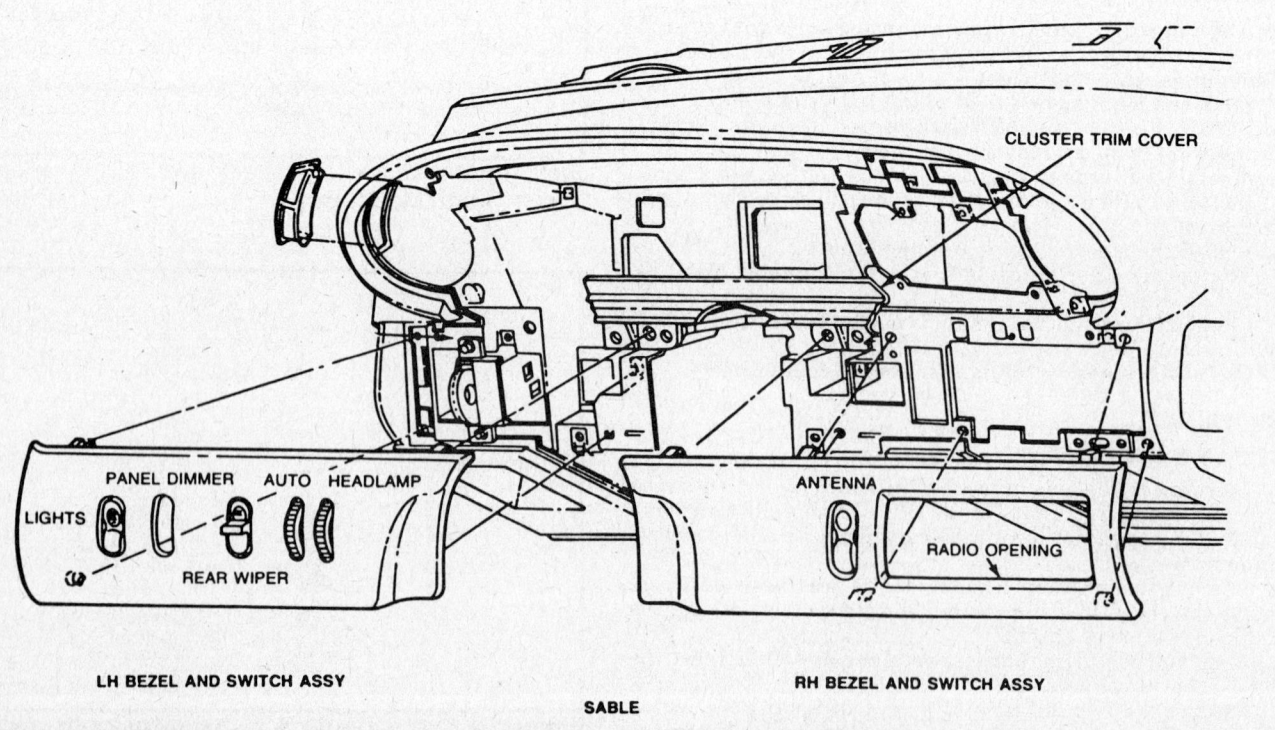

Headlight switch removal and installation—Taurus/Sable

Installation

1. Align the turn signal switch mounting holes with the corresponding holes in the steering column and install two self-tapping screws. Torque the screws to 18–27 in.lbs.
2. Install the three electrical connectors and install the wiring harness retainer.
3. Install the upper and lower steering column shroud and shroud retaining screws, torque the screws to 6–10 inch lbs.
4. Install the ignition lock cylinder. Attach the tilt lever (if so equipped) and torque the tilt lever allen head retaining screw to 6–9 inch lbs.
5. Connect the negative battery cable and check the switch along with the steering column for proper operation.

HORN SWITCH

Removal and Installation

ALL MODELS

NOTE: If the horn switch is installaed in the multi-function switch, refer to the COMBINATION SWITCH ASSEMBLY removal and installation procedure previously outlined in this section.

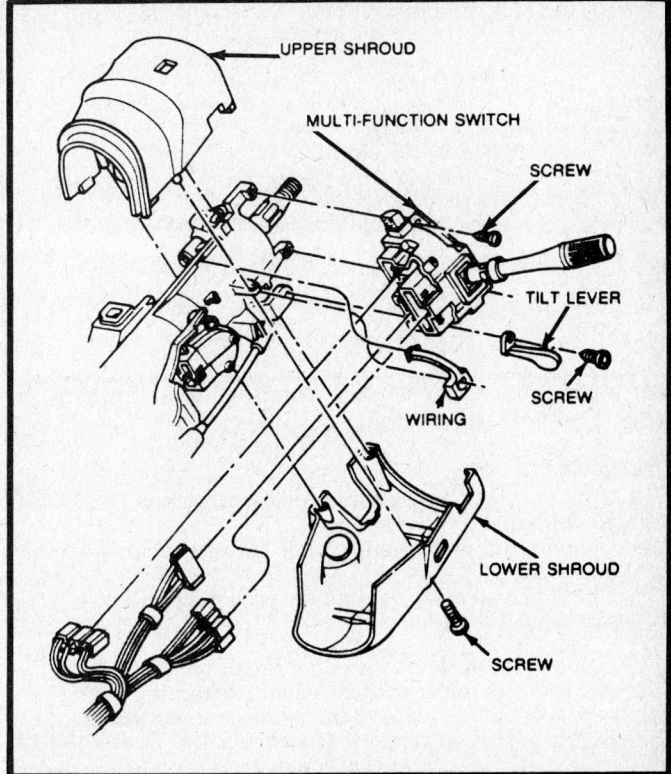

Multi-function switch removal and installation—Taurus/Sable

1. Remove the two screws (four on the later Escort/Lynx models) from the back of the steering wheel and lift off the horn cover pad.
2. Remove the foam pad if so equipped. Remove the wire connectors from the steering wheel terminals and remove the horn switch.
3. Installation is the reverse order of the removal procedure.

WIPER SWITCH

NOTE: The switch handle is an integral part of the switch and can not be removed sparately. On the Taurus/Sable models the wiper switch is incorporated in the multi-function switch on the steering column. If there is any need for repairs to the wiper switch the multi-function switch must be replaced as a assembly.

Removal

ESCORT/EXP, LYNX/LN7

1. Disconnect the negative (ground) battery cable from the battery terminal.
2. Loosen the steering column attaching nuts enough to remove the upper trim shroud.
3. Remove the trim shrouds.
4. Disconnect the quick connect electrical connector.
5. Peel back the foam sight shield. Remove the two hex-head screws holding the switch and remove the wash/wipe switch.

Installation

1. Position the switch on the column and install the two hex-head screws. Replace the foam sight shield over the switch.
2. connect the quick connect electrical connector.
3. Install the upper and lower trim shrouds.

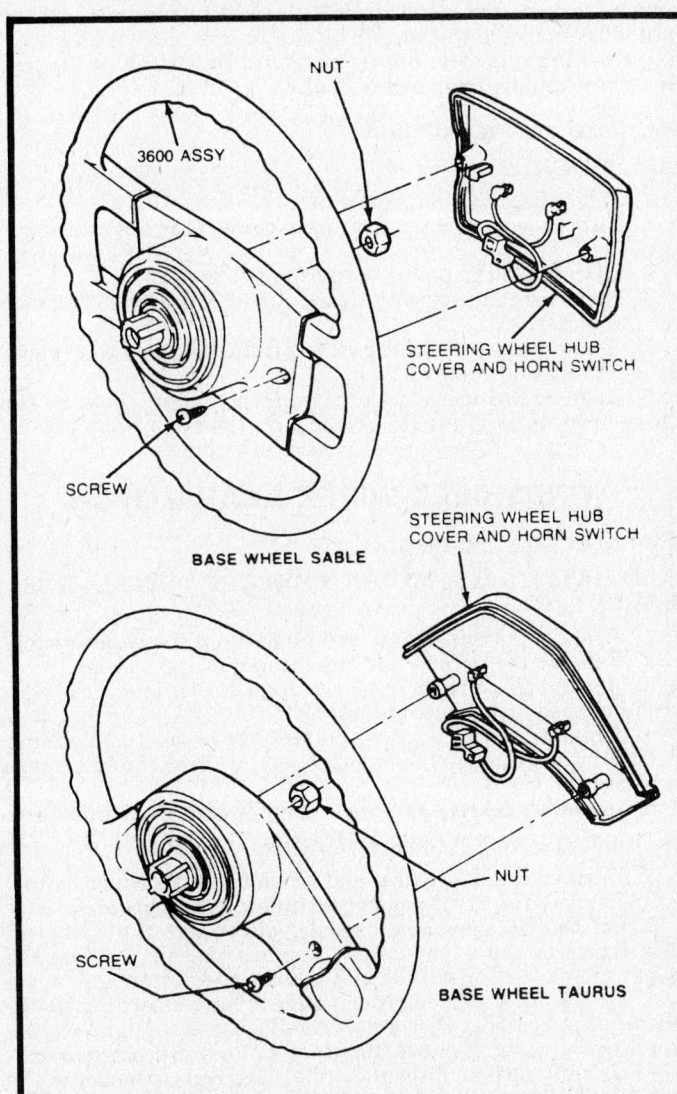

Horn switch removal and installation—Taurus/Sable

FORD MERCURY
FRONT WHEEL DRIVE CARS—ESCORT • EXP • LYNX • TEMPO • TOPAZ • TAURUS • SABLE

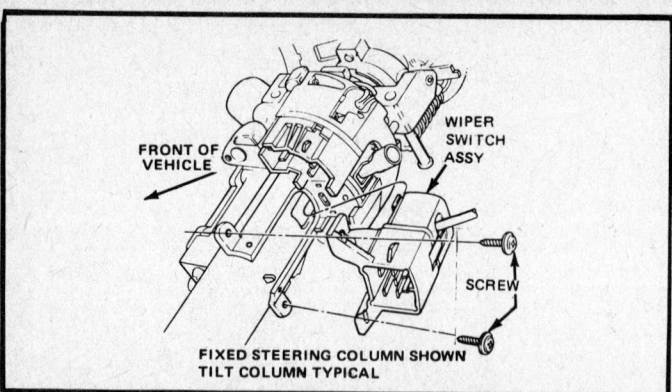

Tempo/Topaz wiper switch removal and installation (© Ford Motor Co.)

4. Tighten the steering column attaching nuts to 17–25 ft. lbs. (23–33 Nm).
5. Connect the negative (ground) battery cable to the battery terminal.
6. Check the steering column for proper operation.

TEMPO/TOPAZ

1. Remove the instrument panel finish panel.
2. Remove the wiper switch housing retaining screws and remove the switch housing from the instrument panel.
3. Remove (pull off) the wiper switch knob. Disconnect the electrical connectors from the switch assembly.
4. Remove the two screws holding the wiper switch in the switch housing plate and remove the switch.
5. Installation is the reverse order of the removal procedure.

INTERVAL GOVERNOR

The interval governor is located on the left-hand side of the steering column support bracket.

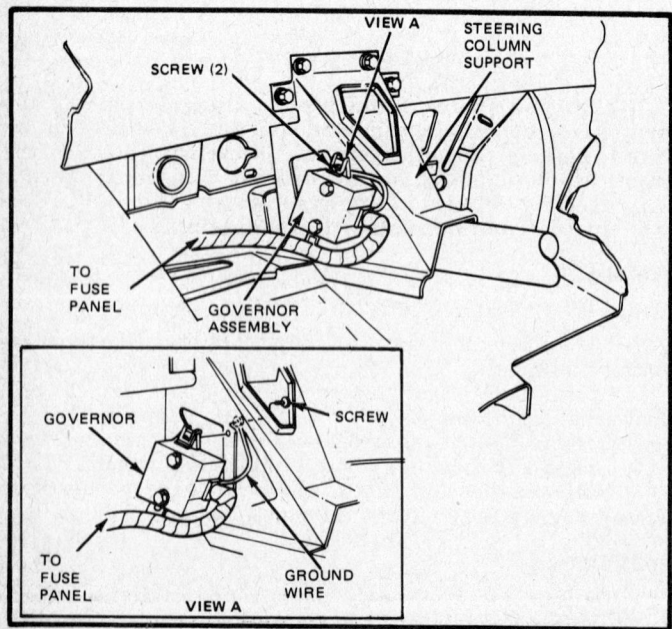

Interval wiper governor removal and installation (© Ford Motor Co.)

Removal and Installation
ALL MODELS

1. Disconnect battery ground cable.
2. Remove steering column shrouds.
3. Disconnect connectors On Tempo/Topaz, the connectors are connected to the fuse panel.
4. Remove two attaching screws (one has ground pigtail under it).

Installation

1. Position interval governor on steering column bracket and install attaching screws.

NOTE: Be sure to install ground wire.

2. Connect harness connectors. On Tempo/Topaz, the connectors are connected to the fuse panel.
3. Connect battery ground cable and check wiper system operation.
4. Install steering column shrouds.

WINDSHIELD WIPER FRONT MOTOR

NOTE: The internal permanent magnets used in the wiper motor are a ceramic (glass-like) material. Care must be exercised in handling the motor to avoid damaging the magnets. The motor must not be struck or tapped with a hammer or other object.

Removal and Installation
ALL MODELS

1. Disconnect the battery cables.
2. Lift the water shield cover from the cowl on the passenger side.
3. Disconnect the power lead from the motor.
4. Remove the linkage retaining clip from the operating arm on the motor.
5. Remove three attaching screws from the motor and bracket assembly and remove.
6. Remove the operating arm from the motor. Unscrew the three bolts an separate the motor form the mounting bracket.
7. To install, reverse the removal procedures.

WINDSHIELD WIPER REAR MOTOR

Removal and Installation
ALL HATCHBACK MODELS EXCEPT THE TAURUS/SABLE

1. Remove the wiper arm and blade from the wiper motor.
2. Remove the pivot shaft attaching nut and spacers.
3. Remove the liftgate inner trim panel. Disconnect the electrical connector to the wiper motor.
4. Remove the three screws holding the bracket to the inner door skin and remove the motor assembly, braket and linkage assembly.
5. Installation is the reverse order of the removal procedure.

ALL STATION WAGON MODELS

1. Remove the wiper arm and blade from the wiper motor.
2. Remove the pivot shaft attaching nut and spacers.
3. On the Taurus/Sable models, disconnect the electrical connectors to the wiper motor. Remove the nut holding the wiper motor to door handle and remove the motor.
4. On all other models, remove the screws attaching the license plate housing. Disconnect the license plate light and remove the housing. Remove the wiper motor and bracket assembly retaining screws, disconnect the electrical connector to the wiper motor and remove the motor.
5. Installation is the reverse order of the removal procedure.

REAR WIPER SWITCH

Removal and Installation
ALL MODELS

1. Remove the two or four cluster opening finish panel retaining screws and remove the finish panel by rocking the upper edge toward the driver.
2. Disconnect the wiring connector from the rear washer switch.
3. Remove the washer switch from the instrument panel. On the Sable models, the switch is attached to the instrument panel with two retaining screws.

Installation

1. Install the cluster opening finish panel and the two or four retaining screws.
2. Connect the wiring connector.
3. Push the rear washer switch into the cluster finish panel until it snaps into place (on the Sable models, install the two retaining screws).

WIPER LINKAGE

Removal and Installation
ALL MODELS

The wiper linkage is mounted below the cowl top panel and can be reached by raising the hood.

1. Remove the wiper arm and blade assembly from the pivot shaft. Pry the latch (on the arm) away from the shaft to unlock the arm from the pivot shaft.
2. Raise the hood and disconnect the negative battery cable. Remove the right and left leaf screens if so equipped.
3. Remove the clip and disconnect the linkage drive arm from the motor crank pin.
4. On Tempo/Topaz remove the cowl top grille.
5. On Tempo/Topaz remove the screws retaining the pivot assemblies to the cow.
6. On Escort/Lynx, EXP/LN7 remove the large pivot retainer nuts from each pivot shaft.
7. On the Taurus/Sable models, remove the screws attaching the pivot assemblies to the cowl panel.
8. Remove the linkage and pivot assembly from the cowl chamber.
9. Installation is the reverse of the removal procedure.

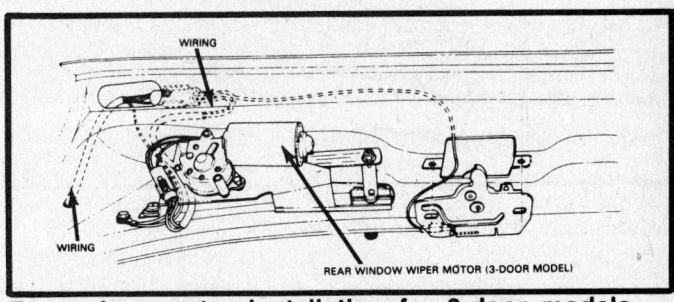
Rear wiper motor installation for 3-door models (© Ford Motor Co.)

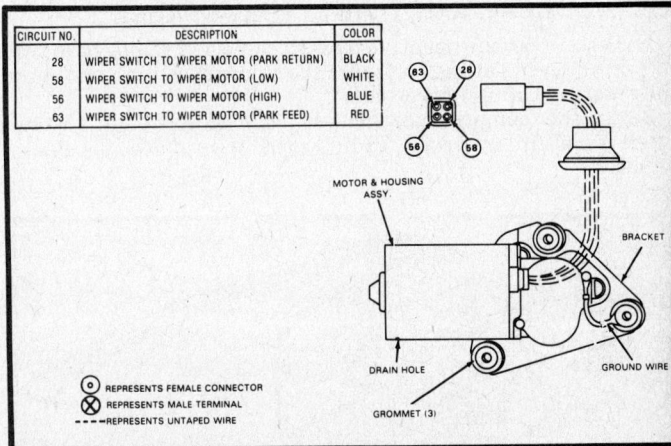
Wiper motor wiring identification and park position measurement (© Ford Motor Co.)

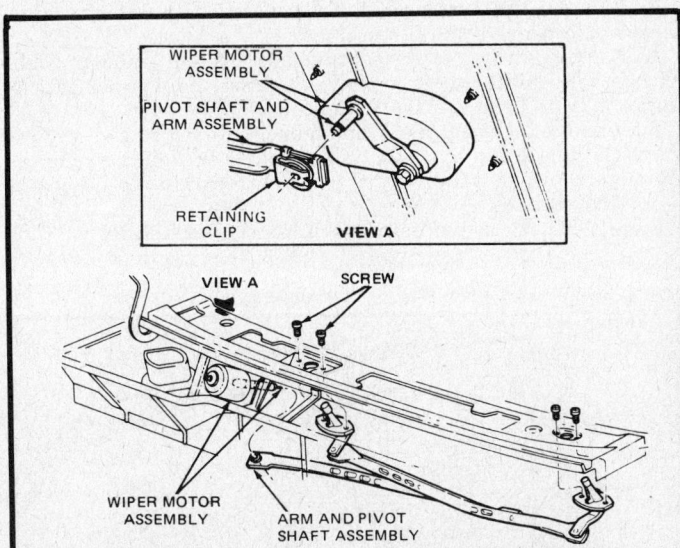
Tempo/Topaz wiper pivot shaft and linkage (© Ford Motor Co.)

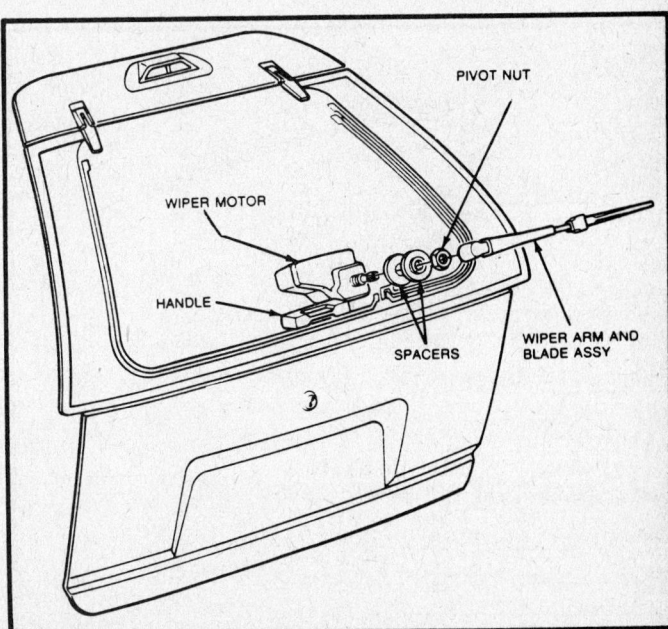
Rear windshield wiper motor—Taurus/Sable station wagon

SECTION 4
FORD MERCURY
FRONT WHEEL DRIVE CARS—ESCORT • EXP • LYNX • TEMPO • TOPAZ • TAURUS • SABLE

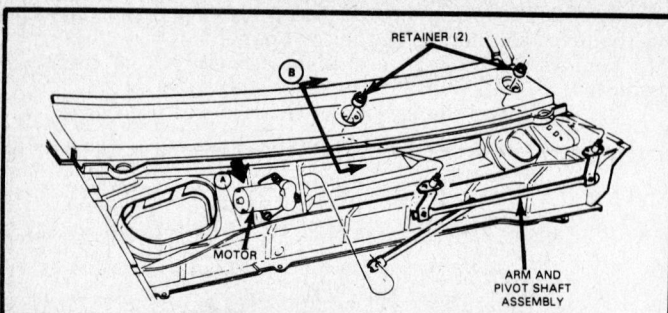

Escort/Lynx, EXP/LN7 wiper motor linkage removal and installation (© Ford Motor Co.)

INSTRUMENT CLUSTER

Removal and Installation

ALL MODELS EXCEPT THE TAURUS/SABLE

1. Disconnect the negative battery cable and remove the two retaining screws at the bottom of the steering column and snap the steering column cover out.
2. On the Tempo/Topaz models, remove the eight instrument panel finish screws, radio knobs and remove the finish panel.

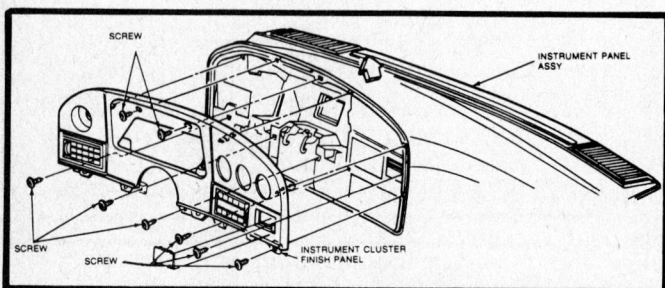

Instrument cluster removal and installation—Taurus

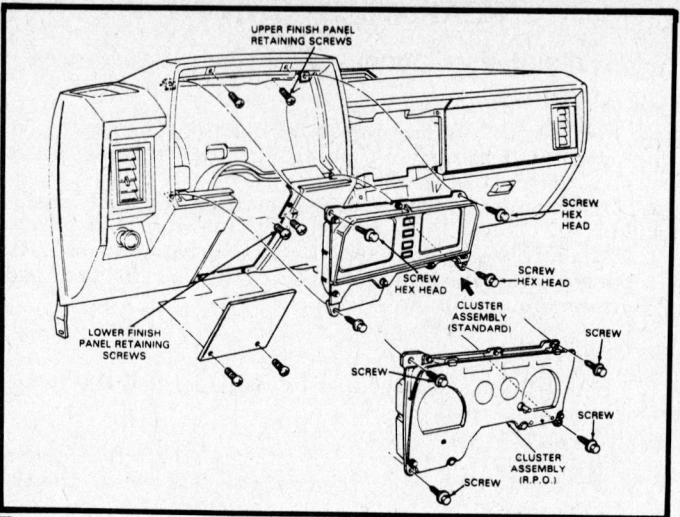

Escort/Lynx, EXP/LN7 instrument cluster assembly (© Ford Motor Co.)

3. On the Escort/Lynx, EXP models remove the four cluster opening finish panel retainer screws and remove the finish panel.
4. Remove the two upper and lower screws, and retaining cluster to remove the instrument panel.
5. From under the instrument panel, disconnect the speedometer cable by pressing the flat surface of the plastic quick connector.
6. Pull the cluster away from the instrument panel and disconnect the electrical feed plug to the cluster from its receptacle in the printed circuit.
7. To install, reverse the removal procedure.

TAURUS/SABLE

1. Disconnect the negative battery cable.
2. Disconnect the speedometer cable by dropping the fuse panel on its hinge to allow access to the speedometer cable latch attachment. Press the cable latch to disengage the cable from the speedometer head, while pulling the cable away from the speedometer.
3. Remove the instrument cluster finish panel retaining screws and remove the finish panel.
4. Remove the steering column shroud. On Sable models with a tachometer cluster, remove the lower trim panel attaching screws and remove the trim panel.
5. Remove the eight mask and lens mounting screws and remove the mask and lens. On Sable models equipped with a tachometer cluster, remove the two lower floodlamp bulb and socket assemblies.
6. Lift the main dial assembly from the backplate.

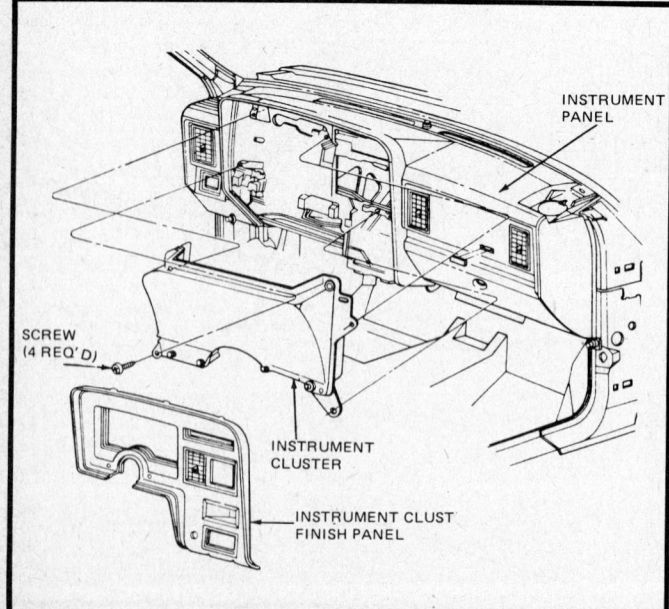

Tempo/Topaz instrument cluster removal and installation (© Ford Motor Co.)

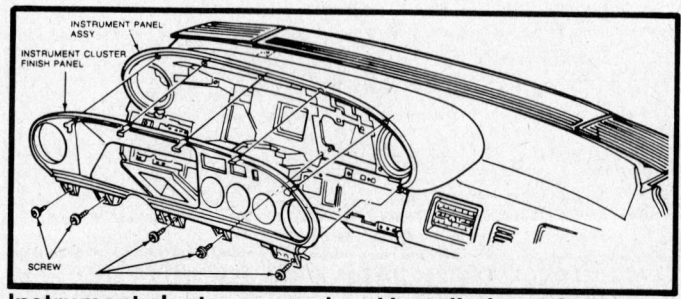

Instrument cluster removal and installation—Sable

Ford Mercury
FRONT WHEEL DRIVE CARS—ESCORT • EXP • LYNX • TEMPO • TOPAZ • TAURUS • SABLE

Section 4

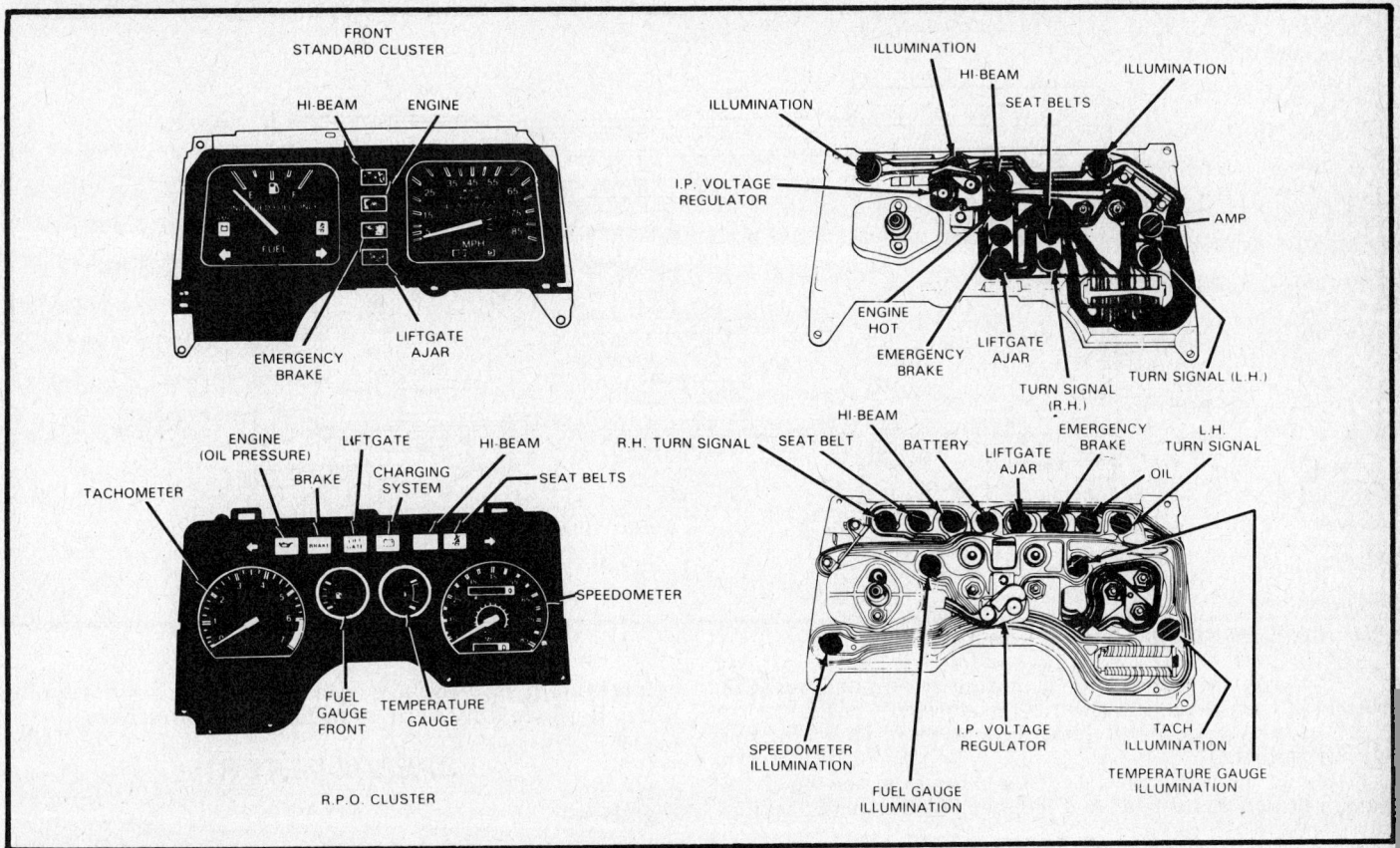

Two types of printed circuits used (© Ford Motor Co.)

NOTE: The speedometer, tachometer and gauges are mounted to the main dial and some effort may be required to pull the quick-connect electrical terminals from the clip.

7. On column shift vehicles only, remove the two screws attaching the transmission selector indicator to the main dial. Remove the transmission selector indicator from the main dial/instrument cluster.
8. Remove the four screws retaining the cluster to the instrument panel and remove the cluster.
9. Installation is the reverse order of the removal procedure.

PRINTED CIRCUIT
Removal
ALL MODELS EXCEPT THE TAURUS/SABLE

1. Disconnect the battery ground cable.
2. Remove the instrument cluster assembly.
3. Unsnap the printed circuit from the instrument voltage regulator (IVR). Remove the IVR attaching screw and remove the IVR.
4. Remove the illumination and indicator bulb and socket assemblies.
5. Remove the two screws retaining the cluster resistor and remove the resistor.
6. Remove the two fuel gauge attaching nuts. Remove the attaching nuts on the temperature gauge and tachometer, if so equipped.
7. Remove the printed circuit.

Installation

1. Position the printed circuit over the locating pins. If equipped with two printed circuits, position the smaller one first on the cluster backplate.
2. Reverse the removal procedure.

TAURUS/SABLE

1. Remove the instrument cluster as previously outlined in this section.
2. Remove the screws attaching the low fuel warning assembly to the instrument cluster and remove the low fuel warning assembly.
3. Remove all bulb and socket assemblies by twisting them out counterclockwise.
4. Remove the instrument dial assembly from the backplate. Remove the clips from the printed circuit board using a pair of needle nose pliers or equivalent.
5. Squeeze both ends of the clip equally so that the locking ears will slide throught the clip opening in the backplate. Push the clip through the opening.
6. Once all the clips have been removed, the printed circuit board can be removed.
7. Installation is the reverse order of the removal procedure.

ELECTRONIC INSTRUMENT CLUSTER
Removal and Installation
TAURUS/SABLE

1. Disconnect the negative battery cable. Remove the two lower panel trim covers.
2. Remove the steering column cover and disconnect the transmission selector indicator cable from the steering column.
3. Remove the cluster trim panel and disconnect the electrical connector to the switch module.

4-25

SECTION 4

Ford Mercury
FRONT WHEEL DRIVE CARS—ESCORT • EXP • LYNX • TEMPO • TOPAZ • TAURUS • SABLE

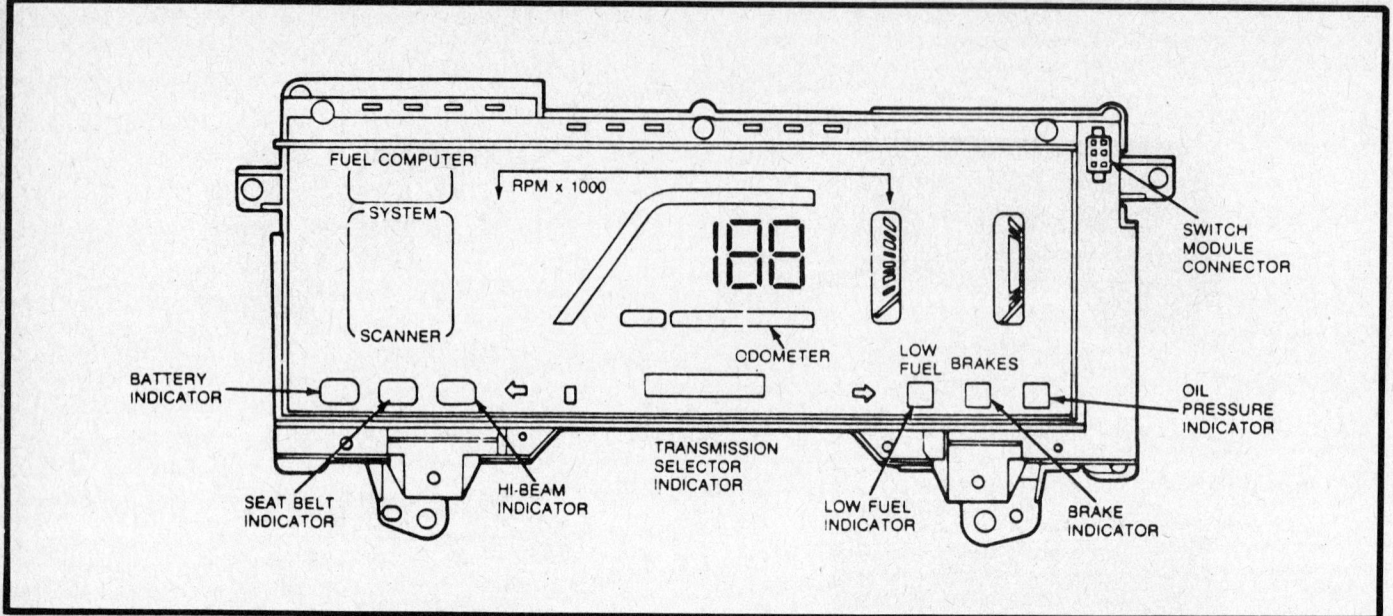

Electronic instrument cluster—Taurus/Sable

4. Remove the four cluster mounting screws and pull the bottom of the cluster out towards the steering wheel.
5. Disconnect the three cluster connectors, from behind the cluster assembly.
6. Swing the bottom of the cluster out to clear the top of the cluster from the crash pad and then remove the cluster assembly from the vehicle.
7. Installation is the reverse order of the removal procedure.

GRAPHIC WARNING DISPLAY MODULE
Removal
1. Remove the console finish trim panel by prying at the bottom to disengage the three retainers.
2. Remove the four module retaining screws.
3. Pull the module outward, disconnect the electrical connectors and remove the module.

Installation
Reverse the removal procedure. Make sure the locator pegs are properly seated in their respective holes before tightening the retaining screws.

— CAUTION —

Do not hook up additional lights or attach external trailer lights on the vehicle. Improper hook-up may result in false warning or no warning. Substitution of headlamp bulbs other than original equipment (such as halogen for conventional) bulbs will result in a false warning or no warning.

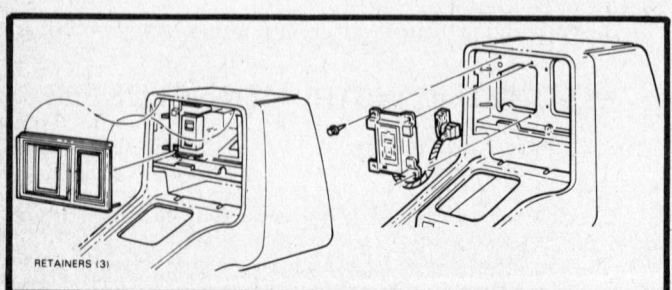

Console graphic warning display module
(© Ford Motor Co.)

NOTE: Do not replace resistance wire with regular wire. Replace only with complete wiring harness.

SPEEDOMETER
Removal
ALL MODELS EXCEPT THE TAURUS/SABLE
1. Disconnect battery ground cable.
2. Reach under the instrument panel and disconnect the speedometer cable by pressing on the flat surface of the plastic connector (quick-connect) and remove the instrument cluster.
3. Remove seven screws that retain the lens and mask to the backplate.
4. Remove screws retaining the fuel gauge and speedometer assembly.

Installation
1. Install speedometer head assembly into cluster.
2. Install seven retaining screws to retain the lens and mask to the backplate.
3. Install instrument cluster.
4. Connect battery ground and check operation of speedometer.

Removal and Installation
TAURUS/SABLE
1. Remove the instrument cluster finish panel retaining screws and remove the finish panel.
2. Remove the eight mask-and-lens mounting screws and remove the mask and lens. On the Sable models, remove the two lower floodlamp bulb and socket assemblies.
3. Remove the entire dial assembly from the instrument cluster by carefully pulling it away from the cluster backplate.

NOTE: The speedometer, tachometer and gauges are mounted to the main dial and some effort may be required to pull the quick-connect electrical terminals from the clip.

4. On column shift vehicles only, remove the two screws attaching the transmission selector indicator to the main dial. Remove the transmission selector indicator from the main dial/

instrument cluster. On the Sable models, remove the odometer drive jack shaft and remove the attachment clip at the odometer, slip the jack shaft out of the odometer bracket and speedometer bridge.

5. Pull the reset knob from the trip odometer, if so equipped. To remove the speedometer from the main dial, manually rotate the speedometer pointer to align it with the slot in the dial. Remove the mounting screws and carefully pull the speedometer away from the dial, making sure to guide the pointer through the slot.

6. Installation is the reverse order of the removal procedure.

SPEEDOMETER CABLE

Removal

1. Reach under the instrument panel and disconnect the speedometer cable housing by pressing on the flat surface of the plastic connector (quick-connect).
2. Pull speedometer cable out of the upper end of the casing.
3. If cable is broken, raise the vehicle on a hoist and remove cable from transaxle or speed control speed sensor if equipped.
4. Remove the lower part of the broken cable from low end of the casing.

Installation

1. Determine the exact length of the old core and cut the new core following the instructions included in the core kit.
2. Install the new cable into casing, inserting it from the speedometer end.
3. Connect the speedometer casing to the transaxle and speedometer.

DUAL WARNING BUZZER LOCATION

The key warning buzzer and the seat belt timer buzzer are combined in one package. The dual buzzer assembly is located behind the instrument panel near the left side of the radio. The Headlamp On warning system also operates the key warning buzzer.

SEAT BELT WARNING LAMP

The warning lamp glows for approximately eight seconds after the ignition switch is turned to the On or Run position, power is supplied through the circuit, the timer buzzer and one side of the seat belt warning lamp through the circuit. The opposite side of the seat belt warning lamp through the circuit. The opposite side of the lamp goes directly to ground.

The timer buzzer goes to ground through the seat belt switch circuit. When the seat belt is engaged, the timer buzzer ground circuit is opened.

KEY IN IGNITION WARNING BUZZER

The warning buzzer sounds when the driver's door is open with the key in the ignition switch. It sounds until the door is closed or the key is removed.

When key is in ignition switch and driver's door is opened, power is supplied through circuit to buzzer and one side of the key switch through the circuit. The opposite side of the key switch goes directly to ground.

CIRCUIT BREAKERS

Circuit breakers are used to protect the various components of the electrical system, such as headlights and windshield wipers. The circuit breakers are located either in the control switch or mounted on or near the fuse panel.

TURN SIGNAL FLASHER, HAZARD WARNING FLASHER AND FUSE BLOCK LOCATION CHART

Ford Motor Co.	1983–87 TSF	1983–87 HWF	1983–87 Fuse Block Location
Escort	①	④	②
Lynx	①	④	③
EXP	①	④	②
LN7	①	④	②
Tempo	①	⑤	③
Topaz	①	⑤	③
Taurus	①	②	⑥
Sable	①	②	⑥

① The turn signal flasher is plugged directly into the fuse block.
② The hazard flasher is plugged directly into the fuse block.
③ The fuse panel is located on the driver's side of the dash panel, adjacent to the parking brake mechanism.
④ The hazard flasher is mounted to the instrument panel and is located between the steering column and fuse block.
⑤ The hazard flasher is located in the rear of the fuse block.
⑥ The fuse block is located in a swing down compartment located below the parking brake release handle.

FUSIBLE LINKS

Fusible links are used to prevent major wire harness damage in the event of a short circuit or an overload condition in the wiring circuits that are normally not fused, due to carrying high amperage loads or because of their locations within the wiring harness. Each fusible link is of a fixed value for a specific electrical load and should a fusible link fail, the cause of the failure must be determine and repaired prior to installing a new fusible link of the same value.

SPEED CONTROL SYSTEM (Automatic Transaxle)

Vehicles equipped with automatic transaxles use a shorting plug instead of a clutch switch.

Actuator Cable Adjustment

TEMPO/TOPAZ AND TAURUS/SABLE WITH 2.5L ENGINE

1. With engine Off, set carburetor so that throttle plate is closed and choke linkage is de-cammed.
2. Remove locking pin.

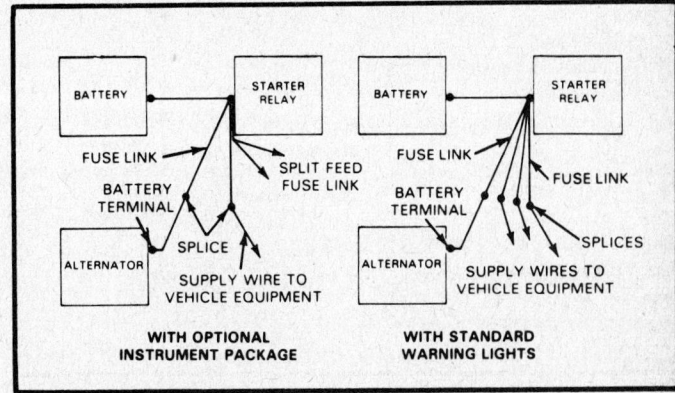

Fusible link locations (© Ford Motor Co.)

Ford Mercury
FRONT WHEEL DRIVE CARS—ESCORT • EXP • LYNX • TEMPO • TOPAZ • TAURUS • SABLE

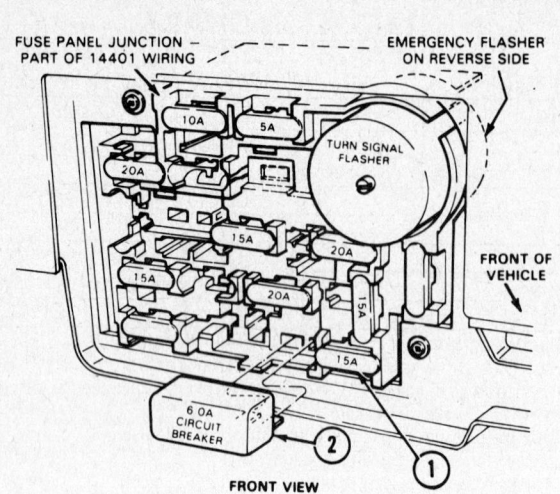

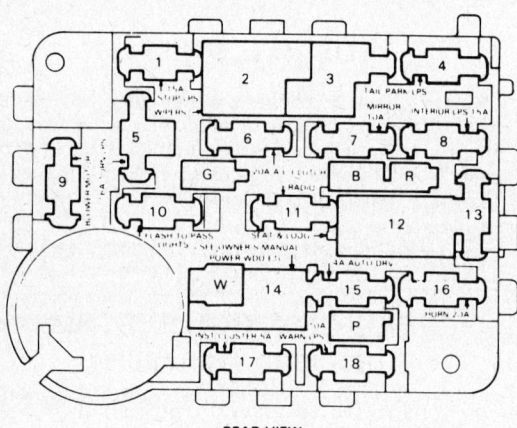

FUSE/CIRCUIT BREAKER USAGE

1. Stop Lamps, Hazard Warning Lamps
   15 Amp Fuse
2. Windshield Wiper, Windshield Washer Pump, Interval Wiper
   6 Amp Circuit Breaker
3. Not Used
4. Taillamps, Parking Lamps, Side Marker Lamps, Cluster Illumination Lamp, License Lamp
   15 Amp Fuse
5. Turn Signal Lamps, Back up Lamps
   15 Amp Fuse
6. Air Conditioner Clutch, Heated Backlite Relay, Liftgate Release, Speed Control Module, Rear Wiper/Washer, Electronic Digital Clock Display, Graphics Display Module, Air Conditioner Throttle Positioner
   20 Amp Fuse
7. Not used
8. Courtesy Lamps, Key Warning Buzzer
   15 Amp Fuse
9. Air Conditioner Blower Motor
   30 Amp Fuse
   Heater Blower Motor
   15 Amp Fuse
10. Flash-to-pass
    20 Amp Fuse
11. Radio, Tape Player, Premium Sound with one Amplifier
    15 Amp Fuse
12. Not Used
13. Not Used
14. Not Used
15. Not Used
16. Horn, Front Cigar Lighter
    20 Amp Fuse
17. Instrument Cluster Illumination Lamps, Radio, Climate Control
    5 Amp Fuse
18. Warning Indicator Lamps, Low Fuel Module, Auto Lamp System, Dual Timer Buzzer, Tachometer

Fuse and circuit breaker locations, typical
(© Ford Motor Co.)

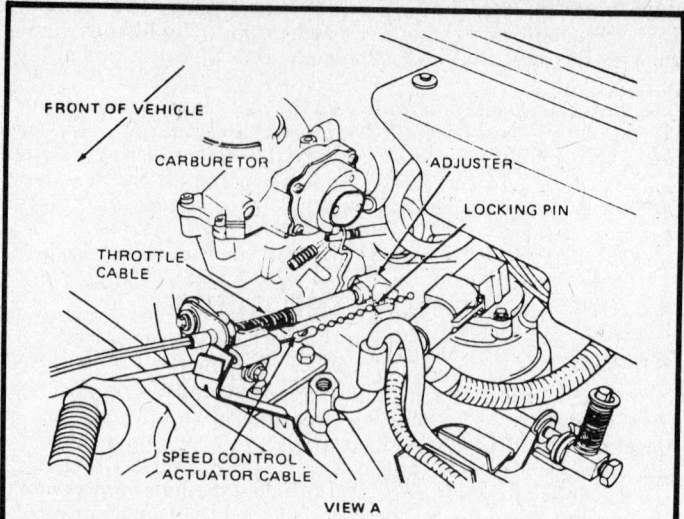

Speed control—Tempo/Topaz, gasoline engine
(© Ford Motor Co.)

3. Pull bead chain through adjuster.
4. Insert locking pin in best hole of adjuster for tight bead chain without opening throttle plate.

ESCORT/LYNX, EXP/LN7 AND TAURUS/SABLE 3.0L ENGINE

1. Remove cable retaining clip.
2. Disengage throttle positioner.
3. Set Carburetor at hot idle.
4. Pull on actuator cable end tube to take up any slack. Maintain a light tension on cable.
5. While holding cable, insert cable retaining clip and snap securely.

VACUUM DUMP VALVE

Adjustment

1. Firmly depress brake pedal and hold in position.
2. Push in dump valve until valve collar bottoms against retaining clip.
3. Place 0.050–0.100 in. (1.27–2.54mm) shim between white button of valve and pad on brake pedal.
4. Firmly pull brake pedal rearward to its normal position allowing dump valve to ratchet backwards in retaining clip.

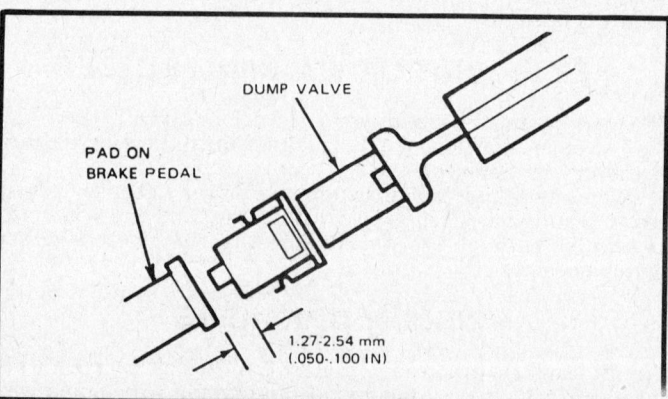

Dump valve—correctly adjusted
(© Ford Motor Co.)

Ford Mercury
FRONT WHEEL DRIVE CARS—ESCORT • EXP • LYNX • TEMPO • TOPAZ • TAURUS • SABLE

CLUTCH SWITCH

Adjustment

1. Prop clutch pedal in full-up position (pawl fully released from sector).
2. Loosen switch mounting screw.
3. Slide switch forward towards clutch pedal until switch plunger cap is 0.030 in. (0.76mm) from contacting switch housing. Then, tighten attaching screw.
4. Remove prop from clutch pedal and test drive for clutch switch cancellation of a speed control.

SERVO ASSEMBLY

Removal

ESCORT/LYNX, EXP

1. Remove air cleaner wing nut and move air cleaner assembly toward left side of vehicle.

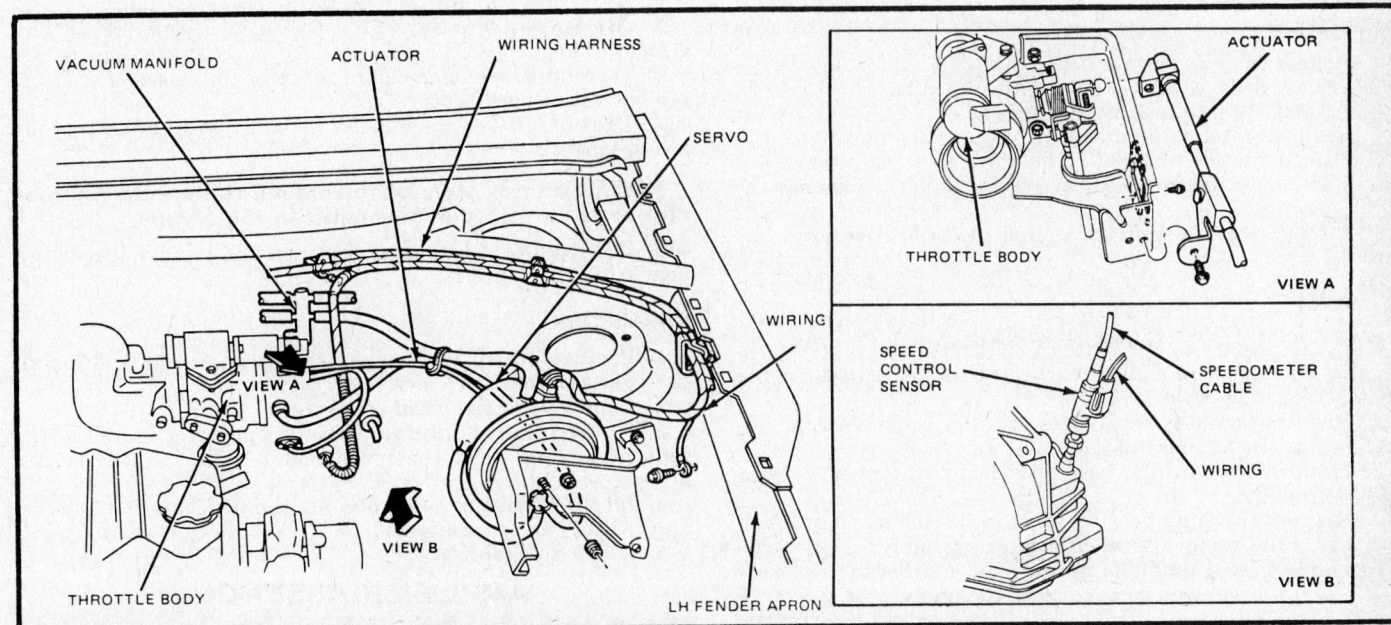
Speed control—Escort/Lynx, EXP—gas engine w/E.F.I. (© Ford Motor Co.)

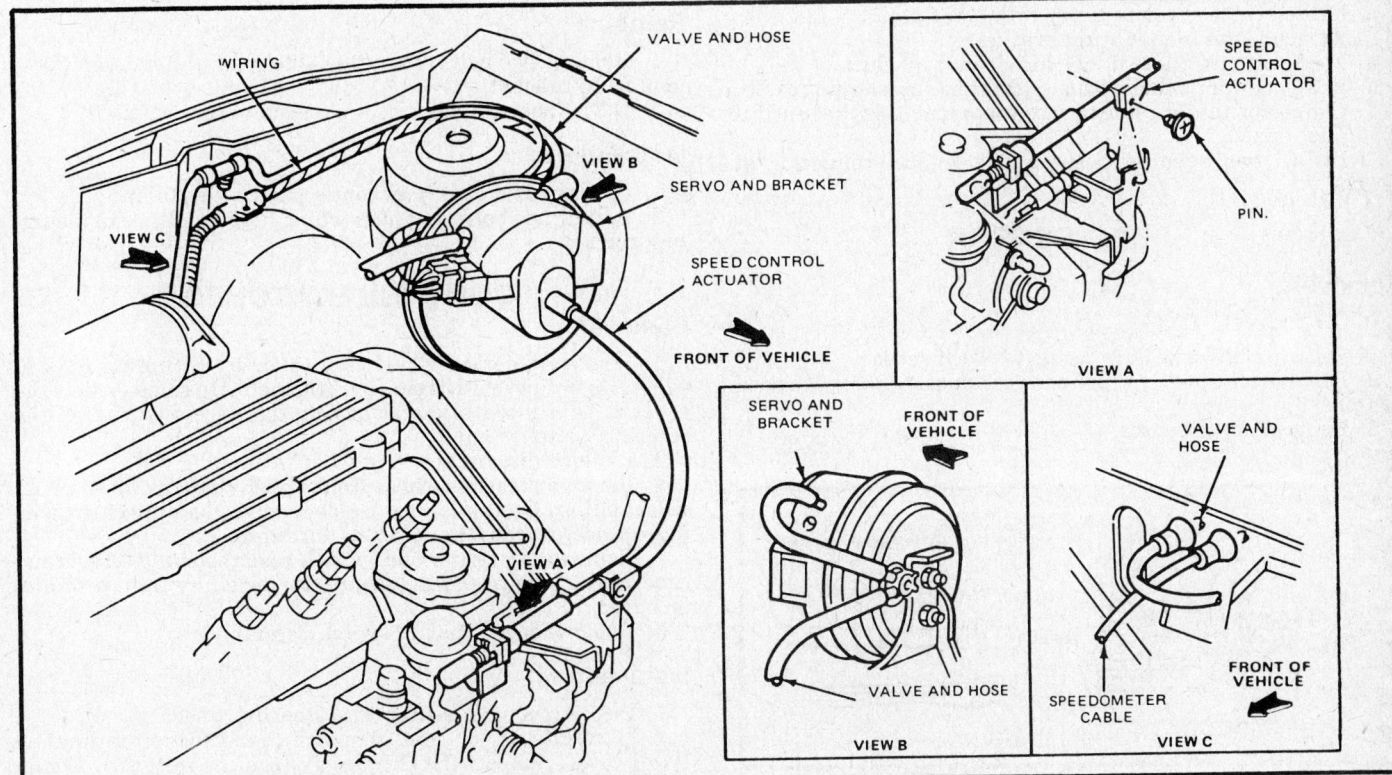
Speed control 2.0L diesel engine (© Ford Motor Co.)

SECTION 4 — FORD MERCURY
FRONT WHEEL DRIVE CARS — ESCORT • EXP • LYNX • TEMPO • TOPAZ • TAURUS • SABLE

2. Remove push pin and disconnect speed control actuator cable from accelerator cable bracket.
3. Disconnect speed control actuator cable with adjuster from accelerator cable.
4. Remove two vacuum hoses and electrical connector from servo assembly.
5. Remove two nuts holding servo to mounting bracket.
6. Carefully remove servo and cable assembly.
7. Remove two nuts holding cable cover to servo.
8. Pull off cover and remove cable assembly.

Installation
1. Attach cable to servo.
2. Attach cable cover to servo with two nuts.
3. Attach servo to mounting bracket.
4. Feed actuator cable under air cleaner air duct.
5. Snap actuator cable with adjuster onto accelerator cable.
6. Connect actuator cable to accelerator cable bucket and install push pin.
7. Install two vacuum hoses and electrical connector at servo.

Removal
TEMPO/TOPAZ AND TAURUS/SABLE
1. Remove screw and disconnect speed control actuator cable from accelerator cable.
2. Disconnect the speed control actuator cable with the adjuster from the accelerator cable.
3. Remove two vacuum hose and electrical connector from servo assembly.
4. Remove two nuts holding servo to its mounting bracket.
5. Carefully remove servo and cable assembly.
6. Remove two nuts holding cable cover to servo.
7. Pull off cover and remove cable assembly.

Installation
1. Attach cable to servo.
2. Attach cable cover to servo with two nuts.
3. Attach servo to mounting bracket.
4. Feed actuator cable under air cleaner air duct.
5. Snap actuator cable with adjuster onto accelerator cable.
6. Connect actuator cable to accelerator cable bucket and install push pin.
7. Install two vacuum hoses and electrical connector at servo.

SPEED SENSOR

Removal
ESCORT/LYNX, EXP
1. Separate electrical connector to speed sensor.
2. Disconnect upper and lower speedometer cables at speed sensor.
3. Remove speed sensor.

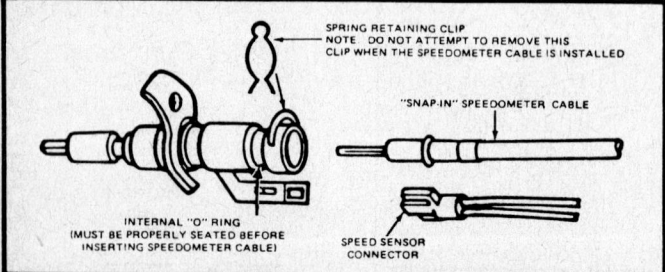
Speed sensor installation (© Ford Motor Co.)

Installation
1. Install speed sensor.
2. Install new O-ring seals on sensor.
3. Connect upper and lower speedometer cables.
4. Connect electrical connector.

Removal
TEMPO/TOPAZ AND TAURUS/SABLE
1. Raise the vehicle on a hoist and remove the bolt retaining the speed sensor mounting clip to the transmission.
2. Remover the sensor and driven gear from the transmission.
3. Disconnect the electrical connector and speedometer cable from the speed sensor.
4. Disconnect the speedometer cable by pulling it out of the speed sensor.

NOTE: Do not attempt to remove the spring retainer clip with the speedometer cable in the sensor.

5. Remove the driven gear retainer and remove the driven gear from the sensor.

Installation
1. Position the driven gear to the speed sensor and install the gear retainer.
2. Connect the electrical connector.
3. Insure that the internal O-ring is properly seated in the sensor housing. Snap the speedometer cable into the sensor housing.
4. Insert the sensor assembly into the transmission housing and install the retaining bolt.
5. Lower the vehicle.

AMPLIFIER ASSEMBLY

The amplifier is located below the steering column on the instrument panel reinforcement.

Removal
1. Remove two bolts and nuts holding amplifier assembly to mounting bracket.
2. Disconnect two electrical connectors at amplifier.

Installation
1. Connect two electrical connectors to amplifier.
2. Install two bolts and nuts which hold amplifier to mounting bracket.

CONTROL SWITCHES

Removal
1. Remove steering wheel hub cover by lifting on outside edges. Do not pry with a sharp instrument. On some models the cover is held in with two attaching screws in the rear of the steering wheel.
2. Remove discard steering wheel attaching nut.
3. Remove steering wheel from upper shaft using steering wheel puller. On the Taurus/Sable models, disconnect the wiring connector from the slip ring terminal.
4. Remove steering wheel to back cover attching screws and separate the control switch connector carefully from terminal on cover.
5. Remove speed control switch assembly.

Installation
1. Position control switch into steering wheel.
2. Carefully attach control switch connector to terminal on lower cover. Support the slip rings at the connector while sliding on connector.

Ford Mercury
FRONT WHEEL DRIVE CARS—ESCORT • EXP • LYNX • TEMPO • TOPAZ • TAURUS • SABLE
SECTION 4

3. Position lower cover to steering wheel (be sure the control switch wire harness is positioned properly in spoke). Install cover retaining screws.
4. Position steering wheel on end of steering shaft. (Be sure index mark on the wheel matches mark on steering shaft.)
5. Install a new steering wheel nut. Tighten nut to 30–40 ft. lbs.(41–54 Nm).
6. Install steering wheel hub cover.

CLUTCH SWITCH

Removal

1. Remove bracket mounting screw.
2. Discount electrical connector.
3. Remove switch and bracket assembly.
4. Remove switch from bracket.

Installation

1. Install switch on bracket.
2. Connect electrical connector.
3. Install bracket mounting screw.
4. Adjust clutch switch as outlined.

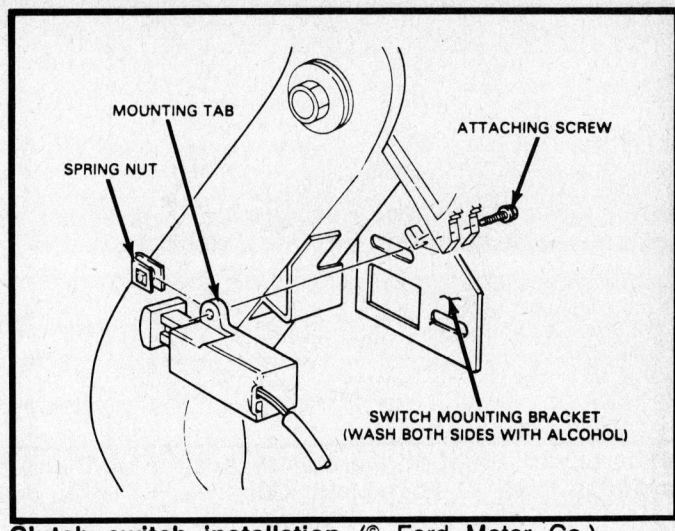
Clutch switch installation (© Ford Motor Co.)

COOLING AND HEATING SECTION

WATER PUMP

Removal and Installation
1.6L AND 1.9L ENGINES

1. Disconnect the negative battery cable. Drain the cooling system.
2. Remove the alternator drive belt. If equipped with air conditioning or power steering, remove the drive belts.
3. Use a wrench on the crankshaft pulley to rotate the engine to TDC of the compression stroke on the number one cylinder.

— **CAUTION** —
Turn the engine only in the direction of normal rotation. Backward rotation will cause the camshaft belt to slip or lose teeth.

4. Remove the timing belt cover.
5. Loosen the belt tensioner attaching bolts, using torque wrench adapter T81P-6254-A or equivalent. Then secure the tensioner over as far as possible.
6. Pull the belt from the camshaft, tensioner, and water pump sprockets. Do not remove it from, or allow it to change its position on, the crankshaft sprocket.

NOTE: Do not rotate the engine with the camshaft belt removed.

7. Remove the camshaft sprocket.
8. Remove the rear timing cover stud. Remove the heater return tube hose connection at the water pump inlet tube.
9. Remove the water pump inlet tube fasteners and the inlet tube and gasket.
10. Remove the water pump to cylinder block bolts and remove the water pump and its gasket.
11. To install, make sure the mating surfaces on the pump and the block are clean.
12. Using a new gasket and sealer, install the water pump and tighten the bolts to 5–7 ft. lbs. Make sure the pump impeller turns freely.
13. Install remaining parts in the reverse order of removal. Use new gaskets and sealer. Install the camshaft sprocket over the cam key.

14. Refer to Engine Section for timing belt installation procedures.

Removal and Installation
2.3L ENGINE

1. Drain engine coolant.
2. Disconnect the negative ground cable at the battery.
3. Loosen thermactor pump adjusting bolt and remove belt.
4. Remove thermactor pump hose clamp located below the thermactor pump.

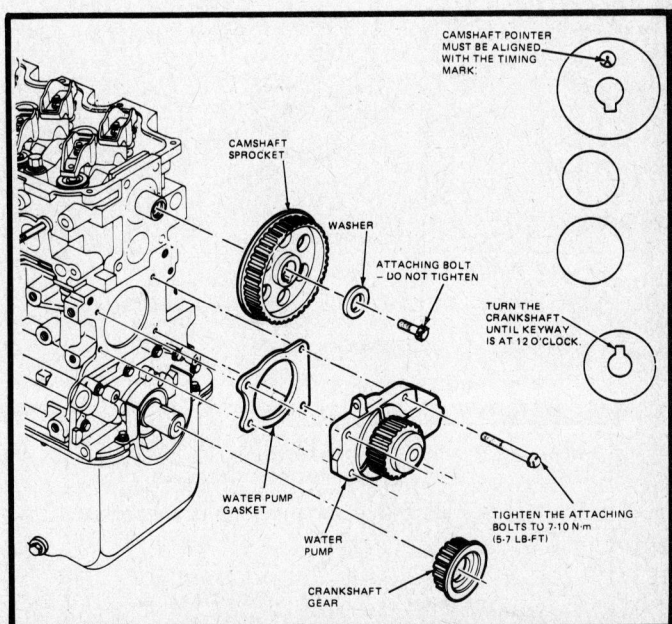
Escort/Lynx, EXP/LN7 water pump location and timing gear alignment for timing belt installation (© Ford Motor Co.)

4-31

Ford Mercury
FRONT WHEEL DRIVE CARS—ESCORT • EXP • LYNX • TEMPO • TOPAZ • TAURUS • SABLE

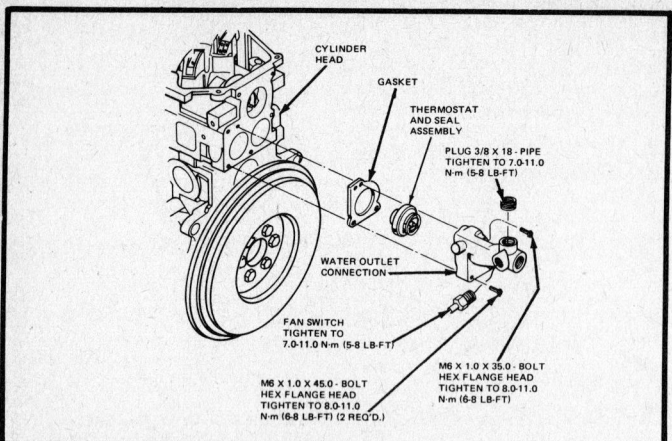

Escort/Lynx, EXP/LN7 thermostat location on the cylinder head (© Ford Motor Co.)

5. Remove three thermactor pump bracket bolts.
6. Remove thermactor pump and bracket as an assembly.
7. Loosen water pump idler pulley and remove the belt from the water pump pulley.
8. Disconnect the heater hose at the water pump.
9. Remove the three water pump bolts.
10. To install, clean both gasket mating surfaces on the water pump and cylinder block.
11. Coat the new gasket on both sides with a water resistant sealer and position on the cylinder block.
12. Install the three water pump bolts. Tighten to 15–22.5 ft. lbs. (20–30 Nm).
13. Connect the heater hose on the water pump.
14. Install water pump belt on the pulley and adjust tension to specification. Install thermactor pump and bracket. Tighten bolts to specification.
15. Install thermactor pump hose located on the bottom of the pump.
16. Install thermactor pump belt to the pulley and adjust belt tension to specification.
17. Connect the negative ground cable.
18. Replace engine coolant. Operate the engine until normal operating temperature is reached. Check for leaks and recheck the coolant level.

2.5L ENGINE

1. Open the hood and disconnect the negative battery cable.
2. Remove the radiator cap and position a drain pan under the bottom radiator hose.
3. Raise and support safely the front of the vehicle. Remove the lower radiator hose from the radiator and drain the coolant into the drain pan.
4. Remove the water pump inlet tube. Loosen the belt tensioner by inserting a 1/2 inch flex handle in the square hole of the tensioner and rotate the tensioner counterclockwise and remove the the belt from the all the pulleys.
5. Disconnect the heater hose from the water pump. Remove the three water pump to engine block bolts and remove the pump from the engine.
6. Installation is the reverse order of the removal procedure and torque the three water pump to engine block bolts to 15 to 22 ft. lbs. Refill the cooling system and check for leaks.

3.0L ENGINE

NOTE: This engine uses aluminum components that require a special corosion inhibitor coolant formulation to avoid radiator damage. The cooling system should be filled with a 50/50 mix of water and antifreeze, with the addition of two cooling system protector pellets D9AZ–19558–A or equivalent.

1. Disconnect the negative battery cable and place a suitable drain pan under the radiator drain cock.

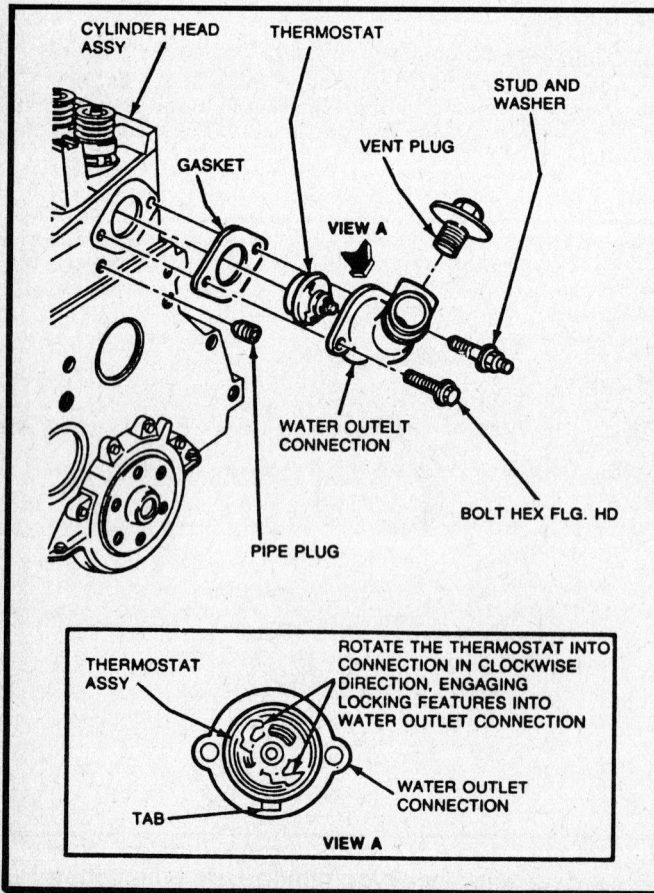

Thermostat removal and installation—2.5L engine

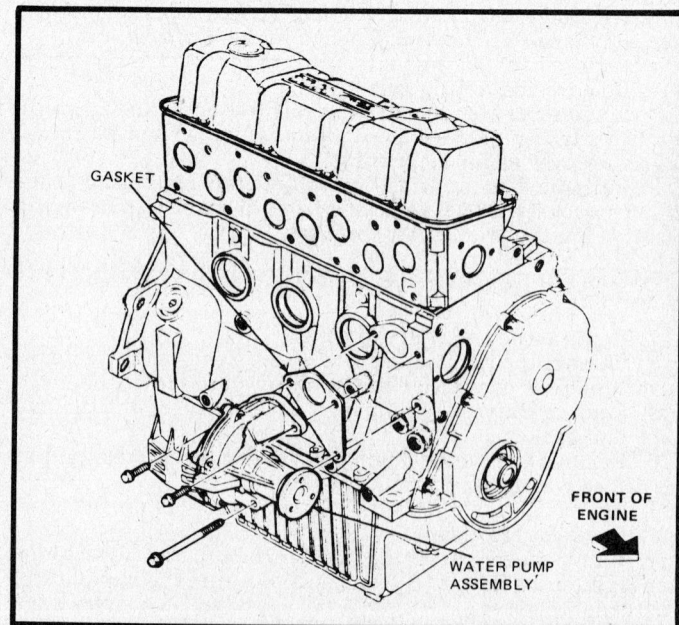

2.3L HSC engine, water pump removal and installation (© Ford Motor Co.)

Ford Mercury
FRONT WHEEL DRIVE CARS—ESCORT • EXP • LYNX • TEMPO • TOPAZ • TAURUS • SABLE

Section 4

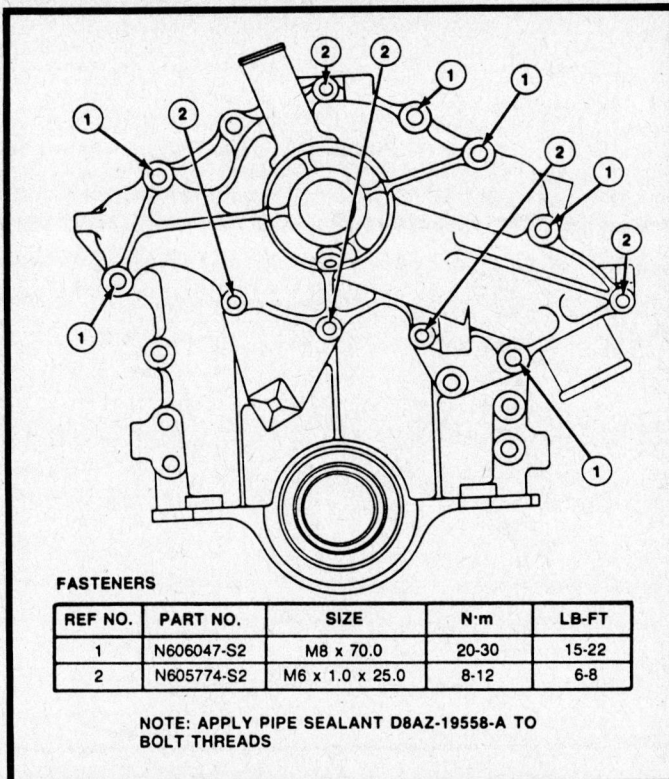

Water pump bolt torque sequence—3.0L engine

REF NO.	PART NO.	SIZE	N·m	LB-FT
1	N606047-S2	M8 x 70.0	20-30	15-22
2	N605774-S2	M6 x 1.0 x 25.0	8-12	6-8

NOTE: APPLY PIPE SEALANT D8AZ-19558-A TO BOLT THREADS

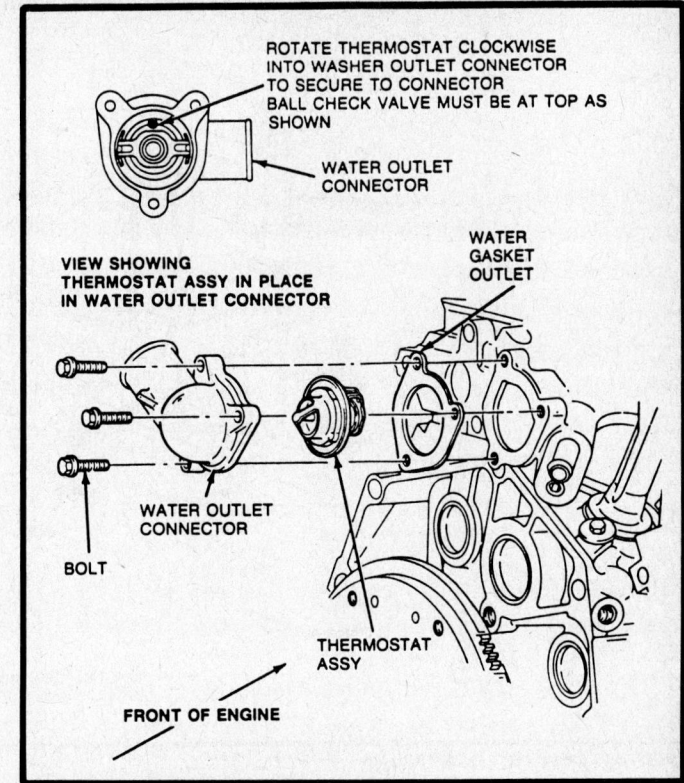

Thermostat removal and installation—3.0L engine

NOTE: Drain the system with the engine cool and the heater temperature control set at the maximum heat position. Attach a $3/8$ inch hose to the drain cock so as to direct the coolant into the drain pan.

2. Remove the radiator cap, open the drain cock on the radiator and drain the cooling system.
3. Loosen the accessory drive belt ideler pulley and remove the drive belts.
4. Remove the two nuts and the one bolt that attach the idler pulley bracket to the engine. Disconnect the heater hose from the water pump.
5. Remove the four pulley to pump hub bolts. The pulley will remain loose on the hub due to the insufficient clearance between the inner fender and the water pump.
6. Remove the eleven water pump to engine block attaching bolts and lift the water pump and pulley out of the vehicle.
7. Installation is the reverse order of the removal procedure. Torque the eleven water pump to engine block bolts as follows: there are two size bolts the metric class M8 bolt (M8 x 70.0mm) which is torqued to 15 to 22 ft. lbs. the other bolt is metric class M6 (M6 x 1.0 x 25.0mm) which is torqued to 6 to 8 ft. lbs. Be sure to apply a suitable thread sealer to the bolts before installing them.

COOLING FAN MOTOR

Removal

1. Open hood and disconnect negative battery cable.
2. Disconnect the wiring connector from the fan motor. Disconnect the wire loom from the clip on the shroud. (Push down on the two lock fingers, pull the connector from the motor end). On the Taurus/Sable models remove the integrated relay control assembly located on the radiator support.
3. Remove the nuts retaining the fan motor and shroud assembly and remove from the vehicle. On the Taurus/Sable models, rotate the fan and shroud assembly and remove them upwards past the radiator.
4. Remove the retaining clip from the motor shaft and remove the fan.

NOTE: A metal burr may be present on the motor shaft after the retaining clip has been removed. If necessary, remove burr to facilitate fan removal.

5. Remove three nuts and washers and withdraw the fan motor from the shroud.

Installation

1. Install the fan motor in position in the fan shroud. Install

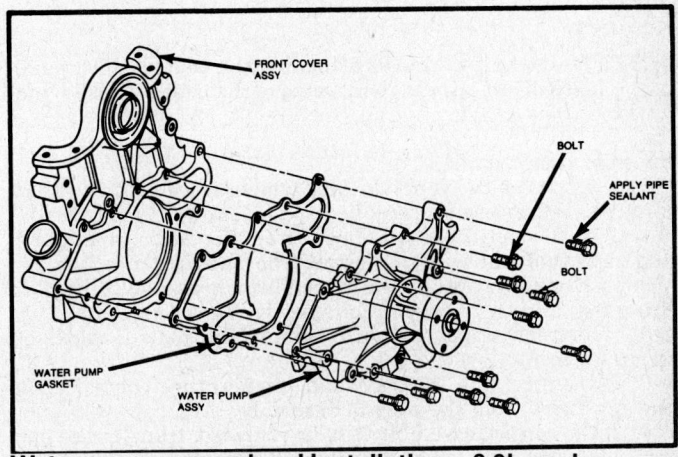

Water pump removal and installation—3.0L engine

4-33

SECTION 4

Ford Mercury
FRONT WHEEL DRIVE CARS—ESCORT • EXP • LYNX • TEMPO • TOPAZ • TAURUS • SABLE

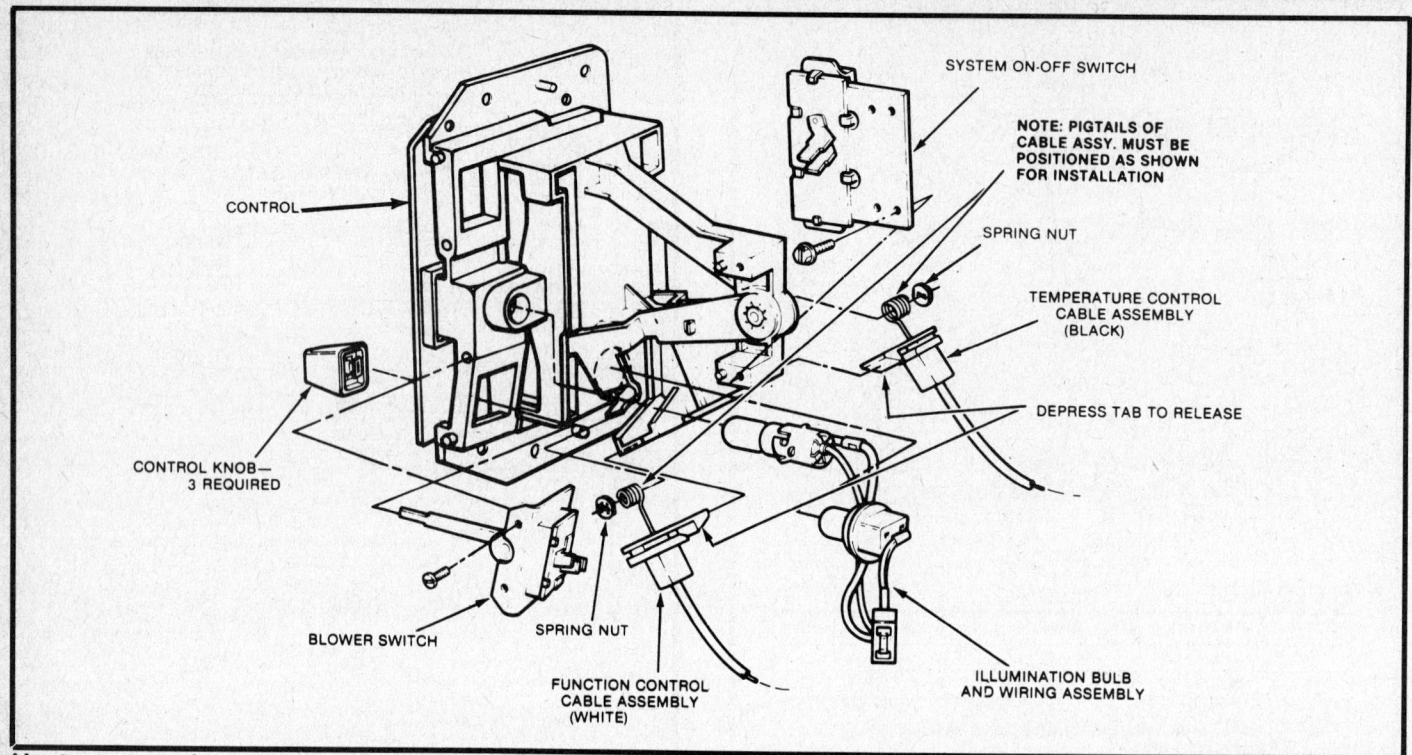

Heater control assembly (© Ford Motor Co.)

three retaining nuts and washers and tighten to 44–66 inch lbs. (5–7 Nm).

2. Position the fan assembly on the motor shaft and install the retaining clip.

3. Position the fan, motor, and shroud as an assembly in the vehicle. Install the retaining nuts and tighten to 35–45 in.lbs. (4–5 Nm) on Escort/Lynx, EXP and 23–33 in.lbs. (2.6–3.7 Nm) on Tempo/Topaz and Taurus/Sable.

4. Install the fan motor wire loom in the clip provided on the fan shroud. Connect the wiring connector to the fan motor. (Be sure the two lock fingers on the connector snap firmly into place.) On the Taurus/Sable models install the integrated relay control assembly located on the radiator support.

5. Reconnect battery cables. Close hood.

6. Check the fan for proper operation.

HEATER CONTROL ASSEMBLY

Removal

1. Remove the two screws attaching the center finish panel to the instrument panel. Then, remove the center finish panel (unsnap).

2. Remove the four screws attaching the control assembly to the instrument panel.

3. Disconnect the function and temperature control cables from the heater case assembly.

4. Pull the control assembly out from the instrument panel and disconnect the wire connectors from the blower switch, the system On-Off switch, the heated back-lite switch (if so equipped) and the illumination wire harness connector.

5. Remove the spring nuts retaining the control cables on the lever arms.

6. Disconnect the function and temperature control cable end retainers from the control assembly.

7. If the control assembly is to be replaced, transfer the necessary components to the new control assembly.

Installation

1. Connect the cable end retainers to the control assembly.

2. Place the end loop of the temperature control cable on the arm of the temperature selector lever and install a new spring nut to retain the cable end loop on the lever arm.

3. Connect the function control cable.

4. Connect the wire connectors to the blower switch, On-Off switch, heated back-lite switch and the illumination wire harness.

5. Position the control assembly to the instrument panel and install the four attaching screws.

6. Install the center finish panel on the instrument panel.

7. Pre-set the self-adjusting clips on the control cables.

8. Connect the control cables to the heater case assembly and adjust the cables.

9. Check the system for proper operation.

SYSTEM ON-OFF SWITCH ASSEMBLY

Removal

1. Remove the control assembly from the instrument panel following the procedure given for Control Assembly Removal.

2. Remove the two screws attaching the on-off switch to the control assembly and remove the switch.

Installation

1. Align the function selector lever tab with the slot of the system on-off switch. Position the switch assembly to the control assembly, taking care to align the locator pins with the holes in the switch.

2. Install the two on-off switch retaining screws and tighten them securely.

3. Install the control assembly following the procedure given for Control Assembly Installation.

BLOWER SWITCH ASSEMBLY

Removal

1983 ESCORT/LYNX, EXP

1. Remove the control assembly from the instrument panel.
2. Remove the blower switch knob from the switch shaft by placing a suitable tool blade between the knob sprig retainer and the control assembly. Then, pull on the tool, applying pressure on the spring retainer, and pull the knob off the switch shaft.
3. Remove one screw attaching the blower switch to the control assembly and remove the switch.

Installation

1. Position the blower switch to the control assembly, engaging the alignment pin with the hole in the switch mounting bracket.
2. Install the switch attaching screw and tighten the screw securely.
3. Install the control assembly following the procedure given for "Control Assembly Installation."
4. Push the control knob on the blower switch shaft.
5. Check the system for proper operation.

Removal and Installation

1984 AND LATER—ALL MODELS

1. Remove the blower switch knob from the switch shaft by pulling the knob straight off the shaft.
2. Remove the instrument cluster as previously outlined in this section.
3. Remove the four screws attaching the control assembly to the instrument panel.
4. Pull the control assembly out from the instrument panel and disconnect the harness connectors from the blower switch and the A/C push button switch.
5. Remove the blower switch and A/C button switch attaching screw and remove the blower switch assembly.
6. Installation is the reverse order of the removal procedure.

BLOWER MOTOR

Removal

ALL MODELS WITHOUT A/C EXCEPT THE TAURUS/SABLE

1. On the Escort/EXP, Lynx/LN7 remove the air inlet duct assembly. On the Tempo/Topaz, remove the right ventilator assembly.

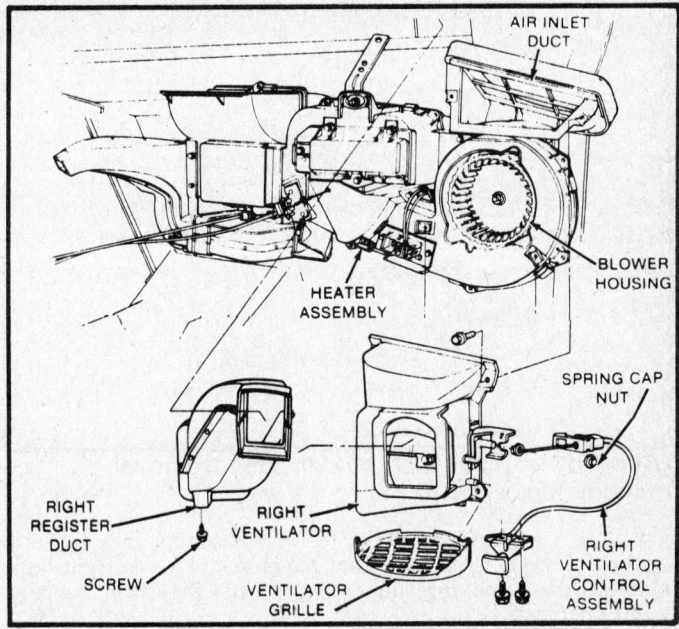

Escort/Lynx, EXP/LN7 heater/blower assembly (© Ford Motor Co.)

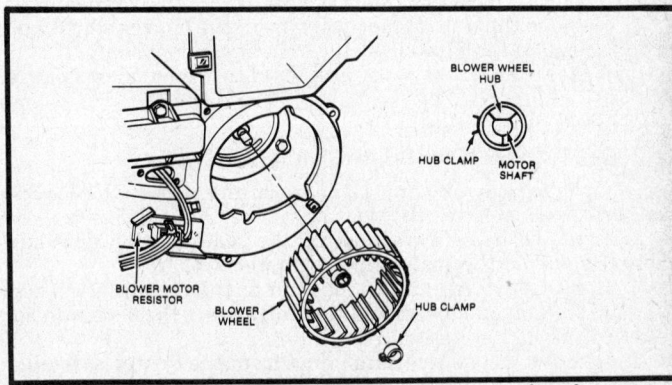

Excort/Lynx, EXP/LN7 blower motor wheel removal (© Ford Motor Co.)

2. Remove the hub clamp spring from the blower wheel hub.
3. Pull the blower wheel from the blower motor shaft.
4. Remove the three blower motor flange attaching screws located inside the blower housing.
5. Pull the blower motor out from the blower housing (heater case) and disconnect the blower motor wires from the motor.

Installation

1. Connect the wires to the blower motor and position the motor in the blower housing.
2. Install the three blower motor attaching screws.
3. Position the blower wheel on the motor shaft and install the hub clamp spring.
4. Install the air inlet duct assembly and the right ventilator assembly.
5. Check the system for proper operation.

Removal and Installation

WITH A/C

1. Empty out the contents of the glove compartment. Remove the glove compartment door.

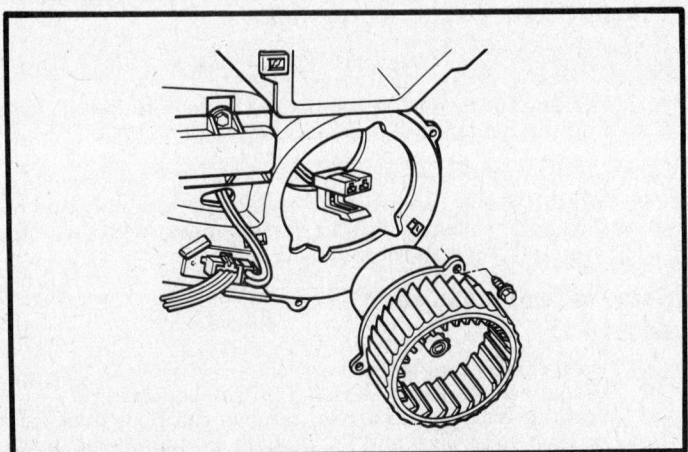

Blower motor assembly (© Ford Motor Co.)

SECTION 4

FORD MERCURY
FRONT WHEEL DRIVE CARS—ESCORT • EXP • LYNX • TEMPO • TOPAZ • TAURUS • SABLE

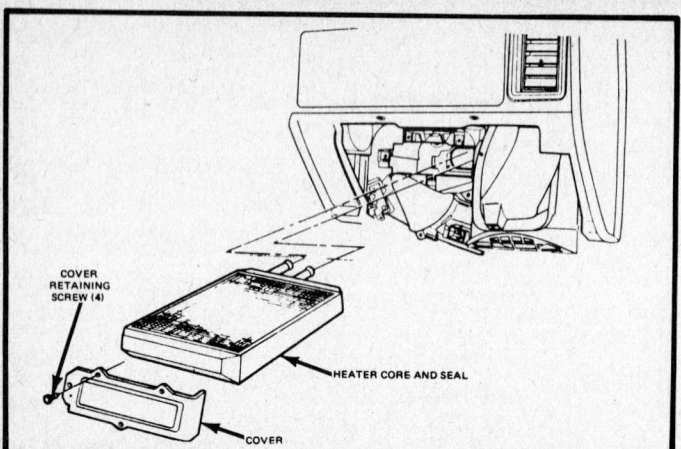

Excort/Lynx, EXP/LN7 heater core removal
(© Ford Motor Co.)

2. Disconnect the blower motor wires from the blower motor resistor. Loosen the instrument panel at the lower right hand side prior to removing the motor through the glove compartment opening.
3. Remove the four screws attaching the blower motor and mounting to the evaporator case.
4. Rotate the motor until the mounting plate flat clears the edge of the clove compartment opening and remove the motor.
5. Remove the hub clamp spring from the blower wheel hub. Then, remove the blower wheel from the motor shaft.
6. Installation is the reverse order of the removal procedure.

Removal and Installation
TAURUS/SABLE WITH OR WITHOUT A/C

1. Open the clove compartment door and release the door retainers so as to lower the door.
2. Remove the screw attaching the recirculation duct support bracket to the instrumnent panel cowl.
3. Remove the vacuum connection to the recirculation door vacuum motor. Remove the screws attaching the recirculation duct to the heater assembly.
4. Remove the recircultaion duct from the heater assembly, lowering the duct from between the instrument panel and the heater case.
5. Disconnect the blower motor electrical lead. Remove the blower motor wheel clip and remove the blower motor wheel.
6. Remove the four blower motor mounting plate screws and remove the blower motor from the evaporator case.
7. Installation is the reverse order of the removal procedure.

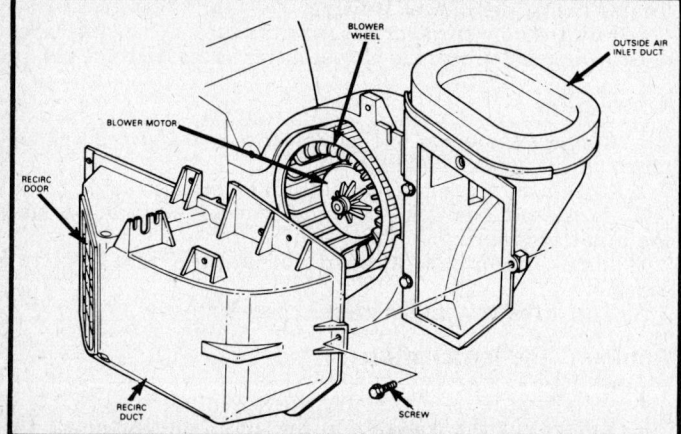

Blower motor removal and installation—Taurus/Sable

HEATER CORE

Removal and Installation
ALL MODELS WITHOUT A/C EXCEPT THE TAURUS/SABLE

1. Drain the cooling system.
2. Loosen the heater hose clamps at the heater core tubes and disconnect the heater hoses from the heater core tubes.
3. Cap the heater core tubes to prevent spilling coolant into the passenger compartment.
4. Remove the glove compartment door, liner and lower reinforcement.
5. Move the temperature control lever to the WARM position.
6. Remove the four screws attaching the heater core cover to the heater assembly and remove the cover.

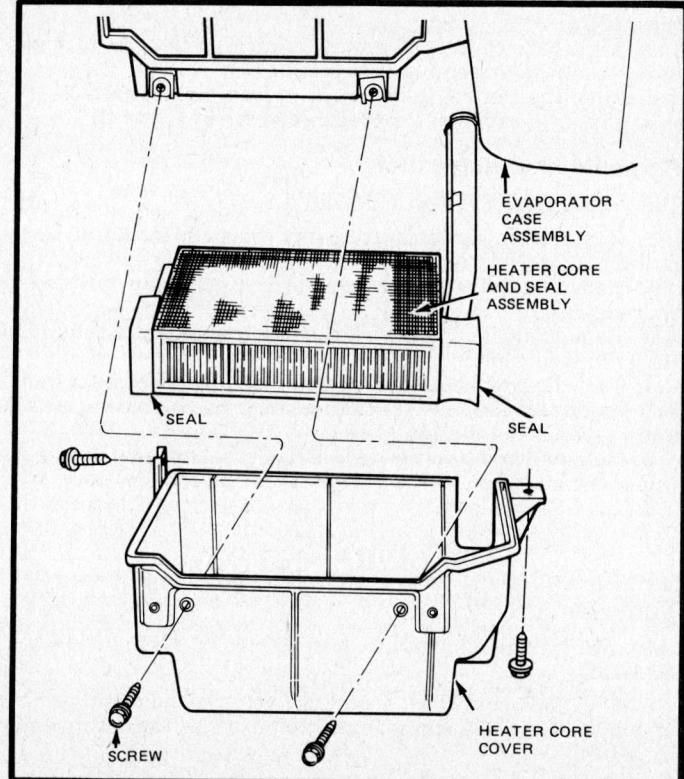

Tempo/Topaz heater core removal
(© Ford Motor Co.)

7. Working in the engine compartment, loosen the two nuts attaching the heater case assembly to the dash panel.
8. Push the heater core tubes toward the passenger compartment to loosen the heater core from the heater case assembly.
9. Pull the heater core from the hater case assembly and remove the heater core through the glove compartment opening.
10. To install, reverse the removal procedure.

Removal and Installation
WITH A/C

1. Drain the coolant from the radiator.
2. Disconnect the heater hoses from the heater core.
3. Working inside the vehicle, remove the floor duct from the plenum (two screws) and the instrument panel (one or two screw) and the evaporator assembly (one screw).

Ford Mercury

FRONT WHEEL DRIVE CARS—ESCORT • EXP • LYNX • TEMPO • TOPAZ • TAURUS • SABLE

Section 4

Escort/Lynx, EXP/LN7 heater and A/C case (© Ford Motor Co.)

NOTE: Most models are equipped with a removable heater core cover to provide access for servicing.

4. Remove the screws attaching the heater core cover to the evaporator case.
5. Remove the heater core and cover from the plenum.
6. Installation is the reverse of removal.

Removal and Installation

TAURUS/SABLE WITH OR WITHOUT A/C

1. Disconnect the negative battery cable and drain the coolant into ta suitable drain pan.
2. Remove the instrument as previously outlined in this section and lay it on the front seat.
3. Disconnect and cap the heater hose from the heater core. Disconnect the vacuum supply hose from the in-line vacuum check valve in the engine compartment.
4. Remove the screw holding the instrument panel shake brace to heater case and remove the instrument panel shake brace.
5. Remove the floor register (or the rear seat adapter) attached by two screws at the bottom of the heater case.
6. Remove the three nuts attaching the heater case to the dash panel in the engine compartment.
7. Remove the two screws attaching the brackets to the cowl top panel. Carefully pull the heater assembly away from the dash panel and remove the heater case assembly from the vehicle.

8. Remove the vacuum source line from the heater core tube seal. Remove the seal from the heater core tubes.
9. Remove the four heater core access cover attaching screws and remove the access cover from the heater case. Lift the heater core and seal from the heater case.
10. Installation is the reverse order of the removal procedure. Be sure to transfer the three foam core seals to the new heater core.

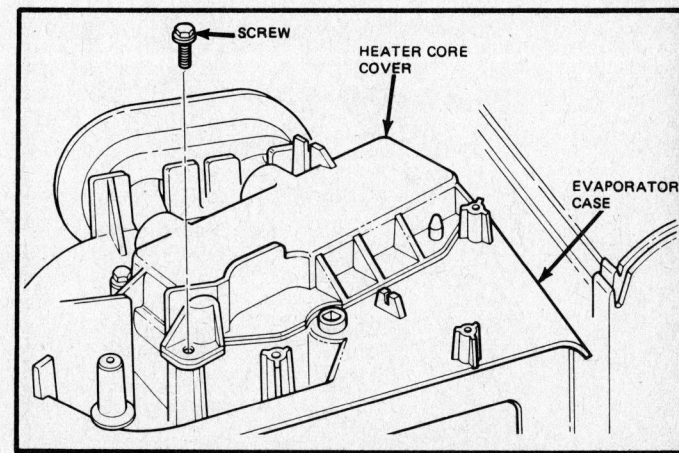

Heater core access cover on the Taurus/Sable

FUEL SYSTEM

ELECTRIC FUEL PUMP

Removal and Installation

ESCORT/LYNX, EXP

NOTE: The pressure in the fuel system must be released before attempting to remove the fuel pump. A special valve is incorporated in the fuel rail assembly for the purpose of relieving the pressure in the fuel system. Remove the air cleaner and attach pressure gauge tool No. T80L–9974–A or equivalent to the fuel pressure valve on the fuel rail assembly and release the pressure from the system.

1. Position the vehicle so it is ready to be raised, depressurized the fuel system and raise and support the vehicle safely.
2. Locate the fuel pump at the right rear, near the fuel tank and remove the assembly from the vehicle by loosening the mounting bolt until the assembly can slide off of the mounting bracket.
3. Remove the parking brake cable from the clip on the pump and disconnect the
electrical connector and fuel pump outlet fitting.
4. Disconnect the fuel pump inlet line and remove the pump from under the vehicle. Be sure to either drain the fuel tank or raise the end of the fuel pump inlet line above the level in the tank to prevent siphon action.

4–37

SECTION 4

FORD MERCURY
FRONT WHEEL DRIVE CARS—ESCORT • EXP • LYNX • TEMPO • TOPAZ • TAURUS • SABLE

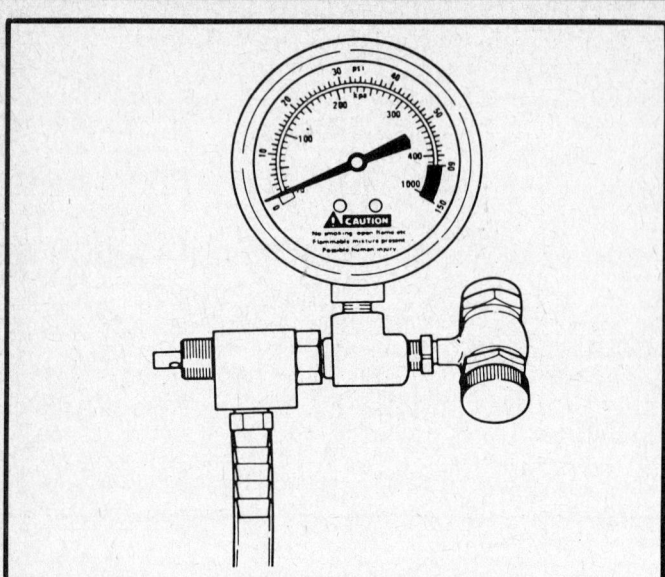
Fuel injection pressure gauge (© Ford Motor Co.)

5. Installation is the reverse order of the removal procedure, also observe the following procedures:

　a. After installation is complete, install the fuel pressure gauge tool No. T80L9974–A or equivalent on the fuel rail pressure fitting.

　b. Turn the ignition switch on and off for two second intervals until the pressure gauge reads 35 psi.

　c. Remove the pressure gauge tool, start the engine and check for fuel leaks.

TEMPO/TOPAZ AND TAURUS/SABLE

1. Position the vehicle so it is ready to be raised, depressurize the fuel system (as previously outlined) and remove the fuel from the fuel tank by pumping it out through the filler neck.

2. Raise and support the vehicle safely and remove the fuel filler tube (neck).

3. Support the fuel tank and remove the fuel tank straps, lower the fuel tank enough to be able to remove the fuel lines, electrical connectors and vent lines from the tank.

4. Remove the fuel tank from under the vehicle and remove any dirt around the fuel pump attaching flange.

5. Turn the fuel pump locking ring counterclockwise ad remove the lock ring.

6. Remove the fuel pump from the fuel tank and discard the flange gasket.

7. Installation is the reverse order of the removal procedure, also observe the following procedures:

　a. Install the fuel pressure gauge and turn the ignition on and off for three second intervals, until the pressure gauge reads 13 psi.

　b. Remove the pressure gauge, start the engine and check for fuel leaks.

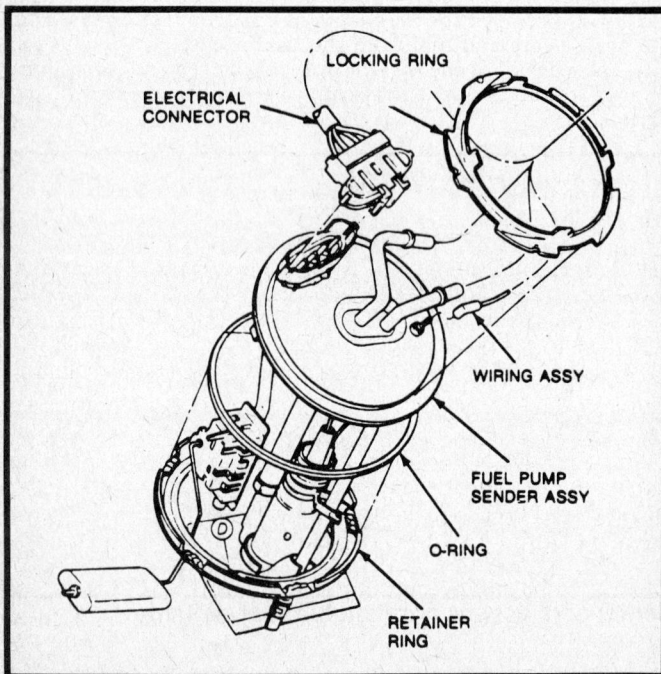
Electronic fuel pump removal and installation Tempo/Topaz, Taurus/Sable

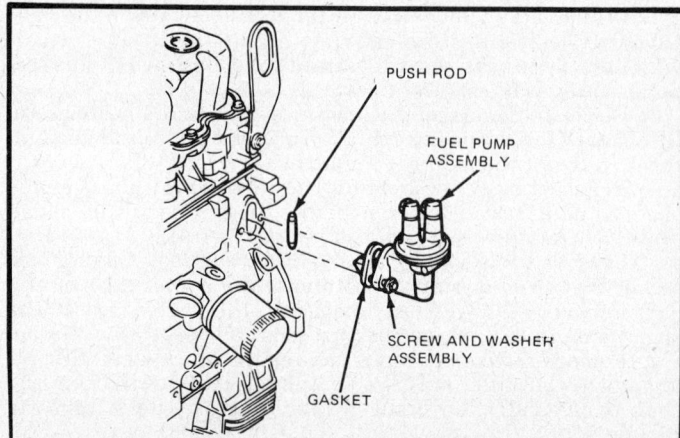
2.3L HSC engine, fuel pump removal and installation (© Ford Motor Co.)

MECHANICAL FUEL PUMP

Removal and Installation

1. Loosen the threaded fuel line connection(s) with the proper size wrench (flare nut wrench preferred) and retighten snugly. Do not remove lines at this time.

2. Loosen mounting bolts two turns. Apply force with hand to loosen fuel pump if gasket is stuck. Rotate the engine, by nudging the starter, until the fuel pump cam lobe is near its low position. The tension on the fuel pump will be greatly reduced at the low cam position.

3. Outlet line is pressurized. Disconnect the fuel pump inlet and outlet lines.

4. Remove the fuel pump attaching bolts and remove the pump and gasket. Discard the old gasket.

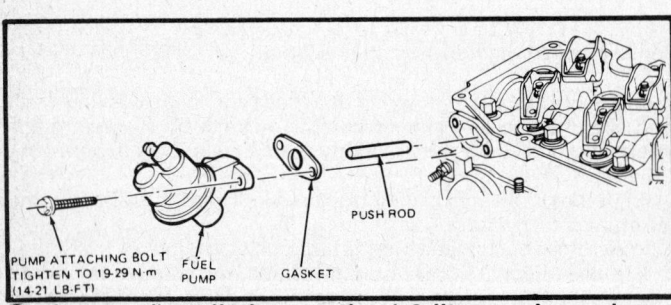
Fuel pump installation on the 1.6 liter engine cylinder head (© Ford Motor Co.)

5. Measure the fuel pump pushrod length. It should be 3.88 in. (98.6mm) minimum on the 1.6L and the 1.9L engines. On the 2.3L engine it should be 2.34 in. (61.7mm) minimum. Replace if worn or out of specification. Reinstall fuel pump and repeat pressure test.

6. To install, remove all fuel pump gasket material from the engine and the fuel pump if installing the original pump.

7. Install the attaching bolts into the fuel pump and install a new gasket on the bolts. Position the fuel pump to the mounting pad. Turn the attaching bolts alternately and evenly and tighten to 11–19 ft.lb. (15–25 Nm).

8. Install fuel lies to fuel pump. Start the threaded fitting by hand to avoid cross threading. Tighten outlet nut to 15–18 ft. lb. (20–24 Nm).

9. Start engine and observe for fuel leaks for two minutes.

10. Stop engine and check all fuel pump fuel line connections for fuel leaks by running a finger under the connections. Check for oil leaks at the fuel pump mounting gasket.

IDLE SPEED AND MIXTURE

1.6L AND 1.9L ENGINES WITH 740–2V – FAST IDLE RPM

1. Place the transmission in Neutral or Park.
2. Bring engine to normal operating temperature.
3. Disconnect the vacuum hose at the EGR and plug.
4. Place the fast idle adjustment screw on the second step of the fast idle cam. Run engine until cooling fan comes on.
5. Check/adjust fast idle rpm to specification. If adjustment is required, loosen locknut, adjust and retighten.

NOTE: Engine cooling fan must be running when checking fast idle rpm.

6. Remove plug from EGR hose and reconnect.

1.6L AND 1.9L ENGINES WITH 740–2V WITHOUT IDLE SPEED CONTROL – CURB IDLE RPM

1. Place the transmission in Neutral or Park.
2. Bring engine to normal operating temperature.
3. Disconnect and plug vacuum hose at thermactor air control valve bypass section.
4. Place the fast idle adjustment screw on the second step of the fast idle cam. Run engine until cooling fan comes on.
5. Slightly depress throttle to allow fast idle cam to rotate. Place transmission in specified gear, and check/adjust curb idle rpm to specification.

NOTE: Engine cooling fan must be running when checking curb idle rpm.

6. Place transmission in Neutral or Park. Rev the engine momentarily. Place transmission in specified position and recheck curb idle rpm. Readjust if required.
7. If vehicle is equipped with a dashpot, check/adjust clearance to specification.
8. Remove plug from hose at thermactor air control valve bypass section and reconnect.
9. If the vehicle is equipped with an automatic transmission and curb idle adjustment is more than 50 rpm, refer to automatic transmission linkage adjustment procedure.

1.6L AND 1.9L ENGINES WITH 740–2V AND MECHANICAL VACUUM IDLE SPEED CONTROL (ISC) – CURB IDLE RPM

1. Place the transmission in Neutral or Park.
2. Bring engine to normal operating temperature.
3. Disconnect and plug vacuum hose at thermactor air control valve by pass section.
4. Place the fast idle adjustment screw on the second step of the fast idle cam. Run engine until cooling fan comes on.
5. Slightly depress throttle to allow fast idle cam to rotate. Place transmission in Drive (fan on) and check curb idle rpm to specification

NOTE: Engine cooling fan must be running when checking curb idle rpm.

If adjustment is required:
- Place transmission in Park, deactivate the ISC by removing the vacuum hose at the ISC and plugging the hose.
- Connect a vacuum pump the ISC and supply sufficient vacuum to retract ISC plunger clear of the ISC adjustment screw.
- Place the transmission in Drive position, if rpm is not at 720 rpm (fan on), adjust rpm by turning the throttle stop adjusting screw.
- Place transmission in Park, remove vacuum pump from ISC, remove plug from ISC vacuum line and reconnect to ISC.
- Place transmission in Drive, if rpm is not at 750 rpm (fan on), adjust by turning the ISC adjustment screw.

6. Place transmission in Neutral or Park. Rev the engine momentarily. Place transmission in specified position and recheck curb idle rpm. Readjust if required.
7. Remove plug from thermactor air control valve bypass section hose and reconnect.
8. If the vehicle is equipped with an automatic transmission and curb idle adjustment is more than 50 rpm, refer to automatic transmission linkage adjustment procedure.

1.6L AND 1.9L ENGINES WITH 740–2V – VACUUM OPERATED THROTTLE MODULATOR (VOTM)

1. Place the transmission in Neutral or Park.
2. Bring engine to normal operating temperature.
3. To check/adjust VOTM rpm:
   a. Place A/C heat selector in Heat position, blower switch on High.
   b. Disconnect vacuum hose from VOTM and plug, install slave vacuum hose from intake manifold vacuum to VOTM.
4. Disconnect and plug vacuum hose at thermactor air control valve-bypass section.
5. Run engine until cooling fan comes on.
6. Place transmission in specified gear, and check/adjust VOTM rpm to specification.

NOTE: Engine cooling fan must be running when checking VOTM rpm. Adjustment rpm by turning screw on VOTM.

7. Remove slave vacuum hose. Remove plug from VOTM vacuum hose and reconnect hose to VOTM.
8. Return intake manifold supply source to original location.
9. Remove plug from vacuum hose at thermactor air control valve by pass section and reconnect.

1.6L AND 1.9L ENGINES WITH ELECTRONIC FUEL INJECTION (EFI) – INITIAL ENGINE RPM ADJUSTMENT (SCI DISCONNECTED)

NOTE: Curb idle RPM is controlled by the EEC IV processor and the Idle Speed Control (ISC) device (part of the fuel charging assembly).

The purpose of this procedure is to provide a means by verifying the initial engine RPM setting with the ISC disconnected. If engine idle RPM is not within specification after performing this procedure, it will be necessary to perform the appropriate 1.6L EFI EEC IV diagnostics.

1. Place the transmission in Neutral or Park.
2. Bring the engine to normal operating temperature and shut off.
3. Disconnect vacuum connector at EGR solenoid and plug both lines.
4. Disconnect idle speed control (ISC) power lead.
5. Electric cooling fan must be on during idle speed set procedure.

Ford Mercury
FRONT WHEEL DRIVE CARS—ESCORT • EXP • LYNX • TEMPO • TOPAZ • TAURUS • SABLE

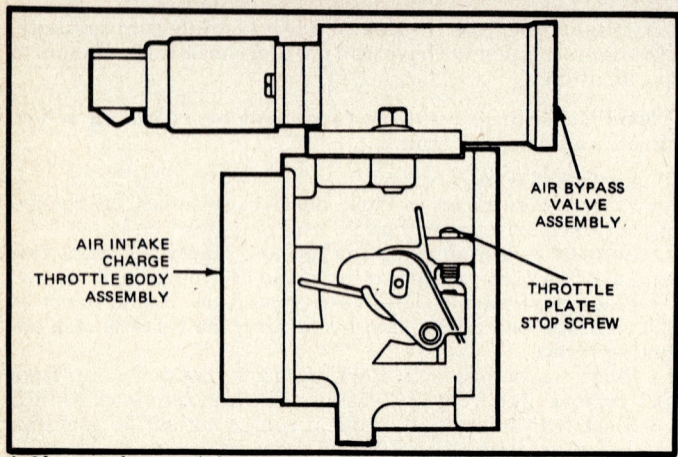

1.6L engine w/electronic fuel injection
(© Ford Motor Co.)

6. Start engine and operate at 2000 rpm for 60 seconds.
7. Set hand brake and place transmission in Neutral for M/T and Drive for A/T, check/adjust initial engine rpm within 120 seconds by adjusting throttle plate screw.
8. If idle adjustment is not completed within 120 second time limit, shut engine Off, restart and repeat Steps 6-7.
9. If vehicle is equipped with an automatic transmission and initial engine rpm adjustment is more than 50 rpm or more or is decreased by any amount, refer to automatic transmission linkage adjustment procedure.
10. turn engine Off and remove plugs from EGR vacuum lines at EGR solenoid and reconnect.
11. Reconnect idle speed control (ISC) power lead.

2.3L ENGINE W/YFA-IV AND YFA/IV FB – FAST IDLE RPM

1. Place transmission in Neutral or Park.
2. Bring engine to normal operating temperature.
3. Turn the ignition key to the Off position.
4. Put A/C selector in the Off position.
5. Disconnect vacuum hose at the EGR valve and plug.
6. If so equipped, disconnect wire to electric PVS.
7. Place the fast idle adjusting screw on the specified step of the fast idle cam.
8. Start engine without touching the accelerator pedal: Check/adjust fast idle rpm to specification.
9. Rev the engine momentarily, allowing engine to return to idle and turn ignition key to Off position.

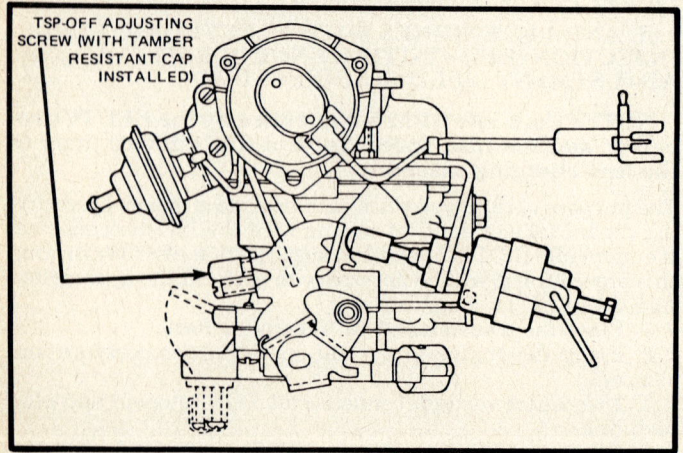

2.3L engine w/YFA-1661 and YFA-1661FB – TSP off adjustment (© Ford Motor Co.)

10. Remove plug from the EGR vacuum hose and reconnect.
11. If so equipped, reconnect wire to electric PVS.

2.3L ENGINE W/YFA-IV AND YFA-IV FB – CURB IDLE RPM

NOTE: "A/C-ON RPM" is non-adjustable "TSP-OFF RPM" is not required.

1. Place the transmission in Neutral or Park.
2. Bring engine to normal operating temperature.
3. Place A/C selector in the Off position.
4. Place transmission in specified position.
5. Check/adjust curb idle rpm. if adjustment is required, turn the hex head adjustment at the rear of the TSP or VOTM/TSP housing.
6. Place the transmission in Neutral or Park. Rev the engine momentarily. Place transmission in specified position and re-check curb idle rpm. Readjust if required.
7. Turn the ignition key to the Off position.
8. Check/adjust the bowl vent setting as follows:
   a. Turn ignition key to the On position to activate the TSP (engine not running). Open throttle so that the TSP plunger extends.
   b. Secure the choke plate in the wide open position.
   c. Open throttle so that the throttle vent lever does not touch the bowl vent rod. Close the throttle to the idle set position and measure the travel of the fuel bowl vent rod from the open throttle position.
   d. Travel of the bowl vent rod should be within specification (0.100-0.150 in.).
   e. If out of specification, bend the throttle vent lever at notch, to obtain required travel.
9. Remove all test equipment and reinstall air cleaner assembly. Tighten holddown bolt to specification.

2.3L WITH YFA 1-V AND YFA 1-V FEEDBACK

Diagnostic Procedure—This adjustment is not required as part of a normal engine idle rpm check/adjustment. It should only be performed on a customer complaint of "engine continues to Run after ignition key is turned to Off position."

1. Place the transmission in neutral or Park.
2. Bring engine to normal operating temperature.
3. Place A/C selector to Off position.
4. Disconnect the electrical lead to the TSP or VOTM/TSP. Check engine rpm to specification (600rpm). If adjustment is required, remove tamper resistant sleeve.
5. Adjust TSP-Off rpm to specification.
6. Shut engine Off, reconnect TSP electrical lead.
7. Reinstall new tamper resistant cap.

2.3L EFI TURBO

1. Apply the parking brake, block the drive wheels and place the vehicle in neutral.
2. Start the engine and let it run until it reaches normal operating temperature, then turn the engine off. Connect a suitable tachometer.
3. Disconnect the idle speed control air bypass valve power lead. Start the engine and run the engine at 2000 rpm for 120 seconds.

NOTE: If the electric cooling fan comes on during the idle speed adjusting procedures, wait for the fan to turn off before proceeding.

4. Let the engine idle and check the base idel, it should be at 750 ± 50 rpm. If it is not adjust as necessary.
5. Adjust the engine rpm to 900 ± 75 rpm by adjusting the throttle stop screw.
6. Shut the engine off and reconnect the power lead to the idle speed control air bypass valve. Disconnect all test equipment.

2.3L HSC ENGINE WITH 1949 CARBURETOR – CURB IDLE RPM

NOTE: Verify that the TSP plunger extends with the ignition key on. The idle specifications can be found on the calibration sticker located under the hood.

1. Apply the parking brake, block the drive wheels and place the vehicle in neutral. Remove the air cleaner assembly, disconnect and plug the throttle kicker vacuum line.
2. Start the engine and let it run until it reaches normal operating temperature, then turn the engine off. Connect a suitable tachometer.
3. Place the A/C selector in the off position and activate the cooling fan by grounding the control wire with a jumper wire.
4. Check and adjust the curb idle rpm. If adjustment is required, turn the curb idle adjusting screw. Rev the engine for a minute and recheck the curb idle rpm. readjust the curb idle if necessary.
5. Reconnect the cooling fan wiring. Turn the ignition key to the off position. reconnect the vacuum line to the throttle kicker and remove all test equipment.

NOTE: If the vehicle is ewquipped with an automatic transaxle and the curb idle adjustment still exceeds 50 rpm, the transaxle linkage must be adjusted.

2.3L AND 2.5L HSC ENGINES WITH CFI AND DC MOTOR IDLE SPEED CONTROL (ISC)

NOTE: If for any reeason the battery is disconnected or the vehicle has to be jump started it may be necessary to perform this following procedure.

1. Apply the parking brake, block the drive wheels and place the vehicle in Neutral.
2. Start the engine and let it run until it reaches normal operating temperature, then turn the engine off. Connect a suitable tachometer.
3. Start the engine and place the transmission in drive or reverse on the Automatic models and neutral on the manual models, let the engine run at idle for 120 seconds. The idle rpm should now return to the the specified idle speed (The idle specifications can be found on the calibration sticker located under the hood).
4. Place the transmission in neutral or park and the engine rpm should increase by approximately 100 rpm. Now lightly step on and off the accelerator. The engine rpm should return to the specified idle speed. If the rpm remains high, repeat the sequence. Remember it may take the the system 120 senconds to adjust. If the vehicle does not act as just outlined, perform the following adjustment.
5. Shut the engine off and remove the air cleaner. Locate the self-test connector and self-test input connector in the engine compartment.
6. Connect a jumper wire between the self-test input connector and the signal return pin (is the top right terminal) on the self-test connector.
7. Place the ignition key in the run position and be careful not to start the engine. The ISC plunger will retract, so wait approxitmately 10 to 15 seconds until the ISC plunger is fully retracted. Turn the ignition key to the off position and wait 10 to 15 secomnds.
8. Remove the jumper wire and unplug the ISC motor from the wire harness. Now perform the throttle stop adjustment as follows:
   a. Remove the Central Fuel Injection (CFI) assembly from the vehicle.
   b. Use a small punch or equivalent to punch through and remove the aluminum plug which covers the throttle stop adjusting screw.
   c. Remove and replace the throttle stop screw.
9. Reinstall the CFI assembly on the vehicle, stabilize the engine and set the idle rpm to the specifications (listed on the calibration decal located under the hood) on the throttle stop adjusting screw.
10. Shut off the engine. Reconnect the ISC motor wire harness, remove all test equipment and reinstall the air cleaner assembly.

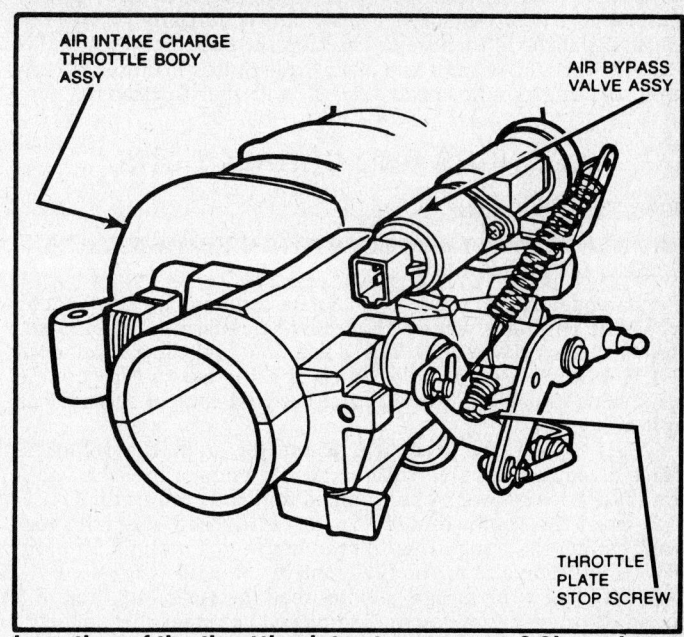

Location of the throttle plate stop screw—3.0L engine

3.0L EFI ENGINE

NOTE: The curb idle speed rpm is controlled by the EEC-IV processor and the idel speed control air bypass valve assembly. The trottle stop screw is factory set and does not directly control the idle speed. Adjustment to this setting should be performed only as part of a full EEC-IV diagnosis of irregular idle conditions or idle speeds. Failure to accurately set the throttle plate stop position as described in the following procedure could result in false idle speed control.

1. Apply the parking brake, block the drive wheels and place the vehicle in neutral.
2. Start the engine and let it run until it reaches normal operating temperature, then turn the engine off. Connect a suitable tachometer and an inductive timing light.
3. Unplug the spout line and verify the ignition timing is at 10° BTDC ± 2°. If the timing is not set to specifications, re-adjust as necessary.
4. Shut the engine off and disconnect the air bypass valve assembly connector. Remove the PCV entry line at the PCV line. Install the orifice tool T86P-9600-A or equivalent in the PCV entry line (0.200 in. orifice diameter).
5. Start the engine and place it in drive or neutral depending on the type of transaxle. Unplug the electric cooling fan.
6. If the idle speed is not at 625 ± 30 rpm, adjust the throttle palte stop screw, after the idle has been adjusted to specifications shut off the engine.
7. Start the engine and reconfirm that the idel speed is now adjusted to specifications, if not adjust as necessary.
8. Shut the engine off, remove all test equipment, remove the orifice and reconnect the PCV entry line. Reconnect the pout line, the ISC motor and the electric cooling fan.
9. Check and see that the throttle plate is not stuck in the bore and that the throttle plate stop screw is setting on the rst

FORD MERCURY
FRONT WHEEL DRIVE CARS—ESCORT • EXP • LYNX • TEMPO • TOPAZ • TAURUS • SABLE

pad with the throttle closed. Correct any condition that will not allow the throttle to close to the stop set position.

10. Restart the engine and after three to five minutes of running, the engine idle speed should be at specifications.

CHANGES AND CORRECTIONS

1984 Tempo/Topaz
PROBLEM: POOR ACCELERATION FROM STEADY SPEED WHEN WARM

Some models may show poor acceleration at steady speeds when the engine is warm. This could be caused by an inoperative fuel control solenoid. There is a new fuel control solenoid (E43Z-9B998-A) available which is designed to correct this condition. Check the condition of the fuel control solenoid as follows:

1. Disconnect the electrical connector from the solenoid. Place a vacuum T valve with a vacuum gaguge into the vacuum ($5/32$) hose between the solenoid and the carburetor.
2. Start the engine and let it run at idle speed. Raed the vacuum gauge, the gauge should read between 1.0 and 2.5 in.Hg. Now apply 12 volts to the fuel control solenoid.
3. The vacuum gauge should read between 4.0 and 5.5 in.Hg. If the vacuum gauge readings do not meet these specifications, replace the fuel control solenoid with the new (E43Z-9B998-A) fuel control solenoid.

CARBURETOR

Removal
MOTORCRAFT MODEL 740

1. Remove the air cleaner assembly.
2. Disconnect the throttle cable and speed control cable, if so equipped.
3. Identify and disconnect: bowl vent tube, altitude compensator tubes (idle, primary and secondary if so equipped), air conditioning and/or power steering vacuum kicker (if so equipped).
4. Identify and disconnect: EGR vacuum tube, venturi vacuum tube, distributor vacuum tube, ISC vacuum tube (if so equipped), choke pulldown motor vacuum tube, and fuel inlet lie at filter.
5. Disconnect the idle solenoid wire an choke cap terminal connectors.
6. Remove the automatic transmission throttle valve (TV) linkage, if so equipped.
7. Remove the four carburetor flange nuts. If so equipped, remove WOT A/C cut out switch.
8. Remove the carburetor from the manifold.

Installation

1. Clean all gasket surfaces. Replace any gasket(s) as necessary.
2. Position the carburetor on the spacer and install the WOT A/C cut out switch, if so equipped and the attaching nuts.
3. Install the automatic transmission throttle valve (TV) linkage, if so equipped.
4. Connect the choke cap and the idle solenoid terminal connectors.
5. Connect the fuel inlet line at the filter and tighten the 22 ft. lbs. (16.5 Nm).
6. Connect the distributor vacuum line, venturi vacuum line, EGR vacuum line, choke pulldown motor line, and ISC vacuum line, if so equipped.
7. Connect the air conditioning and /or power steering kicker vacuum line (if so equipped).
8. Connect the altitude compensator vacuum lines: idle, primary and secondary, if so equipped.

9. Connect the bowl vent line.
10. Connect the throttle cable. Connect the speed control cable.
11. Start the engine and check for leaks.
12. Install the air cleaner assembly.
13. Check and/or adjust the curb idle and fast idle speed as necessary.

MODEL 1949 NON-FEEDBACK AND 6149 FEEDBACK

1. Remove the air cleaner assembly.
2. Dsconnect the throttle cable from the throttle lever.
3. Disconnect the ATX (automatic transaxle) TV rod from the throttle lever, if so equipped.
4. Disconnect the distributor vacuum line, if so equipped, EGR vacuum line, if so equipped, venturi vacuum line, if so equipped, purge vacuum lines, PCV vacuum line, solenoid kicker vacuum line, and fuel line. Use a back-up wrench on the fuel inlet fitting when removing the fuel line to avoid changing the float level.

NOTE: Identify all vacuum lines before removing to aid in installation.

5. Disconnect the TSP electrical connection at the connector. Disconnect the electric choke wire at the connector.
6. Disconnect the canister vent hose at the bowl vent tube.
7. Disconnect the throttle position sensor electrical lead at the connector, Model 6949 carburetor.
8. Disconnect the WOT A/C cut-off switch electrical lead at the connector, Model 1949, if so equipped.
9. Remove EGR sensor wire from clip on pulldown diaphragm assembly mounting screw, Model 6149.
10. Remove two carburetor attaching nuts and remove the carburetor from the intake manifold. Remove carburetor mounting gasket.
11. Clean the gasket mounting surfaces of the intake manifold and the carburetor. Place a new gasket on the intake manifold. Position the carburetor on the gasket and install the attaching nuts. To prevent leakage, distortion, or damage to the carburetor body flange, snug the nuts and then tighten each nut to 20 ft. lbs. (27 Nm).
12. Install EGO sensor wire into clip on pulldown diaphragm assembly mounting screw. Model 6149.
13. Connect WOT A/C cut-off switch electrical lead at the connector, Model 6149.
14. Connect throttle position sensor electrical lead at the connector — Model 6149.
15. Connect the canister vent hose at the bowl vent tube.
16. Connect the TSP electrical connection and the electric choke wire at the connector.
17. Connect the distributor vacuum line, if so equipped, EGR vacuum line, if so equipped, venturi vacuum line, if so equipped, purge vacuum line, solenoid kicker vacuum line, and fuel line. Use a back-up wrench on the fuel inlet fitting when installing the fuel line to avoid changing the float level.
18. Connect the ATX (automatic transaxle) TV rod to the throttle lever.
19. Connect the throttle cable to the throttle lever.
20. Install the air cleaner assembly.
21. Check and adjust if necessary the curb idle speed, idle fuel mixture, and fast idle speed.

MOTORCRAFT 5740 CARBURETOR

1. Disconnect the negative battery cable and remove the air cleaner assembly.
2. Disconnect the throttle cable and speed control cable, if so equipped.
3. Disconnect and tag the bowl vent tube and altitude compensator tubes (idle, primary and secondary if so equipped).
4. Disconnect and tag the EGR vacuum line, distributor vacuum line, ISC vacuum line, choke pulldown motor vacuum line and fuel inlet line at the filter.

5. Disconnect the idle solenoid wire and choke cap terminal connectors. Remove the automatic transmission throttle valve linkage, if so equipped.
6. Remove the four carburetor flange nuts using carburetor wrench T74P-9510-A or equivalent. Remove the wide open throttle A/C cutout switch bracket, if so equipped.
7. Remove the carburetor from the intake manifold. Clean all gasket surfaces. Replace any gaskets as necessary.
8. Position the carburetor on the spacer and install the wide open throttle A/C cutout switch bracket, if so equipped and attaching nuts.

NOTE: To prevent leakage, distortion or damage to the carburetor body flange, alternately tighten each nut to 14 ft. lbs.

9. Install the automatic transmission throttle valve linkage, if so equipped. Connect the choke cap and idle solenoid terminal connectors. Connect the fuel inlet line at the filter and torque it to 22 ft. lbs.
10. Connect all the vacuum lines, the throttle cable, speed control cable and reconnect the negative battery cable. Start the engine and check for fuel leaks.
11. Install the air cleaner assembly.
12. Check and adjust if necessary the curb idle speed, idle fuel mixture, and fast idle speed.

TURBOCHARGER

Operation

A turbocharger lets the engine consume a denser air-fuel mixture. This in turn increases the horsepower and torque, in comparison with a non-turbcharged engine of the same displacement. The turbocharger operates in the following manner; the exhaust gas pressure and heat energy cause the turbine wheel to rotate, which inturn causes the compressor wheel to rotate (both are on a common shaft). A vane air meter then measures the intake air flow and temperature and the rotating compressor wheel compresses the air it receives and delivers it under pressure by way of the turbo air discharge hose to the intake manifold. Fuel is then introduced downstream of the compressor and mixes in with the air charge. The denser air-fuel charge in the combustion chamber develops more horsepower during the combustion cycle and the exhaust gas from the exhaust manifold flows into the turbine. When the intake manifold pressure reaches a set value, the actuator opens the wastegate, allowing some of the exhaust gases to bypass the turbine wheel. The cooled expanded exhaust gases are then directed by the turbine housing to the exhaust system. Boost is controlled by the wastegate and the wastegate closes to maximize vehicle performance, opening only to limit boost to maximum specified levels.

NOTE: For more information on Turbochargers, refer to Unit Repair Secion.

TURBOCHARGER

Removal

1. Disconnect battery ground cable from battery.
2. Remove the radiator shield from the radiator support.
3. Loosen the compressor outlet hose clamp at the throttle housing.
4. Remove the hose from the turbocharger compressor outlet, and rotate the hose up and out of the way.
5. Disconnect the compressor inlet hose from the turbocharger.
6. Remove the alternator and bracket.
7. Disconnect the EGR sensor electrical connector.
8. Raise the vehicle on a hoist.
9. Disconnect the oil return line from the bottom of the turbocharger center housing.
10. Lower the vehicle.
11. Remove the exhaust pipe-to-turbocharger attaching nuts.
12. Remove the bolt attaching the exhaust shield to the water outlet connector.
13. Disconnect the oil feed line at the top of the turbocharger center housing.
14. Remove the nuts attaching the exhaust manifold to the cylinder head. Slide the exhaust manifold and turbocharger away from the cylinder head enough to remove the exhaust shield.
15. Remove the turbocharger and exhaust manifold as an assembly.
16. Remove the four nuts attaching the turbocharger to the exhaust manifold and remove the turbocharger.

Installation

1. Position the turbocharger on the exhaust manifold and tighten the nuts to 16–19 ft. lbs. (21–26 Nm).
2. Install a new exhaust gasket on the cylinder head.
3. Position the exhaust manifold and turbocharger assembly on the cylinder head studs.
4. Position the exhaust shield on the exhaust manifold, and move the exhaust manifold into position on the cylinder head.
5. Install the exhaust manifold nuts and tighten to 16–19 ft. lbs.(21–26 Nm).
6. Install the bolt attaching the exhaust shield to the water outlet housing bracket and tighten to 6–8 ft. lbs. (8–11 Nm).
7. Connect the oil inlet lie to the turbocharger center housing and tighten to 6–8.8 ft. lbs. (8–12 Nm).
8. Position the exhaust pipe on the turbine outlet studs and install the attaching nuts. Tighten the nuts to 6–8.8 ft. lbs. (8–12 Nm).
9. Raise the vehicle.
10. Position the oil return line on the bottom of the turbocharger center housing and install the attaching bolts. Tighten the attaching bolts 6–8 ft. lbs. (8–11 Nm).
11. Lower the vehicle.
12. Connect the EGO sensor electrical connector.
13. Install the alternator bracket and alternator.
14. Install the alternator belt and adjust to specification.
15. Connect the compressor inlet hose to the turbocharger.
16. Connect the compressor outlet hose to the turbocharger. Tighten the clamps at the compressor outlet and throttle body inlet.
17. Connect the battery ground cable to the battery.
18. Start the engine and let idle for 30–60 seconds. Check for oil leaks, exhaust leaks and intake system leaks.

WASTEGATE ACTUATOR

Removal and Installation

1. Remove heat shield and clip attaching actuator rod to wastegate arm.
2. Remove necessary vacuum lines and actuator diaphragm attaching bolts. Remove the actuator assembly.
3. After installing a previously removed unit, verify calibration by following Troubleshooting and System Analysis procedures.
4. To install a new assembly, install the bolts attaching the actuator to the compressor housing. Unscrew the actuator rod end until it just fits over the pin on the wastegate arm while holding it closed (full forward). Install the clip attaching the actuator rod to the wastegate arm. Loctite the rod threads and remove the horsecollar.

Ford Mercury
FRONT WHEEL DRIVE CARS—ESCORT • EXP • LYNX • TEMPO • TOPAZ • TAURUS • SABLE

INTAKE MANIFOLD

Removal and Installation
1.6L AND 1.9L ENGINES

1. Raise and secure the hood in the open position.
2. Install protective fender covers.
3. Disconnect negative cable at the battery.
4. Partially drain the cooling system, and disconnect the heater hose at the fitting located under the intake manifold.
5. Remove air cleaner assembly.
6. Disconnect the vacuum hoses.
7. Disconnect wiring connectors at the following points:
   a. Choke cap wire.
   b. Bowl vent.
   c. Idle fuel solenoid.
8. Remove EGR supply tube.
9. Raise vehicle.
10. Remove the PVS hose connectors. Label the connectors and set aside.
11. Remove the bottom (three) intake manifold nuts, locations numbered two, six and three.
12. Lower vehicle.
13. Disconnect fuel lie at the fuel filter and the return line at the carburetor.
14. Disconnect accelerator and, if equipped, the speed control cable.
15. Disconnect the throttle valve linkage at the carburetor and remove the cable bracket attaching bolts, ATX only.
16. If equipped with power steering, remove the thermactor pump drive belt, the pump, the pump mounting bracket and the thermactor bypass hose.
17. Remove the fuel pump.
18. Remove the (three) remaining intake manifold attaching nuts, intake manifold and gasket. Use wrench T81P-9425-A or equivalent on the center No. 1 position nut.

NOTE: Do not lay the intake manifold flat as the gasket surfaces may be damaged.

19. Upon installation, make sure the mating surfaces on the intake manifold and the cylinder head are clean and free of gasket material.
20. Install intake manifold gasket.
21. Position the intake manifold on the engine and install the attaching nuts. Tighten the nuts to 12–13 ft. lbs. (16–17 Nm). Use wrench T81P-9425-A or equivalent on the No. 1 nut.
22. The balance of installation is the reverse order of removal.

EXHAUST MANIFOLDS

Removal and Installation
1.6L AND 1.9L ENGINES HO AND E.F.I.

1. Disconnect battery cable.
2. Remove air cleaner tray.
3. Disconnect electric fan wire.
4. Remove radiator shroud bolts and radiator shroud.
5. Disconnect EGR tube at the exhaust manifold.
6. Disconnect thermactor tube at the exhaust manifold.
7. Remove exhaust manifold heat stove.
8. Remove exhaust manifold retaining nuts.
9. Raise vehicle.
10. Remove anti-roll brace.
11. Disconnect water tube brackets.
12. Disconnect exhaust pipe at the catalyst.
13. Remove exhaust manifold.
14. Clean gasket areas.
15. Position gasket and exhaust manifold.
16. Installation is the reverse order of removal.

INTAKE AND EXHAUST MANIFOLDS

Removal and Installation
2.3L AND 2.5L ENGINES

1. Open and secure the hood.
2. Disconnect negative ground cable at battery.
3. Drain cooling system.
4. Remove accelerator cable.
5. Remove air cleaner assembly and heat stove tube at heat shield.
6. Remove required vacuum lines.
7. Remove thermactor belt from pulley. Remove hose below thermactor pump. Remove thermactor pump.
8. Disconnect the two exhaust pipe to exhaust manifold retaining nuts.
9. Remove exhaust manifold heat shield.
10. Disconnect EGR sensor wire at connector.
11. Disconnect thermactor check valve hose at tube assembly. Remove bracket to EGR valve attaching nuts.
12. Disconnect water inlet tube at intake manifold.
13. Disconnect EGR tube at EGR valve.
14. Remove intake manifold.
15. Remove exhaust manifold.
To install:
16. Position exhaust manifold to cylinder head using guide bolts in holes 6 and 7.
17. Install the attaching bolts in holes 1 through 5.
18. Rundown attaching bolts until snug, then remove guide bolts and install attaching bolts in holes 6 and 7.
19. Tighten all exhaust manifold bolts to specification using the standard tightening sequence.
20. Install intake manifold gasket and bolts and tighten to specification.
21. Connect water inlet tube at intake manifold.
22. Connect thermactor check valve hose at tube assembly. Install bracket to EGR valve attaching nuts.
23. Connect EGR sensor wire at connector.
24. Connect EGR tube to EGR valve.
25. Install exhaust manifold studs.
26. Connect exhaust pipe to exhaust manifold.

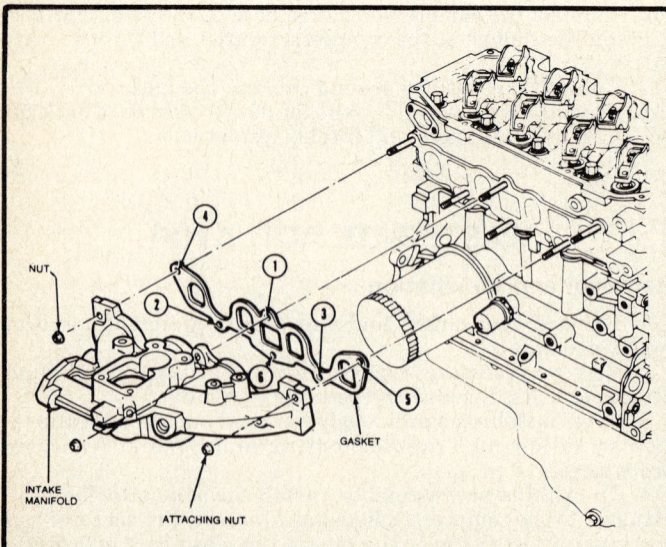

Exhaust manifold removal and installation—1.6L/1.9L engines

27. Install thermactor pump hose to pump. Install thermactor pump and thermactor pump drive belt.
28. Install vacuum lines.
29. Install air cleaner assembly and heat stove tube.
30. Install accelerator cable.
31. Connect negative ground cable.
32. Fill cooling system.
33. Start engine and check for leaks.

3.0L ENGINE

1. Disconnect the negative battery cable and drain the engine cooling system into a suitable drain pan.
2. Loosen the hose clamp attaching the flex hose to the throttle body. Remove the air cleaner flex hose. Remove the throttle.
3. Disconnect and tag all the vacuum connections to the throttle body.
4. Disconnect the EGR valve assembly. Disconnect the throttle linkage, throttle position sensor, air charge temperature sensor and idle speed control.
5. Disconnect the PCV hose and disconnect the alternator support brace.
6. Remove the six throttle body attaching bolts and remove the throttle body.
7. Disconnect the fuel lines. Remove the fuel injection wiring harness from the engine. Disconnect and tag the spark plug wires (for easy installation) and remove the rocker arm covers (It will be necessary to remove the heater hoses to be able to remove the right hand side rocker cover).
8. Disconnect the upper radiator hose, the water outlet heater hose and the thermostat housing. Mark and remove the distributor assembly.
9. Remove the intake manifold attaching bolts and studs. Remove the manifold assembly with the fuel rails and injectors in place. Remove the manifold side gaskets and end seals and discard them.

Installation

Lightly oil all the attaching bolts and stud threads before installation. When using a silcone rubber sealer, assembly must occur within 15 minutes after the sealer has been applied. After this time, the sealer may start to set-up and its sealing quality may be reduced. In high temperature/humidty conditions the sealant will start to set up in approxitmately 5 minutes.

1. The intake manifold, cylinder head, and cylinder block mating surfaces should be clean and free of old silcone rubber sealer. Use a suitable solvent to clean these surfaces.
2. Apply a suitable silcone rubber sealer to the insection of the cylinder block assembly and head assembly on the each corner of the two manifold end seals.
3. Install the front intake manifold gaskets in place and insert the locking tabs over the tabs on the cylinder head gaskets. Apply a suitable silcone sealer over gasket in the same places as before on the manifold end seals.
4. Carefully lower the intake manifold into position on the cylinder block and cylinder heads to prevent smearing the silcone sealer and causing gasket voids.
5. Install the bolts and torque the bolts in two steps, 11 ft.lbs. and 18 ft. lbs.
6. Install the thermostat housing with a new thermostat and gasket, torque the attaching bolts to 6 to 8 ft. lbs.
7. Connect the PCV line at the PCV valve and exhaust manifold. Connect all necessary electrical connections. Connect the EGR valve assembly and all necessary vacuum lines. Apply a suitable silcone sealer to split between the head and the intake manifold (four places).
8. Install the rocker arm covers (with new gaskets), heater hoses and radiator hose.
9. Connect the fuel lines at the fuel charging assembly using

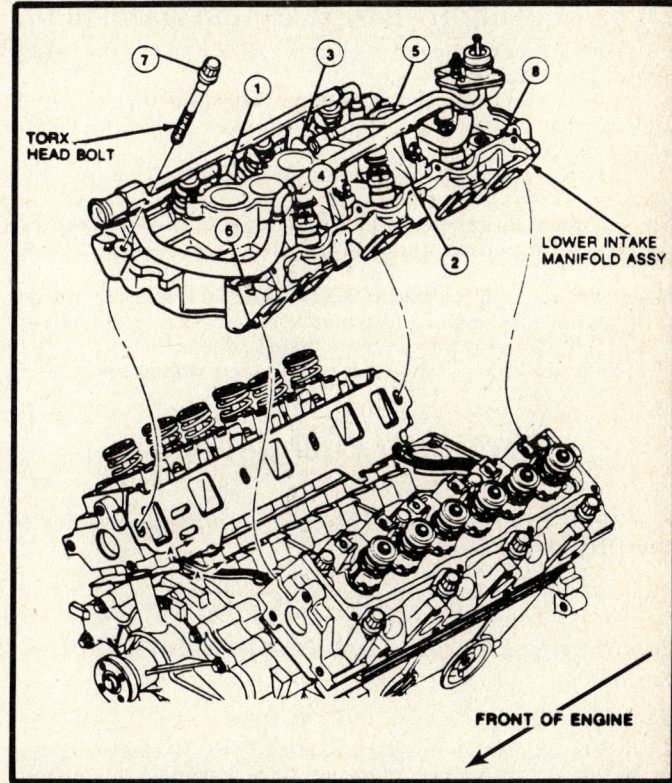

Intake manifold removal and installation—3.0L engine

tube spring lock coupler T83P–19623–C or equivalent. Replace the fuel lines and connector O-rings.
10. Install and the air cleaner assembly and outlet tube. Fill and bleed the cooling system with the specified coolant.

NOTE: This engine uses aluminum components that require a special corosion inhibitor coolant formulation to avoid radiator damage. The cooling system should be filled with a 50/50 mix of water and antifreeze, with the addition of two cooling system protector pellets D9AZ–19558–A or equivalent.

11. Reconnect the negative battery cable, start the engine and check for coolant, fuel and oil leaks.
12. Check and if necessary, adjust the engine idle speed, transmission throttle linkage and speed control.

EXHAUST MANIFOLD

Removal and Installation

3.0L ENGINE (LEFT HAND EXHAUST MANIFOLD)

1. Disconnect the negative battery cable. Remove the oil level indicator support bracket.
2. Remove the power steering pump pressure and return hoses. Remove the manifold exhaust pipe attaching nuts and remove the exhaust pipe from the exhaust manifold.
3. Remove the exhaust manifold attaching bolts and remove the manifold from the vehicle.
4. Clean all mating surfaces and lightly oil all bolt and stud threads pryor to installation. Installation is the reverse order of the removal procedure. Torque the exhaust manifold bolts to 15 to 22 ft. lbs. and torque the exhaust pipe attaching nuts to 16 to 24 ft. lbs.

Ford Mercury
FRONT WHEEL DRIVE CARS—ESCORT • EXP • LYNX • TEMPO • TOPAZ • TAURUS • SABLE

3.0L ENGINE (RIGHT HAND EXHAUST MANIFOLD)

1. Disconnect the negative battery cable. Remove the heater hose support bracket.
2. Disconnect and plug the heater hoses. Remove the EGR tube from the exhaust manifold. Use a back-up wrench on the lower adapter.
3. Remove the manifold to exhaust pipe attaching nuts and remove the pipe from the manifold.
4. Remove the exhaust manifold attaching bolts and remove the exhaust manifold from the vehicle.
5. Clean all mating surfaces and lightly oil all bolt and stud threads pryor to installation. Installation is the reverse order of the removal procedure. Torque the exhaust manifold bolts to 15 to 22 ft. lbs. and torque the exhaust pipe attaching nuts to 16 to 24 ft. lbs. Torque the EGR tube to the exhaust manifold to 25 to 36 ft. lbs.

Electronic Fuel Injection

For More Information on Fuel Injectin System refer to Unit Repair Section.

VEHICLE APPLICATION

Escort/Lynx, EXP and Taurus/Sable With The 3.0L Engine

DESCRIPTION

The Electronic Fuel Injection System (EFI) is classified as a multi-point, pulse time, mass air flow fuel injection system. Fuel is metered into the intake air stream in accordance with engine demand through four injectors mounted on a tuned intake manifold.

An on board vehicle Electronic Engine control (EEC) computer accepts input from various engine sensors to compute the required fuel flow rate necessary to maintain a prescribed air/fuel ratio throughout the entire engine operational range. The computer then outputs a command to the fuel injectors to meter the approximate quantity of fuel.

FUEL CHARGING ASSEMBLY

NOTE: If sub-assemblies are to be serviced and/or removed, with the fuel charging assembly mounted to the engine, the following steps must be taken.

ALL MODELS

1. Open hood and install protective covers.
2. Make sure that ignition key is in Off position.
3. Drain coolant from radiator.
4. Disconnect the negative battery lead an secure it out of the way.
5. Remove fuel cap to relieve fuel tank pressure.
6. Release pressure from the fuel system at the fuel pressure relief valve on the fuel injector manifold assembly. Use Tool T80L-9974-A or equivalent. To gain access to the fuel pressure relief valve, the valve cap must first be removed.
7. Disconnect the push connect fuel supply line. Using a small bladed screwdriver or equivalent inserted under the hairpin clip tab, "pop" the clip free from the push connect tube fitting and disconnect the push connect tube fitting and disconnect the tube. Save the hairpin clip for use in reassembly.
8. Identify and disconnect the fuel return lines and vacuum connections.

NOTE: Care must be taken to avoid combustion from fuel spillage.

9. Disconnect the injector wiring harness by disconnecting the ECT sensor in the heater supply tube under lower intake manifold and the electronic engine control harness.
10. Disconnect air bypass connector from EEC harness.

NOTE: Not all assemblies may be serviceable while on the engine. In some cases, removal of the fuel charging assembly may facilitate service of the various sub-assemblies. To remove the entire fuel charging assembly, the following procedure should be followed.

Removal and Installation

Escort/Lynx, EXP

1. Remove the engine air cleaner outlet tube between the vane air meter and air throttle body by loosening two clamps.
2. Disconnect and remove the accelerator and speed control cables (if so equipped) from the accelerator mounting bracket and throttle lever.
3. Disconnect the top manifold vacuum fitting connections by disconnecting:
   a. Rear vacuum line to the dash panel vacuum tree.
   b. Front vacuum line to the air cleaner and fuel pressure regulator.
4. Disconnect the PCV system by disconnecting the hoses from:
   a. Two large forward facing connectors on the throttle body and intake manifold.
   b. Throttle body port hose at the straight plastic connector.
   c. Canister purge line at the straight plastic connector.
   d. PCV hose at rocker cover.
   e. Unbolt PCV separator support bracket from cylinder head and remove PCV system.
5. Disconnect the EGR vacuum line at the EGR valve.
6. Disconnect the EGR tube from the upper intake manifold by removing the two flange nuts.
7. Withdraw the dipstick and remove the dipstick tube by removing the tube bracket mounting nut and working the tube out of the block hole.
8. Remove the fuel return line.
9. Remove six manifold mounting nuts.
10. Remove the manifold with wiring harness and gasket.
11. Clean and inspect the mounting faces of the fuel charging manifold assembly and the cylinder head. Both surfaces must be clean and flat.
12. Clean and oil manifold stud threads.
13. Install a new gasket.
14. Install manifold assembly to head and secure with top middle nut (tighten nut fingertight only at this time).
15. Install fuel return line to the fitting in the fuel supply manifold. Install two manifold mounting nuts, fingertight.
16. Install dipstick in block and secure with bracket nut fingertight.
17. Install remaining three manifold mounting nuts and tighten all six nuts to 12–15 ft. lbs. observing specified tightening sequence.
18. Install EGR tube with two oil-coated flange nuts tightened to 6–8.5 ft. lbs.
19. Reinstall PCV system.
   a. Mount separator bracket to head.
   b. Install hose on rocker cover, tighten clamps.
   c. Connect vacuum line to canister purge.
   d. Connect vacuum line to throttle body port.
   e. Connect large PCV vacuum line to throttle body.
   f. Connect large PCV vacuum line to upper manifold.
20. Connect manifold vacuum connections:
   a. Rear connection to vacuum tree.
   b. Front connection to fuel pressure regulator and air cleaner.
21. Connect accelerator and speed control cables (if so equipped).

22. Install air supply tube and tighten clamps to 25 in.lbs.
23. Connect the wiring harness at:
    a. ECT sensor in heater supply tube.
    b. Electronic Engine Control harness.
24. Connect the fuel supply hose from the fuel filter to the fuel rail.
25. Connect the fuel return line.
26. Connect negative battery cable.
27. Install engine coolant using prescirbed fill procedure.
28. Start engine and allow to run at idle until engine temperature is stablized. Check for coolant leaks.
29. If necessary, reset idle speed.

INTAKE MANIFOLD, UPPER

Removal and Installation

1. Disconnect the engine air cleaner outlet tube from the air intake throttle body.
2. Unplug the throttle position sensor from the wiring harness.
3. Unplug the air bypass valve connector.
4. Remove three upper manifold retaining bolts.
5. Remove upper manifold assembly and set it aside.
6. Remove and discard the gasket from the lower manifold assembly.

NOTE: If scraping is necessary, be careful not to damage the gasket surfaces of the upper and lower manifold assemblies, or allow material to drop into lower manifold.

7. Ensure that the gasket surfaces of the upper and lower intake manifolds are clean.
8. Place a new service gasket on the lower manifold assembly and mount the upper intake manifold to the lower, securing it with three retaining bolts. Tighten bolts to 15-22 ft. lbs.
9. Ensure the wiring harness in porperly installed.
10. Connect electrical connectors to air bypass valve and throttle position sensor and the vacuum hose to the fuel pressure regulator.
11. Connect the engine air cleaner outlet tube to the throttle body intake securing it with a hose clamp tighten to 15-25 in.lbs.

AIR INTAKE THROTTLE BODY MANIFOLD

Removal and Installation

TAURUS/SABLE WITH 3.0L ENGINE

1. Remove the engine air cleaner outlet tube between the air cleaner and the throttle body.

NOTE: If the fuel rail assembly or injectors must be removed for service, the snow shield and the air intake throttle body must be removed.

2. If required, remove the snow shield by removing the retaining nut on top of the shield and the two bolts on the side of the shield.3. Disconnect and tag the vacuum hoses at the vacuum fittings on the intake manifold. Disconnect and remove the accelerator and speed control cables (if so equipped) from the accelerator mounting bracket and throttle lever.
4. Remove the transmission valve (TV) linkage from the throttle lever (automatic transmission only). Remove the six air intake throttle body manifold retaining bolts and lift the manifold from the quide pins on the lower intake assembly.
5. Remove and discard the gasket from the lower intake manifold assembly.
6. Clean all mating surfaces and lightly oil all bolt and stud threads pryor to installation. Installation is the reverse order of the removal procedure. Torque the all the manifold bolts to 15 to 22 ft. lbs.

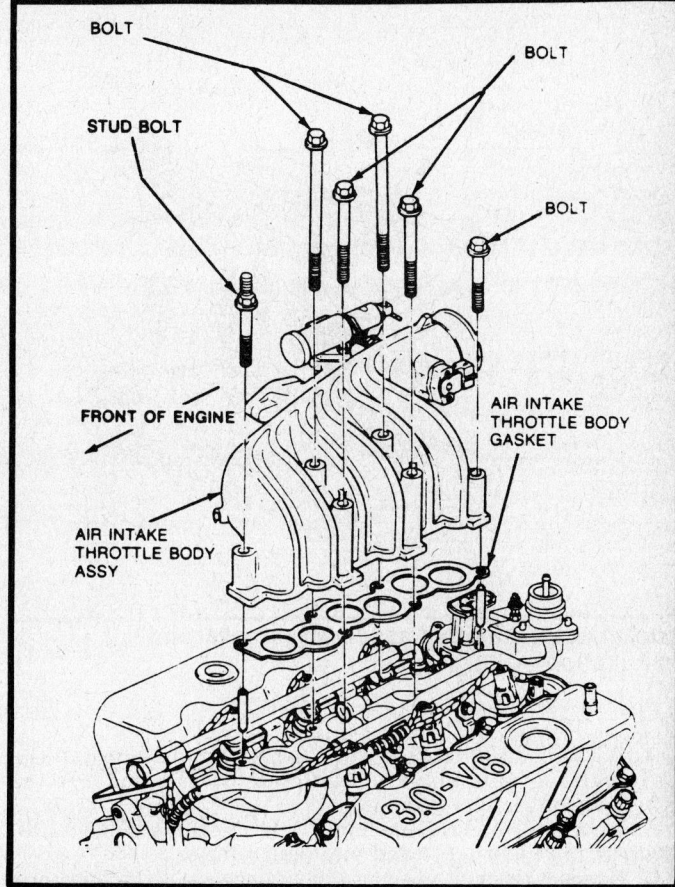

Air intake throttle assembly manifold removal and installation—3.0L engine

FUEL INJECTOR MANIFOLD ASSEMBLY

Removal

TAURUS/SABLE WITH 3.0L ENGINE

1. Remove the air intake throttle body manifold as previously outlined in this section.
2. Disconnect the fuel supply and fuel return lines as previously outlined in this section. Carefully disconnect the wiring harness from the fuel injectors.
3. Disconnect the vacuum line from the fuel pressure regulator valve. Remove the four fuel injector manifold retaining bolts.
4. Carefully disengage the fuel rail assembly from the fuel injectors by lifting and gently rocking the rail.
5. Remove the fuel injectors by lifting while gently rocking the injector from side to side. Place the removed components in a clean container to avoid dirt or other contamination.

Installation

1. Install new O-rings on the injectors (two per injector, lubricate all the O-rings with clean engine oil). Ensure the injector caps are clean and free of contamination or damage.
2. Install the injectors in the fuel rail using a twisting pushing motion.
3. Carefully install the rail assembly and injectors into the lower intake manifold, one side a a time. To ensure that ther O-

Ford Mercury
FRONT WHEEL DRIVE CARS—ESCORT • EXP • LYNX • TEMPO • TOPAZ • TAURUS • SABLE

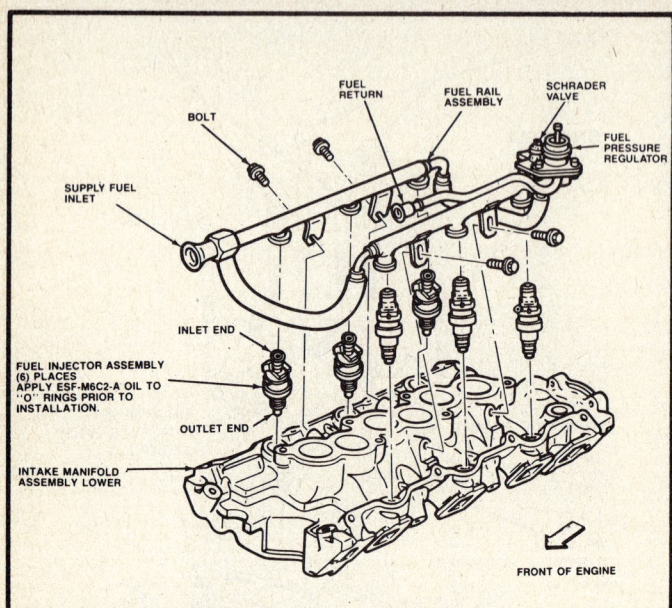

Fuel injector manifold assembly removal and installation—3.0L engine

rings are seated, push down on the fuel rail.
4. While holding the fuel rail assembly in place, install the two retaining bolts finger tight. Repeat Steps 3 and 4 to the other side of the fuel rail.
5. Torque the fuel rail assembly retaining bolts to 6–8 ft. lbs. Connect the fuel supply and fuel return lines.
6. Connect the fuel injector wiring harness at the injectors. Connect the vacuum lines to the fuel pressure regulator and reinstall the air intake throttle body manifold.

FUEL INJECTOR

Removal
ALL MODELS
1. Remove fuel tank cap and release pressure from the fuel system at the fuel pressure relief valve.
2. Disconnect fuel supply and return lines.
3. Remove vacuum line from fuel pressure regulator.
4. Disconnect the fuel injector wiring harness.
5. Remove fuel injector manifold assembly.
6. Carefully remove connectors from individual injectors(s) as required.
7. Grasping the injector's body, pull up while gently rocking the injector from side-to-side.
8. Inspect the injector O-rings (two per injector) for signs of deterioration. Replace as required.
9. Inspect the injector "plastic hat" (covering the injector pintle) and washer for signs of detrioration. Replace as required. If hat is missing, look for it in intake manifold.

Installation
1. Lubricate new O-rings and install two on each injector (use a light grade oil).
2. Install the injector(s). Use a light, twisting, pushing motion to install the injector(s).
3. Carefully seat the fuel injector manifold assembly on the four injectors and secure the manifold with two attaching bolts. Tighten to 15–22 ft. lbs. (20–30 Nm).
4. Connect the vacuum line to the fuel pressure regulator.
5. Connect fuel injector wiring harness.

6. Connect fuel supply and fuel return lines. Tighten fuel return line to 15–18 ft. lbs. (20–25 Nm).
7. Check entire assembly for proper alignment and seating.

Central Fuel Injection

GENERAL INFORMATION

The Ford Central Fuel Injection (CFI) System is a single point, pulse time modulated injection system. Fuel is metered into the air intake stream according to engine demands by two solenoid injection valves. mounted in a throttle body on the intake manifold. Fuel is supplied from the fuel tank by a high pressure, electric fuel pump, either by itself or in addition t a low-pressure, electric fuel pump, either by itself or in addition to a low-pressure pump. The fuel is filtered, and sent to the air throttle body where a regulator keeps the fuel delivery pressure at a constant 39 psi (269 kPa). Two injector nozzles are mounted vertically above the throttle plates and connected in parallel with the fuel pressure regulator. Excess fuel supplied by the pump but not needed by the engine, is returned to the fuel tank by a steel fuel return line.

FUEL CHARING ASSEMBLY

Removal and Installation

TEMPO/TOPAZ WITH 2.3L HSC ENGINE AND TAURUS/SABLE WITH THE 2.5L ENGINE

1. Remove the air tube clamp at the fuel charging assembly air inlet.
2. Remove the electrical connector at the inertial switch located on the right side of the trunk(left hand side on the Taurus/Sable) and release the fuel system pressure by cranking the engine for 15 seconds.
3. Disconnect the throttle cable and transmission throttle valve lever.
4. Disconnect the electrical connector at the idle speed control, throttle position sensor and fuel injector.
5. Disconnect the fuel inlet, outlet connections and PCV vacuum line at the fuel charging assembly.

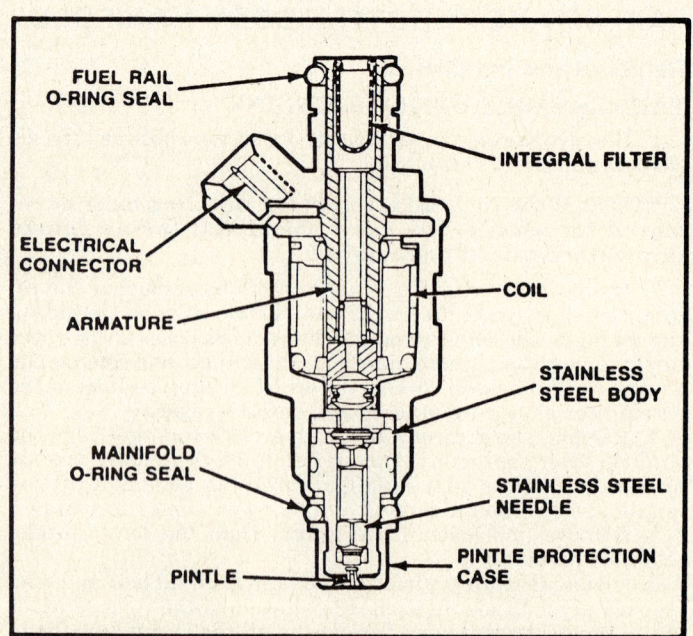

Typical fuel injector (© Ford Motor Co.)

Ford Mercury
FRONT WHEEL DRIVE CARS—ESCORT • EXP • LYNX • TEMPO • TOPAZ • TAURUS • SABLE

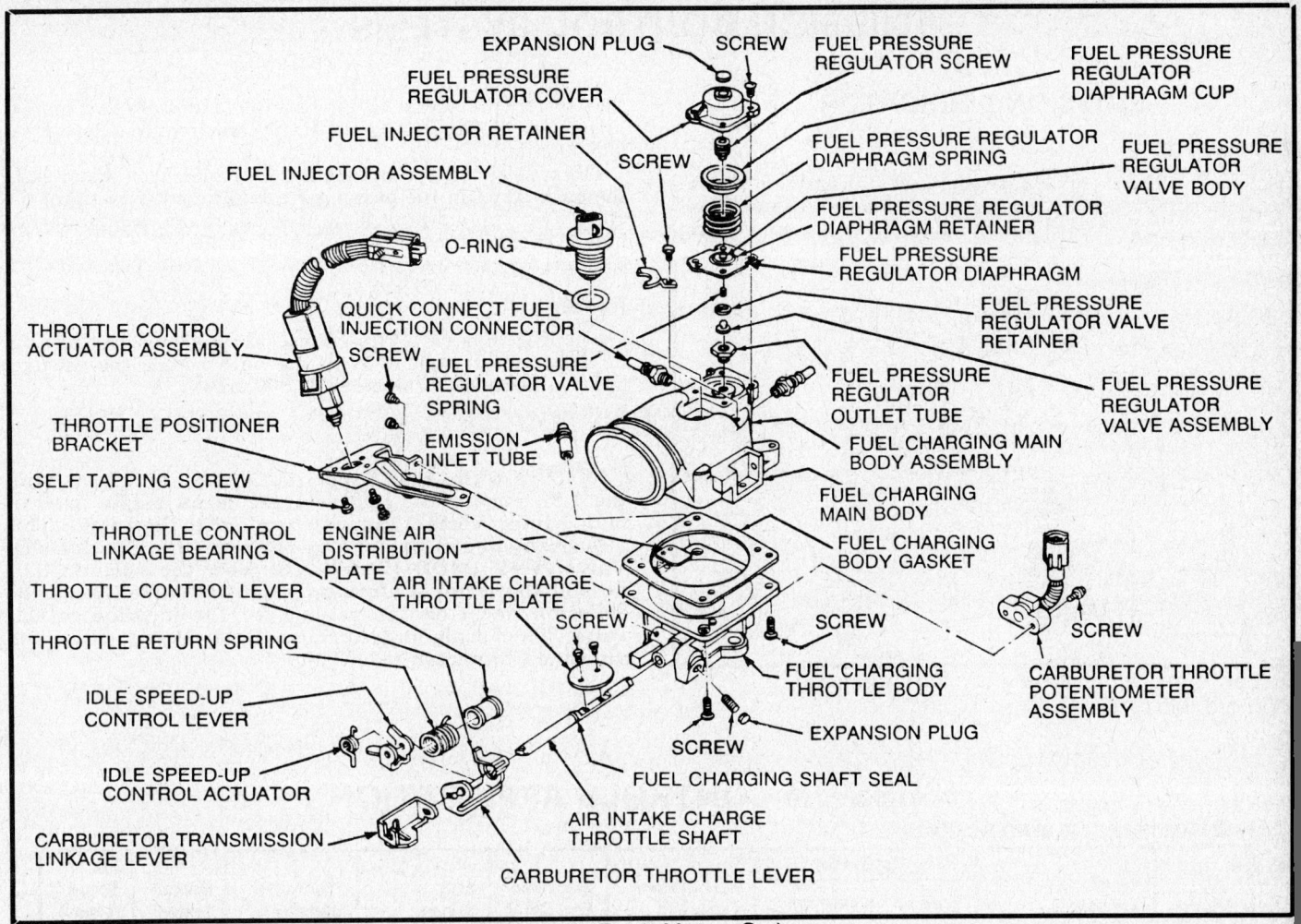

Exploded view of the central fuel injection (© Ford Motor Co.)

6. Remove the fuel charging assembly, two retaining nuts and remove the assembly along with the mounting gasket from the intake manifold.

7. Installation is the reverse order of the removal procedure and torque the fuel charging assembly mounting nuts to 14–16 ft. lbs.

FUEL INJECTOR

Removal and Installation

1. Remove the fuel charging assembly as previously outlined.

2. Remove the four retaining screws holding the throttle body to the main body, and separate the throttle body from the main body.

3. Remove and discard the gasket, and if scraping is necessary, be careful not to damage the mounting surface.

4. Remove the four screws holding the fuel pressure regulator to the assembly.

NOTE: The fuel pressure regulator cover is sprig loaded, so be sure to apply downward pressure when removing the cover to contain all the parts.

5. Remove the regulator cover assembly, cup, spring and diaphragm assembly, also remove the regulator valve seat.

6. Remove the fuel injector retaining screw and retainer, apply finger pressure from below the injector nozzle and remove the injector assembly.

7. Remove the injector lower O-ring from the injector cavity in the main body. Install a new one during installation.

8. Installation is the reverse order of the removal procedure. Torque the injector retainer screws to 18–22 in.lbs. and the fuel pressure regulator retaining screws to 28–32 in.lbs.

NOTE: For information on the 2.0 liter diesel, refer to the diesel section in the unit repair part of this manual.

SECTION 4
FORD MERCURY
FRONT WHEEL DRIVE CARS—ESCORT • EXP • LYNX • TEMPO • TOPAZ • TAURUS • SABLE

EMISSION CONTROL SYSTEMS

EMISSIONS INDICATOR

Escort/Lynx

Some Escort/Lynx vehicles are equipped with an EGR Maintenance Reminder System that consists of a mileage sensor module, an instrument panel warning light and associated wiring.

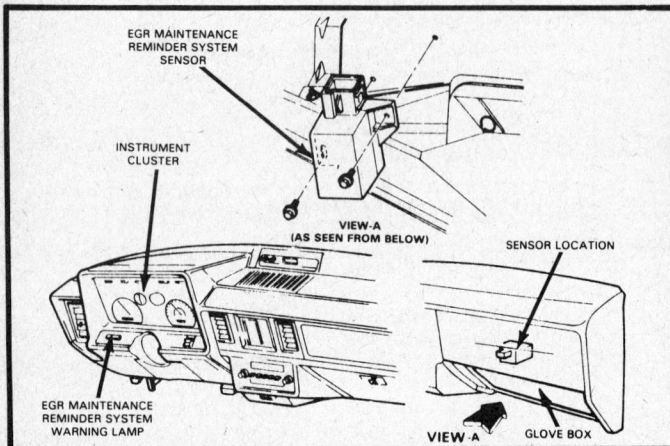

Escort/Lynx emissions indicator system
(© Ford Motor Co.)

This system provides a visual warning to indicate that the Exhaust Gas Recirculating (EGR) System requires service at 30,000 miles.

The mileage sensor module is a blue plastic ox mounted in the dash panel in the passenger compartment forward of the glove box. The warning lamp is snapped into a pre-punched hole in the insturment cluster finish panel, left of the steering column.

Reset

When EGR System Maintenance is completed, replace the mileage sensor module. With the new module the warning light will stay off for another 30,000 mile interval.

NOTE: On the 1983 Escort, EXP, LN7 and Lynx with the 1.6L carbureted engine there is an engine performance improvement that can be made to the engine. This improvement can be done by removing the Spark Delay Valve (VDV D3DE–12A189–AB) from the vacuum harness at the exhaust air supply control valve (check the emission decal on the vehicle for the location of this valve). Then replacing the Spark Delay Valve with Vacuum Line Connector 383003–S.

EMISSION CONTROLS APPLICATION

PASSENGER CAR — 50 STATES/CANADA

Engine	Vehicle Application	Catalyst(s) Type	Catalyst(s) Location	Fuel System Type, Mfg	Electronic Eng Ctrl	EGR System	Thermactor System	Ignition System	Idle Speed Control
1.9L	Escort/Lynx/EXP	TWC & COC	DBUB	740-2V Holley	None	BVT	MTA	TFI-I	M/V
1.9L	Escort/Lynx/EXP	TWC & COC	DBUB	EFI	EEC-IV	BVT	Dual PA	TFI-IV	BPA
2.3L HSC 50 States	Tempo/Topaz	TWC & COC	DBUB	CFI	EEC-IV	ELEC	PA	TFI-IV	DCM
2.3L HSC Canada	Tempo/Topaz	COC	UB	1949-IV Holley	None	Ported	CT	DS-II	TSP
2.5L HSC	Taurus/Sable	TWC & COC	DBUB	CFI	EEC-IV	ELEC	PA	TFI-IV	DCM
3.0L	Taurus/Sable	TWC	UE	EFI	EEC-IV	PFE Canada-None	None	TFI-IV	BPA

ABBREVIATIONS:

- OHC = Overhead Cam
- HSC = High Swirl Combustion
- HO = High Output
- COC = Conventional Oxidation Catalyst
- TWC = Three-Way Catalyst
- TB = Toe Board
- UB = Underbody
- UE = Under Engine
- DBUB = Dual Brick Underbody
- MFG = Manufacturer
- FBC = Feedback Carburetor
- NFB = Non-Feedback Carburetor
- EFI = Electronic Fuel Injection

- ELEC = Electronic Valve
- SEFI = Sequential EFI
- CFI = Central Fuel Injection
- EEC-IV = Electronic Engine Control (System-IV)
- MCU = Microprocessor Control Unit
- EGR = Exhaust Gas Recirculation
- EVP = EGR Valve Position
- EVR = EGR Valve Regulator
- EGRC = EGR Control
- EGRV = EGR Vent
- PFE = Pressure Feedback Electronic
- BP = Backpressure

- IBP = Integral Backpressure
- CT = Conventional Thermactor
- PA = Pulse Air
- MTA = Managed Thermactor Air
- DS-II = Duraspark II
- TFI = Thick Film Ignition
- UIC = Universal Ignition Control
- M/V = Mechanical Vacuum
- BPA = Bypass Air
- DCM = D. C. Motor
- TSP = Throttle Solenoid Positioner
- DP = Dashpot

Ford Mercury
FRONT WHEEL DRIVE CARS—ESCORT • EXP • LYNX • TEMPO • TOPAZ • TAURUS • SABLE
SECTION 4

GASOLINE ENGINE SECTION

ENGINE ASSEMBLY

Removal and Installation

ESCORT/LYNX, EXP

1. Mark position of hood hinges and remove hood.
2. Remove air cleaner, air intake duct and heat tube.
3. Disconnect negative battery cable.
4. Drain cooling system.
5. Remove alternator mounting bolts and lay alternator aside.
6. Disconnect and remove thermactor air pump.
7. Disconnect radiator hoses and oil cooler lies if equipped with ATX transmission.
8. Remove radiator cooling fan and shroud as an assembly.
9. Remove radiator.
10. Disconnect heater hoses, electrical connections and vacuum hoses as necessary.
11. Disconnect kickdown rod at carburetor ATX only.
12. Disconnect accelerator cable at carburetor.
13. Rise vehicle.
14. Remove knee brace at front of starter motor and remove battery cable from starter.
15. disconnect exhaust inlet pipe at manifold.
16. Remove support bracket in front of converter cover ATX, inspection cover MTX transmission, and remove cover.
17. Remove cranskshaft pulley.
18. Remove torque converter to flywheel nuts ATX.
19. Remove timing belt cover lower attaching bolts MTX transmission.
20. Remove converter housing or flywheel housing lower attaching bolts.
21. Disconnect coolant by-pass hose from intake manifold.
22. Remove nut and bolt attaching insulator bracket to the engine bracket at front of engine.
23. Lower vehicle.
24. Install suitable lifting brackets on engine.

NOTE: The top rear bolt attaching the thermactor pump bracket to the engine can be removed and used as a lifting bracket attaching point.

25. Use a suitable lifting device connected to the engine lifting brackets and raise engine just enough to remove the through bolt from the front engine insulator and remove insulator.
26. Remove the remaining timing belt cover bolts and remove the cover, MTX only.
27. Remove insulator attaching bracket from engine.
28. Position a jack under the transaxle. Raise jack just enough to support the weight of the transaxle.
29. Remove the converter housing, flywheel housing upper attaching bolts.
30. Remove engine assembly from vehicle.
31. Installation of the engine assembly can be done by reversing the removal procedure.

ENGINE/TRANSAXLE ASSEMBLY

Removal and Installation

2.3L TEMPO/TOPAZ AND 2.5L TAURUS/SABLE

1. Mark position of hood hinges and remove hood.
2. Remove negative ground cable from battery.
3. Remove air cleaner.
4. Remove lower radiator hose to drain engine coolant.
5. Remove upper radiator hose and disconnect transaxle cooler lines at rubber hoses below radiator.
6. Remove coil, and disconnect coolant fan at electrical connection.
7. Remove radiator shroud and cooling fan as an assembly. Remove radiator.
8. Discharge air conditioning system, if equipped, and remove pressure and suction lines from compressor.

CAUTION
Use extreme care when discharging air conditioning system, as the refrigerant is under high pressure.

---

9. Identify and disconnect all electrical and vacuum lines as necessary.
10. Disconnect TV linkage or clutch cable at transaxle.
11. Disconnect accelerator linkage and fuel lines.
12. Disconnect thermactor pump discharge hose at pump.
13. Disconnect power steering lines at pump if equipped.
14. Install engine support tool to existing engine lifting eye.
15. Raise vehicle on hoist.
16. Remove battery cable from starter and hose off of catalytic converter.
17. Remove bolt attaching exhaust pipe bracket to oil pan an two exhaust pipe to manifold attaching nuts.
18. Pull exhaust system out of rubber insulating grommets and set aside.
19. Remove speedometer cable from transaxle.
20. Remove on heater hose from water pump inlet tube and the other from the steel tube on intake manifold.
21. Remove water pump inlet tube clamp bolt at engine block and two clamp bolts at underside of oil pan. Remove inlet tube.
22. Remove bolts attaching control arms to body. Remove stabilizer bar brackets retaining bolts and remove brackets.
23. Halfshaft assemblies must be removed from transaxle at this time.
24. MTX only, remove roll restrictor nuts from transaxle. Pull roll restrictor from mounting bracket.
25. MTX only, remove shift stabilizer bar to transaxle attaching bolts. Remove shift mechanism to shift shaft attaching nut an bolt at transaxle.
26. ATX only, disconnect manual shift cable clip from lever on transaxle. Remove manual shift linkage bracket bolts from transaxle and remove bracket.
27. Remove the LH rear insulator mount bracket from body bracket by removing the two nuts.
28. Remove the LH front insulator to transaxle mounting bolts.
29. Lower vehicle. Install lifting equipment to the two existing lifting eyes on engine.

CAUTION
Do not allow front wheels to touch floor.

---

30. Remove Engine Support tool.
31. Remove RH No.3A insulator intermediate bracket to engine bracket bolts, intermediate bracket to insulator attaching nuts and the nut on the bottom of the double ended stud which attaches the intermediate bracket to engine bracket. Remove bracket.
32. Carefully lower engine and transaxle assembly to the floor.
33. Installation of the engine/transaxle assembly can be done by reversing the removal procedure.

ENGINE ASSEMBLY

Removal and Installation

TAURUS/SABLE WITH 3.0L ENGINE

1. Disconnect the battery cables and drain the cooling system into a suitable drain pan. Remove the engine hood.
2. Discharge the A/C system. Remove the air cleaner assembly. Remove the battery and the battery tray.
3. Remove the integrated relay controller, cooling fan and radiator with fan shroud. Remove the engine bounce damper bracket on the shock tower.
4. Remove the evaporative emission line, upper radiator hose, starter brace and lower radiator hose.
5. Remove the exhaust pipes from both exhaust manifolds. Remove and plug the power steering pump lines.
6. Remove the fuel lines and remove and tag all necessary vacuum lines.
7. Disconnect the ground strap, heater lines, accelerator cable linkage, throttle valve linkage and speed control cable.
8. Disconnect thwe following wiring connectors; alternator, A/C clutch, oxygen sensor, ignition coil, radio frequency supressor, cooling fan voltage resistor, engine coolant temperature sensor, Thick film ignition module, injector wiring harness, ISC motor wire, throttle position sensor, oil pressure sending switch, ground wire, block heater (if so equipped), knock sensor, EGR sensor and oil level sensor.
9. Remove the engine mount bolts and engine mounts. Remove the transaxle to engine mounting bolts and transaxle brace assembly.
10. Install a suitable engine lifting plate onto the engine and use a suitable engine hoist to remove the engine from the vehicle. Remove the main wire harness from the engine.
11. Installation is the reverse order of the removal procedure. Torque the transaxle brace assewmbly bolts to 40–55 ft. lbs. Torque the engine mount nuts to 55–75 ft. lbs. and torque the engine mount bolts to 40–55 ft. lbs.
12. On the engine mount assembly 6F063 and 6F065 torque the engine mount nuts and engine mount bolts to 70–96 ft. lbs.

ENGINE REAR SUPPORT BRACKET

Removal and Installation

1.6L, 1.9L AND 2.3L ENGINES

1. Remove LH rear No.4 insulator.
2. Remove the three support bracket attaching bolts.
3. To install, position the support bracket. Install the three attaching bolts and tighten to 100–135 Nm (75–100 ft. lbs.).
4. Install LH rear No. 4 insulator.

Valve System

OVERSIZE/UNDERSIZE

Some engines were manufactures with oversize valve tappet bores. When replacing valve tappets, mike old tappet to determine if it is standard or oversize. Standard diameter is 0.874 in. (22.206mm).

Tappet Clearance Check

1.6L AND 1.9L ESCORT/LYNX, EXP

To determine the rocker arm to tappet clearance, make the following check:
1. Connect an auxiliary starter switch in the starting circuit. Crank the engine with the ignition switch Off until the No. 1 piston is on TDC after the compression stroke.
2. With the crankshaft in the position designated in Steps 3 and 4, position the hydraulic lifter compressor tool on the rocker arm. Slowly apply pressure to bleed down the tappet until it

Checking the collapsed tappet clearance

is completely bottom . Hold the tappet in this position and check the available clearance between the rocker arm and the valve stem tip with a feeler gauge. The feeler gauge width must not exceed $3/8$ in., in order to fit between the rails on the rocker arm. If the clearance is less than specifications, check the following for wear:
   a. Fulcrum.
   b. Tappet.
   c. Cam lobe.
   d. Valve tip.
3. With the No. 1 piston on TDC at the end of the compression stroke (Position No. 1), check the following valves:
   a. No. 1 Intake No. 1 Exhaust.
   b. No. 2 Intake.
4. Rotate the crankshaft to Position No. 2 and check the following valves: No. 3 – Intake, No. 3 – Exhaust.
5. Rotate the crankshaft another 180° from Position No. 2 back to TDC and check the following valves:
   a. No. 4 Intake No. 4 Exhaust.
   b. No. 2 Exhaust.
   Collapsed tappet clearance should be 0.059–0.194 in. (1.5–4.95mm).

Collapsed Tappet Gap

2.3L TEMPO/TOPAZ AND 2.5L TAURUS/SABLE

1. Rotate camshaft to position A in illustration. Check intake and exhaust valves on the compression stroke under camshaft position A. Tappet gap should be 0.072–0.174 in. (1.80–4.34mm).
2. Rotate camshaft 180 ° to position B in illustration. Check remaining tappets.

VALVE CLEARANCE

The intake and exhaust valves are driven by the camshaft, working through hydraulic lash adjusters and stamped rocker arms (1.6L and 1.9L engine) or through hydraulic lifters, pushrods and rocker arms (2.3L, 2.5L and 3.0L engine). The hydraulic lash adjusters or lifters eliminate the need for periodic valve lash adjustments.

Ford Mercury

FRONT WHEEL DRIVE CARS—ESCORT • EXP • LYNX • TEMPO • TOPAZ • TAURUS • SABLE

Valve Rocker Assembly

Removal and Installation

1.6L AND 1.9L ENGINES

1. Disconnect the negative battery cable and remove the air cleaner assembly.
2. Remove and tag all necessary vacuum hoses from the rocker cover. Remove the seven screws and washer assemblies retaining the the rocker cover to the cylinder head.
3. Remove the rocker cover and gasket from the engine.
4. Remove the rocker arm nuts, fulcrums, rocker arms, and fulcrum washers. Keep all parts in order so they can be reinstalled to their original position.
5. Before installation, coat the valve tips, rocker arm and fulcrum contact areas with Lubriplate® or equivalent.
6. Rotate the engine until the lifter is on the base circle of the cam (valve closed).

NOTE: Be sure to turn the engine only in the normal rotation. Backward rotation will cause the camshaft belt to slip or lose teeth, altering the valve timing and causing serious engine damage.

7. Install the rocker arm and components and torque the rocker arm nuts to 15–19 ft. lbs. Be sure the lifter is on the base circle of the cam for each rocker arm as it is installed. Adjust the valves as previously outlined.
8. Install guide pins into the cylinder head and guide the gasket and rocker arm cover over the pins. Install the retaining screws and washer and torque the screws to 6–8 ft. lbs.

NOTE: Do not use any glue with the silcone gasket.

Removal and Installation

2.3L AND 2.5L ENGINES

1. Disconnect the negative battery cable and remove the air cleaner assembly.
2. Remove and tag all necessary vacuum hoses from the rocker cover. Remove the oil fill cap and set it aside. Disconnect the PCV hose and set it aside.
3. Disconnect the throttle linkage cable from the top of the rocker arm cover. Disconnect the speed control cable from the top of the rocker arm if so equipped.
4. Remove the nine rocker arm cover bolts. Remove the rocker cover and gasket from the engine.
4. Remove the rocker arm bolts, fulcrums, rocker arms, and fulcrum washers. Keep all parts in order so they can be reinstalled to their original position.
5. Before installation, coat the valve tips, rocker arm and fulcrum contact areas with Lubriplate® or equivalent.
6. Rotate the engine until the lifter is on the base circle of the cam (valve closed).
7. Install the rocker arm and components and torque the rocker arm bolts in two steps the first to 6–8 ft.lbs and the second torque to 20–26 ft. lbs. Be sure the lifter is on the base circle of the cam for each rocker arm as it is installed. Adjust the valves as previously outlined.
8. Install guide pins into the cylinder head and guide the gasket and rocker arm cover over the pins. Install the retaining screws and washer and torque the screws to 7–10 ft. lbs.

NOTE: Do not use any glue with the silcone gasket.

Removal and Installation

3.0L ENGINE

1. Disconnect the negative battery cable. Disconnect and tag the spark plug wires.
2. Remove the ignition wire separators from the rocker arm attaching bolt studs. On the LH cover remove the oil fill cap and disconnect the closure system hose.

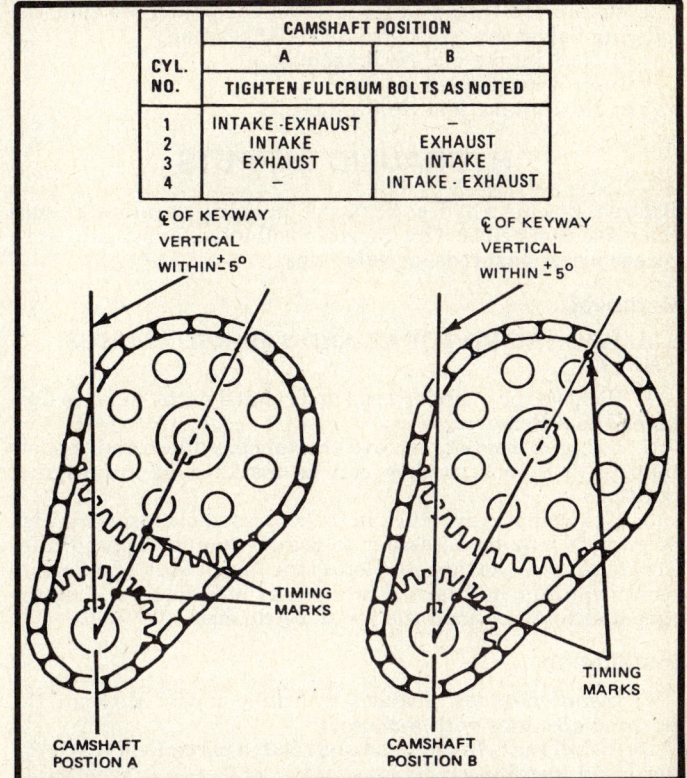

Collapsed tappet clearance 2.3L engine
(© Ford Motor Co.)

CYL. NO.	CAMSHAFT POSITION A	CAMSHAFT POSITION B
	TIGHTEN FULCRUM BOLTS AS NOTED	
1	INTAKE-EXHAUST	—
2	INTAKE	EXHAUST
3	EXHAUST	INTAKE
4	—	INTAKE-EXHAUST

3. On the RH cover, remove the PCV Valve, disconnect the EGR valve and disconnect and plug the heater hose.
4. Remove the rocker arm cover attaching screws and remove the covers and gaskets from the vehicle.
4. Remove the rocker arm bolts, fulcrums, rocker arms, and fulcrum washers. Keep all parts in order so they can be reinstalled to their original position.
5. Before installation, coat the valve tips, rocker arm and fulcrum contact areas with Lubriplate® or equivalent. Lightly oil all the bolt and stud threads before installation.
6. Rotate the engine until the lifter is on the base circle of the cam (valve closed).
7. Install the rocker arm and components and torque the rocker arm fulcrum bolts to 19–29 ft. lbs. Be sure the lifter is on the base circle of the cam for each rocker arm as it is installed. Adjust the valves as previously outlined.
8. Install guide pins into the cylinder head and guide the gaskets and rocker arm covers over the pins. Install the attaching screws and washer and torque the screws to 7–10 ft. lbs. Torque the EGR tube to 25–36 ft. lbs.

NOTE: Apply a bead of RTV silicone sealer or equivalent at the cylinder head to intake manifold rail step (two places per rail) before installing the gasket. Do not use any glue with the silcone (rubber) gasket.

3.0L VALVE TIMING

Test

1. Rotate the engine until the number one cylinder is at top dead center of its compression stroke and check and see that the follwing valves are in the open (down) position.
   a. No.1 intake and No.1 exhaust.
   b. No.3 intake and No.2 exhaust.
   c. No.6 intake and No.4 exhaust.

4–53

FORD MERCURY
FRONT WHEEL DRIVE CARS—ESCORT • EXP • LYNX • TEMPO • TOPAZ • TAURUS • SABLE

2. Rotate the crankshaft 360° and check and see that the follwing valves are in the open (down) position.
   a. No.2 intake and No.3 exhaust.
   b. No.4 intake and No.5 exhaust.
   c. No.5 intake and No.6 exhaust.

HYDRAULIC TAPPETS

Before replacing a hydraulic tappet for noisy operation, be sure the noise is not caused by improper collapsed tappet gap, worn rocker arms, pushrods, or valve tips.

Removal

2.3L HSC TEMPO/TOPAZ AND 2.5L–3.0L TAURUS/SABLE

1. Remove the cylinder head and related parts. Refer to Cylinder Head Removal.
2. Using a magnet, remove the tappets. Place the tappets tappets in a rack so they can be installed in the original positions.
3. If the tappets are stuck in their bores by excessive varnish or gum, it may be necessary to use Hydraulic Tappet Puller Tool to remove the tappets. Rotate the tappet back and forth to loosen any gum and varnish which may have formed. Keep the assemblies intact until the are to be cleaned.

Installation

1. Install new (or cleaned) hydraulic tappet through the pushrod openings with a magnet.
2. Install the cylinder head and related parts. Refer to Cylinder Head Installation.

CYLINDER HEAD

Removal and Installation

1.6L AND 1.9L ESCORT/LYNX, EXP

1. Disconnect the negative cable at the battery.
2. Drain the cooling system and disconnect the heater hose at the fitting located under the intake manifold.
3. Disconnect the raidator upper hose at the cylinder head.
4. disconnect the wiring terminal from the cooling fan switch.

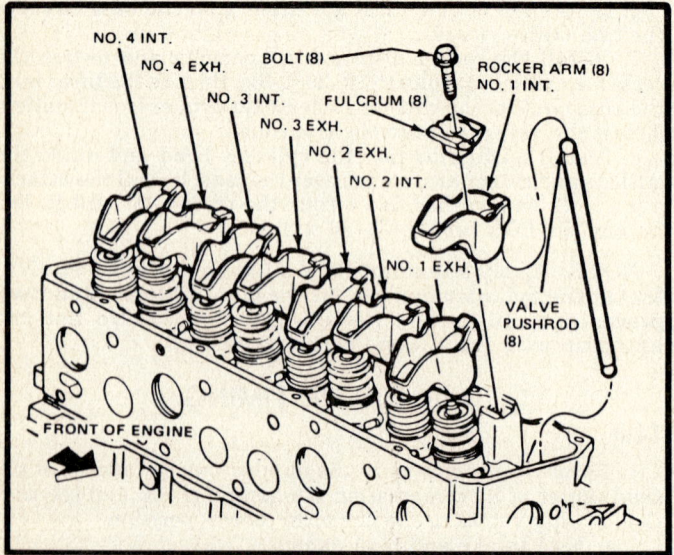

Rocker arm, fulcrum and pushrod removal
(© Ford Motor Co.)

5. Remove the air cleaner assembly.
6. Remove the PVC hose.
7. Disconncet the required vacuum hoses.
8. Remove the rocker arm cover.
9. Disconnect all accessory drive belts.
10. Remove the crankshaft pulley.
11. Remove the timing belt cover.
12. Set the engine No. 1 cylinder to TDC prior to removing the timing belt.
13. Remove the distributor cap and spark plug wires as an assembly.
14. Loosen both belt tensioner attaching blots using torque wrench adapter T81P–6254–A or equivalent.
15. Secure the belt tensioner as far left as possible.
16. Remove the timing belt.
17. Disconnect the EGR tube at the EGR valve.
18. Disconnect the PVS hose connectors, using Tool T81P–8564–A or equivalent. Label the connectors and set aside.
19. Disconnect the choke cap wire.
20. Disconnect the fuel supply and return lines at the metal connectors, located on the right side of the engine, set rubber lines aside.
21. Disconnect the accelerator cable and if equipped, the speed control cable.
22. Disconnect the altitude compensator (if so equipped) from the dash panel and place on the heater/AC air intake.

NOTE: Caution should be taken not to damage the altitude compensator.

23. Disconnect the alternator aid intake tube, and the alternator wiring harness.
24. Remove the alternator and its mounting bracket.
25. If equipped with power steering, remove the thermactor pump drive belt, the pump and the pump mounting bracket.
26. Raise the vehicle.
27. Disconnect the exhaust system at the exhaust pipe.
28. Lower the vehicle.
29. Remove the cylinder head bolts and washers. Discard the bolts. They cannot be reused.
30. Remove the cylinder head with the exhaust and intake manifolds attached.
31. Remove the cylinder head gasket.

CAUTION
Do not lay the cylinder head flat. Damage the the spark plugs or gasket surfaces may result.

Installation

1. Clean all gasket material from the mating surfaces on the cylinder head and block.

NOTE: Rotate the camshaft until the camshaft gear pointer is aligned with the timing mark on the cylinder head and the camshaft keyway is at the 6 o'clock position. Position the No. 1 piston 90° BTDC (pulley keyway at 9 o'clock position), during the cylinder head installation. After the cylinder head has been installed, rotate the crankshaft to bring No. 1 piston the TDC on its compression stroke. The crankshaft keyway should be at the 12 o'clock position. With the distributor cap removed, the rotor should be pointing toward the No.1 spark plug tower in the cap. Install the timing belt and proceed with the cylinder head installation.

2. Position the cylinder head gasket on the cylinder bock.
3. Install the cylinder head and install new bolts and washers in the following order:
   a. Apply a light coat of engine oil to the threads of the new cylinder head bolts and install the new bolts into the head.

Ford Mercury
FRONT WHEEL DRIVE CARS—ESCORT • EXP • LYNX • TEMPO • TOPAZ • TAURUS • SABLE

b. Using the torque sequence in the illustration provided, torque the cylinder head bolts to 44 ft. lbs. (60 Nm).

c. Loosen the cylinder head bolts approximately two turns, and then torque them again to 44 ft. lbs. (60 Nm). using the same torque sequence.

d. After setting the torque again, turn the head bolts 90°, using the same torque sequence and to complete the head bolt installation, turn the head bolts an additional 90° in the same torque sequence.

NOTE: Type cylinder head attaching bolts cannot be tightened to the specified torque more than once and must therefore be replaced when installing a cylinder head.

4. Raise the vehicle.
5. Connect the exhaust system at the exhaust pipe.
6. Lower the vehicle.
7. Install the thermactor pump mounting bracket, pump and drive belt (if removed).

NOTE: Apply Loctite® (or equivalent) to the attaching bolts.

8. Install the alternator mounting bracket and the alternator.
9. Connect the alternator wiring harness, and alternator air intake tube.
10. Connect the altitude compensator (if so equipped).
11. Connect accelerator cable and, if equipped, the speed control cable.
12. Connect the fuel supply and return lines at the metal connector, located on the right side of the engine.
13. Connect the choke cap wire.
14. Connect the EGR tube to the EGR valve.
15. Install the timing belt.
16. Install the timing belt cover.
17. Install the crankshaft pulley.
18. Install the distributor cap and spark plug wires.
19. Apply a 3/16 in. (4.75mm) bead of sealer D6AZ–19562–B or equivalent, to the valve cover flange.

NOTE: Make sure the surfaces on the cylinder head and the valve cover are clean and free of the rocker arm cover on the cylinder head and install the attaching bolts.

20. Tighten the attaching bolts to 6–8 ft. lbs. (8–11 Nm).
21. Connect the required vacuum hoses.
22. Connect the wiring terminal to the cooling fan switch.
23. Connect the radiator upper hose at the cylinder head.
24. Connect the heater hose to the fitting located below the intake manifold.
25. Fill the cooling system to the proper level.

NOTE: Because the cylinder head is an aluminum alloy, the cooling system must be filled only with the specified coolant.

Tighten the attaching bolts to 44 ft. lbs. (60 Nm) in the sequence shown, after tightening turn the bolts 90° in the same sequence. Complete the bolt tightening by turning an additional 90° in the same sequence.

```
    9    3    1    5    7
    O    O    O    O    O    INTAKE
    O    O    O    O    O    EXHAUST
    8    6    2    4   10
```

Use new cylinder head bolts (© Ford Motor Co.)

26. Connect the negative ground cable.
27. Start the engine and check for vacuum, coolant and oil leaks.
28. After engine has reached operating temperature, check and, if necessary, add coolant.
29. Adjust the ignition timing and connect the distributor vacuum line.
30. Install the PVC hose.
31. Install the air cleaner assembly.

CYLINDER HEAD

Removal

2.3L HSC TEMPO/TOPAZ AND 2.5L TAURUS/SABLE

1. Drain cooling system.
2. Remove air cleaner assembly.
3. Remove on heater hose retaining screw to rocker cover.
4. Disconnect distributor cap and spark plug wire and remove assembly.
5. Remove spark plugs.
6. Disconnect required vacuum hoses.
7. Remove dipstick.
8. Remove rocker retaining bolts and remove cover.
9. Remove intake manifold retaining bolts.
10. Loosen alternator retaining bolts, remove belt from the pulley, remove mounting bracket retaining bolts to the head.
11. Disconnect upper radiator hose at both ends and remove from vehicle.
12. Remove cam belt cover four bolts.
13. Loosen cam idler retaining bolts, position idler in the unloaded position and tighten the retaining bolts.
14. Remove cam belt from the cam pulley and auxiliary pulley.
15. Remove heat stove from exhaust manifold the muts and two retaining bolts.
16. Remove the eight exhaust manifold retaining bolts.
17. Remove the cam belt idler and two bracket bolts.
18. Remove cam belt idler spring stop from the cylinder head.
19. Disconnect oil sending unit lead wire.
20. Remove cylinder head retaining bolts.
21. Remove the cylinder head.
22. Clean cylinder head gasket surface at the block.
23. Clean intake manifold gasket surface at the intake manifold.
24. Clean exhaust manifold gasket surface at the exhaust manifold.
25. Clean exhaust manifold gasket surface at the cylinder head.
26. Clean cylinder head gasket surface at the cylinder head.
27. Clean intake manifold gasket surface at the cylinder head.
28. Blow oil out of the cylinder head bolt block holes.
29. Clean camshaft cover gasket surface on the head.
30. Check cylinder head for flatness.

Installation

1. Position head gasket on the block.
2. Clean rocker arm cover (cam cover).
3. Install rocker cover gasket to the rocker cover (use contact cement).
4. Position cylinder head to block.
5. Install cylinder head retaining bolts and tighten to specification.
6. Connect oil sending unit lead wires.
7. Install cam belt idler spring stop to the cylinder head.
8. Position cam belt idler to cylinder head, and install retaining bolts.
9. Install the eight exhaust manifold retaining bolts.
10. Install heat stove to exhaust manifold three nuts and two retaining bolts.

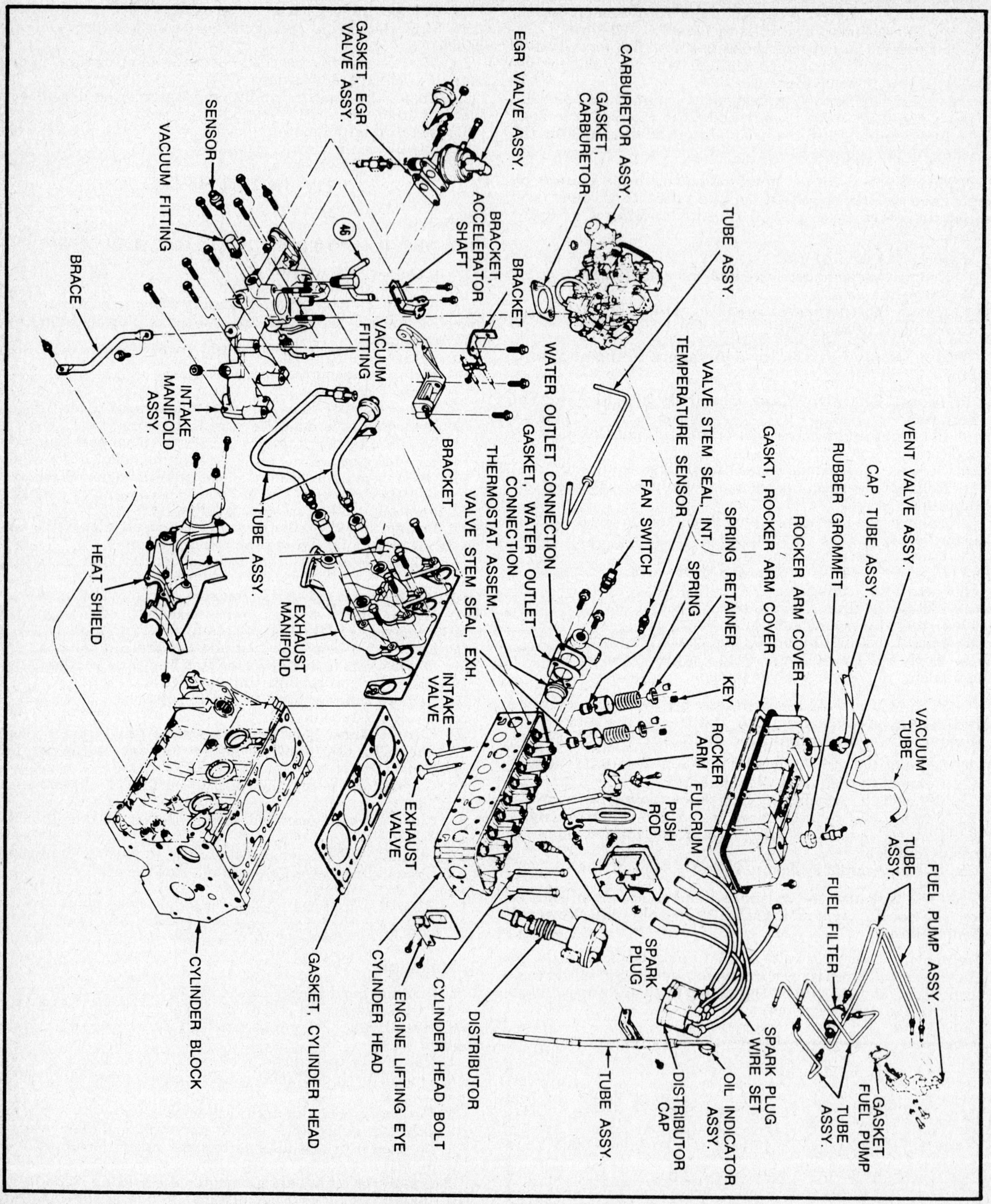

FORD MERCURY
FRONT WHEEL DRIVE CARS—ESCORT • EXP • LYNX • TEMPO • TOPAZ • TAURUS • SABLE

Exploded view 2.3L HSC engine (© Ford Motor Co.)

Ford Mercury
FRONT WHEEL DRIVE CARS—ESCORT • EXP • LYNX • TEMPO • TOPAZ • TAURUS • SABLE

11. Align distributor rotor with number one plug location in the distributor cap.
12. Align cam gear with pointer.
13. Align crank pulley (TDC) with pointer on cam belt cover.
14. Position cam belt to pulleys (cam and auxiliary).
15. Loosen idler retaining bolts, rotate engine and check timing alignment.
16. Adjust belt tensioner and tighten retaining bolts.
17. Install cam belt cover four retaining bolts.
18. Connect upper radiator hose to engine and radiator and tighten retaining clamps.

Removal
3.0L ENGINE

1. Disconnect the negative battery cable. Drain the engine coolant into a suitable drain pan. Remove the air cleaner assembly.
2. Remove the intake manifold as previously outlined. Loosen the accessory drive belt idle pulley, remove the drive belt.
3. When removing the LH cylinder head, remove the alternator adjusting arm, and when removing the RH cylinder head, remove the accessory drive belt idler pulley.
4. If equipped with power steering, remove the pump mounting bracket attaching bolts. Leave the pump hoses connected and position the pump out of the way.
5. When removing the LH cylinder head, remove the coil bracket and dipstick tube. When removing the RH cylinder head, remove the grounding strap throttle cable support bracket.
6. Remove the exhaust manifolds from both heads. Remove the PCV and the rocker arm covers. Loosen the rocker arm fulcrum attaching bolts enough to allow the rocker arm to be lifted off the push rod and rotated to one side.
7. Remove the push rods. Be sure to identify the position of each push rod. The rods should be installed in their original position during reassembly.
8. Remove the cylinder head attaching bolts and remove the cylinder heads from the engine. Remove and discard the old cylinder head gaskets.

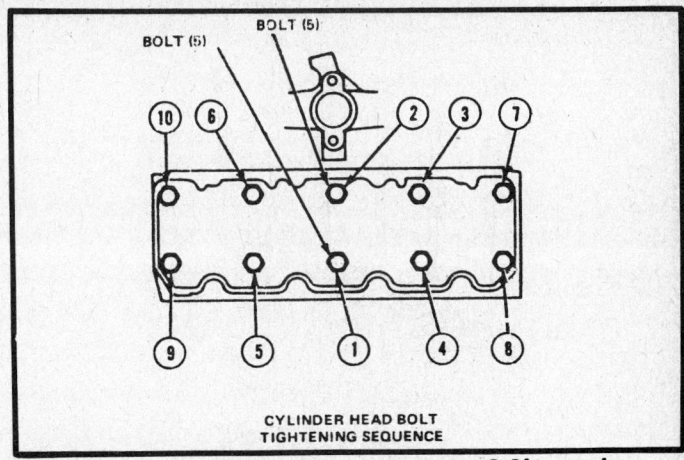

Cylinder head tightening sequence 2.3L engine
(© Ford Motor Co.)

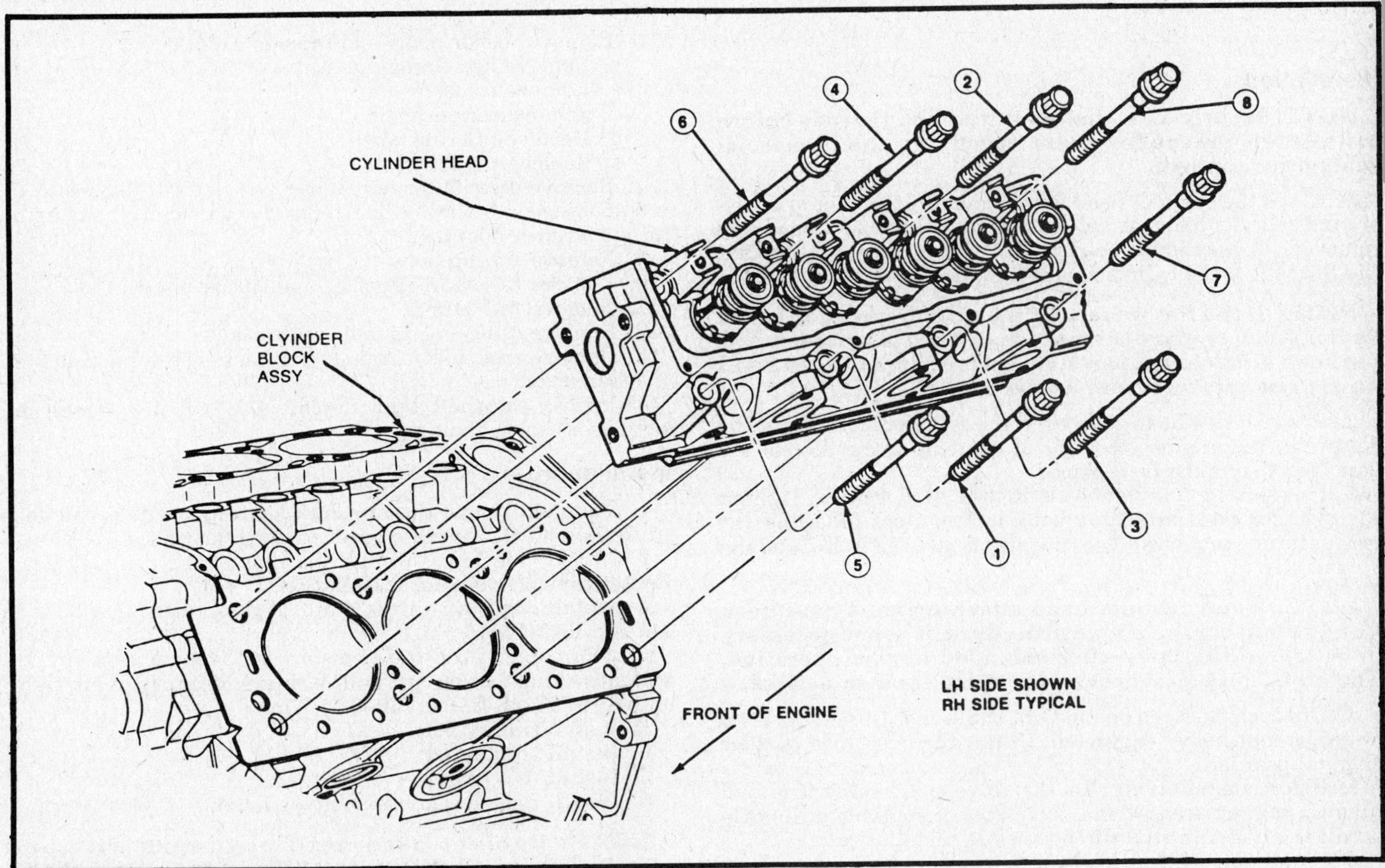

Cylinder head removal and installation—3.0L engine

FORD MERCURY
FRONT WHEEL DRIVE CARS—ESCORT • EXP • LYNX • TEMPO • TOPAZ • TAURUS • SABLE

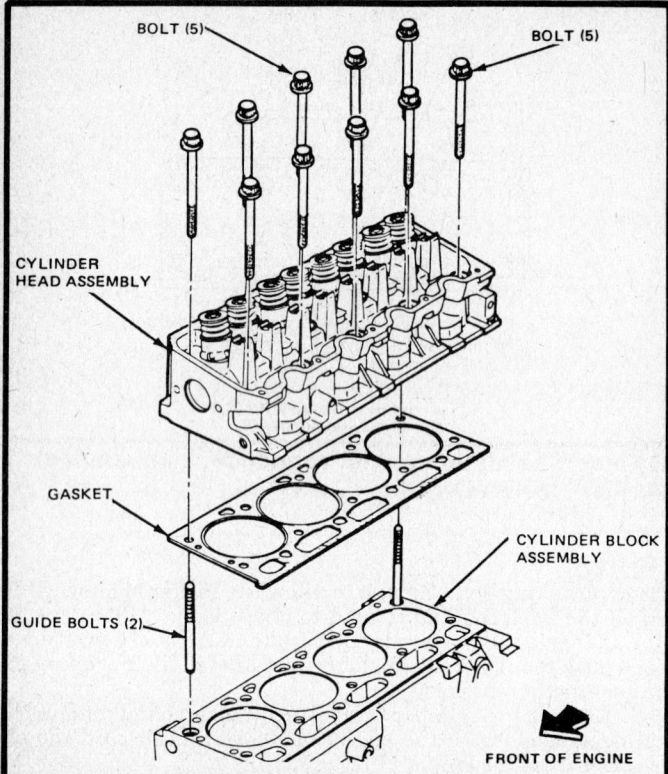

Cylinder head installation 2.3L engine
(© Ford Motor Co.)

Installation

NOTE: **Lightly oil all bolt and stud bolt threads before installation except for those specifying that a special sealant be applied.**

1. Clean the cylinder head, intake manifold, rocker arm cover, and cylinder head gasket surfaces. If the cylinder head was removed for a cylinder head gasket replacement, check that the flatness of the cylinder head and block gasket surfacers.

NOTE: **If the flat surface of the cylinder head is warp, do not plane or grind off more than 0.010 in. (0.254mm). If the head is machined past its resurface limit the head will have to be replaced with a new one.**

2. Position new head gaskets on the cylinder block using the dowels in the engine block for alignment. If the dowels are damaged they must be replaced.
3. Position the cylinder heads on the cylinder block. Tighten the cylinder head attaching bolts in two steps following the proper torque sequence. The first step is 48 to 54 ft. lbs. and the second step is 63 to 80 ft. lbs.

NOTE: **When cylinder head attaching bolts have been tightened using the above procedure, it is not necessary to retighten the bolts after extended engine operation. The bolts can be rechecked for tightness if so desired.**

4. Dip each push rod end in Oil Conditioner D9AZ–19579–C or equivalent heavy engine oil. Install the push rods in their original position.
5. Before installation, coat the valve tips, rocker arm and fulcrum contact areas with Lubriplate® or equivalent. Lightly oil all the bolt and stud threads before installation.
6. Rotate the engine until the lifter is on the base circle of the cam (valve closed).
7. Install the rocker arm and components and torque the rocker arm fulcrum bolts to 19–29 ft. lbs. Be sure the lifter is on the base circle of the cam for each rocker arm as it is installed. Adjust the valves as previously outlined.

NOTE: **The fulcrums must be fully seated in the cylinder head, and the push rods must be seated in the rocker arm sockets prior to the final tightening.**

8. Install the exhaust manifolds, the oil dipstick tube (be sure that the is pushed all the way in). Install the intake manifold. The rest of the installation is the reverse order of the removal procedure.
9. Start the engine and check for coolant, fuel, oil and exhaust leaks.
10. Check and if necessary, adjust the transmission throttle linkage and speed control. Install the air cleaner outlet tube duct.

CAMSHAFT

Removal

1.6L AND 1.9L ESCORT/LYNX, EXP

1. Disconnect negative battery cable.
2. Remove air cleaner, and PCV hose.
3. Remove accessory drive belts, and crankshaft pulley.
4. Remove timing belt cover, and valve cover.
5. Set the engine number one cylinder at TDC prior to removing timing belt.

— CAUTION —
Make sure the crankshaft is positioned at TDC and do not turn the crankshaft until the timing belt is installed.

6. Remove rocker arms and tappets as follows:
   a. Remove hex flange nuts.
   b. Remove fulcurms.
   c. Remove rocker arms.
   d. Remove fulcrum washer.
   e. Remove tappets.
7. Remove distributor assembly.
8. Loosen both timing belt tensioner attaching bolts using torque wrench adapter.
9. Remove timing belt.
10. Remove camshaft sprocket and thrust plate.
11. Remove fuel pump.
12. Remove ignition coil and coil bracket.
13. Remove camshaft through the back of the head toward the transaxle.
14. Inspect camshaft seal. Replace the seal if it shows any signs of wear or damage.

Installation

1. Thoroughly coat the camshaft bearing journals, cam lobe surfaces, and thrust plate groove with lubricant.
2. Install camshaft through the rear of the cylinder head. Rotate camshaft during installation.
3. Install camshaft thrust plate. Tighten attaching bolts to 7–11 ft. lbs. (10–15 Nm).
4. Align and install the cam sprocket over the cam key. Install attaching washer and bolt. While holding camshaft, tighten bolt to 37–46 ft. lbs. (50–62.5 Nm).
5. Install timing belt.
6. Install timing belt cover.
7. Install fuel pump.
8. Install rocker arm assembly as follows:

NOTE: **Replace used hex flange nuts with new ones. Lubricate all the parts with a heavy engine oil before installation.**

a. Install the tappets.
b. Install the fulcrum washers.
c. Install the rocker arms.
d. Install the fulcrums.
e. Install new rocker arm stud hex flange nuts. Tighten to 15–19 ft. lbs. (21–25.5 Nm).
9. Install the distributor assembly.
10. Apply a 3/16 in. (4.75mm) bead of sealer to the valve cover flange.

NOTE: Make sure the surfaces on the cylinder head and valve cover are clean and free of sealant material.

11. Install rocker arm cover attaching bolts and studs. Tighten bolts and studs to 6–8 ft. lbs. (8–11 Nm).
12. Install PCV hose.
13. Install air cleaner assembly.
14. Start engine and set ignition timing to specification.

Removal
2.3 HSC TEMPO/TOPAZ AND 2.5L TAURUS/SABLE

1. With the engine removed from the vehicle and placed on an engine work stand, remove oil dipstick.
2. Assure that the cooling system, fuel system and crankcase have been drained.
3. Remove necessary drive belts and pulleys.
4. Remove cylinder head.
5. Using a magnet, remove the hydraulic tappets and keep them in order so that they can be installed in their original positions. If the tappets are stuck in the bores by excessive varnish, etc., use a Hydraulic Tappet Puller to remove tappets.
6. Loosen and remove the drive belt, fan and pulley, and crankshaft pulley.
7. Remove oil pan.
8. Remove cylinder front cover and gasket.
9. Check the camshaft end play as follows:
   a. Push the camshaft toward the rear of the engine and install dial indicator tool 4201–C or equivalent, so that the indicator point is on the camshaft sprocket attaching screw.
   b. Zero the dial indicator. Position a large screwdriver between the camshaft sprocket or gear and block.
   c. Pull the camshaft forward and release it. Compare the dial indicator reading with the camshaft end play specification of 0.009 in.
   d. If the camshaft end play is over the amount specified, replace the thrust plate.
10. Remove fuel pump, gasket, and fuel pump pushrod.
11. Remove timing chain, sprockets and timing chain tensioner.
12. Remove camshaft thrust plate. Carefully remove the camshaft by pulling it toward the front of the engine. Use caution to avoid damaging bearings, journals, and lobes.

Installation

1. Clean and inspect all parts before installation.
2. Lubricate camshaft lobes and journals with heavy engine oil. Carefully slide the camshaft through the bearings in the cylinder block.
3. Instal thrust plate. Tighten attaching bolts to specification.
4. Install timing chain, sprockets, and timing chain tensioner.
5. Install cylinder front cover and crankshaft pulley.
6. Clean oil pump inlet tube screen, oil pan, and cylinder block gasket surfaces. Prime oil pump by filling the inlet opening with oil and rotate the pump shaft until oil emerges from the outlet tube. Install oil pump, oil pump inlet tube screen, and oil pan.
7. Install accessory drive belts and pulleys.

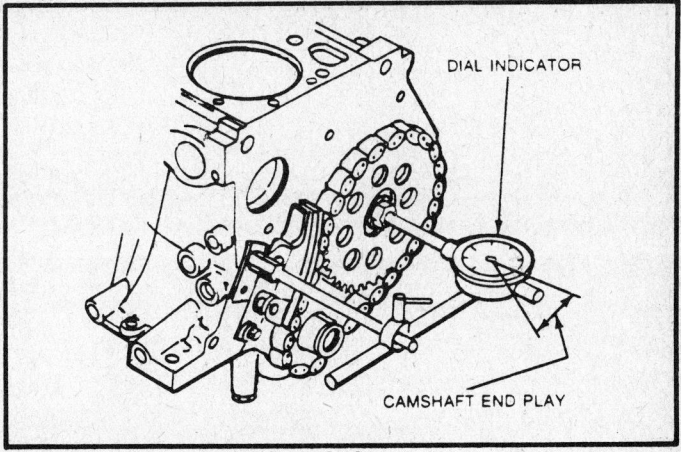

Checking the camshaft end-play

8. Lubricate tappets and tappet bores with heavy engine oil. Install tappets into their original bores.
9. Install cylinder head.
10. Using a new gasket, install fuel pump pushrod and fuel pump. Tighten attaching bolts to specification.
11. Install engine as outlined.
12. Position No. 1 piston at TDC after the compression stroke. Position distributor in the block with the rotor at the No. 1 firing position. Install distributor hold down clamp.
13. Connect engine temperature sending unit wire. Connect coil primary wire. Install distributor cap. Connect spark plug wires and the coil high tension lead.
14. Fill the cooling system. Fill crankcase with the correct viscosity and amount of engine oil.
15. Start engine. Check and adjust ignition timing. Connect distributor vacuum line to distributor. Check for coolant, oil, fuel and vacuum leaks. Adjust engine idle speed and idle fuel mixture.

Removal and Installation
3.0L TAURUS/SABLE

1. Remove the engine from the vehicle (as previously outlined) and place it on a suitable engine stand.
2. Ensure the cooling system, fuel system and crankcase have been drained.
3. Remove the idler pulley and bracket assembly. Remove the drive and accessory belts. Remove the water pump.
4. Remove the crankshaft pulley and damper. Remove the lower radiator hose. Remove the oil pan to timing cover bolts. Unbolt the front timing cover and remove the cover from the engine.
5. Remove and tag the spark plug wires and rocker arm covers. Loosen the rocker arm fulcrum nuts and position the rocker arms to the side for easy access to the pushrods. Remove the pushrods and keep them in their original position.
6. Using a suitable magnet or lifter removal tool, remove the hydraulic tappets and keep them in order so that they can be installed in their original positions. If the tappets are stuck in the bores by excessive varnish use Hydraulic Tappet Puller T70L–6500–A or equivalent, to remove the tappets.
7. Check the camshaft end play as follows:
   a. Push the camshaft toward the rear of the engine and install dial indicator tool 4201–C or equivalent, so that the indicator point is on the camshaft sprocket attaching screw.
   b. Zero the dial indicator. Position a large screwdriver between the camshaft sprocket or gear and block.
   c. Pull the camshaft forward and release it. Compare the dial indicator reading with the camshaft end play specification of 0.009 in.

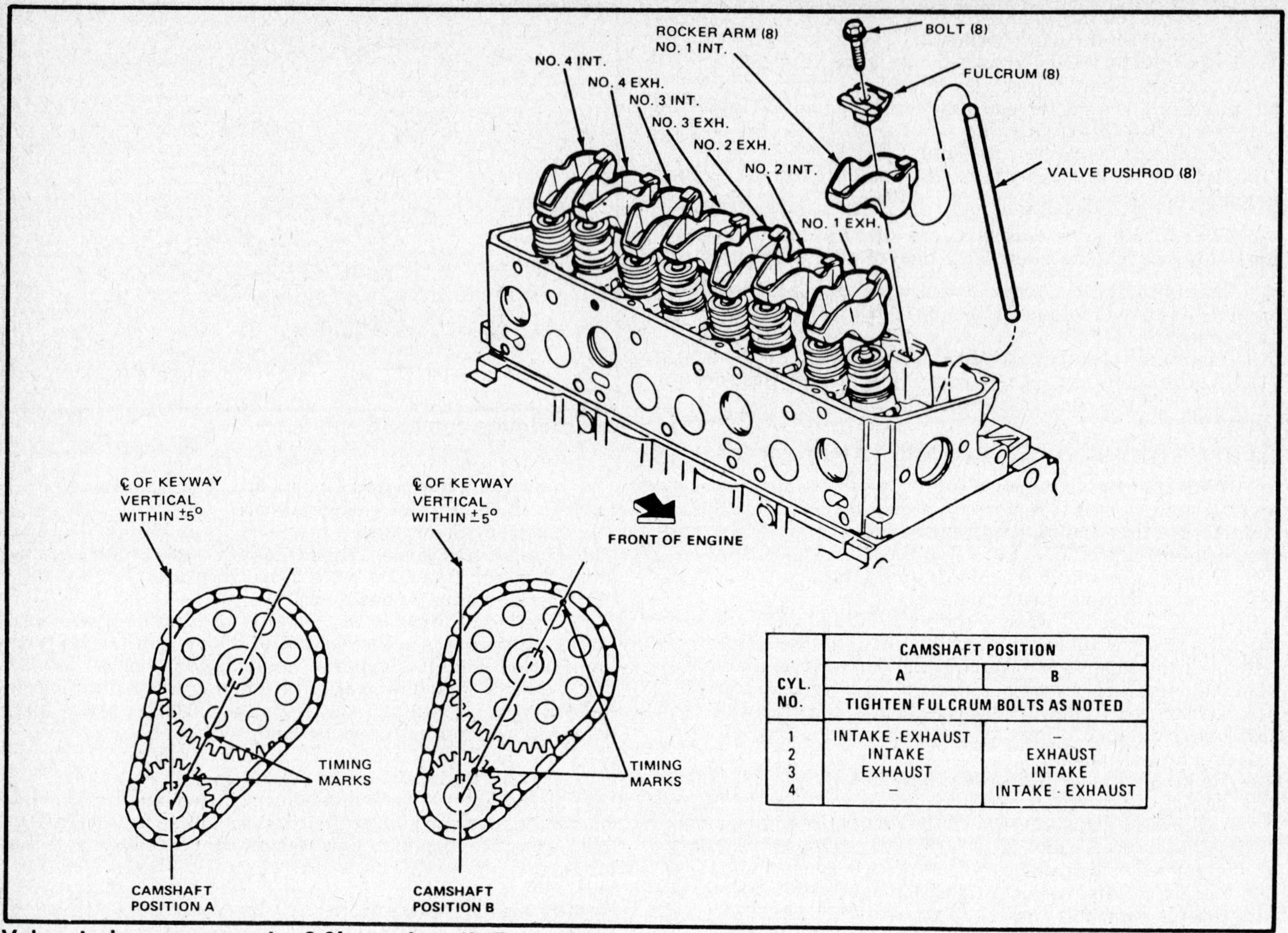

SECTION 4
Ford Mercury
FRONT WHEEL DRIVE CARS—ESCORT • EXP • LYNX • TEMPO • TOPAZ • TAURUS • SABLE

Valve train components 2.3L engine (© Ford Motor Co.)

d. If the camshaft end play is over the amount specified, replace the thrust plate.

8. Remove the timing chain and sprockets.

9. Remove the camshaft thrust plate. Carefully remove the camshaft by pulling it toward the front of the engine. Remove it slowly to avoid damaging the bearings, journals and lobes.

Installation

1. Clean and inspect all parts before installation.
2. Lubricate camshaft lobes and journals with heavy engine oil. Carefully slide the camshaft through the bearings in the cylinder block.
3. Instal thrust plate. Tighten attaching bolts to specification.
4. Install timing chain and sprockets. Check the camshaft sprocket bolt for blockage of drilled oil passages.
5. Install the front timing cover and crankshaft damper and pulley. Install the water pump as previously outlined.
6. Lubricate the tappets and tappet bors with a heavy engine oil. Install the tappets into their original bores. Install the cylinder head throttle body, intake manifold, valve rocker arm, pushrods and rocker arm covers as previously outlined.
7. Install the accessory drive belts and pulleys. install the engine back in the vehicle as previously outlined.
8. Install the spark plug wires. Fill and bleed the cooling system. Fill the crankcase with the correct amount of the proper viscosity engine oil.
9. Start the engine. Check and adjust the ignition timing and engine idle speed as necessary. Check for coolant, oil, fuel and or vacuum leaks of any kind.

PISTONS AND ROD POSITIONING

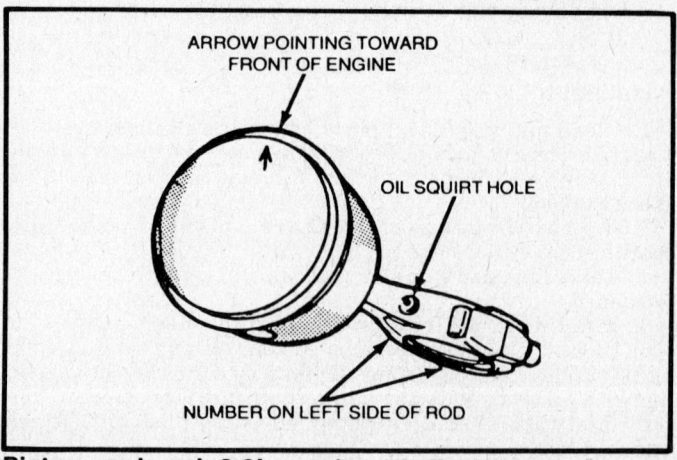

Piston and rod 2.3L engine (© Ford Motor Co.)

Ford Mercury
FRONT WHEEL DRIVE CARS—ESCORT • EXP • LYNX • TEMPO • TOPAZ • TAURUS • SABLE

Piston and rod 1.6L engine (© Ford Motor Co.)

CRANKSHAFT PULLEY

Removal

1.6L and 1.9L ESCORT/LYNX, EXP

1. Disconnect the cable from the battery negative terminal.
2. Loosen alternator bolt on the alternator adjusting arm.
3. Lower alternator to remove the accessory drive belt from the crankshaft pulley.
4. Using crankshaft pulley wrench T81P–6312–A and crankshaft bolt wrench YA–826 or equivalent, remove the crankshaft pulley attaching bolt (12mm).
5. Remove drive plate assembly.
6. Remove crankshaft pulley.

Installation

1. Install crankshaft pulley and pulley drive plate.
2. Install crankshaft pulley attaching bolt.
3. Hold the crankshaft pulley stationary, and tighten the pulley attaching bolt to 74–90 ft. lbs. (100–122 Nm).
4. Position the drive belts over the alternator and crankshaft pulleys. Tighten drive belts to specification.
5. Connect battery cable.

CRANKSHAFT SEAL—FRONT

Removal and Installation

1.6L AND 1.9L ESCORT/LYNX,EXP

1. Remove timing belt as outlined.
2. Remove crankshaft pulley.
3. Remove seal.
4. Install crankshaft seal using Seal Installer Tool.
5. Install crankshaft pulley.
6. Install timing belt as outlined.

OIL SEAL—FRONT COVER

Removal and Installation

2.3L HSC TEMPO/TOPAZ AND 2.5L TAURUS/SABLE

1. Remove bolt and washer at crankshaft pulley.
2. Using damper removal tool No. T77F–4220B1 or equivalent, remove the crankshaft pulley.
3. Using front seal remover tool T74P–6700–A or equivalent, remove the front cover oil seal.
4. Coat a new seal with grease. Using front seal replacer tool, install seal into cover. Drive seal in until it is fully seated. Check the seal after installation to be sure the spring is properly positioned in the seal.
5. Install crankshaft pulley, attaching bolt and washer. Tighten to specification.

CRANKSHAFT PULLEY/FRONT

Removal

3.0L TAURUS/SABLE

1. Disconnect the negative battery cable and loosen the accessory drive belts.
2. Raise and support the front of the vehicle safely and remove the RH front wheel.

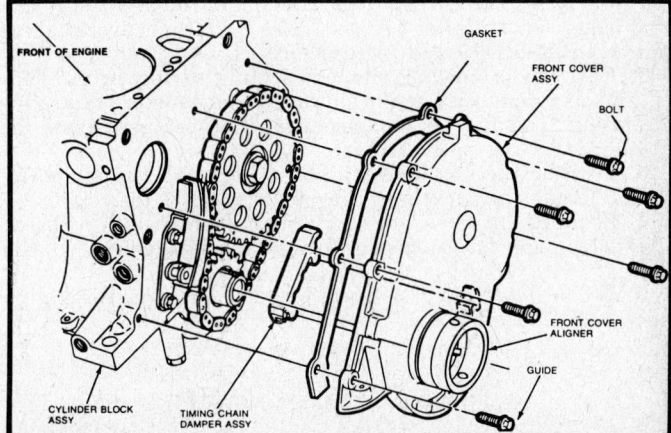

Front cover removal and installation—2.3L and 2.5L engines

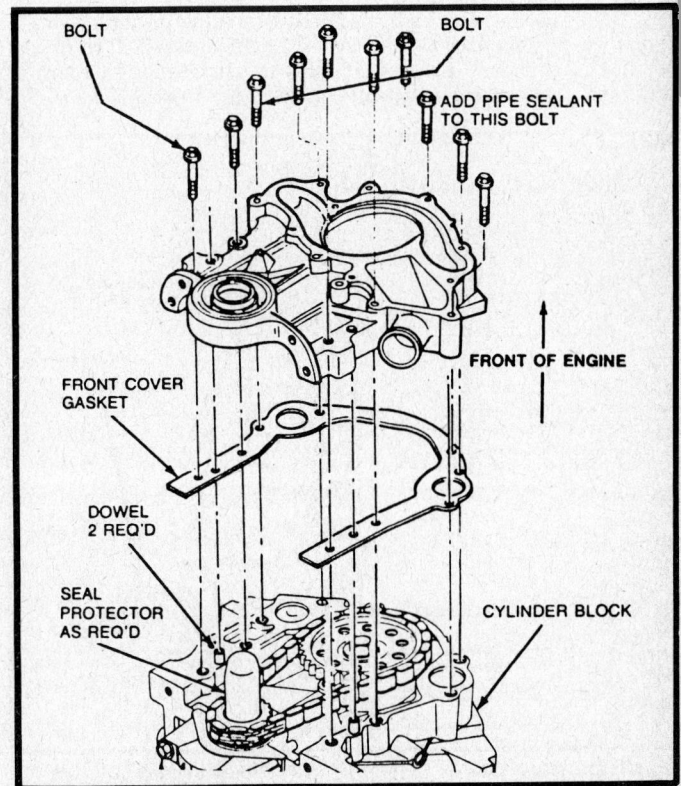

Front cover removal and installation—3.0L engine

Ford Mercury
FRONT WHEEL DRIVE CARS—ESCORT • EXP • LYNX • TEMPO • TOPAZ • TAURUS • SABLE

3. Remove the four pulley to damper attaching bolts. Disengage the accessory drive belts and remove the crankshaft pulley.

4. Remove the damper from the crankshaft using damper removal tool T58P-6316-D or equivalent and also install the damper removal adapter T82L-6316-B or equivalent.

5. Pry the seal from the timing cover with a suitable tool and be careful not to damage the front cover and crankshaft.

Installation

NOTE: Before installation; inspect the front cover and shaft seal surface of the crankshaft damper for damage, nicks, burrs or other roughness which may cause the new seal to fail. Service or replace components as necessary.

1. Lubricate the seal lip with clean engine oil and install the seal using seal installer T82L-6316-A and front cover seal replacer T70P-6B070-A or equivalent.

2. Coat the crankshaft damper sealing surface with clean engine oil. Apply RTV to the keyway of the damper prior to installation. Install the damper using damper seal installer T82L-6316-A or equivalent.

3. Position the crankshaft pulley and install the attaching bolts. Torque the attaching bolts to 19 to 28 ft. lbs.

4. Position the drive belt over the crankshaft pulley. Check the drive belt for proper routing and engagement in the pulleys.

5. Reconnect the negative battery cable and start the engine and checke for oil leaks.

TIMING BELT COVER

Removal and Installation
1.6 LITER ENGINE

1. Disconnect the negative battery cable. Remove the drive belts.

2. Remove the alternator (if needed) to allow enough room to reach the top cover retaining bolts. Position the A/C compressor out of the way (if so equipped) to allow enough room to reach the bottom cover retainer bolts.

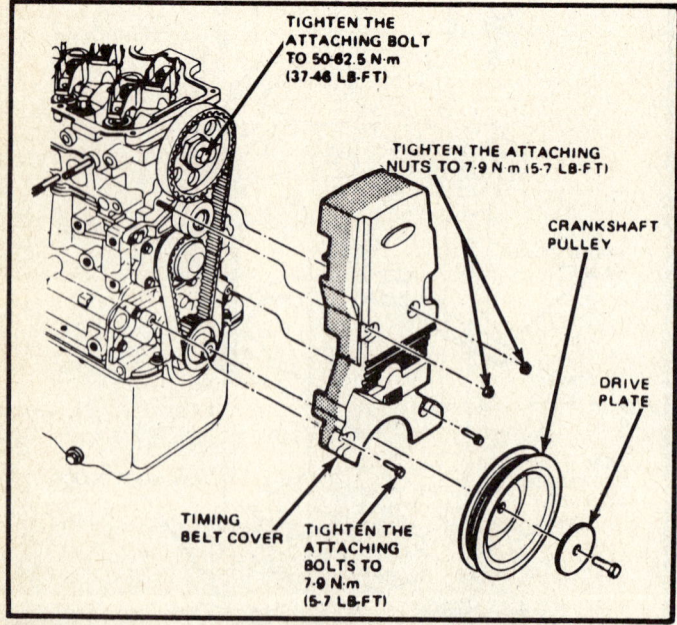

Timing chain cover removal and installation for the 1.6L engine

3. Remove the top two timing cover retaining nuts. Raise and support the vehicle safely.

4. Working from underneath the vehicle, remove the bottom two timing cover retaining screws. Remove the timing cover by prying it loose from the engine block and lifting it straight out.

5. Installation is the reverse order of the removal procedure.

TIMING BELT TENSIONING AND REPLACEMENT PROCEDURES

Removal
1.6L AND 1.9L ESCORT/LYNX, EXP

— CAUTION —
With the timing belt removed and pistons at TDC, DO NOT rotate the camshaft. If the camshaft must be rotated, align the crankshaft pulley to degrees BTC.

1. Disconnect cable from the battery negative terminal.
2. Remove accessory drive belts.
3. Remove timing belt cover.

NOTE: Align timing mark on the camshaft sprocket with the timing mark on the cylinder head.

4. Install the timing belt cover and confirm that the timing mark on the crankshaft pulley aligns with the TDC on the front cover.

5. Remove the timing belt cover.
6. Loosen both timing belt tensioner attaching bolts.
7. Pry belt tensioner away from the belt as far as possible and tighten one of the tensioner attaching bolts.
8. Remove crankshaft pulley if timing belt is to be replaced.

Tensioning/Installation

1. Install timing belt over the sprockets in a counterclockwise direction starting at the crankshaft. Keep the belt span from the crankshaft to the camshaft tight as the belt is installed over the remaining sprocket.

2. Loosen belt tensioner attaching bolts and allow the tensioner to snap against the belt.

3. Tighten one of the tensioner attaching bolts.

4. If timing belt was replaced, install crankshaft pulley, drive plate and pulley attaching bolt. Hold the crankshaft pulley stationary, and tighten the pulley attaching bolt to 74–90 ft. lbs. (100–121 Nm)

5. To seat the belt on the sprocket teeth:
   a. Connect cable to the battery negative terminal.
   b. Crank engine for 30 seconds.
   c. Disconnect cable from the battery negative terminal.
   d. Turn camshaft, as necessary, to align the timing pointer on the cam sprocket with the timing mark on the cylinder head.
   e. Position the timing belt cover n the engine and check to see that the timing mark on the crankshaft aligns with the TDC pointer on the cover. If the timing marks do not align, remove the belt, align the timing marks and return to Step 1.

6. Loosen the belt tensioner attaching blot tightened in Step 3.

7. To prevent rotation of the crankshaft, have an assistant hold the crankshaft. In Step 8 a specified amount of torque will be applied to the camshaft sprocket. While the torque is applied, the crankshaft must not be allowed to turn.

8. With the crankshaft held, turn the cam sprocket counterclockwise. Tighten the belt tensioner attaching bolt when the torque wrench reads as follows:
   a. New Belt: 27–32 ft. lbs. (39–43 Nm)
   b. Used Belt*: 10 ft. lbs. (14 Nm) — *30 days or more in service.

Ford Mercury
FRONT WHEEL DRIVE CARS—ESCORT • EXP • LYNX • TEMPO • TOPAZ • TAURUS • SABLE

SECTION 4

NOTE: The engine must be at ambient temperature when the torque is applied to the cam sprocket. Do not set torque on a hot engine.

9. Intall timing belt cover.
10. Install accessory drive belts and adjust to specification.
11. Connect negative cable at the battery.

FRONT COVER, TIMING CHAIN AND SPROCKETS

Removal

2.3L HSC TEMPO/TOPAZ AND 2.5L TAURUS/SABLE

1. With the engine and transaxle removed from the vehicle as an assembly, remove dipstick.
2. Remove accessory drive pulley, if so equipped, Remove the crankshaft pulley attaching bolt and washer and remove pulley.
3. Remove front cover attaching bolts from front cover. Pry the top of the front cover away from the block.

NOTE: The front cover oil seal must be removed when the front cover is disassembles from the engine in order to use front cover aligner tool T84P-6019-C or equivalent, for proper installation of the front cover.

4. Clean any gasket material from the surfaces.
5. Check timing chain deflection. If the deflection exceeds specification, replace the timing chain and sprockets.
6. Check timing chain tensioner blade for wear depth. If the wear depth exceeds specification, replace tensioner.
7. Turn engine over until the timing marks are aligned. Remove camshaft sprocket attaching bolt and washer. Slide both sprockets and timing chain forward and remove as an assembly.
8. Check timing chain vibration damper for excessive wear. Replace if necessary (the damper is located inside the front cover).
9. Remove oil pan.

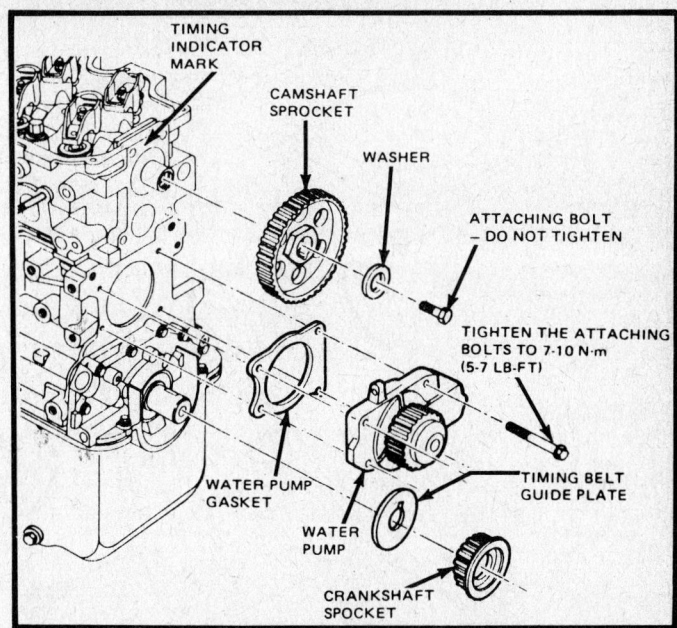

Crankshaft sprocket, camshaft sprocket, water pump installation 1.6L engine (© Ford Motor Co.)

Installation

1. Clean and inspect all parts before installation. Clean oil pan, cylinder block, and front cover of gasket material and dirt.
2. Slide both sprockets and timing chain onto the camshaft and crankshaft with timing marks aligned. Install camshaft bolt and washer and tighten to specification. Oil timing chain, sprockets, and tensioner after installation.
3. Apply oil resistant sealer to a new front cover gasket and position gasket into front cover.
4. Cut two front cover attaching bolt heads off. Install these guide bolts in to cylinder block.
5. Position front cover aligner tool T84P-6019-C or equivalent onto the end of the crankshaft, ensuring the crank key is aligned with the keyway in the tool. Bolt the front cover to the engine. Remove guide bolts and install two new bolts. Tighten all attaching bolts to specification. Remove the front cover aligner tool.
6. Lubricate the hub of the crankshaft pulley with Polyethylene Grease to prevent damage to the seal during installation and initial engine start. Install crankshaft pulley.
7. Install oil pan.
8. Install the accsssory drive pulley, if so equipped.
9. Install crankshaft pulley attaching bolt and washer. Tighten to specification.
10. Remove engine from work stand and install in vehicle.

TIMING CHAIN AND SPROCKETS

Removal

3.0L TAURUS/SABLE

1. Remove the crankshaft pulley and front cover assemblies as previously outlined in this section. Cover the oil pan opening to prevent dirt from entering.
2. Rotate the crankshaft until the number one piston is at TDC on its compression stroke and the timing marks are aligned.
3. Remove the camshaft sprocket attaching bolts and washer. Slide both sprockets and timing chain forward and remove as an assembly.

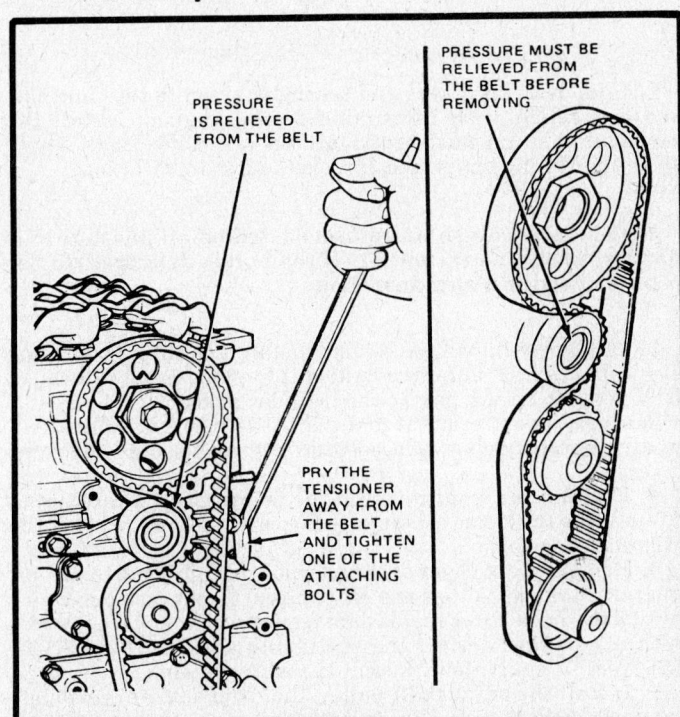

Timing belt tension adjustment 1.6L engine (© Ford Motor Co.)

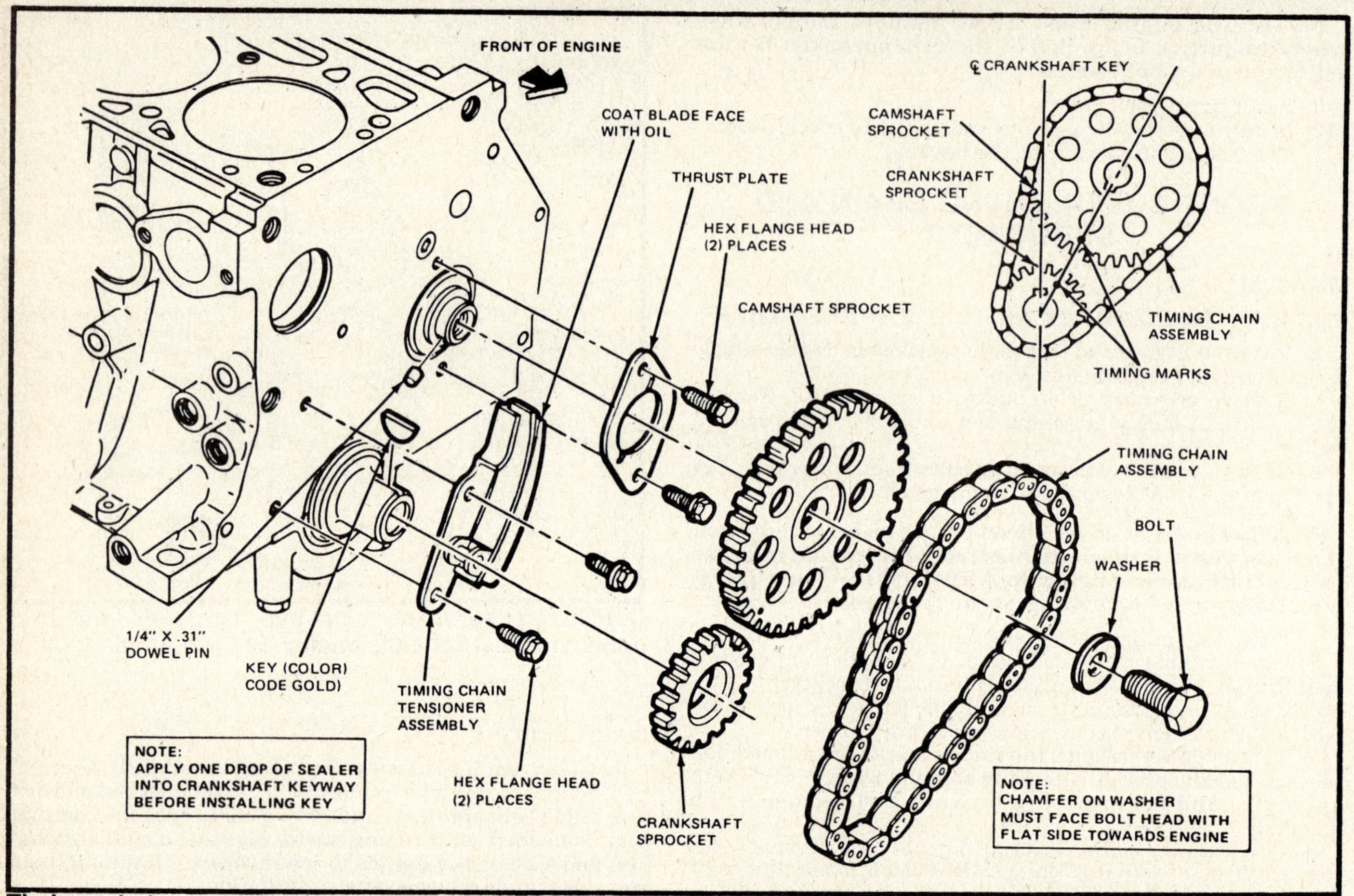

Ford Mercury
FRONT WHEEL DRIVE CARS—ESCORT • EXP • LYNX • TEMPO • TOPAZ • TAURUS • SABLE

Timing chain tensioner, sprockets and timing chain installation 2.3L engine (© Ford Motor Co.)

4. Check the timing chain and sprockets for excessive wear. Replace if necessary.

Installation

NOTE: Before installation, clean and inspect all parts. Clean the gasket material and dirt from the oil pan, cylinder block and front cover.

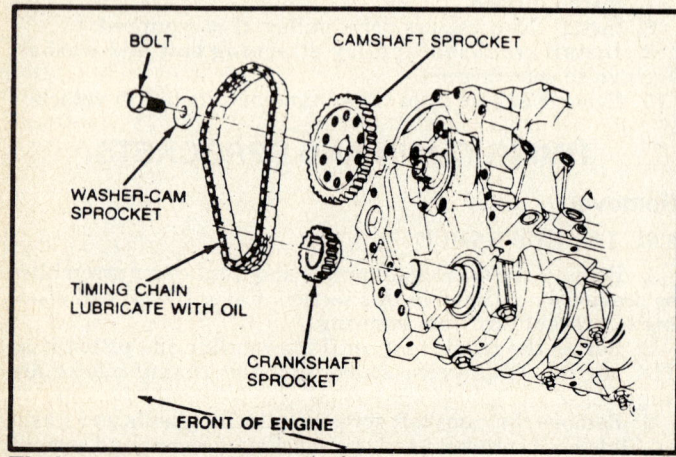

Timing chain installation—3.0L engine

1. Slide both sprockets and timing chain onto the camshaft and crankshaft with the timing marks aligned. Install the camshaft bolt and washer and tighten to specifications. Apply oil to the timing chain and sprockets after installation.

NOTE: The camshaft bolt has a drilled oil passage in it for timing chain lubrication. If the bolt is damaged do not replace it with a standard bolt.

2. Cut a new oil pan gasket and install it on the oil pan using a suitable contact adhesive to hold it in place. Apply a bead of RTV sealant on the gap at the cylinder block.
3. Apply an oil resistant sealer B5A–19554–A or equivalent, to a new front gasket and position the gasket onto the front cover.
4. Position the front cover on the engine taking care not to damage the front seal. Make sure the cover is installed over the alignment dowels.
5. Bolt the front cover to the engine and tighten it to specifications. Make sure that the oil pan seal is not dislodged.
6. If the front cover seal is damaged or worn, replace the seal with a new one. Install the seal using seal installer T70P–6B070–A or equivalent. Install the water pump.
7. Install the crankshaft pulley and front seal as previously outlined. Fill the crankcase with the correct viscosity and amount of engine oil. Fill and bleed the cooling system.
8. Start the engine and check for oil and coolant leaks.

Lubrication

OIL PAN

Removal

1.6L AND 1.9L ESCORT/LYNX, EXP

1. Disconnect negative cable at the battery.
2. Raise the vehicle on a hoist.
3. Drain crankcase.
4. Disconnect cable at the starter.
5. Remove knee-brace located at the front of the starter.
6. Remove starter attaching bolts and starter.
7. Remove knee-braces at the transaxle.
8. Disconnect the exhaust inlet pipe at the manifold and converter. Remove pipe.
9. Remove oil pan retaining bolts and oil pan.
10. Remove oil pan front seal.
11. Remove oil pan rear seal.
12. Remove two oil pan side gaskets.

Installation

1. Clean the oil pan gasket surface and the mating surface on the cylinder block.
2. Remove the clean the oil pump pick up tube and screen assembly. Install tube and screen assembly.
3. Apply sealer approximately 3.0mm wide at the corner of the oil pan front and rear seals and at the seating point of the oil pump to the block retainer joint.
4. Install the front oil pan seal by pressing firmly into the oil pump slot cut into the bottom of the oil pump.
5. Install the oil pan rear seal by pressing firmly into the slot cut into the rear retainer assembly.

NOTE: Install the seals before the sealer has cured (within 10 minutes of application).

6. Apply adhesive evenly to the oil pan flange and to the pan side of the gaskets. Allow the adhesive to dry past the "wet" stage and then install the gaskets on the oil pan.
7. Install the oil pan on the cylinder block.
8. Install the oil pan attaching bolts. Tighten the bolts in the sequence shown in illustration to 6–8 ft lbs. (8–11 Nm).
9. Position the transaxle inspection plate and the rear section of the knee-brace on the transaxle and install two attaching bolts. Tighten bolts to specification.
10. Install starter.
11. Install knee-brace at the starter.
12. Connect starter cable.
13. Install exhaust inlet pipe.
14. Lower vehicle and fill the crankcase with oil.
15. Connect negative cable at the battery.
16. Start engine and check for oil leaks.

OIL PAN

Removal

2.3L HSC TEMPO/TOPAZ AND 2.5L TAURUS/SABLE

1. Disconnect negative ground cable at battery.
2. Raise vehicle.
3. Drain crankcase.
4. Drain coolant by removing lower radiator hose.
5. Remove roll restrictor (MTX only).
6. Disconnect starter cable.
7. Remove starter.
8. Disconnect exhaust pipe from oil pan.
9. Remove engine coolant tube located at the lower radiator hose, at the water pump and at the tabs on the oil pan., Position air conditioner line off to the side. Remove oil pan.

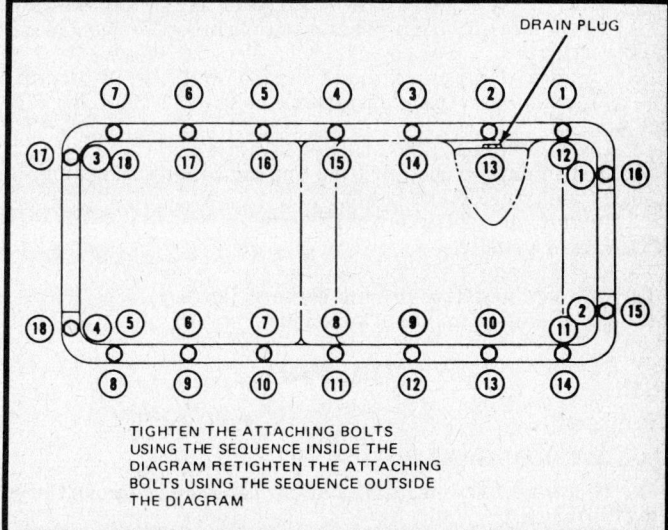

Oil pan bolt tightening sequence 1.6L engine
(© Ford Motor Co.)

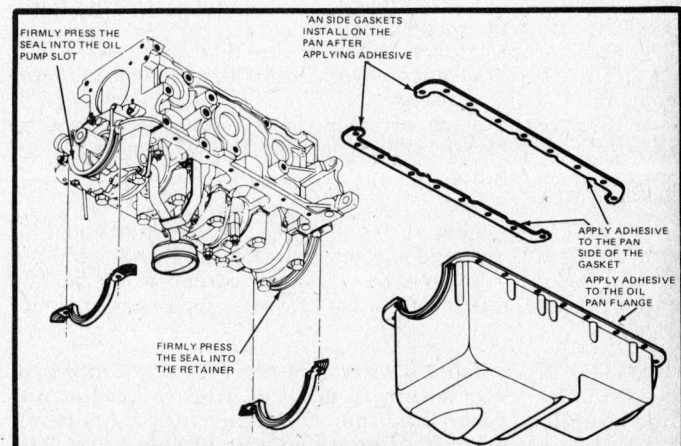

Oil pan removal and installation
(© Ford Motor Co.)

Installation

1. Clean both mating surfaces of oil pan and cylinder block.
2. Remove and clean oil pump pick-up tube and screen assembly. After cleaning, install tube and screen assembly.

NOTE: Before proceeding, a trial installation of the pan to cylinder block must be performed to insure smooth pan installation, thus preventing smearing of sealant. Check again for any residual oil that may have leaked down (particularly the rear of the engine) and re-clean as necessary.

3. Apply a continuous 3/16 in. diameter bead of Silicone Gasket Sealant to grove in oil pan flange.

NOTE: Immediately place the oil pan against the block and transaxle before the sealant "skins" over, approximately 2 minutes.

4. Install oil pan flange bolts tight enough to compress sealant to the point that the two oil pan transaxle hoses are aligned with the two tapped holes in transaxle but loose enough to allow the pan to move relative to the block.

FORD MERCURY
FRONT WHEEL DRIVE CARS—ESCORT • EXP • LYNX • TEMPO • TOPAZ • TAURUS • SABLE

5. Install two oil pan to transaxle bolts. Tighten to 30–39 ft. lbs. (40–50 Nm) to align oil pan with transaxle, then loosen bolts ½ turn.
6. Tighten all oil pan flange bolts to 6–9 ft. lbs. (8–12 Nm).
7. Tighten two oil pan to transaxle bolts to 30–39 ft. lbs. (40–54 Nm).
8. Install exhaust pipe bracket to oil pan.
9. Install engine coolant tube and air conditioning line.
10. Install starter and cable.
11. Install roll restrictor (MTX only).
12. Lower vehicle.
13. Install engine oil and coolant.
14. Connect negative ground cable at battery.
15. Start engine and check for leaks.

OIL PAN

Removal

3.0L TAURUS/SABLE

1. Disconnect the negative battery cable and remove the oil level dipstick.
2. Raise and support the vehicle safely. If equipped with a low level sensor, remove the retainer clip at the sensor. Remove the electrical connector from the sensor.
3. Drain the motor oil from the oil pan into a suitable drain pan. Remove the starter motor and disconnect the electrical connector from the oxygen sensor.
4. Remove the catalyst and pipe assembly. Remove the lower engine/flywheel dust cover from the torque converter housing.
5. Remove the oil pan attaching bolts and slowly remove the oil pan from the engine block. Remove the oil pan gasket.

Installation

1. Clean the gasket surfaces on the cylinder block and oil pan. Apply a ⅕ in. bead of Silcone Sealer No. D6AZ–19562–A or equivalent, to the junction of the rear main bearing cap and cylinder block junction of the front cover assembly and cylinder block.

NOTE: When using a silicone sealer, the assembly process should occur within 15 minutes after the sealer has been applied. After this time, the sealer may start to set-up and its sealing effectivness may be affected.

2. Position the oil pan gasket over the oil pan and secure the gasket with a suitable sealer contact adhesive.
3. Position the oil pan on the engine block and install the oil pan attaching bolts. Torque the bolts to 71 to 106 in.lbs.
4. Install the lower engine/flywheel dust cover to the torque converter housing. Install the catalyst and pip assembly. Connect the oxygen sensor connector.
5. Install the starter motor. Install the low oil level sensor connector to the sensor and install the retainer clip. Lower the vehicle and replace the oil level dipstick.
6. Connect the negative battery cable. Fill the crankcase with the correct viscosity and amount of engine oil. Start the engine and check for oil and exhaust leaks.

OIL PUMP

Removal

1.6L AND 1.9L ESCORT/LYNX, EXP

1. Disconnect the negative cable at the battery.
2. Loosen the alternator bolt on the alternator adjusting arm.
3. Lower the alternator to remove the accessory drivebelt from the crankshaft pulley.
4. Remove the timing belt cover.
5. Loosen both belt tensioner attaching bolts. Using a pry bar of other suitable tool pry the tensioner away from the belt. While holding the tensioner away from the belt, tighten one of the tensioner attaching bolts.

NOTE: Set No. 1 cylinder at TDC prior to timing belt removal.

6. Disengage timing belt from camshaft sprocket, water pump sprocket and crankshaft sprocket.
7. Raise the vehicle on a hoist.
8. Drain crankcase.
9. Using crankshaft pulley wrench T81P–6312–A or equivalent, remove the crankshaft pulley attaching bolt.
10. Remove timing belt.
11. Remove crankshaft drive plate assembly.
12. Remove crankshaft pulley.
13. Remove crankshaft sprocket.
14. Disconnect starter cable at the starter.
15. Remove knee-brace from the engine.
16. Remove starter.
17. Remove rear section of the knee-brace and inspection plate at the transmission.
18. Remove oil pan retaining bolts and oil pan.
19. Remove front and rear oil pan seals.
20. Remove oil pan side gaskets.
21. Remove oil pump attaching bolts, oil pump and gasket.
22. Remove oil pump seal.

Installation

1. Make sure the mating surfaces on the cylinder block and the oil pump are clean and free of gasket material.
2. Remove the oil pick-up tube and screen assembly from the pump for cleaning.
3. Lubricate the outside diameter of the oil pump seal with engine oil.
4. Install the oil pump seal using Seal Installer.
5. Install pick-up tube and screen assembly on the oil pump. Tighten attaching bolts to 6–9 ft. lbs. (8–12 Nm).
6. Lubricate oil pump seal lip with light engine oil.
7. Position oil pump gasket over the locating dowels.
8. Position oil pump. Install attaching bolts and tighten to 5–7 ft. lbs. (7–9 Nm).
9. Apply a bead of sealer approximately 3.0mm wide at the corner of the front and ear oil pan seals, and at the seating point of the oil pump to the block retainer joint.
10. Install front oil pan by pressing firmly into the slot cut into the bottom of the pump.
11. Install the rear oil seal by pressing firmly into the slot cut into rear retainer assembly.

NOTE: Install the seal before the sealer has cured (within 10 minutes of application).

12. Apply adhesive evenly to oil pan flange and to the oil pan side of the gaskets. Allow the adhesive to dry past the "wet" stage and then install the gaskets on the oil pan.
13. Position the oil pan on the cylinder block.
14. Install oil pan attaching bolts. Tighten bolts in the proper sequence to 6–8 ft. lbs. (8–11 Nm).
15. Position the transmission inspection plate and the rear section of the knee-brace on the transmission. Install the two attaching bolts and tighten to specification.
16. Install starter.
17. Install knee-brace.
18. Connect starter cable.
19. Install crankshaft gear.
20. Install crankshaft pulley.
21. Install crankshaft drive plate assembly.
22. Install timing belt over the crankshaft pulley.
23. Using the crankshaft pulley wrench, install the crankshaft pulley attaching bolt. Tighten bolt to specification.

4–66

24. Lower vehicle.
25. Install engine front timing cover.
26. Position the accessory drive belts over the alternator and crankshaft pulleys. Tighten drive belts to specification.
27. Connect negative cable to the battery.
28. Fill crankcase to the proper level with the specified oil.
29. Start the engine and check for oil leaks. Make sure the oil pressure indicator lamp has gone out. If the lamp remains On, immediately shut off the engine, determine the cause and correct the condition.

OIL PUMP

Removal
2.3L HSC TEMPO/TOPAZ AND 2.5L TAURUS/SABLE

1. Remove oil pan as outlined.
2. Remove oil pump attaching bolts and remove oil pump and intermediate driveshaft.

Installation

1. Prime oil pump by filling inlet port with engine oil. Rotate pump shaft until oil flows from outlet port.
2. If screen and cover assembly have been removed, replace gasket. Clean screen and reinstall screen and cover assembly and tighten the two attaching bolts and one nut to specification.
3. Position intermediate driveshaft into distributor socket.
4. Insert intermediate driveshaft into oil pump. Install pump and shaft as an assembly.

――――――――― **CAUTION** ―――――――――
Do not attempt to force the pump into position if it will not seat. The shaft hex may be mis-aligned with the distributor shaft. To align, remove the oil pump and rotate the intermediate driveshaft into a new position.

5. Tighten the two attaching bolts to specification.
6. Install oil pan and all related parts, refer to Oil Pan Installation.

7. Fill crankcase to proper level with recommended engine oil. Start engine and check for oil pressure. Operate engine at fast idle and check for oil leaks.

OIL PUMP

Removal
3.0L TAURUS/SABLE

1. Remove the oil pan as previously described in this section.
2. Remove the oil pump attaching bolts. Lift the oil pump off the engine and withdraw the oil pump driveshaft.

Installation

1. Prime the oil pump by filling either the inlet or the outlet port with engine oil. Rotate the pump shaft to distribute the oil within the oil pump body.
2. Insert the oil pump driveshaft into the block with the pointed end facing inward. The pointed end is the closest to the pressed on flange. Place the oil pump in the proper position with a new gasket and install the attaching bolts.
3. Torque the oil pump attaching bolts to 30–40 ft. lbs. Clean and install the oil pump inlet tube and screen assembly with a new gasket. Torque the oil pump inlet tube to pump bolts to 6–10 ft. lbs. and torque the oil inlet tube support to main baering cap (nut) to 12–15 ft. lbs.
4. Install the oil pan with new gasket as previously outlined in this section.
5. Fill crankcase to proper level with recommended engine oil. Start engine and check for oil pressure. Operate engine at fast idle and check for oil leaks.

CRANKSHAFT OIL SEAL—REAR

Removal
ALL MODELS

1. Remove the transaxle.
2. Remove rear cover plate.
3. Remove flywheel.

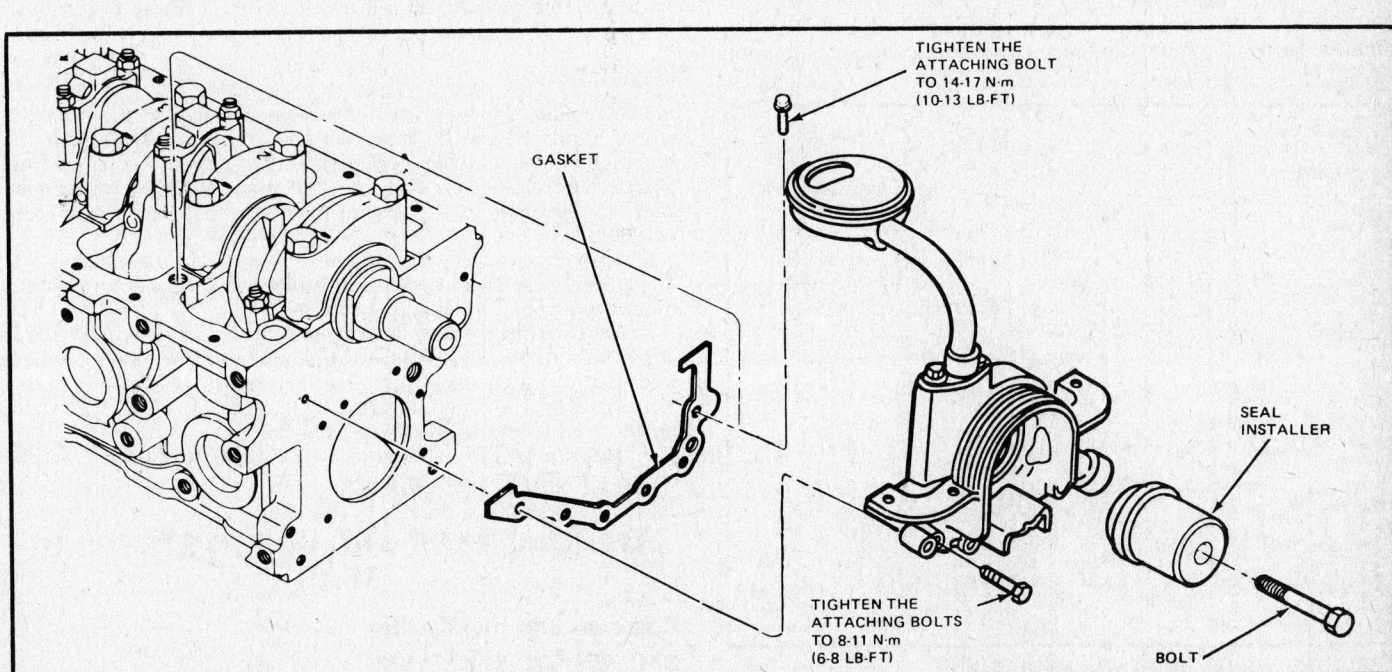

Oil pump installation 1.6L engine (© Ford Motor Co.)

SECTION 4

FORD MERCURY
FRONT WHEEL DRIVE CARS—ESCORT • EXP • LYNX • TEMPO • TOPAZ • TAURUS • SABLE

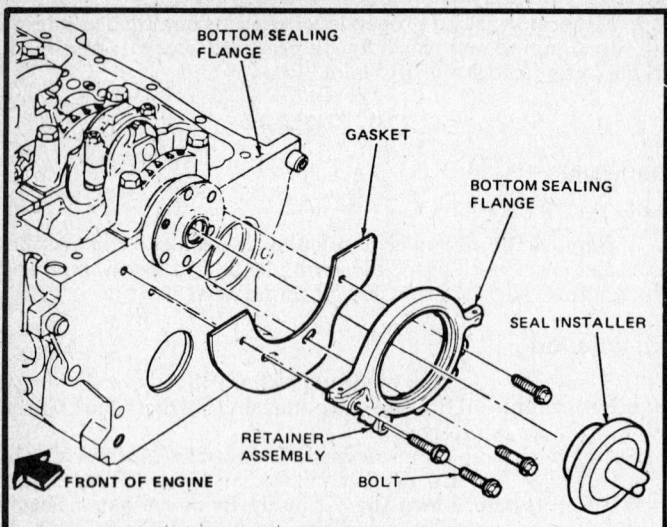

Rear crankshaft seal installation
(© Ford Motor Co.)

4. With a sharp awl, punch a hole into the seal metal surface between the lip and block. Screw in the threaded end of slide hammer tool No. T77L–9533–B or equivalent and use the slide hammer to remove the seal.

NOTE: Use caution to avoid damaging the oil seal surface.

Installation

1. Inspect the crankshaft seal area for any damage which may cause the seal to leak. If damage is evident service or replace the crankshaft as necessary.
2. Coat the crankshaft seal area and the seal lip with engine oil.
3. Using seal installer tool No. T82L–6701–A or equivalent to install the seal. Tighten the two bolts of the seal installer tool evenly so that the seal is straight and seats without misalignment.
4. Install the flywheel. Tighten attaching bolts to 54–64 ft. lbs. (73–87 Nm).
5. Install rear cover plate.
6. Install transaxle.

FRONT SUSPENSION AND STEERING SECTION

For Front Suspension Services refer to Unit Repair Section. For Steering Gear Overhaul refer to Unit Repair Section.

STEERING WHEEL

Removal
ALL MODELS

1. Disconnect the negative battery cable and remove the steering wheel center hub cover.
2. On the 1985 and later models equipped with Air Bag Restraint System, remove the four nuts holding the air bag module to the steering wheel (the nuts are located on the back of the steering wheel).
3. Lift the air bag module from the wheel and disconnect the air bag module to slip-ring clock spring connector.
4. On all models loosen and remove the center mounting nut, and on the models equipped with speed control system remove the electrical connectors.
5. Remove the steering wheel with a crowsfoot type of puller or equivalent. Do not use a knock-off type puller, because it will cause damage to the collapsible steering column. On the Taurus/Sable models, do not use a steering wheel puller, pull the wheel off by hand.

Installation

1. Position the steering wheel on the end of the steering wheel shaft. Align the mark on the steering wheel with the mark on the shaft to assure the straight-ahead steering wheel position corresponds to the straight-ahead steering wheel position corresponds to the straight-ahead position of the front wheels.
2. Install a new service wheel lock-nut and torque it to 30–40 ft. lbs., also reconnect all the electrical connectors on the models equipped with speed control.
3. On the air bag module, connect the air bag module wire to slip ring connector and place the module on the steering wheel with the four attaching nuts, torque the nuts to 35–33 inch lbs.
4. On the other models install the steering wheel hub cover and torque the nuts to 13–20 inch lbs.
5. Reconnect the negative battery cable and check out the operation of the steering wheel.

MANUAL RACK AND PINION STEERING GEAR

Removal and Installation
ESCORT/LYNX, EXP/LN7

1. Disconnect the negative battery cable.

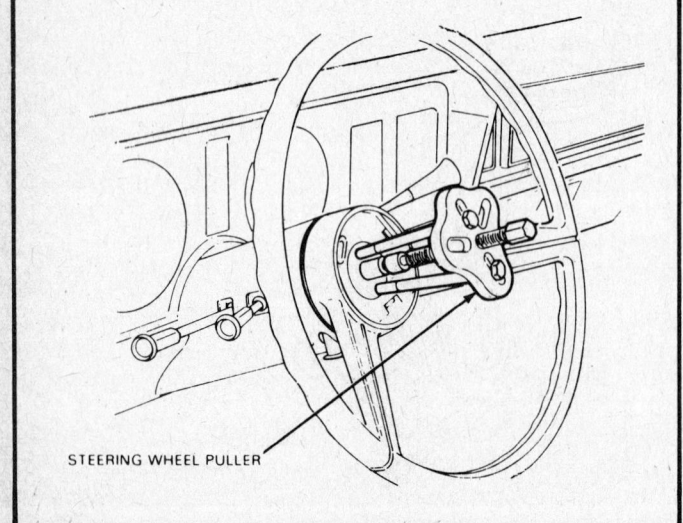

Steering wheel removal with puller
(© Ford Motor Co.)

2. Turn the ignition key to the ON position.
3. Remove the access trim panel from below the steering column.
4. Remove the intermediate shaft bolts at the rack and pinion input shaft and the steering column shaft.
5. Spread the slots enough to loosen the intermediate shaft at both ends. They cannot be separated at this time.
6. Turn the steering wheel to a full left turn so that the tie rod will clear the shift linkage for removal.
7. Separate the tie rod ends from the steering knuckles. Turn the right wheel to the full left turn position.
8. Remove the left tie rod end from the left tie rod and disconnect the speedometer cable at the transmission on automatic transmissions only.
9. Disconnect the secondary air tube at the check valve. Disconnect the exhaust system at the manifold and support the exhaust system to allow clearance for the gear removal.

---- CAUTION ----
Do not allow the exhaust system to hang by the rear support hangers. The system could fall to the floor.

---

10. Remove the exhaust hanger bracket from below the steering gear.
11. Remove the gear mounting brackets and insulators. Keep separated as they are not interchangeable.
12. Separate the gear assembly from the intermediate shaft by pulling upward on the shaft from the inside of the vehicle.
13. Rotate the gear forward and down to clear the input shaft through the dash panel opening.
14. With the gear in the full left turn position, move the gear through the right (passenger side) apron opening until the left tie rod clears the shift linkage and other parts so it may be lowered.
15. Lower the left side of the gear assembly and remove from the vehicle.
16. To install the gear assembly, be sure the gear input shaft is in a full left turn to its stop. Position the right road wheel to the full left turn.
17. Reverse the removal procedure to install the gear assembly back into the vehicle.
18. When assembly is completed, check and adjust the toe to specifications.

TEMPO/TOPAZ

1. Disconnect negative battery cable from battery.
2. Turn ignition key to the RUN position.
3. Remove access panel from dash below the steering column.
4. Remove intermediate shaft bolts at gear input shaft and at the steering column shaft.
5. With a wide blade screwdriver, spread slots enough to loosen intermediate shaft at both ends. The intermediate shaft and gear input shaft cannot be separated at this time.
6. From under vehicle, separate tie rod ends form steering knuckles, using tool No.3290–C and adapter T81P–3504–W or equivalent. Turn right wheel to the full left turn position.
7. Disconnect speedometer cable at transmission (automatic transmission only).
8. Disconnect secondary air tube at check valve. Disconnect exhaust system at exhaust manifold. Remove exhaust system.
9. Remove gear mounting brackets and insulators.

NOTE: Right and left hand brackets and insulators are not interchangeable side to side.

10. Turn steering wheel full left so tie rod will clear shaft linkage during removal.
11. Separate gear from intermediate shaft, with an assistant pulling up on the shaft from inside the vehicle.

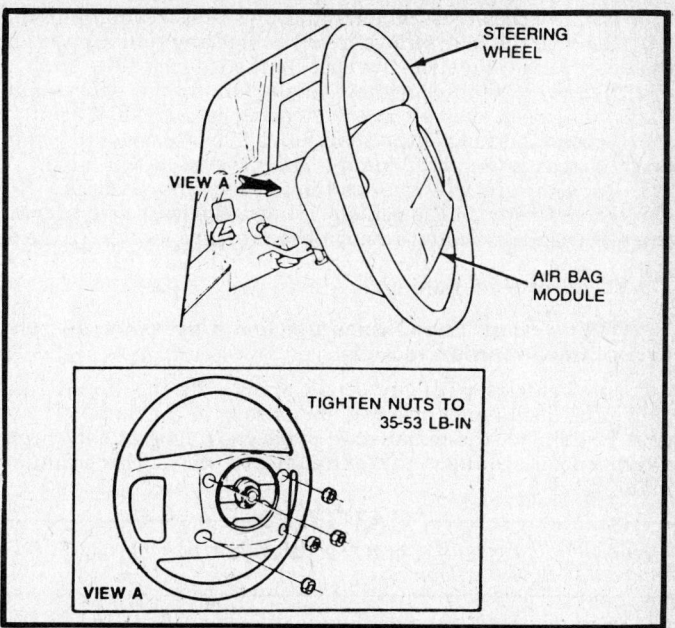

Typical air bag module on new models
(© Ford Motor Co.)

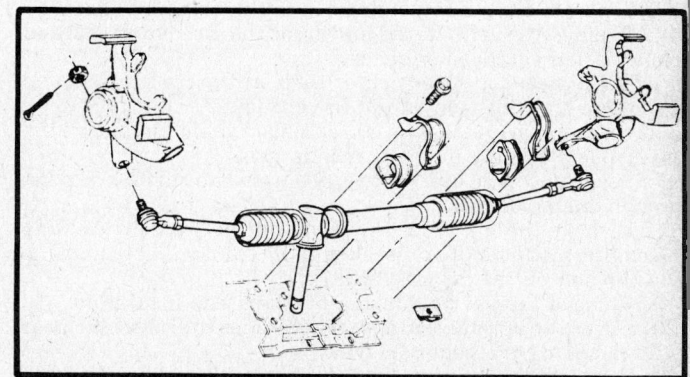

Manual rack and pinion gear assembly
(© Ford Motor Co.)

---- CAUTION ----
Care should be taken during gear removal and installation to prevent tearing or damaging the steering gear bellows.

---

12. Rotate gear forward and down to clear the input shaft through dash panel opening.
13. Make sure input shaft is in full left turn position. Move gear through right (passenger) side apron opening until left tie rod clears shift linkage and other parts so it may be lowered.
14. Lower left side of the gear and remove gear out of the vehicle.
15. Installation is the reverse of removal. Torque the steering gear mounting bolts to 48–55 ft. lbs. (65–75 Nm).

POWER RACK AND PINION STEERING GEAR

Removal and Installation
ALL 1983 MODELS

1. Disconnect the negative battery cable.
2. Turn the ignition switch to the ON position.

Ford Mercury
FRONT WHEEL DRIVE CARS—ESCORT • EXP • LYNX • TEMPO • TOPAZ • TAURUS • SABLE

3. Remove the access panel from below the steering column.
4. Remove the four screws from the steering column boot at the dash panel and slide the boot up the intermediate shaft.
5. Remove the intermediate shaft bolt at the gear input shaft and loosen the bolt at the steering column shaft joint.
6. Spread the slots of the shaft joint. The intermediate shaft and the gear input shaft cannot be separated at this time.
7. Turn the steering gear to the full left turn position.
8. From the top of the vehicle, remove the wire connector to the pressure switch and remove the pressure switch. (All except vehicle with 1.6 liter engine and manual transmission without air conditioning).

NOTE: Tempo/Topaz does not use a pressure switch, except on Canadian models.

9. On vehicles with air conditioning, lift the liquid line above the dash panel opening and wire it to the dash.
10. Disconnect the exhaust secondary air tube at the check valve and disconnect the exhaust system at the exhaust manifold.

---------- CAUTION ----------
Do not allow the exhaust system to hang on the rear hangers. The system could fall to the floor.

11. Remove both exhaust hanger brackets from below the steering gear and from the side apron.
12. Disconnect the pressure and return lines and allow to drain.
13. Separate the tie rod ends form the steering knuckles.
14. Remove the left tie rod end from the tie rod on manual transmission equipped vehicles.
15. Disconnect the speedometer cable at the transmission on automatic transmission equipped vehicles.
16. On automatic transmission equipped vehicles, remove the shift cable assembly at the transmission.
17. Separate the heater water tube from the shake brace below the engine oil pan.
18. Remove the nut from the lower of the two bolts holding the engine mount support bracket to the transmission housing. Tap the bolt out as far as it will go.
19. Remove the gear mounting brackets and insulators.
20. Cover the apron openings on both sides to protect the gear bellows during the gear removal.
21. Separate the intermediate shaft from the column bracket by either pulling the gear downward or pulling upward on the column.
22. Rotate the gear forward and down to clear the input shaft through the dash panel openings.
23. Be sure the input shaft is in a full left turn position and move the gear through the right side apron opening until the left tie rod clears the opening.

Power steering rack and pinion assembly
(© Ford Motor Co.)

24. Lower the gear assembly and remove from the vehicle.
25. To install the gear assembly, have the input shaft in a full left turn against the stop and position the right road wheel to a full left turn. Assembly the gear to the vehicle in the reverse of the removal procedure.
26. Fill the system with fluid, bleed the system and check the toe. Adjust to specifications.

Removal and Installation

1984 AND LATER MODELS EXCEPT THE TAURUS/SABLE

1. Disconnect negative battery cable from battery.
2. Turn the ignition key to the Run position.
3. Remove access panel from dash below the steering column.
4. Remove four screws from steering column boot at the dash panel and slide boot up intermediate shaft.
5. Remove intermediate shaft bolt at gear input shaft and loosen the bolt at the steering column shaft joint.
6. With a wide blade screwdriver, or equivalent, spread the slots enough to loosen intermediates shaft at both ends. The intermediate shaft and gear input shaft cannot be separated at this time.
7. Remove air cleaner.
8. On Escort/Lynx, EXP with A/C, wire the air conditioner liquid line above the dash panel opening. Doing so provides clearance for gear input shaft removal and installation.
9. Separate pressure and return lines at intermediate connections and drain fluid.
10. On Tempo/Topaz non-diesel vehicles, remove pressure switch.
11. Disconnect exhaust secondary air tube at check valve. Disconnect exhaust system at exhaust manifold and remove exhaust systems.
12. Separate tie rod ends from steering knuckles. using tool 3290-C and adapter T81P-3504-W or equivalent.
13. Remove left tie rod end from tie rod on manual transmission vehicles. This will allow tie rod to clear the shift linkage.

NOTE: Mark location of rod end prior to removal.

14. Disconnect speedometer cable at transmission (automatic transmission only).
15. Remove transmission shift cable assembly at transmission (automatic transmission only).
16. Turn steering wheel to full left turn stop for easier gear removal.
17. On Escort/Lynx, EXP, remove two screws holding heater water tube to shake brace below the oil pan.
18. On Escort/Lynx, EXP, remove nut from the lower of two bolts holding engine mount support bracket to transmission housing. Tap bolt out as far as it will go.
19. Remove gear mounting brackets and insulators.
20. Drape cloth towel over both apron opening edges to protect bellows during gear removal.
21. Separate gear from intermediate shaft by either pushing up on shaft with a bar from underneath the vehicle while pulling the gear down, or with a assistant removing the shaft from inside the vehicle.
22. Rotate gear forward and down to clear the input shaft through the dash panel opening.
23. Make sure input shaft is in full left turn position. Move gear through the right (passenger) side apron opening until left tie rod clears left apron opening and other parts so it may be lowered.
24. to install the gear assembly, have the input shaft in a full left turn against the stop and position the right wheel to a full left turn. Assemble the gear to the vehicle in the reverse order of the removal procedure.
25. Fill the system with fluid, bleed the system and check the toe. Adjust to specifications.

Removal and Installation

TAURUS/SABLE

1. Working from inside the vehicle, remove the nuts retaining the steering shaft weather boot to the dash panel.
2. Remove the two bolts retaining the intermidate shaft to the steering coulmn shaft. Set the weather boot aside.
3. Remove the pinch bolt at the steering gear input shaft and remove the interimediate shaft. Raise and support the vehicle safely.
4. Remove the left hand side front wheel assembly. Remove the heat shield. Cut the bundling strap retaining the lines to the gear.
5. Remove the tie rod ends from the spindles. Place a drain pan under the vehicle and remove the hydraulic pressure and return lines from the steering gear.

CAUTION
The pressure and return lines are on the front of the housing. Do not confuse them with the transfer lines on the side of the valve.

6. Remove the nut from the gear mounting bolts. The bolts are pressed into the gear housing and should not be removed during gear removal.
7. Push the weather boot end into the vehicle and lift the gear out of the mounting holes. Rotate the gear so the input shaft will pass between the brake booster and the floor pan. Carefully start working the steering gear out through the LH fender apron opening.
8. Rotate the input shaft so that it clears the LH fender apron opening and complete the removal of the steering gear. If the steering gear seams to be stuck, check the RH tie rod to ensure the stud is not caught on anything.

Installation

1. Install new plastic seals on the hydraulic line fittings.
2. Insert the steering gear through the LH fender apron. Rotate the input shaft forward to completely clear the fender apron opening.
3. To allow the gear to pass between the brake booster and the floorpan, rotate the input shaft rearward. Align the steering gear bolts to the bolt holes. Install the mounting nuts and torque them to 85–100 ft. lbs. Lower the vehicle.
4. Working from the engine compartment, install the hydraulic pressure and return lines. Tighten the pressure line to 20–25 ft. lbs. and the return line to 15–20 ft. lbs. Swivel movement of the lines is normal when the fittings are properly tightened.
5. Raise and support the vehicle safely. Secure the pressure and return lines to the transfer tube with the bundle strap. Install the heat shield.
6. Install the tir rod ends to spindles. Torque the castle nuts to 35 ft. lbs. and if necessary, torque the nuts a little bit more to align the slot in the nut for the cotter pin. Install the cotter pin.
7. Install the LH front wheel assembly and lower the vehicle. Working from inside the vehicle, pull the weather boot end out of the vehicle and install it over the valve housing. Install the intermidiate shaft to the steering gear input shaft. Install the the inner weather boot to the floor pan.
8. Install the intermidiae shaft to the steering column shaft. Fill the power steering system with Motorcraft Type F ® automatic transmission fluid.
9. Check the system for leaks and proper operation. Adjust the toe setting as necessary.

PINION BEARING PRELOAD

Assembly Removed

ALL MODELS

1. Loosen the bolts of the yoke cover to relieve spring pressure on the rack.
2. Remove the pinion cover and gasket. Clean the cover flange area thoroughly.
3. Remove the spacer and shims.
4. Install a new gasket and fit the shims between the upper bearing and spacer until the top of the spacer is flush with the gasket. Check with a straightedge, using light pressure.
5. Add one 0.13mm (0.005 in.) shim to the pack in order to preload the bearings. The spacer must be assembled next to the pinion cover.
6. Remove the oil seal from the cover. Install the cover, using a centering tool.
7. Tighten bolts to specification.
8. Install the pinion oil seal.

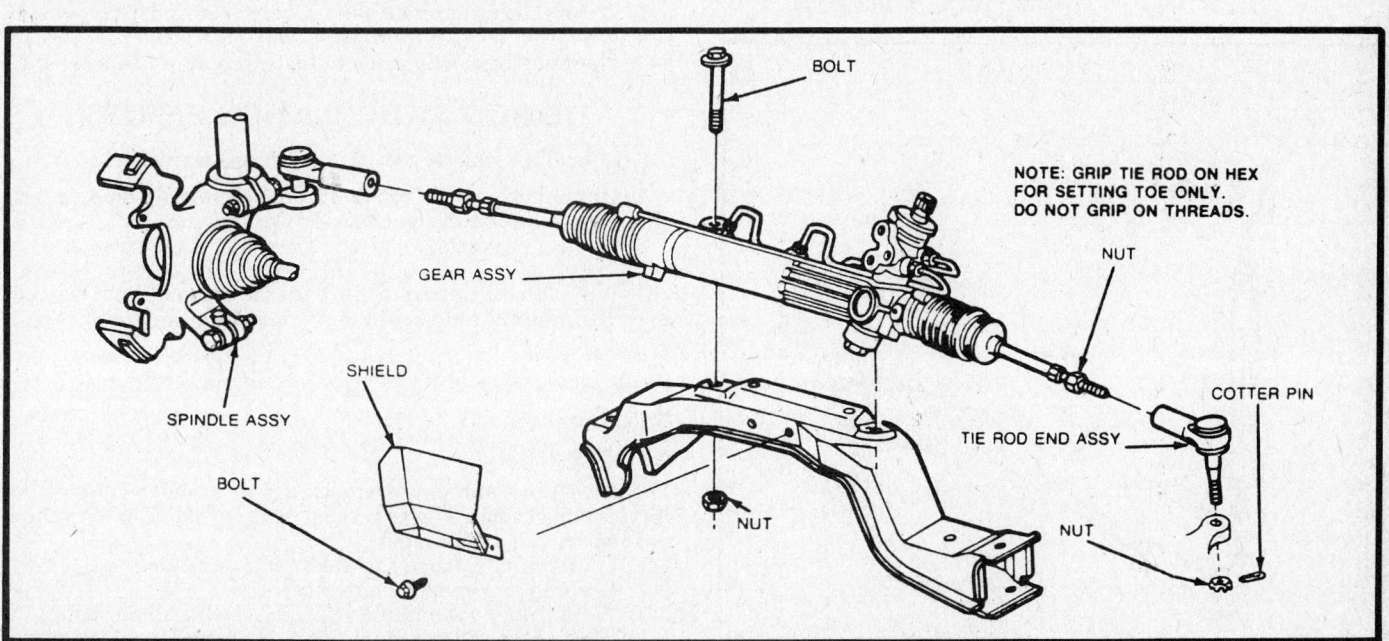

Power rack and pinion steering gear—Taurus/Sable

SECTION 4 — FORD MERCURY
FRONT WHEEL DRIVE CARS—ESCORT • EXP • LYNX • TEMPO • TOPAZ • TAURUS • SABLE

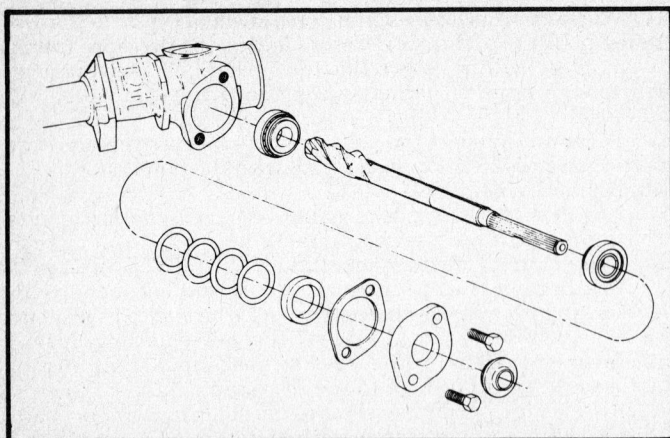

Exploded view of pinion, bearing cover and shims (© Ford Motor Co.)

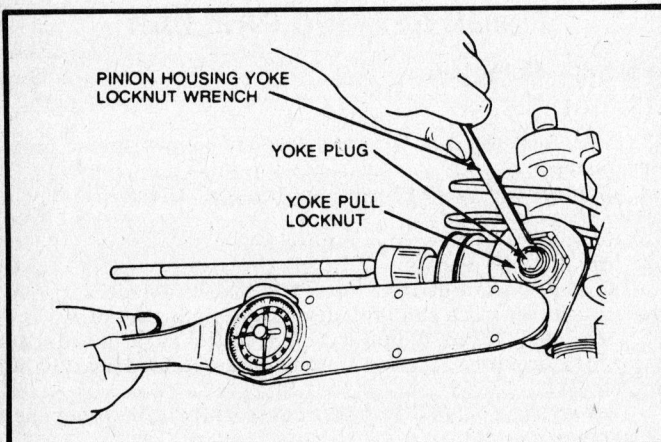

Adjusting the preload—Taurus/Sable

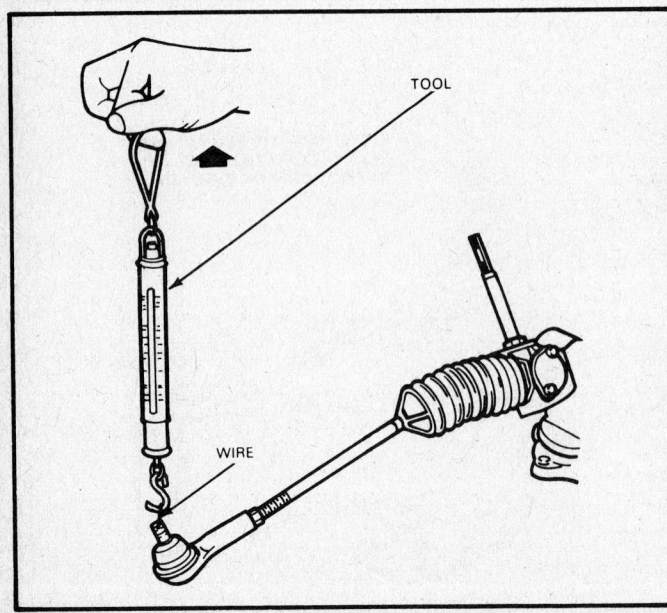

Checking tie rod articulation (© Ford Motor Co.)

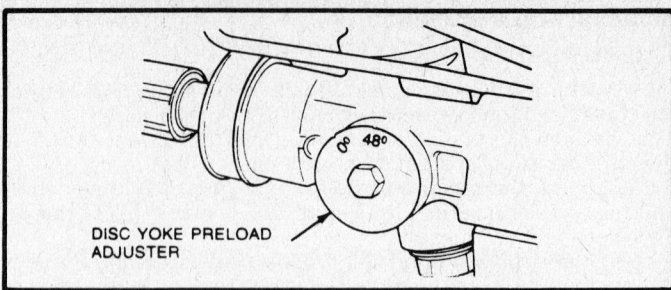

Installing the pre-load adjuster—Taurus/Sable

PINION BEARING PRELOAD

Assembly Removed
TAURUS/SABLE

1. Clean the exterior of the steering gear thoroughly. Mount the steering gear in a suitable holding fixture.
2. To avoid removing the pressed in mounting bolts from the gear, enlarge the mounting holes in the holding fxture with a $\frac{9}{16}$ inch diameter drill bit.
3. Do not remove the extermal pressure lines, unless thet are leaking or damaged. If these lines are removed, they must be replaced with new lines. Drain the the steering gear, by rotating input shaft lock to lock twice using pinion shaft torque djuster T86P–3504–K or equivalent. Position the adapter on the wrench on the input shaft.
4. Loosen the yoke plug locknut with a suitable wrench. With the steering rack at the center of travel, tighten the yoke plug to 45–50 inch lbs. (make sure the threads of the yoke plug are clean).
5. Install the disc-yoke pre-load adjuster T86P–3504–H or equivalent. Mark the location of 0° mark on the housing. Back off the adjuster so that the 48° mark lines up with the 0° mark.
6. Place the pinion housing yoke locknut wrench T86P–3504–E or equivalent on the yoke plug locknut. While holding the yoke plug, tighten the locknut to 40–50 ft. lbs. Do not allow the yoke plug to move while tightening or preload will be affected. Recheck input shaft torque after tightening the locknut.
7. If the external pressure lines were removed, they must be replaced with new service lines. Clean out the old seal threads from the housing ports, prior to installation of the new lines.

TIE ROD ARTICULATION EFFORT

NOTE: This check can be made on the vehicle.

1. Disconnect the tie rod end from the spindle using a suitable tie rod ball stud remover.
2. Hook a pull scale over the tie rod end and measure the force required to remove the tie rod.
3. If the force required to move the tie rod end is not between 2–10 lbs., the tie rod should be removed and replaced.

STEERING GEAR

Adjustment
ALL MODELS

The power rack and pinion steering gear provides for only one service adjustment. The gear must be removed from the vehicle to perform this adjustment.

1. Loosen and remove the yoke plug locknut.
2. Back off the yoke plug one turn.
3. Tighten the yoke plug to 45 inch lbs. (5.8 Nm) using the yoke plug adapter Tool T81P–3504–U and an inch lbs. torque wrench with a full scale reading to 100 inch lbs. maximum.

4. Mark the gear housing in line with the 0 mark on the yoke plug adapter tool.

NOTE: Refer to the Steering chapter in Unit Repair Section for further steering gear information.

POWER STEERING PUMP

Removal and Installation

ALL MODELS EXCEPT THE TAURUS/SABLE

1. Remove the air cleaner, thermactor air pump and belt. Remove the reservoir filler extension and cover the hole to prevent dirt from entering.
2. From under the vehicle, loosen one pump adjusting bolt. Remove one pump to bracket mounting bolt and disconnect the fluid return line.
3. From above the vehicle, loosen one adjusting bolt and the pivot bolt. Remove the drive belt and the two remaining pump to bracket mountning bolts.
4. Remove the pump by passing the pulley through the adjusting bracket pening. Remove the pressure hose from the pump assembly.
5. Reverse the removal procedure to install the pump assembly. Fill the pump with fluid and bleed the system.

TEMPO/TOPAZ

1. Loosen the alternator and remove the drive belt. Pivot the alternator to it most upright position.
2. Remove the radiator overflow bottle. Loosen and remove the power steering pump drive belt. Mark the pulley and pump drive hub with pant or grease pencil for location reference.
3. Remove the pulley retaining bolts and the two pulleys from the pump shaft.
4. Remove the return line from the pump. Be prepared to catch any spilled fluid in a suitable container.
5. Back off the pressure line attaching nut completely. The line will separate from the pump connection when the pump is removed.
6. Remove the three pump mounting bolts and remove the pump.
7. Place the pump in position and connect the pressure line loosely. Install the pump in the reverse order.

DIESEL ENGINE MODELS

1. Remove the drive belts.
2. On air condition models, remove the alternator.
3. Remove both braces from the support bracket on air conditioned models.
4. Disconnect the power steering fluid lines and drain the fluid into a suitable container.
5. Remove the four bracket mounting bolts and remove the pump and bracket assembly.
6. The pulley must be removed before the pump can be separated from the mounting bracket. Tool T65P3A733C or equivalent is required to remove and install the drive pulley.
7. Install the pump and mounting bracket in the reverse order of removal.

Removal and Installation

2.5L ENGINE ON THE TAURUAS/SABLE

1. Disconnect the negative battwry cable. Loosen the tensioner pulley attaching bolts and using the ½ inch drive hole provided in the tensioner pulley, rotate the tensioner pulley clockwise and remove the belt from the alternator and power steering pulley.
2. Position a drain pan under the power steering pump from underneath the vehicle. Disconnect the hydraulic pressure and return lines.

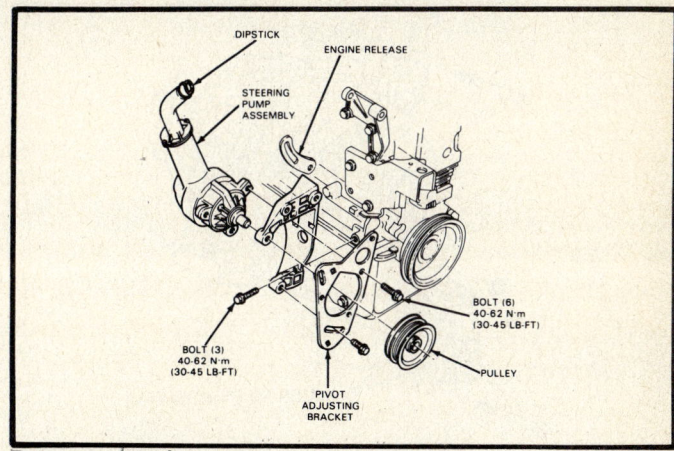

Power steering pump components (© Ford Motor Co.)

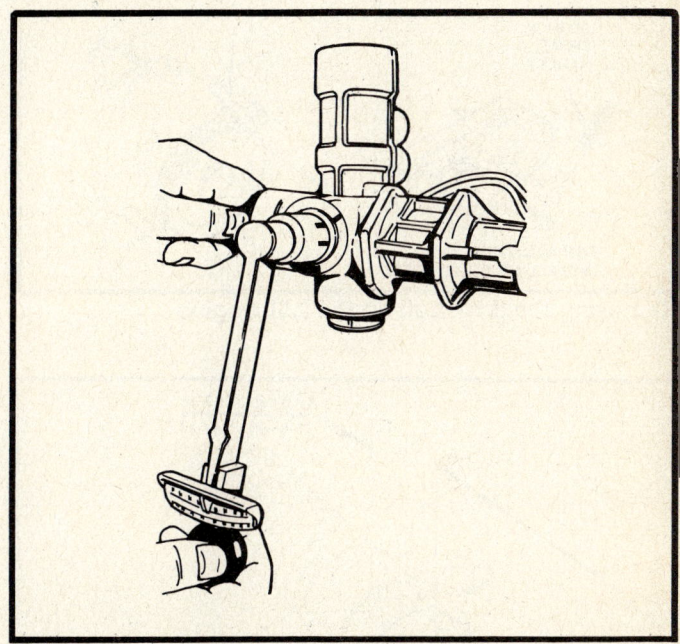

Yoke adjustment (© Ford Motor Co.)

3. Remove the pulley from the pump shaft usinf hub puller T69L–10300–B or equivalent. Remove the three bolts retaining pump to bracket and remove the power steering pump.
4. Installation is the reverse order of the removal procedure.

NOTE: To install the power steering pump pulley, use steering pump pulley replacer T65P–3A733–C or equivalent. When using this tool, the small diameter threads must be fully engaged in the pump shaft before pressing on the pulley. Hold the head screw and turn the nut to install the pulley. Install the pulley face flush with the pump shaft within ± 0.10 in.

3.0L ENGINE ON THE TAURUS/SABLE

1. Disconnect the negative battery cable. Loosen the idler pulley and remove the power steering belt.
2. Disconnect the negative battery cable. Remove the radiator overflow bottle in order to gain access to the three screws attaching the pulleys to the pulley hub.

Ford Mercury
FRONT WHEEL DRIVE CARS—ESCORT • EXP • LYNX • TEMPO • TOPAZ • TAURUS • SABLE

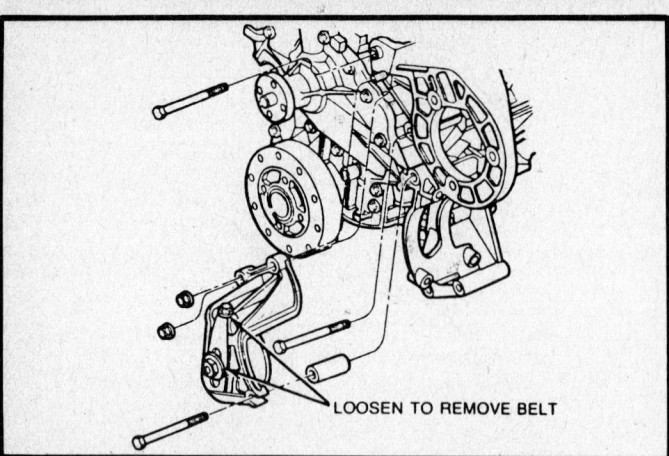

Power steering pump and bracket removal and installation—3.0L engine

Removing the drive belt on the 2.5L engine

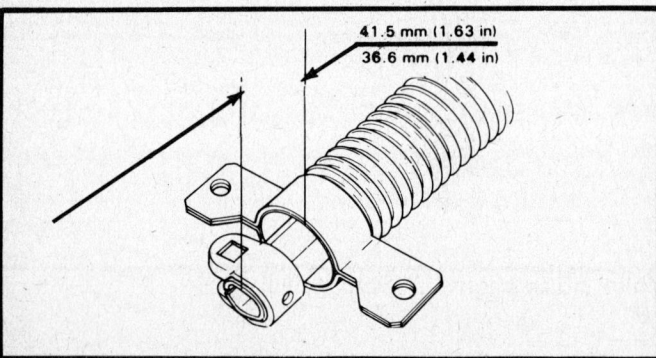

Steering shaft distance from outer tube (© Ford Motor Co.)

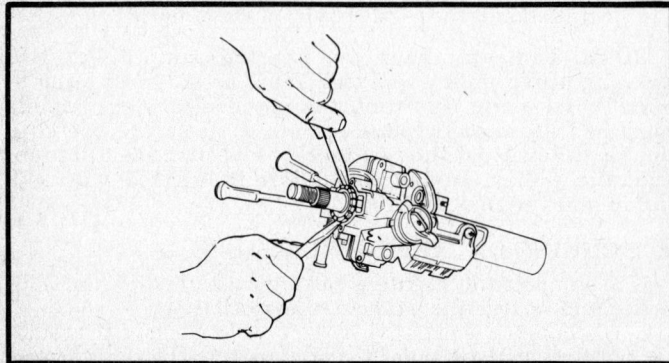

Removing upper shaft bearing (© Ford Motor Co.)

3. Mark both pulley to hub positions with a grease pencil or equivalent, for reassembly to maintain balance.
4. Remove the three bolt and the two pulleys from the pulley hub.
5. Remove the return line from the pump. Be prepared to catch any spilled fluid in a suitable container.
6. Back off the pressure line attaching nut completely. The line will separate from the pump connection when the pump is removed.
7. Remove the three pump mounting bolts and remove the pump.
8. Place the pump in position and connect the pressure line loosely. Install the pump in the reverse order.

STEERING COLUMN

NOTE: All steering column components are assembled with fasteners. They are designed with a thread locking system to prevent loosening due to vibrations assiociated with normal vehicle operation.

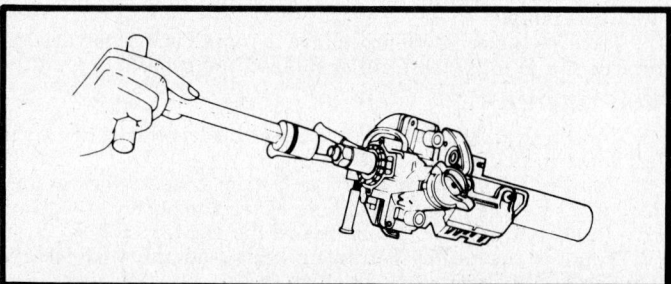

Installing upper shaft bearing (© Ford Motor Co.)

Removal
ALL MODELS EXCEPT THE TAURUS/SABLE

1. Disconnect the negative (ground) battery cable from the battery terminal.
2. Remove the steering column cover on the lower portion of the instrument panel (2 screws) to expose the instrument panel reinforcement section.
3. Remove the instrument panel reinforcement section (2 screws). Remove the speed control module, if so equipped (2 screws).
4. Remove the lower steering column shroud (5 screws).
5. Loosen, but do not remove, the 2 nuts and 2 bolts retaining the steering column to the support bracket. Remove upper shroud.
6. Disconnect all steering column electrical connections (ignition, wash/wipe, turn signal, key warning buzzer and speed control).
7. Loosen the steering column to intermediate shaft clamp connection and remove the bolt or nut.
8. Remove the two nuts and two bolts retaining the steering column to the support bracket (40) and lower the steering column to the floor.
9. Pry open the steering column shaft clamp on each side of the bolt groove with the steering column locked. Open enough to disengage the shaft with a minimal effort. Do not use excessive force, as damage to components may result.
10. Inspect the two steering column bracket clips for damage. If clips have been bent or excessively distorted, they must be replaced.

Installation

1. Check the distance that the steering shaft protrudes past the outer tube assembly. This distance must be between 1.44–1.63 in. (36.6–41.5mm).

Ford Mercury
FRONT WHEEL DRIVE CARS—ESCORT • EXP • LYNX • TEMPO • TOPAZ • TAURUS • SABLE

SECTION 4

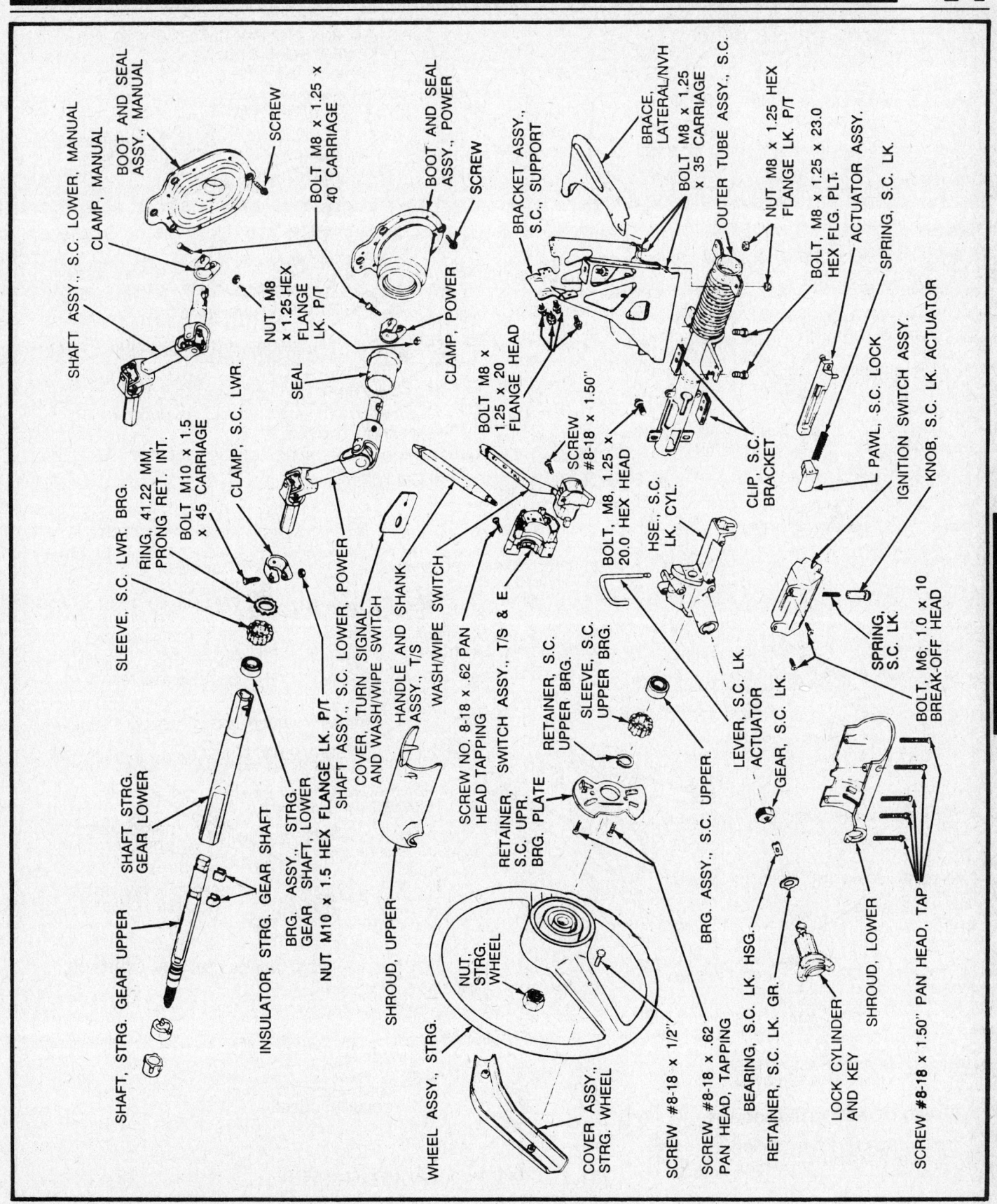

Exploded view of steering column assembly (© Ford Motor Co.)

Ford Mercury
FRONT WHEEL DRIVE CARS—ESCORT • EXP • LYNX • TEMPO • TOPAZ • TAURUS • SABLE

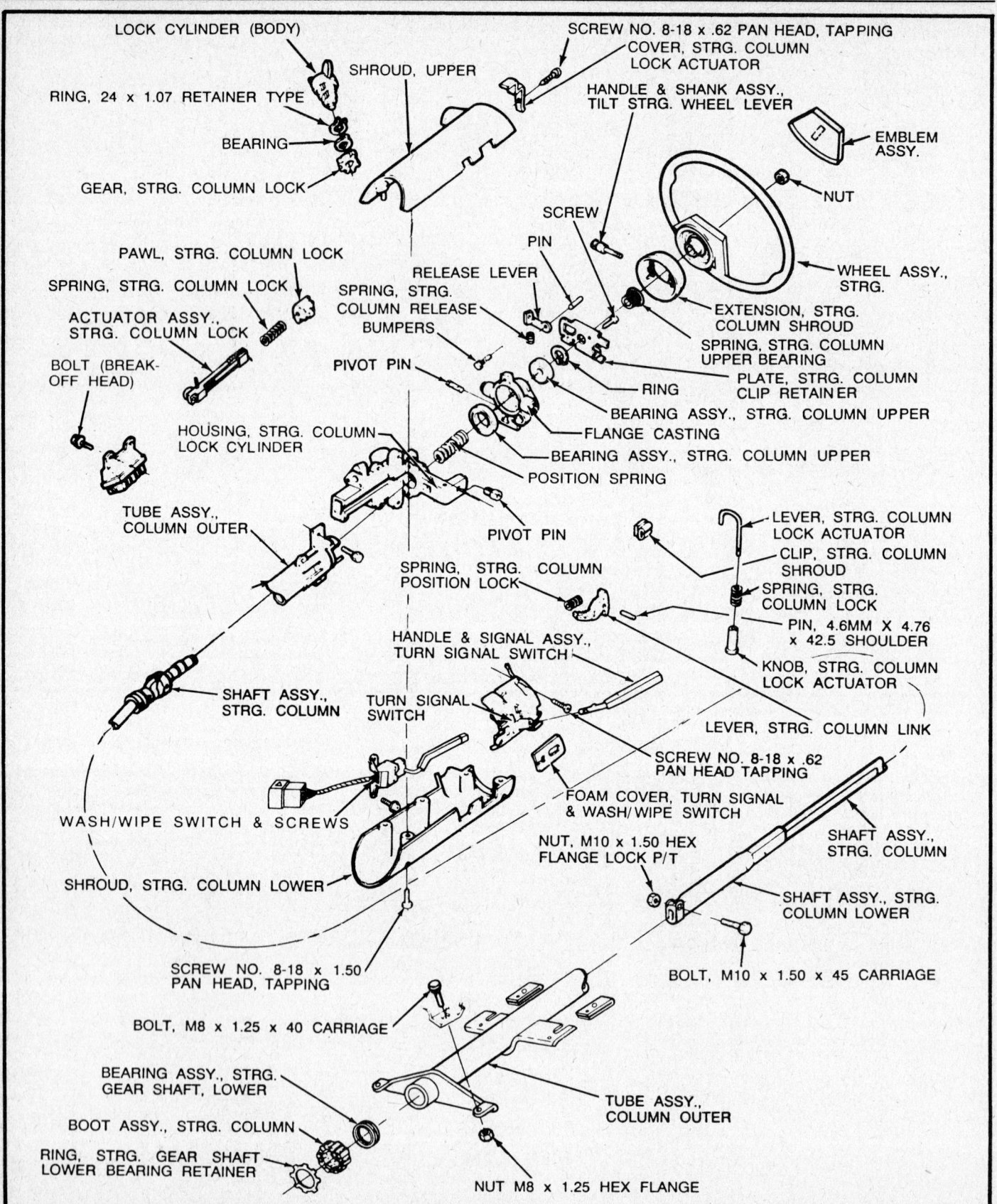

Tilt steering column—exploded view (© Ford Motor Co.)

Ford Mercury
FRONT WHEEL DRIVE CARS—ESCORT • EXP • LYNX • TEMPO • TOPAZ • TAURUS • SABLE
SECTION 4

2. Engage the lower steering shaft to the intermediate shaft and hand start the clamp bolt and nut.
3. Place the steering column under the instrument panel, align the two bolts on the steering column support bracket assembly with the outer tube mounting holes, and hand start the two nuts. Check for the presence of the two clips on the outer bracket. The clips must be present to insure adequate performance of vital parts and systems. Hand start the two bolts through the outer tube upper bracket and clips and into the support bracket nuts.
4. Connect all quick connect electrical connectors (turn signal, wash/wipe, key warning buzzer, ignition, speed control).
5. Install the upper shroud.
6. Tighten the steering column mounting nut and bolts to torque of 17–25 ft. lbs. (23–33 Nm).
7. Cycle the steering column one turn left and one turn right to align the intermediate shaft into the column shaft. (Power steering cars must have the engine running). Torque the steering shaft clamp nut to 20–30 ft. lbs. (27–40 Nm).

TAURUS/SABLE

1. Disconnect the negative battery cable.
2. Remove the steering column cover from lower portion of instrument panel by removing two self-tapping screws.
3. On models equipped with tilt sreering columns, remove the tilt release lever by removing the allen head cap screw that holds the tilt lever to the steering column.
4. Rotate the ignition lock cylinder to the "Run" position and depress the lock cylinder retaining pin through the access hole in the shroud with a $1/8$ in. punch. As you push on the pin pull out on the lock cylinder.
5. Remove horn pad and steering wheel assembly. On the column shift models use the following steps.
   a. Disconnect the PRNDL cable from the lock cylinder housing by removing the retaining screw. Disconnect the PRNDL cable from the shift socket.
   b. Remove the PRNDL cable from the retaining hook on the bottom of the lock cylinder housing.
6. Disconnect the speed control/horn brush wiring connector from the main wiring harness.
7. Remove the multi-function switch wiring harness retainer from the lock cylinder housing by squeezing the end of the retainer and pushing out. Disconnect the multi-function switch connector from the switch and remove the multi-function switch from the lock cylinder housing by removing the two self-tapping screws.
8. Disconnect the key warning buzzer switch wiring connector from the main wiring harness. Disconnect the wiring connector from the ignition switch.
9. Disconnect the steering shaft from the intermediate shaft by removing the two nuts and one U-clamp. On the coulumn shift models use the following steps:
   a. Remove the shift cable plastic terminal from the column selector lever pilot ball using a suitable tool to pry between the plasticterminal and the selector lever. Be sure not to damage the cable during or after assembly.
   b. Remove the shift cable (withthe shift cable still attached) from the lock cylinder housing by removing two retaining screws.
10. For vehicles with an automatic parking brake release mechanism, remove the vacuum hose from the parking brake release switch. On tilt column models only, remove the tilt return spring.
11. Unbolt the column assembly from the mounting bracket by removing the Torx® head retaining bolt.
12. While supporting the column assembly, unbolt the column assembly from the steering column support bracket by removing the two Torx® head bolts. Rotate the column assembly so that the intermediate bracket mounting flanges will pass through the instrument panel opening and slowly pull the column assembly from the instrument panel.

Installation

1. Rotate the column assembly so that the intermidiate bracket mounting flanges will pass through the instrument panel opening and slowly slide the column assembly forward while feeding the steering shaft universal joint tongue over the forward mounting bracket.
2. Rotate the column assembly clockwise and hand start two retaining bolts that attach the column assembly to the column support bracket. Hand start one of the Torx® head bolt that attaches the cloumn assembly to the intermidiate mounting bracket.
3. Center the column assembly in the instrument opening. Torque the Torx® head bolt to 15 to 25 ft. lbs. Torque the remaining two bolts to 15 to 25 ft. lbs.
4. On the tilt columns only, attach the tilt return spring. For the vehicle with an automatic parking brake release mecahnism, install the vacuum hose on the parking brake release switch.
5. On the Column shift models, use the following steps.
   a. Attach the shift cable bracket (with the shift cable attached) to the lock cylinder housing with the two retaining screws. Torque the screws to 30 to 60 in.lbs.
   b. Snap the transmission shift cable terminal to the selector lever pivot ball on the steering column.
6. Connect the steering shaft to the intermidiate shaft with one U-clamp and two hex nuts. Torque them to 15 to 25 ft. lbs. On the tilt columns, the column must be in the middle tilt position before the nuts are tightened.
7. Install the main harness wiring connector to the ignition switch. Install the key warning buzzer switch wiring connector to the main wiring harness.
8. Install the multi-function switch to the lock cylinder housing with the two self-tapping screws. Torque the screws to 18–26 in.lbs. Install the multi-function switch wiring harness retainer over the shroud mounting boss and snap it into the slot in the lock cylinder housing.
9. Connect the speed control/horn brush wiring connector to the main harness. On shift column models, use the following steps:
   a. Install the PRNDL cable into the retaining hook on the cylinder housing. Connect the PRNDL cable to the shift socket.
   b. Loosely install the PRNDL cable onto the lock cylinder housing with one retaining screw. Adjust the PRNDL cable as follows:
   c. Place the shift lever in the D position with the regular transmission and OD position with the overdrive transmission. Adjust the cable until the PRNDL pointer is centered on the D position or the OD position depending on the type of transmission. Tighten the hex head screw to 18–30 inch lbs.
10. Install the steering wheel and horn pad. Install the steering column shrouds with retaining screws. On the tilt columns only, install the tilt release lever with one socket head capscrew.
11. Install the ignition lock cylinder. Install the steering column cover from the lower portion of the instrument panel with two self-tapping screws.
12. Reconnect the negative battery cable and check the steering column and its components for proper operation.

WHEEL BEARINGS

Front wheel bearings are located in the front knuckle, not the rotor. The bearings are protected by inner and outer grease seals and an additional inner grease shield immediately inboard of the inner grease seal. The wheel hub is installed with an interference fit to the constant velocity universal joint outer race shaft. The hub nut and washer are installed and tightened to 180–200 ft. lbs. (240–270 Nm). The rotor fits loosely on the hub assembly and is secured when the wheel and wheel nuts are installed.

4–77

FORD MERCURY
FRONT WHEEL DRIVE CARS—ESCORT • EXP • LYNX • TEMPO • TOPAZ • TAURUS • SABLE

Adjustment

ALL MODELS

The front wheel bearings have a set-right design that requires no scheduled maintenance. The bearing design relies on component stack-up and deformation/torque at assembly to determine bearing setting. Therefore, bearings cannot be adjusted. In addition to maintaining bearing adjustment, the hub nut torque of 180–200 ft. lbs. (240–270 Nm) restricts bearing/hub relative movement and maintains axial position of the hub. Die to the importance of the hub nut torque/tension relationship, certain precautions must be taken during service.

1. The hub nut must be replaced with a new nut whenever the nut is backed off or removed after the nut has been staked. Never re-use the nut.
2. The hub nut must not be backed off after reaching the required torque of 180–200 ft. lbs. (240–270 Nm).
3. The hub nut collar must be staked into the outboard constant velocity joint slot with the proper tool to make sure the required torque is maintained during vehicle operation. The nut collar must not split or crack when staked. If the collar splits or cracks, the nut must be replaced.
4. Impact type tools must not be used to tighten the hub nut or bearing damage will result.
5. The hub and constant velocity joint splines have an interference fit requiring special tools for removal and assembly. The hub nut must not be used to accomplish assembly.
6. To remove the hub nut, apply sufficient torque to the nut to overcome the prevailing torque feature of the crimp in the nut collar. Do not use tools such as a screwdriver or chisel to remove the crimp.

BRAKES

For Brake Service refer to Unit Repair Section.

MASTER CYLINDER

Removal and Installation

STANDARD BRAKES

1. Disconnect the negative battery terminal.
2. Working under the instrument panel, disconnect the master cylinder pushrod from the brake pedal.

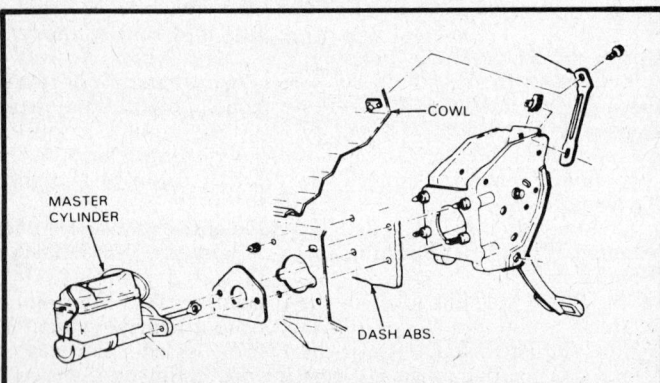

Standard brake master cylinder installation
(© Ford Motor Co.)

3. Disconnect the stoplight switch and remove it.
4. Inside the engine compartment, disconnect the brake lies from the master cylinder.
5. Unbolt the master cylinder from the firewall and remove it. Be careful not to damage the firewall grommet.
6. To install, reverse the removal process, leaving the brake tubes slightly loose at the master cylinder fittings.
7. Fill the master cylinder with fresh brake fluid. Use the foot pedal to bleed the master cylinder. Tighten the brake line fittings. Bleed the system.

POWER BRAKES

1. Disconnect the brake lines from the master cylinder.
2. Unbolt the master cylinder from the booster and remove the cylinder. Disconnect the brake warning lamp wire.
3. To install, mount the aster cylinder on the booster. Attach the brake fluid lines to the master cylinder, but leave the fittings slightly loose. Install the brake warning lamp wire.
4. Fill the reservoirs with fresh brake fluid. Use the foot pedal to bleed the master cylinder. Tighten the brake line fittings. Bleed the system.

HYDRAULIC SYSTEM BLEEDING

All Models

1. Clean all the dirt from around the master cylinder filler cap. If the master cylinder is known or suspected to have air in bore, it must be bleed before any wheel cylinders or calipers.
2. To bleed the master cylinder, loosen the upper secondary left front outlet fitting aprroximately ¾ turn. Have an assisant push the brake pedal down slowly through full travel. Close the outlet fitting, then return the pedal slowly to the full released position. Wait five seconds, then repeat the operation until the air bubbles cease to appear.
3. Loosen the upper primary right front outlet fitting approximately ¾ turn. and repeat Step 3.
4. To continue to bleed the system, remove the rubber cap dust cap from the wheel cylinder bleeder fitting or caliper fitting. Check to make sure the bleeder fitting is positioned at the upper half on the front of the caliper, if not the caliper is located on the wrong side.
5. Place a suitable box wrench on the bleeder fitting and attach the rubber drain tube to the fitting. Submerge the free end of the tube in a container partially filled with clean brake fluid and loosen the bleeder fitting approoitmately ¾ of a turn.
6. Have the assisant push brake pedal down slowly through full travel. Close the bleeder fitting, then return the pedal to the full release position. Wait five seconds, then repeat this op-

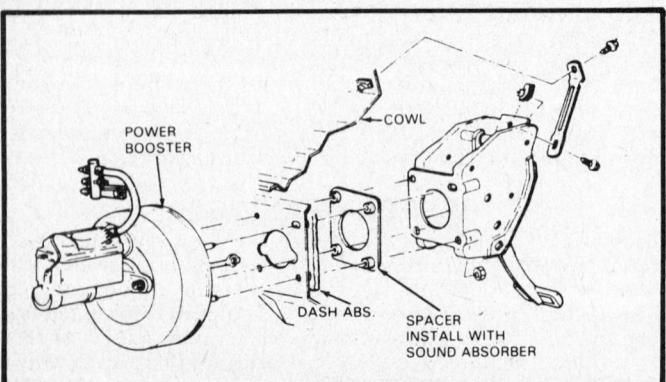

Power brake booster and master cylinder installation (© Ford Motor Co.)

Ford Mercury
FRONT WHEEL DRIVE CARS—ESCORT • EXP • LYNX • TEMPO • TOPAZ • TAURUS • SABLE

SECTION 4

eration until the air bubbles cease to appear at the submerged end of the bleeder tube.

7. When the fluid is completely free of air bubbles, secure the bleeder tube and install the rubber dust cap on the bleeder fitting. Repeat this process on the opposite diagonal system. Refill the master cylinder reservoir after each wheel cylinder or caliper is bled and reinstall the master cylinder cap.

8. When the bleeding operation is completed, the fluid level should be filled to the maximum fill level indicated on the reservoir. Always ensure the disc brake pistons are returned to their normal positions by depressing the brake pedal several times until the normal pedal travel is established. Check the pedal feel. If the pedal feels spongy repeat the bleed procedure.

VACUUM BRAKE BOOSTER

Removal and Installation
ALL MODELS

1. Disconnect the battery ground cable and remove the brake lines from the master cylinder.
2. Remove the two retaining nuts and remove the master cylinder.
3. From under the instrument panel, remove the stoplamp switch wiring connector from the switch. Remove the pushrod retainer and outer nylon washer from the brake pin, slide the stoplamp switch along the brake pedal pin, far enough for the outer hole to clear the pin.
4. Remove the switch by sliding it upward. Remove the booster to dash panel retaining nuts. Slide the booster pushrod and pushrod bushing off the brake pedal pin.

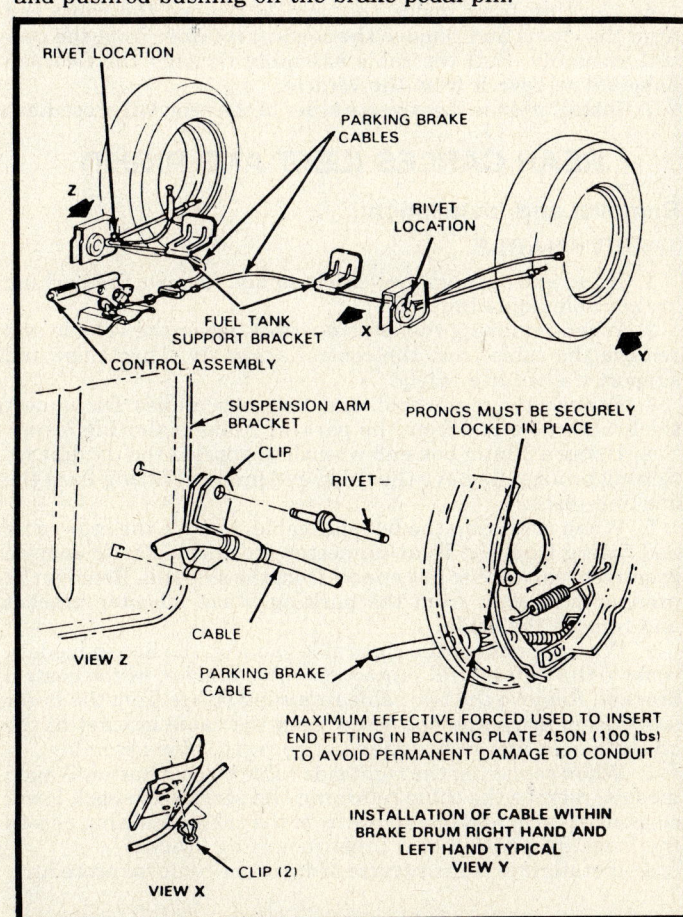

Parking brake cable—Excort/Lynx, EXP
(© Ford Motor Co.)

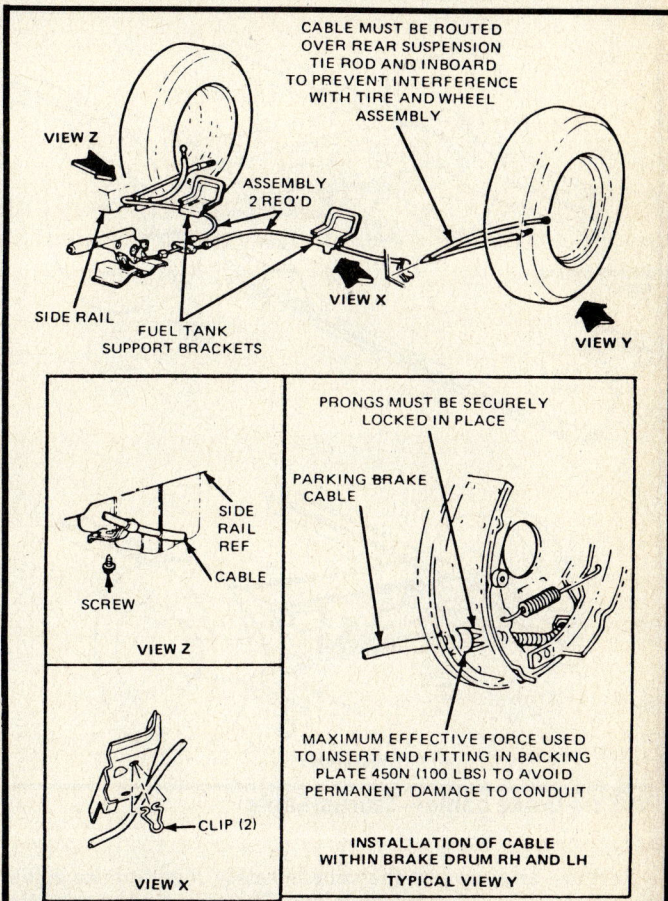

Parking brake cable—Tempo/Topaz
(© Ford Motor Co.)

5. On the Taurus/Sable models, remove the two screws and position the vacuum tee out of the way. Position the wire harness out of the way. Remove the transmission shift cable and bracket.
6. Disconnect the manifold vacuum hose from the booster check valve and move the booster forward until the booster studs clear the dash panel and remove the booster.
7. To install the booster assembly, reverse the removal procedure and bleed the brake system.

PARKING BRAKE

Adjustment
ALL MODELS EXCEPT THE TAURUS/SABLE

1. Apply approximately 100 lbs. pedal effort to the hydraulic service brake three times (with the engine running, on vehicles equipped with power brakes) before adjusting the parking brake.
2. Place the parking brake control assembly in the 12th notch position (two notches from full application). Tighten the adjusting nut until the rear wheel brakes drag slightly when the control assembly is fully released. Repeat as necessary.
3. Repostion the control assembly in the 12th notch. Loosen the adjusting nut just enough to eliminate rear brake drag when the control assembly is fully released.

TAURUS/SABLE

1. Make sure the parking brake is fully released. Place the transmission in the neutral position.

Ford Mercury
FRONT WHEEL DRIVE CARS—ESCORT • EXP • LYNX • TEMPO • TOPAZ • TAURUS • SABLE

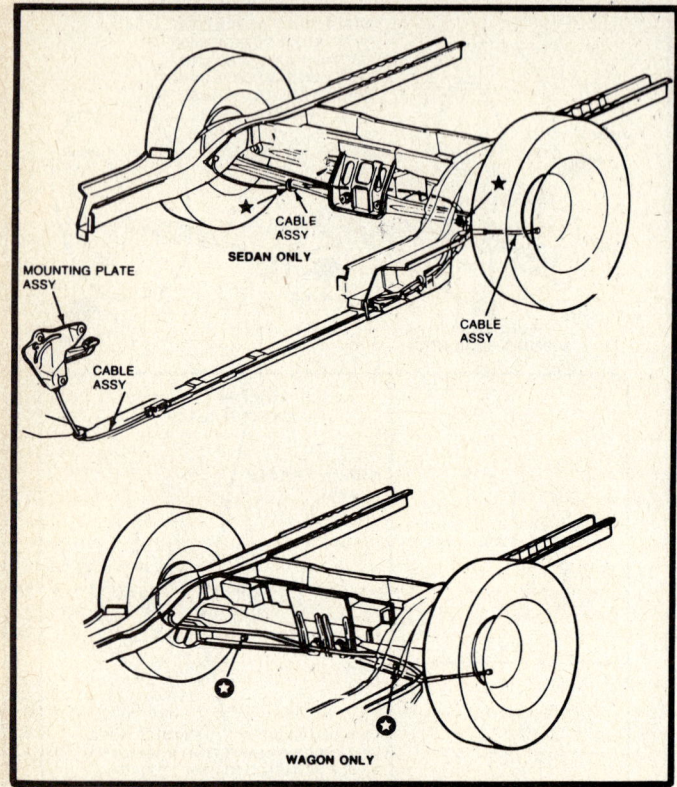

Parking brake cable—Taurus/Sable

2. Raise and support the vehicle safely. Tighten the adjusting nut against the cable equalizer. Then loosen the adjusting nut until the rear brakes are fully released. There should be no brake drag.
3. If the brake cables are replaced in any system having a foot-operated control assembly, stroke the parking brake control with approxitmately a 100 lbs. pedal effort, then release control and repeat this step.
4. Lower the vehicle and check the operation of the parking brake.

REAR CABLE

Removal
ALL MODELS EXCEPT THE TAURUS/SABLE

1. Place control assembly in the seventh notch position and loosen adjusting nut. Completely release control assembly.
2. Raise vehicle and remove the rear parking brake cable from equalizer.
3. Remove the hairpin clip holding cable to floor pan tunnel bracket.
4. Remove wire retainer holding cable to fuel tank mounting bracket. Remove cable from wire retainer.
5. Remove screw (Tempo/Topaz) or drill out pop rivet (Escort/Lynx, EXP), holding cable retaining clip at rear tie rod attaching bracket. Remove cable from clip.
6. Remove wheel and tire assembly, and rear brake drum.
7. Disengage cable end from brake assembly parking brake lever. Depress cable prongs holding cable to backing plate and remove cable through the hole in the backing plate.

Installation

1. Insert cable through the hole in backing plate. Attach cable end to rear brake assembly parking brake lever.
2. Insert conduit end fitting into backing plate. Make sure retention prongs are locked into place.
3. Insert cable into rear attaching clip and attach clip to rear tie rod attaching bracket with screw (Tempo/Topaz) or a new pop rivet (Escort/Lynx, EXP).
4. Route cable through bracket in floor pan tunnel and install hairpin retaining clip.
5. Install cable end into the equalizer.
6. Insert cable into wire retainer and snap retainer into hole in fuel tank mounting bracket.

FRONT CABLE

Removal and Installation
TAURUS/SABLE

1. Raise and support the vehicle safely. Loosen the cable adjuster nut at the adjuster.
2. Lower the vehicle. Disconnect the cable from the control assembly at the clevis. Raise and support the vehicle safely.
3. Disconnect the front cable from the rear cable at the cable connector.
4. Remove the cable and push-in prong retainer from the cable bracket, using a 13mm box end wrench to depress the retaining prongs. Allow the cable to hang.
5. Push the grommet up through the floorpan. Lower the vehicle. Remove the LH cowl side panel.
6. Working from inside the vehicle remove the cable end from the clevis and remove the conduit retainer from the control assembly. Pull the cable assembly through the floorpan hole and remove it from the vehicle.
7. Installation is the reverse order of the removal procedure.

REAR CABLES (LEFT AND RIGHT)

Removal and Installation
TAURUS/SABLE

1. Raise and support the vehicle safely. Remove the parking brake cable adjusting nut.
2. When removing the left side cable, lower the vehicle and remove the cable from the control assembly. Then raise and support the vehicle safely.
3. Remove the rear wheels and drum assemblies. Disconnect the brake cable end from the parking brake actuating lever.
4. Using a 13mm box end wrench to depress the conduit retaining prongs. Remove the cable end pronged fitting from the backing plate.
5. When removing the left side cable, remove the rear cable end fitting from the front connector. Push the plastic snap-in grommet rearward to disconnect from the side rail. Remove the pronged connector from the parking brake adjuster bracket and remove the cable.
6. When removing the right side cable on the Sedan models, remove the differential protection valve bracket at the control bracket. Remove the two cable retaining sttaps from the lower suspension arms and one screw from the cable bracket at the crossmember and remove the entire right cable assembly.
7. When removing the right side cable on the Station Wagon models, remove the cable retaining clip screw from each lower suspension arm and one screw from the cable retaining clip on the lower suspension arm inner mounting bracket.
8. Installation is the reverse order of the removal procedure.

Ford Mercury
FRONT WHEEL DRIVE CARS—ESCORT • EXP • LYNX • TEMPO • TOPAZ • TAURUS • SABLE
SECTION 4

CLUTCH, TRANSAXLE AND DRIVESHAFT SECTION

For overhaul procedures, refer to the unit repair section.

CLUTCH LINKAGE FREE PLAY

The free play in the clutch is adjusted by a built in mechanism that allows the clutch controls to be self-adjusted during normal operation. The self-adjusting feature should be checked every 5000 miles. This is accomplished by insuring that the clutch pedal travels to the top of its upward position. Grasp the clutch pedal with your hand or put your foot under the clutch pedal, pull up on the pedal until it stops. Very little effort is required (about 10 lbs.). During the application of upward pressure, a click may be heard which means an adjustment was necessary and has been accomplished.

CLUTCH ASSEMBLY

Removal and Installation
ALL MODELS

1. Remove the transaxle as outlined in this section.
2. Mark the pressure plate assembly and the flywheel so that they can be assembled in the same position.
3. Loosen the attaching bolts one turn at a time, in sequence, until spring tension is relieved.
4. Support the pressure plate and remove the bolts. Remove the pressure plate and clutch disc.
5. Inspect the flywheel, clutch disc, pressure plate, throwout bearing, and the clutch fork for wear. Replace parts as required. If the flywheel shows any signs of overheating (blue discoloration) or if it is badly grooved or scored, it should be refaced or replaced.
6. Clean the pressure plate and flywheel surfaces thoroughly. Position the clutch disc and pressure plate into the installed position, aligning the marks made previously. Support them with a dummy shaft or clutch aligning tool.
7. Install the pressure plate-to-flywheel bolts. tighten them gradually in a criss-cross pattern. Remove the alignment tool.
8. Lubricate the release bearing and install it in the fork.
9. Install the transaxle.

NOTE: Since the release bearing in this system is constant-running, transmission neutral rollover noise can be detected as such only by disengaging the release bearing from the clutch release fingers. This is best accomplished by disconnecting the cable from the release lever and moving the lever away from the cable. If neutral noise is evident under this condition, it is emanating from the transmission.

Nose associated with the release bearing/clutch system will be evident during all or some portion of pedal travel. During engagement and disengagement of the pawl and sector a "clicking" noise may be heard. This is normal and is in fact assurance that the adjusting mechanism is operating normally.

MANUAL TRANSAXLE

Removal
ESCORT, EXP, LYNX, LN7

1. Remove the two transaxle to engine top mounting bolts.
2. Grasp the clutch cable and pull forward, disconnecting it from the clutch release lever. Remove the clutch cable casing from the rib on the top surface of the transaxle case.
3. Raise the vehicle on a hoist and remove the bolt attaching brake hose routing clip to the suspension strut bracket at both front wheels.

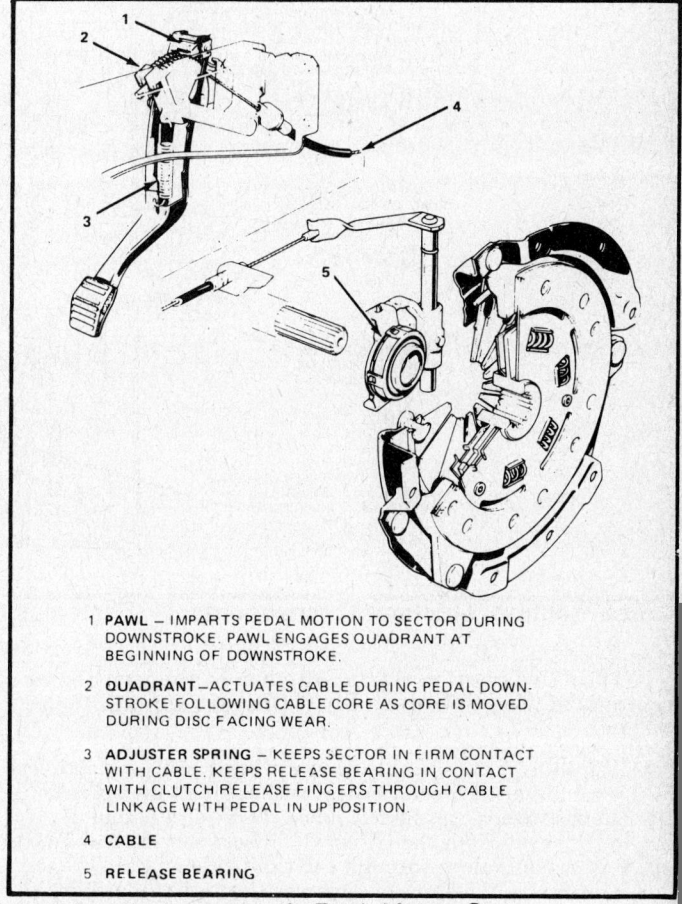

1 PAWL — IMPARTS PEDAL MOTION TO SECTOR DURING DOWNSTROKE. PAWL ENGAGES QUADRANT AT BEGINNING OF DOWNSTROKE.
2 QUADRANT — ACTUATES CABLE DURING PEDAL DOWNSTROKE FOLLOWING CABLE CORE AS CORE IS MOVED DURING DISC FACING WEAR.
3 ADJUSTER SPRING — KEEPS SECTOR IN FIRM CONTACT WITH CABLE. KEEPS RELEASE BEARING IN CONTACT WITH CLUTCH RELEASE FINGERS THROUGH CABLE LINKAGE WITH PEDAL IN UP POSITION.
4 CABLE
5 RELEASE BEARING

clutch components (© Ford Motor Co.)

4. Remove the bolt that secures the lower control arm ball joint to the steering knuckle assembly. Pry the lower control arm away from the knuckle.

NOTE: The plastic shield installed behind the rotor contains a molded pocket into which the lower control arm ball joint fits. When disengaging the control arm from the knuckle, clearance for the ball joint can be provided by bending the shield back toward the rotor. Failure to provide clearance for the ball joint can result in damage to the shield.

CAUTION
The nut and bolt must be discarded.

NOTE: Exercise care not to damage or cut ball joint boot. The pry bar must not contact lower arm.

5. Using a pry bar, pry the right inboard CV-joint assembly from the transaxle.

NOTE: Lubricant will drain from the seal at this time. Install shipping plug T81p–1177–B2 or equivalent to prevent the dislocation of the differential side gears.

Remove the inner CV-joint from the transaxle by grasping the right hand steering knuckle and swinging the knuckle and shaft outward from the transaxle.

Ford Mercury
FRONT WHEEL DRIVE CARS—ESCORT • EXP • LYNX • TEMPO • TOPAZ • TAURUS • SABLE

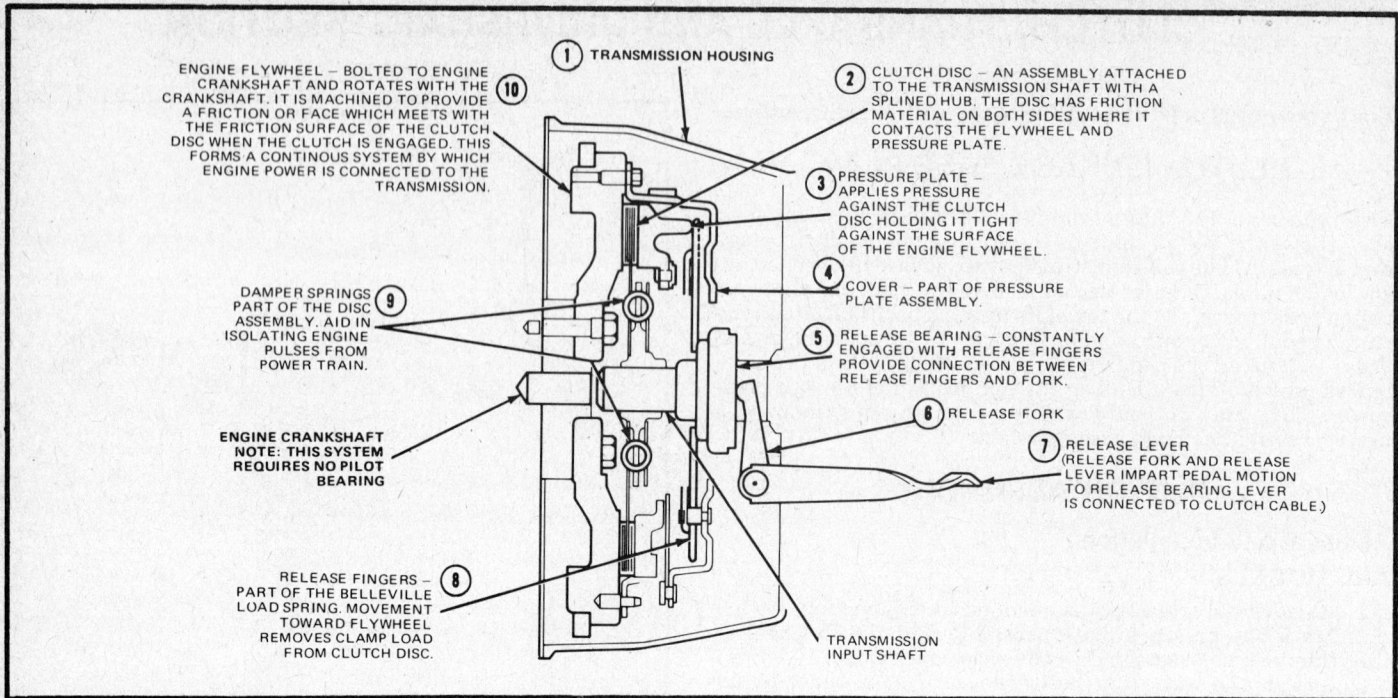

Cross section of clutch components (© Ford Motor Co.)

NOTE: Use caution during the use of the pry bar and removal of the joint assembly to prevent damage to the oil seal.

6. Wire the joint assembly in a near level position to prevent over-extending the assembly during the remaining operations.
7. Repeat Step 5 on the left inboard CV-joint assembly. If it cannot be pried from the transaxle, insert service tool T81P-4026-A or equivalent through the right side and tap the joint out. Remove in the same manner as the right side. Wire the joint assembly as in Step 6.
8. Disconnect the front stabilizer bar at both control arms. Discard the nuts.
9. Remove the two front stabilizer bar mounting brackets. Remove the stabilizer bar. Discard the bolts.
10. Disconnect the speedometer cable from the transaxle.
11. Disconnect the backup lamp switch connector from the transaxle switch.
12. Remove the three nuts from the starter mounting studs which hold the engine roll restrictor bracket.
13. Remove the engine roll restrictor. Remove the starter stud bolts.
14. Remove the two stiffener brace attaching bolts from the lower portion of the clutch housing.
15. Remove the shift mechanism crossover spring.
16. Remove the shift mechanism stabilizer bar to transaxle attaching bolt.
17. Remove the shift mechanism to shift shaft attaching bolt. Remove the shift mechanism from the shift shaft.
18. Position a transmission jack under the transaxle.
19. Loosen the nut on the rear mount stud.
20. Remove the attaching bolt from the bottom of the rear mount and loosen the two bolts at the top of the mount.
21. Remove the three bolts holding the front mount to the transaxle case.
22. Lower the MTX support jack until the transaxle clears the rear mount. Support the engine with a screw-type jack stand underneath the oil pan.
23. Remove the remaining four engine to transaxle attaching bolts.

24. Remove the transaxle from the rear face of the engine and lower from the vehicle.

NOTE: The transaxle case casting may have sharp edges. Wear protective gloves when handling the transaxle assembly.

Installation

1. Using a transmission jack, raise the transaxle into position. Engage the input shaft spline into the clutch disc and work the transaxle onto the dowel sleeves.

NOTE: Make sure the transaxle assembly is flush with the rear face of the engine prior to installation of the attaching bolts.

2. Install the 4 attaching bolts and tighten to specification.

---- CAUTION ----
Do not attempt to start the vehicle prior to installing the CV-oints. Doing so will result in differential side gear dislocation and damage.

3. Connect the speedometer cable.
4. Position the managed air valve bracket and rear mount over the rear mount bolt locations in the case.
5. Install the attaching bolts and tighten to 40-50 ft. lbs. (55-70 Nm).
6. Position the transaxle to tighten the nut on the mount stud. Tighten the nut to 38-41 ft. lbs. (52-56 Nm).
7. Position the transaxle to align with the front mount bracket. Install the three bracket to transaxle case attaching bolts and tighten to 40-50 ft. lbs. (55-70 Nm).
8. Connect the back-up lamp switch harness. Push the connector on until the locking tabs engage. Remove the transaxle jack.
9. Install the two stiffener brace attaching bolts and tighten to 15-21 ft. lbs. (21-28 Nm).
10. Position the starter motor against the engine rear cover plate, insuring that it is correctly piloted in the alignment bore. Install the three starter attaching stud bolts and tighten to 30-40 ft. lbs. (41-54 Nm).

Ford Mercury
FRONT WHEEL DRIVE CARS—ESCORT • EXP • LYNX • TEMPO • TOPAZ • TAURUS • SABLE
SECTION 4

11. Install the engine roll restrictor.
12. Install the three roll restrictor attaching nuts and tighten to 25–30 ft. lbs. (34–40 Nm).
13. Install the shift mechanism stabilizer attaching bolt and tighten to 23–32 ft. lbs. (38–44 Nm).
14. Install the shift mechanism to the input shift rail and tighten the attaching bolt to 7–10 ft. lbs. (9–13 Nm).
15. Install the shift mechanism crossover spring.
16. Remove the seal plugs and install the inner CV-joints into transaxle.

CAUTION

To insure proper installation, the following points must be observed.

---

a. New circlips are required on both inner joints prior to installation.
b. Exercise caution while inserting the shaft into the transaxle to avoid damage to the oil seals.
c. Check to insure that both joints are fully seated in the transaxle. Lightly pry outward to confirm that the retaining rigs are seated. If rings are not seated, the joint will move out of the transaxle.

17. Attach the lower ball joint to the steering knuckle, taking care not to damage or cut the ball joint boot. Insert new service pinch bolt N7801305-S100 and attach new nut N801308. Tighten the nut to 37–44 ft. lbs. (50–60 Nm) torque. DO NOT TIGHTEN THE BOLT.

CAUTION

A new nut and bolt must be installed.

---

18. Position the right brake line routing clip. Install the attaching bolt and tighten to 8 ft. lbs. (11 Nm). Repeat the procedure for the left-hand wheel.
19. Install the new attaching nuts and washers. Do not tighten the nuts.
20. Install both stabilizer mounting brackets. Tighten the new attaching bolts to 40–44 ft. lbs. (54–60 Nm). Tighten the stabilizer to control arm bolts 59–73 ft. lbs. (80–90 Nm).
21. Fill the transaxle with lubricant ESW-M2C33-F (automatic transmission fluid) or equivalent. Tighten the fill plug to 9–15 ft. lbs. (12–20 Nm).
22. Lower the vehicle.
23. Connect the clutch cable.

TEMPO/TOPAZ AND TAURUS/SABLE

1. Wedge a wood block approximately 7 inches long under the clutch pedal to hold the pedal up slightly beyond its normal position. Grasp the clutch cable and pull forward, disconnecting it from the clutch release shaft assembly. Remove the clutch casing from the rib on the top surface of the transaxle case.
2. Using a 13mm socket, remove the two top transaxle-to-engine mounting bolts. Using a 10mm socket, remove the air cleaner.
3. Raise and safely support the car. Remove the front stabilizer bar to control arm attaching nut and washer (drivers side). Discard the attaching nut. Remove the two front stabilizer bar mounting brackets. Discard the bolts.
4. Using a 15mm socket, remove the nut and bolt that secures the lower control arm ball joint to the steering knuckle assembly. Discard the nut and bolt. Repeat this procedure on the opposite side.
5. Using a large pry bar, pry the lower control arm away from the knuckle.

CAUTION

Exercise care not to damage or cut the ball joint boot. Pry bar must not contract the lower arm. Repeat this procedure n the opposite side.

---

6. Using a large pry bar, pry the left inboard CV-joint assembly from the transaxle.

NOTE: Lubricant will drain from the seal at this time. Install shipping plugs (T81P-1177-B or equivalent). Two plugs are required (one for each seal). Remove the inboard CV-joint from the transaxle by grasping the left-hand steering knuckle and swinging the knuckle and halfshaft outward from the transaxle.

CAUTION

Exercise care when using a pry bar to remove the CV joint assembly, If not careful, damage to the differential oil seal may result.

---

7. If the CV-joint assembly cannot be pried from the transaxle, insert differential rotater tool (T81P-4026-A or equivalent), through the left side and tap the joint out. Tool can be used from either side of transaxle.
8. Wire the halfshaft assembly in a rear level position to prevent damage to the assembly during the remaining operations. Repeat this procedure on the opposite side.
9. Using a small pry bar, remove the backup lamp switch connector from the transaxle backup lamp switch.
10. Using a 15mm socket, remove the three nuts from the starter mounting studs which hold the engine roll restrictor bracket. Remove the engine roll restrictor.
11. Using a 13mm deep well socket, remove the three starter stud bolts.
12. Using a 10mm and 12mm socket, remove the shift mechanism to shift shaft attaching nut and bolt and control selector indicator switch arm. Remove the shift shaft.
13. Using a 15mm socket, remove the shift mechanism stabilizer bar to transaxle attaching bolt. Remove the $^7/_{32}$ in. sheet metal screw and the control selector indicator switch and bracket assembly.
14. Using a 22mm ($^7/_8$ in.) crows foot wrench, remove the speedometer cable from the transaxle.
15. Using a 13mm universal socket, remove the two stiffener brace attaching bolts from the oil pan to clutch housing.
16. Position a suitable jack under the transaxle. Using an 18mm socket, remove the two nuts that secure the left hand rear No. 4 insulator to the body bracket.
17. Using a 13mm socket, remove the bolts that secure the left hand front No.1 insulator to the body bracket. Lower the transaxle jack until the transaxle clears the rear insulator. Support the engine with a screw jack stand under the oil pan. Use a 2x4 in. piece of wood top of the screw jack.
18. Using a 13mm socket, remove the four engine to transaxle attaching bolts. One of these bolts holding the ground strap and wiring loom stand off bracket.
19. Remove the transaxle from the rear face of the engine and lower transaxle from the vehicle.
20. Install in reverse order.

WARNING: THE TRANSAXLE CASE CASTING MAY HAVE SHARP EDGES. WEAR PROTECTIVE GLOVES WHEN HANDLING THE TRANSAXLE ASSEMBLY.

SHIFT LEVER ASSEMBLY

Removal
ALL MODELS EXCEPT THE TAURUS/SABLE

1. Remove the shift knob and the locking nut.
2. Remove the shift boot assembly and the inner boot.
3. Through the tunnel opening, remove the four bolts that hold the shift lever assembly to the control assembly mounting bracket. Lift the shift lever assembly out of the mounting bracket and tunnel opening.

Installation

1. Insert the shift lever assembly through the tunnel opening into the control assembly, making sure the lower plastic

Ford Mercury
FRONT WHEEL DRIVE CARS—ESCORT • EXP • LYNX • TEMPO • TOPAZ • TAURUS • SABLE

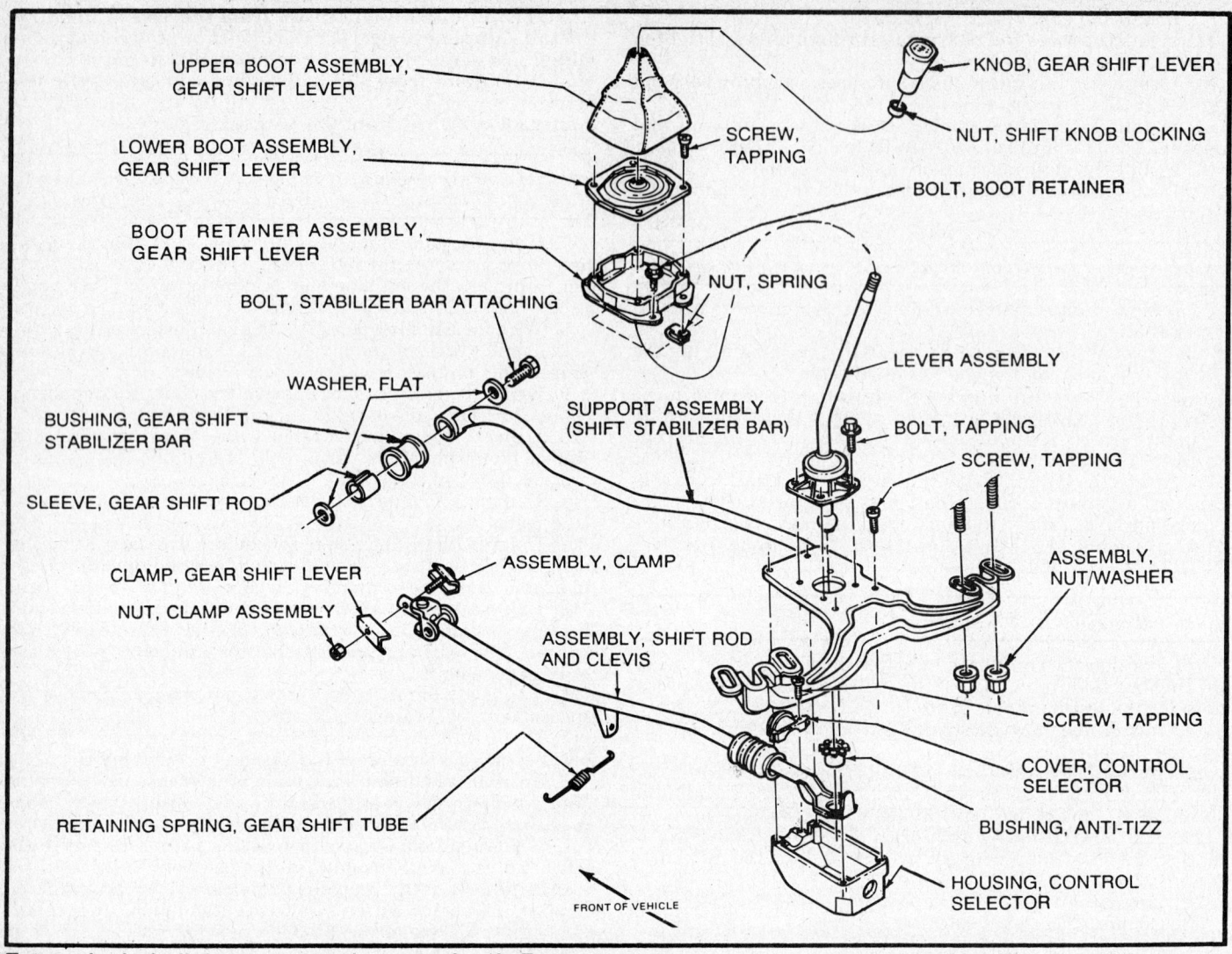

External shaft linkage, manual transaxle (© Ford Motor Co.)

pivot ball on the shift lever is inserted into the round socket on the end of the shift rod.

2. Fasten the shift lever to the control assembly with four self-tapping screws and tighten to 15–20 ft. lbs. (20–27 Nm).
3. Depress the clutch and actuate the shift lever as a check of function and tightness of all fasteners.
4. Install the inner boot and shift boot assembly.
5. Install the locking nut and shift knob.

TARUS/SABLE

1. Remove the snap-in shift knob graphics medallion by prying it out with a suitable tool. Disconnect the shift knob from the shift lever by removing the screw under the medallion.
2. Remove the console applique surrounding the shift boot to expose the four screws which connect the boot to the top of the console.
3. Slide the boot and knob assembly off of the shift lever. Remove the console to expose the shifter assembly.
4. Remove the four bolts holding shifter to floorpan. Pry the two clips holding the shift cables to the control assembly and pry the cable sockets off the control assembly pivot balls using a suitable tool. Do not bend or kink the cable core rods.
5. Remove the cables from the shifter and remove the shifter assembly.

Installation

1. Feed loose ends of cables into the control assembly slots making sure the cables and routed properly.
2. A green paint mark on the shifter and crossover cable will assist. Attach the control assembly to floorpan J-nuts with four bolts. Torque the bolts to 48 to 70 in.lbs.
2. Seat cables insulators into the shifter slots and install the new U-clips using a mallot. Snap the cable sockets onto the shifter pivot balls using pliers. Install the console.
3. Slide the boot and knob assembly over the shift lever. Attach to the console with four screws. Attach the shift knob to the shift lever with one screw. tighten to 44 to 80 in.lbs. Install the shift knob graphics medallion and console applique.

ATX TRANSAXLE

Removal
ALL MODELS

1. Disconnect the cable from the battery negative terminal.

NOTE: Due to ATX case configuration, the right-hand halfshaft assembly must be removed first. The differen-

tial service tool T81P-4026-A or equivalent is then inserted into the transaxle to drive the left-hand inboard CV joint assembly from the transaxle.

2. Remove the bolts attaching the managed air valve to the ATX valve body cover.
3. Disconnect the wiring harness connector from the neutral safety switch.
4. Disconnect the throttle valve linkage and the manual lever cable at their respective levers.
5. Remove the two transaxle to engine upper attaching bolts. The bolts are located below and on either side of the distributor.
6. Remove the nut from the control arm to steering knuckle attaching bolt (at the ball joint).
7. Drive the bolt out of the knuckle using a punch and hammer. Repeat this step on the remaining side.

—————— CAUTION ——————
The nut and bolt must be discarded.

NOTE: Exercise care not to damage or cut ball joint boot. The pry bar must not contact lower arm.

8. Disengage the control arm from the steering knuckle using a pry bar. Repeat this step on the remaining side.

—————— CAUTION ——————
Do not use a hammer on the knuckle to remove the ball joints.

NOTE: The plastic shield installed behind the rotor contains a molded pocket into which the lower control arm ball joint fits. When disengaging the control arm from the knuckle, clearance for the ball joint can be provided by bending the shield back toward to rotor. Failure to provide clearance for the ball joint can result in damage to the shield.

9. Remove the bolts attaching the stabilizer bar bracket to the frame rail. Discard the bolts. Repeat this step on the remaining side.
10. Remove the stabilizer bar to control the arm attaching nut and washer. Discard the nut. Repeat this step on the remaining side.
11. Pull the stabilizer bar to control arms.
12. Remove the bolt attaching the brake hose routing clip to the suspension strut bracket. Repeat this step on the remaining side.
13. Remove the steering gear tie rod to steering knuckle attaching nut and disengage the tie rod from the steering knuckle. Repeat this step on the remaining side.
14. Pry the halfshaft out of the right side of the transaxle. Position the halfshaft on the transaxle housing.

NOTE: It is normal for some transmission fluid to leak from the transaxle when the halfshaft is removed.

15. Disengage the left halfshaft from the differential side gear using driver T81P-4026-A or equivalent.
 a. Pull the halfshaft out of the transaxle.
 b. Support the end of the shaft by suspending if from a convenient underbody component with a length of wire.

NOTE: Do not allow the shaft to hand unsupported, as damage to the outboard CV-joint may result.

16. Install seal plugs T81P-1177-B or equivalent into the differential seals.
17. Remove the starter support bracket and disconnect the starter cable.
18. Remove the starter attaching bolts and the starter.
19. Remove the transaxle support bracket.
20. Remove the dust cover from the torque converter housing.

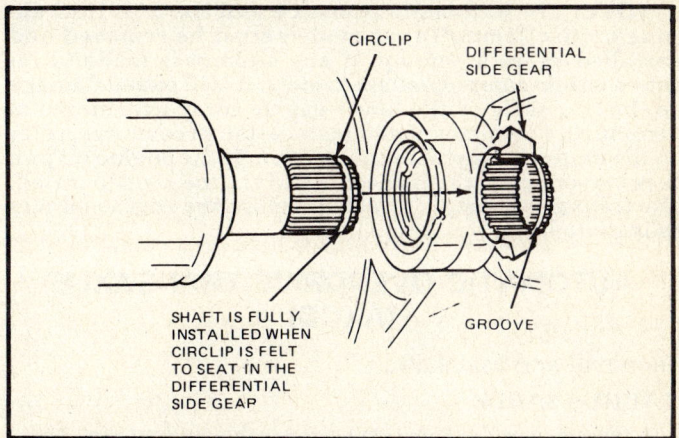
Halfshaft installation into differential side gears
(© Ford Motor Co.)

21. Remove the torque converter to flywheel attaching nuts.
22. Turn the crankshaft pulley bolt to bring the attaching nuts into an accessible position.
23. Remove the nuts attaching the left front insulator to the body bracket.
24. Remove the bracket to body attaching bolts and remove the bracket.
25. Remove the left rear insulator bracket attaching nut.
26. Disconnect the transmission cooler lines.
27. Remove the bolts attaching the manual lever bracket to the transaxle case.
28. Position a transmission jack under the transaxle and remove the four remaining transaxle to engine attaching bolts.
29. Before the transaxle can be lowered out of the vehicle, the torque converter studs must be clear of the flywheel.
30. Insert a suitable tool between the flywheel and the converter and carefully move the transaxle and converter away from the engine. When the converter studs are clear of the flywheel, lower the transaxle slightly (2-3 in.).
31. Disconnect the speedometer cable and finish lowering the transaxle.

NOTE: When moving the transaxle away from the engine, watch the No. 1 insulator. If it contacts the body before the converter studs clear the flywheel, remove the insulator.

Installation

To install the ATX, reverse the removal procedure except for the following.
1. To install the halfshaft in the transaxle, carefully align the splines of the CV-joint with the splines in the differential.
2. Exerting some force, push the CV-joint into the differential until the circlip is felt to seat in the differential side gear.

NOTE: Use care to prevent damage to the differential oil seal.

3. Attach the lower ball joint to the steering knuckle, taking care not to damage or cut the ball joint boot. Insert new service pinch bolt N780305-S100 and attach new nut N801308.
4. Tighten the nut to 37-44 ft. lbs. (50-60 Nm) torque. DO NOT TIGHTEN THE BOLT.

—————— CAUTION ——————
A new nut and bolt must be installed.

SECTION 4

FORD MERCURY
FRONT WHEEL DRIVE CARS—ESCORT • EXP • LYNX • TEMPO • TOPAZ • TAURUS • SABLE

NOTE: The automatic transaxle and the 2.3L HSC engine on the Tempo/Topaz models must be removed and installed as an assembly. If any attempt is made to remove either component separately, it will cause damage to the transaxle or the lower engine compartment metal structure. For removal and installation procedures, refer to the engine removal in this section. If the engine oil pan is removed while the transaxle and engine are separated, the transaxle must be attached before the engine oil pan is installed.

AUTOMATIC OVERDRIVE TRANSAXLE (AXOD)

Removal and Installation

TAURUS/SABLE

1. Disconnect the negative battery cable and raise and support the vehicle safely. Remove the air cleaner assembly.
2. Remove the 13mm bolt retaining the shift cable an bracket assembly to the transaxle.

NOTE: Hold the bracket with the screwdriver in the slot to prevent the bracket from moving.

3. Remove the two 10mm shift cable bracket bolts and bracket from the transmission. Disconnect the electrical connector from the neutral safety switch.
4. Disconnect the electrical bulkhead connector from the rear of the transaxle. Unsnap the throttle valve cable from the throttle body lever. Remove the 8mm bolt securing the throttle valve cable to the transmission case.
5. Carefully pull up on the throttle valve cable and disconnect the throttle valve cable from the T.V. link.

CAUTION

Pulling to hard on the throttle valve may bend the internal T.V. bracket.

---

6. Remove the bolt and nut from the LH engine support strut. Remove the four 15mm torque converter housing bolts from the top of the transmission.
7. Position a suitable engine hoist over the engine and attach the hooks of the hoist to the engine lift points. Lift the engine slightly.
8. Remove both front wheel and tire assemblies. Remove each tie rod end for its spindle.
9. Remove the 18mm bolts and nuts attaching the lower ball joints. Remove the lower ball joints and remove the lower control arms from each spindle. Remove the 18mm nuts from the stabilizer bar.
10. Remove the two 24mm nuts that secure the rack and pinion to the sub frame. Support the steering gear with a piece of wire from the tie rod end to the coil spring to hold the steering gear in position. Secure the housing of the gear to a suitable support to hold it in position.
11. Remove the two 22mm nuts from the engine mounts. Disconnect the oxygen sensor electrical connection. Remove the exhaust Y-pipe from the engine and rear portion of the exhaust system.
12. Remove the sub fram using the following procedure:
    a. Disconnect the exhaust system at the flex coupling and drop it down. Disconnect the lower control arm at the pinch bolts to the ball joints. Remove the two nuts that attach the steering gear to the number two crossmember.
    b. Remove the attaching nuts from the RH front engine mount and RH rear engine mount to subframe. Remove the stabilizer bar link attachment to the stabilizer bar.
    c. Remove the LH engine mount insulator at the through bolts to subframe. Support the subframe with adjustable suitable jack stands at the subframe body mount location points. Remove the four body mount attaching bolts.
    d. With an assisant, lower the adjustable jacks and allow the subframe to lower. Rotate the front of the subframe down and pick up the rear of the subframe off the exhaust pipe. Work the subframe rearward until it can be lowered down past the exhaust pipe.
13. Remove the four 18mm bolts from the sub-frame ataching points. Remove the two 15mm bolts from the LH engine support mount and lower the sub-frame.
14. Position a suitable transmission jack under the oil pan of the transmission. Remove the vehicle speed sensor from the transmission.

NOTE: Vehicles equipped with electronic instrument clusters do not use a speedometer cable.

15. Remove the two 15mm bolts from the transmission mount. Remove the four 15mm bolts from the LH engine support mount and remove the support. Remove the 8mm bolt from the separator plate.
16. Remove the two starter ataching bolts and position the starter out of the way. Remove the separator plate.
17. Rotate the engine with a $1/2$ inch drive rachet and a $7/8$ inch deep socket on the crankshaft pulley bolt to align the torque converter bolts with the starter drive hole. Then remove the four 15mm torque converter to flywheel attaching nuts.
18. Disconnect the transmission cooler lines. Remove the halfshafts as follows:
    a. Screw Extension T86P–3514–A2 or equivalent, into the CV-Joint Puller T86P–3514–A1 or equivalent and install the Slide Hammer D79P–100–A or equivalent into the extension.
    b. Position the puller behind the CV-joint and remove the CV-joint. Do not pry against the case.
19. Remove the last two 15mm torque converter housing bolts. Separate the transmission from the engine and carefully lower the transmission out of the vehicle.
20. Installation is the reverse order of the removal procedure.

THROTTLE LINKAGE

Adjustment

ALL MODELS EQUIPPED WITH AUTOMATIC TRANSAXLE

1. Make sure the curb idle speed is set to specifications and that the carburetor throttle lever is against the hot engine curb idle stop and the choke is off.
2. Set the coupling lever adjustment screw at its approximate mid-range. Make sure that the TV linkage shaft assembly is fully seated upward into the coupling lever.

CAUTION

If adjustment of the linkage is necessary, allow the EGR valve to cool so you won't get burned.

---

3. Loosen the bolt on the sliding trunnion block on the TV control rod assembly one turn minimum.
4. Make sure the trunnion block slides freely on the control rod.
5. Rotate the TV control lever until it is tight against its internal idle stop then tighten the bolt on the trunnion block.
6. Make sure the carburetor throttle lever is still against the hot engine curb idle stop.

ALL MODELS EQUIPPED WITH AUTOMATIC OVERDRIVE TRANSAXLE

NOTE: The throttle valve (TV) cable normally does not need adjusting. The only time the cable should be adjusted is when one of the following components is repaired or replaced; the main control assembly, throttle valve cable, throttle valve cable engine mounting bracket, throttle control lever link or lever assembly, engine throttle body and the transaxle assembly.

Ford Mercury
FRONT WHEEL DRIVE CARS—ESCORT • EXP • LYNX • TEMPO • TOPAZ • TAURUS • SABLE

SECTION 4

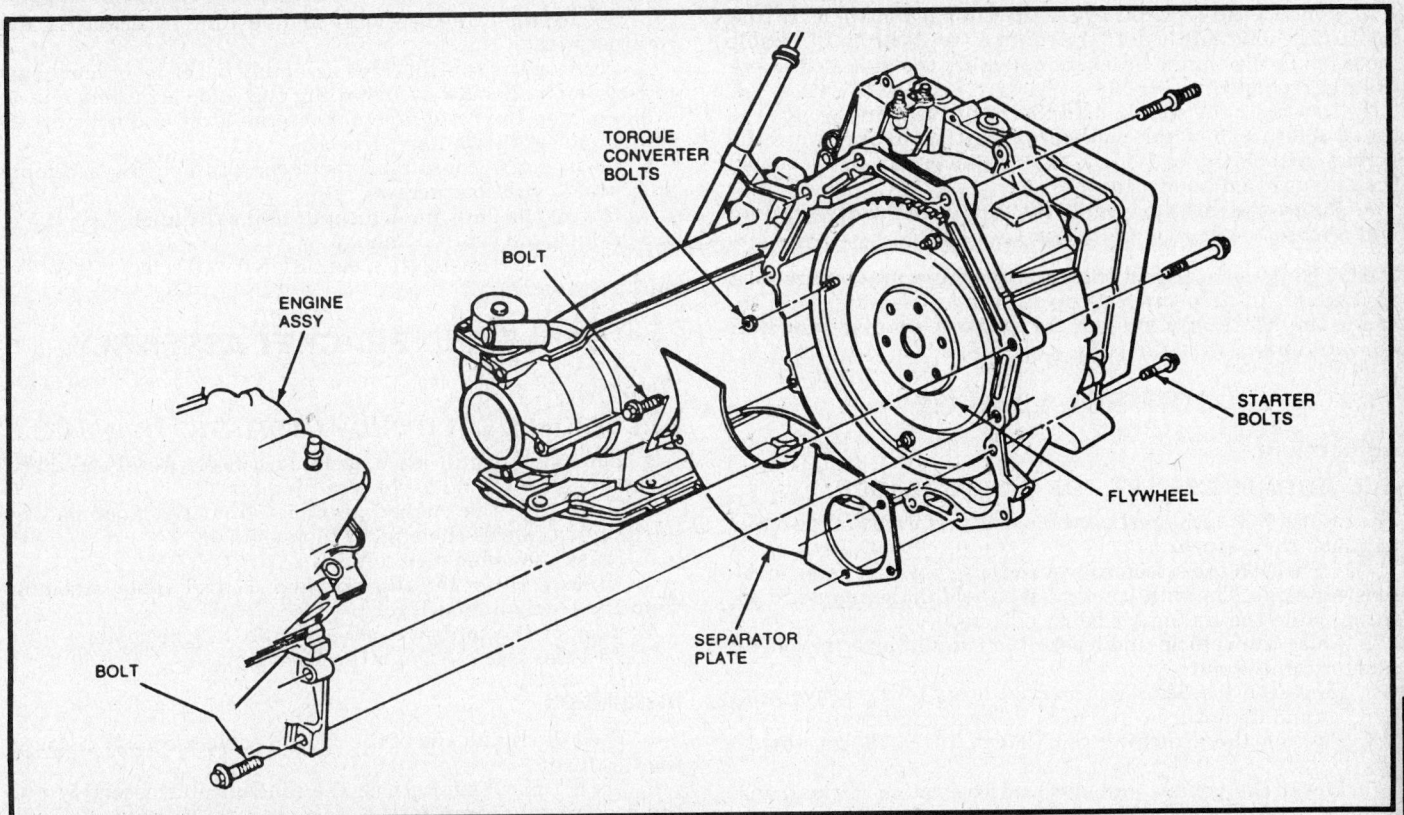

Removing the automatic overdrive transaxle—Taurus/Sable

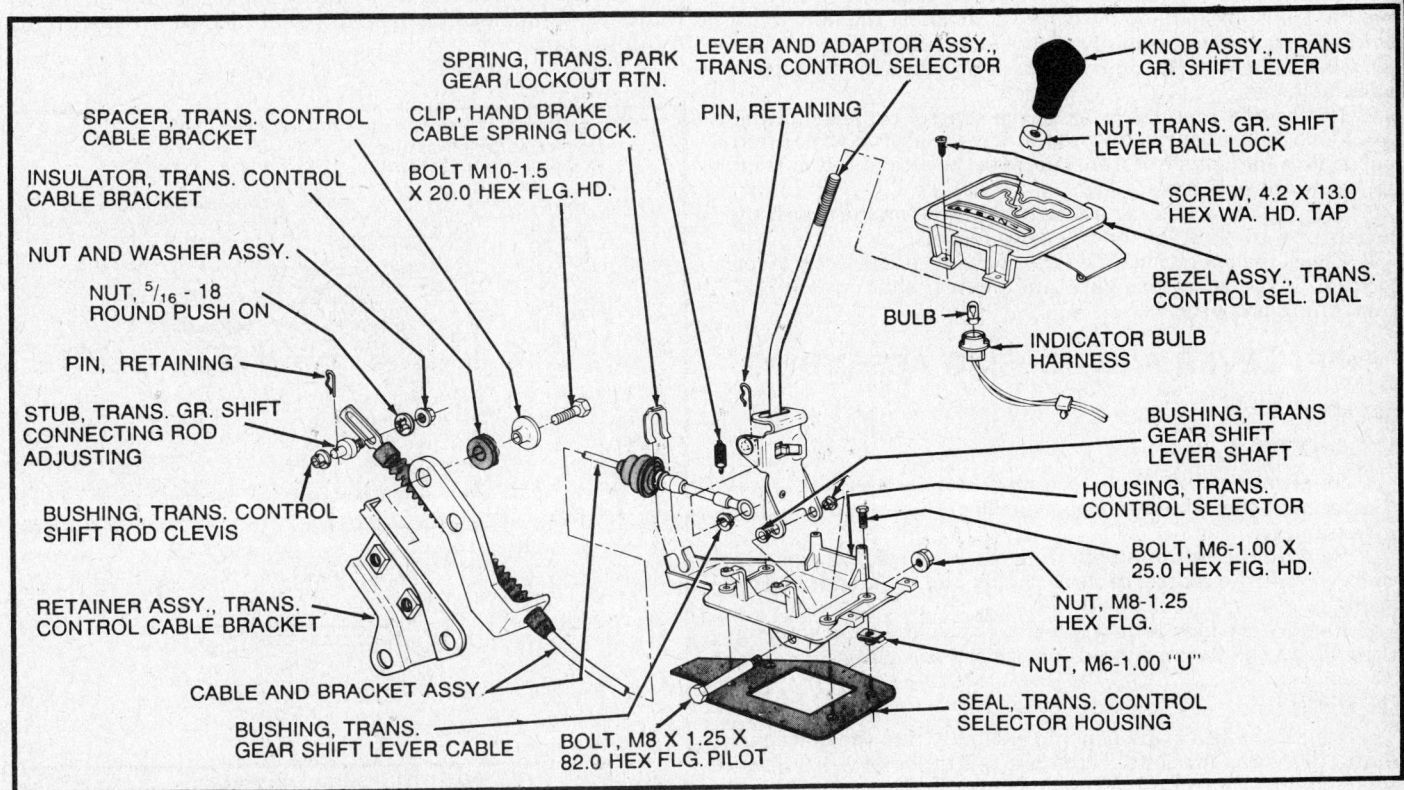

ATX control linkage, exploded view (© Ford Motor Co.)

4-87

FORD MERCURY
FRONT WHEEL DRIVE CARS—ESCORT • EXP • LYNX • TEMPO • TOPAZ • TAURUS • SABLE

1. Connect the TV cable eye to the throttle control lever link and attach the cable boot to the cahin cover. With the TV cable mounted in the engine bracket, make sure the threaded shank id fully retracted.
2. To retract the shank, hold the spring seat and wiggle the top pf the thread shank while pressing the shank toward the spring. Attach the end of the throttle lever to the wide open throttle position and release.
3. Rotate the throttle lever to the wide open throttle position and release.

NOTE: The threaded shank must show movement or a rachet out of grip jaws. If no movement is observed, inspect the TV cable system for broken or disconnected components and repaet the procedure.

CONTROL LINKAGE

Adjustment
ALL MODELS EXCEPT THE TAURUS/SABLE
The control linkage adjustment must be performed in the order in which they appear.
1. Position the selector lever in Drive position against the rearward stop. The shift lever must be held in the rearward position while the linkage is being adjusted.
2. Raise the vehicle and loosen the manual lever to control cable retaining nut.
3. Move the transmission manual lever to the Drive position, second detent from the most rearward position.
4. Tighten the attaching nut (20) to 10–15 ft. lbs. (14–20 Nm).
5. Lower the vehicle and check the operation of the transmission in each selector lever position. Be sure the park mechanism and neutral start switch function properly.

TAURUS/SABLE
1. Position the shift selector in the drive position on the automatic transmission and overdrive position on the automatic overdrive transmission against the rearward stop. The shift lever must be held in the rearward position while the linkage is being adjusted.
2. Loosen the manual lever to the control cable retaining nut. Move the transaxle lever to the drive or overdrive position (depending on the type of transmission), the second detent from the rearward position.
3. Tighten the attaching nut to 10–15 ft.lbs. on the overdrive models and 16–27 ft.lbs. on the drive models.
4. Check the operation of the transaxle in each selector lever position. Make sure that park and neutral start switch and functioning properly.

SHIFT LEVER AND HOUSING ASSEMBLY

Removal
ALL MODELS
1. Remove the shift knob, locknut and bezel assembly.
2. Remove the cable retaining clip from the lever and housing assembly.
3. Remove the retaining pin from the lever and housing assembly. Slide the control cable assembly and bushing from the boss.
4. Remove the four bolts which attach the lever and housing assembly to the floor pan and remove the assembly.

Installation
1. Install the lever and housing assembly into the floor pan and secure with four bolts. Tighten to 3–7 ft. lbs. (4.1–9.5 Nm).
2. Slide the control cable assembly and bushing onto the attaching shaft.
3. Secure the cable assembly and bushing by installing the retainer pin.
4. Position the control cable assembly in the lever and housing assembly. Secure by installing the cable retaining clip.
5. Position the bezel assembly on the lever and housing assembly. Secure with four screws.
6. Position the console on the lever and housing assembly and attach with four screws.
7. Install the shift knob locknut and shift knob.
8. Adjust the control linkage.
9. Check the transmission operation for all selector lever detent positions.

CABLE AND BRACKET ASSEMBLY

Removal
ALL MODELS EQUIPPED AUTOMATIC TRANSAXLE
1. Remove the shift knob, locknut, console, bezel assembly, control cable clip and cable retaining pin.
2. Disengage the rubber grommet from the floor pan by pushing it towards the engine compartment.
3. Raise the vehicle on a hoist.
4. Remove the retaining nut and control cable assembly from the transmission lever.
5. Remove the control cable assembly bracket bolts.
6. Pull the cable through the floor pan.

Installation
1. Feed the round end of the control cable assembly through the floor pan.
2. Press the rubber boot on the control cable assembly into the body panel opening.
3. Lower the vehicle.
4. Position the control cable assembly in the selector lever housing assembly and install the spring clip.
5. Install the bushing and control cable assembly on the selector lever and housing assembly shaft and secure it with the retaining pin.

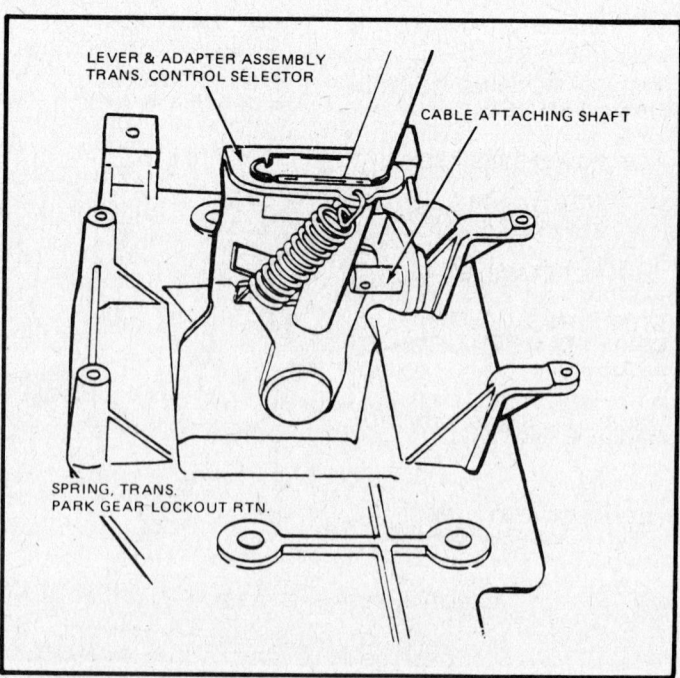

Installing shift control cable assembly
(© Ford Motor Co.)

6. Install the bezel assembly, console, locknut and shift knob.
7. Position the selector in Drive position. the selector lever must be held in this position while attaching the other end of the control cable assembly.
8. Raise the vehicle.
9. Position the control cable bracket on the retainer bracket and secure with two bolts. Tighten to 15–25 ft. lbs. (20–34 Nm).
10. Shift the transmission manual lever into Drive, second detent from the full rearward position.
11. Place the cable end on the transmission manual lever stud, using care to align the flats on the stud with the slot in the cable. Start the attaching nut.
12. Make sure the selector lever has not moved from the Drive detent. Then tighten the nut to (20) to 10–14 ft. lbs. (14–19 Nm).
13. Lower the vehicle and check the transmission operation in each selector lever detent position. Insure Park mechanism and neutral start switch function properly.

TAURUS/SABLE WITH AUTOMATIC OVERDRIVE TRANSMISSION (FLOOR SHIFT)

1. Remove the console. Remove the control cable clip and cable from the plastic snap retainer. Pull back the carpeting.
2. Remove the retainer screw that secures the cable bracket to the dash panel. Disengage the rubber grommet from the floorpan by pushing it towards the passenger compartment.
3. Remove the retaining nut and control cable assembly from the transaxle lever. Remove the cable retaining clip from the cable bracket on the transmission.
4. Remove the control cable assembly from the bracket. Pull the cable through the floorpan into the passenger compartment.

Installation

1. Working from inside the passenger compartment, feed the round end of the control cable assembly through the floorpan. Press the rubber boot on the control cable assembly into the body panel opening. Install the cable bracket and carpeting.
2. Install the bushing and control cable assembly into the snap retainer on the selector lever and housing assembly shaft. Position the control cable assembly in the selector lever housing assembly. Install the spring clip.
3. Install the shift knob. Place the selector lever in overdrive position. The selector lever must be held in this position while attaching the other end of the control cable assembly. Position the cable into the cable bracket on the transmission and install the retainer clip.
4. Attach the cable to the transmission lever and install the retaining nut. Shift the transmission lever into overdrive position, second detent from the full rearward position.
5. Place the cable end on the trnansmission manual lever stud, using care to align the flats on the stud with the slot in the cable. Start the attaching nut, make sure the selector lever has not moved from the overdrive detent and tighten the nut.
6. Check the transmission operation in each selector lever detent position. Ensure park mechanism and neutral start switch function properly.

TAURUS/SABLE WITH AUTOMATIC OVERDRIVE TRANSMISSION (COLUMN SHIFT)

NOTE: Whenever the cable is removed from the cable bracket for any reason, the cable must be replaced. Whenever a steering column, engine or transaxle is removed, do not remove the shift control cable from the retaining brackets. The bracket must be removed with the cable attached.

1. Remove the shift control cable and retaining bracket from the steering column out from under the instrument panel.

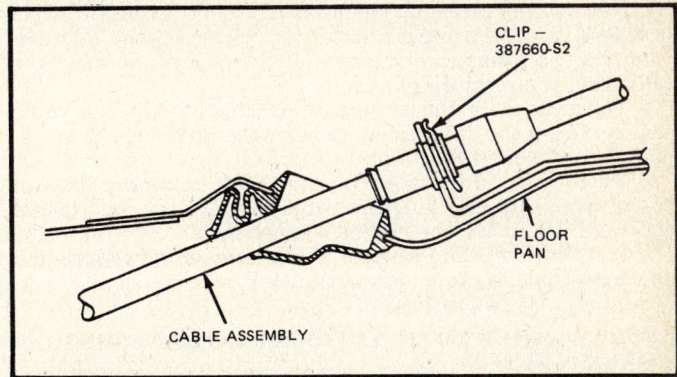
Installation of shift control cable at floor pan (© Ford Motor Co.)

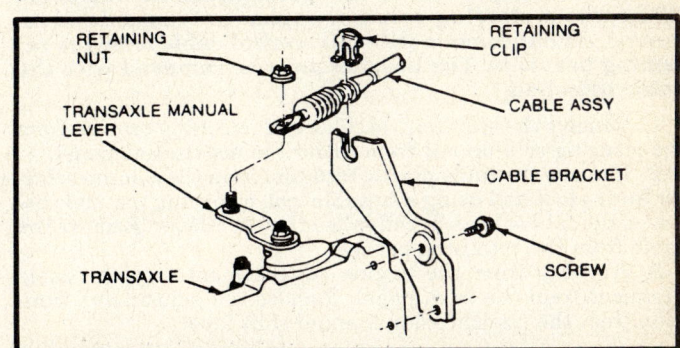
Installing the shift control cable assembly on the AXOD transaxle

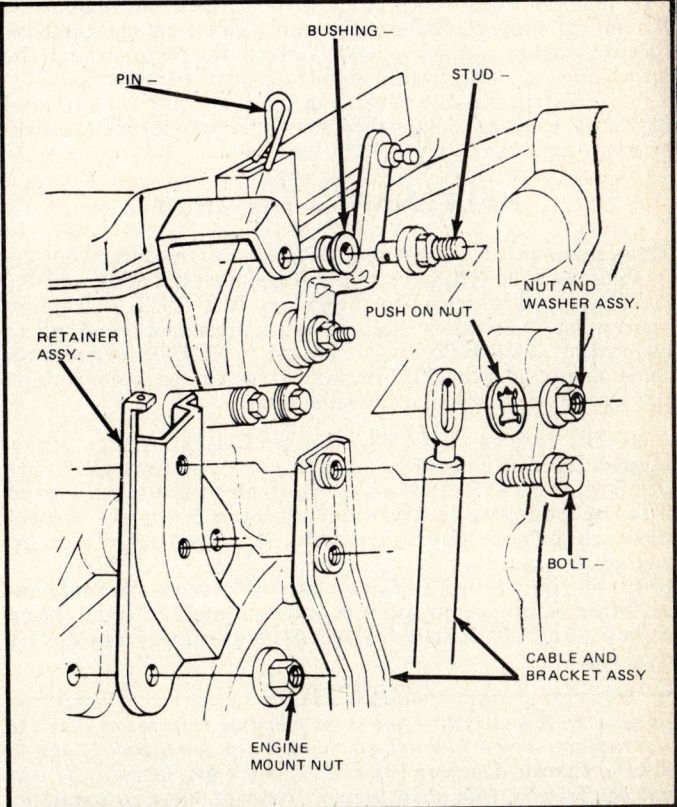
Shift control cable and bracket assembly at ATX transaxle (© Ford Motor Co.)

FORD MERCURY
FRONT WHEEL DRIVE CARS—ESCORT • EXP • LYNX • TEMPO • TOPAZ • TAURUS • SABLE

2. Remove the cable plastic terminal from the column selector lever pivot ball using a suitable tool, by prying the cable between the cable plastic terminal and selector lever. Remove the cable from the retaining bracket.

3. Working from the engine compartment, pry the cable grommet from the dash panel. Remove the nut from the transaxle manual shift lever stud.

4. Remove the shift cable from the cable retaining bracket on the transaxle and pull the cable through the dash panel working from inside the engine compartment.

5. Installation is the reverse of the removal procedure and adjust the cable as previously outlined. Torque the cable bracket retaining screws to 15–24 ft. lbs.

TAURUS/SABLE WITH AUTOMATIC TRANSMISSION (COLUMN SHIFT)

NOTE: Whenever the cable is removed from the cable bracket for any reason, the cable must be replaced. Whenever a steering column, engine or transaxle is removed, do not remove the shift control cable from the retaining brackets. The bracket must be removed with the cable attached.

1. Remove the shift control cable and retaining bracket from the steering column out from under the instrument panel.

2. Remove the cable plastic terminal from the column selector lever pivot ball using a suitable tool, by prying the cable between the cable plastic terminal and selector lever. Remove the cable from the retaining bracket.

3. Working from the engine compartment, pry the cable grommet from the dash panel. Remove the adjustment trunnion from the transmission manual shift lever.

NOTE: A new grommet must be installed in the manual shift lever.

4. Remove the shift cable from the cable retaining clip on the engine support. Remove the shift cable from the cable retaining bracket on the transaxle and pull the cable through the dash panel working from inside the engine compartment.

5. Installation is the reverse of the removal procedure and adjust the cable as previously outlined. Torque the cable bracket retaining screws to 15–24 ft. lbs.

HALFSHAFT ASSEMBLY

These notes and cautions are to be used on all models. When removing both the left and right halfshafts on the MTX and the ATX equipped vehicles, shipping plugs T81P-1177-B or equivalent must be installed. Failure to use these tools can reult in dislocation of the differential side gears. Should the gears become misaligned, the differential will have to be removed from the transaxle to re-align the side gears.

NOTE: Due to the ATX case configuration, the right-hand halfshaft assembly must be removed first. Differential Rotator T81P-4026-A or equivalent is then inserted into the transaxle to drive the left-hand inboard CV-joint assembly from the transaxle. If only the left-hand halfshaft assembly is to be removed for service, remove only the right-hand halfshaft assembly from the transaxle. After removal, support it with a length of wire. Then drive the left-hand halfshaft assembly from the transaxle.

——— CAUTION ———
Do not start this procedure unless the following parts are to known to be available. A new hub nut assembly, a new lower control arm to steering knuckle attaching bolt and nut and a new inboard CV joint stub shaft circlip. Once these parts are removed, these parts must not be re-used during assembly. Their torque holding ability or retension capability is destroyed during removal.

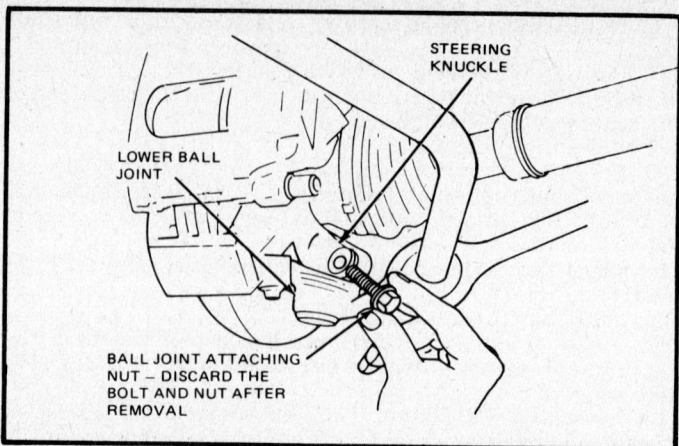

Removing lower ball joint pinch bolt
(© Ford Motor Co.)

Removal
ALL MODELS EXEPT THE TAURUS/SABLE

1. Remove the cap from the hub and loosen the hub nut. Set the parking brake to prevent the car from rolling while the nut is loosened. The nut must be loosened without unstaking. The use of a chisel or similar tool may damage the spindle thread.

2. After raising the vehicle and removing the wheel and tire assembly, remove the hub nut and washer.

——— CAUTION ———
Discard the nut, as it must not be reused.

3. Remove the bolt attaching the brake hose routing clip to the suspension strut.

4. Remove the nut from the ball joint to steering knuckle attaching bolt. Drive the bolt out of the steering knuckle using a punch and hammer.

——— CAUTION ———
Discard the bolt and nut. They are of a torque prevailing design and cannot be reused.

5. Separate the ball joint from the steering knuckle using a pry bar. Position the end of the pry bar outside of the bushing pocket to avoid damage to the bushing. Use care to prevent damage to the ball joint boot.

NOTE: The lower control arm ball joint fits into a pocket formed in the plastic disc brake rotor shield. This shield must be bent back away from the ball joint while prying the ball joint out of the steering knuckle.

6. Remove the halfshaft from the differential housing using a pry bar. Position the pry bar between the case and the shaft, but be careful not to damage the dust deflector location between the shaft and the case.

NOTE: If extreme resistance is encountered when using a prybar to remove the haftshafts from the differential, then do not use the pry bar to remove them. Avoid damage to the transaxle case and oil pan; remove the oil pan and use a large screwdriver to dislodge the circlip from between the pinion shaft and the inboard CV-joint. This will free the haftshaft from the differential.

——— CAUTION ———
Extreme care must be taken not to damage the differential oil seal, the CV-joint boot or the CV-joint dust deflector.

7. Support the end of the shaft by suspending it from a convenient underbody component with a length of wire.

Ford Mercury
FRONT WHEEL DRIVE CARS—ESCORT • EXP • LYNX • TEMPO • TOPAZ • TAURUS • SABLE
Section 4

NOTE: Do not allow the shaft to hang unsupported, as damage to the outboard CV-joint may result.

8. Separate the outboard CV-joint from the hub using puller T81P–1104–C or equivalent, and metric adapters T81P–1104–B and T81P–1104–A or equivalent.

CAUTION
Never use a hammer or separate the outboard CV-joint stub shaft from the hub. Damage to the CV-joint internal components may result.

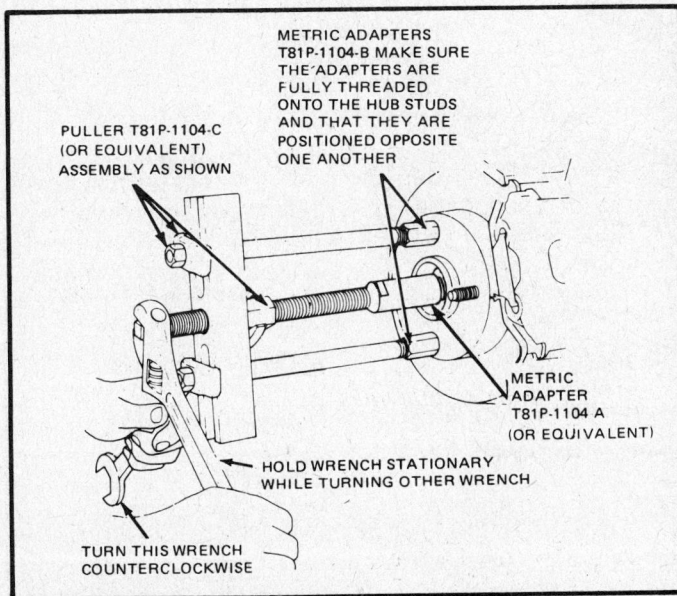

Removing hub from shaft assembly
(© Ford Motor Co.)

Installation

1. Install a new circlip on the inboard CV-joint stub shaft. The outboard CV-joint stub shaft does not have a circlip.

NOTE: To install the circlip properly, start one end in the groove and work the circlip over the stub shaft end and into the groove. This will avoid over expanding the circlip.

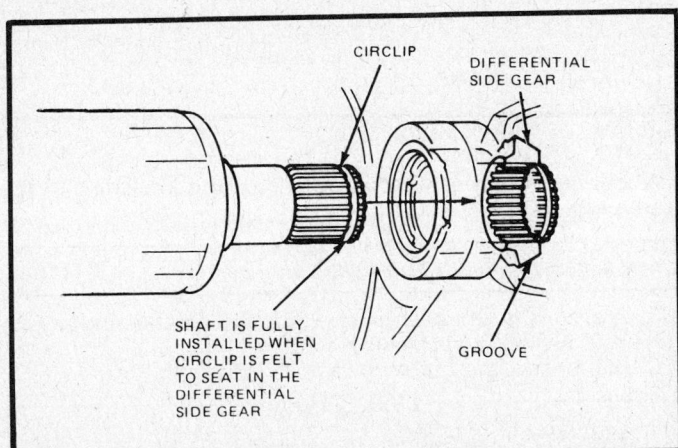

Seating circlip in transaxle differential side gear
(© Ford Motor Co.)

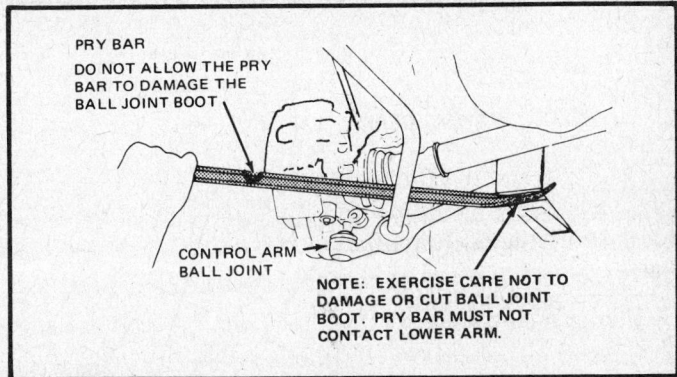

Separating lower ball joint from steering knuckle by prying (© Ford Motor Co.)

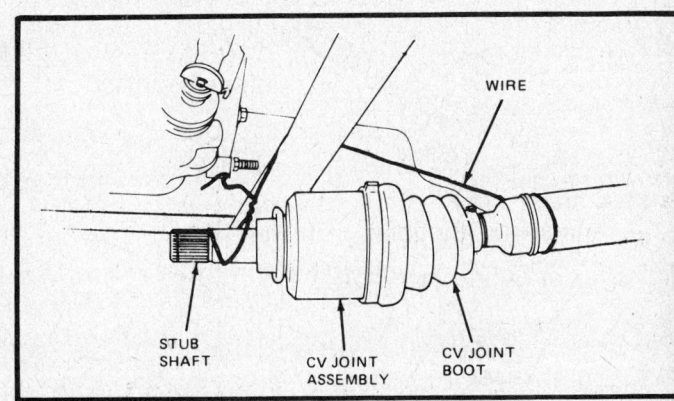

Support halfshaft by wiring to body
(© Ford Motor Co.)

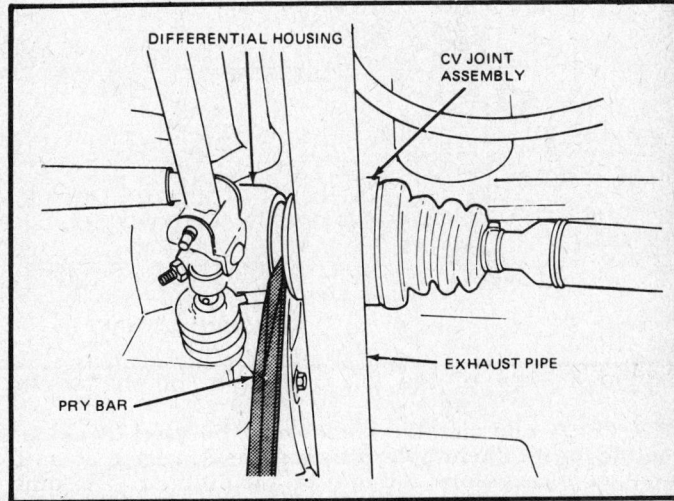

Removing halfshaft from transaxle assembly
(© Ford Motor Co.)

2. Carefully align the splines of the inboard CV-joint stub shaft with the splines in the differential. Exerting some force, push the CV-joint into the differential until the circlip is felt to seat in the differential side gear. Use care to prevent damage to the differential oil seal.

SECTION 4

FORD MERCURY
FRONT WHEEL DRIVE CARS—ESCORT • EXP • LYNX • TEMPO • TOPAZ • TAURUS • SABLE

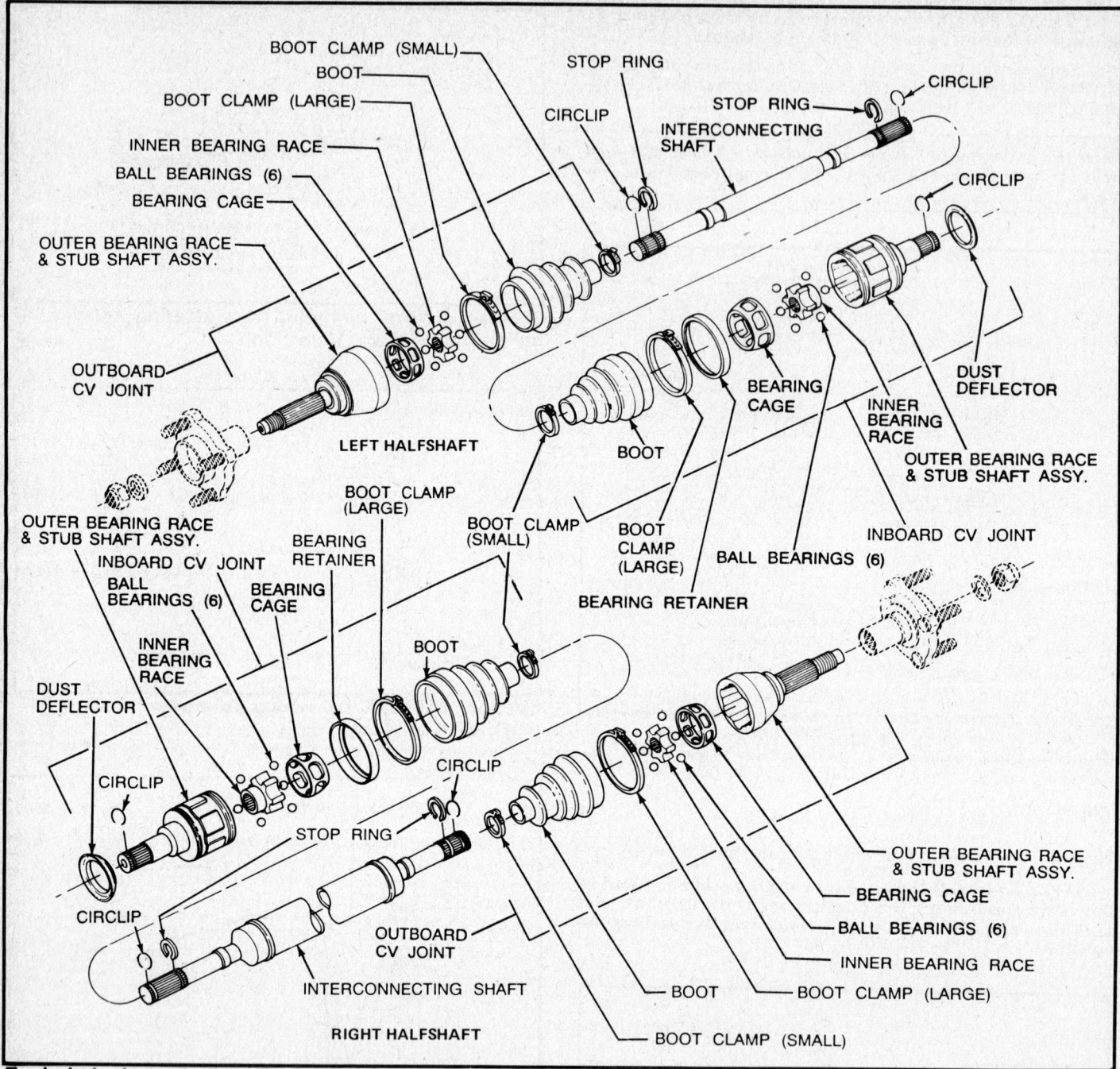

Exploded view of the left and right halfshafts and CV–joints (© Ford Motor Co.)

NOTE: A non-metallic mallet may be used to aid in seating the circlip into the differential side gear groove. if a mallet is necessary, tap only on the outboard CV-joint stub shaft.

3. Carefully align the splines of the outboard CV-joint stub shaft with the splines in the hub and push the shaft into the hub as far as possible. Use puller T81P–1104–C or equivalent and metric adapters T81P–1104–A and T81P–1104–B or equivalent to complete the installation.

— **CAUTION** —

The center thread of puller T81P–1104–C or equivalent must be oiled before installation and tightening. Failure to lubricate the threads could result in an inaccurate torque wrench reading.

4. Connect the control arm to the steering knuckle and install a new nut and bolt.

— **CAUTION** —

A new bolt and nut must be installed.

5. Position the brake hose routing clip on the suspension strut and install the attaching bolts.
6. Install the hub nut washer and a new hub nut.

— **CAUTION** —

A new nut must be installed.

7. Install the wheel and tire assembly and lower the vehicle.
8. Tighten the wheel nuts to specifications.

Ford Mercury
FRONT WHEEL DRIVE CARS—ESCORT • EXP • LYNX • TEMPO • TOPAZ • TAURUS • SABLE

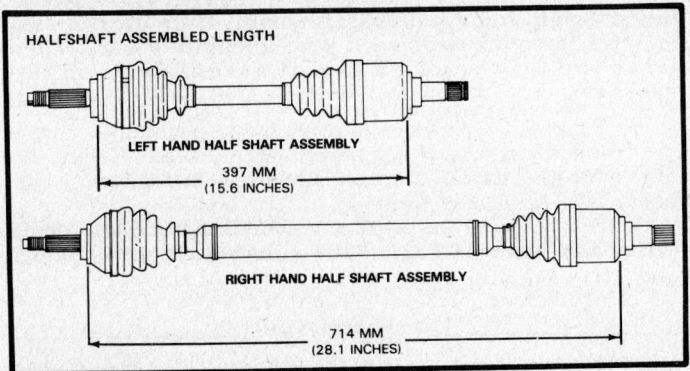

Dimensions for left and right halfshaft assembled lengths (© Ford Motor Co.)

Removal

TAURUS/SABLE

1. Remove the wheel cover/hub cover from the wheel and tire assembly and loosen the wheel nuts. Remove the hub retainer and washer. The nut must be discarded after removal.
2. Raise and support the vehicle safely. Remove the wheel and tire assembly, remove the hub nut and washer. Discard the old hub nut. Remove the nut from the ball joint to steering knuckle attaching bolts.
3. Drive the bolt out of the steering knuckle using a suitable punch and hammer. Discard this bolt and nut after removal. Separate the ball joint from the steering knuckle using a suitable pry bar.
4. Position the end of the pry bar outside of the bushing pocket to avoid damage to the bushing. Use care to prevent damage to the ball joint boot. Remove the stabilizer bar link at the stabilizer bar.
5. The following removal procedure is for the RH side halfshaft/link shaft for the automatic transaxle and the manual transaxle:

   a. Remove the two bolt attaching the bearing to the support to the bracket. Slide the shaft out of the transaxle. Support the end of the shaft by suspending it from a convenient underbody component with a piece of wire. Do not allow the shaft to hang un-supported, damage to the outboard CV-joint may occur.

   b. Separate the outboard CV-joint from the hub using front hub remover T81P-1104-C or equivalent, meteric adapters T83-P-1104-BH, T86P-1104-A1 and T81P-1104-A or equivalent.

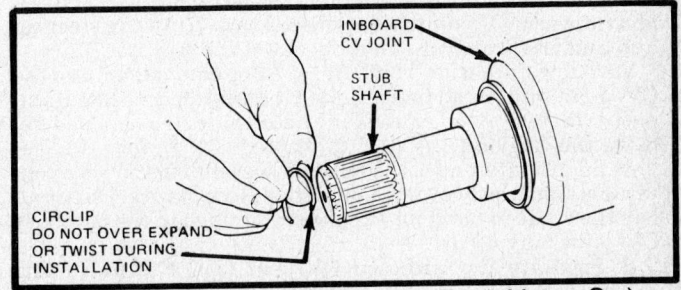

Stub shaft circlip installation (© Ford Motor Co.)

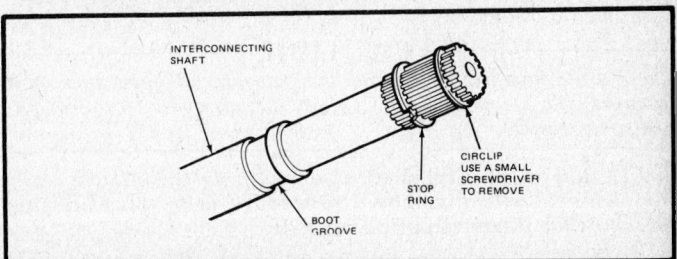

Circlip and stop ring used on the inter connecting shafts (© Ford Motor Co.)

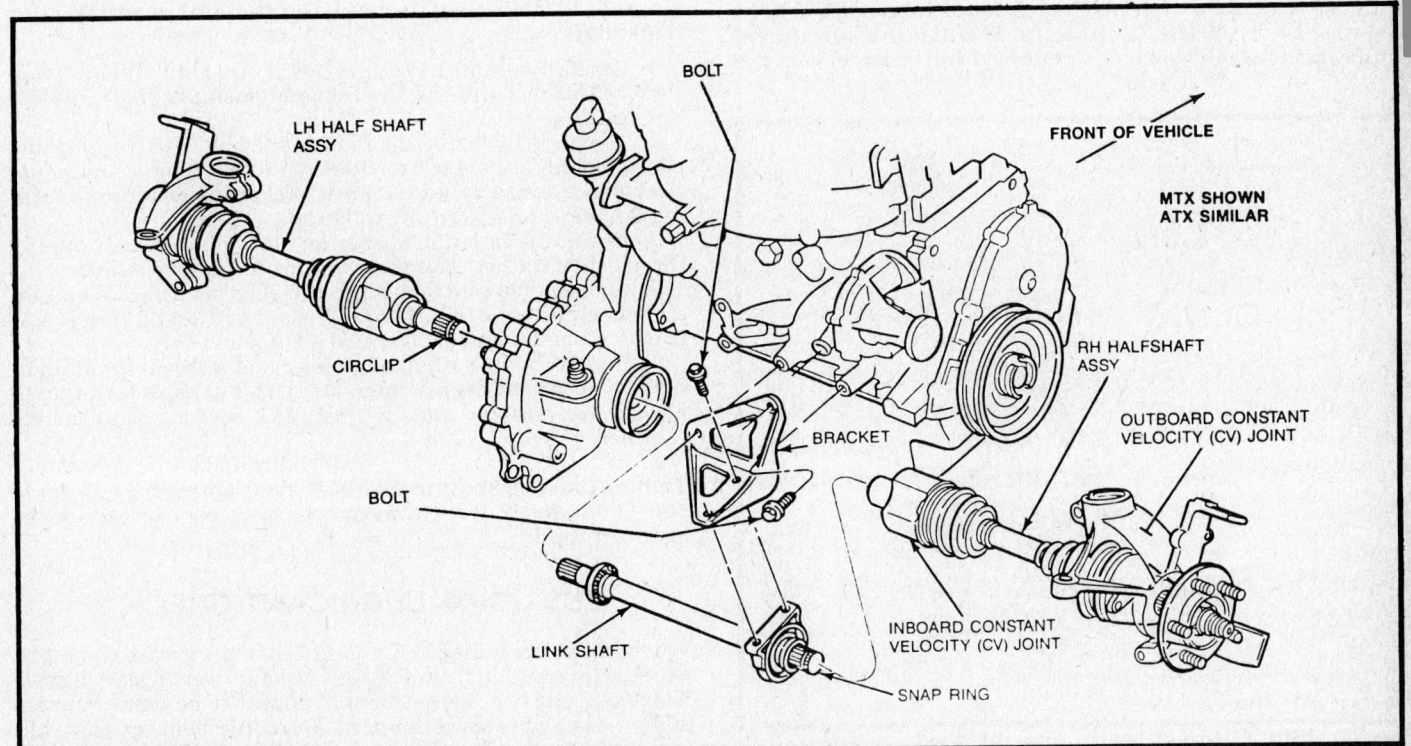

LH and RH halfshaft assembly removal and installation—Taurus/Sable

FORD MERCURY
FRONT WHEEL DRIVE CARS—ESCORT • EXP • LYNX • TEMPO • TOPAZ • TAURUS • SABLE

CAUTION

Never use a hammer to separate the outboard CV–joint stub shaft from the hub. Damage to the CV–joint threads and internal components may result.

NOTE: The RH side link shaft and halfshaft assembly is removed as a complete unit.

6. The following removal procedure is for the RH side halfshaft for the automatic overdrive transaxle and the LH side halfshaft on the manual transaxle:

   a. Install the CV-joint puller T86P-3514-A1 or equivalent between CV-joint and transaxle case. Turn the steering hub and or wire strut assembly out of the way.

   b. Screw Extension T86P-3514-A2 or equivalent, into the CV-Joint puller and hand tighten. Screw Impact Slide Hammer D79-100-A or equivalent onto the extension and remove the CV joint.

   c. Support the end of the shaft by suspending it from a convenient underbody component with a piece of wire. Do not allow the shaft to hang un-supported, damage to the outboard CV-joint may occur.

   d. Separate the outboard CV joint from the hub using Front Hub Remover T81P-1104-C or equivalent, Metric Adapters T83-P-1104-BH, T86P-1104-Al and T81P-1104-A or equivalent.

CAUTION

Never use a hammer to separate the outboard CV–joint stub shaft from the hub. Damage to the CV–joint threads and internal components may result.

---

   e. Remove the halfshaft assembly from the vehicle.

7. The following removal procedure is for the LH side halfshaft for the automatic transaxle:

NOTE: Due to the ATX case configuration, the right-hand halfshaft assembly must be removed first. Differential Rotator T81P-4026-A or equivalent is then inserted into the transaxle to drive the left-hand inboard CV-joint assembly from the transaxle. If only the left-hand halfshaft assembly is to be removed for service, remove only the right-hand halfshaft assembly from the transaxle. After removal, support it with a length of wire. Then drive the left-hand halfshaft assembly from the transaxle.

   a. Support the end of the shaft by suspending it from a convenient underbody component with a piece of wire. Do not allow the shaft to hang un-supported, damage to the outboard CV-joint may occur.

   b. Separate the outboard CV-joint from the hub using fronthub remover T81P-1104-C or equivalent, metric adapters T83-P-1104-BH, T86P-1104-Al and T81P-1104-A or equivalent.

CAUTION

Never use a hammer to separate the outboard CV–joint stub shaft from the hub. Damage to the CV–joint threads and internal components may result.

---

   c. Remove the halfshaft assembly from the vehicle.

Installation

1. Install a new circlip on the inboard CV-joint stub shaft and or link shaft. The outboard CV-joint does not have a circlip. When installing the circlip, start one end in the groove and work the circlip over the stub shaft end into the groove. This will avoid over expanding the circlip.

CAUTION

The circlip must not be re-used. A new circlip must be installed each time the inboard CV-joint is installed into the transaxle differential.

---

2. Carefully align the splines of the inboard CV-joint stub shaft with the splines in the differential. Exerting some force, push the CV-joint into the differential until the circlip is felt to seat in the differential side gear. Use care to prevent damage to the differential oil seal.

NOTE: A non-metallic mallet may be used to aid in seating the circlip into the differential side gear groove. If a mallet is necessary, tap only on the outboard CV-joint stub shaft.

3. Carefully align the splines of the outboard CV-joint stub shaft with the splines in the hub and push the shaft into the hub as far as possible.

4. Temporarily fasten the rotor to the hub with washers and two wheel lug nuts. Insert a steel rod into the rotor and rotate clockwise to contact the knuckle to prevent the rotor from turning during the CV-joint installation.

5. Install the hub nut washer and a new hub nut. Manually thread the retainer onto the CV-joint as far as possible.

6. Connect the control arm to the steering knuckle and install a new nut and bolt. Torque the nut to 37–44 ft. lbs. A new bolt must be installed, do not re-use the old bolt.

7. Install the hub retainer washer and a new hub retainer. Manuualy thread the retainer onto the CV-joint as far as possible. A new retainer must be installed, do not re-use the old retainer.

8. Install the wheel and tire assembly and lower the vehicle. Tighten the wheel nuts to 80–105 ft. lbs. Tighten the hub nut to 180–200 ft. lbs. Fill the transaxle to the proper level with the specified fluid.

CV-JOINT LUBRICANT CHECK

When replacing damaged CV-joint boots, the grease should be checked for contamination. If the CV-joints were operating satisfactorily and the grease does not appear to be contaminated, add grease and replace the boot. If the lubricant appears contaminated, proceed with a complete CV-joint disassembly and inspection.

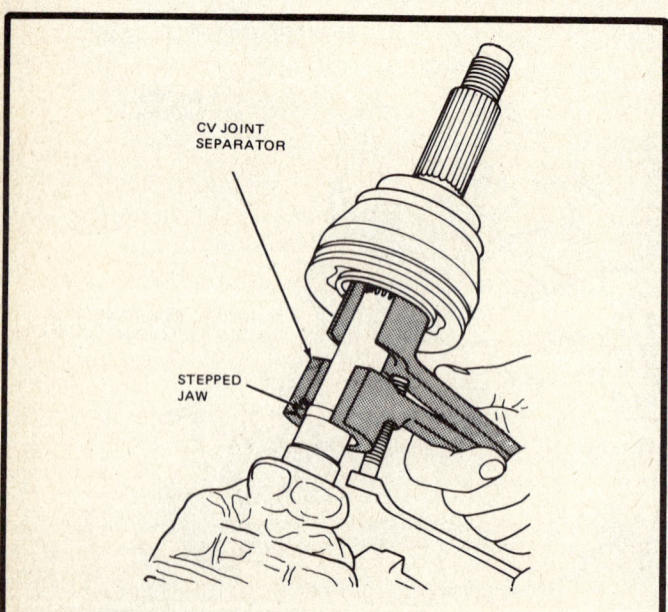

Separating CV-joint with special tool
(© Ford Motor Co.)

Ford Mercury

FRONT WHEEL DRIVE CARS—ESCORT • EXP • LYNX • TEMPO • TOPAZ • TAURUS • SABLE

1. Clamp the halfshaft in a vise. Do not allow the vice jaws to contact the boot or its clamp. The vice should be equipped with jaw caps to prevent damage to any machine surfaces.
2. Cut the large boot clamp using side cutters and peel away from the boot. After removing the clamp, roll the boot back over the shaft.
3. Separate the CV-joint from the shaft using CV-joint separator T81P–3514–A (or equivalent). The boot can now be removed from the shaft if necessary. Cut the remaining clamp and pull the boot from the shaft.
4. Remove the circlip located near the end of the shaft. Discard the circlip. A new clip is supplied with both the boot replacement kit and CV-joint overhaul kit.
5. The stop ring, located just below the circlip, should be removed only if inspection determines it to be damaged, worn or otherwise unserviceable.

CV-JOINT AND BOOT

Removal and Installation

ALL MODELS

1. Clamp the halfshaft in a vise that is equipped with soft jaw covers. Do not allow the vise jaws to contact the boot or boot clamp.
2. Cut the large boot clamp with a pair of side cutters and peel the clamp away from the boot. Roll the boot back over the shaft after the clamp has been removed.
3. Check the grease for contamination by rubbing some between two fingers. If the grease feels gritty, it is contaminated

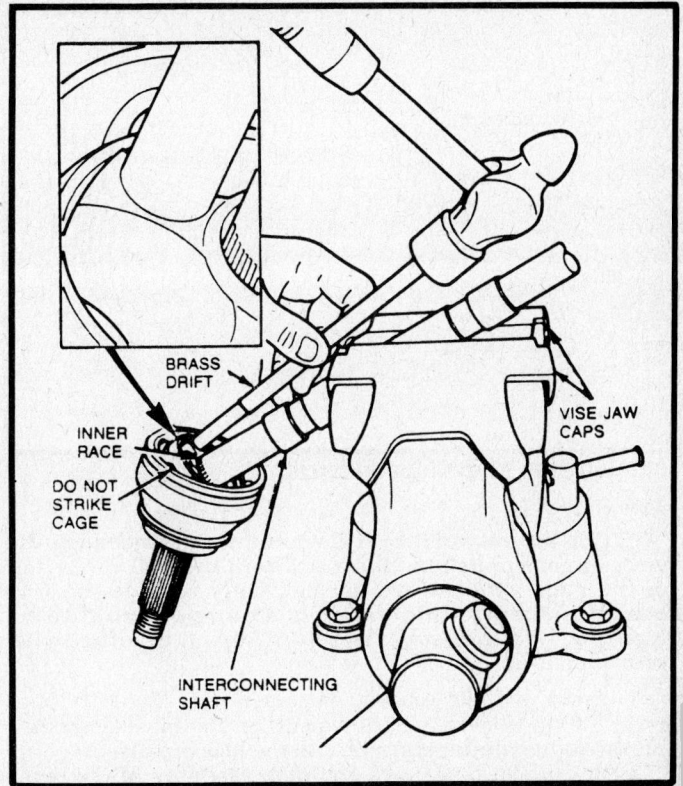

Removing the CV joint from the interconnecting shaft

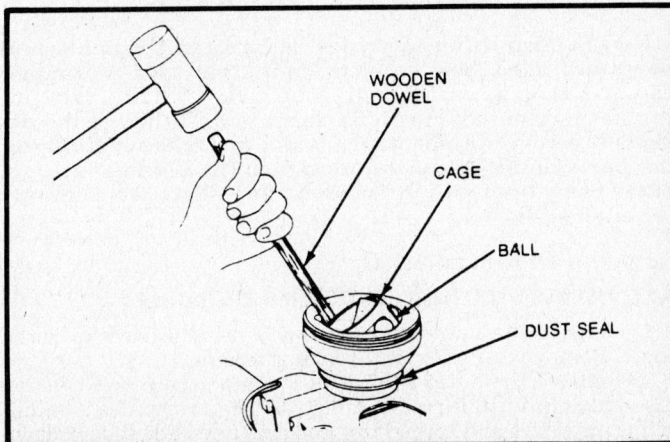

Tilting the bearing assembly to position it for removing the balls from the cage

and the joint will have to be disassembled, cleaned and inspected. If the grease is not contaminated and the CV-joints were operating satisfactorily, repack them with grease and install a new boot, or reinstall the old boot with a new clamp.
4. If disassembly is required, clamp the interconnecting shaft in a soft jawed vise with the CV-joint pointing downward so that the inner bearing race is exposed.
5. Use a brass drift and hammer, give a sharp tap to the inner bearing race to dislodge the internal snap ring and separate the CV-joint from the interconnecting shaft. Take care to secure the CV-joint so that it does not drop on the ground after separation. Remove the clamp and boot from the shaft.
6. Remove and discard the circlip at the end of the interconnecting shaft. The stop ring, located just below the circlip should be removed and replaced only if damaged or worn.
7. Clamp the CV-joint stub shaft in a soft jaw vise with the outer face facing up. Care should be taken not to damage the dust seal. Press down on the inner race until it tilts enough to allow the removal of the ball. A tight assembly can be tilted by tapping the inner race with a wooden dowel and hammer. Do not hit the cage.
8. With the cage sufficiently tilted, remove the ball from the cage. Repaet this step until all six balls are removed. If the balls are tight in the cage, use a suitable tool to pry the balls fron the cage. Be careful not to scratch or cause other damage to the inner race or cage spheres.
9. Pivot the gage and inner race assembly until the it is straight up and down in the outer race. Align the cage windows with the outer race lands while pivoting the bearing. With the cage pivoted and aligned, lift the assembly from the outer race.
10. Rotate the inner race up and out of the cage. Pivot the inner race until it is straight up and down in the cage. Align one of the inner race lands with on of the elongated windows and position the race through the window. Rotate the inner race up and out of the cage.

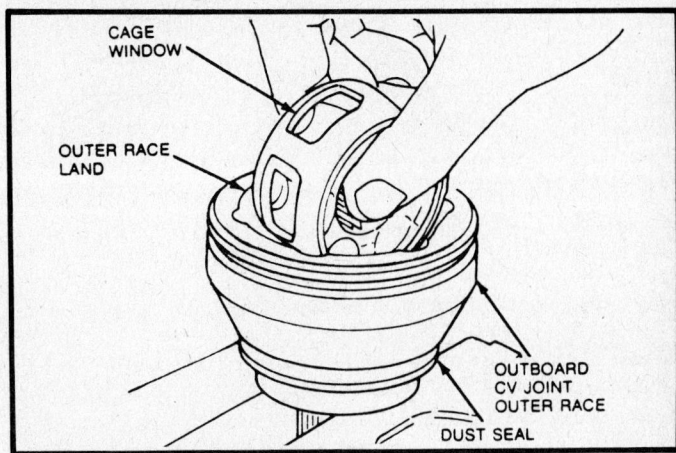

Removing the cage (outer race)

4-95

SECTION 4

FORD MERCURY
FRONT WHEEL DRIVE CARS—ESCORT • EXP • LYNX • TEMPO • TOPAZ • TAURUS • SABLE

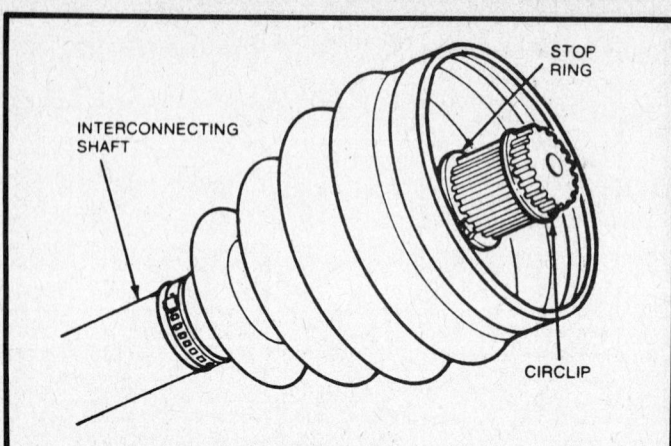

Installing the stop ring and circlip

NOTE: Do not replace a CV-joint merely because the parts appear polished. Shiny areas in the ball races and on the cage spheres are normal. Only replace the CV-joint if inspection determines a component(s) to be cracked, broken, severly pitted, worn or otherwise unserviceable.

11. Apply a light coating of grease (Use Ford CV-joint grease E2FZ–19590–A or equivalent) on the inner and outer ball races. Install the inner race in the bearing cage.

12. Install the inner race and cage assembly in the outer race. Install the assembly vertically and pivot 90 ° into position. Align the bearing cage and inner race with the outer race. Tilt the inner race and cage and install a ball. Repaet this step until all six balls are installed.

13. The LH and RH interconnecting shafts are different, depending on year and model application. The outboard end of the shaft is shorter from the end of the shaft to the end of the boot grove than the inboard end. Take a measurement to insure correct installation.

14. If removed, install a new boot. Make sure the boot is seated in the mounting groove and secure it in position with a new clamp. Tighten the clamp securley, but not to the point where the clamp bridge is cut or the boot is damaged.

15. Clean the interconnecting shaft splines and install a new circlip, and stop ring if removed. To install the circlip correctly, start one end in the groove and work the circlip over the shaft end and into the groove.

16. Pack the CV-joint and boot with the grease supplied in the joint or boot kit. The inboard joint should be packed with about 90 grams of grease; the boot with about 45 grams of grease. The outboard joint should be packed with about 45 grams of grease, and the boot with about 45 grams of grease. If grease from a replacement kit is not on hand, use only grease Ford Number E2FZ–19590–A or equivalent.

17. With the boot peeled back, position the CV-joint on the shaft and tap into position using a plastic tipped hammer. The CV-joint is fully seated when the circlip locks into the groove cut into the CV-joint inner bearing race. Check for seating by attempting to pull the joint away from the shaft.

18. Remove all excess grease form the CV-joint external surface and position the boot over the joint.

19. Before installing the boot clamp, make sure all air pressure that may have built up in the boot is removed. Pry up on the boot lip to allow the air to escape. Refer to the halfshaft length specifications and adjust the shaft to "specs" before tightening the boot clamps.

20. The large end clamp should be installed after making sure of the correct shaft length and that the boot is seated in its groove.

INBOARD CV–JOINTS

NOTE: Two different types of inboard CV-joints and boots are used. The conventional style uses a crimped can on the large end. The tri-lobe style CV-joint does not require a crimped can on the large end. Although the designs are very similar, there is not interchangeability of the parts between the two designs. The CV-joint tripod, outer race, boot and interconnecting shaft are a unique for each style.

Removal and Installation

ALL CONVENTIONAL INBOARD CV-jointS

1. Remove the large clamp and roll the boot back over the shaft. Remove the wire ring bearing retainer.

2. Remove the outer race. Pull the inner race and bearing assembly out until it rests against the snap ring. Use a pair of snap ring pliers and spread the stop ring and slide it back down the shaft.

3. Slide the inner bearing and race assembly down the shaft to allow access to the circlip. Remove the circlip.

4. Remove the inner race and bearing assembly. Remove the stop ring and boot if necessary.

5. With the cage sufficiently tilted, remove the ball from the cage. Repaet this step until all six balls are removed. If the balls are tight in the cage, use a suitable tool to pry the balls fron the cage. Be careful not to scratch or cause other damage to the inner race or cage spheres.

6. Rotate the inner race up and out of the cage. Pivot the inner race until it is straight up and down in the cage. Align one of the inner race lands with on of the elongated windows and position the race through the window. Rotate the inner race up and out of the cage.

7. Clean the interconnecting shaft splines and install a new circlip, and stop ring if removed. To install the circlip correctly, start one end in the groove and work the circlip over the shaft end and into the groove.

8. Pack the CV-joint and boot with the grease supplied in the joint or boot kit. The inboard joint should be packed with about 90 grams of grease; the boot with about 45 grams of

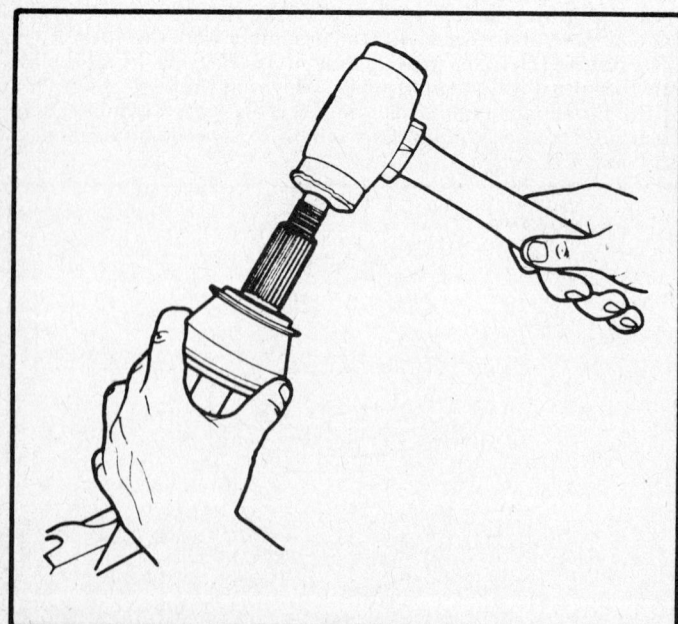

Tapping the CV joint onto the shaft

grease. If grease from a replacement kit is not on hand, use only grease Ford Number E2FZ–19590–A or equivalent.

9. Install the inner race in the bearing cage. The race is installed through the large end of the cage with the circlip counterbort facing the large end of the cage.

10. With the cage and inner race properly aligned, install the balls by pressing them through the cage windows with the heel of the hand. Assemble the inner race and cage assembly into the outer race.

11. Push the inner race and cage assembly by hand, into the outer race. Install the chamfer facing outward. Install the ball retainer into the groove inside of the outer race.

12. Install a new boot and end clamp, fold the boot back, after cleaning the shaft splines. Install the stop ring in position.

NOTE: **The LH interconnecting shaft is the same end for end. The outboard or inboard CV-joint may be installed at either end. The RH interconnecting shaft is different end for end. The tapered faces of the center balance faces outboard.**

13. Position a new stop ring and circlip into the grooves nearest the end of the shaft. Start one end of the circlip in the groove and work the circlip over the end of the shaft into the mounting groove.

14. Fill the boot with about 45 grams of grease and the outer race with about 90 grams of grease. Push the inner race and bearing assembly into the outer race by hand.

15. Position the CV-joint over the shaft and tap down with a plastic hammer until the snap ring locks into the groove. Make sure the splines are aligned before hammering the joint into position.

16. Remove all excess grease from the outside of the CV-joint. Position the boot and secure in retaining groove after removing trapped air and checking for proper length.

Removal and Installation
ALL TRIPOD INBOARD CV-JOINTS

1. Cut and remove the both boot clamps and slide the boot back on the shaft.

NOTE: **On all vehicles, the RH inboard CV-joint requires a re0usable low profile large boot clamp. There is a special pair of boot clamp pliers available to remove this clamp or a pair of crimping pliers may be used. This clamp is then removed by installing the pincer jaws (hooks) of the pliers into the windows of the clamp and drawing them together and then sliding the clamp off of the boot.**

2. Slide the outer race off of the tripod. Move the stop ring back on the shaft using a suitable pair of snap ring pliers. Move the tripod assembly back on the shaft to allow acess to the circlip. Remove the circlip from the shaft and discard the circlip.

NOTE: **It may be necessary to bend the tabs of the outer race to allow the tripod to be separated from the outer race.**

3. Remove the tripod assembly from the shaft. Remove the boot if necessary.

Installation

1. Install the CV-joint boot on the shaft, if removed during disassembly. Make sure the boot is seated in the boot groove on the shaft. Tighten the clamp using a suitable pair of crimping pliers.

2. Install the tripod assembly on the shaft wih chamfered side towards the stop ring. Install a new circlip, do not re-use the old circlip.

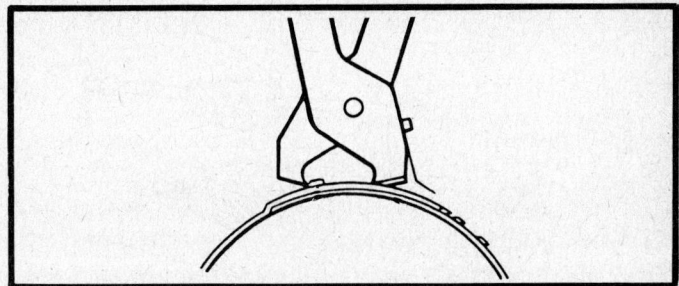
Removing the clamp from the CV joint boot

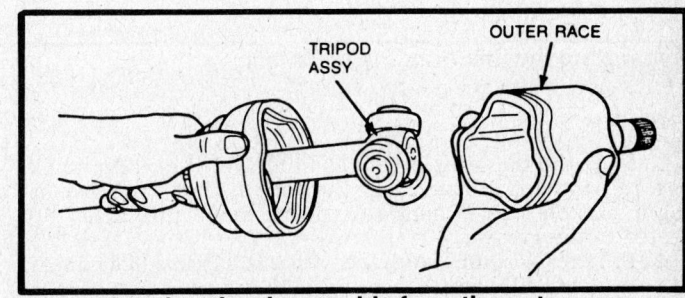
Separating the tripod assembly from the outer race

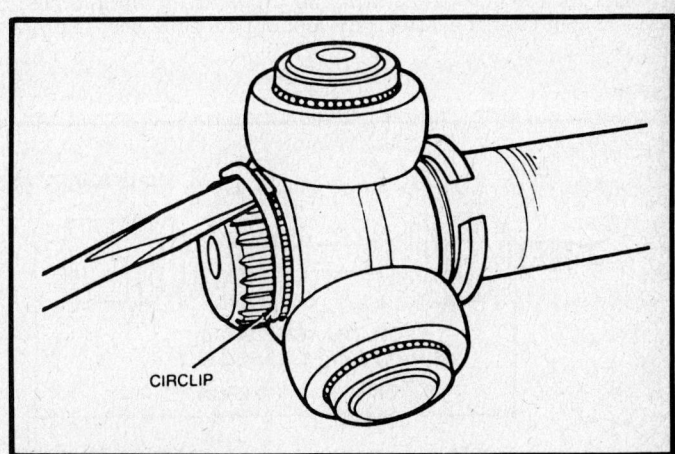
Removing the circlip

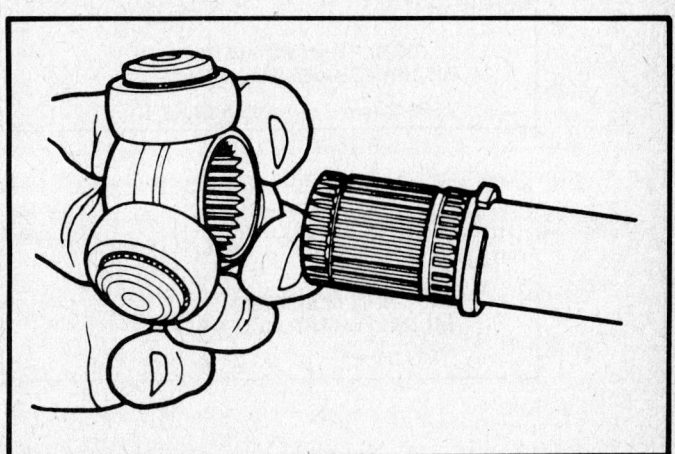
Removing the tripod assembly

SECTION 4

FORD MERCURY
FRONT WHEEL DRIVE CARS—ESCORT • EXP • LYNX • TEMPO • TOPAZ • TAURUS • SABLE

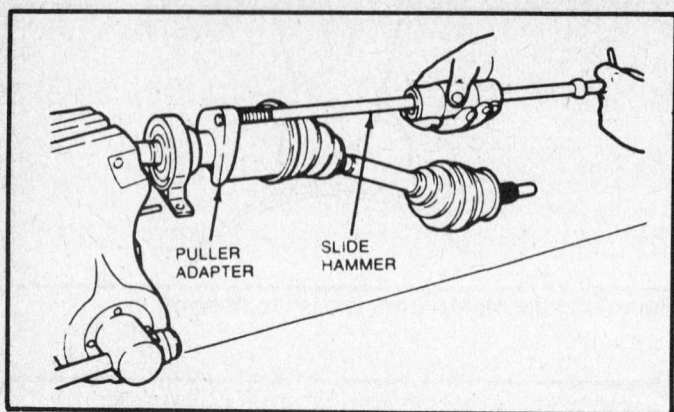

Separating the link from the halfshaft

3. Slide the tripod assembly forward over the circlip to expose the stop ring groove. Make the stop ring into the froove using a suitable pair of snap-ring pliers. make sure it is fully seated in the groove.
4. Fill the CV-joint outer race with a 100 grams (3.5 ounces) of grease and fill the CV boot with 70 grams (2.5 ounces) of grease. If grease from a replacement kit is not on hand, use only grease Ford Number E2FZ–19590–A or equivalent.
5. Install the outer race over the tripod assembly and position the boot over the outer race making sure the boot is properly seated in it groove.

6. Before installing the boot clamp, make sure all air pressure that may have built up in the boot is removed. Pry up on the boot lip to allow the air to escape. Refer to the halfshaft length specifications and adjust the shaft to "specs" before tightening the boot clamps.
7. Seat the boot in the groove and clamp in position using crimping pliers. Secure the clamp by drawing the closing hooks together. When the windows of the clamp are above the locking hooks, the spring tabs will press the windows over the locking hooks and engage the clamp.
8. Install a new circlip, supplied with the service kit

LINK SHAFT/HALFSHAFT

Disassembly and Assembly

TAURUS/SABLE

1. Clamp the link shaft in the vise with the halfshaft supported on the workbench. Using Puller Adapter T86P–3514–A or equivalent and Slide Hammer D79P–100–A or equivalent, separate the link shaft from the halfshaft.
2. Remove the seal from the link shaft by prying it off with a suitable tool. Be careful not to damage to bearing dust shield.
3. Place the shaft assembly in a arbor press or equivalent with the bearing supported and press out the link shaft. Support the link shaft in a press fixture with stop in shaft.
4. Place the bearing on the shaft and press the bearing onto the shaft using a $1\frac{3}{16}$ in. deep well socket until it contacts the stop ring.
5. Place seal on the shaft and press the seal onto the shaft using a deep-well socket until it contacts the bearing.

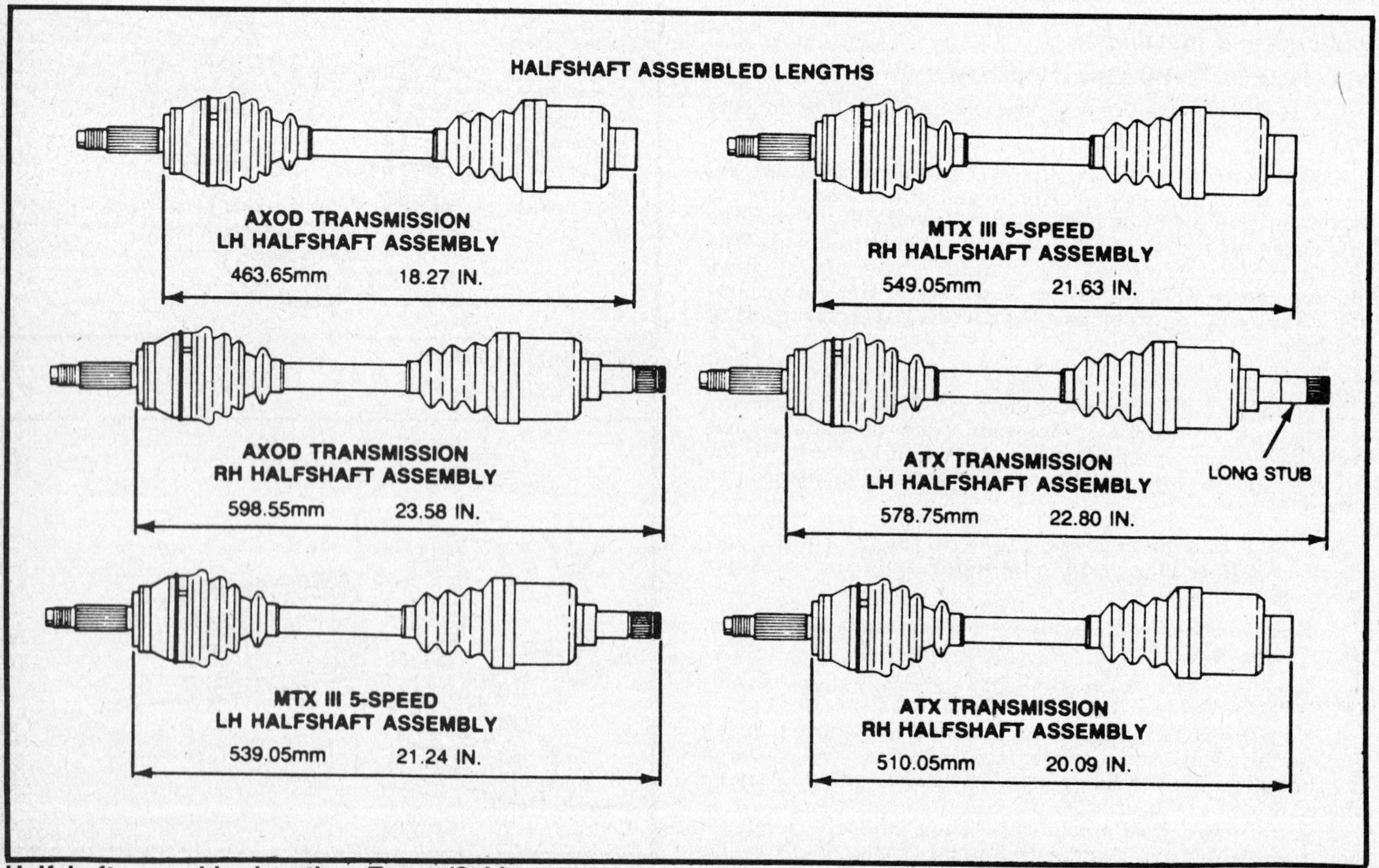

HALFSHAFT ASSEMBLED LENGTHS

AXOD TRANSMISSION LH HALFSHAFT ASSEMBLY — 463.65mm / 18.27 IN.	MTX III 5-SPEED RH HALFSHAFT ASSEMBLY — 549.05mm / 21.63 IN.
AXOD TRANSMISSION RH HALFSHAFT ASSEMBLY — 598.55mm / 23.58 IN.	ATX TRANSMISSION LH HALFSHAFT ASSEMBLY (LONG STUB) — 578.75mm / 22.80 IN.
MTX III 5-SPEED LH HALFSHAFT ASSEMBLY — 539.05mm / 21.24 IN.	ATX TRANSMISSION RH HALFSHAFT ASSEMBLY — 510.05mm / 20.09 IN.

Halfshaft assembles lengths—Taurus/Sable

Ford Mercury

FRONT WHEEL DRIVE CARS—ESCORT • EXP • LYNX • TEMPO • TOPAZ • TAURUS • SABLE

SECTION 4

6. Assemble the halfshaft and link shaft. Before assembly, coat the link shaft spline and seal cavity with CV-joint grease E2FZ–19590–A or equivalent.

Service

NOTE: Disassembly of the CV-joints is necessary when the grease is contaminated. Contamination of the lubricant can damage the parts of the joint, an inspection is necessary to determine if replacement is required.

CV–JOINT SERVICE

Refer to the CV-joint segment of the Unit Repair Section for service procedures.

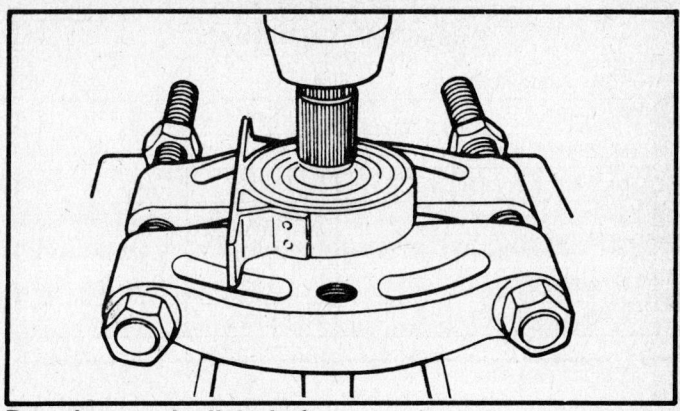
Pressing out the link shaft

REAR AXLE AND SUSPENSION

For Axle Overhaul Procedures and Suspension Services Refer to Unit Repair Section.

REAR SPINDLE

Removal

ALL MODELS EXCEPT THE TEMPO/TOPAZ AND TAURUS/SABLE

1. Raise and support the rear of the vehicle safely. If a frame contact hoist is used, a jack stand must be placed under the lower suspension arm to raise it to curb height.
2. Remove the wheel and tire assembly. Remove the brake drum and wheel bearings as outlined in this section. Remove the brake backing plate assembly from the spindle.
3. Remove the tie rod to spindle nut retainer and two bolts retaining the strut to the spindle. Remove the nut and bolt retaining the lower control arm to spindle and remove the spindle.
4. On the Taurus/Sable models, remove the bolts and nuts attaching the front and rear upper suspension arms to the body crossmember. Remove the bolt, one washer, adjusting cam and nut attaching the spindle to the lower suspension arm.
5. Also on the Taurus/Sable models, Remove the spindle and upper suspension arms from the vehicle as an assembly. Remove the nut attaching the upper suspension arm to the spindle and remove the suspension arms from the spindle.

Installation

1. Install a new tie rod bushing in its place in the spindle and add one new dished washer installed on the tie rod, position the spindle over the end of the tie rod.
2. Attach the spindle to the shock strut tower with a dual nut retainer and two new bolts. The bolts must be installed with the heads toward the rear of the vehicle. Torque the bolts to 70–96 ft. lbs.
3. Attach the lower control arm to the spindle using a new

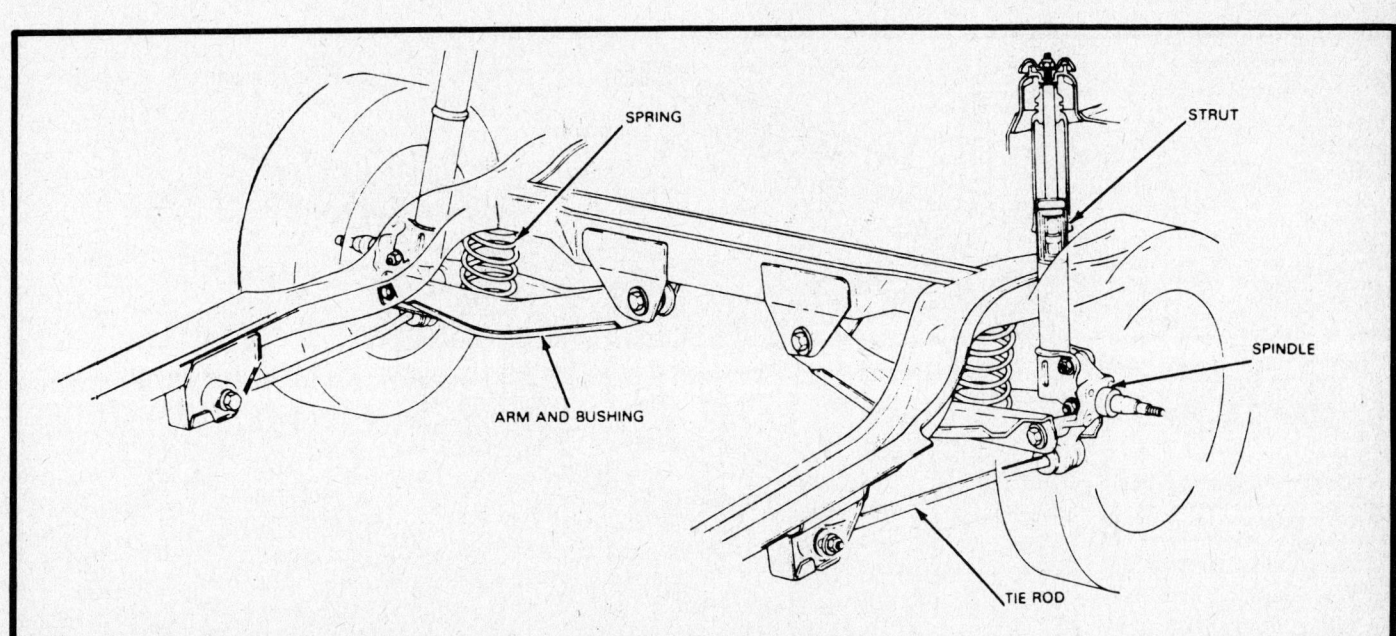
Escort/Lynx, EXP suspension—rear coil springs (© Ford Motor Co.)

SECTION 4

FORD MERCURY
FRONT WHEEL DRIVE CARS—ESCORT • EXP • LYNX • TEMPO • TOPAZ • TAURUS • SABLE

Escort/EXP, LN7/Lynx
TORQUE SPECIFICATIONS

Description	N·m	Lb-Ft
Shock Absorber to Body	47.5-74.6	35-55
Shock Absorber to Spindle	122-135	90-100
Control Arm to Body	88-102	65-75
Control Arm to Spindle	122-135	90-100
Tie Rod to Body	122-135	90-100
Tie Rod to Spindle	88-102	65-75

TORQUE SPECIFICATIONS

Description	N·m	Lb-Ft
Shock Absorber to Body	26-37	19-27
Shock Absorber to Lower Suspension Arm	17-27	12.5-20
Upper Suspension Arms to Body	95-128	70-95
Upper Suspension Arms to Spindle	204-257	150-190
Lower Suspension Arm to Body	54-74	40-55
Lower Suspension Arm to Spindle	81-116	60-86
Tension Strut to Body	54-74	40-55
Tension Strut to Lower Suspension Arm	54-74	40-55
Stabilizer Bar U-Bracket to Lower Suspension Arm	27-40	20-30
Stabilizer Link Assembly to Body	54-74	40-55

Taurus Sable rear suspension torque specifications—Station wagon

bolt, nut and washers. Install the bolt with the head towards the front of the vehicle. Torque the bolt to 70-96 ft. lbs.

4. Install the tie rod to the spindle using a new dished washer and a new nut. Torque the nut to 65-75 ft. lbs. Install the brake backing plate asembly to the spindle. Install the brake drum assembly and bearings.

5. Install the tire and wheel asembly. Remove the jack stand and lower the vehicle.

Removal
TAURUS/SABLE STATION WAGON MODELS

1. Raise and support the rear of the vehicle safely. If a frame contact hoist is used, a jack stand must be placed under the lower suspension arm to raise it to curb height.

2. Remove the wheel and tire assembly. Remove the brake drum and wheel bearings as outlined in this section. Remove the brake backing plate assembly from the spindle.

3. Remove the bolts and nuts attaching the front and rear upper suspension arms to the body crossmember. Remove the bolt, one washer, adjusting cam and nut attaching the spindle to the lower susension arm.

4. Remove the spindle and upper suspension arms from the vehicle as an assembly. Remove the nut attaching the upper suspension arm to the spindle and remove the suspension arms from the spindle.

Installation

1. Install the upper suspension arms on the spindle using a new nut. Do not tighten them at this time. Position the spindle and suspension arm assambly on the lower suspension arm.

2. Install a new bolt, washer, existing adjusting cam and a new nut. Do not tighten them at this time. Position the front and rear upper suspension arm is supported so that the lower suspension arm is at normal curb height.

3. Torque the bolts attaching the front and rear upper suspension arms to body to 70-95 ft. lbs. Torque the nut attaching the upper suspension arms to the spindle to 150-190 ft. lbs. Torque the nut attaching the spindle to the lower suspension arm to 60-86 ft. lbs.

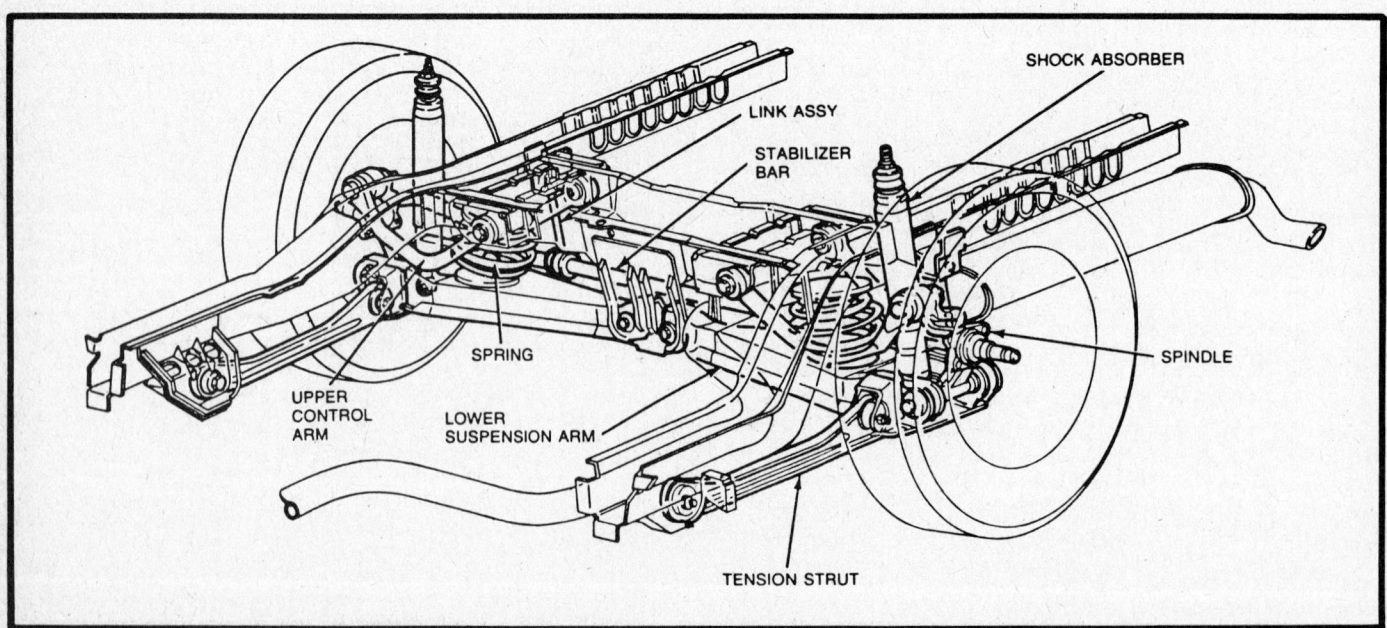

Taurus/Sable rear suspension—Station wagon

Ford Mercury
FRONT WHEEL DRIVE CARS—ESCORT • EXP • LYNX • TEMPO • TOPAZ • TAURUS • SABLE

Section 4

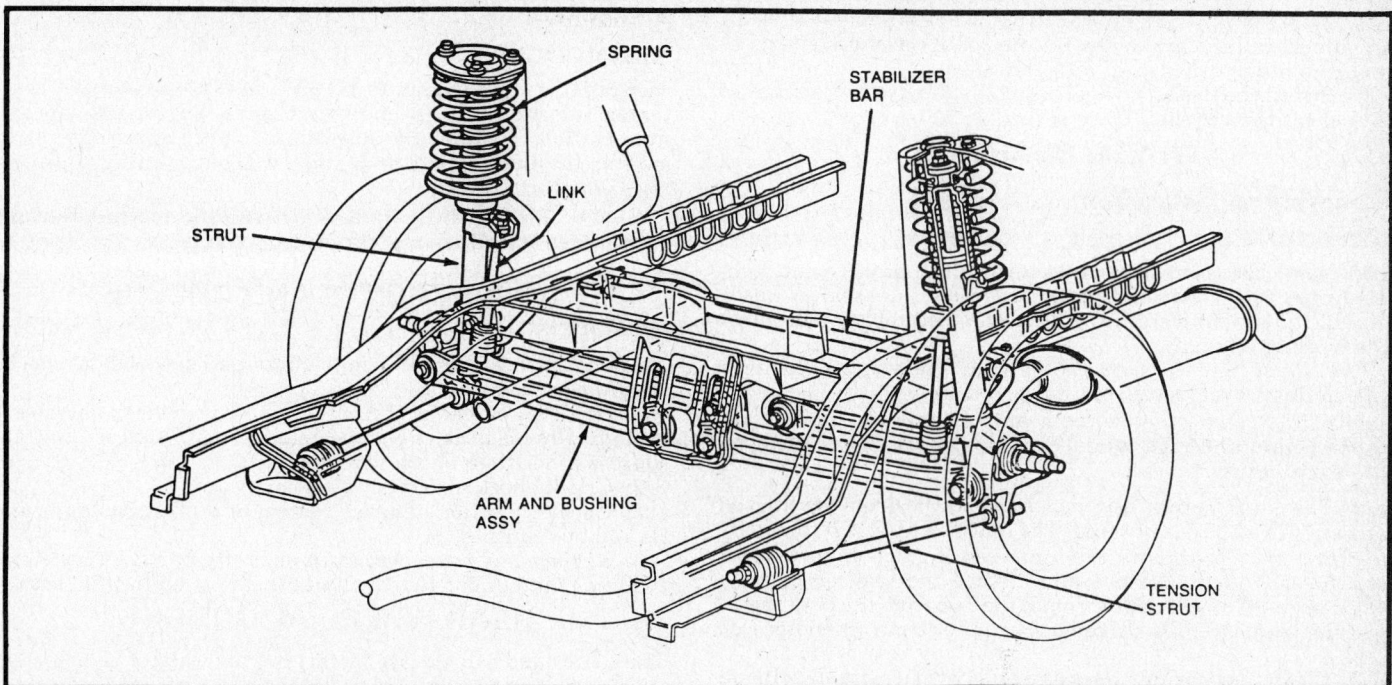

Taurus/Sable rear suspension—Sedan

4. Install the brake backing plate asembly to the spindle. Install the brake drum assembly and bearings.
5. Install the tire and wheel asembly. Remove the jack stand and lower the vehicle.

Removal
TEMPO/TOPAZ AND TAURUS/SABLE SEDAN MODELS

1. Raise and support the rear of the vehicle safely. Do not raise the vehicle by the tension strut.
2. Remove the wheel and tire assembly. Remove the brake drum and wheel bearings as outlined in this section. Remove the clip retaining the brake flex hose to the shock strut bracket. Remove the four bolts retaining the brake backing plate to the spindle.

NOTE: Be careful not to stretch the brake flex hose and or bend the brake tube.

3. Remove the brake backing plate assembly from the spindle and wire it out of the way. Remove the control arm to spindle bolts, washers and nuts.
4. Remove the tension strut nut, washer and bushing. Remove the pinch bolt retaining the spindle to the shock strut and remove the spindle from the vehicle.

Installation

1. Position the spindle onto the tension strut and then onto the shock strut. Insert a new strut to spindle pinch bolt. Do not tighten it at this time.
2. Install the tension strut bushing, washer and new nut. Do not tightne the nut at this time. Install the new control arm to spindle bolts, washers and nuts. Installa jack stand to support the suspension at the normal curb height before tightening the fasteners.
3. Torque the spindle to strut bolt to 55 to 81 ft. lbs. Torque the tension strut nut to 52 to 74 ft. lbs. Torque the control arm to spindle nuts to 52 to 74 ft. lbs.

Tempo/Topaz
TORQUE SPECIFICATIONS

Description	N·m	Lb-Ft
Strut top mount to body	27-41	20-30
Strut to top mount	47-67	35-50
Strut to spindle	95-130	70-96
Control arm to spindle	80-115	60-86
Control arm to body	55-75	40-55
Tie rod to spindle	70-100	52-74
Tie rod to body	70-100	52-74

Description	N·m	Lb-Ft
Shock Absorber to Body	26-37	19-27
Shock Absorber to Lower Suspension Arm	17-27	12.5-20
Upper Suspension Arms to Body	95-128	70-95
Upper Suspension Arms to Spindle	204-257	150-190
Lower Suspension Arm to Body	54-74	40-55
Lower Suspension Arm to Spindle	81-116	60-86
Tension Strut to Body	54-74	40-55
Tension Strut to Lower Suspension Arm	54-74	40-55
Stabilizer Bar U-Bracket to Lower Suspension Arm	27-40	20-30
Stabilizer Link Assembly to Body	54-74	40-55

Taurus Sable rear suspension torque specifications—Sedan

FORD MERCURY
FRONT WHEEL DRIVE CARS—ESCORT • EXP • LYNX • TEMPO • TOPAZ • TAURUS • SABLE

4. Install the brake backing plate asembly to the spindle. Install the brake flex line clip onto the shock strut. Install the brake drum assembly and bearings.

5. Install the tire and wheel asembly. Remove the jack stand and lower the vehicle.

WHEEL BEARINGS

Removal and Installation
ALL MODELS

The rear wheel bearings are located in the brake drum hub. The inner wheel bearing is protected by a grease seal. A washer and spindle nut retain the hub/drum assembly and control the bearing end play.

1. Raise and support the rear of the vehicle. Remove wheel, dust cover, cotter pin nut and drum.

NOTE: **Styled steel wheels and aluminum wheels require removal of the wheel and tire assembly to remove the dust cover.**

2. The outer bearing will be lose when the drum is removed and may be lifted out by hand. The inner bearing is retained by a grease seal. To remove the inner bearing, use seal remover tool or equivalent, remove and discard the seal, or insert a wooden dowel or soft drift through the hub from the outer bearing side and carefully drive out the inner bearing and grease seal.

3. Clean the bearings, cups and hubs with a suitable solvent. Inspect the bearings and cups for damage or heat discoloring. Replace as a set if necessary. Always install a new grease seal.

4. If new bearings are to be used, use a three jawed slidehammer puller to remove the cups from the drum hub. Install the new bearings cups using a suitable driver. Make sure they are fully seated in the hub.

5. Pack the bearings with a multi-purpose grease.

6. Coat the cups with a thin film of grease. Install the inner bearings and grease seal.

7. Coat the bearing surfaces of the spindle with a thin film of grease. Slowly and carefully slide the drum and hub over the spindle and brake shoes. Install the outer bearing over the spindle and into the hub.

8. Install the keyed flat washer and adjusting nut on the spindle.

9. Tighten the adjusting nut to between 17–25 ft. lbs.

10. Back-off the adjusting nut ½ turn. Then retighten it to between 10–15 ft. lbs.

11. Position the nut retainer on the nut and install the cotter pin. Do not tighten the nut to install the cotter pin.

12. Spread the ends of the cotter pin and bend then around the nut retainer. Install the center grease cap.

13. Install the tire and wheel assembly. Lower the car and tighten the wheel lugs.

Adjustment
ALL MODELS

Tighten the adjusting nut to 17–25 ft. lbs. (23–24 Nm) while rotating hub and drum assembly. Back off adjusting nut approximately 100°. Position the nut retainer over adjusting nut so slots are in line with cotter pin hole without rotating adjusting nut. Install cotter pin.

NOTE: **The spindle has a prevailing torque feature that prevents adjusting the nut by hand.**

ADJUSTMENTS AND CHECKS
All Models

At regular intervals, the following rear suspension checks should be made:

1. check for evidence of fluid leaks on rear shock absorbers. (A light film of fluid is permissible. Be sure fluid is not from sources other than shock absorber.)

2. Check shock absorber operation.

3. Check condition of lower control arm pivot bushings and tie rod bushings.

4. Replace any damaged, worn or faulty parts. Use the procedures found under Removal and Installation in this section.

REAR WHEEL ALIGNMENT

The caster and camber are factory set and cannot be adjusted.

Rear Toe Adjustment
ESCORT/EXP, Lynx/LN7

1. Loosen the tie rod nut (that faces the front of the vehicle) and slide the tie rod toward the rear of the vehicle to increase the amount of toe-out.

2. Loosen the tie rod nut (that faces the rear of the vehicle) and slide the tir rod toward the front of the vehicle to increase the amount of toe-in.

3. After adjusting the toe to specifications. Hold the tie rod flat with a wrench and tight tie rod nut (that faces the rear of the vehicle) to 6–12 ft. lbs. and torque the tie rod nut (that faces the front of the vehicle) to 52–74 ft. lbs.

TEMPO/TOPAZ AND TAURUS/SABLE

1. On the Tempo/Topaz models, loosen the bolt attaching the rear control arm to the body and rotate the alignment cam until the required alignment setting is obtained. Torque the control arm attaching bolts to 40–55 ft. lbs.

2. On the Taurus/Sable models, loosen the nut and bolt attaching the spindle to the lower suspension arm. turn the adjusting cam to obtain the alignment setting. While holding the adjusting cam in position. Torque the attaching nut to 60–86 ft. lbs.

REAR WHEEL ALIGNMENT (CURB HEIGHT WITH 1/2 TANK OF FUEL)

Vehicle	Alignment Factors	Units	Nominals	Minimum	Maximum
Escort Lynx (Rear Alignment)	Camber (Rear)	Decimal	−1.188	−2.038	−0.338
		Fractional	−1-3 16	−2-1 32	−11 32
		Minutes	−1.11'	−2 02'	−0 20'
	Camber Difference Side-to-Side (Left Minus Right)	Decimal	0	−1.200	+1.200
		Fractional	0	−1-7 32	+1-7 32
		Minutes	0	−1 12'	+1 12'
	Toe (Individual Sides)	Decimal Inches	+0.090"	−0.240'	+0.060'
		Fractional Inches	+3 32'	−1 4	+1 16
		Decimal Degrees	−0.180	0.280	+0.120
		Millimeters	+2.29mm	−6 10mm	+1.52mm
	Total Toe (Left Plus Right)	Decimal Inches	+0.180	−0.360'	0
		Fractional Inches	+3 16	−3 8'	0
		Decimal Degrees	+0.360	−0.720	0
		Millimeters	+4.57mm	−9 14mm	0

Escort/Lynx rear wheel alignment specifications

Ford Mercury
FRONT WHEEL DRIVE CARS—ESCORT • EXP • LYNX • TEMPO • TOPAZ • TAURUS • SABLE

SECTION 4

REAR WHEEL ALIGNMENT (CURB HEIGHT WITH 1/2 TANK OF FUEL)

Vehicle	Alignment Factors	Units	Nominals	Minimum	Maximum
Tempo Topaz ALL MODELS (Rear Alignment)	Camber (Rear) ①	Decimal Fractional Minutes	-0.281 -9/32 -0 17'	-1.031 -1-1/32 -1 02'	+0.469 +15/32 +0 28'
	Camber Difference Side-to-Side (Left Minus Right) ①	Decimal Fractional Minutes	0 0 0	-1.188 -1-3/16 -1 11'	+1.188 +1-3/16 +1 11'
	Toe (Individual Sides)	Decimal Inches Fractional Inches Decimal Degrees Millimeters	0 0 0 0	-0.250" -1/4" -0.500 -6.35mm	+0.250" +1/4" +0.500 +6.35mm
	Total Toe (Left Plus Right)	Decimal Inches Fractional Inches Decimal Degrees Millimeters	0 0 0 0	-0.250" -1/4" -0.500 -6.35mm	+0.250" +1/4" +0.500 +6.35mm

Tempo/Topaz rear wheel alignment specifications

FIELD WHEEL ALIGNMENT (CURB HEIGHT WITH A 1/2 TANK OF FUEL)

Vehicle	Alignment	Units	Nominals	Minimum	Maximum
TAURUS SEDAN (rear suspension)	Camber ①	Decimal Fractional Minutes	-0.938 -15/16 -0 56'	-1.638 -1-5/8 -1 38'	-0.238 -1/4 -0 14'
	Camber difference ① side-to-side (left minus right)	Decimal Fractional Minutes	-0- -0- -0-	-1.200 -1-7/32 -1 12'	+1.200 +1-7/32 +1 12'
	Toe (individual sides)	Decimal inches Fractional inches Decimal degrees Millimeters	+0.063" +1/16" +0.125 +1.59mm	-0.177" -11/64" -0.355 -4.50mm	+0.303" +19/64" +0.605 +7.70mm
	Total toe (left plus right)	Decimal inches Fractional inches Decimal degrees Millimeters	+0.125" +1/8" +0.250 +3.18mm	-0.205" -13/64" -0.410 -5.21mm	+0.455" +29/64" +0.910 +11.56mm
SABLE SEDAN (rear suspension)	Camber ①	Decimal Fractional Minutes	-0.875 -7/8 -0 52'	-1.575 -1-9/16 -1 35'	-0.175 -3/16 -0 10'
	Camber difference ① side-to-side (left minus right)	Decimal Fractional Minutes	-0- -0- -0-	-1.200 -1-7/32 -1 12'	+1.200 +1-7/32 +1 12'
	Toe (individual sides)	Decimal inches Fractional inches Decimal degrees Millimeters	+0.063" +1/16" +0.125 +1.59mm	-0.177" -11/64" -0.355 -4.50mm	+0.303" +19/64" +0.605 +7.70mm
	Total toe (left plus right)	Decimal inches Fractional inches Decimal degrees Millimeters	+0.125" +1/8" +0.250 +3.18mm	-0.205" -13/64" -0.410 -5.21mm	+0.455" +29/64" +0.910 +11.56mm

Taurus/Sable (Sedan) rear wheel alignment specifications

FIELD WHEEL ALIGNMENT (CURB HEIGHT WITH A 1/2 TANK OF FUEL)

Vehicle	Alignment	Units	Nominals	Minimum	Maximum
TAURUS/SABLE STATION WAGON (rear suspension)	Camber ①	Decimal Fractional Minutes	-0.938 -15/16 -0 56'	-1.638 -1-5/8 -1 38'	-0.238 -1/4 -0 14'
	Camber difference side-to-side (Left minus right)	Decimal Fractional Minutes	-0- -0- -0-	-1.200 -1-7/32 -1 12'	+1.200 +1-7/32 +1 12'
	Toe (Individual sides)	Decimal inches Fractional inches Decimal degrees Millimeters	+0.063" +1/16" +0.125 +1.59mm	-0.177" -11/64" -0.355 -4.50mm	+0.303" +19/64" +0.605 +7.70mm
①Caster and camber are factory set and cannot be adjusted.	Total toe (Left plus right)	Decimal inches Fractional inches Decimal degrees Millimeters	+0.125" +1/8" +0.250 +3.18mm	-0.205" -13/64" -0.410 -5.21mm	+0.455" +29/64" +0.910 +11.56mm

Taurus/Sable (Station wagon) rear wheel alignment specifications

SECTION 5

Ford Lincoln Mercury
REAR WHEEL DRIVE CARS

SPECIFICATIONS

Belt Tension	5–13	Piston & Ring	5–12
Brakes	24–2	Serial Number Identification	5–5
Camshaft	5–9	Torque	5–10
Capacities	5–11	Torque Sequence (Cylinder Heads)	5–61
Crankshaft & Connecting Rod	5–9	Tune-Up	5–6
Firing Order	5–7	Valve	5–8
General engien	5–6	Wheel Alignment	5–12

INDEX

A
Alternator R&R	5–13
Anti-lock Brakes	5–84
Automatic Transmission	
Adjust	5–91
On Car Service	23–2
Assembly R&R	5–90
Axle shaft R&R	5–94

B
Ball Joints	35–2
Belt Tension	5–13
Brake System	5–84
Brake Booster	5–85
Brake Caliper Overhaul	24–2
Braker Caliper R&R	24–2
Brake Drum, Rear	24–2
Brake Master cylinder	5–84
Brake Pad	
Front	24–2
Brake Shoe	
Rear	24–2

C
Camshaft R&R	5–65
Carburetor	5–39
Chassis Electrical	5–17
Clutch	5–87
Adjustment	5–87
R&R	5–87
Comgination switch R&R	5–23
Component Location	5–27
Control Arm R&R	35–2
Cooling Fan Motor	5–37
Cooling System	5–30
Cruise Control	5–29
Cylinder Head	5–61
R&R	5–61

D
Differential	28–2
Inspection	28–2
Dimmer Switch R&R	5–23
Disc Brakes	24–2
Distributor R&R	5–16
Drive Axle	28–2
Drive Belt Tension	5–13
Driveshaft R&R	5–93

E
Electric Fuel Pump	5–38
Electronic Ignition	30–2
Emissions Controls	5–48
Engine	5–50
Identification	5–5
R&R	5–50
Engine Electrical	5–16
Engine Lubrication	5–70
Engine Mechanical	5–50
Engine Mounts R&R	5–56
Exhaust Manifold R&R	5–44

F
Front Suspension	3–52
Alignment	5–12
Anti-lock Brakes	5–84
Fuel Mixture, Adjust	5–39
Fuel Pump R&R	5–37
Fuses/Circuit Breakers	5–27
Fusible Links	5–27

H
Headlight Switch	5–22
Heater Blower R&R	5–31
Heater Core R&R	5–32
Heater Control R&R	5–35
Horn Switch	5–23
High Mount Stoplight	5–21

I
Idle Speed Adjust	5–39
Ignition Switch	5–17
Ignition Timing	5–17
Instrument Cluster R&R	5–24
Intake Manifold R&R	5–42

L, M, N
Lower Control Arm R&R	35–2
Master Cylinder R&R	5–84
Manual Steering Gear R&R	5–76
Manual Transmission	
Overhaul	32–2
Manual Transmission R&R	5–87
Neutral Safety Switch R&R	5–18

O
Oil Pan R&R	5–70
Oil Pump R&R	5–70
Oil Seal R&R	
Rear Main	5–75

P
Parking Brake	5–85
Adjustment	5–85
Piston & Connecting Rod	5–66
Power Brake Unit R&R	5–85
Power Steering Pump R&R	5–79

R
Rear Main Oil seal R&R	5–75
Rear Suspension	35–2
R&R	5–50
Regulator	5–14
Rocker Shaft/Assy R&R	5–59

S
Serial Number	5–5
Engine	5–5
Vehicle	5–5
Shock Absorber R&R	
Front	35–2
Rear	35–2
Starter R&R	5–14
Starter Drive Replacement	5–14
Steering Gear R&R	5–76
Manual	5–76
Power	5–76
Steering Wheel R&R	5–76
Stoplight Switch R&R	5–20
Speedometer R&R	5–26
Suspension R&R	35–2
Service	35–2

T
Throttle Linkage, Adjust	5–93
Timing Belt R&R	5–63
Timing Chain	5–66
Timing Gear Cover	5–63
Oil Seal Replacement	5–69
Transmission Codes	5–5
Tune-Up	5–6
Turbocharger	5–47
Turn Signal Switch R&R	5–23

U, V, Y
U–Joint Overhaul	28–2
Valves, Adjust	5–57
Valve Tappette, R&R	5–59
Valve System	5–57
Voltage Regulator	5–14
Year Identification	5–3

W
Water Pump R&R	5–30
Wheel Alignment	5–12
Front	5–12
Wheel Bearings	
Front	5–80
Rear	5–94
Wheel cylinder	
Rear	24–2
Windshield Wiper	5–24
Linkage R&R	5–24
Motor R&R	5–24
Switch R&R	5–24

BEFORE SERVICING BE CERTAIN TO READ THE SAFETY NOTICE

Ford • Lincoln Mercury
1983–87 Rear Wheel Drive Cars

COUGAR • COUGAR XR7 • COLONY PARK SW
COUNTRY SQUIRE SW • CAPRI • FAIRMONT FUTURA
GRAN MARQUIS • MARQUIS • MARQUIS
BROUGHAM • LINCOLN • LINCOLN CONTINENTAL
LINCOLN TOWN CAR • LTD • MARK VI • VII • MUSTANG
MUSTANG GHIA • MUSTANG COBRA • THUNDERBIRD
ZEPHYR

YEAR IDENTIFICATION

1983–86 Capri

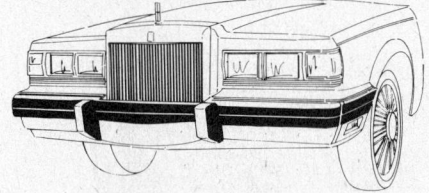
1983 Continental

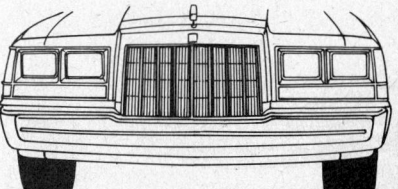
1984–85 Continental

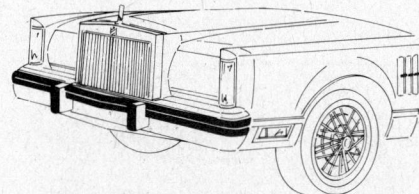
1983 Continental Mark VII LSC

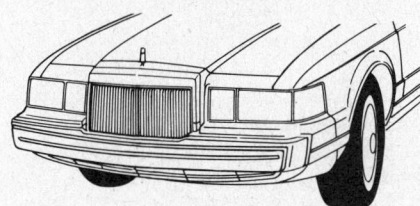
1984–86 Mark VII

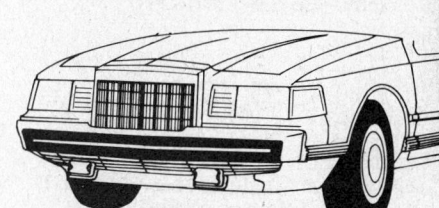
1985–86 Mark VII LSC

1987 Mark VII LSC

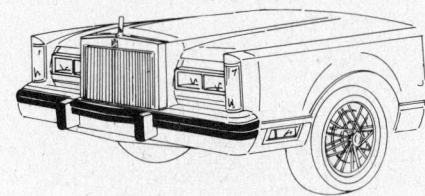
1983–84 Town Car

1985–86 Lincoln Town Car

1987 Lincoln Continental

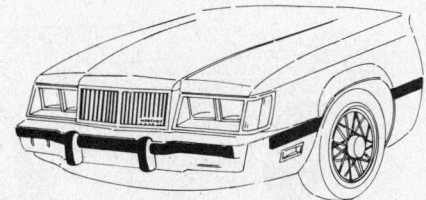
1983–86 Marquis

1983–86 Grand Marquis & Colony Park

5–3

SECTION 5

FORD LINCOLN MERCURY
REAR WHEEL DRIVE CARS

YEAR IDENTIFICATION

1983 Mustang

1984–86 Mustang

1985–86 Mustang GT

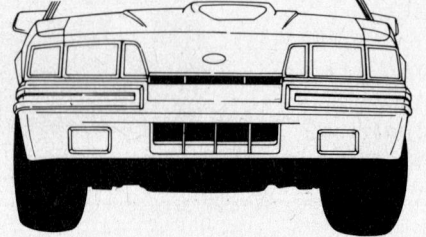
1984–86 Mustang SVO

1987 Mustang GT

1983–86 Thunderbird

1985–86 Thunderbird Turbo Coupe

1987 Thunderbird

1987 Thunderbird Turbo

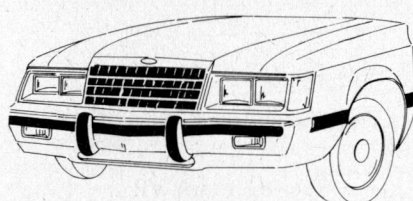
1983 LTD

1984–86 LTD

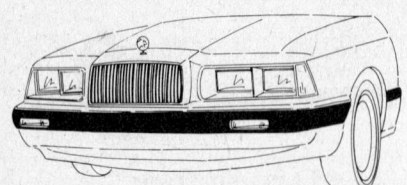
1983–86 Cougar

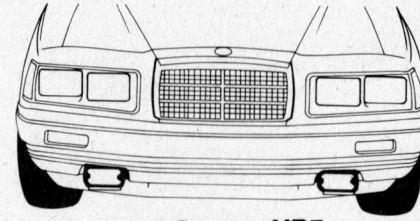
1985 Cougar XR7

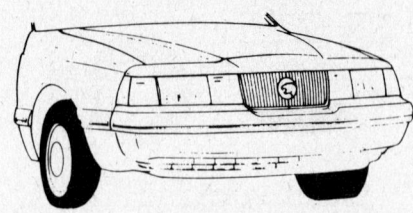
1987 Cougar

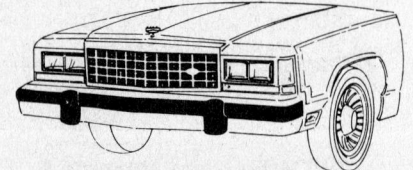
1983–86 Crown Victoria & Country Squire

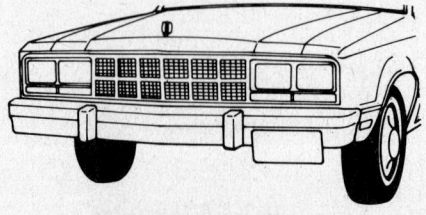
1983 Fairmont Futura

1983 Zephyr

Ford Lincoln Mercury
REAR WHEEL DRIVE CARS
SECTION 5

VEHICLE IDENTIFICATION NUMBER (VIN)

It is important for servicing and ordering parts to be certain of the vehicle and engine identification. The VIN (vehicle identification number) is a 13 or 17 digit number visible through the windshield on the driver's side of the dash and contains the vehicle and engine identification codes. It can be interpreted as follows:

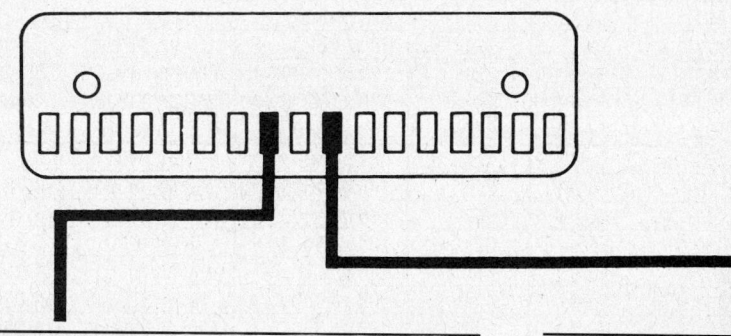

		Engine Code			
Code	Cu. In.	Liters	Cyl.	Carb.	Eng. Mfg.
A	140	2.3	4	1	Ford
W	140-T	2.3	4	Turbo.	Ford
T	140-T SVO	2.3	4	Turbo.	Ford
R	140-HSC	2.3	4	①	Ford
T,B,X	200	3.3	6	1	Ford
3	232	3.8	V6	①	Ford
C	232	3.8	V6	①	Ford
F	302	5.0	V8	1	Ford
M	302-H.O.	5.0	V8	①	Ford
G	351-W	5.8	V8	①	Ford
G	351-H.O.	5.8	V8	①	Ford

Model Year Code	
Code	Year
D	1983
E	1984
F	1985
G	1986
H	1987

The seventeen digit Vehicle Identification Number can be used to determine engine application and model year. The tenth digit indicates the model year, and the eighth digit identifies the engine code.

① EFI, VV, 2 bbl. or 4 bbl. depending on model

TRANSMISSION CODES

1.	Three speed
2.	Five speed overdrive
4.	Four speed overdrive (SROD)
5.	Five speed
5.	Five speed overdrive (RAP)
6.	Four speed (Borg Warner)
7.	Four speed overdrive (RUG)
7.	Four speed (ET) (Hummer)
C	C5 automatic
S.	JATCO automatic
T.	AOD (automatic overdrive),
ZF	ZF-4HP22
U.	C6 automatic
V.	C3 automatic
W.	C4 automatic
X.	FMX automatic
Y.	Borg Warner automatic
Z.	C6 police automatic

Refer to the vehicle certification plate on the driver's door frame for transmission identification code.

SECTION 5

Ford Lincoln Mercury
REAR WHEEL DRIVE CARS

GENERAL ENGINE SPECIFICATIONS

Year	Eng. VIN Code	Engine No. Cyl. Displacement (Cu. In.)	Eng. Mfg.	Carburetor Type	Horsepower @ rpm■	@ rpm (ft lbs)■	Bore × Stroke (in.)	Compression Ratio	Oil Pressure @ 2000 rpm
'83	A	4-140	Ford	2 bbl	88 @ 4800	118 @ 2800	3.781 × 3.126	9.0:1	40–60
	X	6-200	Ford	1 bbl ①	88 @ 3800	154 @ 1400	3.680 × 3.130	8.6:1	30–50
	3	V6-232	Ford	2 bbl	120 @ 3600	250 @ 1600	3.810 × 3.390	8.7:1	40–60
	F	8-302	Ford	EFI ②	130 @ 3200	240 @ 2000	4.000 × 3.000	8.4:1	40–60
	G	8-351	Ford	2 bbl	140 @ 3400	265 @ 2000	4.000 × 3.500	8.3:1	40–60
'84	A	4-140	Ford	1 bbl	88 @ 4000	122 @ 2400	3.781 × 3.126	9.0:1	40–60
	W	4-140-T	Ford	EFI	145 @ 4600	180 @ 3600	3.781 × 3.126	8.0:1	40–60
	T	4-140-T ③	Ford	EFI	175 @ 4400	210 @ 3000	3.781 × 3.126	8.0:1	40–60
	3	V6-232	Ford	CFI ①	120 @ 3600	250 @ 1600	3.810 × 3.390	8.7:1	40–60
	F	8-302	Ford	CFI	140 @ 3200 ④	250 @ 1600 ④	4.000 × 3.000	8.4:1	40–60
	M	8-302 HO	Ford	4 bbl	205 @ 4400	265 @ 3200	4.000 × 3.000	8.3:1	40–60
	G	8-351	Ford	2 bbl	180 @ 3600	285 @ 2400	4.000 × 3.500	8.3:1	40–60
'85	A	4-140	Ford	1 bbl	88 @ 4000	124 @ 2800	3.781 × 3.126	9.0:1	40–60
	W	4-140-T	Ford	EFI	145 @ 4600	180 @ 3600	3.781 × 3.126	8.0:1	40–60
	T	4-140-T ③	Ford	EFI	175 @ 4400	210 @ 3000	3.781 × 3.126	8.0:1	40–60
	R	4-140-H5C	Ford	1/EFI	86 @ 4000	124 @ 2800	3.781 × 3.126	9.0:1	40–60
	3	V6-232	Ford	2 bbl	120 @ 3600	250 @ 1600	3.810 × 3.390	8.7:1	40–60
	C	V6-232	Ford	CFI	120 @ 3600	250 @ 1600	3.810 × 3.390	8.7:1	40–60
	F	8-302	Ford	CFI	165 @ 3200	250 @ 1600	4.000 × 3.000	8.4:1	40–60
	M	8-302	Ford	4 bbl	210 @ 4400	265 @ 3200	4.000 × 3.000	8.3:1	40–60
	G	8-351	Ford	2 bbl	180 @ 3600	285 @ 2400	4.000 × 3.500	8.3:1	40–60
'86–'87	A	4-140	Ford	1 bbl	88 @ 4200	122 @ 2600	3.781 × 3.126	9.0:5	40–60
	T	4-140-T	Ford ⑥	EFI	145 @ 4400	180 @ 3000	3.781 × 3.126	8.0:1	40–60
	W	4-140-T	Ford ⑦	EFI	155 @ 4600	190 @ 2800	3.781 × 3.126	8.0:1	40–60
	3	V6-232	Ford	CFI ①	120 @ 3600	205 @ 1600	3.810 × 3.390	8.7:1	40–60
	F	8-302	Ford	S EFI	150 @ 3200	270 @ 2000	4.000 × 3.000	8.9:1	40–60
	M	8-302 HO	Ford	4 bbl	210 @ 4400	265 @ 3200	4.000 × 3.000	8.3:1	40–60
	G	8-351	Ford	2 bbl	180 @ 3600	285 @ 2400	4.000 × 3.500	8.3:1	40–60

① Some models are equipped with a 2-bbl carburetor
② Some Mustang/Capri models are equipped with a 4-bbl carburetor
③ SVO
④ On models equipped with dual exhaust the horsepower is 155 @ 3600 rpm and the torque is 265 @ 2000 rpm.
⑤ Some models are equipped with EFI
⑥ Manual transmission
⑦ Automatic transmission
T Turbocharger
EFI Electronic fuel injection
SEFI Sequential electronic fuel injection
HO High output
HSC High swirl combustion
CFI Central fuel injection

TUNE-UP SPECIFICATIONS

When analyzing compression test results, look for uniformity among cylinders rather than specific pressures

Year	Eng. VIN Code	Engine No. Cyl. Displacement (cu. in.)	Eng. mfg.	Spark Plugs Orig. Type	Gap (in.)•	Distributor Point Dwell (deg)	Distributor Point Gap (in.)	Ignition Timing (deg) Man. Trans.	Ignition Timing (deg) Auto. Trans.	Valves Intake Opens (deg)	Fuel Pump Pressure (psi)	Idle Speed (rpm) Man. Trans.	Idle Speed (rpm) Auto. Trans.
'83	A	4-140	Ford	AWSF-44	.044	Electronic		①	①	16	5.5–6.5	850	800
	X	6-200	Ford	BSF-92	.050	Electronic		①	①	20	6–8	600	600
	3	V-6-232	Ford	AWSF-52	.044	Electronic		①	①	13	39	550	550
	F	8-302	Ford	ASF-52 ②	.050	Electronic		①	①	16	6–8 ③	—	550
	G	8-351	Ford	ASF-42	.044	Electronic		①	①	23	6–8	—	700/600
'84	A	4-140	Ford	AWSF-44	.044	Electronic		①	①	16	5–7	850	750
	W	4-140-T	Ford	AWSF-32	.034	Electronic		①	①	—	39	①– ④	①– ④
	T	4-140-T ⑤	Ford	AWSF-32	.034	Electronic		①	①	—	39	① ④	① ④
	3	V6-232	Ford	AWSF-54	.044	Electronic		①	①	13	39	—	550
	F	8302	Ford	ASF-52	.050	Electronic		①	①	16	39	550	550
	M	8302HO	Ford	ASF-42	.044	Electronic		①	①	—	6–8	700	700
	G	8-351	Ford	ASF-42	.044	Electronic		①	①	23	6–8	—	600 ⑥

Ford Lincoln Mercury
REAR WHEEL DRIVE CARS
SECTION 5

TUNE-UP SPECIFICATIONS

When analyzing compression test results, look for uniformity among cylinders rather than specific pressures

Year	Engine Eng. VIN Code	Engine No. Cyl. Displacement (cu. in.)	Engine Eng. mfg.	Spark Plugs Orig. Type	Spark Plugs Gap (in.)•	Distributor Point Dwell (deg)	Distributor Point Gap (in.)	Ignition Timing (deg) Man. Trans.	Ignition Timing (deg) Auto. Trans.	Valves Intake Opens (deg)	Fuel Pump Pressure (psi)	Idle Speed (rpm) Man. Trans.	Idle Speed (rpm) Auto. Trans.
'85	A	4-140	Ford	AWSF-44	.044	Electronic		①	①	16	6–8	850	750
	W	4-140T	Ford	AWSF-32	.034	Electronic		①	①	—	39	750	750
	T	4-140-T ⑤	Ford	AWSF-32	.034	Electronic		①	①	—	39	①④	①④
	R	4-140-HSC	Ford	AWSF-52	.044	Electronic		①	①	—	39	800	700
	3	V6-232	Ford	AGSP-52	.044	Electronic		①	①	13	6–8	600	600
	C	V6-232	Ford	AWSF-54	.044	Electronic		①	①	13	39	—	550
	F	8-302	Ford	ASF-52	.050	Electronic		①	①	—	39	550	550
	M	8-302 HO	Ford	ASF-42	.044	Electronic		①	①	—	6–8	700	700
	G	8-351	Ford	ASF-42	.044	Electronic		①	①	—	6–8	—	600 ⑥
'86–'87	A	4-140	Ford	AWSF-44C	.044	Electronic		①	①	16	6–8	750	750
	T	4-140-T	Ford	AWSF-32C	.034	Electronic		①	①	—	39	825/975	825/975
	W	4-140-T	Ford	AWSF-32C	.034	Electronic		①	①	—	39	825/975	825/975
	3	V6-232	Ford	AWSF-54	.044	Electronic		①	①	13	39	—	550
	F	8-302	Ford	ASF-32C	.044	Electronic		①	①	—	39	①④	①④
	M	8-302 HO	Ford	ASF-42	.044	Electronic		①	①	—	6–8	700	700
	G	8-351	Ford	ASF-32C	.044	Electronic		①	①	—	6–8	650	650

NOTE: The underhood calibrations sticker often reflects tune-up specification changes made in production. Sticker figures must be used if they disagree with those in this chart.

T Turbocharger
HO High output
HSC High swirl combustion
① Calibrations vary depending upon the model; refer to the underhood calibration sticker.
② The carbureted models use spark plug ASF-42 (.044) and the idle speed rpm is 700 rpm.
③ On fuel injected models the pressure is 39 psi.
④ Electronic engine control models the ignition timing, idle speed and idle mixture is not adjustable.
⑤ SVO
⑥ 700 rpm with the VOTM on.

FIRING ORDERS

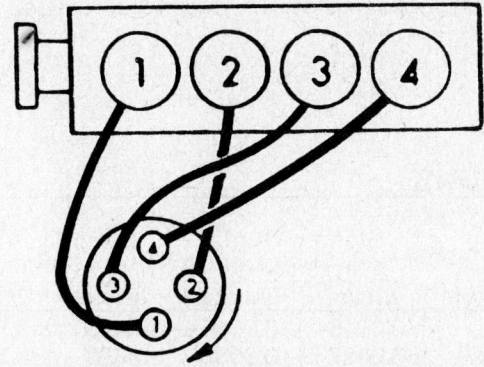

FORD MOTOR CO. 2300 cc 4-cyl.
Engine firing order: 1-3-4-2
Distributor rotation: clockwise

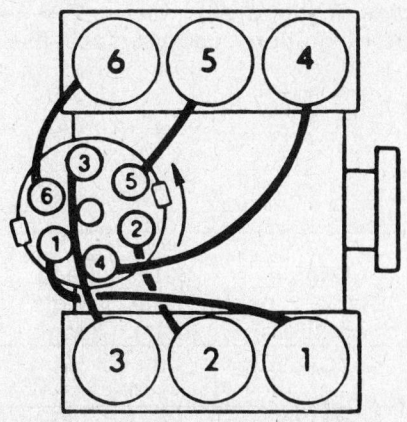

FORD MOTOR CO. 2800cc V6
Engine firing order: 1-4-2-5-3-6
Distributor rotation: Clockwise

SECTION 5: FORD LINCOLN MERCURY
REAR WHEEL DRIVE CARS

FIRING ORDERS

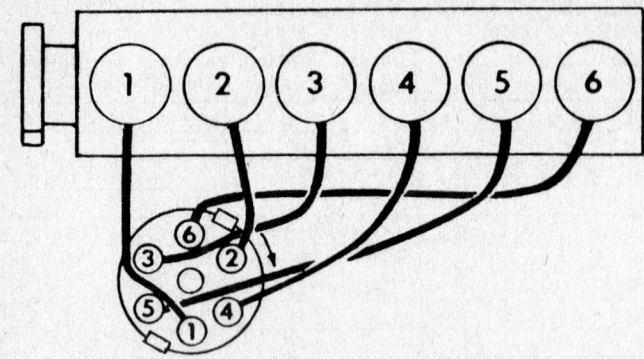

FORD MOTOR CO. 200, 250 6-cyl.
Engine firing order: 1–5–3–6–2–4
Distributor rotation: clockwise

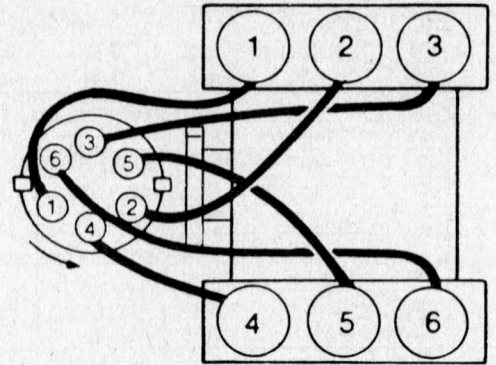

FORD MOTOR CO. 232 V6
Engine firing order 1–4–2–5–3–6
Distributor rotation: counterclockwise

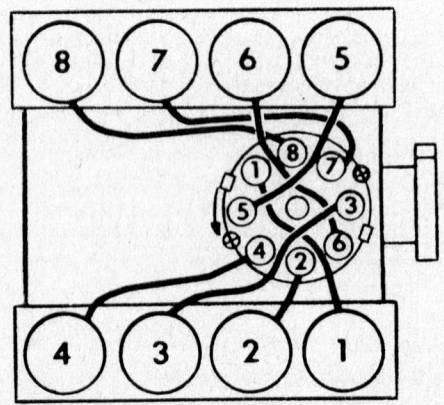

FORD MOTOR CO. 255, 302 (exc. HO) 460 V8
Engine firing order: 1–5–4–2–6–3–7–8
Distributor rotation: counterclockwise

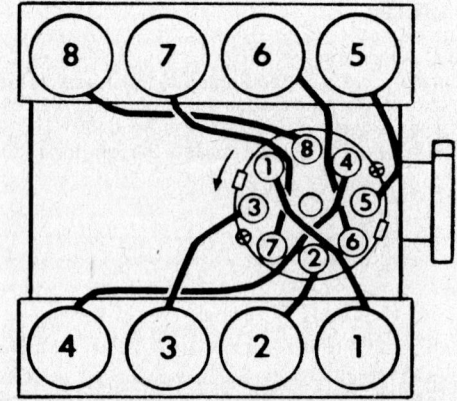

FORD MOTOR CO. 302HO, 351, 400 V8
Engine firing order: 1–3–7–2–6–5–4–8
Distributor rotation: counterclockwise

VALVE SPECIFICATIONS

Year	Engine Displacement cc (liters)	Seat Angle (deg.)	Face Angle (deg.)	Spring Test Pressure (lbs. @ in.)	Spring Installed Height (in.)	Stem-to-Guide Clearance (in.) Intake	Stem-to-Guide Clearance (in.) Exhaust	Stem Diameter (in.) Intake	Stem Diameter (in.) Exhaust
'83–'87	4-140 (2.3L)	45	44	①	1-17/32 – 1-19/32	0.0010–0.0027	0.0015–0.0032	.3416–.3423	.3411–.3418
'85	6-149 (2.4L) Diesel	45	45	②	—	0.010 Limit	0.010 Limit	—	—
'83	6-200 (3.3L)	45	44	③	1.575–1.605	0.0008–0.0025	0.0010–0.0027	.3100–.3107	.3098–.3105
'83–'87	V6-232 (3.8L)	45	44	215 @ 1.79 ④	1.70–1.78 ⑤	0.001–0.0027	0.0015–0.0032	.3423–.3716	.3418–.3411

VALVE SPECIFICATIONS

Year	Engine Displacement cc (liters)	Seat Angle (deg.)	Face Angle (deg.)	Spring Test Pressure (lbs. @ in.)	Spring Installed Height (in.)	Stem-to-Guide Clearance (in.) Intake	Stem-to-Guide Clearance (in.) Exhaust	Stem Diameter (in.) Intake	Stem Diameter (in.) Exhaust
'83-'87	8-302 (5.0L)	45	44	⑥	⑦	0.0010-0.0027	0.0015-0.0032	.3416-.3423	.3411-.3418
'83-'87	8-351 (5.8L)	45	44	⑧	⑨	0.0010-0.0027	0.0015-0.0032	.3416-.3423	.3411-.3418

NOTE: On the 2.4 liter engine the top surface of the valves must be recessed below the gasket surface of the cylinder head at the distance of 0.026-0.033 in. on the intake valves and 0.033-0.041 in. on the exhaust valves.

① Intake 71-79 @ 1.52
   Exhaust 1.52-1.56 @ 1.52
② Install spring in tool # 6513-DD or equivalent and apply torque until a click is heard and multiply the torque reading by two.
③ Intake 51-57 @ 1.59
   Exhaust 142-148 @ 1.222
④ On the 86-87 models 190 @ 1.28
⑤ On the 86-87 models the spring installed height is 2.02 in.
⑥ With the valve closed 74-82 @ 1.78
   With the valve opened 192-214 @ 1.36
⑦ Intake $1^{43}/_{64}-1^{45}/_{64}$
   Exhaust $1^{37}/_{64}-1^{41}/_{64}$
⑧ With the valve closed 71-79 @ 1.60
   With the valve opened 195-215 @ 1.05
⑨ Intake $1^{48}/_{64}-1^{58}/_{64}$
   Exhaust $1^{37}/_{64}-1^{41}/_{64}$

CAMSHAFT SPECIFICATIONS

All measurements in inches

Engine	Journal Diameter 1	Journal Diameter 2	Journal Diameter 3	Journal Diameter 4	Journal Diameter 5	Bearing Clearance	Lobe Lift Intake	Lobe Lift Exhaust	Endplay
4-140 (2.3L)	1.7713-1.7720	1.7713-1.7720	1.7713-1.7720	1.7713-1.7720		.001-.003	.2437 ①	.2437 ①	.001-.007
6-149 (2.4L) Diesel	1.2582-1.2589	1.2582-1.2589	1.2582-1.2589	1.2582-1.2589	1.2582-1.2589	.0039	.374	.376	—
6-200 (3.3L)	1.8095-1.8105	1.8095-1.8105	1.8095-1.8105	1.8095-1.8105		.001-.003	.245	.245	.001-.007
V6-232 (3.8L)	2.0515-2.0505	2.0515-2.0505	2.0515-2.0505	2.0515-2.0505		.001-.003	.240	.241	②
8-302 (5.0L)	2.0805-2.0815	2.0655-2.0665	2.0505-2.0515	2.0355-2.0365	2.0205-2.0215	.001-.003	.2375 ③	.2474 ③	.001-.007
8-351W (5.8L)	2.0805-2.0815	2.0655-2.0665	2.0505-2.0515	2.0355-2.0365	2.0205-2.0205	.001-.003	.2780	.2830	.001-.007

① On the 84 models the lobe lift is .2381 on the intake and exhaust and on the 85-87 models the lobe lift is .400 on the intake and exhaust.
② The endplay is controlled by the button and spring on the camshaft end.
③ On the 83-85 HO engine the intake lobe lift is .2600 and the exhaust is .2780.
   On the 86-87 HO engine the intake lobe lift is .278 and the exhaust is .2780.

CRANKSHAFT AND CONNECTING ROD SPECIFICATIONS

All measurements are given in inches

Year	Engine No. Cyl. Displacement (cu. in.)	Crankshaft Main Brg. Journal Dia	Crankshaft Main Brg. Oil Clearance	Crankshaft Shaft End-Play	Crankshaft Thrust on No.	Connecting Rod Journal Diameter	Connecting Rod Oil Clearance	Connecting Rod Side Clearance
'83	6-200	2.2982-2.2490	.0008-.0015	.004-.008	5	2.1232-2.1240	.0008-.0015	.0035-.0105
'83-'87	4-140	2.3990-2.3982	.0008-.0015	.004-.008	3	2.1232-2.1240	.0008-.0015	.0035-.0105
'83-'87	V6-232	2.5190-2.5198-	.001-.0014-	.004-.008	3	2.3103-2.3111	.001-.0014	.0047-.0114

Ford Lincoln Mercury
REAR WHEEL DRIVE CARS

CRANKSHAFT AND CONNECTING ROD SPECIFICATIONS
All measurements are given in inches

Year	Engine No. Cyl. Displacement (cu. in.)	Crankshaft Main Brg. Journal Dia	Crankshaft Main Brg. Oil Clearance	Crankshaft Shaft End-Play	Crankshaft Thrust on No.	Connecting Rod Journal Diameter	Connecting Rod Oil Clearance	Connecting Rod Side Clearance
'83–'87	8-302	2.2490–2.2482	.0004–.0015 ①	.004–.008	3	2.1228–2.1236	.0008–.0024	.010–.020
'83–'87	8-351	2.9994–3.0002	.0008–.0015	.004–.008	3	2.3103–2.3111	.0007–.0025	.010–.020
'85	6-149 Diesel	②	.0008–.0018	.003–.006	6	—	.0008–.0020	.0024–.0055

① On the 83-84 models the oil clearance for the number one main bearing is .0004–.0025
② Yellow 2.3615–2.3618 Green 2.3613–2.3615 White 2.3610–2.3612

TORQUE SPECIFICATIONS
All readings in ft. lbs.

Year	Engine No. Cyl. Displacement (cu in.)	Cylinder Head Bolts ①	Rod Bolts ①	Main Bolts ①	Crankshaft Pulley or Damper Bolt	Flywheel to Crankshaft Bolts ①	Manifold Intake ①	Manifold Exhaust ①
'83	6-200	70–75	21–26	60–70	85–100	75–85	—	18–24
'83–'87	4-140	80–90	30–36	80–90	100–120	54–64	14–21	16–23
'83–'87	V6-232	②	31–36	65–81	93–121	54–64	18 ③	15–22
'83–'87	8-302	65–72 ④	19–24	60–70	70–90	75–85	23–25	18–24
'83–'87	8-351	105–112	40–45	95–105	70–90	75–85	23–25	18–24
'85	6-149 Diesel	⑤	⑥	43–48	282–311	77–85 ⑦	14–17	14–17

① Torque the bolts in three progressive steps.
② On the 83 to 85 models torque the bolts in four progressive steps to reach a final torque of 59 ft. lbs. On the 86 and later models torque the bolts the same way to reach a final torque of 74 ft. lbs. On all models after the final torque is reached, back off all bolts 2–3 revolutions.
③ On the 84 and later models torque the bolt in three progressive steps to 24 ft. lbs.
④ After assembly retorque with the engine hot.
⑤ Torque the bolts to 22–29 ft. lbs. then to 36–43 ft. lbs. then to 73 ± 3° ft. lbs. After the third step, run the engine for 25 minutes and then put the final torque of 90 ± 5° ft. lbs.
⑥ On the first step torque the bolts to 14 ft. lbs. and on the second step torque the bolts to 70° ft. lbs.
⑦ Apply a suitable thread sealer to the bolts before installation.

CAPACITIES
Mid Size Models

Year	Engine No. Cyl. Displacement (Cu. In.)	Engine Crankcase Add 1 Qt For New Filter	Transmission Pts-to-Refill After Draining Manual 3-Speed	Transmission Pts-to-Refill After Draining Manual 4/5-Speed	Automatic (Total Capacity)	Drive Axle (pts)	Gasoline Tank (gals)	Cooling System (qts) With Heater	Cooling System (qts) With A/C
'83	Cougar XR-7, Thunderbird, Lincoln Continental								
	6-200	4	—	—	22	3.25 ④	21	8.4	8.5
	6-232	4	—	—	24	3.25 ④	21 ①	10.7	10.8
	8-302	4	—	—	24	3.25 ④	22.6	13.0	13.4
'83	Fairmont Futura								
	4-140	4	—	4 ⑦	16	3.25 ④	16	8.6	9.4
	6-200	4	—	—	22	3.25 ④	16	8.4	8.4
'83–'84	LTD/Marquis								
	4-140	4	—	4 ⑦	16	3.25 ④	16	8.6	9.4
	4-140P	4	—	4 ⑦	16	3.25 ④	24	8.6	9.4
	6-200	4	—	—	22	3.25 ④	16	8.4	8.5
	6-232	4	—	—	22 ⑤	3.25 ④	16	10.7	10.8

Ford Lincoln Mercury
REAR WHEEL DRIVE CARS
SECTION 5

CAPACITIES
Mid Size Models

Year	Engine No. Cyl. Displacement (Cu. In.)	Engine Crankcase Add 1 Qt For New Filter	Transmission Pts-to-Refill After Draining — Manual 3-Speed	Transmission Pts-to-Refill After Draining — Manual 4/5-Speed	Automatic (Total Capacity)	Drive Axle (pts)	Gasoline Tank (gals)	Cooling System (qts) With Heater	Cooling System (qts) With A/C
'83–'84	Mustang/Capri								
	4-140	⑥	—	4 ⑦	16	3.25 ④	15.4	8.6	9.4 ⑤
	6-232	4	—	—	22	3.25 ④	15.4	8.4	8.4
	8-302	4	—	4.5	—	3.55	15.4	13.1	13.4
'83–'84	Thunderbird, Cougar Continental								
	4-140 Turbo	4.5 ⑥	—	4.75	—	3.25 ④	18	8.4	8.7
	6-232	4	—	—	22 ⑤	3.25 ④	21	10.4	10.7
	8-302	4	—	—	22 ⑤	3.25 ④	20.7 ㊲	13.3	13.4
	6-149 Diesel	7.1	—	—	12	3.5	26.6	11.8	12
'85–'87	LTD/Marquis								
	4-140	4	—	—	16 ⑧	3.5 ④	16 ⑨	10.0	9.6
	4-140P	4	—	—	16 ⑧	3.5 ④	—	10.0	9.6
	6-232	4	—	—	22 ⑩	3.5 ④	16 ⑨	11.0	11.0
	8-302	4	—	—	24	3.5 ④	16 ⑨	13.7	13.7
'85–'87	Mustang/Capri								
	4-140	4	—	2.8/5.6	16 ⑧	3.5 ④	15.4	10.4	10.2
	6-232	4	—	2.8/5.6	22 ⑩	3.5 ④	15.4	11.5	11.5
	8-302	4	—	5.0	24	3.5 ④	15.4	14.1	14.1
'85–'87	Thunderbird, Cougar Continental								
	4-140 Turbo	4.5 ⑥	—	2.8/5.6	16 ⑧	3.5 ④	18.0	10.0	10.0
	6-232	4	—	2.8/5.6	22 ⑩	3.5 ④	18.8	11.7	11.7
	8-302	4	—	5.0	24	3.5 ④	18.8 ㊲	14.1	14.1

T—Turbocharged
P—Propane
N/A—Specs not available at time of printing
① Continental; 20 gals std; 22.6 optional
② 6.75 in. axle-2.5 pts; 7.5 in. axle-3.5 pts
③ 20 gals optional
④ Traction-Lok; 3.55 pts
⑤ AOD transmission; 24 pts
⑥ 4.5 Turbo add .5 with filter
⑦ 5 speed transmission; 4.75 pts
㊲ 22.3 Continental
⑧ ATX—18 pints
 AOT—25 pints
⑨ LTD/Marquis, the optional sedan is 20 gallons the Crown Victoria and Grand Marquis with the 5.0L engine is 18 gallons
⑩ AOT—24 pints

CAPACITIES
Full Size Models

Year	Engine No. Cyl. Displacement (Cu. In.)	Engine Crankcase Add 1 Qt For New Filter	Automatic Transmission (Total capacity)	Drive Axle (pts)	Gasoline Tank (gals)	Cooling System With Heater	Cooling System With A/C
'83–'87	8-302	4	24	①	22.3	14.1	14.1
'83–'87	8-351	4	24	①	20.0	15.1	15.1

① 7.5 inch axle—3.5
 8.5 inch axle—4.0
add 4 ounces on all models equipped with Traction-Lok differentials.

5–11

SECTION 5: Ford Lincoln Mercury — Rear Wheel Drive Cars

WHEEL ALIGNMENT SPECIFICATIONS

Year	Model	Caster Range (deg)	Caster Pref. Setting (deg)	Camber Range (deg)	Camber Pref. Setting (deg)	Toe-in (in.)	Steering Axis Inclin. (deg)	Wheel Pivot Ratio (deg) Inner Wheel	Wheel Pivot Ratio (deg) Outer Wheel
'83	Fairmont, Futura Zephyr	1/8P to 2 1/8P	1 1/8P	15/16N to 1 13/16P	7/16P	1/16 to 5/16	15 23/32	20	19 27/32
'83	Cougar XR7 Thunderbird	1/2P to 2P	1 1/4P	1/2N to 1P	1/4P	1/16 to 5/16	15 23/32	20	19 23/32
'83–'84	LTD, Marquis (Sedan)	1/8P to 2 1/8P	1 1/8P	15/16N to 1 13/16P	7/16P	1/16 to 5/16	15 23/32	20	19 27/32
'83–'84	LTD, Marquis (Wagon)	1/8N to 1 7/8P	1P	1/4N to 1 1/4P	1/2P	1/16 to 5/16	15 23/32	20	19 27/32
'85–'87	LTD, Marquis (Sedan)	1/8P to 2 1/8P	7/8P	3/8N to 1 1/8P	3/8P	1/16 to 5/16	15 23/32	20	19 27/32
'85–'87	LTD, Marquis (Wagon)	0P to 2P	3/4P	15/16N to 1 13/16P	7/16P	1/16 to 5/16	15 23/32	20	19 27/32
'83–'84	Mustang/Capri	1/2P to 2P	1 1/4P	3/4N to 3/4P	0P	1/16 to 5/16	15 23/32	20	19 27/32
'85–'87	Mustang/Capri	1/4P to 1 3/4P	1P	3/4N to 3/4P	0P	1/16 to 5/16	15 23/32	20	19 27/32
'84	Thunderbird Cougar	1/4P to 1 3/4P	1P	1/2N to 1P	1/4P	1/16 to 5/16	15 23/32	20	19 23/32
'85–'87	Thunderbird Cougar	0P to 1 1/2P	3/4P	1/2N to 1P	1/4P	1/16 to 5/16	15 23/32	20	19 23/32
'83	Continental	3/8P to 2 1/8P	1 1/4P	1/2N to 1 1/4P	3/8P	0 to 1/4	N/A	20	19 1/8
'84	Continental Mark VII ①	7/8P to 2 15/16P	1 3/4P	7/8N to 7/8P	0P	0 to 1/4	11	20	17 1/8
'85–'87	Continental Mark VII ①	5/8P to 2 3/4P	1 1/2P	3/4N to 3/4P	0P	0 to 1/4	11	20	17 1/8
'83–'87	Town Car Mark VI ②	2 1/4P to 4P	3P	1/4N to 1 1/4P	1/2P	1/16 to 3/16	11	20	18 1/2
'83–'87	Ford/Mercury ②	2 1/4P to 4P	3P	1/4N to 1 1/4P	1/2P	1/16 to 3/16	11	20	18 1/2

① Set the vehicle height before making the alignment check.
② On the 84 models the caster range is 2 3/8P to 4 1/8P and the preferred setting is 3 1/8P.

PISTON AND RING SPECIFICATIONS

All measurements in inches

Engine Displacement (cu. in.)	Piston Clearance	Ring Gap Top Compression	Ring Gap Bottom Compression	Ring Gap Oil ① Control	Ring Side Clearance Top Compression	Ring Side Clearance Bottom Compression	Oil Control	Wear Limit
4-140 (2.3L)	0.0014–0.0022	.010–.020	.010–.020	.015–.005	.002–.004	.002–.004	Snug	.006
4-140 (2.3L) ('83–'87 Turbo)	0.0030–0.0038	.010–.020	.010–.020	.015–.005	.002–.004	.002–.004	Snug	.006
6-200 (3.3L)	0.0013–0.0021	.008–.016	.008–.016	.015–.055	.002–.004	.002–.004	Snug	.006
6-232 (3.8L)	0.0014–0.0022 ②	.010–.020	.010–.020	.015–.055	.002–.004	.002–.004	Snug	.006
302 (5.0L) 351W (5.8L)	0.0018–0.0026	.010–.020	.010–.020	.015–.055	.002–.004	.002–.004	Snug	.006
6-149 (2.4L) Diesel	.0010–.0021	.008–.160	.008–.016	.010–.020	.0024–.0055	.0020–.0031	Snug	.006

① Steel rails
② 84 and later 0.0014–0.0032

Ford Lincoln Mercury
REAR WHEEL DRIVE CARS
SECTION 5

ELECTRICAL SECTION

For Overhaul Procedures Refer to Unit Repair Section

Charging System
ALTERNATOR

Removal and Installation

1983-84

NOTE: These models are equipped with either a side terminal or a rear terminal alternator. Removal and installation procedures are the same for both.

1. Disconnect the negative battery cable.
2. Loosen the alternator mounting bolts, remove the alternator to adjusting arm bolt and remove the belt. On models with serpentine belt, lever the tensioner away from the belt.
3. Remove the alternator mounting bolt and spacer, position the alternator so that the wire connectors can be disconnected (label the wires before disconnecting them) and remove the alternator.

4. Reverse the above procedure to reinstall, applying pressure only to the front of the alternator housing when tightening the drive belt. The belt should deflect ¼ to ½ in. between the longest span of pulleys when properly tensioned.

NOTE: Some 1983 and later vehicles with optional automatic overdrive (AOD) transmission and air conditioning are equipped with a 5-rib or 6-rib K-section (V-ribbed) belt and an automatic absorber. A special tool must be fabricated to remove the tension from the absorber assembly arm so that the belt can be removed and installed. Loosen the idler pulley pivot and adjustment bolts before using tool to remove belt.

5. On Mustangs and Capris with the 302 V8 and V6-3.8L engine equipped cars, install the alternator to the bracket, attach the electrical connectors, slide the serpentine belt over the alternator pulley, and release the automatic tensioner. On models equipped with AOD transmission and air conditioning, install the belt over the crankshaft, A/C and absorber pulleys, then place the absorber arm deflection tool on the arm and

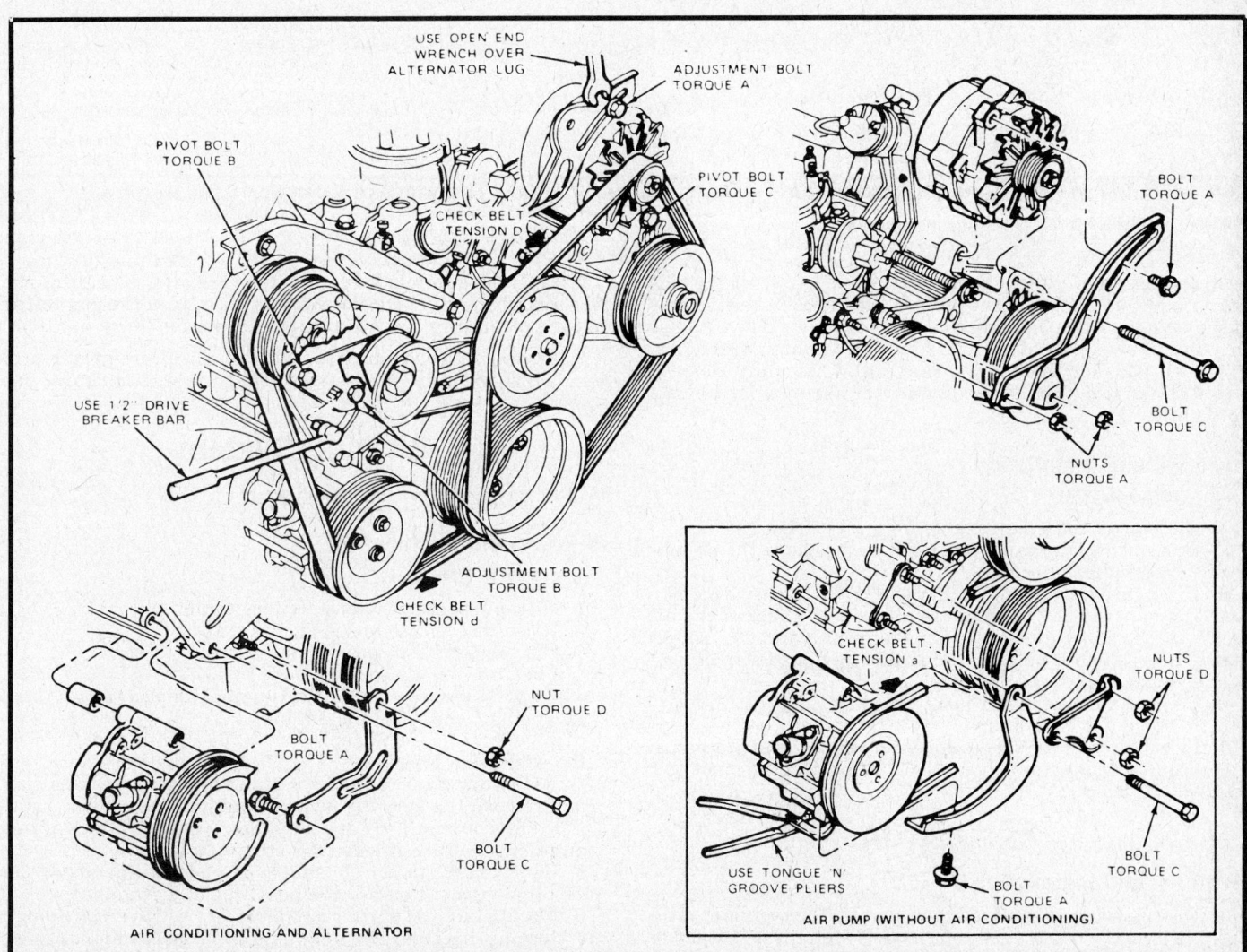

Belt installation and tension adjustment—Lincoln Town Car, Ford Crown Victoria/Mercury Grand Marquis, 5.0L and 5.8L engines (©Ford Motor Co.)

SECTION 5

Ford Lincoln Mercury
REAR WHEEL DRIVE CARS

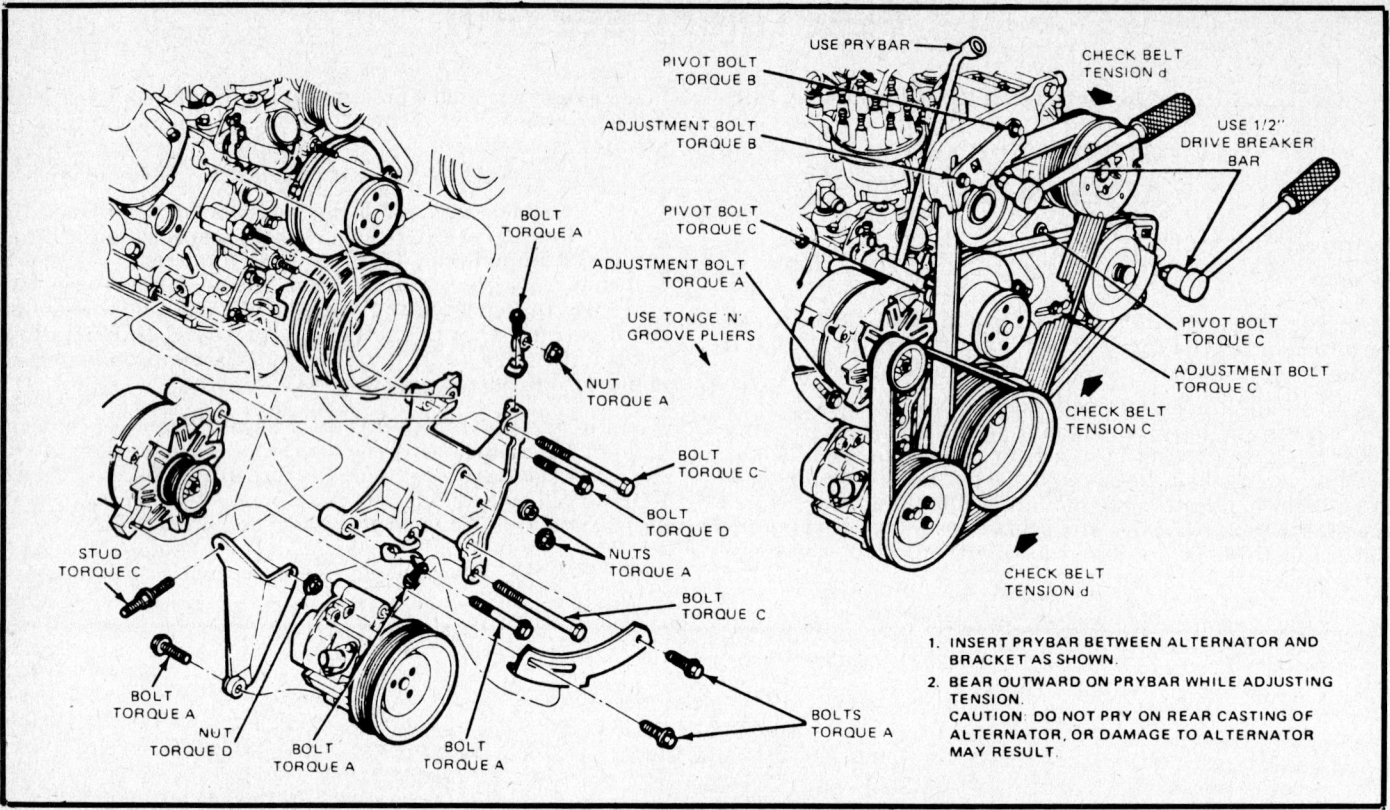

Belt installation and tension adjustments—Mark VII/Continental, Thunderbird/Cougar, 5.0L engine (©Ford Motor Co.)

push the absorber pulley downward to the bottom of the slot (never push on the ribs of the pulley). Fit the belt over the rest of the pulleys. While holding the absorber pulley down, adjust the idler pulley by hand until it is snug and tighten the adjustment bolt and pivot bolt on the idler pulley assembly. Release the deflection tool. The proper tension will be set automatically.

Removal and Installation
1985 AND LATER

1. Disconnect the ground cable from the battery.
2. Loosen the alternator pivot bolt and remove the adjustment arm-to-alternator bolt.
3. Disengage the alternator drive belt from the drive pulley.
4. Disconnect the wiring terminals from the back of the alternator. The stator and field wiring terminals are the push-on type. The push-on type terminal should be pulled straight off the terminal to prevent damage.
5. Remove the alternator pivot bolt.
6. Remove the alternator.
7. Installation is the reverse order of the removal procedure and torque the adjuster bolt to 24–34 ft. lbs. and the pivot bolt to 40–50 ft. lbs.

REGULATOR

Removal and Installation

1. Disconnect the negative battery cable. The regulator is located behind the battery on some models and it is necessary to remove the battery to remove the regulator.
2. Remove the regulator mounting screws, unlock the wire connectors, and remove the regulator.

NOTE: All models have electronic voltage regulators. Always disconnect the connector plug from the regulator before removing the mounting screws on these models.

3. Reverse the procedure to reinstall. On elecro-mechanical regulators, the radio suppression condenser mounts under one screw.

Starting System

STARTER

Removal and Installation
GASOLINE ENGINES

1. Disconnect the negative battery cable.
2. Raise the vehicle and support it safely.
3. Disconnect the starter cable from the starter.
4. Continue as follows:
    a. On Granada with 302 CID engine, remove the right engine mount and raise the engine.
    b. On Fairmont and Zephyr with 200 CID engines, remove the wish-bone brace.
    c. On Mustang, crossmember from under the bell housing and remove the steering gear assembly from the side rail.
    d. On Thunderbirds and Cougars, XR-7s, LTDs Marquis and Continentals, remove the cross brace.
5. Remove the starter housing bolts and crossmember from under the engine. Remove the heat shield, if equipped.
6. Manipulate the starter so that it can be lowered through the steering linkage. On some engine/chassis combinations, this can be accomplished by turning the front wheels either right or left, or by removing the idler arm bracket attaching bolts and lowering the steering linkage away from the engine.

7. Installation of the starter assembly is the reverse of the removal procedure.

2.4 LITER DIESEL

1. Disconnect battery ground cables.
2. Raise vehicle on hoist.
3. Remove starter motor retaining bolts.
4. Lower vehicle from hoist.
5. Disconnect starter motor relay to solenoid wire assembly.
6. Remove oil level indicator tube assembly retaining bolts.
7. Disconnect accelerator pedal to carburetor throttle cable assembly.
8. Remove starter motor.
9. Installation is the reverse order of removal procedure, torque the starter bolts to 40–47 ft. lbs. (54–63 Nm).

Ignition System

Ford utilizes a solid state or breakerless ignition system on all engines. This system eliminates the contact breaker points, replacing them with a permanent magnet, low voltage genera-

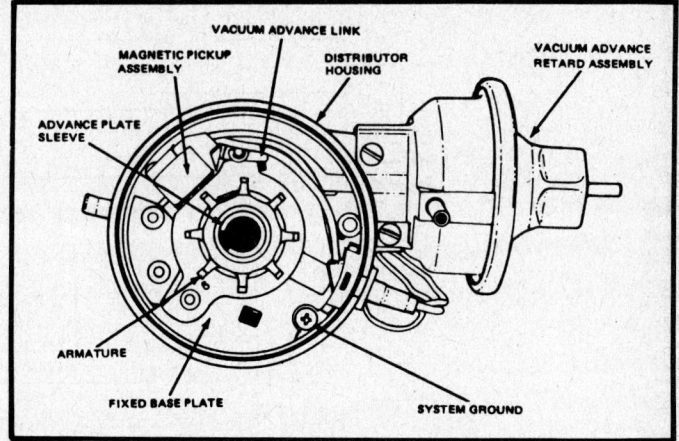

Breakerless ignition distributor used with the eight cylinder engines (©Ford Motor Co.)

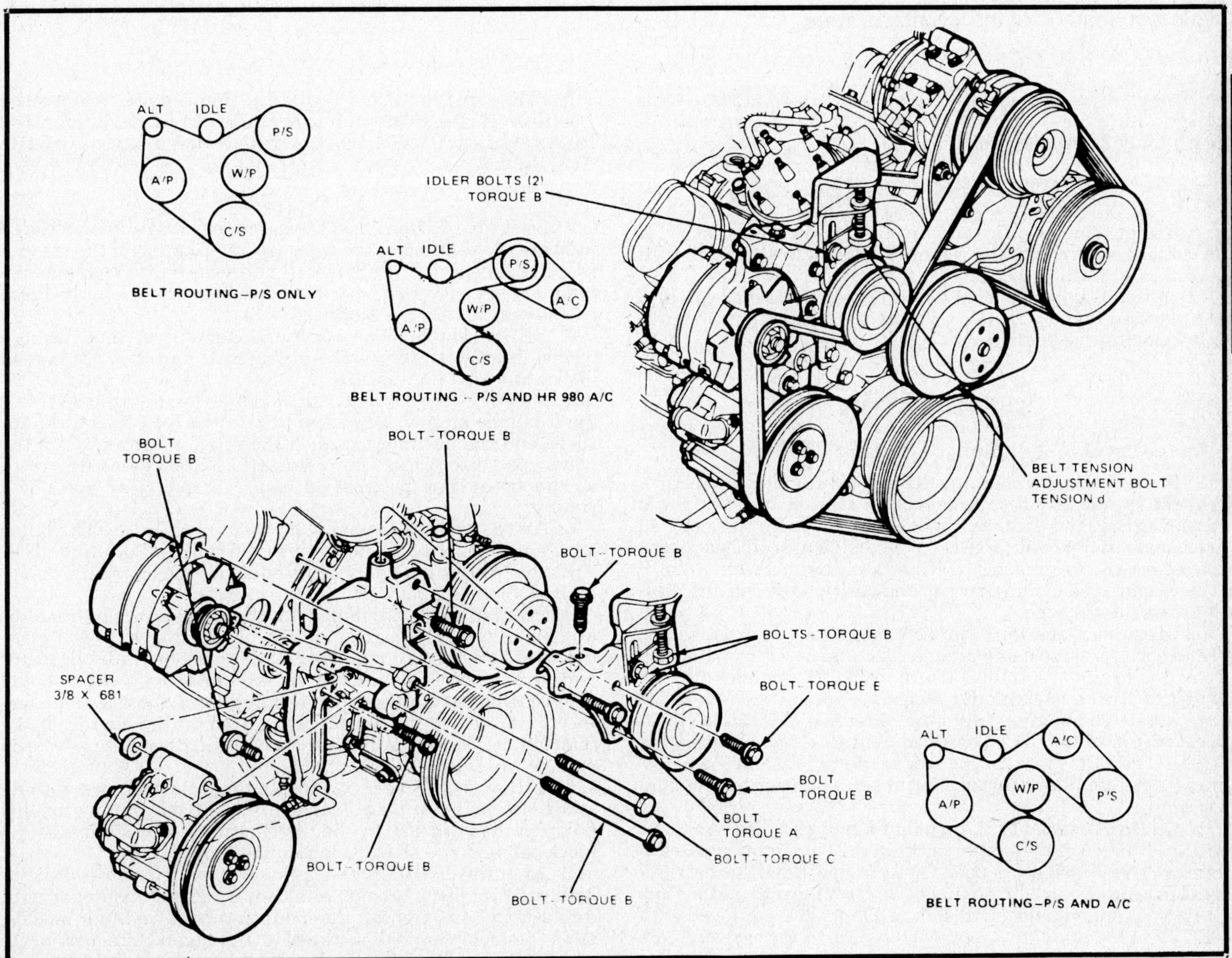

Belt installation and tension adjustments—3.8L engine (©Ford Motor Co.)

Ford Lincoln Mercury
REAR WHEEL DRIVE CARS

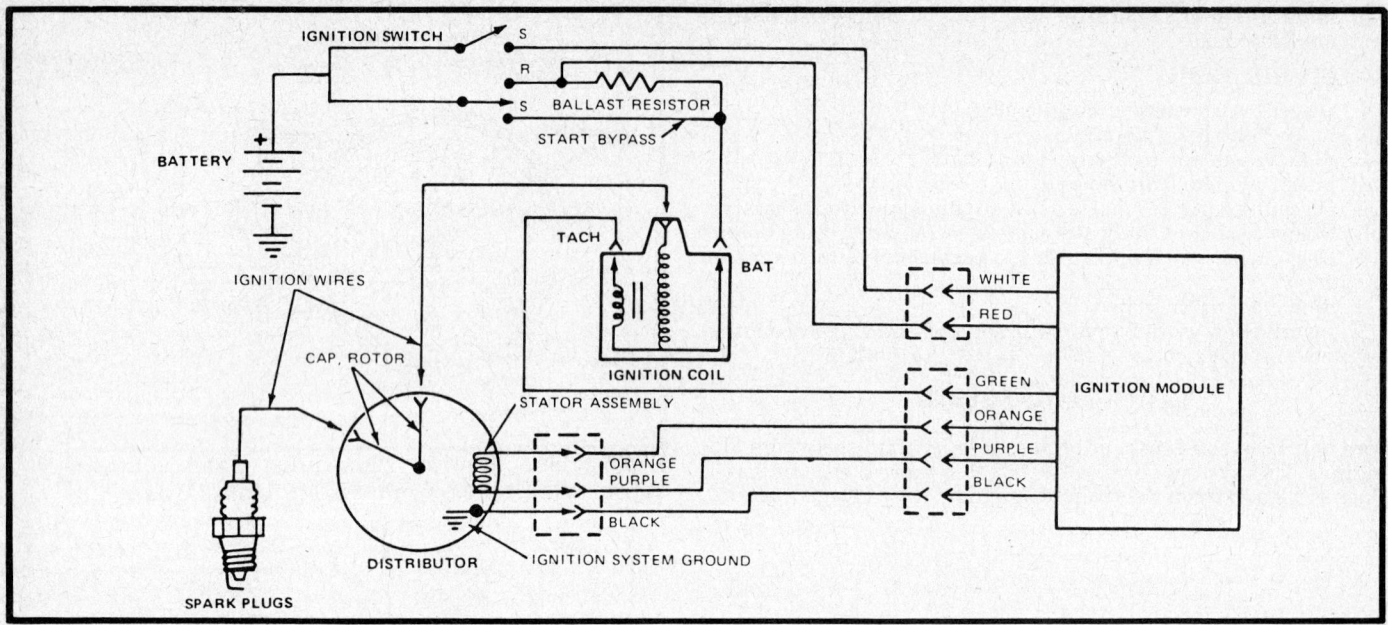

Typical schematic of the ignition system

tor. Complete service information for the Ford Solid State Ignition and Dura Spark ignition can be found in the Electronic Ignition Unit Repair Section.

TACHOMETER CONNECTION

Install a tachometer alligator clip into the Tach Test cavity. If the coil connector must be removed, grasp the wires and pull horizontally until it disconnects from the terminals.

An alligator type clip from the tachometer test lead can also be connected to the DEC (Distributor Electronic Control) without removing the connector.

DISTRIBUTOR

Removal and Installation

1. Remove the air cleaner on V6 and V8 engines. On 4 and 6 cylinder in-line engines, removal of a thermactor (air) pump mounting bolt and drive belt will allow the pump to be moved to the side and permit access to the distributor. If necessary, disconnect the thermactor air filter and lines as well.
2. Remove the distributor cap and position the cap and ignition wires to the side.
3. Disconnect the wire harness plug from the distributor connector. Disconnect and plug the vacuum hoses from the vacuum diaphragm assembly. (DuraSpark III systems are not equipped with a vacuum diaphragm).
4. Rotate the engine (in normal direction of rotation) until No. 1 piston is on TDC (Top Dead Center) of the compression stroke. The TDC mark on the crankshaft pulley and the pointer should align. Rotor tip pointing at No. 1 position on distributor cap.
5. On Dura Spark I or II, turn the engine a slight bit more (if required) to align the stator (pick-up coil) assembly pole with an (the closest) armature pole. On Dura Spark III, the distributor sleeve groove (when looking down from the top) and the cap adaptor alignment slot should align. On models equipped with EEC IV (1984 and later), remove the rotor (2 screws) and note the position of the "polarizing square" and shaft plate for reinstallation reference.

NOTE: On the EEC-IV system make sure to note the position of the shaft plate, armature and rotor locating holes, this will aid in the in the installation of the distributor.

6. Scribe a mark on the distributor body and engine block to indicate the position of the rotor tip and position of the distributor in the engine. DuraSpark III and some EEC IV system distributors are equipped with a notched base and will only locate at one position on the engine.
7. Remove the holddown bolt and clamp located at the base of the distributor. (Some Dura Spark III and EEC IV system distributors are equipped with a special holddown bolt that requires a Torx® head wrench for removal. Remove the distributor from the engine. Pay attention to the direction the rotor turns and the position to which the rotor tip points when the drive gear disengages. For reinstallation purposes, the rotor should be at this position to insure proper gear mesh and timing.
8. Avoid turning the engine if possible, while the distributor is removed. If the engine is turned from TDC position, TDC timing marks will have to be reset before the distributor is installed; Steps 4 and 5.
9. Position the distributor in the engine with the rotor aligned to the marks made on the distributor, or to the place the rotor pointed when the distributor was removed. The stator and armature or "polarizing square" and shaft plate should also be aligned. Engage the oil pump intermediate shaft and insert the distributor until fully seated on the engine. If the distributor does not fully seat, turn the engine slightly to fully engage the intermediate shaft.
10. Follow the above procedures on models equipped with an indexed distributor base. Make sure when positioning the distributor that the slot in the distributor base will engage the block tab and the sleeve/adaptor slots are aligned.
11. After the distributor has been fully seated on the block install the hold down bracket and bolt. On models equipped with an indexed base, tighten the mounting bolt. On other models, snug the mounting bolt so the distributor can be turned for ignition timing purposes.
12. The rest of the installation is in the reverse order of re-

moval. Check and reset the ignition timing on the applicable models.

NOTE: A silicone compound is used on rotor tips, distributor cap contacts and on the inside of the connectors on the spark plugs cable and module couplers. Always apply Silicone Dielectric Compound after servicing any component of the ignition system. Various models use a multi-point rotor which do not require the application of dielectric compound.

IGNITION RETIMING

ENGINE CRANKED WITH DISTRIBUTOR OUT

1. Rotate the engine until No. 1 piston is on TDC of the compression stroke.
2. Align the correct initial timing mark with the pointer.
3. Position the distributor in the block with one of the armature segments aligned with the stator tooth and the rotor at No. 1 firing position.
4. Be sure that the oil pump intermediate shaft properly engages the distributor shaft. Install, but do not tighten, the distributor clamp bolt.
5. Rotate the distributor to advance the timing to a point where the armature tooth is properly aligned. Tighten the clamp.
6. Connect the distributor wiring and check the timing.

IGNITION TIMING

NOTE: Some engines have monolithic timing, set at the factory. The monolithic system uses a timing receptacle on the front of the engine which can be connected to digital read-out equipment, which electronically determines timing. Timing can also be adjusted in the conventional way. Many models are equipped with EEC engine controls. All ignition timing is controlled by the EEC module. Initial ignition timing is not adjustable and no attempt at adjustment should be made on EEC III models, or models equipped with an indexed distributor base. for a description of EEC systems, refer to the Unit Repair sections on "Electronic Ignition Systems" and on "Engine Controls."
NOTE:
Requirements vary from model to model. Always refer to the "Emissions Specifications Sticker" for exact timing procedures.

1. Locate the timing marks and pointer on the lower engine pulley and engine's front cover.
2. Clean the marks and apply chalk or bright-colored paint to the pointer.
3. If the ignition module has (–12A244–) as a basic part number, disconnect the two wire connector (yellow and black wires). On engines equipped with the EEC IV system, disconnect the single white (black on some models) wire connector near the distributor.
4. Attach a timing light and tachometer according to manufacturer's specifications.
5. disconnect and plug all vacuum lines leading to the distributor.
6. Start the engine, allow it to warm to normal operating temperature, then set the idle to the specifications given on the underhood sticker (for timing).
7. On models equipped with the module mentioned in Step 3, jumper the pins in the module connector for the yellow and black wires.
8. Aim the timing light at the timing mark and pointer on the front of the engine. If the marks align when the timing light flashes, remove the timing light, set the idle to its proper specification, and connect the vacuum lines at the distributor. If the marks do not align when the light flashes, turn the engine off and loosen the distributor holddown clamp slightly.

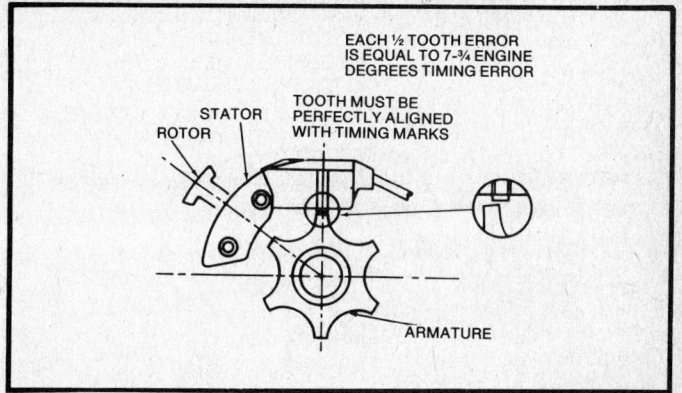

Rotor static timing position, electronic distributor (©Ford Motor Co.)

9. Start the engine again, and observe the alignment of the timing marks. To advance the timing, turn the distributor counterclockwise, on six cylinder engines except the 232 (3.8L) V6, or clockwise, for the 232 (3.8L) V6 and V8 engines. When altering the timing, it is wise to tap the distributor lightly with a wooden hammer handle to move it in the desired direction. Grasping the distributor with your hand may result in a painful electric shock. When the timing marks are aligned, turn the engine off and tighten the distributor holddown clamp. Remove the test equipment, reconnect the vacuum hoses and white (black) single wire connector (EEC IV).
10. On models equipped with the module mentioned in Step 3, remove the jumper connected in Step 7 and reconnect the two wire connector. Test the module operation as follows:
   a. Disconnect and plug the vacuum source hose to the ignition timing vacuum switch.
   b. Using an external vacuum source, apply vacuum greater than 12 in. Hg to the switch, and compare the ignition timing with the requirements below:
   4 cylinder – per specifications less 32°–40°
   6 cylinder – per specifications less 21°–27°
   8 cylinder – per specifications less 16°–20°

Electrical Controls

IGNITION LOCK CYLINDER
Removal and Installation

1. Disconnect the negative battery cable.
2. With a fixed steering column, remove the steering wheel trim pad and the steering wheel. Insert a stiff wire into the hole in the lock cylinder housing. With a tilt wheel, this hole is on the outside of the steering column near the emergency flasher button; it is not necessary to remove the steering wheel. On modular columns, remove the trim shroud and remove the electrical connector from the key warning switch; steering wheel removal is necessary.
3. Place the gear shift lever in Park and turn the ignition key to the ON position.
4. Depress the wire and remove the lock cylinder and wire.
5. Insert the new cylinder into the housing and turn to the OFF position. This will lock the cylinder into position.
6. Reinstall the steering wheel and pad if removed.
7. Connect the negative battery cable.

IGNITION SWITCH
Removal and Installation

1. Disconnect the negative battery cable.
2. Remove the upper shroud below the steering wheel by un-

SECTION 5
FORD LINCOLN MERCURY
REAR WHEEL DRIVE CARS

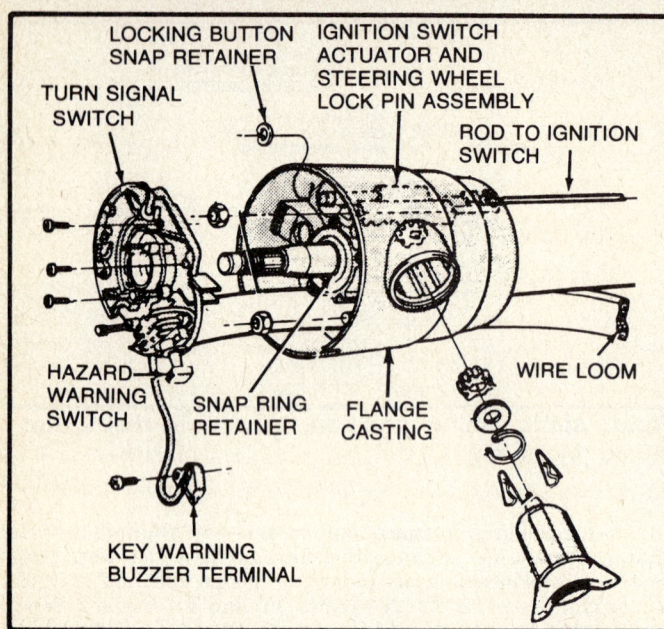

Turnsignal switch and ignition lock cylinder mounting, typical of early type fixed column (©Ford Motor Co.)

housing and into the carrier to restrict movement of the carrier with respect to the switch housing. A new replacement comes with an adjusting pin already installed.
 8. Turn the ignition key to the on position.
 9. Install the ignition switch on the actuator pin.
 10. Install new "brake-off head" bolts and tighten them until the heads break off. Tighten bolts evenly.
 11. Remove the drill bit or adjusting pin.
 12. Connect all electrical connections and the negative battery cable.
 13. Start the car and check for proper operation of the switch.
 14. Install the steering column shroud.

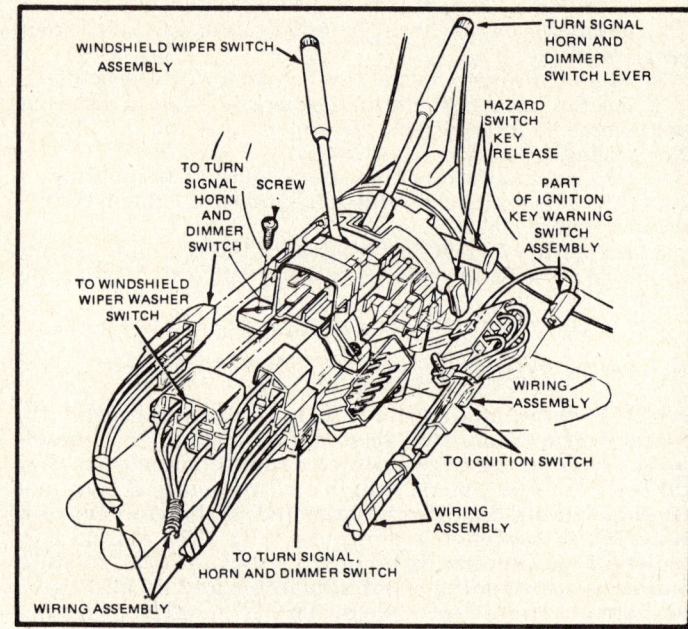

Cluster of switches mounted to steering column (©Ford Motor Co.)

snapping the retaining clips. On the tilt column it will be necessary to remove the five attaching screws.
 3. Disconnect the electrical connector from the ignition switch.
 4. Drill out the bolts holding the switch to the lock cylinder using a $\frac{1}{8}$ in. drill bit.
 5. Remove the bolts using an Easy-Out® bolt extractor.
 6. Disengage the switch from the actuator pin.
 7. Adjust the new ignition switch by sliding the carrier to the on position. Insert a small drill bit through the switch

NEUTRAL START SWITCH (FLOOR SHIFT MODELS ONLY)

Adjustment

NOTE: Models equipped with a column shift lever are not equipped with a neutral start switch. Instead, an ignition lock cylinder-to-shift lever interlock prevents these models from being started in any gear other than Park or Neutral. No adjustment is possible on C3 and AOD transmission.

C4 (1982)

1. Place the transmission selector lever in the Neutral position.
2. Raise the vehicle on a hoist and loosen the two bolts that attach the neutral start switch to the transmission.
3. Rotate the switch until a gauge pin (the shank end of a No. 43 drill bit) can be inserted through the gauge pin holes in the switch. The gauge pin must be inserted a full $\frac{31}{64}$ in. into the switch, through all three holes in the switch.
4. Tighten the switch retaining bolts and remove the pin.

Removal and Installation

C3 AND AOD FLOOR SHIFT MODELS

1. Unplug the connector from the switch and unscrew the switch from the transmission case using a thin-wall socket.

Turnsignal switch and ignition lock cylinder mounting, typical of early tilt column (©Ford Motor Co.)

Ford Lincoln Mercury
REAR WHEEL DRIVE CARS
SECTION 5

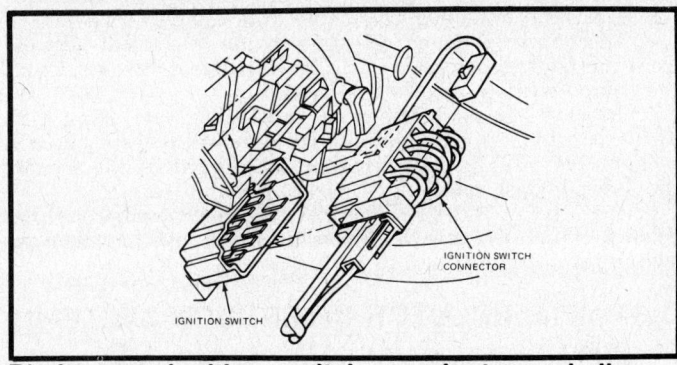

Blade type ignition switch, spade type similar (©Ford Motor Co.)

2. Always install a new O-ring when replacing the switch.
3. Carefully check that the back-up lights work only in Reverse and that the engine will start only in Neutral or Park. No adjustment is required.

C4 and C5 MODELS

1. Raise the car, with the transmission in Neutral, and disconnect the downshift linkage.
2. Remove the neutral switch attaching bolts and remove the switch, then carefully disconnect the wires. Check connectors for corrosion.
3. Install the replacement switch and adjust it as described above.
4. Install the downshift outer lever.
5. Connect the downshift linkage rod to the downshift lever. Check operation.

NEUTRAL START SWITCH

Removal and Installation

Automatic Overdrive Transmissions 1982 FORD MERCURY, LINCOLN, TOWN CAR/CONTINENTAL MARK VI

1. Place the shift selector lever in the manual low (1) position and raise the vehicle on a hoist or stands.
2. Disconnect the throttle valve linkage rod from the transmission throttle valve lever.
3. Disconnect the manual shift linkage from the transmission manual lever.
4. Disconnect the muffler inlet pipe from the catalytic converter.
5. Place a jack under the transmission and raise it enough to remove the weight from the engine rear support.
6. Remove the nuts that secure the engine rear support to the crossmember.
7. Remove the bolts that secure the engine rear support to the transmission extension housing.
8. Remove the bolts that secure the crossmember to the frame and remove the crossmember and rear support.
9. Lower the transmission enough to provide adequate clearance for the removal of the neutral start switch.
10. Disconnect the neutral start switch electrical harness from the neutral switch. Lift the harness straight up off of the switch without side to side motion.
11. Using Neutral Start Switch Socket T74P-77247-A or equivalent, remove the neutral start switch and O-ring seal. Discard the seal and, if damaged, the switch.
12. Installation is the reverse order of the removal procedure and be sure to install a new O-ring on the switch.

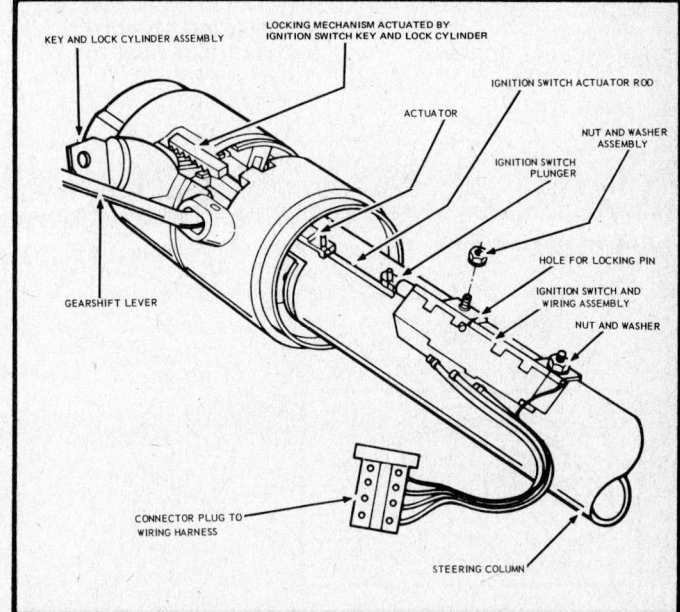

Pin type ignition switch (©Ford Motor Co.)

Mark VII/Continental, Thunderbird/Cougar, LTD/Marquis, Mustang/Capri

1. Place the selector lever in the low position and disconnect the negative battery cable.
2. Raise and support the vehicle safely.

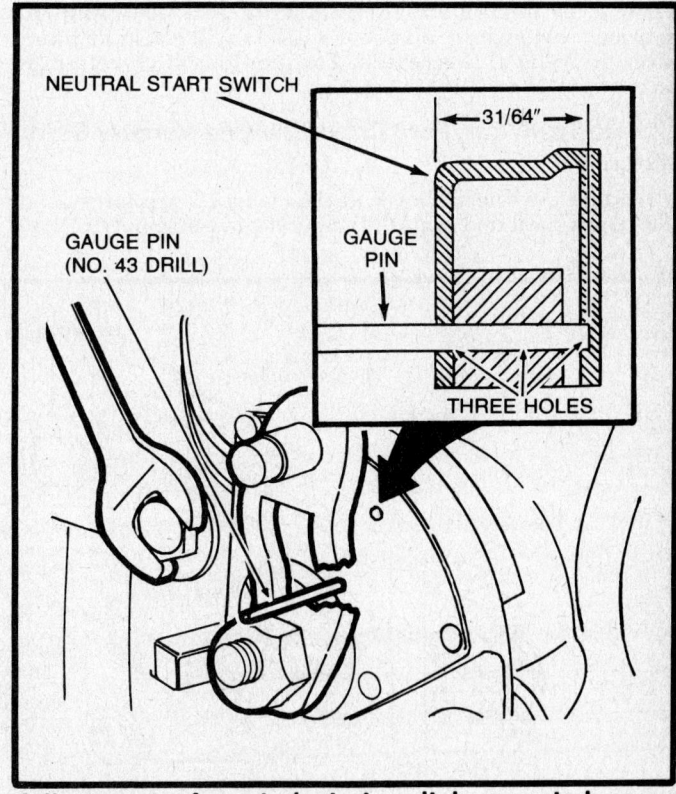

Adjustment of neutral start switch mounted on transmission (©Ford Motor Co.)

5–19

SECTION 5

FORD LINCOLN MERCURY
REAR WHEEL DRIVE CARS

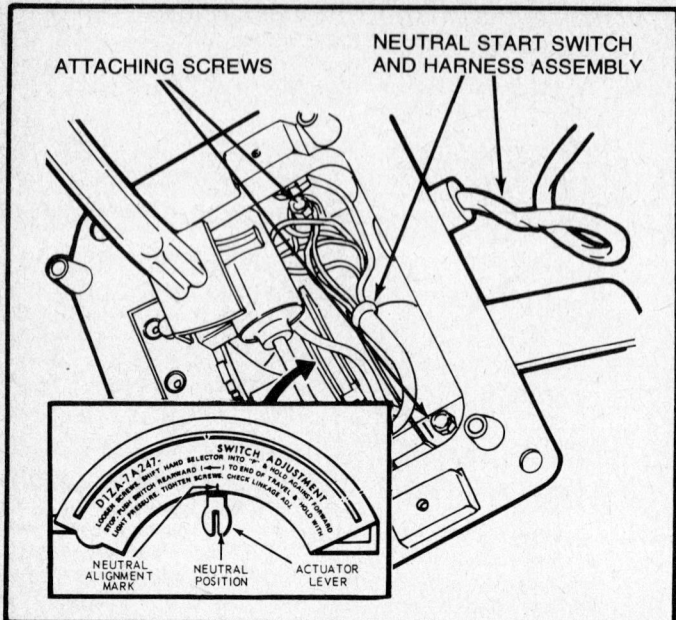

Adjustment of neutral start switch mounted in console (©Ford Motor Co.)

3. Disconnect the neutral start switch electrical harness from the switch and remove the neutral start switch with its O-ring using socket T74P-77247-A or equivalent.
4. Installation is the reverse order of the removal procedure and be sure to install a new O-ring on the switch.

NOTE: It is important to use the special socket T74P-77247-A or equivalent for removing and installing the neutral start switch, all other sockets will crush or puncture the walls of the switch. Torque the switch retaining nut to 8 to 11 ft. lbs. (11–15 Nm).

Lincoln Town Car, Ford Crown Victoria/Mercury Grand Marquis

1. Place the selector lever in the manual low position.
2. Open hood and remove the air cleaner assembly.
3. Disconnect the negative cable from the battery post.
4. Disconnect the neutral start switch electrical harness from the neutral switch by lifting the harness straight up off the switch without side to side motion.
5. Remove the neutral switch and O-ring seal using a 24 inch extension, universal adaptor, and the neutral start switch socket T74P-77247-A or equivalent (access path is the area by the left side dash panel).
6. Installation is the reverse order of the removal procedure, be sure to install a new O-ring on the switch and to torque the switch retaining nut to 8 to 11 ft. lbs. (11–15 Nm).

STARTER/CLUTCH INTERLOCK SWITCH

Removal

1. Disconnect wiring connector.
2. Remove retaining pin from clutch pedal.
3. Remove switch bracket attaching screw.
4. Lift switch and bracket assembly upward to disengage tab from pedal support.
5. Move switch outward to disengage actuating rod eyelet from clutch pedal pin and remove switch from vehicle.

Installation

NOTE: Always install the switch with the self-adjusting clip about 25.4mm (1.0 in.) from the end of the rod. The clutch pedal must be fully up (clutch engaged). Otherwise, the switch may be misadjusted.

1. Place eyelet end of rod onto pivot pin.
2. Swing switch assembly around to line up hole in mounting boss with hole in bracket.
3. Install attaching screw.
4. Replace retaining pin in pivot pin.
5. Connect wiring connector.

STOP LAMP SWITCH

Removal and Installation

EXCEPT WITH VACUUM POWERED BRAKES

1. Disconnect the wire harness at the connector from the switch.
2. Remove the hairpin retainer, slide the stop lamp switch, the push rod and the nylon washers and bushings away from the pedal, and remove the switch.

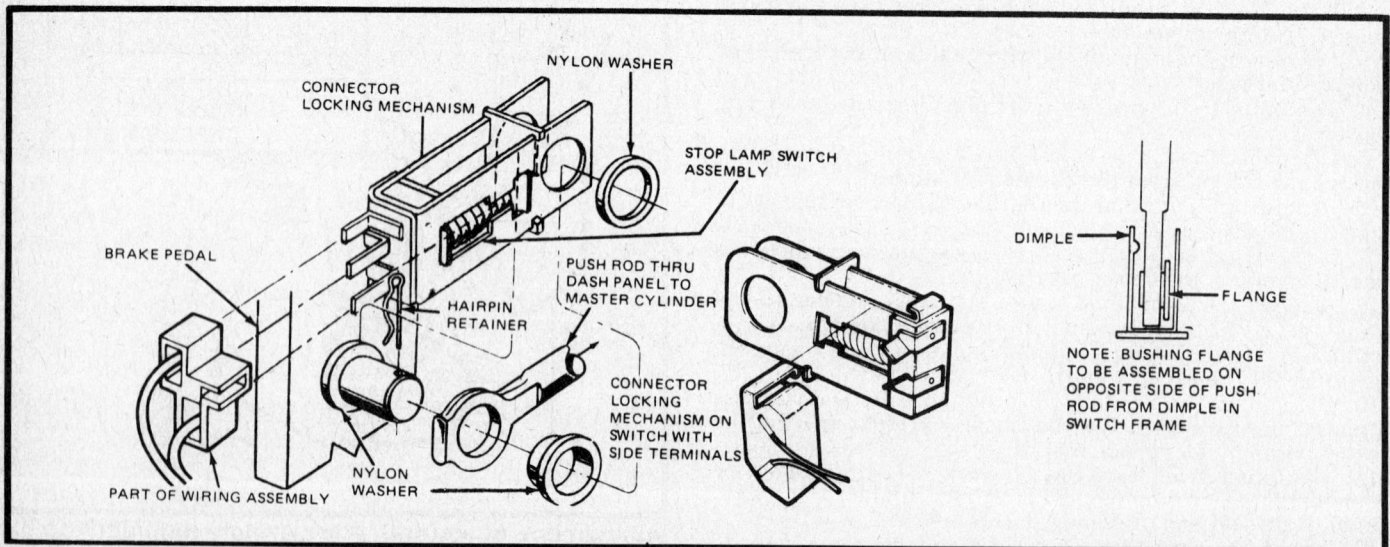

Typical installation of stop lamp switch (©Ford Motor Co.)

Ford Lincoln Mercury
REAR WHEEL DRIVE CARS
SECTION 5

NOTE: Since the switch side plate nearest the brake pedal is slotted, it is not necessary to remove the brake master cylinder pushrod and one spacer-washer from the brake pedal pin.

3. Position the switch, push rod, and busing and washers on the brake pedal pin, and install the hairpin retainer.
4. Assemble the wire harness connector to the switch and install the wires in the retaining clip.

VACUUM-POWERED BRAKES

1. Disconnect the negative battery cable.
2. Disconnect the stop lamp switch wire connector from the switch.
3. **IMPORTANT:** Loosen the brake booster nuts at the pedal support approximately ¼ in. so booster is free to move eliminating binding during switch removal.
4. Remove the hairpin retainer and outer nylon washer from the pedal pin. Slide the stoplamp switch off the brake pedal pin just far enough for the outer arm to clear the pin. Then remove the switch.

NOTE: Since the switch side plate nearest the brake pedal is slotted it is not necessary to remove the brake master cylinder pushrod and one spacer washer from the brake pedal pin.

5. Position the new stop lamp switch so that it straddles the push rod, with the slot on the pedal pin and the switch outer frame hole just clearing the pin. Slide the switch upward onto the pin and pushrod. Slide the assembly inboard toward the brake pedal arm.
6. Install the outer nylon washer and the hairpin retainer.
7. Tighten the booster attaching nuts to specification.
8. Connect the stoplamp switch wire connector to the switch. Connect the negative battery cable.

NOTE: Stoplamp switch wire harness must have sufficient length to travel with switch during full stroke of pedal. If wire length is insufficient, reroute harness or service as required.

9. Check the stoplamps for proper operation.

HIGH-MOUNT STOPLAMP

Removal and Installation

MARK VII AND CONTINENTAL

1. Remove the beauty cap at the front of the lamp assembly. Remove the screw and pull the lamp foward to detach it from the bracket.
2. Locate the wire assembly in the luggage compartment area and remove the wire to allow enough wire length to pull the lamp away from the package tray. Remove the bulb sockets and remove the lamp assembly from the vehicle.
3. Installation is the reverse order of the removal procedure.

LTD/MARGUIS – SEDAN

1. Remove the lamp screw retainer covers. Remove the screws from the retainer and pull the lamp up and forward to detach the retainer bracket. Pull the wire assembly locator from the lamp body on the under side of the lamp.
2. Remove the bulb sockets from the stop lamp and remove the lamp assembly from the vehicle.
3. Installation is the reverse order of the removal procedure.

LTD/MARGUIS – WAGON

1. Remove the two screws from the lens face. Detach the lamp assembly from the bezel housing. Pull the wiring grommet out of the sheet metal and disconnect the lamp wire assembly from the wiring harness.
2. Detach the connector locator from the sheet metal. If nec-

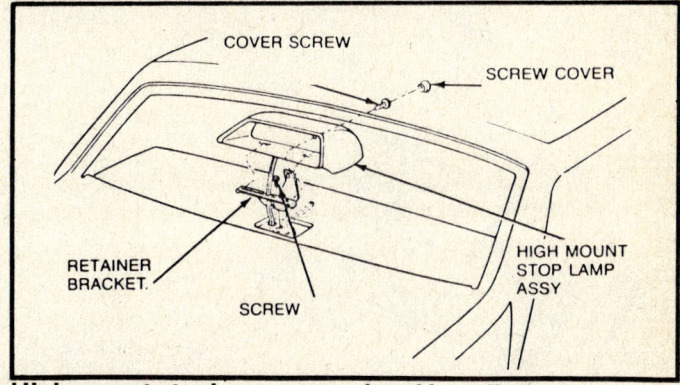

High mount stoplamp removal and installation—Continental

essary remove the bezel by removing the two screws which secure the bezel housing to the vehicle.
3. Installation is the reverse order of the removal procedure.

THUNDERBIRD AND COUGAR

1. Remove the lamp screw retainer covers. Remove the two screws that hold the lamp assembly to the retainer bracket.
2. Lift the lamp assembly up and out of the attaching retainer brackets.
3. Installation is the reverse order of the removal procedure.

MUSTANG (2 DOOR)

1. Locate the wire to the high mount stop lamp under the package tray, which is located inside the luggage compartment. Pull the wire loose from the plastic clip.
2. Remove the beauty cap from the lamp cover. Remove the two lamp retaining screws. Pull the lamp assembly forward, remove the bulbs and remove the lamp assembly.
3. Installation is the reverse order of the removal procedure.

MUSTANG/CAPRI – 2 DOOR HATCHBACK AND CONVERTIBLE

1. On the hatch back models, remove the two retaining screws from the lamp assembly. Pull the lamp assembly rearward from the spoiler.
2. On the convertible models, remove the luggage crossbar. Remove the two retaing screws from the lamp assembly. Lift the lamp assembly up from the decklid.

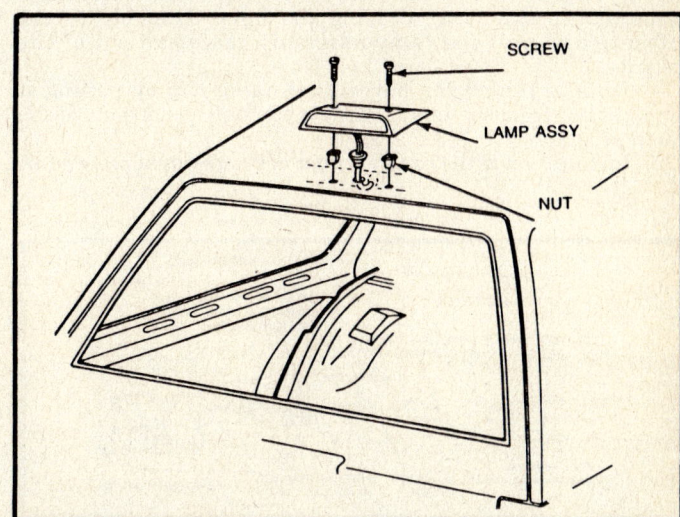

High mount stoplamp removal and installation—LTD/Marquis Wagon

5–21

SECTION 5

FORD LINCOLN MERCURY
REAR WHEEL DRIVE CARS

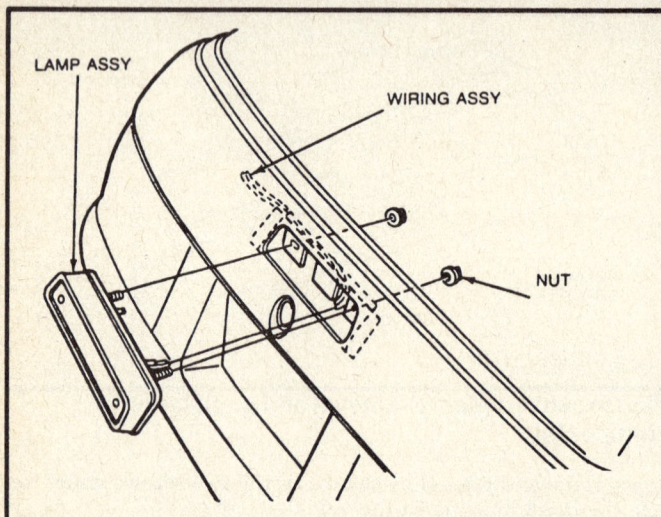

High mount stoplamp removal and installation—Capri

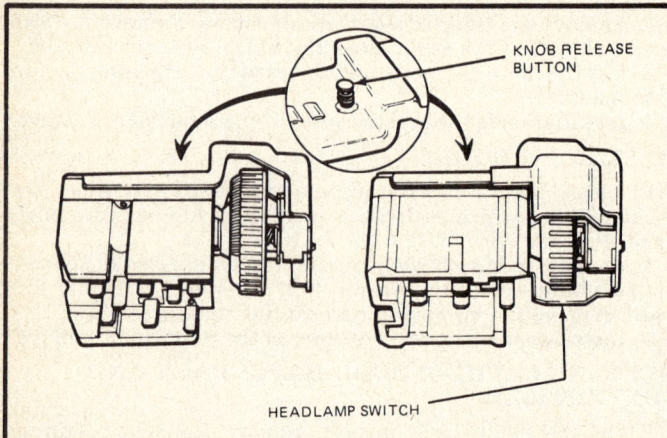

Typical headlamp switch with release button
(©Ford Motor Co.)

HEADLIGHT SWITCH

Removal and Installation
FORD AND MERCURY
1. Disconnect the negative battery cable.
2. Underneath the instrument panel, depress the shaft retaining knob and pull the knob straight out.
3. Unscrew the trim bezel and remove the locknut.
4. Underneath the instrument panel, move the switch toward the front of the car while tilting it downward.
5. Disconnect the wiring from the switch and remove the switch from the car.
6. Installation is the reverse of removal.

1983-84
LINCOLN TOWN CAR/CONTINETAL, MARK VI
1. Disconnect the ground cable from the battery.
2. Remove the headlamp switch knob.
3. Remove the auto dimmer bezel and the autolamp delay bezel, if so equipped.
4. Remove the steering column lower shroud.
5. Remove lower LH instrument panel trim bezel.
6. Remove the five screws that retain the headlamp switch mounting bracket to the instrument panel.
7. Carefully pull the switch and bracket from the instrument panel and disconnect the wiring connector(s) from the headlamp switch.
8. Remove the locknut and one screw that retain the headlamp switch to the switch bracket.
9. Installation is the reverse order of the removal procedure.

3. On the Capri models, remove the lift gate inner trim panel, exposing the two access holes for the high mount stoplamp. Remove the two nuts securing the lamp assembly to the liftgate and pull the lamp assembly rearward out of the liftgate.
4. Remove the wiring harness retaining clip by pulling it straight out from the lamp. Remove the bulbs and remove the lamp assembly.
5. Installation is the reverse order of the removal procedure.

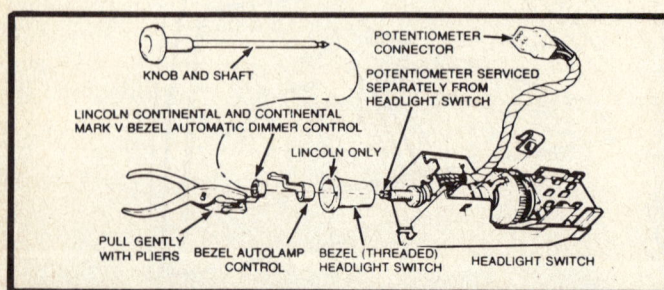

Headlamp switch used with Autolamp system
(©Ford Motor Co.)

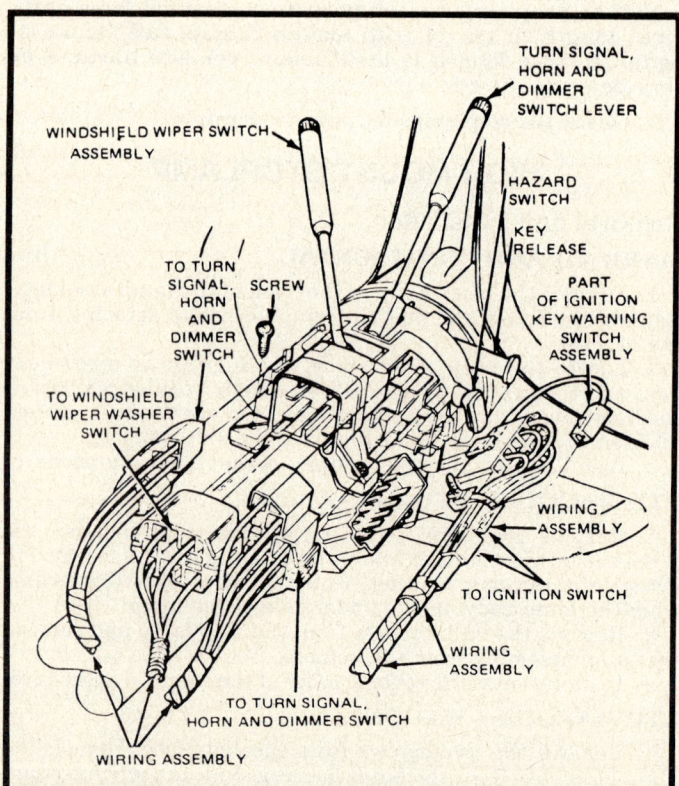

Typical switch cluster wiring connectors, late model steering columns (©Ford Motor Co.)

Ford Lincoln Mercury
REAR WHEEL DRIVE CARS — SECTION 5

1985 and Later
MARK VII/CONTINENTAL, THUNDERBIRD/COUGAR

1. Remove the lens assembly attaching screws and then the lens assembly.
2. Remove the screws securing the switch to the instrument panel and pull the switch out from the panel.

NOTE: On vehicles equipped with the auto lamp/auto dimmer system, remove this control first.

3. Disconnect the electrical connector and remove the switch from the vehicle.
4. Installation is the reverse order of the removal procedure.

LINCOLN, MARK VI, MARK VII WITH HEADLAMP DELAY SYSTEM, AND ALL 1983 AND LATER MODELS

NOTE: The delay system has an additional feature which is the potentiometer, which can be removed from the headlamp switch. Both the headlamp switch and the potentiometer can be replaced separately.

1. Disconnect the negative battery cable and remove the headlight switch as previously outlined.
2. Remove the headlamp switch shaft and knob.
3. Remove the plastic spacer at the rear of the potentiometer by pushing out with a suitable tool.
4. remove the strap securing the wiring harness to the switch.
5. Loosen the potentiometer retaining nut and washer and slide it out of the headlamp switch.
6. Installation is the reverse order of the removal procedure.

HEADLAMP DIMMER SWITCH/HORN SWITCH

Removal and Installation
COLUMN MOUNTED

The dimmer switch is part of the turn/dim/horn multi-switch assembly.
1. Remove the shroud from the steering column.
2. Disconnect the steering column wiring connector plug from the bracket and remove the screws that secure the switch to the column.
3. Installation is the reverse of removal procedures.

FLOOR MOUNTED DIMMER SWITCH

1. Pull the floor carpet back away from the area of the switch and remove the switch mounting screws.
2. Disconnect the three wire connector from the switch.
3. To install new switch, reverse the removal procedure.

AUTOMATIC HEADLAMP DIMMER SWITCH

Removal and Installation
ALL MODELS EXCEPT THOSE LISTED BELOW

1. Disconnect battery ground cable.
2. Remove steering column trim shroud by removing self tapping screws.
3. Remove dimmer switch lever by grasping lever and by using a pulling and twisting motion, pull the lever straight out from the switch.
4. Peel back the foam sight shield from the dimmer switch and disconnect the two electrical connectors.
5. Remove the two self-tapping screws attaching switch to lock cylinder housing.
6. Installation is the reverse of removal procedures.

CONTINENTAL, THUNDERBIRD, COUGAR, FAIRMONT, FUTURA, ZEPHYR, LTD, MARQUIS, MUSTANG, CAPRI

1. Disconnect the battery ground cable.
2. Disconnect wire harness at rear of the sensor-amplifier unit. Do not pull on the cable sheathing as this could damage the leads.
3. Remove the two sensor-amplifier and bracket mounting screws and remove the unit from vehicle.
4. Be certain that headlamp system is properly aimed. Look through the front chamber to see that at least 50 percent of the sensor lens can be seen and is clean.
5. Installation is the reverse of removal procedures.
6. Test unit for proper operation and if necessary, adjust the vertical aiming.

TURN SIGNAL SWITCH

Removal and Installation
FORD, MERCURY, LINCOLN

1. On standard steering columns, remove the upper extension shroud (below the steering wheel) by snapping the shroud from the retaining clip. On tilt columns, remove the trim shroud by removing the five self-tapping screws.
2. Use a pulling and twisting motion, while pulling straight out, to remove the turn signal switch lever.
3. Peel back the piece of foam rubber from around the switch.
4. Disconnect the two switch electrical connectors.
5. Remove the two self-tapping screws which secure the switch to the lock cylinder housing, and disengage the switch from the housing.
6. To install, align the switch mounting holes with the corresponding holes in the lock cylinder housing. Install the two screws.
7. Stick the foam back into place.
8. Align the key on the turn signal lever with the keyway in the switch and push the lever into place.
9. Install the two electrical connectors.
10. Install the trim shrouds.

WIPER SWITCH

Removal and Installation
ALL Models

1. Disconnect the negative battery cable.
2. Remove the split steering column cover retaining screws.
3. Separate the two halves and remove the wiper switch retaining screws.
4. Disconnect the wire connector and remove the wiper switch.
5. The installation of the wiper switch is the reverse of the removal procedure.

REAR WIPER SWITCH

Removal and Installation
1985 AND LATER LTD/MARQUIS

1. Remove the wiper switch knob and the switch retaining bezel.
2. Pull the switch away from the rear of the instrument panel.
3. Disconnect the electrical connector from the switch and remove the switch.
4. Installation is the reverse order of the removal procedure.

5-23

Ford Lincoln Mercury
REAR WHEEL DRIVE CARS

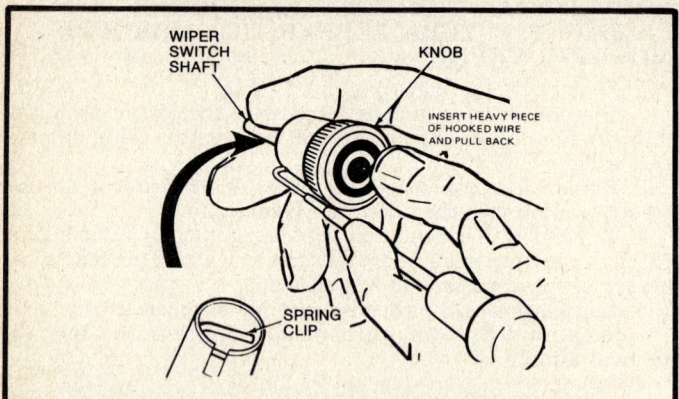

Removing knob from windshield wiper switch shaft (©Ford Motor Co.)

WIPER MOTOR
Removal and Installation
FORD, MERCURY, LINCOLN CONTINENTAL, LINCOLN TOWN CAR, MARK VI AND VII

1. Disconnect the battery ground cable.
2. 1982 and later models, remove the hood seal.
3. Disconnect the right washer nozzle hose and remove the right wiper arm and blade assembly from the pivot shaft.

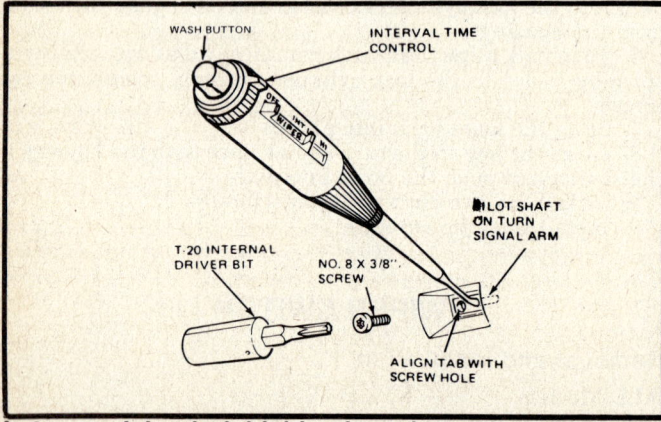

Late model windshield wiper lever installation (©Ford Motor Co.)

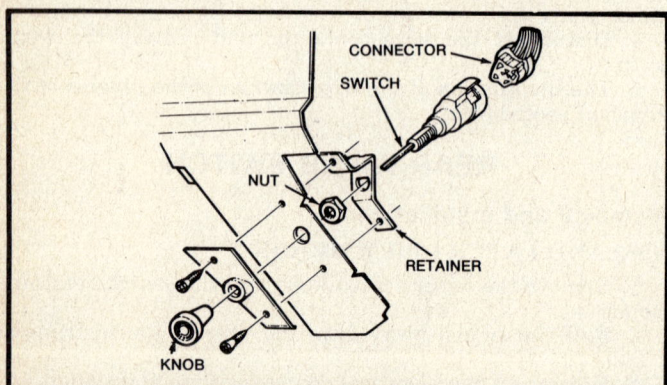

Typical wiper switch installation (©Ford Motor Co.)

4. Remove the windshield wiper motor and linkage cover by removing the two attaching screws.
5. Disconnect the linkage drive arm from the motor output arm crankpin by removing the retaining clip.
6. Disconnect the two push-on wire connectors from the motor.
7. Remove the three bolts that retain the motor to the dash panel extension and remove the motor.
8. To install, be sure the output arm is in the park position and reverse the removal procedure.

FAIRMONT, ZEPHYR, THUNDERBIRD, COUGAR, XR-7, MUSTANG, CAPRI, GRANADA

1. Disconnect the battery ground cable.
2. Remove the right wiper and blade assembly.

NOTE: On Fairmont, Zephyr, Granada and Cougar models, also remove the left wiper arm and blade.

3. Remove the grille on the top of the cowl.
4. Disconnect the linkage drive arm from the motor crankpin after removing the clip.
5. Disconnect the wiper motor electrical connector and remove the three attaching screws from the motor. Pull the motor from the opening.
6. Be sure the motor crank arm is in the park position and reverse the removal procedure to install.

REAR WIPER MOTOR
Removal and Installation
1985 AND LATER LTD/MARQUIS

1. Turn the ignition switch to "Off" or "Lock."
2. Remove the wiper arm and blade.
3. Remove the pivot shaft attaching nut and spacers.
4. Remove the liftgate inner trim panel.
5. Remove the screws that attach the license plate housing.
6. disconnect the license plate lamp wiring and remove the housing.
7. Disconnect the electrical connector to the wiper motor.
8. Remove the linkage arm locking clip, pry off the arm and remove the linkage.
9. Remove the motor and bracket attaching screws and remove the motor and its mounting bracket.
10. Installation is the reverse order of the removal procedure.

WIPER PIVOT SHAFT AND LINKAGE
Removal and Installation

The wiper pivot shafts and linkage can be removed after the motor and wiper arm assemblies have been removed. The pivot shafts are retained to the body with screws and, on certain models, can individually be removed. On other models, the complete left and right pivot shaft and linkage must be removed as a unit.

NOTE: For wiper linkage removal on the models equipped with rear wipers, refer to rear wiper motor removal and installation.

INSTRUMENT CLUSTER
Removal and Installation

--- **CAUTION** ---

Extreme care must be exercised during the removal and installation of the instrument cluster and dash components to avoid damage or breakage. Wooden paddles should be used to separate dash components, if required. Tape or cover dash areas that may be damaged by the removal and installation of the dash components.

Ford Lincoln Mercury
REAR WHEEL DRIVE CARS
SECTION 5

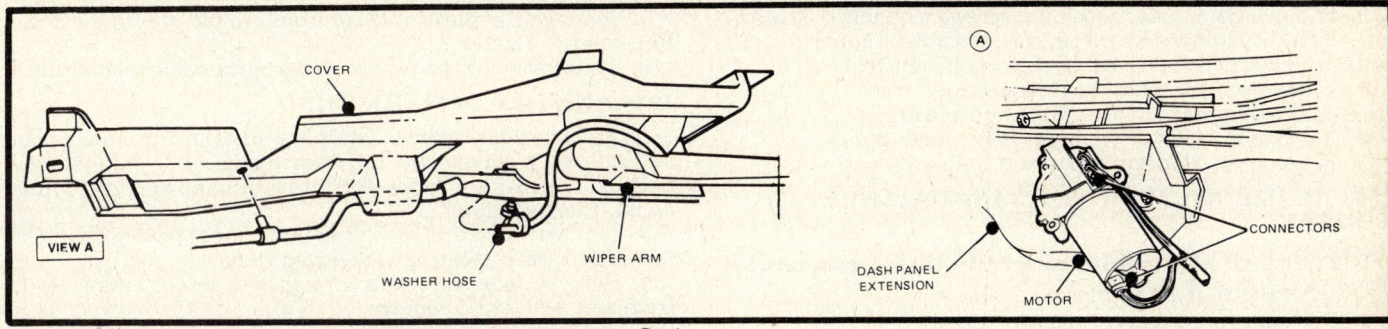

Removal of wiper motor, typical (©Ford Motor Co.)

NOTE: During the removal and installation procedures, slight variations may be required from the general outline, to facilitate the removal and installation of the instrument panel and cluster components, due to slight changes from model year to model year.

FORD, MERCURY, LINCOLN CONTINENTAL, MARK VI, AND LINCOLN TOWN CAR
1983 AND LATER CROWN VICTORIA, GRAND MARQUIS, LINCOLN TOWN CAR, LTD, MARQUIS

1. Disconnect the battery ground cable.
2. remove the lower steering column cove.
3. Remove the instrument cluster trim cover. Remove the bottom half of the steering column shroud.
4. Reach behind the cluster and disconnect the cluster electrical feed plug and the speedometer cable.
5. Unsnap and remove the steering column shroud cover, if not previously done. Disconnect the transmission indicator cable from the tab in the shroud retainer.
6. Remove the attaching screw for the transmission indicator cable bracket to steering column. disconnect the cable loop from the pin on the steering column.
7. Remove the cluster retaining screws and remove the cluster assembly.
8. The installation is the reverse of the removal procedure.

MUSTANG/CAPRI

1. Disconnect battery ground cable.
2. Remove three upper retaining screws from the instrument cluster trim cover and remove the trim cover.
3. Remove four screws retaining instrument cluster to the instrument panel on Mustang SVO, disconnect turbo boost pressure hose at the shake brace.
4. Pull the cluster away from the instrument panel and reach behind the instrument cluster to disconnect the speedometer cable by pressing on the flat surface of the plastic connector (quick connect).
5. Pull the cluster further away from the instrument panel, disconnect the two cluster printed circuit connectors from their receptacles in the cluster backplate.
6. Remove cluster.
7. Installation is the reverse order of the removal procedure.

NOTE: Mustang and Capri models have two printed circuit boards.

1983–86 THUNDERBIRD, COUGAR XR-7 Standard and Electronic Clusters

1. Disconnect the negative battery cable.
2. Disconnect the speedometer cable (standard cluster).
3. Remove the instrument panel trim cover and steering column lower shroud.
4. Remove the cluster retaining screws (Electronic cluster).
5. Remove the attaching screw from the transmission indicator quadrant cable bracket to the steering column. Disconnect the cable loop from the pin on the steering column.

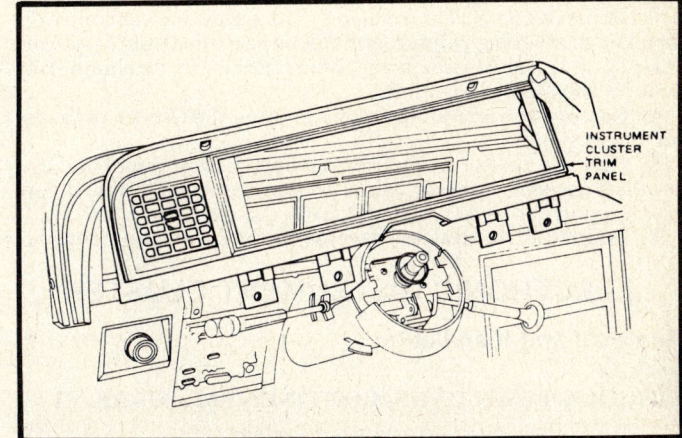

Removing instrument cluster trim panel, typical (©Ford Motor Co.)

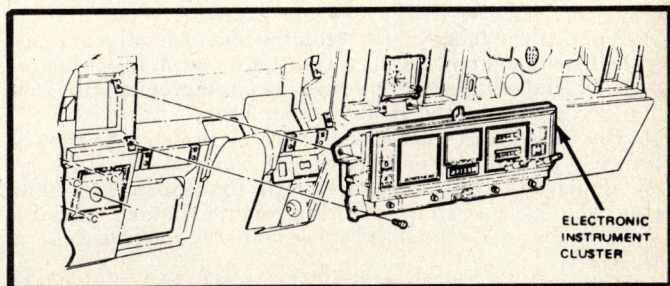

Removing electronic instrument cluster, Thunderbird/Cougar illustrated (©Ford Motor Co.)

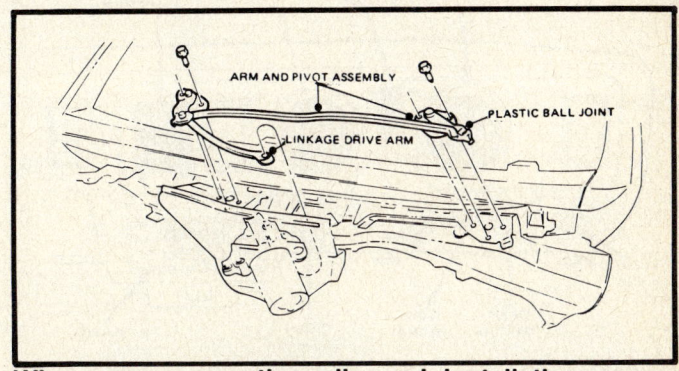

Wiper arm connecting clip and installation procedure (©Ford Motor Co.)

SECTION 5
Ford Lincoln Mercury
REAR WHEEL DRIVE CARS

6. Remove the cluster retaining screws (Standard cluster).
7. Pull the cluster away from the instrument panel and disconnect the speedometer cable (Electronic cluster).
8. Disconnect the electrical connections from the cluster. Disconnect the ground wire (Electronic cluster).
9. Remove the cluster from the instrument panel.
10. Reverse the removal procedure to install.

1983 FAIRMONT, ZEPHYR, GRANADA, AND COUGAR

NOTE: Certain special ordered cluster assemblies have two printed circuits.

1. Disconnect the battery negative cable.
2. Remove the steering column shroud and the cluster trim cover.
3. Remove one screw from the shift quadrant control cable bracket to steering column and disconnect the cable loop from the pin on the shift cane lever. Remove the plastic clamp from around the steering column.
4. Remove the retaining screws holding the cluster to the instrument panel.
5. Pull the cluster away from the instrument panel and disconnect the speedometer cable. Disconnect the electrical connectors and remove the cluster from the dash.
6. To install the cluster, reverse the removal procedure.

ELECTRONIC INSTRUMENT CLUSTER

Removal and Installation

1983-84 LINCOLN TOWN CARS, CONTINENTAL, MARK VI

1. Disconnect the battery ground cable.
2. Remove the steering column cover and lower instrument panel trim cover. Remove the keyboard trim panel and trim panel on left of column.
3. Remove the 10 retaining instrument cluster trim cover screws and remove trim cover.
4. Remove the four screws retaining the instrument cluster to the instrument panel and pull cluster forward. Reach behind the cluster, disconnect both feed plugs and ground wire from their receptacles in the cluster back plate.
5. Disconnect the speedometer cable by pressing on the flat surface of the plastic connector (quick connect).
6. Remove the attaching screw from the transmission indicator cable bracket to the steering column. Detach the cable loop from the pin on the shift cane lever of the steering column.
7. Remove the plastic clamp from around steering column. Remove the cluster.
8. Installation is the reverse order of the removal procedure.

1984 AND LATER MARK VII

1. Remove four screws retaining instrument finish panel and rotate top of panel toward steering wheel. Disconnect electrical and air sensor connectors at right hand portion of finish panel. Remove panel.
2. remove six screws retaining instrument panel pad and rotate pad toward steering wheel and remove.
3. Remove four screws retaining instrument cluster to instrument panel and remove.
4. Disconnect electrical connector at lower left rear corner of cluster.
5. Installation is the reverse order of the removal procedure.

1984 AND LATER CONTINENTAL

1. Remove the steering column shroud.
2. Remove left and right instrument panel mouldings. Mouldings are held in with retaining clips.
3. Remove the two center moulding retaining screws and remove moulding above climate control head.
4. Remove the ash receptacle.
5. Remove the two remaining screws and take out the center moulding.
6. Remove the seventeen screws retaining the instrument cluster finish panel and remove the panel.
7. Disconnect the transmission indicator cable at the steering column.
8. Remove the four screws retaining the cluster to the instrument panel and disconnect the electrical connector at the lower left corner of the cluster.
9. Remove the instrument cluster from the vehicle.
10. Installation is the reverse order of the removal procedure.

SPEEDOMETER (CONVENTIONAL)

Removal and Installation

ALL MODELS

1. Disconnect battery ground cable.
2. Remove instrument cluster.
3. Disconnect speedometer cable by pressing flat surface and pulling cable away from head (quick connect).
4. Remove screws which attach the lens and mask to the cluster and remove lens and mask.
5. Remove two screws attaching speedometer head to cluster and remove speedometer.
6. On Lincoln and Mark VI, remove two screws holding trip odometer reset assembly to the cluster, and remove speedometer. Remove one screw from back of trip odometer mechanism, and unhook trip odometer reset assembly cable from slot in trip odometer.
7. Installation is the reverse order of removal procedures.

SPEEDOMETER (ELECTRONIC)

Removal and Installation

1983

1. Disconnect battery ground cable.
2. Disconnect speedometer cable by pressing flat surface and pulling cable away from head (quick connect).
3. Remove instrument cluster.
4. Remove screws that attach the lens and mask assembly to the cluster backplate and remove lens and mask assembly.
5. Remover terminal nuts from the electronic speedometer housing studs on the back of the cluster terminal.
6. Remove screws attaching speedometer to cluster backplate and remove speedometer assembly.

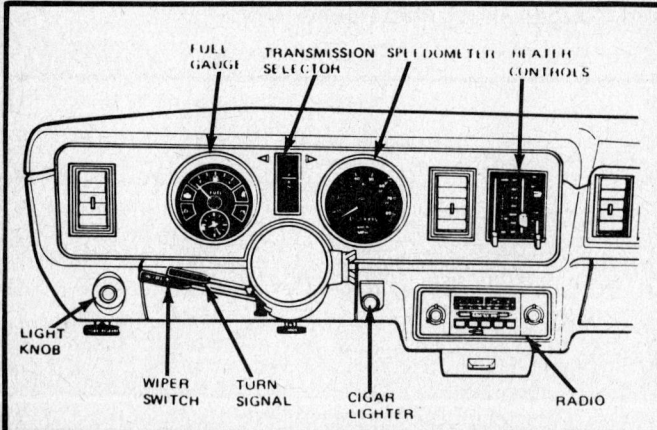

Instrument cluster assembly, Fairmount/Zephyr illustrated (©Ford Motor Co.)

7. Disassemble electronics from mechanical portion of speedometer.
8. Installation is the reverse order of removal procedures.

1984 AND LATER
1. Disconnect the battery ground cable.
2. Remove four screws attaching the lower instrument panel trim cover.
3. Remove steering column cover.
4. Remove six screws that attach the instrument cluster trim panel.
5. Remove four screws that attach the instrument cluster to the instrument panel.
6. Remove the attaching screws from the transmission indicator (PRND) cable bracket to the steering column. Detach the cable loop from the pin of the steering column.
7. Pull the cluster away from the instrument panel.
8. disconnect the speedometer cable by pressing on the flat surface of the plastic connector (quick connect).
9. Disconnect the cluster feed plug and ground wire from their receptacle.
10. Remove cluster assembly.
11. Installation is the reverse order of removal procedures.

SPEEDOMETER CABLE

Removal and Installation
ALL MODELS
1. Disconnect battery ground cable.
2. Remove clip at accelerator bracket stud.
3. Remove screws attaching cluster to instrument panel. Pull cluster rearward to gain access to cable.
4. Disconnect speedometer cable (quick connect) from speedometer head.
5. Pull speedometer cable out of the upper end of casing.
6. If cable is broken, raise vehicle on a hoist and remove the cable casing at the transmission.
7. Remove the cable and driven gear from the transmission, remove driven gear retainer and remove driven gear and core from cable.
8. remove the lower part of cable from the lower end of casing.
9. Installation is the reverse order of removal procedures.
10. Be certain to follow cutting instructions to obtain exact length of new cable.

FUSES, FUSIBLE LINKS AND CIRCUIT BREAKERS

Fusible links are used to protect the main wiring harness and selected branches from complete burn-out, should a short circuit or electrical overload occur.

Circuit breakers are used on certain electrical components requiring high amperage, such as the headlamp circuit, electrical seats and/or windows to name a few. The advantage of the circuit breaker is its ability to open and close the electrical circuit as the load demands, rather than the necessity of a part replacement, should the circuit be opened with another protective device in line.

A fuse panel is used to house the numerous fuses protecting the various branches of the electrical system and is normally the most accessible. The mounting of the fuse panel is usually on the left side of the passenger compartment, under the dash, either on the side kick panel or on the firewall to the left of the steering column. Certain models will have the fuse panel exposed while other models will have it covered with a removable trim cover.

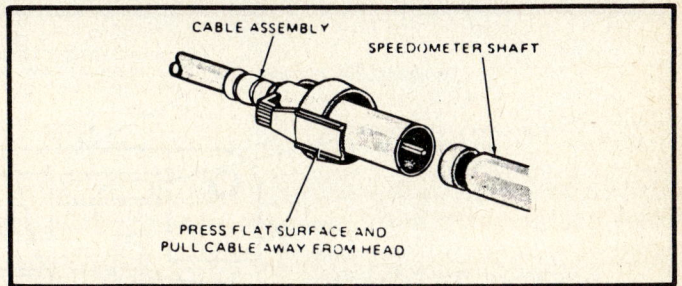

Speedometer cable quick connect
(©Ford Motor Co.)

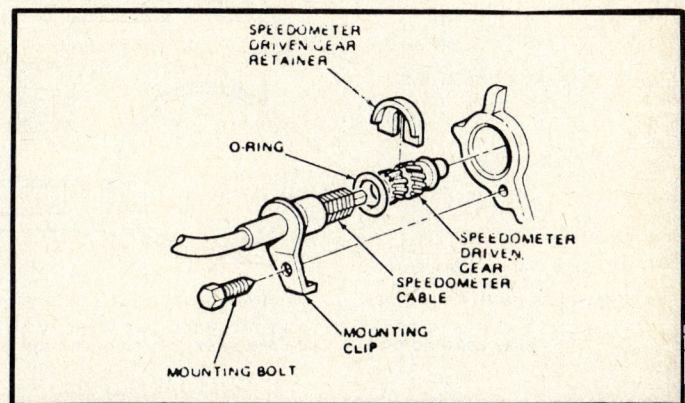

Speedometer cable-to-transmission mounting
(©Ford Motor Co.)

SIGNAL FLASHER, HAZARD WARNING FLASHER AND FUSE BLOCK LOCATION CHART

Model	TSF	HWF	Fuse Block Location
Granada	①	⑤	③
Cougar	①	④	③
Mustang	①	⑤	③
Capri	①	⑤	②
Zephyr	①	⑤	③
Fairmont Futura	①	⑤	③
XR7	①	⑤	③
Thunderbird	①	④	③
Continental	①	④	③
Town Car	①	②	③
LTD	①	②	③
Crown Victoria	①	②	③
Grand Marquis	①	②	③
Continental Mark VI	①	④	③
Continental Mark VII	①	④	③
Marquis	①	④	③

TSF Turn Signal Flasher
HWF Hazard Warning Flasher
① The turn signal flasher is plugged directly into the fuse block.
② The hazard flasher is plugged directly into the fuse block.
③ The fuse panel is located on the drivers side of the dash panel, adjacent to the parking brake mechanism.
④ The hazard flasher is located in the rear of the fuse block.
⑤ The hazard relay is attached to the relay bracket located above the glove box.

SECTION 5
FORD LINCOLN MERCURY
REAR WHEEL DRIVE CARS

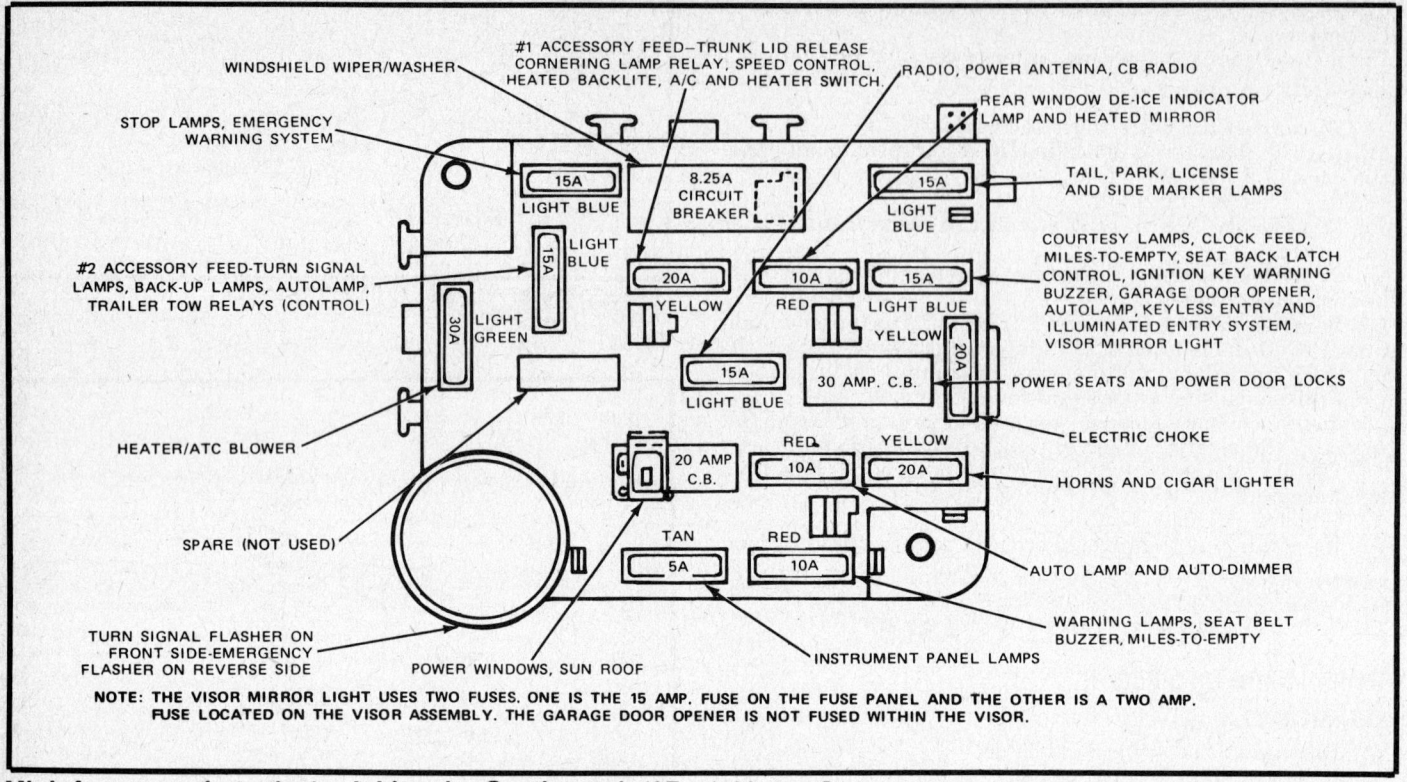

Mini fuse panel, typical of Lincoln Continental (©Ford Motor Co.)

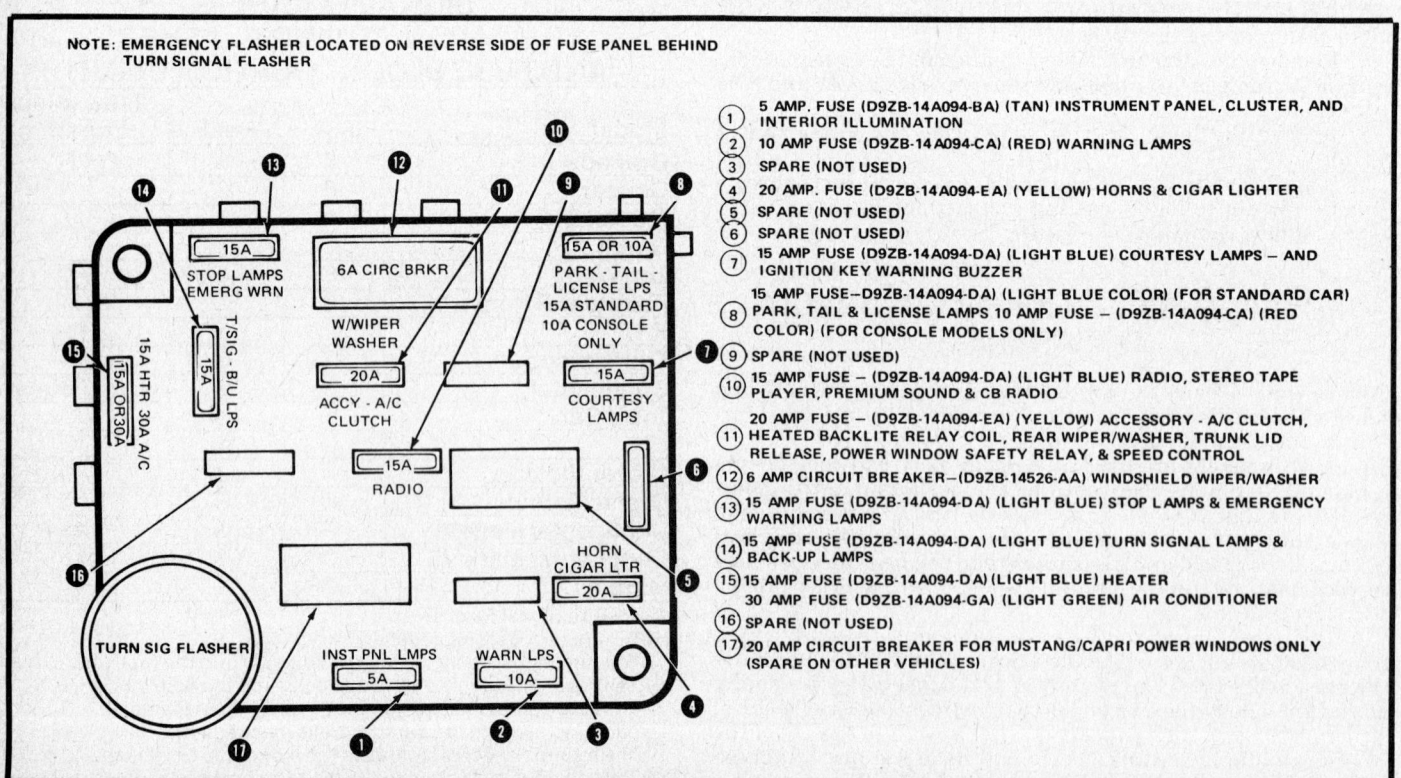

Fuse panel, typical of Fairmont/Zephyr, Mustang/Capri, Granada/Cougar (©Ford Motor Co.)

Ford Lincoln Mercury
REAR WHEEL DRIVE CARS
SECTION 5

Speed Control

ACTUATOR CABLE LINKAGE ADJUSTMENT

1. Set carburetor stroke on hot idle condition with the throttle positioner solenoid disengaged.

NOTE: Omit Step 1 for 2.3L EFI Turbocharged Engine.

2. Remove the speed control cable retaining clip.
3. Push speed control cable through adjuster until a slight tension is felt.
4. Insert the cable retaining clip and snap into place.

VACUUM DUMP VALVE

The vacuum dump valve is movable in its mounting bracket. It should be adjusted so that it is closed (no vacuum leaks) when the brake pedal is in its normal release position (not depressed), and open when the pedal is depressed. Use a hand vacuum pump to make this adjustment.

SERVO ASSEMBLY

Removal

1. Remove the air cleaner.
2. Disconnect speed control actuator cable from accelerator cable.
3. Disconnect servo electrical connector inside engine compartment.
4. Engage emergency brake.
5. Jack up vehicle on front driver's side.
6. Remove tire and wheel (driver's side).
7. Remove inner fender splash shield.
8. Remove two vacuum hoses from servo assembly.
9. Remove two screws holding servo mounting bracket to A-pillar.
10. Remove two nuts from actuator cable cover at the servo. Remove the cable and cover.
11. Remove two nuts attaching the servo to the mounting bracket.
12. If replacing servo with service stock, remove two bolt assemblies from the front of servo.

Installation

1. Attach two bolt assemblies to the front of servo.
2. Attach servo-to-mounting bracket with two nuts. Tighten to 5-7 Nm (45-65 lb-in.).
3. Attach actuator cable to servo plunger. Attach cable cover to servo with two nuts. Tighten to 5-7 Nm (45-65 lb-in).
4. Attach servo and bracket to the A-pillar with two screws.
5. Attach two vacuum hoses to servo in their correct positions.
6. Replace inner fender splash shield.
7. Replace tire and wheel.
8. Lower vehicle.
9. Reconnect servo electrical connector inside engine compartment.
10. Reconnect the speed control actuator cable to the accelerator cable.
11. Replace air cleaner.

ACTUATOR CABLE

To replace the actuator assembly, remove the servo assembly, attach the new actuator cable assembly to the servo, and reinstall the total assembly.

SPEED SENSOR

Removal

1. Raise the vehicle on a hoist and remove the bolt retaining the speed sensor mounting clip to the transmission.
2. Remove the sensor and driven gear from the transmission.
3. Disconnect the electrical connector and speedometer cable from the speed sensor.
4. Disconnect the speedometer cable by pulling it out of the speed sensor.

NOTE: Do not attempt to remove the spring retainer clip with the speedometer cable in the sensor.

5. Remove the driven gear retainer and remove the driven gear from the sensor.

Installation

1. Position the driven gear to the speed sensor and install the gear retainer.

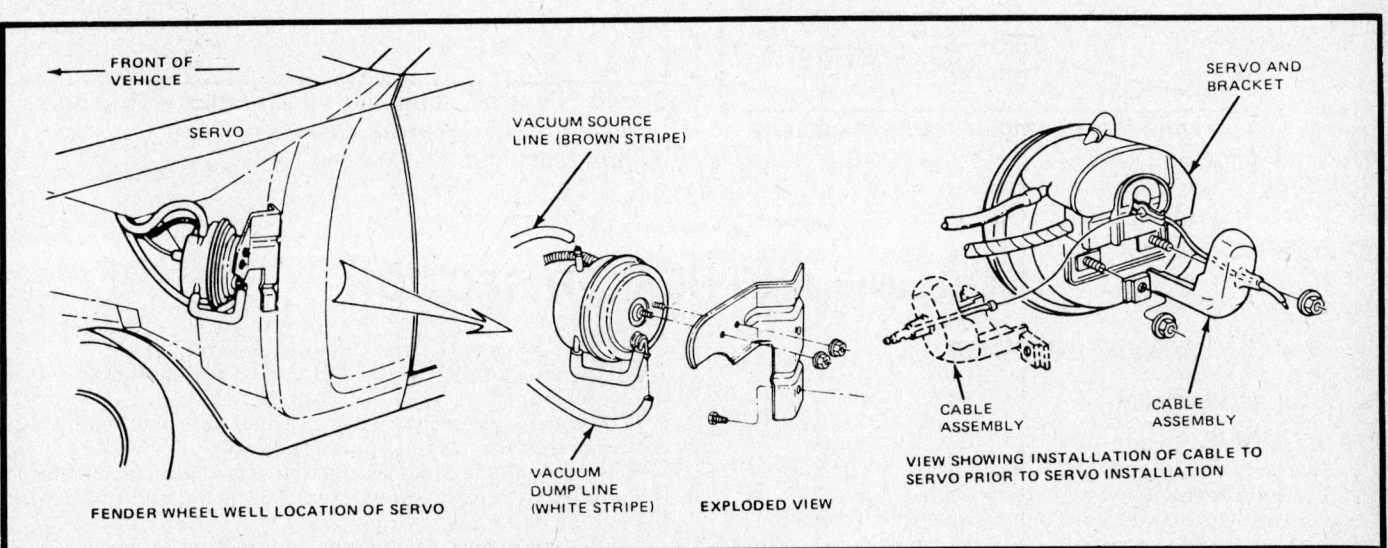

Speed control servo mounting (© Ford Motor Co.)

SECTION 5

Ford Lincoln Mercury
REAR WHEEL DRIVE CARS

2. Connect the electrical connector.
3. Insure that the internal O-ring is properly seated in the sensor housing Snap the speedometer cable into the sensor housing.
4. Insert the sensor assembly into the transmission housing and install the retaining bolt.
5. Lower the vehicle.

AMPLIFIER ASSEMBLY

The amplifier is located just to the left of the steering column inside the passenger compartment.

Removal

1. Remove the screws holding the amplifier assembly to the mounting bracket.
2. Disconnect two electrical connectors at amplifier.

Installation

1. Connect the two electrical connectors to the amplifier.
2. Install the screw which holds the amplifier to the mounting bracket.

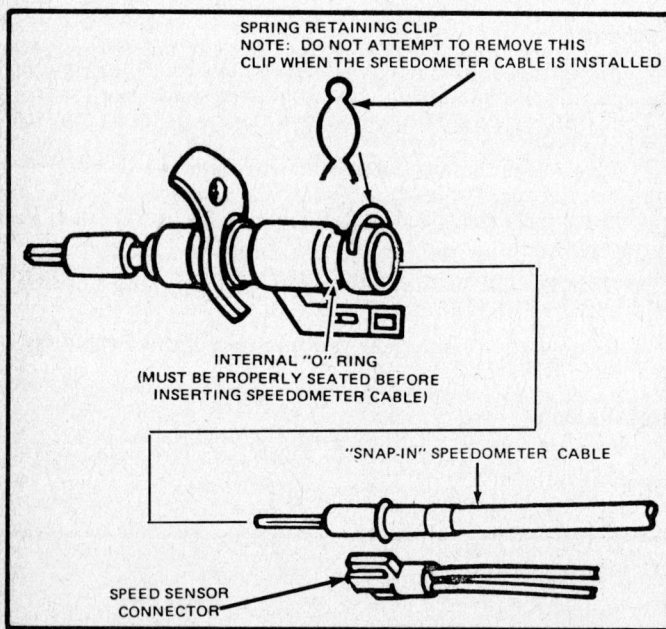

Speed sensor and speedometer cable assembly (©Ford Motor Co.)

VACUUM DUMP VALVE

Removal

1. Remove the vacuum hose from the valve and remove the bracket mounting screw.
2. Remove the valve and bracket assembly.
3. Remove the valve from the bracket.

Installation

1. Install the valve to the bracket.

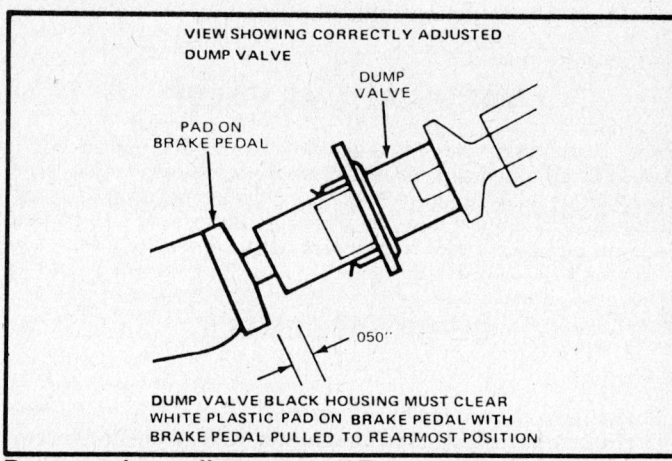

Dump valve adjustment (©Ford Motor Co.)

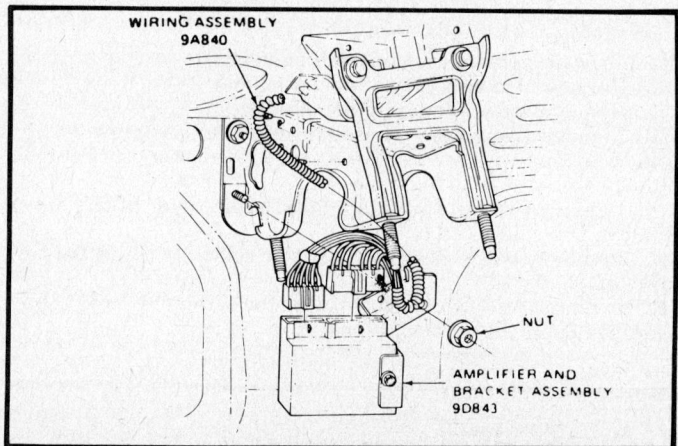

Speed control amplifier installation—Thunderbird/Cougar/LTD/Marquis/Mustang/Capri (©Ford Motor Co.)

COOLING AND HEATER SECTION

WATER PUMP

Removal and Installation
ALL MODELS

1. Drain the cooling system.
2. Disconnect the negative battery cable.
3. On cars with power steering, remove the drive belt.
4. If the vehicle is equipped with air conditioning, remove the idler pulley bracket and air conditioner drive belt.
5. On engines with Thermactor, remove the belt.
6. Disconnect the lower radiator hose and heater hose from the water pump.
7. On cars equipped with a fan shroud, remove the retaining screws and position the shroud rearward.
8. Remove the fan and spacer from the engine, and if the car is equipped with a fan shroud, remove the fan and shroud from the engine as an assembly.
9. On 4-cylinders, remove the cam belt outer cover.
10. On cars equipped with water pump mounted alternators,

5-30

loosen alternator mounting bolts, remove the alternator belt and remove the alternator adjusting arm bracket from the water pump.
11. Loosen bypass hose at water pump, if equipped.
12. Remove water pump retaining screws and remove pump from engine. On 170 cu. in. V6s, the two bolts through the thermostat housing must also be removed; they retain the lower portion of the pump housing.
13. Clean any gasket material from the pump mounting surface.
14. Remove the heater hose fitting from the old pump and install it on the new pump.
15. Coat both sides of the new gasket with a water-resistant sealer, then install the pump reversing the procedure.

BLOWER MOTOR WITH OR WITHOUT A/C

Removal and Installation

FORD AND MERCURY

1. Disconnect the ground cable from the battery.
2. Disconnect the blower motor lead connector from the wiring harness connector.
3. Remove the blower motor cooling tube from the blower motor.
4. Remove the four (4) retaining screws.
5. Turn the motor and wheel assembly slightly to the right so that the bottom edge of the mounting plate follows the contour of the wheel well splash panel. Lift up on the blower and remove it from the blower housing.
6. Installation is the reverse or removal.

BLOWER MOTOR WITHOUT A/C

Removal and Installation

FAIRMONT, ZEPHYR, MUSTANG, CAPRI, GRANADA AND COUGAR

1. Remove right ventilator assembly.
2. Disconnect blower motor lead wire from resistor assembly, push wire back thru hole in case.
3. Remove right side cowl trim panel for access to blower motor ground wire connector and remove retaining screw.
4. Remove blower motor flange retaining screws from inside of housing.

NOTE: Blower wheel may be removed to improve access.

5. Remove blower motor from housing.
6. Reverse procedure for installation.

BLOWER MOTOR WITH A/C

Removal and Installation

LINCOLN CONTINENTAL

1. Disconnect the ground cable from the battery.
2. Disconnect the blower motor lead connector from the wiring harness connector.
3. Remove the four (4) retaining screws.
4. Turn the motor and wheel assembly slightly to the right so that the bottom edge of the mounting plate follows the contour of the wheel well splash panel. Lift up on the blower and remove it from the blower housing.
5. Installation is the reverse of removal.

FAIRMONT, ZEPHYR, MUSTANG, CAPRI, XR7, THUNDERBIRD, GRANADA AND COUGAR

1. Remove the glove box, disconnect outside-recirc door vacuum motor hose.

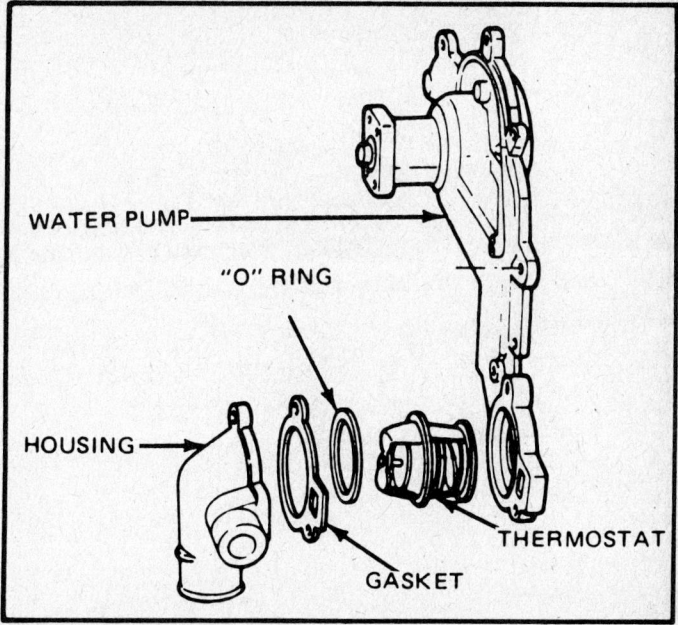
Water pump and thermostat installation, V6 engine (©Ford Motor Co.)

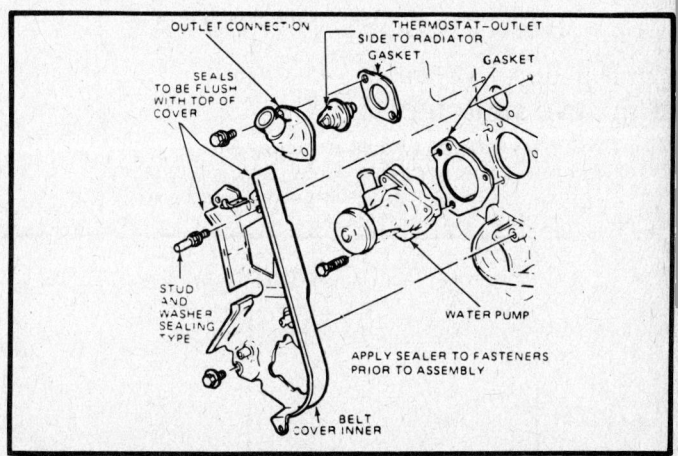
Water pump, thermostat, and inner timing belt cover on 2300 cc engine (©Ford Motor Co.)

2. Remove instrument panel lower right-to-side cowl attaching bolt.
3. Remove support brace to top of air inlet duct retaining screw.
4. Disconnect blower motor lead wire at connector.
5. Remove blower housing lower support bracket to evaporator case retaining nut.
6. Remove side cowl trim panel and remove blower motor ground wire screw.
7. Remove screw securing top of air inlet duct to evaporator case.
8. Remove the air inlet duct and blower housing down and away from evaporator case.
9. Remove four blower motor mounting plate screws and remove blower motor assembly from blower housing.

NOTE: DO NOT remove the mounting plate from the blower motor.

10. Reverse procedure for installation.

5-31

Section 5: Ford Lincoln Mercury
REAR WHEEL DRIVE CARS

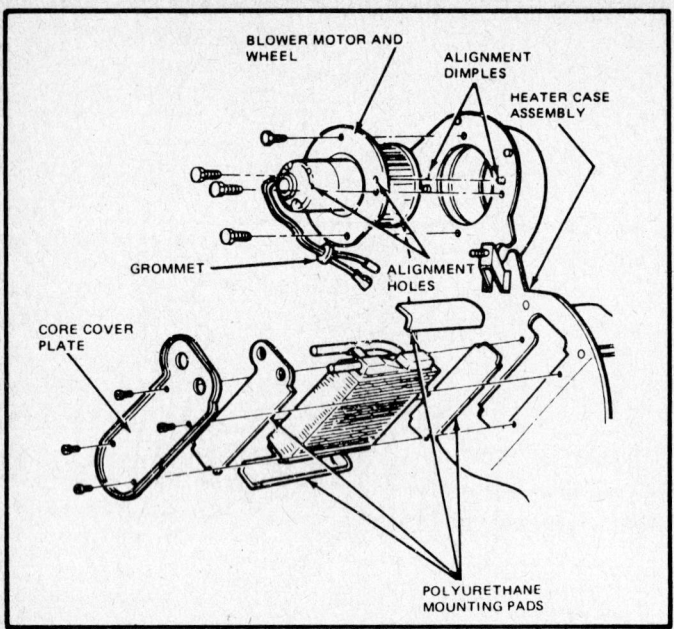

Heater blower and core installation in Cougar, LTD II and Thunderbird—typical (©Ford Motor Co.)

HEATER CORE WITHOUT A/C

Removal and Installation

FORD AND MERCURY

1. Drain the coolant and save for re-use.
2. Disconnect the negative cable from the battery.
3. Remove the heater hoses from the heater core.
4. Plug the heater core tubes to prevent coolant from spilling under the dash during plenum removal.
5. Remove the plenum to dash bolt, located under the windshield wiper motor at the left end of the plenum.
6. Remove the one nut from the heater case (engine side).
7. Disconnect the vacuum supply hose from the vacuum fitting and push the grommet and hose into the pasenger compartment.
8. Remove the glove box assembly.
9. Loosen the right door sillplate and remove the right side cowl trim panel.
10. Remove the lower right instrument panel to side cowl bolt.
11. Remove the instrument panel pad.
12. Remove the temperature control cable from the top of the plenum. Then, disconnect the temperature control cable from the blend door crank arm.
13. Remove the push clip attaching the center register duct bracket to the plenum and rotate the bracket up to the right.
14. Disconnect the vacuum jumper harness at the multiple vacuum connector near the floor air distribution duct.
15. Disconnect the white vacuum hose from the outside air door vacuum motor.
16. Remove the two (2) screws attaching the seat side of the floor air distribution duct to the plenum.

NOTE: It may be necessary to remove the two (2) screws attaching the lower panel door vacuum motor to the mounting bracket to gain access to the floor air distribution duct screw.

17. Remove the plastic push-pin fastener from the floor air distribution duct and remove the duct.
18. Remove the remaining two (2) plenum retaining nuts from the lower flange of the plenum.
19. Move the plenum toward the seat to allow the heater core tubes to clear the holes in the dash panel.

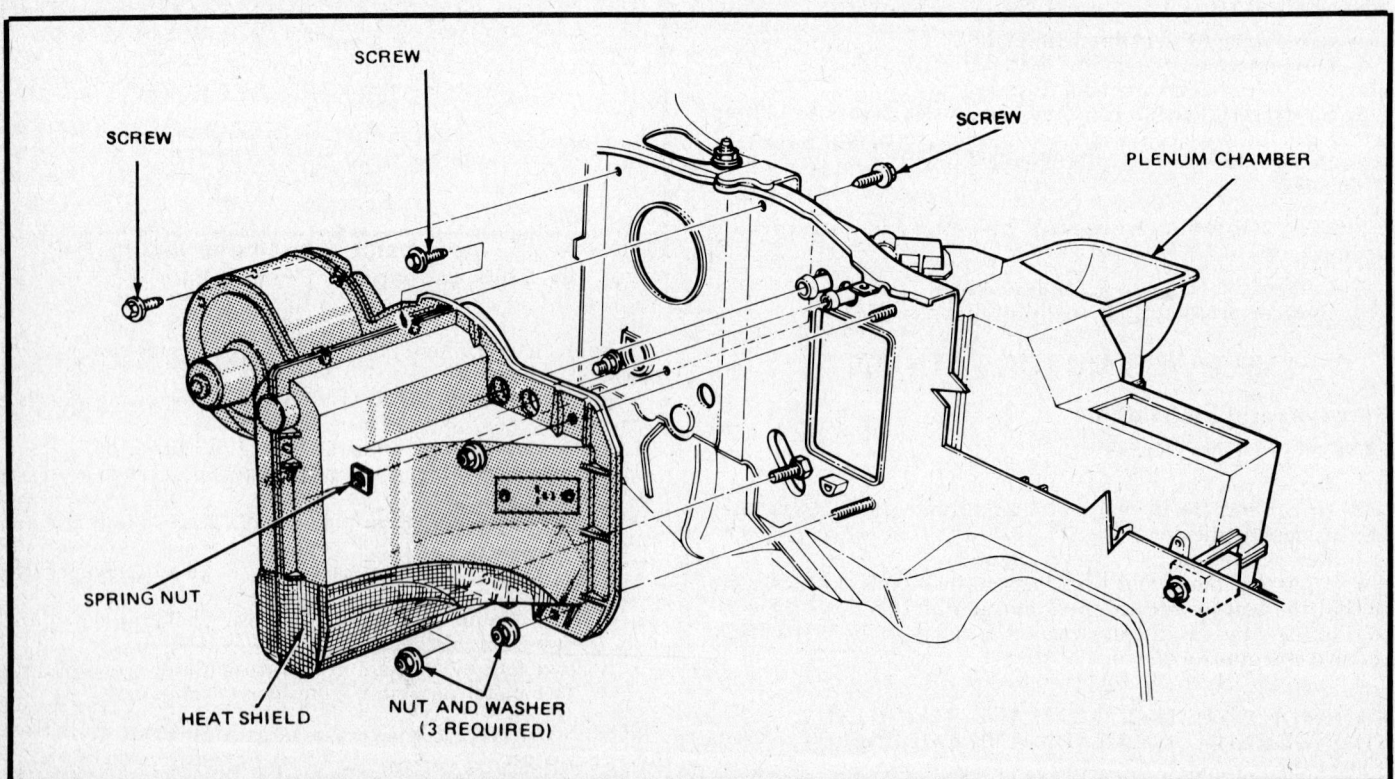

Heater core housing removal, typical of Lincoln (©Ford Motor Co.)

Ford Lincoln Mercury
REAR WHEEL DRIVE CARS
SECTION 5

20. Rotate the top of the plenum down and out from under the instrument panel.
21. Remove the four (4) heater core cover retaining screws and lift off the cover.
22. Remove the heater core tube bracket retaining screw.
23. Pull the heater core and seal from the plenum assembly.
24. Installation is the reverse of removal. Connect the negative battery cable and refill the cooling system. Check heater operation.

FAIRMONT, ZEPHYR, CAPRI, MUSTANG, GRANADA AND COUGAR

1. Drain radiator coolant.
2. Disconnect heater hoses at core connections.
3. Remove glove box.
4. Remove instrument panel-to-cowl brace retaining screws and brace.
5. Move temperature control lever to warm position.
6. Remove four heater core cover retaining screws.
7. Remove heater core cover through glove box opening.
8. In engine compartment, loosen heater case assembly mounting stud nuts. (3).
9. Push heater core tubes and seal toward passenger compartment to loosen heater core assembly from heater case assembly.
10. Remove heater core from heater case assembly through the glove box opening.
11. Reverse procedure for installation.

HEATER CORE WITH A/C INCLUDING AUTOMATIC TEMPERATURE CONTROL

Removal and Installation

1984 AND LATER FORD AND MERCURY, LINCOLN CONTINENTAL

1. Disconnect the negative battery cable.
2. Remove the heater hoses from the core tubes and plug the ends to prevent coolant loss.
3. Plug the heater core tubes to prevent coolant loss during plenum and core removal.
4. In the engine compartment, remove the bolt located under the windshield wiper motor. Remove the nut at the upper left corner (engine side) of the evaporator case.
5. Disconnect the control system vacuum supply hose from the vacuum source and push the grommet and vacuum supply hose in the passenger compartment.
6. Remove the glove box assembly.
7. Loosen the right door sill plate and remove the right side cowl trim panel.
8. Remove the lower right instrument panel to side cowl bolt.
9. Remove the instrument panel.

NOTE: THE FOLLOWING PROCEDURES APPLY TO MODELS WITHOUT AUTOMATIC TEMPERATURE CONTROL SYSTEMS.

10. Remove the bracket from the temperature control cable housing at the top of the plenum assembly. Disconnect the temperature control cable from the blend door crank arm.
11. Remove the push clip attaching the center register duct bracket to the plenum and rotate the bracket up to the right.
12. Disconnect the vacuum jumper harness at the multiple vacuum connector near the floor air distribution duct.
13. Disconnect the white vacuum hose from the outside recirculating door vacuum motor.

NOTE: THE FOLLOWING PROCEDURES APPLY TO MODELS WITH AUTOMATIC TEMPERATURE CONTROL SYSTEMS.

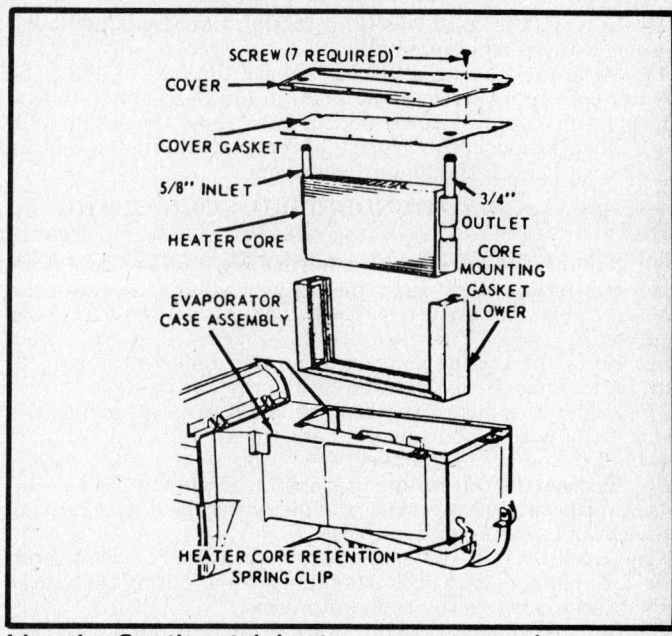

Lincoln Continental heater core removal
(©Ford Motor Co.)

10. Disconnect the temperature control cable from the ATC sensor.
11. Disconnect the vacuum harness connector from the ATC sensor.
12. Disconnect the ATC sensor tube from the sensor and evaporator case connector. Also, disconnect the wire connector from the top end of the electric-vacuum relay, located on the right side of the plenum case.
14. Remove the two (2) attaching screws from the floor air distribution duct, at the seat side of the air distribution duct.
15. Remove the plastic push fastener, holding the air distribution duct to the left of the plenum and remove the air distribution duct.

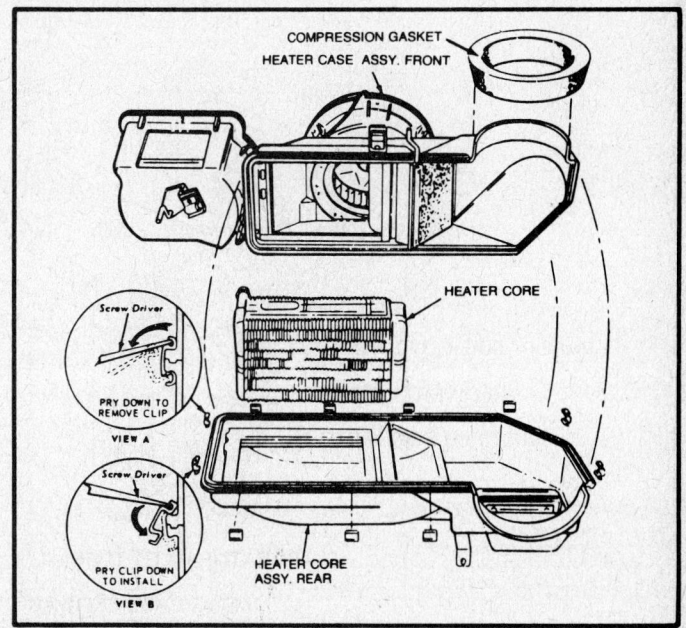

Heater core mounting, typical in subcompact models (©Ford Motor Co.)

5-33

Ford Lincoln Mercury
REAR WHEEL DRIVE CARS

16. Remove the final two (2) retaining nuts from the lower flange of the plenum assembly.
17. Move the plenum assembly toward the seat to allow the heater core tubes to clear the holes in the dash panel. Rotate the plenum assembly down and out from under the dash panel.
18. Installation is the reverse of removal. Refill the cooling system and check the heater operation.

1984 AND LATER THUNDERBIRD, COUGAR AND XR-7

1. Remove the instrument panel and lay it on the front seat.
2. Drain the coolant from the cooling system. Disconnect the heater hoses from the core tubes and plug the tubes to prevent spillage.
3. From the engine compartment side remove the two (2) nuts attaching the evaporator case to the dash panel.
4. Under the dash area remove the screws attaching the evaporator case support bracket and the air inlet duct support bracket to the cowl top panel.
5. Remove the retaining nut from the bracket at the left end of the evaporator case and the nut attaching the heater core access cover to the evaporator case.
6. Carefully pull the evaporator case assembly away from the dash panel to gain access to the screws retaining the heater core access cover to the evaporator case.
7. Remove the heater core cover attaching screws and remove the cover.
8. Lift the heater core and seals from the evaporator case. Remove the two (2) seals from the core tubes.
9. Installation is the reverse of removal. Refill the cooling system and check the heater operation.

MUSTANG/CAPRI

1. Remove instrument panel.
2. Drain radiator coolant.
3. Disconnect heater hoses at core connections.
4. In engine compartment, remove two evaporator case to dash panel retaining nuts.
5. Under dash, remove screws securing evaporator case support bracket and air inlet duct support bracket to the cowl top panel.
6. Remove one nut retaining the bracket at the left end of evaporator case to the dash panel, and one nut securing the bracket below the case to the dash panel.
7. Remove five heater core access cover screws and the cover from the evaporator case.
8. Remove heater core and seals from evaporator case. Remove the two (2) seals from the core tubes.
9. Installation is the reverse of removal. Refill the cooling system and check heater operation.

GRANADA/COUGAR, THUNDERBIRD/XR-7, CONTINENTAL, FAIRMONT/ZEPHYR

NOTE: The instrument panel must be removed for access to the heater core. The A/C system must be evacuated in order to remove the dash panel and gain access to the heater core. It is advisable to remove and replace the A/C receiver drier when the system has been evacuated.

1. Disconnect the negative battery cable.
2. Remove the instrument panel pad:
   a. Remove the screws attaching the instrument cluster trim panel to the pad.
   b. Remove the screw attaching the pad to the panel at each defroster opening.
   c. Remove the screws attaching the edge of the pad to the panel.
3. Remove the steering column opening cover.
4. Remove the nut and bracket holding the steering column to the instrument panel and lay the column across the seat.

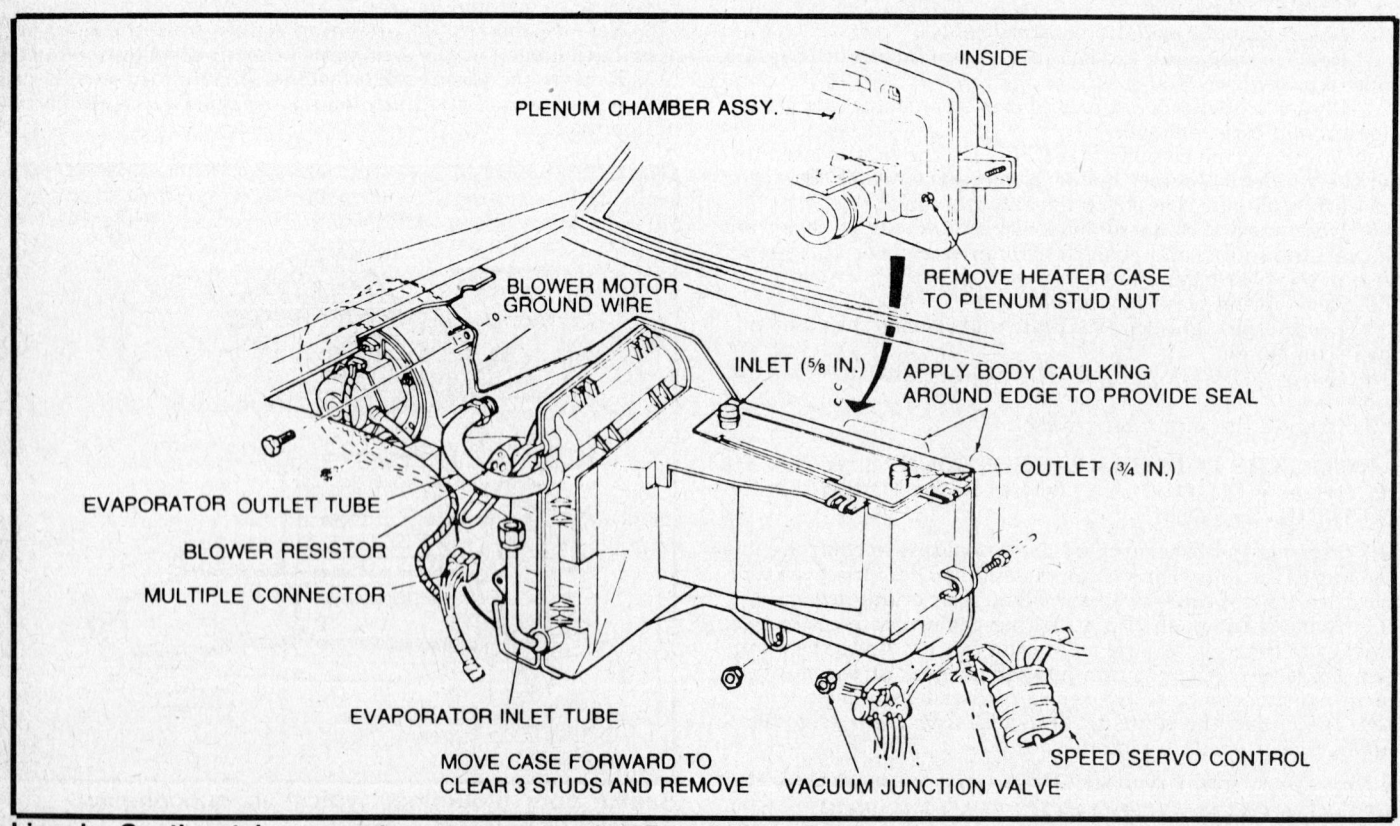

Lincoln Continental evaporator case removal (©Ford Motor Co.)

Ford Lincoln Mercury
REAR WHEEL DRIVE CARS
SECTION 5

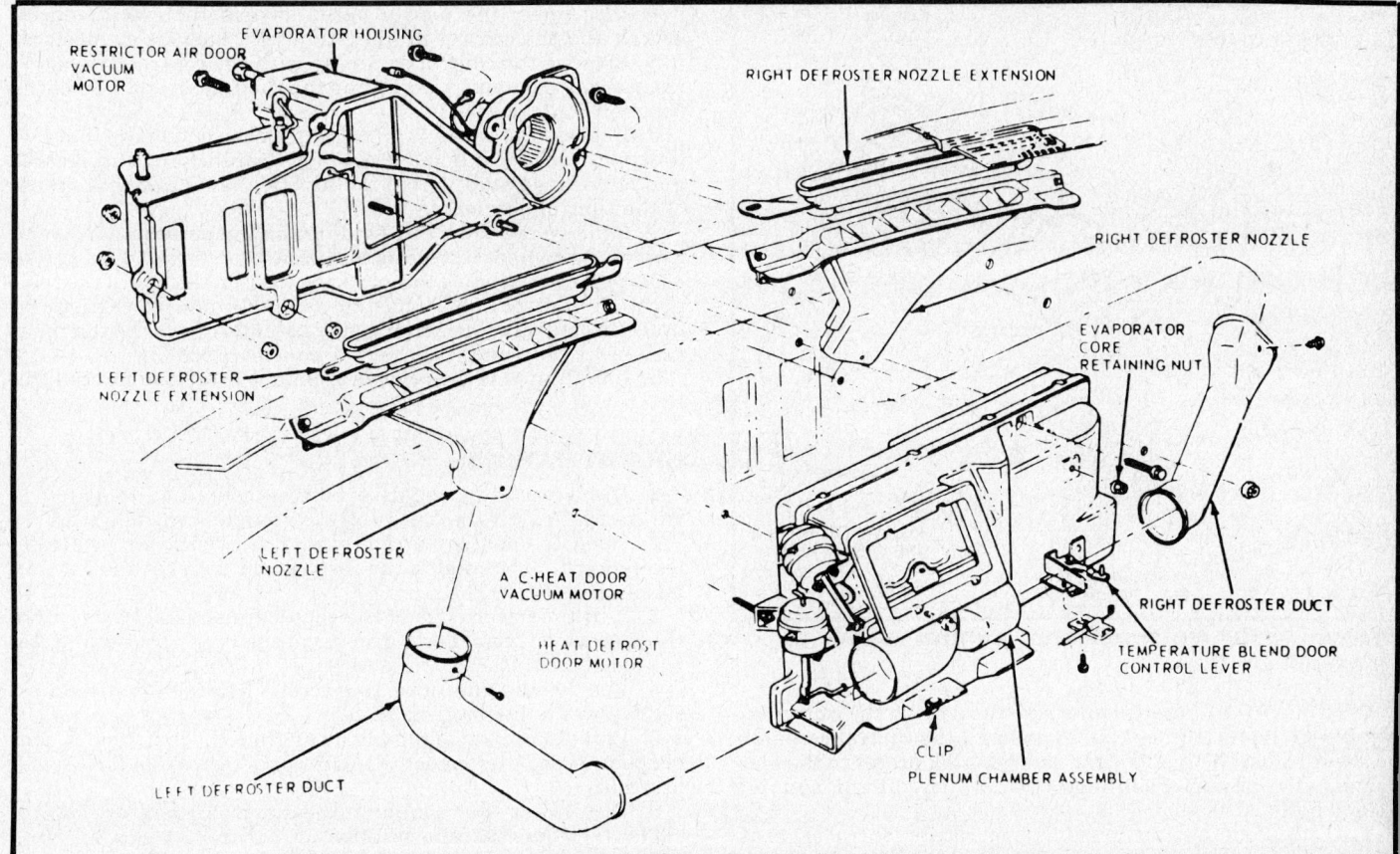

Exploded view of a typical heater/air conditioner assembly used in full sized vehicles (©Ford Motor Co.)

5. Remove the instrument panel to brake pedal support screw at the column opening.
6. Remove the screws attaching the lower brace to the panel below the radio, and below the glove compartment.
7. Disconnect the temperature cable from the door and case bracket.
8. Unplug the seven port vacuum hose connectors at the evaporator case.
9. Disconnect the resistor wire connector and the blower motor feed wire.
10. Remove the screws attaching the top of the panel to the cowl and support the panel while removing the screws.
11. Remove the one screw at each end attaching the panel to the cowl panels.
12. Move the panel rearward and disconnect the speedometer cable and any wires preventing the panel from laying flat on the seat.
13. Drain the coolant and disconnect the heater hoses from the heater core, plug the heater core tubes.
14. Remove the nuts retaining the evaporator case to the firewall in the engine compartment.
15. Remove the case support bracket screws and air inlet duct support bracket.
16. Remove the nut retaining the bracket to the dash panel at the left side of the evaporator case, and the nut retaining the bracket below the case to dash panel.
17. Pull the case assembly away from the panel to get to the screws retaining the heater core cover to the case.
18. Remove the cover screws and cover, lift the hater core and seals out of the case assembly.
19. Installation is the reverse order of the removal procedure.

AC AND/OR HEATER CONTROL ASSEMBLY

The AC and/or heater control assembly is mounted to the instrument panel and is surrounded by a trim or finish panel. In most control assembly removal procedures, the instrument cluster trim panel must be removed as previously outlined in the removal and installation of the Instrument Cluster Assembly, to expose the control assembly retaining screws. In other vehicle model applications, a separate trim cover is used which may incorporate the radio and ash receiver.

The blower switch is part of the control assembly and can be replaced after the control assembly is removed from the instrument panel.

Either vacuum lines and/or connecting cables are used to control the air flow and temperature settings. These controlling links must be disconnected to remove the control assembly from the instrument panel.

NOTE: Certain Lincoln Continental models require the lowering of the steering column.

CONTROL ASSEMBLY

Removal and Installation

GRANADA, COUGAR, FAIRMONT/FUTURA, ZEPHYR, MUSTANG/CAPRI

1. Remove the three attaching screws securing the top edge of the instrument cluster bezel and remove the instrument cluster bezel for access to the control assembly.

5–35

SECTION 5
Ford Lincoln Mercury
REAR WHEEL DRIVE CARS

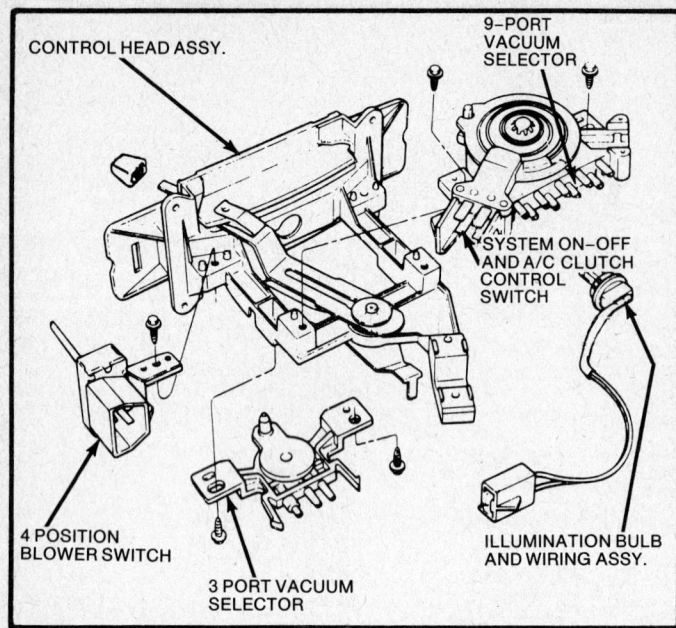

Typical heater/air conditioner control unit (©Ford Motor Co.)

2. Remove the four attaching screws securing the control assembly to the instrument panel and pull the control assembly rearward from the instrument panel to gain access to the electrical wire harness connectors and the control housing attachments.
3. Disconnect the function and temperature control cable assemblies from the heater case assembly.
4. Disconnect the blower speed switch, the system on off switch and the control illumination wire harness connectors.
5. Remove the control assembly with the control cables and remove the push nut holding the function cable end loop of the function control lever.
6. Depress the white locking tang on the end of the function control cable housing and disengage the function control cable and housing assembly from the function lever tang and frame of the control assembly.
7. Remove the push nut holding the temperature cable end loop of the temperature control lever.
8. Depress the black tang locking tang on the end of the temperature control cable housing assembly and disengage the function control cable and housing assembly from the temperature lever tang and frame of the control assembly.
9. Installation is the reverse order of the removal procedure.

FORD MERCURY, TOWN CAR, CROWN VICTORIA, GRAND MARQUIS

1. Disconnect the negative battery cable and if equipped with a radio, pull the knobs off of the radio control shafts.
2. Open the ashtray and remove the two screws attaching the center finish panel to the instrument panel at the ashtray opening.
3. Pull the lower edge of the center finish panel away from the instrument panel and disengage the upper tabs of the finish panel from the instrument panel.
4. Remove the four attaching screws holding the control assembly to the instrument panel.
5. Pull the control assembly away from the instrument panel opening and disconnect the wire connectors from the control assembly.
6. Disconnect the vacuum harness and temperature control cable from the control assembly.
7. Installation is the reverse order of the removal procedure.

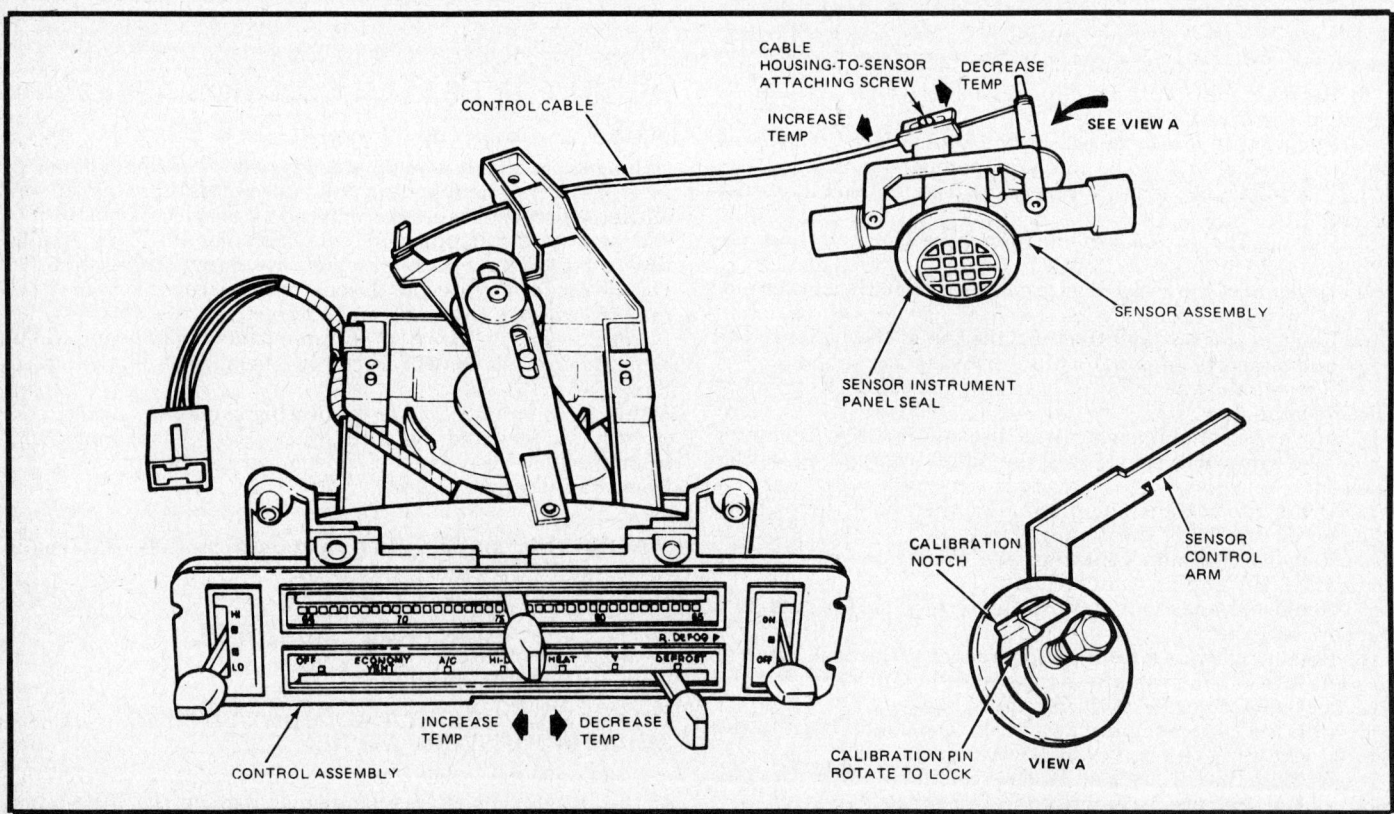

Heater/air conditioner control unit with the automatic temperature control system (©Ford Motor Co.)

5-36

Ford Lincoln Mercury
REAR WHEEL DRIVE CARS
SECTION 5

THUNDERBIRD/XR-7, LTD/MARQUIS 1984-87 COUGAR

1. Disconnect the negative battery cable.
2. Remove the instrument cluster opening finish panel on the 84 and later models.

NOTE: Remove the temperature control knob on the 85 and later models models.

3. Remove the four screws attaching the the control assembly to the instrument panel.
4. Pull the control assembly from the instrument panel opening and disconnect the wire connectors from the control assembly.
5. Disconnect the vacuum harness and the temperature control cable from the control assembly.
6. Installation is the reverse order of the removal procedure.

CONTINENTAL, MARK VI, MARK VII

1. Disconnect the negative battery cable.
2. On the Continental remove the ashtray receptacle and remove the four screws attaching the center finish panel to the instrument at the ashtray opening and at the upper edge of the finish panel.
3. On the Mark VI, and Mark VII remove the finish panel right hand insert attaching screws.
4. Pull the lower edge of the center finish panel (Continental) or finish panel right hand insert (Mark Vl, Mark VII) away from the instrument panel and disengage the upper tabs of the finish panel or insert from the instrument panel.
5. Remove the four attaching screws holding the control assembly to the instrument panel.
6. Slide the control assembly out from the instrument panel opening and disconnect the two harness connectors from the control assembly by disengaging the latches on the bottom of the control.
7. Installation is the reverse order of the removal procedure.

ELECTRIC COOLING FAN

Removal
ALL MODELS

1. Disconnect the negative battery cable and remove the fan wiring harness from the routing clip.
2. Disconnect the wiring harness from the fan motor connector and pull up on the single lock finger to separate the connectors.
3. Remove the four mounting bracket attaching screws and remove the fan assembly from the vehicle.
4. Remove the retaining clip from the end of the motor shaft and remove the fan.
5. Remove the nuts attaching the fan motor to the mounting bracket.

NOTE: After the retaining clip has been removed there may be a small burr left on the shaft, this burr must be removed in order to remove the fan off of the motor shaft.

Installation

1. Position the fan motor on the mounting bracket and torque the attaching nuts to 70-95 in. lbs.
2. Install the fan and retaining clip on the motor shaft and position the fan assembly in the vehicle with the mounting bracket attaching screws.
3. Connect the motor wiring connector to the wiring harness and be sure that the lock finger on the connector snaps firmly into place.
4. Connect the negative battery cable and check the fan for proper operation.

Removal
2.4 Liter Diesel Engine Only

1. Disconnect the negative battery cable and raise and support vehicle safely.
2. Remove the nuts and bolts attaching the mounting brackets to the radiator support.
3. Disconnect the electrical fan and remove the bolts holding the hood latch to the radiator support, place the latch out of the way.
4. Remove the nuts and bolts attaching the mounting brackets to the fan and motor assembly and remove the fan and motor assembly from the vehicle.

Installation

1. Position the fan and motor assembly in the vehicle and position the mounting brackets on the fan and motor assembly. Torque the nuts 4-5 ft. lbs..
2. Install the hood latch and connect the electrical connector to the fan and motor assembly.
3. Position the mounting brackets in the vehicle and torque the mounting bolts to 6-8 ft. lbs.. and the nuts to 4-5 ft. lbs..
4. Lower the vehicle and connect the negative battery cable.

COOLING SYSTEM REFILL

All Models

1. Close the radiator drain cock and install all cylinder block drains.
2. Refill the system with a 50/50 mixture of permanent type coolant and water. Refill the radiator up to approximately 0 to 2 inches below the filler neck seat.
3. Operate the engine until the thermostat opens and the upper radiator hose starts to get hot. Check for any coolant leaks at the hoses, drain cock and block plugs.
4. Stop the engine and add coolant to the filler neck seat and re-install the radiator cap.
5. Fill the coolant recovery tank to the add mark with the specified coolant and add water up to the full hot mark. This is a n easy way to ensure a proper mixture in the coolant recovery tank.

NOTE: On aluminum core radiators add two Cooling System Protector Pellets D9AZ-19558-A or equivalent, to the proper mixture of water and antifreeze.

FUEL SYSTEM

MECHANICAL FUEL PUMP

Removal and Installation

NOTE: Before removing the pump, rotate the engine so that the low point of the cam lobe is against the pump arm. This can be determined by rotating the engine with the fuel pump mounting bolts loosened; when tension is removed from the arm, proceed.

1. Remove the inlet and outlet lines from the pump.
2. Remove the fuel pump retaining screws and remove the pump gasket.

5-37

SECTION 5
Ford Lincoln Mercury
REAR WHEEL DRIVE CARS

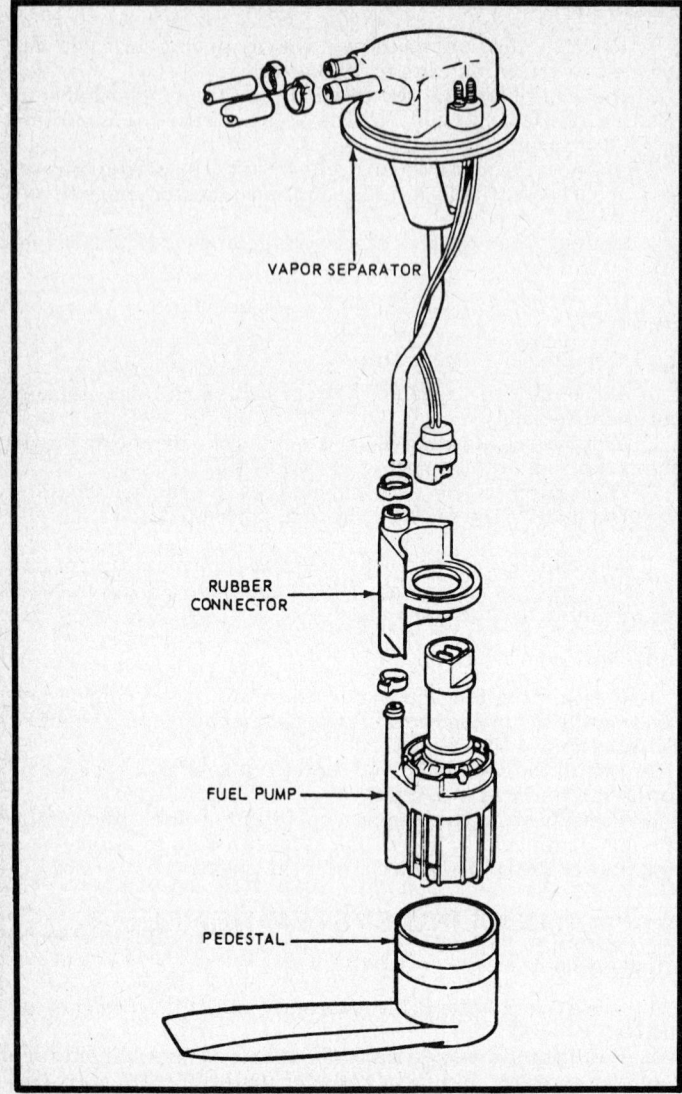

Tank mounted electric fuel pump, typical
(©Ford Motor Co.)

3. Clean all gasket material from the pump mounting surface on the engine, and apply a coat of oil-resistant sealer to the new gasket.
4. Position pump on engine and install retaining screws.
5. Reinstall lines, start engine and check for leaks.

NOTE: If resistance is felt while positioning the fuel pump on the block, the camshaft eccentric is in the high position. To ease installation, connect a remote engine starter switch to the engine and tap the remote switch until resistance fades.

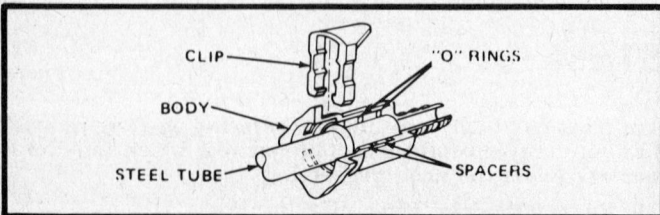

Push connect fitting with "hairpin" clip
(©Ford Motor Co.)

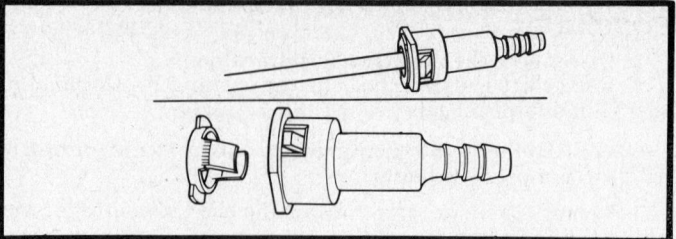

Push connect fitting with "duck bill" clip
(©Ford Motor Co.)

ELECTRIC FUEL PUMP

Removal and Installation

The electric fuel pump used on fuel injected models is mounted in the gas tank.

— CAUTION —
Before servicing any part of the fuel injection it is necessary to depressurize the system. A special tool is available for testing and bleeding the system.

NOTE: Each time the electric fuel pump is removed from the fuel tank, the rubber hoses and clamps must be replaced. Once the air hits the fuel soaked rubber, it will eventually cause the rubber to become brittle and crack.

1. Disconnect the negative battery cable.
2. Depressurize the system by using the following procedure.
  a. Remove the air cleaner assembly. Attach Fuel Pressure Gauge Tool T80L-9974-A or equivalent, to the special service (relief) valve provided on the fuel charging assembly.
  b. With the gauge installed properly release the pressure in the fuel system.
3. Drain as much gas from the tank by pumping out through the filler neck. Raise the back of the car and safely support on jackstands.
4. Disconnect the fuel supply, return the vent lines at the right and left side of the frame.
5. Disconnect the wiring to the fuel pump.
6. Support the gas tank, loosen and remove the mounting straps. Remove the gas tank.
7. Disconnect the lines and harness at the pump flange.
8. Clean the outside of the mounting flange and retaining ring. Turn the fuel pump lock ring counterclockwise and remove.
9. Remove the fuel pump.
10. Clean the mounting surfaces. Put a light coat of grease on the mounting surfaces and on the new sealing ring. Install the new fuel pump.
11. Installation is in the reverse order of removal. Fill the tank with at least 10 gals. of gas. turn the ignition key ON for three seconds. Turn the "OFF" and " ON" for three seconds. Repeat 6 or 7 times until the fuel system is pressurized. Check for any fitting leaks. Start the engine and check for leaks.

PUSH CONNECT FITTINGS

Push connect fittings are designed with two different retaining clips. The fittings used with 3/8 and 5/16 in. fuel lines use a "hairpin" clip and the fittings used with 1/4 in. fuel lines use a "duck bill" clip. Disconnect all push connect fittings from components before component removal.

NOTE: Removal of hairpin type clips is done using hands only. Do not use any tools. The removal of duck bill fittings requires a special tool.

5-38

HIGH PRESSURE IN-LINE PUMP ASSEMBLY

Removal and Installation

1985 AND LATER LTD/MARQUIS AND MUSTANG/CAPRI

1. Depressurize the fuel system. Raise and support the vehicle safely.
2. Disconnect the elctrical connector from the body harness. Remove the inlet and outlet lines from the fuel pump (the fuel pump is in-line with the fuel system and mounted near the fuel filter).
3. The fuel pump can now be removed from the assembly by bending the tab out and sliding the pump out of the ring.
4. The electrical wiring harness may be removed from the assembly by inserting a suitable tool between the connector and the retaining clip and sliding the connector towards the pump inlet.
5. Installation is the reverse order of the removal procedure.

Carburetor

IDLE SPEED

Adjustment

NOTE: Refer to Carburetor Chapter in Unit Repair Section for illustrations.

1983 AND LATER, EXCEPT EEC, EFI AND 7200 VV CARBURETED ENGINES

NOTE: **If equipped with automatic overdrive transmission, see Idle Speed Adjustment section following.**

1. Place the transmission in Park. Apply the emergency brake and block the wheels.
2. Bring the engine to normal operating temperature. Turn off all accessories and connect a tachometer.
3. On carbureted models, disconnect and plug the vacuum hose at the throttle kicker, place the transmission in the gear specified on the underhood sticker and check and adjust the curb idle rpm. Adjust at the curb idle screw at the throttle valve lever or at the saddle bracket adjusting screw.
4. On EFI engines, shut the engine off, restart it and run at 2,000 rpm for 60 seconds in neutral then let the engine idle stabilize for 15 seconds. Place the transmission in drive and check/adjust the curb idle rpm. Adjust at the saddle bracket adjusting screw. If rpm is low, turn the screw clockwise one full turn then repeat Step 4 until correct rpm is reached. If the rpm is high, turn the screw counterclockwise to specific rpm and recheck.
5. On carbureted models, place transmission in Neutral or Park, rev. the engine once, place the transmission in the specified gear (sticker) and recheck the curb idle rpm.
6. On EFI engines, make sure the scribe mark on the throttle position sensor is aligned with the mark on the throttle body. Adjust as necessary.
7. Reconnect the throttle kicker vacuum hose on the 7200 VV carburetor and apply pressure to the nylon nut on the accelerator pump to take up linkage clearance, then adjust the clearance between the top of the accelerator pump and the pump lever to .010 in., using the nylon nut on the pump rod. Turn the pump rod one turn counterclockwise to set the lever lash preload.
8. Reconnect all hoses.
9. To set the throttle kicker speed, set the transmission in Neutral or Park, bring the engine to normal operating temperature and turn off all accessories. Disconnect the vacuum hose at the Vacuum Operated Throttle Modulator (kicker) and connect an external vacuum source (10 in Hg. minimum) to the kicker.

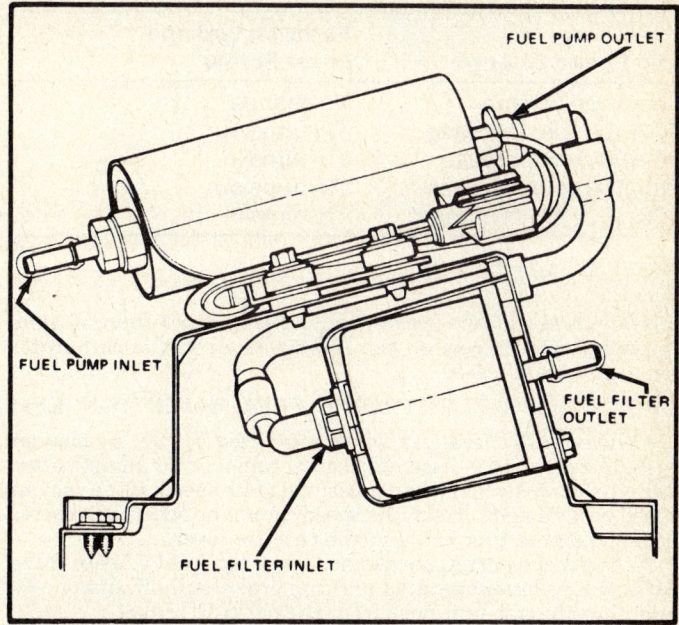

Exploded view of the in-line fuel pump

10. Place the transmission in the gear specified on the underhood sticker (apply parking brake, block wheels).
11. Disconnect the A/C compressor clutch wire, place the A/C selector to max. blower cooling and check/adjust the VOTM kicker speed. If adjustment is required, turn the saddle bracket adjusting screw.
12. Reconnect all components.

NOTE: **1986 5.0 Liter V-8 engine is equipped with sequential electronic fuel injection system with multiport injectors, each timed to deliver precise fuel pulses in sequence with the opening of the associated intake valve, not simultaneously.**

1983 AND LATER WITH EEC

NOTE: **If equipped with automatic overdrive transmission, see the Idle Speed Adjustment Section following.**

1. The air cleaner must be installed. If the engine speed fluctuates, use the average engine speed. Do not depress the brake pedal on models equipped with hydro-boost brakes. On cars with automatic parking brake release, disconnect and plug the vacuum hose at the parking brake pedal. Set the parking brake, turn off all the accessories, warm the engine up to operating temperature and shut it off.
2. Connect a tachometer.
3. Disconnect and plug the EGR line at the EGR valve.
4. Disconnect the evaporative emission purge hose at the intake manifold. Plug the hose connection.
5. Start the engine and allow it to run for at least one minute. Run the engine at 2500 rpm for 15 seconds and place the fast idle lever on the proper step of the fast idle cam (see the underhood sticker). Allow the engine speed to stabilize for abut 15 seconds and measure the fast idle speed. Check the sticker for the proper setting. If it is not within 100 rpm of the specification, rest it and repeat this step to check it.
6. Turn the throttle stop adjusting screw to adjust the idle speed.

AUTOMATIC OVERDRIVE (AOD)

Idle Speed Adjustment

If the car is equipped with Ford's automatic overdrive trans-

5–39

SECTION 5

Ford Lincoln Mercury
REAR WHEEL DRIVE CARS

Idle Speed Change	Turns on Linkage Lever Screw
Less than 50 rpm	No change
500-100 rpm increase	1½ turns out
50-100 rpm increase	1½ turns in
100-150 rpm increase	2½ turns out
100-150 rpm decrease	2½ turns in

mission, and the idle speed is adjusted by more than 50 rpm, the adjustment screw on the linkage lever at the carburetor must also be adjusted:

1983 LATER W/ELECTRONIC FUEL INJECTION (EFI)

1. Leave all hoses and wires connected to the air cleaner case. The air cleaner assembly can be removed for adjustments, but must be installed when measuring idle speed. If the car has speed control and correct idle speed cannot be achieved, disconnect the accelerator cable at the throttle lever.
2. Apply the parking brake and block the front wheels. If the car has a vacuum-operated parking brake pull-off, disconnect and plug the vacuum hose from the parking brake.
3. Turn off all accessories. Start the engine and allow it to reach normal operating temperature. Check the throttle linkage for freedom of movement and correct as necessary. Connect a tachometer to the engine.
4. The throttle stop screw is not to be adjusted.
5. If the throttle speed is high, adjust the Vacuum Operated Throttle Modulator (VOTM) bracket adjusting screw counterclockwise. When the idle speed is as specified, open and close the throttle and recheck.
6. If the rpm is low, shut off the engine. Turn the VOTM bracket adjusting screw one turn clockwise. Start the engine and run at 2000 rpm for ten seconds. Let the idle stabilize for one minute (time not to exceed two minutes) and recheck the idle speed. Repeat as necessary.
7. If the idle speed has been altered more than 50 rpm, the Automatic Overdrive Transmission throttle valve control linkage must be adjusted. See the Automatic Transmissions Unit Repair Section.

1983 AND LATER W/7200 VV CARBURETOR

1. Follow Steps 1–3 of the 302 EFI procedure. Additionally, disconnect and plug the EGR vacuum hose from the EGR valve. Disconnect the evaporative emission (charcoal canister) purge hose from the intake manifold; cap the manifold connection.
2. Curb idle with Cold Start VOTM: Warm the engine to normal operating temperature. If the rpm is higher than specified, adjust the throttle stop-screw counterclockwise. If the rpm is low, shut off the engine, turn the throttle stop adjusting screw one turn clockwise, start the engine, and recheck the adjustment. Open and close the throttle and check the speed. See Step 7 of the 302 EFI procedure.
3. Curb idle with Dashpot: If the car has air conditioning, shut it off. Start the engine and turn the throttle stop adjusting screw until the specified idle speed is reached. Turn the engine off and check the clearance between the dashpot and plunger and the throttle lever pad. Adjust if not correct (see the emission control sticker on the car for proper clearance measurement). Start the engine, open and close the throttle and recheck the idle speed; shut off the engine and recheck the dashpot clearance. See Step 7 of the 302 EFI procedure.
4. Curb Idle without Dashpot: If the car has neither a dashpot nor a VOTM, simply start the engine (A/C off, if equipped) and turn the throttle stop adjusting screw until the specified speed is reached. Open and close the throttle and recheck the adjustment. See Step 7 of the 302 EFI procedure.

2.3L WITH YFA 1–V AND YFA 1–V FEEDBACK

Diagnostic Procedure - This adjustment is not required as part of a normal engine idle rpm check/adjustment. It should only be performed on a customer complaint of "engine continues to "Run after ignition key is turned to Off position."

1. Place the transmission in neutral or Park.
2. Bring engine to normal operating temperature.
3. Place A/C selector to Off position.
4. Disconnect the electrical lead to the TSP or VOTM/TSP. Check engine rpm to specification (600rpm). If adjustment is required, remove tamper resistant sleeve.
5. Adjust TSP-Off rpm to specification.
6. Shut engine Off, reconnect TSP electrical lead.
7. Reinstall new tamper resistant cap.

2.3L ENGINES WITH CFI AND DC MOTOR IDLE SPEED CONTROL (ISC)

NOTE: If for any reason the battery is disconnected or the vehicle has to be jump started it may be necessary to perform this following procedure.

1. Apply the parking brake, block the drive wheels and place the vehicle in neutral.
2. Start the engine and let it run until it reaches normal operating temperature, then turn the engine off. Connect a suitable tachometer.
3. Start the engine and place the transmission in drive or reverse on the Automatic models and neutral on the manual models, let the engine run at idle for 120 seconds. The idle rpm should now return to the the specified idle speed (The idle specifications can be found on the calibration sticker located under the hood).
4. Place the transmission in neutral or park and the engine rpm should increase by approxitmately 100 rpm. Now lightly step on and off the accelerator. The engine rpm should return to the specified idle speed. If the rpm remains high, repeat the sequence. Remember it may take the the system 120 seconds to adjust. If the vehicle does not act as just outlined, perform the following adjustment.
5. Shut the engine off and remove the air cleaner. Locate the self-test connector and self-test input connector in the engine compartment.
6. Connect a jumper wire between the self-test input connector and the signal return pin (is the top right terminal) on the self-test connector.
7. Place the ignition key in the run position and be careful not to start the engine. The ISC plunger will retract, so wait approxitmately 10 to 15 seconds until the ISC plunger is fully retracted. Turn the ignition key to the off position and wait 10 to 15 seconds.
8. Remove the jumper wire and unplug the ISC motor from the wire harness. Now perform the throttle stop adjustment as follows:
   a. Remove the Central Fuel Injection (CFI) assembly from the vehicle.
   b. Use a small punch or equivalent to punch through and remove the aluminum plug which covers the throttle stop adjusting screw.
   c. Remove and replace the throttle stop screw.
9. Reinstall the CFI assembly on the vehicle, stabilize the engine and set the idle rpm to the specifications (listed on the calibration decal located under the hood) on the throttle stop adjusting screw.
10. Shut off the engine. Reconnect the ISC motor wire harness, remove all test equipment and reinstall the air cleaner assembly.

2.3L EFI TURBO

1. Apply the parking brake, block the drive wheels and place the vehicle in neutral.

2. Start the engine and let it run until it reaches normal operating temperature, then turn the engine off. Connect a suitable tachometer.

3. Disconnect the idle speed control air bypass valve power lead. Start the engine and run the engine at 2000 rpm for 120 seconds.

NOTE: If the electric cooling fan comes on during the idle speed adjusting procedures, wait for the fan to turn off before proceeding.

4. Let the engine idle and check the base idel, it should be at 750 ± 50 rpm. If it is not adjust as necessary.

5. Adjust the engine rpm to 900 ± 75 rpm by adjusting the throttle stop screw.

6. Shut the engine off and reconnect the power lead to the idle speed control air bypass valve. Disconnect all test equipment.

3.8L ENGINES WITH CFI AND DC MOTOR IDLE SPEED CONTROL (ISC)

1. Apply the parking brake, block the drive wheels and place the vehicle in neutral.

2. Start the engine and let it run until it reaches normal operating temperature, then turn the engine off. Connect a suitable tachometer.

3. Turn off all accessories and place the transmission in drive or reverse. Let the engine run at idle for 60 seconds. The idle rpm should now return to the specified idle speed (The idle specifications can be found on the calibration sticker located under the hood).

NOTE: The curb and fast idle speeds are controlled by the EEC-IV processor and the idel speed control device. If the control system is operating properly, these speeds are fixed and cannot be changed by traditional adjustment techniques.

4. Place the transmission in neutral or park and the engine rpm should increase by approxitmately 100 rpm. Now lightly step on and off the accelerator. The engine rpm should return to the specified idle speed. If the rpm remains high, repeat the sequence. Remember it may take the the system 120 seconds to adjust. If the vehicle does not act as just outlined, perform the following adjustment.

5. Shut the engine off and remove the air cleaner. Locate the self-test connector and self-test input connector in the engine compartment.

6. Connect a jumper wire between the self-test input connector and the signal return pin (is the top right terminal) on the self-test connector.

7. Place the ignition key in the run position and be careful not to start the engine. The ISC plunger will retract, so wait approxitmately 10 to 15 seconds until the ISC plunger is fully retracted. Turn the ignition key to the off position and wait 10 to 15 secomnds.

NOTE: If the ISC plunger does not retract, the problem is with the EEC-IV system and the diagnostic check of the system should be made.

8. Remove the jumper wire and perform the throttle stop adjustment as follows:
   a. Using a suitable tool, grasp the throttle stop adjusting screw threads and turn the screw until it is removed from the CFI assembly.
   b. Install a new screw.
   c. With the throttle plates closed, turn the new screw inward until there is a .005 in. gap between the screw tip and the throttle lever surface in which it contacts.
   d. Turn the screw inward an additional 1½ turns.

9. Remove all test equipment and reinstall the air cleaner.

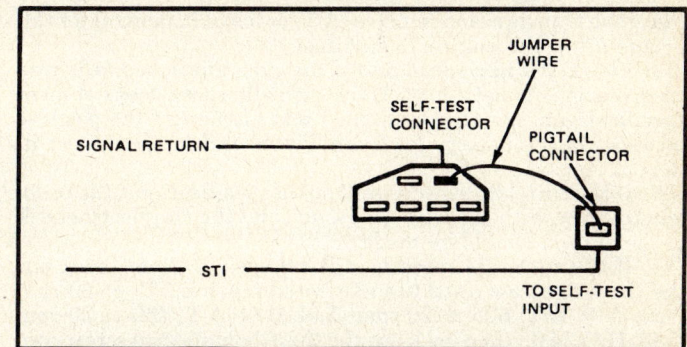

Installing the jumper wire on the 3.8L CFI system

1986-87 5.0L ENGINE WITH SEQUENTIAL ELECTRONIC FUEL INJECTION

NOTE: The curb and fast idle speeds are controlled by the EEC-IV processor and the idel speed control device. If the control system is operating properly, these speeds are fixed and cannot be changed by traditional adjustment.

1. Apply the parking brake, block the drive wheels and place the vehicle in neutral.

2. Start the engine and let it run until it reaches normal operating temperature, then turn the engine off. Connect a suitable tachometer.

3. Turn off all accessories and place the transmission in park or neutral. Check the throttle linkage for freedom of movement and correct as necessary.

4. Check for vacuum leaks. Place the transmission in neutral and operate the engine at 1800 rpm for at least 30 seconds.

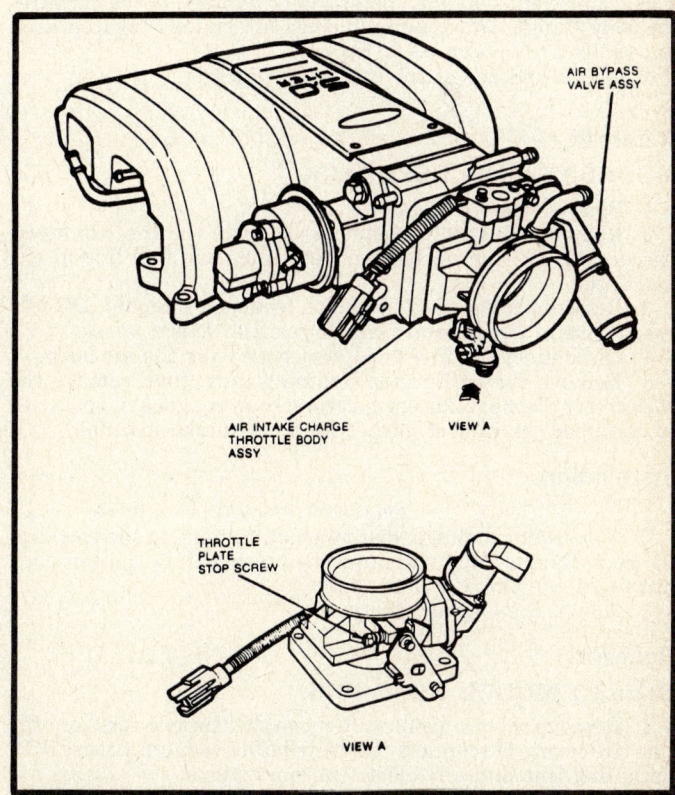

Location of the throttle plate stop screw on the 5.0L SEFI engine

Ford Lincoln Mercury
REAR WHEEL DRIVE CARS

Place the transmission in drive (A/T) or leave in neutral for (M/T) and allow the engine to stabilize.

5. Check the idle speed and if the curb idle speed falls into specification, do not adjust. If the curb idle speed does not meet specifications, turn the engine off and disconnect the positive terminal of the battery for five minutes and ten reconnect it. Repeat steps 4 and 5.

6. If the curb idle speed is still out of specifications, the problem could be with the EEC-IV system and the diagnostic check of the system should be made.

7. If the curb idle speed is still out specifications, back out the throttle screw until the idle speed reaches 575 ± 20 rpm (base 5.0L A/T) 625 ± 20 rpm (5.0L H.O. A/T) 700 ± 20 rpm (5.0L H.O. M/T) then back out the throttle plate stop screw one-half additional turn to bring the throttle plate linkage into the normal operating range of the ISC system.

8. Shut off the engine and remove all test equipment.

CARBURETOR ASSEMBLY

Removal
MODEL YFA 1661

1. Remove the air cleaner.
2. Remove the throttle cable or rod from the throttle lever. Disconnect the vacuum lines, fuel filter tube and the electrical connections for the throttle control, and WOT A/C cut-off switch, if equipped.
3. Disconnect electric choke wire at connector.
4. Remove carburetor retaining nuts; then remove carburetor. Remove carburetor mounting gasket, spacer if equipped, and lower gasket from the intake manifold.

Installation

1. Installation is the reverse of removal procedures.
2. To prevent leakage, distortion or damage to the carburetor body flange, snug the nuts; then alternately tighten each nut to 20–21 Nm (14–13 ft. lbs.).
3. Check and adjust the engine idle speeds.

Removal
MODEL YFA 1661 FEEDBACK

1. Remove the air cleaner.
2. Remove the throttle cable or rod from the throttle lever. Disconnect the appropriate vacuum lines and fuel line at the fuel filter.
3. Disconnect the electric choke, feedback solenoid, DC idle speed control motor, and throttle position sensor wires.
4. Disconnect the fuel bowl vent hose from the air horn.
5. Remove the carburetor retaining nuts; then remove the carburetor. Remove the carburetor mounting gasket, spacer (if so equipped) and lower gasket from the intake manifold.

Installation

1. Installation is the reverse of removal procedures.
2. To prevent leakage, distortion or damage to the carburetor body flange, snug the nuts; then alternately tighten each nut to 17–20 Nm (12–15 ft. lbs.).
3. Adjust the engine idle speed.

Removal
HOLLEY MODEL 4180-C 4BBL

1. Remove the air cleaner. Remove the throttle rod from the throttle lever. Disconnect the distributor vacuum hoses, PCV hose, fuel line and any electrical connections.
2. Disconnect choke heat tube.
3. Remove the carburetor retaining nuts, then remove the carburetor. Remove the spacer from the manifold.

Installation

1. Installation is the reverse of removal procedures.
2. Position carburetor on the manifold and install the lockwashers and nuts. Tighten the nuts alternately to 1927 Nm (14–20 ft. lbs..).
3. Adjust engine idle speed.

Removal
MOTORCRAFT MODEL 7200-VV and 2150 2BBL

1. Remove the air cleaner.
2. Remove the throttle cable and transmission kickdown levers from the throttle lever. Disconnect and mark all vacuum lines, emission hoses, the fuel line and electrical connections to ease installation.
3. Remove the carburetor retaining nuts; then remove the carburetor. Remove the carburetor mounting gasket spacer, if equipped, and lower gasket from the intake manifold.

Installation

1. Installation is the reverse of removal procedures.
2. To prevent leakage, distortion or damage to the carburetor body flange, snug the nuts; then, alternately tighten each nut in a crisscross pattern to 16–20 Nm (12–15 ft. lbs..) on model 7200 and 19–22 Nm (14–16 lb. ft.) on 2150 models.
3. Adjust engine idle speed.

INTAKE MANIFOLD

Removal
2.3L 4CYL ENGINE

1. Disconnect battery cable from negative terminal of battery.
2. Drain cooling system.
3. Remove air cleaner assembly.
4. Disconnect accelerator cable.
5. Disconnect vacuum hose as required.
6. Remove dipstick.
7. Disconnect heat tube at EGR valve.
8. Disconnect fuel line at carburetor (one clamp).

Installation

1. Installation is the reverse of removal procedures.
2. Position intake manifold to head and install retaining bolts. Tighten in sequence in two steps to 15–17 Nm (11–12.5 ft. lbs..), then 19–28 Nm (14–21 ft lbs.).

Removal
3.8L V6 ENGINE

1. Drain engine cooling system.
2. Remove air cleaner assembly including air intake duct and heat tube.
3. Disconnect accelerator cable at the carburetor or fuel charging assembly. Disconnect speed control cable, if equipped.
4. Disconnect the transmission linkage at the carburetor or fuel charging assembly.
5. Remove attaching bolts from accelerator cable mounting bracket and position cables aside.
6. Disconnect thermactor air supply hose at the check valve. The valve is located at the back of the intake manifold.
7. Disconnect fuel lines at carburetor or fuel charging assembly.
8. Disconnect radiator upper hose at thermostat housing.
9. Disconnect coolant bypass hose at manifold.
10. Disconnect heater tube at intake manifold. Remove tube support bracket attaching nut. Remove heater hose at the rear of heater tube. Loosen hose clamp at the heater elbow and re-

Ford Lincoln Mercury
REAR WHEEL DRIVE CARS — SECTION 5

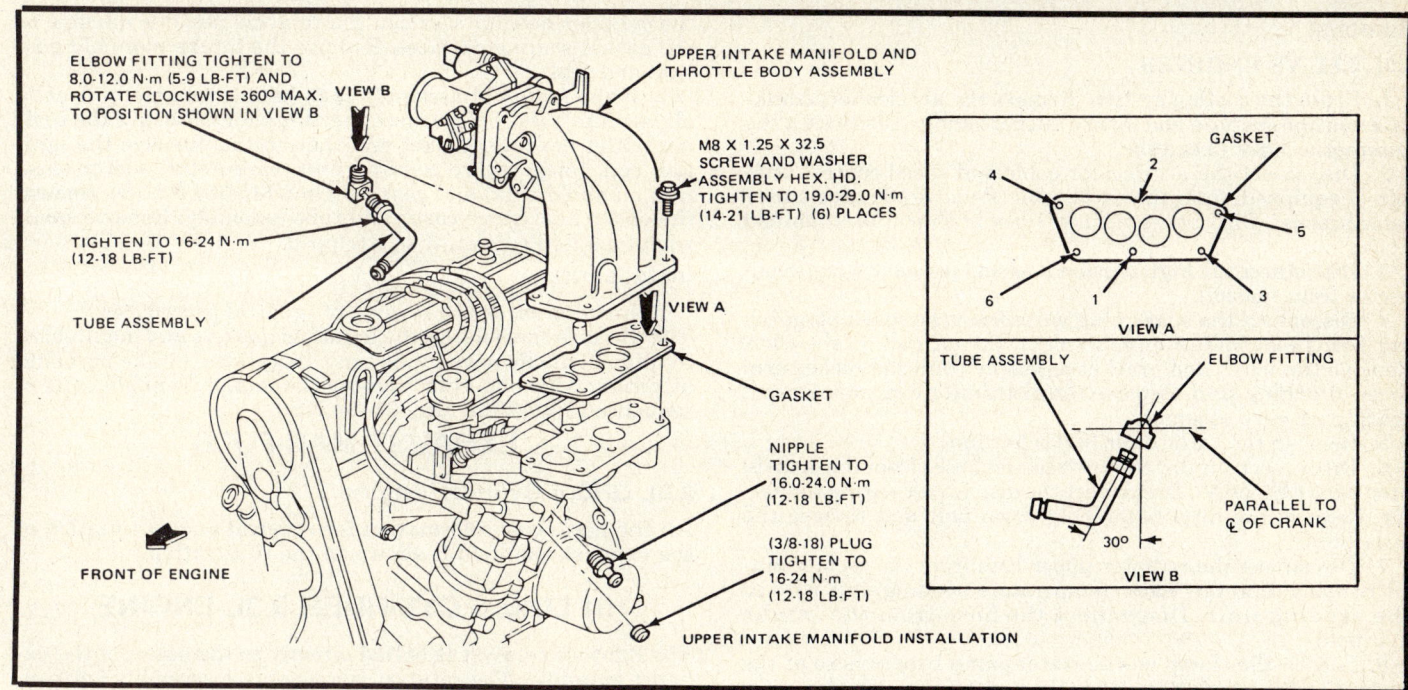

Intake manifold installation—4cyl (©Ford Motor Co.)

move heater tube with hose attached. On CFI applications, remove heater tube with the fuel lines attached and set the assembly aside.

11. Disconnect vacuum lines at the carburetor or fuel charging assembly and intake manifold.
12. Disconnect necessary electrical connectors.
13. If equipped with air conditioning, remove air compressor support bracket attached to left front intake manifold attaching bolt.
14. Disconnect PCV line at the carburetor and at valve. Remove PCV line.
15. Remove carburetor. Discard phenolic gasket.
16. Remove three EGR spacer attaching screws from manifold.
17. With EGR valve attached, work EGR spacer loose from the manifold. Remove spacer assembly. Discard old gasket.
18. Remove the attaching nut and remove wiring retainer bracket located at the LH front of the intake manifold and set aside with spark plug wires.
19. Remove exhaust heat control valve vacuum tube attaching bolt located at the rear of the left cylinder head. Remove attaching nut(s) located on manifold and remove tube(s), if equipped.
20. Remove intake manifold attaching bolts/studs.
21. Remove intake manifold.

NOTE: The manifold is sealed at each end with RTV type sealer. To break the seal, it may be necessary to pry on the front of the manifold with a screwdriver blade. If it is necessary to pry on the manifold use care to prevent damage to machined surfaces.

Installation

1. Installation is the reverse of removal procedure.
2. Apply a 3.0–4.0mm (1/8 in.) bead of Silicone Sealer at each corner where the cylinder head joins the cylinder block.
3. Apply a 3.0–4.0mm (1/8 in.) bead of Silicone Sealer at each end of the cylinder block where the manifold seats against the block.

NOTE: On some 1984-85 Capri, Cougar, LTD, Marquis, Mustang and Thunderbird models with the 3.8L engine, the engine may be making a ticking noise. This problem could be caused by the intake manifold heat control valve. A new intake manifold heat control valve (E4AZ-9G464-A) and speed control bracket (E45Z-9C876-C) are now available for installation. Use the following procedure to test the intake manifold heat control valve.

a. Disconnect the intake manifold heat control valve vacuum hose. Using a suitable 'T' fitting, connect the vacuum reservoir directly to the intake manifold heat control valve.
b. Drive the vehicle and listen for the ticking noise. If the noise has stopped, replace the intake manifold heat control valve and speed control bracket with the newly designed parts as mentioned above.
c. Reconnect the vacuum hose to the new intake manifold heat control valve.

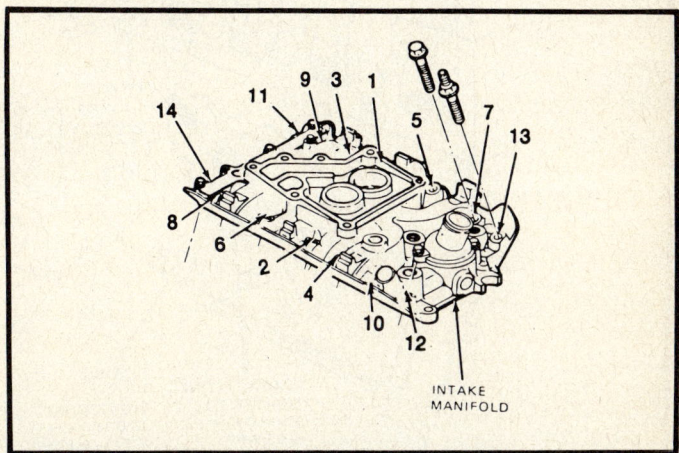

Intake manifold bolts tightening sequence—V6 engine (©Ford Motor Co.)

5-43

Ford Lincoln Mercury
REAR WHEEL DRIVE CARS

Removal

5.0L/5.8L V8 ENGINES

1. Drain the cooling system. Remove the air cleaner, crankcase ventilation hose and intake duct assembly. Disconnect the automatic choke heat tube.
2. Disconnect the accelerator cable and speed control linkage, if equipped, from the carburetor. Remove the accelerator cable bracket. Disconnect vacuum lines, at the intake manifold fitting.
3. Disconnect the high tension lead and primary wiring connector from the coil.
4. Disconnect the spark plug wires from the spark plugs using Tool T74P-6666-A or equivalent. Do not pull on the wire. Remove the wires and bracket assembly from the rocker arm cover attaching stud. Remove the distributor cap, adapter and spark plug wire assembly.
5. Remove the carburetor fuel inlet line.
6. Disconnect the distributor vacuum hoses from the distributor (non-EEC only). Disconnect the distributor wiring connector. Remove the distributor hold down bolt and remove the distributor.
7. Disconnect the radiator upper hose from the coolant outlet housing, and the water temperature sending unit wire at the sending unit. Disconnect the hose from the intake manifold.
8. Loosen the clamp on the water pump bypass hose at the coolant outlet housing and slide the hose off the outlet housing. On EEC IV equipped vehicles, disconnect wires at ECT, ACT and EGR sensors and also disconnect injector wire connections.
9. Disconnect the crankcase vent hose assembly at the valve rocker arm cover. Disconnect fuel evaporative purge tube, if so equipped.
10. Remove the intake manifold and carburetor as an assembly. It may be necessary to pry the intake manifold away from the cylinder head(s). Use caution to avoid possible damage to the gasket sealing surfaces. Remove the intake manifold gaskets and seals.
11. If the manifold assembly is to be disassembled, identify all vacuum hoses before disconnecting them. Remove the coolant outlet housing, gasket and thermostat. Remove the ignition coil, temperature sending unit, carburetor, spacer (case iron manifold only) and gaskets. On 5.8L (351W CID), remove the choke heat stove cover and tube assembly. Remove sandwich type EGR cooler, if so equipped.

Installation

1. Installation is the reverse of removal procedures.
2. Be sure the holes in the manifold gaskets and manifold re in alignment. Remove guide pins. Install the intake manifold attaching bolts and nuts. Tighten the intake manifold bolts in sequence to 23–25 ft. lbs. (31–34 Nm).

EXHAUST MANIFOLD

2.3L OHC 4 Cylinder Engine

All the necessary information for removal and installation of the exhaust manifold is shown in the illustration.

IN LINE 6 CYLINDER 3.3L ENGINE

The light-off catalyst is bolted directly to the outlet of the exhaust manifold. The catalyst is a one-piece assembly between the underbody catalyst and the exhaust manifold outlet. Four studs on the exhaust manifold flange are used to mount the light-off catalyst in place.

Removal

1. Remove the air cleaner assembly and related parts. Disconnect the light-off catalyst from the exhaust manifold.

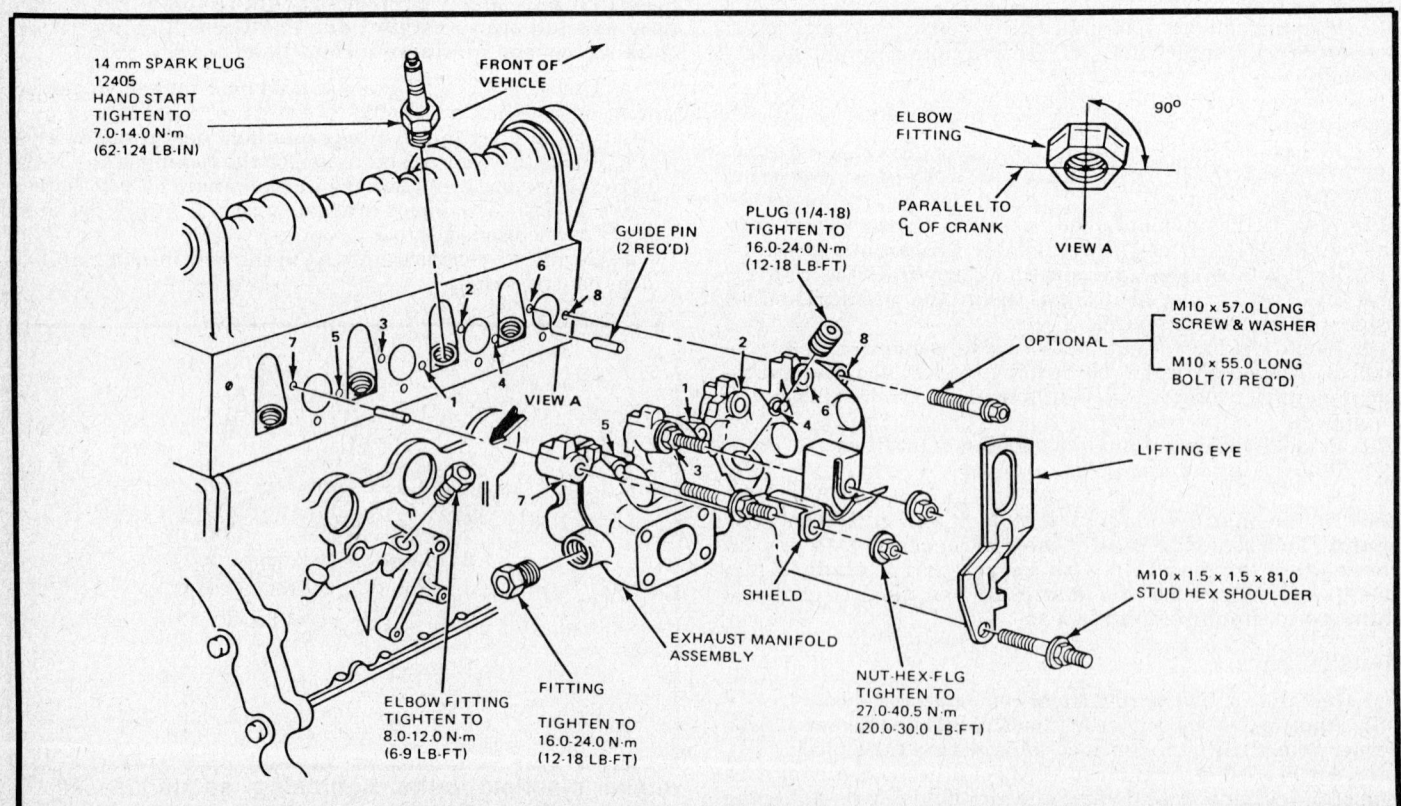

Exhaust manifold installaton—typical 4 cyl (©Ford Motor Co.)

2. Remove or disconnect the EGR tube and all other emission components that interfere with the removal of the exhaust manifold.
3. Remove retaining bolts and nuts. Remove exhaust manifold.

Installation

1. Clean the mating surfaces of the exhaust manifold and cylinder head.
2. Position the exhaust manifold on the cylinder head and install the attaching bolts. Tighten the bolts and studs in the sequence shown in illustration. Tighten the bolts to 18–24 ft. lbs. (23–33 Nm).
3. Position the light-off catalyst to the manifold. Install and tighten the attaching nuts to specification.
4. Install the air cleaner assembly and related parts. Start the engine and check for exhaust leaks.

EXHAUST MANIFOLD

Removal-Left Side

3.8L V6 ENGINE

1. Remove oil level dipstick tube support bracket.
2. Disconnect EGO sensor at the wiring connector, if equipped.
3. Disconnect wires from spark plugs.
4. Raise vehicle.
5. Remove manifold to exhaust pipe attaching nuts.
6. Disconnect exhaust heat control valve vacuum line, if equipped.
7. Lower vehicle.
8. Remove exhaust manifold attaching bolts and manifold.
9. If a new exhaust manifold is being installed, remove EGO sensor, if equipped and exhaust heat control valve, if equipped.

Installation—Left Side

1. Installation is the reverse of removal procedure.
2. If equipped with an EGO sensor, coat the threads with high temperature anti-seize compound. Install the sensor into the exhaust manifold and tighten to 27–33 ft. lbs. (37–45 Nm).
3. Install remaining manifold attaching bolts and tighten to 15–22 ft. lbs. (20–30 Nm).

Removal—Right Side

1. Remove air cleaner assembly and heat tube.
2. Disconnect thermactor hose from the downstream air tube check valve, CFI only).
3. Remove EGO sensor at the wiring connector, if equipped.
4. Disconnect coil secondary wire from the coil and the wires from the spark plugs.
5. Remove spark plugs. Remove outer heat shroud.
6. Raise vehicle.
7. Remove transmission dipstick tube.
8. Remove thermactor downstream air tube. Use EGR Clamp Cutter and Crimping Tool to cut the tube clamp at the underbody catalyst, (CFI only).
9. Remove manifold-to-exhaust pipe attaching nuts.
10. Lower the vehicle.
11. Remove exhaust manifold attaching bolts. Remove manifold and inner heat shroud as an assembly.

Installation—Right Side

1. Installation is the reverse of removal procedures.
2. Install manifold attaching bolts and tighten to 15–25 ft. lbs. (20–30 Nm).
3. Connect exhaust pipe to the manifold, and tighten the attaching nuts to 16–24 ft. lbs. (21–32 Nm).

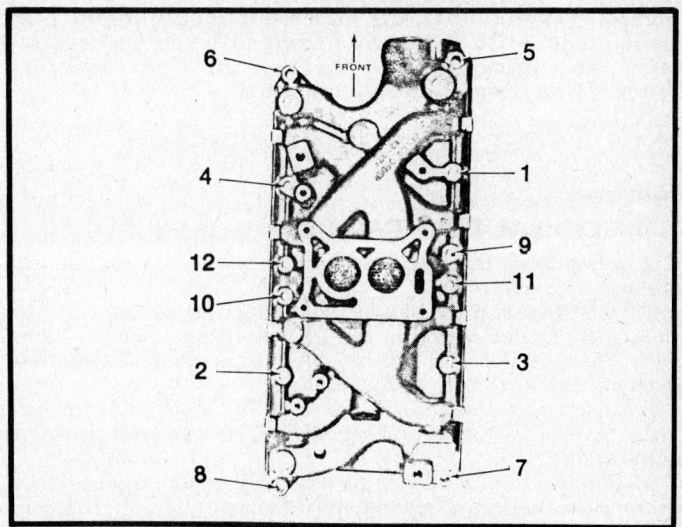

Intake manifold bolts tightening sequence
(©Ford Motor Co.)

EXHAUST MANIFOLD

Removal

5.0L and 5.8L V8 ENGINES

1. On a right exhaust manifold, remove the air cleaner and intake duct assembly and downstream air tube bracket (except Ford Crown Victoria/Mercury Grand Marquis, Lincoln Town Car, Mark VII/Continental). Disconnect the automatic choke heat tubes. On LH exhaust manifolds, remove the oil dipstick and tube assembly, air cleaner and inlet duct assembly (Ford Crown Victoria/Mercury Grand Marquis, Lincoln Town Car, Mark VII/Continental). Remove speed control bracke try, if so equipped.
2. Disconnect the exhaust manifold from the muffler inlet pipe. Remove the attaching nuts and then remove the spark plug wires and spark plugs. Disconnect the exhaust gas oxygen (EGO) sensor if equipped.
3. Remove the attaching bolts and washers and remove the exhaust manifold.

Installation

1. Clean the mating surfaces of the exhaust manifold and cylinder head. Clean the mounting flange of the exhaust manifold and muffler inlet pipe.
2. Position the exhaust manifold on the cylinder head and install the attaching bolts and washers. Working from the center to the ends. tighten the bolts to specifications. Install the spark plugs and spark plug wires. Connect the exhaust gas oxygen sensor (EGO) if equipped.
3. Position the muffler inlet pipe to the manifold. Install the tighten the attaching nuts to specification.
4. Install the automatic choke heat tubes. Install the air cleaner and intake duct assembly. Install downstream air tube bracket.
5. Start the engine and check for exhaust leaks.

Fuel Injection

For Information and Services on Fuel Injection Systems Refer to Unit Repair Sections.

NOTE: The 1986-87 5.0L engine is using a Sequential electronic fuel injection system. This system is classified as a multi-point, pulse time speed denesity control fuel injection system. The fuel is metered into each intake port in sequence with the engine firing order in accordance with the engine demand through the eight injectors mounted on a tuned intake manifold.

FUEL CHARGING ASSEMBLY

Removal

3.8L CENTRAL FUEL INJECTED (CFI) ENGINE

1. Disconnect the negative battery cable. Remove the air cleaner assembly.
2. Release the pressure from the fuel system at the diagnostic (relief) valve on the fuel charging assembly using Fuel Pressure Gauge T80L-9974-A or equivalent. Use care to prevent combustion from fuel spillage.
3. Disconnect the throttle cable and transmission throttle valve lever. Disconnect and tag all fuel, vacuum and electrical connections.
4. Remove the fuel charging assembly retaining nuts, then remove the fuel charging assembly. Remove the mounting gasket from the intake manifold.

Installation

1. Clean the gasket mounting surfaces of spacer and fuel charging assembly. Place the spacer between two new gaskets and position the spacer and gaskets on the intake manifold.
2. Place the charging assembly on the gaskets and spacer. Install the fuel charging assembly retaining nuts and torque them to 12 to 15 ft. lbs.. using a crisscross pattern.
3. Connect the fuel line, electrical connectors, throttle cable and all vacuum hoses. Start the engine and check for any leaks.
4. Adjust the engine idle speed if necessary. Refer to the engine/emission control decal located under the hood for the proper specifications.

NOTE: In order to remove the fuel injectors on this engine, the fuel charging assembly must be removed and disassembled, so as to gain access to the fuel injectors located inside the fuel charging assembly.

UPPER INTAKE MANIFOLD AND THROTTLE BODY

Removal and Installation

1986-87 5.0L ENGINE WITH SEQUENTIAL ELECTRONIC FUEL INJECTION

1. Disconnect the negative battery cable. Remove the fuel cap from the fuel tank.
2. Release the pressure from the fuel system at the diagnostic (relief) valve on the fuel charging assembly using Fuel Pressure Gauge T80L-9974-A or equivalent. Use care to prevent combustion from fuel spillage.
3. Disconnect the electrical connectors at the air bypass valve, throttle position sensor and EGR position sensor.
4. Disconnect the throttle linkage at the throttle ball and the transmission linkage from the throttle body. Remove the two bolts securing the bracket to the intake manifold and position the bracket with cables out of the way.
5. Disconnect the upper intake manifold fitting connections by disconnecting the all vacuum lines to the vacuum tree, vacuum lines to the EGR valve and vacuum line to the fuel pressure regulator.
6. Disconnect the PCV system hose, remove the two canister purge lines from the fittings on the throttle body. Disconnect the EGR tube from the EGR valve by removing the flange nut.
7. Remove the bolt from the upper intake support bracket to the upper manifold. Remove the six upper intake manifold retaining bolts.
8. Remove the upper intake and throttle body as an assembly from the lower intake manifold.
9. Installation is the reverse order of the removal procedure. Torque the upper intake manifold bolts to 12 to 18 ft. lbs..

FUEL RAIL ASSEMBLY

Removal and Installation

1986-87 5.0L ENGINE WITH SEQUENTIAL ELECTRONIC FUEL INJECTION

1. Disconnect the negative battery cable. Remove the fuel cap from the fuel tank.
2. Release the pressure from the fuel system at the diagnostic (relief) valve on the fuel charging assembly using Fuel Pressure Gauge T80L-9974-A or equivalent. Use care to prevent combustion from fuel spillage.
3. Remove the upper intake manifold as previously outlined.
4. Using Spring Lock Coupling Remover Tool T81-19623-G (or G1) or equivalent, disconnect the crossover fuel hose from the fuel rail assembly.
5. Remove the four fuel rail assembly retaining bolts. Carefully disengage the fuel rail from the fuel injectors and remove the fuel rail.

NOTE: It may be easier to remove the injectors with the fuel rail as an assembly.

6. Use a rocking, side to side motion while lifting to remove the injectors from the fuel rail.
7. Installation is the reverse order of the removal procedure.

FUEL INJECTOR

Removal and Installation

1986-87 5.0L ENGINE WITH SEQUENTIAL ELECTRONIC FUEL INJECTION

1. Disconnect the negative battery cable. Remove the fuel cap from the fuel tank.
2. Release the pressure from the fuel system at the diagnostic (relief) valve on the fuel charging assembly using Fuel Pressure Gauge T80L-9974-A or equivalent. Use care to prevent combustion from fuel spillage.
3. Remove the upper intake manifold as previously outlined.
4. Remove the fuel rail assembly as previously outlined.
5. Carefully remove the electrical harness connectors from the individual injector as required.
6. Grasping the injector body, pull up while gently rocking the injector from side to side.

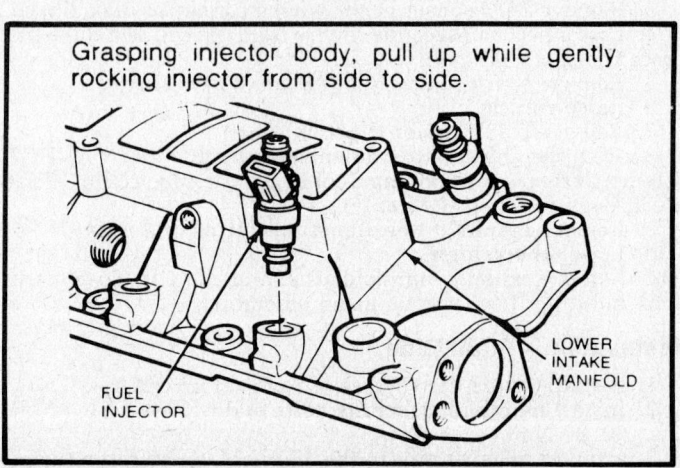

Removing the fuel injector on the 5.0L SEFI engine

7. Replace the injector O-rings (two per injector). Inspect the injector plastic hat (covers the injector pintle) and washer for signs of deterioration. Replace as necessary. If the plastic hat is missing, look for it in the intake manifold.

8. Installation is the reverse order of the removal procedure.

NOTE: After the service is complete and the fuel charging assembly is installed in the engine, the following procedure should used.

a. Install the fuel cap on the fuel tank. Connect the negative battery cable.

b. Add engine coolant if required. Turn the ignition key on and off several times without starting the engine to check for fuel leaks. Check all connections at the fuel rail and all push connections.

CAUTION

The fuel system pressure is normally pressurized to 39 psi.

9. Start the engine and let it reach normal operating temperature. Check for coolant and fuel leaks

Turbocharger System

For More Information on Turbochargers, Refer to Unit Repair Section.

Removal

NOTE: The turbocharger is serviced by replacement only.

1. Remove negative cable from the battery.
2. Remove two hex head bolt retaining throttle body discharge tube to the turbocharger. Also, loosen upper clamp on inlet hose.
3. Identify and disconnect vacuum hose tubes.
4. Disconnect PCV tube from the turbocharger air inlet elbow.
5. Remove throttle body discharge tube and hose as a assembly.
6. Disconnect electrical ground wire from turbocharger air inlet elbow.
7. Remove turbocharger oil supply line.
8. Disconnect oxygen sensor connector at turbocharger.
9. Raise vehicle on hoist.
10. Disconnect exhaust pipe by removing two exhaust pipe-to-turbocharger bolts.
11. Remove two bolts from oil return line located below turbocharger. Do not kink or damage line as it is removed.
12. Remove lower turbocharger bracket-to-block bolt.
13. Lower the vehicle.
14. Remove front lower turbocharger retaining bolt.
15. Simultaneously, remove three remaining nuts as turbocharger is slid off studs.
16. Remove turbocharger assembly from vehicle.

Installation

1. Position a new turbocharger gasket on mounting studs. Be sure the bead faces outward.
2. Install turbocharger assembly on four mounting studs.
3. Install turbocharger bracket on two lower studs. Start two lower retaining nuts followed by two upper retaining nuts.
4. Raise vehicle on hoist.
5. Install lower bracket-to-block bolt and tighten to 28–40 ft. lbs. (38–54 Nm).
6. Install a new oil return line gasket. Bolt oil return line to turbocharger. Tighten bolts to 12–21 ft. lbs. (19–29 Nm).
7. Install exhaust pipe. Tighten retaining nuts to 25–35 ft. lbs. (34–47 Nm).

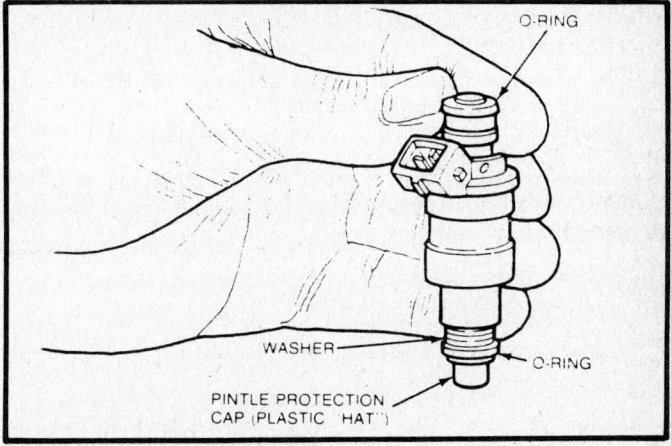

Inspecting the fuel injector

8. Lower vehicle.
9. Using four new nuts, tighten turbocharger-to-exhaust manifold nuts to 28–40 ft. lbs. (38–54 Nm).
10. Install air inlet tube to turbocharger inlet elbow. Tighten bolts to 15–22 ft. lbs. (20–30 Nm). Tighten hose clamp to 15–22 in. lbs. (1.7–2.5 Nm).
11. Install PCV tube fitting and tighten clamp to 15-22 in. lbs. (1.7–2.5 Nm).
12. Connect all vacuum lines.
13. Connect oxygen sensor.
14. Connect electrical ground wire to air inlet elbow.
15. Install turbocharger oil supply lie. Tighten fitting to 9–16 ft. lbs. (12–22 Nm).
16. Install air intake tube and clamp between turbocharger outlet and air intake throttle body. Tighten clamp to 15–20 ft. lbs. (20–27 Nm).
17. Connect ground cable to battery.
18. Start engine and check for leaks.
19. Install hood. Check for proper operation and alignment.

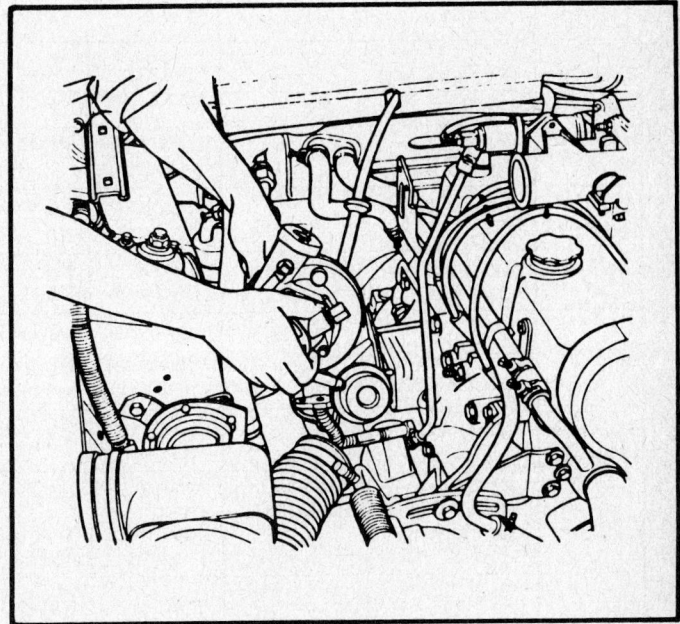

Turbocharger removal (©Ford Motor Co.)

Ford Lincoln Mercury
REAR WHEEL DRIVE CARS

Removal
2.4 LITER DIESEL

1. Remove two bolts attaching exhaust pipe to turbocharger.
2. Remove EGR tube and clamps.
3. Loosen four hose clamps on crossover tube and remove tube.
4. Remove air cleaner assembly and bellows. Cap turbocharger openings using protective caps T84P-9395-B or equivalent.
5. Remove two oil supply line bolts and top of turbocharger center housing.
6. Remove clamp from oil lines.
7. Remove oil return line.
8. Remove bolt and sealing washers attaching oil supply line to oil filter housing.
9. Disconnect and remove EGR valve.
10. Remove four bolts attaching turbocharger to exhaust manifold and remove turbocharger.

Installation

1. Clean mating surfaces of turbocharger and exhaust manifold.
2. Position turbocharger on exhaust manifold and install four mounting bolts. tighten to 17–20 ft. lbs. (23–27 Nm).
3. Install EGR valve. Tighten to 18 ft. lbs. (25 Nm).
4. Install oil supply line using new seals. Tighten bolts to 26–33 ft. lbs. (35–45 Nm).

---- CAUTION ----
Do not overtighten bolt. Oil leaks may occur if overtightened.

5. Install clamp retaining oil lines.
6. Install oil supply line bolts to turbocharger housing and tighten to 15–18 ft. lbs. (20–24 Nm).
7. Remove protective caps from turbocharger and install air cleaner assembly and bellows.
8. Install crossover tube. Tighten hose clamps snug.
9. Install EGR tube clamp.
10. Install two bolts attaching exhaust pipe to turbocharger and tighten to 17–20 ft. lbs. (23–27 Nm).
11. Run engine and check for oil and all leaks.

WASTEGATE ACTUATOR

Removal

1. Disconnect hoses from actuator diaphragm, and remove turbocharger.
2. Remove clip attaching actuator rod to wastegate arm.
3. Remove two bolts attaching actuator diaphragm assembly to compressor housing.

Installation

1. Install two bolts attaching actuator diaphragm assembly to compressor housing. Tighten bolts to 145–165 in. lbs. (16–19 Nm).
2. Unscrew actuator rod end until it just fits over the pin on the wastegate arm, with wastegate arm held closed (full forward).
3. Install clip attaching actuator rod to wastegate arm, and apply Loctite to threads, or crimp the threads on rod.
4. Connect hoses to actuator diaphragm.
5. Remove horse collar.

Emission Control Systems
EMISSION EQUIPMENT USED

1983

ENGINE	USAGE	CATALYST TYPE	CATALYST LOCATION	CARBURETOR MFG	CARBURETOR MODEL	EEC	EGR	THERM-ACTOR AIR	IGNITION
2.3L	49 States A/T	TWC & COC	TB UB	Carter	YFA-1V	No	Ported BF	P/A MTA	DS-II
	49 States M/T								
	50 States	TWC & COC	DBUB	Carter	YFA-1V	MCU & FBC	BP	MTA	DS-II
3.3L (200 CID)	49 States	TWC & COC	FM UB	Holley	1946-1V	No	BP	MTA	DS-II
	California	TWC & COC	FM UB	Holley	1946-1V	No	BP	MTA	DS-II
3.8L (230 CID)	50 States, Thunderbird/XR-7 LTD/Marquis Mustang/Capri	TWC TWC+COC	TB UB	Ford	2150-2V	No	BP	MTA	UIC
5.0L (302 CID)	Mustang/Capri	TWC TWC+COC	TB	Ford	4180C-4V	No	BP	MTA	DS-II
	50 States Lincoln/Mark VI Crown Victoria/Grand Marquis Continental	TWC & COC	UB	Ford	CFI Fuel Charging Ass'y.	EEC-III	Sonic-Cooler	MTA	DS-III
5.8L (351 CID)	49 States Ford/Mercury Police Only	TWC & COC	UB	Ford	7200-VV	MCU & FBC	BP	MTA	UIC

5-48

Ford Lincoln Mercury
REAR WHEEL DRIVE CARS
SECTION 5

EMISSION EQUIPMENT USED

1984

ENGINE	USAGE	CATALYST TYPE	CATALYST LOCATION	CARBURETOR MFG	CARBURETOR MODEL	EEC	EGR	THERMACTOR AIR	IGNITION
2.3L	50 States	TWC & COC	DBUB	Carter	YFA-IV, FB	EEC-IV	BVT	MTA	TFI-IV
2.3L HSC	50 States	TWC & COC	DBUB	Holley	6149-IV, FB	EEC-IV	Sonic	MTA	TFI-IV
2.3L Turbo S.V.O.	50 States A/T & M/T	TWC	DBUB	Bosch/Ford	EFI	EEC-IV	Ported	None	TFI-IV
3.8L (230 CID)	50 States, Thunderbird/Cougar LTD/Marquis Mustang/Capri	TWC TWC & COC	TB UB	Ford	CFI Fuel Charging Assembly	EEC-IV	Sonic	MTA	TFI-IV

EMISSION CONTROLS APPLICATION

PASSENGER CAR — 50 STATES/CANADA

Engine	Vehicle Application	Catalyst(s) Type	Catalyst(s) Location	Fuel System Type, Mfg	Electronic Eng Ctrl	EGR System	Thermactor System	Ignition System	Idle Speed Control
2.3L OHC	Mustang/Capri LTD/Marquis	TWC & COC	DBUB	YFA-1V FBC, Carter	EEC-IV	BVT	MTA	TFI-IV	DCM
2.3L OHC Turbo	SVO Mustang Thunderbird/Cougar Merkur	TWC	UB	EFI	EEC-IV	Ported	None	TFI-IV	BPA
3.8L 50 States	Thunderbird/Cougar LTD/Marquis Mustang/Capri (Canada)	(2) TWC COC	TB UB	CFI	EEC-IV	ELEC	MTA	TFI-IV	DCM
3.8L Canada	Thunderbird/Cougar LTD/Marquis	COC	UB	2150A-2V NFB, Ford	None	IBP	CT	DS-II	TSP/DP
5.0L	Thunderbird/Cougar Cont/Mark VII	(2) TWC COC	TB UB	SEFI	EEC-IV	ELEC	MTA	TFI-IV	BPA
5.0L	Ford/Mercury Lincoln	(2) TWC (2) COC	TB UB	SEFI	EEC-IV	ELEC	MTA	TFI-IV	BPA
5.0L HO	Mustang/Capri Mark VII	(2) TWC (2) COC	TB UB	SEFI	EEC-IV	ELEC	MTA	TFI-IV	BPA
5.8L	Ford/Mercury (Police) Canada Trailer Tow	(2) TWC & COC	DBUB	7200-VV FBC, Ford	MCU	IBP	MTA	UIC	TSP

ABBREVIATIONS:

- OHC = Overhead Cam
- HSC = High Swirl Combustion
- HO = High Output
- COC = Conventional Oxidation Catalyst
- TWC = Three-Way Catalyst
- TB = Toe Board
- UB = Underbody
- UE = Under Engine
- DBUB = Dual Brick Underbody
- MFG = Manufacturer
- FBC = Feedback Carburetor
- NFB = Non-Feedback Carburetor
- EFI = Electronic Fuel Injection
- ELEC = Electronic Valve
- SEFI = Sequential EFI
- CFI = Central Fuel Injection
- EEC-IV = Electronic Engine Control (System-IV)
- MCU = Microprocessor Control Unit
- EGR = Exhaust Gas Recirculation
- EVP = EGR Valve Position
- EVR = EGR Valve Regulator
- EGRC = EGR Control
- EGRV = EGR Vent
- PFE = Pressure Feedback Electronic
- BP = Backpressure
- IBP = Integral Backpressure
- CT = Conventional Thermactor
- PA = Pulse Air
- MTA = Managed Thermactor Air
- DS-II = Duraspark II
- TFI = Thick Film Ignition
- UIC = Universal Ignition Control
- M/V = Mechanical Vacuum
- BPA = Bypass Air
- DCM = D. C. Motor
- TSP = Throttle Solenoid Positioner
- DP = Dashpot

1985-87 Emission equipment used

SECTION 5

FORD LINCOLN MERCURY
REAR WHEEL DRIVE CARS

ENGINE SECTION

For Diesel Engine Service Refer to Unit Repair Section.

ENGINE ASSEMBLY

Removal

2.3L 4 CYL ENGINE

1. Raise the hood and secure it in the vertical position.
2. Drain coolant from the radiator and the oil from the crankcase.
3. On non-turbocharged engines, remove air cleaner and exhaust manifold shroud. On the turbocharged engine, disconnect the zip tube from the turbocharger inlet. Remove the ground strap on the turbocharger inlet elbow.
4. Disconnect the ground cable from the battery.
5. Remove the radiator upper and lower hoses.
6. Remove the radiator and fan. On vehicles equipped with an electric cooling fan, disconnect power lead to fan motor, then remove fan and shroud assembly.
7. Disconnect the heater hose from the water pump and carburetor choke fitting.
8. Disconnect the wires from the alternator and starter. Disconnect the accelerator cable from the carburetor or throttle body (EFI). On a vehicle with air conditioning, remove the compressor from the mounting bracket, and position it out of the way, leaving the refrigerant lines attached.
9. Disconnect the flexible fuel line at the fuel pump line or at the fuel rail (EFI) and plug the fuel line.
10. Disconnect the coil primary wire at the coil. Disconnect the oil pressure and the water temperature sending unit wires from the sending units.
11. Remove the starter.
12. Raise the vehicle. Remove the flywheel or converter housing upper attaching bolts.
13. Disconnect the muffler inlet pipe at the exhaust manifold or turbocharger outlet. Disconnect the engine right and left mounts at the No. 2 crossmember pedestals. Remove the flywheel or converter housing.
On a vehicle with a manual-shift transmission, remove the flywheel housing lower attaching bolts.
On a vehicle with automatic transmission, disconnect the converter from the flywheel. Disconnect transmission oil cooler lines, if attached to engine at pan rail. Remove the converter housing lower attaching bolts.
14. Lower the vehicle. Support the transmission and flywheel or converter housing with a jack.
15. Attach the engine lifting hooks to the existing lifting brackets. Carefully lift the engine out of the engine compartment. Install the engine on a work stand.

Installation

1. Installation is the reverse of removal procedures.
2. On a vehicle with automatic transmission, attach the converter to the flywheel and tighten the attaching nuts to 27-49 ft. lbs. (37-66 Nm).

ENGINE ASSEMBLY

Removal

IN LINE 6 CYL. 3.3L ENGINE

1. Remove the hood.
2. Drain the cooling system and the crankcase.
3. Disconnect the closed crankcase ventilation hose. Remove the air cleaner. Disconnect the canister purge hose from the PCV valve. Disconnect the battery ground cable at the cylinder head and at the battery. Disconnect the radiator upper hose at the water outlet housing and the radiator lower hose at the water pump. On a vehicle with automatic transmission disconnect the transmission oil cooler lines from the radiator.
4. Remove the radiator. Remove the fan, spacer, belt and pulley.
5. Disconnect the heater hoses from the water pump and cylinder block. Disconnect the alternator wires from the alternator, the starter cable from the starter ad the accelerator control cable from the carburetor. On a vehicle with air conditioning, remove the compressor from the mounting bracket, and position it out of the way, leaving the refrigerant lines attached.
6. Disconnect the fuel tank to fuel pump line at the fuel pump and plug the fuel line.
7. Disconnect the coil wires from the coil. Disconnect the oil pressure and water temperature sending unit from the sending units.
8. Remove the starter.
On a vehicle with a manual-shift transmission, disconnect the clutch retracting spring. Disconnect the clutch equalizer shaft and arm bracket at the underbody rail and remove the arm bracket and equalizer shaft.
9. Raise the vehicle. Remove the flywheel or converter housing upper attaching bolts.
10. Disconnect the muffler inlet pipe at the exhaust manifold. Loosen the inlet pipe clamp and slide it off the support bracket on the engine. Disconnect the engine right and left mounts at the No. 2 crossmember pedestals. Remove the flywheel or converter housing cover.
On a vehicle with a manual-shift transmission, remove the flywheel housing lower attaching bolts.
On a vehicle with automatic transmission, disconnect the converter from the flywheel. Remove the converter housing lower attaching bolts.
11. Lower the vehicle. Support the transmission and flywheel or converter housing with a jack.
12. Attach engine lifting hook. Carefully lift the engine out of the engine compartment. Place the engine on a work stand.

Installation

1. Installation is the reverse of removal procedures.

ENGINE ASSEMBLY

Removal

3.8L V6 ENGINES

1. Drain engine cooling system.
2. Disconnect cable from battery negative terminal.
3. If equipped with an underhood lamp, disconnect the wiring connector.
4. Mark position of the hood hinges and remove the hood.
5. Remove air cleaner assembly including the air intake duct and heat tube.
6. Remove fan shroud attaching screws. Remove the fan/clutch assembly attaching bolts.
7. Remove fan/clutch assembly and shroud.
8. Loosen accessory drive belt idler. Remove the drive belt and the water pump pulley.
9. Disconnect radiator upper and lower hoses at radiator.
10. Disconnect thermactor hose from the downstream air tube check valve, (CFI only).
11. Remove downstream air tube bracket attaching bolt at the rear of the right cylinder head.
12. Remove coil secondary wire from the coil.
13. If equipped with power steering, remove the pump mounting brackets' attaching bolts. Leaving the hoses connected,

5-50

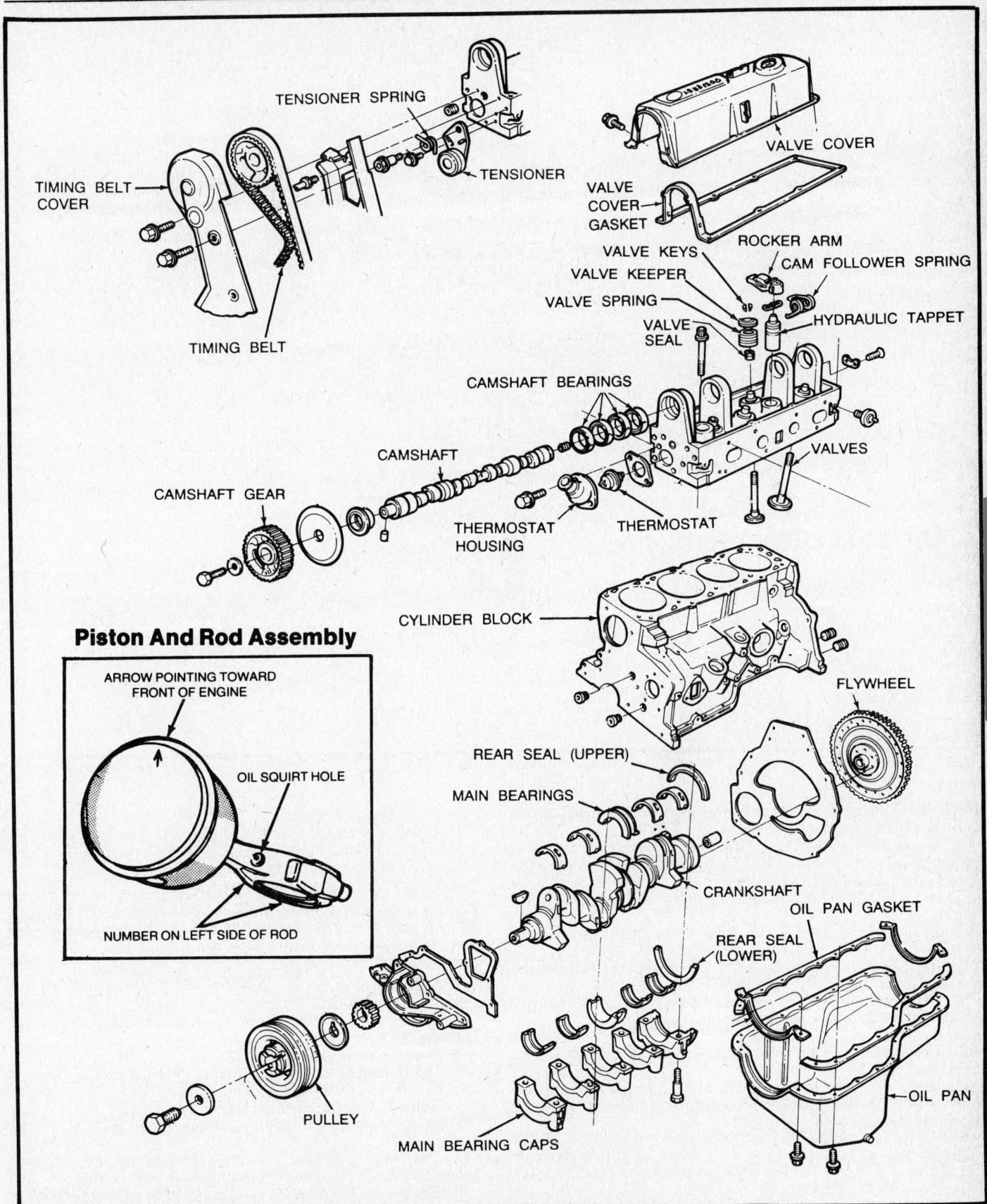

Ford 2.3L 4 cyl-140 cu. in. engine—exploded view (©Ford Motor Co.)

Ford Lincoln Mercury
REAR WHEEL DRIVE CARS

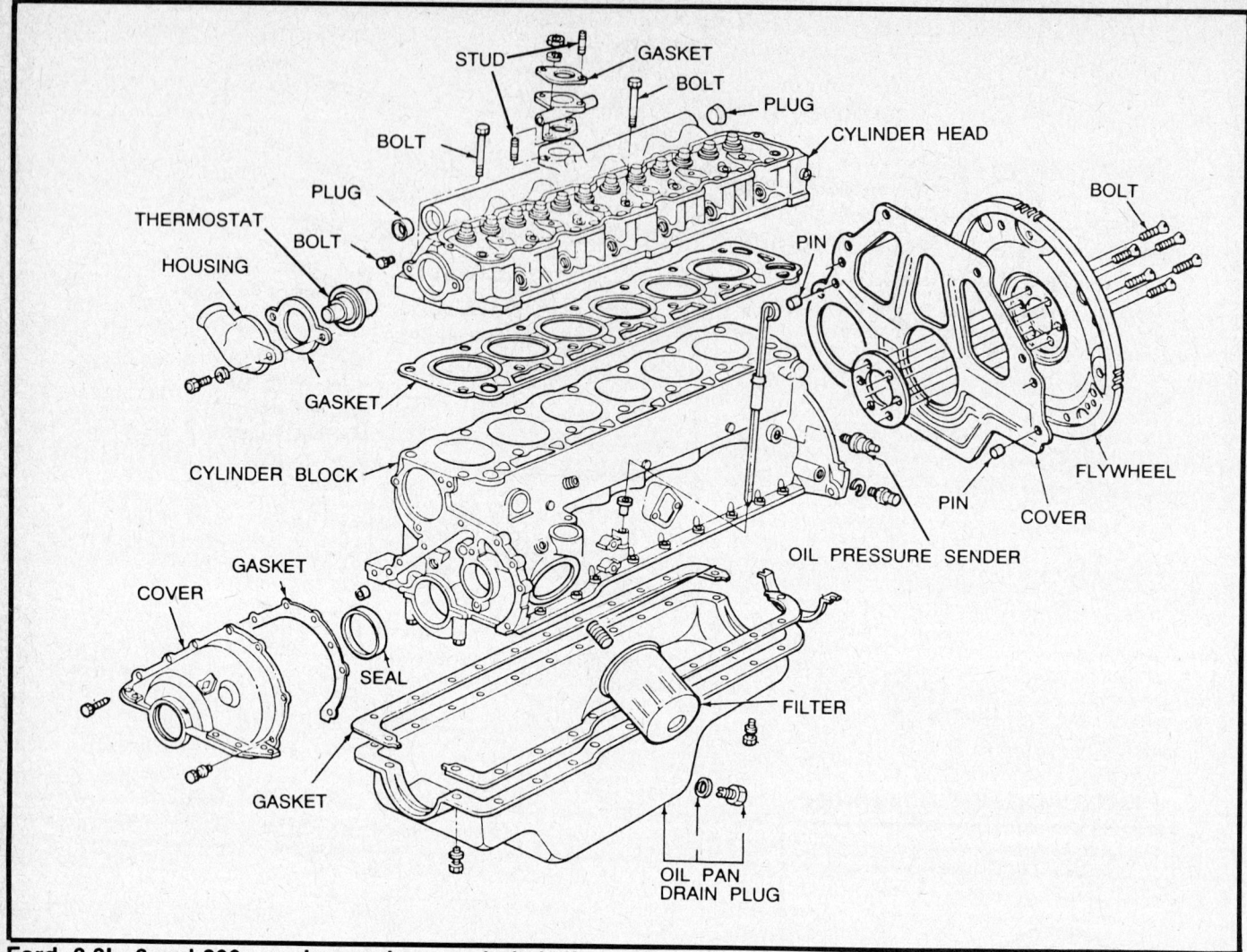

Ford 3.3L 6 cyl-200 cu. in. engine—exploded view (©Ford Motor Co.)

place the pump and bracket assembly aside in a position to prevent the fluid from leaking out.

14. If equipped with air conditioning, remove the mounting brackets' attaching bolts. Leaving hoses connected, secure the compressor to the right shock tower.
15. Remove alternator mounting bolts and set alternator aside.
16. Disconnect heater hoses from heater tube and water pump.
17. If equipped with speed control, disconnect the cable at the carburetor or fuel charging assembly.
18. Disconnect necessary vacuum hoses.
19. Remove screw attaching engine ground strap to dash panel.
20. Disconnect transmission linkage at the carburetor or fuel charging assembly.
21. Disconnect accelerator cable at the carburetor and remove cable routing bracket attaching bolts from the intake manifold (two places).
22. Disconnect necessary electrical connectors.
23. Disconnect fuel line and PCV hose at the carburetor (2150-2V) or flexible fuel lines from steel lines over the rocker arm cover (CFI only).
24. Disconnect flexible fuel inlet lie at the pump (2150-2V only). Plug the lines to prevent fuel leakage.

25. Remove carburetor.
26. Leaving the EGR spacer and phenolic gasket in place, install Engine Lifting Plate T75T–6000–A or equivalent over the carburetor hold-down studs. Tighten nuts securely.

CAUTION

Because the intake manifold is aluminum and of lightweight design, all studs must be used to secure the lifting plate. Do not remove engine with the transmission attached when using lifting plate.

27. Raise vehicle.
28. Drain crankcase.
29. Remove dust shield from the transmission converter housing.
30. Remove flex plate to torque converter attaching nuts.
31. Disconnect battery cable from the starter motor. Remove starter motor attaching bolts and starter.
31. Remove transmission oil cooler line routing clip.
33. Remove exhaust inlet pipe to exhaust manifold attaching nuts.
34. Disconnect exhaust heat control valve vacuum line and remove valve from exhaust manifold studs (if equipped).
35. Remove transmission-to-engine lower attaching bolts (two each side).
36. Remove engine mount-to-crossmember attaching nuts.

Ford Lincoln Mercury
REAR WHEEL DRIVE CARS

37. Lower vehicle.
38. Position a jack under the transmission. Raise the jack just enough to support the weight of the transmission.
39. Remove two transmission-to-engine upper attaching bolts.
40. Position a protective cover (¼ in. plywood) between the engine and the radiator to prevent damage to the radiator.
41. Raise the engine slightly and carefully pull it away from the transmission. Carefully lift the engine out of the engine compartment (avoid bending or damaging the rear cover plate or other components). Install engine on a work stand.

Installation

1. Installation is the reverse of removal procedures.
2. Install engine mount-to-crossmember attaching nuts and tighten to 70–90 ft. lbs. (95–122 Nm).
3. Install flex plate to torque converter attaching nuts and tighten to 20-30 ft. lbs. (28–40 Nm).
4. Install exhaust inlet pipe to exhaust manifold attaching nuts. Tighten nuts to 16–24 ft. lbs. (21–32 Nm).
5. Position starter motor, install attaching bolts and tighten to 15–20 ft. lbs. (20–27 Nm).
6. Install the carburetor or fuel charging assembly and tighten hold-down nuts to 107＝132 in. lbs. (16–20 Nm).

ENGINE ASSEMBLY

Removal
5.0L V8 ENGINES

1. Drain the cooling system and the crankcase.
2. Remove the hood. Disconnect the battery ground cables from the cylinder block.
3. Remove the air cleaner and intake duct assembly.
4. Disconnect the radiator upper hose from the coolant outlet housing and the radiator lower hose at the water pump. Disconnect the transmission oil cooler lines from the radiator. Remove the bolts attaching the fan shroud to the radiator.
5. Remove the radiator. Remove the fan, spacer, belt pulley and shroud.
6. Remove the alternator bolts and position the alternator out of the way.
7. Disconnect the oil pressure sending unit wire from the sending unit, disconnect low oil level sensor wire (if so equipped) at middle of rear oil sump on left hand side of oil pan, and the flexible fuel line at the fuel tank line. Plug the fuel tank line.

NOTE: On EFI and CFI equipped vehicles, relieve pressure in fuel lines before disconnecting.

8. Disconnect the accelerator cable from the carburetor. Disconnect the speed control cable if so equipped. Disconnect the throttle valve vacuum line from the intake manifold (if so equipped). Disconnect the transmission filler tube bracket from the cylinder block. Disconnect the TV rod on the automatic overdrive transmissio models.
On a vehicle with air conditioner, isolate and remove the compressor. On a vehicle with power steering conditioner, isolate and remove the compressor.
vehicle with power steering, disconnect the power steering pump bracket from the cylinder head. Remove the drive belt. Position the power steering pump out of the way and in a position that will prevent the fluid from draining out. On a vehicle with vacuum boosted power brakes, disconnect the brake vacuum line from the intake manifold.

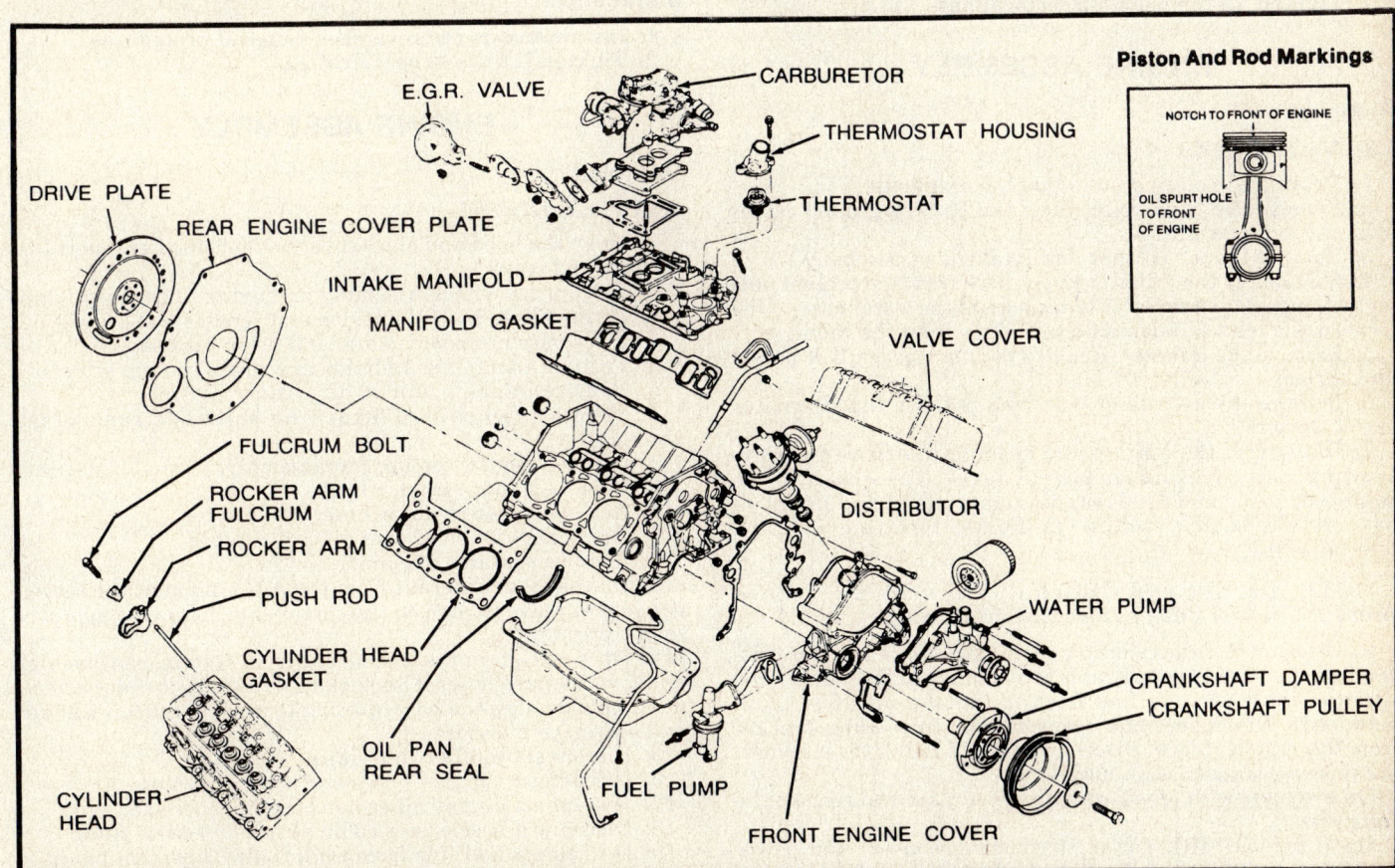

Ford 3.8L V6-230 cu. in. engine—exploded view (©Ford Motor Co.)

FORD LINCOLN MERCURY
REAR WHEEL DRIVE CARS

9. Disconnect the heater hoses from the water pump and intake the manifold. Disconnect the coolant temperature sending unit wire from the sending unit.
10. Remove the flywheel or converter housing to engine upper bolts.
11. Disconnect the primary wire connector from the ignition coil, (except on Continental the coil is located on RH strut tower). Disconnect wiring to ECT, ACT, and EGO sensors on EEC IV equipped vehicles. Disconnect wiring to solenoids on LH rocker cover. Remove the wire harness from the left rocker arm cover and position the wires out of the way. Disconnect the ground strap from the block.
12. Raise the front of the vehicle. Disconnect the starter cable from the starter. Remove the starter.
13. Disconnect the muffler inlet pipes from the exhaust manifolds. Disconnect the engine support insulators from the chassis. Disconnect the downstream Thermactor tubing and check valve frpom the RH exhaust manifold stud is so equipped.Disconnect transmission cooler lines from retainer and remove the converter housing inspection cover. Disconnect the flywheel from the converter. Secure the converter assembly in the housing. Remove the remaining converter housing to engine bolts.
14. Lower the vehicle, and then support the transmission. Attach the engine lifting sling, and hoist to lifting brackets on intake manifolds.
15. Raise the engine slightly and carefully pull it from the transmission. Carefully lift the engine out of the engine compartment (avoid bending or damaging the rear cover plate or other components). Install the engine on a work stand.

Installation

1. Installation is the reverse of removal.
2. Tighten all the bolts to specifications.

ENGINE ASSEMBLY

Removal
5.8L V8 ENGINES

1. Drain the cooling system and the crankcase.
2. Remove the hood. Disconnect the battery ground cables from the cylinder block.
3. Remove the air cleaner and intake duct assembly.
4. Disconnect the radiator upper hose from the coolant outlet housing and the radiator lower hose at the water pump. Disconnect the transmission oil cooler lines from the radiator.
5. Remove the radiator. Remove the fan, spacer, belt pulley and shroud.
6. Remove the alternator bolts and position the alternator out of the way.
7. Disconnect the oil pressure sending unit wire from the sending unit, disconnect low oil level sensor wire (if so equipped) at the middle of rear oil sump on left hand side of oil pan, and the flexible fuel line at the fuel tank line. Plug the fuel tank line.

NOTE: On EFI and CFI equipped vehicles, relieve pressure in fuel lines before disconnecting.

8. Disconnect the accelerator cable from the carburetor. Disconnect the speed control cable if so equipped.Disconnect the throttle valve vacuum line from the intake manifold (if so equipped). Disconnect the transmission filler tube bracket from the cylinder block. Disconnect the TV rod on the automatic overdrive transmission models.
On a vehicle with an air conditioner, isolate and remove the compressor.
On a vehicle with power steering, disconnect the power steering pump bracket from the cylinder head. Remove the drive belt. Position the power steering pump out of the way and

in a position that will prevent the fluid from draining out.On a vehicle with vacuum boosted power brakes, disconnect the brake vacuum line from the intake manifold.

9. Disconnect the heater hoses from the water pump and intake manifold. Disconnect the coolant temperature sending unit wire from the sending unit.
10. Remove the flywheel or converter housing to engine upper bolts.
11. Disconnect the primary wiring connector from the ignition coil, (except on Continental the coil is located on RH strut tower). Disconnect wiring to ECT, ACT and EGO sensors on EEC IV equipped vehicles. Disconnect wiring to solenoids on LH rocker cover. Remove the wire harness from the left rocker arm cover and position the wires out of the way. Disconnect the ground strap from the block.
12. Raise the front of the vehicle. Disconnect the starter cable from the starter. Remove the starter.
13. Disconnect the muffler inlet pipes from the exhaust manifolds. Disconnect the engine support insulators from the chassis. Disconnect the downstream Thermactor tubing and check valve frpom the RH exhaust manifold stud is so equipped. Disconnect transmission cooler lines from retainer and remove the converter housing inspection cover. disconnect the flywheel from the converter. Secure the converter assembly in the housing. Remove the remaining converter housing to engine bolts.
14. Lower the vehicle, and then support the transmission. Attach the engine lifting sling, and hoist to lifting brackets on intake manifolds.
15. Raise the engine slightly and carefully pull it from the transmission. Carefully lift the engine out of the engine compartment (avoid bending or damaging the rear cover plate or other components). Install the engine on a work stand.

Installation

1. Installation is the reverse of removal procedures.
2. Tighten ll bolts to specifications.

ENGINE ASSEMBLY

Removal
2.4 LITER DIESEL

1. Open the hood and place cover on fenders, disconnect battery ground cable.
2. Disconnect wiring assembly on engine underhood lamp.
3. Scribe hinge mark locations and remove hood.
4. Position pan under engine and drain oil pan.
5. Position pan under radiator and drain cooling system.
6. Remove intake manifold air cleaner assembly.
7. Remove fan shroud attaching bolts and remove fan shroud.
8. Remove engine cooling fan assembly.
9. Remove upper radiator hose.
10. Remove lower radiator hose.
11. Disconnect transmission oil cooler tubes.
12. Remove radiator assembly.
13. Discharge refrigerant from the A/C system at the service gauge port valve located on the suction line following approved safety precautions.
14. Once refrigerant is discharged from system, remove high and low pressure hoses. Use backup wrench to prevent component damage. Cap the hose opening to prevent entrance of dirt and excessive moisture.
15. Disconnect muffler inlet pipe.
16. Disconnect vacuum hoses and wiring harness.
17. Disconnect engine oil cooler hoses as outlined.
18. Disconnect accelerator cable at fuel injection pump.
19. Disconnect fuel line from tank to fuel injection pump.
20. Disconnect transmission gear shift linkage.
21. Disconnect battery ground cable at engine.

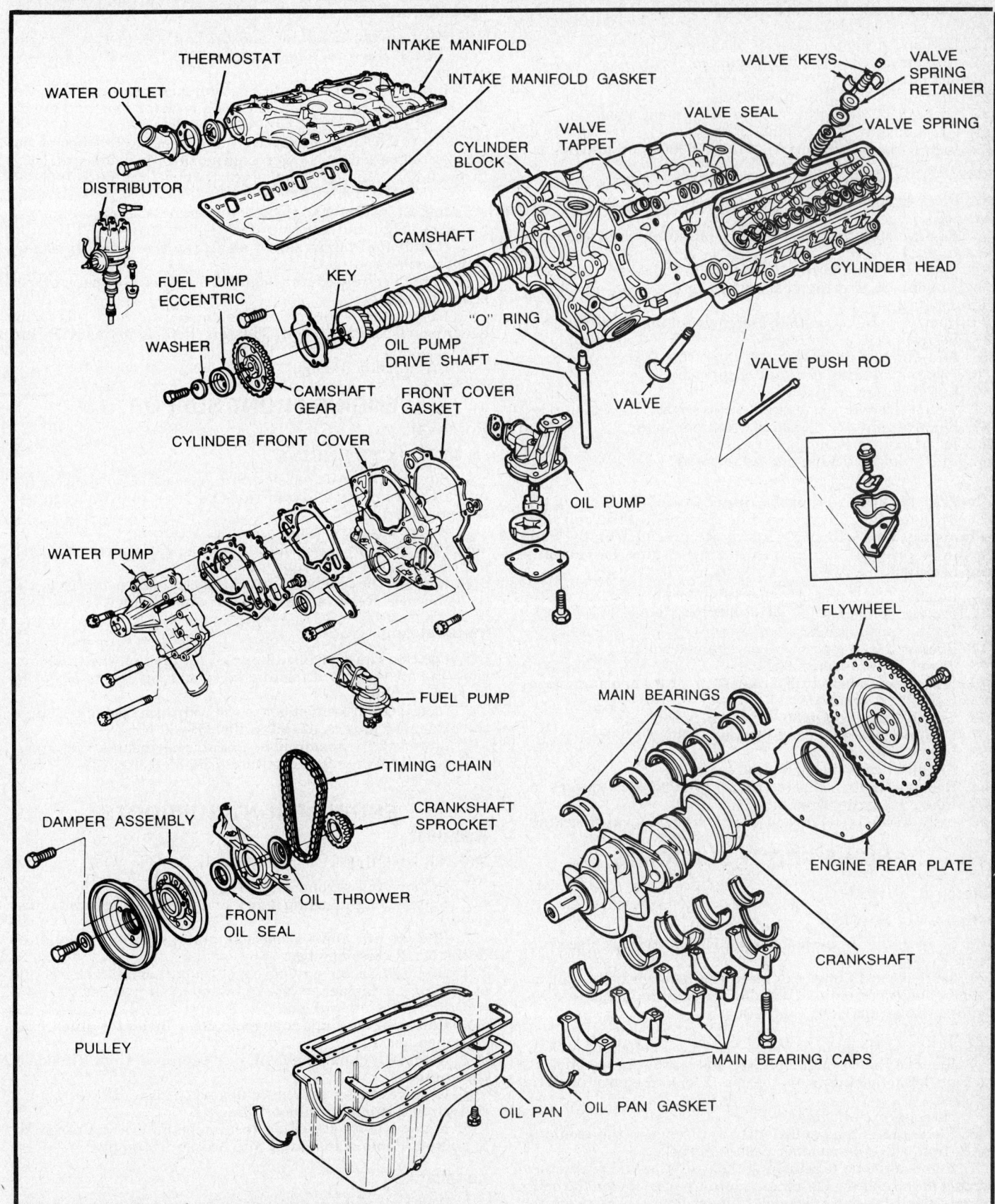

Ford V8 engines—exploded view (©Ford Motor Co.)

22. Remove coolant expansion bottle and position out of the way.
23. Disconnect heater hoses at dash panel.
24. Disconnect wire to A/C compressor clutch.
25. Disconnect power steering pump hose(s).
26. Disconnect fuel line to injectors.
27. Disconnect wiring harness to instrument panel.
28. Disconnect engine ground leads.
29. Install engine support Tool D79F-6000-A or equivalent.
30. Raise vehicle on hoist.
31. Remove muffler inlet pipe.
32. Remove lower engine oil cooler bracket and brace as outlined.
33. Remove stabilizer bar, bracket retaining bolts and position forward.
34. Remove left hand front fender splash shield.
35. Disconnect steering gear input shaft to steering column shaft coupling.
36. Remove retainer nuts to engine insulator supports.
37. Position jack under engine.
38. Raise engine assembly.
39. Position steering gear out of the way.
40. Lower engine assembly.
41. Remove converter housing access cover.
42. Remove converter assembly retainer nuts.
43. Insert pair of locking pliers in converter housing to hold converter in place during engine removal.

NOTE: Make sure that the upper jaw of the locking pliers contacts the converter while clamped to the converter housing. This will apply adequate pressure on the converter to prevent separation during engine movements and removal.

44. Remove No. 3 crossmember retainer nuts.
45. Remove transmission gear shift lever ballcrank.
46. Raise transmission.
47. Remove No. 3 crossmember retainer bolts.
48. Lower the transmission.
49. Remove engine to transmission converter housing retainer bolts.
50. Install No. 3 crossmember retainer bolts.
51. Position jack and drain pan out of the way.
52. Lower vehicle.
53. Install engine lifting equipment.
54. Remove engine support Tool D79T-6000-A or equivalent.
55. Remove engine assembly.
56. Installation is the reverse order of the removal procedure.

ENGINE FRONT SUPPORTS

Removal

2.3L 4 CYL. ENGINE

1. Support the engine using a wood block and jack placed under the engine.
2. Thunderbird/Cougar Remove the through bolts that attach the lower end of the RH and LH engine dampers to the No. 2 crossmember brackets (Fig. 10).
3. LTD/Marquis Remove the bolt that attaches the lower end of the engine damper to the No. 2 crossmember bracket.
4. Remove the through bolt nut and washer assemblies attaching both insulators to the No. 2 crossmember pedestal bracket.
5. Disconnect shift linkage.
6. Raise the engine sufficiently to disengage the insulator studs from the crossmember pedestal bracket.
7. Remove the bolts attaching the insulator and bracket assembly to the engine. On Thunderbird/Cougar, loosen the additional upper damper bracket fasteners. Remove the insulator and bracket assembly.

Installation

1. Position the insulator and bracket assembly to the engine. Install the attaching bolts. Tighten to 33–45 ft. lbs. (45–61 Nm).
2. Lower the engine into position making sure that the insulators are seated flat on the No. 2 crossmember and the insulator studs are at the bottom of the slots.
On 2.3L turbocharged engines, install engine bracket to the No. 2 crossmember. Lower engine into position until the through bolts line up. Hand start, then tighten nuts to 65–85 ft. lbs. (88–119 Nm).
3. Install insulator to the No. 2 crossmember on the insulator studs. Tighten flange nut to 50–65 ft. lbs. (68–89 Nm).
4. Install fuel pump shield attaching screw to LH engine support, if so equipped.
5. Thunderbird/Cougar: Tighten additional upper damper bracket fasteners.
6. LTD/Marquis: Install engine damper to No. 2 crossmember bracket attaching bolt. Tighten the bolt to 35–50 ft. lbs. (40–64 Nm).
7. Install shift linkage.

ENGINE FRONT SUPPORTS

Removal

IN LINE 6 CYL ENGINE

1. Support the transmission with a jack and wood block. Remove the two nuts attaching the rear insulator to the crossmember.
2. Remove the two bolts and nuts attaching the crossmember to the body brackets and remove the crossmember by raising the transmission slightly with a jack.
3. Remove the two bolts attaching the rear insulator to the transmission. Remove the insulator and retainer.

Installation

1. Position the rear insulator and retainer on the transmission. Install the two attaching bolts and tighten to 50–70 ft. lbs. (68–95 Nm).
2. Install the crossmember to the body brackets and tighten the attaching nuts to 35–50 ft. lbs. (48–60 Nm).
3. Lower the transmission, install the insulator to crossmember attaching nuts. Tighten to 25–35 ft. lbs. (34–47 Nm).

ENGINE FRONT SUPPORTS

Removal

3.8L V6 ENGINE

1. Remove fan shroud attaching screws.
2. Support engine using a jack and wood block placed under the engine.
3. Remove nut and washer assemblies attaching insulators to the No. 2 crossmember.
4. On LTD/Marquis, remove bolt that attaches the lower end of the engine damper to No. 2 crossmember bracket.
5. Remove shift linkage.
6. Raise engine high enough to clear insulator studs from crossmember.
7. Remove fuel pump shield, if so equipped, from RH side of the engine.
8. Remove starter ground cable and oil cooler line attaching clips from RH engine support bracket.
9. Remove bolts attaching insulator and bracket assembly to engine. Remove insulator and bracket assembly.

Installation

1. Position insulator and bracket assembly to engine. Install attaching bolts and tighten to 33–45 ft. lbs. (45–61 Nm).

2. Install starter ground cable attaching clip to upper right hand front engine mount support bracket bolt. Tighten to specification.
3. Install fuel pump shield, if so equipped, to RH side of engine.
4. Install screw attaching oil cooler line clip to RH engine mount support bracket.
5. Lower engine into position making sure that insulators are seated flat on the No. 2 crossmember and that insulator studs are at the bottom of the slots.
6. Install insulators to No. 2 crossmember using a flange. On LTD/Marquis, Mustang/Capri, tighten 12 mm nut to 50–65 ft. lbs. (68–89 Nm). On Thunderbird/Cougar, tighten 14mm nut to 80–106 ft. lbs. (110–145).
7. LTD/Marquis, install the bolt which attaches engine damper to No. 2 crossmember bracket. Tighten to 35–50 ft. lbs. (40–64 Nm).
8. Install fan shroud attaching screws and tighten to specification.

ENGINE FRONT SUPPORTS

Removal

LINCOLN TOWN CAR, FORD CROWN VICTORIA/ MERCURY GRAND MARQUIS – V8 ENGINE

1. Remove fan shroud attaching screw.
2. Support the engine using a jack and wood block placed under the engine.
3. Remove the through bolts attaching the insulators to the insulator support bracket.
4. Remove the three bolts attaching the insulator assembly to the frame.
5. Raise the engine slightly with the jack and remove the insulator assembly.

Installation

1. Position the engine insulator assembly to the frame and install the attaching bolts. Tighten the bolts to 26–38 ft. lbs. (35–52 Nm).
2. Lower the engine into position and install the engine insulator assembly to insulator support bracket through bolts. Tighten the through bolts to 33–56 ft. lbs. (45–62 Nm).
3. Install fan shroud attaching screws and tighten to 24–48 in. lbs. (3–5 Nm).

ENGINE FRONT SUPPORTS

Removal

MUSTANG/CAPRI, THUNDERBIRD/COUGAR, MARK VI, MARK VII/CONTINENTAL, LTD/MARQUIS – 5.0L (302 CID) ENGINE

1. Remove fan shroud attaching screws.
2. Support the engine using a jack and wood block placed under the engine.
3. Remove the nuts attaching insulators to the No. 2 crossmember.
4. Disconnect shift linkage.
5. Raise the engine sufficiently with the jack to disengage the insulator studs from the crossmember.
6. Remove the engine insulator and bracket assembly to cylinder block attaching bolts. Remove the engine insulator assembly.

Installation

1. Position the insulator assembly on the engine and install the attaching bolts. Tighten the bolts to 35–60 ft. lbs. (48–81 Nm).
2. Lower the engine into position making sure that the insulators are seated flat on the No. 2 crossmember and the insulator studs are at the bottom of the slots.
3. Install the insulator to the No. 2 crossmember and start the nut assemblies on the insulator studs. On Mustang/Capri, LTD/Marquis, tighten nut to 50–65 ft. lbs. (68–88 Nm). On Thunderbird/Cougar tighten nut to 80–106 ft. lbs. (110–145 Nm).
4. Install the fan shroud attaching screws and tighten to 24–48 ft. lbs.
5. Connect shift linkage.

ENGINE DAMPER

THUNDERBIRD/COUGAR, LTD/MARQUIS – V8 ENGINES

NOTE: Whenever self-locking fasteners are removed, they must be replaced with new self locking fasteners.

Removal

1. Remove the bolt that attaches the lower end of the damper to the No. 2 crossmember bracket.
2. Remove the nut that attaches the upper insulators and washers to the damper.

NOTE: Use the key at the base of the upper joint stem to prevent the damper tube from rotating when removing the nut. DO NOT CLAMP THE DAMPER TUBE.

3. Remove the upper washer and upper insulator.
4. Remove the engine damper.

Installation

1. Position the engine damper with the lower washer and lower insulator on the engine bracket. Position the upper insulator and upper washer on the damper stem. Using the key at the base of the damper stem to prevent the damper tube from rotating, secure the insulator and washers to the engine bracket with a new nut and tighten.
2. Position the engine damper lower joint to line-up with the No. 2 crossmember engine damper bracket. Secure with a new bolt and tighten to specification.

Valve System

Valve Clearance – Hydraulic Valve Lash Adjusters

2.3L 4 CYL ENGINE

1. Position camshaft so that the base circle of lobe is facing the cam follower of the valve to be checked.
2. Using tool slowly apply pressure to the cam follower until the lash adjuster is completely collapsed. Hold follower in this position and insert the proper size feeler gauge between the base circle of the cam and the follower.

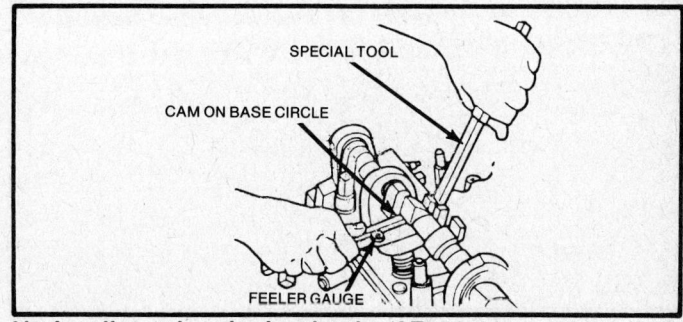

Hydraulic valve lash check (©Ford Motor Co.)

Ford Lincoln Mercury
REAR WHEEL DRIVE CARS

VALVE ADJUSTMENT

IN LINE 6 CYL 3.3L ENGINE

NOTE: A shorter than standard push rod and a longer than standard push rod are available for service to provide a means of compensating for dimensional changes in the valve mechanism.

To determine whether a shorter or a longer push rod is necessary, make the following check:
1. Crank the engine with the ignition switch "OFF" until the No. 1 piston is on TDC after the compression stroke.
2. Position the hydraulic lifter compressor tool on the rocker arm. Slowly apply pressure to bleed down the hydraulic tappet until the plunger is completely bottomed.

If the clearance is above or below specifications, replace the push rod.
Valve stem to valve rocker arm clearance should be within specifications with the hydraulic tappet completely collapsed.

NOTE: Each cylinder should be checked on the compression stroke at T.D.C.

LASH ADJUSTERS

3.8L V6 ENGINE

The configuration of the valve train is identical to that employed in the V8 engines. A hydraulic tapped, providing automatic lash adjustment, rides on a camshaft lobe and transfers its up and down motion to the rocker arm through a pushrod. The rocker arms are pedestal mounted and pivot on folcrums bolted to the cylinder head. The valves are arranged alternately intake/exhaust from the front of the engine.

VALVE CLEARANCE

V8 ENGINES

The valve arrangement of the left bank is E-I-E-I-E-I-E-I and on the right bank is I-E-I-E-I-E-I-E.

A 1.52 mm (0.060 in.) shorter pushrod or a 1.52 mm (0.060 in.) longer pushrod are available for service to provide a means of compensation for dimentional changes in the valve mechanism.

To determine whether a shorter or a longer push rod is necessary, make the following check:

5.0L (302 CID) V8 Engine

1. Install an auxiliary starter switch. Crank the engine with the ignition switch Off until the No. 1 piston is on TDC after the compression stroke.

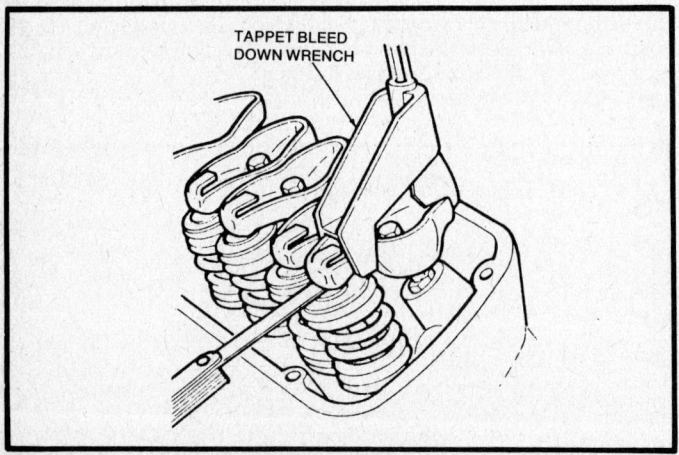

Checking valve clearance (©Ford Motor Co.)

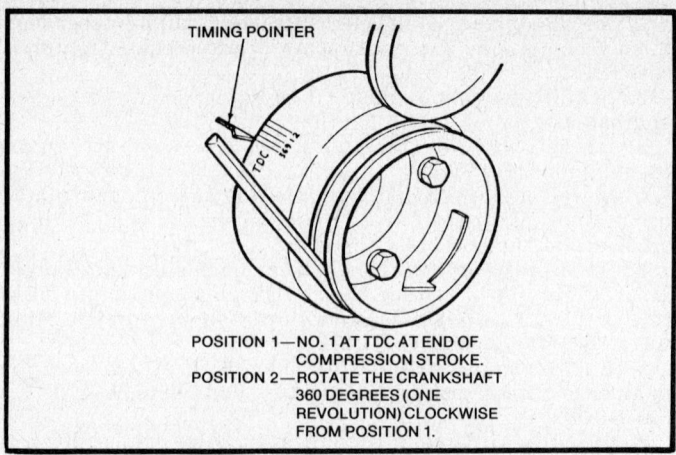

Position of crankshaft for checking and adjusting valve clearance (©Ford Motor Co.)

2. With the crankshaft in the position designated in Steps 3, 4 and 5, position the tappet compressor tool on the rocker arm. Slowly apply pressure to bleed down the tappet until the plunger is completely bottomed. Hold the tappet in this position and check the available clearance between the rocker arm and the valve step tip with a feeler gauge.
3. If the clearance is less than specification, install a shorter push rod. If the clearance is greater than specifications, install a longer push rod.
4. With the No. 1 piston on TDC at the end of the compression stroke, Position 1 in illustration, check the following valves:
   No. 1 Intake No. 1 Exhaust
   No. 7 Intake No. 5 Exhaust
   No. 8 Intake No. 4 Exhaust.
5. Rotate the crankshaft to Position 2 in illustration and check the following valves.
   No. 5 Intake No. 2 Exhaust
   No. 4 Intake No. 6 Exhaust
6. Rotate the crankshaft to Position 3 in illustration and check the following valves.
   No. 2 Intake No. 7 Exhaust
   No. 3 Intake No. 3 Exhaust
   No. 6 Intake No. 8 Exhaust

5.8L (351W CID) V8 Engine

1. Disconnect the brown lead (1 terminal) and the red and blue lead (S terminal) at the starter relay. Install an auxiliary starter switch between the battery and S terminals of the starter relay. Crank the engine with the ignition switch Off until the No. 1 piston is on TDC on the compression stroke.
2. With the crankshaft in the pistons designated in Steps 3, 4 and 5, position the tappet compressor tool on the rocker arm. Slowly apply pressure to bleed down the tappet until the plunger is completely bottomed. Hold the tapped in this position and heck the available clearance between the rocker arm and the valve stem tip with a feeler gauge.
3. With the No. 1 piston on TDC at the end of the compression stroke. Position 1 in illustration, check the following valves:
   No. 1 Intake No. 1 Exhaust
   No. 4 Intake No. 3 Exhaust
   No. 8 Intake No. 7 Exhaust.
4. After these valves have been checked, rotate the crankshaft to Position 2 in illustration and check the following valves:
   No. 3 Intake No. 2 Exhaust
   No. 7 Intake No. 6 Exhaust.

5. After these valves have been checked, rotate the crankshaft to Position 3 in illustration and check the following valves:

No. 2 Intake No. 4 Exhaust
No. 5 Intake No. 5 Exhaust
No. 6 Intake No. 8 Exhaust

If the clearance is less than specified, install a shorter push rod. If the clearance is greater than specification, install a longer push rod.

VALVE ROCKER ARM (CAM FOLLOWER) AND HYDRAULIC LASH ADJUSTER

Removal

2.3L 4 CYL ENGINES

1. Remove the valve rocker arm cover and associated parts as required.
2. Rotate the camshaft so that the base circle of the cam is facing the applicable cam follower.
3. Using tool, collapse the lash adjuster and/or depress the valve sprig if necessary and slide the cam follower over the lash adjuster and out.
4. Lift the hydraulic lash adjuster.

Installation

1. Rotate the camshaft so that the base circle of the cam is facing the applicable cam follower.
2. Place the hydraulic lash adjuster in position in the bore.
3. Using tool, collapse the lash adjuster as necessary to position the cam follower over the lash adjuster and the valve stem. It may also be necessary to compress the valve spring.
4. Before rotating the camshaft to the next position, be sure the lash adjuster just installed is fully compressed and released.
5. Clean the gasket surfaces of the valve cover and cylinder head adhesive. Allow to dry past the "wet" stage, and then install gasket in valve cover. Coat cylinder head contact surfaces with the same adhesive, allowing the adhesive to dry past the "wet" stage. Install the valve cover and gasket, making sure locating tabs are properly positioned in slots in cover.
7. Install eight screws and tighten to 62–97 in lbs. (7–11 Nm).
8. Install the air cleaner and all other hardware removed.
9. Run the engine at fast idle and check for oil leaks.

VALVE SPRING, RETAINER AND STEM SEAL

2.3L 4 CYL ENGINES

If the valve or valve seat has not been damaged; valve springs, seals and retainers may be replaced by holding the affected valve against its seat using compressed air. Use a compressed air line adapter installed in the spark plug hole. A minimum of 965kPa (140 psi) line pressure is required. If air pressure does not hold the valve shut, the valve is damaged or burnt and the cylinder head must be removed and serviced.

Removal

1. Remove the valve rocker arm cover and associated parts as required.
2. Remove the cam follower.
3. Using took, compress the valve spring and remove the retainer locks, spring retainer, and valve spring. Remove and discard the stem seal.
4. If air pressure has forced the piston to the bottom of the cylinder, any removal of air pressure will allow the valve(s) to fall into the cylinder. A rubber band, tape or string wrapped around the end of the valve stem will prevent this condition and will still allow enough travel to check the valve for binds.
5. Inspect the valve stem for damage. Rotate the valve and check the stem tip for eccentric movement. Move the valve up and down through normal travel in the valve guide and check the stem for binds. If the valve has been damaged, it will be necessary to remove the cylinder head and service.

Installation

1. Install a new valve stem seal using a plastic installation cap. Install the valve spring, retainer and locks. Turn off the air and remove the air line and adapter.
2. Apply polyethylene grease to all contact surfaces of the cam follower and install in position. Install the spark plug.

NOTE: Be sure that the effected lash adjuster has been collapsed and released before rotating the camshaft.

3. Install the rocker air cover. Tighten the rocker arm cover bolts to 6–8 ft. lbs. (7–9 Nm).

HYDRAULIC TAPPETS

Removal

IN LINE 6 CYL 3.3L ENGINE

1. Remove the cylinder head and related parts. Refer to Cylinder Head Removal.
2. Using a magnet, remove the tappets. Place the tappets in a rack so they can be installed in the original positions.

If the tappets are stuck in their bores by excessive varnish or gum, it may be necessary to use a plier-type or claw-type tool to remove the tappets. Rotate the tappet back and forth to loosen any gum and varnish which may have formed.

Keep the assemblies intact until they are to be cleaned.

If the tappets are to be tested or disassembled and cleaned, **be sure to fill it with test fluid before installing it in the engine.** New tappets already contain test fluid.

Installation

1. Install new (or cleaned) hydraulic tappets through the pushrod openings with a magnet.
2. Install the cylinder head and related parts.

HYDRAULIC VALVE LIFTERS

Removal

3.8L V6 ENGINES

NOTE: Before replacing a tappet for noisy operation, be sure the noise is not caused by improper valve-to-rocker arm clearance or by worn rocker arm or pushrods.

1. Disconnect secondary ignition wires at the spark plugs.
2. Remove plug wire routing clips from the studs on the rocker arm cover attaching bolts. Lay the plug wires, with the routing clips toward the front of the engine.
3. Remove intake manifold.
4. Remove rocker arm covers.
5. Sufficiently loosen each rocker arm fulcrum attaching bolt to allow the rocker arm to be lifted off the pushrod and rotate to one side.
6. Remove pushrods. The location of each pushrod should be identified. When the engine is assembled each rod should be installed in its original position.
7. Remove tappets using a magnet. The location of each tappet should be identified. When the engine is assembled each tappet should be installed in its original position.

If the tappets are stuck in the bores due to excessive varnish or gum deposits, it may be necessary to use a plier-type tool or a

Ford Lincoln Mercury
REAR WHEEL DRIVE CARS

claw type tool to aid removal. When using a remover tool rotate the tappet back and forth to loosen it from the gum or varnish that may have formed on the tappet.

Installation

1. Installation is the reverse of removal procedures.
2. For each valve rotate the crankshaft until the tappet rests on the heel (base circle) of the camshaft lobe. Position rocker arm over the pushrods. Install fulcrums and tighten fulcrum attaching bolt to 7–15 Nm (62–132 in. lb.).
3. Final tightening fulcrum bolts to 25–35 Nm (19–25 ft.lb.). For final tightening, the camshaft may be in any position.

CAUTION
Fulcrums must be fully seated in cylinder head and pushrods must be seated in rocker arm sockets prior to final tightening.

Removal
V8 ENGINES

1. Remove the intake manifold and related parts.
2. Remove the crankcase ventilation hoses, PCV valve and elbows from the valve rocker arm covers.
3. Remove the valve rocker arm covers. Loosen the valve rocker arm fulcrum bolts and rotate the rocker arms to the side.
4. Remove the valve pushrods and identify them so that they can be installed in their original position.
5. Using a magnet, remove the tappets and place them in a rack so that they can be installed in their original bores. If the tappets cannot be removed from their bores due to excessive varnish, etc., it may be necessary to use a plier-type tool, or a claw type tool to remove them. Rotate the tappet back and forth to loosen it from the gum or varnish that may have formed on the tappet.

NOTE: 1986 5.0 Liter engines are equipped with roller type hydraulic lifters.

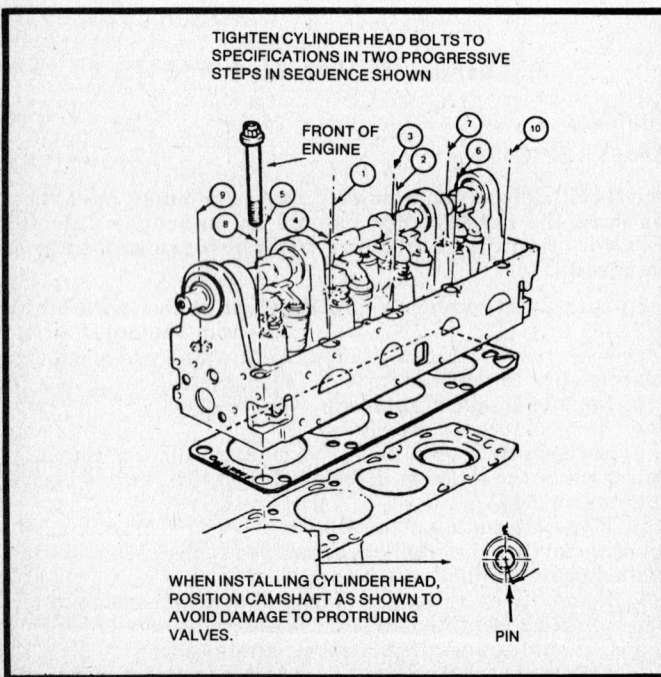

Cylinder head installation – 4cyl (©Ford Motor Co.)

Installation

Tappets and bores are to be lubricated with engine oil SF before installation.
Installation is the reverse of removal procedures.

CYLINDER HEAD

Remove
2.3L 4 CYL OHC ENGINE

1. Drain cooling system.
2. Remove air cleaner assembly.
3. Remove one heater hose retaining screw to rocker cover.
4. Disconnect distributor cap and spark plug wire and remove assembly.
5. Remove spark plugs.
6. Disconnect required vacuum hoses.
7. Remove dipstick.
8. Remove rocker retaining bolts and remove cover.
9. Remove intake manifold retaining bolts.
10. Loosen alternator retaining bolts, remove belt from pulley, remove mounting bracket retaining bolts to the head.
11. Disconnect upper radiator hose at both ends and remove from vehicle.
12. Remove cam belt cover four bolts.
13. Loosen cam idler retaining bolts, position idler in the unloaded position and tighten the retaining bolts.
14. Remove cam belt from the cam pulley and auxiliary pulley.
15. Remove heat stove from exhaust manifold three nuts and two retaining bolts.
16. Remove the eight exhaust manifold retaining bolts.
17. Remove the cam belt idler and two bracket bolts.
18. Remove cam belt idler spring stop from the cylinder head.
19. Disconnect oil sending unit lead wire.
20. Remove cylinder head retaining bolts.
21. Remove the cylinder head.
22. Clean cylinder head gasket surface at the block.
23. Clean intake manifold gasket surface at the intake manifold.
24. Clean exhaust manifold gasket surfaces at the exhaust manifold.
25. Clean exhaust manifold gasket surface at the cylinder head.
26. Clean cylinder head gasket surface at the cylinder head.
27. Clean intake manifold gasket surface at the cylinder head.
28. Blow oil out of the cylinder head bolt block holes.
29. Clean camshaft cover gasket surface on the head.
30. Check cylinder head for flatness.

Installation

1. Position head gasket on the block.
2. Clean rocker arm cover (cam cover).
3. Install rocker cover gasket to the rocker cover (use contact cement).
4. Position cylinder head to block.
5. Install cylinder head retaining bolts and tighten to specification.
6. Connect oil sending unit lead wires.
7. Install cam belt idler spring stop to the cylinder head.
8. Position cam belt idler to cylinder head, and install retaining bolts.
9. Install the eight exhaust manifold retaining bolts.
10. Install heat stove to exhaust manifold three nuts and two retaining bolts.
11. Align distributor rotor with number one plug location in the distributor cap.
12. Align cam gear with pointer.
13. Align crank pulley (TDC) with pointer on cam belt cover.

Ford Lincoln Mercury
REAR WHEEL DRIVE CARS
SECTION 5

14. Position cam belt to pulley (cam and auxiliary).
15. Loosen idler retaining bolts, rotate engine and check timing alignment.
16. Adjust belt tensioner and tighten retaining bolts.
17. Install cam belt cover four retaining bolts.
18. Connect upper radiator hose to engine and radiator and tighten retaining clamps.

CYLINDER HEAD
IN LINE 6 CYL 3.3L ENGINE

1. Drain the cooling system. Remove the air cleaner assembly. Disconnect the radiator upper hose at the engine.
2. Disconnect the muffler inlet pipe at the exhaust manifold. Pull the muffler inlet pipe down. Remove the gasket.
3. Disconnect the accelerator control cable at the carburetor.
4. disconnect the transmission kickdown rod. Disconnect the accelerator control cable at the bracket.
5. disconnect the fuel inlet line at the fuel filter hose. Disconnect the distributor vacuum lines. Disconnect vacuum lines and components as necessary for accessibility and identify them for proper reconnection.
6. Disconnect the carburetor fuel inlet line at the fuel pump. Remove the lines as an assembly.
7. Disconnect the spark plug wires at the spark plugs and the temperature sending unit wire at the sending unit.
8. Remove the crankcase ventilation system. Remove the accelerator control cable bracket.
9. Remove the valve rocker arm cover.
10. Remove the valve rocker arm shaft assembly. Identify and remove the valve push rods in sequence.
11. Remove the remaining cylinder head bolts and remove the cylinder head. Do not pry between the cylinder head and block as the gasket surfaces may become damaged.

Installation

1. Clean the head and block gasket surfaces. If the cylinder head was removed for a gasket change, check the flatness of the cylinder head and block. Install guide studs at each end of the cylinder block.
2. Position the cylinder head gasket over the guide studs on the cylinder block.
3. Install a new gasket on the flange of the muffler inlet pipe.
4. Lift the cylinder head over the guides and slide it down carefully, connect the muffler inlet pipe to the exhaust manifold.
5. Install, but do not tighten two bolts at opposite ends of the head to hold the head and gasket in position. Remove the guides and install the remaining bolts.
6. Cylinder head bolts are tightened in three progressive steps. Tighten all the bolts in sequence to specifications. When cylinder head bolts have been tightened following this procedure, it is not necessary to retighten the bolts after extended operation. However, on cylinder heads with composition gaskets, the bolts may be checked and retightened, if desired. Tighten the exhaust manifold flange attaching nuts to specification.
7. Apply Polyethylene Grease to both ends of the push rods. Install the push rods in the original bores, positioning the lower end of the rods into the tappet sockets. Apply Polyethylene Grease to the valve stem tips and to the rocker arm pads.

CYLINDER HEADS
Removal
3.8L V6 ENGINE

1. Drain the cooling system.
2. Disconnect cable from battery negative terminal.

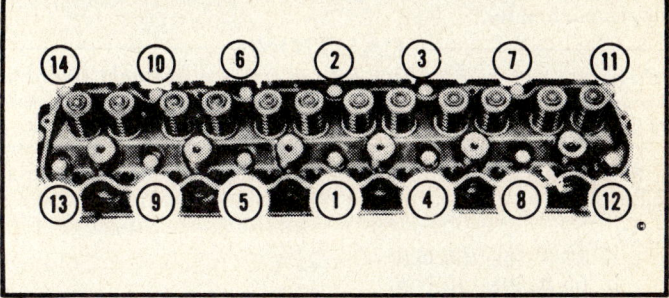

Cylinder head bolt torque sequence—6cyl
(©Ford Motor Co.)

3. Remove air cleaner assembly including the air intake duct and heat tube.
4. Loosen accessory drive belt idler. Remove drive belt.
5. If the left cylinder head is being removed perform the following:
   a. Remove oil fill cap.
   b. If equipped with power steering, remove pump mounting brackets attaching bolts. Leaving the hoses connected, place the pump/bracket assembly aside in a position to prevent the fluid from leaking out.
   c. If equipped with air conditioning, remove mounting brackets' attaching bolts. Leaving hoses connected, position compressor aside.
6. If right cylinder head is being removed perform the following:
   a. Disconnect thermactor air control valve or bypass valve hose assembly at the air pump.
   b. Disconnect thermactor air control valve or bypass valve hose assembly at the air pump.
   c. Disconnect thermactor tube support bracket from the rear of the cylinder head.
   d. Remove accessory drive idler.
   e. Remove alternator.
   f. Remove thermactor pump pulley. Remove thermactor pump.
   g. Remove alternator bracket.

NOTE: If equipped with tripminder, the fuel supply tube (fuel pump to sensor) must be disconnected to gain access to the alternator bracket upper attaching bolt.

   h. Remove PCV valve.
7. Remove intake manifold.
8. Remove valve rocker arm cover attaching screws.
9. Remove exhaust manifold(s).
10. Loosen rocker arm fulcrum attaching bolts enough to allow the rocker arm to be lifted off the pushrod and rotated to one side.
11. Remove pushrods. Identify the position of each rod. The rods should be installed in their original position during assembly.
12. Remove cylinder head attaching bolts and discard.
13. Remove cylinder head(s).

Installation

NOTE: Lightly oil all bolt and stub bolt threads before installation except those specifying special sealant.

1. Clean all mating surfaces.
2. Position new head gasket(s) on the cylinder block using the dowels for alignment.
3. Position cylinder head(s) on block.
4. Apply a thin coating of Pipe Sealant to the threads of the short cylinder head bolts (nearest to the exhaust manifold). Do

5-61

not apply sealant to the long bolts. Install cylinder head bolts (eight each side).

---- **CAUTION** ----

Always use new cylinder head bolts to assure a leak-tight assembly. Torque retention with used bolts can vary, which may result in coolant or compression leakage at the cylinder head mating surface area.

5. Tighten the cylinder head attaching bolts in sequence as follows:

1983
    a. 47 ft. lbs. (65 Nm)
    b. 55 ft. lbs. (75 Nm)
    c. 63 ft. lbs. (85 Nm)
    d. 74 ft. lbs. (101 Nm)
    e. Back-off attaching bolts 2–3 turns.
    f. Repeat Steps a-d.

1984 AND LATER
    a. 37 ft. lbs. (50 Nm)
    b. 45 ft. lbs. (60 Nm)
    c. 52 ft. lbs. (70 Nm)
    d. 59 ft. lbs. (80 Nm)
    e. Back-off the attaching bolts 2–3 turns.
    f. Repeat Steps a-d.

NOTE: When cylinder head attaching bolts have been tightened using the above procedure, it is not necessary to retighten the bolts after extended engine operation. However, the bolts can be checked for tightness if desired.

6. Install pushrods in their original position.
7. For each valve rotate the crankshaft until the tappet rests on the heel (base circle) of the camshaft lobe before tightening the fulcrum attaching bolts. Position rocker arm over the pushrods, install fulcrums, and tighten fulcrum attaching bolts to 61–132 in. lbs. (7–15 Nm).

---- **CAUTION** ----

Fulcrums must be fully seated in cylinder head and pushrods must be seated in rocker arm sockets prior to final tightening.

8. Lubricate all rocker arm assemblies with heavy engine oil.

NOTE: If the original valve train components are being installed, a valve clearance check is not required. If a component has been replaced, perform a valve clearance check.

9. Install exhaust manifold(s).
10. Position cover and new gasket on the cylinder head and install attaching bolts. Note the location of spark plug wire routing clip stud bolts. tighten attaching bolts to 80-106 in. lbs. (9–12 Nm).
11. Install intake manifold.
12. Install spark plugs, if removed.
13. Connect secondary wires to the spark plugs.
14. If left cylinder is being installed, perform the following:
    a. Install oil fill cap.
    b. If equipped with air conditioning, install compressor mounting and support brackets.
    c. If equipped with power steering, install pump mounting and support brackets.
15. If right cylinder head is being installed, perform the following:
    a. Install PCV valve.
    b. Install alternator bracket. Tighten attaching nuts to 30–40 ft. lbs. (40–55 Nm).
    c. If equipped with tripminder, connect fuel supply line (fuel pump to sensor). Tighten fitting securely.
    d. Install thermactor pump and pump pulley.
    e. Install alternator.
    f. Install accessory drive idler.
    g. Install the thermactor air control valve or air bypass valve hose. Tighten the clamps securely to the air pump assembly.
16. Install the accessory drive belt and tighten to specification. Attach the thermactor tube(s) support bracket to the rear of the cylinder head. Tighten attaching bolts to 30–40 ft. lbs. (40–55 Nm).
17. Connect cable to the battery negative terminal.
18. fill cooling system with the specified coolant.

---- **CAUTION** ----

This engine has an aluminum cylinder head and requires a special unique corrosion inhibited coolant formulation to avoid radiator damage.

19. Start engine and check for coolant, fuel and oil leaks.
20. Check and, if necessary, adjust the curb idle speed.
21. Install air cleaner assembly including the air intake duct and heat tube.

CYLINDER HEAD

Removal

V8 ENGINES

1. Remove the intake manifold and carburetor as an assembly.
2. Remove the rocker arm cover(s). If the left cylinder head is to be removed on a vehicle with an air conditioner, isolate and remove the compressor. If the left cylinder head is to be removed on a vehicle with power steering, disconnect the power steering pump bracket from the left cylinder head and remove the drive belt from the pump pulley. Position the power steering pump out of the way and in a position that will prevent the oil from draining out. Remove thermactor crossover tube from rear of cylinder heads.
3. If the right cylinder head is to be removed, remove the alternator mounting mounting bracket bolts and spacer from the right cylinder head assembly.
4. disconnect the exhaust manifold(s) from the muffler inlet pipe(s).
5. Loosen the rocker arm fulcrum bolts so that the rocker arms can be rotated to the side. Remove the push rods in sequence so that they may be installed in their original positions. Remove the exhaust valve stem caps.
6. Install the cylinder head holding fixtures. Remove the cylinder head attaching bolts and lift the cylinder head off the block. If required, remove the exhaust manifolds to gain access to the lower attaching bolts. Remove and discard the cylinder head gasket.

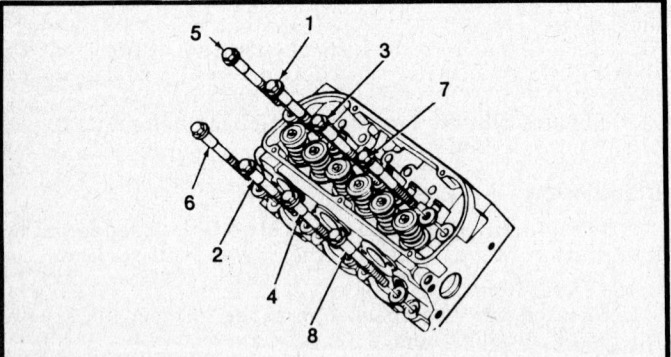

Cylinder head bolt torque sequence – V6 engine
(©Ford Motor Co.)

Installation

1. Clean the cylinder head, intake manifold, valve rocker arm cover and cylinder head gasket surfaces. If the cylinder head was removed for a cylinder head gasket replacement, check the flatness of the cylinder head and block gasket surfaces.
2. Position the new cylinder head gasket over the cylinder dowels on the block. Position the cylinder head on the block and install the attaching bolts. Remove the holding fixtures.
3. the cylinder head bolts are tightened in three progressive steps. Tighten all the bolts in sequence to specifications. when cylinder head bolts have been tightened following this procedure, it is not necessary to retorque the bolts after extended operation. However, the bolts may be checked and retightened if desired. If removed, install the exhaust manifolds and retighten the attaching bolts to specification.
4. Clean the pushrods in a suitable solvent. Blow out the oil passage in the push rod with compressed air. check the ends of the push rods for nicks, grooves, roughness or excessive wear. Visually check the push rods for straightness or check rod runout with a dial indicator. If runout exceeds the maximum limit at any point, discard the rod. **Do not attempt to straighten push rods.**
5. Apply Polyethylene Grease to both ends of the push rods. Install the push rods in their original positions. Apply Polethylene Grease to both ends of the push rods. Install the push rods in their original positions. Apply Polyethylene Grease to the valve stem tips. Install the exhaust valve stem caps.
6. Install the rocker arms. If all original assembly components are installed, a valve clearance adjustment is not necessary. If any valve train components are replaced, perform a valve clearance adjustment.
7. Connect the exhaust manifold(s) at the muffler inlet pipe(s). Tighten nuts to specification.
8. If the right cylinder head was removed, install the alternator attaching bracket on the right cylinder head assembly. Install the alternator. Adjust the drive belt tension to specifications.
9. Clean the valve rocker arm cover(s). Position the valve rocker cover gasket in each cover, making sure that the tabs engage the notches in the cover, making sure that the tabs engage the notches in the cover. Install valve rocker arm cover(s). The valve rocker cover is tightened in two steps. Tighten the bolts to specifications. Two minutes later retighten bolts to the same specifications.
10. If the left cylinder head was removed on a vehicle with an air conditioner, install the compressor. If the left cylinder head was removed on a vehicle with power steering, install the drive belt and power steering pump bracket. Install the bracket attaching bolts. Adjust the drive belt to specifications. Install thermactor crossover tube at rear of cylinder heads.
11. Install the intake manifolds and related parts.

CAMSHAFT TIMING BELT

2.3L 4 CYL ENGINE

Installation information for the complete cam drive mechanism is shown in illustration.

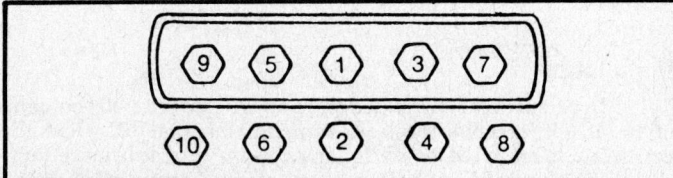

Cylinder head bolt torque sequence—V8 engines (©Ford Motor Co.)

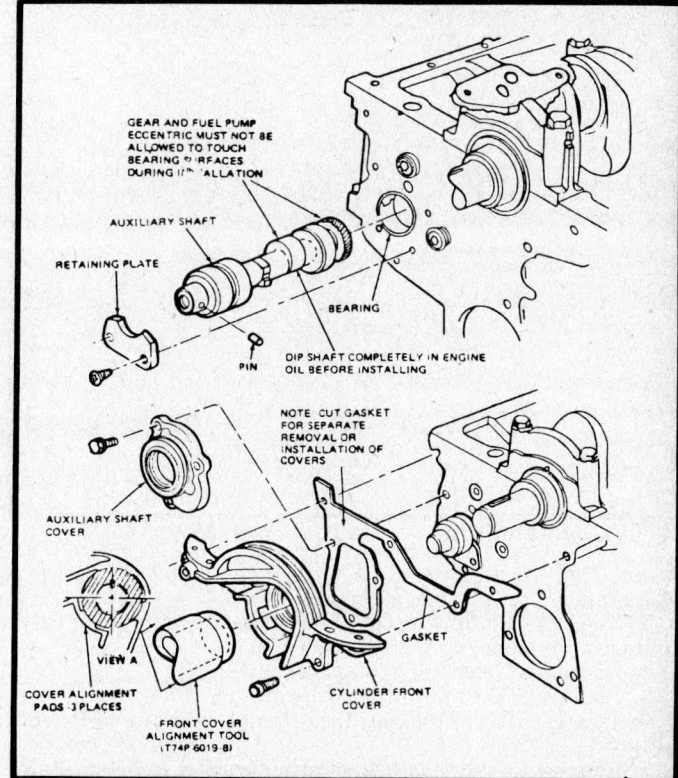

4 cyl auxiliary shaft and bearings and front cover installation (©Ford Motor Co.)

TIMING BELT TENSIONER

2.3L 4 CYL ENGINE

Illustrated instructions for installation of the timing belt tensioner.

AUXILIARY SHAFT AND BEARINGS

2.3L 4 CYL ENGINE

If necessary, the auxiliary shaft bearings can be removed using a slide-hammer, and puller attachment.

Install new bearings using a driver. Be sure to align the oil holes in the bearings with those in the block when installing.

CYLINDER FRONT COVER

2.3L 4 CYL ENGINE

The front seal has been designed so that it is not necessary to remove the cylinder front cover with the engine in the chassis.

When disassembling the engine, first remove the front seal from the cover while the cover is still on the engine.

When assembling the engine, install the cover on the engine without the seal and then use tool to press the seal into place. this will avoid damage to the seal.

Before finally adjusting the cover into position and tightening the attaching bolts, use tool to position the cover in relation to the crankshaft. Tighten the bolts to 8–12 Nm (6–9 lb. ft.) with this tool in place. This will assure that the timing belt does not interfere with the front cover when operating.

CAMSHAFT

Removal

4 CYL ENGINE

1. Drain the cooling system.

Ford Lincoln Mercury
REAR WHEEL DRIVE CARS

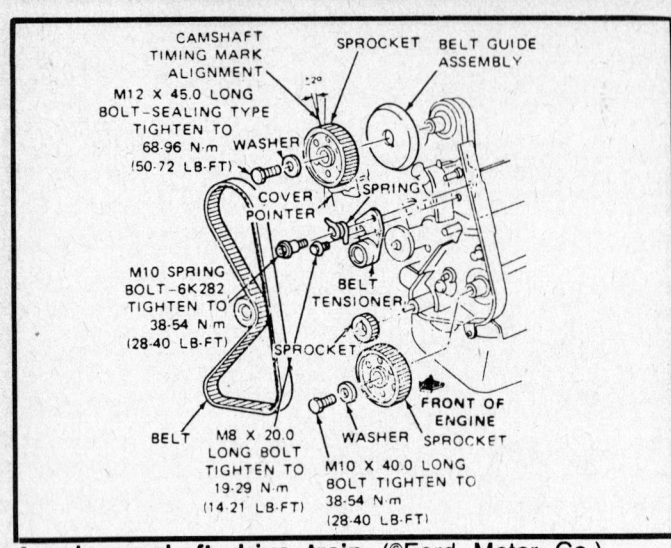

4 cyl camshaft drive train (©Ford Motor Co.)

2. Remove air cleaner assembly.
3. Disconnect plug wires at plugs, disconnect at rocker cover and position aside.
4. Disconnect vacuum hoses as required.
5. Remove rocker retaining bolts and remove cover.
6. Loosen alternator retaining bolts, remove belt from pulley.
7. Remove the alternator mounting bracket to head retaining bolts and position aside.
8. Disconnect the upper radiator hose at both ends and remove from vehicle.

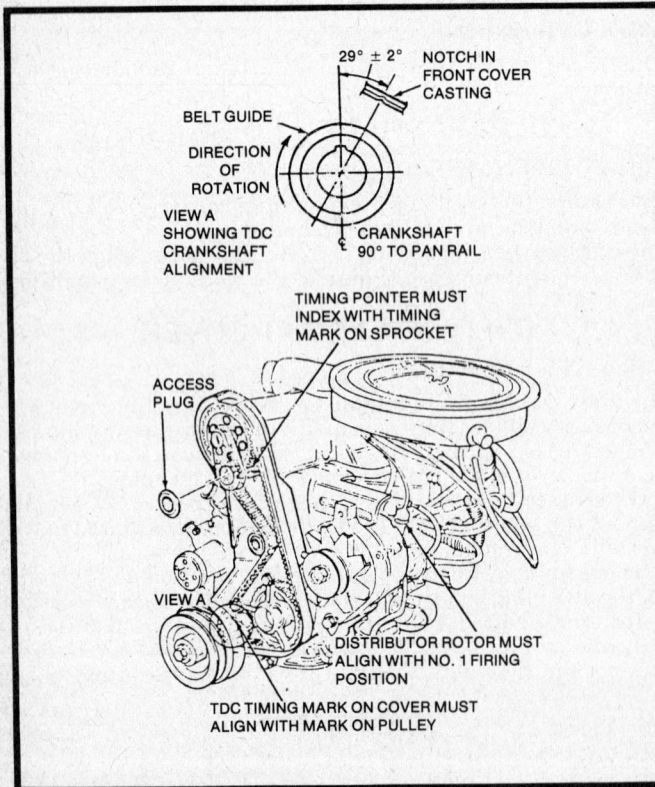

4 cyl camshaft drive train installation (©Ford Motor Co.)

9. Remove four shroud retaining bolts and remove shroud. If equipped with an electric fan, disconnect power lead to fan motor. Remove fan and shroud assembly. Drain the cooling system. Disconnect upper and lower radiator hose at radiator.
10. Remove four cam belt cover bolts. Remove cover.
11. Loosen idler cam retaining bolts, position idler in the unloaded position and tighten retaining bolts.
12. Remove the cam belt from the cam pulley and auxiliary pulley.
13. Raise vehicle on hoist.
14. Remove right and left engine support through bolts, and right and left lower joint-to-bracket retaining bolts.
15. Position a transmission jack under the engine. Position a wood block on the transmission jack. Raise the engine as high as it will go. Place wood blocks between engine mounts and No. 2 crossmember pedestal brackets, and remove jack.
16. Lower vehicle. Using tool, depress valve springs and remove camshaft followers.
17. Remove gear.
18. Remove seal.
19. Remove camshaft rear retainer (two screws).
20. Remove camshaft. Use caution to avoid damaging journals and lobes.

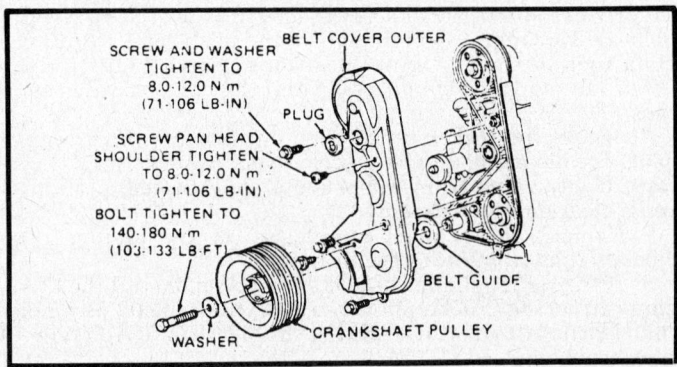

4 cyl timing belt outer cover, crankshaft belt guide and pulley installation (©Ford Motor Co.)

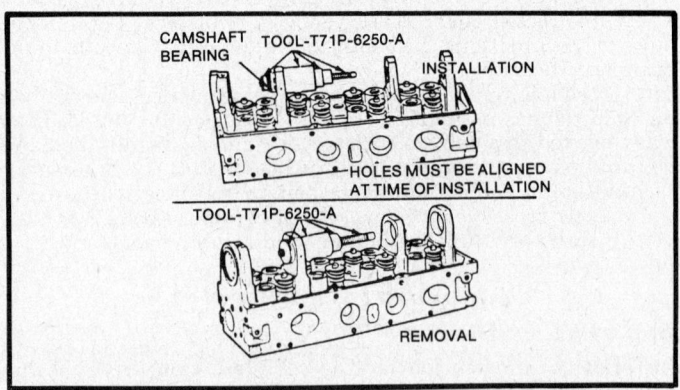

4 cyl camshaft bearings removal or installation—typical (©Ford Motor Co.)

Installation

1. Make sure the threaded plug is in the rear of the camshaft. If not, remove from old camshaft and install. Coat the camshaft lobes with polyethylene grease and lubricate journals with heavy SF oil before installation. Carefully guide the camshaft through the bearings.
2. Installation is the reverse of removal procedure.

Ford Lincoln Mercury
REAR WHEEL DRIVE CARS — SECTION 5

CAMSHAFT

Removal
IN LINE 6 CYL 3.3L ENGINE

1. Drain the cooling system and the crankcase. Remove the air cleaner assembly.
2. disconnect the radiator hoses from the coolant outlet housing and the water pump. Remove the radiator. Remove the grille. On a vehicle with air conditioning, removes the condenser attaching bolts, and position the condenser to one side. Do not disconnect the condenser refrigerant lines.
3. Disconnect the accelerator control cable from the carburetor and from the bracket. disconnect the bracket from the carburetor.
4. Disconnect the fuel inlet line at the fuel filter, and the vacuum hoses and connectors that are connected to the cylinder head directly or indirectly from the carburetor.
5. Disconnect the muffler inlet pipe from the exhaust manifold. Pull the muffler inlet pipe down. Remove the gasket.
6. Disconnect the carburetor fuel inlet line from the fuel pump.
7. Disconnect the spark plug wires from the spark plugs and the coil high tension lead at the coil.
8. Disconnect the engine temperature sending unit wire from the sending unit. Remove the distributor, the fuel pump, and the oil filter.

Remove the crankcase vent hose, regulator valve, valve rocker arm cover and cylinder head by following Steps 8 through 11 under Cylinder Head Removal.

Using a magnet, remove the hydraulic tappets and keep them in order so that they can be installed in their original locations. If the tappets are stuck on the bores by excessive varnish, etc., it may be necessary to use a claw-type tool to remove them.

Loosen and remove the drive belt, fan and pulley. Remove the crankshaft damper using tool.

Remove the cylinder front cover and gasket.

Check camshaft end play. If the end play is excessive, replace the thrust plate.

Remove the timing chain and sprockets.

Remove the camshaft thrust plate. Carefully remove the camshaft by pulling it toward the front of the engine. **Use caution to avoid damaging the bearings, journals and lobes.**

Installation

1. Installation is the reverse of removal procedure.
2. Install the thrust plate with the oil groove toward the rear of the engine and tighten the attaching bolts to 16–24 Nm (12–18 lb. ft.). Replace the crankshaft front oil seal.

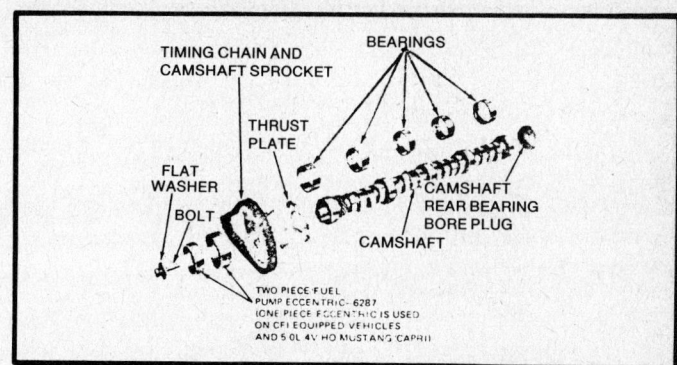

Camshaft and related parts — 6 cyl engine
(©Ford Motor Co.)

CAMSHAFT

Removal
3.8L V6 ENGINE

Lightly oil all attaching bolt and stud threads before installation except those specifying special sealant.

1. Remove radiator.
2. If equipped with air conditioning, remove condenser.
3. Remove grille.
4. Remove intake manifold.
5. Remove tappets as outlined.
6. Remove front cover and timing chain as outlined.
7. Remove oil pan.
8. Remove camshaft through the front of the engine, being careful not to damage bearing surfaces.

Installation

1. Lubricate the cam lobes and bearing surfaces with heavy engine oil.
2. Installation is the reverse of removal procedures.

CAMSHAFT

Removal
V8 ENGINES

1. Remove or reposition radiator, A/C condenser and grille components as necessary to provide clearance to remove camshaft. Remove the cylinder front cover and the timing chain.

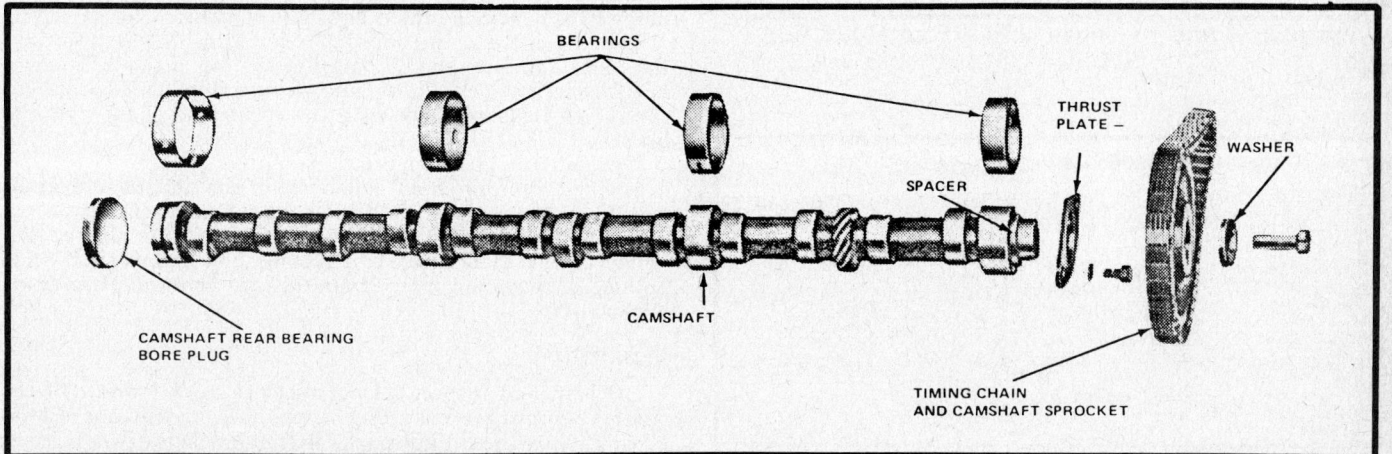

6 cyl camshaft and related parts (©Ford Motor Co.)

Ford Lincoln Mercury
REAR WHEEL DRIVE CARS
SECTION 5

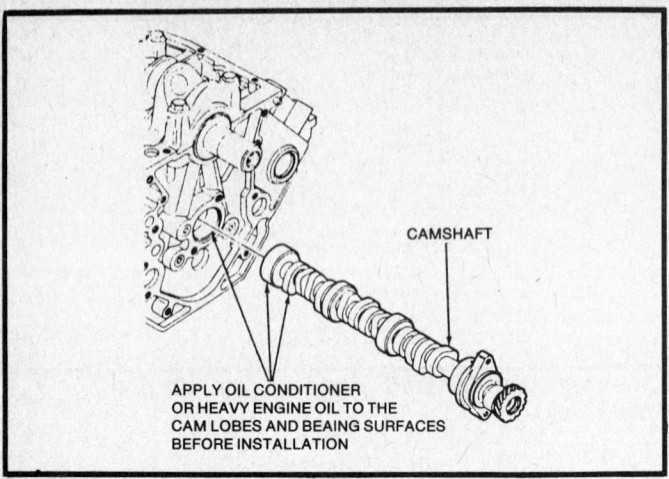

Camshaft installation—V8 engine
(©Ford Motor Co.)

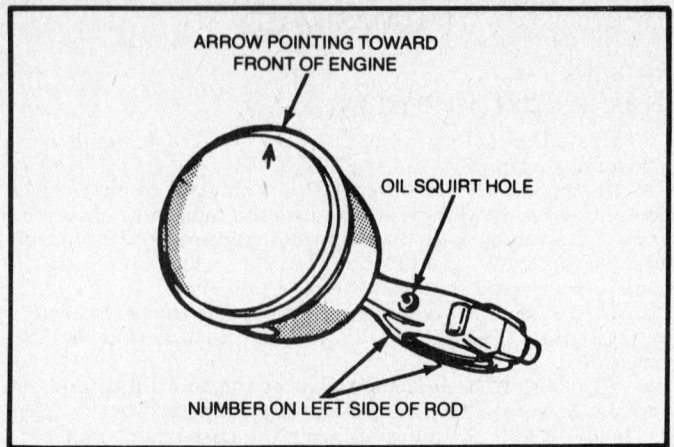

4 cyl piston and rod assembly (©Ford Motor Co.)

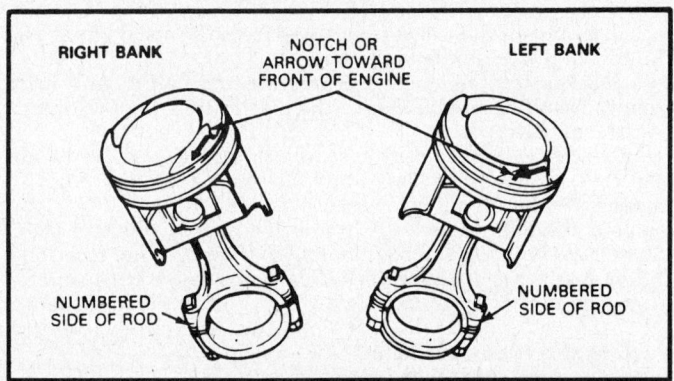

Correct piston and rod positions for the 8 cyl. engine

2. Remove the intake manifold and related parts.
3. Remove the crankcase ventilation valve and tubes from the valve rocker arm covers. Remove EGR cooler, if equipped. Remove the valve rocker arm covers. Loosen the valve rocker arm fulcrum bolts and rotate the rocker arms to the side.
4. Remove the valve pushrods and identify them so that they can be installed in their original positions.
5. Remove the tappets and place them in a rack so that they can be installed in their original bores.
6. Remove the camshaft thrust plate. Carefully remove the camshaft by pulling toward the front of the engine. **Use caution to avoid damaging the camshaft bearings.**

PISTONS AND ROD POSITIONING

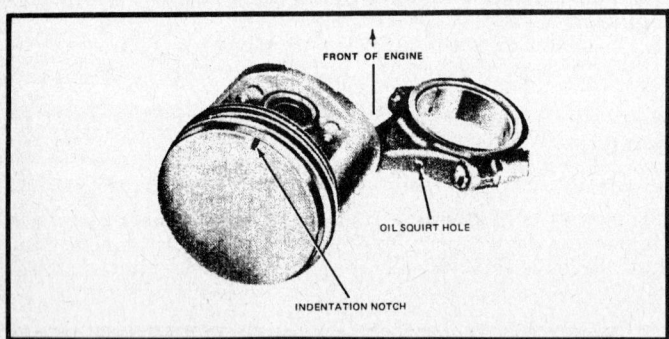

6 cyl piston and rod assembly (©Ford Motor Co.)

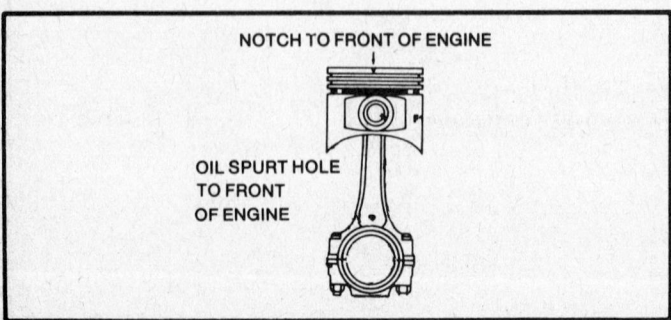

V6 piston and rod assembly (©Ford Motor Co.)

FRONT COVER ASSEMBLY AND TIMING CHAIN

Removal
IN LINE 6 CYL 3.3L ENGINE

1. Drain the cooling system and the crankcase. Remove the radiator. Remove the drive belt, fan and pulley. On a vehicle with air conditioning, remove the condenser attaching bolts and position the condenser forward. **Do not disconnect the refrigerant lines.** Remove the compressor drive belt. If so equipped, remove the accessory drive pulley. Using Tool T-58P-6316-B, remove the crankshaft damper.
2. Remove the cylinder front cover attaching screws from the cover and from the oil pan. Pry the top of the front cover away from the block slightly and, using a thin bladed knife, cut the oil pan gasket flush with the front face of the cylinder block.
3. Clean any gasket material from the surface.
4. Check timing chain deflection. If the deflection exceeds specifications, replace the timing chain and sprockets.
5. Crank the engine until the timing marks are aligned. Remove the camshaft sprocket attaching bolt and washer. Slide both sprockets and timing chain forward and remove them as an assembly.

Installation

1. Clean and inspect all parts before installation. Oil the timing chain after installing it on the camshaft and crankshaft. Be sure the timing marks on the sprockets are positioned properly.

2. Install the camshaft sprocket attaching bolt and washer. Torque the bolt to specifications.
3. Apply oil-resistant sealer to a new cylinder front cover gasket and position the gasket on the cylinder front cover. Apply sealer to the exposed area of the gasket. Coat the gasket surface of the oil pan with oil resistant sealer. cut and position the required portion of a new gasket on the oil pan. Apply sealer to the exposed areas of the gasket, including the corners where they contact the front cover gasket.
4. Install the cylinder front cover.
5. Torque the cover attaching bolts to 12–18 ft. lbs. (17–24 Nm).

FRONT COVER ASSEMBLY AND TIMING CHAIN

Removal

3.8L V6 ENGINE

1. Drain cooling system.
2. Disconnect cable from battery negative terminal.
3. Remove air cleaner assembly and air intake duct.
4. Remove fan shroud attaching screws. Remove fan/clutch assembly attaching bolts.
5. Remove fan/clutch assembly and shroud.
6. Loosen accessory drive belt idler. Remove drive belt and water pump pulley.
7. If equipped with power steering, remove pump mounting brackets' attaching bolts. Leaving the hoses connected, place the pump/bracket assembly aside in a position to prevent the fluid from leaking out.
8. If equipped with air conditioning, remove compressor front support bracket. Leave compressor in place.
9. Disconnect coolant bypass hose at water pump.
10. Disconnect heater hose at water pump.
11. Disconnect radiator upper hose at thermostat housing.
12. Disconnect coil wire from distributor cap and remove cap with the secondary wires attached.
13. Remove distributor hold-down clamp and lift distributor out of the front cover.
14. If equipped with tripminder, remove the fuel flow meter support bracket (the fuel lines will support the flow meter).
15. Raise vehicle.
16. Remove crankshaft damper using puller.
17. Remove fuel pump to carburetor fuel line to fuel pump, (2150–2V only).
20. Remove oil filter.
21. Disconnect radiator lower hose at the water pump.
22. Remove oil pan. Refer to Oil Pan Removal.

CAUTION
The front cover cannot be removed without lowering the oil pan.

---

23. Lower vehicle.
24. Remove front cover attaching bolts. It is not necessary to remove water pump.

CAUTION
Do not overlook the cover attaching bolt located behind the oil filter adapter. the front cover will break if pried upon and all attaching bolts are not removed.

---

25. Remove ignition timing indicator.
26. Remove front cover and water pump as an assembly.
27. Remove cover gasket and discard.
28. Remove camshaft thrust button and spring from the end of the camshaft.
29. Remove camshaft sprocket attaching bolts.
30. Remove camshaft sprocket, crankshaft sprockets and the timing chain.

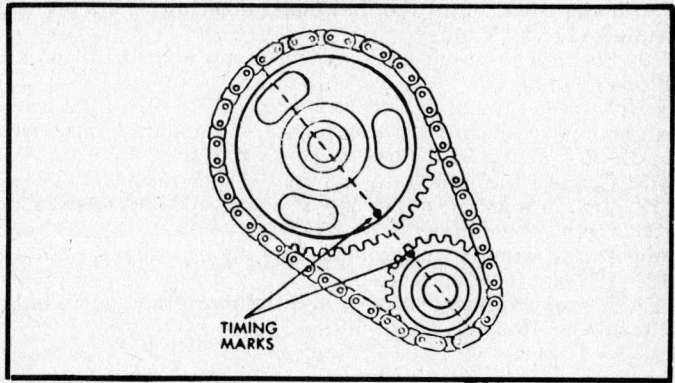
6 cyl engine timing mark alignment
(©Ford Motor Co.)

NOTE: The front cover contains the oil pump and intermediate shaft. If a new front cover is to be installed, remove the water pump, oil pump, oil filter adapter, and intermediate shaft from the old front cover.

Installation

NOTE: Lightly oil all bolt and stud threads before installation except those specifying special sealant.

1. Clean all gasket surfaces on the front cover, cylinder block, and fuel pump.
If re-using the front cover, replace the crankshaft front oil seal.
2. If a new front cover is to be installed:
   a. Install oil pump, oil filter adapter and intermediate shaft.
   b. Clean the water pump gasket surface. Position a new water pump gasket on the front cover and install the water pump. Install pump attaching bolts and tighten to 20–30 Nm (15–22 lb. ft.).
3. Rotate the crankshaft as necessary to position piston No. 1 at TDC and the crankshaft keyway at the 12 o'clock position.
4. Lubricate timing chain with clean engine oil. Install camshaft sprocket, crankshaft sprocket and timing chain. Make sure the marks are positioned across from each other.
5. Install camshaft sprocket attaching bolts and tighten to 20–30 Nm (15–22 ft. lb.).
6. Install camshaft thrust button and spring. (Small end of spring must face toward thrust button.). Lubricate thrust button with polyethylene grease before installation. The thrust button and spring must be bottomed out in the camshaft seat and must not be allowed to fall out during installation of the front cover.
7. Lubricate crankshaft front oil seal with clean engine oil.
8. Position a new cover gasket on the cylinder block and install the front cover/water pump assembly using dowels for proper alignment.
9. Position ignition timing indicator.
10. Install the front cover attaching bolts and tighten to 20–30 Nm (15–22 ft.lb.)

NOTE: The threads of the cover attaching bolt shown in illustration must be coated with Pipe Sealant before installation.

11. Raise vehicle.
12. Install oil pan.
13. Connect radiator lower hose. Tighten clamp securely.
14. Install oil filter.
15. Turn crankshaft clockwise 180° to position the fuel pump eccentric away from the fuel pump actuating arm. Failure to turn the crankshaft can result in the threads being stripped

out of the cover when the fuel pump attaching bolts are installed, (2150-2V only).
16. Position a new gasket on fuel pump and install pump 2150-2V only).
17. Tighten attaching bolts to 20-30 Nm (15-22 ft. lbs.). Install pump crash shield, if so equipped. Tighten attaching nuts to 20-30 Nm (15-22 ft. lbs.) (2150-2V only).
18. Connect fuel line to the pump (2150-2V only).
19. Coat crankshaft pulley key in the crankshaft keyway.
20. Install the damper.
21. Install damper washer and attaching bolt. Tighten bolt to 125-165 Nm (93-121 ft. lbs.).
22. Install crankshaft pulley and tighten attaching bolts to 26-28 Nm (19-28 ft. lbs.).

23. Turn crankshaft 180° counterclockwise to bring piston No. 1 back to TDC.
24. Lower vehicle.
25. Connect coolant bypass. Tighten clamp securely.
26. If equipped with tripminder, install fuel flow meter support bracket. tighten bracket-to-flow meter attaching nuts to 5-7 Nm (4-5 ft .lbs.). Tighten the brcket-to-front cover attaching nuts to 20-30 Nm (15-22 ft. lbs.).
27. Install the distributor with the rotor pointing at the No. 1 distributor cap tower, (2150-2V only).
28. Install distributor cap and coil wire.
29. Connect radiator upper hose at the thermostat housing. Tighten clamp securely.
30. Connect heater hose. Tighten clamp securely.
31. If equipped with air conditioning, install the compressor and mounting brackets. Tighten the attaching bolts to specification.
32. If equipped with power steering, install pump and mounting brackets. tighten attaching bolts to specification.
33. Position accessory drive belt over the pulleys.
34. Install water pump pulley, fan/clutch assembly attaching bolts to 16-24 Nm (12-18 ft. lbs.).
35. Position fan shroud on the radiator and install the attaching screws.
36. Position accessory drive belt over the water pump pulley and tension belt.
37. Connect cable to the battery negative terminal.
38. Fill crankcase to the proper level with the specified oil.
39. Fill cooling system with the specified coolant.

NOTE: This engine uses aluminum components that require a special corosion inhibitor coolant formulation to avoid radiator damage. The cooling system should be filled with a 50/50 mix of water and antifreeze, with the addition of two cooling system protector pellets D9AZ-19558-A or equivalent.

40. Start engine and check for coolant, oil or fuel leaks.
41. Check ignition timing and curb idle speed, adjust as required. Tighten distributor hold-down bolt 27-40 Nm (20-29 ft. lbs.).
42. Install air cleaner assembly and air intake duct.

CYLINDER FRONT COVER AND TIMING CHAIN

Removal

V8 ENGINES

1. Refer to Water Pump Removal. Perform all steps except removal of the pump. Leave water pump attached to the front cover.
2. Drain the crankcase.
3. Remove the crankshaft pulley from the crankshaft vibration damper. Remove the damper attaching screw and washer. Install a puller on the crankshaft vibration damper and remove the vibration damper.
4. Disconnect the fuel pump outlet line from the fuel pump. Remove the fuel pump attaching bolts and lay the pump to one side with the flexible fuel line still attached.
5. Remove fuel line from clip on front cover, is so equipped.
6. Remove the oil pan-to-cylinder front cover attaching bolts. Use a thin blade knife to cut the oil pan gasket flush with cylinder block face prior to separating the cover from the cylinder block. Remove the cylinder front cover and water pump as an assembly.

NOTE: Cover the front oil pan opening while the cover assembly is off to prevent foreign material from entering the pan.

If a new front cover is to be installed, remove the water pump from the old cylinder front cover and install it on the new cover.

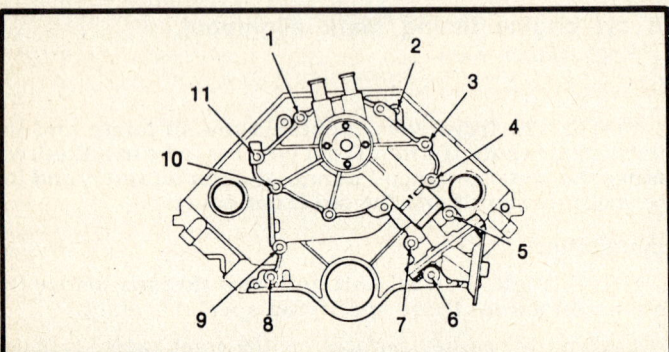
V6 engine front cover (©Ford Motor Co.)

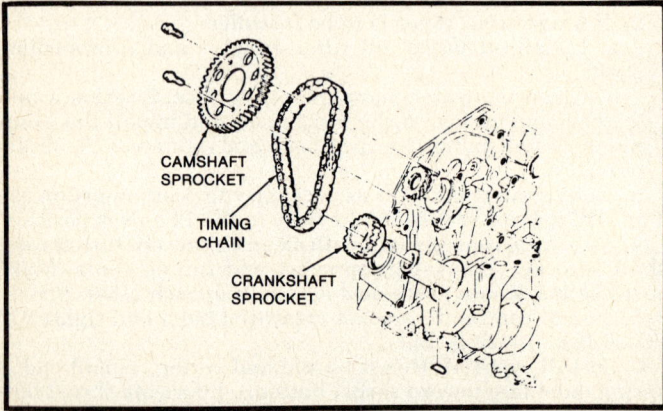
V6 engine timing chain and sprockets
(©Ford Motor Co.)

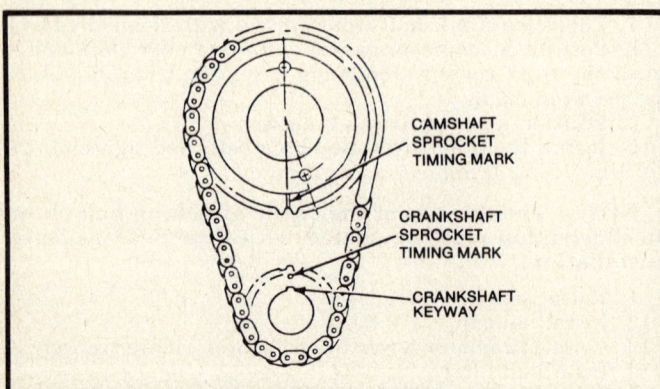
V6 engine timing mark alignment
(©Ford Motor Co.)

7. Discard the cylinder front cover gasket.
8. Check the timing chain deflection.
9. Crank the engine until the timing marks on the sprockets are positioned as shown in illustration.
10. Remove the camshaft sprocket cap screw, washers and fuel pump eccentric. Remove the spacer on Central Fuel Injected (CFI) vehicles. Slide both sprockets and the timing chain forward, and remove them as an assembly.

Installation

1. Position the sprockets and timing chain on the camshaft and crankshaft simultaneously. Be sure the timing marks on the timing marks on the sprockets are positioned as shown in illustration.
2. Install the fuel pump eccentric (install the spacer on Central Fuel Injected (CFI) vehicles, washers and camshaft sprocket cap screw. Tighten the sprocket cap screw to 54–61 Nm (40–45 ft. lbs.).
3. Clean the cylinder front cover, oil pan and the block gasket surfaces.
4. Install a new oil seal in the cylinder front cover.
5. Lubricate the timing chain with engine oil.
6. Coat the gasket surface of the oil pan with sealer, cut and position the required sections of a new gasket on the oil pan, apply sealer at the corners. Install pan seal as required.

NOTE: Contact cement is recommended to hold the seals and gaskets in position during assembly.

Coat the gasket surfaces of the block and cover with sealer, and position a new gasket on the block.

7. Position the cylinder front cover on the cylinder block. Use care when installing the cover to avoid seal damage or possible gasket mislocation.
8. Install the cylinder front cover to seal alignment tool into proper position.
9. It may be necessary to force the cover downward to slightly compress the pan gasket. This operation can be facilitated by using a suitable tool at the front cover attaching hole locations.
10. Coat the threads of the attaching screws with oil resistant sealer and install the screws. While pushing in on the alignment tool, tighten the oil pan to cover attaching screws to 9–11 ft. lbs. (12–15 Nm). Tighten the cover to block attaching screws to specifications. Remove the pilot.
11. Apply polyethylene grease to the oil seal rubbing surface of the vibration damper inner hub to prevent damage to the seal. Apply a coating of polyethylene grease to the front of the crankcase for damper installation.
12. Line up the crankshaft vibration damper keyway with the key on the crankshaft. Install the vibration damper on the crankshaft. Install the capscrew and washer. Tighten the screw to 70–90 ft. lbs. (95–122 Nm). Install the crankshaft pulley.
13. Install the fuel pump using a new gasket. Connect the fuel pump outlet line.
14. Refer to Water Pump Installation. Perform all the required steps except installation of the pump.
15. fill the crankcase with the proper grade and quantity of engine oil.
16. Fill and bleed the cooling system.
17. Operate the engine at fast idle and check for coolant and oil leaks. Check and adjust the ignition timing engine and engine idle speed.

CRANKSHAFT FRONT OIL SEAL

Removal

V6 ENGINES

1. Remove fan shroud attaching screws and position shroud back over the fan.

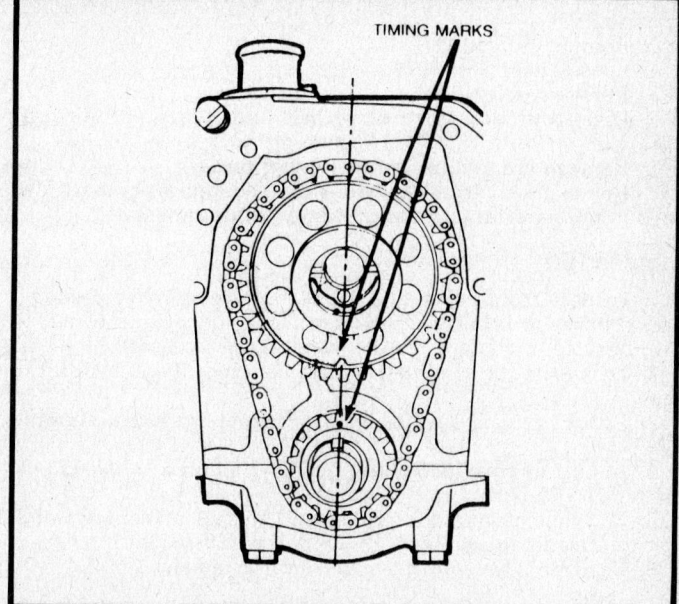
V8 engines timing mark alignment
(©Ford Motor Co.)

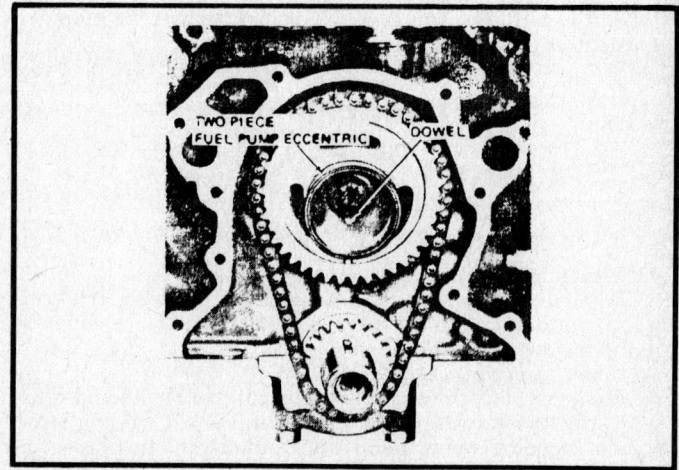
V8 engines fuel pump eccentric installed
(©Ford Motor Co.)

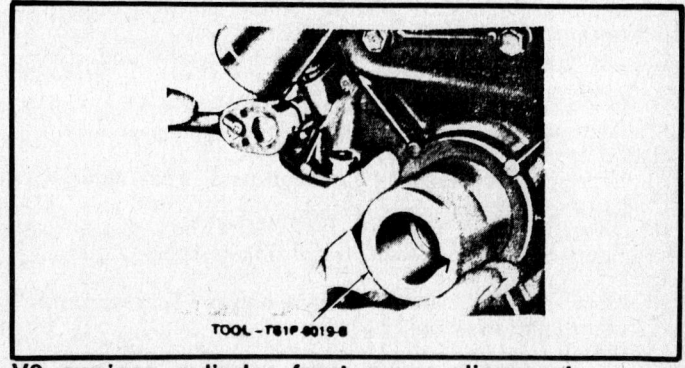
V8 engines cylinder front cover alignment
(©Ford Motor Co.)

Ford Lincoln Mercury
REAR WHEEL DRIVE CARS

2. Remove fan/clutch or electro-drive fan assembly attaching bolts.
3. Remove fan/clutch.
4. Loosen accessory drive belt idler.
5. Raise vehicle.
6. Disengage accessory drive belt and remove crankshaft pulley.
7. Remove crankshaft damper using puller.
8. Remove seal from the front cover using a pry bar. Use care to prevent damage to front cover and crankshaft.

Installation

1. Inspect front cover and crankshaft damper for damage, nicks, burrs or other roughness which may cause the seal to fail. Service or replace the components as necessary.
2. Lubricate the seal lip with clean engine oil and install the seal.
3. Lubricate seal surface on the damper with clean engine oil.
4. Install damper attaching bolt and tighten to 92–121 ft. lbs. (125–165 Nm).
5. Position crankshaft pulley and install attaching bolts. Tighten attaching bolts to 19–28 ft. lbs. (26-38 Nm).
6. Position accessory drive belt over crankshaft pulley.
7. Lower vehicle.
8. Install fan/clutch shroud. Cross tighten the attaching bolts to 12–18 ft. lbs. (16–24 Nm).
9. Position shroud on the radiator and install attaching screws.
10. Check accessory drive belt for proper routing and engagement in the pulleys. Adjust the drive belt to specification.
11. Start engine and check for oil leaks.

Lubrication
OIL PAN

Removal and Installation

MUSTANG/CAPRI 4 CYL 2.3L ENGINE

1. Disconnect the negative battery cable.
2. Remove the fan shroud. If equipped with an electric cooling fan, disconnect the hot lead to the fan motor. Remove the fan and shroud assembly.
3. Drain the crankcase.
4. Remove the right and left engine support bolts and nuts.
5. Using a jack, raise the engine as high as it will go. Place blocks of wood between the mounts and chassis brackets. Remove shake brace. (Mustang and Capri).
6. Remove the sway bar retaining bolts and lower the sway bar.
7. Remove the starter motor.
8. Remove steering gear retaining bolts and lower the gear.
9. Remove the oil pan retaining bolts. Allow the oil pan to drop to the crossmember and remove.
10. Thoroughly clean all gasket mating surfaces and inspect for damage.
11. Install new oil pan gasket and end seals.
12. Position oil pan to the cylinder block and install retaining bolts.
13. Reposition the steering gear and install bolts and nuts.
14. Install starter.
15. raise the engine enough to remove the wood blocks, lower the engine and remove jack. Install shake brace. (Mustang/Capri).
16. Install the right and left engine support bolts and nuts.
17. Install the sway bar.
18. Install the fan shroud.
19. Fill the crankshaft with oil. Replace the filter.
20. Connect battery cable, run engine and check for leak.

FAIRMONT/ZEPHYR/GRANADA/COUGAR/THUNDERBIRD/LTD MARQUIS 4 CYL 2.3L ENGINE

1. Disconnect negative battery cable.
2. Drain the crankcase.
3. Remove the right and left engine support bolts and nuts.
4. Using a jack, raise the engine as far as it will go. Place blocks of wood between the mounts and the chassis brackets. Remove the jack.
5. Remove the steering gear retaining nus and bolts. Remove the bolt retaining the steering flex coupling to the steering gear. Position the steering gear forward and down.
6. Remove the shake brace and starter.
7. Remove the engine rear support to crossmember nuts.
8. Position a jack under the transmission and raise.
9. Remove oil pan retaining bolts. Remove the oil pan.
10. Thoroughly clean all gasket mating surfaces and inspect for damage.
11. Position the new oil pan gasket and end seals to the cylinder block with cement.
12. Position the oil pan to the cylinder block and install its retaining bolts.
13. Lower the jack under the transmission and install the crossmember nuts.
14. Replace the oil filter.
15. Position the flex coupling to the steering gear and install the retaining bolt.
16. Install the steering gear.
17. Install the shakebrace. Install the starter.
18. Raise the engine enough to remove the wood blocks. Lower the engine and remove the jack. Install engine support bolts and nuts.
19. Lower the vehicle and fill the crankcase with oil Replace the filter, if necessary.
20. Connect the battery.
21. Start the engine and check for leaks.

OIL PAN/OIL PUMP

Removal

1983 IN LINE CYL 3.3L ENGINE

1. Disconnect two oil cooler lines at radiator (if equipped).
2. Remove radiator top support tow bolts.
3. Remove oil level dipstick.
4. Raise vehicle on hoist.
5. Drain crankcase.
6. Remove four bolts and nuts attaching sway bar to chassis and allow sway bar to hang down.
7. Remove K brace.
8. Lower front steering rack and pinion.
9. Disconnect battery lead to starter and remove two bolts attaching starter and remove starter.
10. Remove two nuts attaching engine mounts to No. 2 crossmember.
11. Loosen two rear insulator-to-crossmember attaching bolts.
12. Loosen the fan shroud to prevent fan blade damage.
13. raise engine and place one ¼ in. spacer between engine support insulator and chassis bracket.
14. Position jack under transmission and raise slightly.
15. Remove oil pan attaching bolts and lower pan to crossmember.
16. Remove the oil pump, intermediate driveshaft, pick-up tube and screen assembly and allow components to drop into pan.
17. Position transmission cooler lines out of the way and remove oil pan (rotating crankshaft if required).
18. Clean oil pump pick-up tube and screen, oil pan gasket surface at cylinder block and oil pan.
19. Inspect oil pan for damage.

Installation

1. Installation is the reverse of removal procedure.
2. Position oil pan to cylinder block and install attaching bolts. Tighten bolts to 9–1 Nm (7–9 ft. lbs.).

OIL PAN

Removal and Installation

1983 V6 3.8L ENGINE

1. Remove the air cleaner assembly including the air intake duct.
2. Remove the fan shroud attaching bolts and position the shroud back over the fan.
3. Remove the oil level dipstick.
4. Remove the screws attaching the vacuum solenoids to the dash panel. Lay the solenoid on the engine without disconnecting the vacuum hoses or electrical connectors.
5. Remove the exhaust manifold to exhaust pipe attaching nuts.
6. Drain the crankcase.
7. Remove the oil filter.
8. Remove the bolts attaching the shift linkage bracket to the transmission bellhousing.
9. Disconnect the transmission cooler lines at the radiator.
10. Remove the converter cover.
11. On Granada/Cougar and Thunderbird/XR-7 vehicles proceed with the following steps.
    a. Remove the engine damper to No. 2 crossmember bracket attaching bolt. The damper must be disconnected from the crossmember.
    b. Disconnect steering flex coupling. Remove two bolts attaching steering gear to main crossmember and let steering gear rest on the frame away from oil pan.
12. Remove the nut and washer assembly attaching the front engine insulator to the chassis.
13. Raise the engine 2–3 inches and insert wood blocks between the engine mounts and the vehicle frame.

NOTE: On Granada/Cougar and Thunderbird/XR-7 models, it may be necessary to raise the engine as much as 5 inches to provide adequate pan-to-crossmember clearance.

---------------- CAUTION ----------------
Watch the clearance between the transmission dipstick tube and the thermactor downstream air tube. If the tubes contact before adequate pan-to-crossmember clearance is provided, lower the engine and remove the transmission dipstick tube and the downstream air tube.

14. Remove the oil pan attaching bolts. Work the oil pan loose and remove.
15. On Granada/Cougar and Thunderbird/XR-7 models lower the oil pan onto the crossmember. Remove the oil pick-up tube attaching bolts and the tube support bracket attaching nut. Lower the pick-up tube/screen assembly into the pan and remove the oil pan through the front of the vehicle.
16. Remove the oil pan seal from the main bearing cap.
17. Clean the gasket surfaces on the cylinder block, oil pan and oil pick-up tube.
18. Apply ⅛ in. bead of sealer to all matching surfaces of oil pan and engine front cover.
19. Install the oil pan.

NOTE: On Granada/Cougar and Thunderbird/XR-7 models place the oil pick-up tube/screen assembly in the oil pan.

20. Install all other components removed.
21. fill the crankshaft to the correct level with the oil.
22. Start the engine and check the fluid levels in the transmission.
23. Check for engine oil, and transmission fluid leaks.

OIL PAN

Removal

1984 AND LATER V6 3.8L ENGINE

1. Disconnect cable from the battery negative terminal.
2. Remove air cleaner assembly including the air intake duct.
3. Remove fan shroud attaching bolts and position shroud back over the fan.
4. Remove oil level dipstick.
5. If equipped with a low lever oil sensor, remove retainer clip at sensor. Remove electrical connector from sensor.
7. Raise vehicle.
8. Drain crankcase.
9. Remove oil filter.
10. Remove bolts attaching the shift linkage bracket to the transmission bellhousing.
11. Disconnect transmission cooler lines at the radiator.
12. Remove four converter cover retaining bolts and remove cover.
13. On LTD/Marquis and Thunderbird/Cougar, disconnect the steering flex coupling. Remove two bolts attaching steering gear to main crossmember and let steering gear rest on the frame away from the oil pan.
14. Remove nut and washer assembly attaching the front engine insulator to the chassis.
15. Raise engine 2 to 3 in. and insert wood blocks between the engine mounts and the vehicle frame. On LTD/Marquis and Thunderbird/Cougar, it may be necessary to raise the engine as much as 5 in. to provide adequate pan-to-crossmember clearance. When raising the engine in one of these vehicles watch the clearance between the transmission dipstick tube and the thermactor downstream air tube. If the tubes contact before adequate pan-to-crossmember clearance is provided, lower the engine and remove the transmission dipstick tube and the downstream air tube. Clamp Cutter and Crimping Tool will be needed to disconnect the tube from the catalyst.
16. Remove oil pan attaching bolts. Work oil pan loose and remove. On LTD/Marquis and Thunderbird/Cougar lower oil pan onto crossmember. Remove oil pick-up tube attaching bolts and tube support bracket attaching nut. Lower pick-up tube/screen assembly into the pan and remove oil pan through the front of the vehicle.
17. Remove oil seal from the main bearing cap. Discard seal.

Installation

NOTE: When using silicone rubber sealer, assembly must occur within 15 minutes after sealer application. After this time, the sealer may start to set-up, and its sealing effectiveness may be reduced.

1. Clean the gasket surfaces of the cylinder block, oil pan and oil pick-up tube.
2. Trial fit the oil pan to the cylinder block. Make sure enough clearance has been provided to allow the oil pan to be installed without the sealant being scraped off when the pan is positioned under the engine.
3. Remove oil pan.
4. Install oil pan end seal as follows:
   a. Using a small bladed screwdriver, remove any sealer which may have been squeezed into the seal groove when the rear main bearing cap was installed.
   b. Place a ¼ in. drop of sealer into the seal groove where the bearing cap meets the block.
   c. Position seal in the groove. Using a screwdriver, work

Ford Lincoln Mercury
REAR WHEEL DRIVE CARS

the tab on the end of the seal into the cap between rear main cap and cylinder block.
  d. Using a small screwdriver, work the edges of the seal into seal groove.
 5. Install oil pan as follows:
  a. Apply a 4.0–5.0 mm ($1/5$ in.) bead of Silicone Sealer to the seam where the front cover and cylinder block join.
  b. Apply a 4.0–5.0 mm ($1/5$ in.) bead of Silicone Sealer to each end of the rear seal where the rear main cap and cylinder block joint.
  c. Apply a 4.0–5.0 mm ($1/5$ in.) bead of Silicone Sealer along the oil pan rails on the cylinder block as the bead crosses the front cover increase the bead width.
  d. Place oil pick-up tube/screen assembly in the oil pan.
  e. Position oil pan.
  f. Position oil pick-up tube/screen with a new gasket. Install tube attaching bolts and support bracket attaching nut. Tighten to 20–30 Nm (15–22 ft. lbs,).
  g. Install oil pan attaching bolts and tighten to 9–12 Nm (80–106 in. lbs.).
 6. Raise engine, remove wood blocks supporting engine, and lower engine into position.
 7. Install front mount of damper, if equipped LTD/Marquis, attaching bolts and nuts. Tighten attached bolts to specification.
 8. On LTD/Marquis and Thunderbird/Cougar, position the steering gear to the main crossmember. Install two attaching bolts and tighten to specification. Connect steering flex coupling and tighten the attaching nuts to specification.
 9. Position shift linkage bracket and install attaching bolts.
 10. Connect transmission oil cooler lines.
 11. Install a new oil filter.
 12. On LTD/Marquis and Thunderbird/Cougar, install the transmission dipstick tube and the thermactor downstream air tube, if removed. Clamp Cutter and Crimping Tool T78P-9481-A or equivalent will be needed to connect air tube to catalyst.
 13. Lower vehicle.
 14. Install lower level oil sensor connector to the sensor and install retainer clip.
 15. Position fan shroud on the radiator and install attaching bolts.
 16. Connect battery cable.
 17. Fill crankcase to the correct level with the specified oil.
 18. Start engine and check the fluid levels in the transmission. Check for engine oil, and transmission fluid leaks.
 19. Install air cleaner assembly including air intake duct.

OIL PAN

Removal and Installation

1983-84 FORD 5.0L/5.8L (302/351 "W" CID) V-8 ENGINES MUSTANG/CAPRI, FAIRMONT/ZEPHYR, THUNDERBIRD/COUGAR XR-7, GRANADA

NOTE: On vehicles equipped with a dual sump oil pan, both drain plugs must be removed to thoroughly drain the crankcase.

 1. Remove the fan shroud attaching bolts, positioning the fan shroud back over the fan. Remove the dipstick and tube assembly.
 2. Drain the crankcase.
 3. Disconnect steering flex coupling. Remove two bolts attaching steering gear to main crossmember and let steering gear rest on frame away from oil pan.
 4. Remove the idler arm bracket retaining bolts and pull the linkage down and out of the way (Granada only).
 5. Raise the engine and place two wood blocks (2 in. x 4 in.) between the engine mounts and the vehicle frame. Remove converter inspection cover.
 6. Remove rear K-braces (four bolts).
 7. Remove the oil pan attaching bolts and lower oil pan to the frame.
 8. Remove oil pump attaching bolts and the inlet tube attaching nut from the No. 3 main bearing cap stud and lower the oil pump into the oil pan.
 9. Remove the oil pan, rotating the crankshaft as necessary to clear the counterweights.
 10. Clean all gasket mating surfaces and inspect the pan for damage.
 11. Position oil pan gasket and sealer to cylinder block using contact cement.
 12. Position oil pump and inlet tube into oil pan. Slide oil pan into position under the engine. With the oil pump intermediate shaft in position in the oil pump, position the oil pump to the cylinder block, and the inlet tube to the stud on No. 3 main bearing cap attaching bolt. Install the attaching bolts and nut and tighten to specification. Position the oil pan in the engine and install the attaching bolts.
 13. Position the steering gear to the main crossmember. Install the two attaching bolts and tighten to specification. Connect steering flex coupling.
 14. Position rear K braces and install the four attaching bolts.
 15. Raise engine and remove wood blocks.
 16. Install stabilizer bar (Versailles only).
 17. Lower the engine and install engine mount attaching bolts. Tighten to specification. Install converter inspection cover.
 18. Install oil dipstick and tube assembly, and fill crankcase with the specified engine oil Connect the positive battery cable. Install idler arm (Granada/Monarch only).
 19. Connect transmission oil cooler lines.
 20. Position the shroud to the radiator and install the two attaching bolts. Start the engine and check for leaks.

OIL PAN

Removal and Installation

1983 FORD 5.0L/5.8L (302/351 "W" CID) V-8 ENGINES FORD/MERCURY, LINCOLN CONTINENTAL/CONTINENTAL, MARK VI

 1. Remove the air cleaner assembly.
 2. Disconnect the accelerator and kickdown rods at the carburetor.
 3. Remove the accelerator mounting bracket retaining bolts and remove the bracket.
 4. Remove the fan shroud retaining bolts and position the shroud over the fan.
 5. Disconnect wiper motor electrical connector from the wiring harness.
 6. Remove the wiper motor.
 7. Disconnect the windshield washer hose.
 8. Remove the dipstick and retaining bolt at the exhaust manifold.
 9. Remove the thermactor air dump tube retaining clamp.
 10. Remove the thermactor crossover tube at the rear of the engine.
 11. Drain the crankcase.
 12. Remove filler tube from oil pan and drain transmission.
 13. Remove starter motor.
 14. Disconnect the fuel line at the fuel pump.
 15. Disconnect the exhaust pipes from the exhaust manifold.
 16. Remove the exhaust gas oxygen sensor from the exhaust manifold, if equipped.
 17. Remove the thermactor secondary air tube to torque converter housing clamps.
 18. Remove the converter inspection cover.
 19. Disconnect the exhaust pipes to catalytic converter outlet.

Ford Lincoln Mercury
REAR WHEEL DRIVE CARS
SECTION 5

20. Remove the catalytic converter secondary air tube and inlet pipes to exhaust manifold.
21. Loosen the engine rear mount attaching nuts.
22. Remove the dipstick tube from the oil pan.
23. Remove the engine mount through bolts.
24. Remove the shift crossover bolts at the transmission.
25. Remove the brake line retainer from the front crossmember.
26. Disconnect the transmission kickdown rod.
27. Position a jack under the engine and raise it as high as it will go.
28. Place a block of wood between each engine mount and the chassis bracket. When the engine is definitely secured with the wood blocks, remove the jack.
29. Remove the oil pan retaining bolts and lower the oil pan.
30. Remove the three bolts retaining the oil pump pick up tube and screen assembly to the oil pump and cylinder block. Allow the pick up tube assembly to drop into the oil pan.
31. Remove the oil pan.
32. Clean the oil pan and gasket surface on the cylinder block.
33. Position oil pan gaskets and seals on the cylinder block.
34. Place the oil pick up tube and screen assembly in the oil pan and position the oil pan onto the number two crossmember.
35. Position the oil pick up tube and screen assembly and install the retaining bolts.
36. Position the oil pan and install the retaining bolts.
37. Position a jack under the engine and raise the engine enough to remove the wooden blocks.
38. Lower the engine and remove the jack.
39. Install the engine support to chassis through bolts and nuts.
40. Install all other components removed.
41. Fill the crankcase with oil. Start engine and check for leaks.

OIL PAN

Removal
1984 AND LATER FORD CROWN VICTORIA/ MERCURY GRAND MARQUIS – NON-EEC

1. Remove the air cleaner assembly.
2. Disconnect the accelerator and kickdown rods at the carburetor.
3. Remove the accelerator mounting bracket retaining bolts and remove the bracket.
4. Remove the fan shroud retaining bolts and position the shroud over the fan.
5. Disconnect wiper motor electrical connector from the wiring harness.
6. Remove the wiper motor.
7. Disconnect the windshield washer hose.
8. Remove the wiper motor mounting cover.
9. Remove the dipstick.
10. Remove the dipstick retaining bolt at the exhaust manifold.
11. Raise the vehicle.
12. Drain the crankcase.
13. Disconnect the fuel line at the fuel pump.
14. Disconnect the inlet pipes from the exhaust manifold.
15. Loosen the engine rear mount attaching nuts.
16. Remove the engine mount through bolts.
17. Remove the shift crossover bolts at transmission and remove.
18. Disconnect the transmission kickdown rod.
19. Remove the torque converter cover retaining bolts and remove the cover.
20. Remove the brake line retainer from the front crossmember.

21. Position a jack under the engine and raise the engine as high as it will go.
22. Place a wood block between each engine mount and the chassis brackets. When the engine is definitely secured with the wood blocks, remove the jack.
23. Disconnect low oil level sensor on left side of rear oil sump, if so equipped.
24. Remove the oil pan retaining bolts and lower the oil pan.
25. Remove the three bolts retaining the oil pump pick up tube and screen assembly to the oil pump and cylinder block. Allow the pick up tube assembly to drop into the oil pan.
26. Remove the oil pan from the vehicle.
27. Clean the oil pan and inspect for damage.
28. Clean the oil pump pick up tube and screen assembly.
29. Clean the oil pan gasket surface on the cylinder block.

Installation

1. Installation is the reverse order of removal procedures.
2. Position the oil pick up tube and screen assembly and install the retaining bolts. Tighten bolts to 10–15 ft. lbs. (14–20 Nm).
3. Position the oil pan and install the retaining bolts. Tighten bolts to 9–11 ft. lbs. (12–15 Nm).

Removal
1984 AND LATER LINCOLN TOWN CAR, MARK VII/ CONTINENTAL, FORD CROWN VICTORIA/ MERCURY GRAND MARQUIS – WITH EEC

1. Remove the air cleaner assembly.
2. Disconnect the accelerator and kickdown rods at the carburetor.
3. Remove the accelerator mounting bracket retaining bolts and remove the bracket.
4. Remove EGR valve and cooler.
5. Remove the fan shroud retaining bolts and position the shroud over the fan.
6. Disconnect wiper motor electrical connector from the wiring harness.
7. Remove the wiper motor.
8. Disconnect the windshield washer hose.
9. Remove the wiper motor mounting cover.
10. Remove the dipstick.
11. Remove the dipstick retaining bolt at the exhaust manifold.
12. Remove the thermactor air dump tube retaining clamp.
13. Remove the thermactor crossover tube at the rear of the engine.
14. Raise the vehicle.
15. Drain the crankcase.
16. Remove filler tube from oil pan and drain transmission.
17. Disconnect cable from starter motor.
18. Remove starter motor.
19. Disconnect the fuel line at the fuel pump. Vehicles equipped with central fuel injection have a high pressure electrical fuel pump. Pressure must be relieved at the Schrader type valve on the fuel charging assembly before disconnecting fuel supply and return lines.
20. Disconnect the inlet pipes from the exhaust manifold.
21. Remove the exhaust gas oxygen sensor from the exhaust manifold.
22. Remove the thermactor secondary air tube to torque converter housing clamps.
23. Remove the converter inspection cover.
24. Disconnect the exhaust pipes to the catalytic converter outlet.
25. Remove the catalytic converter secondary air tube and inlet pipes to exhaust manifold.
26. Loosen the engine rear mount attaching nuts.
27. Remove the engine mount through bolts.

5-73

28. Remove the shift crossover bolts at the transmission.
29. Remove the brake line retainer from the front crossmember.
30. Disconnect the transmission kickdown rod.
31. Position a jack under the engine and raise the engine as high as it will go.
32. Place a block of wood between each engine mount and the chassis brackets. When the engine is definitely secured with the wood blocks, remove the jack.
33. Disconnect low oil level sensor on left side of rear oil sump, if so equipped.
34. Remove the oil pan retaining bolts and lower the oil pan.
35. Remove the three bolts retaining the oil pump pick up tube and screen assembly to the oil pump and cylinder block. Allow the pick up tube assembly to drop into the oil pan.
36. Remove the oil pan from the vehicle.
37. Clean the oil pan and inspect for damage.
38. Remove and clean the oil pump pick up tube and screen assembly.
39. Clean the oil pan gasket surface on the cylinder block.

Installation

1. Installation is the reverse of removal procedures.
2. Position the oil pick up tube and screen assembly and install the retaining bolts. Tighten bolts to 10–15 ft. lbs. (14–20 Nm).
3. Position the oil pan and install the retaining bolts. Tighten bolts to 9–11 ft. lbs. (12–15 Nm).

Removal

1984 AND LATER THUNDERBIRD/COUGAR

1. Raise hood and cover fenders. Disconnect battery ground cable.
2. Remove oil level indicator from left side of rear oil sump.
3. Remove air cleaner assembly.
4. Remove fan shroud retaining bolts and position shroud over the fan.
5. Raise vehicle on hoist.
6. Drain crankcase and transmission.
7. Remove driveshaft assembly.
8. Disconnect speedometer cable from transmission.
9. Remove gearshift bellcrank lever from transmission.
10. Remove flywheel housing cover retaining bolts and remove cover.
11. Remove flywheel-to-converter attaching bolts.
12. Remove transmission kickdown control shaft.
13. Remove gear selector valve rod.
14. Remove starter motor retaining bolts and electrical connections and remove starter motor from vehicle.
15. Remove exhaust catalyst converter and muffler inlet pipes.
16. Support transmission with suitable transmission jack and remove converter housing to cylinder block attaching bolts.
17. Remove No. 3 crossmember and rear insulator support assemblies.
19. Remove neutral start switch electrical connection at transmission and disconnect transmission oil cooler lines.
20. Remove transmission and converter as an assembly.
21. Remove flywheel attaching bolts.
22. Remove engine rear cover plate.
23. Remove steering gear attaching bolts and position steering gear forward out of the way.
24. Raise and support engine in a position that allows for clearance for oil pan removal.
25. Remove oil pan attaching bolts and lower oil pan to No. 2 crossmember.
26. Remove oil pump and pick-up tube attaching bolts. Allow oil pump and pick up tube assembly to drop into oil pan.
27. Remove oil pan from vehicle.

Installation

1. Installation is the reverse order of removal procedures.
2. Torque all bolts and nuts to specifications.

OIL PUMP

4 CYL ENGINE

Oil pump installation information is shown in illustrations. Prime the oil pump with engine oil when making final installation. Be sure that both the oil pump and strap mounting surfaces are clean prior to assembly and that all bolts are tightened to specification. tighten oil pump mounting bolts to 14–21 ft. lbs. (19–29 Nm). Tighten strap nut to 28–40 ft. lbs. (38–54 Nm).

FRONT COVER ASSEMBLY

V6 ENGINES

The front cover assembly contains three components related to the lubrication system. These components are:
 Oil pump.
 Oil pressure relief valve.
 Pump drive intermediate shaft.

Disassembly

1. If necessary, remove oil filter.
2. Remove oil pump cover attaching bolts and remove the cover.
3. Lift pump gears out of the pocket in the front cover.
4. Remove cover gasket and discard.

Assembly

1. If necessary, remove pump gears from cover. Lightly pack the gear picket with petroleum jelly. Do not use chassis lubricants. Install gears in the cover pocket making sure the petroleum jelly fills all voids between the gears and the pocket.

--- CAUTION ---

Failure to properly coat the oil pump gears may result in failure of the pump to prime when the engine is started.

2. Position cover gasket and install pump cover.zTighten pump cover attaching bolts to 18-2 ft. lbs. (25–30 Nm).

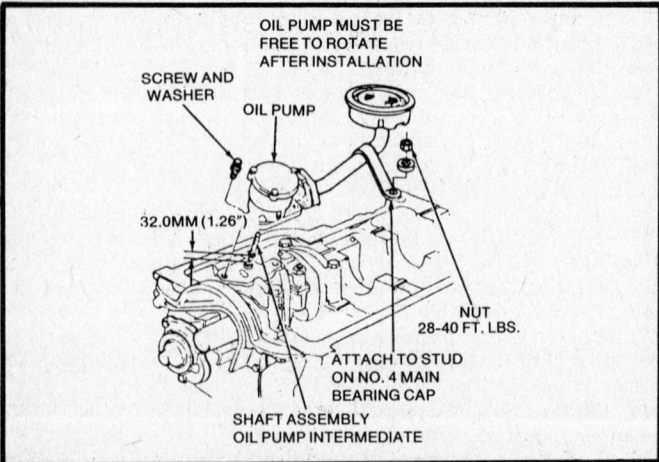

4 cyl oil pump installation (©Ford Motor Co.)

Ford Lincoln Mercury
REAR WHEEL DRIVE CARS
SECTION 5

OIL PUMP

Removal

LINCOLN TOWN CAR, MARK VII/CONTINENTAL, FORD CROWN VICTORIA/MERCURY GRAND MARQUIS

On Thunderbird/Cougar and Mustang/Capri, oil pump removal is described under Oil Pan and Oil Pump Removal.

1. Remove the oil pan and related parts.
2. Remove the oil pump inlet tube and screen assembly.
3. Remove the oil pump attaching bolts and remove the oil pump and intermediate driveshaft.

Installation

1. Prime the oil pump by filling either the inlet or outlet port with engine oil. Rotate the pump shaft to distribute the oil within the pump body.
2. Position the intermediate driveshaft into the distributor socket. With the shaft firmly seated in the distributor socket, the stop on the shaft should touch the roof of the crankcase. Remove the shaft and position the stop as necessary.
3. With the stop properly positioned, insert the intermediate driveshaft into the oil pump. Install the pump and shaft as an assembly. **Do not attempt to force the pump into position if it will not seat readily. The driveshaft hex may be misaligned with the distributor shaft. To align, rotate the intermediate driveshaft into a new position.** Tighten the oil pump attaching screws to 22–32 ft. lbs. (30–42 Nm).
4. Clean and install the oil pump inlet tube and screen assembly.
5. Install the oil pan and related parts as outlined under Oil Pan Installation.

CRANKSHAFT REAR OIL SEAL

Removal

6 CYL AND 5.8L V8 EARLY PRODUCTION ENGINES

A split-lip type crankshaft rear oil seal is provided for service. The complete seal may be replaced without removing the crankshaft.

1. Remove the oil pan and the oil pump (except 3.8L V6 engines) (if required), following procedures under Oil Pan and Oil Pump Removal. On V6 engines, the oil pump is in the front cover assembly. Only the pick up tube and screen assembly is in the oil pan.
2. Loosen all the main bearing cap bolts, thereby lowering the crankshaft slightly but not more than $1/32$ in.
3. Remove the rear main bearing cap, and remove the oil seal from the bearing cap and cylinder block. On the block half of the seal use a seal removal tool, or install a small metal screw in one end of the seal and pull on the screw to remove the seal. Exercise caution to prevent scratching or damaging the crankshaft seal surfaces.
4. Remove the oil seal retaining pin from the bearing cap if so equipped. The pin must not be used with the split-lip seal.

Installation

1. Carefully clean seal grooves in the cap and block with brush and suitable solvent. Also clean the area where sealer is later to be applied. Dry area thoroughly, so no solvent touches the seal.
2. Dip split-lip type seal halves in the clean engine oil.

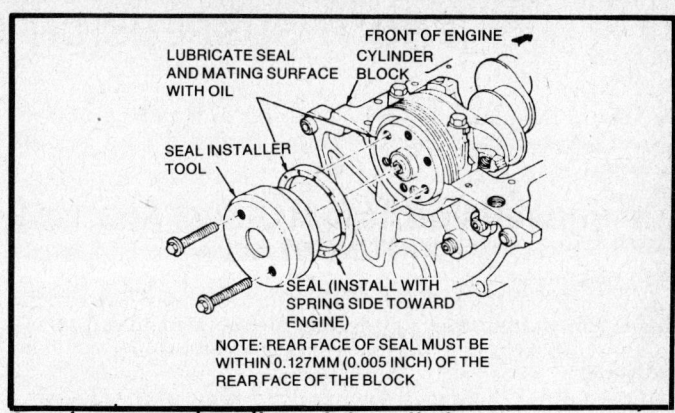

4 cyl rear main oil seal installation
(©Ford Motor Co.)

3. Carefully install the upper seal (cylinder block) into its groove with undercut side of seal toward the front of the engine by rotating it on the seal journal of the crankshaft until approximately $3/8$ in. protrudes below the parting surfaces.

Be sure no rubber has been shaved from OD of the seal by the bottom edge of the groove. Do not allow oil to get on sealer area.

4. Tighten all the bearing cap bolts to specification (except rear main bearing cap).
5. Install the lower seal in the rear main bearing cap with undercut side of seal toward the front of the engine. Allow the seal to protrude approximately $4/8$ in. above the parting surfaces to mate with the upper seal when the cap is installed.
6. Apply an even $1/16$ in. bead of silicone rubber sealer to the areas shown in illustration.

NOTE: Do not delay installation of bearing cap, as this sealer sets up in 15 minutes. Install the rear main bearing cap. Tighten the cap bolts to specification.

7. Install the oil pump and oil pan. Fill the crankcase with the proper amount and viscosity oil.
8. Operate the engine and check for oil leaks.

CRANKSHAFT REAR OIL SEAL

Removal

2.3L, 3.8L, 5.0L AND LATER PRODUCTION 5.8L "W" ENGINES

A one piece crankshaft rear main oil seal is used on these engines.

1. Using a sharp awl, punch one hole into the seal metal surface between the seal lip and the engine block.
2. Screw in the threaded end of Slide Hammer Tool. Use the slide hammer to remove the seal. Use caution to avoid scratching or damaging the oil seal surface.

Installation

1. Lubricate seal with engine oil.
2. Position oil seal on Installer Tool. Position tool and seal on the rear of the engine. Alternate bolt tightening to properly seat the seal.

FORD LINCOLN MERCURY
REAR WHEEL DRIVE CARS

FRONT SUSPENSION AND STEERING SECTION

For Front Suspension Services, Refer to Unit Repair Section. For Steering Gear Overhaul, Refer to Unit Repair Section

AIR SUSPENSION 1984 MARK VII AND 1984 CONTINENTAL

The 1984 Mark VII and Continental are equipped with an air suspension system which replaces the conventional coil spring suspension and provides automatic front and rear load leveling.

When lifting, jacking or towing these vehicles the following caution MUST BE adhered to or damage to the air springs could result.

--- CAUTION ---
The electrical power supply to the air suspension system must be shut off prior to hoisting, jacking or towing an air suspension vehicle. This can be accomplished by disconnecting the battery or turning off the power switch located in the trunk on the LH side. Failure to do so may result in unexpected inflation or deflation of the air springs, which may result in shifting of the vehicle during these operations.

STEERING WHEEL

Removal and Installation

1. Disconnect the negative battery cable.
2. If the vehicle is equipped with a horn ring, remove it by rotating it counterclockwise. If equipped with a steering wheel crash pad, remove the retaining screws from the underside of the steering wheel and then remove the crash pad. Disconnect the horn and speed control (if so equipped) wires from the inside of the steering wheel center.
3. Remove and discard the steering wheel nut, install a steering wheel puller on the end of the shaft, and remove the steering wheel.

--- CAUTION ---
The use of a knockoff type steering wheel puller and a hammer may damage the steering column bearing or (in the case of the collapsible-type steering wheel) the column itself.

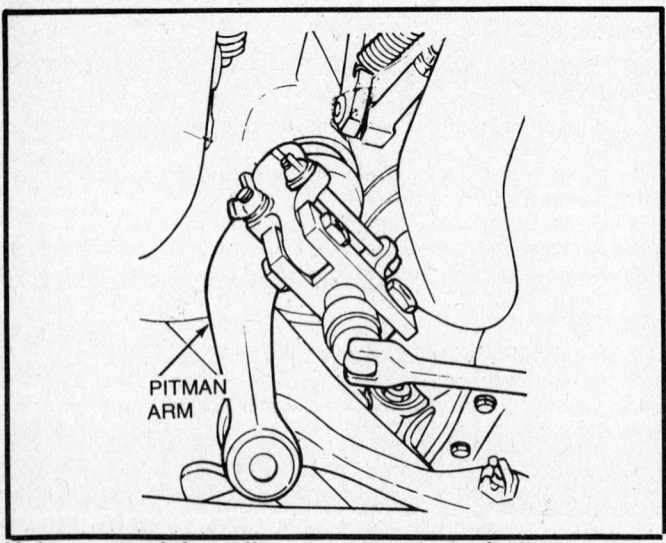

Using special puller to remove pitman arm (©Ford Motor Co.)

4. With the front wheels positioned straight ahead, line up the marks on the steering wheel and column and install the steering wheel and a new locknut. Tighten the nut to 30–40 ft. lbs.
5. Connect the horn and speed control wires and install the horn ring and the crash pad and retaining screws.
6. Connect the negative battery cable.

Manual Steering Gear

WORM AND RECIRCULATING BALL

Removal and Installation

1. Position the steering wheel in the straight ahead position.
2. Remove the bolt(s) retaining the flex coupling to the steering shaft. Match mark the coupling and steering shaft and separate.

NOTE: Separation can be accomplished when the steering gear box is lowered, if necessary.

3. Remove the retaining nut and washer from the pitman arm to sector shaft. Using a puller, separate the pitman arm from the sector shaft.

NOTE: It may be necessary to match mark the two components before separation.

4. It may be necessary to disconnect the clutch linkage on vehicles equipped with manual transmission. V8 models may have to have the exhaust system lowered to provide clearance for the removal of the steering gear.
5. Remove the steering gear to side rail retaining bolts and remove the steering gear from the vehicle.
6. The installation is the reverse of the removal procedure. Match mark the flex coupling with the steering shaft and the pitman arm with the sector shaft.

RACK AND PINION

Removal and Installation

1. Disconnect the battery negative cable.
2. Remove the retaining bolt from the flexible coupling to the steering shaft.
3. Place the ignition switch in the "ON" position and raise the vehicle and support safely.
4. Remove the right and left tie rod retaining nuts and separate the studs from the spindle arms, using a separator tool.
5. Support the steering rack and pinion assembly and remove the retaining nuts, bolts and washers insulators.

NOTE: On the Mustang models, it is necessary to remove the crossmember to allow clearance for the removal of the rack and pinion.

6. Remove the rack and pinion from the vehicle.
7. The installation is the reverse of the removal procedure.

Power Steering Gear

NON-INTEGRAL POWER STEERING

Removal and Installation

CONTROL VALVE ASSEMBLY

1. Raise the vehicle and support safely.
2. Remove the clamp retaining the fluid lines to the outside of the control valve.

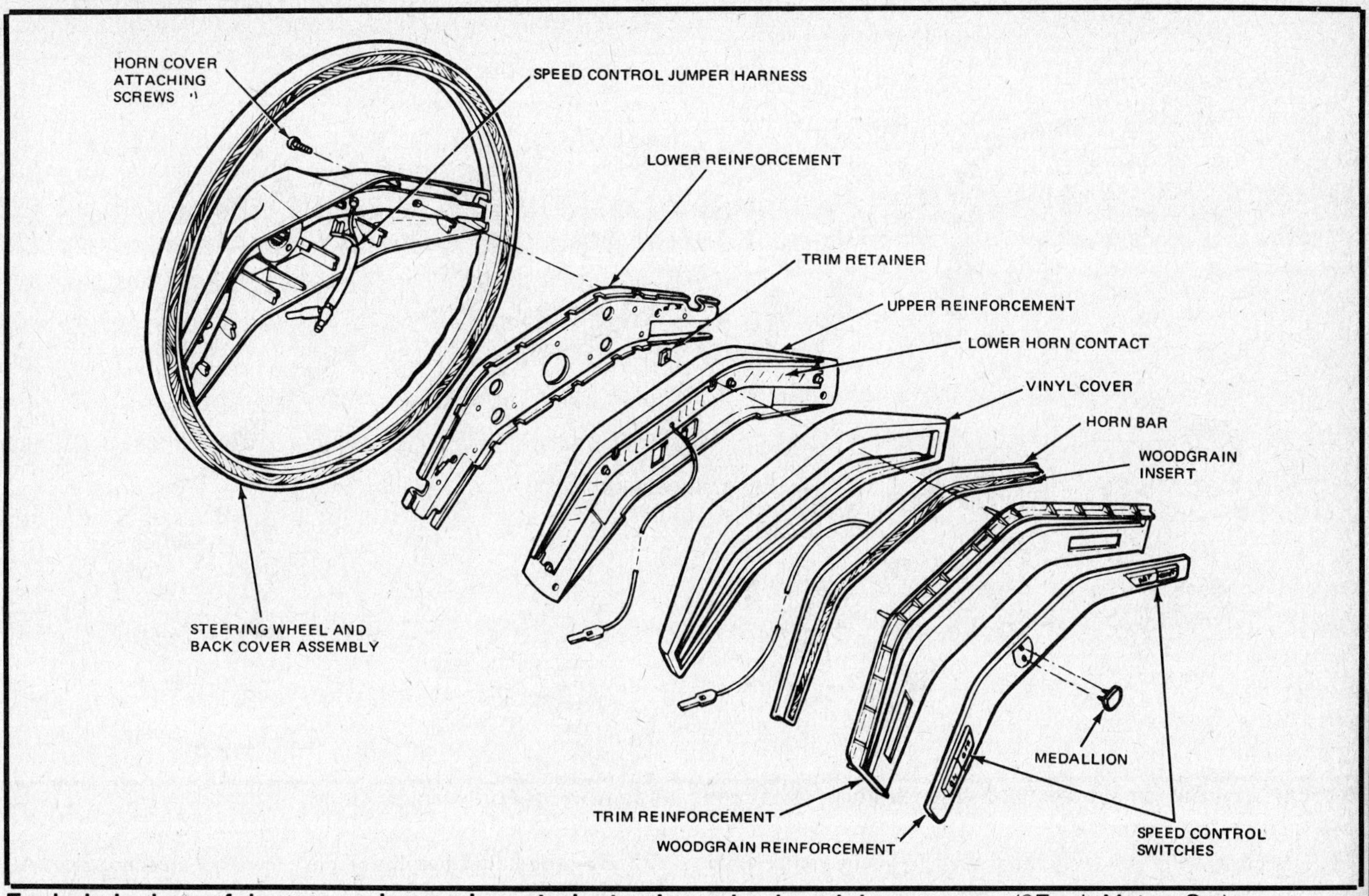

Ford Lincoln Mercury
REAR WHEEL DRIVE CARS — SECTION 5

Exploded view of luxury and speed control steering wheel and horn cover (©Ford Motor Co.)

3. Disconnect the fluid lines after marking each for reassembly. Allow the fluid to drain.
4. Turn the wheels to the left and right several times to force the fluid from the system.
5. Loosen the clamping bolt at the end of the control valve sleeve.
6. Remove the roll-pin from the steering arm to center link through the slot in the control valve sleeve.
7. Remove the cotter pin and the control valve ball stud nut. Remove the ball stud from the sector shaft arm (pitman arm).

NOTE: A special control valve ball stud removing tool should be used to prevent damage to the control valve assembly during removal.

8. Remove the valve assembly from the centerlink by turning the control valve counterclockwise until the valve assembly separates from the centerlink.
9. The installation should follow the outlined procedure:
   a. Thread the control valve on the centerlink until approximately four threads are visible on the centerlink.
   b. Position the ball stud in the sector shaft arm and measure the distance between the center of the left spindle connecting rod hole in the centerlink to the end of the control valve. This distance must be 2.65 to 2.55 in.
   c. If the distance is not correct, disengage the ball stud from the sector shaft arm and turn the control valve on the centerlink to increase or decrease the distance.
   d. When the ball stud is correctly positioned, align the hole in the steering arm to centerlink with the slot near the end of the valve sleeve and install the roll pin.
   e. Complete the assembly in the reverse of the removal procedure, fill with fluid and bleed the system.

POWER CYLINDER
1. Raise the vehicle and support safely.
2. Disconnect the fluid lines from the power cylinder and allow to drain.
3. Remove the PAL crimp nut, washer and the insulator from the end of the power cylinder rod.
4. Remove the cotter pin and nut that retains the power cylinder to the center link.

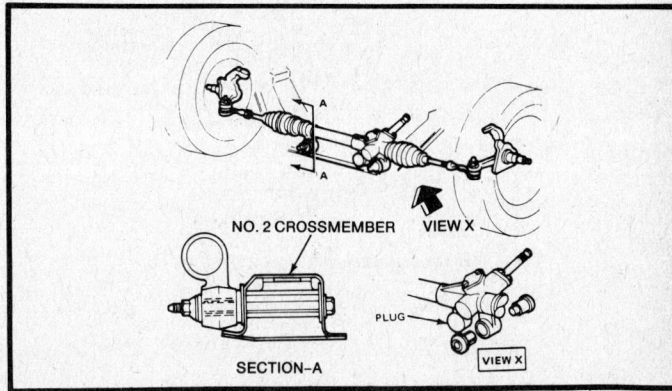

Typical rack and pinion steering gear and linkage (©Ford Motor Co.)

5–77

SECTION 5
Ford Lincoln Mercury
REAR WHEEL DRIVE CARS

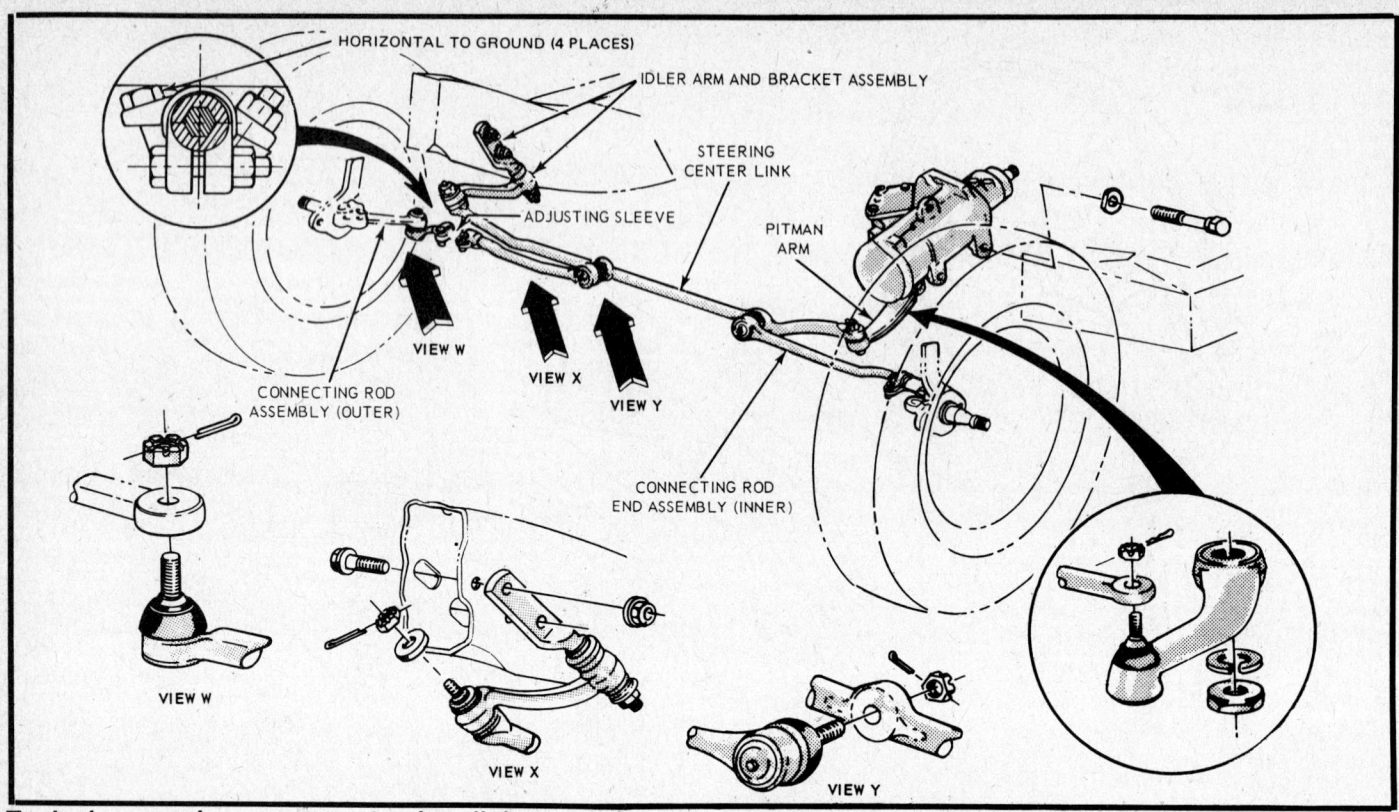

Typical manual or power steering linkage and gear assembly (©Ford Motor Co.)

5. Disconnect the power cylinder stud from the center link by using a steering arm remover tool.

6. Remove the insulator sleeve and washer from the end of the power cylinder rod. Remove the cylinder rod boot and discard the clamp.

7. The installation of the power cylinder is the reverse of the removal procedure. Fill with fluid and bleed the system.

INTEGRAL POWER STEERING GEAR

Removal and Installation

1. Remove the stone shield, if equipped.

2. Tag the fluid lines and remove from the steering gear. Allow to drain.

3. Plug the lines and ports to avoid entry of dirt.

4. Remove the bolts that retain the flexible coupling to the steering column gear.

5. Raise the vehicle and support safely. Remove the sector shaft nut and washer.

6. Remove the pitman arm with a special pulling tool to avoid damage to the shaft.

7. Support steering gear assembly and remove the gear box retaining bolts from the side rail or bracket.

8. Remove the clamping bolt from the flexible coupling and work the steering gear from the flex coupling and remove from the vehicle.

9. The installation of the steering gear is the reverse of the removal procedure. Fill with fluid and bleed the system.

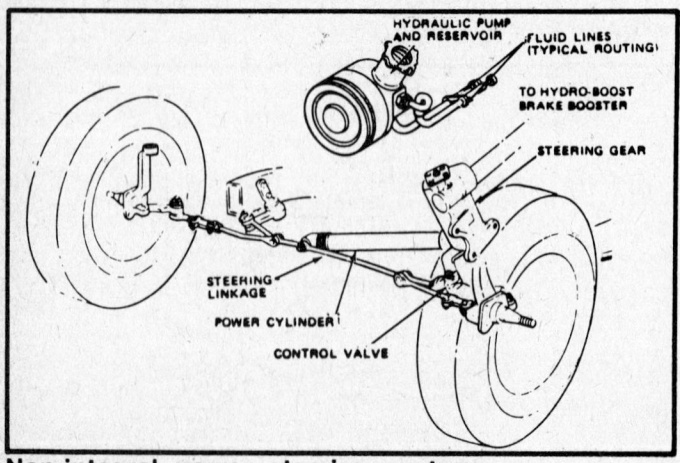

Non-integral power steering system
(©Ford Motor Co.)

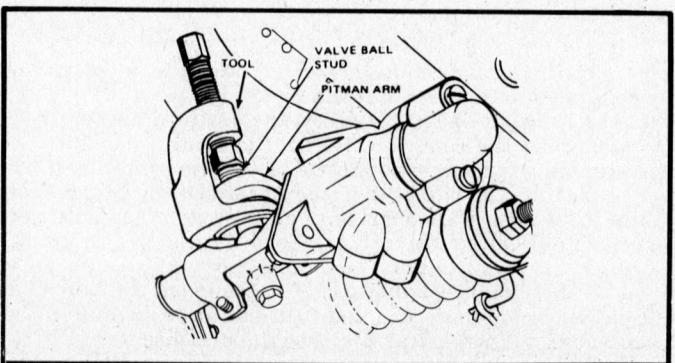

Removing control valve ball stud from the control valve (©Ford Motor Co.)

5-78

Ford Lincoln Mercury
REAR WHEEL DRIVE CARS
SECTION 5

INTEGRAL POWER RACK AND PINION STEERING GEAR

Removal and Installation

1. Disconnect the negative battery cable.
2. Remove the bolt retaining the flexible coupling to the steering input shaft.
3. Place the ignition key in the "ON" position and raise the vehicle and support safely.
4. Remove the two tie rod end retaining nuts and cotter pins. Separate the tie rod stud from the spindle arms with the use of a separator tool.
5. Support the rack and pinion and remove the retaining nuts, washers, and bolts from the rack and pinion to the crossmember.
6. Lower the gear assembly slightly to gain access to the pressure and return line fittings. Disconnect the fittings and plug the openings to prevent the entry of dirt.
7. Remove the rack and pinion gear assembly from the vehicle.
8. The installation of the rack and pinion assembly is the reverse of the removal procedure. Fill with fluid and bleed the system.

Removal and Installation
1985 AND LATER MARK VII/CONTINENTAL

NOTE: To remove the steering gear on models equipped with the 2.4 liter diesel engine, the engine must be raised in order to provide enough clearance between the number two crossmember and the engine oil pan.

1. Turn off the air suspension switch, which is located in the trunk of the vehicle.
2. Disconnect the negative battery cable and turn the ignition switch to the run position.
3. On 2.4 liter engine models, remove the following:
   a. Air cleaner and fan shroud assembly and pull the shroud assembly out of the lower retaining clips.
   b. Raise and support vehicle safely, remove both front engine mount bottom retaining bolts.
   c. Position the fuel line under the fuel-water separator out of the way and lower the vehicle.
   d. Install engine support bar D79P–6000–A or equivalent n a suitable engine lifting device.
   e. Raise the engine at least 2 in. to allow clearance for removal of the steering gear.
4. Raise and support the vehicle safely and position a drain pan under the power steering lines in order to catch the fluid when the lines are removed.
5. Remove one bolt retaining the flexible coupling to the intake shaft.
6. Remove the two tie rod end retaining cotter pins and nuts. Separate the studs from the spindle arms, using ball joint spindle press T57P–3006–B or equivalent.
7. Remove the two nuts, insulator washers, and bolts retaining the steering gear to the number two crossmember.
8. Remove the front rubber insulators and move the gear assembly forward so as to be able to remove the rear rubber insulators.
9. Position the gear to allow access to the hydraulic lines and disconnect the lines.
10. Pull the left hand side of the steering gear forward to clear the mounting spike, and allow it to drop as far as possible without forcing it. Rotate the top of the gear assembly forward to clear the engine oil filter and remove the steering gear.
11. Installation is the reverse order of the removal procedure. Be sure to install a new rubber insulators and also new plastic seals on the hydraulic line fittings, torque the lines to 10–15 ft. lbs. (1420 Nm).

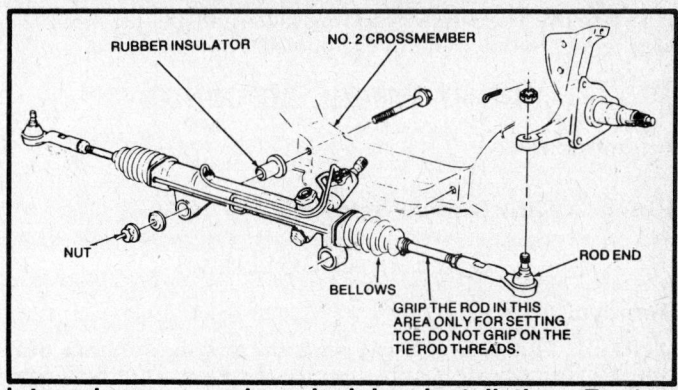

Integral power rack and pinion installation, Ford unit illustrated, TRW unit similar (©Ford Motor Co.)

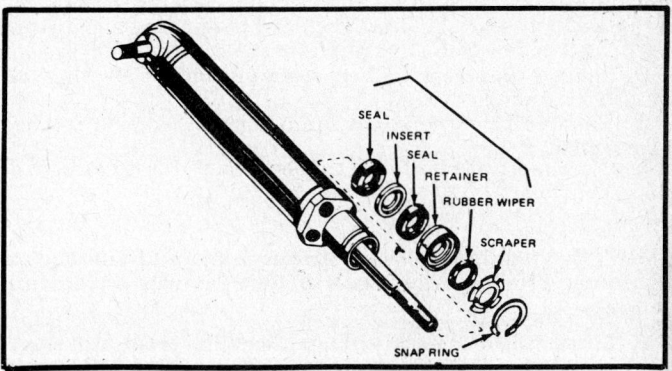

Power cylinder and seal assembly (©Ford Motor Co.)

12. Refill the system with power steering fluid and bleed the system.

POWER STEERING PUMP

Removal and Installation

1. Disconnect the return and pressure lines from the power steering pump and allow to drain into a container. When the system is drained of fluid, plug the openings to avoid entry of dirt into the system.

NOTE: The Ford model CII power steering pump has a fiberglass nylon reservoir, incorporating a pump pressure fitting that allows the pump pressure line to swivel. This is normal and does not indicate a loose fitting.

— CAUTION —
Do not remove the base fitting from the pump reservoir.

2. Loosen the drive belt tensioning nuts or bolts to facilitate the removal of the belt.

NOTE: On the fixed pump system, the alternator must be loosened to remove the pump drive belt.

3. On the fixed pump system, the pump pulley must be removed from the pump shaft with a puller tool, before the pump can be removed from the brackets.

— CAUTION —
Do not hammer on the end of the pump shaft. Internal pump damage can be done.

SECTION 5

Ford Lincoln Mercury
REAR WHEEL DRIVE CARS

4. Remove the pump retaining bolts and/or nuts from the brackets to pump. Remove the pump from the engine.

FRONT WHEEL BEARINGS

Adjustment

Refer to Unit Repair Sections.

STEERING COLUMN

Removal

NOTE: This is a general removal and installation outline. Certain models may require the steps in a different sequence, may or may not have the component as listed.

1. Disconnect the battery negative cable.
2. Remove the retaining nuts from the flexible coupling to the flange on the steering input shaft. Separate the safety strap and bolt assembly from the flexible coupling and disconnect the transmission shift rod from the control shift lever.
3. Remove the steering wheel assembly and the steering column trim shrouds.
4. Remove the steering column cover and hood release mechanism.
5. Disconnect all electrical connections to the steering column switches.

NOTE: To gain access to various nuts and bolts, the instrument cluster may have to be removed on certain models.

6. Loosen the four nuts holding the column to the brake pedal support, allowing the column to be lowered enough to gain access to the shift quadrant indicator cable.

NOTE: Do not lower the column to the point where excessive weight is on the cable or plastic lever. Damage can result.

7. Disconnect the shift quadrant indicator cable from the cleat on the PRND21 lever. Remove the cable from the steering column tube.
8. Remove the four screws holding the dust shield boot to the dash panel.
9. Remove the four attaching bolts holding the column to the brake pedal support and lower the column to clear the mounting bolts.
10. Pull the column out so that the U-joint assembly will pass through the clearance hole in the dash panel.
11. With the column assembly out of the vehicle, the shift lever grommet should be replaced before installing the unit back into the vehicle.

Installation

1. Install the steering column assembly into the dash opening so that the U-joint and lower shift cane clears the opening.
2. Align the four bolts on the brake pedal support with the mounting holes on the column collar and bracket. Attach the nuts loosely and allow the column to hang with a clearance between the column and the instrument panel.
3. Loosely assemble the PRND21 cable clamp to the steering column outer tube.
4. Attach the cable to the PRND21 lever cleat.
5. Tighten the four nuts that hold the column to the brake pedal support. torque to 20–37 ft. lbs.
6. Move the shift selector to the DRIVE position against the drive stop on the insert plate. Rotate the indicator bracket back and forth until the pointer in the instrument cluster points to the center of the letter "D". Tighten the adjusting nut on the bracket.
7. Connect the electrical connectors to the wiring harness.

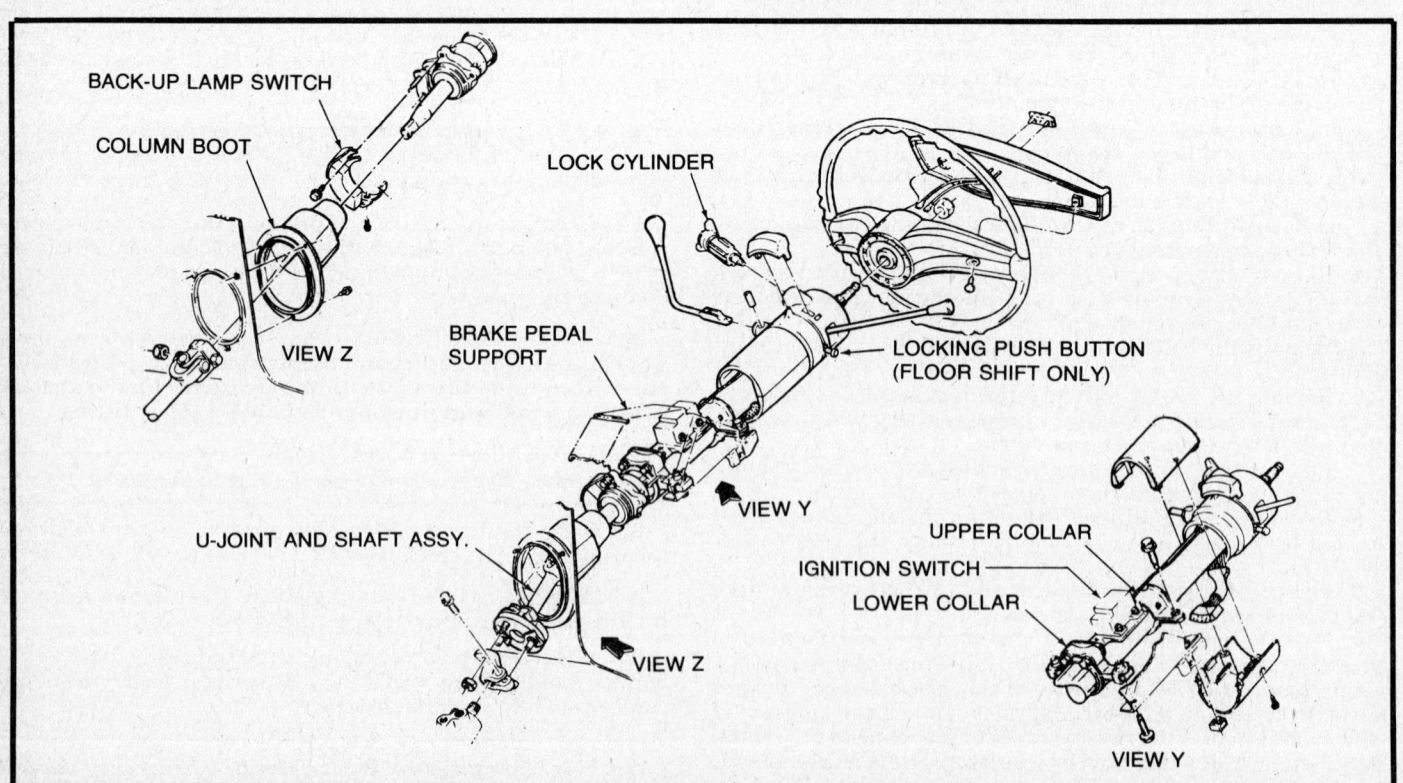

Steering column installation, typical in Lincoln models (©Ford Motor Co.)

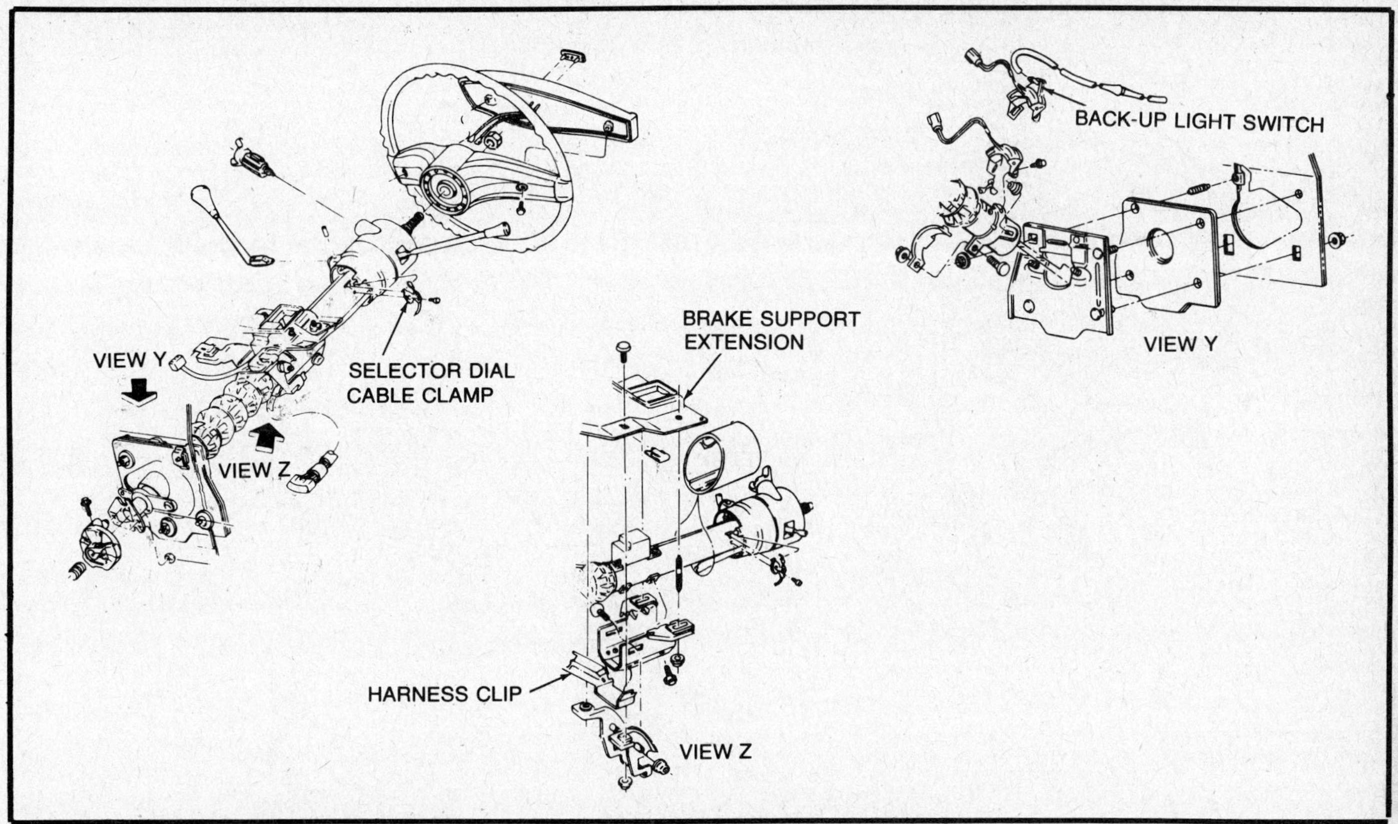

Ford Lincoln Mercury
REAR WHEEL DRIVE CARS
SECTION 5

Steering column installation, typical in full sized car models except Lincoln (©Ford Motor Co.)

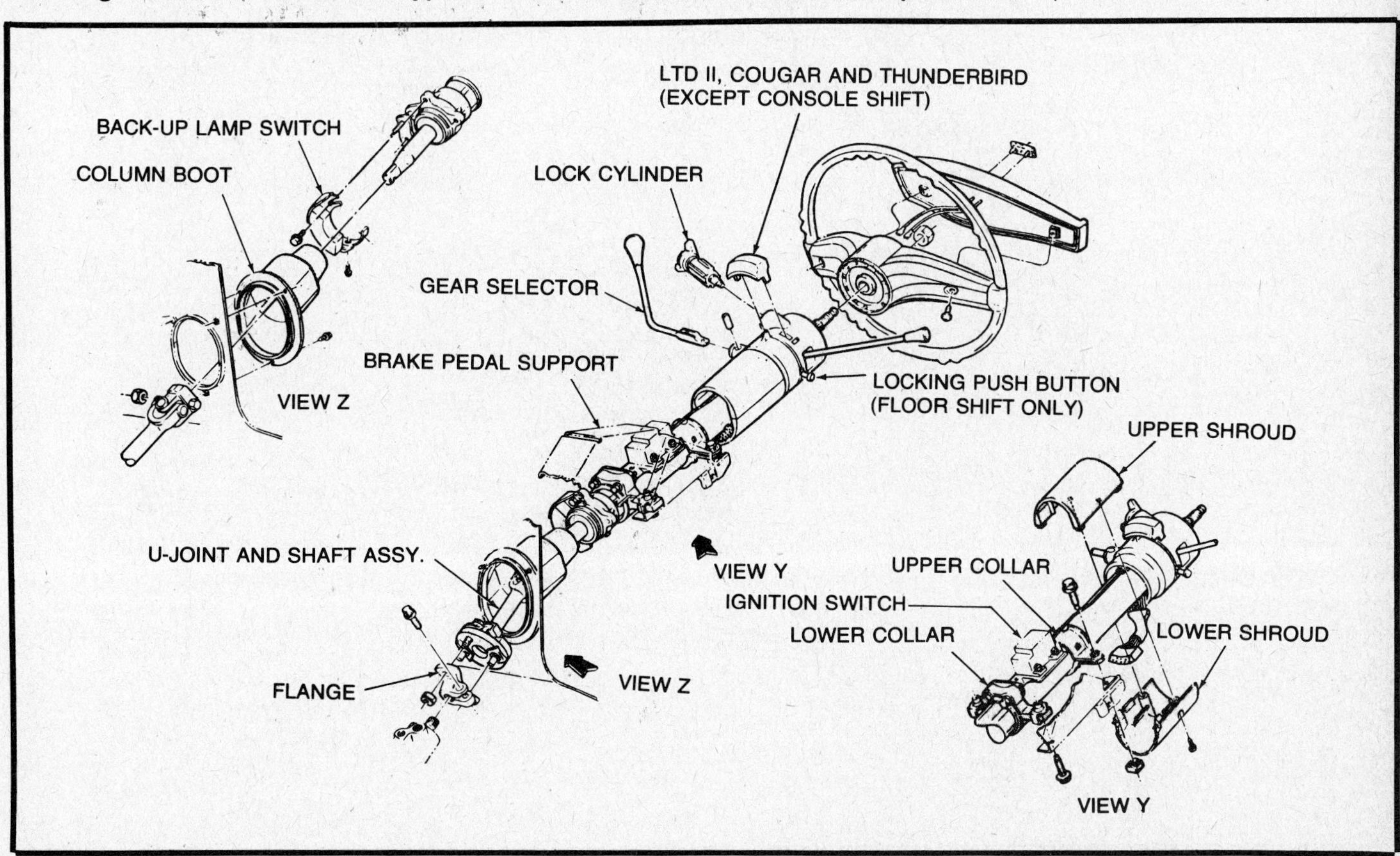

Steering column mounting, typical in Cougar, LTD II and Thunderbird (©Ford Motor Co.)

SECTION 5
Ford Lincoln Mercury
REAR WHEEL DRIVE CARS

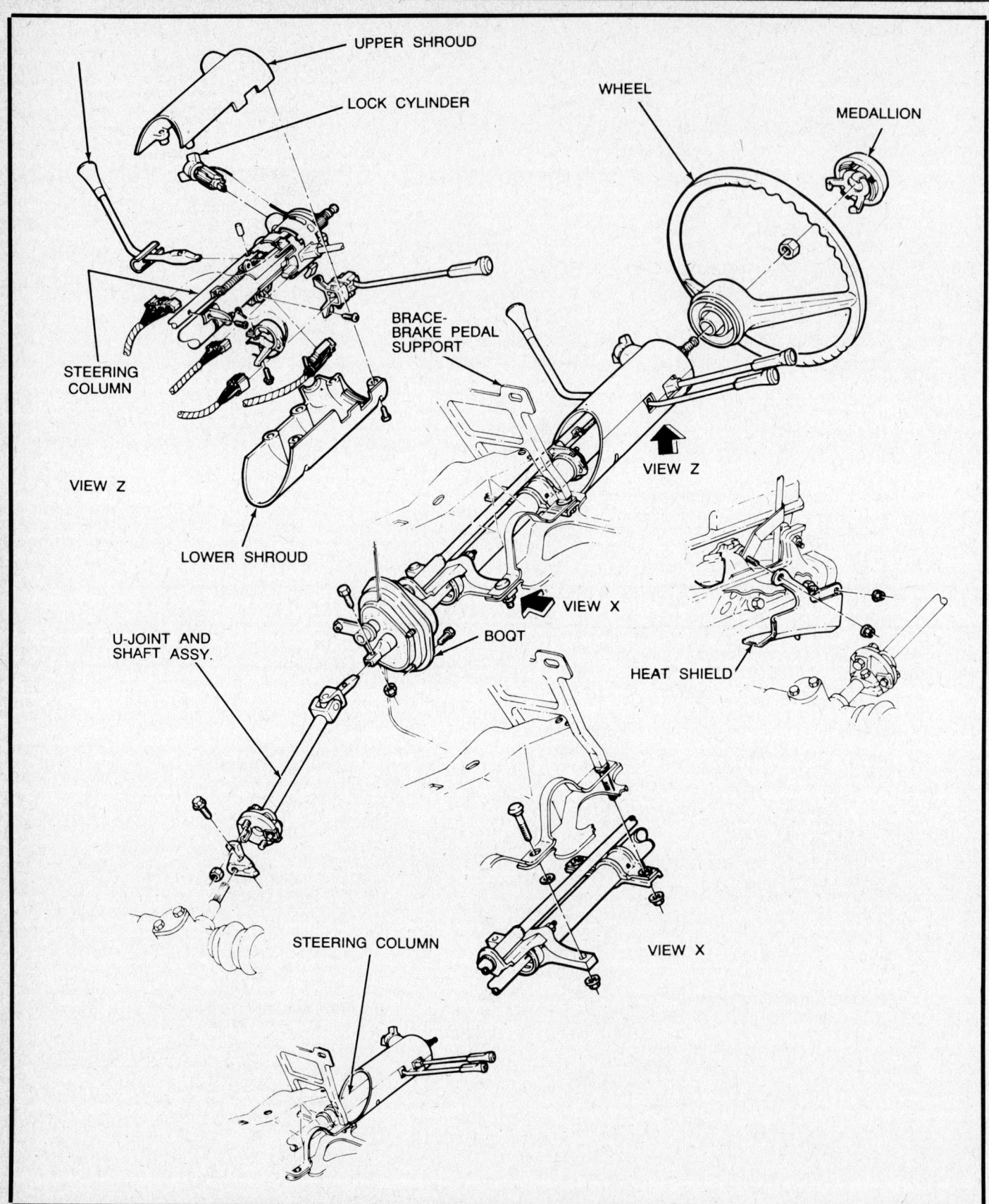

Steering column installation, typical in Fairmont/Zephyr (©Ford Motor Co.)

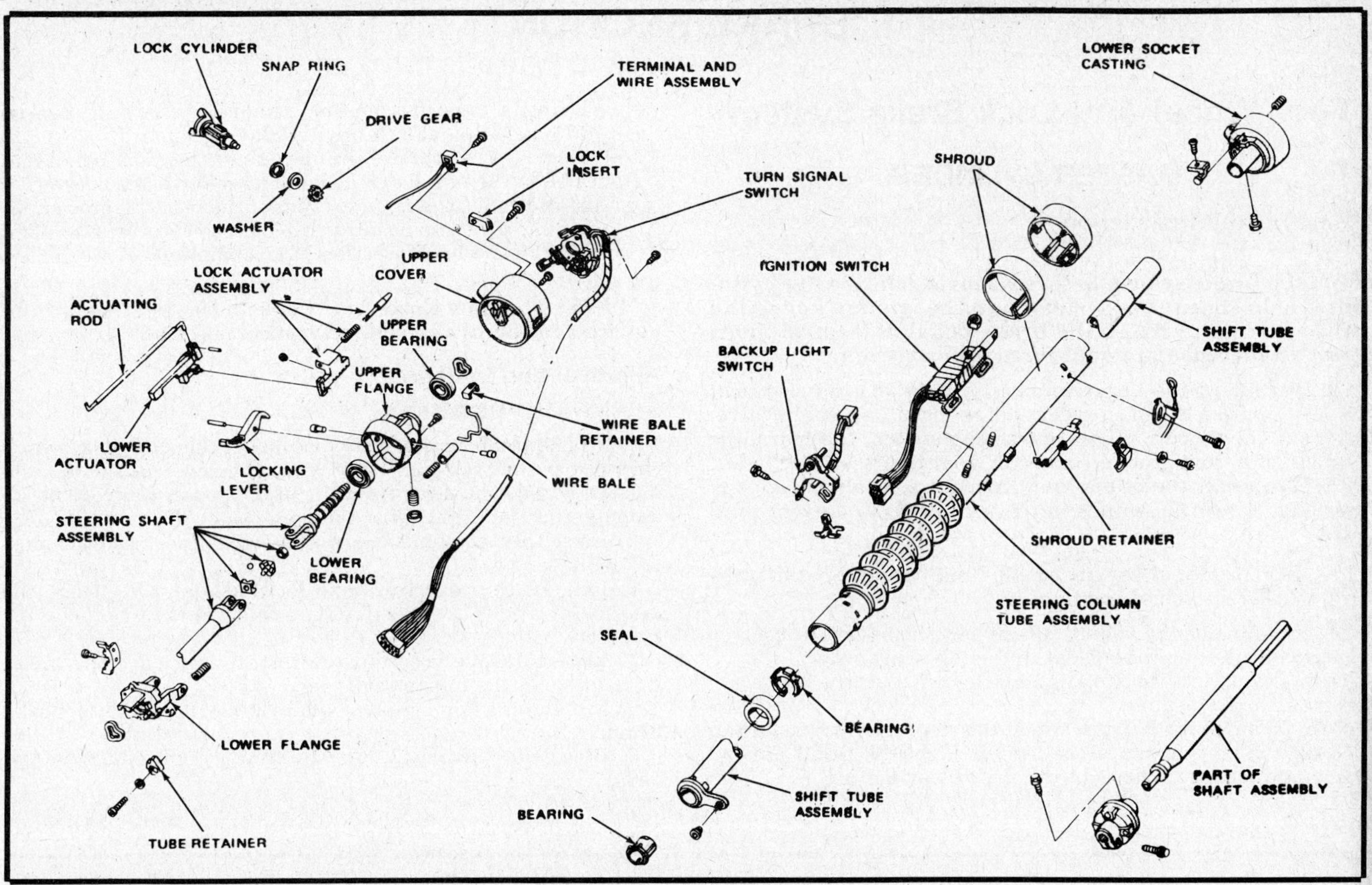

Ford Lincoln Mercury
REAR WHEEL DRIVE CARS

Section 5

Exploded view of typical tilt steering column (©Ford Motor Co.)

8. Engage the safety strap and bolt assembly to the flange on the steering gear input shaft. Tighten the nuts to a torque of 20–37 ft. lbs.

CAUTION
The safety strap must be properly positioned to prevent metal to metal contact after tightening the nuts. The flexible coupling must not be distorted when the nuts are tightened. The flexible coupling must have a 1/8 in. coupling insulator flatness.

9. Connect the shift rod to the shift lever. Adjust the linkage as follows:
   a. Raise the vehicle so that the transmission shift rod adjustment nut can be loosened and the transmission shift lever is in the "DRIVE" position.
   b. Lower the vehicle as necessary to place the column shift lever in the "DRIVE" position.
   c. Hang a weight on the gear shift lever on the columns, to assure the lever is located firmly against the "DRIVE" detent in the steering column. The weight should be: all models, except w/auto overdrive transmission 8 lbs; all models w/ auto overdrive transmission 12 lbs.
   d. Make necessary adjustments on the shift rod adjustment nut and tighten the adjusting nut. Lower the vehicle.
10. Engage the dust boot at the base of the steering column to the dash panel opening. Install the retaining screws.
11. Attach the trim shrouds to the steering column upper end, the hood release mechanism and the steering column cover under the column assembly.
12. Install the steering wheel and remaining components.
13. Connect the negative battery cable.
14. Check the operation of the steering column and operating components.

NOTE: The steering column used with floorshift equipped vehicles is removed and installed in the same basic manner, less the shifting mechanism.

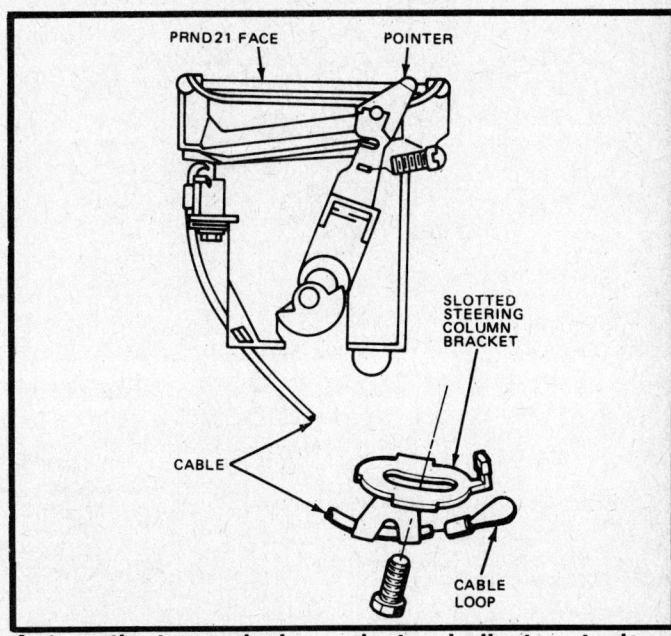

Automatic transmission selector indicator, typical (©Ford Motor Co.)

SECTION 5

Ford Lincoln Mercury
REAR WHEEL DRIVE CARS

BRAKE SECTION

Four Wheel Anti-Lock Brake System

MASTER CYLINDER

Removal and Installation

NOTE: The hydraulic pressure must be discharged from the brake system before removing the master cylinder. To discharge the system, turn the ignition key to the off position and pump the brake pedal at least 20 times until an increase in pedal force is clearly felt.

1. Disconnect the negative battery cable and the electrical connectors from the master cylinder reservoir cap, main valve, solenoid valve body, pressure warning switch, the hydraulic pump motor, and ground connector from the master cylinder.
2. Disconnect the brake lines from the solenoid valve body and plug the line openings in the valve body to prevent fluid loss.

NOTE: Do not allow the brake fluid to leak or spill onto any of the electrical connectors.

3. From inside the vehicle, disconnect the hydraulic booster pushrod from the brake pedal in the following order:
    a. Disconnect the stop light switch wires at the connector on the brake pedal.
    b. Remove the hairpin clip at the stop light switch on the brake pedal and move the switch off of the pedal pin far enough for the switch outer hole to clear the pin.
    c. Using a twisting motion, remove the switch, but be careful not to damage the switch during removal.
    d. Remove the four retaining nuts at the dash panel and from inside the engine compartment remove the booster.
4. Installation is the reverse order of the removal procedure. Also after the unit has been installed bleed the brake system, as outlined in the brake section of this manual.

NOTE: The new Ford Anti-Lock Brake System is fully covered in the brake section of this manual.

Removal and Installation

STANDARD BRAKES

1. Working under the dash, disconnect the stop light switch wires from the stop light switch and remove the switch and master cylinder pushrod from the brake pedal. Use care not to damage the stop light switch during removal.
2. Raise the hood and remove the brake lines from the master cylinder.
3. Remove the capscrews and lockwashers that attach the master cylinder to the firewall and remove the master cylinder.
4. Reverse above procedure to install, but leave the brake lines loose on the master cylinder.
5. Fill the master cylinder with Extra Heavy Duty Brake Fluid.
6. Bleed the master cylinder by slowly depressing the foot pedal.

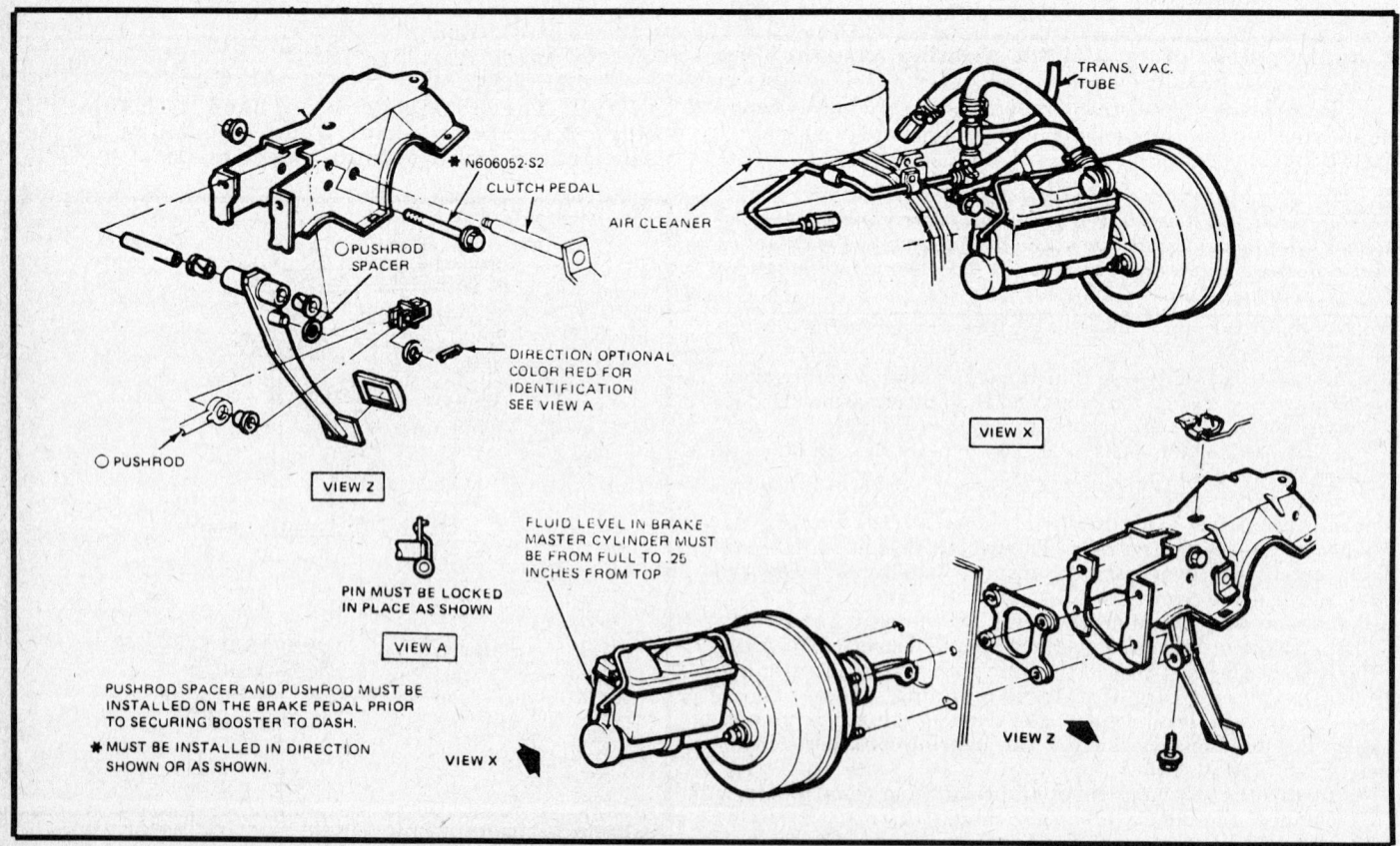

Power brake vacuum unit, typical in Fairmont/Zephyr (©Ford Motor Co.)

7. Refit the master cylinder. Tighten the master cylinder brake lines, then bleed the front and rear brakes.

POWER BRAKES

1. Disconnect the brake lines from the master cylinder.
2. Remove the nuts holding the master cylinder to the booster.
3. Remove the master cylinder.
4. Reverse the procedure for installation. Bleed the system.

VACUUM BRAKE BOOSTER

Removal and Installation

1. From inside the car, remove the stoplight switch connector from the switch; remove the pin retainer and washer from the pedal pin and slide the stoplight switch far enough to clear the pin and remove the switch. Slide the booster push rod, busing and washer off the brake pin.
2. On four and six cylinder models, remove: air cleaner, accelerator cable (at carburetor), accelerator cable bracket, choke water inlet hose (at thermostat), and vacuum hose from EGR valve.
3. Disconnect the manifold vacuum hose from the booster.
4. Remove the primary and secondary brake lines from the outlet ports on the master cylinder. Cap the lines and the master cylinder ports.
5. Remove the master cylinder retaining nuts and remove the master cylinder.
6. From inside the car, remove the booster to firewall retaining nuts. From the engine side, pull the booster until the pushrod clears the firewall, rotate the booster ninety degrees, and pull up until it comes clear.
7. To install, put the booster in position with the check valve on the upper right side. Replace the booster pushrod pin; secure the booster to the firewall and tighten the bolts.
8. Place the stoplight switch on the booster push rod with the slot toward the pedal and the hole just clearing the pin. Be careful not to damage the switch. Install the retaining washer and pin and connect the wiring connector.
9. Reconnect the manifold vacuum hose to the booster unit.
10. Re-attach the master cylinder assembly, reconnect the items removed in Step 2 and bleed the brakes.

HYDRO-BOOST POWER UNIT

Removal and Installation

1. Open the hood and remove the two nuts attaching the master cylinder to the brake booster.
2. Remove the master cylinder from the Hydro-Boost accumulator.
3. Set the master cylinder aside without disturbing the hydraulic lines.
4. Disconnect the pressure, steering and return lines from the accumulator.
5. Plug the lines and ports.
6. Working below the instrument panel, disconnect the Hydro-Boost pushrod from the brake pedal. To do this, disconnect the stoplight switch at the connector. Remove the hairpin retainer. Slide the stoplight switch from the brake pedal pin far enough to clear the switch outer pin hole. Remove the switch from the pin.
7. Loosen the Hydro-Boost attaching nuts and remove the pushrod, washers and bushing from the brake pedal pin.
8. Remove the accumulator.
9. Installation is the reverse of removal. Leave the Hydro-Boost mounting nuts loose until the pushrod and stoplight switch are connected to the brake pedal. After installation, remove the coil wire from the distributor. Fill the power steering reservoir, and while cranking the engine, pump the brake pedal. Do not move the steering wheel until all the air has been pumped out of the system. Check the power steering fluid level, install the coil wire, start the engine and pump the brakes while steering from lock to lock. Check for leaks.

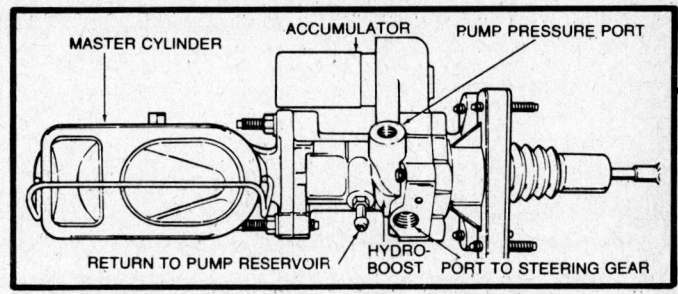

Hydro-boost brake unit (©Ford Motor Co.)

PARKING BRAKE

Adjustment

NOTE: If a new cable is installed, prestretch it by applying and releasing five times before making any adjustments.

REAR DRUM BRAKES

In most cases, a rear brake shoe adjustment will provide satisfactory parking brake action. However, if parking brake cables are excessively loose after releasing the handbrake, proceed as follows:

1. Fully release the parking brake.
2. Loosen locknut on equalizer rod under the car. Then loosen the nut in front of the equalizer, several turns.
3. Turn the locknut forward against the equalizer until the cables are tight enough so that the rear wheels cannot be turned by hand. Then, back off the adjustment until the rear wheels turn freely.
4. When cables are properly adjusted, tighten both nuts against the equalizer.
5. Apply and release the brake and feel for freeness of rear wheels.

DISC BRAKES

1. Fully release the parking brake.
2. Place the transmission in Neutral. If it is necessary to raise the car to reach the adjusting nut and observe the parking brake levers, use an axle hoist or a floor jack positioned beneath the differential. This is necessary so that the rear axle

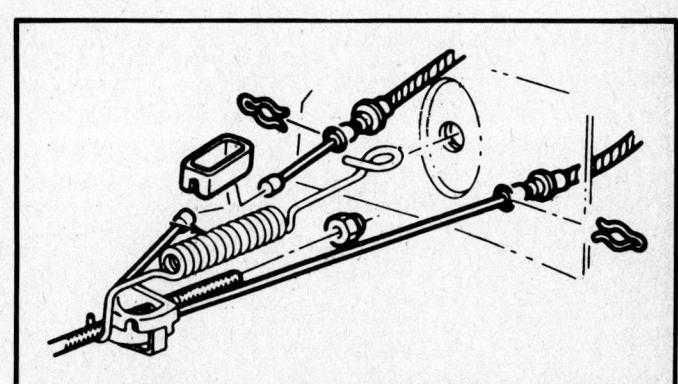

Parking brake cable equalizer used with rear drum brakes (©Ford Motor Co.)

5-85

SECTION 5
Ford Lincoln Mercury
REAR WHEEL DRIVE CARS

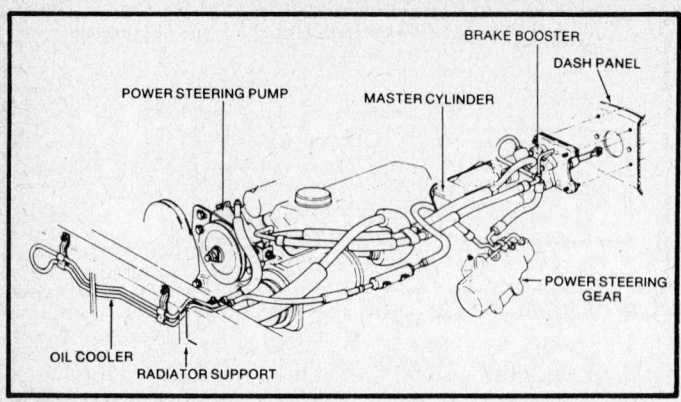
Typical hydro-boost brake system (©Ford Motor Co.)

the rear calipers, tighten the adjusting nut until the levers just begin to move. Then, loosen the nut sufficiently for the levers to fully return to the stop position. The levers are in the stop position when a ¼ in. pin can be inserted past the side of the lever into the holes in the cast iron housing.

4. Check the operation of the parking brake. Make sure the actuating levers return to the stop position by attempting to pull them rearward. If the lever moves rearward, the cable adjustment is too tight, which will cause a dragging rear brake and consequent brake overheating and fade.

remains at the curb attitude, not stretching the parking brake cables.

3. Locate the adjusting nut beneath the car on the driver's side. While observing the parking brake actuating levers on

— CAUTION —
If you are raising the rear of the car only, block the front wheels.

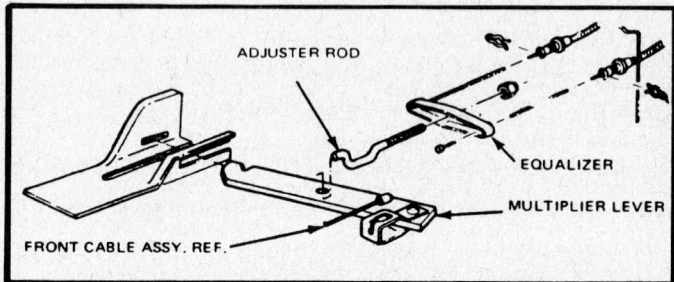
Parking brake cable equalizer used with rar disc brakes (©Ford Motor Co.)

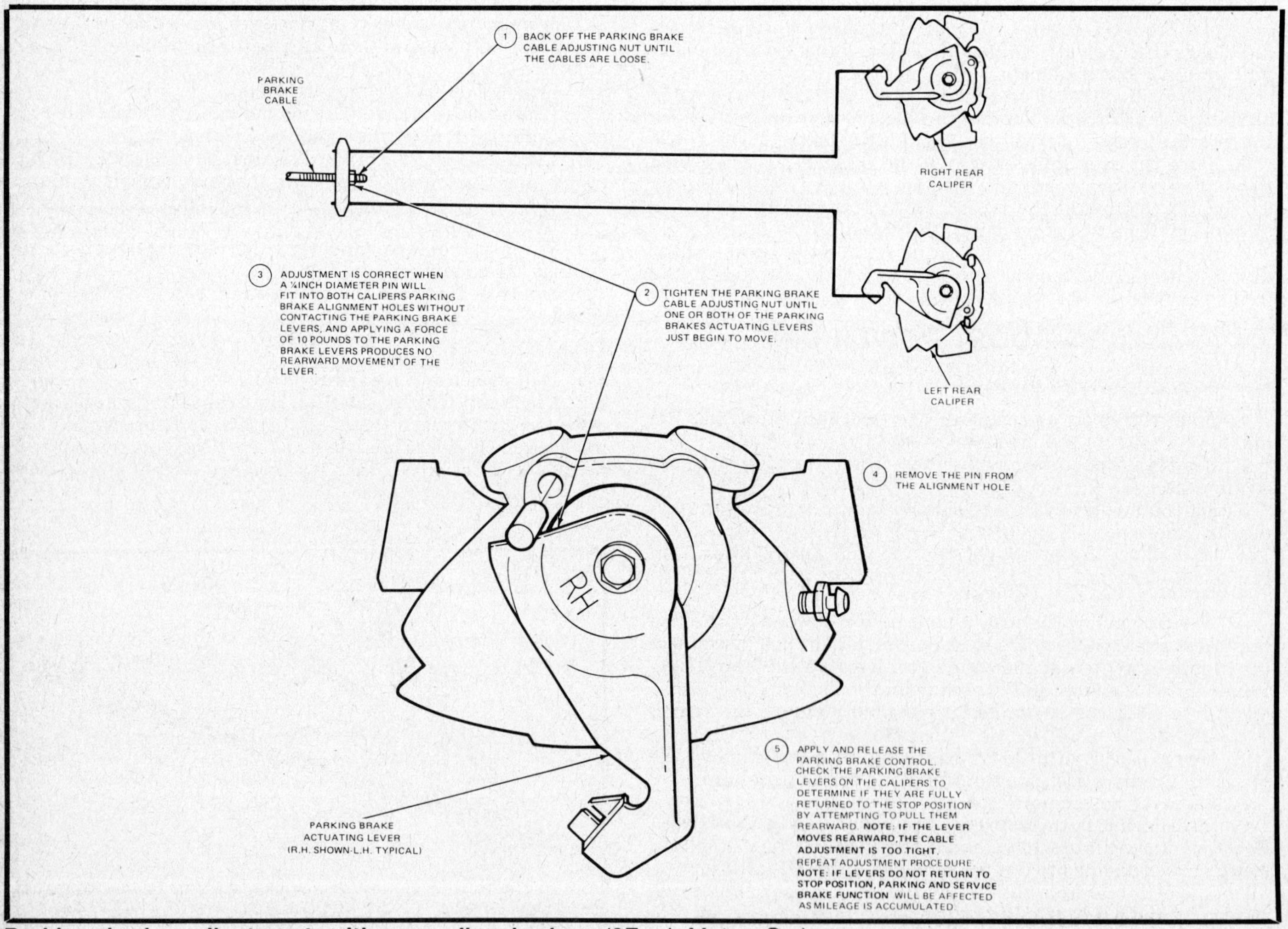

Parking brake adjustment with rear disc brakes (©Ford Motor Co.)

5-86

Ford Lincoln Mercury
REAR WHEEL DRIVE CARS
SECTION 5

CLUTCH, TRANSMISSION AND DRIVESHAFT SECTION

Clutch

CLUTCH LINKAGE AND PEDAL

Adjustment

NOTE: All models have self-adjusting clutches. No adjustments are necessary.

ALL EXCEPT FAIRMONT, ZEPHYR, MUSTANG AND CARPI

1. Disconnect clutch return spring from release lever.
2. Loosen release lever rod locknut and adjusting nut.
3. Move clutch release lever rearward until release bearing lightly contacts clutch pressure plate release fingers.
4. Adjust rod length until rod seats in release lever pocket.
5. Insert specified feeler gauge between adjusting nut and swivel sleeve. Tighten adjusting nut against gauge.
6. Tighten locknut against adjusting nut, taking care not to disturb adjustment. Remove feeler gauge.
7. Install clutch return spring.
8. Check free travel at pedal. Readjust if necessary to obtain specified travel. Moving adjusting nut away from swivel sleeve increases travel. Moving adjusting nut toward swivel sleeve decreases travel.
9. As final check, measure pedal free travel with transmission in neutral and engine running at 3,000 rpm. If pedal travel is not minimum of ½ in., readjust free travel.

FOUR CYLINDER, 255 AND 302 V8

1. Working under the car, remove the dust shield.
2. Loosen the clutch cable locknut. To raise the pedal, turn

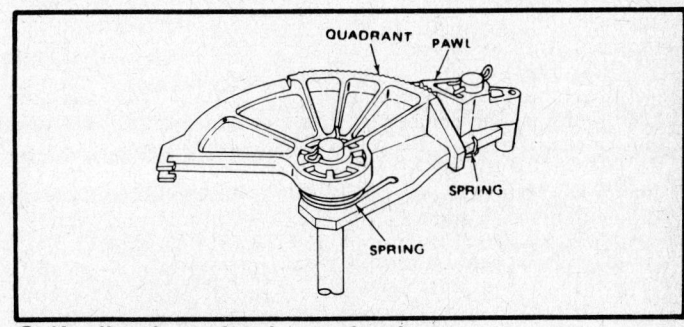

Self-adjusting clutch mechanism
(©Ford Motor Co.)

the adjusting nut clockwise; to lower the pedal, turn it counterclockwise.

3. On the four cylinder engine, adjust the pedal height to 5.3 in; on the 255 and 302 V8 adjust the height to 6.5 in.
4. Tighten the locknut. When the pedal is adjusted properly, the pedal can be raised about 2¾ in. on the V8 to reach the pedal stop.
5. Install the dust shield.

CLUTCH AND/OR MANUAL TRANSMISSION

Removal and Installation

NOTE: This is a general removal and installation outline. Certain model vehicles may require the steps in a different sequence and may or may not have the components as listed.

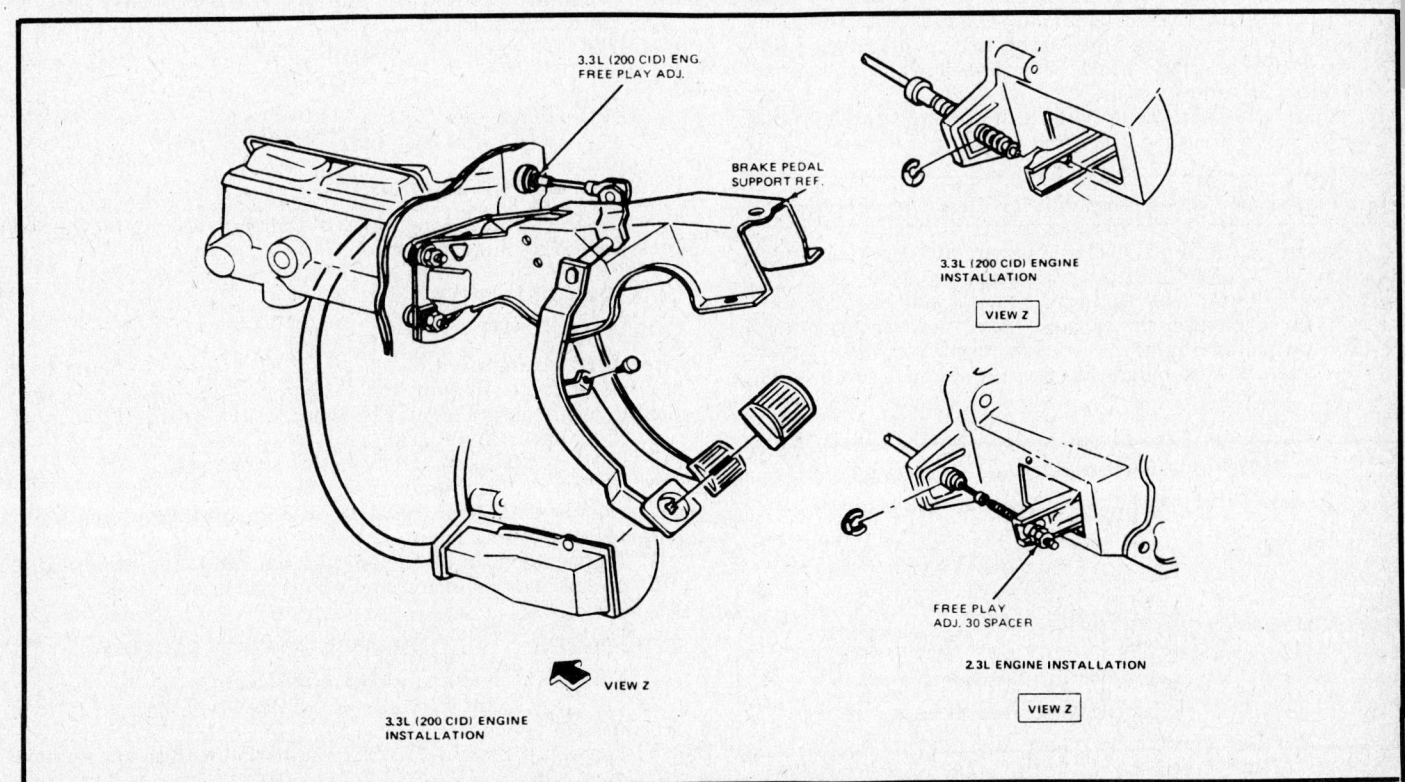

Clutch linkage, typical in Fairmont/Zephyr (©Ford Motor Co.)

5–87

FORD LINCOLN MERCURY
REAR WHEEL DRIVE CARS

1. Disconnect and remove starter and dust ring, if the clutch is to be removed. On floor shift models, remove the boot retainer and shifter lever.
2. On models with the 80ET, 83ET and 85ET four speed transmission: working under the hood, remove the upper clutch housing-to-engine bolts.
3. Raise the car.
4. Matchmark the driveshaft and axle flange for reassembly. Disconnect the driveshaft at the rear universal joint and remove the driveshaft. Plug the extension housing.
5. Disconnect the speedometer cable at the transmission extension. Disconnect the seat belt sensor wires and the back-up lamp switch wires. Remove the clutch lever boot and cable on Fairmonts, Zephyrs, Mustangs, and Capris if so equipped.
6. Disconnect the gear shift rods from the transmission shift levers. If the car is equipped with four speed, remove bolts that secure shift control bracket to extension housing. Support the engine with a jack.
7. Remove the bolt holding the extension housing to the rear support, and remove the muffler inlet pipe bracket to housing bolt.
8. Remove the two rear support bracket insulator nuts from the underside of the crossmember. Remove the crossmember.
9. Place a jack (equipped with a protective piece of wood) under the rear of the engine oil pan. Raise or lower the engine slightly as necessary to provide access to the bolts.
10. Remove transmission-to-flywheel housing bolts.
11. Slide the transmission back and out of the car. It may be necessary to slide the catalytic converter bracket forward to provide clearance on some models.
12. To remove the clutch, remove release lever retracting spring. Disconnect pedal at the equalizer bar, of the clutch cable from the housing, as applicable.
13. Remove bolts that secure engine rear plate to front lower part of bellhousing.
14. Remove bolts that attach bellhousing to cylinder block and remove housing and release lever as a unit. Remove the clutch release lever by pulling it through the window in the housing until the retainer spring disengages from the pivot.
15. Loosen six pressure plate cover attaching bolts evenly to release spring pressure. Mark cover and flywheel to facilitate reassembly in same position.
16. Remove six attaching bolts while holding pressure plate cover. Remove pressure plate and clutch disc.

CAUTION
Do not depress the clutch pedal while the transmission is removed.

---

17. Before installing the clutch, clean the flywheel surface. Inspect the flywheel and pressure plate for wear, scoring, or burn marks (blue color). Light scoring and wear may be cleaned up with emery paper; heavy wear may require refacing of the flywheel or replacement of the damaged parts.
18. Attach the clutch disc and pressure plate assembly to the flywheel. The three dowel pins on the flywheel, if so equipped, must be properly aligned. Damaged pins must be replaced. Avoid touching the clutch plate surface. Tighten the bolts finger tight.
19. Align the clutch disc with the pilot bushing. Torque cover bolts to 12-24 ft. lbs. with the four cylinder, 12-20 ft. lbs. for all others.
20. Lightly lubricate the release lever in the flywheel housing and install the dust shield.
21. Apply very little lubricant on the release bearing retainer journal. Fill the groove in the release bearing hub with grease. Clean all excess grease from the inside bore of the hub to prevent clutch disc contamination. Attach the release bearing and hub on the release lever.
22. Make sure the flywheel housing and engine block are clean. Any missing damaged mounting dowels must be replaced. Install the flywheel housing and torque the attaching bolts to 38-61 ft. lbs. on all V8s and 250 sixes, 38-55 ft. lbs. on 200 sixes, and 28-38 ft. lbs. on fours and 170-V6s. Install the dust cover and torque the bolts to 17-20 ft. lbs.
23. Connect the release rod or cable and the retracting spring. Connect the pedal-to-equalizer rod at the equalizer bar.
24. Install starter and dust ring.
25. After moving the transmission back just far enough for the pilot shaft to clear the clutch housing, move it upward and into position on the flywheel housing. It may be necessary to put the transmission in gear and rotate the output shaft to align the input shaft and clutch splines.
26. Move the transmission forward and into place against the flywheel housing, and install the transmission attaching bolts finger-tight.
27. Tighten the transmission bolts to 37-42 ft. lbs. on all cars.
28. Install the crossmember and torque the mounting bolts to 20-30 ft. lbs. Slowly lower the engine onto the crossmember.
29. Torque the rear mount to 30-50 ft. lbs.
30. Connect gear shift rods and the speedometer cable.
31. Remove the plug from the extension housing and install the driveshaft, aligning the marks made previously.
32. Refill transmission to proper level. On floorshift models, install the boot retainer and shift lever.

MANUAL TRANSMISSION
Removal and Installation
See Clutch, Clutch Housing and Transmission Removal and Installation in this car section.

Linkage Adjustment
COLUMN SHIFT
With the transmission in neutral, the shift lever should be a horizontal plane and parallel to the instrument panel line. Corrective adjustments should be made at the gear shift rods.
1. Place lever in neutral.
2. Loosen two gear shift rod adjustment nuts.
3. Insert 3/16 in. diameter alignment pin through first and reverse gear shift lever and second and third gear shift lever. Align levers to insert pin.
4. Tighten gear shift rod adjustment nuts, and remove pin.
5. Check gear lever for smooth crossover.

THREE-SPEED FLOOR AND CONSOLE SHIFT
1. Loosen three shift linkage adjustment nuts.
2. Install a 1/4 in. diameter alignment pin through control bracket and levers.
3. Tighten three shift linkage adjustment nuts and remove alignment pin.
4. Check gear lever for smooth crossover.

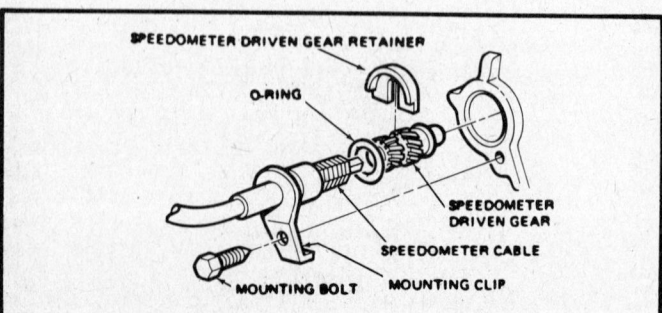

Typical attachment of speedometer driven gear to transmission (©Ford Motor Co.)

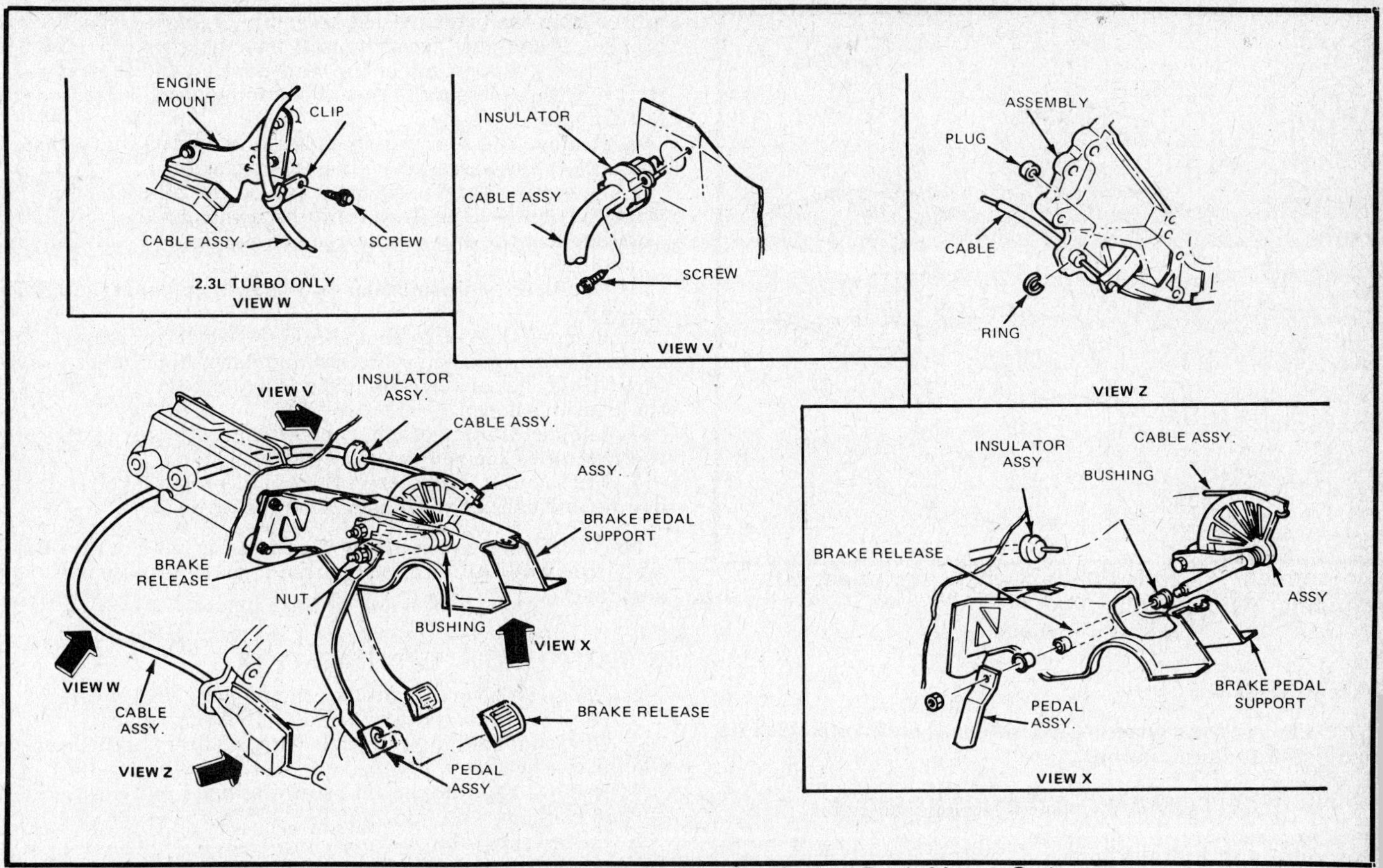

Ford Lincoln Mercury
REAR WHEEL DRIVE CARS
SECTION 5

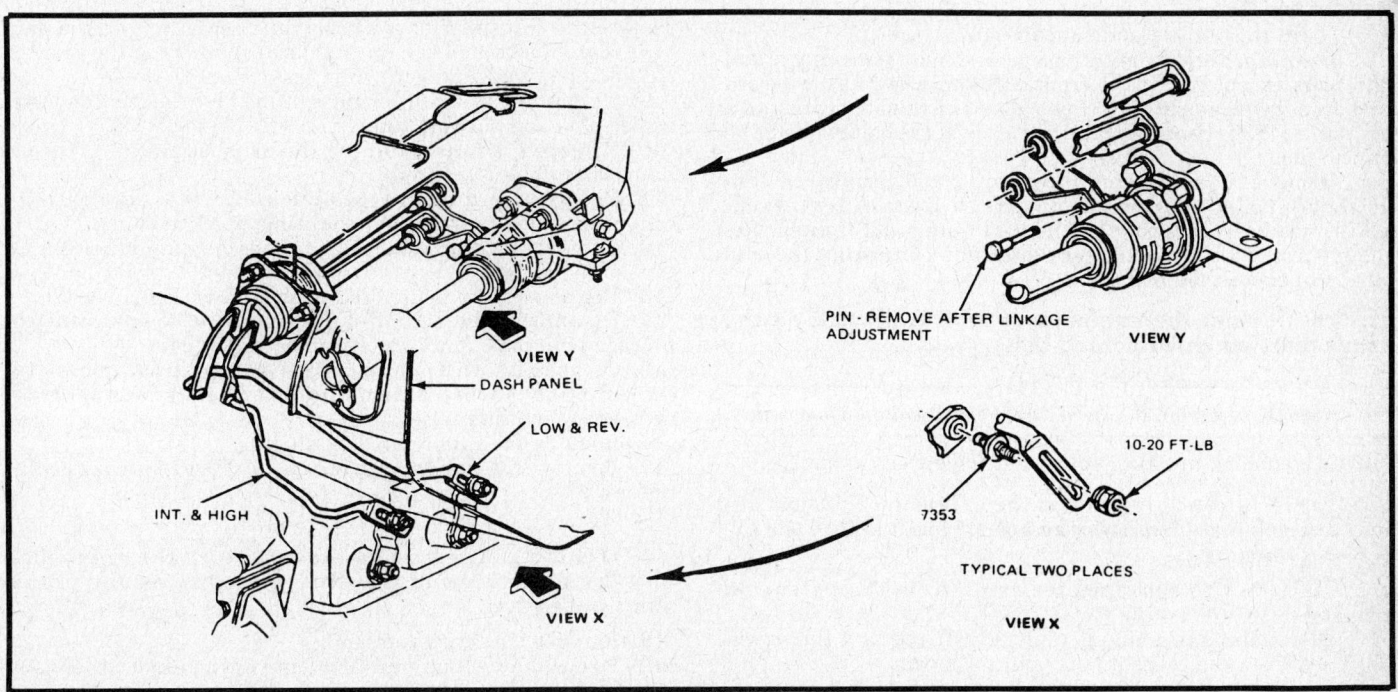

Clutch pedal installation with self-adjusting clutch mechanism (©Ford Motor Co.)

Three speed manual transmission column shift linkage and adjustments (©Ford Motor Co.)

5-89

Ford Lincoln Mercury
REAR WHEEL DRIVE CARS

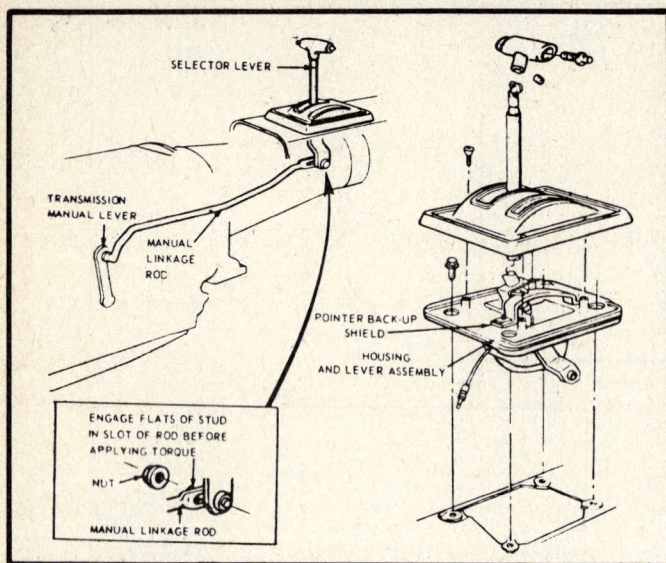

Adjustment of shift linkage when equipped with console (©Ford Motor Co.)

FOUR-SPEED

NOTE: All four speeds have internal shift rails with no provision for adjustment.

AUTOMATIC TRANSMISSION

Removal and Installation

C-3, C-4, C-6, AND AUTOMATIC OVERDRIVE

NOTE: This is a general removal and installation outline. Certain model vehicles may require the steps in a different sequence and may or may not have the components as listed.

1. Raise the vehicle and support safely.
2. Drain the fluid from the transmission by removing all oil pan bolts except two at the front. Loosen the two at the front and drop the oil pan at the rear to allow the fluid to drain into a container. When drained, reinstall a few of the bolts to hold the pan in place.
3. Remove the converter bottom cover and remove the converter drain plug to allow the converter to drain. After the converter has drained, reinstall the drain plug and tighten. Remove the converter to adapter plate bolts by turning the converter to expose the bolts.

NOTE: Crank the engine over with a wrench on the crankshaft pulley attaching bolt.

---- **CAUTION** ----
Never turn the belt drive, overhead cam engine crankshaft backwards.

4. Matchmark and disconnect the drive shaft assembly.

NOTE: Fluid will leak from the extension housing unless a cap is installed over the output shaft and in the extension housing.

5. Remove the speedometer cable from the extension housing.
6. Disconnect the manual control shift rod and the downshift rod from the transmission control levers.
7. Remove the starter cable and remove the starter.
8. Remove the electrical wires and vacuum lines, as required from the transmission assembly. Remove the bellcrank bracket, if equipped from the converter housing.
9. Place a support under the transmission and slightly raise it. It may be necessary to raise the engine hood and loosen the fan shroud.
10. Remove the rear crossmember and engine rear support. Disconnect the necessary exhaust components.
11. Lower the transmission to expose the oil cooler line fittings. Disconnect the lines from the transmission.
12. Support the engine and remove the dipstick tube and all the bell housing retaining bolts except the top two.
13. Chain the transmission to the jack or support unit for safety.
14. Remove the two top bolts from the converter housing and move the transmission rearward and down from under the vehicle. Hold the converter in place to avoid having it drop from the transmission.
15. The installation of the transmission assembly is basically the reverse of the removal procedure.
16. Fill the unit with correct fluid to its proper level, start the engine and check the transmission for leakage.

NOTE: Refer to the fluid dipstick for the correct fluid application for the automatic transmission being serviced.

C-5 AUTOMATIC TRANSMISSION

1. Open the hood and protect the fenders with covers.
2. Disconnect the battery negative battery cable.
3. On Granada/Cougar models with 3.8 liter engine, remove the air cleaner assembly.
4. Remove the fan shroud retaining bolts and position the shroud back over the fan.
5. Loosen the clamp and disconnect the thermactor air injector hose at the catalytic converter check valve on Granada/Cougar models with 3.8 liter engine and on Mustang/Capri models with 4.2 liter engine.
6. On Granada/Cougar models equipped with 3.8 liter engine, remove the two top bell housing to engine bolts from the engine compartment.
7. Raise the vehicle and support safely. Drain the oil pan or remove the transmission with the fluid remaining in the unit.
8. Matchmark and remove the driveshaft. Plug the rear extension opening to prevent fluid loss.
9. Disconnect the muffler pipe from the catalytic converter outlet pipe and support safely.
10. Remove the nuts retaining the exhaust pipe(s) to the exhaust manifold(s).
11. Pull rearward on the catalytic converters to release the converter hangers from the mounting brackets.
12. Remove the speedometer gear assembly from the rear extension housing.
13. Disconnect the neutral start switch wiring harness.
14. Disconnect the shift linkage and kick down rod at the linkage bellcrank and at the transmission lever.
15. On vehicles with floor mounted shift controls, remove the cable routing bracket attaching bolts and disconnect the cable at the transmission.
16. Remove the converter dust shield.
17. Remove the torque converter to drive plate attaching nuts.

NOTE: To gain access to the nuts, turn the crankshaft and drive plate using a socket assembly on the crankshaft pulley nut.

18. Remove the starter assembly.
19. Position a jack or similar lifting device under the transmission and remove the through bolts attaching the number three crossmember to the body brackets.

Ford Lincoln Mercury
REAR WHEEL DRIVE CARS — SECTION 5

NOTE: For safety, chain the transmission to the jack or lifting device.

20. Lower the transmission enough to gain access to the oil cooler lines and disconnect.
21. Remove the remaining bell housing to engine bolts and pull the transmission rearward to disengage the converter studs from the drive plate.
22. Carefully lower the transmission from under the vehicle, being careful not to loosen the converter assembly.
23. The installation of the C-5 transmission is the reverse of the removal procedure.
24. Fill the transmission with the correct fluid (Ford type H) and start the engine. Check for fluid leakage. Correct the fluid level as necessary.

ZF TRANSMISSION

Removal and Installation

1. Remove the kickdown (TV) cable and insert from the injection pump side lever and cable bracket in the engine compartment.
2. Place the transmission selector lever in N (Neutral). Raise the vehicle on a hoist.
3. Remove the outer manual lever and nut from the transmission selector shaft.
4. Remove position sensor from converter housing.
5. Remove the engine brace from the lower end of the converter housing.
6. Place a transmission jack under the transmission.
7. Place a wrench on the crankshaft pulley attaching bolt and turn the converter to gain access to the converter-to-flywheel attaching nuts. Remove the converter-to-flywheel attaching nuts.

NOTE: The converter studs are installed in the converter with Lock-Tite®. During disassembly the nuts may override the Loc-Tite® and the nut and stud come out as a "bolt". This poses no concern. The stud and converter threads should be cleaned, Loc-Tite® applied, and the "bolt" reinstalled and tightened to specification.

8. Disconnect the driveshaft from the rear axle and slide shaft rearward from the transmission.

NOTE: To maintain driveshaft balance, mark the rear driveshaft yoke and axle companion flange so the driveshaft can be installed in its original position. Install a seal installation tool in the extension housing to prevent fluid leakage.

9. Disconnect the neutral start switch electrical connector.
10. Remove the extension housing damper.
11. Remove the rear support-to-crossmember attaching nuts and the two crossmember-to-side support attaching bolts.
12. Remove the two engine rear support-to-extension housing attaching bolts and remove the rear mount from the exhaust system.

NOTE: On some models, exhaust system hardware may have to be removed to facilitate removal of crossmember and transmission.

13. On Continental with column shift, remove the two bolts securing the bellcrank bracket to the engine-to-transmission brace.
14. Disconnect each oil line from the fittings on the transmission using push connect service Tool T82L-9500-AH or equivalent.
15. Disconnect the speedometer wiring harness from the extension housing.
16. Remove the two converter housing to starter motor bolts.
17. Secure the transmission to the jack with a safety chain and lower the jack slightly.
18. Remove the four converter housing-to-cylinder block attaching bolts.
19. Remove the filler tube and dipstick.
20. Carefully move the transmission and converter assembly away from the engine and, at the same time, lower the jack to clear the underside of the vehicle.
21. Mount the transmission in a holding fixture.
22. Place the transmission on the jack. Secure the transmission to the jack with a safety chain.
23. Rotate the converter until the studs are in alignment with the holes in the flywheel and the flexplate.
24. Move the converter and transmission assembly forward into position, using care not to damage the flywheel, flexplate and the converter pilot. The converter face must seat squarely against the flexplate (This indicates that the converter pilot is not binding in the engine crankshaft).
25. Install the filler tube and dipstick, position bracket over the upper right housing to engine bolt holes.
26. Install and tighten the four converter housing-to-engine attaching bolts to 38–48 ft. lbs.
27. Remove the safety chain from around the transmission.
28. Connect the oil cooler lines by pushing them into the fittings on the transmission (located on the intermediate plate).
29. Connect the speedometer wiring harness to the extension housing.
30. Install the extension housing damper with three bolts. Tighten bolts to 18-25 ft. lbs.
21. Install the rear support on the exhaust system.
32. install the crossmember on the side supports and install the attaching bolts and nuts. Position the rear support on the crossmember and tighten the nuts to specification.
33. Secure the engine rear support to the extension housing and tighten the bolts to specification.
34. If removed, install exhaust system hardware.
35. Lower the transmission and the jack.
36. On the Continental equipped with column shift, position the bellcrank to the engine-to-transmission brace and install the two attaching bolts. Tighten the bolts to 10–20 ft. lbs.
37. Guide the kickdown (TV) cable up into the engine compartment.
38. Install the outer manual lever on the transmission selector shaft. Tighten the attaching nut to 10–20 ft. lbs.
39. Install the convert to flywheel attaching nuts (or bolts) and tighten to 20–34 ft. lbs.
40. Install the engine brace on the lower end of the converter housing and engine block. Tighten the bolts to 15–18 ft. lbs.
41. Connect the neutral start switch harness at the transmission.
42. Install position sensor to converter housing.
43. Connect the driveshaft to the rear axle. Install the driveshaft so the index marks, made during removal, are correctly aligned.

NOTE: Lubricate the yoke splines with C1AZ–19590–B or equivalent.

44. Lower the vehicle and adjust the kickdown (TV) cable.
45. Fill the transmission to the correct level with the specified fluid. Start the engine and shift the transmission to all positions, then recheck the fluid level.

SHIFT LINKAGE

Adjustment

COLUMN SHIFT

1. With the engine off, place the gear selector in the D (Drive) position, or D (overdrive) position (AOD). Either hang a weight on the shifter of have an assistant sit in the car and hold the selector against the stop.

SECTION 5
Ford Lincoln Mercury
REAR WHEEL DRIVE CARS

NOTE: Models without AOT – use 8 lb. weight. Models with AOT – use 8–12 lb. weight.

2. Loosen the adjusting nut or clamp at the shift lever so that the shift rod is free to slide. On models with a shift cable, remove the nut from the transmission lever and disconnect the cable from the transmission, except on the Lincoln and Continental VI and VII. On these models, first raise the car, remove the splash shield, then loosen the clamp or cable from underneath.

3. Place the manual shift lever on the transmission in the D (Drive) or D (overdrive) position. This is the second detent position from the full counterclockwise position an all but the Ford/Mercury, Lincoln Continental, Continental Mark VI and VII. On these models, the Drive or Overdrive Position is found by pushing the shift rod down to the bottom position and then pulling up two positions.

4. Tighten the adjusting bolt. On cars with a cable, position the cable end on the transmission lever stud, aligning the flats. Tighten the adjusting nut.

5. Check the pointer alignment and transmission operation for all selector positions. If not correct, adjust linkage.

FLOOR OR CONSOLE SHIFT

1. Position the transmission selector lever in drive against the rearward Drive stop for C–5 transmission and in Overdrive position for AOD transmission.

NOTE: The shifter lever should be held against the rearward Drive/Overdrive stop when the linkage is adjusted.

2. Raise the vehicle and loosen the manual lever shift cable retaining nuts. Move the transmission manual lever to the Drive or Overdrive position (depending on the transmission), second detent position from the full counterclockwise position. On 2.4L floor shift models, move the lever to the third detent position from the rear of the transmission.

3. On all models except those equipped with 2.4L Diesel, with the transmission selector lever and manual lever in the Drive position, tighten the attaching nut to 10–15 lb. ft. On models equipped with 2.4L Diesel, with the transmission selector lever in the Overdrive position, tighten the manual lever shift cable retaining nut to 10–18 lb. ft.

4. Check the operation of the transmission in each selector lever position.

LOCK ROD

Adjustment

1. With the transmission selector lever in the Drive position, loosen the lock rod adjustment nut on the transmission lever.

2. Insert a 0.180 in. diameter rod (No. 15 drill bit) in the gauge pin hole in the steering column socket casting; it is located at the six o'clock position directly below the ignition lock.

3. Manipulate the pin so that the casting will not be moved when the pin is fully inserted.

4. Tighten the lock rod adjustment nut.

5. Remove the pin and check the linkage operation.

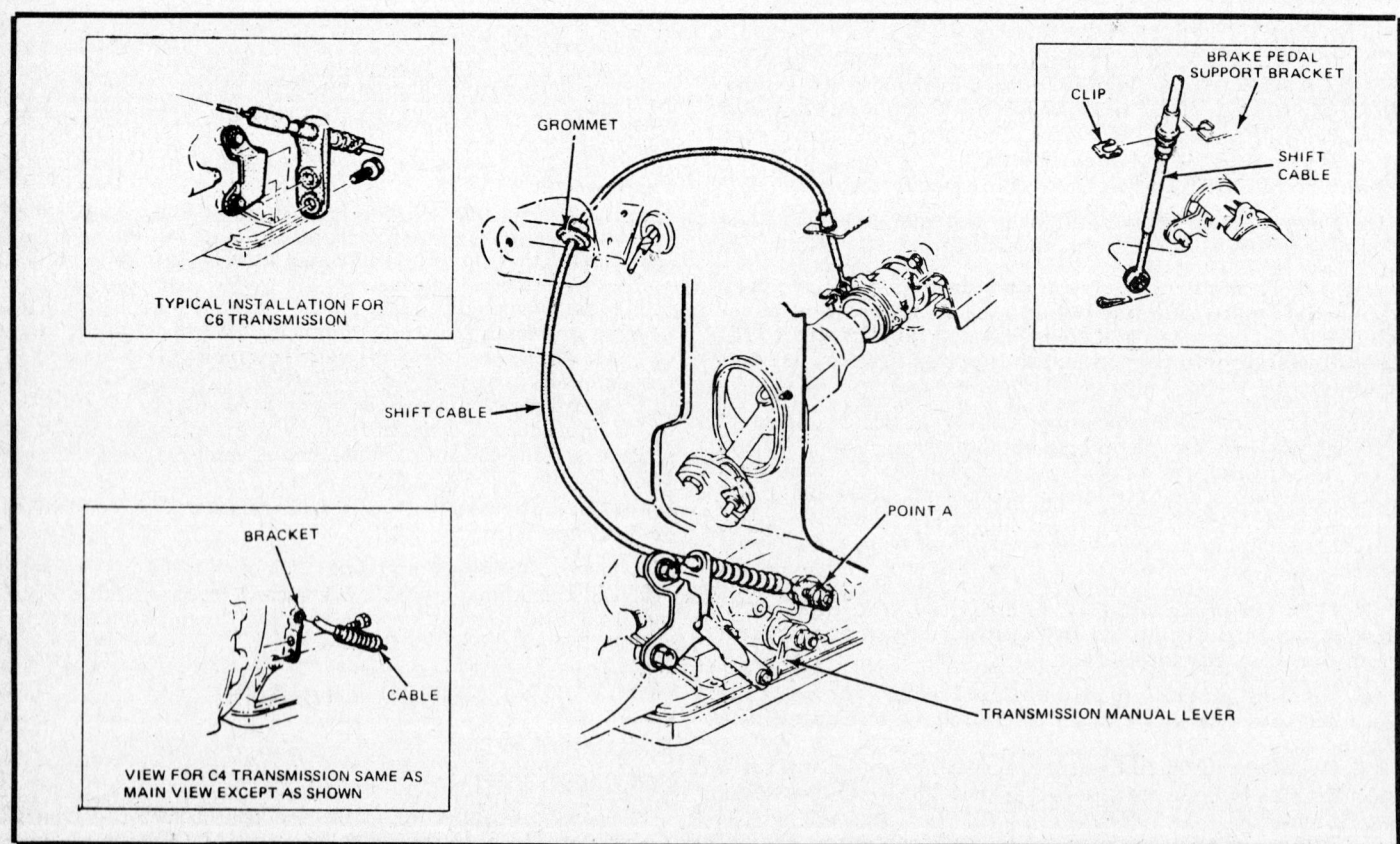

Adjustment points when equipped with column operated shift cable, typical of Cougar, Continental Mark, Granada, LTD II Monarch, Thuderbird and Versailles (©Ford Motor Co.)

DOWNSHIFT (THROTTLE) LINKAGE

Adjustment

ALL MODELS EXCEPT (AOD) AUTOMATIC OVERDRIVE

1. With the engine off, disconnect the throttle and downshift return springs, if equipped.
2. Hold the carburetor throttle lever in the wide open position against the stop.
3. Hold the transmission downshift linkage in the full downshift position against the internal stop.
4. Turn the adjustment screw on the carburetor downshift lever to obtain 0.010–0.080 in. clearance between the screw tip and the throttle shaft lever tab.
5. Release the transmission and carburetor to their normal free positions. Install the throttle and downshift return springs, if removed.

AOD

1. With the engine off, remove the air cleaner and make sure the fast idle cam is released (the throttle lever must be at the idle stop).
2. Turn the linkage lever adjusting screw counterclockwise until the end of the screw is flush with the face of the lever.
3. Turn the linkage adjustment screw in until there is a maximum clearance of .005 in. between the throttle lever and the end of the adjustment screw.
4. Turn the linkage lever adjusting screw clockwise three full turns. A minimum of one turn is permissible if the screw travel is limited.
5. If it is not possible to turn the adjusting screw at least one full turn, or if the initial gap of .005 in. could not be obtained, perform the linkage adjustment in the transmission.

ALTERNATE METHOD, AOD

If unable to adjust the throttle valve control linkage at the carburetor, as described above, proceed as follows:

1. At the transmission, loosen the 8 mm bolt on the throttle valve (TV) control rod sliding trunnion block. Make sure the trunnion block slides freely on the control rod.
2. Push up on the lower end of the TV control rod to insure that the carburetor linkage lever is held against the throttle lever. When the pressure is released, the control rod must stay in position.
3. Force the TV control lever on the transmission against its internal stop. While maintaining pressure tighten the trunnion block bolt. Make sure the throttle lever is at the idle stop.

TV CABLE ADJUSTMENT

ZF TRANSMISSION

1. Set the injection pump lever at the full throttle position.
2. Tighten the rear adjusting nut on the threaded barrel until a gap of 1.54–1.57 in. exists between the edge of the crimped bead on the cable closest to the barrel and the end of the threaded barrel.
3. Tighten the forward adjusting nut to lock the cable assembly to the bracket to 80–106 in. lbs.
4. Recheck the gap and readjust as necessary.

NOTE: Kickdown on this transmission is controlled by the injection pump linkage adjustments.

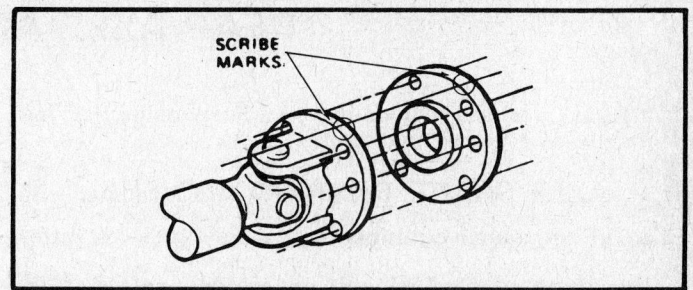

Matching driveshaft to pinion shaft flanges by the scribed marks (©Ford Motor Co.)

SHIFT QUADRANT INDICATOR

Adjustment

Refer to the Steering Column Removal and Installation outline in this chapter for the adjustment procedures.

DRIVESHAFT

Removal and Installation

1. Matchmark the rear driveshaft yoke and the companion flange so that the parts may be reassembled in the same way to maintain balance.
2. Remove the U-bolts and straps or coupling flange nuts and bolts at the rear of the driveshaft, and tape the loose bearing caps to the spider.
3. Allow the rear of the driveshaft to drop down slightly. Pull the driveshaft and slip yoke out of the transmission extension housing.
4. Plug the transmission to prevent fluid leakage.
5. To install, lubricate the yoke splines and install the yoke into the transmission extension housing, aligning the splines. Be careful not to bottom the slip yoke hard against the transmission seal.
6. Rotate the pinion flange as necessary to align the matchmarks made earlier. New bolts should be used and torque the attaching bolts to 70–95 ft. lbs.

On the Versailles, tighten the coupling-to-pinion flange bolts to 70–90 ft. lbs.

The Fairmont, Zephyr, Mustang, Capri, Thunderbird and Cougar XR-7, Granada and Cougar use special was-dipped coupling-to-pinion flange bolts which may not be reused. They must be replaced with special new bolts torqued to 71–96 ft. lbs.

UNIVERSAL JOINT

Removal and Installation

Universal joint and double-cardan joint overhaul procedures are given in the Drive Axles and U-Joints Unit Repair Section.

FORD LINCOLN MERCURY
REAR WHEEL DRIVE CARS

REAR AXLE AND SUSPENSION

For Axle Overhaul Procedures and Suspension Services Refer to Unit Repair Sections.

AXLE SHAFT, BEARING AND SEAL

NOTE: A vehicle equipped with a tractional-lok differential will always have both wheels driving. If, while the vehicle is being serviced, only one wheel is raised off the floor and the rear axle is driven by the engine, the wheel on the fllor could drive the vehicle off the stand or jack. So be sure both rear wheels are off the ground.

Removal and Installation
EXCEPT C-LOCK TYPE

1. Remove the wheel, tire, and brake drum. With disc brakes, remove the caliper, retainer nuts, and rotor. New anchor plate bolts will be needed for reassembly.
2. Remove the nuts holding the retainer plate to the backing plate, or axle shaft retainer bolts from the housing. Disconnect the brake line with drum brakes.
3. Remove the retainer and install nuts, finger-tight, to prevent the brake backing plate from being dislodged.
4. Pull out the axle shaft and bearing assembly, using a slide hammer.

On models with tapered roller bearing, the tapered cup will normally remain in the axle housing when the shaft is removed. The cup must be removed from the housing to prevent seal damage when the shaft is reinstalled. The cup can be removed with a slide hammer and an expanding puller.

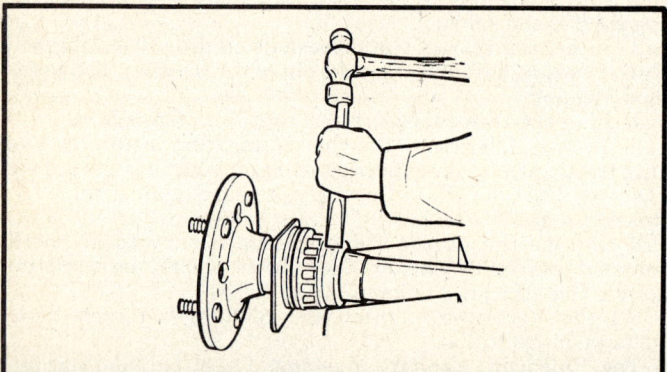
Scoring axle shaft bearing retainer prior to removal (©Ford Motor Co.)

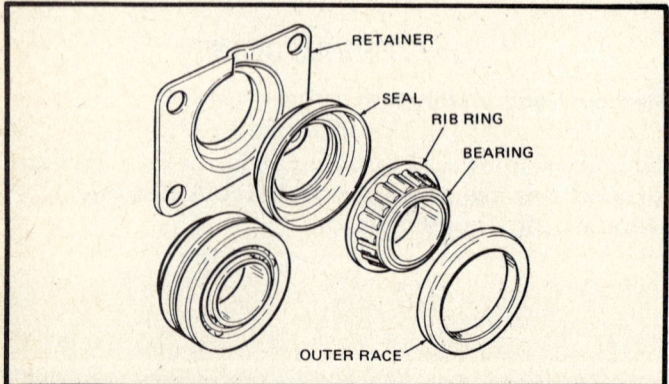
Tapered bearing and retainer-removable carrier axle (©Ford Motor Co.)

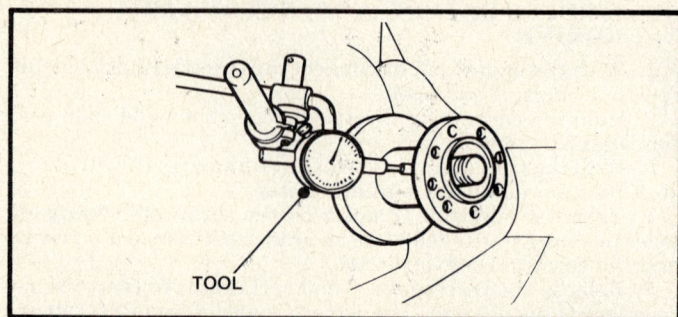
Checking companion flange radial runout typical (©Ford Motor Co.)

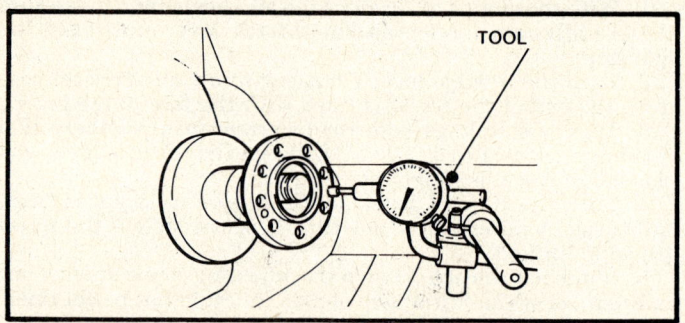
Checking companion flange lateral runout (©Ford Motor Co.)

NOTE: If end-play is found to be excessive, the bearing should be replaced. Shimming the bearing is not recommended as this ignores end-play of the bearing itself and could result in improper seating of the bearing.

5. Using a chisel, nick the bearing retainer in 3 or 4 places. The retainer does not have to be cut, but merely collapsed sufficiently to allow the bearing retainer to be slid from the shaft. On Fords and Mercurys, first drill a ¼ in. hole not more than $^{5}/_{16}$ in. deep in the ring surface.
6. Press off the bearing and install the new one by pressing it into position. With tapered bearings, place the lubricated seal and bearing on the axle shaft (cup rib ring facing the flange). Make sure that the seal is the correct length. Disc brake seal rims are black, drum brake seal rims are grey. Press the bearing and seal onto the shaft.
7. Press on the new retainer.

NOTE: Do not attempt to press the bearing and the retainer on at the same time.

8. On ball bearing models, to replace the seal: remove the seal from the housing with an expanding cone type puller and a slide hammer. The seal must be replaced whenever the shaft is removed. Wipe a small amount of sealer onto the outer edge of the new seal before installation; do not put sealer on the sealing lip. Press the seal into the housing with a seal installation tool.
9. Assemble the shaft and bearing in the housing, being sure that the bearing is seated properly in the housing. On ball bearing models, be careful not to damage the seal with the shaft. With tapered bearings, first install the tapered cup on the bearing, and lubricate the outer diameter of the cup and the seal with axle lube. Then install the shaft and bearing assembly into the housing.

10. Install the retainer, drum or rotor and caliper, wheel and tire. Bleed the brakes.

C-LOCK TYPE

1. Jack up and support the rear of the car.
2. Remove the wheels and tires from the brake drums.
3. Place a drain pan under the housing and drain the lubricant by loosening the housing cover.
4. Remove the locks securing the brake drums to the axle shaft flanges and remove the drums.
5. Remove the housing cover and gasket, if used.
6. Position jackstands under the rear frame member and lower the axle housing. This is done to give easy access to the inside of the differential.
7. Working through the opening in the differential case, remove the side gear pinion shaft lockbolt and the side gear pinion shaft.
8. Push the axle shafts inward and remove the C-locks from the inner end of the axle shafts. Temporarily replace the shaft and lockbolt to retain the differential gears in position.
9. Remove the axle shafts with a slide hammer. Be sure the seal is not damaged by the splines on the axle shaft.
10. Remove the bearing and oil seal from the housing. Both the seal and bearing can be removed with a slide hammer. Two types of bearings are used on some axles, one requiring a press fit and the other a loose fit. A loose fitting bearing does not necessarily indicate excessive wear.
11. Inspect the axle shaft housing and axle shafts for burrs or others irregularities. Replace any worn or damaged parts. A light yellow color on the bearing journal of the axle shaft is normal, and does not require replacement of the axle shaft. Slight pitting and wear is also normal.
12. Lightly coat the wheel bearing rollers with axle lubricant. Install the bearings in the axle housing until the bearing seats firmly against the shoulder.
13. Wipe all lubricant from the oil seal bore, before installing the seal.
14. Inspect the original seals for wear. If necessary, these may be replaced with new seals, which are prepacked with lubricant and do not require soaking.
15. Install the oil seal.

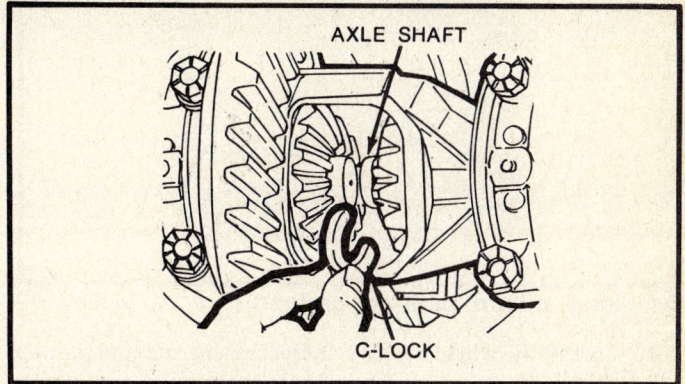

Removing the axle shaft "C" locks
(©Ford Motor Co.)

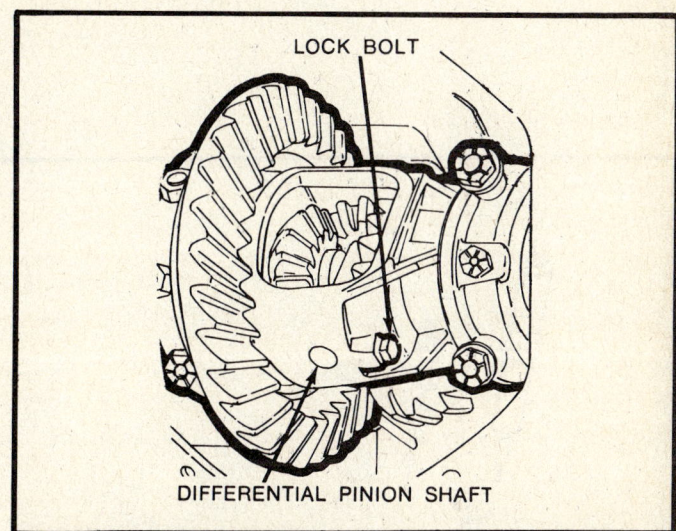

Removing the differential pinion shaft lockbolt
(©Ford Motor Co.)

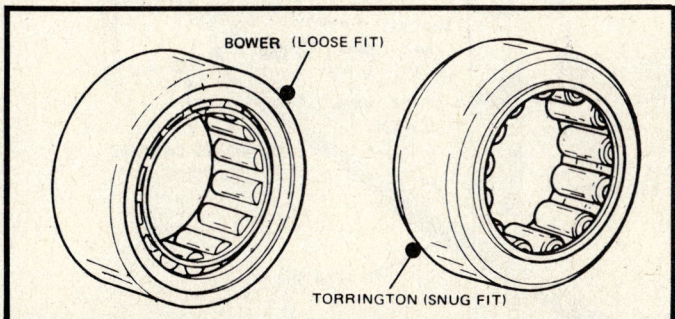

Axle bearing assemblies, used with "C" type locking axle shafts (©Ford Motor Co.)

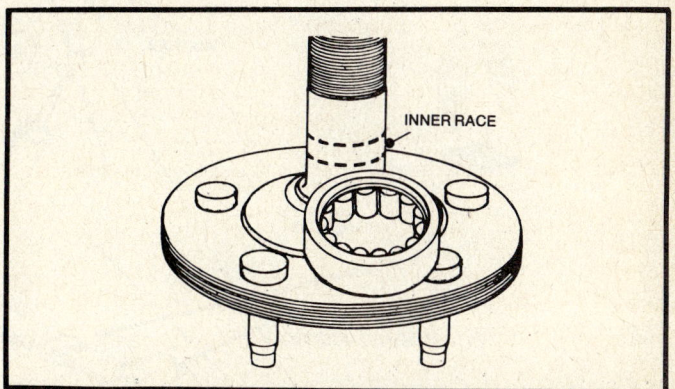

Axle wheel bearing inner race. (© Ford Motor Co.)

CAUTION

Installation of the seal without the proper tool can cause distortion and seal leakage. Oil seals for the right-side are marked with green stripes and the word "RIGHT". Seals for the left-side are marked yellow with the word "LEFT". Do not interchange seals form side to side.

---

16. Remove the lockbolt and pinion shaft. Carefully slide the axle shafts into place. Be careful that you do not damage the seal with the splined end of the axle shaft. Engage the splined end of the shaft with the differential side gears.

17. Install the axle shaft C-locks on the inner end of the axle shafts and seat the C-locks in the counterbore of the differential side gears.
18. Rotate the differential pinion gears until the differential pinion shaft can be installed. Install the differential pinion shaft lockbolt. tighten to 15–22 ft. lbs.
19. Install the brake drum on the axle shaft flange.

SECTION 5
Ford Lincoln Mercury
REAR WHEEL DRIVE CARS

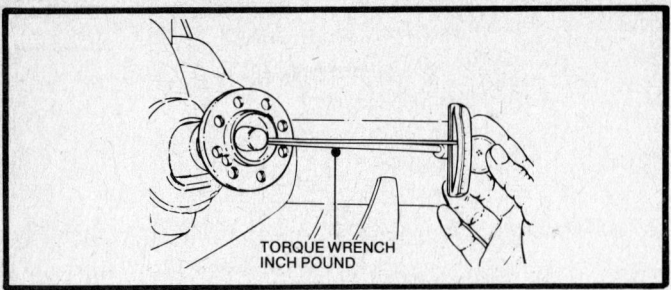

Checking pinion bearing preload (© Ford Motor Co.)

20. Install the wheel and tire on the brake drum and tighten the attaching nuts.
21. Clean the gasket surface of the rear housing and install a new cover gasket and the housing cover. WGY covers do not use a gasket. On these models, apply a bead of silicone sealer on the gasket surface. The bead should run inside of the bolt holes.
22. Raise the rear axle so that it is in the running position. Add the amount of specified lubricant to bring the lubricant level to ½ in. below the filler hole in WER axles, or 1¼ below on the WGY.

NOTE: The axle codes can be determined from the identification tag attached to one of the cover retaining bolts. Be sure to re-attach the tag to the axle assembly after the repairs have been completed. An example of the axle codes are as follows: WGF, WGG 6.75 in. ring gear diameter; WFC, WGX 7.50 in. ring gear diameter; WGY, WFZ 8.50 in. ring gear diameter; WGF, WFV, WFB 9.00 in. ring gear diameter. It is important that the year of the vehicle, the model and the axle code be given when ordering replacement parts of the axle assembly.

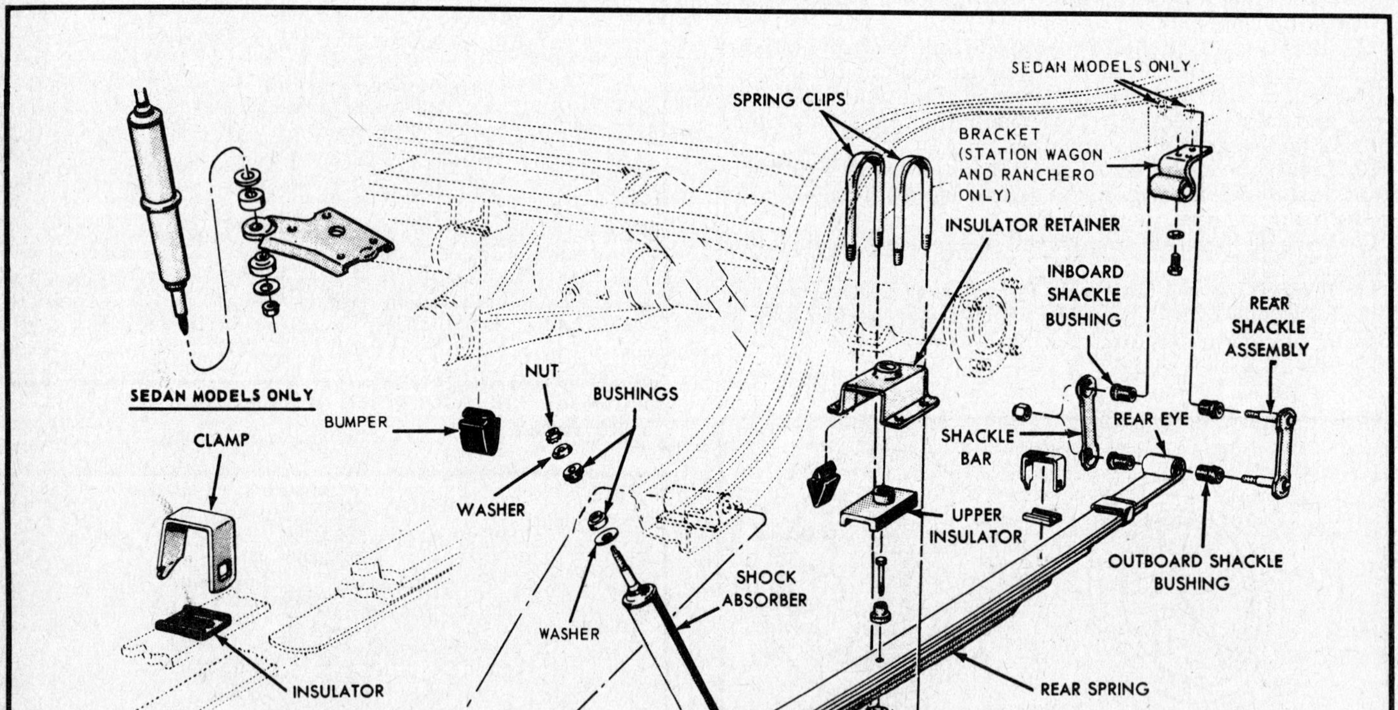

Exploded view of leaf spring rear suspension (©Ford Motor Co.)

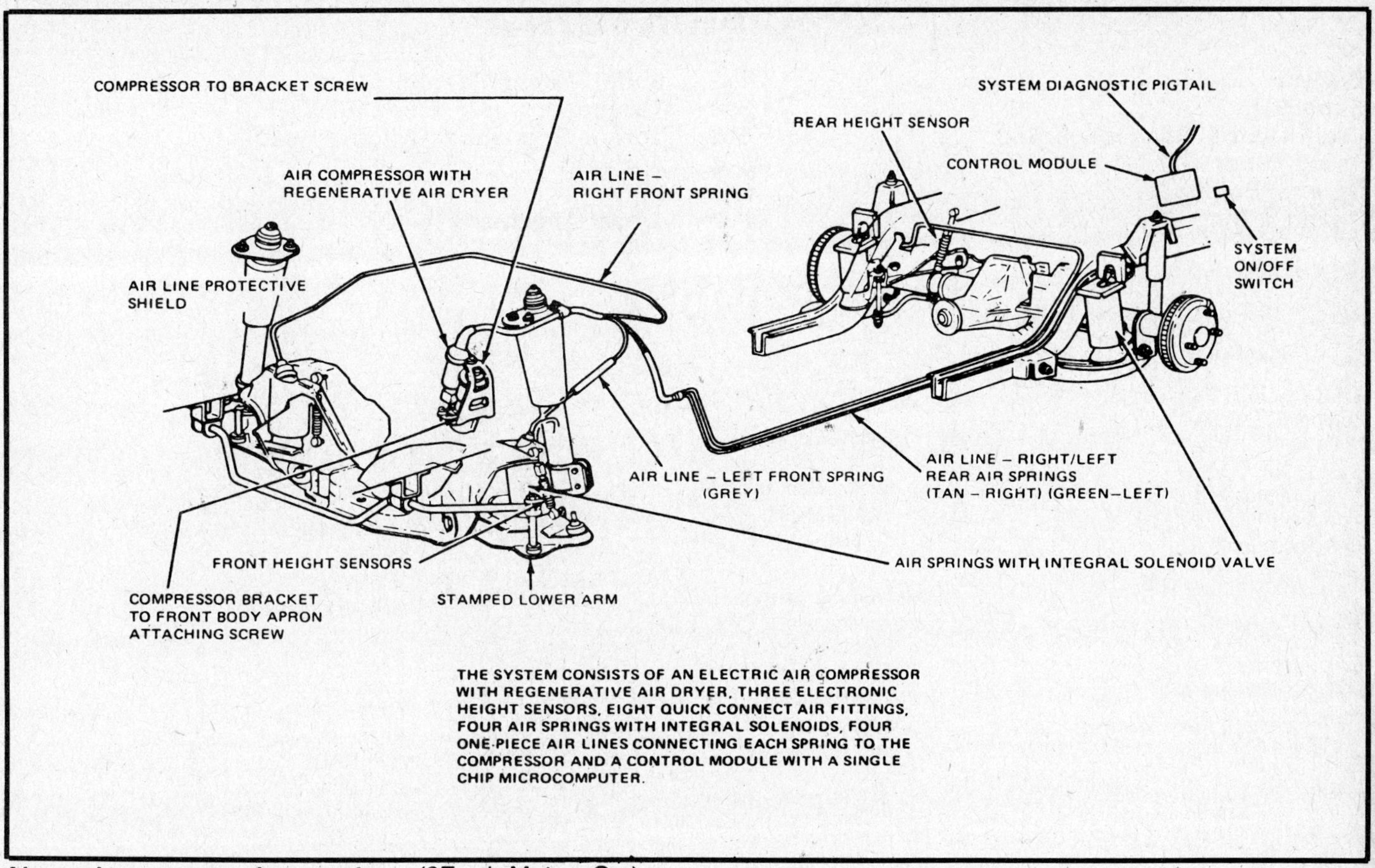

Ford Lincoln Mercury
REAR WHEEL DRIVE CARS
SECTION 5

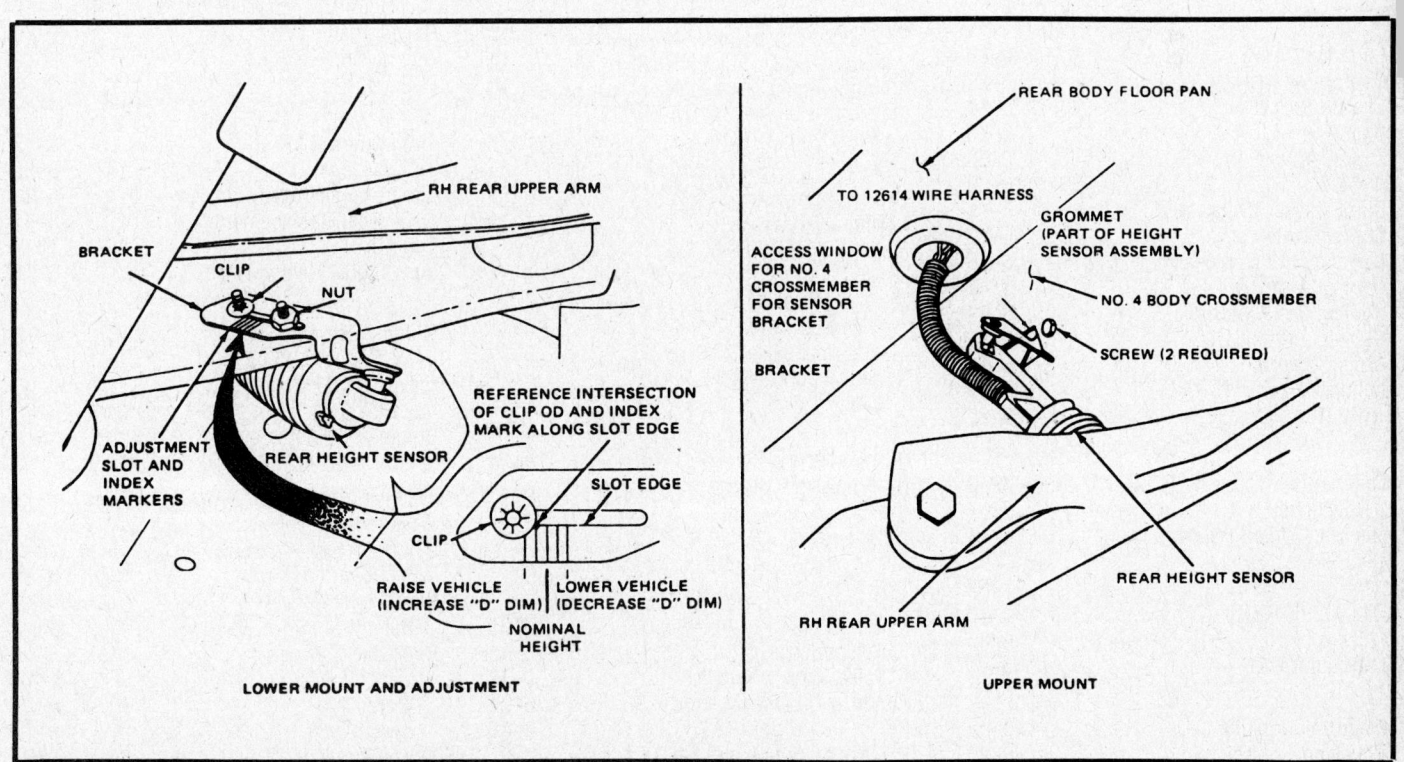

Air spring suspension system (©Ford Motor Co.)

Rear suspension ride height adjustment (©Ford Motor Co.)

SECTION 6
GENERAL MOTORS—"A" AND "X" BODY
FRONT WHEEL DRIVE CARS

SPECIFICATIONS

Brakes	24-2	Serial Number Identification	6-5
Capacities	6-8	Torque	6-9
Crankshaft & Connecting Rod	6-8	Torque Sequence (Cylinder Heads)	6-29
Firing Order	6-6	Tune-Up	6-7
General Engine	6-5	Valve	6-7
Piston & Ring	6-7	Wheel Alignment	6-9

INDEX

A
Alternator R&R ... 6-9
Automatic Transaxle ... 6-39
  On Car Service ... 23-2
  Assembly R&R ... 6-39
Axle Assembly R&R ... 6-40
Axle Shaft R&R ... 6-40
Axle Shaft Boots R&R ... 6-41

B
Ball Joints ... 35-3
Brake System ... 24-2
Brake Booster ... 6-38
Brake Caliper Overhaul ... 24-2
Brake Caliper R&R
  Front ... 24-2
Brake Drum
  Rear ... 24-2
Brake Master Cylinder ... 6-38
Brake Pad
  Front ... 24-2
Brake Shoe
  Rear ... 24-2

C
Camshaft R&R ... 6-30
Carburetor R&R ... 6-22
Chassis Electrical ... 6-14
Clutch ... 6-38
  Adjustment ... 6-38
  R&R ... 6-38
Combination Switch R&R ... 6-11
Starter Switch ... 6-12
Component Locations ... 6-16
Control Arm R&R ... 35-2
Cooling Fan Motor ... 6-19
Cooling System ... 6-19
Cruise Control ... 6-19
Cylinder Head ... 6-29
  R&R ... 6-29

D
Differential ... 32-2
  Inspection ... 32-2
Dimmer Switch R&R ... 6-13
Disc Brakes ... 24-2
  Front ... 24-2
Distributor R&R ... 6-10
Drive Axle ... 6-40
Driveshaft R&R ... 6-40

E
Electronic Ignition ... 30-2
Emission Controls ... 6-25

Engine ... 6-26
  Identification ... 6-5
  R&R ... 6-26
Engine Electrical ... 6-10
Engine Lubrication ... 6-33
Engine Mechanical ... 6-26
Engine Mounts R&R ... 6-28
Exhaust Manifold R&R ... 6-24

F
Front Suspension ... 35-2
  Alignment ... 6-9
Fuel Injection ... 6-24
Fuel Mixture, Adjust ... 6-21
Fuel Pump R&R ... 6-21
Fuses ... 6-19
Fusible Links ... 6-19

H
Head Light Switch ... 6-12
Heater Blower R&R ... 6-20
Heater Core R&R ... 6-20
Heater Unit R&R ... 6-20
Horn Switch ... 6-13

I
Idle Speed Adjust ... 6-22
Ignition Switch ... 6-11
Ignition Timing ... 6-10
Instrument Cluster R&R ... 6-14
Intake Manifold R&R ... 6-22

L, M, N
Lower Control Arm R&R ... 35-2
Master Cylinder R&R ... 6-38
Manual Steering Gear
  R&R ... 6-34
Manual Transaxle
  Overhaul ... 32-2
Manual Transaxle R&R ... 6-39
Neutral Safety Switch
  R&R ... 6-11

O
Oil Pan R&R ... 6-33
Oil Pump ... 6-34
  R&R ... 6-34
Oil Seal R&R
  Rear Main ... 6-34

P
Parking Brake ... 6-38
  Adjustment ... 6-38
  Cable R&R ... 6-38
Piston & Connecting Rod ... 6-31
Power Brake Unit R&R ... 6-38
Power Steering Pump R&R ... 6-37

R
Rear Main Oil Seal R&R ... 6-34
Rear Suspension ... 35-2
Regulator ... 6-9
Rocker Shaft/Assy RR ... 6-28

S
Serial Number ... 6-5
  Engine ... 6-5
  Vehicle ... 6-5
Shock Absorber R&R
  Front ... 35-2
  Rear ... 35-2
Springs
  Front ... 35-2
  Rear ... 35-2
Starter R&R ... 6-9
Starter Drive Replacement ... 6-9
Steering Column R&R ... 6-37
Steering Gear R&R ... 6-34
  Manual ... 6-34
  Power ... 6-34
Steering Wheel R&R ... 6-34
Stop Light Switch R&R ... 6-12
Speedometer R&R ... 6-15
Suspension R&R ... 35-2
  Service ... 35-2

T
Timing Belt R&R ... 6-32
Timing Chain ... 6-32
Timing Gear Cover ... 6-31
  Oil Seal Replacement ... 6-31
Tune-Up ... 6-7
Turn Signal Switch R&R ... 6-13

U, V
U-Joint Overhaul ... 28-2
Valve Tappette R&R ... 6-28
Valve Timing, Adjust ... 6-28
Valve System ... 6-28
Voltage REgulator ... 6-9

W, Y
Water Pump R&R ... 6-19
Wheel Alignment ... 6-9
  Front ... 6-9
Wheel Bearings Front ... 6-37
Wheel Cylinders Rear ... 6-42
  Rear ... 24-2
Windshield Wiper ... 6-14
  Linkage R&R ... 6-14
  Motor R&R ... 6-14
  Switch R&R ... 6-13
Year Identification ... 6-3

BEFORE SERVICING BE CERTAIN TO READ THE SAFETY NOTICE

SECTION 6

GM "A" & "X" Body
Front Wheel Drive Cars

1982-86 "A" BODY—BUICK CENTURY CUSTOM •
CENTURY LIMITED • CHEVROLET CELEBRITY •
OLDSMOBILE CUTLASS CIERA • CIERA-LS • CIERA BROUGHAM
• PONTIAC 6000 • 6000 LE • 6000 STE
1982-86 "X" BODY—BUICK SKYLARK • SKYLARK SPORT •
SKYLARK LIMITED • SKYLARK CUSTOM •
SKYLARK "T" TYPE • CHEVROLET CITATION •
OLDSMOBILE OMEGA • OMEGA BROUGHAM • PONTIAC PHOENIX •
PHOENIX SJ • PHOENIX LJ • PHOENIX SE • PHOENIX LE

YEAR IDENTIFICATION

1983 Omega

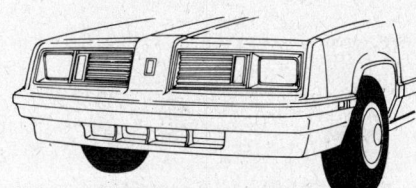

1984 Omega ES

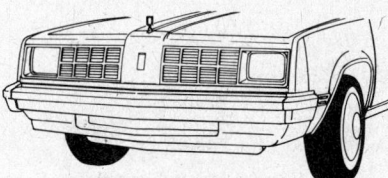

1984 Omega Sedan

1983 Phoenix

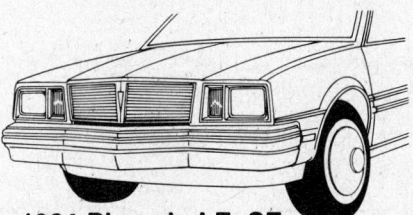

1984 Phoenix LE, SE

1983–85 Citation

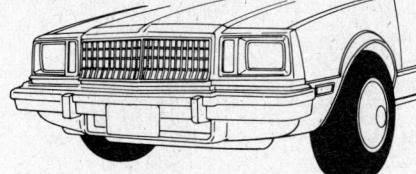

1984–85 Skylark T Type

1981–85 Skylark Sport Coupe

1983 Celebrity

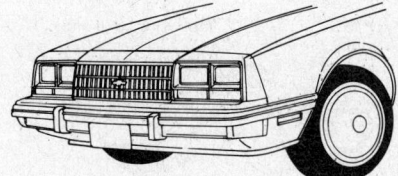

1984–85 Celebrity

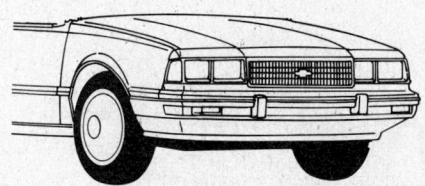

1986–87 Celebrity

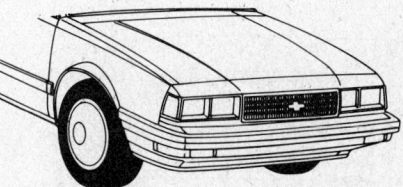

1986–87 Celebrity Eurosport

SECTION 6
GENERAL MOTORS—"A" AND "X" BODY
FRONT WHEEL DRIVE CARS

YEAR IDENTIFICATION

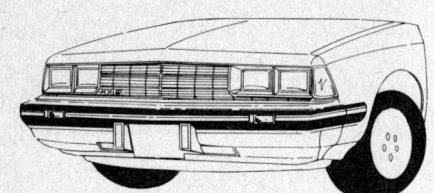
1982–83 Century

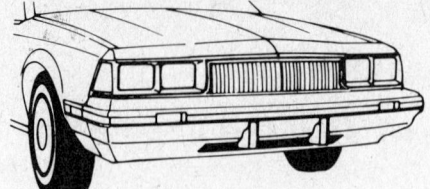
1984–85 Century

1986–87 Century

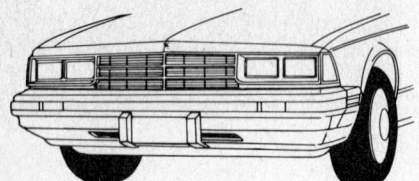
1984 Century T Type

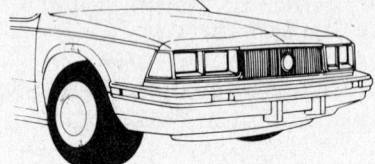
1985 Century T Type

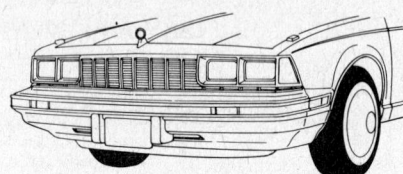
1984 Century Custom, Limited

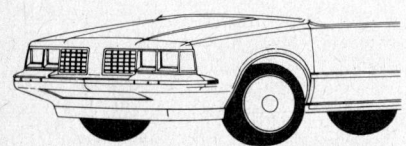
1982–83 Cutlass Ciera

1983 Cutlass Ciera ES

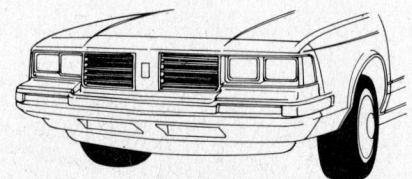
1984 Ciera

1985–86 Cutlass Ciera

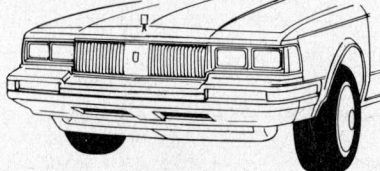
1984–86 Cutlass Cruiser

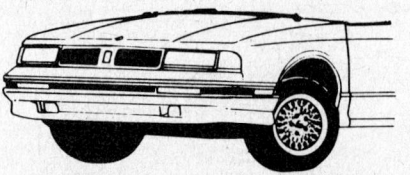
1987 Cutlass Ciera GT

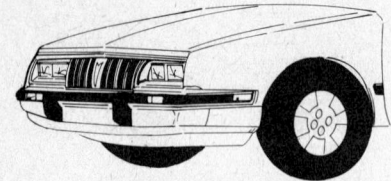
1982–83 6000

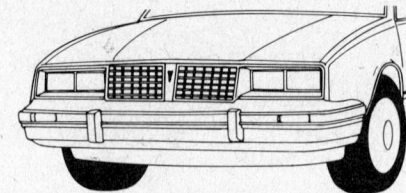
1984 6000, 6000 LE

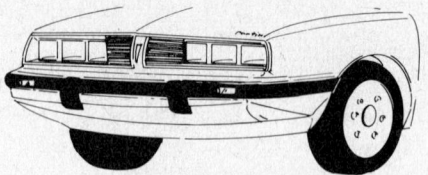
1983–85 6000 STE

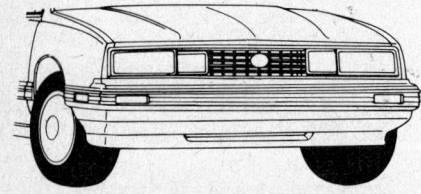
1986 6000 STE

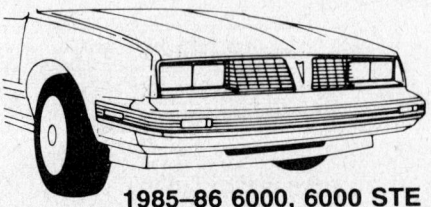
1985–86 6000, 6000 STE

1987 Pontiac 6000 SE

GENERAL MOTORS—"A" AND "X" BODY
FRONT WHEEL DRIVE CARS
SECTION 6

VEHICLE IDENTIFICATION NUMBER (VIN)

It is important for servicing and ordering parts to be certain of the vehicle and engine identification. The VIN (vehicle identification number) is a 13 or 17 digit number visible through the windshield on the driver's side of the dash and contains the vehicle and engine identification codes. It can be interpreted as follows:

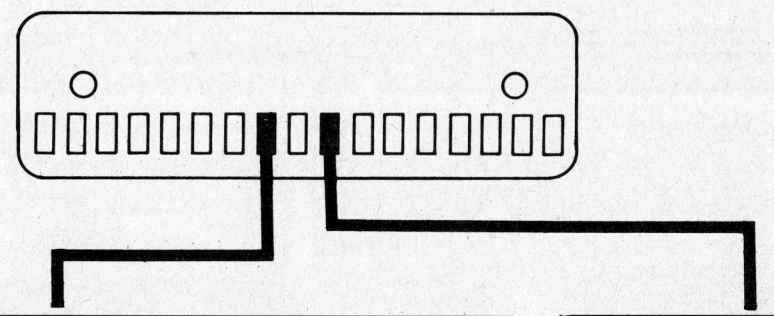

Engine Code						Model Year Code	
Code	Cu. In.	Liters	Cyl.	Carb.	Eng. Mfg.	Code	Year
5	151	2.5	4	2	Pont.	D	1983
R	151	2.5	4	TBI	Pont.	E	1984
X	173	2.8	V6	2	Chev.	F	1985
Z	173(HO)	2.8	V6	2	Chev.	G	1986
E	183	3.0	V6	2	Buick	H	1987
3	231	3.8	V6	MFI	Buick		
T	263	4.3	V6	Diesel	Olds		

The seventeen digit Vehicle Identification Number can be used to determine engine application and model year. The 10th digit indicates the model year and the 8th digit identifies the factory installed engine.
TBI: Throttle Body Injection
MFI: Multi-Point Fuel Injection

GENERAL ENGINE SPECIFICATIONS

Year	VIN Code	Engine No. Cyl. Displ. Cu. In.	Liters	Eng. Mfg.	Fuel Delivery System	Horsepower @ rpm	Torque @ rpm (ft. lbs.)	Bore × Stroke	Compression Ratio	Oil Pressure 2000 @ rpm
'83–'85	R	4-151	2.5	Pont.	T.B.I.	90 @ 4000	132 @ 2800	4.000 × 3.000	8.2:1	36-41
	5	4-151	2.5	Pont.	2-bbl.	90 @ 4000	132 @ 2800	4.000 × 3.000	8.2:1	36-41
	X	6-173	2.8	Chev.	2-bbl.	112 @ 4800	145 @ 3400	3.500 × 3.000	8.5:1	30-45
	Z	6-173 HO	2.8	Chev.	2-bbl.	135 @ 5400	145 @ 2400	3.500 × 3.000	8.9:1	30-45
	E	6-183	3.0	Buick	2-bbl.	110 @ 4800	145 @ 2600	3.800 × 2.660	8.45:1	35-42
	T	6-263	4.3	Olds.	Diesel	85 @ 3600	165 @ 1600	4.057 × 3.385	21.6:1	40-45
	3	6-231	3.8	Buick	MFI	125 @ 4400	195 @ 2000	3.800 × 3400	8.0:1	35-42
'86–'87	R	4-151	2.5	Pont.	T.B.I.	92 @ 4400	132 @ 2800	4.000 × 3.000	8.2:1	36-41
	S	4-151	2.5	Pont.	2-bbl.	92 @ 4400	132 @ 2800	4.000 × 3.000	8.5:1	35-45
	X	6-173	2.8	Chev.	2-bbl.	120-4800	155 @ 3600	3.500 × 3.000	8.5:1	30-45

SECTION 6
GENERAL MOTORS—"A" AND "X" BODY
FRONT WHEEL DRIVE CARS

FIRING ORDERS

NOTE: To avoid confusion, always replace spark plug wires one at a time.

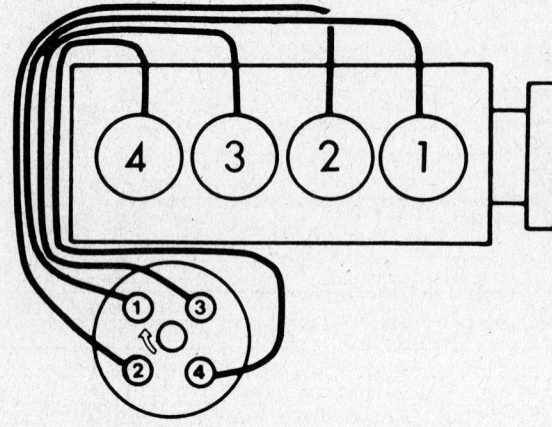

GM (Pontiac) 151-4
Engine firing order: 1-3-4-2
Distributor rotation: clockwise

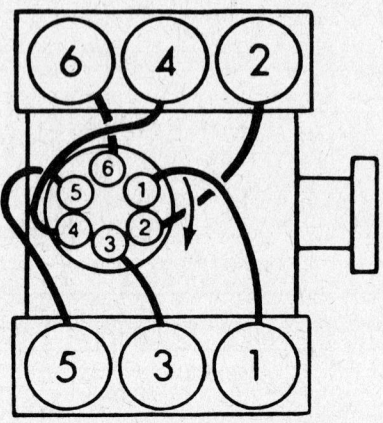

GM (Chevrolet) 173 V6 (2.8L)
Engine firing order: 1-2-3-4-5-6
Distributor rotation: clockwise

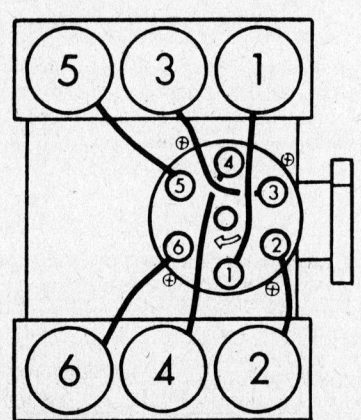

GM (Buick) 183 V8 (3.0L)
Engine firing order: 1-6-5-4-3-2
Distributor rotation: clockwise

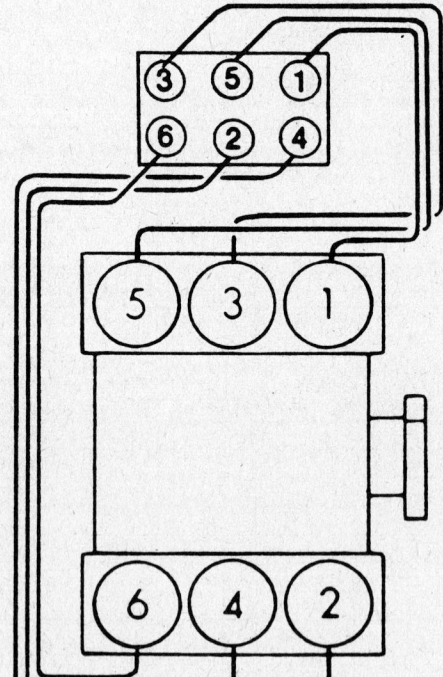

Buick 181 cu. in. V6 (3.0L) C31
Firing order: 1-6-5-4-3-2

6-6

GENERAL MOTORS—"A" AND "X" BODY
FRONT WHEEL DRIVE CARS

TUNE-UP SPECIFICATIONS

When analyzing compression test results, look for uniformity among cylinders rather than specific pressures

Year	VIN Code	Eng. No. Cyl. Displ. Cu. In.	Liters	Eng. Mfg.	hp	Spark Plugs Orig. Type	Gap (in.)	Ignition Timing (deg) ▲ Man. Trans.	Ignition Timing (deg) ▲ Auto. Trans.	Intake Valve Opens (deg.)■	Fuel Pump Pressure (psi)	Idle Speed (rpm) ▲ Man. Trans.	Idle Speed (rpm) ▲ Auto. Trans.
'83-'87	5, R	4-151	2.5	Pont.	90	R-44TSX	0.060	8B	8B	33	6.0–8.0	950 ①	750 ②
	X	6-173	2.8	Chev.	112	R-43CTS	0.045	10B	10B	25	6.0–7.5	800	600
	Z	6-173 HO	2.8	Chev.	135	R-42CTS	0.045	6B	10B	31	6.0–7.5	850 ③	750
	E	6-183	3.0	Buick	110	R-44TS8	0.080	—	15B	16	6.0–8.0	—	see text
	3	6-231	3.8	Buick	125	R-44TS8	0.080	④	④	④	4.0–6.5	④	④
	T	6-263	4.3	Olds.	85	④	④	—	6A	N.A.	5.8–8.7	—	650

NOTE: The underhood specifications sticker often reflects tune-up specification changes made in production. Sticker figures must be used if they disagree with those in this chart.
▲ See text for procedure
■ All figures Before Top Dead Center
B: Before Top Dead Center
A: After Top Dead Center
Part numbers in this chart are not recommendations by Chilton for any product by brand name.
N.A.: Information not available
① Without air conditioning: 850
② Without air conditioning: 680
③ Calif.: 750
④ See underhood specifications sticker

VALVE SPECIFICATIONS

Year	VIN Code	Engine No. Cyl. Displacement (cu. in.)	Liters	Eng. Mfg.	Seat Angle (deg.)	Face Angle (deg.)	Spring Test Pressure (lbs. @ in.)	Spring Installed Height (in.)	Stem-to-Guide Clearance (in.) Intake	Stem-to-Guide Clearance (in.) Exhaust	Stem Diameter (in.) Intake	Stem Diameter (in.) Exhaust
'83-'87	R, 5	4-151	2.5	Pont.	46	45	176 @ 1.254	1.660	0.0010–0.0027	0.0010–0.0027	0.3418–0.3425	0.3418–0.3425
	Z	6-173	2.8	Chev.	46	45	155 @ 1.160	1.610	0.0010–0.0027	0.0010–0.00227	0.3410–0.3416	0.3410–0.3416
	E	6-183	3.0	Buick	45	45	220 @ 1.340	1.727	0.0015–0.0035	0.0015–0.0032	0.3401–0.3412	0.3410–0.3415
	3	6-231	3.8	Buick	45	45	220 @ 1.340	1.727	0.0015–0.0035	0.0015–0.0032	0.3401–0.3412	0.3405–0.3412
	T	6-263	4.3	Olds	①	②	210 @ 1.220	1.670	0.0010–0.0027	0.0015–0.0032	0.3425–0.3432	0.3420–0.3427

① Intake: 45
　 Exhaust: 32
② Intake: 44
　 Exhaust: 30

PISTON AND ING SPECIFICATIONS

All measurements are given in inches. To convert inches to metric units, refer to the Metric Information section.

Year	VIN Code	Engine Type/ Disp. (cu. in.)	Liters	Eng. Mfg.	Piston-to-Bore Clearance	Ring Gap Top Compression	Ring Gap Bottom Compression	Ring Gap Oil Control	Ring Side Clearance Top Compression	Ring Side Clearance Bottom Compression	Oil Control
'83-'85	R, 5	4-151	2.5	Pont.	0.0025–0.0033	0.010–0.022	0.020–0.027	0.015–0.005	0.0015–0.0030	0.0015–0.0030	snug
	X, Z	6-173	2.8	Chev.	0.0017–0.0027	0.0098–0.0197	0.0098–0.0197	0.020–0.055	0.0012–0.0028	0.0016–0.0037	0.008 max.

SECTION 6
GENERAL MOTORS—"A" AND "X" BODY
FRONT WHEEL DRIVE CARS

PISTON AND RING SPECIFICATIONS
All measurements are given in inches. To convert inches to metric units, refer to the Metric Information section.

Year	VIN Code	Engine Type/Disp. (cu. in.)	Liters	Eng. Mfg.	Piston-to-Bore Clearance	Ring Gap Top Compression	Ring Gap Bottom Compression	Ring Gap Oil Control	Ring Side Clearance Top Compression	Ring Side Clearance Bottom Compression	Ring Side Clearance Oil Control
'83–'87	E	6-183	3.0	Buick	0.008–0.0020	0.013–0.023	0.013–0.023	0.015–0.035	0.0030–0.0050	0.0030–0.0050	0.0035 max.
	3	6-231	3.8	Buick	—0.020	0.010–0.020	0.010–0.055	0.015–0.0055	0.0030–0.0050	0.0030–0.0050	0.0035 max.
	T	6-263	4.3	Olds	0.0030–0.0040	0.015–0.025	0.015–0.025	0.015–0.055	0.0050–0.0070	0.0030–0.0070	0.001–0.005

CRANKSHAFT AND CONNECTING ROD SPECIFICATIONS
All measurements are given in inches.

Year	VIN Code	Engine No. Cyl. Displacement (cu. in.)	Liters	Eng. Mfg.	Crankshaft Main Brg Journal Dia.	Crankshaft Main Brg Oil Clearance	Crankshaft Shaft End-Play	Thrust on No.	Connecting Rod Journal Diameter	Connecting Rod Oil Clearance	Connecting Rod Side Clearance
'83–'87	R,5	4-151	2.5	Pont.	2.2995–2.3005	0.0005–0.0022	0.0035–0.0085	5	1.9995–2.0005	0.0005–0.0026	0.006–0.022
	X,Z	6-173	2.8	Chev.	2.4937–2.4946	0.0017–0.0030	0.0020–0.0067	3	1.9984–1.9994	0.0014–0.0036	0.006–0.17
	E	6-183	3.0	Buick	2.4990–2.5000	0.0003–0.0018	0.0030–0.0090	2	2.2487–2.2495	0.0005–0.0026	0.006–0.023
	3	6-231	3.8	Buick	2.4995	0.0003–0.0018	0.003–0.011	2	2.2487–2.2495	0.0005–0.0026	0.006–0.023
	T	6-263	4.3	Olds	2.9993–3.0003	①	0.0035–0.0135	4	2.2490–2.2510	0.0003–0.0025	0.008–0.021

① No. 1, 2, 3: 0.0005–0.00021
No. 4: 0.0020–0.0034

CAPACITIES
A-Body

Year	VIN Code	Engine Displacement (cu. in.)	Liters	Eng. Mfg.	Crankcase (qts.) w/filter	Crankcase (qts.) wo/filter	Transaxle Pints 4 speed	Transaxle Pints Auto.	Gas Tank (gals.)	Cooling System (qts.) w/heater	Cooling System (qts.) w/AC
'83–'87	R	4-151	2.5	Pont.	3.0	2.8	6.0	10.0	16.0	9.5	9.75
	X	6-173	2.8	Chev.	4.0	3.8	6.0	10.0	16.0	11.5	11.75
	E	6-183	3.0	Buick	4.0	3.8	—	10.0	16.0	13.5	14.25
	3	6-231	3.8	Buick	4.0 ①	4.0	—	13.0	16.0	12.25	12.75
	T	6-263	4.3	Olds.	6.0	5.5	—	10.0	16.0	13.25	13.75

① Add as necessary to bring to appropriate level.

CAPACITIES
X-Body

Year	Engine No. Cyl. Displacement (cu. in.)	Liters	Engine Crankcase Add 1 qt. for New Filter■	Transmission (pts to Refill After Draining) Manual 3-Speed	Transmission (pts to Refill After Draining) Manual 4-Speed	Transmission (pts to Refill After Draining) Automatic ●	Drive Axel (pts.)	Gasoline Tank (gals.)	Cooling System (qts.) With heater	Cooling System (qts.) With A/C
'83–'85	4-151 Pont.	2.5	3	—	5.9	10.5	①	14	8.3	8.6
	6-173 Chev.	2.8	4	—	5.9	10.5	①	14	10.6	10.8
	6-173 HO Chev.	2.8	4	—	5.9	10.5	①	14	10.6	10.8

① Transaxle refill given with transmission capacity

GENERAL MOTORS—"A" AND "X" BODY
FRONT WHEEL DRIVE CARS

TORQUE SPECIFICATIONS
All reading in ft. lbs.

Year	VIN Code	Engine No. Cyl. Displacement (cu. in.)	Liters	Eng. Mfg.	Cylinder Head Bolts	Rod Bearing Bolts	Main Bearing Bolts	Crankshaft Bolt	Flywheel-to-Crankshaft Bolts	Manifold Intake	Manifold Exhaust
'83–'87	R,5	4-151	2.5	Pont.	85 ③	32	70	200	44	29	44
	X,Z	6-173	2.8	Chev.	70	37	68	75	50	23	25
	E	6-183	3.0	Buick	80	40	100	225	60	13	25
	3	6-231	3.8	Buick	80	40	100	225	60	13	25
	T	6-263	4.3	Olds	①	42	107	225 ②	76	41	29

① All exc. No. 5, 6, 11, 12, 13, 14: 142
  No. 5, 6, 11, 12, 13, 14: 59
② Range: 160–350 ft. lb.
③ 1984–85: 92

Caution: Verify the correct original equipment engine is in the vehicle by referring to the VIN engine code before torquing any bolts.

WHEEL ALIGNTMENT SPECIFICATIONS

Year	Model	Caster* Range (deg.)	Caster* Pref. Setting (deg.)	Camber Range (deg.)	Camber Pref. Setting (deg.)	Toe-In (in.)	Steering Axis (deg.) Inclination
'83–'87	All	0–4P	2P	1/2N–1/2P	0	13/64 out–13/64 in	14.5

*Caster is not adjustable

ELECTRICAL SECTION

For Overhaul Procedures, refer to Unit Repair Section

Charging System

ALTERNATOR

Removal and installation

1. Disconnect the negative battery cable at the battery.
2. Disconnect the wiring from the unit.
3. Loosen the alternator adjusting bolts and remove the drive belt.
4. Remove the alternator attaching bolts and remove the right front splash shield, if equipped. Remove the alternator from the vehicle.
5. Installation is performed in the reverse of the previous steps.

VOLTAGE REGULATOR

Replacement

Refer to the Alternator segment of the Unit Repair Section for alternator disassembly procedures.

Starting System

STARTER

Removal and installation

ALL EXCEPT DIESEL

1. Disconnect the negative battery cable at the battery.

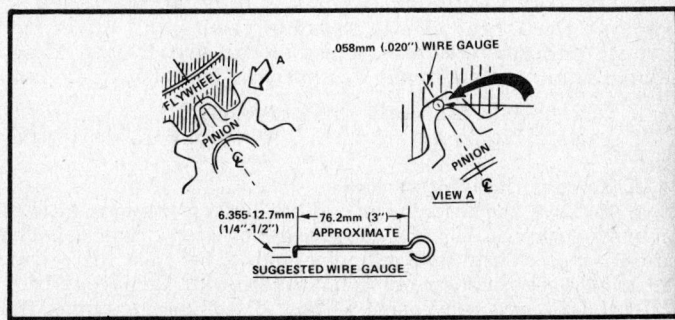

If excessive starter noise is encountered during cranking, check the starter pinion-to-flywheel clearance as shown. Use a screwdriver to mesh the pinion with the flywheel

(© General Motors Corporation)

2. From beneath the vehicle, remove the two starter-to-engine mounting bolts. Carefully lower the starter enough to gain access to the starter wiring.
3. Disconnect the wiring from the starter and remove the unit from the vehicle. Refer to the unit repair section for overhaul procedures.
4. Installation of the starter is performed in the reverse of the previous steps. Remember to install any shims which were present prior to removal.

DIESEL

1. Disconnect the negative battery cable.

SECTION 6

GENERAL MOTORS—"A" AND "X" BODY
FRONT WHEEL DRIVE CARS

2. Install the proper engine holding fixtures, in order to support the vehicle properly.
3. Raise the vehicle on a hoist and support it safely.
4. Remove the left and the center engine mount stud nuts.
5. Move the intermediate shaft seal upward and remove the intermediate shaft to stub shaft pinch bolt. Disconnect the shaft to gear.

NOTE: Failure to disconnect the intermediate shaft from the rack and pinion stud shaft can result in damage to the steering gear and/or intermediate shaft. This damage can cause loss of steering control which could result in a vehicle crash with possible bodily injury.

6. Remove the two front cradle mount bolts and lower the cradle enough to gain access to the flywheel cover bolts.
7. Remove the four flywheel cover bolts. Remove the flywheel cover (two pieces).
8. Remove the starter shield nut at the starter. Remove the flex shield for removal accessibility.
9. Disconnect the wires from the starter assembly. Remove the starter mounting bolts. Remove the starter assembly from the vehicle.
10. Installation is the reverse of removal.

Ignition System

DISTRIBUTOR

Removal and Installation

————————— CAUTION —————————
On Chevrolet V6 models the distributor body is involved in the engine lubricating system. The lubricating circuit to the right-bank valve train can be interrupted by misalignment of the distributor body. See Firing Order illustrations for correct distributor positioning.

NOTE: On 4 cylinder engines, it may be necessary to remove the 2 rear cradle attaching bolts and lower the cradle enough to allow access to the distributor. If so, also disconnect the brake line support from the floor pan.

1. Disconnect the negative battery cable.
2. Tag and disconnect all wires leading from the distributor cap.
3. Remove the ignition coil.
4. Remove the distributor cap by turning the four latches counterclockwise. You may need a stubby screwdriver to get at the latches on the four cylinder engine, because there isn't room between the distributor and the firewall. Remove the distributor cap and set it aside without disconnecting any of the wires.
5. Remove the vacuum hose from the vacuum advance unit.
6. Remove the hold-down clamp and bolt at the base of the V6 distributor. The four cylinder engine has two bolts and a clamp. Remove the outer bolt first, then loosen, but do not remove, the inner bolt. Slide the clamp back and remove it.
7. Before removing the distributor, note the position of the rotor. Scribe a mark on the distributor body indicating the initial position of the rotor.
8. Remove the distributor from the engine. The drive gear on the distributor shaft is helical, and the shaft will rotate slightly as the distributor is removed.

NOTE: Mark the position of the rotor at this second position. Do not crank the engine with the distributor removed.

9. To install the distributor, rotate the distributor shaft until the rotor aligns with the second mark you made (when the shaft stopped moving). Lubricate the drive gear with clean engine oil, then install the distributor into the engine. As the distributor is installed, the rotor should move to the mark you made first, indicating rotor position before the distributor was removed. This will ensure proper timing. If the marks do not align properly, remove the distributor and try again.
10. Install the clamp and hold-down bolt. Tighten them until the distributor can just be moved with a little effort.
11. Connect the ignition wire and tachometer wire, and install the distributor cap. Plug the vacuum advance hose (if so equipped). Set the ignition timing. Connect the vacuum hose.
12. If the engine has been cranked after the distributor has been removed, the following procedure must be used.
13. Turn the crankshaft until the number one cylinder is at the top of its compression stroke. Remove the number one spark plug to feel the compression.
14. Align the timing mark on the vibration damper with the TDC indicator or O mark on the timing scale.
15. With the distributor body oriented in its normal position, hold the rotor pointing toward the number one plug wire location, then turn the rotor approximately 1/8 turn counterclockwise and push the distributor down until it engages the camshaft, rotating the shaft slightly if needed.
16. Press down on the distributor and crank the engine to make sure that the oil pump shaft is engaged.
17. Return the crankshaft to the number one cylinder compression stroke with the timing marks aligned, then tighten the distributor clamp bolt.
18. Install the distributor cap, making sure that the rotor points to the number one terminal. Make sure that the spark plug wires are in their supports and securely connected.
19. Connect the distributor primary wire and the vacuum line if equipped.
20. Start the engine and set the timing.

IGNITION TIMING

Adjustment

Refer to the underhood specifications sticker for a specific timing adjustment procedure for the car you are servicing. When using a timing light, connect an adapter between the number one spark plug and the number one spark plug wire, or use an inductive type pick-up. Do not pierce the plug lead. Once the insulation of the spark plug cable has been broken, voltage will jump to the nearest ground and the spark plug will not fire properly. Always follow tune-up label procedures when adjusting the timing. A magnetic timing probe hole is built in for use with special timing equipment.

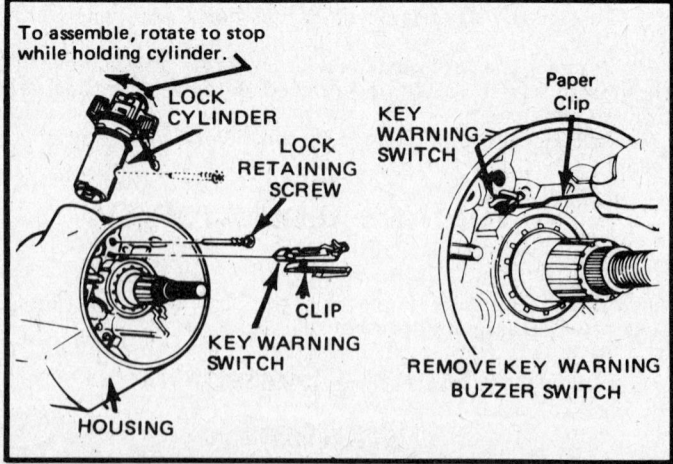

Mounting of the ignition lock cylinder assembly removal of the key warning switch is shown in the inset (General Motors Corporation)

GENERAL MOTORS—"A" AND "X" BODY
FRONT WHEEL DRIVE CARS
SECTION 6

Electrical Controls

IGNITION LOCK

Removal and Installation

1. Place the lock in the Run position. Remove the steering wheel.
2. Remove the lock plate, turn signal switch and buzzer switch.
3. Remove the screw and lock cylinder.

— CAUTION —

If the screw is dropped on removal, it could fall into the column, requiring complete disassembly to retrieve the screw.

4. Rotate the cylinder clockwise to align cylinder key with the keyway in the housing.
5. Push the lock all the way in.
6. Install the screw. Tighten the screw to 14 inch lb. for adjustable columns and 25 inch lb. for standard columns.

IGNITION SWITCH

Removal and installation

1. Lower the steering column; be sure to properly support it.
2. Put the switch in the "Off-Unlocked" position. With the cylinder removed, the rod is in "Lock" when it is in the next to the uppermost detent. "Off-Unlocked" is two detents from the top.
3. Remove the two switch screws and remove the switch assembly.
4. Before installing, place the new switch in "Off-Unlocked" position and make sure the lock cylinder and actuating rod are in "Off-Unlocked" (third detent from the top) position.
5. Install the activating rod into the switch and assemble the switch on the column. Tighten the mounting screws. Use only the specified screws since overlength screws could impair the collapsibility of the column.
6. Reinstall the steering column.

NEUTRAL SAFETY SWITCH

Adjustment

1. After the switch is installed, move the housing towards the low gear position.
2. Shift the gear selector into the park position.
3. The main housing and the housing back should ratchet. This will provide proper switch adjustment.
4. Repeat if necessary.

Removal and Installation

AUTOMATIC TRANSMISSION WITH CONSOLE SHIFT

1. New switches comes with a small plastic alignment pin installed. Leave this pin in place. Position the shifter assembly in Neutral.
2. Remove the old switch and install the replacement, align the pin on the shifter with the slot in the switch, and fasten with the two screws.
3. Move the shifter from the Neutral position. this shears the plastic alignment pin and frees the switch.
4. If the switch is to be adjusted, not replaced insert a 3/32 in. drill bit or similar size pin and align the hole switch. Position switch, adjust as necessary. Remove the pin before shifting from Neutral.

AUTOMATIC TRANSMISSION WITH COLUMN SHIFT

1. Remove wire connectors from the combination back-up and neutral safety switch.
2. Remove two screws attaching the switch to the steering column.
3. Installation is the reverse of removal. To adjust a new switch:

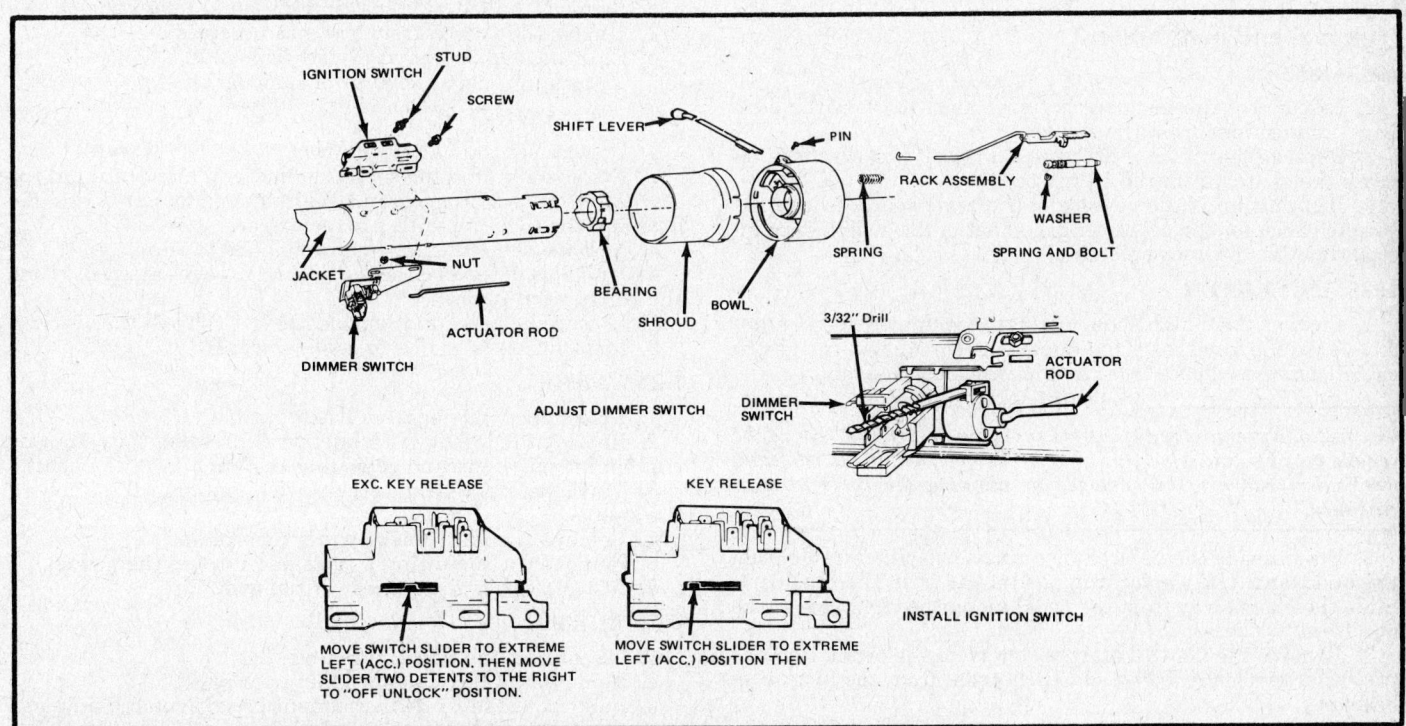

Installation of the ignition switch, showing related parts
(© General Motors Corporation)

6–11

GENERAL MOTORS — "A" AND "X" BODY
FRONT WHEEL DRIVE CARS

a. Position the shift lever in neutral.
b. Loosen the attaching screws. Install a 0.090 in. gauge pin into the outer hole in the switch cover.
c. Rotate the switch until the pin goes into the alignment hole in the inner plastic slide.
d. Tighten the switch to column attaching screws and remove the gauge pin. Torque the screws to 20 inch lbs. maximum.
e. Make sure that the engine starts only in the park and neutral positions.

MECHANICAL NEUTRAL START SYSTEM

Vehicles with this system use a mechanical block rather than an electrical neutral start system. The system only allows the lock cylinder to rotate to the start position when the shift lever is in neutral or park.

STOPLIGHT SWITCH

Adjustment

1. The switch is mounted on the brake pedal bracket.
2. To adjust, depress the pedal and push the switch through the circular retaining clip until it contacts the brake pedal, then pull the pedal up against the internal pedal stop. This places the switch in the correction position within the clip.

CLUTCH START SWITCH

Adjustment

1. Lift the clutch pedal to its uppermost position. Check the operation of the pawl and the quadrant. Make sure that the pawl disengages from the quadrant when the pedal is pulled to this position.
2. Check the quadrant for free rotation in both directions.
3. Depress the clutch pedal slowly several times to set the pawl into mesh with the quadrant teeth.

Removal and Installation

1983–1985

1. Disconnect the negative battery cable. Remove the electrical connections from the switch.
2. Remove the clutch switch retaining bolt and carefully remove the switch from the clutch pedal.
3. Installation is the reverse of the removal procedure. Be sure to check for the proper engagement of the switch once installation has been completed.

1986 AND LATER

1. Support the clutch pedal against the bumper stop in order to release the pawl from the quadrant. Disconnect the clutch cable from the release lever at the transaxle assembly.

--- CAUTION ---
Be careful to prevent the cable from snapping towards the rear of the vehicle possibly causing bodily injury. The quadrant in the adjusting mechanism can also be damaged by allowing the cable to snap rearward.

2. From inside the vehicle, disconnect the clutch cable from the quadrant. Lift the locking pawl away from the quadrant. Slide the cable away from the pedal along the right side of the quadrant.
3. Remove the neutral start switch from the pedal. Remove the pedal pivot nut, bolt and clutch pedal from the mounting bracket.
4. Note the position of the adjusting mechanism, the pawl and quadrant springs. Remove the "E" ring.
5. Inspect the components for tooth damage and replace any components found to be defective.
6. Installation is the reverse of the removal procedure. Check the clutch operation and adjust by lifting the clutch pedal up to allow the mechanism to adjust the cable length. Depress the pedal slowly several times to set the pawl into mesh with the quadrant teeth.

HEADLIGHT SWITCH

Removal and Installation

CITATION

1. Disconnect the negative battery cable.
2. Pull the headlamp switch knob out to the last detent.
3. Remove the spring clip retainer on the knob shaft and remove the shaft.
4. Disconnect all accessory switch connectors.
5. Remove the headlamp switch ferrule nut and push switch forward out of the mounting hole.
6. Lift the switch up and out through the opening above the switch mounting and disconnect the switch electrical connector.
7. Remove the switch from the instrument panel.
8. Installation is the reverse of removal.

CELEBRITY

1. Disconnect the battery ground.
2. Remove the headlamp switch knob.
3. Remove the instrument panel trim pad.
4. Unbolt the switch mounting plate from the instrument panel carrier.
5. Disconnect the wiring from the switch.
6. Remove the switch.
7. Installation is the reverse of removal.

CIERA AND OMEGA

1. Disconnect the negative battery cable.
2. Remove the left side instrument panel trim pad.
3. Unbolt the switch from the instrument panel.
4. Pull the switch rearward and remove it.
5. Installation is the reverse of removal.

6000 AND PHOENIX

1. Disconnect the battery ground.
2. Remove the steering column trim cover and headlight rod and knob by reaching behind the instrument panel and depressing the lock tab with a screwdriver.
3. Remove the left instrument panel trim plate.
4. Unbolt and remove the switch and bracket assembly from the instrument panel.
5. Loosen the bezel and remove the switch from the bracket.
6. Installation is the reverse of removal.

SKYLARK

1. Disconnect the negative battery cable.
2. Remove the light switch knob by depressing the retaining clip behind the knob and removing the knob from the shaft.
3. Turn the sleeve counterclockwise and spin the knob off the shaft.
4. Remove the instrument panel trim plate.
5. Remove the mounting screws and unplug the switch.
6. Installation is the reverse of removal.

CENTURY

1. Disconnect the battery ground.
2. Remove the instrument panel trim plate.
3. Remove the left side instrument panel switch trim panel by removing the three screws and gently rocking the panel out.
4. Remove the three screws and pull the switch straight out.
5. Installation is the reverse of removal.

GENERAL MOTORS—"A" AND "X" BODY
FRONT WHEEL DRIVE CARS
SECTION 6

DIMMER SWITCH

Removal and Installation

1. Disconnect the negative battery cable.
2. Remove the steering wheel. Remove the trim cover.
3. Remove the turn signal switch assembly.
4. Remove the ignition switch stud and screw. Remove the ignition switch.
5. Remove the dimmer switch actuator rod by sliding it from the switch assembly.
6. Remove the dimmer switch bolts and remove the dimmer switch.
7. Installation is the reverse of the removal procedure.
8. Adjust the dimmer switch by depressing the switch slightly and inserting a 3/32 in. drill bit into the adjusting hole. Push the switch up to remove any play and tighten the dimmer switch adjusting screw.

TURN SIGNAL SWITCH

Removal and Installation

1. Remove the steering wheel. Remove the trim cover.
2. Remove the cover off with a suitable tool and lift the cover off the shaft.
3. Position the lockplate compressing tool on the end of the steering shaft and compress the lock plate by turning the shaft nut clockwise. Pry the wire snap ring out of the shaft groove.
4. Remove the tool and lift the lockplate off the shaft.
5. Slip the cancelling cam, upper bearing preload spring, and thrust washer off the shaft.
6. Remove the turn signal lever. Remove the button retaining screw and remove the button, spring and knob.
7. Pull the switch connector out of the mast jacket and tape the upper part to facilitate switch removal. Attach a long piece of wire to the turn signal switch connector. When installing the turn signal switch, feed this wire through the column first, and then use this wire to pull the switch connector into position. On tilt wheels, place the turn signal and shifter housing in low position and remove the harness cover.
8. Remove the three switch mounting screws. Remove the switch by pulling it straight up while guiding the wiring harness cover through the column.
9. Install the replacement switch by working the connector and cover down through the housing and under the bracket. On tilt models, the connector is worked down through the housing, under the bracket, and then the cover is installed on the harness.
10. Install the switch mounting screws and the connector on the mast jacket bracket. Install the column-to-dash trim plate.
11. Install the flasher knob and the turn signal lever.
12. With the turn signal lever in neutral and the flasher knob out, slide the thrust washer, upper bearing preload spring, and cancelling cam onto the shaft.
13. Position the lock plate on the shaft and press it down until a new snap ring can be inserted in the shaft grove. Always use a new snap ring when assembling.
14. Install the cover and the steering wheel.

HORN SWITCH

Removal and Installation
STANDARD STEERING WHEEL

1. Disconnect the negative battery cable.
2. Remove the screws attaching the horn pad assembly from the underside of the steering wheel. Lift the horn pad from the steering wheel.
3. Disconnect the horn contact terminal from the pad. If the contact terminal comes out of or is removed from the turn sig-

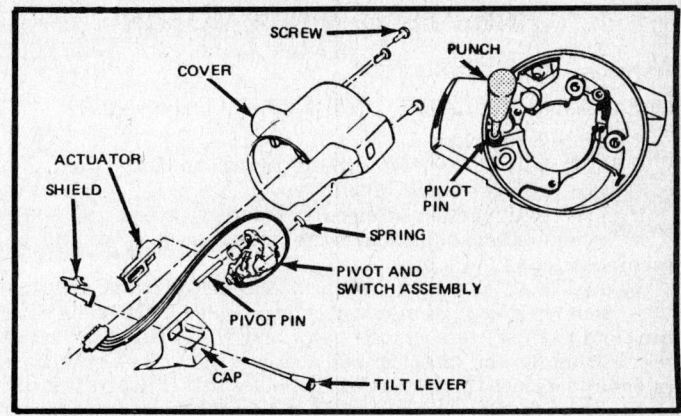

Windshield wiper switch and related components—models with tilt wheel
(© General Motors Corporation)

nal cancelling cam tower, it can be reinstalled by pushing it into the tower and rotating the steering wheel clockwise to lock it into position.

4. Installation is the reverse of the removal procedure. Connect the negative battery cable.

SPORT STEERING WHEEL

1. Disconnect the negative battery cable.
2. Remove the center ornament from the steering wheel.
3. Remove the steering wheel nut and retainer.
4. Remove the horn switch and insulator assembly.
5. Remove the switch retainer screw and separate the switch from the insulator.
6. Installation is the reverse of the removal procedure. Connect the negative battery cable.

WINDSHIELD WIPER SWITCH

Removal and Installation
DASH MOUNTED TYPE

1. Disconnect the negative battery cable.
2. Remove the steering wheel and turn signal switch. It may be necessary to first remove the column mounting nuts and remove the four bracket-to-mast jacket screws, then separate the bracket from the mast jacket to allow the connector clip on the ignition switch to be pulled out of the column assembly.
3. Tag and disconnect the washer/wiper switch lower connector.
4. Remove the screws attaching the column housing to the mast jacket. Be sure to note the position of the dimmer switch actuator rod for reassembly in the same position. Remove the column housing and switch as an assembly.

NOTE: Certain Tilt and Travel columns are equipped with a removable plastic cover on the column housing. This provides access to the wiper switch without removing the entire column housing.

5. Turn upside down and use a drift to remove the pivot pin from the washer/wiper switch. Remove the switch.
6. Place the switch into position in the housing. Install the pivot pin.
7. Position the housing onto the mast jacket and attach by installing the screws. Install the dimmer switch actuator rod in the same position as noted when removed. Check switch operation.
8. Reconnect lower end of the switch assembly.
9. Install remaining components in reverse order of removal. Attach column mounting bracket securely.

6-13

SECTION 6
GENERAL MOTORS—"A" AND "X" BODY
FRONT WHEEL DRIVE CARS

WINDSHIELD WIPER MOTOR
Removal and Installation
CITATION, SKYLARK, OMEGA AND PHOENIX
1. Remove the wiper arms.
2. Remove the lower windshield reveal molding, the front cowl panel and the cowl screen.
3. Disconnect the motor electrical leads.
4. Loosen, but do not remove, the transmission drive link attaching nuts to the motor crank arm.
5. Disconnect the drive link from the motor crank arm.
6. Remove the three motor attaching bolts. On models with air conditioning, remove the bolts and while supporting the motor, remove the motor crank arm nut using lock-ring type pliers and a closed end wrench. The motor attaching bolts must be removed first to avoid damage to the nylon gear inside the motor. On all models, rotate the motor up and out to remove.
7. Reverse the procedure to install.

CELEBRITY, CENTURY, CIERA AND 6000
1. Raise the hood.
2. Remove the air intake grille.
3. Loosen the wiper linkage to drive arm attaching nuts.
4. Remove the transmission link from the drive arm.
5. Disconnect the wiring and hoses from the motor.
6. Unbolt and remove the motor.
7. Installation is the reverse of removal.

WIPER LINKAGE/TRANSMISSION
Removal and Installation
CITATION, SKYLARK, OMEGA AND PHOENIX
1. Remove the lower windshield reveal moulding, wiper arms and the lower front cowl panel.
2. Loosen, but do not remove, the drive link-to-crank arm attaching nuts.
3. Remove the transmission-to-cowl panel attaching screws. Remove the wiper transmission.
4. Installation is performed in the reverse of the previous steps. Torque the attaching bolts to 27–36 inch lbs.

CELEBRITY, CENTURY, CIERA AND 6000
1. Raise the hood and remove the wiper arm and blade assemblies.
2. Loosen, but do not remove, the drive link-to-crank arm attaching nuts.
3. Remove the air intake grille and the cowl vent screen.
4. Disconnect the motor drive link(s) from the motor crank arm.
5. Remove the transmission-to-body attaching screws.
6. Remove the wiper transmission(s).
7. Installation is performed in the reverse of the previous steps. When installing the transmission, position the assembly into the plenum chamber through the upper shroud panel openings.

Instrument Panel
INSTRUMENT CLUSTER
Removal and Installation
CITATION
1. Disconnect the negative battery cable.
2. Remove the radio knobs, shaft nuts, and the clock knob.
3. Remove the instrument cluster bezel trim plate attaching screws. Pull the bezel slightly rearward.
4. Remove the headlamp shaft and knob.
5. Disconnect the accessory switch wiring.
6. Remove the bezel.
7. Remove the four screws holding the instrument cluster to the instrument panel.
8. Disconnect the shift indicator cable from the steering column shift bowl on models with automatic transaxle.
9. Pull the cluster towards you and disconnect the speedometer cable and instrument electrical connections.
10. Remove the instrument cluster. Installation is the reverse.

OMEGA
1. Remove the steering column trim cover.
2. Lower the steering column.
3. Remove the four screws holding the instrument panel trim cover to the panel.
4. Pull the trim cover rearward and disconnect the switch wiring, and the remote control mirror cable, if equipped. Remove the trim panel.
5. Remove the four screws holding the instrument cluster to the panel.

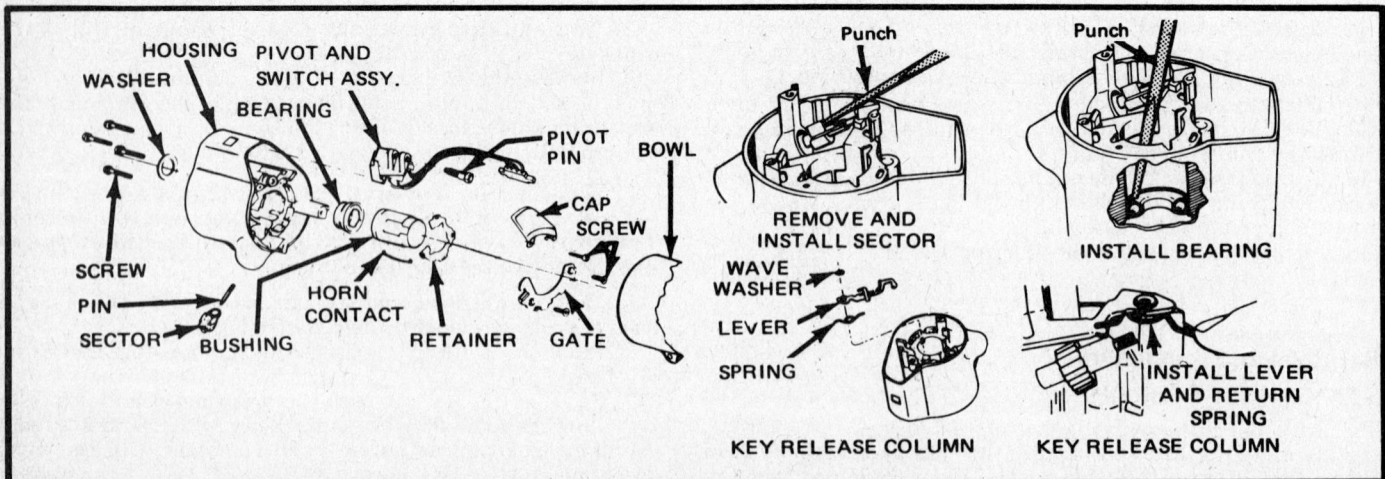

Windshield wiper switch and related components—models without tilt wheel
(© General Motors Corporation)

GENERAL MOTORS—"A" AND "X" BODY
FRONT WHEEL DRIVE CARS

6. Disconnect the shift indicator cable from the steering column shift bowl, if equipped with an automatic transaxle.
7. Pull the cluster towards you and disconnect the speedometer cable and electrical wiring.
8. Remove the instrument cluster. Installation is the reverse.

PHOENIX
1. Disconnect the negative battery cable.
2. Remove the speedometer cluster trim plate.
3. Remove the screws attaching the steering column trim cover to the instrument panel and remove the trim cover.
4. Remove the four cluster attaching screws.
5. With automatic transaxle, disconnect the shift indicator cable, marking the cable location on the steering column shift bowl prior to disconnecting.
6. Disconnect the speedometer cable and pull the cluster toward you. Disconnect the electrical wiring from the back of the cluster and remove the cluster. Installation is the reverse.

SKYLARK
1. Disconnect the negative battery cable.
2. Remove the radio and accessory switch knobs.
3. Remove the instrument panel trim plate.
4. With automatic transaxle, disconnect the shift indicator cable from the steering column shift bowl.
5. Remove the four cluster attaching screws.
6. Disconnect the speedometer cable and electrical wiring from the back of the cluster. Remove the cluster. Installation is the reverse.

CENTURY
1. Disconnect the battery ground.
2. Disconnect the speedometer cable and pull it through the firewall.
3. Remove the left side hush panel by removing the three screws and one nut.
4. Remove the right side hush panel by removing the five screws and two nuts.
5. Remove the shift indicator cable clip.
6. Remove the steering column trim plate.
7. Put the gear selector in LOW, remove the nine retaining screws and gently pull out the instrument panel trim plate.
8. Disconnect the parking brake cable at the lever by pushing it forward and sliding it out of its slot.
9. Unbolt and lower the steering column.
10. Remove the gauge cluster by removing the four screws and pulling the cluster out far enough to disconnect any wires, then pull the cluster out.
11. Installation is the reverse of removal.

CELEBRITY
1. Disconnect battery ground cable.
2. Remove instrument panel hush panel.
3. Remove vent control housing (heater only vehicles).
4. On non A/C cars remove steering column trim cover screws and lower cover with vent cables attached. On A/C equipped vehicles, remove trim cover attaching screws and remove cover.
5. Remove instrument cluster trim pad as outlined in this section.
6. Remove ash tray, retainer and fuse block, disconnect wires as necessary.
7. Remove headlamp switch know and instrument panel trim plate and disconnect electrical connectors of any accessory switches in trim plate.
8. Remove cluster assembly and disconnect speedometer cable. PRNDL and cluster electrical connectors.
9. Installation is the reverse of removal.

CIERA
1. Remove left instrument panel trim pad.
2. Remove instrument panel cluster trim cover.
3. Disconnect speedometer cable at transmission or cruise control transducer if equipped.
4. Remove steering column trim cover.
5. Disconnect shift indicator clip from steering column shift bowl.
6. Remove 4 screws attaching cluster assembly to instrument panel.
7. Pull assembly out far enough to reach behind cluster and disconnect speedometer cable.
8. Remove cluster assembly.
9. Installation is the reverse of removal.

6000
1. Disconnect the negative battery cable.
2. Remove the center and left hand lower instrument panel trim plate.
3. Remove the screws holding the instrument cluster to the instrument panel carrier.
4. Remove the instrument cluster lens to gain access to the speedometer head and gauges.
5. Remove right-hand and left-hand hush panels, steering column trim cover and disconnect parking brake cable and vent cables, if so equipped.
6. Remove steering column retaining bolts and drop steering column.
7. Disconnect temperature control cable, inner to outer A/C wire harness and inner to outer A/C vacuum harness, if so equipped.
8. Disconnect chassis harness behind left lower instrument panel and ECM connectors behind glove box. Disconnect instrument panel harness at cowl.
9. Remove center instrument panel trim plate and remove radio if so equipped.
10. Disconnect neutral switch and brake light switch.
11. Remove six upper instrument panel retaining screws.
12. Remove lower instrument panel retaining screws, nuts and bolts.
13. Pull instrument panel assembly out far enough to disconnect ignition switch, headlight dimmer switch and turn signal switch. Disconnect all other accessory wiring, and vacuum lines necessary to remove instrument panel assembly.
14. Remove instrument panel assembly with wiring harness.
15. Installation is the reverse of removal.

SPEEDOMETER

Removal and Installation
CITATION
1. Disconnect the negative battery cable.
2. Remove the instrument panel trim pad.
3. Remove the screws that attach the cluster lens to the cluster assembly. Remove the cluster lens and the speedometer faceplate.
4. Remove the screws that hold the speedometer to the instrument cluster. Pull the speedometer rearward and disconnect the speedometer cable.
5. Pull the speedometer backward out of the instrument panel.
6. Installation is the reverse of the removal procedure.

OMEGA
1. Disconnect the negative battery cable.
2. Remove the instrument cluster assembly.
3. Remove the screws that hold the cluster lens to the cluster assembly. Remove the lens.
4. Remove the screws on the reverse side of the cluster assembly.

SECTION 6
GENERAL MOTORS—"A" AND "X" BODY
FRONT WHEEL DRIVE CARS

5. Pull the speedometer from the cluster assembly.
6. Remove the speedometer cable clip and disconnect the speedometer cable.
7. Remove the speedometer.
8. Installation is the reverse of the removal procedure.

PHOENIX
1. Disconnect the negative battery cable.
2. Remove the steering column trim cover. Remove the speedometer cluster trim plate.
3. Remove the speedometer cluster attaching screws.
4. Mark the location of the shift indicator detent cable on the steering column shift bowl. Remove the shift indicator detent cable.
5. Remove the speedometer cable clip and disconnect the speedometer cable.
6. Tag and disconnect the wiring harness from the speedometer cluster and remove the cluster with the speedometer.
7. Installation is the reverse of the removal procedure.

SKYLARK
1. Disconnect the negative battery cable.
2. Remove the instrument cluster housing screws. Remove the instrument cluster.
3. Remove the screws holding the lens to the speedometer. Remove the speedometer lens.
4. Remove the screws holding the speedometer head to the instrument housing. Remove the speedometer assembly.
5. Disconnect the speedometer cable by pushing in on the retaining clip and pulling back on the cable.
6. Installation is the reverse of the removal procedure.

CENTURY
1. Disconnect the negative battery cable.
2. Remove the left hand trim plate.
3. Remove the instrument cluster housing screws. Remove the instrument cluster. If the vehicle is equipped with tilt-wheel steering, working room can be gained by removing the tilt-wheel cover.
4. Remove the speedometer lens screws and remove the speedometer lens.
5. Disconnect the speedometer cable by pushing in on the retaining clip and pulling back on the cable.
6. Remove the screws holding the speedometer to the instrument and remove the speedometer assembly.
7. Installation is the reverse of the removal procedure.

CELEBRITY
1. Disconnect the negative battery cable.
2. Remove the cluster trim panel.
3. Remove the cluster lens screws. Remove the cluster lens.
4. Remove the speedometer to cluster attaching screws. Remove the speedometer from the instrument cluster.
5. Disconnect the speedometer cable and remove the speedometer assembly.
6. Installation is the reverse of the removal procedure.

CIERA
1. Disconnect the negative battery cable.
2. Remove the instrument cluster assembly.
3. Remove the vehicle speed sensor screw from the rear of the speedometer. Remove the vehicle speed sensor if equipped.
4. Remove the speedometer lens screws and remove the speedometer lens. Remove the bezel.
5. Remove the screw that hold the speedometer to the instrument cluster.
6. Remove the speedometer head by pulling forward. Disconnect the speedometer cable by prying gently on the retainer and pulling the speedometer cable out of the speedometer head.
7. Installation is the reverse of the removal procedure.

6000
1. Disconnect the negative battery cable.
2. Remove the center and left hand lower instrument panel trim plate.
3. Remove the screws holding the instrument cluster to the instrument panel carrier.
4. Remove the instrument cluster lens to gain access to the speedometer head and gauges.
5. Remove right-hand and left-hand hush panels, steering column trim cover and disconnect parking brake cable and vent cables, if so equipped.
6. Remove steering column retaining bolts and drop steering column.
7. Disconnect temperature control cable, inner to outer A/C wire harness and inner to outer A/C vacuum harness, if so equipped.
8. Disconnect chassis harness behind left lower instrument panel and ECM connectors behind glove box. Disconnect instrument panel harness at cowl.
9. Remove center instrument panel trim plate and remove radio if so equipped.
10. Disconnect neutral switch and brake light switch.
11. Remove six upper instrument panel retaining screws.
12. Remove lower instrument panel retaining screws, nuts and bolts.
13. Pull instrument panel assembly out far enough to disconnect ignition switch, headlight dimmer switch and turn signal switch. Disconnect all other accessory wiring, and vacuum lines necessary to remove instrument panel assembly.
14. Remove instrument panel assembly with wiring harness.
15. Installation is the reverse of removal.

SPEEDOMETER CABLE
Removal and Installation
1. Disconnect the negative battery cable.
2. Remove the steering column trim plate.
3. Remove the speedometer cable casing from the head of the speedometer.
4. Remove the cable from the transaxle assembly.
5. Install the new cable making sure that the bend radius does not exceed 6 in.
6. Installation is the reverse of the removal procedure.

ELECTRICAL COMPONENT LOCATION
Computer
The electronic module is located on the right side of the vehicle. It is positioned under the instrument panel. In order to gain access to the electronic control module, it will be necessary to first remove the trim panel.

Convenience Center and Various Relays
The convenience center is a swing down unit located on the underside of the instrument panel near the fuse panel. It provides a central location for various relays, hazard flasher units and buzzers. All units are easily replaced with plug-in modules.

Turn Signal Flasher
The turn signal flasher is located behind the instrument panel near the steering column. In order to gain access to the component it may first be necessary to remove the under dash padding panel.

Vehicle Speed Sensor
The optic head portion of the vehicle speed sensor (VSS) is located in the speedometer frame. A reflective blade is attached

GENERAL MOTORS—"A" AND "X" BODY
FRONT WHEEL DRIVE CARS
SECTION 6

Servo Test Con't.

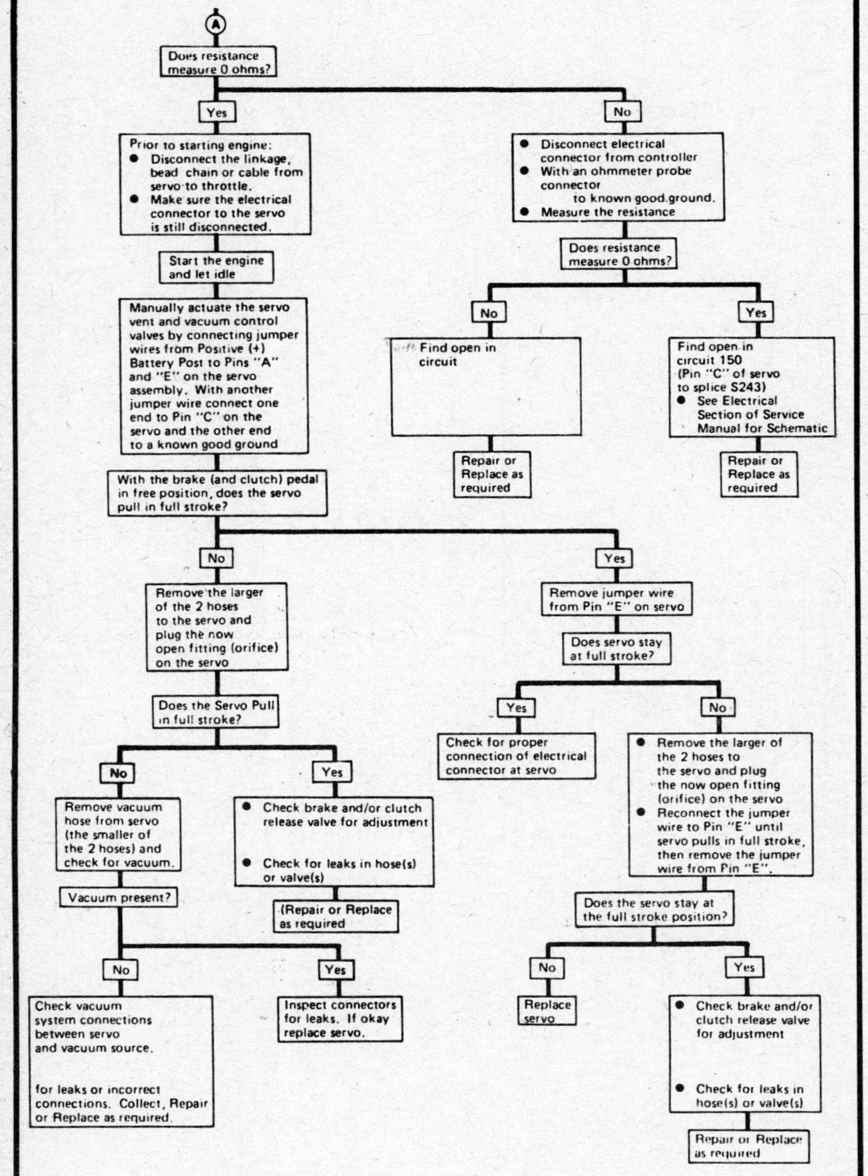

Servo Test

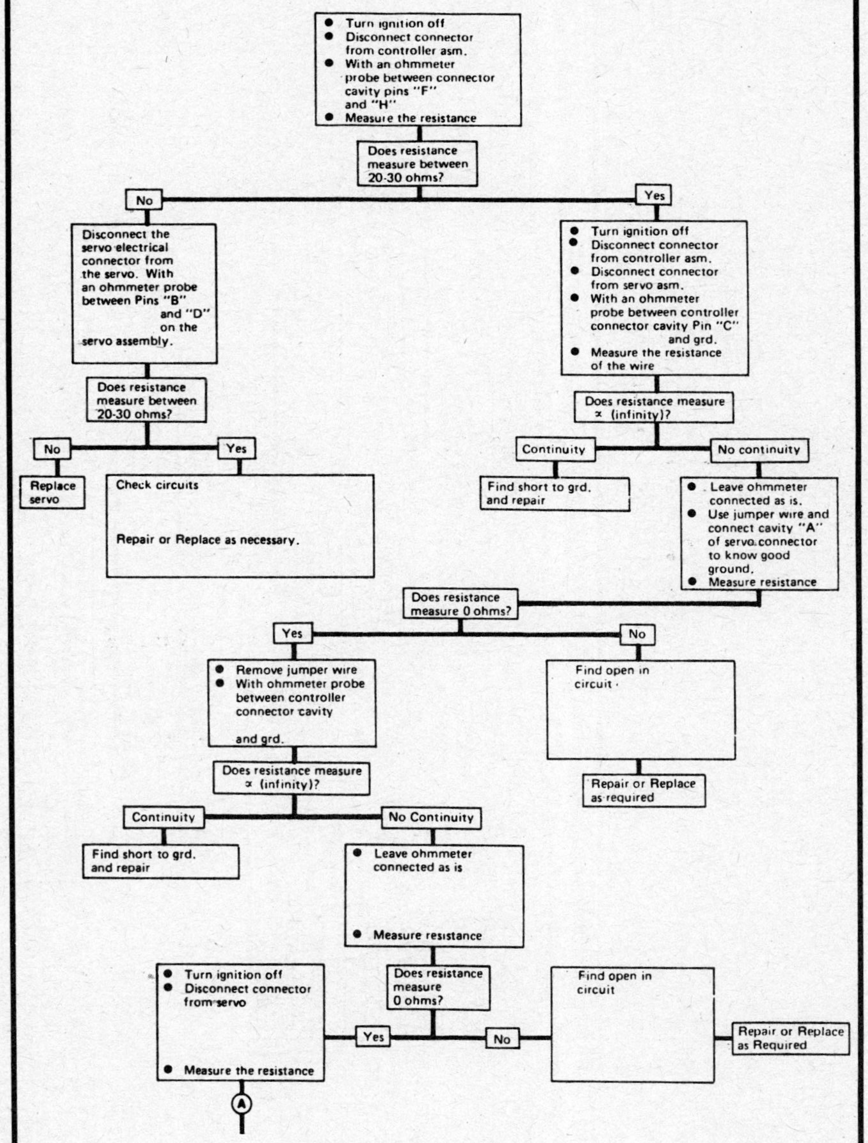

SECTION 6: GENERAL MOTORS — "A" AND "X" BODY
FRONT WHEEL DRIVE CARS

Cruise Control Diagnosis

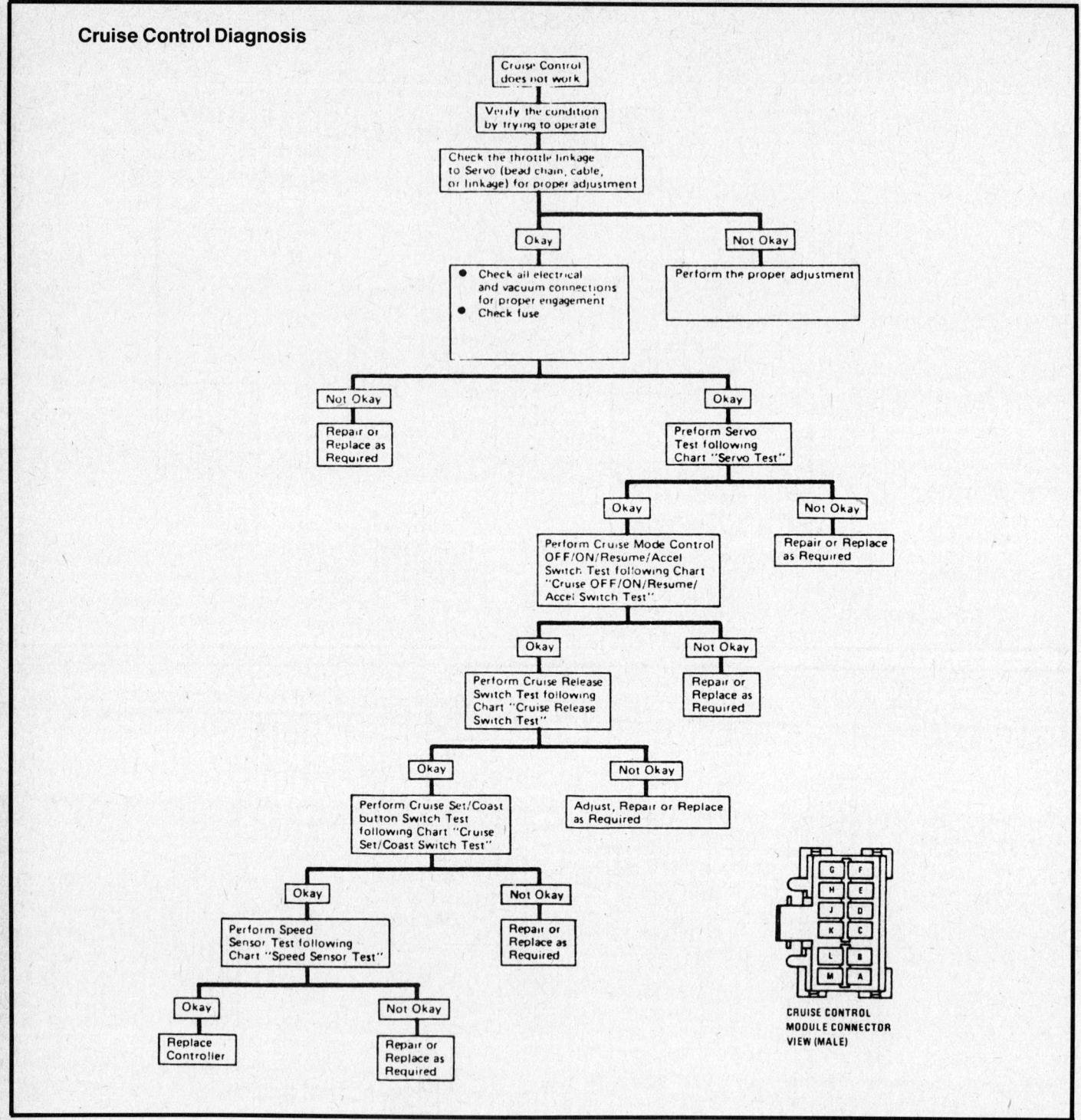

GENERAL MOTORS—"A" AND "X" BODY
FRONT WHEEL DRIVE CARS
SECTION 6

to the speedometer cable/head assembly. The reflective blade spins, with its blades passing through a light beam from a LED in the optic head. As each blade enters the reflective light beam, light is reflected back to a photocell in the optic head causing a low power speed signal to be sent to a buffer for amplification. This signal is then sent to the controller.

CRUISE CONTROL

Adjustments

1. Adjust the throttle lever to the idle position with the engine off. On models equipped with the idle control solenoid, the solenoid must be de-energized.
2. Pull the servo assembly end of the cable towards the servo blade.
3. Line up the holes in the servo blade with the cable pin. Install the cable pin.
4. On vehicles equipped with the 2.8 liter engine, it will be necessary to position the ball of the chain assembly into the chain retainer. This will allow a slight slack to occur not to exceed one ball diameter. Remove the excess chain outside of the chain retainer.

Troubleshooting

Before starting any troubleshooting procedures, a brief visual inspection should be made of the system components. The following components should be inspected:
 a. vacuum hoses; replace any that are kinked, rotted or deteriorated.
 b. servo chain or rod; should be adjusted for minimum slack.
 c. throttle linkage/cable; make sure that the cable or linkage is not binding.
 d. if cruise control is non-operable, inspect the radio fuse, replace as required.

Electrical Circuit Protectors

FUSIBLE LINKS

There are several locations where fusible links can be found. They are located ahead of the left hand front shock tower, near the positive battery connection or at the starter solenoid near the front of the engine.

FUSE PANEL

The fuse panel is located on the left side of the vehicle. It is under the instrument panel assembly. In order to gain access to the fuse panel, it may be necessary to first remove the under dash padding.

COOLING AND HEATING SYSTEMS

WATER PUMP

Removal and Installation

151 (2.5L) AND 173 (2.8L) ENGINES

1. Disconnect the negative battery cable.
2. Remove the drive belts for the accessories.
3. Disconnect the coolant hoses from the pump.
4. Remove the pump mounting bolts. Remove the water pump.

To install
1. If a new pump is being installed, transfer the pulley from the old pump to the new one.
2. No gasket is used. Clean the mating surfaces and apply a 1/8 in. bead of RTV silicone sealer to the water pump sealing surface, and around the mounting stud on the V6.
3. While the sealer is still wet, install the pump onto the engine. Tighten the bolts to 6 ft. lbs. The remainder of the installation is the reverse of the removal procedure. Adjust the drive belts to have no more than 1/2 in. of play on their longest span between pulleys.

183 (3.0L) AND 231 (3.8L) ENGINES

1. Disconnect the negative battery cable.
2. Remove the drive belts from the engine.
3. Remove the water pump attaching bolts.
4. Remove the engine support strut.
5. Position a floor jack under the front crossmember of the cradle. Raise the jack until the front of the vehicle begins to rise.
6. Remove the two front body mount bolts, cushions and retainers. Remove the cushions from the bolts. Thread the body mount bolts into the cage nuts so that the bolts restrain movement of the cradle.
7. Slowly lower the floor jack until the cradle crossmember contact the body mount bolt retainers.

NOTE: Watch and correct any interference between lines, pipes, hoses, cables, etc., while the crossmember is being lowered. When replacing the water pump on a vehicle equipped with the V6 engine, the timing cover must be clamped to the cylinder block prior to tremving the water pump bolts. Certain bolts holding the water pump pass through the front cover, and when removed, may allow the front cover to pull away from the cylinder block, breaking the seal. This may or may not be readily apparent and if left undetected, could allow coolant to enter the crankcase.

8. Remove the water pump from the engine
9. Installation is the reverse of the removal procedure.

DIESEL ENGINE

1. Drain the radiator and disconnect the lower radiator hose from the water pump.
2. Disconnect the heater return hose at the water pump. Remove the heater water return pipe-to-manifold bolt and position the pipe out of the way.
3. On models equipped with air-conditioning, remove the vacuum pump drive belt.
4. Remove the serpentine drive belt.
5. Remove the alternator, A/C compressor, and/or the vacuum pump brackets.
6. Unbolt and remove the water pump unit.

NOTE: If required, the water pump pulley must be removed using a puller.

7. Installation is the reverse of the removal procedure. Coat the new water pump gasket with a thin coat of sealer before installation.

ELECTRIC COOLING FAN

Removal and Installation

1. Disconnect the negative battery cable.
2. Tag and disconnect the electrical connector from the fan motor and fan frame.

6-19

SECTION 6: GENERAL MOTORS—"A" AND "X" BODY
FRONT WHEEL DRIVE CARS

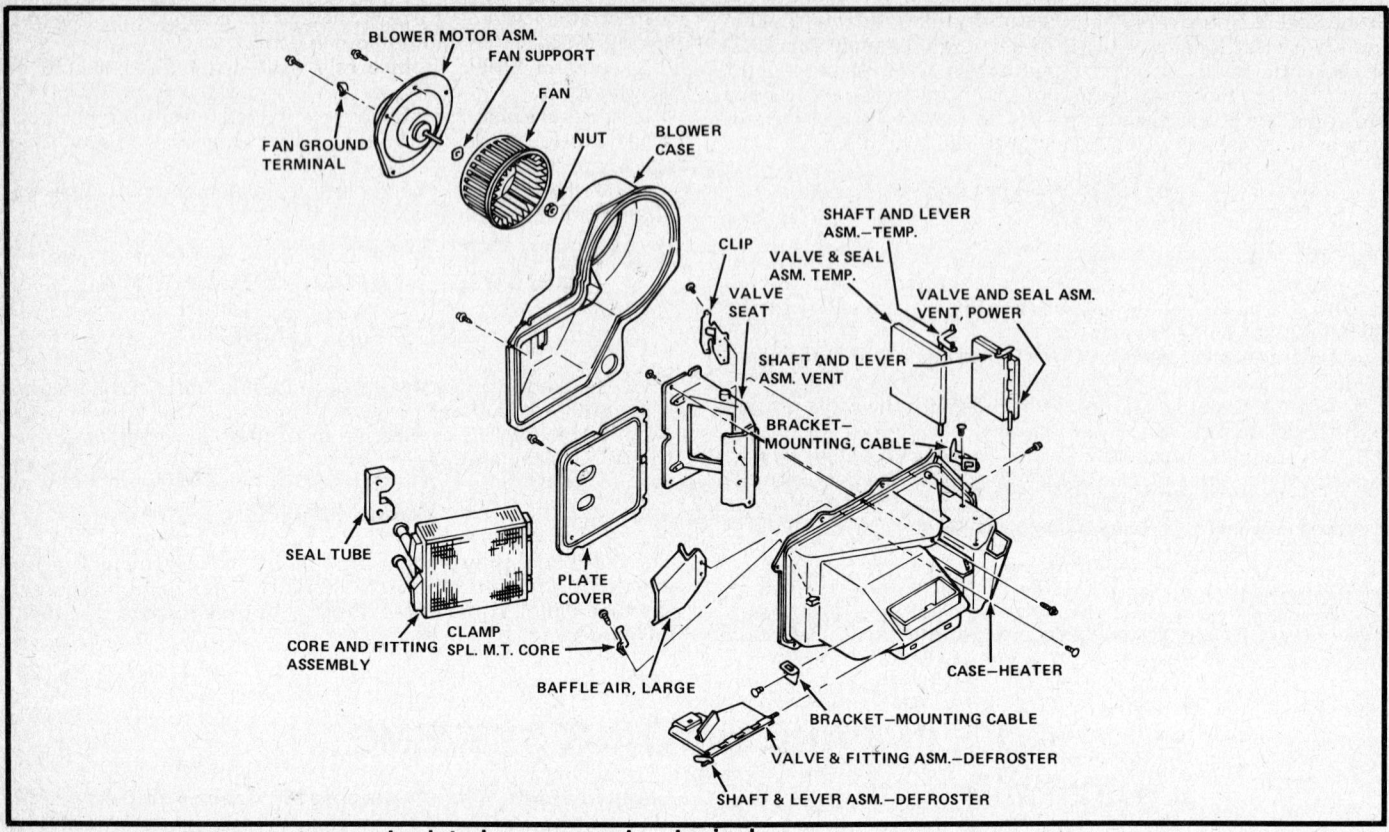

Heater core, blower motor, and related components—typical
(© General Motors Corporation)

3. Remove the fan frame to radiator support bolts.
4. Remove the fan and frame assembly from the vehicle.
5. Installation is the reverse of the removal procedure.

BLOWER MOTOR

Removal and Installation

1. Disconnect the negative battery cable.
2. Tag and disconnect the blower motor electrical leads.
3. Remove the motor retaining bolts and remove the blower motor. On models equipped with the diesel engine it may be necessary to remove the engine support strut.
4. Installation is the reverse of the removal procedure.

HEATER CORE

Removal and Installation
MODELS WITHOUT A/C

1. Drain the cooling system.
2. Remove the heater inlet and outlet hoses.
3. Remove the radio noise suppression strap.
4. Remove the core cover retaining screws. Remove the cover.
5. Remove the core.
6. Installation is the reverse of the removal procedure.

CITATION, SKYLARK, OMEGA AND PHOENIX WITH A/C

1. Drain the cooling system.
2. Remove the heater hoses from the core.
3. Remove the heat duct and heater, the heater case side cover from the instrument panel.
4. Remove the core retaining clamps. Remove the inlet and outlet tube support clamps.
5. Remove the heater core.
6. Installation is the reverse of the removal procedure.

CELEBRITY, CENTURY, CIERA AND 6000 WITH A/C

1. Drain the cooling system.
2. On the diesel, raise and support the vehicle safely.
3. Disconnect the heater hoses at the heater core.
4. On the diesel, remove the instrument panel lower sound absorber.
5. Remove the heater duct and the lower side covers.
6. Remove the lower heater outlet.
7. Remove the two housing cover-to-air valve housing clips.
8. Remove the housing cover bolts. Remove the housing cover.
9. Remove the core retaining straps. Remove the core tubing retainers. Lift out the heater core.
10. Installation is the reverse of the removal procedure.

TEMPERATURE CONTROL/BLOWER SWITCH

Removal and Installation

1. Disconnect the negative battery cable.
2. Remove the necessary trim panels in order to gain access to the control head retaining screws.
3. Remove the control head retaining screws. Pull out and disconnect the cables, vacuum lines and electrical connections from the control head.
4. Remove the control head assembly.
5. Installation is the reverse of the removal procedure.

GENERAL MOTORS—"A" AND "X" BODY
FRONT WHEEL DRIVE CARS
SECTION 6

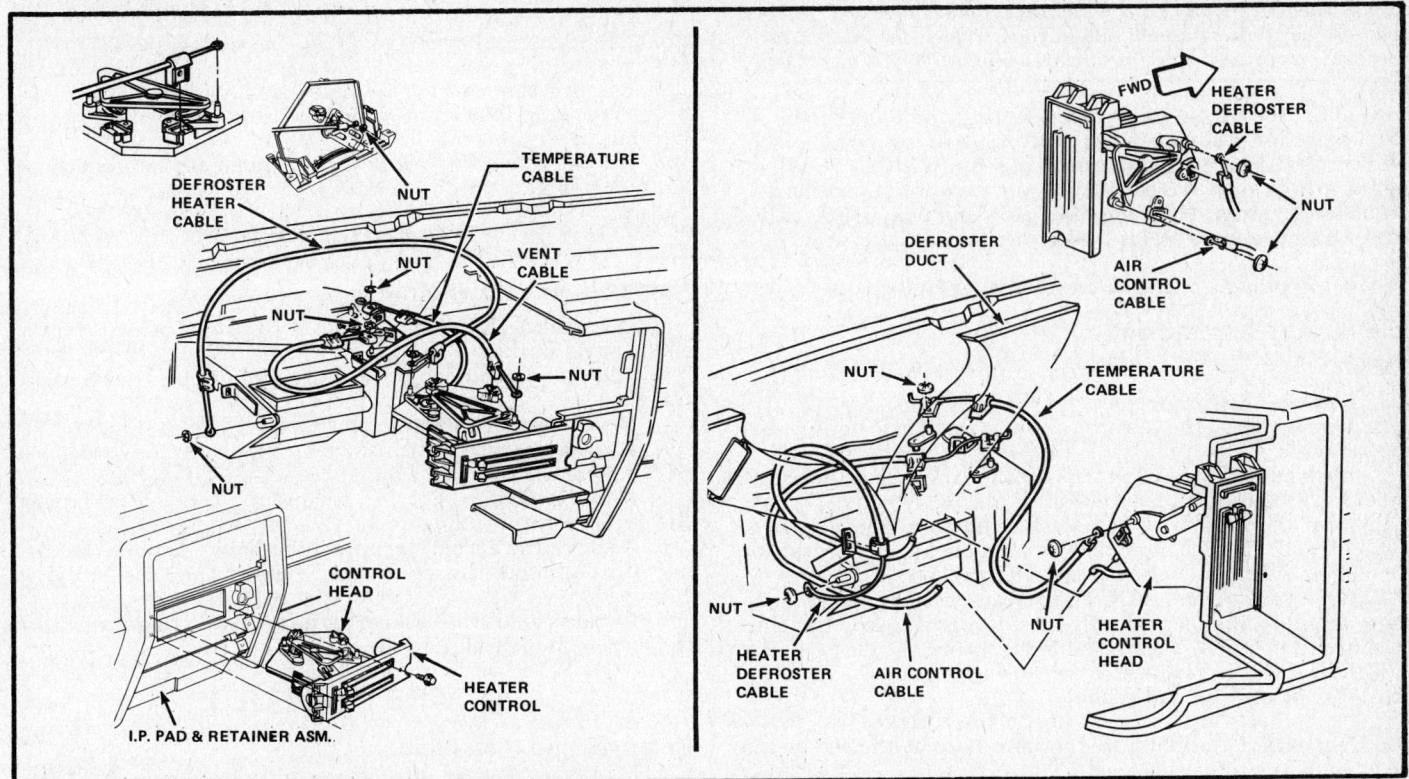

Mounting and cable routing of the horizontal-style heater A/C control unit
(© General Motors Corporation)

Mounting and cable routing of the vertical-style heater A/C control unit
(© General Motors Corporation)

FUEL SYSTEM

FUEL PUMP

Removal and Installation

MECHANICAL PUMP

1. Disconnect the negative battery cable at the battery and raise the vehicle.
2. On V6 models, remove the shields and the oil filter if necessary in order to gain working clearance.
3. Disconnect the hoses from the pump.
4. Loosen the fuel line at the carburetor and disconnect the line from the pump.
5. Remove the attaching bolts and the pump.
6. Installation is performed in the reverse of the previous steps. Tighten the attaching bolts evenly and alternately. Check for leakage after the engine is started.

ELECTRIC PUMP

1. Remove the fuel pump fuse from the fuse panel.
2. Start the engine and let it run until all fuel in the line is used.
3. Crank the starter an additional three seconds to relieve any residual pressure.
4. Disconnect the negative battery cable.
5. Drain the fuel tank.
6. Disconnect wiring from the tank.
7. Remove the ground wire retaining screw from under the body.
8. Disconnect all hoses from the tank.
9. Support the tank on a jack and remove the retaining strap nuts.
10. Lower the tank and remove it.
11. Remove the fuel gauge/pump retaining ring using a spanner wrench such as tool J-24187 or equivalent.
12. Remove the gauge unit and the pump.
13. Installation is the reverse of removal. Always replace the O-ring under the gauge/pump retaining ring.

DIESEL PUMP

1. Disconnect the negative battery cable.
2. Remove the air cleaner.
3. Unplug the leads from the pump assembly.
4. Disconnect the fuel lines from the pump.
5. Remove the pump mounting bracket from the pump. Remove the pump from the vehicle.
6. Installation is the reverse of removal.

CARBURETOR IDLE MIXTURE

Refer to the Carburetor segment of the Unit which has a mixture control solenoid.

—————— CAUTION ——————

Idle mixture screws have been preset at the factory and sealed. Idle mixture should be adjusted only in the case of major carburetor overhaul, throttle body replacement or high emissions as determined by official inspections. Adjusting mixture by other than the following meth-

SECTION 6
GENERAL MOTORS—"A" AND "X" BODY
FRONT WHEEL DRIVE CARS

od may violate Federal and/or California or other state or Provincial laws. Because of the sealed idle mixture screws, the idle mixture, checking procedure requires artificial enrichment by adding propane.

NOTE: Before checking or resetting the carburetor as the cause of poor engine performance or rough idle, check ignition system including distributor, timing, spark plugs and wires. Check air cleaner, evaporative emission system, EFE system, PCV system, EGR valve and engine compression. Also inspect intake manifold vacuum hose gaskets and connections for leaks and check torques of carburetor mounting bolts/nuts.

Idle Mixture Adjustment
E2SE

1. Remove the carburetor.
2. Remove the idle mixture screw plugs, then lightly seal the screws.
3. Back out the screws 5 turns each for the four cylinder engine, 1 1/2 turns each for the V6.
4. Remove the idle air bleed screw plug from the air horn. Lightly seat the air bleed screws, then back it out 3 turns for the four cylinder engine, 5 turns for the V6.
5. Remove the vent stack and screen assembly in order to gain access to the lean mixture screw. Lightly seat the lean mixture screw, then back it out 2 1/2 turns.
6. Reinstall the carburetor on the engine, but DO NOT install the air cleaner and gasket.
7. Disconnect the bowl vent line at the carburetor.
8. Disconnect the plug and vacuum hose at the tee in the bowl vent line (if so equipped).
9. Disconnect the canister purge and EGR line at the carburetor, then plug the carburetor fitting.

NOTE: Steps 10 and 11 pertain only to V6 engines.

10. Remove the thermal vacuum switch (for the secondary vacuum break) from the air cleaner.
11. Disconnect the vacuum hose which connects the thermal vacuum switch to the thermostatic air cleaner sensor, then cap the open port of the thermal vacuum switch.
12. Connect a dwell meter to the mixture control solenoid test lead (green connector) and set the dwell meter to the 6 cylinder position.
13. Connect a tachometer to the distributor TACH lead (brown connector).
14. Block the drive wheels, place the transmission in Park (auto. trans.) or Neutral (man. trans.), and apply the parking brake.
15. Start the engine and allow it to run at fast idle (for at least three minutes) until the engine cooling fan starts to cycle, indicating that the engine is warm and operating in the closed loop mode.
16. Run the engine at 3000 rpm and adjust the lean mixture screw in small increments (allowing the dwell to stabilize after each adjustment) until the average dwell is 35°. If you are unable to adjust to this specification, check the carburetor main metering circuit for leaks, restrictions, etc.

NOTE: It is normal for the dwell to vary about 2 1/2° below and above 35°. The dwell reading may also read 10-15° momentarily due to temporary mixture changes.

17. Allow the engine to return to idle and adjust the idle speed to 700rpm, with the cooling fan in the Off cycle.
18. Adjust the idle mixture screw (in the same manner as in step 16) until a dwell (average) of 25° is obtained. The adjustment is very sensitive the final check must be made with the adjusting tool removed. If you are unable to set the dwell to specification, check the carburetor idle system for leaks, restrictions, etc.

19. Raise the engine rpm to 3000, and make sure that the dwell stabilizes and averages 35° at this rpm. Repeat steps 16-19 if required.
20. Remove the tachometer and dwell meter, reattach the hoses as they were originally, and reinstall the items previously removed.
21. Set the idle speed to the figure given on the underhood emissions label.

CARBURETOR
Removal and Installation

1. Disconnect the negative battery cable. Remove the air cleaner and gasket.
2. Tag and disconnect any electrical connectors. Disconnect the vacuum lines and the fuel supply pipe.
3. Disconnect the accelerator linkage.
4. Disconnect the downshift cable if the vehicle is equipped with automatic transmission.
5. If the vehicle is equipped with cruise control, disconnect the cruise control linkage.
6. Remove the carburetor attaching bolts. Remove the carburetor. Remove the early fuel evaporation assembly, if equipped.
7. Installation is the reverse of the removal procedure. Start the engine and check for leaks.

INTAKE MANIFOLD
Removal and Installation
151 (2.5L) ENGINE

1. Disconnect the negative battery cable. Remove the air cleaner and gasket.
2. Remove the positive crankcase ventilation valve and hose.
3. Disconnect the vacuum hoses and the fuel lines. Drain the coolant from the radiator.
4. If the vehicle is equipped with electronic fuel injection, remove the throttle linkage and wiring.
5. Remove the cruise control linkage and the downshift linkage if equipped.
6. Remove the throttle linkage cable and bellcrank to gain working clearance.
7. Remove the heater hose.
8. Remove the ignition coil and the upper generator bracket.
9. Remove the intake manifold retaining bolts. Remove the intake manifold.
10. Installation is the reverse of the removal procedure. Check for vacuum and fluid leaks.

173 (2.8L), 183 (3.0L) AND 231 (3.8L) ENGINES

1. Disconnect the negative battery cable.

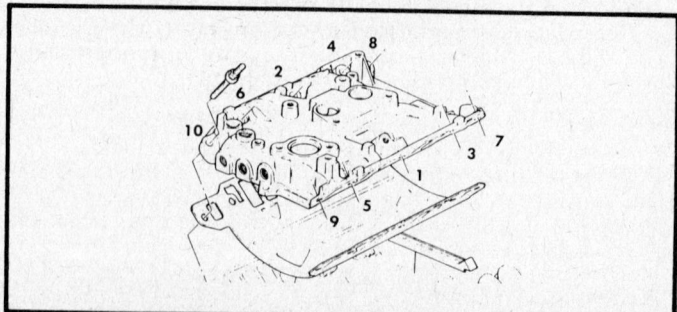

Intake manifold bolt torque sequence—183 and 231 cu. in. gas engine
(© General Motors Corporation)

6-22

GENERAL MOTORS—"A" AND "X" BODY
FRONT WHEEL DRIVE CARS

2. Drain the cooling system.
3. Remove the rocker arm covers. Remove the AIR pump and bracket.
4. Tag and disconnect any necessary wires.
5. Mark the position of the rotor and remove the distributor. Remove the vacuum hose.
6. Remove the power brake vacuum pipe and bracket if equipped.
7. Remove the cruise control assembly if equipped.
8. Remove the manifold retaining bolts. Remove the intake manifold.

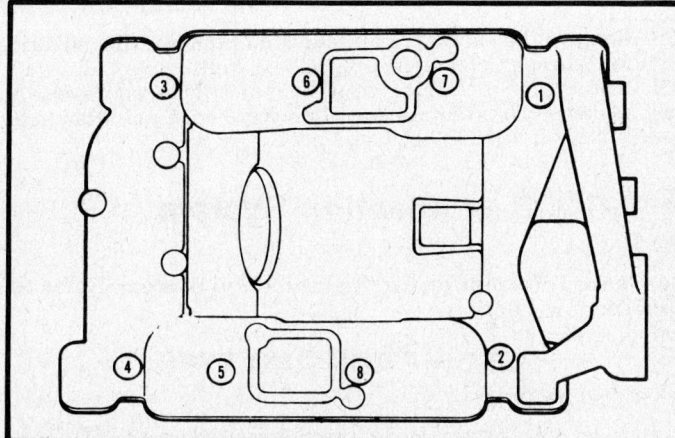

Intake manifold bolt torque sequence—6 cu. in. diesel engine (© General Motors Corporation)

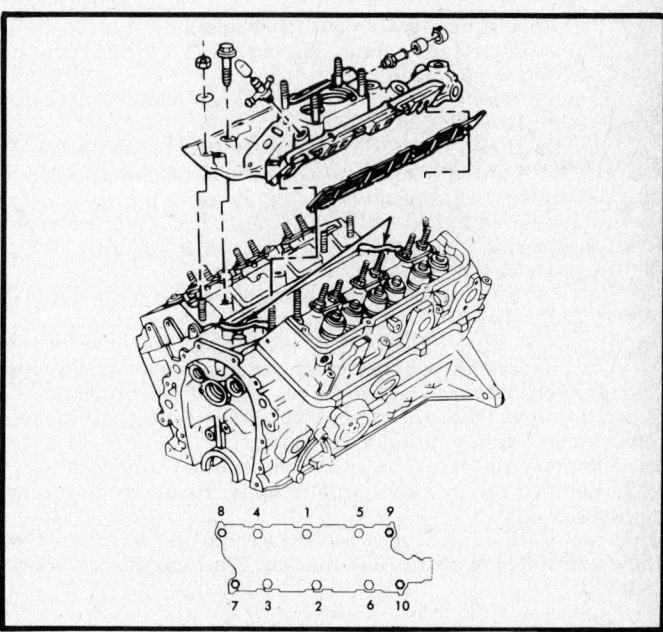

Intake manifold bolt torque sequence—173 cu. in. gas engine (© General Motors Corporation)

Intake manifold bolt torque sequence—151 cu. in. gas engine
(© General Motors Corporation)

9. Installation is the reverse of the removal procedure. Install new manifold gaskets.

263 (4.3L) DIESEL ENGINE

1. Disconnect the negative battery cable.
2. Drain the cooling system. Disconnect the upper radiator hose from the water outlet.
3. Remove the heater outler pipe and the heater inlet hose from the intake manifold.
4. Remove the fuel injection pump and the air crossover. If equipped with cruise control, remove the servo assembly.
5. Disconnect the alternator wiring. Remove the alternator. If the vehicle is equipped with A/C, remove the compressor, position on the side.
6. Disconnect the engine mounting strut.
7. Remove the fuel filter and brackets along with the fuel lines. Cap all lines.
8. Disconnect the wiring to the glow plug controller.
9. Disconnect the exhaust crossover pipe heat shield. Remove the left forward injection lines. Cap all openings.
10. Disconnect the throttle valve cables from the bracket. Remove the intake manifold drain tube.
11. Remove the intermediate pump adapter and seal.
12. Remove the intake manifold bolts. Remove the intake manifold.
13. Installation is the reverse of the removal procedure. Use a new manifold gasket for installation. Start engine and check for leaks.

EXHAUST MANIFOLD

Removal and Installation

151 (2.5L) ENGINE

1. Disconnect the negative battery cable.
2. Remove the air cleaner and the electronic fuel injection pre-heat tube.
3. Remove the torque-strut rod bolts at the radiator.
4. If equipped with air conditioning, remove the compressor and set to one side to gain working clearance.
5. Remove the engine mounting bracket at the cylinder head.
6. Remove the oxygen sensor connector. Disconnect the exhaust manifold from the exhaust pipe.
7. Remove the exhaust manifold nuts. Remove the exhaust manifold.
8. Installation is the reverse of the removal procedure.

173 (2.8L), 183 (3.0L) AND 231 (3.8L) ENGINES

1. Disconnect the negative battery cable.
2. Remove the air cleaner and gasket if equipped.
3. Remove the intermediate pinch bolt and separate the intermediate shaft from the stub shaft on the right side of the engine.
4. Disconnect the crossover pipe. Disconnect the AIR bracket at the exhaust flange. Remove the exhaust pipe.
5. Remove the upper engine support strut.
6. Position a floor jack under the front crossmember and take up the weight of the vehicle.
7. Remove the two front body mount bolts. Remove the cushions from the bolts.
8. Thread the body mount bolts with their retainers into the cage nuts so that the bolts restrict the movement of the engine cradle.
9. Lower the jack until the crossmember contacts the body mount bolt retainers.
10. Remove the bolts that attach the exhaust manifold to the cylinder head. Remove the exhaust manifold.
11. Installation is the reverse of the removal procedure.

263 (4.3L) DIESEL ENGINE

1. Disconnect the negative battery cable.
2. Unbolt the crossover pipe and the manifold from the left side of the vehicle. Remove the left exhaust manifold.
3. Remove the exhaust manifold bolts holding the crossover pipe to the right exhaust manifold.
4. Raise and support the vehicle safely.
5. Remove the exhaust manifold to exhaust pipe bolts.
6. Disconnect the speedometer cable from the transaxle.
7. Remove the right front wheel and tire to gain working clearance.
8. Remove the exhaust manifold bolts. Remove the exhaust manifold through the right front wheel well.
9. Installation is the reverse of the removal procedure. Use a new gasket during installation. Lubricate each manifold bolt with lubricant 1052080 or equivalent.

Fuel Injection System

For More Information on Fuel Injection System, Refer to Unit Repair Section.

DESCRIPTION AND TYPE

GAS ENGINES ONLY

The Model 300 Throttle Body Injection is used on all 151 cu. in. (2.5L) engines. The throttle body injection resembles a carburetor in appearance but does away with much of the carburetor's complexity. The throttle body injection system is centrally located on the intake manifold.

The throttle body injection system is completely controlled by the ECM, which monitors engine temperature, throttle position, vehicle speed and several other engines related conditions then updates the injector opening times in relation to the information given by these sensors.

The throttle body is also equipped with an idle air control motor. The idle air control motor operates pintle valve at the side of the throttle body. The idle air control motor also compensates for accessory loads changing engine friction during break-in. The idle air control motor is controlled by the ECM.

The throttle body injection system is made primarily of aluminum and simple in construction. It contains an electrically operated solenoid, a pressure regulator and an idle air control valve. A fuel return fitting, fuel inlet and throttle position sensor are also included in the throttle body injection system.

FUEL INJECTION PUMP

Removal and Installation

DIESEL ENGINES ONLY

1. Disconnect the negative battery cable.
2. Remove the air cleaner assembly.
3. From the valve covers and air crossover, remove the crankcase ventilation separator/filters and pipes.
4. Remove the air crossover and install intake manifold screen covers J-26996-2 or equivalent.
5. Disconnect the fuel lines. Remove the throttle cable from the throttle lever. Disconnect the throttle return spring.
6. Disconnect the fuel line from the fuel filter. Disconnect the fuel return line from the injection pump.
7. Remove the injection line retaining clamps and remove the injection lines from the pump. Cap all open lines to prevent contamination of inner components.
8. Remove the injection pump retaining bolts.
9. Remove the injection pump from the vehicle. Cap all open lines. Discard the O-ring.

GENERAL MOTORS—"A" AND "X" BODY
FRONT WHEEL DRIVE CARS
SECTION 6

NOTE: The position of the pump drive shaft should be upon removal so the pump can be reinstalled with the drive shaft in its original position.

10. Installation is the reverse of the removal procedure. Install a new O-ring in the pump to flange assembly. Start the engine and check for leaks. Correct as necessary.

FUEL INJECTION PUMP

Timing Procedures

DIESEL ENGINES ONLY

NOTE: The timing specifications located on the vehicle emission control label are based upon using a timing meter that uses a luminosity probe. Any other type of meter that measures something other than luminosity will correspond with the listed specifications and must not be used.

1. Place the selector lever in park, set the parking brake and secure the drive wheels.
2. Start the engine and allow it to reach operating temperature. Shut off the engine.
3. Ground the instrument panel assembly line communication link ground terminal.
4. Remove the air cleaner cover. Remove the manifold absolute pressure sensor retainer. Remove the air cleaner assembly. Clean all dirt from the area.
5. Clean the lens on both ends of the glow plug probe. Clean the photo electric pick-up.
6. Install the RPM probe into the crankshaft RPM counter.
7. Remove the glow plug from the number one cylinder. Install the glowing plug probe in its place. Tighten the probe to 8 ft. lbs. (11 Nm).
8. Connect the timing meter according to manufacturers instructions. Start the engine and set the rpm to the speed indicated on the emission control label.
9. Observe the timing reading at 2 minute intervals. When the readings stabilize, compare that reading to the one specified on the emission control label. The timing reading, when set to specification will be negative (after top dead center).
10. Disconnect the timing meter from the vehicle and install the removed glow plug.

NOTE: Vehicles equipped with aluminum cylinder heads require lubricant 1052771 or equivalent to be applied to the glow plug threads before installation.

11. Install any engine components that were necessary to be removed to adjust timing.

FUEL INJECTION NOZZLE(S)

Removal and Installation

DIESEL ENGINES ONLY

1. Disconnect the negative battery cable.
2. Remove the nozzle from the vehicle by applying torque to the largest hex on the nozzle. When performing work on the right rear bank, it may be necessary to perform the following:

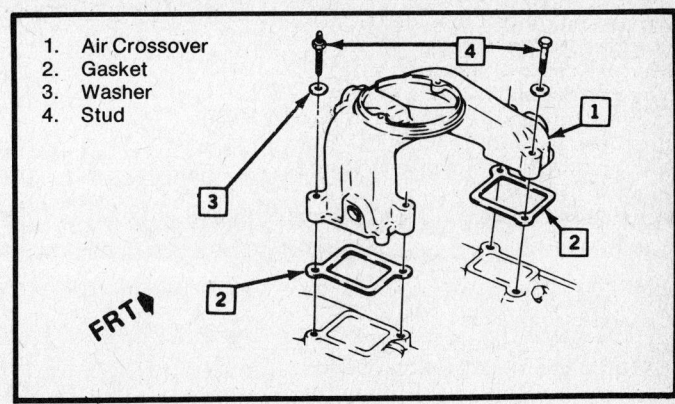

1. Air Crossover
2. Gasket
3. Washer
4. Stud

Air crossover pipe (© General Motors Corporation)

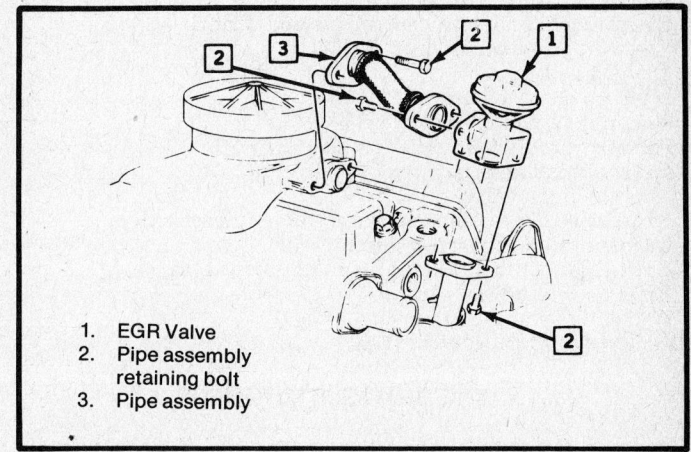

1. EGR Valve
2. Pipe assembly retaining bolt
3. Pipe assembly

EGR valve installation (© General Motors Corporation)

 a. Rotate the intermediate steering shaft so that the steering gear stub shaft clamp bolt is in the up position. Remove the clamp bolt. Disconnect the intermediate shaft from stub shaft.
 b. Remove the engine support strut. Place a floor jack under the front crossmember of the cradle and elevate the jack until the jack just starts to raise the vehicle.
 c. Remove the two front body mount bolts with lower cushions and retainers.
 d. Thread the body mount bolts with retainers into the cage nuts so that bolts restrain cradle movement.
 e. Release the floor jack slowly until the crossmember contact the body mount bolt retainers.
 f. Remove the nozzle assembly from the vehicle as described earlier. Remove the copper nuzzle gasket from the cylinder head if the gasket did not come out with the nozzle.
3. Installation is the reverse of the removal procedure. Tighten the nozzle to 25 ft. lbs. (34 Nm).

EMISSION CONTROL SYSTEMS

1983

Catalytic converter
Early fuel evaporation (EFE)
Exhaust gas recirculation (EGR)
Positive crankcase ventilation (PCV)
Thermostatic air cleaner (THERMAC)
Pulse air injection reaction (PAIR)
Electronic spark timing (EST)
Evaporative emission control system (EECS)

SECTION 6: GENERAL MOTORS—"A" AND "X" BODY
FRONT WHEEL DRIVE CARS

Electronic control module (ECM)
Oxygen sensor
Mixture control solenoid (MCS)
Vacuum regulator valve (VRV)
Exhaust pressure regulator valve (EPRV)
Response vacuum reducer (RVR)
Vacuum modulator valve (VMV)
Idle air bleed valve
Crankcase depression regulator valve (diesel only)

1984 and Later

Catalytic converter
Early fuel evaporation (EFE)
Exhaust gas recirculation (EGR)
Positive crankcase ventilation (PCV)
Thermostatic air cleaner (THERMAC)
Pulse air injection reaction (PAIR)
Electronic spark timing (EST)
Evaporative emission control system (EECS)
Electronic control module (ECM)
Oxygen sensor
Mixture control solenoid (MCS)
Vacuum regulator valve (VRV)
Exhaust pressure regulator valve (EPRV)
Response vacuum reducer (VMV)
Idle air bleed valve
Crankcase depression regulator valve (diesel only)
Transmission converter clutch (TCC)
Shift light control (manual transmissions only)
Electric cooling fan control
A/C wide open throttle control (WOT)
Electronic spark control (ESC)

Emissions Indicator

An emissions indicator flag may appear in the odometer window of the speedometer, on some General Motors vehicles. The flag could say "Sensor", "Emissions" or "Catalyst" depending on the part or assembly that is scheduled for regular emissions maintenance replacement. The word "Sensor" indicates a need for oxygen sensor replacement and the words "Emissions" or "Catalyst" indicate the need for catalytic converter replacement.

Resetting Trouble Indicators
1. Remove the instrument panel trim plate.

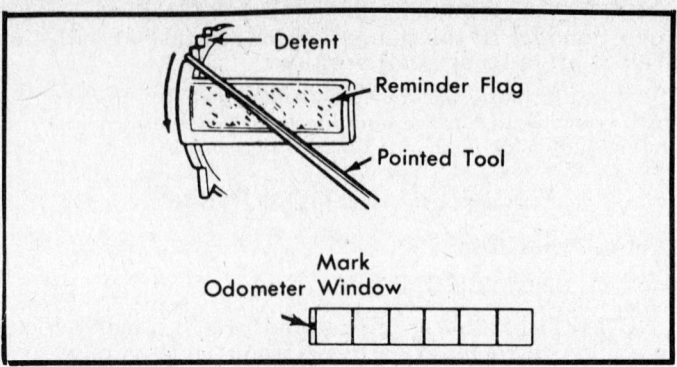

Reseting the maintenance reminder indicator—all GM vehicles except Cadillac
(© General Motors Corporation)

2. Remove the instrument cluster lens.
3. Locate the flag indicator reset notches at the driver side of the odometer.
4. Use a pointed tool to apply light downward pressure on the notches, until the indicator is reset.

NOTE: When the indicator is reset, an alignment mark will appear in the left center of the odometer window.

CLEARING TROUBLE CODES
Procedure

When the electronic control module finds a problem, the "CHECK ENGINE"/"SERVICE ENGINE SOON" light will come on and a trouble code will be recorded in the electronic control module memory. If the problem is not constant, the light will go out after approximately 10 seconds.

The trouble code will stay in the electronic control module memory until the battery voltage to the module is discontinued.

Disconnecting the battery pigtail harness from the positive battery terminal for 10 seconds with the ignition OFF, will clear all stored trouble codes.

NOTE: To prevent damage to the electronic control module, the key must be OFF when disconnecting or reconnecting the power to the module.

ENGINE SECTION

For Diesel Engine service, refer to unit repair section.
For Engine Overhaul procedures, refer to unit repair section

ENGINE ASSEMBLY
Removal and Installation
151 (2.5L)—AUTOMATIC TRANSAXLE

1. Disconnect the battery cables.
2. Drain the cooling system and remove the air cleaner and pre-heat tube. Remove the upper radiator hose.
3. Disconnect the vacuum hoses along with the transaxle and the throttle linkage.
4. Remove the A/C compressor from its brackets if equipped and set aside.
5. Remove the front engine strut assembly.
6. Disconnect the heater hoses at the intake manifold.
7. Remove the two lower transaxle to engine bolts leaving the upper bolts in place.
8. Remove the front cradle mounting bolts. Remove the forward exhaust pipe.
9. Remove the starter motor and the flywheel cover. Remove the bolts holding the flywheel to the torque converter.
10. Remove the power steering pump from its bracket and lay aside.
11. Remove the lower radiator hose.
12. Remove the rear transaxle support bracket bolts.
13. Remove the fuel supply line at the fuel filter.
14. Using a suitable lifting device, raise the engine and remove the remaining transaxle bolts.

GENERAL MOTORS—"A" AND "X" BODY
FRONT WHEEL DRIVE CARS

15. Slide the engine forward and remove the engine from the vehicle.
16. Installation is the reverse of the removal procedure. Make sure that the engine aligns with the transaxle bell housing.

151 (2.5L)—MANUAL TRANSAXLE

1. Disconnect the battery cables.
2. Raise and support the vehicle safely.
3. Remove the front cradle mounting bolts. Remove the front exhaust pipe.
4. Tag and disconnect the starter wires. Remove the starter assembly.
5. Remove the flywheel cover. Lower the vehicle.
6. Remove the air cleaner. Remove the emission hoses.
7. Remove the bell housing bolts. Remove the forward torque reaction rod and the core support.
8. Disconnect the A/C belt and compressor and lay to one side. Remove the power steering hose if equipped.
9. Tag and disconnect the electrical connections at the solenoid.
10. Remove the blower motor.
11. Disconnect the throttle cable.
12. Drain the radiator. Disconnect the heater hoses and the radiator hoses.
13. Disconnect the engine harness at the bulkhead connector.
14. Using a suitable lifting device, lift the engine from the engine compartment.
15. Installation is the reverse of the removal procedure. Check the timing as per emissions label.

173 (2.8L)—AUTOMATIC AND MANUAL TRANSAXLE

1. Disconnect the battery cables.
2. Remove the air cleaner and drain the cooling system. Remove the engine support strut from the radiator and swing rearward.
3. If the vehicle is equipped with A/C, remove the air pump, compressor and the mounting bracket. Lay aside.
4. Disconnect the vacuum hoses from the non-engine components. Remove the heater and radiator hoses.
5. Disconnect the detent cable and the accelerator cable.
6. Tag and disconnect the engine harness from the ECM and left side junction box.
7. Remove the power steering pump and bracket from the engine if equipped.
8. Disconnect the fuel lines from the engine on the left side of the engine.
9. Raise and support the vehicle safely.
10. Remove the front engine mount-to-cradle and mount-to-engine bracket retaining nuts.
11. Remove the battery cables attached to the starter and transaxle housing bolt. Remove the starter.
12. Remove the transaxle inspection cover. Remove the flex plate from the torque converter.
13. Remove the drive belts as required. Remove the lower crankshaft pulley.
14. Disconnect the exhaust pipe.
15. Remove the lower transaxle to engine bolt.
16. Lower the vehicle and disconnect the exhaust crossover pipe.
17. Remove the remaining transaxle to engine bolts. Support the transaxle extension.
18. Using a suitable lifting device, remove the engine from the engine compartment.
19. Installation is the reverse of the removal procedure.

183 (3.0L) AND 231 (3.8L) AUTOMATIC AND MANUAL TRANSAXLE

1. Disconnect the negative battery cable. Remove the air cleaner.
2. Drain the engine coolant and remove the hoses from the radiator. Disconnect the heater hoses from the engine.
3. Remove the alternator. Disconnect the engine harness connector. Remove the engine ground strap located at the forward engine strut.
4. Remove the throttle valve cable and the accelerator linkage from the carburetor lever. Remove the vacuum hosing from the non-engine mounted assemblies.
5. Remove the blower motor.
6. Remove the fuel line from the carburetor.
7. Remove the A.I.R. pump. Remove the pump bracket.
8. Raise and support the vehicle safely.
9. Remove the power steering lines from the steering gear.
10. Remove the exhaust pipe from the exhaust manifold.
11. Remove the bolts that hold the cradle to the front engine.
12. Remove the battery starter cables and the transaxle housing bolts.
13. Disconnect the flywheel cover. Remove the torque converter bolts.

NOTE: Mark the relationship of the flywheel to the torque converter for ease of reassembly.

14. Remove the cylinder block to transaxle support bolts. Lower the vehicle.
15. Position a support under the transaxle rear extension. Remove the cylinder to transaxle retaining bolts.
16. Remove the engine strut bracket from the radiator support.
17. Remove the A/C compressor mounting bracket if equipped.
18. Attach a suitable engine lifting device to the engine. Remove the engine from the engine compartment.
19. Installation is the reverse of the removal procedure. Check for fluid and exhaust leaks.

263 (4.3L)—AUTOMATIC AND MANUAL TRANSAXLE

1. Drain the cooling system. Remove the serpentine drive belt (and vacuum pump drive belt, if A/C equipped).
2. Remove air cleaner and install cover J-26996.
3. Disconnect battery negative cable(s) at batteries and ground wires at inner fender panel. Disconnect engine ground strap, rear (right) head to cowl.
4. Hoist car.
5. Remove the flywheel cover.
6. Remove the flywheel to torque converter bolts.
7. Disconnect the exhaust pipe from the rear exhaust manifold.
8. Remove the engine to transaxle brace.
9. Remove the engine mount to cradle retaining nuts and washers.
10. Disconnect the leads to the starter motor, No. 2 cylinder glow plugs and battery ground cable at transaxle to engine bolt.
11. Disconnect the lower oil cooler hose and cap the openings.
12. Remove the accessible power steering pump bracket fasteners.
13. Lower the car.
14. Remove the remaining power steering pump bracket/brace fasteners and lower the power steering pump with hoses out of the way.
15. Remove heater water return pipe.
16. Disconnect all remaining glow plug leads at the glow plugs.
17. Disconnect all other leads at the engine, disconnect the engine harness at the cowl connector and body mounted relays and position the engine harness aside.
18. If A/C equipped, disconnect the compressor with brackets and lines attached and position aside.
19. Disconnect the fuel and vacuum hoses, cap all fuel line openings.
20. Disconnect the throttle and T.V. cables at the injection pump and cable bracket. Position cables aside.

6-27

GENERAL MOTORS—"A" AND "X" BODY
FRONT WHEEL DRIVE CARS

21. Disconnect the upper oil cooler hose and cap the openings.
22. Remove the exhaust crossover pipe heat shield.
23. Disconnect and move aside the transaxle filler tube.
24. Remove the exhaust crossover pipe.
25. Remove the engine mounting strut and strut brackets.
26. Install a suitable engine lifting device. Make certain that when installing chains to the cylinder heads that washers are used under the chains and bolt heads and that the bolts are torqued to 20 ft. lbs.

CAUTION

Failure to properly secure the engine lift to the aluminum cylinder heads can result in personal injury.

---

27. Position a support under the transaxle rear extension. It may be necessary to raise the support as the engine is being removed.
28. Remove the engine to transaxle bolts and remove the engine.
29. Installation is the reverse of removal. Note the following:
   a. Before installing the flex plate-to-converter bolts, make sure that the weld nuts on the converter are flush with the flex plate, and the converter rotates freely by hand.
   b. Use only new O-rings at all connections.

ENGINE MOUNTS
Removal and Installation

1. Disconnect the negative battery cable.
2. Raise and support the vehicle safely.
3. Using a suitable tool, support the engine and remove the engine mounting bracket nuts.
4. Raise the engine slightly until the engine mount is free from the vehicle chassis.
5. Remove the nuts holding the engine mount to the frame.
6. Remove the engine mounts and discard.
7. Installation is the reverse of the removal procedure.

Valve System

ADJUST VALVES

1. Crank the engine until the timing mark aligns with the "O" mark on the timing scale, and both valves in the number one cylinder are closed.

NOTE: If the valves are moving as the timing marks align, the engine is in the number four firing position. Turn the crankshaft one more revolution.

2. Back off the rocker arm adjusting nut until there is play in the pushrod.
3. Tighten the adjusting nut until the pushrod clearance is eliminated.
4. When the pushrod clearance is eliminated, tighten the adjusting nut one and one half additional turns to place the lifter in the center of its travel.

VALVE LIFTERS
Removal and Installation

1. Disconnect the negative battery cable.
2. Remove the valve cover and the intake manifold to gain working clearance.
3. On vehicles equipped with the diesel motor, remove the valve lifter guide bolts. Remove the valve lifter guide.
4. Remove the pushrod cover and discard the gasket.
5. Loosen the rocker arm adjusting nut and rotate the arm so as to clear the pushrod.
6. Remove the pushrods and valve lifters using tool J3049 or equivalent.
7. Installation is the reverse of the removal procedure. Lubricate the bearing surfaces with Molykote® or its equivalent. Adjust the valves as needed.

VALVE ROCKER ASSEMBLY
Removal and Installation

GASOLINE ENGINE—4 CYLINDER

1. Disconnect the negative battery cable.
2. Remove the air cleaner and the PCV valve and hose.
3. Remove the throttle cables from the EFI assembly.
4. Tag and disconnect the spark plug wires.
5. Remove the valve cover bolts. Remove the valve cover. Discard the gasket.
6. Remove the rocker arm bolts. Remove the valve cover. Discard the gasket.
7. Installation is the reverse of the removal procedure.

GASOLINE ENGINE—6 CYLINDER

1. Disconnect the negative battery cable.
2. Remove the PCV pipe which leads to the air cleaner. Remove the hot air tube.
3. Tag and disconnect any computer command control wires and hoses. Tag and disconnect the spark plug wires.
4. If vehicle is equipped with an upper engine support strut, remove and lay aside.
5. Remove any accessory mounting brackets as needed to gain working clearance.
6. Remove the valve cover bolts. Remove the valve covers. Discard the gaskets.
7. Remove the rocker arm shaft retaining bolts. Remove the shaft assembly.
8. Remove the nylon rocker arm retainers and discard. Remove the rocker arms from the shaft.
9. Installation is the reverse of the removal procedure, using new nylon retainers.

DIESEL ENGINE—6 CYLINDER

1. Disconnect the negative battery cable.
2. Disconnect the fuel injection lines and remove the crankcase ventilation pipes. Remove the filter.
3. Remove the engine support strut if equipped.
4. Place a floor jack under the front crossmember and take up the weight of the engine.
5. Remove the two front body mount bolts. Remove the cushion from the bolts and thread the bolts and retainers into the cage nuts to restrict engine cradle movement.
6. Lower the jack until the crossmember contacts the body mount bolt retainers.
7. Remove the valve cover retaining bolts. Remove the valve covers. Discard the gaskets.
8. Remove the rocker arm retainer bolts. Remove the rocker arm pivot and rocker arms.
9. Installation is the reverse of the removal procedure. Lubricate all wear points with 1050169 lubricant or its equivalent.

VALVE TIMING
Adjustment

Adjustment is made by backing off the rocker arm adjusting nut until there is play in the pushrod. Tighten the nut to remove the pushrod clearance (this can be determined by rotating the pushrod with your fingers while tightening the adjusting nut). When the pushrod cannot be freely turned by hand, tighten the nut 1 additional turn to place the lifter in the center of its travel. No further adjustment is required.

GENERAL MOTORS—"A" AND "X" BODY
FRONT WHEEL DRIVE CARS

VALVE LIFTER BLEED DOWN—DIESEL ENGINES

1. Before installing any removed rocker arms, rotate the engine crankshaft to a position of number 1 cylinder being 32° before TDC. This is a 50mm (2 in.) counterclockwise from the 0° pointer. If only the right valve cover was removed, remove No. 1 cylinder's glow plug to determine if the position of the piston is the correct one. The compression pressure will tell you that you are in the right position.

If the left valve cover was removed, rotate the crankshaft until the number 5 cylinder intake valve pushrod ball is 7.0mm (.28 in.) above the number 5 cylinder exhaust valve pushrod ball.

NOTE: Use only hand wrenches to torque the rocker arm pivot nuts to avoid engine damage.

2. If removed, install the No. 5 cylinder pivot and rocker arms. Torque the nuts alternately between the intake and exhaust valves until the intake valve begins to open, then stop.
3. Install remaining rocker arms except No. 3 exhaust valve (if this rocker arm was removed).
4. If removed, install but do not torque No. 3 valve pivots beyond the point that the valve would be fully open. this is indicated by strong resistance while still turning the pivot retaining bolts. Going beyond this would bend the pushrod. Torque the nuts SLOWLY allowing the lifter to bleed down.
5. Finish torquing No. 5 cylinder rocker arm pivot nut SLOWLY. Do not go beyond the point that the valve would be fully open. This is indicated by strong resistance while still turning the pivot retaining bolts. Going beyond this would bend the pushrod.
6. DO NOT turn the engine crankshaft for at least 45 minutes.
7. Finish reassembling the engine as the lifters are being bled.

NOTE: Do not rotate the engine until the valve lifters have been bled down, or damage to the engine will occur.

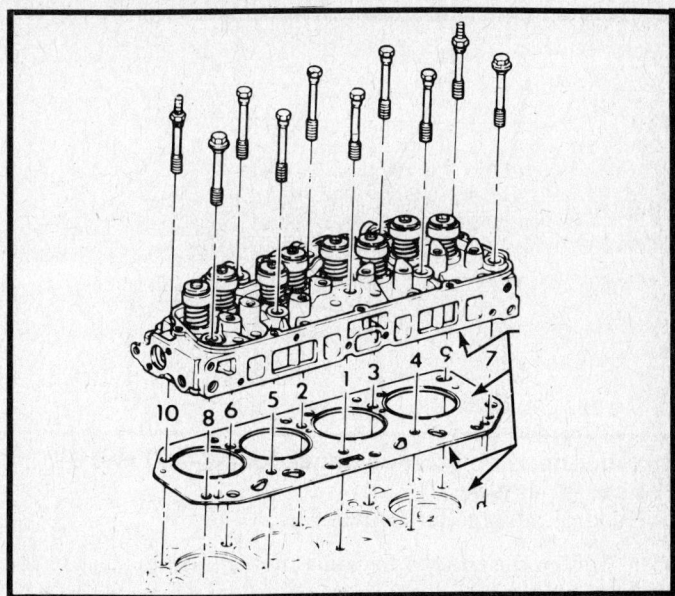

Cylinder head bolt torque sequence—151 cu. in. gas engine (© General Motors Corporation)

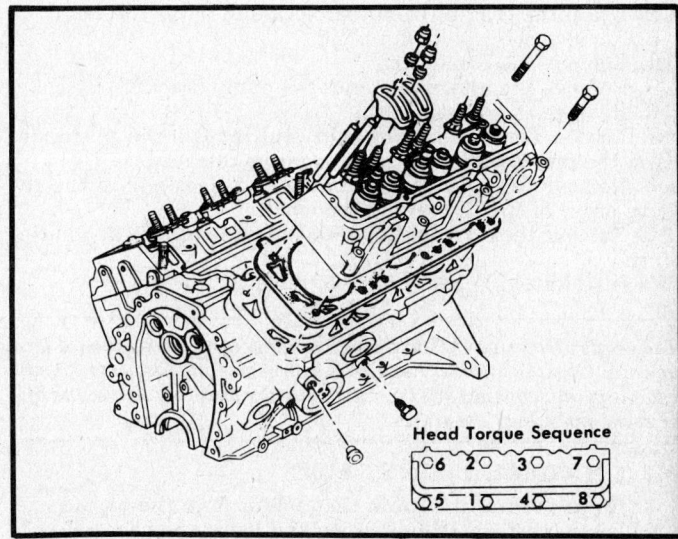

Cylinder head bolt torque sequence—173 cu. in. engine (© General Motors Corporation)

CYLINDER HEADS

Removal and Installation

151 (2.5L) ENGINE

NOTE: On fuel injected engines, relieve the pressure in the fuel system before disconnecting any fuel line connections. The engine should be cold.

1. Drain the cooling system.
2. Remove the air cleaner.
3. Remove the intake and exhaust manifolds as previously outlined.
4. Remove the alternator bracket bolts.
5. Remove the A/C compressor bracket bolts and position the compressor to one side. Do not disconnect any of the refrigerant lines.
6. Disconnect all vacuum and electrical connections from the cylinder head.
7. Disconnect the upper radiator hose.
8. Disconnect the spark plug wires and remove the plugs.
9. Remove the rocker arm cover, rocker arms, and pushrods.
10. Unbolt and remove the cylinder head.
11. Clean the gasket surfaces thoroughly.
12. Install a new gasket over the dowels and position the cylinder head.
13. Coat the head bolt threads with sealer and install finger tight.

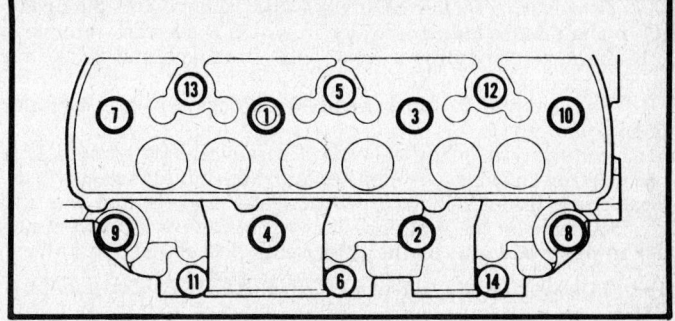

Cylinder head bolt torque sequence—6–263 cu. in. engine (© General Motors Corporation)

6–29

SECTION 6
GENERAL MOTORS—"A" AND "X" BODY
FRONT WHEEL DRIVE CARS

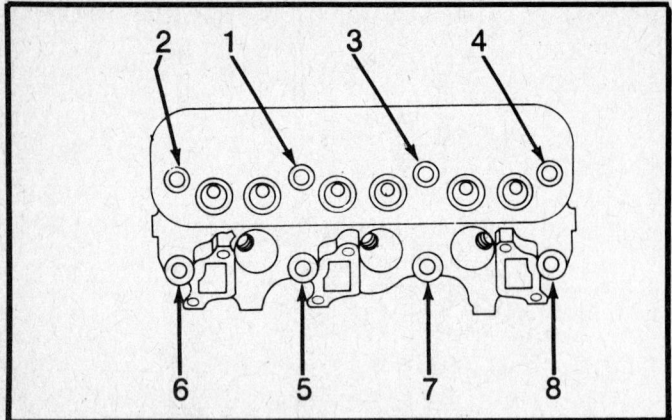

Cylinder head bolt torque sequence—6–183 and 6–231 cu. in. engine
(© General Motors Corporation)

14. Tighten the bolts in sequence, in three equal steps to the specified torque.
15. Install all parts in the reverse of removal.

173 (2.8L) ENGINE/LEFT SIDE

1. Raise and support the car.
2. Drain the coolant from the block and lower the car.
3. Remove the intake manifold.
4. Remove the crossover.
5. Remove the alternator and AIR pump brackets.
6. Remove the dipstick tube.
7. Loosen the rocker arm bolts and remove the pushrods. Keep the pushrods in the same order as removed.
8. Remove the cylinder head bolts in stages and in the reverse order of the tightening sequence.
9. Remove the cylinder head. Do not pry on the head to loosen it.
10. Installation is the reverse of removal.

--- **CAUTION** ---

The words "This Side Up" on the new cylinder head gasket should face upward. Coat the cylinder head bolts with sealer and torque to specifications in the sequence shown. Make sure the pushrods seat in the lifter seats and adjust the valves.

173 (2.8L) ENGINE/RIGHT SIDE

1. Raise the car and drain the coolant from the block.
2. Disconnect the exhaust pipe and lower the car.
3. If equipped, remove the cruise control servo bracket.
4. Remove the air management valve and hose.
5. Remove the intake manifold.
6. Remove the exhaust crossover.
7. Loosen the rocker arm nuts and remove the pushrods. Keep the pushrods in the order in which they were removed.
8. Remove the cylinder head bolts in stages and in the reverse order of the tightening sequence.
9. Remove the cylinder head. Do not pry on the cylinder head to loosen it.
10. Installation is the reverse of removal. The words "This Side Up" on the new cylinder head gasket should face upwards. Coat the cylinder head bolts with sealer and tighten them to specifications in the sequence shown. Make sure the lower ends of the pushrods seat in the lifter seats and adjust the valves.

183 (3.0L) AND 231 (3.8L) ENGINE/RIGHT AND LEFT SIDE

1. Disconnect negative battery cable.
2. Remove intake manifold.
3. Loosen and remove belt(s).
4. When removing LEFT cylinder head;
   a. Remove oil dipstick
   b. Remove air and vacuum pumps with mounting bracket if present, and move out of the way with hoses attached.
5. When removing RIGHT cylinder head;
   a. Remove alternator.
   b. Disconnect power steering gear pump and brackets attached to cylinder head.
6. Disconnect wires from spark plugs, and remove the spark plug wire clips from the rocker arm cover studs.
7. Remove exhaust manifold bolts from head being removed.
8. With air hose and cloths, clean dirt off cylinder head and adjacent area to avoid getting dirt into engine. It is extremely important to avoid getting dirt into the hydraulic valve lifters.
9. Remove rocker arm cover and rocker arm and shaft assembly from cylinder head. Lift out pushrods. If lifters are to be serviced, remove them at this time and place them in a container with numbered holes or a similar device, to keep them identified as to engine position. If they are not to be removed, protect lifters and camshaft from dirt by covering area with a clean cloth.
10. Loosen all cylinder head bolts, then remove bolts and lift off the cylinder head.
11. With cylinder head on bench, remove all spark plugs for cleaning and to avoid damaging them during work on the head.
12. Installation is the reverse of removal. Clean all gasket surfaces thoroughly. Always use a new head gasket. The head gasket is installed with the head downward. Coat the heat bolt threads with thread sealer. Torque the head bolts in three equal stages. Recheck head bolt torque after the engine has been warmed to operating temperature.

263 (4.3L) ENGINE/RIGHT AND LEFT SIDE

NOTE: This procedure requires the complete disassembly of the valve lifters as explained under Diesel Engine Valve Lifter Bleed-Down.

1. Remove intake manifold.
2. Remove valve cover. Loosen or remove any accessory brackets or pipe clamps which interfere.
3. Disconnect glow plug wiring (and block heater lead if so equipped on rear bank).
4. Remove the ground strap from right (rear) cylinder head.
5. Remove rocker arm nuts, pivots, rocker arms and pushrods. Scribe pivots and keep rocker arms separated so they can be installed in their original locations.
6. Disconnect the exhaust crossover pipe from the exhaust manifold on the side being worked on and loosen it on the other.
7. Remove engine block drain plug, from side of the block where head is being removed.
8. Remove pipe plugs covering the upper cylinder head bolts.
9. Remove all the cylinder head bolts and remove the cylinder head.
10. If necessary to remove the pre-chamber, remove the glow plug and injection nozzle, then tap out with a small blunt 1/8 in. drift. Do NOT use a tapered drift.
11. Installation is the reverse of removal. Do not use sealer on the head gasket. If a pre-chamber was replaced, measure the chamber height and grind the new one to within 0.001 in. of the old chamber's height, using #80 grit wet sandpaper to polish it. Coat the heat bolts with sealer.

CAMSHAFT

Removal and Installation

151 (2.5L) ENGINE

NOTE: Relieve the pressure in the EFI system on fuel

GENERAL MOTORS—"A" AND "X" BODY
FRONT WHEEL DRIVE CARS

injected engines before disconnecting the fuel lines leading to the engine.

1. Remove the engine as previously outlined.
2. Remove the rocker cover, rocker arms, and pushrods.
3. Remove the distributor, spark plugs, and fuel pump.
4. Remove the pushrod cover and gasket. Remove the lifters.
5. Remove the alternator, the alternator lower bracket and the front engine mount bracket assembly.
6. Remove the oil pump driveshaft and gear assembly.
7. Remove the crankshaft hub and timing gear cover.
8. Remove the two camshaft thrust plate screws by working through the holes in the gear.
9. Remove the camshaft and gear assembly by pulling it through the front of the block. Take care not to damage the bearings.
10. Install in the reverse order. Torque the thrust plate screws 75 in. lbs.

173 (2.8L) ENGINE

1. Remove the engine from the vehicle.
2. Remove the intake manifold, valve lifters and timing chain. If the vehicle is equipped with A/C, remove the compressor and lay aside. Remove the front crankcase cover.
3. Remove the fuel pump and the fuel pump pushrod.
4. Remove the camshaft sprocket bolts, sprocket and timing chain.
5. Install two bolts in the cam bolt holes and pull the cam from the engine block.
6. Installation is the reverse of the removal procedure. Be sure to align the sprocket timing marks.

183 (3.0L) AND 231 (3.8L) ENGINE

1. Remove the engine from the vehicle.
2. Remove the intake manifold.
3. Remove the rocker arm covers.
4. Remove the rocker arm assemblies, pushrods and lifters.
5. Remove the timing chain and camshaft sprocket.
6. Installation is the reverse of the removal procedure.

263 (4.3L) ENGINE

NOTE: This procedure requires the removal, disassembly, cleaning, reassembly and bleed-down of all the valve lifters.

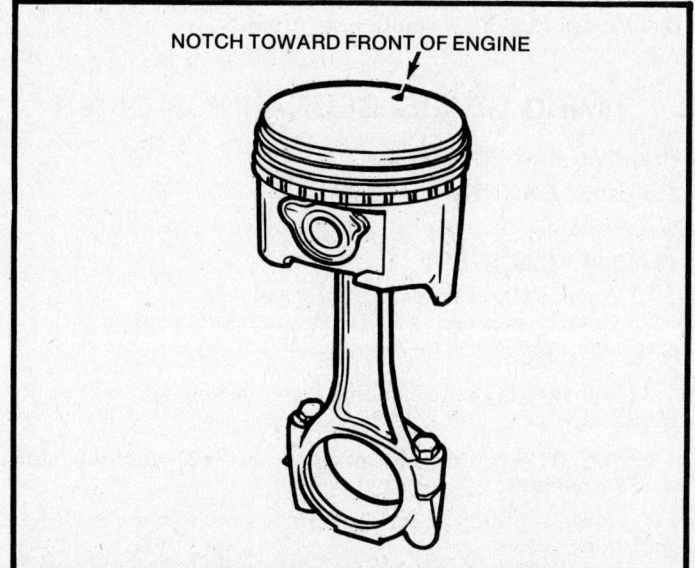

Piston identification—173 cu. in. gas engine
(© General Motors Corporation)

1. Remove the engine as described earlier.
2. Remove the intake manifold.
3. Remove the oil pump drive assembly.
4. Remove the timing chain cover.
5. Align the timing marks.
6. Remove the rocker arms, pushrods and lifters, keeping them in order for reassembly.
7. Remove the timing chain and camshaft sprocket as described earlier.
8. Remove the camshaft bearing retainer.
9. Remove the cam sprocket key.
10. Remove the injection pump drive gear.
11. Remove the injection pump drive gear, intermediate pump adapter and pump adapter. Remove the snap ring and selective washer. Remove the driven gear and spring.
12. Carefully slide the camshaft out of the block.
13. If the camshaft bearings are being replaced, you'll have to remove the oil pan.
14. Installation is the reverse of removal. Perform the complete valve lifter bleed-down procedure mentioned earlier.

PISTONS AND RODS POSITIONING

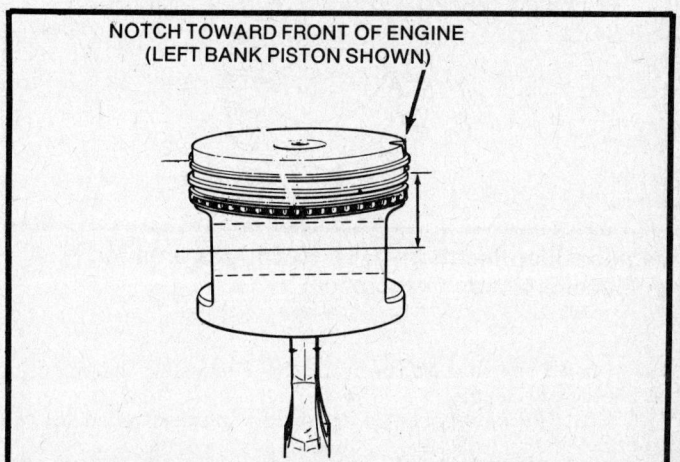

Piston identification—183 cu. in. gas engine
(© General Motors Corporation)

TIMING CASE COVER/OIL SEAL

Removal and Installation

151 (2.5L) ENGINE

NOTE: Relieve the pressure in the EFI system on fuel injected engines before disconnecting the fuel lines leading to the engine.

1. Remove the crankshaft hub. It is necessary to remove the inner fender splash shield.
2. Remove the alternator lower bracket.
3. Remove the front engine mounts.
4. Using a floor jack, raise the engine.
5. Remove the engine mount mounting bracket-to-cylinder block bolts. Remove the bracket and mount as an assembly.
6. Remove the oil pan-to-front cover screws.
7. Remove the front cover-to-block screws.
8. Pull the cover slightly forward, just enough to allow cutting of the oil pan front seal flush with the block on both sides.
9. Remove the front cover and attached portion of the pan seal.
10. Clean the gasket surfaces thoroughly.
11. Cut the tabs from the new oil pan front seal.

6-31

SECTION 6

GENERAL MOTORS—"A" AND "X" BODY
FRONT WHEEL DRIVE CARS

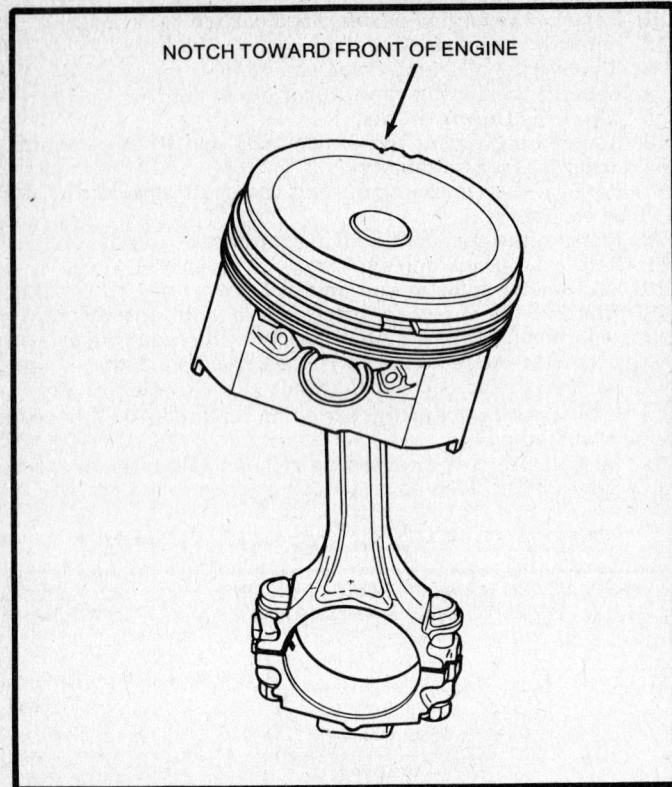

Piston identification—151 cu. in. gas engine
(© General Motors Corporation)

12. Install the seal on the front cover pressing the tips into the holes provided.
13. Coat the new gasket with sealer and position it on the front cover.
14. Apply a 1/8 in. bead of silicone sealer to the joint formed at the oil pan and stock.
15. Align the front cover seal with a centering tool and install the front cover. Tighten the screws. Install the hub.

173 (2.8L) ENGINE

NOTE: The outer ring of the harmonic balancer is bonded to the hub with rubber. Breakage may occur if the balancer is hammered back onto the crankshaft. A press or its equivalent is needed for installation.

1. Remove the water pump.
2. If the vehicle is equipped with A/C, remove the compressor without disconnecting the lines and lay aside.
3. Remove the harmonic balancer using a puller.

NOTE: The balancer must be removed with a puller which acts on the inner hub only. Pulling on the outer portion of the balancer will either break the rubber bond or destroy the tuning of the torsional damper.

4. Remove the lower heater hose and the radiator hose.
5. Remove the timing gear cover attaching bolts, cover and gasket. Discard gasket.
6. Clean all the gasket surfaces on the front cover and block. Apply a 3/32 in. bead of sealer (1052357) or equivalent, to the front cover sealing surface and around the coolant passage ports and central bolt holes.
7. Apply a bead of silicone sealer to the oil pan-to-cylinder block joint.

8. Install a centering tool into the crankshaft snout hole in the front cover and install the cover.
9. Install the front cover bolts finger tight, remove the centering tool and tighten the cover bolts.
10. Install the harmonic balancer, pulley, water pump, belts, radiator and all other parts.

183 (3.0L) AND 231 (3.8L) ENGINES

1. Drain the cooling system.
2. Disconnect the lower radiator hose and the heater hose at the water pump.
3. Remove the water pump pulley and all drive belts.
4. Remove the alternator and brackets.
5. Remove the distributor.
6. Remove the balancer bolt and washer, and using a puller, remove the balancer.
7. Remove the cover-to-block bolts. Remove the two oil pan-to-cover bolts.
8. Remove the cover and gasket.
9. Installation is the reverse of removal. Always use a new gasket coated with sealer. Remove the oil pump cover and pack the area around the gears with petroleum jelly so that no air space is left within the pump. Apply sealer to the cover bolt threads.

263 (4.3L) ENGINE

1. Drain the cooling system.
2. Disconnect the lower radiator hose and the heater hose at the water pump. Disconnect the heater outlet pipe at the manifold.
3. Disconnect the power steering pump, vacuum pump, belt tensioner, air conditioning compressor and alternator brackets.

NOTE: Do not disconnect any of the A/C lines.

4. Remove the crankshaft balancer using a puller.
5. Unbolt and remove the front cover and gasket.
6. Installation is the reverse of removal. Grind a chamfer on the end of each dowel pin to aid in cover installation. Trim 1/8 in. from the ends of the new front pan seal. Apply RTV sealer to the oil pan seal retainer. After the cover gasket is in place, apply sealer to the junction of the pan, gasket and block. When installing the cover, rotate it right and left while guiding the pan seal into place with a small screwdriver.

TIMING GEARS, BELT AND/OR CHAIN

Removal and Installation

151 (2.5L) ENGINE

See the camshaft removal and installation procedure.

173 (2.8L) ENGINE

1. Remove the crankcase front cover.
2. Crank the engine until the marks punched on both sprockets are closest to one another and in line between the shaft centers.
3. Remove the bolts holding the camshaft sprocket to the camshaft.

NOTE: The timing chain will come off with the camshaft sprocket.

4. Using a puller or its equivalent remove the crankshaft sprocket.
5. Installation is the reverse of the removal procedure. Be sure to line up the timing marks as in disassembly. Align the dowel in the camshaft with the dowel hole in the camshaft sprocket.

GENERAL MOTORS—"A" AND "X" BODY
FRONT WHEEL DRIVE CARS
SECTION 6

183 (3.0L) AND 231 (3.8L) ENGINES

1. Remove the timing chain cover. Align the timing marks on the sprockets so they are as close as possible together.
2. Remove the front camshaft oil slinger.
3. Remove the bolts holding the camshaft sprocket to the camshaft. Remove the camshaft sprocket and timing chain.
4. Remove the crankshaft sprocket. Inspect for wear or damage.
5. Installation is the reverse of the removal procedure. Install the oil slinger with the large part of the cone facing the front of the engine.

263 (4.3L) ENGINE

NOTE: The following procedure requires the bleed-down of the valve lifters. Read the procedure before proceeding.

1. Remove the front cover.
2. Loosen all the rocker arms.
3. Remove the crankshaft oil slinger.
4. Remove the camshaft sprocket bolt.
5. Using two prybars, work the camshaft and crankshaft sprockets alternately off their shafts along with the chain. It may be necessary to remove the crankshaft sprocket with a puller.
6. Installation is the reverse of removal. If the engine was turned, make sure that the No. 1 piston is at TDC. Bleed the lifters following the procedure under "Diesel Engine Valve Lifter Bleed-Down."

Lubrication

OIL PAN

Removal and Installation

151 (2.5L) ENGINE

1. Raise the vehicle and support safely. Drain the crankcase.
2. Remove cradle to front engine mount nuts.
3. Disconnect exhaust pipe at manifold and at rear transaxle mount.
4. Disconnect starter and remove flywheel housing inspection cover.
5. Remove upper generator bracket. Remove the splash shield, if equipped, in order to gain working clearance.
6. Install suitable engine support equipment and raise engine.
7. Remove lower generator bracket and engine support bracket.
8. Remove oil pan retaining bolts and remove oil pan.

To Install:
1. Thoroughly clean all gasket sealing surfaces.
2. Install rear oil pan gasket in rear main bearing cap, and apply a small quantity of sealer in depressions where pan gasket engages into block.
3. Install front oil pan gasket on timing gear cover pressing tips into holes provided in cover.
4. Install side gaskets on oil pan using grease as a retainer.
5. Apply a 1/8 in. by 1/4 in. long bead of sealer at split lines of front and side gaskets.
6. Install oil pan. Bolts into timing gear cover should be installed last. They are installed at an angle and holes line up after rest of pan bolts are snugged up.
7. Install all components removed. Fill crankcase with oil, run engine and check for leaks.

173 (2.8L) ENGINE

1. Drain crankcase.
2. Remove exhaust crossover pipe.
3. Remove transaxle converter/starter shield or clutch housing cover, as applicable.
4. Remove starter.
5. If equipped with manual transaxle, remove engine mounting bracket to engine mount retaining nuts and raise front of engine approximately 18mm.
6. Remove oil pan to case and front cover retaining bolts and remove oil pan.

To Install:
1. With clean sealing surfaces, place a 3mm diameter (1/8 in.) bead of sealant on the oil pan sealing flange.
2. Using a new oil pan rear seal, with sealant applied to cap pocket install pan against cylinder case and attach with retaining bolts.
3. Lower front of engine until seated on engine mount, if raised. Install retaining nuts.
4. Install starter.
5. Install converter/starter shield or clutch housing cover, as applicable.
6. Install exhaust crossover pipe.
7. Lower vehicle.
8. Fill crankcase with oil, start engine and check for leaks.

183 (3.0L) AND 231 (3.8L) ENGINE

1. Disconnect the negative battery cable at the battery.
2. Raise the vehicle and drain the engine oil.
3. Remove the flywheel cover.
4. Remove the oil pan.
5. Installation is performed in the reverse of the previous steps. Check for leaks after the engine is started.

263 (4.3L) DIESEL ENGINE

1. Install engine support fixture.
2. Hoist the car but keep the rear slightly lower than the front.
3. Install supports (stands) at the front of the body at the forward lift points.
4. Drain the engine oil pan.
5. Remove the left side steering gear to cradle bolt and loosen the right side steering gear to cradle bolt.
6. Remove the front stabilizer bar.
7. Using a 1/2 in. drill bit, drill through the spot weld located between the rear holes at the left hand front stabilizer bar mounting.
8. Remove the engine and transaxle to cradle mount nuts.
9. Disconnect the left lower ball joint from the knuckle.
10. Position a support (stand) under the transaxle oil pan. Place a wood block between the support and oil pan and raise the transaxle until the mount studs clear the cradle.
11. Remove the bolts securing the front crossmember to the right side of the cradle.
12. Remove the bolts from the left side body mounts.
13. Remove the left side and front crossmember assembly. It will be necessary to lower the rear crossmember below the left side by careful use of a pry bar.
14. Remove the flywheel cover and starter assembly.
15. Remove the engine mount bracket.
16. Remove the oil pan attaching bolts and remove the oil pan.

To Install:
1. Apply sealer to both sides of pan gaskets and install on block. Be certain that the tabs on the gaskets are installed in the notches of the seals.
2. Apply sealer on the front cover oil pan seal retainer.
3. Install front and rear seals (rubber). Apply sealer to each end of the seal where it contacts the cylinder block.
4. Wipe the seal area of the oil pan with engine oil, then install the pan. Torque bolts to 10 ft. lbs. (14 Nm).
5. Install all components removed, fill crankcase with oil, start engine and check for leaks.

6-33

SECTION 6

GENERAL MOTORS—"A" AND "X" BODY
FRONT WHEEL DRIVE CARS

OIL PUMP

Removal and Installation

151 (2.5L) ENGINE
1. Raise and support the vehicle safely.
2. Unbolt the oil pan retaining nuts. Remove the oil pan. Discard the gasket.
3. Remove the oil pump bolts. Remove the main bearing cap bolt.
4. Remove the oil pump and screen assembly.
5. Installation is the reverse of the removal procedure. Install the oil pan with new gaskets.

173 (2.8L) ENGINE
1. Raise and support the vehicle safely.
2. Unbolt the oil pan retaining bolts. Remove the oil pan. Discard the gasket.
3. Remove the oil pump bolts. Remove the drive shaft extension.
4. Remove the oil pump and screen assembly.
5. Installation is the reverse of the removal procedure. Inspect for oil leaks and check oil pressure.

183 (3.0L) AND 231 (3.8L) ENGINES
1. Raise and support the vehicle safely.
2. Remove the oil pan bolts and remove the oil pan. Discard the gasket.
3. Remove the oil filter. Unbolt the oil pump cover from the timing chain cover.
4. Remove the oil pump drive and driven gears. Remove the oil pressure relief valve cap, spring and valve.
5. Installation is the reverse of the removal procedure. Use new gaskets and check for oil leaks.

263 (4.3L) DIESEL ENGINE
1. Raise and support the vehicle safely.
2. Remove the oil pan bolts and remove the oil pan. Discard the gasket.
3. Remove the rear main bearing cap attaching bolts. Remove the oil pump and the drive shaft extension.
4. Installation is the reverse of the removal procedure. Check for oil leaks.

REAR MAIN OIL SEAL

Removal and Installation

151 (2.5L) ENGINE
1. Remove the transaxle and flywheel assembly from the vehicle. Support in a suitable work fixture.
2. Remove the flywheel retaining bolts. Remove the flywheel.
3. Remove the pressure plate and disc if equipped with manual transmission.
4. Without scratching the crankshaft, remove the old seal using a suitable tool.
5. Press the new seal evenly into place. Lubricate with motor oil. Install all other parts in the reverse order of the removal procedure.

173 (2.8L) ENGINE
1. Remove the transaxle assembly from the vehicle and place in a suitable holding fixture.
2. Remove the flex plate or flywheel as applicable.
3. Remove the Remove the oil seal being careful not to damage the crankshaft.
4. Inspect the inside diameter of the bore for damage. Corresct as required. Inspect the crankshaft for burrs which contact the seal. Repair or replace the crankshaft as required.
5. Clean the seal grooves and apply a thin coat of 1050026 or equivalent to the seals. Position the new seal in the cylinder block. Inspect the seal making sure the seal is seated squarely in the bore.
6. The remaining installation is the reverse of the removal procedure. Start the engine and check for leaks.

183 (3.0L), 231 (3.8L), 263 (4.3L) ENGINES
1. Raise and support the vehicle safely.
2. Drain the oil and remove the oil pan.
3. Remove the rear main bearing cap.
4. Using tool BT-6433 or its equivalent, drive the old seal gently into the groove until it is packed tight.
5. Place the new seal in the groove with both ends projecting above the surface of the cap. Push the new seal into the groove until not more than 1/16 in. projects from the groove.
6. Lubricate the new seal with 1050026 or equivalent. The remaining installation is the reverse of the removal procedure.

FRONT SUSPENSION AND STEERING SECTION

For Front Suspension Services Refer to Unit Repair Section. For Steering Gear Overhaul Refer to Unit Repair Section.

STEERING WHEEL

Removal and Installation

Steering wheels on these models are removed and installed in the conventional manner. Note that if a small steering wheel center cap is used, it must be carefully removed; if a full width wheel pad is used, remove the screws from the rear of the wheel to remove the pad.

STEERING RACK

Removal and Installation

1. Move the intermediate shaft seal upward, then remove the intermediate shaft-to-stub shaft pinch bolt.
2. On models with power steering, remove the air, cleaner assembly.
3. Disconnect the power steering pipes from the gear, if so equipped.
4. Raise the vehicle and remove both wheel and tire assemblies.
5. Remove the tie rod cotter pins and nuts, then separate the tie rod ends from the steering knuckles.
6. Place supports under the vehicle body.
7. Remove the air injection pipe bracket bolt from the crossmember, if so equipped.
8. Remove the two rear cradle mount bolts and carefully lower the rear of the cradle 4-5 inches.

CAUTION
Do not lower the cradle too far, as damage to the underhood components may result.

GENERAL MOTORS—"A" AND "X" BODY
FRONT WHEEL DRIVE CARS

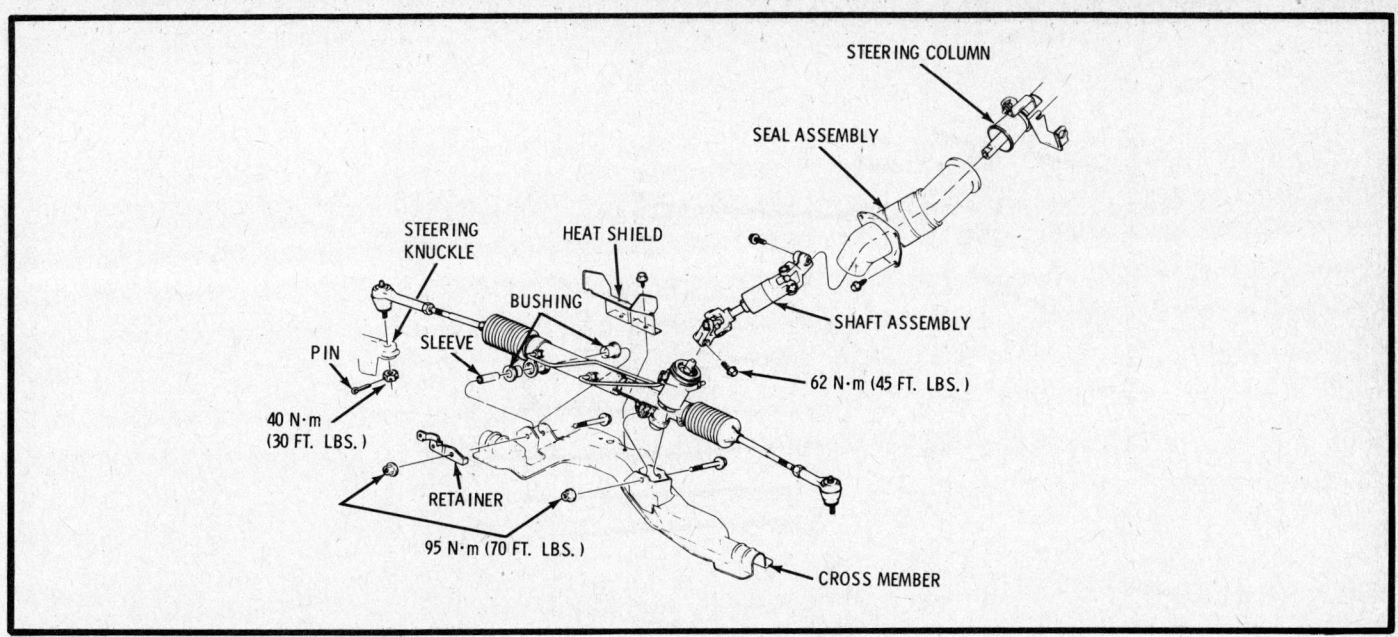

Steering rack and related components (© General Motors Corporation)

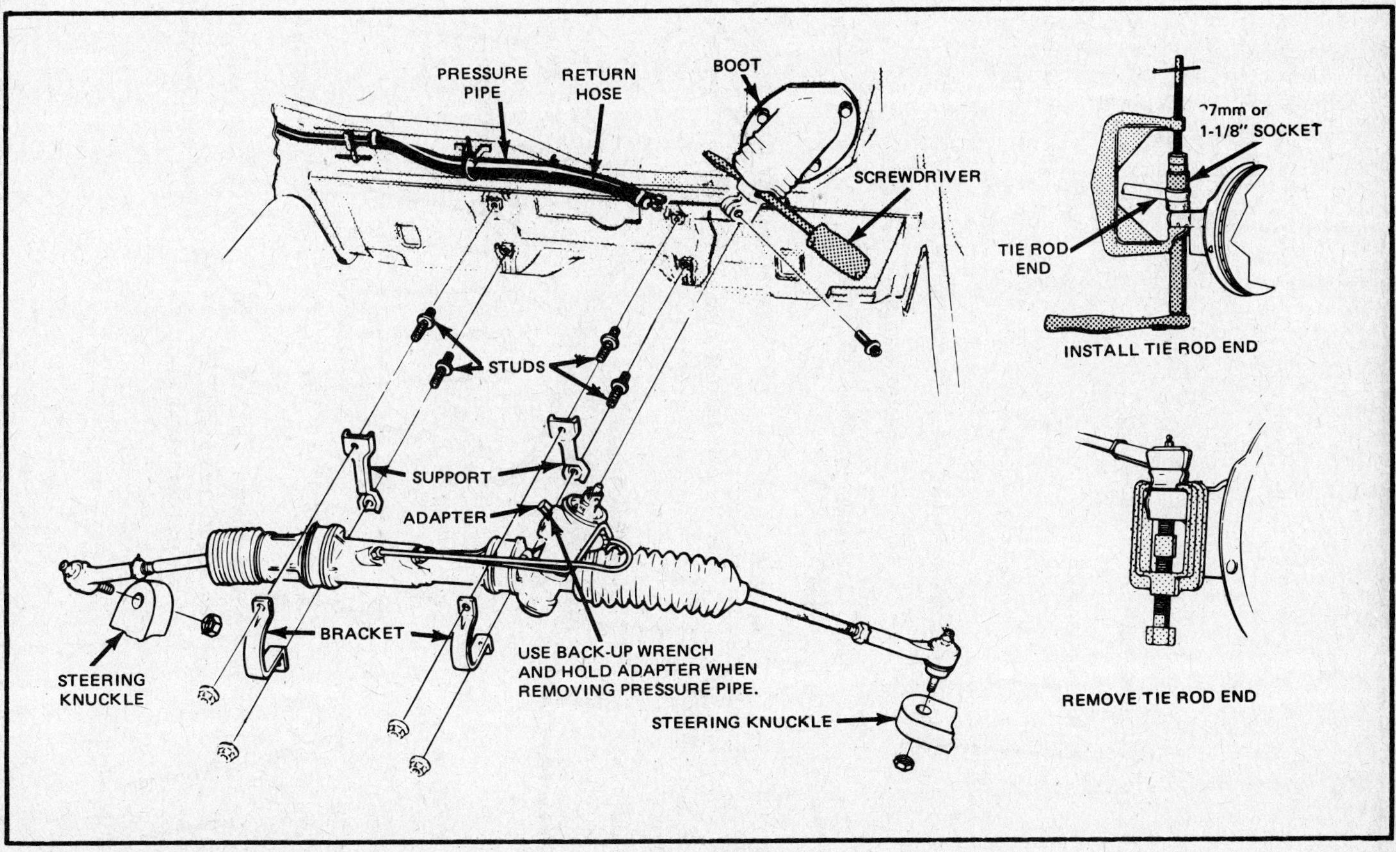

Steering rack and related components—1982 and later models
(© General Motors Corporation)

6-35

SECTION 6: GENERAL MOTORS — "A" AND "X" BODY
FRONT WHEEL DRIVE CARS

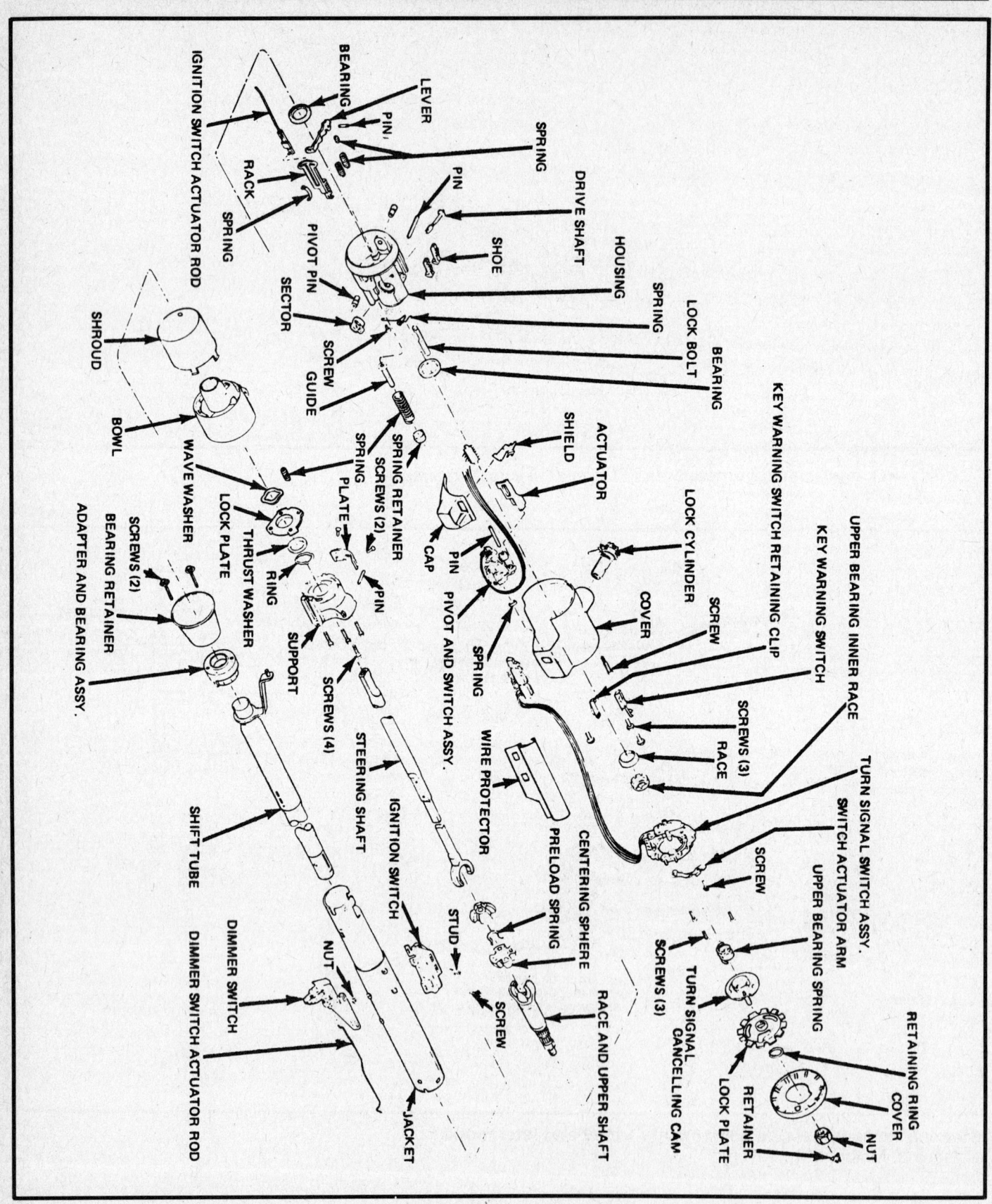

Steering column exploded view – typical (© General Motors Corporation)

GENERAL MOTORS—"A" AND "X" BODY
FRONT WHEEL DRIVE CARS

9. Remove the heat shield, if so equipped.
10. Remove the two steering rack mounting bolts, then remove the rack assembly through the left side wheel opening.
11. Installation is performed in the reverse of the previous steps. After adding the power steering fluid, start the engine and allow it to idle for a minute. Stop the engine and add additional fluid as required. Check for leaks after the engine has been started, then check and adjust the toe-in.

FRONT WHEEL BEARINGS

Adjustment

The only adjustment that can be made to these vehicles after front wheel bearing removal and installation is to lower the vehicle and torque the hub nut to 185 ft. lbs. (260 Nm).

POWER STEERING PUMP

Removal and Installation
FOUR CYLINDER ENGINE

1. Raise and support the vehicle.
2. Remove the pump drive belt and siphon the fluid from the pump reservoir.
3. Disconnect the hydraulic lines from the pump.
4. Remove the radiator hose clamp bolt.
5. Remove the upper and lower bolts (and the upper nut) from the front pump bracket.
6. Remove the pump and bracket from the engine.
7. Installation is performed in the reverse of the previous steps. Be sure to adjust the drive belt tension and bleed the hydraulic system.

V6 GASOLINE ENGINES

1. Disconnect the negative battery cable at the battery. Remove air cleaner if necessary.
2. Disconnect the blower motor wiring and remove the blower motor.
3. Remove the water hose from the water pump.
4. Siphon the fluid out of the pump reservoir, then disconnect the lines from the pump.
5. Place the new seal in the groove with both ends projecting above the surface of the cap. Push the new seal into the groove until not more than 1/16 in. projects from the groove.
6. Lubricate the new seal with 1050026 or equivalent. The remaining installation is the reverse of the removal procedure.
5. Remove the pump drive belt.

6. Remove the one nut which attaches the rear pump bracket to the engine bracket.
7. Remove the two front pump bracket-to-engine bolts, then remove the pump and bracket assembly.
8. See Step 7 of the previous "Four Cylinder Engine" procedure.

V6 DIESEL ENGINE

1. Remove the pump drive belt.
2. Siphon the fluid from the pump reservoir.
3. Raise and support the vehicle.
4. Disconnect the lines from the pump.
5. Remove the three bolts from the front of the pump, through the access holes provided in the pump pulley.
6. Remove the two nuts which attach the lower brace to the engine and remove the brace.
7. Remove the pump and pulley as an assembly.
8. Installation is the reverse of removal.

STEERING COLUMN

NOTE: Once the steering column is removed from the car, the column is extremely susceptible to damage. Dropping the column assembly on its end could collapse the steering shaft or loosen the plastic injections which maintain column rigidity. Leaning on the column assembly could cause the jacket to bend or deform. Any of the above damage could impair the column's collapsible design. If it is necessary to remove the steering wheel, use a standard wheel puller. Under no condition should the end of the shaft be hammered upon, as hammering could loosen the plastic injection which maintains column rigidity.

Removal and Installation

1. Disconnect the negative battery cable.
2. If column repairs are to be made, remove the steering wheel.
3. Remove the nuts and bolts attaching the flexible coupling to the bottom of the steering column. Remove the safety strap and bolt if equipped.
4. Remove the steering column trim shrouds and column covers.
5. Disconnect all wiring harness connectors. Remove the dust boot mounting screws and column mounting bracket bolts.
6. Lower the column to clear the mounting bracket and carefully remove from the car.
7. Install in the reverse order of removal.

SECTION 6: GENERAL MOTORS—"A" AND "X" BODY
FRONT WHEEL DRIVE CARS

BRAKE SECTION

For Anti-Lock Brake Service Refer to the Unit Repair Section

MASTER CYLINDER

Removal and Installation

1. On models with manual brakes, disconnect the master cylinder pushrod from the brake pedal.
2. Disconnect the electrical connector and the hydraulic lines from the master cylinder.
3. Remove the two master cylinder attaching nuts and remove the cylinder.
4. Installation is performed in the reverse of the previous steps.

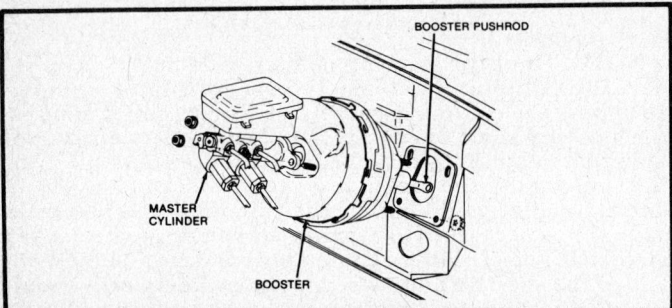

Master cylinder and brake booster mounting—typical (© General Motors Corporation)

VACUUM BRAKE BOOSTER

Removal and Installation

1. Unbolt the master cylinder from the booster and carefully move the cylinder out of the way enough to clear the booster.
2. Disconnect the booster pushrod from the brake pedal.
3. Remove the booster attaching nuts and remove the booster.
4. Installation is the reverse of the previous steps.

HYDRO-BOOST POWER BRAKE UNIT

Removal and Installation

1. Drain the fluid from the reservoir.
2. Remove the master cylinder nuts and move the master cylinder with the lines still attached away from the booster.
3. Remove the hydraulic lines from the booster.
4. Remove the Hydro-Boost pushrod from the brake pedal.
5. Remove the booster to dash panel attaching nuts and remove the booster.
6. Installation is the reverse of the removal procedure.

PARKING BRAKE

Adjustment

1. Depress the parking brake pedal exactly three clicks.
2. Raise and support the vehicle safely.
3. Make sure that the equalizer nut groove is well lubricated with grease.
4. Tighten the parking brake cable adjusting nut until the right rear wheel can be turned counterclockwise with both hands, but locks when clockwise rotation is attempted.
5. Release the parking brake pedal. The rear wheels must be able to turn freely in either direction; if not, repeat the procedure.
6. Lower the vehicle.

PARKING BRAKE CABLE

Removal and Installation

1. Loosen the equalizer nut until the cable tension is released. Depress the retaining tabs and remove the cable from the lever assembly inside the passenger compartment.
2. Raise and support the vehicle safely.
3. Remove the rear wheels. Remove the rear brake drums.
4. Using a suitable tool, move the brake adjuster brackets on the left and right sides to the front and remove the top adjuster bracket rod.
5. Remove the rear hold down springs, actuator levers and return springs from the brake assembly.
6. Remove the adjuster screw spring.
7. Depress the conduit fitting retaining tabs and remove the conduit fitting from the backing plate.

NOTE: On the right rear cable, the cable end button will have to be removed to disconnect the cable.

8. Installation is the reverse of the removal procedure. Adjust the cable as required.

CLUTCH, TRANSMISSION AND DRIVESHAFT SECTION

For Overhaul Procedures Refer to Unit Repair Section.

CLUTCH PEDAL/LINKAGE

Adjustments

The clutch is self-adjusting. Check the self-adjusting mechanism as follows:
1. Depress the clutch pedal and look for the pawl to firmly engage with the teeth in the quadrant.
2. Release the clutch pedal and look for the pawl to be lifted off the quadrant teeth by the bracket stop.

CLUTCH

Removal and Installation

1. Disconnect the clutch cable from the transaxle.
2. Remove the transaxle assembly as outlined later in this section.
3. Mark the relationship between the pressure plate and flywheel.
4. Evenly and carefully loosen the pressure plate bolts until the spring pressure is relieved.
5. Support the pressure plate, then remove the pressure plate bolts.

GENERAL MOTORS—"A" AND "X" BODY
FRONT WHEEL DRIVE CARS

6. Remove the pressure plate and disc.

CAUTION

DO NOT disassemble the pressure plate and disc assembly. If the unit is defective, replace as an assembly.

---

7. Clean and lubricate all parts as required.
8. Installation is the reverse of removal. Note that the disc is installed with the damper springs offset towards the transaxle. Most discs are marked "flywheel side." If the old pressure plate is to be reused, align the marks made during Step 3.

MANUAL TRANSAXLE

Removal and Installation

1. Disconnect the negative battery cable.
2. Disconnect the electrical lead from the horn and remove the attaching bolt. Remove the air cleaner assembly. Disconnect the clutch cable. If equipped with a V6 engine disconnect the fuel lines and fuel line clamps at the clutch cable bracket. Remove the bracket.
3. Remove the clutch cable bracket from the transaxle. Remove the two transaxle strut bracket bolts on the left side of the engine compartment, if equipped.
4. Remove the top four engine-to-transaxle bolts, and the one at the rear near the firewall. The one at the rear is installed from the engine side.
5. Loosen the engine-to-transaxle bolt near the starter, if necessary, but do not remove.
6. Disconnect the speedometer cable at the transaxle, or at the speed control transducer on cars so equipped.
7. Remove the retaining clip and washer from the shift linkage at the transaxle. Remove the clips holding the cables to the mounting bosses on the case.
8. Support the engine with a lifting chain.
9. Unlock the steering column and raise and support the car. Drain the transaxle. Remove the two nuts attaching the stabilizer bar to the left lower control arm. Remove the four bolts which attach the left retaining plate to the engine cradle. The retaining plate covers and holds the stabilizer bar.
10. Loosen the four bolts holding the right stabilizer bracket.
11. Disconnect and remove the exhaust pipe and crossover if necessary.
12. Pull the stabilizer bar down on the left side.
13. Remove the four nuts and disconnect the front and rear transaxle mounts from the engine cradle. Remove the two rear center crossmember bolts.
14. Remove the three right side front cradle attaching bolts. They are accessible under the splash shield.
15. Remove the top bolt from the lower front transaxle shock absorber if equipped.
16. Remove the left front wheel. Remove the front cradle-to-body bolts on the left side, and the rear cradle-to-body bolts.
17. Pull the left side drive shaft from the transaxle. The right side axle shaft will simply disconnect from the case. When the transaxle is removed, the right shaft can be swung out of the way. A boot protector should be used when disconnecting the driveshafts.
18. Swing the cradle to the left side. Secure out of the way, outboard of the fender well.
19. Remove the flywheel and starter shield bolts, and remove the shields.
20. Remove the two transaxle extension bolts from the engine-to-transaxle bracket, if equipped.
21. Place a jack under the transaxle case. Remove the last engine-to-transaxle bolt. Pull the transaxle to the left, away from the engine, then down and out from under the car.
22. Installation is the reverse of removal.
23. Position the right axle shaft into its bore as the transaxle is being installed.
24. When the transaxle is bolted to the engine, swing the cradle into position and install the cradle-to-body bolts immediately. Be sure to guide the left axle shaft into place as the cradle is moved back into position.

SHIFT INDICATOR

Removal and Installation

1. Disconnect the negative battery cable.
2. Remove the instrument cluster assembly screws. Remove the instrument cluster assembly.
3. Remove the screws holding the shift indicator to the instrument cluster.
4. Remove the shift indicator.
5. Installation is the reverse of the removal procedure.

AUTOMATIC TRANSAXLE

Removal and Installation

1. Disconnect the negative battery cable at the transaxle.
2. Remove:
   a. Air cleaner and disconnect the T.V. cable.
   b. T.V. cable lower attaching bolt and disconnect the cable from the transaxle.
   c. Strut shock bracket bolts from the transaxle.
   d. Oil cooler lines from the strut bracket.
   e. Transaxle-to-engine bolts, leaving the bolt near the starter installed loosely.
   f. Shift linkage retaining clip and washer at the transaxle.
   g. Shift linkage bracket bolts.
3. Disconnect the speedometer drive cable at the upper and lower couplings (at the transducer if equipped with cruise control).
4. Disconnect the oil cooler lines at the transaxle.
5. Install the engine support fixture, locating it at the center of the cowl for four cylinder engines and on the strut towers for six cylinder engines.

NOTE: When installing a lift chain onto the aluminum cylinder head of the 4.

3 liter V6 diesel engine, be sure that the bolt is tight or damage to the cylinder head may occur.

6. Rotate the steering wheel to position the steering gear stub shaft bolt in the upward position. Remove the bolt.
7. Raise the vehicle and place a jack under the engine to act as a support during removal and installation.
8. Remove the left front tire and wheel assembly.
9. Remove the power steering line brackets, remove the mounting bolts for the steering rack assembly, and support the assembly.
10. Disconnect the driveline vibration absorber, if so equipped.
11. Disconnect the left side lower ball joint at the steering knuckle.
12. Remove the front stabilizer bar reinforcements and bushings from the right and left cradle side members.
13. Using a drill with a 1/2 in. bit, drill through the spot weld located between the rear holes of the left side front stabilizer bar mounting.
14. Disconnect the engine and transaxle mounts from the cradle.
15. Remove the sidemember-to-crossmember bolts.
16. Remove the bolts from the left side body mounts.
17. Remove the left side and front crossmember assembly. It may be necessary to carefully pry the crossmember loose.
18. Install axle shaft boot protectors, and using the appropri-

SECTION 6: GENERAL MOTORS—"A" AND "X" BODY
FRONT WHEEL DRIVE CARS

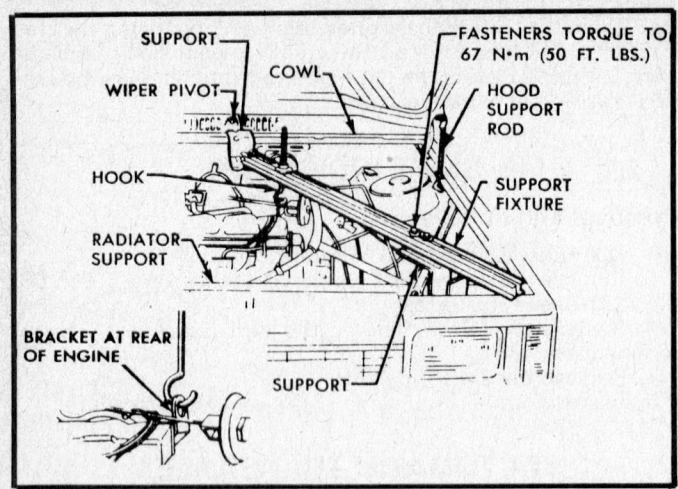

Engine support fixture arrangement—151 (2.5L) engine (© General Motors Corporation)

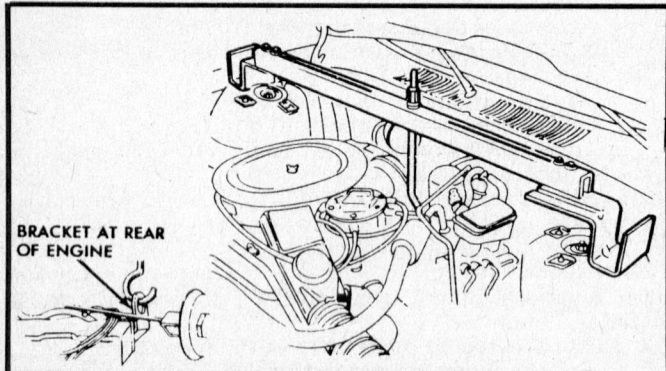

Engine support fixture arrangement—173 (2.8L) engine (© General Motors Corporation)

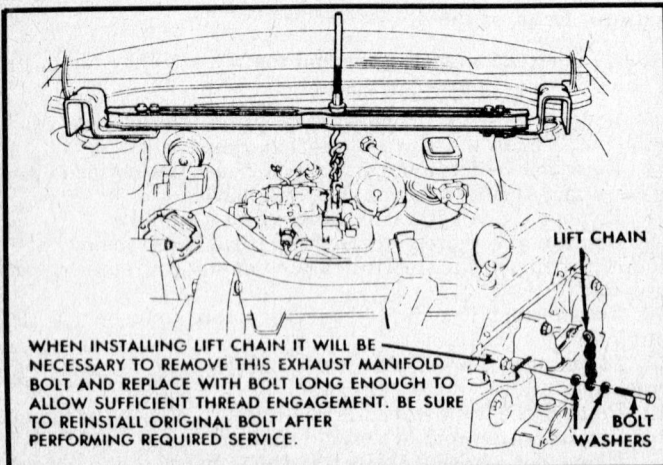

Engine support fixture arrangement—183 (3.0L) engine (© General Motors Corporation)

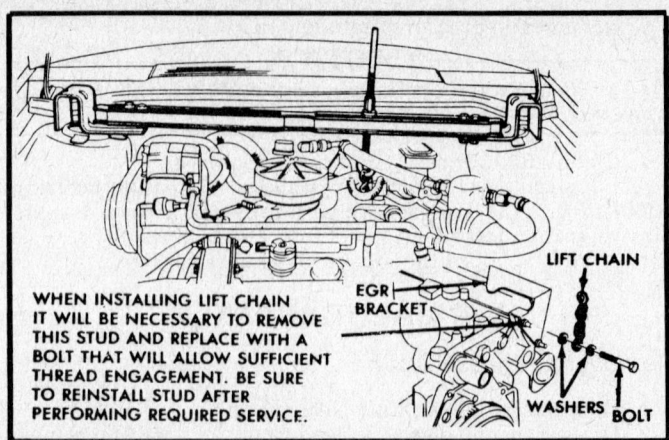

Engine support fixture arrangement—diesel engine (© General Motors Corporation)

ate special tools, pull the axle shaft cones out and away from the transaxle.
19. Pull the left axle shaft out of the transaxle.
20. Rotate the strut assembly so that the axle shaft is out of the way.
21. Remove:
   a. Starter and convertor shields.
   b. Flywheel-to-converter bolts.
   c. Two transaxle extension bolts from the engine-to-transaxle bracket.
   d. Rear transaxle mount bracket assembly. It may be necessary to raise the transaxle slightly.
22. Securely attach a transaxle jack to the transaxle assembly.
23. Remove the two braces to the right end of the transaxle bolts.
24. Remove the remaining transaxle-to-engine bolt.
25. Remove the transaxle by moving it towards the drivers side, away from the engine.
26. Installation is performed in the reverse of the previous steps. Note the following:
   a. When raising the transaxle into place, guide the right side axle shaft into the transaxle.
   b. Check and adjust all front end alignment settings after the installation is complete.
   c. Adjust the transmission detent cable.

FRONT DRIVE AXLE

Removal and Installation

1. Remove the hub nut and discard. A new hub nut must be used for reassembly.
2. Raise the front of the car. Remove the wheel and tire.
3. Install an axle shaft boot seal protector onto the seal.
4. Disconnect the brake hose clip from the MacPherson strut, but do not disconnect the hose from the caliper. Remove the brake caliper from the spindle, and hang the caliper out of the way by a length of wire. Do not allow the caliper to hang by the brake hose.
5. Mark the camber alignment cam bolt for reassembly. Remove the cam bolt and the upper attaching bolt from the strut and spindle.
6. Pull the steering knuckle assembly from the strut bracket.
7. Remove the axle shaft from the transaxle.
8. Using G.M. special tool J-28733 or the equivalent spindle remover, remove the axle shaft from the hub and bearing assembly. Do not allow the axle shaft to hang free, if necessary, support using wire in order to prevent any component damage.

TO INSTALL:

1. If a new drive axle is to be installed, a new knuckle seal should be installed first along with a boot seal protector when necessary.

GENERAL MOTORS—"A" AND "X" BODY
FRONT WHEEL DRIVE CARS

2. Loosely install the drive axle into the transaxle and steering knuckle.
3. Loosely attach the steering knuckle to the suspension strut.
4. The drive axle is an interference fit in the steering knuckle. Press the axle into place, then install the hub nut. When the shaft begins to turn with the hub, insert a drift through the caliper into one of the cooling slots in the rotor to keep it from turning. On some later models, the hub flange has a notch in it which, when one of the hub bearing retainer bolts is removed and a longer bolt put in its place through the notch, can be used to prevent the hub and the shaft from turning. Tighten the hub nut to 70 ft. lbs. to completely seat the shaft.
5. Install the brake caliper. Tighten the bolts to 30 ft. lbs.
6. Load the hub assembly by lowering it onto a jackstand. Align the camber cam bolt marks made during removal, install the bolt and tighten to 140 ft. lbs. Tighten the upper nut to the same valve.
7. Install the axle shaft all the way into the transaxle using a screwdriver inserted into the groove provided on the inner retainer. Tap the screwdriver until the shaft seats in the transaxle. Remove the boot seal protector.
8. Connect the brake hose clip the the strut. Install the tire and wheel, lower the car, and tighten the hub nut to 192 ft. lbs.

INNER AND OUTER BOOTS

Removal and Installation
OUTER BOOT
1. Raise and support the vehicle safely.
2. Remove the front tire and wheel.
3. Remove the caliper bolts and wire the caliper off to the side.
4. Remove the hub nut, washer and wheel bearing.
5. Using a brass drift, lightly tap around the seal retainer to loosen it. Remove the seal retainer.
6. Remove the seal retaining clamp or ring and discard.
7. Using snap ring pliers, remove the race retaining ring from the axle shaft.
8. Pull the outer joint assembly and the outboard seal away from the axle shaft.
9. Installation is the reverse of the removal procedure. Pack the joint assembly with half of the grease provided. Put the remainder of the grease in the seal.

INNER BOOT
1. Raise and support the vehicle safely.
2. Remove the front tire and wheel.
3. Remove the caliper bolts and wire the caliper off to the side of the vehicle.
4. Remove the hub nut, washer and wheel bearing.
5. Remove the front drive axle as outlined earlier in this section. Place in a suitable holding fixture being careful not place undue pressure on the axle shaft.

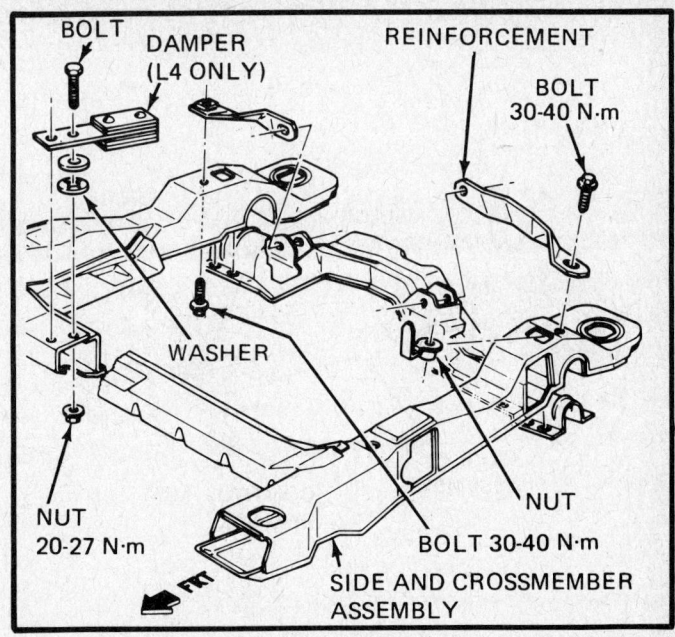

Engine and transaxle support cradle—1982 and later models (© General Motors Corporation)

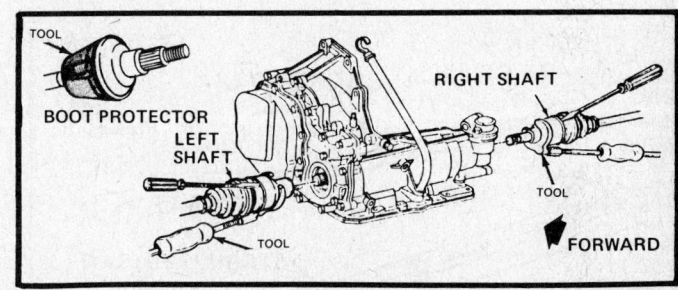

Special tools used for the removal of the axle driveshafts (© General Motors Corporation)

6. Remove the joint assembly retaining ring. Remove the joint assembly.
7. Remove the race retaining ring and remove the seal retainer.
8. Remove the inner seal retaining clamp. Remove the inner joint seal.
9. Installation is the reverse of the removal procedure. Pack the joint assembly with half of the grease provided. Place remainder of the greasse in the seal.

REAR AXLE AND SUSPENSION SECTION

For Axle Overhaul Procedure and Suspension Service. Refer to Unit Repair Section.

REAR AXLE ASSEMBLY

Removal and Installation
1. Raise and support the vehicle safely.

CAUTION
When removing the rear axle on a twin post hoist, the axle assembly must be supported securely otherwise when certain fasteners are removed the axle assembly could slip from the hoist.

---

2. Remove the rear wheels. Remove the rear brake drums. Disconnect the parking brake from the rear axle.

SECTION 6
GENERAL MOTORS—"A" AND "X" BODY
FRONT WHEEL DRIVE CARS

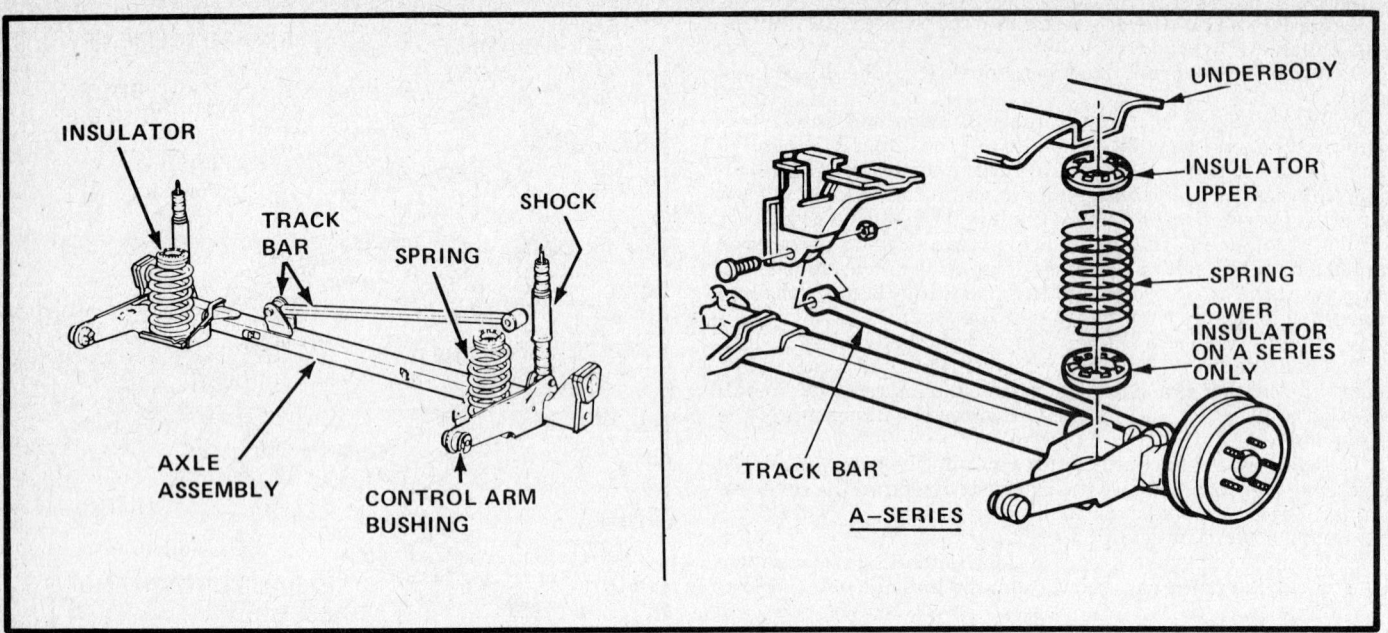

X series rear axle assembly (© General Motors Corp.)

A series rear axle assembly (© General Motors Corp.)

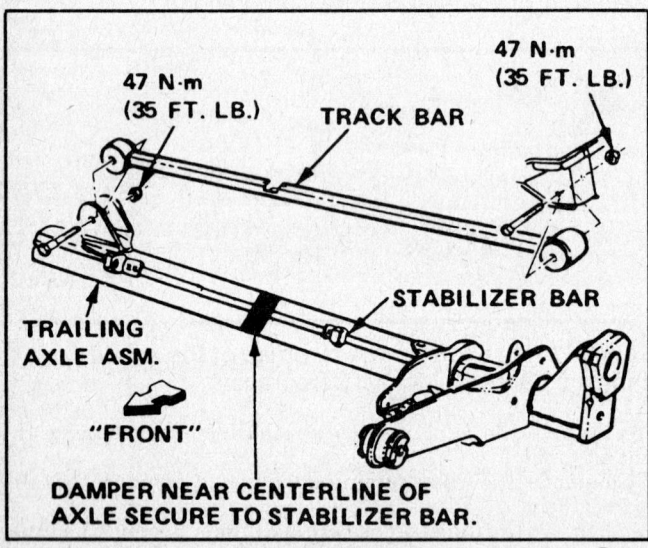

X series track bar attachment (© General Motors Corp.)

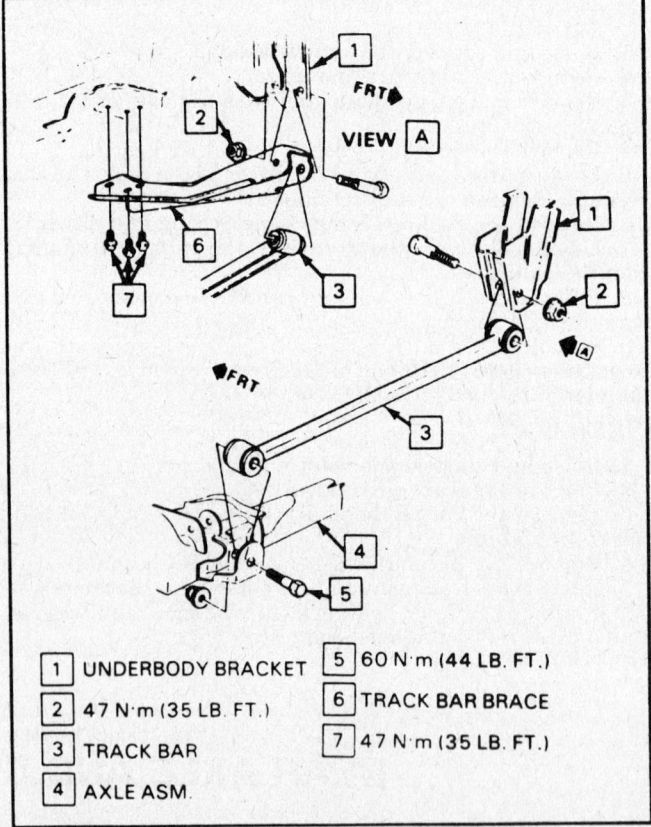

A series track bar attachment (© General Motors Corp.)

REAR WHEEL HUB AND BEARING ASSEMBLY

Removal and Installation

A single unit hub and bearing assembly is bolted to both ends of the rear axle assembly. These take the place of "rear axles" used on rear wheel drive cars. The hub and bearing assembly is a sealed unit which requires no maintenance. The unit be replaced as an assembly and cannot be disassembled or adjusted.

The hub and bearing can be removed by removing the rear brake drum, removing the four hub and bearing-to-axle assembly attaching bolts and pulling the unit out. Installation is the reverse of removal. Tighten the bolts to 35–39 ft. lbs.

3. Remove the brake brackets from the vehicle frame.
4. Remove the rear shock absorbers. Remove the track bar.
5. Disconnect the rear brake hoses.
6. Lower the axle assembly and remove the coil springs and insulators.
7. Remove the hub attaching bolts. Remove the hub and bearing assembly.
8. Remove the control arm bracket attaching bolts. Remove

6–42

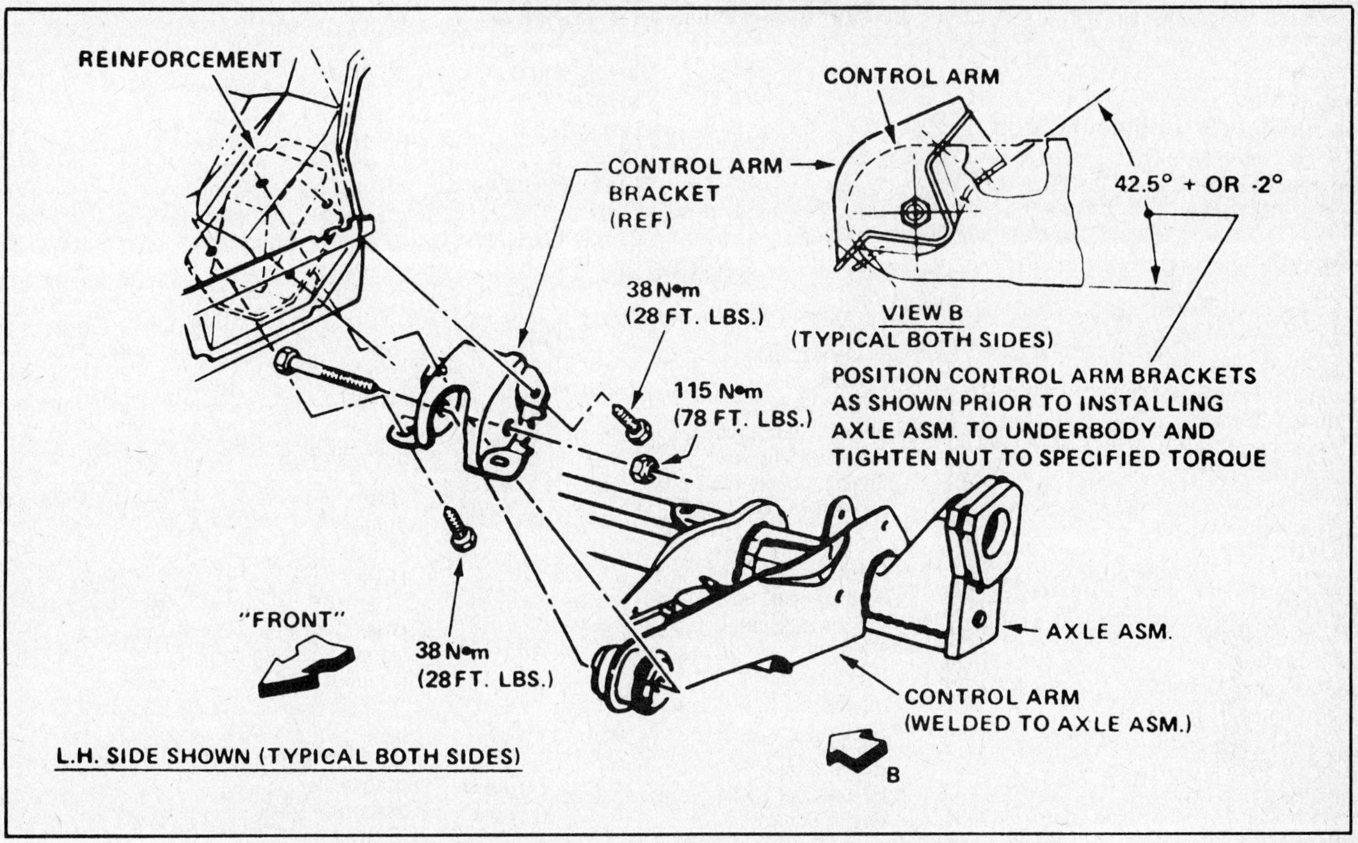

GENERAL MOTORS—"A" AND "X" BODY
FRONT WHEEL DRIVE CARS
SECTION 6

Series control arm attachment to underbody (© General Motors Corp.)

the control arms. Lower the axle from the vehicle.

9. Installation is the reverse of the removal procedure. Bleed the brake system and adjust the parking brake as needed.

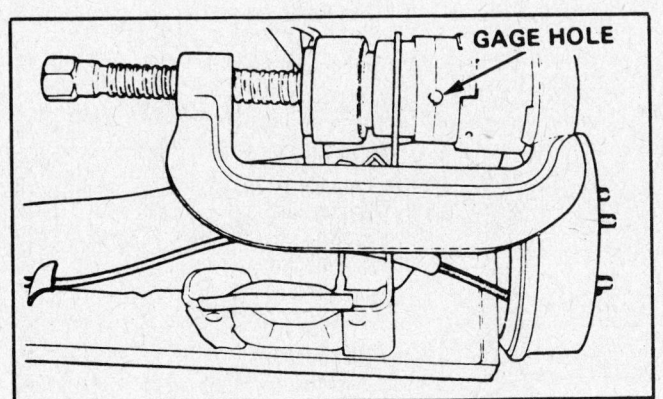

Installing control arm bushing (© General Motors Corp.)

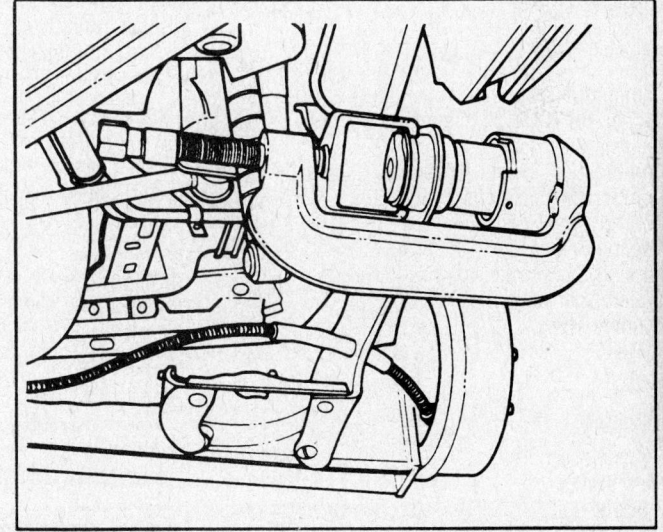

Removing control arm bushing (© General Motors Corp.)

6-43

SECTION 7: GENERAL MOTORS—"C" BODY
FRONT WHEEL DRIVE CARS

SPECIFICATIONS

Brakes	24-2	Serial Number Identification	7-4
Capacities	7-6	Torque	7-6
Crankshaft & Connecting Rod	7-6	Tune-Up	7-4
Firing Order	7-5	Valve	7-5
General Engine	7-4	Wheel Alignment	7-6
Piston & Ring	7-5		

INDEX

A
Alternator	7-7
Automatic Transaxle R&LR	7-27
On Car Service	23-2
Assembly R&R	7-27
Axle Assemby R&R	7-31
Axle Shaft R&R	7-29
Axle Boots R&R	7-29

B
Ball Joints	35-2
Brake System	7-26
Brake Booster	7-26
Brake Caliper Overhaul	24-2
Brake Caliper R&R	
Front	24-2
Brake Drum	
Rear	24-2
Brake Master Cylinder	7-26
Brake Pad	
Front	24-2
Brake Shoe	
Rear	24-2

C
Camshaft R&R	7-23
Carburetor R&R	7-17
Chassis Electrical	7-9
Combination Switch R&R	7-11
Component Locations	7-12
Control Arm R&R	35-2
Cooling Fan Motor	7-15
Cooling System	7-15
Cruise Control	7-12
Cylinder Head	7-22
R&R	7-22

D
Differential	23-2
Inspection	23-2
Disc Brakes	24-2
Front	24-2
Distributor R&R	7-8
Drive Axle	7-27
Driveshaft R&R	7-29

E
Electric Fuel Pump R&R	7-16
Electronic Ignition	30-2
Emission Controls	7-18
Engine	7-19
Identification	7-4
R&R	7-19
Engine Electrical	7-7
Engine Lubrication	7-24
Engine Mechanical	7-19
Engine Mounts R&R	7-22
Exhaust Manifold R&R	7-18

F
Front Suspension	35-2
Alignment	7-6
Fuel Injection	7-18
Fuel Pump R&R	7-16
Fusible Links	7-12

H
Head Light Switch	7-10
Heater Blower R&R	7-16
Heater Core R&R	7-16
Heater Control	7-16

I
Idle Speed Adjust	7-16
Ignition Switch	7-9
Ignition Timing	7-9
Instrument Cluster R&R	7-12
Intake Manifold R&R	7-17

L, M, N
Lower Control Arm R&R	35-2
Master Cylinder R&R	7-26
Neutral Safety Switch	
R&R	7-9

O
Oil Pan R&R	7-24
Oil Pump	7-24
R&R	7-24
Oil Seal R&R	
Rear Main	7-24

P
Parking Brake	7-26
Adjustment	7-26
Cable R&R	7-26
Piston & Connecting Rod	7-23
Power Brake Unit R&R	7-26
Power Steering Pump R&R	7-25

R
Rear Main Oil Seal R&R	7-24
Rear Suspension	35-2
Regulator	7-7
Rocker Shaft/Assembly RR	7-22

S
Serial Number	7-4
Engine	7-4
Vehicle	7-4
Shock Absorber R&R	
Front	35-2
Rear	35-2
Springs	
Front	35-2
Rear	35-2
Starter R&R	7-7
Starter Drive Replacement	7-7
Steering Column R&R	7-26
Steering Gear R&R	7-24
Power	7-24
Steering Wheel R&R	7-24
Stop Light Switch R&R	7-10
Speedometer R&R	7-12
Suspension R&R	35-2
Service	35-2

T
Throttle Linkage, Adjust	7-17
Timing Belt R&R	
Timing Chain	7-23
Timing Gear Cover	7-23
Oil Seal Replacement	7-23
Tune-Up	7-4
Turn Signal Switch R&R	7-10

U, V
U-Joint Overhaul	28-2
Valve Tappette R&R	7-22
Valve Timing, Adjust	7-22
Valve System	7-22
Voltage Regulator	7-7

W, Y
Water Pump R&R	7-15
Wheel Alignment	7-6
Front	7-6
Wheel Bearings Front	7-25
Wheel Cylinders Rear	7-31
Rear	24-2
Windshield Wiper	7-11
Linkage R&R	7-11
Motor R&R	7-11
Switch R&R	7-11
Year Identification	7-3

BEFORE SERVICING BE CERTAIN TO READ THE SAFETY NOTICE

GM "C" Body
1984–87
Front Wheel Drive Cars

BUICK ELECTRA LIMITED • PARK AVENUE • "T" TYPE
CADILLAC FLEETWOOD BROUGHAM • DE VILLE
OLDSMOBILE 98 REGENCY • 98 REGENCY BROUGHAM

YEAR IDENTIFICATION

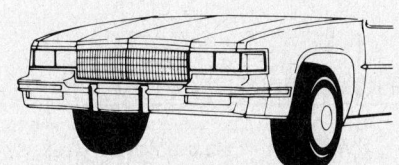

1985–86 Cadillac DeVille, Fleetwood

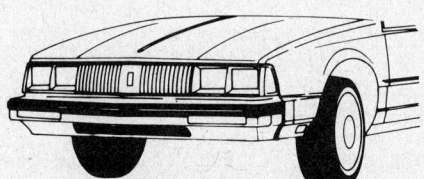

1985–86 Oldsmobile Ninety-Eight Regency Brougham

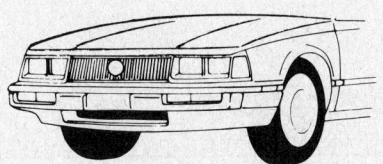

1985–86 Buick Electra, Park Avenue

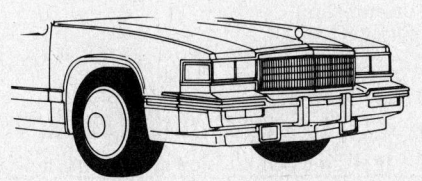

1986–87 Touring Sedan

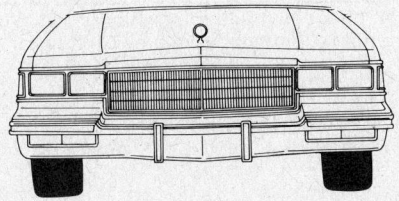

1986–87 Coupe DeVille

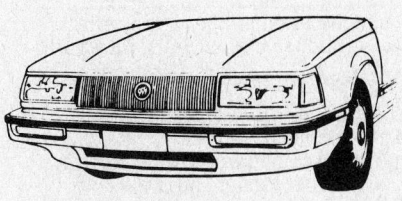

1987 Electra

SECTION 7

GENERAL MOTORS—"C" BODY
FRONT WHEEL DRIVE CARS

VEHICLE IDENTIFICATION NUMBER (VIN)

It is important for servicing and ordering parts to be certain of the vehicle and engine identification. The VIN (vehicle identification number) is a 17 digit number visible through the windshield on the driver's side of the dash and contains the vehicle and engine identification codes. It can be interpreted as follows:

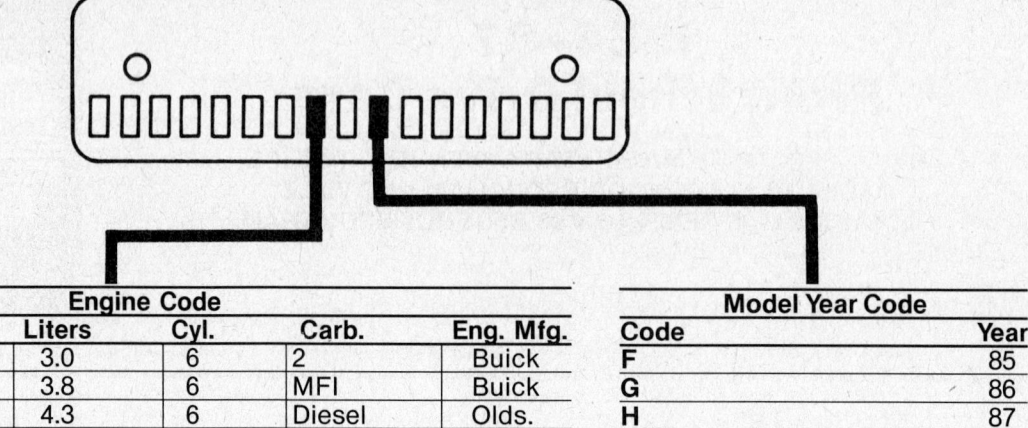

Engine Code

Code	Cu. In.	Liters	Cyl.	Carb.	Eng. Mfg.
E	181	3.0	6	2	Buick
3	231	3.8	6	MFI	Buick
T	263	4.3	6	Diesel	Olds.
8	250	4.1	8	DFI	Cad.

Model Year Code

Code	Year
F	85
G	86
H	87

The seventeen digit Vehicle Identification Number can be used to determine engine application and model year. The 10th digit indicates the model year and the 8th digit identifies the factory installed engine.
MFI Multiport Fuel Injection
DFI Digital Fuel Injection

GENERAL ENGINE SPECIFICATIONS

Year	Eng. VIN Code	Engine Displacement (cu. in.)	Liters	Eng. Mfg.	Fuel Delivery	Horsepower @ rpm■	Torque @ rpm (ft lbs)■	Bore × Stroke (in.)	Compression Ratio	Oil Pressure @ 2000 rpm
'85-'87	E	6-181	3.0	Buick	2bbl	110 @ 4800	145 @ 2600	3.800 × 2.660	8.4:1	35–42
'85-'87	3	6-231	3.8	Buick	MFI	140 @ 4400	200 @ 2000	3.800 × 3.400	8.0:1	35–40
'85-'87	T	6-263	4.3	Olds.	Diesel	85 @ 3600	165 @ 1600	4.057 × 3.385	21.6:1	30–45
'85-'87	8	8-250	4.1	Cad.	DFI	125 @ 4200	190 @ 2000	3.465 × 3.310	8.5:1	30

■ Horsepower and torque are SAE net figures. They are measured at the rear of the transmission with all accessories installed and operating. Since the figures vary when a given engine is installed in different models, some are representative rather than exact.
MFI Multi-Point Fuel Injection
DFI Digital Fuel Injection

GASOLINE ENGINE TUNE-UP SPECIFICATIONS

When analyzing compression test results, look for uniformity among cylinders rather than specific pressures

Year	Eng. VIN Code	No. Cyl. Displacement (cu. in.)	Liters	Eng. Mfg.	Fuel Delivery	Spark Plugs Orig. Type	Spark Plugs Gap (in.)	Distributor Point Dwell (deg.)	Distributor Point Gap (in.)	Ignition Timing (deg.) ▲ Auto. Trans.	Valves Intake Opens ■ (deg.)	Fuel Pump Pressure (psi)	Idle Speed (rpm) ▲ Auto. Trans.
'85-'87	E	6-181	3.0	Buick	2 bbl	R44TSX	.060	Electronic		①②	16	3.9–6.5	①②
'85-'87	3	6-231	3.8	Buick	MFI	R44TS8	.045	Electronic		①②	NA	28–36	①②
'85-'87	8	8-250	4.1	Cad.	DFI	R42CLTS6	.060	Electronic		①②	37	40	①②
'87						See Underhood Specifications Sticker							

NOTE: The underhood specification sticker often reflects tune-up specification changes made in production. Sticker figures must be used if they disagree with those in this chart. Part numbers in this chart are not recommendations by Chilton for any product by brand name.
▲ See text for procedure.
■ All figures Before Top Dead Center
① See Underhood Specifications Sticker
② Only vehicles equipped with computerized emissions systems (which have no distributor vacuum advance unit), the idle speed and ignition timing are controlled by the emissions computer. These adjustments should be performed professionally on models so equipped.

GENERAL MOTORS—"C" BODY
FRONT WHEEL DRIVE CARS

DIESEL ENGINE TUNE-UP SPECIFICATIONS

Year	Engine No. of Cyl.- Displacement- Manufacturer	Liters	Fuel Pump Pressure (psi)	Compression Pressure (psi)	Intake Valve Opens (°BTDC)	Idle Speed (rpm)
'85–Later	6-263-Olds	4.3	5.5–6.5	275 minimum	16	①

Caution: Verify the correct original equipment engine is in the vehicle by referring to the VIN engine code before torquing any bolts.

① See the Underhood Specifications Sticker

FIRING ORDERS

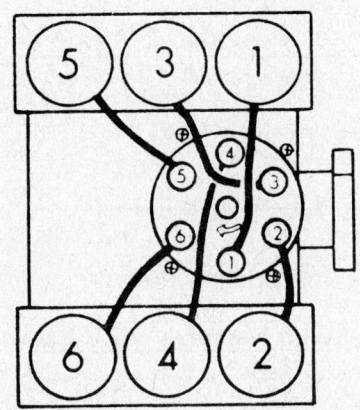

Buick 181, 231, V6 (3.0L, 3.8L)
Engine firing order: 1–6–5–4–3–2
Distributor rotation: clockwise

V 6 harmonic balancers have two timing marks: one is ⅛ in. wide. Use the 1/16 in. mark for timing with a hand held light. The ⅛ in. mark is used only with a magnetic timing pick-up probe.

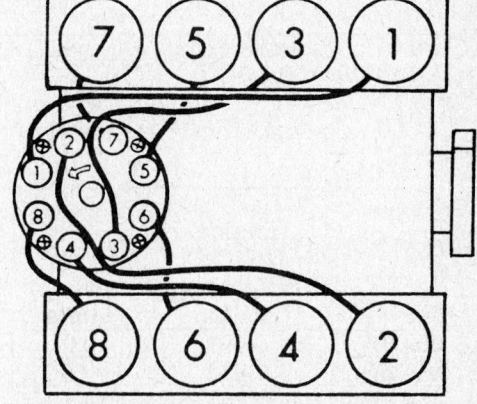

Cadillac 250 V8 (4.1L)
Engine firing order: 1–8–4–3–6–5–7–2
Distributor rotation: counterclockwise

VALVE SPECIFICATIONS

Year	Engine No. Cyl. Displacement (cu. in.)	Liters	Seat Angle (deg.)	Face Angle (deg.)	Spring Test Pressure (lbs @ in.)	Spring Installed Height (in.)	Stem-to-Guide Clearance (in.) Intake	Stem-to-Guide Clearance (in.) Exhaust	Stem Diameter (in.) Intake	Stem Diameter (in.) Exhaust
'85–'87	6-181	3.0	45	45	220 @ 1.340	1.727	0.0015–0.0035	0.0015–0.0032	0.3401–0.3412	0.3405–0.3412
'85–'87	6-231	3.8	45	45	220 @ 1.340	1.727	0.0015–0.0035	0.0015–0.0032	0.3401–0.3412	0.3405–0.3412
'85–'87	6-263	4.3	①	②	210 @ 1.220	1.670	0.0010–0.0027	0.0015–0.0032	0.3425–0.3432	0.3420–0.3427
'85–'87	8-250	4.1	45	44	182 @ 1.280	—	0.001–0.003	0.001–0.003	0.3413–0.3420	0.3411–0.3418

① Intake: 45 Exhaust: 31
② Intake: 44 Exhaust: 30

PISTON AND RING SPECIFICATIONS
All measurements are given in inches.

Year	VIN Code	Engine Type/ Disp. (cu. in.)	Liters	Eng. Mfg.	Piston-to-Bore Clearance	Ring Gap Top Compression	Ring Gap Bottom Compression	Ring Gap Oil Control	Ring Side Clearance Top Compression	Ring Side Clearance Bottom Compression	Ring Side Clearance Oil Control
'85–'87	E	6-181	3.0	Buick	0.0008–0.0020	0.010–0.020	0.010–0.020	0.015–0.055	0.0030–0.0050	0.0030–0.0050	0.0035 max.
'85–'87	3	6-231	3.8	Buick	0.0008–0.0020	0.010–0.020	0.010–0.020	0.015–0.055	0.0030–0.0050	0.0030–0.0050	0.0035 max.
'85–'87	T	6-263	4.3	Olds.	0.0035–0.0045	0.019–0.027	0.013–0.021	0.010–0.022	0.005–0.007	0.003–0.005	0.001–0.005
'85–'87	8	8-250	4.1	Cad.	0.0010–0.0018	0.023–0.025	0.023–0.025	0.010–0.050	0.0016–0.0037	0.0016–0.0037	None (side sealing)

SECTION 7: GENERAL MOTORS – "C" BODY
FRONT WHEEL DRIVE CARS

CRANKSHAFT AND CONNECTING ROD SPECIFICATIONS
All measurements are given in inches

Year	VIN Code	Engine No. Cyl. Displacement (cu. in.)	Liters	Eng. Mfg.	Crankshaft Main Brg. Journal Dia.	Main Brg. Oil Clearance	Shaft End-Play	Thrust on No.	Connecting Rod Journal Diameter	Oil Clearance	Side Clearance
'85–'87	E	6-181	3.0	Buick	2.4990–2.5000	0.0003–0.0018	0.0030–0.0110	2	2.2487–2.2495	0.0005–0.0026	0.006–0.023
'85–'87	3	6-231	3.8	Buick	2.4990–2.5000	0.0003–0.0018	0.0030–0.0110	2	2.2487–2.2495	0.0005–0.0026	0.006–0.023
'85–'87	T	6-263	4.3	Olds.	2.9993–3.0003	①	0.0035–0.0135	4	2.2490–2.2500	0.0005–0.0025	0.008–0.018
'85–'87	8	8-250	4.1	Cad.	2.64	0.0004–0.0027	0.0010–0.0070	3	2.0520–2.0540	0.0005–0.0028	0.008–0.020

① No. 1, 2, & 3: 0.0005–0.0020
No. 4: 0.0020–0.0034

CAPACITIES

Year	Engine No. Cyl. Displacement (cu. in.)	Liters	Engine Crankcase Add 1 qt. for New Filter	Transaxle Automatic Pts. to Refill After Draining •	Gasoline Tank (gals)	Cooling System (qts.) With Heater	With A/C
'85–'87	6-181	3.0	4.0	13	18	13.3	13.6
'85–'87	6-231	3.8	4.0	13	18	13.1	13.2
'85–'87	6-263	4.3	5.5	13	18	13.3	13.3
'85–'87	6-250	4.1	4	13	NA	NA ①	NA ①

• Specifications do not include torque converter
NA Not available at time of publication
① The 4.1L V8 uses a coolant solution specifically designed for use in aluminum engines. Be sure that the coolant you choose meets GM spec. #1825M or is labeled for use in aluminum engines.

TORQUE SPECIFICATIONS
All readings in ft. lbs.

Year	V.I.N. Code	Engine No. Cyl. Displacement (cu. in.)	Liters	Eng. Mfg.	Cylinder Head Bolts	Rod Bearing Bolts	Main Bearing Bolts	Crankshaft Bolt	Flywheel-to-Crankshaft Bolts	Manifold Intake	Exhaust
'85–'87	E	6-181	3.0	Buick	80	40	100	200	60	47	25
'85–'87	3	6-231	3.8	Buick	80	40	100	200	60	47	25
'85–'87	T	6-263	4.3	Olds.	①	42	89	②	76	41	31
'85–'87	8	8-250	4.1	Cad.	③	22	85	18	63	0 ④	18

① All exc. bolt No. 5, 6, 11, 12, 13, 14: 142 } See text
Bolt No. 5, 6, 11, 12, 13, 14: 59
② Crankshaft balancer to crankshaft bolt: 200–350
Crankshaft pulley to balancer bolts: 30
③ See text for proper tightening sequence
④ Bolts No. 1, 2, 3, 4: 15
Bolts No. 5–16: 22

WHEEL ALIGNMENT SPECIFICATIONS

Year	Model	Caster Range (deg.)	Caster Pref. Setting (deg.)	Camber Range (deg.)	Camber Pref. Setting (deg.)	Toe (in.)	Steering Axis (deg.) Inclination
'85–'87	All	1 13/16 – 2 13/16	2 5/16	0–1	1/2	0	—

GENERAL MOTORS—"C" BODY
FRONT WHEEL DRIVE CARS
SECTION 7

ELECTRICAL SECTION

For Overhaul Procedures Refer to the unit Repair Section.

Charging System

ALTERNATOR

Removal and Installation

1. Disconnect the negative battery cable.
2. Tag and disconnect the battery charge wire, 3-prong connector and the ground wire at the back of the alternator.
3. Remove the brace at the back of the alternator (if so equipped).
4. Loosen the adjusting bolt, swivel the alternator in and remove the drive belt.
5. Loosen the power steering pump brace mounting bolts if necessary to gain working clearance.
6. Support the alternator, remove the mounting bolts and then remove the alternator.
7. Installation is in the reverse order of removal. Adjust the drive belt.

VOLTAGE REGULATOR

Removal and Installation

An alternator with an integral voltage regulator is standard equipment. There are no adjustments possible with this unit.

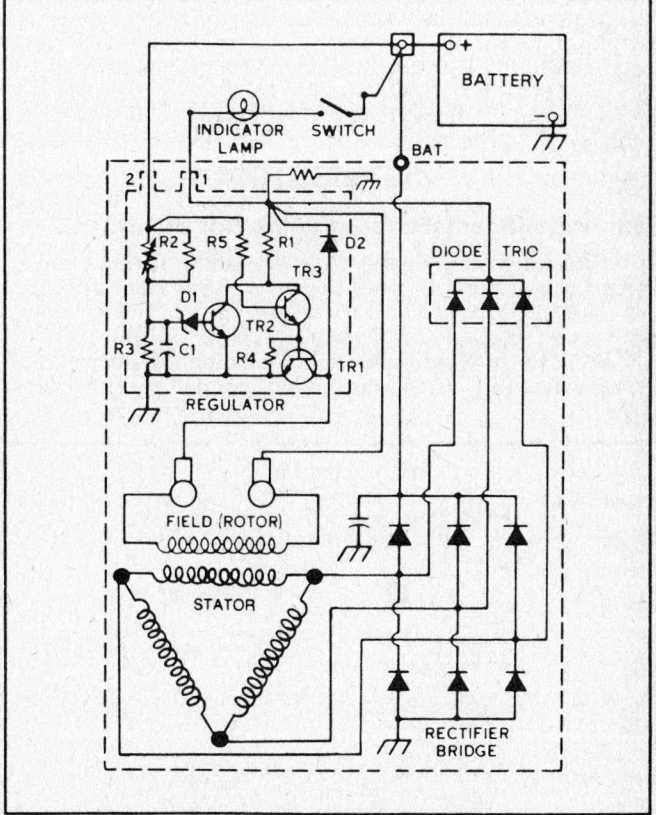

Alternator regulator in charging circuit (© General Motors Corp.)

Starting System

STARTER

Removal and Installation

ALL EXCEPT DIESEL

1. Disconnect the negative battery cable.
2. Raise and support the vehicle safely.
3. Tag and disconnect all wires at the solenoid. Note the color coding of all wires.
4. Remove the starter support bracket mounting bolt. On engines with a solenoid heat shield, remove the front bracket upper bolt and detach the bracket from the starter.
5. Loosen the front bracket bolt or nut and then rotate the bracket clear. Lower and remove the starter. Note the location of any shims so that they may be replaced in the same positions upon installations.

NOTE: On some models it may be necessary to remove the crossover pipe and splash shield if equipped, to complete this procedure.

6. Installation is in the reverse order of removal.

DIESEL

1. Disconnect the negative battery cable.
2. Raise and support the vehicle safely.
3. Remove the lower starter shield nut and then carefully

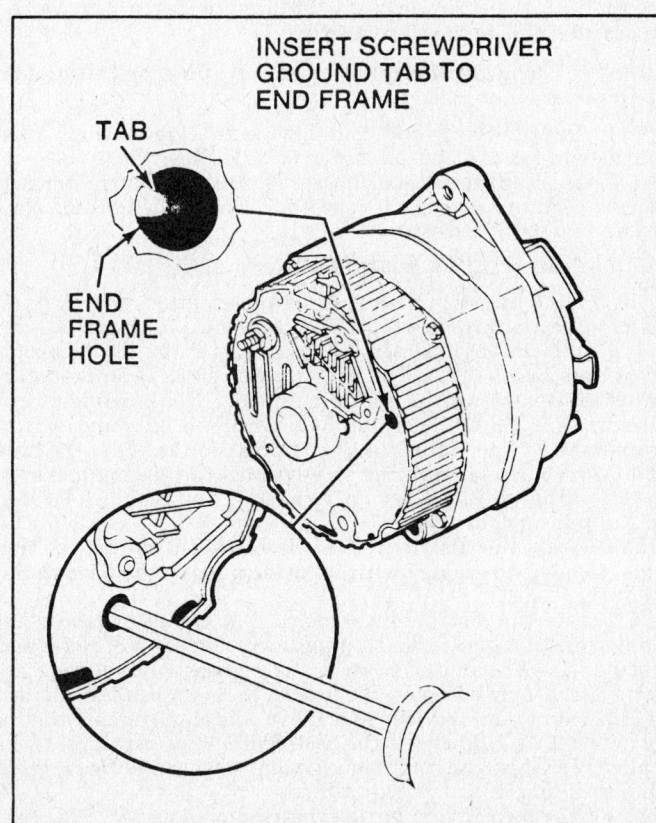

Alternator test hole (© General Motors Corp.)

7-7

bend the shield out of the way. Remove the flywheel cover bolts. Remove the cover in 2 pieces.

4. Tag and disconnect the starter leads at the starter.

5. Remove the front starter bolt. Loosen the rear starter mounting bolt and then remove the starter with the rear bolt still in the housing.

6. Installation is in the reverse order of removal.

Ignition System

DISTRIBUTOR

Removal and Installation (Engine Not Disturbed)

1. Disconnect the negative battery cable. Remove the air cleaner if necessary in order to gain working clearance.

2. Tag and disconnect all wires leading from the distributor cap.

3. Remove the distributor cap by turning the latches counterclockwise. Lift off the distributor cap and carefully set it aside.

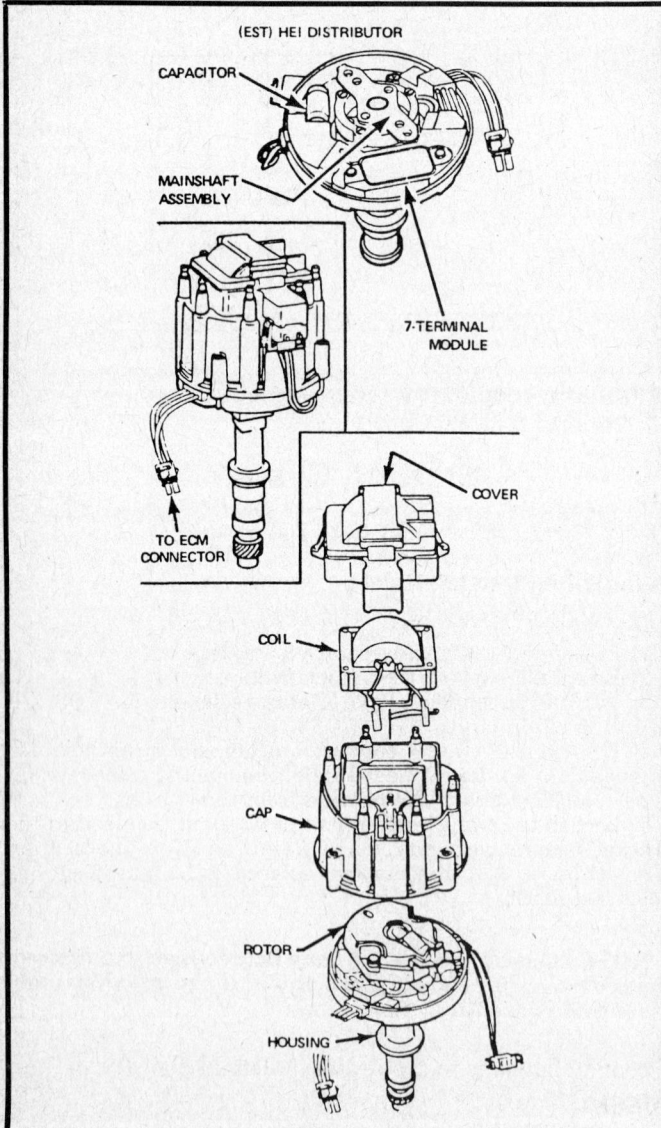

Exploded view of the HEI distributor
(© General Motors Corporation)

NOTE: The location of the distributor cap must be in the same position on reinstallation in order to provide sufficient clearance for adjustment.

4. Disconnect the four terminal ECM connector harness from the distributor if not already done.

5. Loosen, but do not remove, the distributor hold-down clamp.

NOTE: On the 8-250 engine, special tool, No. J-2979, or equivalent, will be required to loosen the hold-down clamp bolt.

6. Scribe a mark on the distributor body to note the initial position of the rotor. Pull the distributor upward until the rotor just stops turning (counterclockwise); note the position of the rotor once again. Remove the distributor.

NOTE: Do not crank the engine with the distributor removed.

7. On certain models, a thrust washer is used between the distributor drive gear and the crankcase. This washer may stick to the bottom of the distributor as it is removed. Always make sure that this washer is at the bottom of the distributor bore before installation.

NOTE: On DFI systems (Digital Fuel Injection), the malfunction trouble codes must be cleared after removal or adjustment of the distributor. This is accomplished by removing battery voltage to terminal "R" for 10 seconds.

8. To install the distributor, rotate the distributor shaft until the rotor aligns with the second rotor positioning mark. Lubricate the drive gear with engine oil, and install the distributor into the engine. As the distributor is installed, the rotor should rotate to the first mark made in Step 6. This will ensure proper timing. If the marks do not align properly, remove the distributor and reinstall correctly.

NOTE: Position the thrust washer when installing the distributor, if so equipped.

9. Install the clamp and hold-down bolt. Tighten them until the distributor can just be moved with a little effort.

10. Connect all wires and hoses. Install the distributor cap and air cleaner assembly if necessary. Check the ignition timing and adjust if necessary.

Installation (Engine Disturbed)

If the engine has been disturbed (cranked) after removing the distributor, perform the following procedure for installation:

1. Crank the engine until No.1 piston is at the top if its compression stroke (TDC). The compression stroke can be determined by removing the spark plug from No. 1 cylinder and placing your thumb over the hole while an assistant slowly cranks the engine. Crank until compresssion is felt at the hole and then continue cranking slowly until the timing mark on the crankshaft pulley lines up with the 0° timing mark located on the timing chain cover.

2. Position the distributor in the block but do not, at this time, allow it to engage with its drive gear at the base of the mounting hole.

3. Rotate the distributor shaft so that the rotor points between No. 1 and No. 8 spark plug towers on the V8, No. 1 and No. 6 on the V6, and push the distributor down to engage the camshaft. It may be necessary to turn the rotor a small amount in either direction in order to achieve this engagement. the rotor will rotate slightly as the distributor gear engages. If installed correctly, the rotor should point toward the No. 1 spark plug terminal in the distributor cap.

4. Press down firmly on the distributor housing. This will ensure that the distributor shaft engages the oil pump shaft, thereby allowing the distributor to fully contact the engine block.

GENERAL MOTORS—"C" BODY
FRONT WHEEL DRIVE CARS
SECTION 7

5. Install the hold-down clamp and tighten the bolt until it is snug.
6. Install the distributor cap, making sure that the rotor points to No. 1 terminal in the cap.
7. Attach all wires and hoses.
8. Start the engine. If it fails to start, or runs roughly, the distributor may be 180° out of time. Lift up on the distributor, turn the rotor one-half revolution, and install the distributor. Repeat Steps 1–8 if the engine continues to run poorly.
9. Check the timing and adjust as necessary.

IGNITION TIMING

Adjustment

NOTE: The 4.1L V8 engine incorporates a magnetic timing probe hole for use with special electronic timing equipment. Consult manufacturer's instructions before using this system.

1. Connect a timing light to the No. 1 spark plug wire according to the light manufacturer's instructions DO NOT PIERCE THE SPARK PLUG WIRE TO CONNECT THE TIMING LIGHT.
2. Follow the instructions on the tune up label located in the engine compartment.
3. On models with Electronic Spark Timing (EST) distributor, disconnect the 4 terminal plug at the distributor. Identification of the EST distributor is given in the emission controls part of this car section, under Computer Command Control.
4. Start the engine and run it at idle speed.
5. Aim the timing light at the degree scale just over the harmonic balancer.
6. Adjust the timing by loosening the securing clamp and rotating the distributor until the desired ignition advance is achieved, then tighten the clamp.

NOTE: On the 4.1L 250 cu. in. V8 engine special tool No. J-29791 or equivalent is used to loosen the hold down nut.

7. Adjust the timing, then replace and tighten the clamp. To advance the timing, rotate the distributor opposite the normal direction of rotor rotation. Retard the timing by rotating the distributor in the normal direction of rotor rotation.

NOTE: On DFI systems (Digital Fuel Injection), the malfunction trouble codes must be cleared after removal or adjustment of the distributor. This is accomplished by removing battery voltage to terminal "R" for 10 seconds.

Electrical Controls

IGNITION LOCK CYLINDER

Removal and Installation

1. Place the lock in the Run position.
2. Remove the lock plate, turn signal switch and buzzer switch.
3. Remove the screw and lock cylinder.

CAUTION

If the screw is dropped on removal, it could fall into the column, requiring complete disassembly to retrieve the screw.

---

4. Rotate the cylinder clockwise to align cylinder key with the keyway in the housing.
5. Push the lock all the way in.
6. Install the screw. Tighten the screws to 14 inch lbs. for adjustable columns and 25 in. lbs. for standard columns.

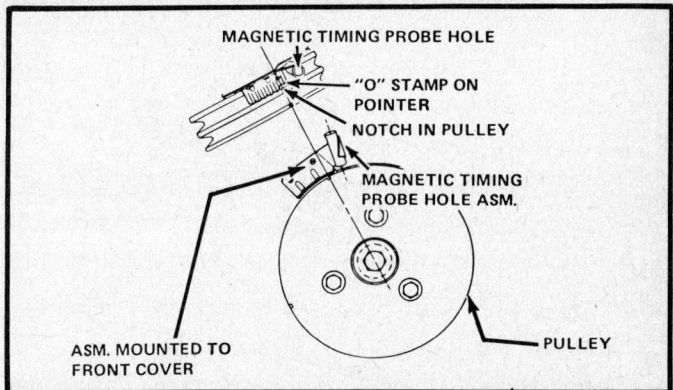

The 4.1L V8 incorporates a special magnetic timing probe hole (© General Motors Corporation)

IGNITION SWITCH

Removal and Installation

The switch is located inside the channel section of the brake pedal support and is completely inaccessible without first lowering the steering column. The switch is actuated by a rod and rack assembly. A gear on the end of the lock cylinder engages the toothed upper end of the rod.

1. Lower the steering column; be sure to properly support it.
2. Put the switch in the "Off-Unlocked" position. With the cylinder removed, the rod is in "Lock" when it is in the next to the uppermost detent. "Off-Unlocked" is two detents from the top.
3. Remove the two switch screws and remove the switch assembly.
4. Before installing, place the new switch in "Off-Unlocked" position and make sure the lock cylinder and actuating rod are in "Off-Unlocked" (third detent from the top) position.
5. Install the activating rod into the switch and assemble the switch on the column. Tighten the mounting screws. Use only the specified screws since overlength screws could impair the collapsibility of the column.

MECHANICAL NEUTRAL START SYSTEM

Vehicles with this system use a mechanical block rather than an electrical neutral start system. The system only allows the

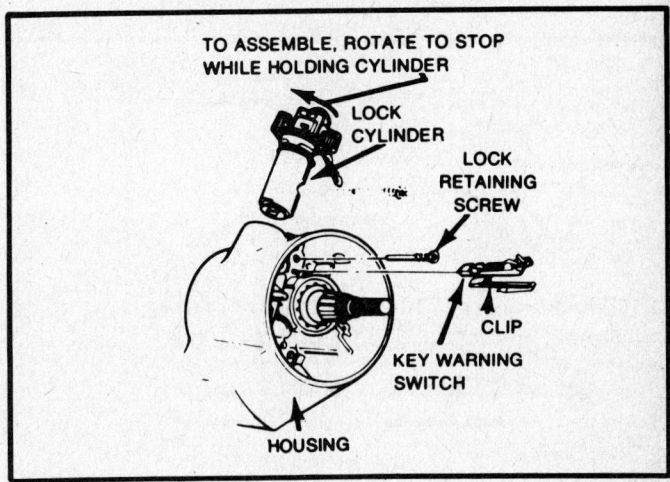

Ignition lock cylinder (© General Motors Corporation)

7-9

SECTION 7: GENERAL MOTORS—"C" BODY
FRONT WHEEL DRIVE CARS

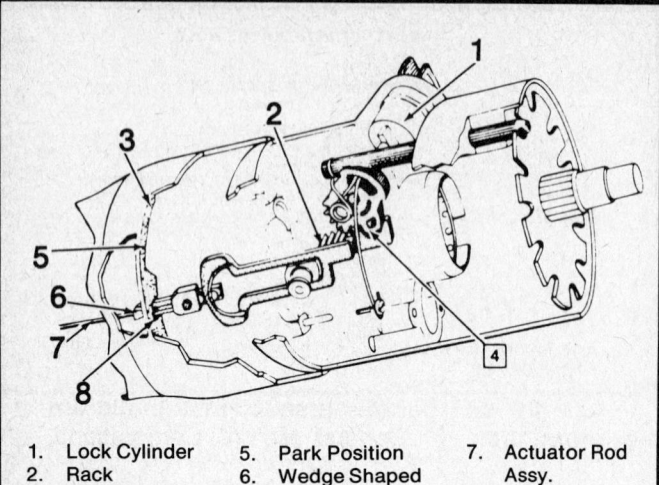

1. Lock Cylinder
2. Rack
3. Bowl Plate
4. Sector
5. Park Position
6. Wedge Shaped Finger
7. Actuator Rod Assy.
8. Neutral Position

Mechanical neutral safety switch
(© General Motors Corporation)

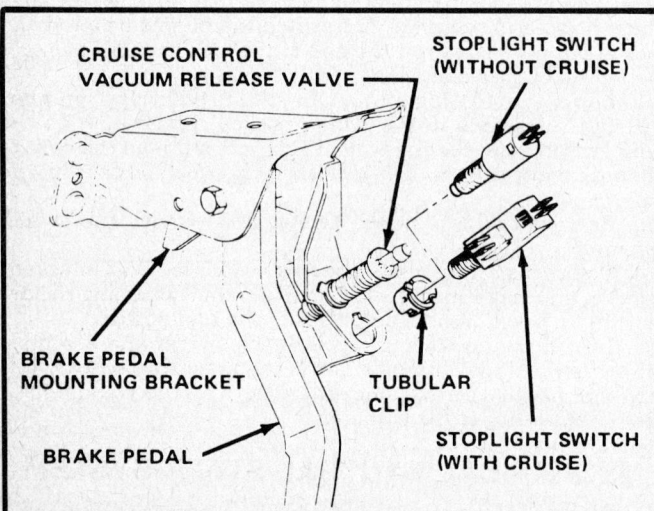

Stoplight switch—typical
(© General Motors Corporation)

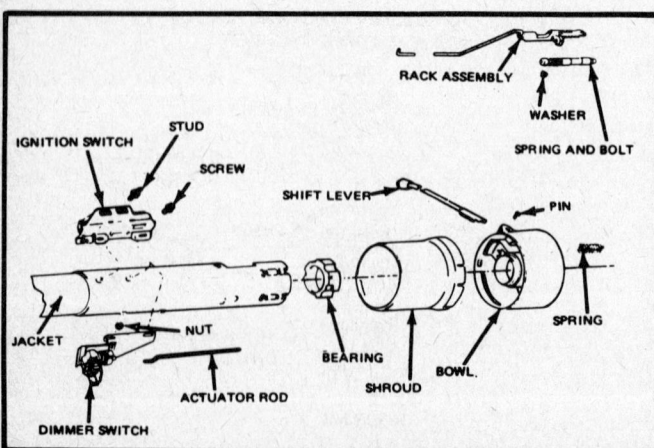

Ignition switch (© General Motors Corporation)

block cylinder to rotate to the start position when the shift lever is in neutral or park.

STOPLIGHT SWITCH

Removal and Installation

1. Disconnect the negative battery cable.
2. Loosen the tubular clip from the stoplight switch assembly.
3. Disconnect the electrical connector from the rear of the switch assembly.
4. Remove the stoplight switch from the vehicle.
5. Installation is the reverse of the removal procedure.

Adjustment

1. Install the switch into the tubular clip until the switch assembly seats itself on the tubular clip.
2. Pull the brake pedal rearward against the pedal stop.
3. The switch will be moved in the tubular clip which will adjust itself properly.

NOTE: Certain 1986–86 models may light up the brake warning light for no apparent reason. After careful inspection of the braking system and no problem is found, the problem may be found in the parking brake mechanism. A small rubber stop may have been lost from the braking mechanism. This allows the brake switch to be compressed, shorting it and causing the brake warning light to operate. If this problem is found, replace the rubber stop with part number 25527682 and install a new switch assembly in the mechanism.

HEADLIGHT SWITCH

Removal and Installation

1. Disconnect the negative battery cable.
2. Remove the instrument trim panel, as required.
3. Remove the headlight switch retaining screws.
4. Pull the switch assembly forward and disconnect the electrical connector. Buick models will automatically disconnect the electrical connector when pulling the switch assembly forward.
5. Remove the switch from the vehicle.
6. Installation is the reverse of the removal procedure.

TURN SIGNAL SWITCH

Removal and Installation

1. Remove the steering wheel. Remove the trim cover.
2. Loosen the cover screws. Remove the cover off with a suitable tool, and lift the cover off the shaft.
3. Position the U-shaped lockplate compressing tool on the end of the steering shaft and compress the lockplate by turning the shaft nut clockwise. Pry the wire snap-ring out of the shaft groove.
4. Remove the tool and lift the lockplate off the shaft.
5. Lift the cancelling cam, upper bearing preload spring, and thrust washer off the shaft.
6. Remove the turn signal lever. Push the flasher knob in and unscrew it. Remove the button retaining screw and remove the button, spring and knob.
7. Pull the switch connector out the mast jacket and tape the upper part to facilitate switch removal. Attach a long piece of wire to the turn signal switch connector. When installing the turn signal switch, feed this wire through the column first, and the use this wire to pull the switch connector into position. On tilt wheels, place the turn signal and shifter housing in low position and remove the harness cover.

GENERAL MOTORS—"C" BODY
FRONT WHEEL DRIVE CARS
SECTION 7

8. Remove the three switch mounting screws. Remove the switch by pulling it straight up while guiding the wiring harness cover through the column.
9. Install the replacement switch by working the connector and cover down through the housing and under the bracket. On tilt models, the connector is worked down through the housing, under the bracket, and then the cover is installed on the harness.
10. Install the switch mounting screws and the connector on the mast jacket bracket. Install the column-to-dash trim plate.
11. Install the flasher knob and the turn signal lever.
12. With the turn signal lever in neutral and the flasher knob out, slide the thrust washer, upper bearing preload spring, and cancelling cam onto the shaft.
13. Position the lock plate on the shaft and press it down until a new snap ring can be inserted in the shaft groove. Always use a new snap ring when assembling.
14. Install the cover and the steering wheel.

WINDSHEILD WIPER SWITCH (MULTI-FUNCTION SWITCH)

Removal and Installation

1. Remove the steering wheel and directional signal switch. It may be necessary to loosen the two column mounting nuts and remove the bracket-to-mast jacket screws, then separate the bracket from the mast jacket to allow the connector clip on the ignition switch to be pulled out of the column assembly.
2. Disconnect the washer/wiper switch lower connector.
3. Remove the screws attaching the column housing to the mast jacket. Be sure to note the position of the dimmer switch actuator rod for reassembly in the same position. Remove the column housing-and-switch as an assembly.

NOTE: The tilt and travel columns have a removable plastic cover on the column housing. This provides access to the wiper switch without removing the entire column housing.

4. Turn upside down and use a drift to remove the pivot pin from the washer/wiper switch. Remove the switch.
5. Place the switch into position in the housing, then install the pivot pin.
6. Position the housing onto the mast jacket and attach by installing screws. Install the dimmer switch actuator rod. Check switch operation.
7. Reconnect lower end of switch assembly.
8. Install remaining components in reverse order of removal. Be sure to attach column mounting bracket in original position.

WINDSHIELD WIPER MOTOR

Removal and Installation

1. Remove the wiper arms.
2. Remove the lower windshield reveal molding, the front cowl panel and the cowl screen as required. Disconnect the washer hose under the screen.
3. Disconnect the motor electrical leads.
4. Loosen, but do not remove, the transmission drive link attaching nuts to the motor crank arm.
5. Disconnect the drive link from the motor crank arm.
6. Remove the motor attaching bolts. On models with air conditioning, it may be necessary to remove the bolts and while supporting the motor, remove the motor crank arm. The motor attaching bolts must be removed first to avoid damage to the nylon gear inside the motor. On all models, rotate the motor up and out to remove.
7. Installation is the reverse of the removal procedure.

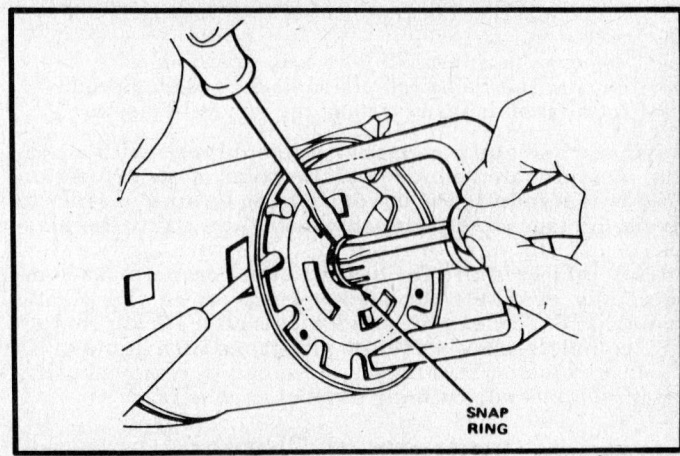
Depress the lockplate and remove the snapring (© General Motors Corporation)

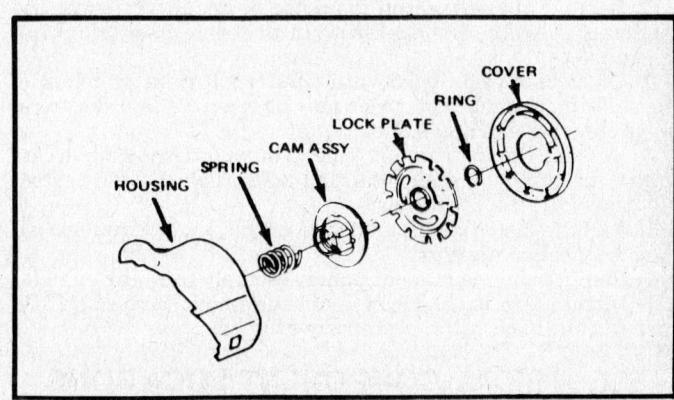
Remove these parts for access to the turn signal switch (© General Motors Corporation)

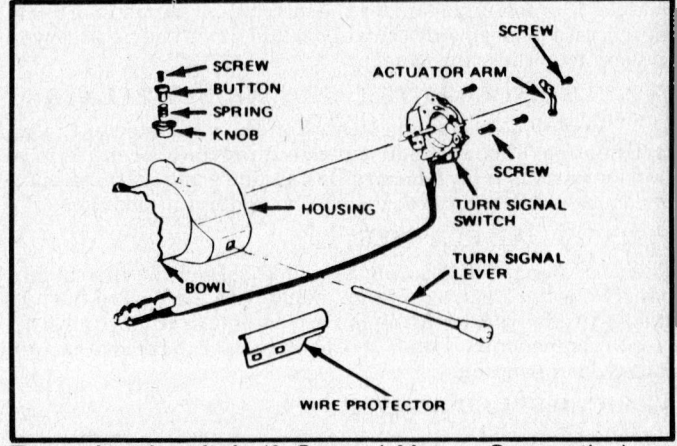
Turn signal switch (© General Motors Corporation)

WIPER LINKAGE/TRANSMISSION

Removal and Installation

1. Disconnect the negative battery cable.
2. Remove the arm blades, lower reveal moulding and the cowl vent screen.

7-11

SECTION 7
GENERAL MOTORS—"C" BODY
FRONT WHEEL DRIVE CARS

3. Disengage the link retainer between the drive link and the crank arm.
4. Remove the transmission to body attaching bolts.
5. Remove the transmission and linkage as an assembly.
6. Installation is the reverse of the removal procedure.

NOTE: Various new models are equipped with a special plastic coated windshield. Removal of the inspection sticker will require the use of a plastic scraper in order to avoid damage to the windshield surface. Using the plastic scraper, lift one corner of the decal, then apply a slow steady pull pressure for best results. Scrapers are commercially available for sticker removal on the plastic windshield. To clean the windshields after sticker removal is complete, use a soft cloth moistened with liquid glass cleaner or water. Stubborn residue can be removed using mineral spirits or rubbing alcohol sparingly.

Instrument Cluster

Removal and Installation

1. Disconnect the negative battery cable.
2. Remove the left sound insulator as required. Lower the steering column, if necessary in order to gain working clearance.
3. On vehicles equipped with Quartz Clusters, removal of the steering column trim cover may be required in order to remove the shift indicator clip.
4. Remove the instrument panel trim in order to gain access to the instrument panel retaining bolts. Remove the instrument panel retaining bolts.
5. Pull the instrument panel forward. Tag and disconnect all the electrical connectors.
6. Remove the instrument panel assembly from the vehicle.
7. Installation is the reverse of the removal procedure. Be sure the shift indicator is properly aligned.

ELECTRICAL COMPONENT LOCATIONS

COMPUTER
The electronic control module is located on the right side of the vehicle. It is positioned under the instrument panel. In order to gain access to electronic control module, it will be necessary to first remove the trim panel.

CONVENIENCE CENTER AND VARIOUS RELAYS
The Convenience center is located on the underside of the instrument panel near the fuse panel. It provides a central location for various relays, hazard flasher units and warning buzzers/chimes. All units are replaced with plug-in modules.

TURN SIGNAL FLASHER
The turn signal flasher unit is located behind the instrument panel near the steering column, along with the hazard flasher. It is secured in place with a plastic retainer. In order to gain access to components, it may first be necessary to remove certain under dash padding.

VEHICLE SPEED SENSOR
The vehicle speed sensor is located on the transaxle housing and is driven directly by the transaxle. The cruise control switch is located on the right side of the instrument panel near the steering column.

CRUISE CONTROL

Adjustments

1. Set the carburetor choke to the slow idle position.
2. Adjust the rod assembly so that the idle load control arm is fully retracted.
3. Install the cruise control retainer bracket.
4. Tighten the cruise control retainer nuts.

Troubleshooting

Before starting any troubleshooting procedures, a brief inspection should be made of the system components. The following components should be inspected:
    a. Servo chain or rod; should be adjusted for minimum slack.
    b. Throttle linkage/cable; make sure that the cable or linkage is not binding.
    c. Vacuum hoses; replace any that are kinked, rotted or deteriorated.

Electrical Circuit Protectors

FUSIBLE LINKS

Fusible links are sections of wire, with special insulation, designed to melt under electrical overload. Replacements are simply spliced into the wire. There may be as many as five of these in the engine compartment wiring harness. These are:
1. Horn relay to the fuse panel circuit.
2. Charging circuit from the starter solenoid to the horn relay.
3. Starter solenoid to the ammeter circuit.
4. Horn relay to the rear window defroster circuit, if equipped.

The fusible links are all two wire gauges smaller than the wires they protect.

NOTE: Most models have fusible links at these locations.

Replacement

1. Disconnect the negative battery cable.
2. Disconnect the fusible link from the junction block or starter solenoid.
3. Cut the harness directly behind the connector in order to remove the damaged fusible link.
4. Strip the harness wire approximately ½ inch.
5. Connect the new fusible link to the harness wire using a crimp on the connector. Solder the connection, if necessary, using resin core solder.
6. Tape all exposed wire using electrical tape.
7. Connect the fusible link to the junction block or starter solenoid and reconnect the negative battery cable.

CIRCUIT BREAKERS

Circuit breakers are incorporated in the wiring of the following systems; headlight switch, horn wiring, power/memory seats, and the Delco-Bose radio systems.

GENERAL MOTORS—"C" BODY
FRONT WHEEL DRIVE CARS

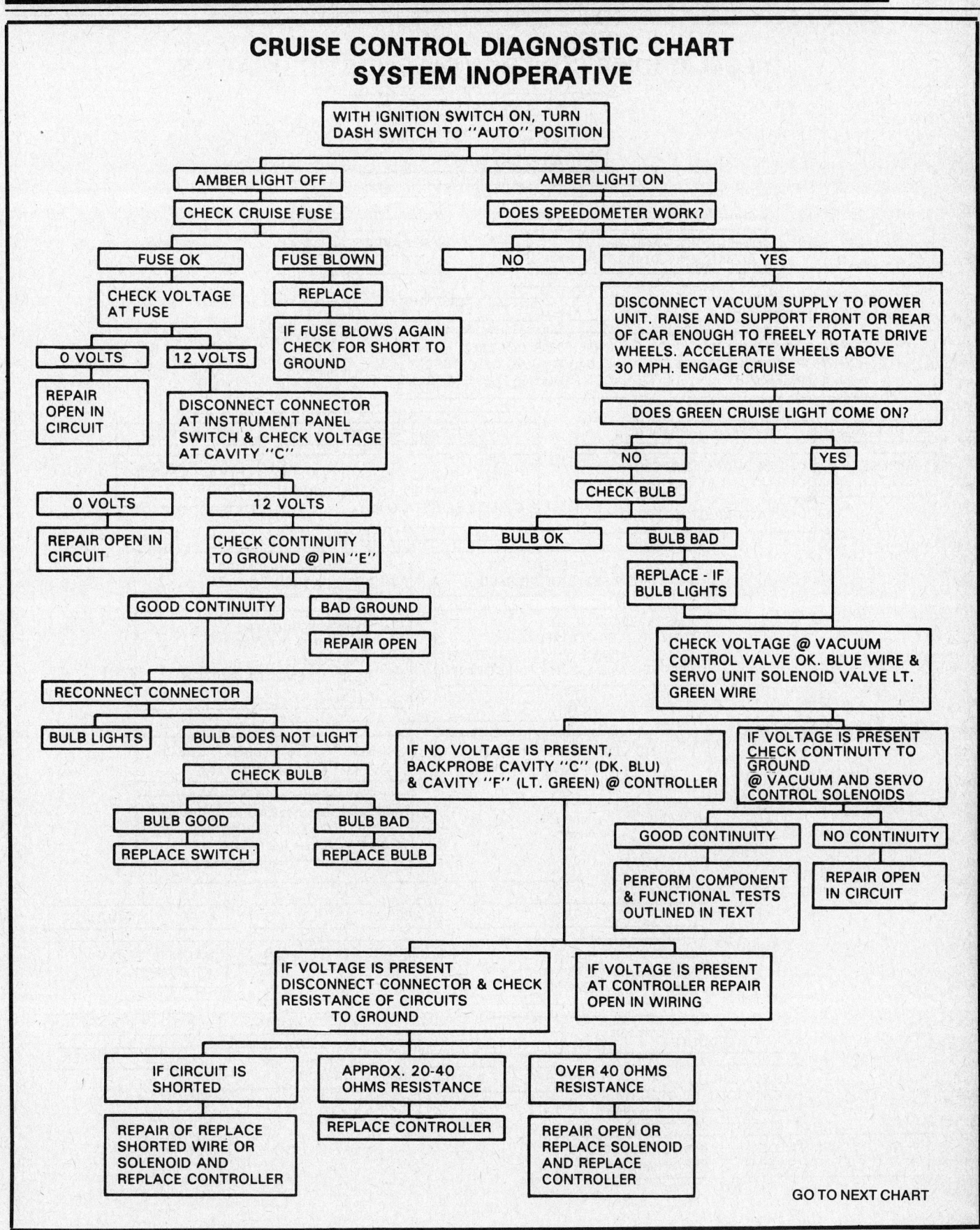

GENERAL MOTORS—"C" BODY
FRONT WHEEL DRIVE CARS

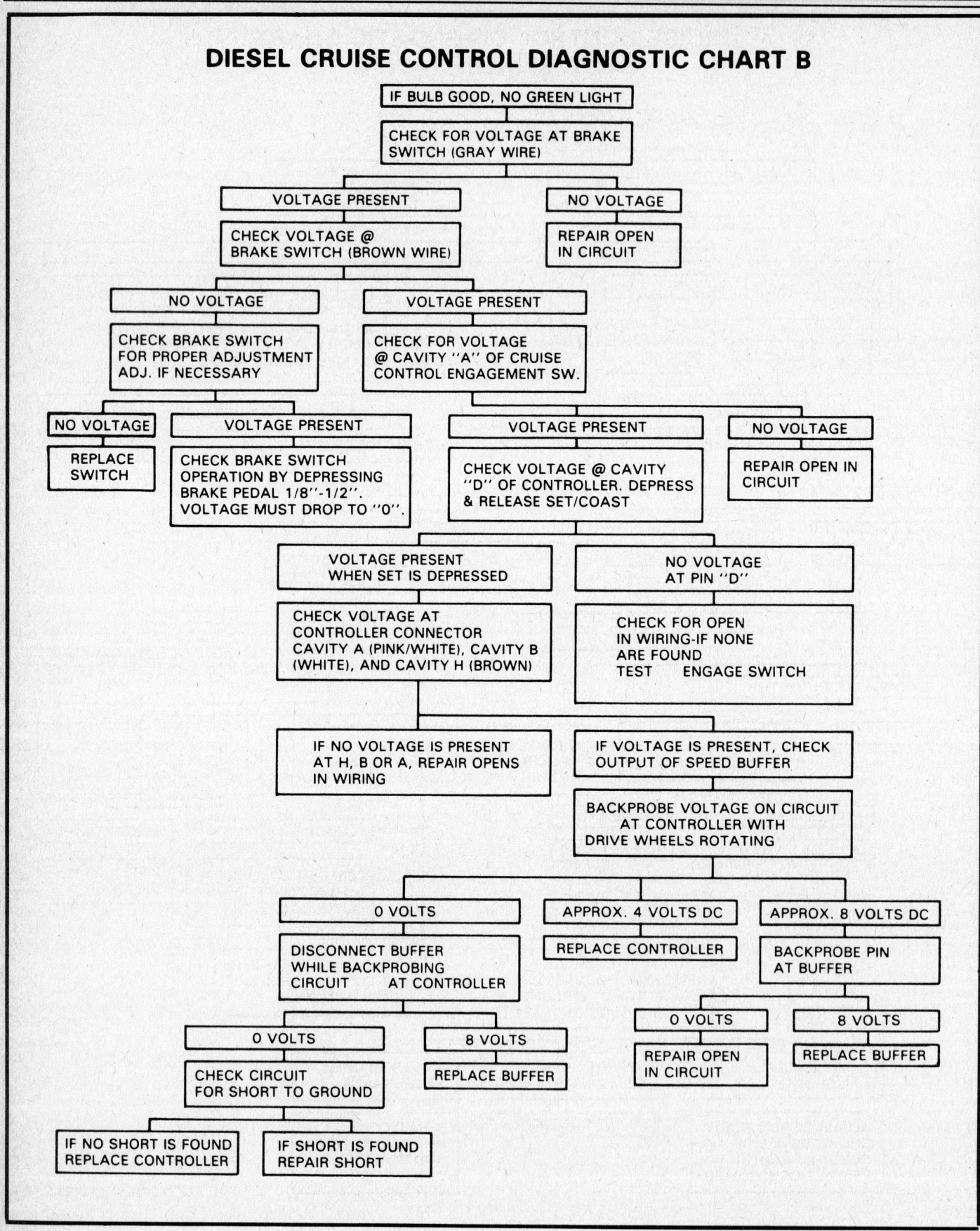

DIESEL CRUISE CONTROL DIAGNOSTIC CHART B

GENERAL MOTORS—"C" BODY
FRONT WHEEL DRIVE CARS

COOLING AND HEATER SECTION

WATER PUMP

Removal and Installation

3.0L V6

1. Disconnect the negative battery cable. Drain the engine coolant.
2. Remove accessory drive belts.
3. Remove water pump attaching bolts.
4. Remove the engine support strut.
5. Place a floor jack under the front crossmember of the cradle and raise the jack until the jack just starts to raise the car.
6. Remove the front two body mount (No. 1 and No.3) bolts with the lower cushions and retainers.
7. Thread the body mount bolts with retainers a minimum of three (3) turns into the cage so that the bolts restrain cradle movement.
8. Release the floor jack slowly until the crossmember contacts the body mount bolt retainers. As the jack is being lowered watch and correct any interference with hoses, lines pipes and cables.

NOTE: Do not lower the cradle without its being restrained as possible damage can occur to the body and underhood items.

9. Remove water pump from engine.
10. Reverse removal procedure.
11. Install pump and torque to 25 ft. lbs.
12. Connect negative battery cable.
13. Fill with coolant and check for leaks.

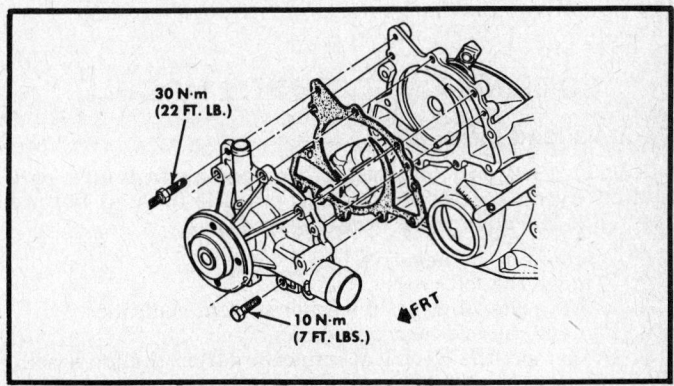

Water pump installation—3.0L V6
(© General Motors Corporation)

3.8L V6

1. Disconnect the negative battery cable. Drain the cooling system. Remove the fan shroud, if necessary for clearance.
2. Loosen the belt of belts, then remove the fan blades and pulley or pulleys from the hub on the water pump shaft. Remove the belt or belts.
3. Disconnect the hose from the water pump inlet and the heater hose from the nipple. Remove the bolts, then remove the pump and gasket from the timing case cover or engine block.

To Install:
1. Install the pump assembly with a new gasket. Bolts and lock washers must be torqued evenly.
2. Connect the radiator hose to the pump inlet and the heater hose to the nipple. Fill the cooling system and check all points for possible coolant leaks.
3. Install the fan pulley or pulleys and the fan blade. Install the belt or belts and adjust for correct tension.

4.1L V8

1. Disconnect the negative battery cable.
2. Drain the coolant.
3. Disconnect the A/C accumulator from its bracket and then position it out of the way.
4. Remove the right side cross-car brace.
5. Remove the drive belt, the idler pulley and the bracket.
6. Unscrew the mounting bolts and remove the water pump pulley.
7. Remove the water pump and gasket.
8. Installation is in the reverse order of removal. Always use a new water pump gasket.

4.3L DIESEL

1. Disconnect the negative battery cable. Drain the cooling system.
2. Remove the hoses from the water pump.
3. Remove the heater return hose from the intake manifold. Position the pipe in order to gain working clearance.
4. Remove the vacuum pump drive belt. Remove the serpentine belt.
5. Remove the alternator and vacuum pump brackets from the vehicle. Remove the A/C compressor from its assembly and wire our of the way.
6. Remove the water pump bolts. Remove the water pump.
7. Installation is the reverse of the removal procedure. Apply a thin coat of sealer, part No. 1050026 or equivalent to hold the gasket during assembly. Apply primer, part No. 1052624 or equivalent in order to avoid coolant leaks.

ELECTRIC COOLING FAN

Removal and Installation

1. Disconnect the negative battery cable.
2. Raise the vehicle and support safely.
3. Disconnect the electrical connectors from the rear of the fan assemblies.
4. Remove the fan attaching bolts from the lower radiator cradle.
5. Lower the vehicle.
6. For right fan removal on vehicle equipped with V8 engines, remove the A/C accumulator to gain working clearance. Remove the air cleaner intake duct.

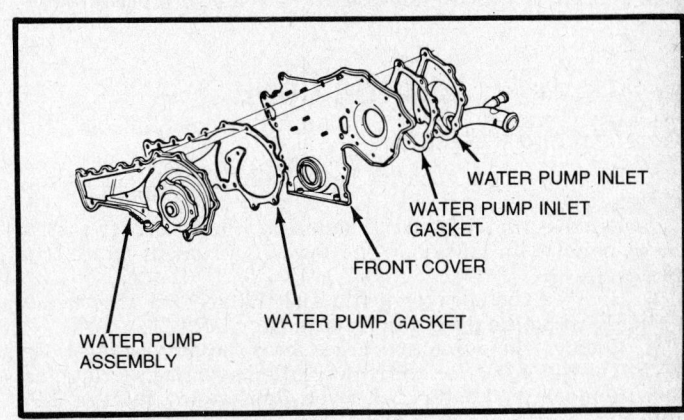

Water pump installation—4.1L V8
(© General Motors Corporation)

GENERAL MOTORS—"C" BODY
FRONT WHEEL DRIVE CARS

7. Remove the upper fan to radiator mounting panel attaching bolts. Remove the upper radiator panel.
8. Remove the cooling fan assemblies.
9. Installation is the reverse of the removal procedure.

COOLING FAN CONTROL MODULE

Removal and Installation

NOTE: **1986 and later Cadillac cooling fans are controlled by an electronic control module located behind the front left cornering lamp assembly.**

1. Disconnect the negative battery cable.
2. Remove the left cross car brace.
3. Remove the windshield washer solvent container.
4. Remove the left cornering lamp assembly.
5. Disconnect the electrical connectors from the fan assemblies. Remove the necessary engine harness connectors.
6. Remove the control module retaining bolts.
7. Remove the control module assembly through the cornering lamp cavity.
8. Installation is the reverse of the removal procedure.

BLOWER MOTOR

Removal and Installation

1. Disconnect the negative battery cable.
2. Tag and disconnect the electrical connections from the blower motor assembly. Remove the heat tube if equipped.
3. Remove the necessary components in order to gain access to the blower motor retaining screws.
4. Remove the blower motor retaining screws. Remove the blower motor.
5. Installation is the reverse of the removal procedure.

HEATER/AC CONTROL AND FAN SWITCH ASSEMBLY

Removal and Installation

1. Disconnect the negative battery cable.
2. Remove the instrument panel trim cover.
3. Remove the control assembly retaining screws. Pull the control assembly forward and disconnect the electrical connections.
4. Remove the control assembly from the vehicle.
5. Installation is the reverse of the removal procedure.

HEATER CORE

Removal and Installation

1. Disconnect the negative battery cable. Drain the cooling system.
2. Remove the right hand sound insulator, center instrument panel trim plate and the lower instrument panel trim plate.
3. Remove the speaker grille and the speaker in order to gain access to the programmer attaching bolt.
4. Remove the wires and hoses form the programmer. Remove the linkage cover and linkage. Remove the programmer.
5. Remove the heater core cover. Remove the splash shield in order to gain access to the heater core form the vehicle.
6. Remove the heater core from the vehicle.
7. Installation is the reverse of the removal procedure.

TEMPERATURE CONTROL/BLOWER SWITCH

Removal and Installation

1. Disconnect the negative battery cable.
2. Remove the necessary trim panels in order to gain access to the control head retaining screws.
3. Remove the control head retaining screws. Pull out and disconnect the cables, electrical connections and vacuum lines from the rear of the control head.
4. Remove the control head assembly form the vehicle.
5. Installation is the reverse of the removal procedure.

Fuel System

FUEL PUMP

Removal and Installation
MECHANICAL PUMP

1. Disconnect the negative battery cable at the battery and raise the vehicle.
2. On V6 models, remove the shields and the oil filter.
3. Disconnect the hoses from the pump.
4. Loosen the fuel line at the carburetor and disconnect the line from the pump.
5. Remove the attaching bolts and the pump.
6. Installation is performed in the reverse of the previous steps. Tighten the attaching bolts evenly and alternately. Check for leakage after the engine is started.

ELECTRIC PUMP

1. Remove the fuel pump fuse from the fuse panel.
2. Start the engine and let it run until all fuel in the line is used.
3. Crank the starter an additional three seconds to relieve any residual pressure.
4. With the ignition "OFF", replace the fuse.
5. Drain the fuel tank.
6. Disconnect wiring from the tank.
7. Remove the ground wire retaining screws from under the body.
8. Disconnect all hoses form the tank.
9. Support the tank on a jack and remove the retaining strap nuts.
10. Lower the tank and remove it.
11. Remove the fuel gauge/pump retaining ring using a spanner wrench such as tool J–24187 or equivalent.
12. Remove the gauge unit and the pump.
13. Installation is the reverse of removal. Always replace the O-ring under the gauge/pump retaining ring.

DIESEL PUMP

1. Disconnect the negative battery cable.
2. Remove the air cleaner.
3. Unplug the leads from the pump assembly.
4. Disconnect the fuel lines from the pump.
5. Remove the pump mounting bracket from the pump. Remove the pump from the vehicle.
6. Installation is the reverse of removal.

IDLE SPEED CONTROL

Adjustment

Adjustment of the Idle Speed Control (ISC) motor is necessary to establish the initial position of the motor after it has been replaced. It may be necessary if the throttle pedal ratchets when the ignition is turned on or off.

GENERAL MOTORS—"C" BODY
FRONT WHEEL DRIVE CARS

1. Remove the air cleaner, run the engine until it reaches normal operating temperature.
2. Connect a tachometer to the engine.
3. Check the throttle position sensor (TPS) adjustment as outlined below.
4. Open the set timing connector.
5. Disconnect the TPS connector.
6. Turn the ignition off for 10 seconds. Observe the plunger movement. It should extend fully.
7. When the ISC plunger is fully extended, disconnect the ISC connector.
8. Reconnect the TPS and start the engine.
9. The idle speed should be 1500 rpm. If not, turn the ISC plunger until the engine reaches 1500rpm.
10. Reconnect the ISC motor and repeat Steps 5–8.
11. Remove the test equipment and make all connections including the set timing connector.
12. Turn the ignition off for ten seconds. The ISC motor should move to the fully extended position.
13. This procudure may have turned on the engine check light, and may have set a trouble code. To clear the code from the ECM system, turn the key on, and press and hold the "OFF" and "HI" buttons in the climate control panel until "E.O.O" appears in the readout. To clear the codes from the Body Computer Module, BCM, depress the "OFF" and "LO" buttons at the same time until "F.O.O" appears.

THROTTLE POSITION SENSOR

Adjustment

1. Remove the air cleaner and run the engine to normal operating temperature.
2. Connect a tachometer and a high impedance voltmeter as follows:
   a. Plus (+) lead to the TPS harness test point which connects to pin A (0.8 dark blue wire).
   b. Negative (-) lead to the TPS harness test point which connects to pin B (0.8 black/white wire).
   c. Select the 2V DC scale.
3. Open the set timing connector.
4. Retract the ISC motor by pressing the plunger (switch activated) in while the throttle is opened to approximately 1500 rpm. When the ISC motor fully retracts, disconnect the ISC connector before releasing the throttle.
5. Jump the ISC harness connector pins A and B together.
6. The ISC plunger should not be touching the throttle lever. If contact is noted, adjust the plunger (turn in) with pliers.
7. The idle speed should now be approximately 375–400 rpm. Adjust the throttle stop screw the the proper rpm if necessary.

8. The digital voltmeter should indicate 0.50 volts. If necessary adjust the TPS as outlined in Steps 9–11. If the voltmeter is correct, proceed to Step 12.
9. Remove the throtle body assembly from the intake manifold. Invert the throttle body assembly to gain access to the spot welds that hold the TPS screws in place. Use a $5/16$ drill bit to drill through the spot welds to gain access to the screws. Loosen the screws enough to permit rotation of the sensor.
10. With the engine idling 375–400 rpm loosen TPS Mounting screws and position the TPS lever so the voltmeter reads 0.50 volts.
11. Tighten the TPS mounting screws with the sensor in this position. Recheck the voltmeter make sure the adjustment has not changed.
12. Remove all test equipment and reconnect all connections including the set timing connector.
13. Turn off the ignition for ten seconds. The ISC motor should move to the extended position.
14. The above procedure may have turned on the (Check Engine) light, and may have set a trouble code. Refer to the procedure at the end of "Idle Speed Control (ISC) Motor Adjustment—DFI" to clear the trouble code from the system.

CARBURETOR

Removal and Installation

1. Remove the air cleaner.
2. Disconnect and plug the fuel line.
3. Remove and tag all vacuum and electrical lines, as required.
4. Remove the carburetor retaining bolts. Remove the carburetor from the vehicle.
5. Installation is the reverse of the removal procedure.

INTAKE MANIFOLD

Removal and Installaion

1. Disconnect the negative battery cable. Drain the cooling system.
2. Remove the accessory drive belt along with the alternator.
3. Tag and disconnect the vacuum lines and electrical connectors as necessary.
4. Remove the heater and radiator hoses as required.
5. If the vehicle is equipped with cruise control, remove the speed control cable.
6. Remove the remaining components in order to gain access to the manifold retaining bolts.

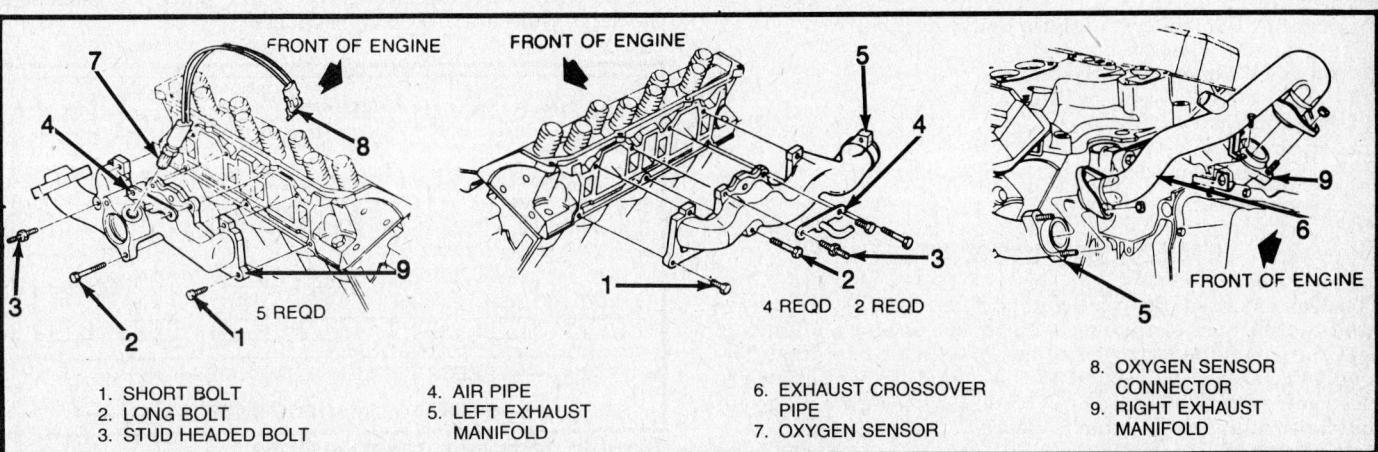

1. SHORT BOLT
2. LONG BOLT
3. STUD HEADED BOLT
4. AIR PIPE
5. LEFT EXHAUST MANIFOLD
6. EXHAUST CROSSOVER PIPE
7. OXYGEN SENSOR
8. OXYGEN SENSOR CONNECTOR
9. RIGHT EXHAUST MANIFOLD

Exhaust manifold removal—4.1L V8 (© General Motors Corporation)

7-17

SECTION 7: GENERAL MOTORS — "C" BODY
FRONT WHEEL DRIVE CARS

3. Remove the manifold retaining bolts. Remove the intake manifold from the vehicle.
4. Installation is the reverse of the removal procedure. Check vehicle for fluid and vacuum leaks.

EXHAUST MANIFOLD

Removal and Installation

1. Disconnect the negative battery cable.
2. Remove all components in order to gain access to the manifold retaining bolts.
3. Remove the exhaust manifold to exhaust flange retaining bolts.
4. Remove the manifold retaining bolts.
5. Remove the exhaust manifold from the vehicle. On some vehicles it may be necessary to raise the engine and remove the manifold from underneath of the vehicle.
6. Installation is the reverse of the removal procedure.

Fuel Injection

For More Information on Fuel Injection, refer to Unit Repair Section.

DIGITAL FUEL INJECTION SYSTEM

The digital fuel injection (DFI) system is a throttle body fuel injection system, on which two solenoid actuated fuel injectors are mounted in the throttle body and inject fuel into the intake manifold. The DFI system controls the air/fuel mixture for combustion by monitoring selected engine operating conditions and electronically metering fuel requirements to meet those conditions.

The DFI system consists of the following subsystems; the fuel delivery system, air induction system, engine sensors, electronic control unit (ECU), electronic spark timing (EST), idle speed control system (ISC), exhaust gas recirculation system (EGR) and a charcoal canister. 1983 and later vehicles also incorporate oxygen sensors and diagnostic readout systems.

FUEL INJECTION PUMP

Removal and Installation

1. Relieve the pressure from the fuel system. Disconnect the negative battery cable.
2. Remove the air cleaner assembly.
3. Remove the crankcase ventilation filters from the valve covers and air crossover. Remove the air crossover.
4. Remove the fuel lines and fuel pump. Remove the fuel filter.
5. Disconnect the throttle link and return spring. Remove the intake manifold brackets holding the throttle cables. Wire out of the way.
6. Remove the fuel return line from the injection pump.
7. Disconnect the injection lines from the pump and cap all lines.
8. Remove the injection pump retaining bolts. Remove the injection pump and discard the O-ring.
9. Installation is the reverse of the removal procedure using a new O-ring.

FUEL INJECTION NOZZLE

Removal and Installation

1. Disconnect the negative battery cable. Relieve fuel system pressure.
2. Tag and disconnect the fuel injector electrical connectors.
3. Remove the fuel rail retaining bolts. Remove the fuel rail.
4. Separate the injector from the fuel rail.
5. Installation is the reverse of the removal procedure. Replace the O-rings when installing the injectors.

EMISSION CONTROL SYSTEMS

EMISSION EQUIPMENT USED — 1983–1987
Positive Crankcase Ventilation
Evaporative Emission Control
Early Fuel Evaporation System
Catalytic Converter
Exhaust Gas Recirculation
Computer Command Control
Deceleration Valve
Computer Controlled Catalytic Converter
Air Injection Reactor
Controlled Combustion System
Transmission Converter Clutch
Electronic Spark Control
Electronic Spark Timing
Thermostatic Air Cleaner

EMISSIONS INDICATOR

The dash mounted "Service Soon" and "Service Now" lights are used to indicated to the mechanic or owner of a malfunction that the computer has detected in the vehicle's operation. The malfunctions can be related to the operating sensors or the electronic control module (ECM). The service light will go out automatically if the trouble is cleared or intermittent.

The ECM, however will automatically store the trouble code until the diagnostic system is "Cleared" or until the ignition has been switched on and off 50 times without the trouble reappearing.

Trouble codes stored in the ECM may be erased (cleared) by entering the diagnostic mode and then pushing the "HI" and "OFF" buttons on the climate control panel at the same time. Hold until "E.O.O." appears.

Trouble codes stored in the Body Computer Module (BCM) can be cleared by depressing the "OFF" and "LO" buttons at the same time until "F.O.O." appears.

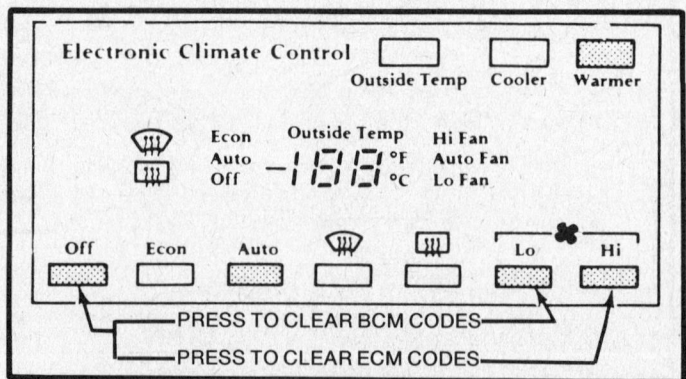

Trouble indicator reset buttons
(© General Motors Corporation)

GENERAL MOTORS—"C" BODY
FRONT WHEEL DRIVE CARS
SECTION 7

GASOLINE ENGINE SECTION

For Diesel Engine Services, refer to Unit Repair Section. For Engine Overhaul procedures, refer to Unit Repair Section

ENGINE ASSEMBLY

Removal and Installation

3.0L V6 AND 3.8L V6

1. Disconnect the negative battery cable.
2. Tag and disconnect the air flow sensor wiring.
3. Disconnect the air intake duct. Drain the engine coolant.
4. Raise the front of the vehicle and support it safely.
5. Remove the retaining bolts and separate the exhaust pipe from the manifold.
6. Loosen and remove the engine mount bolts.
7. Remove the bolts and then disconnect the driveline vibration absorber.
8. Tag and disconnect the starter wiring and remove the starter.
9. Disconnect the A/C compressor and position it out of the way. Do not disconnect the refrigerant lines.
10. Disconnect the hydraulic lines at the power steering pump and wire them out of the way.
11. Loosen and remove the lower transaxle-to-engine bolts.

NOTE: One bolt is located between the transaxle case and the engine block. It is installed in the opposite direction of the other bolts.

12. Remove the flexplate cover. Matchmark the flexplate-to-torque converter relationship to insure porper alignment upon installation. Remove the flexplate-to-torque converter bolts.
13. Disconnect the engine support bracket at the transaxle and then lower the vehicle.
14. Disconnect the radiator and heater hoses at the engine and position them out of the way.
15. Remove the alternator.
16. Disconnect the engine wiring harness.
17. Remove the remaining upper transaxle-to-engine bolts.
18. Install a lifting fixture to the engine and remove the engine from the vehicle.
19. Installation is the reverse of the removal procedure.

4.1L V8

1. Disconnect the negative battery cable. Drain the radiator coolant.
2. Remove the air cleaner. Matchmark the hood to the support brackets and remove the hood.
3. Disconnect the A/C accumulator from its bracket and position it out of the way.
4. Tag and disconnect the canister hoses and ground wire from the accumulator bracket and then remove the bracket itself from the inner strut tower.
5. Disconnect or remove the cooling fans, the drive belt and the radiator and heater hoses.
6. Tag and disconnect the following:
   a. Oil pressure switch
   b. Coolant temperature sensor
   c. Distributor wires
   d. EGR solenoid
   e. Engine temperature switch
   f. Accelerator cable
   g. Cruise control linkage
   h. Transmission TV
7. Remove the cruise control diaphragm and its bracket.
8. Remove the vacuum supply hose and the exhaust crossover pipe.

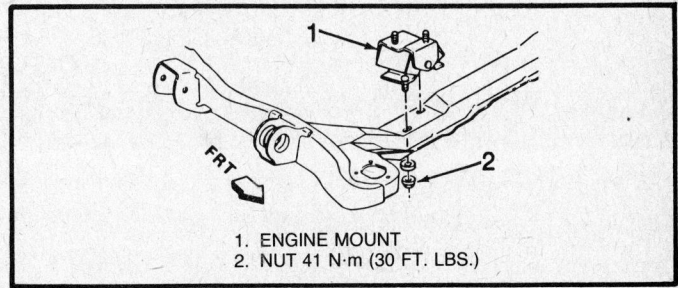

1. ENGINE MOUNT
2. NUT 41 N·m (30 FT. LBS.)

Right side engine mounts—3.0L V6 and 3.8L V6
(© General Motors Corporation)

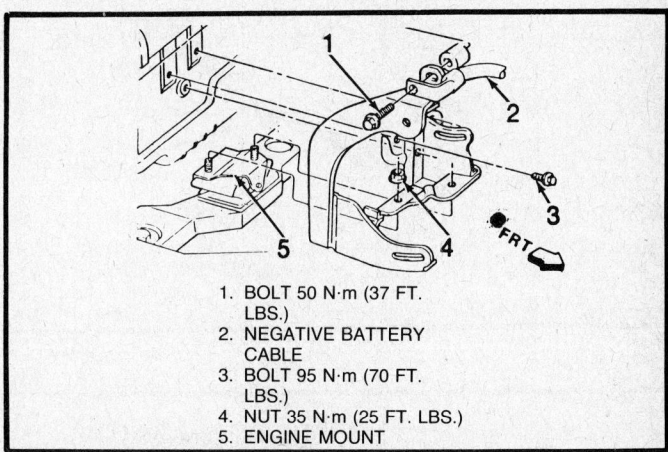

1. BOLT 50 N·m (37 FT. LBS.)
2. NEGATIVE BATTERY CABLE
3. BOLT 95 N·m (70 FT. LBS.)
4. NUT 35 N·m (25 FT. LBS.)
5. ENGINE MOUNT

Left side engine mounts—3.0L V6 and 3.8L V6
(© General Motors Corporation)

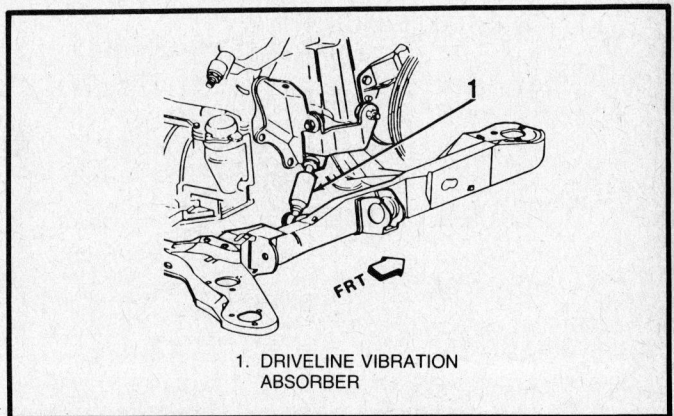

1. DRIVELINE VIBRATION ABSORBER

Typical driveline vibration absorber
(© General Motors Corporation)

9. Disconnect the oil cooler lines at the oil filter adapter, unscrew their mounting bracket at the transaxle and position them out of the way.
10. Remove the air cleaner mounting bracket.
11. CAREFULLY bleed the fuel pressure at the Schraeder valve and then disconnect the fuel lines at the throttle body.

7-19

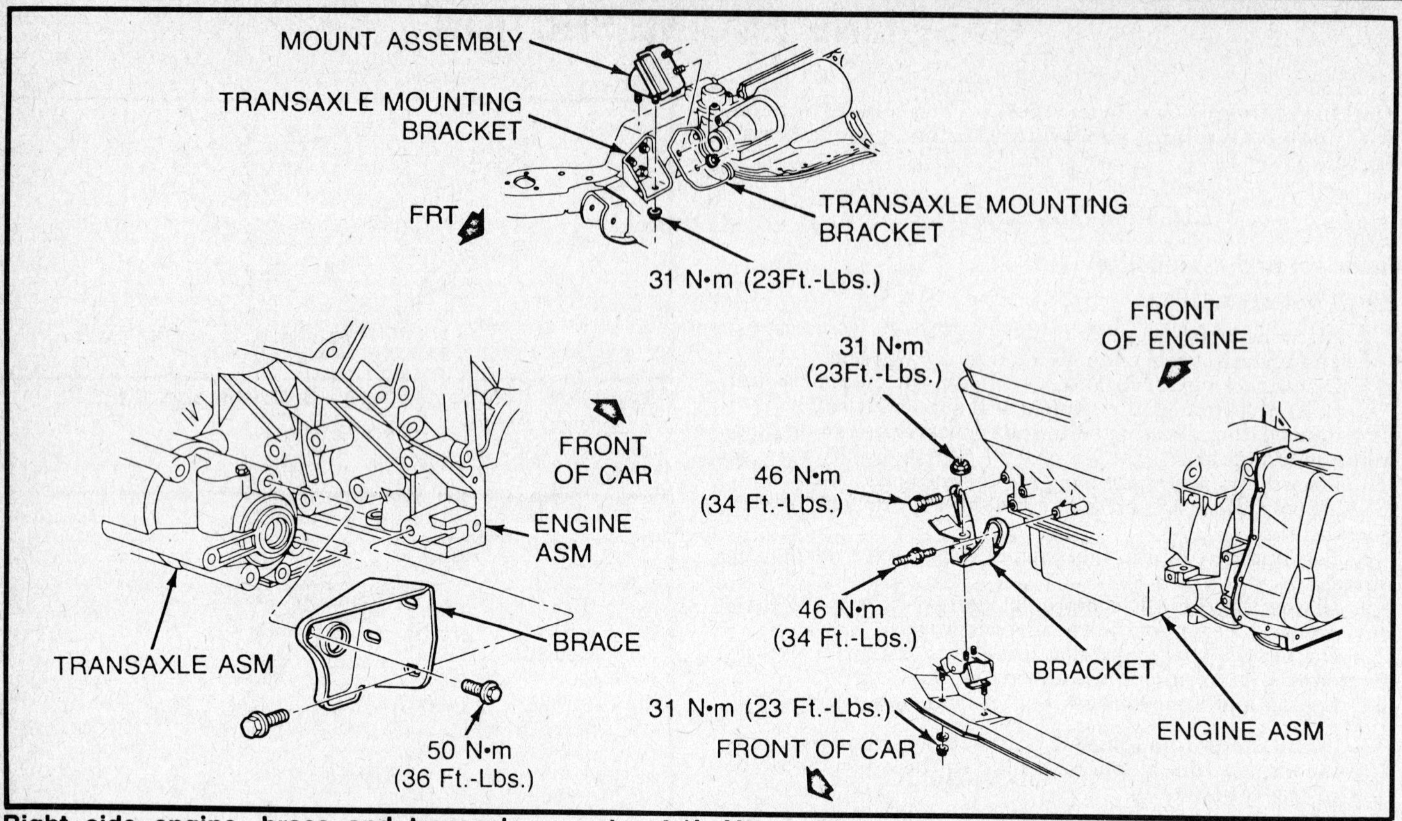

SECTION 7: GENERAL MOTORS—"C" BODY
FRONT WHEEL DRIVE CARS

Right side engine, brace and transaxle mounts—4.1L V8 (© General Motors Corporation)

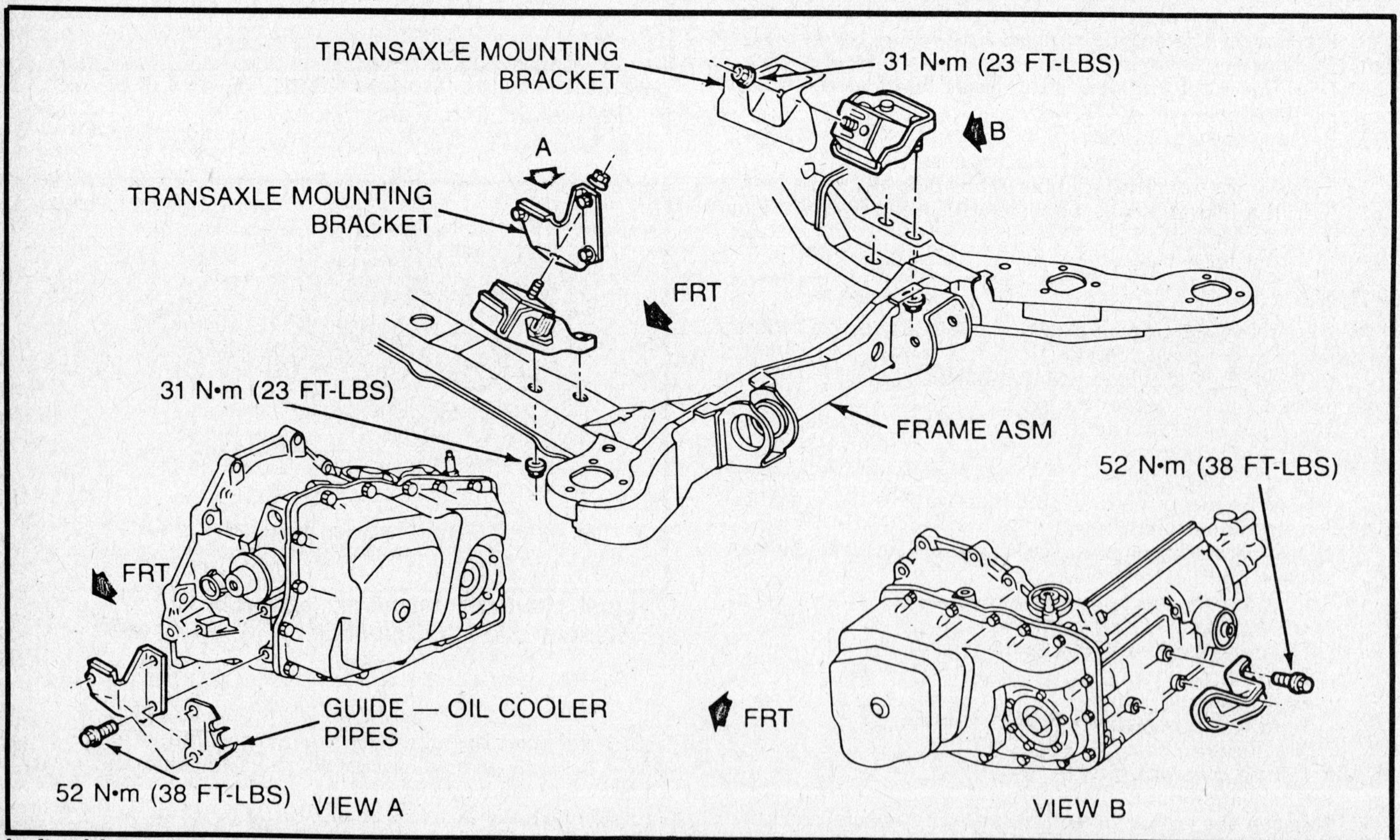

Left side transaxle mounts—4.1L V8 (© General Motors Corporation)

7-20

GENERAL MOTORS—"C" BODY
FRONT WHEEL DRIVE CARS

CAUTION
When bleeding the fuel system, be sure to have a container or rags on hand to catch excess fuel.

---

12. Unscrew the fuel line bracket at the transaxle and wire the fuel lines out of the way.
13. Tag and disconnect the small vacuum line at the brake booster.
14. Tag and disconnect the AIR solenoid electrical and hose connections. Remove the AIR valves and bracket.
15. Tag and disconnect the wires at the following:
    a. ISC
    b. TPS
    c. Fuel injectors
    d. MAT sensor
    e. Oxygen sensor
    f. Throttle body base warmer
    g. Alternator
16. Remove the idler pulley. Remove the power steering pump hose strap from the sud-headed bolt in front of the right cylinder head. Remove the stud-headed bolt.
17. Remove the AIR pipe clip near the No. 2 spark plug.
18. Remove the power steering pump and belt tensioner (with bracket). Wire them out of the way.
19. Raise the vehicle and support it on jack stands.
20. Tag and disconnect the starter wires and the ground wire a the cylinder block.
21. Remove the two flexplate covers. Remove the starter. Remove the three flexplate-to-converter bolts.
22. Remove the A/C compressor lower dust shield.
23. Remove the right front wheel. Remove the outer wheelhouse plastic shield.
24. Remove the A/C compressor mounting bolts and lower the compressor out of the way.
25. Remove the lower radiator hose.
26. Remove the driveline vibration dampener and its brackets from the lower right front of the engine and cradle.
27. Remove the three right front engine-to-transaxle bracket bolts.
28. Disconnect the exhaust pipe at the manifold. Remove the AIR pipe-to-converter bracket from the exhaust manifold stud.

NOTE: Be careful not to lose the springs when detaching the exhaust pipe.

29. Remove the lower right hand bell housing-to-engine bolt. Support the engine with a jack.
30. Remove the five upper bell housing-to-engine bolts. Remove the three left front engine mount bracket-to-engine bolts.
31. Attach a suitable lifting fixture and remove the engine.
32. Installation is in the reverse order of removal.

4.3L V6 DIESEL

1. Disconnect the negative battery cable. Matchmark the hood to the support brackets and then remove the hood. Drain the cooling system.
2. Remove the serpentine drive belt. Remove the vacuum drive belt.
3. Remove the air cleaner. Install an air crossover screen cover (No. J26996–1) or the equivalent.
4. Tag and disconnect the ground wires at the inner fender panel and the engine ground strap.
5. Raise the vehicle and support it on jack stands.
6. Remove the engine-to-transaxle brace.
7. Remove the flywheel cover and then remove the flywheel-to-torque converter bolts.
8. Disconnect the exhaust pipe from the rear exhaust manifold.
9. Remove the engine mount-to-cradle retaining nuts and washers.

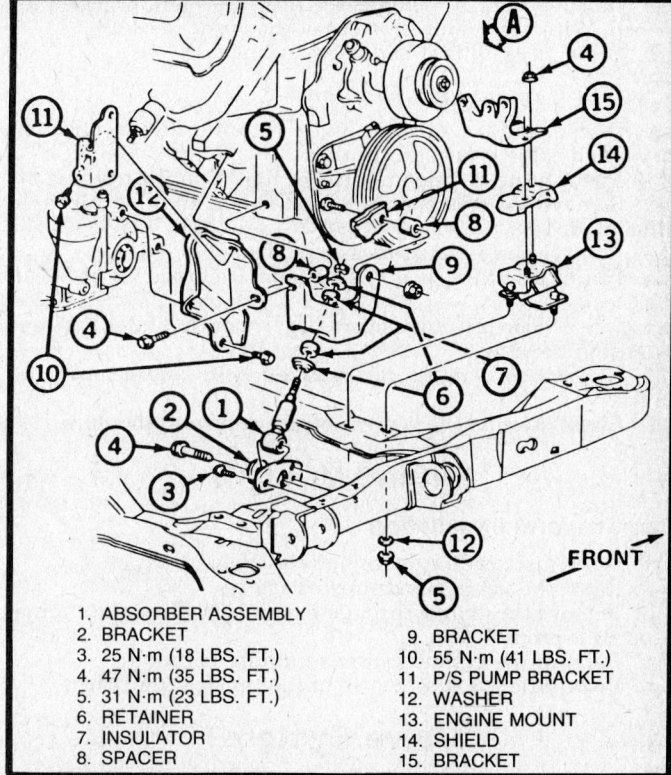

1. ABSORBER ASSEMBLY
2. BRACKET
3. 25 N·m (18 LBS. FT.)
4. 47 N·m (35 LBS. FT.)
5. 31 N·m (23 LBS. FT.)
6. RETAINER
7. INSULATOR
8. SPACER
9. BRACKET
10. 55 N·m (41 LBS. FT.)
11. P/S PUMP BRACKET
12. WASHER
13. ENGINE MOUNT
14. SHIELD
15. BRACKET

Engine mounting—4.3L V6 (diesel)
(© General Motors Corporation)

10. Remove the engine absorbers assembly from the frame bracket.
11. Tag and disconnect the following:
    a. Starter motor wires
    b. Glow plug wire at No. 2 cylinder
    c. Battery ground cable.
12. Disconnect the lower oil cooler hose and cap the opening.
13. Remove the accessible power steering pump bracket fasteners. Lower the vehicle.
14. Remove the remaining power steering pump bracket/brace fasteners and lower the pump (with hoses connected) out of the way.
15. Disconnect the heater water return pipe.
16. Tag and disconnect the remaining glow plug leads and all other electrical leads connected to the engine.
17. Disconnect the engine harness at the cowl connector and body-mounted relays.

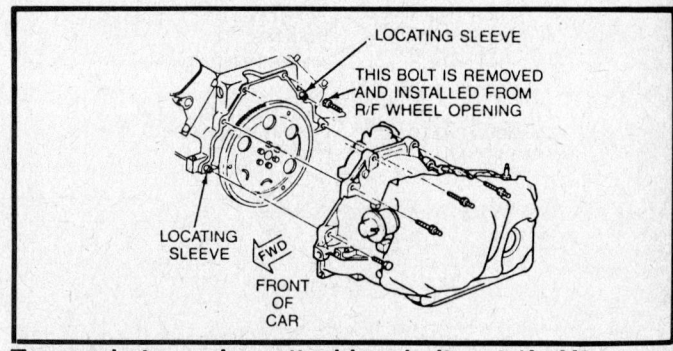

Transaxle-to-engine attaching bolts—4.1L V8
(© General Motors Corporation)

GENERAL MOTORS—"C" BODY
FRONT WHEEL DRIVE CARS

18. Remove the A/C compressor with lines and brackets attached. Wire the compressor out of the way.
19. Disconnect all fuel and vacuum lines.

NOTE: Cap all open fuel lines.

20. Disconnect the throttle and TV cables at the injection pump and cable brackets.
21. Disconnect the upper oil cooler line. Cap the openings.
22. Remove the crossover pipe heat shield and the transaxle filler tube.
23. Remove the exhaust crossover pipe.
24. Install a suitable engine lifting device to the lift hooks on the block.
25. Use a floor jack to support the transaxle under the rear extension housing.
26. Remove the engine to transaxle bolts and remove the engine.
27. Installation is the reverse of the removal procedure.

ENGINE MOUNTS
Removal and Installation

1. Disconnect the negative battery cable.
2. Raise the vehicle and support safely.
3. Remove the engine through mount bolt. Raise the engine, support it properly.
4. Remove the engine mount retaining bolts.
5. Installation is the reverse of the removal procedure.

Valve System

All engines use hydraulic lifters. Valve systems with hydraulic lifters operate with zero clearance in the valve train. The rocker arms are non-adjustable. The lifter itself will compensate if there is slack in the system but if there is excessive play, the entire system should be checked.

If the valve guides are found to be worn past allowable limits, they will have to be rebored and valves with oversize stem installed.

VALVE LIFTERS
Removal and Installation

1. Disconnect the negative battery cable.
2. Drain the coolant from the radiator system.
3. Remove the rocker arm cover. Discard the old gasket material.

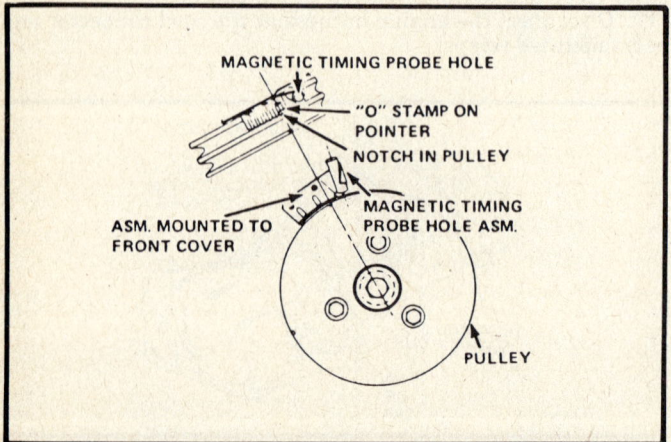

The 4.1L V8 incorporates a special magnetic timing probe hole (© General Motors Corporation)

4. Remove the intake manifold. Remove the rocker arm assemblies.
5. Remove the push rods. Using the proper valve lifter removal tool, remove the valve lifters.
6. Installation is the reverse of the removal procedure. Use new gasket material on the valve covers prior to installation. Be sure to coat the lifters in clean engine oil before installing them.

VALVE ROCKER ASSEMBLY
Removal and Installation

1. Disconnect the negative battery cable.
2. Tag and disconnect any electrical leads or hoses preventing access to the valve cover bolts.
3. Remove the valve cover bolts. Remove the valve covers. Discard the old gasket material.
4. Remove the rocker arm shaft retaining bolts. If only the pushrod is to be replaced, loosen the rocker arm shaft retaining bolts and swing the arm so as to clear the pushrod.
5. Remove the rocker arm shaft assembly.
6. Remove the rocker arms.
7. Installation is the reverse of the removal procedure. Use new gasket material on the valve covers.

VALVE TIMING
Adjustment

NOTE: The 4.1L V8 engine incorporates a magnetic timing probe hole for use with special electronic timing equipment. Consult manufacturer's instructions before using this system.

1. Connect a timing light to the No. 1 spark plug wire according to the light manufacturer's instructions. DO NOT PIERCE THE SPARK PLUG WIRE TO CONNECT THE TIMING LIGHT.
2. Follow the instructions on the tune up label located in the engine compartment.
3. On models with Electronic Spark Timing (EST) distributor, disconnect the 4 terminal plug at the distributor.
4. Start the engine and run it at idle speed.
5. Aim the timing light at the degree scale just over the harmonic balancer.
6. Adjust the timing by loosening the securing clamp and rotating the distributor until the desired ignition advance is achieved, then tighten the clamp.

NOTE: On the 4.1 250 cu. in. V8 engine a special tool No. J–29791 is used to loosen the hold down nut.

7. On the four cylinder, loosen the distributor clamp outer bolt, then slide the clamp back slightly. Do not remove the retaining bolt.
8. Adjust the timing, then replace the tighten the clamp. To advance the timing, rotate the distributor opposite the normal direction of rotor rotation. Retard the timing by rotating the distributor in the normal direction of rotor rotation.

NOTE: On DFI system (Digital Fuel Injection), the malfunction trouble codes must be cleared after removal or adjustment of the distributor. This accomplished by removing battery voltage to terminal "R" for 10 seconds.

CYLINDER HEADS
Removal and Installation

1. Disconnect the negative battery cable.
2. Drain the engine coolant from the radiator. Disconnect the radiator hoses from the intake manifold.

GENERAL MOTORS—"C" BODY
FRONT WHEEL DRIVE CARS

3. Remove the rocker arm covers and the rocker arm assemblies. Remove the pushrods.
4. Remove the mass air flow sensor and air intake duct if equipped. Remove the cruise control cable if equipped.
5. Remove the throttle valve and the accelerator cables if equipped.
6. Disconnect the crankcase ventilation pipe and the vacuum lines. Remove the heater hoses.
7. Remove the intake manifold as described earlier. Remove the cooling fan(s) in order to gain working clearance.
8. Remove the alternator and power steering pump to gain working clearance.
9. Remove the exhaust manifolds from both sides of the vehicle.
10. Tag and disconnect the spark plug wires.
11. Remove the cylinder head bolts. Remove the cylinder head and discard the old gasket material.

NOTE: On vehicles equipped with fuel injection, it may be necessary to remove the fuel rail in order to gain access to the cylinder head bolts.

12. Installation is the reverse of the removal procedure.

CAMSHAFT
Removal and Installation
V6
1. Disconnect the negative battery cable.
2. Remove the engine from the vehicle as previously outlined and place in a suitable work fixture.
3. Remove the intake manifold.
4. Remove the valve covers. Remove the rocker arm shaft assemblies.
5. Remove the push rods. Using a suitable tool, remove the valve lifters.
6. Remove the balancer assembly and the timing chain cover.
7. Align the timing marks of the crankcase and the camshaft sprockets. Remove the timing chain and sprockets.
8. Remove the camshaft from the vehicle. Be careful not to mar the bearing surfaces of the camshaft.
9. Installation is the reverse of the removal procedure.

V8
1. Disconnect the negative battery cable.
2. Remove the engine, timing chain and valve lifters.
3. Temporarily reinstall the camshaft sprockets or a long bolt to use as a handle to slide the camshaft forward until it is out of the engine.

——— CAUTION ———
Extreme care must be exercised to prevent the camshaft lobes from scratching the bearings during removal and installation.

4. Installation is in the reverse order of removal. Apply a thin coat of rear axle lubricant or the equivalent to the camshaft lobes, distributor gear teeth and bearing journals.

CONNECTING ROD
Alignment
Connecting rods are aligned at the factory and do not require alignment in the field. When they are damaged, misalignment can occur. Misalignment can be caused by overheating, lack of oil, etc. If this condition does happen, the piston assembly and rod assembly should be replaced. Damaged connecting rods cannot be straightened and no attempt should be made to do so.

PISTONS AND RODS POSITIONING

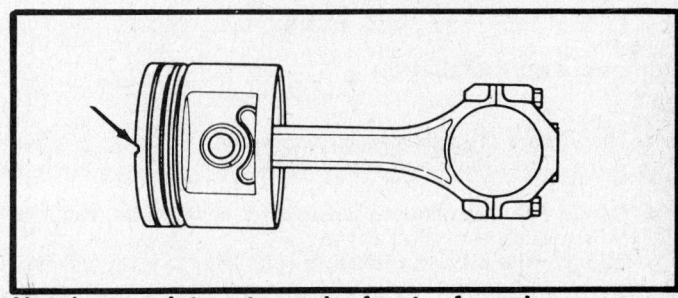

Notch on piston towards front of engine
(© General Motors Corporation)

TIMING CASE COVER/OIL SEAL
Removal and Installation
V6
1. Disconnect the negative battery cable.
2. Drain the engine coolant and remove the lower radiator hose. Remove the heater return hose.
3. Remove the front engine cradle mount bolts and raise the engine using a suitable tool.
4. Remove the belts and the water pump pulley.
5. Tag and disconnect the alternator wiring. Remove the alternator. Remove the alternator bracket.
6. Mark the position of the distributor rotor and remove the distributor.
7. Remove the coolant bypass hose clamp.
8. Remove the balance bolt and washer. Remove the balancer assembly.
9. Remove the bolts holding the timing chain cover to the cylinder block and the oil pan.
10. Remove the timing chain cover. Discard the oil seal.
11. Installation is the reverse of the removal procedure.

V8
1. Disconnect the negative battery cable.
2. Drain the engine coolant. Remove the air cleaner.
3. Remove the serpentine belt.
4. Tag and disconnect the alternator wiring. Remove the alternator. Remove the alternator bracket.
5. Remove the accumulator from the bracket and lay aside. Do not disconnect the fittings on the accumulator.
6. Remove the idler pulley. Remove the water pump pulley. Remove the water pump.
7. Raise the vehicle and support safely.
8. Remove the front cover bolts and remove the front cover.
9. Installation is the reverse of the removal procedure. Use new gasket material on the installation procedure.

TIMING CHAIN
Removal and Installation
1. Disconnect the negative battery cable.
2. Remove the timing case cover as described earlier. Align the timing marks so that they are as close together as possible.
3. Remove the front crankshaft oil slinger or damper as equipped.
4. Remove the camshaft sprocket bolts. Remove the sprocket and chain.
5. Remove the camshaft and crankshaft sprocket.
6. Installation is the reverse of the removal procedure.

SECTION 7: GENERAL MOTORS—"C" BODY
FRONT WHEEL DRIVE CARS

Lubrication

OIL PAN

Removal and Installation

V6

1. Disconnect the negative battery cable.
2. Raise the vehicle and support safely.
3. Drain the engine oil from the vehicle.
4. Remove the transmission converter cover bolts. Remove the transmission converter cover.
5. Remove the oil pan retaining bolts. Remove the oil pan. Discard the old gasket material.
6. Installation is the reverse of the removal procedure. Use new gasket material on the oil pan.

V8

1. Disconnect the negative battery cable.
2. Remove the two flywheel covers.
3. Drain the oil.
4. Remove the mounting bolts and nuts and then remove the oil pan.
5. Seal the oil pan to the block with RTV sealant.
6. Install the mounting bolts and nuts.
7. Installation of the remaining components is in the reverse order of removal.

OIL PUMP

Removal and Installation

1. Disconnect the negative battery cable.
2. Raise the vehicle and support safely.
3. Drain the engine oil.
4. Remove the oil pan as outlined earlier.
5. Remove the oil pump pipe. Remove the bolts holding the oil pump to the engine.
6. Remove the oil pump with the screen.
7. Installation is the reverse of the removal procedure. Use new gasket material on the installation material.

REAR MAIN BEARING OIL SEAL

Removal and Installation

V8

1. Disconnect the negative battery cable.
2. Remove the engine from the vehicle as described earlier. Place in a suitable fixture.
3. Remove the flexplate bolts from the vehicle. Remove the flexplate from the crankshaft.
4. Using a suitable seal removal tool, remove the seal from the vehicle.
5. Using a shop towel, remove any foreign material from the crankshaft and seal bore.
6. Installation is the reverse of the removal procedure. Lubricate the seal lip using wheel bearing grease prior to installation. Use tool J–34604 to press seal into position making sure that it is installed square to the crankshaft.

V6

1. Disconnect the negative battery cable.
2. Raise the vehicle and support safely.
3. Drain the engine oil.
4. Remove the oil pan.
5. Remove the rear main bearing cap.
6. Remove the oil seal from the bearing cap.
7. Installation is the reverse of the removal procedure.

NOTE: When installing the new seal, a small amount of oil applied to the seal surfaces may ease the installation when packing the seal into the cylinder block.

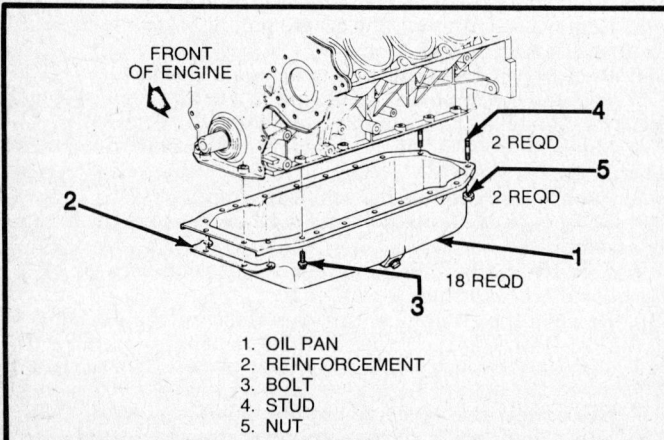

Oil pan installation—4.1L V8
(© General Motors Corporation)

1. OIL PAN
2. REINFORCEMENT
3. BOLT
4. STUD
5. NUT

FRONT SUSPENSION AND STEERING SECTION

For Front Suspension Services, refer to Unit Repair Section. For Steering Gear Overhaul, refer to Unit Repair Section.

STEERING WHEEL

Removal and Installation

CAUTION

Disconnect the battery ground cable before removing the steering wheel. When installing a steering wheel, always make sure that the turn signal lever is in the neutral position.

1. Remove the trim retaining screws from behind the wheel. On wheels with a center cap, pull off the cap.
2. Lift the trim off and pull the horn wires from the turn signal cancelling cam.
3. Remove the retainer and the steering wheel nut.
4. Mark the wheel-to-shaft relationship, and then remove the wheel from the vehicle.
5. Install the wheel on the shaft aligning the previously made marks. Tighten the nut.
6. Insert the horn wires into the cancelling cam.
7. Install the center trim and reconnect the battery cable.

STEERING GEAR

Removal and Installation

1. Raise and support the front end of the car with jackstands

GENERAL MOTORS—"C" BODY
FRONT WHEEL DRIVE CARS

under the frame members. Allow the front suspension to hang freely. Disconnect the power steering hoses form the gear, where equipped.

2. Move the intermediate shaft seal upward and remove the intermediate shaft-to-stub shaft pinch bolt.
3. Remove both front wheels.
4. Remove the cotter pins and nut from both tie rod ends. Disconnect the tie rod ends from the steering knuckles.
5. Remove the line retainer.
6. Remove the outlet and pressure hose.
7. Remove the five rack and pinion assembly mounting bolts.
8. Loosen the front engine cradle mounting bolts. Loosen the rear engine cradle mounting bolts. Install jack stands and then lower the rear of the cradle about 3 in. (76mm).

— **CAUTION** —
Do not lower the rear of the engine cradle too far.

9. Remove the rack and pinion steering assembly.
10. Installation is in the reverse order of removal. Tighten the rack mounting bolts to 50 ft. lbs. (68 Nm). Tighten the tie rod end nut to 35–52 ft. lbs. (50–70 Nm). Bleed the power steering system and check for leaks.

FRONT WHEEL BEARING

Adjustment

All models covered in this section utilize a permanently sealed and lubricated front wheel bearing assembly. No adjustment are either necessary or possible.

POWER STEERING PUMP

Removal and Installation

3.0L V6 AND 3.8L V6

1. Disconnect the negative battery cable.
2. Remove the air cleaner assembly on the 3.0L.
3. Remove the drive belt and tie alternator.
4. Raise the front of the vehicle and support it on jackstands.
5. Disconnect and plug the pressure and return lines at the pump.
6. Remove the rear pump adjustment bracket-to-pump nut.
7. Remove the alternator adjustment bracket and support brace.
8. Remove the rear pump adjustment bracket and then remove the pump assembly.
9. Remove the front pump adjustment bracket and then remove the pulley.
10. Installation in the reverse order of removal. Adjust the drive belts and bleed the power steering system.

4.1L V8

1. Disconnect the negative battery cable.
2. Remove the drive belt and the pulley.
3. Disconnect and plug the high pressure and pump feed lines.
4. Remove the two pump mounting bolts. Remove the power steering pump.
5. Installation is in the reverse order of removal. Tighten the pump mounting bolts to 25 Nm. Adjust the drive belt tension and bleed the power steering system.

4.3L DIESEL

1. Disconnect the negative battery cable.
2. Loosen the power steering pump drive belt. Remove the drive belt from the vehicle.
3. Raise the vehicle and support safely.

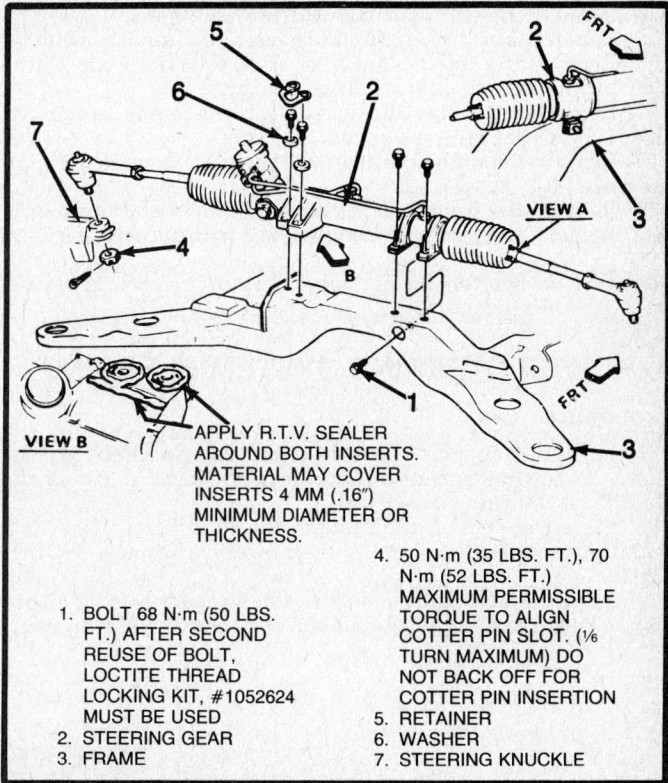

Rack and pinion assembly
(© General Motors Corporation)

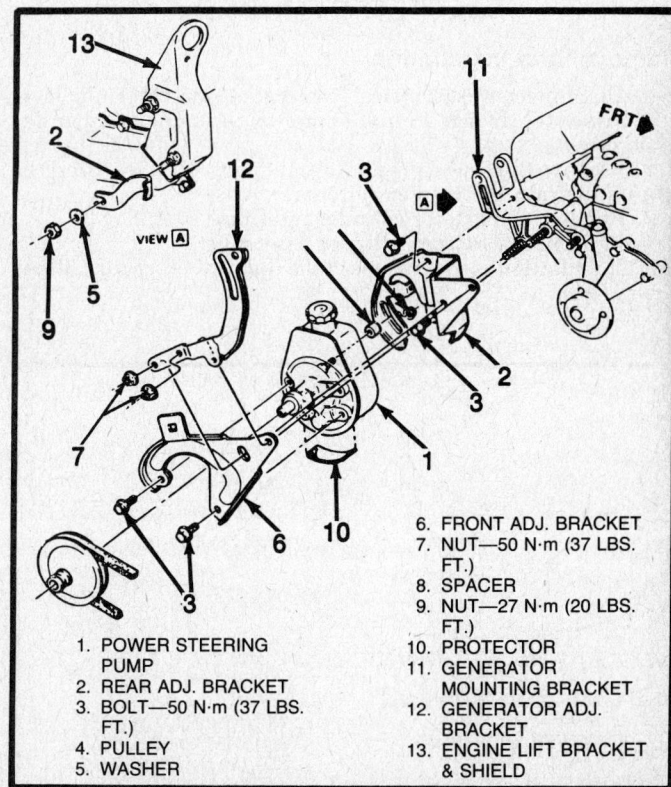

Power steering pump mounting—3.IL V6 and 3.8L V6 (© General Motors Corporation)

GENERAL MOTORS—"C" BODY
FRONT WHEEL DRIVE CARS

4. Remove the engine splash shield if equipped.
5. Remove the crankshaft pulley assembly from the vehicle.
6. Remove the engine absorber assembly from the frame side sill in order to gain working clearance.
7. Remove the reservoir hose from the pump assembly. Drain the power steering pump reservoir.
8. Remove the high pressure hose support. Remove the high pressure hose.
9. Remove the front bracket retaining bolts and nuts.
10. Remove the pump assembly along with the brackets.
11. Installation is the reverse of the removal procedure. Adjust the drive belt tension and bleed the power steering system.

POWER STEERING SYSTEM BLEEDING

Procedure

1. Raise and support the front of the vehicle safely.
2. Add power steering fluid until the "COLD" mark on the fluid level indicator is reached.
3. Start the engine and recheck the fluid level. If needed, add fluid in order to bring the fluid level back to the "COLD" mark.
4. Turn the wheels from side to side without hitting either stop. Check the fluid level and adjust to the "COLD" mark.

NOTE: Fluid which has air in it will appear to have a light tan appearance.

5. Return the wheels to their normal position. Continue to run the engine. Road test the vehicle for normal steering action.
6. Recheck the fluid level after the engine has reached normal operating temperature. Check to insure that the fluid level is at the "HOT" mark after the system has stabilized.

NOTE: When adding fluid to the system, use GM power steering fluid part No. 1050017 or equivalent.

STEERING COLUMN

Removal and Installation

1. Disconnect the negative battery cable.
2. Remove the lower instrument panel trim plates. Remove the left hand sound insulator panel.
3. Remove the shift indicator cable from the shift bowl.
4. Tag and disconnect the electrical connectors from the steering column.
5. Remove the steering column mounting bolts.
7. Remove the bolt holding the steering shaft to the intermediate shaft.
8. Remove the steering column from the vehicle.
9. Installation is the reverse of the removal procedure.

BRAKE SECTION

For Brake Service, refer to Unit Repair Section.

MASTER CYLINDER

Removal and Installation

1. Disconnect the electrical connector from the fluid level sensor switch located on the side of the master cylinder assembly.
2. Remove the brake tube nuts and hydraulic lines. Plug the lines and drain the master cylinder.
3. Remove the master cylinder retaining nuts.
4. Remove the master cylinder assembly.
5. Installation is the reverse of the removal procedure. Bleed the system.

VACUUM BOOSTER

Removal and Installation

1. Disconnect the negative battery cable.
2. Remove the master cylinder assembly.
3. Remove the master cylinder from the booster assembly by removing the retaining nuts.
4. Remove the nuts from the mounting studs which hold the unit to the dash panel.
5. Remove the booster pushrod from the brake pedal.
6. Installation is the reverse of the removal procedure. Check and bleed the brake system.

PARKING BRAKE

Adjustments

1. Depress the parking brake pedal three ratchet clicks.
2. Raise the vehicle and support safely.
3. Check to make sure that the equalizer nut is lubricated.
4. Tighten the adjusting nut until the right rear wheel can just be turned rearward using two hands but is locked in forward rotation.
5. With the mechanism totally disengaged, both rear wheels should turn freely in either direction with no brake drag.

--- CAUTION ---
Do not adjust the parking brake cables so tight as to cause brake drag.

6. Lower the vehicle.

PARKING BRAKE CABLE

Removal and Installation

1. Release the parking brake lever. Remove the tension spring retainer clip. Remove the front cable from the cable connector at the pedal assembly.

1. NUT (20 N·m/14 FT. LB.)
2. SEAL
3. POWER BOOSTER
4. CHECK VALVE
5. MASTER CYLINDER
6. VACUUM SWITCH BRACKET (DIESEL)
7. NUT (30 N·m/22 FT. LB.)
8. VACUUM SWITCH (GAS)

Typical master cylinder and power booster mounting (© General Motors Corporation)

GENERAL MOTORS—"C" BODY
FRONT WHEEL DRIVE CARS

2. Raise and support the vehicle safely.
3. Loosen the equalizer nut until the cable tension is removed. Remove the cable from the equalizer.
4. Remove the clips that hold the parking brake cable to the rear cross member and at each caliper support plate.
5. Remove the cable ends from the parking brake actuator. Remove the control arm hooks and the conduit from the exhaust hanger clip.
6. Installation is the reverse of the removal procedure. Adjust the parking brake as required.

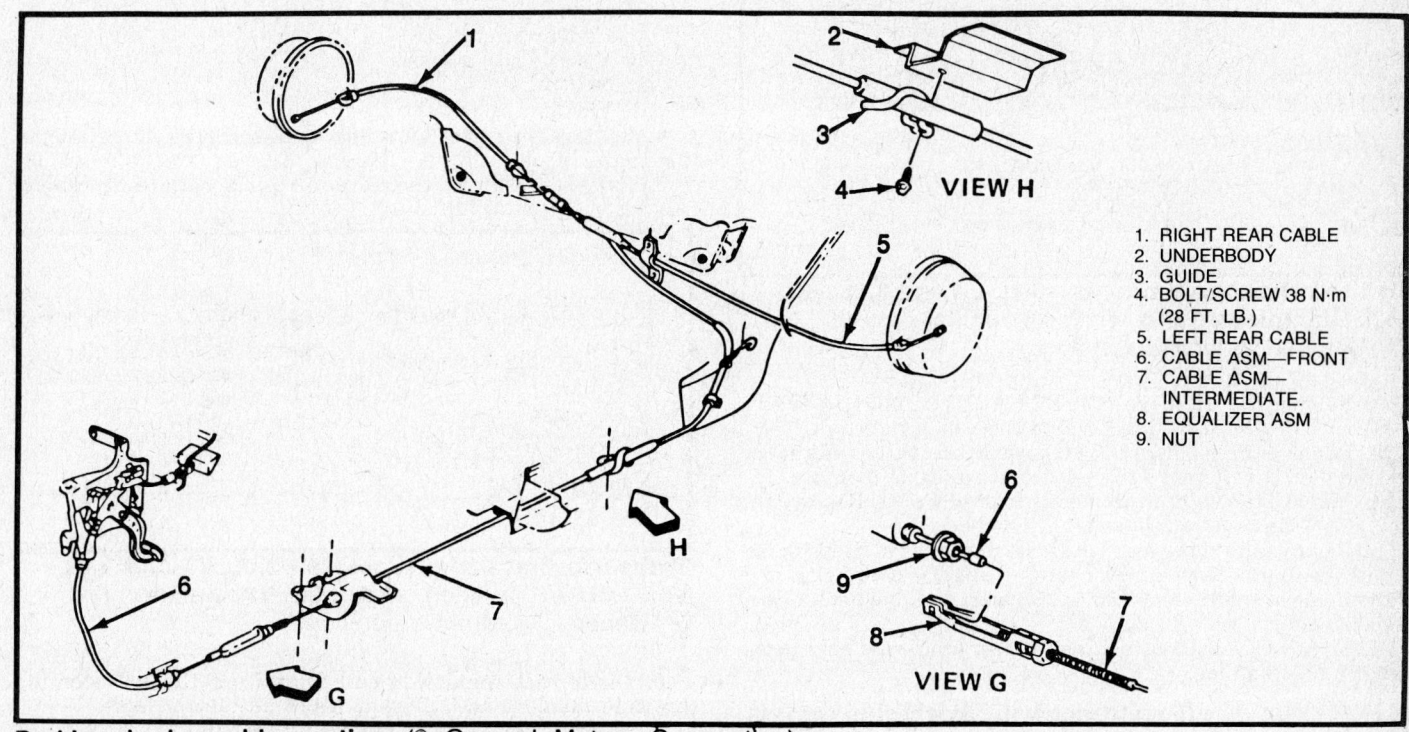

1. RIGHT REAR CABLE
2. UNDERBODY
3. GUIDE
4. BOLT/SCREW 38 N·m (28 FT. LB.)
5. LEFT REAR CABLE
6. CABLE ASM—FRONT
7. CABLE ASM—INTERMEDIATE
8. EQUALIZER ASM
9. NUT

Parking brake cable routing (© General Motors Corporation)

CLUTCH, TRANSMISSION AND DRIVESHAFT SECTION

For Overhaul Procedures, refer to Unit Repair Section.

AUTOMATIC TRANSAXLE

Removal and Installation

V6

1. Disconnect the negative battery cable. Disconnect the wire connector at the mass air flow sensor (3.8L only).
2. Remove the air intake duct and the mass air flow sensor as an assembly.
3. Disconnect the cruise control assembly if equipped. Disconnect the shift control linkage.
4. Tag and disconnect the following:
   a. Park/Neutral switch
   b. Torque converter clutch
   c. Vehicle speed sensor
   d. Vacuum modulator hose at the modulator.

NOTE: Care must be exercised on reassembly of the Park/Neutral switch to ensure a proper fit of both the connector and the T-latch. Failure to do so may result in intermittent loss of switch functions.

5. Remove the three top transaxle-to-engine block bolts. Install an engine support fixture.
6. Remove both front wheels and then turn the steering wheel to the full left position.
7. Remove the right front ball joint nut and separate the control arm from the steering knuckle.
8. Remove the right drive axle as detailed later in this section.

NOTE: Be careful not to allow the drive axle splines to contact any portion of the lip seal.

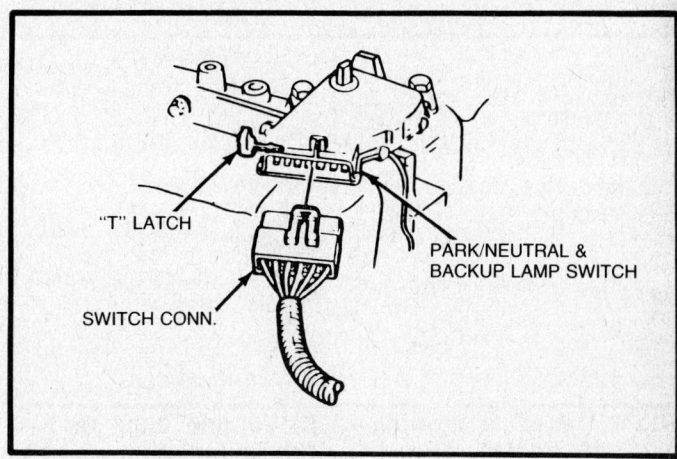

T-latch conector (© General Motors Corporation)

SECTION 7: GENERAL MOTORS—"C" BODY
FRONT WHEEL DRIVE CARS

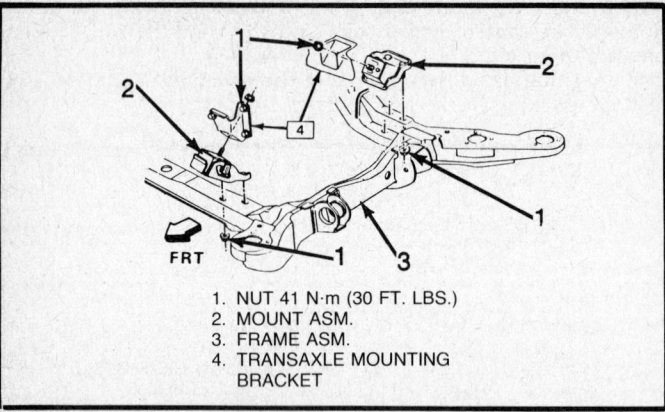

1. NUT 41 N·m (30 FT. LBS.)
2. MOUNT ASM.
3. FRAME ASM.
4. TRANSAXLE MOUNTING BRACKET

Left side transaxle mounts—3.0L V6 and 3.8L V6. 4.3L V6 (diesel) and 4.1L V8 similar
(© General Motors Corporation)

9. Remove the left drive axle. BE CAREFUL NOT TO DAMAGE THE PAN. Install drive axle boot seal protectors.
10. Remove three bolts at the transaxle and three nuts at the cradle member. Remove the left front transaxle mount.
11. Remove the right front mount-to-cradle nuts. Remove the left rear transaxle mount-to-transaxle bolts.
12. Remove the right rear transaxle mount as in Step 10. Remove the engine support bracket-to-transaxle case bolts.
13. Remove the flywheel cover. Remove the flywheel-to-converter bolts.
14. Remove the bolts attaching the rear cradle member to the front cradle dog leg.

NOTE: Be sure to matchmark the flywheel-to-converter relationship for proper alignemt upon reassembly.

15. Remove the front left cradle-to-body bolt. Remove the front left cradle-to-body bolt. Remove the front cradle dog leg-to-right cradle member bolts.
16. Install a transaxle support fixture into position.
17. Remove the cradle assembly by swinging it aside and supporting it with a suitable stand.
18. Disconnect and cap the oil cooler lines at the transaxle.

NOTE: One bolt is located between the transaxle and the engine block and is installed in the opposite direction.

19. Remove the remaining lower transaxle-to-engine bolts and lower the transaxle assembly from the vehicle.
20. Installation is in the reverse order of removal. Check the fluid level and all adjustments.

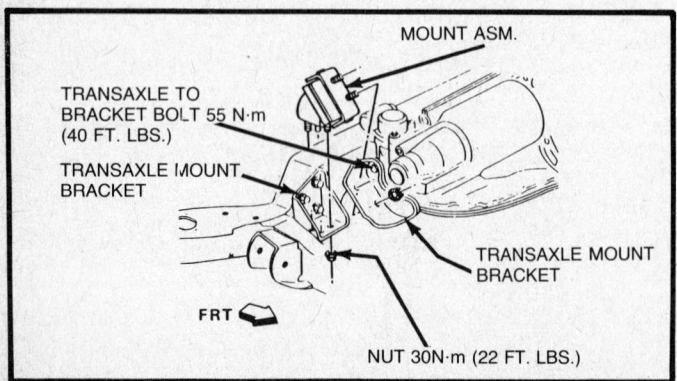

Right transaxle mounts—3.0L V6 and 3.8L V6. 4.3L V6 (diesel) and 4.1L V8 similar
(© General Motors Corporation)

V8

1. Disconnect the negative battery cable, the air cleaner and the TV cable.
2. Disconnnect the shift linkage at the transaxle. Install a suitable engine support fixture.
3. Tag and disconnect the following:
   a. Converter clutch
   b. Vehicle speed sensor
   c. Neutral start/back-up light switch
   d. Vacuum line at the modulator.
4. Remove the upper bolts and studs securing the bell housing to the block.
5. Raise and support the car and remove both front wheels.

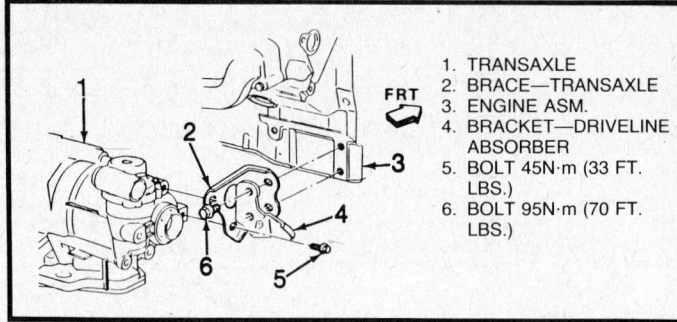

1. TRANSAXLE
2. BRACE—TRANSAXLE
3. ENGINE ASM.
4. BRACKET—DRIVELINE ABSORBER
5. BOLT 45N·m (33 FT. LBS.)
6. BOLT 95N·m (70 FT. LBS.)

Transaxle brace and brackets—3.0L V6 and 3.8L V6. 4.3L V6 (diesel) and 4.3L V8 similar
(© General Motors Corporation)

6. Disconnect the lower ball joint from the left steering knuckle. Remove both drive axles from the transaxle.
7. Remove the stabilizer bar mounting bolt from the left control arm.
8. Remove the left front cradle assembly.
9. Remove the extension housing-to-engine block support bracket.
10. Disconnect and cap the oil cooler lines at the transaxle case.
11. Remove the right and left transaxle mount attachments.
12. Remove the flexplate splash shield. Remove the converter-to-flexplate bolts.
13. Remove all the lower bellhousing bolts except the lower rear one.
14. Position a jack under the transaxle and then remove the last bellhousing bolt.

NOTE: To reach the last bellhousing bolt, a 3 in. socket wrench extension is needed and must be put through the right wheel arch opening.

15. Remove the transaxle assembly.
16. Installation is in the reverse order of removal. Check the fluid level and all adjustments.

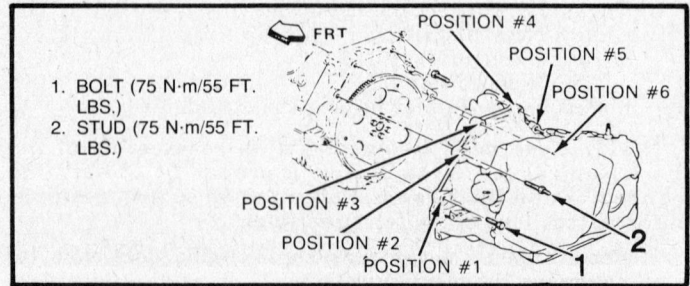

1. BOLT (75 N·m/55 FT. LBS.)
2. STUD (75 N·m/55 FT. LBS.)

Transaxle-to-engine mounting bolts. Remove No. 6 last—4.1L V8 (© General Motors Corporation)

GENERAL MOTORS—"C" BODY
FRONT WHEEL DRIVE CARS

SHIFT INDICATOR

Removal and Installation

1. Disconnect the negative battery cable.
2. Remove the instrument cluster trim plate.
3. Remove the shift indicator clip.
4. Remove the shift indicator.
5. Installation is the reverse of the removal procedure.

FRONT DRIVE AXLE

Removal and Installation

ALL EXCEPT CADILLAC

1. Remove the torque prevailing hub nut. Raise the vehicle and support safely.
2. Remove the wheel and tire.
3. Install an axle shaft boot seal protector or the equivalent onto the seal.
4. Disconnect the brake hose clip from the MacPherson strut, but do not disconnect the hose from the caliper. Remove the brake caliper from the spindle, and hang the caliper out of the way by a length of wire.
5. Remove the strut to steering knuckle attaching bolts.
6. Remove the drive axle from the transaxle using tool J-33008 or equivalent.
7. Pull the drive axle from the transaxle and support properly.
8. Remove the drive axle from the hub and bearing assembly using spindle remover J-28733 or equivalent.
9. Remove the drive axle from the vehicle.

To install:

1. With the drive axle boot seal protector installed, position the drive axle into the steering knuckle.
2. Position the steering knuckle into the strut bracket and install bolts.
3. Install the rotor and brake caliper. Tighten the bolts to 30 ft. lbs.
4. Install a drift in the slot of the rotor to prevent from turning.
5. Install a new torque prevailing hub nut and washer and tighten to 74 ft. lbs.
6. Seat the drive axle into the transaxle making sure the shaft is securely seated.
7. Remove the boot seal protector if installed earlier.
8. Connect the brake hose clip to the strut. Install the tire and wheel, lower the car, and tighten the hub nut to 192 ft. lbs. Check and correct front end alignment if necessary.

CADILLAC

1. Remove the torque prevailing hub nut and washer.
2. Raise the vehicle and support safely.
3. Remove the wheel and tire assemblies.
4. Remove the brake caliper and rotor and wire out of the way in order to gain working clearance.
5. Remove the stabilizer bar from the control arm.
6. Remove the tie rod end from the steering knuckle.
7. Remove the lower ball joint stud from the steering knuckle.
8. Remove the drive axle from the transaxle assembly. Remove the drive axle from hub and bearing assembly using tool J-28733 or equivalent.
9. Remove the drive axle from the vehicle.

To Install:

1. Position the drive axle into the steering knuckle and transaxle.
2. Install the lower ball joint stud to the steering knuckle.
3. Install stabilizer bar to the lower control arm. Install the tie rod end to the steering knuckle.
4. Install the brake caliper and rotor. Install a new torque prevailing nut. Tighten the hub nut to 74 ft. lbs.

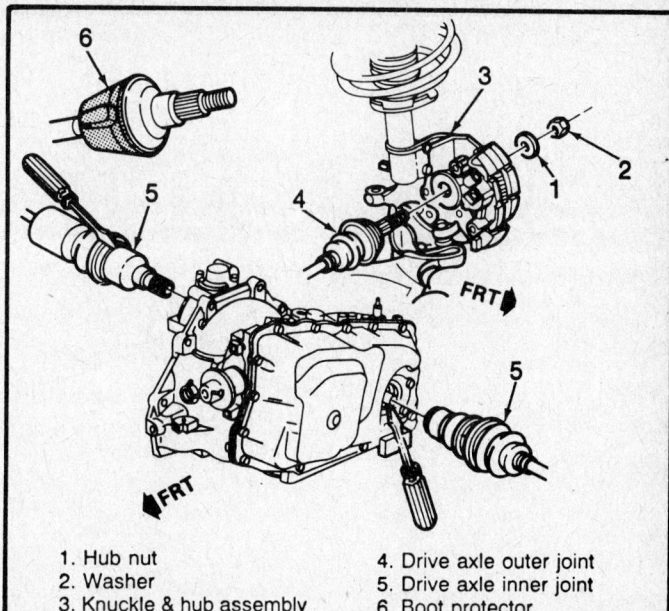

1. Hub nut
2. Washer
3. Knuckle & hub assembly
4. Drive axle outer joint
5. Drive axle inner joint
6. Boot protector

Drive Axle Removal (© General Motors Corporation)

5. Install the drive axle into the drive axle by placing a screwdriver into the groove on the joint housing and lightly tapping until seated.
6. Install the wheel and tire assembly and tighten the hub nut to 183 ft. lbs. Check and correct front end alignment if necessary.

INNER AND OUTER BOOTS

Removal and Installation

OUTER BOOT

1. Raise the vehicle and support safely.
2. Remove the front tire and wheel.
3. Remove the caliper bolts and wire the caliper off to the side of the vehicle.
4. Remove the hub nut, washer and wheel bearing.
5. Using a brass drift, lightly tap around the seal retainer to loosen it. Remove the seal retainer.
6. Remove the seal retainer clamp and discard.
7. Using snap ring pliers, remove the race retaining ring from the axle shaft.
8. Pull the outer joint assembly and the outboard seal away from the axle shaft.
9. Installation is the reverse of the removal procedure. Pack the joint assembly with the grease provided with the new seal.

INNER BOOT

1. Raise the vehicle and support safely.
2. Remove the front tire and wheel.
3. Remove the caliper bolts and wire the caliper off to the side of the vehicle.
4. Remove the hub nut, washer and wheel bearing.
5. Remove the front drive axle as outlined earlier in this section. Place in a suitable holding fixture.
6. Remove the joint assembly retaining ring. Remove the joint assembly.
7. Remove the race retaining ring and remove the seal retainer.
8. Remove the inner seal retainer clamp. Remove the inner joint seal.
9. Installation is the reverse of the removal procedure. Pack the joint assembly with the grease provided.

SECTION 7
GENERAL MOTORS—"C" BODY
FRONT WHEEL DRIVE CARS

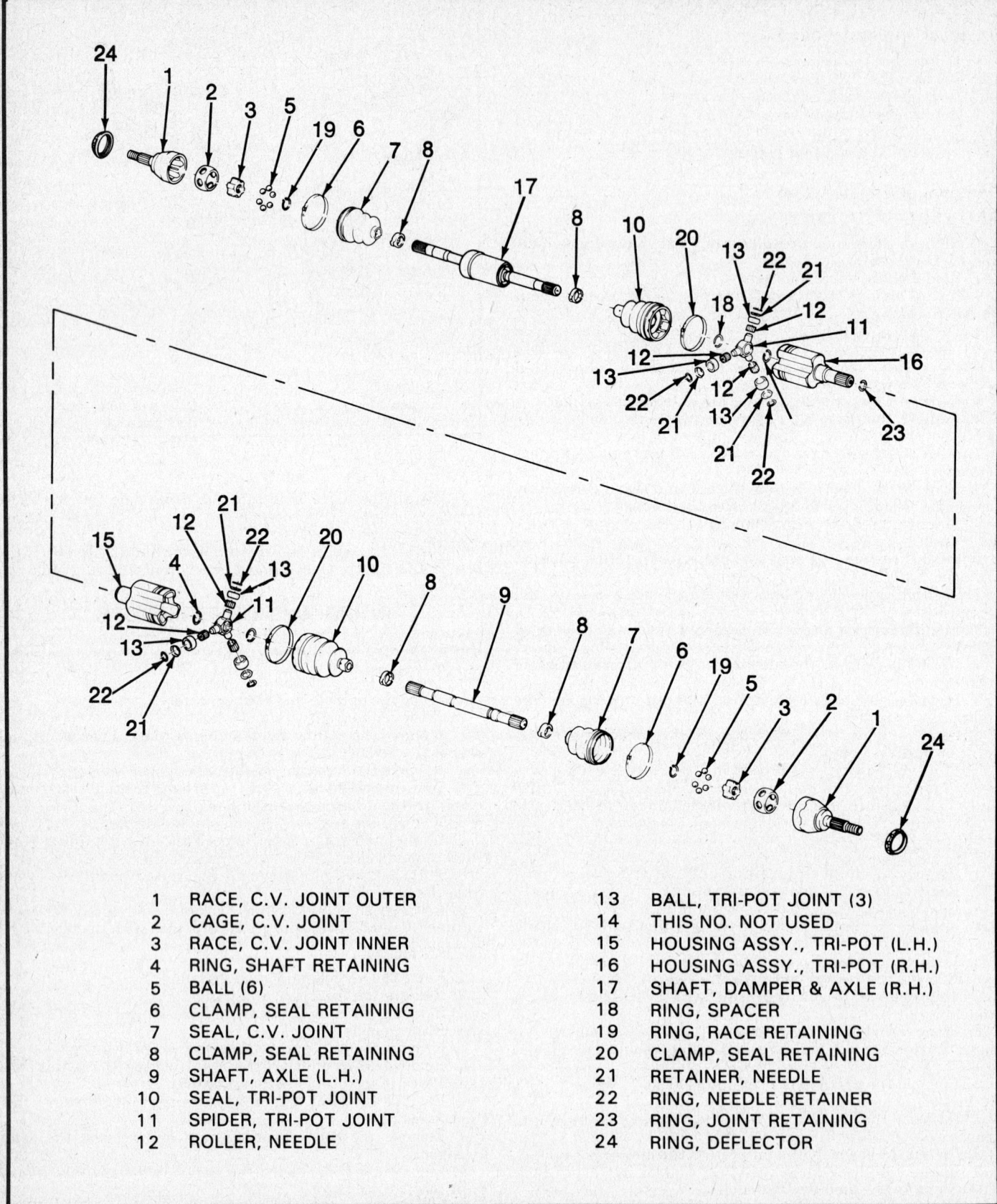

1	RACE, C.V. JOINT OUTER	13	BALL, TRI-POT JOINT (3)
2	CAGE, C.V. JOINT	14	THIS NO. NOT USED
3	RACE, C.V. JOINT INNER	15	HOUSING ASSY., TRI-POT (L.H.)
4	RING, SHAFT RETAINING	16	HOUSING ASSY., TRI-POT (R.H.)
5	BALL (6)	17	SHAFT, DAMPER & AXLE (R.H.)
6	CLAMP, SEAL RETAINING	18	RING, SPACER
7	SEAL, C.V. JOINT	19	RING, RACE RETAINING
8	CLAMP, SEAL RETAINING	20	CLAMP, SEAL RETAINING
9	SHAFT, AXLE (L.H.)	21	RETAINER, NEEDLE
10	SEAL, TRI-POT JOINT	22	RING, NEEDLE RETAINER
11	SPIDER, TRI-POT JOINT	23	RING, JOINT RETAINING
12	ROLLER, NEEDLE	24	RING, DEFLECTOR

Drive Axles—Exploded view (© General Motors Corporation)

GENERAL MOTORS—"C" BODY
FRONT WHEEL DRIVE CARS

REAR AXLE AND SUSPENSION SECTION

For Axle Overhaul Procedures and Suspension Services refer to Unit Repair Section.

REAR AXLE ASSEMBLY

Removal and Installation

In order to gain access to the rear axle assembly, the entire rear suspension must be removed. This Includes the removal of the rear springs, shocks absorbers and if equipped, the electronic leveling control system.

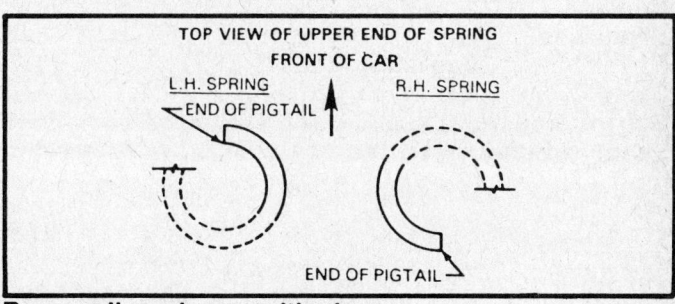

Rear coil spring positioning
(© General Motors Corporation)

Rear hub and bearing assembly—exploded view
(© General Motors Corporation)

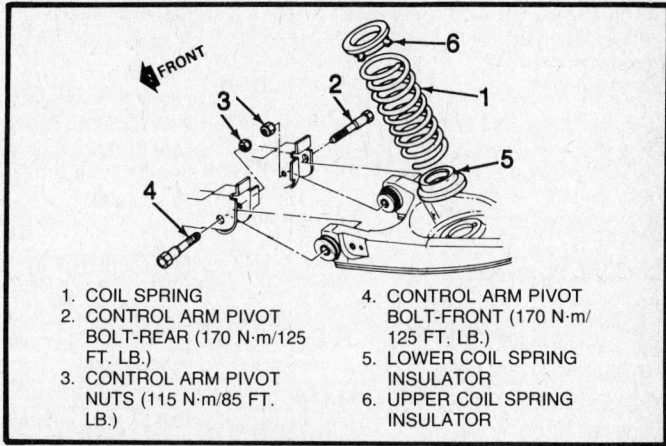

1. COIL SPRING
2. CONTROL ARM PIVOT BOLT-REAR (170 N·m/125 FT. LB.)
3. CONTROL ARM PIVOT NUTS (115 N·m/85 FT. LB.)
4. CONTROL ARM PIVOT BOLT-FRONT (170 N·m/125 FT. LB.)
5. LOWER COIL SPRING INSULATOR
6. UPPER COIL SPRING INSULATOR

Rear coil spring installation
(© General Motors Corporation)

REAR WHEEL HUB AND BEARING ASSEMBLY

Removal and Installation

NOTE: Certain vehicles incorporate Torx® bolts which hold the bearing and hub assembly to the vehicle also supports the brake assembly. Upon removal of these bolts, be sure to support the brake assembly with a wire so it does not hang by the brake cable lines.

1. Raise the vehicle and support safely.
2. Remove the rear tires and wheels.
3. Remove the brake drum from the vehicle. Remove the brake line brackets.
4. Remove the hub and bearing-to-axle assembly attaching bolts. Remove the hub and bearing assembly.
5. Installation is the reverse of the removal procedure. Bleed the brake system as required.

7-31

Section 8: GENERAL MOTORS—"E" AND "K" BODY
FRONT WHEEL DRIVE CARS

SPECIFICATIONS

Brakes	24-2	Serial Number Identification	8-4
Capacities	8-8	Torque	8-8
Crankshaft & Connecting Rod	8-8	Torque Sequence (Cylinder Heads)	8-38
Firing Order	8-6	Tune-Up	8-5
General Engine	8-4	Valve	8-6
Piston & Ring	8-7	Wheel Alignment	8-9

INDEX

A
Alternator R&R	8-9
Automatic Transaxle	8-45
Adjustment	8-45
On Car Service	23-2
Assembly R&R	8-45
Axle Assembly R&R	8-49
Axle Shaft R&R	8-47

B
Ball joints	35-2
Brake System	8-43
Brake Booster	8-43
Brake Caliper Overhaul	24-2
Brake Drum, Rear	24-2
Brake Master cylinder	8-43
Brake Pad	
Front	24-2
Brake shoe	
Rear	24-2

C
Camshaft R&R	8-37
Carburetor R&R	8-31
Chassis Electrical	8-11
Combination Switch R&R	8-13
Component Location	8-17
Control Arm R&R	35-2
Cooling Fan Motor	8-28
Cooling System	8-27
Cruise control	8-17
Cylinder Head	8-37
R&R	8-37

D
Differential	8-45
Inspection	8-45
Dimmer Switch R&R	8-14
Disc Brakes	24-2
Distributor R&R	8-11
Drive Axle	8-45
Driveshaft R&R	8-47

E
Electric Fuel Pump R&R	8-31
Electronic Ignition	30-2
Emission Controls	8-33
Engine	
Identification	8-4
R&R	8-34
Engine Electrical	8-9
Engine Lubrication	8-39
Engine Mechanical	8-34
Engine Mounts R&R	8-35
Exhaust Manifold R&R	8-32

F
Front Suspension	35-2
Alignment	8-9
Final Drive	8-48
Fuel Injection	8-32
Fuel Mixture, Adjust	8-31
Fuel Pump R&R	8-31
Fuses/Circuit Breakers	8-26
Fusible Links	8-26

H
Headlight Switch	8-14
Heater Blower R&R	8-28
Heater Core R&R	8-28
Heater Control	8-30
Horn Switch	8-15

I
Idle Speed, Adjust	8-31
Ignition Switch	8-11
Ignition Timing	8-11
Instrument Cluster R&R	8-16
Intake Manifold R&R	8-32

L, M, N
Lower Control Arm R&R	35-2
Master Cylinder R&R	8-43
Manual Steering Gear R&R	8-41
Neutral Safety Switch R&R	8-13

O
Oil Pan R&R	8-39
Oil Pump R&R	8-40
Oil Seal R&R	
Rear Main	8-40

P
Parking Brake	8-44
Adjustment	8-44
Cable R&R	8-45
Piston & Connection Rod	8-39
Power Brake Unit R&R	8-43
Power Steering Pump R&R	8-42

R
Rear Main Oil Seal R&R	8-40
Rear Suspension	35-2
Regulator	8-9
Rocker Shaft/Assy R&R	8-36

S
Serial Number	8-4
Engine	8-4
Vehicle	8-4
Shock Absorber R&R	
Front	35-2
Rear	35-2
Springs	
Front	35-2
Rear	35-2
Starter R&R	8-10
Starter Drive Replacement	8-10
Steering Column R&R	8-42
Steering Gear R&R	8-41
Manual	8-41
Power	8-41
Steering Wheel R&R	8-40
Stoplight Switch R&R	8-13
Speedometer R&R	8-17
Suspension R&R	35-2
Service	35-2

T
Timing Chain	8-39
Timing Gear Cover	8-38
Oil Seal Replacement	8-39
Tune-Up	8-5
Turn Signal Switch R&R	8-14
Turbocharger	8-33

U, V
U-Joint Overhaul	28-2
Valve tappette R&R	8-36
Valve timing, Adjust	8-37
Valve System	8-36
Voltage Regulator	8-9

W, Y
Water Pump R&R	8-27
Wheel Alignment	8-9
Front	8-9
Wheel bearings	
Front	8-41
Windshield Wiper	8-16
Linkage R&R	8-16
Motor R&R	8-16
Switch R&R	8-16
Year Identification	8-3

BEFORE SERVICING BE CERTAIN TO READ THE SAFETY NOTICE

GM "E" & "K" Body
1983–87 Front Wheel Drive Cars

"E" BODY—BUICK RIVIERA • RIVIERA LUXURY
RIVIERA "T" TYPE • RIVIERA CONVERTIBLE • CADILLAC
ELDORADO • OLDS TORONADO BROUGHAM
"K" BODY—CADILLAC SEVILLE

YEAR IDENTIFICATION

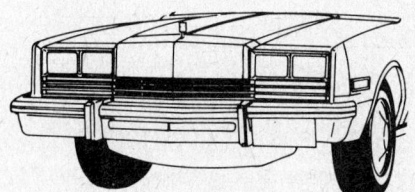
1983–84 Toronado

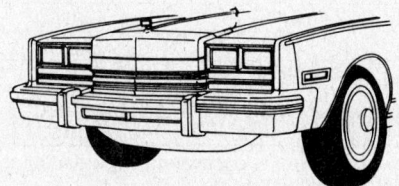
1984–85 Toronado Calienta

1986–87 Toronado

1983–84 Eldorado

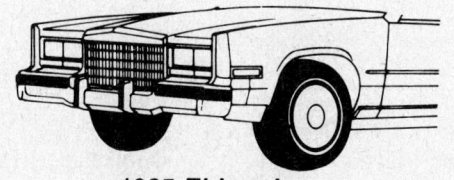
1985 Eldorado

1986–87 Riviera

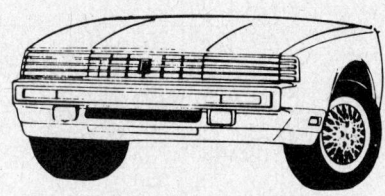
1987 Trofeo

SECTION 8: GENERAL MOTORS—"E" AND "K" BODY
FRONT WHEEL DRIVE CARS

VEHICLE IDENTIFICATION NUMBER (VIN)

It is important for servicing and ordering parts to be certain of the vehicle and engine identification. The VIN (vehicle identification number) is a 13 or 17 digit number visible through the windshield on the driver's side of the dash and contains the vehicle and engine identification codes. It can be interpreted as follows:

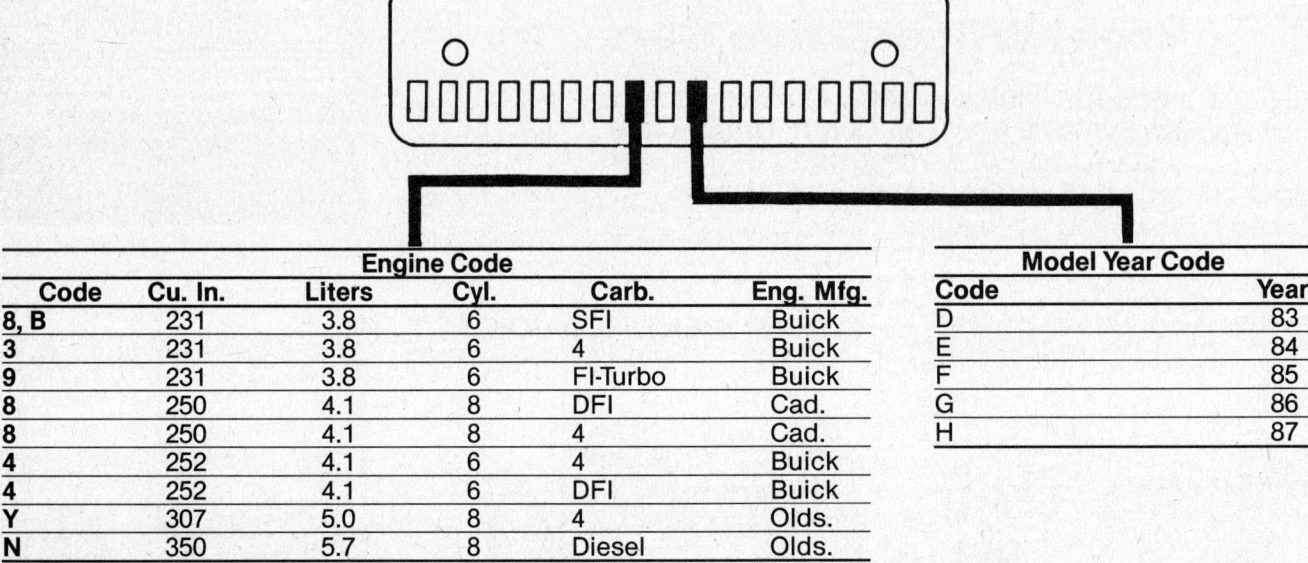

Engine Code

Code	Cu. In.	Liters	Cyl.	Carb.	Eng. Mfg.
8, B	231	3.8	6	SFI	Buick
3	231	3.8	6	4	Buick
9	231	3.8	6	FI-Turbo	Buick
8	250	4.1	8	DFI	Cad.
8	250	4.1	8	4	Cad.
4	252	4.1	6	4	Buick
4	252	4.1	6	DFI	Buick
Y	307	5.0	8	4	Olds.
N	350	5.7	8	Diesel	Olds.

Model Year Code

Code	Year
D	83
E	84
F	85
G	86
H	87

The seventeen digit Vehicle Identification Number can be used to determine engine application and model year. The 10th digit indicates the model year, and the 8th digit identifies the factory installed engine.
EFI Electronic Fuel Injection
DFI Digital Fuel Injection

GENERAL ENGINE SPECIFICATIONS

Year	Eng. Code	Engine No. Cyl. Displacement (cu. in.)	Liters	Carburetor Type	Horsepower @ rpm ■	Torque @ rpm (ft. lbs.)■	Bore × Stroke (in.)	Compression Ratio	Oil Pressure @ 1500 rpm	Eng. Mfg.
TORONADO										
1983	4	6-252	4.1	4 bbl	125 @ 4000	205 @ 2000	3.965 × 3.400	8.0:1	37 ①	Buick
	Y	8-307	5.0	4 bbl	140 @ 3600	240 @ 1600	3.800 × 3.385	8.0:1	40	Olds.
	N	8-350	5.7	Diesel	105 @ 3200	200 @ 1600	4.057 × 3.385	22.5:1	38	Olds.
1984	4	6-252	4.1	4 bbl	125 @ 4000	205 @ 2000	3.965 × 3.400	8.0:1	37 ①	Buick
	Y	8-307	5.0	4 bbl	140 @ 3600	240 @ 1600	3.800 × 3.385	8.0:1	40	Olds.
	N	8-350	5.7	Diesel	105 @ 3200	200 @ 1600	4.057 × 3.385	22.5:1	38	Olds.
1985–'87	Y	8-307	5.0	4 bbl	140 @ 3600	240 @ 1600	3.800 × 3.385	8.0:1	40	Olds.
	N	8-350	5.7	Diesel	105 @ 3200	200 @ 1600	4.057 × 3.385	22.5:1	38	Olds.
1986–'87	B	6-231	3.8	SFI	159 @ 4400	200 @ 2000	3.800 × 3.400	8.0:1	37	Olds.
RIVIERA										
'83	Y	8-307	5.0	4 bbl	140 @ 3600	240 @ 1600	3.736 × 3.385	8.0:1	37	Olds.
	N	8-350	5.7	Diesel	105 @ 3200	200 @ 1600	4.057 × 3.385	22.5:1	38	Olds.
	4	6-252	4.1	4 bbl	125 @ 4000	205 @ 2000	3.965 × 3.400	8.0:1	35 ③	Buick
	8	6-231	3.8	4 bbl Turbo	180 @ 4000	290 @ 2400	3.800 × 3.400	8.0:1	37 ②	Buick
'84	8	6-231	3.8	4 bbl Turbo ④	190 @ 4000	300 @ 2400	3.800 × 3.400	8.0:1	37 ②	Buick
	4	6-252	4.1	4 bbl	125 @ 4000	205 @ 2000	3.965 × 3.400	8.0:1	35 ③	Buick
	Y	8-307	5.0	4 bbl	140 @ 3600	240 @ 1600	3.736 × 3.385	8.0:1	37	Olds.
	N	8-350	5.7	Diesel	105 @ 3200	200 @ 1600	4.057 × 3.385	22.5:1	38	Olds.

GENERAL MOTORS—"E" AND "K" BODY
FRONT WHEEL DRIVE CARS

Section 8

GENERAL ENGINE SPECIFICATIONS (cont'd)

Year	Eng. Code	Engine No. Cyl. Displacement (cu. in.)	Liters	Carburetor Type	Horsepower @ rpm ■	Torque @ rpm (ft. lbs.)■	Bore × Stroke (in.)	Compression Ratio	Oil Pressure @ 1500 rpm	Eng. Mfg.
'85–'87	9	6-231	3.8	4 bbl Turbo ④	190 @ 4000	300 @ 2400	3.800 × 3.400	8.0:1	37 ②	Buick
	Y	8-307	5.0	4 bbl	140 @ 3600	240 @ 1600	3.736 × 3.385	8.0:1	37	Olds.
	N	8-350	5.7	Diesel	105 @ 3200	200 @ 1600	4.057 × 3.385	22.5:1	38	Olds.
1986–'87	B	6-231	3.8	SFI	150 @ 4400	200 @ 2000	3.800 × 3.400	8.0:1	37	Olds.
SEVILLE										
'83	8	8-250	4.1	DFI	135 @ 4200	190 @ 2000	3.465 × 3.307	8.5:1	40	Cadillac
	N	8-350	5.7	Diesel	105 @ 3200	205 @ 1600	4.057 × 3.385	22.5:1	35 ③	Olds.
'84–'87	8	8-250	4.1	DFI	130 @ 4200	200 @ 2200	3.465 × 3.310	8.5:1	40	Cadillac
	N	8-350	5.7	Diesel	105 @ 3200	200 @ 1600	4.057 × 3.385	22.5:1	35 ③	Olds.
ELDORADO										
'83	8	8-250	4.1	DFI	135 @ 4200	190 @ 2000	3.465 × 3.307	8.5:1	40	Cadillac
	N	8-350	5.7	Diesel	105 @ 3200	205 @ 1600	4.057 × 3.385	22.5:1	35 ③	Olds.
'84–'87	8	8-250	4.1	DFI	130 @ 4200	2000 @ 2200	3.465 × 3.310	8.5:1	40	Cadillac
	N	8-350	5.7	Diesel	105 @ 3200	200 @ 1600	4.057 × 3.385	22.5:1	35 ③	Olds.

■ Horsepower and torque are SAE net figures. They are measured at the rear of the transmission with all accessories installed and operating. Since the figures vary when a given engine is installed in different models, some are representative rather than exact.
    EFI Electronic Fuel Injection
    DFI Digital Fuel Injection
    SFI Sequential Fuel Injection
① @ 2400 rpm   ③ @ 2000 rpm
② @ 2600 rpm   ④ @ '85-VIN9, Fuel Injected Turbo

GASOLINE ENGINE TUNE-UP SPECIFICATIONS

When analyzing compression test results, look for uniformity among cylinders rather than specific pressures.

Year	Eng. Code	Engine No. Cyl. Displacement (cu. in.)	Liters	Eng. Mfg.	Spark Plugs Orig. Type	Gap (in.)	Distributor	Ignition Timing (deg.)▲ *Auto Trans.•	Valves Intake Opens (deg.) •	Fuel Pump Pressure (psi)	Idle Speed (rpm)▲ Auto Trans.•
TORONADO											
'83	4	6-252	4.1	Buick	R-45TS8	.080	Electronic	15B	16	6-7.5	①
	Y	8-307	5.0	Olds.	R-46SX	.080	Electronic	15B	20	6-7.5	①
'84–'85	4	6-252	4.1	Buick	R-45TS8	.080	Electronic	①	16	6-7.5	①
	Y	8-307	5.0	Olds.	R-46SX	.080	Electronic	①	20	6-7.5	①
1986–'87	B	231	3.8	Olds.	R44LTS	0.045	Electronic	①	16	34-40	①
RIVIERA											
'83	8	6-231 Turbo	3.8	Buick	R-45TS	.040	Electronic	15B	16	4.2-5.8	①
	4	6-252	4.1	Buick	R-45TS8	.080	Electronic	15B	16	6-7.5	①
	Y	8-307	5.0	Olds.	R-46SX	.080	Electronic	15B @ 1100	20	6-7.5	①
'84–'85	8 ③	6-231 Turbo	3.8	Buick	R-45TS	.040	Electronic	①	16	4.2-5.8	①
	4	6-252	4.1	Buick	R-45TS8	.080	Electronic	①	16	6-7.5	①
	Y	8-307	5.0	Olds.	R-46SX	.080	Electronic	①	20	6-7.5	①
1986–'87	B	231	3.8	Olds.	R44LTS	.045	Electronic	①	16	34-40	①
ELDORADO AND SEVILLE											
'83	8	8-250	4.1	Cadillac	R-43NTS6	.060	Electronic	①	37	40	②
'84–'87	8	8-250	4.1	Cadillac	R-43NTS6 ④	.060	Electronic	①	37	40	②

* Set timing with carburetor adjusted to 1100 rpm, unless sticker specifies otherwise.
▲ See text for procedure
• Where two figures appear separated by a slash, the first is idle speed with solenoid energized, the second is idle speed with solenoid disconnected. Figure in parenthesis indicates California engine.
  B Before Top Dead Center
Part numbers in this chart are not recommendations by Chilton for any product by brand name.
① See Underhood Sticker
② Electronic controlled idle, no adjustment
③ 85; VIN9
④ R42CLTS6

8–5

SECTION 8: GENERAL MOTORS—"E" AND "K" BODY
FRONT WHEEL DRIVE CARS

DIESEL TUNE-UP SPECIFICATIONS

Year	Engine No. Cyl. Displacement (cu. in.)	Liters	Fuel Pump Pressure (psi)	Compression (lbs.)	Intake Valve Opens (deg.)	Idle Speed (rpm)
'82–'87	8-350	5.7	5.5–7.0	275 min.	16	①

NOTE: The underhood specifications sticker often reflects tune-up specification changes made in production. Sticker figures must be used if they disagree with those in this chart.

① See underhood specifications sticker

FIRING ORDERS

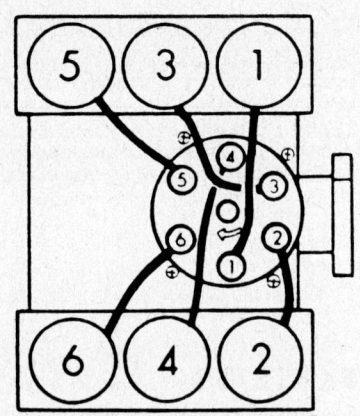

GM (Buick) 231 and 252 V6 (3.8L and 4.1L)
Engine firing order: 1–6–5–4–3–2
Distributor rotation: clockwise
V6 Harmonic balancers have two timing marks: one is 1/8 in. wide, and one is 1/16 in. wide. Use the 1/16 in. mark for timing with a hand held light. The 1/8 in. mark is used only with a magnetic timing pick-up probe.

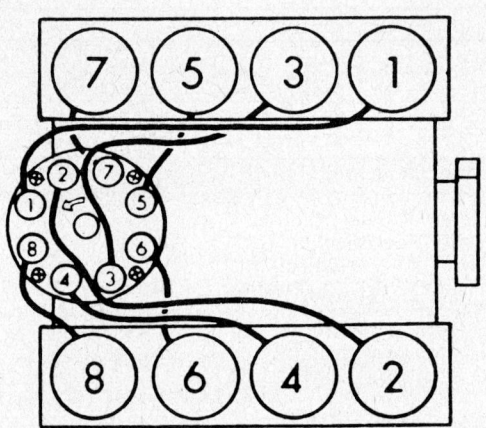

GM 250, 307, 350 V8s, including diesel
Engine firing order: 1–8–4–3–6–5–7–2
Distributor rotation: counterclockwise

VALVE SPECIFICATIONS

Year	Engine No. Cyl. Displacement (cu. in.)	Liters	Seat Angle (deg.)	Face Angle (deg.)	Spring Test Pressure (lbs. @ in.)	Spring Installed Height (in.)	Stem-to-Guide Clearance (in.) Intake	Stem-to-Guide Clearance (in.) Exhaust	Stem Diameter (in.) Intake	Stem Diameter (in.) Exhaust
'83	6-231	3.8	45	45	182 @ 1.34	1 47/64	.0015–.0035	.0015–.0032	.3401–.3412	.3405–.3412
	6-252	4.1	45	45	182 @ 1.34	1 47/64	.0015–.0035	.0015–.0032	.3401–.3412	.3405–.3412
	8-250	4.1	45	44	182 @ 1.28	1 43/64	.001–.003	.001–.003	.3413–.3420	.3411–.3418
	8-307	5.0	45	44	187 @ 1.27	1 43/64	.0010–.0027	.0015–.0032	.3425–.3432	.3420–.3427
	8-350 Diesel	5.7	45 ①	44 ②	210 @ 1.22	1 43/64	.0010–.0027	.0015–.0032	.3425–.3432	.3420–.3427

GENERAL MOTORS—"E" AND "K" BODY
FRONT WHEEL DRIVE CARS
SECTION 8

VALVE SPECIFICATIONS

Year	Engine No. Cyl. Displacement (cu. in.)	Liters	Seat Angle (deg.)	Face Angle (deg.)	Spring Test Pressure (lbs. @ in.)	Spring Installed Height (in.)	Stem-to-Guide Clearance (in.) Intake	Stem-to-Guide Clearance (in.) Exhaust	Stem Diameter (in.) Intake	Stem Diameter (in.) Exhaust
'84–'87	6-231	3.8	45	44	220 @ 1.34	1 47/64	.0015–.0035	.0015–.0032	.3401–.3412	.3405–.3412
	6-252	4.1	45	45	182 @ 1.34	1 47/64	.0015–.0035	.0015–.0032	.3401–.3412	.3405–.3412
	8-250	4.1	45	44	182 @ 1.28	1 43/64	.001–.003	.001–.003	.3413–.3420	.3411–.3418
	8-307	5.0	45	44	187 @ 1.27	1 43/64	.0010–.0027	.0015–.0032	.3425–.3432	.3420–.3427
	8-350 Diesel	5.7	45 ①	44 ②	210 @ 1.22	1 43/64	.0010–.0027	.0015–.0032	.3425–.3432	.3420–.3427

① Exhaust valve seat 31° ② Exhaust valve face 30°

RING SIDE CLEARANCE
All measurements are given in inches.

Year	Engine	Liters	Top Compression	Bottom Compression	Oil Control
'83–'85	8-350 Diesel	5.7	.0040–.0060 ①	.0018–.0038 ②	.0010–.0050
'83–'85	8-307	5.0	.0020–.0040	.0020–.0040	.015–.055
'83–'87	8-250	4.1	.0016–.0037	.0016–.0037	None (side sealing)
'83–'87	6-252	4.1	.0030–.0050	.0030–.0050	.0035 max.
'83–'87	6-231	3.8	.0030–.0050	.0030–.0050	.0035

① '83–'84—.005–.007 ② '83–'84—.003–.005

PISTON CLEARANCE

Year	Engine	Liters	Piston-to-bore Clearance (in.)
'82–'85	8-350 Diesel	5.7	.0050–.0006
'82–'85	8-307	5.0	.00075–.00175
'82–'87	8-250	4.1	.0010–.0018
'82–'85	6-252	4.1	.0008–.0020
'82–'87	6-231	3.8	.0008–.0020 ①

① Measured at skirt top
Turbo engines—.0033–.0034 measured at piston pin centerline.

RING GAP
All measurements are given in inches.

Year	Engine	Liters	Top Compression	Bottom Compression	Oil Control
'83–'86	8-350 Diesel	5.7	.015–.025	.015–.025	.015–.055
'83–'87	6-231	3.8	.010–.020	.010–.020	.015–.055
'83–'85	6-252	4.1	.010–.020	.010–.020	.015–.055
'83–'87	8-250	4.1	.009–.020	.009–.020	.010–.050
'83–'84	8-307	5.0	.009–.019	.009–.019	.015–.055

SECTION 8

GENERAL MOTORS — "E" AND "K" BODY
FRONT WHEEL DRIVE CARS

CRANKSHAFT AND CONNECTING ROD SPECIFICATIONS
All measurements are given in inches.

Year	Engine No. Cyl. Displacement (cu. in.)	Liters	Crankshaft Main Brg. Journal Dia.	Main Brg. Oil Clearance	Shaft End-Play	Thrust on No.	Connecting Rod Journal Diameter	Oil Clearance	Side Clearance
'83	6-231	3.8	2.4995	.0003–.0018	.003–.011	2	2.2491	.0005–.0026	.006–.027
	6-252	4.1	2.4995	.0003–.0018	.003–.011	2	2.2491	.0005–.0026	.006–.023
	8-250	4.1	2.64	.0004–.0027	.001–.007	3	1.929	.0005–.0028	.008–.020
	8-307	5.0	2.4995–2.4990 ③	.0005–.0021 ②	.0035–.0135	3	2.1238–2.1248	.0004–.0033	.006–.020
	8-350 Diesel	5.7	2.9993–3.0003	.0005–.0021 ①	.0035–.0135	3	2.1238–2.1248	.0005–.0026	.006–.020
'84–'87	6-231	3.8	2.4995	.0003–.0018	.003–.011	2	2.2491	.0005–.0026	.003–.015
	6-252	4.1	2.4995	.0003–.0018	.003–.011	2	2.2491	.0005–.0026	.006–.023
	8-250	4.1	2.64	.0004–.0028	.001–.007	3	1.929	.0005–.0028	.008–.020
	8-307	5.0	2.4995–2.4990 ③	.0005–.0021 ②	.0035–.0135	3	2.1238–2.1248	.0004–.0033	.006–.020
	8-350 Diesel	5.7	2.9993–3.0003	.0005–.0021 ①	.0035–.0135	3	2.1238–2.1248	.0005–.0026	.006–.020

① No. 5—.0020–.0034   ② No. 5—.0015–.0031   ③ No. 1—2.4998–2.4993

CAPACITIES

Year	Engine No. Cyl. Displacement (cu. in.)	Liters	Engine Crankcase Add 1 qt. for New Filter	Transmission Pts. to Refill After Draining Automatic •	Drive Axle (pts.)	Gasoline Tank (gals.)	Cooling System (qts.) With A/C	With Heavy Duty
'83	8-307	5.0	4	③	3.25	21	16.2	—
	8-250	4.1	4	③	3.25	20.3	11.8	—
	8-350 Diesel	5.7	7 ①	③	3.25	22.8	18.2	—
	8-252	4.1	4	③	3.25	21.1	13.1	—
	6-231	3.8	4	③	3.25	21.1	13.6	14.1
'84–'87	8-307	5.0	4	③	3.25	21.1	16.2	—
	8-250	4.1	4	③	3.25	20.3 ④	12.6	—
	8-350 Diesel	5.7	7 ①	③	3.25	22.8 ②	18.2	—
	6-252	4.1	4	③	3.25	21.1	12.5	—
	6-231	3.8	5	③	3.25	18	12.9	—

• Does not include torque converter
① Includes mandatory filter change
② Seville: 21, Eldorado: 19.6, Toronado: 22.8
③ Add 6 pts; start engine and allow to warm up. Add fluid necessary to mark on dipstick
④ 1986–later 18.0 gallons

TORQUE SPECIFICATIONS
All readings in ft. lbs.

Year	Engine No. Cyl. Displacement (cu. in.)	Liters	Cylinder Head Bolts	Bearing Bolts Rod	Bearing Bolts Main	Crankshaft Bolt	Flywheel-to-Crankshaft Bolts	Manifold Intake	Exhaust
'83	8-250	4.1	⑤	20	85	20	35	20 ①	20
	8-307	5.0	130 ③	42	80 ②	200–310	60	40 ③	25
	8-350 Diesel	5.7	130 ③	42	120	200–310	60	40 ③	25
'84–'87	6-231	3.8	80	40	100	225	60	30	25
	6-252	4.1	80	40	100	225	60	45	25
	8-250	4.1	⑤	20	85	18 ④	35	20	20
	8-307	5.0	125 ③	42	80 ②	200–310	60	40 ③	25
	8-350 Diesel	5.7	130 ③	42	120	200–310	60	40 ③	25

Caution: Verify the correct original equipment engine is in the vehicle by referring to the VIN engine code before torquing any bolts.
① 12 ft. lbs. for short bolt
② 120 on No. 5
③ Bolts must be oiled before tightening
④ Fan pulley to balancer—18 ft. lbs.
⑤ Pull first to 45 ft. lbs. in sequence, then tighten to 90 ft. lbs. in sequence

GENERAL MOTORS—"E" AND "K" BODY
FRONT WHEEL DRIVE CARS
SECTION 8

WHEEL ALIGNMENT SPECIFICATIONS

Year	Caster Range (deg.)	Caster Pref. Setting (deg.)	Camber Range (deg.)	Camber Pref. Setting (deg.)	Toe in (in.)	Steering Axis Inclin. (deg.)
TORONADO						
'83–'85	1½P to 3½P	2½P	½N to ½P	0	⅛ in to ⅛ out	11
'86–'87	1⁵⁄₁₆P to 3⁵⁄₁₆	2⁵⁄₁₆	¹³⁄₁₆N to ¹³⁄₁₆P	0	³⁄₃₂ to ³⁄₃₂	—
ELDORADO AND SEVILLE						
'83–'87	2P to 3P	2½P	½N to ½P	0	⅛ in to ⅛ out	—
RIVIERA						
'83–'85	2P to 3P	2½P	½N to ½P	0	⅛ in to ⅛ out	—
'86–'87	1¹⁵⁄₁₆ to 3⁵⁄₁₆	2⁵⁄₁₆	¹³⁄₁₆N to ¹³⁄₁₆P	0	³⁄₃₂ to ³⁄₃₂	—

ELECTRICAL SECTION

For Overhaul Procedures, refer to the Unit Repair Section.

Charging System

ALTERNATOR

Removal and Installation

RIVIERA

1. Disconnect the negative battery cable.
2. Tag and disconnect the alternator wiring from the back of the alternator.
3. Remove the bolt holding the alternator to the adjusting bar. On certain models, it may be necessary to first remove the fan shroud and rotate it out of the way to get at the pivot bolt.
4. Push the alternator in towards the engine in order to release the drive belt tension.
5. Remove the alternator from the engine.

NOTE: On vehicles equipped with air conditioning, it will first be necessary to remove the compressor retaining bracket.

6. Installation is the reverse of the removal procedure. Adjust the alternator drive belt to allow ½ in. of play between the longest run of pulleys.

ELDORADO AND SEVILLE EXCEPT 80 AMP AND 100 AMP H.D. ALTERNATOR

1. Disconnect negative battery cable.
2. Disconnect air pump hose at check valve and remove hater hose clip from adjusting link (if so equipped).
3. Remove cap, if installed, from the positive terminal.
4. Disconnect wires from the positive terminal.
5. Unplug the multiple connector.
6. Disconnect black wire from ground terminal (if used).
7. Remove the bracket adjusting screw and raise bracket, then loosen lower alternator mounting bolt and remove V-belt.
8. Remove lower mounting screw, spacer and washer.

NOTE: It may be necessary to twist the alternator toward the fender to do this.

9. Remove the alternator.
10. To install, reverse the removal procedure. Tighten the mounting screw to 17–20 ft. lbs.

80 AMP AND 100 AMP H.D. ALTERNATOR

1. Disconnect the negative battery cable.
2. Disconnect and label all wiring connections from the alternator.
3. Loosen the belt tension adjusting bolts and remove the belt.
4. Remove the 2 nuts and lockwashers from the lower mounting bolts, leaving the bolts in place.
5. Remove the upper mounting bolt and remove the alternator by sliding it rearward off the lower mounting bolts.
6. Installation is the reverse of removal. Adjust the belt tension.

NOTE: On Heavy Duty Alternator ONLY (100 amp with external voltage adjusters): after connecting the negative ground cable, momentarily connect a jumper wire between "Bat" and "R" alternator terminals to reestablish residual magnetism in the rotor. Start the engine and run it at a fast idle for ten seconds; the charge light should go out.

TORONADO

NOTE: Before removing the alternator, disconnect the battery ground cable.

1. Tag and disconnect the wiring from the alternator.
2. Remove the mounting bolt, adjusting bolt, and drive belt.
3. Lift out the alternator.
4. To install, reverse the removal procedure, connect the battery ground cable and tighten the alternator belt. Determine belt tension at a point halfway between the pulleys by pressing on the belt with moderate thumb pressure. If the distance between the pulleys (measured at the pulley center) is 13–16 in., the belt should deflect ½ in. at the halfway point of ¼ in. if the distance is 7–10 in.

VOLTAGE REGULATOR

Removal and Installation

RIVIERA

All gasoline engine Buicks are equipped with a Delcotron 10 SI alternator with internal voltage regulator. The regulator requires no adjustment and is not serviceable without overhauling the alternator.

SECTION 8

GENERAL MOTORS—"E" AND "K" BODY
FRONT WHEEL DRIVE CARS

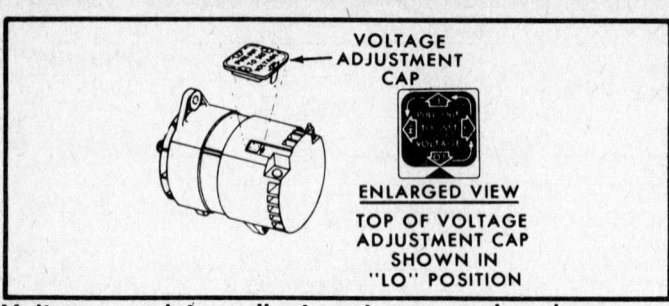

Voltage regulator adjustment cap used on heavy duty alternator (© General Motors Corporation)

ELDORADO AND SEVILLE

The Delcotron alternator voltage regulator is mounted within the slip ring end frame and no adjustment is possible. The heavy duty alternator has a voltage regulator that can be adjusted externally by the repositioning of the voltage regulator adjustment cap in the slip ring end frame.

TORONADO

The alternator must be disassembled to replace the regulator.

Starting System

STARTER

Removal and Installation

RIVIERA

1. Disconnect the negative battery cable.
2. Jack up the car and support it with jack stands. Remove the starter splash shield.
3. Disconnect and label the wires from the solenoid.
4. Remove the starter bolts.
5. Remove the starter.
6. Reverse the steps to install. If the original starter is being installed, put all the mounting pad shims back in their original locations. With a new starter, use shims to establish a clearance of 0.0250–0.060 in. between the tip of one pinion tooth and the root between two flywheel teeth.

SEVILLE AND ELDORADO

1. Disconnect the negative battery cable. Raise the vehicle and support safely.
2. Remove the starter splash shield if equipped.
3. Remove the wiring from the starter solenoid BAT terminal and the S terminal.
4. Release the wiring from the clip attached to the solenoid and position the wiring out of the way.
5. Remove three starter bolts and the starter.
6. Installation is the reverse of removal.

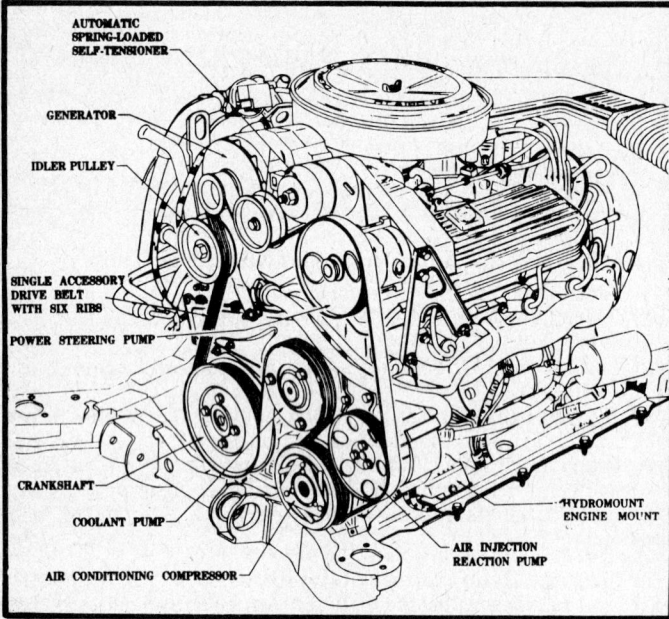

Engine component location—typical

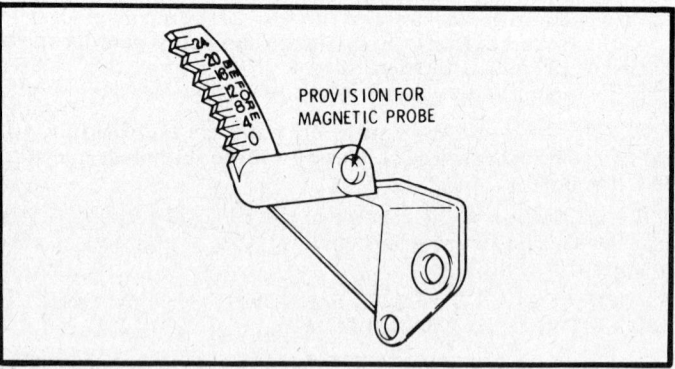

Magnetic timing probe
(© General Motors Corporation)

Correction of Starter Gear Noise

1. To decrease starter noise caused by gear tooth interference loosen all fasteners, and install additional shims as required. (Accumulated thickness of shims not to exceed 0.047 in.).
2. After installation of shims, retighten all fasteners to specified torque. If addition of shims fails to reduce starter noise due to excess clearance, remove all shims (including original shims), and retighten all mounting fasteners to specified torque.
3. To decrease starter gear noise, loosen inboard bolt, re-

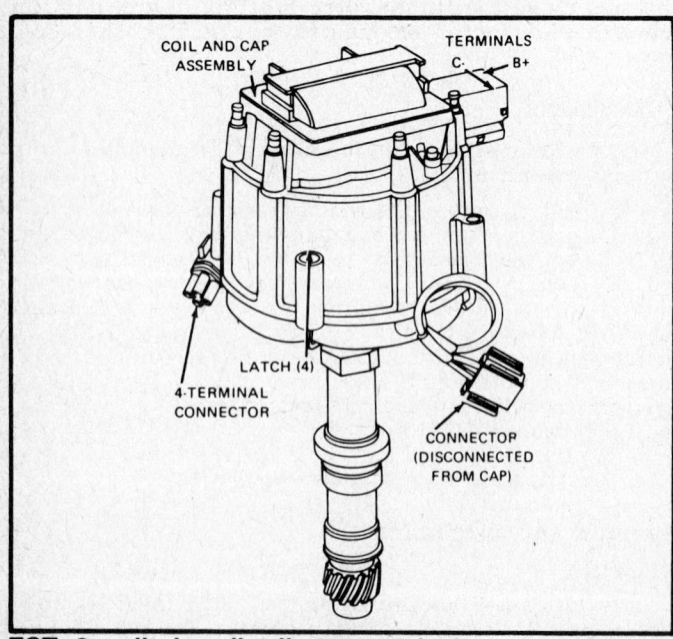

EST 6 cylinder distributor—typical
(© General Motors Corporation)

GENERAL MOTORS—"E" AND "K" BODY
FRONT WHEEL DRIVE CARS
SECTION 8

move outboard bolt and install shim (one shim max.). Retighten bolts to specified torque.

TORONADO

1. Disconnect the negative battery cable.
2. Raise and support the vehicle safely.
3. Remove the upper support attaching bolts. Remove the exhaust crossover pipe if necessary in order to gain working clearance.
4. Remove the front body cross member if equipped.
5. Tag and disconnect the starter wiring.
6. Remove the starter securing bolts. Lower the starter and remove from the vehicle.
7. Installation is the reverse of removal procedure.

NOTE: If starter shims were removed, they must be installed in their original location to assure proper drive pinion-to-flywheel engagement.

Ignition System

DISTRIBUTOR

The Electronic Spark Timing (EST) distributor uses no mechanical or vacuum advance and is easily identified by the absence of a vacuum advance and the presence of a four terminal connector. There are not contact points or condensor to replace, or any cam or rubbing block to wear.

Removal

1. Remove the distributor cap, primary wire and vacuum line at the distributor.
2. Scribe a mark on the distributor body, locating the position of the rotor and scribe another mark on the engine block, showing the position of the body in the block.
3. Remove the hold-down clamp. Mark the position of the rotor, then lift the distributor out of the block until the rotor stops turning. Mark the position of the rotor again and remove the distributor.

Installation

For firing order and cylinder numbering, see the specifications.
1. If the engine has not been disturbed, insert the distributor into the engine, making sure the tip of the rotor is aligned with the marks that were scribed on the distributor housing and the engine block.
2. If the engine has been cranked with the distributor out, remove the No. 1 spark plug and place a finger over the hole. Slowly turn the engine until compression is felt. Align the timing marks so No. 1 cylinder is in firing position. Position the distributor in the block with the rotor at No. 1 firing position. Make sure the oil pump intermediate drive shaft is properly seated in the oil pump.
3. Install the distributor lock but do not tighten.
4. Rotate the distributor body clockwise until the breaker points are just starting to open. Tighten the retaining screw.
5. Connect the primary wire and the vacuum line to the distributor, then install distributor cap.
6. Start the engine and check the timing.

IGNITION TIMING

Adjustment

NOTE: Always consult the underhood sticker before adjusting timing. If the sticker differs from these procedures, follow the sticker.

1. Disconnect the vacuum advance hose from the distributor and plug it.

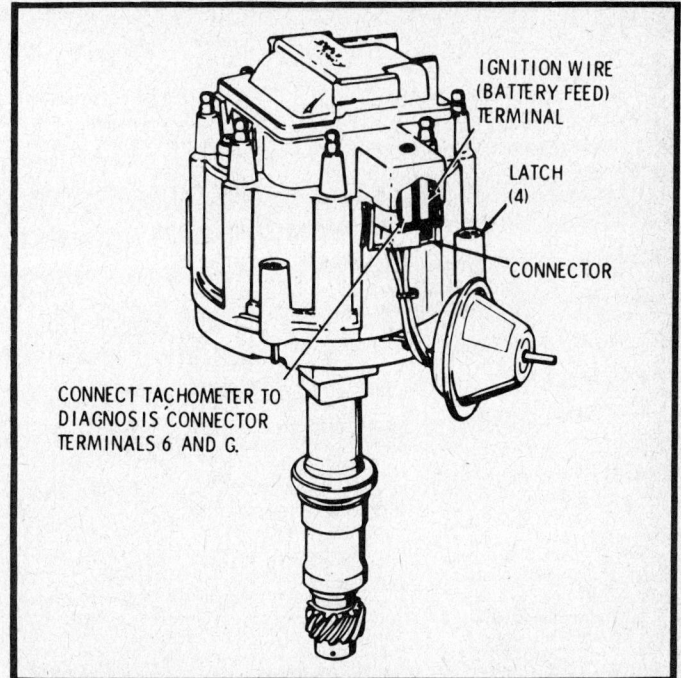

HEI tachometer hook-up at the distributor
(© General Motors Corporation)

NOTE: On models with EST, disconnect the No. 4 terminal connector at the distributor. See the Underhood sticker for identification.

2. Remove the air cleaner and tape over the vacuum hose fitting.
3. Connect the tachometer and adjust the engine speed to specifications.
4. Connect the timing light, loosen the distributor mounting bolt, and turn the distributor until the specified timing is obtained.
5. Tighten the mounting bolt and recheck timing to see if it changed during tightening.
6. Unplug the vacuum advance hose and connect it to the distributor.
7. Remove the tape from the vacuum hose fitting and install and connect the hose, if so equipped.
8. Install the air cleaner.

NOTE: All V6 engines harmonic balancers have two timing marks, one measuring 1/8 in. wide and one measuring the normal 1/16 in. wide. The smaller mark is used for setting the timing with a hand held timing light. The 1/8 in. wide mark is required when using magnetic timing equipment. All engines have a mounting bracket on the front cover which will accept a magnetic timing pick-up probe.

Electrical Controls

IGNITION LOCK

Removal and Installation
STANDARD STEERING COLUMN

1. Remove the steering wheel.
2. Remove the lockplate cover cover assembly.
3. After compressing the lockplate spring, remove the snapring from the groove in the shaft.

8-11

SECTION 8
GENERAL MOTORS—"E" AND "K" BODY
FRONT WHEEL DRIVE CARS

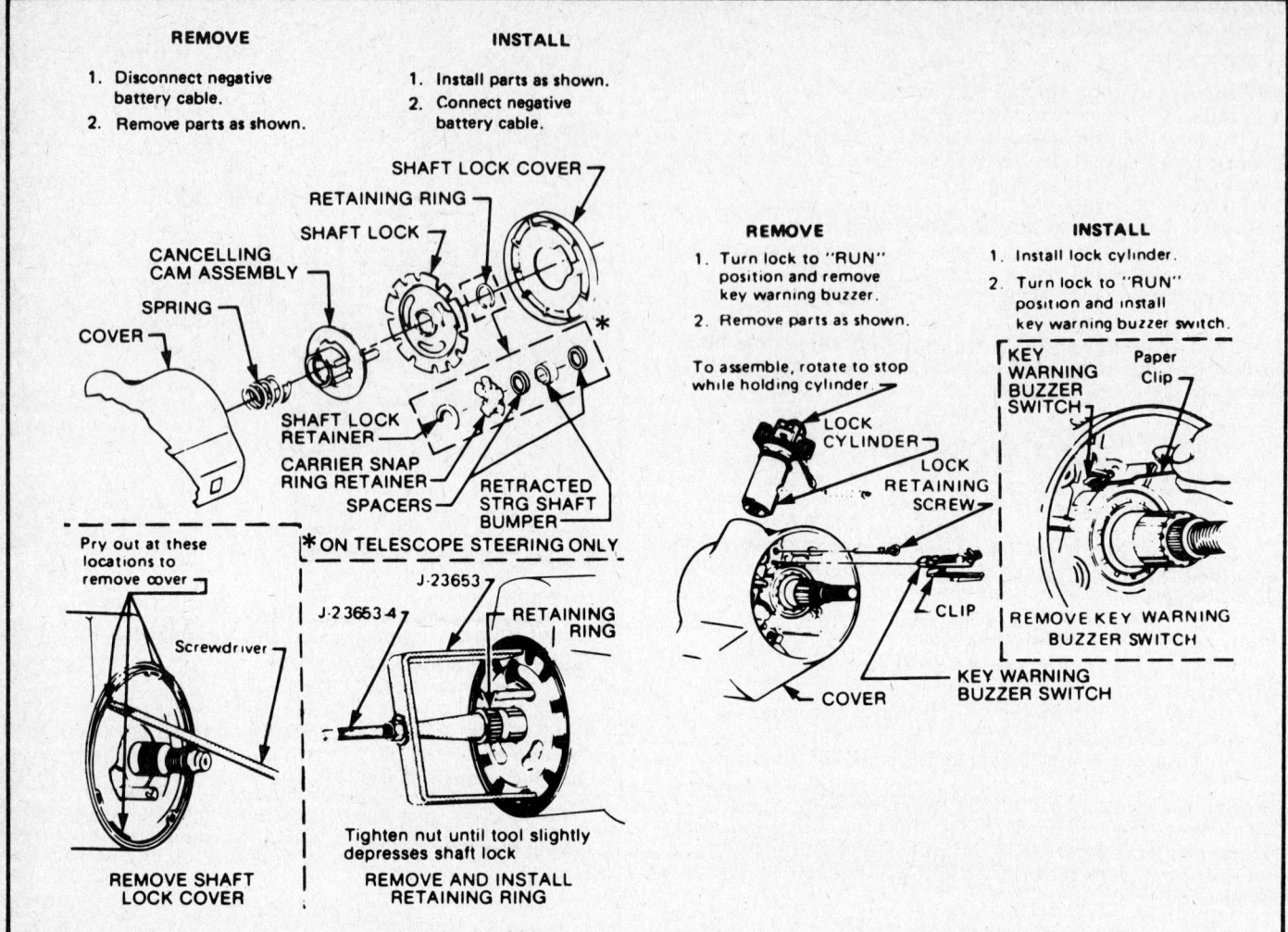

Removal and installation of ignition lock, key warning buzzer, shaft lock and cancelling cam—typical
(© General Motors Corporation)

CAUTION

When the snap-ring is removed do not allow the shaft to slide out the bottom of the column.

---

4. Remove the lockplate and slide the turn signal cam and the upper bearing preload spring off the upper steering shaft.
5. Remove the thrust washer from the shaft.
6. Remove the hazard warning switch from the column along with the turn signal lever.
7. Use the following procedure if the vehicle is equipped with Cruise Control.
   a. Attach a piece of stiff wire to the connector on the cruise control switch harness.
   b. Gently pull the harness up and out of the column.
8. Remove the turn signal switch mounting screws.
9. Slide the switch connector out of the bracket on the steering column.
10. After freeing the switch wiring protector from its mounting, pull the turn signal switch straight up and remove the switch, switch harness and the connector from the column.
11. Turn the ignition switch to on or run and then insert a small drift pin into the slot next to the switch mounting screw boss. Push the lock cylinder tab and remove the lock cylinder.

TILT COLUMN

1. Remove the steering wheel.
2. Remove the rubber sleeve bumper from the steering shaft.
3. Using an appropriate tool, remove the plastic retainer.
4. Using a spring compressor, compress the upper steering shaft spring and remove the C-ring. Release the steering shaft lockplate, the horn contact carrier, and the upper steering shaft preload spring.
5. Remove the four screws which hold the upper mounting bracket and then remove the bracket.
6. Slide the harness connector out of the bracket on the steering column. Tape the upper part of the harness and connector.
7. Disconnect the hazard button and position the shift bowl in Park. Remove the turn signal lever from the column.
8. Use the following procedure for vehicles equipped with cruise control.
   a. Remove the harness protector from the harness.
   b. Attach a piece of piano wire to the switch harness connector.
   c. Before removing the turn signal lever, loop a piece of piano wire and insert it into the turn signal lever opening. Us-

GENERAL MOTORS—"E" AND "K" BODY
FRONT WHEEL DRIVE CARS
SECTION 8

ing the wire, pull the cruise control harness out through the opening.

   d. Pull the rest of the harness up through and out of the column.

   e. Remove the guide wire from the connector and secure the wire to the column.

   f. Remove the turn signal lever.

9. Pull the turn signal switch up until the end connector is within the shift bowl. Remove the hazard flasher lever. Allow the switch to hang.

10. Place the ignition key in the run position.

11. Depress the center of the lock cylinder retaining tab with a screwdriver and then remove the lock cylinder.

12. Installation is the reverse of the removal procedure.

IGNITION SWITCH

Removal and Installation

1. Disconnect negative battery cable.
2. Place ignition switch on Off Unlocked or ACC (tilt wheel).
3. Remove top pan cover (if applicable) and loosen the toe clamp bolts.
4. Remove lower instrument panel trim retaining screws. Remove the panel in order to gain working clearance.
5. Remove automatic transmission shift indicator needle.
6. Remove steering column instrument panel bracket and let steering wheel rest on the driver's seat.
7. Remove the dimmer switch retaining screws and remove the switch.
8. Remove ignition switch attaching screws and lift switch off actuator rod.
9. Tag and disconnect the wiring.
10. To install, check that lock cylinder is still in Off-Unlocked or ACC (tilt wheel), and move sliding portion of switch until switch hole is positioned correctly. Hold the switch in this position with a 0.090 in. pin.
11. Connect the wiring to the switch.
12. Position switch over actuator rod, install attaching screws and remove the 0.090 in. pin.
13. Reverse Steps 1–6 to complete installation.

NEUTRAL SAFETY SWITCH

Removal and Installation

AUTOMATIC TRANSMISSION WITH CONSOLE SHIFT

1. New switches come with a small plastic alignment pin installed. Leave this pin in place. Position the shifter assembly in Neutral.
2. Remove the old switch and install the replacement, align the pin on the shifter with the slot in the switch, and fasten with the two screws.
3. Move the shifter from the Neutral position. This shears the plastic alignment pin and frees the switch.
4. If the switch is to be adjusted, not replaced, insert a 3/32 in. drill bit or similar size pin and align the hole and switch. Position switch, adjust as necessary. Remove the pin before shifting from Neutral.

AUTOMATIC TRANSMISSION WITH COLUMN SHIFT

1. Remove wire connectors from the combination back-up and neutral safety switch.
2. Remove screws attaching the switch to the steering column.
3. Installation is the reverse of removal. To adjust a new switch:

   a. Position the shift lever in Neutral.

   b. Loosen the attaching screws. Install a 0.090 in. gauge pin into the outer hole in the switch cover.

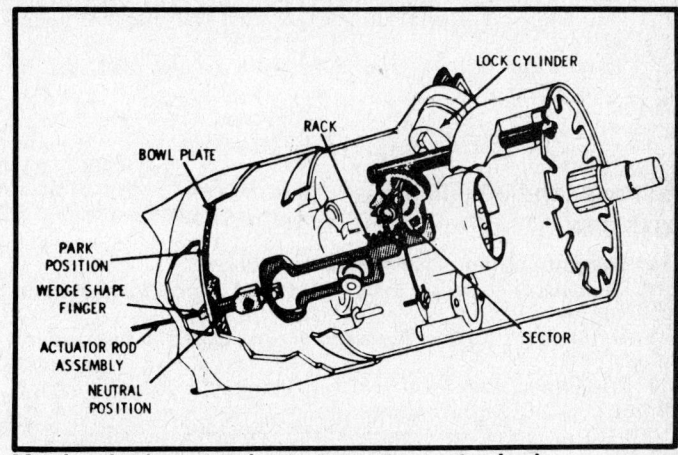

Mechanical neutral start system—typical
(© General Motors Corporation)

   c. Rotate the switch until the pin goes into the alignment hole in the inner plastic slide.

   d. Tighten the switch to column attaching screws and remove the gauge pin. Torque the screws to 20 inch lbs. maximum.

   e. Make sure that the engine starts only in the Park and Neutral positions.

STOPLIGHT SWITCH

Removal and Installation

1. Disconnect the negative battery cable.
2. Locate the stoplight switch on the brake pedal.
3. Remove the tubular retaining clip.
4. Remove the stoplight switch electrical connectors.
5. Remove the switch assembly from the vehicle.
6. Installation is the reverse of the removal procedure.

Adjustment

1. Insert the switch into the retainer until the switch body seats on the tube clip.

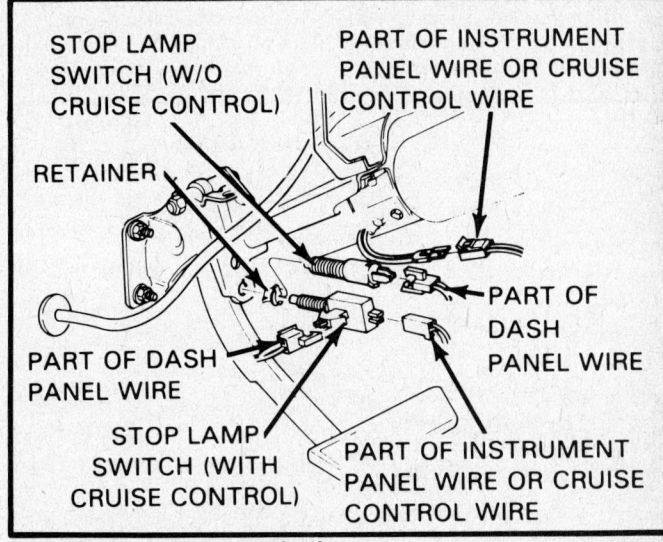

Stoplight switch—typical
(© General Motors Corporation)

SECTION 8

GENERAL MOTORS—"E" AND "K" BODY
FRONT WHEEL DRIVE CARS

2. Pull the brake pedal upward against the internal pedal stop.
3. The switch will be moved in the retainer resulting in proper adjustment.

HEADLIGHT SWITCH

Removal and Installation

RIVIERA

1. Disconnect the negative battery cable.
2. Remove the switch trim cover and the left hand trim cover.
3. Remove the headlight switch screws from the instrument panel.
4. Disconnect any electrical connector and pull the switch forward out of the dash panel.
5. Installation is the reverse of the removal procedure.

ELDORADO AND SEVILLE

1. Disconnect the battery ground.
2. Remove the left instrument panel insert.
3. Remove the screws securing the switch to the instrument panel.
4. On cars equipped with cruise control and twilight sentinel, remove the two screws securing the cruise control switch to the light instrument panel.
5. Slide the cruise control switch forward to remove the light switch.
6. Installation is the reverse of the removal procedure.

TORONADO

1. Remove the left hand trim cover:
   a. Remove the headlight switch knob and the radio knobs.
   b. Remove the steering column trim cover and the four screws beneath the cover.
   c. Remove the left hand sound absorber and carefully pull the trim cover rearward to remove.
2. Remove the screws attaching the switch to the dash frame.
3. Pull the switch rearward to remove.

DIMMER SWITCH

Removal and Installation

1. Disconnect the negative battery cable.
2. Remove the steering wheel. Remove the trim cover.
3. Make sure the switch is in its off position. Remove the turn signal switch assembly.

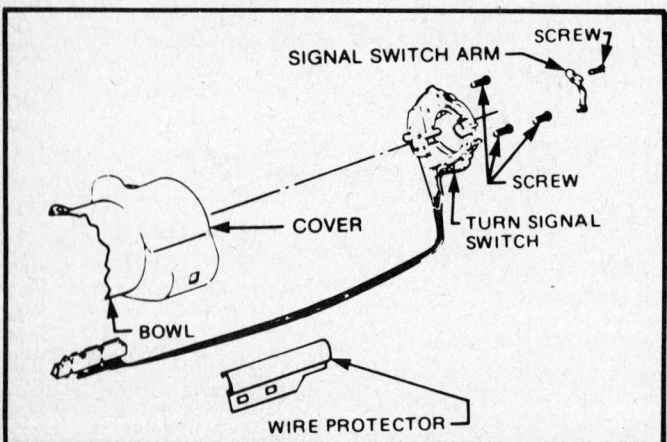

Removal and installation of turn signal switch—typical (© General Motors Corporation)

4. Remove the ignition switch stud and screw. Remove the ignition switch.
5. Remove the dimmer switch actuator rod by sliding it from the switch assembly.
6. Remove the dimmer switch bolts and remove the dimmer switch.
7. Installation is the reverse of the removal procedure.
8. Adjust the dimmer switch by depressing the switch slightly and inserting a $3/32$ in. drill into the adjusting hole. Push the switch up to remove any plat and tighten the dimmer switch adjusting screw.

TURN SIGNAL SWITCH

Removal and Installation

STANDARD STEERING COLUMN

1. Disconnect the negative battery cable.
2. Remove the steering wheel.
3. Insert a thin screwdriver into the lockplate and remove the lockplate cover assembly.
4. Install a spring compressor onto the steering shaft. Tighten the tool to compress the lockplate and the spring. Remove the snap-ring from the groove in the shaft.

--- **CAUTION** ---

When the snap-ring is removed do not allow the shaft to slide out the bottom of the column.

5. Remove the lockplate and slide the turn signal cam and the upper bearing preload spring and the thrust washer off the upper steering shaft.
6. Remove the steering column lower cover.
7. Unscrew the turn signal lever and remove it from the column.
8. On cars with cruise control:
   a. Disconnect the cruise control wire from the harness near the bottom of the column.
   b. Remove the harness protector from the cruise control wire.
   c. Remove the turn signal lever. Do not remove the wire from the column.
9. Remove the two vertical bolts at the steering column upper support. Remove the shim packs. Keep the shims in order for reinstallation.
10. Remove the four screws securing the column upper mounting bracket to the column and remove the bracket.
11. Disconnect the turn signal wiring and remove the wires from the plastic protector.
12. Remove the turn signal switch mounting screws.
13. Slide the switch connector out of the bracket on the steering column.
14. If the switch is known to be bad, cut the wires and discard the switch. Tape the connector of the new switch to the old wires, and pull the new harness down through the steering column while removing the old wires.
15. If the original switch is to be reused, wrap tape around the wire and connector and pull the harness up through the column. It may be helpful to attach a length of wire or string to the harness connector before pulling it up through the column to facilitate installation.
16. After freeing the wiring protector from its mounting, pull the turn signal switch straight up and remove the switch, switch harness, and the connector from the column.
17. To reassemble reverse the removal procedure.

TILT AND TELESCOPIC COLUMNS

1. Disconnect the battery and remove the steering wheel.
2. Remove the rubber sleeve bumper from the steering shaft.

GENERAL MOTORS—"E" AND "K" BODY
FRONT WHEEL DRIVE CARS
SECTION 8

3. Remove the plastic retainer with a screwdriver, disengaging the tabs on the retainer from the C-ring.

4. Compress the upper steering shaft preload spring with a spring compressor and remove the C-ring. When installing the spring compressor, pull the upper shaft up about 1 in. and turn the ignition to the LOCK position to hold the shaft in place.

5. Remove the spring compressor and remove the upper steering shaft lock plate, horn contact carrier and the preload spring.

6. Remove the steering column lower cover.

7. Unscrew and remove the turn signal lever. If equipped with cruise control:
   a. Disconnect the cruise control wire from the harness near the bottom of the steering column.
   b. Slide the protector off the cruise control wire. Remove the lever attaching screw and carefully pull the lever out enough to allow the removal of the turn signal switch.

8. Remove the two nuts and shim packs from the upper column support. Keep the shims together as a unit for reinstallation.

9. Remove the bracket from the steering column by removing the two attaching screws from each side.

10. Disconnect the turn signal wiring harness from the car harness and remove the wires from the plastic protector.

11. Remove the turn signal switch retaining screws and pull the switch up out of the steering column.

12. If the switch is to be replaced, cut the wires from the switch and tape the new switch connector to the old wires. Carefully pull the new harness down through the column as the old wires are removed.

13. If the old switch is to be reused, tape the connector to the wires and carefully pull the harness up out of the columns.

14. Feed the wiring harness down through the steering column to replace the old switch.

15. Secure the switch in the steering column.

16. Install the upper shaft preload spring.

17. Install the lock plate and carrier assembly. Make sure that the flat on the lower end of the steering shaft is pointing up and that the small plastic tab on the carrier is up or nearest the top of the column. The flat surface of the lock plate must be installed facing down against the turn signal switch.

18. Install the spring compressor, compress the preload spring and lock plate and install the C-ring with the wide side toward the keyway.

19. Remove the spring compressor and install the plastic retainer on the C-ring.

20. Install the rubber sleeve bumper over the steering shaft and install the steering wheel.

21. Install the turn signal lever. If the vehicle is equipped with cruise control, secure the lever to the switch with the retaining screw and install the wiring harness.

22. Remove the tape from the end of the harness and connect the switch and cruise control, if so equipped, to the car harness.

23. Cover both harnesses with the plastic protector and position it to the column. The turn signal connector slides on the tabs of the column.

24. Position the steering column upper bracket over the turn signal switch harness plastic protector.

25. Install the mounting bracket nuts and shims in their original positions.

26. Install the steering column lower cover.

HORN SWITCH
Removal and Installation
RIVIERA AND TORONADO

An actuator bar is mounted across the steering wheel. Fastened to the base of the actuator bar, but insulated from it, is a contact plate which is live at all times. When the actuator bar is rocked, the contact plate contacts a ground plate on the steel hub of the steering wheel to ground the horn relay winding, close the relay contacts, and blow the horn. Current is supplied to the contact plate by a spring loaded brush which rides on the contact ring located on the upper end of the steering column. A wire attached to the contact ring runs down the steering column jacket and out under the instrument panel. the wire from

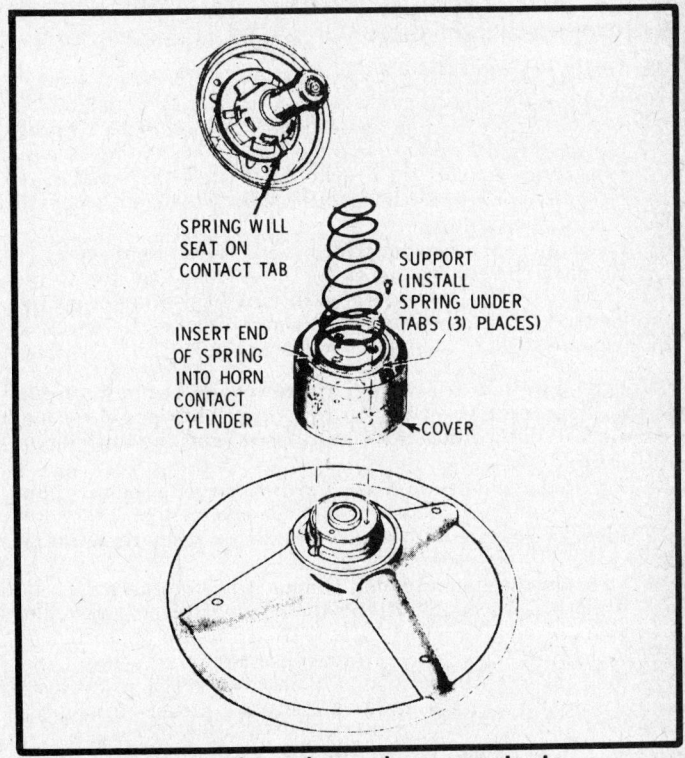

Tilt and telescopic column horn contacts
(© General Motors Corporation)

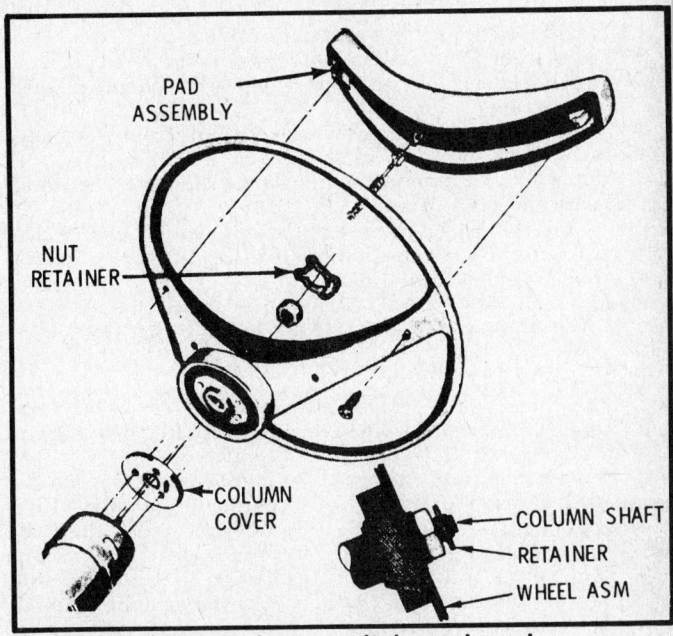

Standard column, horn switch and pad
(© General Motors Corporation)

GENERAL MOTORS—"E" AND "K" BODY
FRONT WHEEL DRIVE CARS

the horn relay connects at this point. Remove the horn pad mounting screws and the steering wheel to gain access to the horn switch assembly.

ELDORADO AND SEVILLE

The horn switch is part of the steering wheel pad and usually riveted or moulded to the pad and cannot be replaced separately.

WINDSHIELD WIPER SWITCH
Removal and Installation
COLUMN MOUNTED TYPE

1. Remove the steering wheel and directional signal switch as outlined earlier. It may be necessary to loosen the two column mounting nuts and remove the four bracket-to-mast jacket screws, then separate the bracket from the mast jacket to allow the connector clip on the ignition switch to be pulled out of the column assembly.
2. Disconnect the washer/wiper switch lower connector.
3. Remove the screws attaching the column housing to the mast jacket. Be sure to note the position of the dimmer switch actuator rod for reassembly in the same position. Remove the column housing-and-switch as an assembly.

NOTE: The tilt and travel columns have a removable plastic cover on the column housing. This provides access to the wiper switch without removing the entire column housing.

4. Turn upside down and use a drift to remove the pivot pin from the washer/wiper switch. Remove the switch.
5. Place the switch into position in the housing, then install the pivot pin.
6. Position the housing onto the mast jacket and attach by installing the screws. Install the dimmer switch actuator rod in the same position as noted earlier. check switch operation.
7. Reconnect lower end of switch assembly.
8. Install remaining components in reverse order of removal. Be sure to attach column mounting bracket in original position.

WINDSHIELD WIPER MOTOR
Removal and Installation

1. Disconnect the negative battery cable.
2. Remove the front cowl panel and screen.
3. Disconnect the washer hoses. Tag and disconnect all electrical connections.
4. Disconnect the transmission drive link from the motor crank arm.
5. Remove the motor attaching bolts. Remove the windshield wiper motor.
6. Installation is the reverse of the removal procedure. Motor must be in the park position before attaching the crank arm to the transmission drive link.

WIPER LINKAGE/TRANSMISSION
Removal and Installation

1. Disconnect the negative battery cable.
2. Remove the front cowl panel and screen. Remove the wiper arm blades.
3. Remove the nuts that hold the motor crank arm to the transmission drive arm. Remove the transmission drive link.
4. Drill out the motor support bracket spot welds. Bend the bracket in order to gain working clearance.
5. Remove the linkage and transmission assembly by sliding it through the plenum chamber opening or under the left side dash panel extension.
6. Installation is the reverse of the removal procedure. Attach the motor with nuts and bolts. Seal all seams with caulk.

Instrument Cluster
Removal and Installation
RIVIERA

1. Disconnect the negative battery cable.
2. Slide the steering column collar upward on the steering column.
3. Remove the headlight knob, escutcheon assembly and all remaining knobs.
4. Depending on the car model, pry either the right or left (or both) trim plates from the instrument panel.

NOTE: Remove the center trim plate by first removing the right and left trim plates. Then remove the radio knob and screws securing the center trim plate.

5. Remove all cluster retaining screws. Pull the cluster out slightly and disconnect the speedometer cable. Remove the instrument cluster assembly.
6. To install, attach the cluster assembly and speedometer cable. Secure the center trim plate. Hold the left and right trim plates in position, press into place and reposition the rubber filler ring and headlight knob assembly.

SEVILLE AND ELDORADO

1. Disconnect the negative battery cable.
2. Remove the left sound insulator.
3. Remove the instrument panel insert and applique trim from the instrument panel.
4. On digital readout speedometer vehicles, remove the filter lens retaining screws. Remove the filter lens.
5. Remove the nuts securing the steering column to the upper mounting bracket and lower the steering column.
6. Remove the screw securing the upper steering column mounting bracket to the cowl and lower the bracket.
7. Remove the cluster retaining screws, disconnect the speedometer cable, printed circuit connector and remove the cluster.
8. The installation is the reverse of removal procedure. Be sure the shift indicator is properly aligned.

1983–1985 TORONADO

NOTE: To remove the left side sound absorber from under the dash take out two screws and one nut. Pull the absorber down to slide from the steering column.

1. Disconnect the A.L.C.L. computer connector, if equipped.
2. Remove 4 screws from bottom side of trim cover.
3. Remove steering column trim cover.
4. Remove headlamp switch knob.
5. Remove radio knobs.
6. Carefully pull left trim cover rearward to remove. Trim cover is retained by clips. It may be necessary to disconnect the shift indicator clip and lower the steering column slightly to obtain clearance needed for trim cover removal.
7. Remove trip odometer knob by turning clockwise.
8. Remove 2 screws attaching cluster lens and face plate to cluster carrier. Remove lens and face plate.
9. Remove 2 screw attaching gage assembly to cluster housing.
10. Pull gauge assembly rearward to remove.
11. Disconnect shift indicator able end at shift indicator pointer.
12. Remove 3 screws attaching speedometer to cluster housing.
13. If printed circuit is to be removed, remove both gauge assemblies now by removing 2 screws attaching upper gauge assemblies to cluster housing. Pull assemblies rearward to remove.
14. Remove 2 screws attaching lower cluster housing to cluster carrier.
15. Disconnect speedometer cable at transmission or at transducer on cars equipped with cruise control.

GENERAL MOTORS—"E" AND "K" BODY
FRONT WHEEL DRIVE CARS
SECTION 8

16. Pull cluster housing rearward far enough to reach behind it and disconnect speedometer cable by depressing speedometer cable clip.
17. Remove screw attaching speed sensor pickup to speedometer head and remove pickup, if equipped.
18. Remove cluster housing and speedometer assembly.
19. Remove 2 screws attaching back of cluster housing to speedometer and remove speedometer.
20. Installation is the reverse of removal.

1986 AND LATER TORONADO

NOTE: These vehicles are equipped with an electronic instrument cluster. Electrostatic discharge can damage the electronic cluster. Do not touch any electrical component or terminal directly, as static discharge can cause damage to the electronic components in this cluster.

1. Disconnect the negative battery cable.
2. Remove the steering column trim cover.
3. Lower the steering column.
4. Remove the instrument panel trim panel retaining screws. Remove the trim panels.
5. Remove the screws retaining the instrument cluster to the instrument panel.
6. Remove the cluster assembly.
7. Installation is the reverse of the removal procedure.

SPEEDOMETER
Removal and Installation
RIVIERA

1. Disconnect the negative battery cable.
2. Remove the left side trim cover. On 1981 models remove the headlight knob.
3. Disconnect the speedometer cable at the transaxle.
4. Remove the instrument cluster lens screws. Remove the cluster lens. Remove the fuel gauge.
5. Remove the lap cooler hoses if equipped. Remove the trim panel.
6. Disconnect the shift indicator wire.
7. Remove the steering column retaining nuts and lower the steering column if necessary in order to gain working clearance.
8. Remove the speedometer retaining bolts. Pull the speedometer out and disconnect the speedometer cable from the rear of the speedometer.
9. Installation is the reverse of the removal procedure.

TORONADO

1. Disconnect the negative battery cable.
2. Remove the left hand trim cover. Remove the face plate lens and housing.
3. Turn the trip odometer knob counterclockwise and remove.
4. Disconnect the shift indicator cable.
5. Remove the speedometer-to-housing screws.
6. If the vehicle is equipped with a printed circuit, remove the screws that hold the upper gauge assembly to the cluster housing. Remove the lower screws.
7. Disconnect the speedometer cable from the transaxle.
8. If the vehicle is equipped with a speed sensor, remove the pick-up at the speedometer head.
9. Reach behind the instrument cluster and disconnect the speedometer cable from the speedometer.
10. Remove the speedometer from the cluster housing. Remove the speedometer.
11. Installation is the reverse of the removal procedure.

ELDORADO AND SEVILLE

1. Disconnect the negative battery cable.
2. Remove the lower instrument cluster trim plate.
3. Remove the screws holding the left and right lens. Remove the instrument cluster lens and retainer.
4. Loosen the shift indicator assembly and lay aside. Remove the coolant temperature indicator.
5. Remove the fuel gauge screws. Remove the fuel gauge.
6. Remove the screws holding the speedometer assembly. Remove the trip odometer reset knob.
7. Remove the vehicle speed sensor pick-up. Disconnect the speedometer cable. Remove the speedometer.
8. Installation is the reverse of the removal procedure.

SPEEDOMETER CABLE
Removal and Installation
RIVIERA AND TORONADO

1. Disconnect the negative battery cable.
2. Remove the speedometer assembly from the instrument cluster.
3. Disconnect the cable casing from the speedometer head.
4. Pull the inner cable from the upper casing.
5. Disconnect the cable from the transaxle. Remove the cable.
6. Installation is the reverse of the removal procedure. Make sure that there are no kinks in the new cable.

ELDORADO AND SEVILLE

1. Disconnect the negative battery cable.
2. Remove the screws holding the instrument cluster trim plate, left and right telltale lens, instrument cluster lens and the transaxle shift indicator assembly. Remove the lens and retainers.
3. Remove the temperature indicator and the fuel gauge.
4. Remove the screws holding the speedometer assembly to the housing. Pull the speedometer head out and disconnect the screw holding the vehicle speed sensor.
5. Remove the speedometer cable. Remove the speedometer.
6. Installation is the reverse of the removal procedure.

ELECTRICAL COMPONENT LOCATION
COMPUTER

The electronic control module is located on the right side of the vehicle. It is positioned under the instrument panel. In order to gain access to the electronic control module, it will first be necessary to remove the trim panels.

CONVENIENCE CENTER AND VARIOUS RELAYS

The convenience center is located on the underside of the instrument panel near the fuse block. It provides a central location for various relays, hazard flasher units and warning chimes. All units are replaced with plug in modules.

TURN SIGNAL FLASHER

The turn signal flasher unit is located behind the instrument panel near the steering column, along with hazard flasher. In order to gain access to the components, it may be necessary to remove certain under dash padding.

VEHICLE SPEED SENSOR

The speed sensor is located on the back of the speedometer cluster. It provides signals to the cruise control module which indicate vehicle speed. It is next to the speedometer cable.

CRUISE CONTROL
Adjustments

1. Set the carburetor choke to the slow idle position.
2. Adjust the rod assembly so that the idle load control arm is fully retracted.
3. Install the cruise control retainer bracket.
4. Tighten the cruise control retainer nuts.

8-17

SECTION 8

GENERAL MOTORS—"E" AND "K" BODY
FRONT WHEEL DRIVE CARS

ECM DIAGNOSTIC CODES

CODE	DESCRIPTION	COMMENTS	CODE	DESCRIPTION	COMMENTS
E013	Open Oxygen Sensor Circuit [Canister Purge]	Ⓐ	E037	MAT Sensor Temperature Too Hi	Ⓐ
E014	Coolant Sensor Temperature Too Hi	Ⓐ/Ⓕ	E038	MAT Sensor Temperature Too Low	Ⓐ
E015	Coolant Sensor Temperature Too Low	Ⓐ/Ⓕ	E040	Open Power Steering Pressure Switch Circuit	Ⓐ
E016	System Voltage Out of Range [All Solenoids]	Ⓐ/Ⓑ	E041	Cam Sensor Circuit	Ⓐ
			E042	Ignition System -(C^3I)	Ⓐ/Ⓙ
E021	Throttle Position Sensor Voltage Too Hi	Ⓐ	E043	ESC System	Ⓐ
E022	Throttle Position Sensor Voltage Too Low	Ⓐ	E044	Lean Exhaust Signal	Ⓐ/Ⓘ
E024	Speed Sensor Circuit [TCC]	Ⓐ	E045	Rich Exhaust Signal	Ⓐ/Ⓘ
E029	Open Fourth Gear Circuit	Ⓐ	E047	BCM-ECM Serial Data [A/C Clutch & Cruise]	Ⓐ
E032	EGR Electrical or Vacuum System	Ⓐ			
E033	MAF Sensor Voltage High	Ⓐ	E051	ECM PROM Error	Ⓐ/Ⓙ/Ⓚ
E034	MAF Sensor Voltage Low	Ⓐ	E052	Calpak Missing	Ⓐ
			E055	Internal ECM Error	Ⓐ

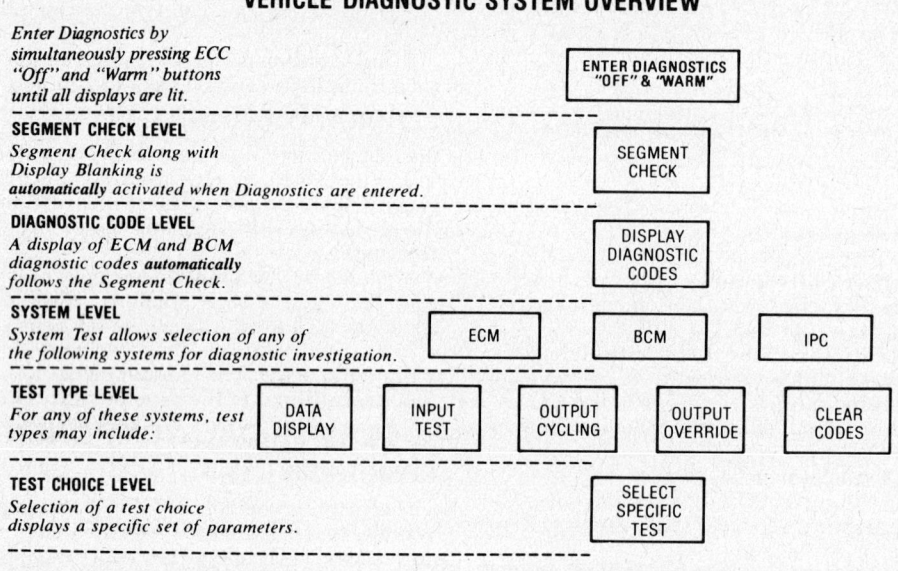

VEHICLE DIAGNOSTIC SYSTEM OVERVIEW

Enter Diagnostics by simultaneously pressing ECC "Off" and "Warm" buttons until all displays are lit. — ENTER DIAGNOSTICS "OFF" & "WARM"

SEGMENT CHECK LEVEL
*Segment Check along with Display Blanking is **automatically** activated when Diagnostics are entered.* — SEGMENT CHECK

DIAGNOSTIC CODE LEVEL
*A display of ECM and BCM diagnostic codes **automatically** follows the Segment Check.* — DISPLAY DIAGNOSTIC CODES

SYSTEM LEVEL
System Test allows selection of any of the following systems for diagnostic investigation. — ECM | BCM | IPC

TEST TYPE LEVEL
For any of these systems, test types may include: — DATA DISPLAY | INPUT TEST | OUTPUT CYCLING | OUTPUT OVERRIDE | CLEAR CODES

TEST CHOICE LEVEL
Selection of a test choice displays a specific set of parameters. — SELECT SPECIFIC TEST

INSTRUCTION KEY

1. • "DASHED" lines when used in the Block Diagrams indicate **automatic** test routes.
   • "SOLID" lines when used in the Block Diagrams indicate **optional** or **elective** test routes.
2. Specific Instructions as they relate to the individual **Test Types** are printed in "Italics".
3. For ease of Reference, **Index Tabs** identify four key areas. Diagnostic Codes, ECM, BCM, IPC.

DIAGNOSTICS — BASIC OPERATION

- ENTER DIAGNOSTICS BY SIMULTANEOUSLY PRESSING ECC "OFF" AND "WARM" BUTTONS UNTIL ALL DISPLAYS ARE LIT
- DIAGNOSTIC CODE LEVEL DISPLAYS ECM CODES FOLLOWED BY BCM CODES
- TO PROCEED TO THE DESIRED TEST LEVEL PRESS AND RELEASE THE INDICATED BUTTON "HI" REFERS TO THE UPPER FAN BUTTON AND "LO" REFERS TO THE LOWER FAN BUTTON
- PRESS "OFF" TO RETURN TO THE NEXT SELECTION IN THE PREVIOUS TEST LEVEL
- EXIT DIAGNOSTICS BY PRESSING "BI-LEV" ON THE ECC PANEL

GENERAL MOTORS—"E" AND "K" BODY
FRONT WHEEL DRIVE CARS
SECTION 8

DIAGNOSTIC CODE COMMENTS

Ⓐ	"Service Engine Soon" Indicator Lights	Ⓗ	Disables CCI
Ⓑ	Displays Diagnostic Message on IPC	Ⓘ	Forces OL Operation
Ⓒ	No Indicator Light or Message	Ⓙ	Causes System to Operate on Bypass Spark
Ⓓ	Displays "ERROR" in Season Odometer	Ⓚ	Causes System to Operate on Back-up Fuel
Ⓔ	Switches Climate Control Mode to ECON, if in AUTO	Ⓛ	ECC Displays 3 Dashes
Ⓕ	Forces Cooling Fans On	[ ]	Functions Within Bracket are Disengaged While Specified Malfunction Remains Current
Ⓖ	Displays "Electrical Problem" Message on IPC		

BCM DIAGNOSTIC CODES

CODE	DESCRIPTION	COMMENTS	CODE	DESCRIPTION	COMMENTS
B110	Outside Air Temperature Circuit	Ⓒ/Ⓗ	B411	Battery Volts Too Low [Cruise]	Ⓑ
B111	A/C High Side Temperature Circuit	Ⓕ	B412	Battery Volts Too High [Cruise]	Ⓑ
B112	A/C Low Side Temperature Circuit [A/C Clutch]	Ⓑ/Ⓔ	B440	Air Mix Door	Ⓒ
			B445	Compressor Clutch Engagement [A/C Clutch]	Ⓑ/Ⓔ
B113	In-Car Temperature Circuit	Ⓒ	B446	Low A/C Refrigerant Condition Warning	Ⓑ
B115	Sunload Temperature Circuit	Ⓒ	B447	Very Low A/C Refrigerant [A/C Clutch]	Ⓑ/Ⓔ
B118	Door Jam/Ajar Circuit	Ⓒ	B448	Very Low A/C Refrigerant Pressure Condition [A/C Clutch]	Ⓑ/Ⓔ
B119	Twilight Sentinel Photosensor Circuit	Ⓒ			
B120	Twilight Sentinel Delay Pot Circuit	Ⓒ	B449	A/C High Side Temperature Too High [A/C Clutch]	Ⓑ/Ⓔ
B122	Panel Lamp Dimming Pot Circuit	Ⓒ	B450	Coolant Temperature Too High [A/C Clutch]	Ⓑ/Ⓔ
B123	Courtesy Lamps On Circuit	Ⓒ	B552	BCM Memory Reset Indicator	
B124	Speed Sensor Circuit [Cruise]	Ⓗ	B556	BCM EEPROM Error	Ⓑ/Ⓓ
B127	PRNDL Sensor Circuit [Cruise]	Ⓒ	B660	Cruise - Transmission Not In Drive [Cruise]	Ⓒ
B131	Oil Pressure Sensor Circuit	Ⓑ	B663	Cruise - Car Speed and Set Speed Difference Too High [Cruise]	Ⓒ
B132	Oil Pressure Sensor Circuit	Ⓑ			
B334	Loss of ECM Serial Data [Cruise and A/C Clutch]	Ⓐ/Ⓔ/Ⓖ	B664	Cruise - Car Acceleration Too High [Cruise]	Ⓒ
B335	Loss of ECC Serial	Ⓛ	B666	Cruise - Engine RPM Too High [Cruise]	Ⓒ
B336	Loss of IPC Serial Data	Ⓖ	B667	Cruise - Cruise Switch Shorted [Cruise]	Ⓒ
B337	Loss of Programmer Serial Data [A/C Clutch]	Ⓒ/Ⓔ	B671	Cruise - Servo Position Sensor Circuit [Cruise]	Ⓒ
B338	Loss of Voice Serial Data	Ⓒ	B672	Cruise - Vent Solenoid Circuit [Cruise]	Ⓒ
B409	Generator Detected Condition	Ⓑ	B673	Cruise - Vacuum Solenoid Circuit [Cruise]	Ⓒ
B410	Charging System Regulator	Ⓑ			

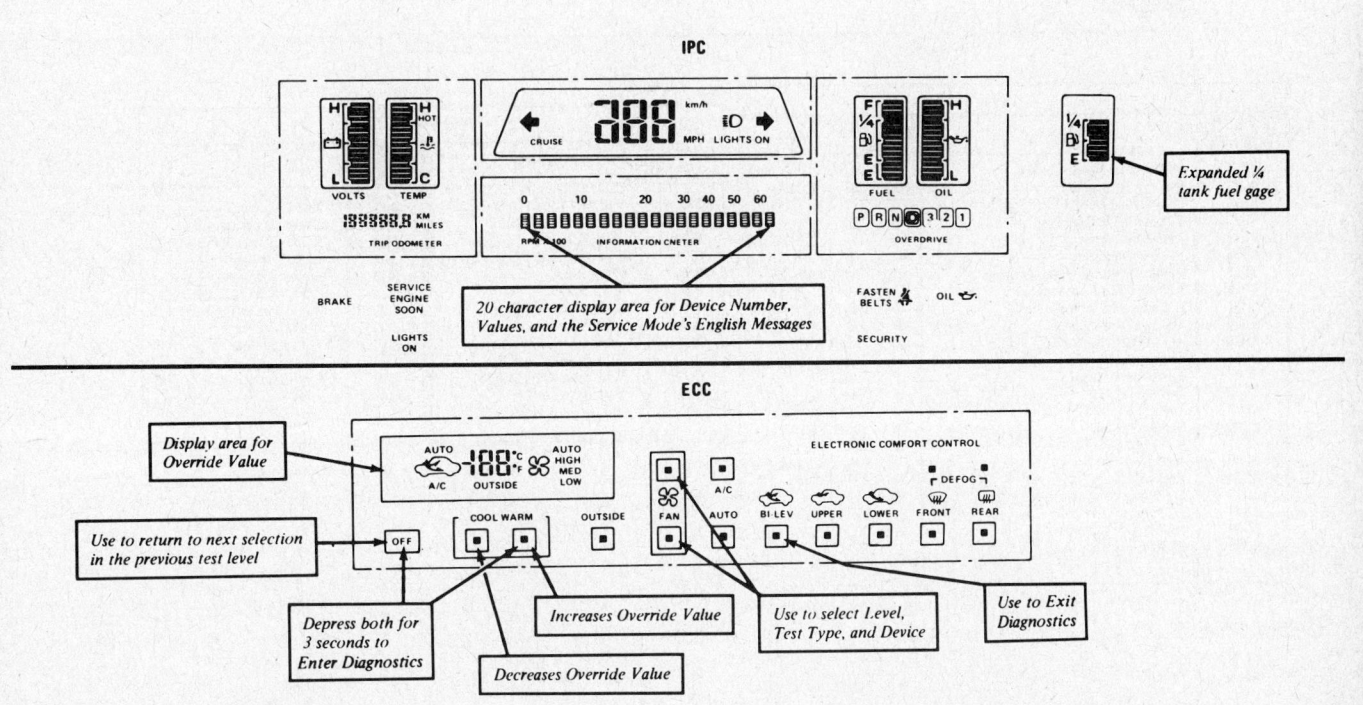

SECTION 8: GENERAL MOTORS — "E" AND "K" BODY
FRONT WHEEL DRIVE CARS

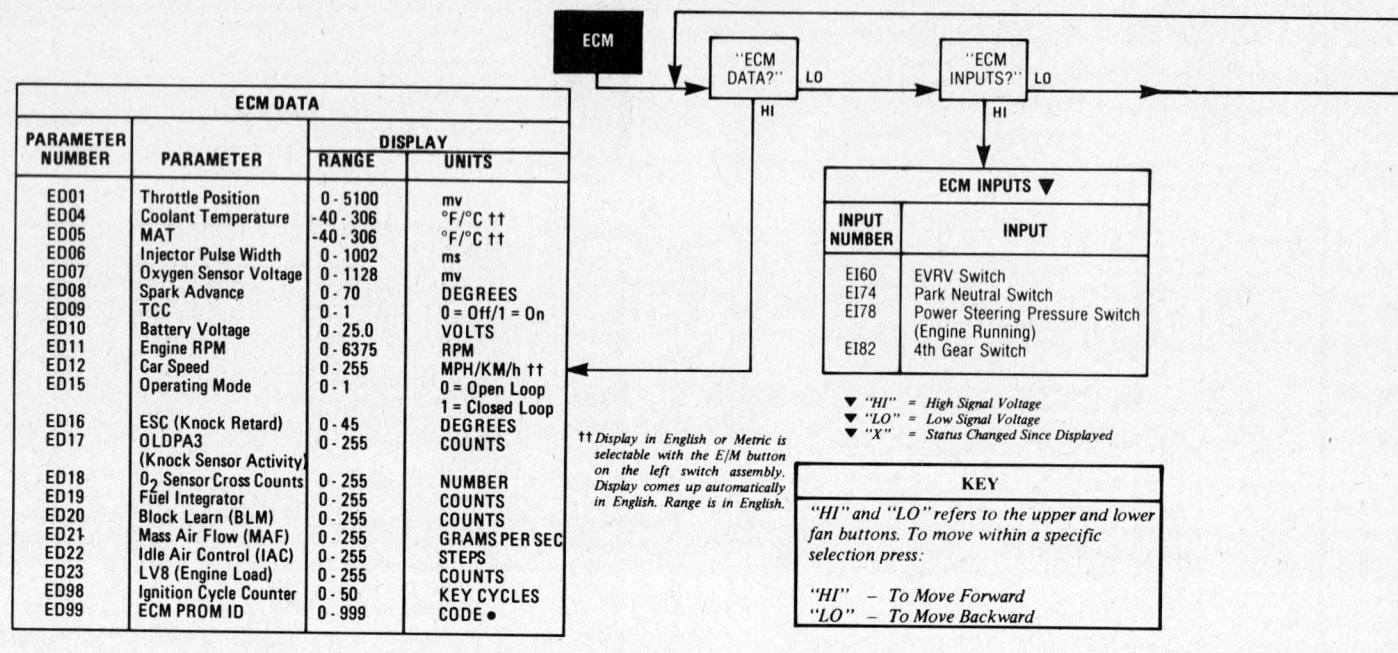

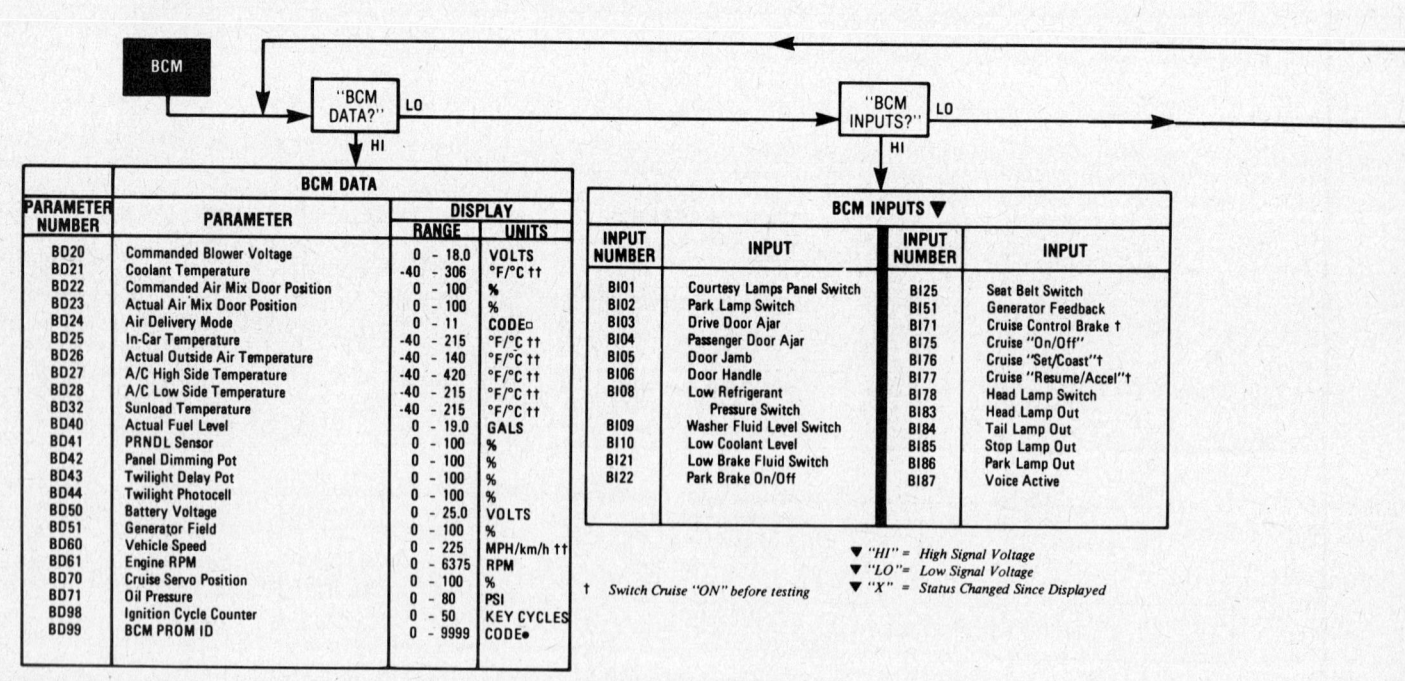

GENERAL MOTORS—"E" AND "K" BODY
FRONT WHEEL DRIVE CARS
SECTION 8

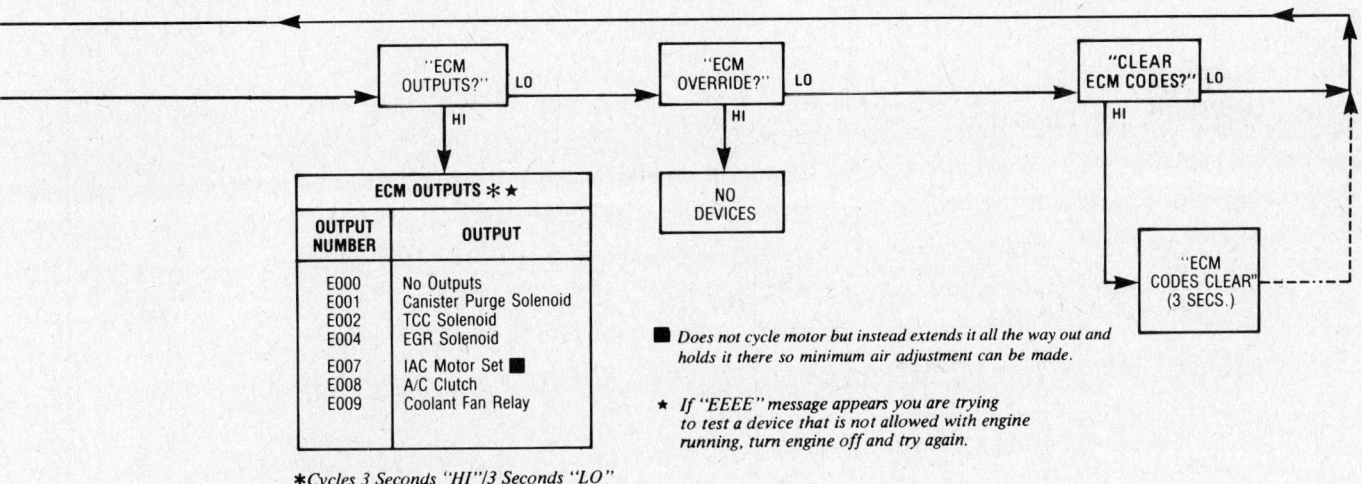

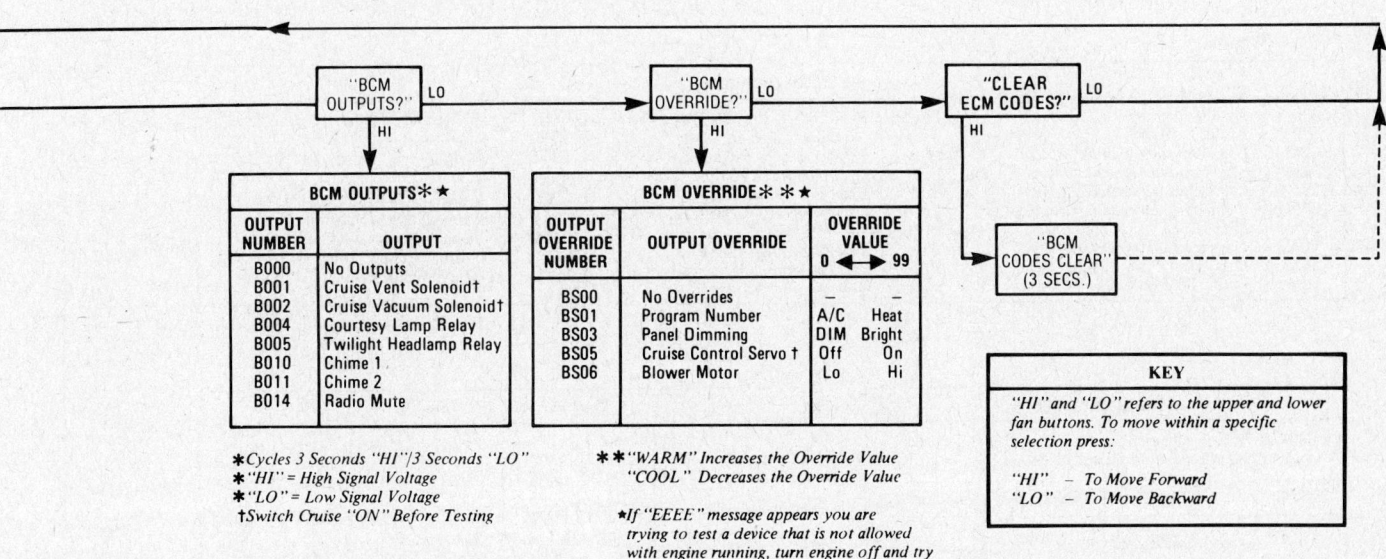

8-21

SECTION 8
GENERAL MOTORS—"E" AND "K" BODY
FRONT WHEEL DRIVE CARS

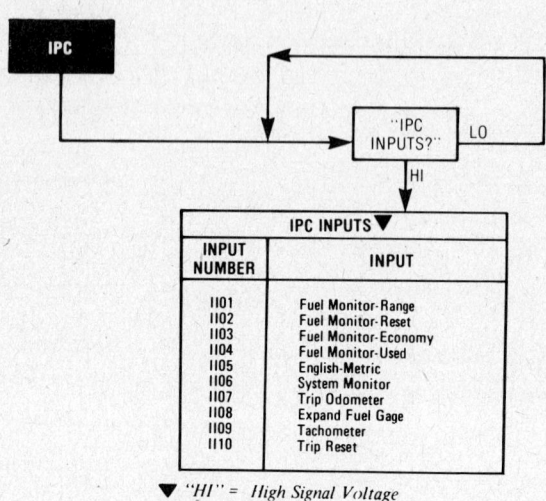

IPC INPUTS ▼	
INPUT NUMBER	INPUT
I101	Fuel Monitor-Range
I102	Fuel Monitor-Reset
I103	Fuel Monitor-Economy
I104	Fuel Monitor-Used
I105	English-Metric
I106	System Monitor
I107	Trip Odometer
I108	Expand Fuel Gage
I109	Tachometer
I110	Trip Reset

▼ "HI" = High Signal Voltage
▼ "LO" = Low Signal Voltage
▼ "X" = Status Changed Since Displayed

KEY
"HI" and "LO" refers to the upper and lower fan buttons. To move within a specific selection press:

"HI" – To Move Forward
"LO" – To Move Backward

ABBREVIATIONS

A/C	Air Conditioning	EEPROM	Electronically Erasable Programmable Read only Memory	MS	Milliseconds
A/D	Analog to Digital			MV	Millivolts
BCM	Body Computer Module	EGR	Exhaust Gas Recirculation	O_2	Oxygen
BLM	Block Learn Multiplier	ESC	Electronic Spark Control	OL	Open Loop
CCI	Continuous Compressor At Idle	EST	Electronic Spark Timing	PROM	Programmable Read Only Memory
C³I	Computer Command Control Ignition	EVRV	Electronic Vacuum Regulator Valve	POT	Potentiometer (Variable Resistor)
CL	Closed Loop	IAC	Idle Air Control	TCC	Transaxle Converter Clutch
ECC	Electronic Climate Control	IPC	Instrument Panel Cluster	TPS	Throttle Position Sensor
ECCP	Electronic Comfort Control Panel	MAF	Mass Air Flow	VF	Vacuum Fluorescent
ECM	Engine Control Module	MAT	Manifold Air Temperature		

AIR DELIVERY MODE
BCM Air Delivery Mode is Parameter BD24 of BCM Data and is displayed as a numerical code as follows:

CODE NO.	MODE	CODE NO.	MODE
0	Auto-Recirc/Max A/C	6	Normal Purge
1	Auto-A/C (Vents)	7	Cold Purge
2	Auto-Bi-Level	8	Defog
3	Auto-HTR-DEG	9	Forced Lower
4	Auto-Max Heat	10	Forced Upper
5	Off	11	Forced Bi-Level

TEMPERATURE CONVERSION

°C	°F	°C	°F	°C	°F	°C	°F
−40	−40	25	77	75	167	140	284
−30	−22	30	86	80	176	150	302
−20	−4	35	95	85	185	160	320
−10	14	40	104	90	194	170	338
−5	23	45	113	95	203	180	356
0	32	50	122	100	212	190	374
5	41	55	131	105	221	200	392
10	50	60	140	110	230	210	410
15	59	65	149	120	248	215	419
20	68	70	158	130	266		

GENERAL MOTORS—"E" AND "K" BODY
FRONT WHEEL DRIVE CARS

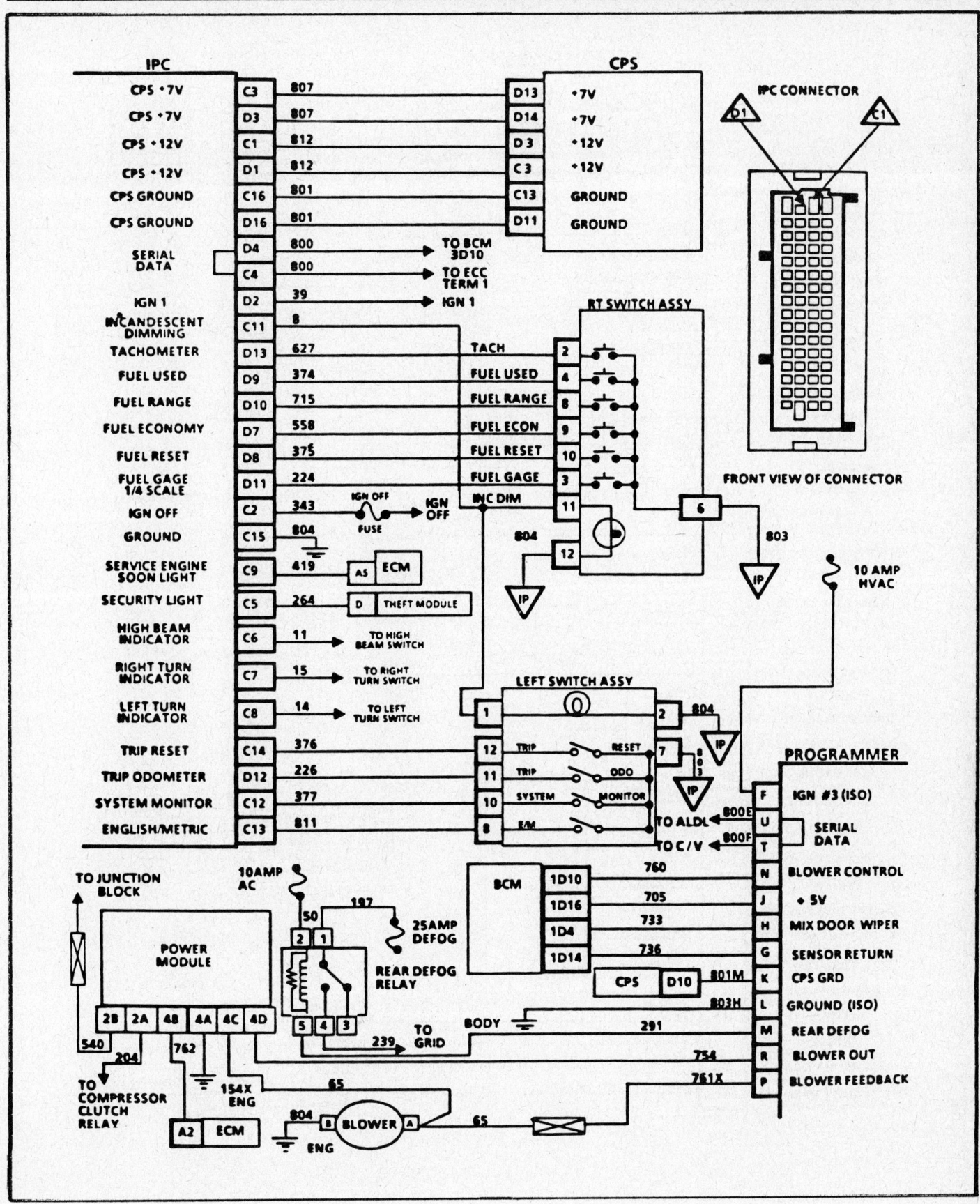

SECTION 8
GENERAL MOTORS—"E" AND "K" BODY
FRONT WHEEL DRIVE CARS

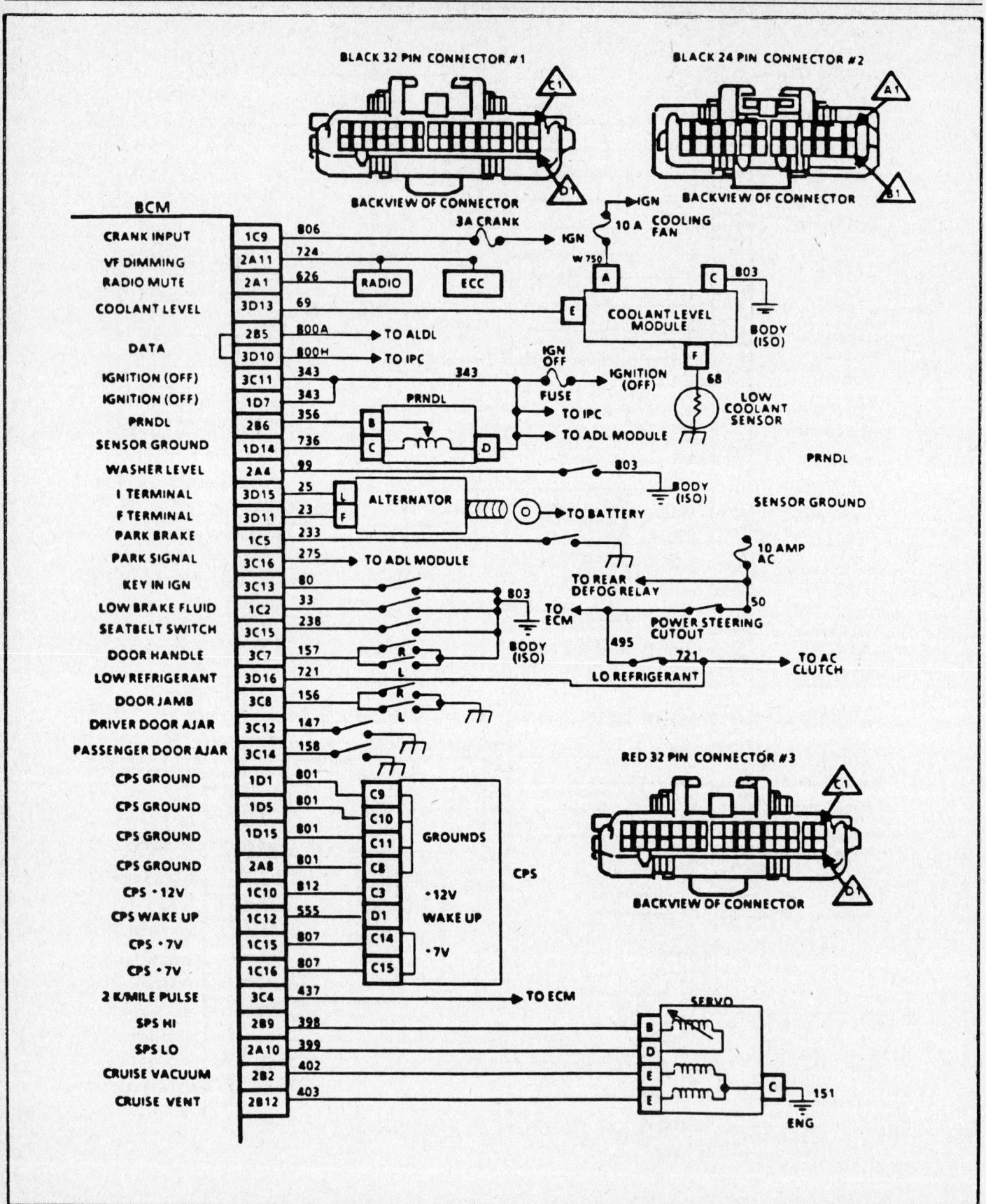

8-24

GENERAL MOTORS – "E" AND "K" BODY
FRONT WHEEL DRIVE CARS
SECTION 8

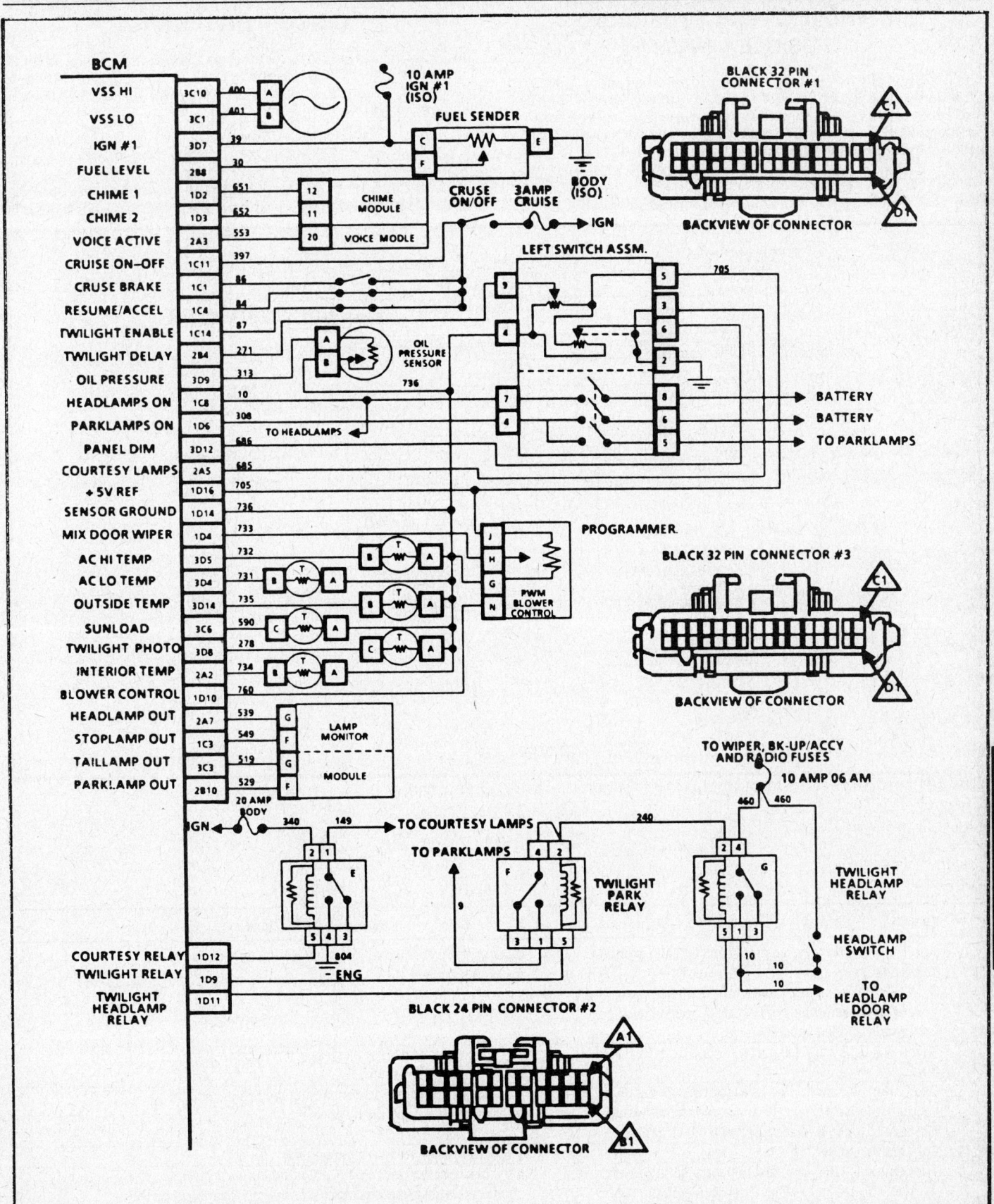

8-25

SECTION 8
GENERAL MOTORS—"E" AND "K" BODY
FRONT WHEEL DRIVE CARS

Electrical Circuit Protectors
FUSIBLE LINKS

The fusible links are located near the starter solenoid. they are attached to the lower ends of the main supply wires. The fusible links serve as additional circuit protection in the event of an electrical overload. In order to gain access to the fusible links, it may be needed to raise the vehicle first.

CIRCUIT BREAKERS

The circuit breakers are located on the left side of the vehicle. They are under the instrument panel. In order to gain access to the circuit breakers, it may first be necessary to remove the under dash padding.

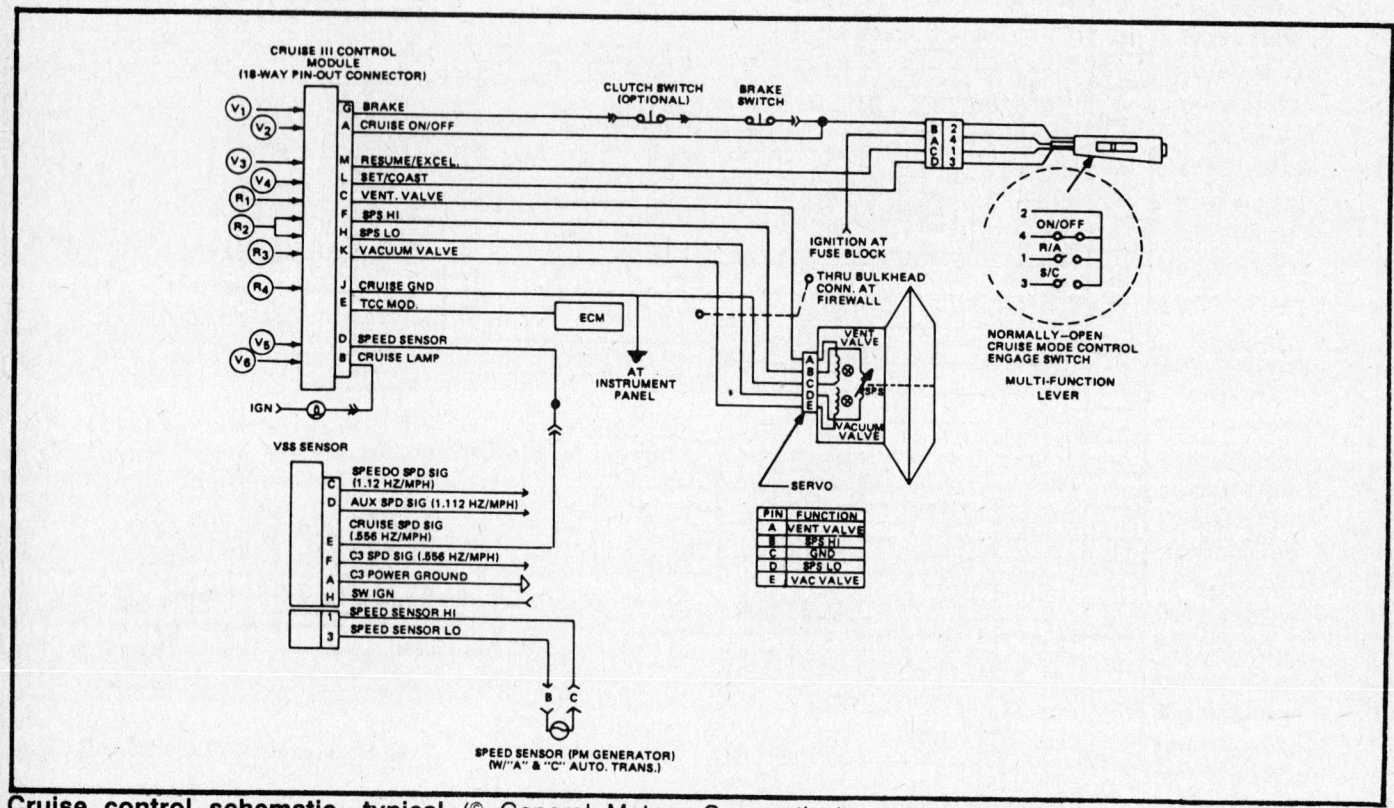

Cruise control schematic—typical (© General Motors Corporation)

TEST	NORMAL REACTION
1 Apply 12 volts dc to servo pins A and E. Then ground servo pin C. NOTE: Pin A to pin C closes the normally-open vent valve; whereas, pin E to pin C opens the normally-closed vacuum valve.	Servo should full stroke. If not, check vacuum hoses to the vacuum supply.
2 Remove the 12 volts dc source voltage from SERVO pin E.	The servo should hold a full stroke. If not, go to step 3. If servo holds, go to step 4.
3 Disconnect vacuum brake release at servo and plug vacuum release port on the servo. Momentarily apply 12 volts dc to pin E to allow servo to full stroke.	If the servo holds its position, adjust the brake vacuum release valve or replace the valve.
4 Turn ignition "ON".	Vacuum release valve should engage.
5 Turn ignition "OFF" and disconnect vacuum valve harness connector at valve. Then turn ignition "ON".	If the brake switch is properly adjusted, battery voltage should be present across the two connector terminals on the switch. No battery voltage indicates an open circuit.

GENERAL MOTORS—"E" AND "K" BODY
FRONT WHEEL DRIVE CARS
SECTION 8

COOLING AND HEATER SECTION

WATER PUMP

Removal and Installation

1. Drain the cooling system. Remove the fan shroud.
2. Unfasten the heater, bypass and lower radiator hoses from the pump.
3. Loosen the drive belts. Remove the fan assembly and the four spacer bolts. On cars with A/C, remove the fan and clutch assembly.

NOTE: Keep the fan in an upright position during removal to prevent the silicone fluid from leaking out of the fan clutch.

4. Remove the alternator, A/C compressor and power steering brackets, if so equipped. Do not disconnect any air conditioning hoses. Remove the front A.I.R. pump bracket and support rod.

5. Unfasten the bolts which secure the water pump and remove it. The long water pump retaining bolt can be removed through the access hole provided in the body side rail.

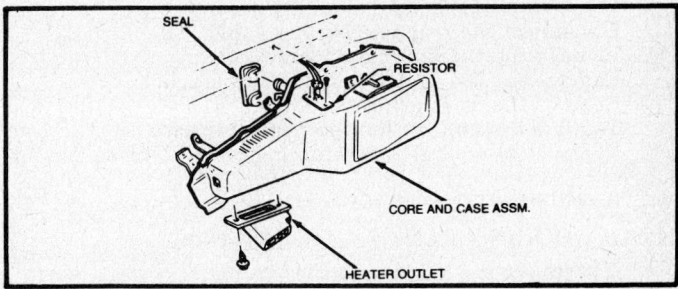
Heater core and case assembly on Riviera (© General Motors Corporation)

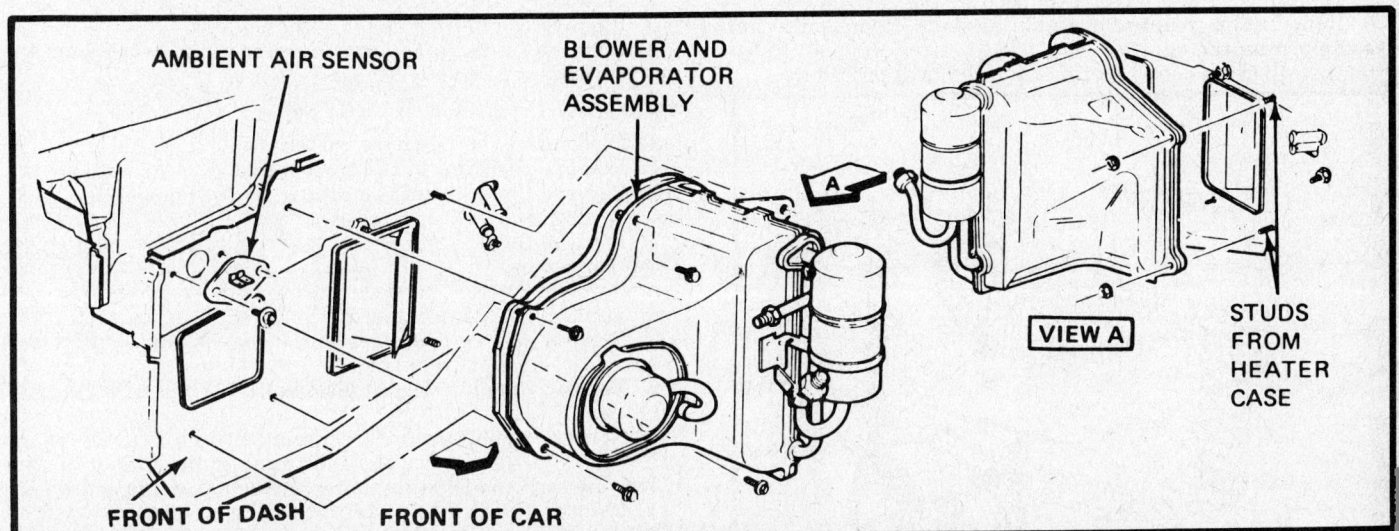
Heater blower and evaporator assembly typical of Eldorado and Seville (© General Motors Corporation)

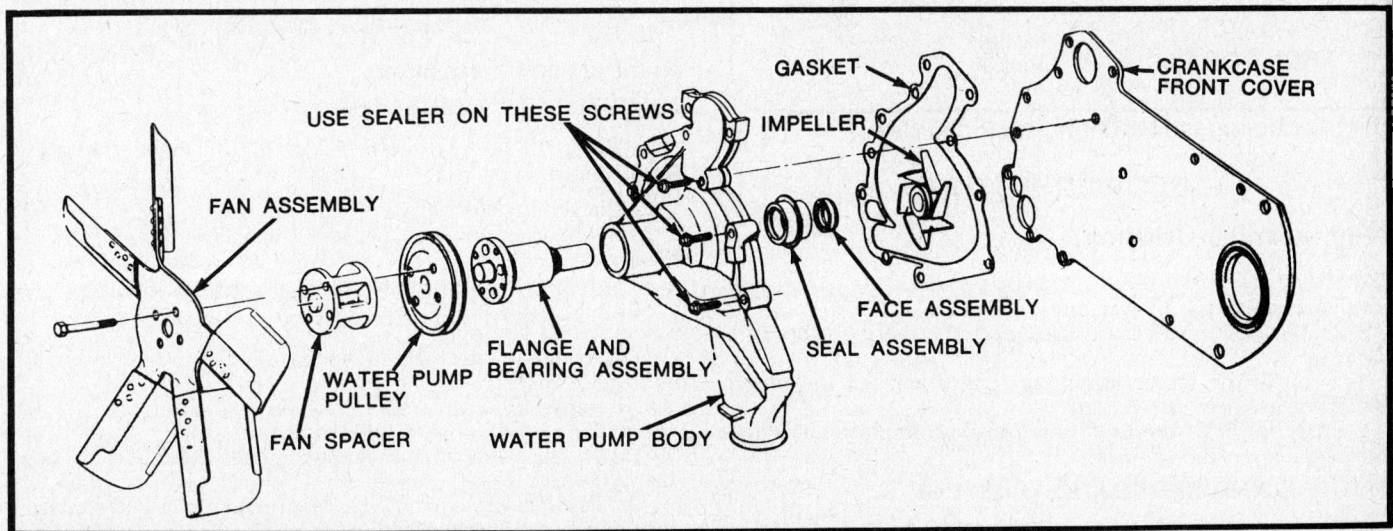
Exploded view of typical water pump (© General Motors Corporation)

SECTION 8: GENERAL MOTORS—"E" AND "K" BODY FRONT WHEEL DRIVE CARS

6. Reverse the removal procedure to install. Properly adjust all belt tensions and refill the cooling system.

ELECTRIC COOLING FAN

Removal and Installation

FRONT COOLING FAN

1. Disconnect the negative battery cable.
2. Remove the radiator cover panel.
3. Remove the fan control module and bracket.
4. Remove the front grille assembly.
5. Tag and disconnect the electrical connector.
6. Remove the cooling fan retaining bolts. Remove the fan assembly.
7. Installation is the reverse of the removal procedure.

REAR COOLING FAN

1. Disconnect the negative battery cable.
2. Disconnect the fresh air cleaner duct if necessary in order to gain working clearance.
3. Remove the A/C hose bracket to gain access to the fan assembly.
4. Disconnect the electrical connector from the fan motor.
5. Remove the cooling fan retaining bolts. Remove the fan assembly from the vehicle.
6. Installation is the reverse of the removal procedure.

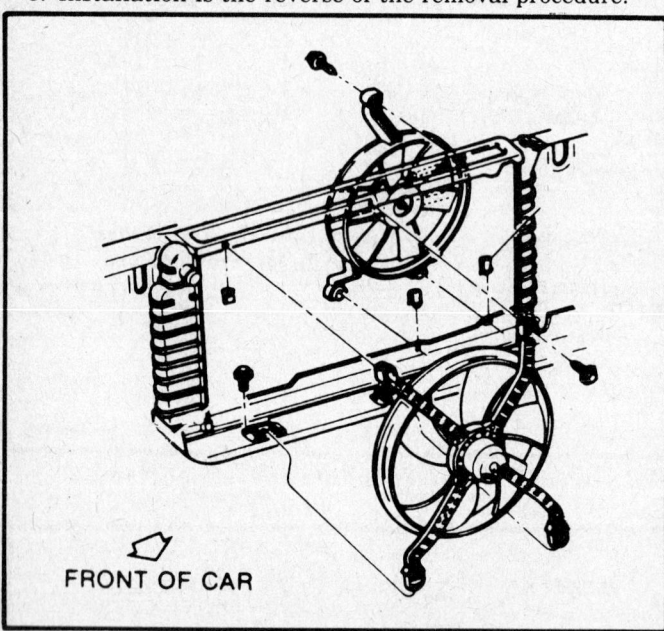

Electric cooling fan mounting-exploded view

BLOWER MOTOR

Removal and Installation

RIVIERA

1. Disconnect the blower motor wires.
2. On A/C equipped cars, disconnect the cooling tube from the case.
3. Remove the motor attaching screws and lift the motor from the case.
4. Installation is the reverse of removal. Replace any damaged sealer.

SEVILLE AND ELDORADO—1983–1985

1. Disconnect the negative battery cable.
2. Disconnect the electrical connections at the blower motor.
3. Disconnect the cooling hose form the blower motor.
4. Remove the mounting screws and remove the motor.
5. Reverse to install. Use a silicone sealer on the blower motor sealing surfaces.

SEVILLE AND ELDORADO—1986 AND LATER

1. Disconnect the negative battery cable.
2. Remove the air cleaner assembly.
3. Remove the cross tower brace.
4. Disconnect the wiring harness support bracket.
5. Tag and disconnect the electrical connector. Remove the cooling hose and mounting screws.
6. Tilt the blower motor in the case and remove the fan from the blower motor.

NOTE: Be careful not to bend the fan upon removal as a fan imbalance will result after reassembly.

7. Remove the blower motor and fan assembly from the vehicle.
8. Installation is the reverse of the removal procedure.

TORONADO—1983–1985

1. Disconnect the battery.
2. Disconnect and remove the Hi-Blower assembly.
3. Remove the blower motor assembly.
4. Installation is the reverse. Be sure the blower mounting has a continuous bead of sealer.

TORONADO—1986 AND LATER

1. Disconnect the negative battery cable.
2. Remove the front of the cowl shield.
3. Remove the bulkhead retaining screw. Remove the bulkhead connector.
4. Remove the Electronic Spark Control (ESC) module electrical connector.
5. Remove the ESC module and bracket assembly.
6. Remove the power steering pump bracket support.
7. Remove the coil bracket nuts. Tag and disconnect the electrical connector from the coil.
8. Remove the plug wire guides. Remove the wiring harness conduit.
9. Remove the blower motor cooling tube.
10. Tag and disconnect the electrical connectors from the blower motor. Remove the blower motor mounting screws.
11. Remove the blower motor mounting screws. Remove the blower motor.
12. Installation is the reverse of the removal procedure.

HEATER CORE

Removal and Installation

RIVIERA AND TORONADO

NOTE: This procedure involves removing the dashboard.

1. Disconnect the negative battery cable.
2. Drain the radiator. Remove the heater hoses from the heater core.
3. Remove the instrument panel sound absorbers which cover the underside of the dash area. Remove the courtesy lamp assemblies if equipped.
4. Loosen and lower the steering column and remove the left hand trim cover.
5. Remove the instrument cluster:
   a. Remove the headlight switch.
   b. Remove the windshield switch, the radio and the heater/AC control.
   c. Remove all cluster electrical connections and disconnect the speedometer cable.
   d. Remove the attaching screws and remove the cluster.

GENERAL MOTORS—"E" AND "K" BODY
FRONT WHEEL DRIVE CARS

SECTION 8

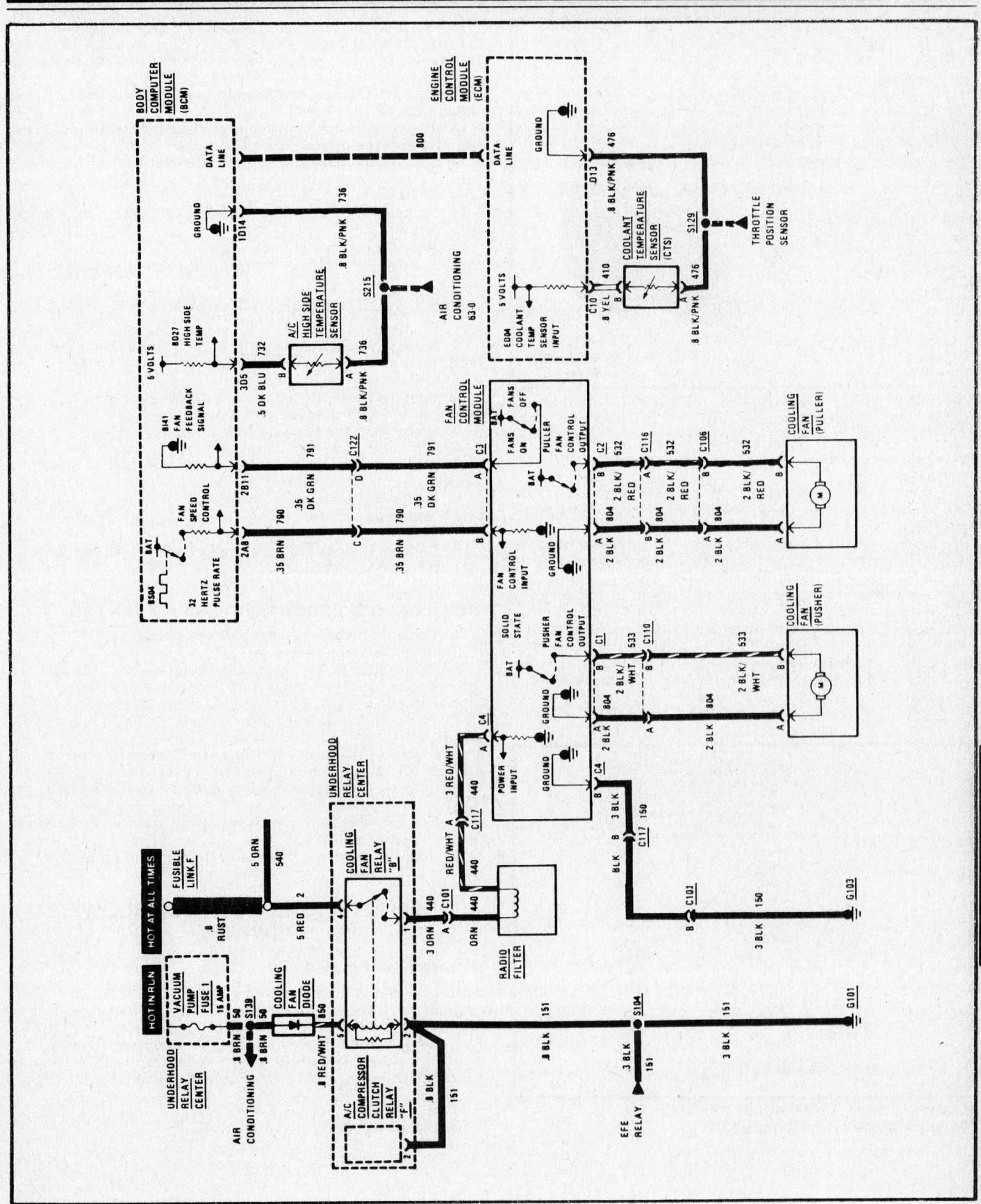

Electric cooling fan schematic

8-29

SECTION 8
GENERAL MOTORS—"E" AND "K" BODY
FRONT WHEEL DRIVE CARS

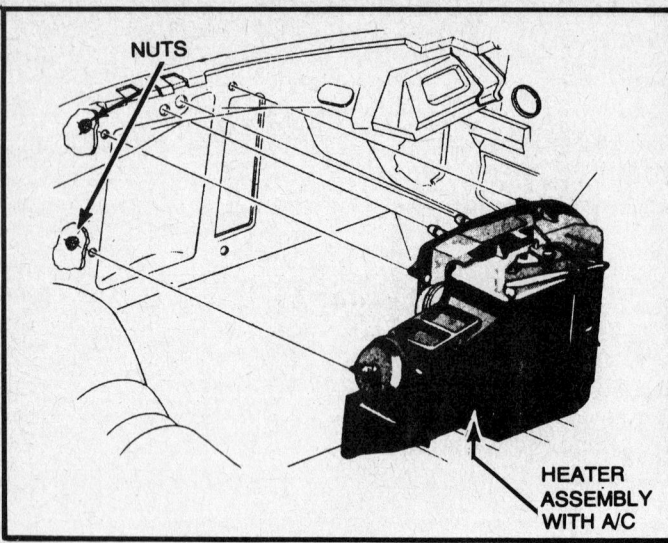

Toronado under-dash heater core mounting
(© General Motors Corporation)

e. Remove the windshield defroster nozzle grilles and deflectors.

6. Remove the front speakers, the screws attaching the manifold to the heater case, the upper and lower instrument panel retaining screws, and disconnect the brake release cable.

7. Disconnect the instrument panel wiring harness from the dash wiring assembly and disconnect the right hand remote control mirror cable from the instrument panel.

8. Disconnect the speedometer cable from its clip and the heater control cable at the heater case.

9. Disconnect all vacuum lines and wiring necessary to remove the instrument panel. If car is equipped with pulse wipers remove the wiper switch, unlock the connector from the cluster carrier and separate the pulse jumper harness from the connector.

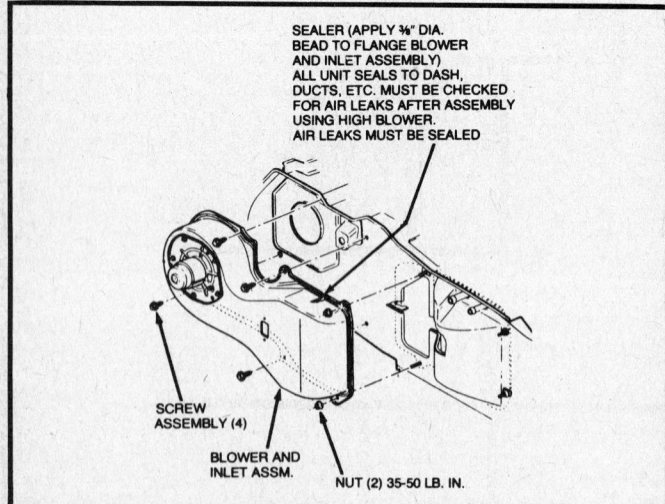

Heater blower installation on Riviera
(© General Motors Corporation)

10. Remove the instrument panel and harness assembly.
11. Remove defroster ducts, disconnect vacuum hoses and temperature cable; remove blower resistor and the heater assembly retaining nuts.
12. Remove the heater assembly-to-dash screw and clip from inside the car.
13. Remove the air conditioner programmer retaining screws and remove the programmer assembly.
14. Remove the power module assembly.
15. Remove the heater core cover screws. Remove the heater core cover.
16. Remove the heater core retaining clip. Remove the heater core screws.
17. Remove the heater core.
18. Installation is the reverse of the removal procedure.

SEVILLE AND ELDORADO—1983–1985

1. Disconnect the negative battery cable. Drain the radiator.
2. Remove the heater hoses from the core and plug the hoses and the nipples to prevent spillage.
3. Remove the instrument panel.
4. Remove the defroster nozzle attaching screws at the cowl and the screw on the case and remove the nozzle.
5. Disconnect the vacuum hoses.
6. Disconnect the electrical connector at the programmer.
7. Under the hood, remove the heater case-to-cowl attaching screws.
8. Under the instrument panel, remove the hater case-to-cowl attaching screws.
9. Remove the heater case.
10. Remove the case-to-core screws and remove the core.
11. Reverse to install.

SEVILLE AND ELDORADO—1986 AND LATER

1. Disconnect the negative battery cable.
2. Drain the engine coolant.
3. Remove the screws retaining the glove box. Tag and disconnect the electrical connectors from the glove box.
4. Remove the glove box assembly from the vehicle.
5. Remove the lower sound insulator to gain working clearance.
6. Remove the screws retaining the Electronic Control Module (ECM), and remove the ECM.
7. Remove the heater core cover. Remove the hoses to the heater core.
8. Remove the heater core retaining screws. Remove the heater core.
9. Installation is the reverse of the removal procedure.

TEMPERATURE CONTROL/BLOWER SWITCH

Removal and Installation

1. Disconnect the negative battery cable.
2. Remove the necessary components preventing access to the control unit such as trim panels, radio, etc.
3. Remove the temperature control mounting screws.
4. Pull the control unit forward and disconnect the vacuum lines, control cables and electrical connections from the back of the unit.
5. Installation is the reverse of the removal procedure. Check the system for proper operation.

GENERAL MOTORS—"E" AND "K" BODY
FRONT WHEEL DRIVE CARS
SECTION 8

FUEL SYSTEM

FUEL PUMP

Removal and Installation
CARBURETED ENGINES

1. Raise and support the car on jackstands.
2. Disconnect the fuel line and the vapor return hose from the fuel pump. Have a towel handy to catch any fuel that leaks out. Plug the hoses.
3. Disconnect the fuel pump-to-carburetor line and position it out of the way.

NOTE: Remove the shields and oil filter on V6 engines.

4. Remove the pump mounting screws and, tipping the pump upward, remove it from the car.
5. Installation is the reverse of the removal procedure. Remember to use a new gasket.

Fuel Injected Engines
CHASSIS-MOUNTED PUMP—EFI SYSTEM

— CAUTION —
Fuel is under high pressure; if the steps below are not followed, the fuel could spray out and result in a fire hazard and possible injury.

1. Disconnect the negative battery terminal.
2. Locate the pressure fitting in the fuel line and remove the protective cap.
3. Loosely install a special valve depressor (GM tool J–5420) or equivalent on the fitting.
4. Wrap a towel around the fitting to block any spray and slowly tighten the tool until the pressure has been relieved.
5. Remove the tool and reinstall the protective cap.
6. Remove the fuel hoses from the pump.
7. Peel back the rubber boot and remove the nuts, one from each electrical terminal. Tag and disconnect the electrical leads.
8. Remove the two screws and flat washers holding the fuel pump to the bracket and remove the pump assembly.
9. Install the fuel pump in the reverse order of removal. Connect the green wire to the positive terminal on the pump and the black wire to the negative terminal. check to make sure the fuel pump is resting evenly on its two mounts and not grounding against the bracket of frame.

IN-TANK PUMP—DFI AND EFE SYSTEMS

1. Remove the fuel pump fuse from the fuel block.
2. Crank the engine until it starts and allow it to run until the remaining fuel supply is exhausted.
3. Engage the starter for an additional 3 seconds to insure the relief of any remaining fuel pressure in the system.
4. Disconnect the negative battery terminal, open the fuel tank filler door and disconnect the sending unit feed wire.
5. Siphon the fuel from the fuel tank. If the rear of the car is raised one foot higher than the front, more fuel can be taken out.
6. Raise the rear of the car and remove the screw securing the ground wire to the crossmember.
7. Disconnect the fuel line, evaporative emission lines and the fuel return lines at the front of the tank.
8. Support the tank with a jack and wooden block and remove one screw on each side securing the fuel tank support straps to the body at the front of the tank.
9. Lower the jack and tank enough so that the fuel pump electrical lead can be disconnected. Disconnect the wire.
10. Remove the fuel tank from the car.
11. Remove the locknuts securing the fuel gauge tank unit and fuel pump feed wires to the tank unit.
12. Turn the cam lock ring counterclockwise. When the lock ring is disengaged, remove it and lift the gauge/pump unit from the tank.
13. Install in the reverse order of removal. Tighten the fuel retaining strap screws to 25 ft. lbs.

CARBURETOR

Adjustments
1983 AND LATER CARBURETORS

1. Run the engine until it reaches normal operating temperature.
2. Prepare the vehicle for adjustment as indicated on the emission label under the hood.
3. Check the ignition timing and adjust as necessary.
4. Reconnect the vacuum advance line.
5. With the A/C off, turn the idle speed screw to obtain the curb idle as specified on the emission label.
6. With the automatic transmission in Drive or the manual transmission in Neutral, disconnect the A/C compressor wire at the compressor and turn the A/C on.
7. Open the throttle slightly to extend the solenoid plunger.
8. Turn the solenoid screw to obtain the correct plunger.
9. Turn the engine off and reconnect the A/C compressor line and all hoses.

Certain models are equipped with an Idle Speed Control (ISC) mounted on the float bowl. Idle speed is computer controlled. On some V8 models, an Idle Load Compensator (ILC) is mounted on the float bowl to control the curb idle speed. The ILC is factory adjusted and capped to prevent readjustment.

On cars that do not include either an ISC or ILC, but are equipped with air conditioning, an idle speed solenoid is used to maintain idle speed.

NOTE: The underhood sticker specifies which idle system each car is equipped with.

FUEL INJECTED ENGINE

Idle Speed Adjustment EFI

NOTE: No idle speed adjustments are possible on the DFI system.

1. Adjust the ignition timing to the correct specifications.
2. Disconnect and plug the distributor vacuum line at the distributor, the parking brake release cylinder vacuum line at the release cylinder, and the air leveling compressor hose at the air cleaner. Set the parking brake and block the wheels.
3. Connect a tachometer to the engine, start it, allow the engine to reach normal operating temperature.
4. Place the transmission selector in Drive, and turn the air conditioning Off.
5. Loosen the lock nut on the idle bypass adjusting screw on the front of the throttle body. A conventional spring-loaded adjusting screw is used.
6. Using an allen wrench, adjust the idle by-pass adjusting screw to obtain the idle speed of 600 rpm for the Eldorado and Seville.
7. Tighten the lock nut on the adjusting screw, stop the engine and remove the tachometer, and install the air cleaner and vacuum hoses.

NOTE: Refer to the Unit Repair section for Fuel Injection information.

SECTION 8: GENERAL MOTORS—"E" AND "K" BODY
FRONT WHEEL DRIVE CARS

CARBURETOR

Removal and Installation

1. Disconnect the negative battery cable.
2. Remove the air cleaner.
3. Disconnect the throttle linkage.
4. Disconnect and label all vacuum hoses.
5. Remove the cruise control if equipped.
6. Disconnect any electrical connection. Tag for ease of reassembly.
7. Disconnect the fuel lines and remove the carburetor retaining bolts.
8. Remove the carburetor.
9. Installation is the reverse of the removal procedure.

INTAKE MANIFOLD

Removal and Installation

V6

1. Disconnect the negative battery cable.
2. Drain the cooling system and remove the upper radiator hose. Remove the heater hoses. Remove the throttle body heater hoses.
3. Remove the air cleaner assembly. Remove the accelerator linkage and the cruise control chain if equipped.
4. Tag and disconnect the vacuum hoses. Remove the transmission vacuum modulator line.
5. Remove the distributor cap and rotor.
6. Remove the accessory drive belt, alternator and bracket.
7. Remove the spark plug wires. Tag for ease of reassembly.
8. If the vehicle is fuel injected, remove the fuel lines, fuel rail and injectors.
9. Remove the intake manifold bolts. Remove the intake manifold.
10. Installation is the reverse of the removal procedure.

V8

1. Disconnect the negative battery cable.
2. Remove the air cleaner assembly. Drain the engine coolant.
3. Remove the right hand cross car brace in order to gain working clearance.
4. Remove the coolant reservoir tank and accessory drive belt.
5. Remove the idler pulley assembly. Remove the power steering brace. Remove the tensioner bracket assembly and position out of the way.
6. Remove the alternator assembly and alternator support bracket.
7. Tag and disconnect the wire connections from the distributor, oil pressure switch connection, coolant sensor if equipped, EGR solenoid, idle speed control motor and the throttle position sensor.
8. Remove the upper radiator hose and heater hoses.
9. If the vehicle is fuel injected, remove the fuel injection assembly.
10. Remove the A/C hose bracket. Remove the distributor.

NOTE: Once the distributor has been removed, DO NOT crank or in any other way rotate the crankshaft.

11. Bleed the fuel pressure at the fuel line schraeder valve. Remove the fuel and vacuum lines from the throttle body.
12. Tag and disconnect the vacuum lines. Remove the valve covers.
13. Remove the rocker arms and pushrods keeping them in order for ease of reassembly.
14. Remove the intake manifold retaining bolts. Remove the intake manifold.
15. Installation is the reverse of the removal procedure.

Clean the sealing surfaces of the intake manifold, cylinder head and cylinder block.

EXHAUST MANIFOLD

Removal and Installation

V6 LEFT

1. Disconnect the negative battery cable.
2. Remove the spark plug wires. Remove the exhaust crossover from the manifold.
3. Remove the cooling fan assembly. Remove the oil level indicator and tube to gain working clearance.
4. Remove any necessary accessory mounting brackets to gain working clearance.
5. Remove the manifold to cylinder head bolts. Remove the exhaust manifold.
6. Installation is the reverse of the removal procedure.

V6 RIGHT

1. Disconnect the negative battery cable.
2. Remove the heater hoses from the heater pipe.
3. Remove the power steering support bracket from the intake manifold and the throttle bracket from the cylinder head.
4. Remove the exhaust crossover bolts from the rear exhaust manifold.
5. Remove the heat shields as necessary to gain working clearance.
6. Raise the vehicle and support safely.
7. Remove the exhaust pipe from the exhaust manifold.
8. Remove the spark plug wires. Remove the oxygen sensor connector.
9. Remove the exhaust manifold bolts and studs. Remove the manifold.
10. Installation is the reverse of the removal procedure.

V8 LEFT

1. Disconnect the negative battery cable.
2. Remove the air cleaner assembly.
3. Remove the A.I.R. hose and pipe from the air pump.
4. Remove the starter heat shield. Remove the accessory drive belt.
5. Remove the power steering tensioner bracket and A/C hose bracket if necessary for working clearance.
6. Remove the cooling fan assembly. Disconnect the spark plug wires.
7. Raise the vehicle and support safely.
8. Remove the exhaust cross under pipe if equipped.
9. Remove the exhaust manifold bolts. Remove the exhaust manifold.
10. Installation is the reverse of the removal procedure.

V8 RIGHT

1. Disconnect the negative battery cable.
2. Remove the air cleaner assembly. Remove the necessary heat shield screws in order to gain working access.
3. Raise the vehicle and support safely.
4. Remove the exhaust crossunder pipe if equipped.
5. Remove the oxygen sensor wire.
6. Remove the exhaust manifold bolts. Remove the exhaust manifold.
7. Installation is the reverse of the removal procedure.

Fuel Injection System

For More Information on Fuel Injection System Refer to Unit Repair Section.

GENERAL MOTORS—"E" AND "K" BODY
FRONT WHEEL DRIVE CARS
SECTION 8

DESCRIPTION

Some vehicles are equipped with either Electronic Fuel Injection (EFI) or Digital Fuel Injection (DFI)

Fuel Injection consists of fuel metering valves, which, when actuated, spray a calculated quantity of fuel into the engine intake manifold. These injectors are mounted on the throttle body with the metering tip pointed into the throttle throats.

FUEL INJECTION NOZZLE

Removal and Installation

1. Disconnect the negative battery cable. Relieve the fuel system pressure.
2. Tag and disconnect the fuel injector electrical connectors.
3. Remove the necessary components in order to gain access to the fuel rail retaining bolts.
4. Remove the fuel rail retaining bolts. Remove the fuel rail.
5. Separate the injector from the fuel rail.
6. Installation is the reverse of the removal procedure. Replace the O-rings when installing the injectors.

Turbocharger System

For More Information on Turbochargers Refer to Unit Repair Section.

DESCRIPTION

A turbocharger is used to increase power on a demand basis, thus allowing a smaller more economical to perform the job of a larger engine. As the load on the engine is increased and the throttle is opened, more air fuel mixture flows into the combustion chambers. As this increased flow is burned, a larger volume of higher energy exhaust gas enters the engine exhaust system and is directed through the turbocharger turbine housing. Some of this energy is used to increase the speed of the turbine wheel. The turbine wheel is connected by a shaft to the compressor wheel. The increased speed of the compressor wheel allows it to compress the air-fuel mixture it receives from the carburetor and delivers it to the intake manifold. The resulting higher pressure in the intake manifold allows a denser charge to enter the combustion chambers.

TURBOCHARGER ASSEMBLY

Removal and Installation

1. Disconnect the negative battery cable.
2. Remove all necessary components in order to gain access to the turbocharger assembly retaining bolts.
3. On some vehicles it may be necessary to first remove the accessory mounting brackets to gain working access to the turbocharger assembly.
4. Remove the turbocharger assembly bolts. Remove the turbocharger assembly from the vehicle.
5. Installation is the reverse of the removal procedure.

TURBOCHARGER WASTEGATE

Removal and Installation

1. Disconnect the hoses. Remove the clip attaching the wastegate linkage to the actuator rod. Remove the mounting bolts and remove the wastegate.
2. Installation is the reverse of the removal procedure.

EMISSION CONTROL SECTION

EMISSION EQUIPMENT USED

Positive Crankcase Ventilation (PCV)
Catalytic Converter
Thermostatic Air Cleaner (THERMAC)
Vapor control Canister System
Early Fuel Evaporation (EFE)
Electric choke
Early Fuel Evaporation-Solenoid (EFE-SOL)
Evaporative Emission Control (EEC)
Electronic Spark Control (ESC)
Oxygen Sensor
Air Induction System
Pulsair Induction Reaction (PAIR)
Air Control Valve
Canister Purge-Control Valve (CP-CV)
Exhaust Gas Recirculation (EGR)
Vacuum Spark Advance
Throttle Position Sensor (TPS)
Electronic Control Module (ECM)
Programmable Read Only Memory (PROM)
Barometric Absolute Pressure Sensor (BARO)
Power Enrichment Control Valve (PECV)
Exhaust Pressure Regulator (EPR)
Exhaust Pressure Regulator-Solenoid (EPR-SOL)
Crankcase Depression Regulator (CDR)
Thermal Vacuum Valve (TVV)
Vacuum Regulator Valve (VRV)

RESETTING TROUBLE INDICATOR

ELECTRONIC DASH DISPLAY

Trouble codes that are stored in the Electronic Control Module (ECM) for 1983–85 vehicles can be erased by pushing the "OFF" and "HI" buttons on the climate control panel at the same time and holding them until ".0.0" appears. The ignition must be turned on for this procedure.

After entering the diagnostic mode on 1986 and later vehicles, the "HI" button will indicate a yes command to the Electronic Control Module (ECM) and Body Computer Module (BCM) while the "LO" button will indicate a no command. To clear codes from the ECM and BCM on 1986 and later vehicles, while in the diagnostic modes, hit the "RESET/RECALL" botton located on the climate control panel. This will return the system to normal functioning.

SECTION 8
GENERAL MOTORS—"E" AND "K" BODY
FRONT WHEEL DRIVE CARS

ENGINE SECTION

For Diesel Engine Services Refer to Unit Repair Section. For Engine Overhaul procedures, refer to Unit Repair Section.

ENGINE ASSEMBLY

Removal and Installation

V6 GAS ENGINE—1983–1985

1. Disconnect the negative battery cable.
2. Remove the hood and cover the fenders.
3. Drain the coolant system.
4. Remove the air cleaner and the fan pulleys and belts. Remove the fan blade.
5. Remove the fan shroud assembly. Remove the radiator and heater hoses.
6. Position the power steering pump out of the way.
7. Remove the fuel line and battery ground cable from the engine.
8. Tag and disconnect all vacuum hosing from non-engine mounted components.
9. Remove the carburetor accelerator linkage.
10. Remove the engine wiring harness connector. Remove the alternator. Remove the engine-to-body ground straps.
11. Remove the crossover pipe from the exhaust pipe.
12. Remove the flywheel cover and torque converter bolts.
13. Remove the starter motor wiring. Remove the starter motor.
14. Remove the transmission-to-cylinder block attaching bolts. Remove the front motor mount bracket bolts.
15. While supporting the engine, install the engine lift fixture. Remove the engine.
16. Installation is the reverse of the removal procedure.

V6 GAS ENGINE—1986 AND LATER

1. Disconnect the negative battery cable. Drain the engine coolant.
2. Remove the hood. Cover the fenders.
3. Remove the radiator hoses and the air inlet hoses.
4. Tag and disconnect the electrical connectors at the following locations:
   a. Fuel rail
   b. engine ground connections
   c. EGR solenoid and oil pressure sending unit
   d. Coolant temperature senders and the throttle body
   e. camshaft and crankshaft sensor
   f. alternator
5. Remove the serpentine belt.
6. Remove the power steering pump and alternator.
7. Remove the heater hoses.
8. If the vehicle is equipped with cruise control, remove the cables from the throttle lever, accelerator and throttle valve assembly.
9. Remove the lines for the fuel supply and return.
10. Remove the cooling fan and and radiator assembly.
11. Remove the exhaust manifold from the front of the engine assembly.
12. Tag and disconnect the engine vacuum connections.
13. Remove the three engine to transaxle bolts. Remove the vibration damper and bracket from the engine.
14. Remove the engine ground bolts and wiring harness hold down bolts.
15. Remove the engine to transaxle bracket.
16. Raise the vehicle and support safely. Remove the A/C compressor from bracket and position out of the way.
17. Remove the exhaust pipe. Tag and disconnect the electrical connections from the starter.
18. Remove the engine mount nuts and the converter cover. Remove the converter bolts.
19. Remove the left wheel and tire assembly.
20. Remove the two remaining engine to transaxle bolts.

NOTE: One of the bolts is located between the transaxle case and engine block and is installed in the opposite direction.

21. Remove the engine to transaxle bracket.
22. Lower the vehicle and install a suitable engine lifting device.
23. Remove the engine assembly from the vehicle.
24. Installation is the reverse of the removal procedure.

V8 GAS ENGINE—1983–1985

1. Disconnect the negative battery cable.
2. Drain the coolant system. Remove the radiator.
3. Remove the air cleaner. Remove the hot air pipe.
4. Remove the hood and cover the fenders against damage.
5. Remove the engine ground strap. Tag and disconnect all electrical connections.
6. Disconnect the power steering pump brackets and the air conditioner compressor bracket and lay aside.
7. Disconnect the throttle cable and the vacuum hoses.
8. Remove the left side through bolt that holds the final drive to the engine.
9. Remove the flywheel shield. Remove the starter wiring and starter motor.
10. Remove the converter to flywheel bolts.
11. Remove the right hand output shaft support bolts.
12. Remove the output shaft support brackets.
13. Attach engine lifting fixture to the engine.
14. Remove the remaining transmission to engine bolts.
15. Lift the engine from the engine compartment.
16. Installation is the reverse of the removal procedure.

V8 GAS ENGINE—1986 AND LATER

1. Disconnect the negative battery cable. Drain the engine coolant.
2. Remove the air cleaner assembly. Remove the hood.
3. Remove the cooling fan and accessory drive belt. Remove the upper radiator hose and heater hose from the thermostat housing.
4. Tag and disconnect all engine electrical connections.
5. If the vehicle is equipped with cruise control, disconnect the accelerator and cruise control cable as well as the transmission T.V. Remove the cruise control diaphragm.
6. Remove the oil and transmission cooler lines from the radiator. Remove the radiator.
7. Remove the oil cooler lines from the oil filter adapter and remove the lines.
8. Remove the air cleaner mounting bracket and oil filter housing adapter. Remove the A.I.R. tubes from the diverter valve.
9. Remove the front right and rear cross car braces. Remove the right front heater hose.
10. Remove the coolant reservoir and air filter box and bracket.
11. Remove the idler pulley.
12. Remove the power steering line brace from the right cylinder head. Remove the power steering tensioner assembly.
13. Diacharge the A/C system. Remove the A/C lines from the accumulator and condensor.

--- **CAUTION** ---
If the following step is not followed, personal injury or fire could result.

GENERAL MOTORS—"E" AND "K" BODY
FRONT WHEEL DRIVE CARS
SECTION 8

14. Bleed the fuel pressure at the fuel line schraeder valve using a suitable tool and container or shop towel to catch fuel.
15. Remove the fuel lines at the throttle body. Remove the fuel line bracket at the transmission. Reposition the fuel lines.
16. Remove the EGR lines and bracket. Remove the vacuum modulator line and fuel air filter.
17. Raise the vehicle and support safely.
18. Remove the starter heat shield. Remove the starter.
19. Remove the exhaust crossunder pipe.
20. Remove the two flexplate covers and three flexplate to converter bolts.
21. Remove the lower dust shield from the A/C compressor.
22. Remove the right front tire and wheel assembly. Remove the outer wheelhouse plastic shield.
23. Remove the right rear trans/engine mounting bolt. Remove the lower engine damper nut. Remove the front engine mount nuts and right rear trans mount bolts.
24. Remove the alternator, oxygen sensor wires and heater bypass bracket from right side of vehicle. Remove the right side engine brace.
25. Lower the vehicle and five top engine/trans mounting bolts.
26. Install a suitable engine lifting device. Remove the engine assembly from the vehicle.
27. Installation is the reverse of the removal procedure.

V8 DIESEL ENGINE

1. Disconnect the negative battery cable.
2. Drain the cooling system and remove the radiator.
3. Remove the air cleaner. Remove the hood. Cover the fenders to protect against damage.
4. Remove the fan assembly.
5. Remove the engine ground strap.
6. Tag and disconnect the heater hoses. Remove the water control valve.
7. Disconnect the upper alternator bracket bolts and remove the alternator bracket with the alternator attached.
8. Remove the power steering pump assembly. Remove the A/C compressor assembly if equipped, and lay aside to gain working room.
9. Tag and disconnect the vacuum hoses and the electrical connections from the engine.
10. Remove the left exhaust pipe from the manifold. Remove the upper heat shield.
11. Remove the final drive-to-engine bolt on the left side of the engine.
12. Raise and support the vehicle safely.
13. Remove the exhaust manifold from the engine.
14. Disconnect the starter wiring and remove the starter.
15. Remove the converter to flywheel bolts.
16. Remove the right hand output shaft support brackets.
17. Remove the right hand transmission to engine bolts. Install final drive support chain.
18. Remove the water control valve.
19. Remove the remaining transmission to engine bolts. A floor jack can be used to raise and lower the transaxle to ease bolt removal or installation.
20. Attach a lifting chain to the engine. Raise the engine from the engine compartment and place in a suitable fixture.
21. Installation is the reverse of the removal procedure.

ENGINE MOUNTS

Removal and Installation

ALL VEHICLES EXCEPT 1986 AND LATER ELDORADO AND SEVILLE

1. Disconnect the negative battery cable.
2. Raise the vehicle and support safely.
3. Remove the engine through mount bolt. Raise the engine and support it properly.
4. Remove the engine mount retaining bolts. Remove the engine mount.
5. Installation is the reverse of the removal procedure.

1986 AND LATER ELDORADO AND SEVILLE (RIGHT SIDE)

1. Disconnect the negative battery cable.
2. Remove the brace from the engine bracket to engine.
3. Remove the two nuts securing the engine bracket to mount.
4. Raise the vehicle and support safely.
5. Remove the nuts securing the engine mount to the frame. Remove the nuts securing the transaxle mount to the frame bracket.
6. Raise the engine using engine support tool J–28467 or equivalent.
7. Raise the engine slowly until the bracket is free from the engine and transaxle mount. Remove the stud and two bolts that secure the bracket to the block. Remove the mount and bracket by pulling forward.
8. Remove the transaxle mounting bracket from the transaxle. Remove the mount assembly.
9. Installation is the reverse of the removal procedure.

1986 AND LATER ELDORADO AND SEVILLE (LEFT SIDE)

1. Disconnect the negative battery cable. Remove the air cleaner assembly.
2. Remove the serpentine belt and discharge the A/C system.
3. Install engine support tool J–28467 or equivalent.
4. Remove the lower center exhaust manifold nut and top nut of the engine damper.
5. Raise the vehicle and support safely.
6. Remove the right side engine compartment splash shield and A/C splash shield.
7. Remove the engine damper. Remove the two A/C compressor brackets. Remove the A/C compressor.
8. Remove the water pipe bracket bolt.
9. Remove the engine mount bracket bolts from the engine block and cradle. Remove the engine mount and bracket through the right hand wheel well.
10. Installation is the reverse of the removal procedure.

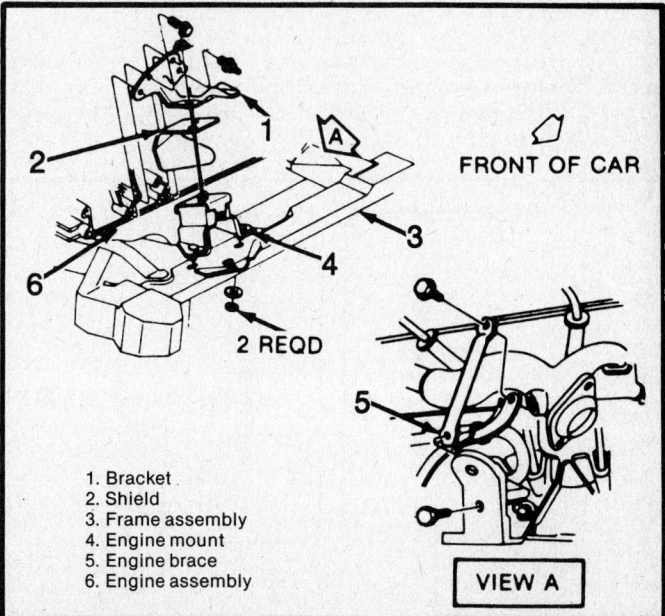

1. Bracket
2. Shield
3. Frame assembly
4. Engine mount
5. Engine brace
6. Engine assembly

VIEW A

Left side engine mount and brace—1986 and later Eldorado and Seville

8-35

SECTION 8

GENERAL MOTORS—"E" AND "K" BODY
FRONT WHEEL DRIVE CARS

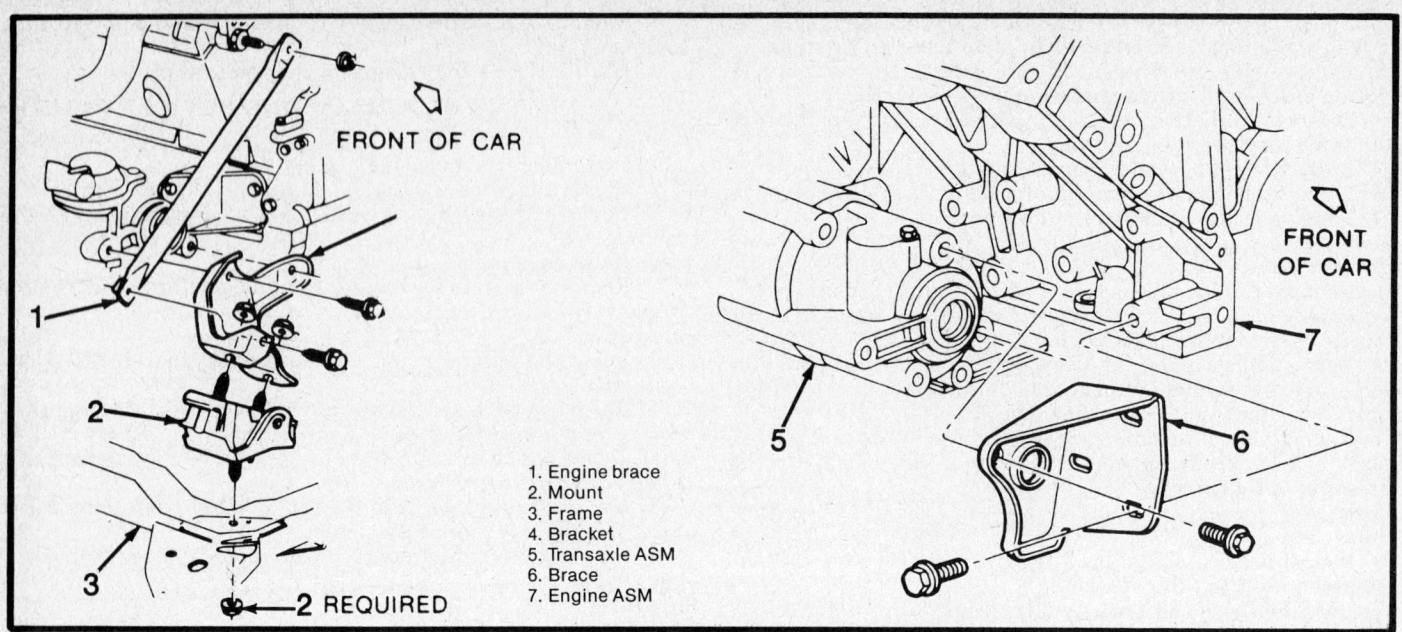

1. Engine brace
2. Mount
3. Frame
4. Bracket
5. Transaxle ASM
6. Brace
7. Engine ASM

Right side transaxle mount and engine brace—1986 and later Eldorado and Seville

Valve System

VALVE ADJUSTMENT

All engines use hydraulic lifters. Valve systems with hydraulic lifters operate with zero clearance in the valve train. The rocker arms are non-adjustable. The lifter itself will compensate if there is a lack in the system but it there is excessive play, the entire system should be checked.

VALVE LIFTERS

Removal and Installation

1. Disconnect the negative battery cable.
2. Remove the intake manifold assembly.
3. Remove the valve cover retaining bolts. Remove the valve covers. Remove the rocker arm assemblies and the push rods.
4. Using the proper valve lifter removal tool, remove the valve lifters.

5. Installation is the reverse of the removal procedure. Be sure to coat the lifters in clean engine oil before installing them.

VALVE ROCKER ASSEMBLY

Removal and Installation

1. Disconnect the negative battery cable.
2. Remove the PCV pipe and the hot air tube. Tag and disconnect any hoses and electrical leads preventing access to the valve cover bolts.
3. Remove the valve cover bolts. Remove the valve covers. Discard the old gaskets.
4. Remove the rocker arm shaft retaining bolts.
5. Remove the rocker arm shaft assembly.
6. Remove the non-reusable nylon rocker arm retainers. Remove the rocker arms.
7. Installation is the reverse of the removal procedure.

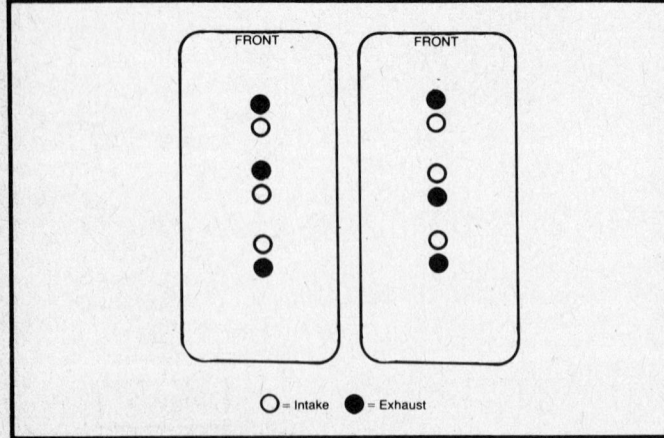

V6 valve arrangement
(© General Motors Corporation)

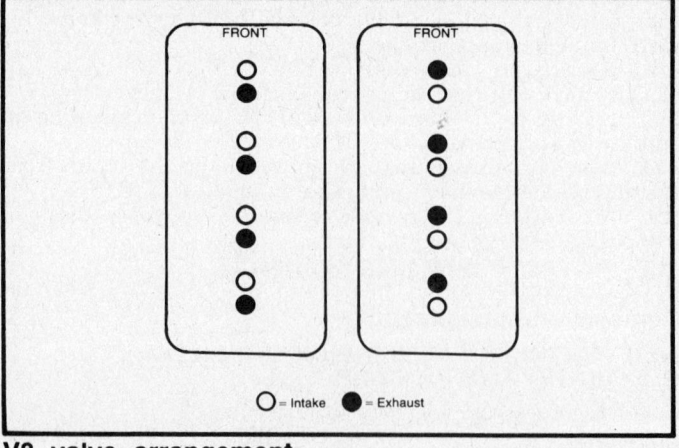

V8 valve arrangement
(© General Motors Corporation)

8-36

GENERAL MOTORS—"E" AND "K" BODY
FRONT WHEEL DRIVE CARS
SECTION 8

VALVE TIMING

Adjustments

Manufacturers recommended procedure for valve timing has not yet been established.

VALVE LIFTER BLEED DOWN

1. Before installing any removed rocker arms, rotate the engine crankshaft to a position of No. 1 cylinder being 32° before top dead center. This is a 2 in. (50 mm) counterclockwise from the 0° pointer. If only the right valve cover was removed, remove No. 1 cylinder's glow plug to determine if the position of the piston is the correct one. The compression pressure will tell you that you are in the right position.

If the left valve cover was removed, rotate the crankshaft until the No. 5 cylinder intake valve pushrod ball is 0.28 in. (7 mm) above the No. 5 cylinder exhaust valve pushrod ball.

NOTE: Use only hand wrenches to torque the rocker arm pivot nuts to avoid engine damage.

2. If removed, install the No. 5 cylinder pivot and rocker arms. Torque the nuts alternately between the intake and exhaust valves until the intake valve begins to open, then stop.
3. Install remaining rocker arms except No. 3 exhaust valve. (If this rocker arm was removed.).
4. If removed, install but do not torque No. 3 valve pivots beyond the point that the valve would be fully open. This is indicated by strong resistance while still turning the pivot retaining bolts. Going beyond this would bend the pushrod. Torque the nuts SLOWLY allowing the lifter to bleed down.
5. Finish torquing No. 5 cylinder rocker arm pivot nut SLOWLY. Do not go beyond the point that the valve would be fully open. This is indicated by strong resistance while still turning the pivot retaining bolts. Going beyond this would bend the pushrod.
6. DO NOT turn the engine crankshaft for at least 45 minutes.
7. Finish reassembling the engine as the lifters are being bled.

NOTE: Do not rotate the engine until the valve lifters have been bled down, or damage to the engine will occur.

CYLINDER HEADS

Removal and Installation

1983–1985

1. Disconnect the negative battery cable.
2. Remove the belts and pulleys to gain working clearance. If the vehicle is equipped with a diesel engine, remove the injection pump and lines.
3. Remove the A/C compressor bracket and the alternator bracket with both units attached and lay aside.
4. Remove the power steering pump and bracket and lay aside to gain working clearance.
5. Tag and remove the spark plug wires.
6. Remove the exhaust manifold bolts. Remove the exhaust manifold.
7. Remove the valve covers. Remove the rocker arm shaft assembly. Remove the push rods.
8. Remove the cylinder head bolts. Remove the cylinder heads.
9. Installation is the reverse of the removal procedure.

V6—1986 AND LATER

1. Disconnect the negative battery cable. Drain the engine coolant.
2. Remove the accessory drive belt. Relieve the fuel pressure in the fuel rail.
3. Remove the alternator.
4. Tag and disconnect the electrical connections from the intake and cylinder head. Remove the upper radiator hose.
5. Remove the air intake duct from the throttle body. Remove the vacuum connector block.
6. Remove the PCV and vapor canister vacuum line.
7. Remove the rear engine left bracket. Remove the front spark plug wiring harness.
8. Disconnect the throttle cables from the throttle body. Remove the heater hose from the water outlet.
9. Remove the fuel rail supply and return lines.
10. Remove the intake manifold.
11. For front cylinder head removal, remove the following:
    a. cooling fan.
    b. oil level indicator assembly.
    c. front exhaust manifold bolts and manifold.
12. For rear cylinder head removal, remove the following:
    a. multi pin connector from the C3I unit.
    b. heat shield to cowl screws.
    c. throttle cable bracket from the cylinder.
    d. belt tensioner/power steering pump bracket.
13. Raise the vehicle and support safely.
14. Remove the heater tube from the manifold studs. Remove the exhaust manifold. Lower vehicle.
15. Remove the valve covers, Remove the rocker arms.
16. Remove the cylinder head bolts. Remove the cylinder head.
17. Installation is the reverse of the removal procedure.

V8—1986 AND LATER (RIGHT HAND)

1. Disconnect the negative battery cable. Drain the engine coolant.
2. Remove the necessary components in order to gain access to the rocker arm covers. Remove the rocker arm covers.
3. Remove the intake manifold. Remove the right hand exhaust manifold.
4. Remove the engine lift bracket and the air injection reaction (AIR) bracket.
5. Remove the cylinder head bolts. Remove the cylinder head.
6. Installation is the reverse of the removal procedure.

V8—1986 AND LATER (LEFT HAND)

1. Disconnect the negative battery cable. Drain the engine coolant.
2. Remove the necessary components in order to gain access to the rocker arm covers. Remove the rocker arm covers.
3. Remove the intake manifold. Remove the left hand exhaust manifold.
4. Remove the engine lift bracket and the dipstick tube.
5. Reposition the AIR bracket in order to gain working clearance.
6. Remove the ten cylinder head bolts. Remove the cylinder head.
7. Installation is the reverse of the removal procedure.

CAMSHAFT

Removal and Installation

V6 ENGINE—1983–1985

1. Disconnect the negative battery cable.
2. Remove the intake manifold.
3. Remove the valve covers, rocker arm shaft assemblies, push rods and valve lifters.
4. Drain the cooling system. Remove the radiator.
5. Remove the A/C compressor if equipped, and lay aside.

8–37

SECTION 8

GENERAL MOTORS—"E" AND "K" BODY
FRONT WHEEL DRIVE CARS

V8 cylinder head bolt tightening sequence
(© General Motors Corporation)

6. Remove the belts and pulleys. Remove the crankshaft balancer as an assembly.
7. Remove the timing chain cover. Remove the timing chain gears.
8. Remove the camshaft from the engine.
9. Installation is the reverse of the removal procedure.

V8 ENGINE—1983–1985

1. Disconnect the negative battery cable.
2. Drain the cooling system. Remove the upper radiator support. Remove the upper radiator hose from the water outlet.
3. Remove the transmission cooler lines from the radiator. Remove the fan shroud, fan and radiator.
4. Remove the air cleaner and the throttle cable from the carburetor.
5. Remove the fuel pump. Remove the alternator assembly.
6. Remove the power steering pump bracket with the pump attached to gain access.
7. If the vehicle is equipped with air conditioning, remove the air conditioner compressor assembly from its bracket and lay aside with the lines still attached.
8. Tag and disconnect all electrical and vacuum connections.
9. Remove the distributor with the cap and wiring intact.
10. Remove the crankshaft pulley and hub.
11. Remove the valve covers and the front engine cover.
12. Remove the intake manifold bolts. Remove the intake manifold.
13. Remove the valve assembly. Remove the oil slinger.
14. Remove the camshaft gear timing chain. Remove the camshaft.

NOTE: In order to gain more working room, the condenser can be removed by first discharging the A/C system, then disconnect the high pressure lines and remove the condenser assembly. The grille can also be removed at this time.

15. Installation is the reverse of the removal procedure. Adjust the fan and accessory drive belt.

V6 AND V8—1986 AND LATER

1. Disconnect the negative battery cable.

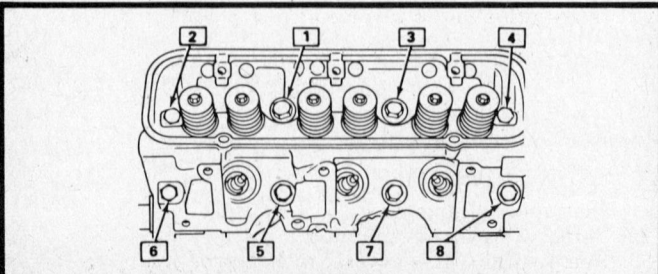

V6 cylinder head bolt tightening sequence
(© General Motors Corporation)

2. Remove the engine assembly as previously outlined.
3. Remove the intake manifold.
4. Remove the valve covers. Remove the rocker arms, pushrods and lifters.
5. Remove the balancer assembly if necessary in order to gain working clearance.
6. Remove the timing chain cover, chain and sprockets.
7. Slide the camshaft forward until it is out of the engine.
8. Installation is the reverse of the removal procedure.

TIMING CASE COVER

Removal and Installation
1983–1985 ENGINES

1. Drain radiator.
2. Disconnect upper and lower radiator hose and heater return hose.
3. Remove fan, fan pulleys and belt(s).
4. Remove fan driving pulley (crankshaft).
5. Disconnect fuel lines and remove fuel pump.
6. Remove generator and brackets.
7. Remove distributor. If timing chain and sprockets are not going to be disturbed, note position of distributor rotor for reinstallation in same position.
8. Loosen the slide front clamp on thermostat by-pass hose rearward.
9. Remove the harmonic balancer.
10. Remove bolts attaching timing chain cover to cylinder block. Remove two oil pan to timing chain cover bolts. Remove timing chain cover assembly and gasket.
11. Installation is the reverse of the removal procedure.

V6–1986 AND LATER

1. Disconnect the negative battery cable. Drain the engine coolant. Remove the accessory drive belt.
2. Install engine support tool J–28467 or equivalent. Remove the lower radiator hose from the water pump. Remove the water pump bolts and remove the water pump.
3. Raise the vehicle and support safely. Remove the wheel and tire assembly. Remove the inner fender splash shields.
4. Remove the crankshaft balancer bolt and slide the balancer forward. Remove the crankshaft sensor bolts and sensor.
5. Remove the engine vibration damper. Remove the rear engine mount nut.
6. Raise the engine so that the crankshaft balancer clears the frame. Remove the crankshaft balancer.
7. Remove the A/C compressor bracket.
8. Remove the cam sensor. Tag and disconnect the electrical connections from the oil pressure sender.
9. Remove the oil filter adapter.
10. Remove the front cover retaining bolts. Remove the front engine cover.
11. Installation is the reverse of the removal procedure.

V8–1986 AND LATER

1. Disconnect the negative battery cable. Drain the engine coolant.
2. Remove the right hand cross car brace. Remove the coolant reservoir.
3. Remove the A.I.R. air filter and bracket.
4. Remove the accessory drive belt. Remove the idler pulley.
5. Remove the water pump assembly.
6. Raise the vehicle and support safely.
7. Remove the crankshaft pulley and hub assembly.
8. Remove the front cover retaining bolts. Remove the front cover.
9. Installation is the reverse of the removal procedure.

8–38

GENERAL MOTORS—"E" AND "K" BODY
FRONT WHEEL DRIVE CARS
SECTION 8

PISTON POSITIONING

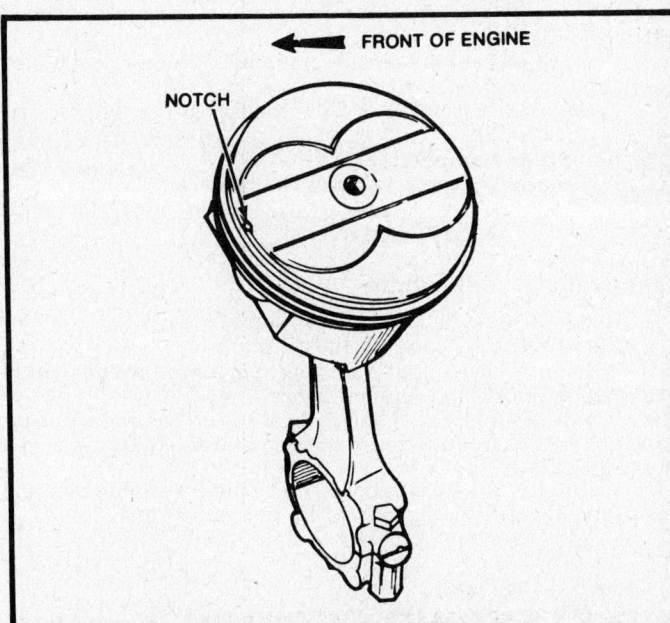

On all engines, the piston assemblies are installed with the notch facing forward
(© General Motors Corporation)

FRONT COVER OIL SEAL

Removal and Installation

1. Remove crankshaft pulley and hub.
2. Using tool J–1859–03 and J–23129, remove oil seal.
3. Installation is the reverse of the removal procedure. Lubricate the new oil seal with engine oil.

TIMING CHAIN

Removal and Installation

1. Remove oil slinger from crankshaft.
2. Rotate the engine until the timing marks line up.
3. Remove screw securing camshaft sprocket to camshaft.
4. Remove camshaft and crankshaft sprocket with chain attached.
5. Installation is the reverse of the removal procedure.

Lubrication

OIL PAN

Removal and Installation

TORONADO V8

1. Disconnect the negative battery cable.
2. Remove the shroud from the upper radiator support. Remove the final drive-to-transmission bolts.
3. Raise the front of the vehicle and support safely.
4. Disconnect the idler and the pitman arms from the relay rod.
5. Remove the bolts attaching the drive axle to the output shaft on the right side and remove the output shaft. Disconnect the right and left side drive axles from their respective output shafts.
6. Disconnect the battery cable bracket from the output shaft support and then disconnect the support itself from the engine block.
7. Remove the remaining final drive-to-transmission bolts, position a transmission jack under the final drive and remove the final drive.
8. Disconnect the starter wiring and remove the starter, remove the splash shield.
9. Drain the oil, remove the oil pan bolts and remove the oil pan.
10. Installation is in the reverse order of removal. Use sealer on both sides of the new gasket and tighten the oil pan bolts to 10 ft. lbs.

ELDORADO AND TORONADO V6

1. Drain the oil pan.
2. Remove the oil pan bolts and remove the oil pan.
3. On 1986 and later Eldorado, remove the two flywheel covers and reposition the exhaust cross under pipe.
4. Clean gasket surface of pan and block and use new gasket or sealer.

SEVILLE

1. Disconnect the negative battery cable.
2. Raise the car on a hoist.
3. Remove the frame brace front attaching bolts from both sides and pivot the braces outward.
4. Remove the securing bolts from the drive axle to the output shaft on both sides. Separate the flanges of the output shaft and drive axles to gain clearance for removal with the shafts attached.
5. Remove the battery cable-to-output shaft retaining screws and remove the screws securing the support to the engine block.
6. Remove the final drive-to-transmission screw that holds the front of the shield. Remove the shield.
7. Remove the remaining final drive-to-transmission bolts.
8. Remove the final support bracket-to-engine block screw.
9. Using a puller, separate the steering linkage intermediate shaft from the pitman arm and the idler arm. Push the linkage toward the front of the car.
10. With the aid of a helper, slide the final drive assembly forward, off the transmission splined shaft, and remove the unit with the output shaft attached. Do not use the shafts as handles, as damage to the seals will occur.
11. Remove the battery cable and the wiring harness connectors from the starter solenoid BAT terminal.
12. Remove the harness connector from the solenoid S terminal.
13. Remove the harness from the clip on the solenoid and position it out of the way.
14. Remove the starter motor attaching bolts and remove the starter.
15. Drain the engine oil.
16. Remove the oil pan attaching screws and remove the oil pan.
17. Reverse to install. Torque the oil pan screws to 10 ft. lbs. When installing the final drive, use the following torque values: final drive-to-transmission bolts—30 ft. lbs.; front support bracket-to-block—50 ft. lbs.; output shaft-to-axle—60 ft. lbs.; steering linkage intermediate shaft-to-pitman arm—60 ft. lbs.

RIVIERA

1. Disconnect negative battery cable.
2. Remove the top three final drive to transmission bolts.
3. Raise and suitably support car.
4. Disconnect two frame braces.
5. disconnect idler arm and pitman arm from relay rod.
6. Disconnect drive axles from output shafts.
7. Disconnect battery cable bracket from output shaft support.

SECTION 8

GENERAL MOTORS—"E" AND "K" BODY
FRONT WHEEL DRIVE CARS

8. Disconnect output shaft support from the engine block.
9. Remove three final drive to transmission bolts.
10. Install transmission jack and remove final drive.
11. Clean gasket material from mating surfaces.
12. Remove splash shield.
13. Disconnect starter wires.
14. Remove starter.
15. Drain oil pan.
16. Remove oil pan bolts and pan.
17. Installation is the reverse of removal. Tighten pan bolts to 10 ft. lbs.

OIL PUMP

Removal and Installation

ALL MODELS EXCEPT 1986 AND LATER V6

1. Raise the vehicle and support safely.
2. Drain the oil pan.
3. Remove the oil pan bolts. Remove the oil pan.
4. Remove the oil pump bolts. Remove the oil pump.
5. Installation is the reverse of the removal procedure.

1986 AND LATER V6

1. Disconnect the negative battery cable.
2. Remove the front cover from the engine as outlined earlier.
3. Remove the engine oil filter adapter, pressure regulator valve and spring.
4. Remove the oil pump cover attaching bolts. Remove the cover.
5. Remove the oil pump gears.
6. Installation is the reverse of the removal procedure.

REAR MAIN OIL SEAL

Removal and Installation

1. Raise the vehicle and support safely.
2. Remove the oil pan and the oil pump.
3. Loosen the bolts that hold the rear main bearing cap to the cylinder block and remove the cap.
4. Rotate the upper seal half by pushing on one end while rotating the crankshaft. Remove the upper seal half from the cylinder block.
5. Installation is accomplished by using a suitable tool and installing the seal with the seal lip facing forward.

FRONT SUSPENSION AND STEERING SECTION

For Front Suspension Services Refer to Unit Repair Section. For Steering Gear Overhaul Refer to Unit Repair Section.

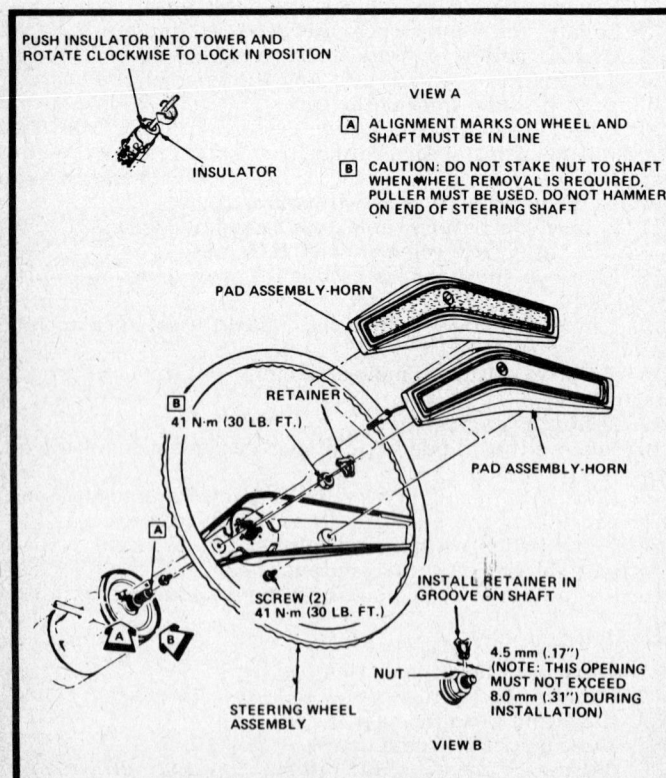

Standard steering wheel—typical
(© General Motors Corporation)

STEERING WHEEL

Removal and Installation

EXCEPT TILT AND TELESCOPE COLUMN

1. Disconnect the negative battery cable. Unplug the horn wire connector from the steering column.
2. On cars with a standard wheel or optional wood-rim wheel, pull off the cap, remove the three screws and the contact, insulator, and spring. On cars with the bar-type horn actuator, remove the screws securing the actuator from the underside of the steering wheel, unhook the lead connector plug, and remove the actuator assembly.
3. Loosen the steering wheel nut.
4. Apply the steering wheel puller and pull the wheel up to the nut. Now remove the puller, nut and steering wheel.

― CAUTION ―
Don't pound on the steering wheel in either direction or the collapsible steering column could collapse, requiring replacement.

On installation:

NOTE: Location marks are provided on the steering wheel an shaft to simplify proper indexing at the time of installation.

1. Install wheel with the location mark aligned with that of the shaft.
2. Install the wheel nut and torque to 30 ft. lbs.
3. Reinstall horn button or actuator assembly.

TILT AND TELESCOPE COLUMN

1. Disconnect the negative battery cable.
2. Remove the attaching screws and lift the pad from the column.
3. Disconnect the horn wire by pushing in the connector and turning it conterclockwise.
4. Push the locking lever counterclockwise until full release is obtained.

GENERAL MOTORS—"E" AND "K" BODY
FRONT WHEEL DRIVE CARS
SECTION 8

5. Mark the lock plate-to-locking lever position and remove the plate and lever.
6. Remove the steering wheel retaining nut and remove the wheel with a puller.
7. Install a $^5/_{16}$ in. x 18 set screw into the upper shaft at the fully extended position and lock it.
8. Install the steering wheel, observing the aligning mark on the hub and the slash mark on the end of the shaft. Make certain that the unattached end of the horn upper contact assembly is seated flush against the top of the horn contact carrier button.
9. Install the nut on the upper steering shaft and torque to 30 ft. lbs.
10. Remove the set screw installed in Step 7.
11. Install the plate assembly finger tight.
12. Position the locking lever in the vertical position and move it counterclockwise until the holes in the plate align with the holes in the lever. Install the attaching screws.
13. Align the pad assembly with the holes in the steering wheel and install the retaining screws.
14. Connect the battery.
15. Make certain that the locking lever securely locks the wheel travel and that the wheel travel is free in the unlocked position.

STEERING GEAR
Removal and Installation

1. Position a fluid catch pan under the steering gear, disconnect the pressure and return lines from the steering gear assembly. Plug the opening to prevent entrance of dirt.
2. If equipped, disconnect the stone shield from the return pipe.
3. Remove the pinch bolt from the flex coupling and disconnect the coupling from the gear.
4. Raise the vehicle and support safely.
5. Remove the pitman arm nut and washer. Remove the pitman arm from the sector shaft with a pitman arm puller tool.
6. Remove the three retaining bolts and washer holding the steering gear to the side rail. Lower the gear assembly from the vehicle.
7. The installation is the reverse of the removal procedure. Tighten the pitman arm nut to 185 ft. lbs., the three mounting bolts to 70 ft. lbs. and the flex coupling pinch bolt to 30 ft. lbs.

Adjustment (On Car)

1. Raise the vehicle and support safely.
2. Turn the steering linkage until the inner tie rod end stud is under the upper control arm bolt.
3. Place a socket on the end of the upper control bolt. Measure from the socket to the center of the inner tie rod end stud on both sides.
4. If the difference between the right and left dimension is more than $^1/_{16}$ in. (2 mm), adjust the linkage at the idler arm.

RACK AND PINION ASSEMBLY
Removal and Installation

1. Disconnect the negative battery cable.
2. Raise the vehicle and support safely.
3. Remove both front tire and wheel assemblies.
4. Remove the intermediate shaft lower pinch bolt.
5. Remove the tie rod ends from the steering knuckles.
6. Remove the line retainer. Remove the outlet and pressure hose.
7. Tag and disconnect the electrical connection at the idle speed power steering switch.

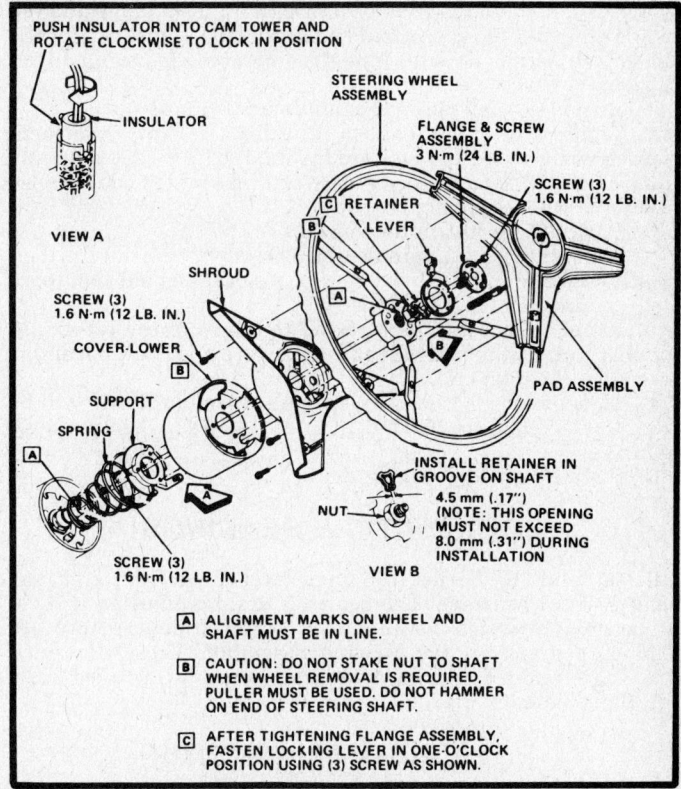

Tilt and telescopic steering wheel—typical
(© General Motors Corporation)

8. Remove the rack and pinion assembly retaining bolts. Remove the rack and pinion assembly.
9. Installation is the reverse of the removal procedure.

FRONT WHEEL BEARINGS
Adjustment
TAPERED ROLLER BEARINGS

The proper functioning of the front suspension cannot be maintained unless the front wheel tapered roller bearings are cor-

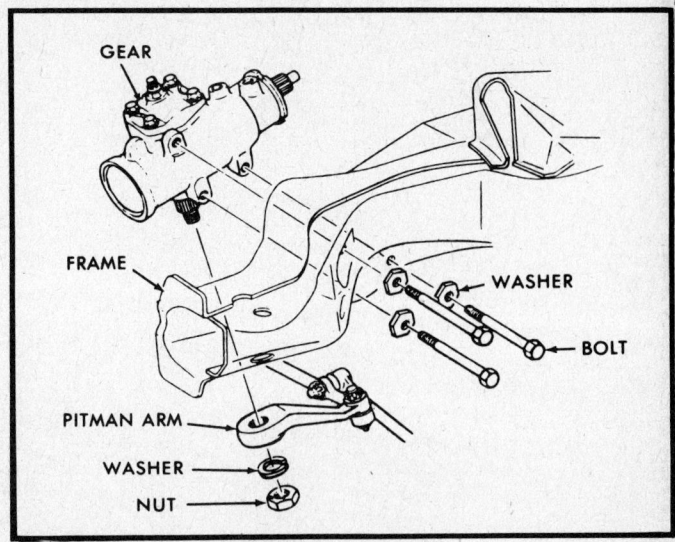

Steering gear installation—typical
(© General Motors Corporation)

8-41

SECTION 8

GENERAL MOTORS—"E" AND "K" BODY
FRONT WHEEL DRIVE CARS

rectly adjusted. Cones must be a slip fit on the spindle and the inside diameter of cones should be lubricated to insure that the cones will creep. Spindle nut must be a free-running fit on threads.

1. Remove cotter pin from spindle and spindle nut.
2. Tighten the spindle nut to 12 ft. lbs. (16 Nm) while turning the wheel assembly forward by hand to fully seat the bearings. This will remove any grease or burrs which could cause excessive wheel bearing play later.
3. Back off the nut to the "just loose" position.
4. Hand tighten the spindle nut. Loosen spindle nut until either hole in the spindle lines up with a slot in the nut (not more than ½ flat).
5. Install new cotter pins. Bend the ends of the cotter pin against nut. Cut off extra length to ensure ends will not interfere with the dust cap.
6. Measure the looseness in the hub assembly. There will be from 0.001–0.005 in. (0.03–0.13 mm) end play when properly adjusted.
7. Install dust cap on hub.

BOLT ON-TYPE BEARINGS

All "E" and "K" Series, 1983 and later, have front and rear sealed wheel bearings. The bearings are pre-adjusted and require no lubrication maintenance or adjustment. There are darkened areas on the bearing assembly. These darkened areas are from a heat treatment process and do not need bearing replacement.

POWER STEERING PUMP

Removal and Installation

NOTE: On some models, it may be necessary to remove the alternator with its adjusting bracket.

V6 ENGINE

1. Disconnect the pressure and return lines from the pump and plug all openings.
2. Loosen the two adjusting screws on the front bracket and one nut on the rear bracket.
3. Remove the power steering pump drive belt and remove the two adjusting screws securing the mounting bracket at the front.
4. Remove one adjusting nut securing the pump to the rear mounting bracket.
5. Remove the pivot bolt and power steering pump assembly with bracket.
6. The installation is the reverse of the removal procedure. Adjust the drive belt tension.

V8 ENGINE

1. Loosen the A/C mounting bracket and vacuum pump bracket. Remove the belts from the pulley.
2. Disconnect the pressure and return lines and plug all openings.
3. Remove two bolts securing the pump to the engine block, through the access holes in the drive pulley. Remove the pump assembly from the vehicle.
4. Install the pump in the reverse order of its removal. Adjust the drive belt.

STEERING COLUMN

Removal and Installation

1983–1985

NOTE: Handle the steering column very carefully. Rapping on the end of it or leaning on it could shear off the inserts which allow the column to collapse in a crash.

1. Disconnect the negative battery cable.
2. Center the steering wheel and remove the upper coupling pinch bolt and nut.
3. Disconnect the transmission shift linkage at the lower shift lever.
4. Remove the steering column lower cover from the instrument panel, exposing the upper support nuts or bolts.
5. Disconnect the turn signal wiring connector. If equipped with cruise control, disconnect the harness.
6. Remove the screw securing the shift cable to the shift bowl.

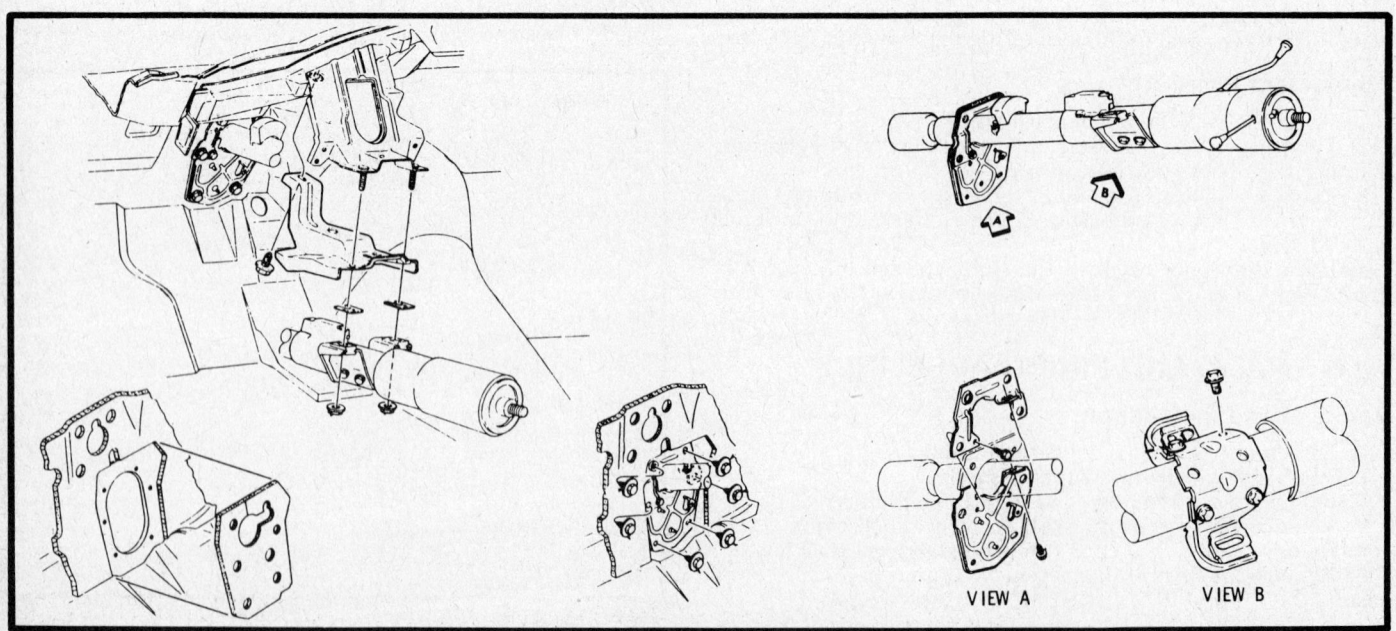

Toronado steering column mounting (© General Motors Corporation)

GENERAL MOTORS—"E" AND "K" BODY
FRONT WHEEL DRIVE CARS

7. Loosen two nuts or bolts at the steering column upper support.

CAUTION
Do not completely remove the upper support nuts or bolts as the steering column could bend under its own weight.

8. Move the rubber carpet seal up the steering column as far as possible and position the carpet to gain access to the toe plate.
9. Remove the screws retaining the toe plate to the floor pan.

NOTE: Seville and Eldorado, remove the lower support bracket assembly before the upper attachment screws are removed, as damage to the column may occur.

Remove the two nuts or bolts at the upper column bracket, disconnect the remaining electrical connectors and vacuum connectors while supporting the column.

10. Carefully pull the steering column up and out of the vehicle. If the shaft hangs up in the upper coupling, secure the upper mounting bracket and free the coupling from the steering shaft. Remove the column assembly.
11. Reverse the removal procedure to install the steering column in the vehicle.
12. A clearance of $5/16$ in. should exist between the shaft and the upper coupling when the installation is complete or lower steering column bearing damage could result.

NOTE: When installing use only the specified hardware. Over-length bolts could prevent the column from properly collapsing in a crash.

1986 AND LATER
1. Disconnect the negative battery cable.
2. Remove the left side sound absorber from the dash area.
3. Remove the steering column trim cover.

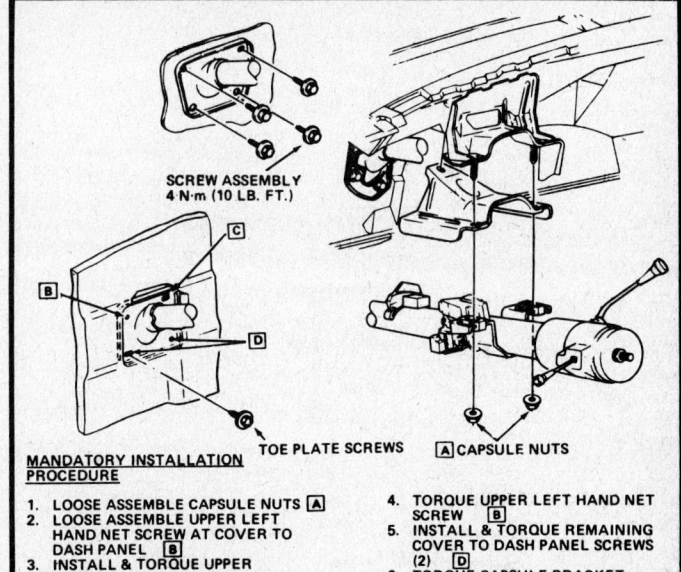

Typical steering column mounting—except Toronado (© General Motors Corporation)

4. Tag and disconnect the electrical connectors from the steering column. Remove the wiring harness protector.
5. Remove the park lock cable from the ignition switch if equipped.
6. Remove the lower column mounting bolts. Remove the pinch bolt from the Toronado.
7. Remove the shift linkage at the column.
8. Remove the column assembly from the vehicle.
9. Installation is the reverse of the removal procedure.

BRAKE SECTION

For Brake Service Refer to Unit Repair Section.

MASTER CYLINDER

Removal and Installation

NOTE: It is possible to remove the master cylinder unit without removing the power booster from the vehicle.

1. Disconnect and plug the front and rear brake lines at the master cylinder.
2. Remove the two securing nuts which hold the master cylinder to the power booster.
3. Remove the master cylinder.
4. To install, reverse the removal procedure. Bleed the hydraulic system.

VACUUM BOOSTER UNIT

Removal and Installation

1. Remove any vacuum from the booster by depressing the bake pedal several times with the engine turned off.
2. Disconnect the front and rear brake outlet lines and electrical connector from the combination valve. Plug the lines and outlets to prevent entry of dirt.
3. Remove the two attaching nuts securing the master cylinder to the booster. Remove the master cylinder and combination valve assembly from the car.
4. Disconnect the booster vacuum hose from the check valve.

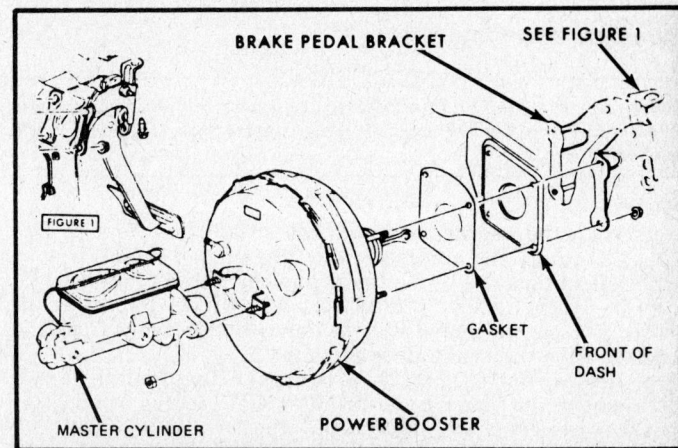

Vacuum power brake unit mounting—typical
(© General Motors Corporation)

SECTION 8
GENERAL MOTORS—"E" AND "K" BODY
FRONT WHEEL DRIVE CARS

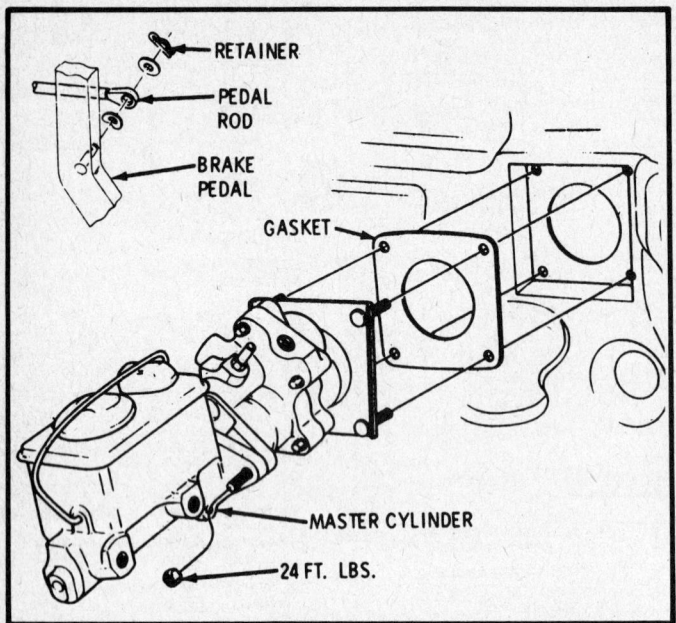

Hydro-boost power brake unit mounting—typical
(© General Motors Corporation)

5. From under the instrument panel, remove the clip and washer from the brake pedal push rod pin. Do not remove the push rod from the brake pedal assembly yet.
6. Remove the two screws retaining the twilight sentinel amplifier, if so equipped, to the brake pedal bracket. Lower the amplifier and discard the connectors.
7. Remove the four booster-to-cowl retaining nuts and discard the nuts. slide the studs through the cowl. Move the booster toward the engine and keep the mounting surface parallel to the cowl. slide the push rod from the brake pedal pin and remove the booster from the car. Do not pry the push rod from the pedal as damage to the booster could result.
8. Install the booster in the reverse order of removal, suing new attaching nuts. tighten the booster-to-cowl nuts to 1 ft. lbs., and the master cylinder-to-booster nuts to 20 ft. lbs.
9. Bleed the brake hydraulic system. Start the engine and check the brake vacuum system for leaks and operation.

HYDRO-BOOST POWER BRAKE UNIT
Removal and Installation

CAUTION

Power steering fluid and brake fluid are incompatible. If brake seals contact steering fluid or steering seals contact brake fluid, the seals will be raised.

1. With the engine off, pump the brake pedal four or five times to empty the accumulator of pressurized fluid.
2. Disconnect the brake lines from the master cylinder and cap the lines. Remove the two master cylinder-to-booster attaching nuts and move the master cylinder away from the booster with the brake lines attached.
3. Remove and plug the three hydraulic lines from the booster. Remove the washer and retainer that secures the booster pedal rod to the brake pedal arm.

NOTE: To avoid booster damage, do not pry the pedal rod off the pedal arm.

4. Remove the four nuts holding the booster to the firewall.
5. Loosen the booster from the firewall and move the booster pedal rod inboard until it disconnects from the brake pedal arm. Remove the spring washer from the brake pedal arm and remove the booster.
6. To install, reverse the removal procedure. Tighten the booster mounting nuts to 30 ft. lbs., and the master cylinder to booster mounting nus to 20 ft. lbs. Bleed the Hyrdo-boost system as explained in the Brakes Unit Repair Section.

PARKING BRAKE

Adjustment—1983–1985
REAR DRUM BRAKES

NOTE: Make certain that the rear brakes are properly adjusted before adjusting the parking brake.

1. Make a check of the parking brake linkage for the free movement of all the cables. Lubricate, if necessary.
2. Depress the parking brake pedal $1\frac{1}{2}$ in.
3. Raise the rear wheels off the ground.
4. While holding the cable stud to keep it from turning, tighten the equalizer nut until a light drag is felt on either wheel when they are spun in the forward direction.

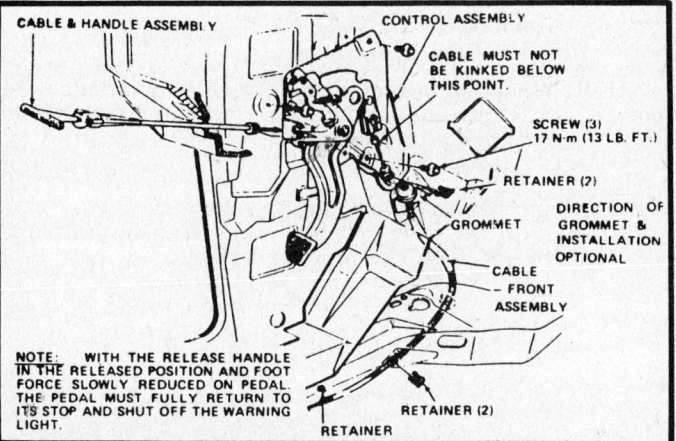

Typical parking brake
(© General Motors Corporation)

5. When the parking brake is released there should be no brake shoe drag.

REAR DISC BRAKES

1. Lubricate the parking brake cables at the underbody rub points, and at the equalizer hooks on Seville.
2. Make sure the parking brake pedal is in the fully released position.
3. Raise the rear wheels.
4. Hold the brake cable stud from turning and tightening the equalizer nut until the cable slack is removed.
5. Make sure the caliper levels are against the stops on the caliper housing after tightening the equalizer nut.
6. If the levers are off the stops, loosen the cable until the levers return to stops.
7. Operate the parking brake several times to check the adjustment.
8. Lower the car.

NOTE: The levers must be on the caliper stops after adjustment. Back off the adjuster if necessary.

GENERAL MOTORS—"E" AND "K" BODY
FRONT WHEEL DRIVE CARS
SECTION 8

Adjustment—1986 and Later

1. Disconnect the negative battery cable. Raise the vehicle and support safely.
2. Inspect the parking brake levers on the rear calipers. Levers should be against the stops on the rear calipers. If levers are not against stops correct by checking for binding in the rear brake cables.
3. Tighten the parking brake cable at the adjuster until one of the levers begins to move off the stop.
4. Loosen the adjuster until the lever which moved off the stop is again resting on the stop. Both levers should be resting on the caliper stops after this step.
5. Operate the parking brake several times to check for adjustment. A firm pedal should be obtained by pumping the pedal less than 3 1/2 full strokes.
6. Check both levers. Both levers must be resting on the stops after adjustment is made.

PARKING BRAKE CABLE

Removal and Installation

1. Release the parking brake lever. Remove the tension spring retainer clip. Remove the front cable form the cable connector at the pedal assembly.
2. Raise the vehicle and support safely.
3. Loosen the equalizer nut until the cable tension is removed. Remove the cable fro the equalizer.
4. Remove the clips that hold the parking brake cable to the rear crossmember and at each caliper support plate.

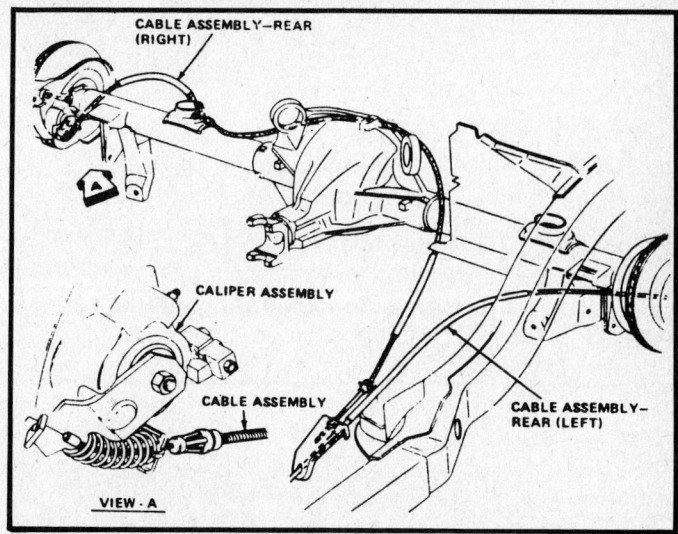

Parking brake cable used with rear disc brakes
(© General Motors Corporation)

5. Remove the cable ends from the parking brake actuator. Remove the control arm hooks and the conduit from the exhaust hanger clip.
6. Installation is the reverse of the removal procedure. Adjust the parking brake as required.

TRANSAXLE AND DRIVESHAFT SECTION

For Overhaul Procedures Refer to Unit Repair Section.

AUTOMATIC TRANSAXLE

Linkage Adjustment

1. Move the shift lever to the neutral position.
2. Place the transaxle lever in the neutral detent.
3. Attach the shift cable to the pin and tighten the retaining nut.
4. On 1983 and later vehicles, assemble the bushing, retainer an shift cable then tighten the attaching nut.

SHIFT INDICATOR

Removal and Installation

1. Disconnect the negative battery cable.
2. Remove the screws holding the instrument cluster trim plate to the instrument panel base. Remove the instrument cluster trim plate.
3. Remove the shift indicator clip. Remove the shift indicator.
4. Installation is the reverse of the removal procedure.

AUTOMATIC TRANSAXLE ASSEMBLY

Removal

1983–85—ALL MODELS EXCEPT BUICK TURBO V6

1. Open hood and disconnect negative battery cable (two cables on diesels).
2. Disconnect the speedometer cable at the transmission. Remove transmission oil dipstick tube.
3. Remove the air cleaner.
4. Disconnect the transmission throttle valve (TV/detent) cable at its upper end. On 400 transmissions, disconnect the linkage by removing one nut from shaft on left side of transmission.
5. Safely support the engine unit from underneath, or install an engine holding fixture between the cowl and radiator support.
6. Remove the top and two upper left final drive to transmission bolts.
7. Remove the remaining accessible engine-to-transmission bolts.
8. Raise the vehicle and support safely.
9. Remove the starter assembly.
10. Disconnect the T.C.C. connector.
11. Disconnect the transmission oil cooler lines and plug the openings.

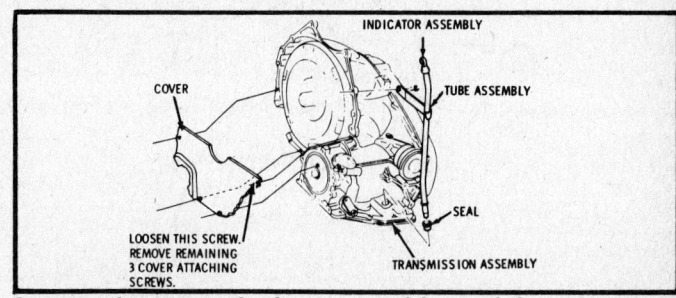

Automatic transmission assembly and front cover —THM 325 shown
(© General Motors Corporation)

8-45

SECTION 8

GENERAL MOTORS—"E" AND "K" BODY
FRONT WHEEL DRIVE CARS

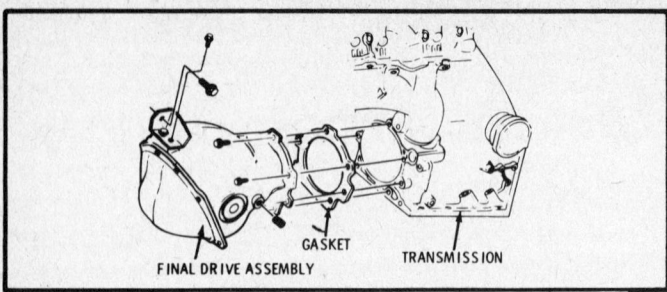

Final drive to transmission mounting—THM 425 shown (© General Motors Corporation)

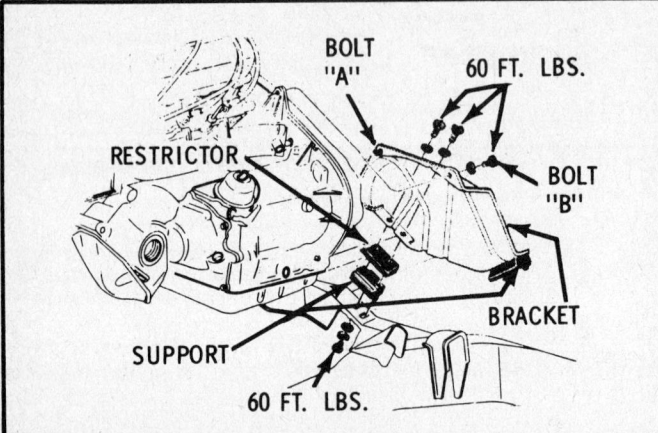

Toronado transmission mount
(© General Motors Corporation)

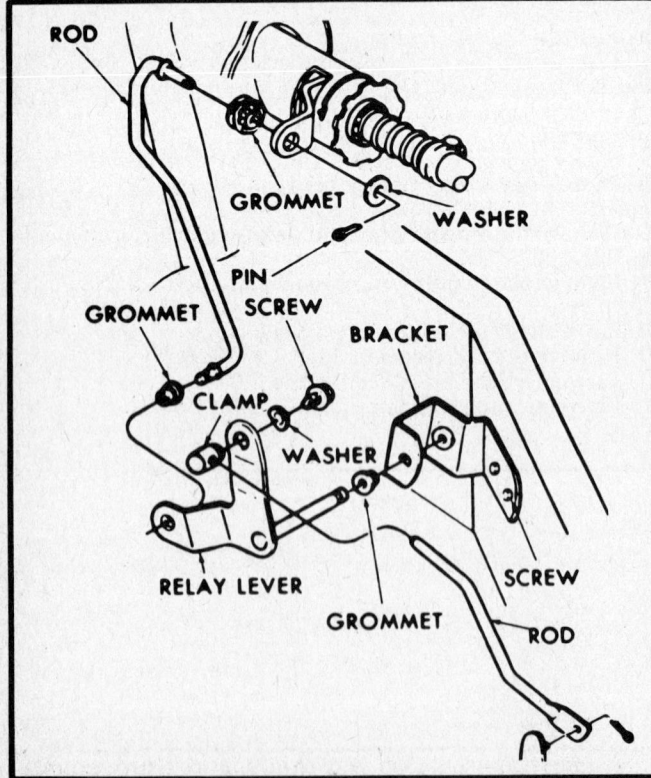

Shift linkage components—Eldorado and Seville
(© General Motors Corporation)

12. Remove the flywheel inspection cover (loosen top left bolt). Matchmark the flywheel-to-converter relationship for later assembly.
13. On V8s, disconnect the exhaust "Y" pipe connection to the left exhaust pipe. On all, disconnect the right exhaust pipe at the manifold. On gasoline cars, disconnect the catalytic converter hanger bolts (2). On all, lower the exhaust system about 5 inches and support the system.
14. Remove the four bolts holding the second frame crossmember.
15. Position a hydraulic floor jack underneath the transmission, with a wooden block on the jack pad to protect the transmission cases. Jack up the transmission slightly.
16. Remove the three remaining final drive to transmission bolts.
17. Remove the converter-to-flywheel bolts.
18. Disconnect the shift linkage to the transmission.
19. Remove the final drive support bracket bolt.
20. Remove the right transmission mount (through bolt and three bracket bolts).
21. Remove the left transmission mount (through bolts and three bracket bolts).
22. Remove the left transmission mount through the bolt. Remove the lower bracket-to-transmission bolt. Raise the transmission assembly about two inches for access to the two remaining upper bracket-to-transmission bolts. Remove the remaining transmission-to-engine bolt.
23. Carefully lower the transmission unit while disengaging the final drive.
24. Install a C-clamp or converter holding clamp in front of the torque converter (attached to the bell housing) to hold the converter in place. Remove the transmission from the car.

BUICK TURBO V6

Removal procedures for the Turbo V6 is the same as the other models, except that the turbocharger unit must be removed from engine early in the removal procedure.

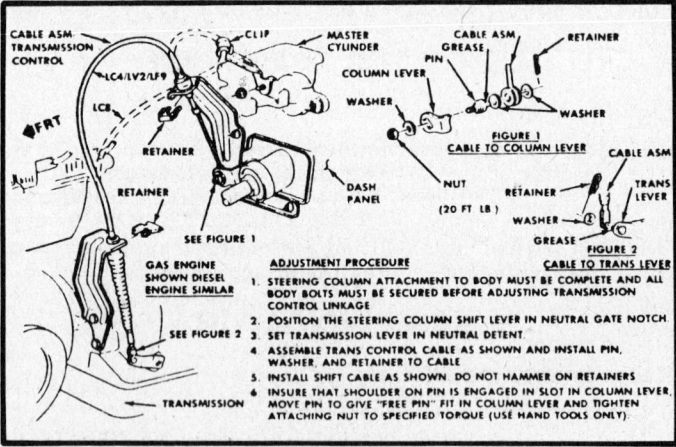

Riviera shift control adjustment
(© General Motors Corporation)

Installation
1983–85 ALL MODELS

To install the transmission, reverse the removal procedure. Always replace the final drive-to-transmission gasket. Use care when engaging the final drive-to-transmission splines—make sure the final drive-to-transmission mounting faces are in alignment with each other. After the splines are engaged, loosely install the two final drive-to-transmission lower attaching bolts. You can save time here by installing two engine-to-transmission bolts from above first to aid alignment.
After the final drive and transmission are mated align the

GENERAL MOTORS—"E" AND "K" BODY
FRONT WHEEL DRIVE CARS
SECTION 8

transmission with the engine and install the remaining attaching bolts. Before the flywheel-to-converter bolts, make sure the weld nuts on the converter are flush with the flywheel and that the converter rotates freely by hand in this position. Then hand start all three bolts and tighten finger tight. This will insure proper converter alignment. Torque the transmission-to-engine bolts to 35 ft. lbs., the final drive-to-transmission bolts to 30 ft. lbs., and the final drive support bracket to final drive bolts to 35 ft. lbs.

REMOVAL AND INSTALLATION
1986 AND LATER

1. Disconnect the negative battery cable. Remove the air cleaner assembly and T.V. cable.
2. Remove the cruise control servo and bracket assembly if equipped. Tag and disconnect the electrical connections from the distributor assembly, oil pressure sender and transaxle.
3. Remove the engine cooling line bracket. Remove the shift linkage bracket from the transaxle.
4. Remove the fuel line bracket and neutral safety switch. Remove the vacuum modulator.
5. Remove the oil cooler line bracket and the four bellhousing bolts from the top of the transaxle. Remove the A.I.R. crossover pipe fitting and reposition the pipe, radiator hose bracket and transaxle mount to bracket nuts. Install a suitable engine support fixture.
6. Raise the vehicle and support safely. Remove both front tire and wheel assemblies.
7. Remove the stabilizer link bolts, ball joint cotter pins and nuts. Remove the ball joints from the steering knuckles. Remove the A/C splash shield if equipped.
8. Remove the A.I.R pipe end hose connections and rear mounting clip. Remove the vacuum hoses and the wire loom from the clips.
9. Remove the engine mount and dampner to cradle attachments, transaxle mount to cradle attachments and the clip to transaxle bracket. Lower the vehicle low enough to raise the transaxle two inches.
10. Raise the vehicle and support safely. Remove the right front and left rear cradle bolts. Remove the left stabilizer mount bolts.
11. Remove the left cradle member assembly. Remove the A.I.R. management valve and bracket assembly.
12. Lower the vehicle and lower the transaxle to its original position. Remove the transaxle mounting bracket.
13. Raise the vehicle and support safely.
14. Remove the bolts from the right rear transaxle mount and engine to transaxle mount.
15. Remove the flywheel covers and torque converter bolts. Position a suitable transaxle lifting device under the transaxle assembly.
16. Remove the remaining bell housing bolts. Remove the cooler lines from the transaxle.
17. Install driveaxle boot seal protector J–34754 or equivalent. Separate the driveaxles from the transaxle assembly and reposition out of the way.
18. Lower the transaxle assembly from the vehicle.
19. Installation is the reverse of the removal procedure.

FRONT DRIVE AXLE
Removal and Installation
RIGHT SIDE

1. Hoist car under lower control arms and remove the wheel.
2. Remove the drive axle cotter pin, retainer, nut and washer from the wheel hub.
3. Remove the oil filter assembly if necessary in order to gain working clearance on V8.
4. Remove inner constant velocity joint attaching bolts.
5. Push inner constant velocity joint outward enough to disengage the right hand final drive output shaft, then move rearward.
6. Remove right hand output shaft bracket bolts to engine and final drive.
7. Remove right hand output shaft and drive axle assembly.

CAUTION

Care must be exercised so that constant velocity joints do not turn to full extremes, and that seals are not damaged against shock absorber or stabilizer bar.

---

8. Carefully place right hand drive axle assembly into lower control arm and enter outer race splines into knuckle.
9. Lubricate final drive output shaft seal, with special seal lubrication.
10. Install right hand output shaft into final drive and attach the support bolts to engine and race. Torque the bolts to 50 ft. lbs.
11. Move right hand drive axle assembly toward front of car and align with right hand output shaft. Install attaching bolts.
12. Install oil filter on V8.
13. Install washer and nut on drive axle. Install the retainer and cotter pin.
14. Remove the floor stands and lower hoist.
15. Check engine oil level on V8.

LEFT SIDE

1. Hoist car under lower control arms.
2. Remove wheel. Remove disc.
3. Remove drive axle cotter pin, nut and washer.
4. Remove tie-rod end cotter pin and nut.
5. Remove the tie-rod end from the knuckle with a puller.
6. Remove bolts from drive axle assembly and left output shaft. Insert a spacer between the axle shaft and lower control arm.
7. Remove upper control arm ball joint cotter pin and nut.
8. Using hammer and brass drift, drive on knuckle until upper ball joint stud is free. Support knuckle.
9. Carefully remove drive axle assembly.

NOTE: Care must be exercised so that constant velocity joints do not turn to full extremes and that seals are not damaged against shock absorber or stabilizer bar.

10. Carefully guide left-hand drive axle assembly onto lower control arm and into position on spacer.

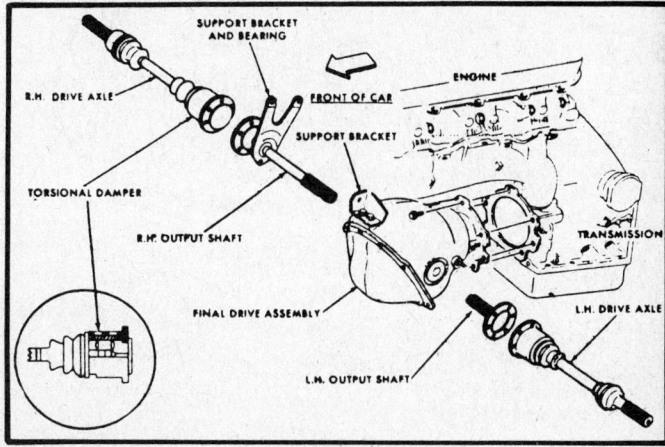

Final drive axle components—typical
(© General Motors Corporation)

8–47

SECTION 8

GENERAL MOTORS—"E" AND "K" BODY
FRONT WHEEL DRIVE CARS

11. Center left-hand drive axle assembly in opening of knuckle and insert upper ball joint stud.
12. Place brake hose clip over upper ball joint stud and install nut. Do not torque.
13. Insert tie rod end stud into knuckle and attach nut. Torque to 35 ft. lbs. on 1983 and later models. Install cotter pin and crimp.
14. Align inner constant velocity joint with output shaft and install attaching bolts. Torque to 60 ft. lbs.
15. Torque upper and lower ball joint stud nuts to 55 ft. lbs. Install cotter pins and crimp.

NOTE: Upper ball joint cotter pin must be crimped toward upper control arm to prevent interference with outer constant velocity joint seal.

16. Install drive axle washer and nut. Torque to 175 ft. lbs. Install cotter pin and crimp.
17. Install wheel.
18. Remove floor stands and lower hoist.
19. Check camber, caster and toe-in and adjust if necessary. Refer to Front End Alignment specifications.

FINAL DRIVE

Removal and Installation

1. Disconnect the negative battery cable and raise the car. Place jackstands underneath the front frame horns and the lower front post.
2. Remove the frame brace attaching bolts and pivot the braces outward in order to gain access.
3. With a drain pan under the final drive cover, loosen the final drive cover screws and allow the fluid to drain. Remove the cover and gasket material.
4. Remove the screws on both sides attaching the output shaft to the drive axle. Separate the flanges of the shaft and axle to obtain clearance. The final drive assembly will be removed with the output shafts installed.
5. Remove the battery cable retaining screws from the right output shaft and the screws securing the support to the engine block. Rotate the support downward for clearance.
6. Remove the screws which attach the final drive shield to the transmission and the support bracket. Remove the shield.
7. Remove the remaining final drive screws.
8. Remove the final drive support-to-engine block attaching screws.
9. Using a puller, separate the steering linkage from the pitman arm. Push the linkage toward the front of the car.

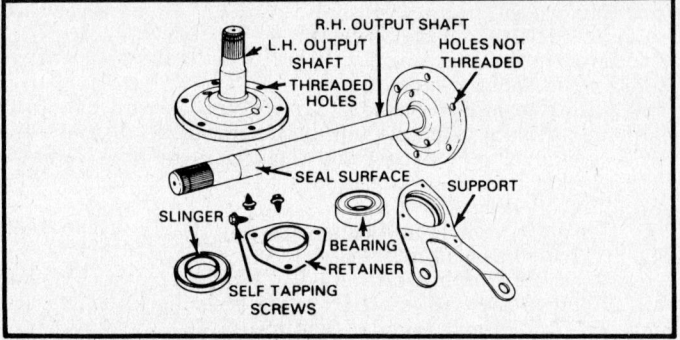

Output shafts and support components
(©General Motors Corporation)

10. Slide the final drive assembly forward, off the transmission shaft and remove the unit. Do not hold the unit by the output shafts as the seals or splines could easily be damaged.
11. To install, thoroughly clean all the gasket surfaces and position a new gasket on the final drive. Do not use a sealer on the gasket.
12. Align the final drive assembly, with the output shafts attached, to the transmission and install all the attaching screws except the one used to hold the shield. Torque in rotation to 30 ft. lbs. in two steps.
13. Loosen the front support bracket screws and install the bracket to the engine block while holding the bracket flush on the housing pad. Torque to 50 ft. lbs.
14. Install the final drive shield. Torque the drive-to-transmission screw to 30 ft. lbs. and the bracket-to-housing screws to 34 ft. lbs.
15. Align the right output shaft support with the attaching holes in the engine block. Do not allow the shaft and support assemblies to hang from the drive unit. By moving the flange end of the shaft up and down and installing the screws and washers loosely, locate the centered position. Torque the screws to 50 ft. lbs.
16. Install the battery cable retainer.
17. Align the right drive axle to the output shaft and install the attaching screws. Torque the screws to 60 ft. lbs. Repeat for the left side.
18. Position a new cover gasket or apply silicone sealer on the final drive cover. Install the cover and torque the screws to 7 ft. lbs. Refill the unit. Torque the filler plug to 30 ft. lbs.
19. Install the steering linkage to the pitman arm and torque to 60 ft. lbs. If the cotter pin hole does not align properly, tighten the nut slightly. Do not loosen to align. Install a new cotter pin.
20. Install the frame braces and torque the nuts to 50 ft. lbs.
21. Lower the car, connect the battery cable, start the car and

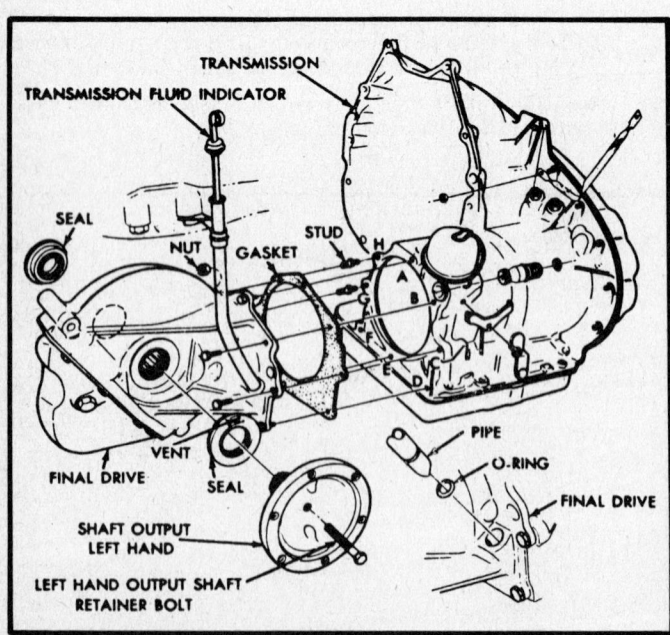

Final drive differential mounting—Toronado
(©General Motors Corporation)

GENERAL MOTORS—"E" AND "K" BODY
FRONT WHEEL DRIVE CARS

check the transmission fluid. When the final drive has reached operating temperature, check it for leaks.

INNER AND OUTER BOOTS

Removal and Installation

OUTER BOOT

1. Raise and support the vehicle safely.
2. Remove the front tire and wheel.
3. Remove the caliper bolts and wire the caliper off to the side of the vehicle.
4. Remove the hub nut, washer and wheel bearing.
5. Using a brass drift, lightly tap around the seal retainer to loosen it. Remove the seal retainer.
6. Remove the seal retaining clamp and discard.
7. Using snap ring pliers, remove the race retaining ring from the axle shaft.
8. Pull the outer joint assembly and the outboard seal away from the axle shaft.
9. Installation is the reverse of the removal procedure. Pack the joint assembly with half of the grease provided with the new seal.

INNER BOOT

1. Raise the vehicle and support safely.
2. Remove the front tire and wheel.
3. Remove the caliper bolts and wire the caliper off to the side of the vehicle.
4. Remove the hub nut, washer and wheel bearing.
5. Remove the front drive axle as outlined earlier in this section. Place in a suitable holding fixture.
6. Remove the joint assembly retaining ring. Remove the joint assembly.
7. Remove the race retaining ring and remove the seal retainer.
8. Remove the inner seal retaining clamp. Remove the inner joint seal.
9. Installation is the reverse of the removal procedure. Pack the joint assembly with half of the grease provided.

REAR SUSPENSION SECTION

For Axle Overhaul Procedures and Suspension Services Refer to Unit Repair Section.

REAR AXLE ASSEMBLY

Removal and Installation

1. Disconnect the negative battery cable. Raise the vehicle partially and support safely. Remove the tire and wheel assemblies.
2. Remove the brake calipers and position out of the way using a length of wire.
3. Remove the necessary suspension components in order to gain access to the Electronic Level Control (ELC) unit.
4. Tag and disconnect the electrical connections from the height sensor and compressor.
5. Remove the air intake filter from the underbody.
6. Remove the parking brake cable from the equalizer and reposition the intermediate cable away from the crossmember assembly.
7. If the vehicle is equipped with a brake crossover tube, remove the retaining bolts and disconnect the crossover tube.
8. Remove the right rear crossover retaining bolt.
9. Support the rear crossmember assembly using jackstands of a suitable length.
10. Remove the crossmember forward arm bolts, upper mounting bolts and lower insulators.
11. With the suspension crossmember supported ony with the jackstands, slowly raise the vehicle away from the crossmember assembly.

NOTE: While raising the vehicle, note the position of the hoses, pipes and brake calipers in order to prevent damage during the removal procedure.

12. Installation is the reverse of the removal procedure.

REAR WHEEL HUB AND BEARING ASSEMBLY

Removal and Installation

1. Raise and support the vehicle safely.
2. Remove the rear tires and wheels.
3. Remove the brake line brackets from the lower control arm.
4. Remove the hub and bearing-to-axle assembly attaching bolts. Remove the hug and bearing assembly.
5. Installation is the reverse of the removal procedure. Bleed the brake system if required.

8-49

SECTION 9

GENERAL MOTORS—"H" BODY
FRONT WHEEL DRIVE CARS—BUICK LE SABRE • OLDSMOBILE 88

SPECIFICATIONS

Brakes	24–2	Serial Number Identification	9–3
Camshaft	9–5	Torque	9–5
Capacities	9–4	Torque Sequence (Cylinder Heads)	9–15
Crankshaft & Connecting Rod	9–5	Tune-Up	9–4
Firing Order	9–4	Valve	9–4
General Engine	9–4	Wheel Alignment	9–6
Piston & Rings	9–5		

INDEX

A
Alternator R&R	9–16
Automatic Transaxle	9–19
On Car SErvice	23–2
Assembly R&R	9–19
Axle Assembly R&R	9–20
Axle Shaft R&R	9–20

B
Ball Joints	35–2
Brake System	9–18
Brake Booster	9–18
Brake Caliper Overhaul	24–2
Brake Caliper R&R	24–2
Brake Drum, Rear	24–2
Brake Master Cylinder	9–18
Brake Pad	
Front	24–2
Brake Shoe	
Rear	24–2

C
Camshaft R&R	9–15
Chassis Electrical	9–7
Combination Switch R&R	9–8
Component Location	9–9
Control Arm R&R	35–2
Cooling Fan Motor	9–10
Cooling System	9–10
Cruise Control	9–10
Cylinder Head	9–15
R&R	9–15

D
Differential	23–2
Inspection	23–2
Disc Brakes	24–2
Drive Axle	9–19
Driveshaft R&R	9–20

E
Electronic Ignition	30–2
Emissions Controls	9–14
Engine	9–14
Identification	9–3
R&R	9–14
Engine Electrical	9–6
Engine Lubrication	9–16
Engine Mechanical	9–14
Engine Mounts R&R	9–15
Exhaust Manifold R&R	9–13

F
Front Suspension	35–2
Alignment	9–6
Fuel Injection	9–14
Fuel Pump R&R	9–13

H
Headlight Switch	9–8
Heater Blower R&R	9–10
Heater Core R&R	9–10
Heater Control	9–12

I
Ignition Switch	9–7
Ignition Timing	9–7
Instrument Cluster R&R	9–9
Intake Manifold R&R	9–13

L, M, N
Lower Control Arm R&R	35–2
Master Cylinder R&R	9–18
Manual Steering Gear R&R	9–17
Neutral Safety Switch R&R	9–8

O
Oil Pan R&R	9–16
Oil Pump R&R	9–16
Oil Seal R&R Rear Main	9–17

P
Parking Brake	9–19
Adjustment	9–19
Cable R&R	9–19
Piston & Connecting Rod	9–16
Power Brake Unit R&R	9–18
Power Steering Pump R&R	9–18

R
Rear Main Oil Seal R&R	9–17
Rear Suspension	35–2
Regulator	9–6
Rocker Shaft/Assy R&R	9–15

S
Serial Number	9–3
Engine	9–3
Vehicle	9–3
Shock Absorber R&R	
Front	35–2
Rear	35–2
Springs	
Front	35–2
Rear	9–21
Starter R&R	9–6
Starter Drive Replacement	9–6
Steering Column R&R	9–17
Steering Gear R&R	9–17
Manual	9–17
Power	9–17
Steering Wheel R&R	9–17
Stoplight Switch R&R	9–8
Speedometer R&R	9–9
Suspension	35–2
Service	35–2

T
Timing Chain	9–16
Timing Gear Cover	9–16
Oil Seal Replacement	9–16
Tune-Up	9–4
Turn Signal Switch R&R	9–8

U, V
U-Joint Overhaul	28–2
Valve Tapppette R&R	9–15
Valve Timing, Adjust	9–15
Valve System	9–15
Voltage Regulator	9–6

W, Y
Water Pump R&R	9–10
Wheel Alignment	9–6
front	9–6
Wheel Bearings	
Front	9–18
Rear	9–21
Wheel Cylinders	
Rear	24–2
Windshield Wiper	9–10
Linkage R&R	9–10
Motor R&R	9–10
Switch R&R	9–10
Year Identification	9–3

BEFORE SERVICING BE CERTAIN TO READ THE SAFETY NOTICE

SECTION 9

GM "H" Body
1986–87
Front Wheel Drive Cars

BUICK LE SABRE
OLDSMOBILE "88"

YEAR IDENTIFICATION

1986 LeSabre Limited

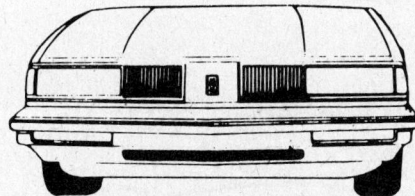

1987 Oldsmobile Delta 88

1987 LeSabre Sedan

VEHICLE IDENTIFICATION NUMBER (VIN)

It is important for servicing and ordering parts to be certain of the vehicle and engine identification. The VIN (vehicle identification number) is a 13 or 17 digit number visible through the windshield on the driver's side of the dash and contains the vehicle and engine identification codes. It can be interpreted as follows:

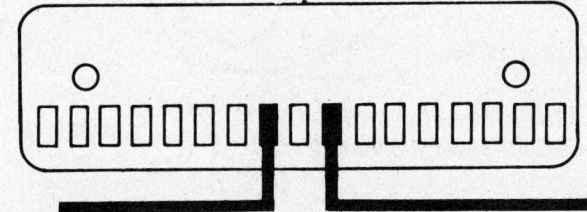

Engine Code						Model Year Code	
Code	Cu. In.	Liters	Cyl.	Fuel Delivery	Eng. Mfg.	Code	Year
L	181	3.0	6	MFI	Buick	G	1986
B,3	231	3.8	6	SFI	Buick	H	1987

The seventeen digit Vehicle Identification Number can be used to determine engine application and model year. The 10th digit indicates the model year and the 8th digit identifies the factory installed engine.
MFI Multiport Fuel Injection
SFI Sequential Fuel Injection

SECTION 9

GENERAL MOTORS—"H" BODY
FRONT WHEEL DRIVE CARS—BUICK LE SABRE • OLDSMOBILE 88

GENERAL ENGINE SPECIFICATIONS

Year	VIN Code	Engine No. Cyl. Displ. (cu. in.)	Eng. Mfg.	Fuel Delivery System	Horsepower @ rpm	Torque ft. lb. @ rpm	Bore × Stroke	Compression Ratio	Oil Pressure @ 2400 rpm
'86–'87	L	6-181	Buick	MFI	125 @ 4900	150 @ 2400	3.80 × 2.66	9.0:1	37
	B,3	6-231	Buick	SFI	150 @ 4400	200 @ 2000	3.80 × 3.40	8.5:1	37

MFI Multiport Fuel Injection
SFI Sequential Fuel Injection

TUNE-UP SPECIFICATIONS

When analyzing compression test results, look for uniformity among cylinders rather than specific pressures

Year	VIN Code	Eng. No. Cyl. Displ. (cu. in.)	Eng. Mfg.	hp	Spark Plugs Orig. Type	Gap (in.)	Ignition Timing (deg.)	Fuel Pump Pressure (psi)	Idle Speed (rpm)
'86	L	6-181	Buick	125	R44LTS	.045	①	34-44	①
	B,3	6-231	Buick	150	R44LTS	.045	①	26-36	①
'87	All				See Underhood Specifications Sticker				

NOTE: The underhood specifications sticker often reflects tune-up specification changes made in production. Sticker figures must be used if they disagree with those in this chart.
Part numbers in this chart are not recommendations by Chilton for any product by brand name.
① Idle speed and ignition timing are computer-controlled and not adjustable

FIRING ORDER

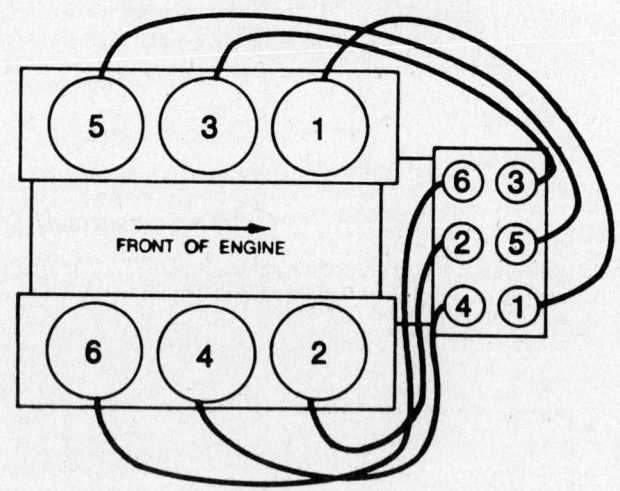

183 cu. in. (3.0L) and 231 cu. in. (3.8L) engines
Firing Order: 1-6-5-4-3-2

CAPACITIES

Year	VIN Code	Engine Displacement (cu. in.)	Eng. Mfg.	Crankcase (qts.) w/filter	wo/filter	Transaxle (pints)	Gas Tank (gals.)	Cooling System (qts.) Standard	HD
'86–'87	L	181	Buick	4.0 ①	4.0	13.0	18	12.1	12.2
	B,3	231	Buick	4.0 ①	4.0	13.0	18	12.5	12.6

① Add as necessary to bring to appropriate level on dipstick

GENERAL MOTORS—"H" BODY
FRONT WHEEL DRIVE CARS—BUICK LE SABRE • OLDSMOBILE 88

VALVE SPECIFICATIONS

Year	VIN Code	Engine No. Cyl. Displacement (cu. in.)	Eng. Mfg.	Seat Angle (deg.)	Face Angle (deg.)	Spring Test Pressure (lbs. @ in.)	Spring Installed Height (in.)	Stem-to-Guide Clearance (in.) Intake	Stem-to-Guide Clearance (in.) Exhaust	Stem Diameter (in.) Intake	Stem Diameter (in.) Exhaust
'86-'87	L	6-181	Buick	45	45	220 @ 1.340	1.727	0.0015-0.0035	0.0015-0.0032	0.3401-0.3412	0.3405-0.3412
	B,3	6-231	Buick	45	45	185 @ 1.340	1.727	0.0015-0.0035	0.0015-0.0032	0.3401-0.3412	0.3405-0.3412

CRANKSHAFT AND CONNECTING ROD SPECIFICATIONS
All measurements are given in inches

Year	VIN Code	Engine No. Cyl. (cu. in.)	Eng. Mfg.	Crankshaft Main Brg. Journal Diameter	Crankshaft Main Brg. Oil Clearance	Crankshaft Shaft End-Play	Thrust on No.	Connecting Rod Journal Diameter	Connecting Rod Oil Clearance	Connecting Rod Side Clearance
'86-'87	L	6-181	Buick	2.4995	0.0003-0.0018	0.003-0.011	2	2.2487-2.2495	0.0005-0.0026	0.006-0.023
	B,3	6-231	Buick	2.4995	0.0003-0.0018	0.003-0.011	2	2.2487-2.2495	0.0005-0.0026	0.006-0.023

CAMSHAFT SPECIFICATIONS
All measurements are given in inches

Year	VIN Code	Engine (cu. in.)	Eng. Mfg.	Journal Diameter 1 2 3 4 5	Bearing Clearance	Lobe Lift Intake	Lobe Lift Exhaust	Camshaft End Play
'86-'87	L	181	Buick	— 1.78-1.7865 —	①	0.358	0.384	—
	B,3	231	Buick	— 1.78-1.7865 —	①	0.368 ②	0.384 ②	—

① No. 1: 0.0005-0.0025
   No. 2-5: 0.0005-0.0035
② VIN B—.392 in.

PISTON AND RING SPECIFICATIONS
All measurements are given in inches

Year	VIN Code	Engine Type/Disp. (cu. in.)	Eng. Mfg.	Piston-to-Bore Clearance	Ring Gap Top Compression	Ring Gap Bottom Compression	Ring Gap Oil Control	Ring Side Clearance Top Compression	Ring Side Clearance Bottom Compression	Ring Side Clearance Oil Control
'86-'87	L	6-181	Buick	①	0.010-0.020	0.010-0.020	0.015-0.055	0.0030-0.0050	0.0030-0.0050	0.0035 max
	B,3	6-231	Buick	①	0.010-0.020	0.010-0.020	0.015-0.055	0.0030-0.0050	0.0030-0.0050	0.0035 max

① Top land—0.046-0.056 in.
   Skirt top—0.0008-0.0020 in.
   Skirt bottom—0.0013-0.0035 in.

TORQUE SPECIFICATIONS
All readings in ft. lbs.

Year	VIN Code	Engine No. Cyl. Displacement (cu. in.)	Eng. Mfg.	Cylinder Head Bolts	Rod Bearing Bolts	Main Bearing Bolts	Crankshaft Bolt	Flywheel-to-Crankshaft Bolts	Manifold Intake	Manifold Exhaust
'86-'87	L	6-181	Buick	①	40	100	200	60	32	37
	B,3	6-231	Buick	①	40	100	200	60	32	37

① See text for angle torque procedure

SECTION 9
GENERAL MOTORS—"H" BODY
FRONT WHEEL DRIVE CARS—BUICK LE SABRE • OLDSMOBILE 88

WHEEL ALIGNMENT SPECIFICATIONS

Year	Model	Caster Range (deg.)	Caster Pref. Setting (deg.)	Camber Range (deg.)	Camber Pref. Setting (deg.)	Toe (in.)
'86–'87	Buick	2–3	2½	L –1–0 R 0–1	½	7/32 ①
'86–'87	Olds	2–3	2½	L –1–0 R 0–1	–½ ½	3/32 ①

L Left
R Right
① In or out. Pref: 0

ENGINE ELECTRICAL

For overhaul procedures, refer to the Unit Repair Section.

Charging System

ALTERNATOR

Removal and Installation

1. Disconnect the negative battery cable.
2. Tag and disconnect the battery charge wire, 3-prong connector and the ground wire at the back of the alternator.
3. Remove the brace at the back of the alternator (if so equipped).
4. Loosen the serpentine belt tensioner and rotate it counterclockwise to remove the drive belt.
5. Support the alternator, remove the mounting bolts and then remove the alternator.

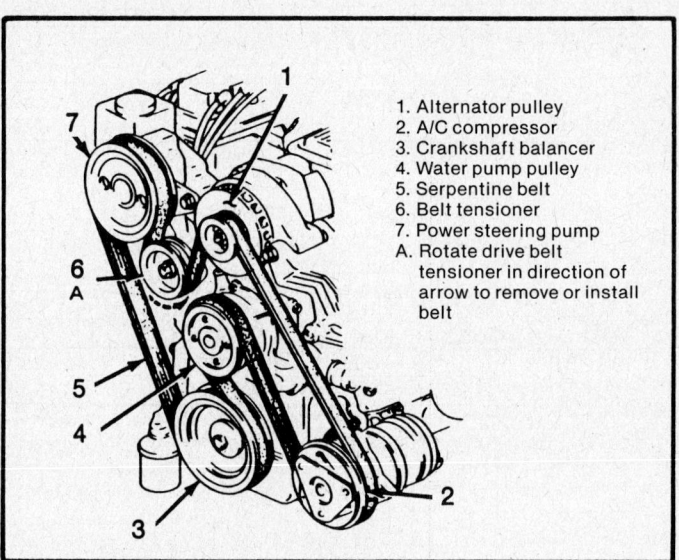

1. Alternator pulley
2. A/C compressor
3. Crankshaft balancer
4. Water pump pulley
5. Serpentine belt
6. Belt tensioner
7. Power steering pump
A. Rotate drive belt tensioner in direction of arrow to remove or install belt

Serpentine drive belt routing

6. Installation is in the reverse order of removal. Tighten the serpentine belt tensioner pulley.

VOLTAGE REGULATOR

An alternator with an integral voltage regulator is standard equipment. There are no adjustments possible with this unit. Testing procedures can be found in the Unit Repair section.

Starting System

STARTER

Removal and Installation

1. Disconnect the negative battery cable.
2. Raise and support the vehicle safely. Remove the starter splash shield and any braces which may be in the way.
3. Remove the two starter mounting bolts and lower the starter slightly to gain access to the wires.
4. Tag and disconnect all wires at the solenoid. Note color coding of wires for reinstallation.
5. Installation is in the reverse order of removal. Install any shims, as required.

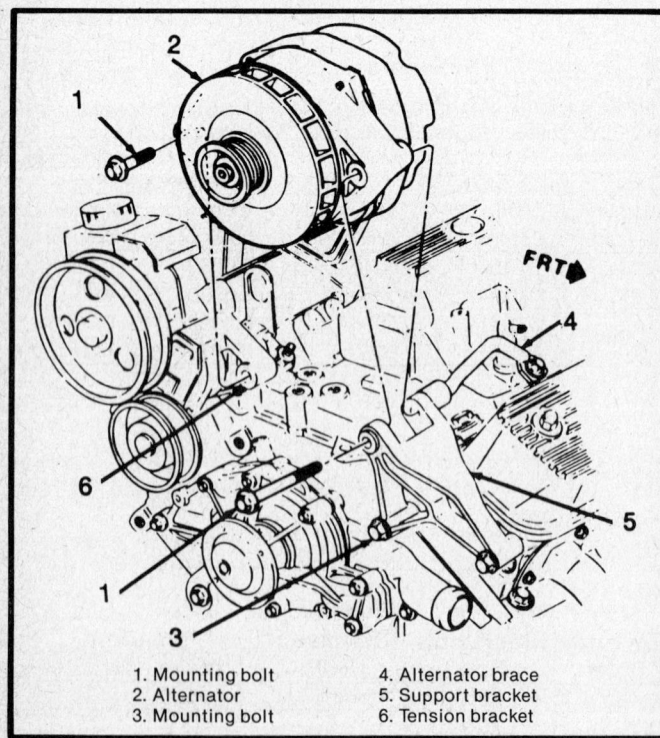

1. Mounting bolt
2. Alternator
3. Mounting bolt
4. Alternator brace
5. Support bracket
6. Tension bracket

Alternator mounting and related components

GENERAL MOTORS—"H" BODY
FRONT WHEEL DRIVE CARS—BUICK LE SABRE • OLDSMOBILE 88

Ignition System

COMPUTER CONTROLLED COIL IGNITION SYSTEM (C3I)

All models are equipped with Computer Controlled Coil Ignition (C3I), which eliminates the distributor. The C3I ignition system consists of a coil pack, ignition module camshaft and crankshaft sensor. There are two types of C3I coils used. Type 1 coils have three plug wires on each side of the coil assembly; Type 2 coils have all six wires connected on one side of the coil. When troubleshooting or replacing components, it is important to determine which C3I system is installed on the engine.

The C3I system consists of the coil pack, ignition module, crankshaft sensor, interruptor rings and electronic control module (ECM). All components are serviced as complete assemblies, although individual coils are available for Type 2 coil packs. Since the ECM controls the ignition timing, no timing adjustments are necessary or possible.

CRANKSHAFT SENSOR

Removal and Installation

1. Disconnect the negative battery cable.
2. Remove the serpentine drive belt.
3. Raise and support the vehicle safely.
4. Remove the right front tire.
5. Remove the inner fender splash shield.
6. Remove the crankshaft balancer bolt and balancer.
7. Remove the mounting bolts and remove the crankshaft sensor from the front cover. Disconnect the electrical connector and remove the sensor from the vehicle.

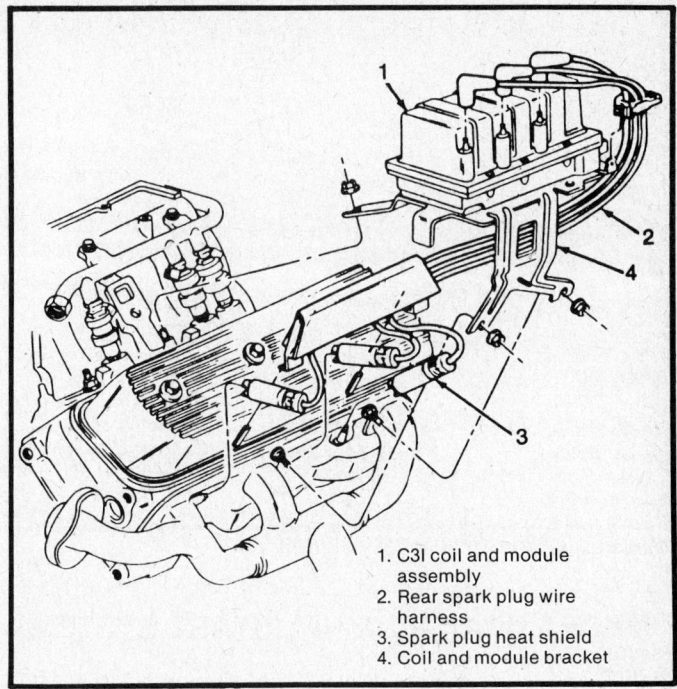

1. C3I coil and module assembly
2. Rear spark plug wire harness
3. Spark plug heat shield
4. Coil and module bracket

C3I ignition system

1. Crankshaft sensor
2. Mounting bolt
3. Camshaft sensor
4. Mounting bolts

Crankshaft and camshaft sensor location

8. Installation is the reverse of removal. Make sure the electrical T-latch connector is assembled properly or an intermittent loss of operation may occur. The sensor must be carefully aligned with the interruptor rings to avoid damage when the engine is cranked. Tighten the crankshaft sensor mounting bolts to 22 ft. lbs. (30 Nm) and the crankshaft balancer bolt to 200 ft. lbs. (270 Nm).

IGNITION TIMING

The C3I ignition system does not require timing adjustments, therefore engine timing is not necessary or available.

Electrical Controls

IGNITION LOCK

Removal and Installation

1. Disconnect the negative battery cable. Place the lock in the RUN position.
2. Remove the lock plate, turn signal switch and buzzer switch.
3. Remove the screw and lock cylinder. If the screw is dropped on removal, it could fall into the column, requiring complete disassembly to retrieve the screw.
4. Rotate the cylinder clockwise to align cylinder key with the keyway in the housing.
5. Push the lock all the way in.
6. Install the screw. Tighten the screw to 14 inch lbs. for adjustable columns and 25 inch lbs. for standard columns.

IGNITION SWITCH

Removal and Installation

1. Disconnect the negative battery cable. Lower the steering column. Be sure to properly support it.
2. Put the switch in the off-unlocked position. With the cylinder removed, the rod is in the lock position when it is in the next to the uppermost detent. The off-unlocked position is two detents from the top.
3. Remove the two switch screws and remove the switch assembly.
4. Before installing, place the new switch in off-unlocked position and make sure the lock cylinder and actuating rod are in off-unlocked (third detent from the top) position.
5. Install the activating rod into the switch and assemble the switch on the column. Tighten the mounting screws. Use only the specified screws since overlength screws could impair the collapsibility of the column.
6. Reinstall the steering column.

SECTION 9
GENERAL MOTORS—"H" BODY
FRONT WHEEL DRIVE CARS—BUICK LE SABRE • OLDSMOBILE 88

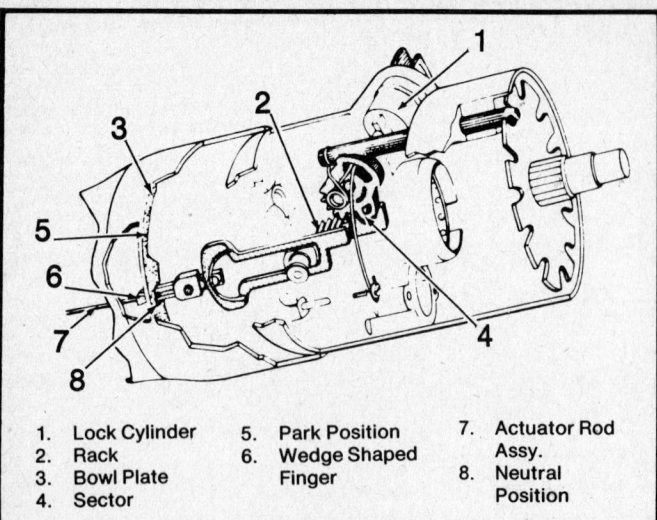

1. Lock Cylinder
2. Rack
3. Bowl Plate
4. Sector
5. Park Position
6. Wedge Shaped Finger
7. Actuator Rod Assy.
8. Neutral Position

Mechanical neutral safety switch

MECHANICAL NEUTRAL START SYSTEM

Vehicles with this system use a mechanical block rather than an electrical neutral start system. The system only allows the lock cylinder to rotate to the start position when the shift lever is in neutral or park.

STOP LIGHT SWITCH

Removal and Installation

1. Disconnect the negative battery cable.
2. Remove the necessary trim panels in order to gain access to the stop light switch mounting bracket.
3. Loosen the tubular clip from the switch assembly.
4. Disconnect the electrical connector from the rear of the switch.
5. Remove the switch assembly from the vehicle.
6. Installation is the reverse of the removal procedure.

HEADLIGHT SWITCH

Removal and Installation

1. Disconnect negative battery cable. Remove the steering column lower cover or the instrument panel trim plate cover-

ing the headlamp switch, if a rocker-type headlamp switch is used.
2. Disconnect wiring harness retainer below headlight switch assembly. On some models the switch connector is integral with the instrument panel, so simply pull the switch outward to disconnect it.
3. On knob type switches, depress spring loaded release button on top of headlight switch and remove switch, knob and rod assembly (switch on).
4. Remove screw with ground wire at bottom of switch housing and any other mounting screws.
5. Pull assembly down and rearward, disconnect wiring harness connectors, bulb(s) and remove assembly.
6. Installation is the reverse of removal.

TURN SIGNAL SWITCH

Removal and Installation

1. Disconnect the negative battery cable. Remove the steering wheel. Remove the trim cover.
2. Loosen the cover screws. Pry the cover off and lift the cover off the shaft.
3. Position the U-shaped lockplate compressing tool on the end of the steering shaft and compress the lock plate by turning the shaft nut clockwise. Pry the wire snapring out of the shaft groove.
4. Remove the tool and lift the lock plate off the shaft.
5. Slip the cancelling cam, upper bearing preload spring, and thrust washer off the shaft.

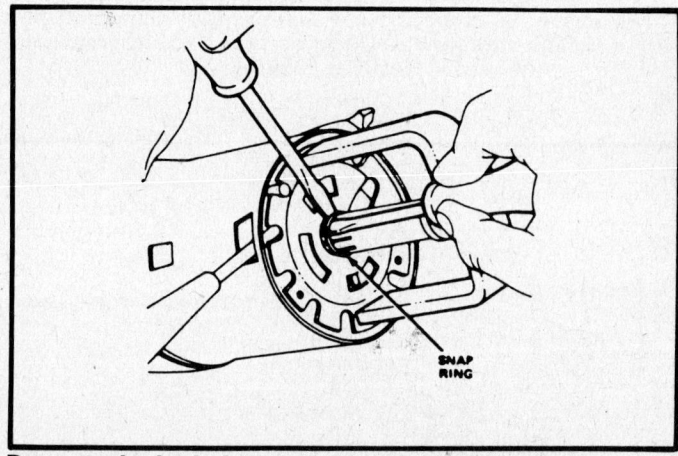

Depress the lockplate and remove the snapring

6. Remove the turn signal lever. Push the flasher knob in and unscrew it. Remove the button retaining screw and remove the button, spring and knob.
7. Pull the switch connector out the mast jacket and tape the upper part to facilitate switch removal. Attach a long piece of wire to the turn signal switch connector. When installing the turn signal switch, feed this wire through the column first, and then use this wire to pull the switch connector into position. On tilt wheels, place the turn signal and shifter housing in low position and remove the harness cover.
8. Remove the three switch mounting screws. Remove the switch pulling it straight up while guiding the wiring harness cover through the column.
9. Install the replacement switch by working the connector and cover down through the housing and under the bracket. On tilt models, the connector is worked down through the housing, under the bracket, and then the cover is installed on the harness.

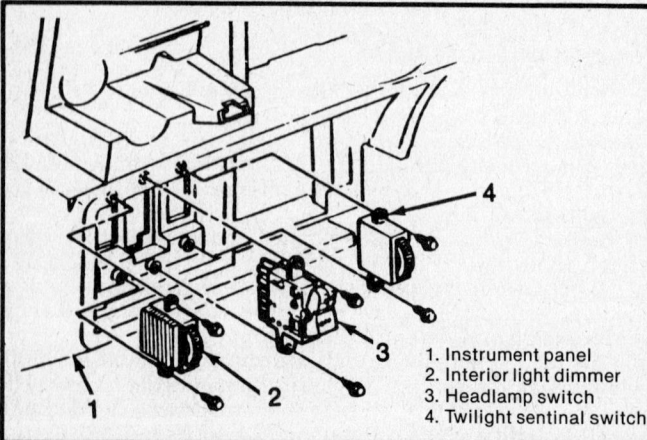

1. Instrument panel
2. Interior light dimmer
3. Headlamp switch
4. Twilight sentinal switch

Light switch assembly

GENERAL MOTORS—"H" BODY
FRONT WHEEL DRIVE CARS—BUICK LE SABRE • OLDSMOBILE 88

10. Install the switch mounting screws and the connector on the mast jacket bracket. Install the column to dash trim plate.
11. Install the flasher knob and the turn signal lever.
12. With the turn signal lever in neutral and the flasher knob out, slide the thrust washer, upper bearing preload spring, and cancelling cam onto the shaft.
13. Position the lock plate on the shaft and press it down until a new snapring can be inserted in the shaft groove. Always use a new snapring when assembling.
14. Install the cover and the steering wheel.

WINDSHIELD WIPER SWITCH
Removal and Installation

1. Disconnect the negative battery cable.
2. Remove the steering wheel and the directional signal switch.
3. It may be necessary to loosen the steering column nuts and remove the bracket to mast retaining screws, then separate the bracket from the mast jacket to allow the connector to clip on the ignition switch to be pulled out of the steering column assembly.
4. Disconnect the washer/wiper switch lower connector.
5. Remove the screws attaching the column housing to the mast jacket. Be sure to note the position of the dimmer switch actuator rod for reassembly. Remove the column housing and switch as an assembly.

NOTE: The tilt and travel columns have a removable plastic cover on the column housing. This provides access to the wiper switch without removing the entire column housing.

6. Remove the pivot pin from the washer/wiper switch using a brass drift. Remove the switch.
7. To install, position the switch in the housing, then install the pivot pin.
8. Position the housing onto the mast jacket and attach it in place with the retaining screws.
9. Install the dimmer switch actuator rod. Check for proper switch operation.
10. Reconnect the lower end of the switch assembly. Continue the installation in the reverse order of the removal procedure.

WINDSHIELD WIPER MOTOR
Removal and Installation

1. Disconnect the negative battery cable. Remove the lower windshield wiper mounding and cowl venting as required.
2. Loosen the linkage drive link to crankarm attaching nuts, and remove the link from the arm.
3. Disconnect the wiring and washer hoses.
4. Remove the three motor attaching screws, guide the crankarm through the hole in the dash, and remove the motor.
5. Installation is the reverse of the removal procedure.

WIPER LINKAGE/TRANSMISSION
Removal and Installation

1. Disconnect the negative battery cable.
2. Remove the wiper arms. Remove the lower reveal moulding and the cowl vent screen.
3. Disengage the link retainer between the drive link and the crank arm.
4. Remove the transmission to body attaching bolts. Remove the wiper transmission and linkage as an assebmly.
5. Installation is the reverse of the removal procedure.

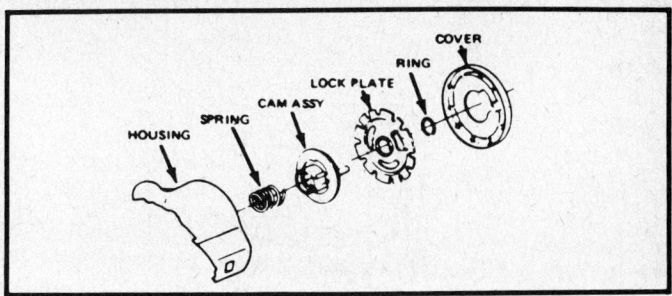
Remove to gain access to the turn signal switch

Instrument Cluster
Removal and Installation

1. Disconnect the negative battery cable.
2. Remove the left sound insulator.
3. Remove the instrument panel insert and applique trim from the instrument panel.
4. Place the shift lever in the Park position and remove the shift indicator clip from the steering column.
5. Remove the nuts securing the steering column to the upper mounting bracket and lower the steering column.
6. Remove the screw securing the upper steering column mounting bracket to the cowl and lower the bracket.
7. Remove the cluster retaining screws, disconnect the speedometer cable, printed circuit connector and remove the cluster.
8. The installation is the reverse of the removal procedure. Be sure the shift indicator is properly aligned.

SPEEDOMETER CABLE
Removal and Installation

1. Disconnect the negative battery cable.
2. Remove the screws holding the instrument cluster trim plate, left and right telltale lens, instrument cluster lens and the transaxle shift indicator assembly. Remove the lens and retainers.
3. Remove the temperature indicator and the fuel gauge.
4. Remove the screws holding the speedometer assembly to the housing. Pull the speedometer head out and disconnect the screw holding the vehicle speed sensor.
5. Remove the speedometer cable. Remove the speedometer.
6. Installation is the reverse of the removal procedure.

ELECTRICAL COMPONENT LOCATIONS
FUSE PANEL

The fuse panel is located on the left side of the instrument panel assembly. In order to gain access to the fuse panel, it is necessary to first remove the cover plate.

ELECTRONIC CONTROL MODULE

The electronic control module is located on the right side of the vehicle. It is positioned up behind the glovebox. In order to gain access to the assembly you must first remove the trim panel and/or glovebox assembly.

TURN SIGNAL AND HAZARD FLASHER

The turn signal and hazard flasher is located directly under the steering column of the vehicle. It is secured in place with a plastic retainer. In order to gain access to the components, it may first be necessary to remove the under dash padding.

SECTION 9

GENERAL MOTORS—"H" BODY
FRONT WHEEL DRIVE CARS—BUICK LE SABRE • OLDSMOBILE 88

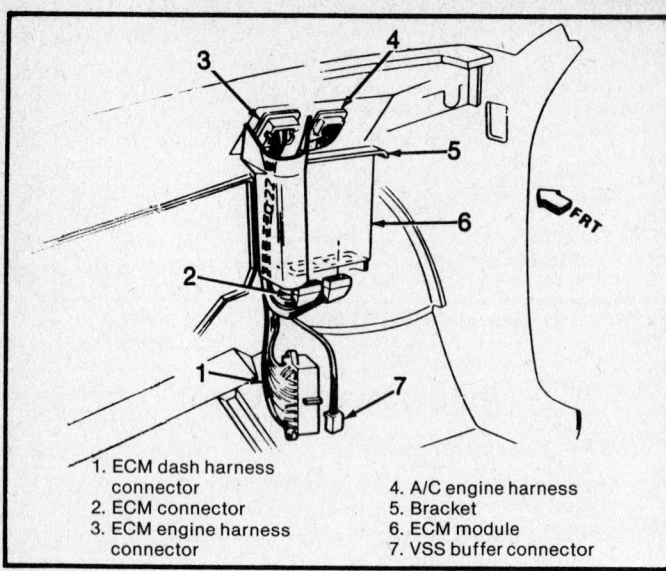

1. ECM dash harness connector
2. ECM connector
3. ECM engine harness connector
4. A/C engine harness
5. Bracket
6. ECM module
7. VSS buffer connector

Typical electronic control module (ECM) mounting

CONVENIENCE CENTER
If equipped, the convenience center is located on the right side of the vehicle. It is positioned under the dash panel. In order to gain access to the convenience center it may be necessary to remove instrument panel sound absorber.

CIRCUIT BREAKER
A circuit breaker is an electrical switch which breaks the circuit during an electrical overload. The circuit breaker will remain open until the short or overload condition in the circuit is corrected. Circuit breakers are located in the fuse box.

FUSIBLE LINKS
Fusible links are sections of wire, with special insulation, designed to melt under electrical overload. Replacements are simply spliced into the wire. There may be as many as five of these in the engine compartment wiring harnesses.

SPEED CONTROLS
For detailed information on vehicles equipped with cruise control, refer to the "A" and "X" body section of this manual.

COOLING AND HEATER SYSTEMS

WATER PUMP

Removal and Installation
1. Disconnect the negative battery cable.
2. Drain the cooling system.
3. Remove the serpentine drive belt.
4. Disconnect the coolant hoses at the water pump.
5. Remove the water pump pulley bolts. The long bolt is removed through the access hole provided in the body side rail. Remove the pulley.
6. Remove the water pump attaching bolts and remove the water pump from the engine.
7. Installation is the reverse of removal. Clean all gasket mating surfaces and use a new gasket. Torque the short water pump mounting bolts to 8 ft. lbs. and the long mounting bolts to 29 ft. lbs.

ELECTRIC COOLING FAN
All vehicles are equipped with an electric cooling fan. If the vehicle is equipped with air condition an additional cooling fan may also be used.

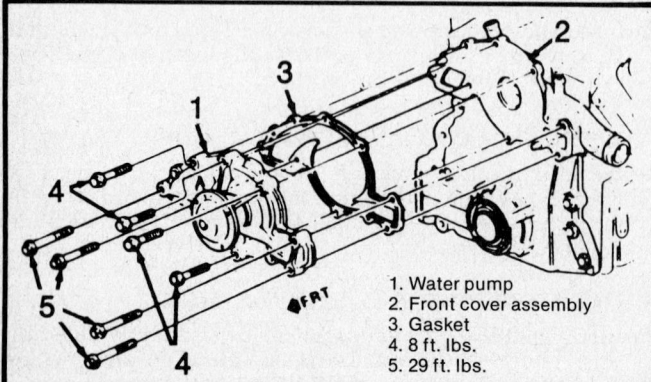

1. Water pump
2. Front cover assembly
3. Gasket
4. 8 ft. lbs.
5. 29 ft. lbs.

Typical water pump mounting

Removal and Installation
1. Disconnect the negative battery cable.
2. Remove all the necessary components in order to gain access to the radiator fan retaining bolts. Disconnect the electrical connectors.
3. Remove the radiator fan bolts and remove the fan assembly from the vehicle.
4. Installation is the reverse of the removal procedure.

BLOWER MOTOR

Removal and Installation
1. Disconnect the negative battery cable.
2. Disconnect the electrical connections at the blower motor.
3. Disconnect the cooling hose from the blower motor.
4. Remove the mounting screws and remove the motor.
5. Reverse to install. Use a silicone sealer on the blower motor sealing surfaces.

HEATER CORE

Removal and Installation
1. Disconnect the negative battery cable. Drain the radiator.
2. Remove the heater hoses from the core and plug the hoses and the nipples to prevent spillage.
3. Remove the instrument panel.
4. Remove the four defroster nozzle attaching screws at the cowl and the screw on the case and remove the nozzle.
5. Disconnect the vacuum hoses.
6. Disconnect the electrical connector at the programmer.
7. Under the hood, remove the heater case to cowl attaching screws.
8. Under the instrument panel, remove the heater case to cowl attaching screw.
9. Remove the heater case.
10. Remove the four case to core screws and remove the core.
11. Installation is the reverse of removal.

GENERAL MOTORS — "H" BODY
FRONT WHEEL DRIVE CARS — BUICK LE SABRE • OLDSMOBILE 88

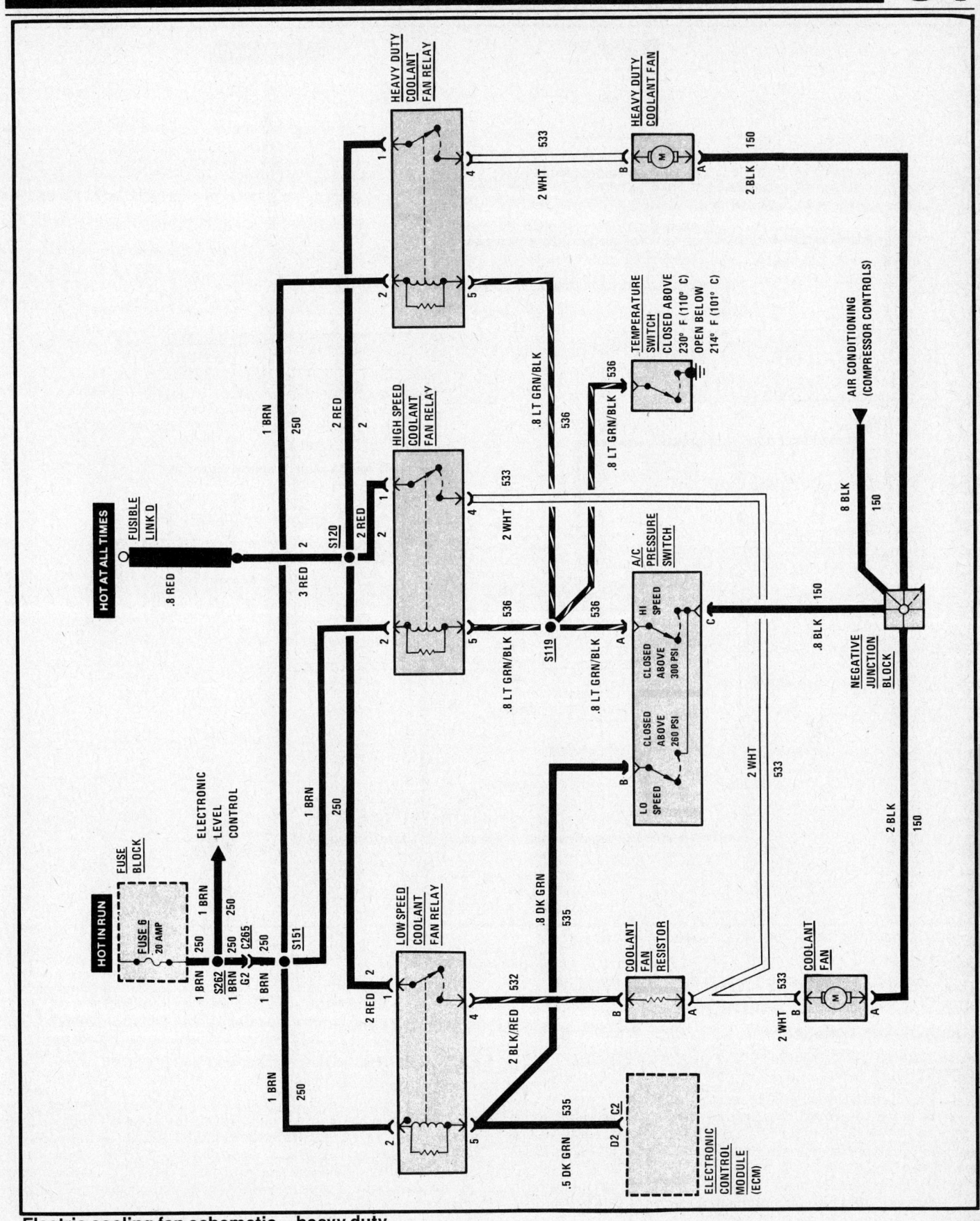

Electric cooling fan schematic — heavy duty

SECTION 9

GENERAL MOTORS—"H" BODY
FRONT WHEEL DRIVE CARS—BUICK LE SABRE • OLDSMOBILE 88

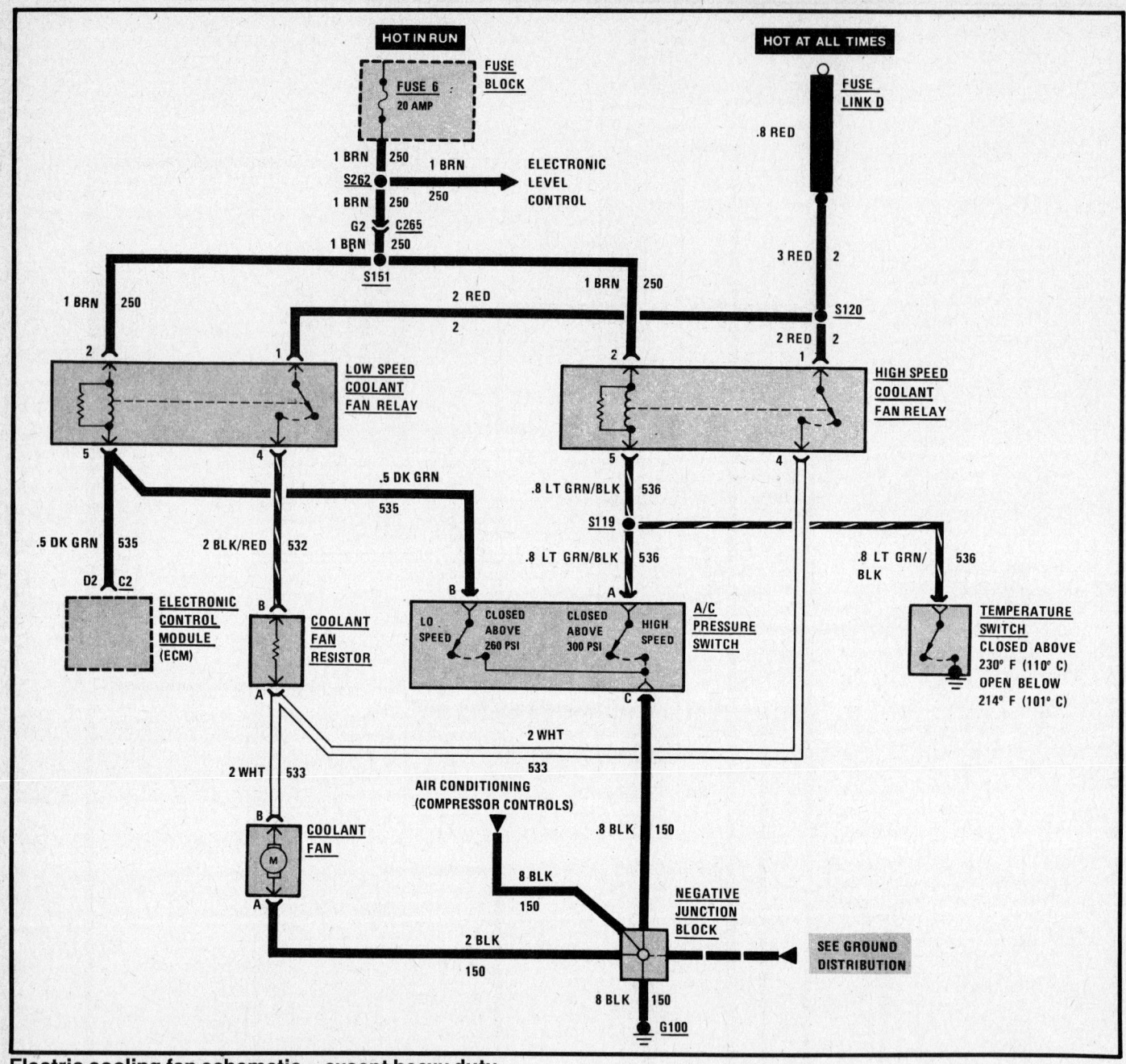

Electric cooling fan schematic—except heavy duty

TEMPERATURE CONTROL/BLOWER SWITCH

Removal and Installation

ALL EXCEPT ELECTRONIC TOUCH CLIMATE CONTROL

1. Disconnect the negative battery cable.
2. Remove the instrument panel trim cover as required to gain access to the control head retaining screws. Remove the attaching screws that retain the control head to the instrument panel carrier.
3. Pull the control head out far enough and turn the bulb socket assembly while pulling back. Remove the bulb from the socket.
4. Disconnect all electrical and vacuum connections as required. Disconnect the control cables as required.
5. Remove the control head assembly from the vehicle.
6. Installation is the reverse of the removal procedure.

ELECTRONIC TOUCH CLIMATE CONTROL

1. Disconnect the negative battery cable.
2. Remove the instrument panel trim cover as required to gain access to the control head retaining screws. Remove the attaching screws that retain the control head to the instrument panel carrier.
3. Carefully push from the rear of the control head assembly on the electrical prongs and slide the assembly out from the case.
4. Installation is the reverse of the removal procedure.

GENERAL MOTORS—"H" BODY
FRONT WHEEL DRIVE CARS—BUICK LE SABRE • OLDSMOBILE 88

FUEL SYSTEM

FUEL PUMP

Removal and Installation

ELECTRIC

Fuel system pressure must be relieved before attempting any service procedures. Remove the fuel pump fuse from the fuse box, then start and run the engine until it stalls. Crank the engine for three more seconds to make sure all fuel is exhausted from the lines, then turn the ignition switch to the off position and replace the fuse. Take precautions to avoid the risk of fire.

1. Relieve the fuel system pressure.
2. Disconnect the negative battery cable.
3. Raise and support the vehicle safely.
4. Drain and remove the fuel tank.
5. Remove the fuel lever sending unit and pump assembly by turning the cam lock ring counterclockwise and lifting the assembly from the fuel tank.
6. Pull the fuel pump up into the attaching hose while pulling outward away from the bottom support. Take care to prevent damage to the rubber sound insulator and strainer during removal. Once the pump assembly is clear of the bottom support, pull it out of the rubber connector.
7. Installation is the reverse of removal. Use a new O-ring when installing the assembly into the fuel tank. When installing the fuel tank, make sure all rubber sound isolators or spacers are replaced in their original locations.

FUEL FILTER

Removal and Installation

NOTE: The Fuel system is under pressure. Relieve fuel pressure before attempting to remove any fuel lines.

The fuel injection system uses an inline filter located in the fuel feed line under the hood, attached to the frame rail, or on the rear crossmember of the vehicle. Always use a backup wrench on the fittings any time a fuel filter is removed or installed, and never replace a metal fuel line with a rubber insert. The high pressure fuel system used with all fuel injection systems requires metal fuel lines to contain the pressure. Replace the O-ring at the connection and torque the fuel fitting to 22 ft. lbs.

INTAKE MANIFOLD

Removal and Installation

1. Disconnect the negative battery cable.
2. Remove the mass air flow sensor and air intake duct.
3. Remove the serpentine drive belt, alternator and bracket.
4. Remove the C3I ignition module and wiring.
5. Tag and disconnect all vacuum hoses and wiring connectors as necessary.
6. Disconnect the throttle, cruise control and throttle valve cables from the throttle body.
7. Drain the cooling system.
8. Disconnect the heater hoses from the throttle body.
9. Disconnect the upper radiator hose from the intake manifold.
10. Depressurize the fuel system and remove the fuel lines, fuel rail and injectors as an assembly.
11. Remove the intake manifold bolts in reverse of the torque sequence and lift off the intake manifold.
12. Installation is the reverse of removal. Clean all gasket mating surfaces and apply sealer if a steel gasket is used. Torque the intake manifold bolts in the proper sequence to 32 ft. lbs.

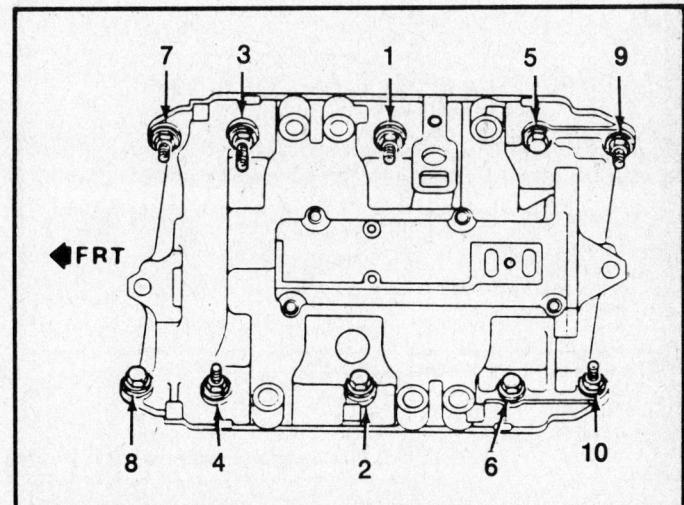

Intake manifold bolt torque sequence

EXHAUST MANIFOLD

Removal and Installation

LEFT SIDE

1. Disconnect the negative battery cable.
2. Remove the mass air flow sensor, air intake duct and crankcase ventilation pipe.
3. Remove the two bolts attaching the exhaust crossover pipe to the manifold.
4. Tag and disconnect the spark plug wires.
5. Remove the mounting bolts and remove the manifold.

NOTE: The oil dipstick tube may have to be removed to provide access to the manifold bolts.

6. Installation is in the reverse order of removal.

Right Side

1. Disconnect the negative battery cable.

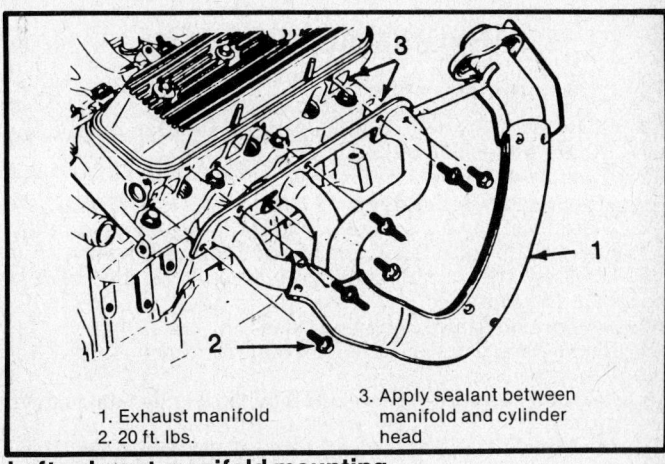

1. Exhaust manifold
2. 20 ft. lbs.
3. Apply sealant between manifold and cylinder head

Left exhaust manifold mounting

SECTION 9
GENERAL MOTORS—"H" BODY
FRONT WHEEL DRIVE CARS—BUICK LE SABRE • OLDSMOBILE 88

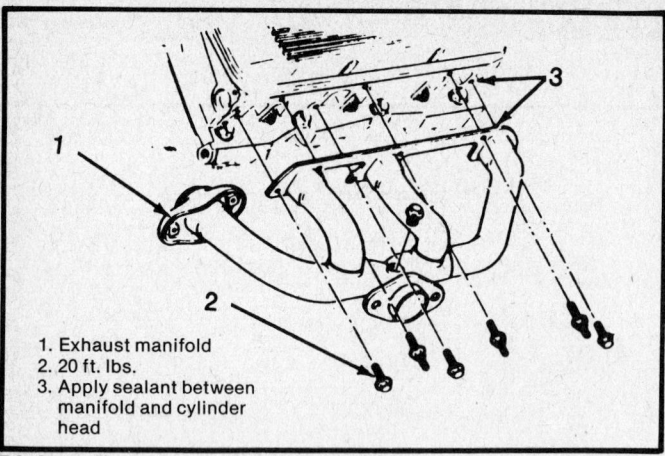

1. Exhaust manifold
2. 20 ft. lbs.
3. Apply sealant between manifold and cylinder head

Right exhaust manifold mounting

2. Remove components as required to gain access to manifold retaining bolts.
3. Disconnect the IAC connector at the throttle body (3.8L only).
4. Tag and disconnect the spark plug wires and the oxygen sensor lead.
5. Disconnect the heater inlet pipe from the manifold studs.
6. Remove the exhaust crossover pipe.
7. Remove the front alternator support bracket.
8. Remove the exhaust manifold mounting bolts. Raise and support the front of the vehicle.
9. Disconnect the exhaust pipe from the manifold.
10. Remove the front exhaust pipe. Remove the manifold.
11. Installation is in the reverse order of removal.

Fuel Injection System

For overhaul procedures, refer to the Unit Repair Section.

EMISSION CONTROL SYSTEMS

3.0 LITER ENGINE

Oxygen sensor
Coolant temperature sensor
Throttle position sensor
Vehicle speed sensor
Air temperature sensor
EGR valve
EGR vacuum control solenoid
Electronic control module
Mass air flow sensor
Electronic spark control system
Prom
Calpak

Fuel injectors
Fuel rail
Throttle body assembly
Idle air control valve
Vapor canister
Canister purge solenoid
Computer controlled coil ignition system (C^3I)
ESC knock sensor
ESC module
Torque converter clutch
PCV system
Catalytic converter

GASOLINE ENGINE SECTION

For engine overhaul procedures refer to the Unit Repair Section.

ENGINE ASSEMBLY

Removal and Installation

1. Disconnect the negative battery cable. Matchmark the hood hinges and remove the hood.
2. Tag and disconnect the air flow sensor wiring. Depressurize the fuel system.
3. Disconnect the air intake duct. Drain the engine coolant.
4. Raise the front of the vehicle and support it safely.
5. Unscrew the retaining bolts and separate the exhaust pipe from the manifold.
6. Loosen and remove the engine mount bolts.
7. Remove the bolts and then disconnect the driveline vibration absorber.
8. Tag and disconnect the starter wiring and then remove the starter.
9. Disconnect the A/C compressor and position it out of the way. Do not disconnect the refrigerant lines.
10. Disconnect the hydraulic lines at the power steering pump and wire them out of the way.
11. Loosen and remove the lower transaxle to engine bolts.

NOTE: One bolt is situated between the transaxle case and the engine block. It is installed in the opposite direction of the other bolts.

12. Remove the flexplate cover. Matchmark the flexplate to torque converter relationship to insure proper alignment upon installation. Remove the flexplate to torque converter bolts.
13. Disconnect the engine support bracket at the transaxle and then lower the vehicle.
14. Disconnect the radiator and heater hoses at the engine and position them out of the way.
15. Remove the alternator.
16. Either disconnect the engine wiring harness at the electronic control unit, then feed the main connector through the firewall and lay it across the engine, or tag and disconnect all engine sensor connectors from the wiring harness.
17. Remove the remaining upper transaxle to engine bolts.
18. Install a lifting fixture to the engine and remove the en-

GENERAL MOTORS—"H" BODY
FRONT WHEEL DRIVE CARS—BUICK LE SABRE · OLDSMOBILE 88

gine from the vehicle. Lift the engine slowly and make sure no wiring or hoses are snagged as the engine is removed.

19. Installation is the reverse of the removal procedure.

ENGINE MOUNTS

Removal and Installation

1. Disconnect the negative battery cable. Properly support the engine assembly, using tool J-28467 or equivalent.
2. Raise and support the vehicle safely. Remove the engine mount to engine mount bracket retaining nuts.
3. Raise the engine slightly. Remove the engine mount to frame retaining nuts.
4. Remove the engine mount from the vehicle.
5. Installation is the reverse of the removal procedure.

Valve System

All engines use hydraulic valve lifters. Valve systems with hydraulic lifters operate with zero clearance in the valve train. The rocker arms are non adjustable. The lifter itself will compensate if there is slack in the system. If there is excessive play in the valve train system the entire system should be checked.

VALVE LIFTERS

Removal and Installation

1. Disconnect the negative battery cable.
2. Drain the engine coolant. Drain the engine oil. Remove the valve covers.
3. Remove the rocker arm assemblies. Remove the pushrods.
4. Remove the intake manifold. Remove the hydraulic valve lifters using the proper tools.
5. Installation is the reverse of the removal procedure. Be sure to use new gaskets as required.

VALVE ROCKER ASSEMBLY

Removal and Installation

1. Disconnect the negative battery cable. Remove the valve cover.
2. Remove the rocker arm pedestal retaining bolts. Note the positions of the double ended bolts for reassembly.
3. Remove the pedestal and rocker arm assembly. Place the assemblies in order on a clean workbench so they can be reassembled in their original locations.
4. Installation is the reverse of removal. Torque the rocker arm pedestal bolts to 45 ft. lbs. and the valve cover bolts to 7 ft. lbs.

VALVE TIMING

Adjustment

Manufacturers recommended procedure for valve timing has not yet been established.

CYLINDER HEAD

Removal and installation

1. Disconnect the negative battery cable. Drain the cooling system.
2. Remove the intake manifold.
3. Disconnect the exhaust crossover pipe.
4. Remove the exhaust manifold.
5. Remove the valve covers, rocker arms and pushrods. Keep all parts in order so they may be reassembled in their original locations.

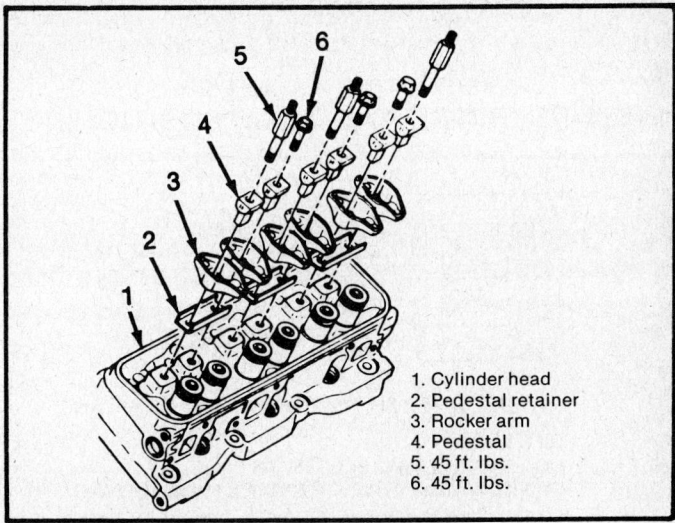

1. Cylinder head
2. Pedestal retainer
3. Rocker arm
4. Pedestal
5. 45 ft. lbs.
6. 45 ft. lbs.

Exploded view of rocker arm assembly

6. Loosen the cylinder head bolts in reverse of the torque sequence, then remove the bolts and lift off the cylinder head.
7. Clean all gasket mating surfaces and the cylinder head bolt holes in the block.
8. Installation is the reverse of removal. Torque the cylinder head bolts in the sequence shown to 25 ft. lbs.
9. Tighten each cylinder head bolt ¼ turn (90°) in sequence.
10. Tighten each cylinder head bolt an additional ¼ turn in sequence.

NOTE: Should you reach 60 ft. lbs. of torque at any time in Steps 9 and 10, stop tightening the bolt at this point. Do not complete the balance of the 90° turn.

Camshaft

Removal and Installation

1. Disconnect the negative battery cable.
2. Remove the engine from the vehicle an position it in a suitable holding fixture.
3. Remove the valve covers, rocker assemblies and push rods.
4. Remove the intake manifold. Remove the valve lifters.
5. Remove the front cover. Remove the timing chain and timing gear.

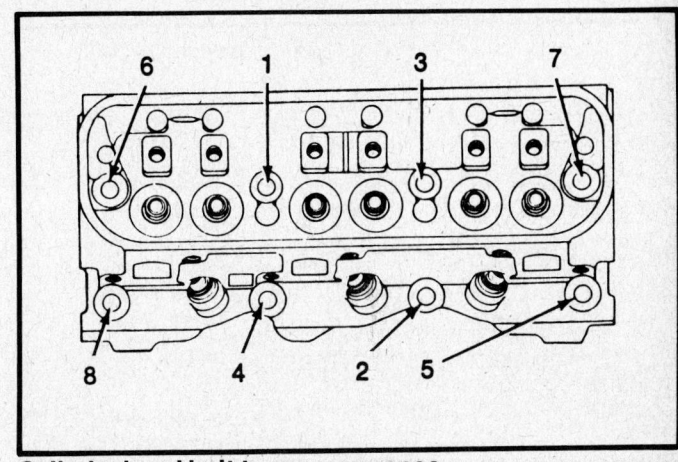

Cylinder head bolt torque sequence

SECTION 9
GENERAL MOTORS—"H" BODY
FRONT WHEEL DRIVE CARS—BUICK LE SABRE • OLDSMOBILE 88

6. Carefully remove the camshaft from the engine.
7. Installation is the reverse of the removal procedure. Be sure to use new gaskets as required.

PISTONS, RINGS AND RODS POSITIONING

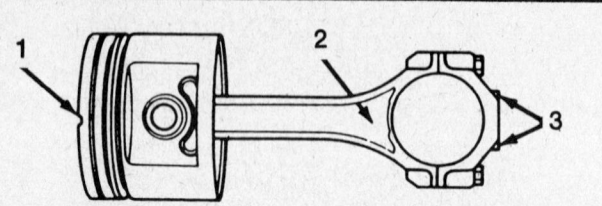

1 — NOTCH ON PISTON TOWARDS FRONT OF ENGINE
LEFT BANK
2 — NO. 1, 3 & 5 TWO BOSSES ON ROD TOWARDS REAR OF ENGINE (NOT SHOWN)
3 — CHAMFERED CORNERS ON ROD CAP TOWARDS FRONT OF ENGINE
RIGHT BANK
2 — NO. 2, 4 & 6 TWO BOSSES ON ROD TOWARDS FRONT OF ENGINE (NOT SHOWN)
3 — CHAMFERED CORNERS ON ROD CAP TOWARDS REAR OF ENGINE

Piston and connecting rod positioning

TIMING CASE COVER/OIL SEAL
Removal and Installation

1. Disconnect the negative battery cable. Drain the cooling system and disconnect the upper and lower radiator hoses.
2. Disconnect the heater return hose.
3. Remove the two nuts from the front engine mount a the cradle and raise the engine slightly with a suitable lifting device.
4. Remove the serpentine drive belt and the water pump pulley.
5. Remove the alternator and mounting bracket.
6. Remove the front clamp on the coolant bypass hose.
7. Remove the right front tire and the inner fender splash shield, then remove the crankshaft balancer and pulley assembly.
8. Remove the timing chain cover mounting bolts at the block and oil pan.
9. Remove the timing chain cover. Clean all gasket mating surfaces and pry out the old oil seal with a suitable tool. Install a new oil seal using tool J-35354 or equivalent.
10. Installation is the reverse of removal.

TIMING GEARS AND CHAIN
Removal and Installation

1. Rotate the engine until the No. 1 cylinder is at TDC/compression using a remote starter. Disconnect the negative battery cable.
2. Remove the front cover.
3. Remove the timing chain dampener.
4. Remove the camshaft sprocket bolts, then remove the camshaft sprocket, timing chain and crankshaft sprocket.
5. Installation is the reverse of removal. Align the timing marks and install the sprockets and timing chain together. Torque the camshaft sprocket bolts to 19 ft. lbs.

Lubrication
OIL PAN
Removal and Installation

1. Disconnect the negative battery cable.
2. Raise and support the vehicle safely.
3. Drain the engine oil into a suitable container and discard.
4. Remove the transmission converter cover.
5. Remove the oil pan mounting bolts and lower the oil pan. Clean all gasket mating surfaces.
6. Installation is the reverse of removal. Use a new oil pan gasket and tighten the retaining bolts to 7 ft. lbs.

OIL PUMP
Removal and Installation

1. Disconnect the negative battery cable.
2. Remove the front cover from the engine.
3. Remove the oil filter adapter, pressure regulator valve and valve spring.
4. Remove the oil pump cover retaining screws and cover.
5. Remove the oil pump gears.
6. Installation is the reverse of removal.

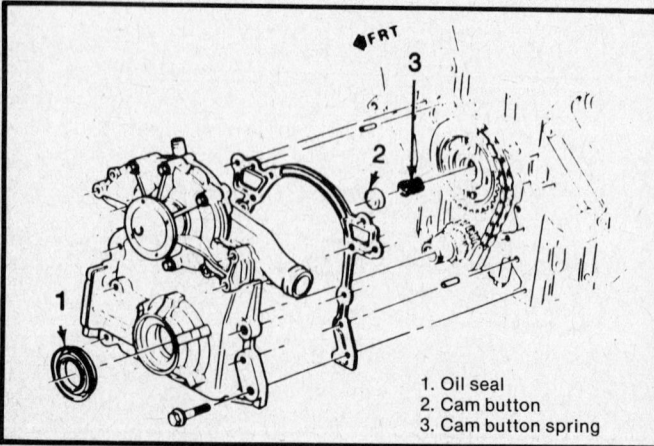

1. Oil seal
2. Cam button
3. Cam button spring

Timing chain cover

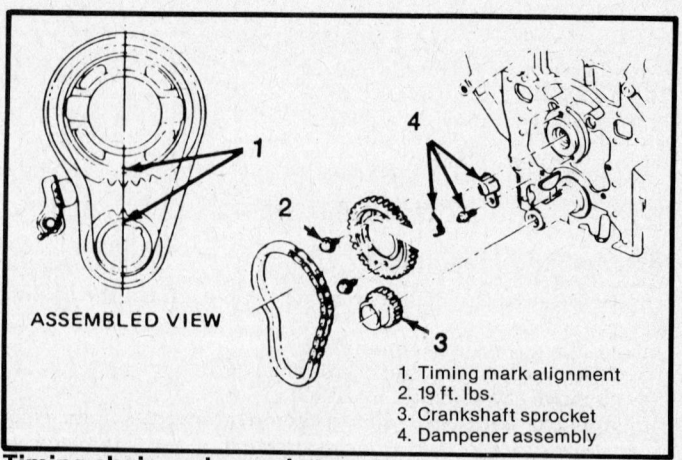

1. Timing mark alignment
2. 19 ft. lbs.
3. Crankshaft sprocket
4. Dampener assembly

Timing chain and sprockets

GENERAL MOTORS—"H" BODY
FRONT WHEEL DRIVE CARS—BUICK LE SABRE • OLDSMOBILE 88

REAR MAIN SEAL

Removal and Installation

1. Disconnect the negative battery cable. Raise and support the vehicle safely.
2. Drain the engine oil and remove the oil pan.
3. Remove the rear main bearing cap.
4. Remove the old seal from the bearing cap.
5. Insert packing tool J-21526-2 or equivalent against one end of the seal in the cylinder block. Pack the old seal into the groove until it is packed tight, then repeat the procedure on the other end of the seal.
6. Measure the amount the seal was driven up, then add approximately $1/16$ in. Cut this length from the old seal removed from the lower bearing cap, then repeat for the other side. Use the lower bearing cap as a holding fixture when cutting the short lengths with a razor blade.
7. Install seal packer guide J-21526-1 or equivalent onto the cylinder block.
8. Using the packing tool, work the short pieces into the guide tool and pack into the cylinder block until the tool hits the built in stop.

NOTE: It may help to use oil on the short seal pieces when packing into the block.

9. Repeat Steps 7 and 8 for the other side.
10. Remove the guide tool.
11. Install a new rope seal into the lower bearing cap.
12. Install the lower main bearing cap and torque the bolts to 100 ft. lbs. (135 Nm).
13. Install the remaining components in the reverse order of removal. Fill the crankcase with engine oil, start the engine and check for leaks.

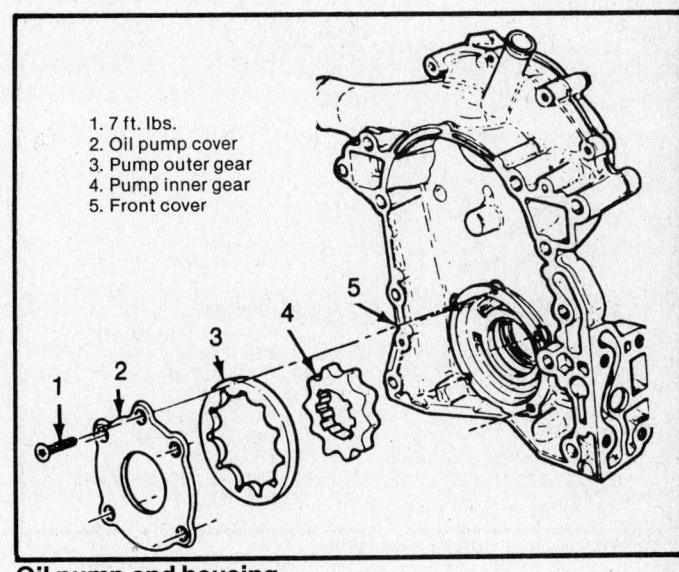

1. 7 ft. lbs.
2. Oil pump cover
3. Pump outer gear
4. Pump inner gear
5. Front cover

Oil pump and housing

FRONT SUSPENSION AND STEERING SECTION

For Front Suspension services refer to the Unit Repair Section. For Steering Gear Overhaul, refer to the Unit Repair Section.

STEERING WHEEL

Removal and Installation

1. Disconnect the negative battery cable. Remove the trim retaining screws from behind the wheel. On wheels with a center cap, pull off the cap.
2. Lift the trim off and pull the horn wires from the turn signal cancelling cam.
3. Remove the retainer and the steering wheel nut.
4. Mark the wheel to shaft relationship, and then remove the wheel with a puller.
5. Install the wheel on the shaft aligning the previously made marks. Tighten the nut. When installing a steering wheel, always make sure that the turn signal lever is in the neutral position.
6. Insert the horn wires into the cancelling cam.
7. Install the center trim and reconnect the battery cable.

STEERING RACK

Removal and Installation

1. Raise and support the vehicle safely. If equipped, disconnect the power steering hoses.
2. Move the intermediate shaft seal upward and remove the intermediate shaft to stub shaft pinch bolt.
3. Remove both front wheels.
4. Remove the cotter pins and nut from both tie-rod ends. Disconnect the tie-rod ends from the steering knuckles.

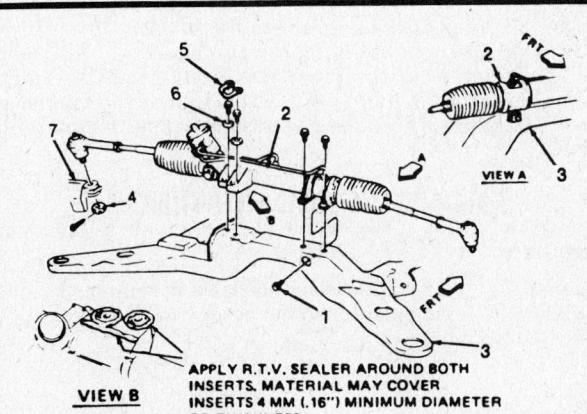

1. BOLT 68 N·m (50 LBS. FT.) AFTER SECOND REUSE OF BOLT, LOCTITE THREAD LOCKING KIT, #1052624 MUST BE USED
2. STEERING GEAR
3. FRAME
4. 50 N·m (35 LBS. FT.), 70 N·m (52 LBS. FT.) MAXIMUM PERMISSIBLE TORQUE TO ALIGN COTTER PIN SLOT. (¹⁄₆ TURN MAXIMUM) DO NOT BACK OFF FOR COTTER PIN INSERTION
5. RETAINER
6. WASHER
7. STEERING KNUCKLE

APPLY R.T.V. SEALER AROUND BOTH INSERTS. MATERIAL MAY COVER INSERTS 4 MM (.16") MINIMUM DIAMETER OR THICKNESS.

Rack and pinion assembly

SECTION 9

GENERAL MOTORS—"H" BODY
FRONT WHEEL DRIVE CARS—BUICK LE SABRE • OLDSMOBILE 88

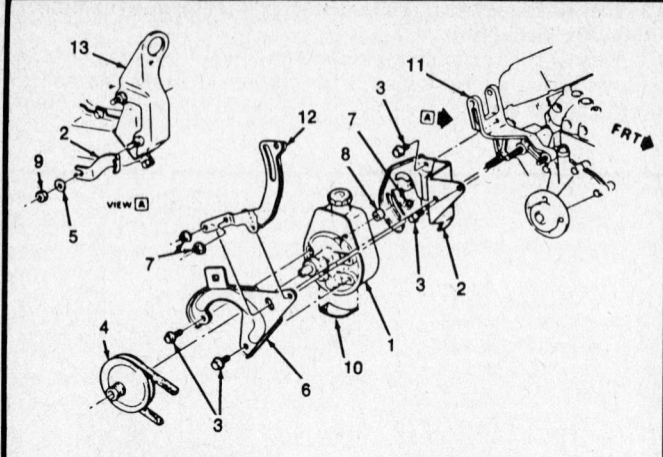

1. POWER STEERING PUMP
2. REAR ADJ. BRACKET
3. BOLT—50 N·m (37 LBS. FT.)
4. PULLEY
5. WASHER
6. FRONT ADJ. BRACKET
7. NUT—50 N·m (37 LBS. FT.)
8. SPACER
9. NUT—27 N·m (20 LBS. FT.)
10. PROTECTOR
11. GENERATOR MOUNTING BRACKET
12. GENERATOR ADJ. BRACKET
13. ENGINE LIFT BRACKET & SHIELD

Power steering pump mounting

5. Remove the line retainer.
6. Remove the outlet and pressure hose.
7. Remove the five rack and pinion assembly mounting bolts.
8. Loosen the front engine cradle mounting bolts. Install jack stands and the lower the rear of the cradle about 3 in. Do not lower the rear of the engine cradle too far.
9. Remove the rack and pinion assembly.
10. Installation is in the reverse order of removal. Tighten the rack mounting bolts to 50 ft. lbs. Tighten the tie-rod end nut to 35–52 ft. lbs. Bleed the power steering system and check for leaks.

FRONT WHEEL BEARINGS

Adjustment

All models covered in this section utilize a permanently sealed and lubricated front wheel bearing assembly. No adjustments are necessary or possible.

POWER STEERING PUMP

Removal and Installation

1. Disconnect the negative battery cable.
2. Remove the air cleaner assembly, as required.
3. Remove the drive belt and then the alternator itself.
4. Raise and support the vehicle safely.
5. Disconnect and plug the pressure and return lines at the pump.
6. Remove the rear pump adjustment bracket to pump nut. Remove the power steering belt. Lower the vehicle.
7. Remove the alternator adjustment bracket and support brace.
8. Remove the rear pump adjustment bracket and then remove the pump assembly.
9. Remove the front pump adjustment bracket and then remove the pulley.
10. Installation is in the reverse order of removal. Adjust the drive belts and bleed the power steering system.

BLEEDING THE POWER STEERING SYSTEM

1. Fill the fluid reservoir.
2. Let the fluid stand undisturbed for two minutes, then crank the engine for about two seconds. Refill reservoir if necessary.
3. Repeat Steps 1 and 2 above until the fluid level remains constant after cranking the engine.
4. Raise the front of the car until the wheels are off the ground, then start the engine. Increase the engine speed to about 1500 rpm.
5. Turn the wheels lightly against the stops to the left and right, checking the fluid level and refilling if necessary.

STEERING COLUMN

Removal and Installation

1. Disconnect the negative battery cable.
2. Remove the lower trim plate from the center of the steering wheel, as required.
3. Detach the shift indicator cable from the steering column shift bowl.
4. Remove the insulator pad from under the dash.
5. Remove the steering column retaining bolts and lower the column carefully.
6. Remove the bolt holding the steering shaft to the rack assembly.
7. Disconnect all electrical connections from the steering column assembly.
8. Carefully remove the steering column from the vehicle.
9. Installation is the reverse of the removal procedure.

BRAKE SECTION

For brake service, refer to the Unit Repair section.

MASTER CYLINDER

Removal and Installation

1. Disconnect the negative battery cable. Disconnect and plug hydraulic lines, and drain the cylinder.
2. Remove the attaching nuts and remove the master cylinder from the power booster unit.
3. Reverse to install. Bleed the system.

POWER BOOSTER

Removal and Installation

1. Disconnect the negative battery cable. From inside the vehicle, detach the brake pushrod from the brake pedal.
2. Disconnect the hydraulic lines from the front of the master cylinder.
3. Remove the nuts from the mounting studs which hold the unit to the dash panel. Remove the unit and clean it prior to installation.

GENERAL MOTORS—"H" BODY
FRONT WHEEL DRIVE CARS—BUICK LE SABRE • OLDSMOBILE 88

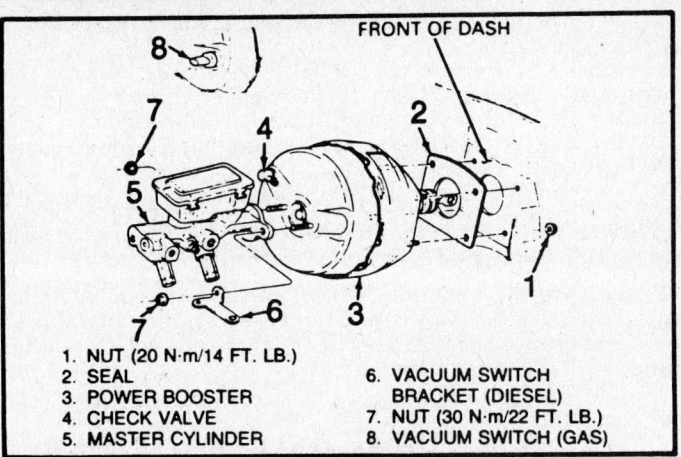

1. NUT (20 N·m/14 FT. LB.)
2. SEAL
3. POWER BOOSTER
4. CHECK VALVE
5. MASTER CYLINDER
6. VACUUM SWITCH BRACKET (DIESEL)
7. NUT (30 N·m/22 FT. LB.)
8. VACUUM SWITCH (GAS)

Typical master cylinder and power booster mounting

2. Remove the front cable from the cable connector at the pedal assembly.
3. Raise and support the vehicle safely.
4. Loosen the equalizer nut until the cable tension is removed than remove the cable from the equalizer.

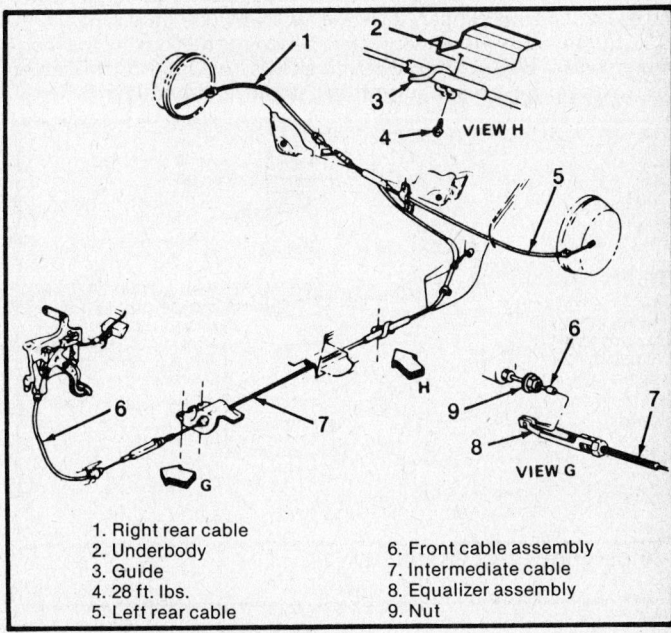

1. Right rear cable
2. Underbody
3. Guide
4. 28 ft. lbs.
5. Left rear cable
6. Front cable assembly
7. Intermediate cable
8. Equalizer assembly
9. Nut

Parking brake cable assembly

4. Installation is the reverse of removal. Bleed the brake system.

PARKING BRAKE

Adjustment

1. Depress the parking brake pedal 1½ in.
2. Raise and support the vehicle safely.
3. Tighten the adjusting nut until the left rear wheel can just be turned to the rear with both hands, but is locked when forward rotation is attempted.
4. With the mechanisms totally disengaged, both rear wheels should turn freely in either direction with no brake drag. Do not adjust the parking brake cable so tight as to cause brake drag.
5. Lower the vehicle.

PARKING BRAKE CABLE

Removal and Installation

1. Release the parking brake lever. Remove the tension spring retainer clip.

5. Remove the clips that hold the parking brake cable to the rear crossmember and at each caliper support plate.
6. Remove the cable ends from the parking brake actuator.
7. Remove the control arm hooks and the conduit from the exhaust hanger clip.
8. Installation is the reverse of the removal procedure. Adjust the parking brake, as required.

TRANSAXLE AND DRIVESHAFT SECTION

For Overhaul Procedures, refer to the Unit Repair Section.

AUTOMATIC TRANSAXLE

Automatic Transmission

NOTE: Any inaccuracies in shift linkage adjustments may result in premature failure of the transmission due to operation without the controls in full detent. Such operation results in reduced fluid pressure and in turn, partial engagement of the affected clutches. Partial engagement of the clutches, with sufficient pressure to permit apparently normal vehicle operation will result in failure of the clutches and/or other internal parts after only a few miles of operation.

1. Disconnect the negative battery cable. Disconnect the wire connector at the mass air flow sensor.
2. Remove the air intake duct and the mass air flow sensor as an assembly.
3. Disconnect the cruise control assembly. Disconnect the shift control linkage.
4. Tag and disconnect the Park/Neutral switch, torque converter clutch, vehicle speed sensor and vacuum modulator hose at the modulator.

NOTE: Care must be exercised on reassembly of the Park/Neutral switch to ensure a proper fit of both the connector and the T-latch. Failure to do so may result in intermittent loss of switch functions.

5. Remove the three top transaxle to engine block bolts. Install an engine support fixture.
6. Remove both front wheels and then turn the steering wheel to the full left position.
7. Remove the right front ball joint nut and separate the control arm from the steering knuckle.
8. Remove the right drive axle. Be careful not to allow the drive axle splines to contact any portion of the lip seal.
9. Remove the left drive axle using a suitable pry bar. Be

careful not to damage the pan. Install drive axle boot seal protectors.

10. Remove three bolts at the transaxle and three nuts at the cradle member. Remove the left front transaxle mount.
11. Remove the right front mount to cradle nuts. Remove the left rear transaxle mount to transaxle bolts.
12. Remove the right rear transaxle mount as in Step 10. Remove the engine support bracket to transaxle case bolts.
13. Remove the flywheel cover. Remove the flywheel to converter bolts. Be sure to matchmark the flywheel to converter relationship for proper alignment upon reassembly.
14. Remove the bolts attaching the rear cradle member to the front cradle dog leg.
15. Remove the front left cradle to body bolt. Remove the front cradle dog leg to right cradle member bolts.
16. Install a transaxle support fixture into position.
17. Remove the cradle assembly by swinging it aside and supporting it with a suitable stand.
18. Disconnect and cap the oil cooler lines at the transaxle.

NOTE: One bolt is located between the transaxle and the engine block and is installed in the opposite direction.

19. Remove the remaining lower transaxle to engine bolts. And then lower the transaxle assembly away from the vehicle.
20. Installation is in the reverse order or removal. Check the fluid level and all adjustments.

DRIVE AXLE

Removal and Installation

1. Use care when removing the drive axle. Tri-pots can be damaged if the drive axle is over extended. Remove the hub nut.
2. Raise the front of the car. Remove the wheel and tire.
3. Install an axle shaft boot seal protector, GM special tool No. J-28712 or equivalent, onto the seal.
4. Disconnect the brake hose clip from the MacPherson strut, but do not disconnect the hose from the caliper. Remove the brake caliper from the spindle, and hang the caliper out of the way by a length of wire. Do not allow the caliper to hang by the brake hose.
5. Mark the camber alignment cam bolt for reassembly. Remove the cam bolt and the upper attaching bolt from the strut and spindle.
6. Pull the steering knuckle assembly from the strut bracket.
7. Using GM special tool J-28733 or the equivalent spindle remover, remove the axle shaft from the hub and bearing assembly.
8. If a new drive axle is to be installed, a new knuckle seal should be installed first.
9. Loosely install the drive axle into the transaxle and steering knuckle.
10. Loosely attach the steering knuckle to the suspension strut.
11. The drive axle is an interference fit in the steering knuckle. Press the axle into place, then install the hub nut. When the shaft begins to turn with the hub, insert a drift through the caliper into one of the cooling slots in the rotor to keep it from turning. Insert a long bolt in the hub flange to prevent the shaft from turning. Tighten the hub nut to 70 ft. lbs. to completely seat the shaft.
12. Install the brake caliper. Tighten the bolts to 30 ft. lbs.
13. Load the hub assembly by lowering it onto a jackstand. Align the camber cam bolt marks made during removal, install the bolt and tighten to 140 ft. lbs. Tighten the upper nut to the same value.
14. Install the axle shaft all the way into the transaxle using a screwdriver inserted into the groove provided on the inner retainer. Tap the screwdriver until the shaft seats in the transaxle. Remove the boot seal protector.
15. Connect the brake hose clip to the strut. Install the tire and wheel, lower the car, and tighten the hub nut to 185 ft. lbs.

CONSTANT VELOCITY JOINT

OVERHAUL

Please refer to the "U-Joint" section of the Unit Repair section.

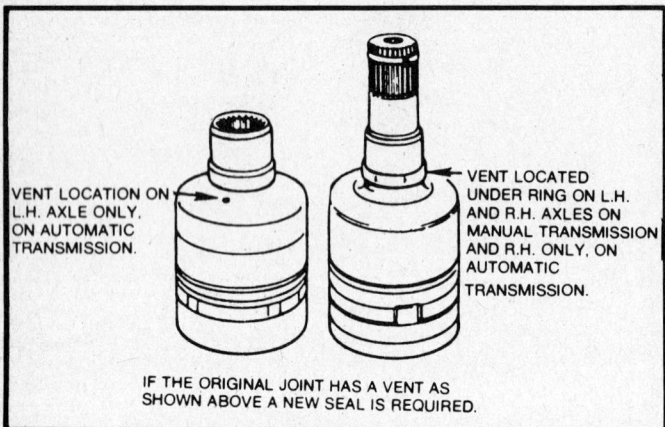

T-latch connector assembly

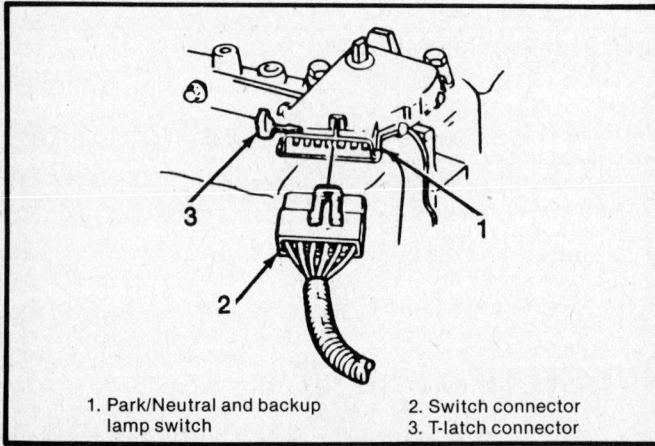

Comparison of old and new style CV joints

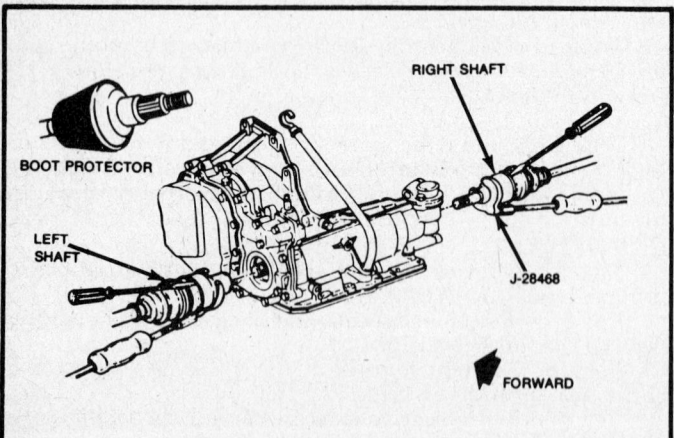

Halfshaft removal using special tools

GENERAL MOTORS—"H" BODY
FRONT WHEEL DRIVE CARS—BUICK LE SABRE • OLDSMOBILE 88

REAR AXLE AND SUSPENSION

HUB

REMOVAL & INSTALLATION

A single unit hub and bearing assembly is bolted to both ends of the rear axle assembly. These take the place of rear axles used on rear wheel drive cars. The hub and bearing assembly is a sealed unit which requires no maintenance. The unit must be replaced as an assembly and cannot be disassembled or adjusted.

The hub and bearing can be removed by removing the rear brake drum, removing the four hub and bearing to axle assembly attaching bolts and pulling the unit out. Installation is the reverse of removal. Tighten the bolts to 35–39 ft. lbs.

SUPERLIFT STRUT

Removal and installation

1. Remove the inner trunk side cover.
2. Raise and support the rear of the vehicle. Remove the wheels and tires.
3. Disconnect and plug the ELC air line.
4. Remove the strut tower mounting nuts from inside the trunk.
5. Remove the strut anchor bolts, washers and nuts from the rear knuckle and knuckle bracket.
6. Remove the strut.
7. Installation is in the reverse order of removal. Tighten the strut tower mounting nuts to 19 ft. lbs. (25 Nm). Tighten the strut anchor nuts to 144 ft. lbs. (195 Nm). Lightly pressurize the ELC system by momentarily grounding the compressor test lead in the engine compartment. Check rear wheel alignment.

COIL SPRINGS

Removal and Installation

1. Raise the rear of the vehicle and support it so that the control arms hang free. Remove the rear wheels.
2. Separate the rear stabilizer bar from the knuckle bracket and remove it.
3. Disconnect the ELC height sensor link (right control arm) and/or the parking brake cable retaining clip (left control arm).
4. Position the special tool J-23028-01 or its equivalent, so as to cradle the control arm bushings. Special tool J-23028-01 should be secured to a suitable jack.
5. Raise the jack to remove the tension from the control arm pivot bolts. Secure a chain around the spring and through the control arm as a safety precaution.
6. Remove the rear control arm pivot bolt and nut.
7. Slowly maneuver the jack so as to relieve any tension in the front control arm pivot bolt and then remove the bolt and nut.
8. Lower the jack to allow the control arm to pivot downward.
9. When all pressure is removed from the coil spring, remove the safety chain, spring and insulators. The spring insulators should be inspected for cuts or tears. They should be replaced if the vehicle has over 50,000 miles.
10. Snap the upper insulator onto the spring. Position the lower insulator and the spring in the control arm. Install the coil springs so that the upper ends are positioned as indicated.
11. Installation of the remaining components is in the reverse order of removal. Control arm mounting nuts should not be tightened until the vehicle is unsupported and resting on its wheels at normal trim height.

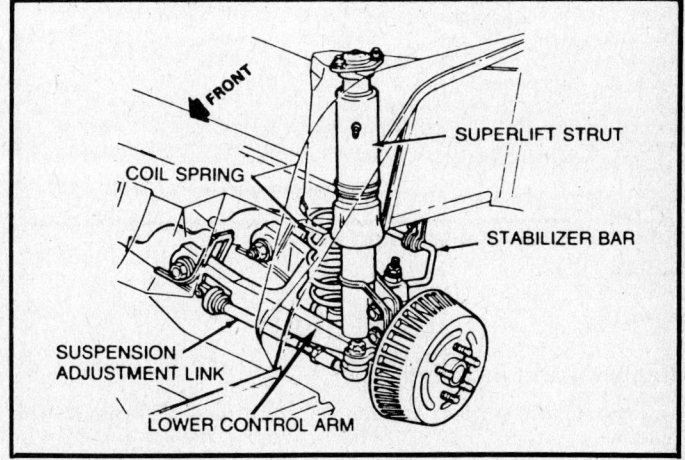
Rear suspension

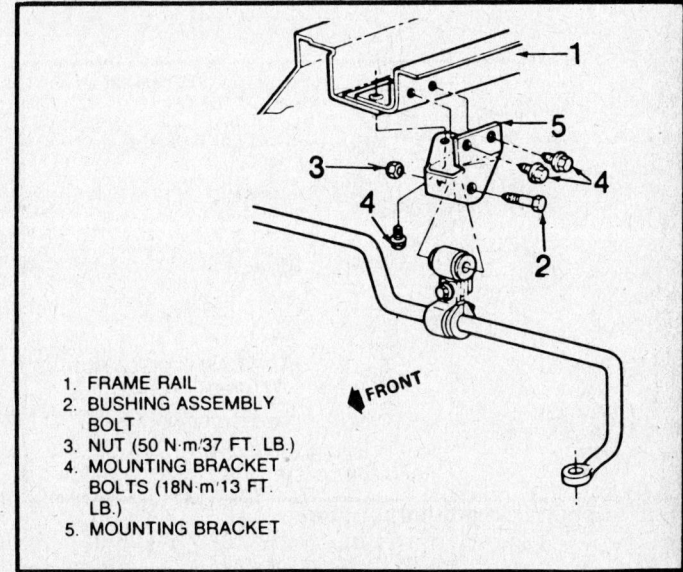

1. FRAME RAIL
2. BUSHING ASSEMBLY BOLT
3. NUT (50 N·m/37 FT. LB.)
4. MOUNTING BRACKET BOLTS (18N·m/13 FT. LB.)
5. MOUNTING BRACKET

Rear stabilizer bar mounting bracket

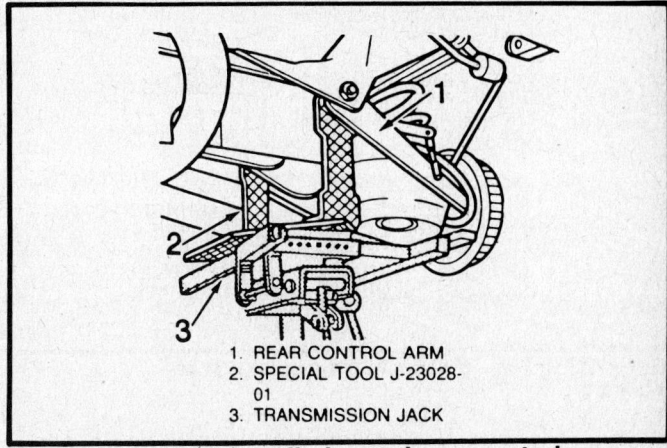

1. REAR CONTROL ARM
2. SPECIAL TOOL J-23028-01
3. TRANSMISSION JACK

Transmission jack installation on lower control arm

GENERAL MOTORS—"H" BODY
FRONT WHEEL DRIVE CARS—BUICK LE SABRE • OLDSMOBILE 88

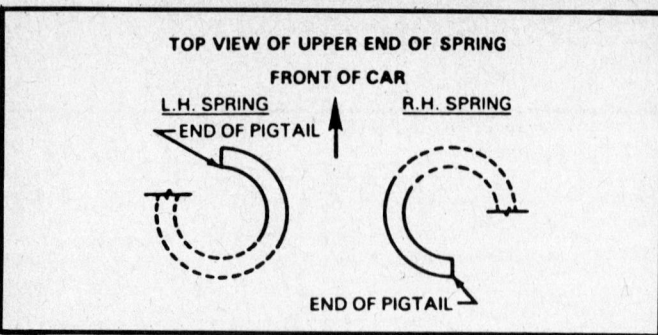
Rear coil spring positioning

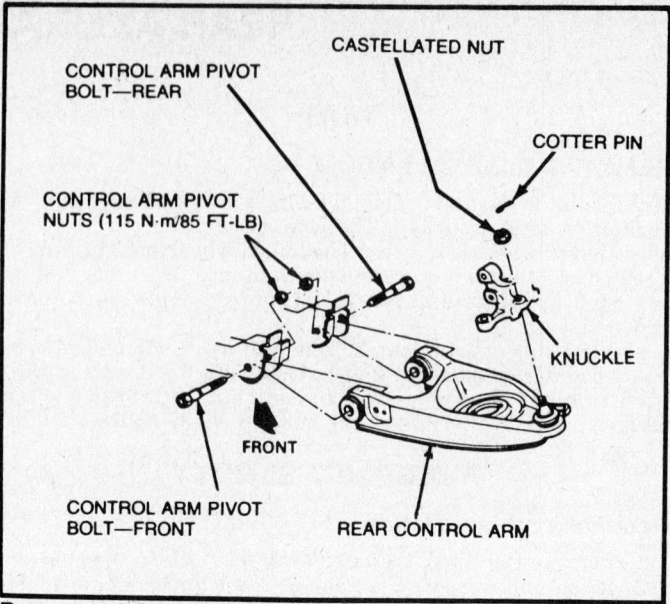
Rear control arm assembly

BALL JOINT

Removal and installation

1. Raise and support the rear of the vehicle and remove the wheels.
2. Disconnect the ELC height sensor link (right control arm) and/or the parking brake cable retaining link (left control arm).
3. Remove the cotter pin and castellated nut from the outer suspension adjustment link.
4. Separate the outer suspension link from the knuckle.
5. Support the control arm with a suitable jack. The lower control arm must be supported to prevent the coil spring from forcing the control arm downward.
6. Remove the ball stud cotter pin.
7. Remove the castellated nut and then reinstall it with the flat side facing upward. Do not tighten the nut.
8. Install a ball joint separator tool and separate the knuckle from the ball stud by backing off the inverted nut against the tool.
9. Separate the ball joint from the control arm.
10. Installation is in the reverse order of removal. Tighten the new castellated nut to 7.5 ft. lbs. Tighten the nut an additional 2/3 of a turn. Align the slot in the nut to the cotter pin hole by tightening only. Do not loosen the nut to align the holes.

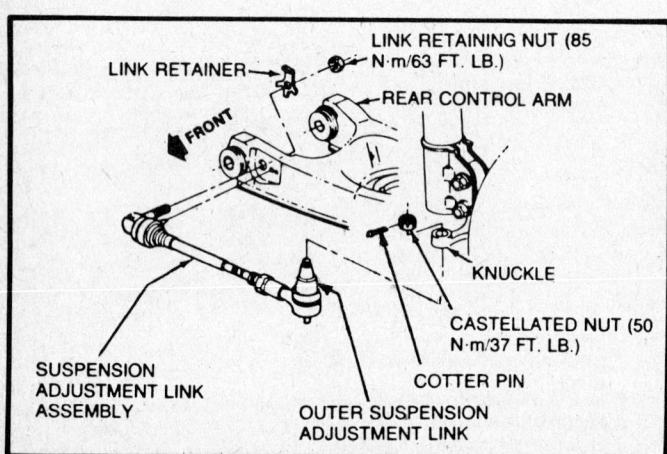
Rear suspension adjustment link

CONTROL ARM

Removal and installation

1. Raise and support the rear of the vehicle and remove the wheels. Disconnect the ELC height sensor link (right control arm) and/or the parking brake cable retaining link (left control arm).
2. Remove the suspension adjustment link retaining nut and retainer.
3. Separate the link assembly from the control arm.
4. Remove the coil spring.
5. Remove the ball stud cotter pin. Remove the castellated nut and then reinstall it with the flat side facing upward. Do not tighten the nut. Install a ball joint separator tool and separate the knuckle from the ball stud by backing off the inverted nut against the tool. Separate the ball joint from the control arm.
6. Remove the control arm.
7. Installation is in the reverse order of removal.

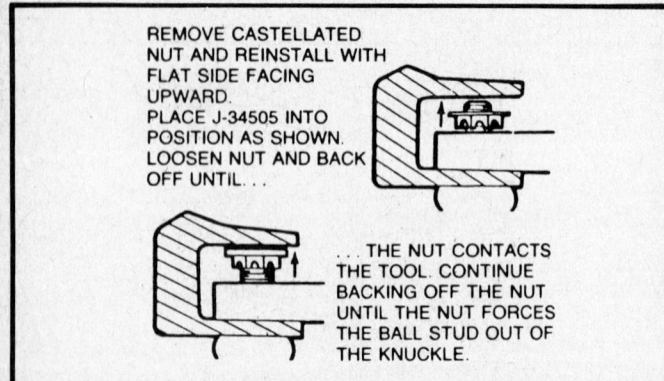
Separating ball joint from steering knuckle

9-22

GENERAL MOTORS – "H" BODY
FRONT WHEEL DRIVE CARS – BUICK LE SABRE • OLDSMOBILE 88

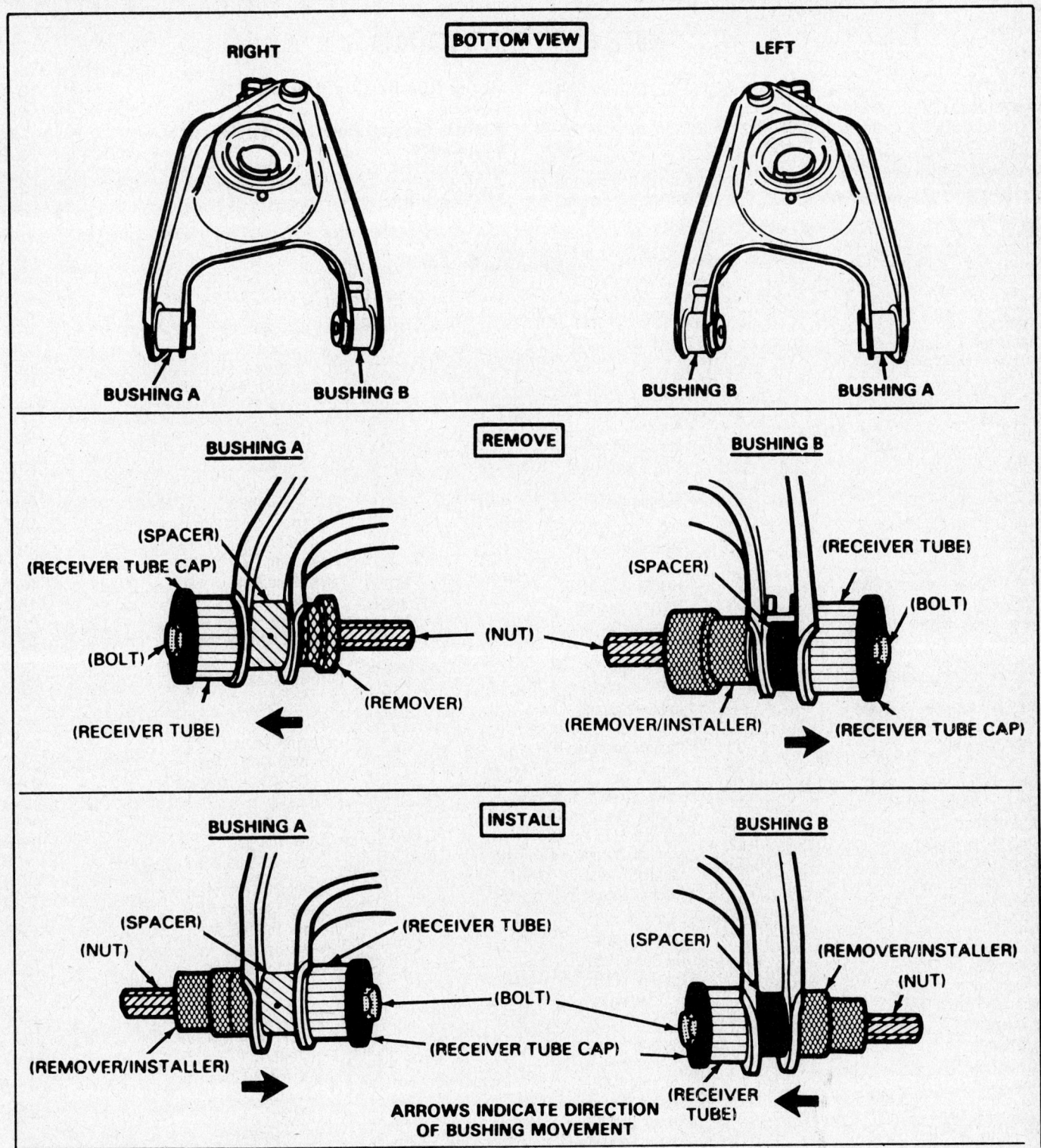

Remove/Install Control Arm Bushings – C & H Series

SECTION 10

GENERAL MOTORS—"J" BODY
FRONT WHEEL DRIVE CARS

SPECIFICATIONS

Brakes	24–2	Serial Number Identification	10–4
Capacities	10–6	Torque	10–7
Crankshaft & Connecting Rod	10–6	Torque Sequence (Cylinder Heads)	10–22
Firing Order	10–5	Tune-Up	10–5
General Engine	10–4	Valve	10–6
Piston & Ring	10–6	Wheel Alignment	10–7

INDEX

A
- Alternator R&R ... 10–7
- Automatic Transaxle ... 23–2
  - On car service ... 23–2
  - Assembly R&R ... 10–31
- Axle Assembly R&R ... 10–33
- Axle Shaft R&R ... 10–32

B
- Ball Joints ... 35–2
- Brake System ... 10–28
- Brake Booster ... 10–28
- Brake Caliper Overhaul ... 24–2
- Brake Caliper R&R ... 24–2
- Brake Drum, Rear ... 24–2
- Brake Master Cylinder ... 10–28
- Brake Pad Front ... 24–2
- Brake Shoe Rear ... 24–2

C
- Camshaft R&R ... 10–23
- Carburetor R&R ... 10–17
- Chassis Electrical ... 10–8
- Clutch ... 10–30
  - Adjustment ... 10–30
  - R&R ... 10–30
- Combination Switch R&R ... 10–10
- Component Locators ... 10–11
- Control Arm ... 35–2
- Cooling Fan motor ... 10–12
- Cooling System ... 10–12
- Cruise Control ... 10–11
- Cylinder Head ... 10–22
  - R&R ... 10–22

D
- Differential ... 23–2, 33–2
  - Inspection ... 23–2, 33–2
- Dimmer Switch R&R ... 10–10
- Disc Brakes ... 24–2
- Distributor R&R ... 10–7
- Drive Axle ... 10–30
- Driveshaft R&R ... 10–32

E
- Electronic Ignition ... 30–2
- Emission Controls ... 10–19
- Engine ... 10–19
  - Identification ... 10–4
  - R&R ... 10–19
- Engine Electrical ... 10–7
- Engine Lubrication ... 10–25
- Engine Mechanical ... 10–19
- Engine Mounts R&R ... 10–20
- Exhaust Manifold ... 10–18

F
- Front Suspension ... 35–2
  - Alignment ... 10–7
- Fuel Injection ... 10–18
- Fuel Mixture Adjust ... 10–15
- Fuel Pump R&R ... 10–15
- Fuses/Circuit Breakers ... 10–11
- Fusible Links ... 10–11

H
- Headlight Switch ... 10–9
- Heater BLower R&R ... 10–12
- Heater Core R&R ... 10–14
- Heater Control ... 10–15
- Horn Switch ... 10–10

I
- Idle Speed Adjust ... 10–15
- Ignition Switch ... 10–8
- Ignition Timing ... 10–8
- Instrument Cluster R&R ... 10–11
- Intake Manifold R&R ... 10–17

L, M, N
- Lower Control Arm R&R ... 35–2
- Master Cylinder R&R ... 10–28
- Manual Steering Gear R&R ... 10–26
- Manual Transaxle Overhaul ... 32–2
- Manual Transaxle R&R ... 10–30
- Neutral Safety Switch R&R ... 10–8

O
- Oil Pan R&R ... 10–25
- Oil Pump R&R ... 10–25
- Oil Seal R&R
  - Rear Main ... 10–25

P
- Parking Brake ... 10–29
  - Adjustment ... 10–29
  - Cable R&R ... 10–29
- Piston Connecting Rod ... 10–23
- Power Brake Unit R&R ... 10–28
- Power Steering Pump R&R ... 10–28

R
- Rear Main Oil Seal R&R ... 10–25
- Rear Suspension ... 35–2
- Regulator ... 10–7
- Rocker Shaft/Assy R&R ... 10–22

S
- Serial Number ... 10–4
  - Engine ... 10–4
  - Vehicle ... 10–4
- Shock Absorber R&R
  - Front ... 35–2
  - Rear ... 35–2
- Springs
  - Front ... 35–2
  - Rear ... 35–2
- Starter R&R ... 10–7
- Starter Drive Replacement ... 10–7
- Steering column R&R ... 10–26
- Steering Gear R&R ... 10–26
  - Manual ... 10–26
  - Power ... 10–26
- Steering Wheel R&R ... 10–26
- Stop Light Switch R&R ... 10–9
- Speedometer R&R ... 10–11
- Suspension R&R ... 35–2
  - Service ... 35–2

T
- Timing Chain ... 10–24
- Timing Gear Cover ... 10–23
  - Oil Seal Replacement ... 10–23
- Tune-Up ... 10–5
- Turn Signal Switch R&R ... 10–10
- Turbocharger ... 10–18

U, V
- U-Joint Overhaul ... 28–2
- Valve Tappetts R&R ... 10–21
- Valve Timing, Adjust ... 10–22
- Valve System ... 10–21
- Voltage Regulator ... 10–7

W, Y
- Water Pump R&R ... 10–12
- Wheel Alignment ... 10–7
  - Front ... 10–7
- Wheel Bearings
  - Front ... 10–27
  - Rear ... 10–33
- Wheel Cylinders
  - Rear ... 24–2
- Windshield wiper ... 10–10
  - Linkage R&R ... 10–10
  - Motor R&R ... 10–10
  - Switch R&R ... 10–10
- Year Identification ... 10–3

BEFORE SERVICING BE CERTAIN TO READ THE SAFETY NOTICE

GM "J" Body
1983–87
Front Wheel Drive Cars

BUICK SKYHAWK • SKYHAWK CUSTOM • SKYHAWK LIMITED • SKYHAWK "T" TYPE
CADILLAC CIMARRON
CHEVROLET • CAVALIER
OLDSMOBILE FIRENZA • FIRENZA "S", SX & LX
PONTIAC J2000 • J2000 LE • J2000 SE

YEAR IDENTIFICATION

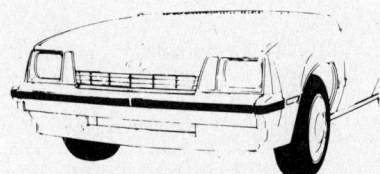
1983 Cavalier

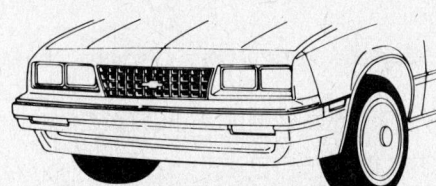
1984–87 Cavalier

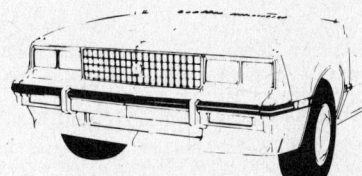
1983 Cimarron

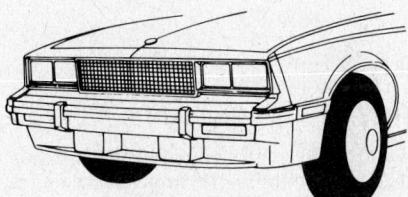
1984–85 Cimarron

1983 Firenza

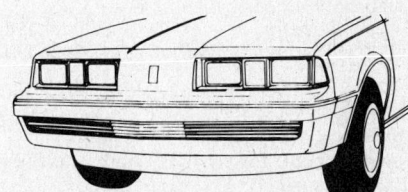
1984 Firenza

1984–87 Firenza GT

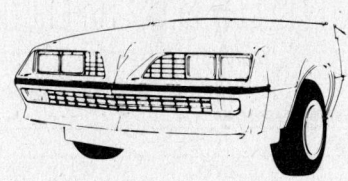
1983 2000

1984 2000 Sunbird

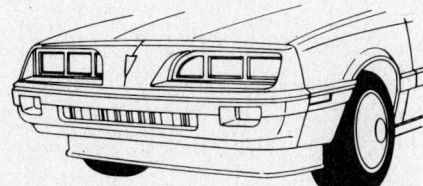
1984–85 2000 Sunbird LE, SE

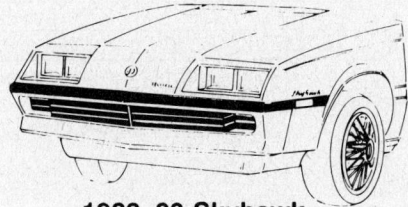
1982–83 Skyhawk

1984–85 Skyhawk

SECTION 10: GENERAL MOTORS—"J" BODY
FRONT WHEEL DRIVE CARS

YEAR IDENTIFICATION

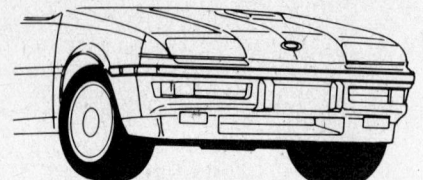
1986–87 Skyhawk

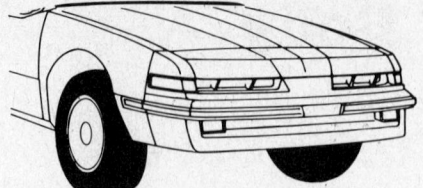
1986–87 Sunbird GT

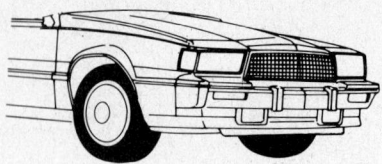
1986–87 Cimarron

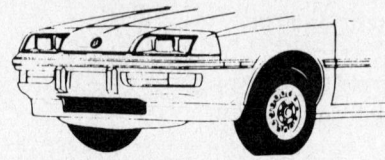
1986–87 Skyhawk Sedan

GENERAL ENGINE SPECIFICATIONS

Year	Engine No. Cyl. Displ. Cu. In.	Liters	Engine VIN Code	Fuel Delivery System	Engine Mfg.	Horsepower @ rpm	Torque @ rpm (ft. lb.)	Bore × Stroke	Compression Ratio	Oil Pressure 2400 rpm
1983–87	4-110	1.8	G	2-bbl	Chev.	88 @ 5100	100 @ 2800	3.50 × 2.91	9.0:1	45
	4-110	1.8	O	TBI	Pont.	84 @ 5200	102 @ 2800	3.34 × 3.13	8.8:1	45
	4-110	1.8	J	MFI ①	Pont.	150 @ 5600	150 @ 2800	3.34 × 3.13	8.0:1	65 ③
	4-122	2.0	P	EFI	Chev.	86 @ 4900	100 @ 3000	3.50 × 3.15	9.3:1	68 ②
	4-122	2.0	B	TBI	Chev.	90 @ 5100	111 @ 2800	3.50 × 3.15	9.0:1	45
	6-173	2.8	W	MFI	Chev.	135 @ 5500 ④	145 @ 3400 ⑤	3.50 × 3.00	8.5:1	30–45

① Turbocharged
② @ 1200 rpm
③ @ 2500 rpm
④ 120 @ 4800 for 1987
⑤ 155 @ 3600 for 1987

VEHICLE IDENTIFICATION NUMBER (VIN)

It is important for servicing and ordering parts to be certain of the vehicle and engine identification. The VIN (vehicle identification number) is a 13 or 17 digit number visible through the windshield on the driver's side of the dash and contains the vehicle and engine identification codes. It can be interpreted as follows:

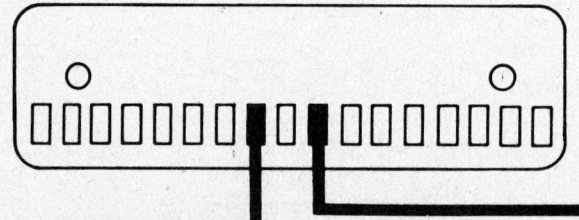

Engine Code						Model Year Code	
Code	Cu. In.	Liters	Cyl.	Carb.	Eng. Mfg.	Code	Year
G	110 (OHV)	1.8	4	2 bbl.	Chev.	D	1983
O	110 (OHC)	1.8	4	TBI	Pontiac	E	1984
J	110 (OHC)	1.8	4	MFI (Turbo)	Pontiac	F	1985
B	122	2.0	4	TBI	Chev.	G	1986
P	122	2.0	4	EFI	Chev.	H	1987
W	173	2.8	6	MFI	Chev.		

The seventeen digit Vehicle Identification Number can be used to determine engine application and model year. The 10th digit indicates the model year, and the 8th digit identifies the factory installed engine.
OHV—Overhead valve engine
OHC—Overhead cam engine
TBI—Throttle Body Injection
MFI—Multi-Port Fuel Injection
NOTE: Some 1983–85 Canadian models with the 2.0 Liter engine use a 2 bbl. carburetor.

GENERAL MOTORS—"J" BODY
FRONT WHEEL DRIVE CARS
SECTION 10

TUNE-UP SPECIFICATIONS

When analyzing compression test results, look for uniformity among cylinders rather than specific pressures.

Year	Eng. VIN Code	Engine No. Cyl. Displacement (cu. in.)	Liters	Eng. Mfg.	hp	Spark Plugs Orig Type	Gap (in.)	Ignition Timing (deg)▲ Man. Trans.	Auto. Trans.	Valves Intake Opens (deg)■	Fuel Pump Pressure (psi)	Idle Speed (rpm)▲ Man. Trans.	Auto. Trans.
1983–87	G	4-110	1.8	Chev.	88	R-42TS	0.045 ①	12B	12B	30	4.5–6.0	4F32	②
	O	4-110	1.8	Pont.	84	R-42XLS6 ④	0.060	8B	8B	N.A.	9–13	②	②
	B	4-122	2.0	Chev.	90	R-42CTS	0.035	—	12B	30	4.5–6.0 ③	②	②
	P	4-122	2.0	Chev.	86	R-42CTS	0.035	②	②	N.A.	12	②	②
	J	4-110	1.8	Pont.	150	R-42CXLS	0.035	②	②	N.A.	12	②	②
	W	6-173	2.8	Chev.	112	R42CTS	0.045	6B	10B	31	6.0	850	750

NOTE: The underhood specifications sticker often reflects tune-up specification changes made in production. Sticker figures must be used if they disagree with those in this chart.
Part numbers in this chart are not recommendations by Chilton for any product by brand name.
① Certain models may use 0.035 in. Gap—see underhood specifications sticker to be sure
② See underhood specifications sticker
③ 1983–84 w/T.B.I.—12 psi
④ 1984–85—R44XLS
N.A.: Not Available

▲ See text for procedure
■ All figures Before Top Dead Center
B Before Top Dead Center

FIRING ORDERS

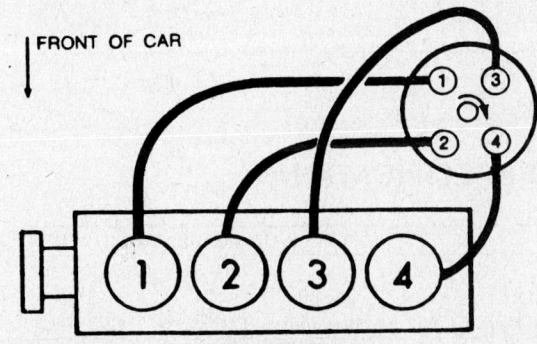

GM (Chevrolet) 110 and 122 overhead valve (OHV)
Engine firing order: 1–3–4–2
Distributor rotation: clockwise

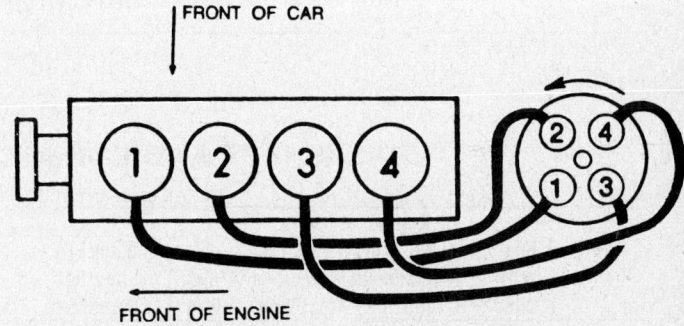

GM (Pontiac) 110 overhead camshaft (OHC)
Engine firing order: 1–3–4–2
Distributor rotation: counterclockwise

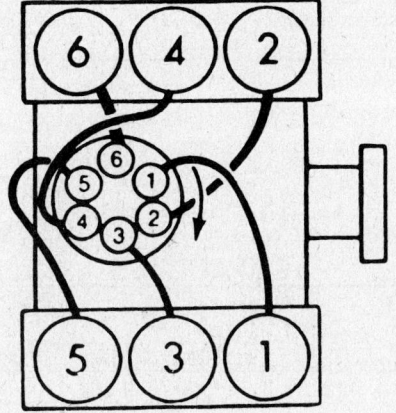

GM (Chevrolet) 173 V6 (2.8L)
Engine firing order: 1–2–3–4–5–6
Distributor rotation: clockwise

GENERAL MOTORS—"J" BODY
FRONT WHEEL DRIVE CARS

VALVE SPECIFICATIONS

Year	Eng. VIN Code	Engine No. Cyl. Displacement (cu. in.)	Liters	Eng. Mfg.	Seat Angle (deg)	Face Angle (deg)	Spring Test Pressure (lbs.@in.)	Spring Installed Height (in.)	Stem-to-Guide Clearance (in.) Intake	Stem-to-Guide Clearance (in.) Exhaust	Stem Diameter (in.) Intake	Stem Diameter (in.) Exhaust
1983–86	G	4-110	1.8	Chev.	46	45	183 @ 1.33	1.60	.0011–.0026	.0014–.0031	.3139–.3144	.3129–.3136
	O,J	4-110	1.8	Pont.	46	45	N.A.	N.A.	.0006–.0016	.0012–.0024	N.A.	N.A.
	B,P	4-122	2.0	Chev.	46	45	183 @ 1.33	1.60	.0011–.0026	.0014–.0031	.3139–.3144	.3129–.3136
	W	6-173	2.8	Chev.	46	45	155 @ 1.160	1.61	.0010–.0027	.0010–.0027	.3410–.3416	.3110–.3416

PISTON AND RING SPECIFICATIONS
All measurements are given in inches.

Year	Eng. VIN Code	Engine No. Cyl. Disp. (cu. in.)	Liters	Eng. Mfg.	Piston-to-Bore Clearance	Ring Gap Top Compression	Ring Gap Bottom Compression	Ring Gap Oil Control	Ring Side Clearance Top Compression	Ring Side Clearance Bottom Compression	Ring Side Clearance Oil Control
1983–86	G	4-110	1.8	Chev.	0.0008–0.0018	0.0098–0.0197	0.0098–0.0197	snug	0.0012–0.0027	0.0012–0.0034	0.0078
	O,J	4-110	1.8	Pont.	0.0008 ①	0.0010–0.0020	0.0010–0.0020	0.0010–0.0020	0.0010–0.0030	0.0010–0.0024	snug
	B,P	4-122	2.0	Chev.	0.0008 ② 0.0018	0.0098–0.0197	0.0098–0.0197	snug	0.0012–0.0027	0.0012–0.0034	0.078
	W	6-173	2.8	Chev.	0.0017–0.0027	0.0098–0.0197	0.0098–0.0197	0.020–0.055	0.0012–0.0028	0.0016–0.0037	0.008

① Code J: 0.0004–0.0012
② 1984–1985: 0.0007–0.0017

CRANKSHAFT AND CONNECTING ROD SPECIFICATIONS
All measurements are given in inches.

Year	Eng. VIN Code	Engine No. Cyl. Displacement (cun. in.)	Liters	Eng. Mfg.	Crankshaft Main Brg. Journal Diameter	Crankshaft Main Brg. Oil Clearance	Crankshaft Shaft End-Play	Thrust on No.	Connecting Rod Journal Diameter	Connecting Rod Oil Clearance	Connecting Rod Side Clearance
1983–87	G	4-110	1.8	Chev.	2.4944–2.4954 ②	0.0006– ③ 0.0018	0.0019–0.0071	4	1.9983–1.9993	0.0009–0.0031	0.0039–0.0240
	O,J	4-110	1.8	Pont.	①	0.0006–0.0016	0.0118–0.0027	3	1.9278–1.9286	0.0007–0.0024	0.0027–0.0095
	B,P	4-122	2.0	Chev.	2.4944–2.4954 ②	0.0006– ③ 0.0018	0.0019–0.0071	4	1.9983–1.9993	0.0009–0.0031	0.0039–0.0240 ④
	W	6-173	2.8	Chev.	2.4937–2.4946	0.0017–0.0030	0.0020–0.0067	3	1.9984–1.9994	0.0014–0.0036	0.006–0.0017

① Bearing are identified by color:
 Brown 2.2830–2.2832
 Green 2.2827–2.2830
② #5: 2.4936–2.4946
③ #5: 0.0014–0.0027
④ '84–'85: .004–.015

CAPACITIES

Year	Eng. VIN Code	Engine Displacement (Cu. In.)	Liters	Eng. Mfg.	Crankcase Quarts (Liters) w/filter	Crankcase Quarts (Liters) wo/filter	Transaxle Pints (L) 4 speed	Transaxle Pints (L) 5 speed	Transaxle Pints (L) Auto	Gas Tank Gal (L)	Cooling System Qts (L) w/heater	Cooling System Qts (L) w/AC
1983–87	G	110	1.8	Chev.	4.0(3.8)	4.0(3.8)	5.9(2.8)	—	10.5(5.0)	14(53)	8.0(7.57)	8.0(7.57)
	O,J	110	1.8	Pont.	①	①	5.—	2.5((5.3)	10.5(5.0)	14(53)	7.8(7.4)	7.9(7.5)
	B,P	122	2.0	Chev.	4.0(3.8)	4.0(3.8)	5.9(2.8)	—	10.5(5.0)	14(53)	8.3(7.7)	8.3(7.7)
	W	173	2.8	Chev.	4.0(3.8)	3.0(2.8)	6.0(2.9)	—	10.0(4.9)	16(61)	11.5(13)	11.75(13)

① Add 3 qts, check oil level at dipstick and add as necessary.

GENERAL MOTORS—"J" BODY
FRONT WHEEL DRIVE CARS
SECTION 10

TORQUE SPECIFICATIONS
All readings in ft. lbs.

Year	Eng. VIN Code	Engine No. Cyl Displacement (cu. in.)	Liters	Eng. Mfg.	Cylinder Head Bolts	Rod Bearing Bolt	Main Bearing Bolt	Crankshaft Pully Bolt	Flywheel to Crankshaft Bolts	Manifold Intake	Manifold Exhaust
1983-87	G	4-110	1.8	Chev.	65-75	34-40	63-74	66-84	45-55	20-25	22-28
	O,J	4-110	1.8	Pont.	①	39	57	115	45	25	16
	B,P	4-122	2.0	Chev.	65-75	34-43	63-77	66-89	② 45-63	18-25	20-30
	W	6-173	2.8	Chev.	70	37	68	75	45	23	25

① Torque bolts to 18 ft. lb., then turn each bolt 60°, in sequence, 3 times for a 180° rotation, then run the engine to normal operating termpuature and turn each bolt, in sequence, an additional 30°-50°.

② Auto. trans.: 45-59.

CAUTION: Verify the correct original equipment engine is in the vehicle by referring to the VIN engine code before torquing any bolts.

WHEEL ALIGNMENT SPECIFICATIONS

Year	Camber (postive) Range (degrees)	Camber (postive) Preferred (degrees)	Toe Range (degrees)	Toe Preferred (degrees)
'83	7/32 to 1-7/32	23/32	5/16 to 1/16	1/8 ①
'84-'85	3/16 to 1³⁄₁₆	11/16	1/4 to 0	1/8 ①
'85-'86	7/32 to 1¹⁄₂	23/32 ②	5/16 to 1/16	1/8

① Out   ② except '86 Firenza—27/32

ELECTRICAL SECTION

For Overhaul Procedures Refer to Unit Repair Sections.

Charging System
ALTERNATOR
Removal and Installation

1. Disconnect the negative battery cable at the battery.
2. Disconnect the two terminal plug and the battery leads from the rear of the alternator.
3. Loosen the mounting belts and remove the the drive belt. remove all necessary components to gain access to the mounting hardware.
4. To install, place the alternator in its brackets and install the mounting bolts.
6. Slip the belts over the pulley. Pull outwards on the unit and adjust the belt tension. Tighten the mounting and adjusting bolts.
7. Install the electrical leads.
8. Install the negative battery cable.

VOLTAGE REGULATOR
REMOVAL AND INSTALLATION

The voltage regulator is incorporated within the alternator assembly. There is no adjustment procedure. Should the regulator require service the alternator must be disassembled.

Starting System
STARTER
REMOVAL AND INSTALLATION

1. Disconnect the negative battery cable.
2. Disconnect the solenoid wires and battery cable.
3. Remove the rear motor support bracket. Remove the A/C compressor support rod (if so equipped).
4. Working under the car, remove the two starter-to-engine bolts, and allow the starter to drop down. Note the location and number of any shims. Remove the starter.
5. Installation is the reverse. Tighten the mounting bolts.

Ignition System
DISTRIBUTOR
REMOVAL AND INSTALLATION

1. Disconnect the negative battery cable.
2. Disconnect all wires leading from distributor cap.
3. Remove the air cleaner housing.
4. Remove the distributor cap.
5. Disconnect the AIR pipe-to-exhaust manifold hose at the air management valve.
6. Unscrew the rear engine lift bracket bolt and nut, lift it

10-7

SECTION 10
GENERAL MOTORS—"J" BODY
FRONT WHEEL DRIVE CARS

off the stud and then position the entire assembly out of the way to facilitate better access to the distributor.

7. Mark the position of the distributor, relative to the engine block and then scribe a mark on the distributor body indicating the initial position of the rotor.

8. Remove the hold-down nut and clamp from the base of the distributor. Remove the distributor from the engine. The drive gear on the distributor shaft is helical and the shaft will rotate slightly as the distributor is removed. Note and mark the position of the rotor at this second position. Do not crank the engine while the distributor is removed.

9. To install the distributor, rotate the shaft until the rotor aligns with the second mark you made (when the shaft stopped moving). Lubricate the drive gear with clean engine oil and install the distributor into the engine. As the distributor is installed, the rotor should move to the first mark you made. This will ensure proper timing. If the marks do not align properly, remove the distributor and reinstall.

10. Install the clamp and hold-down nut.

11. Installation of the remaining components is in the reverse order of removal, check the ignition timing.

12. If the engine was distributed during removal, remove the NO. 1 spark plug and crank the engine until compression is felt.

13. Align the timing mark on the crankshaft pulley with the 0 degree mark on the timing scale attached to the front of the engine. This places the engine at TDC of the compression stroke.

14. Turn the distributor shaft until the rotor points to the NO. 1 spark plug tower on the cap. Rotate shaft counterclockwise slightly away from the NO. 1 position so the gear will mesh with the drive.

15. Install the distributor into the engine. Be sure to align the distributor-to-engine block mark made earlier.

16. Perform Steps 10–11 of the preceding removal and installation procedure.

IGNITION TIMING

Adjustment

1. Refer to instruction on the emission control sticker inside the engine compartment. Follow all instructions on the label.

2. Locate the timing marks on the crankshaft pulley and the front of the engine.

3. Clean off the marks so that you can see them. Chalk or white paint will help to make them more visible.

4. Attach a tachometer to the engine.

5. Disconnect the 4–terminal EST connector at the distributor so that the engine will switch to the bypass timing mode.

6. Attach a timing light as per the manufacturers instructions. Clamp the inductive pick-up on the wire, it may be necessary to peel back the protective plastic cover which encases the wire.

7. Loosen the distributor clamp bolt slightly so that the distributor may be rotated as necessary to adjust timing.

8. Check that all wires are clear of the fan and then start the engine. allow the engine to reach normal operating temperature.

9. Aim the timing light at the marks. A slight jiggling of the notch on the pulley may appear due to the fact that each cylinder is being displayed as it fires. The apparent notch 'width' cannot be reduced by a timing adjustment.

10. Center the total apparent notch 'width' to the correct timing mark on the indicator by rotating the distributor housing. This will insure that the average cylinder timing is as close to specifications as possible. Once again, the apparent notch 'width' cannot be reduced by timing adjustment.

11. Turn off the engine and tighten the distributor lock bolt. Start the engine and re-check the timing.

12. Turn off the engine and disconnect the timing light and the tachometer. Reconnect the 4-terminal EST connector.

Electrical Controls

IGNITION LOCK CYLINDER

REMOVAL AND INSTALLATION

1. Remove the steering wheel.
2. Turn the lock to the run position.
3. Remove the lock plate, turn signal switch or combination switch, and the key warning buzzer switch. The warning buzzer switch can be fished out with a bent paper clip.
4. Remove the lock cylinder retaining screw and lock cylinder.

─────────── CAUTION ───────────
If the screw is dropped on removal, it could fall into the column, requiring complete disassembly to retrieve the screw.

5. Rotate the cylinder clockwise to align the cylinder key with the keyway in the housing.
6. Push the lock all the way in.
7. Install the screw. Tighten to 15 inch lbs.
8. The rest of the installation is the reverse of the removal. Turn the lock to run to install the key warning buzzer switch, which is simply pushed down into place.

IGNITION SWITCH

Removal and Installation

The switch is located inside the channel section of the brake pedal support and is completely inaccessible without first lowering the steering column. The switch is actuated by a rod and rack assembly. A gear on the end of the lock cylinder engages the toothed upper end of the rod.

1. Lower the steering column; be sure to properly support it.
2. Put the switch in the 'Off-Unlocked' position. With the cylinder removed, the rod is in 'Off-Unlocked' position when it is in the next to the uppermost detent.
3. Remove the two switch screws and remove the switch assembly.
4. Before installing, place the new switch in 'Off-Unlocked' position and make sure the lock cylinder and actuating rod are in 'Off-Unlocked' position (second detent from the top).
5. Install the activating rod into the switch and assemble the switch on the column. Tighten the mounting screws. Use only the specified screws, since overlength screws could impair the collapsability of the column.
6. Install the steering column.

NEUTRAL SAFETY/REVERSE LIGHT SWITCH

Removal and Installation

1983–1985

The neutral safety switch is self adjusting and must be replaced rather than adjusted if malfunctioning.

1. Disconnect the negative battery cable.
2. Apply the parking brake and place the gear selector in neutral. Remove the front ash tray and the torx screws under the ash tray.
3. Gently pry the emblem from the center of the shift knob and remove the snap ring securing the shift knob. Lift the trim plate assembly by pulling the front end up first. Disconnect the wiring harness.
4. Remove the screws under the trim plate. Remove the rear ash tray and the screw located under the ash tray.

GENERAL MOTORS—"J" BODY
FRONT WHEEL DRIVE CARS
SECTION 10

5. Lift the console up and off.
6. Disconnect the wiring and removal the neutral safety switch from the side of the shift assembly.
7. Install the new switch and the console in the reverse order of the removal.

1986 AND LATER

1. Disconnect the negative battery cable.
2. Remove the console trim plates and retaining screws.
3. Tag and disconnect the wiring from the switch assembly. The switch is located at the side of the shifter arm.
4. To install a new switch; position the transmission control shifter assembly in the neutral notch in the detent plate.
5. Position the switch in the transmission control shifter assembly by inserting the carrier tang into the hole in the shifter lever assembly.
6. Tighten the mounting screws and move the transmission lever in order to shear the internal plastic pin.

NEUTRAL SAFETY/REVERSE LIGHT SWITCH

Adjustment

1. Place the trnasmission control shift lever in the neutral position.
2. Loosen the switch attaching screws.
3. Rotate the switch on the shifter assembly in order to align the service adjustment hole with the carrier tang hole.
4. Insert 2.34 diameter gauge pin to a depth of 15 mm. Tighten the screws and remove the pin.
5. Install the console assembly.

STARTER SAFETY SWITCH

Removal and Installation

The starter safety switch is used on cars equipped with a manual transaxle. The switch prevents the engine from starting unless the clutch pedal is depressed.
1. Disconnect the negative battery cable.
2. Unbolt the switch from the clutch pedal assembly, disconnect the wiring.
3. Install the new switch in reverse order of removal.

STOPLIGHT SWITCH—CRUISE CONTROL SWITCH

Removal and Installation

The stoplight, cruise control and cruise control vacuum switch are all located on the brake pedal mounting bracket and are adjusted in an identical manner.
1. Remove wiring or vacuum source from the switch. Remove the switch.
2. Install by pushing new switch well into the tubular retaining clip. Pull the brake pedal up just enough to reach the normal released position, this will automatically adjust the switch.
3. Rotate each switch $\frac{1}{2}$ turn counterclockwise to make sure the brake pedal is not applied. Reconnect wires or vacuum source.

HEADLIGHT SWITCH

Removal and Installation
CAVALIER, 2000 AND CIMARRON

1. Disconnect the negative battery cable.
2. Pull knob out fully. Remove knob from rod by depressing retaining clip from underside knob.
3. Remove trimplate.
4. Remove switch by removing nut, rotating switch 180 degrees, then tilting forward and pulling out. Disconnect wire harness.
5. To install, reverse removal procedures.

SHYHAWK AND FIRENZA

1. Disconnect the negative battery cable.
2. Remove the left side trim cover.
3. Remove the screws attaching the headlight switch to the instrument panel.
4. Pull the switch rearward in order to remove it from the vehicle.
5. Installation is the reverse from removal.

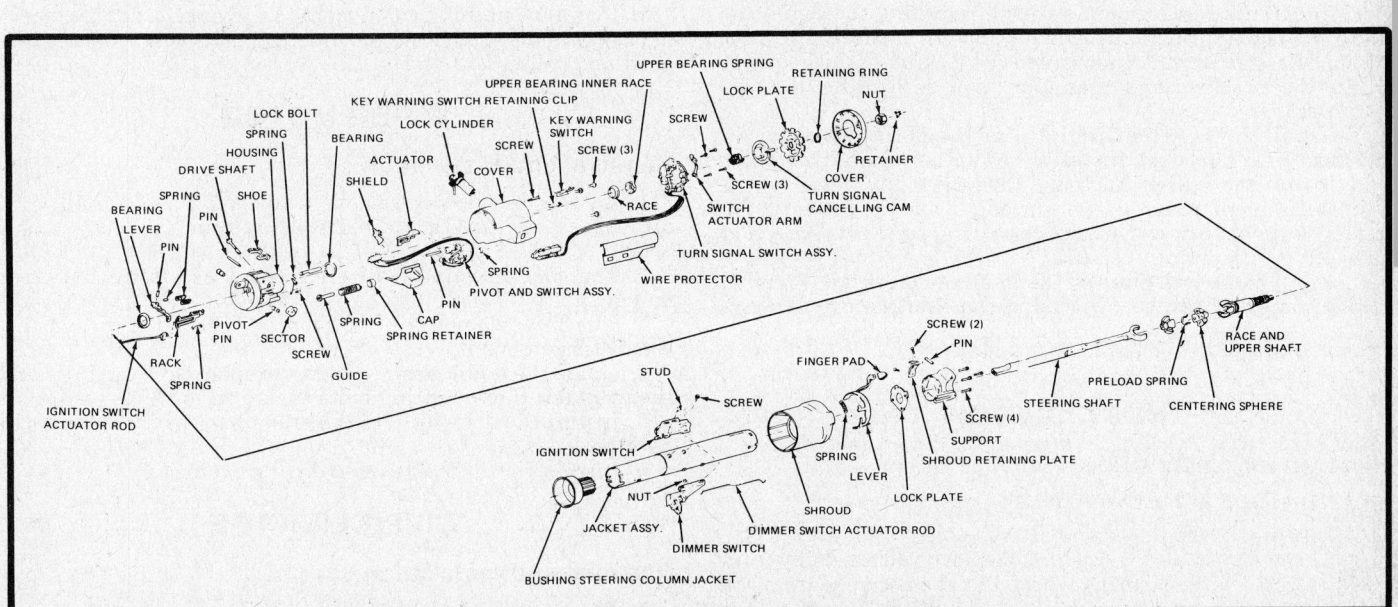

Key release tilt wheel steering column (© General Motors Corporation)

GENERAL MOTORS—"J" BODY
FRONT WHEEL DRIVE CARS

DIMMER SWITCH

Removal and Installation

1. Remove the steering wheel. Remove the trim cover.
2. Remove the turn signal switch assembly.
3. Remove the ignition switch stud and screw. Remove the ignition switch.
4. Remove the dimmer switch actuator rod by sliding it from the switch assembly.
5. Remove the dimmer switch bolts and remove the dimmer switch.
6. Installation is the reverse of the removal procedure.
7. Adjust the dimmer switch by depressing the switch slightly and inserting a $3/32$ inch drill bit into the adjusting hole. Push the switch up to remove any play and tighten the dimmer switch adjusting screw.

TURN SIGNAL SWITCH

Removal and Installation

NOTE: Before removing the turn signal switch, be sure the lever is in the off or center position.

1. Remove the steering wheel. Remove the trim cover.
2. Pry the cover from the steering column.
3. Position a U-shaped lockplate compressing tool on the end of the steering shaft nut clockwise. Pry the wire snap-ring on the shaft groove.
4. Remove the tool and lift the lockplate off the shaft.
5. Slip the cancelling cam, upper bearing preload spring, and thrust washer off the shaft.
6. Remove the turn signal lever. Remove the hazard flasher button retaining screw and remove the button, spring and knob.
7. Pull the switch connector out of the mast jacket and tape the upper part to facilitate switch removal. Attach a long piece of wire to the turn signal switch connector. When installing the turn signal switch, feed this wire through the column first, and then use this wire to pull the switch connector into position. On tilt wheels, place the turn signal and shifter housing in low position and remove the harness cover.
8. Remove the three switch mounting screws. Remove the switch by pulling it straight up while guiding the wire harness cover through the column.
9. Install the replacement switch by working the connector and cover down through the housing and under the bracket. On tilt models, the connector is worked down through the housing, under the bracket, and then the cover is installed on the harness.
10. Install the switch mounting screws and the connector on the mast jacket bracket. Install the column-to-dash trim plate.
11. Install the flasher knob and turn the signal lever.
12. With the turn signal lever in neutral and the flasher knob out, slide the thrust washer, upper bearing preload spring, and cancelling cam onto the shaft.
13. Position the lock plate on the shaft and press it down until a new snap-ring can be inserted in the shaft groove. Always use a new snap-ring when assembling.
14. Install the cover and steering wheel.

HORN SWITCH

Removal and Installation
STANDARD STEERING WHEEL

1. Disconnect the negative battery cable.
2. Remove the screws attaching the horn pad assembly from the underside of the steering wheel. Lift the horn pad from the steering wheel.
3. Disconnect the horn contact terminal from the pad. If the contact terminal comes out of or is removed from the turn signal cancelling cam tower it can be re-installed by pushing it into the tower and rotating the steering wheel clockwise to lock it into position.
4. Installation is the reverse of removal. Connect the negative battery cable.

SPORT STEERING WHEEL

1. Disconnect the negative battery cable.
2. Pull up on the center ornament assembly and remove it from the steering wheel.
3. Remove the steering wheel nut and retainer nut.
4. Remove the horn switch and insulator assembly.
5. Remove three screws and separate the switch from the insulator.
6. Installation is the reverse of the removal. Install the negative battery cable.

WIPER SWITCH

Removal and Installation

1. Remove the steering wheel and directional signal switch, It may be necessary to loosen the two column mounting nuts and remove the four bracket-to-mast jacket to allow the connector clip on the ignition switch to be pulled out of the column assembly.
2. Disconnect the washer/wiper switch lower connector.
3. Remove the screws attaching the column housing to the mast jacket. Be sure to note the position of the dimmer switch actuator rod for reassembly in the same position. Remove the column housing-and-switch as an assembly.

NOTE: The tilt and travel columns have a removable plastic cover on the column housing. This provides access to the wiper switch without removing the entire column housing.

4. Turn upside down and use a drift to remove the pivot pin from the washer/wiper switch. Remove the switch.
5. Place the switch into the position in the housing, then install the pivot pin.
6. Position the housing onto the mast jacket and attach by installing the screws. Install the dimmer switch actuator rod in the same position as noted earlier. Check switch operation.
7. Reconnect lower end of switch assembly.
8. Install remaining components in reverse order of removal. Be sure to attach column mounting bracket in original position.

WIPER MOTOR

Removal and Installation

1. Loosen (but do not remove) the drive link-to-crank arm attaching nuts to detach the drive link from the motor crank arm.
2. Tag and disconnect all electrical leads from the wiper motor.
3. Unscrew the mounting bolts, rotate the motor up and outward and remove it.
4. Guide the crank arm through the opening in the body and then tighten the mounting bolts to 4–6 ft. lbs.
5. Install the drive link to the crank arm with the motor in park position.
6. Installation is the reverse order or removal.

WIPER LINKAGE

Removal and Installation

1. Remove the wiper arms.
2. Remove the shroud top vent grille.

3. Loosen (but do not remove) the drive link-to-crank arm attaching nuts.
4. Unscrew the linkage-to-cowl panel retaining screws and remove the linkage.
5. Installation is the reverse order of removal.

Instrument Cluster

Removal and Installation
SKYHAWK AND FIRENZA
1. Disconnect the negative battery cable.
2. Remove the steering column trim cover. Remove the left and right hand trim cover.
3. Remove the cluster trim cover.
4. Remove the screws attaching the lens and bezel to the cluster carrier.
5. Lower the steering wheel column by removing the two upper steering column attaching bolts.
6. Remove the screws attaching the cluster housing to the cluster carrier. Pull the cluster out slightly from the instrument panel and disconnect the speedometer cable. Disconnect all others connectors.
7. Remove the cluster housing from the vehicle.
8. Installation is the reverse of removal.

CIMARRON, CAVALIER AND 2000
1. Disconnect the negative battery cable.
2. Remove the speedometer cluster trimplate.
3. Remove the speedometer cluster attaching screws.
4. Lower the steering column. Pull the cluster away from the instrument panel and disconnect the speedometer cable.
5. Disconnect the vehicle speed sensor connector from the cluster. Disconnect all other electrical connectors as required.
6. Remove the cluster housing from the vehicle.
7. Installation is the reverse of removal.

SPEEDOMETER

Removal and Installation
1. Disconnect the negative battery cable.
2. Remove the left side trim panels from the underside of the dash assembly. Remove the lower air conditioning duct if so equipped.
3. Remove the steering column trim cover. Remove the screws holding the steering column to the dash assembly.
4. Lower the steering column and remove the speedometer cluster from its housing.
5. Disconnect the case assembly and speedometer cable from the transaxle assembly or cruise control transducer if equipped.
6. Remove the case assembly from the vehicle.
7. Installation is the reverse of removal procedure.

ELECTRONIC COMPONENT LOCATION

Electronic Control Module
The electronic control module (ECM) is located on the right side of the vehicle. It is positioned in front of the right hand kick panel. In order to gain access to the assembly, you must first remove the trim panel.

Convenience Center and Various Relays
The convenience center is located on the underside of the instrument panel near the fuse panel. It provides a central location for various relays, hazard flasher units and buzzers. All units are easily replaced with plug in modules.

Turn Signal Flasher
The turn signal flasher is located directly under the steering column of the vehicle. It is secured in place by means of a plastic retainer. In order to gain access to the component it may be necessary to remove the underdash padding panel.

Vehicle Speed Sensor
The optic head portion of the vehicle speed sensor(VSS) is located in the speedometer frame. A reflective blade is attached to the speedometer cable head assembly. The reflective blade spins, with its blade passing through a light beam, light is reflected back to a photocell in the optic head causing a low power speed signal to be sent to a buffer for amplification. This signal is then sent to the controller.

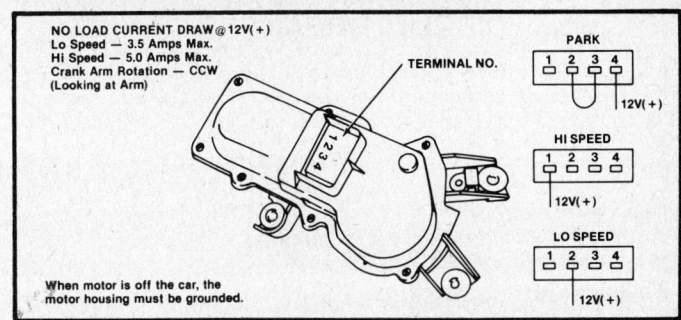

Connections to operate wiper motor independent of vehicle wiring and column switch
(© General Motors Corporation)

CRUISE CONTROL

Adjustments
RELEASE SWITCH AND VALVUE
1. Depress the clutch or brake pedal and insert the vacuum release valve into the retainer until a click is heard indicating that the valve switch is seated.
2. Allow the brake pedal to travel rearward to the positive stop.
3. Allow the clutch pedal to return to normal operating position.
4. The valve switch will be moved through the retainer into the proper position.

SERVO LINKAGE
1. Install the cable into the engine bracket. Route the cable assembly to the servo bracket.
2. Pull the servo end of the cable towards the servo assembly without moving the throttle lever.
3. Line up the pin in the end of the cable with one of the holes in the servo assembly tab.
4. Insert the cable pin into one of the six holes in the servo bracket. Install the retainer.

NOTE: Do not stretch the cable to make a certain connection as this will prevent the engine from returning to idle. Use the next closest hole.

Electrical Circuit Protectors

FUSIBLE LIKS

Fusible links are used to prevent major wire harness damage in the event of short circuit or an overload condition in the wiring circuits which are normally not fused, due to carrying high amperage loads or because of their locations within the wiring harness. Each fusible link is of a fixed value for a specific electrical load and should a link fail, the cause of failure must be determined and repaired prior to installing a new fusible link of the same value.

SECTION 10: GENERAL MOTORS—"J" BODY
FRONT WHEEL DRIVE CARS

CIRCUIT BREAKERS

Circuit breakers are used along with the fusible links to protect the various components of the electrical system, such as headlights, the windshield wipers and electric windows. The circuit breakers are located either in the switch or mounted on or near the lower lip of the instrument panel, to the right or left of the steering column.

COOLING AND HEATER SECTION

WATER PUMP

Removal and Installation

OHC ENGINE

1. Disconnect the negative battery cable.
2. Drain the cooling system.
3. Remove the engine timing belt.
4. Remove the timing belt rear protective covers.
5. Remove the hose from the water pump.
6. Remove the water pump retaining bolts. Remove the pump and the sealing ring from the vehicle.
7. Installation is the reverse of removal.

OHV ENGINE

1. Disconnect the negative battery cable.
2. Drain the cooling system.
3. Remove all accessory drive belts.
4. Remove the alternator.
5. Unscrew the water pump pulley mounting bolts and then pull off the pulley.
6. Remove the mounting bolts and remove the water pump.
7. Place a $\frac{1}{8}$ inch bead of RTV sealant on the water pump sealing surface. While the sealer is still wet, install the pump and tighten the bolts to 13–18 ft. lbs. (18–24 Nm).
8. Installation of the remaining components is in the reverse order of removal.

ELECTRIC COOLING FAN

The coolant fan relay is activated by the Electronic Control Module (ECM) when the Coolant Temperature Sensor recognizes temperature readings above 234° celcius (112°F). The ECM also activates the coolant fan relay when the A/C is on and the vehicle speed is less than 40 mph. The coolant fan is also activated if a coolant temperature sensor failure is detected or if the ECM is in the back up mode. The ECM will also activate the relay on V6 engines when the A/C pressure exceeds 233 psi.

Testing

COOLANT FAN DOES NOT RUN

1. Turn the ignition switch to the run position. Ground the diagnostic terminal "B" of the assembly line communication link.
2. If the coolant fan runs, replace the ECM. If the coolant fan does not run, refer to the next step.
3. Remove the connector from the coolant fan relay which is located on the left front fender forward of the shock tower. Connect a test lamp to terminal "C" of the connector and ground. Turn the ignition switch to the run position.
4. If the test lamp does not light, inspect the brown and white wire for an open. Repair as necessary.
5. If the test lamp lights, move the test light from terminal "C" to terminal "E" of the coolant fan relay connector.
6. If the test lamp does not light, inspect the red wire and fusible link "C", located on the engine harness near the starter solenoid. Repair as necessary.
7. If the test lamp lights, connect a fused jumper between terminals "E" and "A" of the coolant fan relay connector.
8. If the coolant fan runs, replace the coolant fan relay. If the coolant fan does not run, go to the next step.
9. With the fused jumper still in place, remove the coolant fan connector and connect a test lamp to terminal "B" of the connector and ground.
10. If the lamp does not light, inspect the wiring for an open and repair as necessary. If the lamp lights, go to the next step.
11. Move the test lamp ground lead to terminal "A" of the coolant fan connector. If the test lamp does not light, check wire for an open and repair as necessary.

COOLANT FAN RUNS CONTINUOUSLY WITH THE IGNITION SWITCH IN RUN

1. Check for diagnostic code 14 or 15. If either of these codes are present, replace the coolant sensor. If no code is present, go to the next step.
2. Inspect the dark green and white wire for an open and repair as necessary. If the wire appear normal on the 4 cylinder, replace the coolant fan relay, For V6 engine, go to the next step.
3. For the V6 engine, remove the connector from the fan temperature back up switch and turn the ignition switch to run.
4. If the coolant fan runs, replace the coolant fan relay. If the coolant fan does not run, replace the fan temperature back up switch located between the coolant fan relay and the ECM.

COOLANT FAN RUNS CONTINUOUSLY WITH THE IGNITION SWITCH IN OFF

1. Remove the connector from the coolant fan relay.
2. If the coolant fan runs, check for a short to battery voltage. Repair as necessary.
3. If the coolant fan stops running, replace the coolant fan relay.

Removal and Installation

1. Disconnect the negative battery cable.
2. Tag and disconnect the wiring harness from the fan frame and motor assembly.
3. Remove the fan assembly retaining bolts. Remove the fan and motor assembly from the vehicle.
4. Installation is the reverse of the removal procedure.

BLOWER MOTOR

Removal and Installation

1. Disconnect the negative battery cable.
2. Disconnect the electrical connections at the blower motor and blower resistor.
3. Remove the plastic water shield from the right side of the cowl.

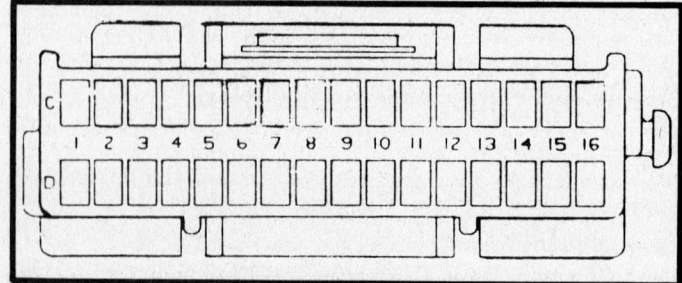

To electronic control module (ECM) (C2)

GENERAL MOTORS — "J" BODY
FRONT WHEEL DRIVE CARS
SECTION 10

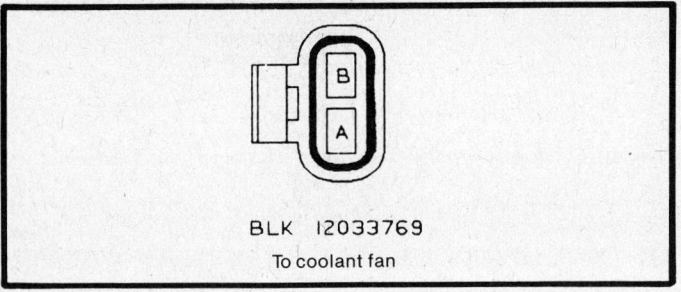

Coolant fan connector

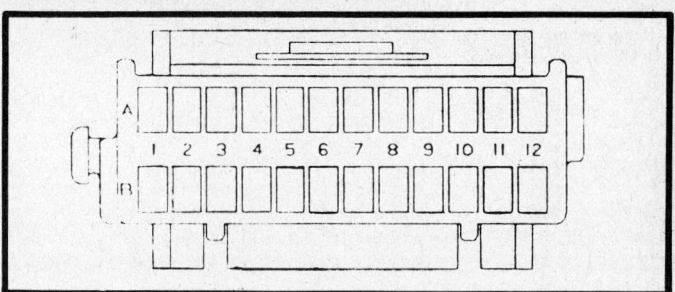

To electronic control module (ECM) (C1)

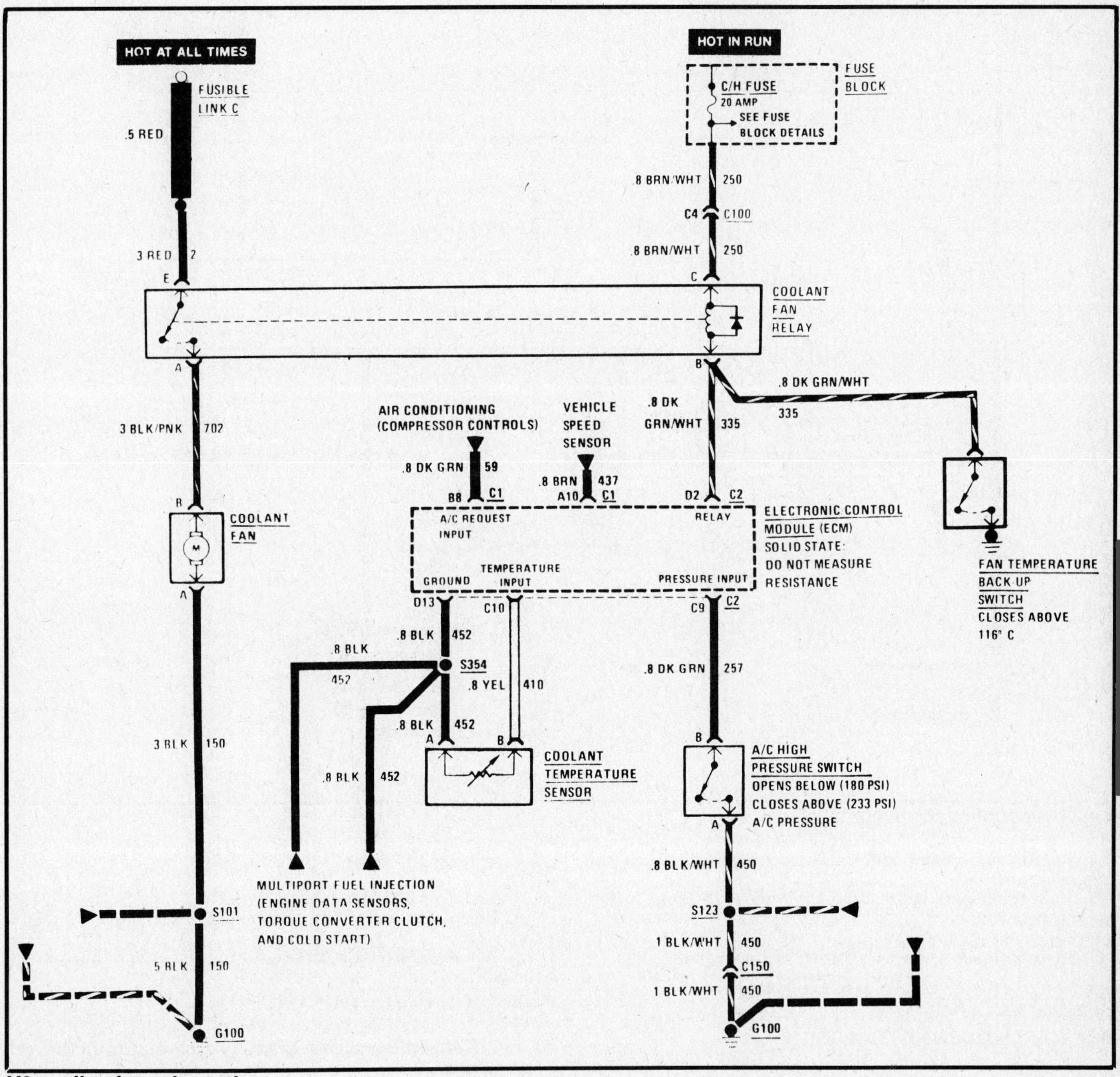

V6 cooling fan schematic

10-13

Section 10: GENERAL MOTORS—"J" BODY
FRONT WHEEL DRIVE CARS

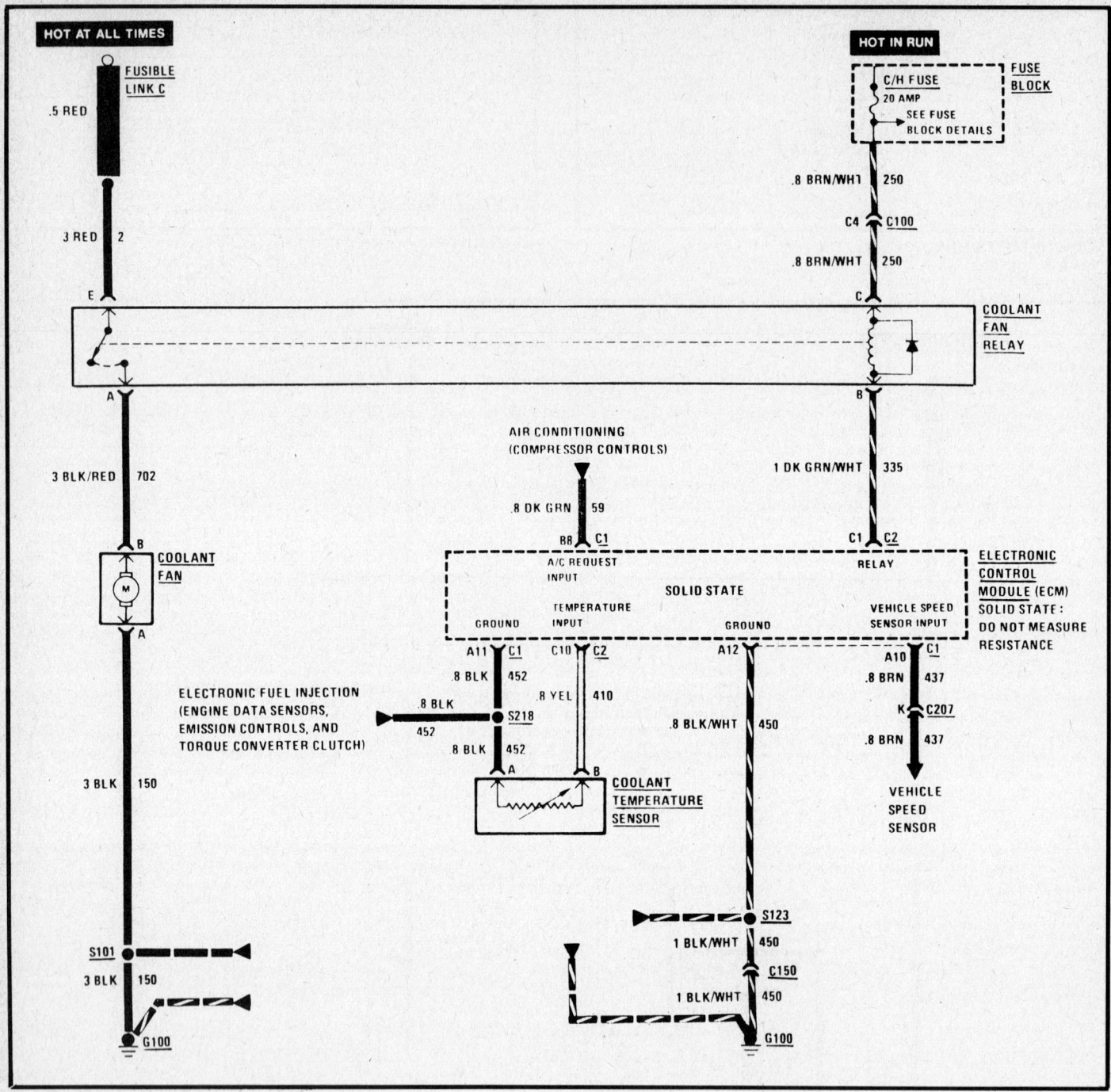

4 cylinder cooling fan schematic

4. Remove the blower motor retaining screws and then pull the motor and cage out.
5. Hold the blower motor cage and remove the cage retaining nut from the blower motor shaft.
6. Remove the blower motor and cage.
7. Installation is the reverse order of removal.

HEATER CORE
Removal and Installation
WITHOUT AIR CONDITIONING

1. Disconnect negative battery cable and drain the cooling system.

2. Remove the heater inlet and outlet hoses from the heater core.
3. Remove the heater outlet deflector.
4. Remove the retaining screws and then remove the heater core cover.
5. Remove the heater core retaining straps and then remove the heater core.

WITH AIR CONDITIONING

1. Disconnect the negative battery cable and drain the cooling system.
2. Raise and support the front of the vehicle.

10-14

GENERAL MOTORS—"J" BODY
FRONT WHEEL DRIVE CARS
SECTION 10

3. Disconnect the drain tube from the heater case.
4. Remove the heater hoses from the heater core.
5. Lower the car. Remove the right and left hush panels, the steering column trim cover, the heater outlet duct and the glove box.
6. Remove the heater core cover. Be sure to pull the cover straight to the rear so as not to damage the drain tube.
7. Remove the heater core clamps and then remove the core.
8. Installation is the reverse order of removal.

TEMPERATURE CONTROL/BLOWER SWITCH

NOTE: If the vehicle is equipped with touch climate control air conditioning, extreme care should be used when disconnecting the electrical connections from the unit.

Removal and Installation
SKYHAWK, FIRENZA AND 2000

1. Disconnect the negative battery cable.
2. Remove the right hush panel, glove box and lower right side of the heater outlet duct.
3. Disconnect the temperature cable at the temperature door and at the vacuum actuator.
4. Remove the cigarette lighter and the control assembly trim plate.
5. Remove the control panel screws. Remove the control panel from the dashboard.
6. Tag and disconnect the vacuum and electrical connections from the rear or the control unit. Remove the control unit.
7. Installation is the reverse of the removal procedure.

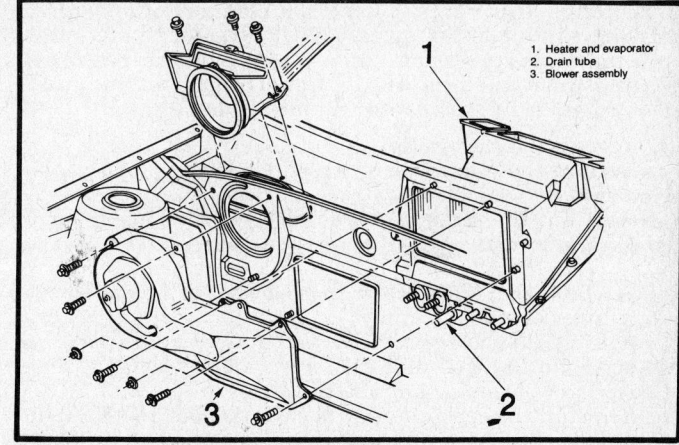

Heater evaporator assembly, blower assembly and air inlet assembly installation
(© General Motors Corporation)

CIMARRON AND CAVALIER

1. Disconnect the negative batter cable.
2. Remove the steering column cover if necessary in order to gain working clearance.
3. Remove the right hand trim cover.
4. Remove the screws attaching the control assembly to the instrument panel.
5. Pull the control assembly out far enough in order to disconnect the electrical connectors and vacuum lines. Disconnect the necessary cables.
6. Remove the control assembly from the vehicle.
7. Installation is the reverse of the removal procedure. Check the system for proper operation.

FUEL SYSTEM

FUEL PUMP

Removal and Installation
MECHANICAL PUMP

1. Disconnect the negative cable at the battery. Raise and support the car.
2. Disconnect the inlet hose from the pump. Disconnect the vapor return hose, if equipped.
3. Loosen the fuel line at the carburetor, then disconnect the outlet pipe from the pump.
4. Remove the two mounting bolts and remove the pump from the engine.
5. To install, place a new gasket on the pump on the engine. Tighten the two mounting bolts alternately and evenly.
6. Install the pump outlet pipe. This is easier if the pipe is disconnected from the carburetor. Tighten the fitting while backing up the pump nut with another wrench. Install the pipe at the carburetor.
7. Install the inlet and vapor hoses. Lower the car, connect the negative battery cable, start the engine, and check for leaks.

ELECTRIC PUMP

1. Remove the fuel pump fuse from its location in side the fuse block.
2. Crank the engine, the engine will start and run until all fuel is consumed. Crank the starter for three seconds to be sure all fuel pressure is relieved.

3. Disconnect the negative battery cable.
4. Raise the vehicle and support it safely.
5. Remove the fuel tank from the vehicle.
6. Remove the fuel pump from the tank.
7. Installation is the reverse of removal. Install the fuse in the fuse block. Start the engine and check for leaks.

CARBURETOR ADJUSTMENTS
IDLE MIXTURE—E2SE CARBURETOR

NOTE: Refer to the Carburetor segment of the Unit Repair Section for carburetor specifications and overhaul adjustments. A E2SE carburetor is used with a Computer Command Control system (CCC), the carburetor is equipped with a mixture control solenoid.

--- CAUTION ---
Idle mixture screws have been preset at the factory and sealed. Idle mixture should be adjusted only in the case of major carburetor overhaul, throttle body replacement of high emissions as determined by official inspections. Adjusting mixture by other than the following method may violate Federal and/or California or other state or Provincial laws. Because of the sealed idle mixture screws, the idle mixture checking procedure requires artificial enrichment by adding propane.

NOTE: Before checking or resetting the carburetor as the cause of poor engine performance or rough idle, check ignition system including distributor, timing,

10-15

SECTION 10
GENERAL MOTORS—"J" BODY
FRONT WHEEL DRIVE CARS

spark plugs and wires. Check air cleaner, evaporative emission system, EFE system, PCV system, EGR valve and engine compression. Also inspect intake manifold vacuum hose gaskets and connections for leaks and check torques of carburetor mounting bolts/nuts.

1. Remove the carburetor.
2. Remove the idle mixture screw plugs, then lightly seat the screws.
3. Back out the screws 5 turns each for the four cylinder engine.
4. Remove the idle air bleed screw plug from the air horn. Lightly seat the air bleed screw, then back it out 3 turns for the four cylinder engine.
5. Remove the vent stack and screen assembly in order to gain access to the lean mixture screw. Lightly seat the lean mixture screw, then back it out 2 ½ turns.
6. Reinstall the carburetor on the engine, but DO NOT install the air cleaner and gasket.
7. Disconnect the bowl vent line at the carburetor.
8. Disconnect and plug the vacuum hose at the tee in the bowl vent line (if so equipped).
9. Disconnect the canister purge and EGR lie at the carburetor, then plug the carburetor fitting.
10. Connect a dwell meter to the mixture control solenoid test lead (green connector) and set the dwell meter to the 6 cylinder position.
11. Connect a tachometer to the distributor TACH lead (brown connector).
12. Block the drive wheels, place the transmission in Park (auto. trans.) or Neutral (man. trans.), and apply the parking brake.
13. Start the engine cooling fan starts to cycle, indicating that the engine is warm and operating in the closed loop mode.
14. Run the engine at 3000 rpm and adjust the lean mixture screw in small increments (allowing the dwell to stabilize after each adjustment) until the average dwell is 35°. If you are unable to adjust to this specification, check the carburetor main metering circuit for leaks, restrictions, etc.

NOTE: It is normal for the dwell to vary about 2 ½ below and above 35°. The dwell reading may also read 10–15° momentarily due to temporary mixture changes.

15. Allow the engine to return to idle and adjust the idle speed to 700 rpm, with the cooling fan in the Off cycle.
16. Adjust the idle mixture screw (in the same manner as in Step 14.) until a dwell (average) of 25° is obtained. The adjustment is very sensitive-the final check must be made with the adjusting tool removed. If you are unable to set the dwell to specification, check the carburetor idle system for leaks, restrictions, etc.
17. Raise the engine rpm to 3000, and make sure that the dwell stabilizes and averages 35° at this rpm. Repeat Steps 14–17 if required.

18. Remove the tachometer and dwell meter, reattach the hoses as they were originally, and reinstall the items previously removed.
19. Set the idle speed to the figure given on the underhood emissions label.

IDLE SPEED CONTROL (ISC)

The idle speed control (ISC) is controlled by the electronic control module (ECM), which has the desired idle speed programmed in its memory. The ECM compares the actual idle speeder is moved in or out. This automatically adjusts the throttle to hold an idle rpm independent of the engine loads.

An integral part of the ISC is the throttle contact switch. The position of the switch determines whether or not the ISC should control idle speed. When the throttle lever is resting against the ISC plunger, the switch contacts are closed, at which time the ECM moves the ISC to the programmed idle speed. When the throttle lever is not contacting the ISC plunger, the switch contacts are open; the ECM stops sending idle speed commands and the driver controls engine speed.

Adjustments

NOTE: Before starting engine, place transmission selector lever in park or neutral, set parking brake, and block drive wheels.

When a new ISC assembly is installed, a base (minimum authority) and high (minimum authority) rpm speed check must be performed and adjustment made as required. These adjustment limit the low and high rpm speeds to the ECM. When making a low and high speed adjustment, the low speed adjustment is always made first. DO NOT use the ISC plunger to adjust curb idle speed as the idle speed is controlled by the ECM.

NOTE: Do not disconnect or connect ISC connector with ignition on as damage to the ECM may occur.

1. Connect tachometer (distributor side of tach filter, if used).
2. Connect dwell meter to mixture control (M/C) solenoid dwell lead. Remember to set dwell meter on the six cylinder scale, regardless of the engine being tested.
3. Turn A/C off.
4. Start engine and run until stabilized by entering "closed loop" (dwell meter needle starts to vary).
5. Turn ignition off.
6. Unplug connector from ISC motor.
7. Fully retract ISC plunger by applying 12 volts DC (battery voltage) to terminal "C" of the ISC motor connection and ground lead to terminal "D" of the ISC motor connection. It may be necessary to install jumper leads from the ISC motor in order to make proper connections.

NOTE: Do not apply battery voltage to motor longer than necessary to retract ISC plunger. Prolonged contact will damage motor. Also, never connect voltage source across terminals "A" and "B" as damage to the internal throttle contact switch will result.

8. Start engine and wait until dwell meter needle starts to vary, indicating "closed loop" operation.
9. With parking brake applied and drive wheels blocked, place transmission in Drive (Neutral, manual transmission models).
10. With ISC plunger fully retracted, adjust carburetor base (slow) idle stop screw to the specified rpm (see specifications). ISC plunger should not be left in full retracted position.
11. Place transmission in Park or Neutral and fully extend ISC plunger by applying 12 volts DC to terminal "D" of the ISC motor connection and ground lead to terminal "C" of the ISC motor connection.

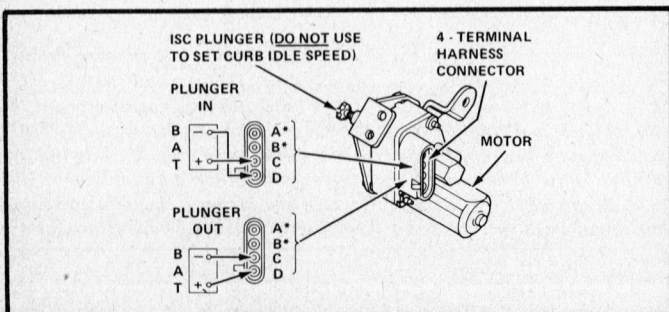

Idle motor (© General Motors Corporation)

10-16

GENERAL MOTORS—"J" BODY
FRONT WHEEL DRIVE CARS

NOTE: Never connect voltage source across terminal "A" and "B" as damage to the internal throttle contact switch will result.

12. With ISC plunger fully extended, using Tool J–29831 or equivalent, turn ISC plunger to obtain ISC adjustment rpm. Verify ISC adjustment rpm with voltage applied to motor will ratchet in and out.

    Auto trans. only; place transmission in Drive and readjust ISC plunger to ISC adjustment rpm.

13. Place transmission in Park or Neutral and turn ignition off. Disconnect 12 volt DC power source, jumper leads, ground lead, tachometer, and dwell meter.
14. Reconnect four terminal harness connector to ISC motor.
15. "Tricking" the ISC motor as described will cause the "Check Engine" light to come on and an ISC motor trouble code to be set. By restoring the system to normal operation, the light will go out, but the trouble code will continue to be stored as an intermittent problem. In this case, it will be necessary to clear the diagnostic trouble code.

FAST IDLE ADJUSTMENT

1. Prepare the car for adjustment as specified on the underhood emission label. Place the transmission in Park or Neutral.
2. Place the fast idle screw on the highest step of the fast idle cam.
3. Turn the fast idle screw in or out to obtain the specified fast idle speed.

CARBURETOR

Removal and Installation

1. Remove the air cleaner and gasket.
2. Disconnect the fuel line and all vacuum lines.
3. Tag and disconnect all electrical connections.
4. Disconnect the downshift cable.
5. If equipped with cruise control, disconnect the linkage.
6. Unscrew the carburetor mounting bolts and remove the carburetor.
7. Before installing the carburetor, fill the float bowl with gasoline to reduce the battery strain and the possibility of backfiring when the engine is started again.
8. Inspect the EFE heater for damage. Be sure that the throttle body and the EFE mating surfaces are clean.
9. Install the carburetor and tighten the nuts alternately to the proper specifications.
10. Installation of the remaining components is in the reverse order of removal.

INTAKE MANIFOLD

Removal and Installation

4 CYLINDER

1. Disconnect the negative cable at the battery.
2. Remove the air cleaner and drain the coolant from the radiator.
3. Remove the idler pulley and the power steering belt.
4. Disconnect the power steering pump and the power steering adjusting bracket.
5. Tag and disconnect all electrical connections and vacuum lines Disconnect the fuel lines.
6. If the vehicle is equipped with fuel injection, remove the fuel injection linkage and assembly.
7. Disconnect the heater hose and the condenser from the bottom of the intake manifold.
8. Remove the distributor.

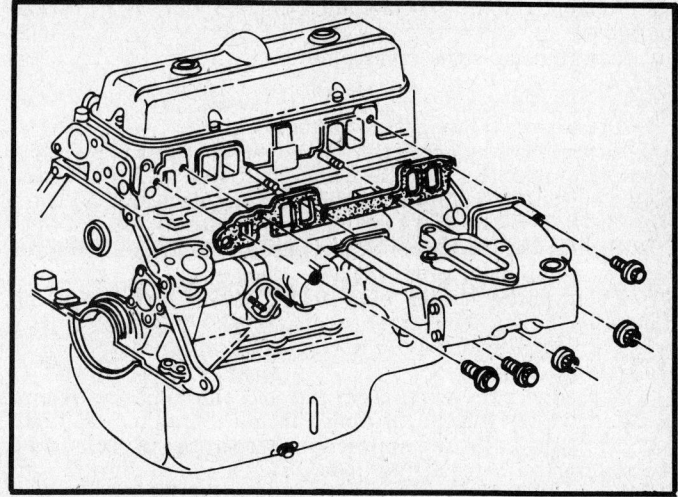
Intake manifold (© General Motors Corporation)

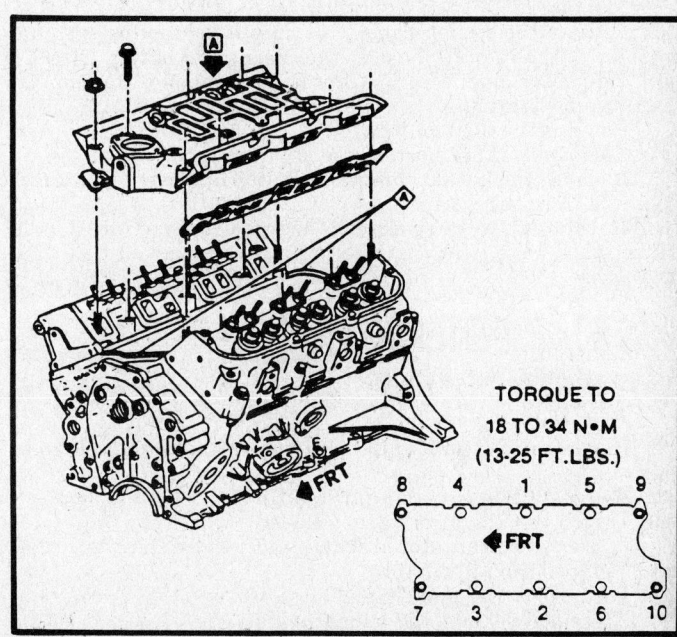
Intake manifold tightening sequence—V6 engine (© General Motors Corporation)

TORQUE TO 18 TO 34 N•M (13-25 FT.LBS.)

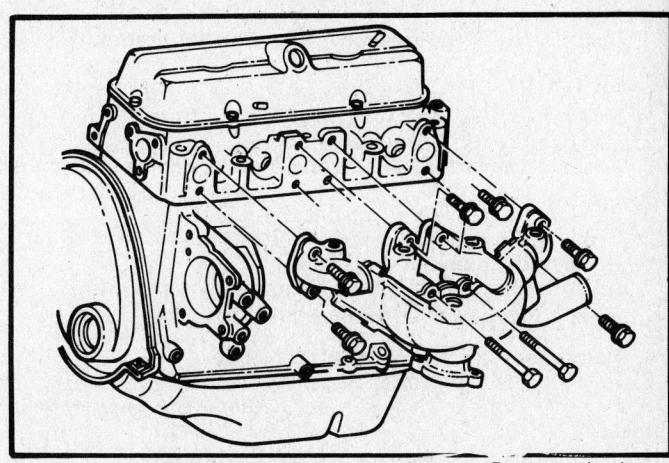
Exhaust manifold (© General Motors Corporation)

10-17

SECTION 10
GENERAL MOTORS—"J" BODY
FRONT WHEEL DRIVE CARS

9. Remove the intake bolts and nuts and remove the intake manifold.
10. Installation is the reverse of removal.

V6

1. Disconnect the negative battery cable.
2. Disconnect the accelerator cable bracket at the plenum.
3. Disconnect the throttle body. Disconnect the EGR pipe from the EGR valve. Remove the plenum assembly.
4. Disconnect the fuel pipe along the fuel rail.
5. Disconnect the serpentine drive belt. Remove the power steering pump mounting bracket.
6. Remove the heater pipe at the power steering pump bracket.
7. Tag and disconnect the wiring at the alternator. Remove the alternator.
8. Disconnect the wires from the cold start injector assembly. Remove the injector assembly from the intake manifold.
9. Disconnect the idle air vacuum hose at the throttle body. Disconnect the wires at the injectors.
10. Remove the fuel rail, breather tube and the fuel runners from the engine.
11. Tag and disconnect the coil wires.
12. Remove the rocker arm covers. Drain the cooling system. Disconnect the radiator hose at the thermostat outlet. Disconnect the heater pipe from the thermostat housing. Disconnect the thermostat wiring.
13. Remove the distributor.
14. Remove the thermostat assembly housing.
15. Remove the intake manifold bolts. Remove the intake manifold from the engine.
16. Installation is the reverse of the removal procedure. Upon installation, take note that the gaskets are marked Left and Right Side.

EXHAUST MANIFOLD

Removal and Installation

4 CYLINDER

1. Remove the exhaust pipe heat shield and the air cleaner duct.
2. Remove the engine oil dipstick tube.
3. Disconnect the oxygen sensor lead.
4. Loosen the alternator brackets and remove the alternator belt. Remove the alternator.
5. Disconnect the pulsair pipe.
6. Raise the vehicle and support safely.
7. Disconnect the exhaust pipe from the exhaust manifold. Lower the vehicle.
8. Remove the exhaust manifold bolts. Remove the exhaust manifold.
9. Installation is the reverse of the removal procedure.

V6 LEFT SIDE

1. Disconnect the negative battery cable.
2. Remove the air cleaner assembly.
3. Remove the air flow sensor. Remove the engine heat shield.
4. Remove the crossover pipe at the manifold.
5. Remove the exhaust manifold bolts.
6. Remove the exhaust manifold.
7. Installation is the reverse of the removal procedure.

V6 RIGHT SIDE

1. Disconnect the negative battery cable.
2. Remove the air cleaner assembly.
3. Remove the air flow sensor. Remove the engine heat shield.
4. Disconnect the crossover pipe at the manifold.
5. Disconnect the accelerator and throttle valve cable at the throttle lever and the plenum. Move aside to gain working clearance.
6. Disconnect the power steering line at the power steering pump.
7. Remove the EGR valve assembly.
8. Raise the vehicle and support safely.
9. Disconnect the exhaust pipe at the exhaust manifold.
10. Lower the vehicle.
11. Remove the manifold bolts. Remove the exhaust manifold.
12. Installation is the reverse of the removal procedure.

Fuel Injection

For More Information on the Fuel Injection System Refer to the Unit Repair Section.

THROTTLE BODY INJECTION—MODEL 500

Throttle Body injection is used on all vehicles equipped with the 2.0 liter engine, VIN Code "P". The throttle body injector is located on the center of the intake manifold where air and fuel are mixed and then routed through a single bore in the throttle body into the intake manifold. The throttle body injector is made of aluminum and consists of two major assemblies, the fuel metering body and the throttle body.

FUEL INJECTION NOZZLE

Removal and Installation

1. Disconnect the negative battery cable. Relieve the fuel system pressure.
2. Tag and disconnect the fuel injection electrical connections.
3. Remove the necessary components in order to gain access to the fuel rail retaining bolts.
4. Remove the fuel rail retaining bolts. Remove the fuel rail assembly.
5. Separate the fuel injector from the fuel rail.
6. Installation is the reverse of the removal procedure. Replace the O-rings when installing the injectors.

Turbocharger System

For More Information on Turbochargers Refer to the Unit Repair Section.

DESCRIPTION AND TYPE

The turbocharger is basically an air compressor or air pump. It consists of a turbine or hot wheel, as shaft, a compressor or cold wheel, a turbine housing, a compressor housing and a center housing which contains bearings, a turbine seal assembly and a compressor seal assembly.

Turbochargers are installed on an engine to put more and denser air into the engine combustion chambers. Because of the increased volume and weight of compressed air more fuel can be scheduled to produced more horsepower from a given size engine. The turbocharged version of an engine will also maintain a higher lever of power output than the non-turbocharged version when operated at altitudes above sea level.

TURBOCHARGER ASSEMBLY

Removal and Installation

1. Disconnect the negative battery cable. Raise the vehicle and support safely.

GENERAL MOTORS—"J" BODY
FRONT WHEEL DRIVE CARS
SECTION 10

2. Remove the exhaust pipe to gain working clearance. Remove the lower fan retaining bolt.
3. Remove the rear air conditioner support bracket. Disconnect the engine to turbocharger support bracket.
4. Remove the oil drain hose at the turbocharger and drain the turbocharger. Lower the vehicle.
5. Disconnect the coolant recovery pipe and lay aside. Remove the induction tube.
6. Remove the coolant fan and the oxygen sensor. Disconnect the turbocharger oil feed pipe.
7. Disconnect the vacuum hose at the actuator and the intake duct.
8. Remove the four turbocharger mounting nuts. Remove the turbocharger.
9. Installation is the reverse of the removal procedure. Make sure that all mating surfaces of the turbocharger are clean prior to installation.

TURBOCHARGER WASTEGATE
Removal and Installation

1. Remove the induction tube.
2. Remove the clip attaching the wastegate linkage to the actuator rod.
3. Disconnect the vacuum hose. Remove the wastegate mounting bolts and remove the wastegate actuator.
4. Installation is the reverse of the removal procedure.

EMISSION CONTROL SECTION

Emission Equipment Used
1983 AND LATER

Positive crankcase ventilation (PCV)
Exhaust gas recirculation (EGR)
Thermostatic air cleaner (THERMAC)
Computer command control (CCC)
Electronic control module (ECM)
Throttle position sensor (TPS)
Electronic spark timing (EST)
Air management
Evaporative emission control system (EECS)
Early fuel evaporation (EFE)
Coolant sensor
Oxygen sensor
Vacuum sensor
Air injection control system
Pulseair system
Catalytic converter

EMISSIONS INDICATOR
Clearing Trouble Codes

When the electronic control module (ECM) finds a problem, the "CHECK ENGINE" light will come on and a trouble code will be stored in the ECM memory. If the problem is not a regular one, the light will go out after 10 seconds. In order to clear the stored trouble code it is necessary to remove the battery voltage for 10 seconds. This will clear all stored codes in ECM memory. Do this by disconnecting the ECM harness from the positive battery cable with the ignition in the off position, or by removing the ECM fuse.

NOTE: In order to prevent damage to the ECM, the key must be off when connecting or disconnecting power to the ECM.

ENGINE SECTION

For Diesel Engine services, Refer to Unit Repair Section.

ENGINE ASSEMBLY
Removal and Installation
4 CYLINDER OVERHEAD VALVE

1. Disconnect the negative battery cable.
2. Remove the air cleaner. Drain the cooling system.
3. Remove the power steering pump (if so equipped) and position it out of the way. Leave the lines connected. Remove the windshield washer bottle.
4. If the car is equipped with A/C, remove the relay bracket at the bulkhead connector. Remove the bulkhead connector and then separate the wiring harness connections.
5. If equipped with cruise control, remove the servo bracket and position it out of the way.
6. Tag and disconnect all vacuum hoses and wires.
7. Remove the master cylinder at the vacuum booster.
8. Remove all heater and radiator hoses and then position them out of the way.
9. Remove the fan assembly. Remove the horn.
10. Disconnect the carburetor linkage. Raise the front of the car and support it.
11. Disconnect the fuel line at the intake manifold.
12. Remove the air conditioning brace (if so equipped).
13. Remove the exhaust shield. Remove the starter.
14. Disconnect the exhaust pipe at the manifold. Remove the wheels.
15. Disconnect the stabilizer bar from the lower control arms. Remove the ball joints from the steering knuckle.
16. Remove the drive axles at the transaxle and then remove the transaxle strut.
17. If equipped with A/C, remove the inner fender shield. Remove the drive belt, tag and disconnect the wires and then remove the compressor.

NOTE: Do not disconnect any of the refrigerant lines.

18. Remove the rear engine mount nuts and plate.
19. If equipped with an automatic transaxle, remove the oil filter.
20. Disconnect the speedometer cable and lower the vehicle.
21. If equipped with an automatic transaxle, remove the oil cooler at the transaxle.

10-19

SECTION 10
GENERAL MOTORS—"J" BODY
FRONT WHEEL DRIVE CARS

22. Remove the front engine mount nuts.
23. Disconnect the clutch cable on the manual transaxle. Disconnect the detent cable on the automatic transaxle.
24. Install an engine lifting device, remove the transaxle mount and bracket. Lift the engine out of the car.
25. Lower the engine into the car, leaving the lifting device attached.
26. Install the transaxle bracket. Install the mount to the side frame and secure with new mounting bolts.
27. With the weight not yet on the mounts, tighten the transaxle bolts. Tighten the right front mounting bolts.
28. Lower the engine onto the mounts, remove the lifting device and then raise the front of the car.
29. Installation of the remaining components is in the reverse order of removal. Check the powertrain alignment bolt; if excessive force is required to remove the bolt, loosen the transaxle adjusting bolts and realign the powertrain. Adjust the drive belts and the clutch cable (if equipped with manual transaxle).

4 CYLINDER OVERHEAD CAM

1. Remove the negative battery and the air cleaner.
2. Drain the cooling system.
3. Disconnect the engine electrical harness at the bulkhead.
4. Disconnect the electrical connector at the break cylinder.
5. Remove the throttle cable from the bracket and remove the electronic fuel injection assembly.
6. Remove the power steering high pressure hose at the cut-off switch.
7. Remove the vacuum hoses at the map sensor.
8. Disconnect the power steering return hose from the power steering pump.
9. Remove the ECM wire connections and feed the harness through the bulkhead.
10. Remove the upper and lower radiator hoses from the engine.
11. Remove the electrical connections from the temperature switch at the thermostat housing.
12. Disconnect the transmission shift cable at the transmission.
13. Raise the vehicle and support safely.
14. Remove the speedometer cable at the transmission and bracket.
15. Disconnect the exhaust pipe at the exhaust manifold.
16. Remove the exhaust pipe from the converter and the heater hoses from the heater core.
17. Remove the transmission cooler lines and the fuel lines at the flex hoses.
18. Remove the front wheels.
19. Remove the right hand spoiler section if equipped.
20. Remove the front brake calipers and support with wire.
21. Remove the left and right tie rod ends.
22. Remove the A/C compressor connections. Remove the A/C compressor assembly.
23. Remove the front suspension support attachment bolts.
24. Lower the vehicle and support the front of the vehicle by placing two short jack stands under the radiator core support.
25. Position front post hoist to the rear of the cowl.
26. Position a 4" x 4" x 6" timber on the front of the post hoist.
27. Raise the vehicle enough to remove the jack stands.
28. Position a 4-wheel dolly under the engine and transaxle assembly.
29. Position three 4" x 4" x 12" blocks under the engine and transaxle assembly and lower the vehicle slightly onto the 4-wheel dolly.
30. Remove the rear transaxle mounting bolts.
31. Remove the left front engine mount attachment bolts.
32. Remove the engine support to body attachment bolts behind the right hand inner axle universal joint.
33. Disconnect the attaching bolt and nut from the right hand chassis side rail to engine mount bracket.
34. Remove the six strut attachment nuts.
35. Raise the vehicle allowing the engine, transaxle and suspension to rest on the dolly.

Reverse removal procedure for engine installation with the following exception is:
1. Position engine and transaxle assembly in chassis.
2. Install transaxle and left front mounts to side rail bolts loosely.
3. Install alignment bolt in left front mount to prevent powertrain misalignment.
4. Torque transaxle mount bolts to 42 ft. lb. and left front mount bolts to 18 ft. ft.
5. Install right rear mount to body bolts and torque to 38 lb. ft.
6. Install right rear mount to chassis side rail bolt and nut torque to 38 lb. ft.
7. Place a floor jack under control arms, jack struts into position and install retaining nuts.
8. Raise vehicle.
9. Using a transmission jack or suitable lifting equipment, raise control arms and attach tie rod ends.

V6

1. Disconnect the negative battery cable. Drain the cooling system. Remove the air cleaner assembly.
2. Remove the air flow sensor. Remove the exhaust crossover heat shield. Remove the exhaust crossover pipe.
3. Remove the serpentine belt tensioner and the serpentine belt.
4. Remove the power steering pump mounting bracket. Disconnect the heater pipe at the power steering pump mounting bracket.
5. Disconnect the radiator hoses from the engine.
6. Disconnect the accelerator and throttle valve cable at the throttle valve.
7. Remove the alternator. Tag and disconnect the wiring harness at the engine.
8. Disconnect the fuel hoses. Disconnect the coolant by-pass hoses and the overflow hoses at the engine.
9. Remove the necessary vacuum hoses leading to the engine.
10. Raise the vehicle and support safely.
11. Remove the inner fender splash shield. Remove the harmonic balancer.
12. Remove the flywheel cover. Remove the starter bolts. Tag and disconnect the electrical connections from the starter. Remove the starter.
13. Disconnect the wires at the oil sending unit.
14. Remove the A/C compressor and related brackets.
15. Disconnect the exhaust pipe at the rear of the exhaust manifold.
16. Remove the flexplate to torque converter bolts.
17. Remove the transaxle to engine bolts. Remove the engine to rear mount frame nuts.
18. Disconnect the shift cable bracket at the transaxle. Remove the lower bell housing bolts.
19. Lower the vehicle and disconnect the heater hoses at the engine.
20. Install a suitable engine lifting device and while supporting the engine and transaxle, remove the upper bell housing bolts.
21. Remove the front mounting bolts.
22. Remove the master cylinder.
23. Remove the engine from the vehicle.
24. Installation is the reverse of the removal procedure.

ENGINE MOUNTS

Removal and Installation—Front

1. Disconnect the negative battery cable.
2. Raise the vehicle and support safely.

GENERAL MOTORS—"J" BODY
FRONT WHEEL DRIVE CARS
SECTION 10

3. Using a suitable fixture, support the engine and remove the engine mount nuts.
4. Remove the inner fender shield.
5. Remove the engine mount bolts. The manufacturer recommends discarding the engine mount bolts. Note the location and length of each bolt for reassembly.
6. Remove the engine mount.
7. Installation is the reverse of the removal procedure.

Removal and Installation—Rear

1. Disconnect the negative battery cable.
2. Raise the vehicle and support safely.
3. If equipped with manual transmission, remove the oil filter in order to gain working clearance.
4. Using a suitable fixture, support the engine and remove the engine mounting nuts.
5. Remove the engine mounting bolts. Remove the engine mount.
6. Installation is the reverse of the removal procedure.

Valve System

VALVE ADJUSTMENT

4 CYLINDER

1. Crank the engine until the mark on the crank pulley lines up with the "O" mark on the timing tab.
2. Determine that the engine is in the number 1 firing position. Place fingers on the number 1 rocker arm as the mark on the crank pulley comes near the "O" mark. If the valves are not moving the engine is in the number 1 firing position.

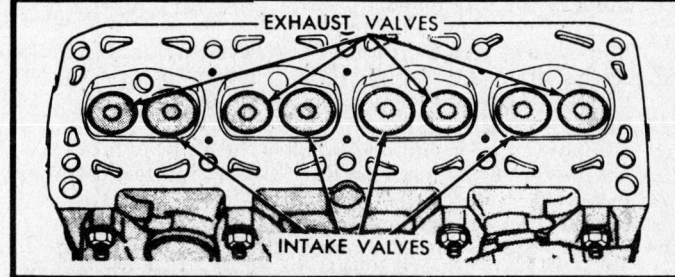

Valve arrangement—4 cylinder
(© General Motors Corporation)

3. The following valves may be adjusted in the number 1 firing position, exhaust valves 1 and 3, and intake valves 1 and 2.
4. Loosen the adjusting nut until lash is felt at the push rod. Turn the adjusting nut clockwise until all lash is removed.
5. Crank the engine one revolution. Line up the crank pulley with the "O" mark. This is the number 4 firing position. Adjustment can be made to exhaust valves 2 and 4, and intake valves 3 and 4.
6. Install the rocker arm covers. Start the engine and check the timing and idle speed.

V6

1. Crank the engine until the mark on the torsional damper lines up with the "O" mark on the timing tab.
2. Determine that the engine is in the number 1 firing position. This can be done by placing the fingers on the #1 rocker arms as the damper mark comes near the "O" mark. If the valves are not moving, the engine is in the #1 firing position. If the valves move as the mark comes up to the timing tab, the engine is in the #4 firing position. The engine should be turned one revolution to be in the #1 firing position.
3. With the engine in the number 1 firing position the following valves may be adjusted: Intake 1,5,6 Exhaust 1,2,3

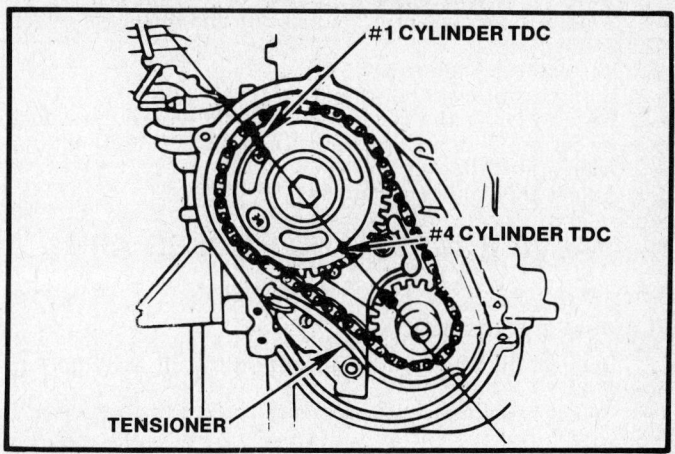

Timing mark—4 cylinder
(© General Motors Corporation)

4. Back the adjusting nut out until lash is felt at the pushrod. Turn the adjusting until all lash is removed.
5. When all lash has been removed, turn the adjusting nut 1 ½ additional turns.
6. Crank the engine one revolution until the timing tab "O" mark and torsional damper mark are in alignment. This will bring up the number 4 firing position. While the engine is in this position the following valves may be adjusted: Intake 2,3,4 Exhaust 4,5,6
7. Install the rocker arm covers. Start the engine and check idle speed and timing.

VALVE LIFTERS

Removal and Installation

NOTE: Certain V6 engines will require the removal of the intake manifold in order to gain access to the valve mechanism.

1. Remove the rocker arm cover.

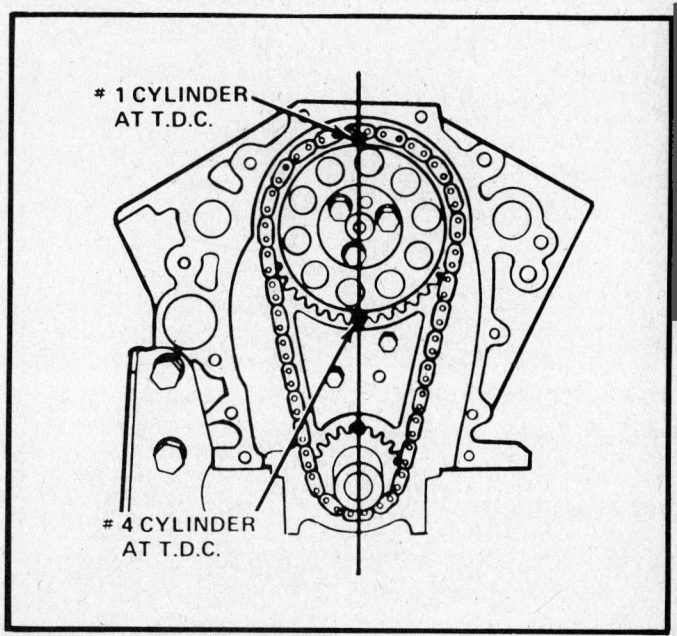

Timing marks—V6 engine
(© General Motors Corporation)

10-21

SECTION 10
GENERAL MOTORS—"J" BODY
FRONT WHEEL DRIVE CARS

2. Loosen the rocker arm holding nut and move the rocker arm to the side.
3. Remove the push rod.
4. Using a suitable tool, remove the valve lifter.
5. Installation is the reverse of removal procedure. Lubricate the bottom of the valve lifter with Molykote® or its equivalent prior to installation.
6. Adjust the valve mechanism.

VALVE ROCKER AND ROCKER ARM COVER ASSEMBLY

Removal and Installation

1. Remove the air cleaner. Disconnect the negative battery cable.
2. Remove the distributor cap with the spark plug wires.
3. Disconnect the vacuum hoses at the alternator bracket, P.C.V. valve, and at the front of the valve cover.
4. Remove the ground wire for the oxygen sensor.
5. Loosen the accelerator linkage bracket.
6. Remove the rocker arm cover bolts and remove the rocker arm cover.
7. Remove the rocker arm nuts and the rocker arm balls. Remove the rocker arms and push rods.
8. Installation is the reverse of the removal procedure. Lubricate the rocker with "Molykote" or its equivalent prior to installation. Use new gaskets on the rocker arm cover.

VALVE TIMING

Adjustments

Further information on valve timing adjustments can be found under Valve System Adjustments.

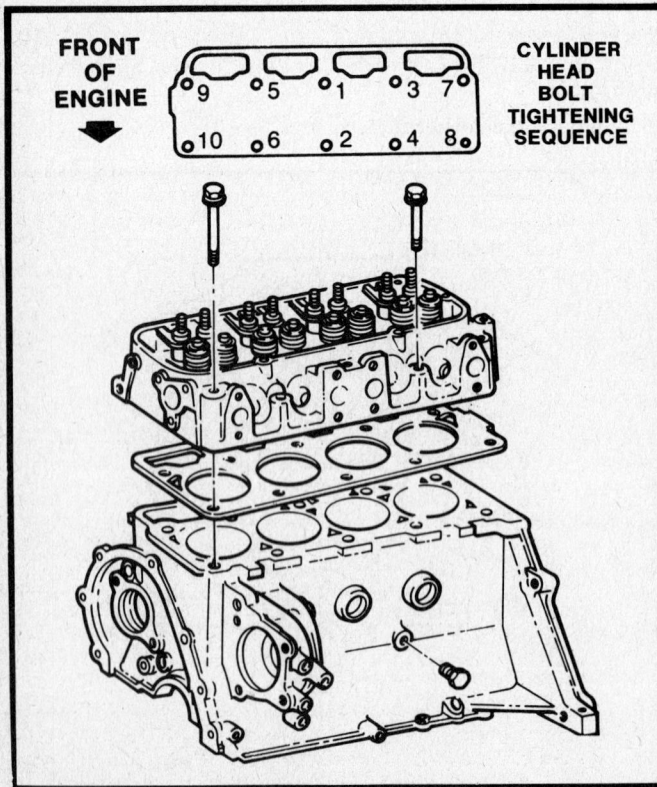

Cylinder head—4 cylinder
(© General Motors Corporation)

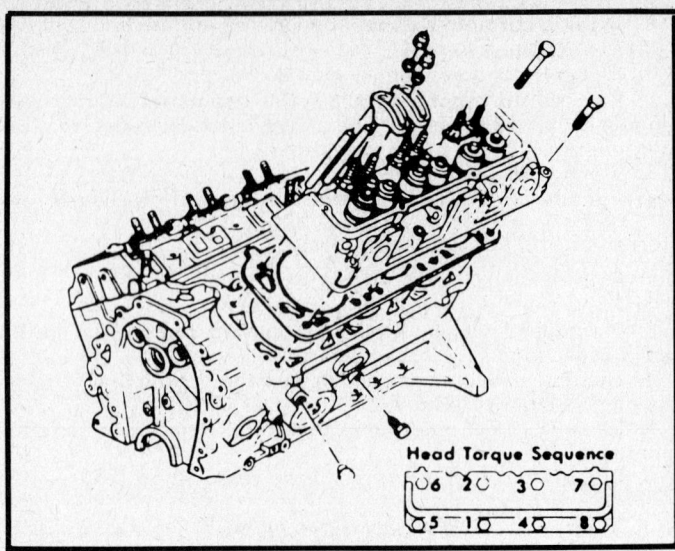

V6 cylinder head installation
(© General Motors Corporation)

CYLINDER HEAD

Removal and Installation

4 CYLINDER

1. Disconnect the negative battery cable.
2. Drain the cooling system.
3. Remove the air cleaner.
4. Raise the vehicle and support safely.
5. Remove the exhaust pipe and the exhaust shield from the exhaust manifold.
6. Remove the heater hose from the intake.
7. Remove the distributor.
8. Disconnect the vacuum manifold a the alternator bracket. Remove the remaining vacuum lines at the thermostat and intake manifold.
9. Remove the appropriate emission control assemblies.
10. Remove the carburetor linkage. If the vehicle is equipped with throttle body injection, remove the accelerator linkage from the accelerator linkage bracket.
11. Tag and disconnect any necessary wires.
12. Remove the upper radiator hose from the thermostat location.
13. Remove the bolt which holds the dipstick tube and the hot water bracket.
14. If the vehicle is equipped with power steering, remove the power steering assembly and lay aside.
15. Disconnect the fuel lines.
16. Disconnect the alternator with the wires and lay aside. Disconnect the alternator brackets from the cylinder head.
17. Remove the rocker arm cover along with the rocker arms and push rods.
18. Remove the cylinder head bolts from the cylinder head. Carefully lift the cylinder head from the engine block. The cylinder head will include the throttle body injection if equipped, the exhaust manifold and the intake manifold.
19. Installation is the reverse of the removal procedure. Be sure that both mating surfaces are clean of any nicks, burrs or remaining gasket material.
20. Any damaged valves should be refaced or replaced.

V6

1. Disconnect the negative battery cable.
2. Remove the intake manifold.
3. Remove the exhaust manifold.

GENERAL MOTORS—"J" BODY
FRONT WHEEL DRIVE CARS
SECTION 10

4. Tag and disconnect the spark plug wires. Remove the spark plugs.
5. Remove the pushrods.
6. Remove the cylinder head bolts. Remove the cylinder head from the vehicle.
7. Installation is the reverse of the removal procedure. Take note to install the cylinder head gaskets with the note "This Side Up" showing. Use sealer #1052080 or equivalent on the cylinder head bolt threads.

CAMSHAFT

Removal and Installation

4 CYLINDER

1. Remove the engine from the vehicle as described earlier in this chapter.
2. Remove the valve lifters as outlined under valve lifters.
3. Remove the crankcase front cover bolts and remove the crankcase cover.
4. Use a suitable tool, remove the front hub.
5. Note the position of the rotor and mark its location using a felt marker. Remove the distributor.
6. Remove the timing chain and sprocket.
7. Grasp the camshaft and pull the camshaft out of the engine.
8. Installation of the camshaft is the reverse of the removal procedure.

V6

1. Disconnect the negative battery cable. Remove the engine assembly from the vehicle.
2. Remove the intake manifold as described earlier.
3. Remove the rocker arm covers. Remove the rocker arm nuts, rocker arm balls, rocker arms and pushrods.
4. Remove the upper front cover bolts. Remove the lower cover bolts. Remove the front cover.
5. Remove the camshaft sprocket bolts. Remove the camshaft sprocket and timing chain.
6. Remove the camshaft. Measure the camshaft bearing journals using a micrometer and replace the camshaft if the journals exceed 0.025mm out of round.
7. Installation is the reverse of the removal procedure.

PISTON AND ROD POSITIONING

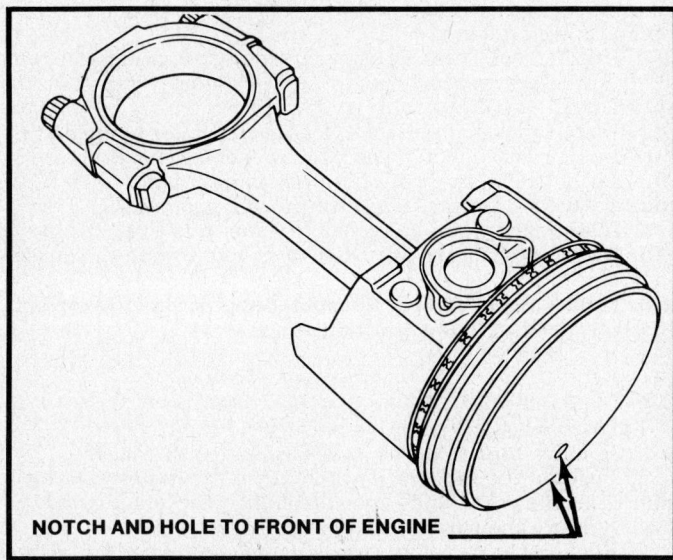

Piston positioning (© General Motors Corporation)

NOTE: When installing a new camshaft, lubricate the camshaft lobes with General Motors E.O.S. or equivalent.

TIMING CASE COVER/OIL SEAL

Removal and Installation

4 CYLINDER

1. Remove the engine drive belts.
2. Although not absolutely necessary, removal of the right front inner fender splash shield will facilitate access to the front cover.
3. Unscrew the center bolt from the crankshaft pulley and slide the pulley and hub from the crankshaft.
4. Remove the lower alternator bracket.
5. Remove the oil pan to front cover bolts.
6. Remove the front cover to block bolts. Remove the front cover.
7. Remove the vibration damper bolts and remove the vibration damper.
8. The surfaces of the block and front cover must be clean and free of oil. Apply a $\frac{1}{8}$ in. bead of RTV sealant to the cover. The sealant must be wet to the touch when the bolts are torqued.

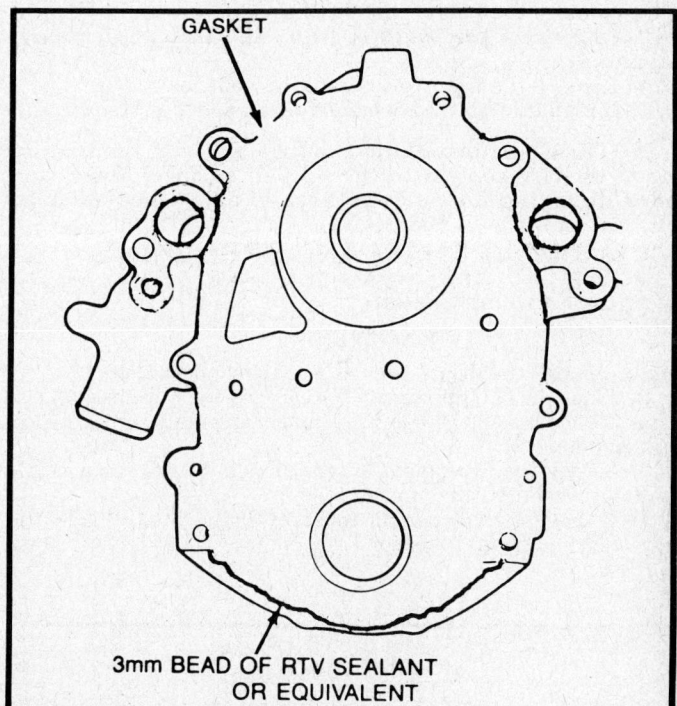

Front cover sealant placement—V6
(© General Motors Corporation)

NOTE: When applying RTV sealant, be sure not to get any in the bolts holes.

9. Installation is the reverse of the removal procedure.

V6

1. Disconnect the negative battery cable.
2. Drain the cooling system. Remove the coolant recovery tank from the vehicle.
3. Disconnect the manifold and EGR sensor solenoids.
4. Remove the serpentine belt and adjusting pulley.
5. Tag and disconnect the alternator wiring. Remove the alternator.
6. Disconnect the heater pipe at the power steering bracket.

10-23

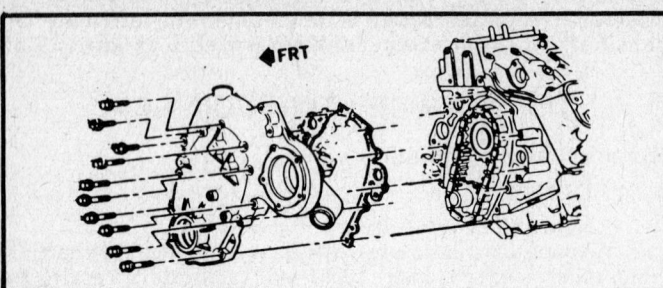

Timing case cover—V6
(© General Motors Corporation)

7. Raise the vehicle and support safely.
8. Remove the inner fender splash shield. Remove the air conditioning compressor belt. Remove the flywheel cover at the transaxle.
9. Remove the harmonic balancer if necessary to gain working clearance.
10. Remove the pan to block bolts. Remove the lower cover bolts.
11. Lower the vehicle and disconnect the radiator hoses at the water pump.
12. Remove the heater pipe from the goose neck.
13. Disconnect the overflow hoses and the canister purge hose.
14. Remove the front cover from the vehicle.
15. Installation is the reverse of the removal procedure.

NOTE: Upon installation, apply a 3 mm continuous bead of RTV sealant to the oil pan surface. Make sure that all mating surfaces are clean of old gasket material.

TIMING CHAIN AND SPROCKETS

Removal and Installation

4 CYLINDER OHV ENGINES

1. Remove the front cover as previously detailed.
2. Place the No. 1 piston at TDC of the compression stroke so that the marks on the camshaft and crankshaft sprockets are in alignment.
3. Loosen the timing chain tensioner nut as far as possible without actually removing it.
4. Remove the camshaft sprocket bolts and remove the sprocket and chain together.

Timing gears and camshaft removal
(© General Motors Corporation)

5. Use a gear puller (J–2288–8–20) and remove the crankshaft sprocket.
6. Press the crankshaft sprocket back onto the crankshaft.
7. Install the timing chain over the camshaft sprocket and then around the crankshaft sprocket. Make sure that the marks on the two sprockets are in alignment. Lubricate the thrust surface with Molykote® or its equivalent.
8. Align the dowel in the camshaft with the dowel hole in the sprocket and then install the sprocket on to the camshaft. Use the mounting bolts to draw the sprocket onto the camshaft and then tighten them to 27–33 ft. lb.
9. Lubricate the timing chain with clean engine oil. Tighten the chain tensioner.
10. Installation of the remaining components is in the reverse order of removal.

V6

1. Disconnect the negative battery cable.
2. Remove the front cover from the crankcase.
3. Place the number 1 piston at TDC with the marks on the camshaft and crankshaft sprocket aligned.
4. Remove the camshaft sprocket bolts. Remove the camshaft sprocket and chain.
5. Installation is the reverse of the removal procedure.

TIMING BELT/CHAIN

Removal and Installation

4 CYLINDER OHC ENGINES

1. Remove the timing belt front cover.
2. Rotate the crankshaft so that the timing mark on the crankshaft pulley lines up with 10° BTDC mark on the indicator scale. The mark on the camshaft sprocket must line up with mark on the camshaft carrier.
3. Remove the crankshaft pulley as previously described.
4. Remove timing prove holder.
5. Loosen the water pump retaining bolts and rotate the water pump to loosen the timing belt.
6. Remove the timing belt.
7. Install timing belt on sprockets.
8. Install the crankshaft pulley.
9. Check if the mark on the camshaft sprocket lines up with mark on the camshaft carrier. The timing mark on the crankshaft pulley should line up at 10° BTDC on the indicator scale.
10. Rotate the water pump clockwise using Tool J–33039 until all slack is removed from the belt. Slightly tighten the water pump retaining bolts.
11. Install Tool J–26486 between the water pump and camshaft sprockets so that the pointer is midway between the sprockets.
12. If the tension is incorrect, loosen the water pump and rotate it using Tool J–33039 until the proper tension is obtained.
13. Fully torque the water pump retaining bolts to 19 ft. lb. taking care not to further rotate the water pump.
14. Install timing probe holder. Torque nuts to 19 ft. lb.
15. Install the timing belt front cover and torque the attaching bolts to 5 ft. lb.
16. Install and adjust the alternator and power steering belt. Refill the cooling system, if necessary.

V6

1. Disconnect the negative battery cable.
2. Remove the crankcase cover as described earlier.
3. Position the number 1 piston at top dead center with the marks on the crankshaft and camshaft sprockets aligned.
4. Remove the camshaft sprocket bolts.
5. Remove the camshaft sprocket and chain from the front of the engine.

NOTE: If the sprocket does not move freely from the camshaft, a light blow using only a plastic hammer on the lower edge of the sprocket should dislodge it.

6. Installation is the reverse of the removal procedure. Draw the camshaft sprocket onto the camshaft using the mounting bolts. Lubricate the timing chain with engine oil prior to installation.

Lubrication

OIL PAN

Removal and Installation

4 CYLINDER OHC ENGINE

1. Raise the vehicle on the hoist and support it safely.
2. Remove the right front tire and wheel. Remove the right hand splash shield.
3. Remove the lower A/C bracket strut rod attaching bolt in order to gain working clearance. Position the assembly aside.
4. Remove the flywheel cover. Remove the exhaust pipe to manifold attaching bolts.
5. Drain the engine oil. Remove the oil pan retaining bolts. Remove the oil pan from the vehicle.
6. Installation is the reverse of removal.

4 CYLINDER OHV ENGINE

1. Disconnect the negative battery cable.
2. Raise and support the front of the vehicle. Drain the crankcase.
3. Remove the A/C brace if so equipped.
4. Remove the exhaust shield and disconnect the exhaust pipe at the manifold.
5. Remove the starter motor and position it out of the way.
6. Remove the flywheel cover. Remove the right support bolts and lower the support in order to gain clearance for oil pan removal.
7. Remove the oil pan retaining bolts. Remove the oil pan.

NOTE: Prior to oil pan installation, check that the sealing surfaces on the pan, cylinder block and front cover are clean and free of oil. If installing the old pan, be sure that all old RTV or gasket material has been removed.

8. Apply a $1/8$ in. bead of RTV sealant to the oil pan sealing surface or install a new pan gasket (if originally equipped). Use a new oil pan front and/or rear seal, and install the pan in place. Tighten the bolts to 9–13 ft. lbs.
9. Installation of the remaining components is in the reverse order of removal.

V6

1. Disconnect the negative battery cable.
2. Raise the vehicle and support safely.
3. Drain the oil from the crankcase.
4. Remove the flywheel dust cover.
5. Tag and disconnect the electrical connections at the starter motor.
6. Remove the starter retainer bolts. Remove the starter.
7. Remove the oil pan bolts. Remove the oil pan.
8. Installation is the reverse of the removal procedure. Start engine and check for leaks.

OIL PUMP

Removal and Installation

4 CYLINDER OHV ENGINES

1. Remove the engine oil pan.
2. Remove the pump attaching bolts and carefully lower the oil pump.

3. Installation is the reverse of the removal procedure. To ensure immediate oil pressure on start-up, the oil pump gear cavity should be packed with petroleum jelly.

4 CYLINDER OHC ENGINES

1. Remove the crankshaft sprocket.
2. Remove the timing belt rear covers.
3. Disconnect and tag the oil pressure wires.
4. Remove the oil pan.
5. Remove the oil filter.
6. Unbolt and remove the oil pick-up tube.
7. Unbolt and remove the oil pump.
8. Installation is the reverse of the removal procedure.

V6

1. Disconnect the negative battery cable.
2. Remove the oil pan as described earlier.
3. Remove the bolt holding the rear main bearing cap.
4. Remove the oil pump and extension shaft.
5. Installation is the reverse of the removal procedure.

REAR MAIN OIL SEAL

Removal and Installation

4 CYLINDER OHV ENGINES – 1983–1985

1. Remove the oil pan and pump.
2. Remove the rear main bearing cap.
3. Gently pack the upper seal into the groove approximately $1/4$ inch on each side.
4. Measure the amount the seal was driven in on one side and add $1/16$ in. Cut this length from the old lower cap seal. Be sure to get a sharp cut. Repeat for the other side.
5. Place the piece of cut seal into the groove and pack the seal into the block. Do this for each side.
6. Install a piece of Plastigage or the equivalent on the bearing journal. Install the rear cap and tighten to 75 ft. lbs. Remove the cap and check the gauge for bearing clearance. If out of specification, the ends of the seal may be frayed or not flush, preventing the cap from proper seating. Correct as required.
7. Clean the journal, and apply a thin film of sealer to the mating surfaces of the cap and tighten to 70 ft. lbs. Install the pan and pump.

1986 AND LATER

1. Disconnect the negative battery cable.
2. Support the engine and remove the transaxle assembly as described elsewhere in this chapter.
3. Remove the flywheel and verify that the leak is originating from the rear main seal.
4. Remove the seal from the dust lip.
5. Clean the cylinder block and crankshaft sealing surface.
6. Inspect the crankshaft for damage. Coat the seal and engine mating surface with engine oil.
7. Install the new seal using seal installation tool J–34686 or equivalent. For remainder of installation, reverse Steps 3 through 1 of the removal procedure.

4 CYLINDER OHC ENGINES

1. Remove engine as previously outlined.
2. Remove flywheel dust cover.
3. Remove flexplate to torque converter attachment bolts on automatic vehicles.
4. Remove bellhousing bolts and separate engine from transaxle assembly.
5. Remove flexplate on automatic transaxle vehicles.
6. Remove pressure plate, clutch disc and flywheel on manual transaxle vehicles.
7. Using a screwdriver or suitable tool, remove rear main oil seal.
8. Clean cylinder block and crankshaft sealing surface.

9. Inspect crankshaft for nicks, scratches, etc.
10. Coat seal and engine mating surfaces with engine oil.
11. Position seal on Protector (J–33084–2) and place onto crankshaft flywheel flange.
12. Install Seal Installer (J–33084) on crankshaft flywheel flange, starting the three bolts EVENLY in a rotational sequence until the seal bottoms in the block.
13. For remainder of installation reverse Steps 6 through 1 of removal procedure.

V6

1. Disconnect the negative battery cable.
2. Support the engine and remove the transaxle assembly as described elsewhere in this chapter.
3. Remove the flywheel and verify that the leak is originating from the rear main seal.
4. Remove the seal from the dust lip.

NOTE: Care must be exercised during removal so as not to damage the crankshaft outside diameter area.

5. Clean the cylinder block and crankshaft sealing surface.
6. Inspect the crankshaft for nicks, burrs, scratches, etc.
7. Coat the seal using seal installation tool J–34686 or equivalent. Follow manufacturers instructions supplied with the seal installation tool.
8. Install the new seal using seal installation tool J–34686 or equivalent. Follow manufacturers instructions supplied with the seal installation tool.
9. For remainder of installation, reverse Steps 3 through 1 of the removal procedure.

FRONT SUSPENSION AND STEERING SECTION

For Front Suspension Services Refer to Unit Repair Section. For Steering Gear Overhaul Refer to Unit Repair Section.

STEERING WHEEL

Removal and Installation

SPORT WHEEL

1. Disconnect the negative cable at the battery.
2. Pry the center cap from the wheel.
3. Remove the retainer (if so equipped).
4. Remove the shaft nut.
5. If the wheel and shaft do not have factory-installed alignment marks, matchmark the parts before removal of the wheel.
6. Install a puller and remove the wheel. A horn spring, eyelet and insulator are underneath; don't lose the parts.
7. Install the spring, eyelet and insulator into the tower on the column.
8. Align the matchmarks and install the wheel onto the shaft. Install the retaining nut and tighten to 30 ft. lbs. (40 Nm).
9. Install the retainer. Install the center cap. Connect the negative battery cable.

STANDARD WHEEL

1. Disconnect the negative cable at the battery.
2. Pull the pad from the wheel. The horn lead is attached to the pad at one end; the other end of the pad has a wire with a spade connector. The horn lead is disconnected by pushing and turning; the spade connector is unplugged.
3. Remove the retainer under the pad (if so equipped).
4. Remove the steering shaft nut.
5. There should be alignment marks already present on the wheel and shaft. If not, matchmark the parts.
6. Remove the wheel with a puller.
7. Install the wheel on the shaft, aligning the matchmarks. Install the shaft nut and tighten to 30 ft. lbs. (40 Nm).
8. Install the retainer.
9. Plug in the spade connector, and push and turn the horn lead to connect. Install the pad. Connect the negative battery cable.

STEERING RACK

Removal and Installation

MANUAL STEERING ASSEMBLY

1. Disconnect the negative battery cable.
2. Remove the driver's side sound insulator.
3. Remove the seal assembly from under the steering column. Remove the upper pinch bolt.
4. Remove the air cleaner and the windshield washer reservoir assembly.
5. Raise the vehicle and support safely. Remove the wheel and tire assemblies.
6. Disconnect both tie rods from the support struts.
7. Disconnect the left and right hand mounting clamp from the vehicle chassis.
8. Remove the lower pinch bolt from the flexible coupling. Separate the flexible coupling from the rack assembly.
9. Remove the dash seal from the rack assembly.
10. Remove the splash shield from the driver's side inner fender if equipped.
11. Slide the rack and pinion assembly through the driver's side fender opening.
12. Installation is in the reverse order of removal. Check and adjust toe setting as needed.

POWER STEERING ASSEMBLY

1. Disconnect the negative battery cable.
2. Remove the driver's side sound insulator.
3. Remove the seal assembly from under the steering column. Remove the upper pinch bolt.

Inner tie rod and pivot bushing, removal and installation (© General Motors Corporation)

GENERAL MOTORS—"J" BODY
FRONT WHEEL DRIVE CARS
SECTION 10

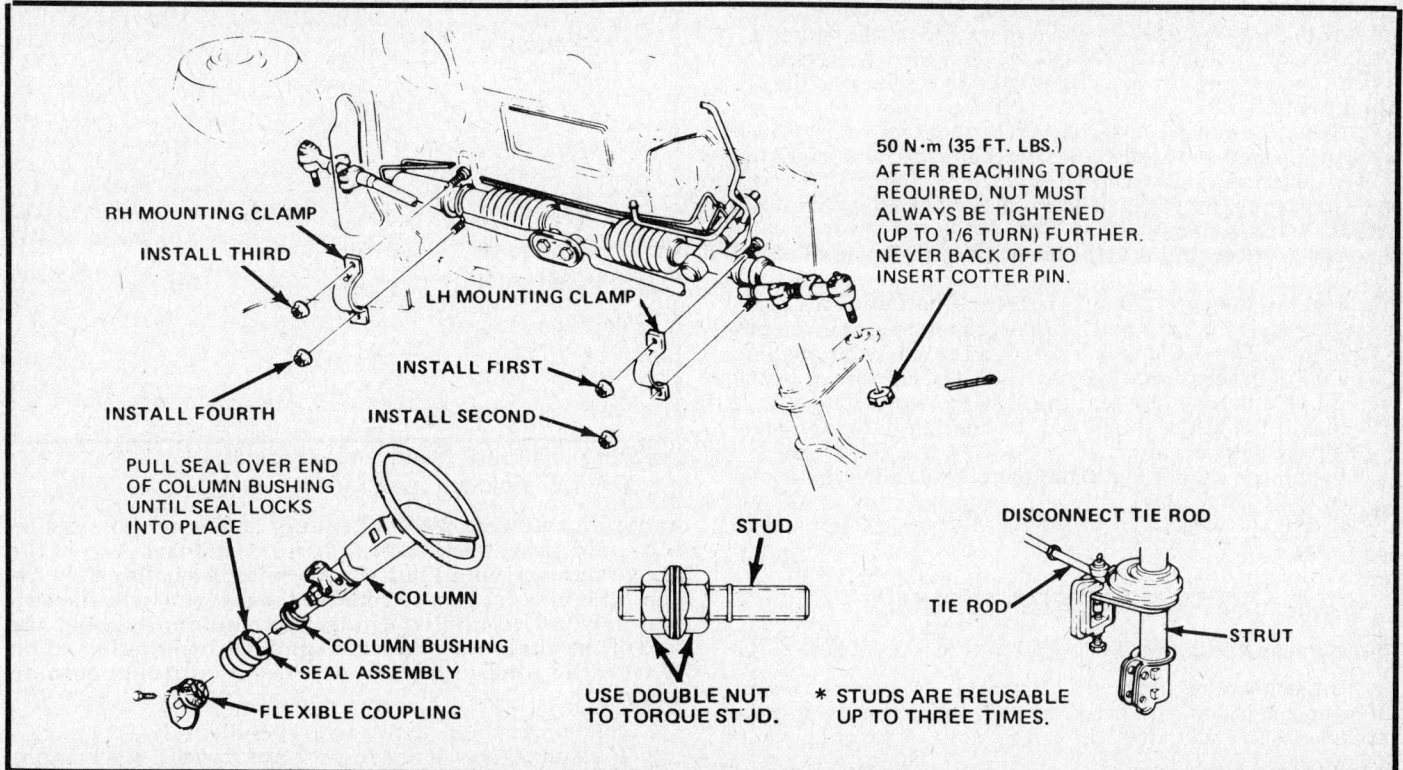

Power rack and pinion unit mounting (© General Motors Corporation)

4. Remove the air cleaner and the windshield washer reservoir assembly if necessary to gain working clearance.
5. Disconnect the pressure line from the rack assembly and the switch block. Remove the pressure line to gain access to the return line fitting.
6. Disconnect the return line from the rack assembly.
7. Raise the vehicle and support safely. Remove the wheel and tire assemblies.
8. Disconnect the both tie rods from the support struts.
9. Disconnect the left and right hand mounting clamp from the vehicle chassis.
10. Remove the lower pinch bolt from the flexible coupling. Separate the flexible coupling from the rack assembly.
11. Remove the dash seal from the rack assembly.
12. Remove the splash shield from the driver's side inner fender.
13. Slide the rack and pinion assembly through the driver's side fender opening.
14. Installation is in the reverse order of removal. Check and adjust toe setting as needed.

FRONT WHEEL BEARINGS

The front wheel bearings are sealed, non-adjustable units which require no periodic attention. They are bolted to the steering knuckle by means of an integral flange.

Removal and Installation

1. Remove the wheel cover, loosen the hub nut, and raise and support the car safely. Remove the front wheel.
2. Install the boot cover protector.
3. Remove the hub nut.
4. Remove the brake caliper and rotor.

—— **CAUTION** ——
Do not allow the brake caliper to hang from the brake hose.

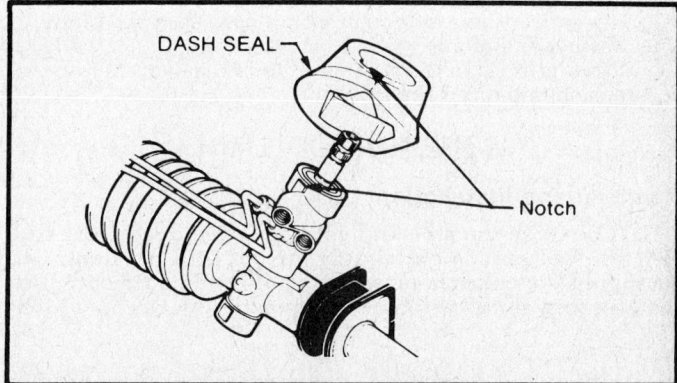

Steering column dash seal, removal and installation (© General Motors Corporation)

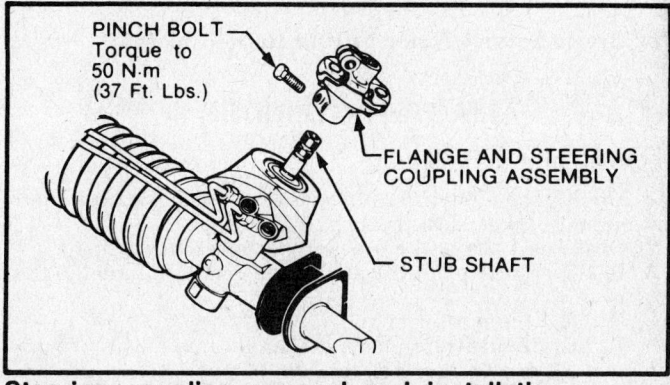

Steering coupling removal and installation
(© General Motors Corporation)

10–27

SECTION 10: GENERAL MOTORS—"J" BODY
FRONT WHEEL DRIVE CARS

5. Remove the three hub and bearing attaching bolts. If the old bearing is to be reused, match mark the bolts and holes.
6. Attach a puller, and remove the bearing. If corrosion is present, make sure the bearing is loose in the knuckle before using the puller.
7. Clean the mating surfaces of all dirt and corrosion. Check the knuckle bore and knuckle seal for damage. If a new bearing is to be installed, remove the old knuckle seal and install a new one. Grease the lips of the new seal before installation; install with a seal driver.
8. Push the bearing onto the halfshaft. Install a new washer and hub nut.
9. Tighten the new hub nut on the halfshaft until the bearing is seated. If the rotor and hub start to rotate as the hub nut is tightened, insert a long bolt through the cut out in the hub assembly to prevent rotation. Do not apply full torque to the hub nut at this time-just seat the bearing.
10. Install the brake shield and the bearing retaining bolts. Tighten the bolts evenly.
11. Install the caliper and rotor. Install the caliper bolts and tighten to 21–35 ft. lbs.
12. Install the wheel. Lower the car. Tighten the hub nut to 185 ft. lbs.

POWER STEERING PUMP
Removal and Installation

1. Disconnect the negative battery cable. Remove the necessary components to gain access to the power steering pump.
2. Loosen the adjusting bolt and turn the pump on the bolt. Remove the drive belt.
3. Remove the three pump to bracket bolts and remove the adjusting bolt.
4. Remove the high pressure fitting from the pump.
5. Disconnect the reservoir to pump hose from the pump.
6. Remove the pump.
7. Installation is in the reverse order of removal. Adjust the belt tension and bleed the system.

STEERING COLUMN
Removal and Installation

NOTE: Once the steering column is removed from the car, the column is extremely susceptible to damage. Dropping the column assembly on its end could collapse the steering shaft or loosen the plastic injections which

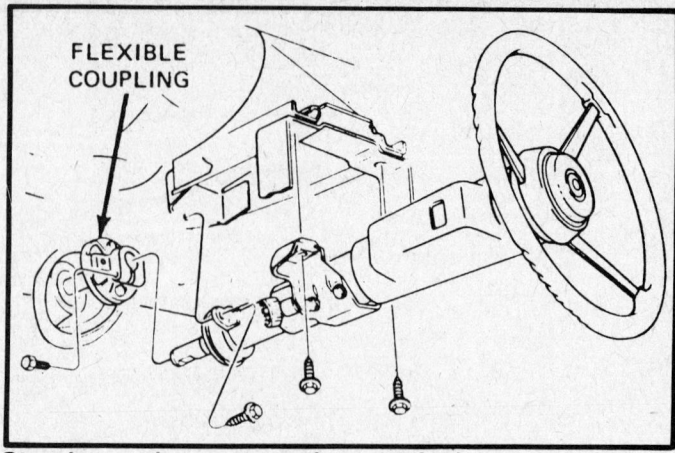

Steering column mounting—typical
(© General Motors Corporation)

maintain column rigidity. Leaning on the column assembly could cause the jacket to bend or deform. Any of the above damage could impair the column's collapsible design. If it is necessary to remove the steering wheel, use a standard wheel puller. Under no condition should the end of the shaft be hammered upon, as hammering could loosen the plastic injection which maintains column rigidity.

1. Disconnect the negative battery cable.
2. If column repairs are to be made, remove the steering wheel.
3. Remove the hush panels as necessary to gain access to the steering column retaining bolts.
4. Remove the nuts and bolts attaching the flexible coupling to the bottom of the steering column. Remove the safety strap and bolt if equipped.
5. Remove the steering column trim shrouds and column covers.
6. Disconnect all wiring harness connectors. Remove the dust boot mounting screws and column mounting bracket bolts.
7. Remove the shift cable at the actuator and housing holder.
8. Lower the column to clear the mounting bracket and carefully remove from the car.
9. Install in the reverse order of removal.

BRAKE SECTION

For Brake Service Refer to Unit Repair Section.

MASTER CYLINDER
Removal and Installation

1. Unplug the electrical connector from the master cylinder. On manual brakes, disconnect push rod.
2. Disconnect the brake tubes from the master cylinder.
3. Remove the two nuts attaching the master cylinder to the booster or firewall.
4. Remove the master cylinder.
5. To install, attach the master cylinder to the booster with the nuts. Torque to 22–30 ft. lbs. (30–45 Nm).
6. Connect the electrical lead.
7. Bleed the brakes.

VACUUM PUMP

The vacuum pump is designed to aid the engine in maintaining a proper vacuum level for the power brake system. The vacuum pump will maintain a vacuum of 47 ± 6 kPa (13.0 ± 1.8 in. Hg) in the system. When the vacuum decreases 47 ± 6 kPa, the vacuum pump is activated for 5–10 seconds to bring the vacuum back to proper level.

VACUUM BOOSTER
Removal and Installation

1. Remove the master cylinder from the booster. It is not necessary to disconnect the lines from the master cylinder. Just move the cylinder aside.

GENERAL MOTORS—"J" BODY FRONT WHEEL DRIVE CARS
SECTION 10

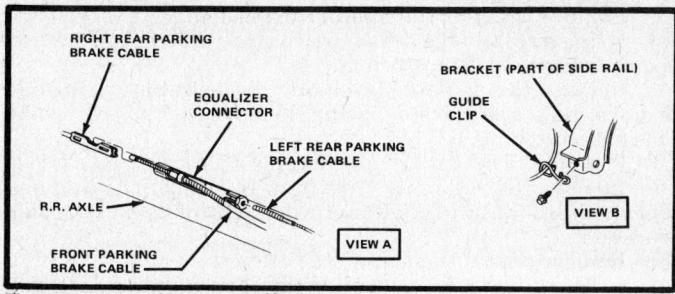

Parking brake equalizer
(© General Motors Corporation)

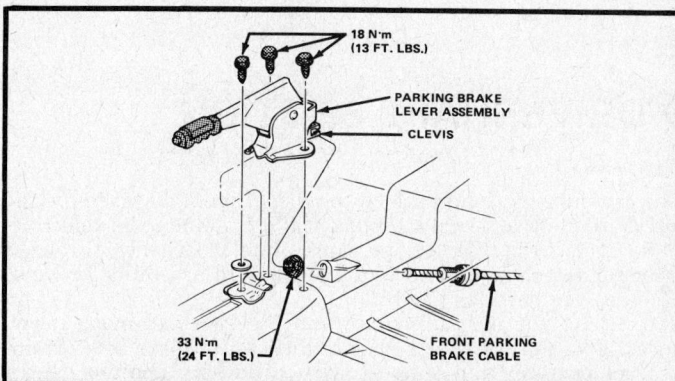

Parking brake lever (© General Motors Corporation)

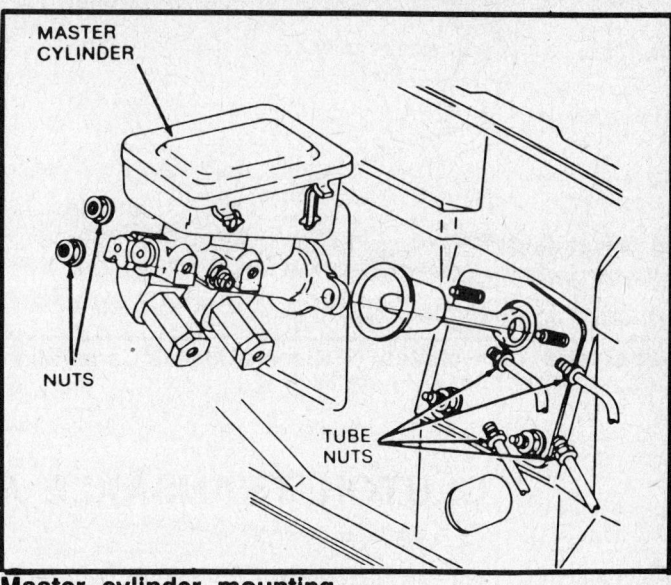

Master cylinder mounting
(© General Motors Corporation)

2. Disconnect the vacuum booster pushrod from the brake pedal inside the vehicle.
3. Remove the attaching nuts from inside the car. Remove the booster.
4. Install the booster on the firewall. Tighten the mounting nuts to 22–28 ft. lbs. (30–45 Nm).
5. Connect the pushrod to the brake pedal.
6. Install the master cylinder. Mounting torque is 22–33 ft. lbs. (30–45 Nm).

PARKING BRAKE

Adjustments

1. Raise and support the vehicle with both rear wheels off the ground.
2. Pull the parking brake lever exactly five clicks.
3. Loosen the equalizer locknut, then tighten the adjusting nut until the left rear wheel can just be turned backwards using two hands, but is locked in the forward rotation. On 1986 and later vehicles, use the right rear wheel.
4. Tighten the locknut.
5. Release the parking brake. Rotate the rear wheels-there should be no drag.
6. Lower the vehicle.

PARKING BRAKE CABLE

Removal and Installation
FRONT CABLE

1. Remove the console. Disconnect the parking brake cable from the parking brake lever.
2. Raise the vehicle and support safely.
3. Loosen the parking brake cable equalizer nut.
4. Remove the parking brake cable retaining nut and bracket.

5. Loosen the catalytic converter shield, if necessary, and remove the brake cable from the vehicle body.
6. Disconnect the cable from the equalizer assembly.
7. Installation is the reverse of the removal procedure. Adjust the parking brake cable as needed.

LEFT AND RIGHT REAR CABLE

1. Raise the vehicle and support safely.
2. Loosen the equalizer nut until the parking brake cable tension is eliminated.

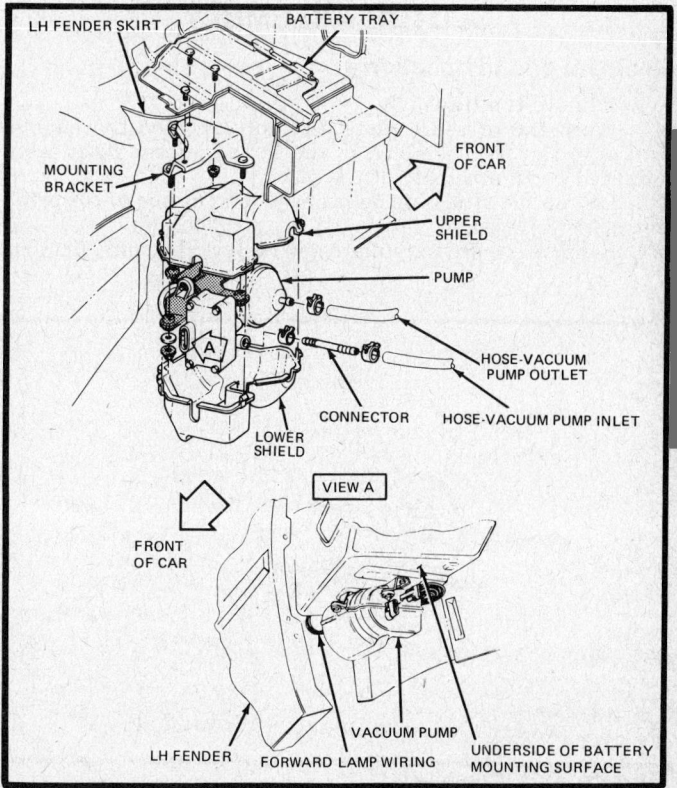

Brake vacuum pump (© General Motors Corporation)

SECTION 10
GENERAL MOTORS—"J" BODY
FRONT WHEEL DRIVE CARS

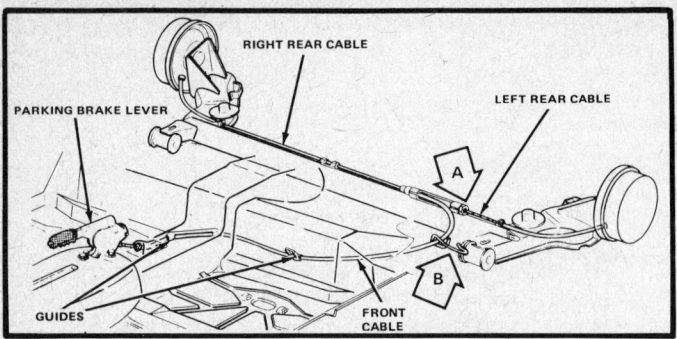

Front and rear cables (© General Motors Corporation)

3. Remove the rear tires and brake drums.
4. Using a suitable tool, remove the top adjuster bracket rod and the rear hold down spring.
5. Remove the actuator lever and the lever return spring. Remove the screw adjuster spring. Remove the top rear brake shoe return spring.
6. Disconnect the brake cable from the parking brake lever.
7. Remove the retaining clips from the conduit fitting and remove the conduit fitting from the backing plate and the axle bracket.
8. Remove the cable end from the connector (right side only).
9. Installation is the reverse of the removal procedure. Adjust cable as required.

CLUTCH, TRANSAXLE AND DRIVESHAFT SECTION

For Overhaul Procedure Refer to Unit Repair Section.

CLUTCH PEDAL—LINKAGE

Adjustments

The J-series vehicles have a self-adjusting clutch mechanism located on the clutch pedal, eliminating the need for periodic free play adjustments. The self-adjusting mechanism should be inspected periodically as follows:
1. Depress the clutch pedal and look for pawl on the self-adjusting mechanism to firmly engage the teeth on the ratchet.
2. Release the clutch. The pawl should be lifted off of the teeth by the metal stop on the bracket.

CLUTCH ASSEMBLY

Removal and Installation

1. Remove the transaxle.
2. Mark the pressure plate assembly and the flywheel so that they can be assembled in the same position. They were balanced as an assembly at the factory.
3. Loosen the attaching bolts one turn at a time until spring tension is relieved.
4. Support the pressure plate and remove the bolts. Remove the pressure plate and the clutch disc. Do not disassemble the pressure plate assembly; replace it if it is found to be defective.
5. Inspect the flywheel, pressure plate, clutch disc, throwout bearing and the clutch fork and pivot shaft assembly for wear. Replace the parts as needed.
6. Clean the pressure plate and the flywheel mating surfaces. Position the clutch disc and pressure plate into the installed position and support with a dummy shaft of clutch aligning tool. The clutch plate is assembled with the damper springs offset toward the transaxle.
7. Install the pressure plate-to-flywheel bolts. Tighten them in a criss-cross pattern.
8. Lubricate the outside grooves and the inside recess of the release bearing with high temperature grease. Wipe off any excess. Install the release bearing.
9. Install the transaxle.

MANUAL TRANSAXLE

Removal and Installation

1. Disconnect the negative battery cable.
2. Install an engine holding bar so that one end is supported on the cowl tray over the wiper motor and the other end rests on the radiator support. Use padding and be careful not to damage the paint or body work with the bar. Attach a lifting hook to the engine lift ring and raise the engine enough to take the pressure of the motor mounts.

NOTE: If a lifting bar and hook is not available, a chain hoist can be used, however, during the procedure the vehicle must be raised, at which time the chain hoist must be adjusted to keep tension on the engine/transaxle assembly.

3. Remove the heater hose clamp at the transaxle mount bracket. Disconnect the electrical connectors and remove the horn assembly.
4. Remove the transaxle mount attaching bolts. Discard the bolts attaching the mount to the side frame. New bolts must be used at installation.
5. Disconnect the clutch cable from the clutch release lever. Remove the transaxle mount bracket attaching bolts and nuts.
6. Disconnect the shift cable and retaining clips at the transaxle. Disconnect the ground cables at the transaxle mounting studs.
7. Remove the upper transaxle to engine mounting bolts.
8. Raise the vehicle and support safely. Remove the front tire and wheel assemblies.

Clutch and flywheel
(© General Motors Corporation)

10-30

GENERAL MOTORS—"J" BODY
FRONT WHEEL DRIVE CARS
SECTION 10

9. Remove the left front inner splash shield. Remove the transaxle strut and bracket.
10. Remove the clutch housing cover bolts.
11. Disconnect the speedometer cable at the transaxle.
12. Disconnect the stabilizer bar at the left suspension support and control arm.
13. Disconnect the ball joint from the steering knuckle.
14. Remove the left suspension attaching bolts and remove the support and control arm as an assembly.
15. Install boot protectors and disengage the drive axles at the transaxle. Remove the left side shaft from the transaxle.
16. Position a jack under the transaxle case, remove the lower two transaxle to engine mounting bolts and remove the transaxle by sliding it towards the drivers side away from the engine. Carefully lower the jack, guiding the right shaft out of the transaxle.
17. When installing the transaxle, guide the right drive axle into its bore as the transaxle is being raised. The right drive axle cannot be readily installed after the transaxle is connected to the engine. Installation if the remaining components is in the reverse order of the removal procedure with the following notes. When installing the bolts attaching the mount to transaxle bracket, check the alignment bolt at the engine mount. If excessive effort if required to remove the alignment bolt. realign the powertrain components and tighten the bolts to 40 foot pounds and then remove the alignment bolts.

SHIFT INDICATOR

Removal and Installation

1. Remove the trim button in the center of the shift knob. Remove the shift knob snap ring. Remove the knob.
2. Remove the console trim cover along with the shift indicator lens and the shift indicator.
3. Installation is the reverse of the removal procedure.

AUTOMATIC TRANSAXLE

Removal and Installation

1. Disconnect the negative battery cable.
2. Insert a $\frac{1}{4} \times 2$ in. bolt into the hole in the right front motor mount to prevent any mislocation during the transaxle removal.
3. Remove the air cleaner. Disconnect the T.V. cable at the carburetor.
4. Unscrew the bolt securing the T.V. cable to the transaxle. Pull up on the cable cover at the transaxle until the cable can be seen. Disconnect the cable from the transaxle rod.
5. Remove the wiring harness retaining bolt at the top of the transaxle.
6. Remove the hose from the air management valve and then pull the wiring harness up and out of the way. Remove the speed sensor wiring.
7. Install an engine support bar. Raise the engine just enough too take the pressure off the motor mounts.

CAUTION
The engine support bar must be located in the center of the cowl and the bolts must be tightened before attempting to support the engine.

8. Remove the transaxle mount and bracket assembly. It may be necessary to raise the engine slightly to aid in removal.
9. Disconnect the shift control linkage from the transaxle.
10. Remove the top transaxle-to-engine mounting bolts. Loosen, but do not remove, the transaxle-to-engine bolt nearest to the starter.
11. Unlock the steering column. Raise and support the front of the car. Remove the front wheels.
12. Pull out the cotter pin and loosen the castellated ball joint

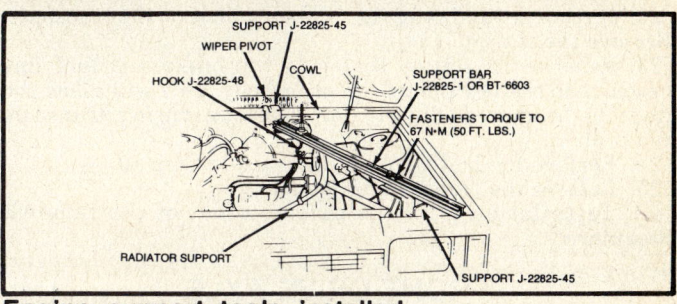

Engine support tools installed
(© General Motors Corporation)

nut until the ball joint separates from the control arm. Repeat on the other side of the car.
13. Disconnect the stabilizer bar from the left lower control arm. Drain the transaxle fluid.
14. Remove the six bolts that secure the left front suspension support assembly.
15. Connect an axle shaft removal tool (J–28468) or equivalent, to a slide hammer.
16. Position the tool behind the axle shaft cones and then pull the cones out and away from the transaxle. Remove the axle shafts and plug the transaxle bores to reduce fluid leakage.
17. Remove the nut that secures the transaxle control cable bracket to the transaxle, then remove the engine-to-transaxle stud.
18. Disconnect the speedometer cable at the transaxle.
19. Disconnect the transaxle strut at the transaxle.
20. Remove the four retaining screws and remove the torque converter shield.
21. Remove the three bolts securing the torque converter to the flex plate.

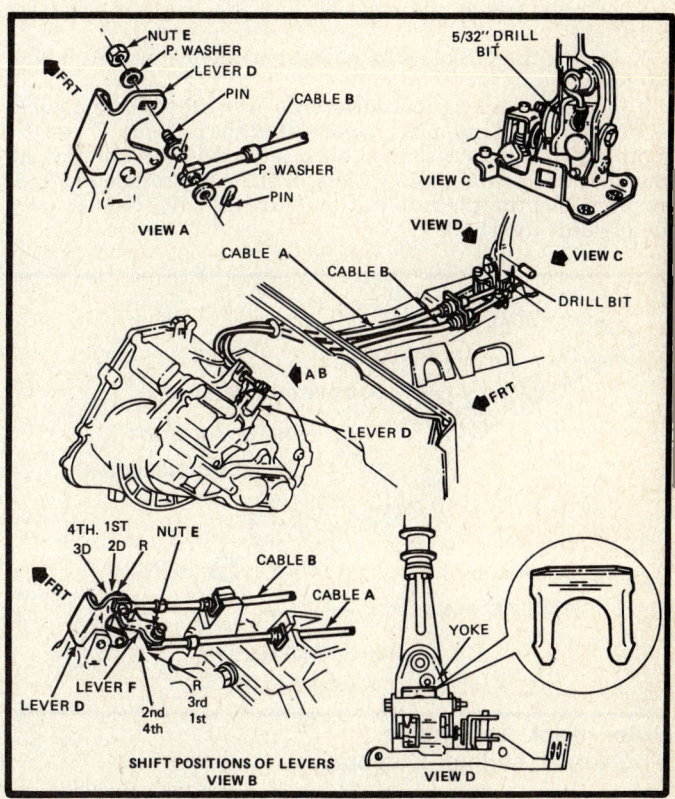

Manual transaxle on car adjustment
(© General Motors Corporation)

10-31

Section 10: GENERAL MOTORS—"J" BODY
FRONT WHEEL DRIVE CARS

22. Disconnect and plug the oil cooler lines at the transaxle. Remove the starter.
23. Remove the screws that hold the brake and fuel line brackets to the left side of the underbody. This will allow the lines to be moved slightly for clearance during transaxle removal.
24. Remove the bolt that was loosened in Step 10.
25. Remove the transaxle to the left.
26. Installation is in the reverse order of the removal procedure.

FRONT DRIVE AXLE

Removal and Installation

1. Remove the hub nut.
2. Raise the front of the car. Remove the wheel and tire.
3. Install an axle shaft boot seal protector onto the seal.
4. Disconnect the brake hose clip from the MacPherson strut, but do not disconnect the hose from the caliper. Remove the brake caliper from the spindle, and hang the caliper out of the way by a length of wire. DO NOT ALLOW THE CALIPER TO HANG BY THE BRAKE HOSE.
5. Mark the camber alignment cam bolt for reassembly. Remove the cam bolt and the upper attaching bolt from the strut and spindle.
6. Pull the steering knuckle assembly from the strut bracket.
7. Remove the axle shaft from the transaxle.
8. Remove the axle shaft from the hub and bearing assembly.

To install:
1. If a new drive axle is to be installed, a new knuckle seal should be installed first.
2. Loosely install the drive axle into the transaxle and steering knuckle.
3. Loosely attach the steering knuckle to the suspension strut.
4. Install the brake caliper. Tighten the bolts to 30 ft. lbs. (40 Nm).
5. The drive axle is an interference fit in the steering knuckle. Press the axle into place, then install the hub nut. When the shaft begins to turn with the hub, insert a drift through the caliper into one of the cooling slots in the rotor to keep it from turning. Tighten the hub nut to 70 ft. lbs. (100 Nm) to completely seat the shaft.

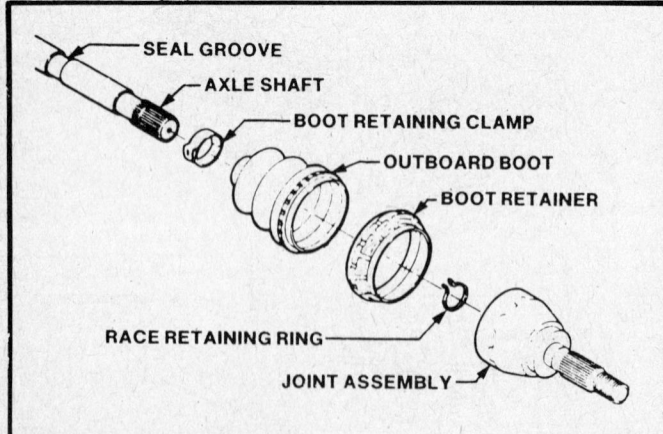

Outer boot assembly
(© General Motors Corporation)

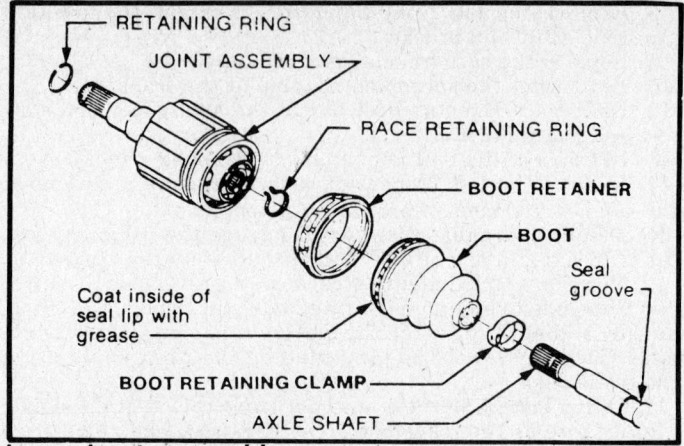

Inner boot assembly
(© General Motors Corporation)

6. Load the hub assembly by lowering it onto a jackstand. Align the camber cam bolt marks made during removal, install the bolt and tighten to 140 ft. lbs. (190Nm). Tighten the upper nut to the same value.
7. Install the axle shaft all the way into the transaxle using a screwdriver inserted into the groove provided on the inner retainer. Tap the screwdriver until the shaft seats in the transaxle.
8. Connect the brake hose clip to the strut. Install the tire and wheel, lower the car, and tighten the hub nut to 225 ft. lbs. (305 Nm).

OUTER AND INNER BOOT

Removal and Installation

OUTER BOOT

1. Disconnect the negative battery cable. Raise and support the vehicle safely.
2. Remove the front tire and wheel.
3. Remove the brake caliper and rotor. Support the brake caliper.
4. Slide the outer joint assembly off of the axle shaft.
5. Remove the race retaining ring. Remove the boot retainer and the boot retaining clamp.
6. Remove the outer boot.
7. Installation is the reverse of the removal procedure. Pack the new boot with grease prior to installation.

INNER BOOT

1. Disconnect the negative battery cable. Raise and support the vehicle safely.
2. Remove the front tire and wheel. Remove the brake caliper and rotor. Support the brake caliper.
3. Remove the outer boot assembly.
4. Remove the boot retaining clamps. Remove the spacer ring.
5. Slide the axle and the spider bearing assembly out of the tri-pot housing. Install the spider bearing retainer onto the spider bearing assembly.
6. Remove the spider assembly and the boot from the axle.
7. Installation is the reverse of the removal procedure. Pack the new boot with grease prior to installation.

GENERAL MOTORS—"J" BODY
FRONT WHEEL DRIVE CARS
SECTION 10

REAR AXLE AND SUSPENSION SECTION

For Axle Overhaul Procedures and Suspension Services Refer to Unit Repair Section.

REAR AXLE ASSEMBLY

Removal and Installation

1. Disconnect the negative battery cable. Raise the vehicle and support safely.
2. Remove the rear wheel and tire assemblies. Remove the brake drum. Remove the stabilizer bar from the axle assembly if equipped.

NOTE: Do not hammer on the brake drum as bearing assembly damage could result.

3. Remove the lower shock absorber bolts and disconnect the control arm.
4. Remove the parking brake cable from the axle assembly.
5. Carefully lower the rear axle and remove the coil springs and insulators. Remove the control arm bolts and lower the axle.
6. Remove the hub attaching bolts and remove the bearing, backing plate and hub.
7. Installation is the reverse of the removal procedure. Bleed the brake system as needed and refill the reservoir. Check the parking brake for possible adjustment.

REAR WHEEL HUB AND BEARING ASSEMBLY

Removal and Installation

1. Disconnect the negative battery cable. Raise and support the vehicle safely.

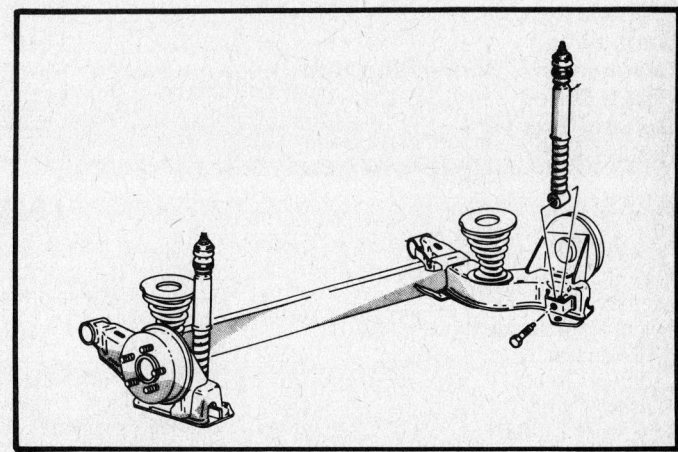

Rear axle assembly (© General Motors Corporation)

2. Remove the wheel and tire. Remove the brake drum.

— **CAUTION** —

Do not hammer on the brake drum as damage to the assembly could result.

3. Remove the four bolts which hold the hub and bearing assembly to the rear axle. Remove the hub and bearing assembly from the axle.
4. Installation is the reverse of the removal procedure.

SECTION 11: GENERAL MOTORS – "N" BODY
BUICK SOMERSET REGAL • OLDS CALAIS • PONTIAC GRAND AM

SPECIFICATIONS

Brakes 24–2	Serial Number Identification 11–3
Camshaft 11–5	Torque 11–6
Capacities 11–5	Torque Sequence (Cylinder Heads) 11–18
Crankshaft & Connecting Rod 11–5	Tune-up 11–4
Firing Order 11–4	Valve 11–5
General Engine 11–4	Wheel Alignment 11–6
Piston & Ring 11–5	

INDEX

A
Alternator R&R 11–6
Automatic Transaxle
   Adjustment 23–2
   On Car Service 23–2
   Assembly R&R 11–23
Axle Assembly R&R 11–23
Axle Shaft R&R 11–23

B
Ball Joints 35–2
Brake System 11–22
Brake Booster 11–22
Brake Caliper Overhaul 24–2
Brake Caliper R&R 24–2
Brake Drum Rear 24–2
Brake Master Cylinder 11–22
Brake Pad Front 24–2
Brake Shoe Rear 24–2

C
Camshaft R&R 11–18
Chassis Electrical 11–9
Clutch 11–22
   Adjustment 11–22
   R&R 11–22
Combination Switch R&R 11–8
Component Locators 11–9
Control Arm R&R 35–2
Cooling System 11–9
Cruise Control 11–9
Cylinder Head 11–17
   R&R 11–17

D
Differential 32–2
   Inspection 32–2
Dimmer Switch R&R 11–8
Disc Brakes 24–2
Distributor R&R 11–7
Drive Axle 11–23
Driveshaft R&R 11–23

E
Electronic Ignition 30–2
Emission Controls 11–15
Engine 11–15
   Identification 11–3
   R&R 11–15
Engine Electrical 11–6
Engine Lubrication 11–19
Engine Mechanical 11–15

Engine Mounts R&R 11–16
Exhaust Manifold R&R 11–11

F
Front Suspension 35–2
   Alignment 11–6
   Fuel Injection 11–12
Fuel Pump R&R 11–10
Fuel pump R&R 11–10
Fuses 11–9
Fusible Links 11–9

H
Headlight switch 11–8
Heater Blower R&R 11–10
Heater Core R&R 11–10
Heater Control 11–10

I
Ignition Switch 11–7
Ignition Timing 11–7
Instrument Cluster R&R 11–9
Intake Manifold R&R 11–10

L, M, N
Lower Control Arm R&R 35–2
Master Cylinder R&R 11–22
Manual Steering Gear
   R&R 11–21
Manual Transaxle
   Overhaul 32–2
Manual Transaxle R&R 11–22
Neutral Safety Switch
   R&R 11–7

O
Oil Pan R&R 11–19
Oil Pump R&R 11–20

P
Parking Brake 11–22
   Adjustment 11–22
Piston & Connecting Rod 11–18
Power Brake Unit R&R 11–22
Power Steering Pump R&R 11–21

R
Rear Suspension 35–2
Regulator 11–6
Rocker Shaft/Assy R&R 11–16

S
Serial Number 11–3
   Engine 11–3
   Vehicle 11–3
Shock Absorber R&R
   Front 35–2
   Rear 35–2
Springs
   Front 35–2
   Rear 35–2
Starter R&R 11–6
Starter Drive Replacement 11–6
Steering Column R&R 11–21
Steering Gear R&R 11–21
Steering Wheel R&R 11–21
Stop Light Switch R&R 11–8
Speedometer R&R 11–9
Suspension R&R 35–2

T
Timing Chain 11–19
Timing Gear Cover 11–19
   Oil Seal ReEplacement 11–19
Tune up 11–4
Turn Signal Switch R&R 11–8

U, V
U–Joint Overhaul 28–2
Valves Adjust 11–16
Valves Tapetts R&R 11–16
Valve Timing, Adjust 11–17
Valve System 11–16
Voltage Regulator 11–6

W
Water Pump R&R 11–9
Wheel Alignment 11–6
   Front 11–6
Wheel Bearings 11–24
Wheel Cylinders
   Rear 24–2
Windshield wiper 11–9
   Linkage R&R 11–9
   Motor R&R 11–9
   Switch R&R 11–9

Y
Year Identification 11–3

BEFORE SERVICING BE CERTAIN TO READ THE SAFETY NOTICE

GM "N" Body
1985–87
Front Wheel Drive Cars

BUICK SOMERSET REGAL • OLDSMOBILE CALAIS
PONTIAC GRAND AM

YEAR IDENTIFICATION

1985–86 Grand Am

1985–86 Calais

1985–86 Somerset

1986 Calais

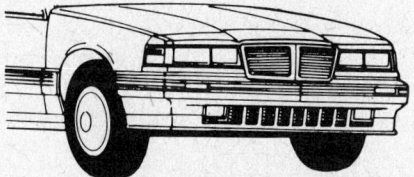
1986–87 Grand Am SE

1987 Calais GT

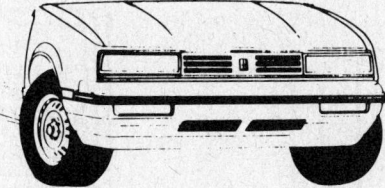
1987 Calais Supreme Coupe

VEHICLE IDENTIFICATION NUMBER (VIN)

It is important for servicing and ordering parts to be certain of the vehicle and engine identification. The VIN (vehicle identification number) is a 17 digit number visible through the windshield on the driver's side of the dash and contains the vehicle and engine identification codes. It can be interpreted as follows:

Engine Code						Model Year Code	
Code	Cu. In.	Liters	Cyl.	Carb.	Eng. Mfg.	Code	Year
U	151	2.5	4	TBI	Pont.	F	1985
L	183	3.0	V6	MFI	Buick	G	1986
						H	1987

The seventeen digit Vehicle Identification Number can be used to determine engine application and model year. The 10th digit indicates the model year and the 8th digit identifies the factory installed engine.
TBI Throttle Body Injection
MFI Multi-Port Fuel Injection

SECTION 11
GENERAL MOTORS — "N" BODY
BUICK SOMERSET REGAL • OLDS CALAIS • PONTIAC GRAND AM

GENERAL ENGINE SPECIFICATIONS

Year	Engine No. Cyl. Displ. (cu. in.)	Engine VIN Code	Fuel Delivery System	Engine Mfg.	Horsepower @ rpm	Torque @ rpm (ft. lb.)	Bore × Stroke	Compression Ratio	Oil Pressure @ rpm
'85–'87	4-151	U	TBI	Pont.	92 @ 4500	138 @ 2400	4.00 × 3.00	9.0:1	36–41 @ 2000
	6-181	L	MFI	Buick	125 @ 4900	150 @ 2400	3.80 × 2.66	9.0:1	37 @ 2400

TUNE-UP SPECIFICATIONS

Year	Eng. VIN Code	Engine No. Cyl. Displacement (cu. in.)	Eng. Mfg.	Spark Plugs Orig. Type	Spark Plugs Gap (in.)	Ignition Timing (deg.) Man. Trans.	Ignition Timing (deg.) Auto. Trans.	Valves Intake Opens (deg.)	Fuel Pump Pressure (psi)	Idle Speed (rpm) Man. Trans.	Idle Speed (rpm) Auto. Trans.
'85–'86	U	4-151	Pont.	R43TSX	0.060	8B	8B	NA	12	①	①
	L	6-181	Buick	R44LTS	0.040	15B	15B	NA	34–44	①	①
'87	All			See Underhood Specifications Sticker							

NOTE: The underhood specifications sticker often reflects tune-up specification changes made in production. Sticker figures must be used if they disagree with those in this chart.
B Before Top Dead Center
Part numbers in this chart are not recommendations by Chilton for any product by brand name.
NA Not Available at time of publication
① See underhood sticker

FIRING ORDERS

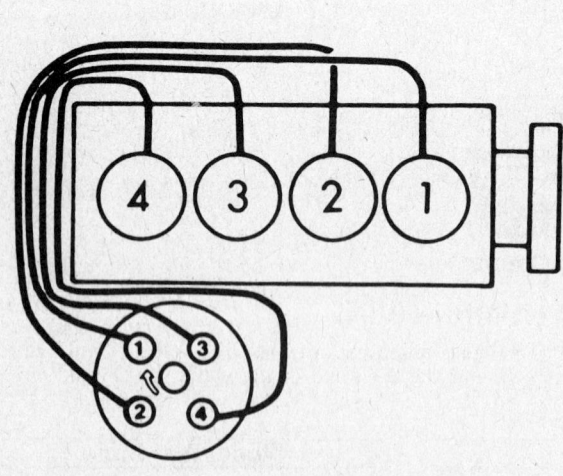

Pontiac-built 151-4 cylinder engine
Engine firing order: 1–3–4–2
Distributor rotation: clockwise

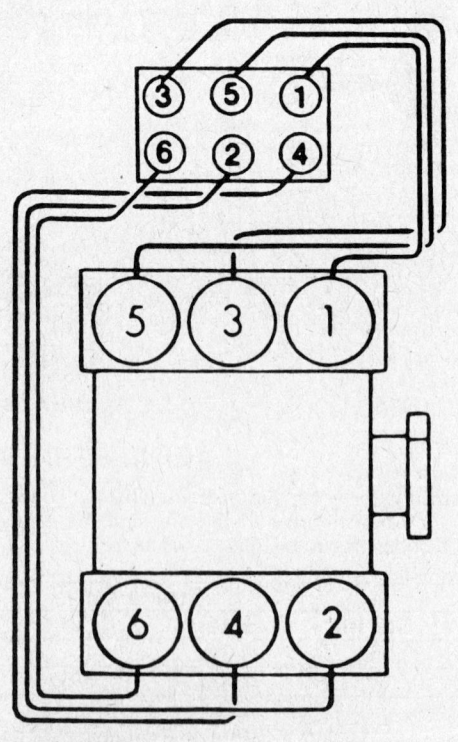

GM (Buick) 181 V6 (3.0L)
Engine firing order: 1–6–5–4–3–2
Distributor rotation: clockwise

GENERAL MOTORS—"N" BODY
BUICK SOMERSET REGAL • OLDS CALAIS • PONTIAC GRAND AM

SECTION 11

CAPACITIES

Year	Eng. VIN Code	Engine Displacement (cu. in.)	Eng. Mfg.	Crankcase (qts.) w/filter	Crankcase (qts.) wo/filter	Transaxle (pints) 5 speed	Transaxle (pints) Auto.	Gas Tank Gal	Cooling System (qts.) w/heater	Cooling System (qts.) w/AC
'85–'87	U	4-151	Pont.	①	3	5.3	8 ②	13.6	7.8	7.9
	L	6-181	Buick	①	4	5.3	8 ②	13.6	7.8	7.9

① Fill to mark on dipstick
② 12 pts. if drained completely

VALVE SPECIFICATIONS

Year	Eng. VIN Code	Engine No. Cyl. Displacement (cu. in.)	Eng. Mfg.	Seat Angle (deg.)	Face Angle (deg.)	Spring Test Pressure (lbs. @ in.)	Spring Installed Height (in.)	Stem-to-Guide Clearance (in.) Intake	Stem-to-Guide Clearance (in.) Exhaust	Stem Diameter (in.) Intake	Stem Diameter (in.) Exhaust
'85–'87	U	4-151	Pont.	46	45	78–86 @ 1.66	1.69	0.0010–0.0027	0.0010–0.0027 ①	0.3420–0.3430	0.3420–0.3430
	L	6-181	Buick	45	45	210–230 @ 1.340	1.727	0.0015–0.0035	0.0015–0.0032	0.3401–0.3412	0.3405–0.3412

CAMSHAFT SPECIFICATIONS
All measurements in inches

Year	Eng. VIN Code	Engine	Eng. Mfg.	Journal Diameter 1 2 3 4 5	Bearing Clearance	Lobe Lift Intake	Lobe Lift Exhaust	Camshaft End Play
'85–'87	U	4-151	Pont.	1.869	0.0007–0.0027	0.398	0.398	0.0015–0.0050
	L	6-181	Buick	1.785–1.786	0.0005–0.0025	NA	NA	NA

NA Not available at time of publication.

CRANKSHAFT AND CONNECTING ROD SPECIFICATIONS
All measurements are given in inches

Year	Eng. VIN Code	Engine No. Cyl. Displacement (cu. in.)	Eng. Mfg.	Crankshaft Main Brg Journal Dia	Crankshaft Main Brg Oil Clearance	Crankshaft Shaft End-Play	Thrust on No.	Connecting Rod Journal Diameter	Connecting Rod Oil Clearance	Connecting Rod Side Clearance
'85–'87	U	4-151	Pont.	2.30	0.0005–0.0022	0.0035–0.0085	5	2.00	0.0005–0.0022	0.006–0.022
	L	6-181	Buick	2.4995	0.0003–0.0018	0.0030–0.0110	2	2.487	0.0005–0.0026	0.003–0.015

PISTON AND RING SPECIFICATIONS
All measurements are given in inches

Year	Eng. VIN Code	Engine No. Cyl. Disp. (cu. in.)	Eng. Mfg.	Piston-to-Bore Clearance	Ring Gap Top Compression	Ring Gap Bottom Compression	Ring Gap Oil Control	Ring Side Clearance Top Compression	Ring Side Clearance Bottom Compression	Ring Side Clearance Oil Control
'85–'87	U	4-151	Pont.	0.0014–0.0022 ①	0.010–0.020	0.010–0.020	0.020–0.060	0.002–0.003	0.001–0.003	0.015–0.055
	L	6-181	Buick	0.008–0.0020 ②	0.010–0.020	0.010–0.020	0.015–0.055	0.010–0.020	0.010–0.020	0.015–0.055

① Measured 1.8 inches from piston top
② Measured at the top of the skirt

11–5

SECTION 11: GENERAL MOTORS — "N" BODY
BUICK SOMERSET REGAL • OLDS CALAIS • PONTIAC GRAND AM

TORQUE SPECIFICATIONS
All readings in ft. lbs.

Year	VIN Code	Engine No. Cyl. Displacement (cu. in.)	Eng. Mfg.	Cylinder Head Bolts	Rod Bearing Bolts	Main Bearing Bolts	Crankshaft Bolt	Flywheel to Crankshaft Bolts	Manifold Intake	Manifold Exhaust
'85–'87	U	4-151	Pont.	②	32	70	200	55	32	37
	L	6-181	Buick	①	40	100	200	60	32	37

Caution: Verify the correct original equipment engine is in the vehicle by referring to the VIN engine code before torquing any bolts.

① Torque bolts to 25 lb. ft. in sequence. Turn each bolt 1/4 turn (90°) in sequence. Turn each bolt an additional 1/4 turn (90°). Should you reach 60 lb. ft. at any time, you should stop at this point. Do not complete the balance of the 90° turn.

② Cylinder head bolts gradually with torque wrench to 18 lb. ft. in sequence. Repeat sequence, bringing torque to 22 lb. ft. on all bolts except number 9. Torque number 9 to 29 lb. ft. Repeat sequence. Turn all bolts, except number 9, 120 degrees (two flats). Turn number 9 1/4 turn (90 degrees).

WHEEL ALIGNMENT SPECIFICATIONS

Year	Model	Caster Range (deg)	Caster Pref. Setting (deg)	Chamber Range (deg)	Chamber Pref. Setting (deg)	Toe-In (in.)
'85	All	2/3P to 2 2/3P	1 2/3P	1/5P to 1 1/2P	5/6P	1/8 OUT
'86–'87	All	3/4P to 2 3/4P	1 3/4P	1/4P to 1 3/8P	13/16P	1/16 OUT

ELECTRICAL SECTION

For Overhaul Procedures, refer to Unit Repair Section.

Charging System

ALTERNATOR

Removal and Installation

1. Disconnect the negative battery cable.
2. Remove the two terminal plug and the battery lead from the back of the alternator assembly.
3. Remove the necessary components in order to gain access to the alternator retaining bolts. Loosen the adjusting bolts. Remove the alternator belt.
4. Remove the alternator retaining bolts. Remove the alternator assembly from the vehicle.
5. Installation is the reverse of the removal procedure. Check for the proper belt tension.

VOLTAGE REGULATOR

Removal and Installation

The voltage regulator is incorporated within the alternator assembly. There is no adjustment procedure. Should the regulator require service the alternator must be disassembled.

Starting System

STARTER

Removal and Installation

1. Disconnect the negative battery cable. Raise the vehicle and support it safely.
2. Disconnect the starter wiring.
3. Remove the three dust cover bolts. Pull the dust cover back to gain access to the front starter bolt.
4. Remove the front starter bolt.
5. Remove the rear support bracket.
6. Pull the rear dust cover back to gain access to the rear starter bolt. Remove the bolt.
7. Push the dust cover back into place and pull the starter assembly back and out.
8. Installation is the reverse of the removal procedure.

Ignition System

Two types of ignition systems are being used on the N-body vehicles. The HEI system is being used on the four cylinder engine and the Computer Controlled Coil Ignition system is being used on the six cylinder engine.

GENERAL MOTORS — "N" BODY
BUICK SOMERSET REGAL • OLDS CALAIS • PONTIAC GRAND AM

The C³I system does not use a distributor. The C3I ignition system consists of a coil pack, ignition module camshaft and crankshaft sensor. There are two types of C3I coils used. Type 1 coils have three plug wires on each side of the coil assembly; Type 2 coils have all six wires connected on one side of the coil. When troubleshooting or replacing components, it is important to determine which C3I system is installed on the engine.

The C3I system incorporates a coil pack, ignition module, crankshaft sensor, interruptor rings and electronic control module (ECM). All components are serviced as complete assemblies, although individual coils are available for Type 2 coil packs. Since the ECM controls the ignition timing, no timing adjustments are necessary or possible.

DISTRIBUTOR

Removal and Installation

EXCEPT C3I SYSTEM

1. Disconnect the negative battery cable.
2. Disconnect the ignition switch battery feed wire and the tachometer lead, if equipped, from the distributor cap.
3. Release the coil connectors from the cap. Remove the distributor cap, and position it out of the way.
4. Disconnect the four terminal ECM harness from the distributor.
5. Remove the distributor clamp screw and hold down clamp.
6. Note position of rotor, then pull distributor up until rotor just stops turning counterclockwise and again note position of rotor.
7. If the engine was accidentally cranked after the distributor was removed, the following procedure can be used for installing:
8. Remove No. 1 spark plug. Place finger over No. 1 spark plug hole and crank engine slowly until compression is felt.
9. Align timing mark on pulley to "O" on engine timing indicator. Turn rotor to point between No. 1 and No. 4.
10. Install distributor and connect ignition feed wire.
11. Install distributor cap and spark plug wires.
12. Check engine timing.

CRANKSHAFT SENSOR- C3I SYSTEM

Removal and Installation

1. Disconnect the negative battery cable.
2. Remove the serpentine drive belt.
3. Raise and support the vehicle safely.
4. Remove the right front tire.
5. Remove the inner fender splash shield.
6. Remove the crankshaft balancer bolt and balancer.
7. Remove the mounting bolts and remove the crankshaft sensor from the front cover. Disconnect the electrical connector and remove the sensor from the vehicle.
8. Installation is the reverse of removal. Make sure the electrical T-latch connector is assembled properly or an intermittent loss of operation may occur. The sensor must be carefully aligned with the interruptor rings to avoid damage when the engine is cranked. Tighten the crankshaft sensor mounting bolts to 22 ft. lbs. (30 Nm) and the crankshaft balancer bolt to 200 ft. lbs. (270 Nm).

IGNITION TIMING

Adjustment

EXCEPT C3I SYSTEM

1. Refer to the vehicle control information label which is located on the radiator support panel, for the proper timing information.

2. If the engine timing requires adjustment, loosen the distributor hold down bolt and rotate the distributor slowly in either direction, to advance or retard the engine timing.
3. Tighten the hold down bolt and recheck the engine timing.
4. Some engines incorporate a magnetic timing probe hole which is used when setting the engine timing with special electronic equipment. Consult manufacturers instructions if using this form of timing equipment.

C3I SYSTEM

The C3I ignition system does not require timing adjustments, therefore engine timing is not necessary or available.

Electrical Controls

IGNITION LOCK CYLINDER

Removal and Installation

1. Disconnect the negative battery cable. Position the ignition lock cylinder in the Run position.
2. Remove the steering wheel. Remove the lock plate, turn signal switch and the buzzer switch.
3. Remove the lock cylinder retaining screw. Remove the lock cylinder.
4. To install, rotate the lock cylinder clockwise to align the cylinder key with the keyway in the lock housing.
5. Push the lock all the way in. Install the screw.
6. Continue the installation in the reverse order of the removal procedure.

IGNITION SWITCH

Removal and Installation

1. Disconnect the negative battery cable. Lower the steering column and properly support it.
2. Put the switch in the "Off-Unlocked" position. With the cylinder removed, the rod is in "Lock" when it is in the next to the uppermost detent. "Off-Unlocked" is two detents from the top.
3. Remove the two switch screws and remove the switch assembly.
4. Before installing, place the new switch in "Off-Unlocked" position and make sure the lock cylinder and actuating rod are in "Off-Unlocked" (third detent from the top) position.
5. Install the activating rod into the switch and assemble the switch on the column. Tighten the mounting screws. Use only the specified screws since over-length screws could impair the collapsibility of the column.
6. Reinstall the steering column.

NEUTRAL START SYSTEM

All steering columns contain a mechanical neutral start system. This system relies on a mechanical block, rather than the starter safety switch to prevent starting the engine in other than Park or Neutral.

The mechanical block is achieved by a cast in finger added to the switch actuator rack, which interferes with the bowl plate in all shift positions except Neutral or Park. This interference prevents rotation of the lock cylinder into the "start" position.

In either "P" or "N", this finger passes through the bowl plate slots, allowing the lock cylinder full rotational travel into the "Start" position.

11-7

SECTION 11

GENERAL MOTORS—"N" BODY
BUICK SOMERSET REGAL • OLDS CALAIS • PONTIAC GRAND AM

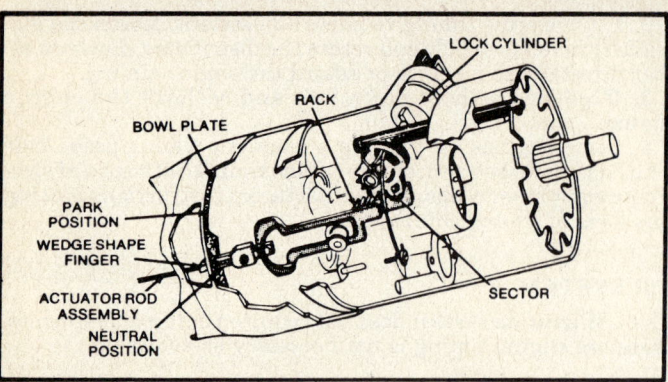

Mechanical neutral start system—typical
(© General Motors Corporation)

CLUTCH START SWITCH

Adjustment

1. Lift the clutch pedal to its uppermost position. Check the operation of the pawl and the quandrant. Make sure that the pawl disengages from the quandrant when the pedal is pulled to this position.
2. Check the quandrant for free rotation in both directions.
3. Depress the clutch pedal slowly several times to set the pawl into mesh with the quandrant teeth.

Removal and Installation

1. Disconnect the negative battery cable. Remove the electrical connections from the switch.
2. Remove the clutch switch retaining bolt and carefully remove the switch from the clutch pedal.
3. Installation is the reverse of the removal procedure. Be sure to check for the proper engagement of the switch once installation has been completed.

STOPLIGHT SWITCH

Adjustment

1. The switch is mounted on the brake pedal bracket.
2. To adjust, depress the pedal and push the switch through the circular retaining clip until it contacts the brake pedal, then pull the pedal up against the internal pedal stop. This places the switch in the correct position within the clip.

HEADLIGHT SWITCH

Removal and Installation

CALAIS

1. Disconnect the negative battery cable.
2. Remove the lower steering column collar.
3. Remove the instrument panel cluster trim plate.
4. Remove the headlight switch mounting screws. Pull the switch assembly rearward and unplug both electrical connections.
5. Remove the headlight switch from the vehicle.
6. Installation is the reverse of the removal procedure.

GRAND AM

1. Disconnect the negative battery cable.
2. Remove the headlight switch trim plate.
3. Remove the headlight switch retaining screws. Pull the switch assembly rearward and unplug the electrical connections.
4. Remove the headlight switch from the vehicle.
5. Installation is the reverse of the removal procedure.

SOMERSET REGAL AND SKYLARK

1. Disconnect the negative battery cable.
2. Remove the instrument panel trim cover.
3. Remove the headlight switch trim panel.
4. Remove the switch retaining screws.
5. Remove the switch from the vehicle.
6. Installation is the reverse of the removal procedure.

DIMMER SWITCH

Removal and Installation

1. Disconnect the negative battery cable. Remove the steering wheel. Remove the trim cover.
2. Remove the turn signal switch assembly.
3. Remove the ignition switch stud and screw. Remove the ignition switch.
4. Remove the dimmer switch actuator rod by sliding it from the switch assembly.
5. Remove the dimmer switch bolts and remove the dimmer switch.
6. Installation is the reverse of the removal procedure.
7. Adjust the dimmer switch by depressing the switch slightly and inserting a 3/32" drill bit into the adjusting hole. Push the switch up to remove any play and tighten the dimmer switch adjusting screw.

TURN SIGNAL SWITCH

Removal and Installation

1. Disconnect the negative battery cable. Remove the steering wheel. Remove the trim cover.
2. Pry the cover from the steering column.
3. Position a U-shaped lockplate compressing tool on the end of the steering shaft and compress the lock plate by turning the shaft nut clockwise. Pry the wire snapring out of the shaft groove.
4. Remove the tool and lift the lockplate off the shaft.
5. Slip the canceling cam, upper bearing preload spring, and thrust washer off the shaft.
6. Remove the turn signal lever. Remove the hazard flasher button retaining screw and remove the button, spring and knob.
7. Pull the switch connector out of the mast jacket and tape the upper part to facilitate switch removal. Attach a long piece of wire to the turn signal switch connector. When installing the turn signal switch, feed this wire through the column first, and then use this wire to pull the switch connector into position. On tilt wheels, place the turn signal and shifter housing in low position and remove the harness cover.
8. Remove the three switch mounting screws. Remove the switch by pulling it straight up while guiding the wiring harness cover through the column.
9. Install the replacement switch by working the connector and cover down through the housing and under the bracket. On tilt models, the connector is worked down through the housing, under the bracket, and then the cover is installed on the harness.
10. Install the switch mounting screws and the connector on the mast jacket bracket. Install the column to dash trim plate.
11. Install the flasher knob and the turn signal lever.
12. With the turn signal lever in neutral and the flasher knob out, slide the thrust washer, upper bearing preload spring, and canceling cam onto the shaft.
13. Position the lock plate on the shaft and press it down until a new snapring can be inserted in the shaft groove. Always use a new snapring when assembling.

14. Install the cover and the steering wheel.

WINDSHIELD WIPER SWITCH

Removal and Installation

CALAIS
1. Disconnect the negative battery cable.
2. Remove the lower steering column collar.
3. Remove the instrument panel cluster trim plate.
4. Remove the wiper switch mounting screws. Pull the switch assembly rearward and unplug both electrical connections.
5. Remove the windshield wiper switch from the vehicle.
6. Installation is the reverse of the removal procedure.

GRAND AM
1. Disconnect the negative battery cable.
2. Remove the wiper switch trim plate.
3. Remove the wiper switch retaining screws. Pull the switch assembly rearward and unplug the electrical connectors.
4. Remove the wiper switch from the vehicle.
5. Installation is the reverse of the removal procedure.

SOMERSET REGAL AND SKYLARK
1. Disconnect the negative battery cable.
2. Remove the instrument panel trim cover.
3. Remove the wiper switch trim panel.
4. Remove the wiper switch retaining screws.
5. Remove the wiper switch from the vehicle.
6. Installation is the reverse of the removal procedure.

WINDSHIELD WIPER MOTOR

Removal and Installation
1. Disconnect the negative battery cable.
2. Remove the wiper arm assemblies.
3. Loosen, but do not remove the retaining nuts that secure the transmission drive link to the motor crank arm.
4. Remove the air inlet screw panel. Remove the transmission drive link from the motor crank arm.
5. Remove the wiper motor retaining bolts. Remove the wiper motor and linkage by guiding it through the access hole in the upper shroud panel.
6. Installation is the reverse of the removal procedure.

Instrument Cluster

Removal and Installation

CALAIS
1. Disconnect the negative battery cable.
2. Remove the steering column collar. Remove the screws from the steering column opening filler.
3. Remove the screws from the cluster trim plate. Remove the trim plate.
4. Remove the bolts from the steering column support. Lower the steering column.
5. Remove the screws retaining the cluster to the instrument panel pad. Remove the cluster from the vehicle, by pulling it rearward.
6. Installation is the reverse of the removal procedure.

GRAND AM, SOMERSET REGAL AND SKYLARK
1. Disconnect the negative battery cable.
2. Remove the cluster lower trim plate.
3. Lower the steering column, as required.
4. Remove the upper cluster trim plate.
5. Remove the cluster retaining screws. Remove the cluster from the vehicle, by pulling it rearward.
6. Installation is the reverse of the removal procedure.

ELECTRICAL COMPONENT LOCATIONS

Electronic Control Module
The electronic control module is located on the right side of the vehicle, underneath the dash pad. To gain access to this component you may first have to remove the right dash pad trim panel.

Convenience Center
The convenience center, on some vehicles, is a swing down unit that is located on the underside of the instrument panel. This component provides a central location and easy access to buzzers, relays and flasher units.

SPEED CONTROLS

Adjustment
For cruise control information refer to the diagnostic charts in the "A" and "X" body section of this repair manual.

Electrical circuit protectors

FUSE PANEL
The fuse panel is located on the left side of the vehicle. It is under the instrument panel assembly. In order to gain access to the fuse panel it may be necessary to first remove the under dash padding.

FUSEABLE LINKS
Fusible links are used to prevent major wire harness damage in the event of a short circuit or an overload condition in the wiring circuits which are normally not fused, due to carrying high amperage loads or because of their locations within the wiring harness. Each fusible link is of a fixed value for a specific electrical load and should a link fail, the cause of the failure must be determined and repaired prior to installing a new fusible link of the same value.

COOLING AND HEATER SYSTEMS

WATER PUMP

Removal and Installation

NOTE: Special pulley removal and installation tools will be required to remove and install the water pump pulley on the 2.5 liter engine.

1. Disconnect the negative battery cable. Drain the cooling system. Remove the drive belts.
2. Remove the fan, pulley and radiator shroud, as required.
3. Remove all the necessary components in order to gain access to the water pump retaining bolts.
4. Remove the radiator hose from the water pump. Remove the heater hose from the pump, as required.

SECTION 11

GENERAL MOTORS—"N" BODY
BUICK SOMERSET REGAL • OLDS CALAIS • PONTIAC GRAND AM

5. Remove the water pump retaining bolts. On the V6 engine, the long bolt is removed through the access hole that is provided in the body side rail.
6. Remove the water pump from the vehicle.
7. Installation is the reverse of the removal procedure. Be sure to use a new gasket or RTV sealant, as required.

BLOWER MOTOR

Removal and Installation

1. Disconnect the negative battery cable.
2. Remove the electrical connectors from the blower motor.
3. Remove the blower motor retaining screws. Slide the blower motor far enough away from the housing to remove the fan retaining nut.
4. Slide the fan into the housing. Remove the blower motor from the vehicle.
5. Installation is the reverse of the removal procedure.

HEATER CORE

Removal and Installation

1. Disconnect the negative battery cable. Drain the cooling system.
2. Raise the vehicle and support it safely.
3. Remove the heater hoses at the heater core. Remove the drain tube.
4. Lower the vehicle. Remove the instrument panel sound insulator.
5. Lower the heating duct and hoses.
6. Remove the heater core cover retaining screws and remove both core covers.
7. Remove the heater core from the vehicle.
8. Installation is the reverse of the removal procedure.

TEMPERATURE CONTROL/BLOWER SWITCH

Removal and Installation

CALAIS

1. Disconnect the negative battery cable.
2. Remove the lower steering column trim and collar. Remove the center trim. Remove the instrument panel compartment insert.
3. Remove the right instrument panel trim. Remove the lower instrument panel trim.
4. Remove the control assembly retaining bolts. Pull the assembly forward.
5. Disconnect the temperature cable at the control head. Disconnect all vacuum and electrical connections from the control assembly. Remove the control head from the vehicle.
6. Installation is the reverse of the removal procedure.

GRAND AM

1. Disconnect the negative battery cable.
2. Remove the radio trim plate. Remove the right hush panel.
3. Remove the console extension.
4. Remove the control assembly retaining bolts. Pull the control assembly out far enough to disconnect all electrical and vacuum and cable connections.
5. Remove the control assembly from the vehicle.
6. Installation is the reverse of the removal procedure.

SOMERSET REGAL AND SKYLARK

1. Disconnect the negative battery cable.
2. Remove the temperature control trim plate.
3. Remove the temperature control retaining screws. Pull the control assembly forward.
4. Disconnect the control cable, and all electrical and vacuum connections from the control assembly.
5. Remove the control assembly from the vehicle.
6. Installation is the reverse of the removal procedure.

FUEL SYSTEM

FUEL PUMP

Removal and Installation

1. To relieve the fuel system pressure, remove the fuel pump fuse which is located in the fuse block.
2. Crank the engine. The engine will run until all fuel that is in the fuel lines has been consumed. Once the engine cuts off engage the starter for three seconds to assure relief of any remaining fuel pressure.
3. Disconnect the negative battery cable.
4. Raise and support the vehicle safely. Drain the fuel tank.
5. Remove the fuel tank from the vehicle.
6. Remove the sending unit along with the electric fuel pump.
7. Installation is the reverse of the removal procedure.

INTAKE MANIFOLD

Removal and Installation

2.5 LITER ENGINE

1. Disconnect the negative battery cable.
2. Remove the air cleaner and the heat stove pipe.
3. Remove the PCV valve and hose at the throttle body injection system.
4. Drain the coolant. Remove the fuel lines and vacuum lines.
5. Remove the wiring and throttle linkage from the throttle body injection system.
6. Disconnect the transaxle downshift linkage and cruise control linkage if equipped.
7. Disconnect the throttle linkage and bell crank. Position the assembly to the side for clearance.
8. Disconnect the heater hose. Disconnect and remove the upper bracket on the power steering pump.
9. Remove the ignition coil.
10. Remove the intake manifold retaining bolts. Remove the intake manifold from the vehicle.
11. Installation is the reverse of the removal procedure. Be sure to torque the retaining bolts to specification.

3.0 LITER ENGINE

1. Disconnect the negative battery cable.
2. Disconnect the mass air flow sensor and remove the air intake duct.
3. Remove the serpentine accessory drive belt, alternator and bracket.
4. Remove the C3I ignition module and wiring.
5. Remove all vacuum lines and wiring connectors as required.

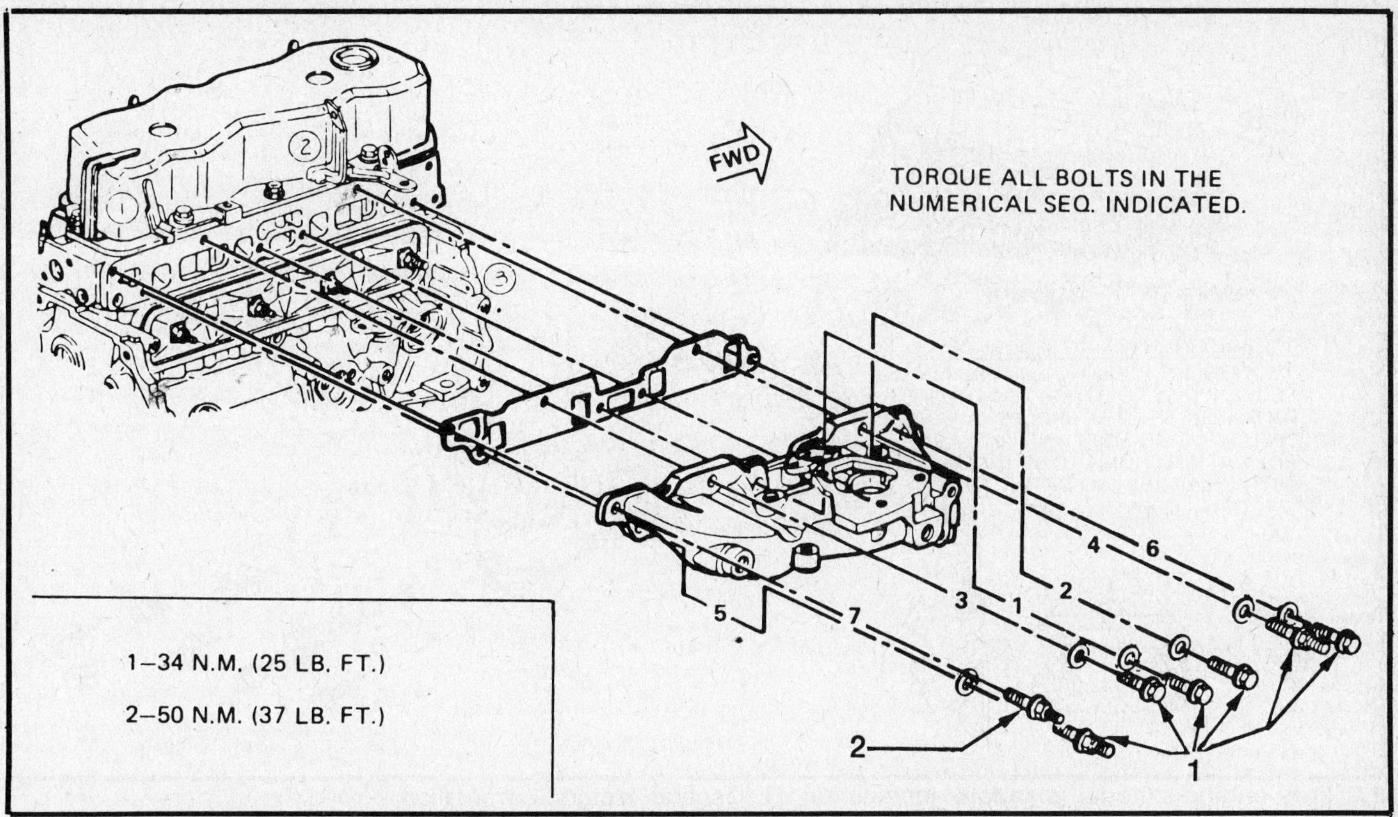

GENERAL MOTORS—"N" BODY
BUICK SOMERSET REGAL • OLDS CALAIS • PONTIAC GRAND AM

SECTION 11

TORQUE ALL BOLTS IN THE NUMERICAL SEQ. INDICATED.

1—34 N.M. (25 LB. FT.)
2—50 N.M. (37 LB. FT.)

2.5 liter engine-intake manifold bolt torque sequence (© General Motors Corporation)

6. Remove or disconnect as required, throttle, cruise control and TV cables from the throttle body assembly.
7. Drain the engine coolant. Disconnect the heater hoses from the throttle body.
8. Remove the upper radiator hose.
9. Remove the fuel lines, fuel rail and the fuel injectors. Remove the spark plug wires.
10. Remove the intake manifold retaining bolts. Remove the intake manifold.
11. Installation is the reverse of the removal procedure. Be sure to torque the retaining bolts to specification.

EXHAUST MANIFOLD

Removal and Installation

2.5 LITER ENGINE

1. Disconnect the negative battery cable.
2. Remove the air cleaner and the heat stove tube.
3. Remove the alternator top mounts and position the unit to the side.
4. Disconnect the oxygen sensor connector.
5. Raise and support the vehicle safely.
6. Disconnect the exhaust pipe from the exhaust manifold retaining flange.
7. Lower the vehicle.
8. Remove the exhaust manifold retaining bolts. Remove the exhaust manifold from the engine.
9. Installation is the reverse of the removal procedure. Be sure to torque the retaining bolts to specification.

3.0 LITER ENGINE

1. Disconnect the negative battery cable.
2. Raise and support the vehicle safely.

3. Remove the exhaust pipe to manifold flange retaining bolts.
4. Lower the vehicle. Remove the oxygen sensor electrical connector. Remove the spark plug wires.
5. Remove the two nuts retaining the crossover pipe to the manifold.
6. Remove all the necessary components in order to gain access to the exhaust manifold retaining bolts.
7. Remove the manifold retaining bolts. Remove the manifold.
8. Installation is the reverse of the removal procedure. Be sure to torque the retaining bolts to specification.

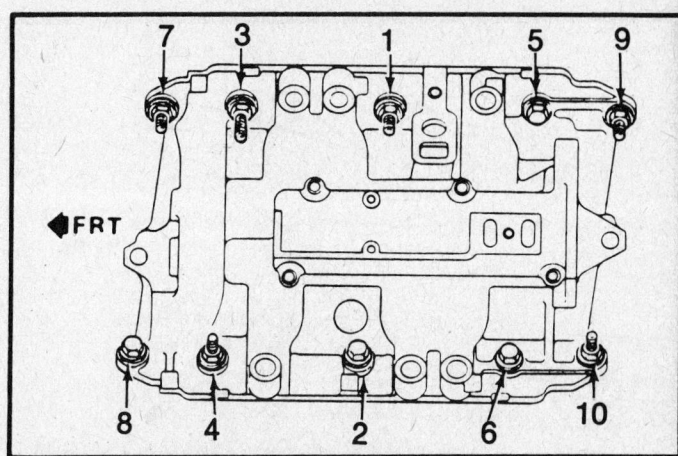

3.0 liter engine-intake manifold torque sequence (© General Motors Corporation)

11-11

SECTION 11

GENERAL MOTORS—"N" BODY
BUICK SOMERSET REGAL • OLDS CALAIS • PONTIAC GRAND AM

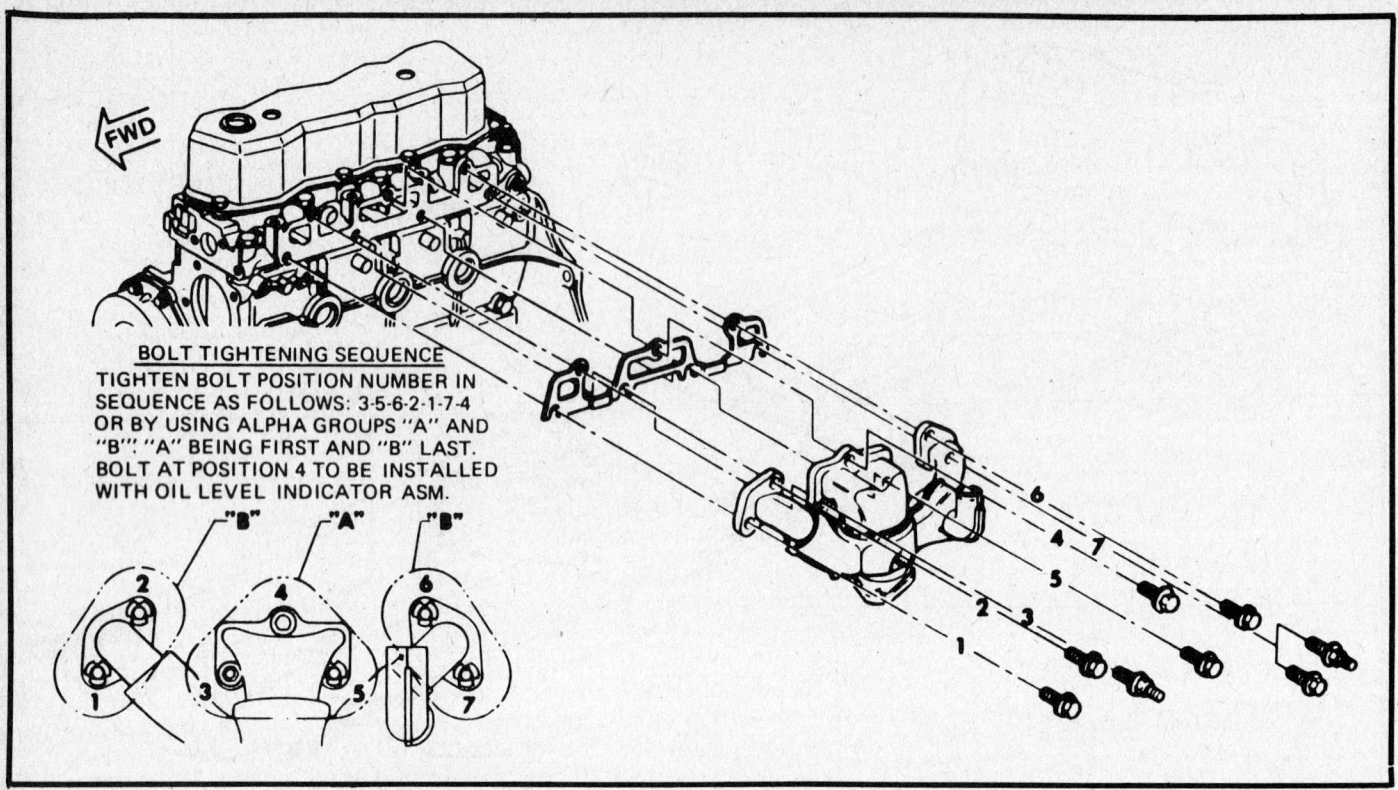

2.5 liter engine-exhaust manifold installation (© General Motors Corporation)

Fuel Injection System

For more information on Fuel Injection System, refer to Unit Repair Section

DESCRIPTION AND TYPE

Throttle Body Injection (2.5 Liter Engine)

With throttle body injection (TBI), an injection unit is placed on the intake manifold where the carburetor is normally mounted. The TBI unit is computer controlled and supplies the correct amount of fuel during all engine operating conditions.

In this throttle body system, a single fuel injector mounted at the top of the throttle body sprays fuel down through the throttle valve and into the intake manifold. The throttle body resembles a carburetor in appearance but does away with much of the carburetor's complexity (choke system and linkage, power valves, accelerator pump, jets, fuel circuits, etc.), replacing these with the electrically operated fuel injector.

The injector is actually a solenoid which when activated lifts a pintle valve off its seat, allowing the pressurized (10 psi) fuel behind the valve to spray out. The nozzle of the injector is designed to atomize the fuel for complete air/fuel mixture.

The activating signal for the injector originates with the electronic control module (ECM), which monitors engine temperature, throttle position, vehicle speed and several other en-

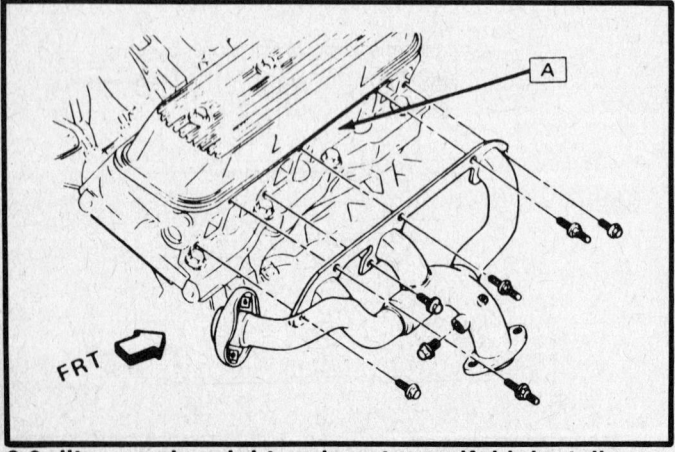

3.0 liter engine-right exhaust manifold installation (© General Motors Corporation)

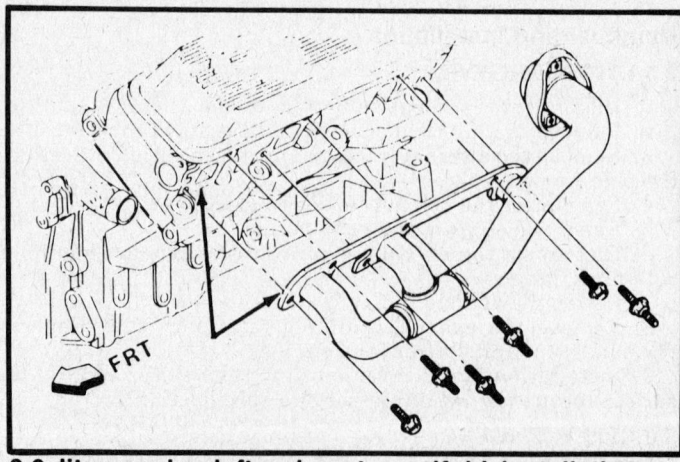

3.0 liter engine-left exhaust manifold installation (© General Motors Corporation)

GENERAL MOTORS—"N" BODY
BUICK SOMERSET REGAL • OLDS CALAIS • PONTIAC GRAND AM

gine-related conditions then continuously updates injector opening times in relation to the information given by these sensors.

The throttle body is also equipped with an idle air control motor. The idle air control motor operates a pintle valve at the side of the throttle body. When the valve opens it allows air to bypass the throttle, which provides the additional air required to idle at elevated speed when the engine is cold. The idle air control motor also compensates for accessory loads and changing engine friction during break-in. The idle speed control motor is controlled by the ECM.

Fuel pressure for the system is provided by an in-tank fuel pump. The pump is a two-stage turbine design powered by a DC motor. It is designed for smooth, quiet operation, high flow and fast priming. The design of the fuel inlet reduces the possibility of vapor lock under hot fuel conditions. The pump sends fuel forward through the fuel line to a stainless steel high-flow fuel filter mounted on the engine. From the filter the fuel moves to the throttle body. The fuel pump inlet is located in a reservoir in the fuel tank which insures a constant supply of fuel to the pump during hard cornering and on steep inclines. The fuel pump is controlled by a fuel pump relay, which in turn receives its signal from the ECM. A fuel pressure regulator inside the throttle body maintains fuel pressure at 10 psi and routes unused fuel back to the fuel tank through a fuel return line. On the dual throttle body system, a fuel pressure compensator is used on the second throttle body assembly to compensate for a momentary fuel pressure drop between the two units.

This constant circulation of fuel through the throttle body prevents component overheating and vapor lock.

The electronic control module (ECM), also called a microcomputer, is the brain of the fuel injection system. After receiving inputs from various sensing elements in the system, the ECM commands the fuel injector, idle air control motor, EST distributor, torque converter clutch and other engine actuators to operate in a pre-programmed manner to improve driveability and fuel economy while controlling emissions. The sensing elements update the computer every tenth of a second for general information and every 12.5 milli-seconds for critical emissions and driveability information.

The ECM has limited system diagnostic capability. If certain system malfunctions occur, the diagnostic "check engine" light in the instrument panel will light, alerting the driver to the need for service. Since both idle speed and mixture are controlled by the ECM on this system, no adjustments are possible or necessary.

Multi-Port Fuel Injection (3.0 Liter Engine)

The multi-port fuel injection (MFI) system is controlled by an electronic control module which monitors engine operations and generates output signals to provide the correct air/fuel mixture, ignition timing and engine idle speed control. Input to the control unit is provided by an oxygen sensor, coolant temperature sensor, detonation sensor, hot film air mass sensor and throttle position sensor. The ECM also receives informa-

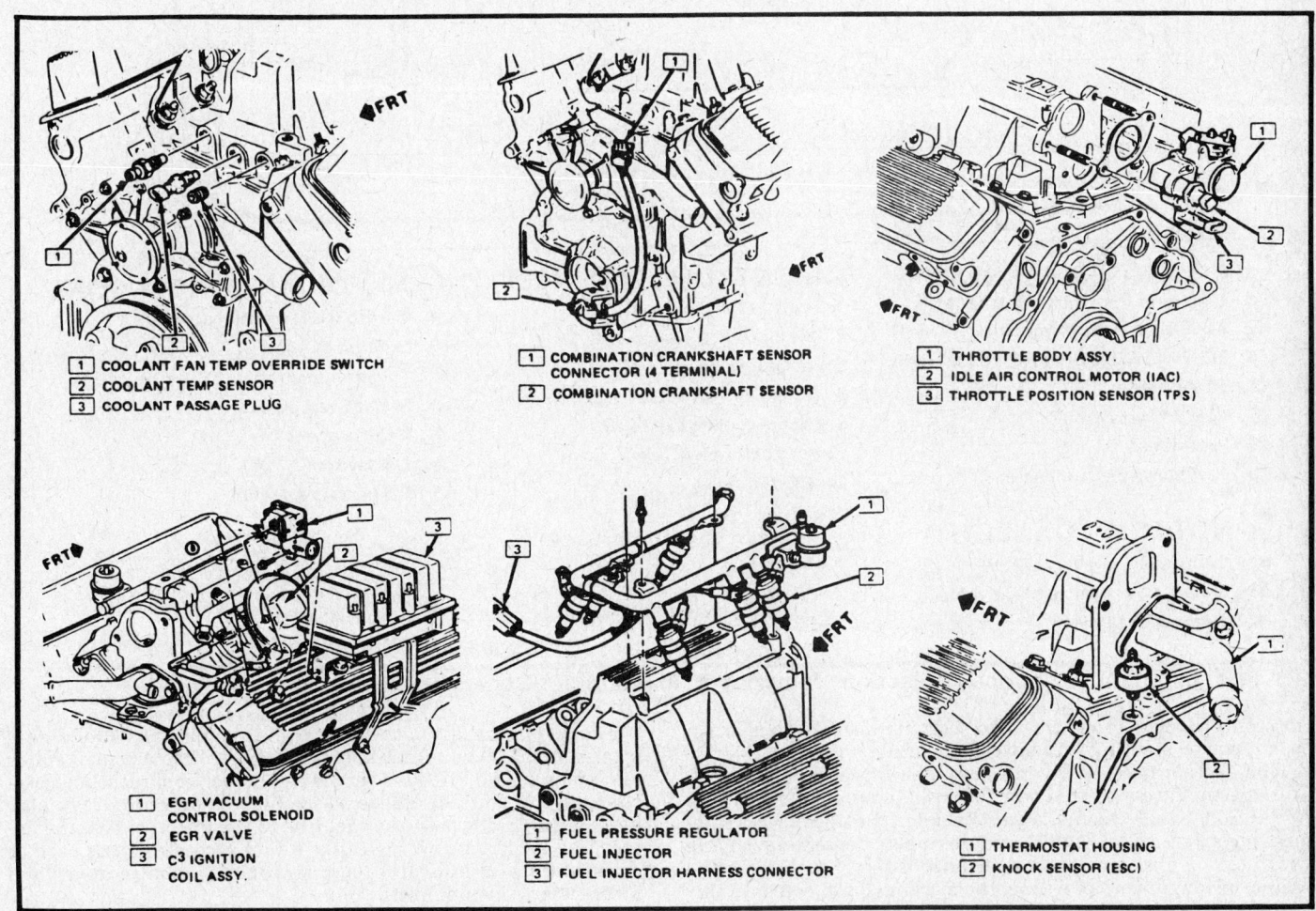

3.0 liter engine—fuel injection components

SECTION 11

GENERAL MOTORS—"N" BODY
BUICK SOMERSET REGAL • OLDS CALAIS • PONTIAC GRAND AM

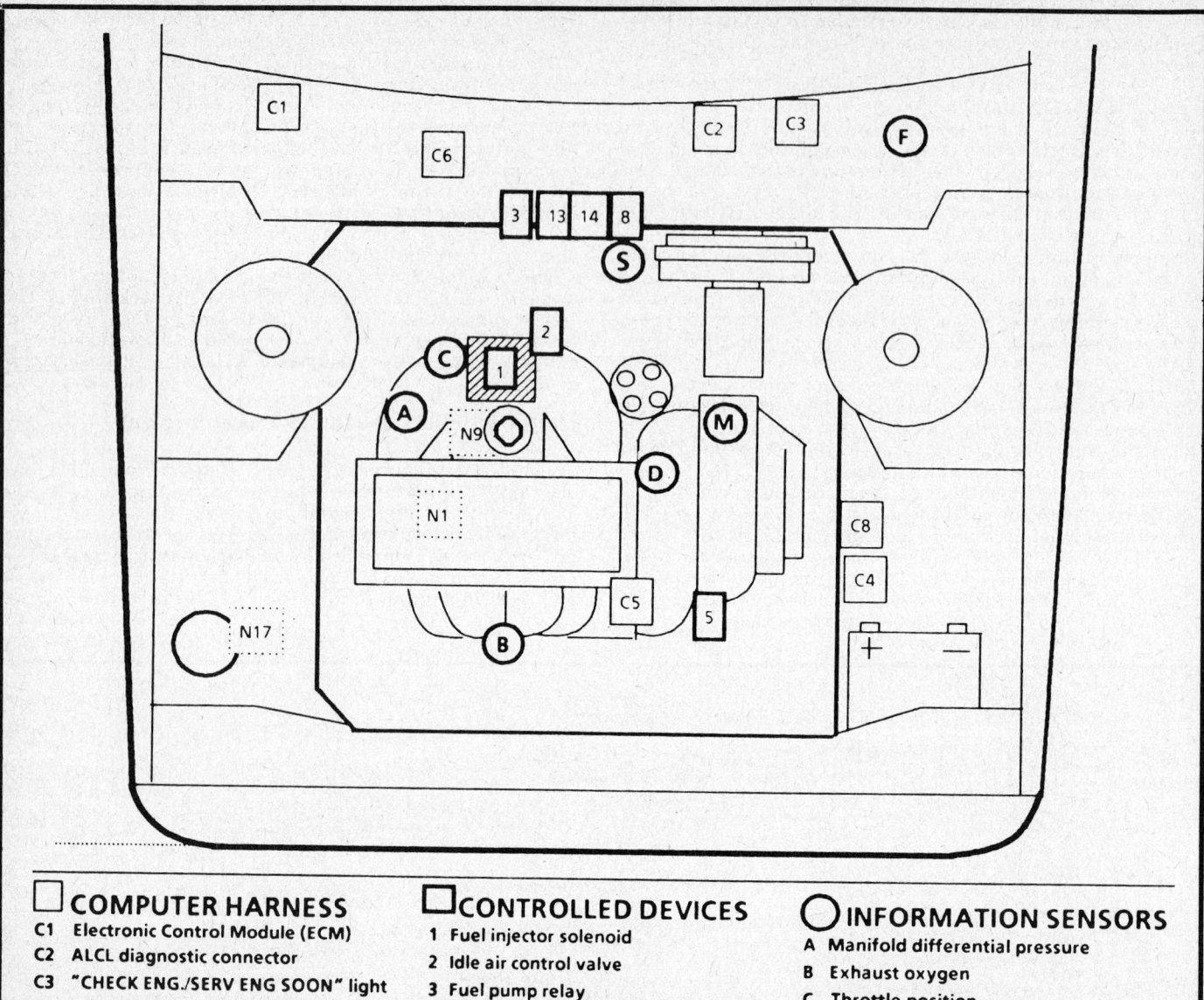

☐ **COMPUTER HARNESS**
- C1 Electronic Control Module (ECM)
- C2 ALCL diagnostic connector
- C3 "CHECK ENG./SERV ENG SOON" light
- C4 ECM power
- C5 ECM harness ground
- C6 Fuse panel
- C8 Fuel pump test connector

▨ **NOT ECM CONNECTED**
- N1 Crankcase vent valve (PCV)
- N9 Exhaust Gas Recirculation valve
- N17 Fuel vapor canister

☐ **CONTROLLED DEVICES**
- 1 Fuel injector solenoid
- 2 Idle air control valve
- 3 Fuel pump relay
- 5 Trans. Converter Clutch connector
- 8 Engine cooling fan relay
- 13 A/C compressor relay
- 14 A/C fan relay

⬡ Exhaust Gas Recirculation valve

○ **INFORMATION SENSORS**
- A Manifold differential pressure
- B Exhaust oxygen
- C Throttle position
- D Coolant temperature
- F Vehicle speed
- M P/N switch
- S P/S pressure switch

2.5 liter engine-throttle body injection component location (© General Motors Corporation)

tion concerning engine rpm, road speed, transmission gear position, power steering and air conditioning.

This system uses Bosch injectors, one at each intake port. The injectors are mounted on a fuel rail and are activated by a signal from the electronic control module. The injector is a solenoid operated valve which remains open depending on the width of the electronic pulses (length of the signal) from the ECM; the longer the open time, the more fuel is injected. In this manner, the air/fuel mixture can be precisely controlled for maximum performance with minimum emissions.

Fuel is pumped from the tank by a high pressure fuel pump, located inside the fuel tank. It is a positive displacement roller vane pump. The impeller serves as a vapor separator and precharges the high pressure assembly. A pressure regulator maintains 28-36 psi in the fuel line to the injectors and the excess fuel is fed back to the tank. A fuel accumulator is used to dampen the hydraulic line hammer in the system created when all injectors open simultaneous.

The mass air flow sensor is used to measure the mass of air that is drawn into the engine cylinders. It is located just ahead

GENERAL MOTORS—"N" BODY
BUICK SOMERSET REGAL • OLDS CALAIS • PONTIAC GRAND AM

of the air throttle in the intake system and consists of a heated film which measures the mass of air, rather than just the volume. A resistor is used to measure the temperature of the incoming air and the air mass sensor maintains the temperature of the film at 75 degrees above ambient temperature. As the ambient (outside) air temperature rises, more energy is required to maintain the heated film at the higher temperature and the control unit uses this difference in required energy to calculate the mass of the incoming air. The control unit uses this information to determine the duration of fuel injection pulse, timing and EGR.

The throttle body incorporates an idle air control (IAC) that provides for a bypass channel through which air can flow. It consists of an orifice and pintle which is controlled by the ECM through a stepper motor. The IAC provides air flow for idle and allows additional air during cold start until the engine reaches operating temperature. As the engine temperature rises, the opening through which air passes is slowly closed.

The throttle position sensor (TPS) provides the control unit with information on throttle position, in order to determine injector pulse width and hence correct mixture. The TPS is connected to the throttle shaft on the throttle body and consists of a potentiometer with one end connected to a 5 volt source from the ECM and the other to ground. A third wire is connected to the ECM to measure the voltage output from the TPS which changes as the throttle valve angle is changed (accelerator pedal moves). At the closed throttle position, the output is low (approximately .4 volts); as the throttle valve opens, the output increases to a maximum 5 volts at wide open throttle (WOT). The TPS can be misadjusted open, shorted, or loose and if it is out of adjustment, the idle quality or WOT performance may be poor. A loose TPS can cause intermittent bursts of fuel from the injectors and an unstable idle because the ECM thinks the throttle is moving. This should cause a trouble code to be set. Once a trouble code is set, the ECM will use a preset value for TPS and some vehicle performance may return. A small amount of engine coolant is routed through the throttle assembly to prevent freezing inside the throttle bore during cold operation.

EMISSION CONTROL SYSTEMS

3.0 LITER ENGINE

Oxygen sensor
Coolant temperature sensor
Throttle position sensor
Vehicle speed sensor
Air temperature sensor
EGR valve
EGR vacuum control solenoid
Electronic control module
Mass air flow sensor
Electronic spark control system
Prom
Calpak
Fuel injectors
Fuel rail
Throttle body assembly
Idle air control valve
Vapor canister
Canister purge solenoid
Computer controlled coil ignition system (C^3I)
ESC knock sensor
ESC module
Torque converter clutch
PCV system
Catalytic converter

2.5 LITER ENGINE

Electronic control module
Oxygen sensor
Coolant temperature sensor
Throttle position sensor
Vehicle speed sensor
Map sensor
Idle air control
Electronic spark timing
Prom
Distributor reference signal
Torque converter clutch
Throttle body injection assembly
Idle air control valve
Charcoal canister
EGR valve
PCV system
Thermostatic air cleaner
Catalytic converter

GASOLINE ENGINE SECTION

For Diesel Engine services, refer to the unit repair section. For Engine Overhaul procedures, refer to the Unit Repair section.

ENGINE ASSEMBLY

NOTE: Be sure to relieve fuel pump pressure before disconnecting the fuel lines.

Removal and Installation
2.5 LITER ENGINE

NOTE: The following procedure is for removing the engine and transaxle as one unit.

1. Disconnect the battery cables. Remove the hood. Drain the engine coolant. Remove the air cleaner.
2. Disconnect the electronic control module connections and feed harness through the bulkhead and lay the wires across the engine.
3. Disconnect the engine wiring harness and lay it across the engine.
4. Disconnect the heater hoses, radiator hoses and all required vacuum hoses.
5. Disconnect the air condition compressor from its mounting on the engine.
6. Remove the power steering pump from its mounting on the engine. Remove the bracket from the engine.
7. Remove the front transaxle strut.

SECTION 11
GENERAL MOTORS—"N" BODY
BUICK SOMERSET REGAL • OLDS CALAIS • PONTIAC GRAND AM

8. If equipped with manual transaxle, remove the clutch and transaxle linkage. Remove the throttle cable at the TBI.
9. If equipped with automatic transaxle, remove the transaxle cooler lines, shifter linkage, downshift cable and the throttle cable at the TBI.
10. Disconnect the redundant ground and multi relay bracket.
11. Raise and support the vehicle safely.
12. Remove the front wheels. Remove the calipers and tie them out of the way. Remove the rotors.
13. Remove the knuckle to strut bolts, two per side.
14. Disconnect the exhaust pipe at the manifold and position it aside.
15. Remove the four body to cradle bolts at the lower control arms. Loosen the remaining eight body to cradle bolts at their ends. Remove one bolt at each end of each cradle side, leaving one bolt per corner.
16. Place stands under front of body. Mmove the hoist back to the body pan with a 6'4" × 4" timber between hoist and vehicle.
17. Lift hoist and remove jack stands.
18. Place dolly under engine/transaxle assembly with 4" × 4" blocks to maintain position on dolly.
19. Lower vehicle, allowing engine transaxle assembly to rest on dolly.
20. Remove the engine mount bolts and the right front bracket. Remove the remaining four cradle to body bolts.
21. Remove the engine and transaxle assembly from the vehicle. Separate the engine from the transaxle.
22. Installation is the reverse of the removal procedure.

3.0 LITER ENGINE

1. Disconnect the negative battery cable. Remove the hood. Raise the vehicle and support it safely. Drain the radiator.
2. Remove the starter. Remove the torque converter cover.
3. Remove the torque converter bolts. Match mark the torque converter to the flywheel for reassembly.
4. Disconnect the A/C compressor wiring and the unit, position it to the side. Disconnect the heater hoses.
5. Remove the lower radiator hose.
6. Remove the front motor mount bolts. Remove the right inner fender splash shield.
7. Remove the transaxle to engine mount bolt located between the transaxle and the cylinder block.
8. Remove the two right rear motor mount nuts.
9. Disconnect the exhaust pipe from the exhaust manifold flange.
10. Lower the vehicle.
11. Remove the serpentine drive belt, alternator wiring and the alternator.
12. Remove the power steering pump and the fluid lines.
13. Disconnect the mass air flow sensor and the air intake duct. Disconnect the top radiator hose.
14. Disconnect the electric fan wiring and remove the fan assembly. Remove the radiator.
15. Install the engine lifting device. Remove the left upper transaxle mount.
16. Disconnect and remove the master cylinder, as required.
17. Disconnect and remove the fuel lines at the fuel rail, as required.
18. Disconnect the throttle, T.V. and cruise control cables at the throttle body.
19. Remove the remaining engine to transaxle retaining bolts. Remove the engine from the vehicle.
20. Installation is the reverse of the removal procedure.

ENGINE MOUNTS

NOTE: Before removing any engine mounts the engine and transaxle must be used. This special tool must be located in the center of the cowl and be properly fastened before the engine mounts are removed.

Removal and Installation
2.5 LITER ENGINE

1. Disconnect the negative battery cable.
2. Properly support the engine using the special tool. Raise the vehicle and support it safely.
3. Remove the bolts securing the engine mount to the chassis.
4. Remove the nuts securing the mount to the engine bracket.
5. Remove the engine mount from the vehicle.
6. Installation is the reverse of the removal procedure.

3.0 LITER ENGINE

1. Disconnect the negative battery cable.
2. Properly support the engine using the special tool. Raise the vehicle and support it safely.
3. Remove the engine mount to bracket nuts. Raise the engine slightly.
4. Remove the mount to frame nuts.
5. Remove the engine mount from the vehicle.
6. Installation is the reverse of the removal procedure.

Valve System

VALVE ADJUSTMENT

Hydraulic valve lifters are used in all engines produced by General Motors Corporation. No adjustment is possible.

VALVE LIFTERS

NOTE: If required, be sure to relieve fuel pump pressure before disconnecting fuel lines.

Removal and Installation
2.5 LITER ENGINE

1. Disconnect the negative battery cable.
2. Remove the valve cover.
3. Remove the intake manifold.
4. Remove the engine side cover.
5. Loosen the rocker arms and rotate them in order to clear the pushrods. This must be done in pairs so that the lifter guide can be removed.
6. Remove the push rods, retainer and guide from each cylinder.
7. Remove the valve lifters. Be sure to keep them in order if they are going to be reused.
8. Installation is the reverse of the removal procedure. Prime lifter with clean engine oil before installation.

3.0 LITER ENGINE

1. Disconnect the negative battery cable.
2. Drain the radiator. Remove the valve covers.
3. Remove the intake manifold.
4. Remove the rocker arms, pedestals, and pushrods. Keep these components in order for reinstallation.
5. Remove the valve lifters. Be sure to keep them in order if they are going to be reused.
6. Installation is the reverse of the removal procedure. Prime lifter with clean engine oil before installation.

VALVE ROCKER ASSEMBLY

NOTE: If required, be sure to relieve fuel pump pressure before disconnecting any fuel lines.

Removal and Installation
2.5 LITER ENGINE

1. Disconnect the negative battery cable.

GENERAL MOTORS—"N" BODY
BUICK SOMERSET REGAL • OLDS CALAIS • PONTIAC GRAND AM
SECTION 11

2. Remove all the necessary components in order to gain access to the valve cover retaining bolts.
3. Remove the valve cover retaining bolts. Remove the valve cover.
4. Remove the rocker arm bolt and ball. Remove the rocker arm, push rod and guide.
5. Installation is the reverse of the removal procedure. Be sure to coat new components with fresh engine oil before installation.

3.0 LITER ENGINE (LEFT FRONT COVER)

1. Disconnect the negative battery cable.
2. Remove all the necessary components in order to gain access to the valve cover retaining bolts.
3. Remove the valve cover retaining bolts. Remove the valve cover.
4. Remove the rock arm pedestal retaining bolts. Remove the rocker arm and pedestal assembly.
5. Installation is the reverse of the removal procedure. Be sure to coat new components with clean engine oil before installation.

3.0 LITER ENGINE (RIGHT REAR COVER)

1. Disconnect the negative battery cable.
2. Remove the C3I ignition coil module. Remove the spark plug wires, electrical connectors and EGR solenoid wiring and vacuum hoses.
3. Remove the serpentine belt, alternator wiring, rear alternator bracket mounting bolt. Rotate the alternator toward the front of the vehicle.
4. Remove the power steering pump from the belt tensioner and remove the tensioner assembly.
5. Remove the engine lift bracket and the rear alternator brace.

6. Drain the radiator below the heater hose level. Remove the throttle body heater hoses.
7. Remove the valve cover retaining bolts. Remove the valve cover from the engine.
8. Remove the rocker arm pedestal retaining bolts. Remove the rocker arm and pedestal assembly.
9. Installation is the reverse of the removal procedure. Be sure to coat new components with clean engine oil before installation.

VALVE TIMING

Adjustment

Manufacturers recommended procedure for valve timing has not yet been established.

CYLINDER HEADS

Removal and Installation

2.5 LITER ENGINE

NOTE: Be sure to relieve fuel pump pressure before disconnecting any fuel lines.

1. Disconnect the negative battery cable.
2. Drain the radiator. Remove the oil level indicator tube. Remove the air cleaner.
3. Disconnect the exhaust pipe to manifold flange.
4. Remove the electrical wiring and the throttle linkage from the TBI assembly.
5. Remove the heater hose from the intake manifold.
6. Remove the ignition coil. Disconnect all wiring connections from the intake manifold and the cylinder head.

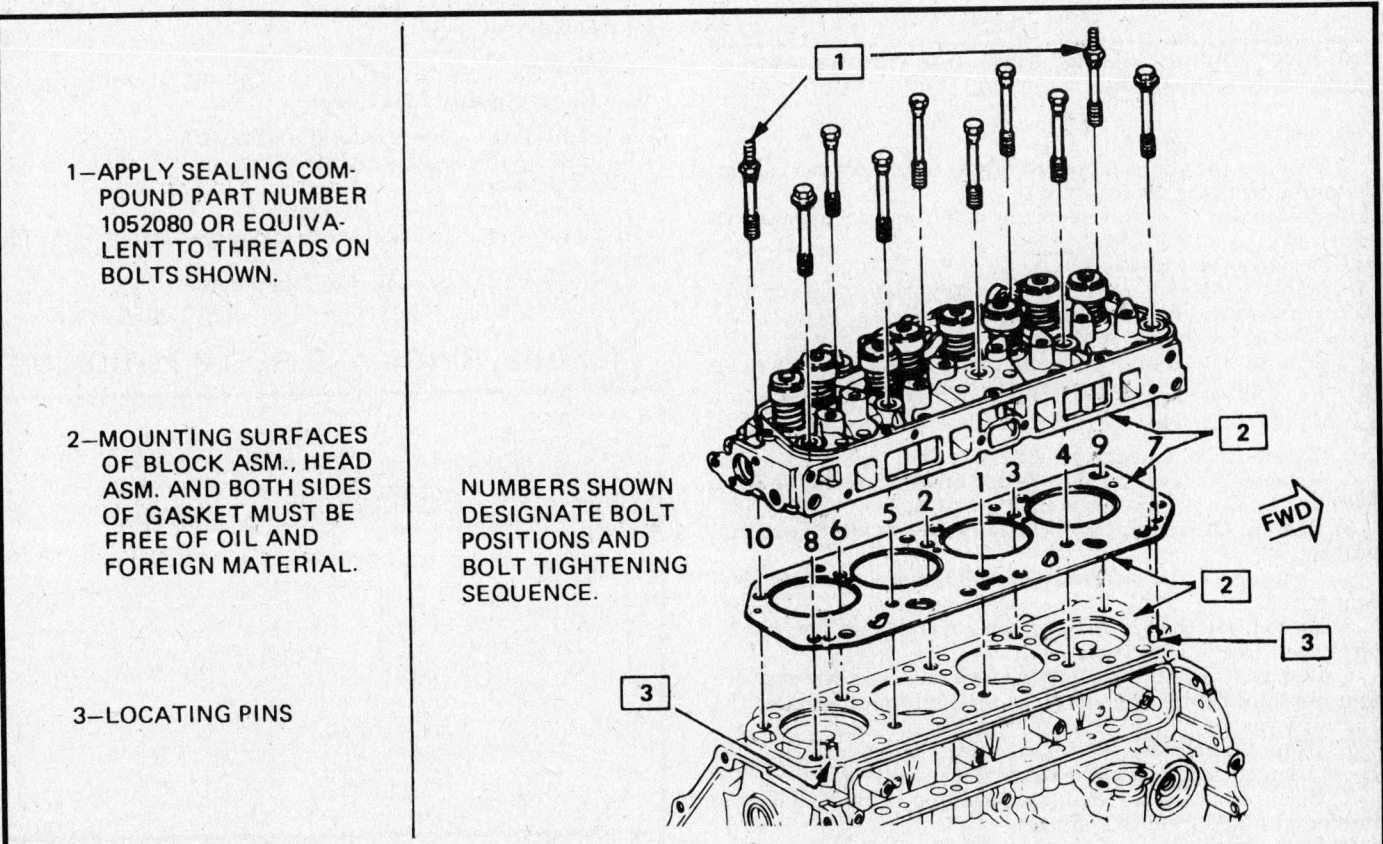

1—APPLY SEALING COMPOUND PART NUMBER 1052080 OR EQUIVALENT TO THREADS ON BOLTS SHOWN.

2—MOUNTING SURFACES OF BLOCK ASM., HEAD ASM. AND BOTH SIDES OF GASKET MUST BE FREE OF OIL AND FOREIGN MATERIAL.

3—LOCATING PINS

NUMBERS SHOWN DESIGNATE BOLT POSITIONS AND BOLT TIGHTENING SEQUENCE.

2.5 liter engine—cylinder head bolt torque sequence

Section 11: GENERAL MOTORS—"N" BODY
BUICK SOMERSET REGAL • OLDS CALAIS • PONTIAC GRAND AM

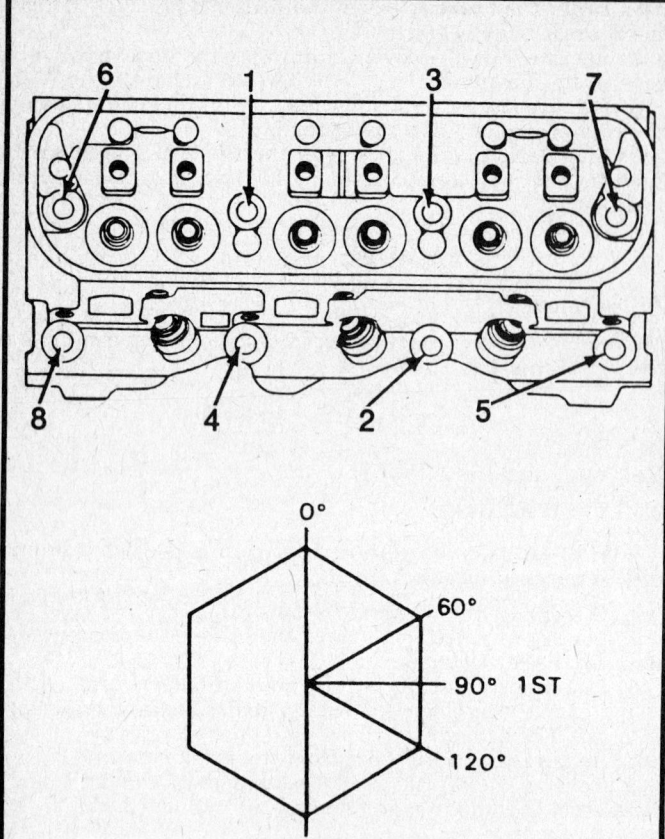

3.0 liter engine-cylinder head bolt torque and tightening procedure (© General Motors Corporation)

7. Remove the A/C compressor brackets, compressor assembly and alternator, as required.
8. Remove the power steering pump upper bracket as required.
9. Remove the radiator hoses.
10. Remove the rocker arm cover, rocker arms and push rods.
11. Remove the cylinder head retaining bolts. Remove the cylinder head from the engine.
12. Installation is the reverse of the removal procedure. Be sure to torque the retaining bolts to specification.

3.0 LITER ENGINE

1. Disconnect the negative battery cable.
2. Remove the mass air flow sensor and the air intake duct. Remove the C³I ignition module and wiring.
3. Remove the serpentine belt. Remove the alternator and bracket.
4. Remove all the necessary vacuum lines and electrical connections.
5. Disconnect the throttle, cruise control and T.V. cables from the throttle body assembly.
6. Remove the fuel lines and the fuel rail. Be sure to relieve fuel pressure before disconnecting the fuel lines. Remove the spark plug wires.
7. Drain the radiator. Remove the heater hoses and radiator hoses from the throttle body and intake manifold.
8. Remove the intake manifold retaining bolts. Remove the intake manifold from the engine.
9. Remove the valve covers. Remove the rocker arms, pedestals and push rods. Remove the radiator and the cooling fan.
10. Remove the left exhaust manifold.
11. Remove the power steering pump. Remove the engine oil level indicator and tube.
12. Remove the left cylinder head retaining bolts. Remove the left cylinder head from the vehicle.
13. Raise and support the vehicle safely. Remove the right exhaust manifold flange retaining bolts.
14. Remove the right cylinder head retaining bolts. Remove the right cylinder head from the vehicle.
15. Installation is the reverse of the removal procedure. Be sure to torque the retaining bolts to specifications.

CAMSHAFT

Removal and Installation

2.5 LITER ENGINE

NOTE: Be sure to relieve fuel pressure before disconnecting any fuel lines.

1. Remove the engine from the vehicle.
2. Remove the rocker cover, rocker arms, and pushrods.
3. Remove the distributor, spark plugs, and fuel pump.
4. Remove the pushrod cover and gasket. Remove the lifters.
5. Remove the alternator, the alternator lower bracket and the front engine mount bracket assembly.
6. Remove the oil pump driveshaft and gear assembly.
7. Remove the crankshaft hub and timing gear cover.
8. Remove the two camshaft thrust plate screws by working through the holes in the gear.
9. Remove the camshaft and gear assembly by pulling it through the front of the block. Take care not to damage the bearings.
10. Install in the reverse order. Torque the thrust plate screws to 75 in. lbs.

3.0 LITER ENGINE

NOTE: Be sure to relieve fuel pump pressure before disconnecting any fuel lines.

1. Remove the engine from the vehicle.
2. Remove the intake manifold. Remove the valve covers, rocker arm assemblies, push rods and lifters.
3. Remove the balancer assembly.
4. Remove the front cover. Remove the timing chain and sprockets.
5. Remove the camshaft from the engine.
6. Installation is the reverse of the removal procedure.

PISTONS, RINGS AND ROD POSITIONING

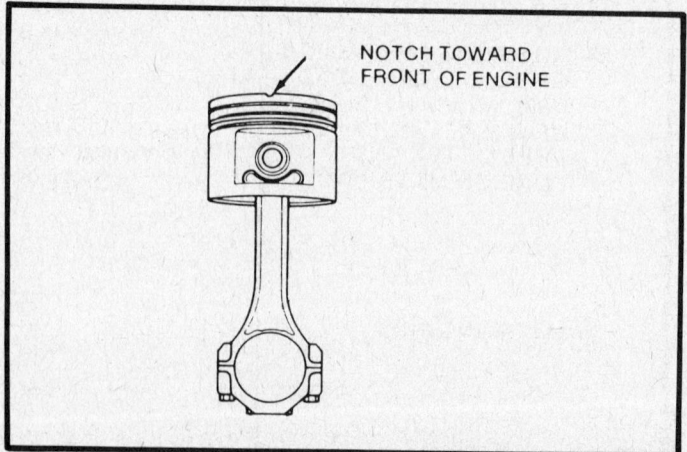

3.0 liter engine-piston indentification (© General Motors Corporation)

GENERAL MOTORS—"N" BODY
BUICK SOMERSET REGAL • OLDS CALAIS • PONTIAC GRAND AM
SECTION 11

TIMING GEAR COVER/OIL SEAL

Removal and Installation

2.5 LITER ENGINE

1. Disconnect the negative battery cable.
2. Remove the inner fender splash shield.
3. Remove the fan pulley and the crankshaft hub.
4. Remove the front cover retaining bolts. Remove the front cover.
5. Installation is the reverse of the removal procedure.
6. Apply a 3/8 in. wide by 3/16 in. thick bead of RTV sealant to the joint of the oil pan and timing gear cover.
7. Apply a 1/4 in. wide by 1/8 in. thick bead of TRV sealant to the timing gear cover at the engine block mating surfaces.
8. Using tool J34995 or equivalent, install the timing gear cover.

NOTE: Tool J34995 is a centering tool which fits over the crankshaft seal and is used to correctly position the timing cover.

9. Partially tighten the two timing case cover opposing screws. Tighten the remaining cover screws. Remove the tool.
10. Continue the installation in the reverse order of the removal procedure.

3.0 LITER ENGINE

1. Disconnect the negative battery cable. Drain the radiator.
2. Loosen, but do not remove the water pump pulley bolts. Remove the serpentine belt. Remove the water pump pulley.
3. Remove the water pump retaining bolts. Remove the water pump.
4. Raise and support the vehicle safely. Remove the right tire and wheel assembly. Remove the right inner fender splash shield.
5. Remove the crankshaft balancer. Drain the engine oil and remove the oil filter.
6. Remove the radiator and the heater hoses.
7. Remove the crankshaft sensor. Remove the engine oil pan.
8. Remove the front cover retaining bolts. Remove the front cover and gasket.
9. Installation is the reverse of the removal procedure. Be sure to apply thread sealer to all front cover bolts.

TIMING GEARS/CHAIN

Removal and Installation

2.5 LITER ENGINE

NOTE: If the camshaft gear is to be replaced the engine must be removed from the vehicle. The crankshaft gear can be replaced with the engine in the vehicle.

1. Disconnect the negative battery cable.
2. If replacing the camshaft gear, remove the engine. Remove the timing cover bolts and remove the cover. Remove the camshaft and press the gear off of the cam.
3. If removing the crankshaft gear, remove the timing cover. Remove the crankshaft gear.
4. Installation is the reverse of the removal procedure. Be sure to properly align the timing marks.

3.0 LITER ENGINE

1. Disconnect the negative battery cable.
2. Remove the timing cover.
3. Align the timing marks on the sprockets, as close together as possible.
4. Remove the camshaft sprocket bolts. Remove the camshaft sprocket and chain.
5. Remove the crankshaft sprocket.

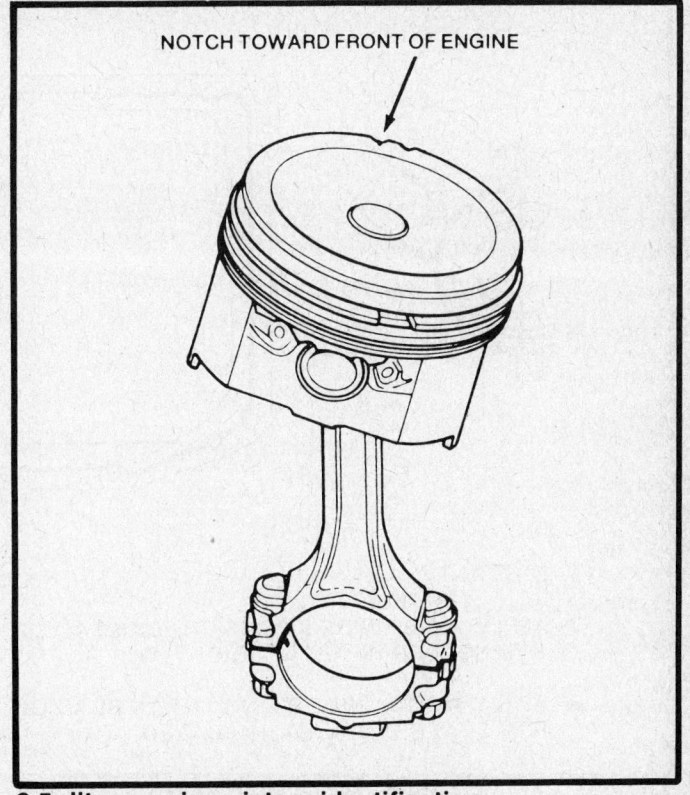

2.5 liter engine-piston identification
(© General Motors Corporation)

6. Installation is the reverse of the removal procedure.

Lubrication

OIL PAN

Removal and Installation

2.5 LITER ENGINE

1. Disconnect the negative battery cable. Raise and support the vehicle safely. Drain the engine oil.
2. Remove the cradle to front engine mount nuts.

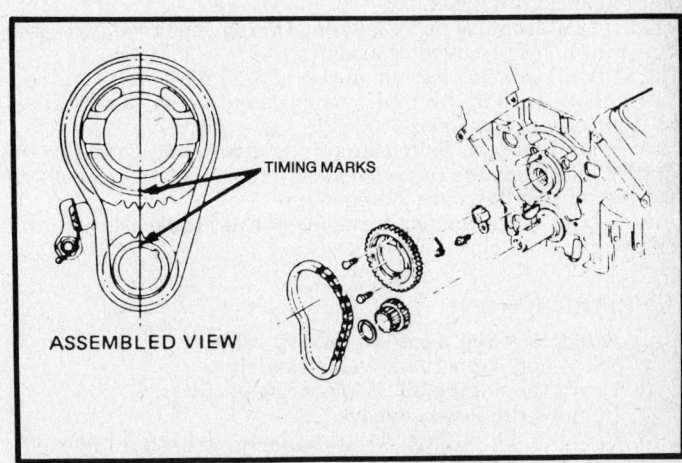

2.5 liter engine-oil pan installation
(© General Motors Corporation)

11-19

SECTION 11
GENERAL MOTORS—"N" BODY
BUICK SOMERSET REGAL • OLDS CALAIS • PONTIAC GRAND AM

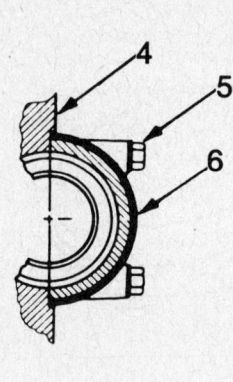
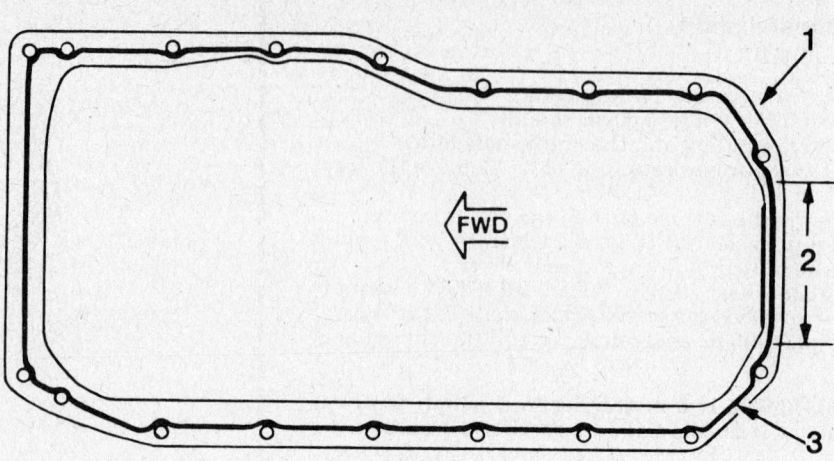

1—OIL PAN

2—APPLY A 3/8" WIDE BY 3/16" THICK BEAD OF RTV SEALER IN AREA INDICATED

3—APPLY A 3/16" WIDE BY 1/8" THICK BEAD OF RTV SEALER IN AREA INDICATED

4—ENGINE BLOCK ASSEMBLY

5—REAR BEARING

6—GROOVE IN MAIN BEARING CAP MUST BE FILLED FLUSH TO 1/8" ABOVE SURFACE WITH RTV

3.0 liter engine timing mark alignment (© General Motors Corporation)

3. Disconnect exhaust pipe at manifold and at rear transaxle mount.
4. Disconnect starter and remove flywheel housing inspection cover.
5. Remove upper generator bracket.
6. Install suitable engine support equipment and raise engine. J22825-40
7. Remove lower generator bracket and engine support bracket.
8. Remove oil pan retaining bolts and remove oil pan.
9. Thoroughly clean all gasket sealing surfaces.
10. Install rear oil pan gasket in rear main bearing cap, and apply a small quantity of sealer in depressions where pan gasket engages into block.
11. Install front oil pan gasket on timing gear cover pressing tips into holes provided in cover.
12. Install side gaskets on oil pan using grease as a retainer.
13. Apply a 1/8 in. by 1/4 in. long bead of sealer at split lines of front and side gaskets.
14. Install oil pan. Bolts into timing gear cover should be installed last. They are installed at an angle and holes line up after rest of pan bolts are snugged up.
15. Install all components removed. Fill crankcase with oil, run engine and check for leaks.

3.0 LITER ENGINE
1. Disconnect the negative battery cable.
2. Raise and support the vehicle safely.
3. Drain the engine oil. Remove the oil filter.
4. Remove the flywheel cover.
5. Remove the oil pan retaining bolts and the oil pan tensioner spring, which is located behind the oil filter adapter.
6. Remove the oil pan from the vehicle.
7. Installation is the reverse of the removal procedure.

OIL PUMP

Removal and Installation
2.5 LITER ENGINE
1. Disconnect the negative battery cable.
2. Remove the oil pan.
3. Remove the oil pump from its mounting.
4. Installation is the reverse of the removal procedure.

3.0 LITER ENGINE
1. Disconnect the negative battery cable.
2. Remove the engine front cover.
3. Remove the oil filter adapter, pressure regulator valve and valve spring.
4. Remove the oil pump cover retaining screws and cover.
5. Remove the oil pump gears.
6. Installation is the reverse of the removal procedure.

OIL FILTER ADAPTER AND PRESSURE VALVE

Removal and Installation
3.0 LITER ENGINE
1. Disconnect the negative battery cable.
2. Remove the front cover.
3. Remove the four bolts retaining the oil filter adapter to the front cover.
4. Remove the oil filter adapter, gasket, oil pressure valve and spring.
5. Installation is the reverse of the removal procedure.

GENERAL MOTORS—"N" BODY
BUICK SOMERSET REGAL • OLDS CALAIS • PONTIAC GRAND AM

OIL PUMP DRIVESHAFT

Removal and Installation

2.5 LITER ENGINE

1. Disconnect the negative battery cable.
2. Raise and support the vehicle safely.
3. Disconnect the bracket from the retainer plate stud.
4. Remove the retainer plate bolts, pump driveshaft and bushing.
5. Installation is the reverse of the removal procedure. Apply a 1/16 in. bead of RTV sealant to the retaining plate.

FRONT SUSPENSION AND STEERING SECTION

For Front Suspension services, refer to Unit Repair Section.
For Steering Gear Overhaul, refer to Unit Repair Section.

STEERING WHEEL

Removal and Installation

1. Disconnect the negative battery cable. Unplug the horn wire connector from the steering column.
2. On vehicles with a standard wheel or optional wood rim wheel, pull off the cap, remove the three screws and the contact, insulator, and spring. On vehicles with the bar type horn actuator, remove the screws securing the actuator from the underside of the steering wheel, unhook the lead connector plug, and remove the actuator assembly.
3. Loosen the steering wheel nut.
4. Apply the steering wheel puller and pull the wheel up to the nut. Now remove the puller, nut and steering wheel. Location marks are provided on the steering wheel and shaft to simplify proper indexing at the time of installation.
5. Install wheel with the location mark aligned with that of the shaft.
6. Install the wheel nut and torque to 30 ft. lbs.
7. Reinstall horn button or actuator assembly.

POWER STEERING RACK

Removal and Installation

1. Disconnect the negative battery cable.
2. Remove the left sound insulator. Remove the upper pinch bolt on the coupling assembly. Remove the three clamp nuts.
3. Raise and support the vehicle safely.
4. Remove the other clamp nut.
5. Remove the front tires.
6. Using tool J-24319-01 or equivalent, and remove the tie rod ends from the knuckles.
7. Lower the vehicle. Disconnect the line retainer.
8. Disconnect and cap the power steering lines at the gear.
9. Move the gear forward and remove the lower pinch bolt on the coupling assembly. Remove the coupling from the gear.
10. Remove the rack and pinion assembly with the dash seal through the left wheel opening.
11. Installation is the reverse of the removal procedure.

POWER STEERING PUMP

Removal and Installation

1. Disconnect the negative battery cable.
2. Remove the belt. Disconnect and plug the fluid lines. On the 2.5 liter engine it may be necessary to remove the pump before disconnecting the fluid lines.
3. If the vehicle is equipped with a 3.0 liter engine, remove the front adjustment bracket to rear adjustment bracket bolt. Remove the front adjustment bracket to engine bolt and spacer.
4. Remove the power steering pump retaining bolts. Remove the pump from the vehicle.
5. Installation is the reverse of the removal procedure. After installation bleed the system.

POWER STEERING SYSTEM BLEEDING

1. With the wheels turned all the way to the left, add power steering fluid to the "COLD" mark on the fluid level indicator.
2. Start the engine. With the engine running at fast idle, recheck the fluid level. If necessary, add fluid to bring the level to the "COLD" mark.
3. Bleed the system by turning the wheels from side to side, without reaching the stop at either end. Keep the fluid level just above the internal pump casting, or at the "COLD" mark. Fluid with air in it has a light tan or red appearance. This air must be eliminated from the fluid before normal steering action can be obtained.
4. Return the wheels to the center position. Continue running the engine for two or three minutes.
5. Road test the car to be sure the steering functions normally and is free from noise.
6. Recheck the fluid level. Make sure the fluid level is at the "HOT" mark after the system has stabilized at its normal operating temperature.

STEERING COLUMN

Removal and Installation

1. Disconnect the negative battery cable.
2. If column repairs are to be made, remove the steering wheel.
3. Remove the nuts and bolts attaching the flexible coupling to the bottom of the steering column. Remove the safety strap and bolt if equipped.
4. Remove the steering column trim shrouds and column covers.
5. Disconnect all wiring harness connectors. Remove the dust boot mounting screws and column mounting bracket bolts.
6. Lower the column to clear the mounting bracket and carefully remove from the vehicle.
7. Install in the reverse order of removal.

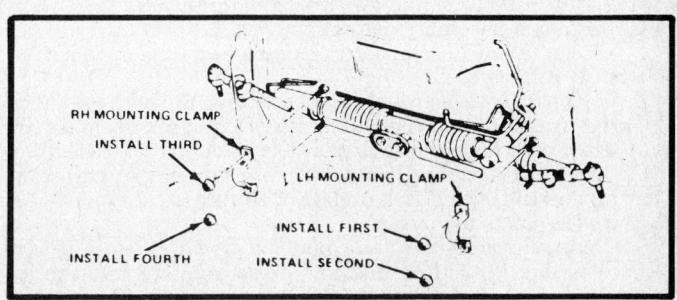

Typical rack and pinion assembly
(© General Motors Corporation)

11–21

SECTION 11

GENERAL MOTORS—"N" BODY
BUICK SOMERSET REGAL • OLDS CALAIS • PONTIAC GRAND AM

BRAKE SECTION

For Brake Service, refer to Unit Repair Section

MASTER CYLINDER

Removal and Installation

1. Disconnect the negative battery cable.
2. If equipped with manual brakes, disconnect the pushrod from the brake pedal.
3. Remove the electrical connector at the warning switch.
4. Disconnect and cap the brake fluid lines.
5. Remove the master cylinder retaining bolts. Remove the master cylinder.
6. Installation is the reverse of the removal procedure. Bleed the brake system, as required.

POWER BRAKE BOOSTER

Removal and Installation

1. Disconnect the negative battery cable.
2. Remove the master cylinder from the booster.
3. Remove the booster retaining nuts from the fire wall.
4. Remove the brake pedal push rod.
5. Remove the booster assembly from the vehicle.
6. Installation is the reverse of the removal procedure.

PARKING BRAKE

Adjustments

1. Raise and support the vehicle with both rear wheels off the ground.
2. Pull the parking brake lever exactly five clicks.
3. Loosen the equalizer locknut, then tighten the adjusting nut until the left rear wheel can just be turned backwards using two hands, but is locked in the forward rotation.
4. Tighten the locknut.
5. Release the parking brake. Rotate the rear wheels--there should be no drag.
6. Lower the vehicle.

CLUTCH, TRANSAXLE AND DRIVESHAFT SECTION

For Overhaul Procedures, refer to Unit Repair Section

CLUTCH/PEDAL/LINKAGE

Adjustment

N-body vehicles have a self-adjusting clutch mechanism located on the clutch pedal. This mechanism eliminates the need for periodic clutch adjustments.

As the clutch friction material wears, the clutch cable must be lengthened. This is done by pulling the clutch pedal up to its rubber bumper. This action forces the pawl against its stop and rotates it out of mesh with the detent teeth, allowing the cable to play out until the detent spring load is balanced against the load applied to the release bearing.

CLUTCH ASSEMBLY

Removal and Installation

1. Remove the transaxle.
2. Mark the pressure plate assembly and the flywheel so that they can be assembled in the same position. They were balanced as an assembly at the factory.
3. Loosen the attaching bolts one turn at a time until spring tension is relieved.
4. Support the pressure plate and remove the bolts. Remove the pressure plate and the clutch disc. Do not disassemble the pressure plate assembly, replace it if it is found to be defective.
5. Inspect the flywheel, pressure plate, clutch disc, throwout bearing and the clutch fork and pivot shaft assembly for wear. Replace the parts as needed.
6. Clean the pressure plate and the flywheel mating surfaces. Position the clutch disc and pressure plate into the installed position and support with a dummy shaft or clutch aligning tool. The clutch plate is assembled with the damper springs offset toward the transaxle.
7. Install the pressure plate to flywheel bolts. Tighten them in a crisscross pattern.
8. Lubricate the outside grooves and the inside recess of the release bearing with high temperature grease. Wipe off any excess. Install the release bearing. 9.Install the transaxle.

MANUAL TRANSAXLE

Removal and Installation

1. Disconnect the negative battery cable.
2. Install an engine holding bar so that one end is supported on the cowl tray over the wiper motor and the other end rests on the radiator support. Use padding and be careful not to damage the paint or body work with the bar. Attach a lifting hook to the engine lift ring and to the bar and raise the engine enough to take the pressure off the motor mounts.

NOTE: If a lifting bar and hook is not available, a chain hoist can be used, however, during the procedure the vehicle must be raised, at which time the chain hoist must be adjusted to keep tension on the engine/transaxle assembly.

3. Remove the hush panel from inside of the vehicle.
4. Remove the transaxle mount attaching bolts. Discard the bolts attaching the mount to the side frame: New bolts must be used at installation.
5. Disconnect the clutch cable from the clutch release lever. Remove the transaxle mount bracket attaching bolts and nuts.
6. Disconnect the shift cables and retaining clips at the transaxle. Disconnect the ground cables at the transaxle mounting stud.
7. Remove the four upper transaxle to engine mounting bolts. Remove the air management valve attaching bolts, in order to gain clearance to remove the right upper transaxle to engine bolt.
8. Raise the vehicle and support it on stands. Remove the left front wheel.

11-22

GENERAL MOTORS—"N" BODY
BUICK SOMERSET REGAL • OLDS CALAIS • PONTIAC GRAND AM
SECTION 11

9. Remove the left front inner splash shield. Remove the transaxle strut and bracket.
10. Remove the clutch housing cover bolts.
11. Disconnect the speedometer cable at the transaxle.
12. Disconnect the stabilizer bar at the left suspension support and control arm.
13. Disconnect the ball joint from the steering knuckle.
14. Remove the left suspension support attaching bolts and remove the support and control arm as an assembly.
15. Install boot protectors and disengage the drive axles at the transaxle. Remove the left side shaft from the transaxle.
16. Position a jack under the transaxle case, remove the lower two transaxle to engine mounting bolts and remove the transaxle by sliding it towards the driver's side, away from the engine. Carefully lower the jack, guiding the right shaft out of the transaxle.
17. When installing the transaxle, guide the right drive axle into its bore as the transaxle is being raised. The right drive axle cannot be readily installed after the transaxle is connected to the engine. Installation of the remaining components is in the reverse order of removal with the following notes: Tighten the transaxle to engine mounting bolts to 55 ft. lbs. Tighten the suspension support to body attaching bolts to 75 ft. lbs. and the clutch housing cover bolts to 10 ft. lbs. Using new bolts, install and tighten the transaxle mount to side frame to 40 ft. lbs. When installing the bolts attaching the mount to transaxle bracket, check the alignment bolt at the engine mount. If excessive effort is required to remove the alignment bolt, realign the engine components and torque the bolts to 40 ft. lbs. Remove the alignment bolt.

SHIFT QUADRANT POINTER

Removal and Installation

1. Disconnect the negative battery cable.
2. Remove the shifter knob.
3. Remove the console trim cover and related components.
4. Installation is the reverse of the removal procedure.

AUTOMATIC TRANSAXLE

Removal and Installation

1. Disconnect the negative battery cable.
2. Remove the air cleaner assembly. Remove the mass air flow and air intake duct, if equipped.
3. Disconnect the T.V. cable at the throttle lever and the transaxle.
4. Remove the transaxle fluid level indicator and the fill tube.
5. Install the engine support tool J-28467 or equivalent. Insert a $\frac{1}{4}$ inch by 2 in. bolt in the hole at the right motor mount to maintain driveline alignment.
6. Remove the nut securing the wiring harness to the automatic transaxle assembly. Disconnect the wring connectors at the speed sensor, TCC connector, and back up lamp switch.

NOTE: When servicing requires that the "T" latch type wiring connector be disconnected from the switch, care must be taken to ensure proper reassembly of both the connector and the "T" latch. Failure to do so may result in intermittent loss of switch functions.

7. Remove the shift linkage from the transaxle.
8. Remove the top two transaxle to engine bolts and the left upper transaxle mount along with the bracket assembly.
9. Remove the rubber hose from the transaxle vent pipe. Remove the remaining upper engine to transaxle bolts.
10. Raise and support the vehicle safely. Remove both front tires. Drain the transaxle fluid.
11. Remove the shift linkage and bracket from the transaxle.
12. Install drive axle boot seal protector J-33162 or equivalent on the inner seals.

NOTE: Some vehicles may use a silicone (gray) boot on the inboard axle joint. Use J-33162 on these boots, all other boots are made from a thermo plastic material (black) and do not require use of a boot seal protector.

13. Remove both ball joints from the control arms. Remove both drive axles. Support these drive axles properly.
14. Remove the transaxle mounting strut. Remove the left stabilizer bar link pin bolt, frame bushing clamp nuts and frame support assembly.
15. Remove the transaxle converter cover. Remove the torque converter to flex plate retaining bolts. Match mark the flex plate and the torque converter to aid in installation.
16. Disconnect and plug the transaxle oil cooler lines.
17. Remove the transaxle to engine support bracket. Install the transaxle removal jack.
18. Remove the remaining transaxle to engine retaining bolts. Remove the transaxle from the vehicle.
19. Installation is the reverse of removal procedure. Be sure to fill the transaxle with the proper grade and type automatic transmission fluid.

FRONT DRIVE AXLE

Removal and Installation

1. Disconnect the negative battery cable.
2. Remove the hub nut. Raise and support the vehicle safely. Remove the wheel.

NOTE: Install drive axle seal boot protector J-28712 or equivalent on the inner and outer seals for vehicles using the double offset design. Install drive axle seal protector J-28712 or equivalent on the outer seal and J-33162 or equivalent on the inner seal for vehicles using the tri pot design.

3. Remove and support the brake caliper. Remove the rotor.
4. Remove the strut to steering knuckle attaching bolts. Pull the steering knuckle assembly out of the strut bracket.
5. Using tools J-33008 and J-29794 or equivalent, carefully remove the drive axle from the transaxle assembly.
6. Once the drive axle has been pulled from the transaxle it must be supported horizontally until it is disconnected from the hub and bearing.
7. Using spindle remover tool J-28733 or equivalent, remove the drive axle from the hub and bearing assembly.
8. Remove the drive axle from the vehicle.
9. Installation is the reverse of the removal procedure.

OUTER AND INNER BOOT

Removal and Installation

OUTER BOOT

1. Disconnect the negative battery cable. Raise and support the vehicle safely.
2. Remove the front tire and wheel.
3. Remove the brake caliper and rotor. Support the brake caliper.
4. Slide the outer joint assembly off of the axle shaft.
5. Remove the race retaining ring. Remove the boot retainer and the boot retaining clamp.
6. Remove the outer boot.
7. Installation is the reverse of the removal procedure. Pack the new boot with grease prior to installation.

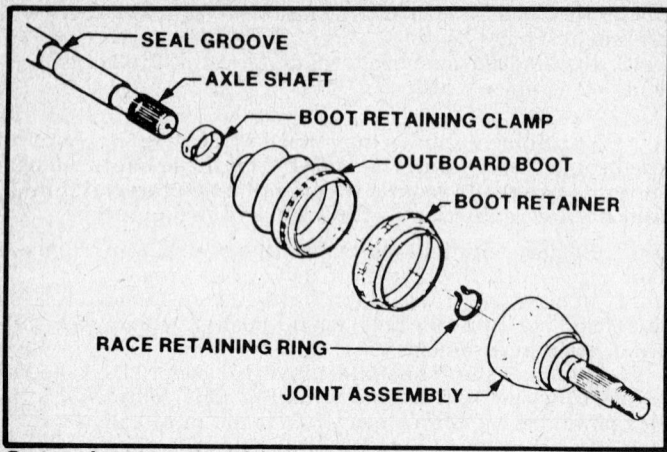

Outer boot assembly (© General Motors Corporation)

INNER BOOT

1. Disconnect the negative battery cable. Raise and support the vehicle safely.
2. Remove the front tire and wheel. Remove the brake caliper and rotor. Support the brake caliper.
3. Remove the outer boot assembly.

4. Remove the boot retaining clamps. Remove the spacer ring.
5. Slide the axle and the spider bearing assembly out of the tri pot housing. Install the spider bearing retainer onto the spider bearing assembly.
6. Remove the spider assembly and the boot from the axle.
7. Installation is the reverse of the removal procedure. Pack the new boot with grease prior to installation.

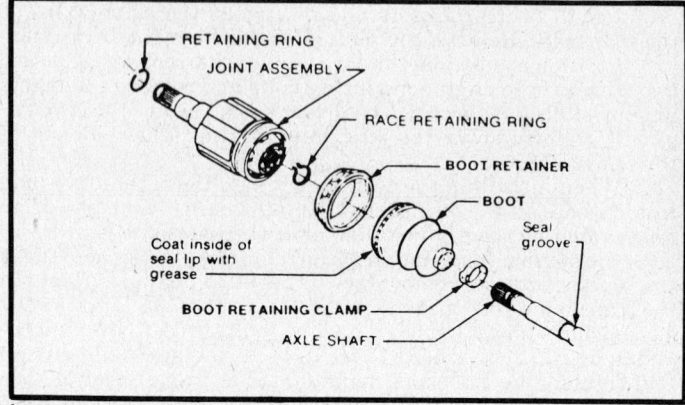

Inner boot assembly
(© General Motors Corporation)

REAR AXLE AND SUSPENSION

For Axle Overhaul Procedures and Suspension Services, refer to Unit Repair

REAR AXLE ASSEMBLY

Removal and Installation

1. Disconnect the negative battery cable. Raise the vehicle and support safely.

Rear axle assembly
(© General Motors Corporation)

2. Remove the wheel and tire. Remove the brake drum. Remove the stabilizer bar if equipped. Do not hammer on the brake drum as bearing assembly damage could result.
3. Remove the lower shock absorber bolts and disconnect the control arm.
4. Remove the parking brake cable from the axle assembly.
5. Carefully lower the rear axle and remove the coil springs and insulators. Remove the control arm bolts and lower the axle.
6. Remove the hub attaching bolts and remove the bearing, backing plate and hub.
7. Installation is the reverse of the removal procedure. Bleed the brake system as needed. Check the parking brake for possible adjustment.

REAR WHEEL HUB AND BEARING ASSEMBLY

Removal and Installation

1. Disconnect the negative battery cable. Raise and support the vehicle safely.
2. Remove the wheel and tire. Remove the brake drum.
3. Remove the four bolts which hold the hub and bearing assembly to the rear axle. Remove the hub and bearing assembly from the axle.
4. Installation is the reverse of the removal procedure.

GENERAL MOTORS—"N" BODY
BUICK SOMERSET REGAL • OLDS CALAIS • PONTIAC GRAND AM
SECTION 11

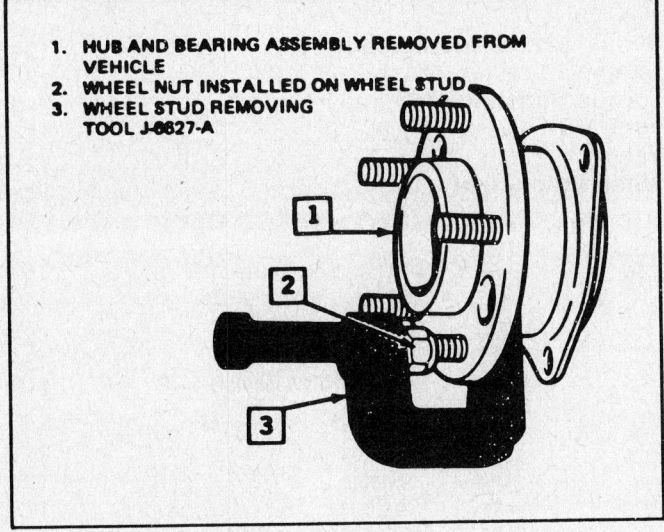

Removing Wheel Stud (© General Motors Corporation)

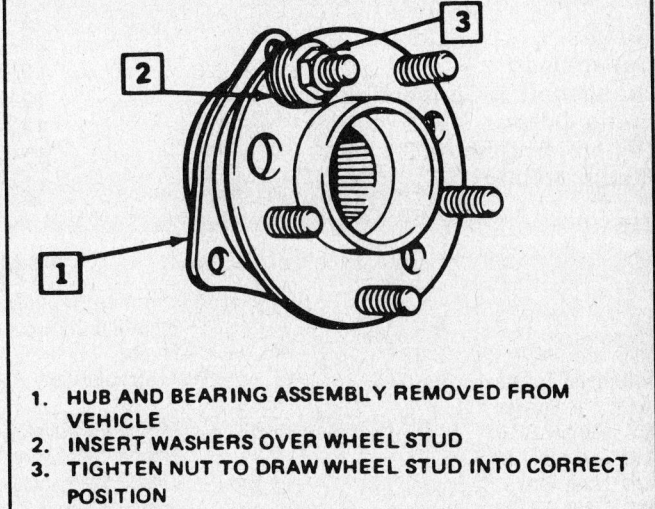

Installing Wheel Stud (© General Motors Corporation)

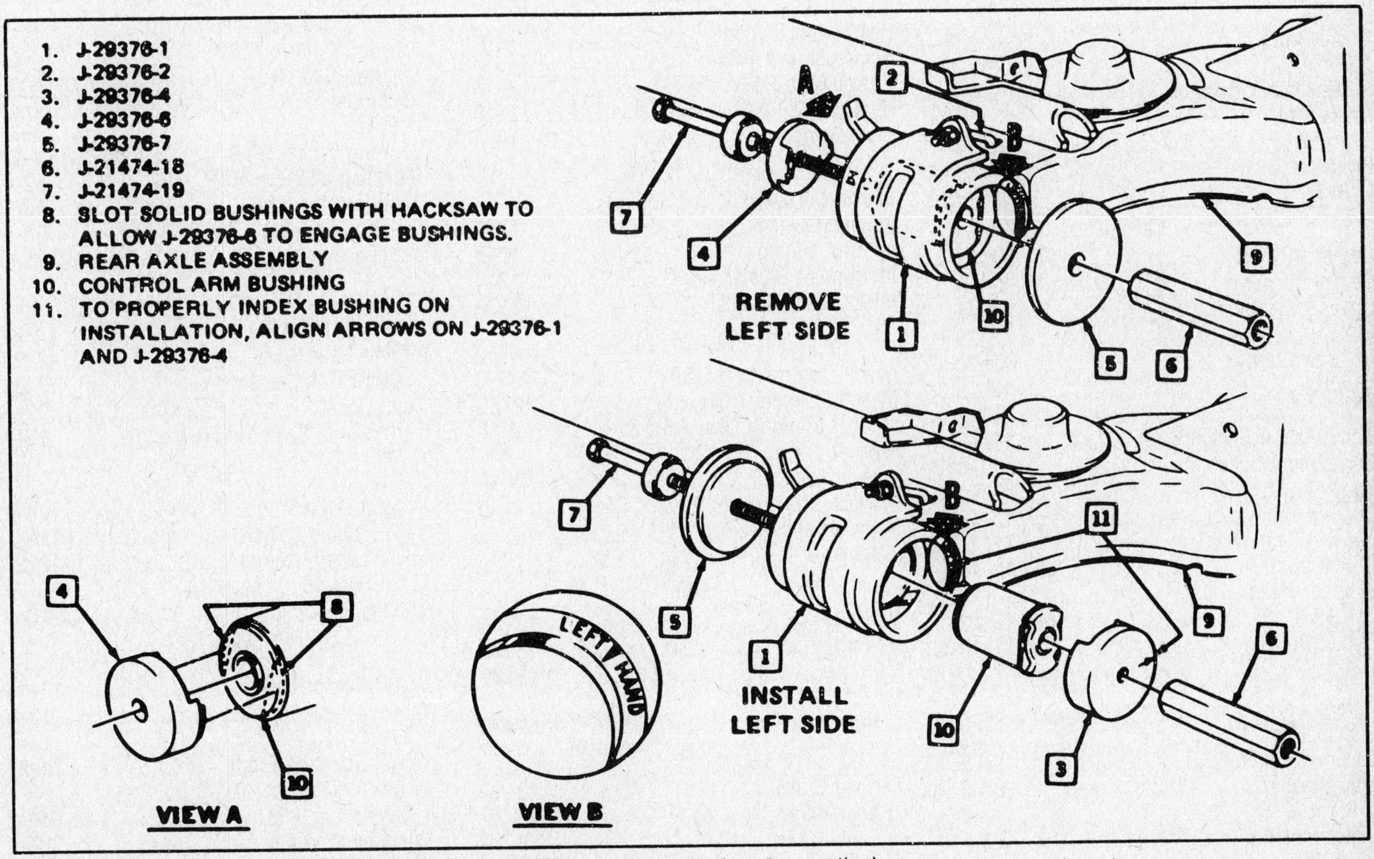

Remove/Install Control Arm Bushings – N Series (© General Motors Corporation)

11-25

SECTION 12

GENERAL MOTORS—"S" BODY
CHEVROLET NOVA

SPECIFICATIONS

Brakes	24–2	Serial Number Identification	12–5
Capacities	12–4	Torque	12–4
Crankshaft & Connecting Rod	12–4	Torque Sequence (Cylinder Heads)	12–23
Firing Order	12–4	Tune-Up	12–3
General Engine	12–3	Valve	12–3
Piston & Ring	12–4	Wheel Alignment	12–5

INDEX

A
Alternator R&R	12–5
Automatic Transaxle	12–30
On Car Service	23–2
Assembly R&R	12–30
Axle Assembly R&R	12–31
Axle Shaft Boots R&R	12–31
Axle Shaft R&R	12–32

B
Ball Joints	35–2
Brake System	12–29
Brake Booster	24–2
Brake Caliper Overhaul	24–2
Brake Caliper R&R	
Front	24–2
Brake Drum	
Rear	24–2
Brake Master Cylinder	12–29
Brake Pad	
Front	24–2
Brake Shoe	
Rear	24–2

C
Camshaft R&R	12–23
Carburetor R&R	12–19
Chassis Electrical	12–7
Clutch	12–29
Adjustment	12–29
R&R	12–29
Start Switch	12–7
Combination Switch R&R	12–8
Component Locations	12–8
Control Arm R&R	35–2
Cooling Fan Motor	12–18
Cooling System	12–18
Cruise Control	12–10
Cylinder Head	12–22
R&R	12–22
Circuit Breakers	12–10

D
Differential	32–2
Inspection	32–2
Dimmer Switch R&R	12–8
Disc Brakes	24–2
Front	24–2
Distributor R&R	12–5
Drive Axle	12–31

E
Electronic Ignition	30–2
Emission Controls	12–20
Engine	12–20
Identification	12–5
R&R	12–20
Engine Electrical	12–5
Engine Lubrication	12–24
Engine Mechanical	12–20
Engine Mounts R&R	12–21
Exhaust Manifold R&R	12–20

F
Front Suspension	35–2
Alignment	12–5
Fuel Pump R&R	12–18

H
Head Light Switch	12–8
Heater Blower R&R	12–18
Heater Core R&R	12–18
Heater Unit R&R	12–18
Horn Switch	12–8

I
Idle Speed Adjust	12–18
Ignition Switch	12–7
Ignition Timing	12–7
Instrument Cluster R&R	12–8
Intake Manifold R&R	12–20

L, M, N
Lower Control Arm R&R	35–2
Master Cylinder R&R	12–29
Manual Steering Gear R&R	12–16
Manual Transaxle	
Overhaul	32–2
Manual Transaxle R&R	12–30
Neutral Safety Switch	
R&R	12–7

O
Oil Pan R&R	12–24
Oil Pump	12–25
R&R	12–25
Oil Seal R&R	
Rear Main	12–26

P
Parking Brake	12–29
Adjustment	12–29
Cable R&R	12–29
Piston & Connecting Rod	12–23

R
Rear Main Oil Seal R&R	12–26
Rear Suspension	35–2
Regulator	12–5
Rocker Shaft/Assembly R&R	12–21

S
Serial Number	12–5
Engine	12–5
Vehicle	12–5
Shock Absorber R&R	
Front	35–2
Rear	35–2
Springs	
Front	35–2
Rear	35–2
Starter R&R	12–5
Starter Drive Replacement	12–5
Steering Column R&R	12–28
Steering Gear R&R	12–26
Manual	12–26
Power	12–27
Steering Wheel R&R	12–26
Stop Light Switch R&R	12–7
Speedometer R&R	12–8
Suspension R&R	35–2
Service	35–3

T
Timing Belt R&R	12–24
Timing Gear Cover	12–23
Oil Seal Replacement	12–23
Tune-Up	12–3
Turn Signal Switch R&R	12–8

U, V
U-Joint Overhaul	28–2
Valve Tappette R&R	12–21
Valve Timing Adjust	12–22
Valve System	12–21
Voltage Regulator	12–5

W, Y
Water Pump R&R	12–18
Wheel Alignment	12–5
Front	12–5
Wheel Bearings Front	12–27
Wheel Cylinders	
Rear	24–2
Windshield Wiper	12–8
Linkage R&R	12–8
Motor R&R	12–8
Switch R&R	12–8
Year Identification	12–3

BEFORE SERVICING BE CERTAIN TO READ THE SAFETY NOTICE

Chevrolet
1985 1/2-86
Front Wheel Drive Cars
NOVA

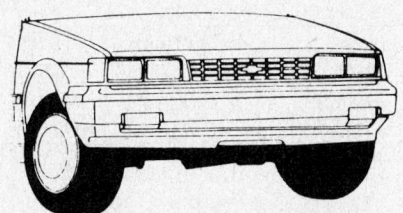

1985–87 Nova

GENERAL ENGINE SPECIFICATIONS

Year	VIN Code	Engine No. Cyl. Disp. Cu. In.	Liters	Fuel Delivery System	H.P. @ rpm	Torque @ rpm (ft. lb.)	Bore × Stroke	Compression Ratio	Oil Pressure @ 2000 rpm
'85–'87	①	97	1.5	2-bbl.	70 @ 4800	86 @ 2800	3.19 × 3.03	9.0	34 psi

① See vehicle identification illustration.

TUNE-UP SPECIFICATIONS

Year	Engine Type	Spark Plugs Type	Spark Plugs Gap (in.)	Distributor Point Dwell (deg)	Distributor Point Gap (in)	Ignition Timing (deg) MT	Ignition Timing (deg) AT	Compression Pressure	Fuel Pump Pres.	Idle Speed (rpm) MT	Idle Speed (rpm) AT	Valve Clearance (in) Intake	Valve Clearance (in) Exhaust
'85–'87	4A-LC	BRP5EY11	0.043	Electronic		5B	5B	160	2.5–3.5	650	800	.008	.012

NOTE: If the information given in this chart disagrees with the information on the emission control specification decal located under the hood, use the specifications on the decal.

VALVE SPECIFICATIONS

Year	VIN Code	Engine No. Cyl. Displacement (cu. in.)	Liters	Eng. Mfg.	Seat Angle (deg)	Face Angle (deg)	Spring Test Pressure (lbs. @ in.)	Spring Installed Height (in.)	Stem-to-Guide Clearance (in.) Intake	Stem-to-Guide Clearance (in.) Exhaust	Stem Diameter (in.) Intake	Stem Diameter (in.) Exhaust
'85–'87	①	97	1.5	Chev.	45	45.5	52	1.52	0.008–0.0024	0.0012–0.0026	0.2744–0.2750	0.2742–0.2748

① See vehicle identification illustration.

SECTION 12
GENERAL MOTORS—"S" BODY
CHEVROLET NOVA

FIRING ORDER

Firing order: 1-3-4-2

PISTON AND RING SPECIFICATIONS
All measurements in inches

Year	Engine Size (cu. in.)	Liters	Piston Clearance	Ring Gap			Ring Side Clearance		
				Top Compression	Bottom Compression	Oil Control	Top Compression	Bottom Compression	Oil Control
'85–'87	97	1.5	0.0039–0.0047	0.0079–0.0157	0.0059–0.0138	0.0039–0.0236	0.0016–0.0031	0.0012–0.0028	snug

CRANKSHAFT AND CONNECTING ROD SPECIFICATIONS
All measurements in inches

Year	Engine Size (cu. in.)	Liters	Crankshaft				Connecting Rod		
			Main Brg. Journal Dia.	Main Brg. Oil Clearance	Shaft End-Play	Thrust on No.	Journal Diameter	Oil Clearance	Side Clearance
'85–'87	97	1.5	1.8892–1.8898	0.0005–0.0019	0.0008–0.0073	3	1.5742–1.5748	0.0008–0.0020	0.0059–0.0098

CAPACITIES

Year	Engine Size (cu. in.)	Liters	Crankcase (qt)		Transmission (qt)		Drive Axle (pt)	Fuel Tank (gal)	Cooling System w/Heater (qt)
			W/Filter	W/O Filter	Manual	Automatic			
'85–'87	97	1.5	3.5	3.2	2.7	5.8	①	13.2	6.3

TORQUE SPECIFICATIONS
All readings in ft. lbs.

Year	Engine Size (cu. in.)	Liters	Cylinder Head Bolts	Rod Bearing Bolts	Main Bearing Bolts	Crankshaft Pulley Bolt	Flywheel-to-Crankshaft Bolts	Manifold	
								Intake	Exhaust
'85–'87	97	1.5	40–45	①	40–47	80–94	55–61	15–21	15–21

Caution: Verify the correct original equipment engine is in the vehicle by referring to the VIN engine code before torquing any bolts.
① 1985—29 ft. lbs.   1986 & Later—36 ft. lbs.

GENERAL MOTORS—"S" BODY
CHEVROLET NOVA
SECTION 12

WHEEL ALIGNMENT SPECIFICATIONS

	Caster		Camber		Toe-in (mm)	
	Range (deg.)	Pref. (deg.)	Range (deg.)	Pref. (deg.)	Range	Pref.
Front	0°53 ± 45'	0°53 ± 30	–30 ± 45'	–30 ± 30	0 ± 4	0 ± 1
Rear	NA	NA	–31 ± 45'	–31 ± 30	3.8 ± 4	3.8 ± 2

NA Not adjustable

VEHICLE IDENTIFICATION NUMBER (VIN)

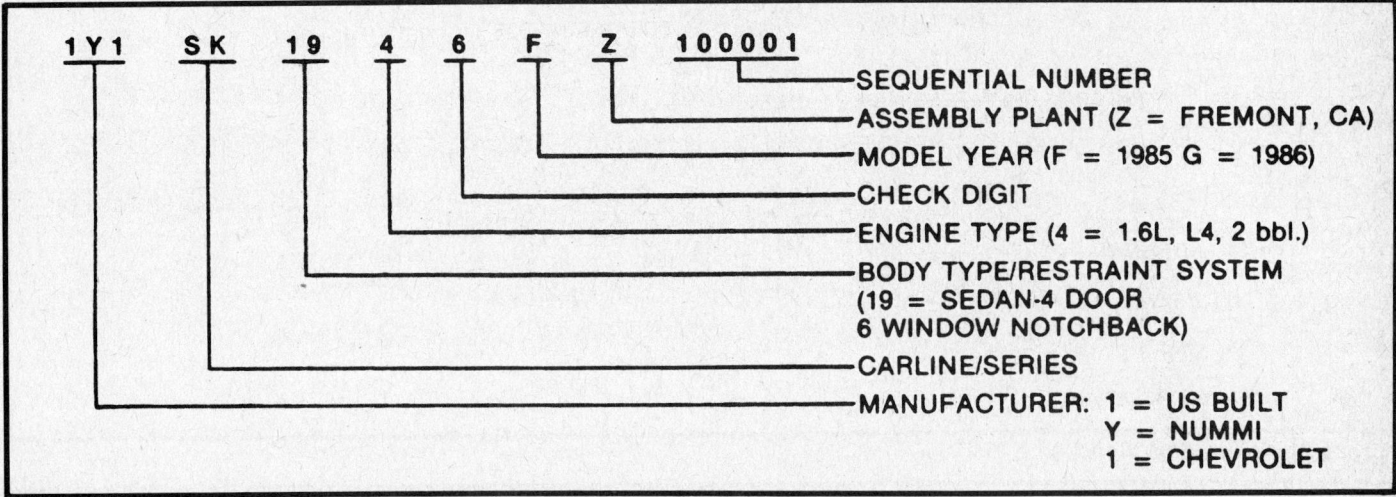

```
1Y1 SK 19 4 6 F Z 100001
                        └─ SEQUENTIAL NUMBER
                      └─── ASSEMBLY PLANT (Z = FREMONT, CA)
                    └───── MODEL YEAR (F = 1985 G = 1986)
                  └─────── CHECK DIGIT
                └───────── ENGINE TYPE (4 = 1.6L, L4, 2 bbl.)
             └──────────── BODY TYPE/RESTRAINT SYSTEM
                           (19 = SEDAN-4 DOOR
                            6 WINDOW NOTCHBACK)
         └──────────────── CARLINE/SERIES
     └──────────────────── MANUFACTURER: 1 = US BUILT
                                         Y = NUMMI
                                         1 = CHEVROLET
```

ELECTRICAL SECTION

For Overhaul Procedures, refer to Unit Repair Section

Charging System

ALTERNATOR

Removal and Installation

1. Disconnect the negative battery cable.
2. Tag and disconnect the wiring from the alternator.
3. Loosen the alternator adjusting bracket and remove the alternator drive belt.
4. Remove the alternator retaining bolts. Remove the alternator from the vehicle.
5. Installation is the reverse of the removal procedure.

Starting System

STARTER

Removal and Installation

1. Disconnect the negative battery cable.
2. If vehicle is equipped with automatic transmission, remove the oil filler tube.
3. Raise the vehicle and support safely.
4. Tag and disconnect the wiring from the starter motor.
5. Remove the starter retaining bolts. Remove the starter from the vehicle.
6. Installation is the reverse of the removal procedure.

VOLTAGE REGULATOR

Removal and Installation

NOTE: The voltage regulator is located within the alternator assembly. Replacement of the voltage regulator requires disassembly of the alternator.

1. Remove the alternator from the vehicle as outlined earlier.
2. Mount the alternator assembly in a suitable holding fixture.
3. Remove the alternator rear cover screws. Remove the rear cover.
4. Remove the brush holder assembly.
5. Remove the regulator retaining screws. Remove the voltage regulator.
6. Installation is the reverse of the removal procedure.

Ignition System

DISTRIBUTOR

Removal and Installation—Timing Not Disturbed

1. Disconnect the negative battery cable.
2. Disconnect the ignition assembly wiring from the distributor.
3. Tag and disconnect the vacuum hoses. Disconnect the vacuum advance unit.
4. Tag and disconnect the spark plug wires.
5. Remove the distributor hold down bolts. Remove the distributor.

Section 12: GENERAL MOTORS – "S" BODY
CHEVROLET NOVA

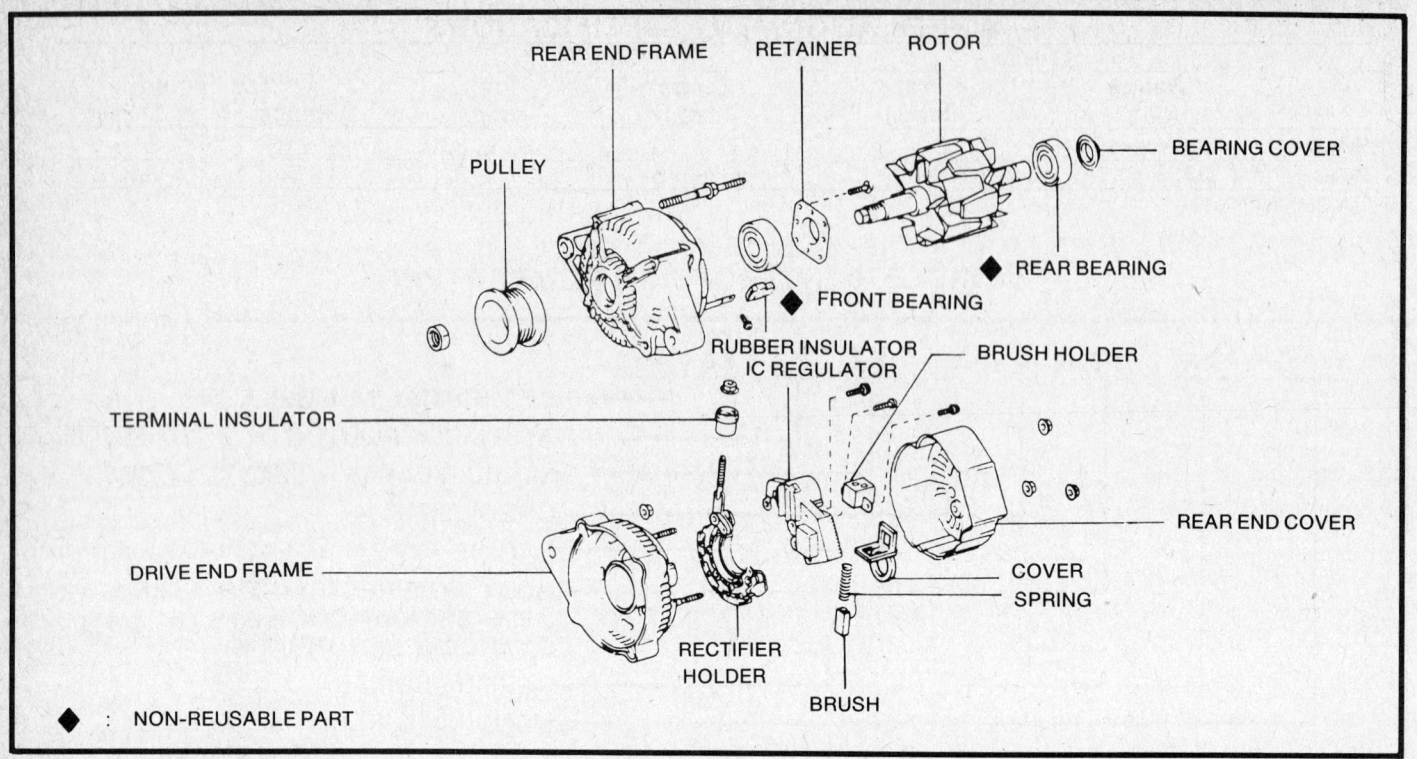

Alternator-exploded view

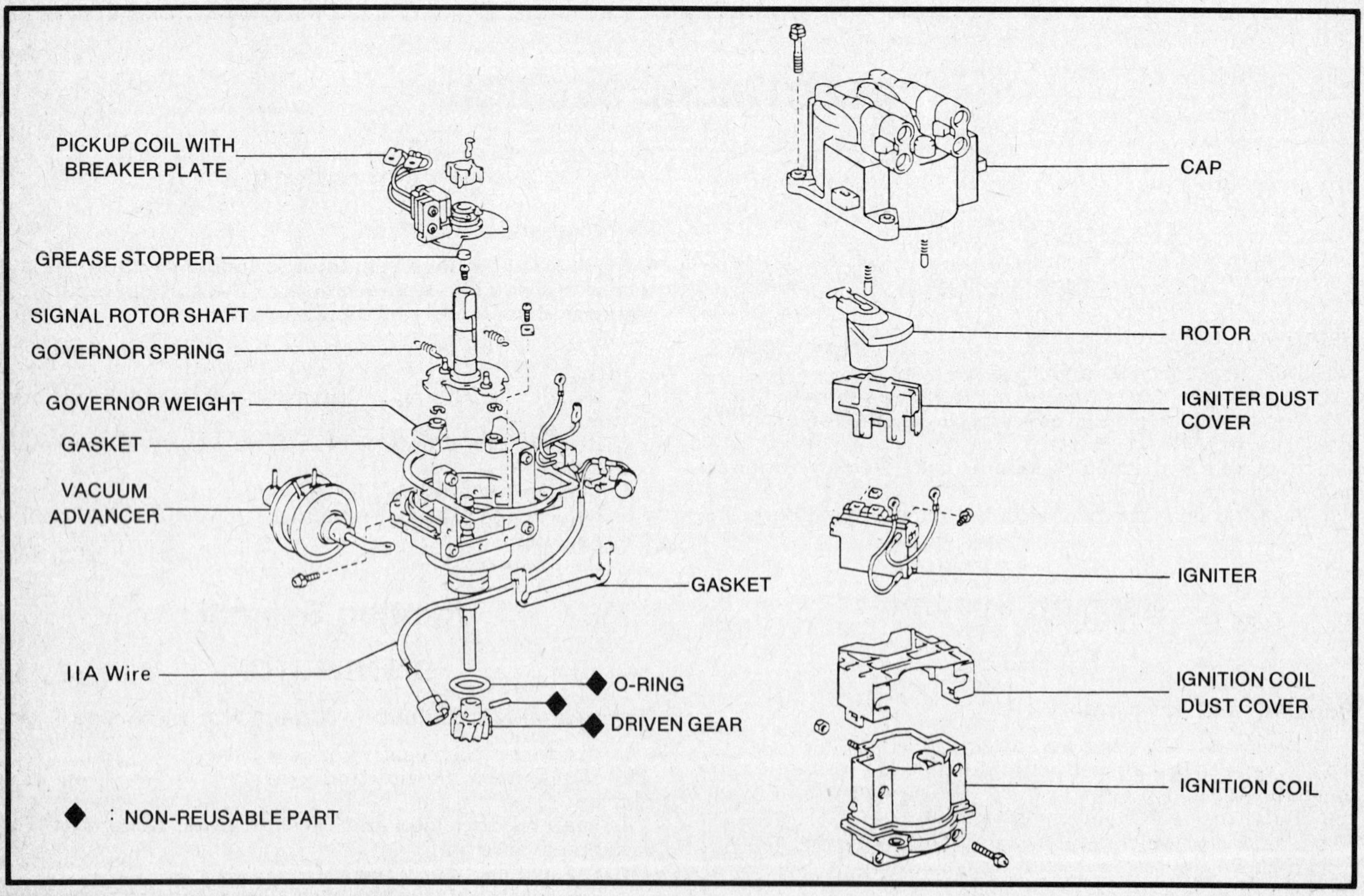

Distributor-exploded view-typical

GENERAL MOTORS – "S" BODY
CHEVROLET NOVA

6. Installation is the reverse of the removal procedure.

Installation – Timing Disturbed

1. Remove the No. 1 spark plug.
2. Place a finger over the spark plug hole and bring the engine up until pressure if felt. The engine is now at top dead center (TDC).
3. Install the removed spark plug.
4. Install the distributor in the engine. Install the distributor hold down bolts.
5. Connect the spark plug wires and vacuum hoses.
6. Connect the negative battery cable.

IGNITION TIMING

Adjustment

1. Connect a timing light according to manufacturers instructions.
2. Disconnect the vacuum hoses from the ignition assembly diaphragm and plug the hoses.
3. Slowly turn the ignition assembly, using the timing light, until the timing mark on the crankshaft pulley is in alignment with the 5° mark.
4. Tighten the distributor bolts and recheck the ignition timing. Ignition timing should be as follows: BTDC @ 950 rpm max. (transmission in Neutral and vacuum advance off).

Electrical Controls

IGNITION LOCK/SWITCH

Removal and Installation

1. Disconnect the negative battery cable.
2. Remove the steering wheel.
3. Unfasten the ignition switch connector located under the instrument panel.
4. If necessary, remove the upper and lower halves of the steering column to gain working clearance.
5. Withdraw the lock cylinder from the lock housing while depressing the stop tab.
6. To remove the ignition switch, unfasten the securing screws and withdraw the switch from the lock housing.

Installation is performed in the following order:
1. Align the locking cam with the hole in the locking switch and insert the switch into the lock housing.
2. Secure the switch with the screws.
3. Make sure that the lock cylinder and the column lock are in the "ACC" position.
4. Slide the cylinder into the lock housing until the stop tab engages the hole in the lock.
5. The rest of the installation is performed in the reverse order of the removal.

NEUTRAL SAFETY SWITCH

Adjustment

1. Locate the neutral safety switch on the side of the transaxle housing.
2. Loosen the switch bolt.
3. Move the gear selector to the neutral position.
4. Disconnect the neutral start switch connector.
5. Connect the ohmmeter between the terminals of the switch.
6. Adjust the switch until there is continuity between the terminals.
7. Connect the neutral start switch connector. Tighten the switch bolt to 48 inch lbs. (5.4 Nm).

Removal and Installation

1. Disconnect the negative battery cable.
2. Locate the neutral safety switch on the side of the transaxle housing.
3. Disconnect the neutral start switch wiring.
4. Remove the switch retaining bolt. Remove the switch from the vehicle.
5. Installation is the reverse of the removal procedure. Adjust as outlined above.

CLUTCH START SWITCH

Removal and Installation

NOTE: The clutch start switch is located in the passenger compartment under the dash assembly on the drivers side of the vehicle. The clutch switch has no adjustment and must be replaced if thought to be defective.

1. Disconnect the negative battery cable.
2. Remove the necessary trim panels in order to gain access to the clutch switch retaining screws.
3. Remove the clutch switch retaining screws.
4. Pull the switch down from its retainer and disconnect the electrical connections.
5. Installation is the reverse of the removal procedure.

STOPLIGHT SWITCH

Removal and Installation

1. Disconnect the negative battery cable.
2. Loosen the stoplight switch retaining nut located on the brake pedal.
3. Disconnect the electrical connections from the stoplight switch.
4. Remove the stoplight switch from the vehicle.
5. Installation is the reverse of the removal procedure.

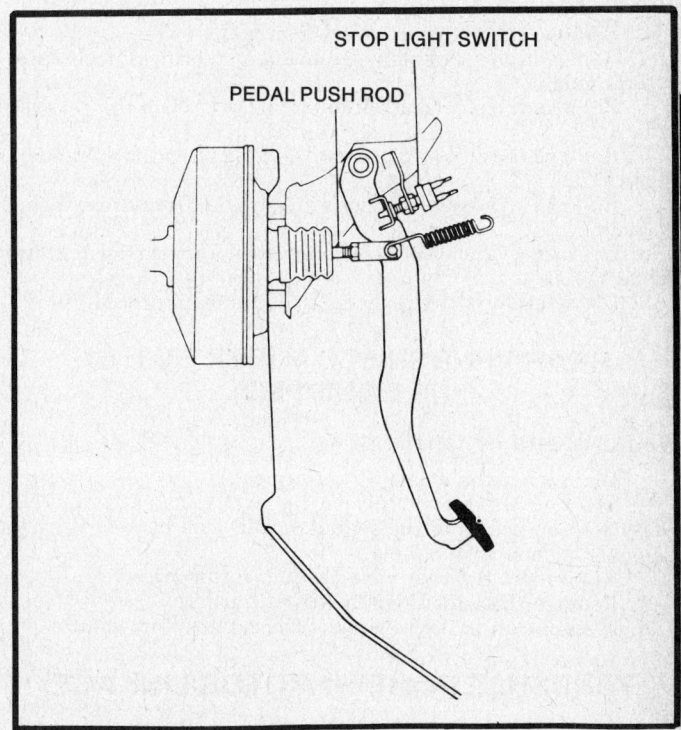

Stoplight switch loction

SECTION 12

GENERAL MOTORS — "S" BODY
CHEVROLET NOVA

HEADLIGHT/DIMMER/TURN SIGNAL SWITCH

Removal and Installation

1. Disconnect the negative battery cable.
2. Unfasten the horn and turn signal connector located at the base of the steering column shroud.
3. Loosen the trim pad retaining screws from the back of the steering wheel.
4. Lift the trim pad and horn assemblies from the wheel.
5. Remove the steering wheel hub retaining nut.
6. Scratch matchmarks on the hub and shaft to aid in correct installation.
7. Use a steering wheel puller to remove the steering wheel.
8. Disconnect the ignition switch and turn signal switch wiring.
9. Remove the combination switch which includes the headlight/dimmer/turn signal switch from the vehicle.
10. Installation is the reverse of the removal procedure.

HORN SWITCH

Removal and Installation

1. Disconnect the negative battery cable.
2. Loosen the trim pad retaining screws from the rear of the steering wheel.
3. Lift the trim pad from the steering wheel.
4. Remove the horn wiring assembly from the steering wheel hub.
5. Installation is the reverse of the removal procedure.

FRONT WINDSHIELD WIPER SWITCH

Removal and Installation

1. Disconnect the negative battery cable.
2. Unfasten the trim pad retaining screws from the back of the steering wheel.
3. Remove the steering wheel trim pad.
4. Remove the steering wheel using a steering wheel puller or equivalent.
5. Remove the steering column trim cover from the steering column.
6. Remove the retaining screws holding the windshield wiper switch.
7. Pull the windshield wiper switch away from the steering column.
8. Disconnect the electrical connectors from the switch. Remove the switch.
9. Installation is the reverse of the removal procedure.

REAR WINDSHIELD WIPER SWITCH (IF EQUIPPED)

Removal and Installation

1. Disconnect the negative battery cable.
2. The rear wiper switch is located in the dash assembly. In order to gain access to the switch, it will first be necessary to remove various trim panels.
3. Disconnect the rear wiper switch retaining screws.
4. Remove the wiper switch wiring harness.
5. Installation is the reverse of the removal procedure.

WINDSHIELD WIPER MOTOR/LINKAGE

Removal and Installation

1. Disconnect the negative battery cable.
2. Remove the necessary trim panels in order to gain access to the wiper motor/linkage retaining bolts.
3. Remove the retaining bolts from the wiper/linkage assembly.
4. Tag and disconnect the electrical connections from the motor.
5. Remove the wiper/linkage from the vehicle.
6. Installation is the reverse of the removal procedure.

Instrument Cluster and Speedometer

Removal and Installation

1. Disconnect the negative battery cable.
2. Remove the steering wheel.
3. Remove the left side speaker grille by removing the retaining clip.
4. Remove the lower steering column trim cover.
5. Remove the hood release lever.
6. Remove the necessary components in order to gain access to the heater duct. Remove the heater duct.
7. Remove the top panel from the instrument cluster. Remove the A/C vents.
8. Remove the lower underdash trim panels.
9. Remove the two retaining screw from the right speaker grille. Remove the grille and bracket assembly.
10. Disconnect the electrical connector from the speaker assembly and remove the speaker.
11. Remove the glove compartment.
12. Remove the center cluster trim panel. Remove the radio.
13. Remove the heater control retaining screws. Pull the heater control panel forward enough to disconnect the electrical and vacuum connectors. Remove the heater control panel.
14. Remove the side defroster nozzle and remove the instrument panel from the vehicle.
15. Installation is the reverse of the removal procedure.

SPEEDOMETER CABLE

Removal and Installation

1. Disconnect the negative battery cable.
2. Remove the speedometer assembly from the instrument cluster.
3. Disconnect the cable casing from the speedometer head assembly.
4. Remove the inner cable from the upper casing.
5. Raise and support the vehicle safely.
6. Disconnect the speedometer cable from the transaxle. Remove the cable.
7. Installation of the new cable is the reverse of the removal procedure. Check the new cable for kinks upon installation and remove when routing the cable.

ELECTRICAL COMPONENT LOCATION

COMPUTER

The electronic control module is located towards the center of the vehicle under the instrument panel. In order to gain access to the electronic control module, it will first be necessary to remove various trim panel assemblies.

VARIOUS RELAYS (ENGINE COMPARTMENT)

The starter, air conditioning, fan and main engine relays are located in the engine compartment at the front of the vehicle. In order to gain access to these electrical components, it may be necessary to remove the grille assembly from the vehicle.

VARIOUS RELAYS (PASSENGER COMPARTMENT)

The defogger, heater, charge light and seat belt relay are located on the passenger side of the vehicle under the dash assem-

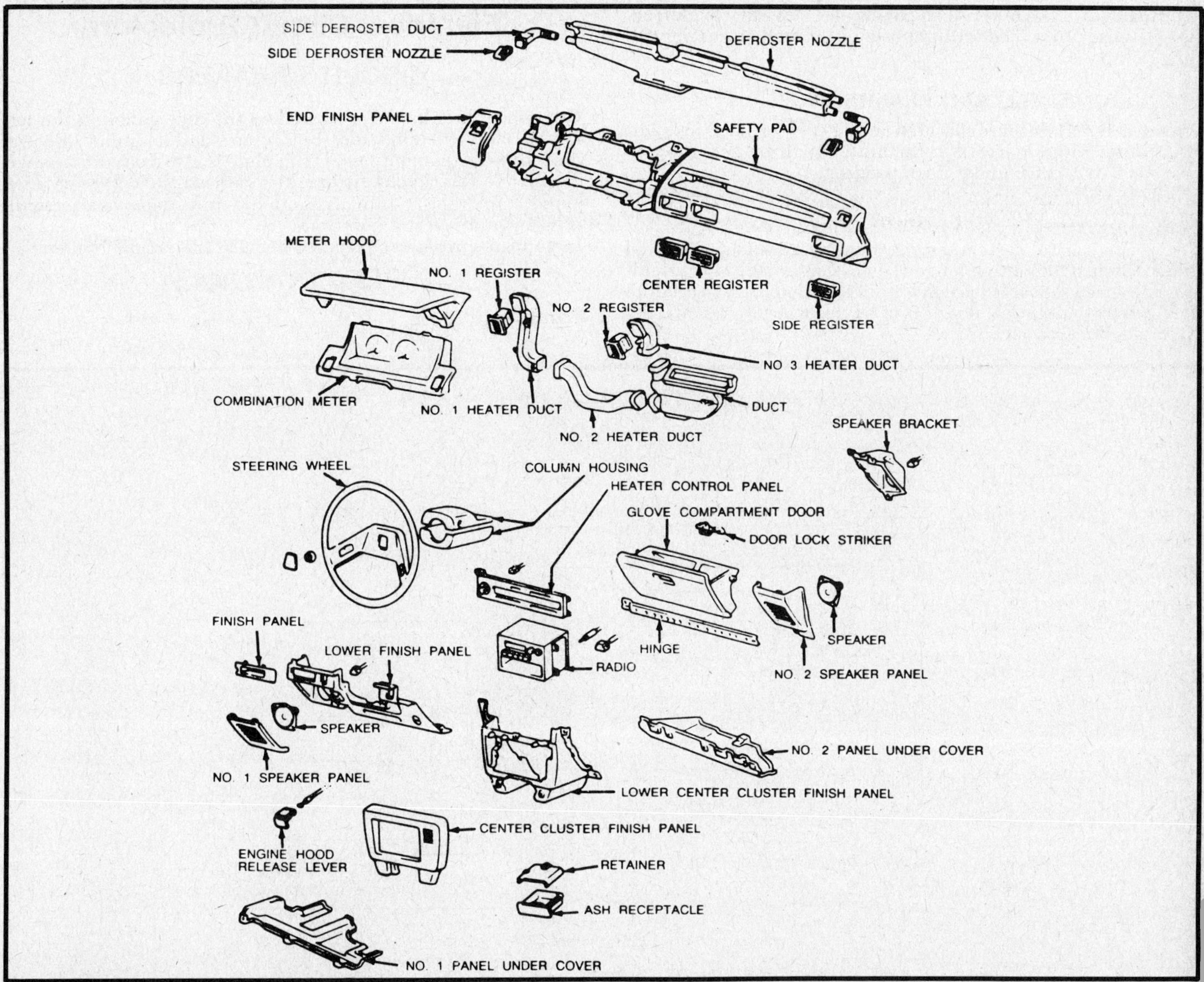

GENERAL MOTORS—"S" BODY
CHEVROLET NOVA

SECTION 12

Instrument panel—exploded view

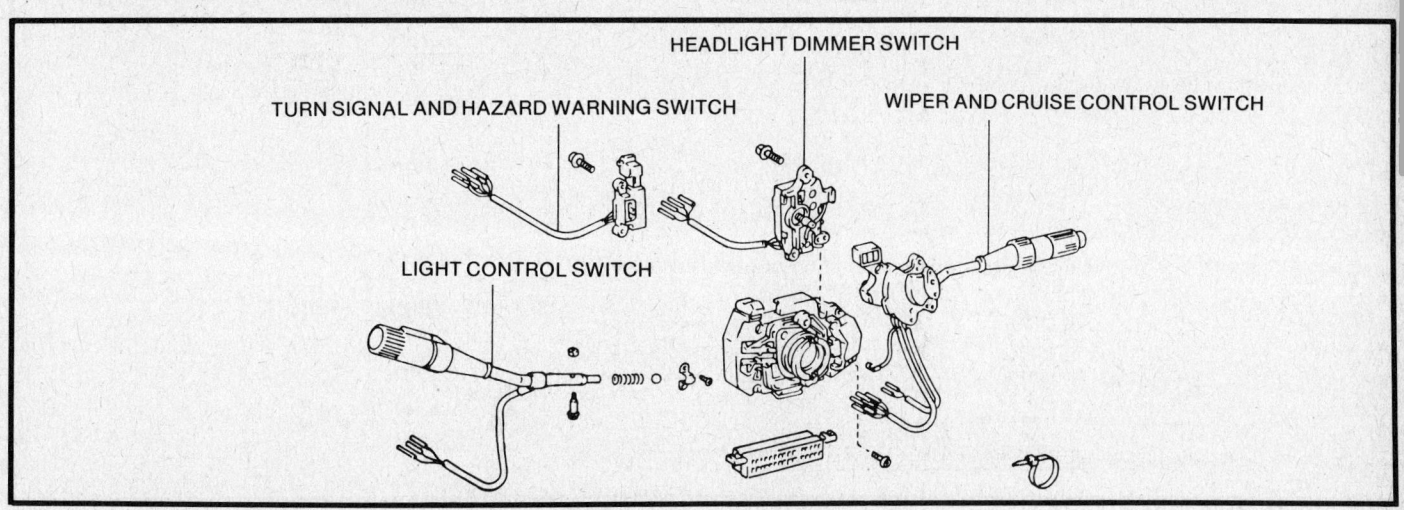

Steering column mounted switches—exploded view

SECTION 12: GENERAL MOTORS—"S" BODY
CHEVROLET NOVA

bly. Removal of the lower hush panels are necessary to gain access to these units. The taillight relay is located on the drivers side kick panel.

TURN SIGNAL/HAZARD FLASHER

The turn signal flasher is located on the drivers side kick panel. In order to gain access to the unit, it will be necessary to first remove certain under dash padding.

ELECTRICAL SPEED SENSOR

The cruise control system is controlled by a computer located under the instrument panel on the passenger side of the vehicle. The speed sensor is located within the computer. In order to gain access to the unit, it will first be necessary to remove the right side kick panel.

Electrical Circuit Protectors

CIRCUIT BREAKERS

The circuit breakers are located in the fuse panel on the left side of the vehicle behind the driver side kick panel. Behind the center instrument panel trim plate is also a circuit breaker. In order to reset a circuit breaker, remove the necessary kick panel(s) in order to gain access to the unit. Remove the circuit breaker and insert a non-conductive probe into the reset hole. Install the circuit breaker and replace the circuit breaker.

SPEED CONTROLS

Troubleshooting

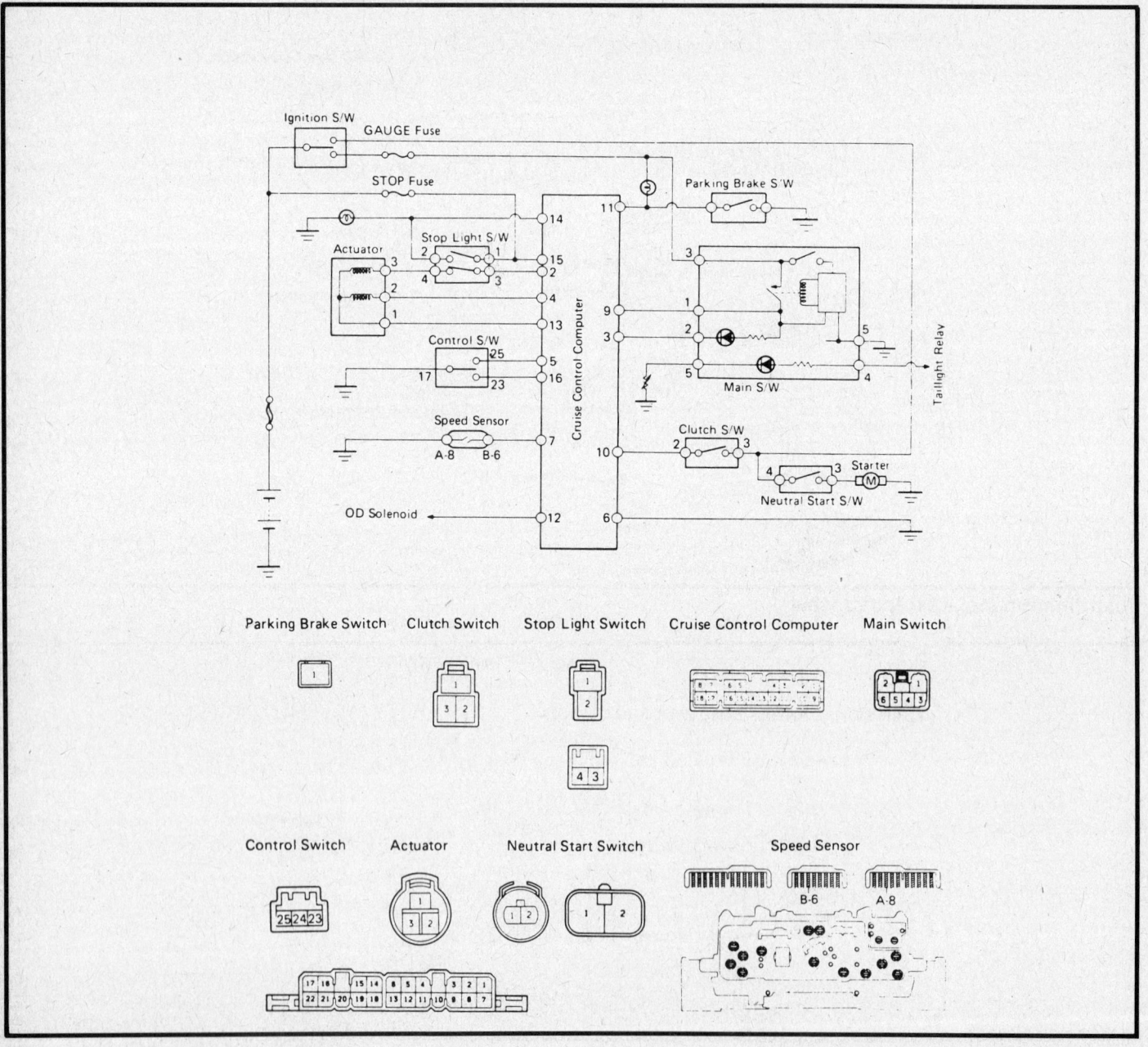

Cruise control electrical schematic

GENERAL MOTORS – "S" BODY
CHEVROLET NOVA
SECTION 12

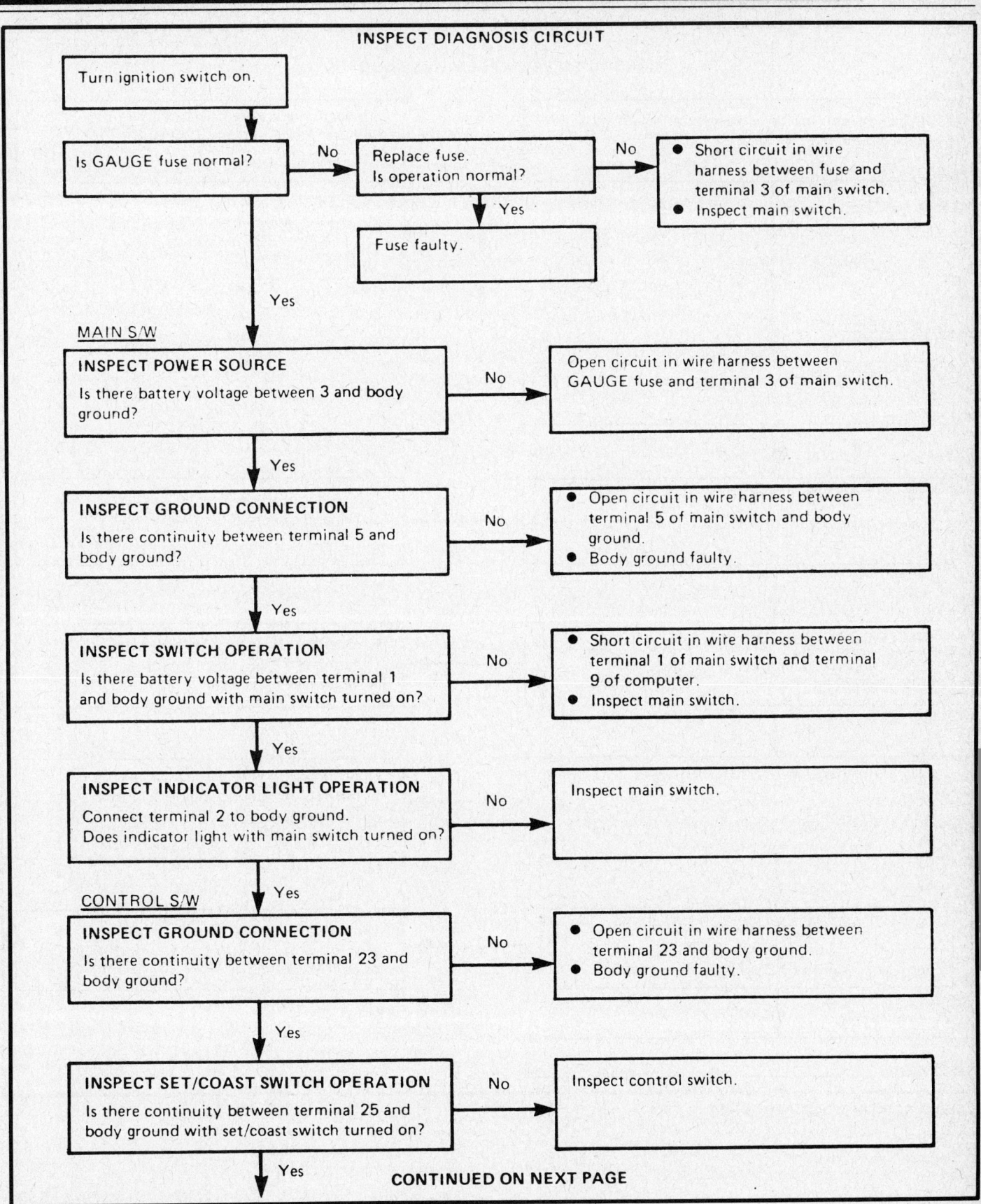

Cruise control troubleshooting

12-11

SECTION 12
GENERAL MOTORS—"S" BODY
CHEVROLET NOVA

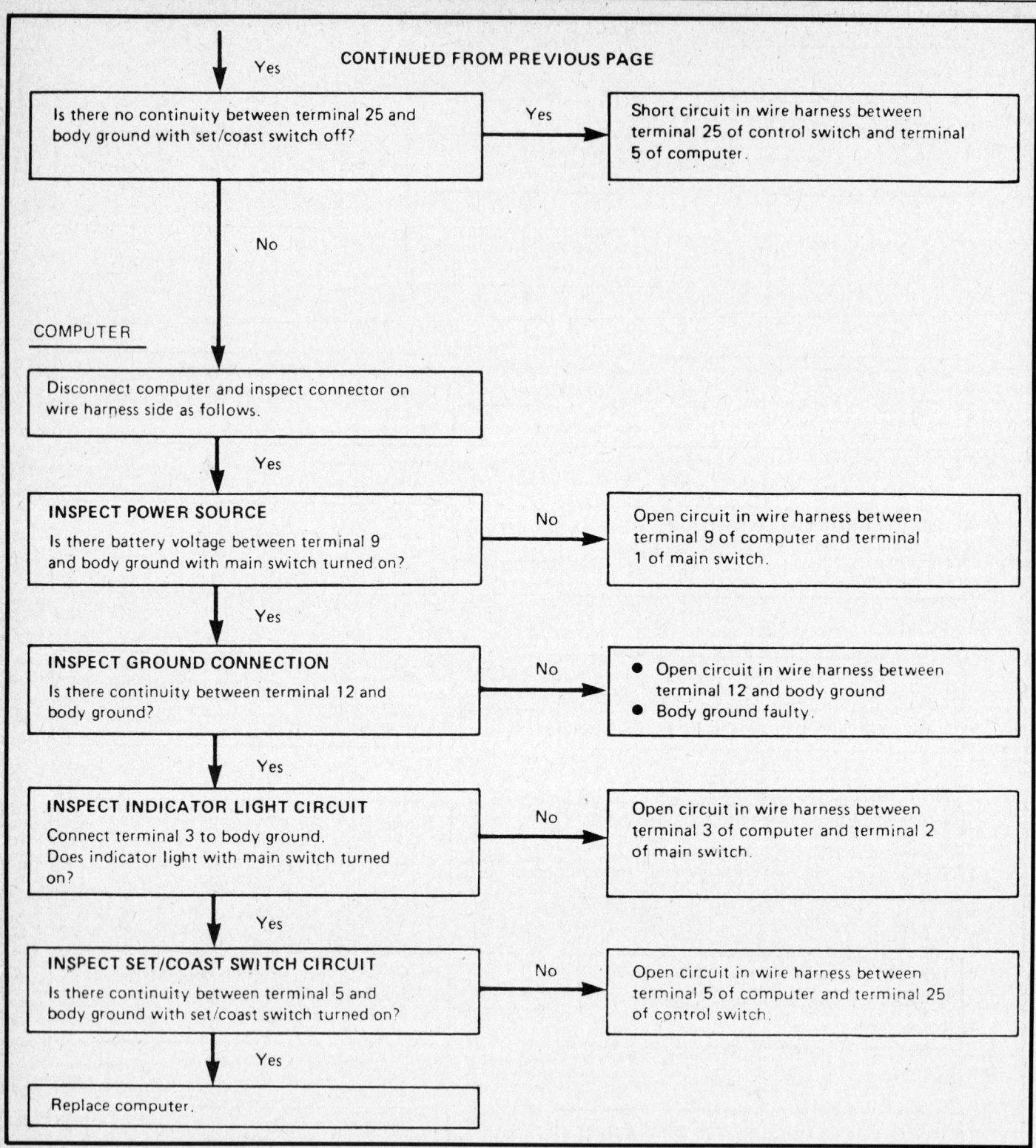

Cruise control troubleshooting

GENERAL MOTORS – "S" BODY
CHEVROLET NOVA
SECTION 12

A INSPECTION OF SET/COAST SWITCH CIRCUIT

CONTROL S/W

INSPECT SET/COAST SWITCH OPERATION
Is there continuity between terminal 25 and body ground with set/coast switch turned off?

— Yes → Inspect control switch.

↓ No

COMPUTER

INSPECT SET/COAST SWITCH CIRCUIT
Disconnect connector from computer.
Is there continuity between terminal 5 and body ground with set/coast switch turned off?

— Yes → Short circuit in wire harness between terminal 5 of computer and terminal 25 of control switch.

↓ No

Replace computer.

B INSPECTION OF ACCEL/RESUME SWITCH CIRCUIT

CONTROL S/W

INSPECT ACCEL/RESUME SWITCH OPERATION
Is there continuity between terminal 23 and body ground with accel/resume switch turned off?

— Yes →
- Short circuit in wire harness between terminal 23 of control switch and terminal 16 of computer.
- Inspect control switch.

↓ No

Is there continuity between terminal 23 and body ground with accel/resume switch turned on?

— No → Inspect control switch.

↓ Yes

COMPUTER

INSPECT ACCEL/RESUME SWITCH CIRCUIT
Is there continuity between terminal 16 and body ground with accel/resume switch turned on?

— No → Open circuit in wire harness between terminal 16 of computer and terminal 23 of control switch.

↓ Yes

Replace computer.

Cruise control troubleshooting

12-13

SECTION 12 GENERAL MOTORS—"S" BODY
CHEVROLET NOVA

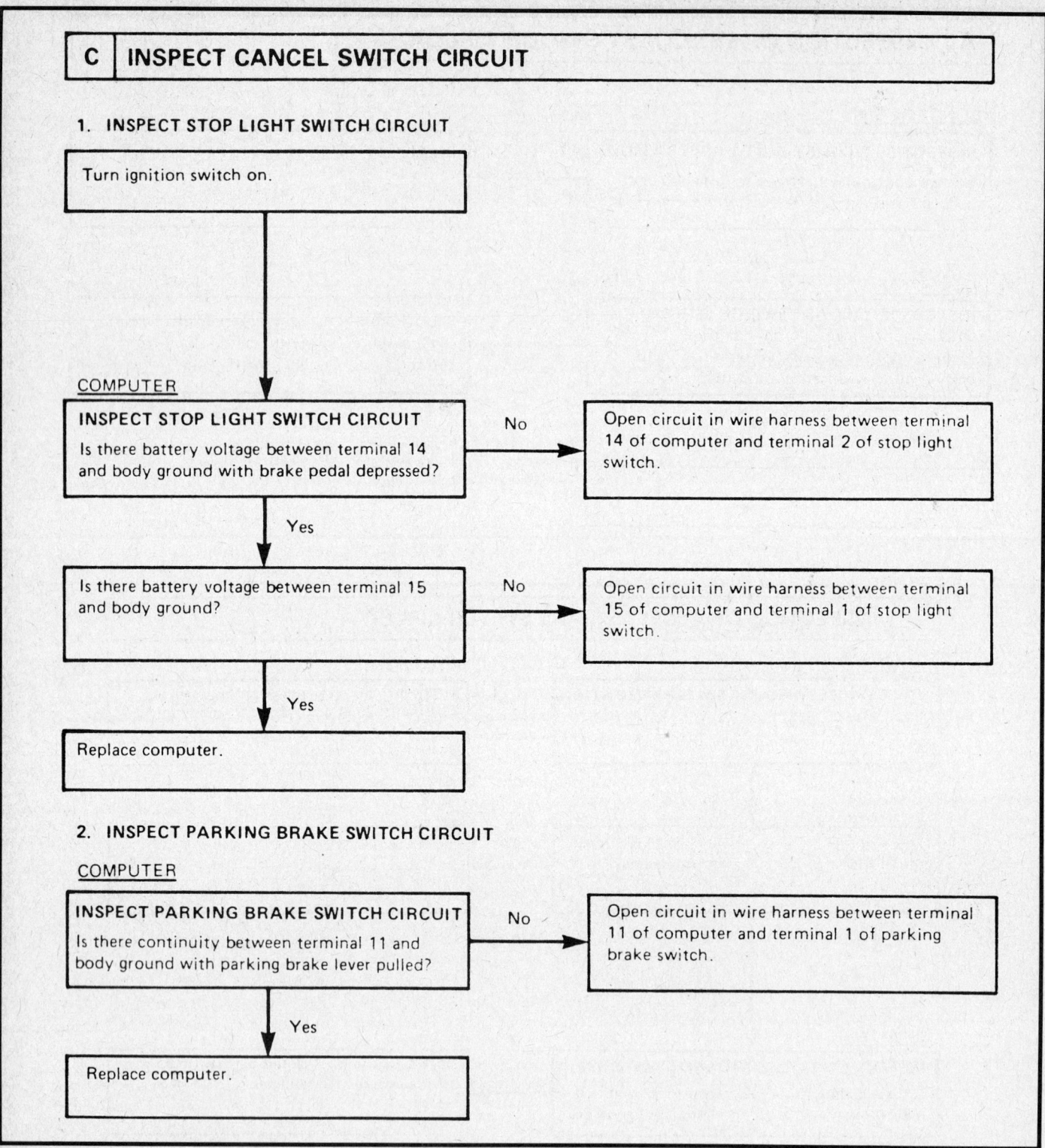

Cruise control troubleshooting

GENERAL MOTORS – "S" BODY
CHEVROLET NOVA

3. INSPECT CLUTCH SWITCH CIRCUIT (M/T)

CLUTCH S/W

INSPECT GROUND CONNECTION
Is there continuity between terminal 3 and body ground?
— No →
- Open circuit in wire harness between terminal 3 and body ground.
- Body ground faulty.

↓ Yes

INSPECT CLUTCH SWITCH CONTINUITY
Is clutch switch normal? (See On-Car Service)
— No → Replace clutch switch.

↓ Yes

COMPUTER

INSPECT CLUTCH SWITCH CIRCUIT
Is there continuity between terminal 10 and body ground with clutch pedal depressed?
— No → Open circuit in wire harness between terminal 10 of computer and terminal 2 of clutch switch.

↓ Yes

Is there continuity between terminal 10 and body ground with clutch pedal returned?
— Yes → Short circuit in wire harness between terminal 10 of computer and terminal 2 of clutch switch.

↓ No

Replace computer.

4. INSPECT NEUTRAL START SWITCH CIRCUIT (A/T)

COMPUTER

INSPECT NEUTRAL START SWITCH CIRCUIT
Disconnect connector from computer.
Is there continuity between terminal 10 and body ground with neutral start switch turned to "N" range?
— No → Open circuit in wire harness between terminal 10 of computer and terminal 4 of neutral start switch.

↓ Yes

Replace computer.

Cruise control troubleshooting

GENERAL MOTORS — "S" BODY
CHEVROLET NOVA

D | INSPECTION OF SPEED SENSOR CIRCUIT

SPEED SENSOR

INSPECT GROUND CONNECTION
Disconnect combination meter.
Is there continuity between terminal of wire harness side and body ground?

→ No →
- Open circuit in wire harness between terminal of combination meter and body ground.
- Body ground faulty.

↓ Yes

INSPECT SPEED SENSOR OPERATION
Is speed sensor normal?

→ No → Replace speed sensor.

↓ Yes

COMPUTER

INSPECT SPEED SENSOR CIRCUIT
Disconnect connector from combination meter.
Is there continuity between terminal 7 and body ground?

→ Yes → Short circuit in wire harness between terminal 7 of computer and terminal of combination meter.

↓ No

Is there continuity between terminal 7 of computer and terminal of combination meter?

→ No → Open circuit in wire harness between terminal 7 of computer and terminal of combination meter.

↓ Yes

Replace computer.

Cruise control troubleshooting

E | INSPECTION OF ACTUATOR OPERATION

ACTUATOR

INSPECT ACTUATOR OPERATION
Remove actuator.
Is actuator normal?
(See On-Car Service)

→ No → Replace actuator.

↓ Yes

Replace computer.

Cruise control troubleshooting

12-16

GENERAL MOTORS – "S" BODY
CHEVROLET NOVA
SECTION 12

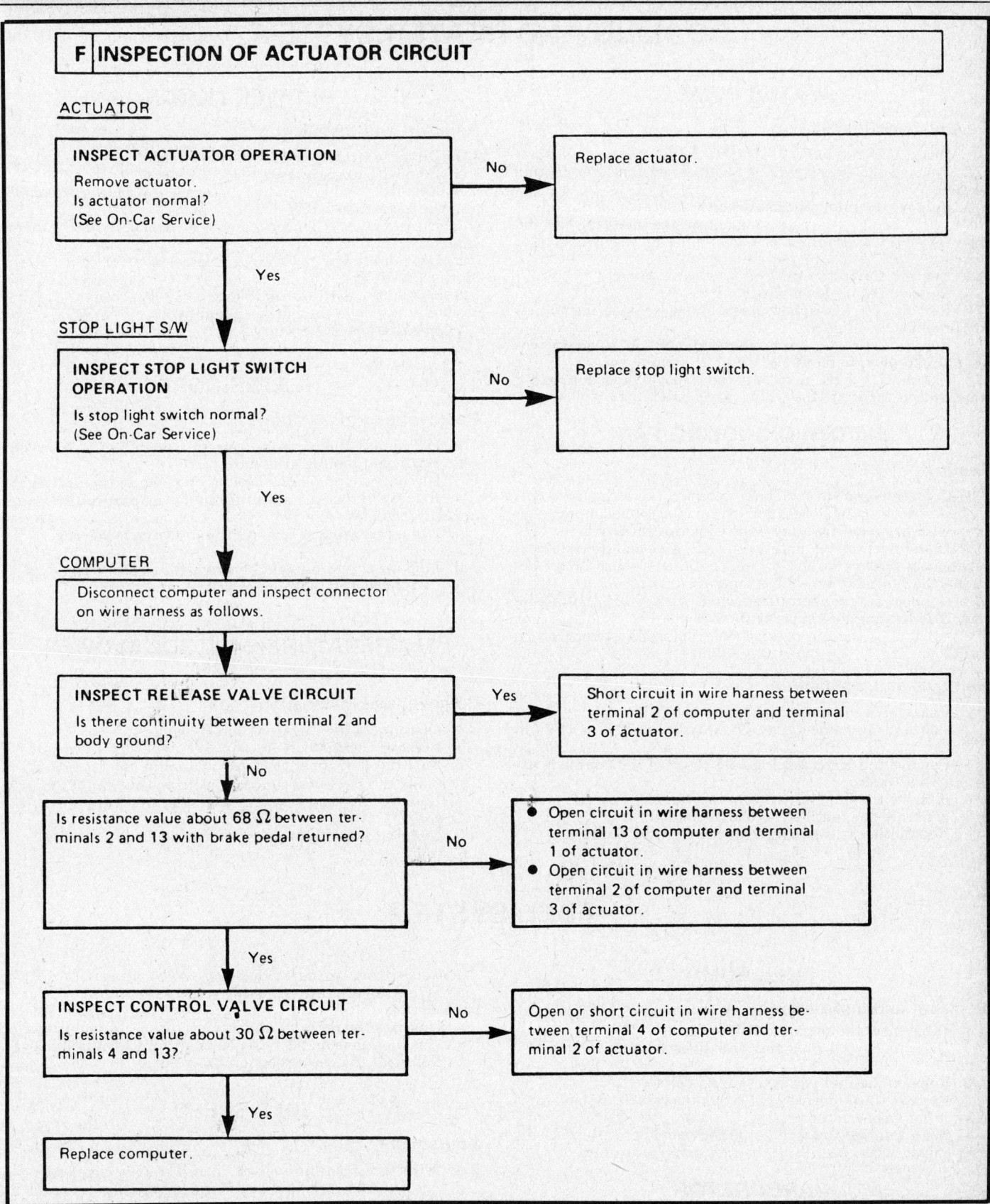

Cruise control troubleshooting

12–17

SECTION 12

GENERAL MOTORS—"S" BODY
CHEVROLET NOVA

COOLING AND HEATER SYSTEM

WATER PUMP

Removal and Installation

1. Disconnect the negative battery cable.
2. Remove the upper timing cover as outline later in this section.
3. Remove the inlet pipe mounting bolt located on the side of the engine. Remove the retaining nuts at the inlet pipe and the pipe "O" ring. Disconnect the inlet pipe at the water inlet housing.
4. Remove the inlet pipe from the water pump.
5. Remove the oil level gauge.
6. Remove the right splash shield and power steering adjusting bracket, if equipped.
7. Remove the water pump retaining bolts. Remove the water pump pulley. Remove the water pump and gasket.
8. Installation is the reverse of the removal procedure using a new gasket. Torque the water pump bolts to 11 ft. lbs.

ELECTRIC COOLING FAN

Testing

1. Turn the ignition switch on to confirm that the fan stops. If the fan doesn't stop, check for a separated connector or a severed wire between the relay and temperature switch.
2. Disconnect the temperature switch wire and check for fan rotation. If the fan doesn't rotate, check for a short circuit between the fan relay and the temperature switch.
3. Connect the temperature switch wire. Start the engine and raise the engine temperature to above 194°. Confirm that the fan runs. If the fan doesn't run, replace the temperature switch.

Removal and Installation

1. Disconnect the negative battery cable.
2. Tag and disconnect the electrical connector at the fan motor.
3. Remove the fan retaining bolt. Remove the fan blade assembly and spacer.
4. Remove the fan shroud from the vehicle.
5. Separate the fan blade from the motor.
6. Installation is the reverse of the removal procedure.

BLOWER MOTOR

Removal and Installation

1. Disconnect the negative battery cable.
2. Remove the glove box.
3. Remove the blower duct between the blower assembly and the heater assembly.
4. Disconnect the blower motor wire connector at the motor case.
5. Disconnect the air source selector control cable at the blower assembly.
6. Loosen the two nuts and the one bolt attaching the blower assembly. Remove the blower assembly.
7. Installation is the reverse of the removal procedure.

HEATER CORE

Removal and Installation

1. Disconnect the negative battery cable.
2. Drain the cooling system.
3. Disconnect the heater hose at the engine compartment.
4. Remove the clips retaining the lower part of the heater unit case. Remove the lower part of the case.
5. Use a screwdriver to carefully open the lower part of the case.
6. Remove the core assembly from the heater case.
7. Installation is the reverse of the removal procedure.

TEMPERATURE CONTROL/BLOWER SWITCH

Removal and Installation

1. Disconnect the negative battery cable.
2. Remove the instrument panel center cluster assembly.
3. Pull the instrument cluster assembly out far enough to disconnect the electrical connections from the rear of the unit.
4. Remove the temperature control/blower switch from the vehicle.
5. Installation is the reverse of the removal procedure.

FUEL SYSTEM

FUEL PUMP

Removal and Installation

1. Disconnect the negative battery cable.
2. Disconnect and plus the fuel lines leading to the fuel pump.
3. Remove the fuel pump retaining bolts.
4. Remove the pump assembly from the vehicle. Remove any remaining gasket material.
5. Installation is the reverse of the removal procedure. Use a new gasket when installing the fuel pump assembly.

CARBURETOR

Idle Mixture Adjustment

1. Remove the carburetor from the vehicle.
2. Remove the mixture adjusting screws plug.
3. Screw the mixture adjusting screw fully into the carburetor body.
4. Unscrew the mixture adjusting screw 3 $\frac{1}{4}$ revolutions for USA specifications and 2 $\frac{1}{2}$ revolutions for Canadian models.
5. Reinstall the carburetor on the vehicle.

IDLE SPEED

Adjustment

1. With the choke fully open, install the air cleaner.
2. All accessories should be off and all vacuum lines should be connected.
3. Make sure that the ignition timing is properly set according to the underhood emissions sticker.

GENERAL MOTORS—"S" BODY
CHEVROLET NOVA

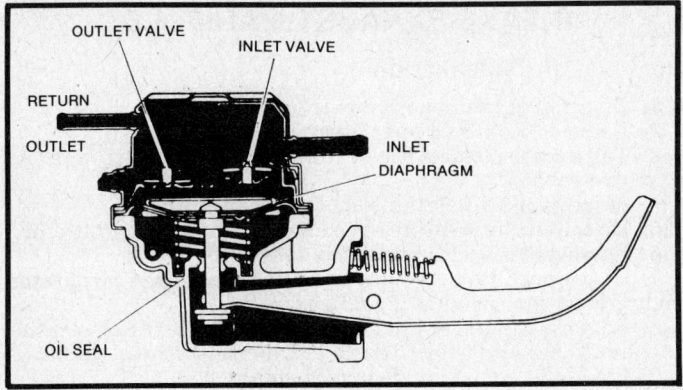

Fuel pump-cross section

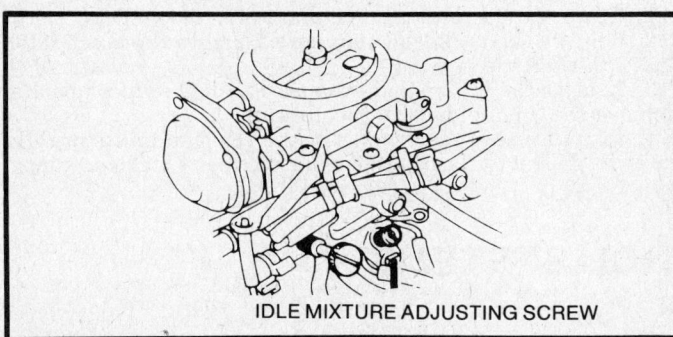

Idle mixture adjusting screw location

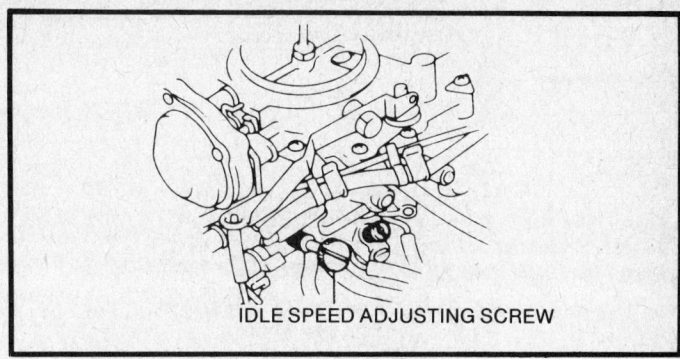

Idle speed adjusting screw location

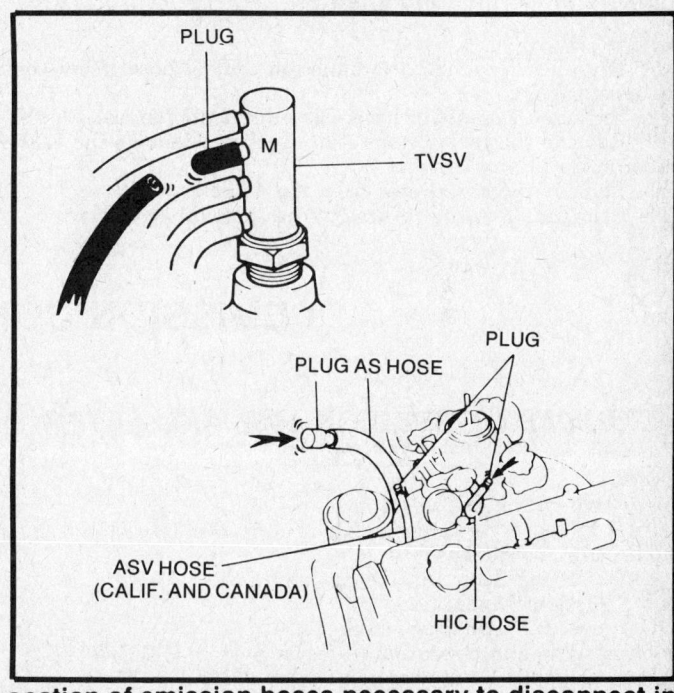

Location of emission hoses necessary to disconnect in order to set the fast idle speed

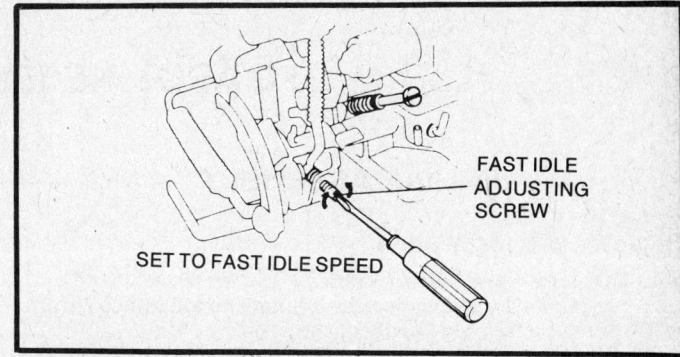

Fast idle speed adjusting screw location

4. Place the transmission in the "N" range with the wheels blocked securely.
5. Start the engine and allow it to reach normal operating temperature.
6. Fuel level should be centered in the carburetor sight glass.
7. Connect a tachometer according to manufacturers instructions.
8. Adjust the idle speed until it reaches: 650 rpm-manual transmission, 800 rpm-automatic transmission (1985), 750 rpm-automatic transmission (1986)

FAST IDLE SPEED

Adjustment

1. Stop the engine and remove the air cleaner.
2. Disconnect and plug the hot idle compensator hose in order to prevent rough idling.
3. Disconnect the hose from the Thermo Vacuum Switching Valve "M" port.
4. While holding the throttle slightly open, push the choke valve closed, and hold it closed while releasing the throttle valve.
5. Start the engine, but do not press the accelerator pedal.
6. Set the fast idle speed to 3000 rpm by turning the fast idle adjusting screw.

CARBURETOR

Removal and Installation

1. Disconnect the negative battery cable.
2. Disconnect the air intake hose. Tag and disconnect the emission control hoses from the air cleaner assembly.
3. Remove the air cleaner assembly from the vehicle.
4. Disconnect the accelerator cable from the carburetor.
5. Disconnect the throttle cable from the automatic transmission if equipped.
6. Disconnect the electrical connector for for the carburetor.

12-19

SECTION 12: GENERAL MOTORS—"S" BODY
CHEVROLET NOVA

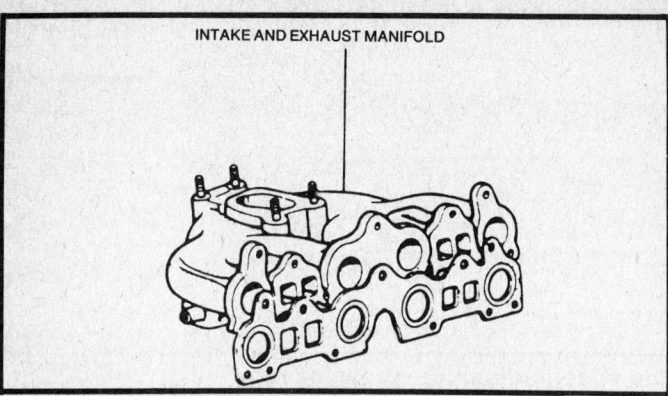

Intake and exhaust manifold

7. Tag and disconnect the emission control hoses from the carburetor body.
8. Remove the canister hose. Disconnect the fuel inlet hose.
9. Remove the carburetor retaining nuts. Remove the EGR vacuum modulator bracket.
10. Remove the carburetor from the vehicle.
11. Installation is the reverse of the removal procedure.

INTAKE/EXHAUST MANIFOLD

Removal and Installation

1. Disconnect the negative battery cable.
2. Remove the air cleaner assembly.
3. Tag and disconnect the vacuum hoses. Remove the throttle valve cable.
4. Remove the accelerator cable.
5. Disconnect any electrical connections at the carburetor.
6. Remove the fuel line at the fuel pump.
7. Disconnect the necessary vacuum hoses at the carburetor and remove the carburetor and gasket.
8. Remove the Early Fuel Evaporation gasket. Remove the vacuum line and dashpot bracket. Remove the heat shield.
9. Raise the vehicle and support safely.
10. Remove the exhaust pipe retaining bolt at the manifold. Remove the exhaust pipe. Remove the exhaust bracket located at the engine.
11. Remove the converter pipe and lower the vehicle.
12. Remove the brake vacuum hose. Remove the accelerator and throttle cable bracket.
13. Remove the intake and exhaust manifold retaining bolts. Remove the manifolds with the gaskets.
14. Installation is the reverse of the removal procedure. Be sure the gasket surfaces are clean and free of nicks or burrs.

EMISSION CONTROL SYSTEMS

EQUIPMENT USED ON 1985 AND LATER MODELS

Positive Crankcase Ventilation (PCV)
Fuel Evaporative Emission Control System (EVAP)
Throttle Positioner (TP)
Exhaust Gas Recirculation System (EGR)
Air Suction System (AS)
Carburetor Feedback System
Three Way and Oxidation Catalyst System (TWC-OC)
High Altitude Compensation System (HAC)
Automatic Hot Air Intake System (HAI)
Hot Idle Compensation System (HIC)
Automatic Choke System
Choke Breaker System (CB)
Choke Opener System
Auxiliary Acceleration Pump (AAP)
Deceleration Fuel Cut System
Heat Control Valve
Cold Mixture Heater System (CMH)

RESETTING TROUBLE INDICATORS

Recommended manufacturers procedure has not been established at the time of publication.

GASOLINE ENGINE SECTION

ENGINE ASSEMBLY

Removal and Installation

1. Disconnect the battery cables.
2. Scribe marks on the hood and hinges to aid in hood alignment during assembly. Remove the hood.
3. Drain the cooling system.
4. Drain the transmission fluid or gear oil.
5. Remove the air cleaner assembly.
6. Disconnect the upper radiator hose and the overflow hose. Disconnect the coolant hose at the cylinder head rear coolant pipe and thermostat housing.
7. Disconnect the fuel lines from the fuel pump.
8. Remove the accessory drive belts.
9. Tag and disconnect the electrical and vacuum connections from the engine. Disconnect the transaxle wiring and the speedometer cable.
10. Raise the vehicle and support safely.
11. Disconnect the exhaust pipe at the manifold. Disconnect the air hose at the converter pipe, if equipped.
12. Remove the transaxle cooler lines from the radiator.
13. Remove the under body splash shields.
14. If the vehicle is equipped with power steering, remove the pump assembly and wire out of the way.
15. Disconnect the A/C compressor, if equipped.
16. Disconnect the cable and bracket at the transaxle.
17. Remove the steering knuckles from the lower control arms.
18. Disconnect the drive shafts at the transaxle. Remove the flywheel cover.
19. Remove the flexplate-to-torque converter bolts.

GENERAL MOTORS—"S" BODY
CHEVROLET NOVA

20. Remove the front and rear mounting assemblies at the center member. Disconnect the cable and remove the center member.
21. Lower the vehicle.
22. Remove the radiator and fan assembly.
23. Install a suitable engine lifting device.
24. Remove the right hand motor mount through bolt.
25. Remove the left hand transaxle mount bolt and mount.
26. Lift the engine/transaxle assembly out of the vehicle. Place the engine in a suitable engine holding fixture.
29. Installation is the reverse of the removal procedure. Install and adjust the accessory drive belts. Adjust all transmission and carburetor linkages. Install and adjust the hood. Replenish the fluid levels in the engine, radiator and transmission before attempting to start the engine.

ENGINE MOUNTS

Removal and Installation

1. Disconnect the negative battery cable.
2. Raise the vehicle and support safely.
3. Loosen the engine mounting center and lower the vehicle. Install a suitable engine support fixture and remove the disconnect the engine mount at the engine.
4. Raise the engine in order to relieve engine weight from the mount.
5. Remove the engine mount from the vehicle.
6. Installation is the reverse of the removal procedure.

Valve System

VALVES

Adjustment

1. Start the engine and allow it to reach normal operating temperature.
2. Stop the engine. Remove the air cleaner assembly. Remove any other hoses or cables which are attached to or in the way of the cylinder head cover. Remove the cylinder head cover.
3. Turn the crankshaft until the point or notch on the pulley aligns with the "O" or "T" mark on the timing scale. This will insure that the engine is at top dead center.
4. Retighten the cylinder head bolts to the proper torque specification. Retighten the valve rocker support bolts.
5. Using a flat feeler gauge, check the clearance between the bottom of the rocker arm and the top of the valve stem. Check only the valves listed under "First" in the accompanying valve arrangement illustration.
6. If the valves are not within specification, loosen the locknut on the end of the rocker arm and, still holding the nut with an open end wrench turn the adjustment nut to achieve the proper clearance.
7. Once the correct valve clearance is achieved, keep the adjustment screw from turning using a screwdriver. Tighten the locknut. Recheck the valve clearance.
8. Turn the engine one complete revolution (360°) and adjust the remaining valves. Follow Steps 5–7 and use the valve arrangement illustration marked "Second."
9. Using a new gasket, install the cylinder head cover. Install any other components which were removed in Step 2.

VALVE LIFTERS

Removal and Installation

1. Disconnect the negative battery cable. Drain the cooling system.
2. Remove the air cleaner assembly with the accompanying hoses.

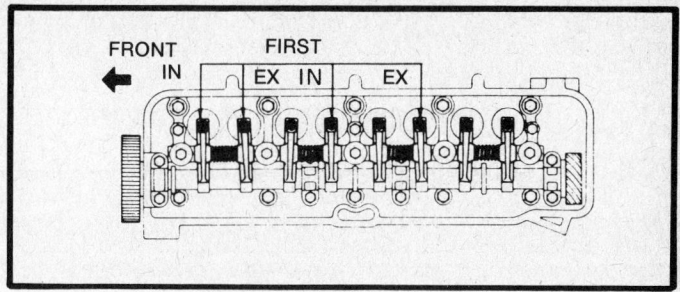

Adjust these valves first

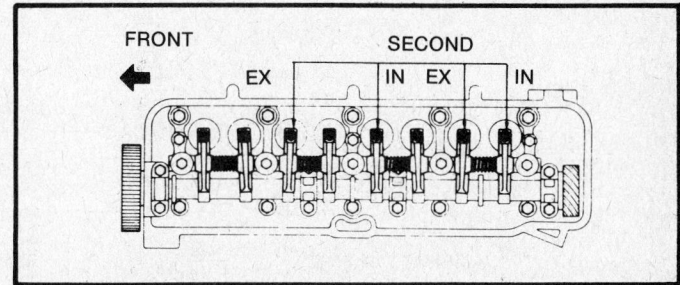

Adjust these valves second

3. Tag and disconnect the vacuum lines which run from the vacuum switching valve to the various emission control devices mounted on the cylinder head.
4. Unfasten the water hose clamps and remove the hoses from the water pump. Remove the water valve. Detach the heater temperature control cable from the water valve.
5. Detach the water temperature sender wiring.
6. Remove the choke stove pipe. Remove the intake pipe.
7. Remove the PCV hose from the intake manifold.
8. Tag and disconnect the fuel and vacuum lines from the carburetor if necessary to gain working room.
9. Remove the cylinder head cover.
10. Remove the valve rocker support retaining bolts and nuts. Lift out the valve rocker assembly.
11. Remove the pushrods. Remove the cylinder head retaining bolts.
12. Remove the cylinder head assembly. Lift out the valve lifters.
13. Installation is the reverse of the removal procedure.

VALVE ROCKER ASSEMBLY

Removal and Installation

1. Disconnect the negative battery cable. Drain the cooling system.
2. Remove the air cleaner assembly with the accompanying hoses.
3. Tag and disconnect the vacuum lines which run from the vacuum switching valve to the various emission control devices mounted on the cylinder head.
4. Unfasten the water hose clamps and remove the hoses from the water pump. Remove the water valve.
5. Detach the water temperature sender wiring.
6. Remove the choke stove pipe. Remove the intake pipe.
7. Remove the PCV hose from the intake manifold.
8. Tag and disconnect the fuel and vacuum lines from the carburetor if necessary to gain working room.
9. Remove the cylinder head cover.
10. Remove the valve rocker support retaining bolts and nuts. Lift out the valve rocker assembly.

Section 12: GENERAL MOTORS—"S" BODY
CHEVROLET NOVA

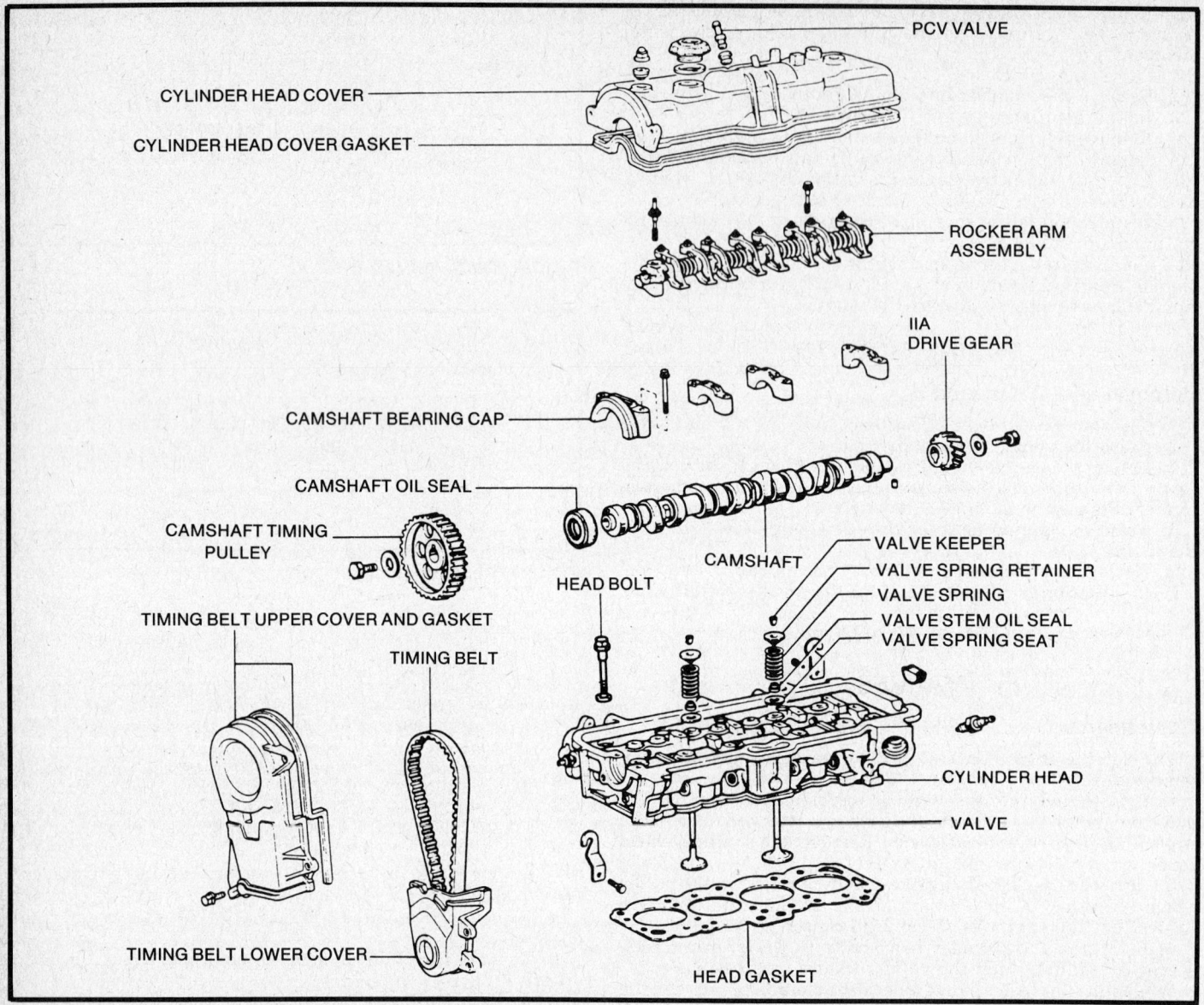

Cylinder head and related components-exploded view

11. Installation is the reverse of the removal procedure. Use a new gasket when installing the valve cover assembly.

VALVE TIMING

Adjustment

1. Warm up the engine and set the parking brake. Check the engine idle speed and adjust if necessary to the specifications.
2. Connect a timing light to the engine as outlined in the instructions supplied by the manufacturer of the light.
3. Disconnect the vacuum line from the distributor vacuum unit and plug the line. If a vacuum advance retard distributor is used, plug both vacuum lines from the distributor.
4. Allow the engine to run at idle speed with the gear shift in "Neutral" for vehicles with manual transmissions, and in "D" for vehicles with automatics. Be sure that the drive wheels of the vehicle are securely blocked and that the parking brake is firmly applied.
5. Point the timing light at the timing marks. With the engine at idle, the timing should be at the specification given in the tune up chart. If not, loosen the pinch bolt at the base of the distributor and rotate the distributor to advance or retard the timing as required.
6. Stop the engine and tighten the pinch bolt. Start the engine and recheck the timing.
7. Stop the engine and disconnect the timing light and the tachometer is used. Connect the vacuum lines.

CYLINDER HEAD

Removal and Installation

1. Disconnect the negative battery cable.
2. Drain the cooling system.
3. Remove the air cleaner assembly.
4. Raise the vehicle and support safely. Drain the engine oil.
5. Remove the exhaust pipe at the manifold and the bracket from the engine.
6. Remove the hose at the converter pipe.

GENERAL MOTORS—"S" BODY
CHEVROLET NOVA

7. If the vehicle is equipped with power steering, loosen the pivot bolt and remove the adjusting bracket. Lower the vehicle.
8. Remove the accelerator and throttle cable at the carburetor and bracket. 9. Disconnect the wires from the cowl, distributor and oxygen sensor. Disconnect the vacuum hoses.
10. Remove the fuel lines from the fuel pump.
11. Remove the upper radiator hose. Remove the Remove the water outlet at the head. Remove the heater hose.
12. Tag and disconnect the spark plug wires from the distributor and remove the distributor. Remove the PCV valve.
13. Remove the upper timing cover bolts.
14. Remove the cylinder head cover and gasket.
15. Remove the alternator belt.
16. Remove the water pump pulley bolts.
17. Remove the upper timing cover and gasket.
18. Mark the position of the crankshaft timing pulley and the timing belt rotational direction.
19. Loosen the idler pulley, and reposition in order to release timing belt tension. Tighten the pulley bolt slightly.
20. Pull the timing belt away from the camshaft timing pulley.
21. Loosen the head bolts gradually in three passes in the numerical order shown.

CAUTION
Head warpage and/or cracking could result from removing in an incorrect manner.

---

22. Remove the cylinder head with the intake and exhaust manifold.
23. Installation is the reverse of the removal procedure.

CAMSHAFT

Removal and Installation

1. Disconnect the negative battery cable.
2. Remove the air cleaner assembly along with the accompanying emission hoses.
3. Remove the cylinder head cover. Discard the used gasket material.
4. Drain the coolant system. Loosen the water pump pulley bolts.
5. Remove the alternator belt.
6. Raise the vehicle and support safely.
7. Remove the power steering pivot bolt, if equipped. Remove the bolts that pass through the upper and lower timing covers.
8. Lower the vehicle and remove the power steering belt, if equipped.
9. Disconnect the coolant pump pulley and remove the upper radiator hose at the outlet.
10. Remove the upper timing cover.
11. Tag and disconnect the spark plug wires, electrical connections and vacuum hoses from the distributor. Remove the distributor.
12. Disconnect the fuel pump lines and remove the fuel pump.
13. Remove the distributor gear bolt. Remove the rocker arm assembly.
14. Turn the crankshaft clockwise and set the number one piston at TDC.

NOTE: If the rocker arms on the number one piston are not loose, turn the crankshaft one full turn.

15. Matchmark the camshaft timing pulley and belt. Loosen the idler pulley bolt and push the idler pulley as far as possible to the left and temporarily tighten it.

NOTE: The belt must be held securely in order for the crankshaft timing pulley and timing belt not to shift.

16. Remove the camshaft bearing caps. Remove the camshaft. Remove the distributor drive gear.
17. Installation is the reverse of the removal procedure.

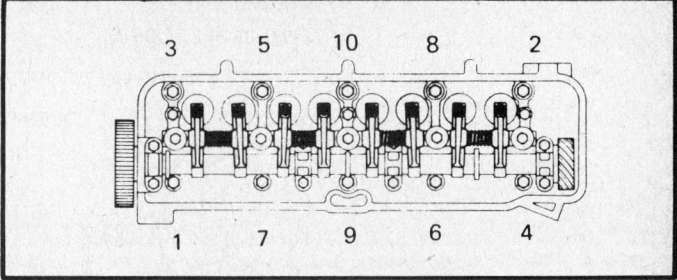
Cylinder head bolt removal sequence

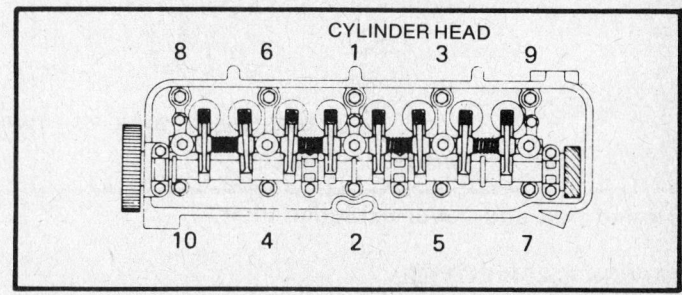
Cylinder head bolt tightening sequence

PISTON AND ROD POSITIONING

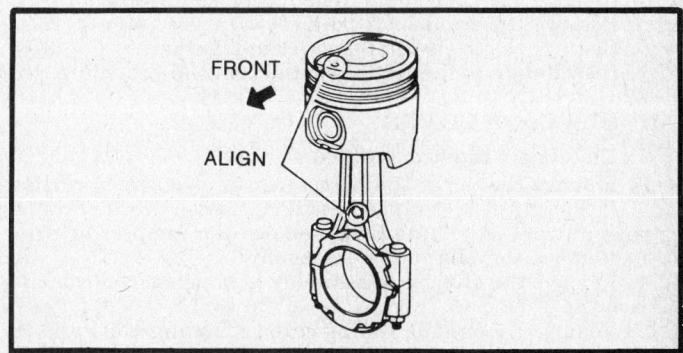
Piston and rod positioning

TIMING CASE COVER

NOTE: The timing belt cover is three individual covers with each one having its own gasket and removal and installation procedure as outlined below.

Removal and Installation

UPPER CASE COVER

1. Disconnect the negative battery cable.
2. Loosen the coolant pump pulley bolts. Remove the alternator belt.
3. Remove the power steering belt, if equipped.
4. Disconnect the coolant pump pulley. Drain the cooling system.
5. Disconnect the upper radiator hose.
6. Tag and disconnect the necessary vacuum hoses in order to gain working clearance. Remove the top bolts on the upper timing cover.
7. Raise the vehicle and support safely.
8. Remove the lower bolts on the cover. Lower the vehicle and remove the cover.
9. Installation is the reverse of the removal procedure.

12-23

SECTION 12

GENERAL MOTORS—"S" BODY
CHEVROLET NOVA

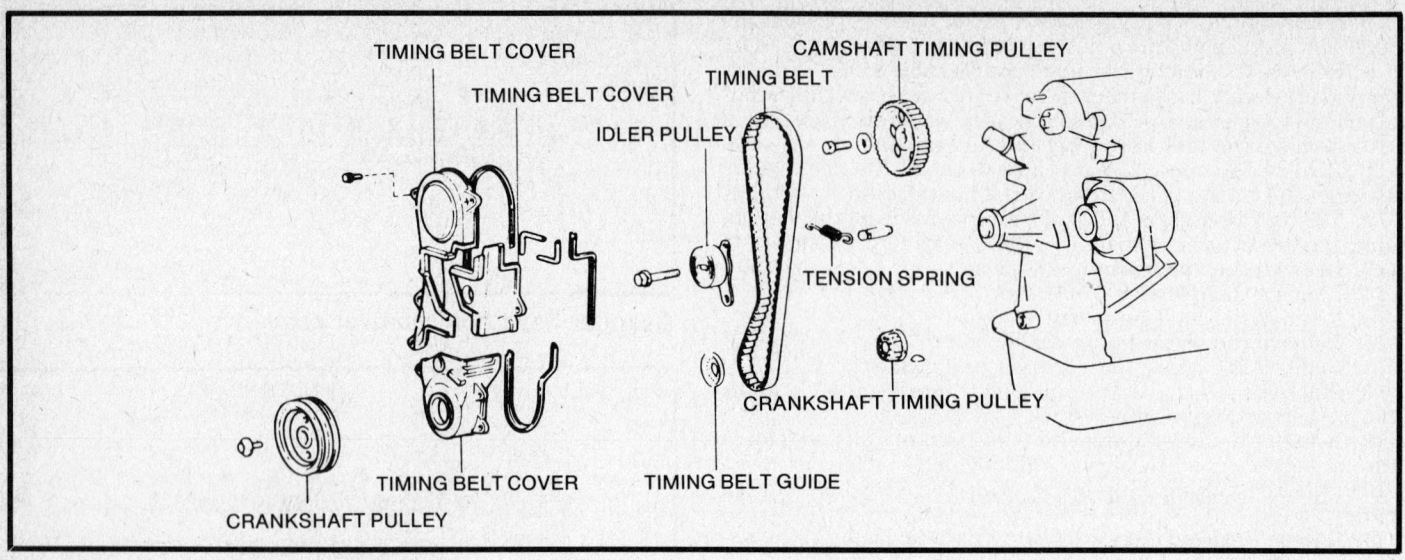

Timing belt and cover-exploded view

LOWER CASE COVER

1. Disconnect the negative battery cable.
2. Remove the alternator belt. Remove the A/C belt, if equipped.
3. Raise the vehicle and support safely.
4. Remove the right hand under cover and flywheel cover.
5. Remove the crankshaft pulley.
6. Remove the lower timing cover and gasket.
7. Installation is the reverse of the removal procedure.

MIDDLE CASE COVER

1. Disconnect the negative battery cable.
2. Remove the upper timing case cover as outlined earlier.
3. If the vehicle is equipped with A/C, loosen the idler pulley mount nut and adjusting bolt. Remove the compressor drive belt. Remove the idler pulley assembly.
4. Remove the alternator assembly in order to gain working clearance.
5. Remove the middle timing cover retaining bolts and remove the cover and gasket.
6. Installation is the reverse of the removal procedure.

TIMING GEARS AND BELT

Removal and Installation

1. Disconnect the negative battery cable.
2. Drain the coolant system. Loosen the coolant pump pulley bolts.
3. Remove the alternator belt and the power steering belt, if equipped.
4. Remove the coolant pump pulley.
5. If the vehicle is equipped with air conditioning, remove the idler pulley mount assembly and drive belt.
6. Raise the vehicle and support safely.
7. Remove the right side splash shield and flywheel cover. Remove the crankshaft pulley.
8. Remove the lower timing case cover. Disconnect the center engine mounting bracket.
9. Lower the vehicle and disconnect the upper radiator hose.
10. Tag and disconnect the necessary vacuum hoses in order to gain working clearance.
11. Remove the upper timing cover.
12. Tag and disconnect the wiring from the alternator. Remove the alternator assembly.
13. Remove the remaining timing cover. Support the engine using a suitable support fixture.
14. Set the number one piston to TDC.
15. Disconnect the right side engine mount.
16. Loosen the idler pulley in order to relieve timing belt tension. Lower the engine and remove the timing belt.

NOTE: If the same timing belt is to be used upon installation, mark the location of the belt and pulleys before removing.

17. Installation is the reverse of the removal procedure.

LUBRICATION

OIL PAN

Removal and Installation

1. Disconnect the negative battery cable. Raise the vehicle and support safely.
2. Drain the engine oil from the oil pan.
3. Remove the right side under cover.
4. Remove the oil pan nuts and bolts.
5. Separate the oil pan from the cylinder block.
6. When removing the oil pan, be careful not to bend or distort the pan flange.
7. Installation is the reverse of the removal procedure. Use a new oil pan gasket upon installation.

GENERAL MOTORS—"S" BODY
CHEVROLET NOVA

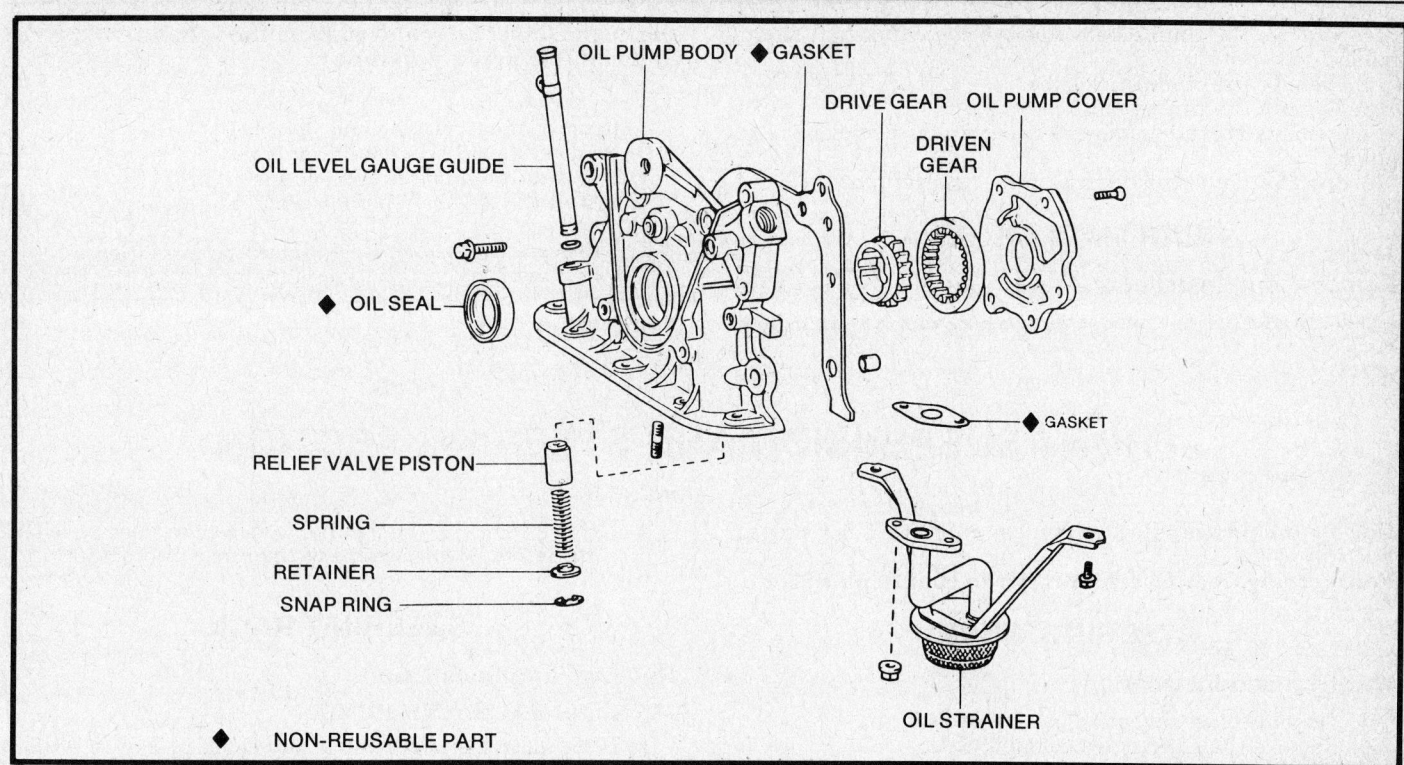

Oil pump-exploded view

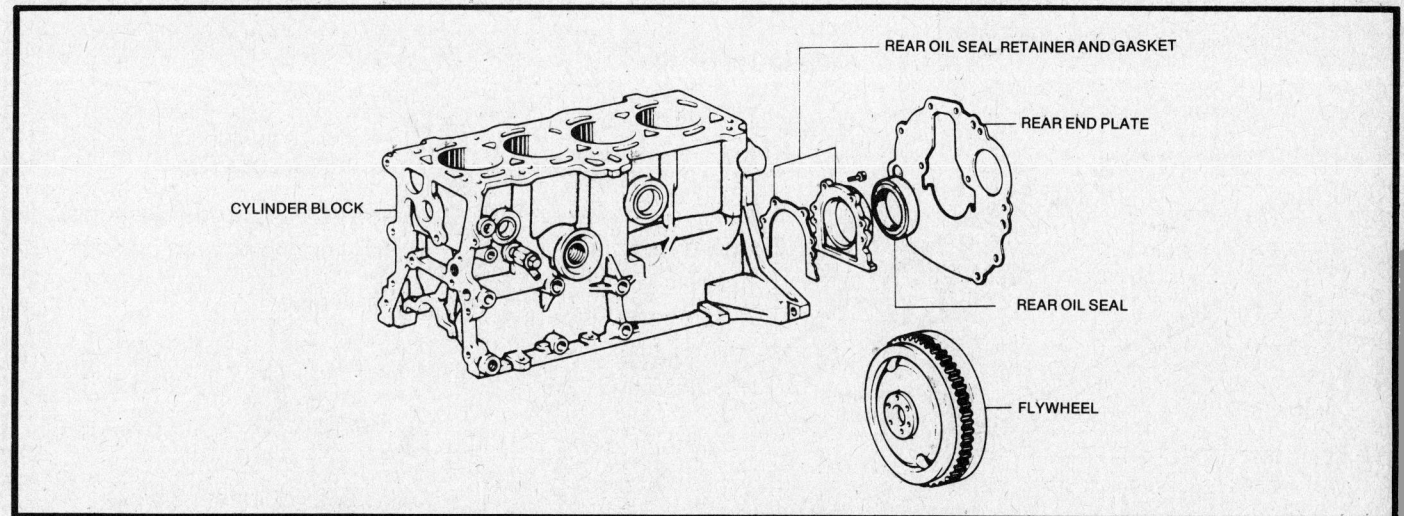

Cylinder block with exploded view of rear main oil seal placement

OIL PUMP

Removal and Installation

1. Disconnect the negative battery cable. Drain the cooling system.
2. Remove the oil strainer and loosen the water pump pulley bolts.
3. Remove the alternator drive belt and power steering belt if equipped.
4. If the vehicle is equipped wit A/C, loosen the A/C idler pulley mount and remove the A/C belt. Remove the idler pulley.
5. Loosen the alternator retaining bolts and position the alternator to one side.
6. Disconnect the water pump pulley. Remove the upper radiator hose from the outlet.
7. Tag and disconnect the necessary vacuum hoses in order to gain working clearance.
8. Remove the upper and middle timing case covers as outlined earlier.
9. Position the number one piston to TDC.
10. Raise the vehicle and support safely.
11. Remove the right side under cover and flywheel cover. Remove the crankshaft pulley.
12. Matchmark the crankshaft and camshaft timing pulleys and timing belt direction.
13. Loosen the idler pulley bolt and slide the pulley in order to relieve belt tension. Tighten the pulley bolt.

12–25

SECTION 12
GENERAL MOTORS—"S" BODY
CHEVROLET NOVA

14. Remove the timing belt. Remove the crankshaft timing pulley.
15. Remove the oil dipstick tube.
16. Remove the timing belt idler pulley.
17. Remove the oil pump retaining bolts. Remove the oil pump.
18. Installation is the reverse of the removal procedure.

REAR MAIN OIL SEAL

Removal and Installation

NOTE: Before the above procedure can be attempted, the engine must be removed from the vehicle and placed in a suitable holding fixture.

1. Remove the transaxle and flywheel.
2. Remove the oil seal retaining plate.
3. Use a suitable tool to remove the oil seal.
4. Install the new seal being careful not to distort the seal when seating.
5. Lubricate the seal lips using multipurpose grease.
6. The remaining installation is the reverse of the removal procedure. Check engine oil level and start engine inspecting for leaks.

FRONT SUSPENSION AND STEERING SECTION

For Front Suspension services, refer to Unit Repair Section
For Steering Gear Overhaul, refer to Unit Repair Section

STEERING WHEEL

Removal and Installation

1. Disconnect the negative battery cable.
2. Remove the steering wheel trim pad.
3. Remove the steering wheel retaining nut.
4. Using a steering wheel puller, remove the steering wheel.
5. Installation is the reverse of the removal procedure.

STEERING RACK

Removal and Installation
MANUAL RACK AND PINION

1. Disconnect the negative battery cable.
2. Remove the intermediate shaft cover.

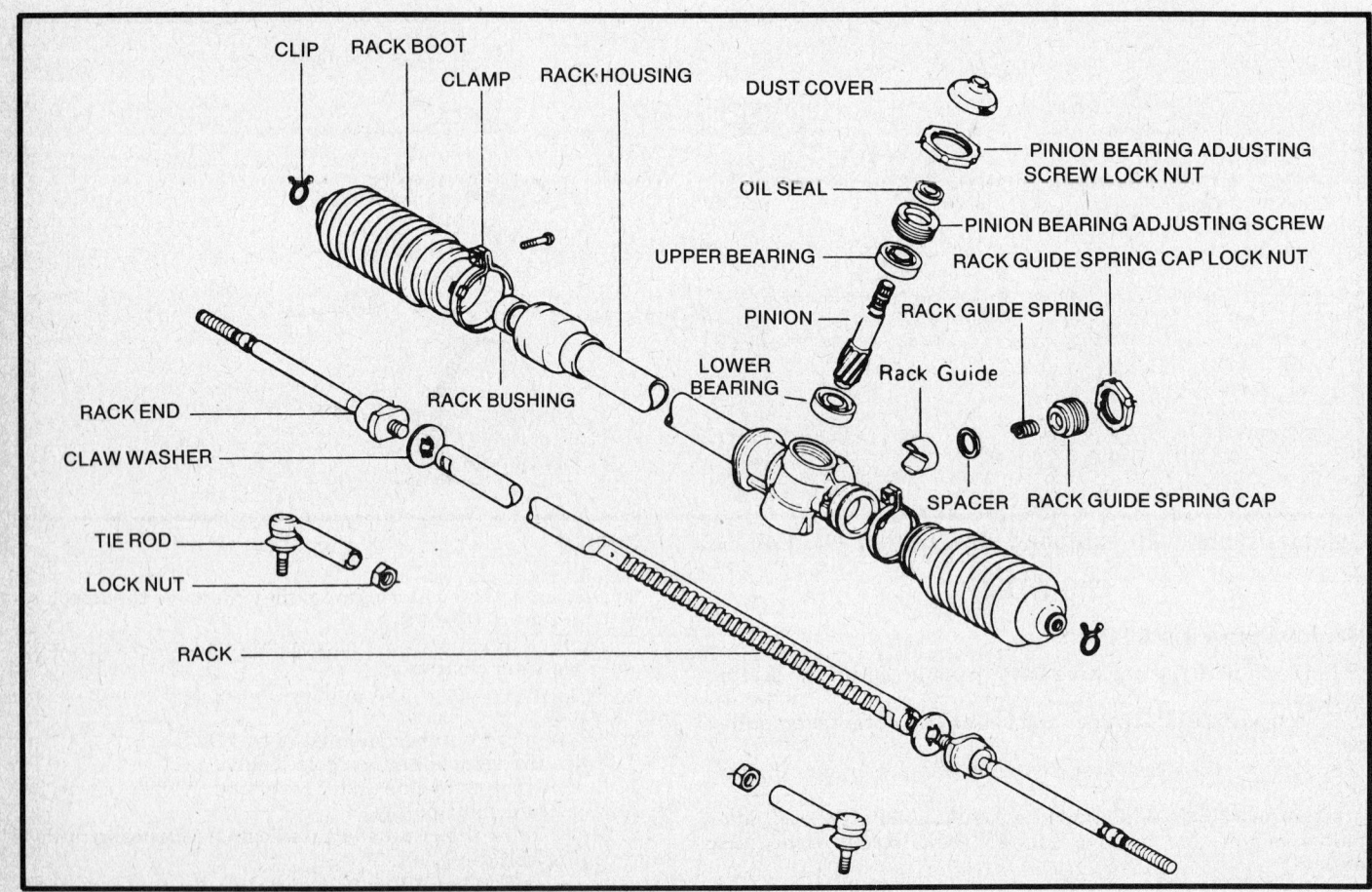

Manual steering rack housing—exploded view

GENERAL MOTORS—"S" BODY
CHEVROLET NOVA
SECTION 12

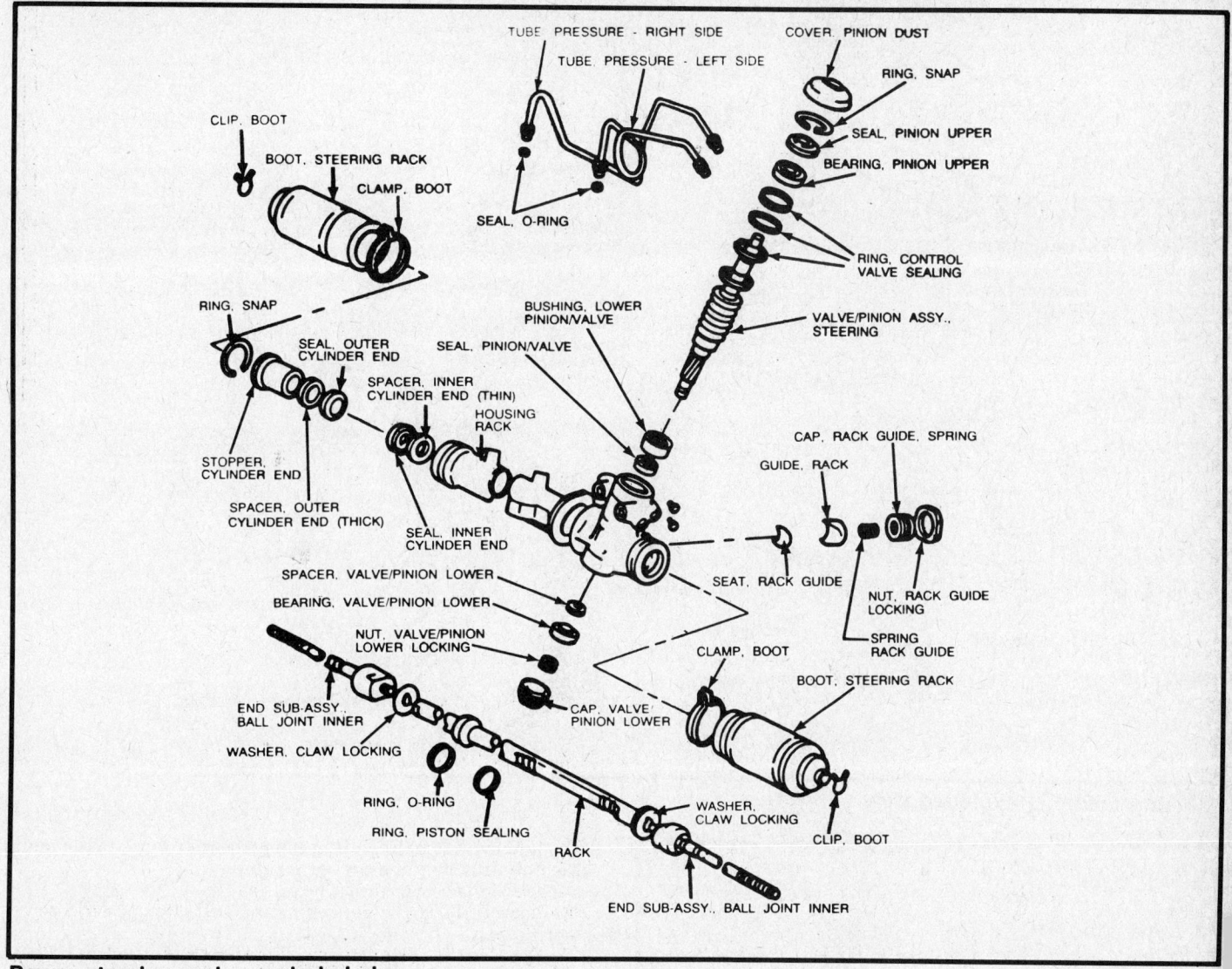

Power steering rack—exploded view

3. Loosen the upper pinch bolt. Remove the lower pinch bolt from the pinion shaft.
4. Raise the vehicle and support safely. Remove the wheel and tire assemblies.
5. Remove the cotter pins from the tie rod ends. Remove both tie rod ends from the steering knuckles.
6. Remove the steering gear to body mounting bolts.
7. Remove the rack and pinion assembly through the access hole.
8. Installation is the reverse of the removal procedure.

POWER RACK AND PINION

1. Disconnect the negative battery cable.
2. Remove the intermediate shaft protector. Remove the lower intermediate shaft pinch bolts.
3. Place a drain pan below the gear assembly in order to catch fluid.
4. Raise the vehicle and support safely. Remove the wheel and tire assemblies.
5. Remove the tie rod ends from the knuckles. Support the transaxle using a suitable fixture.
6. Remove the rear center engine mounting member bolts. Remove the rear engine mount bracket attaching nut and bolt.
7. Raise and lower the rear of the transaxle in order to gain access to the steering gear to body attaching bolts and nuts.
8. Disconnect the pressure and return lines at the steering gear.
9. Remove the gear to body mounting bolts and nuts.
10. Remove the steering gear assembly through the access hole.
11. Installation is the reverse of the removal procedure. Add fluid, check for leaks and bleed the system.

FRONT WHEEL BEARINGS

Removal and Installation

1. Raise and support the front of the vehicle safely.
2. Remove the wheel and tire assemblies.
3. Remove the brake caliper and wire it out of the way to gain access to the bearing assembly.
4. Remove the bearing cap, cotter pin, locknut and nut.
5. Installation is the reverse of the removal procedure. Torque the caliper bolts to 65 ft. lbs. and the bearing locknut to 137 ft. lbs.

12-27

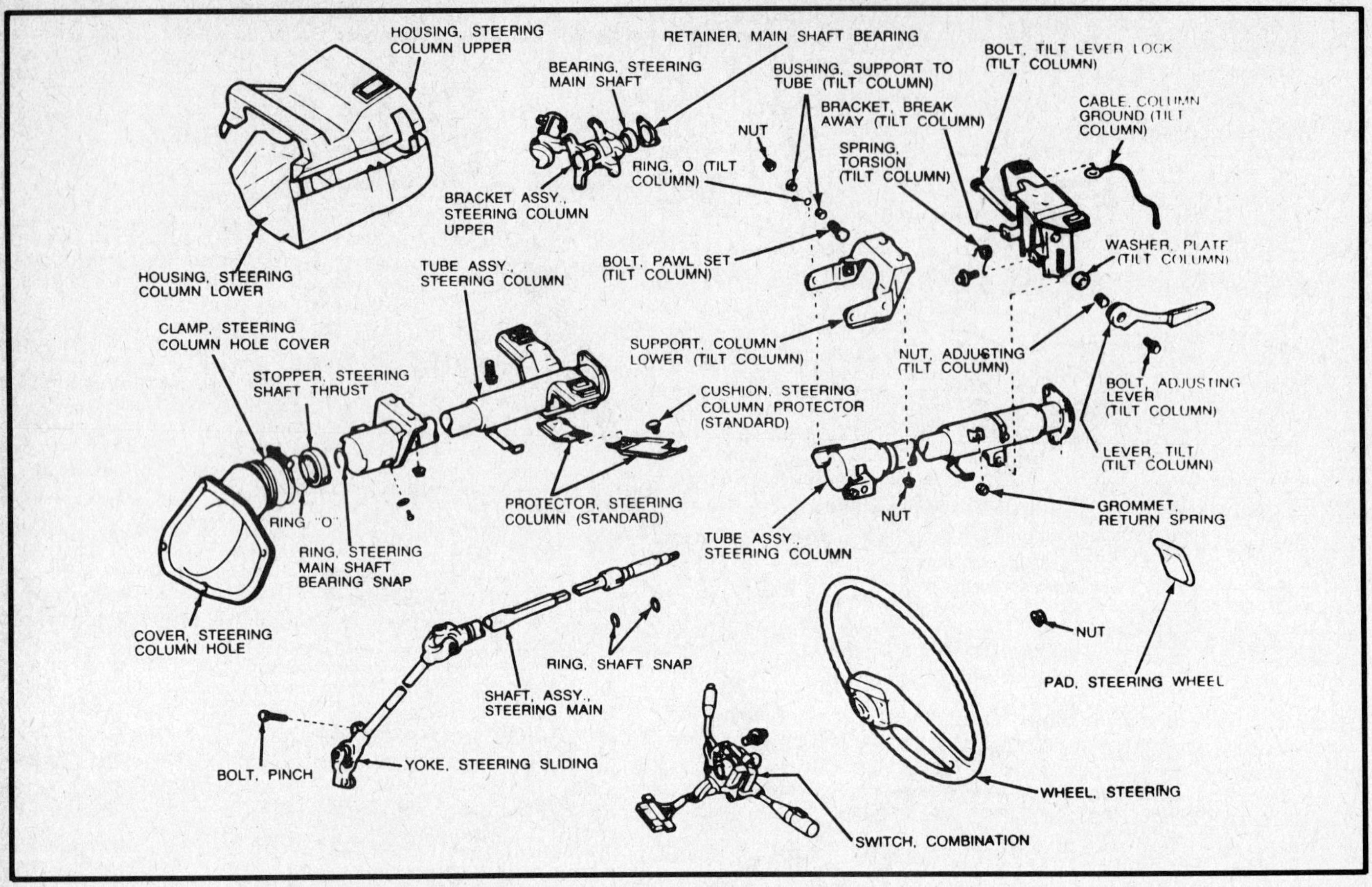

Section 12: GENERAL MOTORS—"S" BODY
CHEVROLET NOVA

Steering column—exploded view

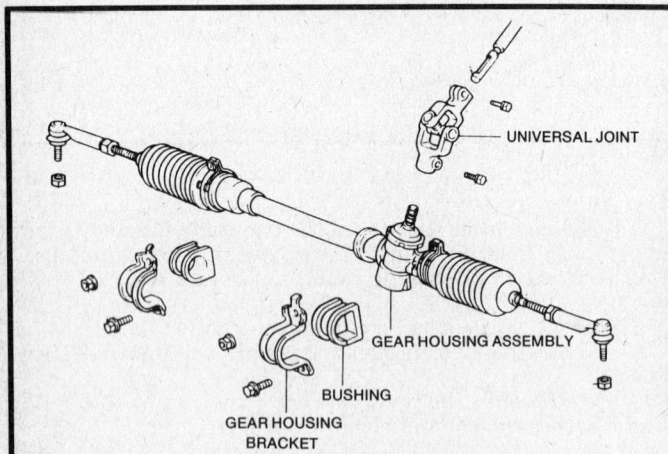

Steering rack mounting bracket location

POWER STEERING PUMP

Removal and Installation

1. Drain the fluid from the reservoir. This can be accomplished by using a syringe or other similar device.
2. Remove the bolt holding the pressure tubing to the pump assembly. Remove the pressure tubing.
3. Disconnect the return hose.
4. Loosen the drive belt adjusting bolt. Remove the power steering belt.
5. Remove the power steering pump retaining bolts and nuts from the brackets.
6. Remove the power steering pump.
7. Installation is the reverse of the removal procedure. Bleed the air from the system.

STEERING COLUMN

Removal and Installation

1. Disconnect the negative battery cable.
2. Remove the two set bolts securing the universal joint to the jack housing and the steering column shaft. Remove the universal joint.
3. Remove the steering wheel as outlined earlier.
4. Remove the lower instrument panel trim cover. Remove the lower steering column trim cover.
5. Tag and disconnect the electrical connector for the ignition switch.
6. Remove the upper steering column cover. Remove the switch assembly.
7. Remove the steering column mounting bolts.
8. Remove the steering column from the vehicle.
9. Installation is the reverse of the removal procedure.

12-28

GENERAL MOTORS—"S" BODY
CHEVROLET NOVA
SECTION 12

BRAKE SECTION

For Brake Service, refer to Unit Repair Section

MASTER CYLINDER

Removal and Installation

NOTE: **Be careful not to spill brake fluid on the painted surfaces of the vehicle; it will damage the paint.**

1. Disconnect the negative battery cable. Disconnect the brake level warning switch connector.
2. Drain the brake fluid from the master cylinder.
3. Remove the two brake lines from the master cylinder. Plug the ends.
4. Remove the masster cylinder retaining nuts. Remove the master cylinder.
5. Installation is the reverse of the removal procedure. Bleed the brake system.

PARKING BRAKE

Adjustment

1. Check that the parking brake is in need of adjustment. To do this release the lever and pull the lever up slowly counting the number of clicks heard. The proper number of clicks should be between 4–7.
2. If the brake needs adjusting, remove the console.
3. Loosen the lock nut and turn the adjusting nut until the travel is correct.

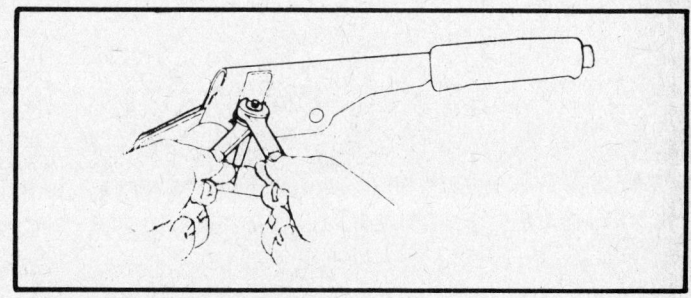

Adjusting lock nut location

4. Tighten the lock nut. Install the console.

PARKING BRAKE CABLE

Removal and Installation

1. Release the parking brake lever. Remove the console. Remove the parking brake lock nut. Remove the cable from the parking brake lever.
2. Raise and support the vehicle safely.
3. Remove the attaching clips from the parking brake cable.
4. Disconnect the cable from the rear brake assembly.
5. Remove the brake cable assembly from the vehicle.
6. Installation is the reverse of the removal procedure. Adjust the parking brake as required.

CLUTCH, TRANSMISSION AND DRIVESHAFT SECTION

For Overhaul Procedures, refer to Unit Repair Section

CLUTCH PEDAL

Adjustment

1. Check that the pedal height is adjusted properly. Pedal height should be 5.650–6.043 in. (143.5–153.5mm).
2. If adjustment is necessary, remove the lower dash assembly trim panel.
3. Loosen the lock nut and turn the stopper nut until the correct pedal height is reached.

PEDAL FREEPLAY

Adjustment

1. Depress the clutch pedal until the beginning of clutch resistance is felt. Pedal freeplay should be 0.51–0.91 in. (13–23mm).
2. If adjustment is necessary, loosen the lock nut and turn the pushrod until the pedal freeplay is correct.
3. Tighten the lock nut.
4. Check the pedal height, Install any trim panels which may have to have been removed in order to gain access to the lock nut.

CLUTCH ASSEMBLY

Removal and Installation

1. Remove the transaxle.

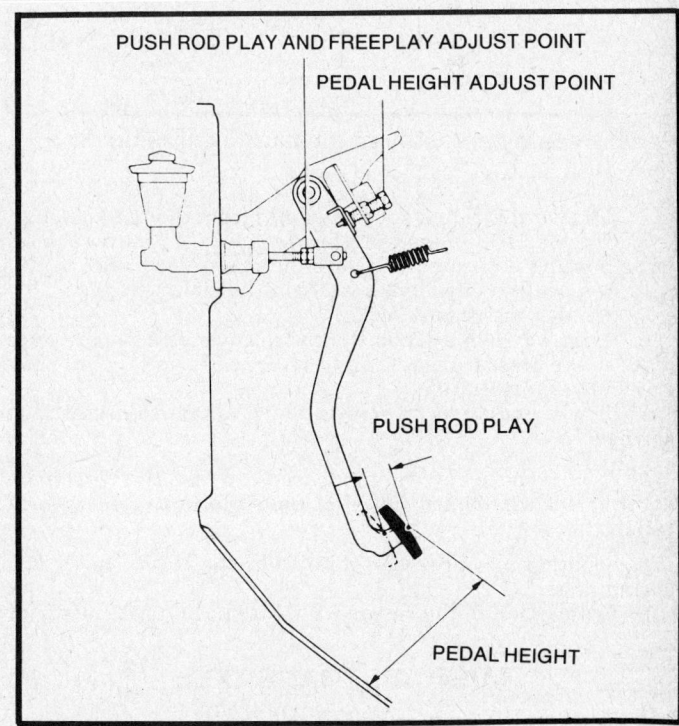

Clutch pedal adjusting points

SECTION 12

GENERAL MOTORS—"S" BODY
CHEVROLET NOVA

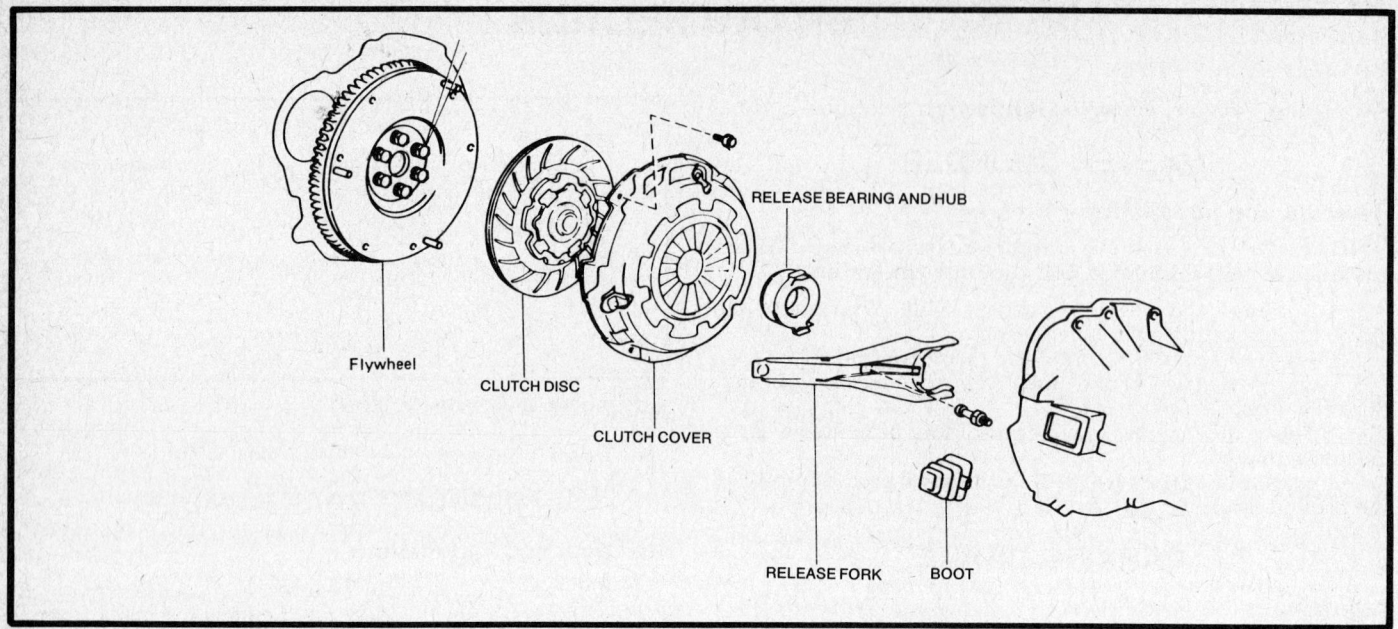

Clutch assembly-exploded view

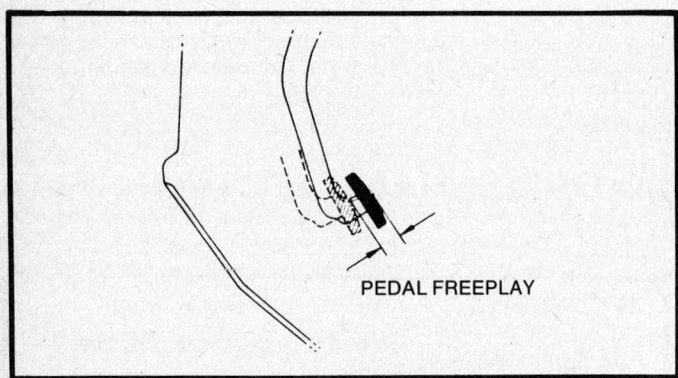

Pedal freeplay adjustment measurement location

2. Remove the clutch cover and disc from the bellhousing.
3. Unfasten the release fork bearing clips. Withdraw the release bearing hub, complete with the release bearing.
4. Remove the tension spring from the clutch linkage.
5. Remove the release fork.
6. Punch matchmarks on the clutch cover and the pressure plate so the pressure plate can be returned to its original position during installation.
7. Slowly unfasten the screws which attach the retracting springs.

NOTE: If the screws are released too fast, the clutch assembly will fly apart, causing possible injury or loss of parts.

8. Separate the pressure plate from the clutch cover and spring assembly.
9. Installation is the reverse of the removal procedure.

MANUAL TRANSAXLE

Removal and Installation

1. Disconnect the negative battery cable.
2. Remove the air inlet tube and disconnect the speedometer cable.
3. From the transaxle, disconnect the ground wire and the thermostat housing.
4. Disconnect the clutch slave cylinder and lay aside.
5. Disconnect the clutch cables and the back up light switch.
6. Remove the two upper bellhousing bolts. Remove the upper transaxle mounting bolt.
7. Install a suitable engine supporting fixture.
8. Raise the vehicle and support safely.
9. Remove the left wheel and tire assembly.
10. Remove the left, center and right splash shield.
11. Remove the center vehicle beam. Remove the inspection cover.
12. Remove both lower control arms from the spindles. Remove the right and left axle shafts at the transaxle.
13. Remove the starter assembly.
14. While supporting the transaxle with a suitable fixture, remove the three backside engine to transaxle bolts.
15. Remove the one remaining mounting bolt.
16. Remove the transaxle from the vehicle.
17. Installation is the reverse of the removal procedure.

SHIFT QUANDRANT POINTER

Removal and Installation

The factory procedure for removal and installation of the shift quandrant pointer has not been established by the manufacturer at the time of publication.

AUTOMATIC TRANSAXLE

Removal and Installation

1. Disconnect the negative battery cable.
2. Remove the air cleaner assembly.
3. Disconnect the neutral start switch.
4. Disconnect the speedometer cable.
5. Remove the thermostat housing from the transaxle. Remove the ground cable.
6. Remove the upper mounting bracket bolt.

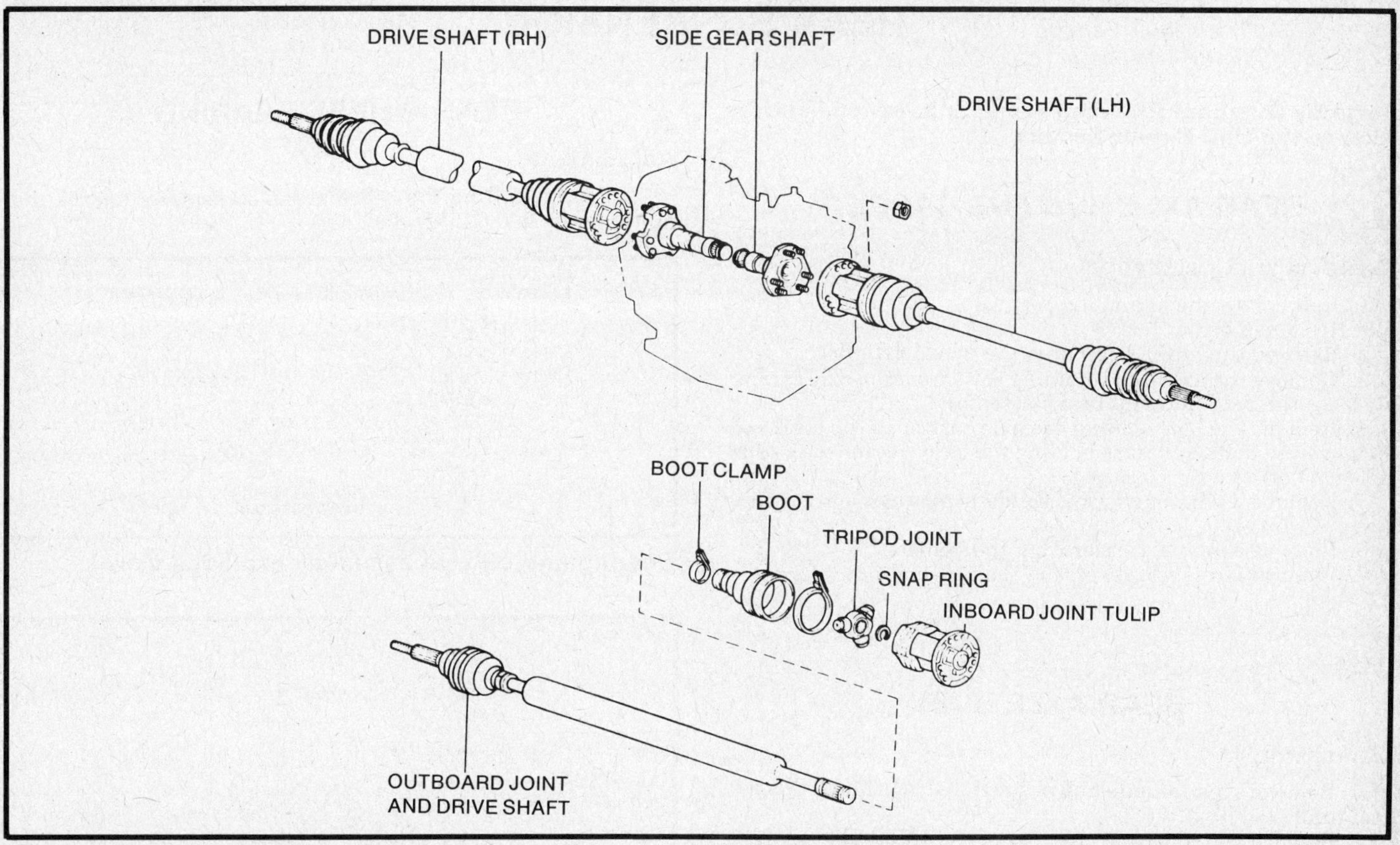

GENERAL MOTORS—"S" BODY
CHEVROLET NOVA

Front drive axle-exploded view

7. Tag and disconnect any necessary electrical connections in order to gain working clearance.
8. Remove the T.V. cable at the carburetor.
9. Remove the upper bellhousing bolts.
10. Support the engine using a suitable fixture. Raise and support the vehicle safely.
11. Remove the left wheel and tire assembly. Remove the splash shields.
12. Remove the center support beam.
13. Disconnect the shift cables from the transaxle. Remove the shift cable bracket.
14. Disconnect the transaxle cooler lines. Remove the transaxle inspection cover and converter bolts.
15. Remove the control arms at the ball joints.
16. Remove the right and left axle shafts at the transaxle.
17. Remove the starter assembly.
18. Remove the three rear transaxle bolts. Support the transaxle using a suitable fixture.
19. Remove the remaining mounting and bellhousing bolts.
20. Remove the transaxle from the vehicle.
21. Installation is the reverse of the removal procedure.

FRONT DRIVE AXLE

Removal and Installation

1. Raise and support the vehicle safely. Remove the front tire and wheel assemblies.
2. Remove the cotter pin, locknut cap and locknut from the hub assembly.
3. Remove the lower control arm to ball joint attaching nuts.
4. Remove the tie rod ball joint from the knuckle.
5. Remove the brake caliper and support it out of the way with wire.

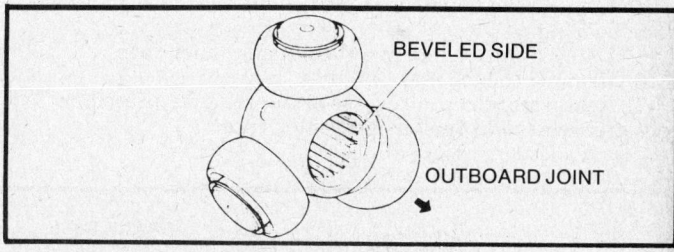

Beveled side faces the outboard joint

6. Remove the rotor.
7. Using a puller, pull the hub from the halfshaft.
8. Remove the halfshaft.
9. Installation is the reverse of the removal procedure. Torque the steering knuckle nut to 47 ft. lbs.; the caliper bolts to 65 ft. lbs.; the drive axle nut to 137 ft. lbs.

INNER AND OUTER BOOTS

Removal and Installation

1. Remove the front drive axle as previously outlined. Place the axle assembly in a suitable holding fixture.
2. Remove the boot retaining clamps.
3. Remove the inboard joint tulip.
4. Remove the tripod joint snap ring. Remove the tripod joint from the drive shaft.
5. Remove the inboard and outboard joint boots.
6. Installation is the reverse of the removal procedure. Note the following; the inboard joint and clamp is larger than the outboard clamp. Face the beveled side of the tripod axial spline towards the outboard joint.

12–31

SECTION 12

GENERAL MOTORS—"S" BODY
CHEVROLET NOVA

REAR SUSPENSION

For Axle Overhaul Procedures and Suspension Services refer to the Unit Repair Section.

REAR AXLE HUB AND CARRIER

Removal and Installation

1. Raise the vehicle and support safely. Remove the wheel and tire assembly.
2. Remove the brake tube from the wheel cylinder.
3. Remove the axle hub retaining bolts from the axle carrier. Remove the axle hub and brake assembly.
4. Remove the bolt holding the axle carrier to the strut rod. Remove the bolts and nuts holding the axle carrier to the suspensions arms.
5. Remove the lower shock absorber to axle carrier retaining nuts.
6. Remove the axle carrier from the vehicle.
7. Installation is the reverse of the removal procedure.

REAR AXLE HUB

Disassembly

1. Remove the rear axle hub as previously outlined. Place in a suitable holding fixture.
2. Remove the nut from the rear of the axle hub.
3. Using a puller, remove the axle shaft from the axle hub.
4. Remove the inside bearing, inside inner race and the outside bearing.
5. Using a puller, remove the outside inner race.
6. Remove the oil seal.
7. Reassembly is the reverse of the removal procedure. Apply grease around the bearing outer race.

REAR WHEEL BEARING

Adjustment

1. After installing the bearing and oil seal, torque the rear nut to 90 ft. lbs. (123 Nm).

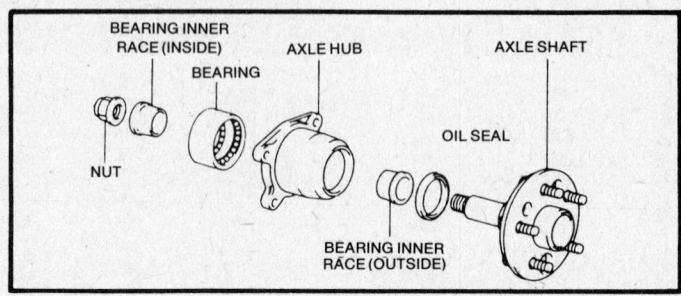

Bearing and oil seal assembly-exploded view

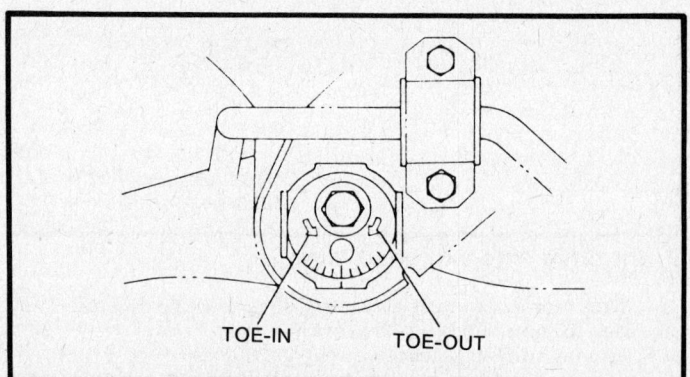

Rear wheel alignment adjusting bolt

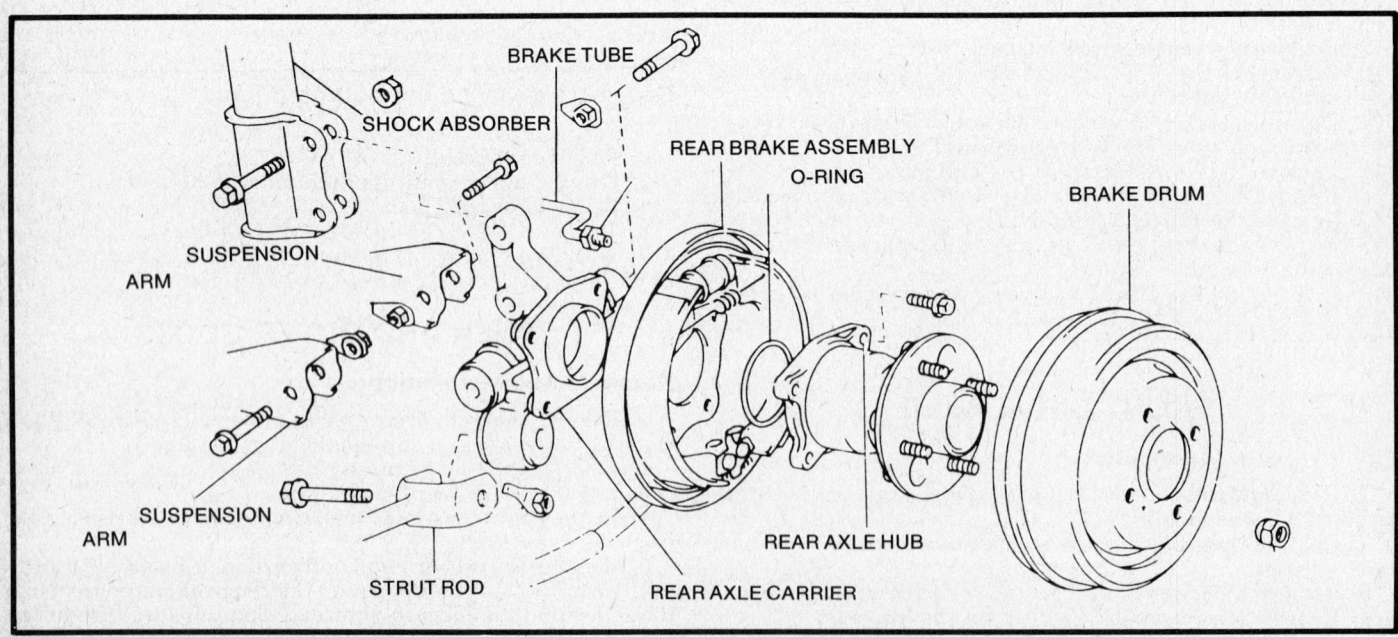

Rear axle hub assembly-exploded view

GENERAL MOTORS—"S" BODY
CHEVROLET NOVA

2. Using a hammer and chisel, stake the nut.
3. Install the bearing assembly onto the axle shaft.

REAR WHEEL ALIGNMENT

Adjustment

1. Check the tires for size, proper inflation and wear.
2. Check the wheel runout. Lateral runout should be less than 0.047 in. (1.2mm).
3. Check the rear suspension for looseness.
4. Adjust the toe-in. Left-right error should be less than 0.12 in. (3mm).
5. On a flat surface, move the vehicle forward approximately 10 feet with the front wheels facing forward.
6. Mark the center of each rear tread and measure the distance between the marks of the left and right tires.
7. Move the vehicle forward until the marks on the rear side of the tires comes to the front.
8. Measure the distance between the marks on the front side of the tires. Toe-in should be 0.150 ± 0.16 in. (3.8 ± 4mm).
9. If not within specification, adjust by turning the left and right adjusting nuts an equal amount, but in opposite directions.
10. The toe-in will change about 0.08 in. (2mm). Torque the nut to 64 ft. lbs. (87 Nm).

SECTION 13

BUICK
ELECTRA · ESTATE WAGON · LE SABRE · REGAL

SPECIFICATIONS

Alternator Output 13–9	Serial Number Identification 13–4
Brakes 24–2	Torque 13–8
Capacities 13–8	Torque Sequence (Cylinder Heads) 13–37
Crankshaft & Connecting Rod 13–7	Tune-Up 13–5
Firing Order 13–6	Valve 13–6
General Engine 13–4	Wheel Alignment 13–8
Piston & Ring 13–7	

INDEX

A
Alternator R&R 13–9
Automatic Transmission 13–49
   Adjustment 13–49
   On Car Service 23–2
   Assembly R&R 13–49
Axle Assembly R&R 13–51

B
Ball Joints 35–2
Brake System 13–46
Brake Booster 13–46
Brake Caliper Overhaul 24–2
Brake Caliper R&R
   Front 24–2
Brake Drum
   Rear 24–2
Brake Master Cylinder 13–46
Brake Pad
   Front 24–2
Brake Shoe
   Rear 24–2

C
Camshaft R&R 13–38
Carburetor R&R 13–28
Chassis Electrical 13–11
Combination Switch R&R 13–12
Component Locations 13–16
Control Arm R&R 35–2
Cooling System 13–21
Cruise Control 13–18
Cylinder Head 13–37
   R&R 13–37

D
Differential 28–2
   Inspection 28–2
Dimmer Switch R&R 13–12
Disc Brakes 24–2
   Front 24–2
Distributor R&R 13–10
Drive Axle 28–2
Driveshaft R&R 13–50

E
Electric Fuel Pump R&R 13–22
Electronic Ignition 30–2
Emission Controls 13–33
Engine 13–34
   Identification 13–4
   R&R 13–34

Engine Electrical 13–10
Engine Lubrication 13–41
Engine Mechanical 13–34
Engine Mounts R&R 13–35
Exhaust Manifold R&R 13–29

F
Front Suspension 35–2
   Alignment 13–8
Fuel Injection 13–30
Fuel Pump R&R 13–22
Fuel Mixture, Adjust 13–24
Fuses 13–17

H
Head Light Switch 13–11
Heater Blower R&R 13–21
Heater Core R&R 13–22
Heater Control 13–21
Horn Switch 13–12

I
Idle Speed Adjust 13–23
Ignition Switch 13–11
Ignition Timing 13–10
Instrument Cluster R&R 13–13
Intake Manifold R&R 13–28

L, M, N
Lower Control Arm R&R 35–2
Master Cylinder R&R 13–46
Neutral Safety Switch
   R&R 13–11

O
Oil Pan R&R 13–41
Oil Pump 13–42
   R&R 13–42
Oil Seal R&R
   Rear Main 13–42

P
Parking Brake 13–48
   Adjustment 13–48
   Cable R&R 13–48
Piston & Connecting Rod 13–38
Power Brake Unit R&R 13–46
Power Steering Pump R&R 13–43

R
Rear Main Oil Sear R&R 13–42
Rear Suspension 35–2

Regulator 13–9
Rocker Shaft/Assembly R&R 13–36

S
Serial Number 13–4
   Engine 13–4
   Vehicle 13–4
Shock Absorber R&R
   Front 35–2
   Rear 35–2
Springs
   Front 35–2
   Rear 35–2
Starter R&R 13–9
Starter Drive Replacement 13–9
Steering Column R&R 13–46
Steering Gear R&R 13–43
   Power 13–43
Steering Wheel R&R 13–43
Speedometer R&R 13–15
Suspension R&R 35–2
   Service 35–2

T
Throttle Linkage, Adjust 13–50
Timing Gears 13–40
Timing Gear Cover 13–39
   Oil Seal Replacement 13–39
Tune-Up 13–5
Turbocharger R&R 13–30
Turn Signal Switch R&R 13–12

U, V
U-Joint Overhaul 28–2
Valve Tappetts R&R 13–36
Valve Timing, Adjust 13–36
Valve System 13–36
Voltage Regulator 13–9

W, Y
Water Pump R&R 13–21
Wheel Alignment 13–8
   Front 13–8
Wheel Bearings Front 13–43
Wheel Cylinders
   Rear 24–2
Windshield Wiper 13–13
   Linkage R&R 13–13
   Motor R&R 13–13
   Switch R&R 13–12
Year Identification 13–3

BEFORE SERVICING BE CERTAIN TO READ THE SAFETY NOTICE

SECTION 13

Buick
1983–87 Rear Wheel Drive Cars

REGAL • REGAL LIMITED • REGAL SPORT COUPE
LE SABRE • LE SABRE CUSTOM • LE SABRE LIMITED
ELECTRA • ESTATE WAGON

YEAR IDENTIFICATION

1983 Electra

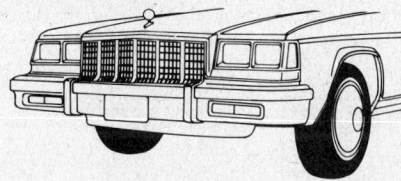
1984 Electra

1983 LeSabre

1984–85 LeSabre

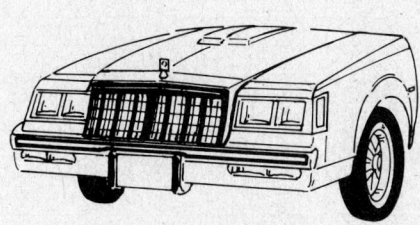
1983 Regal

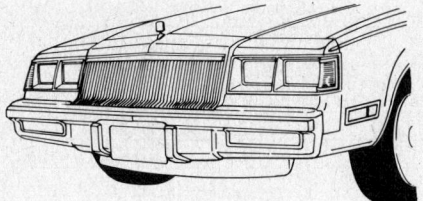
1984 Regal

1985–87 Regal

13–3

SECTION 13

BUICK
ELECTRA • ESTATE WAGON • LE SABRE • REGAL

VEHICLE IDENTIFICATION NUMBER (VIN)

The Vehicle Identification Number (VIN) is a seventeen digit number visible through the windshield on the driver's side of the dash and contains the vehicle and engine identification codes. The eight digit identifies the original equipment engine and the tenth digit identifies the model year.

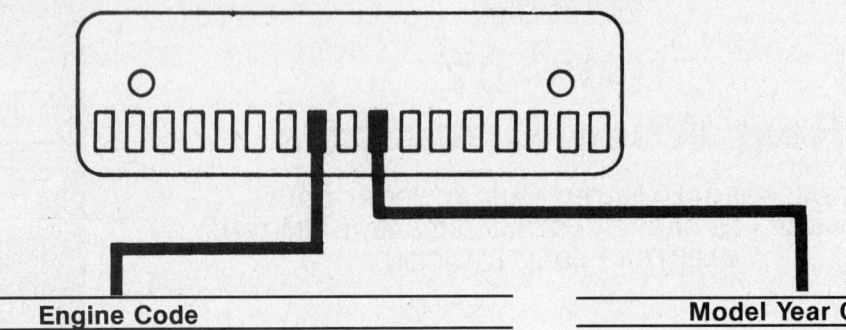

Year	VIN Code	Cu. In.	Liters	Cyl.	Carb. (bbls)	Eng. Mfg.
'83	A	231	3.8	V6	2	Buick
	8	231	3.8	V6	4/Turbo	Buick
	4	252	4.1	V6	4	Buick
	V	263	4.3	V6	Diesel	Olds
	Y	307	5.0	V8	4	Olds
	N	350	5.0	V8	Diesel	Olds
'84	A	231	3.8	V6	2	Buick
	9	231	3.8	V6	SFI/Turbo	Buick
	4	252	4.1	V6	4	Buick
	V	263	4.3	V6	Diesel	Olds
	Y	307	5.0	V8	4	Olds
	N	350	5.7	V8	Diesel	Olds
'85-'87	A	231	3.8	V6	2	Buick
	9	231	3.8	V6	MFI/Turbo	Buick
	V	263	4.3	V6	Diesel	Olds
	Y	307	5.0	V8	4	Olds
	N	350	5.7	V8	Diesel	Olds
	7	231	3.8	V6	SFI	Buick

Model Year Code	
Code	Year
C	82
D	83
E	84
F	85
G	86
H	87

MFI—Multiport Fuel Injection (Injectors opened in groups)
SFI—Sequential Fuel Injection (Injectors opened individually)

GENERAL ENGINE SPECIFICATIONS

Year	Engine VIN Code	Engine Type	Engine Manufacturer	Fuel Delivery	Horsepower @ rpm ①	Torque @ rpm (ft. lbs.) ①	Bore × Stroke (in.)	Compression Ratio	Oil Pressure (psi @ rpm)
'83-'84	A	6-231	Buick	2 bbl	110 @ 3800	190 @ 1600	3.800 × 3.400	8.0:1	37 @ 2400
	8	6-231 ②	Buick	4 bbl	170 @ 3800	275 @ 2600	3.800 × 3.400	8.0:1	37 @ 2400
	9	6-231 ②	Buick	SFI	190 @ 4000	300 @ 2480	3.800 × 3.400	8.0:1	37 @ 2400
	4	6-252	Buick	4 bbl	125 @ 4000	205 @ 2000	3.965 × 3.400	8.0:1	37 @ 2400
	V	6-263	Olds.	Diesel	85 @ 3600	165 @ 1600	4.057 × 3.385	21.6:1 ③	30-45 @ 1500
	Y	8-307	Olds.	4 bbl	150 @ 3800	260 @ 2400	3.800 × 3.385	8.5:1	30-45 @ 1500
	N	8-350	Olds.	Diesel	105 @ 3200	200 @ 1600	4.057 × 3.385	22.5:1	30-45 @ 1500
'85	A	6-231	Buick	2 bbl	110 @ 3800	190 @ 1600	3.800 × 3.400	8.0:1	37 @ 2400
	9	6-231 ②	Buick	SFI	190 @ 4000	300 @ 2400	3.800 × 3.400	8.0:1	37 @ 2400
	V	6-263	Olds.	Diesel	85 @ 3600	165 @ 1600	4.057 × 3.385	22.5:1	30-45 @ 1500
	Y	8-307	Olds.	4 bbl	140 @ 3600	240 @ 1600	3.800 × 3.385	8.0:1	30-45 @ 1500
	N	8-350	Olds.	Diesel	105 @ 3200	200 @ 1600	4.057 × 3.385	22.5:1	30-45 @ 1500

BUICK
ELECTRA · ESTATE WAGON · LE SABRE · REGAL
SECTION 13

GENERAL ENGINE SPECIFICATIONS

Year	Engine VIN Code	Engine Type	Engine Manufacturer	Fuel Delivery	Horsepower @ rmp ①	Torque @ rpm (ft. lbs.) ①	Bore × Stroke (in.)	Compression Ratio	Oil Pressure (psi @ rpm)
'86–'87	A	6-231	Buick	2 bbl	110 @ 3800	190 @ 1600	3.800 × 3.400	8.0:1	37 @ 2400
	7	6-231	Buick	SFI	235 @ 4400	330 @ 2800	3.800 × 3.400	8.0:1	37 @ 2400
	Y	8-307	Olds.	4 bbl	140 @ 3200	255 @ 2000	3.800 × 3.385	7.99:1	30 @ 1500

NA—Not available at time of publication.
SFI—Sequential Fuel Injection

① Horsepower and torque are SAE net figures. They are measured at the rear of the transmission with all accessories installed and operating. Since the figures vary when a given engine is installed in different models, some are representative rather than exact.
② Turbocharged engine
③ 1984—22.5:1

TUNE-UP SPECIFICATIONS
Gasoline Engines

When analyzing compression test results, look for uniformity among cylinders rather than specific pressures

Year	Engine VIN Code	Engine Type	Liters	Engine Manufacturer	Spark Plugs Type ①	Gap (in.)	Ignition timing (deg. B.T.D.C.) ② Automatic Transmission ④	Intake Valve Opens (°B.T.D.C.)	Fuel Pump Pressure (psi)	Idle Speed (rmp) Automatic Transmission ④
'83	A	6-231	3.8	Buick	R45TS8	.080	③	16	5½–6½	③
	3	6-231	3.8 ⑤	Buick	R45TSX	.060	③	16	5½–6½	③
	4	6-252	4.1	Buick	R45TS8	.080	③	16	5½–6½	③
	Y	8-307	5.0	Olds	R46SX	.080	③	20	5½–6½	③
'84	A	6-231	3.8	Buick	R45TSX	.060	③	16	5½–6½	③
	9	6-231	3.8 ⑥	Buick	R44TS	.045	③	16	26–51	③
	4	6-252	4.1	Buick	R45TSX	.060	③	16	5½–6½	③
	Y	8-307	5.0	Olds	R46SX	.080	③	20	5½–6½	③
'85–'87	A	6-231	3.8	Buick	R45TSX	.060	③	16	5½–6½	③
	7,9	6-231	3.8 ⑦	Buick	R44TS	.045	③	16	26–51	③
	Y	8-307	5.0	Olds	R45TS	.060	③	20	5½–6½	③

NOTE: The underhood specifications sticker often reflects tune-up specification changes made in production. Sticker figures must be used if they disagree with those in this chart.
B.T.D.C.—Before top dead center
C.I.D.—Cubic inch displacement
Min.—Minimum
Part numbers in this chart are not recommendations by Chilton for any product by brand name.

① All models use electronic ignition systems.
② On some models, the engine must be held at a specific rpm to accurately check and adjust the ignition timing. See the text for specific procedures.
③ On vehicles equipped with computerized emissions systems (which have no distributor vacuum advance unit), the idle speed and ignition timing are controlled by the emissions computer.
④ Manual transmissions not used with 1982 and later Buick rear wheel drive vehicles.
⑤ Turbo
⑥ SFI-Sequential Fuel Injection
⑦ MFI—Multiport Fuel Injection

TUNE-UP SPECIFICATIONS
Diesel Engines

Year	Engine VIN Code	Engine No. of cyl.- Displacement- Manufacturer	Liters	Fuel Pump Pressure (psi) ③	Injection Nozzle Pressure (psi)	Compression Pressure (psi) ②	Injection Pump Setting (deg)	Intake Valve Opens (°B.T.D.C.)	Idle Speed (rpm)
'83–'85	N	8-350-Olds	5.7	5.5–6.5	1225	275 minimum	④	16	①
'83–'85	V	6-263-Olds	4.3	5.8–8.7	⑤	275 minimum	6ATDC	16	①

NOTE: The underhood specifications sticker often reflects tune-up specification changes made in production. Sticker figures must be used if they disagree with those in this chart.
B.T.D.C.—Before top dead center (No. 1 cylinder)
① See the underhood specifications sticker.
② The lowest cylinder reading must not be less than 70% of the highest cylinder reading.
③ Fuel transfer pump pressure given. Injection pump reading should be 8–12 psi @ 1000 rpm taken at injection pump pressure tap.
④ 4ATDC on 1982 and later models
⑤ Injector opening pressure:
New nozzle (green band/no color)—1000 psi New nozzle (red band)—800 psi
Used nozzle—200 psi less than new

SECTION 13 BUICK
ELECTRA • ESTATE WAGON • LE SABRE • REGAL

FIRING ORDERS

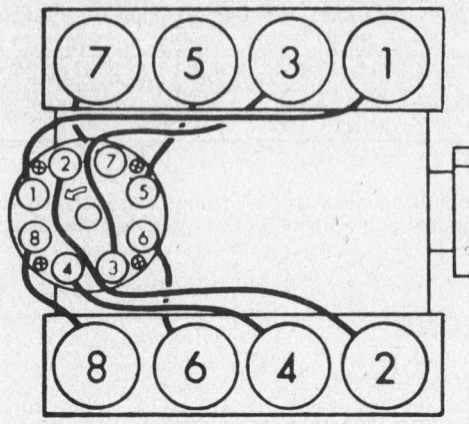

Oldsmobile 307, 350 cu. in. V8 (5.0, 5.7L)
Firing order: 1-8-4-3-6-5-7-2
Distributor rotation: counterclockwise

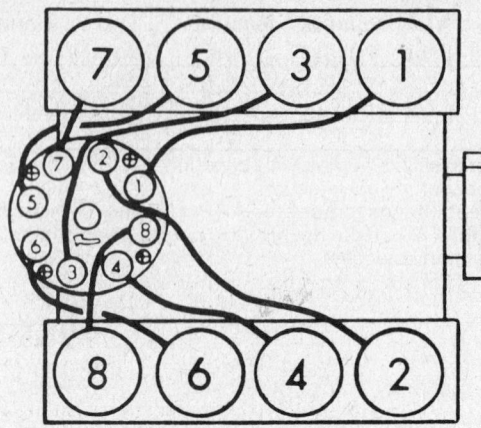

Chevrolet 267, 305 cu. in. V8 (4.3, 5.0L)
Firing order: 1-8-4-3-6-5-7-2
Distributor rotation: clockwise

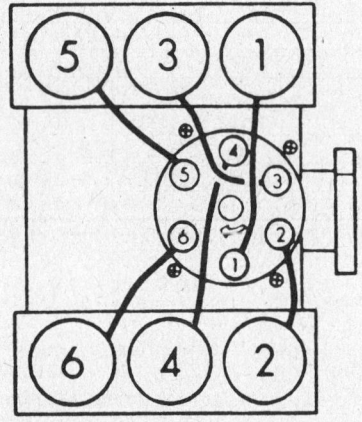

Buick 231, 252 cu. in. V6 (3.8, 4.1L)
Firing order: 1-6-5-4-3-2
Distributor rotation: clockwise

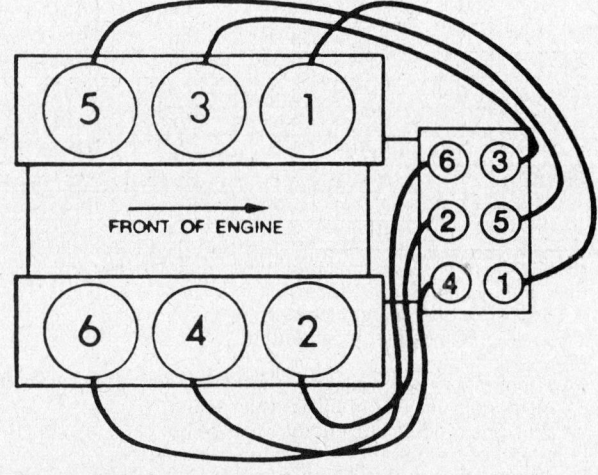

Buick 181 cu. in. V6 (3.0L) C3I
Firing order: 1-6-5-4-3-2

VALVE SPECIFICATIONS

Year	VIN Code	Engine No. Cyl. Displacement (cu. in.)	Liter and Mfg.	Seat Angle (deg)	Face Angle (deg)	Spring Test Pressure (lbs @ in.)	Spring Installed Height (in.)	Stem-to-Guide Clearance (in.)		Stem Diameter (in.)	
								Intake	Exhaust	Intake	Exhaust
'83	A-8	6-231	3.8 Buick	45	45	182 @ 1.34	1⁴⁷⁄₆₄	.0015-.0035	.0015-.0032	.3401-.3412	.3405-.3412
	4	6-252	4.1 Buick	45	45	182 @ 1.34	1⁴⁷⁄₆₄	.0015-.0035	.0015-.0032	.3401-.3412	.3405-.3412
	V	8-307	5.0 Olds	45 ①	44 ①	187 @ 1.27	1⁴⁷⁄₆₄	.0010-.0027	.0015-.0032	.3425-.3432	.3420-.3427
	Y	6-263 Diesel	4.3 Olds	45 ①	44 ①	209 @ 1.22	—	.0010-.0027	.0015-.0032	.3425-.3432	.3420-.3427
	N	8-350 Diesel	5.7 Olds	45 ①	44 ①	209 @ 1.22	1⁴⁷⁄₆₄	.0010-.0027	.0015-.0032	.3425-.3432	.3420-.3427
'84	A-9	6-231	3.8 Buick	45	45	182 @ 1.34	1⁴⁷⁄₆₄	.0015-.0035	.0015-.0032	.3401-.3412	.3405-.3412
	4	6-252	4.1 Buick	45	45	182 @ 1.34	1⁴⁷⁄₆₄	.0015-.0035	.0015-.0032	.3401-.3412	.3405-.3412
	Y	8-307	5.0 Olds	45 ①	44 ①	187 @ 1.27	1⁴⁷⁄₆₄	.0010-.0027	.0015-.0032	.3425-.3432	.3420-.3427
	V	6-263 Diesel	4.3 Olds	45 ①	44 ①	209 @ 1.22	—	.0010-.0027	.0015-.0032	.3425-.3432	.3420-.3427
	N	8-350 Diesel	5.7 Olds	45 ①	44 ①	209 @ 1.22	1⁴⁷⁄₆₄	.0010-.0027	.0015-.0032	.3425-.3432	.3420-.3427

BUICK
ELECTRA · ESTATE WAGON · LE SABRE · REGAL

VALVE SPECIFICATIONS

Year	VIN Code	Engine No. Cyl. Displacement (cu. in.)	Liter and Mfg.	Seat Angle (deg)	Face Angle (deg)	Spring Test Pressure (lbs @ in.)	Spring Installed Height (in.)	Stem-to-Guide Clearance (in.) Intake	Stem-to-Guide Clearance (in.) Exhaust	Stem Diameter (in.) Intake	Stem Diameter (in.) Exhaust
'85-'87	A-9,7	6-231	3.8 Buick	45	45	182 @ 1.34 ②	1⁴⁷⁄₆₄	.0015-.0035	.0015-.0032	.3401-.3412	.3405-.3412
	Y	8-307	5.0 Olds	45 ①	44 ①	187 @ 1.27	1⁴⁷⁄₆₄	.0010-.0027	.0015-.0032	.3425-.3432	.3420-.3427
	V	6-263 Diesel	4.3 Olds	45 ①	44 ①	209 @ 1.22	—	.0010-.0027	.0015-.0032	.3425-.3432	.3420-.3427
	N	8-350 Diesel	5.7 Olds	45 ①	44 ①	209 @ 1.22	1⁴⁷⁄₆₄	.0010-.0027	.0015-.0032	.3425-.3432	.3420-.3427

① Exhaust valve seat angle—31°
    exhaust valve face angle—30°
② 6-231 with Sequential Fuel Injection—185 @ 1.34

CRANKSHAFT AND CONNECTING ROD SPECIFICATIONS

All measurements are given in inches

Year	Liter	Code	Engine No. Cyl. Displacement (cu. in.)	Crankshaft Main Brg. Journal Dia	Crankshaft Main Brg. Oil Clearance	Crankshaft Shaft End-Play	Thrust on No.	Connecting Rod Journal Diameter	Connecting Rod Oil Clearance	Connecting Rod Side Clearance
'83	3.8	A-8	6-231 Buick	2.4995	.0003-.0018	.003-.011	2	2.2487-2.2495	.0005-.0026	.006-.023
	4.1	4	6-252 Buick	2.4995	.0003-.0018	.003-.011	2	2.2487-2.2495	.0005-.0026	.006-.023
	5.0	Y	8-307 Olds	2.4990-2.4995 ①	.0005-.0021 ③	.0035-.0135	3	2.1238-2.1248	.0004-.0033	.006-.020
	4.3	V	6-263 Olds Diesel	2.9993-3.0003	.0005-.0021 ⑤	.0035-.0135	3	2.2490-2.2510	.0005-.0026	.006-.020
	5.7	N	8-350 Olds Diesel	2.9993-3.0003	.0005-.0021	.0035-.0135	3	2.2495-2.2500	.0005-.0026	.006-.020
'84	3.8	A-9	6-231 Buick	2.4995	.0003-.0018	.003-.011	2	2.2487-2.2495	.0005-.0026	.006-.023
	4.1	4	6-252 Buick	2.4995	.003-.0018	.0003-.011	2	2.2487-2.2495	.0005-.0026	.006-.023
	5.0	Y	8-307 Olds	2.4990-2.4995 ①	.0005-.0021 ③	.0035-.0135	3	2.1238-2.1248	.0004-.0033	.006-.020
	4.3	V	6-263 Olds Diesel	2.9993-3.0003	.0005-.002 ⑤	.0035-.0135	3	2.2490-2.2500	.0005-.0026	.006-.020
	5.7	N	8-350 Olds Diesel	2.9993-3.0003	.0005-.0021 ⑥	.0035-.0135	3	2.2495-2.2500	.0005-.0026	.006-.020
'85-'87	3.8	A-9-7	6-231 Buick	2.4995	.0003-.0018	.003-.011	2	2.2487-2.2495	.0005-.0026	.006-.023
'86	5.0	Y	8-307 Olds	2.4985-2.4995 ②	.0005-.0021 ④	.0035-.0135	3	2.1238-2.1248	.0004-.0033	.006-.020
	4.3	V	6-263 Olds Diesel	2.9993-3.0003	.0005-.002 ⑤	.0035-.0135	3	2.2490-2.2500	.0004-.0026	.008-.021
	5.7	N	8-350 Olds Diesel	2.9993-3.0003	.0005-.0021 ⑥	.0035-.0135	3	2.2495-2.2500	.0005-.0026	.006-.020

① No. 1: 2.4973-2.4998 inch
② No. 1: 2.4998-2.4998 inch
③ No. 5: .0015-.0031 inch
④ No. 5: .0016-.0032 inch
⑤ No. 4: (rear) .0020-.0034 inch
⑥ No. 5: .0020-.0034 inch

PISTON AND RING SPECIFICATIONS

All measurements are given in inches. To convert inches to metric units, refer to the Metric Conversion Chart

Year	VIN Code	Engine Type/ Disp. cu. in. (Liters)	Eng. Mfg.	Piston-to-Bore Clearance	Ring Gap Top Compression	Ring Gap Bottom Compression	Ring Gap Oil Control	Ring Side Clearance Top Compression	Ring Side Clearance Bottom Compression	Ring Side Clearance Oil Control
'83-'87	A, 3, 7, 8, 9	6-231 (3.8)	Buick	.0008-.0020 ①	.010-.020	.010-.020	.015-.055	.0030-.0050	.0030-.0050	.0035 max
'83-'84	4	6-252 (4.1)	Buick	.0008-.0020	.010-.020	.010-.020	.015-.055	.0030-.0050	.0030-.0050	.0035 max
'83-'85	V	6-263 (4.3)	Olds Diesel	.0035-.0045	.019-.027	.013-.021	.015-.055	.0050-.0070	.0030-.0050	.001-.005
'83-'87	Y	8-307 (5.0)	Olds	.0008-.0018	.009-.019 ②	.009-.019 ②	.015-.055 ③	.0020-.0040	.0020-.0040	.0010-.0050
'83-'85	N	8-350 (5.7)	Olds Diesel	.0035-.0045	.015-.025	.015-.025	.015-.055	.0040-.0060 ④	.0018-.0038 ⑤	.0010-.0050

SECTION 13

BUICK
ELECTRA • ESTATE WAGON • LE SABRE • REGAL

CAPACITIES

Year	Engine Liter	Engine No. Cyl. Displacement (cu. in.)	VIN Code	Engine Crankcase Add 1 Qt For New Filter	Transmission Pts to Refill After Draining Manual	Transmission Pts to Refill After Draining Automatic •	Drive Axle (pts)	Gasoline Tank (gals)	Cooling System (qts) With Heater	Cooling System (qts) With A/C	Cooling System (qts) Heavy Duty
'83-'84	3.8	6-231 Buick	A-8-9	4	—	③	①	19.0	13	13	13
	4.1	6-252 Buick	4	4	—	③	①	19.0	13	13	13
	5.0	8-307 Olds	Y	4	—	③	①	25.0	15.4	16.2	16.1
	4.3	6-263 Diesel Olds	V	6	—	③	①	19.0	13.6	14.4	14.4
	5.7	8-350 Diesel Olds	N	6	—	③	①	25.0	17.9	17.9	18.3
'85-'87	3.8	6-231 Buick	A-9-7	4	—	7	①	19.0	13	13	13
	5.0	8-307 Olds	Y	4	—	7	①	19.0	15.4	16	16
	4.3	6-263 Diesel Olds	V	6	—	7	①	19.0	13.6	14.4	14.4
	5.7	8-350 Diesel Olds	N	6	—	7	①	19.0	17.9	17.9	18.3

• Specifications do not include torque convertor
—: Not applicable
① 7.5 in. ring gear—3.5;
  8.5 in. ring gear—4.25;
  8.75 in. ring gear—5.4
② Not used
③ THM 200 & 200R-4—7 pts.;
  THM 250C—8 pts.;
  THM 350C—6.3 pts.

TORQUE SPECIFICATIONS
Buick Rear Wheel Drive (1982-86)
All readings in ft. lbs.

Year	Liter	Code	Engine No. Cyl. Displacement (cu. in.)	Cylinder Head Bolts	Rod Bearing Bolts	Main Bearing Bolts	Crankshaft Bolt	Flywheel-to-Crankshaft Bolts	Manifold Intake	Manifold Exhaust
'83	3.8	A-8	6-231 Buick	80	40	100	225	60	45	25
	4.1	4	6-252 Buick	80	40	100	225	60	45	25
	5.0	Y	8-307 Olds	125 ①	42	80 ②	200-310	60	40 ①	25
	4.3	V	6-263 Olds Diesel	142 ④	42	105	203-305	57	41	29
	5.7	N	8-350 Olds Diesel	130 ①	42	120	200-310	60	40 ①	25
'84	3.8	A-9-7	6-231 Buick	80	40	100	225	60	45	25
	4.1	4	6-252 Buick	80	40	100	225	60	45	25
	5.0	Y	8-307 Olds	125 ①	42	80 ②	200-310	60	40 ①	25
	4.3	V	6-263 Olds Diesel	142 ④	42	105	203-350	57	41	31
	5.7	N	8-350 Olds Diesel	130 ①	42	120	200-310	60	40 ①	25
'85-'87	3.8	A-9	6-231 Buick	80	40	100	200	60	47	25
	5.0	Y	8-307 Olds	125 ①	42	80 ②	200-310	60	40 ①	25
	4.3	V	6-263 Olds Diesel	142 ④	42	89 ⑤	203-350	57	41	28
	5.7	N	8-350 Olds Diesel	130 ①	42	120	200-310	60	40 ①	25

Caution: Verify correct original equipment engine is in vehicle by referring to the VIN engine code before torquing any bolts.
① Clean and dip entire bolt in engine oil before tightening to obtain a correct torque reading.
② Rear main bearing cap bolts—120 ft. lbs.
③ Not Used
④ No. 5, 6, 11, 12, 13 and 14 cylinder head bolts—59 ft. lbs.
⑤ No. 2 and 3 main bearing cap retaining outer bolts—52 ft. lbs. (Type II—Has four bolts retaining no. 2 and 3 main bearing caps).

WHEEL ALIGNMENT SPECIFICATIONS

Year	Model	Caster Range (deg)	Caster Pref Setting (deg)	Camber Range (deg)	Camber Pref Setting (deg)	Toe-in ① Inch (deg)
'83-'87	Regal	2P to 4P	3P	5/16N to 1 5/16P	1/2P	1/16P to 1/4P (1/8P to 1/2P)
'83-'87	All	2P to 4P	3P	0P to 1 5/8P	13/16P	1/16P to 1/4P (1/8P to 1/2P)

BUICK 13
ELECTRA • ESTATE WAGON • LE SABRE • REGAL
SECTION

ELECTRICAL SECTION

For Overhaul Procedures refer to the Unit Repair Section.

Charging System

ALTERNATOR

Removal and Installation

1. Disconnect the negative battery cable.
2. Remove the two terminal plug and the battery lead from the back of the alternator assembly.
3. Loosen the adjusting bolts. Remove the alternator belt.
4. Remove the alternator retaining bolts. Remove the alternator assembly from the vehicle.
5. Installation is the reverse of the removal procedure. Once the alternator belt is installed, check for the proper belt tension.

VOLTAGE REGULATOR

Removal and Installation

The voltage regulator is incorporated within the alternator assembly. There is no adjustment procedure. Should the regulator require service, the alternator must be disassembled.

Starting System

STARTER

Removal and Installation

1. Disconnect the negative battery cable.
2. Raise the vehicle and support it safely.
3. Remove the starter braces, shields or anything else that may stop the starter assembly from being removed.
4. Remove the starter mounting bolts. Remove the electrical wires from the solenoid assembly.
5. Remove the starter from the vehicle.
6. Installation is the reverse of the removal procedure. If any shims were removed along with the starter assembly be sure to reinstall them where removed.

Ignition System

1982–83

The High Energy Ignition (HEI) system is used on all models.

NOTE: 1985 3.8L 231 CID V6 engines (VIN A), a color change was made during the model year to the ignition

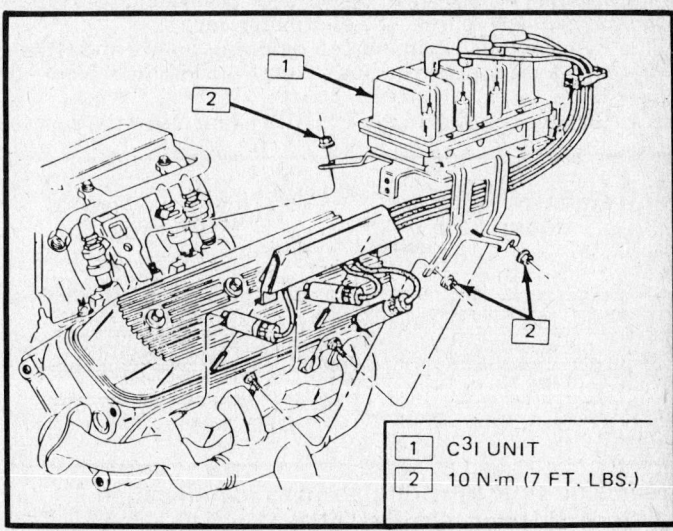

| 1 | C³I UNIT |
| 2 | 10 N·m (7 FT. LBS.) |

C31 System ignition coil assembly—V6 shown
(©General Motors Corporation)

ALTERNATOR OUTPUT SPECIFICATIONS

Alternator Number	AMPS	Cold Output Approx RPM	AMPS	Approx RPM	Hot Output AMPS **
1100231	25	2,000	38	5,000	42
1100206, 1100239	37	2,000	60	7,000	56
1100208, 1105562, 1100247	38	2,000	70	7,000	66
1100200, 1100217, 1100257, 1100260, 1105028, 1105494	51	2,000	81	7,000	78
1105466	52	2,000	72	5,000	80
1105197	55	2,000	70	5,000	70
1105441, 1105443, 1105444, 1104446, 1105447, 1105493, 1105496, 1105541, 1105447, 1105592, 1105617	56	2,000	103	7,000	94
1105200, 1105552, 1105329, 1105548	57	2,000	85	5,000	85
1105428	63	2,000	103	7,000	94
1105553	75	2,000	115	7,000	97
1105085, 1105497, 1105509	75	2,000	115	7,000	108

VOLTMETER NOT NEEDED FOR COLD OUTPUT CHECK.
LOAD BATTERY WITH CARBON PILE TO OBTAIN MAXIMUM OUTPUT.
** At maximum operating speed.

13-9

SECTION 13
BUICK
ELECTRA • ESTATE WAGON • LE SABRE • REGAL

wiring, leading to the distributor. The new wires are all black in color with a color stripe for identification.

1984 AND LATER

Two types of ignition systems are used. The HEI system is used on all engines except the 3.8L 231 CID, V6 SFI turbo engines (VIN 9), which uses the Computer Controlled Coil Ignition System, (C I). With the C I system, no distributor is used. The system utilizes a coil pack, ignition module, crankshaft and camshaft sensors.

HEI DISTRIBUTOR

Removal and Installation

1. Remove all the necessary components in order to gain access to the distributor assembly.
2. Remove all electrical connections from the unit. Release the coil connectors from the distributor cap.
3. Remove the distributor cap retaining screws and remove the cap. Disconnect the four terminal harness from the distributor.
4. Remove the distributor hold down bolt. Note the position

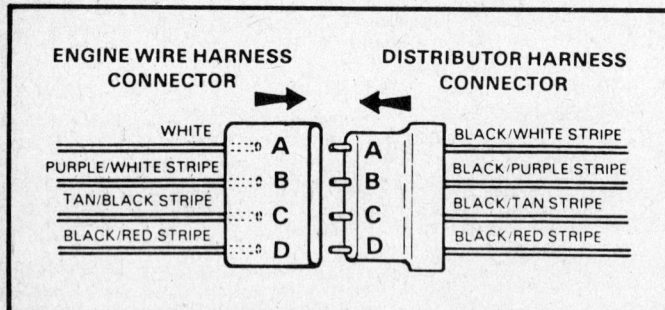

1985 3.8L (VIN A) wiring harness Identification
(© General Motors Corporation)

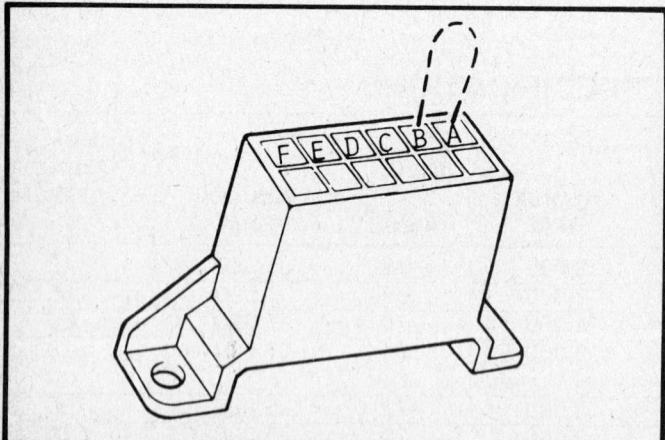

Grounding of the ALCL connector
(© General Motors Corporation)

of the rotor and then pull the distributor assembly from the engine until the rotor just stops turning counterclockwise, and again note position of rotor.

5. To insure correct ignition timing the distributor must be installed with the rotor in the same position as it was removed.
6. Installation is the reverse of the removal procedure.
7. If the engine has been cranked after the distributor has been removed, the following procedure must be used:

8. Remove the No. 1 spark plug. Place your finger over the spark plug hole and crank the engine slowly until compression is felt.
9. Align the timing mark on the pulley to "0" on the engine timing indicator. Position the rotor between No. 1 and No. 8 spark plug towers on V8 engines, between No. 1 and No. 6 spark plug towers on all V6 engines except the 3.8L which should be positioned, between No. 1 and No. 2.
10. The distributor can now be correctly installed in the engine. Be sure rotor points to No. 1 spark plug terminal when installed.
11. Once the distributor has been installed, check the engine timing and adjust as required.

IGNITION TIMING

Adjustment

EXCEPT 3.8L (VIN A, 3, 8, 9) AND 5.0L (VIN Y)

1. Refer to the vehicle control information label which is located on the radiator support panel, for the proper timing information.
2. If the engine timing requires adjustment, loosen the distributor hold down bolt and rotate the distributor slowly in either direction, to advance or retard the engine timing.
3. Tighten the hold down bolt and recheck the engine timing.
4. Some engines incorporate a magnetic timing probe hole which is used when setting the engine timing with special electronic equipment. Consult manufacturers instructions if using this form of timing equipment.

NOTE: Some engines will incorporate a magnetic timing probe hole for the use with special electronic timing equipment. Be sure to consult the manufactures instructions for the use of this equipment.

Adjustment

3.8L (VIN A,3,8,9)

1. With engine at operating temperature, air cleaner installed and air conditioning off (if equipped), connect timing light or meter and verify "Check Engine" light is not on.
2. Disconnect distributor four wire electrical connector. "Check Engine" light will come on.
3. Set ignition timing to specification shown on EMISSION LABEL by loosening the distributor clamp bolt and rotating the distributor until the specification is obtained.
4. Tighten the distributor clamp bolt and recheck timing to make sure distributor was not moved during tightening of the bolt.
5. Reconnect distributor electrical connector.
6. With engine off, momentarily disconnect battery to cancel any stored trouble codes.

Adjustment

5.0L (VIN Y)

1. With engine RUNNING at operating temperature, choke fully open and air conditioning off (if equipped), ground the diagnostic terminal of the 12 terminal ALCL.
2. With use of a timing light or meter, set timing at specified rpm (shown on the EMISSION LABEL) by loosening the distributor clamp bolt and rotating the distributor until specified timing is obtained.
3. Tighten the distributor clamp bolt and recheck timing to make sure distributor was not moved during tightening of the bolt.
4. With the engine still running, unground the diagnostic terminal (if done before engine is shut off), no trouble codes will be stored.

BUICK 13
ELECTRA • ESTATE WAGON • LE SABRE • REGAL

5. Make carburetor adjustments as required. Remove the plugs from any disconnected vacuum hoses and reconnect hoses.

Electrical Controls

IGNITION LOCK CYLINDER

Removal and Installation

1. Disconnect the negative battery cable. Position the ignition lock cylinder in the Run position.
2. Remove the steering wheel. Remove the lock plate, turn signal switch and the buzzer switch.
3. Remove the lock cylinder retaining screw. Remove the lock cylinder.
4. To install, rotate the lock cylinder clockwise to align the cylinder key with the keyway in the lock housing.
5. Push the lock all the way in. Install the screw.
6. Continue the installation in the reverse order of removal procedure.

IGNITION SWITCH

Removal and Installation

1. Disconnect the negative battery terminal.
2. Loosen the toe pan screws on the steering column, as required.
3. Remove the column to instrument panel trim plates and attaching nuts, as required.
4. Lower the steering column. Be sure that the steering column is supported at all times in order to prevent damage to the column. Disconnect the switch wire connectors.
5. Remove the switch attaching screws and remove the switch.
6. Move the switch slider to the extreme left (acc.) position. Then move the slider two detents to the right (off-unlock) position. If equipped with Park-Lock system (cable operated), move the slider one detent to the left (off-lock) position.
7. Install the switch with the rod in the hole.
8. Position and reassemble the steering column in reverse of the disassembly procedure, as required.

BACK-UP LIGHT SWITCH

The back-up light switch still remains on the steering column and looks similar to the previous switches except for the electrical terminals.

Removal

1. Remove wire connectors from the back-up light switch.
2. Remove two screws attaching the switch to the steering column.

Installation

1. Place the gear selector in the neutral position.
2. Align the actuator on the switch with the hole in the shift column tube.
3. Position the rearward portion of the switch (connector side) to fit into the cutout in the lower jacket.
4. Push down on the front of the switch and the two tangs on the housing will snap into place in the rectangular holes in the jacket.
5. Adjust by moving the gear selector to the Park position. The main housing and the housing back should ratchet, providing the proper switch adjustment.
6. To adjust the switch with the assembly installed, move the switch housing all the way towards Low position and repeat Step 5.

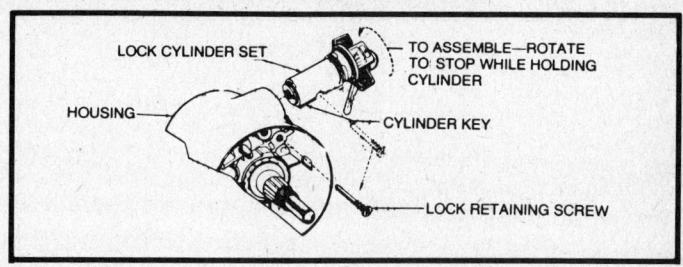

Ignition lock assembly (© General Motors Corporation)

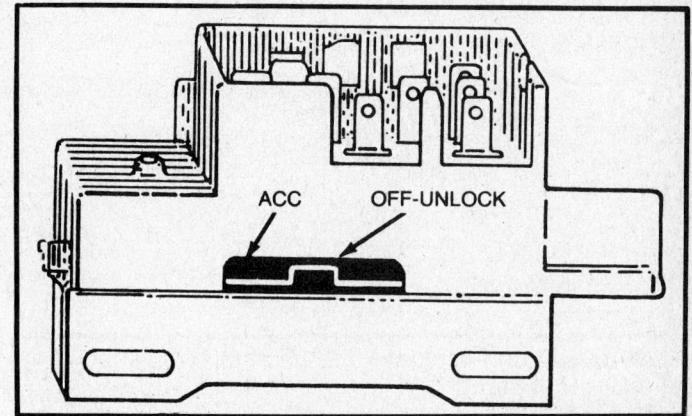

Typical ignition switch assembly (© General Motors Corporation)

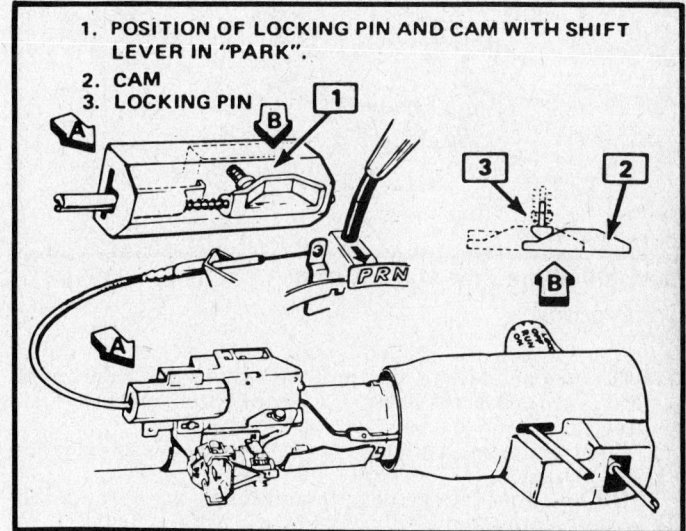

Park Lock system (© General Motors Corporation)

NEUTRAL SAFETY SWITCH

A mechanical neutral start switch is used and is located in the steering column bowl, between the lock and the transmission selector and is non-adjustable.

HEADLIGHT SWITCH

Removal and Installation

1. Disconnect the negative battery cable. On all vehicles ex-

SECTION 13

BUICK
ELECTRA • ESTATE WAGON • LE SABRE • REGAL

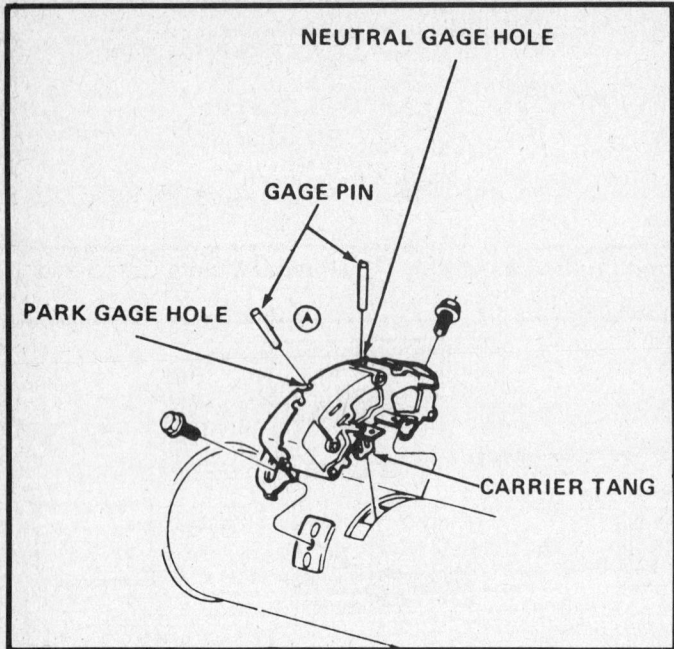

Back-up switch—typical (© General Motors Corporation)

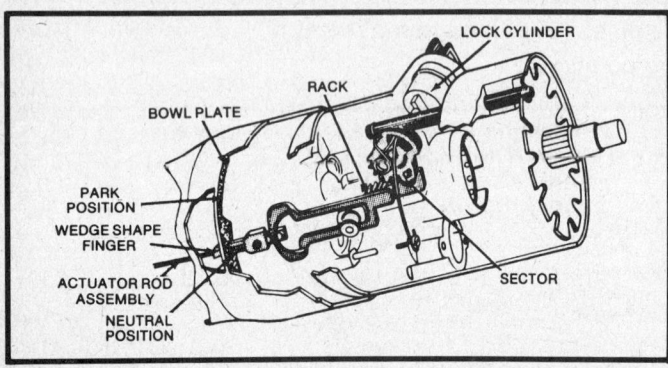

Mechanical neutral start system (© General Motors Corporation)

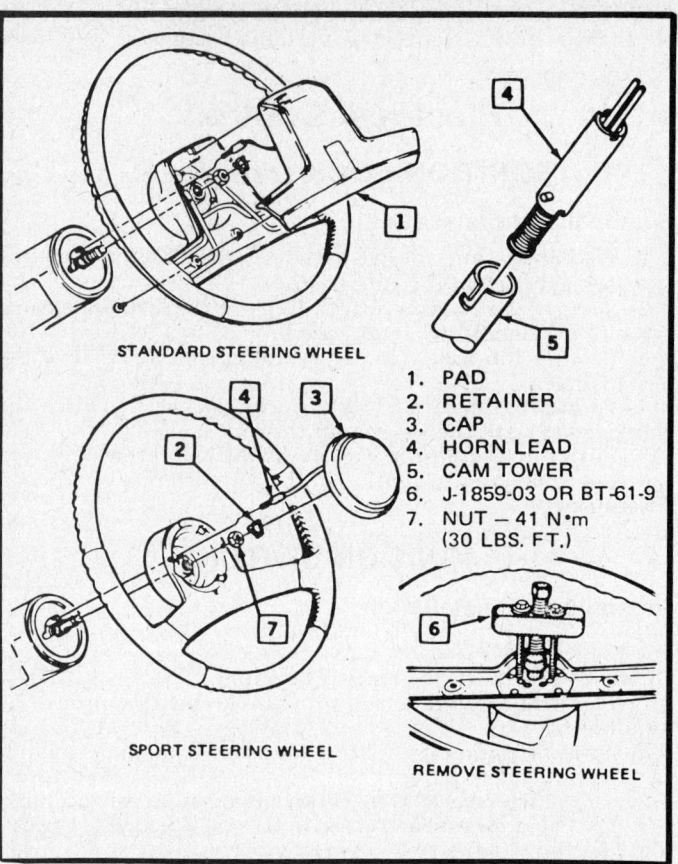

Steering wheel and horn contact assembly with standard steering column (© General Motors Corporation)

1. PAD
2. RETAINER
3. CAP
4. HORN LEAD
5. CAM TOWER
6. J-1859-03 OR BT-61-9
7. NUT – 41 N·m (30 LBS. FT.)

cept the 1984 and later Regal, pull the light switch knob out to the last detent. Depress the spring loaded button on the switch and remove the knob.

2. Remove the left hand trim cover. Remove the sound insulator, if equipped.
3. On Regal models, remove the retaining screws and pull the switch straight out. This will also disconnect all electrical connections.
4. On all other models, remove the lower air conditioning duct. Disconnect the switch electrical connections.
5. Remove the retaining nut from the front of the headlight switch and push the switch assembly in and down to remove.
6. Installation is the reverse of the removal procedure.

HORN SWITCH

Removal and Installation

1. Disconnect the negative battery cable.
2. Remove the horn pad. Remove the contact assembly and all other related components.
3. If the vehicle is equipped with tilt and telescopic steering column, remove the lock lever and plate.
4. Installation is the reverse of the removal procedure.

MULTI-FUNCTION SWITCH

All models use the multi-function lever. This lever operates the turn signals, headlamp beam changer, cruise control, if equipped and the windshield washer/wipers.

Removal and Installation

1. Disconnect the negative battery cable. Remove the steering wheel. Remove the turn signal switch.
2. It may be necessary to loosen the two column mounting nuts and remove the four bracket-to-mast jacket screws, then separate the bracket from the mast jacket to allow the connector clip on the ignition switch to be pulled out of the column assembly.
3. Disconnect the washer/wiper switch lower connector.
4. Remove the screws attaching the column housing to the mast jacket. Be sure to note the position of the dimmer switch actuator rod for reassembly in the same position. Remove the column housing and switch as an assembly.

NOTE: The tilt and travel columns have a removable plastic cover on the column housing. This provides access to the wiper switch without removing the entire column housing.

5. Turn upside down and use a drift to remove the pivot pin from the washer/wiper switch. Remove the switch.

BUICK 13
ELECTRA · ESTATE WAGON · LE SABRE · REGAL

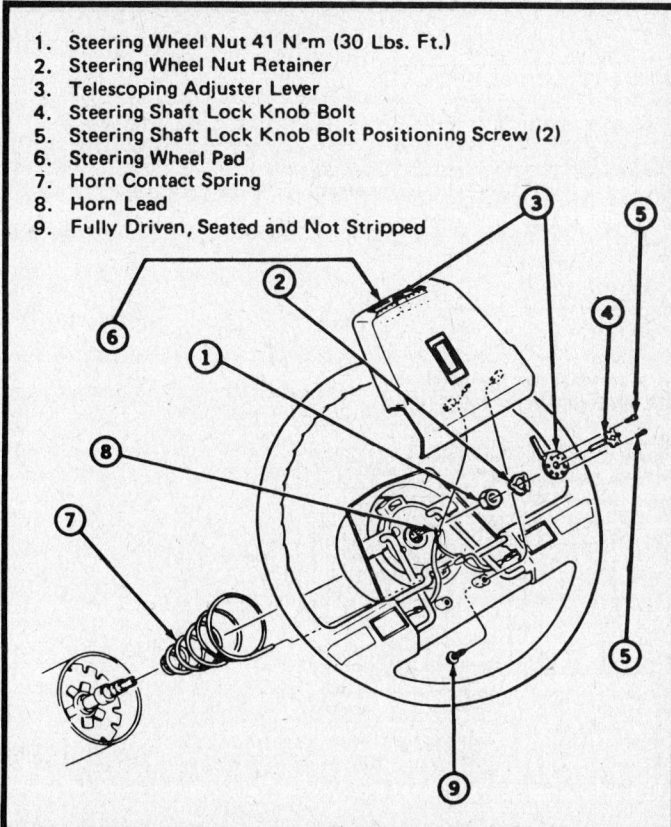

1. Steering Wheel Nut 41 N·m (30 Lbs. Ft.)
2. Steering Wheel Nut Retainer
3. Telescoping Adjuster Lever
4. Steering Shaft Lock Knob Bolt
5. Steering Shaft Lock Knob Bolt Positioning Screw (2)
6. Steering Wheel Pad
7. Horn Contact Spring
8. Horn Lead
9. Fully Driven, Seated and Not Stripped

Steering wheel and horn contact assembly with tilt and telescoping wheel (© General Motors Corporation)

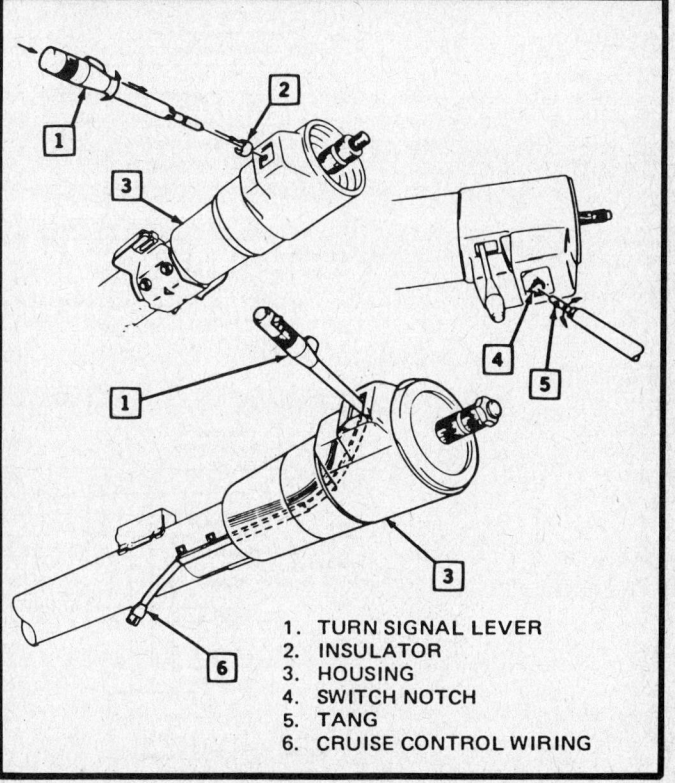

1. TURN SIGNAL LEVER
2. INSULATOR
3. HOUSING
4. SWITCH NOTCH
5. TANG
6. CRUISE CONTROL WIRING

Multifunction turnsignal lever assembly, typical
(© General Motors Corporation)

6. Place the switch into position in the housing, then install the pivot pin.
7. Position the housing onto the mast jacket and attach by installing the screws. Install the dimmer switch actuator rod in the same position as noted earlier. Check switch operation.
8. Reconnect lower end of switch assembly.
9. Install remaining components in reverse order of removal. Be sure to attach column mounting bracket in original position.

WINDSHIELD WIPER MOTOR

Removal and Installation

1. Disconnect the negative battery cable.
2. Raise the hood and remove the cowl screen.
3. Loosen the transmission drive link to crank arm retaining bolts. Remove the drive link from the motor crank arm.
4. Disconnect the electrical wiring and the washer hoses from the motor assembly.
5. Remove the motor retaining screws. Remove the windshield wiper motor while guiding the crank arm through the hole.
6. Installation is the reverse of the removal procedure. The motor must be in the Park position before assembling the crank arm to the drive link.

WIPER LINKAGE/TRANSMISSION

Removal and Installation

1. Disconnect the negative battery cable.
2. Raise the hood and remove the cowl vent screen. Remove both wiper arms and blade assemblies. Remove windshield lower reveal moulding.
3. Loosen, but do not remove the retaining nuts securing the transmission drive link to the motor crank arm.
4. Disconnect the transmission drive link from the motor crank arm. Remove the transmission to body retaining screws.
5. Remove the transmission and linkage assembly by guiding it through the plenum chamber opening or to the left side under the dash panel extension.
6. Installation is the reverse of the removal procedure.
7. Check wiper operation, pattern and Park position.

Instrument Panel

INSTRUMENT CLUSTER

Removal and Installation

1983 REGAL

1. Disconnect the negative battery cable.
2. Remove the headlight switch knob and retainer. Lower the steering column, as required. Disconnect the shift indicator clip if necessary.
3. Pry out and remove the left hand instrument panel trim plate.
4. Remove the instrument panel retaining screws. Pull the panel forward and disconnect all the electrical connections and the speedometer cable. Remove the instrument panel from the vehicle.
5. Installation is the reverse of the removal procedure.

1984 AND LATER REGAL (STANDARD CLUSTER)

1. Remove the left side trim cover.

13-13

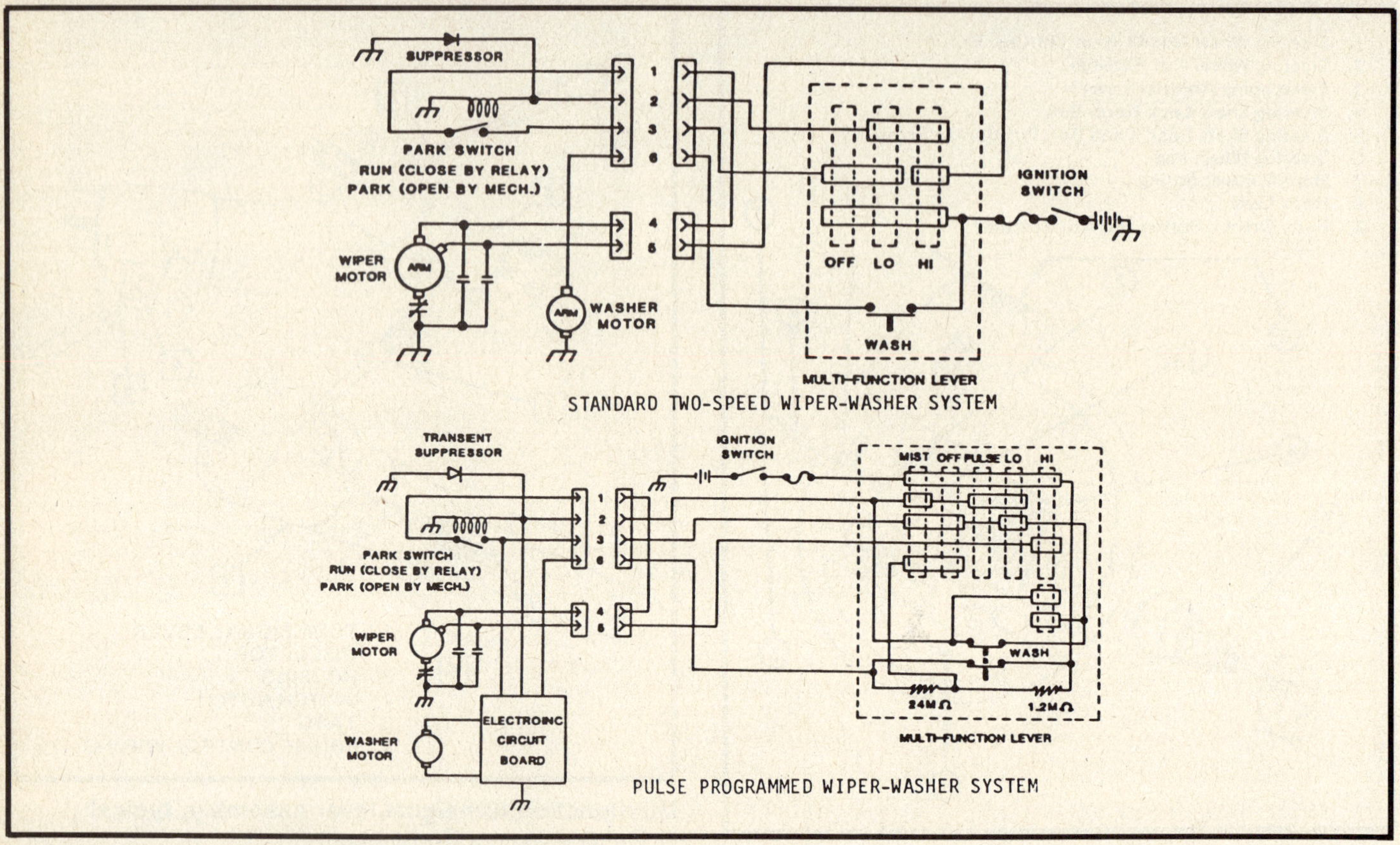

Section 13

BUICK
ELECTRA • ESTATE WAGON • LE SABRE • REGAL

Standard and pulse wiper motor circuit diagrams (© General Motors Corporation)

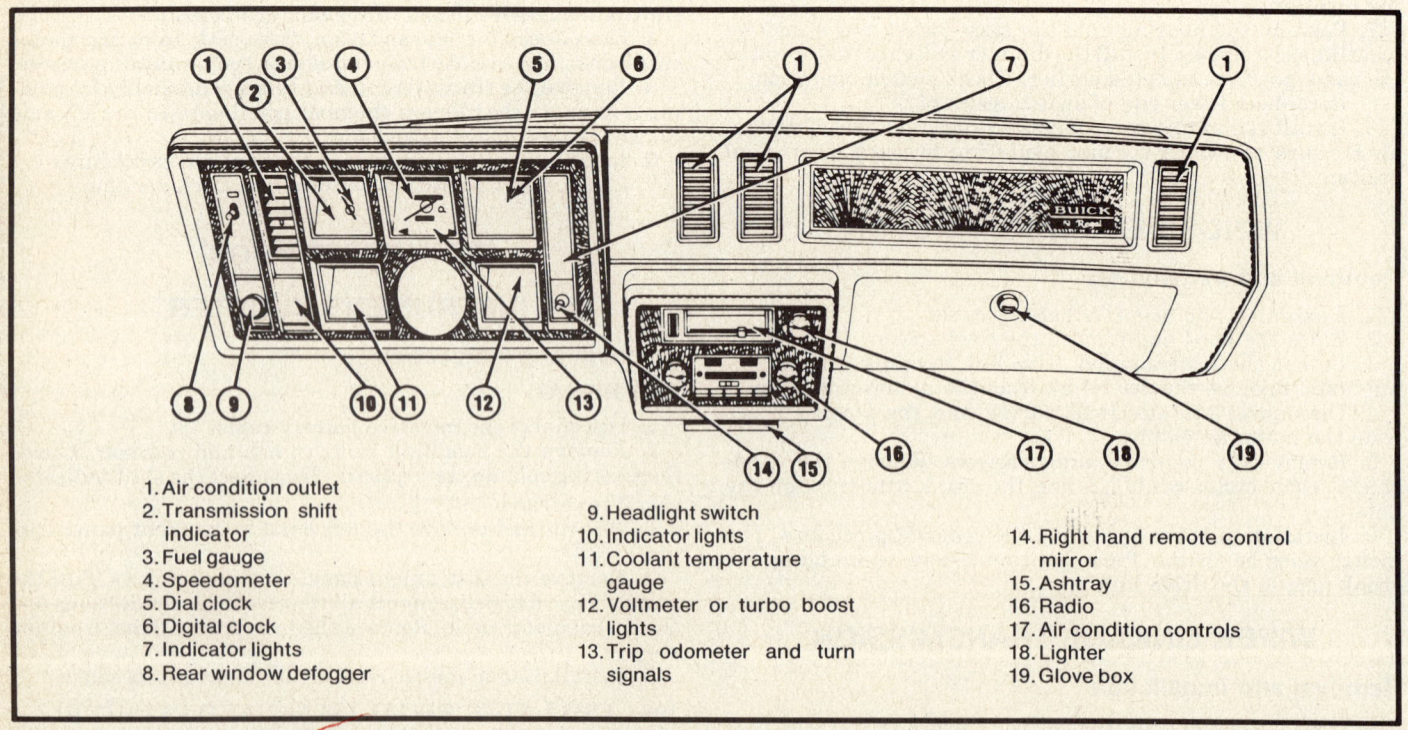

1. Air condition outlet
2. Transmission shift indicator
3. Fuel gauge
4. Speedometer
5. Dial clock
6. Digital clock
7. Indicator lights
8. Rear window defogger
9. Headlight switch
10. Indicator lights
11. Coolant temperature gauge
12. Voltmeter or turbo boost lights
13. Trip odometer and turn signals
14. Right hand remote control mirror
15. Ashtray
16. Radio
17. Air condition controls
18. Lighter
19. Glove box

Instrument cluster assembly, typical of Century and Regal models to 1983 (© General Motors Corporation)

BUICK

ELECTRA • ESTATE WAGON • LE SABRE • REGAL

SECTION 13

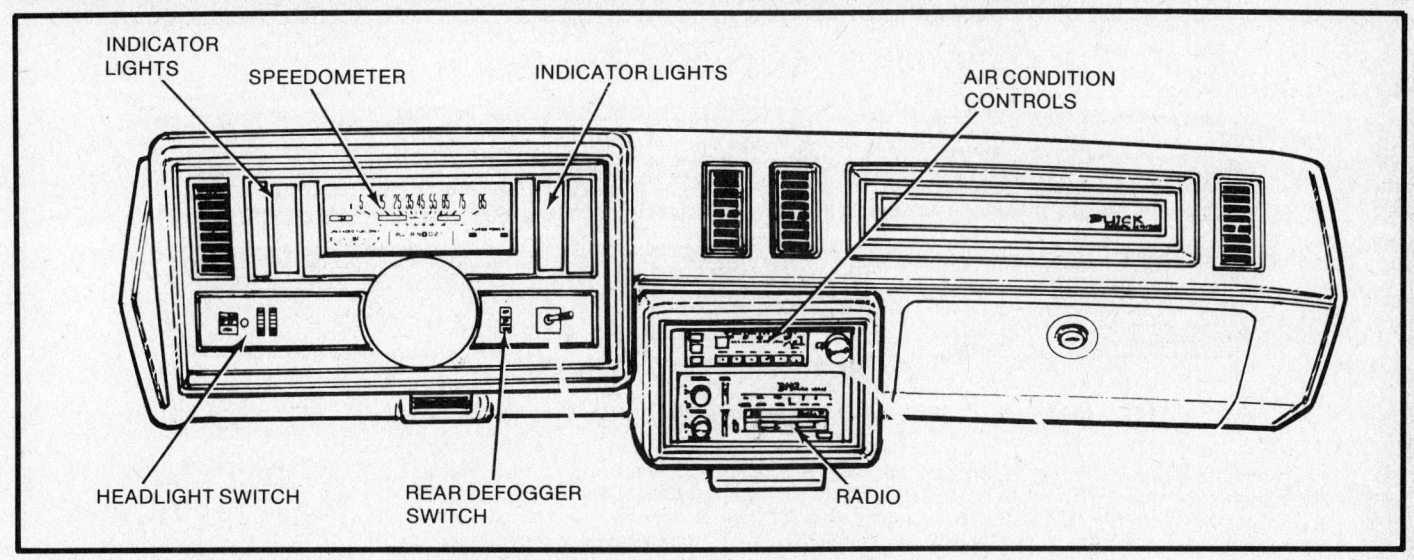

Instrument cluster assembly—Regal model 1984 and later (© General Motors Corporation)

2. Remove the retaining screws holding the cluster carrier to the instrument panel.
3. Disconnect the speedometer cable from the split in the engine compartment, if a two piece cable is used.
4. Remove the steering column trim cover.
5. Disconnect the shift indicator clip.
6. Lower the steering column. If the vehicle is equipped with a tilt wheel it will be necessary to lower the wheel as far as possible and then unscrew the tilt lever.
7. Pull the instrument cluster forward enough to disconnect the speedometer cable from the rear of the cluster. Disconnect the wiring connectors.
8. Pull the gear selector lever down into the Low position.
9. Pull the cluster out far enough to remove the screw retaining the Vehicle Speed Sensor (VSS) to the head of the speedometer.
10. Remove the cluster.
11. The installation of the cluster assembly is the reverse of the removal procedure.

1984 AND LATER REGAL (DIGITAL CLUSTER)

1. Disconnect the negative battery cable. Remove the left hand trim panel.
2. Remove the instrument cluster housing as previously outlined. Pull the cluster out far enough to remove the screw retaining the Vehicle Speed Sensor (VSS) to the head of the speedometer.
3. Disconnect the two edgeboard connectors on the printed circuit from the tube and circuit board assembly. Remove the four screws from the face of the cluster and remove the lense and bezel. All pushbuttons must be removed first, by pulling them straight out.
4. Remove the six screws holding the tube and circuit board to the cluster carrier. Remove the tube and circuit board.
5. Remove the two regular screws to remove the mecahnical odometer from the tube and circuit board.
6. Remove the two telltale lenses and pads from the face plate. The shift indicator needle, spring and cable stay with the tube and circuiot board. Do not remove.
7. Installation is the reverse order of the removal procedure.

1983 LESABRE AND ELECTRA

1. Disconnect the negative battery cable.
2. Pull the steering column filler forward.
3. Remove the headlamp switch knob and bezel. The bezel screws out unless the vehicle is equipped with the twilight sentinel system. Then the bezel is removed by pulling straight out.

NOTE: The headlamp switch knob is removed with the use of a screwdriver type tool to push forward in the slot on the knob to release the retaining clip.

4. Remove the left hand instrument panel trim plate by grasping and gently pulling the panel outward to clear the opening.
5. The installation is the reverse of the removal procedure.

1984 AND LATER LESABRE AND ELECTRA

1. Disconnect the negative battery cable. Remove the defroster grille.
2. Remove the 10 screws retaining the instrument panel top cover to the instrument panel.
3. If the vehicle is equipped with a twilight sentinel, pop up the photocell retainer and turn the photocell counterclockwise in the retainer and pull it down and out.
4. Slide the instrument panel top cover out far enough to disconnect the aspirator hose, electrical connector to the in-car sensor and the electrical connector to the electroluminescent inverter.
5. Remove the instrument panel top cover from the instrument panel. On models equipped with Quartz clusters, remove the steering coulmn trim cover, so that the shift indicator can be removed.
6. Remove the 5 screws from the instrument cluster to the instrument panel carrier. Pull the cluster housing assembly straight out, this will also separate the electrical connectors to the cluster.

NOTE: It may be helpful to tilt the wheel all the way down and pull the gear select lever to low. When removing the cluster.

7. Installation is the reverse order of the removal procedure.

SPEEDOMETER

Removal and Installation

1983 REGAL

1. Disconnect the negative battery cable.
2. Remove the headlight switch knob and retainer (1982). Remove the left hand trim cover.

13-15

BUICK
ELECTRA • ESTATE WAGON • LE SABRE • REGAL

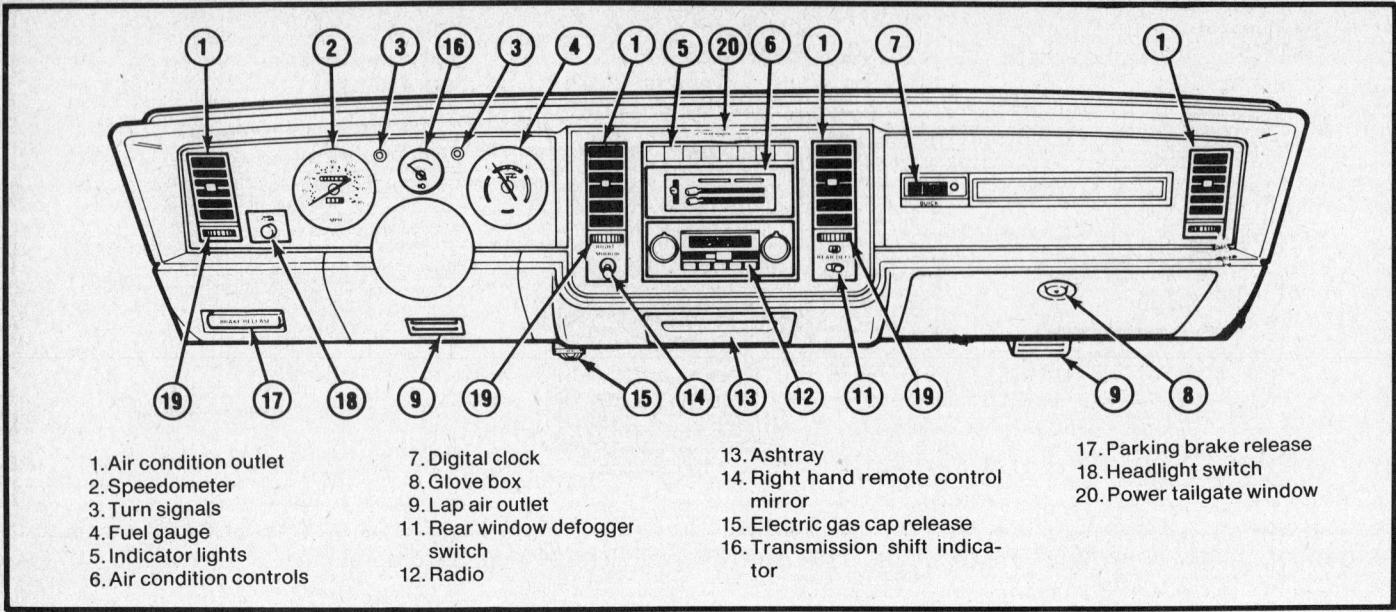

1. Air condition outlet
2. Speedometer
3. Turn signals
4. Fuel gauge
5. Indicator lights
6. Air condition controls
7. Digital clock
8. Glove box
9. Lap air outlet
11. Rear window defogger switch
12. Radio
13. Ashtray
14. Right hand remote control mirror
15. Electric gas cap release
16. Transmission shift indicator
17. Parking brake release
18. Headlight switch
20. Power tailgate window

Instrument cluster assembly—LeSabre and Electra models (© General Motors Corporation)

3. Unscrew the knob on the trip odometer reset. Remove the lens and bezel.
4. Remove the clock. Remove the fuel gauge.
5. Remove the speedometer retaining screws. Pull the assembly out far enough to gain access to the speedometer cable and electrical connectors.
6. Disconnect the speedometer cable at the head. To gain slack it may be necessary to disconnect the cable at the cruise control transducer or at the transmission. Remove Vehicle Speed Sensor (VSS), if equipped.
7. Remove the speedometer assembly from the vehicle.
8. Installation is the reverse of the removal procedure.

LESABRE, ELECTRA AND 1984 AND LATER REGAL

1. Disconnect the negative battery cable. Remove the instrument cluster (left hand side) trim plate.
2. Remove the four screws holding the lenses to the cluster assembly and remove the lenses, on the tilt columns remove the tilt lever.
3. Remove the speedometer retaining screws. Pull the assembly forward in order to disconnect the speedometer cable and electrical connectors. To gain slack it may be necessary to disconnect the cable at the cruise control transducer or the transmission. Remove Vehicle Speed Sensor (VSS), if equipped.
4. Remove the speedometer assembly from the vehicle.
5. Installation is the same as the removal procedure.

ELECTRONIC COMPONENT PRECAUTIONS

Special precautions **MUST** be taken while servicing any electronic devices to preclude damaging or degrading these components as a result of static electricity. Degradation of unprotected electronic parts is possibly by electrostatic voltages as low as 30 volts generated by an ungrounded person just sliding across the car seat. Depending on the percentage of Relative Humidity present, just walking on a carpet across the room can generate an electrostatic voltage as high as 30,000 volts!

Therefore, when servicing electronic components sensitive to electrostatic discharge (ESD), certain standard industry practices must be adhered to. These recommended practices include:

1. Transporting static sensitive parts in protective packaging.
2. Requiring that service personnel wear a wrist strap connected to ground through a one megohm resistor.
3. Using a static-protected work station free of static producing material (such as plastic styrofoam, etc.) when servicing the electronic components.
4. Using a floor mat to stand on that is grounded to earth ground through a one megohm resistor.
5. Working in a dust free work area where the Relative Humidity is kept at a minimum of 30%.
6. Using an approved mat covering the work (surface) area that is grounded through a one megohm resistor to earth ground.

QUARTZ ELECTRONIC SPEEDOMETER (OPTIONAL)

1984 AND LATER

The Quartz Electronic Speedometer is a sealed unit that must be replaced as a unit, should a malfunction occur. A speed sensor is located on the transmission and generates vehicle speed information, in place of the conventional speedometer cable. The assembly is removed and installed in the conventional manner.

ELECTRICAL COMPONENT LOCATION

Electronic Control Module

The electronic control module is located on the right side of the vehicle. It is positioned in front of the right hand kick panel. In order to gain access to the assembly you must first remove the trim panel.

Fusible Links

All vehicles are equipped with fusible links. The links are attached to the lower ends of the main supply wires and connect to the starter solenoid. One of the main wires is a No. 12 red wire which supplies the headlight circuit and the other is a No. 10 red which supplies all electrical units except the headlights.

BUICK SECTION 13
ELECTRA · ESTATE WAGON · LE SABRE · REGAL

TURN SIGNAL FLASHER, HAZARD WARNING FLASHER AND FUSE BLOCK LOCATION CHART

Buick	1983-87 TSF	1983-87 HWF	1983-87 Fuse Block Location
Century	1	2	3
Skylark	1	2	3
Skyhawk	1	2	4
Electra	1	5	4
Park Avenue	1	2	4
Riviera	1	2	6
Somerset Regal	1	2	4
Regal	1	5	4
LaSabre	1	2	4

1. The turn signal flasher is located under the left side of the instrument panel on or near the steering column support.
2. The hazard flasher is located on the right hand side of the instrument panel, on the convenience center. On some of the later models it is located on the right hand side of the steering column brace.
3. The fuse block is located on the right hand side of the instrument panel.
4. The fuse block is located on the cowl under the left side of the instrument panel (behind the trim panel on some of the later models).
5. The hazard flasher is plugged directly into the fuse block.
6. The fuse block is located on the cowl under the left side of the instrument panel. On the later models the fuse block is located in the center of the instrument panel in the front of the console.

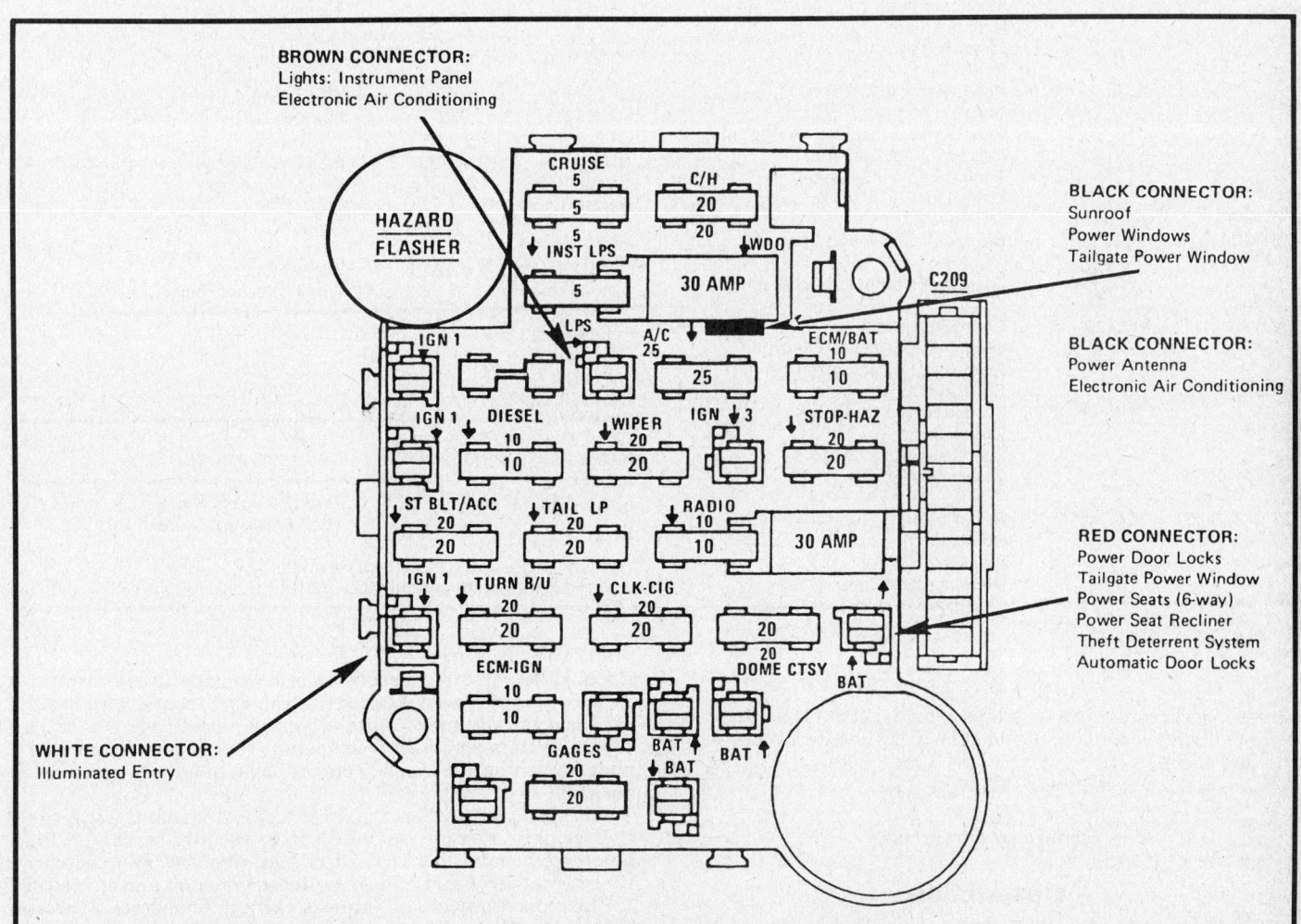

Typical fuse panel and circuit identification (© General Motors Corporation)

13-17

SECTION 13

BUICK
ELECTRA • ESTATE WAGON • LE SABRE • REGAL

FUSE	COLOR (AMPS)	SCHEMATICS
A/C	WHT (25)	Air Conditioning Heater Trunk Release
C/H	YEL (20)	Choke Heater (Gasoline)
CIG-CLK	YEL (20)	Clock Electronic Air Conditioning Front Cigar Lighter Glove Box Light Warnings: Ignition Key Warnings: Lights-On Power Antenna Radio Warnings: Seatbelt Theft Deterrent System
CRUISE	TAN (5)	Cruise Control
DIESEL	RED (10)	Air Conditioning Glow Plugs Fuel Control Indicators (Instrument Panel, Diesel)
DOME CTSY	YEL (20)	Automatic Door Locks Illuminated Entry Interior Lights Memory Seats Power Door Locks Power Remote Mirrors Rear Cigar Lighter Rear Dome Light (Station Wagon) Indicators: Tailgate Ajar Theft Deterrent System Trunk Light
ECM/BAT	RED (10)	Computer Command Control
ECM-IGN	RED (10)	Computer Command Control
GAGES	YEL (20)	Charging System Computer Command Control Electronic Level Control Emission Controls And Torque Converter Clutch (Diesel Only) Fuel Gage and Indicators (Instrument Panel)
ST BLT/ACC	YEL (20)	Brake Warning System Defogger Illuminated Entry Warnings: Seatbelt

FUSE	COLOR (AMPS)	SCHEMATICS
		Theft Deterrent System
INST LPS	TAN (5)	Electronic Air Conditioning Lights: Instrument Panel
PWR ACCY (Circuit Breaker)	GRN (30)	Defogger Power Door Locks Automatic Door Locks Power Seats Power Seats Recliner Memory Seats Tailgate Power Window Theft Deterrent System
RADIO	RED (10)	Power Antenna Radio
STOP-HAZ	YEL (20)	Computer Command Control Lights: Stop/Hazard

TAIL LP	YEL (20)	Lights: Cornering/Front Park/
		  Front Marker/License/
		  Radio/Tail/Rear Marker/
		  Engine Compartment/
		  Opera
		Twilight Sentinel

TURN B/U	YEL (20)	Automatic Door Locks Back Up Lights Turn Lights Memory Seats
WDO (Circuit Breaker)	GRN (30)	Fuel Cap Release Power Windows Sunroof Tailgate Power Window
WIPER	WHT (20)	Wiper/Washer Wiper/Washer (Pulse)

In Line Fuse Data*

NAME	SIZE (AMPS)	CIRCUITS PROTECTED
A	(25)	Theft Deterrent System
B	(25)	Theft Deterrent System

*(In-Line Fuses A and B are located under the LH side of the I/P near the fuse block)

Convenience Center

Some vehicles are equipped with a convenience center. This center incorporates various relays and flashers. If the vehicle is equipped with a convenience center it will be located next to the fuse block.

Cruise Control

Description

1983

Cruise control with resume is a speed control system which maintains a desired car speed under normal driving conditions. However, steep grades up or down may cause variations in the selected speeds. Cruise control with resume also has the capability to resume to a pre-set speed upon driver demand after the system has been disengaged. This is done by moving a slide switch on the cruise control lever handle to the resume position.

The main parts of the cruise control system are the transducer assembly, resume solenoid valve, vacuum servo and linkage, engagement switch button and off/on/resume switch on turn signal lever and release switches (vacuum and electrical).

The cruise control system uses vacuum to operate a throttle servo unit. The servo unit maintains a desired car speed by receiving a controlled amount of vacuum from the transducer unit to regulate throttle position. A speedometer cable from the

BUICK 13
ELECTRA · ESTATE WAGON · LE SABRE · REGAL

TEST		NORMAL REACTION
1	Apply 12 volts dc to servo pins A and E. Then ground servo pin C. NOTE: Pin A to pin C closes the normally-open vent valve; whereas, pin E to pin C opens the normally-closed vacuum valve.	Servo should full stroke. If not, check vacuum hoses to the vacuum supply.
2	Remove the 12 volts dc source voltage from SERVO pin E.	The servo should hold a full stroke. If not, go to step 3. If servo holds, go to step 4.
3	Disconnect vacuum brake release at servo and plug vacuum release port on the servo. Momentarily apply 12 volts dc to pin E to allow servo to full stroke.	If the servo holds its position, adjust the brake vacuum release valve or replace the valve.
4	Turn ignition "ON".	Vacuum release valve should engage.
5	Turn ignition "OFF" and disconnect vacuum valve harness connector at valve. Then turn ignition "ON".	If the brake switch is properly adjusted, battery voltage should be present across the two connector terminals on the switch. No battery voltage indicates an open circuit.

Cruise III system vacuum servo tests (© General Motors Corporation)

transmission drives the transducer, and a second speedometer cable from the transducer drives the speedometer. The cruise control transducer contains a low speed limit switch that prevents system engagement below a minimum speed, about 30 mph (50 km/h) depending on the transducer used. The operation of the transducer unit is controlled by an engagement switch button located in the end of the directional signal lever and the off/on/resume slide switch. To disengage the system, two release switches are provided. An electrical release switch mounted on the brake pedal bracket (and clutch pedal bracket on cars equipped with manual transaxle) disengages the system electrically when the brake pedal (or clutch pedal) is depressed. A vacuum release valve, mounted on the brake pedal bracket, (and clutch pedal bracket on cars equipped with manual transaxle), vents controlled vacuum to the atmosphere when the brake pedal (or clutch pedal) is depressed, allowing the servo unit to quickly return the throttle to idle position.

1984 AND LATER

Prior to 1984 cruise control systems for maintaining a desired vehicle speed under normal driving conditions were electromechanical. In 1984 the electronically-controlled Cruise III system with a memory was introduced. Vacuum-controlled valving was retained to operate the throttle servo unit since Cruise III can effectively operate at the lower manifold vacuum levels of the 1984 and later, more fuel efficient engines.

Cruise III operates in one of three modes:
1. Steady-state cruise ("COAST").
2. Accelerate ("TAP UP").
3. Decelerate ("TAP DOWN").

The driver can disengage the cruise control system by braking the vehicle and resume a pre-set speed merely by moving the 3 position slide switch on the multi-function lever to the RESUME position. Steep grades, up or down, however, may cause variations between the selected and actual vehicle speeds.

In addition to the multi-function switch on the steering column, the Cruise III Speed Control System includes:
1. An electronic control module (controller).
2. A two-valve (vent and vacuum) servo unit containing two solenoids.
3. An electrical switch and a vacuum release valve.
4. A vacuum supply.
5. A speed sensing system.
6. Electrical and vacuum harness.

The servo unit maintains a desired car speed by trapping vacuum in the servo unit at the proper servo-throttle position. The controller: (1) monitors vehicle speed and servo position, and (2) operates the vacuum and vent valves in the servo to maintain desired speed. The controller has a low speed control limit which prevents system engagement below a 25 mph minimum speed. An electrical release switch disengages the cruise system; on vehicles equipped with automatic transmission the switch is mounted on the brake pedal bracket. On cars equipped with a manual transaxle the release switch is on the clutch pedal bracket. The cruise control system is disengaged electrically when the brake (or clutch) pedal is depressed.

A vacuum release valve, also mounted on the brake pedal bracket, vents vacuum trapped in the servo to the atmosphere when the brake pedal is depressed and allows the throttle to return quickly to the idle position.

NOTE: Special testing tools are available to test the electronic circuits.

Adjustments

1983 – 4.3L GAS ENGINE (267 CID, VIN CODE J)

1. Position the carburetor choke in the hot idle position.
2. With the cable installed to the manifold bracket servo assembly bracket and carburetor, pull the servo assembly end of the cable toward the servo assembly as far as it will go.
3. If one of the four holes in the servo assembly tab then lines up with the cable pin, connect pin to tab with retainer.
4. If a tab hole does not line up with the pin, move the cable away from servo assembly until the next closest tab hole lines up and connect pin to tab with retainer.
5. Do not stretch the cable in order to make a tab hole connect to the pin. If this is done it will prevent the engine from returning to idle.

5.0L GAS ENGINE (305, 307 CID, VIN CODE H, Y)

1. Adjust the rod length to the minimum slack with the carburetor lever on the slow idle screw.
2. Be sure that the engine is not running.
3. The idle load control must be fully retracted when the retainer is installed.

1983 – 3.8 (231 CID, VIN CODE A, 3, 8) AND 4.1L (252 CID, VIN CODE 4) GAS ENGINES

1. Assemble the chain to be taut with the carburetor in the hot idle position. Be sure that the idle control solenoid is not energized.

13–19

BUICK
ELECTRA • ESTATE WAGON • LE SABRE • REGAL

CRUISE CONTROL WITH RESUME TROUBLE DIAGNOSIS
1982-83 Models

Condition	Possible Cause	Correction
System inoperative but cruise light comes on	1) Throttle linkage from servo unit to throttle disconnected.	1) Connect throttle linkage and adjust.
	2) Large vacuum leak. Vacuum hose disconnected.	2) Check all vacuum lines and connections. Check for torn or leaking servo unit. Repair or replace as required.
	3) Restricted or plugged vacuum line. Faulty vacuum regulator (diesel only) or incorrect check valve orientation (vacuum pump and aspirator).	3) Check for kinks or collapsed vacuum line. Remove restriction. Replace vacuum regulator or correct check valve orientation.
	4) Brake pedal vacuum release valve or brake electrical switch out of adjustment.	4) Adjust or replace as necessary.
	5) Resume solenoid valve inoperative.	5) Check for voltage at solenoid (2 volts with ignition on). If voltage, check ground wire and repair. Investigate "engage" circuit for 12 volts or possible faulty solenoid. If no voltage, check for proper adjustment of brake switch wiring or engage switch. Repair as necessary.
System inoperative and cruise light stays off	1) Loose electrical connections or open wiring.	1) Check and secure all electrical connectors, transducer, cruise engage switch, fuse block, and repair cut or open wiring.
	2) Fuse blown.	2) Replace fuse.
	3) Malfunctioned turn signal and engage switch assembly.	3) Substitute new turn signal and engage switch assembly by plugging into connector at bottom of steering column. Check operation and, if satisfactory, install new turn signal and engage switch assembly.
	4) Malfunctioned transducer.	4) Replace.
Speed increases after engagement	1) Speedometer cable (needle) fluctuates due to speedo cable or housing bent, kinked or misrouted.	1) Correct as necessary.
	2) Transducer orifice tube out of adjustment.	2) Adjust.
	3) Transducer malfunction.	3) Replace.
Speed drops off after engagement	1) Throttle linkage too loose. Vacuum leak or restriction.	1) Check for damaged, disconnected, pinched, or kinked hoses. Repair or replace as required. Adjust throttle linkage.
	2) Transducer orifice tube out of adjustment.	2) Adjust.
Surging	1) Check for restricted vacuum line from engine to transducer.	1) Repair or replace.
	2) Check to insure that servo unit will full stroke.	2) Replace servo unit.
	3) Transducer malfunction.	3) Replace.
	4) Check valve stuck closed (vacuum pump and aspirator only) or missing.	4) Install or re-orient check valve as necessary.

BUICK 13
ELECTRA • ESTATE WAGON • LE SABRE • REGAL

CRUISE CONTROL WITH RESUME TROUBLE DIAGNOSIS (Cont.)
1982-83 Models

Condition	Possible Cause	Correction
Speed Drops Off Excessively on Inclines	1) Throttle linkage too loose.	1) Adjust.
	2) Vacuum source hose restricted.	2) Repair or Replace.
	3) Cruise system not connected to auxiliary vacuum pump or aspirator.	3) Correct.
	4) Check valve reversed or stuck open (vacuum or aspirator pump only).	4) Re-orient or replace as necessary.
	5) AIR management valve is diverting (aspirator equipped cars only) causes line pressure to aspirator to be reduced.	5) Check vacuum line to AIR management valve (if so specified) diverter line muffler should have pressure regulator.

2. Place the chain into the swivel cavities which permit the chain to have slight slack.
3. Place the retainer over the swivel and chain assembly. The retainer must be positioned between the balls.
4. Cut off the chain flush with the side of the swivel, to remove excess chain length.
5. Chain slack must not exceed one half the diameter of the ball stud when measured at the hot idle position (3.8L, VIN A). When making this measurement be sure that the idle control solenoid is not energized and that the swivel is disconnected from the ball stud.

1984 AND LATER 3.8L (231 CID, VIN CODE A, 9) AND 4.1L (252 CID, VIN CODE 4) GAS ENGINES

1. Set the fast idle cam to the off position. Be sure that the engine is not running.
2. Retract the idle speed motor. Check that the throttle is closed.
3. Install the rod on the throttle stud at the large end of the slot.
4. Adjust the length so that the stud is at the end of the slot in the rod assembly. Be sure that the rod is aligned with the hole in the servo.
5. Install the retainer. Insert the rod end of the rod through the holes and snap the retainer in place.

4.3L (263 CID, VIN CODE V) AND 5.7L (350 CID, VIN CODE N) DIESEL ENGINES

1. Adjustment is made with the engine not running.
2. Adjust the rod length to minimum slack with the pump on slow idle screw.

COOLING AND HEATER SECTION

WATER PUMP

Removal and Installation
GENERAL, ALL ENGINES

1. Disconnect the negative battery cable. Drain the cooling system. Remove the fan shroud, if required.
2. Remove all the necessary components in order to gain access to the water pump assembly.
3. Remove the fan and pulley. Disconnect all hoses from the water pump.
4. Remove the water pump retaining bolts. Remove the water pump from the engine.
5. Installation is the reverse of the removal procedure. Be sure to clean the engine to water pump mating surface before installing the pump.
6. Use a new gasket when installing the pump assembly. Tighten all belts to specifications.

BLOWER MOTOR

Removal and Installation

1. Disconnect the negative battery cable.
2. Disconnect the electrical connections from the blower motor.
3. Remove the blower motor flange screws. Remove the blower motor assembly from the heater case.
4. Installation is the reverse of removal.

HEATER/AC CONTROL ASSEMBLY

NOTE: If the vehicle is equipped with touch climate control air condition, extreme care should be used when disconnecting the electrical connections from the unit.

Removal and Installation

The removal and installation of the dash mounted temperature control unit is general in the vehicle models. The outlined steps may not be in the correct order for a specific model. Rearrange the steps to relate to the vehicle being repaired.

1. Disconnect the negative battery cable.
2. Remove the necessary instrument panel trim.
3. Remove the radio and/or knobs, radio speaker, ash tray, cigar lighter, and the floor console trim plate, as required.
4. After exposing the control retaining screws, remove them and pull the control away from the dash. Disconnect the bowden cable, electrical and/or vacuum connections.
5. Remove the control unit.
6. The installation is the reverse of the removal procedure.

SECTION 13

BUICK
ELECTRA • ESTATE WAGON • LE SABRE • REGAL

HEATER CORE

Removal and Installation

1983 AND LATER REGAL WITHOUT A/C

1. Disconnect the negative battery cable. Drain the cooling system.
2. Remove the heater hoses from the heater core. Disconnect and or remove all electrical connections and wires from the heater core housing.
3. Remove the retaining screws that secure the heater core cover to the heater core housing.
4. Remove the heater core cover and remove the heater core from the vehicle.
5. Installation is the revere order of the removal procedure.

1983 AND LATER LESABRE/ELECTRA

1. Disconnect the negative battery cable. Drain the cooling system.
2. Remove the right side insulator, the center instrument panel trim plate and the lower instrument poanel trim plate.
3. Remove the right speaker grille and speaker. Remove the electrical connections, wires and hoses from the programmer.
4. Remove the programmer linkage cover and linkage. Remove the programmer.
5. Remove the heater core cover retaining screws and then the heater core cover.
6. Remove the splash cover to gain access to the heater core hoses. Remove the heater core hoses and remove the heater core.
7. Installation is the reverse order of the removal procedure.

1983 AND LATER ESTATE

1. Remove the negative battery cable, resistor and blower motor wires.
2. Remove the heater core ground strap from the dash panel. Drain the cooling system and disconnect both heater hoses.
3. Remove the seven heater and blower case to plenum case screws and remove the case. It may be necessary at this time to remove the temperature air valve.
4. Remove the four heater core shroud screws and remove the shroud and heater core assembly.
5. Remove the three screws and heater core mounting clamps to separate the core from the shroud.
6. Installation is the reverse order of the removal procedure.

HEATER CORE WITH A/C

Removal and Installation

1983 AND LATER ESTATE/REGAL

1. Disconnect the negative battery cable.
2. Disconnect all electrical connections from the heating unit. Disconnect the heater core ground strap.
3. Remove the right hood seal and the air inlet screens. Remove the case to dash bolts, upper to lower case screws around the flange and the case screws inside the air intake plenum.
4. Disconnect the heater hoses, after draining the radiator. Remove the upper cover case.
5. Remove the heater core assembly by lifting it straight up and out of the case.
6. Installation is the reverse of the removal procedure.

1983 AND LATER LESABRE/ELECTRA

1. Disconnect the negative battery cable. Drain the cooling system.
2. Remove the right side insulator, the center instrument panel trim plate and the lower instrument poanel trim plate.
3. Remove the right speaker grille and speaker. Remove the electrical connections, wires and hoses from the programmer.
4. Remove the programmer linkage cover and linkage. Remove the programmer.
5. Remove the heater core cover retaining screws and then the heater core cover.
6. Remove the splash cover to gain access to the heater core hoses. Remove the heater core hoses and remove the heater core.
7. Installation is the reverse order of the removal procedure.

FUEL SYSTEM

FUEL PUMP

Removal and Installation

MECHANICAL

1. Disconnect the negative battery cable.
2. Remove all components in order to gain access to the fuel pump.
3. Remove the inlet and outlet hoses from the pump assembly.
4. Remove the fuel pump retaining bolts. Remove the fuel pump from the engine.
5. Discard the fuel pump gasket. Scrape the block gasket surface before installing the fuel pump.
6. Installation is the reverse of the removal procedure. Be sure to correctly install the fuel pump push rod and mounting plate, if used.

ELECTRIC – EXCEPT V6 DIESEL ENGINE

1. Remove the fuel pump fuse from its location inside the fuse block.
2. Crank the engine, the engine will start and run until all the fuel is consumed. Crank the starter for three seconds to be sure all fuel pressure is relieved.
3. Disconnect the negative battery cable.
4. Raise the vehicle and support it safely.
5. Using a suitable jack, support the fuel tank and remove the two fuel tank mounting straps. Lower the tank fall enough to disconnect the sending unit wire wire, hoses and ground strap if so equipped. Remove the fuel tank from the vehicle.
6. Remove the fuel pump from the tank, by turning the cam lock ring on the fuel sending unit counterclockwise. Lift the assembly from the fuel tank and remove the fuel pump from the fuel sending unit.
7. Installation is the reverse of removal. Install the fuse in the fuse block. Start the engine and check for leaks.

ELECTRIC – V6 DIESEL ENGINE

NOTE: The fuel pump used on the V6 diesel engine is located at the front of the engine next to the fuel heater.

1. Disconnect the negative battery cable.
2. Remove the inlet and outlet fuel lines. Disconnect all electrical connectors from the pump assembly.
3. Remove the fuel pump retaining bolts. Remove the fuel pump from its mounting on the engine.
4. Installation is the reverse of the removal procedure. Be sure to torque the retaining bolts to 18 ft.lbs..

CARBURETOR

Adjustments

CHECKING CHOKE – HOT AIR TYPE

1. With parking brake applied, drive wheels blocked, transmission in park or neutral, start engine and allow engine to warm up, visually checking to be certain choke valve opens fully.
2. If choke valve fails to open fully, momentarily touch choke housing and hot air inlet pipe or hose to determine if sufficient heat is reaching the choke coil.

NOTE: The choke housing and hot air inlet pipe or hose are hot to the touch. Use care to prevent burning of hands.

3. If choke housing and/or heat inlet are cool to the touch, check for loss of vacuum to the housing, restricted heat inlet in the choke housing or choke heat pipe, collapsed or deteriorated heat inlet hose, or restricted passages in the manifold choke heat stove.
4. Replace or correct as necessary.

CHECKING CHOKE – ELECTRIC TYPE

NOTE: This test should be performed between 60° and 80°F.

1. Allow the engine to cool so that when the throttle is opened slightly, the choke blade fully closes.
2. Start the engine and determine a time for the choke blade to reach the full open position.
3. If the choke blade fails to open fully after 3.5 minutes, check the voltage at the choke heater connection.
4. If the voltage is approximately 12–15 volts, replace the electric choke unit.
5. If the voltage is low or zero, check all wires and connections. If any connections in the oil pressure switch circuitry are faulty, or if pressure switch is failed open, the oil warning light will be on with the engine running. Repair wires or connectors as required.
6. If the problem is still not corrected, replace the oil pressure switch. No gasket is used between the choke cover and the choke housing due to grounding requirements.

COMPUTER COMMAND CONTROL SYSTEM (CCC)

CARBURETOR MODELS

1983 – E2ME, E2SE, E4ME
1984 – E2SE, E2ME, E4ME, E4MC
1985–87 – E2SE, E2ME, E4MC

Mixture Control Adjustments
The Computer Command Control System provides precise control of carburetor air/fuel mixtures during all ranges of engine operation. Because of this System control, the below listed mixture control adjustment procedures are to be used if required. The previously used propane enrichment or lean drop methods of idle mixture adjustment may not be used when adjusting carburetors used with this system because system control will change air/fuel mixtures to lean or rich as the mixture needles are adjusted rich or lean respectively.
The computer command control system is sensitive to any change in mixture control adjustment which, if improperly set, can impair the ability of the system to maintain precise control of air/fuel mixtures. Plugs are installed in the carburetor air horn and over the idle mixture needles in the throttle body to seal the factory settings. For this reason, the mixture control adjustment points should never be changed from the original factory setting. However, if in diagnosis the system indicates the carburetor to be the cause of a driver performance complaint or emissions failure or critical parts such as air horn, float bowl, or throttle body are replaced, then the plugs may be removed and mixture control adjustments made, carefully following factory recommended procedures. After adjustment, replacement plugs (supplied in applicable service kits) must be installed.

Checking Mixture Control Solenoid Travel

Before proceeding, it will be necessary to modify float gauge J–9789–130, BT7720, or equivalent (used to externally check float level setting) by filling or grinding sufficient material off the gauge to allow insertion down the vertical vent ("D" shaped hole in the air horn casting next to the idle air bleed valve cover).
Check that gauge freely enters "D" vent hole and does not bind. The gauge will be used to determine total mixture control solenoid travel.
With engine off, air cleaner removed, measure mixture control solenoid travel as follows:

a. Insert modified float gauge down "D" shaped vent hole. Press down on gauge and release, observing that gauge moves freely and does not bind. With gauge released (solenoid up position), reading at eye level record mark on gauge (in inches) that lines up with top of air horn casting (upper edge).
b. Then, lightly press down on gauge until bottomed (solenoid down position). Record in inches mark on gauge that lines up with top of air horn casting.
c. Subtract gauge up dimension (item "a") from gauge down position (item "b") and record difference (in inches). The difference in dimensions is total solenoid travel.
d. If total solenoid travel (difference in item "c") is not within $3/32$–$5/32$ in. – 1982, and $2/32$ in.–$6/32$ in. – 1983 and later vehicles, make mixture control solenoid adjustments as noted below. If difference is within the above specifications, proceed to idle air bleed valve adjustment.

Mixture Control Solenoid Adjustments

1983 AND LATER

1. Remove air horn, mixture control solenoid plunger, air horn gasket and plastic filler block, using normal service procedures.

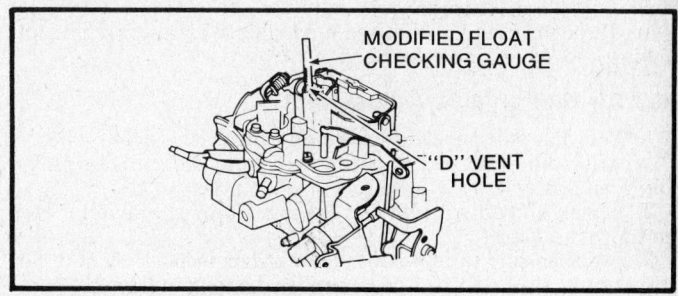

Location of "D" vent hole
(© General Motors Corporation)

2. Remove throttle side metering rod. Install mixture control solenoid gaging tool J–33815–1 and BT–8253-A, or equivalent over throttle side metering jet rod guide, and temporarily reinstall the solenoid plunger into the solenoid body.
3. Holding the solenoid plunger in the down position, use tool J–28696–10 and BT-7928, or equivalent, to turn lean mixture (solenoid) screw counterclockwise until the plunger breaks contact with the gauging tool. Turn slowly clockwise until the plunger just contacts the gauging tool. The adjust-

BUICK
ELECTRA • ESTATE WAGON • LE SABRE • REGAL

ment is correct when the solenoid plunger is contacting both the solenoid stop and the gauging tool.

If the total difference in adjustment required less than ¾ turn of the lean mixture (solenoid) screw, the original setting was within the manufacturer's specifications.

4. Remove solenoid plunger and gauging tool, and reinstall metering rod and plastic filler block.

5. Invert air horn and remove rich mixture stop screw and (if used) the rich authority adjusting spring from bottom side of air horn, using tool J–28696-4 and BT7967A or equivalent.

6. Remove lean mixture screw plug and the rich mixture stop screw plug from air horn, using a suitable sized punch.

7. Reinstall rich mixture stop screw and (if used) the rich authority adjusting spring in air horn and bottom lightly, then back screw out ¼ turn.

8. Reinstall air horn gasket, mixture control solenoid plunger and air horn to carburetor.

9. Insert external float gauge in vent hole and, with tool J–28696-10 and BT-7928, or equivalent, adjust rich mixture stop screw to obtain $^4/_{32}$ in. total plunger travel.

10. With solenoid plunger travel correctly set, install the plugs (supplied in service kits) in the air horn.

11. To install the lean mixture plug, position it hollow end down into the access hole of the lean mixture screw (solenoid), and use a suitably sized punch to drive plug into the air horn until the top of the plug is even with the lower plug.

12. To install the rich mixture stop screw, position it hollow end down, over the rich mixture stop screw access hole, and drive plug into place so that the top of the plug is $^1/_{16}$ in. below the surface of the air horn casting.

Idle Mixture & Speed Adjustment

Idle mixture screws are sealed with hardened caps covering the screws during original equipment production. These plugs are not to be removed unless required for cleaning or part replacement.

Before suspecting the carburetor as the cause of poor engine performance or rough idle, check ignition system including distributor, timing, spark plugs and wires. Inspect air cleaner, evaporative emission system, EFE system, PCV system, EGR system and engine compression. Also inspect intake manifold, vacuum hoses and connections for leaks and check torque of carburetor mounting bolts.

In the case of major carburetor repair, throttle body replacement or high idle CO as indicated by state or local emission inspection, idle mixture may be adjusted. Adjusting mixture by other than the Propane method may violate emissions. The following procedure must be used.

Idle Air Bleed Valve Adjustment

1. Position the parking brake and block the drive wheels. Disconnect and plug the vacuum hose from the canister purge valve and plug it.

2. Check and adjust ignition timing. Connect a dwell meter and a tachometer.

3. Start engine, and with transmission in park or neutral, run engine at idle until fully warm and a varying dwell is noted on the dwell meter. It is essential that the engine is operated for a sufficient length of time to ensure that the engine coolant sensor, and the oxygen sensor in the exhaust, are at full operational temperature.

4. Check engine idle speed and compare to specifications on the underhood label. If necessary, adjust curb idle speed. On models with idle speed control (ISC) or idle load compensator (ILC), no adjustment is possible.

5. With engine idling in drive (neutral for manual transmission), observe dwell reading on the 6 cylinder scale. If varying within the 10–50° range, adjustment is correct. If not, perform the following.

6. Remove the idle air bleed valve cover. If the cover is

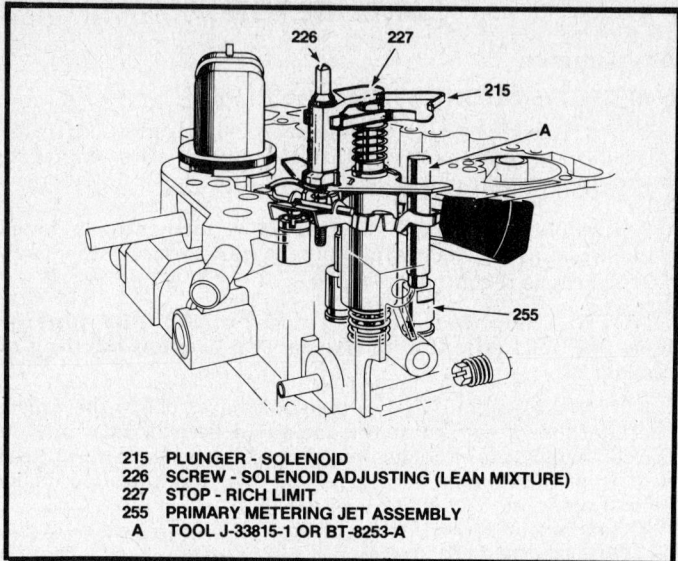

215 PLUNGER - SOLENOID
226 SCREW - SOLENOID ADJUSTING (LEAN MIXTURE)
227 STOP - RICH LIMIT
255 PRIMARY METERING JET ASSEMBLY
A TOOL J-33815-1 OR BT-8253-A

Installing mixture control solenoid gauge, typical
(© General Motors Corporation)

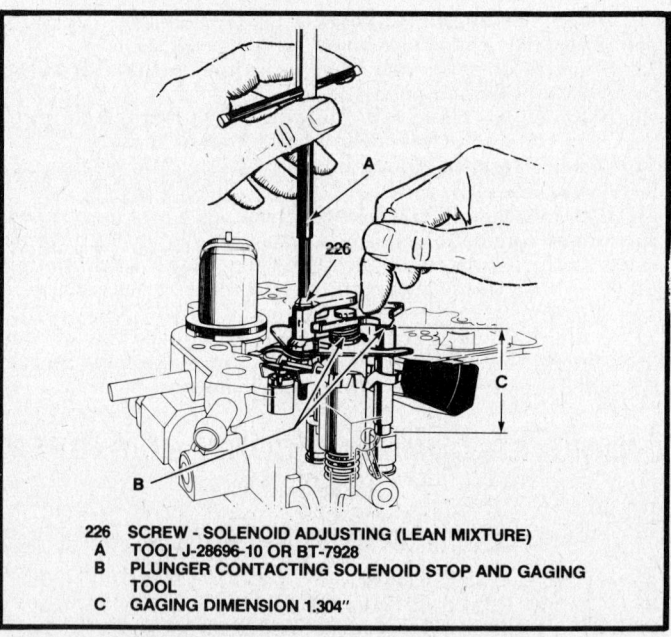

226 SCREW - SOLENOID ADJUSTING (LEAN MIXTURE)
A TOOL J-28696-10 OR BT-7928
B PLUNGER CONTACTING SOLENOID STOP AND GAGING TOOL
C GAGING DIMENSION 1.304"

Adjusting the solenoid lean mixture screw
(© General Motors Corporation)

staked in place, pry it off using a suitable tool and an allen wrench.

7. If the cover is riveted, cover the internal bowl vents to the bleed valve with masking tape. Cover the carburetor air intakes with masking tape in order to prevent metal chips from entering the engine.

8. Cover carburetor air intakes with masking tape to prevent metal chips from entering carburetor and engine.

9. Carefully align a No. 35 (0.110") drill bit on one of the steel rivet heads holding the idle air bleed valve cover in place. Drill only enough to remove rivet head. Drill the remaining rivet head located on the other side of the tower. Use a drift and small hammer to drive the remainder of the rivets out of the idle air bleed valve tower in the air horn casting. Use care in drilling to prevent damage to the air horn casting.

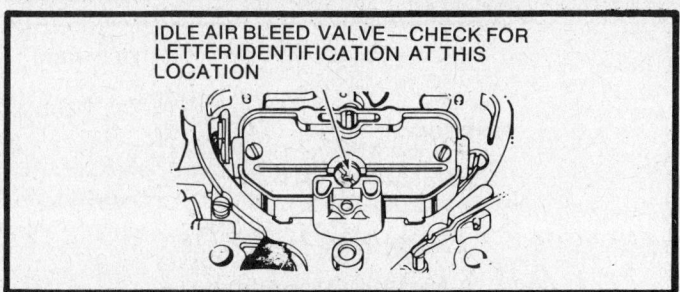

Air bleed valve—letter identification
(© General Motors Corporation)

10. Lift out cover over the idle air bleed valve and remove the rivet pieces from inside the idle air bleed valve tower.
11. Using shop air, carefully blow out any remaining chips from inside the tower. Discard cover after removal. A missing cover indicates that the idle air bleed valve setting has been changed from its original factory setting.
12. With cover removed, look for presence (or absence) of a letter identification on top of idle air bleed valve.
13. If an identifying letter appears on top of the valve proceed to the procedure outlined under type two. If an identifying letter does not appear on the top of the valve proceed to the procedure outlined under Type One.

Type One

1. Presetting the idle air bleed valve to a gauge dimension if the idle air bleed valve was serviced prior to on-vehicle adjustment.
   a. Install idle air bleed valve gauge tool J–33815–2, BT–8253–B, or equivalent, in throttle side "D" shaped vent hole in the air horn casting. The upper end of the tool should be positioned over the open cavity next to the idle air bleed valve.
   b. While holding the gauge tool down lightly, so that the solenoid plunger is against the solenoid stop, adjust the idle air bleed valve so that the gauge tool will pivot over and just contact the top of the valve. The valve is now preset for on-vehicle adjustment.
   c. Remove the gauging tool.

NOTE: 1985 and Later—The above procedures are the only idle air bleed valve adjustments required on carburetors E2ME, E2SE and E4MC.

2. Adjusting the idle air bleed valve on the vehicle to obtain correct dwell reading.
   a. Start engine and allow it to reach normal operating temperature.
   b. While idling in drive, use a suitable tool to slowly turn valve counterclockwise or clockwise, until the dwell reading varies within the 25–35° range, attempting to be as close to 30° as possible. Perform this step carefully. The air bleed valve is very sensitive and should be turned in $1/8$ turn increments only.
   c. If, after performing Steps a and b above, the dwell reading does not vary and is not within the 25–35° range, it will be necessary to remove the plugs and to adjust the idle mixture needles.
3. Idle mixture needle plug removal, only if necessary.
   a. Remove the carburetor from the engine, following normal service procedures, to gain access to the plugs covering the idle mixture needles.
   b. Invert carburetor and drain fuel into a suitable container.
   c. Place carburetor on a suitable holding fixture, with manifold side up. Use care to avoid damaging linkage, tubes, and parts protruding from air horn.
   d. Make two parallel cuts in the throttle body, one on each side of the locator points beneath the idle mixture needle plug (manifold side), with a hacksaw.
   e. The cuts should reach down to the steel plug, but should not extend more than $1/8$ in. beyond the locator points. The distance between the saw cuts depends on the size of the punch to be used.
   f. Place a flat punch near the ends of the saw marks in the throttle body. Hold the punch at a 45° angle and drive it into the throttle body until the casting breaks away, exposing the steel plug.
   g. The hardened plug will break, rather than remaining intact. It is not necessary to remove the plug in one piece, but remove the loosen pieces.
   h. Repeat this procedure with the other mixture needle.
4. Setting the idle mixture needles (if necessary) where correct dwell reading could not be obtained with idle air bleed valve adjustment.
   a. Using tool J–29030, BT–7610B, or equivalent, turn both idle mixture needles clockwise until they are lightly seated, then turn each mixture needle counterclockwise the number of turns specified.
   b. Reinstall carburetor on engine using a new flange mounting gasket, but do not install air cleaner and gasket at this time.
5. Readjusting idle air bleed valve to finalize correct dwell reading.
(This is only necessary if idle mixture needles required setting in Step 4, above.)
   a. Start engine and run until fully warm, and repeat "Idle Air Bleed Valve Adjustment", Step 2, above.
   b. If unable to set dwell to 25–35°, and the dwell is below 25°, turn both mixture needles counterclockwise an additional turn. If dwell is above 35°, turn both mixture needles clockwise an additional turn. Readjust idle air bleed valve to obtain dwell limits.
   c. After adjustments are complete, seal the idle mixture needle openings in the throttle body, using silicone sealant, RTV rubber, or equivalent. The sealer is required to discourage unnecessary adjustment of the setting, and to prevent fuel vapor loss in that area.
   d. On vehicles WITHOUT a carburetor-mounted idle speed control or idle load compensator, adjust curb idle speed if necessary.
   e. Check, and only if necessary adjust, fast idle speed as described on emission control information label.

Type Two

1. Setting the idle air bleed valve to a gauge dimension, and:
   a. Install air bleed valve gauging tool J–33815–2, BT–8253–B, or equivalent, in throttle side "D" shaped vent hole in the air horn casting. The upper end of the tool should be positioned over the open cavity next to the idle air bleed valve.
   b. While holding the gauging tool down lightly, so that the solenoid plunger is against the solenoid stop, adjust the idle air bleed valve so that the gauging tool will pivot over and just contact the top of the valve. The valve is now set properly. No further adjustment of the valve is necessary.
   c. Remove gauging tool.
2. Adjusting the idle mixture needles on the vehicle to obtain correct dwell readings.
   a. Remove idle mixture needle plugs, following instructions in the information given for Type One.
   b. Using tool J–29030–B, BT–7610–B, or equivalent, turn each idle mixture needle clockwise until lightly seated, then turn each mixture needle counterclockwise three turns.
   c. Reinstall carburetor on engine, using a new flange mounting gasket, but do not install air cleaner or gasket at this time.

SECTION 13 BUICK
ELECTRA • ESTATE WAGON • LE SABRE • REGAL

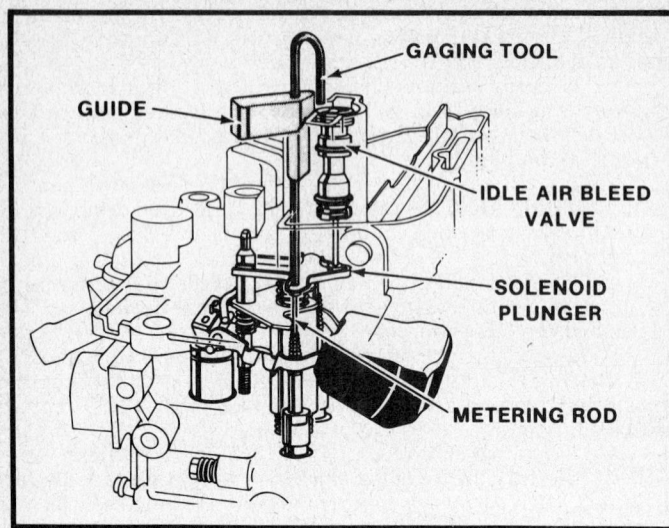

Installing idle air bleed valve gauge
(© General Motors Corporation)

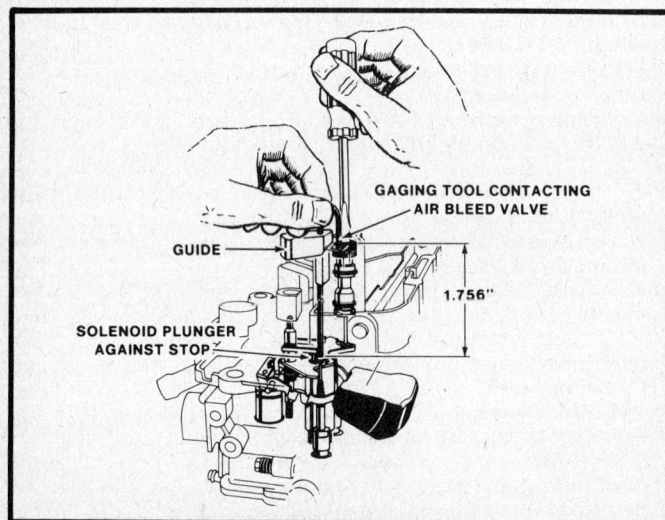

Positioning of the idle air bleed valve
(© General Motors Corporation)

d. Start engine and allow it to reach normal operating temperature.

e. While idling in drive (neutral for manual transmission), adjust both mixture needles equally, in 1/8 turn increments, until dwell reading varies within the 25–35° range, attempting to be as close to 30° as possible. If reading is too high, turn mixture needles clockwise. Allow time for dwell reading to stabilize after each adjustment.

f. After adjustments are complete, seal the idle mixture needle openings in the throttle body, using silicone sealant, RTV rubber, or equivalent. The sealer is required to discourage unnecessary readjustment of the setting, and to prevent fuel vapor loss in that area.

g. On vehicles without a carburetor-mounted idle speed control or idle load compensator, adjust curb idle speed if necessary.

h. Check, and if necessary, adjust fast idle speed, as described on the emission control information label.

Throttle Position Sensor (TPS) Adjustment

The plug covering the TPS adjustment screw is used to provide

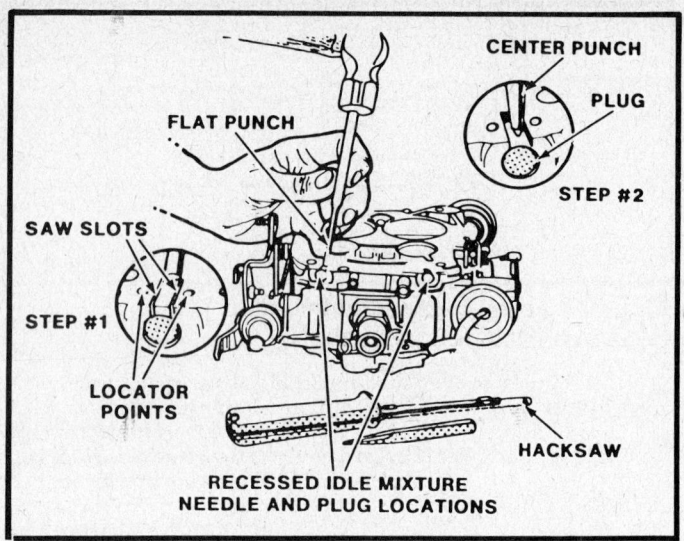

Removal of idle mixture screw plugs
(© General Motors Corporation)

a tamper-resistant design and retain the factory setting during vehicle operation. Do not remove the plug unless diagnosis indicates that the TPS Sensor is not adjusted correctly or it is necessary to replace the air horn assembly, float bowl TPS Sensor to TPS adjustment screw. This is a critical adjustment that must be performed accurately and carefully to ensure proper vehicle performance and control of exhaust emissions.

If necessary to adjust the TPS sensor:

a. Using a 5mm ($5/64$ in.) drill, drill hole in aluminum plug covering TPS adjustment screw drilling only enough to start self-tapping screw (approximate drilling depth $1/16$ in.–$1/8$ in.). Use care in drilling to prevent damage to adjustment screw head.

b. Start a No. 8 $1/2$ in. long self-tapping screw in drilled hole in plug turning screw in only enough to ensure good thread engagement in hole.

c. Placing a wide-blade section of screwdriver between screw head and air horn casting, pry against screw head to remove plug. Discard plug.

d. Using tool J–28696, BT7967A or equivalent, remove screw.

e. Connect digital voltmeter (such as J–29125) or equivalent from TPS connector center terminal (B) to bottom terminal (C).

NOTE: After TPS screw is adjusted, a new plug should be installed. If a new plug is not available, a locking type of sealer should be placed on the screw threads to prevent movement of the screw after installation.

f. With ignition on, engine stopped, reinstall TPS adjustment screw and with tool J–28696, BT7967A or equivalent turn screw to obtain specified voltage at specified throttle position with A/C off. (Refer to Unit Repair Section, Carburetor Repair and to C-3 System, Engine Controls.)

g. After adjustment, install new plug (supplied in service kits) into the air horn, driving plug in place until flush with raised pump lever boss on casting.

Idle Load Compensator (ILC) Adjustment

1. Prepare vehicle for adjustments—see emission label.
2. Connect tachometer (distributor side of TACH filter, if used).
3. Remove air cleaner and plug vacuum hose to thermal vacuum valve (TVV).
4. Disconnect and plug vacuum hose to EGR.

5. Disconnect and plug vacuum hose to canister purge port.
6. Disconnect and plug vacuum hose to ILC.
7. Back out idle stop screw on carburetor 3 turns.
8. Turn A/C Off.

CAUTION
Before starting engine, place transmission in Park, set parking brake, and block drive wheels.

9. With engine running (engine warm, choke off), transmission in drive, and ILC plunger fully extended (no vacuum applied), using tool J–29607, BT–8022, or equivalent, adjust plunger to obtain 750 rpm E2MC models, 725 rpm E4MC models. Jam nut on plunger must be held with wrench to prevent damage to guide tabs.
10. Remove plug from vacuum hose, reconnect hose to ILC and observe idle speed. Idle speed should be 500 rpm in Drive.
11. If rpm in Step 10 is correct, proceed to Step 13. No further adjustment of the ILC is necessary.
12. If rpm in Step 10 is not correct:
   a. Stop engine and remove the ILC. Plug vacuum hose to ILC.
   b. With the ILC removed, remove the rubber cap from the center outlet tube and then remove the metal plug (if used) from this same tube.
   c. Install ILC on carburetor and re-attach throttle return spring and any other related parts removed during disassembly. Remove plug from vacuum hose and reconnect hose to ILC.
   d. Using a spare rubber cap with hole punched to accept a 0.090 in. ($3/32$ in.) hex key wrench, install cap on center outlet tube (to seal against vacuum loss) and insert wrench through cap to engage adjusting screw inside tube. Start engine and turn adjusting screw with wrench to obtain 550 rpm in Drive. Turning the adjusting screw will change the idle speed approximately 75–100 rpm for each complete turn. Turning the screw counterclockwise will increase the engine speed.
   e. Remove wrench and cap (with hole) from center outlet tube and install new rubber cap.
   f. Engine running, transmission in drive, observe idle speed. If a final adjustment is required, it will be necessary to repeat Steps 12a through 12e.
13. After adjustment of the ILC plunger, measure distance from the jam nut to tip of the plunger, dimension must not exceed 25mm (1 in.).
14. Disconnect and plug vacuum hose to ILC. Apply vacuum source such as hand vacuum pump J–23768, BT–7517 or equivalent to ILC vacuum inlet tube to fully retract the plunger.
15. Adjust the idle stop on the carburetor float bowl to obtain 500 rpm in drive.
16. Place transmission in park and stop engine.
17. Remove plug from vacuum hose and install hose on ILC vacuum inlet tube.
18. Remove plugs and reconnect all vacuum hoses.
19. Install air cleaner and gasket.
20. Remove block from drive wheels.

Differential Vacuum Delay Valve (DVDV) Adjustment
1983 AND LATER

The DVDV is located in the vacuum line between the idle load compensator (ILC) and the vacuum source. It is used on all 5.0L engines (engine code Y).

The DVDV acts as cushioning device by slightly delaying the operation of the ILC until a constant vacuum change has occurred. Without the DVDV the ILC would react too quickly to changes in engine vacuum, causing a stalling or run-on condition.

To check the operation of the DVDV, install a vacuum gauge with a "T" into the hose from the DVDV to the ILC. Install a

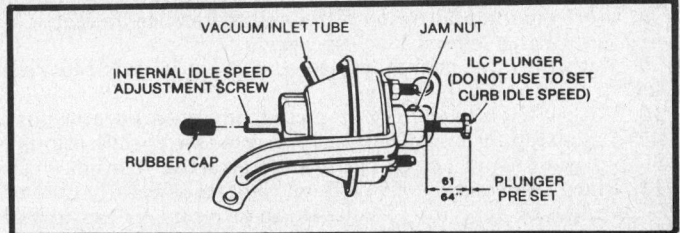

Typical idle load compensator ILC
(© General Motors Corporation)

vacuum pump to port 1 of the DVDV and apply 17.8 in. of vacuum while watching the other vacuum gauge, it should take 6–9 seconds for the vacuum to rise to 16.9 in. Remove the vacuum gauge with "T", install the vacuum pump to port 2 and leave port 1 open. Air should flow through the valve after 0.5 in. is applied.

Idle Speed Control (ISC) Adjustment

The idle speed control (ISC) is controlled by the electronic control module (ECM), which has the desired idle speed programmed in its memory. The ECM compares the actual idle speeder is moved in or out. This automatically adjusts the throttle to hold an idle rpm independent of the engine loads. An integral part of the ISC is the throttle contact switch. The position of the switch determines whether or not the ISC should control idle speed. When the throttle lever is resting against the ISC plunger, the switch contacts are closed, at which time the ECM moves the ISC to the programmed idle speed. When the throttle lever is not contacting the ISC plunger, the switch contacts are open; the ECM stops sending idle speed commands and the drive controls engine speed.

NOTE: Before starting engine, place transmission selector lever in park or neutral, set parking brake, and block drive wheels.

When a new ISC assembly is installed, a base (minimum authority) and high (maximum authority) rpm speed check must be performed and adjustments made as required. These adjustments limit the low and high rpm speeds to the ECM. When making a low and high speed adjustment, the low speed adjustment is always made first. DO NOT use the ISC plunger to adjust curb idle speed as the idle speed is controlled by the ECM.

NOTE: Do not disconnect or connect ISC connector with ignition on as damage to the ECM may occur.

1. Connect tachometer (distributor side of tach filter, if used).
2. Connect dwell meter to mixture control (M/C) solenoid dwell lead. Remember to set dwell meter on the six cylinder scale, regardless of the engine being tested.
3. Turn A/C off.
4. Start engine and run until stabilized by entering "closed loop" (dwell meter needle starts to vary).
5. Turn ignition off.
6. Unplug connector from ISC motor.
7. Fully retract ISC plunger by applying 12 volts DC (battery voltage) to terminal "C" of the ISC motor connection and ground lead to terminal "D" of the ISC motor connection. It may be necessary to install jumper leads from the ISC motor in order to make proper connections.

NOTE: Do not apply battery voltage to motor longer than necessary to retract ISC plunger. Prolonged contact will damage motor. Also, never connect voltage source across terminals "A" and "B" as damage to the internal throttle contact switch will result.

13-27

BUICK
ELECTRA • ESTATE WAGON • LE SABRE • REGAL

8. Start engine and wait until dwell meter needle starts to vary, indicating "closed loop" operation.
9. With parking brake applied and drive wheels blocked, place transmission in Drive.
10. With ISC plunger fully retracted, adjust carburetor base (slow) idle stop screw to the specified rpm (see specifications). ISC plunger should not be left in full retracted position.
11. Place transmission in Park or Neutral and fully extend ISC plunger by applying 12 volts DC to terminal "D" of the ISC motor connection and ground lead to terminal "C" of the ISC motor connection.

NOTE: Never connect voltage source across terminals "A" and "B" as damage to the internal throttle contact switch will result.

12. Automatic Transmission—with transmission in Park, using Tool J-29607 or BT-8022 or equivalent, preset ISC plunger to obtain 1500 rpm.
13. With parking brake set and drive wheels blocked, place transmission in Drive. Using tool J-29607 or BT-8022 or equivalent, turn ISC plunger to obtain ISC adjustment rpm (maximum authority).
14. Recheck ISC Maximum Authority Adjustment rpm with voltage applied to motor. Motor will ratchet at full extension with power applied.
15. Fully retract ISC plunger. Place transmission in park or neutral and turn ignition off. Disconnect 12 volt power source, ground lead, tachometer and dwell meter. With ignition "off", reconnect four terminal harness connector to ISC motor. To prevent internal damage to ISC, apply finger pressure to ISC plunger while retracting.
16. Remove block from drive wheels.

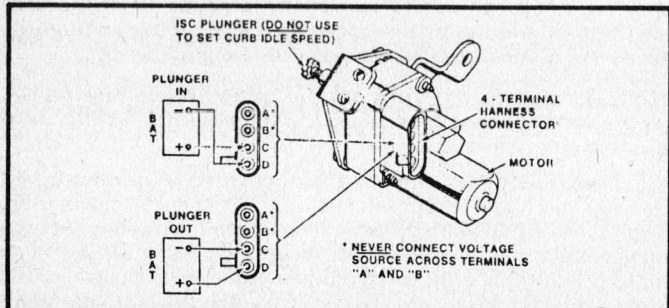

Idle speed control check ISC (© General Motors Corporation)

CARBURETOR
Removal and Installation
1. Remove air cleaner.
2. Disconnect accelerator linkage.
3. Disconnect transmission detent cable.
4. Disconnect cruise control, if equipped.
5. Disconnect all necessary electrical connectors.
6. Disconnect all necessary vacuum lines.
7. Disconnect fuel line at carburetor inlet.
8. Remove the attaching bolts and remove carburetor.
9. Reverse removal procedure to install.
10. Check idle speeds.

INTAKE MANIFOLD
Removal and Installation
GAS ENGINE
1. Disconnect the negative battery cable. Drain the radiator.
2. Remove the air cleaner assembly.
3. Disconnect the upper radiator hose and the heater hose at the manifold.
4. Disconnect the accelerator linkage at the carburetor and the linkage bracket at the manifold. Remove the cruise control chain or cable, if so equipped.
5. Remove the fuel line from the carburetor and the booster vacuum pipe from the manifold. Remove turbocharger, if so equipped.
6. Disconnect and label the transmission vacuum modulator line, idle stop solenoid wire (if so equipped), distributor wires and the temperature sending unit wire.
7. Disconnect and mark the vacuum hoses at the distributor and the carburetor.
8. Disconnect the coolant bypass hose at the manifold.
9. On 6 cylinder models, it may be necessary to remove the distributor cap and wires to gain access to the Torx head bolt. Remove the bolt.
10. Remove the throttle linkage springs.
11. Remove the A/C compressor top bracket, if so equipped.
12. Remove the manifold.
13. Installation is the reverse of the removal procedure. Be sure to use new gaskets or RTV sealant as required.

DIESEL ENGINE
1. Remove the air cleaner.
2. Drain the radiator. Loosen the upper bypass hose clamp, remove the thermostat housing bolts, and remove the housing and the thermostat from the intake manifold.

ISC CONTROL PLUNGER ADJUSTMENT CHART

Plunger Identification	Plunger Length Dimension "A"	Dimension "B" Must Not Exceed
None	9/16 inch	7/32 inch
None	41/64 inch	5/16 inch
X	47/64 inch	25/64 inch
A	49/64 inch	27/64 inch
Y	51/64 inch	15/32 inch
S	27/32 inch	1/2 inch
Z	7/8 inch	35/64 inch
G	29/32 inch	37/64 inch
E	1 inch	43/64 inch
L	13/32 inch	3/4 inch
J	13/16 inch	27/32 inch
N	1 17/64 inch	59/64 inch
T	1 11/32 inch	1 inch

BUICK 13
ELECTRA · ESTATE WAGON · LE SABRE · REGAL

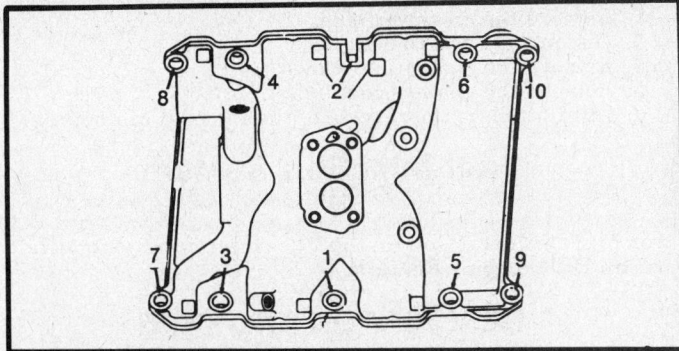

V6 gas intake manifold torque sequence
(© General Motors Corporation)

3. Remove the breather pipes from the rocker covers and the air crossover. Remove the air crossover.
4. Disconnect the throttle rod and the return spring. If equipped with cruise control, remove the servo.
5. Remove the hairpin clip at the bell-crank and disconnect the cables. Remove the throttle cable from the bracket on the manifold; position the cable away from the engine. Disconnect and label any wiring as necessary.
6. Remove the alternator bracket if necessary. On the 350 cu. in. engine, if equipped with air conditioning, remove the compressor mounting bolts and move the compressor aside, without disconnecting any of the hoses. Remove the compressor mounting bracket from the intake manifold.
7. Disconnect the fuel line from the pump and the fuel filter. Remove the fuel filter and bracket.
8. Remove the fuel injection pump and lines.
9. Disconnect and remove the vacuum pump or oil pump drive assembly from the rear of the engine.
10. Remove the intake manifold drain tube.
11. Remove the intake manifold bolts and remove the manifold. Remove the adapter seal. Remove the injection pump adapter.
12. Clean the mating surfaces of the cylinder heads and the intake manifold.
13. Coat both sides of the gasket surface that seal the intake manifold to the cylinder heads with GM sealer No. 1050026 or the equivalent. Position the intake manifold gaskets on the cylinder heads. Install the end seals, making sure that the ends are positioned under the cylinder heads.
14. Carefully lower the intake manifold into place on the engine.
15. Clean the intake manifold bolts thoroughly, then dip them in clean engine oil. Install the bolts and on the V8 engine tighten to 15 ft.lbs.. in the sequence shown. Next, tighten all the bolts to 30 ft.lbs.. in sequence, and finally tighten to 40 ft.lbs.. in sequence. On the V6 engine tighten to 15 ft. lbs. in the sequence shown, then retorque to 41 ft.lbs..
16. Install the intake manifold drain tube and clamp.
17. Install the injection pump adapter. Install the injection pump.
18. Install the vacuum pump or coil pump drive assembly. Do not operate the engine without the vacuum pump/oil pump assembly in place as this unit drives the engine oil pump.
19. Continue the installation in the reverse order of the removal procedure. Adjust the throttle rod and the transmission cable as required.

EXHAUST MANIFOLD

Removal and Installation

GAS ENGINE – LEFT SIDE

1. Disconnect the negative battery cable. On some vehicles

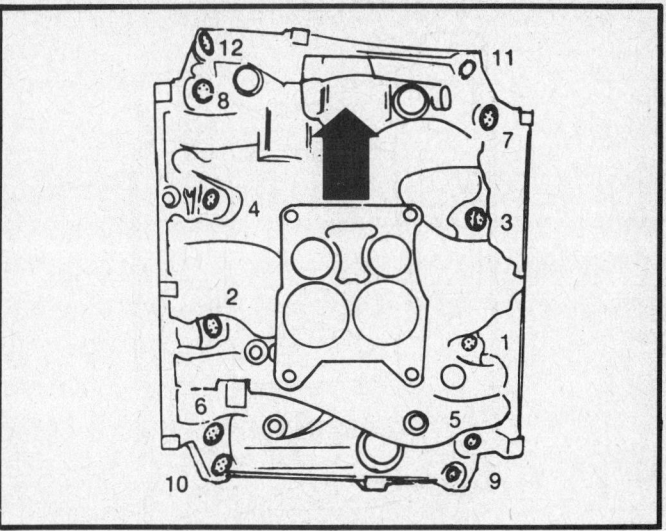

V8 gas intake manifold torque sequence
(© General Motors Corporation)

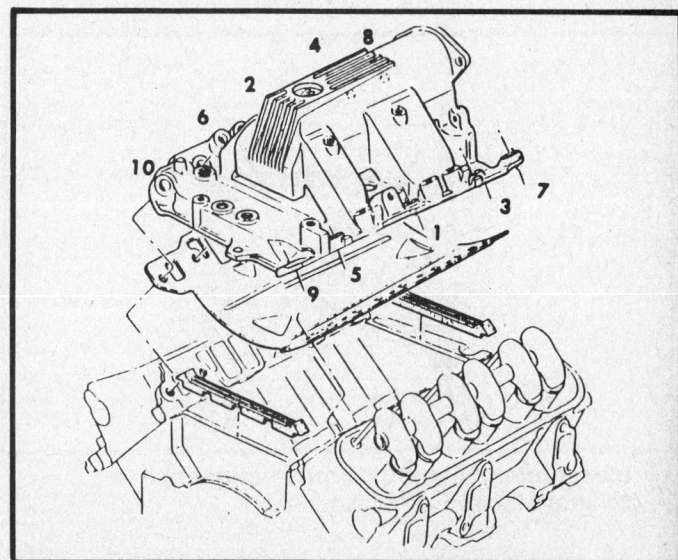

V6 gas intake manifold torque sequence with turbocharger (© General Motors Corporation)

it may be necessary to remove the air cleaner assembly.
2. If equipped, disconnect the EFE pipe and flatten the exhaust manifold lock tabs.
3. Disconnect the exhaust pipe at the exhaust manifold flange.
4. On "G" series vehicles it may be necessary to remove or disconnect the intermediate steering colum shaft.
5. Remove the hot air shroud, if equipped. If necessary, remove the lower alternator bracket.
6. Remove the exhaust manifold retaining bolts. Remove the exhaust manifold from the vehicle.
7. Installation is the reverse of the removal procedure. If equipped, be sure to bend the lock tabs after installation of the manifold retaining bolts.

GAS ENGINE – RIGHT SIDE

1. Disconnect the negative battery cable.
2. If equipped, disconnect the oxygen sensor and flatten the exhaust manifold lock tabs.

13–29

SECTION 13

BUICK
ELECTRA • ESTATE WAGON • LE SABRE • REGAL

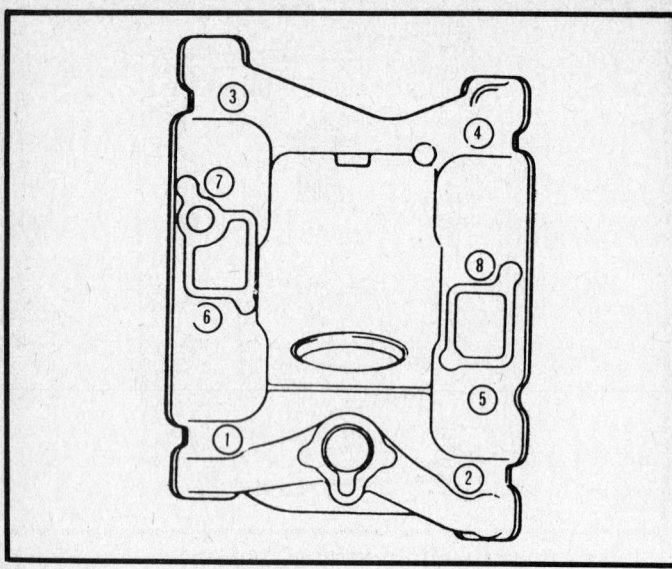

V6 diesel intake manifold torque sequence
(© General Motors Corporation)

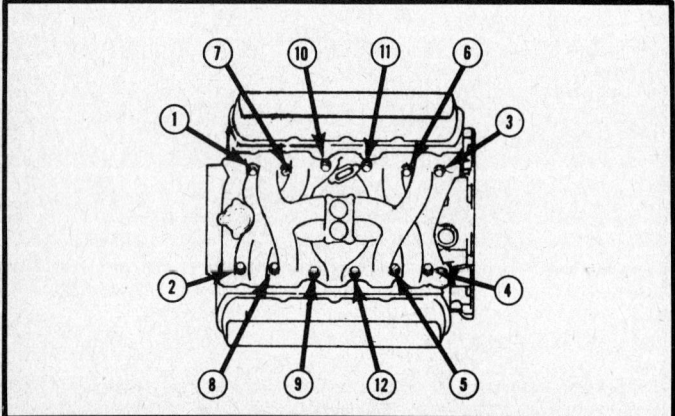

V8 diesel intake manifold torque sequence
(© General Motors Corporation)

3. Disconnect the exhaust pipe at the exhaust manifold flange.
4. On some vehicles it may be necessary to remove the right front tire.
5. Remove the exhaust manifold retaining bolts. Remove the exhaust manifold from the vehicle.
6. Installation is the reverse of the removal procedure. If equipped, be sure to bend the lock tabs after installation of the exhaust manifold retaining bolts.

DIESEL ENGINES – LEFT SIDE

1. Remove the air cleaner. Disconnect the negative battery cable.
2. Remove the alternator lower bracket.
3. Raise and support the car.
4. Remove the crossover pipe.
5. Lower the car.
6. Remove the exhaust manifold.
7. Installation is the reverse of the removal procedure.

DIESEL ENGINE – RIGHT SIDE

1. Disconnect the negative battery cable. Raise and support the car.
2. Remove the crossover pipe.
3. Disconnect the exhaust pipe.
4. Remove the right front wheel.
5. Remove the exhaust manifold from under the car.
6. Installation is the reverse of the removal procedure.

Fuel Injection System

For More Information on the Fuel Injection System Refer to the Unit Repair Section.

DESCRIPTION AND TYPE

Throttle Body Injection

The Throttle Body Injection (TBI) system has the carburetor type fuel delivery unit mounted on the intake manifold. The TBI unit is computer controlled and supplies the correct amount of fuel during all engine operating conditions. There are two TBI units used, the 300 and 500 models.

Port Fuel Injection

Two Port Fuel Injection systems are used, the Multiport Fuel Injection system where the injectors are opened in groups at each crankshaft revolution, and the Sequential Fuel Injection system where each injector is opened independently of each other, once every two revolutions of the crankshaft and prior to the opening of the intake valve for the cylinder to be fired. The Electronic Control Modules in complete control of both systems during all phases of engine operation.

Turbocharger System

For More Information on Turbochargers Refer to the Unit Repair Section.

DESCRIPTION AND TYPE

The turbocharger is basically an air compressor or air pump. It consists of a turbine or hot wheel, a shaft, a compressor or cold wheel, a turbine housing, a compressor housing, and a center housing which contains bearings, a turbine seal assembly and a compressor seal assembly.

Turbochargers are installed on an engine to put more and denser air into the engine combustion chambers. Because of the increased volume and weight of compressed air more fuel can be scheduled to produce more horsepower from a given size engine. The turbocharged version of an engine will also maintain a higher level of power output than the non-turbocharged version when operated at altitudes above sea level.

TURBOCHARGER ASSEMBLY

Removal and Installation

1983

1. Disconnect exhaust inlet and outlet pipes at the turbocharger.
2. Disconnect oil feed pipe from center housing rotating assembly.
3. Remove air intake elbow.
4. Disconnect accelerator, cruise and detent linkages at carburetor. Disconnect linkage bracket from plenum.
5. Remove bolts attaching plenum to side bracket.
6. Disconnect carburetor fuel and vacuum lines.
7. Drain the cooling system and disconnect coolant hoses from plenum.
8. Disconnect plenum from bracket by removing the attaching bolt at the intake manifold.

BUICK

ELECTRA · ESTATE WAGON · LE SABRE · REGAL

SECTION 13

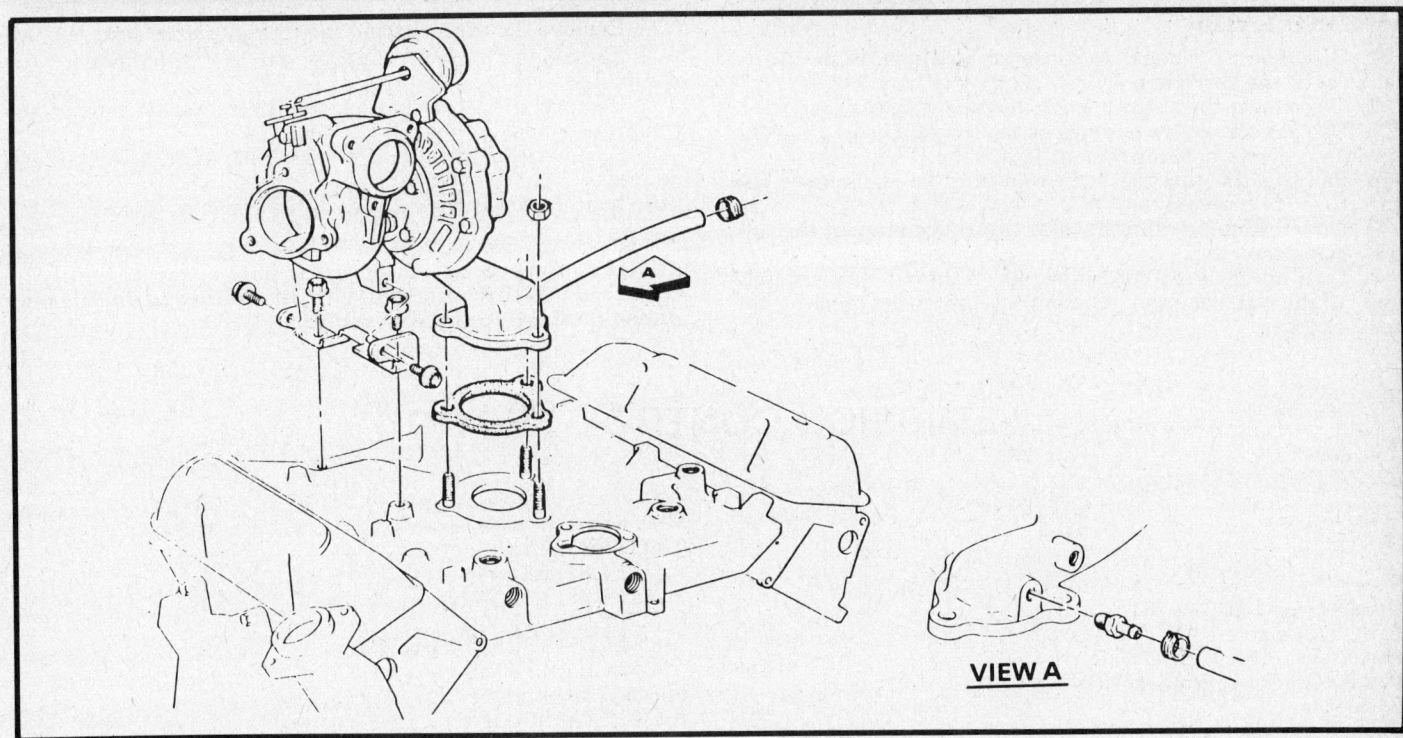

Turbocharger assembly, through 1983 (© General Motors Corporation)

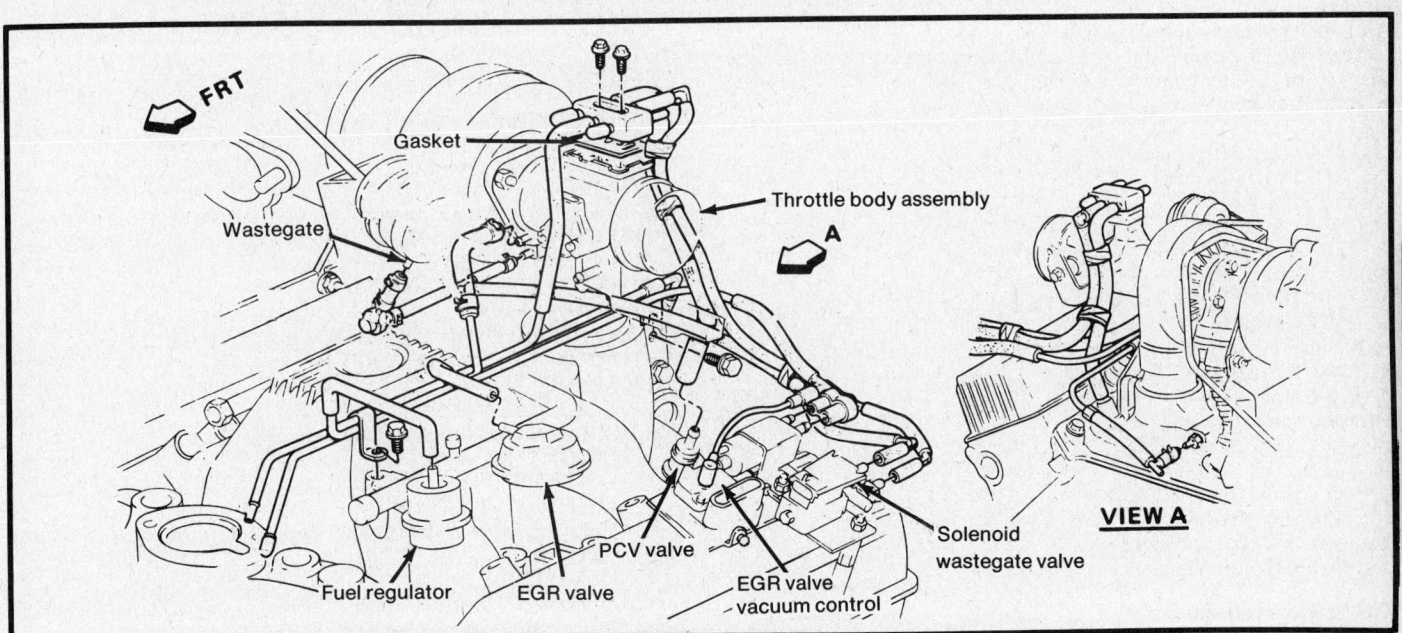

Turbocharger assembly—1984 and Later (© General Motors Corporation)

9. Remove bolts attaching turbine housing to bracket on intake manifold.
10. Remove bolts attaching EGR valve manifold to plenum. Loosen the bolts attaching EGR valve manifold to the intake manifold.
11. Remove AIR bypass-to-pipe-to-check valve hose.
12. Remove bolts attaching compressor housing to intake manifold.
13. Remove turbocharger and actuator, still attached to carburetor and plenum, from the engine. Separate components as necessary.
14. Installation is the reverse of removal.

NOTE: Before installing the turbocharger assembly be sure that it is first charged with oil. Failure to do this may cause damage to the assembly.

SECTION 13

BUICK
ELECTRA · ESTATE WAGON · LE SABRE · REGAL

1984 AND LATER

1. Disconnect the negative battery cable. Remove the air inlet tube at the throttle body.
2. Disconnect the throttle body vacuum harness connector.
3. Disconnect the water lines at the throttle body. Plug the lines in order to prevent coolant loss.
4. Remove the throttle body retaining bolts. Remove the throttle body assembly.
5. Disconnect and plug the oil pressure feed line at the turbocharger assembly.
6. Disconnect the exhaust inlet pipe at the exhaust manifold and at the turbocharger. Disconnect the outlet pipe at the turbocharger.
7. Remove the turbocharger mounting bracket nuts that attach the upper to lower bracket on the right side of the assembly.
8. Remove the turbocharger stabilizer bracket bolt at the compressor housing on the left side.
9. Remove the turbocharger assembly from the manifold adapter.
10. Installation is the reverse of the removal procedure.

NOTE: Before installing the turbocharger assembly be sure that it is first charged with oil. Failure to do this may cause damage to the assembly.

EMISSION CONTROL SECTION

1983

Catalytic converter
Early fuel evaporation (EFE)
Exhaust gas recirculation (EGR)
Positive/crankcase ventilation (PCV)
Electric choke
Thermostatic air cleaner (TAC)
Evaporative emission control (EEC)
Computer Command Control (CCC)
Oxygen sensor
Air management system (MAIR)
   The following additional emissions devices may be found on these carbureted gasoline engines as listed:
AIR management valve
   (171 CID) 2.8L V-6 A/T
   (171 CID) 2.8L V-6 M/T
   (181 CID) 3.0L V-6
   (231 CID) 3.8L V-6
Wastegate actuator
   (231 CID) 3.8L V-6 Turbo
AIR switching valve
   (231 CID) 3.8L V-6 Turbo
   (252 CID) 4.1L V-6
AIR control valve
   (231 CID) 3.8L V-6 Turbo
   (252 CID) 4.1L V-6
Deceleration valve
   (171 CID) 2.8L V-6 A/T
   (171 CID) 2.8L V-6 M/T
   (181 CID) 3.0L V-6
   (231 CID) 3.8L V-6
Vacuum delay valve (VDV)
   (307 CID) 5.0L V-8
CCC system vacuum sensor
   (171 CID) 2.8L V-6 A/T
   (171 CID) 2.8L V-6 M/T
   (181 CID) 3.0L V-6
   (231 CID) 3.8L V-6
Manifold absolute pressure sensor (MAP)
   (231 CID) 3.8L V-6
   (231 CID) 3.8L V-6 Turbo
   (252 CID) 4.1L V-6
Secondary vacuum break-thermal vacuum switch (SVB-TVS)
   (171 CID) 2.8L V-6 A/T
   (171 CID) 2.8L V-6 M/T
   (181 CID) 3.0L V-6
   (231 CID) 3.8L V-6
Vacuum check valves
   (171 CID) 2.8L V-6 A/T
   (171 CID) 2.8L V-6 M/T
   (181 CID) 3.0L V-6
   (231 CID) 3.8L V-6
   (231 CID) 3.8L V-6 Turbo
   (252 CID) 4.1L V-6
Idle load compensator (ILC)
   (307 CID) 5.0L V-8
Thermostatic air cleaner—temperature sensor (TAC-TS)
   (171 CID) 2.8L V-6 A/T
   (171 CID) 2.8L V-6 M/T
   (181 CID) 3.0L V-6
   (231 CID) 3.8L V-6
   (231 CID) 3.8L V-6 Turbo
   (252 CID) 4.1L V-6
Thermal vacuum delay valve (TVDV)
   (231 CID) 3.8L V-6 A/T
   (231 CID) 3.8L V-6 M/T
   (252 CID) 4.1L V-6
Thermostatic air cleaner thermal vacuum switch (TAC-TVS)
   (171 CID) 2.8L V-6 A/T
   (181 CID) 3.0L V-6
   (231 CID) 3.8L V-6 Turbo
   (307 CID) 5.0L V-8
Canister control valve (CCV)
   (231 CID) 3.8L V-6 Turbo
   (252 CID) 4.1L V-6
   (307 CID) 5.0L V-8
Exhaust gas recirculation—solenoid (EGR-SOL)
   (171 CID) 2.8L V-6 A/T
   (181 CID) 3.0L V-6
   (231 CID) 3.8L V-6 Turbo
Early fuel evaporation/exhaust gas recirculation—Solenoid (EFE/EGR-SOL)
   (231 CID) 3.8L V-6
   (252 CID) 4.1L V-6
Fuel tank pressure control valve (FTPCV)
   (171 CID) 2.8L V-6 A/T
   (171 CID) 2.8L V-6 M/T
   (181 CID) 3.0L V-6
Canister purge—solenoid (CP-SOL)
   (171 CID) 2.8L V-6 A/T
   (171 CID) 2.8L V-6 M/T
   (181 CID) 3.0L V-6
Carburetor fuel bowl vent valve
   (231 CID) 3.8L V-6 Turbo
   (252 CID) 4.1L V-6
Canister purge—thermal vacuum switch (CP-TVS)
   (252 CID) 4.1L V-6
   (307 CID) 5.0L V-8

BUICK SECTION 13
ELECTRA • ESTATE WAGON • LE SABRE • REGAL

Throttle Body Injection Engines
Emissions Devices
Manifold absolute pressure sensor (MAP)
   (TBI) 1.8L L4
   (151 CID) 2.5L L4
Thermostatic air cleaner—vacuum switch (TAC-VS)
   (TBI) 1.8L L4
   (151 CID) 2.5L L4 TBI
Canister purge control valve (CPCV)
   (151 CID) 2.5L L4 TIB

DIESEL ENGINES
Emissions Devices
Exhaust gas recirculation
   (263 CID) 4.3L V-6 Diesel
   (350 CID) 5.7L V-8 Diesel
Exhaust gas recirculation—control valve (EGR-CV)
   (263 CID) 4.3L V-6 Diesel
   (350 CID) 5.7L V-8 Diesel
Vacuum regulator valve (VRV)
   (263 CID) 4.3L V-6 Diesel
   (350 CID) 5.7L V-8 Diesel
Exhaust pressure regulator (EPR)
   (263 CID) 4.3L V-6 Diesel
Crankcase depression regulator (CDR)
   (263 CID) 4.3L V-6 Diesel
   (350 CID) 5.7L V-8 Diesel

1984-1985

GASOLINE CARBURETED ENGINES
The emissions system for most gasoline carbureted engines consists of the following:
Calibrated carburetion
Catalytic converter
Early fuel evaporation (EFE)
Exhaust gas recirculation (EGR)
Positive/crankcase ventilation (PCV)
Electric choke
Thermostatic air cleaner (TAC)
Evaporative emission control (EEC)
Computer Command Control (CCC)
Oxygen sensor
Air management system (MAIR)
Electronic control module (ECM)
Assembly line communication link (ALCL)
Mixture control
Idle speed relay
Early fuel evaporation relay
Heated grid EFE
Transmission converter clutch connection
Electric spark timing
Air injection pump
Air control solenoid valve
Air switching solenoid valve
EGR valve
EGR solenoid valve
Canister purge solenoid valve
Vapor canister
Fuel bowel vent solenoid
Differential pressure sensor
Exhaust oxygen sensor
Throttle position sensor
Coolant sensor
Barometric pressure sensor
Vehicle speed sensor

   The following additional emissions devices may be found on these carbureted gasoline engines as listed:
A/C compressor relay
   (186 CID) 3.0L V6
   (231 CID) 3.8L V6

Manifold pressure sensor (MAP)
   (250 CID) 4.1L V6
Electronic spark control knock sensor
   (250 CID) 4.1L V6
Remote lamp driver
   (307 CID) 5.0L V8
Cold start module
   (307 CID) 5.0L V8
Rear vacuum brake
   (307 CID) 5.0L V8
Rear vacuum brake solenoid
   (307 CID) 5.0L V8
Idle lead compensator
   (307 CID) 5.0L V8

THROTTLE BODY INJECTION ENGINES EMISSIONS DEVICES
Idle air control
   (111 CID) 1.8L L4
   (121 CID) 2.0L L4
Fuel pump relay
   (111 CID) 1.8L L4
   (121 CID) 2.0L L4
Park and Neutral switch
   (111 CID) 1.8L L4
   (121 CID) 2.0L L4
Pulse air control
   (121 CID) 2.0L L4

PORT FUEL INJECTION ENGINES EMISSIONS DEVICES
Fuel injectors jumper
Idle air meter
Cooling fan relay
Turbo charger
Wastegate solenoid
Manifold air temperature sensor
Knock sensor
   (111 CID) 1.8L L4
   (231 CID) 3.8L V6
Brake sensor switch
Mass air flow system
   (231 CID) 3.8L V6

DIESEL ENGINES EMISSIONS DEVICES
Thermostatic vacuum switch (TVS)
   (263 CID) 4.3L V6 Diesel
   (350 CID) 5.7L V8 Diesel
EGR cutoff solenoid
   (263 CID) 4.3L V6 Diesel
   (350 CID) 5.7L V8 Diesel
Altitude vacuum reducer vane (AVRV)
   (263 CID) 4.3L V6 Diesel
   (350 CID) 5.7L V8 Diesel
EGR quick vacuum response valve
   (263 CID) 4.3L V6 Diesel
   (350 CID) 5.7L V8 Diesel
Exhaust gas recirculation
   (263 CID) 4.3L V6 Diesel
   (350 CID) 5.7L V8 Diesel
Exhaust gas recirculation—control valve (EGR-CV)
   (263 CID) 4.3L V6 Diesel
   (350 CID) 5.7L V8 Diesel
Vacuum regulator valve (VRV)
   (263 CID) 4.3L V6 Diesel
   (350 CID) 5.7L V8 Diesel
Exhaust pressure regulator (EPR)
   (263 CID) 4.3L V6 Diesel
Crankcase depression regulator (CDR)
   (263 CID) 4.3L V6 Diesel
   (350 CID) 5.7L V8 Diesel

   NOTE: Some or all carry-over for 1986 models. Lists not available at time of publication.

SECTION 13 BUICK
ELECTRA • ESTATE WAGON • LE SABRE • REGAL

EMISSIONS INDICATOR

"Check Engine" or "Service Engine Soon" Light

Although this light may indicate either wording depending on the vehicle, it has the same function in either case. The terms are interchangeable. This light is on the instrument panel and has 2 functions:

1. It is used to tell the driver that a problem has occurred, and that the vehicle should be taken for service as soon as reasonably possible.
2. It is used by the technician to read out "Trouble Codes" to help diagnosis system problems.

As a bulb and system check, the "Check Engine/Service Engine Soon" light will come on with the key on and the engine not running. When the engine is started, the "Check Engine/Service Engine Soon" light will turn off.

If the "Check Engine/Service Engine Soon" light remains on, the self-diagnostic system has detected a problem. If the problem goes away, the light will go out in most cases after 10 seconds, but a Trouble Code will remain stored in the ECM.

Clearing Trouble Codes

When the ECM finds a problem, the "Check Engine/Service Engine Soon" light will come on and a trouble code will be recorded in the ECM memory. If the problem is intermittent, the "Check Engine/Service Engine Soon" light will go out after 10 seconds, when the fault goes away. However, the trouble code will stay in the ECM memory until the battery voltage to the ECM is removed. Removing battery voltage for 10 seconds will clear all stored trouble codes. Do this by disconnecting the ECM harness from the positive battery pigtail for 10 seconds with the ignition off, or by disconnecting the ECM fuse, designated ECM or ECM/Bat., from the fuse holder.

NOTE: To prevent ECM damage, the key must be OFF when disconnecting or reconnecting power to ECM (for example battery cable, ECM pigtail, ECM fuse, jumper cables, etc.).

ECM Learning Ability

The ECM has a "learning" ability. If the battery is disconnected to clear diagnostic codes, or for repair, the "learning" process has to begin all over again. A change may be noted in the vehicle's performance to "teach" the vehicle, make sure the vehicle is at operating temperature, and drive at part throttle, with moderate acceleration and idle conditions, until normal performance returns.

NOTE: For further service information on the C-3 system, refer to the Engine Control Section in the Unit Repair or refer to Chilton's Electronic Engine Control Manual.

NOTE: Some 1983 Regal models may have problems with the A.I.R pipes. The pipes in question go from the check valve to the intake manifold. These pipes may rust through from the inside out. This condition is caused by corrosive exhaust gases. To cut down on this problem, a stainless steel pipe will be used for service parts (it is also installed in the 84 and later models).

Catalytic Converter A.I.R. Pipe Problem

Some 1984 LeSabres and Electras with the 5.0L engines may make a noise that sounds like an exhaust system hitting the floor pan. This condition may be caused by the A.I.R. pipe to converter touching the bdy heat shield. To correct this condition, use the following procedure:

1. Loosen the A.I.R. pipe to converter clamp, reposition the A.I.R pipe away fromt he heat shield and tighten the clamp.
2. There should be ½ in. clearance at the heat shield.

ENGINE SECTION

For Diesel Engine Services Refer to the Unit Repair Section.

ENGINES

NOTE: General Motors Parts release a 3.8L V6 Goodwrench engine (part number 25528795, replacing the part number 25525217) for 1986 and prior model year usage. Numerous differences exist and must be considered during installation. Use the following as quide for installation.

1. A thicker cylinder head gasket is used to improve the cylinder head to block sealing.
2. To accomm odate the new cylinder head gasket, the block deck height has been lowered approximately 0.038 in. To identify this Goodwrench engine block, a code "6-GW" is stamped next to the three digit julian date on the front on the engine block.
3. New cylinder head bolts are used to improve the clamping of the cylinder head to the block.
4. New, low tension piston ring expanders are used, reducing internal engine friction.
5. Due to the engine changes in the cylinder head area, the cylinder head service label must be installed as per instructions provided with the replacement engine. Failure to do so could result in the incorrect usage of parts or service procedures, should they become necessary at a later date.

ENGINE ASSEMBLY

Removal and Installation

V6—GAS ENGINE

1. Remove the hood.
2. Disconnect battery.
3. Drain coolant into a suitable container.
4. Remove air cleaner.
5. On vehicles equipped with air conditioning, disconnect

BUICK
ELECTRA • ESTATE WAGON • LE SABRE • REGAL
SECTION 13

compressor ground wire from the mounting bracket. Remove the electrical connector from the compressor clutch, remove the compressor to mounting bracket attaching bolts, and position the compressor out of the way.
6. Remove fan blade, pulleys, and belts.
7. Disconnect radiator and heater hoses from engine.
8. Remove fan shroud assembly.
9. Remove power steering pump to mounting bracket bolts and position pump assembly out of the way.
10. Disconnect fuel pump hoses and plug.
11. Disconnect battery ground cable from engine.
12. Disconnect the vacuum supply hose from carburetor to the vacuum manifold. On vehicles so equipped, the vacuum modulator, load leveler, and power brake vacuum hoses should all be disconnected at the engine.
13. Disconnect accelerator cable at carburetor.
14. Disconnect alternator, oil and coolant sending unit switch connections at the engine. Remove the alternator.
15. Disconnect engine to body ground strap(s) at engine.
16. Raise the vehicle, disconnect the cable shield from the engine (if so equipped).
17. Disconnect exhaust pipes from exhaust manifolds.
18. Remove lower flywheel or converter cover.
19. Remove flywheel to converter attaching bolts. Scribe chalk mark on the flywheel and converter for reassembly alignment.
20. Remove transmission to engine attaching bolts.
21. Remove motor mount through bolts and cruise control bracket if equipped.
22. Lower the vehicle and support the automatic transmission.
23. Attach a lifting device to the engine and raise the engine enough so mounting through-bolts can be removed. Make certain wiring harness, vacuum hoses, and other parts are free and clear before lifting engine out of the vehicle.
24. Raise engine far enough to clear engine mount, raise transmission support accordingly and alternately until engine can be disengaged from the transmission and removed.
25. Installation is the reverse of the removal procedure.

V8 – GAS ENGINE
1. Drain cooling system.
2. Remove air cleaner and hot air pipe.
3. Remove hood from hinges, mark hood for reassembly.
4. Disconnect battery negative cable at battery and ground wire at inner fender panel. Disconnect engine ground strap, right head to cowl.
5. Disconnect radiator hoses, automatic transmission cooler lines, heater hoses, vacuum hoses, power steering hose bracket from engine, air conditioning compressor with brackets and hoses attached, fuel hose from fuel line, wiring and throttle cable.
6. Remove upper radiator support and radiator.
7. Raise and support the vehicle.
8. Disconnect exhaust pipes at manifold.
9. Remove torque converter cover and the bolts holding converter to flywheel.
10. Remove engine mount bolts or nuts.
11. Remove three bolts, transmission to engine on the right side. Remove starter with wires attached, then support the starter with the frame.
12. Lower the vehicle. Secure lift chain to engine.
13. Place board on top of jack and slightly raise transmission. Remove 3 left transmission to engine bolts. Remove engine.
14. Installation is the reverse of the removal procedure.

V6 – DIESEL ENGINE
1. Drain the cooling system.
2. Remove air cleaner and install cover J–26996 or equivalent.
3. Remove hood from hinges, mark hood for reassembly.
4. Disconnect battery negative cables at batteries and ground wires at inner fender panel. Disconnect engine ground strap, right head to cowl.
5. Disconnect radiator hoses, cooler lines, heater hoses, vacuum hoses, power steering pump hoses at power steering gear, air conditioning compressor with brackets sand hoses attached, fuel hoses from fuel pump inlet line and injection pump return line.
6. Disconnect all engine wiring except at starter.
7. Disconnect the throttle cable.
8. Disconnect the transmission T.V. or detent cable at the injection pump and engine brackets.
9. Remove upper radiator support and radiator.
10. Raise the vehicle and support it safely.
11. Disconnect exhaust pipes at manifolds.
12. Remove the torque converter (flywheel) cover and the three torque converter to flywheel bolts.
13. Remove the starter motor.
14. Remove the engine mount through bolts.
15. Remove the three engine to transmission bolts on the right side.
16. Lower the vehicle.
17. Secure an engine lift chain to the engine.
18. Place a board on top of a jack and slightly raise the transmission. Remove the 3 left transmission to engine bolts. Remove engine.
19. Installation is the reverse of the removal procedure.

V8 – DIESEL ENGINE
1. Drain cooling system.
2. Remove air cleaner and install cover screen J–26996 or equivalent.
3. Mark hood hinges and remove hood.
4. Disconnect negative battery cables at batteries and ground wires at inner fender panel. Disconnect engine ground strap, right head to cowl.
5. Disconnect radiator hoses, cooler lines, heater hoses, vacuum hoses, power steering pump hoses at power steering gear, air conditioning compressor with brackets and hoses attached, fuel hose from fuel pump and wiring.
6. Remove hairpin clip at bellcrank.
7. Remove throttle and T.V. cables from intake manifold brackets, then position cables away from engine.
8. Remove upper radiator support and radiator.
9. Raise the vehicle and support it safely.
10. Disconnect exhaust pipes at manifold.
11. Remove torque converter cover and three bolts holding converter to flywheel.
12. Remove engine mount bolts or nuts.
13. Remove three bolts, transmission to engine on the right side. Disconnect wires from starter and remove starter.
14. Lower the vehicle. Secure lift chain to engine.
15. Place board on top of jack and slightly raise transmission. Remove 3 left transmission to engine bolts. Remove engine.
16. Installation is the reverse of the removal procedure.

ENGINE MOUNTS
Removal and Installation
1. Disconnect the negative battery cable. Raise and support he vehicle safely.
2. Properly support he weight of the engine at the forward edge of the oil pan.
3. Remove the mount to engine block bolts. Raise the engine slightly and remove the mount to mount bracket bolt and nut. Remove the engine mount.
4. Installation is the reverse of the removal procedure.

13-35

BUICK
ELECTRA • ESTATE WAGON • LE SABRE • REGAL

Valve System

VALVE ADJUSTMENT

Hydraulic valve lifters are used in all engines produced by General Motors Corporation. No adjustment is possible.

VALVE LIFTERS

Removal and Installation
1. Disconnect the negative battery cable.
2. Remove the intake manifold assembly.
3. Remove the rocker arm covers. Remove the rocker arm assembly. Remove the push rods. Be sure to keep them in order as they must be installed in the same bores as they were removed.
4. On diesel engines, remove the valve lifter guide retaining bolts. Remove the valve lifter guide.
5. Remove the valve lifters using the proper valve lifter removal tool.
6. Installation is the reverse of the removal procedure. Be sure to use new gaskets as required. Be sure to coat the lifter assemblies with clean engine oil prior to installation.

VALVE ROCKER ASSEMBLY

Removal and Installation

V6 – GAS ENGINE
1. Disconnect the negative battery cable.
2. Remove the rocker arm cover. Remove the rocker arm and shaft assembly from the cylinder head.
3. Remove the nylon rocker arm retainers and separate the rocker arms from the rocker shaft.
4. Installation is the reverse of the removal procedure. Be sure to use new valve cover gaskets, where required.
5. When installing the rocker arms on to the rocker shaft, be sure to position them in the correct sequence.

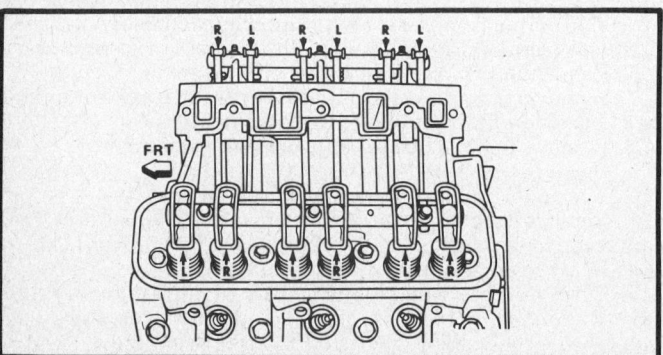

V6 gas engine rocker arm assembly
(© General Motors Corporation)

V8 – GAS ENGINE
1. Disconnect the negative battery cable.
2. Remove the valve cover.
3. Remove the rocker arm retaining bolts, rocker arm pivot and rocker arms. On 4.3L (267 cu. in.) engine remove the rocker arm retaining nut and then remove the rocker arm.
4. Installation is the reverse of the removal procedure. BE SURE to use new valve cover gaskets, as required.

V6 AND V8 – DIESEL ENGINES
1. Disconnect the negative battery cable.
2. Remove the valve cover.
3. Remove the rocker arm retaining bolts. Remove the rocker arm pivot. Remove the rocker arms.
4. Installation is the reverse of the removal procedure. Be sure to use new valve cover gaskets as required.

VALVE TIMING

Adjustment

Manufacturers recommended procedure for valve timing has not been established, except for the 5.0L (307 cu. in.) Oldsmobile produced V8 engine.

5.0L (307 cu. in.) ENGINE
1. Remove the distributor cap. Remove the right valve cover. Remove the No. 4 intake and exhaust rocker arm assembly.
2. Remove the wire from the BAT terminal of the distributor cap.
3. Turn ignition switch on. Crank engine until rotor is in line with No. 4 spark plug wire position. No. 4 piston will be approximately at the top of cylinder.
4. Measure from pivot boss on head surface to top of Number Four intake push rod. Record measurement.
5. Slowly turn engine 1½ revolutions until rotor approaches No. 1 spark plug wire position. Continue to turn engine until timing mark on crank puller is aligned with 0 on indicator. This is TDC of the No. 1 piston.
6. Again measure from pivot boss surface to top of No. 4 cylinder intake push rod.
7. Measurement should increase over the first measurement.
8. If measurement increase is not within $1/32$ in. of first measurement, camshaft is advanced or retarded.

VALVE LIFTER BLEED DOWN – DIESEL ENGINES

If the intake manifold has been removed and if any rocker arms have been loosened or removed; remove those valve lifters, disassemble, drain, then reassemble them.

If the intake manifold has not been removed but rocker arms have been loosened or removed, valve lifters can be bled down by the following procedure:
1. Before reinstalling rocker arms, rotate the crankshaft until number 1 cylinder is at 32° BTDC. This is 2 in. counterclockwise from the 0° pointer. If only the right valve cover was removed, remove No. 1 glow plug to determine if the position of the piston is the correct one. The compression pressure will tell you that you are in the right position.
If the left valve cover was removed, rotate the crankshaft until the No. 5 cylinder intake valve push rod ball is 0.28 in. above the No. 5 cylinder exhaust valve pushrod ball.

NOTE: Use only hand wrenches to torque the rocker arm pivot nuts or bolts to avoid engine damage.

2. If removed, install the No. 5 cylinder pivot and rocker arms. Torque the nuts or bolts alternately between the intake and exhaust valves until the intake valve begins to open, then stop.
3. Install remaining rocker arms except No. 3 exhaust valve. (If this rocker arm was removed).
4. If removed, install but do not torque No. 3 valve pivots beyond the point that the valve would be fully open. This is indicated by strong resistance while still turning the pivot retaining nuts or bolts. Going beyond this would bend the push rod. Torque the nuts or bolts slowly allowing the lifter to bleed down.
5. Finish torquing No. 5 cylinder rocker arm pivot nut or bolt slowly. Do not go beyond the point that the valve would be fully open. This is indicated by strong resistance while still turning the pivot retaining nuts or bolts. Going beyond this would bend the push rod.
6. Do not turn the engine crankshaft for at least 45 minutes.

BUICK
ELECTRA • ESTATE WAGON • LE SABRE • REGAL
SECTION 13

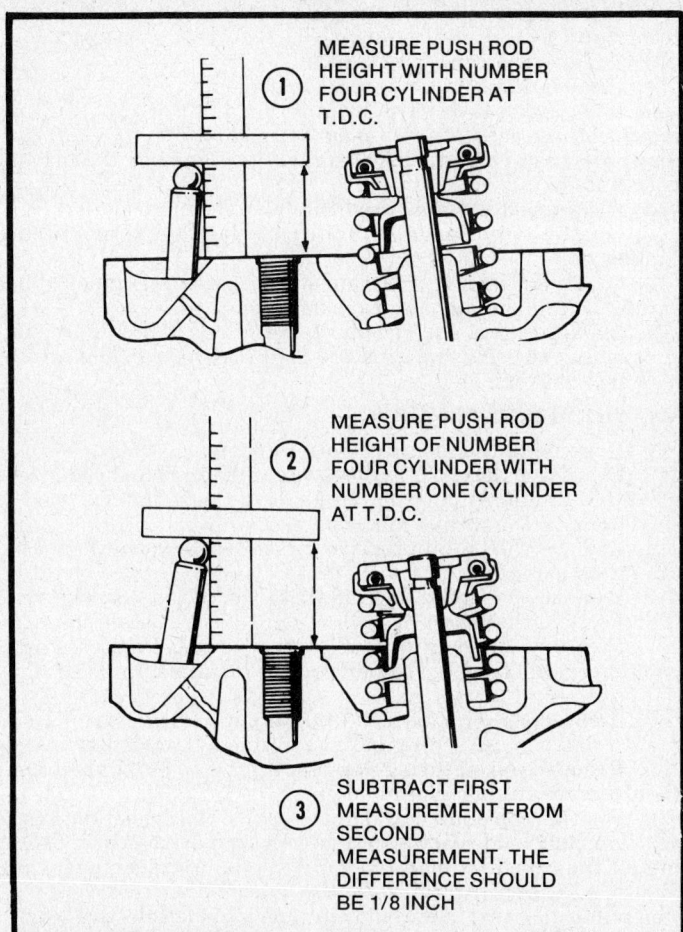

Checking valve timing—5.0L 307 cu. in. engine
(© General Motors Corporation)

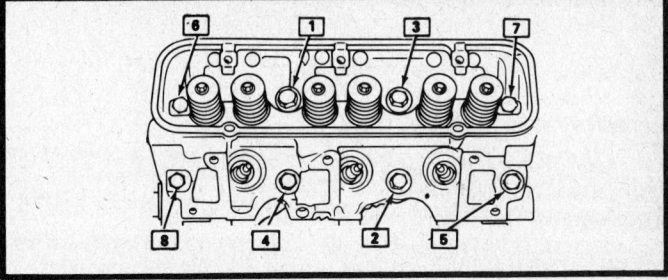

V6 gas engine cylinder head bolt torque sequence
(© General Motors Corporation)

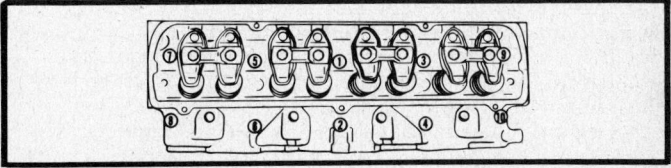

V8 gasoline and diesel engine cylinder head bolt torque sequence (© General Motors Corporation)

NOTE: Do not rotate the engine until the valve lifters have been bled down, or damage to the engine will occur.

CYLINDER HEADS

Removal and Installation

V6—GAS ENGINE

1. Disconnect negative battery cable.
2. Remove intake manifold.
3. Loosen and remove belt(s).
4. When removing left cylinder head:
   a. Remove oil dipstick.
   b. Remove air and vacuum pumps with mounting bracket if present, and move out of the way with hoses attached.
5. When removing right cylinder head:
   a. Remove alternator.
   b. Disconnect power steering gear pump and brackets attaching to cylinder head.
6. Disconnect wires from spark plugs, and remove the spark plug wire clips from the rocker arm cover studs.
7. Remove exhaust manifold bolts from head being removed.
8. With air hose and cloths, clean dirt off cylinder head and adjacent area to avoid getting dirt into engine.
9. Remove rocker arm cover and rocker arm and shaft assembly from cylinder head. Lift out push rods.
10. Loosen all cylinder head bolts, then remove bolts and lift off the cylinder head.
11. Installation is the reverse of the removal procedure. Refer to Torque Specification Chart for correct torque values.

V8—GAS ENGINE

1. Disconnect the negative battery cable. Drain the radiator.
2. Remove the intake manifold. Remove the exhaust manifold.
3. Remove the valve cover. Remove the ground strap from the left cylinder head.
4. Remove rocker arm bolts, pivots, rocker arms and push rods. Scribe pivots and keep rocker arms separated so they can be installed in their original locations.
5. Remove cylinder head bolts and remove cylinder head.
6. Installation is the reverse of the removal procedure. Refer to Torque Specifications Chart for correct torque values.

V6 AND V8—DIESEL ENGINES

1. Disconnect the negative battery cable. Drain the cooling system.
2. On the V8 diesel engine remove the injection pump and lines.
3. Remove the intake manifold. Remove the valve cover.
4. Disconnect glow plug wiring.
5. Remove ground strap from right cylinder head.
6. Remove rocker arm bolts, pivots, rocker arms, and push rods. Scribe pivots and keep rocker arms separated so they can be installed in their original locations.
7. Disconnect the exhaust manifold from the head. Leave it attached to the crossover pipe.
8. Remove engine block drain plug, from side of the block where head is being removed.
9. Remove cylinder head bolts and remove cylinder head.
10. If necessary to remove pre-chamber, remove the glow plug and injection nozzle, then tap out with a small blunt drift.
11. Installation is the reverse of the removal procedure.
12. If the vehicle is equipped with a V8 diesel (VIN N), torque the cylinder head bolts to 100 ft.lbs. and then retorque the head to 130 ft.lbs.
13. If the vehicle is equipped with a V6 diesel (VIN V), torque the cylinder heads in the following manner:
14. Torque all cylinder head bolts in sequence except No. 5, 6, 11, 12, 13 and 14 to 100 lbs. ft. Torque No. 5, 6, 11, 12, 13 and 14 to 41 lbs. ft.
15. Retorque in sequence all cylinder head bolts except No. 5,

SECTION 13
BUICK
ELECTRA • ESTATE WAGON • LE SABRE • REGAL

6, 11, 12, 13 and 14 to 142 lbs. ft. Retorque No. 5, 6, 11, 12, 13 and 14 to 59 lbs. ft.

CAMSHAFT

Removal and Installation

V6 – GAS ENGINE

1. Disconnect the negative battery cable. Drain the radiator.
2. Remove the intake manifold. Remove the rocker covers. Remove the rocker arm assemblies, push rods and valve lifters.
3. Remove the radiator and the air condition condenser, as required.
4. Remove timing chain cover, timing chain and sprocket.
5. Align timing marks of camshaft and crankshaft sprocket. This avoids burring of the camshaft journals by the crankshaft during removal. Slide camshaft forward out of bearing bores carefully to avoid marring the bearing surfaces.
6. Installation is the reverse of the removal procedure.
7. Before installing the camshaft and the lifters, be sure to coat them with clean engine oil.
8. Be sure to use new gaskets and seals as required.

V8 – GAS ENGINE

1. Disconnect the negative battery cable. Drain the radiator. Remove the upper radiator baffle.
2. Disconnect the upper radiator hose.
3. Remove the radiator.
4. Disconnect the fuel line at the fuel pump.
5. Remove the air cleaner. Disconnect the throttle cable.
6. Remove the alternator belt. Remove the alternator bracket attaching bolts.
7. Remove power steering pump bracket attaching bolts and remove pump.
8. Remove air conditioning compressor mounting bracket attaching bolts and support compressor to side for access. The air conditioning lines at the compressor are flexible and should be left attached to the compressor.
9. Disconnect thermostat bypass hose at water pump. Disconnect electrical and vacuum connections. Remove distributor with cap and wiring intact.
10. Remove balancer pulley. Remove balancer.
11. Remove engine front cover. Remove both valve covers.
12. Remove intake manifold and gasket, front and rear seal.
13. Remove rocker arms, push rods and valve lifters. Parts position should be noted so they will be installed in their original position.
14. If equipped with air conditioning, discharge the system, remove condenser attaching bolts and remove condenser.
15. Remove bolt securing fuel pump eccentric, remove eccentric, camshaft gear, oil slinger and timing chain.
16. Remove camshaft by carefully sliding it out the front of the engine.
17. Installation is the reverse of the removal procedure. Be sure to coat the camshaft and the lifters with clean engine oil prior to installation. Be sure to use new gaskets, as required.

V6 – DIESEL ENGINE

1. Disconnect the negative battery cable.
2. Drain the radiator. Remove the radiator fan shroud. Remove the radiator upper baffle. Remove the radiator.
3. Remove the intake manifold assembly.
4. Remove the oil pump drive assembly.
5. Remove the front cover. Remove the rocker covers.
6. Rotate the crankshaft so that the timing marks are in alignment.
7. Remove all rocker arms, pivots, push rods, and lifters. Parts position should be noted so that the parts can be installed in their original position.
8. Remove the bolt securing the camshaft sprockets and remove the camshaft and crankshaft sprockets and timing chain.
9. Remove the bolts retaining the front camshaft bearing retainer and remove the retainer.
10. Remove the cam sprocket key.
11. Remove the injection pump drive gear.
12. If necessary to remove the injection pump driven gear, remove the intermediate pump adapter and pump adapter. Remove the snap ring and selective washer. Remove the driven gear and spring.
13. If equipped with air conditioning, discharge the system, remove the condenser attaching bolts and remove the condenser.
14. Carefully remove the camshaft from the engine being careful not to damage any camshaft bearings.
15. Installation is the revere of the removal procedure. Be sure to coat the camshaft and the lifters with clean engine oil. Use new gaskets, as required.

V8 – DIESEL ENGINE

1. Disconnect the negative battery cable.
2. Drain the radiator. Remove the radiator fan shroud. Remove the radiator upper baffle. Remove the radiator.
3. Remove the intake manifold assembly.
4. Remove the oil pump drive assembly. Remove the vacuum pump assembly.
5. Remove the front cover. Remove the rocker covers.
6. Remove the balancer pulley. Remove the balancer.
7. Remove rocker arms, push rods, and valve lifters. Parts position should be noted so they will be installed in their original position.
8. If equipped with air conditioning, discharge system, remove condenser attaching bolts, and remove condenser.
9. Remove bolt securing camshaft gear and timing chain, then remove timing gears and chain.
10. Position camshaft dowel pin at the 3 o'clock position. With the camshaft held rearward, remove pump drive gear by sliding off the camshaft while rocking the pump driven gear.
11. If necessary to remove pump driven gear, remove injection pump adapter, then remove snap ring and selective washer. Remove the driven gear and spring.
12. Remove camshaft by carefully sliding it out the front of the engine.
13. Installation is the reverse of the removal procedure.
14. Be sure to coat the camshaft and the lifters with clean engine oil. Use new gaskets, as required.

PISTON AND ROD POSITIONING

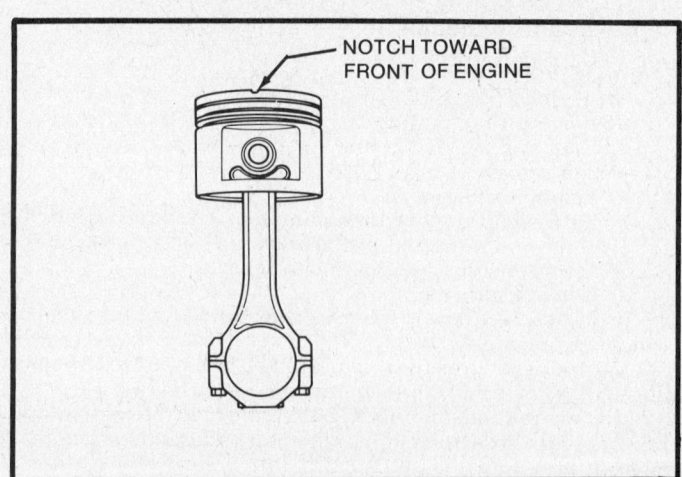

V6 gas engine – piston assembly
(© General Motors Corporation)

BUICK 13

ELECTRA • ESTATE WAGON • LE SABRE • REGAL

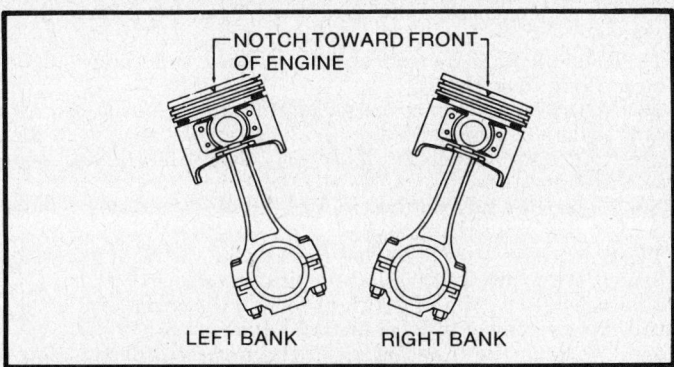

V8 gasoline engine piston assembly
(© General Motors Corporation)

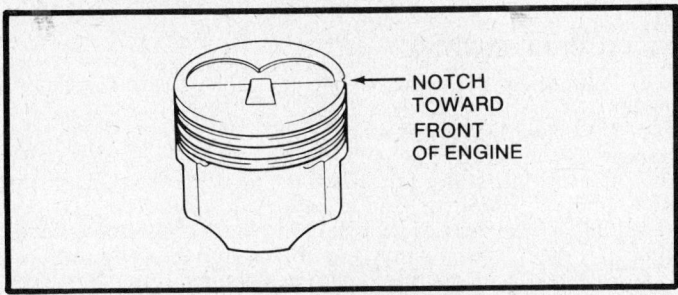

V6 and V8 diesel engine 1982 and later — piston assembly (© General Motors Corporation)

── **CAUTION** ──

Always match-mark pistons and connecting rods to assure correct installation of re-used or new components. Relationship of connecting rods to crankshaft should be noted before disassembly.

TIMING CASE COVER/OIL SEAL

Removal and Installation

V6 – GAS ENGINE

1. Disconnect the negative battery cable. Drain the radiator.
2. Disconnect the radiator hoses and the heater return hose at the water pump.
3. Remove the fan assembly and pulleys. Remove the crankshaft vibration damper.
4. Remove the fuel pump. Remove the alternator.
5. Remove the distributor. If timing chain and sprockets are not going to be disturbed, note position of distributor rotor for reinstallation in same position.
6. Loosen and slide front clamp on thermostat bypass hose rearward.
7. Remove bolts attaching timing chain cover to cylinder block. Remove 2 oil pan to timing chain cover bolts. Remove timing chain cover assembly and gasket.
8. Thoroughly clean the cover, taking care to avoid damage to the gasket surface.
9. Installation is the reverse of the removal procedure.
10. Remove oil pump cover and pack the space around the oil pump gears completely full of petroleum jelly. There must be no air space left inside the pump. Reinstall cover using new gasket.
11. To replace the front oil seal, use a punch and drive out the old seal and shedder. Drive the seal out from the front toward the rear of the timing chain cover.
12. Coil new packing around opening so ends of packing are at top. Drive in shedder using suitable punch. Stake the shedder in place in at least 3 places.
13. Size the packing by rotating a hammer handle or similar tool around the packing until the balancer hub can be inserted through the opening.
14. Torque the front cover retaining bolts to 28 ft.lbs..

V8 – GAS ENGINE

1. Disconnect the negative battery cable. Drain the cooling system. Disconnect the radiator hoses and the bypass hose.
2. Remove the radiator upper support. Remove the radiator.
3. Remove all belts, fan and fan pulley, crankshaft pulley and harmonic balancer.
4. Remove cover to block attaching bolts and remove cover, timing indicator and water pump assembly.
5. Remove front cover and both dowel pins. It may be necessary to grind a flat on the pins to get a rough surface for gripping.
6. To install, grind a chamfer on one end of each dowel pin.

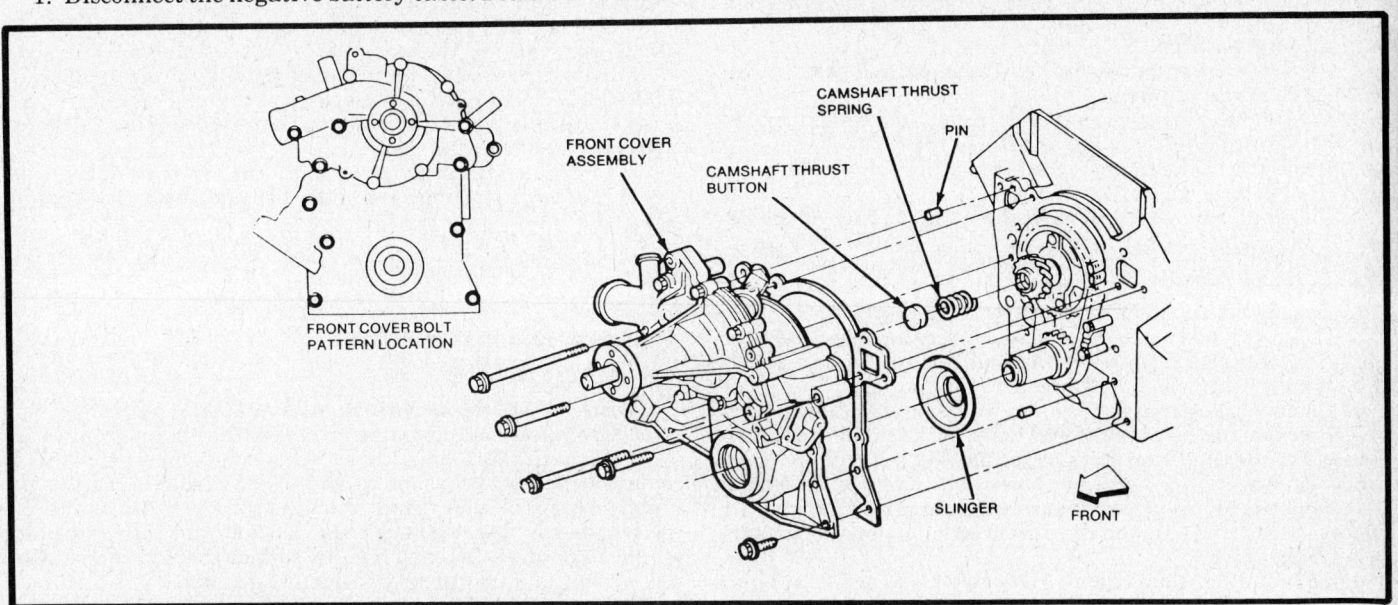

V6 gas engine timing cover and related components (© General Motors Corporation)

BUICK
ELECTRA • ESTATE WAGON • LE SABRE • REGAL

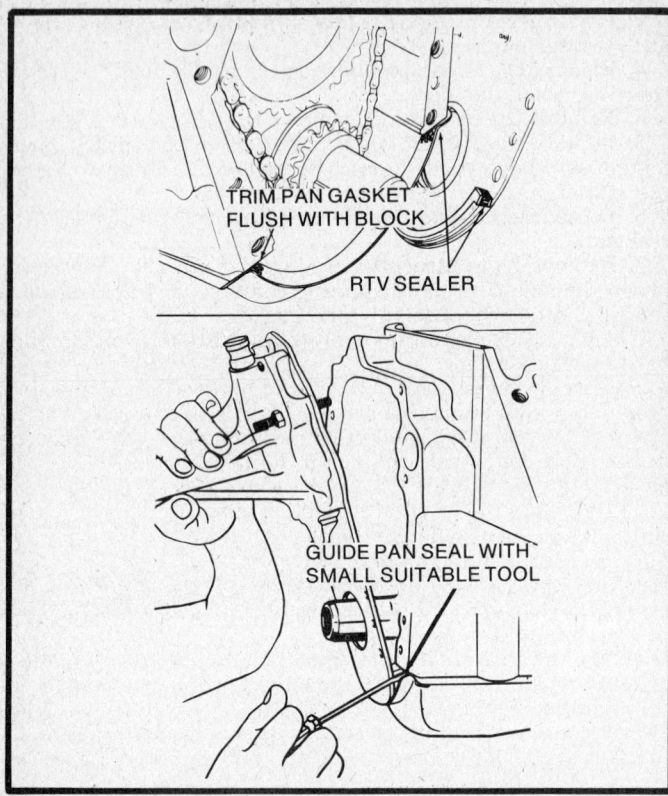

V6 and V8 diesel engine and V8 gasoline engine timing cover installation (© General Motors Corporation)

7. Cut excess material from front end of oil pan gasket on each side of engine block.
8. Clean block, oil pan and front cover mating surfaces with solvent.
9. Trim about 1/8 in. from each end of new front pan seal, using a sharp tool.
10. Install new front cover gasket on engine block and new front seal on front cover. Apply sealer to gasket around coolant holes and place on block. Apply RTV sealer or equivalent to both mating surfaces.
11. Place the cover on the front of the block and press downward to compress the seal.
12. Rotate the cover to the left and then to the right and guide the seal into the cavity using a suitable tool.
13. Install two bolts finger tight to hold the cover in place. Install the 2 dowel pins, chamfered end first.
14. Continue the installation in the reverse order of the removal procedure.

V6 – DIESEL ENGINE

1. Disconnect the negative battery cable.
2. Drain the cooling system. Disconnect the lower radiator hose. Disconnect the heater outlet and the bypass hoses.
3. Remove the crankshaft balancer and pulley.
4. Remove the fan assembly and water pump pulley.
5. Remove the alternator, power steering pump, belt tensioner and air condition compressor brackets, if equipped.
6. Remove the front cover to block bolts and probe holder.
7. Remove the front cover and both dowel pins. It may be necessary to grind a flat on the pins in order to get a rough surface for gripping.
8. To install, grind a chamfer on one end of each dowel pin.
9. Cut excess material from front end of oil pan gasket on each side of engine block.

10. Clean block, oil pan and front cover mating surfaces with solvent.
11. Trim about 1/8 in. from each end of new front pan seal, using a sharp tool.
12. Install new front cover gasket on engine block and new front seal on front cover. Apply sealer to gasket around coolant holes and place on block. Apply RTV sealer or equivalent to both mating surfaces.
13. Place the cover on the front of the block and press downward to compress the seal.
14. Rotate the cover to the left and then to the right and guide the seal into the cavity using a suitable tool.
15. Install two bolts finger tight to hold the cover in place. Install the two dowel pins, chamfered end first.
16. Continue the installation in the reverse order of the removal procedure.
17. To replace the front cover oil seal, pry it from the front cover. Before installing a new oil seal coat it with clean engine oil.

V8 – DIESEL ENGINE

1. Disconnect the negative battery cable. Drain the cooling system.
2. Disconnect the radiator hoses. Disconnect the bypass hose.
3. Remove all belts, fan and fan pulley, crankshaft pulley and harmonic balancer, and accessory brackets.
4. Remove cover to block attaching bolts and remove cover, timing indicator, and water pump assembly.
5. Remove front cover and both dowel pins. It may be necessary to grind a flat on the pins to get a rough surface for gripping.
6. To install, grind a chamfer on one end of each dowel pin.
7. Cut excess material from front end of oil pan gasket on each side of engine block.
8. Clean block, oil pan and front cover mating surfaces with solvent.
9. Trim about 1/8 in. from each end of new front pan seal, using a sharp tool.
10. Install new front cover gasket on engine block and new front seal on front cover. Apply sealer to gasket around coolant holes and place on block. Apply RTV sealer or equivalent to both mating surfaces.
11. Place the cover on the front of the block and press downward to compress the seal.
12. Rotate the cover to the left and then to the right, and guide the seal into the cavity using a suitable tool.
13. Install two bolts finger tight to hold the cover in place. Install the 2 dowel pins, chamfered end first.
14. Continue the installation in the reverse order of the removal procedure.
15. To replace the front cover oil seal, pry it from the front cover. Before installing a new oil seal coat it with clean engine oil.

TIMING GEARS

Removal and Installation

V6 – GAS ENGINE

1. Disconnect the negative battery cable.
2. Drain the cooling system. Remove the engine front cover.
3. With timing chain cover removed, temporarily install balancer bolt and washer in end of crankshaft. Turn crankshaft so that the timing marks on the sprockets are as close together as possible. Remove balancer bolt and washer using a sharp blow on the wrench handle, so that the bolt can be started out without changing position of sprockets.
4. Remove front crankshaft oil slinger. Remove the camshaft sprocket bolts.

5. Use two large suitable tools to alternately pry the camshaft sprocket then the crankshaft sprocket forward until the camshaft sprocket is free, then remove the camshaft sprocket and chain and finish working crankshaft sprocket off crankshaft.
6. Thoroughly clean the timing chain, sprockets, distributor drive gear, fuel pump eccentric and crankshaft oil slinger.
7. If the pistons have not been moved in the engine, go to Step 10. If the engine has been turned over or the pistons moved, start with Step 1.
8. Turn crankshaft so that No. 1 piston is at top dead center.
9. Turn camshaft so with sprocket temporarily installed, timing mark is straight down. Remove sprocket.
10. Assemble timing chain on sprockets and slide the sprocket and chain assembly on the shafts with the timing marks in their closest together position and in line with the sprocket hubs.
11. Assemble slinger on crankshaft with large part of cone to front of engine.
12. Install camshaft sprocket bolts. Torque to specification.
13. Install camshaft thrust button and spring and timing chain dampers.
14. Install timing chain cover. Continue the installation in the reverse order of the removal procedure.

V8 – GAS ENGINE

1. Disconnect the negative battery cable.
2. Drain the cooling system. Remove the engine front cover.
3. Remove the fuel pump eccentric, oil slinger, cam gear and timing chain.
4. Remove the key. Remove the crankshaft gear.

NOTE: Remove crankshaft key, if possible, before using puller because keyway is machined only part way in crankshaft gear and breakage could occur.

5. Install camshaft gear, crankshaft gear and timing chain together, and align timing marks.
6. When the two marks are in alignment, No. 6 is at TDC. To obtain TDC for No. 1 cylinder, slowly rotate crankshaft one rotation, this will bring the cam mark to the top, No. 1 then will be in firing position.
7. Install fuel pump eccentric with flat side rearward.
8. Drive key in with a brass hammer until it bottoms in gear. Install oil slinger.
9. Continue the installation in the reverse order of the removal procedure.

V6 – DIESEL ENGINE

1. Disconnect the negative battery cable. Drain the cooling system.
2. Remove the engine front cover.
3. Loosen all rocker arm pivot bolts evenly so that lash exists between the rocker arms and valves.
4. Remove the crankshaft oil slinger.
5. Remove the camshaft sprocket to camshaft bolt and washer.
6. Remove the timing chain, camshaft an crankshaft sprockets.
7. If the camshaft sprocket to cam key should come out with the camshaft sprocket, remove the front camshaft bearing retainer and install the key into the injection pump drive gear. Install the bearing retainer and torque the bolts to 48 ft.lbs..
8. Install the key in the crankshaft, if removed.
9. Install camshaft sprocket, crankshaft sprocket and timing chain together, and align timing marks.
10. Torque camshaft sprocket bolt to 64 ft.lbs.. Install the oil slinger.
11. After installing the front cover, it is necessary to bleed down the valve lifters.
12. Install the valve covers.
13. Check and reset if necessary, the injection pump timing.
14. Continue the installation in the reverse order of the removal procedure.

V8 – DIESEL ENGINES

1. Disconnect the negative battery cable. Drain the cooling system.
2. Remove the engine front timing cover.
3. Remove the oil slinger. Remove the cam sprocket, crankshaft sprocket and timing chain.
4. Remove the fuel pump eccentric from the crankshaft if necessary.
5. Install the key in the crankshaft, if removed. Install the fuel pump eccentric, if removed.
6. Install camshaft sprocket, crankshaft sprocket and timing chain together, and align timing marks.
7. Torque camshaft sprocket bolt to 65 ft.lbs..
8. When the two marks are in alignment, No. 6 cylinder is at TDC. To obtain TDC for No. 1 cylinder, slowly rotate crankshaft 1 rotation. This will bring the cam mark to the top, No. 1 will be in firing position.
9. Install oil slinger.
10. Continue the installation in the reverse order of the removal procedure. Be sure to bleed down the valve lifters, as required.

Lubrication

OIL PAN

Removal and Installation

V6 – GAS ENGINE

1. Disconnect the negative battery cable.
2. Raise the vehicle and support it safely. Drain the engine oil.
3. Remove the flywheel cover and the engine crossover pipe.
4. Remove the oil pan bolts. Remove the oil pan from the engine assembly.
5. Installation is the reverse of removal.

V8 – GAS ENGINE

1. Disconnect the negative battery cable. Remove the engine oil dipstick.
2. Remove the fan shroud attaching screws. Raise and support the vehicle safely. Remove distributor cap and align rotor in the No. 1 firing position. This positions the crankshaft counter weights and connecting rods for the least amount of interference with the oil pan.
3. Drain the engine oil from the oil pan into a suitable drain pan. Remove the flywheel cover and crossover pipe.
4. Remove the starter. Using a jack, with a block of wood on top, place it under the crankshaft hub to support the engine. Remove the engine mounts at the cylinder block.
5. Raise the front of engine as high as possible. Remove the oil pan retaining bolts and remove the oil pan from the engine.
6. Clean all the gasket material from the pan and the block mating surfaces. Use a new gasket kit and sealer. Make sure the seals are firmly positioned on the flange surfaces with each seal properly located in the cut-out notches of the pan gasket.
7. Installation is the reverse of the removal procedure.

V6 AND V8 – DIESEL ENGINES

1. Disconnect the negative battery cable.
2. Remove the oil pump drive and the vacuum pump.
3. Raise vehicle and support safely. Drain engine oil. Remove dipstick.
4. Remove the upper radiator support and fan shroud attaching screws.
5. Remove the flywheel cover and the engine crossover pipe.

6. Disconnect the oil cooler lines at the filter adapter. Remove the starter assembly.

7. Remove engine mounts and support the engine. Remove the oil pan bolts. Remove the engine oil pan.

8. Installation is the reverse of removal. Apply RTV sealant to both sides of the oil pan. Be sure that the tabs on the gaskets are installed in the notches of the seals.

OIL PUMP

Removal and Installation

V6—GAS ENGINE

1. Disconnect the negative battery cable. Drain the engine oil. Remove the oil filter.
2. Unbolt the pump cover assembly from the timing chain cover.
3. Remove the cover assembly and slide out the pump gears.
4. Remove the oil pressure relief valve cap, spring, and valve. Do not remove the oil filter bypass valve and spring.
5. Check that the relief valve spring isn't worn on its side or collapsed. Check that the relief valve is no more than an easy slip fit in its bore in the cover. If there is any perceptible sideplay, replace the valve. If there is still sideplay, replace the cover.
6. Check the filter bypass valve for good condition.

To assemble the pump:

7. Lubricate and install the pressure relief valve and spring in the cover bore. Install the gasket and cap, torquing the cap to 35 ft.lbs..
8. Install the gears and check that gear-to-cover end clearance is between 0.002–0.006 in. If the clearance is less, check the timing cover gear pocket for wear.
9. Remove the gears and pack the gear pocket full of petroleum jelly. Don't use grease.
10. Install the gears. Install a new gasket and the cover. Torque the bolts evenly to 10 ft.lbs.. Replace the filter.

V8—GAS ENGINE, V6 and V8 DIESEL ENGINES

1. Disconnect the negative battery cable. Drain the engine oil. Remove the engine oil pan.
2. Remove pump attaching screws and carefully lower the pump.

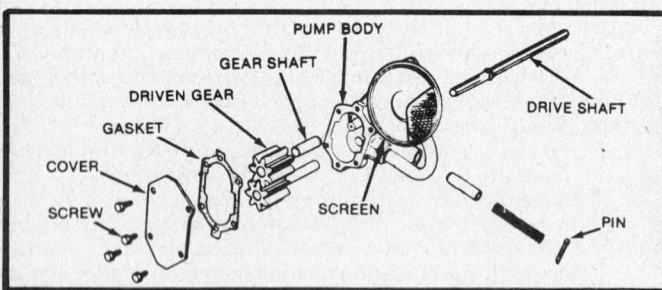

Oil pump—exploded view except V6 gas engine
(© General Motors Corporation)

V6 gas engine oil pump—exploded view
(© General Motors Corporation)

3. Reinstall in reverse order. To ensure immediate oil pressure on start-up, the oil pump gear cavity should be packed with petroleum jelly.

REAR MAIN OIL SEAL

NOTE: On the 5.0L engine, the rear main seal should br replaced with the crankshaft out of the engine. However there is a kit available to repair the rear main bearing upper seal if it should develop a leak.

Removal and Installation

1. Remove the oil pan, and pump where required, and remove the rear main bearing cap.
2. Pry the lower seal out of the bearing cap with a screwdriver, being careful not to gouge the cap surface.
3. Remove the upper seal by lightly tapping on one end with a brass pin punch until the other end can be grasped and pulled out with pliers.
4. Clean the bearing cap, cylinder block, and crankshaft mating surfaces with solvent. Inspect all these surfaces for gouges, nicks, and burrs.
5. Apply light engine oil on the seal lips and bead, but keep the seal ends clean.
6. Insert the tip of the installation tool between the crankshaft and the seal of the cylinder block. Place the seal between the tip of the tool and the crankshaft, so that the bead contacts the tip of the tool.
7. Be sure that the seal lip is facing the front of the engine, and work the seal around the crankshaft using the installation tool to protect the seal from the corner of the cylinder block.

NOTE: Do not remove the tool until the opposite end of the seal is flush with the cylinder block surface.

8. Remove the installation tool, being careful not to pull the seal out at the same time.
9. Using the same procedure, install the lower seal into the bearing cap. Use your finger and thumb to lever the seal into the cap.
10. Apply sealer to the cylinder block only where the cap mates to the surface. Do not apply sealer to the seal ends.
11. Install the rear cap and torque the bolts to specifications.

5.0L Engine

REAR MAIN BEARING UPPER OIL SEAL REPAIR (ENGINE IN CAR)

1. Disconnect the negative battery cable. Remove the oil pan as previously outlined in this section. Remove the rear main bearing cap.
2. Using packing tool BT-6433 or J-25282-2 or equivalent, drive both side of the old seal gently into the groove until it is packed tight.
3. Measure the amount of the seal that was driven up on one side; add $1/16$ in., then cut this length from the old seal removed from the main bearing cap with a suitable cutting tool.
4. Measure the amount of the seal that was driven up on the other side. Add a $1/16$ in. and cut another length from the old seal. Use the main bearing cap as a holding fixture when cutting the seal.
5. Work these two pieces of the seal into the cylinder block (one piece on each side) with two suitable tools. Using the packing tool, pack these short pieces up into the block using tool BT-6436 or equivalent or a sharp blade.
6. Place a piece of shim stock between the seal and the crankshaft to protect the bearing surface before triming the seal.
7. Form a new rope seal in the rear main bearing cap. Place a drop of a suitable sealer on each end of the seal and cap. Install the main bearing cap.

BUICK SECTION 13
ELECTRA • ESTATE WAGON • LE SABRE • REGAL

NOTE: Do not use the attaching bolts to pull down the bearing cap. Tap gently into place with a suitable tool.

8. Install the oil pan and fill with the proper oil to the specified amount.

FRONT SUSPENSION AND STEERING SECTION

For Front Suspension Services Refer to the Unit Repair Section.
For Steering Gear Overhaul Refer to the Unit Repair Section.

STEERING WHEEL

Removal and Installation

EXCEPT TILT AND TELESCOPE COLUMN

1. Disconnect the horn wire connector from the steering column.
2. On vehicles with a standard wheel or optional wood rim wheel, pull off the cap, remove the three screws and the contact, insulator, and spring. On vehicles with the bar-type horn actuator, remove the screws securing the actuator form the underside of the steering wheel, unhook the lead connector plug, and remove the actuator assembly.
3. Loosen the steering wheel nut.
4. Apply the steering wheel puller and pull the wheel up to the nut. Now remove the puller, nut and steering wheel.

NOTE: Location marks are provided on the steering wheel and shaft to simplify proper indexing at the time of installation.

5. Install wheel with the location mark aligned with that of the shaft.
6. Install the wheel nut and torque to 30 ft.lbs..
7. Reinstall horn button or actuator assembly.

TILT AND TELESCOPE COLUMN

1. Remove the attaching screws and lift the pad from the column.
2. Disconnect the horn wire by pushing in the connector and turning it counterclockwise.
3. Push the locking lever counterclockwise until full release is obtained.
4. Mark the lock plate-to-locking lever position and remove the plate and lever.
5. Remove the steering wheel retaining nut and remove the wheel with a puller.
6. Install a $^5/_{16}$ in. x 18 set screw into the upper shaft at the fully extended position and lock it.
7. Install the steering wheel, observing the aligning mark on the hub and the slash mark on the end of the shaft. Make certain that the unattached end of the horn upper contact assembly is seated flush against the top of the horn contact carrier button.
8. Install the nut on the upper steering shaft and torque to 30 ft.lbs..
9. Remove the set screw installed in Step 6.
10. Install the plate assembly finger tight.
11. Position the locking lever in the vertical position and move it counterclockwise until the holes in the plate align with the holes in the lever. Install the attaching screws.
12. Align the pad assembly with the holes in the steering wheel and install the retaining screws.
13. Make certain that the locking lever securely locks the wheel travel and that the wheel travel is free in the unlocked position.

STEERING GEAR

Removal and Installation

1. Remove the flexible coupling shield by sliding it up on the column.
2. On vehicles equipped with power steering, disconnect the hoses from the gear and cap the hose fittings.
3. Raise and support the vehicle safely.
4. Remove the pitman shaft nut, then disconnect the pitman arm from the pitman shaft using a pitman arm puller.
5. Remove the gear to frame rail attaching bolts and lift out the steering gear.

NOTE: If the gear mounting threads are stripped, do not repair. Replace the steering gear housing.

6. Installation is the reverse of removal.

FRONT WHEEL BEARINGS

Adjustment

1. Raise the vehicle and support it safely.
2. Remove the dust cap from the hub.
3. Remove the cotter pin and discard it.
4. Tighten the spindle nut to 12 ft.lbs.. while turning the wheel, then back off the nut ¼–½ turn.
5. Retighten the nut by hand until it is finger tight.
6. Loosen the nut no more than $^1/_6$ of a turn until the nearest hole in the spindle lines up with the slot in the spindle nut, and insert a new cotter pin.
7. Feel the looseness in the hub assembly. There should be 0.001–0.005 in. end play.
8. Replace the dust cover and lower the vehicle.

POWER STEERING PUMP

Removal and Installation

V6 ENGINES

1. Disconnect the negative battery cable. Remove the power steering pump belt.
2. Loosen the bolts and nuts attaching the AIR pump bracket. If equipped with a vacuum pump remove the AIR pump/vacuum pump bracket.
3. Remove the three bolts attaching the power steering pump front bracket to the power steering and AIR mounting bracket.
4. Remove the nut from the stud on the back of the pump. Move the pump and bracket assembly forward to gain access to the power steering lines.
5. Disconnect and plug the power steering lines. Remove the pump and bracket assembly from the vehicle. Remove the pulley and bracket from the pump.
6. Installation is the reverse order of the removal procedure.

REGAL (3.8L SFI-Turbo)

1. Disconnect the negative battery cable. Turn the steering wheel all the way to the left.
2. Remove the serpentine belt. Remove the left intercooler bracket bolts and bracket.

SECTION 13 BUICK
ELECTRA • ESTATE WAGON • LE SABRE • REGAL

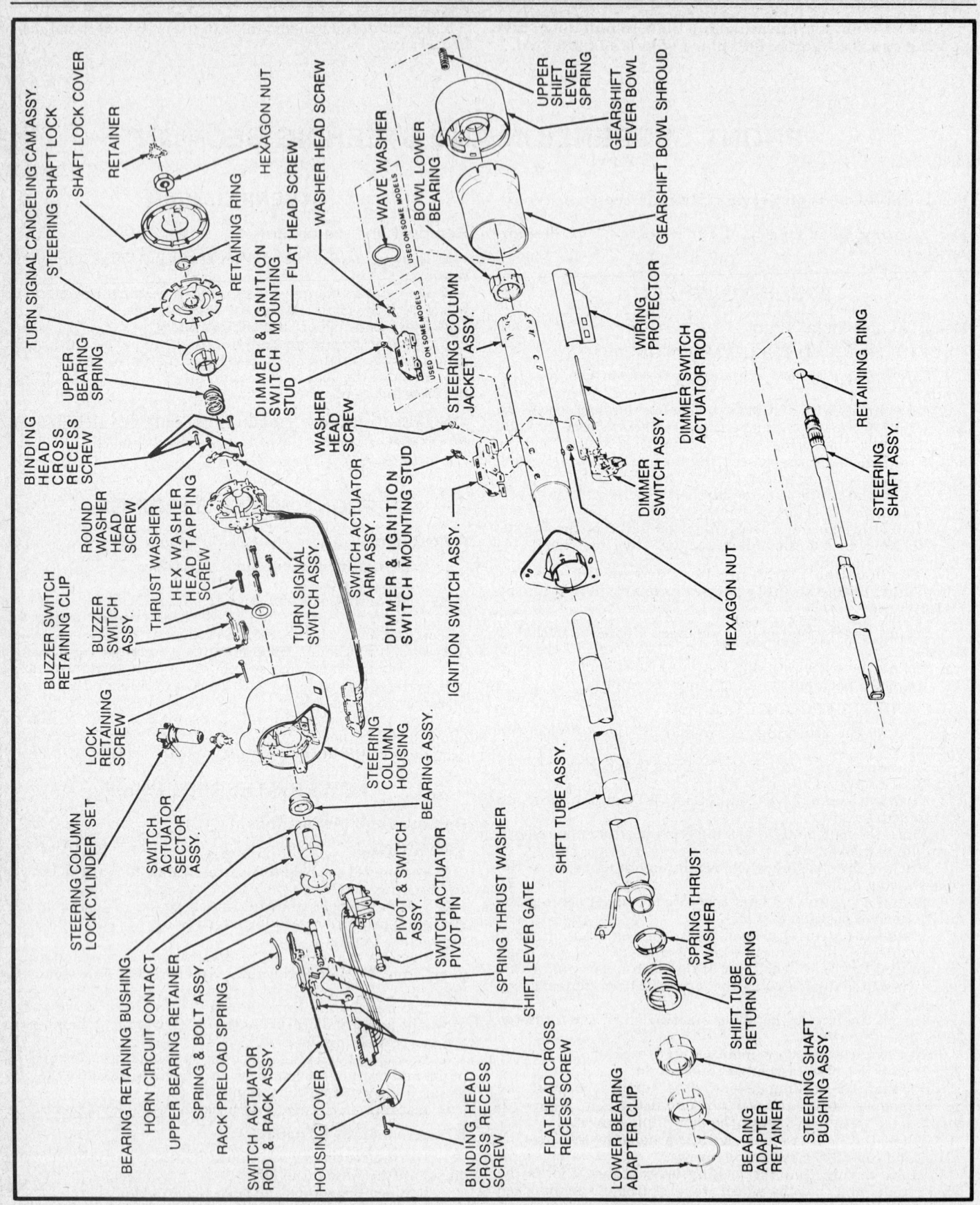

Exploded view of typical standard steering column (© General Motors Corporation)

BUICK 13
ELECTRA • ESTATE WAGON • LE SABRE • REGAL

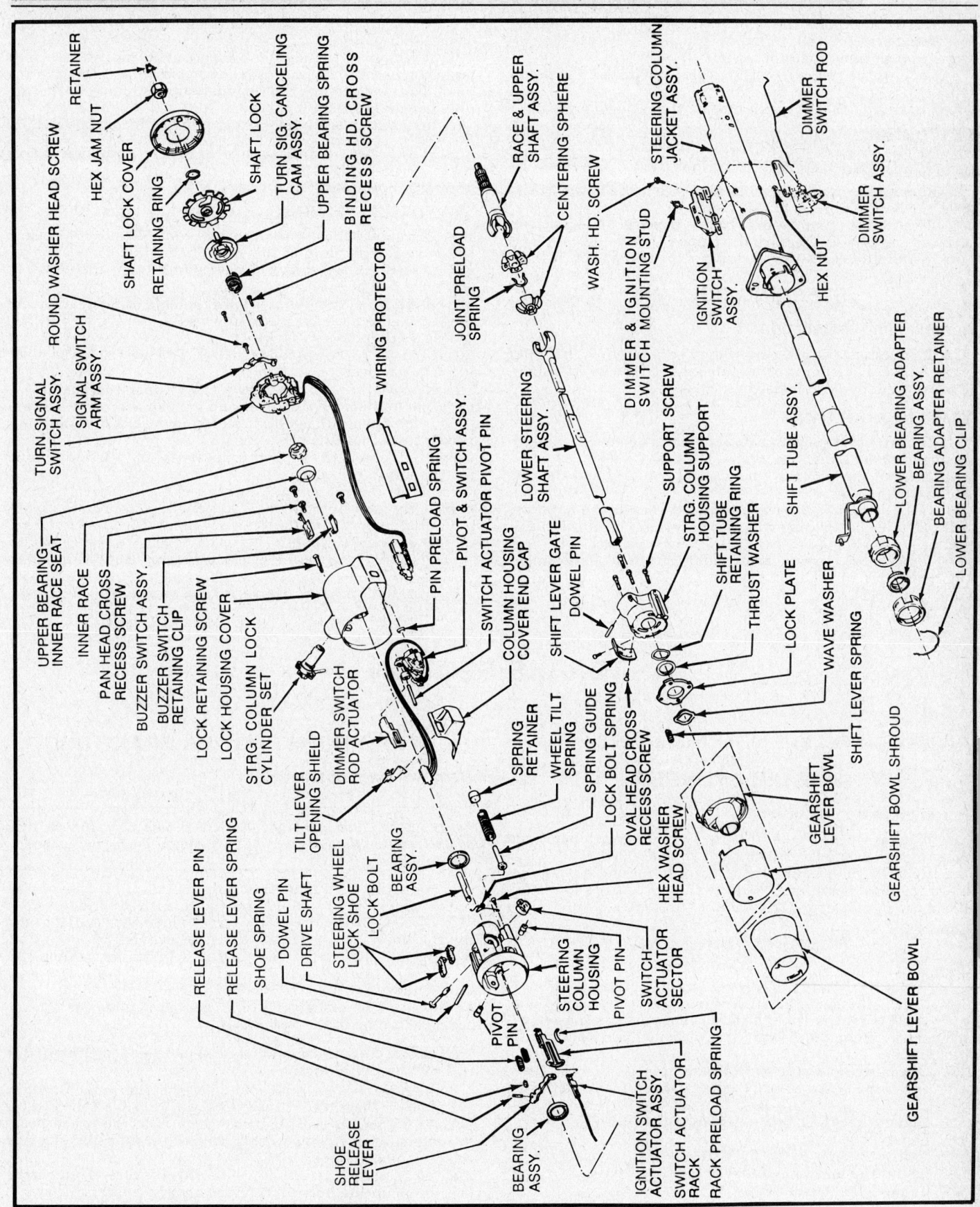

Exploded view of typical tilt wheel steering column (© General Motors Corporation)

SECTION 13

BUICK
ELECTRA • ESTATE WAGON • LE SABRE • REGAL

3. Raise and support the vehicle safely. Disconnect the power steering pressure hose fron the pump pipe and drain the system into a suitable container.
4. Remove the pump mounting bolts, disconnect the pump return hose and remove the pump.
5. Installation is the reverse order of the removal procedure.

V8 ENGINE

1. Disconnect the negative battery cable. Loosen all the drive belts.
2. Remove the pump pulley (as described in the Power Steering Unit Repair Section of this manual).
3. Remove the pump bracket bolts. Disconnect and plug the power stering hoses. Remove the pump from the vehicle.
4. Installation is the reverse order of the removal procedure.

STEERING COLUMN

Removal and Installation

NOTE: Handle the steering column very carefully. Rapping on the end of it or leaning on it could shear off the inserts which allow the column to collapse in a crash.

FLEXIBLE COLUMNS

1. Disconnectthe negative battery cable. Remove the left instrument panel sound absorber.
2. Remove the left instrument panel trim pad and steering column trim collar.
3. If the column is to be disassembled, remove the horn contact pad and the steering wheel as previously outlined in this section.
4. Remove the steering shaft to intermediate shaft connections. Remove the column support bracket bolts and column support bracket nut.
5. Remove the shift indicator cable. Remove all electrical connections and shift cable at the actuator and housing holder.
6. Working in the engine compartment, move the plastic protector to gain access to the lower pinch bolt. Remove the pinch bolt and remove the flexible coupling. Remove the column assembly from the vehicle.
7. Installation is the reverse order of the removal procedure.

NOTE: When installing use only the specified hardware. Over-length bolts could prevent the column from properly collapsing in a crash.

STANDARD STEERING COLUMN

1. Disconnect the negative battery cable. Remove the clamp bolt from the coupling at the lower end of the column shaft.
2. Disconnect the shift linkage from the shift tube lever at the lower end of the steering column.
3. If the steering column is to be replaced or repaired (out of the vehicle) remove the steering wheel as previously outlined in this section.
4. Remove the left sound insulator. Remove the lower steering column cover.
5. Remove the trim cap or lower trim panel from the instrument panel. Remove the cover and toe-pan attaching screws.
6. If equipped with a column shift, remove the shift indicator needle from the shift bowl. Remove the two steering column support nuts from the support bracket assembly, while holding the column in position.
7. Lower the column and disconnect the electrical connections to the steering column. If spacers were used on the steering column support bolts, retain them for use when reinstalling the steering column.
8. Carefully remove the steering column from inside of the vehicle.
9. Installation is the reverse order of the removal procedure.

BRAKE SECTION

For Brake Service Refer to the Unit Repair Section.

MASTER CYLINDER

Removal and Installation

1. Disconnect the brake lines from the master cylinder and tape the end of the lines to prevent entrance of dirt.
2. Remove the master cylinder-to-dash retaining bolts. Remove the master cylinder. Reverse the above steps to install. Bleed the master cylinder after it is reinstalled.

POWER BRAKE UNIT

Removal and Installation

1. Unbolt the master cylinder from the power unit. Being careful not to kink or bend the brake lines, pull the master cylinder away from the power unit without disconnecting the brake lines.
2. Disconnect and plug the vacuum hose.
3. Disconnect the power brake pushrod from the brake pedal.
4. Unbolt the power brake unit from the firewall.
5. Remove the unit.
6. Mount the unit to the firewall.
7. Install the master cylinder to the power unit.
8. Connect the vacuum hose.
9. Connect the power brake pushrod to the brake pedal.

HYDRO-BOOST POWER BRAKE UNIT

Removal and Installation

--- **CAUTION** ---
Power steering fluid and brake fluid are incompatible. If brake seals contact steering fluid or steering seals contact brake fluid, the seals will be ruined.

1. With the engine off, pump the brake pedal four or five times to empty the accumulator of pressurized fluid.
2. Disconnect the brake lines from the master cylinder and cap the lines. Remove the two master cylinder-to-booster attaching nuts and move the master cylinder away from the booster with the brake lines attached.
3. Remove and plug the three hydraulic lines from the booster. Remove the washer and retainer that secures the booster pedal rod to the brake pedal arm.

NOTE: To avoid booster damage, do not pry the pedal rod off the pedal arm.

4. Remove the four nuts holding the booster to the firewall.
5. Loosen the booster from the firewall and move the booster pedal rod inboard until it disconnects from the brake pedal arm. Remove the spring washer from the brake pedal arm and remove the booster.
6. To install, reverse the removal procedure. Tighten the booster mounting nuts to 30 ft.lbs.. and the master cylinder to booster mounting to 20 ft.lbs.. Bleed the system.

POWERMASTER POWER BRAKE UNIT

Description

The Powermaster unit is a complete, integral power brake apply system, consisting of an electro-hydraulic pump, fluid, accumulator, pressure switch, fluid reservoir and a hydraulic booster, with an integral dual master cylinder. The nitrogen charged accumulator stores fluid at 510–675 psi for the hydraulic booster operation. The electro-hydraulic operates between pressure limits with the ignition switch on. When the pressure switch senses accumulator pressure is below 510 psi, the 12 volt pump operates to increase the accumulator fluid pressure to 675 psi. When the brake pedal is depressed, fluid from the accumulator acts on the booster power piton to apply the master cylinder which functions in the same manner as the conventional dual master cylinder.

--- **CAUTION** ---

Because of the excessively high draulic pressure, the system must be depressurized before any service operations are performed on the system. Failure to depressurize could result in personal injury and/or damage to the vehicle's painted surfaces.

DEPRESSURIZING THE POWERMASTER SYSTEM

1. With the ignition switch in the Off position, apply and release the brake pedal a minimum of 10 times, using approximately 50 lbs. of force on the brake pedal.
2. When loosening hoses or pipe fittings, wrap shop towels close to the fittings to prevent spraying of residual pressurized fluid.

Removal

1. Disconnect the power lead from the pressure switch.
2. Disconnect the electrical connector from the electro-hydraulic pump.
3. Disconnect the brake tubing fittings from the Powermaster unit.
4. Remove the two retaining nuts for the unit to dash panel.
5. Remove the brake pedal pushrod.
6. Remove the Powermaster unit from the vehicle.

Installation

1. Install the Powermaster unit, the brake pedal pushrod and install the two retaining nuts. Torque to 22–30 ft.lbs..
2. Install the brake pipes to the unit.
3. Install the electrical connections to the unit.

Bleeding of Unit

FLUID FILLING OF POWERMASTER

NOTE: Bench bleed the master cylinder portion of the Powermaster unit before installing the assembly on the vehicle.

1. Fill both sides of the master cylinder reservoir with approved brake fluid.
2. Turn the ignition switch to the On position. With the pump running, the brake fluid level in the booster side of the reservoir should decrease as fluid is moved to the accumulator. If the booster side of the reservoir begins to run dry, add fluid to cover the reservoir pump port until the pump stops.

NOTE: The pump must turn off within 20 seconds.

3. Turn the ignition switch to the Off position after the 20 seconds have elapsed. Check for leaks or flow back to the reservoir from the booster return port. Install reservoir cover.

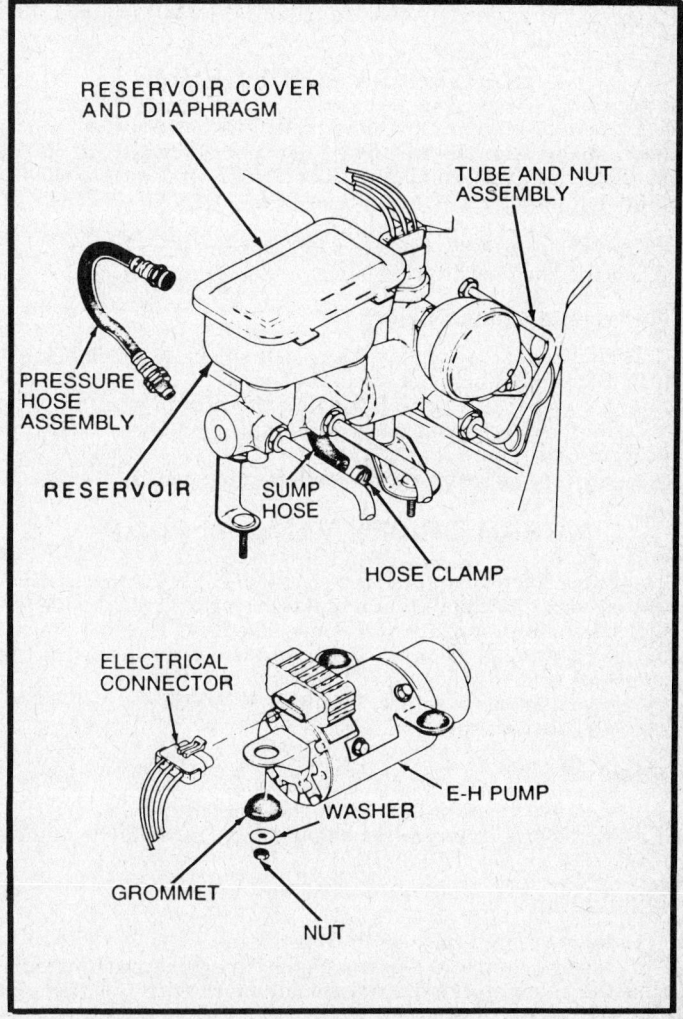

Exploded view of power Master power brake unit
(© General Motors Corporation)

4. With the ignition Off, apply and release the brake pedal at least 10 times. Recheck and correct booster fluid level to the full mark.
5. Turn the ignition switch to the On position. The pump will run and refill the accumulator. Be sure the pump does not run over 20 seconds and the fluid level remains above the pump sump port in the reservoir.
6. Reinstall the reservoir cover. With the ignition switch in the On position, apply and release the brake pedal to cycle the pump on and off for at least 10–15 cycles. Do not allow the pump to run longer than 20 seconds. This will remove air from the booster section.
7. Recheck the fluid level and brake system operation.
8. Should further diagnosis and/or repairs be needed, refer to the Unit Repair, Brake section for disassembly and assembly procedures.

CONVENTIONAL BRAKE BLEEDING

The brake system is bled in the conventional manner, either manually or by pressure. It must be remembered not to have the ignition switch on during the bleeding operation.

Vacuum Pumps

Vacuum pumps are used on selective engines to aid the engine

BUICK
ELECTRA • ESTATE WAGON • LE SABRE • REGAL

in maintaining a proper level of vacuum for the power brake system.

ELECTRIC VACUUM PUMP

The vacuum pump is mounted under the battery tray on the left hand side of the car. The inlet hose is connected to the booster check valve and the outlet hose is connected to the intake manifold.

A low vacuum warning light switch is located in the inlet hose line operating a warning light on the instrument panel when the vacuum drops below a predetermined level.

Removal and Installation

1. Raise vehicle and remove splash shield, left side of car.
2. Disconnect hoses at vacuum pump.
3. Disconnect electrical connector at vacuum pump.
4. Remove three units securing pump assembly to mounting bracket and remove pump.
5. Reverse procedure for installation of vacuum pump.

GEAR DRIVEN VACUUM PUMP

The gear driven vacuum pump is a diaphragm pump which requires no periodic maintenance. It is driven by a cam inside the drive assembly in which it mounts. The drive housing assembly has a drive gear on the lower end which meshes with the camshaft gear in the engine. This drive gear causes the cam in the drive housing to rotate. The drive gear also powers the engine oil lubricating pump.

Removal

1. Remove vacuum hose from vacuum pump inlet.
2. Remove bolt and clamp holding drive assembly to engine block.

Installation

1. Remove protective cloth from engine.
2. Insert pump and drive assembly in engine, making sure that the gears on the drive assembly mesh with the gears on the engine camshaft.
3. Rotate the pump into position so the bracket and bolt can be installed.
4. Install clamp and bolt.
5. Install vacuum hose to pump.

BELT DRIVEN VACUUM PUMP

The pump has a pulley attached and is driven by a belt. With the exception of the pulley, the vacuum pump is serviced as an assembly.

Removal and Installation

1. Loosen the retaining bolts for the vacuum pump and remove the drive belt.
2. Remove the retaining bolts and hoses/lines to the assembly and remove from the vehicle.
3. The installation is the reverse of the removal procedure.

Parking Brake

Adjustment

Adjustment of the parking brake is necessary whenever the rear brake cables have been disconnected or the parking brake pedal can be depressed more than eight ratchet clicks under heavy foot pressure. The vehicle should first be raised on a lift.

1. Make sure that the service brakes are properly adjusted.
2. Depress the parking brake pedal two ratchet clicks on all models.
3. Loosen the jam nut on the equalizer adjusting nut. Tighten the adjusting nut until the left rear wheel can just be turned rearward by hand, but not forward.
4. Release the ratchet one click; the rear wheel should rotate rearward freely and forward with a slight drag.
5. Release the ratchet fully; the rear wheel should turn freely in either direction.

PARKING BRAKE CABLE

Removal and Installation

FRONT

1. Raise and suitably support car.
2. Loosen adjuster nut and disconnect front cable from connector. Compress retainer fingers and loosen at frame.
3. Remove supports and lower car.
4. Remove lower rear bolt from wheelhouse panel and pull panel out to gain access to front cable.
5. Disconnect cable from parking brake pedal assembly. Compress retainer fingers and remove cable.
6. Install cable by reversing removal procedure. Make sure cable is routed properly and securely retained.
7. Adjust parking brake cable.

LEFT REAR

1. Raise and suitably support car.
2. Loosen adjuster nut and compress retainer fingers at equalizer and loosen cable.
3. Disconnect cable from connector and remove from equalizer.
4. Mark relationship of wheel to axle flange and remove wheel and tire assembly.
5. Remove brake drum.
6. Remove primary shoe return spring and parking brake strut.
7. Compress retainer fingers and loosen cable from backing plate. Disconnect cable from parking brake lever and remove cable.
8. Installation is the reverse of the removal procedure.
9. Adjust the parking brake cable.

RIGHT REAR

1. Raise and suitably support car.
2. Remove adjuster nut at equalizer and compress retainer fingers and loosen cable from retainers at frame and from axle housing clip.
3. Mark relationship of wheel to axle flange and remove wheel and tire assembly.
4. Remove brake drum.
5. Remove primary shoe return spring, parking brake strut, and secondary shoe hold down spring.
6. Compress retainer fingers and loosen cable from backing plate. Disconnect cable from parking brake lever and remove cable.

Install cable by reversing removal procedure. Make sure cable is routed properly and securely retained.
Adjust parking brake cable.

BUICK 13
ELECTRA • ESTATE WAGON • LE SABRE • REGAL

TRANSMISSION AND DRIVE SHAFT SECTION

Automatic Transmission

Removal and Installation

Because of the varied applications of the automatic transmission used in the Buick models, a general transmission removal and installation is outlined. the removal steps can be rearranged as required by the technician.
1. Disconnect the battery.
2. Disconnect detent cable (if so equipped) from accelerator lever or carburetor.
3. Remove, disconnect or relocate any of the following necessary for removal:
   a. Exhaust crossover pipe
   b. Drive shaft
   c. Oil cooler lines
   d. Transmission crossmember (support engine and transmission as needed)
   e. Speedometer cable
   f. Shift linkage
   g. Electrical connections
   h. Flywheel cover pan
4. Mark flywheel and converter for installation reference.
5. Remove mounting bolts, and slide transmission back and out of vehicle.

NOTE: some 1983 LeSabres equipped with the THM 250C (M31) transmission with serial numbers between B3CO3D and BCD12D, may experience a condition of a torque converter shudder or early clutch engagement. If this condition is encountered, the cause may be a restriction in the torque converter clutch (T.C.C.) solenoid assembly which prevents it from exhausting.

This causes the T.C.C. solenoid to function as if it were being applied at all times. This will cause the torque converter clutch to apply whenever the 2-3 shift ios made and will not release until the transmission is downshifted to a lower gear. To correct this condition, replace the T.C.C. solenoid.

AUTOMATIC TRANSMISSION MANUAL LINKAGE

Adjustment

1. Adjust the linkage so the shift lever positions correspond exactly to the transmission positions.
2. Some linkage arrangements have adjustment gauge pin holes. In these a free pin fit will insure proper adjustment.
3. After linkage adjustment, check operation of the neutral start switch, backup lights and automatic parking brake release.

SHIFT ROD

Adjustment

1. With shift rod clamp screw loosened, set transmission outer lever in neutral position.
2. Hold upper shift lever against neutral position stop in upper steering column. Do not raise lever.
3. Tighten screw in clamp on lower end of shift rod to specified torque.
4. Check operation. With key in Run position and transmission in Reverse be sure that the key cannot be removed and that the steering wheel is not locked. With key in Lock position and shift lever in Park, be sure that the key can be removed, that the steering wheel is locked and that the transmission remains in park when the steering column is locked. With brakes firmly applied, check to make sure that the starter will not work in any shift lever position except Neutral and Park.

SHIFT CABLE

Adjustment

1. Loosen shift rod clamp screw, loosen pin in transmission manual lever.
2. Place shift lever in Park position. Place transmission manual lever in Park position and ignition key in Lock position.

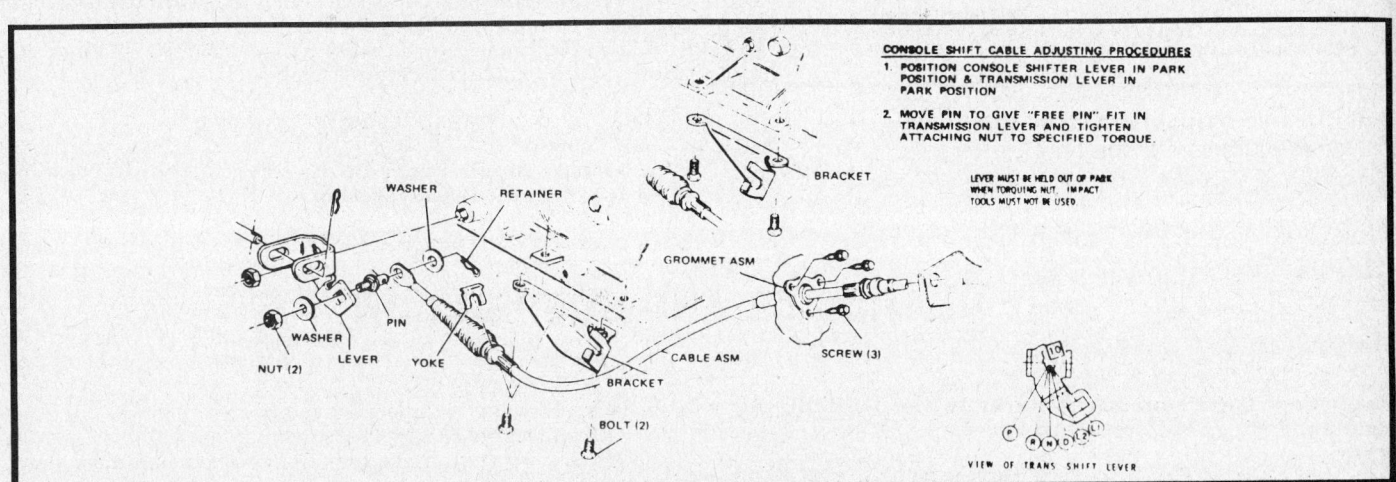

Linkage adjustment console shift (© General Motors Corporation)

SECTION 13 BUICK
ELECTRA • ESTATE WAGON • LE SABRE • REGAL

3. Tighten cable pin nut to 20 ft.lbs..
4. Rotate the transmission manual lever full against the Park stop, then release the lever.
5. Pull shift rod down against lock stop to eliminate lash and tighten clamp screw to 20 ft.lbs..
6. Check operation. Move shift handle into each gear position and see that transmission manual lever is also in detent position. With key in Run position and transmission in Reverse be sure that the key cannot be removed and that steering wheel is not locked. With key in Lock position and transmission in Park, be sure that key can be removed and that steering wheel is locked. Engine must start in Park and Neutral. With brakes firmly applied, check to make sure that the starter will not work in any shift lever position except Neutral and Park.

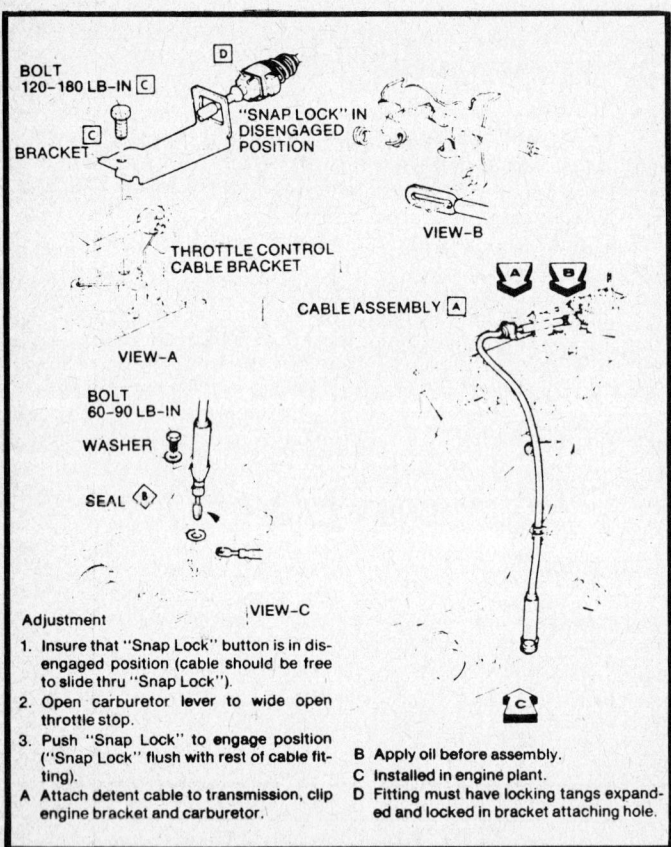

Detent cable adjustment in all car models
(© General Motors Corporation)

MANUAL TYPE T.V. CABLE
Adjustment
1. Stop engine.
2. Unlock T.V. cable snap-lock button.
3. Rotate carburetor lever by hand to wide open throttle and hold open.
4. Engage T.V. cable snap-lock button.

SELF-ADJUSTING TYPE T.V. CABLE
Adjustment
1. Stop engine.
2. Depress lock tab. Move slider back through fitting in direction away from throttle body or pump lever until slider stops against fitting.
3. Release lock tab.
4. Open carburetor lever to Full Throttle Stop position to automatically adjust T.V. cable. Release carburetor lever.
5. Check T.V. cable for sticking and binding.
6. When the T.V. cable adjustment is made and locked, the cable housing will extend through the cable snap lock assembly about 2.57–7.95mm ($1/16$–$5/16$ in.).

SHIFT QUADRANT POINTER
Adjustment
1. With the engine off, set the transmission selector lever in neutral.
2. If the pointer does not align with the Neutral indicator position, move the clip on the shift bowl, so that the pointer lines up with the Neutral.

NOTE: The Manual linkage must be adjusted properly before changing the shift quadrant adjustment.

DRIVESHAFT
Removal and Installation
1. Mark the driveshaft rear yoke and the differential flange to assure correct alignment upon reassembly.
2. Remove the bolts and straps from the differential flange.
3. Remove the driveshaft assembly by first sliding the driveshaft sufficiently forward to disengage the differential flange and then slide the shaft downward and rearward to disengage the front splined yoke from the transmission output shaft.
4. Installation is the reverse of removal. Be sure to align the match marks made before disassembly.

UNIVERSAL JOINTS
For U-joint repair procedures, refer to the drive axles and U-joint unit repair section.

REAR AXLE AND SUSPENSION

For Overhaul Procedures Refer to the Unit Repair Section.

REAR AXLE ASSEMBLY
Removal and Installation
1. Raise the vehicle and support it safely. Be sure that the rear axle assembly is supported safely.
2. Disconnect shock absorbers from axle.
3. Mark drive shaft and pinion flange, then disconnect drive shaft and support out of the way.
4. Remove brake line junction block bolt at axle housing, then disconnect brake lines at junction block. On Regal models disconnect brake line at wheel cylinder.

13-50

BUICK
ELECTRA · ESTATE WAGON · LE SABRE · REGAL
SECTION 13

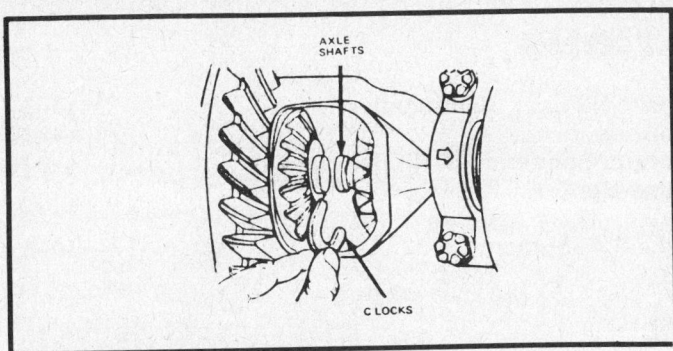

Removing or installing "C" locks
(© General Motors Corporation)

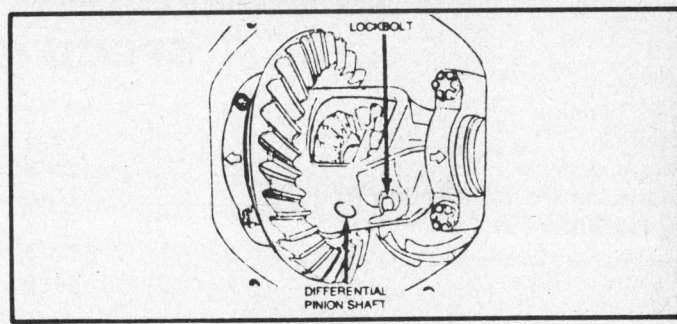

Differential pinion shaft and lock bolt
(© General Motors Corporation)

5. Disconnect upper control arms from axle housing.
6. Lower rear axle assembly on hoist and remove springs.
7. Remove rear wheels and drums.
8. Remove rear axle cover bolts and remove cover.
9. Remove the axle shaft. Disconnect the brake lines from the axle housing clips.
10. Remove backing plates.
11. Disconnect lower control arms from axle housing.
12. Remove rear axle housing.
13. Installation is the reverse of the removal procedure.
14. Be sure to bleed the brake system, as required.

AXLE SHAFT

Removal and Installation

1. Raise vehicle and support it safely. Remove the tire and wheel assembly. Remove the brake drum.
2. Drain the fluid. Remove the rear carrier cover. Discard the gasket.
3. Remove the rear axle pinion shaft lock screw and the rear axle pinion shaft.
4. Push flanged end of axle shaft toward center of the vehicle and remove C-lock from button end of shaft.
5. Remove axle shaft from housing, being careful not to damage oil seal.
6. Installation is the reverse of the removal procedure. Be sure to fill the rear assembly with the proper grade and type gear oil.

OIL SEAL/BEARING

Removal and Installation

1. Remove the axle shaft.

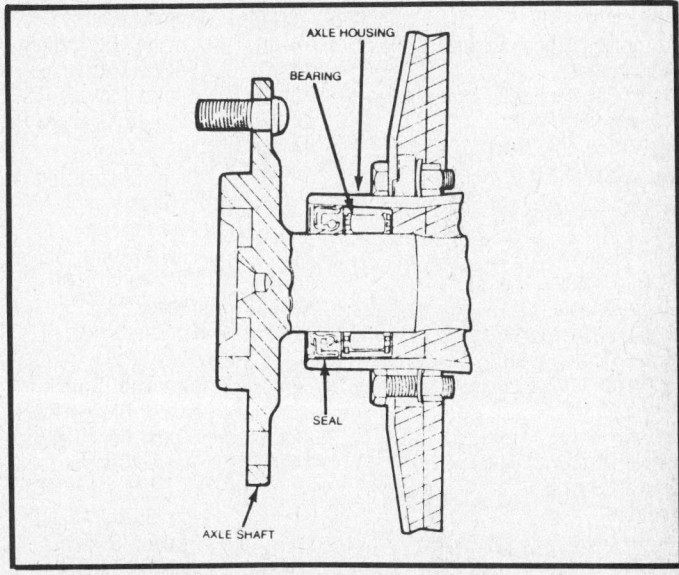

Bearing and seal used with "C" lock type axle
(© General Motors Corporation)

2. Remove seal from housing with a pry bar behind steel case of seal, being careful not to damage housing.
3. Insert tool J-23689 or equivalent into bore and position it behind bearing so that tangs on tool engage bearing outer race. Remove bearing, using slide hammer.
4. Lubricate the bearing with gear lubricant and install bearing so that tool bottoms against shoulder in housing, using tool J-23690 or equivalent.
5. Lubricate seal lips with gear lubricant. Position seal on tool J-21128 or equivalent and position seal into housing bore. Tap seal into place so that it is flush with axle tube.

13-51

SECTION 14

CADILLAC
DE VILLE • FLEETWOOD

SPECIFICATIONS

Belt Tension	14-19	Serial Number Identification	14-3
Brakes	24-2	Torque	14-6
Capacities	14-6	Torque Sequence (Cylinder Heads)	14-31
Crankshaft & Connecting Rod	14-5	Tune-Up	14-4
Firing Order	14-5	Valve	14-4
General Engine	14-4	Wheel Alignment	14-6
Piston & Ring	14-6		

INDEX

A
Alternator R&R	14-8
Automatic Transmission	14-46
Adjustment	14-47
On Car Service	23-2
Assembly R&R	14-46
Axle Assembly R&R	14-49
Axle Shaft R&R	14-49

B
Ball Joints	35-2
Belt Tension	14-19
Brake System	14-45
Brake Booster	14-45
Brake Baliper Overhaul	24-2
Brake Caliper R&R	
Front	24-2
Brake Drum	
Rear	24-2
Brake Master Cylinder	14-45
Brake Pad	
Front	24-2
Brake Shoe	
Rear	24-2

C
Camshaft R&R	14-32
Carburetor R&R	14-21
Chassis Electrical	14-10
Combination Switch R&R	14-2
Component Locations	14-15
Control Arm R&R	35-2
Cooling System	14-18
Cruise Control	14-17
Cylinder Head	14-31
R&R	14-31

D
Differential	28-2
Inspection	28-2
Disc Brakes	24-2
Front	24-2
Distributor R&R	14-9
Drive Axle	14-49
Driveshaft R&R	14-48

E
Electronic Ignition	30-2
Emisssion Controls	14-27
Engine	14-29
Identification	14-3
R&R	14-29
Engine Electrical	14-9
Engine Lubrication	14-39
Engine Mechanical	14-29
Engine Mounts R&R	14-29
Exhaust Manifold R&R	14-21

F
Front Suspension	14-41
Alignment	14-6
Fuel Injection	14-24
Fuel Mixture, Adjust	14-20
Fuel Pump R&R	14-19
Fuses	14-17
Fusible Links	14-16

H
Headlight Switch	14-12
Heater Blower R&R	14-19
Heater Core R&R	14-19
Heater Control	14-18

I
Idle Speed Adjust	14-20
Ignition Switch	14-11
Ignition Timing	14-20
Instrument Cluster R&R	14-15
Intake Manifold R&R	14-22

L, M, N
Lower Control Arm R&R	35-2
Master Cylinder R&R	14-45
Neutral Safety Switch	
R&R	14-12

O
Oil Pan R&R	14-39
Oil Pump	14-39
R&R	14-39
Oil Seal R&R	
Rear Main	14-40

P
Parking Brake	14-45
Adjustment	14-45
Cable R&R	14-46
Piston & Connecting Rod	14-38
Power Brake Unit R&R	14-45
Power Steering Pump R&R	14-42

R
Rear Main Oil Seal R&R	14-40
Rear Suspension	35-2
Regulator	14-8
R&R	14-29
Rocker Shaft/Assembly R&R	14-30

S
Serial Number	14-3
Engine	14-3
Vehicle	14-3
Shock Absorber R&R	
Front	35-2
Rear	35-2
Springs	
Front	35-2
Rear	35-2
Starter R&R	14-8
Starter Drive Replacement	14-8
Steering Column R&R	14-42
Steering Gear R&R	14-41
Power	14-41
Steering Wheel R&R	14-42
Stop Light Switch R&R	14-12
Speedometer R&R	14-15
Suspension R&R	35-2
Service	35-2

T
Throttle Linkage, Adjust	14-21
Timing Chain	14-32
Timing Gear Cover	14-33
Oil Seal Replacement	14-36
Tune-Up	14-4
Turn Signal Switch R&R	14-13

U, V
U-Joint Overhaul	28-2
Valve Tappette R&R	14-29
Valve Timing, Adjust	14-30
Valve System	14-29
Voltage Regulator	14-8

W, Y
Water Pump R&R	14-18
Wheel Alignment	14-6
Front	14-6
Wheel Bearings Front	14-42
Wheel Cylinders Rear	14-49
Rear	24-2
Windshield Wiper	14-14
Linkage R&R	14-14
Motor R&R	14-14
Switch R&R	14-14
Year Identification	14-3

BEFORE SERVICING BE CERTAIN TO READ THE SAFETY NOTICE

Cadillac
1983–87 Rear Wheel Drive Cars
DEVILLE • FLEETWOOD

1983–87 Cadillac

VEHICLE IDENTIFICATION NUMBER (VIN)

It is important for servicing and ordering parts to be certain of the vehicle and engine identification. The VIN (vehicle identification number) is a 17 digit number visible through the windshield on the driver's side of the dash and contains the vehicle and engine identification codes. It can be interpreted as follows:

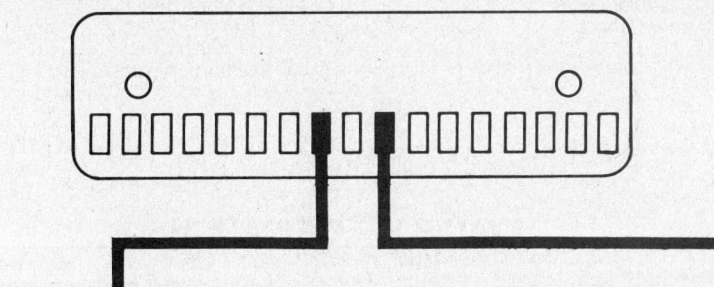

Engine Code						Model Year Code	
Code	Cu. In.	Liters	Cyl.	Carb.	Eng. Mfg.	Code	Year
8	250 ①	4.1	V8	DFI	Cad.	D	83
Y	305	5.0	V8	4 bbl	Olds.	E	84
N	350	5.7	V8	Diesel	Olds.	F	85
9	368	6.0	V8	DFI	Cad.	G	86
6	368	6.0	V8	4 bbl	Cad.	H	87

The seventeen digit Vehicle Identification Number can be used to determine engine application and model year. The 10th digit indicates the model year, and the 8th digit identifies the factory installed engine.
① HT4100 engine

14–3

SECTION 14

CADILLAC
DE VILLE • FLEETWOOD

GENERAL ENGINE SPECIFICATIONS

Year	Eng. V.I.N. Code	Cyl.	Engine Displacement Cu. In.	Liters	Eng. Mfg.	Fuel Delivery	Horsepower @ rpm■	Torque @ rpm (ft lbs)■	Bore × Stroke (in.)	Compression Ratio	Oil Pressure @ 2000 rpm
'83–'87	8	V8	250 ①③	4.1	Cad.	DFI	135 @ 4200	190 @ 2000	3.465 × 3.307	8.5:1	30
	6	V8	368 ②	6.0	Cad.	4 bbl	150 @ 3800	265 @ 1600	3.800 × 4.060	8.2:1	35
	N	V8	350	5.7	Olds.	Diesel	105 @ 3200	205 @ 1600	4.057 × 3.385	22.5:1	40
	9	V8	368 ②	6.0	Cad.	DFI	140 @ 3800	265 @ 1400	3.800 × 4.060	8.2:1	35
	Y	V8	305	5.0	Olds.	4 bbl	140 @ 3600	255 @ 2000	3.800 × 3.390	8.0:1	35

■ Horsepower and torque are SAE net figures. They are measured at the rear of the transmission with all accessories installed and operating. Since the figures vary when a given engine is installed in different models, some are representative rather than exact.
DFI Digital Fuel Injection
① HT4100 engine
② 6.0L (368) V8 engines used in limousine and commercial chassis only from 1983 and later.
③ 9.0:1—With swirl cylinder heads

TUNE-UP SPECIFICATIONS

When analyzing compression test results, look for uniformity among cylinders rather than specific pressures

Year	VIN Code	Cyl.	Engine Displacement cu. in.	Liters	Mfg.	Fuel Delivery	Spark Plugs Orig. Type♦	Gap (in.)	Distributor Point Dwell (deg)	Point Gap (in.)	Ignition Timing (deg) ▲ Auto. Trans.	Valves Intake Opens ■(deg)	Fuel Pump Pressure (psi)	Idle Speed (rpm) ▲ Auto. Trans.
'83	N	V8	350	5.7	Olds.	Diesel	—	—	—		②	16	5.5–6.5	②
	8	V8	250 ①	4.1	Cad.	D.F.I.	R43NTS6	.060	Electronic		10B	20	12–14	450
	9	V8	368	6.0	Cad.	D.F.I.	R45NSX	.060	Electronic		10B	11	12–14	450
	6	V8	368	6.0	Cad.	4 bbl	R45NSX	.060	Electronic		10B	11	5.5–6.5	450
'84	N	V8	350	5.7	Olds.	Diesel	—	—	—		Electronic	②	16	5.5–6.5	②
	8	V8	250 ①	4.1	Cad.	D.F.I.	R42CLTS6	.060	Electronic		10B	20	12–14	450
	6	V8	368	6.0	Cad.	4 bbl	R45NSX	.060	Electronic		10B	11	5.5–6.5	550/650
'85	N	V8	350	5.7	Olds.	Diesel	—	—	—		②	16	5.5–6.5	②
	8	V8	250 ①	4.1	Cad.	D.F.I.	R44LTS6	.060	Electronic		10B	20	12–14	450
	6	V8	368	6.0	Cad.	4 bbl	R45NSX	.060	Electronic		10B	11	5.5–6.5	550/650
'86–'87	8	V8	250 ①	4.1	Cad.	D.F.I.	R42CLTS6	.060	Electronic		10B	20	12–14	450
	6	V8	368	6.0	Cad.	4 bbl	R45NSX	.060	Electronic		10B	11	5.5–6.5	550/650
	Y	V8	307	5.0	Olds.	4 bbl	FR3LS6	.060	Electronic		20B	N/A	5.5–6.5	425/475

NOTE: The underhood specifications sticker often reflects tune-up specification changes made in production. Sticker figures must be used if they disagree with those in this chart. Part numbers in this chart are not recommendations by Chilton for any product by brand name.
▲ See text for procedure
■ All figures Before Top Dead Center
♦ See the Spark Plug Replacement Chart
DFI Digital Fuel Injection
—Not applicable

B Before top dead center
N/A Not available
① HT4100 engine
② See underhood sticker

VALVE SPECIFICATIONS

Year	Cyl.	Engine Displacement cu. in.	Liters	Seat Angle (deg)	Face Angle (deg)	Spring Test Pressure (lbs @ in.)	Spring Installed Height (in.)	Stem-to-Guide Clearance (in.) Intake	Exhaust	Stem Diameter (in.) Intake	Exhaust
'83–'87	V8	368	6.0	45	44	160 @ 1.50	1^{15}/$_{32}$	.0010–.0027	.0010–.0027	.3417	.3417
'83–'84	V8	250 ③	4.1	45	44	167 @ 1.34	1^{43}/$_{64}$	.001–.003	.001–.003	.3413–.3420	.3411–.3418
'83–'85	V8	350 Diesel	5.7	①	②	210 @ 1.22	1^{47}/$_{64}$	.0010–.0027	.0015–.0032	.3425–.3432	.3420–.3427
'85–'86	V8	250 ③	4.1	45	44	182 @ 1.28	1^{47}/$_{64}$	.001–.003	.001–.003	.3413–.3420	.3413–.3420
'86–'87	V8	307	5.0	45	44	76–84 @ 1.67	1^{47}/$_{64}$	.0010–.0027	.0015–.0032	.3429	.3425

① Intake 45°; exhaust 31°
② Intake 44°; exhaust 30°
③ HT4 100 engine

CADILLAC 14
DE VILLE • FLEETWOOD

FIRING ORDERS

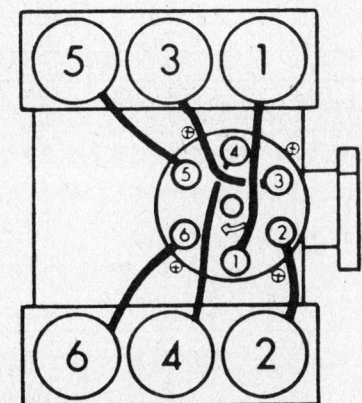

GM (Buick) 252 (4.1L) V6
Engine firing order: 1-6-5-4-3-2
Distributor rotation: clockwise

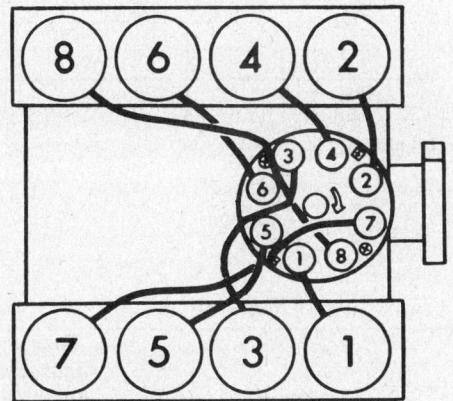

GM (Cadillac) 250 (4.1L) V8
Engine firing order: 1-8-4-3-6-5-7-2
Distributor rotation: counterclockwise

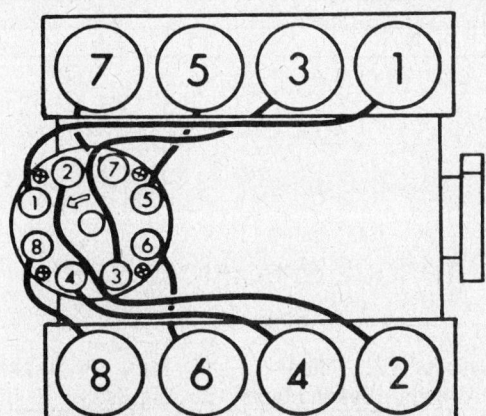

GM (Cadillac) 368
V8 Engine firing order: 1-5-6-3-4-2-7-8
Distributor rotation: clockwise

CRANKSHAFT AND CONNECTING ROD SPECIFICATIONS
All measurements are given in inches

Year	Cyl.	Engine Displacement cu. in.	Liters	Crankshaft Main Brg. Journal Dia	Main Brg. Oil Clearance	Shaft End-Play	Thrust on No.	Connecting Rod Journal Diameter	Oil Clearance	Side Clearance
'83–'87	V8	368	6.0	3.250	.0001–.0026	.002–.012	3	2.5000	.0005–.0028	.008–.020
'83–'87	V8	250 ③	4.1	2.64	.0008.0039	.001–.007	3	2.052–2.054	.0005–.0028	.008–.020
'83–'85	V8	350 Diesel	5.7	2.9993–3.0003	.0005–.0021 ②	.004–.014	3	2.1238–2.1248	.0005–.0026	.006–.020
'86–'87	V8	307	5.0	2.4985–2.4995 ①	.0005–.0021 ②	.0035–.0135	3	2.1238–2.1248	.0004–.0033	.006–.020

① No. 1—2.4988–2.4998 in.
② No. 5—.0015–.0031 in.
③ HT4100 engine

SECTION 14

CADILLAC
DE VILLE • FLEETWOOD

PISTON AND RING SPECIFICATIONS

Year	Cyl.	Engine Displ. Cu. In.	Liters	Piston-Bore Clearance	Ring Side Clearance			Ring Gap		
					Top Compression	Bottom Compression	Oil Control	Top Compression	Bottom Compression	Oil Control
'83–'87	V8	368	6.0	.0006–.0014	.0017–.0040	.0017–.0040	None ①	.013–.023	.013–.023	.015–.055
'83–'87	V8	8-250 ②	4.1	.0010–.0018	.0016–.0037	.0016–.0037	None ①	.015–.025	.015–.025	.010–.050
	V8	8-350 Diesel	5.7	.0035–.0045	.005–.007	.003–.005	.001–.005	.019–.027	.013–.021	.010–.022
'86–'87	V8	8-307	5.0	.0075–.00175	.0018–.0038	.0018–.0038	.001–.005	.009–.019	.009–.019	.015–.055

① Side sealing
② HT 4100 engine

CAPACITIES

Year	Cyl.	Engine Displacement Cu. In.	Liters	Engine Crankcase Add 1 Qt For New Filter	Transmission Automatic Pts To Refill After Draining •	Drive Axle (pts)	Gasoline Tank (gals)	Cooling System (qts)	
								With Heater	With A/C
'83–'87	V8	368	6.0	4	8	4.25	25	21.4	21.4
'83–'87	V8	250 ①	4.1	4	10	3.5	24.5	11	11
'83–'85	V8	350 Diesel	5.7	6	10.6	3.5	26	23.7	23.7
'86–'87	V8	305	5.0	4	10.5	3.5	24.5	15.3	15.3

• Specifications do not include torque converter
① HT4100 engine

TORQUE SPECIFICATIONS
All readings in ft. lbs.

Year	Cyl.	Engine Displacement cu. in.	Liters	Cylinder Head Bolts	Rod Bearing Bolts	Main Bearing Bolts	Crankshaft Bolt	Flywheel-to-Crankshaft Bolts	Manifold	
									Intake	Exhaust
'83–'85	V8	350 Diesel	5.7	130 ①	42	120	200–310	60	40	25
'83–'87	V8	368	6.0	95 ①	40	90	Press-Fit	75	30	④
'83–'87	V8	250	4.1	②	22	85	Press-Fit	37 ⑤	③	18
'86–'87	V8	307	5.0	125 ①	42	80 ⑥	200–310	60	40	25

① Dip bolt in oil before tightening
② Tighten all bolts in sequence to 45 ft. lbs., then in sequence to 90 ft. lbs.
③ Tighten bolts 1, 2, 3, 4, in sequence to 11–15 ft. lbs.; tighten bolts 5 thru 16 to 18–22 ft. lbs., Retighten all bolts in sequence to 18–22 ft. lbs.
④ Long bolt—35, short bolt—12
⑤ 17mm Head is torqued to 63 ft. lbs.
⑥ No. 5 is torqued to 120 ft. lbs.

WHEEL ALIGNMENT SPECIFICATIONS

Year	Model	Caster		Camber		Toe-in (in.)	Steering Axis Inclin. (deg)
		Range (deg)	Pref Setting (deg)	Range (deg)	Pref Setting (deg)		
'83–'87	Cadillac (RWD)	2P to 4P	3P	5/16N to 1 5/16P	1/2P	1/8	10 19/32

N Negative
P Positive

CADILLAC
DE VILLE • FLEETWOOD
SECTION 14

ITEM	SET TO SPEC. (1)	FIELD SERVICE AND STATIC CHECKING (CURB) ***		
		TOLERANCES		
		(1) CUSTOMER SERVICE SETTING	(2) WARRANTY DIAGNOSIS	(3) PERIODIC INSPECTION
CAMBER	+0.50°	±0.40°	±0.80°	±1.50°
CROSS-CAMBER (LH MINUS RH)	0.0°	±0.50°	±1.00°**	—
CASTER	+4.00°	±0.50°	±1.00°	±2.00°
CROSS-CASTER (LH MINUS RH)	0.0°	±0.50°	±1.00°**	—
TOE PER WHEEL	0.12°	±0.06°	±0.12°*	±0.38°
SPOKE ANGLE	0.0°	±5.00°	±10.00°	—

** CROSS-CAMBER AND CROSS-CASTER NOT TO EXCEED 1° MAX. PER VEHICLE
* 1/8" TOE IS EQUIVALENT TO AN ANGLE MEASUREMENT OF .12° PER WHEEL
*** CURB HEIGHT INCLUDES FULL TANK OF FUEL OR EQUIVALENT COMPENSATING WEIGHT.

SUGGESTED SHIM CHANGE TO CORRECT CASTER – CAMBER ALIGNMENT
(TOTAL THICKNESS CHANGE IN THOUSANDTHS OF AN INCH)

MEASURED CAMBER READING (CURB) ***		MEASURED CASTER READING (CURB) ***						
		+4½°	+4°	+3½°	+3°	+2½°	+2°	+1½°
+1½°	FRONT	+.27	+.24	+.21	+.18	+.15	+.12	+.09
	REAR	+.045	−.09	+.135	+.18	+.225	+.27	+.315
+1°	FRONT	+.18	+.15	+.12	+.09	+.06	+.03	.00
	REAR	−.045	.00	+.045	+.09	+.135	+.18	+.225
+½°	FRONT	+.09	+.06	+.03	.00	−.03	−.06	−.09
	REAR	−.135	−.09	+.045	.00	+.045	+.09	+.135
+0°	FRONT	.00	−.03	−.06	−.09	−.12	−.15	−.18
	REAR	−.225	−.18	−.135	−.09	−.045	.00	+.045
−½°	FRONT	−.09	−.12	−.15	−.18	−.21	−.24	−.27
	REAR	−.315	−.27	−.225	−.18	−.135	−.09	−.045
−1°	FRONT	−.18	−.21	−.24	−.27	−.30	−.33	−.36
	REAR	−.405	−.36	−.315	−.27	−.225	−.18	−.135

(+) = ADD SHIMS AND (−) = REMOVE SHIMS. SHIM USAGE THICKNESS DIFFERENCE BETWEEN FRONT AND REAR ATTACHMENT SHOULD NOT EXCEED .40 IN. MAXIMUM SHIM USAGE IN FRONT AND/OR REAR LOCATION NOT TO EXCEED .60 IN.

Wheel alignment specifications and shim applications for the 1983 and later Brougham

SECTION 14

CADILLAC
DE VILLE • FLEETWOOD

ELECTRICAL SYSTEM

For Overhaul Procedures Refer to the Unit Repair Section.

Charging System

ALTERNATOR

The basic charging system used on the Cadillac RWD model vehicles are the 10S1, 15S1 and 27S1 integral regulator equipped alternators, which provide different electrical outputs at idle and at maximum rpms, tailored to the electrical demands of the vehicle.

Removal and Installation

1. Disconnect negative battery cable.
2. Disconnect the electrical leads from the alternator.
3. Remove the screw from the alternator adjusting bracket.
4. Remove the screw from the rear of the alternator, retaining the shims for reinstallation.
5. Loosen the alternator pivot bolt and remove the drive belt.
6. Remove the air pump pulley for access to the pump bolt behind the pulley.
7. Loosen the two screws securing the front bracket to the engine.
8. Remove the alternator, spacer and lower through bolt by twisting the alternator toward the fender for clearance.
9. Install the alternator in the reverse order of removal.

VOLTAGE REGULATOR

Removal and Installation

The voltage regulator is incorporated within the alternator on all models.
Refer to the Overhaul Procedures in the Unit Repair Section.

Starting System

STARTER

Five types of starter motors are used. Models 5MT, 10MT and 27MT are used on gasoline engines. Model 15MT/GR is used on

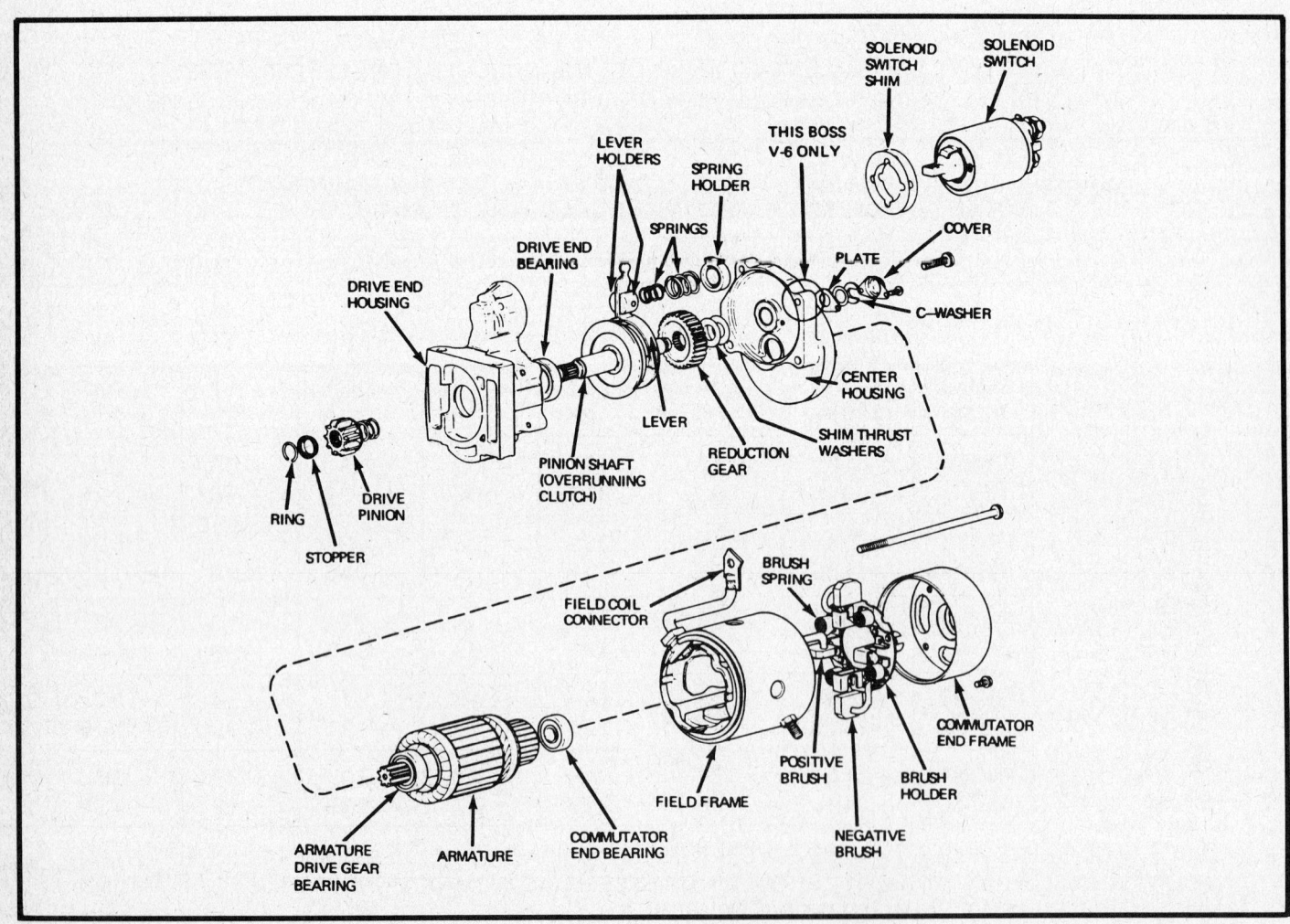

Exploded veiw of aluminum/GR starter assembly (© General Motors Corporation)

14-8

the 5.7L diesel engine through 1983 and the model Aluminum/GR is used on the 1984 and later 5.7 diesel engines.

Removal and Installation

1. Disconnect the negative battery lead at the battery.
2. Raise the vehicle and support safely.
3. Remove the starter braces, shields, flywheel housing cover and other items that may interfere with the starter removal.
4. Remove the starter motor to engine block retaining bolts and allow the starter to be lowered.
5. Remove the solenoid wires and the battery cable while supporting the starter. Be sure to note the position of the wires and remove the starter.
6. To install the starter, reverse the removal procedure and install any shims that may have been removed with the starter.
7. If another starter has been installed, the pinion teeth to flywheel teeth clearance should be measured. A clearance of 0.020 in. (0.058 mm) should exist.

Ignition System

DISTRIBUTOR

Removal and Installation

1. Disconnect the ignition switch battery feed wire from the distributor cap, along with the coil connectors.

CAUTION
Do not use a screwdriver or other tool to release the locking tabs.
---

2. Remove the distributor cap by removing the four bolts. Move the cap out of the way and if necessary, remove the secondary wires from the cap, by releasing the wiring harness latches.
3. Disconnect the 4 terminal ECM harness from the distributor.
4. Remove the distributor clamp screw or nut and the hold-down clamp. Use special tool J-29791 or its equivalent to remove the hold-down nut on the 4.1L engine.
5. Note and mark the position of the rotor electrode, then pull the distributor upward until the rotor stops turning and again note the position of the rotor electrode. Mark each position to distributor body for ease of installation and remove the distributor.
6. Note that a thrust washer is used between the distributor drive gear and the crankcase. This washer may stick to the bottom of the distributor as it is removed. Before distributor installation, verify that the thrust washer is located in the crankcase at the bottom of the distributor bore.
7. To install the distributor, place the rotor electrode in the last position as marked and lower the assembly into the distributor bore of the engine. When the distributor rotor stops turning as the unit is seated, the rotor electrode should be pointing to the first mark made.
8. If the engine has been accidently cranked with the distributor out, the following procedure can be used to correctly time the engine and distributor.
   a. Remove number one spark plug.
   b. Place finger over the number one spark plug hole and crank the engine slowly until a compression build-up can be felt in the cylinder.
   c. Carefully align the timing mark on the crankshaft pulley to "O" on the timing indicator on the engine.
   d. On the V8 engines, turn the rotor electrode to point between the No. 1 and No. 8 spark plug towers on the distributor cap. On the V6 engines, the rotor electrode must point between the between No. 1 and No. 6 towers.

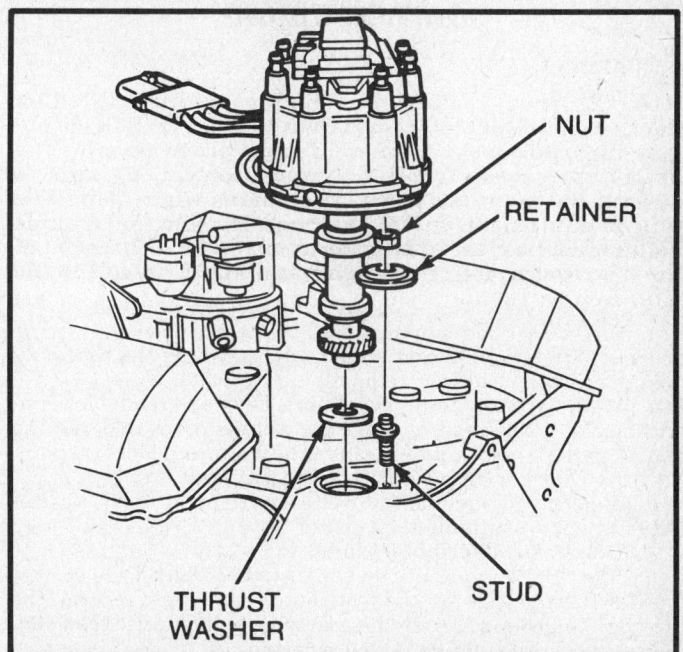

Thrust washer location on distributor shaft of HT4100 engine (© General Motors Corporation)

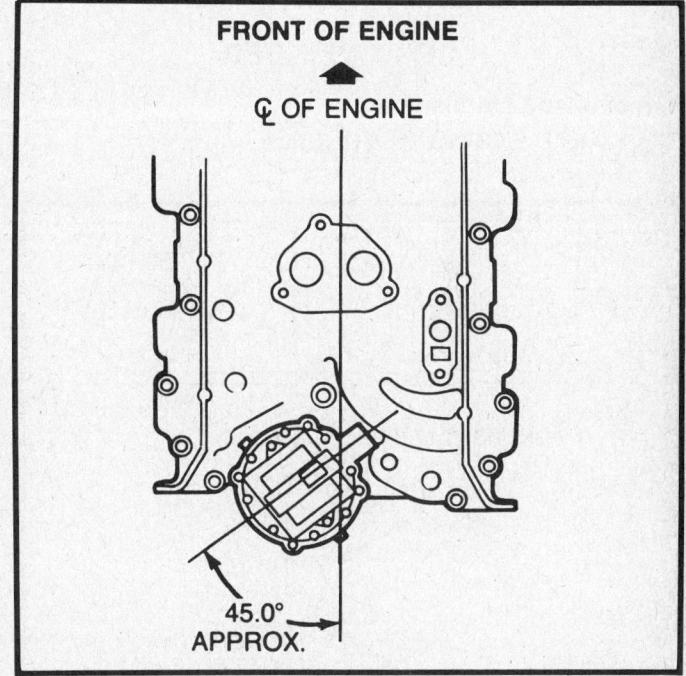

Correct positioning of distributor in the HT4100 engine (© General Motors Corporation)

   e. Install the distributor and connect the ignition feed wire.
   f. Install the distributor cap and the spark plug wires.
   g. Start the engine and adjust the ignition timing.

NOTE: On DFI systems, malfunction trouble codes must be cleared after the removal or adjustment of the distributor. Refer to Engine and Fuel Controls in the Unit Repair Section.

SECTION 14

CADILLAC
DE VILLE • FLEETWOOD

IGNITION TIMING

Adjustment

NOTE: Always follow the timing procedures listed on the Emission Control Information Label. The HT4100 engine incorporates a magnetic timing probe hole for the use of special electronic timing equipment. Be sure to consult the manufacturers instructions when using this type of equipment. On DFI systems, malfunction trouble codes must be cleared after the removal or adjustment of the distributor. Refer to Engine and Fuel Controls in the Unit Repair Section.

1. Disconnect the four terminal connector from the wiring harness. On the 1986 and later models, ground the assembly line diagnostic lead connector.
2. Make sure the timing marks are clean and readable. Timing marks are located on the front engine cover and one the harmonic balancer or pulley. Start the engine and let it run until it reaches normal operating temperature.
3. Stop the engine and connect a timing light to No.1 cylinder. Connect a suitable tachometer.
4. Loosen the distributor clamp.
5. Start the engine. Rotate the distributor until the correct marks line up. Tighten the distributor clamp and recheck the timing. Unground the the assembly line diagnostic lead connector while the engine is still running.
6. Reconnect the four terminal connector and adjust the engine idle rpm if necessary.

Electrical Controls

LOCK CYLINDER

Removal and Installation
STANDARD STEERING COLUMN

1. Remove the steering wheel.

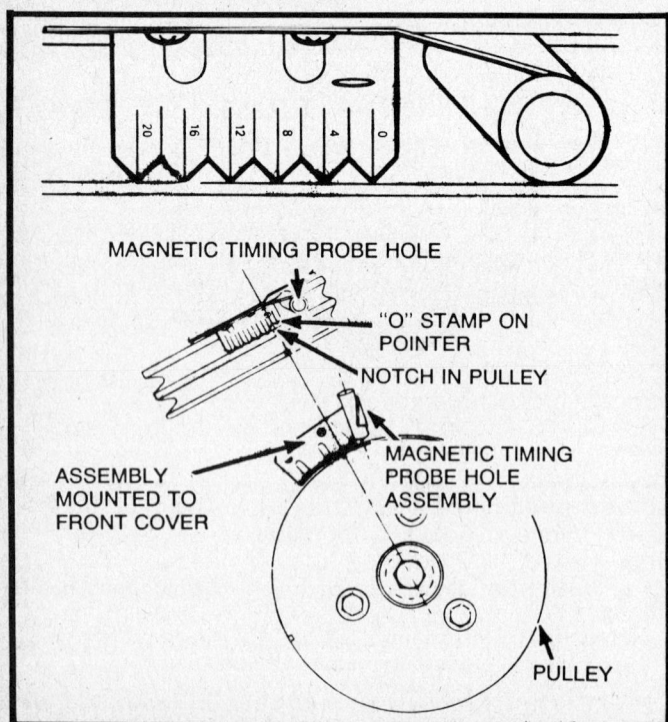

Exploded view of the magnetic timing probe hole—HT4100 V8 engine

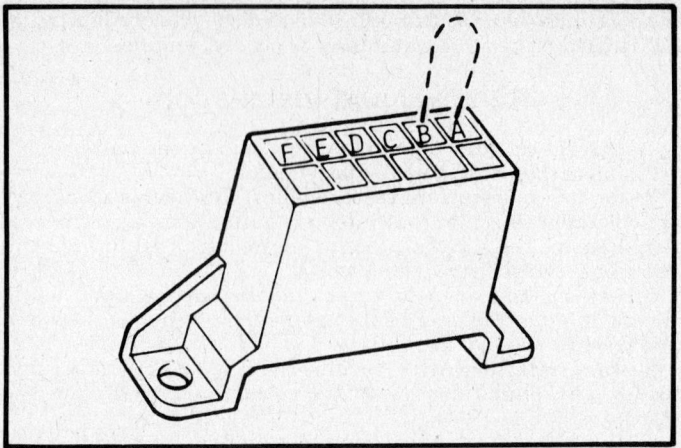

Grounding out the assembly line diagnostic lead connector

2. Remove the lockplate cover assembly.
3. After compressing the lockplate spring, remove the snapring from the groove in the shaft.

--- **CAUTION** ---

If the column is out of the vehicle when the snap-ring is removed do not allow the shaft to slide out the bottom of the column.

4. Remove the lockplate and slide the turn signal cam and the upper bearing preload spring off the upper steering shaft.
5. Remove the thrust washer from the shaft.
6. Remove the hazard warning switch knob from the column along with the turn signal lever.
7. Use the following procedure if the vehicle is equipped with cruise control:
   a. Attach a piece of mechanic's wire to the connector on the cruise control switch harness.
   b. Gently pull the harness up and out of the column.
8. Remove the turn signal switch mounting screws.
9. Slide the switch connector out of the bracket on the steering column.
10. After freeing the switch wiring protector from its mounting, pull the turn signal switch straight up and remove the switch, switch harness and the connector from the column.
11. Turn the ignition switch to on or run and then insert a small drift pin into the slot next to the switch mounting screw boss. Push the lock cylinder tab and remove the lock cylinder.

TILT COLUMN

1. Remove the steering wheel.
2. Remove the rubber sleeve bumper from the steering shaft.
3. Using an appropriate tool, remove the plastic retainer.
4. Using a spring compressor, compress the upper steering shaft spring and remove the C-ring. Release the steering shaft lockplate, the horn contact carrier, and the upper steering shaft preload spring.
5. Remove the four screws which hold the upper mounting bracket and then remove the bracket.
6. Slide the harness connector out of the bracket on the steering column. Tape the upper part of the harness and connector.
7. Disconnect the hazard button and position the shift bowl in park. Remove the turn signal lever from the column.
8. Use the following procedure for vehicles with cruise control:
   a. Remove the harness protector from the harness.
   b. Attach a piece of mechanic's wire to the switch harness connector.

CADILLAC
DE VILLE · FLEETWOOD
SECTION 14

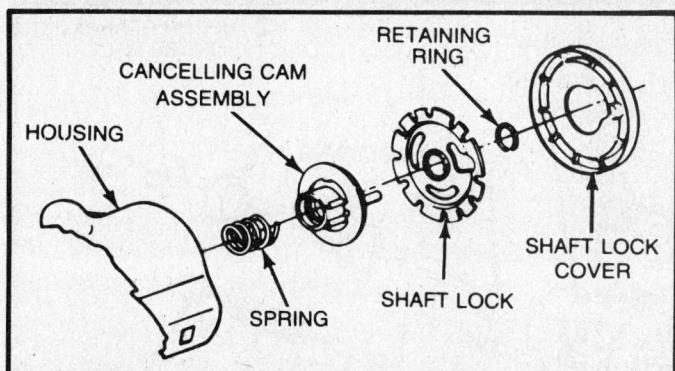

Positioning of shaft lock and canceling cam assembly, standard Column
(© General Motors Corporation)

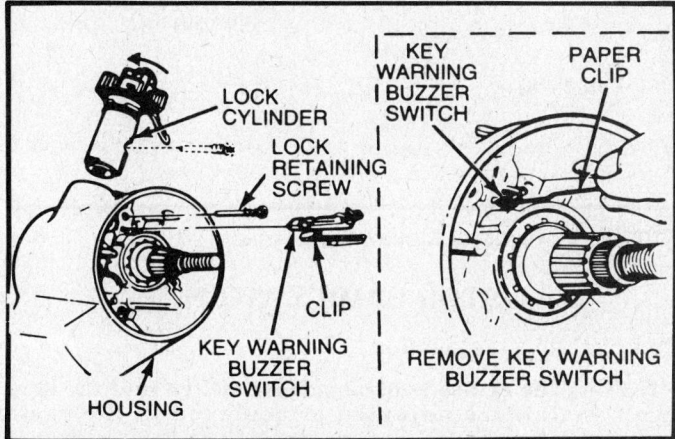

Removal and installation of lock cylinder
(© General Motors Corporation)

c. Before removing the turn signal lever, loop a piece of mechanic's wire and insert it into the turn signal lever opening. Using the wire, pull the cruise control harness out through the opening.
d. Pull the rest of the harness up through and out of the column.
e. Remove the guide wire from the connector and secure the wire to the column.
f. Remove the turn signal lever.
9. Pull the turn signal switch up until the end connector is within the shift bowl. Remove the hazard flasher lever. Allow the switch to hang.
10. Place the ignition key in the run position.
11. Depress the center of the lock cylinder retaining tab with a suitable tool and then remove the lock cylinder.
12. To install reverse the procedure.

IGNITION SWITCH

Removal and Installation

1. Disconnect the negative battery terminal.
2. Position lock cylinder in lock position.
3. Remove steering column lower cover.
4. Loosen 2 nuts on upper steering column, allowing column to drop and support on the seat.
5. Disconnect ignition switch connector at switch.
6. Remove 2 screws securing the dimmer switch and ignition switch to steering column. Position the dimmer switch out of the way and remove the one screw securing the ignition switch to the steering column. Remove switch.
7. To install, first assemble ignition switch on actuator rod and adjust to lock position as follows:
    a. Standard column—hold switch actuating rod stationary with one hand while moving switch toward bottom of column until switch reaches end of travel (Acc. position). Back off 2 detents to the right (Off-Unlock position), then with key also in Off-Unlock position, tighten 2 switch mounting screws to 35 inch lbs.
    b. Tilt column—hold switch actuating rod stationary with one hand while removing switch toward upper end of column until switch reaches end of travel (Acc. position). Back off 1

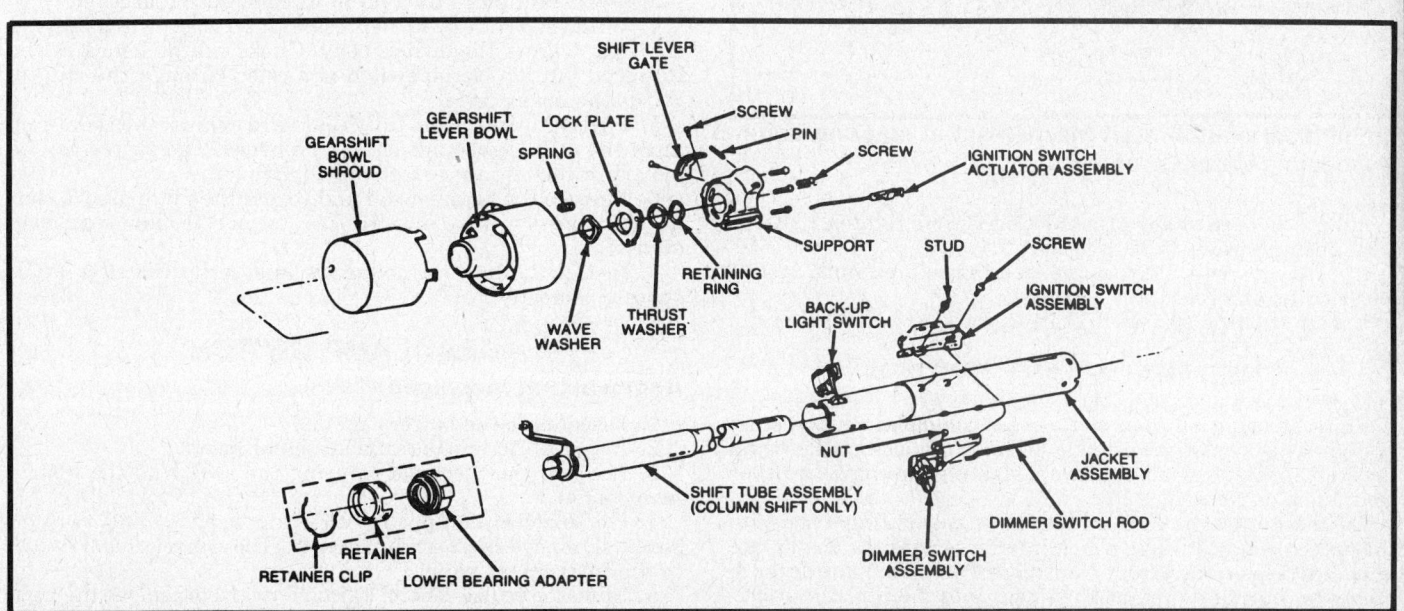

Exploded view of tilt and telescoping column bowl assembly and location of switches
(© General Motors Corporation)

14-11

SECTION 14

CADILLAC
DE VILLE • FLEETWOOD

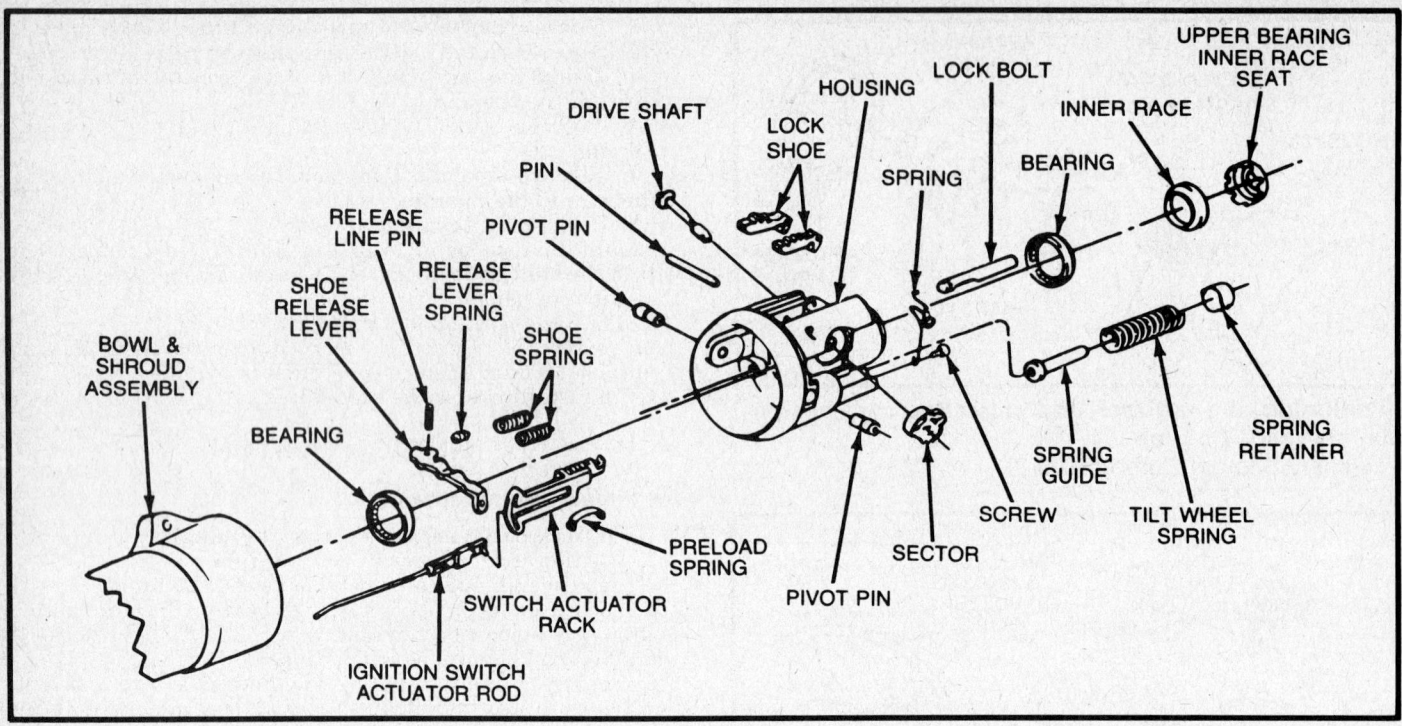

Exploded view of tilt and telescoping column housing assembly (© General Motors Corporation)

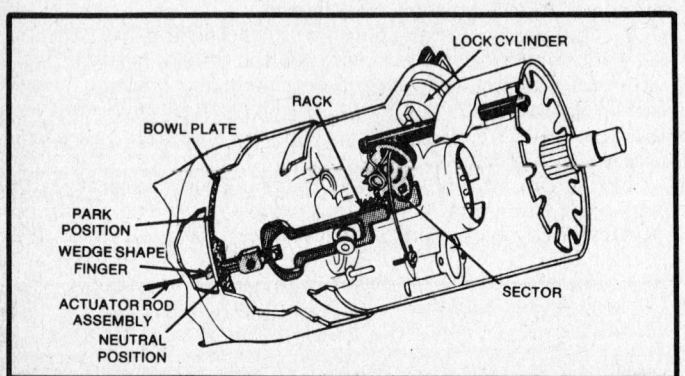

Mechanical neutral start mechanism in steering column (© General Motors Corporation)

detent, then, with key also in lock position, tighten 2 switch mounting screws to 35 inch lbs.
8. Connect wires, tighten two steering column nuts, install lower cover and reconnect battery.
9. Test starting system to start in Park and Neutral only.

NEUTRAL START SYSTEM

Cadillac steering columns contain a mechanical neutral start system. This system relies on a mechanical block, rather than the starter safety switch to prevent starting the engine in other than Park or Neutral.

The mechanical block is achieved by a cast in finger added to the switch actuator rack, which interferes with the bowl plate in all shift positions except Neutral or Park. This interference prevents rotation of the lock cylinder into the Start position.

In either Park or Neutral, this finger passes through the bowl plates lots allowing the lock cylinder full rotational travel into the Start position.

STOP LAMP SWITCH

Removal and Installation

NOTE: **The cruise control release switch and the stop lamp switch are adjusted or replaced in the same manner.**

1. Disconnect the wire harness connector from the switch.
2. Remove the switch from the clip and then remove the clip from the bracket.
3. To install, place the clip in its bore on the bracket.
4. With the brake pedal depressed, insert the switch into the clip and depress the switch body. Clicks can be heard as the threaded portion of the switch is pushed through the clip towards the brake pedal.
5. Pull the brake pedal fully rearward against the pedal stop until the clicking sounds cannot be heard. The switch can be moved in the clip to correct the adjustment.
6. Release the brake pedal and repeat Step 5 to assure that no clicking sounds remain. The switch is now correctly adjusted.
7. Install the harness connector and verify the stop lamps operate correctly.

HEADLAMP SWITCH

Removal and Installation

1. Disconnect the battery ground.
2. Remove the left instrument panel insert.
3. Remove the 3 screws securing the switch to the instrument panel.
4. On vehicles equipped with cruise control and twilight sentinel remove the 2 screws securing the cruise control switch to the instrument panel.
5. Slide the cruise control switch forward to remove the light switch. Disconnect the two-piece connector from the headlight switch. Disconnect the Guidematic and twilight sentinel, is so equipped, under the instrument panel.

CADILLAC
DE VILLE · FLEETWOOD
SECTION 14

6. Remove the switch rod. Remove the switch by unthreading the nut from the front of the lens housing.
7. Installation is the reverse of the removal procedure.

TURN SIGNAL SWITCH

Removal and Replacement

STANDARD STEERING COLUMN

1. Disconnect the negative battery cable.
2. Remove the steering wheel.
3. Insert a suitable tool into the lockplate and remove the lockplate cover assembly.

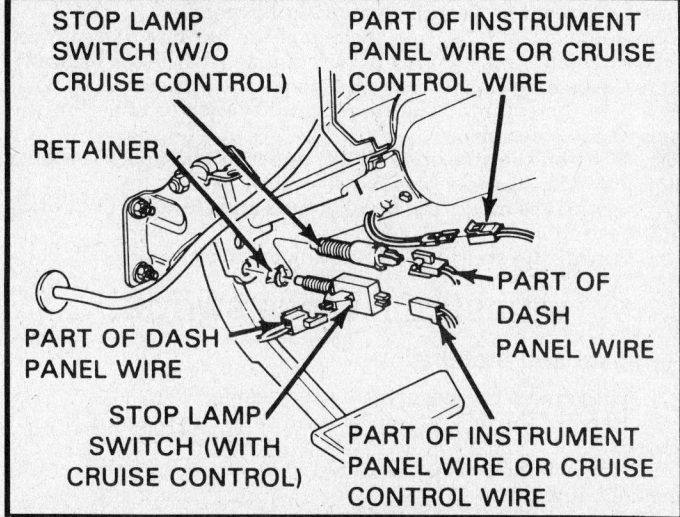

Location of stoplight switch, with or without cruise control (© General Motors Corporation)

4. Install a spring compressor onto the steering shaft. Tighten the tool to compress the lockplate and the spring. Remove the snap-ring from the groove in the shaft.

CAUTION
If the column is out of the vehicle when the snap-ring is removed do not allow the shaft to slide out the bottom of the column.

5. Remove the lockplate and slide the turn signal cam and the upper bearing preload spring and the thrust washer off the upper steering shaft.
6. Remove the steering column lower cover.
7. Unscrew the turn signal lever and remove it from the column.
8. On vehicles equipped with cruise control:
   a. Disconnect the cruise control wire from the harness near the bottom of the column.
   b. Remove the harness protector from the cruise control wire.
   c. Remove the turn signal lever. Do not remove the wire from the column.
9. Remove the 2 vertical bolts at the steering column upper support. Remove the shim packs. Keep the shims in order for reinstallation.
10. Remove the 4 screws securing the column upper mounting bracket to the column and remove the bracket.
11. Disconnect the turn signal wiring and remove the wires from the plastic protector.
12. Remove the turn signal switch mounting screws.
13. Slide the switch connector out of the bracket on the steering column.
14. If the switch is known to be bad, cut the wires and discard the switch. Tape the connector of the new switch to the old wires, and pull the new harness down through the steering column while removing the old wires.
15. If the original switch is to be reused, wrap tape around the wire and connector and pull the harness up through the column. It may be helpful to attach a length of mechanic's wire to

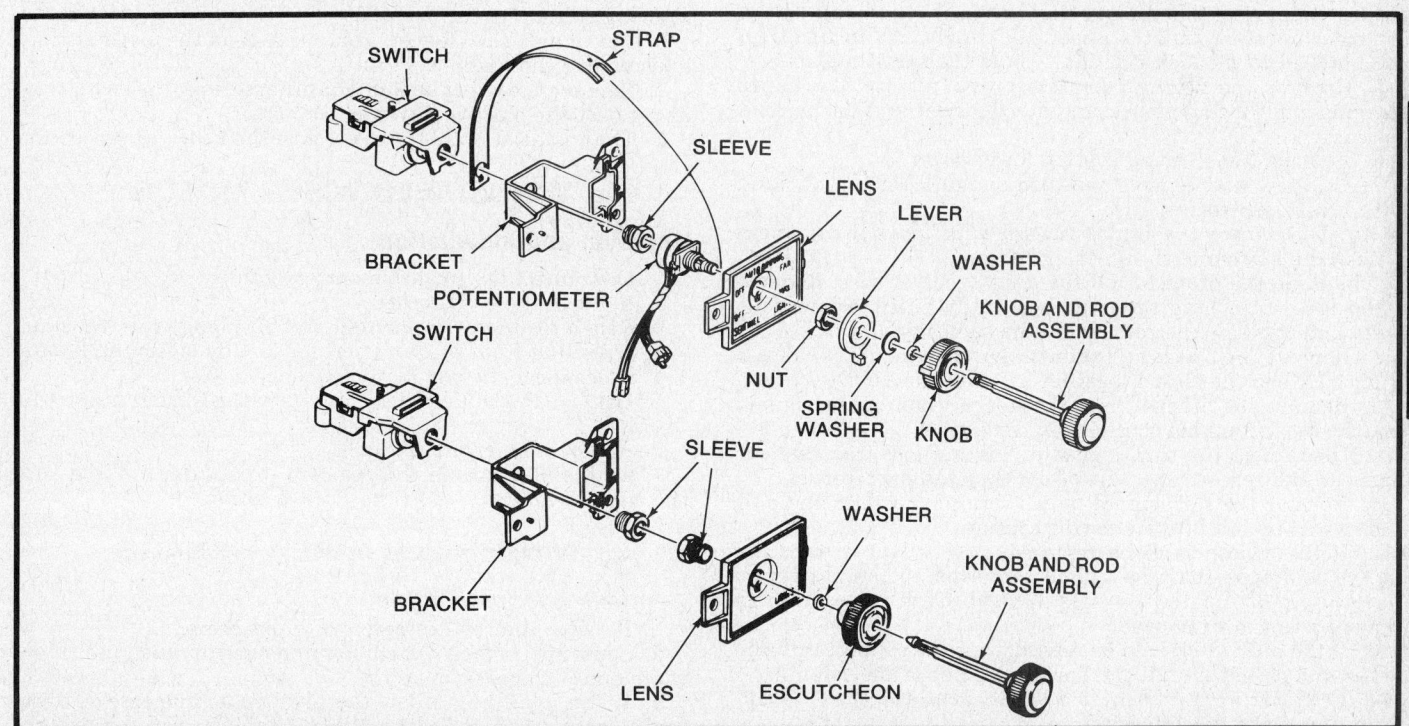

Cadillac light switches, typical exploded view (© General Motors Corporation)

14–13

CADILLAC
DE VILLE • FLEETWOOD

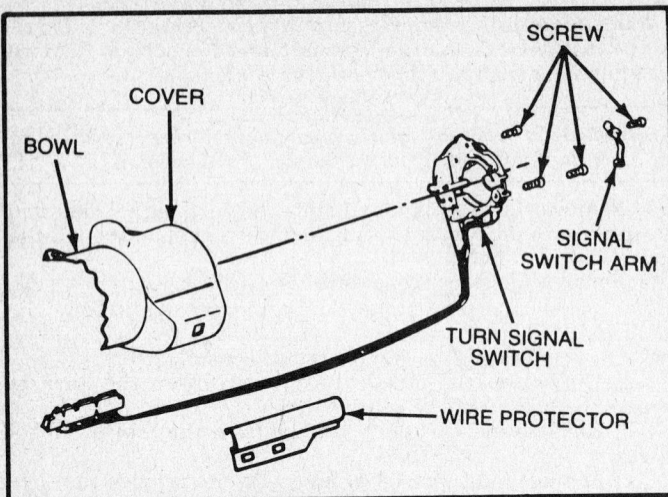

Turnsignal switch assembly on standard column
(© General Motors Corporation)

the harness connector before pulling it up through the column to facilitate installation.

16. After freeing the switch wiring protector from its mounting, pull the turn signal switch straight up and remove the switch, switch harness, and the connector from the column.

17. To reassemble reverse the removal procedure.

TILT AND TELESCOPIC COLUMNS

1. Disconnect the battery and remove the steering wheel.
2. Remove the rubber sleeve bumper from the steering shaft.
3. Remove the plastic retainer with a screwdriver, disengaging the tabs on the retainer from the C-ring.
4. Compress the upper steering shaft preload spring with a spring compressor and remove the C-ring. When installing the spring compressor, pull the upper shaft up about 1 in. and turn the ignition to the lock position to hold the shaft in place.
5. Remove the spring compressor and remove the upper steering shaft lock plate, horn contact carrier and the preload spring.
6. Remove the steering column lower cover.
7. Unscrew and remove the turn signal lever. If equipped with cruise control:
   a. Disconnect the cruise control wire from the harness near the bottom of the steering column.
   b. Slide the protector off the cruise control wire. Remove the lever attaching screw and carefully pull the lever out enough to allow the removal of the turn signal switch.
8. Remove the 2 nuts and shim packs from the upper column support. Keep the shims together as a unit for reinstallation.
9. Remove the bracket from the steering column by removing the two attaching screws from each side.
10. Disconnect the turn signal wiring harness from the car harness and remove the wires from the plastic protector.
11. Remove the turn signal switch retaining screws and pull the switch up out of the steering column.
12. If the switch is to be replaced, cut the wires from the switch and tape the new switch connector to the old wires. Carefully pull the new harness down through the column as the old wires are removed.
13. If the old switch is to be reused, tape the connector to the wires and carefully pull the harness up out of the column.
14. Feed the wiring harness down through the steering column to replace the old switch.
15. Secure the switch in the steering column.
16. Install the upper shaft preload spring.
17. Install the lock plate and carrier assembly. Make sure that the flat on the lower end of the steering shaft is pointing up and that the small plastic tab on the carrier is up or nearest the top of the column. The flat surface of the lock plate must be installed facing down against the turn signal switch.
18. Install the spring compressor, compress the preload spring and lock plate and install the C-ring with the wide side toward the keyway.
19. Remove the spring compressor and install the plastic retainer on the C-ring.
20. Install the rubber sleeve bumper over the steering shaft and install the steering wheel.
21. Install the turn signal lever. If the vehicle is equipped with cruise control, secure the lever to the switch with the retaining screw and install the wiring harness.
22. Remove the tape from the end of the harness and connect the switch and cruise control, if so equipped, to the car harness.
23. Cover both harnesses with the plastic protector and position it to the column. The turn signal connector slides on the tabs of the column.
24. Position the steering column upper bracket over the turn signal switch harness plastic protector.
25. Install the mounting bracket nuts and shims in their original positions.
26. Install the steering column lower cover.

WINDSHIELD WIPER SWITCH

Removal and Installation

1. Disconnect the negative battery cable.
2. Remove the left A/C outlet door knob by loosening the set screw.
3. Remove the left A/C outlet grill by depressing the retaining tabs inward.
4. Remove the bezel retaining screws.

NOTE: One screw is located inside of A/C outlet.

5. Remove upper and lower retaining screws in the lower steering column cover.
6. Disconnect the steering column seal on the lower surface and remove the bezel.
7. Remove the wiper switch retaining screws, the switch and disconnect the electrical wiring connector.
8. The installation is the reverse of the removal procedure.

WINDSHIELD WIPER MOTOR

Removal and Installation

1. Disconnect the negative battery cable.
2. Remove the cowl screen.
3. Reach through the opening and disengage the transmission drive link from the wiper crank arm by loosening 2 nuts.
4. Disconnect the wiring and washer hoses.
5. Remove the bolts that secure the wiper/washer unit to the firewall.
6. Remove the entire assembly.
7. To install, reverse the removal procedure, making sure the wiper crank arm is in the Park position.

WINDSHIELD WIPER LINKAGE

Removal and Installation

1. Remove the cowl screen and wiper arms.
2. Separate linkage from motor and mounts, and guide it out the plenum chamber opening.
3. When installing, allow the pivot attaching screws to remain loose until the drive links-to-crank arm screws are tightened.
4. To install, reverse the removal procedure.

CADILLAC
DE VILLE • FLEETWOOD
SECTION 14

Instrument Panel

INSTRUMENT CLUSTER

Removal and Installation

1. Disconnect the negative battery cable.
2. Remove the retaining screws and the left hand instrument panel and applique.
3. With the shift lever in the Park position, remove the shift indicator cable and clip retaining screw from the steering column.
4. Remove the upper and lower (2 inboard) cluster assembly retaining screws. Remove 1 screw directly above the steering column, retaining the cluster to the speedometer mounting plate.
5. Pull the cluster outward to disengage the speedometer cable and circuit board connectors.
6. If equipped, disconnect the speed control sensor from the cluster assembly. Disconnect other connectors as required.
7. Place the shift lever in the Low position, and if equipped with tilt wheel, place the wheel in its lowest position. Remove the cluster assembly from the dash.
8. The installation is the reverse of the removal procedure. Set the shift, indicator cable in the Neutral position and adjust the cable accordingly.

SPEEDOMETER CABLE

Removal and Installation

1. Remove the left instrument panel.
2. Disconnect the battery ground.
3. Place the shift lever in park and remove the screw securing the shift indicator cable to the column.
4. Remove the two upper screws securing the cluster assembly to the panel horizontal support.
5. Remove the two lower inside screws securing the cluster to the horizontal support.
6. Remove the screw located directly above the steering column securing the cluster to the speedometer mounting plate.
7. Pull the cluster outward to disengage the cable and remove the cluster. Placing the shift lever in the low range and tilting the steering wheel all the way down will help during removal.
8. Disconnect the cable housing from the locking spring on the mounting plate and pull it through the firewall.
9. Pull the core from the cable. If the core is broken or frayed on the transmission end, raise and support the car and disconnect the cable the transmission. Be sure the entire cable has been removed.
10. Installation is the reverse of removal.

ELECTRICAL COMPONENT LOCATION

FUSE PANEL

The fuse panel is located on the left side of the vehicle. It is under the instrument panel assembly. In order to gain access to

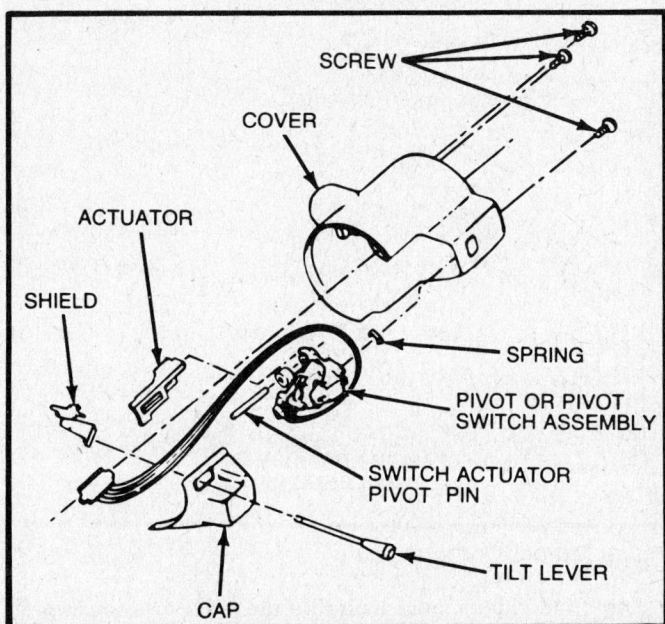

Turnsignal switch assembly on tilt and telescoping column (© General Motors Corporation)

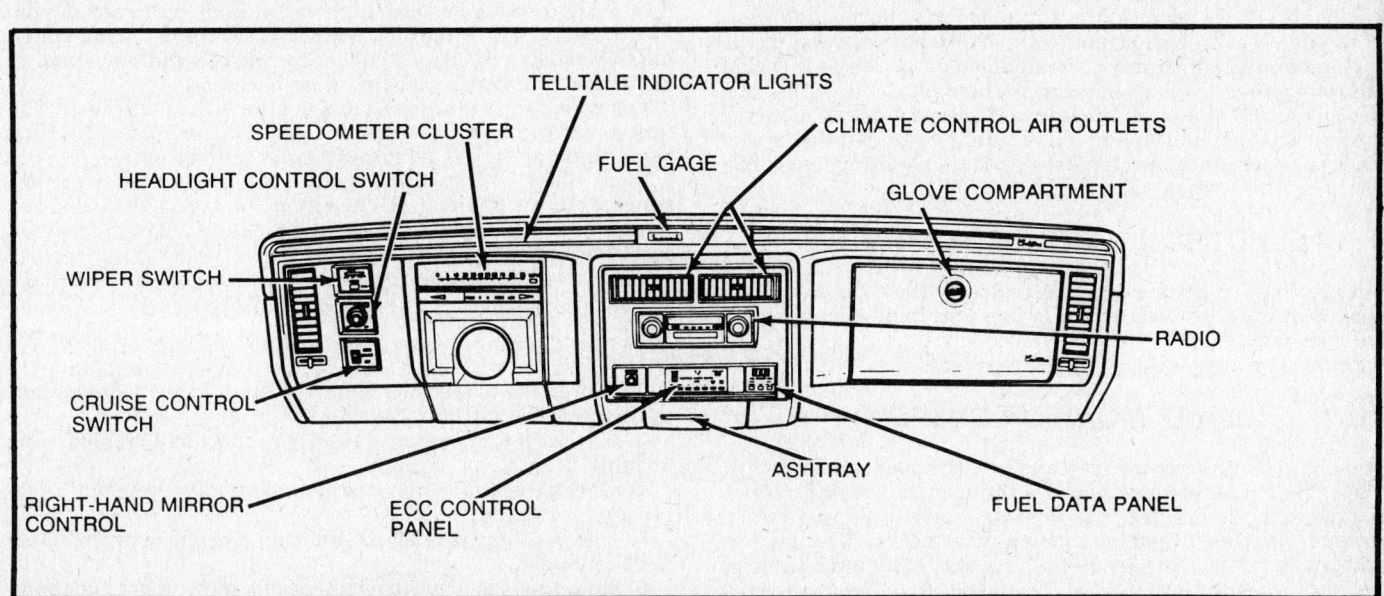

Typical dash assembly with component location (© General Motors Corporation)

14–15

SECTION 14

CADILLAC
DE VILLE • FLEETWOOD

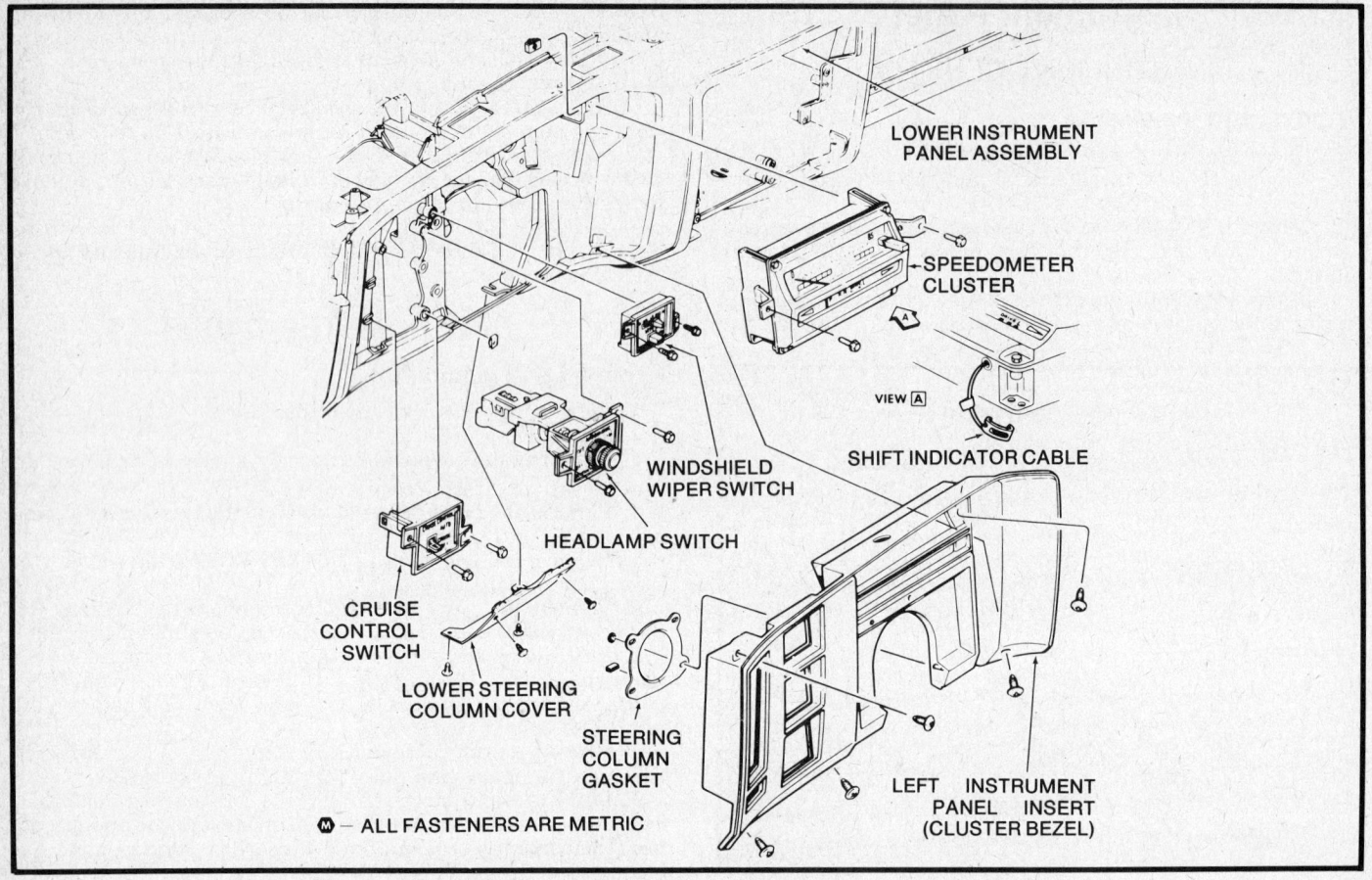

Instrument cluster and components, DeVille models (© General Motors Corporation)

the fuse panel it may be necessary to first remove the under dash padding.

FUSIBLE LINKS

Fusible links are used to prevent major wire harness damage in the event of a short circuit or an overload condition in the wiring circuits which are normally not fused, due to carrying high amperage loads or because of their locations within the wiring harness. Each fusible link is of a fixed value for a specific electrical load and should a link fail, the cause of the failure must be determined and repaired prior to installing a new fusible link of the same value.

ELECTRONIC CONTROL MODULE

The electronic control module is located on the right side of the vehicle. It is positioned in front of the right hand kick panel. In order to gain access to the assembly you must first remove the trim panel.

LAMP MONITOR SYSTEM

The Lamp Monitor system is standard equipment on all cars. It allows the driver to visually check the operation of the exterior lamps without leaving the vehicle. This is accomplished through the use of light conductors (fiber optics). The conductors are used to transfer light from the individual exterior lamp to its respective monitor. The system does not use electrical power in order to operate, nor does it have any moving parts.

Three individual lamp monitors are used. One monitor is mounted on top of each front fender, and one at the center of the headliner, immediately above the rear window.

The front lamp monitor high beam headlamp indicator lens is blue and thus matches the high beam headlamp indicator in the speedometer face. The high beam fiber optic has a blue identification marking near each end. The fiber optic transmits the light directly from the low beam headlamps and is identified by a white marking near each end.

The park and turn signal lamp monitor lens is also clear. The fiber optic transmits the amber light from the park and turn signal lamp. There is no marking on the fiber optic.

Each lamp monitored, except headlamps, has a pickup mounted in the housing; the headlamp pickup is located in the connector on the wiring harness and picks up the light from the sealed beam unit nipple.

The rear monitor indicates each tail lamp on the respective side of the vehicle.

Diagnosis

1. Check bulb in lamp connected to inoperative monitor.
2. If bulb is burned out, replace bulb. If lamp operates normally, proceed with further checks.
3. Check for proper installation of conductors to sealed beam or lamp housing as required.
4. Check conductor harness mounting to lamp monitors for proper attachment.
5. Check conductor harness routing for pinched or severely bent condition.
6. If none of the above checks reveals the inoperative condition, the conductor light fibers have probably been damaged. Replace conductors as required.

CADILLAC
DE VILLE · FLEETWOOD
SECTION 14

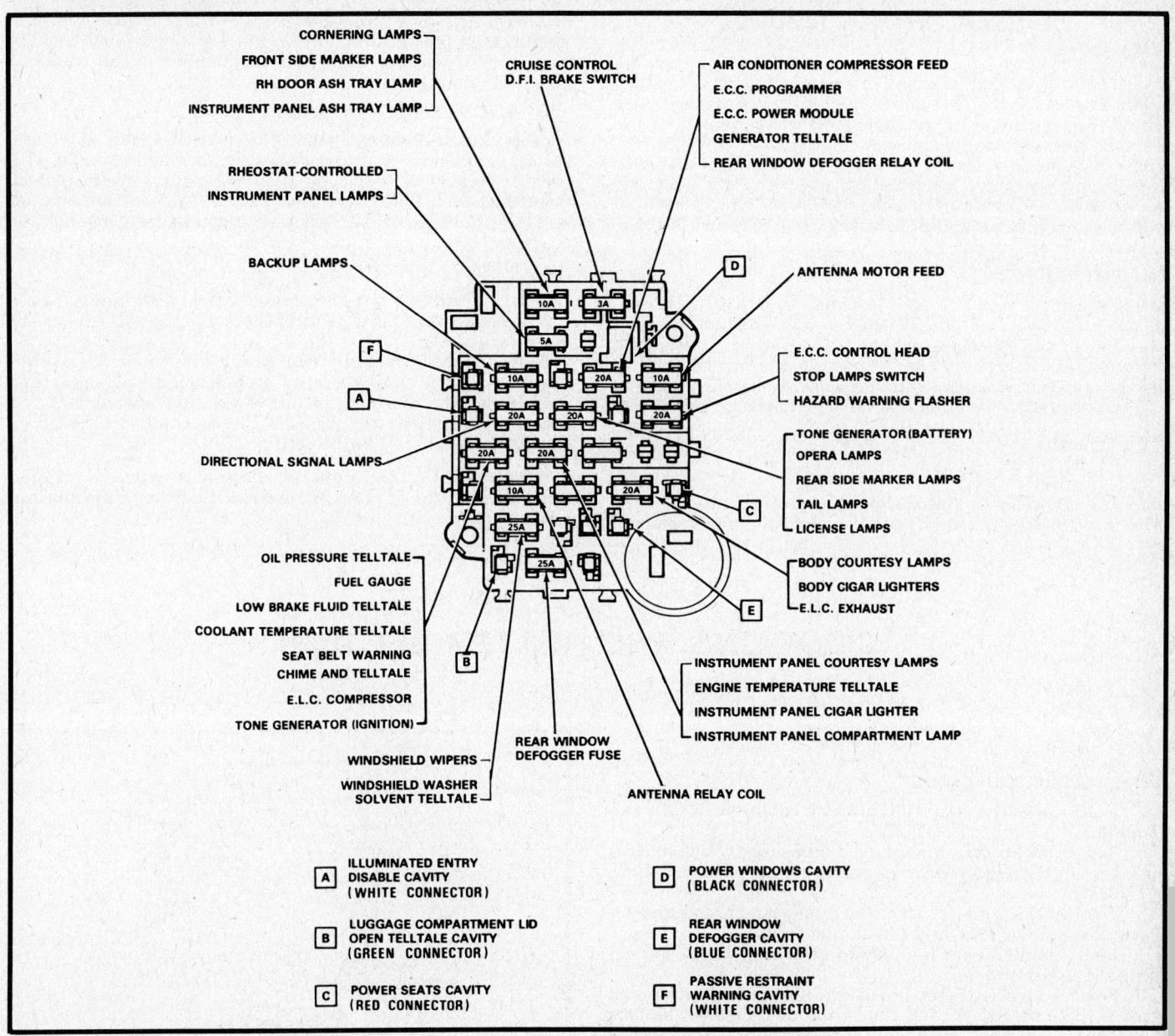

Typical fuse panel with circuits indicated (© General Motors Corporation)

Electronic Cruise Control

Cruise Control is a speed control system that uses vacuum from a vacuum pump to actuate the throttle power unit, or servo. The servo unit moves the throttle when its diaphragm is subjected to varying amounts of vacuum. The amount of vacuum to the servo unit is controlled by a solenoid valve which constantly modulates vacuum to the servo unit in response to commands from the electronic controller. The controller receives signals from the engagement and instrument panel switches, electric brake release switch and speed sensor. The speed sensor is located on the back of the speedometer cluster and provides signals representative of car speed to the control system. A wire harness connects the speed sensor to the electronic controller.

Input signals received from the sensor by the electronic control module are used to control the servo unit solenoid valve which regulates the amount of vacuum to the servo unit to control the speed of the car.

A two position (off, on-auto) switch, located on the instrument panel and an engagement switch, located at the end of the turn signal lever, control the operation of the system.

Two systems for brake release are provided:

1. An electric switch mounted on the brake pedal support cancels the controller signal by shutting off power to the system and vents the servo diaphragm vacuum to atmosphere through the servo unit solenoid valve.

2. A vacuum release valve also is mounted on the brake pedal bracket and vents the servo diaphragm vacuum to atmosphere as a second disengagement system.

14-17

CRUISE CONTROL MODULE

D.F.I. ONLY

Cruise control operation is one of the many functions which ECM controls. The ECM receives input signals from the cruise control engagement switches, the instrument panel switch, the brake release switch and the speed sensor.

The ECM processes these cruise control inputs together with the DFI engine control information and transmits command signals to the vacuum control solenoid valve to provide vacuum to the system and servo unit solenoid valve to control vehicle speed.

EXCEPT D.F.I.

A cruise control module receives signals from the cruise engagement switch, instrument panel switch, electric brake release switch and speed sensor. The cruise control module then processes this information and transmits command signals to the vacuum control valve to provide vacuum to the system and signals to the servo unit solenoid valve to control vehicle speed.

Adjustments

1983–V6 GAS ENGINE

Install bead chain into throttle lever clip and lock into position. With throttle lever in hot idle position and idle control solenoid de-energized, place bead chain into swivel cavity. The ball swivel must be installed on the inboard side of lever. Chain slack should not exceed one half the diameter of ball stud. Cut off excess chain.

1983 AND LATER – V8 GAS ENGINE

A combination cable and bead chain is used. Install cable into throttle clip and lock into position. Chain should be taut with throttle body lever in hot idle position and idle speed solenoid fully retracted. Place bead into swivel, then install retainer and lock into place. Chain slack should not exceed one half the diameter of ball stud. Cut off excess chain.

ALL DIESEL ENGINES

1. Insert rod end into the servo assembly bushing.
2. Assemble the plastic end of the rod to the ball stud on the accelerator lever.
3. Adjust the rod length to minimum slack with the accelerator lever on the slow idle screw and the engine not operating.
4. Install the retainer pin in the rod after adjustment.
5. Check for free operation of the assembly to wide open throttle position and to the return.

NOTE: For cruise control diagnosis when equipped with DFI, refer to the Unit Repair Section, Engine Control chapter.

COOLING AND HEATER SECTION

WATER PUMP

Removal and Installation

1. Disconnect the negative battery cable and drain the radiator.
2. Remove two screws from the radiator support rods on each side. Loosen 1 screw on each side and move the support rod out of the way.
3. Remove the 2 screws from the upper fan shroud and remove the radiator hose brace-to-shroud screw.
4. Drill out the upper fan shroud attaching rivets and remove the upper shroud.
5. Remove all drive belts. Loosen the alternator bracket and remove the pulley so the fan can be rotated. Remove the four screws attaching the fan hub to the water pump. Remove the fan assembly from the engine.
6. Partially remove the A/C compressor unit from the engine mounting brackets. Do not remove the high and low pressure lines from the compressor head.
7. Remove the alternator and supprt bracket from the engine. Remove the power steering pump pulley with tool J-25034 or equivalent. On the 86 and later models remove the power steering pump adjusting bracket and the air pump bracket.
8. Loosen the clamps and disconnect the water pump inlet and outlet hoses at the pump. Disconnect the by-pass hose at the water pump. Remove the A?C Bracket at the water pump.
9. Remove the timing mark tab from the front cover. Remove the watr pump mounting bolts and remove the water pump. Remove all old gasket material.
10. Reverse to install, using a new gasket and applying a suitable RTv sealant on the gasket. Install the drive belts and tighten them to the proper tension. Refill the cooling system with the correct mixture of antifreeze and water. Run the engine and check for leaks.

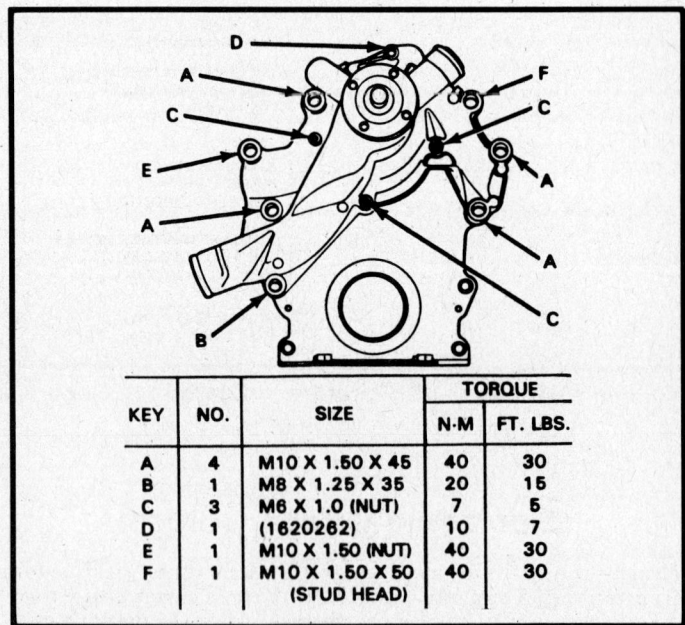

Water pump mounting bolts installation—1983-85 V8 engines

HEATER/AC CONTROL AND FAN SWITCH ASSEMBLY

Removal and Installation

The center instrument panel insert must be removed. Depend-

CADILLAC
DE VILLE · FLEETWOOD
SECTION 14

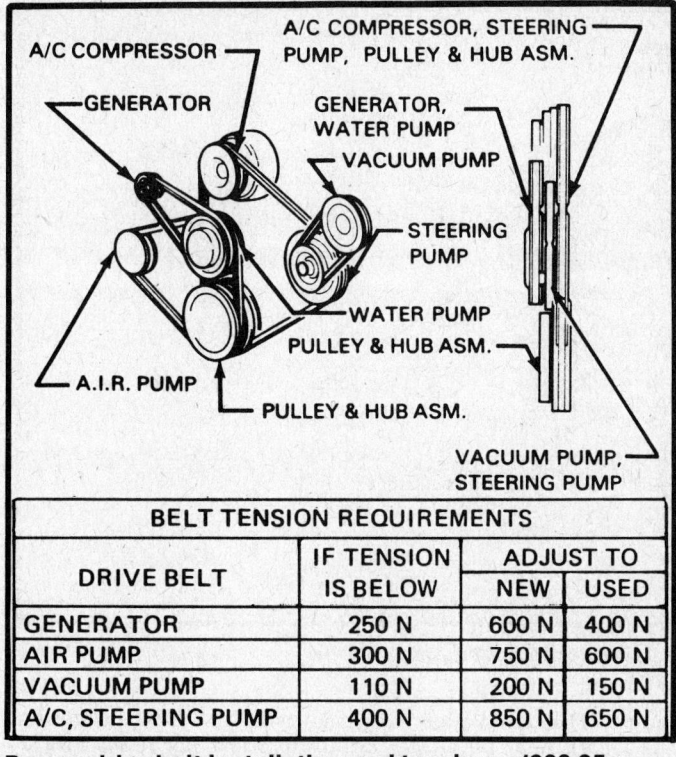

BELT TENSION REQUIREMENTS			
DRIVE BELT	IF TENSION IS BELOW	ADJUST TO NEW	ADJUST TO USED
GENERATOR	250 N	600 N	400 N
AIR PUMP	300 N	750 N	600 N
VACUUM PUMP	110 N	200 N	150 N
A/C, STEERING PUMP	400 N	850 N	650 N

Proper drive belt installation and tension—1983-85 V8 engines

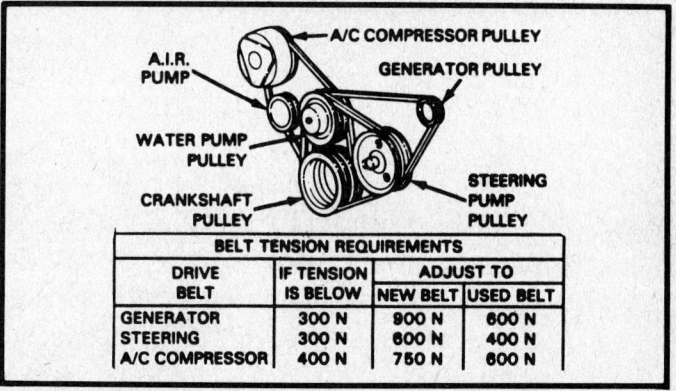

BELT TENSION REQUIREMENTS			
DRIVE BELT	IF TENSION IS BELOW	ADJUST TO NEW BELT	ADJUST TO USED BELT
GENERATOR	300 N	900 N	600 N
STEERING	300 N	600 N	400 N
A/C COMPRESSOR	400 N	750 N	600 N

Proper drive belt installation and tension—1986 and later V8 engines

ing upon the vehicle model, the radio knobs and retaining nuts must be removed, along with the 2 center A/C outlet grills to obtain access to one screw located in each outlet. Remove the control unit retaining screws, disconnect the electrical and vacuum lines and remove the control unit.

The installation is accomplished by the reverse of the removal procedure.

BLOWER MOTOR

Removal and Installation

1. Disconnect the negative battery cable.
2. Remove the rubber cooling hose from the nipple and blower motor.
3. Disconnect the electrical connector.
4. Remove the screws that secure the motor to the case, then twist the motor 180° and pull out.

HEATER CORE

Removal and Installation

1. Disconnect the negative battery cable. Disconnect wiring from the blower, power module, resistors, compressor cycling switch and radio lead-in connections. Position the wiring harness out of the way.
2. Remove the right windshield washer nozzle.
3. Remove the right air inlet screen from the plenum. Partially remove the rubber molding above the plenum (one screw on the right hand side). Drain the radiator.
4. Remove the remaining screws and remove the primary inlet screen. Remove the blower motor.
5. Remove the two screws holding the compressor cycling switch to the module and carefully reposition the switch off of the module cover.
6. Remove the 16 screws holding the A/c module cover and remove the cover. Remove and plug the heater hoses from the heater core nipples.
7. Remove one screw and retainmer holding the heater core to the frame at the top.
8. With the temperature door in the max/hot position, reach through the temperature housing and push the lower forward corner of the heater core away from the housing.
9. Rotate the core parallel to the housing. This will cause the core to snap out of the lower clamp. The core can now be removed in a vertical direction due to the configuration of the lower core tank, lower calmp and temperature housing.
10. Installation is the reverse order of the removal procedure. Be sure to install a new heater-A/C module cover seal.

FUEL SYSTEM

FUEL PUMP

1983-85 CARBURETED ENGINES

1. Raise and support the vehicle safely.
2. Disconnect the fuel line and the vapor return hose from the fuel pump.
3. Disconnect the fuel pump-to-carburetor line and position it out of the way.
4. Remove the pump mounting screws and, tipping the pump upward, remove it from the vehicle.
5. Installation is the reverse of removal. Use a new gasket.

1986 AND LATER BROUGHAM

1. Disconnect the negative battery cable . Remove the A/C compressor drive belt.
2. If equipped with an air injection system the following procedure should be used:
   a. Loosen the air pump pulley bolts. and remove the air pump hoses and electrical leads to the air pump.
   b. Remove the air pump pulley and remove the air pump from the engine.
3. Remove the compressor front bracket. Remove the fuel in-

14—19

SECTION 14

CADILLAC
DE VILLE • FLEETWOOD

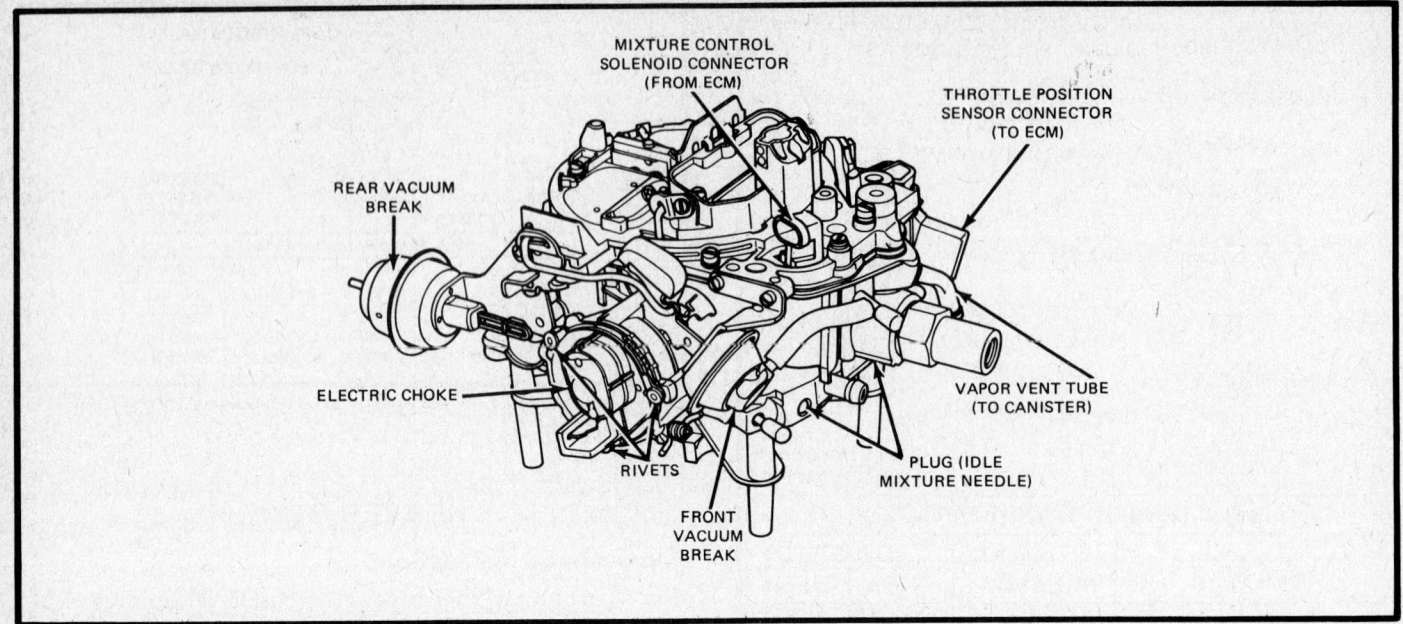

Carburetor components, E4ME illustrated, others similar (© General Motors Corporation)

let hose from the fuel pump. Alos disconnect the vapor return hose, if so equipped.

4. Remove the fuel outlet pipe. Remove the two ½ inch hex head bolts or nuts securing the fuel pump to the engine. Remove the fuel pump.

5. Installationm is the reverse order of the removal procedure.

FUEL INJECTED ENGINES

CAUTION

Fuel is under high pressure; if the steps below are not followed, the fuel could spray out and result in a fire hazard and possible injury.

IN-TANK PUMP: DFI SYSTEMS

1. Disconnect the negative battery terminal, open the fuel tank filler door and disconnect the sending unit feed wire.

2. Siphon the fuel from the fuel tank. If the rear of the vehicle is raised 1 ft. higher than the front, more fuel can be taken out.

3. Raise the rear of the vehicle and remove the screw securing the ground wire to the crossmember.

4. Disconnect the fuel line, evaporative emission lines and the fuel return lines at the front of the tank.

5. Support the tank with a jack and wooden block and remove 1 screw on each side securing the fuel tank support straps to the body at the front of the tank.

6. Lower the jack and tank enough so that the fuel pump electrical lead can be disconnected. Disconnect the wire.

7. Remove the fuel tank from the vehicle.

8. Remove the locknuts securing the fuel gauge tank unit and fuel pump feed wires to the tank unit.

9. Turn the cam locking ring counterclockwise with a soft non-ferrous punch and hammer (there is tool #J-24187 available). When the lock ring is disengaged, remove it and lift the gauge/pump unit from the tank.

10. Install in the reverse order of removal. Tighten the fuel retaining strap screws to 25 ft. lbs.

CARBURETOR

The 1986-87 Fleetwood Brougham is equipped with a 307 V8 engine. This particular engine is using a E4MC carburetor. The E4ME and the E4MC carburetors are also being used in the 1983-84 commercial chassis. For more detailed information on these carburetors, refer to the Carburetor Chapter in the Unit Repair Section of this manual.

Adjustments

IDLE SPEED AND MIXTURE

All carburetors have mixture needles concealed under staked-in plugs. Mixture adjustments are possible only during carburetor overhaul or extreme circumstances.

Vehicles equipped with the computer command control system can not use the propane enrichment or lean drop methods of idle mixture adjustment.

Carburetor Adjustment

1. Place the transmission in the park position, set the parking brake and block the drive wheels. Connect a suitable tachometer to the engine. Remove the air cleaner assembly and plug the vacuum hose to the Thermal Vacuum Valve (TVV).

2. Disconnect and plug the vacuum hose to the EGR valve and the vacuum hose to the canister purge port.

3. Disconnect and plug the vacuum hose to the idle load compensator (ILC). Back out the idle stop screw on the carburetor three turns.

4. Turn the A/C to the "OFF" position. With the engine running and at normal operating temperature, place the transmission in the "DRIVE" position. Fully extend the idle load compensator plunger (no vacuum applied).

5. Using tool J-29607, Bt-8022 or equivalent, adjust the ILC plunger to obtain a 725 ± 50 rpm. The jam nut on the plunger must be held with a suitable wrench to prevent damge to the guide tabs.

6. Measure the distance from the jam nut to the tip of the plunger. The dimension must not exceed 1 inch. If the dimension does exceed 1 inch, check for a low idle condition. Remove the pluf from the ILC vacuum hose and plug the hose back into the ILC. The idle speed should be 450 ± 25 rpm in the "DRIVE" position.

7. If the idle speed is correct then the adjustment is over. If

CADILLAC
DE VILLE • FLEETWOOD
SECTION 14

the idle spped does not meet specifications perform the following steps:

a. Stop the engine and remove the idle load compensator. It will not be necessary to remove the idle load compensator if a hex wrench is modified to clear the obstructions.

b. Remove the rubber cap from the center outlet tube. Using a $3/32$ in. hex key wrench, insert it through the open center tube to engage the idle speed adjusting screw inside the tube.

c. If the idle speed was low, turn the adjusting screw counterclockwise one turn for every 75-100 rpm low. If the idle was too high, turn the adjusting screw clockwise one turn for every 75-100 rpm high. Re-install the plug on the center of the outlet tube.

d. Re-install the idle load compensator on the carburetor and reattach the the throttle return spring and other related parts removed. Recheck the idle speed in the "DRIVE" position and closed loop mode. If the idle speed is still not within specification, repeat steps a through c.

e. Disconnect the power feed (fuse) to the ECM with the ignition off, for ten seconds. This will allow the ECM to re-set the throttle position sensor value.

8. Disconnect and plug the vacuum source to the ILC. Apply a vacuum source using a hand held vacuum pump or equivalent to the ILC vacuum inlet tube to fully retract the plunger.

9. Adjust the idle stop screw on the carburetor float bowl to obtain a 450 rpm in the "DRIVE" position. Place the transmission in "PARK" and stop the engine.

10. Remove the plug from the vacuum hose and install the hose on the ILC vacuum inlet tube. Remove all the plugs from the disconnected vacuum lines and reconnect the vacuum lines to their proper ports.

11. Install the air cleaner and gasket, remove the blocks from the drive wheels and road test the vehicle.

Throttle Position Sensor Adjustment
5.0L ENGINE

NOTE: Before the throttle position sensor voltage output setting can be checked or adjusted, the idle rpm settinga must have been set to specifications. The throttle position sensor adjustment should only be required if the voltage readings are above .70 volts.

1. Remove the air cleaner assembly.
2. Disconnect the throttle position sensor harness from the throttle position sensor.
3. Using three jumper wires connect the throttle position sensor harness to the throttle position sensor.
4. With the ignition on and the engine stopped. Disconnect the electrical connector from the idle solenoid (plunger retracted). Be sure the throttle lever is against the idle speed screw.
5. Use a (10 megohm) digital voltmeter to measure the voltage between between terminals "B" and "C". If adjustment is required, remove the throttle position sensor plug to allow adjustment as follows:

a. Using a $5/64$ in. drill bit, drill a $1/16$ to $1/8$ in. deep hole in the aluminum plug covering the throttle position sensor adjustment screw. Be careful when drilling not to damage the adjustment screw head.

b. Start a (number eight) ½ in. long self-tapping screw into the drilled hole turning the screw in only enough to ensure good thread engagemant in the hole.

c. Plcaing a suitable tool between the screw head and the air horn casting, pry against the screw head to remove the plug.

d. Using tool J-28696, BT-7967-A or equivalents, adjust the throttle position sensor to obtain .46 volts.

e. After adjustment, install a new plug (usally supplied in the service kit) into the air horn, driving the plug into place

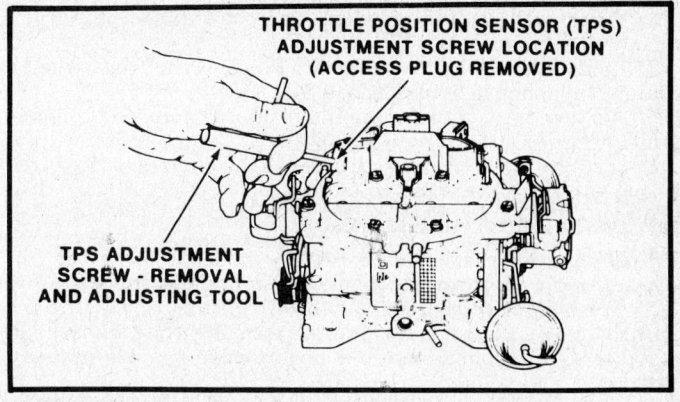

Making the throttle position sensor adjustment

until it is flush with the raised pump lever boss on the casting.

6. Clear any trouble code memory after adjustment and disconnect all test equipment.

NOTE: The plug must be installed to retain the throttle position sensor adjustment screw setting. If a plug is not available, remove the adjustment screw and and apply a suitable threadlock sealant to the screw threads, then repeat the adjustment.

CARBURETOR
Removal and Installation

1. Disconnect the negative battery cable. Remove the air cleaner assembly and disconnect the accelerator linkage.
2. Disconnect the transmission detent cable, if so equipped. Disconnect the cruise control linkage, if so equipped.
3. Remove and tag all vacuum and electrical lines to the carburetor. Disconnect the choke heat pipe.
4. Remove the fuel line at the carburetor inlet. Remove the four carburetor mounting bolts. Remove the carburetor from the manifold.
5. Installation is the reverse order of the removal procedure. Install a new carburetor base gasket and torque the mounting bolts to 12 ft. lbs.

EXHAUST MANIFOLD
Removal and Installation
5.0L ENGINES (Left Side)

1. Disconnect the negative battery cable and remove the air cleaner assembly.
2. Raise and support the vehicle safely. Flaten the exhaust manifold bolt lock tabs.
3. Remove the exhaust pipe from the exhaust manifold. Lower the vehicle.
4. Remove the hot air shroud. Loosen the generator bracket bolts and lower the generator bracket.
5. Remove the exhaust manifold reatining bolts and remove the exhaust manifold from the engine.
6. Installation is the reverse order of the removal procedure. Be sure to install new gaskets.

5.0L ENGINE (Right Side)

1. Disconnect the negative battery cable and remove the air cleaner assembly.
2. Remove the oxygen sensor lead wire. Raise and support the vehicle safely.

SECTION 14
CADILLAC
DE VILLE • FLEETWOOD

3. Remove the crossover ppipe. and the exhaust pipe from the exhaust manifold.
4. Remove the oil filter adapter. Remove the front wheel. Flaten the exhaust manifold bolt lock tabs.
5. Remove the exhaust manifold retaining bolts and remove the exhaust manifold from the engine.
6. Installation is the reverse order of the removal procedure. Be sure to install new gaskets.

HT4100 ENGINE (LEFT SIDE)

1. Disconnect the negative battery cable. Remove the air cleaner and tube assembly from the air preheat stove.
2. Remove the screw securing the oil dipstick tube to the air preheat stove. Remove the screws securing the air orcheat stove to the exhaust manifold and remove the air preheat stove.
3. Remove the nust from the two stud/bolts securing the transmission linkage support to the manifold. Disconnect the "Y" pipe from the exhaust manifold.
4. Remove the oxygen sensor using a suitable box end wrench. Special tools such as J-29533 are available to perform this operation.
5. Remove the bolts securing the exhaust manifold to the cylinder head. Remove the manifold from the engine compartment.
6. Installation is the reverse order of the removal procedure. Be sure to install new gaskets.

HT4100 ENGINE (Right Side)

1. Remove the nut from the stud/bolt securing the transmission cooler line bracket to the exhaust manifold.
2. Remove the two nuts securing the air valve bracket to the exhaust manifold. Remove the upper exhaust manifold to head bolts.
3. Raise and support the vehicle safely. Remove the lower exhaust manifold to head bolts.
4. Disconnect the "Y" pipe from the exhaust manifold. Remove the exhaust manifold from the engine compartment.
5. Installation is the reverse order of the removal procedure. Be sure to install new gaskets.

6.0L ENGINES

1. Disconnect the negative battery cable.
2. Remove all the necessary equipment in order to gain access to the exhaust manifold retaining bolts.
3. Remove the exhaust manifold retaining bolts. Remove the exhaust manifold to crossover pipe flange bolts.
4. On some vehicles it may be necessary to raise the engine in order to gain clearance to remove the manifold.
5. Remove the exhaust manifold from the vehicle. On some vehicles it may be necessary to raise the vehicle and remove the manifold from underneath of the engine.
6. Installation is the reverse of the removal procedure. Be sure to install new gaskets.

5.7L DIESEL ENGINE (LEFT SIDE)

1. Disconnect the negative battery cable. Remove the air cleaner assembly and then install the air crossover cover.
2. Remove the lower generator braket. Raise and support the vehicle safely.
3. Remove the crossover pipe. Lower the vehicle.
4. Remove the exhaust manifold retaining bolts and remove the exhaust manifold from the engine.
5. Installation is the reverse order of the removal procedure.

5.7L DIESEL ENGINE (RIGHT SIDE)

1. Disconnect the negative battery cable. Raise and support the vehicle safely.
2. Remove the crossover pipe. Disconnect the exhaust pipe from the exhaust manifold.
3. Remove the right front wheel assembly. Remove the exhaust manifold retaining bolts and remove the exhaust manifold from underneath the vehicle.
4. Installation is the reverse order of the removal procedure.

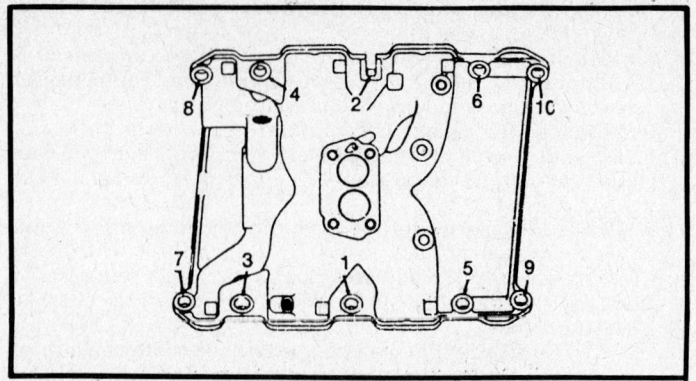

Intake manifold torque sequence—V6
(© General Motors Corporation)

INTAKE MANIFOLD

Removal and Installation

5.0L ENGINE

1. Disconnect the negative battery cable. Drain the coolant into a suitable drain pan.
2. Remove the air cleaner assembly. Remove the upper radiator hose, thermostat by-pass hose at the water pump, heater hose at the rear of the manifoild. Remove and tag all fuel lines and vacuum lines from the intake manifold.
3. Remove all the air injection pump hoses from the intake manifold area. Remove the throttle cable and the T.V. cable.
4. Remove the drive belts, generator rear brace, A/C compressor rear brace and all necessary electrical leads.
5. Remove the computer command control solenoid assembly and the idle load compensator with bracket assembly. Remove the EGR valve.
6. Remove the intake manifold retaining bolts and remove the intake manifold from the vehicle.
7. Installation is the reverse order of the removal procedure. Be sure to apply a suitable RTV sealant to the head side of the manifold gasket and to the corners of the front and rear manifold seals.

HT4100 ENGINE

NOTE: Some 1984-85 Cadillac models equipped with the HT4100 V8 engine have been experiencing oil leakage at the intake manifold-to-block seal, due to a split intake manifold seal. When repairing this leak, replace the old seal with a new silcone seal (Part #3634619) The new seal is easily identified by its gray color.

1. Disconnect the negative battery cable. Drain the coolant into a suitable drain pan and disconnect the upper radiator hose from the thermostat housing.
2. Disconnect the following electrical connections and position the wiring harness out of the way; coolant sensor, mass airflow temperature sensor, throttle position sensor, four-way connector at the distributor, idle speed control motor and fuel injectors.
3. Disconnect the heater hose from the nipple at the rear of the intake manifold. Disconnect the fuel inlet and return lines from the throttle body.
4. Remove the distributor as previously outlined in this section. Remove both rocker arm covers. Remove the rocker arm support with the rocker arms intact by first alternately and

CADILLAC
DE VILLE • FLEETWOOD

evenly removing the four bolts followed by the five nuts. Keep the pushrods in sequence so they may be reassembled in their original positions.

5. Partially remove the A/C compressor and do not discharge the A/C system. Remove the vacuum harness connections from the TVS at the rear of the intake manifold.

6. Remove the 16 intake manifold bolts and remove the two bolts securing the lower thermostat hgousing to the front cover. Remove the engine lift brackets or bend them out of the way.

7. Remove the intake manifold and lower the thermostat housing as an assembly by lifting it straight up off of the dowels.

8. Installation is the reverse order of the removal procedure. Apply a suitable RTV Sealant to the four corners where the end seals will meet the side gaskets, place the end seals into position, then again apply the RTV selant to the four corners. Apply a suitable thread sealer to the manifold retaining bolts.

NOTE: The right intake manifold gasket for the 1985 and later models, contains a restrictor which controls the flow of the exhaust gas into the intake manifold. The gaskets that do not have this restrictor are identified by a tab which protrudes from between the cylinder head ans the intake manifold. On the left side of the engine the tab will protrude from the rear of the engine. If a gasket without a restrictor is used ont he right side of the engine the tab will protrude from the front of the engine. The manifold gasket with the restrictor has "Right Bank" printed on it to aid identification when the gasket is out of the vehicle.

6.0L ENGINE

1. Disconnect the negative battery cable. Drain the cooling system.

2. Remove all the necessary components in order to gain access to the intake manifold retaining bolts.

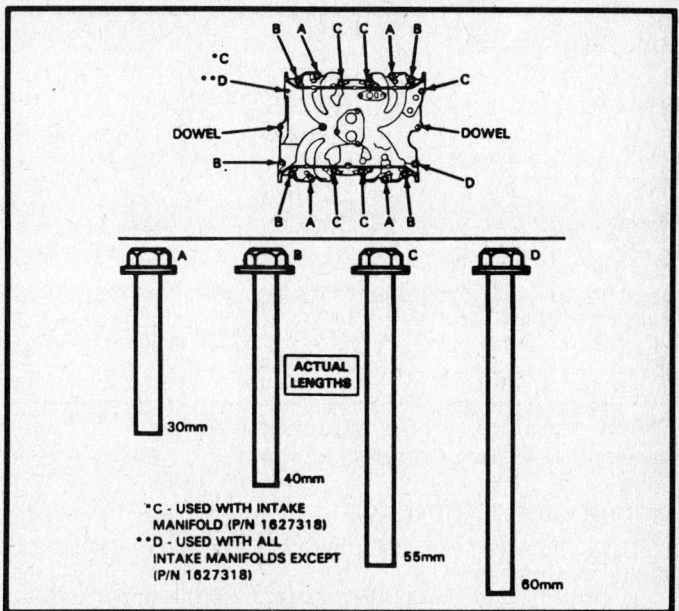

Intake manifold bolt size and installation sequence—1985 and later HT4100 V8 engine

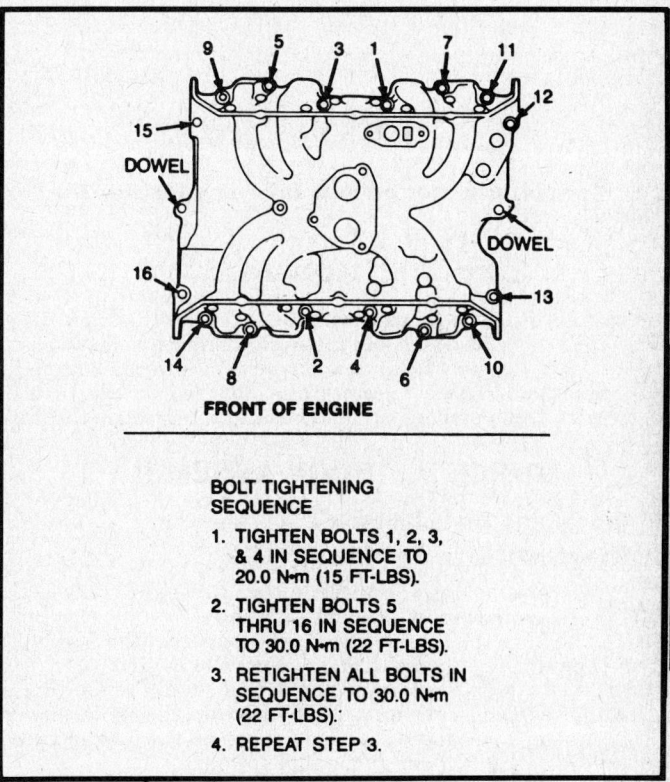

Intake manifold bolt torque sequence—HT4100 V8 engine

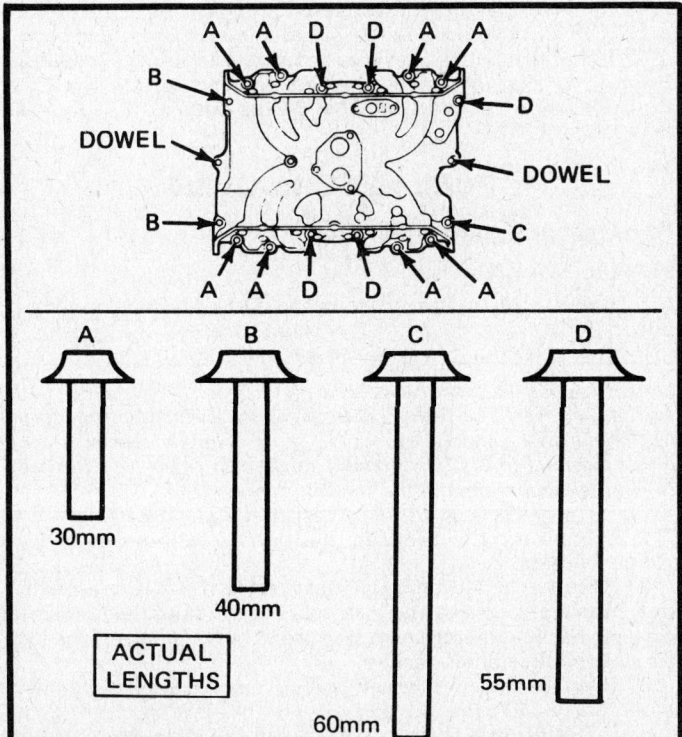

Intake manifold bolt size and installation sequence—1983-84 HT4100 V8 engine

3. On some vehicles it may be necessary to remove the distributor assembly or discharge the air condition.

4. Remove the intake manifold retaining bolts. Remove the intake manifold from the vehicle.

5. Installation is the reverse of the removal procedure. Be sure to torque the manifold retaining bolts to specification.

SECTION 14

CADILLAC
DE VILLE • FLEETWOOD

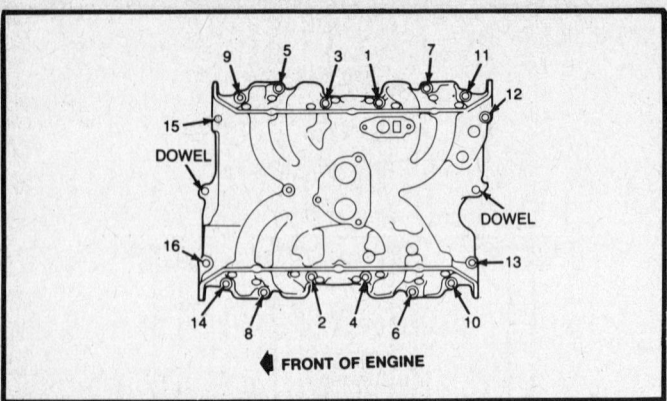

Intake manifold torque sequence—V8
(© General Motors Corporation)

5.7L DIESEL ENGINE

1. Disconnect the negative battery cable and remove the air cleaner assembly.
2. Drain the radiator, then disconnect the upper radiator hose and thermostat bypass hose from the coolant outley. Also disconnect the heater hose and vacuum hose from the water control valve.
3. Remove the breather pipes from the valve covers and air crossover. Remove the air crossover and cap the intake manifold with a suitable cover.
4. Disconnect the throttle rod and return spring. If equipped with cruise control remove the servo.
5. Remove the clip at the bellcrank, disconnect the cables, then remove the throttle and T.V. or detent cable brackets on the intake manifold and position the cables out of the way.
6. Disconnect and tag all necessary wiring. Disconnect and or remove the generator and air conditioning compressor brackets as necessary. The air conditioning lines at the compressor are flexible and should be left attached to the compressor.
7. Disconnect the fuel line from the fuel pump and fuel filter and remove the fuel filter bracket.
8. Disconnect the fuel line at the injector nozzles, using a back-up wrench on all the nozzles. Remove the injection pump and cap all open fuel lines and fittings on the injection pump, filter and nozzles. Do not bend injection lines.
9. Disconnect the fuel return line from the injection pump. Disconnect the vacuum lines at the vacuum pump and remove the drain tube.
10. Remove the intake manifold bolts, then remove the intake manifold. Remove the adapter seal.
11. Installation is the reverse order of the removal procedure. Refer to the diesel unit repair section in this book for the injection pump timing.

Fuel Injection System

For More Information on Fuel Injection, Refer to the Unit Repair Section.

DESCRIPTION AND TYPE

Most vehicles are equipped with Digital Fuel Injection (DFI). Fuel Injection consists of fuel metering valves, which, when actuated, spray a calculated quantity of fuel into the engine intake manifold. These injectors are mounted on the throttle body with the metering tip pointed into the throttle throats.

THROTTLE BODY ASSEMBLY

Removal and Installation

HT4100 ENGINE

1. Before removing the throttle body assembly, relieve the fuel pressure in the fuel system as follows:
   a. Remove the fuse marked fuel pump from the fuse block in the passenger compartment. Start the engine.
   b. Let the engine run until the fuel supply remaining in the fuel system is exhausted. When the engine stalls, engage the starter three more times to be sure all the fuel and pressure has been run out of the fuel system.
   c. Turn the ignition to the off position and replace the fuel pump fuse.
2. Disconnect thenegative battery cable and the following electrical connections at the following components; throttle position sensor, idle speed control motor and both fuel injectors.
3. Remove the throttle return springs, cruise control and the throttle linkage along with the downshift cable.
4. Disconnect the lines and or vacuum hose from the following components; fuel inlet line, fuel return line, brake booster vacuum line, manifold absolute pressure sensor vacuum hose and all necessary air injection lines.
5. Disconnect and tag the PCV, EGR and other emission hoses from the front of the throttle body.
6. Remove the three throttle body mounting bolts and remove the throttle body assembly along with the old gasket.
7. Installation is the reverse order of the removal procedure. Be sure to install a new base gasket and torque the three mounting bolts to 11 ft. lbs. Make any adjustment as necessary.

FUEL METER COVER

Removal and Installation

HT4100 ENGINE

1. Relieve the fuel pressure in the fuel system as previously outlined.

──────────── **CAUTION** ────────────
Do not remove the four screws securing the pressure regulator to the fuel meter cover. The fuel pressure regulator includes a large spring under a heavy compression which, if accidentally released, could cause personal injury. Disassembly might also cause a fuel leak between the diaphragm and the regulator container.

2. Disconnect the negative battery cable. Remove the air cleaner assembly.
3. Remove the electrical connections to the fuel injector. Remove the eight screws and lockwashers securing the fuel meter cover to the fuel meter body. Be sure to make a note of the location of the four short screws.
3. Remove the fuel meter cover from the fuel meter body assembly.
4. Installation is the reverse order of the removal procedure. Be sure to install a new dust seal into the recess on the fuel meter body. Install a new fuel return passage gasket and torque the retaining screws to 28 in. lbs.

CADILLAC
DE VILLE · FLEETWOOD
SECTION 14

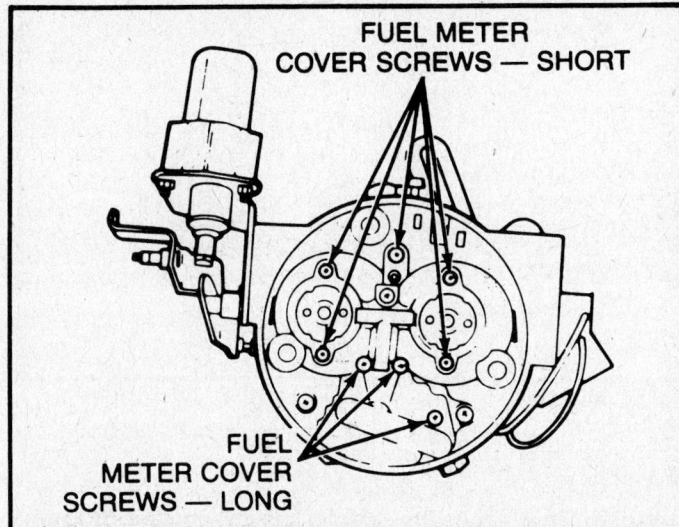

Removing the fuel meter cover

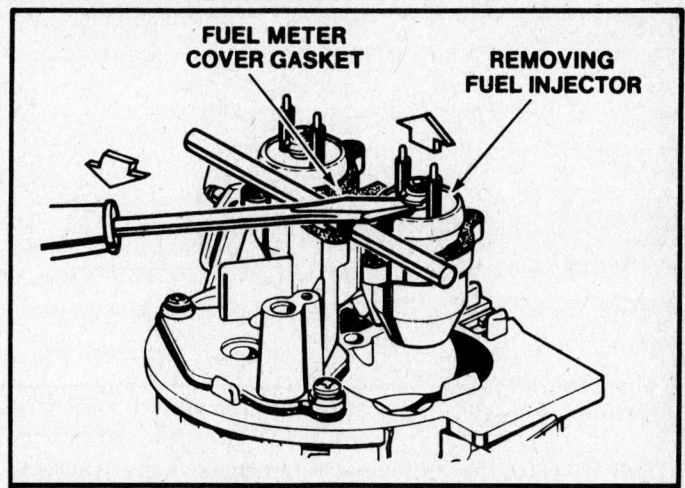

Fuel injector removal

FUEL INJECTOR

Removal and Installation

HT4100 ENGINE

1. Relieve the fuel pressure in the fuel system as previously outlined. Disconnect the negative battery cable. Remove the air cleaner assembly.
2. Disconnect the electrical connector from the fuel injector. Remove the fuel meter cover as previously outlined.
3. With the fuel meter cover in place to prevent damage to the casting, use a suitable tool and lift the injector carefully until it is free from the fuel meter body.
4. Remove the small O-ring from the nozzle end of the injector. Carefully rotate the injector fuel filter back and forth and remove the filter from the base of the injector. Remove and discard the fuel meter cover gasket.
5. Remove the large O-ring and steel back-up washer from the top counterbore of the fuel meter body injector cavity. Remove the other injector in the same way.
6. Installation is the revere order of the removal procedure. Be sure to install all new gaskets, O-rings and washers. The back-up washer and large O-ring must be installed before the injector, or improper seating of the large O-ring could cause a fuel leak.

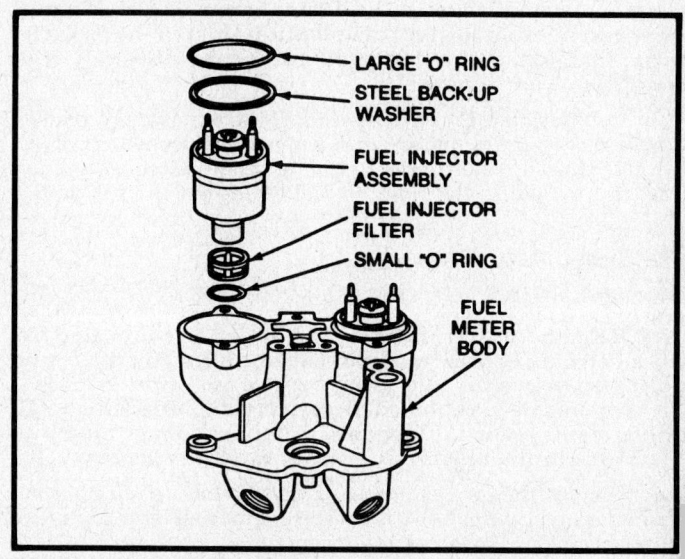

Exploded view of the fuel injector components

FUEL METER BODY

Removal and Installation

HT4100 ENGINE

1. Relieve the fuel pressure in the fuel system as previously outlined.

---- CAUTION ----

Do not remove the four screws securing the pressure regulator to the fuel meter cover. The fuel pressure regulator includes a large spring under a heavy compression which, if accidentally released, could cause personal injury. Disassembly might also cause a fuel leak between the diaphragm and the regulator container.

2. Disconnect the negative battery cable. Remove the air cleaner assembly.
3. Remove the electrical connections to the fuel injector. Remove the eight screws and lockwashers securing the fuel meter cover to the fuel meter body. Be sure to make a note of the location of the four short screws.

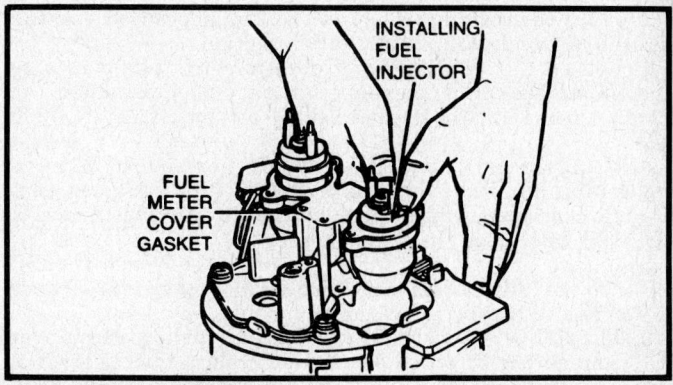

Fuel injector installation

3. Remove the fuel meter cover from the fuel meter body assembly.
4. Remove the fuel injectors as previously outlined. Remove the fuel inlet and fuel outlet nuts and gaskets from the fuel meter body.

14-25

SECTION 14

CADILLAC
DE VILLE • FLEETWOOD

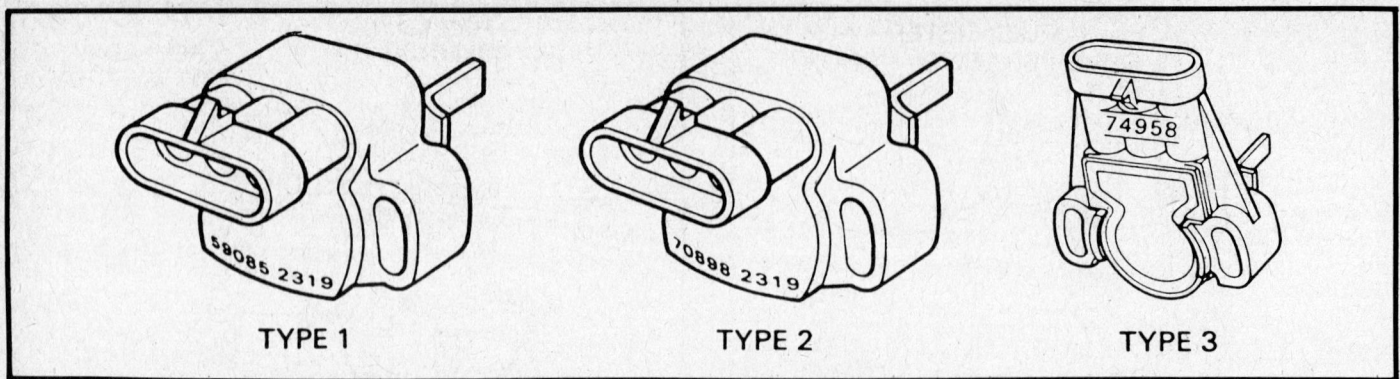

Three different types of throttle position sensors used on Cadillac models

5. Remove the three screws and lockwashers, then remove the fuel meter body from the throttle body assembly, along with the fuel meter body insulator gasket.

NOTE: Do not remove the center screw and staking at each end holding the fuel distribution shirt in the throttle body. The skirt is an integral part of the throttle body and is not serviced separately.

6. Installation is the reverse order of the removal procedure. Install new gaskets and O-rings where ever needed. Apply a suitable thread sealer to the retaining screws. Torque the fuel inlet nut to 30.0 ft. lbs. and the fuel outlet nut to 21.0 ft. lbs.

Idle Speed Adjustment
HT4100 ENGINE

NOTE: The 4.1L DFI engine idle speed, is controlled by the electronic control module. The idle adjustment is only necessary when the idle speed control motor or the throttle body has been replaced. Before making this idle speed adjustment, record, diagnosis, repair and clear all trouble codes in the electronic control module memory.

1. Remove the air cleaner assembly. Connect a suitable tachometer and timing light. Start the engine and let it run until it reaches normal operating temperature.
2. Turn the A/C and all the accessories off. Check and adjust the ignition timing (the cooling fan should not be running during any adjustments).
3. Place the steering wheel in the center position and the transmission selector in the "Park" position.
3. Retract the idle speed control motor (ISC) plunger. to do this, unlock the ISC motor connector, but do not disconnect the motor. Open the throttle and hold it at approximately 1500 rpm.
4. Using the same hand, close the throttle switch by depressing the ISC plunger. When the plunger is fully retracted, continue to hold the throttle open and the throttle switch closed, while disconnecting the ISC motor.
5. Return the throttle to idle. Be sure not to power the ISC motor in the fully retracred position for more than four seconds or damage to the elctronic control module may occur.
6. The ISC plunger should now be retracted. If the plunger still contacts the throttle lever, turn the plunger in so it is not touching. With the ISC plunger fully retracted and not touching the throttle lever, the idle speed should be 450 rpm.
7. Check the throttle position sensor adjustment. With the ISc motor fully retracted and the throttle against the stop screw. Turn the ISC plunger adjustment screw to obtain a .160 in. gap between the throttle lever and the plunger.
8. Shut the engine off, disconnect all the test equipment and plug in all harness connectors. Turn the ignition off for a least 10 seconds. Start the engine and check the ISC motor for proper operation.

NOTE: This procedure could have recorded intermittent trouble codes in the DFI computer. After all the connections have been made and the system is restored to normal operations, these codes must be cleared.

Throttle Position Sensor
HT4100 ENGINE

NOTE: The throttle position adjustment screw is factiry sealed. There should be no adjustment necessary, unless indicated by the Computer Command Control System performance check. It will be necessary to use a high impedance digital volymeter to measure the voltages during the following adjustment procedure.

1. Place the ignition switch in the "ON" position, but do not start the engine. With the throttle closed against the stop screw, measure and record the voltage at the throttle position sensor terminals "B" the gray wire and "C" the black & white wire.
2. Connect the positive lead of the voltmeter to the throttle position sensor harness test point at terminal "A" the dark blue wire. Connect the negative lead to terminal "B" the gray wire. Set the voltmeter on the two volt DC scale. Measure and record the throttle position sensor voltage between the terminals "A" and "B".
3. The following list should be used to determine the correct throttle position sensor voltage:
   a. If the voltage is less 4.90, the throttle position sensor voltage should be .48 volts at idle.
   b. If the voltage is 4.90 to 5.10, the throttle position sensor voltage should be .50 at idle.
   c. If the voltage is 5.11 to 5.30, the throttle position sensor voltage should be .52 at idle.
   d. If the voltage is more than 5.30, the throttle position sensor voltage should be .54 at idle.
4. Determine the correct throttle position sensor voltage by using the list outlined above. To adjust the throttle position sensor voltage, loosen the attaching screws and rotate the throttle position sensor, until the correct voltage is obtained. Recheck the throttle position sensor voltage after tightening the attaching screws and re-adjust if necessary.

NOTE: The 1981-85 Cadillac models equipped with Digital Fuel Injection (DFI), may expierence a high idle and or an intermittent code 26. This problem could be caused by the installation of the wrong throttle position sensor. To correct the problem, check the throttle position sensor on the vehicle in question and be sure it is the right throttle position sensor mfor that vehicle. The foolowing are the proper throttle position sensors:

14-26

CADILLAC
DE VILLE • FLEETWOOD
SECTION 14

a. Type one is for the 1981-84 6.0L (368) V-8-6-4, the part number is 17067979 and the throttle position sensor identification number is 59085. This one is used on all 1981 models and the 1981 and later limousine models.

b. Type two is for the HT4100 engine, the part number is 17078259 and the throttle position sensor identification number is 70898. This one is used on all 1981 and later FWD models, except the limousine.

c. Type three is for the HT4100 engine, the part number is 17110352 and the throttle position sensor identification number is 74958. This one is used on all 1981 and later Eldorado/Seville FWD models, 1981 and later Deville and Fleetwood (and the Fleetwood Brougham) RWD models.

EMISSION CONTROL SYSTEM

CARBURETOR MODELS

Calibrated Carburetion
Catalytic Converter
Early Fuel Evaporation (EFE)
Exhaust Gas Recirculation (EGR)
Positive Crankcase Ventilation (PCV)
Electric Choke
Thermostatic Air Cleaner (TAC)
Evaporative Emissions Control (EEC)
Computer Command Control (CCC)
Electronic Spark Timing (EST)
Oxygen Sensor
Manifold Absolute Pressure Sensor (MAP)
Air Management System
Air Injection Reactor (AIR)
Air Control Valve (ACV)
Air Management Valve (AMgV)
Air Solenoid Valve (ASV)
Air Temperature Sensor (ATS)
Back Pressure EGR (BPEGR)
Charcoal Canister
Canister Purge (CP)
Deceleration Valve (DV)
EGR Control Solenoid (EGRCS)
Pulse Air Injector (PAIR)
Pulse Air Solenoid (PAS)
Pulse Air Shutoff Valve (PSV)
Pulse Air Valve (PV)
Thermal Vacuum Switch (TVS)
Thermal Vacuum Valve (TVV)
Vacuum Pump (VP)

DIESEL MODELS

EGR Vacuum Switch (EGRVS)
Vacuum Pump (VP)
Exhaust Gas Recirculation (EGR)
Exhaust Pressure Regulator (EPR)
Flow Control Valve
EGR Solenoid (EGR-SOL)
EPR Solenoid (EPR-SOL)
Transmission Vacuum Valve (TRV)
Thermal Vacuum Valve (TVV)
Vacuum Regulator Valve (VRV)

DIGITAL FUEL INJECTION MODELS

Calibrated Carburetion
Catalytic Converter
Early Fuel Evaporation (EFE)
Exhaust Gas Recirculation (EGR)
Positive Crankcase Ventilation (PCV)
Electric Choke
Thermostatic Air Cleaner (TAC)
Evaporative Emission Control (EEC)
Manifold Absolute Pressure Sensor (MAP)
Manifold Air Temperature Sensor (MAT)
Oxygen Sensor (OXS)
Air Management System
Air Pump-Control Valve (AP-CV)
Air Switching Valve (ASV)
Check Valve (CV)
Canister Purge - Solenoid (CP-SOL)
Exhaust Gas Recirculation - Solenoid (EGR-SOL)
Exhaust Gas Recirculation - Signal Solenoid (EGR-S/SOL)
Early Fuel Evaporation - Thermal Vacuum Switch (EFE-TVS)

SCHEDULE I

Follow Schedule I if your car is mainly operated under one or more of the following conditions:
- When most trips are less than 4 miles (6 kilometers).
- When most trips are less than 10 miles (16 kilometers) and outside temperatures remain below freezing.
- Idling for extended periods and/or low-speed operations such as found in delivery, police, rental or taxi operation.
- Towing a trailer.
- Operating in dusty areas.

ITEM NO.	TO BE SERVICED	WHEN TO PERFORM Miles (Kilometers) or Months, Whichever Occurs First	MILES (000)	3	6	9	12	15	18	21	24	27	30	33	36	39	42	45	48
			KILOMETERS (000)	5	10	15	20	25	30	35	40	45	50	55	60	65	70	75	80
1	Engine Oil & Oil Filter Change*	Every 3,000 mi. (5 000 km) or 3 mos.		•	•	•	•	•	•	•	•	•	•	•	•	•	•	•	•
2	Chassis Lubrication	Every other oil change			•		•		•		•		•		•		•		•
3	Carburetor Choke and Hose Inspection*	At 6,000 mi. (10 000 km) and every 30,000 mi. (50 000 km)			•								•••						
4	Carb. or Throttle Body Mtg. Bolt Torque*	At 6,000 mi. (10 000 km) only		••															
5	Vac. or A.I.R. Pump Drive Belt Insp.*	Every 30,000 mi. (50 000 km) or 24 mos.											•••						
6	Cooling System Service*														•				

14-27

SECTION 14

CADILLAC
DE VILLE • FLEETWOOD

SCHEDULE I

Follow Schedule I if your car is mainly operated under one or more of the following conditions:
- When most trips are less than 4 miles (6 kilometers).
- When most trips are less than 10 miles (16 kilometers) and outside temperatures remain below freezing.
- Idling for extended periods and/or low-speed operations such as found in delivery, police, rental or taxi operation.
- Towing a trailer.
- Operating in dusty areas.

ITEM NO.	TO BE SERVICED	WHEN TO PERFORM Miles (Kilometers) or Months, Whichever Occurs First	The services shown in this schedule up to 48,000 miles (80 000 km) are to be performed after 48,000 miles at the same intervals														
		MILES (000)	3	6	9	12	15	18	21	24	27	30	33	36	39	42	45	48
		KILOMETERS (000)	5	10	15	20	25	30	35	40	45	50	55	60	65	70	75	80
7	Wheel Bearing Repack (Rear Wheel Drive Cars Only)	See explanation for service interval in text.																
8	Transmission/Transaxle Service																	
9	Spark Plug and Wire Service*	Every 30,000 mi. (50 000 km)										•**						
10	PCV Valve Insp.*											•						
11	EGR System Service*	Every 30,000 mi. (50 000 km) or 36 mos.										•						
12	Air Cleaner & PCV Filter Repl.*											•**						
13	Eng. Timing Check*											•						
14	Fuel Tank, Cap & Lines Insp.*	Every 30,000 mi. (50 000 km)										•						
15	Thermostatically Controlled Air Cleaner*											•						

SCHEDULE II

Follow Schedule II only if none of the above conditions apply.

ITEM NO.	TO BE SERVICED	WHEN TO PERFORM Miles (Kilometers) or Months, Whichever Occurs First	The services shown in this schedule up to 45,000 miles (75 000 km) are to be performed after 45,000 miles at the same intervals					
		MILES (000)	7.5	15	22.5	30	37.5	45
		KILOMETERS (000)	12.5	25	37.5	50	62.5	75
1	Engine Oil Change*	Every 7,500 mi. (12 500 km) or 12 mos.	•	•	•	•	•	•
	Oil Filter Change*	At first and every other oil change	•		•		•	
2	Chassis Lubrication	Every 7,500 mi. (12 500 km) or 12 mos.	•	•	•	•	•	•
3	Carburetor Choke and Hose Inspection*	At 7,500 mi. (12 500 km) and then every 30,000 mi. (50 000 km)	•			•**		
4	Carb. or Throttle Body Mtg. Bolt Torque*	At 7,500 mi. (12 500 km) only	•**					
5	Vac. or A.I.R. Pump Drive Belt Insp.*	Every 30,000 mi. (50 000 km) or 24 mos.				•**		
6	Cooling System Service*					•		
7	Wheel Bearing Repack (Rear Wheel Drive Cars Only)	Every 30,000 mi. (50 000 km)				•		
8	Transmission/Transaxle Service	See explanation for service interval in text.						
9	Spark Plug and Wire Service*	Every 30,000 mi. (50 000 km)				•**		
10	PCV Valve Insp.*					•		
11	EGR System Service*	Every 30,000 mi. (50 000 km) or 36 mos.				•**		
12	Air Cleaner & PCV Filter Repl.*					•		
13	Eng. Timing Check*	Every 30,000 mi. (50 000 km)				•		
14	Fuel Tank, Cap & Lines Insp.*					•		
15	Thermostatically Controlled Air Cleaner*					•		

*An Emission Control Service.
**In California, these are the minimum Emission Control Maintenance Services an owner must perform according to the California Air Resources Board. General Motors, however, urges that all Emission Control Maintenance Services shown above be performed. To maintain your other new car warranties, all services shown in this booklet should be performed.

NORMAL CAR USE

The maintenance items shown in Schedules I and II are based on the assumption that your car will be used as designed:
- To carry passengers and cargo within the limits shown on the tire label located on the edge of the driver's door,
- On paved road surfaces within legal driving limits,
- On unleaded gasoline.

Emission equipment maintenance schedule

CADILLAC
DE VILLE • FLEETWOOD
SECTION 14

GASOLINE ENGINE SECTION

NOTE: When servicing the 4.1L V8 engine which is constructed largely of aluminum, particular care must be exercised to accommodate the characteristics of this material. Refer to the Diesel Section, Unit Repair, For Overhaul Information on 5.7L (350) V8 Diesel Engine.

ENGINE ASSEMBLY

Removal and Installation

V8 – GAS ENGINE

1. Disconnect the negative battery cable.
2. Remove hood, after scribing hood hinge outline for proper alignment.
3. Re000027ir cleaner and heat shroud.
4. Drain cooling system. Unfasten the fender struts from the radiator shroud.
5. Remove radiator hose bracket, radiator cover and fan.
6. Remove upper radiator hose.
7. Disconnect throttle and cruise control linkage at carburetor.
8. Disconnect the brake vacuum hose from the vacuum pipe. Remove cruise control power unit on cars so equipped.
9. Disconnect power steering pump bracket and swing pump out of way with hoses still connected. Position power steering fluid cooler out of the way.
10. Remove A/C compressor bracket bolts and swing compressor out of way with hoses still connected. Do not discharge system.
11. Disconnect temperature sender wire, idle speed-up wire (if so equipped), ignition primary wire, downshift switch wire, S.C.S. solenoid (if so equipped) and anti-dieseling solenoid wires, electronic ignition connector, block temperature sender lead, and all ground straps. On fuel injected engines, disconnect the EFI manifold harness and all necessary wires, move them out of the way.
12. Bend back clips and position wiring harness out of the way.
13. Disconnect all vacuum hoses, and purge hose from E.L.C. canister. Disconnect the automatic level control line, on models so equipped.
14. Disconnect alternator, heater switch and oil pressure sender wires.
15. Remove wiring harness from clips.
16. Remove water hose from fitting at rear of right-hand cylinder head.
17. Looses and remove alternator and A.I.R. pumps and remove belts.
18. Disconnect tie struts and swing out of the way.
19. Raise the car and support safely. Remove the six engine-to-transmission bolts and remove each engine mount through bolt.
20. Relieve fuel pressure on fuel injected cars.
21. Support the engine and transmission with separate jacks.
22. Remove starter motor, then disconnect exhaust pipes from manifolds.
23. Remove the four bolts attaching the flywheel inspection cover to the transmission and remove the cover.
24. Remove the bolts attaching the flywheel to the converter.
25. Disconnect and plug the fuel line and the vapor return line at the fuel pump.
26. Lower the car to the ground.
27. Connect a lifting bracket to the engine.
28. Support transmission with a wood-padded floor jack.
29. Raise engine slightly and pull forward to disengage from transmission, then pull engine up and out.
30. Installation is the reverse of removal.

V8 – DIESEL ENGINE

1. Drain cooling system.
2. Remove air cleaner.
3. Mark hood hinges and remove hood.
4. Disconnect negative battery cables at batteries and ground wires at inner fender panel. Disconnect engine ground strap, right read to cowl.
5. Disconnect radiator hoses, cooler lines, heater hoses, vacuum hoses, power steering pump hoses at power steering gear, air conditioning compressor with brackets and hoses attached, fuel hose from fuel pump and wiring.
6. Remove hairpin clip at bellcrank.
7. Remove throttle and T.V. cables from intake manifold brackets, then position cables away from engine.
8. Remove upper radiator support and radiator.
9. Raise car and support safely.
10. Disconnect exhaust pipes at manifold.
11. Remove torque converter cover and 3 bolts holding converter to flywheel.
12. Remove engine mount bolts or nuts.
13. Remove 3 bolts, transmission to engine on the right side. Disconnect wires from starter and remove starter.
14. Lower car. Secure lift chain to engine.
15. Place board on top of jack and slightly raise transmission. Remove three left transmission to engine bolts. Remove engine.
16. Installation is the reverse of the removal procedure.

ENGINE MOUNTS

Removal and Installation

HT4100 Engine

1. Disconnect the negative battery cable.
2. Remove the two screws on each side securing the radiator cover to the strut support rods. Loosen the one screw on each side and position the support rods out of the way.
3. Remove the two screws securing the upper radiator shroud to the radiator cover. Remove the clip securing the upper shroud to the lower shroud and position the upper shroud so the fan will not hit when the engine is raised.
4. Raise the vehicle and support it safely.
3. Remove the engine through mount bolt. Raise the engine and support it properly.
4. Raise the engine until the bracket is free from the engine mount. Remove the engine mount retaining nuts and bolts. Remove the engine mount by pulling it straight back.
5. Installation is the reverse of the removal procedure.

Valve System

VALVE ADJUSTMENT

All Cadillac engines use hydraulic lifters. Valve systems with hydraulic lifters operate with zero clearance in the valve train. The rocker arms are nonadjustable. The lifter itself will compensate if there is slack in the system but if there is excessive play, the entire system should be examined.

VALVE LIFTERS

Removal and Installation

1. Disconnect the negative battery cable.
2. Remove the intake manifold assembly.

3. Remove the valve covers. Remove the rocker arm assemblies and the push rods.
4. Using the proper valve lifter removal tool, remove the valve lifters.
5. Installation is the reverse of the removal procedure. Be sure to coat the lifters in clean engine oil before installing them.

VALVE ROCKER ASSEMBLY OR ROCKER ARM PIVOT

Removal and Installation

4.1L (HT 4100) V8 ENGINE

1. Remove the rocker arm covers and necessary components.
2. Remove the valve train support by removing 5 nuts from the stud-headed cylinder head bolts and remove the valve train support with the rocker arms and pivots attached as an assembly.

NOTE: This method of removal is preferred as the pivot assemblies may be damaged if the pivot bolt torque is not removed evenly against the valve spring tension.

3. Secure the support assembly in a vise or other holder and individually remove the rocker arms and pivots.
4. When installing new components, thoroughly lubricate all parts.
5. With the valve train support secured in a vise or other holder, position the rocker arms and pivots to the valve train support. Loosely install the pivot bolts on all studs and torque each to 20 ft. lbs. (30 Nm).
6. Position the pushrod into the seat of each rocker arm and loosely install the five retaining nuts.
7. Recheck the pushrods for being seated correctly. Tighten the five nuts alternately and evenly, checking the position of the pushrods while tightening.
8. When the nuts have been seated and the pushrods are correct, tighten the nuts to 35 ft. lbs. (50Nm) torque.
9. Install the valve cover and necessary components.

6.0L (368) V8 ENGINES

These engines feature a modulated displacement design that can operate 8, 6 or 4 cylinders depending on driving requirements. The selective operation of the number of cylinders is controlled by a microprocessor that operates 4 engine valve selector units. The selector units are electromechanical devices which can deactivate both the intake and exhaust valves of a cylinder.

NOTE: The modulated displacement engine is used in limousine and commercial chassis only from 1982 and later.

5.0L ENGINE

1. Disconnect the negative battery cable.
2. Tag and disconnect any electrical leads or hoses preventing access to the valve cover bolts.
3. Remove the valve cover bolts. Remove the valve covers. Discard the old gasket material.
4. Remove the rocker arm shaft retaining bolts. If only the push rod is to be replaced, loosen the rocker arm shaft retaining bolts and swing the arm so as to clear the push rod.
5. Remove the rocker arm shaft assembly.
6. Remove the rocker arms.
7. Installation is the reverse of the removal procedure. Use new gasket material on the valve covers. When ever new rocker arms and/or rockers rocker arm balls are being installed, coat the bearing surface of the rocker arm and rocker balls with a thin even coating of Molykote® or equivalent.

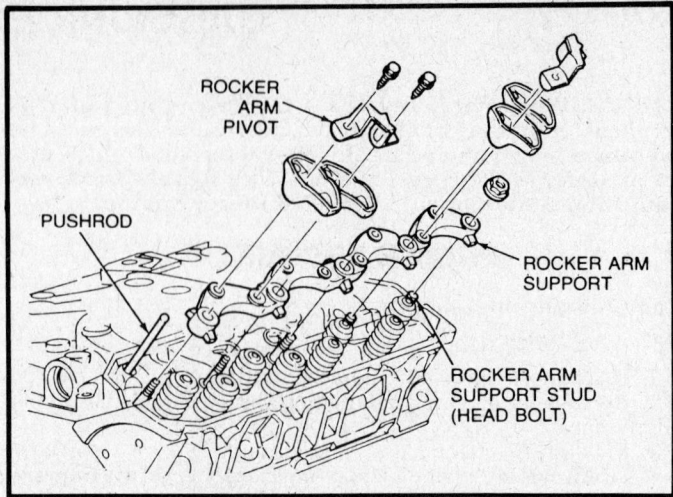

Rocker arm assembly, 4.1L (HT4100) V8 engine
(© General Motors Corporation)

5.7L DIESEL

1. Remove the valve covers.
2. Remove the rocker arm flanged bolts, pivot and rocker arms.
3. Remove each set, 1 per cylinder, as a unit.
4. To install, position 1 set of rocker arms, for 1 cylinder, in their proper location.
5. Bleed the lifters down prior to rocker arm installation or before starting the engine to avoid valve to piston interference.
6. Lubricate all wear points and install the bolts.
7. Torque the bolts to 28 ft. lbs. (38 Nm).
8. Install the valve covers.

VALVE LIFTER BLEED DOWN

If the intake manifold has been removed, and if any rocker arms have been loosened or removed; it will be necessary to remove those valve lifters, disassemble, drain, then reassemble the lifters.

If the intake manifold has not been removed, but rocker arms have been loosened or removed, valve lifters can be bled down by the following procedure:

1. Before installing any removed rocker arms, rotate the engine crankshaft to a position of No. 1 cylinder being 32° before top dead center. This is 2.0 in. (50 mm) counter clockwise from the 0° pointer. It may be necessary to remove No. 1 cylinder's glow plug to determine if the position of the piston is correct. The compression pressure will tell if it is in the right position.

NOTE: Use only hand wrenches to torque the rocker arm pivot bolts to avoid engine damage.

2. If removed, install remaining rocker arms except No. 3 exhaust valve (if this rocker arm was removed).
3. If removed, install but do not torque No. 3 exhaust valve pivot beyond the point that the valve would be fully open. This is indicated by strong resistance while still turning the pivot retaining bolts. Going beyond this would bend the push rod. Torque the bolts SLOWLY, allowing the lifter to bleed down.
4. Finish torquing No. 5 cylinder rocker arm pivot bolt SLOWLY. Do not go beyond the point that the valve would be fully open. This is indicated by strong resistance while still turning the pivot retaining bolts. Going beyond this would bend the push rod.
5. DO NOT turn the engine crankshaft for at least 45 minutes.

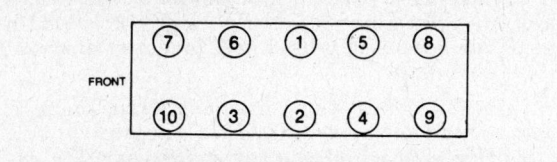

Cylinder head bolt torque sequence—V8
(© General Motors Corporation)

6. Finish reassembling the engine as the lifters are being bled.

NOTE: Do not rotate the engine until the valve lifters have been bled down, or damage to the engine will occur.

VALVE TIMING

Adjustment

Engine valve timing can be checked by referring to the intake valve opening specifications and checking this specification when either the number one or the number six cylinder pistons are at TDC, at the beginning of their respective firing strokes. Measure the intake valve opening on the particular cylinder that is on its firing stroke.

CYLINDER HEAD

Removal and Installation

4.1L (HT 4100) V8 ENGINE

1. Disconnect the negative battery cable. Drain the engine coolant.
2. Remove the intake and exhaust manifolds.
3. Disconnect all electrical and ground connections from the cylinder head.
4. When removing the left cylinder head, partially remove the power steering pump.
5. When removing the right cylinder head, remove the alternator and the heater hose from the rear of the head.
6. Remove the A.I.R. pump, if so equipped.
7. Remove bolts holding the rocker arm cover to the heads and remove the cover.
8. Remove nuts holding the rocker arm support to cylinder head, then remove the support and rocker arm assemblies. Store these assemblies so that they may be reinstalled in their correct locations.
9. Remove pushrods and store them with their respective rocker arm assemblies.
10. Remove 10 cylinder head bolts.
11. Lift cylinder head off the block.

NOTE: Install cylinder liner holders to prevent loss of bottom seal.

12. Remove all gasket material from the cylinder head and block mating surfaces.
13. Install by reversing removal procedures.
14. When torquing the head bolts, use the three-step method. Torque the bolts to $1/3$ of the total torque listed in the sequence shown. Once this is done, repeat the same procedure, this time torquing all the bolts to $2/3$ of the total listed torque. Finally torque the bolts to the recommended torque of 90 ft. lbs.

5.0L AND 6.0L ENGINES

1. Disconnect the negative battery cable.
2. Drain the engine coolant from the radiator. Disconnect the radiator hoses from the intake manifold.
3. Remove the intake manifold as described earlier. Remove the exhaust manifold as outlined earlier.

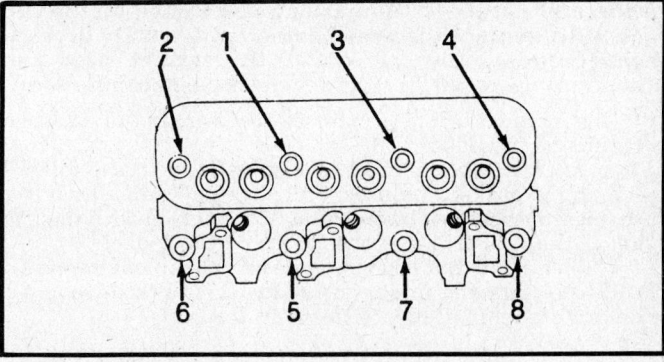

Cylinder head bolt torque sequence—V6
(© General Motors Corporation)

4. Remove the alternator lower mounting bolt and lay aside to gain working clearance.
5. If the vehicle is equipped with power steering, remove the pump and bracket to gain access.
6. Remove the rocker arm covers and the rocker assemblies. Remove the push rods.

NOTE: If the rear cylinder head bolts or push rods (number 7 and 8 cylinders) can not be removed without interference. Remove them together with the cylinder head.

7. Remove all vacuum hoses from the engine assembly. Tag and disconnect spark plug wires.
8. Remove the cylinder head bolts. Remove the cylinder head and discard the old gasket material.
9. Installation is the reverse of the removal procedure. Install the head gasket over the dowel pins, with the note "This Side Up" showing. On engines using a steel gasket, coat both sides with a suitable sealer. Spread the sealer evenly with a paint roller or equivalent. Too much sealer may hold the gasket away from the head or block thus causing a bad seal. Carefully guide the cylinder head over the dowel pins and onto the cylinder block. Apply engine oil to the threads of the head bolts and tighten the head bolts finger tight. Torque the cylinder head bolts gradually and evenly until a they reach the specified torque.

5.7L (350) DIESEL ENGINE

1. Remove the injection pump and lines. Drain cooling system.
2. Remove the intake manifold.
3. Remove the valve covers. Remove any accessory brackets which could interfere with the cylinder head removal or installation.
4. Disconnect the glow plug wiring and remove the ground strap from the right cylinder head.
5. Remove the rocker arm bolts, pivots, rocker arms and the pushrods. Mark the components so that each can be installed in their original positions.
6. Disconnect the exhaust manifolds from the heads and leave them attached to the cross-over pipe.
7. Remove the cylinder head bolts and remove the cylinder head assembly.
8. If necessary to remove the pre-chamber, remove the glow plug and the injection nozzle, then tap the pre-chamber out with a blunt drift.
9. If the pre-chamber was removed, re-install it or a new chamber and seat it to a depth of 0.004 inch below the cylinder head.

NOTE: When replacement of the pre-chamber is necessary, clean the flat surface of the chamber that faces the

piston and not if a 0.010 marking is stamped on the surface. If so, replace the pre-chamber with a 0.010 oversize (deeper) unit. Failure to install the correct sized pre-chamber will result in cylinder head gasket failure.

10. The installation of the cylinder heads are in the reverse of the removal procedure.
11. Guide to correct cylinder head installation are as follows:
   a. Head gaskets are used with a special composition that requires no sealant. Instructions are included with the gasket package or noted on the cylinder head gaskets.
   b. Clean and dip the cylinder head bolts in engine oil. Install the bolts and torque to 100 ft. lbs. in proper sequence and retorque, in sequence to 130 ft. lbs.

CAMSHAFT

Removal and Installation

ALL EXCEPT THE 5.0L ENGINE

1. Drain the cooling system and remove the radiator.
2. Remove the engine front cover and the distributor from the rear of the engine on 4.1L, (HT4100 engines).
3. Remove the oil pump and the oil slinger from the crankshaft.
4. Remove the fuel pump and the fuel pump eccentric from the camshaft.
5. Remove the camshaft sprocket and the timing chain.

NOTE: Make certain that the marks on the 2 sprockets are correctly aligned before removing the timing chain.

6. Remove the lifters and slide the camshaft carefully out of the engine block.

NOTE: Do not allow the camshaft lobes to scratch the camshaft bearings.

7. To install the camshaft, reverse the procedure. Before installation, the camshaft should be lubricated with a thin coat of engine oil and then carefully inserted to avoid bearing damage.
8. The camshaft sprocket screws should be torqued to 18 ft. lbs. while the fuel pump eccentric screw is tightened to 35 ft. lbs.

5.0L ENGINE

1. Disconnect the negative battery cable and drain the cooling system into a suitable drain pan.
2. Remove the intake manifold as previously outlines. Remove the rocker covers, rocker arm assemblies, push rods, and lifters (be sure to note the location of each component for proper installation) as previously outlined.
3. Remove and tag all necessary wires, hoses and vacuum lines. Remove the distributor cap and wiring intact. Disconnect the upper and lower transmission cooler lines.
4. Remove the radiator shroud assembly and radiator. Remove the front grille if necessary. Remove the cooling fan and water pump pulley.
5. Remove the power steering pump if so equipped. Remove the drive belts, alternator, crankshaft pulley and torsional damper.
6. Discharge the A/C system and remove the A/C compressor mount bolts, brackets, accumulator, condensor and compressor (if so equipped) and position it out of the way. Remove the air injection pump with brackets and set it aside.
7. Remove the water pump assembly, remove the front engine cover. Remove the fuel pump and fuel pump push rod. Remove the camshaft thrust button and spring. Rotate the crankshaft and align the timing marks.
8. Remove the camshaft retaining bolt(s), gear and chain. Remove the camshaft retaining plate and camshaft flange adapter and carefully remove the camshaft.

NOTE: The camshaft sprocket is a light fit. If the sprocket does not come off easily a light blow on the lower edge of the sprocket with a soft face mallet should dislodge the sprocket.

9. Installation is the reverse order of the removal procedure. Lubricate the camshaft journals with a suitable engine oil supplement, before installing the camshaft. Once the camshaft has been installed, install the chain on the camshaft sprocket. Hold the sprocket vertically with the chain hanging down and align the marks on the camshaft and crankshaft sprockets.
10. Align the dowel in the camshaft sprocket with the dowel hole in the camshaft sprocket then install the sprocket on the camshaft. Draw the camshaft sprocket onto the camshaft using the mounting bolts. Torque the mounting bolts to specifications.

TIMING CHAIN COVER, CHAIN, AND SPROCKET

Removal and Installation

6.0L (368) V8 ENGINE

NOTE: On 368 cu. in. engines with nylon oil pans, the pan must be removed from the engine, not just loosened.

1. Disconnect negative battery cable and drain cooling system.
2. Detach upper radiator hose retainer from cradle and position hose out of the way.
3. Remove the fan, alternator and power steering belts.
4. Remove four capscrews that secure crank pulley to harmonic balancer, then remove the pulley.
5. Remove the plug from the end of the crankshaft. Install the puller and remove the harmonic balancer.
6. Drain the engine oil. Loosen the oil pan bolts enough to allow the front of the oil pan to drop slightly.

NOTE: It may be necessary to remove the starter to gain access to the bolts that are directly behind it.

7. Disconnect lower radiator hose from water pump, then remove the screws that hold front cover to engine. Remove cover with water pump attached.
8. Remove distributor and fuel pump.
9. Remove oil slinger and fuel pump eccentric.
10. Remove capscrews that secure camshaft sprocket.
11. Remove camshaft sprocket along with timing chain.
12. To install, reverse removal procedure. Mount the timing chain over the camshaft and the crankshaft sprocket and start the camshaft sprocket over the shaft, being certain the aligning dowel is in a position where it will enter the hole in the camshaft freely. Make certain that the timing marks on the sprockets are in line between shaft centers.
13. Camshaft sprockets are a tight fit. However, a comparatively easy way to install a tight-fitting sprocket is to draw it on carefully with 2 bolts somewhat longer than the regular mounting bolts. By drawing alternately against each bolt, and tapping gently with a plastic hammer, even a very tight camshaft gear sprocket can be installed.
14. When the camshaft is secured, turn the engine 2 full revolutions until the timing marks again assume the original position. Check to make certain that the punch marks, which are stamped into the front face of the sprockets, are in line between the shaft centers.

4.1L (HT4100) V8 ENGINE

1. Disconnect the negative battery cable and drain the radiator.
2. On the Fleetwood and Deville models, remove the 2 screws on each side of the radiator securing the support rod. Move the support rods out of the way.

CADILLAC
DE VILLE • FLEETWOOD
SECTION 14

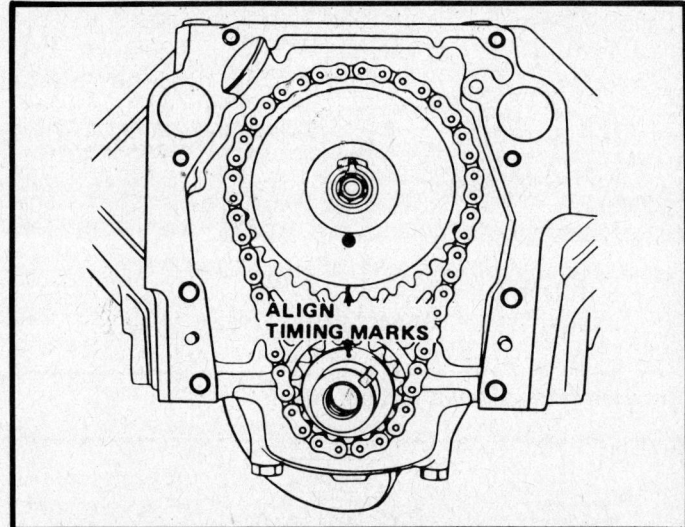

Alignment of timing marks on sprockets, typical
(© General Motors Corporation)

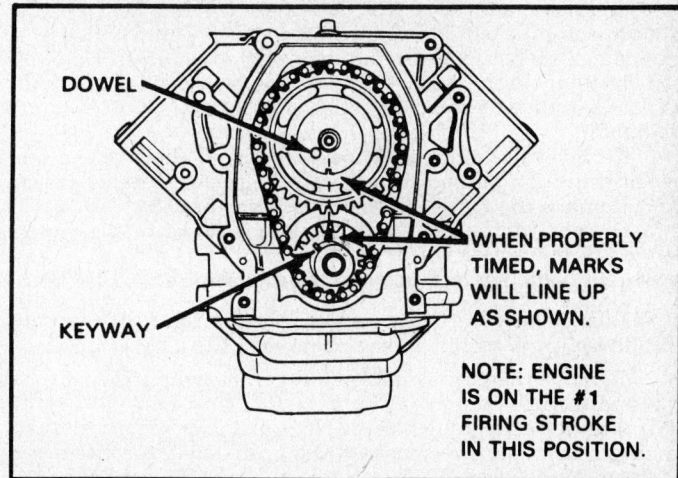

The proper alignment of the timing marks—HT4100 V8 engine

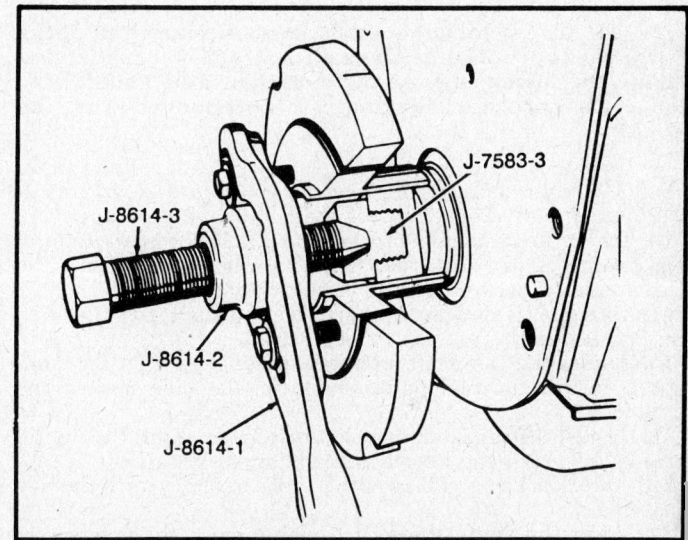

Removing the crankshaft hub—5.0L engine

3. Remove the wiring harness from the upper fan shroud clamps.
4. Remove the power steering pump reservoir from the upper radiator shroud.
5. Remove the upper fan shroud from the lower fan shroud by removing the staples.
6. Remove the clutch fan assembly.
7. Remove the generator, A.I.R. Pump, vacuum pump, and A/C pump drive belts.
8. Partially remove the A/C compressor from the engine mounting brackets without discharging the system.
9. Remove the alternator and support bracket from the engine.
10. Loosen the clamp and disconnect the coolant reservoir to water pump hose at the pump.
11. Disconnect the inlet and outlet hoses at the water pump.
12. Drain the crankcase by either removing the crankcase plugs (one on each side) or by elevating the rear wheels. This will prevent coolant from draining into the oil pan as the front cover is removed.
13. Remove the water pump and crankcase pulleys.
14. Remove the A/C bracket at the water pump.
15. Remove the timing mark tab from the front cover.
16. Remove the crankcase pulley to hub bolts and separate the pulley from the hub.
17. Remove the plug from the end of the crankshaft. Install a puller and remove the hub.
18. Remove the remaining front cover attaching screws and remove the cover with the water pump and lower thermostat housing as an assembly.
19. The timing chain and sprocket may now be removed as follows:
20. Remove the oil slinger from the crankshaft.
21. Rotate the engine and line up the timing marks as shown in the illustration.
22. Remove the screw securing the camshaft sprocket to the camshaft, then remove the camshaft and crankshaft sprocket with the chain attached.
23. Installation is the reverse of removal. After installing the timing chain over the camshaft sprocket rotate the crankshaft until the timing mark on the crank sprocket is positioned straight up.
24. Install the cam sprocket and timing chain over the crankshaft so that the timing marks are aligned.
25. Hold the camshaft sprocket in position against the end of the camshaft and press the sprocket on the camshaft by hand. Make sure the index pin in the camshaft is lined up with the index hole in the sprocket.
26. If necessary, keep the engine from rotating while torquing the camshaft sprocket screw to 35 ft. lbs.

NOTE: Engine timing has been set so that the No. 1 cylinder is in the TDC firing position. If for some reason the distributor was removed make sure the rotor is set so that cylinder No. 1 is in the firing position.

27. Install the oil slinger on the crankshaft with the smaller end of the slinger against the crankshaft sprocket.
28. Install the engine front cover by reversing the removal procedure.

5.0L ENGINE

1. Disconnect the negative battery cable. Drain the cooling system into a suitable drain pan.
2. Remove the drive belts and accessory belts. Remove the fan assembly and fan pulley. Using Hub Balancer Puller J-8614 or equivalent remove the hub balancer.
3. On vehicles equipped with A/C, remove the rear A/C com-

pressor braces and lower the A/C mount bolts. Remove the compressor bracket and nuts at the water pump. Slide the mounting bracket forward and remove the compressor mount bolt. Disconnect the wires at the compressor and lay the unit aside. Disconnect the air injection hose at the right exhaust manifold.

4. Remove the compressor mount bracket. Remove the upper air injection pump bracket with the power steering reservoir. Remove the lower air injection pump bracket.

5. Disconnect the heater and radiator hoses to the water pump. Remove the water pump. Remove the front cover reatining bolts, timing indicator, front cover and old gasket.

NOTE: It may be necessary to grind a flat surfacxe on the dowel pins to aid in the removal of the front cover.

6. Remove the crankshaft oil slinger, camshaft thrust button and spring.

7. Crank the engine until the No. 1 piston is at TDC and the timing marks on the camshaft and crankshaft sprockets are aligned (No.4 firing).

8. Remove the fuel pump, gasket and fuel pump eccentric. Remove the camshaft sprocket bolts and remove the camshaft sprocket and chain.

NOTE: The sprocket is a light fit on the camshaft. If the sprocket does not come off easily, use a plastic mallet and strike the lower edge of the sprocket. This should dislodge the sprocket allowing it to be removed from the shaft.

9. To remove the crankshaft gear, first remove the crankshaft key, then using puller BT-6812, or J-25287 and J-21052-2 or equivalent. Remove the crankshaft sprocket.

10. Insert the camshaft sprocket and crankshaft sprocket into the timing chain, with the timing marks aligned. Lube the thrust surface with Molykote or equivalent.

11. Grasp both sprockets and the timing chain together and put them into there prospective places.

12. Rotate the camshaft sprocket and engage it on the camshaft. Install the fuel pump eccentric, flat side toward the engine.

13. Install the camshaft sprocket bolt finger tight. Rotate the crankshaft until the keyways are aligned. Install the crankshaft sprocket key, tap it in with a brass hammer until the key bottoms.

14. When the timing marks are in alignment, the number six cylinder should be at top dead center. When both timing marks are on the top, the number one cylinder is at top dead center of the compression stroke.

15. Slowly and evenly draw the camshaft sprocket onto the camshaft using the mounting bolt and torque the bolt to 65 ft. lbs.

16. Lubricate the timing chain and finish the installation by reversing the order of the removal procedure.

17. When installing the front cover, apply a suitable RTV sealant around the coolant holes of the new front cover. Be sure to trim the ends of the oil pan seal and install the seal onto the timing chain cover.

FRONT COVER

Removal

5.7L (350) DIESEL ENGINE

1. Drain the cooling system. Disconnect the radiator hoses and the by-pass hose.
2. Remove all belts, the fan and fan pulley, crankshaft pulley and harmonic balancer assembly and the accessory brackets.
3. Remove cover to block attaching bolts and remove cover, timing indicator, and water pump assembly.

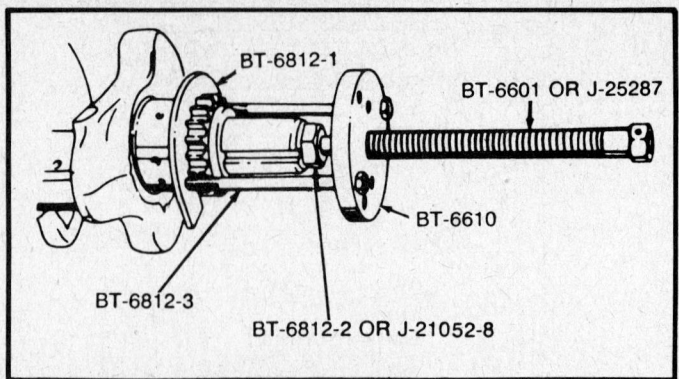

Removing the crankshaft sprocket

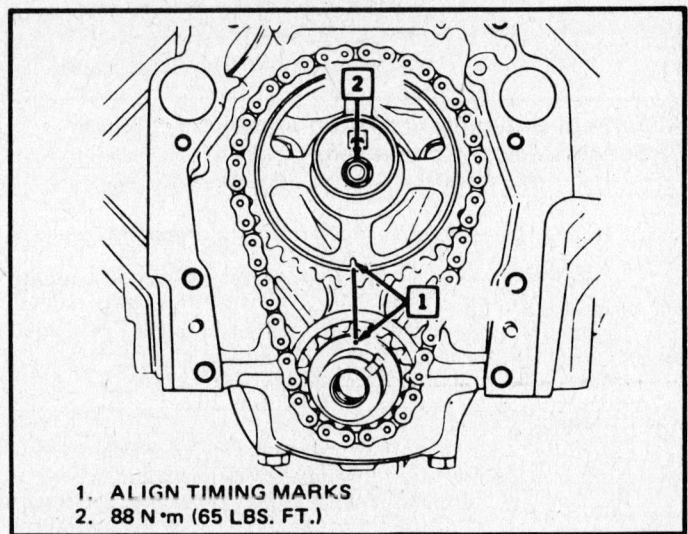

1. ALIGN TIMING MARKS
2. 88 N·m (65 LBS. FT.)

Aligning the timing marks—5.0L engine

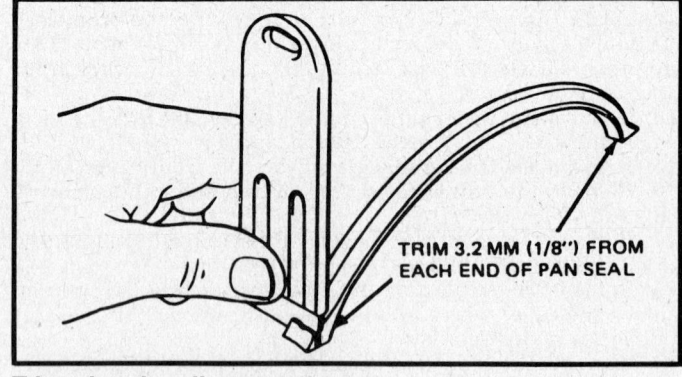

TRIM 3.2 MM (1/8") FROM EACH END OF PAN SEAL

Trimming the oil pan seal

4. Remove front cover and both dowel pins. It may be necessary to grind a flat on the pins to get a rough surface for gripping.

Installation

1. Grind a chamfer on 1 end of each dowel pin.
2. Cut excess material front front end of oil pan gasket on each side of engine block.
3. Clean block, oil pan, and front cover mating surfaces with solvent.

CADILLAC
DE VILLE · FLEETWOOD
SECTION 14

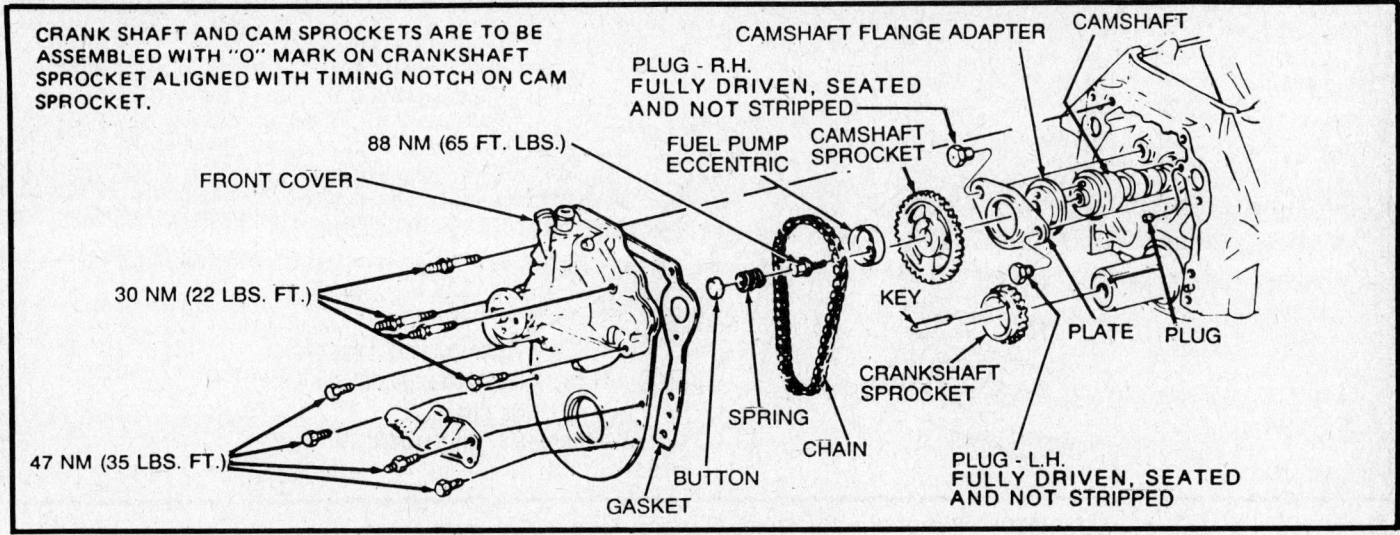

Exploded view of the front timing chain cover removal and installation

4. Trim about 1/8 in. from each end of new front pan seal, using a sharp tool.
5. Apply R.T.V. sealer on the front cover oil pan seal retainer.
6. Install a new front cover gasket on engine block and new front seal on front cover. Apply sealer to gasket around coolant holes and place on block.
7. Apply R.T.V sealer at junction of block, pan and front cover.
8. Place cover on front of block and press downward to compress seal. Rotate cover left and right and guide pan seal into cavity using a small flat blade tool.
9. Apply engine oil to bolts (threads and heads).
10. Install two bolts finer tight to hold cover in place.
11. Install two dowel pins (chamfered end first).
12. Install timing indicator and water pump assembly. Then torque bolts evenly.

NOTE: If 2 lower water pump bolts were removed, seal threads with sealer.

13. Apply lubricant on balancer seal surface.
14. Install balancer and balancer bolt. Torque from 200–310 ft. lbs. (271–420 Nm).
15. Install necessary brackets.
16. Connect by-pass hose and radiator hoses.
17. Install crankshaft pulley and four attaching bolts. Torque to 20 ft. lbs. (27 Nm).
18. Install fan pulley, fan, and four attaching bolts. Torque bolts to 20 ft. lbs. (27 Nm).
19. Install belts and adjust, using Tool J-23600 or equivalent.
20. Fill radiator.
21. Road test car and check for leaks.

TIMING CHAIN AND SPROCKETS

Removal

5.7L (350) DIESEL ENGINE

1. Remove front cover as previously described.
2. Remove oil slinger, cam sprocket, crank sprocket, and timing chain.
3. Remove fuel pump eccentric from crankshaft, if replacement is necessary.

Installation

1. Install key in crankshaft, if removed.
2. Install fuel pump eccentric, if removed.
3. Install camshaft sprocket, crankshaft sprocket and timing chain together, and align timing marks.
4. Torque camshaft sprocket bolt to 65 ft. lbs. (88 Nm). When the two marks are in alignment, No. 6 is at TDC. To obtain TDC for No. 1 cylinder, slowly rotate crankshaft 1 rotation. This will bring the cam mark to the top, No. 1 will be firing position.
5. Install oil slinger. Anytime the timing chain and sprockets are replaced, it will be necessary to retime the engine.

CAMSHAFT, INJECTION PUMP DRIVE AND DRIVEN GEARS

Removal

5.7L (350) DIESEL ENGINE

1. Disconnect battery.
2. Drain radiator coolant.
3. Remove upper radiator baffle.
4. Disconnect upper radiator hose at water outlet.
5. Disconnect upper radiator hose support clamp.
6. Disconnect cooler lines at radiator.
7. Remove radiator fan shroud.
8. Remove radiator.
9. Remove the oil pump drive and vacuum pump assembly.
10. Remove intake manifold and gasket, front and rear seal.
11. Remove balancer pulley.
12. Remove balancer attaching bolt.
13. Remove balancer.
14. Remove engine front cover.
15. Remove bolt valve covers.
16. Remove rocker arms, push rods, and valve lifters. Parts position should be noted so they can be installed in their original position.
17. Discharge A/C system, remove condenser attaching bolts, and remove condenser.
18. Remove bolt securing camshaft gear and timing chain, then remove timing gears and chain.
19. Position camshaft dowel pin at the 3 o'clock position.
20. With the camshaft held rearward, remove pump drive gear by sliding off the camshaft while rocking the pump driven gear.

CADILLAC
DE VILLE · FLEETWOOD

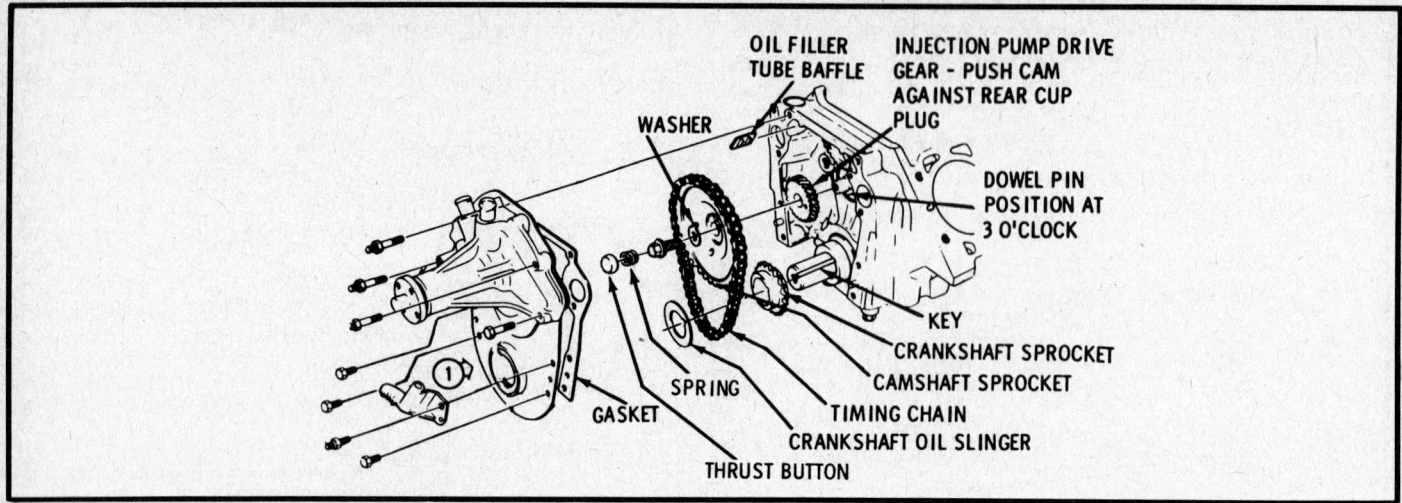

Front cover assembly 5.7L (350) V8 diesel engine (© General Motors Corporation)

21. If necessary to remove pump driven gear, remove injection pump adapter, then remove snap ring and selective washer. Remove the driven gear and spring.
22. Remove camshaft by carefully sliding it out the front of the engine. Do not force shaft as damage can occur to camshaft bearings.
23. If cam bearings are being replaced, it is necessary to remove oil pan.

Installation

1. Any time the injection pump adapter is replaced or if pump drive or driven gears or timing chain and gears are replaced, it is necessary to remark the timing mark on the adapter.
2. If either the pump drive or driven gears are to be replaced, replace both gears.
3. Coat camshaft and bearings liberally with lubricant before installing. Camshaft sprocket and crankshaft sprocket must be aligned.
4. Check the injection pump driven gear bushing. Install the injection pump driven gear, spring, shim and snap ring. Check the gear end play. If not within 0.002 to 0.006 in., replace the shim to obtain the clearance.
5. Shims are available from 0.080 to 0.115 inch in 0.003 increments.
6. Position the camshaft dowel pin at 3 o'clock, align the "O" marks on the pump drive and driven gears. Then, with the camshaft held in the rearward position, slide the pump drive gear on the camshaft.
7. Timing indicator attaching stud must be installed and properly torqued before installing power steering pump bracket. Bleed valve lifters—see "Valve Lifter Bleed-Down." Start engine, recharge A/C system, and check for possible leaks.

TIMING COVER OIL SEAL

Removal and Installation

6.0L ENGINE

1. Disconnect the battery and remove the air cleaner.
2. Remove the power steering pump drive belt.
3. Remove the alternate drive belt.
4. On air conditioned cars and cars equipped with the A.I.R. system remove the pump drive belts.
5. Raise and support the front of the car on jack stands. Remove the fan.

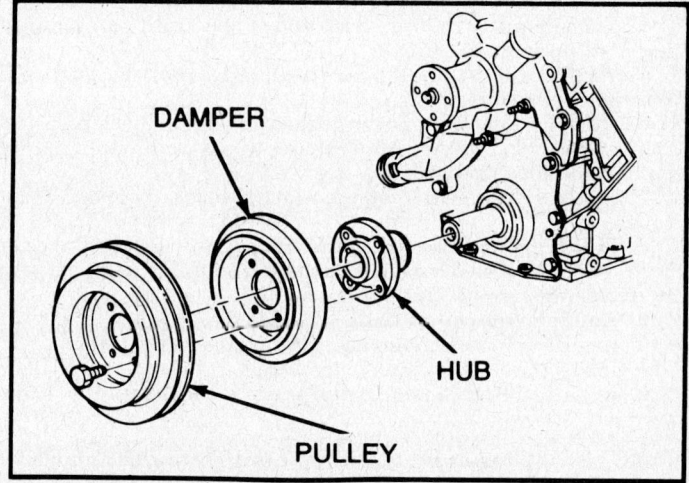

Removing the crankshaft pulley and damper

6. Remove pulley and harmonic balancer.
7. With a suitable tool, pry out front cover oil seal.
8. Lubricate new oil seal with wheel bearing grease. Position the seal on the end of the crankshaft with the garter spring side toward the engine.
9. Using a seal installer, drive the front seal into the front cover until it bottoms.
10. Assemble and install the remaining parts in reverse order of disassembly.

NOTE: If there are any difficulties in removing the crankshaft hub or the front cover seal, refer to the timing cover oil seal removal and installation for the HT4100 engine.

HT4100 ENGINE

1. Disconnect the negative battery cable. Remove the A.I.R. pump belt, power steering pump belt and vacuum belt.
2. Remove the four screws that hold crankshaft pulley. Remove the damper to hub and remove the pulley and damper. Remove the plug from the end of the crankshaft.
3. Install Puller Pilot J-21052-4 or equivalent, in the bore in end of the crankshaft.
4. Install the Holding Base J-21052-02 or equivalent, on the front hub, lining up the two holes on the base with two tapped

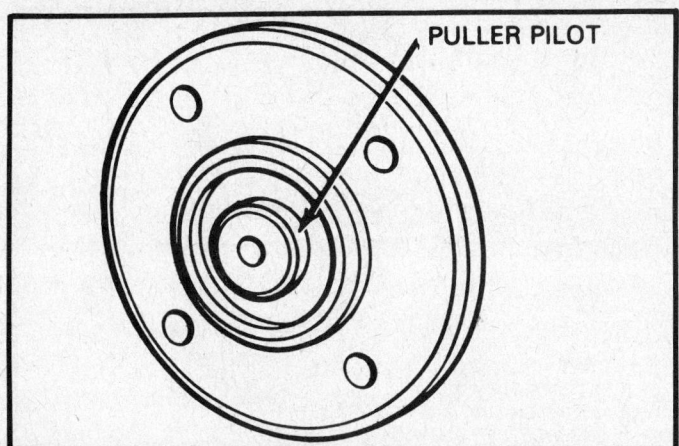
Balancer hub pilot installation

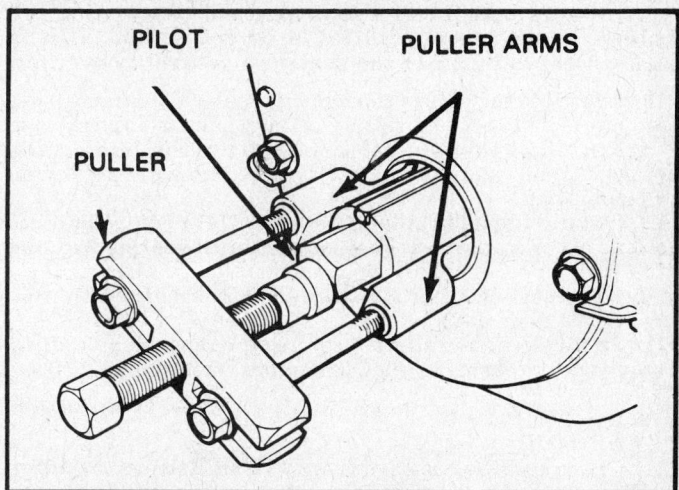
Removal of the front cover oil seal

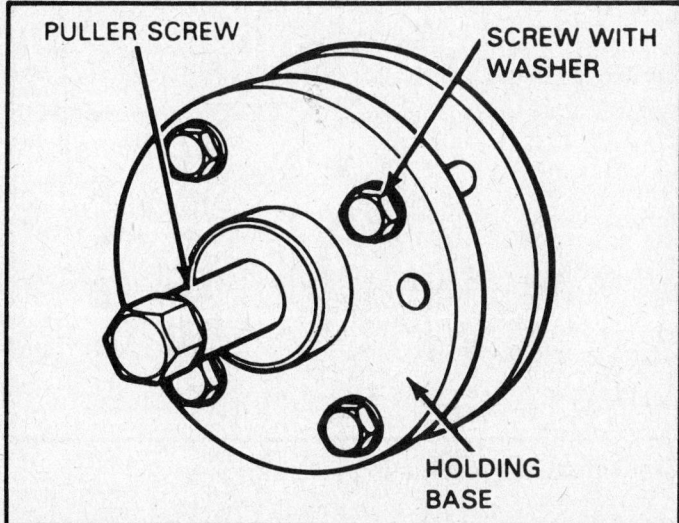
Balancer hub removal

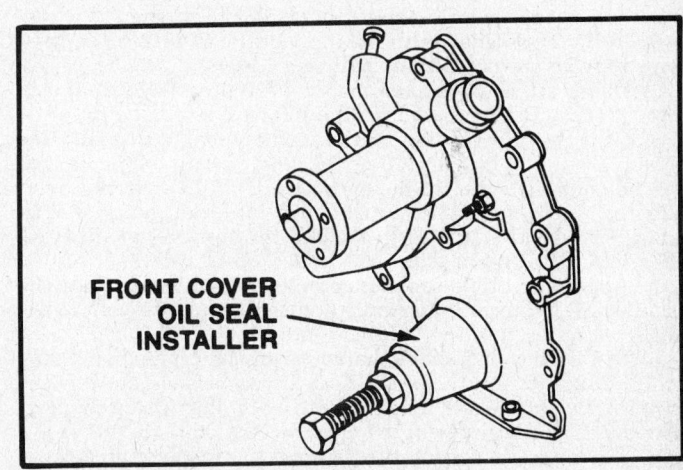
Installation of the front cover oil seal.

holes in the hub and install the two screws with washers finger tight.

5. Thread the puller J-21052-2 or equivalent, into the base until the screw contact point. Using a suitable wrench, remove the hub from the crankshaft by tightening the screw.

NOTE: The use of compressed air pressure to hold one piston within its compression stroke may bne necessary to remove the hub with out turning the crankshaft. Remove a spark plug and install Adapter J-22794 or equivalent into the spark plug port (finger tight) and apply air pressure to the hold piston within its compression stroke. The adapter should not be tightened with a wrench.

6. Remove the pilot from the end of the crankshaft and remove the puller from the hub.

7. With the crankshaft pulley and hub removed. Use tools J-1859-03 and J-23129 or equivalent and remove the oil seal.

8. Lubricate the new oil seal lips with engine oil and position the seal on the end of the crankshaft with the garter spring side toward the engine.

9. Using seal installer J-29662 or equivalent, use a hammer and drive the seal into the front cover until the tool bottoms out against the front cover.

NOTE: The tool J-29662 is designed is such a way that

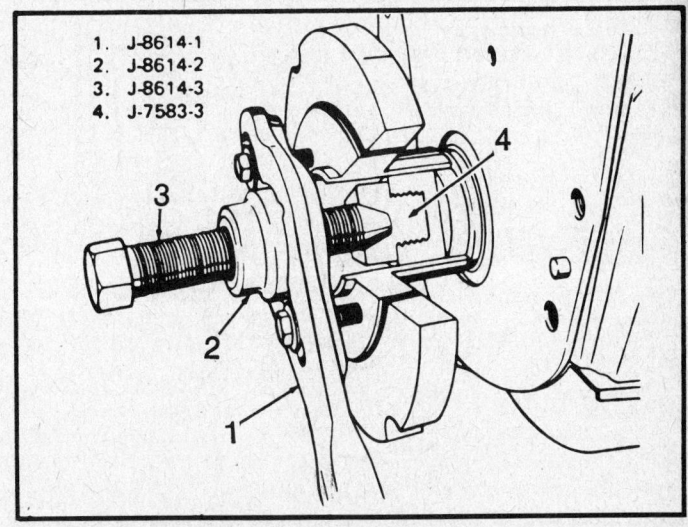
Crankshaft hub removal—5.0L engine

14-37

CADILLAC
DE VILLE • FLEETWOOD

the front cover seal can also be pressed on by using the balancer hub installer J-29774 or equivalent, if it is incovenient to hammer the seal onto the front cover.

10. Lubricate the bore of the hub and seal with extreme pressure lubricant to prevent seizure to the crankshaft and provide lubrication of the oil seal lip. Position the hub on the cranksahft, lining up the key slot in the hub with the key on the crankshaft.

11. Install Thread Installer Screw J-29774 or equivalent into the end of the crankshaft. Position the thrust bearing with the inner race forward, washer next and Installer Nut last. Using a suitable wrench install the hub on the crankshaft by tightening the installer nut.

12. To finish the installation reverse the removal procedure. Torque the crankshaft pulley to damper screws to 20 ft. lbs.

5.0L ENGINE

1. Disconnect the negative battery cable. Remove the upper radiator support.
2. Remova all drive belts. Remove the fan, fan clutch and water pump pulley.
3. Remove the crankshaft pulley bolts and the cranksahft pulley. Remove the crankshaft hub bolt and washer.
4. Using crankshaft hub balancer puller J-8614 or equivalent, remove the crankshaft balancer hub.
5. Using oil seal remover tools BT-6406 or J-23129 and J-185903 or equivalent, remove the front cover oil seal.
6. Coat the outside diameter of the new seal with a suitable sealer. Using tools BT-6405 or J-25264 or equivalent, install the oil seal with the lip facing outward into the front cover. Tighten the seal installer until a .005 in. feeler gauge will fit snug between the seal installer and the front cover. Remove ther seal installation tool.
7. Apply a suitable sealer to crankshaft key and inside the brankshaft balancer hub. Apply a suitable seal lubricant to the seal contact area of the balancer hub.
8. Install the crankshaft balancer on the crankshaft using tool J-25288 or equivalent. Check the clearance betwen the front of the engine and balancer hub while installting the hub. The proper balncer to engine clearance is .0007 to .001 in.
9. To finish the installation reverse the removal procedure. Torque the crankshaft hub bolt to 200-310 ft. lbs. and torque the cranksahft pulley bolts to 28 ft. lbs.

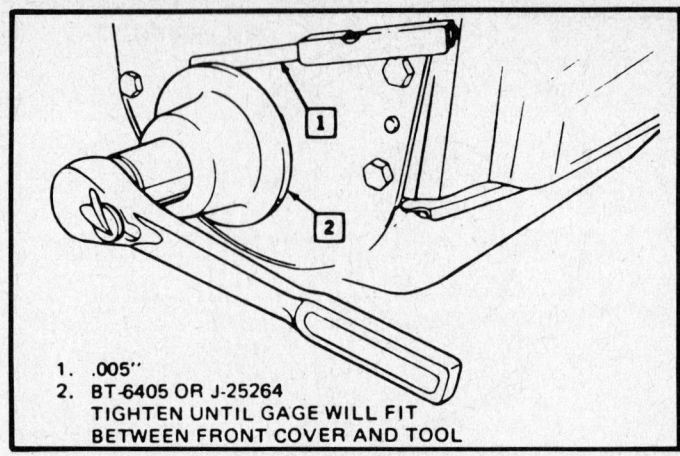

1. .005"
2. BT-6405 OR J-25264 TIGHTEN UNTIL GAGE WILL FIT BETWEEN FRONT COVER AND TOOL

Front cover oil seal installation—5.0L engine

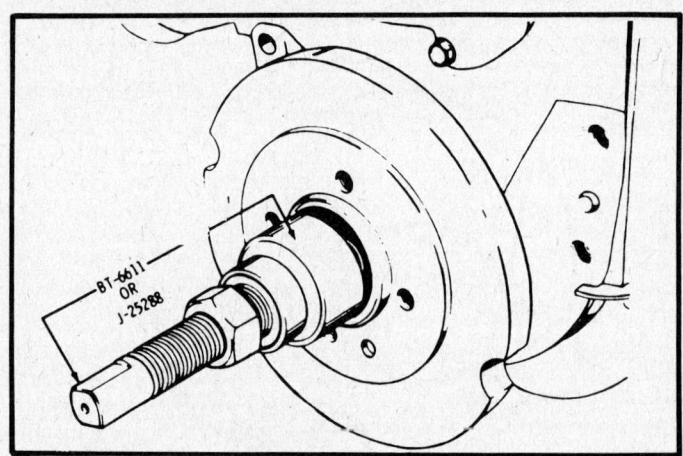

BT-6611 OR J-25288

Crankshaft hub installation—5.0L engine

PISTON & CONNECTING ROD POSITIONING

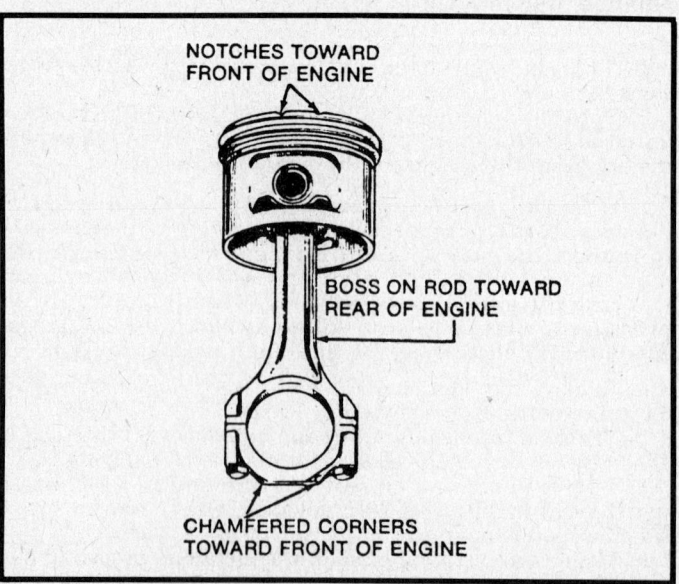

NOTCHES TOWARD FRONT OF ENGINE

BOSS ON ROD TOWARD REAR OF ENGINE

CHAMFERED CORNERS TOWARD FRONT OF ENGINE

Piston identification, V8 (HT4100) engines
(© General Motors Corporation)

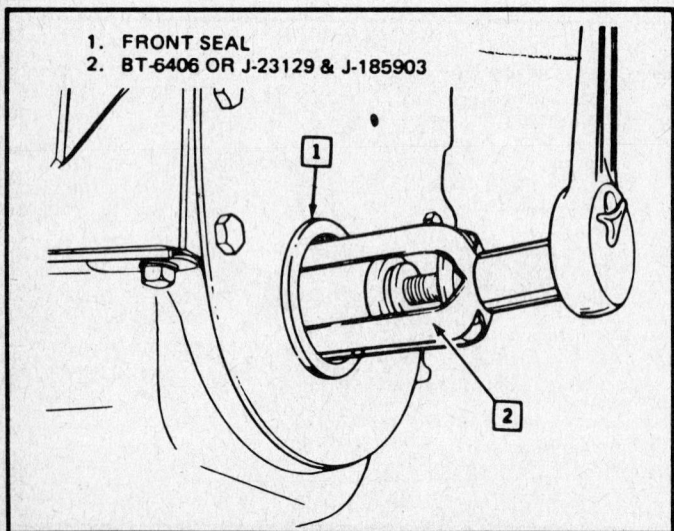

1. FRONT SEAL
2. BT-6406 OR J-23129 & J-185903

Front cover oil seal removal—5.0L engine

CADILLAC
DE VILLE · FLEETWOOD
SECTION 14

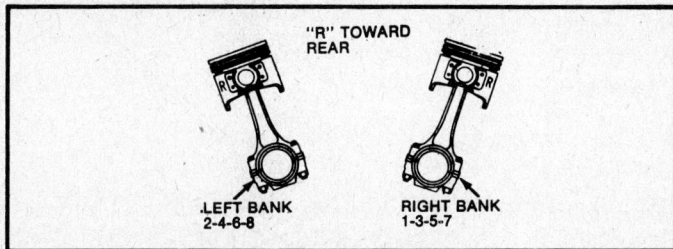

Piston Identification—V8 (368 cu. In.)
(© General Motors Corporation)

Lubrication

OIL PAN

Removal and Installation

4.1L (HT4100) V8 ENGINE AND DIESEL ENGINE

1. Disconnect the negative battery cable.
2. Jack the car up, and support it with jack stands.
3. Drain the engine oil and remove the oil filter.
4. Remove the flywheel inspection cover and support struts.
5. Disconnect the exhaust "Y" pipe at the exhaust manifolds and remove the 1 bolt at the catalytic converter bracket.
6. Remove the oil pan screws, lower the exhaust pipe, and remove the oil pan.

NOTE: If the pan is difficult to remove lightly tap the edges of the pan with a plastic hammer.

7. Seal the oil pan to the block with RTV sealant.
8. Tighten the oil pan retaining screws and nuts to 11 ft. lbs.
9. The remainder of the installation is the reverse of removal.

6.0L (368) V8 ENGINE

1. Remove the wheel housing struts from the fenders. Disconnect the negative battery terminal.
2. Remove the 3 screws from the upper radiator shroud, 2 securing the shroud, and one securing the top radiator hose. Drill out the rivets securing the upper shroud to the lower one and remove the shroud. Use bolts and nuts to replace the rivets when reinstalling the shroud.
3. Loosen the drive belts and remove the crankshaft pulley.
4. Jack up your car and support it with jackstands.
5. Remove the through-bolt from each motor mount.
6. Remove the crossover pipe and the converter as an assembly.
7. Remove the starter.
8. Remove the torque converter cover.
9. Drain the oil pan.
10. Using a jack, with a block of wood on top, place it under the crankshaft hub. Jack up the engine, remove the pan bolts and the pan.
11. Clean all the gasket material from the pan and the block mating surfaces. Use a new gasket kit and sealer. Make sure the seals are firmly positioned on the flange surfaces with each seal properly located in the cut-out notches of the pan gasket.
12. Installation is the reverse of the removal procedure.

5.0L ENGINE

1. Disconnect the negative battery cable. Remove the engine oil dipstick.
2. Remove the fan shroud attaching screws. Raise and support the vehicle safely.
3. Drain the engine oil from the oil pan into a suitable drain pan. Remove the flywheel cover and crossover pipe.
4. Remove the starter. Using a jack, with a block of wood on top, place it under the crankshaft hub to support the engine. Remove the engine mounts at the cylinder block.
5. Raise the front of engine as high as possible. Remove the oil pan retaining bolts and remove the oil pan from the engine.
6. Clean all the gasket material from the pan and the block mating surfaces. Use a new gasket kit and sealer. Make sure the seals are firmly positioned on the flange surfaces with each seal properly located in the cut-out notches of the pan gasket.
7. Installation is the reverse of the removal procedure.

OIL PUMP

Removal and Installation

HT4100 V8 ENGINE

1. Jack up the car and support it with jack stands.
2. Remove the oil pan.
3. Remove the 2 screws and 1 nut securing the oil pump to the engine.
4. To disassemble, remove the 4 screws holding the oil pump cover to the housing, then slide the drive shaft, drive gear and driven gear out of the pump housing.
5. Remove the oil pressure regulator valve and spring from the bore in the housing assembly.
6. Inspect the oil pressure regulator valve for nicks and burrs.
7. Measure the free length of the regulator valve spring. It should be 2.57–2.69 in.
8. Inspect the drive gear and driven gear for nicks and burrs.
9. Assemble the pump drive gear over the drive shaft so that the retaining ring is inside the gear. Position the drive gear over the pump housing shaft closest to the pressure regulator bore.

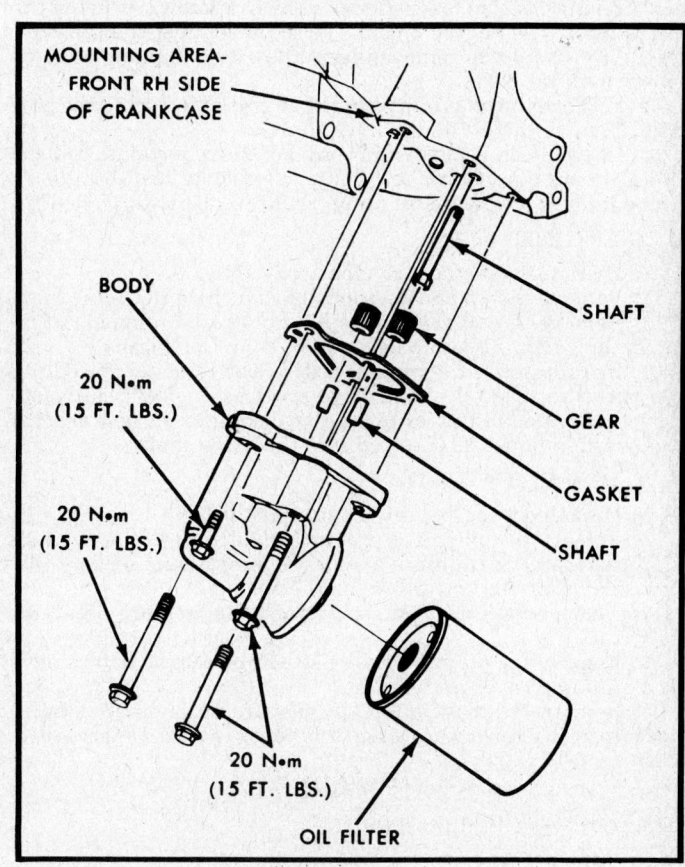

Oil pump removal—6.0L engine

14-39

SECTION 14

CADILLAC
DE VILLE • FLEETWOOD

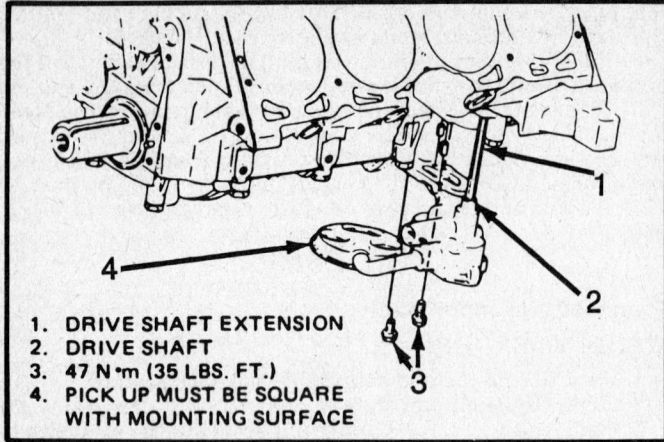

1. DRIVE SHAFT EXTENSION
2. DRIVE SHAFT
3. 47 N·m (35 LBS. FT.)
4. PICK UP MUST BE SQUARE WITH MOUNTING SURFACE

Oil pump removal—5.0L engine

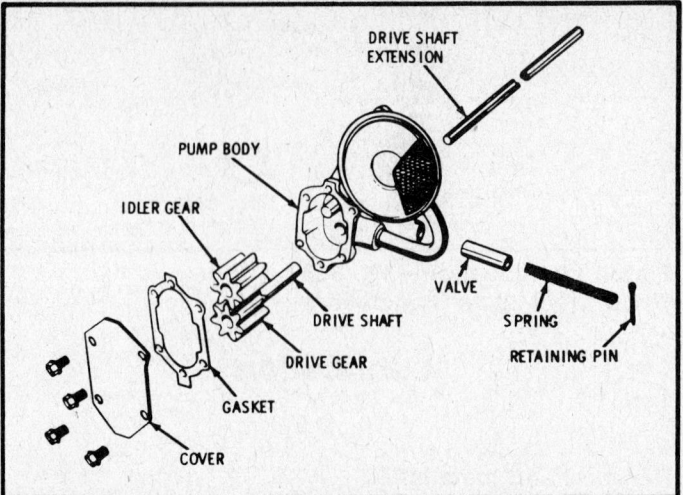

Exploded view of the diesel engine oil pump

10. Slide the driven gear over the remaining shaft in the pump housing, meshing the driven gear with the drive gear.
11. Install the oil pressure regulator spring and valve in the bore of the pump housing assembly.
12. Install the pump cover and four retaining screws.
13. Install the oil pump assembly to the block, engaging the drive shaft to the distributor gear. Tighten the nut to 22 ft. lbs. and the 2 screws to 15 ft. lbs.
14. Install the oil pan and lower the car.

6.0L ENGINE

1. Disconnect the negative battery cable. Raise and support the vehicle safely.
2. Remove the oil filter. Remove the five screws securing the oil pump to the engine block. The screw nearest the pressure regulator should be removed last, allowing the pump to come down with the screw.
3. Remove the oil pump from the engine and discard the gasket. Remove the oil pump drive shaft.
4. Installation is the reverse order of the removal procedure. Pack the oil pump with petroleum jelly before installing it on the engine. Torque the oil pump retaining bolts to 15 ft. lbs.

5.0L ENGINE

1. Disconnect the negative battery cable.
2. Remove the oil pan as previously outlined in this section.
3. Remove the oil pump retaining bolts and remove the oil assembly with the pump drive shaft from the engine.
4. Installation is the reverse orderof the removal procedure. Be sure that the oil pump drive shaft extension is fully engaged. The end of the oil pump drive shaft extension nearest the washers must be inserted into the drive shaft.

5.7L DIESEL ENGINE

1. Disconnect the negative battery cable.
2. Remove the oil pan as previously outlined in this section.
3. position the thumb iver the pressure regulator bore, before removing the cotter pin, as the spring is under pressure. Then remove the cotter pin, spring and the pressure regulator valve.
4. Remove the oil pump cover attaching screws and remove the oil pump cover and gasket.
5. Remove the drive and idler gear from the pump body.
6. Installtion is the reverse order of the removal procedure.

REAR MAIN SEAL

Removal and Installation

ALL MODELS

NOTE: On the new 5.0L engine, the rear main seal should br replaced with the crankshaft out of the engine. However there is a kit available to repair the rear main bearing upper seal if it should develop a leak.

1. Disconnect the negative battery cable.
2. Drain the oil pan. Remove the oil pan.
3. Remove the rear main bearing cap.
4. Remove the oil seal from the bearing cap.
5. To remove the upper half of the seal, use a small hammer to tap a brass pin punch on one end of the seal until it prodtrudes far enough to be removed with a suitable pair of needle nose pliers.

Installation

NOTE: Before going on with the installation procedure, fabricate a seal installer using a piece of .004 in. shim stock (refer to the illustration).

1. Clean all sealant and foreign material from the cylinder case bearing cap and crankshaft, using non-abrrasive cleaner. Inspect the components for nicks, scratches, burrs, and machining defects at all sealing surfaces, case assembly and crankshaft.
2. Coat the new seal lips and seal bead with a light engine oil, use care to prevent the oil from reaching the seal mating ends.
3. Position the tip of the of the installation tool between the crankshaft and the seal seat in the cylinder case.
4. Position the seal between the crankshaft and the tip of the tool so that the seal bead is in contact with the tip of the tool. Be sure that the oil seal lip is positioned toward the front of the engine.
5. Roll the seal around the crankshaft using the tool as a "shoe-horn", feeding the seal into the cap using light pressure with the thumb and finger. Install the bearing cap to the case with a sealant applied to the cap to case interface being careful to keep the sealant off the seal split line.
6. Install the rear main bearing cap (with new seal) and torque to 10-12 ft. lbs. Tap the end of the cranksahft rearward then forward with a lead hammer. This will line up the thrust surfaces. Retorque the bearing cap to specifications. Complete the installation by revering the removal procedure.

5.0L Engine

REAR MAIN BEARING UPPER OIL SEAL REPAIR (ENGINE IN CAR)

1. Disconnect the negative battery cable. Remove the oil pan

CADILLAC
DE VILLE • FLEETWOOD
SECTION 14

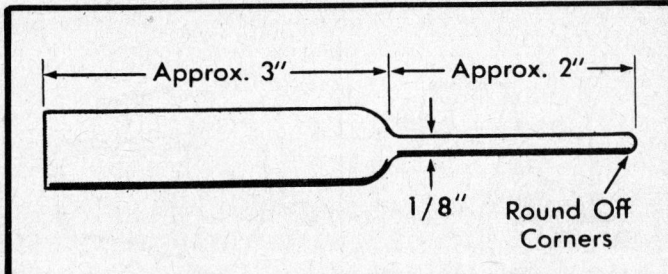

"Home Made" rear main seal installation tool

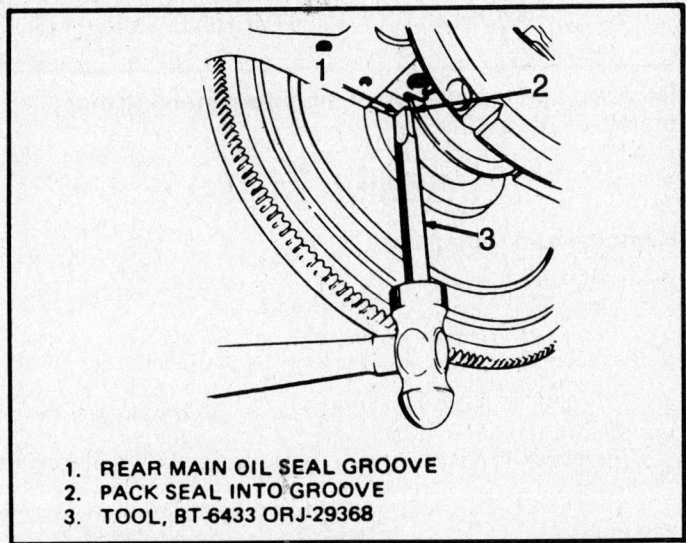

1. REAR MAIN OIL SEAL GROOVE
2. PACK SEAL INTO GROOVE
3. TOOL, BT-6433 OR J-29368

Packing the rear main upper oil seal—5.0L engine

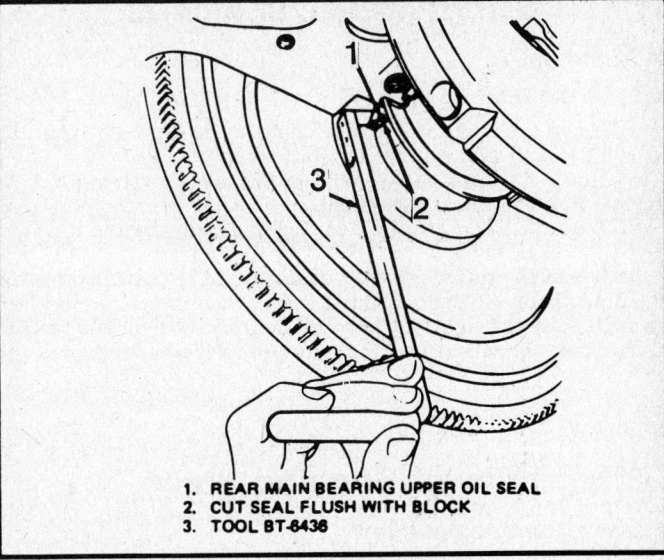

1. REAR MAIN BEARING UPPER OIL SEAL
2. CUT SEAL FLUSH WITH BLOCK
3. TOOL BT-6436

Trimming off the upper seal—5.0L engine

as previously outlined in this section. Remove the rear main bearing cap.

2. Using packing tool BT-6433 or J-25282-2 or equivalent, drive both side of the old seal gently into the groove until it is packed tight.

3. Measure the amount of the seal that was driven up on one side; add $1/16$ in., then cut this length from the old seal removed from the main bearing cap with a suitable cutting tool.

4. Measure the amount of the seal that was driven up on the other side. Add a $1/16$ in. and cut another length from the old seal. Use the main bearing cap as a holding fixture when cutting the seal.

5. Work these two pieces of the seal into the cylinder block (one piece on each side) with two suitable tools. Using the packing tool, pack these short pieces up into the block using tool BT-6436 or equivalent or a sharp blade.

6. Place a piece of shim stock between the seal and the crankshaft to protect the bearing surface before triming the seal.

7. Form a new rope seal in the rear main bearing cap. Place a drop of a suitable sealer on each end of the seal and cap. Install the main bearing cap.

NOTE: Do not use the attaching bolts to pull down the bearing cap. Tap gently into place with a suitable tool.

8. Install the oil pan and fill with the proper oil to the specified amount.

FRONT SUSPENSION AND STEERING SECTION

For Front Suspension Services refer to the Unit Repair Section. For Steering Gear Overhaul refer to the Unit Repair Section.

STEERING GEAR

Removal and Installation

ALL MODELS

1. Position a fluid catch pan under the steering gear, disconnect the pressure and return lines from the steering gear assembly. Plug the opening to prevent the entrance of dirt.

2. If equipped, disconnect the stone shield from the return pipe.

3. Remove the pinch bolt from the flex coupling, and disconnect the coupling from the gear.

NOTE: Failure to disconnect the flexible coupling from the steering gear stub shaft can result in damage to the steering gear and or the intermidiate shaft. This damage can cause the lost of steering control which could result in a vehicle crash and bodily injuries.

4. Raise the vehicle, and support safely.

5. Remove the pitman arm nut and washer. Remove the pitman arm from the sector shaft with a pitman arm puller tool.

6. Remove the 3 retaining bolts and washers holding the steering gear to the side rail. Lower the gear assembly from the vehicle.

7. The installation is the reverse of the removal procedure. Tighten the pitman arm nut to 185 ft. lbs., the 3 mounting bolts to 70 ft. lbs. and the flex coupling pinch bolt to 30 ft. lbs.

SECTION 14

CADILLAC
DE VILLE • FLEETWOOD

FRONT WHEEL BEARINGS

Adjustment
ALL MODELS

1. Raise the front of the car. Remove the dust cap from the wheel bearing and remove the cotter pin.
2. While spinning the wheel, tighten the adjusting nut to 12 ft. lbs. Stop spinning the wheel.
3. Back off the nut until it is free and then tighten it finger tight.
4. Insert the cotter pin. If the pin cannot be installed in this position, back off the nut until the holes align. Make certain that the pin fits tightly. Ther will be from .001 to .005 in. end play when the wheel bearings are properly adjusted.

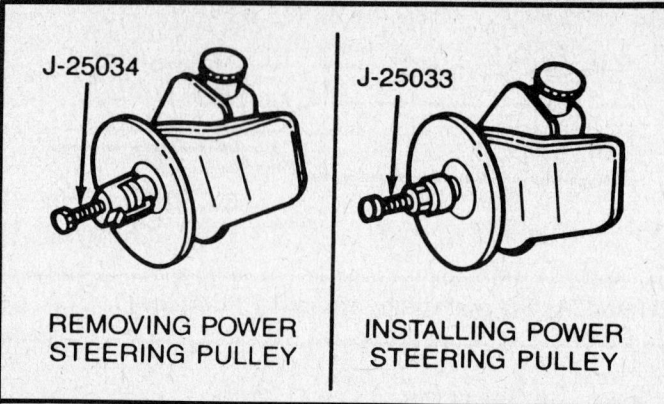

Removal and installation of the power steering pump pulley—5.0L engine

Power Steering Pump

Removal and Installation
HT4100 AND 6.0L ENGINES

1. Disconnect and plug the fluid lines at the pump. Remove the vacuum pump if so equipped.
2. Remove the nut securing the pump mounting bracket to the cylinder head mounting stud. Remove A/C brackets as required.
3. Remove the steering pump bracket attaching bolt from the front of the cylinder block.
4. Remove the drive belts and remove the bottom pivot bolt and remove the pump with the bracket and filter attached.
5. Reverse the removal procedure to install.
6. The adjustment of the power steering pump drive belts are to be made with the use of a tension gauge. Proper tension for a new belt is 125 lbs. and 90 lbs. for a belt that has been previously tensioned.

DIESEL ENGINE

1. Partially remove the cruise control servo, if so equipped.
2. Partially remove the generator, leave the throughbolt in and tilt the generator up and out of the way.
3. Remove the generator adjusting bracket(s). Disconnect the pressure and return lines from the pump. Plug all openings to prevent a loss of fluid and entrance of dirt into the system.
4. Loosen the pump adjusting bolt, pivot the bolt and pivot the nut. Remove the belt form the pulley.
5. Remove the two nuts and spacer securing the pump mounting bracket to the water pump and timing chain cover. Remove the bracket joining bolt and remove the pump with the bracket attached.
6. Installation is the reverse order of the removal procedure. Be sure to bleed the air from the system.

5.0L ENGINE

1. Disconnect and relocate the air cleaner inlet tube and the upper radiator hose to gain access to the pump.
2. Loosen the generator mounting bolts except for the long bolt. Rotate the generator upward to gain access by pivoting the long bolt.
3. Remove and plug the pressure and return hoses from the pump. Remove the front pump bracket mounting bolts and spacer. Remove the rear pump mounting nut.
4. Remove the pump and bracket from the engine as an assembly. Remove thepulley using tool J-25034-B or equivalent and remove the bracket from the pump.
5. Installation is the reverse order of the removal procedure. Be sure to bleed the air from the system.

STEERING WHEEL

Removal and Installation
ALL MODELS

1. Disconnect the negative battery cable.
2. Remove the screws on the underside of the steering wheel spokes near the center and remove the pad assembly.
3. Remove the horn contact wire from the plastic tower by pushing it on the wire and turning it counterclockwise. Turning the ignition on will facilitate the removal.
4. Remove the nut holding the steering wheel to the steering shaft.
5. On tilt wheels, remove locking lever and flange and screw assembly.
6. Matchmark the shaft and wheel for installation in the original position and use a puller to remove the steering wheel.
7. On installation, tighten the steering shaft nut to 30 ft. lbs. on the Deville and 35 ft. lbs. on the Fleetwood Brougham.

STEERING COLUMN

Removal and Installation
ALL MODELS

1. Disconnect the negative battery cable.
2. Center the steering wheel and remove the upper coupling pinch bolt and nut.
3. Disconnect the transmission shift linkage at the lower shift lever.
4. Remove the steering column lower cover from the instrument panel, exposing the upper support nuts or bolts.
5. Disconnect the turn signal wiring connector. If equipped with cruise control, disconnect the harness.
6. Remove the screw securing the shift cable to the shift bowl.
7. Loosen 2 nuts or bolts at the steering column upper support.

— CAUTION —
Do not completely remove the upper support nuts or bolts as the steering column could bend under its own weight.

8. Move the rubber carpet seal up the steering column as far as possible and position the carpet to gain access to the toe plate.
9. Remove the screws retaining the toe plate to the floor pan.
10. Remove the two nuts or bolts at the upper column bracket, disconnect the remaining electrical connectors and vacuum connectors while supporting the column.

14-42

CADILLAC
DE VILLE • FLEETWOOD

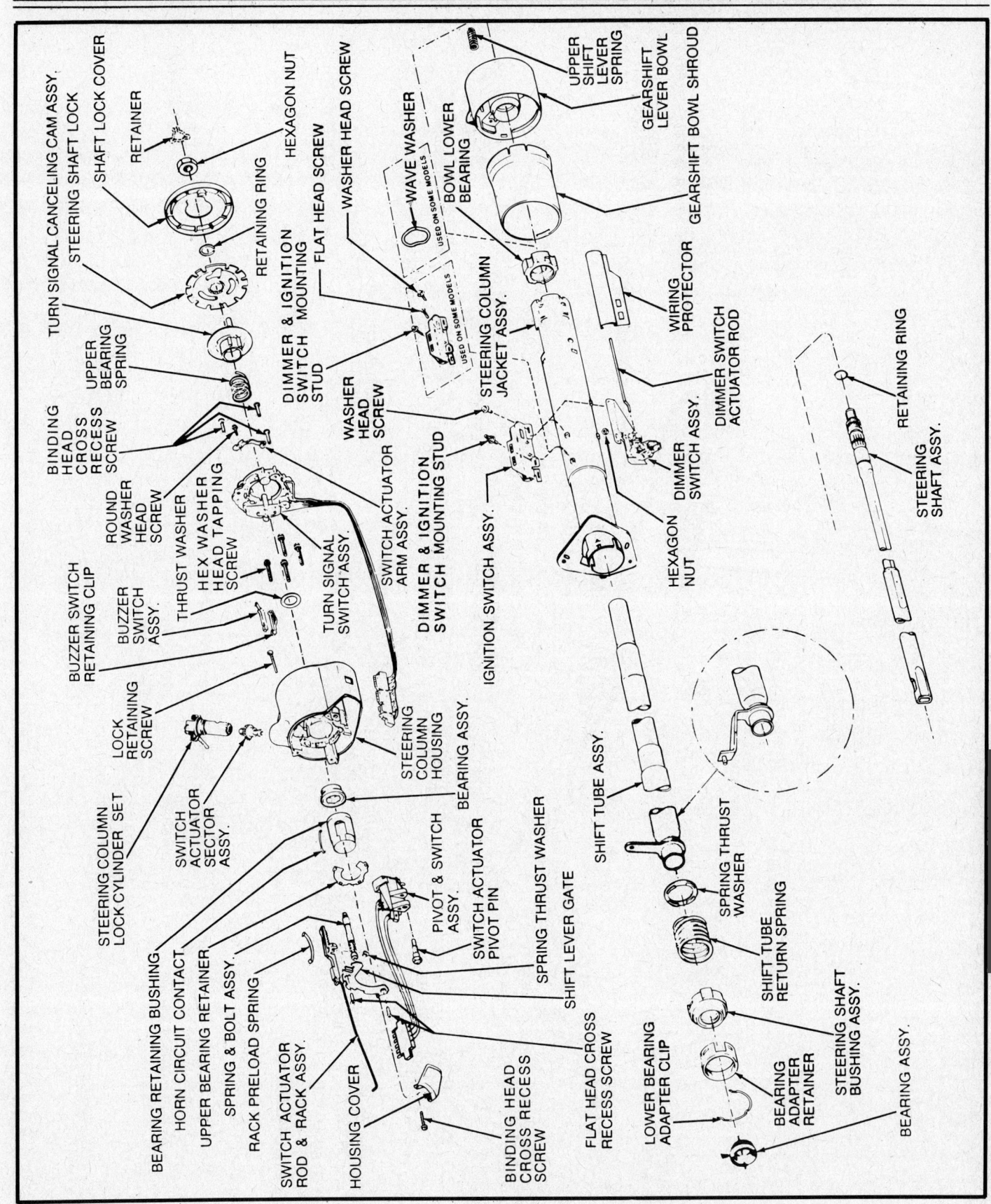

Exploded view of standard column assembly (© General Motors Corporation)

Section 14

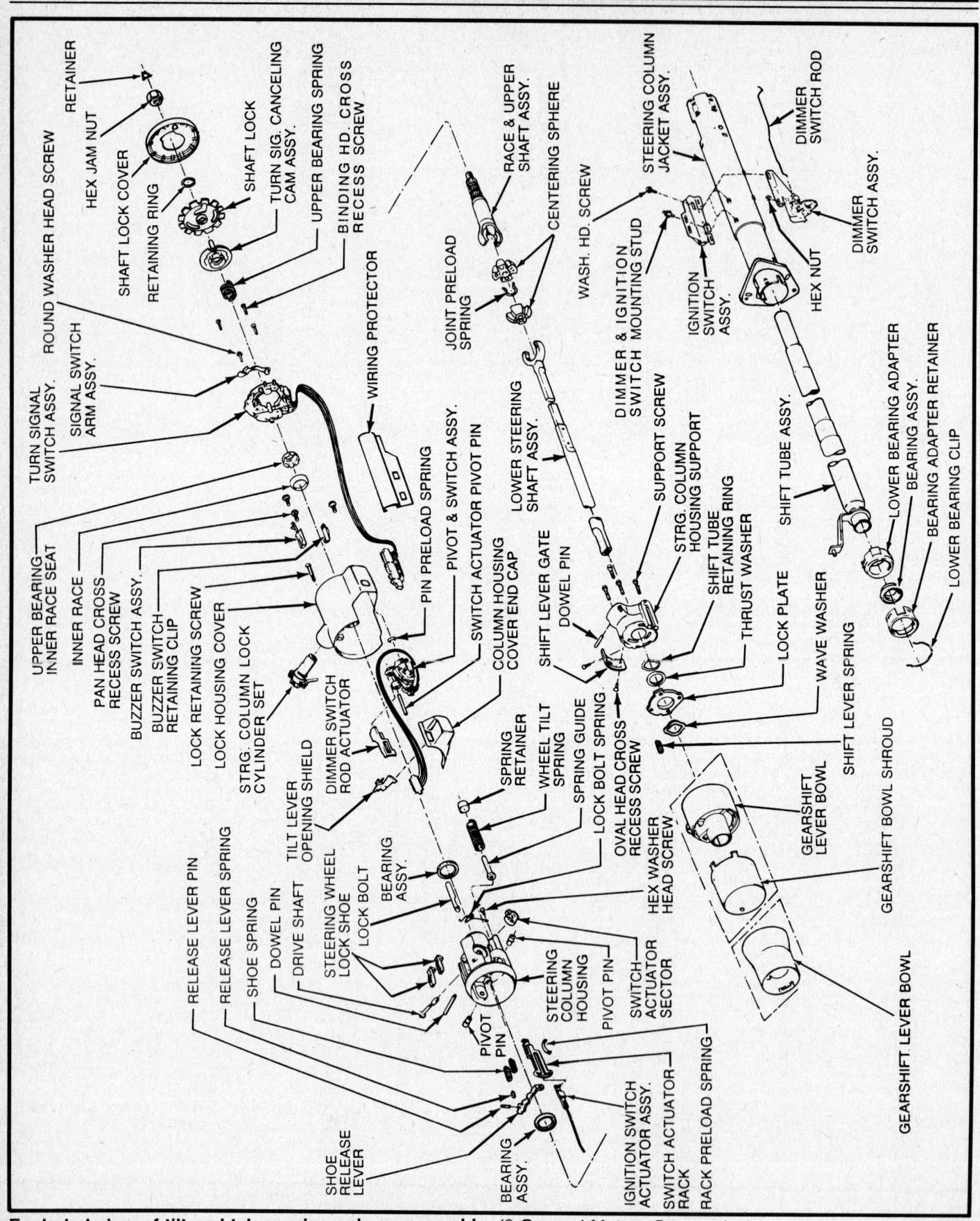

Exploded view of tilt and telescoping column assembly (© General Motors Corporation)

CADILLAC
DE VILLE • FLEETWOOD
SECTION 14

11. Carefully pull the steering column up and out of the vehicle. If the shaft hangs up in the upper coupling, resecure the upper mounting bracket and free the coupling from the steering shaft. Remove the column assembly.

12. Reverse the removal procedure to install the steering column in the vehicle.

13. A clearance of 5/16 in. should exist between the shaft and the upper coupling when the installation is complete or lower steering column bearing damage could result.

BRAKE SECTION

For Brake Service refer to the Unit Repair Section.

MASTER CYLINDER

Removal and Installation

ALL MODELS

NOTE: It is possible to remove the master cylinder unit without removing the power booster from the vehicle.

1. Disconnect and plug the front and rear brake lines at the master cylinder.
2. Remove the 2 securing nuts which hold the master cylinder to the power booster.
3. Remove the master cylinder.
4. To install, reverse the removal procedure. Bleed the hydraulic system.

VACUUM PUMP

A belt driven vacuum pump is used on the 4.1L (HT4100) V8 engine, while a gear driven vacuum pump is used on the 5.7L (350) V8 Diesel engine. This is to aid in the correct operation of the power brakes, air conditioning, etc. Should a malfunction occur in the unit, both pumps are only serviced as an assembly.

VACUUM POWER BRAKE UNIT

Removal and Installation

1. Disconnect and cap hydraulic lines from master cylinder.
2. Disconnect vacuum line from vacuum check valve on unit.
3. Remove steering lower cover.
4. Remove cotter pin, washer and spring spacer that secure power unit pushrod to brake pedal arm.
5. Remove the four nuts that secure power unit to firewall, then remove power unit.
6. To install, reverse removal procedure. Bleed the hydraulic system.

HYDRO-BOOST POWER BRAKE UNIT

Removal and Installation

— CAUTION —
Power steering fluid and brake fluid are incompatible. If brake seals contact steering fluid or steering seals contact brake fluid, the seals will be ruined.

1. With the engine off pump the brake pedal 4 or 5 times to empty the accumulator of pressurized fluid.
2. Disconnect the brake lines from the master cylinder and cap the lines.
3. Remove and plug the three hydraulic lines from the booster. Remove the washer and retainer that secures the booster pedal rod to the brake pedal arm.

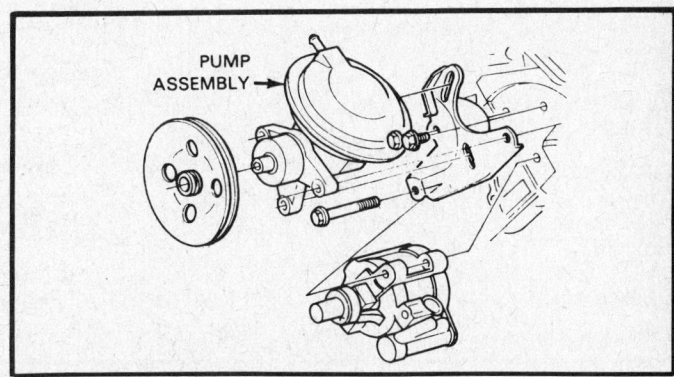

Belt driven vacuum pump
(© General Motors Corporation)

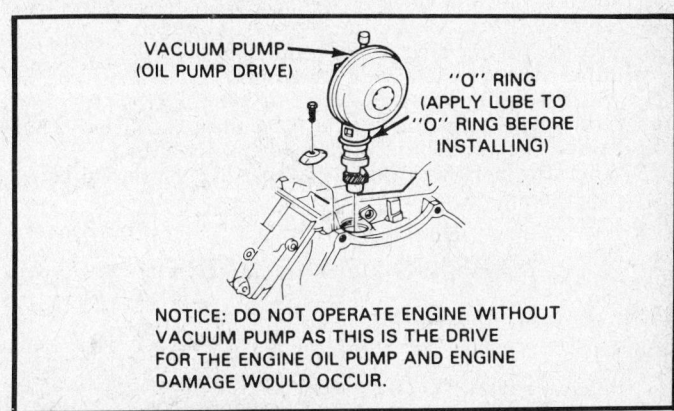

Gear driven vacuum pump
(© General Motors Corporation)

NOTE: To avoid booster damage, do not pry the pedal off the pedal arm.

4. Remove the four nuts holding the booster to the firewall.
5. Loosen the booster from the firewall and move the booster pedal rod inboard until it disconnects from the brake pedal arm. Remove the spring washer from the brake pedal arm and remove the booster.
6. To install, reverse the removal procedure. Tighten the booster mounting nuts to 20 ft. lbs. Bleed the hydro-boost system.

PARKING BRAKE

Adjustment

REAR DRUM BRAKES

NOTE: Make certain that the rear brakes are properly adjusted before adjusting the parking brake.

14-45

SECTION 14

CADILLAC
DE VILLE · FLEETWOOD

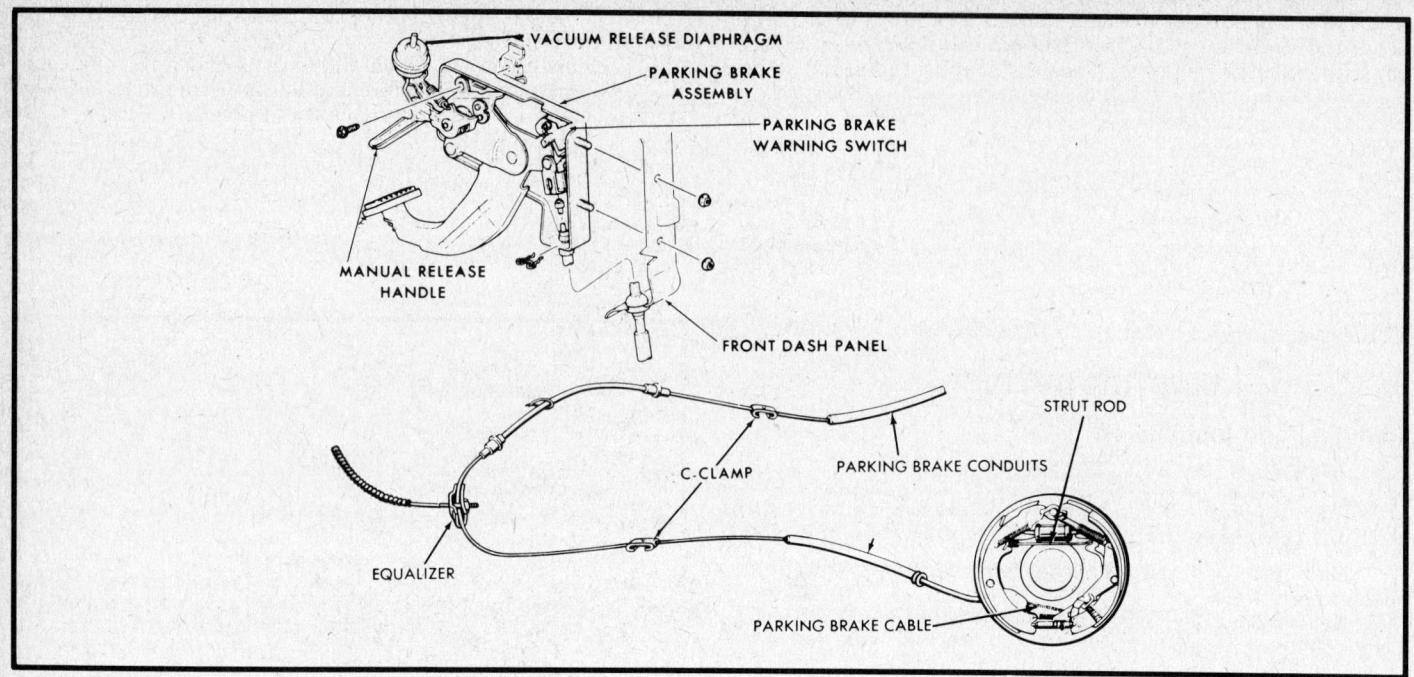

Parking brake cable, typical of drum brakes (© General Motors Corporation)

1. Make a check of the parking brake linkage for the free movement of all the cables. Lubricate, if necessary.
2. Depress the parking brake pedal 1½ in.
3. Raise the rear wheels off the ground.
4. While holding the cable stud to keep it from turning, tighten the equalizer nut until a light drag is felt on either wheel when they are spun in the forward direction.
5. When the parking brake is released there should be no brake shoe drag.

PARKING BRAKE CABLE

Removal and Installation
FRONT
1. Release parking brake.
2. Raise the vehicle and support it safely.
3. Disconnect cable stud at equalizer by removing equalizer nut and separating cable stud from equalizer.
4. Remove front cable from cable connector.
5. Loosen adjuster nut and disconnect front cable from connector. Compress retainer fingers using worm screw hose clamp and loosen at frame.
6. Remove cable at pedal assembly. Follow procedure in Step 5.
7. Remove cable end from parking brake assembly clevis.
8. Pull cable through hole in frame and remove from car.
9. Installation is the reverse of the removal procedure.

REAR
1. Release parking brake.
2. Raise rear of car and place on jack stands.
3. Remove rear wheel and drum on same side of car as parking brake cable being replaced.
4. Remove equalizer nut and retainer. Separate equalizer from right rear cable stud.
5. Remove end of left rear cable from cable connector and equalizer.
6. Remove clip securing right rear cable to control arm bracket and remove cable from bracket by pulling rearward.
7. Remove cable from brake backing plate. Removal can be assisted by compressing multiple prong retainer with worm screw hose clamp.
8. Remove pawl spring and pawl lever from actuating lever.
9. Remove cable end from operating lever and remove cable from backing plate.
10. Installation is the reverse of the removal procedure.

AUTOMATIC TRANSMISSION AND DRIVESHAFT SECTION

AUTOMATIC TRANSMISSION

Removal and Installation

Because of the varied applications of the Turbo Hydra-Matic transmissions used in the Cadillac models, a general transmission removal and installation procedure is outlined. The removal steps can be rearranged as required by the repairman.

1. Disconnect the negative battery cable. Place the shift selector lever in the Neutral position.
2. If necessary, remove the dipstick and the upper bolt on the dipstick tube.
3. Raise the vehicle and support safely.
4. Remove the shift linkage from the transmission shift lever, the bolt retaining the TV cable or the vacuum hose to the transmission modulator.

CADILLAC
DE VILLE • FLEETWOOD
SECTION 14

5. Disconnect the speedometer cable and electrical connection at the detent solenoid, if equipped.
6. Disconnect the oil cooler lines and any exhaust/converter brackets or pipes as required.
7. Remove the flywheel pan and mark the flywheel and converter. Remove the converter retaining bolts.
8. Mark and remove the drive shaft assembly.
9. Support the engine from either on top or with the use of an adjustable jack under the vehicle.
10. With the weight off the transmission, remove the rear mount and/or the rear crossmember.
11. Lower the transmission enough to gain access to the bell housing bolts and remove the bolts.

NOTE: It may be necessary to remove the starter with the bell housing bolts.

12. With the transmission safely chained to a transmission type jack, remove the unit from under the vehicle.

— CAUTION —
Do not allow the converter to fall from the transmission bell housing during the removal or installation of the transmission.

13. The installation is the reverse of the transmission removal procedure.
14. Fill the transmission with the correct fluid, start the engine and check for leakage and correction operation.

COLUMN SHIFT LINKAGE
Adjustment

Manual linkage should be adjusted so that the engine will start in the Park and Neutral positions only.

With the selector lever in the park position, the parking pawl should freely engage within the rear/reaction internal gear lugs or output ring gear lugs. The pointer on the indicator quandrant should line up properly with the range indicators in all ranges.

If the linkage is not adjusted properly, an internal leak could occur at the manual valve which could cause a clutch and/or band failure.

1. Loosen adjusting screw.
2. Working under car, pull trunnion lever up to position transmission shift valve in park, then pull lever down to the third (Neutral) step. Make sure lever is centered in this detent position.
3. Position selector lever in Neutral detent in steering column.
4. Tighten adjusting screw.
5. Check operation of selector lever by performing the following steps:
   a. Lift lever and move to neutral detent. (This is the detent in the transmission.) Release the lever and check to make sure that the lever fits into neutral notch in steering column.
   b. Move lever to drive detent. There should be a slight travel of the lever beyond this detent until the drive stop in the steering column is reached.
   c. Move lever to Reverse detent and check as in Step b above.

TRANSMISSION DOWNSHIFT SWITCH
Adjustment

1. Remove carburetor air cleaner.
2. Make certain that carburetor is adjusted to specification and that throttle linkage is at low speed idle setting.
3. Loosen 2 mounting screws and insert a No. 42 (0.094 in.) wire gauge size drill into the calibrating hole below lower wire terminal. Adjust position of switch so that lever just touches

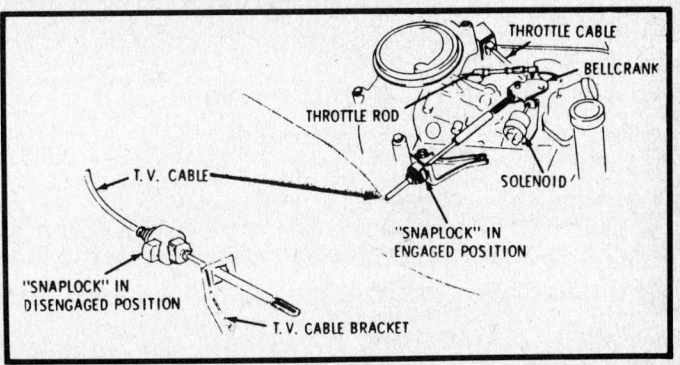

Throttle valve (T.V.) adjustment, 200 series automatic transmission with diesel engine
(© General Motors Corporation)

the carburetor adapter (stud on 6L). With this adjustment the downshift switch should make contact above 60° throttle.

4. With switch positioned, tighten mounting screws and remove No. 42 gauge from calibrating hole through switch.
5. Repeat Step 3, if necessary.
6. Install air cleaner.

T.V. CABLE
Adjustment
ADJUSTING MANUAL TYPE T.V. CABLE (DIESEL ENGINE ONLY)

1. Stop engine.
2. Remove cruise control rod (if equipped).
3. Unlock T.V. cable snap-lock button.
4. Remove T.V. cable from bell crank.
5. Remove throttle rod from bell crank.
6. Rotate bell crank to full throttle stop and hold open.
7. Hold throttle rod and pump lever at full throttle stop; adjust throttle rod to meet bell crank pin at full throttle stop (Do Not Connect). Release bell crank.
8. Reconnect T.V. cable to bell crank.
9. Rotate bell crank to full throttle stop and hold open.
10. Engauge T.V. cable snap-lock button. Release bell crank.
11. Connect throttle rod and cruise control.

ADJUSTING MANUAL TYPE T.V. CABLE (GASOLINE ENGINE ONLY)

1. Stop engine.
2. Unlock T.V. cable snap-lock button.
3. Rotate carburetor lever by hand to wide open throttle and hold open.
4. Engage T.V cable snap-lock button.

ADJUSTING SELF-ADJUSTING TYPE T.V. CABLE (GASOLINE ENGINE ONLY)

1. Stop engine.
2. Depress lock tab. Move slider back through fitting in direction away from throttle body or pump lever until slider stops against fitting.
3. Release lock tab.
4. Open carburetor lever to "full throttle stop" position to automatically adjust T.V. cable. Release carburetor lever.
5. Check T.V. cable for sticking and binding.
6. When the T.V. cable adjustment is made and locked, the cable housing will extend through the cable snap-lock assembly about 1.57–7.95 mm ($^{1}/_{16}$–$^{5}/_{16}$ in.).

SECTION 14 CADILLAC
DE VILLE • FLEETWOOD

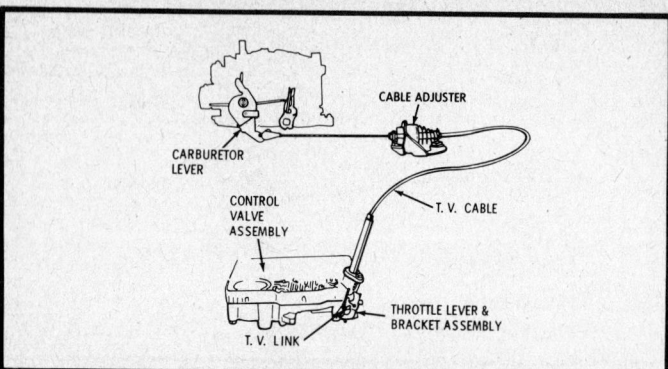

Throttle valve (T.V.) cable and linkage between carburetor and control valve body, typical
(© General Motors Corporation)

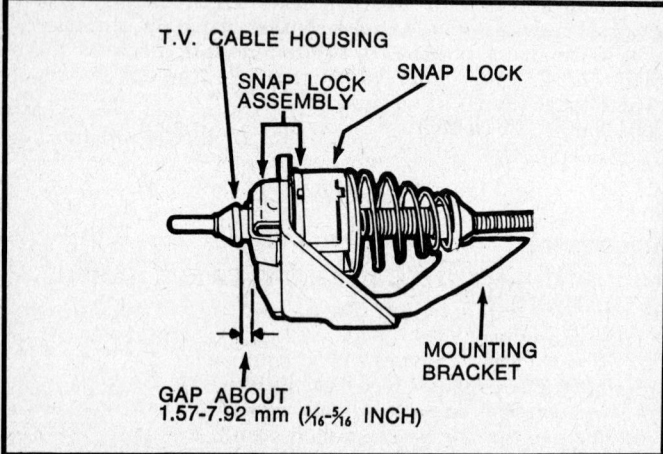

Adjusting T.V. cable to specifications
(© General Motors Corporation)

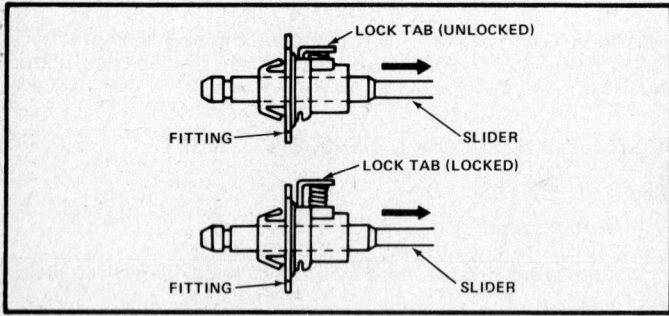

Self adjusting type T.V. cable bracket assembly
(© General Motors Corporation)

DOWNSHIFT (DETENT) CABLE

Adjustment

1. Insure that snap-lock button is in disengaged position (cable should be free to slide thru snap-lock).
2. Open carburetor lever to wide open throttle stop.
3. Push snap-lock to engage position (snap-lock flush with rest of cable fitting).

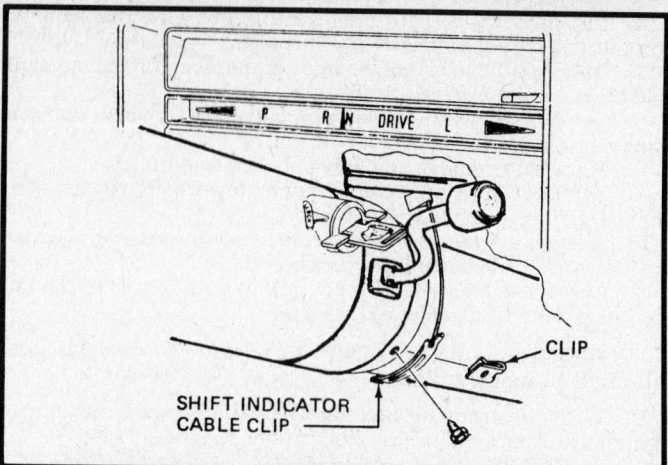

Adjusting the shift indicator quadrant pointer
(© General Motors Corporation)

Adjustment

1. Disconnect the negative battery cable.
2. Remove the left hand instrument cluster bezel, from in front of the speedometer.
3. Loosen the shift indicator cable clip screw on the steering column.

NOTE: Make sure that the automatic transmission control linkage is properly adjusted before adjusting the shift quandrant indicator.

4. Position the shift lever in the detented neutral position.
5. Adjust the cable clip so that the indicator pointer is centered on Neutral.
6. Secure the cable clip screw and move the transmission shift lever from Park to Low to check for full pointer travel from Park to Low.
7. Install the instrument cluster bezel and the negative battery cable.

DRIVESHAFT

Removal and Installation

1. Put the transmission in Neutral, then jack up your car and support it with jack stands.
2. Remove the 2 accessible rear U-joint flange capscrews.
3. Rotate the driveshaft and remove the other two capscrews, while supporting the shaft. Never let the full weight of the driveshaft be supported only by the front universal joint.
4. Push shaft forward to clear pinion flange, then pull rearward to disengage slip yoke from transmission. Plug transmission to prevent oil leakage or entry of dirt.
5. Lubricate slip yoke inside diameter with gear lube, outside of splines with A.T.F.
6. To install, reverse removal procedure, tightening rear U-joint fasteners to 70 ft. lb. Place transmission in Park to hold shaft while tightening capscrews.

UNIVERSAL JOINTS

Refer to the Unit Repair Section for the overhaul information.

CADILLAC
DE VILLE · FLEETWOOD
SECTION 14

REAR AXLE AND SUSPENSION

For Axle Overhaul Procedures and Suspension Services refer to the Unit Repair Section.

AXLE SHAFT, BEARING, AND SEAL

Removal and Installation

1. Raise the car on a hoist and remove the wheel and brake drum.
2. Clean any dirt from the differential cover and loosen the cover attaching bolts, allowing the lubricant to drain out into a suitable container.
3. Remove the pinion cross shaft lockscrew and remove the cross shaft.
4. Push in on the flanged end of the axle shaft and remove the C-lock from the splined end of the axle shaft.
5. Remove the axle shaft from the housing, being cautious not to damage the oil seal.
6. Use a suitable tool to pry the oil seal out of the bore. Use an axle shaft bearing puller on a slide hammer to remove the axle bearing from the bearing bore.
7. Lubricate the new bearing with gear lubricant. Use bearing installer J-23690 or equivalent, and install the bearing so that the tool bottoms out against the shoulder in the housing. Lubricate the lips of the seal with gear lubricant. Position the new seal on seal installer J-23771 or equivalent, and position the seal into the housing bore. Tap the seal into place so that it is flush with the axle tube.
8. Slide the axle shaft into the housing until the splines on the end of the shaft engage the splines of the differential side gear. Handle the shaft gently when trying to engage to splines.
9. Install the axle shaft C-lock on the splined end of the axle shaft in the differential. Push the shaft outward so that the shaft lock seats in the counterbore of the differential side gear.
10. Install the pinion cross shaft through the differential case and pinion gears. Align the lock screw hole and install the lock screw, tightening it to 25 ft. lbs.
11. Clean the differential housing and cover mating surfaces and install the cover with a new gasket.
12. Fill the differential with lubricant, install the brake drum and wheel, and lower the car.

REAR AXLE ASSEMBLY

Removal and Installation

1. Hoist or jack car and support car at frame. Hoist or jack must remain under rear axle housing.
2. Disconnect shock absorbers from axle.
3. Mark drive shaft and pinion flange, then disconnect drive shaft and support out of the way.
4. Remove brake line junction block bolt at axle housing, then disconnect brake lines at junction block.
5. Disconnect upper control arms from axle housing.
6. Lower rear axle assembly on hoist or jack and remove springs.
7. Remove rear wheels and drums.
8. Remove rear axle cover bolts and remove cover.
9. Remove axle.
10. Disconnect brake lines from axle housing clips.
11. Remove backing plates.
12. Disconnect lower control arms from axle housing.

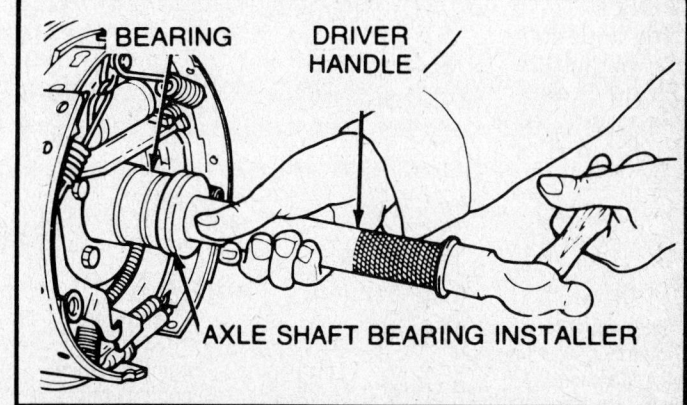

Installation of the rear axle shaft bearing

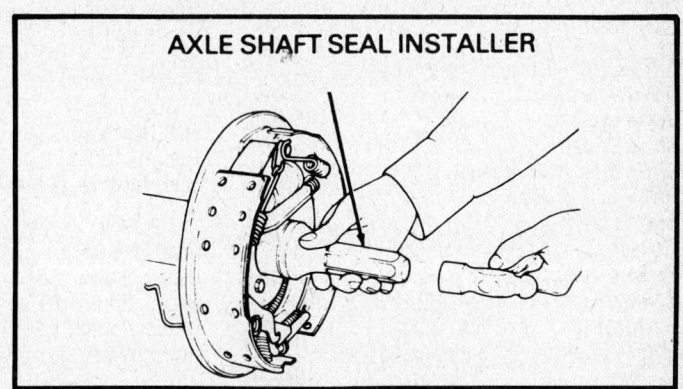

Installation of the rear axle shaft seal

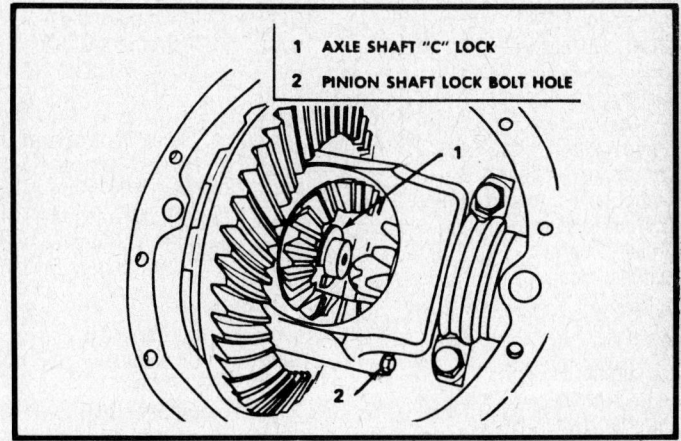

Location of axle "C" lock in the differential housing (© General Motors Corporation)

13. Remove rear axle case assembly and drive pinion, refer to rear axle case and drive pinion removal.
14. Installation is the reverse of the removal procedure.

14–49

SECTION 15 — CHEVROLET
CAPRICE CLASSIC • CORVETTE • MALIBU • MONTE CARLO • IMPALA

SPECIFICATIONS

Brakes	24–2	Serial Number Identification	15–4
Capacities	15–10	Torque	15–9
Crankshaft & Connecting Rod	15–8	Torque Sequence (Cylinder Heads)	15–31
Firing Order	15–6	Tune-Up	15–5
General Engine	15–5	Valve	15–7
Piston & Rings	15–8	Wheel Alignment	15–11

INDEX

A
Alternator R&R	15–11
Automatic Transmission	
Adjustment	15–43
On car Service	23–2
Assembly R&R	15–43
Axle Assembly R&R	15–45
Axle Shaft R&R	15–46

B
Ball Joints	35–2
Brake system	15–41
Brake Booster	15–40
Brake Caliper Overhaul	24–2
Brake Caliper R&R	24–2
Brake Drum	
Rear	24–2
Brake Master Cylinder	15–41
Brake Pad	
Front	24–2
Brake shoe	
Rear	24–2

C
Camshaft R&R	15–32
Carburetor R&R	15–23
Chassis Electrical	15–12
Clutch	
Adjustment	15–42
R&R	15–43
Combination Switch R&R	15–14
Component Location	15–16
Computer command Control	15–19
Cooling System	15–17
Cruise Control	15–16
Cylinder Head	15–31
R&R	15–31

D
Differential	28–2
Inspection	28–2
Dimmer Switch R&R	15–14
Disc Brakes	24–2
Distributor R&R	15–12
Drive Axle	28–2
Driveshaft R&R	15–45

E
Electronic Ignition	30–2
Emission Controls	15–27
Engine	15–27
Identification	15–4
R&R	15–27
Engine Electrical	15–11
Engine Lubrication	15–36
Engine Mechanical	15–27
Engine Mounts R&R	15–29
Exhaust Manifold R&R	15–25

F
Front Suspension	35–2
Alignment	15–11
Fuel Injection	15–21
Fuel Pump R&R	15–18
Fuel, Mixture, Adjust	15–19

H
Headlight switch	15–13
Heater Blower R&R	15–17
Heater Core R&R	15–18
Heater Control R&R	15–17
Horn Switch	15–13

I
Idle Speed Adjust	15–20
Ignition Switch	15–12
Ignition Timing	15–12
Instrument Cluster R&R	15–14
Intake Manifold R&R	15–23

L, M, N
Lower Control Arm R&R	35–2
Master Cylinder R&R	35–2
Manual Steering Gear R&R	15–40
Manual Transmission Overhaul	32–2
Manual Transmission R&R	15–43
Neutral Safety Switch R&R	15–12

O
Oil Pan R&R	15–36
Oil Pump	15–37
R&R	15–37
Oil Seal	
Rear Main	15–37

P
Parking Brake	15–41
Adjustment	15–41
Cable R&R	15–42
Piston & Connecting Rod	15–33
Power Brake Unit R&R	15–40
Power Steering Pump R&R	15–40

R
Rear Main Oil Seal R&R	15–37
Rear Suspension	35–2
Regulator	15–11
Rocker Shaft/Assembly R&R	15–29

S
Serial Number	15–4
Engine	15–4
Vehicle	15–4
Shock Absorber R&R	
Front	35–2
Rear	35–2
Springs	
Front	35–2
Rear	35–2
Starter R&R	15–12
Starter Drive Replacement	15–12
Steering Column R&R	15–40
Steering Wheel R&R	15–38
Speedometer R&R	15–16
Suspension R&R	35–2

T
Timing Chain	15–35
Timing Gear cover	15–34
Oil Seal Replacement	15–34
Tune-Up	15–5
Turn Signal Switch R&R	15–14

U, V
U-Joint Overhaul	28–2
Valve Tappetts R&R	15–29
Valve Timing, Adjust	15–30
Valvey System	15–29
Voltage Regulator	15–11

W, Y
Water Pump R&R	15–17
Wheel alignment	15–11
Front	15–11
Wheel Bearings	
Front	15–40
Rear	15–47
Wheel Cylinders	15–47
Rear	24–2
Windshield Wiper	15–14
Linkage R&R	15–14
Motor R&R	15–14
Switch R&R	15–13
Year Identification	15–3

BEFORE SERVICING BE CERTAIN TO READ THE SAFETY NOTICE

Chevrolet
1983–87 Rear Wheel Drive Cars
CAPRICE CLASSIC • CORVETTE • MALIBU
MONTE CARLO • IMPALA

YEAR IDENTIFICATION

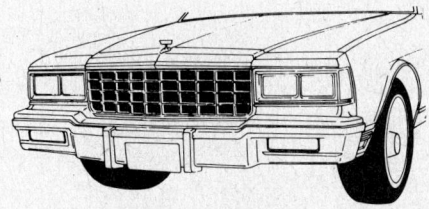

1983–87 Caprice

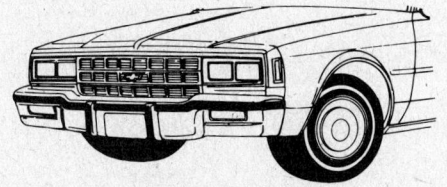

1983–84 Impala

1983 Malibu

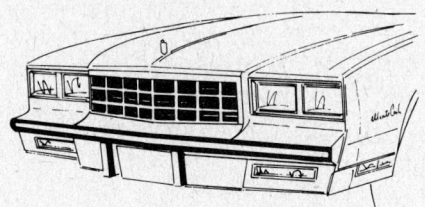

1983–86 Monte Carlo

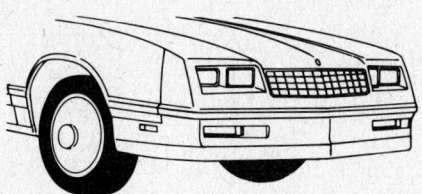

1984–87 Monte Carlo SS

SECTION 15
CHEVROLET
CAPRICE CLASSIC • CORVETTE • MALIBU • MONTE CARLO • IMPALA

VEHICLE IDENTIFICATION NUMBER (VIN)
All Except Corvette

It is important for servicing and ordering parts to be certain of the vehicle and engine identification. The VIN (vehicle identification number) is a 13 or 17 digit number visible through the windshield on the driver's side of the dash and contains the vehicle and engine identification codes. It can be interpreted as follows:

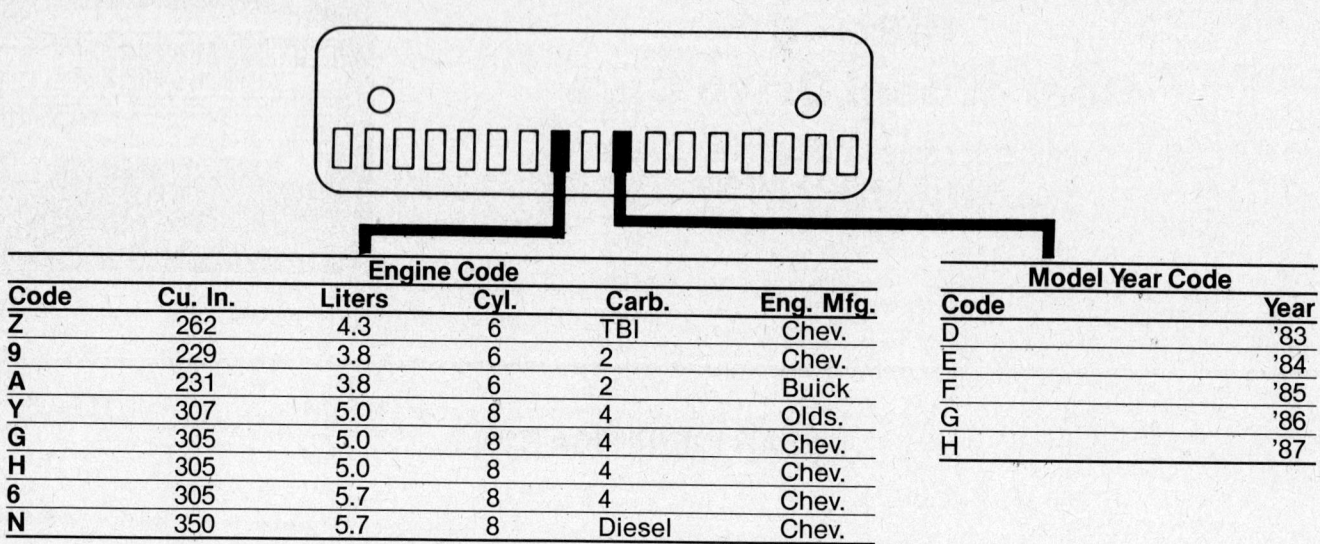

Engine Code						Model Year Code	
Code	Cu. In.	Liters	Cyl.	Carb.	Eng. Mfg.	Code	Year
Z	262	4.3	6	TBI	Chev.	D	'83
9	229	3.8	6	2	Chev.	E	'84
A	231	3.8	6	2	Buick	F	'85
Y	307	5.0	8	4	Olds.	G	'86
G	305	5.0	8	4	Chev.	H	'87
H	305	5.0	8	4	Chev.		
6	305	5.7	8	4	Chev.		
N	350	5.7	8	Diesel	Chev.		

VEHICLE IDENTIFICATION NUMBER (VIN)
Corvette

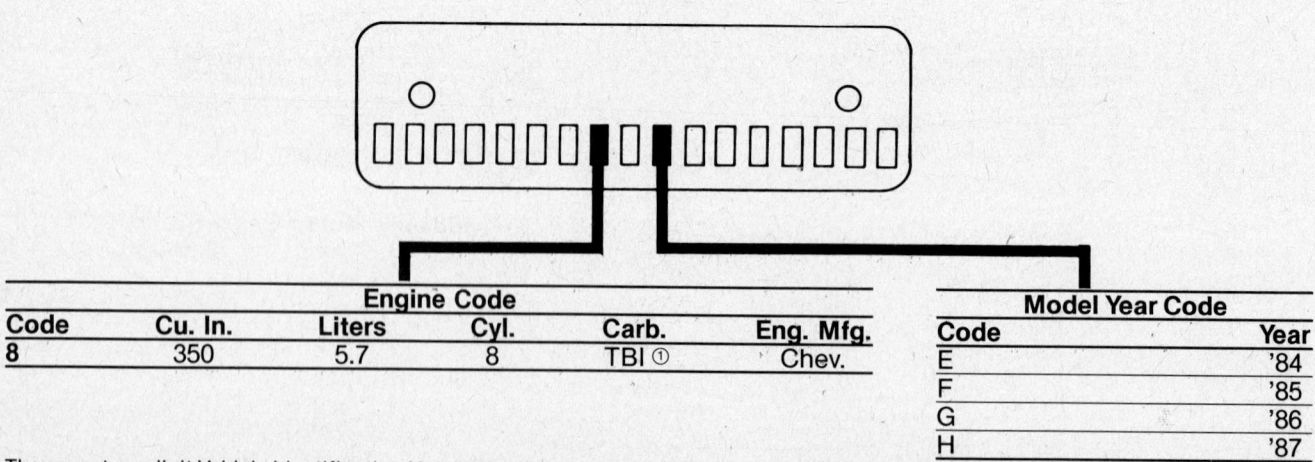

Engine Code						Model Year Code	
Code	Cu. In.	Liters	Cyl.	Carb.	Eng. Mfg.	Code	Year
8	350	5.7	8	TBI ①	Chev.	E	'84
						F	'85
						G	'86
						H	'87

The seventeen digit Vehicle Identification Number can be used to determine engine application and model year. The 10th digit indicates the model year, and the 8th digit identifies the factory installed engine. There is no 1983 Corvette model.
TBI—Throttle body (fuel) injection
① Tuned Port Injection (TPI) on 1985 and later.

CHEVROLET
CAPRICE CLASSIC • CORVETTE • MALIBU • MONTE CARLO • IMPALA
SECTION 15

GENERAL ENGINE SPECIFICATIONS
All Except Corvette

Year	Eng. VIN Code	Engine No. Cyl. Displacement Cu. In.	Liter	Eng. Mfg.	Carburetor Type	Horsepower @ rpm ■	Torque @ rpm (ft. lbs.) ■	Bore × Stroke (in.)	Compression Ratio	Oil Pressure @ 2000 rpm
'83	9	6-229	3.8	Chev.	2 bbl	115 @ 4000	170 @ 2000	3.736 × 3.480	8.6:1	45
	A	6-231	3.8	Buick	2 bbl	110 @ 2800	190 @ 1600	3.800 × 3.400	6.0:1	45
	V	6-263	4.3	Olds.	Diesel	85 @ 3200	111 @ 1600	4.057 × 3.385	21.6:1	45 ①
	H	8-305	5.0	Chev.	4 bbl	150 @ 3800	240 @ 2400	3.736 × 3.480	8.6:1	45
	N	8-350	5.7	Olds.	Diesel	105 @ 3200	205 @ 1600	4.057 × 3.385	22.5:1	30–45 ①
'84	9	6-229	3.8	Chev.	2 bbl	115 @ 4000	170 @ 2000	3.736 × 3.480	8.6:1	45
	A	6-231	3.8	Buick	2 bbl	110 @ 3800	190 @ 1600	3.800 × 3.400	8.0:1	45
	G	8-305	5.0	Chev.	4 bbl	190 @ 4800	240 @ 3200	3.736 × 3.480	9.5:1	45
	H	8-305	5.0	Chev.	4 bbl	150 @ 3800	240 @ 2400	3.736 × 3.480	8.6:1	45
	N	8-350	5.7	Olds.	Diesel	105 @ 3200	205 @ 1600	4.057 × 4.485	22.5:1	30–45 ①
	6	8-350	5.7	Chev.	4 bbl	205 @ 4200	290 @ 4200	4.000 × 3.480	8.2:1	45
'85	Z	V6-262	4.3	Chev.	TBI	110 @ 4000	190 @ 1600	4.000 × 3.480	9.3:1	45
	G	8-305	5.0	Chev.	4 bbl	105 @ 3200	240 @ 2400	3.736 × 3.480	9.5:1	45
	H	8-305	5.0	Chev.	4 bbl	105 @ 3200	240 @ 2400	3.736 × 3.480	8.6:1	45
	6	8-350	5.7	Chev.	4 bbl	205 @ 4200	290 @ 4200	4.000 × 3.480	8.2:1	45
	N	8-350	5.7	Olds.	Diesel	105 @ 3200	205 @ 1600	4.057 × 3.385	22.46:1	30–45 ①
'86–'87	Z	V6-262	4.3	Chev.	TBI	110 @ 4000	190 @ 1600	4.000 × 3.480	9.3:1	45
	G	8-305	5.0	Chev.	4 bbl	105 @ 3200	240 @ 2400	3.736 × 3.480	9.5:1	45
	H	8-305	5.0	Chev.	4 bbl	105 @ 3200	240 @ 2400	3.736 × 3.480	8.6:1	45
	6	8-350	5.7	Chev.	4 bbl	205 @ 4200	290 @ 4200	4.000 × 3.480	8.2:1	45
	Y	8-307	5.0	Olds.	4 bbl	148 @ 3800	250 @ 2400	3.800 × 3.385	8.0:1	40 ①

■ Horsepower and torque are SAE net figures. They are measured at the rear of the transmission with all accessories installed and operating. Since the figures vary when a given engine is installed in different models, some are representative rather than exact.
① @ 1500

GENERAL ENGINE SPECIFICATIONS
Corvette

Year	No. of Cyl. Displacement (Cu. In.)	Engine V.I.N. Code	Fuel Delivery	Horsepower @ rpm ①	Torque @ rpm (ft. lbs.) ①	Bore × Stroke (in.)	Compression Ratio	Oil Pressure @ 2000 rpm
'84	8-350	8	TBI	205 @ 4300	290 @ 2800	4.000 × 3.480	9.0:1	50–65
'85	8-350	8	MFI	NA	NA	4.000 × 3.480	9.0:1	50–65
'86–'87	8-350	8	TPI	230 @ 4000	330 @ 3200	4.000 × 3.480	9.0:1	50–65

NOTE: All engines used in the Corvette are manufactured by Chevrolet Motor Division, G.M. Corp.
NA—Not available at time of publication
TPI—Tuned Port Injection
TBI—Throttle body fuel injection system
MFI—Multiport fuel injection system
① Horsepower and torque are SAE net figures. They are measured at the rear of the transmission with all accessories installed and operating. Since the figures vary when a given engine is installed in different models, some are representative rather than exact.

TUNE-UP SPECIFICATIONS
All Except Corvette

Year	Eng. VIN Code	Engine No. Cyl. Displacement	Eng. Mfg.	Spark Plugs Orig. Type	Gap. (in.)	Distributor	Ignition Timing (deg) ▲ Auto. Trans.	Valves Intake Opens ■ (deg)	Fuel Pump Pressure (psi)	Idle Speed (rpm) ▲ Auto. Trans.
'83	9	6-229	Chev.	R-45TS	.045	Electronic	0B ①	42	4.5–6.0	475/850
	A	6-231	Buick	R-45TS	.045	Electronic	15B ①	16	4.25–5.75	450/900
	H	8-305	Chev.	R-45TS	.045	Electronic	6B ①	44	5.5–7.0	500/650
	N	8-350	Olds.	—	—	—	4A ①	16	5.5–6.5	600/750
	V	6-263	Olds	—	—	—	①	16	5.5–6.5	①

15-5

SECTION 15

CHEVROLET
CAPRICE CLASSIC • CORVETTE • MALIBU • MONTE CARLO • IMPALA

TUNE-UP SPECIFICATIONS
All Except Corvette

Year	Engine VIN Code	Engine No. Cyl. Displacement	Engine Mfg.	Spark Plugs Orig. Type	Spark Plugs Gap. (in.)	Distributor	Ignition Timing (deg)▲ Auto. Trans.	Valves Intake Opens ■(deg)	Fuel Pump Pressure (psi)	Idle Speed (rpm)▲ Auto. Trans.
'84	9	6-229	Chev.	R-45TS	.045	Electronic	0B ①	42	4.5–6.0	475
	A	6-231	Buick	R-45TS8	.060	Electronic	15B ①	16	4.25–5.75	600/700
	H	8-305	Chev.	R-45TS	.045	Electronic	6B ①	44	5.5–7.0	500/650
	N	8-350	Olds.	—	—	—	4A ①	16	5.5–6.5	600/750
	G	8-305	Chev.	R-45TS	.045	Electronic	6B ①	44	5.5–7.0	①
'85	Z	V6-262	Chev.	R-43CTS	.035	Electronic	6B ①	16	5.5–6.5	450/900
	G	8-305	Chev.	R-45TS	.045	Electronic	6B ④	44	5.5–7.0	500/650
	H	8-305	Chev.	R-45TS	.045	Electronic	6B ①	44	5.5–7.0	500/650
	6	8-350	Chev.	R-45TS	.045	Electronic	6B ①	16	5.5–6.5	475
	N	8-350	Olds.	—	—	—	4A ①	16	5.5–6.5	600/750
'86–'87	Z	V6-262	Chev.	R-43CTS ③	.035	Electronic	6B ①	16	5.5–6.5	450/900
	G	8-305	Chev.	R-45TS ②	.045 ②	Electronic	6B ①	44	5.5–7.0	500/650
	H	8-305	Chev.	R-45TS ②	.045 ②	Electronic	6B ①	44	5.5–7.0	500/650
	6	8-350	Chev.	R-45TS	.045	Electronic	6B ①	16	5.5–6.5	475
	Y	8-307	Olds.	FR3LS6	.060	Electronic	①	—	6.0–7.5	①

NOTE: The underhood specifications sticker often reflects tune-up specification changes made in production. Sticker figures must be used if they disagree with those in this chart.
▲ See text for procedure
■ All figures Before Top Dead Center
B Before Top Dead Center
TDC Top Dead Center
— Not applicable
Part numbers in this chart are not recommendations by Chilton for any product by brand name.
① See underhood specifications sticker
② '86 Caprice: R-44TS—.035 gap
③ '86 Monte Carlo: R-43TS—.035 gap

FIRING ORDERS

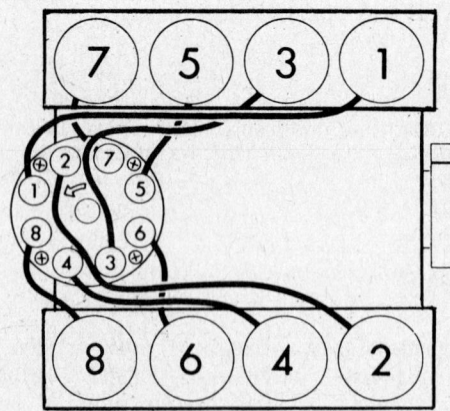

GM (Oldsmobile) 307
Engine firing order: 1–8–4–3–6–5–7–2
Distributor rotation: counterclockwise

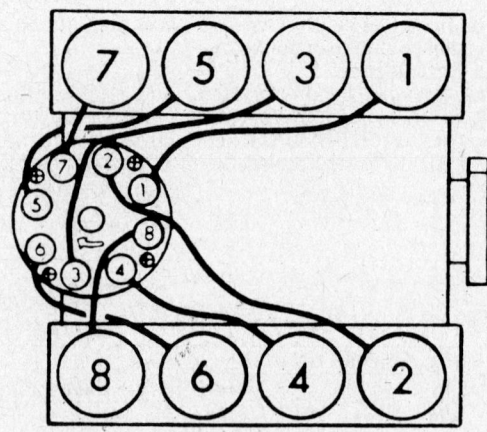

GM (Chevrolet) V8
Engine firing order: 1–8–4–3–6–5–7–2
Distributor rotation: clockwise

CHEVROLET
CAPRICE CLASSIC • CORVETTE • MALIBU • MONTE CARLO • IMPALA

SECTION 15

FIRING ORDERS

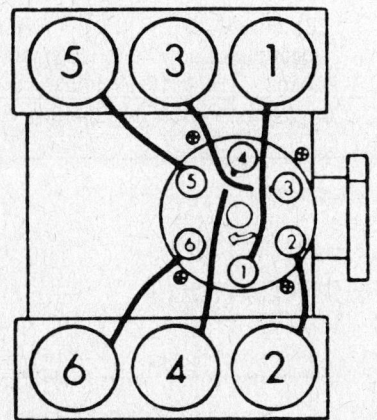

GM (Buick) 231 V6
Engine firing order: 1–6–5–4–3–2
Distributor rotation: clockwise

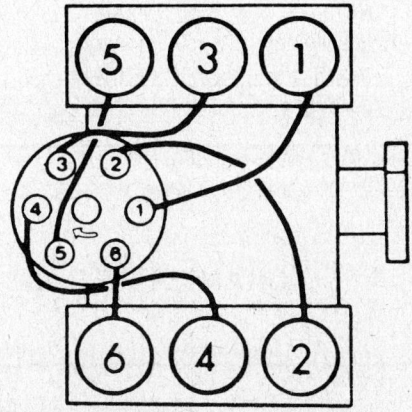

Chevrolet-built V6 engine
Engine firing order: 1–6–5–4–3–2
Distributor rotation: clockwise

TUNE-UP SPECIFICATIONS
Corvette

	Engine			Spark Plugs		Ignition Timing (deg) ②		Valves Intake Opens (deg) ③	Fuel Pump Pressure (psi)	Idle Speed (rpm) ②	
Year	No. of Cyl. Displacement (Cu. In.)	V.I.N. Code	Option Code	Type (A.C.)	Gap (in.)	Man. Trans.	Auto. Trans.			Man. Trans.	Auto. Trans.
'84	8-350	8	L83	R45TS	.045	①	①	32	9–13	①	475
'85	8-350	8	L98	R45TS	.045	①	①	32	9–13	400	450
'86–'87	8-350	8	L98	R45TS	.045	①	①	32	9–13	400	450

NOTE: The underhood specifications sticker often reflects tuneup specification changes made in production. Sticker figures must be used if they disagree with those in this chart. Part numbers in this chart are not recommendations by Chilton for any product by brand name.
B—Before Top Dead Center
① See Underhood Sticker
② See text for procedure
③ All figures Before Top Dead Center

VALVE SPECIFICATIONS
All Except Corvette

	Engine No. Cyl. Displacement (cu. in.)	Seat Angle (deg)	Face Angle (deg)	Spring Test Pressure (lbs. @ in.)	Spring Installed Height (in.)	Stem-to-Guide Clearance (in.)		Stem Diameter (in.)	
Year						Intake	Exhaust	Intake	Exhaust
'83–'87	6-229 Chev.	46	45	200 @ 1.25	1.70	.0010–.0027	.0010–.0027	.3414	.3414
	6-231 Buick	45	45	168 @ 1.32	1.72	.0015–.0032	.0015–.0032	.3407	.3409
	6-262 Chev.	46	45	200 @ 1.25	1.70	.0010–.0027	.0010–.0027	.3414	.3414
	6-263 Olds. Diesel	45 ①	44 ①	210 @ 1.22	1.67	.0010–.0027	.0015–.0032	.3429	.3424
	8-307 Olds.	45	44	187 @ 1.27	1.67	.0010–.0027	.0015–.0032	.3429	.3429
	8-305 Chev.	46	45	200 @ 1.25	1.70	.0010–.0027	.0010–.0027	.3414	.3414
	8-350 Chev.	46	45	200 @ 1.25	1.70	.0010–.0027	.0010–.0027	.3414	.3414
	8-350 Olds. Diesel	45 ②	44 ③	205 @ 1.300	1.67	.0010–.0027	.0015–.0032	.3429	.3424

① Exhaust: Face 30°; Seat 31°
② Exhaust: 31°
③ Exhaust: 30°

15-7

SECTION 15

CHEVROLET
CAPRICE CLASSIC • CORVETTE • MALIBU • MONTE CARLO • IMPALA

VALVE SPECIFICATIONS
Corvette

Year	Engine No. Cyl. Displacement (cu. in.)	Seat Angle (deg)	Face Angle (deg)	Spring Test Pressure (lbs. @ in.)	Spring Installed Height (in.)	Stem-to-Guide Clearance (in.) Intake	Stem-to-Guide Clearance (in.) Exhaust	Stem Diameter (in.) Intake	Stem Diameter (in.) Exhaust
'84–'87	8-350	46	45	194–206 @ 1.25 ②	1 23/32 ①	.0010–.0027	.0010–.0027	.3410–.3417	.3410–.3417

① 1 19/32 for the exhaust valve spring
② 1.16 exhaust valve

CRANKSHAFT AND CONNECTING ROD SPECIFICATIONS
All Except Corvette
All measurements are given in inches

Year	Engine No. Cyl. Displacement (cu. in.)	Crankshaft Main Brg. Journal Dia.	Crankshaft Main Brg. Oil Clearance	Crankshaft Shaft End-Play	Crankshaft Thrust on No.	Connecting Rod Diameter Journal	Connecting Rod Clearance Oil	Connecting Rod Clearance Side
'83–'87	6-229 Chev.	2.4484–2.4493 ①	.0008–.0020 ②	.002–.006	4	2.0986–2.0998	.0013–.0035	.006–.014
	6-231 Buick	2.4995	.0004–.0015	.004–.008	2	2.2495–2.2487	.0005–.0026	.006–.027
	6-262 Chev.	2.4484–2.4493 ①	.0008–.0020 ②	.002–.006	4	2.0986–2.0998	.0013–.0035	.006–.014
	6-263 Olds.	2.9993–3.0003	.0005–.0021 ③	.0035–.0135	3	2.2490–2.2510	.0005–.0026	.006–.020
	8-305 Chev. 8-350 Chev.	2.4484–2.4493 ①	.0008–.0020 ②	.002–.006	5	2.0986–2.0998	.0013–.0035	.006–.014
	8-350 Olds.	2.9993–3.0003	.0005–.0021 ④	.0035–.0135	3	2.1238–2.1248	.0005–.0026	.006–.020
	8-307 Olds.	2.4990–2.4995 ⑤	.0005–.0021 ⑥	.0035–.0135	3	2.1238–2.1248	.0004–.0033	.006–.020

① Intermediate—2.4481–2.4490
   Rear—2.4479–2.4488
② Intermediate—.0011–.0020
   Rear—.0017–.0032
③ No. 4:.0020–.0034
④ No. 5:.0015–.0031
⑤ No. 1—2.4993–2.4998
⑥ No. 5—.0015–.0031

CRANKSHAFT AND CONNECTING ROD SPECIFICATIONS
Corvette
All measurements are given in inches

Year	Engine No. Cyl. Displacement (Cu. In.)	Crankshaft Main Brg. Journal Dia.	Crankshaft Main Brg. Oil Clearance	Crankshaft Shaft End-Play	Crankshaft Thrust on No.	Connecting Rod Journal Diameter	Connecting Rod Oil Clearance	Connecting Rod Side Clearance
'83–'87	8-350	2.4484–2.4493 ①	.0008–.0020 ②	.002–.006	5	2.0988–2.0998	.0013–.0035	.008–.014 ③

① Nos. 2, 3, 4—2.4481–2.4490; No. 5—2.4479–2.4488
② Nos. 2, 3, 4—.0011–.0023; No. 5—.0017–.0032
③ 1986 and Later: .006–.014

PISTON AND RING SPECIFICATIONS
Corvette
All measurements are given in inches

Year	Engine No. of Cyl. Displacement (Cu. In.)	Ring Gap Top Compression	Ring Gap Bottom Compression	Ring Gap Oil Control	Ring Side Clearance Top Compression	Ring Side Clearance Bottom Compression	Ring Side Clearance Oil Control	Piston-to-Bore Clearance (in.)
'84–'87	8-350	.010–.020	.010–.025	.015–.055	.0012–.0032	.0012–.0032	.002–.007	.00025–.00035

CHEVROLET
CAPRICE CLASSIC • CORVETTE • MALIBU • MONTE CARLO • IMPALA
SECTION 15

PISTON AND RING SPECIFICATIONS
All Except Corvette

Year	VIN Code	Engine Type/ Disp. cu. in.	Piston-to-Bore Clearance	Ring Gap			Ring Side Clearance		
				Top Compression	Bottom Compression	Oil Control	Top Compression	Bottom Compression	Oil Control
'83–'84	9	6-229	0.0012	0.010–0.020	0.010–0.025	0.010–0.055	0.0012–0.0032	0.0012–0.0032	0.0020–0.0070
'85–'87	Z	6-262	0.0012	0.010–0.020	0.010–0.025	0.015–0.055	0.0012–0.0032	0.0012–0.0032	0.0020–0.0070
'83	V	6-263	0.0030–0.0040	0.015–0.025	0.015–0.025	0.015–0.035	0.005–0.007	0.003–0.005	0.001–0.005
'83–'87	H	8-305	0.0012	0.010–0.020	0.010–0.025	0.015–0.055	0.0012–0.0032	0.0012–0.0032	0.0020–0.0070
'84–'87	G	8-305	0.0012	0.010–0.020	0.010–0.025	0.015–0.055	0.0012–0.0032	0.0012–0.0032	0.0020–0.0070
'86–'87	Y	8-307	0.0008–0.0018	0.009–0.019	0.009–0.019	0.015–0.055	0.0020–0.0040	0.0020–0.0040	0.000–0.0035
'83–'85	N	8-350	0.0050–0.0060	0.015–0.025	0.015–0.025	0.015–0.055	0.005–0.007	0.003–0.005	0.0010–0.0050
'83–'84	A	6-231	0.0012	0.010–0.020	0.010–0.025	0.015–0.055	0.0012–0.0032	0.0012–0.0032	0.0020–0.0070

TORQUE SPECIFICATIONS
All Except Corvette
All readings in ft. lbs.

Year	Engine No. Cyl. Displacement (cu. in.)	Cylinder Head Bolts	Rod Bearing Bolts	Main Bearing Bolts	Crankshaft Bolt	Flywheel to Crankshaft Bolts	Manifold Intake	Manifold Exhaust
'83–'87	6-229, 8-305	65	45	70 ⑥	60	60	30	20 ④
'83–'84	6-231	80	40	100	175 ②	60	45	25
'85–'87	6-262	60–75	45	80	70	70	45	20
'83–'85	8-350 Diesel	130 ①	42	120	310	60	40 ①	25
'83	6-263 Diesel	142 ③	42	107	160–350	48	41	29
'86–'87	8-307	125 ①	42	⑤	200–310	46	40 ①	25

① Dip bolt in oil before tightening
② '83–'85: 225 ft. lbs.
③ Bolts No. 5, 6, 11, 12, 13, 14: 59 ft. lbs.
④ 8-305 inside bolts: 25 ft. lbs.
⑤ No. 1 thru 4; 80 ft. lbs., No. 5: 120 ft. lbs.
⑥ '85–'87: 70-85

TORQUE SPECIFICATIONS
Corvette
All readings in ft. lbs.

Year	Engine No. of Cyl. Displacement (Cu. In.)	Cylinder Head Bolts	Rod Bearing Bolts	Main Bearing Bolts	Crankshaft Balancer Bolt	Flywheel to Crankshaft Bolts	Manifold Intake	Manifold Exhaust
'84–'87	350	65	45	80	60	60	35	20

Caution: Verify the correct original equipment engine is in the vehicle by referring to the VIN engine code before torquing any bolts.

SECTION 15

CHEVROLET
CAPRICE CLASSIC • CORVETTE • MALIBU • MONTE CARLO • IMPALA

CAPACITIES
Monte Carlo, Malibu

Year	Engine No. Cyl. Displacement (Cu. In.)	Engine Crankcase Add 1 Qt For New Filter ■	Transmission (Pts To Refill After Draining) Automatic ●	Drive Axle (pts)	Gasoline Tank (gals)	Cooling System (qts) With Heater	Cooling System (qts) With A/C
'83	6-229 Chev.	4	6.0	3.5	18.1	15.0	15.0
	6-231 Buick	4	6.0	3.5	18.1	15.0	15.0
	6-263 Diesel	6 ③	6.0	3.5	18.1	15.0	15.0
	8-305 Chev.	4	6.0	3.5	18.1	15.0	15.0
	8-350 Diesel	7 ③	6.0	3.5	18.1	18.0	18.0
'84	6-229 Chev.	4	6.0	3.5	18.1	15.0	15.0
	6-231 Buick	4	6.0	3.5	18.1	15.0	15.0
	8-350 Chev. ⑧	4	6.0	3.5	18.1	16.6	16.6
	8-305 Chev.	4	6.0	3.5	18.1	16.3	16.3
	8-350 Diesel	7 ③	6.0	3.5	19.8	17.3	17.3
'85-'87	6-262	4 ③	7.0	⑤	17.6	12.0	12.0
	8-305	4 ③	7.0	⑤	18.1	16.3	16.3
	8-305 ⑧	4 ③	7.0	⑤	18.1	16.6	16.6

● Specifications do not include torque converter
Add just enough fluid to fill the transmission to the proper level. It takes only one pint to raise the level from "ADD" to "FULL" with a hot transmission. Do not overfill.
■ On models with micro oil filters, capacity is the same with or without new filter
③ Includes mandatory filter change
⑤ With 7.5 inch ring gear: 3.5
  with 8.5 inch ring gear: 4.25
  with 8.75 inch ring gear: 5.4
⑧ Eng. Code G

CAPACITIES
Impala, Caprice

Year	Engine No. Cyl. (Cu. In.) Displacement	Engine Crankcase Add 1 Qt For New Filter	Transmission Pts To Refill After Draining Automatic ●	Drive Axle (pts)	Gasoline Tank (gals)	Cooling System (qts) With Heater	Cooling System (qts) With A/C
'83	6-229	4	6.0	⑥	⑦	—	14¼ ④
	6-231	4	6.0	⑥	⑦	—	11¾ ④
	8-305	4	6.0 ⑧	⑥	⑦	—	15½
	8-350 Diesel	6	6.0	⑥	⑦	—	18.3
'84	6-229	4	6.0	⑥	⑦	—	14¼
	6-231	4	6.0	⑥	⑦	—	11¾
	8-305	4	6.0 ⑧	⑥	⑦	—	15½
	8-350 Diesel	6	6.0 ⑧	⑥	⑦	—	18.3
'85	6-262	4 ③	7.0 ⑧	⑥	⑦	—	14.0 ⑩
	8-305	4	7.0 ⑧	⑥	⑦	—	15.3 ⑪
	8-350 Diesel	6	7.0 ⑧	⑥	⑦	—	18.3
'86-'87	6-262	4 ③	7.0 ⑧	⑥	⑦	12.2	12.5
	8-305	4	7.0 ⑧	⑥	⑦	16.8	17.5
	8-307	4	7.0 ⑧	⑥	⑦	17.1	17.6

● Specifications do not include torque converter
Add just enough fluid to fill the transmission to the proper level. It takes only one pint to raise the level from "ADD" to "FULL" with a hot transmission. Do not overfill.
— Not applicable
③ 4 qt. with filter change
④ Cooling system capacity. Station wagon heavy duty capacity 16¾ qts.
⑥ 7.5" ring gear: 3.5 pts
  8.5" ring gear: 4.25 pts
  8.75" ring gear: 5.0 pts
⑦ Gasoline coupe and sedan—25 gal;
  Diesel coupe and sedan—26 gal.
  All station wagons—22 gal.
⑧ Automatic Overdrive; 10 pts
⑩ With H.D. cooling: 14.6
⑪ With H.D. cooling: 16.1

CHEVROLET 15
CAPRICE CLASSIC • CORVETTE • MALIBU • MONTE CARLO • IMPALA

CAPACITIES
Corvette

Year	Engine No. of Cyl. Displacement (Cu. In.)	Engine Crankcase (Add 1 Qt For New Filter)	Transmission (Pts-to-Refill After Draining)			Gasoline Tank (gals)	Cooling System (qts)	
			Manual 4-Speed	Automatic ①	Drive Axle (pts)		With Heater	With A/C
'84-'87	8-350	4	3.5 ②	10	3.75	20	14	14

① For pan removal and filter change only
② Four speed overdrive uses Dexron II in the overdrive section and 80WGL5 lube in the transmission section

WHEEL ALIGNMENT SPECIFICATIONS
Impala, Caprice

Year	Model	Caster Range (deg)	Caster Pref. Setting (deg)	Camber Range (deg)	Camber Pref. Setting (deg)	Toe-in (in.)
'83-'87	Chevrolet	2P-4P	3P	0-1.6	4/5P	1/16-1/4

N Negative   P Positive   — Not specified

WHEEL ALIGNMENT SPECIFICATIONS
Malibu, Monte Carlo

Year	Model	Caster Range (deg)	Caster Pref. Setting (deg)	Camber Range (deg)	Camber Pref. Setting (deg)	Toe-In (in.)	Steering Axis (deg) Inclination
'83-'87	Monte Carlo, Manual Steer.	0 to 2P	1P	3/10N to 1 3/10P	1/2P	1/16 to 1/4	7 7/8
	Monte Carlo, Pow. Steer.	2P to 4P	3P	3/10N to 1 3/10P	1/2P	1/16 to 1/4	7 7/8

N Negative   P Positive

WHEEL ALIGNMENT SPECIFICATIONS
Corvette

Year	Front Wheel Caster Range	Front Wheel Caster Preferred	Front Wheel Camber Range	Front Wheel Camber Preferred	Rear Wheel Camber Range	Rear Wheel Camber Preferred	Toe-In (in.) Front Wheel	Toe-In (in.) Rear Wheel
'84-'87	2 1/2P-3 1/2P	3P	5/16P-1 5/16P	13/16P	1/32N ± 29/32 ①	13/32 ②	0 – 1/4P	3/32 ± 7/32

N—Negative   ① 1984—1/2N-1/2P
P—Positive   ② 1984—0

ELECTRICAL SECTION

For Overhaul Procedures Refer to the Unit Repair Section.

Charging System

ALTERNATOR

Removal and Installation

1. Disconnect the negative battery cable. Remove all necessary components in order to gain access to the alternator assembly.
2. Disconnect the two terminal plug and the battery lead from the back of the alternator assembly.
3. Loosen the adjusting bolts. Remove the alternator belt.
4. Remove the alternator retaining bolts. Remove the alternator assembly from the vehicle.
5. Installation is the reverse of the removal procedure. Once the alternator belt is installed, check for the proper belt tension.

VOLTAGE REGULATOR

Removal and Installation

The voltage regulator is incorporated within the alternator assembly. There is no adjustment procedure. Should the regulator require service the alternator must be disassembled.

15-11

SECTION 15

CHEVROLET
CAPRICE CLASSIC • CORVETTE • MALIBU • MONTE CARLO • IMPALA

Starting System

STARTER

Removal and Installation

1. Disconnect the negative battery cable.
2. Raise the vehicle and support it safely.
3. Remove the starter braces, shields or anything else that may stop the starter assembly from being removed.
4. Remove the starter mounting bolts. Remove the electrical wires from the solenoid assembly.
5. Remove the starter from the vehicle.
6. Installation is the reverse of the removal procedure. If any shims were removed along with the starter assembly be sure to reinstall them where removed.

Ignition System

DISTRIBUTOR

Removal and Installation

1. Disconnect the negative battery cable. Remove all the necessary components in order to gain access to the distributor assembly.
2. Remove all electrical connections from the unit. Release the coil connectors from the distributor cap.
3. Remove the distributor cap retaining screws and remove the cap. Disconnect the four terminal harness from the distributor.
4. Remove the distributor hold down bolt. Note the position of the rotor and then pull the distributor assembly from the engine.
5. To insure correct ignition timing the distributor must be installed with the rotor in the same position as it was removed.
6. Installation is the reverse of the removal procedure.
7. If the engine has been cranked after the distributor has been removed, the following procedure must be used.
8. Remove the number one spark plug. Place your finger over the spark plug hole and crank the engine slowly until compression is felt.
9. Align the timing mark on the pulley to "O" on the engine timing indicator. Position the rotor between number one and number eight spark plug towers on V8 engines and between number one and number six spark plug towers on V6 engines.
10. The distributor can now be correctly installed in the engine.
11. Once the distributor has been installed, check the engine timing and adjust as required.

IGNITION TIMING

Adjustment

1. Refer to the vehicle control information label which is located on the radiator support panel, for the proper timing information.
2. If the engine timing requires adjustment, loosen the distributor hold down bolt and rotate the distributor slowly in either direction, to advance or retard the engine timing.
3. Tighten the hold down bolt and recheck the engine timing.
4. Some engines incorporate a magnetic timing probe hole which is used when setting the engine timing with special electronic equipment. Consult manufacturer's instructions if using this form of timing equipment.

Electrical Controls

IGNITION LOCK CYLINDER

Removal and Installation

1. Disconnect the negative battery cable. Position the ignition lock cylinder in the Run position.
2. Remove the steering wheel. Remove the lock plate, turn signal switch and the buzzer switch.
3. Remove the lock cylinder retaining screw. Remove the lock cylinder.
4. To install, rotate the lock cylinder clockwise to align the cylinder key with the keyway in the lock housing.
5. Push the lock all the way in. Install the screw.
6. Continue the installation in the reverse order of the removal procedure.

IGNITION SWITCH

Removal and Installation

1. Disconnect the negative battery terminal.
2. Loosen the toe pan screws on the steering column.
3. Remove the column to instrument panel trim plates and attaching nuts.
4. Lower the steering column. Be sure that the steering column is supported at all times in order to prevent damage to the column. disconnect the switch wire connectors.
5. Remove the switch attaching screws and remove the switch.
6. To replace, move the key lock to the LOCK position.
7. Move the actuator rod hole in the switch to the LOCK position.
8. Install the switch with the rod in the hole.
9. Position and reassemble the steering column in reverse of the disassembly procedure.

Adjustment

STANDARD COLUMN

1. Place the switch in the OFF position.
2. Position the switch on the column, then move the slider to the extreme left (toward the wheel).
3. Move the slider back two positions to the right of ACCESSORY position.
4. Place the key in any run position and shift the transmission into any position but Park.
5. Position the lock toward ACCESSORY with a light finger pressure and secure the switch.

TILT COLUMN

1. Place the key in ACCESSORY position and leave the key in the lock.
2. Loosen the switch mounting screws.
3. Push the switch upward toward the wheel to make certain it is in ACCESSORY detent.
4. Hold the key in full counterclockwise ACCESSORY position and tighten the switch mounting screws.
5. Check for proper switch installation.

NEUTRAL SAFETY/BACK–UP–SWITCH

Removal and Installation

NOTE: The neutral safety switch is incorporated into the steering column bowl and is nonadjustable. The back-up light switch still remains on the steering column and looks similar to the previous switches except for the electrical terminals.

CHEVROLET
CAPRICE CLASSIC · CORVETTE · MALIBU · MONTE CARLO · IMPALA
SECTION 15

COLUMN MOUNTED SHIFTER
1. Disconnect the negative battery cable. Remove wire connectors from the back-up light switch.
2. Remove two screws attaching the switch to the steering column.
3. Installation is the reverse of removal.
4. To adjust the switch, position the shift lever in neutral. Loosen the attaching screws. Install a 0.090 in. gauge pin into the outer hole in the switch cover.
5. Rotate the switch until the pin goes into the alignment hole in the inner plastic slide. Tighten the switch to column attaching screws and remove the gauge pin.
6. Torque the screws to 20 inch lbs. maximum.

FLOOR MOUNTED SHIFTER
1. Disconnect the negative battery cable.
2. Remove the floor console cover.
3. Disconnect all the electrical connectors on the switch assembly.
4. Position the shift lever in the "N" detent. Remove the screws securing the switch, and remove the unit from the vehicle.
5. Installation is the reverse of removal. Be sure that the new switch is installed with the selector lever in the neutral position.
6. After installation move the selector from the "N" position in order to shear the retaining pin.

CORVETTE WITH MANUAL TRANSMISSION
1. Disconnect the negative battery cable. Raise the vehicle and support it safely.
2. Pull electrical connector from switch which is located at rear of the transmission.
3. Remove switch from the transmission case.
4. Install the back-up light switch and gasket.
5. Push on electrical connector and lower vehicle.
6. Turn on ignition switch and place transmission in reverse detent to check operation of back-up lights.

CLUTCH START SWITCH

Removal and Installation
CORVETTE
1. Disconnect the negative battery cable. Remove the hush pad from under the dash panel.
2. Remove the bolt and switch from the clutch bracket and rotate the switch slightly so that the actuating shaft retainer can be pulled from the hole of the clutch pedal.
3. Place a new switch in position so that the actuating shaft retainer is in line with the hole in the clutch pedal and reinstall the bolt.
4. Connect the electrical connector to the switch and depress the clutch pedal fully to the floor to adjust the switch.

NOTE: The clutch operated starting switch is self-adjusting. If there is a readjustment necessary, depress the detent on the adjuster block and slide the block to the full forward position on the switch rod. Depress clutch pedal fully to the floor to adjust the clutch switch

HEADLIGHT SWITCH

Removal and Installation
IMPALA AND CAPRICE
1. Disconnect the negative battery cable.
2. Pull the headlamp switch to the "ON" position.
3. Depending upon the switch mechanism, pull the trim knob from the switch by either reaching under the dash and depressing the switch shaft release button while pulling the knob and shaft from the light switch or by using a suitable tool and pushing the tang under the trim knob while pulling the knob from the shaft.
4. Remove the ferrule nut retaining the switch to the dash panel. Disconnect the electrical connector and remove the switch.
5. Installation is the reverse of the removal procedure.

MALIBU AND MONTE CARLO
1. Disconnect the negative battery cable.
2. Remove six screws and instrument panel pad.
3. Remove the 3 windshield wiper/light switch mounting screws.
4. Depending upon the switch mechanism, pull the trim knob from the switch by either reaching under the dash and depressing the switch shaft release button while pulling the knob and shaft from the light switch or by using a suitable tool and pushing the tang under the trim knob while pulling the knob from the shaft.
5. Remove ferrule nut and switch assembly from instrument panel.
6. Installation is the reverse of the removal procedure.

CORVETTE
1. Disconnect the negative battery terminal.
2. Remove the left air distribution duct.
3. Remove the instrument cluster attaching screws and pull the cluster rearward.
4. Disconnect the speedometer cable, electrical connectors and remove the cluster.
5. Remove the instrument panel to left door pillar attaching screws and pull the left side of the instrument panel slightly forward for access.
6. Depress the shaft retainer, pull the knob and shaft assembly out and remove the switch bezel.
7. Disconnect all connections from the switch, tagging them for installation.
8. Pry the connector from the switch and remove the switch from the panel.
9. Installation is the reverse of the removal procedure.

HORN SWITCH

Removal and Installation
1. Disconnect the negative battery cable.
2. Remove the horn pad, contact assembly and all other related components.
3. On tilt-telescopic columns, remove the lock lever and plate.
4. Installation is the reverse of removal.

WINDSHIELD WIPER SWITCH—DASH MOUNTED EXCEPT CORVETTE

Removal and Installation
1. Disconnect the negative battery cable.
2. Remove all required trim and instrument panel bezels in order to remove the switch.
3. Disconnect the electrical connectors from the switch assembly.
4. Remove the switch retaining screws. Remove the switch.
5. Installation is the reverse of removal.

CORVETTE

Removal and Installation
1. Disconnect the negative battery cable.
2. Remove the drivers door panel, as required.

CHEVROLET
CAPRICE CLASSIC • CORVETTE • MALIBU • MONTE CARLO • IMPALA

3. Disconnect the electrical connections from the switch.
4. Remove the switch retaining screws. Remove the switch from the panel.
5. Installation is the reverse of the removal procedure.

TURN SIGNAL SWITCH

Removal and Installation

NOTE: This procedure is for vehicles not equipped with the multi-function switch.

1. Disconnect the negative battery cable.
2. Remove the steering wheel, using the proper wheel removal tool.
3. Pry the lock plate cover off, using a suitable tool.
4. Place a lock plate removal tool over the steering shaft and tighten the nut to depress the lock plate. Remove the snap ring retainer.
5. Remove the lock plate and the cancelling cam.
6. Remove the upper bearing preload spring. With the turn signal lever in the right turn position, remove the lever attaching screw and the lever. Remove the actuator arm screw and the arm. Remove the turn signal lever. Remove the three turn signal switch screws.
7. Push in the hazard switch knob and remove the retaining screw and the knob. On tilt columns, position the housing in the center position.
8. Remove the lower trim panel from the instrument panel and disconnect the turn signal connector from the wiring harness. Remove the connector.
9. Remove the bolts attaching the surrounding bracket assembly to the jacket. On some column shift automatics it may be necessary to remove the shift indicator needle attaching screw and remove or disconnect the needle.
10. Hold the steering column in place and remove the two attaching nuts from below. Remove the bracket assembly and the wire protector. Loosely reinstall the nuts to hold the column in place.
11. Carefully remove the turn signal switch and the wiring.
12. To install, place the switch in the right turn position and push the switch in until it is properly seated. Torque the three attaching nuts to 35 inch lbs. Return the switch to the neutral position and reverse the removal procedure.

MULTI—FUNCTION SWITCH

Removal and Installation

1. Disconnect the negative battery cable. Remove the steering wheel. Remove the turn signal switch.
2. It may be necessary to loosen the two column mounting nuts and remove the four bracket-to-mast jacket screws, then separate the bracket from the mast jacket to allow the connector clip on the ignition switch to be pulled out of the column assembly.
3. Disconnect the washer/wiper switch lower connector.
4. Remove the screws attaching the column housing to the mast jacket. Be sure to note the position of the dimmer switch actuator rod for reassembly in the same position. Remove the column housing and switch as an assembly.

NOTE: The tilt and travel columns have a removable plastic cover on the column housing. This provides access to the wiper switch without removing the entire column housing.

5. Turn the assembly upside down and use a drift to remove the pivot pin from the washer/wiper switch. Remove the switch.
6. Place the switch into position in the housing, then install the pivot pin.

7. Position the housing onto the mast jacket and attach by installing the screws. Install the dimmer switch actuator rod in the same position as noted earlier. Check switch operation.
8. Reconnect lower end of switch assembly.
9. Install remaining components in reverse order of removal. Be sure to attach column mounting bracket in original position.

WINDSHIELD WIPER MOTOR

Removal and Installation
EXCEPT CORVETTE

1. Disconnect the negative battery cable.
2. Raise the hood and remove the cowl screen.
3. Loosen the transmission drive link to crank arm retaining bolts. Remove the drive link from the motor crank arm.
4. Disconnect the electrical wiring and the washer hoses from the motor assembly.
5. Remove the motor retaining screws. Remove the windshield wiper motor while guiding the crank arm through the hole.
6. Installation is the reverse of the removal procedure. The motor must be in the park position before assembling the crank arm to the drive link.

CORVETTE

1. Disconnect the negative battery cable.
2. Remove wiper arms.
3. Remove air inlet leaf screen.
4. Turn ignition on, and activate motor with wiper switch. Allow motor crank arm to rotate to point to a position between 4 and 5 o'clock as viewed from passenger compartment. Stop crank arm in this position by turning off ignition switch.
5. Disconnect battery ground cable.
6. Disconnect upper motor electrical connectors.
7. Remove motor mounting bolts.
8. With crank arm in position described in Step 4 above, motor may now be removed from vehicle. Lower electrical connector may be disconnected as motor is partially removed.
9. Installation is the reverse of the removal procedure.

WIPER LINKAGE/TRANSMISSION

Removal and Installation

1. Disconnect the negative battery cable. Raise the hood and remove the cowl vent screen.
2. Remove the right and left wiper arm and blade.
3. Loosen but do not remove, the attaching nuts securing the transmission drive links to the motor crank arm.
4. Disconnect the transmission drive link from the motor crank arm.
5. Remove the wiper transmission to body attaching screws.
6. Remove the wiper transmission and linkage by guiding it through the plenum chamber opening or to the left side under the dash panel extension.
7. To install, reverse the removal procedure.

Instrument Panel

INSTRUMENT CLUSTER

Removal and Installation
IMPALA AND CAPRICE

1. Disconnect battery ground cable.
2. Remove four steering column lower cover screws and the cover.
3. If equipped with automatic transmission, disconnect shift indicator cable from steering column.

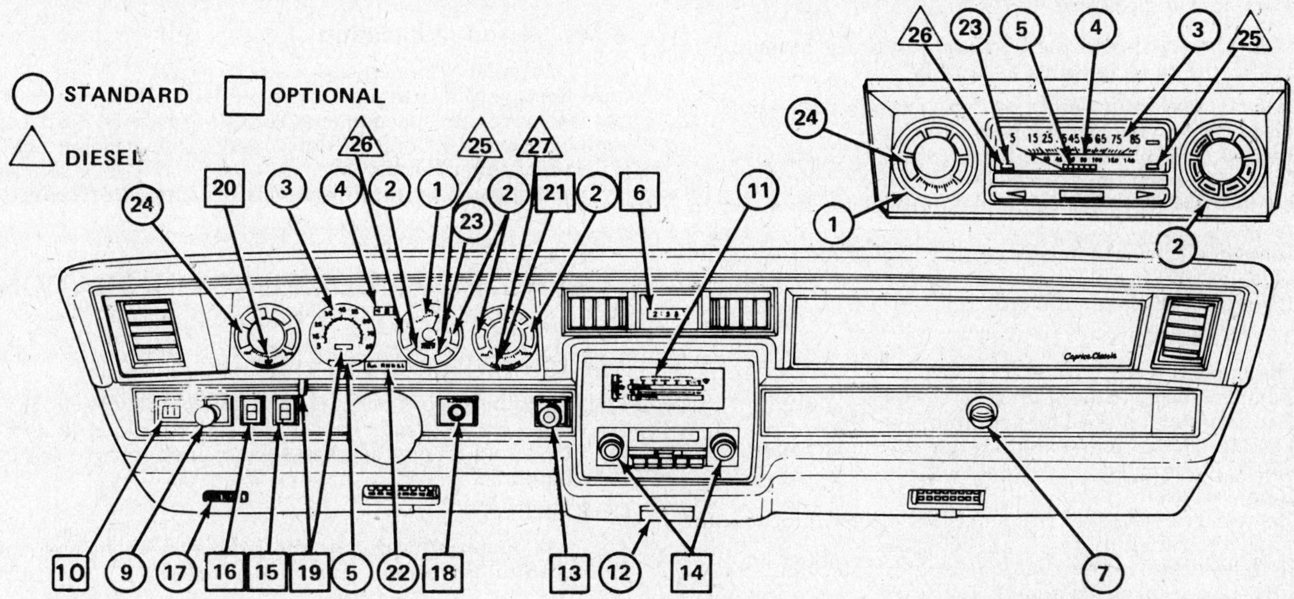

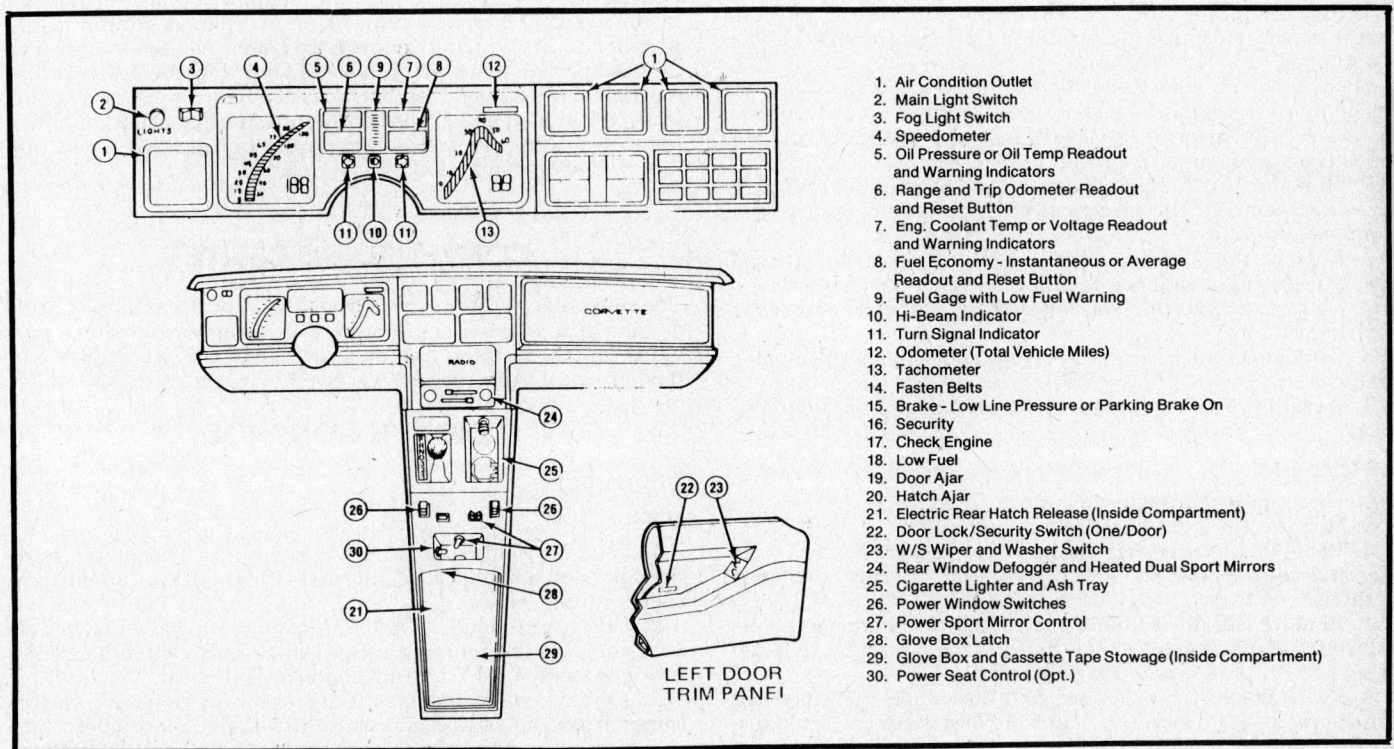

CHEVROLET
CAPRICE CLASSIC • CORVETTE • MALIBU • MONTE CARLO • IMPALA

4. Remove two steering column to instrument panel screws and lower steering column.

NOTE: Use extreme care when lowering steering to prevent damage to column assembly.

5. Remove six screws and the three snap-in fasteners from the perimeter of the instrument cluster lens.
6. Remove two screws from lower corner of cluster.
7. Remove two stud nuts from lower corner of cluster.
8. Disconnect speedometer cable and pull cluster from instrument panel.
9. Disconnect electrical connectors from cluster and remove the vehicle.
10. Reverse procedure to install.

MALIBU—STANDARD CLUSTER

1. Disconnect battery ground cable.
2. Remove clock set stem knob, if equipped.
3. Remove instrument bezel retaining screws.
4. Pull bezel from panel slightly and disconnect rear defogger switch, if equipped.
5. Remove bezel.
6. Remove two screws at transmission selector indicator and lower indictor assembly to disconnect cable.
7. Remove three screws at windshield wiper/light switch mounting plate and pull assembly rearward for access to lower left cluster attaching bolt and nut.
8. Remove nuts attaching cluster to instrument panel.
9. Pull cluster rearward and disconnect the speedometer cable and all wiring and cables.
10. Remove cluster from vehicle.
11. Reverse procedure to install.

MALIBU—OPTIONAL CLUSTER AND MONTE CARLO

1. Disconnect the negative battery cable. Remove the clock set stem knob.
2. Remove the instrument bezel retaining screws.
3. Slightly pull the bezel rearward. Disconnect the rear defogger switch. Remove the remote control mirror control knob, if equipped.
4. Remove the dash panel bezel. Remove the speedometer assembly retaining screws. Pull the assembly from the cluster, disconnect the speedometer cable from the assembly and remove the speedometer from the vehicle.
5. Remove the fuel gauge or the tachometer retaining screws, disconnect the electrical connectors and remove the components.
6. Remove the clock or voltmeter retaining screws, disconnect the electrical connectors and remove the components.
7. Disconnect the transmission shift indicator cable from the steering column.
8. Disconnect all wiring connectors and remove the cluster case.
9. Installation is the reverse of the removal procedure.

CORVETTE

1. Disconnect the negative battery cable.
2. Remove the light switch knob and nut.
3. Remove the steering column trim cover. Remove the steering column bolts and lower the column. Be sure to support it safely.
4. Remove the cluster bezel attaching bolts. Remove the bezel from the instrument panel. Remove the four bezel to panel screws.
5. Pull the cluster rearward and disconnect all electrical connections. Metal retaining clips are located at the back side of the connectors.
6. Installation is the reverse of removal.

SPEEDOMETER
Removal and Installation

1. Disconnect the negative battery cable.
2. Remove the instrument cluster trim plate.
3. Remove the speedometer retaining screws. Pull the assembly forward in order to disconnect the speedometer from the rest of the assembly.
4. Installation is the reverse of the removal procedure.

ELECTRICAL COMPONENT LOCATION
Fuse Panel
ALL EXCEPT CORVETTE

The fuse panel is located on the left side of the vehicle. It is under the instrument panel assembly. In order to gain access to the fuse panel it may be necessary to first remove the under dash padding.

CORVETTE

The fuse panel is located at the right end of the instrument panel behind the access door labeled fuses.

Electronic Control Module

The electronic module is located on the right side of the vehicle. It is positioned in front of the right hand kick panel. In order to gain access to the assembly you must first remove the trim panel.

Turn Signal Flasher

The turn signal flasher is located inside the convenience center.

Fusible Links

Fusible links are used to prevent major wire harness damage in the event of a short circuit or an overload condition in the wiring circuits which are normally not fused, due to carrying high amperage loads or because of their locations within the wiring harness. Each fusible link is of a fixed value for a specific electrical load and should a link fail, the cause of the failure must be determined and repaired prior to installing a new fusible link of the same value.

CONVENIENCE CENTER

The convenience center is a swing-down unit located on the underside of the instrument panel. The swing-down feature provides central location and each access to buzzers, relays and flasher units. All units are serviced by plug-in replacement.

CRUISE CONTROL
Adjustment
1983

1. With air conditioning off, adjust engine curb hot idle, with the idle stop solenoid disconnected (if equipped), to 500 rpm, then shut off engine.
2. Check bead chain slack by unsnapping swivel from ball stud and holding chain taut at ball stud; center of swivel should extend 1/8 in. beyond center of ball stud.
3. Adjust bead chain slack if necessary, by removing the retainer from the swivel and chain assembly. Place chain into swivel cavities which permits chain to have slight slack. Place retainer over swivel and chain assembly.

CHEVROLET
CAPRICE CLASSIC • CORVETTE • MALIBU • MONTE CARLO • IMPALA
SECTION 15

1984 AND LATER IMPALA, CAPRICE AND MONTE CARLO WITH 350 V8 DIESEL ENGINE

1. Adjust engine idle.
2. Adjust the length of the rod to achieve minimum slack with the injection pump on the slow idle screw.

1984 AND LATER IMPALA, CAPRICE AND MONTE CARLO WITH 321 V6 GAS ENGINE

1. Turn ignition off. Position fast idle cam in the off position.
2. Be sure that the idle speed motor is retracted and that the throttle is closed.
3. Install the rod on the throttle stud at the large end of the slot.
4. Adjust length so stud is at end of slot and rod is aligned with hole in servo.
5. Install retainer, insert rod end of rod through holes and snap retainer in place.

1984 AND LATER MONTE CARLO WITH 299 CU.IN. ENGINE

1. With cable connected to throttle lever and the other end of cable sleeve snapped into bracket, select hole in servo blade based on minimum cable slack.

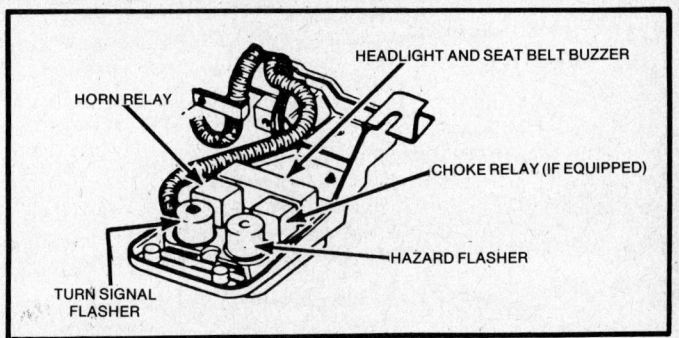

Convenience center — typical
(© General Motors Corporation)

CORVETTE

1. With servo cable installed to servo bracket, place second ball on chain on cable end.
2. With throttle completely closed (Ignition off and fast idle cam off), adjust cable jamnuts until cable sleeve at the T.B.I. is tight but not holding throttle open. Tighten jamnuts.

COOLING AND HEATER SECTION

WATER PUMP

Removal and Installation

ALL EXCEPT CORVETTE

1. Disconnect the negative battery cable. Drain the cooling system. Remove the fan shroud, as required.
2. Remove all the necessary components in order to gain access to the water pump assembly.
3. Remove the fan and pulley. Disconnect all hoses from the water pump.
4. Remove the water pump retaining bolts. Remove the water pump from the engine.
5. Installation is the reverse of the removal procedure. Be sure to clean the engine to water pump mating surface before installing the pump.
6. Use a new gasket when installing the pump assembly.

CORVETTE

1. Disconnect the negative battery cable, drain the cooling system and remove the drive belts.
2. Remove the water pump pulley and the AIR pump pulley along with the air management valve adapter.
3. Remove the air pump and disconnect the fuel inlet and return lines.
4. Remove the rear A/C compressor braces and the lower A/C compressor mounting bolt.
5. Remove the A/C compressor and the idler pulley bracket nuts. Disconnect the A/C compressor wires.
6. Slide the mounting bracket forward and remove the rear A/C compressor bolt along with the compressor.
7. Remove the right and left air injection filter hoses at the check valve and remove the AIR pipe at the intake and power steering reservoir bracket including the top alternator bolt.
8. Remove the lower AIR bracket on the water pump and the lower radiator and heater hose at the water pump.
9. Remove the water pump and gasket from the vehicle.
10. Installation is the reverse order of the removal procedure, be sure to use a new gasket and RTV sealant as needed.

BLOWER MOTOR

Removal and Installation

IMPALA, CAPRICE, MALIBU AND MONTE CARLO

1. Disconnect the negative battery cable.
2. Disconnect the electrical connections from the blower motor.
3. Remove the blower motor flange screws. Remove the blower motor assembly from the heater case.
4. Installation is the reverse of removal.

CORVETTE

1. Disconnect the negative battery cable.
2. Remove the front wheel hose rear panel. Move the wheel hose seal aside.
3. Remove the heat motor cooling tube. Remove the heater motor relay.
4. Remove the motor retaining screws and remove the motor assembly from the vehicle.
5. Installation is the reverse of removal.

HEATER/AC CONTROL ASSEMBLY

Removal and Installation

IMPALA, CAPRICE, MALIBU AND MONTE CARLO

The removal and installation of the dash mounted temperature control unit is general in the vehicle models. The outlined steps may not be in the correct order for specific model. Rearrange the steps to relate to the vehicle being repaired.

1. Disconnect the negative battery cable.
2. Remove the necessary instrument panel trim.
3. Remove the radio and/or knobs, radio speaker, ash tray, cigar lighter, and the floor console trim plate (if equipped).
4. After exposing the control retaining screws, remove them and pull the control away from the dash. Disconnect the bowden cable, electrical and/or vacuum connections.
5. Remove the control unit.

15–17

SECTION 15

CHEVROLET
CAPRICE CLASSIC • CORVETTE • MALIBU • MONTE CARLO • IMPALA

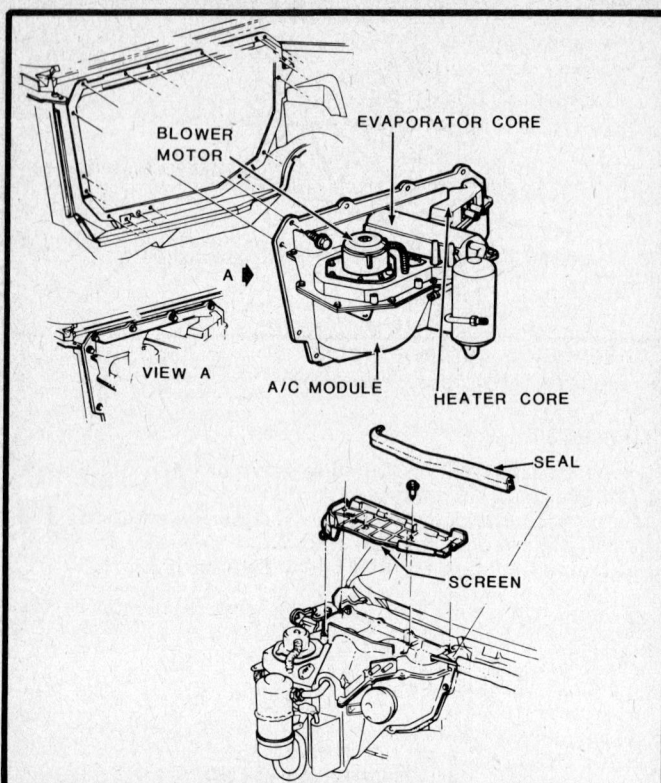

Typical air conditioning module mounting
(© General Motors Corporation)

6. The installation of the control is the reverse of the removal procedure.

CORVETTE

1. Disconnect the negative battery cable.
2. Remove the cluster bezel. Remove the tilt wheel lever.
3. Remove the center bezel above the console assembly.
4. Remove the screws attaching the control assembly to its carrier.
5. Rotate the control assembly to gain access to the electrical connectors, temperature control cable and vacuum hoses.
6. Installation is the reverse of the removal procedure.

HEATER CORE

Removal and Installation

IMPALA, CAPRICE, MALIBU AND MONTE CARLO

1. Disconnect the battery negative cable. Drain the cooling system.
2. Disconnect heater hoses.
3. Remove retaining bracket and ground strap.
4. Pull off module rubber seal. Remove screws from module leaf screen and remove screen.
5. Remove right hand windshield wiper arm.
6. Remove diagnostic connector, high blower relay and thermostatic switch mounting screws.
7. Disconnect all electrical connections at the module top.
8. Remove heater core.
9. Reverse procedure for installation. Reseal with strip type caulking.

CORVETTE

1. Disconnect the negative battery cable.

2. Remove the instrument cluster bezel, tilt wheel pad and the instrument panel pad.
3. Remove the A/C distributor duct. Disconnect the flex hose.
4. Remove the right side hush panel. Remove the side window defroster flex hose.
5. Remove the side window defroster to heater cover screws and disconnect the extension.
6. Remove the temperature control cable and bracket assembly at the heater cover. Disconnect the heater door control shaft.
7. Remove the electronic control module and disconnect all electrical connections.
8. Remove the tubular support brace from the door pillar to the aluminum instrument panel reinforcement brace.
9. Remove the heater core cover attaching screws. Remove the heater pipe. Remove the heater water control bracket attaching screws.
10. Cut the heater hose at the heater core pipes.
11. Remove the heater core assembly from the vehicle.
12. Installation is the reverse of removal.

FUEL SYSTEM

FUEL PUMP

Removal and Installation

MECHANICAL

1. Disconnect the negative battery cable.
2. Remove all necessary components in order to gain access to the fuel pump.
3. Remove the inlet and outlet lines from the unit.
4. Remove the fuel pump retaining bolts. Remove the pump from the vehicle.
5. Installation is the reverse of the removal procedure.

ELECTRIC EXCEPT CORVETTE AND V6 DIESEL

1. To relieve the fuel system pressure, remove the fuel pump fuse which is located in the fuse block.
2. Crank the engine until all the fuel that is left in the fuel lines is consumed. Once the engine cuts off, engage the starter for three seconds to assure relief of any remaining fuel pressure.
3. Disconnect the negative battery cable and raise ad support the vehicle safely.
4. Remove the fuel tank from the vehicle and remove the sending unit along with the electric fuel pump.
5. Installation is the reverse order of the removal procedure, be sure to use a new gasket on the fuel sending unit.

ELECTRIC CORVETTE

1. Disconnect the negative battery cable.
2. Remove the fuel filler door. Remove the fuel cap.
3. Remove the fuel tank filler neck housing. Disconnect the drain hose.
4. Remove the screws attaching the fuel pump to the gas tank.
5. Disconnect the fuel lines, fuel vapor line and the electrical connector.
6. Remove the fuel pump and gasket.
7. Installation is the reverse of the removal procedure.

ELECTRIC V6 DIESEL

NOTE: The fuel pump used on the V6 diesel engine is located at the front of the engine next to the fuel heater.

1. Disconnect the negative battery cable.
2. Remove the inlet and outlet fuel lines. Disconnect all of the electrical connectors from the pump assembly.

3. Remove the fuel pump retaining bolts. Remove the fuel pump from its mounting on the engine.
4. Installation is the reverse of the removal procedure. Torque the retaining bolts to 18 ft. lbs.

CARBURETOR

Adjustments

CHECKING CHOKE – HOT AIR TYPE

1. With parking brake applied, drive wheels blocked, transmission in park or neutral, start engine and allow engine to warm up, visually checking to be certain choke valve opens fully.
2. If choke valve fails to open fully, momentarily touch choke housing and hot air inlet pipe or hose to determine if sufficient heat is reaching the choke coil.
3. If the choke housing and/or heat inlet are cool to the touch, check for loss of vacuum to the housing, restricted heat inlet in the choke housing or choke heat pipe, collapsed or deteriorated heat inlet hose, or restricted passages in the manifold choke heat stove.
4. Replace or correct as necessary.

CHECKING CHOKE – ELECTRIC TYPE

NOTE: This test should be performed between 60 and 80 degrees F.

1. Allow the engine to cool so that when the throttle is opened slightly, the choke blade fully closes.
2. Start the engine and determine a time for the choke blade to reach the full open position.
3. If the choke blade fails to open fully after 3.5 minutes, check the voltage at the choke heater connection.
4. If the voltage is approximately 12 to 15 volts, replace the electric choke unit.
5. If the voltage is low or zero, check all wires and connections. If any connections in the oil pressure switch circuitry are faulty, or if pressure switch is failed open, the oil warning light will be on with the engine running. Repair wires or connectors as required.
6. If the problem is still not corrected, replace the oil pressure switch. No gasket is used between the choke cover and the choke housing due to grounding requirements.

COMPUTER COMMAND CONTROL SYSTEM (CCC)

Mixture Control Adjustment

The computer command control System provides precise control of carburetor air/fuel mixtures during all ranges of engine operation. Because of this system control, the below listed mixture control adjustment procedures are to be used if required. The previously used propane enrichment or lean drop methods of idle mixture adjustment may not be used when adjusting carburetors used with this system because system control will change air/fuel mixtures to lean or rich as the mixture needles are adjusted rich or lean respectively.

The computer command control system is sensitive to any change in mixture control adjustment which, if improperly set, can impair the ability of the system to maintain precise control of air/fuel mixtures. Plugs are installed in the carburetor air horn and over the idle mixture needles in the throttle body to seal the factory settings. For this reason, the mixtures control adjustment points, should never be changed from the original factory setting. However, if in diagnosis the system indicates the carburetor to be the cause of a driver performance complaint or emissions failure or critical parts such as air horn, float bowl, or throttle body are replaced, then the plugs may be removed and mixture control adjustments made, carefully following factory recommended procedures. After adjustment, replacement plugs (supplied in applicable service kits) must be installed.

Checking Mixture Control Solenoid Travel

Before proceeding, it will be necessary to modify float gage J-9789-130, BT7720, or equivalent (used to externally check float level setting) by filing or grinding sufficient material off the gage to allow insertion down the vertical vent ("D" shaped hole in the air horn casting next to the idle air bleed valve cover).

Check that gage freely enters "D" vent hole and does not bind. The gage will be used to determine total mixture control solenoid travel. With engine off, air cleaner removed, measure mixture control solenoid travel as follows:

a. Insert modified float gage down "D" shaped vent hole. Press down on gage and release, observing that gage moves freely and does not bind. With gage released (solenoid up position), reading at eye level record mark on gage (in inches) that lines up with top of air horn casting (upper edge).

b. Then, lightly press down on gage until bottomed (solenoid down position). Record in inches mark on gage that lines up with top of air horn casting.

c. Subtract gage up dimension (item "a") from gage down position (item "b") and record difference (in inches). The difference in dimensions is total solenoid travel.

d. If total solenoid travel (difference in item "c") is not within 2/32 to 6/32 in., make mixture control solenoid adjustments as noted below. If difference is within specification, proceed to Idle Air Bleed Valve Adjustment.

Mixture Control Solenoid Adjustment

1. Remove air horn, mixture control solenoid plunger, air horn gasket and plastic fuller block, using normal service procedures.
2. Remove throttle side metering rod. Install mixture control solenoid gaging tool J-33815-1 and BT8253-A, or equivalent over throttle side metering jet rod guide, and temporarily reinstall the solenoid plunger into the solenoid body.
3. Holding the solenoid plunger in the down position, use tool J-28696-10 and BT-7928, or equivalent, to turn lean mixture (solenoid) screw counterclockwise until the plunger breaks contract with the gauging tool. Turn slowly clockwise until the plunger breaks contact with the gauging tool. Turn slowly clockwise until the plunger just contracts the gauging tool. the adjustment is correct when the solenoid plunger is contacting both the solenoid stop and the gauging tool. If the total difference in adjustment required less than 3/4 turn of the lean mixture (solenoid) screw, the original setting was within the manufacturer's specifications.
4. Remove solenoid plunger and gauging tool, and reinstall metering rod and plastic filler block.
5. Invert air horn and remove rich mixture stop screw and (if used) the rich authority adjusting spring from bottom side of air horn, using tool J-28696-4 and BT7967A or equivalent.
6. Remove lean mixture screw plug and the rich mixture stop screw plug from air horn, using a suitable sized punch.
7. Reinstall rich mixture stop screw and (if used) the rich authority adjusting spring in air horn and bottom lightly, then back screw out 1/4 turn.
8. Reinstall air horn gasket, mixture control solenoid plunger and air horn to carburetor.
9. Insert external float gage in vent hole and, with tool J-28696-10 and BT7928, or equivalent, adjust rich mixture stop screw to obtain 4/32 in. total plunger travel.
10. With solenoid plunger travel correctly set, install the plugs (supplied in service kits) in the air horn.
11. To install the lean mixture plug, position it, hollow end down, into the access hole of the lean mixture screw (solenoid),

SECTION 15 CHEVROLET
CAPRICE CLASSIC • CORVETTE • MALIBU • MONTE CARLO • IMPALA

and use a suitably sized punch to drive plug into the air horn until the top of the plug is even with the lower plug.

12. To install the rich mixture stop screw, position it, hollow end down, over the rich mixture stop screw access hole, and drive plug into place so that the top of the plug is 1/16 in. below the surface of the air horn casting.

Idle Mixture and Speed Adjustment

Idle mixture screws are sealed with hardened caps covering the screws during original equipment production. These plugs are not to be removed unless required for cleaning or part replacement.

Before suspecting the carburetor as the cause of poor engine performance or rough idle, check ignition system including distributor, timing, spark plugs and wires. Inspect air cleaner, evaporative emission system, EFE system, PCV system, EGR system and engine compression. Also inspect intake manifold, vacuum hoses an connections for leaks and check torque of carburetor mounting bolts.

In the case of major carburetor repair, throttle body replacement or high idle CO as indicated by state or local emission inspection, idle mixture may be adjusted. Adjusting mixture by other than the proper method may violate emissions. The following procedure must be used.

Idle Air Bleed Valve Adjustment

1. Position the parking brake and block the drive wheels. Disconnect and plug the hoses as directed on the vehicle emission control label.
2. Check and adjust ignition timing. Connect a dwell meter and a tachometer.
3. Start engine, and with transmission in park or neutral, run engine at idle until fully warm and a varying dwell is noted on the dwell meter. It is essential that the engine is operated for a sufficient length of time to ensure that the engine coolant sensor, and the oxygen sensor in the exhaust, are at full operational temperature.
4. Check engine idle speed and compare to specifications on the underhood label. If necessary, adjust curb idle speed. On models with idle speed control (ISC) or idle load compensator (ILC), no adjustment is possible.
5. With engine idling in drive (neutral for manual transmission), observe dwell reading on the 6 cylinder scale. If varying within the 10 to 0° range, adjustment is correct. If not, perform the following.
6. Remove the idle air bleed valve cover. If the cover is staked in place, pry it off using a suitable tool and a allen wrench.
7. If the cover is riveted, cover the internal bowl vents to the bleed valve with masking tape. Cover the carburetor air intakes with masking tape in order to prevent metal chips from entering the engine.
8. Cover carburetor air intakes with masking tape to prevent metal chips from entering carburetor and engine.

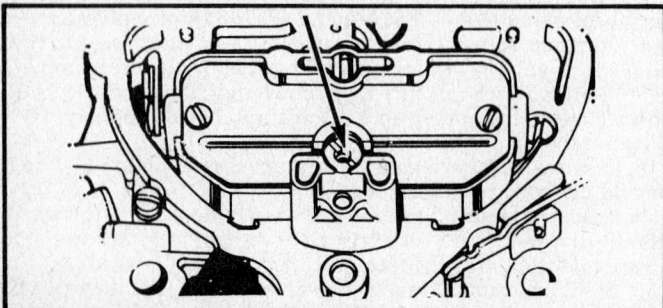

Idle air bleed valve location
(© General Motors Corporation)

9. Carefully align a No. 35 (.110 in.) drill bit on one of the steel rivet heads holding the idle air bleed valve cover in place. Drill only enough to remove rivet head. Drill the remaining rivet head located on the other side of the tower. Use a drift and small hammer to drive the remainder of the rivets out of the idle air bleed valve tower in the air horn casting. Use care in drilling to prevent damage to the air horn casting.
10. Lift out cover over the idle air bleed valve and remove the rivet pieces from inside the idle air bleed valve tower.
11. Using shop air, carefully blow out any remaining chips from inside the tower. Discard cover after removed. A missing cover indicates that the idle air bleed valve setting has been changed from its original factory setting.
12. With cover removed, look for presence (or absence) of a letter identification on top of idle air bleed valve.
13. If an identifying letter appears on top of the valve proceed to the procedure outlined under type two. If an identifying letter does not appear on the top of the valve proceed to the procedure outlined under type one.

Type One

1. Presetting the idle air bleed valve to a gauge dimension if the idle air bleed valve was serviced prior to on-vehicle adjustment.
2. Install idle air bleed valve gauging tool J-33815-2, BT-8253-B, or equivalent, in throttle side "D" shaped vent hole in the air horn casting. The upper end of the tool should be positioned over the open cavity next to the idle air bleed valve.
3. While holding the gauging tool down lightly, so that the solenoid plunger is against the solenoid stop, adjust the idle air bleed valve so that the gauging tool will pivot over and just contact the top of the valve. The valve is now preset for on-vehicle adjustment. Remove the gauging tool.
4. Adjusting the idle air bleed valve on the vehicle to obtain correct dwell reading.
5. Start engine and allow it to reach normal operating temperature. While idling in drive (neutral for manual transmission), use a suitable tool to slowly turn valve counterclockwise or clockwise, until the dwell reading varies within the 25 to 35° range, attempting to be as close to 30° as possible. Perform this step carefully. The air bleed valve is very sensitive and should be turned in 1/8 turn increments only.
6. If, after performing the steps above, the dwell reading does not vary and is not within the 25 to 35° range, it will be necessary to remove the plugs and to adjust the idle mixture needles.
7. Idle mixture needle plug removal, only if necessary. Remove the carburetor from the engine, following normal service procedures, to gain access to the plugs covering the idle mixture needles.
8. Invert carburetor and drain fuel into a suitable container. Place carburetor on a suitable holding fixture, with manifold side up. Use care to avoid damaging linkage, tubes, and parts protruding from air horn.
9. Make two parallel cuts in the throttle body, one on each side of the locator points beneath the idle mixture needle plug (manifold side), with a hacksaw.
10. The cuts should reach down to the steel plug, but should not extend more than 1/8 in. beyond the locator points. The distance between the saw cuts depends on the size of the punch to be used.
11. Place a flat punch near the ends of the saw marks in the throttle body. Hold the punch at a 45° angle and drive it into the throttle body until the casting breaks away, exposing the steel plug.
12. The hardened plug will break, rather than remaining intact. It is not necessary to remove the plug in one piece, but remove the loose pieces. Repeat this procedure with the other mixture needle.
13. Setting the idle mixture needles (if necessary) where cor-

CHEVROLET
CAPRICE CLASSIC • CORVETTE • MALIBU • MONTE CARLO • IMPALA

SECTION 15

rect dwell reading could not obtained with idle air bleed valve adjustment.

14. Using tool J-29030, BT-7610B, or equivalent, turn both idle mixture needles clockwise until they are lightly seated, then turn each mixture needle counterclockwise the number of turns specified. Reinstall carburetor on engine using a new flange mounting gasket, but do not install air cleaner and gasket at this time.

15. Readjusting idle air bleed valve to finalize correct dwell reading. Start engine and run until fully warm, and adjust the air bleed valve.

16. If unable to set dwell to 25 to 35°, and the dwell is below 25°, turn both mixture needles counterclockwise an additional turn. If dwell is above 35°, turn both mixture needles clockwise an additional turn. Readjust idle air bleed valve to obtain dwell limits.

17. After adjustments are complete, seal the idle mixture needle openings in the throttle body, using silicone sealant, RTV rubber, or equivalent. The sealer is required to discourage unnecessary adjustment of the setting, and to prevent fuel vapor loss in that area.

18. On vehicles without a carburetor mounted idle speed control or idle load compensator, adjust curb idle speed if necessary. Check, and only if necessary, adjust fast idle speed as described on emission control information label.

Type Two

1. To sett the idle air bleed valve to a gauge dimension, install air bleed valve gauging tool J-33815-2, BT-8253-B, or equivalent, in throttle side "D" shaped vent hole in the air horn casting. The upper end of the tool should be positioned over the open cavity next to the idle air bleed valve.

2. While holding the gauging tool down lightly, so that the solenoid plunger is against the solenoid stop, adjust the idle air bleed valve so that the gauging tool will pivot over and just contact the top of the valve.

3. The valve is now set properly. No further adjustment of the valve is necessary. Remove gauging tool.

4. Adjusting the idle mixture needles on the vehicle to obtain correct dwell readings. Remove idle mixture needle plugs, following instructions in the information given for Type 1.

5. Using tool J-29030-B, BT-7610-B, or equivalent, turn each idle mixture needle clockwise until lightly seated, then turn each mixture needle counterclockwise three turns.

6. Reinstall carburetor on engine, using a new flange mounting gasket, but do not install air cleaner or gasket at this time. Start engine and allow it to reach normal operating temperature.

7. While idling in drive (neutral for manual transmission), adjust both mixture needles equally, in 1/8 turn increments, until dwell reading varies within the 25 to 35° range, attempting to be as close to 30° as possible. If reading is too low, turn mixture needles counterclockwise. If reading is too high, turn mixture needles clockwise. Allow time for dwell reading to stabilize after each adjustment.

8. After adjustments are complete, seal the idle mixture needle openings in the throttle body, using silicone sealant, RTV rubber, or equivalent. The sealer is required to discourage unnecessary readjustment of the setting, and to prevent fuel vapor loss in that area.

9. On vehicles without a carburetor-mounted idle speed control or idle load compensator, adjust curb idle speed if necessary. Check, and if necesary, adjust fast idle speed, as described on the emission control information label.

Throttle Position Sensor (TPS) Adjustment

The plug covering the TPS adjustment screw is used to provide a tamper-resistant design and retain the factory setting during vehicle operation. Do not remove the plus unless diagnosis indicates that the TPS Sensor is not adjusted correctly or it is necessary to replace the air horn assembly, float bowl, TPS Sensor to TPS adjustment screw. This is a critical adjustment that must be performed accurately and carefully to ensure proper vehicle performance and control of exhaust emissions.

If necessary to adjust the TPS sensor proceed as follows. Using a 5mm (5/64 in.) drill, drill hole in aluminum plug covering TPS adjustment screw, drilling only enough to start self-tapping screw (approximate drilling depth 1/16 in. to 1/8 in.). Use care in drilling to prevent damage to adjustment screw head. Start a No. 8 1/2 in. long self tapping screw in drilled hole in plug, turning screw in only enough to ensure good thread engagement in hole. Placing a suitable tool between the screw head and air horn casting, pry against screw head to remove plug. Discard plug. Using tool J-28696, BT7967A or equivalent, remove screw. Connect digital voltmeter (such as J-29125) or equivalent from TPS connector center terminal (B) to bottom terminal (C). Jumpers for access can be made using terminals 12014836 and 12014837). After TPS screw is adjusted, a new plug should be installed. If a new plug is not available, a locking type of sealer should be placed on the screw threads to prevent movement of the screw after installation. With igniton on, engine stopped, reinstall TPS adjustment screw and with tool J-28696, BT7967A, or equivalent turn screw to obtain specified voltage at specified throttle position with A/C off. After adjustment, install new plug (supplied in service kits) in air horn, driving plug in place until flush with raised pump lever boss on casting.

TUNED PORT INJECTION

Throttle Position Sensor Adjustment

1985 AND LATER CORVETTE

1. Install three jumper wires between the TPS harness and the TPS connector.
2. With the ignition switch in the on position, connect a digital voltmeter to terminals A and B.
3. Adjust the TPS to reach .54 volts and torque the TPS screws to 18 inch lbs. Recheck the adjustment to be sure it has not changed.
4. With the ignition switch in the off position, remove the jumper wires and reconnect the TPS harness.

Idle Speed Adjustment

1985 AND LATER CORVETTE WITH TUNED PORT INJECTION

NOTE: The idle speed should only be adjusted if it is absolutely necessary.

1. Using an awl or equivalent, pierce the idle stop plug and remove it.
2. Leave the idle air control motor connected and ground the diagnostic lead. Turn the ignition to the on position, but do not start the engine.
3. Wait 30 seconds, and with the ignition switch still in the on position disconnect the idle air control connector.
4. Remove the ground from the diagnostic lead and start the engine.
5. Allow the engine to go into the closed loop mode and adjust the idle screw to specifications (5.0 and 5.7 liter engines with automatic transmissions is 400 rpm, manual transmission models are 450 rpm.
6. Turn the ignition off and reconnect the idle speed control connector.
7. Adjust the throttle position sensor, start the engine and check the engine for proper idle operation.

Idle Load Compensator (ILC) Adjustment

1. Prepare vehicle for adjustments according to the emission label.

15-21

SECTION 15

CHEVROLET
CAPRICE CLASSIC • CORVETTE • MALIBU • MONTE CARLO • IMPALA

2. Connect tachometer (distributor side of TACH filter, if used).
3. Remove air cleaner and plug vacuum hose to thermal vacuum valve (TVV).
4. Disconnect and plug vacuum hose to EGR.
5. Disconnect and plug vacuum hose to canister purge port.
6. Disconnect and plug vacuum hose to ILC.
7. Back out idle stop screw on carburetor 3 turns.
8. Turn A/C "OFF".
9. Before starting engine, place transmission in PARK, set parking brake, and block drive wheels. With engine running (engine warm, choke off), transmission is drive, and ILC plunger fully extended (no vacuum applied), using tool J-29607, BT-8022, or equivalent, adjust plunger to obtain 750 rpm. E2MC models, 725 rpm E4MC models. Jam nut on plunger must be held with wrench to prevent damage to guide tabs.
10. Remove plug from vacuum hose, reconnect hose to ILC and observe idle speed. Idle speed should be 500 rpm in drive.
11. If rpm in Step 10 is correct proceed to Step 13. No further adjustment of the ILC is necessary.
12. If rpm in Step 10 is not correct, proceed as follows. Stop engine and remove the ILC. Plug vacuum hose to ILC. With the ILC removed, remove the rubber cap from the center outlet tube and then remove the metal plug (IF USED) from this same tube. Install ILC on carburetor and reattach throttle return spring and any other related parts removed during disassembly. Remove plug from vacuum hose and reconnect hose to ILC.
13. Using a spare rubber cap with hole punched to accept a .090 in. (3/32 in.) hex key wrench, install cap on center outlet tube (to seal against vacuum loss) and insert wrench through cap to engage adjusting screw inside tube. Start engine and turn adjusting screw with wrench to obtain 550 rpm in drive. Turning the adjusting screw will change the idle speed approximately 75 to 100 rpm for each complete turn. Turn the screw counterclockwise will increase the engine speed.
14. Remove wrench and cap (with hole) from center outlet tube and install new rubber cap. Engine running, transmission in drive, observe idle speed. If a final adjustment is required, it will be necessary to repeat Steps 12a 12e.
15. After adjustment of the ILC plunger, measure distance from the jam nut to tip of the plunger, dimension must not exceed 25mm (1 in.).
16. Disconnect and plug vacuum hose to ILC. Apply vacuum source such as hand vacuum pump J-23768, BT-7517 or equivalent to ILC vacuum inlet tube to fully retract the plunger.
17. Adjust the idle speed on the carburetor float bowl to obtain 500 rpm in drive. Place transmission in park and stop engine.
18. Remove plug from vacuum hose and install hose on ILC vacuum inlet tube. Remove plugs and reconnect all vacuum hoses. Install air cleaner and gasket. Remove block from drive wheels.

Differential Vacuum Delay Valve (DVDV) Adjustment

The DVDV is located in the vacuum line between the idle load compensator (ILC) and the vacuum source. It is used on all 5.0L engines (engine code Y). The DVDV acts as cushioning device by slightly delaying the operation of the ILC until a constant vacuum change has occurred. Without the DVDV the ILC would react too quickly to changes in engine vacuum, causing a surging condition or if too restrictive to vacuum flow, it would cause a stalling or run-on condition.

To check the operation of the DVDV, install a vacuum gage with a "T" into the hose form the DVDV to the ILC. Install a vacuum pump to port 1 of the DVDV and apply 17.8 in. of vacuum while watching the other vacuum gage, it should take six to nine seconds for the vacuum to rise to 16.9 in. Remove the vacuum gauge with "T", install the vacuum pump to port 2 and leave port 1 open. Air should flow through the valve after .5 in. is applied.

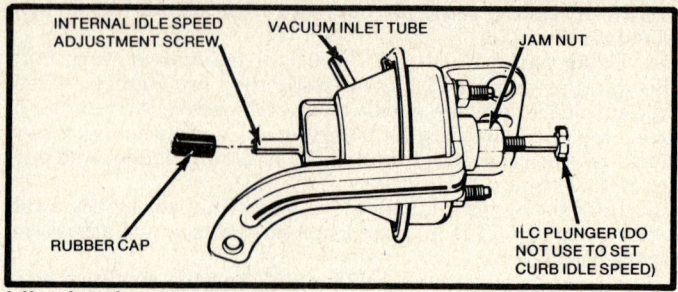

Idle load compensator
(© General Motors Corporation)

Idle Speed Control (ISC) Adjustment

The idle speed control (ISC) is controlled by the electronic control module (ECM), which has the desired idle speed programmed in its memory. The ECM compares the actual idle speeder is moved in or out. This automatically adjusts the throttle to hold an idle rpm independent of the engine loads.

An integral part of the ISC is the throttle contact switch. The position of the switch determines whether or not the ISC should control idle speed. When the throttle lever is resting against the IASC plunger, the switch contacts are closed, at which time the ECM moves the ISC to the programmed idle speed. When the throttle lever is not contacting the ISC plunger, the switch contacts are open; the ECM stops sending idle speed commands and the driver controls engine speed. Before starting engine, place transmission selector lever in park or neutral, set parking brake, and block drive wheels.

When a new ISC assembly is installed, a base (minimum authority) and high (maximum authority) rpm speed check must be performed and adjustment made as required. These adjustments limit the low and high rpm speeds to the ECM. When making a low and high speed adjustment, the low speed adjustment is always made first. DO NOT use the ISC plunger to adjust curb idle speed as the idle speed is controlled by the ECM. Do not disconnect or connect ISC connector with ignition on as damage to the ECM may occur.

1. Connect tachometer (distributor side of tach filter, if used).
2. Connect dwell meter to mixture control (M/C) solenoid dwell lead. Remember to set dwell meter on the six cylinder scale, regardless of the engine being tested.
3. Turn A/C off.
4. Start engine and run until stabilized by entering "closed loop" (dwell meter needle starts to very).
5. Turn ignition off.
6. Unplug connector from ISC motor.
7. Fully retract ISC plunger by applying 12 volts DC (battery voltage) to terminal "C" of the ISC motor connection and ground lead to terminal "D" of the ISC motor connection. It may be necessary to install jumper leads from the ISC motor in order to make proper connections.

NOTE: Do not apply battery voltage to motor longer than necessary to retract ISC plunger. Prolonged contact will damage motor. Also, never connect voltage source across terminals "A" and "B" as damage to the internal throttle contact switch will result.

8. Start engine and wait until dwell meter needle starts to very, indicating "closed loop" operation.
9. With parking brake applied and drive wheels blocked, place transmission in Drive (Neutral, manual transmission models).
10. With ISC Plunger fully retracted, adjust carburetor base (slow) idle stop screw to the specified rpm (see specifications). ISC plunger should not be left in full retracted position.

15-22

CHEVROLET
CAPRICE CLASSIC • CORVETTE • MALIBU • MONTE CARLO • IMPALA
SECTION 15

11. Place transmission in Park or Neutral and fully extend ISC plunger by applying 12 volts DC to terminal "D" or the ISC motor connection and ground lead to terminal "C" of the ISC motor connection. Never connect voltage source across terminals "A" and "B" as damage to the internal throttle contact switch will result.

12. Manual transmission: Using tool J-29607 or BT-8022 or equivalent, turn ISC Plunger to obtain ISC adjustment RPM (Maximum Authority).

13. Automatic Transmission: With Transmission in park, using tool J-29607 or BT-8022 or equivalent, preset ISC plunger to obtain 1500 RPM. With parking brake set and drive wheels blocked, place transmission in drive. Using tool J-29607 or BT-8022 or equivalent, turn ISC Plunger to obtain ISC adjustment RPM (Maximum Authority).

14. Recheck ISC Maximum Authority Adjustment RPM with voltage applied to motor. Motor will ratchet at full extension with power applied. After adjustment of ISC plunger, measure distance from back side of plunger head to ISC nosepiece, Dimension "B", Figure 6C1-8C. Dimension must not exceed that shown by plunger type as either identified by plunger length or letter identification.

15. Fully retract ISC Plunger. Place transmission in park or neutral and turn ignition "Off". Disconnect 12 volt power source, ground lead, tachometer and dwell meter. With ignition "Off", reconnect four terminal harness connector to ISC motor. To prevent internal damage to ISC, apply finger pressure to ISC plunger while retracting.

16. Remove block from drive wheels.

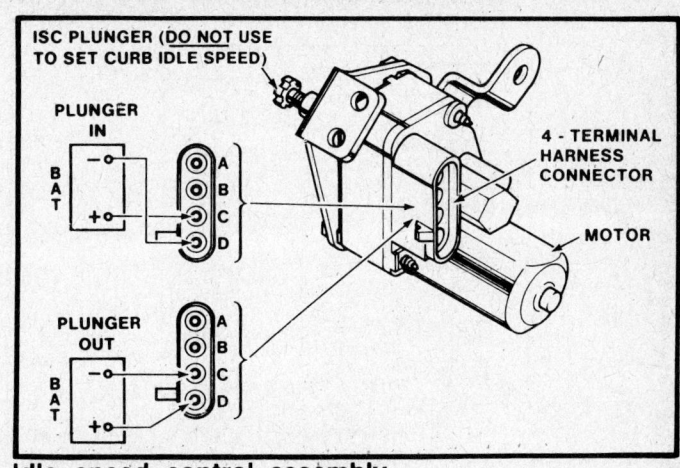

Idle speed control assembly
(© General Motors Corporation)

CARBURETOR
Removal and Installation

1. Disconnect the negative battery cable. Remove air cleaner.
2. Disconnect accelerator linkage.
3. Disconnect transmission detent cable.
4. Disconnect cruise control, if equipped.
5. Disconnect all necessary electrical connectors.
6. Disconnect all necessary vacuum lines.
7. Disconnect fuel line at carburetor inlet.
8. Remove the attaching bolts and remove carburetor.
9. Installation is the reverse of the removal procedure.
10. Check idle speed.

INTAKE MANIFOLD
Removal and Installation
GASOLINE ENGINE – 1983

1. Disconnect the negative battery cable. Drain the radiator.
2. Remove the air cleaner assembly.
3. Disconnect the upper radiator hose and the hose at the manifold.
4. Disconnect the accelerator linkage at the carburetor and the linkage bracket at the manifold. Remove the cruise control chain or cable, if so equipped.

ISC CONTROL PLUNGER ADJUSTMENT CHART

Plunger Identification	Plunger Length Dimension "A"	Dimension "B" Must Not Exceed
None	9/16 inch	7/32 inch
None	41/64 inch	5/16 inch
X	47/64 inch	25/64 inch
A	49/64 inch	27/64 inch
Y	51/64 inch	15/32 inch
S	27/32 inch	1/2 inch
Z	7/8 inch	35/64 inch
G	29/32 inch	37/64 inch
E	1 inch	43/64 inch
L	13/32 inch	3/4 inch
J	13/16 inch	27/32 inch
N	1 17/64 inch	59/64 inch
T	1 11/32 inch	1 inch

15-23

SECTION 15 CHEVROLET
CAPRICE CLASSIC • CORVETTE • MALIBU • MONTE CARLO • IMPALA

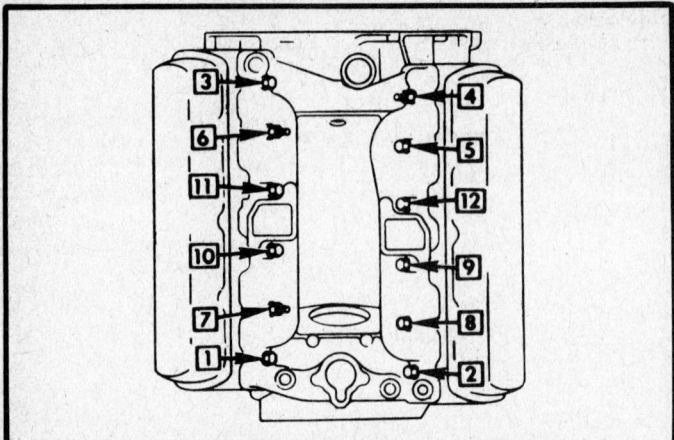
Diesel engine intake manifold torque sequence

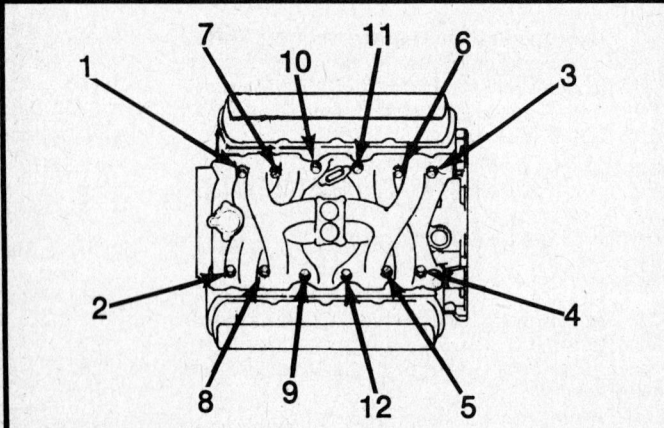
Intake manifold sequence—1986 and later 307 V8 gas engine

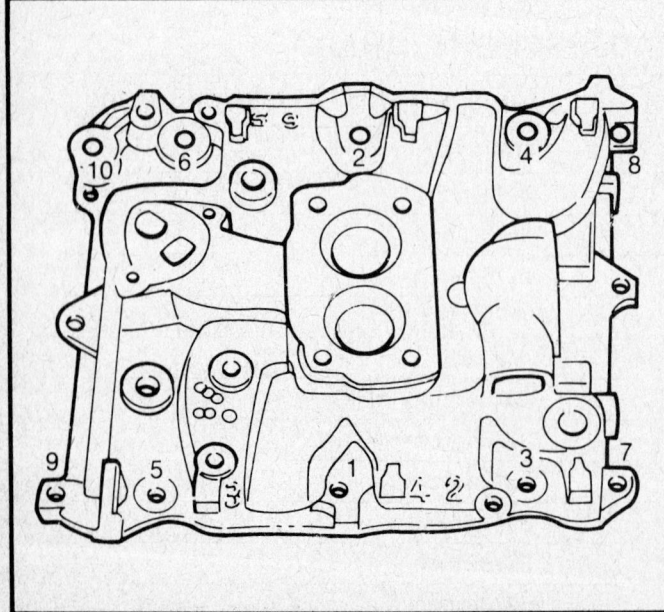
Intake manifold bolt torque sequence—231 cu.in. V6 gas engine (© General Motors Corporation)

5. Remove the fuel line from the carburetor and the booster vacuum pipe from the manifold. Remove turbocharger, if so equipped.
6. Disconnect and label the transmission vacuum modulator line, idle stop solenoid wire (if so equipped), distributor wires and the temperature sending unit wire.
7. Disconnect and mark the vacuum hoses at the distributor and the carburetor.

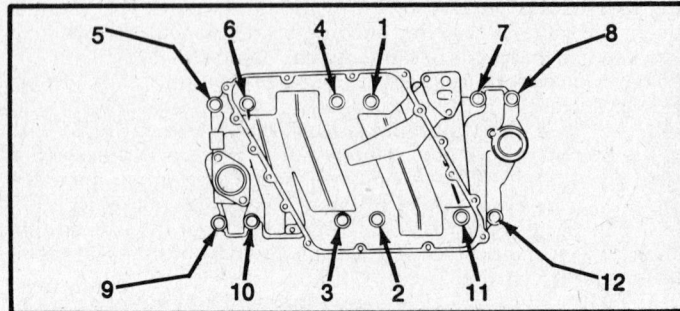
Intake manifold bolt torque sequence—Corvette
(© General Motors Corporation)

8. Disconnect the coolant bypass hose at the manifold. If required, remove the distributor.
9. On six cylinder models, it may be necessary to remove the distributor cap and wires to gain access to the Torx® head bolt. Remove the bolt.
10. Remove the throttle linkage springs.
11. Remove the A/C compressor top bracket, if so equipped.
12. Remove the manifold.
13. Installation is the reverse of the removal procedure. Be sure to use new gaskets or RTV sealant as required.

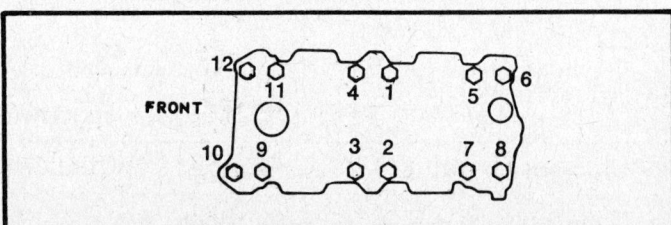
Small block V8 intake manifold torque sequence

GASOLINE ENGINE—1984 AND LATER EXCEPT CORVETTE AND 1986 AND LATER 307 V8

1. Disconnect the negative battery cable, drain the cooling system and remove the air cleaner.
2. On the V8 models disconnect the computer command control harness and lay it to the side out of the way.
3. Remove the heater hose and radiator hose and remove the upper alternator bracket.
4. Disconnect the fuel line and brake pipes at the carburetor on the V8 models and on the V6 models, disconnect the fuel line clips and fuel lines at the throttle body injector.
5. Disconnect the accelerator and T.V. cables and on the V8 models, remove the spark plug wires at the right cylinder head and exhaust manifold.
6. Remove the distributor cap, and mark the position of the rotor, then remove the distributor.

7. On the V6 models remove the coil and on the V8 models remove the carburetor.
8. Remove the A/C brace and disconnect the A/C bracket at the intake manifold.
9. Remove the manifold bolts and remove the intake manifold.
10. Installation is the reverse order of the removal procedure. Be sure to use new gaskets and RTV sealant as required when installing the manifold and torque the manifold to 25 to 45 ft. lbs.

GASOLINE ENGINE – CORVETTE

1. Disconnect the negative battery cable, drain the cooling system and remove the air cleaner.
2. Remove the fuel injection subassembly, mass air flow sensor, plenum, runners and the fuel rail assembly if so equipped.
3. Disconnect and mark all necessary vacuum and electrical connections.
4. Remove the distributor cap, mark the position of the rotor and the distributor and remove the distributor.
5. Disconnect the heater hose at the rear of the intake manifold and remove the serpentine belt.
6. Remove the air pump bracket and bolts and remove the air pump.
7. Disconnect the electrical connection at the coolant temperature sensor.
8. Remove the manifold bolts and remove the intake manifold.
9. Installation is the reverse order of the removal procedure. Be sure to use new gaskets and RTV sealant as required when installing the intake manifold. Torque the manifold bolts to 35 ft. lbs.

GASOLINE ENGINE – 1986 AND LATER 307 V8

1. Disconnect the negative battery cable. Drain the radiator. Remove the air cleaner.
2. Disconnect the upper radiator hose and the heater hose at the manifold.
3. Disconnect the accelerator linkage at the carburetor and the linkage bracket at the manifold.
4. Remove the cruise control chain or cable, if so equipped.
5. Remove the fuel line from the carburetor. Remove the brake booster vacuum pipe from the manifold.
6. Disconnect and label the transmission vacuum modulator line, idle stop solenoid wire (if so equipped).
7. Disconnect and mark the vacuum hoses at the distributor and the carburetor.
8. Disconnect the coolant bypass hose at the manifold. If required, remove the distributor.
9. Remove the throttle linkage springs.
10. Remove the A/C compressor top bracket, if so equipped.
11. Remove the intake manifold from the engine.
12. Installation is the reverse of the removal procedure. Be sure to use new gaskets or RTV sealant as required.

DIESEL ENGINE

1. Disconnect the negative battery cable. Remove the air cleaner.
2. Drain the radiator. Loosen the upper bypass hose clamp, remove the thermostat housing bolts, and remove the housing and the thermostat from the intake manifold.
3. Remove the breather pipes form the rocker covers and the air crossover. Remove the air crossover.
4. Disconnect the throttle rod and the return spring. If equipped with cruise control, remove the servo.
5. Remove the hairpin clip at the bellcrank and disconnect the cables. Remove the throttle cable from the bracket on the manifold; position the cable away from the engine. Disconnect and label any wiring as necessary.

6. Remove the alternator bracket if necessary. On the 350 cu. in. engine, if equipped with air conditioning, remove the compressor mounting bolts and move the compressor aside, without disconnecting any of the hoses. Remove the compressor mounting bracket from the intake manifold.
7. Disconnect the fuel line from the pump and the fuel filter. Remove the fuel filter and bracket.
8. Remove the fuel injection pump and lines.
9. Disconnect and remove the vacuum pump or oil pump drive assembly from the rear of the engine.
10. Remove the intake manifold drain tube.
11. Remove the intake manifold bolts and remove the manifold. Remove the adapter seal. Remove the injection pump adapter.
12. Clean the mating surfaces of the cylinder heads and the intake manifold.
13. Coat both sides of the gasket surface that seal the intake manifold to the cylinder heads with G.M. sealer #1050026 or the equivalent. Position the intake manifold gaskets on the cylinder heads. Install the end seals, making sure that the ends are positioned under the cylinder heads.
14. Carefully lower the intake manifold into place on the engine.
15. Clean the intake manifold bolts throughly, then dip them in clean engine oil. Install the bolts and on the V8 engine tighten to 15 ft. lbs. in the sequence shown. Next, tighten all the bolts to 30 ft. lbs., in sequence, and finally tighten to 40 ft. lbs. in sequence. On the V6 engine tighten to 15 ft. lbs. in the sequence shown, then retorque to 41 ft. lbs.
16. Install the intake manifold drain tube and clamp.
17. Install the injection pump adapter. Install the injection pump.
18. Install the vacuum pump or coil pump drive assembly. Do not operate the engine without vacuum pump/oil pump assembly in places as this unit drives the engine oil pump.
19. Continue the installation in the reverse order of the removal procedure. Adjust the throttle rod and the transmission cable as required.

EXHAUST MANIFOLD

Removal and Installation

GASOLINE ENGINE – 1983 V6 EXCEPT 229 CU. IN. V6

1. Disconnect the negative battery cable. Raise the vehicle and support it safely.
2. Remove the exhaust crossover pipe.
3. If remove the left exhaust manifold, disconnect the EFE pipe.
4. Remove the exhaust manifold retaining bolts. Remove the exhaust manifold from the vehicle.
5. Installation is the reverse of the removal procedure.

GASOLINE ENGINE – 1983 V8 AND 229 CU. IN. V6

1. Disconnect the negative battery cable. Remove the air cleaner. Remove the heat stove pipe, as required.
2. Raise the vehicle and support it safely.
3. Discinnect the exhaust pipe flange from the manifold.
4. Lower the vehicle.
5. Disconnect the spark plug wires, heat shields, EFE valve vacuum hose and all the necessary equipment in order to remove the exhaust manifold.
6. On the 299 cu. in. V6 gas engine, remove the oil dipstick tube retainer, when removing the right exhaust manifold.
7. Remove the air conditioner compressor and bracket, as required. Remove the power steering pump bracket, as required.
8. Remove the manifold retaining bolts and remove the manifold from the vehicle.
9. Installation is the reverse of the removal procedure.

SECTION 15

CHEVROLET
CAPRICE CLASSIC • CORVETTE • MALIBU • MONTE CARLO • IMPALA

GASOLINE ENGINE – 1984 AND LATER V6

1. Disconnect the negative battery cable and raise and support the vehicle safely.
2. Disconnect the exhaust pipe from the exhaust manifold.
3. Remove the following components on the right side. Lower the vehicle and disconnect the air management valve bracket. Disconnect the AIR hoses and AIR converter pipe. Disconnect the AIR pipe at the cylinder heads and at the manifold. Disconnect the spark plug wires.
4. Remove the following components on the left side. Remove the A/C compressor and the power steering pump. Remove the rear A/C adjusting brace and the lower power steering adjusting brace. Disconnect the spark plug wires.
5. Remove the exhaust manifold bolts and remove the exhaust manifold.
6. Installation is the reverse order of the removal procedure, be sure to use new gaskets and to torque the manifold bolts to 20 to 25 ft. lbs.

GASOLINE ENGINE – 1984 AND LATER V8 EXCEPT 1986 AND LATER 307 V8 ENGINE

1. Disconnect the negative battery cable and raise and support the vehicle safely.
2. Disconnect the exhaust pipe from the exhaust manifold and lower the vehicle.
3. On the models on the right side, remove the air cleaner, spark plugs and disconnect the vacuum hoses at the early fuel evaporator canister.
4. On the left side remove the power steering pump and loosen the A/C bracket at the front of the head, remove the rear A/C bracket and the A/C compressor. Remove the lower power steering adjusting bracket.
5. Remove the vacuum hose at the air injection reactor (AIR) valve.
6. On the right side, remove the alternator belt and lower alternator bracket, also remove the AIR valve. Disconnect the converter AIR pipe at the back of the manifold.
7. Remove the exhaust manifold bolts, and on the left side remove the wire loom holder at the valve cover, remove the exhaust manifold.
8. Installation is the reverse order of the removal procedure, and torque the manifold bolts to 20 to 25 ft. lbs.

GASOLINE ENGINE – 1986 AND LATER 307 V8

1. Disconnect the negative battery cable.
2. Remove all the necessary components in order to gain access to the manifold retaining bolts.
3. Remove the exhaust manifold retaining bolts.
4. Remove the exhaust manifold to exhaust pipe flange retaining bolts.
5. Remove the exhaust manifold from the vehicle. On some vehicles, it may be necessary to raise the engine in order to gain clearance.
6. Installation is the reverse of the removal procedure.

GASOLINE ENGINE – CORVETTE (RIGHT SIDE)

1. Disconnect the negative battery cable. Remove the air cleaner.
2. Drain the cooling system.
3. Remove the rear air condition compressor brace. Disconnect the AIR hose at the exhaust check valve. Disconnect the AIR hose at the converter pipe check valve.
4. Disconnect the heater hose at the rear of the intake manifold.
5. Disconnect the spark plug wires at the valve cover. Remove the spark plugs.
6. Remove the temperature sending unit at the right cylinder head.
7. Raise the vehicle and support it safely.
8. Disconnect the exhaust pipe at the exhaust manifold.
9. Disconnect the AIR pipe at the exhaust manifold.
10. Remove the two rear exhaust manifold bolts. Disconnect the dipstick tube at the exhaust manifold.
11. Lower the vehicle.
12. Remove the remaining exhaust manifold retaining bolts. Remove the exhaust manifold from the vehicle.
13. Installation is the reverse of the removal procedure.
14. Torque the exhaust manifold retaining bolts to specification.

GASOLINE ENGINE – CORVETTE (LEFT SIDE)

1. Disconnect the battery negative cable.
2. Remove the air cleaner.
3. Disconnect the PCV hose from intake and rocker cover.
4. Disconnect AIR hose at the exhaust check valve.
5. Disconnect rear alternator brace at the manifold.
6. Raise the vehicle.
7. Disconnect the exhaust pipe at manifold.
8. Lower the vehicle.
9. Remove manifold bolts. Remove manifold.
10. Installation is the reverse of the removal procedure.

DIESEL ENGINE

1. Disconnect the negative battery cable.
2. Remove the air cleaner. Remove the lower alternator bracket, as required.
3. Raise the vehicle and support it safely.
4. Remove the exhaust crossover pipe.
5. If removing the right exhaust manifold, remove the right front wheel. Disconnect the exhaust pipe at the manifold flange and remove the exhaust manifold retaining bolts. Remove the manifold from underneath of the vehicle.
6. If removing the left exhaust manifold, lower the vehicle. Remove the exhaust manifold retaining bolts and remove the manifold from the vehicle.
7. Installation is the reverse of the removal procedure.

Fuel Injection System

For More Information of Fuel Injection System Refer to the Unit Repair Section.

DESCRIPTION AND TYPE

All Corvettes are equipped with fuel injection. The Model 400 Throttle Body Injection System (TBI) includes a pair of throttle body injection units, mounted in front and rear positions on a single manifold cover. This arrangement allows each TBI unit to supply the correct air/fuel mixture through a tuned crossover runner in the intake manifold to the bank of cylinders on the opposite side of the engine, thus the name "Crossfire Injection" or "CFI". In addition, a throttle bore tube or "Swirl plate" is located under the manifold cover, below each throttle valve, to aid in mixture distribution.

TUNED PORT INJECTION (TPI)

This system can be found on the Corvette with the 5.7 liter V8 engine. The introduction of this new TPI system to these engines has improved the torque and power from both engines. The induction system for the TPI is made up of large forward mounted air cleaners, a new mass airflow sensor, a cast aluminum throttle body assembly with dual throttle blades, a large extended cast aluminum plenum, individial aluminum tuned runners and a protruding dual fuel rail assembly with computer controlled injectors, The base plate is cast aluminum and incorporates the crossover portion of the tuned runners. The base plate also seves as a mounting for the fuel injectors. The individual aluminum runners ar designed to provde the best tuning or frequency of air pulses within the runners and for the optimum throttle response throughout the driving range, thus the name Tuned Port Injection. The runners are selected by length and size so to take advantage of the air pulses set up by

CHEVROLET
CAPRICE CLASSIC • CORVETTE • MALIBU • MONTE CARLO • IMPALA
SECTION 15

the opening and closing of the intake valves. The high pressure pulses result in denser air at each intake valve, and timing the pressure pulses to occure during the valve open period forces more air into the combustion chamber, which results in a more efficient cylinder charging and improved volumetric efficiency.

Turbocharger System

For more information on the turbocharger system refer to the Unit Repair Section.

EMISSION CONTROL SECTION

Electronic control module
Fuel control system
Oxygen sensor
Mixture control solenoid
Coolant sensor
Throttle position sensor (TPS)
Idle speed control throttle switch
Early fuel evaporation (EFE)
Early fuel evaporation-thermal vacuum switch
Catalytic converter
Positive crankcase ventilation (PCV)
Barometric pressure sensor (BARO)
Manifold absolute pressure sensor (MAP)
Differential pressure sensor (DPS)
Thermostatic air cleaner (THERMAC)
Electronic spark timing (EST)
Electonic spark control (ESC)
Air injection reaction (AIR)
Air management valve
Deceleration valve
Canister purge valve check
Transmission converter clutch (TCC)
Vehicle speed sensor

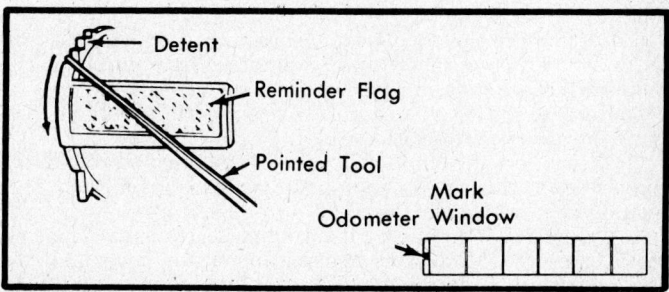

Resetting the maintenance reminder indicator
(© General Motors Corporation)

EMISSIONS INDICATOR

An emissions indicator flag may appear in the odometer window of the speedometer on some vehicles. The flag could say "Sensor", "Emissions" or "Catalyst" depending on the part or assembly that is scheduled for regular emissions maintenance replacement. The word "Sensor" indicates a need for oxygen sensor replacement and the words "Emissions" or "Catalyst" indicate the need for catalytic converter catalyst replacement.

Reset

1. Remove the instrument panel trim plate.
2. Remove the instrument cluster lens.
3. Locate the flag indicator reset notches at the drivers side of the odometer.
4. Use a pointed tool to apply light downward pressure on the notches, until the indicator is reset.
5. When the indicator is reset an alignment mark will apear in the left center of the odometer window.

ENGINE SECTION

For Diesel Engine Services Refer to the Unit Repair Section.

ENGINE ASSEMBLY

Removal and Installation

GASOLINE ENGINE – V6 EXCEPT 229 CU. IN.

1. Disconnect the negative battery cable. Remove the hood. Raise and support the vehicle safely.
2. Disconnect the exhaust pipe at the manifold and remove the flywheel cover.
3. Disconnect the transmission oil cooler lines at the oil pan and remove the left motor mount securing bolt and loosen the right.
4. Remove the flywheel to torque converter bolts and remove the bellhousing bolts.
5. Disconnect the computer command control (CCC) wiring harness at the transmission and disconnect the knock sensor.
6. Disconnect the fuel lines at the frame and remove the lower fan shroud and lower the vehicle.
7. Disconnect the CCC wiring harness at the engine and remove the windshield washer bottle.
8. Disconnect and tag all necessary wiring and vacuum hoses and remove the air cleaner.
9. Remove the upper fan shroud, the accelerator and T.V. cables and drain the cooling system.
10. Remove the heater hoses and radiator hoses, remove the A/C compressor and position it out of the way.
11. Remove the power steering pump and tie it off to the fender skirt.
12. Disconnect the transmission cooler lines at the radiator, the overflow tube and the radiator.
13. Disconnect the A/C hose from the alternator and position it out of the way.
14. Remove the alternator adjusting brace and disconnect the battery cables at the frame.
15. Remove the hood from its hinges and mark the hood for easy reassembly.
16. Support the transmission with a suitable jack, and using an engine lifting device, raise the engine and remove it from the vehicle.

CHEVROLET
CAPRICE CLASSIC • CORVETTE • MALIBU • MONTE CARLO • IMPALA

17. Installation is the reverse order of the removal procedure.

GASOLINE ENGINE – 229 CU. IN.

1. Disconnect the negative battery cable. Remove the air cleaner assembly.
2. Remove the hood from its hinges, but mark the hinges for easy reassembly.
3. Drain the cooling system and remove the following, radiator hoses, heater hoses, fan shroud, radiator, drive belts and pulleys.
4. Disconnect and tag all electrical wiring, vacuum hoses and fuel lines that must be removed in order to remove the engine.
5. Disconnect the accelerator cable and if so equipped remove the A/C compressor and power steering pump from the mounting brackets and position them out of the way.
6. Remove the alternator, raise and support the vehicle safely and drain the crankcase.
7. Disconnect the exhaust pipe at the exhaust manifold and converter bracket (if so equipped) at the transmission rear mount. Remove the starter.
8. On models equipped with automatic transmissions, remove the torque converter housing inspection cover and the converter to flex plate bolts. Remove the engine to transmission attaching bolts. On models equipped with manual transmission the transmission is removed with the engine.
9. Remove the motor mount securing bolts and the cruise control bracket (if so equipped), support the transmission and lower the vehicle.
10. Install a suitable lifting device to the engine and raise the engine high enough to allow it to be removed from the vehicle.
11. Installation is the reverse order of the removal procedure.

GASOLINE ENGINE – V8

1. Disconnect the negative battery cable. Remove the hood. Remove the air cleaner assembly. Drain the cooling system.
2. Remove the radiator hoses, upper fan shroud, fan assembly and heater hoses.
3. Remove the power steering pump and the A/C compressor and position them out of the way.
4. Disconnect the cooler lines at the radiator and remove the radiator from the vehicle.
5. Disconnect the vacuum lines, CCC wiring harness, AIR hoses and remove the windshield washer bottle.
6. Disconnect the engine wiring harness and all necessary wiring.
7. Remove the hood from its hinges and mark the hinges for easy reassembly.
8. Remove the distributor cap, disconnect the cruise control and the positive battery cable from the frame.
9. Disconnect the negative battery cable at the A/C hose bracket on the alternator bracket.
10. Raise the vehicle and support it safely, remove the crossover pipe and catalytic converter as an assembly.
11. Remove the flywheel cover and the torque converter bolts.
12. Remove the motor mount securing bolts and disconnect the fuel hose at the fuel pump.
13. Disconnect the torque converter clutch wiring at the transmission (if so equipped) and disconnect the transmission cooler lines at the clip on the engine oil pan.
14. Remove the transmission to engine bolts and support the transmission with a suitable jack.
15. Lower the vehicle and install a lifting device to the engine and raise and remove the engine from the vehicle.
16. Installation is the reverse order of the removal procedure.

GASOLINE ENGINE – CORVETTE

1. Disconnect the negative battery cable. Remove the hood. Remove the air cleaner. Drain the cooling system.
2. Disconnect all hoses at the air management check valve.
3. Remove the air condition compressor rear braces. Disconnect the compressor electrical wiring.
4. Remove the air management pulley and the valve adapter at the air pump. Remove the air pump retaining bolts and remove the air pump.
5. Remove the radiator upper hose at the thermostat outlet and the power steering reservoir brace.
6. Remove the alternator.
7. Remove the air pipe at the intake manifold and power steering reservoir brace.
8. Remove the power steering reservoir brace. Remove the power steering pump lower bracket.
9. Move the reservoir and brace, power steering pump and A/C wire loom to front.
10. Remove fuel inlet and return lines.
11. Remove A/C compressor and idler pulley bracket nuts at water pump.
12. Remove A/C lower mounting bolt. Move bracket forward and remove A/C compressor upper bolt. Remove compressor and lay aside.
13. Remove fuel lines lower bracket at former fuel pump cover plate. Remove idler pulley bracket.
14. Remove lower radiator hose at water pump. Remove heater hose at water pump.
15. Disconnect accelerator, TV and cruise control cables from brackets and from TBI.
16. Disconnect brake vacuum and PCV at intake manifold.
17. Disconnect electrical connections at TBI, front ground stud, coolant sensor and EGR solenoid. Disconnect vacuum lines.
18. Remove wiring harness from valve cover clip. Move air management valve, air pipe and wiring harness to back right of engine.
19. Remove tach filter and ground wires from intake cover stud. Disconnect connections and wire from distributor cap.
20. Disconnect spark plug wires and remove distributor cap.
21. Remove heater hose from intake manifold.
22. Mark and remove distributor. Remove oil sending unit.
23. Remove rear intake manifold bolt and remove wire bracket.
24. Remove crankshaft pulley for clearance.
25. Raise vehicle and support it safely.
26. Remove crossover pipe at manifold. Remove crossover pipe at converter. Remove hanger from crossover.
27. Remove converter air management pipe from right exhaust manifold.
28. Remove starter wires and sensor wire.
29. Disconnect coolant sensor wire at head and bracket on block.
30. Disconnect wire harness from oil pan, front of block, temperature sensor, oil temperature and oxygen sensor.
31. Disconnect battery ground and engine ground from rear of block above oil filter.
32. Remove flywheel cover. Remove torque converter bolts.
33. Remove bellhousing bolts on right side. Remove lower bolt, then upper in order to gain access to center bolt. Remove bolts on left side including ground wire.
34. Support engine.
35. Remove motor mount to block bolts.
36. Lower vehicle. Support transmission.
37. Attach lifting device and remove engine. Disconnect wires at rear left head.
38. Installation is the reverse of the removal procedure.

DIESEL ENGINE – V6

1. Drain the cooling system.
2. Remove air cleaner and install cover J-26996 or equivalent.
3. Remove hood from hinges, mark hood for reassembly.
4. Disconnect battery negative cables at batteries and

CHEVROLET
CAPRICE CLASSIC • CORVETTE • MALIBU • MONTE CARLO • IMPALA
SECTION 15

ground wires at inner fender panel. Disconnect engine ground strap, right head to cowl.

5. Disconnect radiator hoses, cooler lines, heater hoses, vacuum hoses, power steering pump hoses at power steering gear, air conditioning compressor with brackets and hoses attached, fuel hoses from fuel pump inlet line and injection pump return line.
6. Disconnect all engine wiring except at starter.
7. Disconnect the throttle cable.
8. Disconnect the transmission T.V. or detent cable at the injection pump and engine brackets.
9. Remove upper radiator support and radiator.
10. Raise the vehicle and support it safely.
11. Disconnect exhaust pipes at manifolds.
12. Remove the torque converter (flywheel) cover and the three torque converter to flywheel bolts.
13. Remove the starter motor.
14. Remove the engine mount through bolts.
15. Remove the three engine to transmission bolts on the right side.
16. Lower the vehicle.
17. Secure an engine lift chain to the engine.
18. Place a board on top of a jack and slightly raise the transmission. Remove the three left transmission to engine bolts. Remove engine.
19. Installation is the reverse of the removal procedure.

DIESEL ENGINE—V8

1. Drain cooling system.
2. Remove air cleaner and install cover screen J-26996 or equivalent.
3. Mark hood hinges and remove hood.
4. Disconnect negative battery cables at batteries and ground wires at inner fender panel. Disconnect engine ground strap, right head to cowl.
5. Disconnect radiator hoses, cooler lies, heater hoses, vacuum hoses, power steering pump hoses at power steering gear, air conditioning compressor with brackets and hoses attached, fuel hose from fuel pump and wiring.
6. Remove hairpin clip a bellcrank.
7. Remove throttle and T.V. cables from intake manifold brackets, then position cables away from engine.
8. Remove upper radiator support and radiator.
9. Raise the vehicle and support it safely.
10. Disconnect exhaust pipes a manifold.
11. Remove torque converter cover and three bolts holding converter to flywheel.
12. Remove engine mount bolts or nuts.
13. Remove three bolts, transmission to engine on the right side. Disconnect wires from starter and remove starter.
14. Lower the vehicle. Secure lift chain to engine.
15. Place board on top of jack and slightly raise transmission. Remove three left transmission to engine bolts. Remove engine.
16. Installation is the reverse of the removal procedure.

ENGINE MOUNTS

Removal and Installation

1. Disconnect the negative battery cable. Raise and support the vehicle safely. On Corvette, disconnect the catalytic converter air pipe.
2. Properly support the weight of the engine at the forward edge of the oil pan.
3. Remove the mount to engine block bolts. Raise the engine slightly and remove the mount to mount bracket bolt and nut. Remove the engine mount.
4. Installation is the reverse of the removal procedure.

VALVE SYSTEM

Valve Adjustment

Hydraulic valve lifters are used in all engines produced by General Motors Corporation. Valve adjustments are not possible on the V6 or V8 diesel engine or on the 321 cu. in. V6 gas engine.
1. Remove the valve covers.
2. Tighten the rocker arm nuts until all lash is eliminated.
3. Adjust the valves when the lifter is on the base circle of the camshaft lobe by cranking the engine until the mark on the vibration damper lines up with the center or "O" mark on the timing tab fastened to the crankcase front cover and the engine is in the No.1 firing position.

NOTE: This may be determined by placing your fingers on the No. 1 valve as the mark on the damper comes near the "O" mark on the crankcase front cover. If the valves move as the mark comes up to the timing tab, the engine is in the No. 6 (No. 4-V6) firing position and should be turned over one more time to reach to No. 1 firing position.

4. With the engine in the No. 1 firing position, adjust the following valves. V6 engine:exhaust—1,5,6 intake—1,2,3. V8 engine: exhaust—1,3,4,8 intake—1,2,5,7.
5. Back out adjusting nut until lash is felt at the push rod then turn in adjusting nut until all lash is removed. This can be determined by rotating push rod while turning adjusting nut. When play has been removed, turn adjusting nut in one full additional turn.
6. Crank the engine one revolution until the pointer "O" mark and the vibration damper mark are again in alignment. This is the No. 6 (No.4-V6) firing position.
7. With the engine in this position, adjust the following valves. V6 engine: exhaust—2,3,4 intake—4,5,6. V8 engine: exhaust—2,5,6,7 intake—3,4,6,8.
8. Install the rocker arm covers.
9. Start the engine and adjust the idle speed as required.

VALVE LIFTERS

Removal and Installation

1. Disconnect the negative battery cable.
2. Remove the intake manifold assembly.
3. Remove the rocker arm covers. Remove the rocker arm assembly. Remove the push rods. Be sure to keep them in order as they must be installed in the same bores as they were removed.
4. As required, remove the valve lifter guide retaining bolts. Remove the valve lifter guide.
5. Remove the valve lifters using the proper valve lifter removal tool.
6. Installation is the reverse of the removal procedure. Be sure to use new gaskets as required. Be sure to coat the lifter assemblies with clean engine oil prior to installation.

VALVE ROCKER ASSEMBLY

Removal and Installation

GASOLINE ENGINE—V6 EXCEPT 229 CU.IN

1. Disconnect the negative battery cable.
2. Remove the rocker arm cover. Remove the rocker arm and shaft assembly from the cylinder head.
3. Remove the nylon rocker arm retainers and separate the rocker arms from the rocker shaft.
4. Installation is the reverse of the removal procedure. Be sure to use new valve cover gaskets, where required.

15—29

CHEVROLET
CAPRICE CLASSIC • CORVETTE • MALIBU • MONTE CARLO • IMPALA

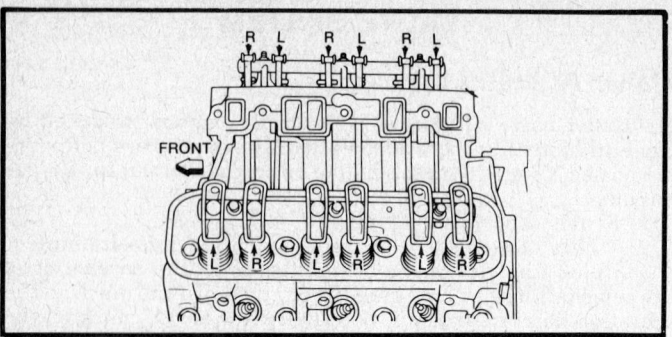

V6 gas engine rocker arm installation sequence—except 229 cu.in. engine
(© General Motors Corporation)

5. When installing the rocker arms on to the rocker shaft, be sure to position them in the correct sequence.

GASOLINE ENGINE—V8 AND 229 CU. IN. EXCEPT 1986 AND LATER 307 V8 ENGINE

1. Disconnect the negative battery cable.
2. Remove the air cleaner. Disconnect the necessary hoses and wires in order to gain access to the valve cover retaining bolts.
3. Remove the EGR solenoid and bracket. If the vehicle is equipped with a four barrel carburetor, remove the EGR valve.
4. Disconnect the spark plug wires. Remove the AIR hoses. Remove the PCV valve tube. Remove the idle speed solenoid. If removing the left valve cover, remove the power brake vacuum pipe.
5. If the vehicle is equipped with the axial six air condition compressor, remove the upper rear bracket and belt in order to position the compressor to the side.
6. If the vehicle is equipped with air condition and cruise control, remove the compressor, as required.
7. Remove the valve covers.
8. Remove the rocker arm nuts, rocker arm balls and rocker arms.
9. Installation is the reverse of the removal procedure. Be sure to use new valve cover gaskets as required.

GASOLINE ENGINE—1986 and LATER 307 V8

1. Disconnect the negative battery cable. Remove the valve cover.
2. Remove the rocker arm retaining bolts, rocker arm pivot and rocker arms.
3. Installation is the reverse of the removal procedure. Be sure to use new valve cover gaskets as required.

GASOLINE ENGINE—CORVETTE

1. Disconnect the negative battery cable. Remove the air cleaner.
2. If removing the left valve cover, disconnect the PCV valve and hose. Disconnect the power brake booster vacuum line. Remove the alternator.
3. If removing the right valve cover, disconnect the air hose from the exhaust check valve. Remove the fuel inlet and return lines from the throttle body. Remove the air condition compressor.
4. Remove the valve cover retaining bolts. Remove the valve covers.
5. Remove the rocker arm nuts, rocker arm balls and the rocker arms.
6. Installation is the reverse of the removal procedure. Be sure to use new valve cover gaskets as required.

DIESEL ENGINE

1. Disconnect the negative battery cable.
2. Remove the valve cover.

3. Remove the rocker arm retaining bolts. Remove the rocker arm pivot. Remove the rocker arms.
4. Installation is the reverse of the removal procedure. Be sure to use new valve cover gaskets as required.

VALVE TIMING

Adjustment

Manufacturers recommended procedure for valve timing has been established and recommended for only the 5.0L (307 cu. in.) Oldsmobile produced V8 engine.

5.0L (307 CU.IN.) ENGINE

1. Remove the distributor cap. Remove the right valve cover. Remove the number four intake and exhaust rocker arm assembly.
2. Remove the wire from the BAT. terminal of the distributor cap.
3. Turn ignition switch on. Crank engine until rotor is in line with Number Four spark plug wire position. Number Four piston will be approximately at the top of cylinder.
4. Measure from pivot boss on head surface to top of Number Four intake pushrod. Record measurement.
5. Slowly turn engine one and one half revolutions until rotor approaches Number One spark plug wire position. Continue to turn engine until timing mark on crank puller is aligned with 0 on indicator. This is top dead center of Number One piston.
6. Again measure from pivot boss surface to top of Number Four cylinder intake pushrod.
7. Measurement should increase over the first measurement.
8. If measurement increase is not within 1/32 in. of first measurement, camshaft is advanced or retarded.

DIESEL ENGINE VALVE LIFTER BLEED DOWN

If the intake manifold has not been removed but rocker arms have been loosened or removed, valve lifters can be bled down by the following procedure.

1. Before reinstalling rocker arms, rotate the crankshaft until No.1 cylinder is at 32 degrees before top dead center. This is 2 in. counterclockwise from the o degrees pointer. If only the right valve cover was removed, remove No. 1 glow plug to determine if the position of the piston is the correct one. The compression pressure will tell you that you are in the right position.
2. If the left valve cover was removed, rotate the crankshaft until the No. 5 cylinder intake valve push rod ball is 28 in. above the No. 5 cylinder exhaust valve pushrod ball. Use only hand wrenches to torque the rocker arm pivot nuts or bolts to avoid engine damage.
3. If removed, install the No. 5 cylinder pivot and rocker arms. Torque the nuts or bolts alternately between the intake and exhaust valves until the intake valve begins to open, then stop. Install remaining rocker arms except No. 3 exhaust valve. (If this rocker arm was removed.)
4. If removed, install but do not torque No. 3 valve pivots beyond the point that the valve would be fully open. This is indicated by strong resistance while still turning the pivot retaining nuts or bolts. Going beyond this would bend the push rod. Torque the nuts or bolts slowly allowing the lifter to bleed down.
5. Finish torquing No. 5 cylinder rocker arm pivot nut or bolt slowly. Do not go beyond the point that the valve would be fully open. This is indicated by strong resistance while still turning the pivot retaining nuts or bolts. Going beyond this would bend the push rod.

CHEVROLET
CAPRICE CLASSIC • CORVETTE • MALIBU • MONTE CARLO • IMPALA
SECTION 15

6. Do not turn the engine crankshaft for at least 45 minutes. Do not rotate the engine until the valve lifters have been bled down, or damage to the engine will occur.

CYLINDER HEADS

Removal and Installation

GASOLINE ENGINE – V6 EXCEPT 299 CU. IN.

1. Disconnect negative battery cable.
2. Remove intake manifold.
3. Loosen and remove belt(s).
4. When removing left cylinder head, remove oil dipstick and move the air and vacuum pumps with mounting bracket if present, out of the way with hoses attached.
5. When removing right cylinder head, remove the alternator and disconnect the power steering gear pump and brackets attaching to cylinder head.
6. Disconnect wires from spark plugs, and remove the spark plug wire clips from the rocker arm cover studs.
7. Remove exhaust manifold bolts from head being removed.
8. With air hose and cloths, clean dirt off cylinder head and adjacent area to avoid getting dirt into engine.
9. Remove rocker arm cover and rocker arm and shaft assembly from cylinder head. Lift out push rods.
10. Loosen all cylinder head bolts, then remove bolts and lift off the cylinder head.
11. Installation is the reverse of the removal procedure. Torque the cylinder head bolts to 80 ft. lbs., torque the exhaust manifold bolts to 25 ft. lbs. and torque the intake manifold bolts to 45 ft. lbs.

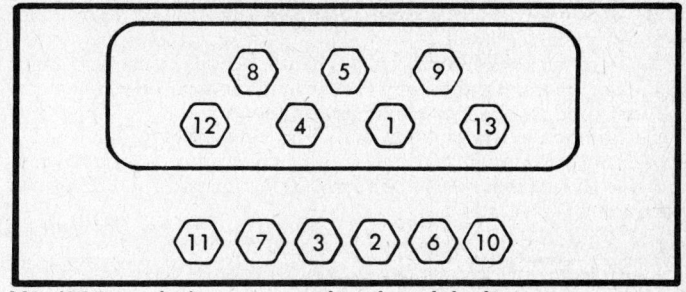

V6 (229 cu.in.) – gas engine head bolt torque sequence (© General Motors Corporation)

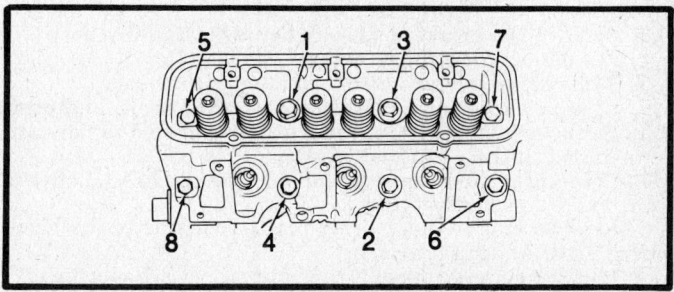

V6 (231 cu.in.) – gas engine head bolt torque sequence (© General Motors Corporation)

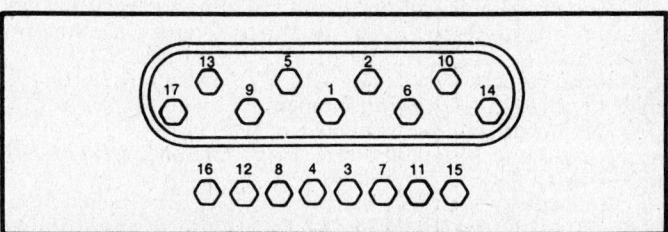

Small block V8 cylinder head torque sequence

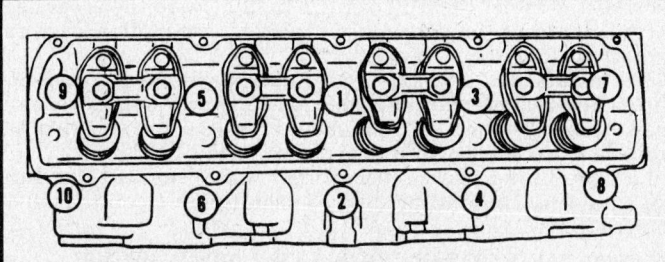

Diesel engine cylinder head torque sequence

GASOLINE ENGINE – V8 AND 299 CU. IN. EXCEPT 1986 AND LATER 307 V8 ENGINE

1. Disconnect the negative battery cable.
2. Remove the intake manifold. Remove the alternator. Remove the air condition compressor and power steering pump as required.
3. Remove the exhaust manifolds. Remove all electrical and ground connections.
4. Remove the rocker covers. Remove the valve train mechanism.
5. Remove the diverter valve, except Corvette. On Corvette, remove the spark plugs when removing the right cylinder head.
6. Remove the cylinder head retaining bolts. Remove the cylinder head from the engine.
7. Installation is the reverse of the removal procedure. Torque the cylinder head bolts to specification.

GASOLINE ENGINE – 1986 AND LATER 307 V8

1. Disconnect the negative battery cable. Drain the radiator.
2. Remove the intake manifold. Remove the exhaust manifold.

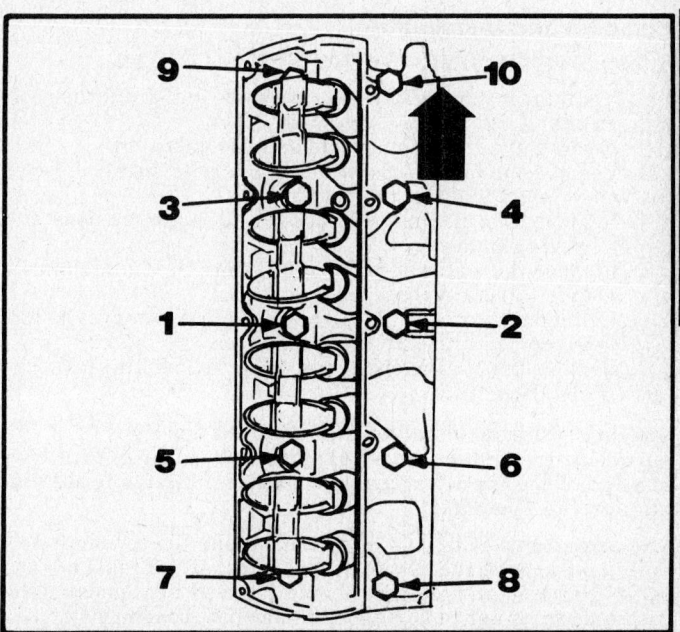

V8 (307 cu. in.) gas engine cylinder head bolt torque sequence

15-31

CHEVROLET
CAPRICE CLASSIC • CORVETTE • MALIBU • MONTE CARLO • IMPALA

3. Remove the valve cover. Remove the ground strap from the left cylinder head.
4. Remove rocker arm bolts, pivots, rocker arms and push rods. Scribe pivots and keep rocker arms separated so they can be installed in their original locations.
5. Remove cylinder head bolts and remove cylinder head.
6. Installation is the reverse of the removal procedure. Torque the cylinder head bolts to 100 ft. lbs. and then to a final torque of 130 ft. lbs.

DIESEL ENGINE

1. Disconnect the negative battery cable. Drain the cooling system.
2. On the V8 diesel engine remove the injection pump and lines.
3. Remove the intake manifold. Remove the valve cover.
4. Disconnect glow plug wiring.
5. Remove ground strap from right cylinder head.
6. Remove rocker arm bolts, pivots, rocker arms, and push rods. Scribe pivots and keep rocker arms separated so they can be installed in their original locations.
7. Disconnect the exhaust manifold from the head. Leave it attached to the crossover pipe.
8. Remove engine block drain plug, from side of the block where head is being removed.
9. Remove cylinder head bolts and remove cylinder head.
10. If necessary to remove pre-chamber, remove the glow plug and injection nozzle, then tap out with a small blunt drift.
11. Installation is the reverse of the removal procedure.
12. If the vehicle is equipped with a V8 diesel torque the cylinder head bolts to 100 ft. lbs. and then retorque the head to 130 ft. lbs.
13. If the vehicle is equipped with a V6 diesel torque the cylinder heads in the following manner.
14. Torque all cylinder head bolts in sequence except number 5,6,11,12,13 and 14 to 100 lbs. ft. Torque number 5,6,11,12,13 and 14 to 41 lbs. ft.
15. Retorque in sequence all cylinder head bolts except number 5,6,11,12,13 and 14 to 142 lbs. ft. Retorque number 5,6,11,12,13 and 14 to 59 lbs. ft.

CAMSHAFT

Removal and Installation

GASOLINE ENGINE – V6 EXCEPT 229 CU. IN.

1. Disconnect the negative battery cable and drain the cooling system.
2. Remove the intake manifold and the valve covers.
3. Remove the upper fan shroud, drive belts, heater hose at the water pump and the radiator hoses.
4. Remove the alternator bracket and brace, remove the power steering pump.
5. Remove the water pump and fan, align the timing marks and remove the crankshaft pulley.
6. Using pulley tool #J-23523 or equivalent, remove the torsional damper and remove the front cover.
7. Remove the timing chain and gear, remove the pushrods and lifters.

NOTE: The sprocket on the camshaft is a light fit, if the sprocket does not come off easily a light blow on the lower edge of the sprocket (using a plastic mallet) should disengage the sprocket.

8. Install two 5/16 inch-18x4 inch bolts in the camshaft bolt holes and remove the camshaft. All camshaft journals are the same diameter and caution should be used in removing the camshaft so as not to damage the camshaft bearings.
9. Installation is the reverse order of the removal procedure, be sure to coat the lifters and camshaft with clean engine oil before installation.

GASOLINE ENGINE 229 CU. IN.

1. Disconnect the negative battery cable and drain the cooling system.
2. Remove the intake manifold and valve covers.
3. Remove the rocker arm assemblies, push rods and lifters.
4. Remove the radiator, grille, water pump and front engine cover.
5. Remove the fuel pump push rod.
6. Install two 5/16 × 4 inch bolts into the camshaft bolt holes and carefully remove the camshaft.
7. Installation is the reverse order of the removal procedure, be sure to coat the lifters and the camshaft with clean engine oil before installation.

GASOLINE ENGINE – V8 EXCEPT 1986 AND LATER 307 V8 ENGINE

1. Disconnect the negative battery cable and drain the cooling system.
2. Remove the intake manifold and the valve covers.
3. Remove the upper fan shroud, drive belts, heater hose at the water pump and the radiator hoses. Disconnect the oil cooler lines and remove the radiator.
4. Remove the alternator bracket and brace, remove the power steering pump and AIR pump bracket.
5. Remove the water pump and fan, align the timing marks and remove the crankshaft pulley.
6. Using pulley tool #J-23523 or equivalent, remove the torsional damper and remove the front cover. Remove the timing chain and gear.
7. Disconnect the fuel lines and remove the fuel pump.
8. Purge and evacuate the A/C system and remove the A/C condenser.
9. Disconnect the grille support rods, remove the push rods and lifters. The sprocket on the camshaft is a light fit, if the sprocket does not come off easily a light blow on the lower edge of the sprocket (using a plastic mallet) should disengage the sprocket.
10. Install two 5/16 inch-18 × 4 inch bolts in the camshaft bolt holes and remove the camshaft. All camshaft journals are the same diameter and caution should be used in removing the camshaft so as not to damage the camshaft bearings.
11. Installation is the reverse order of the removal procedure, be sure to coat the lifters and camshaft with clean engine oil before installation.

GASOLINE ENGINE – 1986 AND LATER 307 V8

1. Disconnect the negative battery cable. Drain the radiator. Remove the upper radiator baffle.
2. Disconnect the upper radiator hose.
3. Remove the radiator.
4. Disconnect the fuel line at the fuel pump.
5. Remove the air cleaner. Disconnect the throttle cable.
6. Remove the alternator belt. Remove the alternator bracket attaching bolts.
7. Remove power steering pump bracket attaching bolts and remove the pump.
8. Remove air conditioning compressor mounting bracket attaching bolts and support compressor to side for access. The air conditioning lines at the compressor are flexible and should be left attached to the compressor.
9. Disconnect thermostat bypass hose at water pump. Disconnect electrical and vacuum connections. Remove distributor with cap and wiring intact.
10. Remove balancer pulley. Remove balancer.
11. Remove engine front cover. Remove both valve covers.
12. Remove intake manifold and gasket, front and rear seal.
13. Remove rocker arms, push rods and valve lifters.
14. Parts position should be noted so they will be installed in their original position.
15. If equipped with air conditioning, discharge the system, remove condenser attaching bolts and remove condenser.

16. Remove bolt securing fuel pump eccentric, remove eccentric, camshaft gear, oil slinger and timing chain.
17. Remove camshaft by carefully sliding it out the front of the engine.
18. Installation is the reverse of the removal procedure. Be sure to coat the camshaft and the lifters with clean engine oil prior to installation. Be sure to use new gaskets, as required.

GASOLINE ENGINE—CORVETTE

1. Disconnect the negative battery cable.
2. Remove the intake manifold.
3. Remove the crankshaft pulley and the vibration damper.
4. Remove the power steering line in order to gain access to the vibration damper for installation.
5. Remove the air conditioning compressor brackets and position the compressor to the side. Remove the air pump.
6. Disconnect radiator hoses at water pump. Remove radiator hoses.
7. Remove front cover bolts. Remove front cover.
8. Rotate crankshaft and align timing marks.
9. Remove cam gear bolts remove chain and gear.
10. Remove alternator bolts and position the unit to the side.
11. Disconnect spark plug wires at spark plugs, remove rockers cover bolts. Remove rocker covers.
12. Remove all push rods. Remove lifters.
13. Disconnect air conditioning accumulator from shroud and lay aside.
14. Disconnect upper transmission cooler line at radiator. Disconnect fan wire at fan and fan shroud. Remove cooling fan. Disconnect lower transmission cooler line and remove fitting at radiator.
15. Remove upper fan shroud bolts and remove shroud. Remove radiator.
16. Disconnect air conditioning high pressure line bracket at right frame rail. Swing air conditioning condenser up and rest on top of lower shroud.
17. Remove camshaft, using care not to damage the camshaft bearings.
18. Installation is the reverse of the removal procedure.

DIESEL ENGINE—V6

1. Disconnect the negative battery cable.
2. Drain the radiator. Remove the radiator fan shroud. Remove the radiator upper baffle. Remove the radiator.
3. Remove the intake manifold assembly.
4. Remove the oil pump drive assembly.
5. Remove the front cover. Remove the rocker covers.
6. Rotate the crankshaft so that the timing marks are in alignment.
7. Remove all rocker arms, pivots, push rods, and lifters. Parts position should be noted so that the parts can be installed in their original position.
8. Remove the bolt securing the camshaft sprockets and remove the camshaft and crankshaft sprockets and timing chain.
9. Remove the bolts retaining the front camshaft bearing retainer and remove the retainer.
10. Remove the cam sprocket key.
11. Remove the injection pump drive gear.
12. If necessary to remove the injection pump driven gear, remove the intermediate pump adapter and pump adapter. Remove the snap ring and selective washer. Remove the driven gear and spring.
13. If equipped with air conditioning, discharge the system, remove the condenser attaching bolts and remove the condenser.
14. Carefully remove the camshaft from the engine being careful not to damage any camshaft bearings.
15. Installation is the reverse of the removal procedure. Be sure to coat the camshaft and the lifters with clean engine oil. Use new gaskets, as required. Bleed the valve lifters as required.

DIESEL ENGINE—V8

1. Disconnect the negative battery cable.
2. Drain the radiator. Remove the radiator fan shroud. Remove the radiator upper baffle. Remove the radiator.
3. Remove the intake manifold assembly.
4. Remove the oil pump drive assembly. Remove the vacuum pump assembly.
5. Remove the front cover. Remove the rocker covers.
6. Remove the balancer pulley. Remove the balancer.
7. Remove rocker arms, push rods, and valve lifters. Parts position should be noted so they will be installed in their original position.
8. If equipped with air conditioning, discharge system, remove condenser attaching bolts, and remove condenser.
9. Remove bolt securing camshaft gear and timing chain, then remove timing gears and chain.
10. Position camshaft dowel pin at the 3 o'clock position. With the camshaft held rearward, remove pump drive gear by sliding off the camshaft while rocking the pump driven gear.
11. If necessary to remove pump driven gear, remove injection pump adapter, then remove snap ring and selective washer. Remove the driven gear and spring.
12. Remove camshaft by carefully sliding it out the front of the engine.
13. Installation is the reverse of the removal procedure.
14. Be sure to coat the camshaft and the lifters with clean engine oil. Use new gaskets, as required. Bleed the valve lifters as required.

PISTON AND ROD POSITIONING

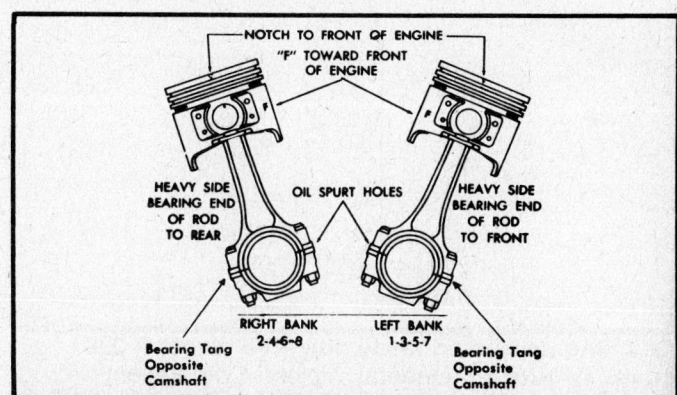

Gas engine piston assembly—V8 and 229 cu.in. engine (© General Motors Corporation)

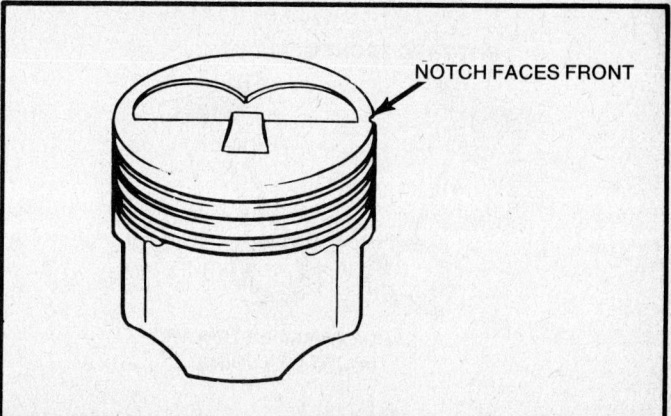

Diesel engine piston assembly (© General Motors Corporation)

CHEVROLET
CAPRICE CLASSIC • CORVETTE • MALIBU • MONTE CARLO • IMPALA

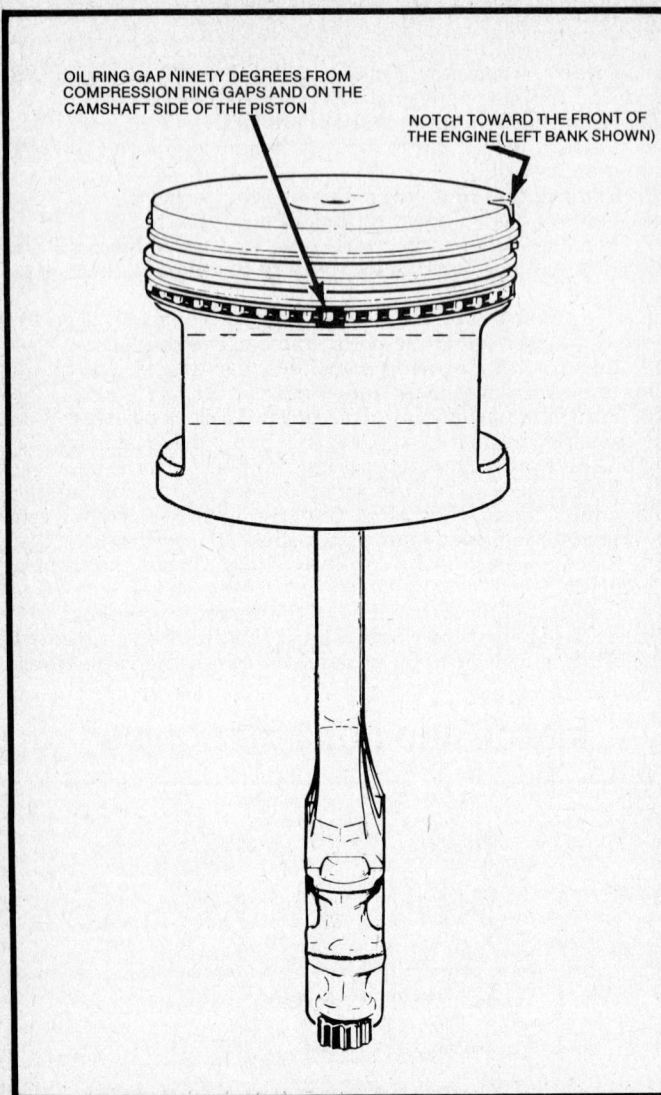

Gas engine piston assembly—V6 except 229 cu.in. engine (© General Motors Corporation)

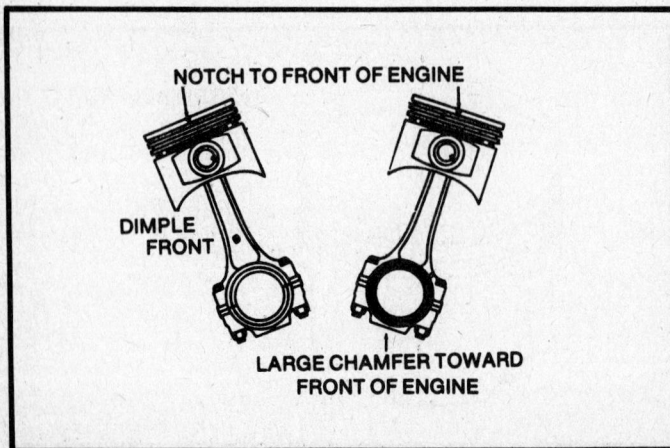

Gas engine piston assembly—1986 and later 307 V8 gas engine

TIMING CASE COVER/OIL SEAL

Removal and Installation

GASOLINE ENGINE—V6 EXCEPT 229 CU. IN.

1. Disconnect the negative battery cable. Drain the radiator.
2. Disconnect the radiator hoses and the heater return hose at the water pump.
3. Remove the fan assembly and pulleys. Remove the crankshaft vibration damper.
4. Remove the fuel pump. Remove the alternator.
5. Remove the distributor. If timing chain and sprockets are not going to be disturbed, note position of distributor rotor for reinstallation in same position.
6. Loosen and slide front clamp on thermostat by-pass hose rearward.
7. Remove bolts attaching timing chain cover to cylinder block. Remove two oil pan to timing chain cover bolts. Remove timing chain cover assembly and gasket.
8. Throughly clean the cover, taking care to avoid damage to the gasket surface.
9. Installation is the reverse of the removal procedure.
10. Remove oil pump cover and pack the space around the oil pump gears completely full of petroleum jelly. There must be no air space left inside the pump. Reinstall cover using new gasket.
11. To replace the front oil seal, use a punch and drive out the old seal and shedder. Drive the seal out from the front toward the rear of the timing chain cover.
12. Coil new packing around opening so ends of packing are at top. Drive in shedder using suitable punch. Stake the shedder in place in at least three places.
13. Size the packing by rotating a hammer handle or similar tool around the packing until the balancer hub can be inserted through the opening.
14. Torque the front cover retaining bolts to 28 ft. lbs.

GASOLINE ENGINE—V8 AND 299 CU. EXCEPT 1986 AND LATER 307 V8 ENGINE

1. Disconnect the negative battery cable.
2. Remove the vibration damper assembly.
3. Remove the water pump.
4. Remove the crankcase front cover retaining bolts. Remove the front cover and discard the gasket.

GASOLINE ENGINE—1986 AND LATER 307 V8

1. Disconnect the negative battery cable. Drain the cooling system. Disconnect the radiator hoses and the bypass hose.
2. Remove the radiator upper support. Remove the radiator.
3. Remove all belts, fan and fan pulley, crankshaft pulley and harmonic balancer.
4. Remove cover to block attaching bolts and remove cover, timing indicator and water pump assembly.
5. Remove front cover and both dowel pins. It may be necessary to grind a flat on the pins to get a rough surface for gripping.
6. Remove the timing chain and gears, as required.
7. Installation is the reverse of the removal procedure.
8. To install the cover, grind a chamfer on one end of each dowel pin.
9. Cut excess material from front end of oil pan gasket on each side of engine block.
10. Clean block, oil pan and front cover mating surfaces with solvent.
11. Trim about 1/8 in. from each end of new front pan seal, using a sharp tool.
12. Install new front cover gasket on engine block and new front seal on front cover. Apply sealer to gasket around coolant holes and place on block. Apply RTV sealer or equivalent to both mating surfaces.

CHEVROLET
CAPRICE CLASSIC • CORVETTE • MALIBU • MONTE CARLO • IMPALA
SECTION 15

13. Place the cover on the front of the block and press downward to compress the seal.
14. Rotate the cover to the left and then to the right and guide the seal into the cavity using a suitable tool.
15. Install two bolts finger tight to hold the cover in place. Install the two dowel pins, chamfered end first.
16. Continue the installation in the reverse order of the removal procedure.
17. To replace the front cover oil seal, pry it from the front cover. Before installing a new oil seal coat it with clean engine oil.

GASOLINE ENGINE – CORVETTE

1. Disconnect the negative battery cable.
2. Remove the vibration damper assembly.
3. Remove the air pump. Disconnect the fuel inlet and outlet pipes at the throttle body.
4. Disconnect the air condition compressor mounting brackets and position the unit to the side.
5. Remove the air pump brackets, power steering brackets and the air condition compressor brackets.
6. Drain the radiator. Remove the water pump.
7. Remove the front cover attaching bolts. Remove the front cover and discard the gasket.
8. Installation is the reverse of the removal procedure.

DIESEL ENGINE – V6

1. Disconnect the negative battery cable.
2. Drain the cooling system. Disconnect the lower radiator hose. Disconnect the heater outlet and the bypass hoses.
3. Remove the crankshaft balancer and pulley.
4. Remove the fan assembly and water pump pulley.
5. Remove the alternator, power steering pump, belt tensioner and air condition compressor brackets, if equipped.
6. Remove the front cover to block bolts and probe holder.
7. Remove the front cover and both dowel pins. If may be necessary to grind a flat on the pins in order to get a rough surface for gripping.
8. To install, grind a chamfer on one end of each dowel pin.
9. Cut excess material from front end of oil pan gasket on each side of engine block.
10. Clean block, oil pan and front cover mating surfaces with solvent.
11. Trim about 1/8 in. from each end of new front pan seal, using a sharp tool.
12. Install new front cover gasket on engine block and new front seal on front cover. Apply sealer to gasket around coolant holes and place on block. Apply /RTV sealer or equivalent to both mating surfaces.
13. Place the cover on the front of the block and press downward to compress the seal.
14. Rotate the cover to the left and then to the right and guide the seal into the cavity using a suitable tool.
15. Install two bolts finger tight or hold the cover in place. Install the two dowel pins, chamfered end first.
16. Continue the installation in the reverse order to the removal procedure.
17. To replace the front cover oil seal, pry it from the front cover. Before installing a new oil seal coat it with clean engine oil.

DIESEL ENGINE – V8

1. Disconnect the negative battery cable. Drain the cooling system.
2. Disconnect radiator hoses. Disconnect the bypass hose.
3. Remove all belts, fan and fan pulley, crankshaft pulley and harmonic balancer, and accessory brackets.
4. Remove cover to block attaching bolts and remove cover, timing indicator, and water pump assembly.
5. Remove front cover and both dowel pins. It may be necessary to grind a flat on the pins to get a rough surface for gripping.
6. To install, grind a chamfer on one end of each dowel pin.
7. Cut excess material from front end of oil pan gasket on each side of engine block.
8. Clean block, oil pan and front cover mating surfaces with solvent.
9. Trim about 1/8 in. from each end of new front pan seal, using a sharp tool.
10. Install new front cover gasket on engine block and new front seal on front cover. Apply sealer to gasket around coolant holes and place on block. Apply RTV sealer or equivalent to both mating surfaces.
11. Place the cover on the front of the block and press downward to compress the seal.
12. Rotate the cover to the left and then to the right and guide the seal into the cavity using a suitable tool.
13. Install two bolts finger tight to hold the cover in place. Install the two dowel pins, chamfered end first.
14. Continue the installation in the reverse order of the removal procedure.
15. To replace the front cover oil seal, pry it from the front cover. Before installing a new oil seal coat it with clean engine oil.

TIMING GEARS

Removal and Installation

GASOLINE ENGINE – V6 EXCEPT 229 CU. IN.

1. Disconnect the negative battery cable.
2. Drain the cooling system. Remove the engine front cover.
3. With timing chain cover removed, temporarily install balancer bolt and washer in end of crankshaft. Turn crankshaft so that the timing marks on the sprockets are as close together as possible. Remove balancer bolt and washer using a sharp blow on the wrench handle, so that the bolt can be started out without changing position of sprockets.
4. Remove front crankshaft oil slinger. Remove the camshaft sprocket bolts.
5. Use two large suitable tools to alternately pry the camshaft sprocket then the crankshaft sprocket forward until the camshaft sprocket is free, then remove the camshaft sprocket and chain and finish working crankshaft sprocket off crankshaft.
6. Throughly clean the timing chain, sprockets, distributor drive gear, fuel pump eccentric and crankshaft oil slinger.
7. If the pistons have not been moved in the engine, go to Step 10. If the engine has been turned over or the pistons moved, start with Step 1.
8. Turn crankshaft so that No. 1 piston is at top dead center.
9. Turn camshaft so with sprocket temporarily installed, timing mark is straight down. Remove sprocket.
10. Assemble tuning chain on sprockets and slide the sprocket and chain assembly on the shafts with the timing marks in their closets together position and in line with the sprocket hubs.
11. Assemble slinger on crankshaft with large part of cone to front of engine.
12. Install camshaft sprocket bolts. Torque to specification.
13. Install camshaft thrust button and spring and timing chain dampers.
14. Install timing chain cover.
15. Continue the installation in the reverse order of the removal procedure.

GASOLINE ENGINE – V8 AND 299 CU. IN.

1. Disconnect the negative battery cable.
2. Remove the engine front cover. Rotate the crankshaft and align the timing marks.

15-35

SECTION 15
CHEVROLET
CAPRICE CLASSIC • CORVETTE • MALIBU • MONTE CARLO • IMPALA

3. Remove the camshaft gear bolts. Remove the camshaft gear.
4. Remove the timing chain.
5. Remove the crankshaft gear sprocket, as required.
6. Installation is the reverse of the removal procedure.

DIESEL ENGINE—V6

1. Disconnect the negative battery cable. Drain the cooling system.
2. Remove the engine front cover.
3. Loosen all rocker arm pivot bolts evenly so that lash exists between the rocker arms and valves.
4. Remove the crankshaft oil slinger.
5. Remove the camshaft sprocket to camshaft bolt and washer.
6. Remove the timing chain, camshaft and crankshaft sprockets.
7. If the camshaft sprocket to cam key should come out with the camshaft sprocket, remove the front camshaft bearing retainer and install the key into the injection pump drive gear. Install the bearing retainer and torque the bolts to 48 ft. lbs. (65 Nm).
8. Install the key in the crankshaft, if removed.
9. Install camshaft sprocket, crankshaft sprocket and timing chain together, and align timing marks.
10. Torque camshaft sprocket bolt to 64 ft. lbs. Install the oil slinger.
11. After installing the front cover, it is necessary to bleed down the valve lifters.
12. Install the valve covers.
13. Check and reset if necessary, the injection pump timing.
14. Continue the installation in the reverse order of the removal procedure. Be sure to bleed down the valve lifters, as required.

DIESEL ENGINE—V8

1. Disconnect the negative battery cable. Drain the cooling system.
2. Remove the engine front timing cover.
3. Remove the oil slinger. Remove the cam sprocket, crankshaft sprocket and timing chain.
4. Remove the fuel pump eccentric from the crankshaft if necessary.
5. Install the key in the crankshaft, if removed. Install the fuel pump eccentric, if removed.
6. Install camshaft sprocket, crankshaft sprocket and timing chain together, and align timing marks.
7. Torque camshaft sprocket bolts to 65 ft. lbs.
8. When the two marks are in alignment, No. 6 cylinder is a T.D.C. To obtain T.D.C. for number on cylinder, slowly rotate crankshaft one rotation. This will bring the cam mark to the top, number one will be in firing position.
9. Install oil slinger. Any time the timing chain and sprockets are replaced, it will be necessary to retime the engine. Refer to the diesel engine section of this manual for the proper information.
10. Continue the installation in the reverse order of the removal procedure. Be sure to bleed down the valve lifters, as required.

Lubrication

OIL PAN

Removal and Installation

GASOLINE ENGINE—V6 EXCEPT 229 CU. IN.

1. Disconnect the negative battery cable.
2. Raise the vehicle and support it safely. Drain the engine oil.
3. Remove the flywheel cover. Remove the exhaust crossover pipe.
4. Lift the engine in order to gain access for pan removal clearance.
5. Remove the oil pan retaining bolts. Remove the oil pan from the engine.
6. Installation is the reverse of the removal procedure. Be sure to use a new gasket or RTV sealant as required.

GASOLINE ENGINE—V8 AND 229 CU. IN. ENGINE EXCEPT 1986 AND LATER 307 V8 ENGINE

1. Disconnect the negative battery cable.
2. Drain the engine oil. On some vehicles it will be necessary to remove the upper fan shroud.
3. If equipped, remove the cruise control servo bracket.
4. Raise the vehicle and support it safely.
5. Remove the exhaust crossover retaining bolts at the exhaust manifold and lower the crossover pipe.
6. Remove the starter. Remove the flywheel cover.
7. Remove the left side mount through bolt. Loosen the right side mount through bolt. Raise the engine and reinstall the left side mount through bolt.
8. Remove the oil pan retaining bolts. Remove the oil pan from the engine.
9. Installation is reverse of the removal procedure. Be sure to use new gaskets or RTV sealant, as required.

GASOLINE ENGINE—1986 AND LATER 307 V8

1. Disconnect the negative battery cable.
2. Raise the vehicle and support it safely.
3. Remove distributor cap and align rotor in the number one firing position. This positions the crankshaft counter weights and connecting rods for the least amount of interference with the oil pan.
4. Remove upper radiator support and fan shroud attaching screws.
5. Remove flywheel cover and drain oil.
6. Disconnect exhaust and crossover pipes.
7. Remove starter assembly.
8. Remove engine mounts from engine block, then jack front of engine up as far as possible.
9. Remove oil pan.
10. Apply sealer to both sides of pan gasket.
11. Apply sealer to front cover.
12. Install front and rear rubber pan seals.
13. Wipe seal with engine oil then install pan and torque bolts to 10 ft. lbs. Reverse the removal procedure. Fill the crankcase. Start engine and check for leaks.

GASOLINE ENGINE—CORVETTE

1. Disconnect the negative battery cable. Raise the vehicle and support it safely. Drain the engine oil.
2. Remove the starter. Remove the flywheel cover.
3. Remove the oil pan retaining bolts. Remove the oil pan from the engine.
4. Installation is the reverse of the removal procedure. Be sure to use a new gasket, as required.

DIESEL ENGINE

1. Disconnect the negative battery cable. Remove the vacuum pump and the oil pump drive.
2. Remove the dipstick.
3. Remove the upper radiator support and fan shroud.
4. Raise and support the car. Drain the oil.
5. Remove the flywheel cover.
6. Disconnect the exhaust and crossover pipes.
7. Remove the oil cooler lines at the filter base.
8. Remove the starter assembly. Support the engine with a jack.

CHEVROLET

CAPRICE CLASSIC • CORVETTE • MALIBU • MONTE CARLO • IMPALA

SECTION 15

9. Remove the engine mounts from the block.
10. Raise the front of the engine and remove the oil pan.
11. Installation is the reverse of removal.

OIL PUMP

Removal and Installation

GASOLINE ENGINE – V6 EXCEPT 229 CU. IN.

1. Disconnect the negative battery cable. Drain the engine oil. Remove the oil filter.
2. Unbolt the pump cover assembly from the timing chain cover.
3. Remove the cover assembly and slide out the pump gears.
4. Remove the oil pressure relief valve cap, spring, and valve. Do not remove the oil filter by-pass valve and spring.
5. Check that the relief valve spring isn't worn on its side or collapsed. Check that the relief valve is no more than an easy slip fit in its bore in the cover. If there is any perceptible sideplay, replace the valve. If there is still side-play, replace the cover.
6. Check the filter by-pass valve for good condition.
7. Before assembling the pump, lubricate and install the pressure relief valve and spring in the cover bore. Install the gasket and cap, torquing the cap to 35 ft. lbs.
8. Install the gears and check that gear-to-cover end clearance is between 0.002 to 0.006 in. If the clearance is less, check the timing cover gear pocket for wear.
9. Remove the gears and pack the gear pocket full of petroleum jelly. Don't use grease.
10. Install the gears. Install a new gasket and the cover. Torque the bolts evenly to 10 ft. lbs. Replace the filter.

ALL OTHERS ENGINES

1. Disconnect the negative battery cable. Drain the engine oil. Remove engine oil pan.
2. Remove pump attaching screws and carefully lower the pump.
3. Reinstall in reverse order. To ensure immediate oil pressure on start-up, the oil pump gear cavity should be packed with petroleum jelly.

REAR MAIN OIL SEAL

Removal and Installation

ALL EXCEPT ONE PIECE SEAL

1. Remove the oil pan. Remove the oil pump where required. Remove the rear main bearing cap.
2. Pry the lower seal out of the bearing cap with a suitable tool, being careful not to gouge the cap surface.
3. Remove the upper seal by lightly tapping on one end with a brass pin punch until the other end can be grasped and pulled out with pliers.
4. Clean the bearing cap, cylinder block, and crankshaft mating surfaces with solvent. Inspect all these surfaces for gouges, nicks, and burrs.
5. Apply light engine oil on the seal lips and bead, but keep the seal ends clean.
6. Insert the tip of the installation tool between the crankshaft and the seal of the cylinder block. Place the seal between the crankshaft and the seal of the cylinder block. Place the seal between the tip of the tool and the crankshaft, so that the bead contacts the tip of the tool.
7. Be sure that the seal lip is facing the front of the engine, and work the seal around the crankshaft using the installation tool to protect the seal from the corner of the cylinder block.

NOTE: Do not remove the tool until the opposite end of the seal is flush with the cylinder block surface.

8. Remove the installation tool, being careful not to pull the seal out at the same time.
9. Using the same procedure, install the lower seal into the bearing cap. Use your finger and thumb to lever the seal into the cap.

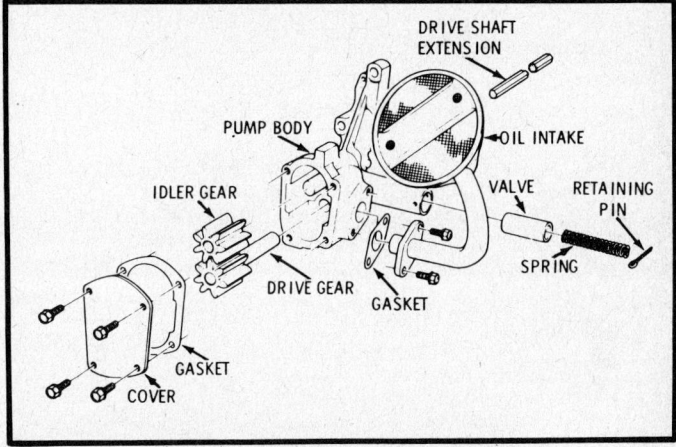
Diesel engine oil pump – exploded view
(© General Motors Corporation)

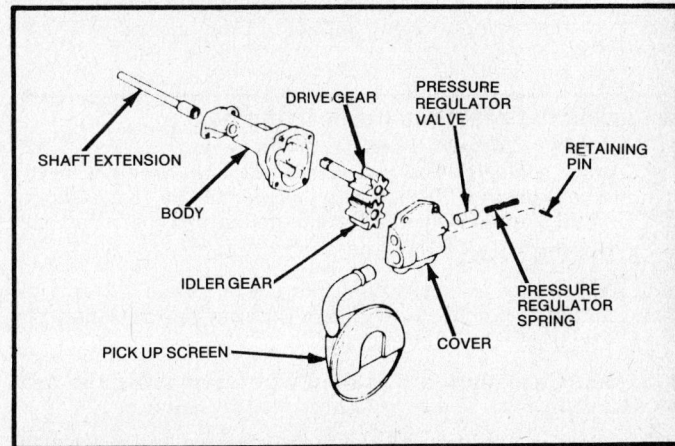
Gas engine oil pump (except 231 cu.in.) – exploded view (© General Motors Corporation)

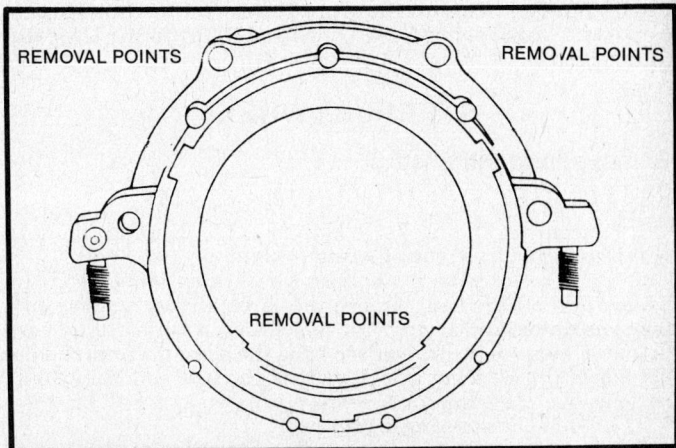
One piece rear main oil seal removal procedure

SECTION 15

CHEVROLET
CAPRICE CLASSIC • CORVETTE • MALIBU • MONTE CARLO • IMPALA

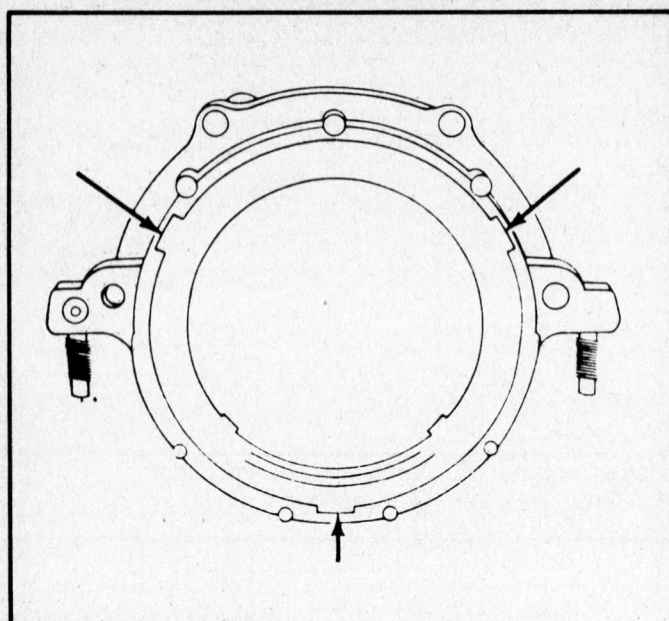

Removing the seal from the seal retainer

this is to insure that the seal will be installed squarely over the crankshaft. Tighten the tool wing nut until it bottoms.
5. Remove the tool from the crankshaft.
6. Install the transmission.

ONE PIECE SEAL RETAINER AND GASKET
Removal and Installation

1. Remove the transmission from the vehicle.
2. Remove the oil pan bolts. Lower the oil pan.
3. Remove the retainer and seal assembly.
4. Remove the gasket.

NOTE: Whenever the retainer is removed a new retainer gasket and rear main seal must be installed.

5. Installation is the reverse of the removal procedure. Once the oil pan has been installed the new rear main oil seal can be installed.

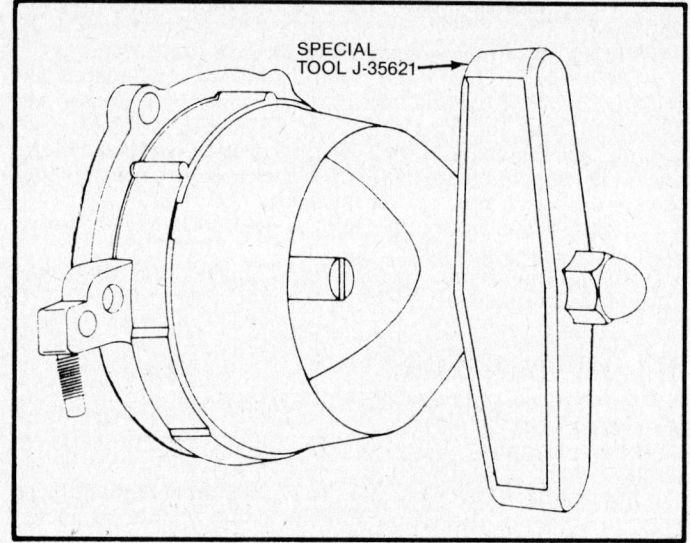

One piece rear main oil seal removal tool

10. Apply sealer to the cylinder block only where the cap mates to the surface. Do not apply sealer to the seal ends.
11. Install the rear cap and torque the bolts to specifications.

ONE PIECE SEAL

1. Remove the transmission from the vehicle.
2. Using the notches provided in the rear seal retainer, pry out the seal using the proper tool.

NOTE: Care should be taken when removing the seal so as not to nick the crankshaft sealing surface.

3. Before installation lubricate the new seal with clean engine oil.
4. Install the seal on tool J-3561 or equivalent. Thread the tool into the rear of the crankshaft. Tighten the screws snugly,

FRONT SUSPENSION AND STEERING SECTION

For Front Suspension Services Refer to the Unit Repair Section. For Steering Gear Overhaul Refer to the Unit Repair Section.

STEERING WHEEL

Removal and Installation

EXCEPT TILT AND TELESCOPE COLUMN

1. Disconnect the negative battery cable. Unplug the horn wire connector from the steering column.
2. On vehicles with a standard wheel or optional wood rim wheel, pull off the cap, remove the three screws and the contact, insulator, and spring. On vehicles with the bar type horn actuator, remove the screws securing the actuator from the underside of the steering wheel, unhook the lead connector plug, and remove the actuator assembly.
3. Loosen the steering wheel nut.
4. Apply the steering wheel puller and pull the wheel up to the nut. Now remove the puller, nut and steering wheel.

NOTE: Location marks are provided on the steering wheel and shaft to simplify proper indexing at the time of installation.

5. Install wheel with the location mark aligned with that of the shaft.
6. Install the wheel nut and torque to 30 ft. lbs.
7. Reinstall horn button or actuator assembly.

TILT AND TELESCOPE COLUMN

1. Disconnect the negative battery cable.
2. Remove the attaching screws and lift the pad from the column.
3. Disconnect the horn wire by pushing in the connector and turning it counterclockwise.
4. Push the locking lever counterclockwise until full release is obtained.
5. Mark the lock plate to locking lever position and remove the plate and lever.

CHEVROLET

CAPRICE CLASSIC • CORVETTE • MALIBU • MONTE CARLO • IMPALA

SECTION 15

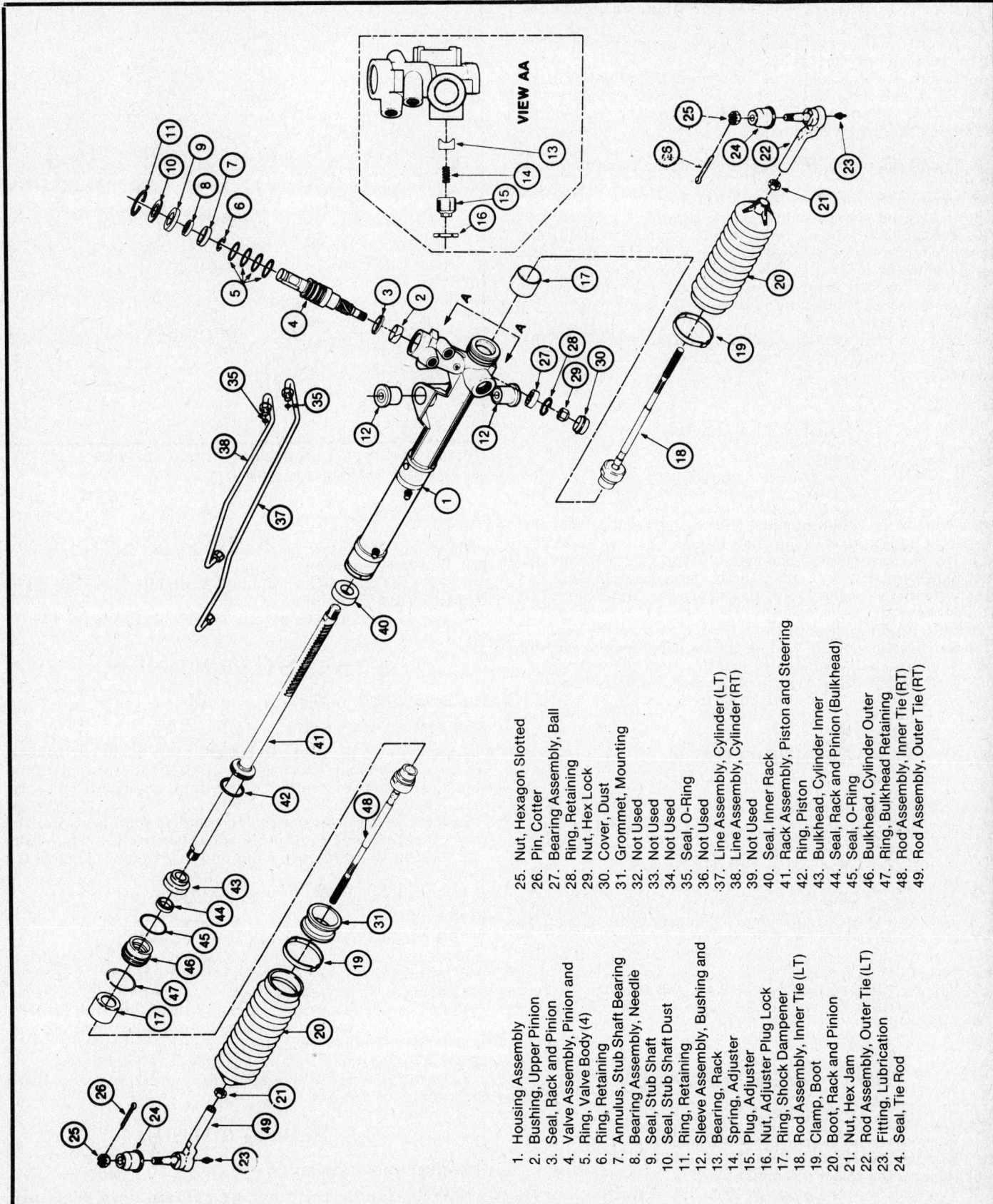

1. Housing Assembly
2. Bushing, Upper Pinion
3. Seal, Rack and Pinion
4. Valve Assembly, Pinion and
5. Ring, Valve Body (4)
6. Ring, Retaining
7. Annulus, Stub Shaft Bearing
8. Bearing Assembly, Needle
9. Seal, Stub Shaft
10. Seal, Stub Shaft Dust
11. Ring, Retaining
12. Sleeve Assembly, Bushing and
13. Bearing, Rack
14. Spring, Adjuster
15. Plug, Adjuster
16. Nut, Adjuster Plug Lock
17. Ring, Shock Dampener
18. Rod Assembly, Inner Tie (LT)
19. Clamp, Boot
20. Boot, Rack and Pinion
21. Nut, Hex Jam
22. Rod Assembly, Outer Tie (LT)
23. Fitting, Lubrication
24. Seal, Tie Rod
25. Nut, Hexagon Slotted
26. Pin, Cotter
27. Bearing Assembly, Ball
28. Ring, Retaining
29. Nut, Hex Lock
30. Cover, Dust
31. Grommet, Mounting
32. Not Used
33. Not Used
34. Not Used
35. Seal, O-Ring
36. Not Used
37. Line Assembly, Cylinder (LT)
38. Line Assembly, Cylinder (RT)
39. Not Used
40. Seal, Inner Rack
41. Rack Assembly, Piston and Steering
42. Ring, Piston
43. Bulkhead, Cylinder Inner
44. Seal, Rack and Pinion (Bulkhead)
45. Seal, O-Ring
46. Bulkhead, Cylinder Outer
47. Ring, Bulkhead Retaining
48. Rod Assembly, Inner Tie (RT)
49. Rod Assembly, Outer Tie (RT)

Steering rack—exploded view (© General Motors Corporation)

15–39

SECTION 15
CHEVROLET
CAPRICE CLASSIC • CORVETTE • MALIBU • MONTE CARLO • IMPALA

6. Remove the steering wheel retaining nut and remove the wheel with a puller.
7. Install a 5/16 in. × 18 set screw into the upper shaft at the fully extended position and lock it.
8. Install the steering wheel, observing the aligning mark on the hub and the slash mark on the end of the shaft. Make certain that the unattached end of the horn upper contact assembly is seated flush against the top of the horn contact carrier button.
9. Install the nut on the upper steering shaft and torque to 30 ft. lbs.
10. Remove the set screw installed in Step 7.
11. Install the plate assembly finger tight.
12. Position the locking lever in the vertical position and move it counterclockwise until the holes in the plate align with the holes in the lever. Install the attaching screws.
13. Align the pad assembly with the holes in the steering wheel and install the retaining screws.
14. Connect the battery.
15. Make certain that the locking lever securely locks the wheel travel and that the wheel travel is free in the unlocked position.

STEERING GEAR

Removal and Installation

1. Disconnect the negative battery cable. Remove coupling shield, if equipped.
2. Remove the retaining nuts, lock washers and bolts at the steering coupling to steering shaft flange.
3. Disconnect and plug the pressure and return lines from the steering gear box. Plug the hoses and gearbox openings.
4. Remove the pitman arm nut and washer. Matchmark the arm to the shaft.
5. With a puller, remove the pitman arm from the shaft.
6. Remove the bolts retaining the steering gear box to the side frame rail and remove the gear box from the vehicle.
7. Installation is the reverse of the removal procedure.
8. Fill and bleed the hydraulic system.

STEERING RACK

Removal and Installation

1. Disconnect the negative battery cable.
2. Raise and support the vehicle safely.
3. Remove the left wheel and tire assembly.
4. Disconnect the power steering hoses. Disconnect the tie rod ends on both sides.
5. Remove the upper and lower mounting bolts on the left side. Remove the mounting bolt on the right side.
6. Remove the intermediate shaft lower flexible joint at the rack and pinion assembly.
7. Remove the stabilizer bar. Remove the electric fan.
8. Remove the steering rack assembly from the vehicle.
9. Installation is the reverse of the removal procedure.

FRONT WHEEL BEARINGS

Adjustment

1. Raise the vehicle and support if safely.
2. Remove the dust cap from the hub.
3. Remove the cotter pin and discard it.
4. Tighten the spindle nut to 12 ft. lbs. while turning the wheel. Then back off the nut 1/4 to 1/2 turn.
5. Retighten the nut by hand until it is finger tight.

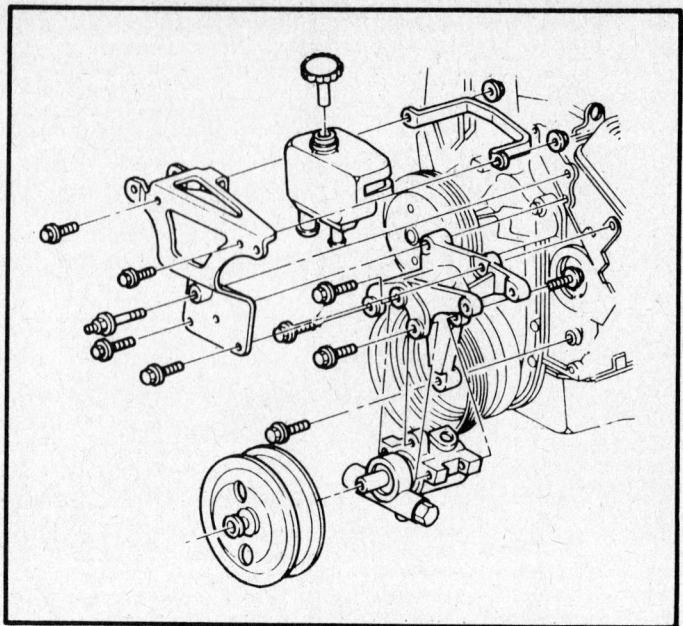

Power steering pump assembly—Corvette
(© General Motors Corporation)

6. Loosen the nut no more than 1/6 of a turn until the nearest hole in the spindle lines up with the slot in the spindle nut, and insert a new cotter pin.
7. Feel the looseness in the hub assembly. There should be 0.001 to 0.005 in. endplay.
8. Replace the dust cover and lower the vehicle.

POWER STEERING PUMP

Removal and Installation

EXCEPT CORVETTE

1. Disconnect the negative battery cable. Remove the hoses at the pump and tape the openings shut to prevent contamination. Position the disconnected lines in a raised position to prevent leakage.
2. Remove any components in order to gain access to the power steering pump retaining bolts. Remove the pump belt.
3. Loosen the retaining bolts and any braces. Remove the pump.
4. Installation is the reverse of removal.

CORVETTE

1. Disconnect the negative battery cable.
2. Remove all the necessary components in order to gain access to the power steering pump retaining bolts.
3. Remove the serpentine belt.
4. Remove the reservoir assembly along with its bracket. Cap the lines to prevent dirt from entering the system.
5. Remove the power steering retaining bolts. Remove the power steering pump from the vehicle.
6. Installation is the reverse of the removal procedure. Bleed the system as required.

STEERING COLUMN

Removal and Installation

NOTE: Handle the steering column very carefully. Rapping on the end of it or leaning on it could shear off the inserts which allow the column to collapse in a crash.

CHEVROLET
CAPRICE CLASSIC • CORVETTE • MALIBU • MONTE CARLO • IMPALA
SECTION 15

1. Disconnect the negative battery cable. Remove the nut and bolt from the upper intermediate shaft coupling. Separate the coupling from the lower end of steering column.
2. Disconnect the shift linkage from the lower shift lever, as required.
3. Disconnect all electrical connectors from the column assembly.
4. Remove the screws securing the toe pan cover to the floor.
5. Remove the nuts securing the bracket to the instrument panel. Disconnect the shift position indicator pointer (where applicable), then withdraw column.
6. Installation is the reverse of the removal procedure. Use only the specified hardware. Overlength bolts could prevent the column from properly collapsing in a crash.

BRAKE SECTION

For Brake Service Refer to the Unit Repair Section

MASTER CYLINDER

Removal and Installation

1. Disconnect hydraulic lines at master cylinder.
2. Remove the retaining nuts and lockwashers that hold cylinder to the brake booster.
3. Remove the master cylinder, gasket and rubber boot.
4. Install the cylinder on the booster.
5. Install nuts and lockwashers.
6. Install hydraulic lines then check brake pedal free play.
7. Bleed brakes.

POWER BRAKE UNIT

Removal and Installation

1. Disconnect vacuum hose from vacuum check valve.
2. Unbolt the master cylinder and carefully move it aside without disconnecting the hydraulic lines.
3. Disconnect pushrod at brake pedal assembly.
4. Remove nuts and lockwashers that secure booster to firewall and remove booster from engine compartment.
5. Install by reversing removal procedure. Make sure to check operation of stop lights. Allow engine vacuum to build before applying brakes.

HYDRO—BOOST POWER BRAKE UNIT

Removal and Installation

NOTE: Power steering fluid and brake fluid are incompatible. If brake seals contact steering fluid or steering seals contact brake fluid, the seals will be ruined.

1. With the engine off, pump the brake pedal four or five times to empty the accumulator of pressurized fluid.
2. Disconnect the master cylinder to booster retaining bolts.
3. Remove and plug the three hydraulic lines from the booster. Remove the washer and retainer that secures the booster pedal rod to the brake pedal arm. To avoid booster damage, do not pry the pedal rod off the pedal arm.
4. Remove the four nuts holding the booster to the firewall.
5. Loosen the booster from the firewall and move the booster pedal rod inboard until it disconnects from the brake pedal arm. Remove the spring washer from the brake pedal arm and remove the booster.
6. To install, reverse the removal procedure. Tighten the master cylinder to booster mounting nuts to 20 ft. lbs. Bleed the system, as required.

POWERMASTER POWER BRAKE UNIT

Description

The Powermaster unit is a complete, integral power brake apply system, consisting of an electro-hydraulic pump, fluid accumulator, pressure switch, fluid reservoir and hydraulic booster, with an integral dual master cylinder. The nitrogen charged accumulator stores fluid between 510 and 675 psi for the hydraulic booster operation. The electro-hydraulic operates between pressure limits with the ignition switch" on". When the pressure switch senses accumulator pressure is below 510 psi, and 12 volt pump operates to increase the accumulator fluid pressure to 675 psi. When the brake pedal is depressed, fluid from the accumulator acts on the booster power piston to apply the master cylinder which functions in the same manner as the conventional dual master cylinder. Because of the excessively high hydraulic pressure, the system must be depressurized before any service operations are performed on the system. Failure to depressurize could result in personal injury and/or damage to the vehicle's painted surfaces.

Depressuring the powermaster system

1. With the ignition switch in the OFF position, apply and release the brake pedal a minimum of ten (10) times, using approximately 50 pounds of force on the brake pedal.
2. When loosening hoses or pipe fittings, wrap shop towels close to the fittings to prevent spraying of residual pressurized fluid.

Removal and Installation

1. Disconnect the power lead from the pressure switch.
2. Disconnect the electrical connector from the electro-hydraulic pump.
3. Disconnect the brake tubing fittings from the Powermaster unit.
4. Remove the two retaining nuts for the unit to dash panel.
5. Remove the brake pedal pushrod.
6. Remove the Powermaster unit from the vehicle.
7. Install the Powermaster unit, the brake pedal pushrod and install the two retaining nuts. Torque 22 to 30 ft. lbs.
8. Install the brake pipes to the unit.
9. Install the electrical connections to the unit.

Bleeding the Unit

The brake system is bled in the conventional manner, either manually or by pressure. It must be remembered not to have the ignition switch on during the bleeding operation.

PARKING BRAKE

Adjustment

ALL EXCEPT CORVETTE

Adjustment of the parking brake is necessary whenever the rear brake cables have been disconnected or the parking brake pedal can be depressed more than eight ratchet clicks under heavy foot pressure.

1. Raise and support the vehicle safely. Make sure that the service brakes are properly adjusted.

15—41

SECTION 15

CHEVROLET
CAPRICE CLASSIC • CORVETTE • MALIBU • MONTE CARLO • IMPALA

2. Depress the parking brake pedal two ratchet clicks on all models.
3. Loosen the jam nut on the equalizer adjusting nut. Tighten the adjusting nut until the left rear wheel can just be turned rearward by hand, but not forward.
4. Release the ratchet one click, the rear wheel should rotate rearward freely and forward with a slight drag.
5. Release the ratchet fully, the rear wheel should turn freely in either direction.

CORVETTE

1. Raise the vehicle and remove the rear wheels, place two wheel lug nuts opposite of each other to insure correct disc/drum position.
2. Back the caliper piston into its bore.
3. Loosen the park brake cable so that there is no tension on the park brake shoes.
4. Rotate the disc so that the hole in the disc/drum face will align with the star adjuster.
5. To make the adjustment, insert a brake adjusting spoon through the hole in the disc face.
6. For the driver's side, move the handle of the tool towards the ceiling to adjust the shoes out and towards the floor to adjust the shoes in.
7. For the passenger side, move the handle of the tool towards the floor to adjust the shoes out and towards the ceiling to adjust them in.
6. Adjust one side at a time until there is no rotation of the disc/drum, then back the star adjuster off 5 to 7 notches. Then go to the opposite side and do the same procedure.
7. Apply the park brake lever two notches.
8. Adjust the cable at the equalizer so that the wheel has a drag.
9. Release the park brake lever and check the wheel for free rotation.
10. Correct adjustment will result in no drag on the wheel.

PARKING BRAKE CABLE
Removal and Installation

FRONT – EXCEPT CORVETTE

1. Raise and support the vehicle safely.
2. Loosen adjuster nut and disconnect front cable from connector. Compress retainer fingers and loosen at frame.
3. Lower the vehicle.
4. Remove lower rear bolt from wheelhouse panel and pull panel out to gain access to front cable.
5. Disconnect cable from parking brake pedal assembly, compress retainer fingers and remove cable.
6. Install cable by reversing removal procedure. Make sure cable is routed properly and securely retained.
7. Adjust parking brake cable.

LEFT REAR – EXCEPT CORVETTE

1. Raise and support the vehicle safely.
2. Loosen adjuster nut and compress retainer fingers at equalizer and loosen cable.
3. Disconnect cable from connector and remove from equalizer.
4. Mark relationship of wheel to axle flange and remove wheel and tire assembly.
5. Remove brake drum.
6. Remove primary shoe return spring and parking brake strut.
7. Compress retainer fingers and loosen cable from backing plate.
8. Installation is the reverse of the removal procedure.
9. Adjust the parking brake cable.

RIGHT REAR – EXCEPT CORVETTE

1. Raise and support the vehicle safely.
2. Remove adjuster nut at equalizer and compress retainer fingers and loosen cable from retainers at frame and from axle housing clip.
3. Mark relationship of wheel to axle flange and remove wheel and tire assembly.
4. Remove brake drum.
5. Remove primary shoe return spring, parking brake strut, and secondary shoe hold down spring.
6. Compress retainer fingers and loosen cable from backing plate. Disconnect cable from parking brake lever and remove cable.
7. Install cable by reversing removal procedure. Make sure cable is routed properly and securely retained. Adjust parking brake cable.

FRONT – CORVETTE

1. Raise the vehicle and support it safely.
2. Disconnect the left rear cable at the equalizer.
3. Disconnect the right rear cable at the retainer.
4. Lower the vehicle in order to remove the lower door sill moulding.
5. Remove the cable nut, cable guide and cable, in the sequence given.
6. Installation is the reverse of the removal procedure. Adjust the parking brake, as required.

LEFT REAR – CORVETTE

1. Raise the vehicle and support it safely.
2. Disconnect the left rear cable at the equalizer.
3. Remove the cable at the frame. Remove the caliper mounting bracket and parking brake lever at the wheel.
4. Installation is the reverse of the removal procedure. Adjust the parking brake, as required.

RIGHT REAR – CORVETTE

1. Raise the vehicle and support it safely.
2. Remove enough tension at the equalizer to disconnect the right rear parking brake at the retainer.
3. Remove the cable at the frame. Remove the caliper mounting bracket and the parking brake lever at the wheel.
4. Installation is the reverse of the removal procedure. Adjust the parking brake as required.

CLUTCH, TRANSMISSION AND DRIVESHAFT SECTION

For Overhaul Procedures, Refer to the Unit Repair Section

CLUTCH PEDAL
Adjustment

1. Fill the master cylinder reservoir with the proper grade and type brake fluid.
2. Raise the vehicle and support it safely.
3. Remove the clutch slave cylinder attaching bolts.
4. Hold the slave cylinder at about a forty five degree angle with the bleeder valve at the highest point.
5. Fully depress the clutch pedal and open the bleeder valve. Close the bleeder valve and release the clutch pedal.
6. Repeat the above step until all air is expelled from the system.
7. Check the fluid reservoir as required.

CHEVROLET
CAPRICE CLASSIC • CORVETTE • MALIBU • MONTE CARLO • IMPALA
SECTION 15

CLUTCH

Removal and Installation

1. Remove the transmission. Remove the slave cylinder attaching bolts.
2. Remove the pedal return spring from the clutch fork.
3. Remove the flywheel housing.
4. Remove the throw out bearing from the clutch fork.
5. Disconnect the clutch fork from the ball stud.
6. Mark the clutch cover and the flywheel to assure proper balance on reassembly.
7. Loosen the clutch cover to flywheel bolts one turn at a time until the spring pressure is released.
8. Support the pressure plate and cover assembly while removing the last bolts, then remove the cover assembly and the driven plate.
9. Inspect the flywheel for scoring, grooves, or signs of overheating (discoloration). Reface or replace the flywheel as necessary.
10. Install the clutch by reversing the removal procedure. Use a clutch aligning pilot or a spare transmission input shaft through the hub of the driven plate and into the pilot bushing. Be sure to align the clutch cover to flywheel index marks.

LINKAGE

Adjustment

1. Disconnect the negative battery cable.
2. Remove the left seat.
3. Remove the shift knob. Remove the console cover. Remove the glove box lock. Remove the left side panel from the console. Remove the shifter cover.
4. Loosen the adjuster nuts on the shifter rods.

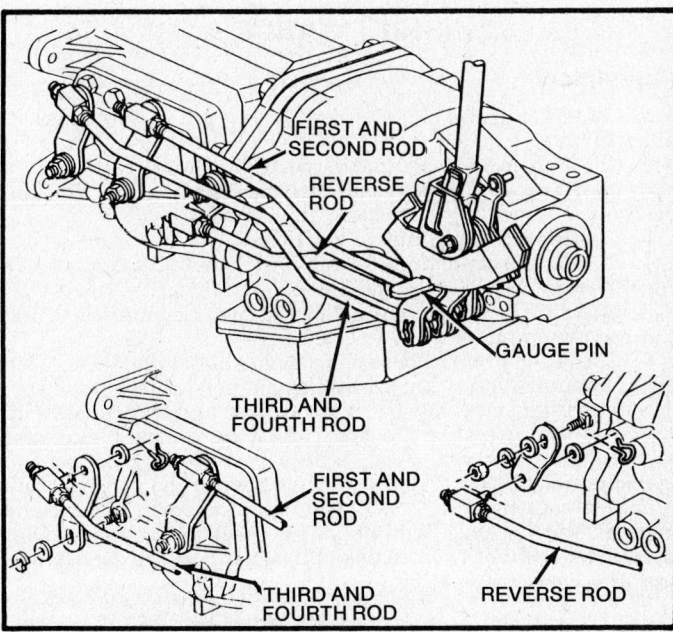

Shift linkage adjustment—Corvette
(© General Motors Corporation)

5. With the transmission in the neutral position, install the alignment pin into the bottom of the shifter.
6. Equalize the swivels on all three shifter rods. Hand tighten the rear and forward adjusting nuts at the same time and with equal force.
7. Do this for all three rods and then torque them to specification.
8. Reinstall the components that were removed in order to perform the operation.

MANUAL TRANSMISSION

Removal and Installation

1. Disconnect the negative battery cable.
2. Remove the air cleaner. Disconnect the throttle valve cable at the left of the throttle body unit. Remove the distributor cap.
3. Raise the vehicle and support it safely.
4. Remove the complete exhaust system. Remove the exhaust hanger at the transmission.
5. Support the transmission assembly using the proper equipment.
6. Remove the bolts attaching the driveline beam at the axle and transmission. Remove the driveline beam from the vehicle.
7. Mark the relationship of the propeller shaft to the axle companion flange. Remove the trunnion bearing straps and disengage the rear universal joint from the axle. Slide the propeller shaft slip yoke out from the overdrive unit and remove shaft from the vehicle.
8. Disconnect the transmission cooler lines at the overdrive unit. Disconnect the throttle valve at the overdrive unit. Disconnect the shift linkage at the side cover.
9. Disconnect the electrical connectors at the side cover. Disconnect the back up light switch, overdrive unit and speedometer sensor switch.
10. Lower the transmission and support the engine.
11. Remove the bolts attaching the transmission to the bellhousing. Slide the transmission rearward to disengage the input shaft from the clutch. Remove the transmission from the vehicle.
12. Installation is the reverse of the removal procedure. Refill the transmission with the proper grade and type fluid.

AUTOMATIC TRANSMISSION

Removal and Installation

1. Disconnect the negative battery cable.
2. Disconnect detent cable (if so equipped) from accelerator lever or carburetor.
3. Remove, disconnect or relocate any of the following necessary for removal. Exhaust crossover pipe. Complete exhaust system on the Corvette. Drive shaft, oil cooler lines, transmission crossmember, speedometer cable, shift linkage, electrical connections and flywheel cover pan.
4. Mark flywheel and converter for installation reference.
5. Remove mounting bolts, and slide transmission back and out of vehicle.
6. Reverse the removal procedure to install.

AUTOMATIC TRANSMISSION MANUAL LINKAGE

Adjustment

1. Adjust the linkage so the shift lever positions correspond exactly to the transmission positions.
2. Some linkage arrangements have adjustment gage pin holes. In these a free pin fit will insure proper adjustment.
3. After linkage adjustment, check operation of the neutral start switch, backup lights and automatic parking brake release.

15–43

SECTION 15

CHEVROLET
CAPRICE CLASSIC • CORVETTE • MALIBU • MONTE CARLO • IMPALA

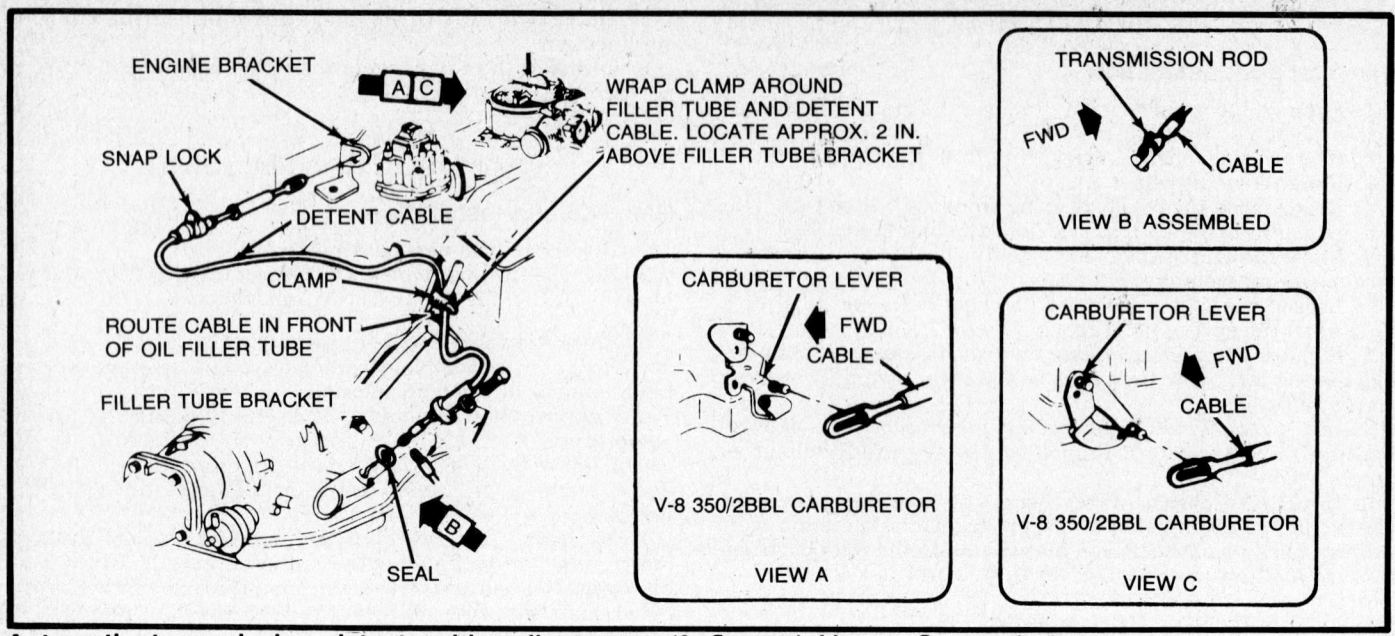

Automatic transmission detent cable adjustment (© General Motors Corporation)

SHIFT ROD

Adjustment

1. With shift rod clamp screw loosened set transmission outer lever in neutral position.
2. Hold upper shift lever against neutral position stop in upper steering column. Do not raise lever.
3. Tighten screw in clamp on lower end of shift rod to specified torque.
4. Check for proper operation. With key in "run" position and transmission in "reverse" be sure that the key cannot be removed and that the steering wheel is not locked. With key in "lock" position and shift lever in "park", be sure that the key can be removed, that the steering wheel is locked and that the transmission remains in park when the steering column is locked. With brakes firmly applied, check to make sure that the starter will not work in any shift lever position except neutral and park.

SHIFT CABLE

Adjustment

1. Loosen shift rod clamp screw, loosen pin in transmission manual lever.
2. Place shift lever in "park" position. Place transmission manual lever in "park" position and ignition key in lock position.
3. Tighten cable pin nut to 20 ft. lbs.
4. Rotate the transmission manual lever full against the "park" stop, then release the lever.
5. Pull shift rod down against lock stop to eliminate lash and tighten clamp screw to 20 ft. lbs.
6. Check for proper operation. Move shift handle into each gear position and see that transmission manual lever is also in detent position. with key in "run" position and transmission in "reverse" be sure that the key cannot be removed and that steering wheel is not locked. With key in "lock" position and transmission in "park", be sure that key can be removed and that steering wheel is locked. Engine must start in park and neutral. With brakes firmly applied, check to make sure that the starter will not work in any shift lever position except neutral and park.

Typical downshift cable adjustment
(© General Motors Corporation)

MANUAL TYPE T.V. CABLE

Adjustment

1. Stop engine.
2. Unlock T.V. cable "snap-lock" button.
3. Rotate carburetor lever by hand to wide open throttle and hold open.
4. Engage T.V. cable "snap-lock" button.

CHEVROLET
CAPRICE CLASSIC · CORVETTE · MALIBU · MONTE CARLO · IMPALA
SECTION 15

SELF—ADJUSTING TYPE T.V. CABLE
Adjustment
1. Stop engine.
2. Depress lock tab. Move slider back through fitting in direction away from throttle body or pump lever until slider stops against fitting.
3. Release lock tab.
4. Open carburetor lever to "full throttle stop" position to automatically adjust T.V. cable. Release carburetor lever.
5. Check T.V. cable for sticking and binding.
6. When the T.V. cable adjustment is made and locked, the cable housing will extend through the cable snap lock assembly about 1/16 to 5/16 in.

SHIFT INDICATOR
Adjustment
1. With the engine off set the transmission selector lever in neutral.
2. If the pointer does not align with the "N" indicator position, move the clip on the shift bowl so that the pointer lines up with the "N". The manual linkage must be adjusted properly before changing the shift quadrant adjustment.

DRIVESHAFT
Removal and Installation
ALL EXCEPT CORVETTE
1. Raise and support the vehicle safely. Remove the driveshaft rear yoke and the differential flange to assure correct alignment upon reassembly.
2. Remove the bolts and straps from the differential flange.
3. Remove the driveshaft assembly by first sliding the driveshaft sufficiently forward to disengage the differential flange and then slide the shaft downward and rearward to disengage the front splined yoke from the transmission output shaft.
4. Installation the reverse of removal. Be sure to align the match marks made before disassembly.

CORVETTE
1. Raise the vehicle and support it safely.
2. Remove the complete exhaust system.
3. Remove the bolts attaching the support beam at the axle and transmission. Remove support beam from the vehicle.
4. Mark relationship of shaft to companion flange and disconnect the rear universal joint by removing trunnion bearing straps. Tape bearing cups to trunnion to prevent dropping and loss of bearing rollers.
5. Slide slip yoke from the transmission and remove shaft. Watch for oil leakage from transmission output shaft housing.
6. Installation the reverse of the removal procedure.

UNIVERSAL JOINTS
For U-Joint Repair Procedures, Refer to the Drive Axles and U-Joint Unit Repair Section.

REAR AXLE AND SUSPENSION

For Overhaul Procedures Refer to the Unit Repair Section.

REAR AXLE ASSEMBLY
Removal and Installation
ALL EXCEPT CORVETTE
1. Raise the vehicle and support it safely. Be sure that the rear axle assembly is supported safely.
2. Disconnect shock absorbers from axle.
3. Mark drive shaft and pinion flange, then disconnect drive shaft and support out of the way.
4. Remove brake line junction block bolt at axle housing, then disconnect brake lines at junction block or disconnect brake line at wheel cylinder.
5. Disconnect upper control arms from axle housing.
6. Lower rear axle assembly and remove springs.
7. Remove rear wheels and drums.
8. Remove rear axle cover bolts and remove cover.
9. Remove axle.
10. Disconnect brake lines from axle housing clips.
11. Remove backing plates.
12. Disconnect lower control arms from axle housing.
13. Remove rear axle housing.
14. Installation is the reverse of the removal procedure.
15. Be sure to bleed the brake system, as required.

CORVETTE
1. Remove air cleaner.
2. Disconnect distributor cap from distributor.
3. Raise and support the vehicle safely.
4. Remove spare tire.
5. Remove spare tire cover by removing support hooks.
6. Remove the complete exhaust system as an assembly.
7. Disconnect leaf spring at the knuckles and remove attaching bolts at the cover. Remove leaf spring from vehicle.
8. Scribe mark on cam bolts and mounting bracket so they can be realigned in the same position. Remove cam bolts and then mounting bracket from carrier.
9. Disconnect both tie rod ends from the knuckles.
10. Remove the axle shaft union straps from the side gear yokes. Push wheel and tire assemblies outboard to disengage the trunnions from the side gear yokes.
11. Remove prop shaft trunnion straps at pinion flange. Push

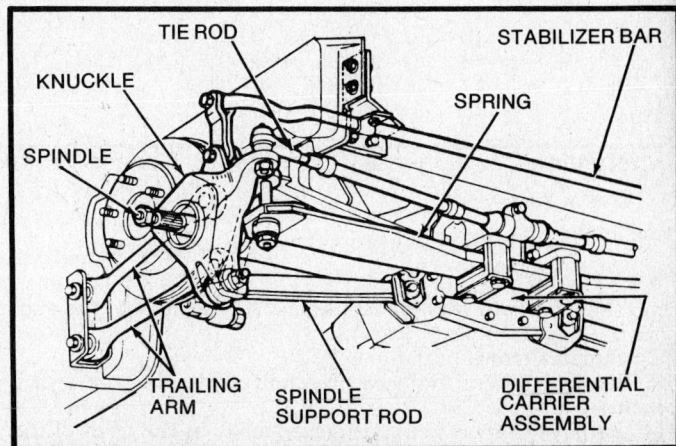

Rear suspension and related components-Corvette
(© General Motors Corporation)

15-45

SECTION 15 CHEVROLET
CAPRICE CLASSIC • CORVETTE • MALIBU • MONTE CARLO • IMPALA

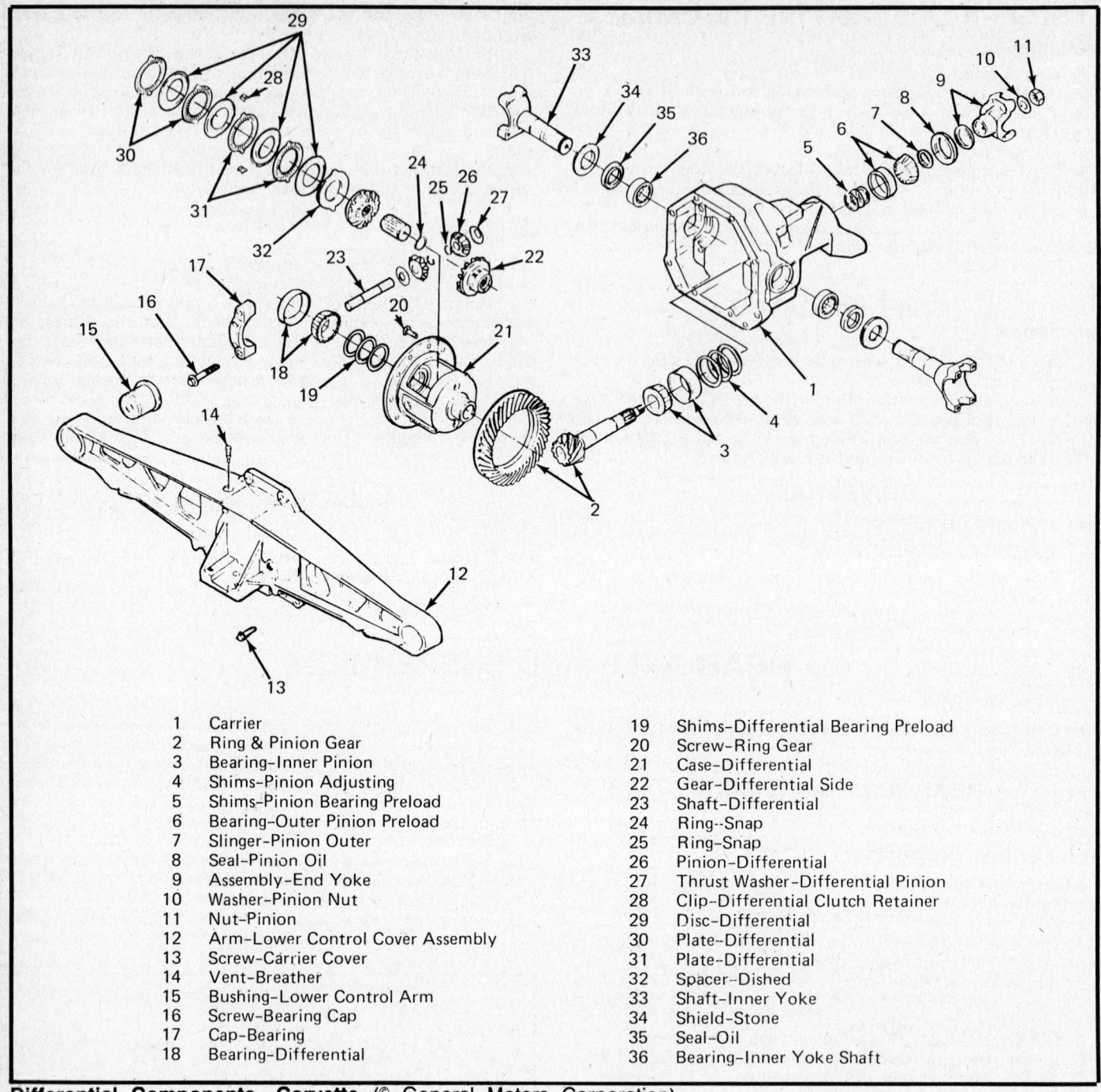

1	Carrier	19	Shims-Differential Bearing Preload
2	Ring & Pinion Gear	20	Screw-Ring Gear
3	Bearing-Inner Pinion	21	Case-Differential
4	Shims-Pinion Adjusting	22	Gear-Differential Side
5	Shims-Pinion Bearing Preload	23	Shaft-Differential
6	Bearing-Outer Pinion Preload	24	Ring--Snap
7	Slinger-Pinion Outer	25	Ring-Snap
8	Seal-Pinion Oil	26	Pinion-Differential
9	Assembly-End Yoke	27	Thrust Washer-Differential Pinion
10	Washer-Pinion Nut	28	Clip-Differential Clutch Retainer
11	Nut-Pinion	29	Disc-Differential
12	Arm-Lower Control Cover Assembly	30	Plate-Differential
13	Screw-Carrier Cover	31	Plate-Differential
14	Vent-Breather	32	Spacer-Dished
15	Bushing-Lower Control Arm	33	Shaft-Inner Yoke
16	Screw-Bearing Cap	34	Shield-Stone
17	Cap-Bearing	35	Seal-Oil
18	Bearing-Differential	36	Bearing-Inner Yoke Shaft

Differential Components—Corvette (© General Motors Corporation)

prop shaft forward into transmission and tie shaft to the support beam.
12. Support transmission.
13. Remove differential cover/beam attaching bolts at frame brackets.
14. Remove support beam attaching bolts at the front of the differential carrier. Remove differential carrier assembly from the vehicle.
15. Installation is the reverse of removal.

AXLE SHAFT

Removal and Installation
ALL EXCEPT CORVETTE

1. Raise vehicle and support it safely. Remove the tire and wheel assembly. Remove the brake drum.
2. Drain the fluid. Remove the rear carrier cover. Discard the gasket.

CHEVROLET
CAPRICE CLASSIC • CORVETTE • MALIBU • MONTE CARLO • IMPALA

SECTION 15

3. Remove the rear axle pinion shaft lock screw and the rear axle pinion shaft.
4. Push flanged end of axle shaft toward center of vehicle and remove "C" lock from button end of shaft.
5. Remove axle shaft from housing, being careful not to damage oil seal.
6. Installation is the reverse of the removal procedure. Be sure to fill the rear assembly with the proper grade and type gear oil.

CORVETTE

1. Raise the vehicle and support it safely.
2. Disconnect the leaf spring from the knuckle. Disconnect the tie rod end from the knuckle.
3. Scribe mark on cam bolt and on mounting bracket so they can be realigned in the same position.
4. Remove cam bolt and separate the spindle support rod from the mounting bracket at the carrier.
5. Remove axle shaft trunnion straps at the spindle and at the side gear yoke.
6. Push out on the wheel and tire assembly and remove the axle shaft.
7. Installation is the reverse of the removal procedure.

OIL SEAL/BEARING

Removal and Installation
ALL EXCEPT CORVETTE

1. Remove the axle shaft.
2. Remove seal from housing with a pry bar behind steel case of seal, being careful not to damage housing.
3. Insert tool J-24689 or equivalent, into bore and position it behind bearing so that tangs on tool engage bearing outer race. Remove bearing, using slide hammer.
4. Lubricate the new bearing with gear lubricant and install bearing so that tool bottoms against shoulder in housing, using tool J-23690 or equivalent.
5. Lubricate seal lips with gear lubricant. Position seal on tool J-21128 or equivalent, and position seal into housing bore. Tap seal into place so that it is flush with axle tube.

REAR WHEEL BEARING

Removal and Installation
CORVETTE

1. Raise the vehicle and support it safely.
2. Remove the tire and wheel. Remove the center cap.
3. Remove the cotter pin, spindle nut and washer.
4. Remove the brake caliper and support. Remove the rotor.
5. Disconnect the tie rod end from the knuckle. Disconnect the transverse spring from the knuckle.
6. Scribe a mark on the dam bolt and mounting bracket.
7. Remove the cam bolt and separate the spindle support rod from the mounting bracket.
8. Remove the trunnion straps at the side gear yoke shaft. Separate and remove the axle shaft.
9. Remove the hub and bearing mounting bolts using a number 45 Torx® head socket, or equivalent.
10. Remove the hub and bearing from the vehicle. Be sure to support the parking brake backing plate.
11. Installation is the reverse of removal.

WHEEL BEARING END PLAY

Adjustment
CORVETTE

The rear wheel bearing should have end play of .0001 to .008 inches. When necessary, adjust them using the following procedure.
1. Raise and support the vehicle safely.
2. Remove the tire and wheel assembly.
3. Remove the axle drive shaft.
4. Mark the camber cam in relation to the bracket. Loosen and turn the camber bolt until the strut rod forces the torque control arm outward.
5. Mount a dial indicator on the torque control surface and rest the pointer on the flange end.
6. Grasp the rotor and move it in and out. If the bearing movement is with the
specifications no adjustment is necessary. If the adjustment is not within these limits you must add or subtract shims accordingly.

SECTION 16

GENERAL MOTORS—"F" BODY
CAMARO • CAMARO BERLINETTA • FIREBIRD • TRANS AM • SE

SPECIFICATIONS

Brakes	24–2	Serial Number Identification	16–4
Camshaft	16–8	Torque	16–11
Capacities	16–12	Torque Sequence (Cylinder Heads)	16–33
Crankshaft & Connecting Rod	16–9	Tune-Up	16–6
Firing Order	16–13	Valve	16–7
General Engine	16–5	Wheel Alignment	16–12
Piston & Ring	16–10		

INDEX

A
Alternator R&R 16–14
Automatic Transmisssion
  Adjustment 16–45
  On Car Service 23–2
  Assembly R&R 16–46
  Axle Assembly R&R 16–47
  Axle Shaft R&R 16–47

B
Ball Joints 35–2
Brake System 24–2
Brake Booster 16–42
Brake Caliper Overhaul 24–2
Brake Caliper R&R
  Front 24–2
Brake Drum
  Rear 24–2
Brake Master Cylinder 16–42
Brake Pad
  Front 24–2
Brake Shoe
  Rear 24–2

C
Camshaft R&R 16–34
Carburetor R&R 16–26
Chassis Electrical 16–16
Clutch 16–43
  Adjustment 16–43
  R&R 16–44
Component Locations 16–20
Control Arm R&R 35–2
Cooling System 16–20
Cruise Control 16–20
Cylinder Head 16–33
  R&R 16–33

D
Differential 28–2
  Inspection 28–2
Dimmer Switch R&R 16–17
Disc Brakes 24–2
  Front 24–2
Distributor R&R 16–15
Drive Axle 28–2
Driveshaft R&R 16–46

E
Electronic Ignition 30–2
Emisssion Controls 16–30
Engine 16–31
  Identification 16–4
  R&LR 16–31
Engine Electrical 16–14

Engine Lubrication 16–37
Engine Mechanical 16–31
Engine Mounts R&R 16–31
Exhaust Manifold R&R 16–27

F
Front Suspension 35–2
  Alignment 16–12
Fuel Injection 16–28
Fuel Mixture, Adjust 16–25
Fuel Pump R&R 16–22
Fuses 16–20
Fusible Links 16–20

H
Head Light Switch 16–17
Heater Blowe R&R 16–20
Heater Core R&R 16–21
Heater Controls 16–21
Horn Switch 16–18

I
Idle Speed Adjust 16–23
Ignition Switch 16–16
Ignition Timing 16–15
Instrument Cluster R&R 16–18
Intake Manifold R&R 16–26

L, M, N
Lower Control Arm R&R 35–2
Master Cylinder R&R 16–42
Manual Steering Gear
  R&R 16–40
Manual Transmission
  Overhaul 32–2
Manual Transmission R&R 16–45
Neutral Safety Switch
  R&R 16–16

O
Oil Pan R&R 16–37
Oil Pump 16–38
  R&R 16–38
Oil Seal R&R
  Rear Main 16–38

P
Parking Brake 16–43
  Adjustment 16–43
  Cable R&R 16–43
Piston & Connecting Rod 16–35
Power Brake Unit R&R 16–42
Power Steering Pump R&R 16–41

R
Rear Main Oil Seal R&R 16–38
Rear Suspension 35–2
Regulator 16–14
Rocker Shaft/Assy R&R 16–32

S
Serial Number 16–4
  Engine 16–4
  Vehicle 16–4
Shock Absorber R&R
  Front 35–2
  Rear 35–2
Springs
  Front 35–2
  Rear 35–2
Starter R&R 16–14
Starter Drive Replacement 16–14
Steering Column R&R 16–41
Steering Gear R&R 16–40
  Manual 16–40
  Power 16–40
Steering Wheel R&R 16–40
Speedometer R&R 16–19
Suspension R&R 35–2
  Service 35–2

T
Timing Chain 16–36
Timing Gear Cover 16–35
  Oil Seal Replacement 16–35
Tune-Up 16–6
Turn Signal Switch R&R 16–17

U, V
U-Joint Overhaul 28–2
Valve Tappette R&R 16–32
Valve System 16–32
Voltage Regulator 16–14

W, Y
Water Pump R&R 16–20
Wheel Alignment 16–12
  Front 16–12
Wheel Bearings Front 16–41
Wheel Cylinders Rear 16–47
  Rear 24–2
Windshield Wiper 16–18
  Linkage R&R 16–18
  Motor R&R 16–18
  Switch R&R 16–18
Year Identification 16–3

BEFORE SERVICING BE CERTAIN TO READ THE SAFETY NOTICE

GM "F" Body
1983–87
Rear Wheel Drive Cars

CAMARO • CAMARO BERLINETTA • FIREBIRD
FIREBIRD TRANS AM • SE

YEAR IDENTIFICATION

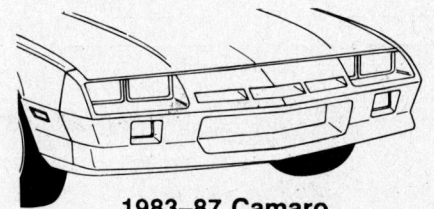

1983–87 Camaro

1983–87 Camaro Z–28

1985–87 Camaro IROC

1987 Firebird Formula

1983–87 Firebird

1985–87 Trans Am

SECTION 16
GENERAL MOTORS—"F" BODY
CAMARO • CAMARO BERLINETTA • FIREBIRD • TRANS AM • SE

VEHICLE IDENTIFICATION NUMBER (VIN)

It is important for servicing and ordering parts to be certain of the vehicle and engine identification. The VIN (vehicle identification number) is a 17 digit number visible through the windshield on the driver's side of the dash and contains the vehicle and engine identification codes. It can be interpreted as follows:

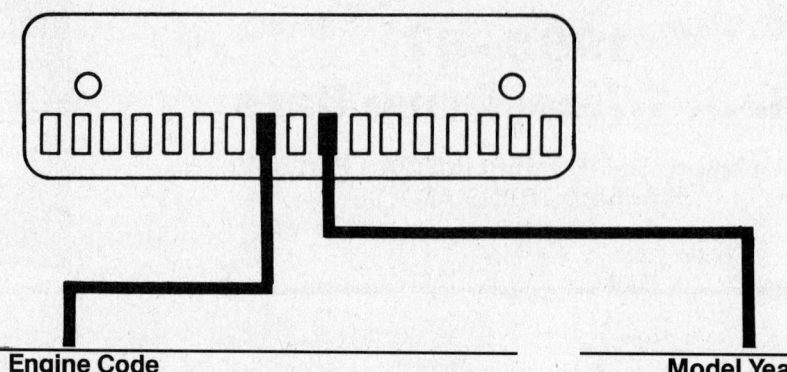

	Engine Code				
Code	Cu. In.	Liters	Cyl.	Carb.	Eng. Mfg.
		CAMARO			
2	151	2.5	4	T.B.I.	Pont.
F	151	2.5	4	2	Pont.
1	173	2.8	V-6	2	Chev.
L	173	2.8	V-6	2	Chev.
S	173	2.8	V-6	M.F.I.	Chev.
K	229	3.8	6	2	Chev.
A	231	3.8	V-6	2	Buick
J	267	4.4	8	2	Chev.
H	305	5.0	8	4	Chev.
7	305	5.0	8	T.B.I.	Chev.
G	305	5.0	8	4	Chev.
F	305	5.0	8	T.B.I.	Chev.
		FIREBIRD			
2	151	2.5	4	T.B.I.	Pont.
F	151	2.5	4	2	Pont.
1	173	2.8	V-6	2	Chev.
L	173	2.8	V-6	2	Chev.
S	173	2.8	V-6	M.F.I.	Chev.
A	231	3.8	V-6	2	Buick
W	301	4.9	8	4	Pont.
T	301 ①	4.9	8	4	Pont.
H	305	5.0	8	4	Chev.
7	305	5.0	8	T.B.I.	Chev.
G	305	5.0	8	4	Chev.
F	305	5.0	8	T.B.I.	Chev.

Model Year Code	
Code	Year
B	1981
C	1982
D	1983
E	1984
F	1985
G	1986
H	1987

The seventeen digit Vehicle Identification Number can be used to determine engine application and model year. The 10th digit indicates the model year, and the 8th digit identifies the factory installed engine.
① Turbocharged engine
T.B.I.—Throttle body (fuel) injection
M.F.I.—Multi-Pont fuel injection
NOTE: Some 1985-and later Camaro and Firebird models are equipped with Tuned Port Injection (TPI).

GENERAL MOTORS – "F" BODY
CAMARO • CAMARO BERLINETTA • FIREBIRD • TRANS AM • SE
SECTION 16

GENERAL ENGINE SPECIFICATIONS
Camaro

Year	Engine VIN Code	Engine No. of Cyl. Displacement (Cu. In.)	Engine Manufacturer	Fuel Delivery	Horsepower @ rpm ①	Torque @ rpm (ft. lbs.) ①	Bore and Stroke (in.)	Compression Ratio	Oil Pressure @ 2000 rpm
'83	2	4-151	Pont.	TBI	92 @ 4000	134 @ 2400	4.000 × 3.000	8.2:1	36–41
	F	4-151	Pont.	2 bbl.	92 @ 4200	130 @ 2800	4.000 × 3.000	8.2:1	36–41
	1	6-173	Chev.	2 bbl.	102 @ 4800	145 @ 2400	3.503 × 2.992	8.5:1	40
	H	8-305	Chev.	4 bbl.	145 @ 4000	240 @ 2400	3.736 × 3.480	8.6:1	40
	7	8-305	Chev.	4 bbl.	190 @ 4800	240 @ 3200	3.736 × 3.480	9.5:1	40
	S	8-305	Chev.	T.B.I.	175 @ 4200	250 @ 2800	3.736 × 3.480	9.5:1	50–65
'84	2	4-151	Pont.	1 EFI	92 @ 4000	134 @ 2800	4.000 × 3.000	9.0:1	36–41
	F	4-151	Pont.	2 bbl.	92 @ 4000	134 @ 2800	4.000 × 3.000	9.0:1	36–41
	1	6-173	Chev.	2 bbl.	107 @ 4800	145 @ 2100	3.503 × 3.000	8.5:1	50–65 ②
	G	8-305	Chev.	4 bbl.	150 @ 4000	240 @ 2400	3.736 × 3.480	9.5:1	50–65
	H	8-305	Chev.	4 bbl.	150 @ 4000	240 @ 2400	3.736 × 3.480	8.6:1	50–65
'85	2	4-151	Pont.	EFI	92 @ 4000	134 @ 2800	4.000 × 3.000	9.0:1	36–41
	S	6-173	Chev.	MFI	135 @ 5100	165 @ 3600	3.503 × 3.000	8.9:1	50–65 ②
	F	8-305	Chev.	TPI	190 @ 4800	240 @ 3200	3.740 × 3.480	9.5:1	50–65
	G	8-305	Chev.	4 bbl.	165 @ 4400	250 @ 2000	3.740 × 3.480	9.5:1	50–65
	H	8-305	Chev.	4 bbl.	150 @ 4000	240 @ 2400	3.736 × 3.480	8.6:1	50–65
'86–'87	2	4-151	Pont.	EFI	92 @ 4000	134 @ 2800	4.000 × 3.000	9.0:1	36–41
	S	6-173	Chev.	MFI	135 @ 5100	165 @ 3600	3.503 × 3.000	8.9:1	50–65 ②
	F	8-305	Chev.	TPI	190 @ 4800	240 @ 3200	3.740 × 3.480	9.5:1	50–65
	G	8-305	Chev.	4 bbl.	165 @ 4400	250 @ 2000	3.740 × 3.480	9.5:1	50–65
	H	8-305	Chev.	4 bbl.	150 @ 4000	240 @ 2400	3.736 × 3.480	8.6:1	50–65
	6	8-350	Chev.	TPI	230 @ 4000	330 @ 3200	4.000 × 3.480	9.5:1	50–65

TBI Throttle Body Injection
EFI Electronic Fuel Injection
MFI Multi-Point Fuel Injection
TPI Tuned Port Injection

① Horsepower and torque are SAE net figures. They are measured at the rear of the transmission with all accessories installed and operating. Since the figures vary when a given engine is installed in different models, some are representative, rather than exact.
② Oil Pressure at 1200 rpm

GENERAL ENGINE SPECIFICATIONS
Firebird

Year	Engine VIN Code	Engine No. of Cyl. Displacement (Cu. In.)	Engine Manufacturer	Fuel Delivery	Horsepower @ rpm ①	Torque @ rpm (ft. lbs.) ①	Bore and Stroke (in.)	Compression Ratio	Oil Pressure @ 2050 rpm
'83	2	4-151	Pont.	TBI	90 @ 4000	134 @ 2400	4.000 × 3.000	8.2:1	36–41 ②
	F	4-151	Pont.	2 bbl.	92 @ 4200	130 @ 2800	4.000 × 3.000	8.2:1	36–41
	1	6-173	Chev.	2 bbl.	102 @ 4800	145 @ 2400	3.503 × 2.992	8.5:1	40
	L	6-173	Chev.	2 bbl.	125 @ 5400	145 @ 2400	3.503 × 2.992	8.9:1	50–65
	H	8-305	Chev.	4 bbl.	145 @ 4000	240 @ 2400	3.736 × 3.480	8.6:1	40
	7	8-305	Chev.	4 bbl.	190 @ 4800	240 @ 3200	3.736 × 3.480	9.5:1	40
	S	8-305	Chev.	TBI	175 @ 4200	250 @ 2800	3.736 × 3.480	9.5:1	50–65
'84	2	4-151	Pont.	TBI	92 @ 4000	134 @ 2800	4.000 × 3.000	9.0:1	36–41
	F	4-151	Pont.	2 bbl.	92 @ 4000	134 @ 2800	4.000 × 3.000	9.0:1	36–41
	X	V6-173	Chev.	2 bbl.	107 @ 4800	145 @ 2100	3.504 × 2.992	8.5:1	50–65 ②
	Z	V6-173	Chev.	2 bbl.	125 @ 5400	145 @ 2400	3.504 × 2.992	8.9:1	50–65 ②
	G	8-305	Chev.	4 bbl.	165 @ 4400	250 @ 2000	3.736 × 3.480	9.5:1	50–65
	H	8-305	Chev.	4 bbl.	150 @ 4000	240 @ 2400	3.736 × 3.480	8.6:1	50–65
'85	2	4-151	Pont.	TBI	92 @ 4000	134 @ 2800	4.000 × 3.000	9.0:1	36–41
	5	V6-173	Chev.	MFI	135 @ 5100	165 @ 3600	3.503 × 3.000	8.9:1	50–65 ②
	F	8-305	Chev.	EFI	190 @ 4800	240 @ 3200	3.736 × 3.480	9.5:1	50–65
	G	8-305	Chev.	4 bbl.	165 @ 4400	250 @ 2000	3.736 × 3.480	9.5:1	50–65
	H	8-305	Chev.	4 bbl.	150 @ 4000	240 @ 2400	3.736 × 3.480	8.6:1	50–65

16–5

SECTION 16
GENERAL MOTORS—"F" BODY
CAMARO • CAMARO BERLINETTA • FIREBIRD • TRANS AM • SE

GENERAL ENGINE SPECIFICATIONS
Firebird

Year	Engine VIN Code	Engine No. of Cyl. Displacement (Cu. In.)	Engine Manufacturer	Fuel Delivery	Horsepower @ rpm ①	Torque @ rpm (ft. lbs.) ①	Bore and Stroke (in.)	Compression Ratio	Oil Pressure @ 2050 rpm
'86–'87	2	4-151	Pont.	TBI	92 @ 4000	134 @ 2800	4.000 × 3.000	9.0:1	36–41
	S	V6-173	Chev.	MFI	135 @ 5100	165 @ 3600	3.503 × 3.000	8.9:1	50–65 ②
	F	8-305	Chev.	MFI	190 @ 4800	240 @ 3200	3.736 × 3.480	9.5:1	50–65
	G	8-305	Chev.	4 bbl.	165 @ 4400	250 @ 2000	3.740 × 3.480	9.5:1	50–65
	H	8-305	Chev.	4 bbl.	150 @ 4000	240 @ 2400	3.736 × 3.480	8.6:1	50–65
	8	8-350	Chev.	MFI	230 @ 4000	330 @ 3200	3.736 × 3.480	9.5:1	50–65

TBI Throttle Body Injection
EFI Electronic Fuel Injection
MFI Multi-Point Fuel Injection
① Horsepower and torque are SAE net figures. They are measured at the rear of the transmission with all accessories installed and operating. Since the figures vary when a given engine is installed in different models, some are representative, rather than exact.
② Oil pressure at 2000 rpm

TUNE-UP SPECIFICATIONS
Camaro

Year	Engine VIN Code	Engine No. of Cyl. Displacement (Cu. In.)	Engine Manufacturer	Spark Plugs Type	Spark Plugs Gap (in.)	Ignition Timing (deg) ①② Man Trans	Ignition Timing (deg) ①② Auto Trans	Intake Valve Opens (deg) ③	Fuel Pump Pressure (psi)	Idle Speed (rpm) ①② Man Trans	Idle Speed (rpm) ①② Auto Trans
'83	2	4-151	Pont.	R-44TSX	0.060	8	8	NA	9–13	750–800	475–525
	F	4-151	Pont.	R-44TSX	0.060	8	8	NA	5½–6½	750–800	475–525
	1	6-173	Chev.	R-43CTS	0.045	10	10	NA	5½–6½	775–1100	600–750
	H	8-305	Chev.	R-45TS	0.045	6	6	NA	5½–6½	700–800	500–650
	7	8-305	Chev.	R-45TS	0.045	6	6	NA	9–13	700–800	500–650
	S	8-305	Chev.	R-45TS	0.045		6	NA	9–13		475
'84	2	4-151	Pont.	R-44TSX	0.060	8	8	NA	9–13	775	500
	F	4-151	Pont.	R-44TSX	0.060	8	8	NA	5½–6½	775	500
	1	6-173	Chev.	R-43CTS	0.045	10	10	NA	5½–6½	800–1100	600–750
	H	8-305	Chev.	R-45TS	0.045	6	6	NA	5½–6½	700–800	500–650
	G	8-305	Chev.	R-45TS	0.045	6	6	NA	9–13	700–800	500–650
'85	2	4-151	Pont.	R-43TSX	0.060	8	8	NA	9–13	775	500
	S	V6-173	Chev.	R-42CTS	0.045	10	10	NA	6–7.5	④	④
	F	8-305	Chev.	R-43CTS	0.045		6	NA	9–13		500
	G	8-305	Chev.	R-43CTS	0.045	6	6	NA	9–13	700–800	500–650
	H	8-305	Chev.	R-43CTS	0.045	6	6	NA	9–13	700–800	500–650
'86–'87	2	4-151	Pont.	R-43TSX	0.060	④	④	NA	9–13	④	④
	S	V6-173	Chev.	R-42CTS	0.045	④	④	NA	6–7.5	④	④
	F	8-305	Chev.	R-43CTS	0.045	④	④	NA	9–13	④	④
	G	8-305	Chev.	R-43CTS	0.045	④	④	NA	9–13	④	④
	H	8-305	Chev.	R-43CTS	0.045	④	④	NA	9–13	④	④
	6	8-350	Chev.	R-43CTS	0.045	④	④	NA	9–13	④	④

NOTE: The underhood specifications sticker often reflects tune-up specification changes made during the production run. Sticker figures must always be used if they disagree with those in this chart. Part numbers in this chart are not recommendations by Chilton for any product by brand name.
All models use electronic ignition systems.
B Before Top Dead Center
TDC Top Dead Center
—Not applicable
NA—Not available
① See text for procedure
② Figure in parenthesis indicates California engine
③ All figures Before Top Dead Center (B.T.D.C.)
④ These functions are controlled by the emissions computer. In rare instances when adjustment is necessary, refer to the underhood emissions sticker for specifications.

GENERAL MOTORS—"F" BODY
CAMARO • CAMARO BERLINETTA • FIREBIRD • TRANS AM • SE

SECTION 16

TUNE-UP SPECIFICATIONS
Firebird

Year	Engine VIN Code	Engine No. of Cyl. Displacement (Cu. In.)	Engine Manufacturer	Spark Plugs Type	Gap (in.)	Ignition Timing (deg) ①② Man Trans	Auto Trans	Intake Valve Opens (deg) ③	Fuel Pump Pressure (psi)	Idle Speed (rpm) ①② Man Trans	Auto Trans
'83	2	4-151	Pont.	R-44TSX	0.060	8	8	NA	9-13	750-800	475-525
	F	4-151	Pont.	R-44TS	0.060	8	8	NA	5½-6½	750-800	475-525
	1	6-173	Chev.	R-43CTS	0.045	10	10	NA	5.5-6.5	775-1100	600-750
	L	6-173HO	Chev.	R-42CTS	0.045	10	10	NA	6-7½	800-1100	725-850
	H	8-305	Chev.	R-45TS	0.045	6	6	NA	5.5-6.5	700-800	500-650
	7	8-305	Chev.	R-45TS ⑤	0.045	6	6	NA	9-13	700-800	500-650
	S	8-305	Chev.	R-45TS	0.045		6	NA	9-13		475
'84	2	4-151	Pont.	R-44TSX	0.060	8	8	NA	9-13	775	500
	F	4-151	Pont.	R-44TSX	0.060	8	8	NA	5½-6½	775	500
	X	6-173	Chev.	R-43CTS	0.045	10	10	NA	5½-6½	800-1100	600-750
	Z	6-173	Chev.	R-42CTS	0.045	10	10	NA	6-7½		④
	H	8-305	Chev.	R-45TS	0.045	6	6	NA	5½-6½	700-800	500-650
	G	8-305	Chev.	R-45TS	0.045	6	6	NA	9-13	700-800	500-650
'85	2	4-151	Pont.	R-43TSX	0.060	8	8	NA	9-13	775	500
	S	6-173	Chev.	R-42CTS	0.045	10	10	NA	6-7½	④	④
	F	8-305	Chev.	R-43CTS	0.045		6	NA	9-13		500
	G	8-305	Chev.	R-44TS	0.045	6	6	NA	9-13	700-800	500-650
	H	8-305	Chev.	R-44TS	0.045	6	6	NA	9-13	700-800	500-650
'86-'87	2	4-151	Pont.	R-43TSX	0.060	④	④	NA	9-13	④	④
	S	V6-173	Chev.	R-42CTS	0.045	④	④	NA	6-7.5	④	④
	F	8-305	Chev.	R-43CTS	0.045	④	④	NA	9-13	④	④
	G	8-305	Chev.	R-43CTS	0.045	④	④	NA	9-13	④	④
	H	8-305	Chev.	R-43CTS	0.045	④	④	NA	9-13	④	④
	8	8-350	Chev.	R-43CTS	0.045	④	④	NA	9-13	④	④

NOTE: The underhood specifications sticker often reflects tune-up specification changes made during the production run. Sticker figures must always be used if they disagree with those in this chart. Part numbers in this chart are not recommendations by Chilton for any product by brand name.
All models use electronic ignition systems.
B Before Top Dead Center
TDC Top Dead Center
— Not applicable
NA—Not available
① See text for procedure
② Figure in parenthesis indicates California engine
③ All figures are in degrees Before Top Dead Center. Where two figures appear, the first represents timing with manual transmission, the second with automatic transmission.
  Auto—29
  Trans Am—16
④ These functions are controlled by the emissions computer. In rare instances when adjustment is necessary, refer to the underhood emissions sticker for specifications.

VALVE SPECIFICATIONS
Camaro

Year	Engine No. Cyl. Displacement (cu. in.)	Seat Angle (deg)	Face Angle (deg)	Spring Test Pressure (lbs. @ in.)	Spring Installed Height (in.)	Stem-to-Guide Clearance (in.) Intake	Exhaust	Stem Diameter (in.) Intake	Exhaust
'83	4-151	46	45	122-180 @ 1.25	1.69	.0010-.0027	.0010-.0027 ①	.3418-.3425	.3418-.3425
	6-173	46	45	194 @ 1.18	1.57	.0010-.0026	.0010-.0026	.3410-.3420	.3410-.3420
	8-305	46	45	194-206 @ 1.25	1²³⁄₃₂	.0010-.0027	.0010-.0027	.3410-.3420	.3410-.3420

16-7

SECTION 16: GENERAL MOTORS — "F" BODY
CAMARO • CAMARO BERLINETTA • FIREBIRD • TRANS AM • SE

VALVE SPECIFICATIONS
Camaro

Year	Engine No. Cyl. Displacement (cu. in.)	Seat Angle (deg)	Face Angle (deg)	Spring Test Pressure (lbs. @ in.)	Spring Installed Height (in.)	Stem-to-Guide Clearance (in.) Intake	Stem-to-Guide Clearance (in.) Exhaust	Stem Diameter (in.) Intake	Stem Diameter (in.) Exhaust
'84–'87	4-151	46	45	122–180 @ 1.25	1.69	.0010–.0027	.0010–.0027 ①	.3418–.3425	.3418–.3425
	6-173	46	45	194 @ 1.18	1.57	.0010–.0026	.0010–.0026	.3410–.3420	.3410–.3420
	8-305 8-350	46	45	194–206 @ 1.25	1²³⁄₃₂	.0010–.0027	.0010–.0027	.3410–.3420	.3410–.3420

① Figure given is measured at the top of the guide; .0020–.0037 is measured at the bottom of the guide.

VALVE SPECIFICATIONS
Firebird

Year	Engine No. Cyl. Displacement (cu. in.)	Seat Angle (deg) ①	Face Angle (deg) ②	Spring Test Pressure (lbs. @ in.)	Spring Installed Height (in.)	Stem-to-Guide Clearance (in.) Intake	Stem-to-Guide Clearance (in.) Exhaust	Stem Diameter (in.) Intake	Stem Diameter (in.) Exhaust
'83	4-151 Pont.	46	45	122–180 @ 1.25	1.69	.0010–.0027	.0010–.0027 ③	.3418–.3425	.3418–.3425
	6-173 Chev.	46	45	194 @ 1.18	1.57	.0010–.0026	.0010–.0026	.3410–.3420	.3410–.3420
	8-305 Chev.	46	45	194–206 @ 1.25	1²³⁄₃₂	.0010–.0027	.0010–.0027	.3410–.3420	.3410–.3420
'84–'87	4-151 Pont.	46	45	122–180 @ 1.25	1.69	.0010–.0027	.0010–.0027 ③	.3418–.3425	.3418–.3425
	6-173 Chev.	46	45	194 @ 1.18	1.57	.0010–.0026	.0010–.0026	.3410–.3420	.3410–.3420
	8-305 Chev. 8-350	46	45	194–206 @ 1.25	1²³⁄₃₂	.0010–.0027	.0010–.0027	.3410–.3420	.3410–.3420

NA: Not available
① Intake valve seat angles are shown. All exhaust valve seat angles are 45° unless otherwise indicated.
② Intake valve face angles are shown. All exhaust valve face angles are 44° unless otherwise indicated.
③ Figure given is measured at the top of the guide; .0020–.0037 is measured at the bottom of the guide.

CAMSHAFT SPECIFICATIONS
Camaro

All measurements in inches. To convert inches to metric units, refer to Metric Information section

Year	Engine Type/Disp. L (cu. in.)	Journal Diameter 1 2 3 4 5	Lobe Lift Intake	Lobe Lift Exhaust	Camshaft End Play
'83	2.5(4-151)	All 1.8690	0.3980	0.3980	0.0015–0.0050
	2.8(6-173)	All 1.8976–1.8996	0.2350	0.2660	NA
	5.0(8-305)	All 1.8682–1.8692	0.2340 ②③	0.2570 ②③	0.004–0.012
'84–'87	2.5(4-151)	All 1.8690	0.3980	0.3980	0.0015–0.0050
	2.8(6-173)	All 1.8976–1.8996	0.2350	0.2660	NA
	5.0(8-305)	All 1.8682–1.8692	0.2340 ②③	0.2570 ②③	0.004–0.012
'84–'87	5.7(8-350)	All 1.8682–1.8692	0.2730	0.2820	0.004–0.012

NA—Not available
① TBI engine 0.2600 intake—0.2730 exhaust
② TBI engine 0.2570 intake—0.2690 exhaust
③ 4-bbl. High Output engine 0.2690 intake—0.2760 exhaust

GENERAL MOTORS – "F" BODY
CAMARO • CAMARO BERLINETTA • FIREBIRD • TRANS AM • SE

CAMSHAFT SPECIFICATIONS
Firebird
All measurements in inches. To convert inches to metric units, refer to Metric Information section

Year	Engine Type/Disp. L (cu. in.)	Journal Diameter 1 2 3 4 5	Lobe Lift Intake	Lobe Lift Exhaust	Camshaft End Play
'83	2.5(4-151)	All 1.8690	0.3980	0.3980	0.0015–0.0050
	2.8(6-173)	All 1.8976–1.8996	0.2350	0.2660	NA
	5.0(8-305)	All 1.8682–1.8692	0.2340 ②③	0.2570 ②③	0.004–0.012
'84–'87	2.5(4-151)	All 1.8690	0.3980	0.3980	0.0015–0.0050
	2.8(6-173)	All 1.8976–1.8996	0.2350	0.2660	NA
	5.0(8-305)	All 1.8682–1.8692	0.2340 ②③	0.2570 ②③	0.004–0.012
'86–'87	5.7(8-350)	All 1.8682–1.8692	0.2730	0.2820	0.004–0.012

NA—Not available
① TBI engine 0.2600 intake—0.2730 exhaust
② TBI engine 0.2570 intake—0.2690 exhaust
③ 4-bbl. High Output engine 0.2690 intake—0.2760 exhaust

CRANKSHAFT AND CONNECTING ROD SPECIFICATIONS
Camaro
All measurements are given in inches

Year	Engine No. Cyl. Displacement (cu. in.)	Crankshaft Main Brg Journal Dia.	Crankshaft Main Brg Oil Clearance	Crankshaft Shaft End-Play	Crankshaft Thrust on No.	Connecting Rod Journal Diameter	Connecting Rod Oil Clearance	Connecting Rod Side Clearance
'83	4-151	2.300	.0005–.0022	.0035–.0085	5	2.000	.0005–.0026	.0060–.0020
	6-173	2.493–2.494	.0017–.0029	.0019–.0066	3	1.998–1.999	.0014–.0035	.0060–.0170
	8-305	①	②	.0020–.0060	5	2.098–2.099	.0018–.0039	.0080–.0140
'84–'87	4-151	2.300	.0005–.0022	.0035–.0085	5	2.000	.0005–.0026	.0060–.0220
	6-173	2.493–2.494	.0017–.0029	.0019–.0066	3	1.998–1.999	.0014–.0035	.0060–.0170
	8-305	①	②	.0020–.0060	5	2.098–2.099	.0018–.0039	.0080–.0140
'86–'87	8-350	①	②	.002–.006	5	2.098–2.099	.0013–.0035	.006–.014

① No. 1—2.4484–2.4493
Nos. 2, 3, 4—2.4481–2.4490
No. 5—2.4479–2.4488
② No. 1—0.0008–0.0020
Nos. 2, 3, 4—0.0011–0.0023
No. 5—0.0017–0.0032

CRANKSHAFT AND CONNECTING ROD SPECIFICATIONS
Firebird
All measurements are given in inches

Year	Engine Displacement (cu. in.)	Crankshaft Main Brg. Journal Dia.	Crankshaft Main Brg. Oil Clearance	Crankshaft Shaft End-Play	Crankshaft Thrust on No.	Connecting Rod Journal Diameter	Connecting Rod Oil Clearance	Connecting Rod Side Clearance
'83	4-151	2.300	.0005–.0022	.0035–.0085	5	2.000	.0005–.0026	.0060–.0020
	6-173	2.493–2.494	.0017–.0029	.0019–.0066	3	1.998–1.999	.0014–.0035	.0060–.0170
	8-305	①	②	.0020–.0060	5	2.098–2.099	.0018–.0039	.0080–.0140
'84–'87	4-151	2.300	.0005–.0022	.0035–.0085	5	2.000	.0005–.0026	.0060–.0220
	6-173	2.493–2.494	.0017–.0029	.0019–.0066	3	1.998–1.999	.0014–.0035	.0060–.0170
	8-305	①	②	.0020–.0060	5	2.098–2.099	.0018–.0039	.0080–.0140

SECTION 16
GENERAL MOTORS—"F" BODY
CAMARO • CAMARO BERLINETTA • FIREBIRD • TRANS AM • SE

CRANKSHAFT AND CONNECTING ROD SPECIFICATIONS
Firebird
All measurements are given in inches

Year	Engine Displacement (cu. in.)	Crankshaft Main Brg. Journal Dia.	Crankshaft Main Brg. Oil Clearance	Crankshaft Shaft End-Play	Crankshaft Thrust on No.	Connecting Rod Journal Diameter	Connecting Rod Oil Clearance	Connecting Rod Side Clearance
'86–'87	8-350	①	②	.002–.006	5	2.098–2.099	.0013–.0035	.006–.014

① No. 1: 2.4484–2.4493
 Nos. 2, 3, 4: 2.4481–2.4490
 No. 5: 2.4479–2.4488
② No. 1: .0008–.0020
 Nos. 2, 3, 4: .0011–.0023
 No. 5: .0017–.0033
⑦ No. 1: .001–.0015
 Nos. 2, 3, 4: .001–.0025
 No. 5: .0025–.0035

RING SPECIFICATIONS
Camaro
All measurements are given in inches

Year	Engine No. Cyl. Displacement (Cu. In.)	Ring Gap Top Compression	Ring Gap Bottom Compression	Ring Gap Oil Control	Ring Side Clearance Top Compression	Ring Side Clearance Bottom Compression	Ring Side Clearance Oil Control
'83	4-151	.0100–.0020	.0100–.0270	.0150–.0550	.0015–.0030	.0015–.0030	.0010–.0050
'83	6-173	.0098–.0196	.0098–.0196	.0020–.0550	.0011–.0027	.0015–.0037	.0078 max.
'83	305	.0200	.0250	.0500	.0032	.0032	.0070
'84–87	4-151	.0100–.0020	.0100–.0270	.0150–.0550	.0015–.0030	.0015–.0030	.0010–.0050
	6-173	.0098–.0196	.0098–.0196	.0020–.0550	.0011–.0027	.0015–.0037	.0078 max.
	8-305 8-350	.0100–.0200	.0100–.0250	.0150–.0550	.0012–.0032	.0012–.0032	.0020–.0070

RING SPECIFICATIONS
Firebird
All measurements are given in inches

Year	Engine No. Cyl. Displacement (Cu. In.)	Ring Gap Top Compression	Ring Gap Bottom Compression	Ring Gap Oil Control	Ring Side Clearance Top Compression	Ring Side Clearance Bottom Compression	Ring Side Clearance Oil Control
'83	4-151 Pont.	.0100–.0020	.0100–.0270	.0150–.0550	.0015–.0030	.0015–.0030	.0010–.0050
'83	6-173 Chev.	.0098–.0196	.0098–.0196	.0200–.0550	.0011–.0027	.0015–.0037	.0078 max.
'84–87	4-151	.0100–.0020	.0100–.0270	.0150–.0550	.0015–.0030	.0015–.0030	.0010–.0050
	6-173	.0098–.0196	.0098–.0196	.0020–.0550	.0011–.0027	.0015–.0037	.0078 max.
	8-305 8-350	.0100–.0200	.0100–.0250	.0150–.0550	.0012–.0032	.0012–.0032	.0020–.0070

GENERAL MOTORS—"F" BODY
CAMARO • CAMARO BERLINETTA • FIREBIRD • TRANS AM • SE
SECTION 16

PISTON CLEARANCE
Firebird

Year	Engine	Piston-to-Bore Clearance (in.)
'83	4-151 Pont.	.0017–.0033 ④
	6-173 Chev.	.0016–.0027
	8-305 Chev.	.0007–.0027 ③
'84–'87	4-151	.0017–.0033 ②
	6-173	.0016–.0027
	8-305	.0007–.0027 ①
'86–'87	8-350	.0025–.0045

① .75" below piston pin C/L
② Top of skirt
③ 2.5" from top of cylinder (bore); across piston pin centerline (piston)
④ 2.25" from top of cylinder (bore); 1¹³⁄₁₆" from top of piston

PISTON CLEARANCE
Camaro

Year	Engine No. Cyl Displacement (cu. in.)	Piston-to-Bore Clearance (in.)
'83	4-151	.0017–.0033 ②
	6-173	.0016–.0027
	8-305	.0007–.0027 ①
'84–'87	4-151	.0017–.0033 ②
	6-173	.0016–.0027
	8-305	.0007–.0027 ①
'86–'87	8-350	.0025–.0045

① .75" below piston pin centerline
② 2.25" from top of cylinder (bore); 1¹³⁄₁₆" from top of piston

TORQUE SPECIFICATIONS
Camaro
All readings in ft. lbs.

Year	Engine No. Cyl. Displacement (cu. in.)	Cylinder Head Bolts	Rod Bearing Bolts	Main Bearing Bolts	Crankshaft Pulley Bolts	Flywheel-to Crankshaft Bolts	Manifold Intake	Manifold Exhaust
'83–'84	4-151	85	32	70	160	44	29	44
	6-173	65-75	34-40	63-74	66-84	45-55	20-25	22-28
	8-305	65	45	70	60	60	30	20
'85–'87	4-151	92	32	70	200 ③	44 ④	29 ①	44
	6-173	65-90	34-45	63-83	67-85	45-55	13-25	19-31
	8-305/8-350	60-75	42-47	60-75 ⑤	60	50-70 ⑥	25-45	②

① Bolt and Nuts on the EFI assembly to the manifold—15 ft. lbs.
② Outer 4 bolts—14-26 ft. lbs.
  Inner 2 bolts—20-32 ft. lbs.
③ 86-87—162 ft. lbs.
④ 86-87—55 ft. lbs.
⑤ 86-87—Inner—70-85 ft. lbs.
  Outer—60-75 ft. lbs.
⑥ 86-87—63-85 ft. lbs.

TORQUE SPECIFICATIONS
Firebird
All readings in ft. lbs.

Year	Engine No. Cyl. Displacement (cu. in.)	Cylinder Head Bolts	Rod Bearing Bolts	Main Bearing Bolts	Crankshaft Bolt	Flywheel-to Crankshaft Bolts	Manifold Intake	Manifold Exhaust
'83	4-151 Pont.	85	32	70	160	44	29 ①	44
	6-173 Chev.	65-75	34-40	63-74	66-84	45-55	20-25	22-28
	8-305 Chev.	65	45	70	60	60	30	20
'84–'86	4-151 Pont.	92	32	70	200 ④	44 ⑤	29 ①	44
	6-173 Chev.	65-75 ③	34-45	63-83	67-85	45-55	13-25	19-31
	8-305/350 Chev.	60-75	42-47	60-75 ⑥	60	50-70 ⑦	25-45	②

Caution: Verify the correct original equipment engine is in the vehicle by referring to the VIN engine code before torquing any bolts.
① Bolt and Nuts on the EFI assembly to the manifold—15 ft. lbs.
② Outer bolts—14-26 ft. lbs.
  Inner bolts—20-32 ft. lbs.
③ 85-87—65-90 ft. lbs.
④ 86-87—162 ft. lbs.
⑤ 86-87—55 ft. lbs.
⑥ 86-87—Inner—70-85 ft. lbs.
  Outer—60-75 ft. lbs.
⑦ 86-87—63-85 ft. lbs.

SECTION 16
GENERAL MOTORS – "F" BODY
CAMARO • CAMARO BERLINETTA • FIREBIRD • TRANS AM • SE

CAPACITIES
Camaro

Year	Engine No. Cyl. Displacement (cu. in.)	Engine Crankcase Add 1 qt for New Filter	Transmission Pts to Refill After Draining — Manual 3-Speed	Manual 4-Speed	Automatic ①	Drive Axle (pts)	Gasoline Tank (gals)	Cooling System (qts) With Heater	With A/C
'83	4-151	3 ②	—	4.3 ⑤	8.5 ⑥	3.5	16	12.8	13.0
	6-173	4 ②	—	4.3 ⑤	8.5 ⑥	3.5	16	12.8	12.8
	8-305 ③	4	—	4.3 ⑤	8.5 ⑥	3.5	16	17.2	17.2
	8-305 ④	4	—	4.3 ⑤	8.5 ⑥	3.5	16	15.9	15.9
'84-'87	4-151	3 ②	—	3.5 ⑤	8.5 ⑥	3.5	16	8.8	9.1
	6-173	4 ②	—	3.5 ⑤	8.5 ⑥	3.5	16	12.5	12.5
	8-305 ③	4	—	3.5 ⑤	8.5 ⑥	3.5	16	15.0	15.0
	8-305 ④	4	—	3.5 ⑤	8.5 ⑥	3.5	16	15.0	15.0

— Not applicable
① Drain and refill only—does not include torque convertor
② Capacity same with or without filter change
③ With 4 bbl. carburetor
④ With throttle body fuel injection
⑤ 5-speed—5.3 pints—85 and later 6.6 pints
⑥ Overdrive transmission—9.9 pints; Add 4 pints, run engine and check dipstick—fill as necessary

CAPACITIES
Firebird

Year	Engine No. Cyl. Displacement (Cu. In.)	Engine Crankcase (Add 1 Qt For New Filter)	Transmission (Pts to Refill After Draining) Manual 3 Spd.	Manual 4 Spd.	Automatic (Pts.) ①	Drive Axle (pts)	Gasoline Tank (gals)	Cooling System (qts) With Heater	With A/C
'83	4-151 Pont.	3 ②	—	4.3 ③	8.5 ④	3.5	16.0	12.8	13.0
	6-173 Chev.	4 ②	—	4.3 ③	8.5 ④	3.5	16.0	12.8	12.8
	8-305 Chev. ⑤	4	—	4.3 ③	8.5 ④	3.5	16.0	17.2	17.2
	8-305 Chev. ⑥	4	—	4.3 ③	8.5 ④	3.5	16.0	15.9	15.9
'84-'87	4-151 Pont.	3 ②	—	3.5 ③	8.5 ④	3.5	16.0	8.8	9.1
	6-173 Chev.	4 ②	—	3.5 ③	8.5 ④	3.5	16.0	12.5	12.5
	8-305 Chev. ⑤	4	—	3.5 ③	8.5 ④	3.5	16.0	15.0	15.0
	8-305 Chev. ⑥	4	—	3.5 ③	8.5 ④	3.5	16.0	15.0	15.0

— Not applicable
① Drain and refill only—does not include torque convertor
② Capacity same with or without filter change
③ 5-speed—5.3 pints—85 and later 6.6 pints
④ Overdrive transmission—9.9 pints. Add 4 pints, run engine and check dipstick—fill as necessary
⑤ With 4 bbl. carburetor
⑥ With throttle body injection

WHEEL ALIGNMENT SPECIFICATIONS

Year	Caster Range (deg)	Caster Pref. Setting (deg)	Camber Range (deg)	Camber Pref. Setting (deg)	Toe-in (in.)	Steering Inclin. (deg)
Camaro						
'83-'84	2P to 4P	3P	3/16P to 1 13/16P	1P	3/32 to 5/16	N/A
Z-28	2P to 4P	3P	3/16P to 1 13/16P	1P	1/16 to 1/4	N/A
'85-'87	2 1/2P to 3 1/2P	3P	1/2P to 1 1/2P	1P	1/16 to 1/4	N/A
Z-28	3P to 4P	3 1/2P	1/2P to 1 1/2P	1P	1/16 to 1/4	N/A
Firebird						
'83	2P to 4P	3P	1/8P to 1 13/16P	1P	3/32 to 5/16	N/A
Trans Am	2P to 4P	3P	1/8P to 1 13/16P	1P	1/16 to 1/4	N/A
'84	2P to 4P	3P	3/16P to 1 13/16P	1P	3/32 to 5/16	N/A
Trans Am	2P to 4P	3P	3/16P to 1 13/16P	1P	1/16 to 1/4	N/A
'85	2 5/16P to 3 5/16P	2 13/16P	1/2P to 1 1/2P	1P	1/32 to 1/4	N/A
'86-'87	3P to 4P	3 1/2P	1/2P to 1 1/2P	1P	1/32 to 1/4	N/A

GENERAL MOTORS—"F" BODY
CAMARO • CAMARO BERLINETTA • FIREBIRD • TRANS AM • SE
SECTION 16

FIRING ORDERS

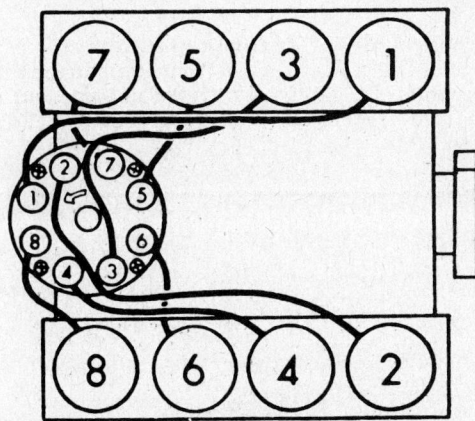

Pontiac-built V8 engines
Engine firing order: 1-8-4-3-6-5-7-2
Distributor rotation: counterclockwise

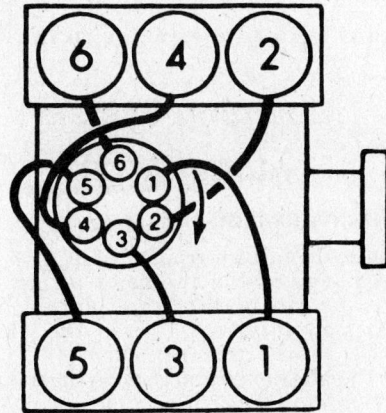

Chevrolet-built 173 V6 engine
Engine firing order: 1-2-3-4-5-6
Distributor rotation: clockwise

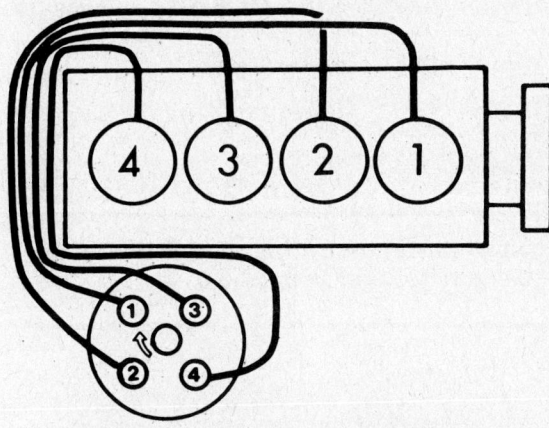

Pontiac-built 151-4 cylinder engine
Engine firing order: 1-3-4-2
Distributor rotation: clockwise

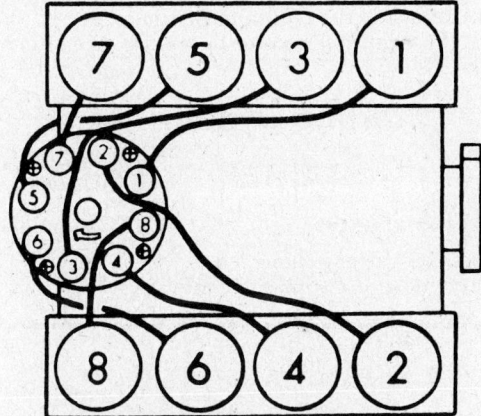

Chevrolet-built V8 engines
Engine firing order: 1-8-4-3-6-5-7-2
Distributor rotation: clockwise

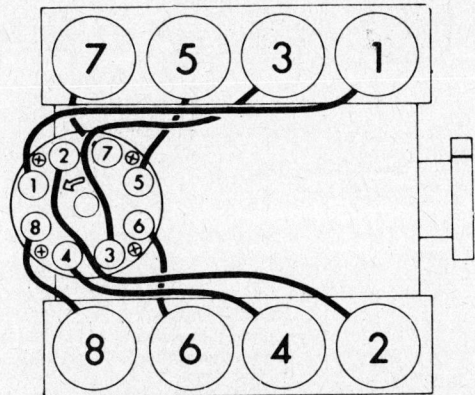

Oldsmobile-built V8 engines
Engine firing order: 1-8-4-3-6-5-7-2
Distributor rotation: counterclockwise

SECTION 16

GENERAL MOTORS—"F" BODY
CAMARO • CAMARO BERLINETTA • FIREBIRD • TRANS AM • SE

ELECTRICAL SECTION

For Overhaul Procedures refer to the Unit Repair Section.

Charging System

ALTERNATOR

Removal and Installation

1. Disconnect the battery ground cable.
2. Tag and disconnect the alternator wiring.
3. Remove the alternator brace bolt. If the vehicle is equipped with power steering, loosen the pump brace and mount nuts. Detach the drive belt(s).
4. Support the alternator and remove the mount bolt(s). Remove the unit from the vehicle.
5. Installation is the reverse of the previous steps. Tighten belt enough to allow approximately ½ in. of play on the longest run between pulleys.

VOLTAGE REGULATOR

The voltage regulator is electronic and is housed within the alternator. Adjustments to the regulator are not possible. Should replacement of the regulator become necessary, the alternator must be disassembled.

Starting System

STARTER

Removal and Installation

1. Disconnect the battery cable.
2. Raise the vehicle and support it safely.
3. Disconnect all wiring from the starter.
4. Remove the front bracket from the starter and the two mounting bolts. On engines with a solenoid heat shield, remove the front bracket upper bolt and detach the bracket from the starter.

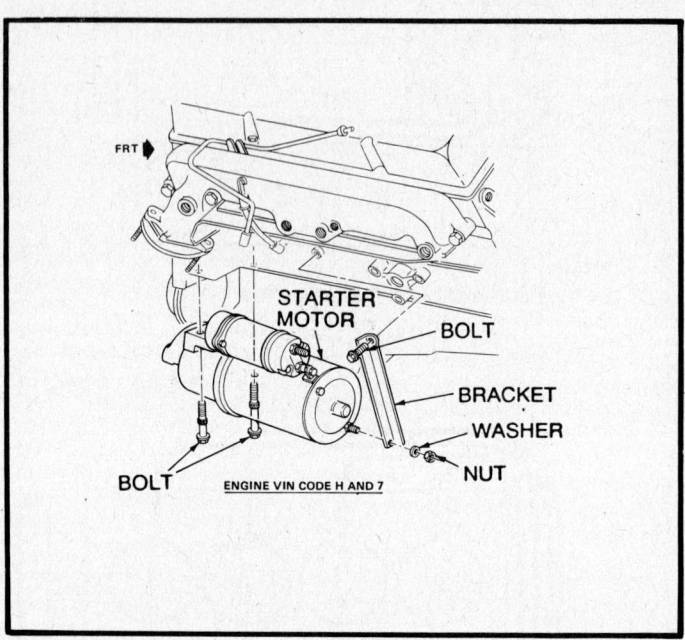

Typical starter motor installation
(© General Motors Corporation)

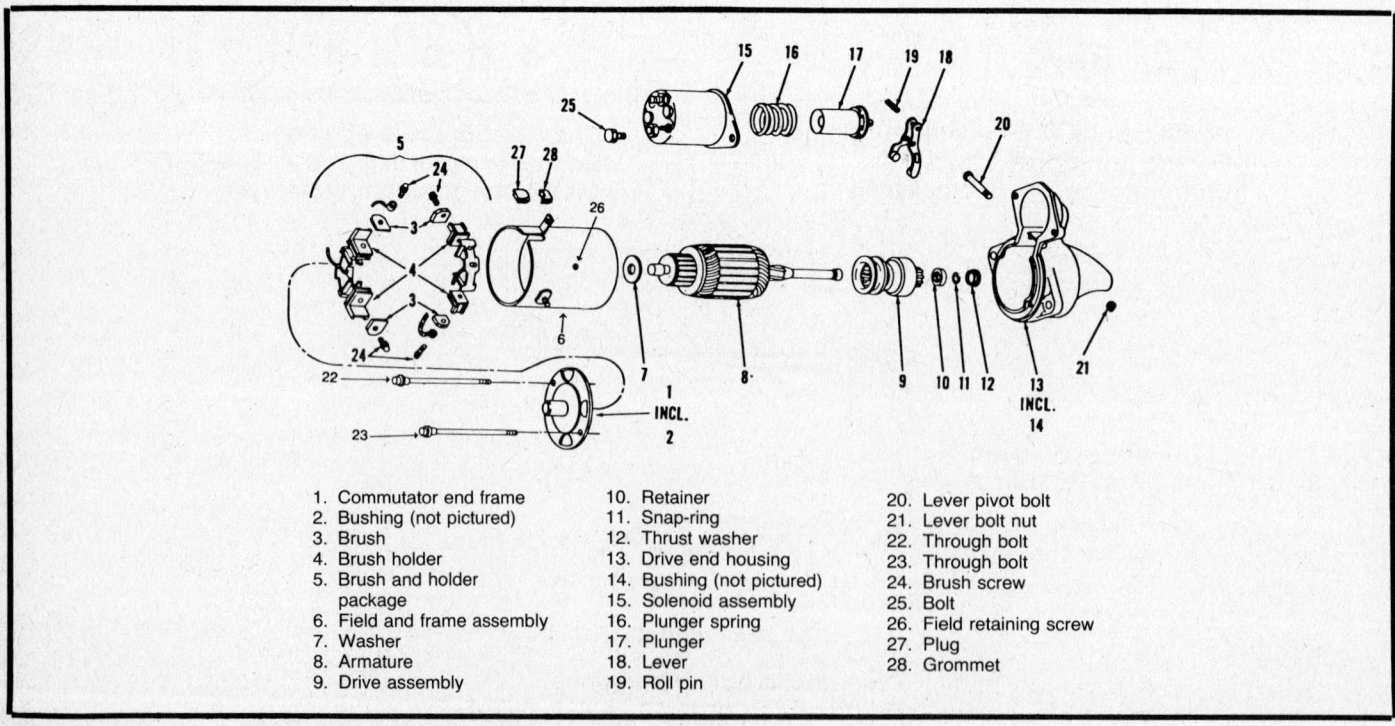

1. Commutator end frame
2. Bushing (not pictured)
3. Brush
4. Brush holder
5. Brush and holder package
6. Field and frame assembly
7. Washer
8. Armature
9. Drive assembly
10. Retainer
11. Snap-ring
12. Thrust washer
13. Drive end housing
14. Bushing (not pictured)
15. Solenoid assembly
16. Plunger spring
17. Plunger
18. Lever
19. Roll pin
20. Lever pivot bolt
21. Lever bolt nut
22. Through bolt
23. Through bolt
24. Brush screw
25. Bolt
26. Field retaining screw
27. Plug
28. Grommet

Exploded view of a typical starter (© General Motors Corporation)

GENERAL MOTORS—"F" BODY
CAMARO • CAMARO BERLINETTA • FIREBIRD • TRANS AM • SE.
SECTION 16

NOTE: Starter removal on certain models may necessitate the removal of the frame support. This support runs from the corner of the frame to the front crossmember.

5. Remove the front bracket bolt or nut. Lower the starter front end first, and then remove the unit from the car.
6. Reverse the removal procedures to install the starter. Torque the two mounting bolts to 25–35 ft.lbs.

NOTE: If shims were placed between the starter and engine block, they must be replaced in their original locations.

1984 AND LATER FIREBIRD

1. Disconnect the negative battery cable and remove the engine harness bracket from the motor mount brace.
2. Disconnect the upper starter bolt and raise and support the vehicle safely.
3. Disconnect the fuel lines from the bracket and loosen the fuel lines at the fuel regulator.
4. Remove the rear starter bracket and disconnect the cover and wiring to the solenoid and negative battery cable grounding bolt.
5. Remove lower starter bolt and starter.
6. Installation is the reverse order of the removal procedure.

Ignition System

DISTRIBUTOR

Removal and Installation

1. Disconnect the ground cable from the battery.
2. Tag and disconnect the feed and module terminal connectors from the distributor cap. Disconnect all required connectors.
3. Disconnect a hose at the vacuum advance unit, if so equipped.
4. Depress the release the 4 distributor cap-to-housing retainers and lift off the cap assembly.
5. Using crayon or chalk, make locating marks on the rotor and module and on the distributor housing and engine for installation purposes.
6. Loosen and remove the distributor clamp bolt and clamp, and lift the distributor out of the engine. Noting the relative position of the rotor and module alignment marks, make a second mark on the rotor to align it with the one mark on the module.
7. With a new O-ring on the distributor housing and the second mark on the rotor aligned with the mark on the module, install the distributor, taking care to align the mark on the housing with the one on the engine. It may be necessary to lift the distributor and turn the rotor slightly to align the gears and the oil pump driveshaft.
8. With the respective marks aligned, install the clamp and bolt finger-tight.
9. Install and secure the distributor cap.
10. Connect the feed and module connectors to the distributor cap.
11. Connect a timing light to the engine and plug the vacuum hose.
12. Connect the ground cable to the battery.
13. Start the engine and set the timing.
14. Turn the engine off and tighten the distributor clamp bolt. Disconnect the timing light and unplug and connect the hose to the vacuum advance.

NOTE: If equipped with electronic spark timing (no vacuum advance) the four wire connector must be separated before initial timing can be adjusted.

15. If the engine has been disturbed, proceed as follows:

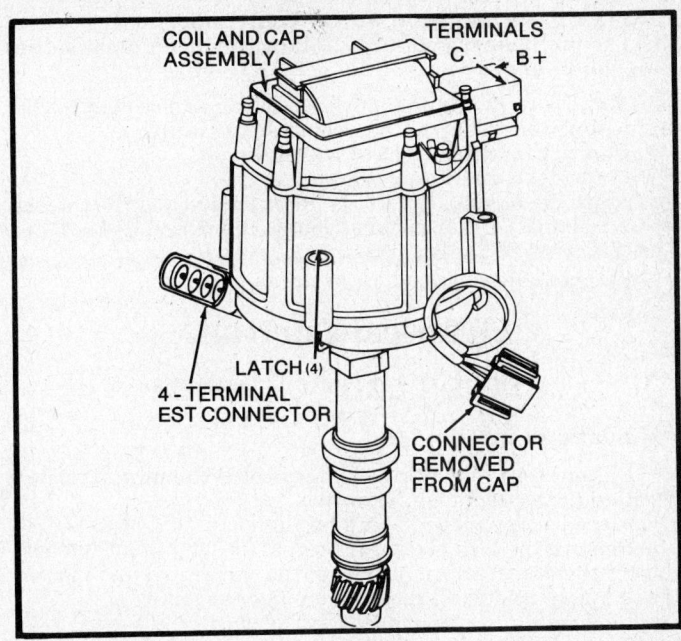

HEI distributor with four-terminal electronic spark timing connector (© General Motors Corporation)

16. Turn the crankshaft until the No. 1 cylinder is at the top if its compression stroke. Remove the No.1 spark plug to feel the compression.
17. Align the timing mark on the vibration damper with the TDC indicator or 0 mark on the timing scale.
18. With distributor body oriented in its normal position, hold the rotor pointing toward the No. 1 plug wire location, then turn the rotor approximately 1/8 turn counterclockwise and push the distributor down until it engages the camshaft, rotating the shaft slightly if necessary.
19. Press down on the distributor and crank the engine to make sure the oil pump shaft is engaged.
20. Return the crankshaft to No. 1 cylinder compression stroke with the timing marks aligned, then tighten the distributor clamp bolt.
21. Install the distributor cap, checking that the rotor points to the No.1 terminal. Make sure that the spark plug wires are in their supports and are securely connected.
22. Connect distributor vacuum line and primary wire.
23. Start engine and set the timing.

IGNITION TIMING

NOTE: On models equipped with Electronic Spark Timing (EST) it will be necessary to put the EST in the bypass mode by disconnecting the single wire timing connector. This wire is tan with a black tracer and breaks out of the wiring harness conduit near the rear of the right hand valve cover. Also on the EST equipped models, when adjusting the timing do not disconnect the four wire connector to the distributor.

Adjustment

Timing marks are located on the front engine cover and one the harmonic balancer or pulley.

1. Disconnect the distributor vacuum advance hose from the distributor and plug the hose.
2. On models without Electronic Spark Timing (EST), disconnect the four terminal connector from the wiring harness.

16-15

SECTION 16

GENERAL MOTORS—"F" BODY
CAMARO • CAMARO BERLINETTA • FIREBIRD • TRANS AM • SE

NOTE: If the instructions on your underhood sticker differ from these procedures, follow the directions on the underhood sticker.

3. Make sure the timing marks are clean and readable. The engine must be at normal operating temperature.
4. Connect a timing light to No.1 cylinder.
5. Loosen the distributor clamp.
6. Start the engine. Rotate the distributor until the correct marks line up. Tighten the distributor clamp and recheck the timing.
7. Reconect the vacuum hose or the four terminal connector.

Electrical Controls

IGNITION LOCK CYLINDER

Removal and Installation

1. Disconnect the negative battery cable. Remove steering wheel and directional signal switch.
2. Place lock cylinder in Run position.
3. Remove the lock plate, turn signal switch (be sure to disconnect the electrical connectors of the turnsignal and buzzer switch before removing them) and buzzer switch.
4. Remove the screw and lock cylinder.

NOTE: To remove the lock plate it will be necessary to use special tool J-23653-4 with J-23653 or equivalent to remove the retaining (snap) ring that secures the lock plate to the steering wheel shaft.

---------- **CAUTION** ----------
If the screw is dropped on removal, it could fall into the column. Complete disassembly would be required to retrieve the screw.

5. Rotate the cylinder clockwise to align cylinder key with the keyway in the housing.
6. Push the lock all the way in.
7. Install the screw. Tighten the screw to 14 inch lbs. for adjustable columns and 25 inch lbs. for standard columns.

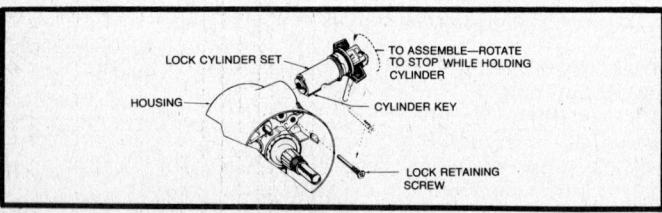

Removing the lock cylinder
(© General Motors Corporation)

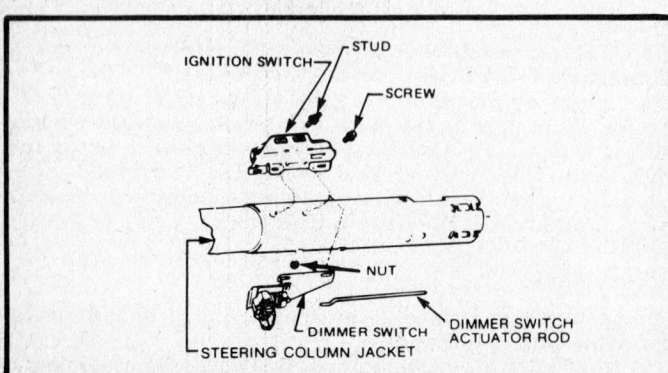

Removing ignition and dimmer switch
(© General Motors Corporation)

IGNITION SWITCH

Removal and Installation

1. Disconnect the negative battery cable. Lower the steering column; be sure to properly support it.
2. Put the switch in the Off-Locked position. With the cylinder removed, the rod is in Lock when it is in the next to the upper-most detent. Off-Unlocked is 2 detents from the top.
3. Remove the two switch screws and remove the switch assembly.
4. Before installing, place the new switch in the Off-Unlocked position and make sure the lock cylinder and actuating rod are in the Off-Unlocked (third detent from the top) position.
5. Install the activating rod into the switch and assemble the switch on the column. Tighten the mounting screws. Use only the specified screws since overlength screws could impair the collapsibility of the column.
6. Reinstall the steering column.

NEUTRAL SAFETY SWITCH

Removal and Installation

AUTOMATIC TRANSMISSION

1. New switches come with a small plastic alignment pin installed. Leave this pin in place. Position the shifter assembly in neutral.
2. Remove the old switch and install the replacement, align the pin on the shifter with the slot in the switch, and fasten with the two screws.
3. Move the shifter from the neutral position. This shears the plastic alignment pin and frees the switch.

If the switch is to be adjusted, not replaced, insert a $^3/_{32}$ in. drill bit or similar size pin and align the hole and switch. Position switch, adjust as necessary. Remove the pin before shifting from neutral.

MANUAL TRANSMISSION

1. Remove the wiring connector and the bolt attaching the switch assembly to the brake pedal bracket.
2. Installation is the reverse of removal. To adjust, set the switch to supply current for starting the clutch pedal fully depressed to the floor.

NOTE: Manual transmission vehicles equipped with cruise control will have a combination clutch switch/clutch cruise release valve. Depressing the brake pedal or the clutch pedal on these models disengages the cruise control.

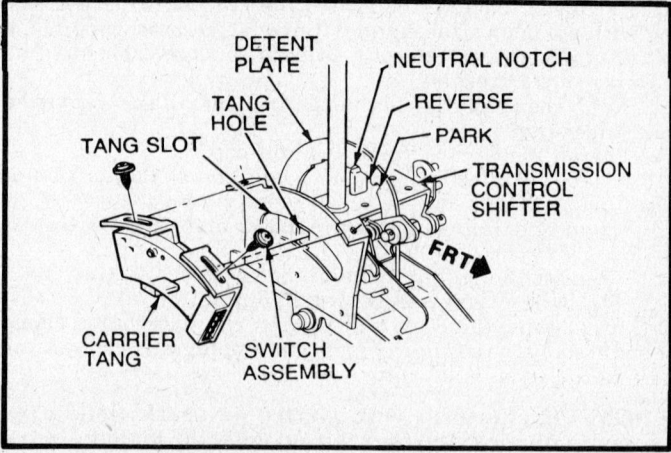

Console mounted neutral safety switch
(© General Motors Corporation)

GENERAL MOTORS—"F" BODY
CAMARO • CAMARO BERLINETTA • FIREBIRD • TRANS AM • SE

HEADLIGHT SWITCH

Removal and Installation

1983 CAMARO

1. Disconnect the negative battery cable at the battery.
2. Remove the four screws from inside the defroster duct (instrument panel pad securing screws).
3. Removal the screws which are under the lip of the instrument panel pad.
4. Remove the instrument panel pad.
5. On models equipped with air conditioning, remove the instrument panel cluster bezel and the cluster.
6. Remove the radio speaker bracket.
7. Pull the headlamp switch knob to the On position, depress the locking button for the knob and shaft (located on the switch), and remove the knob and shaft.
8. Remove the switch bezel (retainer).
9. Disconnect the wiring from the switch and remove the switch.
10. Installation is performed in the reverse of the previous steps.

1984 AND LATER CAMARO

1. Disconnect the negative battery cable and remove the left and right lower trim plates.
2. Remove the instrument panel trim plate and the two switch assembly retaining screws.
3. Depress the side tangs and remove the switch from the instrument panel.
4. Installation is the reverse order of the removal procedure.

1984 AND LATER BERLINETTA

NOTE: The headlight switch on the Berlinetta is located in the left pod assembly. In order to replace the switch assembly, the pod assembly must be removed as a unit.

1. Disconnect the negative battery cable.
2. Remove the instrument panel trim plate screws. Remove the instrument panel trim plate.
3. Remove the lower steering column trim cover.
4. Remove the left control head attaching screw at the bottom front. Release the holding tab.
5. Disconnect the electrical connector located below the instrument panel.
6. Remove the pod assembly. Slide the control off the track to remove.
7. Installation is the reverse of the removal procedure.

FIREBIRD

1. Remove the right and left lower trim plates.

NOTE: Removal of the instrument panel lower cover(s) is not required.

2. Remove the instrument panel cluster trim plate.
3. Remove the two switch mounting screws.
4. Depress the side tangs of the switch and pull the switch out of the instrument panel.
5. The individual switches of the headlamp switch assembly are now serviceable. Installation of the switch is performed in the reverse order of the previous steps.

DIMMER SWITCH

Removal and Installation

1. Disconnect the negative battery cable.
2. Remove the steering wheel. Remove the trim cover.
3. Remove the turn signal switch assembly.
4. Remove the ignition switch stud and screw. Remove the ignition switch.
5. Remove the dimmer switch actuator rod by sliding it from the switch assembly.
6. Remove the dimmer switch bolts. Remove the dimmer switch.
7. Installation is the reverse of the removal procedure.
8. Adjust the dimmer switch by depressing the switch slightly and inserting a $3/32$ in. drill into the adjusting hole. Push the switch up to remove any play and tighten the dimmer switch adjusting screw.

TURN SIGNAL SWITCH

Removal and Installation

1. Remove the steering wheel trim cover.
2. Remove the steering wheel.
3. Position the GM lockplate compressing tool on the end of the steering shaft and compress the lock plate by turning the shaft nut clockwise. Pry the wire snapring out of the shaft groove.
4. Remove the tool and lift the lockplate off the shaft.
5. Slip the cancelling cam, upper bearing preload spring and thrust washer off the shaft.
6. Remove the turn signal lever. Push the flasher knob in and unscrew it. On models equipped with a button and a knob, remove the button retaining screw, then remove the button, spring, and knob.
7. Pull the switch connector out the mast jacket and tape the upper part to facilitate switch removal. Attach a long piece of wire to the turn signal switch connector. When installing the turn signal switch, feed this wire through the column first, and then use this wire to pull the switch connector into position. On tilt wheels, place the turn signal and shifter housing in low position and remove the harness cover.
8. Remove the three switch mounting screws. Remove the switch by pulling it straight up while guiding the wiring harness cover through the column.
9. Install the replacement switch by working the connector and cover down through the housing and under the bracket. On tilt models, the connector is worked down through the housing, under the bracket, and then the cover is installed on the harness.
10. Install the switch mounting screws and the connector on the mask jacket bracket. Install the column-to-dash trim plate.
11. Install the flasher knob and the turn signal lever.
12. With the turn signal lever in neutral and the flasher knob out, slide the thrust washer, upper bearing preload spring, and cancelling cam onto the shaft.
13. Position the lock plate on the shaft and press it down until a new snapring can be inserted in the shaft groove. Always use a new snapring when assembling.
14. Install the cover and the steering wheel.

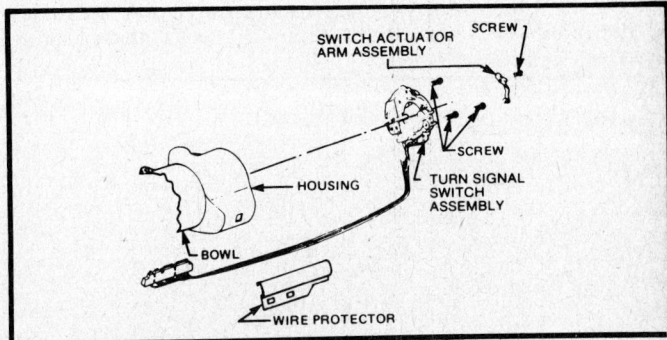

Removing the turnsignal switch all models
(© General Motors Corporation)

16–17

SECTION 16

GENERAL MOTORS—"F" BODY
CAMARO • CAMARO BERLINETTA • FIREBIRD • TRANS AM • SE

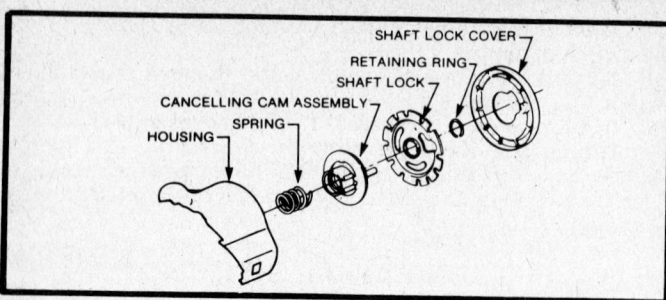

Remove components to reach turnsignal switch
(© General Motors Corporation)

HORN SWITCH

Removal and Installation

1. Disconnect the negative battery cable.
2. Remove the horn pad. Remove the contact assembly and all other related components.
3. Installation is the reverse of the removal procedure.

WINDSHIELD WIPER SWITCH

Removal and Installation
ALL MODELS

1. Remove the steering wheel and directional signal switch. It may be necessary to loosen the two column mounting nuts and remove the four bracket-to-mast jacket screws, then separate the bracket from the mast jacket to allow the connector clip on the ignition switch to be pulled out of the column assembly.
2. Disconnect the washer/wiper switch lower connector.
3. Remove the screws attaching the column housing to the mast jacket. Be sure to note the position of the dimmer switch actuator rod for reassembly in the same position. Remove the column housing-and-switch as an assembly.

NOTE: The Tilt and Travel columns have a removal plastic cover on the column housing. This provides access to the wiper switch without removing the entire column housing.

4. Turn upside down and use a drift to remove the pivot pin from the washer/wiper switch. Remove the switch.
5. Place the switch into position in the housing, then install the pivot pin.
6. Position the housing onto the mast jacket and attach by installing the screws. Install the dimmer switch actuator rod in the same position as noted earlier. Check switch operation.
7. Reconnect lower end of switch asembly.
8. Install remaining components in reverse order of removal. Be sure to attach column mounting bracket in original position.

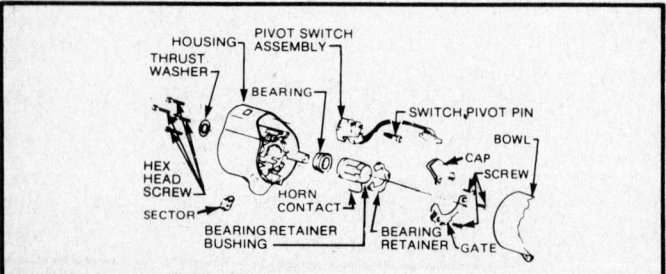

Removing the column mounted wiper switch
(© General Motors Corporation)

WIPER MOTOR

Removal and Installation

1. Disconnect the negative battery cable at the battery.
2. Raise the hood.
3. Remove the screen or grill that covers the cowl area.
4. Working under the hood, disconect the motor wiring. Then, reach through the cowl opening and loosen, but do not remove, the nuts which attach the transmission drive link to the motor crank arm. Then, disconnect the drive link from the crank arm.
5. Remove the three motor attaching screws, and remove the motor, guiding the crank arm through the hole.
6. Installation is in the reverse order of removal. The motor must be in the park position before assembling the crank arm to the transmission drive link(s).

WIPER LINKAGE

Removal and Installation

1. Remove the wiper arms and blades. Remove the cowl screen or grill.
2. Disconnect the wiring from the wiper motor. Loosen, but do not remove the nuts which attach the transmission drive link from the arm.
3. Remove the transmission-to-body attaching screws from both the right and left sides of the car.
4. Guide the transmissions and linkage out through the cowl opening.
5. Installation is the reverse of removal.

INSTRUMENT CLUSTER

Removal and Installation
CAMARO/FIREBIRD – EXCEPT BERLINETTA

1. Disconnect negative battery cable.
2. Remove instrument cluster bezel.
3. Remove six cluster attachment screws, pull cluster back and disconnect speedo cable and electrical connections.

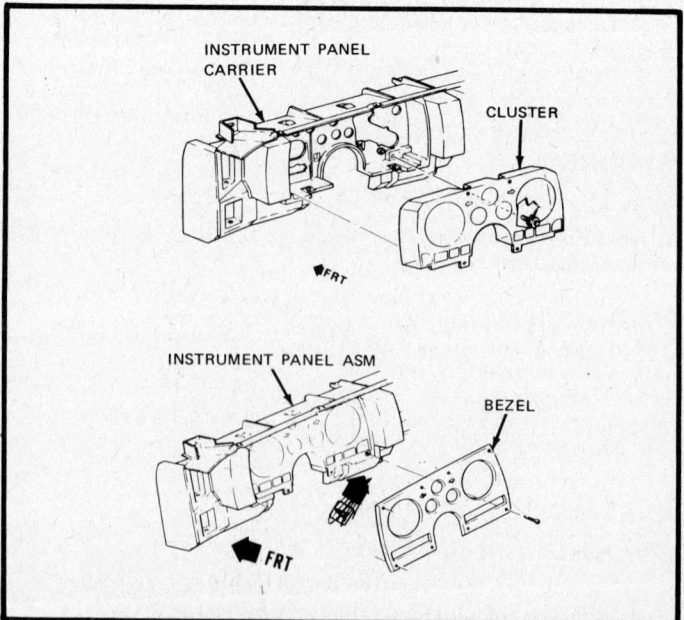

Instrument panel cluster and trim
(© General Motors Corporation)

16–18

GENERAL MOTORS—"F" BODY
CAMARO • CAMARO BERLINETTA • FIREBIRD • TRANS AM • SE

SECTION 16

4. Remove trip odometer, reset knob (if so equipped) and remove the cluster lens.
5. Individual gages and/or speedometer head are not accessible for service or replacement. If service is intended for only gauges or tachometer, skip Step 3.
6. Reverse removal procedure to reinstall.

BERLINETTA

1. Disconnect the negative battery cable.
2. Remove the screws holding the steering column trim cover to the instrument panel. Remove the trim cover.
3. Remove the screws at the bottom of the right hand pod. Pull the pod rearward and disconnect the electrical connector.
4. Slide the pod from the track as a unit.
5. Repeat Step 3 for removal of the left hand pod. Disconnect the electrical connector from under the instrument panel.
6. Remove the cluster bezel screws and remove the bezel. Remove the cluster lens screws and remove the cluster lens.
7. Remove the steering column bolts and lower the column to gain working clearance.
8. Pull the cluster rearward and disconnect the cluster electrical connection.
9. Installation is the reverse of the removal procedure.

SPEEDOMETER

Removal and Installation
EXCEPT BERLINETTA

1. Disconnect the negative battery cable.

2. Remove the instrument cluster bezel.
3. Remove the headlight switch by depressing the shaft retainer button located under the dash and pulling on the switch knob.
4. Remove the cluster attaching screws and pull the instrument cluster rearward. Disconnect the speedometer cable.
5. Remove any other necessary components in order to gain access to the speedometer assembly.
6. Remove the speedometer assembly from the instrument panel.
7. Installation is the reverse of the removal procedure.

BERLINETTA

1. Disconnect the negative battery cable.
2. Remove the screws form the bottom of the instrument cluster lens and the top of the lens.
3. Remove the bezel assembly.
4. Remove the hex nut screws holding the dial and applique assembly to the instrument panel.
5. Remove the screws holding the gauge assembly and pull the gauge assembly outward.
6. Disconnect the speedometer wiring. Remove the speedometer assembly.
7. Installation is the reverse of the removal procedure.

SPEEDOMETER CABLE

Removal and Installation

1. Disconect the negative battery cable.

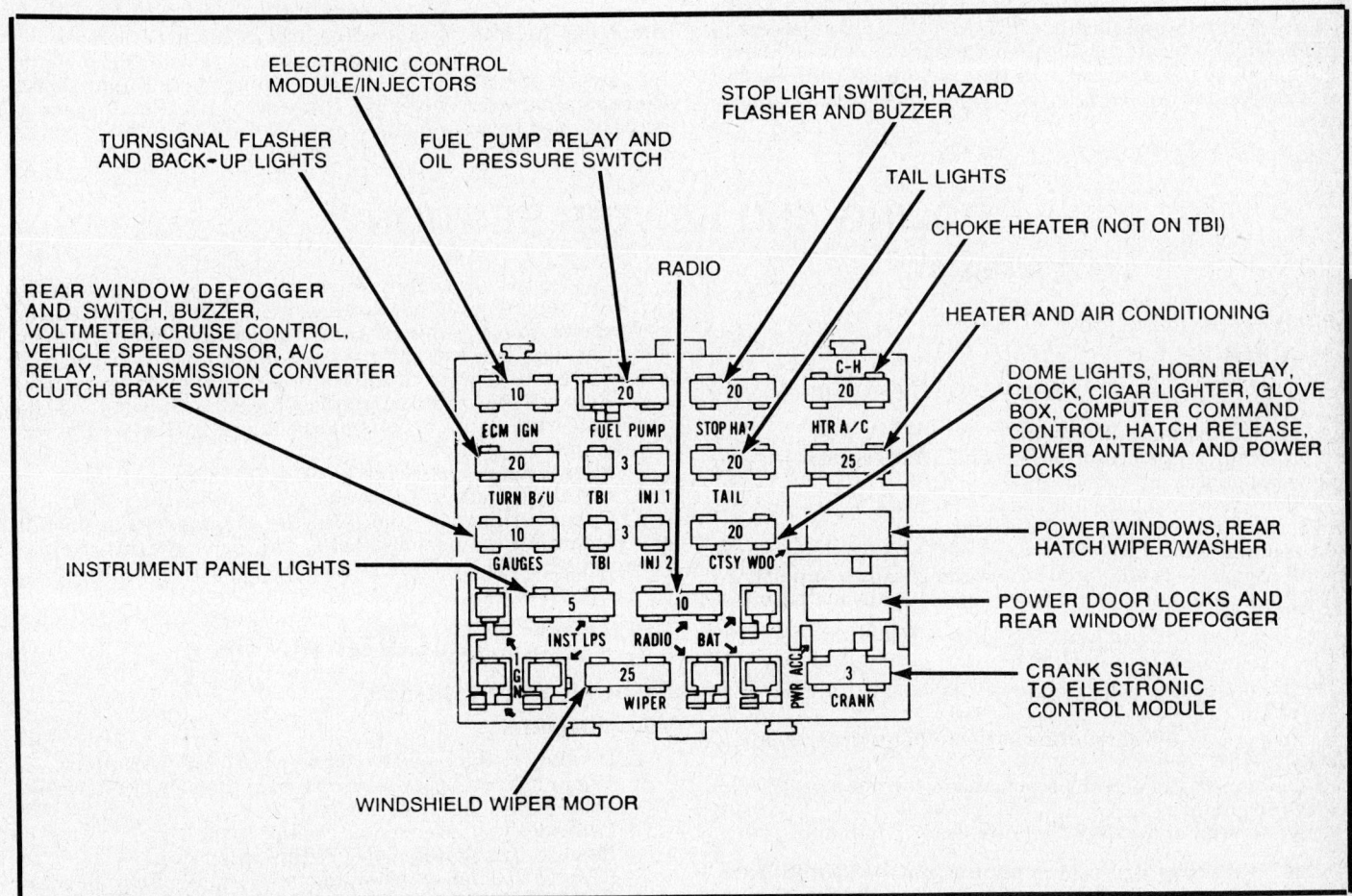

Typical fuse panel (© General Motors Corporation)

SECTION 16
GENERAL MOTORS—"F" BODY
CAMARO • CAMARO BERLINETTA • FIREBIRD • TRANS AM • SE

2. On non-cruise control equipped vehicles, disconnect the speedometer cable strap at the power brake booster. On cruise control equipped vehicles, disconnect the speedometer cable at the cruise control transducer.

3. Pull the cluster out far enough to gain access to the back of the speedometer. Disconnect the speedometer cable form the speedometer head.

4. Slide the cable out from the casing. Install the new cable after it has been well lubricated.

5. When replacing the speedometer cable and case, proper routing must be followed to insure its functioning.

6. The remaining installation is the reverse of the removal procedure.

ELECTRICAL COMPONENT LOCATION

Fuse Panel

The fuse panel is located on the cowl under the left side of the instrument panel (behind the trim panel on some later models).

Electronic Control Module

The electronic control module is located on the right side of the vehicle. It is positioned under the instrument panel. In order to gain access to the electronic control module it may be necessary to remove the under dash padding.

Convenience Center

The convenience center is located on the underside of the instrument panel. It is a swing down unit which provides access to buzzers, relays and flasher units. In order to gain access to the convenience center it may be necessary to remove instrument panel sound absorber. On the later models the flasher units are located on the right hand side of the steering column brace.

FUSIBLE LINKS

The fusible links are located near the starter solenoid. They are attached to the lower ends of the main supply wires. The fusible links serve as additional circuit protection in the event of an electrical overload. In order to gain access to the fusible links, it may be needed to raise the vehicle.

Circuit Breakers

The circuit breakers are located on the left side of the vehicle. They are under the instrument panel. In order to gain access to the circuit breakers, it may be necessary to remove the under dash padding.

FUSIBLE LINKS

Removal and Installation

1. Disconnect the negative battery cable.
2. Disconnect the fusible link from either the junction block or the starter solenoid.
3. Remove the damaged fusible link. Strip approximately 1½ in. from the wiring harness.
4. Install the new fusible link and crimp the wire.
5. Connect the fusible link to the terminal it was attached to. Connect the negative battery cable.

Speed Controls
ADJUSTMENTS

Assemble chain to be taut with carb. in the hot idle position and with the idle control solenoid de-energized. Place chain into swivel cavities which permit chain to have slight slack. Place retainer over swivel and chain assembly. Retainer must be positioned between balls.

COOLING AND HEATER SECTION

WATER PUMP

Removal and Installation
2.5L ENGINE

1. Disconnect the negative battery cable and drain the cooling system.
2. Loosen the fan pulley bolts.
3. Disconnect the heater hose(s) and lower radiator hose, at the water pump.
4. Remove the water pump to cylinder block attaching bolts and remove the pump from the engine.
5. Installation is the reverse order of the removal procedure. Install new gaskets and torque the water pump attaching bolts to 15 ft. lbs. The water pump bolts should also be coated with a suitable RTV sealer to avoid coolant leaks.

2.8L AND 5.0L/5.7L ENGINES

1. Disconnect the negative battery cable and drain the cooling system.
2. Remove the fan shroud and or the radiator upper support, as applicable.
3. Disconnect the heater hose(s) and lower radiator hose, at the water pump.
Remove the fan and pulley from the water pump hub.

NOTE: Viscous drive fans should not be stored horizontally. The silicone fluid can leak out of the fan assembly if it is not kept upright.

4. Loosen the alternator swivel bolt (remove the upper brace on V8s) and remove the alternator drive belt and accessory drive belts. Remove the alternator upper and lower brackets, air brace and bracket and if so equipped, the power steering pump lower bracket from the water pump and swing it aside.
5. Remove the water pump-to-cylinder block bolts and the power steering-to-pump bolts (if so equipped). Remove the water pump.
6. Install the pump on the block with a new gasket.
7. Install the pump pulley and the fan onto the pump.
8. Connect the hoses and refill the cooling system. Install the remaining components, bolts, and belts. 9. Start the engine, replenish the cooling system, and check for leaks.

BLOWER MOTOR

Removal and Installation
ALL MODELS

1. Disconnect the negative battery cable at the battery.
2. Tag and disconnect the wiring from the blower motor and the resistor.
3. Remove the blower motor cooling tube.
4. Remove the blower motor retaining screws.
5. Remove the blower motor and fan assembly from the case.
6. Installation of the motor is performed in the reverse of the previous steps.

GENERAL MOTORS—"F" BODY
CAMARO • CAMARO BERLINETTA • FIREBIRD • TRANS AM • SE
SECTION 16

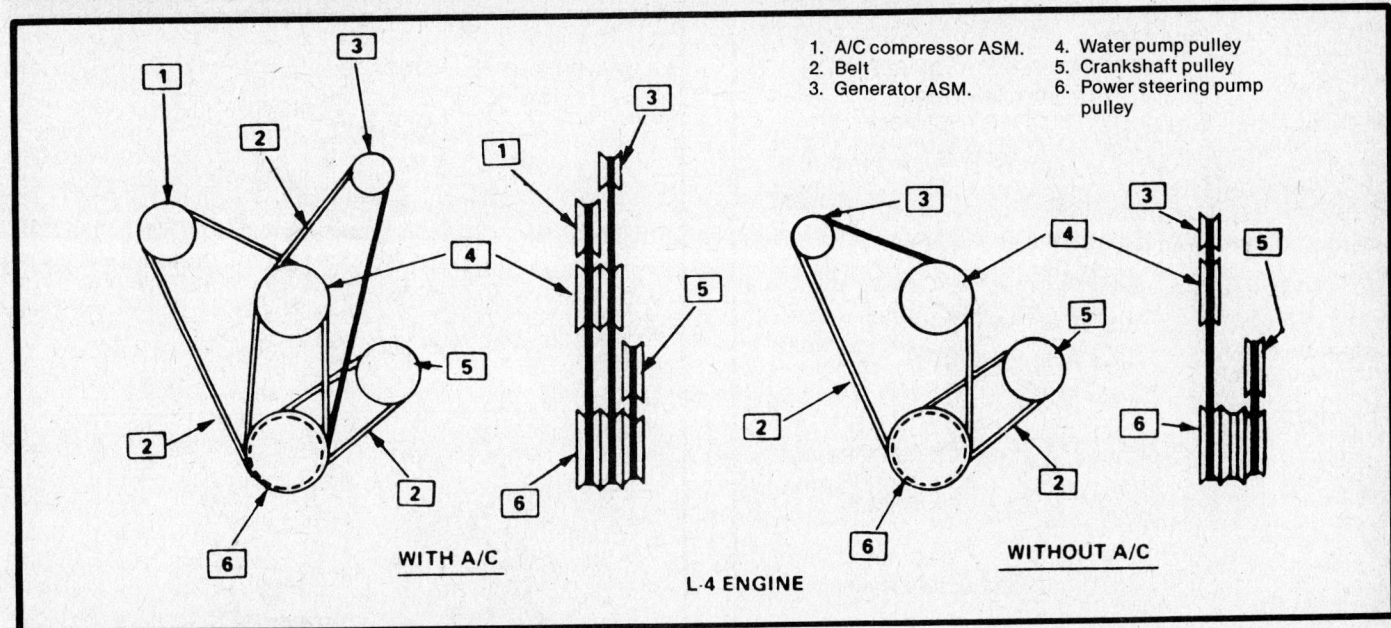

Proper belt installation for the 2.5L 4 cyl. engine

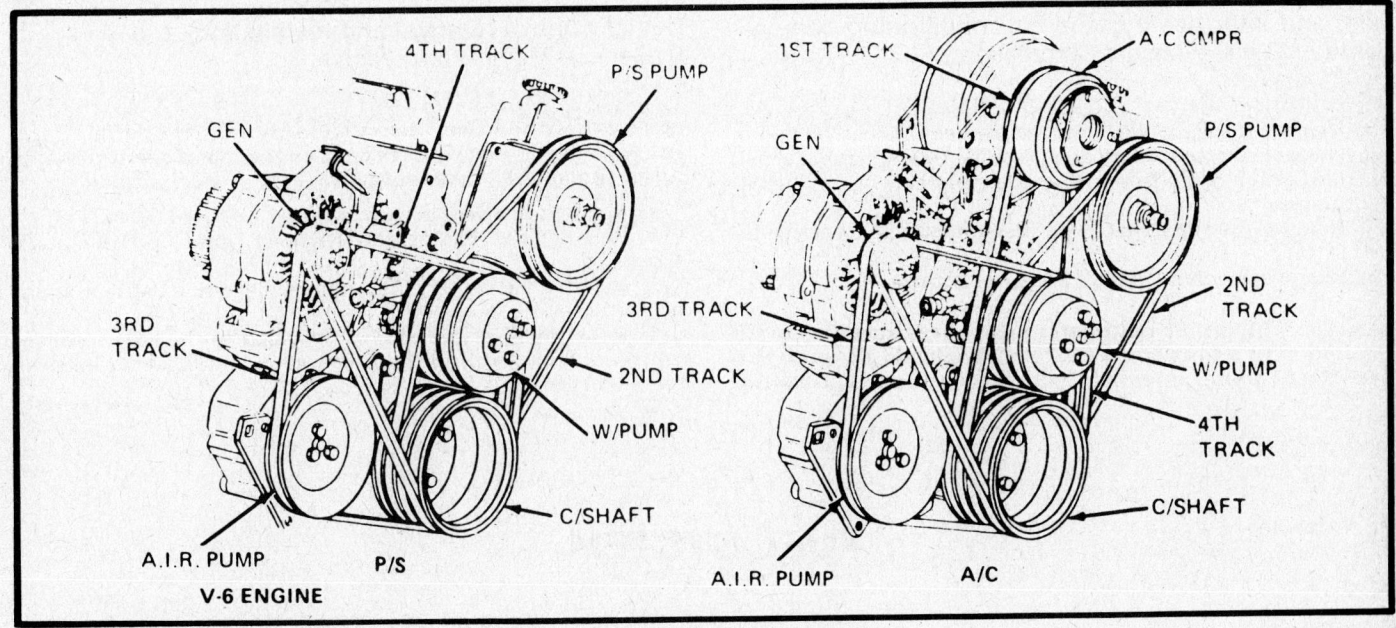

Proper belt installation for the 2.8L V6 engine and the 5.0L 8 cyl. engine

HEATER/AC CONTROL AND FAN SWITCH ASSEMBLY

Removal and Installation
ALL MODELS

1. Disconnect the negative battery cable.
2. Remove the instrument padding from under the dash.
3. Remove the temperature control/radio console trim plate.
4. Remove the control retaining bolts and pull the control arm from the console.
5. Tag the disconnect all control cables and electronic connections from the unit.

6. Installation is the reverse of the removal procedure. Fully cycle the controls to adjust the opening and closing of the mode doors.

HEATER CORE

Removal and Installation
ALL MODELS

1. Disconnect the negative battery cable at the battery.
2. Drain the cooling system.
3. Disconnect the coolant hoses from the heater core.
4. Remove the right side lower hush panel.

16-21

SECTION 16

GENERAL MOTORS—"F" BODY
CAMARO • CAMARO BERLINETTA • FIREBIRD • TRANS AM • SE

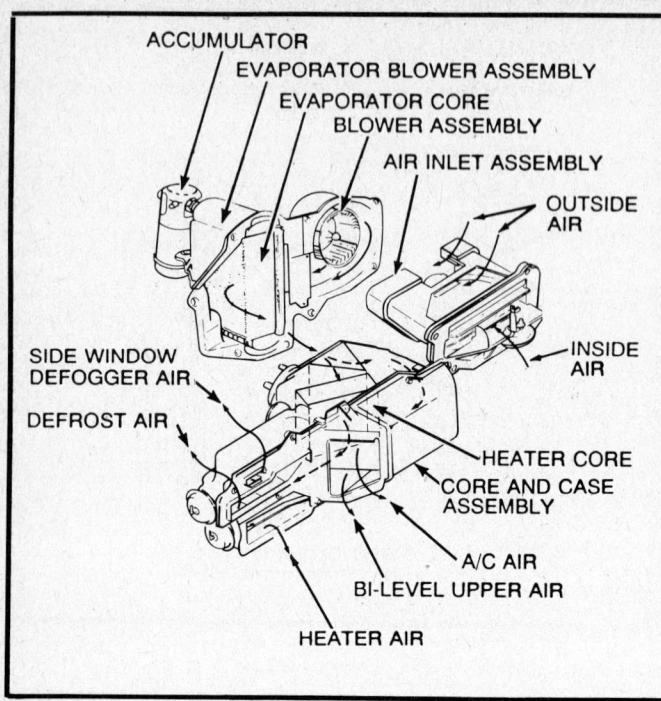

1982 and later heating and air conditioning components (© General Motors Corporation)

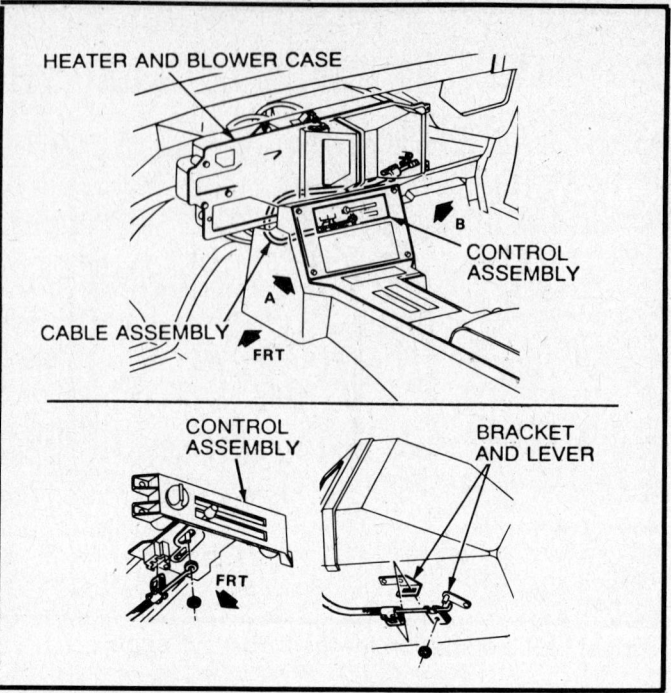

Heater control removal and installation (© General Motors Corporation)

5. Remove the right side lower instrument panel trim panel.
6. On fuel-injected V8 models, remove the electronic spark control (ESC) module from under the right side of the instrument panel.
7. Remove the right side lower instrument panel carrier-to-cowl screw.
8. Remove the four heater case cover screws.

NOTE: The upper left heater case cover screw may be reached with a long socket extension placed through the instrument panel openings which were exposed by the removal of the lower instrument panel trim panel. Carefully lift the lower right corner of the instrument panel to align the socket extension.

9. Remove the heater case cover.
10. Remove the heater core support plate and the baffle screws.
11. Remove the heater core, support plate, and baffle from the heater case.
12. Installation of the core is peformed in the reverse of the previous steps. Refill the cooling system and check for leaks after the engine has been started.

FUEL SYSTEM

FUEL PUMP

Removal and Installation

CARBURETED ENGINES—MECHANICAL PUMP

1. Disconnect the negative battery cable at the battery.
2. Disconnect the fuel intake and outlet lines at the pump and plug the pump intake line.
3. On Chevrolet V6 and V8 engines remove the upper bolt from the right front mounting boss. Insert a longer bolt (3/8–16 x 2 in.) in this hole to hold the fuel pump pushrod.
4. Remove the two pump mounting bolts and lockwashers; remove the pump and its gasket.
5. If the rocker arm pushrod is to be removed from V6 or V8, remove the two adapter bolts and lockwashers and remove the adapter and its gasket.

6. Install the fuel pump with a new gasket reversing the removal procedure. Coat the mating surfaces with sealer.
7. Connect the fuel lines and check for leaks.

FUEL INJECTED ENGINES—ELECTRONIC PUMP

The electric pump used with fuel injected models is an integral part of the fuel tank (gauge) sending unit. The pump may be serviced separately after the pump/sending unit assembly is removed from the tank.
1. Relieve the fuel pressure from the fuel system as follows:
   a. Remove the fuel pump fuse from the fuse block located in the passenger compartment.
   b. Start the engine and allow it to run until it stalls due to lack of fuel.
   c. Engage the starter for a few seconds to make sure that all presure has been relieved.

GENERAL MOTORS—"F" BODY
CAMARO • CAMARO BERLINETTA • FIREBIRD • TRANS AM • SE
SECTION 16

d. Turn the ignition off.
2. Disconnect the negative battery cable at the battery.
3. Remove the fuel filler cap and drain the fuel from the fuel tank.
4. Disconnect the exhaust pipe at the catalytic convertor and the rear hanger. Allow the exhaust system to hang over the rear axle assembly.
5. Remove the tailpipe and muffler heat shields.
6. Remove the fuel filler neck shield from behind the left rear tire.
7. Remove the rear suspension track bar and the track bar brace.
8. Disconnect the fuel pump/sending unit electrical connector, at the body harness connector.

CAUTION

DO NOT pry up on the cover connector, as the pump/sending unit wiring harness is an integral part of the sending unit.

---

9. Disconnect the fuel pipes.
10. Remove the fuel pipe retaining bracket on the left side and the brakeline clip from the retaining bracket.
11. Position a jack under the rear axle assembly in order to support the rear axle.
12. Disconnect the lower ends of the shock absorbers, lower the axle assembly enough to release the tension on the coil springs. Remove the coil springs.
13. Lower the rear axle assembly as far as possible without causing damage to the brake lines and cables.
14. Remove the fuel tank strap bolts.
15. Remove the tank by rotating the front of the tank downward and sliding it to the right side.
16. Remove the fuel pump/sending unit from the tank, by loosening the cam nut (refer to the CAUTION below). Remove the O-ring from beneath the unit. Replace the O-ring if defective.

CAUTION

Use EXTREME care when working around fuel. Do not smoke or use a drop light in the area. When removing the cam nut, use brass tools to tap the nut loose. DO NOT use standard metal tools, as sparks could be generated.

---

17. Separate the fuel pump from the sending unit and install the new pump in the same manner.
18. Installation of the fuel pump/sending unit is performed in the reverse of Steps 1–17.

NOTE: The 1985 Camaro with the 2.5L engine, may experience a no run/no start condition and/or a blown fuel pump fuse due to a short in the Radio Frequency Interference (RFI) filter. The filter is located on the electrical input terminals of the in-tank electrical fuel pump. If this no run/start condition occurs, this filter should also be checked along with the other normal diagnostic tests.

CARBURETOR

Idle Speed Adjustment
ALL BUT V8-350

1. Run the engine to normal operating temperature.
2. Make sure that the choke is fully opened, turn the A/C Off, set the parking brake, block the drive wheels and connect a tachometer to the engine according to the manufacturer's instructions.
3. Disconnect and plug the vacuum hoses at the EGR valve and the vapor canister.
4. Place the transmission in Park (AT) or Neutral (MT).
5. Disconnect and plug the vacuum advance hose at the distributor. Check and adjust the timing.

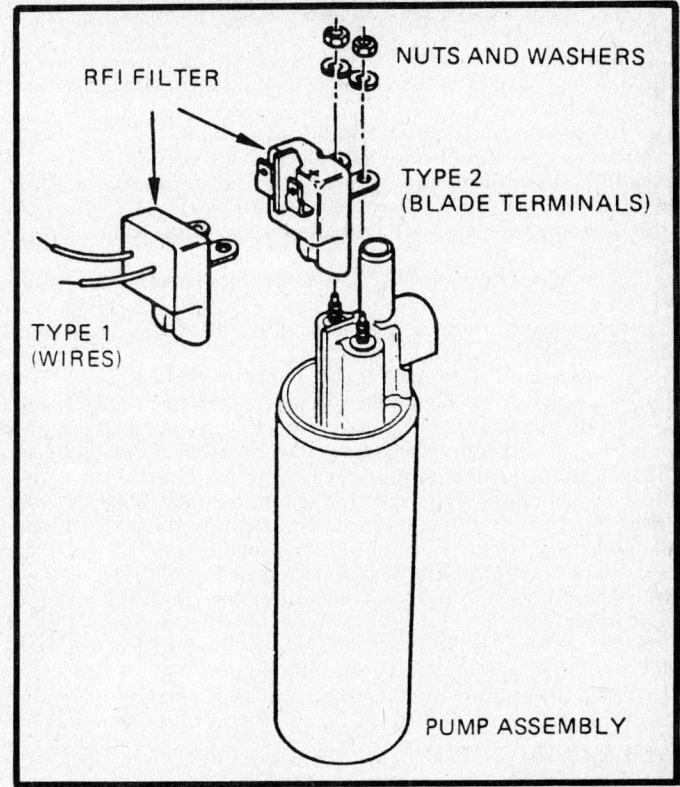

Location of the Ratio Frequency Interference Filter

6. Connect the distributor vacuum line.
7. Manual transmission cars without A/C an without solenoid: place the idle speed screw on the low step of the fast idle cam and turn the screw to achieve the specified idle speed. Cars with A/C: set the idle speed screw to the specified rpm. Disconnect the compressor clutch wire and turn the A/C On. Open the throttle momentarily to extend the solenoid plunger. Turn the solenoid screw to obtain the specified rpm.

Automatic transmission cars without A/C; manual transmission cars without A/C, solenoid-equipped carburetor: momentarily open the throttle to extend the solenoid plunger. Turn the solenoid screw to obtain the specified rpm. Disconnect the solenoid wire and turn the idle speed screw to obtain the slow engine idle speed.

V8-350

1. Run the engine to normal operating temperature.
2. Set the parking brake and lock the drive wheels.
3. Connect a tachometer to the engine according to the manufacturer's instructions.
4. Disconnect and plug the purge hose at the vapor canister. Disconnect and plug the EGR vacuum hose at the EGR valve.
5. Turn the A/C off.
6. Place the transmission in Park (AT) or Neutral (MT).
7. Disconnect and plug the vacuum advance line at the distributor. Check and adjust the timing.
8. Connect the vacuum advance line. Place the automatic transmission in Drive.
9. Manual transmission cars without A/C: adjust the idle stop screw to obtain the specified rpm. Cars with A/C: with the A/C off, adjust the idle stop screw to obtain the specified rpm. Disconnect the compressor clutch wire and turn the A/C on. Open the throttle slightly to allow the solenoid rpm listed on the underhood emission sticker.
10. Connect all hoses and remove tachometer.

16-23

SECTION 16: GENERAL MOTORS—"F" BODY
CAMARO • CAMARO BERLINETTA • FIREBIRD • TRANS AM • SE

V6–231, V8–305

1. Run the engine until it reaches normal operating temperature. Make sure that the choke is open and the air conditioning is OFF.
2. Connect a tachometer and a timing light.
3. Set the parking brake and block the wheels.
4. Tag, disconnect and plug all carbon canister and EGR vacuum hoses.
5. Disconnect the air conditioner compressor clutch connector.
6. Start the engine and place the transmission in Drive or Neutral.
7. Disconnect and plug the distributor vacuum advance line. Set the ignition timing.
8. Unplug and reconnect the distributor vacuum line.
9. On cars with A/C, adjust the idle stop screw to the specified rpm, turn the A/C ON and disconnect the electrical connector at the A/C compressor. Open the throttle momentarily to ensure that the solenoid plunger is fully extended. Adjust the idle speed solenoid to the speed given on the underhood sticker. Turn the A/C Off. On cars without air conditioning; turn the idle speed screw until you obtain the specified rpm.
10. Place the automatic transmission in Park.
11. Disconnect and plug the vacuum hose running from the EGR valve.
12. Adjust the fast idle screw on the second step of the fast idle cam until you obtain the specified rpm.
13. Stop the engine and reconnect the EGR vacuum hose, the vapor canister hose and the A/C compressor clutch connector.

CAMARO/FIREBIRD

The underhood label should be referred to for preparation procedures. Check the timing. Block the drive wheels and set the parking brake before performing idle adjustments.

WITH A/C

1. Turn the base idle speed screw to obtain the specified rpm.
2. Disconnect the A/C solenoid lead and open the throttle slightly to extend the solenoid plunger.
3. Turn the solenoid screw to the specified solenoid rpm.

WITHOUT A/C

1. Open the throttle slightly to fully extend the solenoid plunger if equipped.
2. Turn the solenoid screw to obtain the specified rpm (solenoid energized, if equipped).
3. Disconnect the solenoid electrical lead and turn the base idle speed screw to the specified base rpm.

2.5 LITER ENGINE WITH FUEL INJECTION

NOTE: The throttle stop screw that is used to adjust the idle speed of the vehicle, is adjusted to specifications at the factory. The throttle stop screw is then covered with a steel plug to prevent the unnecessary readjustment in the field. If it is necessary to gain access to the throttle stop screw without removing the TBI unit from the manifold.

1. Using a small punch or equivalent mark over the center line of the throttle stop screw. Drill a 5/32 in. diameter hole through the casting to the hardened steel plug.
2. Using a 1/16 in. diameter punch or equivalent punch out the steel plug.
3. With the vehicle in the park position, the parking brake applied and the drive wheels blocked, remove the air cleaner and plug the thermac vacuum port.
4. Remove the transmission T.V. cable from the throttle control bracket in order to gain access to the minimum air adjustment screw (automatic transmission only).
5. Connect a tachometer to the engine and disconnect the idle air control motor connector.
6. Start the engine and let the engine reach normal operating temperature and the rpm to stabilize.
7. Install the special tool No. J–3307 or equivalent to the idle air passage of the throttle body.
8. Using a No. 20 torx head bit or equivalent, turn the throttle stop screw until the rpm reachers specifications (500 ± 25 rpm on the automatic models and 775 ± 25 on the manual transmission models.
9. Re-install the transmission T.V. cable into the throttle control bracket (automatic transmission only).
10. Shut down the engine and remove the special tool or equivalent from the throttle body.
11. Reconnect the idle air control motor connector and seal the drilled hole through the throttle body housing with solicone sealant or equivalent.
12. Check the throttle position sensor voltage (as outlined in the fuel injection section of this manual) and reinstall the air cleaner and thermac vacuum lines.

1985 AND LATER FIREBIRD AND CAMARO WITH TUNED PORT INJECTION

NOTE: The idle speed should only be adjusted if it is absolutely necessary.

1. Using an awl or equivalent, pierce the idle stop plug and remove it.
2. Leave the idle air control motor connected and ground the diagnostic lead. Turn the ignition on but do not start the engine.
3. Wait thirty seconds, and with the ignition switch still in the on position, disconnect the idle air control connector.
4. Remove the ground from the diagnostic lead and start the engine.
5. Allow the engine to go into the closed loop mode and adjust the idle screw to specifications (400 rpm on automatic transmissions and 450 rpm on manual transmissions).
6. Turn the ignition off and reconnect the idle speed control connector.
7. Adjust the throttle position sensor, start the engine and check the engine for proper idle operation.

NOTE: The above procedure is also used on the 2.8 liter Multi-port Injection system. 600 rpm (in drive) on automatic transmissions, and 800 rpm (in neutral) on the manual transmissions.

Idle Mixture Adjustment

1. If the enriched idle speed is within the enriched idle specification, the mixture is corrected. Do no further testing or adjustment.
2. If the enriched idle speed is not within specifications, remove mixture screw plug following procedures.
3. Lightly seat screws, then back out equally, just enough so engine will run.
4. Place transmission in Drive (automatic) or Neutral (manual).
5. Back each screw out (richen 1/8 turn at a time until maximum idle speed is obtained). Then set idle speed to the enriched idle specification.
6. Turn each mixture screw in (clockwise) 1/8 turn at a time until idle speed reaches value given on Emission Contol Information Label.
7. Recheck enriched speed with propane. If not within specification, repeat adjustment beginning with Step 4.
8. Check and adjust fast idle as described on Emission Control Information Label.
9. Turn off engine. Remove propane tool, connect crankcase ventilation tube. Re-connect vacuum hoses.

GENERAL MOTORS—"F" BODY
CAMARO • CAMARO BERLINETTA • FIREBIRD • TRANS AM • SE
SECTION 16

Mixture Adjustments

ROCHESTER E2ME AND E4ME CARBURETORS

The computer controlled carburetor systems are designed to provide precise control of carburetor air/fuel mixtures during all ranges of engine operation. Because of this system control, new mixture control adjustment procedures are required. For example; the previously used propane enrichment or lean drop methods of idle mixture adjustment may not be used when adjusting carburetors with a computer system because system control will change air/fuel mixtures to lean or rich as the mixture screws are adjusted rich or lean, respectively.

The system is sensitive to any change in mixture control adjustment which, if improperly set, can impair the ability of the system to maintain precise control of carburetor air/fuel mixtures. Plugs are installed in the carburetor air horn and over the idle mixture needles in the throttle body to seal the factory settings. For this reason, the mixture control adjustment points should never be changed from the original factory setting. However, if in diagnosis, the 'preliminary system performance check' indicates the carburetor to be the cause a driver performance complaint or emissions failure, or critical parts such as air horn, float bowl, throttle body, needle and seat, may be removed and the mixture control adjustments made, carefully following factory recommended procedures outlined below.

External Gauge Check

Before proceeding, a check of mixture control solenoid adjustments can be made on the vehicle. It will be necessary to modify Float Gauge J-9789-130 (used to externally check float level setting on Dualjet and Quadrajet models) by filing or grinding sufficient material off the gage to allow insertion down the vertical vent 'D' shaped hole in the air horn casting (next to the Idle Air Bleed Valve Plug).

Check that gauge freely enters 'D' vent hole and does not bind. The gauge will be used to determine total mixture control solenoid travel.

With engine off, air cleaner and gasket removed, measure mixture control solenoid travel as follows:

1. Insert modified Float Gauge J-9789-130 down 'D' shaped vent hole. Press down on gage and release, observing that gage moves freely and does not bind. With gage released (solenoid up position), reading at eye level record mark on gauge (in inches) that lines up with top of air horn casting.
2. Than, lightly press down on gauge until bottom (Solenoid down positon). Record in inches mark on gage that lines up with top of air horn casting.
3. Subtract gauge up dimension (Step 1) from gauge down dimension (Step 2) and record difference (in inches). The difference in dimensions is total Solenoid travel.
4. If total solenoid travel (Step 3 is greater or less than $3/32 \pm 1/32$ in., make mixture control Solenoid adjustments as noted below.

Mixture Control Solenoid Adjustments

If external gauge check shows the total solenoid travel is incorrect, proceed as follows:

1. Remove air horn following normal service procedures.
2. Using tool No. J-28696 or equivalent, on upper end of mixture control solenoid screw (in float bowl), turn screw clockwise until bottom lightly in bowl, counting number of turns until screw is bottomed. If number of turns counted is greater than 2½ turns, or less than 1½ turns, solenoid travel was incorrect. In this case, reset mixture control solenoid screw (see Step 3). If solenoid screw setting is correct (1½ to 2½ turns), it will be necessary to reset solenoid stop screw to air horn (see Step 4). Return solenoid screw back in previous position.

NOTE: Do not bottom Solenoid screw by forcing. To do so may result in breakage of the screw head. Do not use pliers, which would damage or break the screw.

3. From bottomed position, turn solenoid screw counterclockwise until the screw is backed out of the bowl exactly 2 turns.
4. Invert air horn and using a suitable wrench, solenoid stop screw, and spring (if used), from air horn. With stop screw removed, drive out small plug located between 'D' shaped vent holes to gain access to the solenoid stop screw (when installed). Reinstall solenoid stop screw, and spring (if used), in air horn until screw is bottomed lightly.
5. Reinstall air horn and new gasket on float bowl.
6. Install external gage in vent hole and with a suitable tool inserted in small hole in air horn, turn mixture control solenoid stop screw clockwise until total solenoid travel is within specified limits.

NOTE: The mixture control solenoid on the E2SE carburetor is not adjustable.

Idle Air Bleed Valve Adjustment

1. Before proceeding:
   a. Set parking brake and block drive wheels
   b. Disconnect and plug hoses as directed on the Emission Control Information Label under the hood.
   c. Check ignition timing as shown on the Emission Control Information Label.
   d. Connect dwell meter and tachometer to engine and mixture solenoid.
2. Start engine and run at idle until fully warm and a varying dwell is noted on the dwell meter.

It is absolutely essential that the engine is operated for a sufficient length of time to ensure the engine coolant sensor, and the oxygen sensor in the exhaust, are at full operational temperature.

3. Adjust curb idle speed, if necessary. With engine idling, observe dwell reading on the 6 cylinder scale. If within, or varying between 25–35° range, no further adjustment is necessary. If dwell does not vary and/or falls outside of the 10–50° range, perform the following:
   a. With engine off, cover primary and secondary carburetor air intake with a shop cloth to prevent metal chips from entering carburetor and engine, also place masking tape over side air top vents on bleed valve tower.
   b. Carefully align a No.35 drill (0.110 in.) on the steel rivet head holding the idle air bleed valve cover in place and drill only enough to remove rivet head. Use a drift and small hammer to drive the remainder of the rivets out of the idle air bleed value tower in the air horn casting. Use care in drilling to prevent damage to the air horn casting.
   c. Remove idle air bleed valve cover and remove remainder of rivets from inside tower in air horn casting. Discard cover after removal. Carefully blow-out any chips or dirt which may be in air bleed valve cavity. A missing cover indicates the idle air bleed valve setting has been changed from its original factory setting.
   d. While idling in drive or neutral, slowly turn valve up or down until dwell reading varies within the 25–35° range, attempting to be as close to 30° as possible. Perform this step carefully. The idle air bleed valve is very sensitive and should be turned only in ⅛ turn increments.
   e. If ater performing Step d, the dwell reading does not vary and is not within the 25–35° range, it will be necessary to remove the carburetor to gain access to the plug covering the idle mixture needles and readjust the idle mixture.

Idle Mixture Adjustment Procedure

If total solenoid travel and the idle air bleed valve dwell are correct, proceed with idle mixture adjustment.

SECTION 16 — GENERAL MOTORS—"F" BODY
CAMARO • CAMARO BERLINETTA • FIREBIRD • TRANS AM • SE

1. Remove carburetor from engine following normal service procedures, to gain access to the plugs covering the idle mixture needles.
2. Invert carburetor and drain fuel in container.
3. Place inverted carburetor on suitable holding fixture (manifold side up.) Use car to avoid damaging linkage, tubes and parts protruding from air horn. Remove idle mixture needle plug as follows:
  a. Using a punch between the 2 locator points in throttle body beneath idle mixture need plus (manifold side), break out throttle body to gain access to the idle mixture needle plug. Then, drive out hardened steel plug covering mixture needle. Hardened plus will shatter rather than remaining intact. It is not necessary to remove the plug completely; instead, remove loose pieces to allow use of the Idle Mixture Adjusting Tool J-29030 or equivalent.
  b. Use same procedure for both plugs over idle mixture needles.
4. Using Tool J-29030 or equivalent, turn each idle mixture needle inward until lightly seated. Then, back out of each mixture needle $4\frac{1}{2}$ turns.
5. Reinstall carburetor, except do not install air cleaner and gasket.
6. Start engine, run until fully warm, and repeat Idle Air Bleed Valve Adjustment until dwell reading is varying and within specified limits. If unable to achieve varying dwell and specified limits, turn each mixture needle out an additional $\frac{1}{2}$ turn. Then, reset idle air bleed valve to obtain dwell limit specifications.
7. If necessary, reset curb idle speed to specifications as shown on Emission Control Information Label.
8. Check and, if necessary, adjust fast idle speed as described on Emission Control Information Label.
9. Disconnect dwell meter and tachometer.
10. Unplug and reconnect vacuum hoses.
11. Reinstall air cleaner and gasket.

NOTE: Do not attempt to adjust the throttle position sensor (TPS) on the 2.5L engine. The TPS supplies the elctronic control module with a variable voltage. If the TPS voltage is not .45-1.25 volts (1982-84) or less than 1.25 volts (l985 and later) at the idle position, replace the TPS.

CARBURETOR

Removal and Installation

1. Disconnect the negative battery cable and remove the air cleaner assembly.
2. Disconnect the accelerator linkage and the detent cable (if equipped).
3. Separate the necessary electrical connectors and remove vacuum lines. Mark the vacuum lines for easier installation.
4. Remove the fuel line at the carburetor inlet.
5. Remove the four attaching bolts and remove the carburetor and insulator (base gasket).
6. Installation is the reverse of removal. Use a new insulator. Torque the bolts to 12 ft. lbs. (16 Nm), when using a new insulator. When retorquing an old insulator, if bolts are less than 5 ft. lbs. (7 Nm), then retorque them to 8 ft. lbs (11 Nm). If the bolts are at more than 5 ft. lbs. (7Mn), then do not retorque.

INTAKE MANIFOLD

Removal and Installation
FOUR CYLINDER

1. Disconnect the negative battery cable.
2. Remove the air cleaner, PCV valve and hose.
3. Drain the cooling system. Tag and disconnect the vacuum hoses.

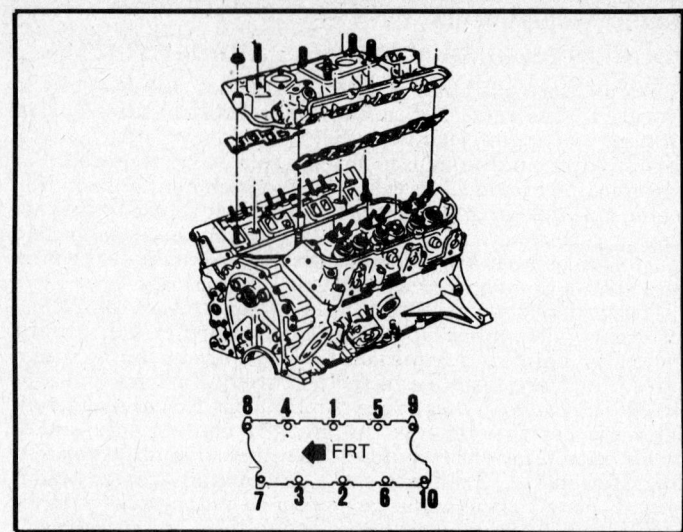

Intake manifold bolt tightening sequence for the 173 V6 engine (© General Motors Corporation)

4. Disconnect the fuel lines from the carburetor.
5. If the vehicle is equipped with EFI, remove the throttle linkage and wiring.
6. Disconnect the transmission downshift linkage.
7. Disconnect the cruise control linkage if needed.
8. Remove the heater hoses to gain working clearance.
9. Disconnect the alternator bracket and lay aside.
10. Disconnect the ignition coil assembly.
11. Remove the intake manifold retaining bolts and remove the intake manifold.
12. Installation is the reverse of the removal procedure. Fill the cooling system and check for leaks.

V6 ENGINES

1. Disconnect the negative battery cable, remove the air cleaner and drain the coolant system.
2. On models equipped with fuel injection remove the following subassemblies. The plenum, fuel rail and runner. (Refer to the fuel injection section for aid in the removal of these assemblies.)
3. Remove the spark plug wires from the spark plugs and disconnect the coil wires.
4. Remove the distributor cap along with the spark plug wires, mark the position of the distributor, remove the distributor hold down bolt and lift the distributor out of the vehicle.
5. Remove the air management hose and bracket (manual transmission only).
6. Disconnect the emission canister hoses. Remove the pipe bracket on the front left valve cover and remove the left valve cover.
7. Remove the right valve cover and the upper radiator hose. Disconnect the coolant switches.
8. Remove the manifold bolts along with the intake manifold. Discard the old gaskets and any loose RTV sealant from the front and rear ridges of the cylinder case.
9. Installation is the reverse order of the removal procedure. Be sure to apply a $\frac{3}{16}$ bead of RTV sealant on the front and rear ridge of the cylinder case.

V8 ENGINES

1. Disconnect the negative battery cable.
2. Remove the air cleaner.

GENERAL MOTORS—"F" BODY
CAMARO • CAMARO BERLINETTA • FIREBIRD • TRANS AM • SE
SECTION 16

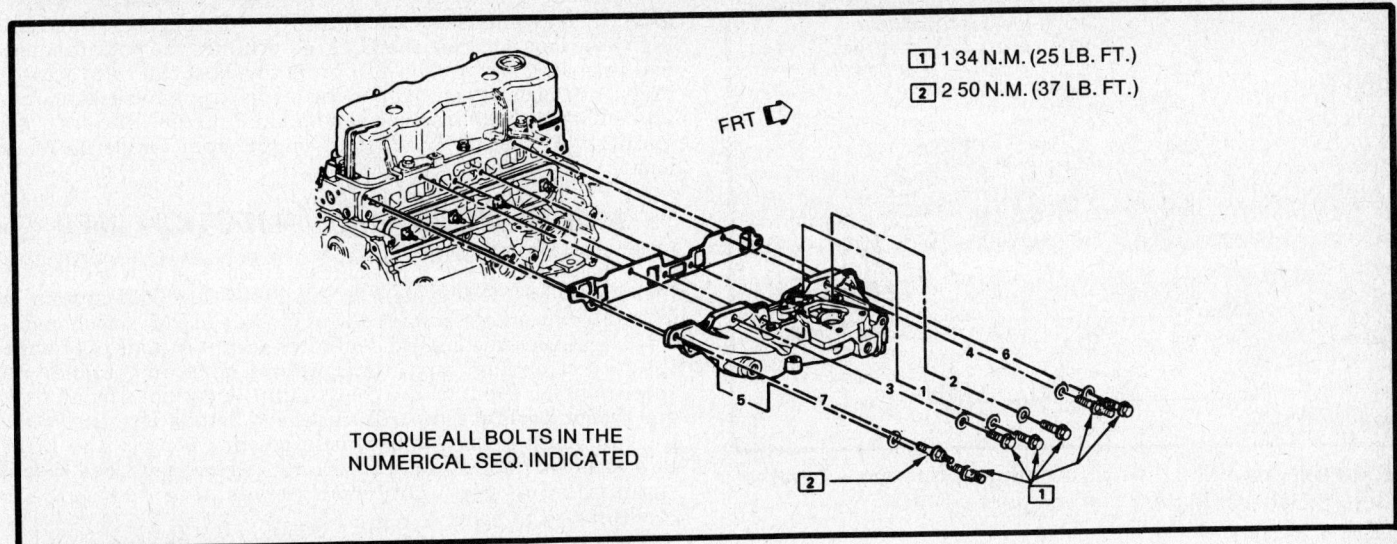

Intake manifold bolt tightening sequence—4 cylinder
(© General Motors Corporation)

3. Drain the radiator. Disconnect the upper radiator hose and the heater hoses at the manifold.
4. Disconnect the carburetor linkage and fuel line at the carburetor. Remove and tag the spark plug wires on the right side and remove all necessary wires and hoses.
5. Remove the distributor cap. Mark the position of the rotor and remove the distributor.
6. If the vehicle is equipped with A/C and/or cruise control, remove the A/C compressor with brackets and the cruise control servo assembly with bracket.
7. Loosen the alternator belt and remove the upper mounting bracket.
8. Remove the EGR solenoids and brackets. Remove the vacuum brake line.
9. Remove the intake manifold attaching bolts and remove the intake manifold.
10. Installation is the reverse of the removal procedure. Adjust the ignition timing if needed. Be sure to apply a $^{3}/_{16}$ bead of RTV sealant on the front and rear ridge of the cylinder case.

EXHAUST MANIFOLD

Removal and Installation

FOUR CYLINDER

1. Disconnect the negative battery cable.
2. Remove the air cleaner and EFI preheat tube if equipped. Remove the oxygen sensor if equipped.
3. Remove the exhaust pipe from the exhaust manifold.
4. Remove the oil dipstick tube to gain working clearance.
5. Remove the exhaust manifold bolts. Remove the exhaust manifold.
6. Installation is the reverse of the removal procedure. Inspect for exhaust leaks.

V6 ENGINES

1. Disconnect the negative battery cable and raise and support the vehicle safely.
2. Disconnect the exhaust pipe from the exhaust manifold.
3. Remove the following components on the right side.
   a. Lower the vehicle and disconnect the air management valve bracket.
   b. Disconnect the AIR hoses and AIR converter pipe.
   c. Disconnect the AIR pipe at the cylinder heads and at the manifold. Disconnect the spark plug wires.
4. Remove the following components on the left side:
   a. Remove the A/C compressor and the power steering pump.

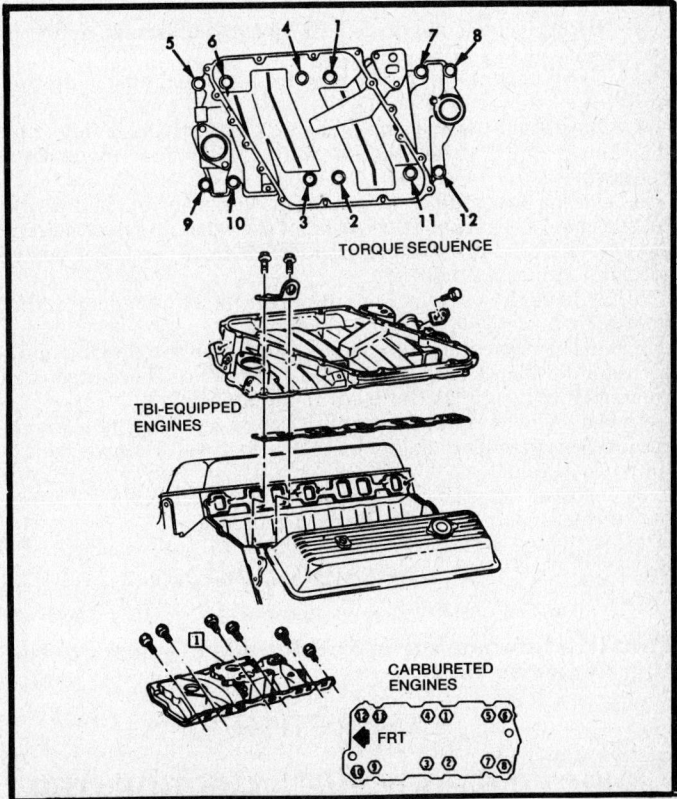

Intake manifold bolt tightening sequence of all Chevrolet-built V8 engines. Note that the lower sequence is used for all carbureted engines, whereas the upper sequence is used for all TBI—equipped engines (© General Motors Corporation)

16-27

SECTION 16
GENERAL MOTORS—"F" BODY
CAMARO • CAMARO BERLINETTA • FIREBIRD • TRANS AM • SE

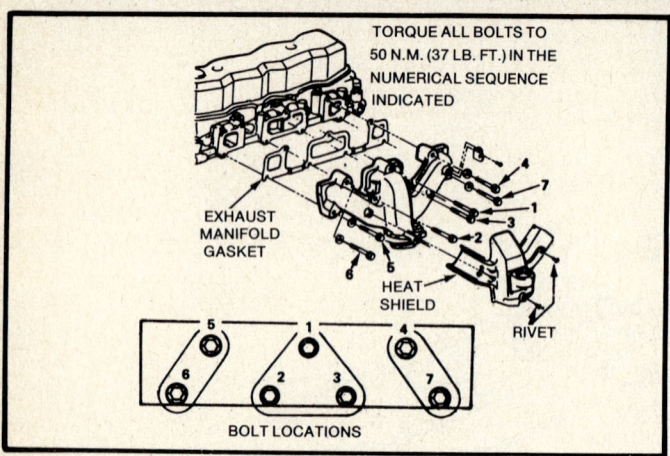

Exhaust manifild bolt tightening sequence—4 cylinder (© General Motors Corporation)

b. Remove the rear A/C adjusting brace and the lower power steering adjusting brace. Disconnect the spark plug wires.
5. Remove the exhaust manifold bolts and remove the exhaust manifold.
6. Installation is the reverse order of the removal procedure. Be sure to use new gaskets and to torque the manifold bolts to specifications.

V8 ENGINES
1. Disconnect the negative battery cable and raise and support the vehicle safely.
2. Disconnect the exhaust pipe from the exhaust manifold and lower the vehicle.
3. On the right side, remove the air cleaner, spark plugs and disconnect the vacuum hoses at the early fuel evaporator canister.
4. On the left side, remove the power steering pump and loosen the A/C bracket at the front of the head, remove the rear A/C bracket and the A/C compressor. Remove the lower power steering adjusting bracket.
5. Remove the vacuum hose at the air injection reactor (AIR) valve.
6. On the right side, remove the alternator belt and lower alternator bracket, also remove the AIR valve. Disconnect the converter AIR pipe at the back of the manifold.
7. Remove the exhaust manifold bolts, and on the left side remove the wire loom holder at the valve cover, remove the exhaust manifold.
8. Installation is the reverse order of the removal procedure, and torque the manifold bolts to specifications.

Fuel Injection System

For More Information on Fuel Injection System refer to Unit Repair Section.

DESCRIPTION

THROTTLE BODY FUEL INJECTION (TBI)

The TBI system, on Camaro/Firebird 4 cylinders and V8s (optional), is a completely electronic system which meters and delivers precise amounts of fuel and air to the engine, according to the exact engine operating requirements at any given time. The system is controlled by the same on-board computer (ECM) used with the emissions systems (CCC). Through the monitoring of various sensors, the EMC determines the optimum air/fuel ratio and signals the TBI units to adjust the ratio accordingly. TBI is designed to offer the owner trouble-free starting, immediate throttle response, and maximum fuel efficiency; regardless of weather conditions, engine rpm temperature or load.

MULTI—PORT FUEL INJECTION (MFI)

On 1984 and later non-turbocharged models, a new multi-port fuel injection (MFI) system is available. The MFI system is controlled by an electronic control module (ECM) which monitors engine operations and generates output signals to provide the correct air fuel mixture, ignition timing and engine idle speed control. Input to the control unit is provided by an oxygen sensor, coolant temperature sensor, detonation sensor, hot film air mass sensor and throttle position sensor. The ECM also receives information concerning engine rpm, road speed, transmission gear position, power steering and air conditioning.

TURNED PORT INJECTION (TPI)

This system is new for 1985 and can be found in the Camaro/Firebird with the 5.0 liter V8 engine. The introduction of this new TPI system to these engines has improved the torque and power from both engines. The induction system for the TPI is made up of large forward mounted air cleaners, a new mass airflow sensor, a cast aluminum throttle body assembly with dual throttle blades, a large extended cast aluminum plenum, individual aluminum tuned runners and a protruding dual fuel rail assembly with computer controlled injectors. The base plate is cast aluminum and incorporates the crossover portion of the tuned runners. The base plate also serves as as mounting for the fuel injectors. The individual aluminum runners are designed to provide the best tuning or frequency of air pulses within the runners and for the optimum throttle response through the driving range, thus the size so as to take advantage of the air pulses set up by the opening and closing of the intake valves. The high pressure pulses result in denser air at each intake valve, and timing the pressure pulses to occur during the value open period forces more air into the combustion chamber, which results in a more efficient cylinder charging and improved volumetric efficiency.

NOTE: On some 1985 Firebird models with the 2.8 liter multi-port fuel engine, there have been some poor start or no start conditions due to fuel fouled spark plugs. The cause of the fouled spark plugs may be a poor spray pattern from the fuel injectors. To correct this problem, remove and replace the old injectors with the new improved (part No. 17111297) which are available at the manufacturers. The new injectors have a revised pintle which in turn allows a better spray pattern to prevent the fouling of spark plugs.

FUEL INJECTOR
Removal and Installation
2.5L ENGINE WITH TBI FUEL INJECTION

1. Before removing the fuel injector assembly, relieve the fuel pressure in the fuel system as follows:
a. Remove the fuse marked fuel pump from the fuse block in the passenger compartment. Start the engine.
b. Let the engine run until the fuel supply remaining in the fuel system is exhausted. When the engine stalls, engage the starter three more times to be sure all the fuel and pressure has been run out of the fuel system.

GENERAL MOTORS – "F" BODY
CAMARO • CAMARO BERLINETTA • FIREBIRD • TRANS AM • SE

c. Turn the ignition to the off position and replace the fuel pump fuse.

CAUTION
Do not remove the four screws securing the pressure regulator to the fuel meter cover. The fuel pressure regulator includes a large spring under a heavy compression which, if accidentally released, could cause personal injury. Disassembly might also cause a fuel leak between the diaphragm and the regulator container.

2. Disconnect the negative battery cable. Remove the air cleaner assembly.
3. Remove the electrical connections to the fuel injector. Remove the five screws and lockwashers securing the fuel meter cover to the fuel meter body. Be sure to make a note of the location of the two short screws. Remove the fuel meter cover from the throttle body assembly.
4. With the fuel meter cover in place to prevent damage to the casting, use a suitable tool and lift the injector carefully until it is free from the fuel meter body.
5. Remove the small O-ring from the nozzle end of the injector. Carefully rotate the injector fuel filter back and forth and remove the filter from the base of the injector. Remove and discard the fuel meter cover gasket.
6. Remove the large O-ring and steel back-up washer from the top counterbore of the fuel meter body injector cavity.
7. Installation is the revere order of the removal procedure. Be sure to install all new gaskets, O-rings and washers. The back-up washer and large O-ring must be installed before the injector, or improper seating of the large O-ring could cause a fuel leak.

FUEL RAIL ASSEMBLY
Removal and Installation
2.8L MULTI–PORT INJECTION ENGINE

1. Before removing the fuel rail assembly, relieve the fuel pressure in the fuel system as follows:
   a. Connect fuel gauge J-34730-1 or equivalent to the fuel pressure valve (located on the fuel rail assembly). Wrap a shop towel around the fitting while connecting the gauge to avoid spillage.
   b. Install a bleed hose into a suitable container and open the fuel pressure valve to let the fuel pressure bleed off into the container.
2. Disconnect the negative battery cable. Remove the air inlet duct at the throttle body. Remove the two throttle body retaining bolts.

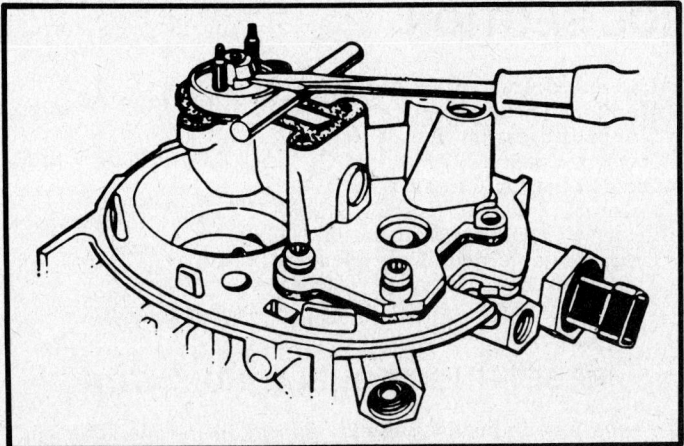

Fuel injector removal for the 2.5L TBI engine

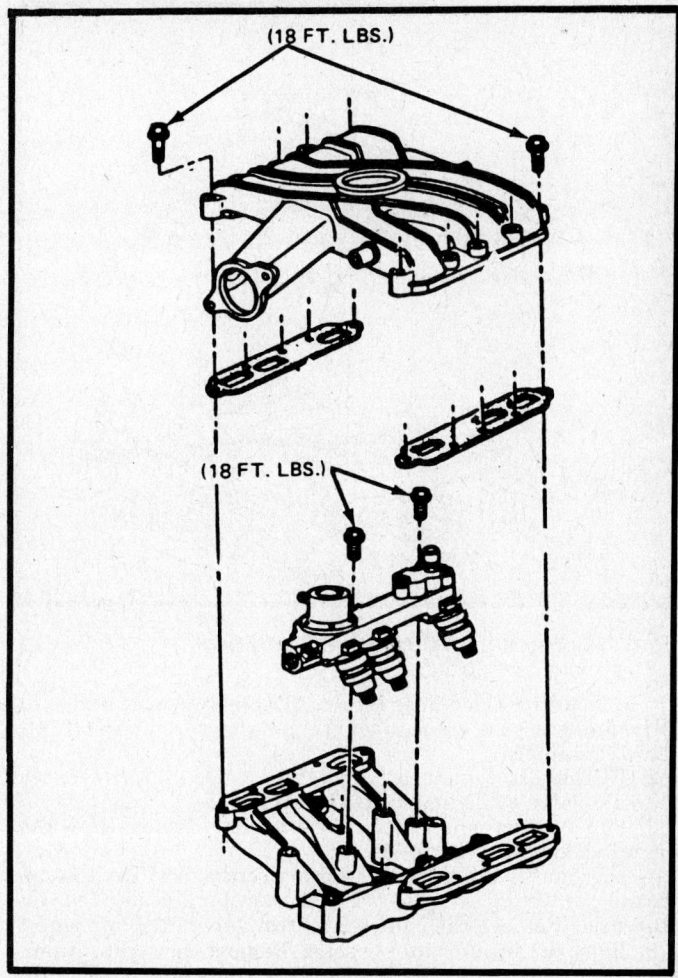

Plenum removal on the 2.8L MPI engine

3. Remove the two EGR pipe bolts. Remove the throttle cable bracket.
4. Remove the eight plenum retaining bolts and remove the plenum.
5. Remove the fuel lines. Remove the distributor cap and remove the cold start valve retaining bolt. Remove the cold start valve from the fuel rail.
6. Remove the vacuum line from the fuel pressure regulator. Remove the fuel rail retaining bolts.
7. Remove the fuel injector harness connectors. Remove the fuel rail assembly with injectors from the engine.
8. Installation is the reverse order of the removal procedure. Torque the plenum bolts to 18 ft. lbs. Replace all necessary O-rings and washers. After installation is completed, cycle the ignition on and off several times and inspect the fuel system for leaks.

FUEL RAIL ASSEMBLY
Removal and Installation
5.0L/5.7L TUNED–PORT INJECTION ENGINE

1. Before removing the fuel rail assembly, relieve the fuel pressure in the fuel system as follows:
   a. Connect fuel gauge J-34730-1 or equivalent to the fuel pressure valve (located on the fuel rail assembly). Wrap a shop towel around the fitting while connecting the gauge to avoid spillage.

SECTION 16: GENERAL MOTORS—"F" BODY
CAMARO • CAMARO BERLINETTA • FIREBIRD • TRANS AM • SE

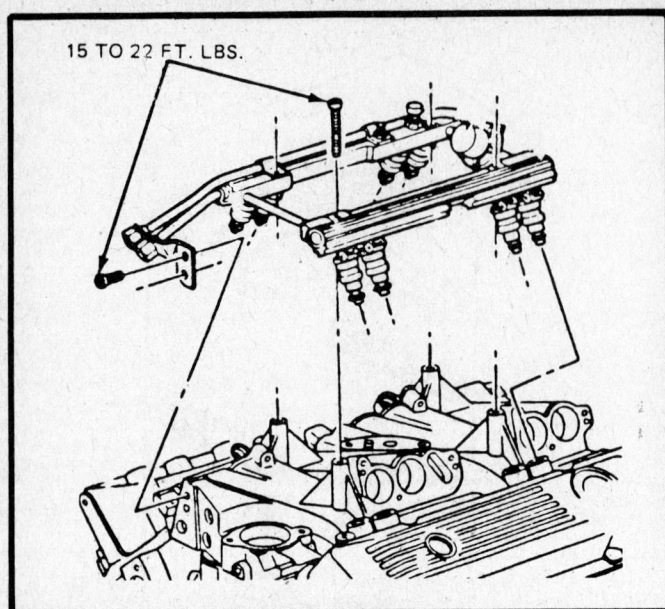

Fuel rail removal on the 5.0L TPI engine

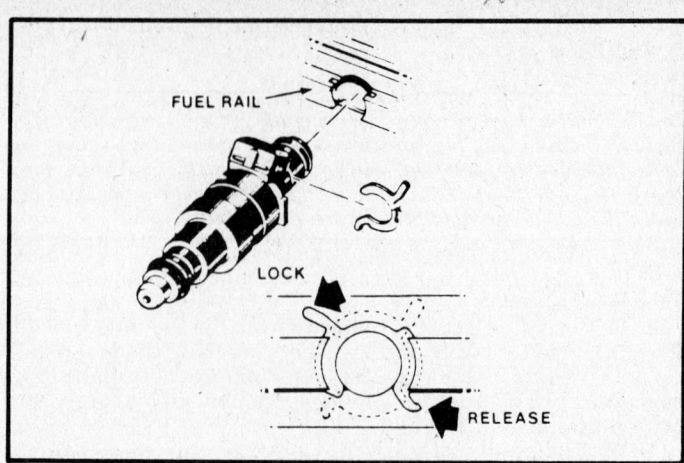

Fuel injector removal and installation

    b. Install a bleed hose into a suitable container and open the fuel pressure valve to let the fuel pressure bleed off into the container.

    2. Disconnect the negative battery cable, throttle cable, Throttle valve cable and cruise control cable.

    3. Remove the cable retaining bracket. Remove the four throttle body retaining bolts.

    4. Disconnect the throttle position sensor and the idle air control connectors. Remove the brake booster pipe and the vacuum hose. Remove the canister control valve fresh air pipe.

    5. Remove the alternator bracket. Remove the right runners and plenum retaining bolts. Remove the plenum from the engine.

    6. Remove the fuel lines. Remove the distributor cap and remove the cold start valve line and retaining bolt. Remove the cold start valve from the fuel rail.

    7. Remove the fuel injector harness connectors. Remove the left side runners. Remove the fuel rail assembly and injectors as an assembly.

    8. Installation is the reverse order of the removal procedure. Torque the fuel rail retaining bolts to 15-22 ft. lbs. Replace all necessary O-rings and washers. After installation is completed, cycle the ignition on and off several times and inspect the fuel system for leaks.

FUEL INJECTOR

Removal and Installation
ALL PORT INJECTED MODELS

    1. Remove the fuel rail assembly as previously outlined.

    2. Once the fuel rail assembly is removed, rotate the injector retaining clip(s) to the unlock position.

    3. Remove the injector from the fuel rail.

    4. Install new O-rings on the injector and lubricate them with clean engine oil before installation.

    5. Place the injector into the fuel rail and rotate the injector retainer clip(s) to the locking position. Reinstall the fuel rail assembly.

EMISSION CONTROL SECTION

1982 AND LATER

Air Injector System (AIR)
Assembly Line Communication Link (ALCL)
Barometric Absolute Pressure Sensor (BARO)
Computer Command Control (CCC)
Controlled Canister Purge (CCP)
Closed Loop Carburetor Control (CLCC)
Coolant Temperature Sensor (CTS)
Catalytic Converter
Electric Air Control (EAC)
Electric AIr Switching (EAS)
Electronic Control Module (ECM)
Exhaust Gas Recirculation (EGR)
Evaporative Emissions Control System (EECS)
Electronic Module Retard (EMR)
Electronic Spark Control (ESC)
Idle Air Bleed Valve (IABV)
Idle Speed Control Motor (ISC)
Manifold Vacuum Sensor
Manifold Pressure Sensor (MAP)
Mixture Control Solenoid (M/C)
Oxygen Sensor, Exhaust
Pulse Air Injection Reactor System (PAIR)
Positive Crankcase Ventilation (PCV)
Programmable Read Only Memory (PROM)
Thermostatic Air Cleaner (THERMAC)
Throttle Position Sensor (TPS)

RESETTING TROUBLE INDICATOR

An emissions indicator flag may appear in the odometer window of the speedometer, on General Motors vehicles. The flag could say "Sensor," "Emissions" or "Catalyst" depending on

GENERAL MOTORS—"F" BODY
CAMARO • CAMARO BERLINETTA • FIREBIRD • TRANS AM • SE

the part or assembly that is scheduled for regular emissions maintenance replacement. The word "Sensor" indicates a need for oxygen sensor replacement and the words "Emissions" or "Catalyst" indicate the need for catalytic converter catalyst replacement.

Reset

1. Remove the instrument panel trim plate.
2. Remove the instrument cluster lens.
3. Locate the flag indicator reset notches at the drivers side of the odometer.
4. Use a pointed tool to apply light downward pressure on notches, until the indicator is reset.

NOTE: When the indicator is reset an alignment mark will appear in the left center of the odometer window.

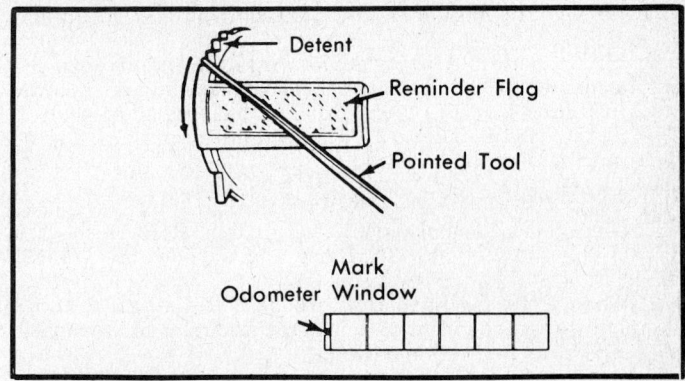

Resetting the maintenance reminder indicator—all GM vehicles (© General Motors Corporation)

ENGINE SECTION

NOTE: In the middle of the 1986 year General Motors will introduce a limited addition (1000) Camaro IROC, equipped with the 350 5.7L engine similar to the Corvette engine. There is no information on that particular vehicle at the time of the publication. If information is need on the that particular engine, refer to the Corvette section in this book.

ENGINE ASSEMBLY

Removal and Installation

FOUR CYLINDER

1. Disconnect the negative battery cable.
2. Mark the location of the hood on the hood hinges and remove the hood.
3. Drain the cooling system.
4. Remove the A/C compressor and any necessary brackets to gain working clearance.
5. Remove the radiator hoses from the engine. Remove the fan assembly. Remove the radiator shroud and radiator.
6. If the vehicle is equipped with power steering, remove the power steering pump.
7. Tag and disconnect the electrical connector at the bulkhead connector.
8. Disconnect the fuel lines at the carburetor.
9. Remove the brake hoses from the filter and the ground strap from the rear of the cylinder head.
10. Working from inside the vehicle, remove the right-hand hush panel and the ECM harness at the main ECM connector. Remove the right-hand splash shield from the right fender and feed the ECM harness out from inside the vehicle.
11. Disconnect the heater hoses from the heater core. Remove the canister hose and the throttle cable from the electronic fuel injection if equipped.
12. Raise the vehicle and support safely. Disconnect the electrical connections from the transmission.
13. Remove the flywheel dustcover. If the vehicle is an automatic, remove the torque converter to flywheel holding bolts.
14. Remove the bolts holding the bellhousing to the engine. Remove the bellhousing to engine exhaust pipe support.
15. Remove the exhaust pipe at the manifold. Remove the catalytic converter assembly.
16. Remove the starter assembly.
17. Remove the clutch fork return spring if vehicle is equipped with a manual transmission.
18. Remove the motor mount bolts.
19. Lower the vehicle and install a suitable engine lifting device.
20. Position a floor jack under the transmission to support the transmission.
21. Lift the engine from the vehicle and place in a suitable engine holding fixture.
22. Installation is the reverse of the removal procedure.

V6 AND V8

1. Disconnect the negative battery cable.
2. Mark the location of the hood and remove the hood from the vehicle.
3. Drain the cooling system. Remove the lower raditor hose and the upper fan shroud. Remove the fan assembly.
4. Remove the upper radiator hose and the coolant recovery hose. Remove the radiator.
5. Remove the transmission cooler lines.
6. Remove the heater hoses.
7. Disconnect the carburetor linkage. If the vehicle is equipped with cruise control, disconnect the detent cable.
8. Remove the vacuum brake booster line.
9. Remove the distributor cap and lay aside with the wiring to gain working clearance.
10. Disconnect all necessary wires and hoses.
11. Remove the power steering pump and lay aside.
12. Raise the vehicle support safely.
13. Remove the exhaust pipes from the manifold. Remove the dust cover from the vehicle. Remove the converter bolts.
14. Disconnect the starter wires and remove the starter assembly.
15. Remove the bellhousing bolts. Remove the motor mount through bolts.
16. Disconnect the fuel lines at the fuel pump.
17. Lower the vehicle and support the transmission using a suitable fixture.
18. Remove the air injection reaction system if equipped.
19. Attach a suitable engine lifting device and remove the engine from the vehicle.
20. Installation is the reverse of the removal procedure.

ENGINE MOUNTS

Removal and Installation

2.5L ENGINE

1. Disconnect the negative battery cable. Raise and support the vehicle safely.

16-31

SECTION 16
GENERAL MOTORS—"F" BODY
CAMARO • CAMARO BERLINETTA • FIREBIRD • TRANS AM • SE

2. Remove the engine to mount attachment bolt on the left and right side.
3. Using a suitable lifting device, raise the engine until the engine mount is clear. Remove the mount bolts and the mount.
4. Installation is the reverse order of the removal procedure. Torque the mount bolt to 34 ft. lbs. and torque the engine mount attaching bolt to 48 ft. lbs.

2.8L ENGINE

1. Disconnect the negative battery cable. Remove the top half of the radiator shroud. Raise and support the vehicle safely.
2. Remove the engine mount through bolt. Using a suitable engine lift, raise the front of the engine and remove the mount to engine bolts and remove the mount.

NOTE: Raise the engine only enough for sufficient clearance. Check for interference between the rear of the engine and the cowl panel which could cause distributor damage.

3. Installation is the reverse order of the removal procedure.

5.0L/5.7L ENGINE

1. Disconnect the negative battery cable.
2. Raise the vehicle and support safely.
3. Remove the engine mount retaining bolt from below the the frame mounting bracket.
4. Using a suitable engine lift, raise the front of the engine and remove the mount to engine bolts and remove the mount.

NOTE: Raise the engine only enough for sufficient clearance. Check for interference between the rear of the engine and the cowl panel which could cause distributor damage.

5. Installation is the reverse of the removal procedure.

Valve System

VALVE ADJUSTMENT

All engines use hydraulic lifters. Valve systems with hydraulic lifters operate with zero clearance in the valve train. The rocker arms are non-adjustable. The lifter itself will compensate if there is slack in the system but if there is excessive play, the entire system should be checked. There are two kinds of lifters in use, the Flat Tappet Valve Lifter (no roller) and the Roller Tappet Valve Lifter.

VALVE LIFTERS

Removal and Installation

1. Disconnect the negative battery cable.
2. Remove the intake manifold assembly.
3. Remove the valve cover bolts. Remove the valve covers. Discard the gasket material.
4. Loosen the rocker rams on 4 cylinder engines and turn to 1 side to clear the push rod. On V6 and V8 engines, remove the rocker arm assemblies.
5. Remove the push rods. Using the proper valve lifter removal tool, remove the valve lifters.
6. Installation is the reverse of the removal procedure. Be sure to coat the lifters in clean engine oil before installing them. Use the new gasket material on the valve covers prior to installation.

VALVE ROCKER ASSEMBLY

Removal and Installation

1. Disconnect the negative battery cable.
2. Tag and disconnect any electrical leads or hoses preventing access to the valve cover bolts.
3. Remove the valve cover bolts. Remove the valve covers. Discard the old gasket material.
4. Remove the rocker arm shaft retaining bolts. If only the push rod is to be replaced, loosen the rocker arm shaft retaining bolts and swing the arm so as to clear the push rod.
5. Remove the rocker arm shaft assembly.
6. Remove the rocker arms.
7. Installation is the reverse of the removal procedure. Use new gasket material on the valve covers. When ever new rocker arms and/or rockers rocker arm balls are being installed, coat the bearing surface of the rocker arm and rocker balls with a thin even coating of Molykote® or equivalent.

VALVE ADJUSTMENT

NOTE: The 2.5L four cylinder engine has no valve adjustment. After the rocker arm assembly has been installed, the rocker arm nut/bolt is to be torqued to 20 ft. lbs.

V6 and V8 Engines

1. After the rocker arm assembly has been installed, tighten the rocker arm nuts until all the lash is eliminated.
2. Adjust the valves when the lifter is on the base circle of the camshaft lobe as follows.
3. Crank the engine until the mark on the vibration damper lines up with '0' mark on the timing tab. The engine should be in the number one firing position. This can be determined by placing fingers on the number one rocker arms as the mark on the damper comes near the '0' mark.
4. If the valves are not moving, the engine is in the number one firing position. If the valves move as the mark comes up to the timing tab, the engine is in the number four firing position (number six firing position on the V8 engine) and should be rotated one revolution to reach the number one position.
5. With the engine in the number one firing position on the V6 engine, the following valves may be adjusted:
    a. Exhaust Valves - one, two and three.
    b. Intake Valves - one, five and six.
6. With the engine in the number one firing position on the V8 engine, the following valves may be adjusted:
    a. Exhaust Valves - one, three, four and eight.
    b. Intake Valves - one, two, five and seven.

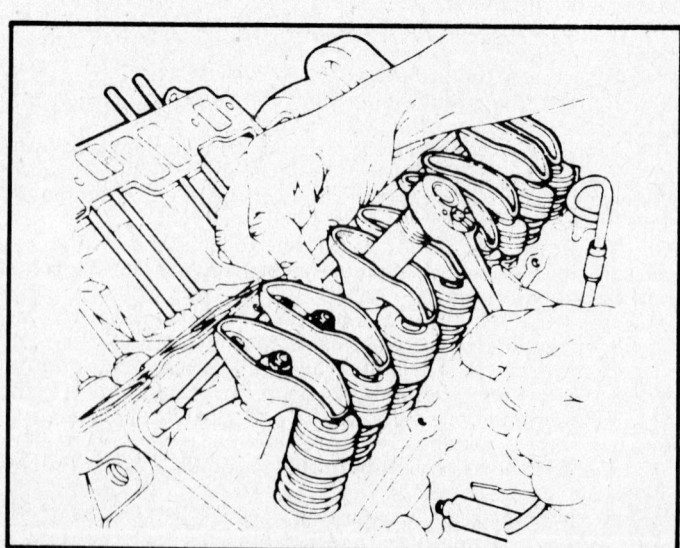

Typical valve adjustment on a V8 engine

16-32

GENERAL MOTORS—"F" BODY
CAMARO • CAMARO BERLINETTA • FIREBIRD • TRANS AM • SE

7. Back out the adjusting nut until the lash is felt at the push rod, then turn in the adjusting nut until all the lash is removed. This can be determined by rotating the push rod while turning the adjusting nut.

8. When the lash has been removed, turn the adjusting nut in one and half additional turns (this will center the lifter plunger).

9. Crank the engine one revolution until ther timing tab '0' mark and the vibration damper mark are aligned again. This is the number four firing position (number six firing position on the V8 engine).

10. With the engine in the number four position on the V6 engine, the following valves may be adjusted:
    a. Exhaust Valves - four, five and six.
    b. Intake Valves - two, three and four.

11. With the engine in the number six position on the V8 engine, the following valves may be adjusted:
    a. Exhaust Valves - two, five , six and seven.
    b. Intake Valves - three, four, six and eight.

12. Install the rocker arm covers. Start the engine and check the timing and idle speed.

CYLINDER HEADS

Removal and Installation

FOUR CYLINDER

1. Disconnect the negative battery cable.
2. Drain the engine coolant from the radiator.
3. Raise the vehicle and support safely. Disconnect the exhaust pipe. Lower the vehicle.
4. Remove the air cleaner and the oil dipstick tube.
5. Tag and disconnect any carburetor electrical connections and fuel lines. Remove any vacuum hoses. On models equipped with TBI, disconnect the throttle linkage and electrical wiring.
6. Remove the EGR baseplate if equipped and the heater hose from the intake manifold.
7. Remove the ignition coil and any other wiring connections from the intake manifold and cylinder head.
8. Remove the A/C compressor and brackets and lay side to working clearance. Remove the alternator and bracket for same reason. Remove the power steering upper bracket if so equipped.
9. Remove the throttle valve and throttle cables at the intake manifold.
10. Remove the radiator hoses and valve cover.
11. Remove the rocker arms and push rods as outlined earlier. Remove the cylinder head bolts.
12. Remove the cylinder head and discard the used gasket material.
13. Installation is the reverse of the removal procedure. Use new gasket material prior to installing the cylinder head. Apply a suitable thread sealer to the stud-bolts at both ends of the head. Torque the cylinder head bolts gradually and evenly until a final torque of 92 ft. lbs. has been reached.

V6 AND V8

1. Disconnect the negative battery cable.
2. Drain the engine coolant from the radiator. Disconnect the radiator hoses from the intake manifold.
3. Remove the intake manifold as described earlier. Remove the exhaust manifold as outlined earlier.
4. Remove the alternator lower mounting bolt and lay aside to gain working clearance.
5. If the vehicle is equipped with power steering, remove the pump and bracket to gain access.
6. Remove the rocker arm covers and the rocker assemblies. Remove the push rods.
7. Remove all vacuum hoses from the engine assembly. Tag and disconnect spark plug wires.
8. Remove the cylinder head bolts. Remove the cylinder head and discard the old gasket material.

9. Installation is the reverse of the removal procedure. Install the head gasket over the dowel pins, with the note "This Side Up" showing. On engines using a steel gasket, coat both

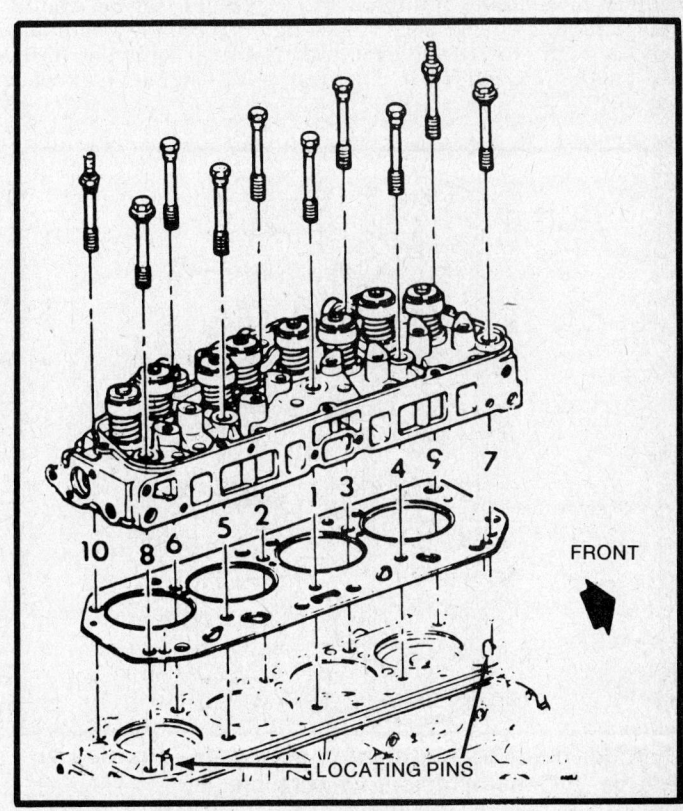

Cylinder head bolt tightening sequence — 4 cylinder
(© General Motors Corporation)

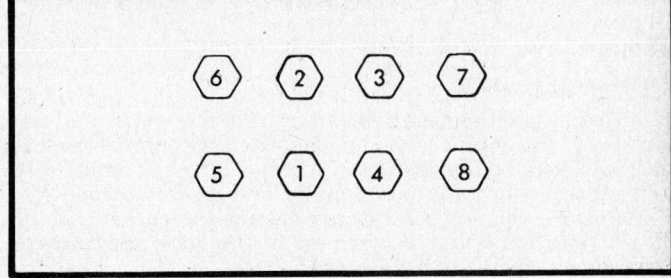

Cylinder head bolt tightening sequence — V6 engine (© General Motors Corporation)

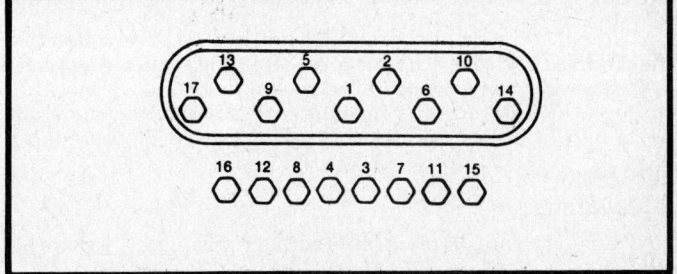

Cylinder head bolt tightening sequence — Chevrolet V8 engine (© General Motors Corporation)

16-33

SECTION 16: GENERAL MOTORS — "F" BODY
CAMARO • CAMARO BERLINETTA • FIREBIRD • TRANS AM • SE

sides with a suitable sealer. Spread the sealer evenly with a paint roller or equivalent. Too much sealer may hold the gasket away from the head or block thus causing a bad seal. Carefully guide the cylinder head over the dowel pins and onto the cylinder block. Apply a suitable thread sealer to the head bolts and tighten the head bolts finger tight. Torque the cylinder head bolts gradually and evenly until a final torque of 70 ft. lbs. on the V6 and 75 ft. lbs. on the V8 engines has been reached.

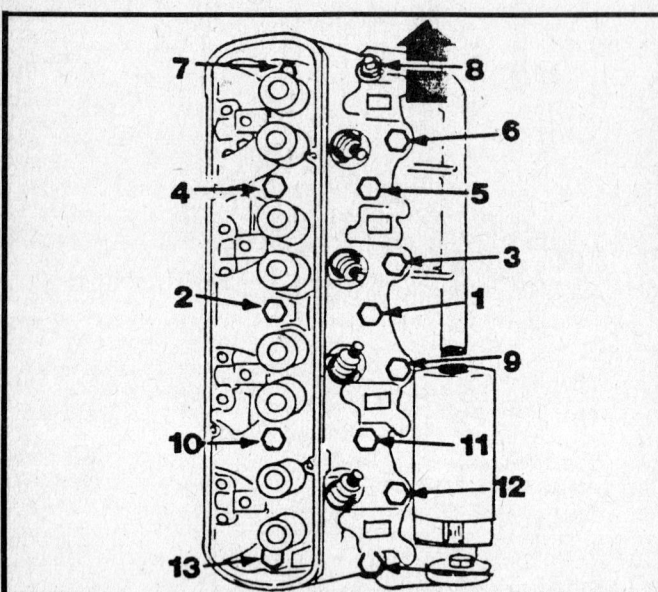

Cylinder head bolt tightening sequence — Pontiac V8 engine (© General Motors Corporation)

CAMSHAFT

Removal and Installation

FOUR CYLINDER

1. Disconnect the negative battery cable.
2. Drain the engine oil and coolant from the engine. Remove the radiator (if equipped with A/C, remove the A/C condenser).
3. Remove the water pump pulley and the fan assembly.
4. Remove the valve cover and discard the gasket. Loosen the valve rocker bolts and turn the rocker bolts and turn the rocker arms to clear the push rods.
5. Remove the oil pump drive shaft and gear assembly. (remove the spark plugs on the 83-84 models).
6. Mark the location of the distributor and remove it.
7. Remove the push rod cover, push rods, guides and valve lifters.
8. Remove the crankshaft pulley and hub assembly. Remove the timing gear cover. Remove the timing chain and gears.
9. Remove the two camshaft thrust plate screws, by working through the holes in the camshaft gear. Remove the camshaft assembly by pulling it out through the front of the engine block.

Installation

1. Coat the camshaft journals with a high quality engine oil supplement.
2. Install the camshaft assembly into the engine block, being careful not to damage the bearings or the cam.
3. Turn the crankshaft and camshaft so that the valve timing marks on the gear teeth will line up. The engine is now up on the number four cylinder firing position.
4. Install the thrust plate the engine block retaining screws and torque the screws to 88 ft. lbs. Install the timing gear cover as outlined in this section.
5. Line up and slide the crankshaft hub onto the shaft. Install the center bolt and torque it to 162 ft. lbs.
6. Install the valve lifters, push rods, push rod cover, oil pump shaft and gear assembly. Install the distributor.
7. Turn the crankshaft 360 degrees to the firing position of the number one cylinder (number one exhaust and intake valve lifters both are on the base circle of the camshaft and timing mark on the harmonic balancer indexed with the top dead center mark on the timing pad). Install the distributor in the original position and align the shaft with the rotor arm towards the number one plug contact.
8. Position the push rods and install the rocker arms and rocker arm bolts. Torque the rocker arm bolts to 20 ft. lbs.
9. Install the water pump pulley and fan assembly. Install the A/C condenser and recharge the A/C system. Install the radiator and shroud assembly. Refill engine coolant and engine oil to specifications.
10. Start the vehicle and check for leaks, and check for proper operation.

V6 ENGINE

1. Remove the engine from the vehicle and place n a suitable holding fixture.
2. Remove the valve covers and remove the valve lifters assemblies.
3. Remove the crankshaft front cover from the engine.
4. Remove the fuel pump bolts. Remove the fuel pump and push rod.

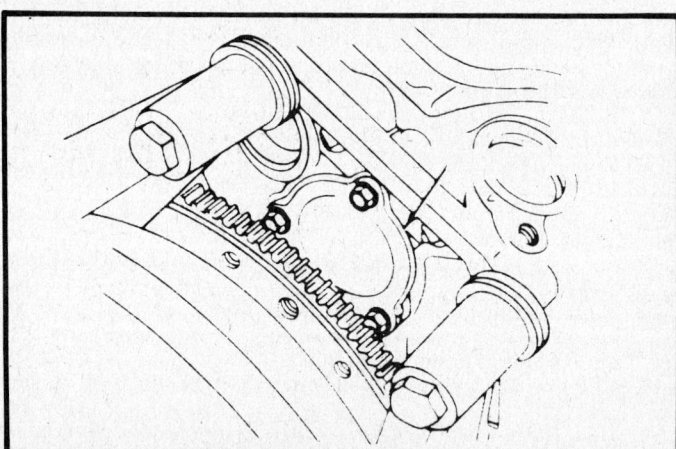

Location of the camshaft rear cover

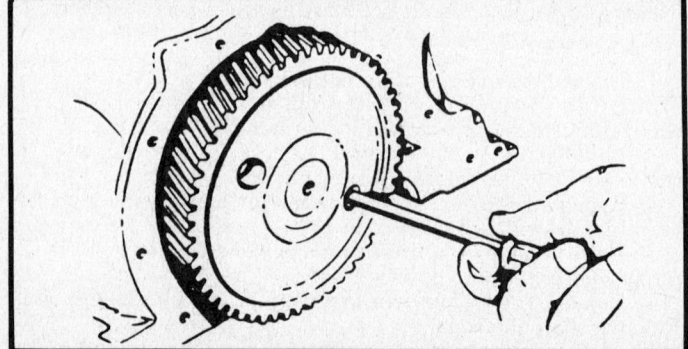

Removing the two thrust plate retaining screws

16-34

GENERAL MOTORS—"F" BODY
CAMARO • CAMARO BERLINETTA • FIREBIRD • TRANS AM • SE
SECTION 16

5. Remove the timing chain and the sprocket.
6. Remove the camshaft rear cover. Remove the camshaft from the engine.
7. Installation is the reverse of the removal procedure. Lubricate the camshaft with engine oil before installing. Be sure to seal the camshaft rea cover with a suitable sealant.

V8 ENGINES

1. Disconnect the negative battery cable and drain the cooling system into a suitable drain pan.
2. Remove the intake manifold as previously outlines. Remove the rocker covers, rocker arm assemblies, push rods, and lifters (be sure to note the location of each component for proper installation) as previously outlined.
3. Remove all necessary wires and hoses. Disconnect the upper and lower transmission cooler lines.
4. Remove the radiator shroud assembly and radiator. Remove the front grille if necessary. Remove the cooling fan.
5. Remove the power steering pump if so equipped. Remove the drive belts, crankshaft pulley and torsional damper.
6. Remove the A/C compressor mount bolts, brackets, accumulator and compressor (if so equipped) and position it out of the way. Remove the air injection pump with brackets and set it aside.
7. Remove the water pump assembly, remove the front engine cover. Remove the fuel pump push rod. Rotate the crankshaft and align the timing marks.
8. Remove the camshaft bolts, gear and chain. Install two $\frac{5}{16}$ in. x 4 in. bolts in the camshaft bolt holes and carefully remove the camshaft.

NOTE: The camshaft sprocket is a light fit. If the sprocket does not come off easily a light blow on the lower edge of the sprocket with a soft face mallet should dislodge the sprocket.

9. Installation is the reverse order of the removal procedure. Lubricate the camshaft journals with a suitable engine oil supplement, before installing the camshaft. Once the camshaft has been installed, install the chain on the camshaft sprocket. Hold the sprocket vertically with the chain hanging down and align the marks on the camshaft and crankshaft sprockets.
10. Align the dowel in the camshaft sprocket with the dowel hole in the camshaft sprocket then install the sprocket on the camshaft. Draw the camshaft sprocket onto the camshaft using the mounting bolts. Torque the mounting bolts to 13-23 ft. lbs.

PISTON AND ROD POSITIONING

Typical piston and rod positioning with piston notches facing forward
(© General Motors Corporation)

Piston and rod positioning for the V6 engine

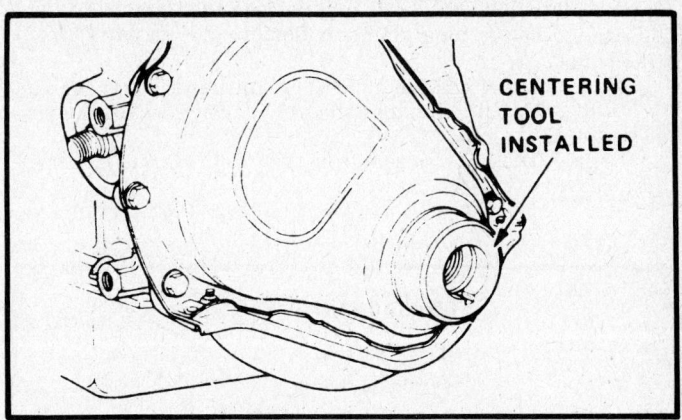

Installing the front cover on the 2.5L engine

TIMING CASE COVER/OIL SEAL

Removal and Installation
FOUR CYLINDER

1. Disconnect the negative battery cable. Drain the cooling system and remove the drive belts.
2. Remove the center bolt and slide the hub and pulley(s) from the crankshaft. Remove the alternator lower bracket. Remove the front engine mount to cradle nuts.
3. Install the Engine Support Fixture J-28467 or equivalent and raise the engine. Remove the engine to mount bolts and remove the support bracket and mount as an assembly. Remove the oil pan-to-front cover attaching screws.
4. Remove the front cover-to-block attaching screws. Pull the cover slightly forward enough to allow cutting of the front oil seal.
5. Using a suitable cutting tool, cut the front oil pan seal flush with the cylinder block on both sides of the timing case cover.
6. Remove the front cover and the attached portion of the front oil pan seal. Remove the front cover gasket.

Installation

1. Clean the mating surfaces of the engine block and front cover. Using a suitable cutting tool, cut the tabs off of the new oil pan front gasket. Install the gasket, coated with sealer on, onto the front cover. Be sure to press the tips into the holes pro-

16–35

SECTION 16: GENERAL MOTORS—"F" BODY
CAMARO • CAMARO BERLINETTA • FIREBIRD • TRANS AM • SE

vided in the cover. Apply a suitable silcone sealer to the joint at the oil pan and engine block and on the timing gear cover at block mating surfaces.

2. Install Crankshaft Seal Seal Centering Fixture J-3499 or equivalent in the front cover seal. Install the front cover on the block. Install and temporarily tighten the two oil pan to front cover bolts. Install the front cover to block bolts and torque them to 90 in. lbs. Remove the centering tool and finish the installation by reversing the removal procedure.

V6 ENGINE

1. Disconnect the negative battery cable.
2. Remove the drive belts and pulley. If equipped with A/C, remove the compressor from the mounting bracket and lay it aside. Then remove the compressor mounting bracket. Remove the A.I.R. pump and bracket if so equipped.
3. Drain the cooling system. Disconnect the lower radiator hose at the front cover and the heater at the water pump. Remove the water pump. Raise the vehicle and support safely.
4. Remove the crankshaft pulley. Remove the torsional damper retaining bolt.
5. Install tool J–23523 or equivalent on the torsional damper. Remove the torsional damper. Remove the oil pan to front cover bolts.
6. Lower the vehicle. Remove the remaiming front cover-to-block attaching bolts. Remove the front cover. Discard the gasket material.
7. Remove the front oil seal from the front cover using a suitable tool.

8. Installation is the reverse of the removal procedure. Be sure to apply a continuous bead of a suitable sealant to the front cover sealing surface. Then apply a continuous bead of a suitable sealer to the oil pan surface of the front cover. Alos be sure to install the components within five minutes of sealant application. Install the new oil seal so that the open end of the seal is facing the inside of the cover.

V8 ENGINES

1. Disconnect the negative battery cable. Drain the cooling the system into a suitable drain pan.
2. Remove the drive belts and accessory belts. Remove the fan assembly and fan pulley. Using Torsional Damper Puller J-23523 or equivalent remove the torsional damper.
3. On engines equipped with TBI, remove the air injection pump pulley and air management valve adapter, then remove the air injection pump. Disconnect the fuel inlet and outlet lines at the TBI unit.
4. On vehicles equipped with A/C, remove the rear A/C compressor braces and lower the A/C mount bolts. Remove the compressor bracket and nuts at the water pump. Slide the mounting bracket forward and remove the compressor mount bolt. Disconnect the wires at the compressor and lay the unit aside. Disconnect the air injection hose at the right exhaust manifold.
5. Remove the compressor mount bracket. Remove the upper air injection pump bracket with the power steering reservoir. Remove the lower air injection pump bracket.
6. Disconnect the heater and radiator hoses to the water pump. Remove the water pump. Remove the front cover reatining bolts, cover and old gasket.

Installation

1. Clean the gasket surfaces. Apply a suitable sealer to the new gasket. Apply a suitable RTV sealant to the joint formed where the oil pan meets the cylinder block, be sure to trim the excess material the sticks out from the junction. Place the gasket on the cover and install the cover to oil pan seal. The rest of the installation procedure is the reverse order of the removal procedure.

TIMING GEARS

Removal and Installation
FOUR CYLINDER

1. Disconnect the negative battery cable.
2. Remove the camshaft as prviously outlined.
3. With the camshaft removed, use a press plate and Adapter J-971 or equivalent on the press to remove the timing gear from the camshaft. Be sure to place the camshaft through the opening in the tools on the table of the press and press the camshaft out of the timing gear. Position the thrust plate so that the woodruff key in the camshaft does no damage during removal.
4. If the crankshaft gear needs to be replaced, use a suitable gear puller to remove it from the crankshaft.

Installation

1. Support the camshaft at the back of the front journal in a arbor press using the press plate adaptors. Install the spacer ring and thrust plate over the end of the camshaft.
2. Install the woodruff key in the shaft keyway. Install the timing gear on the camshaft until it bottoms against the gear ring spacer ring. Measure the end clearance of the thrust plate. The clearance should be .0015-.0050 in.
3. If the clearance is less than specified, replace the spacer ring. If the clearance is more than specified, replace the thrust plate.

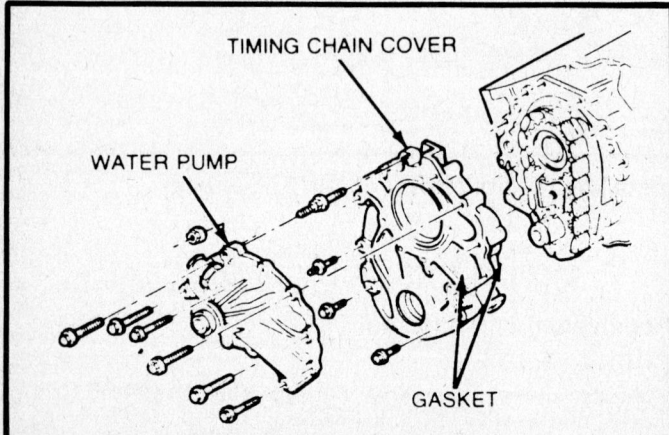

Front cover installation on the V6 engine

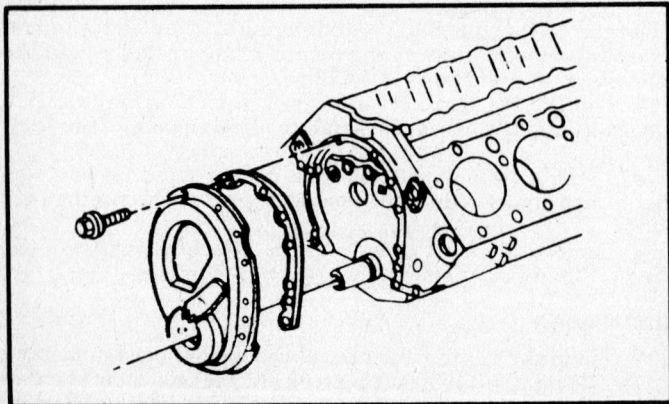

Front cover removal on the V8 engine

GENERAL MOTORS—"F" BODY
CAMARO • CAMARO BERLINETTA • FIREBIRD • TRANS AM • SE

4. Coat the camshaft journals with a high quality engine oil supplement.
5. Install the camshaft assembly into the engine block, being careful not to damage the bearings or the cam.
6. Turn the crankshaft and camshaft so that the valve timing marks on the gear teeth will line up. The engine is now up on the number four cylinder firing position.
7. Install the thrust plate the engine block retaining screws and torque the screws to 88 ft. lbs. Install the timing gear cover as outlined in this section.
8. Line up and slide the crankshaft hub onto the shaft. Install the center bolt and torque it to 162 ft. lbs.
9. Install the valve lifters, push rods, push rod cover, oil pump shaft and gear assembly. Install the distributor.
10. To install the distributor, turn the crankshaft 360 degrees to the firing position of the number one cylinder (number one exhaust and intake valve lifters both are on the base circle of the camshaft and timing mark on the harmonic balancer indexed with the top dead center mark on the timing pad) Install the distributor in the original position and align the shaft with the rotor arm towards the number one plug contact.
11. Position the push rods and install the rocker arms and rocker arm bolts. Torque the rocker arm bolts to 20 ft. lbs.
12. Install the water pump pulley and fan assembly. Install the A/C condenser and recharge the A/C system. Install the radiator and shroud assembly. Refill engine coolant and engine oil to specifications.

V6 AND V8

1. Remove the timing chain cover as previously outlined in this section. Remove the crankshaft oil slinger if so equipped.
2. Crank the engine until the No. 1 piston is at TDC and the timing marks on the camshaft and crankshaft sprockets are aligned (No.4 firing).
3. Remove the camshaft sprocket bolts and remove the camshaft sprocket and chain.

NOTE: The sprocket is a light fit on the camshaft. If the sprocket does not come off easily, use a plastic mallet and strike the lower edge of the sprocket. This should dislodge the sprocket allowing it to be removed from the shaft.

4. Install the timing chain on the camshaft sprocket and lube the thrust surface with Molykote or equivalent.
5. Hold the sprocket vertically with the chain hanging down and align the marks on the camshaft and crankshaft sprockets.
6. Align the dowel in the camshaft with the dowel hole in the camshaft sprocket, and install the sprocket on the camshaft.
7. Slower and evenly draw the camshaft sprocket onto the camshaft using the mounting bolts and torque the bolts to specifications.

NOTE: Do not drive the sprocket onto the camshaft, for this could cause the rear freeze plug to be dislodged.

8. Lubricate the timing chain and install the timing chain cover as previous outlined.

Lubrication

OIL PAN

Removal and Installation

2.5L FOUR CYLINDER ENGINE

1. Disconnect the negative battery cable at the battery.
2. Raise the vehicle and support it safely with jackstands.

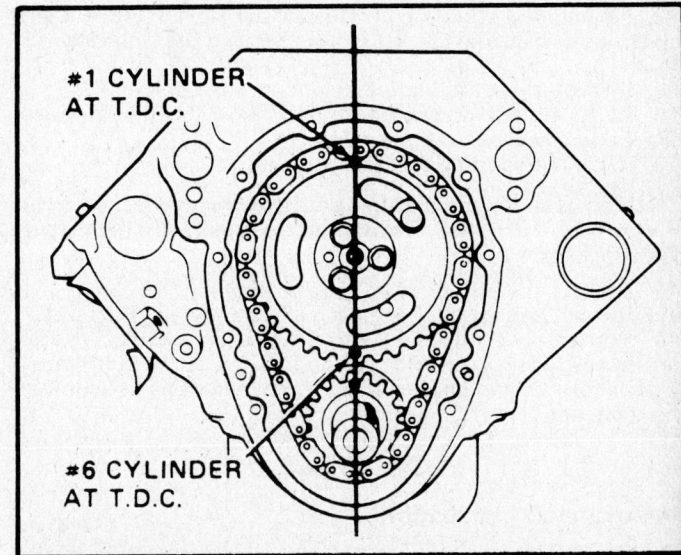

Aligning the timing gears on the V6 engine

Aligning the timing gears on the V8 engine

3. Drain the engine oil.
4. Disconnect the exhaust pipe at the manifold.
5. Loosen the exhaust pipe at the manifold.
6. Remove the starter assembly, if necessary.
7. Remove the flywheel dust cover, if necessary.
8. Remove the front engine mount through-bolts.
9. Carefully raise the engine enough to provide sufficient clearance to lower the oil pan.
10. Remove the oil pan retaining bolts and remove the oil pan.
11. Clean all old RTV from the mating surfaces.
12. Install the rear gasket into the rear main bearing cap and apply a small amount of RTV where the gasket engages into the engine block.
13. Install the front gasket.
14. Install the side gaskets, using grease as retainer. Apply a small amount of RTV where the side gaskets meet the front gasket.
15. Install the oil pan.

16-37

SECTION 16

GENERAL MOTORS—"F" BODY

CAMARO • CAMARO BERLINETTA • FIREBIRD • TRANS AM • SE

NOTE: Install the oil pan-to-timing cover bolts last, as these holes will not align until the other pan bolts are snug.

16. The remainder of the installation procedure is performed in the reverse of removal.

V6 AND V8

1. Disconnect the negative battery cable at the battery. Remove the air cleaner assembly. Remove the distributor cap and lay it aside.
2. Remove the upper half of the fan shroud assembly.
3. Raise the vehicle and support it safely with jackstands.
4. Drain the engine oil.

CAUTION
Be sure that the catalytic convertor is cool before proceeding.

5. Remove the air injection pipe at the catalytic convertor. remove the catalaytic converter hanger bolts. Remove the torque converter dust shield.

NOTE: On some vehicles equipped with manual transmissions, it may be necesary to remove the oil filter in order to remove the dust shield.

6. Remove the exhaust pipe at the manifolds.
7. Remove the starter bolts, loosen the starter brace, then lay the starter aside. On V8 models remove the front starter brace.
8. Remove the front engine mount through bolts.
9. Raise the engine enough to provide sufficient clearance for oil pan removal.
10. Remove the oil pan bolts.

NOTE: If the front crankshaft throw prohibits removal of the pan, turn the crankshaft to position the throw horizontally.

11. Remove the oil pan from the vehicle.
12. Remove all old RTV from the oil pan and engine block.
13. Run a ⅛ in. bead of RTV found the oil pan sealing surface. Remember to keep the RTV on the INSIDE of the bolt holes.
14. Install the pan and reverse the removal steps to complete the operation.

OIL PUMP

Removal and Installation

ALL MODELS

1. Raise the vehicle and support safely.
2. Drain the oil pan.
3. Remove the oil pan as described earlier in this section. Discard the old gasket material.
4. Remove the oil pump bolts and the bolt or nuts from the main bearing cap. Remove the oil pump. On the V6 and V8 models remove the pump with the extension shaft.
5. Installation is the reverse of the removal procedure. Use a new gasket or equivalent prior to installing. All parts should be coated with clean engine oil before installation.

REAR MAIN OIL SEAL

Removal and Installation

FOUR CYLINDER

1. Disconnect the negative battery cable and raise and support vehicle safely.
2. Remove the transmission assembly and if the vehicle is equipped with a manual transmission remove the clutch assembly also.
3. Remove the bell housing and the flywheel.

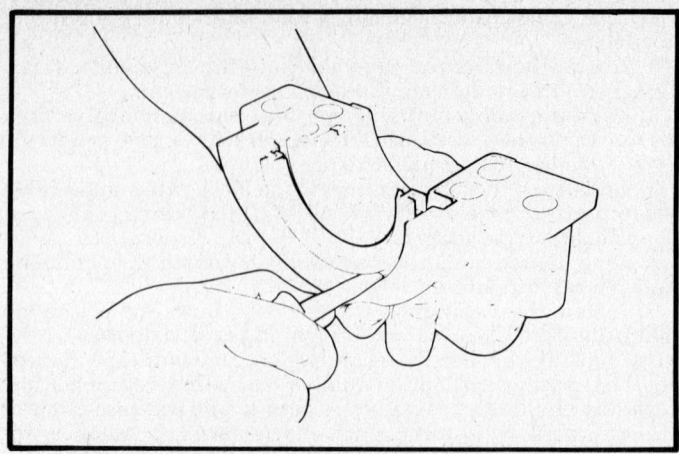

Removing the bottom half of the seal

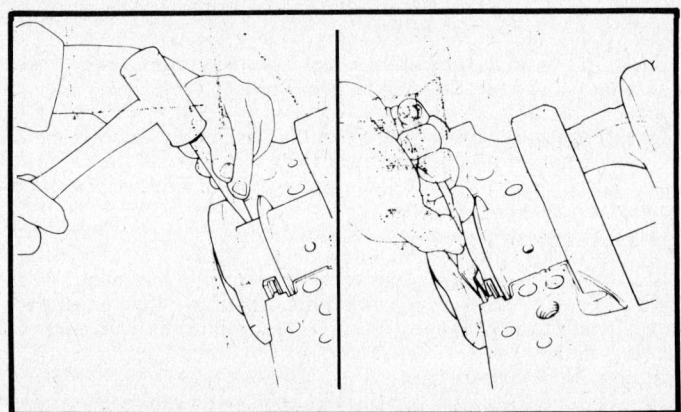

Removing the top half of the seal

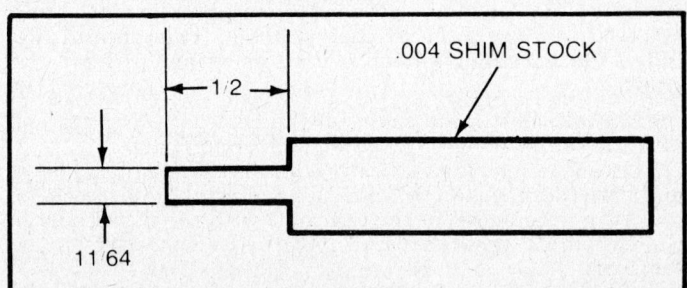

Rear oil seal installation tool

4. Using a suitable tool pry the old seal out of the engine block, be careful not to scratch or gouge the crankshaft or the seal surface.
5. Clean the block to seal mating surface. Installation is the reverse of the removal procedure. Be sure to coat the outside surface of the seal with engine oil and install the seal with the lip toward the engine.

1983-84 V6 AND 1983-85 V8 ENGINES

1. Disconnect the negative battery cable.
2. Drain the oil pan. Remove the oil pan.
3. Remove the rear main bearing cap.
4. Remove the oil seal from the bearing cap.
5. To remove the upper half of the seal, use a small hammer to tap a brass pin punch on one end of the seal until it

GENERAL MOTORS—"F" BODY
CAMARO • CAMARO BERLINETTA • FIREBIRD • TRANS AM • SE

prodtrudes far enough to be removed with a suitable pair of needle nose pliers.

Installation

NOTE: Before going on with the installation procedure, fabricate a seal installer using a piece of .004 in. shim stock (refer to the illustration).

1. Clean all sealant and foreign material from the cylinder case bearing cap and crankshaft, using non-abrasive cleaner. Inspect the components for nicks, scratches, burrs, and machining defects at all sealing surfaces, case assembly and crankshaft.
2. Coat the new seal lips and seal bead with a light engine oil, use care to prevent the oil from reaching the seal mating ends.
3. Position the tip of the of the installation tool between the crankshaft and the seal seat in the cylinder case.
4. Position the seal between the crankshaft and the tip of the tool so that the seal bead is in contact with the tip of the tool. Be sure that the oil seal lip is positioned toward the front of the engine.
5. Roll the seal around the crankshaft using the tool as a "shoe-horn", feeding the seal into the cap using light pressure with the thumb and finger. Install the bearing cap to the case with a sealant applied to the cap to case interface being careful to keep the sealant off the seal split line.
6. Install the rear main bearing cap (with new seal) and torque to 10-12 ft. lbs. Tap the end of the cranksahft rearward then forward with a lead hammer. This will line up the thrust surfaces. Retorque the bearing cap to specifications. Complete the installation by revering the removal procedure.

1985 AND LATER V6 ENGINE

1. Disconnect the negative battery cable and raise and support the vehicle safely.
2. Remove the transmission assembly and if the vehicle is equipped with a manual transmission, remove the clutch assembly also.
3. Remove the bell housing assembly and flywheel.
4. Insert a suitable seal puller through the dust lip in the seal and pry out the seal by pulling the handle of the seal puller towards the crankshaft. Be careful not to scratch or gouge the crankshaft outer diameter with the seal removal tool.
5. Clean the seal mating surface. To install the seal special tool J–34686 or equivalent.

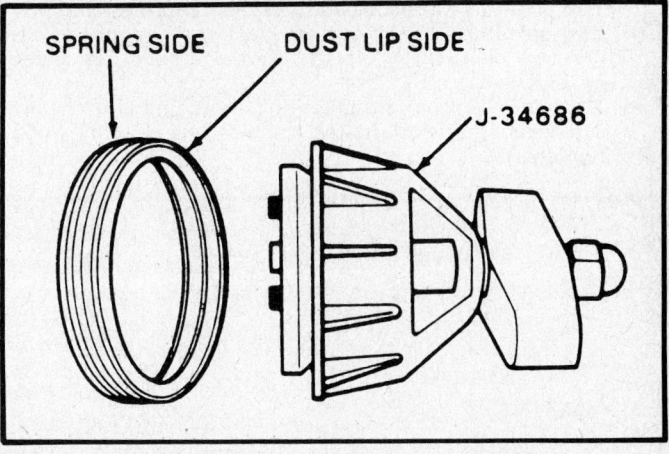

Installing the rear main seal on the seal installation tool (© General Motors Corporation)

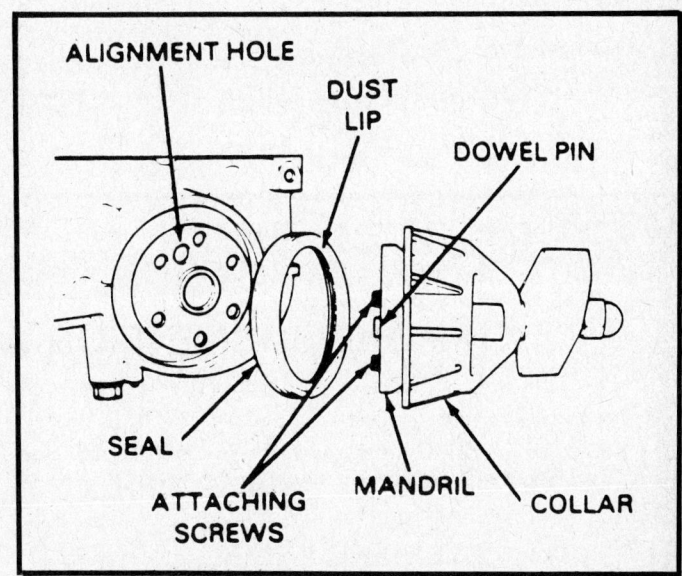

Installing the rear main seal
(© General Motors Corporation)

6. Apply a light coat of oil to the inner diameter of the new seal and install the seal over the seal installer and slide the seal up on the seal installer until back of the seal (dust lip) bottoms out squarely against the collar of the tool.
7. Align the dowel pin of the tool with the dowel pin hole in the crankshaft and attach the tool to the crankshaft. Torque the attaching screw by hand to 2–5 ft. lbs.
8. Turn the "T" handle of the tool so that the collar of the tool pushed the seal into the bore. Turn the handle until the collar is tight against the engine case. This will insure that the seal is sealed properly.
9. Loosen the "T" handle of the tool until it comes to a stop and remove the attaching screw. Make sure that the seal is seated squarely in its bore.
10. The installation of the other components is the reverse order of the removal procedure.

1986 AND LATER V8 ENGINES

1. Remove the transmission as outlined in this section.
2. Remove the flywheel from the crankshaft.

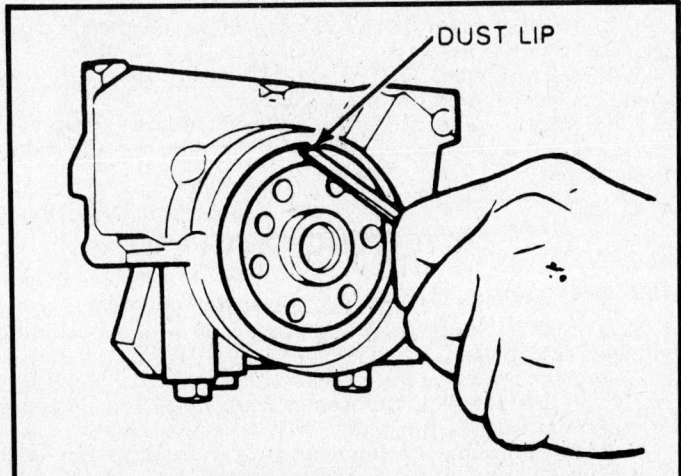

Removing the rear main seal
(© General Motors Corporation)

16–39

SECTION 16

GENERAL MOTORS—"F" BODY
CAMARO • CAMARO BERLINETTA • FIREBIRD • TRANS AM • SE

3. Using the notches provided in the seal retainer on the engine, use a suitable tool and pry the seal out of the retainer. Be careful not to nick or scratch the crankshaft sealing surface when removing the seal.

4. Lubricate the inner diameter and out diameter of the new seal with clean engine oil. Install the new seal on tool J-35621 or equivalent.

5. Thread the screws of the seal installer into the crankshaft. Tighten the screws snugly to insure that the seal will be installed squarely over the crankshaft.

6. Tighten the wing nut on the seal installer unitl it bottoms out. Remove the seal installer from the crankshaft.

7. Install the flywheel and transmission as outlined in this section.

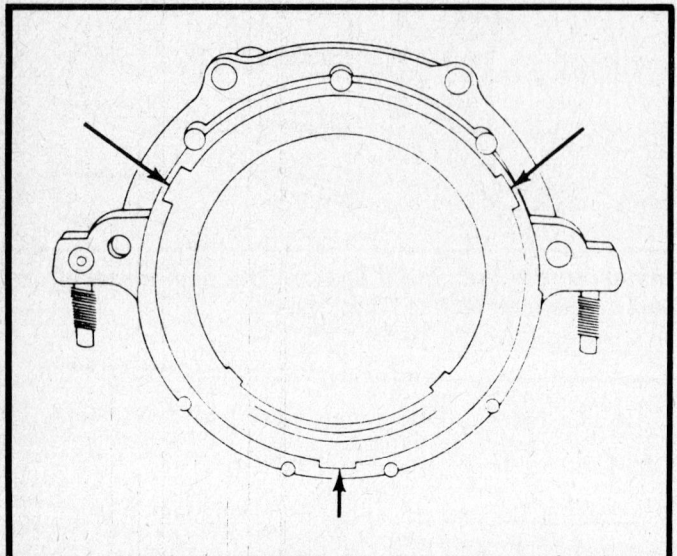

Removing the seal from the seal retainer

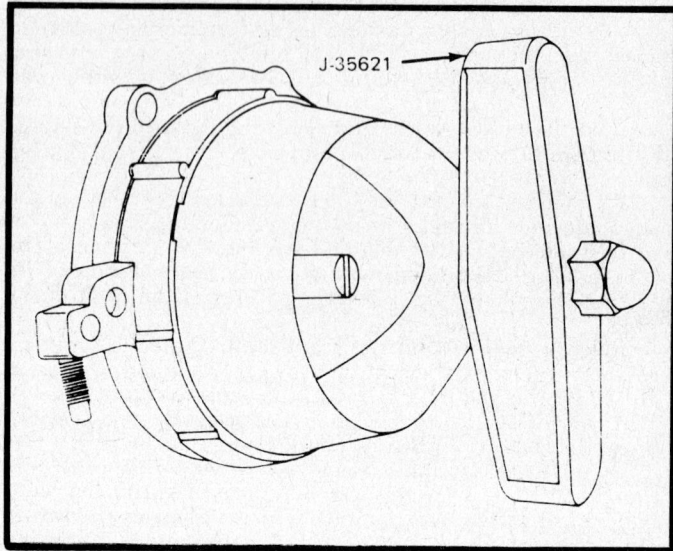

Installing the rear main seal

FRONT SUSPENSION AND STEERING SECTION

For Front Suspension Services refer to Unit Repair Section. For Steering Gear Overhaul refer to Unit Repair Section.

STEERING WHEEL

Removal and Installation
STANDARD WHEEL

CAUTION

Disconnect the battery ground cable before removing the steering wheel. When installing a steering wheel, always make sure that the turn signal lever is in the Neutral position.

1. Remove the trim retaining screws from behind the wheel. On wheels with a center cap, pull off the cap.
2. Life the trim off and pull the horn wires from the turn signal cancelling cam.

NOTE: On the tilt-telescope wheel, remove the three upper contact retaining screws, the contact and shim if used. Then remove the center star screw and lever.

3. Remove the shaft snap-ring. Remove the steering wheel nut.
4. Mark the wheel-to-shaft relationship, and then remove the wheel with a puller.

PADDED RIM WHEEL

1. Pry out the center cap and retaining. Remove the shaft snap-ring.

NOTE: One the tilt-telescope wheel, remove the three upper contact retaining screws, the contact and shim if used. Then remove the center star screw and lever.

2. Remove the steering wheel nut and washer.
3. Remove the three receiving cup screws and remove the cup belleville spring, bushing, and pivot ring.
4. Mark the wheel-to-shaft relationship, and then remove the wheel with a puller.
5. Install the wheel on the shaft, aligning the previously made marks. Tighten the nut to 30 ft. lbs.
6. Install the belleville spring (dished side up), pivot ring, bushing, and receiving cup. Install the center cap and reconnect the battery.

STEERING GEAR

Removal

1. Disconnect battery ground cable and remove coupling shield if so equipped.
2. Remove retaining nuts, lock washers, and bolts at steering coupling to steering shaft flange. Disconnect and plug power steering lines, if equipped.
3. Remove pitman arm nut and washer from pitman shaft and mark relation of arm position to shaft.
4. Remove pitman arm with Tool J-6632 or equivalent.
5. Remove screws securing steering gear to frame and remove gear from vehicle.

16-40

Installation

NOTE: The original equipment type of grade of fasteners must be maintained in order to retain vehicle safety standards.

1. Place gear into position so that steering coupling mounts properly to flanged end of steering shaft. Secure gear to frame with washers and bolts. Torque all gear to frame fasteners to 70 ft. lbs.

NOTE: Be sure the coupling reinforcement is bottomed on the wormshaft so that the coupling bolt passes through the undercut on the wormshaft.

2. Secure steering coupling to flanged end of steering column with lockwashers and nuts. Maintain coupling adjustments. Torque nuts to 20 ft. lbs.

NOTE: To check for proper steering column to flange clearance and coupling adjustments refer to steering column removal and installation procedures.

3. Install pitman arm, aligning marks made during removal, and with washer and retaining nut. Torque to 185 ft. lbs.
4. Install coupling shield and connect battery ground cable. Connect power steering lines, if equipped. Bleed the system.

Bleeding The Hydraulic System

1. Fill the fluid reservoir to the proper level and let remain undisturbed for at least two minutes. Start vthe engine and let it run momentarily. shut the engine of and add to the fluid if needed. Keep repeating this procedure until the fluid level remains constant after running the engine.
2. Raise and support safely the front of the vehicle so that the wheels are off the ground. Increase the engine speed to approxitmately 1500 rpm.
3. Turn the wheels to the right and left lightly contacting the wheel stops. Lower the vehicle and turn the wheel right and left.
4. Shut the engine off, check the fluid level and add as necessary. If the fluid is extremely foamy, allow the vehicle to stand a few minutes with the engine off and then repeat the above procedure again.

FRONT WHEEL BEARINGS

Adjusment

1. Remove dust cap from hub.
2. Remove cotter pin from spindle and spindle nut.
3. Tighten the spindle nut to 16 Nm (12 ft. lbs.) while turning the wheel assembly forward by hand to fully seat the bearings. This will remove any grease or burrs which could cause excessive wheel bearing play later.
4. Back off the nut to the 'just loose' position.
5. Hand tighten the spindle nut. Loosen spindle nut until either hole in the spindle lines up with a slot in the nut, not more than half flat.
6. Install new cotter pin. Bend the ends of the cotter pin against nut, cut off extra length to ensure ends will not interfere with the dust cap.
7. Measure the looseness in the hub assembly. There will be from 0.001–0.005 in. (0.03–0.13 mm) end play when properly adjusted.
8. Install dust cap on hub.

POWER STEERING PUMP

Removal and Installation

1. Remove the hoses at the pump and tape the openings shut to prevent contamination. Position the disconnected lines in a raised position to prevent leakage.
2. Remove the pump belt.
3. Loosen the retaining bolts and any braces, and remove the pump.
4. Install the pump on the engine with the retaining bolt handtight.
5. Connect and tighten the hose fittings.
6. Refill the pump with fluid and bleed by turning the pulley counterclockwise (viewed from the front). Stop the bleeding when air bubbles no longer appear.
7. Install the pump belt on the pulley and adjust the tension.

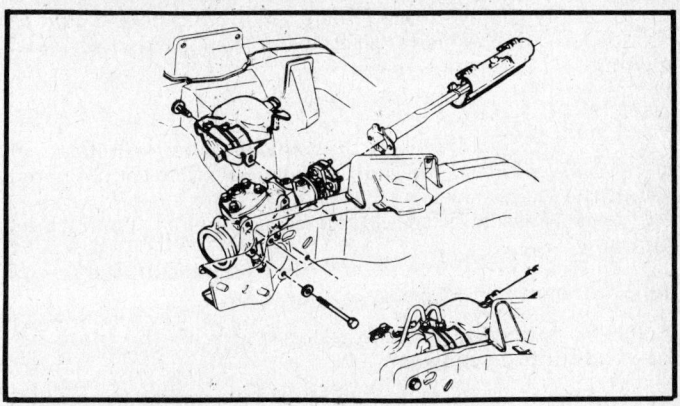

Typical steering gear mounting
(© General Motors Corporation)

STEERING COLUMN

Removal

NOTE: Once the steering column is removed from the car, the column is susceptible to damage. Dropping the column assembly on its end could collapse the steering shaft or loosen the plastic injections, which maintain column rigidity. Leaning on the mast jacket could cause jacket to bend or deform. Any of the above damage could impair the column's collapsible design. If it is necessary to remove the steering wheel, use standard wheel puller. Do not hammer on end of shaft, as hammering could loosen plastic injections which maintain column ridigity.

1. Front of dash mounting plates must be loosened whenever the column is to be lowered from the instrument panel.
2. Disconnect the battery ground cable.
3. Remove the steering wheel.
4. Remove the nut and bolt from the upper intermediate shaft coupling. Separate coupling from lower end of steering column.
5. Disconnect the transmission control linkage (backdrive linkage on floor shift models) from the column shift tube levers.
6. Disconnect the steering column harness at the connector. Disconnect all electrical connectors.
7. Remove the floor pan trim cover screws and remove the cover.
8. Remove the column plate floor pan screws.
9. Remove the ash tray assembly, as required.
10. Remove the (6) steering column panel to instrument panel screws and carefully lower the panel and heater (or air conditioning control) as an assembly.
11. Remove the transmission indicator cable, if so equipped.
12. Move the front seat as far back as possible to provide maximum clearance.
13. Remove the two column bracket-to-instrument panel nuts

16–41

SECTION 16
GENERAL MOTORS—"F" BODY
CAMARO • CAMARO BERLINETTA • FIREBIRD • TRANS AM • SE

and carefully remove from vehicle. Additional help should be obtained to guide the lower shift levers through the dash panel opening.

Installation

1. Position the column in the vehicle, install all electrical connections, position the shaft flange to flexible coupling and install the lockwashers and nuts.
2. Loosely assemble the column support to instrument panel stud nuts.
3. Position the column plate to floor pan, install the screws tighten them to 35 inch lbs.

NOTE: Align the column plate seal with the plate before tightening screws.

4. Tighten the column support to instrument panel stud nuts to 20 ft.lbs.
5. Install the floor pan screws in the slotted locations and tighten to 35 inch lbs.

CAUTION
With the column installed, the following requirements must be met:

a. The flexible coupling must not be distorted due to the pot joint bottoming in either direction.
b. The steering wheel should be free to rotate from stop to stop (front wheels off the ground) with no lumpiness, stickiness or binding.
c. Steering column intermediate shaft to supper control ram forward bolt clearance must be 0.15 in. minimum.
d. If any of the above conditions exist, the column must be removed and checked for bent or damaged parts, incorrectly installed components or possible frame damage.
e. After correcting the complaint, repeat Installation Steps 1–5.

6. Install the floor pan trim cover.
7. Install the steering column panel assembly to the instrument panel.
8. Install the ash tray, if necessary. Install all electrical connections.
9. Install the steering wheel.
10. Connect the transmission control linkage (back-drive linkage on floor shift models).
11. Connect the battery ground cable.

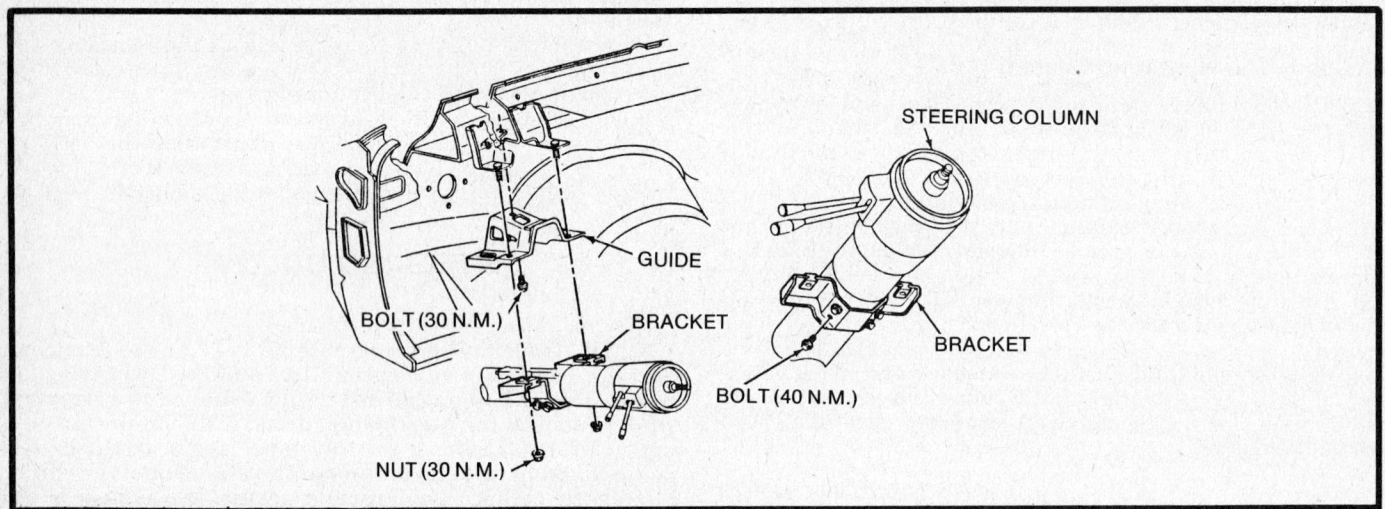

Steering column installation (© General Motors Corporation)

BRAKE SECTION

For Brake Service refer to Unit Repair Section.

MASTER CYLINDER

Removal and Installation

1. Disconnect hydraulic lines at master cylinder.
2. Remove the retaining nuts and lock-washers that hold cylinder to firewall or the brake booster. Disconnect pushrod at brake pedal (non-power brakes only).
3. Remove the master cylinder, gasket and rubber boot.
4. On non-power brakes, position master cylinder on firewall, making sure pushrod goes through the rubber boot into the piston. Reconnect pushrod clevis to brake pedal. With power brakes, install the cylinder on the booster.
5. Install nuts and lockwashers.
6. Install hydraulic lines then check brake pedal free play.
7. Bleed brakes.

NOTE: Cars having disc brakes do not have a check valve in the front outlet port of the master cylinder. If one is installed, front discs will quickly wear out due to residual hydraulic pressure holding pads against rotor.

VACUUM POWER BRAKE BOOSTER

Removal and Installation

1. Disconnect vacuum hose from vacuum check valve.
2. Unbolt the master cylinder and carefully move it aside without disconnecting the hydraulic lines.
3. Disconnect pushrod at brake pedal assembly.
4. Remove nuts and lockwashers that secure booster to firewall and remove booster from engine compartment.
5. Install by reversing removal procedure. Make sure to check operation of stop lights. Allow engine vacuum to build before applying brakes.

PARKING BRAKE

Adjustment

MODELS WITH REAR DRUM BRAKES

1. Depress the parking brake pedal exactly two ratchet clicks.
2. Raise the rear of the vehicle and support safely with jackstands.
3. Tighten the brake cable adjusting nut until the left rear wheel can be turned rearward with both hands, but locks when forward rotation is attempted.
4. Release the parking brake pedal; both rear wheels must turn freely in either direction without brake drag. Be sure that the parking brake cables arenot adjusted too tightly causing the brakes to drag.
5. Lower the vehicle.

MODELS WITH REAR DISC BRAKES

1. Check for free movement of the parking brake cables and lubricate the underbody rub points of the cables. Also lubricate the equalizer hooks.
2. Release the parking brake pedal completely.
3. Raise the rear of the vehicle and support it safely with jackstands.
4. Hold the brake cable stud from turning, then tighten the adjusting nut until all cable slack is taken up.

NOTE: Check that the parking brake levers on the rear calipers are against the stops on the caliper housing. If the levers are not contacting the stops, loosen the cable adjusting nut until the levers just contact the stops.

5. Operate the parking brake cable several times. Parking brake pedal travel should be 14 clicks with approximately 150 ± 20 lbs. of forced applied to the pedal.
6. Readjust if necessary.
7. Make sure that the levers contact the caliper stops after adjustment.
8. Lower the vehicle.

PARKING BRAKE CABLE

Removal and Installation

FRONT CABLE

1. Raise and support the vehicle safely. Remove the adjusting nut at the equalizer.
2. Remove the spring retainer clip from the bracket. Lower the car and remove the upper console for access to cable retainer at the hand lever.
3. Remove the cable retainer pin, cable retainer and remove the cable.
4. Installation is the reverse order of the removal procedure. Adjust the parking brake cable.

REAR CABLE (DRUM BRAKES)

1. Raise and support the vehicle safely. Remove the adjusting nut at the equalizer.
2. Disengage the rear cable at the connector. Mark the relationship of the wheel to the axle flange and remove the wheel assembly and brake drum.
3. Bend the retainer fingers. Disengage the cable at the brake shoe operating lever.
4. Install the new cable by reversing the removal procedure. Adjust the parking brake cable.

REAR CABLE (REAR DISC BRAKES)

1. Raise and support the vehicle safely. Remove the adjusting nut at the equalizer.
2. Disengage the rear cable at the connector. Push forward on the caliper parking brake apply lever. This will allow the cable to be removed from the tang in the lever. Release the lever.
3. Installation is the reverse order of the removal procedure. Adjust the parking brake. Apply the parking brake three times with heavy pressure and repeat the adjustment.

CLUTCH, TRANSMISSION AND DRIVESHAFT SECTION

For Overhaul Procedures refer to Unit Repair Section.

CLUTCH PEDAL

Adjustment

1. Disconnect the return spring at the clutch fork.

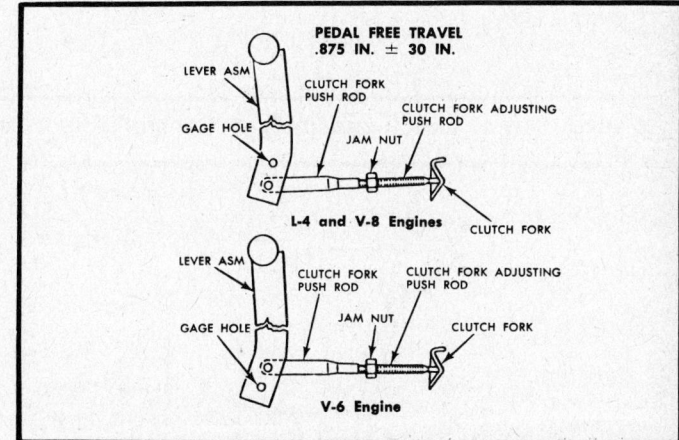

1982 and later clutch pedal free play adjustment
(© General Motors Corporation)

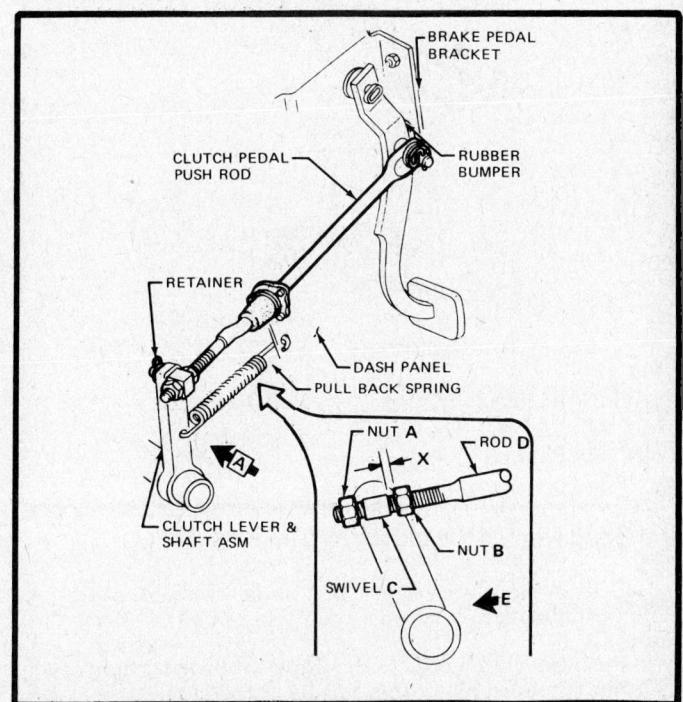

Clutch linkage adjustment
(© General Motors Corporation)

SECTION 16
GENERAL MOTORS—"F" BODY
CAMARO • CAMARO BERLINETTA • FIREBIRD • TRANS AM • SE

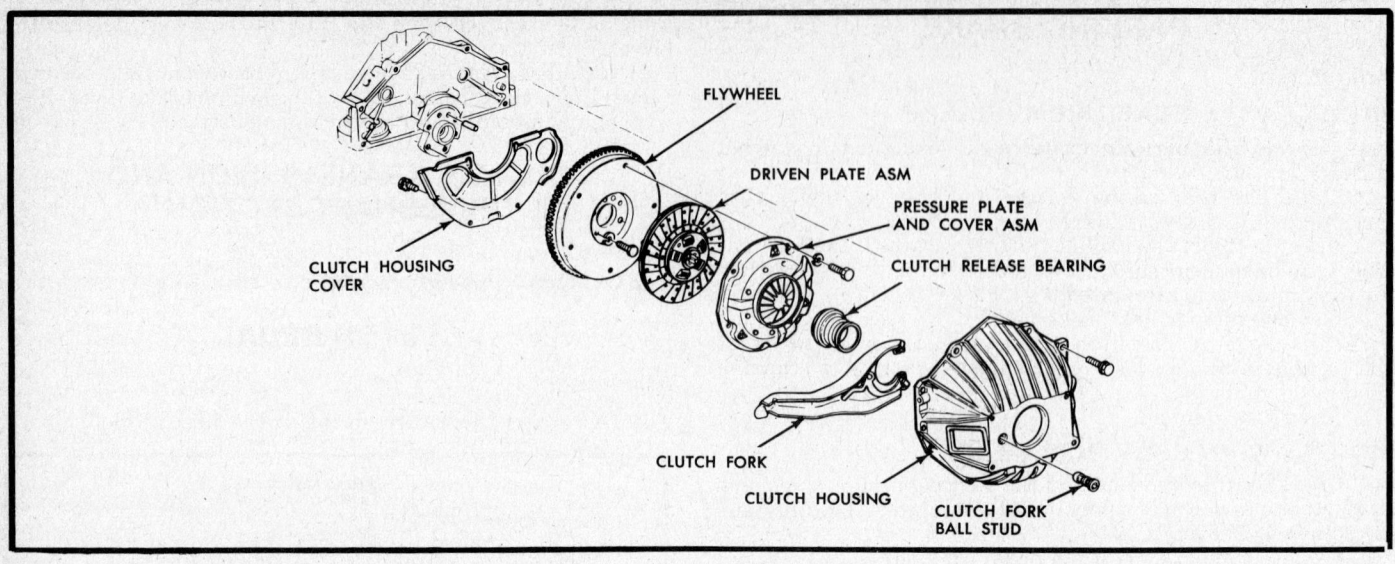

Exploded view of clutch assembly (© General Motors Corporation)

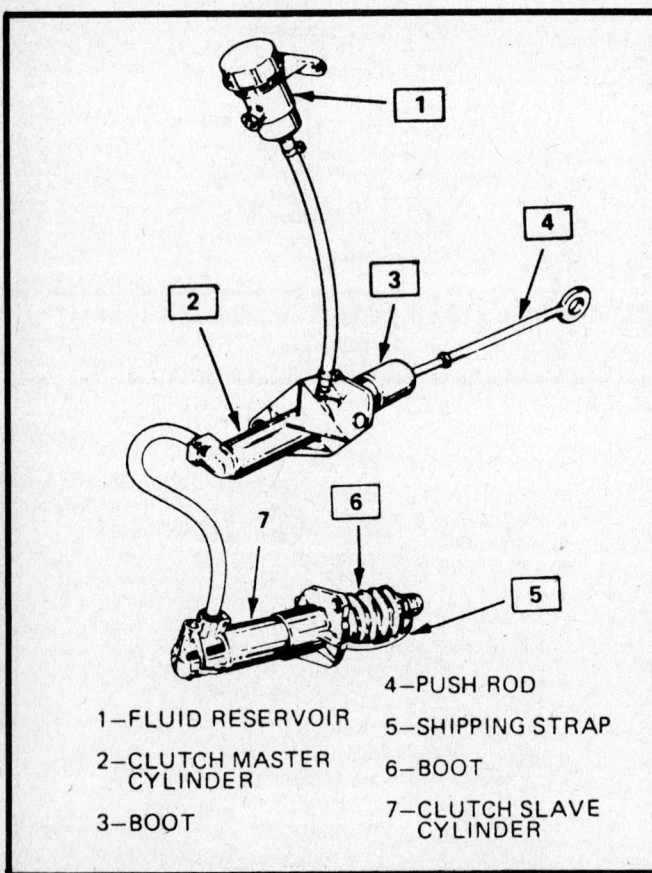

1—FLUID RESERVOIR
2—CLUTCH MASTER CYLINDER
3—BOOT
4—PUSH ROD
5—SHIPPING STRAP
6—BOOT
7—CLUTCH SLAVE CYLINDER

Exploded view of the clutch hydraulic system

2. Rotate the clutch lever and shaft assembly until the clutch pedal is firmly against the rubber bumper on the dash brace.
3. Push the clutch fork so the throwout bearing lightly contacts the pressure plate fingers.
4. Loosen the locknut and adjust the length of the rod so that the swivel or rod can slip freely into the gauge hole in the lever. Increase the length of the rod until all free-play is removed.

5. Remove the rod or swivel from the gauge hole and insert it in the other (original) hole on the lever. Install the retainer and tighten the locknut.
6. Install the return spring and check free-play measurement from the floor mat to top of the pedal pad. It should measure: $7/8-1 1/8$ in. for 1982–83.

CLUTCH
Removal and Installation

1. Support engine and remove the transmission.
2. Disconnect the clutch fork push rod and spring.
3. Remove the flywheel housing.
4. Slide the clutch fork from the ball stud and remove the fork from the dust boot. The ball stud is threaded into the clutch housing and may be replaced, if necessary. On models equipped with a slave cylinder, remove the clutch forx from the slave cylinder.
5. Install an alignment tool to support the clutch assembly during removal. Mark the flywheel and clutch cover for reinstallation, if they do not already have "X" marks.
6. Loosen the clutch-to-flywheel attaching bolts evenly, one turn at a time, until spring pressure is released. Remove the bolts and clutch assembly.
7. Installation is the reverse of removal. Be sure to install the driven disc is installed with the damper springs facing the transmission. Adjust clutch as required.

CLUTCH HYDRAULIC SYSTEM
Removal and Installation
1984 AND LATER MODELS

1. Disconnect the negative battery cable. Remove the steering column trim cover and hush panel.
2. Remove the master cylinder push rod from the clutch pedal.
3. Remove the clutch master cylinder to cowl nuts.
4. Remove the brake booster to cowl nuts. Remove the clutch fluid reservoir from the bracket.
5. Pull the brake master cylinder forward for access to the clutch master cylinder. Remove the clutch master cylinder from the cowl.
6. Raise and support the vehicle safely. Remove the slave cylinder heat shield.

GENERAL MOTORS—"F" BODY
CAMARO • CAMARO BERLINETTA • FIREBIRD • TRANS AM • SE
SECTION 16

7. Disconnect the slave cylinder from the clutch forx. Remove the slave cylinder retaining bolts and remove the slave cylinder from the bell housing.
8. Lower the vehicle and remove the complete clutch hydraulic system from the engine compartment.
9. Installation is the reverse order of the removal procedure. Bleed the system as outlined in this section.

Bleeding Clutch Hydraulic System

1. Clean all dirt and grease from the cap to make sure that no foreign subtances enter the system.
2. Remove rthe cap and diaphragm and fill the reservoir to the top with the approved DOT 3 brake fluid. Fully loosen the bleed screw which is in the slave cylinder body next to the inlet connection.
3. At this point bubbles of air will appear at the bleed screw outlet. When the slave cylinder is full and a steady stream of fluid comes out of the slave cylinder bleeder, tighten the bleed screw.
4. Assemble the diaphragm and cap to the reservoir, fluid in the reservoir should be level with the step. Exert a light load (approxitmately 20 lbs.) to the slave cylinder piston by pushing the release lever towards the cylinder and loosen the bleed screw. Maintain a constant light load, fluid and any air that is left will be expelled through the bleed port. Tighten the bleed screw when a steady flow of fluid and no air is being expelled.
5. Fill the reservoir fluid level back to normal capacity and if necessary repeat Step 4.
6. Exert a light load to the release lever (but do not open the bleeder screw) the piston in the slave cylinder will move slowly down the bore . Repeat this operation 2-3 times, the fluid movement will force any ait left in the system into the reservoir. The hydraulic system should now be fully bled.
7. Check the the operation of the clutch hydraulic system and repeat this procedure if necesary. Check the push rod travel at the slave cylinder to insure the minimum travel 0.57 in.

MANUAL TRANSMISSION

Removal and Installation
FOUR SPEED

1. Disconnect the negative battery cable at the battery.
2. Raise the vehicle and support it safely.
3. Drain the lubricant from the transmission.
4. Remove the torque arm from the vehicle.
5. Mark the driveshaft and the rear axle pinion flange to indicate their relationship. Unbolt the rear universal joint straps. Lower the rear of the driveshaft, being careful to keep the universal joint caps in place. Withdraw the driveshaft from the transmission and remove it from the vehicle.
6. Disconnect the speedometer cable and the electrical connectors from the transmission.
7. Remove the exhaust pipe brace.
8. Remove the transmission shifter support attaching bolts from the transmission.
9. Disconnect the shift linkage at the shifter.
10. Raise the transmission slightly with a jack, then remove the crossmember attaching bolts.
11. Remove the transmission mount attaching bolts and remove the mount and crossmember from the vehicle.
12. Remove the transmission attaching bolts, and with the aid of an assistant, **move** the transmission rearward and downward out of the vehicle.
13. Installation is performed in the reverse order of the previous steps. Note the following during installation.
    a. Apply a light coating of high temperature grease to the main drive gear bearing retainer and to the splined portion of the main drive gear. This will assure free movement of the clutch and transmission components during assembly.
    b. Adjust the shift linkage.
    c. Refill the transmission with the proper amount and quality of transmission lubricant.
    d. Observe the following torque specifications:
    Filler plug—15 ft.lbs.
    Transmission-to-clutch housing bolts—55 ft.lbs.
    Crossmember-to-body bolts—35 ft.lbs.
    Mount-to-crossmember bolts—35 ft.lbs.
    Mount-to-transmission bolts—35 ft.lbs.
    Shifter bracket-to-extension housing—25 ft.lbs.

FIVE SPEED

1. Disconnect the negative battery cable at the battery.
2. Remove the shift lever boot attaching screws and slide the boot up the shift lever.
3. Remove the shift lever from the transmission.
4. Raise the vehicle and support it safely.
5. Drain the lubricant from the transmission.
6. Remove the torque arm from the vehicle as outlined under 'Rear Suspension'.
7. Mark the driveshaft and the rear axle pinion flange to indicate their relationship. Unbolt the rear universal joint straps. Lower the rear of the driveshaft, being careful to keep the universal joint caps in place. Withdraw the driveshaft from the transmission and remove it from the vehicle.
8. Disconnect the speedometer cable and the electrical connectors from the transmission.
9. Disconnect the clutch cable at the transmission.
10. Remove the catalytic converter hanger.
11. Remove the exhaust pipe brace.
12. Remove the transmission shifter support attaching bolts from the transmission.
13. Disconnect the shift linkage at the shifter.
14. Raise the transmission slightly with a jack, then remove the crossmember attaching bolts.
15. Remove the transmission mount attaching bolts and remove the mount and crossmember from the vehicle.
16. Remove the transmission attaching bolts, and with the aid of an assistant, move the transmission rearward and downward out of the vehicle.
17. Installation is performed in the reverse order of the previous steps. Note the following during installation:
    a. Apply a light coating of high temperature grease to the main drive gear bearing retainer and to the splined portion of the main drive gear. This will assure free movement of the clutch and transmission components during assembly.
    b. Refill the transmission with the proper amount and quality of transmission lubricant.
    c. Observe the following torque specifications:
    Filter plug—20 ft.lbs.
    Transmission-to-clutch housing bolts—55 ft.lbs.
    Crossmember-to-body bolts—35 ft.lbs.
    Mount-to-crossmember bolts—35 ft.lbs.
    Mount-to-transmission bolts—35 ft.lbs.

AUTOMATIC TRANSMISSION

Linkage Adjustments

There are 2 procedures that can be used, depending on the shape of the transmission end of the shifter cable. On early models, the cable ends in a straight rod with a clamp (trunnion) bolt. On later models, the cable ends in a flattened eye with a fixed bolt through it.

1. Loosen the trunnion bolt at the transmission end of the cable on early models. On later models, pull the clip from the cable housing at the side of the transmission.
2. Set the console shift lever against the Drive stop on early models. On later models, set it in the Park detent.
3. Set the transmission shift lever in the drive position on early models. This is the third position from the back. On later

SECTION 16
GENERAL MOTORS—"F" BODY
CAMARO • CAMARO BERLINETTA • FIREBIRD • TRANS AM • SE

models, set it in the Park, or most forward, position.

4. On early models, tighten the trunnion bolt against the cable end. On later models, replace the clip to hold the cable housing in position.

5. Place the console shift lever in the Park position.

6. Set the console shift lever in Park. Loosen the clamp at the bottom of the back drive rod (the one that goes to the steering column). Push the back drive rod up against the stop and tighten the clamp screw.

Throttle Valve (T.V.) Cable Adjustment

1. Depress the re-adjust tab on the T.V. cable. Move the slider back through the fitting in the direction away from the throttle body until the slider stops against the fitting.

2. Release re-adjust tab.

AUTOMATIC TRANSMISSION

Removal and Installation

1. Disconnect the negative battery cable.
2. Remove the air cleaner assembly.
3. Disconnect the throttle valve (TV) control cable at the carburetor.
4. Remove the transmission oil dipstick. Unbolt and remove the dipstick tube.
5. Raise the vehicle and support it safely.
6. Mark the relationship between the driveshaft and the rear pinion flange so that the driveshaft may be reinstalled in its original position.
7. Unbolt the universal joint straps from the pinion flange (use care to keep the universal joint caps in place), lower and remove the driveshaft from the vehicle.
8. Disconnect the catalytic convertor support bracket at the transmission.

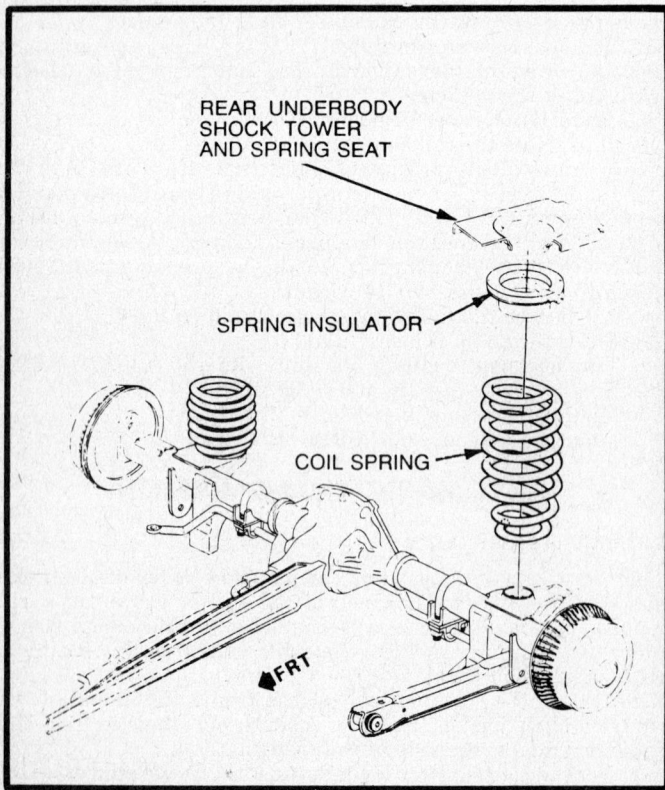

Coil Springs and insulator
(© General Motors Corporation)

9. Disconnect the speedometer cable, electrical connectors and the shift control table from the transmission.

CAUTION
During the next step, rear spring force will cause the torque arm to move toward the floor pan. When disconnecting the arm from the transmission, carefully place a piece of wood between the floor pan and the torque arm. This will prevent possible personal injury and/or floor pan damage.

10. Remove the torque arm-to-transmission bolts.
11. Remove the flywheel cover, then mark the relationship between the torque convertor and the flywheel.
12. Remove the torque convertor-to-flywheel attaching bolts.
13. Support the transmission with a jack, then remove the transmission mount bolt.
14. Unbolt and remove the transmission crossmember.
15. Lower the transmission slightly. Disconnect the TV cable and oil cooler lines from the transmission.
16. Support the engine. Remove the transmission-to-engine mounting bolts.
17. Remove the transmission from the vehicle. Keep the rear of the transmission lower than the front to avoid the possibility of the torque convertor disengaging from the transmission.
18. Installation is performed in the reverse of the previous steps. Note the following points during installation.
   a. Before installing the convertor-to-flywheel bolts, be sure that the weld nuts on the convertor are flush with the flywheel, and that the convertor rotates freely by hand in this position.
   b. Install a NEW dipstick tube O-ring before installing the tube.

SHIFT INDICATOR

Removal and Installation

1. Disconnect the negative battery cable.
2. Remove the screws holding the console trim plate to the console assembly base.
3. Disconnect any clips holding the shift indicator to the lower console assembly. Remove the indicator.
4. Installation is the reverse of the removal procedure.

NOTE: On the Berlinetta console, be careful when removing the indicator so as not to damage the radio head assembly which is located at the front of the console.

DRIVESHAFT

Removal and Installation

The driveshaft may be held to the differential pinion flange by a circular mounting flange, or the bearing cups may be retained to the pinion flange by U-bolts or straps.

1. Raise and support the car. Matchmark the pinion flange and driveshaft for assembly. The parts were balanced at the factory and should be assembled in the same relationship.
2. Unbolt the flange or remove the U-bolts or straps. If straps or U-bolts are used, tape the bearing cups in place.
3. Drop the driveshaft down at the rear, then pull it backwards out from the transmission extension housing. The transmission housing should be plugged to prevent leakage.
4. Before installation, inspect the transmission yoke seal. Replace if necessary. Apply a light coat of transmission lubricant to the sliding spines.
5. Insert the front yoke of the driveshaft into the transmission. Do not allow the yoke to bang into the transmission seal.
6. Raise the rear of the driveshaft into place and align the matchmarks made during removal. Bolt the driveshaft to the pinion flange.

GENERAL MOTORS—"F" BODY
CAMARO • CAMARO BERLINETTA • FIREBIRD • TRANS AM • SE
SECTION 16

UNIVERSAL JOINTS

Refer to Unit Repair Section.

REAR AXLE AND SUSPENSION SECTION

For Axle Overhaul Procedures and Suspension Services refer to Unit Repair Section.

REAR AXLE ASSEMBLY

Removal and Installation

1983-85 MODELS

1. Raise the vehicle and support safely. Using a suitable tool, support the rear axle assembly.
2. Disconnect both shock absorbers from the vehicle.
3. Remove the bolt that holds the left side of the tracking bar to the axle assembly.
4. Remove the bolt holding the brake line junction block to the axle housing. Disconnect the brake lines from the junction block.
5. Lower the rear axle assembly and disconnect the springs.
6. Remove the rear wheels and drums. Remove the rear axle cover. Drain the gear lube.
7. Remove the axle shafts and disconnect the brake lines from the housing clips.
8. Remove the brake backing plates and disconnect the lower control arms.
9. Disconnect the torque arm. Mark the companion flange and the propeller shaft for reassembly. Disconnect the propeller shaft.
10. Remove the rear axle housing.
11. Installation is the reverse of the removal procedure. Bleed the brake system as required.

1986 AND LATER MODELS

1. Disconnect the negative battery cable. Raise the rear of the vehicle using a suitable hoist. Suport the vehicle at the frame and leave the hoist connect under the rear axle housing.
2. Disconnect the shock absorbers from the axle. Mark the drive shaft and the pinion companion flange, disconnect the drive shaft and position it out of the way.
3. Remove the brake line junction block bolt at the axle carrier and the brake lines at the junction block. On the "G" models, disconnect the brake lines at the wheel cylinder.
4. Disconnect the upper control arms from the axle carrier. Lower the rear axle assembly on a hoist and remove the springs.
5. Remove the rear wheels and drums/rotors. Remove the rear axle cover bolts and remove the axle cover.
6. Remove the axle shaft. Refer to axle shaft removal in outlined in this section.
7. Disconnect the brake lines from the axle carrier clips. If equipped with brake drums, remove the brake backing plates.
8. Disconnect the lower control arms from the axle carrier.
9. Remove the rear axle carrier by lowering it from the vehicle.
10. Installation is the reverse order of the removal procedure.

AXLE SHAFT, BEARING/OIL SEAL

Removal and Installation

1. Raise the vehicle and support safely. Remove the rear wheels and drums.
2. Remove the carrier cover and drain the lube.
3. Remove the rear axle pinion shaft lock screw. Remove the rear axle pinion shaft.
4. Remove the C-lock clip from the bottom end of the pinion shaft.
5. Remove the axle shaft from the axle housing.
6. Using a suitable tool, remove the oil seal from the axle housing. Be careful not to damage the housing.
7. Install tool No. J–22813-01 or equivalent into the bore of the axle housing making sure that it engages the bearing outer race. Remove the bearing using slide hammer.
8. Installation is the reverse of the removal procedure. Lubricate the new bearing with gear lube before installing.

REAR SUSPENSION, REAR SHOCK ABSORBERS

The rear suspension components and the rear shock absorber information, removal and installation procedure are found in the Suspension segment of the Unit Repair Section.

NOTE: Some 1982–85 Firebird models have experienced a squawking noise from the rear suspension stabilizer bar. The probable cause of this noise is dried out stabilizer bar bushings. This problem can be corrected by removing the old bushings and installing new stabilizer bar bushings with Teflon liners. When installing the new bushings be sure to position the new bushings with the slit toward the rear of the stabilizer bar.

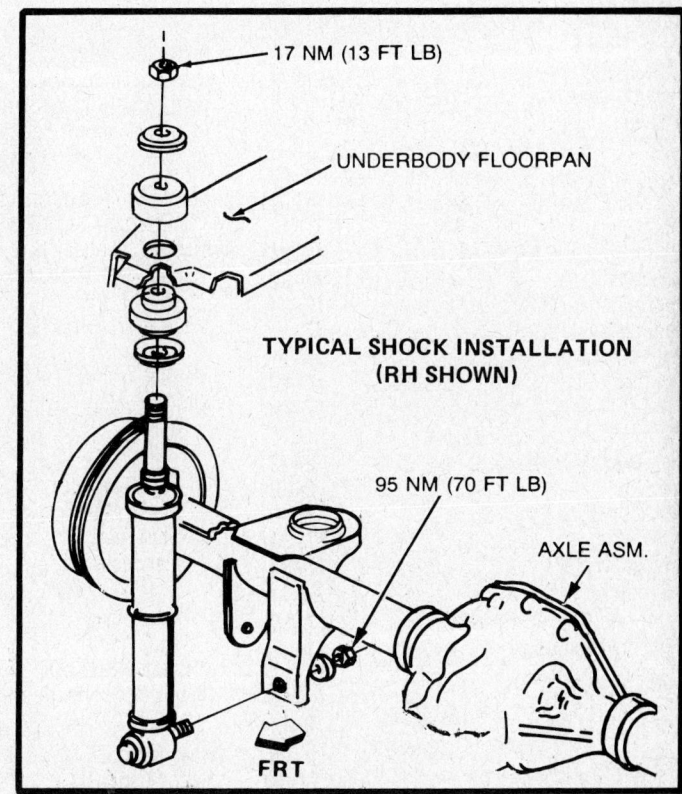

Shock absorber (© General Motors Corporation)

16–47

SECTION 17
GENERAL MOTORS—"P" BODY
PONTIAC FIERO • FIERO SE

SPECIFICATIONS

Brakes	24-2	Serial Number Identification	17-3
Camshaft	17-5	Torque	17-5
Capacities	17-4	Torque Sequence (Cylinder Heads)	17-19
Crankshaft & Connecting Rod	17-5	Tune-Up	17-4
Firing Order	17-4	Valve	17-4
General Engine	17-4	Wheel Alignment	17-5
Piston & Ring	17-5		

INDEX

A
Alternator R&R	17-6
Automatic Transmission	17-31
Adjustment	17-32
On Car Service	23-2
Assembly R&R	17-31
Axle Assembly R&R	17-33
Axle Shaft R&R	17-33

B
Ball Joints	35-2
Brake System	24-2
Brake Caliper Overhaul	24-2
Brake Caliper R&LR	24-2
Brake Drum	
Rear	24-2
Brake Master Cylinder	17-30
Brake Pad	
Front	24-2
Brake Shoe	
Rear	24-2

C
Camshaft R&R	17-20
Chassis Electrical	17-7
Clutch	
Master Cyl R&R	17-31
R&R	17-30
Control Arm R&R	17-24
Cooling System	17-11
Cruise Control	17-11
Cylinder Head	17-19
R&R	17-19

D
Disc Brakes	24-2
Front	24-2
Distributor R&R	17-6
Drive Axle	17-33
Driveshaft R&R	17-33

E
Electronic Fuel Pump R&R	17-14
Electronic Ignition	30-2
Emission Controls	17-16
Engine	17-17
Identification	17-3
R&R	17-17
Engine Electrical	17-6
Engine Lubrication	17-21
Engine Mechanical	17-17
Exhaust Manifold R&R	17-15

F
Front Suspension	35-2
Alignment	17-5
Fuel Injection	17-16
Fuel Pump R&R	17-14
Fuses	17-9
Fusible Links	17-10

H
Head Light Switch	17-9
Heater Blower R&R	17-12
Heater Core R&R	17-12
Heater Control	17-12

I
Ignition Switch	17-7
Ignition Timing	17-7
Instrument Cluster R&R	17-9
Intake Manifold R&R	17-14

L, M, N
Lower Control Arm R&R	17-24
MacPherson Strut R&R	17-35
Master Cylinder R&R	17-30
Manual Steering Gear	
R&R	17-23
Manual Transmission	
Overhaul	32-2
Manual Transmission R&R	17-31
Neutral Safety Switch	
R&R	17-8

O
Oil Pan R&R	17-21
Oil Pump R&R	17-22
Oil Seal R&R	
Rear Main	17-22

P
Parking Brake	17-30
Adjustment	17-30
Cable R&R	17-30
Piston & Connecting Rod	17-21

R
Rear Main Oil Seal R&R	17-22
Rear Suspension	17-33
Alignment	17-35
Regulator	17-6
Rocker Shaft/Assy RR	17-17

S
Serial Number	17-3
Engine	17-3
Vehicle	17-3
Shock Absorber R&R	
Front	17-24
Rear	17-33
Springs	
Front	17-24
Rear	17-33
Starter R&R	17-6
Starter Drive Replacement	17-6
Steering Column R&R	17-25
Steering Gear R&R	17-23
Manual	17-23
Steering Wheel R&R	17-23
Stop Light Switch R&R	17-8
Speedometer R&R	17-9
Spindle R&R	17-25
Suspension R&R	35-2
Service	35-2

T
Timing Chain	17-21
Timing Gear Cover	17-20
Oil Seal Replacement	17-20
Tune-Up	17-4
Turn Signal Switch R&R	17-8

U, V
U-Joint Overhaul	28-2
Valve System	17-19
Voltage Regulator	17-6

W, Y
Water Pump R&R	17-11
Wheel Alignment	17-5
Front	17-5
Wheel Bearings Front	17-25
Wheel Cylinders Rear	17-35
Rear	24-2
Windshield Wiper	17-9
Linkage R&R	17-9
Motor R&R	17-9
Year Identification	17-3

BEFORE SERVICING BE CERTAIN TO READ THE SAFETY NOTICE

SECTION 17

GM "P" Body
1984–87
Rear Wheel Drive Cars
PONTIAC FIERO • FIERO SE

YEAR IDENTIFICATION

1984–85 Fiero

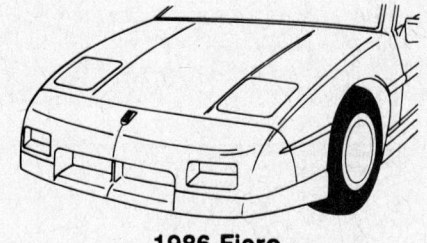

1986 Fiero

VEHICLE IDENTIFICATION NUMBER (VIN)

It is important for servicing and ordering parts to be certain of the vehicle and engine identification. The VIN (vehicle identification number) is a 17 digit number visible through the windshield on the driver's side of the dash and contains the vehicle and engine identification codes. It can be interpreted as follows:

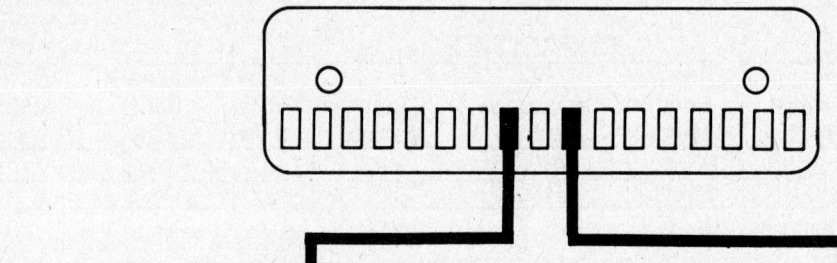

Engine Code						Model Year Code	
Code	Cu. In.	Liters	Cyl.	Carb.	Eng. Mfg.	Code	Year
R	151	2.5	4	TBI	Pontiac	E	1984
9	173	2.8	6	MFI	Chev.	F	1985
						G	1986
						H	1987

The seventeen digit Vehicle Identification Number can be used to determine engine application and model year. The 10th digit indicates the model year, and the 8th digit identifies the factory installed engine.
TBI (Throttle body injection)

17-3

SECTION 17
GENERAL MOTORS — "P" BODY
PONTIAC FIERO • FIERO SE

GENERAL ENGINE SPECIFICATIONS

Year	Eng. VIN Code	Engine Displacement Cu. In.	Eng. Mfg.	Fuel Delivery	Horsepower @ rpm■	Torque @ rpm (ft lbs)	Bore × Stroke (in.)	Compression Ratio	Oil Pressure @ 2000 rpm
'83–'85	R	151	Pont.	TBI	90 @ 4000	132 @ 2800	4.000 × 3.000	9.0:1	36–41
'86–'87	R	151	Pont.	TBI	92 @ 4400	134 @ 2800	4.000 × 3.000	9.0:1	36–41
'85	9	173	Chev.	MFI	130 @ 5400	160 @ 3600	3.500 × 3.000	8.5:1	30–45
'86–'87	9	173	Chev.	MFI	140 @	170 @ 3600	3.500 × 3.000	8.5:1	30–45

TUNE-UP SPECIFICATIONS

Year	VIN Code	Eng. No. Cyl. Displ. Cu. In.	Eng. Mfg.	hp	Spark Plugs Orig Type	Spark Plugs Gap (in.)	Ignition Timing (deg)▲ Man. Trans.	Ignition Timing (deg)▲ Auto. Trans.	Intake Valve Opens (deg)■	Fuel Pump Pressure (psi)	Idle Speed (rpm)▲ Man. Trans.	Idle Speed (rpm)▲ Auto. Trans.
'84–'85	R	151	Pont	90	R43CTS	.060	①	①	33	6–8	①	①
'86–'87	R	151	Pont	92	R43CTS6	.060	①	①	33	6–8	①	①
'85–'87	9	173	Chev	130	R42CTS	.045	①	①	25	6–8	①	①

FIRING ORDER

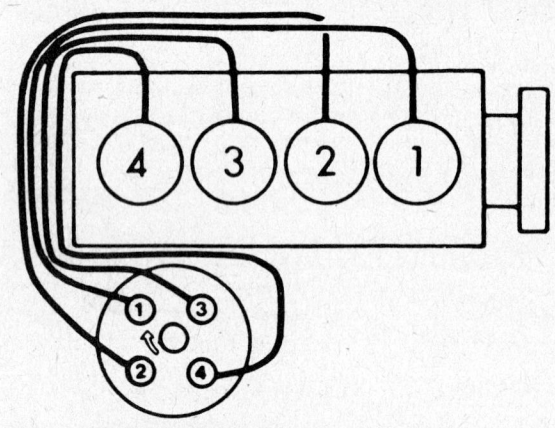

GM (Pontiac) 151–4
Engine firing order: 1–3–4–2
Distributor rotation: clockwise

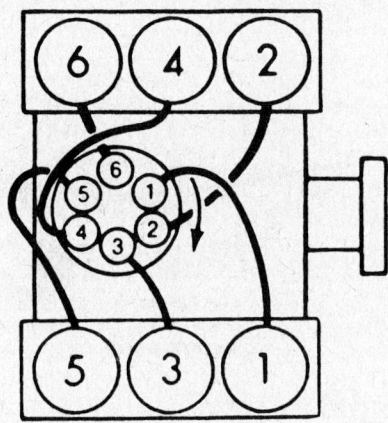

GM (Chevrolet) 173 V6 (2.8L)
Engine firing order: 1–2–3–4–5–6
Distributor rotation: clockwise

CAPACITIES

Year	VIN Code	Engine Displacement Cu. In.	Eng. Mfg.	Crankcase Quarts	Transaxle Pints Manual	Transaxle Pints Auto	Gas Tank Gal	Cooling System Qts
'84–'87	R	151	Pont.	3 ①	6.0	8.0	10.5	13.8
'85–'87	9	173	Chev.	4 ①	5.9	8.0	10.3	13.8

① With or without filter change

VALVE SPECIFICATIONS

Year	VIN Code	Eng. No. Cyl. Displacement (cu. in.)	Eng. Mfg.	Seat Angle (deg)	Face Angle (deg)	Spring Test Pressure (lbs. @ in.)	Spring Installed Height (in.)	Stem to Guide Clearance (in.) Intake	Stem to Guide Clearance (in.) Exhaust	Stem Diameter (in.) Intake	Stem Diameter (in.) Exhaust
'84–'87	R	4-151	Pont.	45	45	176 @ 1.26	1.69	0.0010–0.0027	0.0010–0.0027	0.3418–0.3425	0.3418–0.3425
'85–'87	9	6-173	Chev.	46	45	195 @ 1.181	1.57	0.0010–0.0027	0.0010–0.0027	0.3410–0.3416	0.3410–0.3416

GENERAL MOTORS—"P" BODY
PONTIAC FIERO • FIERO SE

SECTION 17

CRANKSHAFT AND CONNECTING ROD SPECIFICATIONS

All measurements are given in inches.

Year	V.I.N. Code	Engine No. Cyl. Displacement (cu. in.)	Eng. Mfg.	Crankshaft Main Brg. Journal Dia.	Crankshaft Main Brg. Oil Clearance	Crankshaft Shaft End-Play	Crankshaft Thrust on No.	Connecting Rod Journal Diameter	Connecting Rod Oil Clearance	Connecting Rod Side Clearance
'84–'87	R	4-151	Pont.	2.2995–2.3005	0.0005–0.0022	0.0035–0.0085	5	1.9995–2.0005	0.0005–0.0026	0.006–0.022
'85–'87	9	6-173	Chev.	2.4937–2.4946	0.0016–0.0031	0.0023–0.0082	3	1.9984–1.9994	0.0014–0.0037	0.006–0.17

CAMSHAFT SPECIFICATIONS

All measurements in inches.

Year	VIN Code	Engine	Eng. Mfg.	Journal Diameter 1	Journal Diameter 2	Journal Diameter 3	Bearing Clearance	Lobe Lift Intake	Lobe Lift Exhaust	Camshaft End Play
'84–'87	R	4-151	Pont.	1.869	1.869	1.869	0.0007–0.0027	0.398	0.398	0.0015–0.0050
'85–'87	9	6-173	Chev.	1.869	1.869	1.869	0.0010–0.0040	0.231	0.263	—

PISTON AND RING SPECIFICATIONS

All measurements are given in inches. To convert inches to metric units, refer to the Metric Information section.

Year	V.I.N. Code	Engine Type/Disp. cu. in.	Eng. Mfg.	Piston-to-Bore Clearance	Ring Gap Top Compression	Ring Gap Bottom Compression	Ring Gap Oil Control	Ring Side Clearance Top Compression	Ring Side Clearance Bottom Compression	Ring Side Clearance Oil Control
'84	R	4-151	Pont.	0.0025–0.0033	0.010–0.022	0.010–0.027	0.015–0.055	0.002–0.003	0.002–0.003	snug
'85–'87	R	4-151	Pont.	0.0014–0.0022 ①	0.010–0.020	0.010–0.020	0.020–0.060	0.002–0.003	0.001–0.003	0.015–0.055
'85–'87	9	6-173	Chev.	0.0007–0.0017	0.0098–0.0197	0.0098–0.0197	0.020–0.055	0.0012–0.0028	0.0016–0.0037	.008 max.

① Measured 1.8 inch down from piston top

TORQUE SPECIFICATIONS

All readings in ft. lbs.

Year	V.I.N. Code	Engine Cyl. Displacement (cu. in.)	Eng. Mfg.	Cylinder Head Bolts	Rod Bearing Bolts	Main Bearing Bolts	Crankshaft Bolt	Flywheel to Crankshaft Bolts	Manifold Intake	Manifold Exhaust
'84–'85	R	4-151	Pont.	92	32	70	200	44	①	44
'86–'87	R	4-151	Pont.	①	32	70	162	44	①	44
'85–'87	9	6-173	Chev.	65–90	34–40	63–74	66–84	45–55	20–25	22–28

① See text and illustration for procedure and specifications.

WHEEL ALIGNMENT SPECIFICATIONS

Year	Model	Caster Range (deg)	Caster Pref. Setting (deg)	Camber Range (deg)	Camber Pref. Setting (deg)	Toe-in (in.)	Steering Axis (deg) Inclination
'84–'87	All	3P–7P	5P	5/16N–1 5/16P	1/2P	1/16 ± 1/32	—

17–5

SECTION 17: GENERAL MOTORS—"P" BODY
PONTIAC FIERO • FIERO SE

ELECTRICAL SECTION

For Overhaul Procedures Refer to Unit Repair Section

Charging System

ALTERNATOR

Removal and Installation

1. Disconnect the negative battery cable.
2. Remove the air cleaner.
3. Disconnect the upper strut mount.
4. Disconnect the alternator adjusting bolts, upper adjusting bracket and drive belt.
5. Disconnect the wiring from the back of the alternator.
6. Lower the alternator mounting bracket and remove the alternator from the bottom of the vehicle.
7. Installation is the reverse of removal.

VOLTAGE REGULATOR

An alternator with an integral voltage regulator is standard equipment. There are no adjustments possible with this unit. The alternator must be disassembled in order to service the regulator.

Starting System

STARTER

Removal and Installation

1. Disconnect the negative battery cable.
2. Raise and support the vehicle safely.
3. Disconnect all wires at solenoid terminals. Note color coding of wires for reinstallation.
4. Remove starter support bracket mount bolts.
5. Loosen the front bracket bolt or nut and rotate bracket clear. Lower and remove starter. Note the location of any shims so that they may be replaced in the same positions upon installation.
6. Reverse procedure to install.

Ignition System

DISTRIBUTOR

Removal and Installation

1. Disconnect the negative battery cable.
2. Tag and disconnect all wires leading from the distributor cap.
3. Remove the external ignition coil.
4. Remove the distributor cap.
5. Remove the vacuum hose from the vacuum advance unit. Mark the position of the vacuum advance unit in relation to the engine for correct installation.
6. The four cylinder engine has two bolts and a clamp. Remove the outer bolt first, then loosen, but do not remove, the inner bolt. Slide the clamp back and remove it.
7. Before removing the distributor, note the position of the rotor. Scribe a mark on the distributor body indicating the initial position of the rotor.
8. Remove the distributor from the engine. The drive gear on the distributor shaft is helical, and the shaft will rotate slightly as the distributor is removed. Note and mark the position of the rotor at this second position. Do not crank the engine with the distributor removed.
9. To install the distributor, rotate the distributor shaft until the rotor aligns with the second mark you made (when the shaft stopped moving). Lubricate the drive gear with clean engine oil, then install the distributor into the engine.
10. Install the clamp and hold-down bolt. Tighten them until the distributor can just be moved with a little effort.
11. Connect the ignition wire and tachometer wire, and install the distributor cap.
12. Check engine timing.

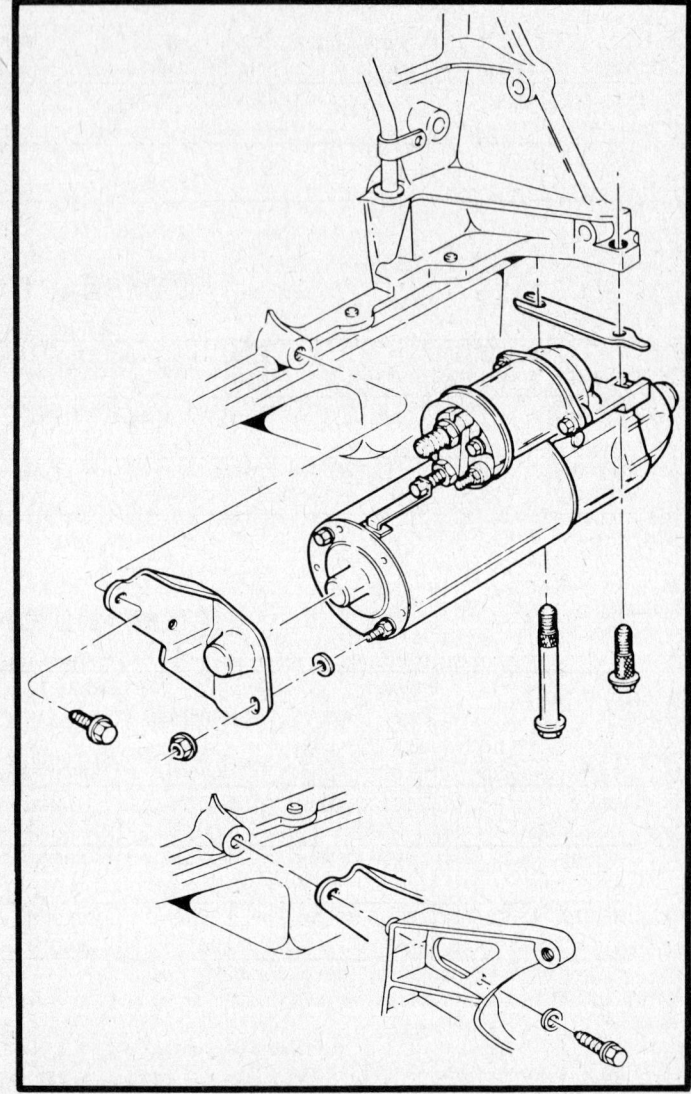

Starter motor mounting
(© General Motors Corporation)

Installation If The Engine Was Disturbed

If the engine was cranked while the distributor was removed, you will have to place the engine on TDC of the compression stroke to obtain proper ignition timing.

GENERAL MOTORS—"P" BODY
PONTIAC FIERO • FIERO SE

Alternator mounting (© General Motors Corporation)

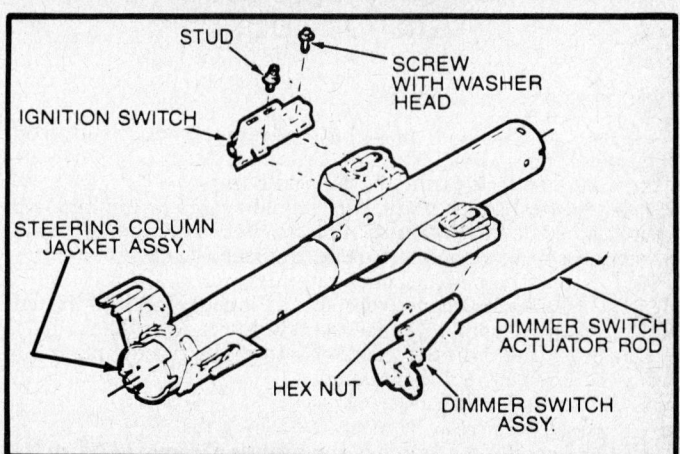

Ignition switch removal
(© General Motors Corporation)

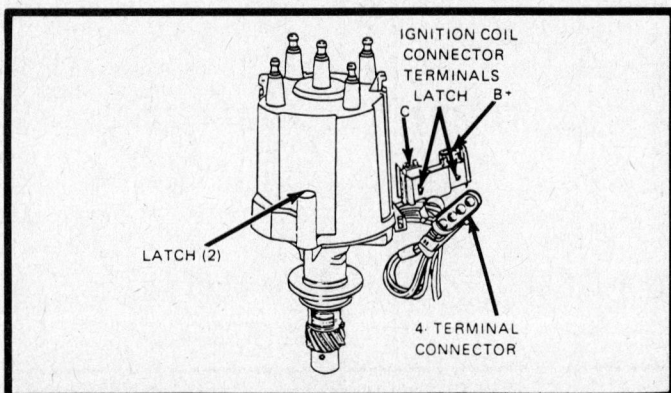

Typical distributor used with a separately mounted coil (© General Motors Corporation)

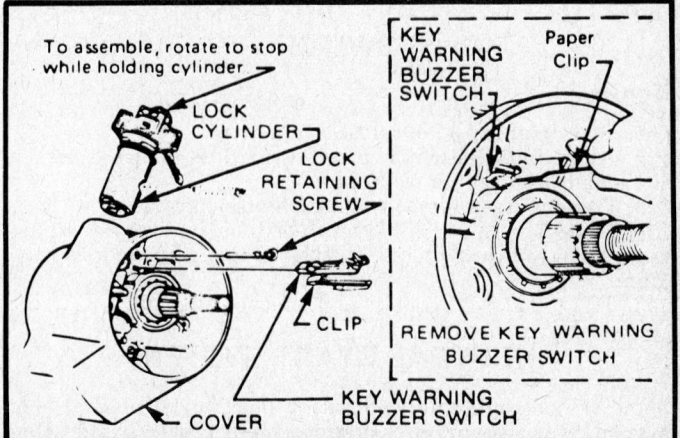

Ignition lock cylinder removal
(© General Motors Corporation)

1. Remove the No. 1 spark plug.
2. Place your thumb over the spark plug hole. Crank the engine slowly until compression is felt.
3. Align the timing mark on the crankshaft pulley with the 0° mark on the timing scale attached to the front of the engine. This places the engine at TDC of the compression stroke.
4. Turn the distributor shaft until the rotor points between the No. 1 and No. 3 spark plug towers on the cap for the four cylinder engine. If equipped with the V6 engine turn the distributer shaft until the rotor points between the No. 1 and No. 6 spark plug towers on the cap.
5. Install the distributor into the engine.
6. Continue the distributer installation procedure.

IGNITION TIMING

1. Connect a timing light to the No. 1 spark plug wire according to the manufacturer's instructions.
2. Follow the instructions on the underhood engine decal.
3. Disconnect the 4 terminal connector at the distributor.
4. Start the engine and run it at idle speed.
5. Aim the timing light at the degree scale just over the harmonic balancer.
6. Adjust the timing by loosening the securing clamp and rotating the distributor until the desired ignition advance is achieved, then tighten the clamp.
7. Loosen the distributor clamp outer bolt, then slide the clamp back slightly. Do not remove the retaining bolt.

8. Adjust the timing, then replace and tighten the clamp. To advance the timing, rotate the distributor opposite the normal direction of rotor rotation. Retard the timing by rotating the distributor in the normal direction of rotor rotation.

Electrical Controls

IGNITION SWITCH

Removal and Installation

1. Disconnect the negative battery cable. Lower the steering column and support it properly.
2. Put the switch in the 'Off-Unlocked' position. with the cylinder removed, the rod is n an 'Off-Unlocked' position when it is in the next to the uppermost detent.
3. Remove the two switch screws and remove the switch assembly.
4. Before installing, place the new switch in 'Off-Unlocked' position and make sure the lock cylinder and actuating rod are in 'Off-Unlocked' position (second detent from the top).
5. Install the activating rod into the switch and assemble the switch on the column. Tighten the mounting screws. Use only the specified screws, since overlength screws could impair the collapsibility of the column.
6. Reinstall the steering column.

17-7

SECTION 17 GENERAL MOTORS—"P" BODY
PONTIAC FIERO • FIERO SE

IGNITION LOCK

Removal and Installation

1. Disconnect the negative battery cable. Remove the steering wheel.
2. Turn the lock to the 'RUN' position.
3. Remove the lock plate, turn signal switch or combination switch, and the key warning buzzer switch. The warning buzzer switch can be fished out using a suitable tool.
4. Remove the lock cylinder retaining screw and lock cylinder. If the screw is dropped on removal, it could fall into the column, requiring complete disassembly to retrieve the screw.
5. Rotate the cylinder clockwise to align the cylinder key with the keyway in the housing.
6. Push the lock all the way in.
7. Install the screw. Tighten to 15 inch lbs.
8. The rest of installation is the reverse of removal. Turn the lock to 'RUN' and install the key warning buzzer switch, which is simply pushed down into place.

NEUTRAL SAFETY AND BACKUP LAMP SWITCH

Adjustment

1. Place transmission selector in neutral.
2. Align flats in switch insert with flats on transmission shaft and push switch over shaft.
3. Loosely assemble bolts to transmission case.
4. Insert shank end of 3/32 inch drill bit into service adjustment hold. Rotate switch until the drill bit drops to a depth of 9mm.
5. Tighten attaching bolts and remove gauge pin or drill bit.

NEUTRAL START SYSTEM

Some vehicles are equipped with a mechanical neutral start system. This system relies on a mechanical block rather than the starter safety switch to prevent starting the engine in any gear except Park or Neutral.

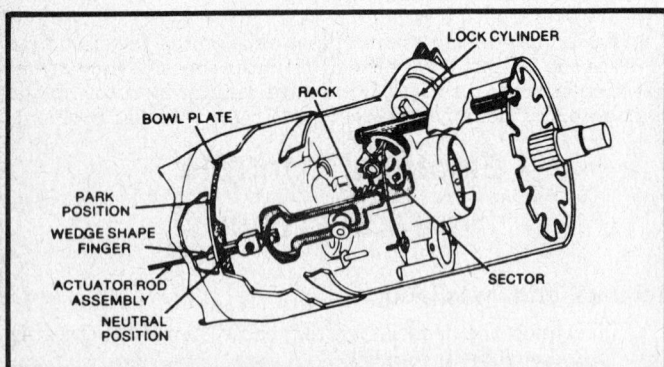

Mechanical neutral start system

CLUTCH START SWITCH

Removal and Installation

1. Disconnect the negative battery cable. Disconnect the electrical connect at the clutch switch, which is located at the top of the clutch pedal.
2. Remove the bolt attaching the switch to the clutch bracket.
3. Rotate the clutch switch slightly to disconnect the shaft from the clutch pedal hole.

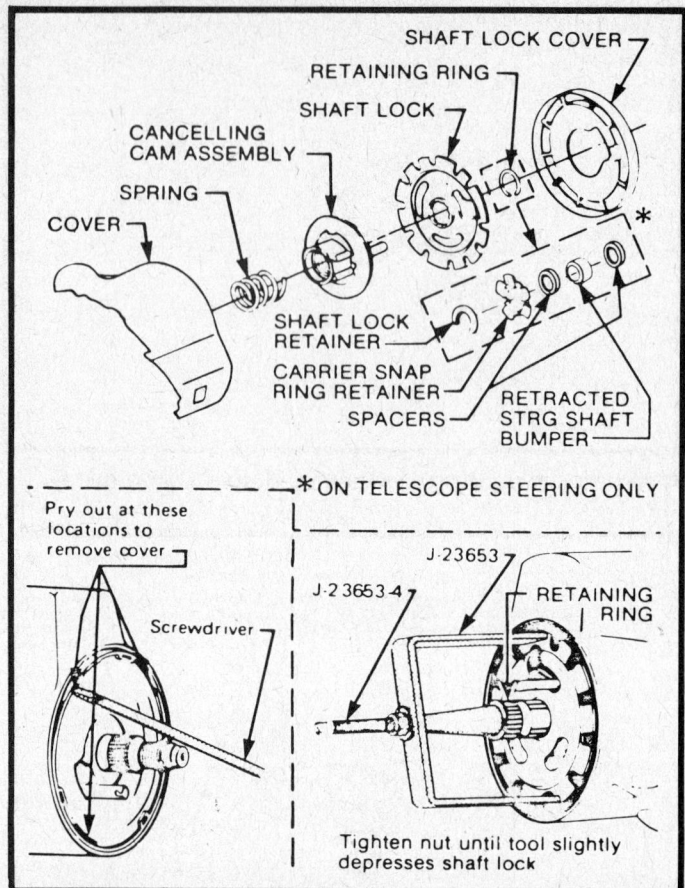

These parts must be removed to remove the turn signal switch (© General Motors Corporation)

4. Installation is the reverse order of the removal procedure.

STOP LIGHT SWITCH

Removal and Installation

1. Disconnect the negative battery cable. Disconnect the wiring harness from the switch which is located under the instrument panel at the brake pedal support.
2. Remove the retaining nut from the switch and remove the switch from the bracket.
3. Installation is the reverse order of the removal procedure.

TURN SIGNAL SWITCH

Removal and Installation

1. Disconnect the negative battery cable. Remove the steering wheel. Remove the trim cover.
2. Pry the cover from the steering column.
3. Position a U-shaped lockplate compressing tool on the end of the steering shaft and compress the lock plate by turning the shaft nut clockwise. Pry the wire snapring out of the shaft groove.
4. Remove the tool and lift the lockplate off the shaft.
5. Slip the canceling cam, upper bearing preload spring, and thrust washer off the shaft.
6. Remove the turn signal lever. Remove the hazard flasher button retaining screw and remove the button, spring and knob.

GENERAL MOTORS—"P" BODY
PONTIAC FIERO • FIERO SE
SECTION 17

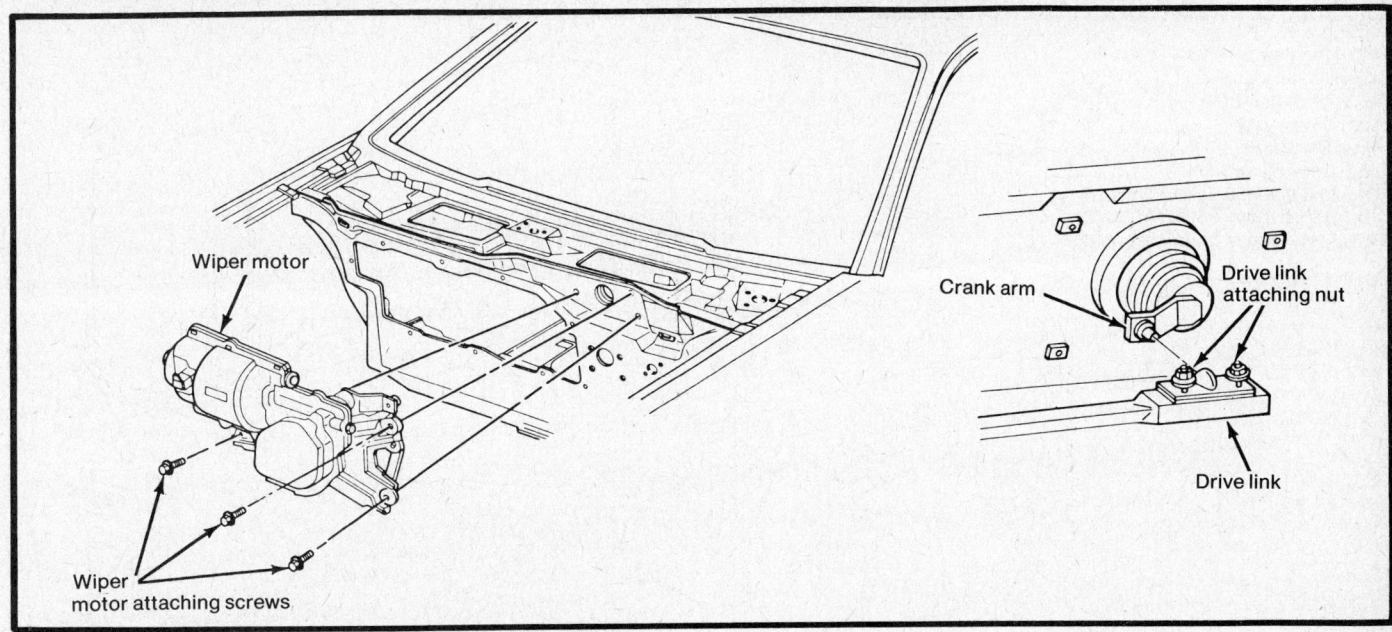

Wiper motor removal (© General Motors Corporation)

7. Pull the switch connector out of the mast jacket and tape the upper part to facilitate switch removal. Attach a long piece of wire to the turn signal switch, feed this wire through the column first, and then use this wire to pull the switch connector into position. On vehicles equipped with tilt wheel, place the turn signal and shifter housing in low position and remove the harness cover.
8. Remove the three switch mounting screws. Remove the switch by pulling it straight up while guiding the wiring harness cover through the column.
9. Install the replacement switch by working the connector and cover down through the housing and under the bracket. On tilt models, the connector is worked down through the housing, under the bracket, and then the cover in installed on the harness.
10. Install the switch mounting screws and the connector on the mast jacket bracket. Install the column to dash trim plate.
11. Install the flasher knob and the turn signal lever.
12. With the turn signal lever in neutral and the flasher knob out, slide the thrust washer, upper bearing preload spring, and canceling cam onto the shaft.
13. Position the lock plate on the shaft and press it down until a new snapring can be inserted in the shaft groove. Always use a new snapring when assembling.
14. Install the cover and the steering wheel.

HEADLAMP SWITCH
Removal and Installation

1. Disconnect the negative battery cable.
2. Remove the headlight/dimmer switch trim plate screws.
3. Disconnect the electrical connector and remove the switch assembly.
4. Installation is the reverse of the removal.

WINDSHIELD WIPER MOTOR
Removal and Installation

1. Disconnect the negative battery cable. Remove the wiper arms.
2. Remove the shroud top vent screen.
3. Remove the drive link from the crank arm.
4. Disconnect the electrical leads.
5. Remove the three attaching screws and remove the wiper motor.
6. Installation is the reverse of removal. Make sure the wiper motor is in the park position before installing the wiper arms and the shroud top screen.

WINDSHIELD WIPER TRANSMISSION
Removal and Installation

1. Remove wiper arms.
2. Remove shroud top vent screen.
3. Remove drive link from crank arm.
4. Remove the transmission to cowl panel attaching bolts.
5. Remove wiper transmission.
6. Installation is the reverse of the removal procedure.

Instrument Panel
INSTRUMENT CLUSTER
Removal and Installation

1. Disconnect the negative battery cable.
2. Remove the rear cluster cover.
3. Remove the front trim plate.
4. Remove the steering column cover.
5. Remove the cluster attaching screws. Disconnect the wiring harness and remove the cluster assembly.
6. The speedometer, tach, and gauges may be serviced by removing the front cluster lens.

Circuit Protection
FUSE BLOCK

The fuse block is a swing-down unit located in the underside of

SECTION 17
GENERAL MOTORS—"P" BODY
PONTIAC FIERO • FIERO SE

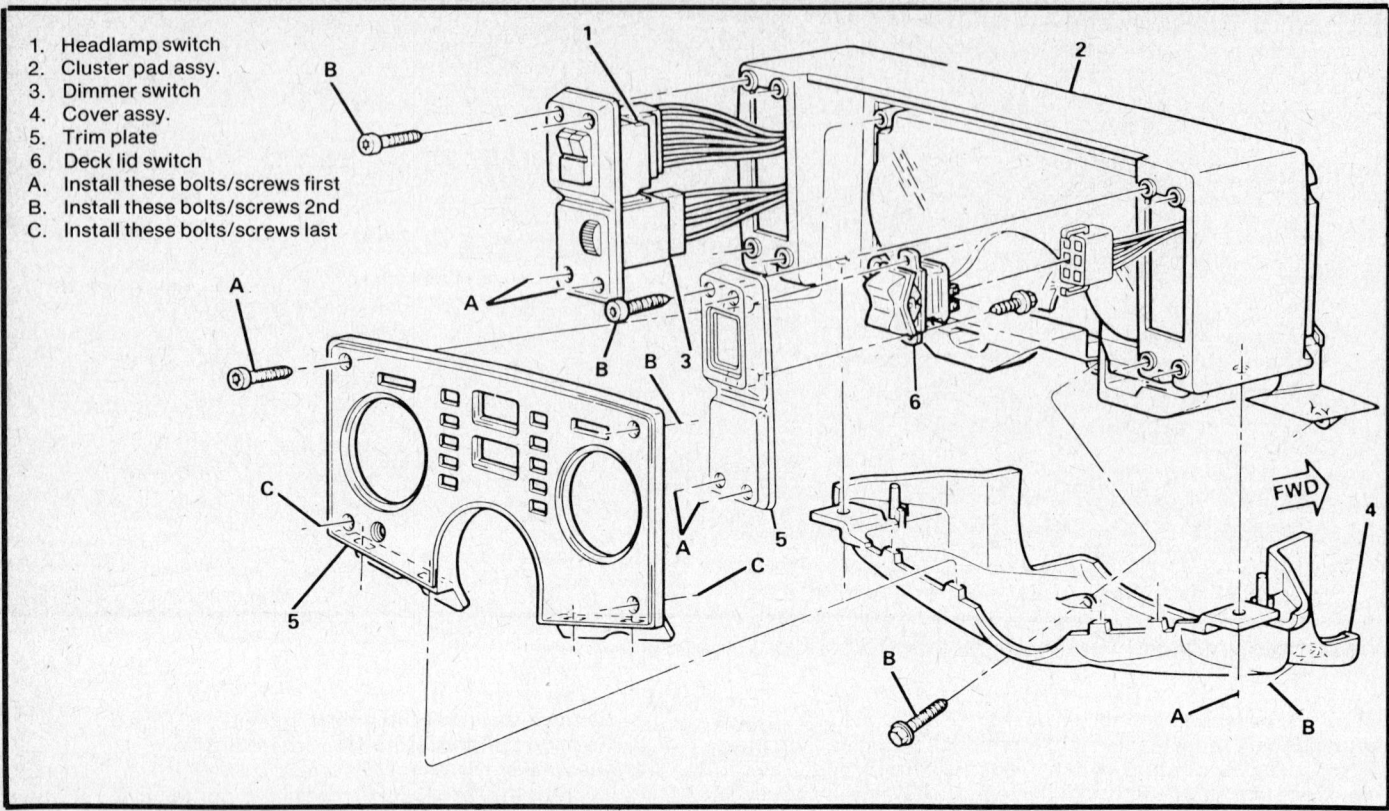

1. Headlamp switch
2. Cluster pad assy.
3. Dimmer switch
4. Cover assy.
5. Trim plate
6. Deck lid switch
A. Install these bolts/screws first
B. Install these bolts/screws 2nd
C. Install these bolts/screws last

Instrument cluster trim plates (© General Motors Corporation)

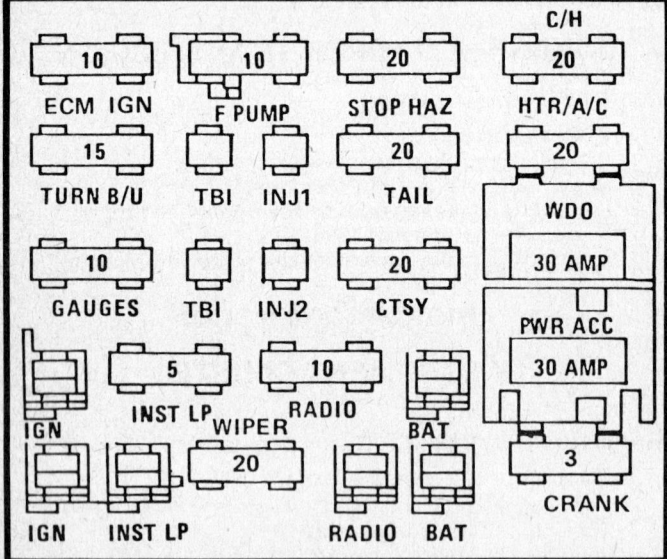

Front face of fuse block
(© General Motors Corporation)

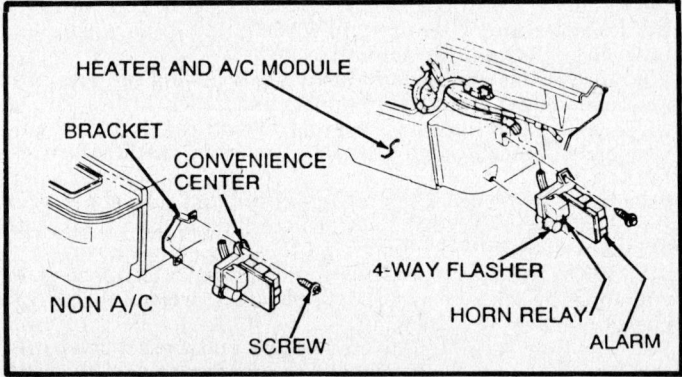

Convenience center and components
(© General Motors Corporation)

CONVENIENCE CENTER

The Convenience Center is a stationary unit. It is located on the right side of the heater or A/C module in the vehicle under the instrument panel. This location provides easy access to the audio alarm, hazard warnings, the horn relay and the seatbelt key and headlamp warning alarm. All units are serviced by plug-in replacement.

FUSIBLE LINK

Added protection is provided in all battery feed circuits and other selected circuits by a fusible link. This link is a short piece of copper wire approximately 4 inches long inserted in series with the circuit and acts as a fuse. The link is two or more

the instrument panel left of the steering column. The fuse block uses miniaturized fuses, designed for increased circuit protection and greater reliability. Various convenience connectors, which snap-lock into the fuse block, add to the serviceability of this unit.

GENERAL MOTORS—"P" BODY
PONTIAC FIERO • FIERO SE

gages smaller in size than the circuit wire it is protecting and will burn out without damage to the circuit in case of current overload.

Fusible Link Replacement

1. Disconnect the negative battery cable.
2. Locate burned out link.
3. Strip away all melted harness insulation.
4. Cut burned link ends from circuit wire.
5. Strip circuit wire back approximately 1/2" to allow soldering of new link.
6. Using fusible link four gages smaller than protected circuit (approximately 10 in. long), solder a new link into circuit.

NOTE: Use only resin core solder. Under no circumstances should an acid solder be used nor should the link be connected in any other manner except by soldering. Use of acid core solder may result in corrosion.

7. Tape the soldered ends securely using suitable electrical tape.
8. After taping wire, tape the harness leaving an exposed loop of wire approximately 5 inches in length.
9. Reconnect the negative battery cable.

Cruise Control
SERVO CABLE

Adjustment

1. With cable assembly installed in bracket install cable end on to stud of E.F.I. lever. Secure with retainer.
2. Pull servo assembly end of cable toward servo without moving E.F.I. lever.
3. If one of the six holes in the servo assembly tab lines up with cable pin. Connect pin to tag with retainer.
4. If a tab hole does not line up with the pin, move the cable away from the servo assembly, until the next closest tab hole lines up and connect pin to tab with retainer.
5. Do not stretch cable so as to make a particular tab hole connect to pin. This will prevent engine from returning to idle.

COOLING AND HEATER SECTION
WATER PUMP

Removal and Installation
EXCEPT V6 ENGINE

1. Disconnect battery negative cable. Drain the engine coolant.
2. Remove accessory drive belts. Remove all components in order to gain access to the water pump retaining bolts.
3. Remove water pump attaching bolts and remove pump.
4. If installing a new water pump, transfer pulley from old unit. With sealing surfaces cleaned, place a 1/8 inch bead of sealant #1052289 or equivalent on the water pump sealing surface. While sealer is still wet, install pump and torque bolts to 6 ft. lbs.
5. Install accessory drive belts.
6. Connect battery negative cable.

V6 ENGINE

1. Disconnect the negative battery cable. Drain the engine coolant.
2. Remove the fan shroud and the drive belts. Remove all the necessary components in order to gain access to the water pump retaining bolts.

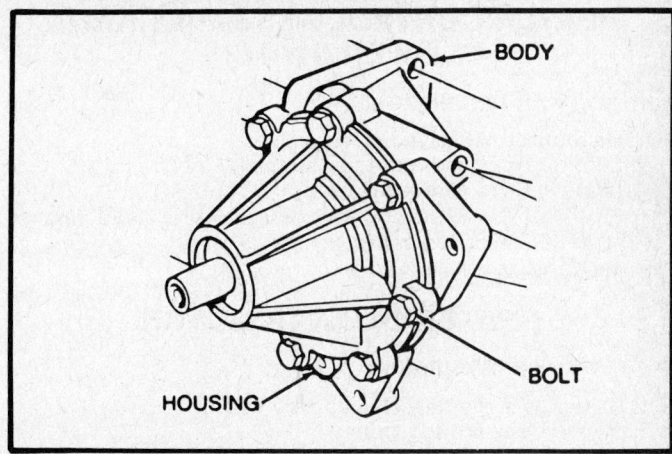

Water pump mounting
(© General Motors Corporation)

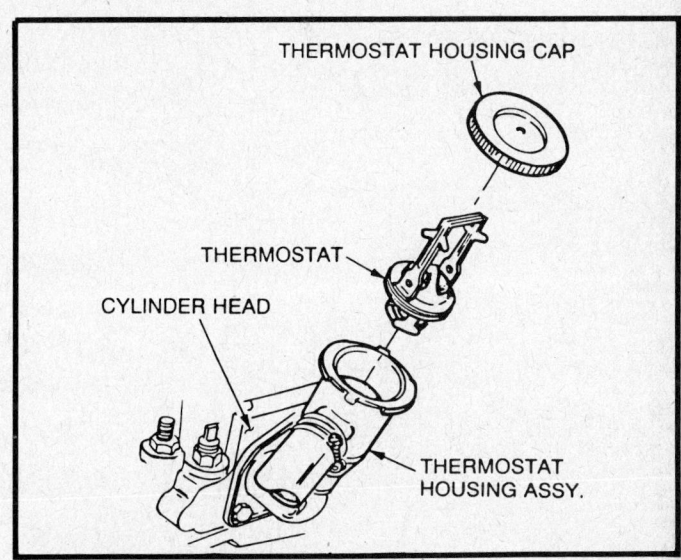

Thermostat and housing
(© General Motors Corporation)

3. Remove the radiator hoses and the heater hose running to the water pump.
4. Remove the bolts attaching the water pump to the engine block and remove the water pump and gasket.
5. Installation is the reverse order of the removal procedure, be sure to apply a thin bead of RTV sealant to the water pump mounting surface and the water pump bolts. Torque the bolts to 6–9 ft. lbs. Do not over torque the water pump bolts, because the pump is aluminum and will crack very easily.

THERMOSTAT

Removal and Installation

1. Remove the thermostat cap.
2. Grasp the thermostat handle and gently pull up.
3. Before installing, clean the thermostat housing and O-ring. Apply a suitable lubricant to the O-ring for easier installation.
4. Push the thermostat down into the housing until it is properly seated and install the cap.

SECTION 17

GENERAL MOTORS—"P" BODY
PONTIAC FIERO • FIERO SE

HEATER CONTROL ASSEMBLY AND BLOWER SWITCH

Removal and Installation

1. Disconnect negative battery cable.
2. Remove front pad and trim plate assembly.
3. Remove the 3 controller retaining screws.
4. Disconnect electrical connection at switch and remove blower switch from controller.
5. Installation is the reverse of removal procedure.

HEATER BLOWER MOTOR

Removal and Installation

1. Disconnect the negative battery cable.
2. Remove the cooling tube.
3. Disconnect all electrical connections.
4. Remove the heater motor retaining screws. Remove the heater motor and cage assembly.
5. Installation is the reverse of removal.

HEATER CORE

Removal and Installation
WITH A/C

1. Disconnect the negative battery cable. Disconnect and plug the heater hoses at the heater.
2. Remove the speaker grille and the speaker.
3. Remove the heater core cover retainers and the heater core.
4. Installation is the reverse of removal. Refill the cooling system as required.

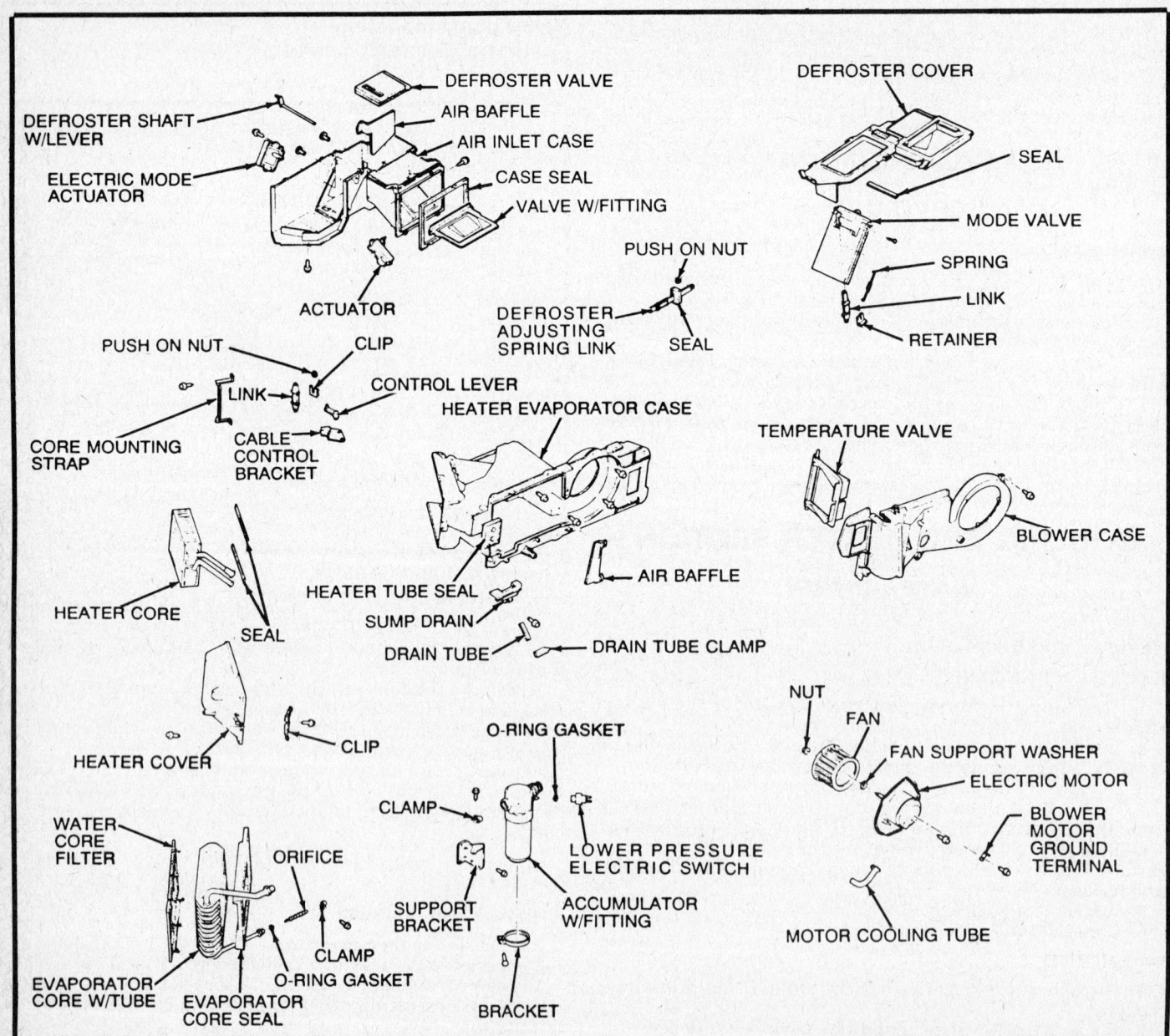

Exploded view of A/C module (© General Motors Corporation)

GENERAL MOTORS—"P" BODY
PONTIAC FIERO • FIERO SE

WITHOUT A/C
1. Disconnect the negative battery cable.
2. Disconnect the following wire connections, heater relay, heater blower resistor, heater blower switch, heater ground connection and forward courtesy lamp socket.
3. Remove the windshield washer fluid container.
4. Disconnect the heater core inlet and outlet hoses.
5. Remove the heater core grommets.
6. Remove the heater case cover.
7. Remove the heater core retainer and remove the heater core.
8. Installation is the reverse of removal. Refill the cooling system as required.

FUEL SYSTEM

The TBI (Throttle Body Injection) system used by the Fiero uses an electric fuel pump. The fuel pump is located in the gas tank.

FUEL PRESSURE RELIEF PROCEDURE

All Except V6 with MFI

Before opening any part of the fuel system, the pressure must be relieved. Follow the procedure below to relieve the pressure.
1. Remove the fuel pump fuse from the fuse panel.

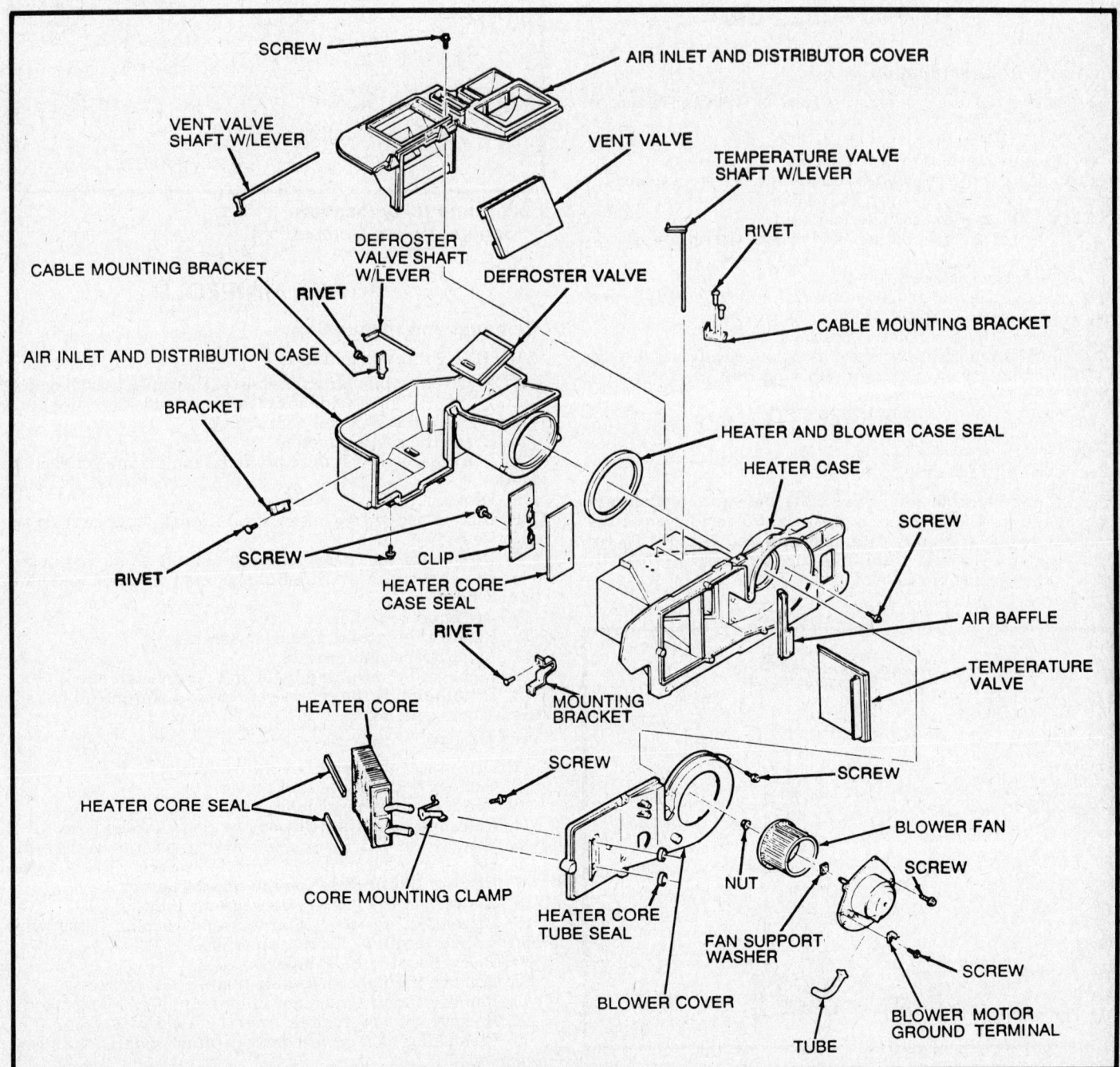

Exploded view of heater module (© General Motors Corporation)

17-13

SECTION 17
GENERAL MOTORS – "P" BODY
PONTIAC FIERO • FIERO SE

2. Start the engine and let it run until all fuel in the line is used.
3. Crank the starter an additional three seconds to relieve any residual pressure.
4. With the ignition OFF replace the fuse.

V6 Engine with MFI

1. Connect the fuel gauge J-34730-1 or equivalent to the fuel pressure valve, located on the fuel rail.
2. Wrap a shop towel around the fitting while connecting the gauge to avoid any spillage.
3. Install the bleed hose into a suitable container and open the valve to bleed off the fuel pressure.

ELECTRIC FUEL PUMP

Removal and Installation

1. Relieve the fuel system pressure. Disconnect the negative battery cable.
2. Drain the fuel tank.
3. Disconnect wiring from the tank.
4. Remove the ground wire retaining screw from under the body.
5. Disconnect all hoses from the tank.
6. Support the tank on a jack and remove the retaining strap nuts.
7. Lower the tank and remove it.
8. Remove the fuel gauge/pump retaining ring using a spanner wrench such as tool J-24187 or equivalent.
9. Remove the gauge unit and the pump.
10. Installation is the reverse of removal. Always replace the O-Ring under the gauge/pump retaining ring.

FUEL FILTER

Removal and Installation

The filter is an inline unit ahead of the fuel injectors. Before removal relieve the fuel pump pressure. To remove the filter, make sure the engine is cold, unclamp and remove the fuel hose, then unscrew the filter from the steel fuel line. Installation is the reverse of removal.

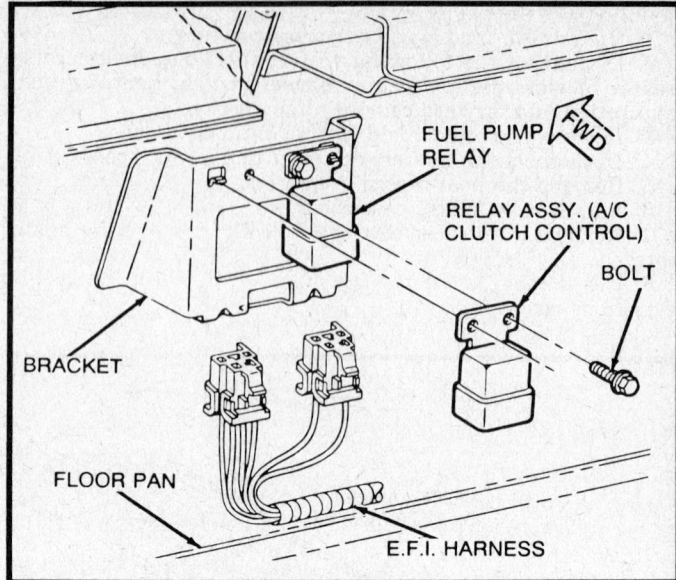

Fuel pump relay location
(© General Motors Corporation)

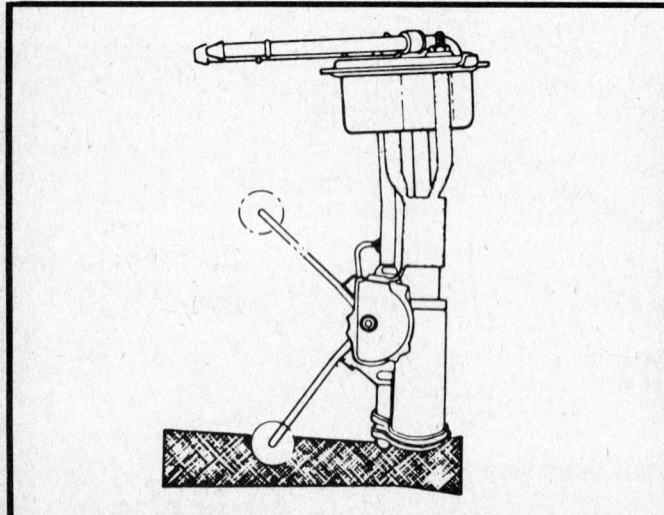

Typical electric fuel pump and sending unit
(© General Motors Corporation)

INTAKE MANIFOLD

Removal and Installation

ALL EXCEPT V6 ENGINE

1. Relieve the fuel pump pressure. Disconnect the negative battery cable. Remove the air cleaner assembly.
2. Remove the PCV valve and hose.
3. Drain the cooling system.
4. Relieve the fuel system pressure and disconnect the fuel lines.
5. Disconnect the vacuum hoses.
6. Disconnect the wiring and the throttle linkage from the throttle body assembly.
7. Disconnect the cruise control and linkage, if so equipped.
8. Disconnect the throttle linkage and bell crank and place to one side.
9. Disconnect the heater hose.
10. Remove the generator upper bracket.
11. Remove the ignition coil.
12. Remove the retaining bolts and remove the manifold.
13. Installation is the reverse of removal. Torque all bolts in the proper sequence.

V6 ENGINE

1. Disconnect the negative battery cable.
2. Remove both rocker arm covers.
3. Drain the engine coolant.
4. Disconnect the throttle body to elbow intake hose.
5. Remove the distributor and mark the position of the rotor.
6. Disconnect the shift and throttle linkage.
7. Remove the throttle body to upper plenum.
8. Disconnect the heater and radiator hoses.
9. Disconnect all wiring harness and vacuum hoses while noting their locations for reassembly.
10. Disconnect the EGR pipe.
12. Remove the upper manifold plenum and gaskets.
13. Remove the intermediate intake manifold and gasket.
14. Remove the lower intake manifold and gaskets.
15. Clean all gasket surfaces on the intake manifolds and cylinder head.
16. Install the lower intake manifold and gasket and torque to specification in the proper sequence.

GENERAL MOTORS—"P" BODY
PONTIAC FIERO • FIERO SE
SECTION 17

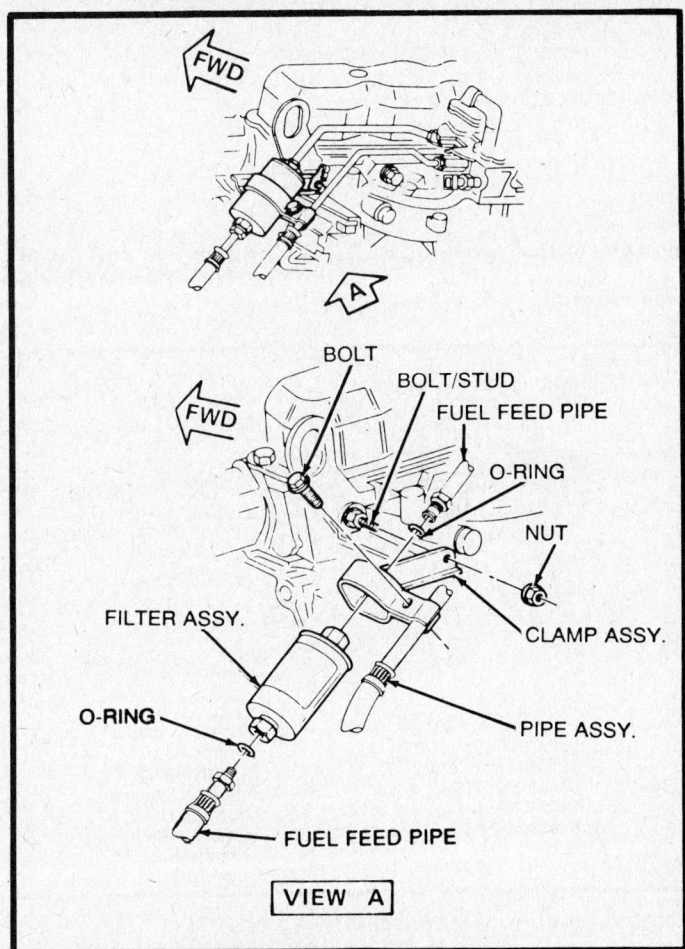

Fuel filter (© General Motors Corporation)

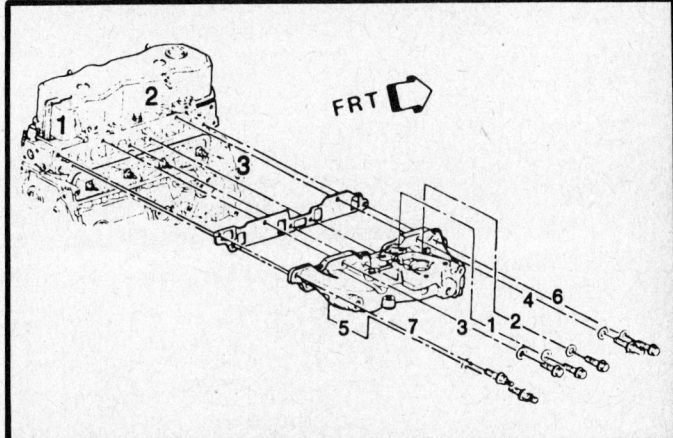

Intake manifold torque sequence
(© General Motors Corporation)

17. Install the intermediate intake manifold and gaskets and torque in sequence to specification.
18. Install the upper manifold plenum and gaskets and torque in sequence.
19. The remainder of the installation is the reverse of the removal. Check engine timing, coolant level and for leaks.

EXHAUST MANIFOLD

Removal and Installation

ALL EXCEPT V6 ENGINE

1. Disconnect the negative battery cable. Remove the air cleaner and the EFI bracket tube.
2. Raise and support the vehicle safely.
3. Remove the exhaust pipe and lower the vehicle.
4. Remove the retaining bolts and washers and remove the exhaust manifold and gasket.
5. Installation is the reverse of removal. Clean the sealing surfaces and use a new gasket. Torque the retaining bolts in sequence.

V6 ENGINE (FRONT)

1. Disconnect the negative battery cable.
2. Remove the rear compartment lid. Do not remove the torsion rod retaining bolts.
3. Remove the brake volume hose.
4. Remove the manifold heat shield.
5. Remove the front crossover bolts.

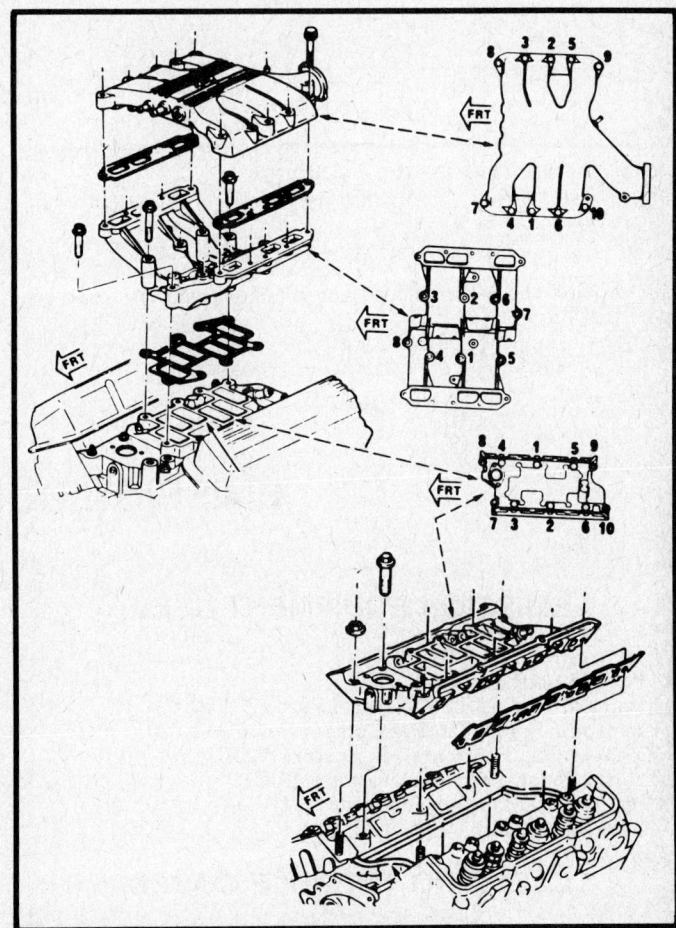

Intake manifold installation—V6 engine

6. Raise the car and remove the front converter heat shield and the lower manifold bolts.
7. Lower the vehicle and remove the upper manifold bolts then remove the manifold.
8. Install the manifold and torque the bolts to specification.
10. Install the front converter heat shield.

17–15

SECTION 17: GENERAL MOTORS—"P" BODY
PONTIAC FIERO • FIERO SE

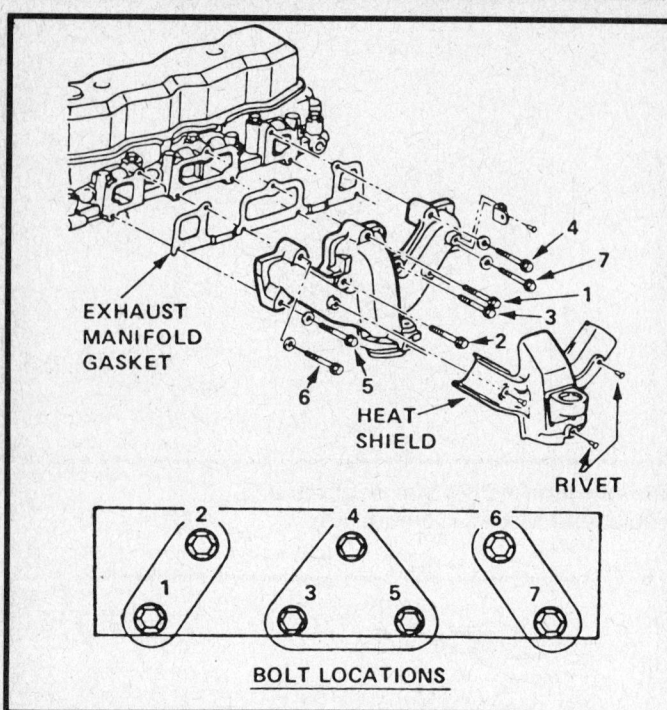

Exhaust manifold torque sequence
(© General Motors Corporation)

11. Lower the vehicle and torque the crossover bolts to specification.
12. The remainder of the installation is the reverse of the removal. Check for exhaust or vacuum leaks.

V6 ENGINE (REAR)
1. Disconnect the manifold to crossover bolts.
2. Remove the manifold bolts then remove the manifold.
3. Installation is the reverse of removal. Torque the manifold bolts to specification.

Fuel Injection

For all service procedures, including removal and installation of the TBI unit, refer to the Fuel Injection section of this manual.

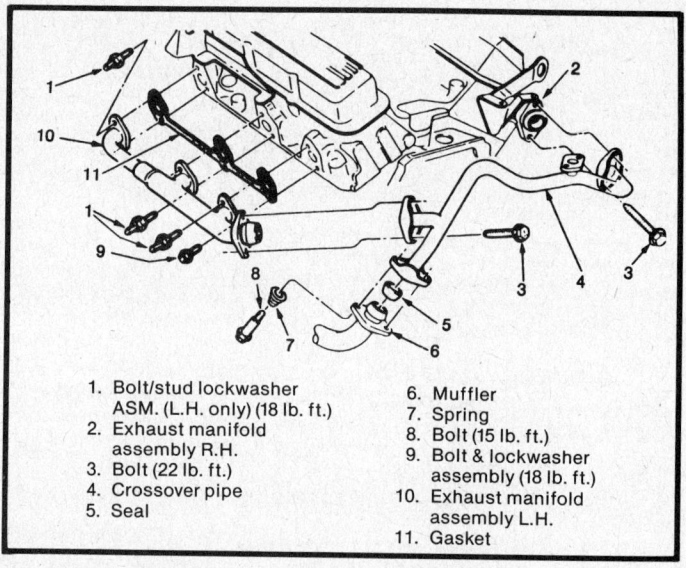

1. Bolt/stud lockwasher ASM. (L.H. only) (18 lb. ft.)
2. Exhaust manifold assembly R.H.
3. Bolt (22 lb. ft.)
4. Crossover pipe
5. Seal
6. Muffler
7. Spring
8. Bolt (15 lb. ft.)
9. Bolt & lockwasher assembly (18 lb. ft.)
10. Exhaust manifold assembly L.H.
11. Gasket

Exhaust manifold installation—V6 engine

EMISSION CONTROL SYSTEMS

EMISSION EQUIPMENT USED

Electronic Control Module
Throttle Body Injection
Evaporative Emission Control System (EEEC)
Electronic Spark Timing Control System (EST)
Exhaust Gas Recirculation System (EGR)
Transmission Converter Clutch (TCC)
Positive Crankcase Ventilation (PCV)
Thermostatic Air Cleaner (TAC)

CLEARING TROUBLE CODES

When the ECM finds a problem, the 'CHECK ENGINE' light will come 'ON' and a trouble code will be recorded in the ECM memory. If the problem is intermittent, the 'CHECK ENGINE' light will go out after 10 seconds, when the fault goes away. However, the trouble code will stay in the ECM memory until the battery voltage to the ECM is removed. Removing battery voltage for 10 seconds will clear all stored trouble codes. Do this by disconnecting the ECM harness from the positive battery pigtail for 10 seconds with the key 'off', or by removing the 'ECM' fuse.

Trouble Codes should be cleared after repairs have been completed on a problem. Also, some Diagnostic Charts will tell you to clear the codes before using the chart. This allows the ECM to set the code while going thru the chart, which will help to find the cause of the problem more quickly. To prevent ECM damage, the key must be 'OFF' when disconnecting or reconnecting power to ECM (for example battery cable, ECM pigtail, ECM fuse, jumper cables, etc.).

ECM LEARNING ABILITY

The ECM has a 'learning' ability. If the battery is disconnect to clear diagnostic codes, or for repair, the 'learning' process has to begin all over again. A change may be noted in the vehicle's performance. To 'teach' the vehicle, make sure the vehicle is at operating temperature, and drive at part throttle, with moderate acceleration and idle conditions, until normal performance returns.

GENERAL MOTORS—"P" BODY
PONTIAC FIERO • FIERO SE
SECTION 17

ENGINE SECTION

ENGINE ASSEMBLY

Removal and Installation

NOTE: The engine assembly is removed from underneath the vehicle.

1. Disconnect the battery cables.
2. Drain the engine coolant.
3. Remove the rear compartment lid and also the side panels on the V6 engine. Do not remove the torsion rod retaining bolts.
4. Remove the air cleaner assembly.
5. Disconnect the throttle and shift cables.
6. Disconnect the heater hose at the intake manifold.
7. Disconnect the vacuum hoses from all non-engine components.
8. Disconnect the fuel lines and filter.
9. Disconnect the fuel pump relay and the oxygen sensor.
10. On models equipped with automatic transaxle, disconnect the transaxle cooler lines.
11. Disconnect the slave cylinder from the manual transaxle equipped vehicles.
12. Disconnect the engine to chassis ground strap.
13. Disconnect the A/C system, if so equipped, then disconnect the A/C lines at the compressor and seal the end. Be careful when disconnecting the refrigerant lines, escaping refrigerant will freeze any surface it contacts, including your skin and eyes.
12. Remove the rear console.
15. Remove the ECM haness through the bulkhead panel.
16. Install an engine support fixture.
17. Remove the engine strut bracket and mark the bolt and bracket for reassembly.
18. Raise and support the vehicle safely.
19. Remove the rear wheels.
20. On models equipped with an automatic transaxle, remove the torque converter bolts.
21. Remove the parking brake cable and calipers. Do not disconnect the brake hoses. Support the caliper out of the way.
22. Remove the strut bolts and mark the struts for realignment.
23. Disconnect the A/C wiring, if so equipped.
24. Loosen the four engine cradle bolts.
25. On the 4 cylinder engine, release the parking rake cables at the cradle. A special tool No. J-34065 is available for this procedure.

NOTE: Support the engine/transaxle and cradle assembly on a jack. Be sure to support the outboard ends of the lower control arms. Disconnect the engine support fixture.

26. Lower the vehicle and attach the engine/transaxle assembly to a dolly. Remove the cradle bolts. Raise the vehicle and roll the dolly from under the vehicle.
27. Separate the engine and transaxle.
28. Installation is the reverse of removal.

ROCKER ARM AND PUSH ROD

Removal and Installation

ALL EXCEPT V6

1. Disconnect the negative battery cable. Remove the air cleaner.
2. Remove the PCV valve and hose.
3. Remove the valve cover bolts.

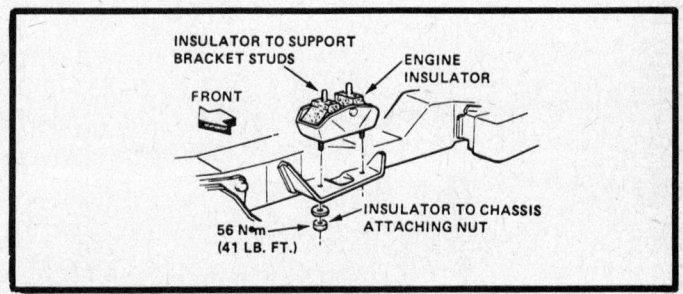

Engine mount to crossmember
(© General Motors Corporation)

4. Disconnect the wires from the spark plugs and clips.
5. Remove the valve cover by tapping lightly with a rubber hammer. Prying on the cover could cause damage to the sealing surfaces.
6. Remove the rocker arm bolt.
7. If replacing the push rod only, loosen the rocker arm bolt and swing the arm clear of the push rod.
8. Remove the rocker arm and push road.
9. Installation is the reverse of removal. Torque the rocker arm bolt to 20 ft. lbs. Apply a continuous $3/16$ in. diameter bead of RTV sealant or equivalent around the cylinder head sealant surfaces inboard at the bolt holes.

V6 ENGINE

1. Disconnect the negative battery cable.
2. Remove the engine compartment lid and both side covers. Do not remove the torsion rod retaining bolts.
3. Disconnect the vacuum boost line and tube.
4. Disconnect the throttle and downshift cables and bracket.
5. Disconnect the cruise control cable, if applicable.
6. Disconnect the ground cable.
7. Remove the PCV from the cover.
8. Remove the oil dip stick tube.
9. Disconnect the plug wires and bracket.
10. Remove the engine lift hook.
11. Remove the rocker arm cover bolts and carefully remove cover by bumping with your hand or a rubber mallet. If prying is necessary do not distort the sealing flange.
12. Remove the rocker arm nuts. Keep all components in order so that they may be reinstalled in the same location.
13. Remove the rocker arm pivot balls, arms and push rods.
14. Before installation, coat the bearing surfaces of the rocker arms and pivot balls with 'Molykote' or equivalent.
15. Insert the push rods, rocker arms and pivot balls. Make sure the push rods are seated in the valve lifters.
16. Adjust the rocker arm nuts until lash is eliminated. Rotate the engine until the mark on the torsional damper lines up with the '0' mark on the timing tab, with the engine in the No.1 firing position. This may be determined by placing fingers on the No. 1 rocker arms as the mark on the damper comes near the '0' mark. If the valves are not moving, the engine is in the No.1 firing position. With the engine in the No.1 firing position the following valves may be adjusted, Exhaust - 4, 5, 6; Intake - 2, 3, 4.
17. Install the rocker arm covers. Clean the surfaces on the cylinder head and rocker arm cover. Place a 1/8 inch) dot of RTV sealer, at the intake manifold and cylinder head split line. Install the rocker arm cover gasket, using care to line up the holes in the gasket with the bolt holes in the cylinder head.
18. Install the rocker arm cover bolts and torque to 90 inch lbs.

17-17

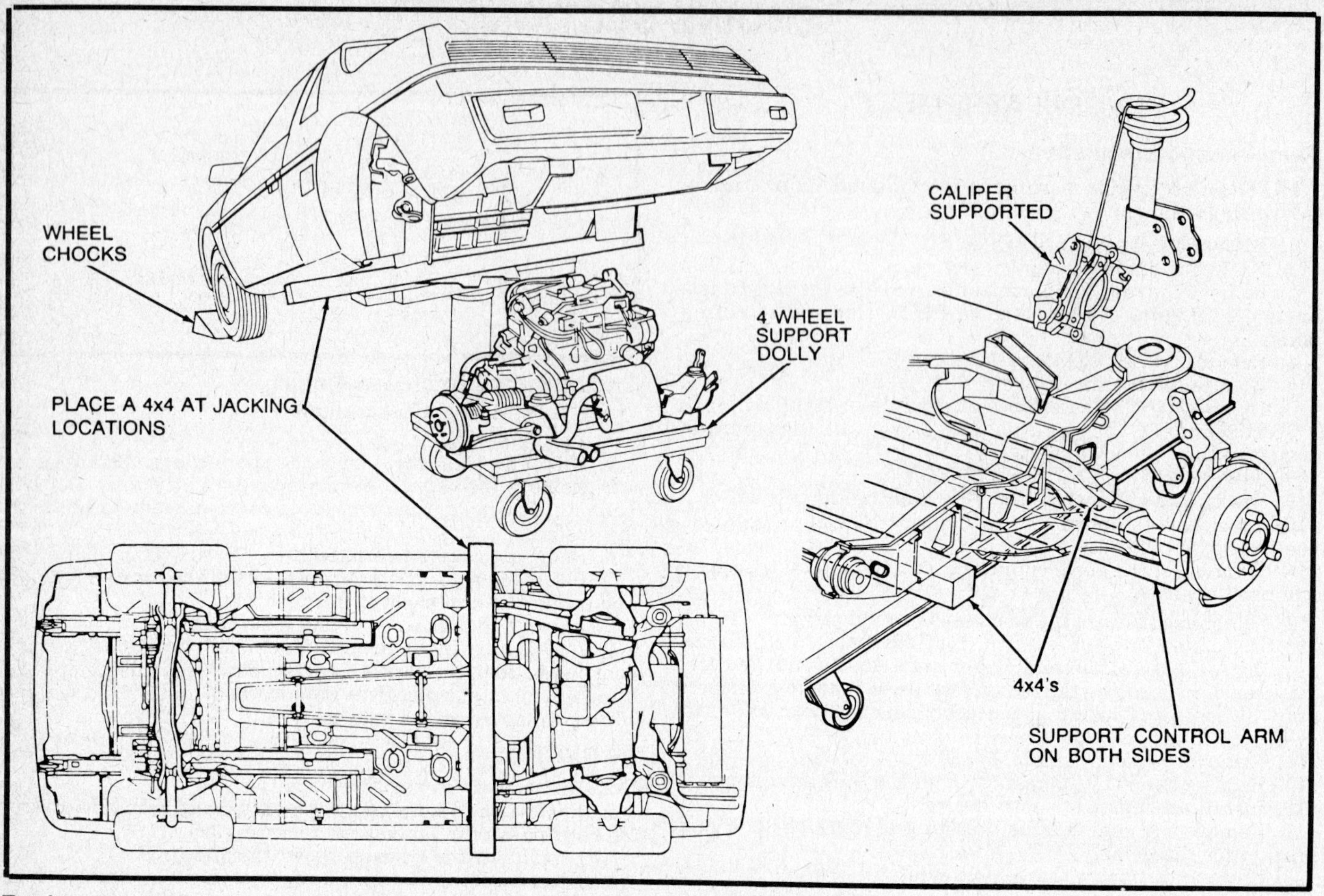

SECTION 17 — GENERAL MOTORS—"P" BODY
PONTIAC FIERO • FIERO SE

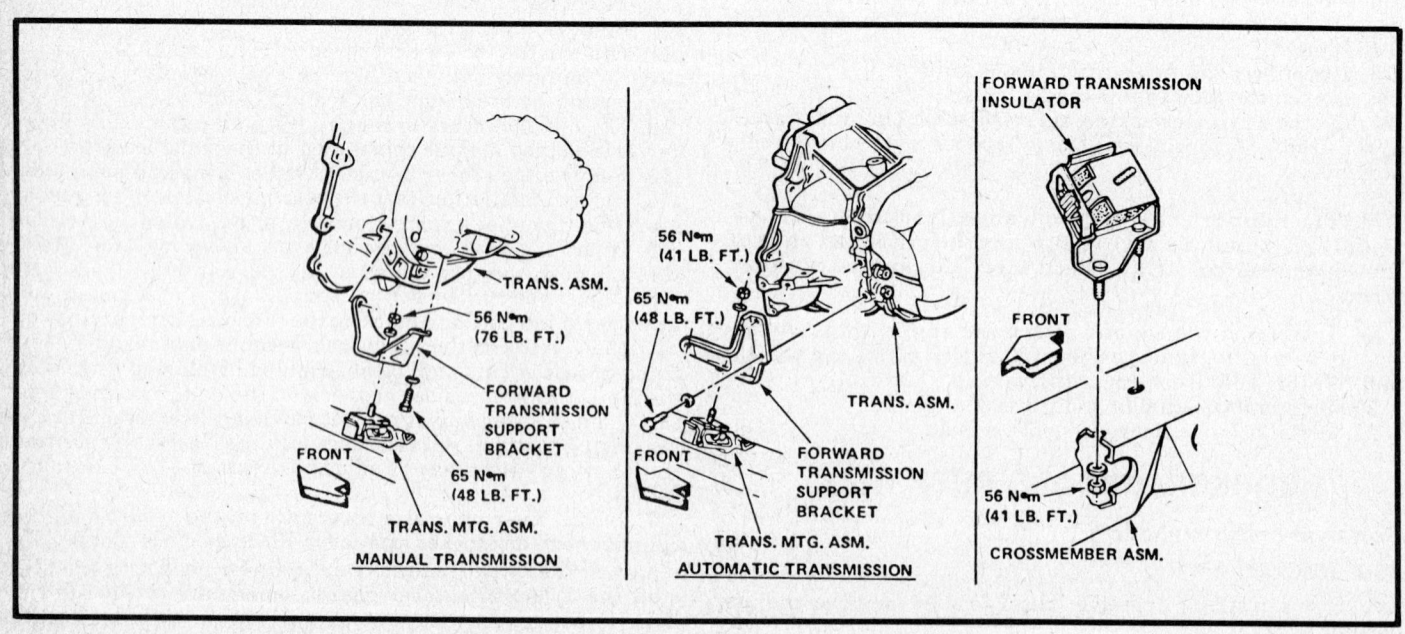

Engine removal and cradle support points (© General Motors Corporation)

Forward transaxle mount and mounting brackets (© General Motors Corporation)

17–18

GENERAL MOTORS—"P" BODY
PONTIAC FIERO · FIERO SE
SECTION 17

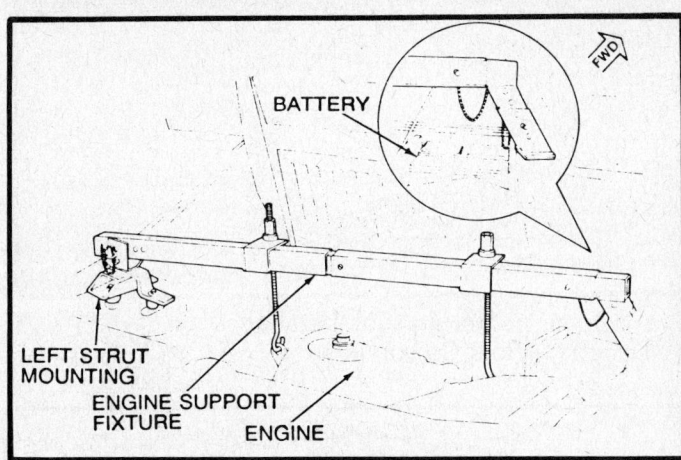

Engine holding fixture mounting
(© General Motors Corporation)

19. The remainder of the installation is the reverse of removal.

VALVE LASH ADJUSTMENT

No routine adjustment is necessary.

CYLINDER HEAD

Removal and Installation

ALL EXCEPT V6 ENGINE

1. Disconnect the negative battery cable. Drain the cooling system.
2. Raise the vehicle and support it safely.
3. Remove the exhaust pipe.
4. Lower the vehicle.
5. Remove the oil level indicator tube.
6. Remove the air cleaner assembly.
7. Disconnect the E.F.I. electrical connections and vacuum hoses.
8. Remove the EGR base plate.
9. Remove the heater hose from the intake manifold.
10. Remove the ignition coil lower mounting bolt and wiring connections.
11. Remove all wiring connections from the intake manifold and cylinder head.
12. Remove the engine strut bolt from the upper support.
13. Remove the generator belt.
14. Remove the throttle cables from the intake manifold.
15. Remove the valve cover, rocker arms and push rods.
16. Remove the cylinder head bolts and remove the cylinder head.
17. Before installing, clean the gasket surfaces of the head and block.
18. Make sure the retaining bolt threads and the cylinder block threads are clean since dirt could affect bolt torque.
19. Install a new gasket over the dowel pins in the cylinder block.
20. Install the cylinder head into place over the dowel pins.
21. Coat the cylinder head bolt threads with sealing compound and install finger tight.
22. Tighten the cylinder head bolts gradually in the proper sequence and torque to 92 ft. lbs. on vehicles through 1985.
23. On 1986 and later vehicles tighten the cylinder head bolts in the proper sequence to 18 ft. lbs. Repeat the sequence and torque the bolts to 22 ft. lbs. on all bolts except number nine. Toeque that bolt to 29 ft. lbs. Turn all bolts, except number nine, 120 degrees. Turn bolt number nine ninety degrees.

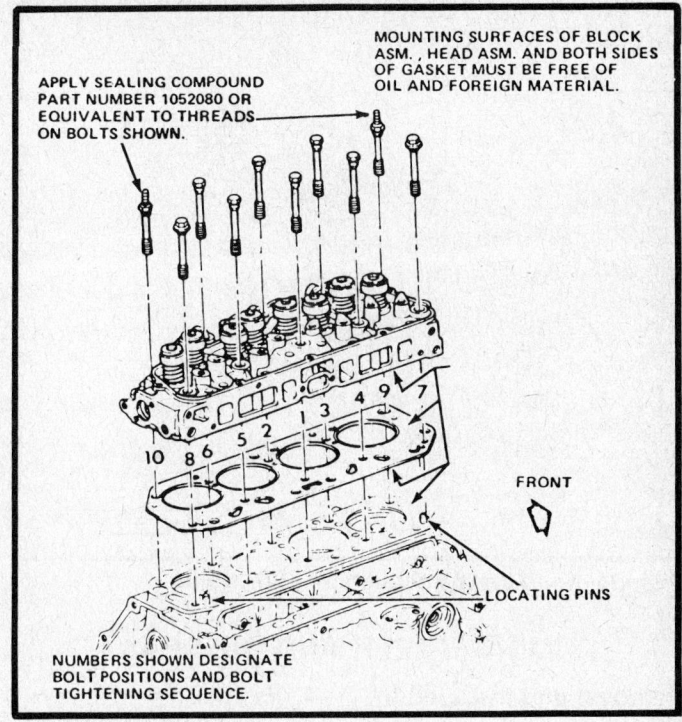

Cylinder head torque sequence
(© General Motors Corporation)

24. The remainder of the installation is the reverse of removal.

V6 ENGINE (LEFT SIDE)

1. Disconnect the negative battery cable. Raise the vehicle and support it safely. Drain the coolant from the block.
2. Lower the vehicle.
3. Remove the intake manifold.
4. Disconnect the exhaust crossover pipe.
5. Disconnect the generator bracket.
6. Remove the oil level indicator tube.
7. Loosen the rocker arms until you're able to remove the push rods.
8. Remove the cylinder head bolts then remove the cylinder head.
9. Before installing, clean the gasket surfaces on the head, cylinder head and intake manifold.
10. Place the gasket in position over the dowel pins with the note 'This Side UP' showing.
11. Place the cylinder head into position.
12. Coat the cylinder head bolts threads with a sealer and install the bolts. Tighten the bolts in sequence to 66 ft. lbs.
13. Install the push rods and loosely retain with the rocker arms. Make sure the lower ends of the push rods are in the lifter seals then adjust the valve lash.
14. The remainder of the installation is the reverse of the removal.

V6 ENGINE (RIGHT SIDE)

1. Disconnect the negative battery cable. Raise the vehicle and support it safely. Drain the cooling system.
2. Disconnect the exhaust pipe.
3. Lower the vehicle.
4. Disconnect the cruise control servo bracket.
5. Remove the intake manifold.
6. Disconnect the exhaust crossover pipe.
7. Follow Steps 7 thru 14 of the left side cylinder head procedure above.

SECTION 17

GENERAL MOTORS—"P" BODY
PONTIAC FIERO • FIERO SE

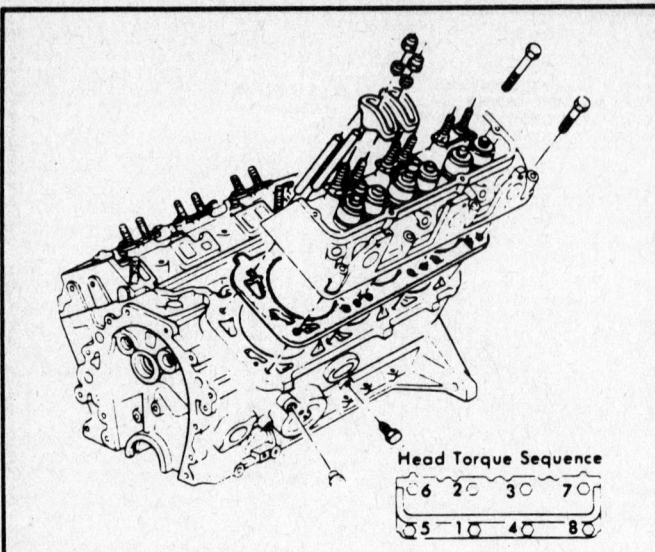

Cylinder head torque sequence—V6 engine

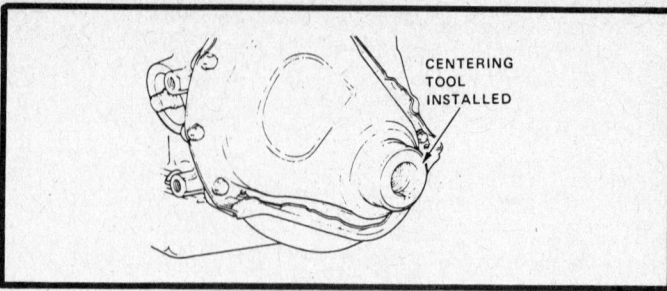

Front cover centering tool installed
(© General Motors Corporation)

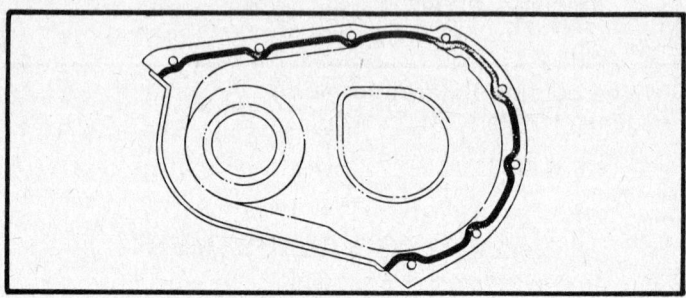

Timing cover sealer application
(© General Motors Corporation)

Removing camshaft thrust screws
(© General Motors Corporation)

TIMING COVER AND OIL SEAL

Removal and Installation

ALL EXCEPT V6 ENGINE

1. Disconnect the negative battery cable. Remove the crankshaft hub. It is necessary to remove the inner fender splash shield.
2. Remove the alternator flower bracket.
3. Remove the front engine mounts.
4. Raise the engine.
5. Remove the engine mount mounting bracket to cylinder block bolts. Remove the bracket and mount as an assembly.
6. Remove the oil pan to front cover screws.
7. Remove the front cover to block screws.
8. Pull the cover slightly forward, just enough to allow cutting of the oil pan front seal flush with the block on both sides.
9. Remove the front cover and attached portion of the pan seal.
10. Clean the gasket surfaces thoroughly.
11. Cut the tabs from the new oil pan front seal.
12. Install the seal on the front cover, pressing the tips into the holes provided.
13. Coat the new gasket with sealer and position it on the front cover.
14. Apply a ⅛ inch bead of silicone sealer to the joint formed at the oil pan and block.
15. Align the front cover seal with a centering tool and install the front cover. Tighten the screws.
16. Install the hub and torque the hub bolt to 160 ft. lbs.

V6 ENGINE

1. Disconnect the negative battery cable.
2. Remove the A/C compressor and bracket, without disconnecting the refrigerant lines, and position out of the way.
3. Remove the water pump.
4. Raise the vehicle and support it safely.
5. Remove the torsional damper. Pry out the seal using a suitable tool. When installing a new seal, ubricate the seal with clean engine oil. Insert the seal in the front cover with the lip facing the engine. Using Tool No. J23042 Seal Install, or equivalent, drive the seal into place.
6. Remove the oil pan to cover bolts.
7. Lower the vehicle and remove the front cover.
8. Before installing, clean the sealing surfaces on the front cover and cylinder block. Install a new gasket and apply a ⅛ inch bead of RTV sealer to the oil pan sealing surface of the front cover.
9. Place the front cover on the engine and install the stud bolt and bolts.
10. The remainder of the installation is the reverse of removal.

CAMSHAFT AND TIMING GEAR

Removal and Installation

ALL EXCEPT V6 ENGINE

1. Remove the engine from the vehicle.
2. Install the engine on a stand.
3. Remove the rocker arm cover, loosen valve rocker arm bolts and pivot rocker arms clear of push rods.
4. Remove the distributor, and fuel pump.
5. Remove the push rod cover, push rods and valve lifters.
6. Remove the generator, lower generator bracket and front engine mount bracket assembly.
7. Remove the oil pump drive shaft and gear assembly.
8. Remove the front pulley hub and timing gear cover.

GENERAL MOTORS—"P" BODY
PONTIAC FIERO • FIERO SE

9. Remove the two camshaft thrust plate screws by working through holes in the camshaft gear.
10. Remove the camshaft and gear assembly by pulling it out through the front of the block. (Support shaft carefully when removing so as not to damage camshaft bearings).
11. If the gear must be removed from the shaft, use press plate and adaptor J-971 on press.
12. Place tools on table of a press. Place the camshaft through the opening in the tools. Press shaft out of gear using socket or other suitable tool. Thrust plate must be so positioned that woodruff key in shaft does not damage it when the shaft is pressed out of gear.
13. To install, assemble the camshaft gear, thrust plate and gear spacer ring to camshaft, proceed as follows. Firmly support shaft at back of front journal in an arbor press using press plate adaptors. Place gear spacer rin and thrust plate over end of shaft, and install woodruff key in the shaft anyway. Install camshaft gear and press it only the shaft until it bottoms against the gear spacer ring. The end clearance of the thrust plate should be 0.0015 to 0.0050 inch If less than 0.0015 inch, the spacer ring should be replaced. If more than 0.0050 inch, the thrust plate should be replaced.
14. Thoroughly coat the camshaft journals with a high quality engine oil supplement.
15. Install the camshaft assembly in the engine block, bearing careful not to damage bearings or cam.
16. Turn crankshaft and camshaft so that the valve timing marks on the gear teeth will line up. engine is now in the number 4 cylinder firing position. Install camshaft thrust plate to block screws and tighten to 75 inch lbs.
17. Install timing gear cover and gasket. Line up keyway in hub with key on crankshaft and slide hub onto shaft. Install center bolt and torque to 160 ft. lbs. (212 Nm).
18. Install the valve lifters, push rods, push rod cover, oil pump shaft and gear assembly and fuel pump.
19. Install distributor as follows. Turn crankshaft 360° to firing position of number one cylinder (number one exhaust and intake valve lifters both on base circle of camshaft and timing mark on harmonic balancer indexed with top dead center mark on timing pad.) Install distributor in its original position and align shaft so that rotor arm points toward number one cylinder spark plug contact.
20. Pivot rocker arms over push rods. With lifters on base circle of camshaft, tighten rocker arm bolt to 20 ft. lbs. (27 Nm). Do not overtorque.
21. Install front mount assembly lower generator bracket and generator.
22. Install the engine.

TIMING CHAIN AND SPROCKETS
Removal and Installation
V6 ENGINE

1. Disconnect the negative battery cable. Remove the crankcase front cover.
2. Remove the No. 1 piston at top dead center, with the marks on the camshaft and crankshaft sprockets aligned.
3. Remove the camshaft sprocket and chain. It may be necessary to use a plastic mallet on the lower edge of the sprocket to dislodge it.
4. Remove the camshaft sprocket with Tool No. J5825 or equivalent.
5. Install the sprocket with Tool No. J5590 or equivalent.
6. Apply 'Molykote' or equivalent to the sprocket thrust surface.
7. Hold the sprocket with the chain hanging down and align the marks on the camshaft and crankshaft sprockets.
8. Align the dowel in the camshaft with the dowel hole in the camshaft sprocket.

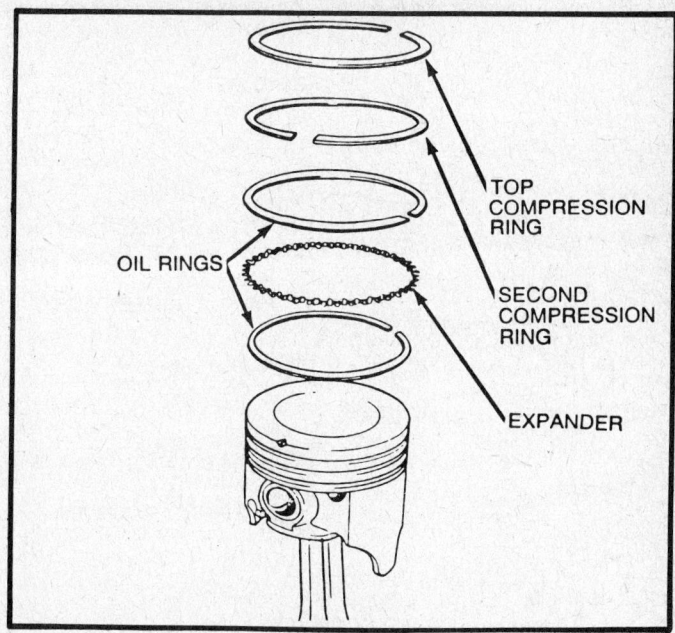

Typical piston and rod assembly
(© General Motors Corporation)

9. Draw the camshaft sprocket onto the camshaft, using the mounting bolts and torque 15 to 25 ft. lbs.
10. Lubricate the timing chain with engine oil.
11. Install the crankcase front cover.

CAMSHAFT
Removal and Installation
V6 ENGINE

1. Remove the engine.
2. Remove the valve lifters.
3. Remove the crankcase front cover.
4. Remove the timing chain and sprocket.
5. Remove the rear cover.
6. Carefully remove the camshaft to avoid damage to the bearings.
7. Before installation, lubricate the camshaft journals with engine oil. If a new camshaft is to be installed, coat the lobes with clean engine oil.
8. The remainder of the installation is the reverse of removal.

PISTON AND CONNECTING ROD POSITION

See the accompanying illustration to properly install the piston and connecting rod assembly. Align the piston and connecting rod assembly with the piston mark (notch) toward the front of the engine.

Lubrication
OIL PAN
Removal and Installation
ALL EXCEPT V6 ENGINE

1. Remove the engine cradle. The cradle can be removed from the vehicle without removing the engine or transaxle.
2. Using engine support fixture J-28467 or equivalent, raise the engine enough to take tension off the engine mounts.

SECTION 17
GENERAL MOTORS—"P" BODY
PONTIAC FIERO • FIERO SE

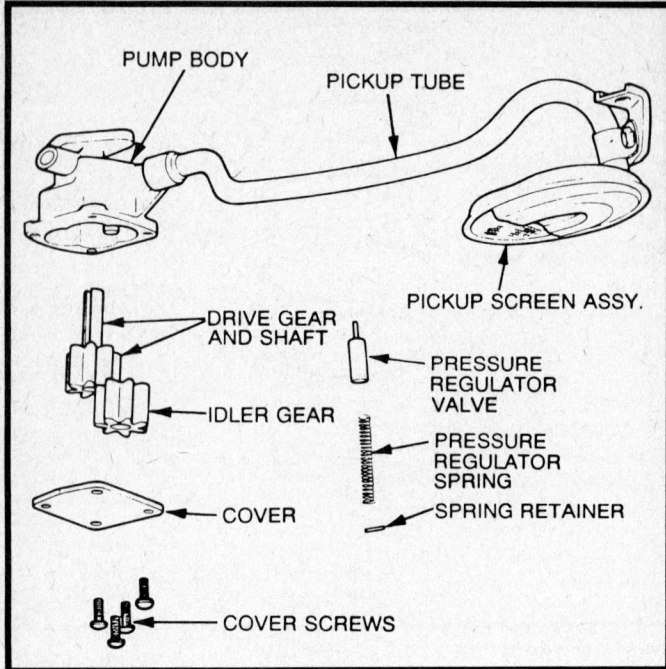

Oil pump-exploded view
(© General Motors Corporation)

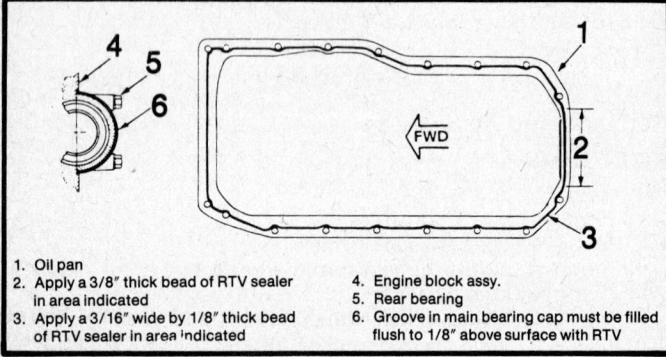

1. Oil pan
2. Apply a 3/8" thick bead of RTV sealer in area indicated
3. Apply a 3/16" wide by 1/8" thick bead of RTV sealer in area indicated
4. Engine block assy.
5. Rear bearing
6. Groove in main bearing cap must be filled flush to 1/8" above surface with RTV

Oil pan sealer application
(© General Motors Corporation)

3. Raise the vehicle and support it safely. If using a twin post hoist, place safety stands at the rear most point. If using a single post hose place two safety stands in the front and two in the rear.
4. Remove the exhaust pipe bolts at the manifold. Remove the rear wheels and tire assemblies. Remove both lower control arms at the knuckle.
5. Remove both toe-link rods at the knuckle. Remove the emergency brake cable at the cradle. Remove the engine and transmission mounting bolts. Remove the cradle bolts and remove the cradle assembly.
6. Drain the engine oil. Remove the nuts from the engine mount to the support bracket. Disconnect the exhaust pipe at the manifold and the rear transaxle mount. Remove the starter and flywheel cover. Remove the upper generator bracket and engine support bracket.
7. Support the engine with Tool J28467 or equivalent.
8. Remove the lower generator bracket and engine support bracket.

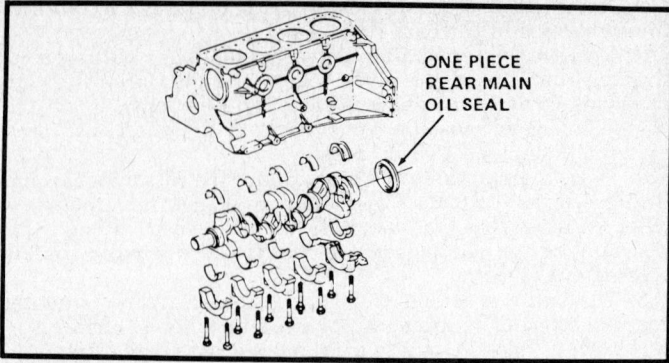

Crankshaft bearings and rear seal
(© General Motors Corporation)

9. Remove the oil pan retaining bolts and remove the oil pan.
10. Installation is the reverse of removal. Apply RTV sealer or equivalent as shown in the illustration. The two bolts in the timing gear cover should be installed last after the pan bolts are tight.

V6 ENGINE

1. Disconnect the negative battery cable.
2. Raise the vehicle and support it safely.
3. Drain the crankcase.
4. Remove the flywheel shield or clutch housing cover.
5. Remove the starter.
6. Remove the oil pan.
7. Before installation, clean all mating surfaces.
8. Place a 1/8 inch bead of RTV sealant on the oil pan sealing flange.
9. Install the oil pan and torque the 1 inch bolts 6 to 9 ft. lbs. and the 1.5 inch bolts 14 to 22 ft. lbs.
10. The remainder of the installation is the reverse of removal.

OIL PUMP

Removal and Installation

ALL EXCEPT V6 ENGINE

1. Remove the oil pan.
2. Remove the two flange mounting bolts and the nut from the main bearing cap bolt.
3. Remove the pump and screen as an assembly.
4. Installation is the reverse of removal. Align the pump shaft with the drift shaft tang. Torque the pump retaining bolts to 20 ft. lbs.

V6 ENGINE

1. Remove the oil pan.
2. Remove the pump and driveshaft extension.
3. To install, engage the driveshaft extension in the cover end of the distributor drive gear.
4. Install the pump to rear bearing cap bolt and torque 26 to 35 ft. lbs.
5. Install the oil pan and refill with oil.

REAR MAIN OIL SEAL

Removal and Installation

ALL EXCEPT V6 ENGINE

NOTE: This is a one piece seal and can be replaced without removal of the oil pan or crankshaft.

17-22

GENERAL MOTORS—"P" BODY
PONTIAC FIERO • FIERO SE
SECTION 17

1. Remove the transaxle assembly.
2. Remove the flywheel.
3. If equipped with a manual transaxle, remove the pressure plate and disc.
4. Pry out of the rear main seal.
5. Before installing, clean the block and crankshaft to seal mating surfaces.
6. Lubricate the outside of the seal for ease of installation and press into the block with fingers.
7. Install the flywheel and torque the bolts to 44 ft. lbs.
8. Install the transaxle assembly.

V6 ENGINE (THIN SEAL)

1. Remove the engine and mount on a suitable stand.
2. Remove the oil pan and oil pump assembly.
3. Remove the front cover, then the lock chain tensioner with a pin.
4. Rotate the crankshaft until the timing marks on the cam and crank sprockets align.
5. Remove the camshaft bolt, cam sprocket and timing chain.
6. Rotate the crankshaft to the horizontal position.
7. Remove the rod bearing nuts, caps and bolts.
8. Remove the crankshaft and the old oil seal.
9. Apply a light coat of G.M. 1052726 or equivalent to the outside of the seal.
10. Install the new seal and tool in the rear area of the crankshaft.
11. Install the crankshaft and tool in the engine.
12. Position the seal tool sot hat the arrow points towards the cylinder block and remove the tool.
13. Put a light coat of oil on the crankshaft journals.
14. Seal the rear main bearing split line surface with G.M. 1052726 or equivalent.
15. The remainder of the installation is the reverse of removal. Torque to specifications.

V6 ENGINE (THICK SEAL)

1. Remove the transaxle. If equipped with a manual transaxle, remove the pressure plate and the clutch.
2. Remove the flywheel from the crankshaft.
3. Using a small pry bar, pry the rear oil seal from the housing. When prying the oil seal from the housing, be careful not to damage the machined surfaces.
4. Using the seal installation tool J-34686 or equivalent, lubricate the new oil seal lip and slide it onto the installation (dust lip side against the tool) until it seats against the tool.
5. Align the installation tool's dowel pin with the dowl pin hole in the crankshaft. Torque the mounting screws to 2–5 ft. lbs.
6. Turn the 'T' handle and push the seal into the housing, until it bottoms out against the housing.
7. Loosen the 'T' handle until it comes to a stop. Remove the mounting screws of the installation tool.
8. Check the seal and make sure that it is squarely seated in the bore.
9. To complete the installation reverse the removal procedures. Torque the flywheel bolts to 50 ft. lbs.

FRONT SUSPENSION AND STEERING SECTION

STEERING WHEEL

Removal and Installation

1. Disconnect the negative battery cable. Pry off the center cap and remove the retainer clip and nut.
2. Remove the wheel using a steering wheel puller.
3. When installing, align the index mark on the steering wheel with the index mark on the steering shaft. Torque the retaining nut to 35 ft. lbs.
4. The canceling cam tower must be centered in the slot of the lock plate cover before assembling the wheel.

STEERING RACK AND PINION ASSEMBLY

Removal and Installation

1. Raise the vehicle and support it safely.
2. Disconnect both front crossmember braces.
3. Disconnect the flexible coupling pinch bolt to the shaft.
4. Remove the outer tie rod cotter pins and nuts on the left and right sides.
5. Disconnect the tie rods from the steering knuckle.
6. Remove the four bolts retaining the steering assembly to the cross member and remove the steering assembly.
7. Installation is the reverse of removal. Tighten the flexible coupling bolt to 46 ft. lbs., the four new steering assembly bolts to 21 ft. lbs., the four cross member brace bolts to 20 ft. lbs., and the tie rod nut at each knuckle to 29 ft. lbs. then turn to align the cotter pin.

OUTER TIE ROD

Removal and Installation

1. Loosen the jam nut and remove the tie rod from the steer-

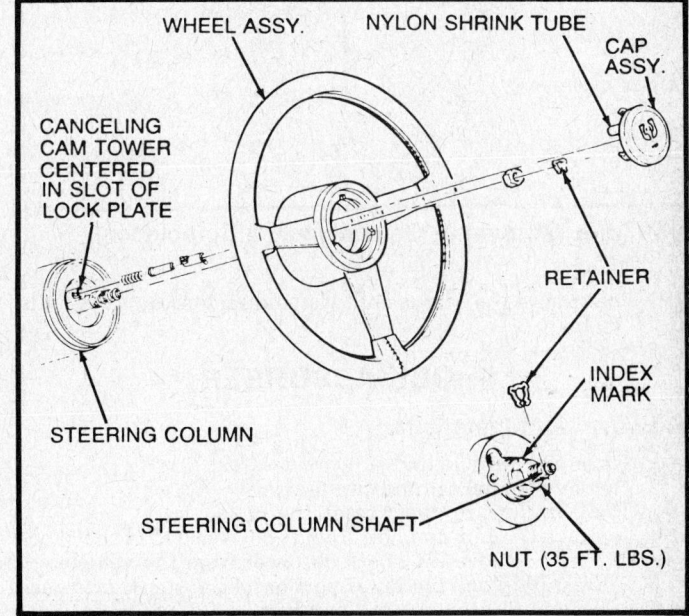

Steering wheel removal
(© General Motors Corporation)

ing knuckle. General Motors recommends a special tool for this procedure. Tool No. J-24319-01 or BT 7101 or equivalent.
2. Remove the outer tie rod.
3. Install the outer tie rod in the reverse of removal. Do not tighten the jam nut.
4. Adjust the toe-in by turning the inner tie rod.

SECTION 17
GENERAL MOTORS—"P" BODY
PONTIAC FIERO • FIERO SE

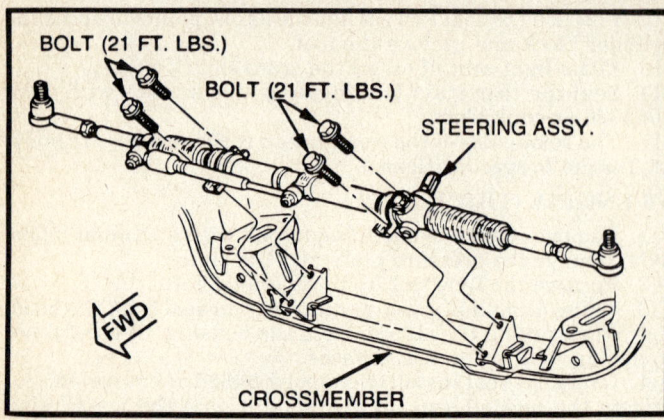

Rack and pinion assembly
(© General Motors Corporation)

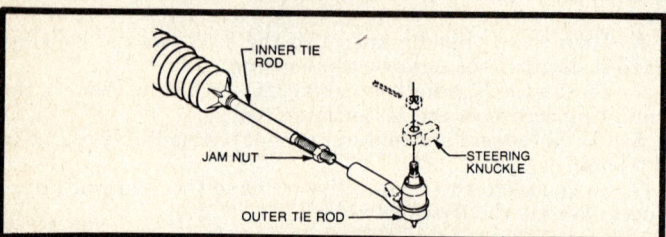

Outer tie rod end (© General Motors Corporation)

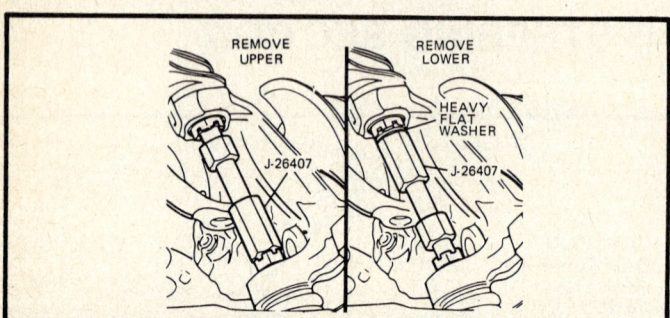

Ball joint removal (© General Motors Corporation)

5. Make sure the boot is not twisted then torque the jam nut to 50 ft. lbs.

SHOCK ABSORBER

Removal and Installation

1. Raise the vehicle and support it safely.
2. Remove the wheel and tire assembly.
3. Remove the two upper retaining bolts.
4. Remove the nut and bolt from the lower end of the shock absorber and remove the shock absorber from the vehicle.
5. To install, place the lower portion of the shock into position and hand tighten the nut and bolt.
6. Extend the shock up into the shock absorber support and torque both bolts to 20 ft. lbs.
7. Torque the lower nut and bolt to 20 ft. lbs.
8. Replace the wheel and tire assembly.

BALL JOINTS

Inspection

1. Raise the front of the vehicle and position a lift placed un-

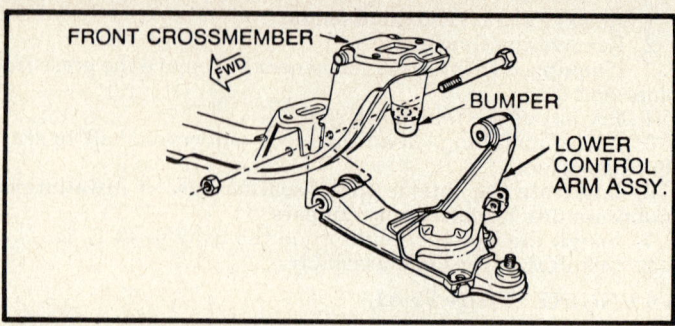

Lower control arm (© General Motors Corporation)

der the engine cradle. The front wheel should be clear of the ground.
2. Grasp the wheel at the top and bottom and shake the wheel in and out.
3. If any movement is seen of the steering knuckle relative to the control arm, the ball joints are defective and must be replaced. Note that movement elsewhere may be due to loose wheel bearings or other troubles, watch the knuckle to control arm connection.
4. If the ball stud is disconnected from the steering knuckle and any looseness is noted, often the ball joint stud can be twisted in its socket with your fingers, replace the ball joints.

Removal and Installation
UPPER

1. Raise the vehicle and support it safely.
2. Remove the tire and wheel assembly.
3. Support the lower control arm with a floor jack.
4. Remove upper ball stud nut then reinstall nut finger tight.
5. Install Tool J-26407 or equivalent, with the cup end over the lower ball stud nut.
6. Turn the threaded end of tool until upper ball stud is free of steering knuckle.
7. Remove tool and remove nut from ball stud.
8. Remove two nuts and bolts attaching ball joints to upper control arm. Note which way the flat of the ball joint is pointing before removing it. The direction of this flat on the ball joint flanges should be in the same direction as the one removed unless a change in camber is desired.
9. Remove ball joint.
10. Inspect the tapered hole in the steering knuckle. Remove any dirt and if any out of roundness, deformation, or damage is noted, the knuckle must be replaced.
11. Install bolts and nuts attaching ball joint to upper control arm and torque to 28 lb.ft., then mate the upper control arm ball stud to the steering knuckle.
12. Install the ball stud nut and torque to 35 lb.ft. Then turn to align cotter pin.
13. Install cotter pin. Install the tire and wheel assembly.
14. Lower the vehicle to the floor. The toe must now be checked and adjusted as necessary.

LOWER

The lower ball joint is welded to the lower control arm and cannot be serviced separately. Replacement of the entire lower control arm will be necessary if the lower ball joint requires replacement.

FRONT SPRING/LOWER CONTROL ARM

Removal and Installation

1. Raise the vehicle and support it on the crossmember.

GENERAL MOTORS—"P" BODY
PONTIAC FIERO • FIERO SE
SECTION 17

2. Remove the wheel and tire assembly.
3. Disconnect the stabilizer bar from the lower control arm.
4. Disconnect the tie rod from the steering knuckle.
5. Disconnect the shock absorber at the lower control arm.
6. Support the lower control arm with a jack.
7. Remove the nut from the lower ball joint, then use tool J-26407 or its equivalent, to press the ball joint out of the knuckle.
8. Swing the knuckle and hub out of the way.
9. Loosen the lower control arm pivot bolts.
10. Install a chain through the coil spring as a safety precaution. The coil spring is under load and could result in personal injury if it were released to quickly. Be sure to install a chain and to slowly lower the jack.
11. Slowly lower the jack and remove the spring.
12. Remove the pivot bolts at the chassis and the crossmember and remove the lower control arm. Removal of the pivot bolt at the crossmember may require the loosening or removal of the steering assembly mounting bolts.
13. Install the lower control arm and pivot bolts at crossmember and body. Tighten slightly but do not torque.
14. Position the spring and install the spring into the upper pocket. Align the spring bottom to the lower control arm pocket.
15. Install the spring lower end onto lower control arm. It may be necessary to have an assistant help you compress the spring far enough to slide it over the raised area of the lower control arm seat.
16. Use a jack to raise the lower control arm and compress the coil spring. Install the ball joint through the lower control arm and into the steering knuckle. Install nut to ball joint stud and torque to 55 lb.ft. Install a new cotter pin.
17. Connect the stabilizer bar and torque the bolt to 16 lb.ft. Connect the tie rod and torque to 29 lb.ft. Install the shock absorber to the lower control arm and torque the bolt to 35 lb.ft.
18. If the bolts were removed or loosened at the steering assembly, replace with new bolts and torque to 21 lb.ft.
19. With the suspension system in its normal standing height, torque the lower control arm to body bolt at 62 lb.ft. and the lower control arm to crossmember nut at 52 lb.ft.
20. Check and set alignment as necessary.

UPPER CONTROL ARM

Removal and Installation

1. Raise the vehicle and support safely.
2. Remove the tire and wheel assembly.
3. Remove the rivet holding brake line clip to upper control arm.
4. Support the lower control arm with a floor jack.
5. Remove upper ball joint from steering knuckle.
6. Remove control arm pivot bolt and remove the control arm from vehicle.
7. Transfer the ball joint is not damaged or worn. Washers and shims must be reinstalled as removed unless a change in geometry is desired.
8. Install the upper control arm and pivot bolt to the vehicle. The inner pivot bolt must be installed with the bolt head toward the front.
9. Install the pivot bolt nut. Position the control arm in a horizontal plane and torque the nut to 66 lb. ft. The bolt may turn when torqued to minimum if nut is not backed up with a wrench. This does not mean the joint is loose.
10.. Install the ball joint to upper control arm and to steering knuckle. Install the nut, torque to 35 lb.ft. Install a new cotter pin.
11. Install the wheel and tire. Lower the vehicle to the floor.

STEERING KNUCKLE

Removal and Installation

1. Raise the vehicle and support the lower control arm properly. This keep the coil spring compressed. Use care to support adequately, or personal injury could result.
2. Remove the tire and wheel assembly.
3. Remove the disc brake caliper. Secure the caliper to the suspension using wire. Do not allow the caliper to hang by the brake hose. Insert a piece of wood between the shoes to hold the piston in the caliper bore. (The block of wood should be about the same thickness as the brake disc).
4. Remove the hub and disc. Remove the splash shield. Remove both ball stud nuts. Remove the tie rod end from the steering knuckle.
5. Using Tool J-26407 or its equivalent, press the upper ball stud from the steering knuckle.
6. Reverse tool to the other ball stud and press the lower all stud from the steering knuckle. Remove the ball stud nuts and remove the steering knuckle.
7. Place the steering knuckle in position and insert the upper and lower ball studs into knuckle bosses.
8. Install the ball stud nuts and tighten to specifications. Lower, torque to 55 lb.ft. Upper, torque to 35 lb.ft. Install new cotter pins.
9. Install the splash shield to the steering knuckle. Torque to 7 lbs.ft. Install the tie rod end to the steering knuckle. Torque to 29 lb.ft., and install the cotter pin.
10. Repack the wheel bearings. Then install the hub and disc, bearings and nut. Torque to specifications. Install the brake caliper. Install the tire wheel assembly.
11. Lower the vehicle to the floor.

FRONT WHEEL BEARING

ADJUSTMENT

1. Raise the vehicle and support it safely.
2. Remove the wheel.
3. Remove the dust cap from the hub.
4. Remove cotter pin from spindle and spindle nut.
5. Tighten the spindle nut to 12 lb.ft. while turning the wheel assembly forward by hand to fully seat the bearings. This will remove any grease or burrs which could cause excessive wheel bearing play later.
6. Back off the nut to the just loose position.
7. Hand tighten the spindle nut. Loosen the spindle nut until either hole in the spindle lines up with a slot in the nut. (Not more than ½ flat).
8. Install new cotter pin. Bend the ends of the cotter pin against nut, cut off extra length to ensure ends will not interfere with the dust cap.
9. Measure the looseness in the hub assembly. There will be from 0.001 inch to 0.005 inch end play when properly adjusted.
10. Install the dust cap on the hub.
11. Replace the wheel cover or hub cap.
12. Lower the vehicle to the floor.

STEERING COLUMN

Removal and Installation

1. Disconnect battery negative cable.
2. Remove steering column cover.
3. Remove bolt at flex joint.
4. Remove two nuts from lower support and two bolts from upper support.
5. Disconnect all electrical connectors and remove steering column.

17-25

SECTION 17 GENERAL MOTORS—"P" BODY
PONTIAC FIERO • FIERO SE

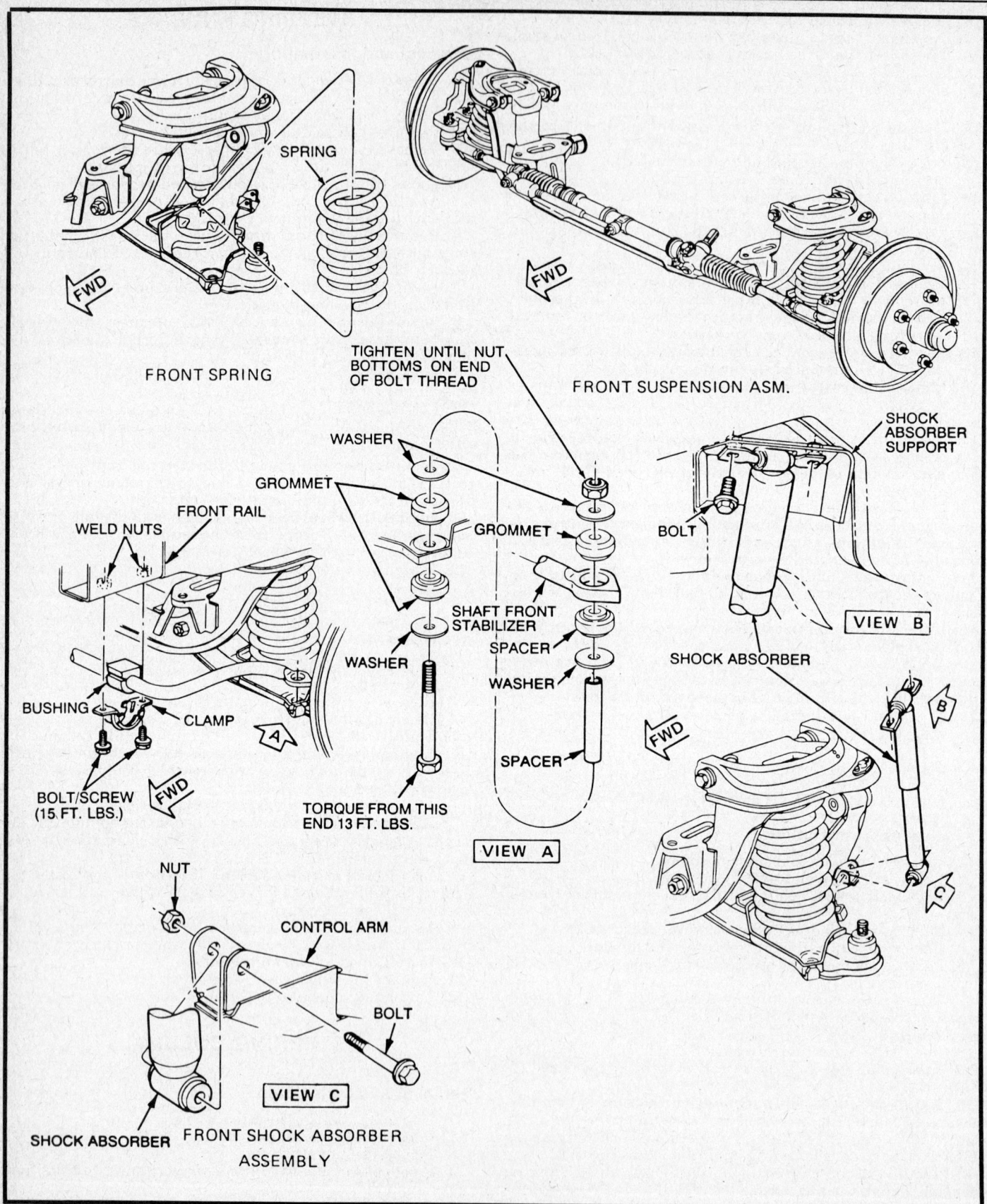

Front suspension (© General Motors Corporation)

17-26

GENERAL MOTORS—"P" BODY
PONTIAC FIERO • FIERO SE

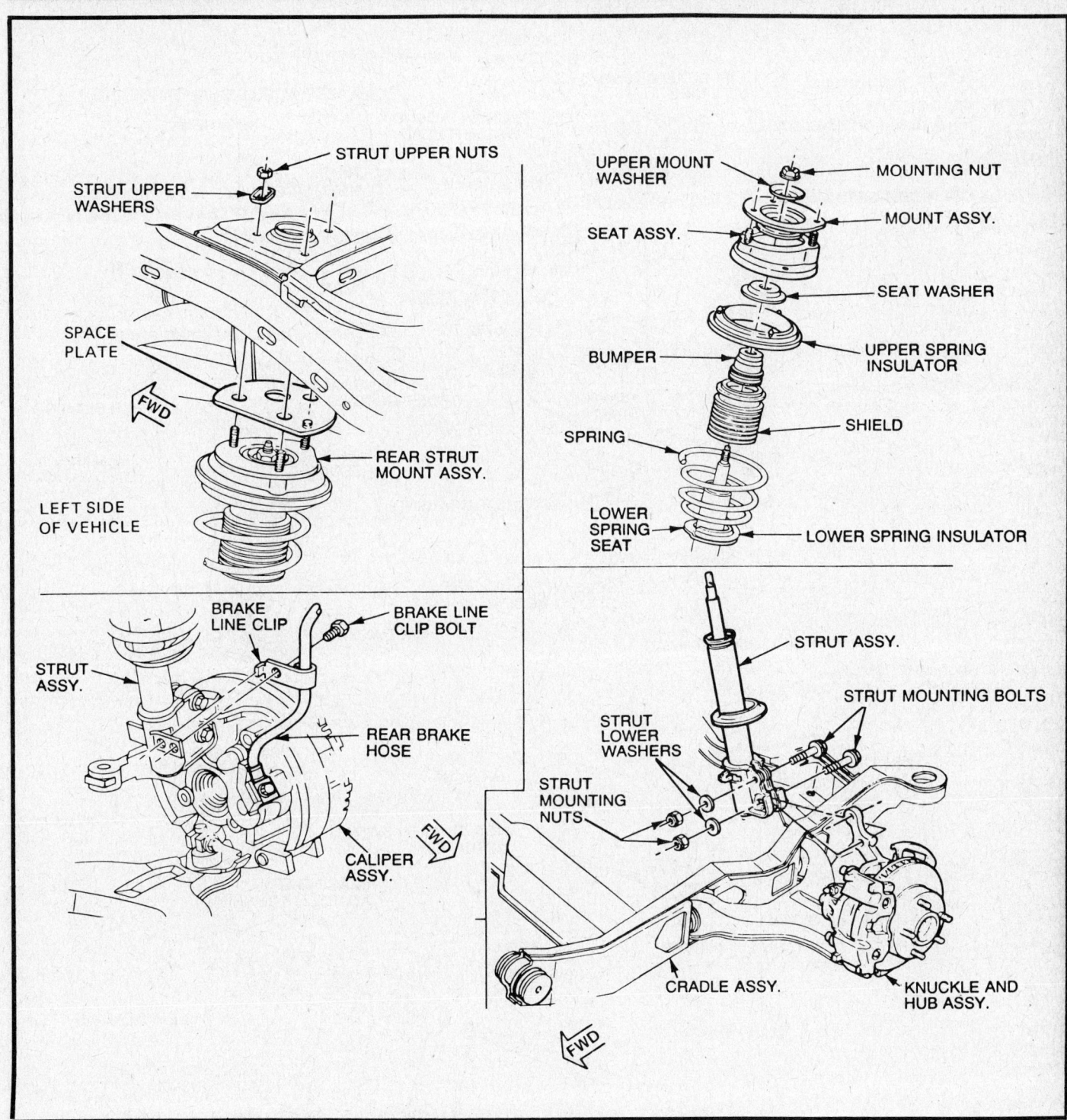

Exploded view of strut assembly (© General Motors Corporation)

6. Installation is the reverse of removal procedure.
7. Center the steering shaft within the steering column jacket bushing and tighten lower attaching bolt. This can be done by moving the steering column jacket assembly up and down or side to side until the steering shaft is centered.

SECTION 17 GENERAL MOTORS—"P" BODY
PONTIAC FIERO • FIERO SE

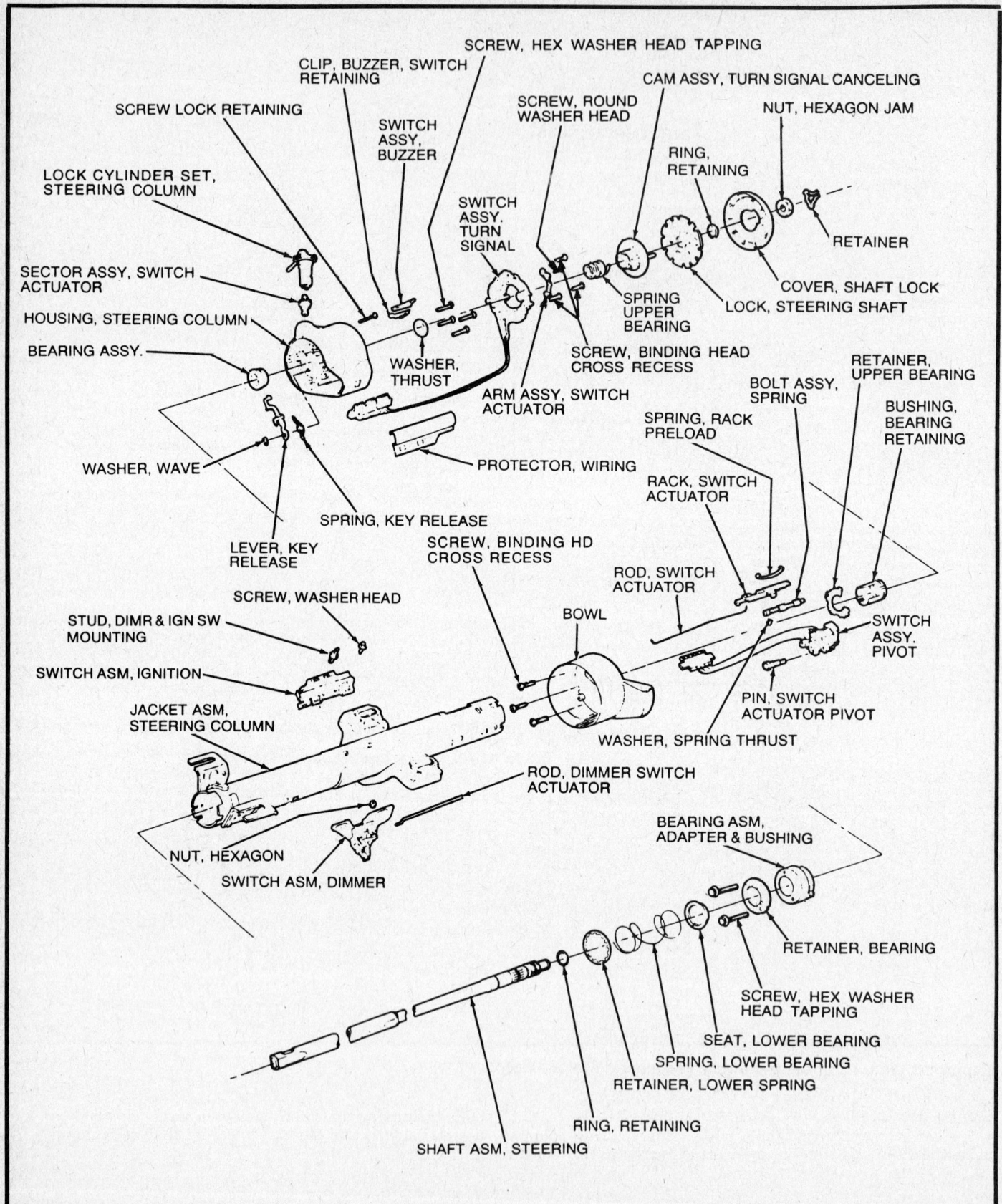

Exploded view of standard steering column (© General Motors Corporation)

GENERAL MOTORS – "P" BODY
PONTIAC FIERO • FIERO SE
SECTION 17

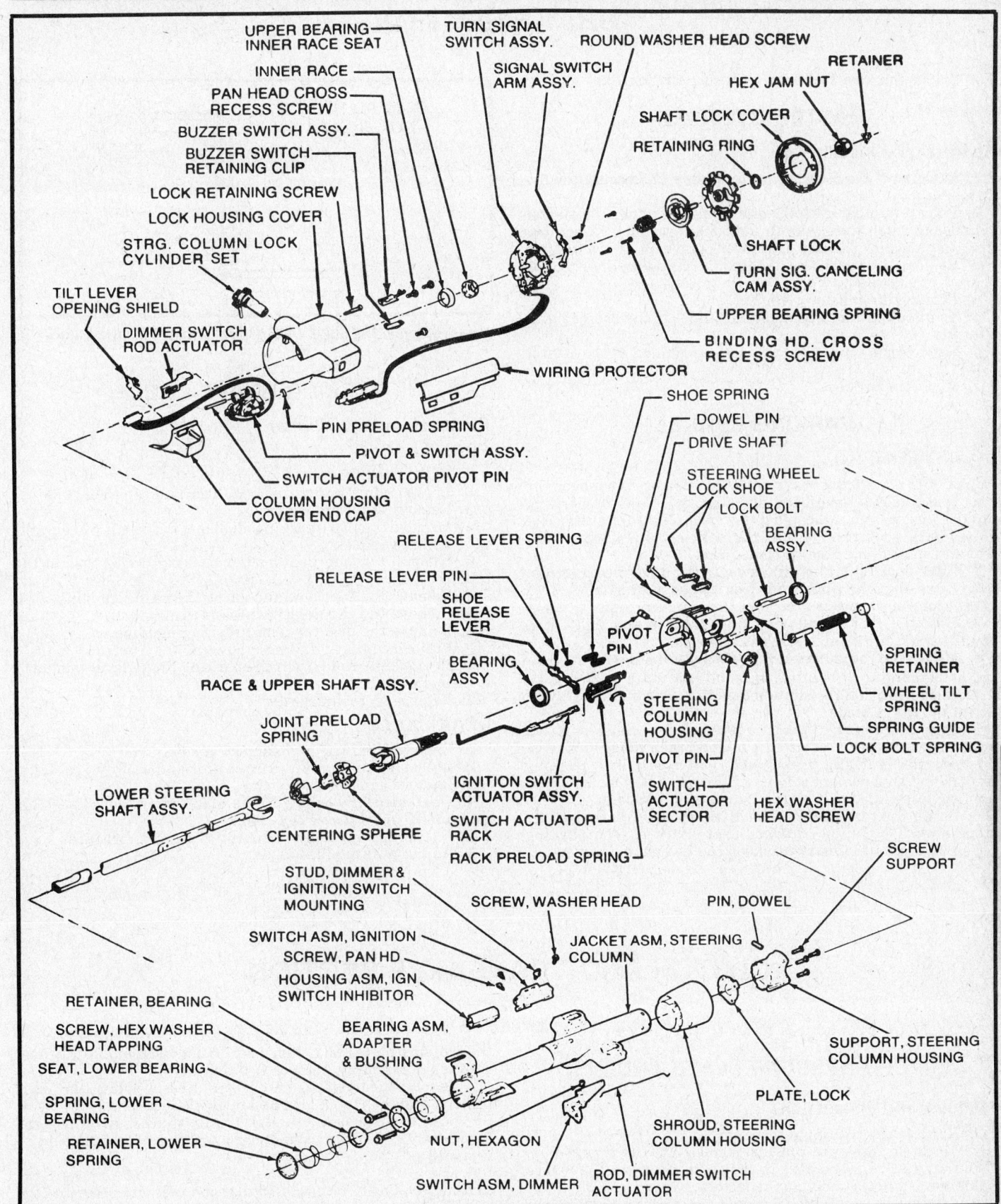

Exploded view of tilt steering column (© General Motors Corporation)

17-29

SECTION 17: GENERAL MOTORS—"P" BODY
PONTIAC FIERO • FIERO SE

BRAKE SECTION

For Brake Service Refer to Unit Repair Section

MASTER CYLINDER

Removal and Installation

1. Disconnect the negative battery cable. Disconnect the hydraulic lines at the master cylinder.
2. Place a number of cloths or a container under the master cylinder to catch the brake fluid. Disconnect the brake tubes from the master cylinder. Tape over open ends of the tubes.
3. Remove the two nuts attaching the master cylinder to the booster or firewall.
4. Remove the master cylinder.
5. To install, attach the master cylinder to the booster with the nuts.
6. Remove the tape from the lines and connect to the master cylinder.
7. Bleed the brakes.

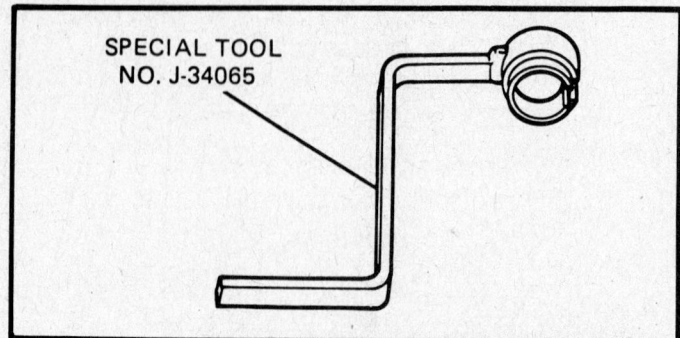

Special tool J–34065 (© General Motors Corporation)

PARKING BRAKE

ADJUSTMENT

Adjustment of parking brake cable is necessary whenever the rear brake cables have been disconnected. Need for parking brake adjustment is indicated if the hydraulic brake system operates with good reserve, but the parking brake hand level travel is more than nine ratchet clicks.

1. Place parking brake hand lever in the unapplied position.
2. Raise the rear wheels off floor and support safely.
3. Apply lubricant to groove in the equalizer nut.
4. Hold the brake cable stud from turning and tightening equalizer nut until cable slack is removed.
5. Make sure the caliper levers are against stops on the caliper housing after tightening the equalizer nut.
6. If levers are off the stops, loosen the cable until the levers do return to the stops.
7. Operate the parking brake lever several times to check adjustment. Properly adjusted parking brake shoes and properly adjusted parking brake cable will result in a parking brake handle movement of five to eight notches when a force is applied perpendicularly at the handle grip midpoint.
8. Lower the rear wheels. The levers must be on the caliper stops after completion of adjustment. Back off the parking brake adjuster if necessary to keep the levers on the stops.

PARKING BRAKE CABLE

Removal and Installation

FRONT CABLE

1. Raise the vehicle and support it safely.
2. Loosen adjusting nut at equalizer and separate cables.
3. Remove clip from cable.
4. Remove the two retaining clip bolts in the left wheel well.
5. Lower vehicle.
6. Unsnap the clip holding the parking brake boot to the lever.
7. Remove the seat bolt and carpet finishing molding.
8. Remove the shoulder harness retaining bolt.
9. Remove the quarter trim finishing molding.
10. Pull carpet back and note how cable is routed.
11. Remove the cable from the parking brake lever and push it through the body.
12. Replace in reverse order.

REAR CABLES

1. Raise the vehicle and support it safely.
2. Loosen adjusting nut at equalizer and separate cables.
3. Remove cables at calipers.
4. Disconnect the cables at the cradle with tool J-34065 or equivalent, and remove the cables.
5. Install new cable by reversing removal procedure.
6. Adjust parking brake.

CLUTCH AND TRANSAXLE SECTION

For Overhaul Procedures Refer to Unit Repair Section

CLUTCH PRESSURE PLATE AND DISC

Removal and Installation

1. Remove the transaxle.
2. Mark the pressure plate assembly and the flywheel so that they can be assembled in the same position. They were balanced as an assembly at the factory.
3. Loosen the attaching bolts one turn at a time until spring tension is relieved.
4. Support the pressure plate and remove the bolts. Remove the pressure plate and clutch disc. Do not disassemble the pressure plate assembly, replace it if defective.
5. Inspect the flywheel, clutch disc, pressure plate, throwout bearing and the clutch fork and pivot shaft assembly for wear. Replace the parts as required. If the flywheel shows any signs of overheating, or if it is badly grooved or scored, it should be replaced.
6. Clean the pressure plate and flywheel mating surfaces thoroughly. Position the clutch disc and pressure plate into the installed position, and support with a dummy shaft or clutch aligning tool. The clutch plate is assembled with the damper

GENERAL MOTORS—"P" BODY
PONTIAC FIERO • FIERO SE

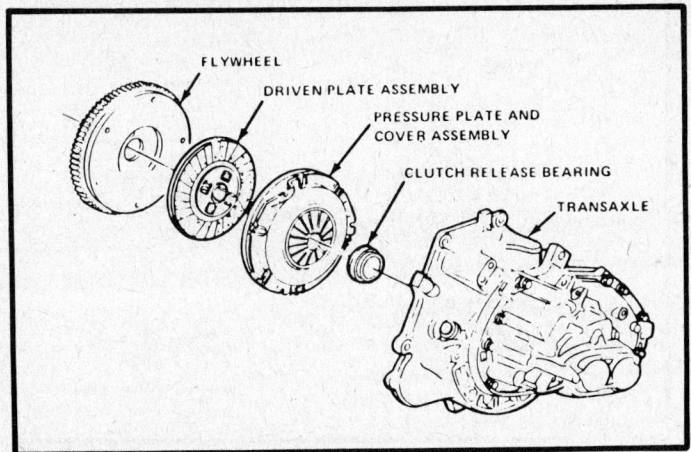

Exploded view of clutch assembly
(© General Motors Corporation)

springs offset toward the transaxle. One side of the factory-supplied clutch disc is stamped 'flywheel side'.
  7. Install the pressure plate to flywheel bolts. Tighten them gradually in a crisscross pattern.
  8. Lubricate the outside groove and the inside recess of the release bearing with high temperature grease. Wipe off any excess. Install the release bearing.
  9. Install the transaxle.

CLUTCH MASTER CYLINDER

Removal and Installation

  1. Disconnect the negative battery cable. Disconnect the cylinder push rod at the clutch pedal.
  2. Disconnect the hydraulic line at the master cylinder.
  3. Remove the nuts attaching the cylinder to the cowl, then remove the cylinder.
  4. Position the cylinder push rod through the cowl and loosely install the cylinder to cowl nuts.
  5. Connect the cylinder push rod to the clutch pedal with the spring clip.
  6. Tighten the cylinder to cowl nuts to 13 ft. lbs.
  7. Connect the hydraulic line the master cylinder and torque to 13 ft. lbs.
  8. Fill the clutch master cylinder with the proper fluid and bleed the system.

CLUTCH SLAVE CYLINDER

NOTE: Prior to any vehicle that requires removal of the slave cylinder, the master cylinder push rod must be disconnected from the clutch pedal. If it is not disconnected, permanent damage to the slave cylinder will occur to the slave cylinder if the clutch pedal is depressed while the slave cylinder is disconnected.

Removal and installation

  1. Disconnect the hydraulic line at the slave cylinder.
  2. Remove the slave cylinder to bracket bolts and remove the slave cylinder.
  3. Place the slave cylinder at the mounting bracket and position the cylinder push rod into the clutch release lever.
  4. Install the slave cylinder to racket nuts to tighten to 16 ft. lbs.
  5. Install the hydraulic line to the slave cylinder and tighten to 13 ft. lbs.

  6. Fill the clutch master cylinder with the recommended fluid and bleed the system.

BLEEDING THE CLUTCH SYSTEM

NOTE: It is extremely important that cleanliness be maintained throughout the bleeding operation.

  1. Fill the reservoir directly from an unused can of Delco Supreme No.11 brake fluid or an equivalent brand fluid conforming to DOT3 specifications. Never use fluid which has been bled from a system to fill the reservoir as it may be aerated or contain moisture or possibly be contaminated. Also, during the bleeding operation, never let the fluid level in the reservoir fall to a point where air may be admitted into the hydraulic system.
  2. Unscrew the bleedscrew at the slave cylinder enough to ally fluid (usually a half turn) to be pumped out.
  3. Push the pedal all the way down one full stroke, followed by three short rapid strokes.
  4. Allow the pedal to return quickly to its stop by removing your foot from the pedal.
  5. Repeat the above procedure until all air is dispelled at the bleedscrew.
  6. Close the bleedscrew immediately after the downward stroke of the pedal when air bubbles no longer appear.

TRANSAXLE (MANUAL OR AUTOMATIC)

Removal and Installation

  1. Remove the air cleaner assembly.
  2. Disconnect the negative battery cable.
  3. Disconnect the ground cable at the transaxle.
  4. Disconnect the shift and select cable at the transaxle.
  5. Remove the upper transaxle to engine bolts.
  6. Install an engine support fixture J-28467 or equivalent.
  7. Raise and support the vehicle safely.
  8. Remove the rear wheels and tires.
  9. Remove the axle shafts.
  10. Remove the heat shield from the catalytic converter.
  11. Disconnect the exhaust pipe at the exhaust manifold.
  12. Remove the engine mount to cradle nuts.
  13. Support the cradle with an adjustable stand.
  14. Remove the rear cradle to body bolts.
  15. Remove the forward cradle to body through bolts.
  16. Lower the cradle and move out of the way.
  17. Remove the starter and inspection cover shields and remove the starter.
  18. Remove the flywheel to converter bolts.
  19. Disconnect and plug cooler lines, if equipped with an automatic transaxle.
  20. Position a transmission stand under the transaxle.
  21. On manual transmissions remove the lower transaxle to engine bolts and remove the transaxle.
  22. On automatic transaxles remove the transaxle to support mounting bolts on the right side.
  23. Install the starter and the inspection cover shields. Hoist the cradle into position. Lower the cradle at the front and raise the car. Work cradle at rear into position on mounts then raise the front into position.
  24. The remainder of the installation is the reverse of removal. Torque the retaining nuts to the following specifications. Starter to engine 32 ft. lbs. Front cradle to body nuts 67 ft. lbs. Rear cradle to body bolts 76 ft. lbs. Exhaust pipe to exhaust manifold 25 ft. lbs. Transaxle mounts to cradle nuts, rear 18 ft. lbs., front 36 ft. lbs. Engine mount to cradle nuts 40 ft. lbs. Upper trnsaxle to engine bolts 55 ft. lbs. Cooler lines 20 ft. lbs. Support bracket to transaxle (automatic) 37 ft. lbs.

SECTION 17 GENERAL MOTORS—"P" BODY
PONTIAC FIERO • FIERO SE

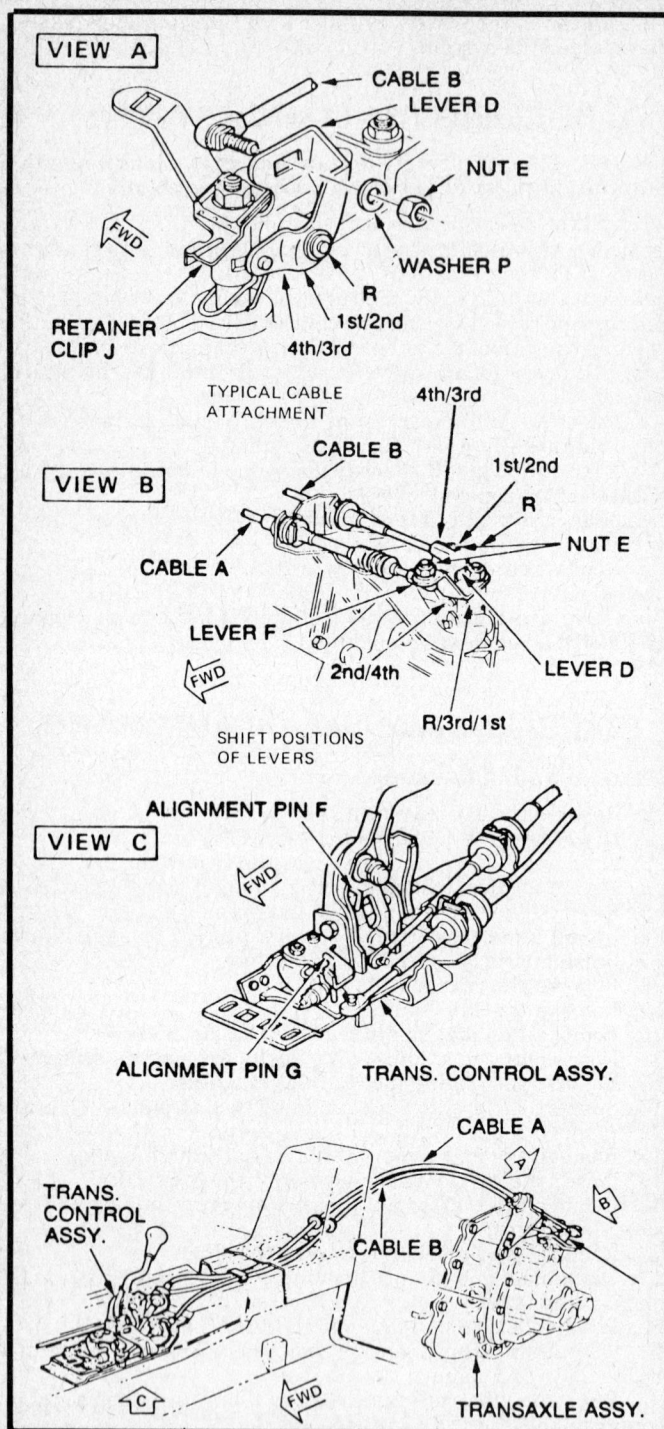

Manual transaxle cable adjustment
(© General Motors Corporation)

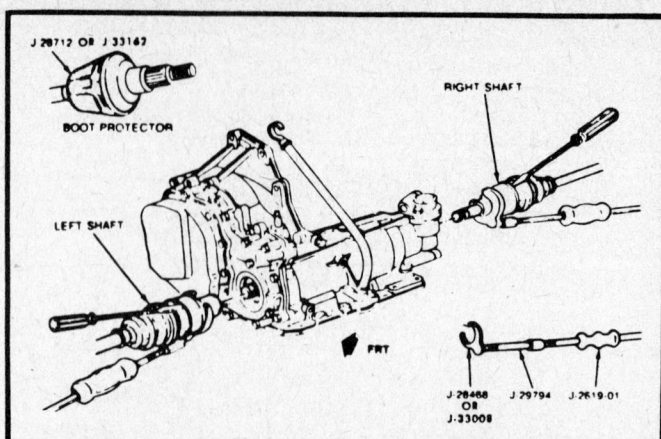

Removing the drive axle from the transaxle
(© General Motors Corporation)

4. Remove the console and trim plates as required for access to shifter.
5. With the shifter lever in first gear position (pulled to left and held against stop), insert alignment pins F and G as shown in view D.
6. Remove the lash from transaxle by first compressing select cable (B) and then tightening nut (3). Levers (D) and (F) should be kept from moving during this process. Similarly, shift cable (A) is first compressed and nut (E) then tightened. Again levers (D) and (F) remain stationary. Nut (E) on levers (D) and (F) tightened to 20 ft. lbs. (27 Nm).
7. Ensure that the reverse inhibit cam is against roller and align if necessary.
8. Remove the alignment pins F and G at shifter assembly. While cycling from 1 to 2 and 2 to 1, the select cable should not move. Difficulty in shifting transaxle to reverse may be corrected by biasing select lever (D) inboard toward 1-3-R position during shift cable (A) adjustment.

TRANSMISSION CONTROL CABLE
Adjustment

1. Place the shift lever in the 'N' (neutral) position.
2. Place the transmission lever in the 'N' (neutral) position. Obtain the 'neutral' position by rotating the transmission lever clockwise from 'park' through 'R' into 'N' (neutral).
3. Insert the threaded pin (part of the shift cable assembly) upward thru the slotted hole in the lever and hand start nut. The lever must be held out of park when torquing the nut. Torque the nut 15 to 25 ft. lbs.

NEUTRAL SAFETY AND BACK UP LIGHT SWITCH
Adjustment

1. Place the transmission shaft in the 'NEUTRAL' position.
2. Loosen the bolts attaching the switch to the transmission case.
3. Insert a 2.34 diameter gauge pin (or rounded shank of a 3/32 inch drill bit) into the service adjustment hole. Rotate the switch until the gage pin drops to a depth of 9mm.
4. Tighten the attaching bolts and remove the gauge pin.

T.V. CABLE
Adjustment

1. After installation of the cable to transmission, engine

MANUAL TRANSAXLE CABLE
Adjustment

1. Disconnect the negative battery cable.
2. Place the transaxle in first gear.
3. Loosen the shift cable attaching nuts (E) at transaxle levers (D) and (F) shown in illustration.

GENERAL MOTORS—"P" BODY
PONTIAC FIERO • FIERO SE
SECTION 17

bracket, and throttle lever, check to ensure that the cable slider is in the zero or fully readjusted position. If not, please refer to the readjustment procedure.

2. Rotate the throttle lever to the 'full travel stop' position.
3. The slider must move (ratchet) toward the idler lever when the idler lever is rotated to the full travel stop position.

ReAdjustment Procedure

In case readjustment is necessary because of inadvertent adjustment before or during assembly, perform the following.
1. Depress and hold the metal readjust tab.
2. Move the slider back through the fitting in the direction away from the throttle lever until the slider stops against the fitting.
3. Release the metal readjust tab.
4. Rotate the throttle lever to the 'full travel stop' position.

Drive Axles and CV-Joint

DRIVE AXLE

Removal and Installation
1. Remove the hub nut and discard.
2. Raise the vehicle and remove the wheel and tire.
3. Drive boot seal protector No. J-28712 or its equalivent on the outer seal.
4. Disconnect the toe link rod at the knuckle assembly.
5. Disconnect the parking brake cables at the cradle.
6. Disconnect the brake line bracket at the underbody in the inner wheel housing opening.
7. Using tool No. J-28733 or its equivalent, hub spindle remover, remove the axle shaft from the hub and bearing assembly.
8. Support the axle shaft.
9. Remove the clamp bolt from the lower control arm ball stud.
10. Separate the knuckle from the lower control arm.
11. Pull the strut, knuckle and caliper assembly away from the body and secure in this position.
12. Using tool No. J-33008 and No. J-2619-01 or their equivalents, disengage the snap rings which are retaining the drive axle at the transaxle and remove the drive axle. If the drive axle is being replaced, replace the knuckle seal.
13. When installing the drive to the transaxle seat the axle positioning a suitable tool inside the groove provided on the inner retainer. The remainder of the installation is the reverse of removal. Torque the hub nut to 225 ft. lbs.

REAR SUSPENSION

MacPHERSON STRUT

Removal and Installation
1. Remove the engine compartment cover.
2. Remove the three upper strut nuts and washers.
3. Loosen the wheel lug nuts.
4. Raise the vehicle and support the rear control arm.
5. Remove the wheel and tire.
6. Remove the brake line clip.
7. Scribe the strut and knuckle. Using a sharp tool, scribe the knuckle along the lower outboard strut radius, as in view A. Scribe the strut flange on the inboard side, along the curve of the knuckle, as in view B. Make a chisel mark across the strut/knuckle interface, as shown in view C.
8. Remove the two strut mounting nuts and bolts and remove the strut assembly and spacer plate.
9. Installation is the reverse of removal. Align the scribe marks on the strut and knuckle and replace the bolts in the same order in which they were removed. Tighten the strut mounting nuts to 18 ft. lbs.

REAR COIL SPRING

Removal and Installation

NOTE: Special tool No. J-26584 or its equivalent must be used to disassemble and assemble strut damper. Care must be taken not to damage the special coating on the coil springs, or damage could occur to the coils.

1. Clamp strut compressor tool in vise.
2. Place strut assembly in bottom adapter of compressor and install tool (be certain adapter captures the strut and locating pins are engaged).
3. Rotate strut assembly to align top mounting assembly with strut compressor support notch.
4. Insert tool top adapter on the top spring seal. Position top adapters so that the long stud is at high location to strut flange.
5. Using a ratchet with 1 inch socket, turn compressor forcing screw clockwise until top support flange contacts the top

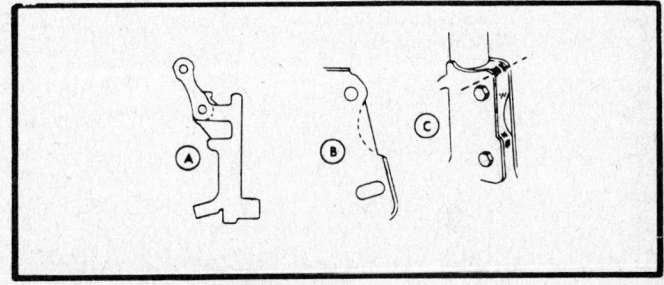

Scribing strut and knuckle
(© General Motors Corporation)

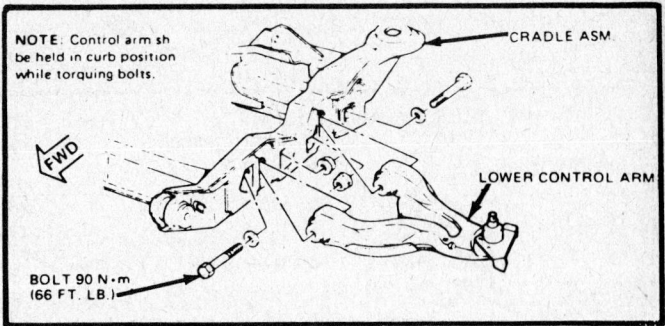

Rear control arm mounting
(© General Motors Corporation)

adapter of the tool. Continue turning the screw compressing the strut spring.
6. Place tool top adapter over the spring seat assembly.
7. Turn the strut compressor forcing screw counterclockwise until the strut spring tension is relieved, remove the adapters and remove strut.
8. Clamp strut compressor tool in vise. Place the strut as-

17-33

Section 17: GENERAL MOTORS—"P" BODY
PONTIAC FIERO • FIERO SE

sembly in bottom adapter of compressor and install tool. (Be certain adapter captures strut and locating pins are engaged).

9. Rotate the strut assembly until mounting flange is facing out, directly opposite the compressor tool forcing screw.

10. Position the spring and components on the strut. Be certain spring is properly seated on the bottom spring plate.

11. Install the strut spring seat assembly on top of spring. The long stud must be 180° from the strut mounting flange.

12. Place compressor tool top adapter over the spring seat assembly. Turn the compressor tool forcing screw until the compressor top support just contacts the top adapters (do not compress spring at this time).

13. Install strut alignment rod through the top spring seat and thread the rod onto the damper shaft, hand tight.

14. Compress the spring by turning the screw clockwise until enough of the damper shaft is exposed to where the nut can be threaded securely, and tighten nut on damper shaft. Do not compress spring until it bottoms. Be sure that the damper shaft comes through the center of the spring seat opening or damage could occur.

15. Remove the alignment rod and position the strut mount over the damper shaft and spring seat studs. Install the washer and nut.

16. Turn the tool forcing screw counterclockwise to back off support and remove the strut assembly from the compressor tool.

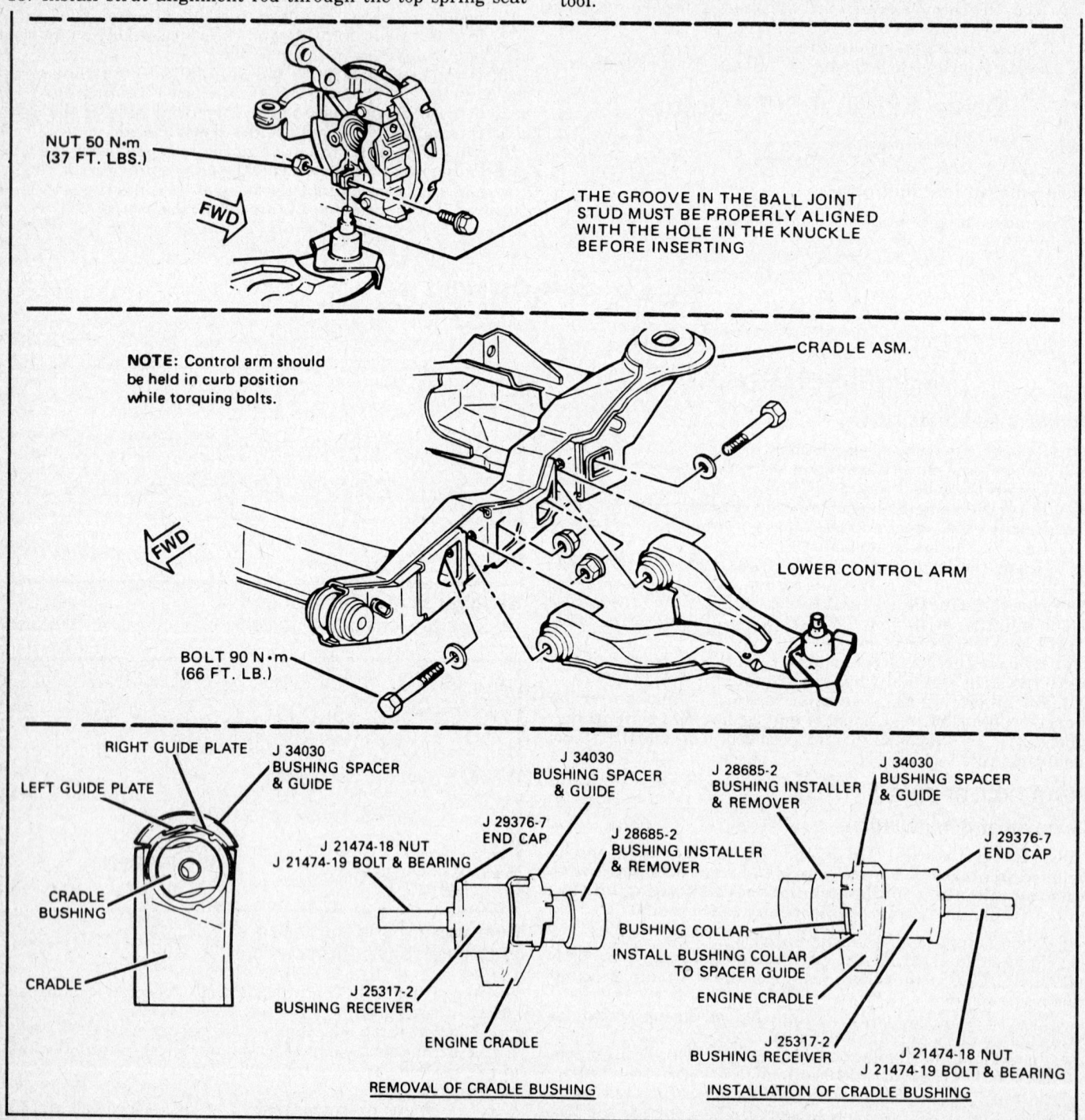

Remove/Install Lower Control Arm

GENERAL MOTORS—"P" BODY
PONTIAC FIERO • FIERO SE

LOWER CONTROL ARM

Removal and Installation

1. Raise the vehicle and support it safely.
2. Remove the ball joint clamping bolt.
3. Separate the knuckle from the ball joint.
4. Remove the lower control arm pivot bolts at the frame and remove the control arm.
5. Installation is the reverse of removal. The toe-in and camber settings should be checked and adjusted as required.

LOWER BALL JOINT

Removal and Installation

1. Raise the vehicle and support it safely. Remove the wheel.
2. Remove the clamp bolt from the lower control arm ball stud.
3. Disconnect the ball joint from the knuckle. It may be necessary to tap the ball stud with a mallet.
4. Using a ⅛ inch drill, drill the rivets approximately ¼ inch deep in the center of the rivet.
5. Use a ½ inch drill and drill just deep enough to remove the rivet head.
6. Remove the rivets using a hammer and a punch.
7. The ball joint is replaced using nuts and bolts. Torque to 13 ft. lbs. Check the toe-in setting and adjust as necessary.

REAR WHEEL BEARING

Removal and Installation

1. Remove the hub cap and loosen the hub nut. On models equipped with 14 inch aluminum wheels, set the parking brake.
2. Raise and support the vehicle safely and remove the tire and wheel assembly.
3. Install the drive axle boot protectors #J-33162 or equivalent and remove the and discard the hub nut.
4. Remove the caliper and rotor and remove the hub and bearing attaching bolts. If the bearing assembly is being reused, mark the attaching bolts and corresponding holes for installation.
5. Install tool #J-28733 or equivalent and remove the hub and bearing assembly.
6. If installing a new bearing, be sure to replace the knuckle seal. Clean and inspect the bearing mating surfaces and knuckle bore for dirt, nicks and burrs.
7. If installing a knuckle seal, use tool #J-28671 or equivalent and apply grease to the seal and knuckle bore.
8. Push the hub and bearing on the axle shaft and install any other components at this time.
9. Apply a torque of 74 ft. lbs. to the new hub nut, until the hub and bearing assembly is seated properly.
10. Install the rotor and caliper and apply a final torque of 200 ft. lbs. to the hub nut.
11. Install the tire and wheel assembly and lower the vehicle.

REAR WHEEL ALIGNMENT

The rear alignment refers to the angular relationship between the rear wheels, the rear suspension attaching parts and the ground. Camber and toe are the only adjustments required.

CAMBER ADJUSTMENT

The camber can be adjusted by loosening both the strut to knuckle bolts enough to allow movement between the strut and knuckle and grasping the top of the tire and moving it inboard or outboard until the correct camber is obtained.

TOE ADJUSTMENT

Toe-in is adjusted by loosening the jam nuts on the toe link rods then rotating the toe link rods to adjust to specifications.

SECTION 18

GENERAL MOTORS—"T" BODY
CHEVETTE • CHEVETTE SCOOTER • PONTIAC T1000 • 1000

SPECIFICATIONS

Brakes	24–2	Serial Number Identification	18–3
Camshaft	18–5	Torque	18–5
Capacities	18–6	Torque Sequence (Cylinder Heads)	18–16
Crankshaft & Connecting Rod	18–5	Tune-Up	18–4
Firing Order	18–4	Valve	18–5
General Engine	18–4	Wheel Alignment	18–6
Piston & Ring	18–5		

INDEX

A
- Alternator R&R 18–6
- Automatic Transmission 18–24
  - Adjustment 18–24
  - On Car Service 23–2
  - Assembly R&R 18–24
- Axle Assembly R&R 18–25
- Axle Shaft R&R 18–25

B
- Ball Joints 35–2
- Brake System 18–22
- Brake Booster 18–22
- Brake Caliper Overhaul 24–2
- Brake Caliper R&R 24–2
- Brake Drum
  - Rear 24–2
- Brake Master Cylinder 18–22
- Brake Pad
  - Front 24–2
- Brake Shoe
  - Rear 24–2

C
- Camshaft R&R 18–16
- Carburetor R&R 18–13
- Chassis Electrical 18–8
- Clutch 18–22
  - Adjustment 18–22
  - R&R 18–22
- Component Locations 18–10
- Control Arm R&R 35–2
- Cooling System 18–11
- Cruise Control 18–10
- Cylinder Head 18–15
  - R&R 18–15

D
- Differential 32–2
  - Inspection 32–2
- Disc Brakes 24–2
- Distributor R&R 18–7
- Drive Axle 32–2
- Driveshaft R&R 18–23

E
- Electronic Ignition 30–2
- Emission Controls 18–13
- Engine 18–14
  - Identification 18–3
  - R&R 18–14
- Engine Electrical 18–6
- Engine Lubrication 18–18
- Engine Mechanical 18–14
- Engine Mounts R&R 18–14
- Exhaust Manifold R&R 18–13

F
- Front Suspension 35–2
  - Alignment 18–6
- Fuel Mixture, Adjust 18–12
- Fuel Pump R&R 18–12
- Fuses 18–10

H
- Head Light Switch 18–9
- Heater Blower R&R 18–11
- Heater Core R&R 18–11
- Heater Control 18–11

I
- Idle Speed Adjust 18–12
- Ignition Switch 18–8
- Ignition Timing 18–7
- Instrument Cluster R&R 18–10
- Intake Manifold R&R 18–13

L, M, N
- Lower Control Arm R&R 35–2
- Master Cylinder R&R 18–22
- Manual Steering Gear
  - R&R 18–23
- Manual Transmission
  - Overhaul 32–2
- Manual Transmission R&R 18–23
- Neutral Safety Switch
  - R&R 18–8

O
- Oil Pan R&R 18–18
- Oil Pump R&LR 18–19
- Oil Sear R&R
  - Rear Main 18–20

P
- Parking Brake 18–22
  - Adjustment 18–22
  - Cable R&R 18–22
- Piston & Connecting Rod 18–17
- Power Brake Unit R&R 18–22
- Power Steering Pump R&R 18–21

R
- Rear Main Oil Seal R&R 18–20
- Rear Suspension 35–2
- Regulator 18–6
- Rocker Shaft/Assy RR 18–15

S
- Serial Number 18–3
  - Engine 18–3
  - Vehicle 18–3
- Shock Absorber R&R
  - Front 35–2
  - Rear 35–2
- Springs
  - Front 35–2
  - Rear 35–2
- Starter R&R 18–6
- Starter Drive Replacement 18–6
- Steering Column R&R 18–21
- Steering Gear R&R 18–20
  - Manual 18–20
  - Power 18–20
- Steering Wheel R&R 18–20
- Speedometer R&R 18–10
- Suspension R&R 35–2
  - Service 35–2

T
- Throttle Linkage, Adjust 18–24
- Timing Belt R&R 18–17
- Timing Belt 18–17
- Timing Belt Cover 18–17
- Oil Seal Replacement 18–17
- Tune-Up 18–4
- Turn Signal Switch R&R 18–9

U, V
- U-Joint Overhaul 28–2
- Valve Tappette R&R 18–15
- Valve Timing, Adjust 18–15
- Valve System 18–15
- Voltage Regulator 18–6

W, Y
- Water Pump R&R 18–11
- Wheel Alignment 18–6
  - Front 18–6
- Wheel Bearings Front 18–21
- Wheel Cylinders Rear 18–25
  - Rear 24–2
- Windshield Wiper 18–10
  - Linkage R&R 18–10
  - Motor R&R 18–10
  - Switch R&R 18–9
- Year Identification 18–3

BEFORE SERVICING BE CERTAIN TO READ THE SAFETY NOTICE

18 SECTION

GM "T" Body
1983–87
Rear Wheel Drive Cars

CHEVETTE • CHEVETTE SCOOTER
PONTIAC T1000 • 1000

YEAR IDENTIFICATION

1983–87 Chevette

1983 1000

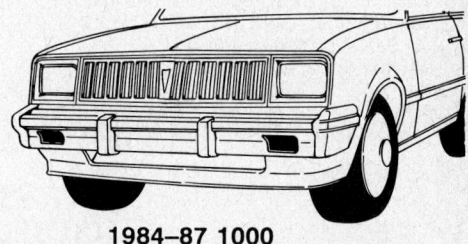
1984–87 1000

VEHICLE IDENTIFICATION NUMBER (VIN)

It is important for servicing and ordering parts to be certain of the vehicle and engine identification. The VIN (vehicle identification number) is a 13 or 17 digit number visible through the windshield on the driver's side of the dash and contains the vehicle and engine identification codes. It can be interpreted as follows:

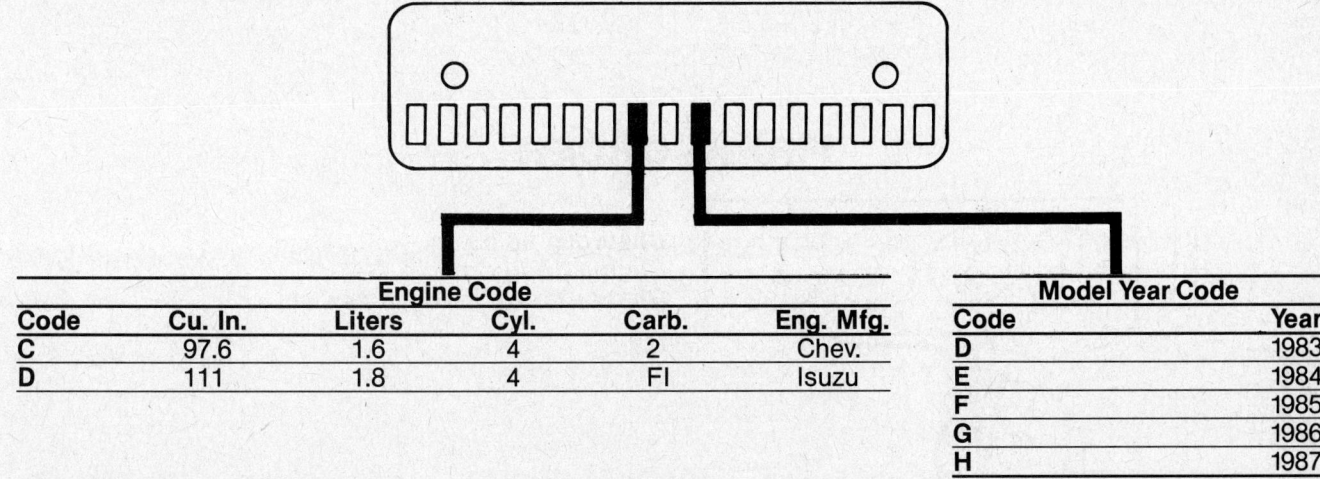

Engine Code						Model Year Code	
Code	Cu. In.	Liters	Cyl.	Carb.	Eng. Mfg.	Code	Year
C	97.6	1.6	4	2	Chev.	D	1983
D	111	1.8	4	FI	Isuzu	E	1984
						F	1985
						G	1986
						H	1987

The seventeen digit Vehicle Identification Number can be used to determine engine application and model year. The 10th digit indicates the model year, and the 8th digit identifies the factory installed engine.

18–3

SECTION 18

GENERAL MOTORS—"T" BODY
CHEVETTE • CHEVETTE SCOOTER • PONTIAC T1000 • 1000

GENERAL ENGINE SPECIFICATIONS

Year	Eng. V.I.N. Code	Engine No. Cyl. Displacement liters (cu. in.)	Mfg.	Carburetor Type	Horsepower @ rpm ■	Torque @ rpm (ft lbs.) ■	Bore × Stroke (in.)	Compression Ratio	Oil Pressure @ 2000 rpm
'83–'87	C	4-1.6	Chev.	2 bbl	65 @ 5200	80 @ 2400	3.228 × 2.980	9.0:1	55
'83–'87 Diesel	D	4-1.8	Isuzu	Fuel Injection	51 @ 5000	72 @ 2000	3.310 × 3.230	22.0:1	64 ①

■ Horsepower and torque are SAE net figures. They are measured at the rear of the transmission with all accessories installed and operating. Since the figures vary when a given engine is installed in different models, some are representative rather than exact.
① @ 5000

GASOLINE ENGINE TUNE-UP SPECIFICATIONS

Year	Eng. V.I.N. Code	Engine No. Cyl Displacement (liters)	Mfg.	Spark Plugs Orig. Type	Gap. (in.)	Distributor	Ignition Timing (deg) ▲ Man. Trans.	Auto. Trans.	Valves Intake Opens ■ (deg)	Fuel Pump Pressure (psi)	Idle Speed (rpm) ▲ Man. Trans.	Auto. Trans.
'82–'87		4-1.6	Chev.	R42CTS	.035	Electronic	8B	8B	—	5.5–6.5	800	700

NOTE: The underhood specifications sticker often reflects tune-up specification changes made in production. Sticker figures must be used if they disagree with those in this chart. Product numbers in this chart are not recommendations by Chilton for any product by brand name.
▲ See text for procedure
■ All figures Before Top Dead Center

DIESEL ENGINE TUNE-UP SPECIFICATIONS

Year	Engine No. Cyl. Displacement (liters)	Static Injection Timing	Fuel Injection Order	Compression (lbs)	Injection Nozzle Opening Pressure (psi)	Intake Valve Opens (deg)	Idle Speed ▲ (rpm) Man.	Auto.
'83–'87	L-4-1.8	11°B	1-3-4-2	441 ①	1707	32	620	720

NOTE: The underhood specifications sticker often reflects changes made in production. Sticker figures must be used if they disagree with those in the above chart.
▲ See underhood sticker for fast idle speed.
① At 200 rpm

FIRING ORDER

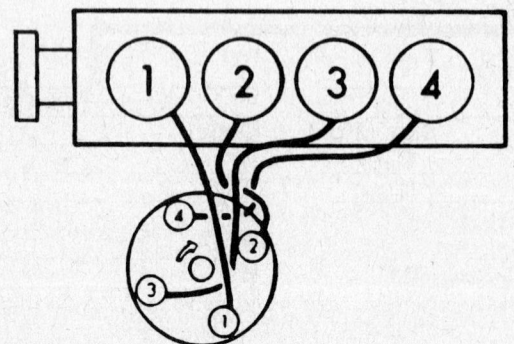

Chevrolet 98 cu. in. (1.6L) 4 cyl.
Engine firing order: 1-3-4-2
Distributor rotation: clockwise

GENERAL MOTORS—"T" BODY
CHEVETTE • CHEVETTE SCOOTER • PONTIAC T1000 • 1000

SECTION 18

VALVE SPECIFICATIONS

Year	Engine No. Cyl. Displacement (liters)	Seat Angle (deg)	Face Angle (deg)	Spring Test Pressure (lbs @ in.)	Spring Installed Height (in.)	Stem-To-Guide Clearance (in.) Intake	Stem-To-Guide Clearance (in.) Exhaust	Stem Diameter (in.) Intake	Stem Diameter (in.) Exhaust
'83–'87	4-1.6	45	46	173 @ .886	1.25	.0006–.0017	.0014–.0025	.3141	.3133
'83–'87	4-1.8	45	45	108 @ 1.24 ①	1.61	.0015–.0028	.0018–.0030	.3128–.3134	.3126–.3132

① Exhaust 112 @ 1.22; Innter spring test pressures—intake 58 @ 1.14
   exhaust 60 @ 1.12

CRANKSHAFT AND CONNECTING ROD SPECIFICATIONS
All measurements are given in inches.

Year	Engine No. Cyl. Displacement (liters)	Crankshaft Main Brg. Journal Dia	Crankshaft Main Brg. Oil Clearance	Crankshaft Shaft End-Play	Thrust on No.	Connecting Rod Journal Diameter	Connecting Rod Oil Clearance	Connecting Rod Side Clearance
'83–'87	4-1.6	2.0078–2.0088	①	.004–.008	4	1.809–1.810	.0014–.0031	.004–.012
'83–'87	4-1.8	2.2010–2.2020	.0015–.0027	.0024–.0094	3	1.927–1.928	.0016–.0032	.008–.020

① #5—.0009–.0026
  All others—.0005–.0018

CAMSHAFT SPECIFICATIONS
All measurements in inches.

Year	Engine Type/Disp. L(cu. in.)	Journal Diameter 1	2	3	4	5	Bearing Clearance	Lobe Lift Intake	Lobe Lift Exhaust	Camshaft End Play
'83–'87	4-1.6	1.7682–1.7697	1.7584–1.7598	1.7485–1.7500	1.7387–1.7402	1.1816–1.1837	.0020–.0044	.2410	.2410	.0067–.0169
'83–'87	4-1.8	1.102	1.102	1.102	1.102	1.102	.0008–.0035	N/A	N/A	NA

NA—Not Available

PISTON AND RING SPECIFICATIONS
All measurements are given in inches.

Year	Engine Type/Disp. (liters)	Piston-to-Bore Clearance	Ring Gap Top Compression	Ring Gap Bottom Compression	Ring Gap Oil Control	Ring Side Clearance Top Compression	Ring Side Clearance Bottom Compression	Ring Side Clearance Oil Control
'83–'87	4-1.6	.0008–.0016	.009–.019	.008–.018	.015–.055	.0012–.0027	.0012–.0032	.0000–.0050
'83–'87	4-1.8	.0002–.0017	.0078–.0157	.0078–.0157	.0078–.0157	.0035–.0049	.0019–.0033	.0012–.0028

TORQUE SPECIFICATIONS
All readings in ft. lbs.

Year	Engine No. Cyl. Displacement (liters)	Cylinder Head Bolts	Rod Bearing Bolts	Main Bearing Bolts	Crankshaft Pulley Bolt	Flywheel to Crankshaft Bolts	Manifold Intake	Manifold Exhaust
'83–'87	4-1.6	70–80	34–40	40–52	75–100	40–52	13–18	①
'83–'87	4-1.8	②	65	75	N/A	40	30	30

N/A Not Available
① Center bolts—13–18; end bolts—19–25
② First tighten to 21–36 ft. lbs. then retighten to 83–98 (new bolt),
  90–105 (reused bolt)

Section 18: GENERAL MOTORS—"T" BODY
CHEVETTE • CHEVETTE SCOOTER • PONTIAC T1000 • 1000

CAPACITIES

Year	Engine No. Cyl. Displacement (liters)	Engine Crankcase	Transmission Pts. to Refill After Draining			Drive Axle (pts)	Gasoline Tank (gals)	Cooling System (qts)	
			Manual		Automatic •			With Heater	With A/C
			4-Speed	5-Speed					
'83–'87	4-1.6	4	3	4	6	1³⁄₄	12.5	9	9¹⁄₄
'83–'87	4-1.8	6 ①	3	3¹⁄₄	6	1³⁄₄	12.5	8.5	9.0

• Specificaitons do not include torque converter
① With filter change

WHEEL ALIGNMENT SPECIFICATIONS

Year	Model	Caster		Camber		Toe-in (in.)	Steering Axis Inclination (deg)
		Range (deg)	Pref Setting (deg)	Range (deg)	Pref Setting (deg)		
'83–'87	All	4P–6P	5P	1/4P–1/2P	1/4P	1/16P	—

P Positive

ELECTRICAL SECTION

For Overhaul Procedures Refer to the Unit Repair Section.

Charging System

ALTERNATOR

Removal and Installation

1. Disconnect the negative battery cable. Disconnect the alternator wiring.
2. If equipped with a diesel engine, remove the fan shroud and fresh air duct. Disconnect the oil and vacuum lines at the vacuum pump.
3. Remove the brace bolt. Remove the alternator drive belt.
4. Support the alternator and remove the mounting bolt. Remove the alternator assembly from the vehicle.

NOTE: If equipped with a diesel engine the alternator mounting bolts are removed from underneath of the vehicle, below the car.

5. Installation is the reverse of the removal procedure. Adjust the alternator belt as required.

VOLTAGE REGULATOR

Removal and Installation

The voltage regulator is incorporated within the alternator assembly. There is no adjustment procedure. Should the regulator require service the alternator must be disassembled.

Starting System

STARTER

Removal and Installation

GAS ENGINE (WITHOUT POWER BRAKES)

1. Disconnect the battery negative cable.

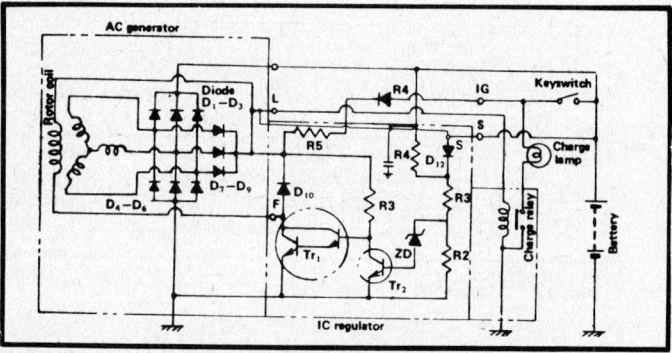

Electrical schematic of Hitachi charging system, used with diesel engines
(© General Motors Corporation)

2. Remove the air cleaner.
3. Disconnect the gas line at the carburetor and move to one side.
4. Disconnect the vacuum hose at the carburetor.
5. Remove the splash shield from the distributor coil and move to one side.
6. Remove the upper and lower starter bolts.
7. Disconnect the starter wiring.
8. Remove the master cylinder mounting nuts to gain access for removing the starter.
9. Installation is the reverse of removal.

GAS ENGINE (WITH POWER BRAKES)

1. Disconnect the battery ground cable.
2. Remove the air cleaner.
3. Disconnect the gas line at the carburetor and move to one side.
4. Remove the splash shield from the distributor coil and move to one side.
5. Remove the upper starter bolt.

GENERAL MOTORS—"T" BODY
CHEVETTE • CHEVETTE SCOOTER • PONTIAC T1000 • 1000
SECTION 18

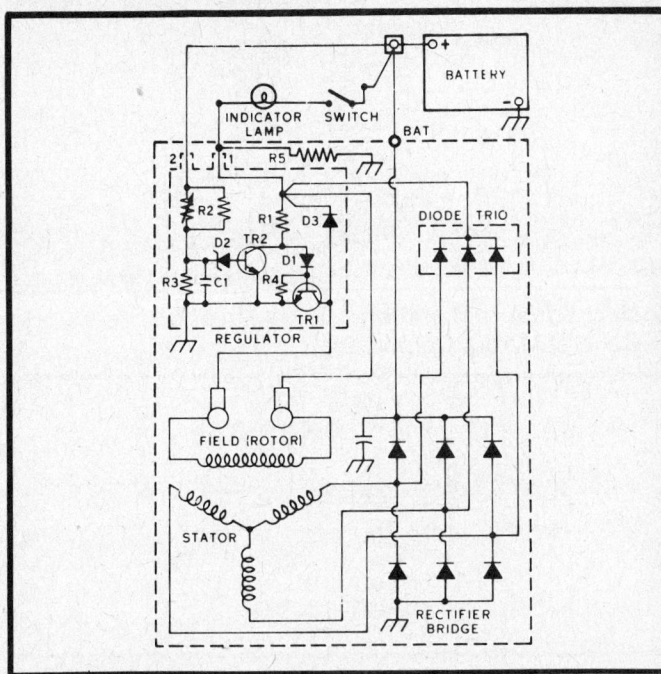

Electrical schematic of Delcotron charging system
(© General Motors Corporation)

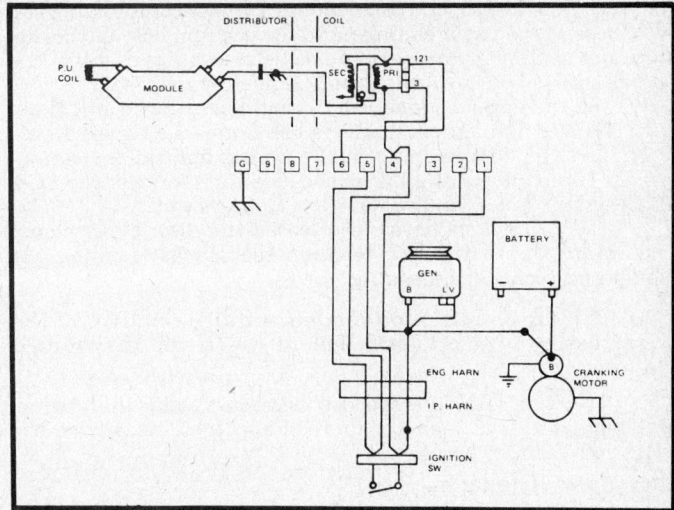

Ignition and starting circuits
(© General Motors Corporation)

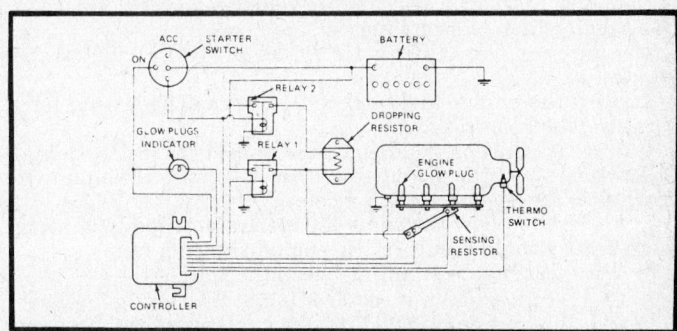

Diesel engine electrical circuit schematic
(© General Motors Corporation)

6. Remove the steering column cover screws and remove the cover.
7. Remove the steering column upper nuts and toe pan screw.
8. Raise the vehicle safely and remove the steering shaft from the steering coupling.
9. Lower the vehicle and move the steering column from inside the car to gain access to the starter.
10. Disconnect the starter wiring.
11. Remove the starter lower bolt and remove the starter.
12. Installation is the reverse of removal.

DIESEL ENGINE
1. Disconnect the negative battery cable.
2. Disconnect the starter wiring.
3. Remove the upper mounting nut and the lower mounting bolt, then remove the starter.
4. Installation is the reverse of removal.

Ignition System

DISTRIBUTOR

Removal and Installation
1. Disconnect the negative battery cable.
2. If the vehicle is air conditioned, disconnect the electrical lead at the air conditioning compressor.
3. Remove the compressor mounting thru bolt and two adjusting bolts.
4. Remove two bolts and remove the compressor upper mounting bracket. Raise and support the vehicle safely. Remove the two bolts securing the compressor lower mounting bracket and pull the bracket outward for clearance. Lower the vehicle.
5. Remove the air cleaner.
6. Remove the distributor cap.
7. Remove the ignition coil cover.
8. Remove the ignition coil mounting bracket bolts.

9. Disconnect the electrical connector with red and brown wires that goes from the ignition coil to the distributor.
10. Remove the fuel pump, gasket, and push rod, noting the direction in which push rod was installed.
11. Scribe a mark on the engine in line with the distributor rotor. Note the approximate position of the distributor housing in relation to the engine.
12. Remove the distributor hold down bolt and clamp and remove the distributor.
13. If the engine has not been disturbed with the distributor removed, simply reverse the installation procedure to install, aligning the marks made during removal.
14. If the engine has been disturbed, remove the No. 1 spark plug and place your thumb or finger over the spark plug hole. Manually turn the engine in the normal direction of operation until compression is felt and the timing marks point to TDC. Align the marks made during removal and install the distributor.

IGNITION TIMING

Adjustment

WITHOUT EST DISTRIBUTOR

NOTE: Refer to the underhood sticker before any adjustments are made with respect to engine timing.

1. Bring the engine to normal operating temperature. Stop

18-7

the engine and connect a tachometer. Disconnect and plug the PCV hose at the vapor canister and the vacuum hose at the distributor vacuum advance unit on models so equipped. Start the engine and check curb idle speed. Adjust as necessary.

2. Stop the engine, clean the timing marks and mark them with chalk to make them more visible. Connect a timing light.

3. Start the engine and aim the timing light at the timing marks. If the marks align, stop the engine, reconnect the PCV and vacuum hoses, and remove the timing light.

4. If adjustment is necessary, loosen the distributor clamp and rotate the distributor to align the marks. Tighten the clamp and recheck the timing.

NOTE: Air conditioned models require removal of the compressor, bracket, and belt to reach the distributor clamp.

5. Reset the curb idle speed if necessary, stop the engine, and remove the tachometer and timing light. Reconnect the PCV and vacuum hoses.

WITH EST DISTRIBUTOR

NOTE: Vehicles equipped with the EST distributor can be identified by the absence of a vacuum and a mechanical spark advance on the distributor assembly.

1. Follow all instructions on the vehicle emissions information label, which is located under the hood.
2. Connect the timing light, as per manufacturers instructions.
3. Start the engine and be sure that normal operating temperature has been reached.
4. Increase the engine idle and disconnect the four terminal EST connector at the distributor. This will cause the engine to operate in the bypass timing mode.
5. Failure to allow the engine to reach the proper operating temperature could result in the engine shutting off.
6. With the engine running, check the timing.
7. Correct the timing as required. Once the timing has been adjusted, shut the engine and reconnect all wires and hoses as required.

NOTE: If the vehicle is equipped with air conditioning, it will be necessary to remove the compressor and position it to the side in order to check the timing.

Electrical Controls

IGNITION LOCK CYLINDER

Removal and Installation

1. Disconnect the negative battery cable. Remove the steering wheel and turn signal switch.
2. Do not remove the buzzer switch or damage to the lock cylinder will result.
3. Place the lock cylinder in the RUN position. Remove the securing screw and remove the cylinder.
4. To install the lock cylinder, hold the cylinder sleeve and rotate knob (key in) clockwise to stop, this retracts the actuator. Insert the cylinder into the housing bore with the key on the cylinder sleeve aligned with the keyway in the housing. Push the cylinder in until it bottoms. Install the retaining screw.
5. Install the turn signal switch and the steering wheel.

IGNITION SWITCH

Removal and Installation

1. Disconnect the negative battery cable.
2. Remove the steering wheel.

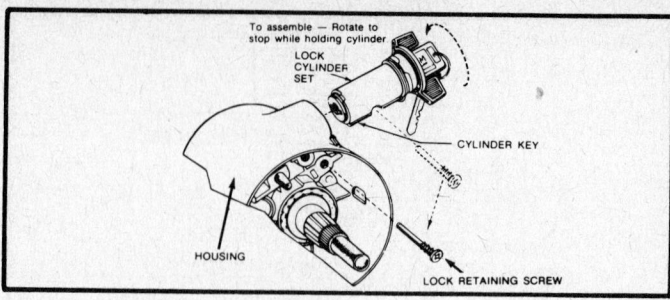

Lock cylinder installation
(© General Motors Corporation)

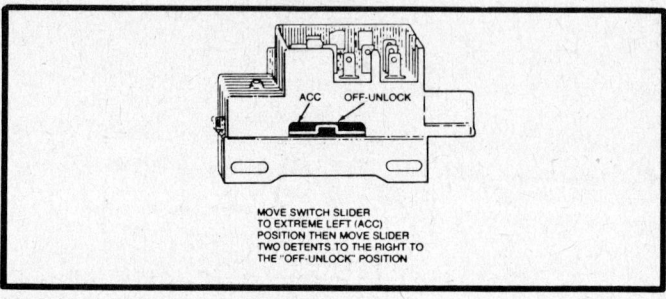

Ignition switch positioning
(© General Motors Corporation)

3. Move the driver's seat as far back as possible.
4. Remove the floor pan bracket screw.
5. Remove the two column bracket to instrument panel nuts and lower the column far enough to disconnect the ignition switch wiring harness. Be sure that the steering column is properly supported before proceeding.
6. The switch should be in the Lock position before removal. If the lock cylinder has already been removed, the actuating rod to the switch should be pulled up until there is a definite stop, then moved down one detent to the Lock position.
7. Remove the two mounting screws and remove the ignition switch. In certain vehicles, the dimmer switch may have to be removed with the ignition switch.
8. Install the lock cylinder as required.
9. Turn the cylinder clockwise to stop and then counterclockwise to stop, then counterclockwise again to stop (Off-Unlock position).
10. Place the ignition switch in the Off-Unlock position. Move the slider two positions to the right from Accessory to the Off-Unlock position.
11. Fit the actuator rod into the slider hole and install the switch on the column. Be sure to use only the correct screws. Be careful not to move the switch out of its detent.
12. Check the dimmer switch adjustment.
13. Connect the ignition switch wiring harness.
14. Loosely install the column bracket to instrument panel nuts.
15. Install the floor pan bracket screw and tighten it to 20 ft. lbs.
16. Tighten the column bracket to instrument panel nuts to 22 ft. lbs.
17. Install the steering wheel.
18. Connect the battery negative cable.

NEUTRAL START SWITCH

Removal and Installation

MANUAL TRANSMISSION

1. Remove the electrical connection from the switch.

GENERAL MOTORS—"T" BODY
CHEVETTE • CHEVETTE SCOOTER • PONTIAC T1000 • 1000
SECTION 18

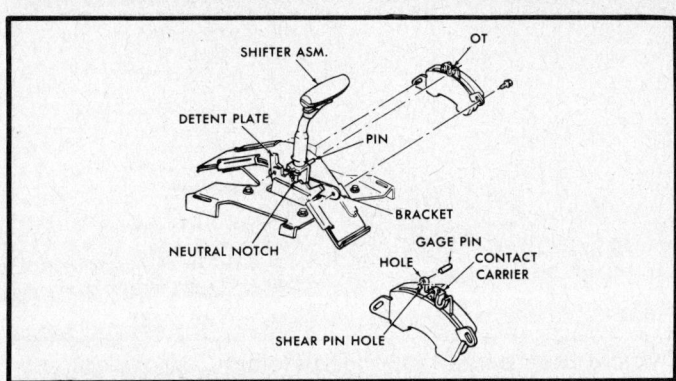

Neutral start switch position on automatic transmission shift console
(© General Motors Corporation)

2. Compress the switch retainer and remove the safety switch from the bracket. Rotate the switch slightly so that the actuating shaft retainer can be pulled from the hole of the clutch pedal. Place the new switch in position so that the actuating shaft retainer is in line with the hole of the clutch pedal and then pop the switch into the hole of the clutch bracket.
4. Reconnect the electrical connection.

NOTE: The engine will only start with the clutch depressed and the ignition switch in the START position.

AUTOMATIC TRANSMISSION

1. Remove the floor console cover and disconnect the electrical connectors of the backup, seat belt warning and neutral start from the switch assembly.
2. Position the shift lever in the neutral position and remove the two switch retaining screws. Remove the switch.
3. To install switch, be sure the shift lever is in the neutral position. Place the replacement switch in position on the shift lever, making sure that the pin on the shift lever is in the slot of the neutral start switch.
4. Secure the switch with the two retaining screws and torque the screws to 14-19 inch lbs.
5. Shift the lever from the neutral position in order to shear the plastic positioning pin in the switch.
6. Install the electrical connections and verify that the switch operates in its proper modes.
7. If the plastic positioning pin has been sheared, align the hole in the contact carrier with the hole in the back of the switch and insert a 0.092 in. gauge pin in both holes.
8. Installation is the reverse of the removal procedure. Be sure to remove the gauge pin before the shift lever is moved.

HEADLIGHT SWITCH

Removal and Installation

1. Disconnect the negative battery cable.
2. Pull the headlight switch control knob on the On position.
3. Reach up under the instrument panel and depress the switch shaft retainer button while pulling on the switch control shaft knob.
4. Remove the three screws and remove the headlight switch trim plate.
5. Use a suitable tool to remove the light switch ferrule nut from the front of the instrument panel.
6. Disconnect the multi ontact connector from the bottom of the headlight switch.
7. Installation is the reverse of removal.

TURN SIGNAL SWITCH

Removal and Installation

1. Disconnect the negative battery cable. Remove the steering wheel.
2. Position a suitable tool into one of the three cover slots. Pry up and out (at least two slots) to free the cover.
3. Press down on the lockplate, but do not relieve the full load of the spring because the ring will rotate and make removal difficult. Pry the round wire snapring out of the shaft groove and discard it. Lift the lockplate off the end of the shaft.
4. Slide the turn signal canceling cam, upper bearing preload spring, and thrust washer off the end of the shaft.
5. Remove the multi function lever by rotating it clockwise to its stop (off position), then pull the lever straight out to disengage it.
6. Push the hazard warning knob in and unscrew the knob.
7. Remove the two screws, pivot arm, and spacer.
8. Wrap the upper part of the connector with tape to prevent snagging the wires during switch removal.
9. Remove the three switch mounting screws and pull the switch straight up, guiding the wiring harness through the column housing.
10. Position the switch into the housing.
11. Install the three switch mounting screws. Replace the spacer and pivot arm. Be sure that the spacer protrudes through the hole in the arm and that the arm finger encloses the turn signal switch frame.
12. Install the hazard warning knob.
13. Make sure that the turn signal switch is in the neutral position and that the hazard warning knob is out. Slide the thrust washer, upper bearing preload spring, and the canceling cam into the upper end of the shaft.
14. Place the lockplate and a new snapring onto the end of the shaft. Compress the lockplate as far as possible. Slide the new snapring into the shaft groove and remove the lockplate compressor tool.
15. Install the multi function lever, guiding the wire harness through the column housing. Align the lever pin with the switch slot. Push on the end of the lever until it is seated securely.
16. Install the steering wheel.

WINDSHIELD WIPER/WASHER SWITCH

Removal and Installation

1. Disconnect the negative battery cable. Remove the steering wheel and directional signal switch. It may be necessary to loosen the two column mounting nuts and remove the four bracket to mast jacket screws, then separate the bracket from the mast jacket to allow the connector clip on the ignition switch to be pulled out of the column assembly.
2. Disconnect the washer/wiper switch lower connector.
3. Remove the screws attaching the column housing to the mast jacket. Be sure to note the position of the dimmer switch actuator rod for reassembly in the same position. Remove the column housing and switch as an assembly.
4. Turn upside down and use a drift to remove the pivot pin from the washer/wiper switch. Remove the switch.
5. Place a new switch into position in the housing, then install the pivot pin.
6. Position the housing onto the mast jacket and attach by installing the screws. Install the dimmer switch actuator rod in the same position as noted earlier. Check switch operation.
7. Reconnect lower end of switch assembly.
8. Install remaining components in reverse order of removal. Be sure to attach column mounting bracket in original position.

18-9

SECTION 18

GENERAL MOTORS—"T" BODY
CHEVETTE • CHEVETTE SCOOTER • PONTIAC T1000 • 1000

WIPER MOTOR

Removal and Installation

1. Disconnect the negative battery cable. Working inside the car, reach up under the instrument panel above the steering column and loosen, but do not remove, the transmission drive link to motor crank arm attaching nuts.
2. Disconnect the transmission drive link from the wiper motor crank arm.
3. Raise the hood and disconnect the wiper motor wiring.
4. Remove the three motor attaching bolts.
5. Remove the motor while guiding the crank arm through the hole.
6. To install, align the sealing gasket to the base of the motor and reverse the rest of the removal procedure.

WIPER LINKAGE/TRANSMISSION

Removal and Installation

1. Remove or loosen the instrument panel cover, the instrument panel cluster housing.
2. On units equipped with air conditioning, remove screws and push left air conditioning duct aside for better access to transmission attaching bolts (left side). Remove the left side air outlet duct the speedometer cable shield and the instrument panel brace (left side).
3. Working from inside the car, loosen transmission drive link to motor crank arm attaching nuts and disengage drive link.
4. Remove wiper arm and blade assemblies. Remove transmission to dash panel attaching bolts.
5. Move transmission assembly to the left while rotating the assembly, work it out through instrument panel access hole at right upper center of instrument panel.
6. Load transmission assembly through instrument panel access hole and insert serrated shafts through holes in upper dash panel, then install the attaching bolts.
7. Cycle motor to insure that motor crank arm is in the park position.
8. Attach transmission drive link to motor crank arm.

Instrument Panel

INSTRUMENT CLUSTER

Removal and Installation

1. Disconnect the negative battery cable.
2. If equipped remove the clock stem knob.
3. Remove four screws and remove instrument cluster bezel and lens.
4. Remove two nuts securing instrument cluster to instrument panel and pull instrument cluster slightly forward.
5. Disconnect electrical connector and speedometer cable from instrument cluster and remove cluster.
6. Install replacement instrument cluster in reverse order of removal.

SPEEDOMETER

Removal and Installation

1. Disconnect the negative battery cable. Remove the instrument cluster assembly.

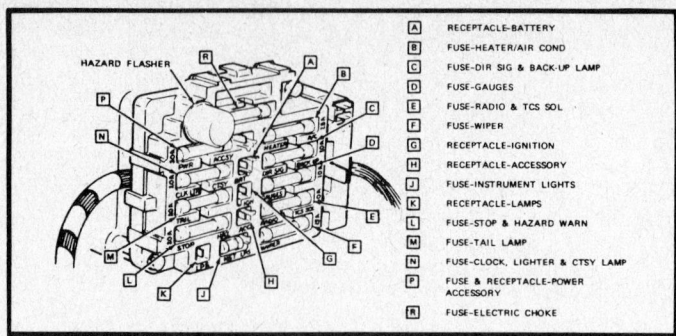

Typical fuse panel (© General Motors Corporation)

2. Remove the speedometer retaining screws from the instrument cluster.
3. Separate the speedometer head from the instrument cluster.
4. Installation is the reverse of the removal procedure.

SPEEDOMETER CABLE

Removal and Installation

1. Disconnect the negative battery cable. Remove the instrument cluster assembly.
2. Pull the core from the speedometer cable housing. If the core is broken in the middle, it will be necessary to disconnect the speedometer cable at the transmission and insert the new core through the top of the housing.
3. Attach the cable housing to the transmission and insert the new core through the top of the housing.
4. Attach the speedometer cable to the rear of the speedometer.
5. Install the instrument cluster assembly.

ELECTRICAL COMPONENT LOCATION

Fuse Panel

The fuse panel is located under the left-hand side of the instrument panel. The fuse amperage and the circuit protected is marked on the fuse panel.

Electronic Control Module

The electronic control module is located below the right hand side of the instrument panel.

Turn Signal Flasher

The turn signal flasher is located above the brake pedal bracket and to the left of the steering column.

Fusible Link

The fusible link is incorporated into the wiring system. The fusible link is a sixteen gauge red wire located at the battery terminal of the starter solenoid. Also, on diesel models a fourteen gauge brown fusible link is located between the battery and the glow plug relay.

SPEED CONTROL

For information on speed control refer to the "A" and "X" body section of this manual.

GENERAL MOTORS—"T" BODY
CHEVETTE • CHEVETTE SCOOTER • PONTIAC T1000 • 1000
SECTION 18

COOLING AND HEATER SYSTEMS

Water Pump

Removal and Installation
GAS ENGINE

1. Disconnect the negative battery cable. Remove the alternator, and air conditioner compressor drive belts.
2. Remove the engine fan, spacer (air conditioned models), and the pulley.
3. Remove the timing belt front cover by removing the two upper bolts, center bolt, and two lower nuts. Remove the timing belt lower cover retaining nut and remove the cover.
4. Drain the coolant.
5. Remove the lower radiator hose and the heater hose at the water pump.
6. Turn the crankshaft pulley so that the mark on the pulley is aligned with the 0 mark on the timing scale and so that a $1/8$ in. drill bit can be inserted through the timing belt upper rear cover and camshaft sprocket.
7. Remove the idler pulley and pull the timing belt off the sprocket. Don't disturb crankshaft position.
8. Remove the water pump retaining bolts and remove the pump and gasket from the engine.
9. Clean all the old gasket material from the cylinder case.
10. With a new gasket in place on the water pump, position the water pump in place on the cylinder case and install the water pump retaining bolts.
11. Install the timing belt onto the cam sprocket.
12. Apply sealer to the idler pulley attaching bolt and install the bolt and the idler pulley. Turn the idler pulley counterclockwise on its mounting bolt to remove the slack in the timing belt.
13. Use a tension gauge to adjust timing belt tension. Check belt tension midway between the tensioner and the cam sprocket on the idler pulley side. Correct belt tension is 70 lbs. Torque the idler pulley mounting bolt 13 to 18 ft. lbs.
14. Remove the $1/8$ in. drill bit from the upper rear timing belt cover and cam sprocket.
15. Install the lower radiator hose and the heater hose to the water pump.
16. Install the timing belt front covers.
17. Install the water pump pulley, spacer (if equipped), and engine fan.
18. Install the engine drive belt(s).
19. Refill the cooling system.
20. Connect the battery negative cable.
21. Start the engine and check for leaks. Run the engine with the heater on until the thermostat opens, then recheck the coolant level.

DIESEL ENGINE

1. Disconnect the negative battery cable. Drain the cooling system.
2. Remove the fan shroud, fan assembly and the accessory drive belt.
3. Unscrew the retaining bolts and remove the damper pulley.
4. Remove the upper and lower halves of the front cover and then remove the bypass hose at the pump.
5. Unscrew the pump retaining bolts and remove the pump assembly.
6. Installation is in the reverse order of removal.

BLOWER MOTOR

Removal and Installation

1. Disconnect the negative battery cable.
2. Disconnect the electrical lead from the blower motor.
3. Scribe a mark to reference the blower motor flange to case position.
4. Remove the blower motor to case attaching screws and remove the blower motor and wheel as an assembly. Pry the flange gently if the sealer acts as an adhesive.
5. Remove the blower wheel retaining nut and separate the motor and wheel.
6. To install, reverse the removal procedure. Be sure to align the scribe marks made during removal. Assemble the blower wheel to the motor with the open end of the wheel away from the motor. If necessary, replace the sealer at the motor flange.

HEATER CORE

Removal and Installation
WITH AIR CONDITIONING

1. Disconnect the negative battery cable.
2. Disconnect the heater hoses at the heater core. Plug the hoses to prevent spillage.
3. Remove the A/C hose bracket.
4. Remove the heater core case cover and remove the core from the case.
5. Installation is the reverse of the removal procedure.

HEATER/AC CONTROL AND FAN SWITCH ASSEMBLY

Removal and Installation

1. Disconnect the negative battery cable.
2. Remove the four screws from the center trim panel, above and below the heater/air conditioning control.
3. Remove the knobs and other necessary hardware from the radio controls, if equipped.
4. Remove the section of instrument panel surrounding the radio and heater controls. On air conditioned equipped vehicles, remove the instrument panel bezel.
5. Remove the three heater/air conditioning control to instrument panel screws.
6. Slide the control unit from the dash opening. Do not kink the bowden cables or damage the electrical connectors. When the control unit is out of the dash, disconnect the cables and the electrical connections.
7. The installation is the reverse of the removal procedure.

SECTION 18
GENERAL MOTORS—"T" BODY
CHEVETTE • CHEVETTE SCOOTER • PONTIAC T1000 • 1000

FUEL SYSTEM

FUEL PUMP

Removal and Installation
GAS ENGINE
1. Disconnect the negative battery cable. Remove the air cleaner as required. Remove the air condition compressor, as required. Do not disconnect the refrigerant lines.
2. Remove the distributor cap and the spark plug wiring retaining clip.
3. Remove the coil assembly.
4. Disconnect the fuel pump hoses and remove the retaining bolts. Remove the fuel pump.
5. The installation is the reverse of the removal procedure.

DIESEL ENGINE
The fuel pump is part of the diesel fuel injection pump, on vehicles equipped with a diesel engine.

CARBURETOR

Adjustments
CHECKING CHOKE OPERATION
1. Remove air cleaner. With engine off, hold throttle half open. Open and close choke several times. Watch linkage to be certain all links are connected and there are no signs of damage.
2. If choke or linkage binds, sticks or works sluggishly, clean with choke cleaner or equivalent. Use cleaner as directed.
3. Visually inspect carburetor to be certain all vacuum hoses are securely connected. Inspect hoses for cracks, abrasion, hardness or signs of deterioration. Replace as necessary.
4. Check vacuum break. If vacuum break does not hold vacuum, replace vacuum break, diaphragm and shaft.

CHECKING ELECTRIC CHOKE MECHANISM
1. Check voltage at the choke heater connection with the engine running. If voltage is between 12 and 15 volts, replace the electrical choke unit.
2. If the voltage is low or zero, check all wires and connections. If the connection at the oil pressure switch is faulty, the temperature pressure warning light will be off with the key "on" and the engine not running. Repair wires as required.
3. If the above steps do not solve the problem, replace oil pressure switch.

CHECKING MIXTURE CONTROL SOLENOID
1. With engine off, remove air cleaner.
2. Check for proper electrical connection at mixture control solenoid.
3. Turn ignition key to the on position, but do not start engine.
4. Ground diagnostic "test" terminal.
5. Listen for movement (cycling) of the plunger inside the mixture control solenoid.
6. If no sound can be heard, remove solenoid and check for plugged passage in bottom of solenoid.
7. If passage is plugged blow out with compressed air.
8. If compressed air will not clear opening, replace solenoid.
9. If passage is clear and solenoid still does not cycle, replace solenoid and recheck.

IDLE MIXTURE ADJUSTMENT
NOTE: The idle mixture needle has been preset at the factory and sealed. Do not remove the plug during normal engine maintenance. Idle mixture should be adjusted only in the case of major carburetor overhaul, throttle body replacement or high emissions.

1. Remove the carburetor.
2. Place inverted carburetor on a suitable holding fixture, manifold side up. Use care to avoid damaging linkage tubes and parts protruding from air horn.
3. Remove the idle mixture needle plug as follows. Position a punch in locator point of throttle body, beneath idle mixture needle plug (manifold side). Drive out hardened steel plug covering mixture needle. Using tool J-29030 or equivalent, lightly seat needle and then back out 2 turns as a preliminary idle mixture adjustment.
4. Install carburetor.
5. Perform idle mixture needle adjustment.
6. After adjustment is complete, seal the idle mixture needle setting using silicone sealant, RTV or equivalent.
7. If necessary, reset idle speed.

THROTTLE POSITION SENSOR
1. Connect the voltmeter from the TPS "B" terminal to terminal "C".
2. Remove the adjustment screw.
3. Apply thread lock adhesive or equivalent to the TPS adjustment screw.
4. With the ignition in the On position, the engine stopped and the air conditioning off, install the adjustment screw.
5. Quickly adjust the screw to specification with the adjustment screw on the high step of the fast idle cam.
6. Install a new plug or silicone sealer over the TPS adjustment screw.

STEPPED SPEED CONTROL
The SSC system consists of three major components. They are a throttle lever actuator, solenoid vacuum control valve and an electronic speed sensor.

The throttle lever actuator is mounted as part of the carburetor assembly, this device open the primary throttle blades to a preset amount in excess of the curb idle when engine vacuum is applied. This actuating vacuum is controlled by a separate solenoid control valve.

The solenoid vacuum control valve is mounted separately from the carburetor. The valve, when open, allows a manifold vacuum signal to be applied to the SSC throttle lever actuator. This valve is held open when energized by any of the following conditions. If the engine speed is above the calibrated value of the electronic speed sensor (vehicles with manual transmission only). If time after engine start up on vehicles with air condition is less than ten seconds. If the air conditioning compressor clutch is engaged. If the power steering pump output pressure exceeds power steering pressure switch calibration. If the engine coolant temperature light is on (vehicles with air conditioning only).

The electronic speed sensor is mounted separately from the solenoid vacuum control valve, this switching device monitors engine speed at the distributor and supplies a continuous electrical signal to the solenoid vacuum control valve as long as the present engine speed is exceeded.

GENERAL MOTORS—"T" BODY
CHEVETTE • CHEVETTE SCOOTER • PONTIAC T1000 • 1000
SECTION 18

CARBURETOR

Removal and Installation

1. Disconnect the negative battery cable. Remove air cleaner.
2. Disconnect the fuel and vacuum lines from the carburetor.
3. Disconnect the accelerator linkage and the electrical connectors.
4. Remove the carburetor attaching nuts and remove the carburetor.
5. Remove the electric EFE heater and the insulator gasket.
6. Be sure the throttle body and intake manifold sealing surfaces are clean.
7. Install a new EFE heater and an insulator gasket on the manifold.
8. Install the carburetor over the manifold studs.
9. Install the vacuum lines and loosely connect the fuel line.
10. Install and tighten the attaching nuts.
11. Tighten the fuel inlet nut to 25 ft. lbs.
12. Connect the accelerator linkage and the electrical connectors.
13. Check and adjust the idle speed as required.
14. Install the air cleaner.

INTAKE MANIFOLD

Removal and Installation
GAS ENGINE

1. Disconnect the battery ground.
2. Drain the cooling system.
3. Remove the air cleaner.
4. Disconnect the upper radiator hose. Disconnect the heater hoses.
5. Remove the EGR valve.
6. Disconnect all electrical wiring, vacuum hoses and the accelerator linkage from the carburetor.
7. Disconnect the fuel line from the carburetor.
8. Remove the coil.
9. Remove the intake manifold retaining bolts.
10. Remove the manifold.
11. If installing a new manifold, transfer all good parts. Always use a new gasket. Installation is the reverse of removal. Torque all bracket bolts to 30 ft. lbs. and the intake manifold bolts to 15 ft. lbs.

DIESEL ENGINE

1. Disconnect the negative battery cable.
2. Disconnect the fresh air hose and the vent hose. Remove the fuel separator.
3. Tag and disconnect all electrical connectors, the accelerator linkage and the flow plug wires.
4. Disconnect the injector lines at the injection pump and at the injector nozzles. Remove the injector lines and clamps.
5. Remove the glow plug line at the cylinder head.
6. If equipped with power steering, remove the drive belt, the idler pulley and the bracket.
7. Remove the upper half of the front cover and the bracket.
8. Unscrew the mounting bolts and remove the intake manifold.
9. Place a new gasket over the mounting studs on the cylinder head and install the manifold. Tighten the bolts to 30 ft. lbs.
10. Installation of the remaining components is in the reverse order of removal.

EXHAUST MANIFOLD

Removal and Installation

1. Disconnect the battery ground.
2. Raise the vehicle and support it safely.
3. Disconnect the exhaust pipe from the flange.
4. Lower the vehicle.
5. On the diesel, remove the power steering belt, the flex hose and the power steering pump (if so equipped).
6. Remove the carburetor heat tube on the gas engine.
7. Remove the pulse air tubing, if so equipped.
8. Remove the manifold.
9. Installation is the reverse of removal. Install the two upper inner bolts first, to properly position the manifold. Tighten the bolts to the specified torque.

EMISSION CONTROL SYSTEMS

Emission Equipment

Closed positive crankcase ventilation (PCV)
Emission calibrated carburetor
Emission calibrated distributor
Thermostatic air cleaner (TAC)
Evaporative emission control vapor canister (EEC)
Exhaust gas recirculation (EGR)
Catalytic converter
Electric EFE grid
Electric choke
Pulse air reduction reaction (PAIR)
Deceleration valve
Pulse air shut off valve
Vacuum delay valve
Distributor/canister purge thermal vacuum switch (D/CP-TVS)
Vacuum regulator valve
Vacuum break delay valve
Fuel tank presssure control valve
Transmission converter clutch switch (TCC-S)
Transmission converter clutch delay valve (TCC-DV)
Vacuum pump
Low vacuum switch
Vacuum switching valve
Fast idle actuator
Electronic control module

EMISSIONS INDICATOR

An emissions indicator flag may appear in the odometer window of the speedometer, on some General Motors vehicles. The flag could say "Sensor", "Emissions" or "Catalyst" depending on the part or assembly that is scheduled for regular emissions maintenance replacement. The word "Sensor" indicates a need for oxygen sensor replacement and the words "Emissions" or "Catalyst" indicate the need for catalytic converter catalyst replacement.

Reset

1. Remove the instrument panel trim plate.
2. Remove the instrument cluster lens.

SECTION 18: GENERAL MOTORS—"T" BODY
CHEVETTE • CHEVETTE SCOOTER • PONTIAC T1000 • 1000

3. Locate the flag indicator reset notches at the drivers side of the odometer.
4. Use a pointed tool to apply light downward pressure on the notches, until the indicator is reset. When the indicator is reset an alignment mark will appear in the left center of the odometer window.

GASOLINE ENGINE SECTION

For Diesel Engine Services Refer to the Unit Repair Section.

ENGINE ASSEMBLY
Removal and Installation

1. Remove the hood.
2. Disconnect the battery cables.
3. Remove the battery cable clips from the frame rail.
4. Drain the cooling system. Disconnect the radiator hoses from the engine and the heater hoses at the heater.
5. Tag and disconnect any wires leading from the engine.
6. Remove the radiator upper support and remove the radiator and engine fan. On the diesel, remove the oil cooler.
7. Remove the air cleaner assembly.
8. Disconnect the fuel line at the rubber hose along the left frame rail. On the diesel, disconnect and plug the fuel lines at the injector pump and position them out of the way. Disconnect the automatic transmission throttle valve linkage. Disconnect the accelerator cable.
9. On air conditioned vehicles, remove the compressor from its mount and lay it aside. If equipped with power steering, remove the power steering pump and bracket and lay it aside.
10. Raise the vehicle and support it safely.
11. Remove the engine strut on the diesel.
12. Disconnect the exhaust pipe at the exhaust manifold.
13. Remove the flywheel dust cover on manual transmission vehicles or the torque converter underpan on automatic transmission vehicles.
14. On automatic transmission vehicles, remove the torque converter to flywheel bolts.
15. Remove the converter housing or flywheel housing to engine retaining bolts and lower the vehicle.
16. Position a floor jack or other suitable support under the transmission.
17. Remove the safety straps from the front engine mounts and remove the mount nuts.
18. Remove the oil filter on the diesel.
19. Install the engine lifting apparatus.
20. Remove the engine by pulling forward to clear the transmission while lifting slowly. Check to make sure that all necessary disconnections have been made and that proper clearance exists with surrounding components. Remove the lifting apparatus.
21. Install the engine lifting apparatus and install guide pins in the engine block.
22. Install the engine in the vehicle by aligning the engine with the transmission housing.
23. Install the front engine mount nuts and safety straps.
24. Raise the vehicle and support it with jackstands.
25. Install the engine to transmission housing bolts. Tighten to 25 ft. lbs.
26. On automatic transmission vehicles, install the torque converter to the flywheel. Torque the bolts to 35 ft. lbs.
27. Install the flywheel dust cover or torque converter underpan as applicable.
28. Install the engine strut on the diesel.
29. Install the exhaust pipe to the exhaust manifold and lower the vehicle.
30. Install the air conditioning compressor or the power steering pump if necessary, and adjust drive belt tension.
31. Connect the fuel lines. Connect the automatic transmission throttle valve linkage. Connect the accelerator cable.
32. Install the air cleaner.
33. Install the engine fan, radiator, and radiator upper support. Install the oil cooler if so equipped.
34. Connect all wires previously disconnected.
35. Connect the radiator and heater hoses and fill the cooling system.
36. Install the battery cable clips along the frame rail.
37. Install the engine hood.
38. Connect the battery cables. Start the engine and check for leaks.

ENGINE MOUNTS
Removal and Installation
GAS ENGINE (FRONT)

1. Disconnect the negative battery cable.
2. Remove the heater assembly and position it on top of the engine.
3. Remove the upper radiator support.
4. Remove the engine mount nuts and retaining wire.
5. Raise the vehicle and support it safely. Using the proper tool raise the engine.
6. Remove the mount to engine bracket. Remove the engine mount from the vehicle.
7. Installation is the reverse of the removal procedure.

GAS ENGINE (REAR)

1. Disconnect the negative battery cable.
2. Raise the vehicle and support it safely.
3. Remove the crossmember to mount bolts and nuts.
4. Raise the transmission and take the weight off of the mount.
5. Remove the mount to transmission retaining bolts.
6. Remove the rear mount from its mounting on the crossmember.
7. Installation is the reverse of the removal procedure.

DIESEL ENGINE (RIGHT)

1. Disconnect the negative battery cable.
2. Raise the vehicle and support it safely.
3. Remove the one bolt from the bottom of the engine side mount.
4. Remove the strut from the engine mount.
5. Lower the vehicle. Remove the separator and position it to one side.
6. Remove the engine mount nut and retaining wire. Remove the mount using the proper removal tool.
7. Installation is the reverse of the removal procedure.

DIESEL ENGINE (LEFT)

1. Disconnect the negative battery cable.
2. Remove the engine mount nut and the retaining wire.
3. Raise the vehicle and support it safely. Raise the engine to take the weight off of the mount.
4. Remove the engine mount using the proper mount removal tool.
5. Installation is the reverse of the removal procedure.

GENERAL MOTORS—"T" BODY
CHEVETTE • CHEVETTE SCOOTER • PONTIAC T1000 • 1000

Valve System

VALVE ADJUSTMENT

Gas Engine

Adjustment of the hydraulic valve lash adjusters is not possible. Cleanliness should be exercised when handling the valve lash adjusters. Before installation of lash adjusters, fill them with oil and check the lash adjuster oil hole in the cylinder head to make sure that it is free of foreign matter.

DIESEL ENGINE

NOTE: The rocker arm shaft bracket bolts and nuts should be tightened to 20 ft. lbs. before adjusting the valves.

1. Unscrew the retaining bolts and remove the rocker cover.
2. Rotate the crankshaft until the No. 1 and No. 4 piston is at TDC of the compression stroke.
3. Start with the intake valve on the No. 1 cylinder and insert a feeler gauge of the correct thickness (intake-0.01 in., exhaust-0.014 in.) into the gap between the valve stem cap and the rocker arm. If adjustment is required, loosen the lock nut on top of the rocker arm and turn the adjusting screw clockwise to decrease the gap and counterclockwise to increase it. When the proper clearance is reached, tighten the lock nut and then recheck the gap. Adjust the remaining three valves in the same manner.
4. Rotate the crankshaft one complete revolution and then adjust the remaining valves accordingly.

VALVE LIFTERS

Removal and Installation

GAS ENGINE

1. Disconnect the negative battery cable. Remove the carburetor, as required.
2. Remove the camshaft housing cover and gasket.
3. Remove the valve rocker arm, using the proper rocker arm removal tool.
4. Remove the valve lash and guide.
5. Installation is the reverse of the removal procedure. Be sure to use a new gasket as required.

VALVE ROCKER ASSEMBLY

Removal and Installation

GAS ENGINE

1. Disconnect the negative battery cable. Remove the camshaft cover.
2. Using the special valve spring compressor tool, compress the valve springs and remove the rocker arms. Keep the rocker arms and guides in order so that they can be installed in their original locations.
3. To install the rocker arms, compress the valve springs and install the rocker arm guides.
4. Position the rocker arms in the guides and on the valve lash adjusters.
5. Install the camshaft cover.

DIESEL ENGINE

1. Disconnect the negative battery cable.
2. Remove the cylinder head cover.
3. Remove the rocker arm shaft bracket bolts and nuts. Remove the rocker arm shaft bracket and the rocker arm assembly.
4. Remove the rocker arms.

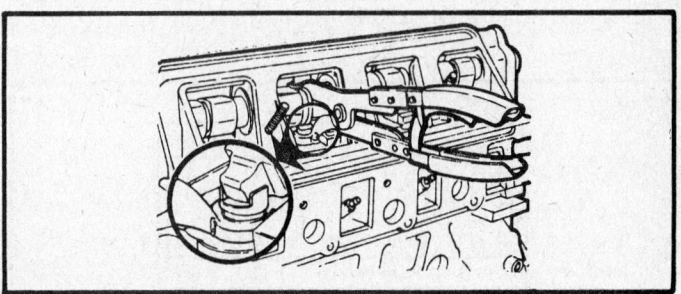

CYLINDER NO.	1		2		3		4	
VALVES	I	E	I	E	I	E	I	E
STEP. 1	O	O	O		O			
STEP. 2				O	O		O	O

I: INTAKE VALVE
E: EXHAUST VALVE

Valve adjustment sequence for the diesel engine
(© General Motors Corporation)

Depressing the valve spring using the special tool
(© General Motors Corporation)

5. Apply a generous amount of clean engine oil to the rocker arm shaft, rocker arms and the valve stem end caps.
6. Install the rocker arm shaft assembly and then tighten the bolts to 20 ft. lbs.
7. Adjust the valves as required.
8. Install the cylinder head cover.

VALVE TIMING

Adjustment

Manufacturers recommended procedure for valve timing has not yet been established.

CYLINDER HEAD

Removal and Installation

GAS ENGINE

1. Disconnect the negative battery cable.
2. Remove all accessory drive belts.
3. Remove the engine fan, timing belt cover and the timing belt.
4. Remove the air cleaner.
5. Drain the cooling system and disconnect the upper radiator hose and heater hose at the intake manifold.
6. Remove the accelerator cable support bracket.
7. Disconnect and label the spark plug wires.
8. Disconnect and label the wires from the idle solenoid, choke, temperature sender, and alternator.
9. Disconnect the exhaust pipe from the exhaust manifold.
10. Remove the dipstick tube bracket to manifold attaching bolt.
11. Disconnect the fuel line at the carburetor.
12. Take off the coil cover. Remove the coil bracket bolts and lay the coil aside.
13. Remove the camshaft cover.
14. Remove the camshaft cover to camshaft housing attaching studs.
15. Remove the rocker arms, rocker arm guides, and valve lash adjusters. Keep the parts in order so that they can be installed in their original locations.
16. Remove the camshaft carrier bolts and remove the camshaft carrier. A sharp wedge may be necessary to separate the

SECTION 18

GENERAL MOTORS—"T" BODY
CHEVETTE • CHEVETTE SCOOTER • PONTIAC T1000 • 1000

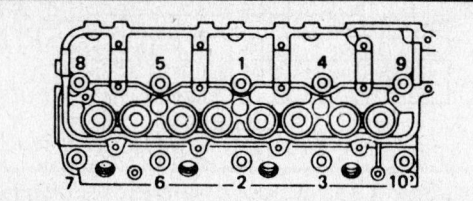

Diesel engine cylinder head torque sequence
(© General Motors Corporation)

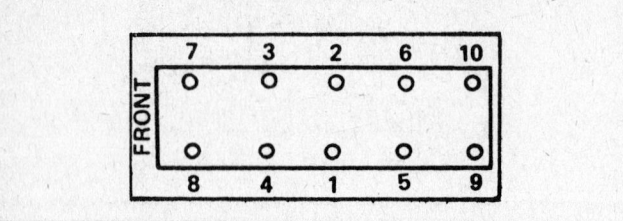

Gas engine cylinder head torque sequence
(© General Motors Corporation)

camshaft carrier from the cylinder head. Be very cautious not to damage the mating surfaces.
17. Remove the manifold and cylinder head assembly.
18. Install a new cylinder head gasket with the words This Side Up facing up over dowel pins in the block. Make sure that the gasket is clean.
19. Install the manifold and cylinder head assembly.
20. Apply a light, thin continuous bead of sealant to the joining surfaces of the cylinder head and the camshaft carrier and install the camshaft carrier. Clean any excess sealer from the cylinder head. Apply sealing compound to the camshaft carrier/cylinder head bolts and install the bolts finger tight. Tighten the bolts a little at a time and in the proper sequence until the final specified torque figure is reached.
21. Install the camshaft cover to camshaft housing attaching studs.
22. Install the valve lash adjusters and rocker arm guides. Prelube the rocker arms with engine assembly lubricant and install the rocker arms.
23. Using new gaskets, install the camshaft covers.
24. Install the coil bracket mounting bolt.
25. Connect the fuel line to the carburetor.
26. Install the dipstick tube bracket to manifold attaching bolt.
27. Attach the exhaust pipe to the exhaust manifold.
28. Connect the wires to the idle solenoid, choke, temperature sender, and alternator.
29. Connect the spark plug wires.
30. Apply teflon tape or equivalent to the threads of the accelerator cable support bracket attaching bolts and install the bracket.
31. Install the air cleaner.
32. Connect the upper radiator hose and heater hose to the intake manifold.
33. Fill the cooling system.
34. Install the timing belt, timing belt cover, engine fan, drive belts and connect the negative battery cable.

DIESEL ENGINE

1. Disconnect the negative battery cable.
2. Drain the cooling system.
3. Remove the cylinder head cover.
4. Disconnect the bypass hose. Remove the upper half of the front cover.
5. Loosen the tension pulley bolts and slide the timing belt off of the two upper gears.
6. Unscrew the bearing cap bolts and then remove the camshaft.
7. Tag and disconnect the glow plug resistor wire.
8. Disconnect the injector lines at the injector pump and at the injector nozzles and then remove the injector lines. Disconnect and plug the fuel leak-off hose.
9. Disconnect the exhaust pipe at the manifold.
10. Remove the oil feed pipe from the rear of the cylinder head.
11. Disconnect the upper radiator hose and position it out of the way.
12. Remove the head bolts and then remove the cylinder head with the intake and exhaust manifolds installed.

NOTE: The gasket surfaces on both the head and the block must be clean of any foreign matter and free of nicks or heavy scratches. Cylinder bolt threads in the block and on the bolt must also be clean.

13. Place a new gasket over the dowel pins with the word "TOP" facing up.
14. Apply engine oil to the threads and the seating face of the cylinder head bolts, install them and then tighten them in the proper sequence.
15. Install the camshaft and rocker arm assembly. Loosen the adjusting screws so that the entire rocker arm assembly is held in a free state.
16. Reinstall the timing belt.
17. Connect the upper radiator hose and the oil feed pipe.
18. Connect the exhaust pipe to the manifold.
19. Install the fuel leak-off hose. Connect the injector lines.
20. Connect the glow plug resistor wire.
21. Adjust the valve clearance. Install the cylinder head cover.
22. Refill the cooling system.

CAMSHAFT

Removal and Installation

GAS ENGINE

NOTE: A special valve spring compressor (tool no. J-25477) is necessary for this procedure. If replacing the camshaft or rocker arms, prelube new parts with engine assembly lubricant.

1. Disconnect the negative battery cable.
2. Remove engine accessory drive belts.
3. Remove the engine fan and pulley.
4. Remove the upper and lower front timing belt covers.
5. Loosen the idler pulley and remove the timing belt from the camshaft sprocket.
6. Remove the camshaft sprocket attaching bolt and washer and remove the camshaft sprocket.
7. Remove the camshaft cover. Using the special valve spring compressor, remove the rocker arms and guides. Keep the rocker arms and guides in order so that they can be installed in their original locations.
8. Remove any components necessary to gain working clearance.
9. Remove the camshaft carrier rear cover.
10. Remove the camshaft thrust plate bolts. Slide the camshaft slightly to the rear and remove the thrust plate.
11. Remove the engine mount nuts and wire retainers.
12. Raise the front of the engine.
13. Remove the camshaft from the camshaft carrier.
14. Install the camshaft into the camshaft carrier.
15. Lower the engine.
16. Install the engine mount nuts and attach the retaining wires.

GENERAL MOTORS—"T" BODY
CHEVETTE • CHEVETTE SCOOTER • PONTIAC T1000 • 1000
SECTION 18

17. Slide the camshaft slightly to the rear and install the thrust plate. Slide the camshaft forward and install the carrier rear cover.
18. Position and align a new gasket over the end of the camshaft, against the camshaft carrier.
19. Install any components which were removed to gain working clearance.
20. Install the valve rocker arms and guides in their original locations using the special valve spring compressor. Install the camshaft covers.
21. Align the dowel in the camshaft sprocket with the hole in the end of the camshaft and install the sprocket.
22. Apply thread locking compound to the sprocket retaining bolt threads and install the bolt and washer. Torque the sprocket retaining bolt 65 to 85 ft. lbs.
23. Turn the crankshaft clockwise to bring the No. 1 cylinder to top dead center. Make sure that the distributor rotor is in position to fire the No. 1 spark plug. Align the hole in the camshaft sprocket with the hole in the upper rear timing belt cover and install the timing belt on the camshaft sprocket.
24. Adjust timing belt tension.
25. Install the upper and lower front timing belt covers.
26. Install the engine fan and pulley.
27. Install the engine accessory drive belts.
28. Connect the negative battery cable.

DIESEL ENGINE

1. Remove the rocker cover.
2. Remove the timing belt. Remove the plug.
3. Install the fixing plate into the slot at the rear of the camshaft.
4. Remove the camshaft gear retaining bolt and then use a puller to remove the cam gear.
5. Remove the rocker arms and shaft.
6. Unscrew the bolts attaching the front head plate and then remove the plate.
7. Unscrew the camshaft bearing cap retaining bolts and remove the bearing caps with the cap side bearings.
8. Lift out the camshaft oil seal and then remove the camshaft.
9. Coat the cam and cylinder head journals with clean engine oil.
10. Position the camshaft back in the cylinder head with a new oil seal.
11. Apply a suitable liquid gasket to the cylinder head face of the No. 1 camshaft bearing cap.
12. Install the remaining bearing caps. Install the rocker arm shaft assembly, leaving the adjusting screws loose.
13. Install the front head plate.
14. Install the timing belt.
15. Adjust the valve clearance to specification. Install the cylinder head cover.

PISTON AND ROD POSITIONING

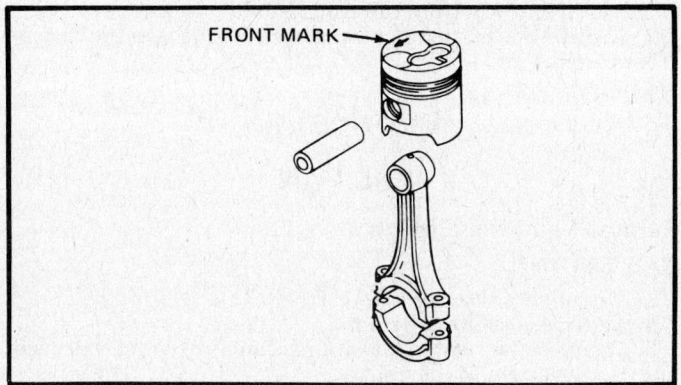
FRONT MARK

TIMING BELT COVER

Removal and Installation
DIESEL ENGINE UPPER FRONT COVER

1. Disconnect the negative battery cable. Remove the radiator upper mounting panel on models without A/C or fan shroud on models with A/C.
2. Remove the bypass hose.
3. Remove the engine fan.
4. Remove the cover retaining screws and nuts and remove the cover.
5. To install the cover, align the screw slots on the upper and lower parts of the cover.
6. Install the cover retaining screws and nuts.
7. Install the engine fan.
8. Install the bypass hose.
9. Connect the negative battery cable.

DIESEL ENGINE LOWER FRONT COVER

1. Disconnect the negative battery cable.
2. Loosen the alternator and the A/C compressor bolts, if so equipped. Remove the drive belt.
3. Remove the damper pulley to crankshaft bolt and washer and remove the pulley.
4. Remove the upper front timing belt cover.
5. Remove the lower cover retaining diesel. Remove the lower cover.
6. To install the cover, align the cover with the studs on the engine block.
7. Install the lower front cover retaining nut or bolts.
8. Install the upper front timing belt cover.
9. Install the crankshaft damper pulley. Torque the retaining bolt to the specified torque.
10. Install the drive belt and tighten the alternator and compressor mounting bolts.
11. Connect the negative battery cable.

GAS ENGINE UPPER REAR COVER

1. Crank the engine so that No. 1 cylinder is at TDC of the compression stroke.
2. Disconnect the negative battery cable.
3. Remove the upper and lower front cover, the timing belt, and the camshaft timing sprocket.
4. Remove the three screws retaining the camshaft sprocket cover to the camshaft carrier.
5. Inspect the condition of the cam seal.
6. Position and align a new gasket over the end of the camshaft and against the camshaft carrier.
7. Install the three camshaft sprocket cover retaining screws.
8. Install the camshaft sprocket, timing belt, and the upper and lower front covers.
9. Connect the negative battery cable.

TIMING BELT SPROCKETS

Removal and Installation
GAS ENGINE

NOTE: Rotate the engine to bring No. 1 cylinder to TDC. The timing mark should be at the 0° mark on the timing scale. With No. 1 cylinder at TDC, a 1/8 in. drill bit may be inserted through a hole in the timing belt upper rear cover into a hole in the camshaft drive sprocket. These holes are provided to facilitate and verify camshaft timing. Aligning these holes now will make installation of the new belt much easier.

1. Disconnect the negative battery cable.

SECTION 18

GENERAL MOTORS—"T" BODY
CHEVETTE • CHEVETTE SCOOTER • PONTIAC T1000 • 1000

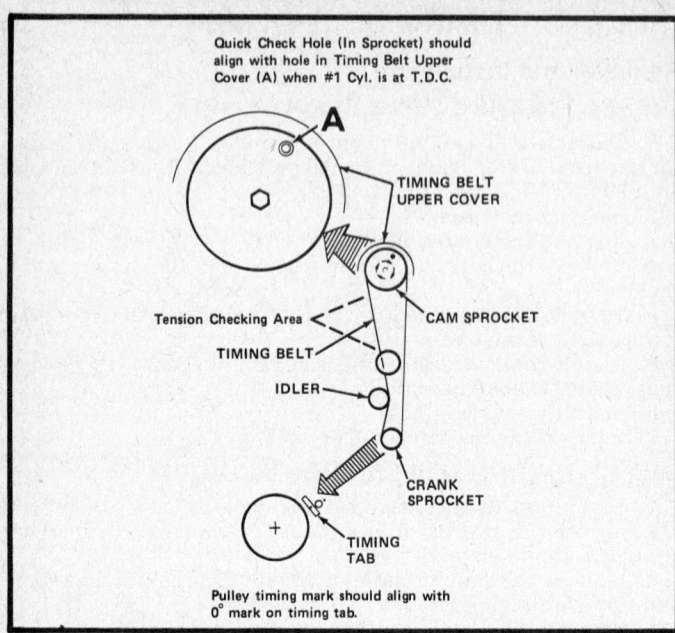

Timing belt installation—1.6L chevette. When camshaft is aligned at No. 1 cylinder TDC compression stroke, a $1/8$ in. drill bit should fit throught rear timing belt cover and into quick check hole in sprocket (© General Motors Corporation)

2. Remove the alternator and air conditioning compressor drive belts.
3. Remove the engine fan and pulley.
4. Remove the engine upper and lower front timing belt covers.
5. Remove the timing belt idler pulley.
6. Remove the timing belt from the camshaft and crankshaft timing sprockets.
7. With the distributor cap off, mark the location of the rotor in the No. 1 spark plug firing position on the distributor housing. On air conditioned vehicles, remove the compressor and lower its mounting bracket.
8. Remove the camshaft timing sprocket bolt and washer and remove the camshaft sprocket.
9. Remove the crankshaft sprocket.
10. Place the crankshaft sprocket on the crankshaft making sure that the locating tabs face outward.
11. Install the crankshaft sprocket.
12. Align the camshaft sprocket dowel with the hole in the end of the camshaft and install the sprocket on the camshaft.
13. Apply thread locking compound to the camshaft sprocket retaining bolt and washer and torque 65 to 85 ft. lbs.
14. Position the timing belt over the crankshaft sprocket.
15. Install the crankshaft pulley.
16. Align the crankshaft pulley timing mark with the 0 mark on the timing scale and the distributor rotor with the scribed mark on the distributor housing.
17. Align the hole in the camshaft sprocket with the hole in the upper rear timing belt cover. Insert a $1/8$ in. drill bit to hold the sprocket in alignment.
18. Install the timing belt on the camshaft and crankshaft sprockets.
19. Adjust the timing belt tension as required.
20. Install the distributor cap. On air conditioned vehicles, install the lower compressor bracket and the compressor.
21. Install the upper and lower front timing belt covers.
22. Install the engine fan and pulley.
23. Install the alternator and, if necessary, the air conditioning compressor drive belts.
24. Connect the negative battery cable.

DIESEL ENGINE

1. Disconnect the negative battery cable.
2. Drain the cooling system.
3. Remove the fan shroud, cooling fan and the pulley.
4. Disconnect the bypass hose and then remove the upper half of the front cover.
5. With the No. 1 piston at TDC of the compression stroke, make sure that the notch mark on the injection pump gear is aligned with the index mark on the front plate. If so, thread a lock bolt (8mm × 1.25) through the gear and into the front plate.
6. Remove the cylinder head cover and install a fixing plate (J-29761 or equivalent) in the slot at the rear of the cam. This will prevent the cam from rotating during the procedure.
7. Remove the crankshaft damper pulley and check to make sure that the No. 1 piston is still at TDC.
8. Remove the lower half of the front cover and then remove the timing belt holder from the bottom of the front plate.
9. Remove the tension spring behind the front plate, next to the injection pump.
10. Loosen the tension pulley and slide the timing belt off the pulleys.
11. Remove the camshaft gear retaining bolt, install a gear puller and remove the gear.
12. Reinstall the cam gear loosely so that it can be turned smoothly by hand.
13. Slide the timing belt back over the gears and note the following: the belt should be properly tensioned between the pulleys, the cogs on the belt and the gears should be properly engaged, the crankshaft should not be turned and the belt slack should be concentrated at the two tension pulleys. Push the tension pulley in with your finger and install the tension spring.
14. Partially tighten the tension pulley bolts in sequence (top first, bottom second) so as to prevent any movement of the pulley.
15. Tighten the camshaft gear retaining bolt to 45 ft. lbs. Remove the injection pump gear lock bolt.
16. Remove the fixing plate from the end of the cam.
17. Install the crankshaft damper pulley and then check that No. 1 piston is still at TDC. Do not try to adjust it by moving the crankshaft.
18. Check that the marks on the injection pump gear and the front plate are still aligned and that the fixing plate still fits properly into the slot on the camshaft.
19. Loosen the tensioner pulley and plate bolts, concentrate the looseness of the timing belt around the tensioner and then tighten the bolts.
20. Belt tension should be 46 to 63 lbs., checked at a point midway between the upper two pulleys.
21. Remove the damper pulley again and install the belt holder in position away from the timing belt.
22. Installation of the remaining components is in the reverse order of removal.

Lubrication

OIL PAN

Removal and Installation

GAS ENGINE

1. Disconnect the negative battery cable.
2. Drain the cooling system.
3. Remove the heater housing assembly from the firewall and rest it on top of the engine.

GENERAL MOTORS—"T" BODY
CHEVETTE • CHEVETTE SCOOTER • PONTIAC T1000 • 1000
SECTION 18

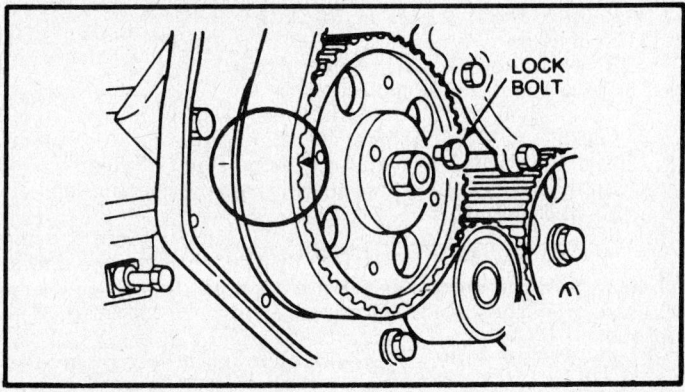

Injection gear setting mark

4. Remove the upper radiator support. On vehicles equipped with air conditioning, remove the upper half of the fan shroud.
5. Remove the radiator hoses. On vehicles equipped with automatic transmission, disconnect and plug the cooler lines from the radiator.
6. Remove the radiator. On some vehicles it may be necessary to remove the grille.
7. If the vehicle is equipped with air conditioning, remove the condenser from its supporting bracket. Lay the condenser on top of the engine. Do not disconnect any of the refrigerant lines.
8. Remove the motor mount nuts and clips.
9. Raise the vehicle and support it safely. Drain the engine oil.
10. Remove the flywheels splash shield, if equipped.
11. On all models with the 200 automatic transmission, loosen the catalytic converter to exhaust pipe clamp bolts. On other models, disconnect the exhaust pipe at the manifold.
12. Remove the body to crossmember braces, if so equipped.
13. Remove the rack and pinion unit from the crossmember and the steering shaft. Pull the unit down and out of the way.
14. Raise the front of the engine.
15. Remove the oil pan bolts.
16. Pull the oil pan down and remove the oil pump suction pipe and the screen.
17. Remove the oil pan.
18. Clean all of the old sealer that is loose off the oil pan mating surface. It is not necessary to clean all of the sealer material off. Reverse the above procedure to install. Tighten the oil pan attaching bolts to 55 inch lbs.

DIESEL ENGINE

1. Remove the engine.
2. Support the engine in a stand.
3. Unscrew the nuts and bolts attaching the oil pan to the crankcase and then remove the pan.
4. Clean the mating surfaces of the oil pan and the block. Apply a suitable liquid gasket to the front and rear mating surfaces and then install a new gasket.
5. Install the oil pan retaining bolts and tighten them to 5 ft. lbs.
6. Reinstall the engine.

OIL PUMP

Removal and Installation
GAS ENGINE

1. Disconnect the negative battery cable. Remove the ignition coil attaching bolts and lay the coil aside.
2. Remove the fuel pump, pushrod, and gasket.
3. Remove the distributor. On air conditioned vehicles, re-

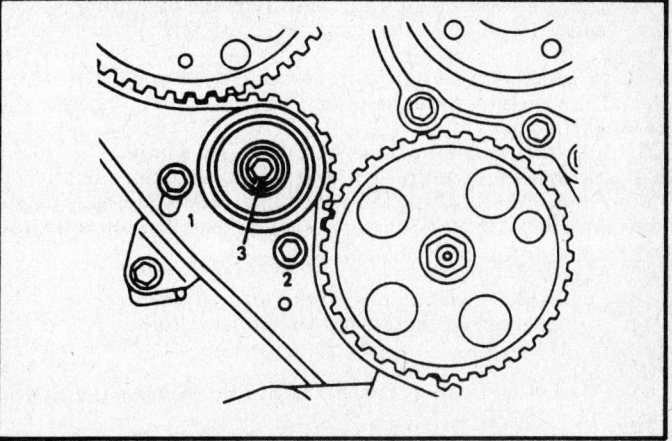

Tighten the tension pulley bolts in sequence

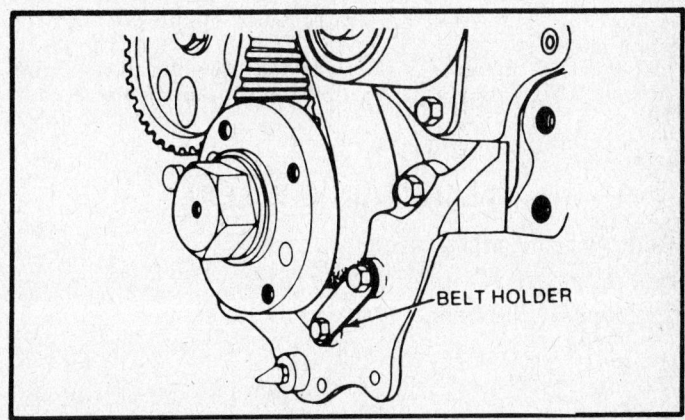

Diesel engine timing belt holder must be removed before the timing belt can be removed

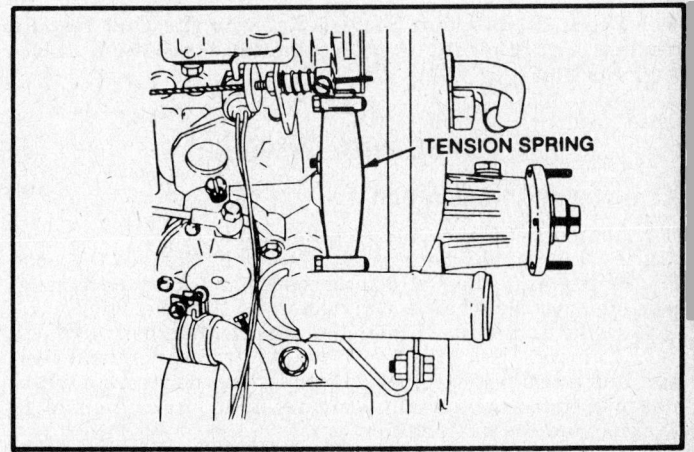

Diesel engine tension spring

move the compressor mounting bolts and lay it aside. Do not disconnect any refrigerant lines.
4. Raise the vehicle and support it safely. Remove the oil pan.
5. Remove the oil pump pipe and screen assembly clamp and remove the bolts attaching the pipe and screen assembly.
6. Remove the pipe and screen assembly from the oil pump.

18–19

SECTION 18

GENERAL MOTORS—"T" BODY
CHEVETTE • CHEVETTE SCOOTER • PONTIAC T1000 • 1000

7. Remove the pick-up tube seal from the oil pump.
8. Remove the oil pump attaching bolts and remove the oil pump.
9. Install the oil pump. Torque the oil pump bolts to 15 ft. lbs. Make certain that the pilot on the oil pump engages the case.
10. Install the pick-up tube seal in the oil pump.
11. Install the pick-up pipe and screen assembly in the oil pump and install the pick-up pipe and screen clamp. Torque the clamp bolt 70 to 95 inch lbs. Torque the pick-up tube and screen mounting bolt 19 to 25 ft. lbs.
12. Install the oil pan.
13. Install the fuel pump with gasket and pushrod.
14. Install the distributor and the ignition coil.

DIESEL ENGINE

1. Disconnect the negative battery cable. Remove the timing belt.
2. Unscrew the four allen bolts attaching the oil pump to the front plate and remove the pump complete with the pulley.
3. Coat the vane with clean engine oil and then install it with the taper side toward the cylinder body.
4. Install a new O-ring, coated with engine oil, into the pump housing.
5. Position the rotor in the vane and then install the pump body together with the pulley. Tighten the Allen bolts to 15 ft. lbs.
6. Install the timing belt.

REAR MAIN OIL SEAL

Removal and Installation
GAS ENGINE

1. Remove the engine. Place it in a stand.
2. Remove the flywheel or flexplate.
3. Remove the oil pan.
4. Remove the rear main bearing cap.
5. Clean the bearing cap and case.
6. Check the crankshaft seal for excessive wear.
7. Install a new crankshaft seal. Make sure that it is properly seated against the rear main bearing seal bulkhead.
8. Apply RTV sealer or its equivalent to the bearing cap horizontal split line.
9. With the sealer still wet, install the rear main bearing cap. Tighten the bearing bolts 10 to 12 ft. lbs. Tap the crankshaft toward the rear, then toward the front to be sure everything is properly seated. Retorque the cap bolts to the specified torque.
10. Apply RTV sealer or its equivalent in the vertical grooves of the rear main bearing cap.
11. Remove any excess sealer and install the oil pan. Torque the oil pan bolts 45 to 60 inch lbs.
12. Install the engine in the vehicle.

DIESEL ENGINE

1. Remove the transmission. If equipped with a manual transmission remove the clutch.
2. Unscrew the flywheel retaining bolts in a diagonal pattern and then remove the flywheel.
3. Pry off the old oil seal.
4. Coat the lipped portion and the fitting face of the new oil seal with engine oil and install it into the crankshaft bearing. Make sure that the seal is properly seated.
5. Coat the threads of the new mounting bolts with Loctite® and install the flywheel. Tighten the bolts to 40 ft. lbs. in a diagonal sequence. Do not reuse the old bolts, they must be new.
6. Installation of the remaining components is in the reverse order of removal.

FRONT SUSPENSION AND STEERING SECTION

For Front Suspension Service Refer to the Unit Repair Section. For Steering Gear Overhaul Refer to the Unit Repair Section.

STEERING WHEEL

Removal and Installation

1. Disconnect the negative battery cable.
2. Pull up on the horn cap to remove it. Remove the horn ring-to-steering wheel attaching screws and remove the ring.
3. Remove the wheel nut retainer and the wheel nut.
4. Using a steering wheel puller, remove the steering wheel.
5. To install, place the turn signal lever in the neutral position and install the steering wheel. Torque the steering wheel nut to 30 ft. lbs. and install the nut retainer. Use caution not to over expand the nut retainer.
6. Connect the negative battery cable.

STEERING RACK

Removal and Installation

1. Raise the vehicle and support it safely.
2. Remove the bolts and shield.
3. Remove the outer tie rod cotter pins and nuts on both sides.

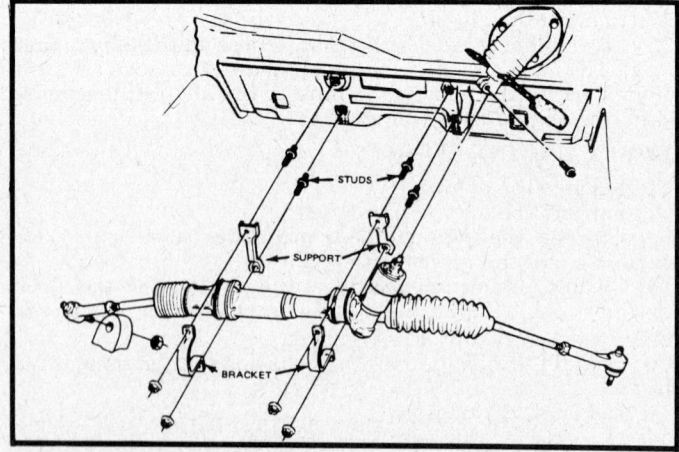

Rack and pinion attaching location—typical
(© General Motors Corporation)

4. Using a tie rod separating tool, disconnect the tie rods from the steering knuckles.
5. On power steering models remove the two hydraulic lines from the steering gear.
6. Remove the flexible coupling pinch bolt to the shaft.

GENERAL MOTORS—"T" BODY
CHEVETTE • CHEVETTE SCOOTER • PONTIAC T1000 • 1000
SECTION 18

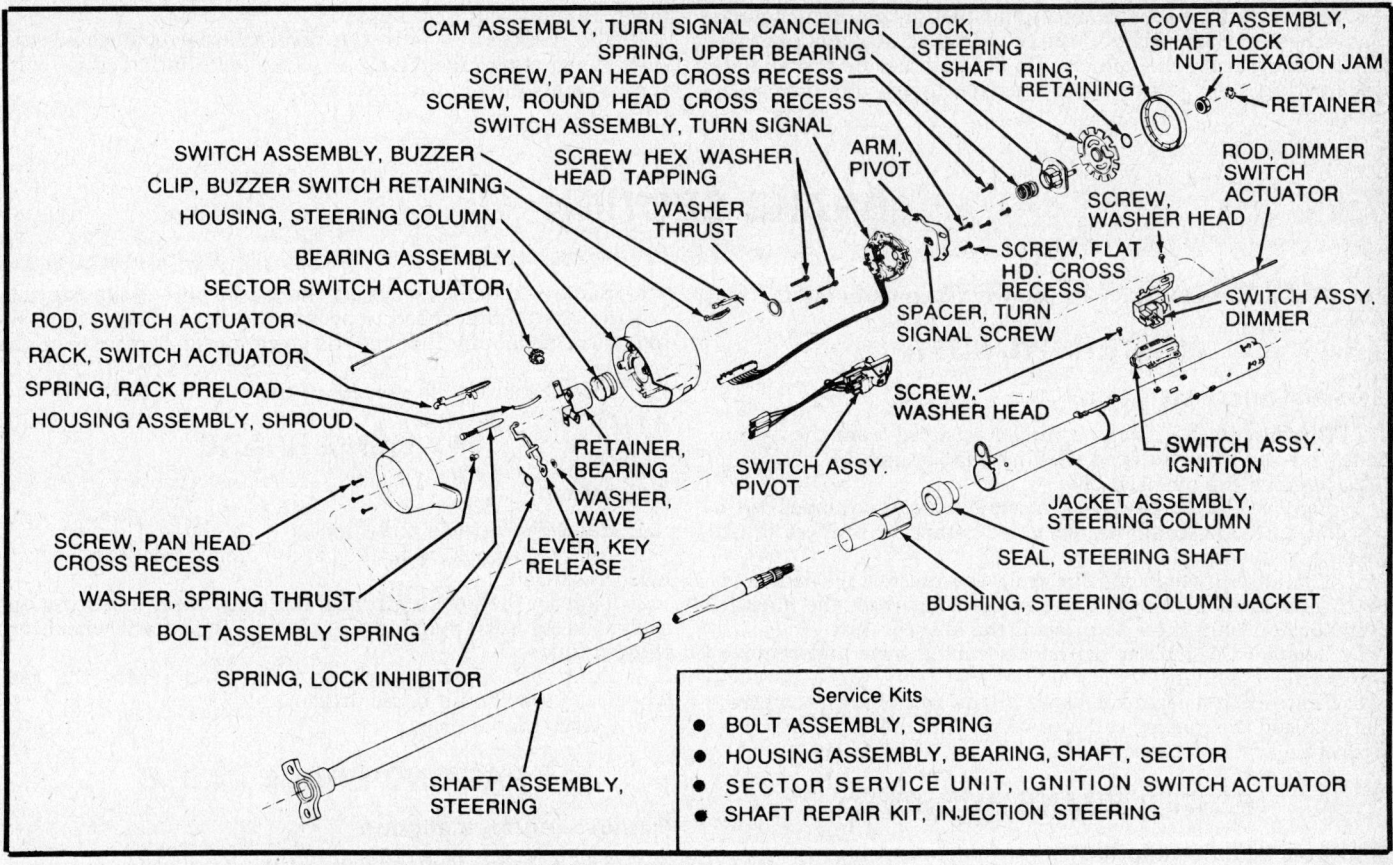

Steering column and related components (© General Motors Corporation)

7. Remove the four bolts at the clamps, and remove the assembly from the vehicle.
8. Position the assembly to the vehicle with the stub shaft in position with the flexible coupling, and install the clamps and four new bolts.
9. Install the flexible coupling pinch bolt to the shaft.
10. Install the tie rods into the steering knuckles and torque the nuts to 30 ft. lbs. Install a new cotter pin.
11. On power steering models install the two hydraulic hoses and bleed the system.
12. Install the bolts and shield. Lower the vehicle.

FRONT WHEEL BEARINGS
Adjustment
1. Raise the vehicle and support at the front lower control arm.
2. Remove the hub cap or wheel cover from the wheel. Remove the dust cap from the hub.
3. Remove the cotter pin from the spindle and spindle nut.
4. Spin the wheel forward by hand and tighten the spindle nut to 12 ft. lbs. This will fully seat the bearings.
5. Back off the nut to a just loose position.
6. Hand-tighten the spindle nut. Loosen the spindle nut until either hole in the spindle aligns with a slot in the nut, but not more than 1/2 flat.
7. Install a new cotter pin, bend the ends of the pin against the nut, and cut off any extra length to avoid interference with the dust cap.
8. Proper bearing adjustment should give 0.001-0.005 in. of end-play.
9. Install the dust cap on the hub and the hub cap or wheel cover on the wheel.

10. Lower the vehicle.

POWER STEERING PUMP
Removal and Installation
1. Disconnect the negative battery cable. Remove the upper adjusting bolt.
2. Remove the lower brace bolt to pump bracket.
3. Remove the left hand crossmember brace to body.
4. Remove the pressure line and the reservoir line at the pump.
5. Remove the rear pump adjusting bracket.
6. Remove the front pivot bolt at the pump and remove the bolt.
7. Remove the front pump bracket at the bolt to engine. Remove the bracket and pump.
8. Installation is the reverse of the removal procedure. In addition, adjust the belt tension, fill the reservoir and bleed the system.

STEERING COLUMN
Removal and Installation
1. Disconnect the battery ground cable.
2. Remove the steering wheel and move the front seat rearward as far as possible.
3. Remove the floor pan bracket screws. Remove bolts securing steering column to rack and pinion assembly.
4. Remove the two column bracket to instrument panel nuts and lower the column far enough to disconnect the wiring harnesses.

GENERAL MOTORS—"T" BODY
CHEVETTE • CHEVETTE SCOOTER • PONTIAC T1000 • 1000

6. Disconnect the directional signal and ignition switch wiring harnesses. Carefully pull the column rearward and remove the assembly from the vehicle. Do not hammer on the end of the steering shaft. The plastic injection break-way pins will shear, causing shaft collapse.

7. The installation is in the reverse order of the removal. Special attention must be given to the installation of the bolts and brackets during the assembly.

BRAKE SECTION

For Brake Service Refer to the Unit Repair Section.

MASTER CYLINDER

Removal and Installation

1. Disconnect the master cylinder pushrod from the brake pedal, on vehicles equipped with manual brakes.
2. Remove the pushrod boot.
3. Remove the air cleaner. On some vehicles equipped with power brakes the combination valve retaining bracket must first be removed.
4. Thoroughly clean all dirt from the master cylinder and the brake lines. Disconnect the brake lines from the master cylinder and plug them to prevent the entry of dirt.
5. Remove the master cylinder securing nuts and remove the master cylinder.
6. Installation is the reverse of the removal procedure. Bench bleed the master cylinder before installation. Bleed the hydraulic system, as required.

POWER BRAKE BOOSTER

Removal and Installation

1. Remove the air cleaner.
2. Disconnect the vacuum hose from the check valve.
3. Remove the master cylinder brace. On some vehicles it may be necessary to remove the combination valve retaining bracket.
4. Remove the master cylinder to power cylinder nut, and pull forward on the master cylinder until it clears the power cylinder mounting studs. Move the master cylinder aside and support it, being careful of the brake lines.
5. Remove the nuts securing the power unit to the firewall.
6. Remove the pushrod to pedal retainer and slip the pushrod off the pedal pin. Remove the power brake booster from the vehicle.
7. Installation is the reverse of removal.

PARKING BRAKE

Adjustment

1. Raise the vehicle and support it safely.
2. Apply the parking brake three notches from the fully released position.
3. Tighten the parking brake cable equalizer adjusting nut under the car until a light drag is felt when the rear wheels are rotated forward.
4. Fully release the parking brake and rotate the rear wheels. There should be no drag.
5. Lower the vehicle.

PARKING BRAKE CABLE

Removal and Installation

1. Raise the vehicle and support it safely.
2. Disconnect the parking brake equalizer spring and equalizer.
3. Remove the cable from the underbody mounting brackets.
4. Remove the tires and wheels. Remove the brake drums.
5. Remove the parking brake cable from the parking brake lever.
6. Remove the spring locking clip and push out the cable grommets at the backing plate entry hole. Withdraw the cable.
7. Installation is the reverse of the removal procedure.

CLUTCH, TRANSMISSION AND DRIVESHAFT SECTION

For Overhaul Procedures Refer to the Unit Repair Section

CLUTCH PEDAL

Adjustment

Adjustment is made at the firewall end of the outer clutch cable. Pedal free-play should be ½ in. at the pedal.
1. Pull the adjusting ring clip from the cable at the firewall.
2. To increase free-play, move the cable into the firewall, one notch at a time, and replace the clip.
3. To decrease free-play, pull the cable out, one notch at a time, and replace the clip.
4. If, after the adjustment, the pedal won't return tight against the bumper, the ball stud will have to be adjusted.

CLUTCH ASSEMBLY

Removal and Installation

1. Raise the vehicle and support it safely.
2. Remove the transmission.
3. Remove the throwout bearing from the clutch fork by sliding the fork off the ball stud against spring tension. If the ball stud is to be replaced, remove the locknut and stud from the bellhousing.
4. If the balance marks on the pressure plate and the flywheel are not easily seen, remark them with paint or a centerpunch.
5. Alternately loosen the pressure plate to flywheel attaching bolts one turn at a time until spring tension is released.

GENERAL MOTORS—"T" BODY
CHEVETTE • CHEVETTE SCOOTER • PONTIAC T1000 • 1000
SECTION 18

6. Support the pressure plate and cover assembly, then remove the bolts and the clutch assembly.

7. Check the pressure plate, clutch plate and flywheel for wear. If the flywheel is scored, worn or discolored from overheating, it should be either refaced or replaced. Replace the clutch plate as necessary.

8. Align the balance marks on the clutch assembly and the flywheel. Place the clutch disc on the pressure plate with the long end of the splined hub facing forward and the damper springs inside the pressure plate. Insert a dummy shaft through the cover and clutch disc.

9. Position the assembly against the flywheel and insert the dummy shaft into the pilot bearing in the crankshaft.

10. Align the balance marks and install the pressure plate to flywheel bolts finger tight. Tighten all bolts evenly and gradually until tight to avoid possible clutch distortion. Torque the bolts to 18 ft. lbs. (14 lbs. on diesel engine) and remove the dummy shaft.

11. Pack the groove on the inside of the throwout bearing with graphite grease. Also coat the fork groove and ball stud depression with the lubricant.

12. Install the throwout bearing and release fork assembly in the bellhousing with the fork spring hooked under the ball stud and the fork spring fingers inside the bearing groove.

13. Position the transmission and clutch housing and install the clutch housing attaching bolts and lockwashers. Torque the bolts to 25 ft. lbs.

14. Complete the transmission installation. Check the position of the engine in the front mounts and realign as necessary. A special gauge (J-23644) is necessary to adjust ball stud position if it has been removed.

15. Adjust clutch pedal free-play as required.

16. Lower the vehicle and check operation of the clutch and transmission.

BALL STUD

Initial Adjustment

1. Install throw-out bearing assembly, clutch fork and ball stud to transmission.
2. Mount and secure transmission to engine.
3. Cycle clutch one time.
4. Place gauge J-28449 so flat end is against front face of clutch housing and the hooked end is aligned with the bottom depression in the clutch fork.
5. Turn ball stud clockwise by hand until clutch release bearing makes contact with clutch spring and fork is snug on gauge.
6. Install lock nut and tighten to 25 ft. lbs., being careful not to change ball stud adjustment.
7. Remove gauge by pulling outward at housing end.

MANUAL TRANSMISSION

Removal and Installation
FOUR SPEED (70MM)

1. Remove the floor console and the boot retainer.
2. Lift up the boot in order to gain access to the locknut on the shift lever. Loosen the locknut and unscrew the upper portion of the shift lever with the knob attached.
3. Remove the foam insulator.
4. Remove the threes bolts on the extension and remove the control assembly.
5. Carefully remove the retaining clip.
6. Remove the locknut, the boot retainer and the seat from the threaded end of the control lever.
7. Remove the spring and the guide from the forked end of the control lever.

8. Raise the vehicle and support it safely. Drain the lubricant from the transmission.
9. Remove the driveshaft.
10. Disconnect the speedometer cable and back-up light switch.
11. Disconnect the return spring and clutch cable at the clutch release fork.
12. Remove the crossmember to transmission mount bolts.
13. Remove the exhaust manifold nuts and converter to tailpipe bolts and nuts. Remove the converter to transmission bracket bolts and remove the converter.
14. Remove the crossmember to frame bolts and remove the crossmember.
15. Remove the dust cover.
16. Remove the clutch housing to engine retaining bolts, slide the transmission and clutch housing to the rear, and remove the transmission.
17. Place the transmission in gear, position the transmission and clutch housing, and slide forward. Turn the output shaft to align the input shaft splines with the clutch hub.
18. Install the clutch housing retaining bolts and lockwashers. Torque the bolts to 25 ft. lbs.
19. Install the dust cover.
20. Position the crossmember to the frame and loosely install the retaining bolts. Install the crossmember to transmission mounting bolts. Torque the center nuts to 33 ft. lbs.; the end nuts to 21 ft. lbs. Torque the crossmember to frame bolts to 40 ft. lbs.
21. Install the exhaust pipe to the manifold and the converter bracket on the transmission.
22. Connect the clutch cable. Adjust clutch pedal free-play.
23. Connect the speedometer cable and back-up light switch.
24. Install the driveshaft.
25. Fill the transmission to the correct level with SAE 80W or SAE 80W-90GL-5 gear lubricant. Lower the car.
26. Install the shift lever and check operation of the transmission.

FIVE SPEED (69.5MM)

1. Disconnect the negative battery cable.
2. Unscrew the retaining screws and then remove the shift lever console.
3. Remove the mounting screws and remove the shift lever assembly.
4. Unscrew and remove the upper starter mounting bolts.
5. Raise the front of the vehicle and drain the lubricant from the transmission.
6. Remove the drive shaft.
7. Disconnect the speedometer and the back-up light switch wires.
8. Disconnect the return spring and clutch cable at the clutch release fork.
9. Remove the starter lower bolt and support the starter.
10. Unscrew the retaining bolts and disconnect the exhaust pipe from the manifold.
11. Remove the flywheel inspection cover.
12. Unscrew the rear transmission support mounting bolt. Support the transmission underneath the case and then remove the rear support from the frame.
13. Lower the transmission approximately four in.
14. Remove the transmission housing-to-engine block bolts. Pull the transmission straight back and away from the engine.
15. Installation is the reverse of removal.

5 SPEED (77MM)

1. Disconnect the negative battery cable.
2. Remove the shift boot attaching screws. Slide the boot up the shift lever.
3. Remove the shift lever from the transmission assembly.
4. Raise the vehicle and support it safely.

18-23

SECTION 18

GENERAL MOTORS—"T" BODY
CHEVETTE • CHEVETTE SCOOTER • PONTIAC T1000 • 1000

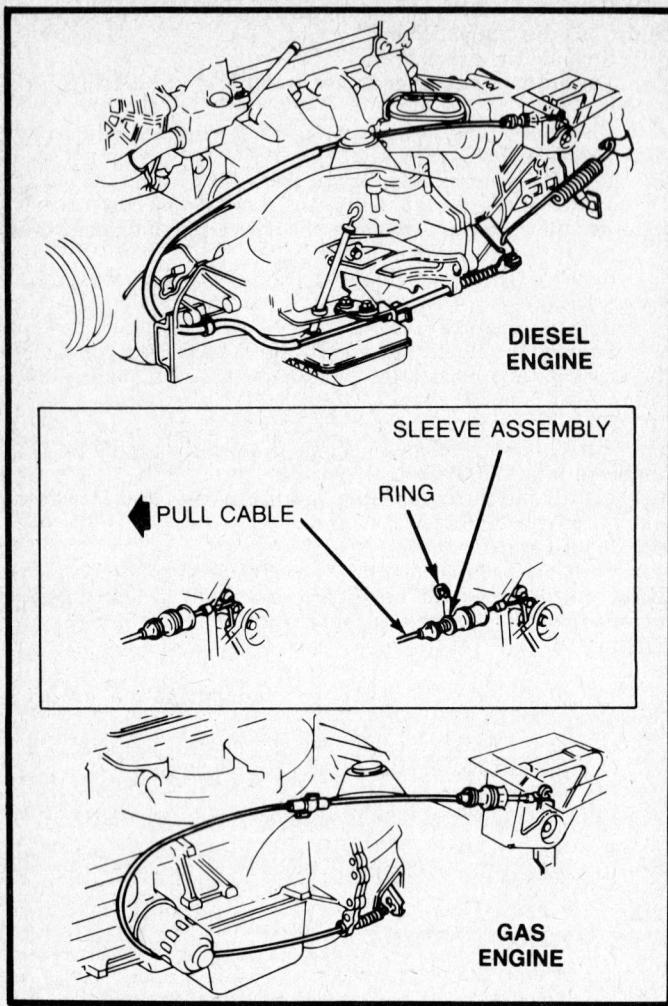

Detent cable adjustment (© General Motors Corporation)

5. Remove the drive shaft. Be sure to match mark the component to aid in reinstallation.
6. Disconnect the speedometer cable. Disconnect all electrical connections from the transmission.
7. Disconnect the clutch cable from the transmission.
8. Support the transmission. Remove the transmission mount retaining bolts.
9. Remove the exhaust manifold nuts. Remove the catalytic converter to tailpipe nuts and bolts.
10. Remove the catalytic converter to transmission bracket bolts and remove the catalytic converter from the vehicle. Remove the converter hanger.
11. Remove the crossmember attaching bolts. Remove the crossmember.
12. Remove the dust cover bolts. Remove the dust cover.
13. Remove the transmission to engine retaining bolts. Carefully remove the transmission from the vehicle.
14. Installation is the reverse of the removal procedure. Be sure to fill the transmission with the proper grade and type fluid.

AUTOMATIC TRANSMISSION

Removal and Installation

1. Before raising the vehicle, disconnect the negative battery cable and the T.V./detent cable at the bracket and carburetor or pump.
2. Remove the air cleaner and dipstick.
3. On vehicles with air conditioning, remove the heater core cover screws from the heater assembly. Disconnect the wire connector and with hoses attached, place the heater core cover out of the way.
4. Raise vehicle and remove propeller shaft.
5. Disconnect speedometer cable, electrical lead to case connector and oil cooler pipes.
6. Disconnect shift control linkage.
7. Support transmission with suitable transmission jack and remove the rear transmission support bolts.
8. Remove the nuts holding the converter bracket to the support.
9. Disconnect the exhaust pipe at the rear of the catalytic converter.
10. Disconnect exhaust pipe at manifold and remove the exhaust pipe, catalytic converter and converter bracket as an assembly.
11. Remove the torque converter under pan, if equipped.
12. Remove converter to flexplate bolts.
13. Lower transmission until jack is barely supporting it and remove transmission to engine mounting bolts.
14. Raise transmission to its normal position, then place a 2 in. block of wood between the rack-and-pinion housing and the engine oil pan, then support engine with jack and slide transmission rearward from engine and lower it away from vehicle. The use of a converter holding tool J-5384 or equivalent, is necessary when lowering the transmission or keep the rear of the transmission lower than the front so not to lose the converter.
15. Installation is the reverse of removal and includes the following. Before installing the flex plate to converter bolts, make certain that the weld nuts on the converter are flush with the flex plate and the converter rotates freely by hand in this position. Hand start the three bolts and tighten finger tight, then torque to specifications. This will insure proper converter alignment. Install new oil seal on oil filler tube before installing tube. Make all linkage adjustments.

THROTTLE VALVE CABLE

Adjustment

GAS ENGINE

1. Disengage the snap lock, and position the carburetor in the full open position.
2. Push the snap lock on the cable down until the top is flush with the cable.

DIESEL ENGINE

1. Loosen pump rod lock nut and shorten rod by several turns.
2. Push the snap lock on the cable down until the top is flush
3. Lengthen pump rod until the pump lever touches the full throttle stop.
4. Release lever assembly and tighten pump rod lock nut.

SHIFT INDICATOR

Adjustment

1. Disconnect the negative battery cable.
2. Remove the floor console.
3. Adjust the shift indicator pointer as necessary.
4. Installation of the removed components is the reverse of the removal.

MANUAL LINKAGE

Adjustment

1. Place the shift lever in neutral.

GENERAL MOTORS—"T" BODY
CHEVETTE • CHEVETTE SCOOTER • PONTIAC T1000 • 1000
SECTION 18

2. Disconnect the rod from the lower end of the shift lever, and place the transmission lever in neutral.
3. Adjust the rod until the hole aligns with the pin on the shift lever. Install the rod and secure.

DRIVESHAFT
Removal and Installation

1. Raise the vehicle and support it safely. Scribe matchmarks on the driveshaft and the companion flange and disconnect the rear universal joint by removing the trunnion bearing straps.
2. Move the driveshaft to the rear under the axle to remove the slip yoke from the transmission. Watch for leakage from the transmission output shaft housing.
3. Install the driveshaft in the reverse order of removal. Tighten the trunnion strap bolts to 16 ft. lbs.

REAR AXLE AND SUSPENSION

For Axle Overhaul Procedures and Suspension Services Refer to the Unit Repair Section.

REAR AXLE EXTENSION
Removal and Installation

1. Raise the vehicle and support it safely.
2. Disconnect the driveshaft from the companion flange and remove it from the transmission.
3. Position a jackstand under the front of the rear axle carrier housing.
4. Be sure to support the extension assembly before removing it.
5. Disconnect the center support bracket from the underbody.
6. Disconnect the extension housing flange from the rear axle housing.
7. Remove the extension housing from the vehicle. It may be necessary to pry the extension housing from the axle housing.
8. Installation is the reverse of the removal procedure.

REAR AXLE ASSEMBLY
Removal and Installation

1. Raise vehicle and support it safely.
2. Place adjustable lifting device under axle.
3. Disconnect right and left shock absorbers from axle.
4. Remove the driveshaft.
5. Disconnect stabilizer bar, tie-rod, and rear axle extension bracket. Support axle extension so that it does not swing down rapidly when disconnected from body bracket.
6. Remove right and left wheel and tire.
7. Remove right and left brake drums.
8. Disconnect brake lines from clips on axle tubes.
9. Remove differential cover and gasket. Drain lubricant.
10. Unscrew differential pinion lock screw. Remove pinion shaft and axle shaft C-locks. Reinstall pinion shaft and tighten lock screw to retain differential gears.
11. Remove both axle shafts.
12. Remove brake backing plate retaining nuts (both sides); remove backing plates (with shoes and brake lines attached) and wire to frame. Exercise caution not to damage or bend brake lines.
13. Remove right and left lower control arm pivot bolts at axle.
14. Lower axle assembly slowly until coil spring tension is released then remove axle from vehicle.

AXLE SHAFT, BEARING, AND SEAL
Removal and Installation

1. Raise the vehicle and support it safely. Remove the wheel and tire assembly and the brake drum.
2. Clean the area around the differential carrier cover.
3. Remove the differential carrier cover to drain the rear axle lubricant.
4. Use a metric Allen wrench to unscrew the differential pinion shaft lockscrew and remove the differential pinion shaft. It may be necessary to shorten the Allen wrench to do this.
5. Push the flanged end of the axle shaft toward the center of the vehicle and remove the C-lock from the inner end of the shaft.
6. Remove the axle shaft from the housing making sure not to damage the oil seal.
7. If replacing the seal only, remove the oil seal by using the inner end of the axle shaft. Insert the end of the shaft behind the steel case of the oil seal and carefully pry the seal out of the bore.
8. To remove bearings, insert a bearing and seal remover into the bore so that the tool head grasps behind the bearing. Slide the washer against the seal or bearing and turn the nut against the washer. Attach a slide hammer and remove the bearing.
9. Lubricate a new bearing with hypoid lubricant and install it into the housing with a bearing installer tool. Make sure that the tool contacts the end of the axle tube to ensure that the bearing is at the proper depth.
10. Lubricate the cavity between the seal lips with a high melting point wheel bearing grease. Place a new oil seal on the seal installation tool and position the seal in the axle housing bore. Tape the seal into the bore flush with the end of the housing.
11. To install the axle shaft, slide the axle shaft into place making sure that the splines on the end of the shaft do not damage the oil seal and that they engage the splines of the differential side gar. Install the C-lock on the inner end of the axle shaft and push the shaft outward so that the shaft lock seats in the counterbore of the differential side gear.
12. Position the differential pinion shaft through the case and pinions, aligning the hole in the shaft with the lockscrew hole. Install the lockscrew.
13. Clean the gasket mounting surfaces on the differential carrier and the carrier cover. Install the carrier cover using a new gasket and tighten the cover bolts in a crosswise pattern to 22 ft. lbs.
14. Fill the rear axle with lubricant to the bottom of the filler hole.
15. Install the brake drum and the wheel and tire assembly.
16. Lower the vehicle.

18-25

SECTION 19

OLDSMOBILE
CUTLASS • DELTA 88 • CUSTOM CRUISER • OLDS 98 • HURST OLDS

SPECIFICATIONS

Brakes	24–2	Serial Number Identification	19–4
Capacities	19–8	Torque	19–10
Crankshaft & Connecting Rod	19–7	Torque Sequence (Cylinder Heads)	19–26
Firing Order	19–6	Tune-Up	19–5
General Engine	19–5	Valve	19–7
Piston & Ring	19–10	Wheel Alignment	19–8

INDEX

A
Alternator R&R	19–11
Automatic Transmission	19–33
Adjustment	19–34
On Car Service	23–2
Assembly R&R	19–33
Axle Assembly R&R	19–35
Axle Shaft R&R	19–37

B
Ball Joints	35–2
Brake System	19–32
Brake Booster	19–32
Brake Caliper Overhaul	24–2
Brake Caliper R&R	24–2
Brake Drum	
Rear	24–2
Brake Master Cylinder	19–32
Brake Pad	
Front	24–2
Brake Shoe	
Rear	24–2

C
Camshaft R&R	19–27
Carburetor R&R	19–23
Chassis Electrical	19–12
Component Locations	19–16
Control Arm R&R	35–2
Cooling System	19–17
Cruise Control	19–16
Cylinder Head	19–26
R&R	19–26

D
Differential	23–2
Inspection	23–2
Dimmer Switch R&LR	19–13
Disc Brakes	24–2
Front	24–2
Distributor R&R	19–11
Drive Axle	23–2
Driveshaft R&R	19–35

E
Electric Fuel Pump R&R	19–18
Electronic Ignition	30–2
Emission Controls	19–24
Engine	19–24
Identification	19–4
R&R	19–24
Engine Electrical	19–11
Engine Lubrication	19–28
Engine Mechanical	19–24
Engine Mounts R&R	19–25
Exhaust Manifold R&R	19–23

F
Front Suspension	35–2
Alignment	19–8
Fuel Mixture, Adjust	19–19
Fuel Pump R&R	19–18
Fuses	19–16

H
Head Light Switch	19–13
Heater Blower R&R	19–17
Heater Core R&R	19–17
Heater Control	19–17
Horn Switch	19–13

I
Idle Speed Adjust	19–20
Ignition Switch	19–12
Ignition Timing	19–11
Instrument Cluster R&IR	19–14
Intake Manifold R&R	19–23

L, M, N
Lower Control Arm R&R	35–2
Master Cylinder R&R	19–32
Manual Steering Gear	
R&R	19–29
Neutral Safety Switch	
R&R	19–13

O
Oil Pan R&R	19–28
Oil Pump R&R	19–29
Oil Seal R&R	
Rear Main	19–29

P
Parking Brake	19–33
Adjustment	19–33
Cable R&R	19–33
Piston & Connecting Rod	19–27
Power Brake Unit R&R	19–32
Power Steering Pump R&R	19–29

R
Rear Main Oil Seal R&R	19–29
Rear Suspension	35–2
Regulator	19–11
Rocker Shaft/Assy R&R	19–26

S
Serial Number	19–4
Engine	19–4
Vehicle	19–4
Shock Absorber R&R	
Front	35–2
Rear	35–2
Springs	
Front	35–2
Rear	35–2
Starter R&R	19–11
Starter Drive Replacement	19–11
Steering Column R&R	19–31
Steering Gear R&R	19–29
Manual	19–29
Power	19–29
Steering Wheel R&R	19–30
Speedometer R&R	19–14
Suspension R&R	35–2
Service	35–2

T
Throttle Linkage, Adjust	19–21
Timing chain	19–27
Timing Gear Cover	19–27
Oil Seal Replacement	19–27
Tune-Up	19–5
Turn Signal Switch R&R	19–13

U, V
U-Joint Overhaul	28–2
Valve Tappette R&R	19–25
Valve Timing, Adjust	19–26
Valve System	19–25
Voltage Regulator	19–11

W, Y
Water Pump R&R	19–17
Wheel Alignment	19–8
Front	19–8
Wheel Bearings Front	19–29
Wheel Cylinders Rear	19–37
Rear	24–2
Windshield Wiper	19–14
Linkage R&R	19–14
Motor R&R	19–14
Switch R&R	19–13
Year Identification	19–3

BEFORE SERVICING BE CERTAIN TO READ THE SAFETY NOTICE

Oldsmobile
1983–87 Rear Wheel Drive Cars

CUTLASS SUPREME • CUTLASS SALON • CUTLASS SUPREME BROUGHAM • CUTLASS CALAIS • DELTA 88 DELTA 88 ROYALE • DELTA 88 ROYALE BROUGHAM CUSTOM CRUISER • OLDS 98 • OLDS 98 REGENCY OLDS 98 REGENCY BROUGHAM • HURST OLDS

YEAR IDENTIFICATION

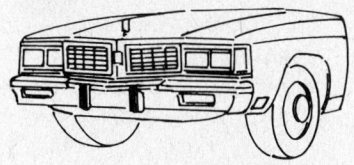

1983–84 Delta 88

1985 Delta 88 Royale Coupe

1985 Delta 88 Royale Brougham LS Sedan

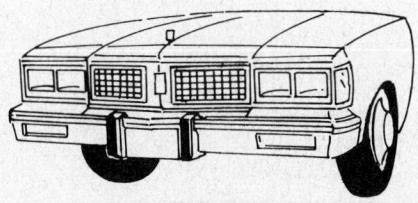

1983–84 98

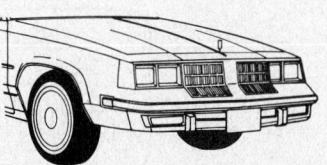

1983 Cutlass Supreme

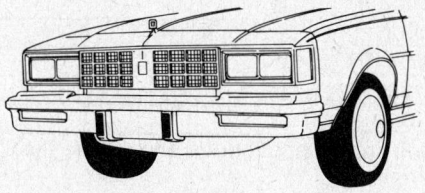

1984 Cutlass Supreme Sedan

1985–87 Cutlass Supreme

SECTION 19 OLDSMOBILE
CUTLASS • DELTA 88 • CUSTOM CRUISER • OLDS 98 • HURST OLDS

YEAR IDENTIFICATION

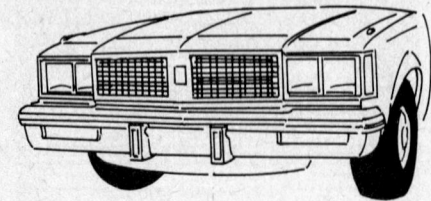
1983 Cutlass Supreme Brougham Sedan

1985-87 Cutlass Supreme Brougham

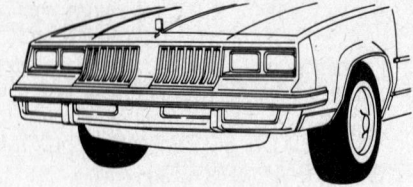
1984 Cutlass Supreme Coupe

1986 Cutlass Salon

1987 Cutlass Cruiser

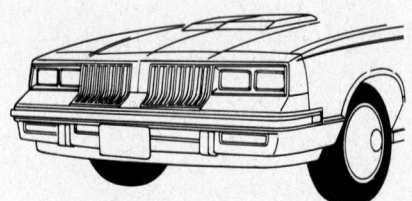
1984-87 Hurst Olds

VEHICLE IDENTIFICATION NUMBER (VIN)

It is important for servicing and ordering parts to be certain of the vehicle and engine identification. The VIN (vehicle identification number) is a 13 or 17 digit number visible through the windshield on the driver's side of the dash and contains the vehicle and engine identification codes. It can be interpreted as follows:

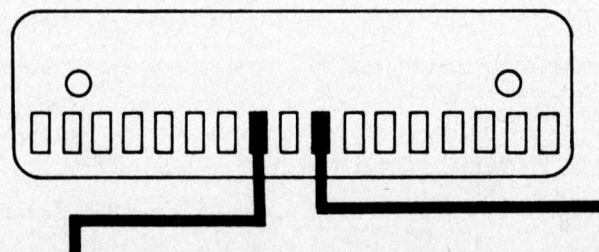

Engine Code						Model Year Code	
Code	Cu. In.	Liters	Cyl.	Carb.	Eng. Mfg.	Code	Year
A	231	3.8	6	2bbl	Buick	D	1983
4	252	4.1	6	4bbl	Buick	E	1984
V	263	4.3	6	Diesel	Olds.	F	1985
Y	307	5.0	8	4bbl	Olds.	G	1986
N	350	5.7	8	Diesel	Olds.	H	1987

The seventeen digit Vehicle Identification Number can be used to determine engine application and model year. The 10th digit indicates the model year and the 8th digit identifies the factory installed engine.

OLDSMOBILE
CUTLASS • DELTA 88 • CUSTOM CRUISER • OLDS 98 • HURST OLDS

SECTION 19

GENERAL ENGINE SPECIFICATIONS

Year	Eng. VIN Code	Engine No. Cyl. Displacement (cu. in.)	Liter	Eng. Mfg.	Carburetor Type	Horsepower @ rmp ■	Torque @ rpm (ft lbs) ■	Bore × Stroke (in.)	Compression Ratio	Oil Pressure PSI
'83	A	6-231	3.8	Buick	2 bbl	110 @ 3800	190 @ 1600	3.800 × 3.400	8.0:1	37 ②
	4	6-252	4.1	Buick	4 bbl	125 @ 4000	205 @ 2000	3.965 × 3.400	8.0:1	37 ②
	V	6-260	4.3	Olds.	Diesel	85 @ 3600	165 @ 1600	4.057 × 3.385	21.6:1	30 ③
	9 ①	8-307	5.0	Olds.	4 bbl	148 @ 3800	250 @ 2400	3.800 × 3.385	8.5:1	30 ③
	Y	8-307	5.0	Olds.	4 bbl	148 @ 3800	250 @ 2400	3.800 × 3.385	8.5:1	30 ③
	N	8-350	5.7	Olds.	Diesel	125 @ 3600	225 @ 1600	4.057 × 3.385	22.5:1	30 ③
'84	A	6-231	3.8	Buick	2 bbl	110 @ 3800	190 @ 1600	3.800 × 3.400	8.0:1	37 ②
	4	6-252	4.1	Buick	4 bbl	125 @ 4000	205 @ 2000	3.965 × 3.400	8.0:1	37 ②
	V	6-260	4.3	Olds.	Diesel	85 @ 3600	165 @ 1600	4.057 × 3.385	22.5:1	30 ③
	N	8-350	5.7	Olds.	Diesel	125 @ 3600	225 @ 1600	4.057 × 3.385	22.5:1	30 ③
	9 ①	8-307	5.0	Olds.	4 bbl	148 @ 3800	250 @ 2400	3.800 × 3.385	8.5:1	30 ③
	Y	8-307	5.0	Olds.	4 bbl	148 @ 3800	250 @ 2400	3.800 × 3.385	8.5:1	30 ③
'85	A	6-231	3.8	Buick	2 bbl	110 @ 3800	190 @ 1600	3.800 × 3.400	8.0:1	37 ②
	9 ①	8-307	5.0	Olds.	4 bbl	140 @ 3200	225 @ 2000	3.800 × 3.385	7.99:1	30-45 ③
	Y	8-307	5.0	Olds.	4 bbl	140 @ 3200	240 @ 1600	3.800 × 3.385	8.0:1	30-45 ③
	N	8-350	5.7	Olds.	Diesel	105 @ 3200	200 @ 1600	4.057 × 3.385	22.73:1	30-45 ③
'86	A	6-231	3.8	Buick	2 bbl	110 @ 3800	190 @ 1600	3.800 × 3.400	8.0:1	37 ②
	Y	8-307	5.0	Olds.	4 bbl	140 @ 3200	255 @ 2000	3.800 × 3.385	7.99:1	30-45 ③
	9 ①	8-307	5.0	Olds.	4 bbl	140 @ 3200	255 @ 2000	3.800 × 3.385	7.99:1	30-45 ③
'87					Specifications not available at time of printing					

Horsepower and torque are SAE net figures. They are measured at the rear of the transmission with all accessories installed and operating. Since the figures vary when a given engine is installed in different models, some are representative rather than exact.
① Hurst/Olds Package
② @ 2400 rpm
③ @ 1500 rpm

TUNE-UP SPECIFICATIONS
Gasoline Engines

When analyzing compression test results, look for uniformity among cylinders rather than specific pressures

Year	Eng. VIN Code	Engine No. Cyl. Displacement (cu. in.)	Liter	Eng. Mfg.	Spark Plugs Orig. Type	Gap (in.)	Distributor Point Dwell (Deg.)	Point Gap (in.)	Ignition Timing (deg.) ▲ Auto. Trans.	Fuel Pump Pressure (psi)	Idle Speed (rpm) ▲ Auto. Trans.
'83	A	6-231	3.8	Buick	R-45TS8	.080	Electronic		①	5.6-6.5	①
	4	6-252	4.1	Buick	R-45TS8	.080	Electronic		①	5.6-6.5	①
	Y	8-307	5.0	Olds.	R-46SX	.080	Electronic		①	5.6-6.5	①
	9 ②	8-307	5.0	Olds.	R-46SX	.080	Electronic		①	5.5-6.5	①
'84	A	6-231	3.8	Buick	R45TSX	0.060	Electronic		①	5.5-6.5	①
	4	6-252	4.1	Buick	R45TSX	0.060	Electronic		①	5.5-6.5	①
	9	8-307	5.0	Olds.	R46SX ④	0.080	Electronic		①	5.5-6.5	①
	Y	8-307	5.0	Olds.	R46SX ④	0.080	Electronic		①	5.5-6.5	①
'85	A	6-231	3.8	Buick	R45TSX	0.060	Electronic		①	5.5-6.5	①
	9	8-307	5.0	Olds.	R46SZ	0.060	Electronic		①	5.5-6.5	①
	Y	8-307	5.0	Olds.	FR3LS6	0.060	Electronic		①	5.5-6.5	①
'86	A	6-231	3.8	Buick	R45TSX	0.060	Electronic		①	5.5-6.5	①
	Y	8-307	5.0	Olds.	FR3LS6 ⑤	0.060	Electronic		①	6.0-7.5	①
	9	8-307	5.0	Olds.	FR3LS6 ⑤	0.060	Electronic		①	6.0-7.5	①

19-5

SECTION 19

Oldsmobile
CUTLASS • DELTA 88 • CUSTOM CRUISER • OLDS 98 • HURST OLDS

TUNE-UP SPECIFICATIONS
Gasoline Engines

When analyzing compression test results, look for uniformity among cylinders rather than specific pressures

Year	Eng. VIN Code	Engine No. Cyl. Displacement (cu. in.)	Liter	Eng. Mfg.	Spark Plugs Orig. Type	Gap (in.)	Distributor Point Dwell (Deg.)	Point Gap (in.)	Ignition Timing (deg.) ▲ Auto. Trans.	Fuel Pump Pressure (psi)	Idle Speed (rpm) ▲ Auto. Trans.
'87	Refer to the Underhood Emission Label and/or Owner's Manual General Specifications										

NOTE: The underhood specifications sticker often reflects tuneup specification changes made in production. Sticker figures must be used if they disagree with those in this chart. Part numbers in this chart are not recommendations by Chilton for any product by brand name.

▲ See text for procedure
■ All figures are in degrees Before Top Dead Center
① See Underhood Emission Label
② Hurst/Olds Package
③ Type of driving mode may necessitate a change of heat range application and reference number of the spark plugs as listed in the above specifications
④ Or R46SZ
⑤ Or FR3CLS6

FIRING ORDERS

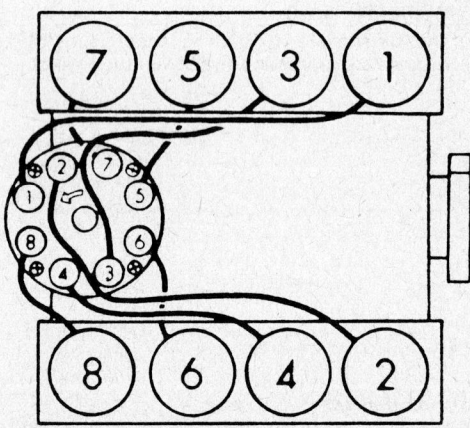

GM (Oldsmobile) 307, 350
Engine firing order: 1–8–4–3–6–5–7–2
Distributor rotation: counterclockwise

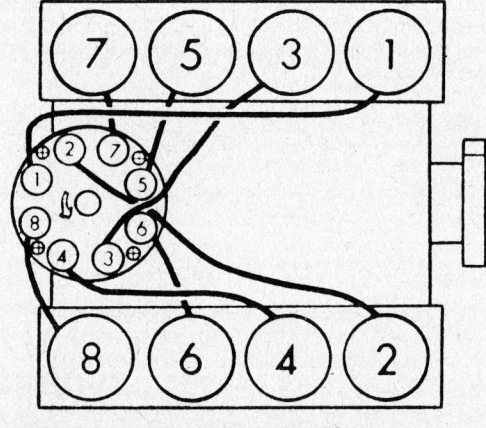

GM (Oldsmobile) 260 V8
Engien firing order 1–8–4–3–6–5–7–2
Distributor rotation: counterclockwise

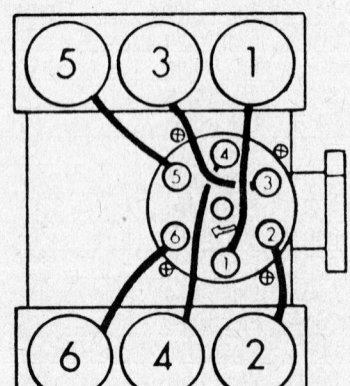

GM (Buick) 231, 252 V6
3.8L, 4.1L)
Engine firing order: 1–6–5–4–3–2
Distributor rotation: clockwise

V6 harmonic balancers have two timing marks: one is 1/8 in. wide, and one is 1/16 in. wide. Use the 1/16 in. mark for timing with a hand held light. The 1/8 in. mark is used only with a magnetic timing pick-up probe

OLDSMOBILE 19
CUTLASS • DELTA 88 • CUSTOM CRUISER • OLDS 98 • HURST OLDS

VALVE SPECIFICATIONS

Year	Eng. VIN Code	Engine No. Cyl. Displacement (cu. in.)	Liter	Seat Angle (deg)	Face Angle (deg)	Spring Test Pressure (lbs @ in.)	Spring Installed (Height (in.))	Stem-to-Guide Clearance (in.) Intake	Stem-to-Guide Clearance (in.) Exhaust	Stem Diameter (in.) Intake	Stem Diameter (in.) Exhaust
'83–'84	A	6-231	3.8	45	45	210–220 @ 1.340	1.727	0.0015–0.0035	0.0015–0.0032	0.3401–0.3412	0.3405–0.3412
	4	6-252	4.1	45	45	210–220 @ 1.340	1.727	0.0015–0.0035	0.0015–0.0032	0.3401–0.3412	0.3405–0.3412
	V	6-263 ②	4.3	45 ②	44 ③	203–217 @ 1.220	1.670	0.0010–0.0027	0.0015–0.0032	0.3425–0.3432	0.3420–0.3427
	N	8-350 ①	5.7	45 ②	44 ③	144–158 @ 1.300	1.670	0.0010–0.0027	0.0015–0.0032	0.3425–0.3432	0.3420–0.3427
	Y	8-307	5.0	45 ②	44 ③	180–194 @ 1.270	1.670	0.0010–0.0027	0.0015–0.0032	0.3425–0.3432	0.3420–0.3427
	9	8-307	5.0	45 ②	44 ③	203–217 @ 1.220	1.670	0.0010–0.0027	0.0015–0.0032	0.3425–0.3432	0.3420–0.3427
'85	A	6-231	3.8	45	45	210–220 @ 1.340	1.727	0.0015–0.0035	0.0015–0.0032	0.3401–0.3412	0.3405–0.3412
	Y	8-307	5.0	45 ②	44 ③	180–194 @ 1.270	1.670	0.0010–0.0027	0.0015–0.0032	0.3425–0.3432	0.3420–0.3427
	9	8-307	5.0	45 ②	44 ③	203–217 @ 1.220	1.670	0.0010–0.0027	0.0015–0.0032	0.3425–0.3432	0.3420–0.3427
	N	8-350 ①	5.7	45 ②	44 ③	144–158 @ 1.300	1.670	0.0010–0.0027	0.0015–0.0032	0.3425–0.3432	0.3420–0.3427
'86–'87	A	6-231	3.8	45	45	210–220 @ 1.340	1.727	0.0015–0.0035	0.0015–0.0032	0.3401–0.3412	0.3405–0.3412
	Y	8-307	5.0	45 ②	44 ③	180–194 @ 1.270	1.670	0.0010–0.0027	0.0015–0.0032	0.3425–0.3432	0.3420–0.3427
	9	8-307	5.0	45 ②	44 ③	203–217 @ 1.220	1.670	0.0010–0.0027	0.0015–0.0032	0.3425–0.3432	0.3420–0.3427

① Diesel Engine
② Exhaust 31 degrees
③ Exhaust 30 degrees

CRANKSHAFT AND CONNECTING ROD SPECIFICATIONS
All measurements are given in inches.

Year	VIN Code	Engine No. Cyl. Displacement (cu. in.)	Liter	Crankshaft Main Brg. Journal Dia.	Crankshaft Main Brg. Oil Clearance	Crankshaft Shaft End-Play	Crankshaft Thrust on No.	Connecting Rod Journal Diameter	Connecting Rod Oil Clearance	Connecting Rod Side Clearance
'83	A	6-231	3.8	2.4995	.0003–.0018	.003–.011	2	2.2487–2.2495	.0005–.0026	.006–.015
	4	6-252	4.1	2.4995	.0003–.0018	.003–.011	2	2.2487–2.2495	.0005–.0026	.006–.015
	V	6-26	4.3	2.9993–3.0003	.0005–.0021 ④	.0035–.0135	3	2.2490–2.2510	.0005–.0026	.006–.020
	Y-9	8-307	5.0	2.4990–2.4995 ①	.005–.0021 ②	.0035–.0135	3	2.1238–2.1248	.0004–.0033	.006–.020
	N	8-350	5.7	2.9993–3.0003	.0005–.0021 ⑤	.0035–.0135	3	2.2495–2.2500	.0005–.0026	.006–.020
'84	A	6-231	3.8	2.4995	.0003–.0018	.003–.011	2	2.2487–2.2495	.0005–.0026	.006–.015
	4	6-252	4.1	2.4995	.0003–.0018	.003–.011	2	2.2487–2.2495	.0005–.0026	.006–.015
	V	6-26	4.3	2.9993–3.0003	.0005–.0021 ④	.0035–.0135	3	2.2490–2.2510	.0005–.0026	.006–.020
	Y-9	8-307	5.0	2.4990–2.4995 ③	.0005–.0021 ②	.0035–.0135	3	2.1238–2.1248	.0004–.0033	.006–.020
	N	8-350	5.7	2.9993–3.0003	.0005–.0021 ⑤	.0035–.0135	3	2.2495–2.2500	.0005–.0026	.006–.020
'85	A	6-231	3.8	2.4995	.0003–.0018	.003–.011	2	2.2487–2.2495	.0005–.0026	.006–.023
	Y-9	8-307	5.0	2.4985–2.4995 ⑥	.0015–.0021 ②	.0035–.0135	3	2.1238–2.1248	.0004–.0033	.006–.020
	N	8-350	5.7	2.9993–3.0003	.0005–.0021 ⑤	.0035–.0135	3	2.2495–2.2500	.0005–.00256	.006–.020

SECTION 19
OLDSMOBILE
CUTLASS • DELTA 88 • CUSTOM CRUISER • OLDS 98 • HURST OLDS

CRANKSHAFT AND CONNECTING ROD SPECIFICATIONS
All measurements are given in inches.

Year	VIN Code	Engine No. Cyl. Displacement (cu. in.)	Liter	Crankshaft Main Brg. Journal Dia.	Crankshaft Main Brg. Oil Clearance	Crankshaft Shaft End-Play	Thrust on No.	Connecting Rod Journal Diameter	Connecting Rod Oil Clearance	Connecting Rod Side Clearance
'86–	A	6-231	3.8	2.4995	.0003–.0018	.003–.011	2	2.2487–2.2495	.0005–.0026	.006–.023
'87	Y-9	8-307	5.0	2.4985–2.4995 ⑥	.0015–.0021 ②	.0035–.0135	3	2.1238–2.1248	.0004–.0033	.006–.020

① #1—2.4993–2.4998
② #5—.0015–.0031
③ #1—2.4973–2.4998
④ #4—.0020–.0034
⑤ #5—.0020–.0034
⑥ #1—2.4988–2.4998

CAPACITIES
Oldsmobile 88, 98

Year	Eng. VIN Code	Engine No. Cyl. Displacement (cu. in.)	Liter	Engine Crankcase Add 1 Qt for New Filter	Transmission Pts. to Refill After Draining Automatic•	Drive Axle (pts.)	Gasoline Tank (gals.)	Cooling System (qts) With Heater	Cooling System (qts) With A/C
'83	A	6-231	3.8	4	①	②	③	13.00	13.0 w/EC
	Y-9	8-307	5.0	4	①	②	③	15.50	15.25 / 16.25 w/EC / 16.00 w/HC
	N	8-350 Diesel	5.7	6	①	②	③	18.25	18.00 w/HC
	4	6-252	4.1	4	①	②	③	12.50	12.50 w/EC
'84	A	6-231	3.8	4	①	②	③	13.00	13.00
	Y-9	8-307	5.0	4	①	②	③	15.50 ④	15.25 / 16.25 w/EC / 16.00 w/HC
	N	8-350 Diesel	5.7	6	①	②	③	18.25	18.00 w/HC
'85	A	6-231	3.8	4	①	②	③	13.00	13.00
	Y-9	8-307	5.0	4	①	②	③	15.60	15.30 / 16.30 w/EC / 16.00 w/HC
	N	8-350 Diesel	5.7	6	①	②	③	18.30	18.00

EC Extra Cooling Capacity
HC High Cooling Capacity

① THM 200C 1983–86:
    Drain and Refill —7.0 pts.
    Overhaul —19.0 pts.
  THM 250C 1983–84:
    Drain and Refill —8.0 pts.
    Overhaul —20.0 pts.
  THM 350C 1983:
    Drain and Refill —6.5 pts.
    Overhaul —20.0 pts.
  THM 200-4R 1983–86:
    Drain and Refill —7.0 pts.
    Overhaul —22.0 pts.

② 7½ Ring gear—3.5 pts.
  8½ Ring gear—4.25 pts.
  8¾ Ring gear (83 only)—5.25 pts.

③ Cutlass Series 1983–86
  Coupe and Sedan:
    Except Diesel—18.25 gal. (1983–84)
    Except Diesel—18.10 gal. (1985–86)
    With Diesel —19.75 gal. (1983–85)
  Cutlass Cruiser:
    18.25 gal. (1983)
    22.00 gal. (1986)

④ Not Used
⑤ VIN 9–15.50 Qts.
⑥ Custom Cruiser

OLDSMOBILE
CUTLASS • DELTA 88 • CUSTOM CRUISER • OLDS 98 • HURST OLDS
SECTION 19

CAPACITIES
Cutlass

Year	Eng. VIN Code	Engine No. Cyl. Displacement (cu. in.)	Liter	Engine Crankcase Add 1 qt For New Filter	Transmission Pts. to Refill After Draining Automatic•	Drive Axle (pts.)	Gasoline Tank (gals.)	Cooling System (qts) With Heater	Cooling System (qts) With A/C
'83	A	6-231	3.8	4	①	②	③	13.00 w/EC	13.25 w/HC
	V	6-263 Diesel	4.3	5	①	②	③	13.75	14.25 w/HC
	Y-9	8-307	5.0	4	①	②	③	14.75	15.50 w/EC, HC
	N	8-350 Diesel	5.7	6	①	②	③	17.50	17.50 w/HC
'84	A	6-231	3.8	4	①	②	③	13.00	13.25 w/HC
	V	6-263 Diesel	4.3	5	①	②	③	13.75	14.25
	Y-9	8-307	5.0	4	①	②	③	14.75	15.50
	N	8-350	5.7	6	①	②	③	17.50	17.50
'85	A	6-231	3.8	4	①	②	③	13.00	13.50 w/HC
	Y-9	8-307	5.0	4	①	②	③	14.90	15.60 w/EC 15.50 w/HC ⑤
	N	8-350	5.7	6	①	②	③	17.40	17.40
'86	A	6-231	3.8	4	①	②	③	13.00	13.50
	Y-9	8-307	5.0	4	①	②	③	14.90	15.60 w/EC 15.50 w/HC
	Y ⑥	8-307	5.0	4	①	②	③	15.30	16.30 w/EC 16.00 w/HC
'87	Information not available at time of printing								

PISTON RING GAP SPECIFICATIONS
All specifications given in inches.

Year	Engine VIN Code	Engine	Liter	Top Compression	Bottom Compression	Oil Control
'83	A	6-231	3.8	0.010–0.020	0.010–0.020	0.015–0.055
	4	6-252	4.1	0.010–0.020	0.010–0.020	0.015–0.055
	Y-9	8-307	5.0	①	①	②
	V	6-263 Diesel	4.3	0.019–0.027	0.013–0.021	0.015–0.053
	N	8-350 Diesel	5.7	0.019–0.027	0.013–0.021	0.015–0.055
'84	A	6-231	3.8	0.010–0.020	0.010–0.020	0.015–0.055
	4	6-252	4.1	0.010–0.020	0.010–0.020	0.015–0.055
	Y-9	8-307	5.0	①	①	②
	V	6-263 Diesel	4.3	0.019–0.027	0.013–0.021	0.010–0.022
	N	8-350 Diesel	5.7	0.019–0.027	0.013–0.021	0.010–0.022
'85	A	6-231	3.8	0.010–0.020	0.010–0.020	0.015–0.055
	Y-9	8-307	5.0	0.009–0.019	0.009–0.019	0.015–0.055
	N	8-350 Diesel	5.7	0.015–0.025	0.015–0.025	0.015–0.055
'86	A	6-231	3.8	0.010–0.020	0.010–0.020	0.015–0.055
	Y-9	8-307	5.0	0.009–0.019	0.009–0.019	0.015–0.055
'87	1987 information not available at time of printing					

① Sealed Power Rings: .009–.019 in.
   TRW Rings: .010–.020 in.
② Sealed Power Rings: .015–.055 in.
   TRW Rings: .010–.020 in.

19–9

WHEEL ALIGNMENT

Year	Model	Caster Range (deg.)	Caster Pref Setting (deg.)	Camber Range (deg.)	Camber Pref. Setting (deg.)	Toe (in.)	Steering Axis Inclin. (deg.)	Wheel Pivot Ratio (deg.) Inner Wheel	Wheel Pivot Ratio (deg.) Outer Wheel
'83	Cutlass w/Power Steering	2P to 4P	3P	5/16N to 1 5/16P	1/2P	1/16 to 1/4	7	NA	NA
	w/Manual Steering	0 to 2P	1P	5/16N to 1 5/16P	1/2P	1/16 to 1/4	7	NA	NA
'84–'85	Cutlass	2P to 4P	3P	5/16N to 1 5/16P	1/2P	1/16 to 1/4	7	NA	NA
'86	Cutlass	1 13/16P to 3 13/16P	2 13/16P	0 to 1 5/8P	13/16P	1/16 to 1/4	NA	NA	NA
'83–'85	88–98 Series	2P to 4P	3P	0 to 1 5/8P	3/16P	1/16 to 1/4	10 9/16	NA	NA

NA Not Available
N Negative
P Positive

TORQUE SPECIFICATIONS

All readings in ft. lbs.

Year	Engine VIN Code	Engine	Liter	Cylinder Head Bolts	Rod Bearing Bolts	Main Bearing Bolts	Crankshaft Bolt	Flywheel-to-Crankshaft Bolts	Manifold Intake	Manifold Exhaust
'83	A	6-231	3.8	80	40	100	225	60 ①	45	25
	4	6-252	4.1	80	40	100	225	60 ①	45	25
	Y-9	8-307	5.0	125 ②	42	80 ④	200–310	60	40 ②	25
	V	6-263 Diesel	4.3	③	42	89	160–350	57	41 ②	29
	N	8-350 Diesel	5.7	130 ②	42	120	200–310	60	40 ②	25
'84	A	6-231	3.8	80	40	100	225	60	45	25
	4	6-252	4.1	80	40	100	225	60	45	25
	Y-9	8-307	5.0	125 ②	42	80 ④	200–310	60	40 ②	25
	V	6-263 Diesel	4.3	③	42	89	203–350	57	41	31
	N	8-350 Diesel	5.7	130 ②	42	120	200–310	60	40 ②	25
'85	A	6-231	3.8	72	40	97	200 ⑤	60	35	20
	Y-9	8-307	5.0	125 ②	42	80 ④	200–310	60	35	20
	N	8-350 Diesel	5.7	130 ②	42	120	200–310	60	40 ②	25
'86	A	6.231	3.8	72	40	97	200 ⑤	60	35	20
	Y-9	8-307	5.0	125 ②	42	80 ④	200–310	60	40 ②	25

OLDSMOBILE 19
CUTLASS • DELTA 88 • CUSTOM CRUISER • OLDS 98 • HURST OLDS

TORQUE SPECIFICATIONS
All readings in ft. lbs.

Year	Engine VIN Code	Engine	Liter	Cylinder Head Bolts	Rod Bearing Bolts	Main Bearing Bolts	Crankshaft Bolt	Flywheel-to-Crankshaft Bolts	Manifold Intake	Exhaust
'87				1987 information not available at time of printing						

① Automatic and Manual transmissions
② Clean and dip the entire bolt in engine oil before tightening to obtain correct torque reading
③ 142 ft. lbs. on numbers 1, 2, 3, 4, 7, 8, 9, 10 and 11 bolts
   59 ft. lbs. on numbers 5, 6, 11, 12, 13 and 14 bolts
④ Number five bearing cap—120 ft. lbs.
⑤ Minimum

ELECTRICAL SECTION

For Overhaul Procedures, refer to the Unit Repair Section.

Charging System

ALTERNATOR

Removal and Installation

1. Disconnect the negative battery cable. Disconnect the wiring from the alternator.
2. Remove the mounting bolt, adjusting bolt, and drive belt.
3. Lift out the alternator.
4. To install, reverse the removal procedure, connect the battery ground cable and tighten the alternator belt. Determine belt tension at a point halfway between the pulleys by pressing on the belt with moderate thumb pressure.
5. If the distance between the pulleys (measured at the pulley center) is 13–16 in., the belt should deflect ½ in. at the halfway point.
6. If the distance is 7–10 in., the belt should deflect ¼ in. at the halfway point.

VOLTAGE REGULATOR

Removal and Installation

The voltage regulator is incorporated within the alternator assembly. There is no adjustment procedure. Should the regulator require service, the alternator must be disassembled.

Starting System

STARTER

Removal and Installation

1. Disconnect the negative battery cable. Raise and support the vehicle safely.
2. Remove upper support attaching bolts and the brace and wire guide tube bolt, if equipped.
3. Remove the flywheel housing cover, as required. On some vehicles, it may be necessary to remove the exhaust crossover pipe.
4. Remove two starter mounting bolts, if so equipped. On some vehicles, it may be necessary to disconnect the transmission oil cooler lines.
5. Lower starter, disconnect wiring, and remove starter. If equipped with dual exhausts, it may be necessary to remove the lefthand exhaust pipe.
6. Install by reversing the procedure. If shims were removed, they must be installed in their original location to assure proper drive pinion-to-flywheel engagement.

Ignition System

DISTRIBUTOR

Removal and Installation

1. Remove all the necessary components in order to gain access to the distributor assembly.
2. Remove all electrical connections from the unit. Release the coil connectors from the distributor cap.
3. Remove the distributor cap retaining screws and remove the cap. Disconnect the four terminal harness from the distributor.
4. Remove the distributor hold down bolt. Note the position of the rotor and then remove the distributor assembly from the engine. Again, note the position of the rotor.
5. To insure correct ignition timing, the distributor must be installed with the rotor in the same position as when it was removed.
6. Installation is the reverse of the removal procedure.
7. If the engine has been cranked after the distributor has been removed, the following procedure must be used.
8. Remove the number one spark plug. Place your finger over the spark plug hole and crank the engine slowly until compression is felt.
9. Align the timing mark on the pulley to "0" on the engine timing indicator.
10. Position the rotor between number one and number eight spark plug towers on V8 engines and between number one and number six spark plug towers on V6 engines.
11. The distributor can now be correctly installed in the engine.
12. Once the distributor has been installed, check the engine timing and adjust as required.

IGNITION TIMING

Adjustment

V6

1. Run the engine until normal operating temperature is reached. Be sure that the air cleaner is installed and the air conditioner is off.
2. Connect a timing light according to the manufacturers instructions.

19–11

Oldsmobile
CUTLASS • DELTA 88 • CUSTOM CRUISER • OLDS 98 • HURST OLDS

3. Disconnect the four wire electrical connector at the distributor. The check engine light will come on.
4. If the timing requires adjustment, loosen the distributor and set the timing to the specifications as noted on the vehicle emission label.
5. Once the timing has been set, turn the engine off and disconnect the battery to cancel any stored trouble codes.

V8

1. Run the engine until operating temperature has been reached. Be sure that the choke is fully open and the air conditioner is off.
2. With the engine running, ground the twelve terminal ALCL connector at point B and A.
3. Connect the timing light according to the manufacturers instructions.
4. If the timing requires adjustment, loosen the distributor and set the timing to the specifications noted on the vehicle emission label.
5. Once the timing has been set and with the engine still running, unground the diagnostic terminal.

Electrical Controls

IGNITION LOCK CYLINDER

Removal and Installation

1. Disconnect the negative battery cable. Position the ignition lock cylinder in the RUN position.
2. Remove the steering wheel. Remove the lock plate, turn signal switch and the buzzer switch.
3. Remove the lock cylinder retaining screw. Remove the lock cylinder.
4. To install, rotate the lock cylinder clockwise to align the cylinder key with the keyway in the lock housing.
5. Push the lock all the way in. Install the screw.
6. Continue the installation in the reverse order of the removal procedure.

IGNITION SWITCH

Removal and Installation

1. Disconnect the negative battery terminal.
2. Loosen the toe pan screws on the steering column.
3. Remove the column to instrument panel trim plates and attaching nuts.

4. Lower the steering column. Be sure that the steering column is supported at all times in order to prevent damage to the column. Disconnect the switch wire connectors.
5. Remove the switch attaching screws and remove the switch.
6. To replace, move the key lock to the LOCK position.
7. Move the actuator rod hole in the switch to the LOCK position.
8. Install the switch with the rod in the hole.
9. Position and reassemble the steering column in reverse of the disassembly procedure.

Adjustment

STANDARD COLUMN

1. Place the switch in the OFF position.
2. Position the switch on the column, then move the slider to the extreme left (toward the wheel).
3. Move the slider back two positions to the right of ACCESSORY position.
4. Place the key in any RUN position and shift the transmission into any position but PARK for automatics. Put it in REVERSE for manual.
5. Position the lock toward ACCESSORY with a light finger pressure and secure the switch.

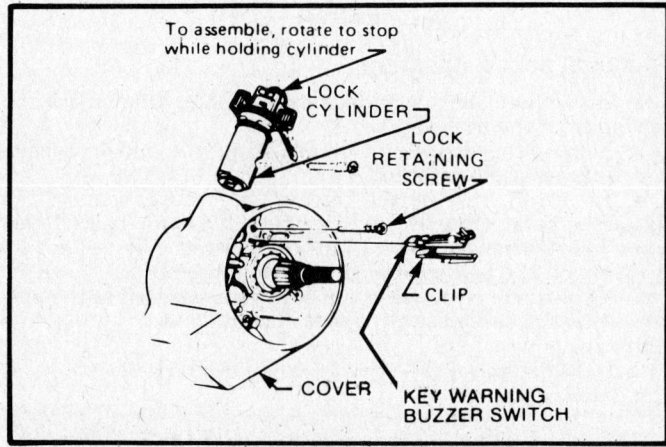

Remove and install ignition lock and key warning buzzer (© General Motors Corporation)

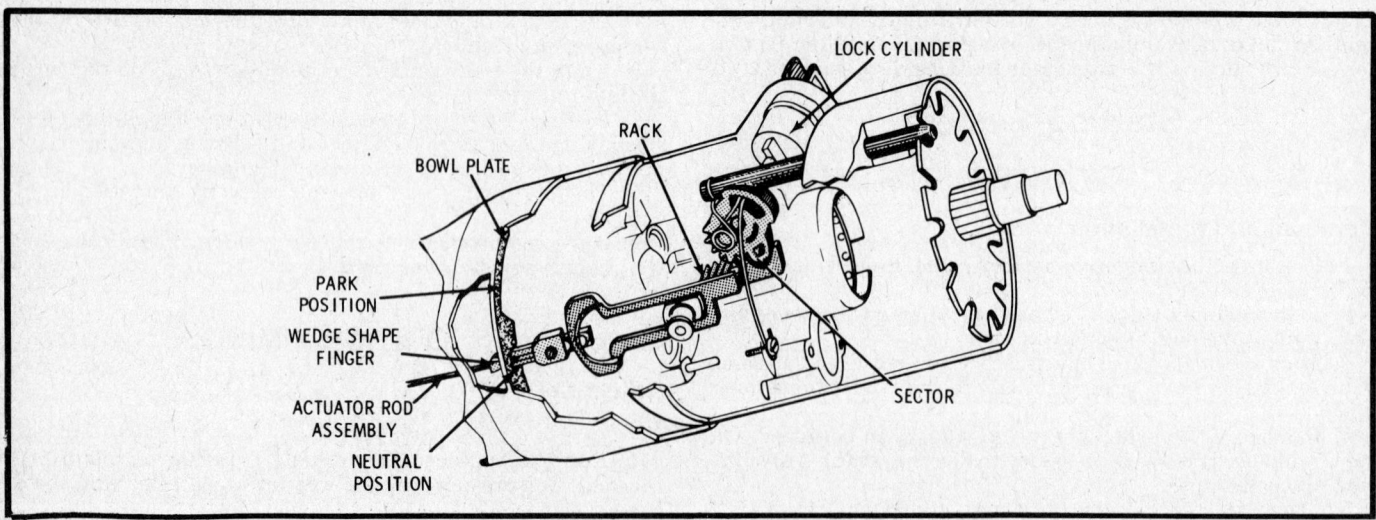

Mechanical neutral start system (© General Motors Corporation)

19-12

OLDSMOBILE

CUTLASS • DELTA 88 • CUSTOM CRUISER • OLDS 98 • HURST OLDS

TILT COLUMN

1. Place the key in ACCESSORY position; leave the key in the lock.
2. Loosen the switch mounting screws.
3. Push the switch upward toward the wheel to make certain it is in ACCESSORY detent.
4. Hold the key in full counterclockwise ACCESSORY position and tighten the switch mounting screws.
5. The switch is properly adjusted if it will go into ACCESSORY position, the key can be removed when in lock, and the switch will go into START position.

NEUTRAL SAFETY/BACK-UP SWITCH

Removal and Installation

COLUMN MOUNTED SHIFTER

A mechanical neutral safety switch is incorporated into the steering column bowl, between the lock and the transmission selector and is non-adjustable.

The mechanical block is achieved by a wedge shaped finger added to the ignition switch actuator rod. The finger will only pass through the bowl plate when in the "P" and "N" quadrant positions. This prevents the lock cylinder from being turned to the START position when in other quadrant positions. When in either "P" or "N" quadrant positions, the finger is allowed to pass through the bowl plate notches, allowing the lock cylinder to rotate to the START position.

The back-up light and park/neutral (for computer use) switch still remains on the lower steering column and looks similar to the previous switches except for the electrical terminals.

1. Place the gear selector in the NEUTRAL position.
2. Remove wire connectors from the combination back-up and park/neutral switch.
3. Apply pressure to the locking tangs on the front of the switch and remove the switch from the column.
4. To install the switch, be sure the shift lever is in the NEUTRAL position.
   a. Align the actuator on the switch with the hole in the shift tube.
   b. Position the rearward portion of the switch (connector side) to fit into the cutout of the lower column jacket.
   c. Push down on the front of the switch until the two tangs on the switch housing will snap into place in the rectangular holes in the column jacket.
5. To adjust a new switch, move the gear selector to the PARK position. The switch main housing and the housing back should rachet, providing proper switch adjustment.
6. Should a re-adjustment be necessary, move the switch housing all the way towards the LOW position and move the gear selector to the PARK position, as in Step 5.

HEADLIGHT SWITCH

Removal and Installation

CUTLASS

1. Disconnect the negative battery cable.
2. Remove the instrument cluster pad.
3. Remove the two switch mounting screws and remove the switch.
4. Installation is the reverse of the removal procedure.

88 AND 98

1. Disconnect the negative battery cable.
2. Remove steering column trim cover. Remove the trim cover.
3. Remove 2 screws attaching mounting plate to cluster carrier.

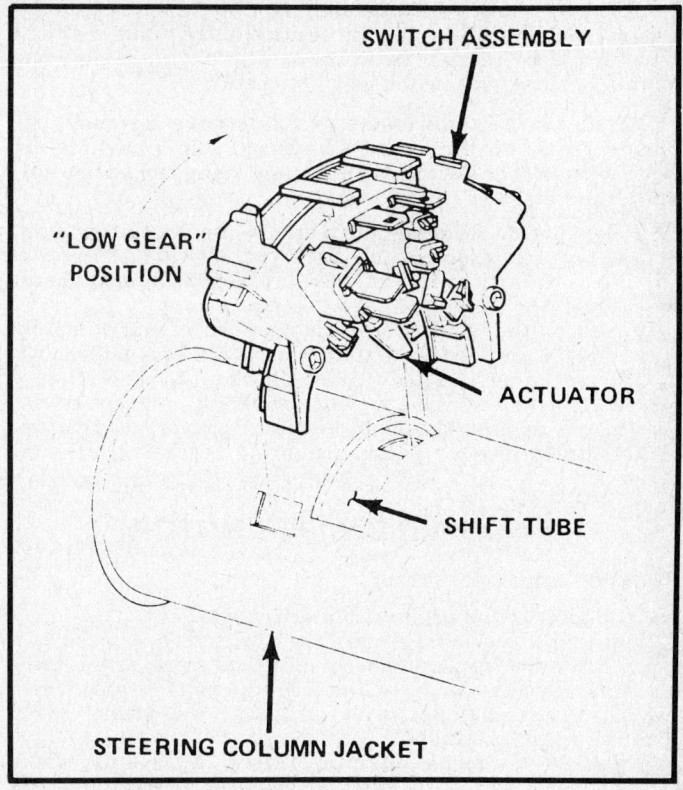

Back-up light and park/neutral switch (© General Motors Corp.)

4. Pull switch and mounting plate rearward and disconnect wiring connector.
5. Separate mounting plate from switch by removing nut.

HORN SWITCH

Removal and Installation

1. Disconnect the negative battery cable.
2. Remove the horn pad.

NOTE: The horn pad is assembled to the steering wheel by either screws or clips. Check the steering wheel spokes for screws through the spokes and into the pad. If none are used, the pad can be snapped off with the use of a non-marring wooden type tool. Exercise caution to avoid damage to the covered pad.

3. Remove the contact assembly and all other related components.
4. If the vehicle is equipped with tilt and telescopic steering column, remove the lock lever and plate.
5. Installation is the reverse of the removal procedure.

MULTI-FUNCTION SWITCH

Removal and Installation

1. Disconnect the negative battery cable. Remove the steering wheel.
2. It may be necessary to loosen the two column mounting nuts and remove the four bracket-to-mast jacket screws, then separate the bracket from the mast jacket to allow the connector clip on the ignition switch to be pulled out of the column assembly.
3. Disconnect the washer/wiper switch lower connector.

19-13

SECTION 19

OLDSMOBILE
CUTLASS • DELTA 88 • CUSTOM CRUISER • OLDS 98 • HURST OLDS

4. Remove the screws attaching the column housing to the mast jacket. Be sure to note the position of the dimmer switch actuator rod for reassembly in the same position. Remove the column housing and switch as an assembly.

NOTE: The tilt and travel columns have a removable plastic cover on the column housing. This provides access to the wiper switch without removing the entire column housing.

5. Turn upside down and use a drift to remove the pivot pin from the washer/wiper switch. Remove the switch.
6. Place the switch into position in the housing and install the pivot pin.
7. Position the housing onto the mast jacket and attach by installing the screws. Install the dimmer switch actuator rod in the same position as noted earlier. Check switch operation.
8. Reconnect lower end of switch assembly.
9. Install remaining components in reverse order of removal. Be sure to attach column mounting bracket in original position.

WINDSHIELD WIPER MOTOR

Removal and Installation

1. Disconnect the negative battery cable.
2. Raise the hood and remove the cowl screen.
3. Loosen the transmission drive link to crank arm retaining bolts. Remove the drive link from the motor crank arm.
4. Disconnect the electrical wiring and the washer hoses from the motor assembly.
5. Remove the motor retaining screws. Remove the windshield wiper motor while guiding the crank arm through the hole.
6. Installation is the reverse of the removal procedure. The motor must be in the park position before assembling the crank arm to the drive link.

WIPER LINKAGE/TRANSMISSION

Removal and Installation

1. Disconnect the negative battery cable.
2. Raise the hood and remove the cowl vent screen. Remove both wiper arms and blade assemblies.
3. Loosen, but do not remove, the retaining nuts securing the transmission drive link to the motor crank arm.
4. Disconnect the transmission drive link from the motor crank arm. Remove the transmission to body retaining screws.
5. Remove the transmission and linkage assembly by guiding it through the plenum chamber opening or to the left side under the dash panel extension.
6. Installation is the reverse of the removal procedure. Be sure to seal all broken seams and cut welds with body caulk.
7. Check wiper operation, pattern and park position.

Instrument Panel

INSTRUMENT CLUSTER

Removal and Installation

88 AND 98

1. Disconnect the negative battery cable. Slide steering column collar up steering column.
2. Pull steering column trim cover rearward to remove. It is snapped into place.
3. Remove screws attaching gauge cluster to left hand trim cover.
4. Pull gauge cluster rearward far enough to reach behind it and disconnect gage wiring connectors and both lamp sockets.
5. Remove gauge cluster.
6. Remove trip odometer knob, if equipped.
7. Remove screws attaching speedometer lens to cluster carrier. Remove speedometer lens.
8. Remove screws attaching face plate and adapter plate to cluster carrier. Remove both plates.
9. Remove headlamp switch knob by depressing retaining clip with a small suitable tool while pulling on knob rearward.
10. Remove screws attaching right hand trim cover to cluster carrier.
11. Remove right hand trim cover rearward to remove. Trim cover is held in place by clips.
12. Remove screws attaching speedometer to cluster carrier.

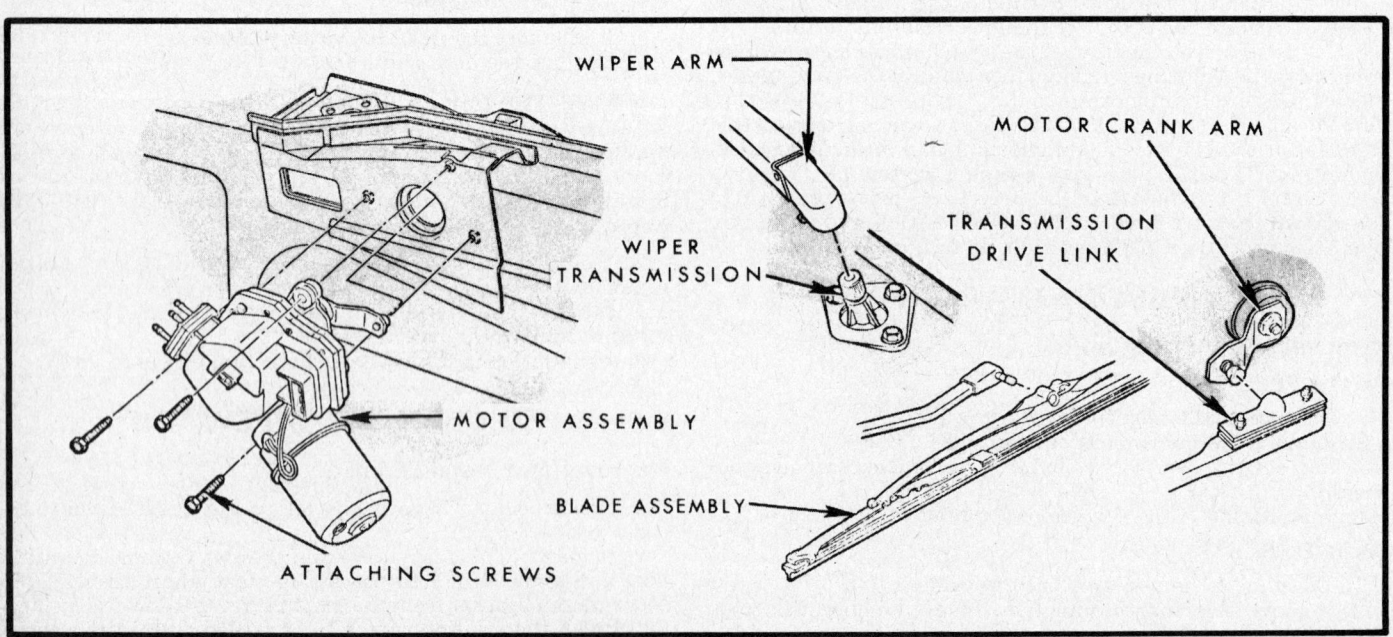

Windshield wiper motor installation—typical (© General Motors Corp.)

OLDSMOBILE

CUTLASS • DELTA 88 • CUSTOM CRUISER • OLDS 98 • HURST OLDS

SECTION 19

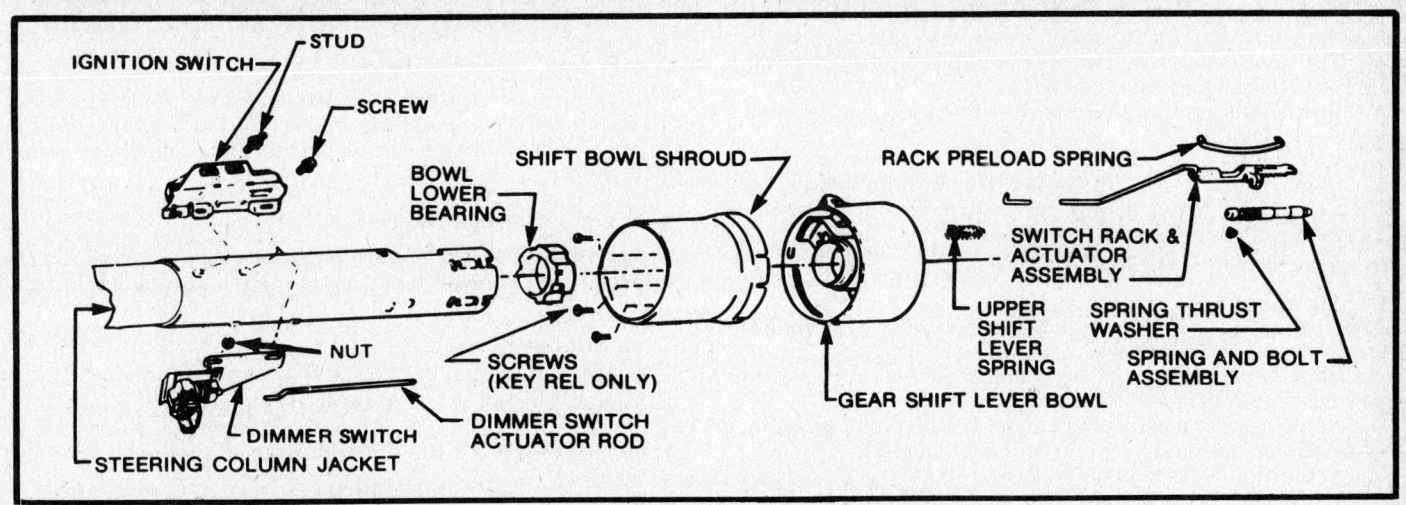

Ignition and dimmer switch installation on the lower steering column
(© General Motors Corporation)

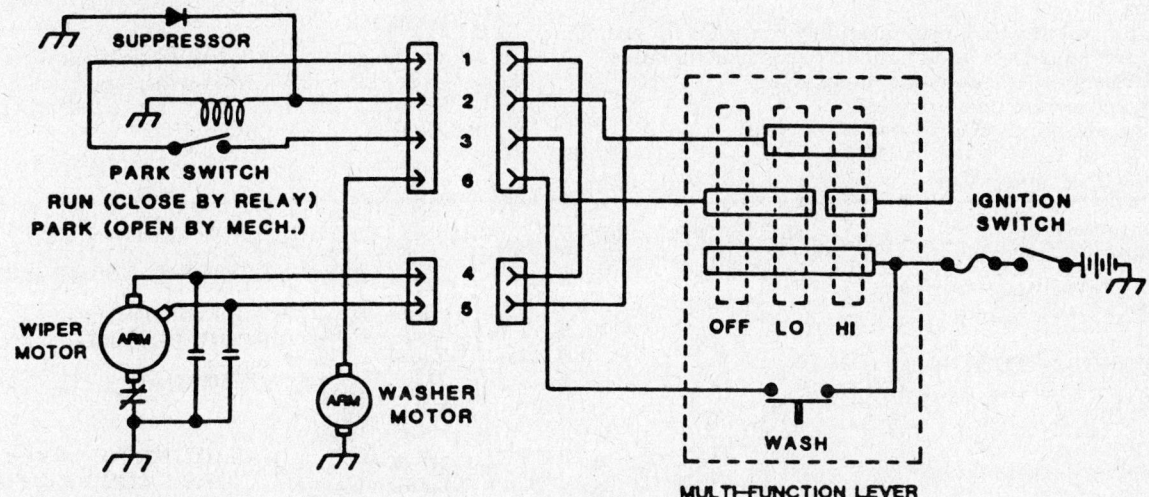

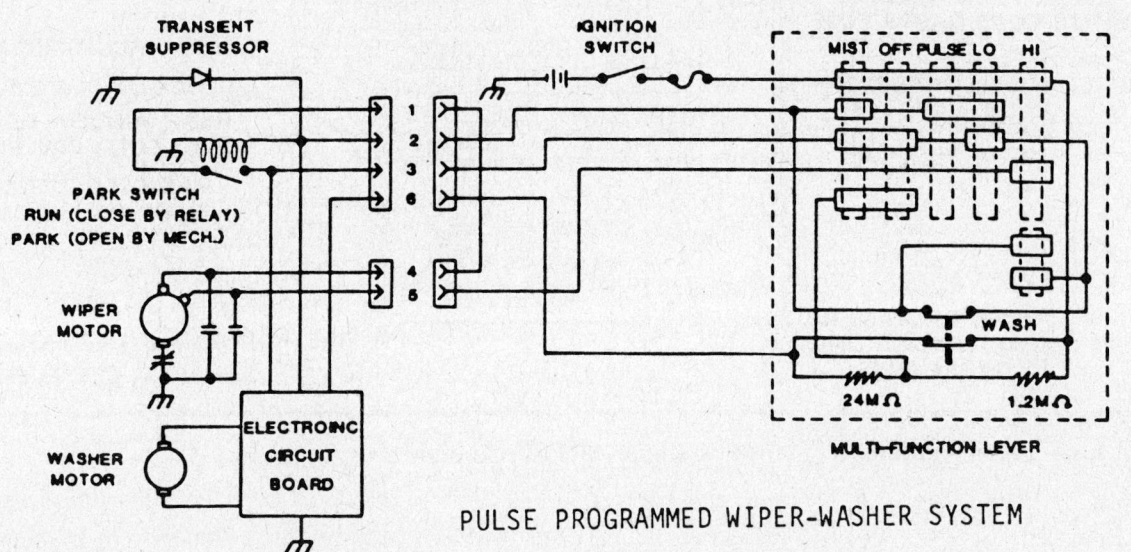

Electrical schematic of standard and pulse wiper circuits (© General Motors Corp.)

SECTION 19

OLDSMOBILE
CUTLASS • DELTA 88 • CUSTOM CRUISER • OLDS 98 • HURST OLDS

13. Disconnect speedometer cable end at transmission or at transducer on vehicles equipped with cruise control.
14. Pull speedometer rearward far enough to reach behind it and release speedometer cable clip.
15. Remove screw attaching speed sensor pickup to speedometer head, if equipped.
16. Remove speedometer.
17. Remove instrument cluster lamps by pulling straight out.
18. Remove screws attaching gas gage to cluster carrier.
19. Pull gas gauge rearward to remove.
20. Installation is the reverse of removal.

CUTLASS

1. Disconnect speedometer cable at transducer on vehicles equipped with cruise control.
2. Remove the right and left hand trim covers by pulling outward. The covers are retained by clips.
3. Remove screws attaching cluster pad to panel adapter.
4. Pull pad assembly away from panel adapter.
5. Remove pad assembly.
6. Remove steering column trim cover.
7. Disconnect shift indicator clip from steering column shift bowl.
8. Remove screws holding instrument cluster to panel adapter.
9. Pull instrument cluster assembly rearward far enough to reach behind cluster and disconnect speedometer cable.
10. Disconnect speed sensor, if equipped.
11. Remove instrument cluster.
12. Installation is the reverse of removal.

ELECTRICAL COMPONENT LOCATION

Fuse Panel

The fuse panel is located on the left side of the vehicle. It is under the instrument panel assembly. In order to gain access to the fuse panel it may be necessary to first remove the under dash padding.

Electronic Control Module

The electronic control module is located on the right side of the vehicle. It is positioned near the right hand kick panel. In order to gain access to the assembly, remove the trim panel.

Turn Signal Flasher

The turn signal flasher is located directly under the steering column of the vehicle. It is secured in place with a plastic retainer. In order to gain access to the component, it may first be necessary to remove the under dash padding panel.

SPEED CONTROLS

Adjustments
ROD–TYPE

Adjust the rod length to minimum slack with the carburetor lever on the slow idle screw and the engine not running. The idle load control must be fully retracted when the retainer is installed.

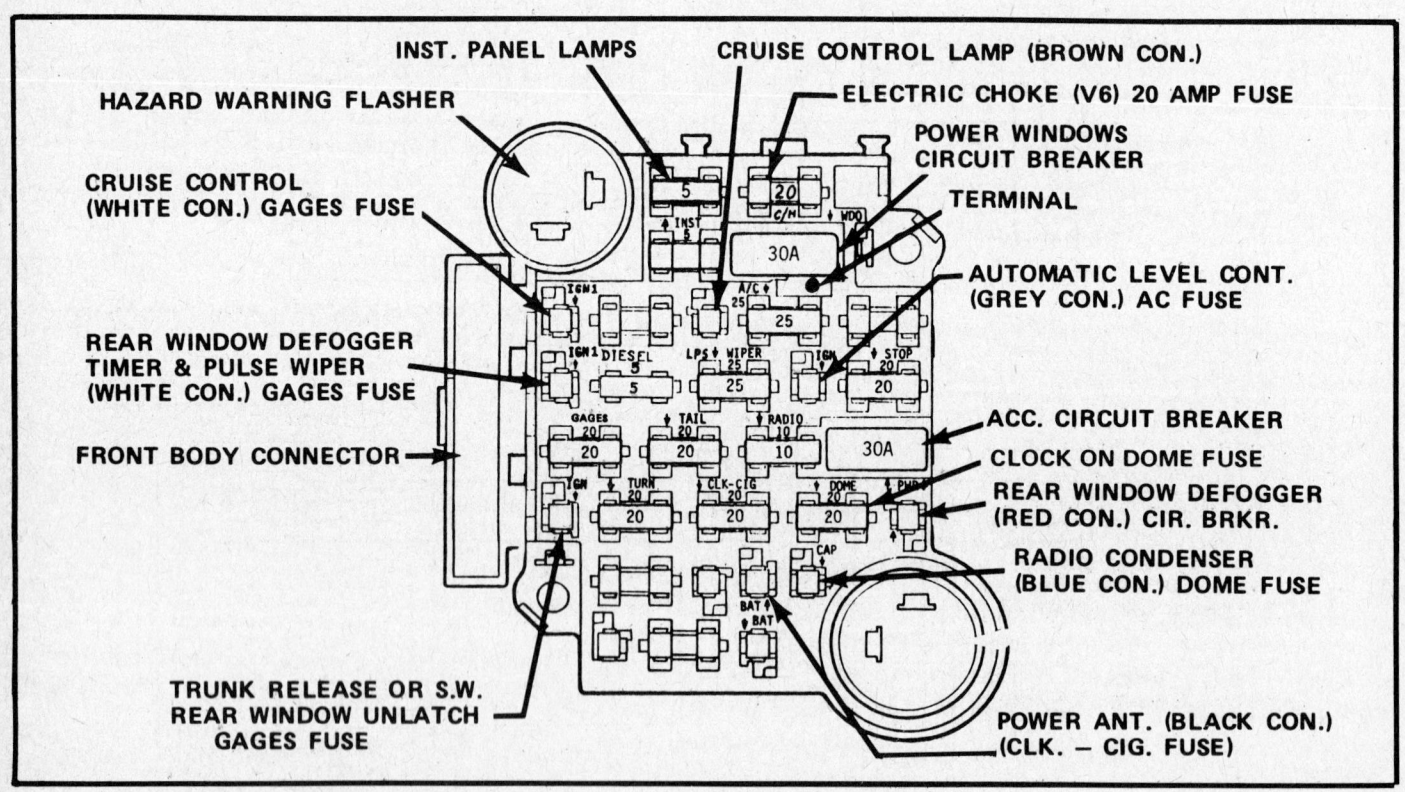

Cutlass fuse panel—others similar (© General Motors Corporation)

OLDSMOBILE
CUTLASS • DELTA 88 • CUSTOM CRUISER • OLDS 98 • HURST OLDS

SECTION 19

COOLING AND HEATER SYSTEMS

WATER PUMP

Removal and Installation

1. Disconnect the negative battery cable. Drain the cooling system.
2. Unfasten the heater, bypass, and lower radiator hoses from the pump.
3. Loosen the drive belts and remove the fan assembly and the four spacer bolts. On vehicles with A/C, remove the fan and clutch assembly.

NOTE: **Keep the fan in an upright position during removal to prevent the silicone fluid from leaking out of the fan clutch.**

4. Remove the alternator, A/C compressor and power steering brackets, if so equipped.
5. Unfasten the bolts which secure the water pump and remove it.
6. Installation is the reverse of the removal procedure.

BLOWER MOTOR

Removal and Installation

1. Disconnect the battery ground.
2. Disconnect the blower wiring.
3. Unbolt and remove the motor.
4. Installation is the reverse of removal. Replace any damaged sealer.

HEATER CORE

Removal and Installation

88 AND 98

1. Disconnect the battery ground. Drain the radiator.
2. Disconnect the blower wiring.
3. Remove the thermostatic switch and diagnostic connector.
4. Remove the right end of the hood seal and the air inlet screen screws.
5. Remove the case-to-firewall screws at the top, upper case-to-lower case screws at the flange and two more at the plenum.
6. Lift the upper case straight up and off. Remove the pipe bracket screws from the case. Disconnect the hoses and position them to prevent spillage.
7. Disconnect and lift out the heater core.
8. Installation is the reverse of removal. Replace any damaged sealer.

CUTLASS

1. Drain the cooling system. Disconnect the negative battery cable.
2. Disconnect the hoses at the core pipes.
3. Remove the retaining bracket and ground strap.
4. Remove the module rubber seal.
5. Remove the module screen.
6. Remove the right windshield wiper arm.
7. Remove the diagnostic connector, high blower relay and thermostatic switch mounting screws.
8. Disconnect all electrical connections at the module.
9. Remove the module top cover.
10. Lift out the core.
11. Installation is the reverse of removal. Replace all insulation.

HEATER A/C CONTROL AND FAN SWITCH ASSEMBLY

Removal and Installation

CUTLASS

1. Disconnect the negative battery cable.
2. Remove the instrument panel lower trim cover.
3. Remove the control mounting screws. Pull the control out

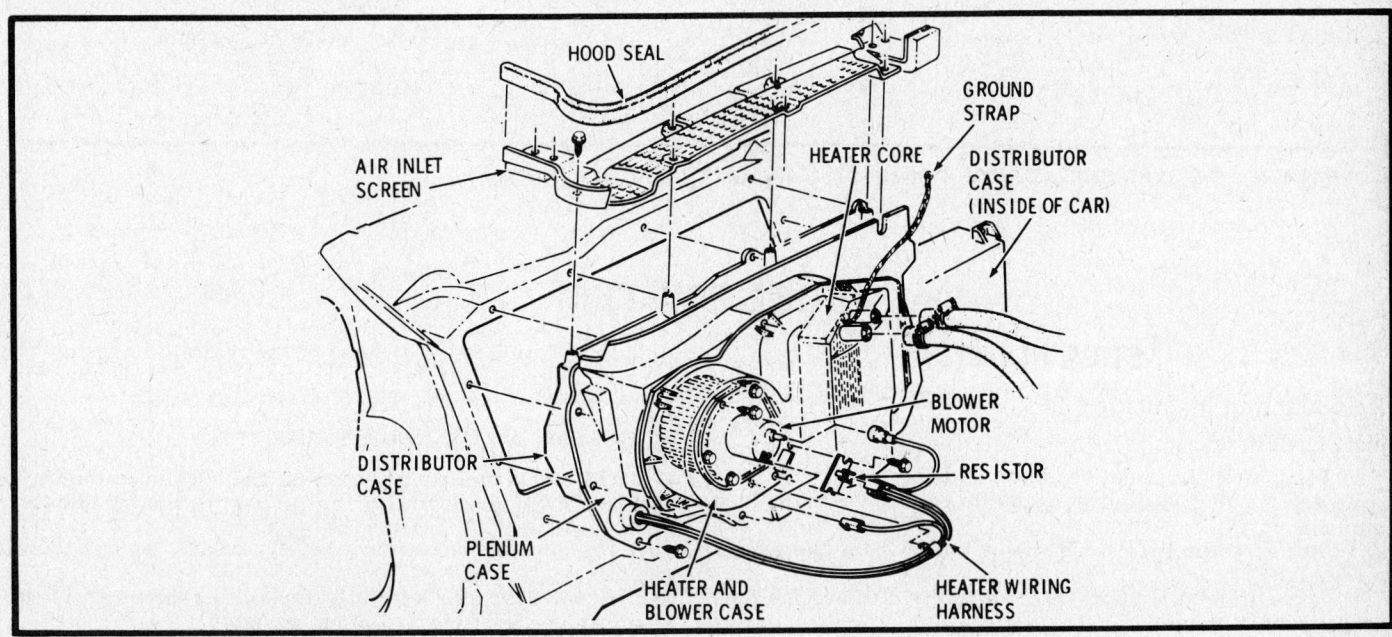

Heater module mounting—88 and 98 models (© General Motors Corporation)

SECTION 19 OLDSMOBILE
CUTLASS • DELTA 88 • CUSTOM CRUISER • OLDS 98 • HURST OLDS

far enough and disconnect all the electrical connectors, vacuum lines and cables.

4. Remove the control from the vehicle.
5. Installation is the reverse of the removal procedure.

DELTA 88 AND 98

1. Disconnect the negative battery cable.
2. Remove the right hand trim panel.
3. Remove the heater and A/C control to cluster carrier attaching screws.
4. Pull the control assembly rearward and disconnect the lamp socket, wiring connectors, cables and vacuum lines.
5. Remove the control from the vehicle.
6. Installation is the reverse of the removal procedure.

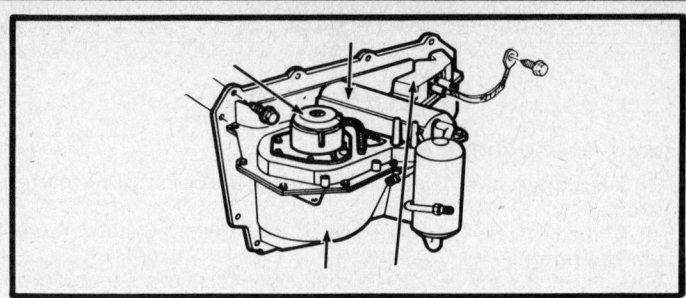

Heater module mounting — Cutlass
(© General Motors Corporation)

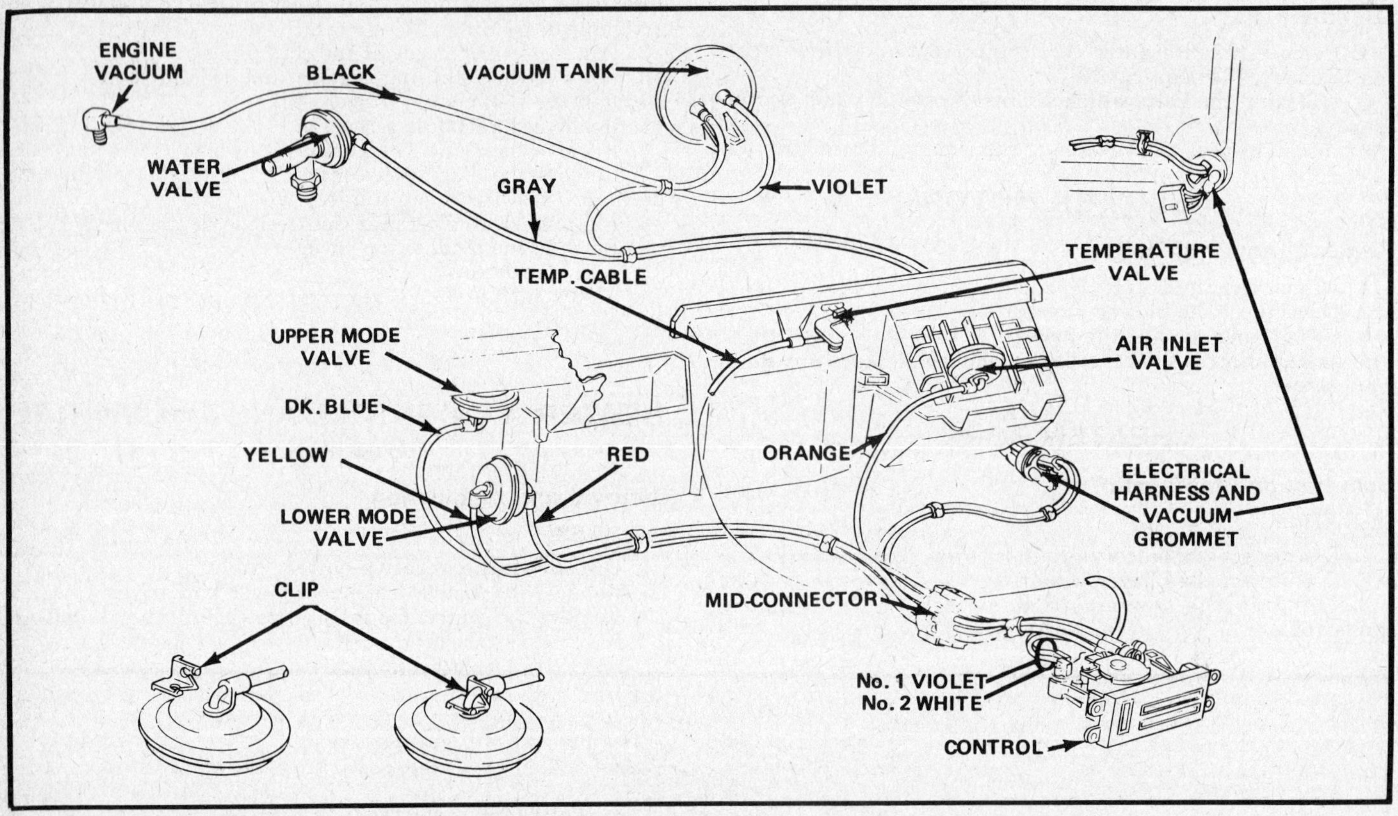

Heater and A/C vacuum control hoses (© General Motors Corporation)

FUEL SYSTEM

FUEL PUMP

Removal and Installation

MECHANICAL

1. Disconnect the negative battery cable.
2. Remove all components in order to gain access to the fuel pump.
3. Remove the inlet and outlet hoses from the pump assembly.
4. Remove the fuel pump retaining bolts. Remove the fuel pump from the engine.
5. Discard the fuel pump gasket. Scrape the block gasket surface before installing the fuel pump.
6. Installation is the reverse of the removal procedure. Be sure to correctly install the fuel pump push rod and mounting plate, if used.

ELECTRIC–V6 DIESEL ENGINE

NOTE: The fuel pump used on the V6 diesel engine is located at the front of the engine next to the fuel heater.

1. Disconnect the negative battery cable. Remove the air cleaner.
2. Remove the inlet and outlet fuel lines. Disconnect all electrical connectors from the pump assembly.
3. Remove the fuel pump retaining bolts. Remove the fuel pump from its mounting on the engine.

4. Installation is the reverse of the removal procedure. Be sure to torque the retaining bolts to 18 ft. lbs.

CARBURETOR

Adjustments

CHECKING CHOKE–HOT AIR TYPE

1. With parking brake applied, drive wheels blocked, transmission in park or neutral, start engine and allow engine to warm up, visually checking to be certain choke valve opens fully.
2. If choke valve fails to open fully, momentarily touch choke housing and hot air inlet pipe or hose to determine if sufficient heat is reaching the choke coil.

NOTE: The choke housing and hot air inlet pipe or hose are "hot" to the touch. Use care to prevent burning of hands.

3. If choke housing and/or heat inlet are cool to the touch, check for loss of vacuum to the housing, restricted heat inlet in the choke housing or choke heat pipe, collapsed or deteriorated heat inlet hose, or restricted passages in the manifold choke heat stove.
4. Replace or correct as necessary.

CHECKING CHOKE–ELECTRIC TYPE

NOTE: This test should be performed between 60 and 80 degrees F.

1. Allow the engine to cool so that when the throttle is opened slightly, the choke blade fully closes.
2. Start the engine and determine a time for the choke blade to reach the full open position.
3. If the choke blade fails to open fully after 3.5 minutes, check the voltage at the choke heater connection.
4. If the voltage is approximately 12–15 volts, replace the electric choke unit.
5. If the voltage is low or zero, check all wires and connections. If any connections in the oil pressure switch circuitry are faulty, or if pressure switch is failed open, the oil warning light will be on with the engine running. Repair wires or connectors as required.
6. If the problem is still not corrected, replace the oil pressure switch. No gasket is used between the choke cover and the choke housing due to grounding requirements.

Computer Command Control System (CCC)

MIXTURE CONTROL

The Computer Command Control System provides precise control of carburetor air/fuel mixtures during all ranges of engine operation. Because of this System control, the below listed mixture control adjustment procedures are to be used if required. The previously used propane enrichment or lean drop methods of idle mixture adjustment may not be used when adjusting carburetors used with this system because system control will change air/fuel mixtures to lean or rich as the mixture needles are adjusted rich or lean respectively.

The computer command control system is sensitive to any change in mixture control adjustment which, if improperly set, can impair the ability of the system to maintain precise control of air/fuel mixtures. Plugs are installed in the carburetor air horn and over the idle mixture needles in the throttle body to seal the factory settings. For this reason, the mixture control adjustment points should never be changed from the original factory setting.

However, if in diagnosis the system indicates the carburetor to be the cause of a driver performance complaint or emissions failure or critical parts such as air horn, float bowl, or throttle body are replaced, then the plugs may be removed and mixture control adjustments made, carefully following factory recommended procedures. After adjustment, replacement plugs (supplied in applicable service kits) must be installed.

MIXTURE CONTROL

Checking Mixture Control Solenoid Travel

1. Before proceeding, it will be necessary to modify float gauge J–9789–130, BT7720, or equivalent (used to externally check float level setting) by filing or grinding sufficient material off the gauge to allow insertion down the vertical vent ("D" shaped hole in the air horn casting next to the idle air bleed valve cover).
2. Check that gauge freely enters "D" vent hole and does not bind. The gauge will be used to determine total mixture control solenoid travel.
3. With engine off, air cleaner removed, measure mixture control solenoid travel as follows:
    a. Insert modified float gauge down "D" shaped vent hole. Press down on gauge and release, observing that gauge moves freely and does not bind. With gauge released (solenoid up position), reading at eye level, record mark on gauge that lines up with top of air horn casting (upper edge).
    b. Lightly press down on gauge until bottomed (solenoid down position). Record the results of the mark on gauge that lines up with top of air horn casting.
    c. Subtract gauge up dimension (item "a") from gauge down position (item "b") and record difference. The difference in dimensions is total solenoid travel.
    d. If total solenoid travel (difference in item "c") is not within $2/32$–$6/32$ in., make mixture control solenoid adjustments as noted below. If difference is within the above specifications, proceed to idle air bleed valve adjustment.

Mixture Control Solenoid Adjustments

1. Remove air horn, mixture control solenoid plunger, air horn gasket and plastic filler block, using normal service procedures.
2. Remove throttle side metering rod. Install mixture control solenoid gauging tool J–33815–1 and BT–8253–A, or equivalent over throttle side metering jet rod guide and temporarily reinstall the solenoid plunger into the solenoid body.
3. Holding the solenoid plunger in the down position, use tool J–28696–10 and BT–7928, or equivalent, to turn lean mixture (solenoid) screw counterclockwise until the plunger breaks contact with the gauging tool. Turn slowly clockwise until the plunger just contacts the gauging tool. The adjustment is correct when the solenoid plunger is contacting both the solenoid stop and the gauging tool.

NOTE: If the total difference in adjustment required less than ¾ turn of the lean mixture (solenoid) screw, the original setting was within the manufacturer's specifications.

4. Remove solenoid plunger and gauging tool, and reinstall metering rod and plastic filler block.
5. Invert air horn and remove rich mixture stop screw and (if used) the rich authority adjusting spring from bottom side of air horn, using tool J–28696–4 and BT7967A or equivalent.
6. Remove lean mixture screw plug and the rich mixture stop screw plug from air horn, using a suitable sized punch.
7. Reinstall rich mixture stop screw and (if used) the rich authority adjusting spring in air horn and bottom lightly, then back screw out ¼ turn.

8. Reinstall air horn gasket, mixture control solenoid plunger and air horn to carburetor.
9. Insert external float gauge in vent hole and, with tool J–28696–10 and BT–7928, or equivalent, adjust rich mixture stop screw to obtain $4/32$ in. total plunger travel.
10. With solenoid plunger travel correctly set, install the plugs (supplied in service kits) in the air horn.
11. To install the lean mixture plug, position it hollow end down into the access hole of the lean mixture screw (solenoid), and use a suitably sized punch to drive plug into the air horn until the top of the plug is even with the lower plug.
12. To install the rich mixture stop screw, position it hollow end down, over the rich mixture stop screw access hole, and drive plug into place so that the top of the plug is $1/16$ in. below the surface of the air horn casting.

IDLE MIXTURE AND SPEED ADJUSTMENT PROCEDURES

Idle mixture screws are sealed with hardened caps covering the screws during original equipment production. These plugs are not to be removed unless required for cleaning or part replacement.

Before suspecting the carburetor as the cause of poor engine performance or rough idle, check ignition system including distributor, timing, spark plugs and wires. Inspect air cleaner, evaporative emission system, EFE system, PCV system, EGR system and engine compression. Also inspect intake manifold, vacuum hoses and connections for leaks and check torque of carburetor mounting bolts.

In the case of major carburetor repair, throttle body replacement or high idle CO as indicated by state or local emission inspection, idle mixture may be adjusted. Adjusting mixture by other than the proper method may violate emissions.

IDLE AIR BLEED VALVE

Adjustment

1. Position the parking brake and block the drive wheels. Disconnect and plug the hoses as directed on the vehicle emission control label.
2. Check and adjust ignition timing. Connect a dwell meter to the carburetor mixture solenoid and a tachometer to the engine's distributor electrical system.
3. Start engine and with transmission in park or neutral, run engine at idle until fully warm and a varying dwell is noted on the dwell meter (engine now in closed loop operation). It is essential that the engine is operated for a sufficient length of time to ensure that the engine coolant sensor and the oxygen sensor in the exhaust, are at full operational temperature.
4. Check engine idle speed and compare to specifications on the underhood Emission Label. If necessary, adjust curb idle speed. On models with idle speed control (ISC) or idle load compensator (ILC), idle speeds are controlled by signals from the computer.
5. With engine idling in drive (neutral for manual transmission), observe dwell reading on the 6 cylinder scale. If varying within the 10–50° range, adjustment is correct. If not, perform the following.
6. Remove the idle air bleed valve cover. If the cover is staked in place, pry it off using a suitable tool.
7. If the cover is riveted, cover the internal bowl vents to the bleed valve with masking tape.
8. Cover carburetor air intakes with masking tape to prevent metal chips from entering carburetor and engine.
9. Carefully align a No. 35 (0.110 in.) drill bit on one of the steel rivet heads holding the idle air bleed valve cover in place. Drill only enough to remove rivet head. Drill the remaining rivet head located on the other side of the tower. Use a drift and small hammer to drive the remainder of the rivets out of the idle air bleed valve tower in the air horn casting. Use care in drilling to prevent damage to the air horn casting.
10. Lift out cover over the idle air bleed valve and remove the rivet pieces from inside the idle air bleed valve tower.
11. Using shop air, carefully blow out any remaining chips from inside the tower. Discard cover after removal. A missing cover indicates that the idle air bleed valve setting has been changed from its original factory setting.
12. With cover removed, look for presence (or absence) of a letter identification on top of idle air bleed valve.
13. If an identifying letter appears on top of the valve proceed to the procedure outlined under type two. If an identifying letter does not appear on the top of the valve proceed to the procedure outlined under type one.

TYPE ONE

1. Presetting the idle air bleed valve to a gauge dimension if the idle air bleed valve was serviced prior to on-vehicle adjustment.
   a. Install idle air bleed valve gauging tool J–33815–2, BT–8253–B, or equivalent, in throttle side "D" shaped vent hole in the air horn casting. The upper end of the tool should be positioned over the open cavity next to the idle air bleed valve.
   b. While holding the gauging tool down lightly, so that the solenoid plunger is against the solenoid stop, adjust the idle air bleed valve so that the gauging tool will pivot over and just contact the top of the valve. The valve is now preset for on-vehicle adjustment.
   c. Remove the gauging tool.
2. Adjusting the idle air bleed valve on the vehicle to obtain correct dwell reading.
   a. Start engine and allow it to reach normal operating temperature.
   b. While idling in drive (neutral for manual transmission), use a suitable tool to slowly turn valve counterclockwise or clockwise, until the dwell reading varies with the 25–35° range, attempting to be as close to 30° as possible. Perform this step carefully. The air bleed valve is very sensitive and should be turned in $1/8$ turn increments only.
   c. If, after performing Steps a and b above, the dwell reading does not vary and is not within the 25–35° range, it will be necessary to remove the plugs and to adjust the idle mixture needles.
3. Idle mixture needle plug removal, only if necessary.
   a. Remove the carburetor from the engine, following normal service procedures, to gain access to the plugs covering the idle mixture needles.
   b. Invert carburetor and drain fuel into a suitable container.
   c. Place carburetor on a suitable holding fixture, with manifold side up. Use care to avoid damaging linkage, tubes, and parts protruding from air horn.
   d. Make two parallel cuts in the throttle body, one on each side of the locator points beneath the idle mixture needle plug (manifold side), with a hacksaw.
   e. The cuts should reach down to the steel plug, but should not extend more than $1/8$ in. beyond the locator points. The distance between the saw cuts depends on the size of the punch to be used.
   f. Place a flat punch near the ends of the saw marks in the throttle body. Hold the punch at a 45° angle and drive it into the throttle body until the casting breaks away, exposing the steel plug.
   g. The hardened plug will break, rather than remaining intact. It is not necessary to remove the plug in one piece, but remove the loose pieces.
   h. Repeat this procedure with the other mixture needle.
4. Setting the idle mixture needles (if necessary) where correct dwell reading could not be obtained with idle air bleed valve adjustment.
   a. Using tool J–29030, BT–7610B, or equivalent, turn

both idle mixture needles clockwise until they are lightly seated, then turn each mixture needle counterclockwise the number of turns specified.
  b. Reinstall carburetor on engine using a new flange mounting gasket, but do not install air cleaner and gasket at this time.
  5. Readjusting idle air bleed valve to finalize correct dwell reading.
(Only necessary if idle mixture needles required setting in Step 4, above).
  a. Start engine and run until fully warm and repeat "Adjusting the Air Bleed Valve", Step 2 above.
  b. If unable to set dwell to 25–35° and the dwell is below 25°, turn both mixture needles counterclockwise an additional turn. If dwell is above 35°, turn both mixture needles clockwise an additional turn. Readjust idle air bleed valve to obtain dwell limits.
  c. After adjustments are complete, seal the idle mixture needle openings in the throttle body, using silicone sealant, RTV rubber, or equivalent. The sealer is required to discourage unnecessary adjustment of the setting, and to prevent fuel vapor loss in that area.
  d. On vehicles WITHOUT a carburetor-mounted idle speed control or idle load compensator, adjust curb idle speed if necessary.
  e. Check and only if necessary, adjust the fast idle speed as described on emission control information label.

TYPE TWO

1. Setting the idle air bleed valve to a gauge dimension.
  a. Install air bleed valve gauging tool J–33815–2, BT–8253–B, or equivalent in throttle side "D" shaped vent hole in the air horn casting. The upper end of the tool should be positioned over the open cavity next to the idle air bleed valve.
  b. While holding the gauge tool down lightly, so that the solenoid plunger is against the solenoid stop, adjust the idle air bleed valve so that the gauging tool will pivot over and just contact the top of the valve.
  c. The valve is now set properly. No further adjustment of the valve is necessary.
  d. Remove the gauging tool.
2. Adjusting the idle mixture needles on the vehicle to obtain correct dwell readings.
  a. Remove idle mixture needle plugs, following instructions in information given for Type One.
  b. Using tool J–29030–B, BT–7610–B, or equivalent, turn each idle mixture needle clockwise until lightly seated, then turn each mixture needle counterclockwise three turns.
  c. Reinstall carburetor on engine, using a new flange mounting gasket, but do not install air cleaner or gasket at this time.
  d. Start engine and allow it to reach normal operating temperature.
  e. While idling in drive (neutral for manual transmission), adjust both mixture needles equally, in $1/8$ turn increments, until dwell reading varies within the 25–35° range, attempting to be as close to 30° as possible. If reading is too low, turn mixture needles counterclockwise. If reading is too high, turn mixture needles clockwise. Allow time for dwell reading to stabilize after each adjustment.
  f. After adjustments are complete, seal the idle mixture needle openings in the throttle body, using silicone sealant, RTV rubber, or equivalent. The sealer is required to discourage unnecessary readjustment of the setting and to prevent fuel vapor loss in that area.
  g. On vehicles without a carburetor-mounted idle speed control or idle load compensator, adjust curb idle speed if necessary.
  h. Check and if necessary, adjust fast idle speed, as described on the emission control information label.

THROTTLE POSITION SENSOR (TPS)

Adjustment

NOTE: The plug covering the TPS adjustment screw is used to provide a tamper-resistant design and retain the factory setting during vehicle operation. Do not remove the plug unless diagnosis indicates that the TPS Sensor is not adjusted correctly or it is necessary to replace the air horn assembly, float bowl, TPS Sensor to TPS adjustment screw. This is a critical adjustment that must be performed accurately and carefully to ensure proper vehicle performance and control of exhaust emissions.

1. If necessary to adjust the TPS sensor:
a. Using a 5mm ($5/64$ in.) drill, drill hole in aluminum plug covering TPS adjustment screw, drilling only enough to start self-tapping screw (approximate drilling depth $1/16 - 1/8$ in.).
  b. Use care in drilling to prevent damage to adjustment screw head.
  c. Start a No. 8 1/2 in. long self-tapping screw in drilled hole in plug, turning screw in only enough to ensure good thread engagement in hole.
  d. Placing a wide-blade section of screwdriver between screw head and air horn casting, pry against screw head to remove plug. Discard plug.
  e. Using tool J–28696, BT7967A or equivalent, remove screw.
  f. Connect digital voltmeter (such as J–29125) or equivalent from TPS connector center terminal (B) to bottom terminal (C). (Jumpers for access can be made using terminals 12014836 and 12014837.)

NOTE: After TPS screw is adjusted, a new plug should be installed. If a new plug is not available, a locking type of sealer should be placed on the screw threads to prevent movement of the screw after installation.

  g. With ignition on, engine stopped, reinstall TPS adjustment screw and with tool J–28696, BT7967A, or equivalent turn screw to obtain specified voltage at specified throttle position with A/C off.
  h. After adjustment, install new plug (supplied in service kits) in air horn, driving plug in place until flush with raised pump lever boss on casting.

IDLE LOAD COMPENSATOR (ILC)

Adjustment

1. Prepare vehicle for adjustments. Refer to the Emission label for specific instructions.
2. Connect tachometer (distributor side of TACH filter, if used).
3. Remove air cleaner and plug vacuum hose to thermal vacuum valve (TVV).
4. Disconnect and plug vacuum hose to EGR.
5. Disconnect and plug vacuum hose to canister purge port.
6. Disconnect and plug vacuum hose to ILC.
7. Back out idle stop screw on carburetor 3 turns.
8. Turn A/C "OFF".

--- **CAUTION** ---
Before starting engine, place transmission in PARK, set parking brake, and block drive wheels.

9. With engine running (engine warm, choke off), transmission in drive and ILC plunger fully extended (no vacuum applied), using tool J–29607, BT–8022 or equivalent, adjust plunger to obtain 750 rpm E2MC models, 725 rpm E4MC models. Jam nut on plunger must be held with wrench to prevent damage to guide tabs.
10. Remove plug from vacuum hose, reconnect hose to ILC

19-21

OLDSMOBILE
CUTLASS • DELTA 88 • CUSTOM CRUISER • OLDS 98 • HURST OLDS

and observe idle speed. Idle speed should be 500 rpm in drive.

11. If rpm in Step 10 is correct, proceed to Step 13. No further adjustment of the ILC is necessary.

12. If rpm in Step 10 is not correct:

   a. Stop engine and remove the ILC. Plug vacuum hose to ILC.

   b. With the ILC removed, remove the rubber cap from the center outlet tube and then remove the metal plug (IF USED) from this same tube.

   c. Install ILC on carburetor and re-attach throttle return spring and any other related parts removed during disassembly. Remove plug from vacuum hose and reconnect hose to ILC.

   d. Using a spare rubber cap with hole punched to accept a .090 in. (3/32 in.) hex key wrench, install cap on center outlet tube (to seal against vacuum loss) and insert wrench through cap to engage adjusting screw inside tube. Start engine and turn adjusting screw with wrench to obtain 550 rpm in drive. Turning the adjusting screw will change the idle speed approximately 75–100 rpm for each complete turn. Turning the screw counterclockwise will increase the engine speed.

   e. Remove wrench and cap (with hole) from center outlet tube and install new rubber cap.

   f. Engine running, transmission in drive, observe idle speed. If a final adjustment is required, it will be necessary to repeat Steps 12a–12e.

13. After adjustment of the ILC plunger, measure distance from the jam nut to tip of the plunger, dimension must not exceed 1 in. (25mm).

14. Disconnect and plug vacuum hose to ILC. Apply vacuum source such as hand vacuum pump J–23768, BT–7517 or equivalent to ILC vacuum inlet tube to fully retract the plunger.

15. Adjust the idle stop on the carburetor float bowl to obtain 500 rpm in drive.

16. Place transmission in park and stop engine.

17. Remove plug from vacuum hose and install hose in ILC vacuum inlet tube.

18. Remove plugs and reconnect all vacuum hoses.

19. Install the air cleaner and gasket.

20. Remove block from drive wheels.

DIFFERENTIAL VACUUM DELAY VALVE (DVDV)

Adjustment

The DVDV is located in the vacuum line between the idle load compensator (ILC) and the vacuum source. It is used on all 5.0L engines (engine code Y).

The DVDV acts as cushioning device by slightly delaying the operation of the ILC until a constant vacuum change has occurred. Without the DVDV, the ILC would react too quickly to changes in engine vacuum, causing a surging condition or if too restrictive to vacuum flow, it would cause a stalling or run-on condition.

1. To check the operation of the DVDV, install a vacuum gage with a "T" into the hose from the DVDV to the ILC.

2. Install a vacuum pump to port 1 of the DVDV and apply 17.8 in. Hg. while watching the other vacuum gauge.

3. It should take six to nine seconds for the vacuum to rise to 16.9 in. Hg.

4. Remove the vacuum gauge with "T", install the vacuum pump to port 2 and leave port 1 open.

5. Air should flow through the valve after 5 in. Hg. is applied.

IDLE SPEED CONTROL (ISC)

Adjustment

The idle speed control (ISC) is controlled by the electronic control module (ECM), which has the desired idle speed programmed in its memory. The ECM controls the idle speed by moving the idle speed control stem in or out. This automatically adjusts the throttle to hold an idle rpm independent of the engine loads.

An integral part of the ISC is the throttle contact switch. The position of the switch determines whether or not the ISC should control idle speed. When the throttle lever is resting against the ISC plunger, the switch contacts are closed, at which time the ECM moves the ISC to the programmed idle speed. When the throttle lever is not contacting the ISC plunger, the switch contacts are open; the ECM stops sending idle speed commands and the driver controls engine speed.

NOTE: Before starting engine, place transmission selector lever in park or neutral, set parking brake, and block drive wheels.

When a new ISC assembly is installed, a base (minimum authority) and high (maximum authority) rpm speed check must be performed and adjustments made as required. These adjustments limit the low and high rpm speeds to the ECM. When making a low and high speed adjustment, the low speed adjustment is always made first. DO NOT use the ISC plunger to adjust curb idle speed as the idle speed is controlled by the ECM.

---------- CAUTION ----------

Do not disconnect or connect ISC connector with ignition on as damage to the ECM may occur.

---

1. Connect tachometer (distributor side of tach filter, if used).

2. Connect dwell meter to mixture control (M/C) solenoid dwell lead. Remember to set dwell meter on the six cylinder scale, regardless of the engine being tested.

3. Turn A/C off.

4. Start engine and run until stabilized by entering "closed loop" (dwell meter needle starts to vary).

5. Turn ignition off.

6. Unplug connector from ISC motor.

7. Fully retract ISC plunger by applying 12 volts DC (battery voltage) to terminal "C" of the ISC motor connection and ground lead to terminal "D" of the ISC motor connection. It may be necessary to install jumper leads from the ISC motor in order to make proper connections.

NOTE: Do not apply battery voltage to motor longer than necessary to retract ISC plunger. Prolonged contact will damage motor. Also, never connect voltage source across terminals "A" and "B" as damage to the internal throttle contact switch will result.

8. Start engine and wait until dwell meter needle starts to vary, indicating "closed loop" operation.

9. With parking brake applied and drive wheels blocked, place transmission in Drive (Neutral, manual transmission models).

10. With ISC plunger fully retracted, adjust carburetor base (slow) idle stop screw to the specified rpm (see specifications). ISC plunger should not be left in full retracted position.

11. Place transmission in Park or Neutral and fully extend ISC plunger by applying 12 volts DC to terminal "D" of the ISC motor connection and ground lead to terminal "C" of the ISC motor connection.

NOTE: Never connect voltage source across terminals "A" and "B" as damage to the internal throttle contact switch will result.

12. Manual transmission: Using tool J–29607 or BT–8022 or equivalent, turn ISC plunger to obtain ISC adjustment rpm (maximum authority).

13. Automatic transmission:

   a. With transmission in park, using tool J–29607 or BT–

OLDSMOBILE
CUTLASS • DELTA 88 • CUSTOM CRUISER • OLDS 98 • HURST OLDS

8022 or equivalent, preset ISC plunger to obtain 1500 rpm.

b. With parking brake set and drive wheels blocked, place transmission in drive. Using tool J–29607 or BT–8022 or equivalent, turn ISC plunger to obtain ISC adjustment rpm (maximum authority).

14. Recheck ISC maximum authority adjustment rpm with voltage applied to motor. Motor will ratchet at full extension with power applied.
15. After adjustment of ISC plunger, measure distance from back side of plunger head to ISC nosepiece, Dimension "B". Dimension must not exceed that shown by plunger type as either identified by plunger length or letter identification.
16. Fully retract ISC plunger. Place transmission in park or neutral and turn ignition "Off". Disconnect 12 volt power source, ground lead, tachometer and dwell meter. With ignition "Off", reconnect four terminal harness connector to ISC motor. To prevent internal damage to ISC, apply finger pressure to ISC plunger while retracting.
17. Remove block from drive wheels.

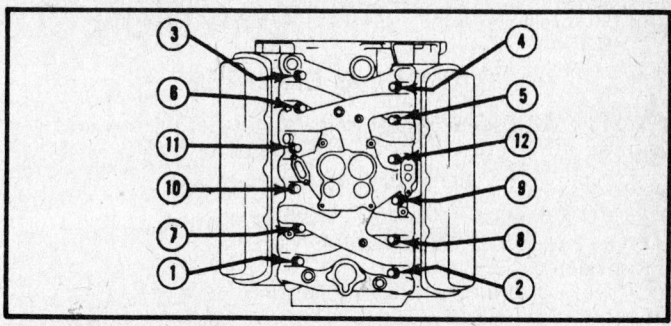

V6 intake manifold torque sequence
(© General Motors Corporation)

CARBURETOR

Removal and Installation

1. Remove air cleaner.
2. Disconnect accelerator linkage.
3. Disconnect transmission detent cable.
4. Disconnect cruise control, if equipped.
5. Disconnect all necessary electrical connectors.
6. Disconnect all necessary vacuum lines.
7. Disconnect fuel line at carburetor inlet.
8. Remove the attaching bolts and remove carburetor.
9. Reverse removal procedure to install.
10. check idle speeds.

INTAKE MANIFOLD

Removal and Installation

GASOLINE ENGINE

1. Disconnect the negative battery cable. Drain the radiator.
2. Remove the air cleaner assembly.
3. Disconnect the upper radiator hose and the heater hose at the manifold.
4. Disconnect the accelerator linkage at the carburetor and the linkage bracket at the manifold. Remove the cruise control chain or cable, if so equipped.
5. Remove the fuel line from the carburetor and the booster vacuum pipe from the manifold.
6. Disconnect and label the transmission vacuum modulator line, idle stop solenoid wire (if so equipped).
7. Disconnect and mark the vacuum hoses at the distributor and the carburetor.
8. Disconnect the coolant bypass hose at the manifold. If required, remove the distributor.
9. On six cylinder models, it may be necessary to remove the distributor cap and wires to gain access to the Torx head bolt. Remove the bolt.
10. Remove the throttle linkage springs.
11. Remove the A/C compressor top bracket, if so equipped.
12. Remove the manifold.

V8 intake manifold Torque sequence
(© General Motors Corporation)

13. Installation is the reverse of the removal procedure.
14. Be sure to use new gaskets or RTV sealant as required.

EXHAUST MANIFOLD

Removal and Installation

1. Disconnect the negative battery cable.
2. Remove all the necessary components in order to gain access to the manifold retaining bolts.
3. Remove the exhaust manifold retaining bolts.
4. Remove the exhaust manifold to exhaust pipe flange retaining bolts.
5. Remove the exhaust manifold from the vehicle. On some vehicles, it may be necessary to raise the engine in order to gain clearance.
6. Installation is the reverse of the removal procedure.

SECTION 19

Oldsmobile
CUTLASS • DELTA 88 • CUSTOM CRUISER • OLDS 98 • HURST OLDS

EMISSION CONTROL SYSTEM

GASOLINE ENGINES

NOTE: All listed components or systems may not appear on all engines.

COMPONENTS AND SYSTEMS

Emission calibrated carburetor
Emission calibrated distributor
Closed positive crankcase ventilation
Catalytic converter
Thermostatic air cleaner (TAC)
Vapor control, canister storage
Exhaust gas recirculation (EGR)
Early fuel evaporation (EFE)
Electric choke
Early fuel evaporation–solenoid (EFE–SOL)
Evaporative emission control (EEC)
Electronic spark control
Oxygen sensor
Computer command control
Air management system
Air control valve (ACV)
Air switching valve (ASV)
Air temperature sensor (ATS)
Back pressure EGR (BPEGR)
Charcoal canister (CAN)
Canister purge (CP)

Coolant temperature sensor (CTS)
Deceleration valve (DV)
EGR control solenoid (EGRCS)
Manifold pressure sensor (MAP)
Pulse air shut off valve (PSV)
Thermal vacuum switch (TVS)
Vacuum pump (VP)
Vacuum sensor (VS)
Vacuum solenoid valve (VSV)

DIESEL ENGINES

NOTE: All listed components on systems may not appear on all diesel engines.

COMPONENTS AND SYSTEMS

EGR vacuum switch (EGRVS)
Vacuum pump (VP)
Exhaust gas recirculation (EGR)
Exhaust pressure regulator (EPR)
Flow control valve
EGR solenoid (EGR–SOL)
EPR solenoid (EPR–SOL)
Transmission vacuum valve (TRV)
Thermal vacuum valve (TVV)
Vacuum regulator valve (VRV)

GASOLINE ENGINE SECTION

For Diesel Engine Services, Refer to the Unit Repair Section.

ENGINE ASSEMBLY

General Motors Parts released a 3.8L V6 Goodwrench engine (part number 25528795, replacing part number 25525217) for 1986 and prior model year usage. Numerous differences exist and must be considered during its installation.

1. A thicker cylinder head gasket is used to improve cylinder head to block sealing.
2. To accommodate the new cylinder head gasket, the block deck height has been lowered approximately 0.038 in. To identify this Goodwrench engine block, a code of "6GW" is stamped next to the three digit julian date on the front of the engine block.
3. New cylinder head bolts are used to improve the clamping of the cylinder head to the block.
4. New, low tension piston ring expanders are used, reducing internal engine friction.
5. Due to the engine changes in the cylinder head area, the Cylinder Head Service Label must be installed as per the instructions provided with the replacement engine. Failure to do so could result in the incorrect usage of parts or service procedures, should they become necessary at a later date.

Removal and Installation
V6 GASOLINE ENGINE

1. Remove the hood.
2. Disconnect battery.
3. Drain coolant into a suitable container.
4. Remove air cleaner.
5. On vehicles equipped with air conditioning, disconnect compressor ground wire from the mounting bracket. Remove the electrical connector from the compressor clutch, remove the compressor to mounting bracket attaching bolts and position the compressor out of the way.
6. Remove fan blade, pulleys and belts.
7. Disconnect radiator and heater hoses from engine.
8. Remove fan shroud assembly.
9. Remove power steering pump to mounting bracket bolts and position pump assembly out of the way.
10. Disconnect fuel pump hoses and plug.
11. Disconnect battery ground cable from engine.
12. Disconnect the vacuum supply hoses that supply all non-engine mounted components with engine vacuum. On vehicles so equipped, the vacuum modulator, load leveler and power brake vacuum hoses should all be disconnected at the engine.
13. Disconnect accelerator cable at carburetor.
14. Disconnect generator, oil and coolant sending unit switch connections at the engine. Remove the alternator.
15. Disconnect engine to body ground strap(s) at engine.
16. Raise the vehicle, disconnect the cable shield from the engine (if so equipped).
17. Disconnect exhaust pipes from exhaust manifolds.
18. Remove lower flywheel or converter cover.
19. Remove flywheel to converter attaching bolts. Scribe chalk mark on the flywheel and converter for reassembly alignment.
20. Remove transmission to engine attaching bolts (automatic transmission).
21. Remove motor mount through bolts and cruise control bracket if equipped.
22. Lower the vehicle and support the automatic transmission.

OLDSMOBILE
CUTLASS • DELTA 88 • CUSTOM CRUISER • OLDS 98 • HURST OLDS
SECTION 19

23. Attach a lifting device to the engine and raise the engine enough so mounting through-bolts can be removed. Make certain wiring harness, vacuum hoses and other parts are free and clear before lifting engine out of the vehicle.
24. Raise engine far enough to clear engine mounts, raise transmission support accordingly and alternately until engine can be disengaged from the transmission and removed.
25. Installation is the reverse of the removal procedure.

V8 GASOLINE ENGINE

1. Drain cooling system.
2. Remove air cleaner and hot air pipe.
3. Remove hood from hinges, mark hood for reassembly.
4. Disconnect battery negative cable at battery and ground wire at inner fender panel. Disconnect engine ground strap, right head to cowl.
5. Disconnect radiator hoses, automatic transmission cooler lines, heater hoses, vacuum hoses, power steering hose bracket from engine, air conditioning compressor with brackets and hoses attached, fuel hose from fuel line, wiring and throttle cable.
6. Remove upper radiator support and radiator.
7. Raise and support the vehicle.
8. Disconnect exhaust pipes at manifold.
9. Remove torque converter cover and the bolts holding converter to flywheel.
10. Remove engine mount bolts or nuts.
11. Remove the transmission to engine retaining bolts on the right side. Remove the starter.
12. Lower the vehicle. Secure lift chain to engine.
13. Place board on top of jack and slightly raise transmission. Remove three left transmission to engine bolts. Remove engine.
14. Installation is the reverse of the removal procedure.

V6 DIESEL ENGINE

1. Drain the cooling system.
2. Remove air cleaner and install cover J—26996 or equivalent.
3. Remove hood from hinges, mark hood for reassembly.
4. Disconnect battery negative cables at batteries and ground wires at inner fender panel. Disconnect engine ground strap, right head to cowl.
5. Disconnect radiator hoses, cooler lines, heater hoses, vacuum hoses, power steering pump hoses at power steering gear, air conditioning compressor with brackets and hoses attached, fuel hoses from fuel pump inlet line and injection pump return line.
6. Disconnect all engine wiring except at starter.
7. Disconnect the throttle cable.
8. Disconnect the transmission T.V. or detent cable at the injection pump and engine brackets.
9. Remove upper radiator support and radiator.
10. Raise the vehicle and support it safely.
11. Disconnect exhaust pipes at manifolds.
12. Remove the torque converter (flywheel) cover and the three torque converter to flywheel bolts.
13. Remove the starter motor.
14. Remove the engine mount through bolts.
15. Remove the three engine to transmission bolts on the right side.
16. Lower the vehicle.
17. Secure an engine lift chain to the engine.
18. Place a board on top of a jack and slightly raise the transmission. Remove the three left transmission to engine bolts. Remove engine.
19. Installation is the reverse of the removal procedure.

V8 DIESEL ENGINE

1. Drain cooling system.
2. Remove air cleaner and install cover screen J—26996 or equivalent.
3. Mark hood hinges and remove hood.
4. Disconnect negative battery cables at batteries and ground wires at inner fender panel. Disconnect engine ground strap, right head to cowl.
5. Disconnect radiator hoses, cooler lines, heater hoses, vacuum hoses, power steering pump hoses at power steering gear, air conditioning compressor with brackets and hoses attached, fuel hose from fuel pump and wiring.
6. Remove hairpin clip at bellcrank.
7. Remove throttle and T.V. cables from intake manifold brackets, then position cables away from engine.
8. Remove upper radiator support and radiator.
9. Raise the vehicle and support it safely.
10. Disconnect exhaust pipes at manifold.
11. Remove torque converter cover and three bolts holding converter to flywheel.
12. Remove engine mount bolts or nuts.
13. Remove the transmission to engine retaining bolts on the right side. Remove the starter.
14. Lower the vehicle. Secure lift chain to engine.
15. Place board on top of jack and slightly raise transmission. Remove three left transmission to engine bolts. Remove engine.
16. Installation is the reverse of the removal procedure.

ENGINE MOUNTS

Removal and Installation

1. Disconnect the negative battery cable. Raise and support the vehicle safely.
2. Properly support the weight of the engine at the forward edge of the oil pan.
3. Remove the mount to engine block bolts. Raise the engine slightly and remove the mount to mount bracket bolt and nut. Remove the engine mount.
4. Installation is the reverse of the removal procedure.

Valve System

VALVE ADJUSTMENT

The engines produced for use in the Oldsmobile vehicle models use only hydraulic lifters, which are not adjustable. The rocker arm shaft assembly or the rockers, with pivot, are bolted to the cylinder head with a specific torque pressure, automatically positioning the lifter internal components for correct hydraulic operation.

TORQUE SPECIFICATIONS

Gasoline Engines
Code A, 3.8L – Rocker shaft assembly bolts – 30 ft. lbs.
Code 4, 4.1L – Rocker shaft assembly bolts – 30 ft. lbs.
Code Y-9, 5.0L – Rocker arm pivot bolt to cylinder head – 28 ft. lbs.

Diesel Engines
Code V, 4.3L – Rocker arm pivot bolt to cylinder head – 28 ft. lbs.
Code N, 5.7L – Rocker arm pivot bolt to cylinder head – 28 ft. lbs.

VALVE LIFTERS

Removal and Installation

1. Disconnect the negative battery cable.
2. Remove the intake manifold assembly.
3. Remove the rocker arm covers. Remove the rocker as-

sembly or the rocker and pivot. Remove the push rods. Be sure to keep them in order as they must be installed in the same bores as they were removed.

4. On diesel engines, remove the valve lifter guide retaining bolts. Remove the valve lifter guide.

5. Remove the valve lifters, using the proper valve lifter removal tool.

6. Installation is the reverse of the removal procedure. Be sure to use new gaskets as required. Be sure to coat the lifter assemblies with clean engine oil prior to installation.

VALVE ROCKER ASSEMBLY

Removal and Installation

V6 GASOLINE ENGINE

1. Disconnect the negative battery cable.
2. Remove the rocker arm cover. Remove the rocker arm and shaft assembly from the cylinder head.
3. Remove the nylon rocker arm retainers and separate the rocker arms from the rocker shaft.
4. Installation is the reverse of the removal procedure. Be sure to use new valve cover gaskets, where required.
5. When installing the rocker arms onto the rocker shaft, be sure to position them in the correct sequence.

V8 GASOLINE ENGINE, V6 and V8 DIESEL ENGINES

1. Disconnect the negative battery cable.
2. Remove the valve cover.
3. Remove the rocker arm retaining bolts, rocker arm pivot and rocker arms.
4. Installation is the reverse of the removal procedure. Refer to the torque specifications as listed under Valve Adjustment. Be sure to use new valve cover gaskets, as required.

NOTE: Refer to the 4.3L and 5.7L Diesel Engine Chapters in the Unit Repair Section of this manual for lifter bleed down procedures, necessary before starting the engines.

VALVE TIMING

Adjustment

Manufacturers recommended procedure for valve timing has been established and recommended for only the 5.0L (307 cu. in.) Oldsmobile produced V8 engine.

5.0L (307 CU.IN.) ENGINE

1. Remove the distributor cap. Remove the right valve cover. Remove the number four intake and exhaust rocker arm assembly.
2. Remove the wire from the BAT. terminal of the distributor cap.
3. Turn ignition switch on. Crank engine until rotor is in line with Number Four spark plug wire position. Number Four piston will be approximately at the top of cylinder.
4. Measure from pivot boss on head surface to top of Number Four intake push-rod. Record measurement.
5. Slowly turn engine one and one half revolutions until rotor approaches Number One spark plug wire position. Continue to turn engine until timing mark on crank puller is aligned with 0 on indicator. This is top dead center of Number One piston.
6. Again measure from pivot boss surface to top of Number Four cylinder intake push-rod.
7. Measurement should increase over the first measurement.
8. If measurement increase is not within 1/32 in. of first measurement, camshaft is advanced or retarded.

CYLINDER HEAD

Removal and Installation

V6 GASOLINE ENGINE

1. Disconnect negative battery cable.
2. Remove intake manifold.
3. Loosen and remove belt(s).
4. When removing left cylinder head;
   a. Remove oil dipstick.
   b. Remove air and vacuum pumps with mounting bracket if present, and move out of the way with hoses attached.
5. When removing right cylinder head;
   a. Remove alternator.
   b. Disconnect power steering gear pump and brackets attaching to cylinder head.
6. Disconnect wires from spark plugs, and remove the spark plug wire clips from the rocker arm cover studs.
7. Remove exhaust manifold bolts from the head being removed.

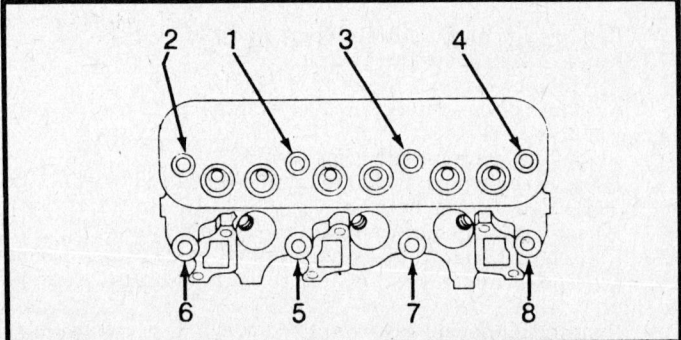

V6 gas engine—cylinder head bolt torque sequence (© General Motors Corporation)

8. With air hose and cloths, clean dirt off cylinder head and adjacent area to avoid getting dirt into engine.
9. Remove rocker arm cover and rocker arm and shaft assembly from cylinder head. Lift out push rods.
10. Loosen all cylinder head bolts, then remove bolts and lift off the cylinder head.
11. Installation is the reverse of the removal procedure. Torque the cylinder head bolts to 80 ft. lbs., torque the exhaust manifold bolts to 25 ft. lbs. and torque the intake manifold bolts to 45 ft. lbs.

V8 GASOLINE ENGINE

1. Disconnect the negative battery cable. Drain the radiator.
2. Remove the intake manifold. Remove the exhaust manifold.
3. Remove the valve cover. Remove the ground strap from the left cylinder head.

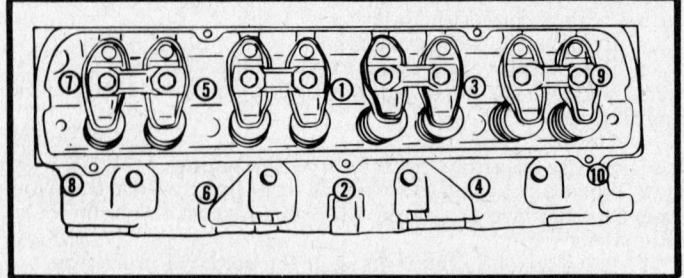

V8 gas engine—cylinder head bolt torque sequence (© General Motors Corporation)

OLDSMOBILE
CUTLASS • DELTA 88 • CUSTOM CRUISER • OLDS 98 • HURST OLDS

SECTION 19

4. Remove rocker arm bolts, pivots, rocker arms and push rods. Scribe pivots and keep rocker arms separated so they can be installed in their original locations.
5. Remove cylinder head bolts and remove cylinder head.
6. Installation is the reverse of the removal procedure. Torque the cylinder head bolts to 100 ft. lbs. and then to a final torque of 130 ft. lbs.

CAMSHAFT

Removal and Installation

V6 GASOLINE ENGINE

1. Disconnect the negative battery cable. Drain the radiator.
2. Remove the intake manifold. Remove the rocker covers. Remove the rocker arm assemblies, push rods and valve lifters.
3. Remove the radiator and the air condition condenser, as required.
4. Remove timing chain cover, timing chain and sprocket.
5. Align timing marks of camshaft and crankshaft sprocket. This avoids burring of the camshaft journals by the crankshaft during removal. Slide camshaft forward out of bearing bores carefully to avoid marring the bearing surfaces.
6. Installation is the reverse of the removal procedure.
7. Before installing the camshaft and the lifters, be sure to coat them with clean engine oil.
8. Be sure to use new gaskets and seals as required.

V8 GASOLINE ENGINE

1. Disconnect the negative battery cable. Drain the radiator. Remove the upper radiator baffle.
2. Disconnect the upper radiator hose.
3. Remove the radiator.
4. Disconnect the fuel line at the fuel pump.
5. Remove the air cleaner. Disconnect the throttle cable.
6. Remove the alternator belt. Remove the alternator bracket attaching bolts.
7. Remove power steering pump bracket attaching bolts and remove pump.
8. Remove air conditioning compressor mounting bracket attaching bolts and support compressor to side for access. The air conditioning lines at the compressor are flexible and should be left attached to the compressor.
9. Disconnect thermostat bypass hose at water pump. Disconnect electrical and vacuum connections. Remove distributor with cap and wiring intact.
10. Remove balancer pulley. Remove balancer.
11. Remove engine front cover. Remove both valve covers.
12. Remove intake manifold and gasket, front and rear seal.
13. Remove rocker arms, push rods and valve lifters.
14. Parts position should be noted so they will be installed in their original position.
15. If equipped with air conditioning, discharge the system, remove condenser attaching bolts and remove condenser.

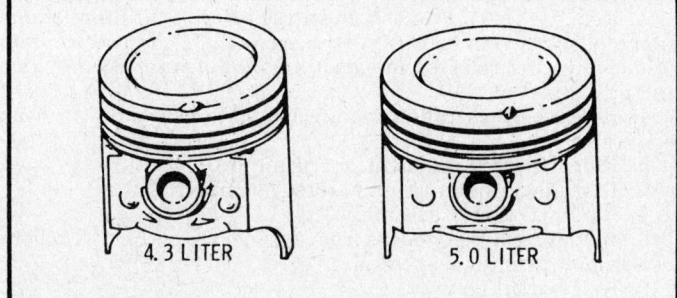

V8 Gas engine—piston ring identification
(© General Motors Corporation)

16. Remove bolt securing fuel pump eccentric, remove eccentric, camshaft gear, oil slinger and timing chain.
17. Remove camshaft by carefully sliding it out the front of the engine.
18. Installation is the reverse of the removal procedure. Be sure to coat the camshaft and the lifters with clean engine oil prior to installation. Be sure to use new gaskets, as required.

PISTON AND CONNECTING ROD POSITIONING

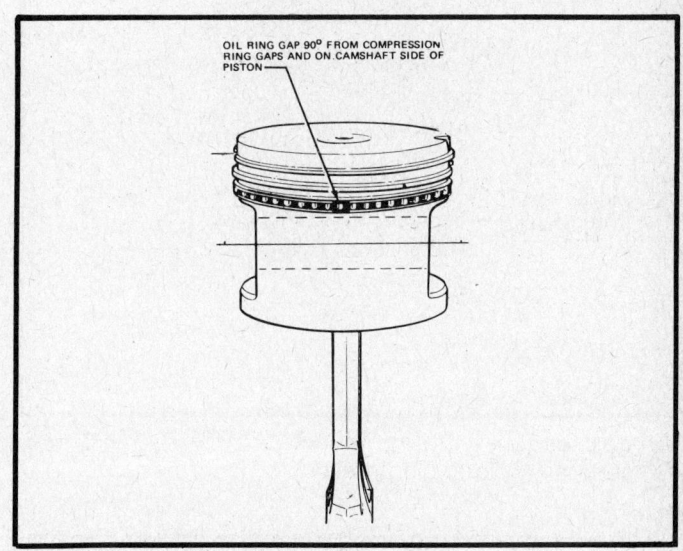

V6 gas engine—piston identifiction
(© General Motors Corporation)

TIMING CASE COVER/OIL SEAL CHAIN AND GEARS

Removal and Installation

V6 GASOLINE ENGINE

1. Disconnect the negative battery cable. Drain the radiator.
2. Disconnect the radiator hoses and the heater return hose at the water pump.
3. Remove the fan assembly and pulleys. Remove the crankshaft vibration damper.
4. Remove the fuel pump. Remove the alternator.
5. Remove the distributor. If timing chain and sprockets are not going to be disturbed, note position of distributor rotor for reinstallation in same position.
6. Loosen and slide front clamp on thermostat bypass hose rearward.
7. Remove bolts attaching timing chain cover to cylinder block. Remove two oil pan to timing chain cover bolts. Remove timing chain cover assembly and gasket.
8. Thoroughly clean the cover, taking care to avoid damage to the gasket surface.
9. Remove the timing chain and gears, as required.
10. Installation is the reverse of the removal procedure.
11. Remove oil pump cover and pack the space around the oil pump gears completely full of petroleum jelly. There must be no air space left inside the pump. Reinstall cover using new gasket.
12. To replace the front oil seal, use a punch and drive out the old seal and shedder. Drive the seal out from the front toward the rear of the timing chain cover.

19-27

OLDSMOBILE
CUTLASS • DELTA 88 • CUSTOM CRUISER • OLDS 98 • HURST OLDS

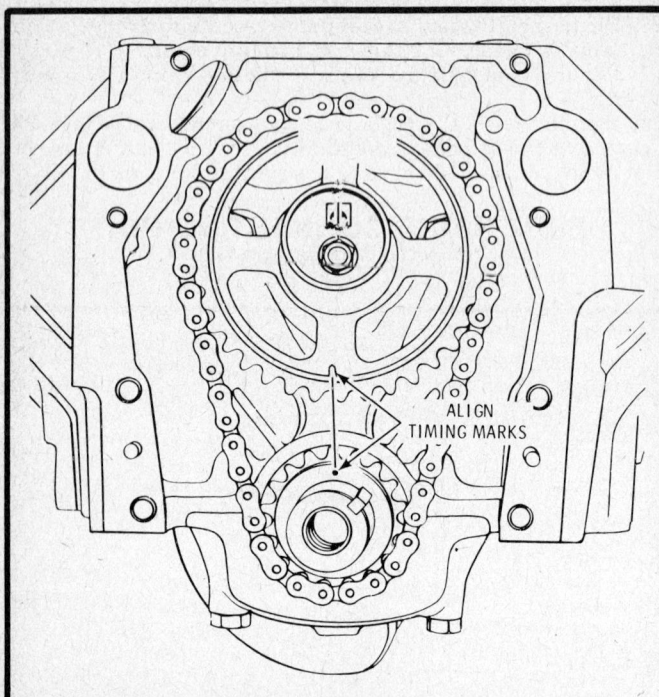

V8 gas engine – timing marks
(© General Motors Corporation)

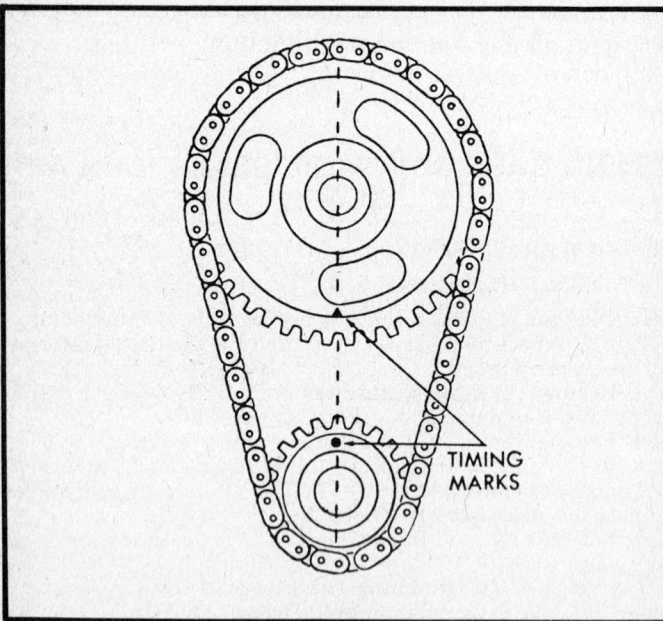

V6 gas engine – timing marks
(© General Motors Corporation)

13. Coil new packing around opening so ends of packing are at top. Drive in shedder using suitable punch. Stake the shedder in place in at least three places.
14. Size the packing by rotating a hammer handle or similar tool around the packing until the balancer hub can be inserted through the opening.
15. Torque the front cover retaining bolts to 28 ft. lbs.

V8 GASOLINE ENGINE

1. Disconnect the negative battery cable. Drain the cooling system. Disconnect the radiator hoses and the bypass hose.
2. Remove the radiator upper support. Remove the radiator.
3. Remove all belts, fan and fan pulley, crankshaft pulley and harmonic balancer.
4. Remove cover to block attaching bolts and remove cover, timing indicator and water pump assembly.
5. Remove front cover and both dowel pins. It may be necessary to grind a flat on the pins to get a rough surface for gripping.
6. Remove the timing chain and gears, as required.
7. Installation is the reverse of the removal procedure.
8. To install the cover, grind a chamfer on one end of each dowel pin.
9. Cut excess material from front end of oil pan gasket on each side of engine block.
10. Clean block, oil pan and front cover mating surfaces with solvent.
11. Trim about $1/8$ in. from each end of new front pan seal, using a sharp tool.
12. Install new front cover gasket on engine block and new front seal on front cover. Apply sealer to gasket around coolant holes and place on block. Apply RTV sealer or equivalent to both mating surfaces.
13. Place the cover on the front of the block and press downward to compress the seal.
14. Rotate the cover to the left and then to the right and guide the seal into the cavity using a suitable tool.
15. Install two bolts finger tight to hold the cover in place. Install the two dowel pins, chamfered end first.
16. Continue the installation in the reverse order of the removal procedure.
17. To replace the front cover oil seal, pry it from the front cover. Before installing a new oil seal coat it with clean engine oil.

Lubrication

OIL PAN

Removal and Installation

V6 GASOLINE ENGINE

1. Disconnect the negative battery cable.
2. Raise the vehicle and support it safely. Drain the engine oil.
3. Remove the flywheel cover and the engine crossover pipe.
4. Remove the oil pan bolts. Remove the oil pan from the engine assembly.
5. Installation is the reverse of removal.

V8 GASOLINE ENGINE

1. Disconnect the negative battery cable.
2. Raise the vehicle and support it safely.
3. Remove distributor cap and align rotor in the number one firing position. This positions the crankshaft counter weights and connecting rods for the least amount of interference with the oil pan.
4. Remove upper radiator support and fan shroud attaching screws.
5. Remove flywheel cover and drain oil.
6. Disconnect exhaust and crossover pipes.
7. Remove starter assembly.
8. Remove engine mounts from engine block, then jack front of engine up as far as possible.
9. Remove oil pan.
10. Apply sealer to both sides of pan gasket.
11. Apply sealer to front cover.
12. Install front and rear rubber pan seals.

OLDSMOBILE
CUTLASS • DELTA 88 • CUSTOM CRUISER • OLDS 98 • HURST OLDS
SECTION 19

13. Wipe seal with engine oil then install pan and torque bolts to 10 ft. lbs. (14 Nm). Reverse the removal procedure. Fill crankcase. Start engine and check for leaks.

OIL PUMP

Removal and Installation

V6 GASOLINE ENGINE

1. Disconnect the negative battery cable. Drain the engine oil. Remove the oil filter.
2. Unbolt the pump cover assembly from the timing chain cover.
3. Remove the cover assembly and slide out the pump gears.
4. Remove the oil pressure relief valve cap, spring, and valve. Do not remove the oil filter bypass valve and spring.
5. Check that the relief valve spring isn't worn on its side or collapsed. Check that the relief valve spring is no more than an easy slip fit in its bore in the cover. If there is any perceptible sideplay, replace the valve. If there is still sideplay, replace the cover.
6. Check the filter bypass valve for good condition.
7. Lubricate and install the pressure relief valve and spring in the cover bore. Install the gasket and cap, torquing the cap to 35 ft. lbs.
8. Install the gears and check that gear-to-cover end clearance is between 0.002–0.006 in. If the clearance is less, check the timing cover gear pocket for wear.
9. Remove the gears and pack the gear pocket full of petroleum jelly. Don't use grease.
10. Install the gears. Install a new gasket and the cover. Torque the bolts evenly to 10 ft. lbs. Replace the filter.

V8 GASOLINE ENGINE

1. Disconnect the negative battery cable. Drain the engine oil. Remove the engine oil pan.
2. Remove pump attaching screws and carefully lower the pump.
3. Reinstall in reverse order. To ensure immediate oil pressure on start-up, the oil pump gear cavity should be packed with petroleum jelly.

REAR MAIN OIL SEAL

Removal and Installation

1. Remove the oil pan, and pump, where required, and remove the rear main bearing cap.
2. Pry the lower seal out of the bearing cap with a suitable tool, being careful not to gouge the cap surface.
3. Remove the upper seal by lightly tapping on one end with a brass pin punch until the other end can be grasped and pulled out with pliers.
4. Clean the bearing cap, cylinder block, and crankshaft mating surfaces for gouges, nicks, and burrs.
5. Apply light engine oil on the seal lips and bead, but keep the seal ends clean.
6. Insert the tip of the installation tool between the crankshaft and the seal of the cylinder block. Place the seal between the tip of the tool and the crankshaft, so that the bead contacts the tip of the tool.
7. Be sure that the seal lip is facing the front of the engine, and work the seal around the crankshaft using the installation tool to protect the seal from the corner of the cylinder block.

NOTE: Do not remove the tool until the opposite end of the seal is flush with the cylinder block surface.

8. Remove the installation tool, being careful not to pull the seal out at the same time.
9. Using the same procedure, install the lower seal into the bearing cap. Use finger and thumb to lever the seal into the cap.
10. Apply sealer to the cylinder block only where the cap mates to the surface. Do not apply sealer to the seal ends.
11. Install the rear cap and torque the bolts to specifications.

FRONT SUSPENSION AND STEERING SECTION

For Front Suspension Services refer to the Unit Repair Section. For Steering Gear Overhaul refer to the Unit Repair Section.

STEERING GEAR

Removal and Installation

1. Remove the flexible coupling shield by sliding it up on the column.
2. Disconnect the power steering hoses from the gear and cap the hose fittings.
3. Raise the vehicle and support it safely.
4. Remove the pitman shaft nut, then disconnect the pitman arm from the pitman shaft using a pitman arm puller.
5. Remove the gear to frame rail attaching bolts and lift out the steering gear.

NOTE: If the gear mounting threads are stripped, do not repair. Replace the steering gear housing.

6. Installation is the reverse of removal.

FRONT WHEEL BEARINGS

Adjustment

1. Raise and support the vehicle safely.
2. Remove the dust cap from the hub.
3. Remove the cotter pin and discard it.
4. Tighten the spindle nut to 12 ft. lbs. while turning the wheel. Then back off the nut $1/4$–$1/2$ turn.
5. Retighten the nut by hand until it is finger tight.
6. Loosen the nut no more than $1/6$ of a turn until the nearest hole in the spindle lines up with the slot in the spindle nut, and insert a new cotter pin.
7. Feel the looseness in the hub assembly. There should be 0.001–0.005 in. end play.
8. Replace the dust cover and lower the vehicle.

POWER STEERING PUMP

Removal and Installation

1. Remove the pump belt. Remove the pump pulley, if necessary. Disconnect and plug both power steering hoses.
2. Remove all the necessary components in order to gain access to the pump retaining bolts. Loosen the retaining bolts and any braces and remove the pump.
3. Install the pump on the engine with the retaining bolts hand-tight.
4. Connect and tighten the hose fittings.
5. Refill the pump with fluid and bleed by turning the pulley counterclockwise (viewed from the front). Stop the bleeding when air bubbles no longer appear.

SECTION 19 OLDSMOBILE
CUTLASS • DELTA 88 • CUSTOM CRUISER • OLDS 98 • HURST OLDS

6. Install the pump belt on the pulley and adjust the tension.

STEERING WHEEL

Removal and Installation

EXCEPT TILT AND TELESCOPE MODELS

1. Disconnect the battery ground cable.
2. On the stock wheel, remove the two screws attaching the horn pad assembly to the wheel. Disconnect the horn contact from the pad assembly.
On the deluxe wheel, remove the pad attaching screws, lift up the pad, and disconnect the horn wire by pushing on the insulator and turning counterclockwise.
On the sport steering wheel, pull up on the emblem to remove it. Remove the contact assembly attaching screws and the contact assembly.
3. On all models remove the steering wheel nut retainer.
4. Remove the retaining nut and the steering wheel, using a puller.
5. Installation is the reverse of removal. Align the marks on the wheel hub and the steering shaft. If the spokes of the wheel are not horizontal, it is necessary to adjust the tie rod ends. Torque the attaching bolt to 30 ft. lbs.

TILT AND TELESCOPE MODELS

1. Disconnect the battery ground.
2. Remove the three pad attaching screws, lift off the pad assembly and disconnect the horn wire.
3. Push the locking lever counterclockwise to full release.
4. Mark the plate assembly where the two attaching screws

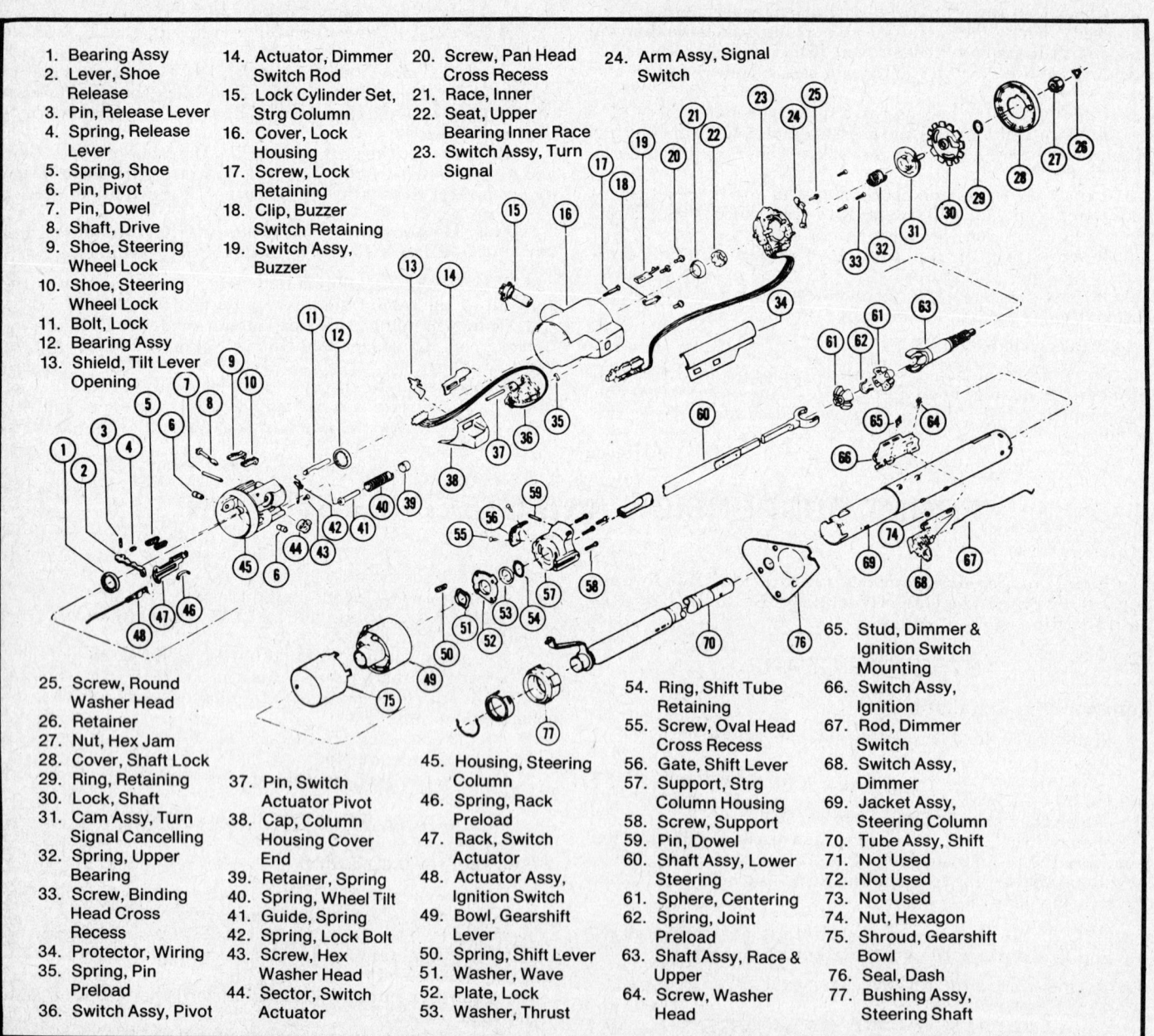

1. Bearing Assy
2. Lever, Shoe Release
3. Pin, Release Lever
4. Spring, Release Lever
5. Spring, Shoe
6. Pin, Pivot
7. Pin, Dowel
8. Shaft, Drive
9. Shoe, Steering Wheel Lock
10. Shoe, Steering Wheel Lock
11. Bolt, Lock
12. Bearing Assy
13. Shield, Tilt Lever Opening
14. Actuator, Dimmer Switch Rod
15. Lock Cylinder Set, Strg Column
16. Cover, Lock Housing
17. Screw, Lock Retaining
18. Clip, Buzzer Switch Retaining
19. Switch Assy, Buzzer
20. Screw, Pan Head Cross Recess
21. Race, Inner
22. Seat, Upper Bearing Inner Race
23. Switch Assy, Turn Signal
24. Arm Assy, Signal Switch
25. Screw, Round Washer Head
26. Retainer
27. Nut, Hex Jam
28. Cover, Shaft Lock
29. Ring, Retaining
30. Lock, Shaft
31. Cam Assy, Turn Signal Cancelling
32. Spring, Upper Bearing
33. Screw, Binding Head Cross Recess
34. Protector, Wiring
35. Spring, Pin Preload
36. Switch Assy, Pivot
37. Pin, Switch Actuator Pivot
38. Cap, Column Housing Cover End
39. Retainer, Spring
40. Spring, Wheel Tilt
41. Guide, Spring
42. Spring, Lock Bolt
43. Screw, Hex Washer Head
44. Sector, Switch Actuator
45. Housing, Steering Column
46. Spring, Rack Preload
47. Rack, Switch Actuator
48. Actuator Assy, Ignition Switch
49. Bowl, Gearshift Lever
50. Spring, Shift Lever
51. Washer, Wave
52. Plate, Lock
53. Washer, Thrust
54. Ring, Shift Tube Retaining
55. Screw, Oval Head Cross Recess
56. Gate, Shift Lever
57. Support, Strg Column Housing
58. Screw, Support
59. Pin, Dowel
60. Shaft Assy, Lower Steering
61. Sphere, Centering
62. Spring, Joint Preload
63. Shaft Assy, Race & Upper
64. Screw, Washer Head
65. Stud, Dimmer & Ignition Switch Mounting
66. Switch Assy, Ignition
67. Rod, Dimmer Switch
68. Switch Assy, Dimmer
69. Jacket Assy, Steering Column
70. Tube Assy, Shift
71. Not Used
72. Not Used
73. Not Used
74. Nut, Hexagon
75. Shroud, Gearshift Bowl
76. Seal, Dash
77. Bushing Assy, Steering Shaft

Exploded view of the Cutlass "G Body" tilt steering column
(© General Motors Corporation)

OLDSMOBILE
CUTLASS • DELTA 88 • CUSTOM CRUISER • OLDS 98 • HURST OLDS

attach the plate assembly to the locking lever and remove the two screws.

5. Unscrew and remove the plate assembly. Remove the steering wheel nut.
6. Using a puller, remove the steering wheel.
7. Install a 5/16 in. x 18 set screw into the upper shaft at the full extended position and lock.
8. Install the steering wheel, observing the aligning mark on the hub and the slash mark on the end of the shaft. Make certain that the unattached end of the horn upper contact assembly is seated flush against the top of the horn contact carrier button.
9. Install the nut on the upper steering shaft and torque to 30 ft. lb.
10. Remove the set screw installed in Step 7.
11. Install the plate assembly finger tight.
12. Position the locking lever in the vertical position and move it counterclockwise until the holes in the plate align with the holes in the lever. Install the attaching screws.
13. Align the pad assembly with the holes in the steering wheel and install the retaining screws.
14. Connect the battery.
15. Make certain that the locking lever securely locks the wheel travel and that the wheel travel is free in the unlocked position.

STEERING COLUMN

Removal and Installation

CAUTION

Disconnect the battery cable to insure against accidental deployment of the air cushion restraint system on vehicles so equipped.

NOTE: Handle the steering column very carefully. Rapping on the end of it or leaning on it could shear off the inserts which allow the column to collapse in a crash.

1. Disconnect battery.
2. Disconnect flexible coupling.
3. Remove cover and toe-pan attaching screws.
4. If necessary, remove instrument panel lower trim.
5. Disconnect shift linkages, wiring, etc.
6. Remove lower column mounts, then upper column mounts, and pull column up and out of the vehicle.
7. When installing, check that flexible coupling alignment is correct.

NOTE: When installing, use only the specified hardware. Overlength bolts could prevent the column from properly collapsing in a crash.

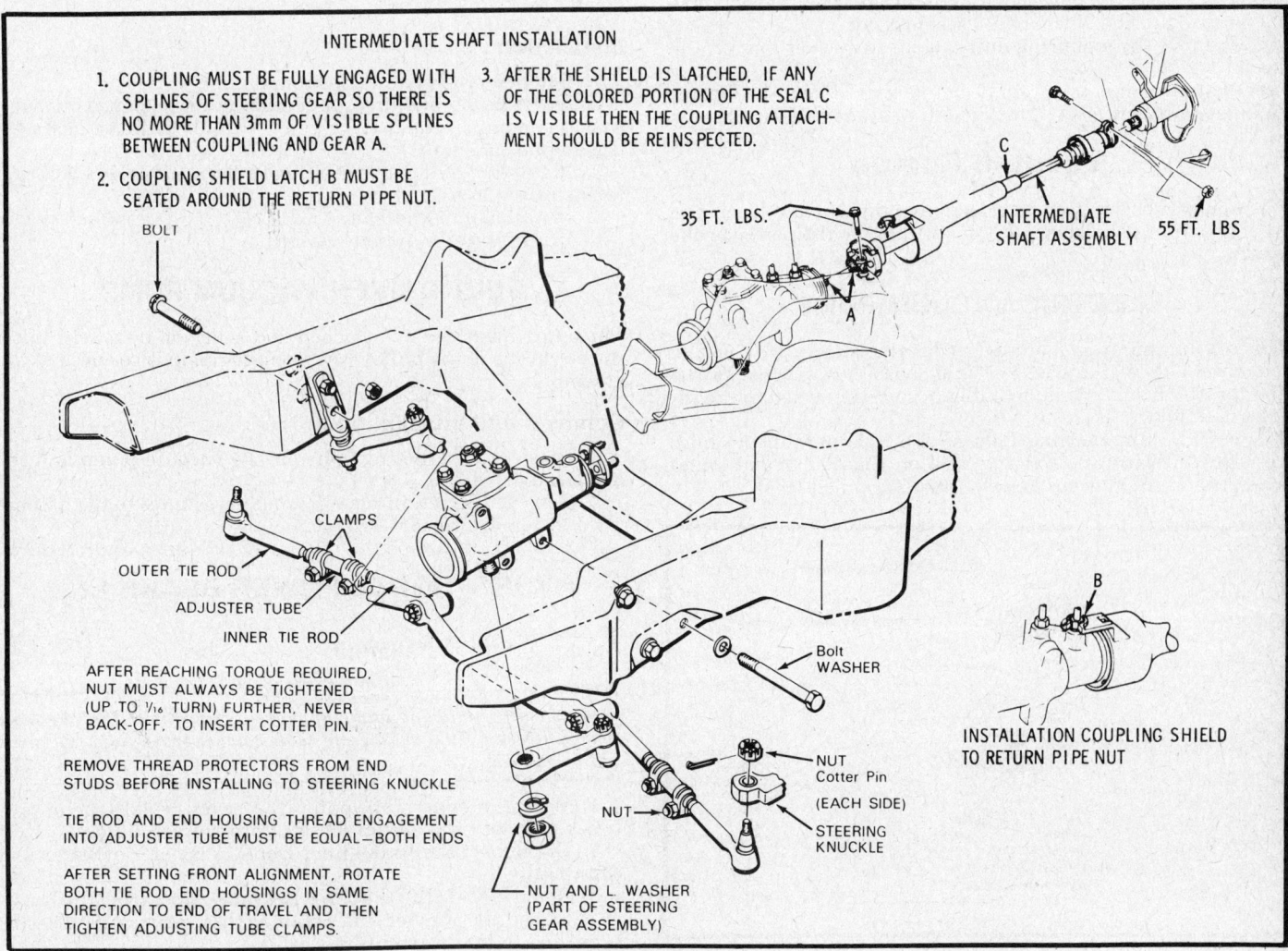

Typical steering linkage and steering gear mounting
(© General Motors Corporation)

SECTION 19
OLDSMOBILE
CUTLASS • DELTA 88 • CUSTOM CRUISER • OLDS 98 • HURST OLDS

BRAKE SECTION

For Brake Service refer to the Unit Repair Section.

MASTER CYLINDER

Removal and Installation

1. Disconnect and cap or plug hydraulic lines. Disconnect the electrical lead, if so equipped.
2. Remove the attaching bolts and master cylinder.
3. Install in the reverse order of removal. Fill with fluid and bleed.

POWER BRAKE BOOSTER

Removal and Installation

1. Remove the two nuts holding the master cylinder to the power unit. Carefully position the master cylinder out of the way, being careful not to kink any of the hydraulic lines. It is not necessary to disconnect the brake lines.
2. Disconnect the vacuum hose from the vacuum check valve on the front housing. Plug the hose.
3. Loosen the nuts that hold the power unit to the firewall.
4. Disconnect the pushrod from the brake pedal. Do not force the pushrod to the side when disconnecting.
5. Remove the mounting nuts and lift the power unit off the studs.
6. Installation is the reverse of removal. Torque the master cylinder-to-power brake unit mounting studs to 24 ft. lbs.

Vacuum Pumps

Vacuum pumps are used on selective engines to aid the engine in maintaining a proper level of vacuum for the power brake system.

ELECTRIC VACUUM PUMP

The vacuum pump is mounted under the battery tray on the left hand side of the car. The inlet hose is connected to the booster check valve and the outlet hose is connected to the intake manifold.

A low vacuum warning light switch is located in the inlet hose line operating a warning light on the instrument panel when the vacuum drops below a predetermined level.

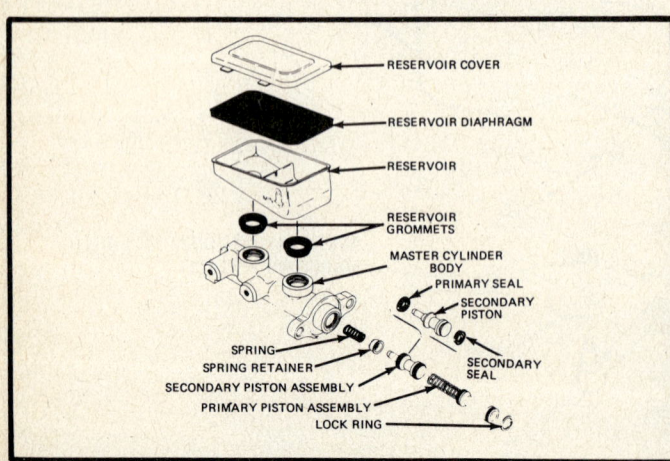

Master cylinder—exploded view
(© General Motors Corporation)

Removal and Installation

1. Raise vehicle and remove splash shield, L.H. side of car.
2. Disconnect hoses at vacuum pump.
3. Disconnect electrical connector at vacuum pump.
4. Remove three nuts securing pump assembly to mounting bracket and remove pump.
5. Reverse procedure for installation of vacuum pump.

GEAR DRIVEN VACUUM PUMP

The gear driven vacuum pump is a diaphragm pump which requires no periodic maintenance. It is driven by a cam inside the drive assembly to which it mounts. The drive housing assembly has a drive gear on the lower end which meshes with the camshaft gear in the engine. This drive gear causes the cam in the drive housing to rotate. The drive gear also powers the engine oil lubricating pump.

Removal

1. Remove vacuum hose from vacuum pump inlet.
2. Remove bolt and clamp holding drive assembly to engine block.

Installation

1. Remove protective cloth from engine.
2. Insert pump and drive assembly in engine, making sure that the gears on the drive assembly mesh with the gears on the engine camshaft.
3. Rotate the pump into position so the bracket and bolt can be installed.
4. Install clamp and bolt.
5. Install vacuum hose to pump.

BELT DRIVEN VACUUM PUMP

The pump has a pulley attached and is driven by a belt. With the exception of the pulley, the vacuum pump is serviced as an assembly.

Removal and Installation

1. Loosen the retaining bolts for the vacuum pump and remove the drive belt.
2. Remove the retaining bolts and hoses/lines to the assembly and remove from the vehicle.
3. The installation is the reverse of the removal procedure.

HYDRO–BOOST POWER BRAKE UNIT

Removal and Installation

CAUTION

Power steering fluid and brake fluid are incompatible. If brake seals contact steering fluid or steering seals contact brake fluid, the seals will be ruined.

---

1. With the engine off, pump the brake pedal four or five times to empty the accumulator of pressurized fluid.
2. Disconnect the brake lines from the master cylinder and cap the lines.
3. Remove and plug the three hydraulic lines from the booster. Remove the washer and retainer that secures the booster pedal rod to the brake pedal arm.

NOTE: To avoid booster damage, do not pry the pedal rod off the pedal arm.

OLDSMOBILE
CUTLASS • DELTA 88 • CUSTOM CRUISER • OLDS 98 • HURST OLDS
SECTION 19

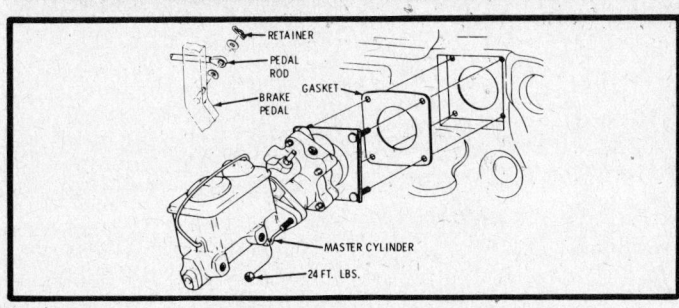

Hydro-boost power brake unit mounting
(© General Motors Corporation)

4. Remove the four nuts holding the booster to the firewall.
5. Loosen the booster from the firewall and move the booster pedal rod inboard until it disconnects from the brake pedal arm. Remove the spring washer from the brake pedal arm and remove the booster.
6. To install, reverse the removal procedure. Tighten the booster mounting nuts to 20 ft. lbs. Bleed the system.

POWER MASTER BRAKE SYSTEM

If the vehicle is equipped with Power Master Brake System, refer to the Buick Rear Wheel Drive Section of this Manual.

PARKING BRAKE

Adjustment

1. Make sure that the service brakes are properly adjusted. Raise and support the vehicle safely.
2. Depress the parking brake pedal two ratchet clicks on all models.
3. Loosen the jam nut on the equalizer adjusting nut. Tighten the adjusting nut until the left rear wheel can just be turned rearward by hand, but not forward.
4. Release the ratchet one click; the rear wheel should rotate rearward freely and forward with a slight drag.
5. Release the ratchet fully; the rear wheel should turn freely in either direction.

PARKING BRAKE CABLE

Removal and Installation

FRONT

1. Raise the vehicle and support it safely.
2. Loosen adjuster nut and disconnect front cable from connector. Compress retainer fingers and loosen at frame.
3. Remove supports and lower the vehicle.
4. Remove lower rear bolt from wheelhouse panel and pull panel out to gain access to front cable.
5. Disconnect cable from parking brake pedal assembly, compress retainer fingers and remove cable.
6. Install cable by reversing removal procedure. Make sure cable is routed properly and securely retained.
7. Adjust parking brake cable.

LEFT REAR

1. Raise and support the vehicle safely.
2. Loosen adjuster nut and compress retainer fingers at equalizer and loosen cable.
3. Disconnect cable from connector and remove from equalizer.
4. Mark relationship of wheel to axle flange and remove wheel and tire assembly.
5. Remove brake drum.
6. Remove primary shoe return spring and parking brake strut. Disconnect cable from parking brake lever and remove cable.
7. Installation is the reverse of the removal procedure.
8. Adjust the parking brake cable.

RIGHT REAR

1. Raise and support the vehicle safely.
2. Remove adjuster nut at equalizer and compress retainer fingers and loosen cable from retainers at frame and from axle housing clip.
3. Mark relationship of wheel to axle flange and remove wheel and tire assembly.
4. Remove brake drum.
5. Remove primary shoe return spring, parking brake strut, and secondary shoe hold down spring.
6. Compress retainer fingers and loosen cable from backing plate. Disconnect cable from parking brake lever and remove cable.
7. Install cable by reversing removal procedure. Make sure cable is routed properly and securely retained.
8. Adjust parking brake cable.

AUTOMATIC TRANSMISSION AND DRIVESHAFT SECTION

For Overhaul Procedures, refer to the Unit Repair Section.

AUTOMATIC TRANSMISSION

Removal and Installation

1. Disconnect the battery.
2. Disconnect detent cable (if so equipped) from accelerator lever or carburetor.
3. Remove, disconnect or relocate any of the following necessary for removal:
   a. Exhaust crossover pipe
   b. Drive Shaft
   c. Oil cooler lines
   d. Transmission crossmember (support engine and transmission as needed)
   e. Speedometer cable
   f. Shift linkage
   g. Electrical connections
   h. Flywheel cover pan
4. Mark flywheel and converter for installation reference.
5. Remove mounting bolts, and slide transmission back and out of vehicle.

NOTE: Transmission and torque converter are removed as an assembly.

6. Installation is the reverse of removal.

19-33

SECTION 19

OLDSMOBILE
CUTLASS • DELTA 88 • CUSTOM CRUISER • OLDS 98 • HURST OLDS

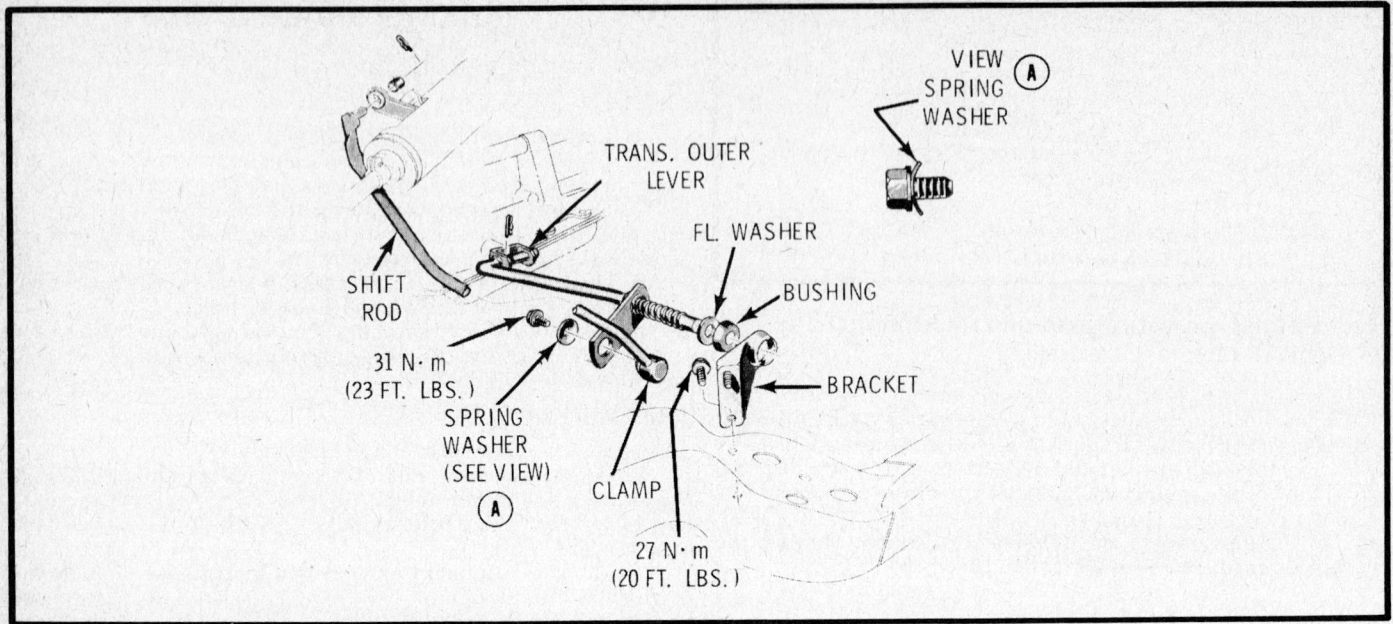

Automatic transmission column shift controls and shift rod adjustment
(© General Motors Corporation)

AUTOMATIC TRANSMISSION MANUAL LINKAGE

Adjustment

1. Adjust the linkage so the shift lever positions correspond exactly to the transmission positions.
2. Some linkage arrangements have adjustment gauge pin holes. In these, a free pin fit will insure proper adjustment.
3. After linkage adjustment, check operation of the neutral start switch, backup lights and automatic parking brake release.

SHIFT ROD

Adjustment

1. With shift rod clamp screw loosened, set transmission outer lever in neutral position.
2. Hold upper shift lever against neutral position stop in upper steering column. Do not raise lever.
3. Tighten screw in clamp on lower end of shift rod to specified torque.
4. Check operation. With key in "run" position and transmission in "reverse", be sure that the key cannot be removed and that the steering wheel is not locked. With key in "lock" position and shift lever in "park", be sure that the key can be removed, that the steering wheel is locked and that the transmission remains in park when the steering column is locked.
5. With brakes firmly applied, check to make sure that the starter will not work in any shift lever position except neutral and park.

SHIFT CABLE

Adjustment

1. Loosen shift rod clamp screw, loosen pin in transmission manual lever.
2. Place shift lever in "park" position. Place transmission manual lever in "park" position and ignition key in lock position.
3. Tighten cable pin nut to 20 ft. lbs.
4. Rotate the transmission manual lever fully against the "park" stop, then release the lever.
5. Pull shift rod down against lock stop to eliminate lash and tighten clamp screw to 20 ft. lbs.
6. Check operation. Move shift handle into each gear position and see that transmission manual lever is also in detent position. With key in "run" position and transmission in "reverse", be sure that the key cannot be removed and that steering wheel is not locked. With key in "lock" position and transmission in "park", be sure that key can be removed and that steering wheel is locked. Engine must start in park and neutral.
7. With brakes firmly applied, check to make sure that the starter will not work in any shift lever position except neutral and park.

FLOOR SHIFTER OPERATION

HURST/OLDS

The Hurst/Olds uses a three lever floor mounted shifter. The left hand lever controls Park, Reverse, Neutral, Overdrive and Drive functions. Placing the left hand lever in the overdrive position will allow the transmission to shift from first through overdrive.

The center lever is used to lock in second gear. The right hand lever is used to lock in first gear. To use the lock in feature for first and second gear the left hand lever must be positioned in the drive position.

To lock in second gear, push the button on the center lever down and pull the lever back. To lock in first gear, push the button on the right hand lever down and pull the lever back. When the first and second lock in levers are being used, it is necessary to manually upshift the transmission. This is done by moving the right hand lever, first gear, and the center lever, second gear, forward respectively.

To manually downshift the transmission from drive to sec-

OLDSMOBILE
CUTLASS • DELTA 88 • CUSTOM CRUISER • OLDS 98 • HURST OLDS
SECTION 19

ond gear, push the button on the center lever down and pull the lever back. To manually downshift to first gear, downshift to second, then push the button the right hand lever down and pull it back.

SELF–ADJUSTING TYPE T.V. CABLE

Adjustment

1. Stop engine.
2. Depress lock tab. Move slider back through fitting in direction away from throttle body or pump lever until slider stops against fitting.
3. Release lock tab.
4. Open carburetor lever to "full throttle stop" position to automatically adjust T.V. cable. Release carburetor lever.
5. Check T.V. cable for sticking and binding.
6. When the T.V. cable adjustment is made and locked, the cable housing will extend through the cable snap lock assembly about $1/16-5/16$ in. (2.57-7.95 mm).

SHIFT QUADRANT POINTER

Adjustment

1. With the engine off, set the transmission selector lever in neutral.
2. If the pointer does not align with the "N" indicator position, move the clip on the shift bowl, so that the pointer lines up with the "N".

NOTE: The Manual linkage must be adjusted properly before changing the shift quadrant adjustment.

DRIVESHAFT

Removal and Installation

1. Matchmark the relationship of the driveshaft to the differential flange.
2. Unbolt the straps or flange. Tape the bearing caps in place to prevent losing the bearing rollers. Support the driveshaft to prevent excessive strain on the universal joint.
3. Pull the shaft back and remove it. Be careful not to damage the splines at the transmission end.
4. If the transmission splined slip yoke does not have a vent hole at the center, it should be lubricated for installation with engine oil. If it does have a vent hole, it should be lubricated with grease. Slide the slip yoke into place.
5. Align the matchmarks and tighten the bolts. Tighten the U-bolts to 16 ft. lbs.

UNIVERSAL JOINT

See the Drive Axles and U-Joints Unit Repair Section for overhaul procedures.

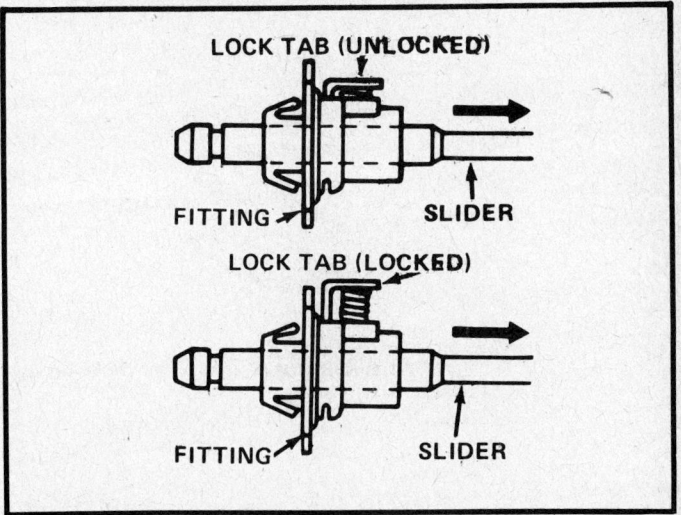

Self-adjusting throttle valve cable
(© General Motors Corporation)

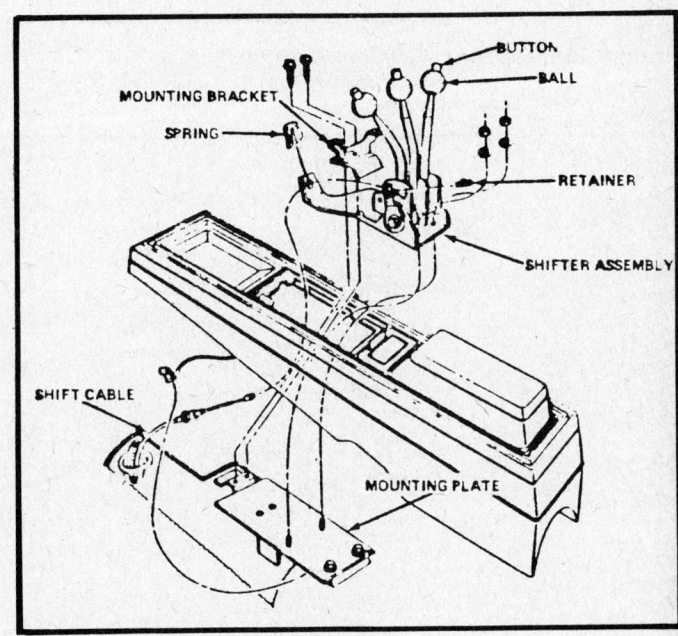

Hurst/Olds shifter mounting
(© General Motors Corporation)

REAR AXLE AND SUSPENSION

For Overhaul Procedures refer to the Unit Repair Section.

REAR AXLE ASSEMBLY

Removal and Installation

1. Raise the vehicle and support it safely. Be sure that the rear axle assembly is supported safely.
2. Disconnect shock absorbers from axle.
3. Mark drive shaft and pinion flange, then disconnect drive shaft and support it out of the way.
4. Remove brake line junction block bolt at axle housing, then disconnect brake lines at junction block. On some vehicles, disconnect brake line at wheel cylinder.
5. Disconnect upper control arms from axle housing.
6. Lower rear axle assembly on hoist and remove springs.
7. Remove rear wheels and drums.

19-35

SECTION 19 OLDSMOBILE
CUTLASS • DELTA 88 • CUSTOM CRUISER • OLDS 98 • HURST OLDS

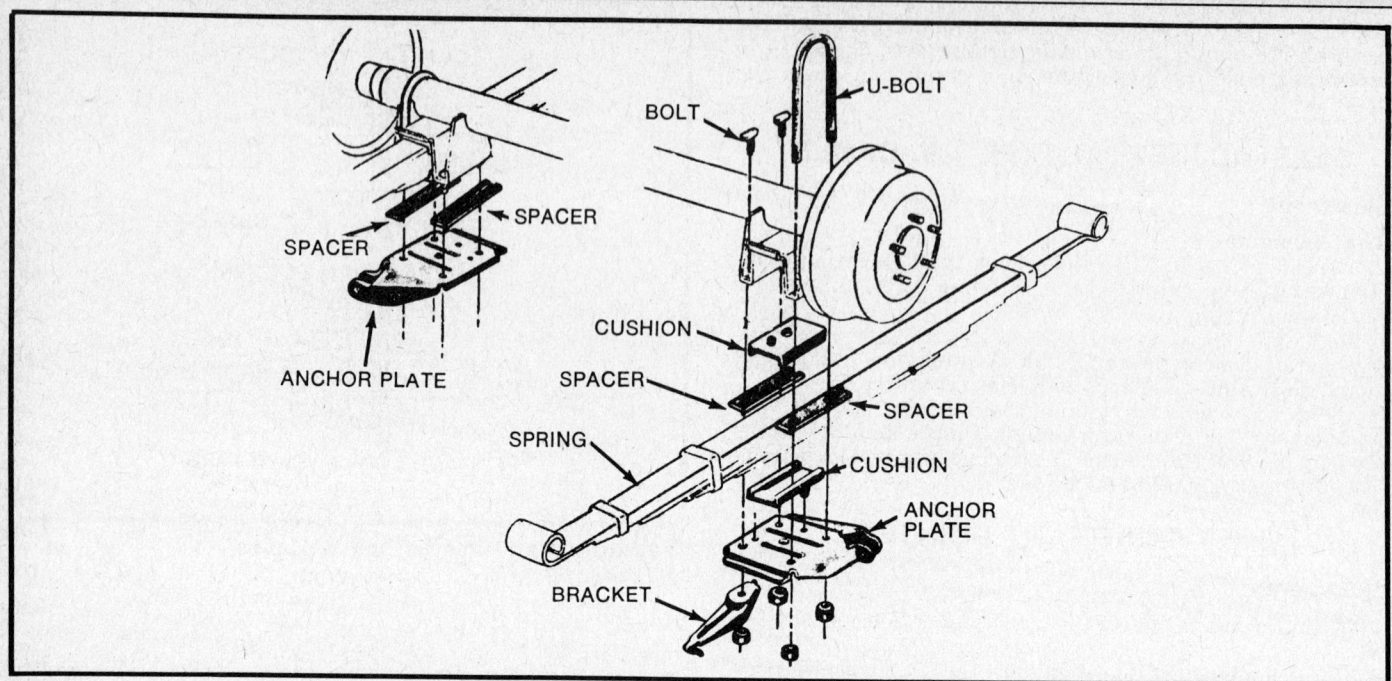

Omega leaf spring rear suspension—Custom Cruiser similar
(© General Motors Corporation)

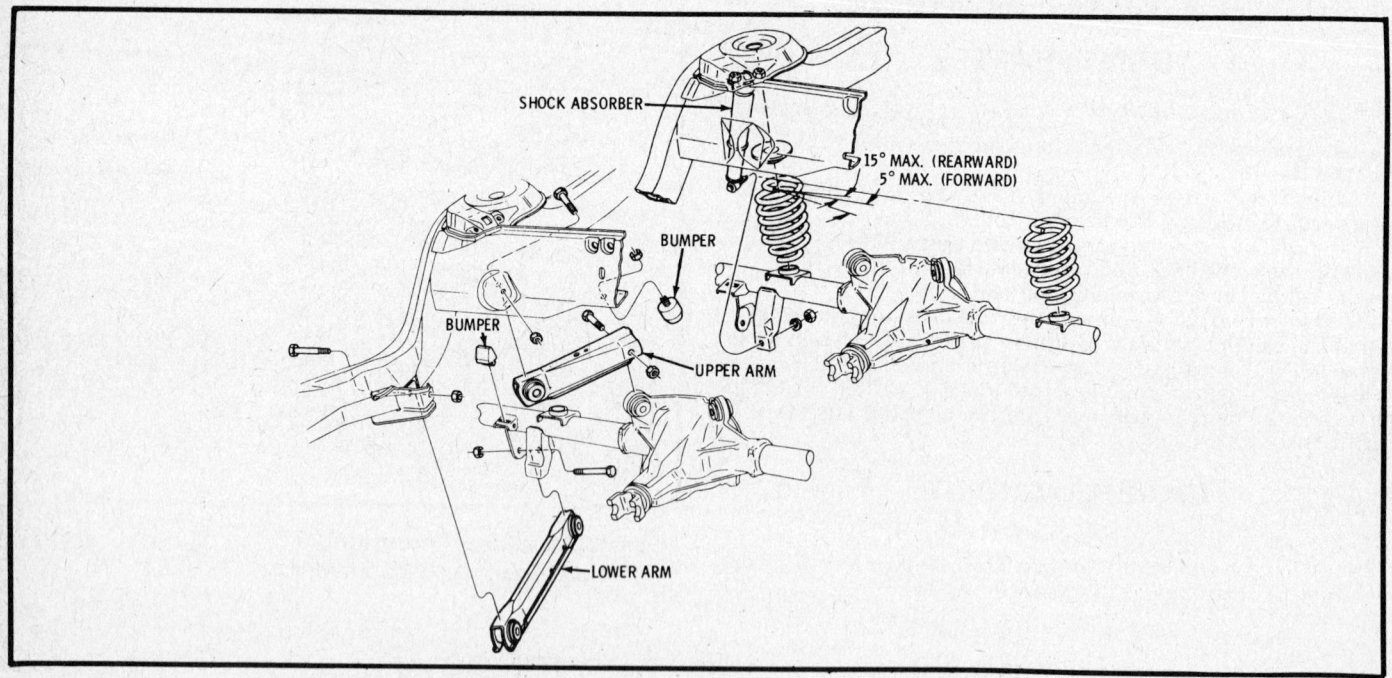

Cutlass, 88 and 98 rear suspension (except wagon)
(© General Motors Corporation)

OLDSMOBILE
CUTLASS • DELTA 88 • CUSTOM CRUISER • OLDS 98 • HURST OLDS

8. Disconnect brake lines from axle housing clips.
9. Disconnect lower control arms from axle housing.
10. Remove rear axle housing.
11. Installation is the reverse of the removal procedure.
12. Be sure to bleed the brake system, as required.

AXLE SHAFT

Removal and Installation

1. Raise vehicle and support it safely. Remove the tire and wheel assembly. Remove the brake drum.
2. Drain the fluid. Remove the rear carrier cover. Discard the gasket.
3. Remove the rear axle pinion shaft lock screw and the rear axle pinion shaft.
4. Push flanged end of axle shaft toward center of the vehicle and remove "C" lock from button end of shaft.
5. Remove axle shaft from housing, being careful not to damage oil seal.
6. Installation is the reverse of the removal procedure. Be sure to fill the rear assembly with the proper grade and type gear oil.

OIL SEAL/BEARING

Removal and Installation

1. Remove the axle shaft.
2. Remove seal from housing with a pry bar behind steel case of seal, being careful not to damage housing.
3. Insert tool J–23689 or equivalent into bore and position it behind bearing so that tangs on tool engage bearing outer race. Remove bearing, using slide hammer.
4. Lubricate the new bearing with gear lubricant and install bearing so that tool bottoms against shoulder in housing, using tool J–23690 or equivalent.
5. Lubricate seal lips with gear lubricant. Position seal on tool J–21128 or equivalent and position seal into housing bore. Tap seal into place so that it is flush with axle tube.

SECTION 20 PONTIAC
BONNEVILLE • GRAND PRIX • SAFARI • PARISIENNE

SPECIFICATIONS

Belt Tension	20-8	Serial Number Identification	20–4
Brakes	24–2	Torque	20–7
Capacities	20–7	Torque Sequence (Cylinder Heads)	20–25
Crankshaft & Connecting Rod	20–6	Tune-Up	20–5
Firing Order	20–5	Valve	20–6
General Engine	2–4	Wheel Alignment	20–7
Piston & Ring	20–6		

INDEX

A
Alternator R&R	20–8
Automatic Transmission	
Adjust	20–33
On Car Service	23–2
Assembly R&R	20–33
Axle Assembly R&R	20–33
Axle Shaft R&R	20–33

B
Ball joints	35–2
Belt Tension	20–8
Brake System	20–31
Brake Booster	20–31
Brake Caliper Overhaul	24–2
Brake Caliper R&R	24–2
Brake Drum	
Rear	24–2
Brake Master Cylinder	20–31
Brake Pad	
Front	24–2
Brake Shoe	
Rear	24–2

C
Camshaft R&R	20–25
Carburetor R&R	20–16
Chassis Electrical	20–9
Combination Switch R&R	20–11
Component Locations	20–12
Control Arm R&R	35–2
Computer Command Control	20–16
Cooling system	20–15
Cruise Control	20–12
Cylinder Head	20–25
R&R	20–25

D
Differential	28–2
Inspection	28–2
Dimmer Switch R&R	20–11
Disc Brakes	24–2
Distributor R&R	20–8
Drive Axle	28–2
Drive Belt Tension	20–8
Driveshaft R&R	20–33

E
Electronic Ignition	30–2
Emissions Controls	20–22
Engine	20–23
Identification	20–4
R&R	20–23
Engine Electrical	20–8
Engine Lubrication	20–27
Engine Mechanical	20–23
Engine Mounts R&R	20–23
Exhaust Manifold R&R	20–22

F
Front Suspension	35–2
Alignment	20–7
Fuel Injection	20–22
Fuel Pump R&R	20–16
Fuel Mixture, Adjust	20–16
Fuses	20–12

H
Headlight Switch	20–11
Heater Blower R&R	20–15
Heater Core R&R	20–15
Heater Control	20–15
Horn Switch	20–11

I
Idle Speed, Adjust	20–21
Ignition Switch	20–9
Ignition Timing	20–9
Instrument Cluster R&R	20–12
Intake Manifold R&R	20–12

L, M, N
Lower Control Arm R&R	35–2
Master Cylinder R&R	20–31
Manual Steering Gear R&R	20–29
Neutral Safety Switch R&R	20–9

O
Oil Pan R&R	20–27
Oil Pump R&R	20–27
Oil Seal R&R	
Rear Main	20–28

P
Parking Brake	20–32
Adjustment	20–32
Cable R&R	20–32
Piston & Connecting Rod	20–27
Power Brake Unit R&R	20–31
Power Steering Pump R&R	20–29

R
Rear Main Oil Seal R&R m	
Rear Suspension	3–52
Regulator	20–8
R&R	20–23
Rocker Shaft/Assembly R&R	20–24

S
Serial Number	20–4
Engine	20–4
Vehicle	20–4
Shock Absorber R&R	
Front	35–2
Rear	35–2
Springs	
Front	35–2
Rear	35–2
Starter R&R	20–8
Starter Drive Replacement	20–8
Steering Column R&R	20–31
Steering Gear R&R	20–29
Manual	20–29
Power	20–29
Steering Wheel R&R	20–29
Speedometer R&R	20–12
Suspension R&R	35–2
Service	35–2

T
Throttle Linkage, Adjust	20–20
Timing Chain	20–26
Timing Gear Cover	20–25
Oil Seal Replacement	20–25
Tune-Up	20–5
Turn Signal switch R&R	20–11

U, V
U-joint Overhaul	28–2
Valves, Adjust	20–23
Valve Tappette R&R	20–24
Valve Timing, Adjust	20–25
Valve System	20–23
Voltage Regulator	20–8

W, Y
Water Pump R&R	20–15
Wheel Alignment	20–7
Front	20–7
Wheel Bearings	
Front	20–31
Rear	20–33
Wheel Cylinders	24–2
Windshield Wiper	
Linkage R&R	20–11
Motor R&R	20–11
Switch R&R	20–11
Year Identification	20–3

BEFORE SERVICING BE CERTAIN TO READ THE SAFETY NOTICE

Pontiac
1983–87
Rear Wheel Drive Cars

BONNEVILLE • BONNEVILLE LE • BONNEVILLE BROUGHAM • GRAND PRIX • GRAND PRIX LE GRAND PRIX BROUGHAM • SAFARI SW PARISIENNE • PARISIENNE BROUGHAM PARISIENNE BROUGHAM WAGON

YEAR IDENTIFICATION

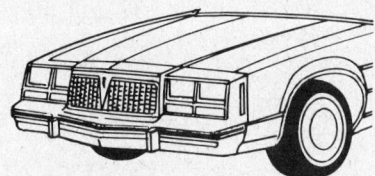
1983–84 Bonneville

1985–87 Bonneville

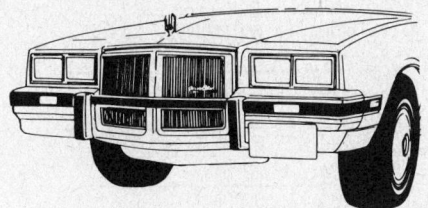
1983–84 Grand Prix

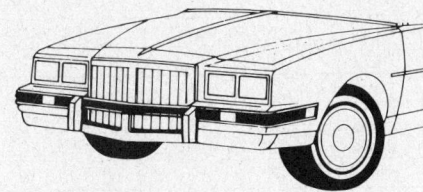
1985–86 Grand Prix

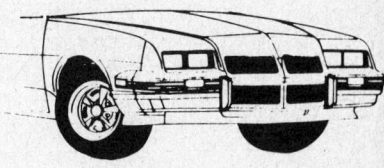
1987 Grand Prix

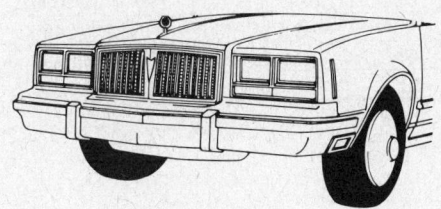
1984–87 Parisienne

SECTION 20

PONTIAC
BONNEVILLE • GRAND PRIX • SAFARI • PARISIENNE

VEHICLE IDENTIFICATION NUMBER (VIN)

It is important for servicing and ordering parts to be certain of the vehicle and engine identification. The VIN (vehicle identification number) is a 17 digit number visible through the windshield on the driver's side of the dash and contains the vehicle and engine identification codes. It can be interpreted as follows:

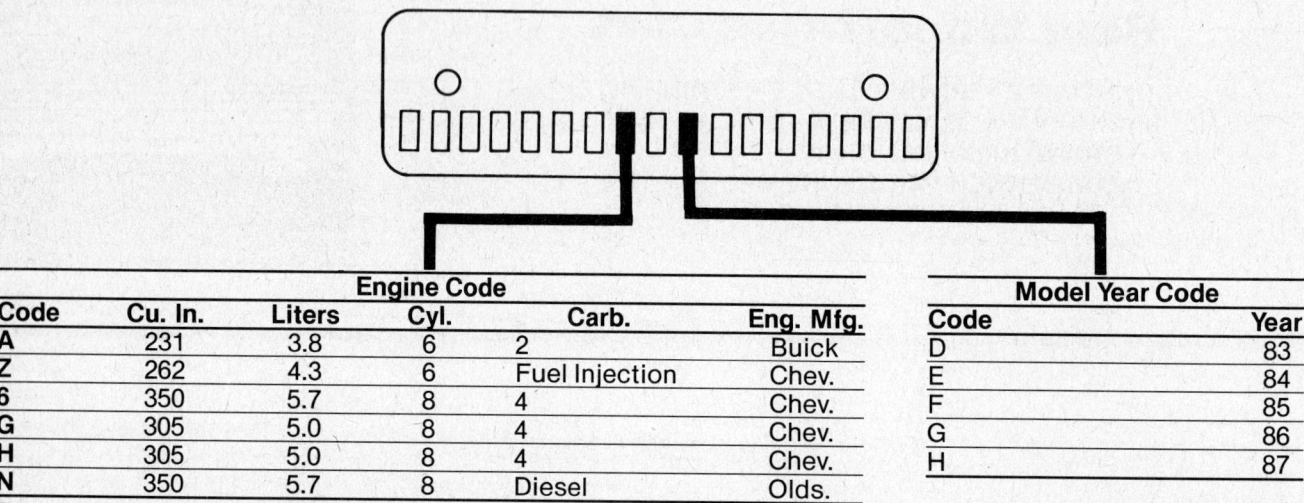

		Engine Code			
Code	Cu. In.	Liters	Cyl.	Carb.	Eng. Mfg.
A	231	3.8	6	2	Buick
Z	262	4.3	6	Fuel Injection	Chev.
6	350	5.7	8	4	Chev.
G	305	5.0	8	4	Chev.
H	305	5.0	8	4	Chev.
N	350	5.7	8	Diesel	Olds.

Model Year Code	
Code	Year
D	83
E	84
F	85
G	86
H	87

The seventeen digit Vehicle Identification Number can be used to determine engine application and model year. The 10th digit indicates the model year, and the 8th digit identifies the factory installed engine.

GENERAL ENGINE SPECIFICATIONS

Year	Eng. VIN Code	Engine No. Cyl. Displacement Cu. In.	Liter	Eng. Mfg.	Carburetor Type	Horsepower @ rpm	Torque @ rpm (ft lbs)	Bore × Stroke (in.)	Compression Ratio	Oil Pressure
'83	A	6-231	3.8	Buick	2 bbl	110 @ 3800	190 @ 1600	3.800 × 3.400	8.0:1	37 ①
	H	8-305	5.0	Chev.	4 bbl	150 @ 3800	240 @ 2400	3.736 × 3.480	8.6:1	45 ③
	N	8-350	5.7	Olds.	Diesel	105 @ 3200	200 @ 1600	4.057 × 3.385	22.5:1	35 ②
'84	A	6-231	3.8	Buick	2 bbl	110 @ 3800	190 @ 1600	3.800 × 3.400	8.0:1	37 ①
	H	8-305	5.0	Chev.	4 bbl	150 @ 3800	240 @ 2400	3.736 × 3.480	8.6:1	45 ③
	G	8-305	5.0	Chev.	4 bbl	190 @ 4800	240 @ 3200	3.736 × 3.480	8.6:1	45 ③
	N	8-350	5.7	Olds.	Diesel	105 @ 3200	200 @ 1600	4.057 × 3.385	22.5:1	30 ④
'85	A	6-231	3.8	Buick	2 bbl	110 @ 3800	190 @ 1600	3.800 × 3.400	8.0:1	37 ①
	Z	6-262	4.3	Chev.	F.I. ⑤	110 @ 4000	190 @ 1600	4.000 × 3.480	9.3:1	45 ③
	H	8-305	5.0	Chev.	4 bbl	105 @ 3200	240 @ 2400	3.736 × 3.480	8.6:1	45 ③
	G	8-305	5.0	Chev.	4 bbl	105 @ 3200	240 @ 2400	3.736 × 3.480	8.6:1	45 ③
	6	8-350	5.7	Chev.	4 bbl	205 @ 4200	290 @ 4200	4.000 × 3.480	8.2:1	45 ③
	N	8-350	5.7	Olds.	Diesel	105 @ 3200	205 @ 1600	4.057 × 3.385	22.5:1	30-45 ④
'86-'87	A	6-231	3.8	Buick	2 bbl	110 @ 3800	190 @ 1600	3.800 × 3.400	8.0:1	37 ①
	G	8-305	5.0	Chev.	4 bbl	105 @ 3200	240 @ 2400	3.736 × 3.480	8.6:1	45 ③
	H	8-305	5.0	Chev.	4 bbl	150 @ 4200 ⑥	235 @ 2000 ⑦	3.736 × 3.480	9.5:1	45 ③
	Z	6-262	4.3	Chev.	F.I. ⑤	110 @ 4000	190 @ 1600	4.000 × 3.480	9.3:1	45 ③

① at 2400 rpm
② at 1500-3000 rpm
③ at 2000 rpm
④ at 1500 rpm
⑤ Electronic Fuel Injection
⑥ Parisienne—165hp @ 4200 rpm
⑦ Parisienne—245 lbs. ft. @ 2400 rpm

PONTIAC 20
BONNEVILLE • GRAND PRIX • SAFARI • PARISIENNE

TUNE-UP SPECIFICATIONS

When analyzing compression test results, look for uniformity among cylinders rather than specific pressures.

Year	Eng. VIN Code	Engine No. Cyl. Displacement Cu. In.	Liter	Eng. Mfg.	Spark Plugs Orig. Type•	Gap (in.)	Distributor Point Dwell (deg)	Distributor Point Gap (in.)	Ignition Timing (deg)▲ Auto. Trans.	Intake Valve Opens ■(deg)	Fuel Pump Pressure (psi)	Idle Speed• (rpm) Auto. Trans.
'83	A	6-231	3.8	Buick	R-45TS8	.080	Electronic		15B	16	4.25–5.75	500
	H	8-305	5.0	Chev.	R-45TS	.045	Electronic		6B	—	5.5–7.0	500/650
	N	8-350	5.7	Olds.	—	—	—		4A	16	5.5–6.5	600/750
'84	A	6-231	3.8	Buick	R-45TS8	.080	Electronic		15B	16	4.25–5.75	500
	H	8-305	5.0	Chev.	R-45TS	.045	Electronic		6B	44	5.5–7.0	500/650
	G	8-305	5.0	Chev.	R-45TS	.045	Electronic		6B	44	5.5–7.0	500/650
	N	8-350	5.7	Olds.	—	—	—		4A	16	5.5–6.5	600-750
'85	A	6-231	3.8	Buick	R-45TS8	.080	Electronic		15B	16	4.25–5.75	500
	Z	6-262	4.3	Chev.	R-43CTS	.035	Electronic		6B	16	5.5–6.5	450/900
	H	8-305	5.0	Chev.	R-45TS	.045	Electronic		6B	44	5.5–7.0	500/650
	G	8-305	5.0	Chev.	R-45TS	.045	Electronic		6B	44	5.5–7.0	500/650
	6	8-350	5.7	Chev.	R-45TS	.045	Electronic		6B	16	5.5–6.5	475
	N	8-350	5.7	Olds.	—	—	—		4A	16	5.5–6.5	600-750
'86	A	6-231	3.8	Buick	R-45TS8	.080	Electronic		①	16	5.5–6.5	①
	G	8-305	5.0	Chev.	R45TS	.045	Electronic		①	44	5.5–7.0	①
	H	8-305	5.0	Chev.	R45TS	.045	Electronic		①	44	5.5–7.0	①
	Z	6-262	4.3	Chev.	R43CTS	.035	Electronic		①	16	5.5–6.5	①
'87					Refer to Underhood Emission Information Decal							

NOTE: The underhood specifications sticker often reflects tune-up specification changes made in production. Sticker figures must be used if they disagree with those in this chart.
Part numbers in this chart are not recommendations by Chilton for any product by brand name.
• Figure in parentheses indicates California engine. Where two idle speeds appear separately by a slash, the second is with the solenoid disconnected.
■ All figures are in degrees Before Top Dead Center.
① Refer to Underhood Emission Information Decal

FIRING ORDERS

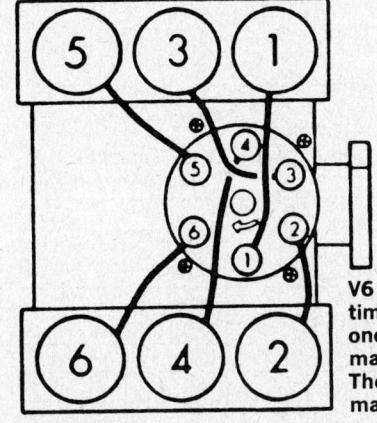

V6 harmonic balancers have two timing marks: one is 1/8 in. wide, and one is 1/16 in. wide. Use the 1/16 in. mark for timing with a hand held light. The 1/8 in. mark is used only with a magnetic timing pick-up probe.

GM (Buick) 231 V6 engine
GM (Chevrolet) 262 V6 engine
Firing order: 1–6–5–4–3–2
Distributor rotation: clockwise

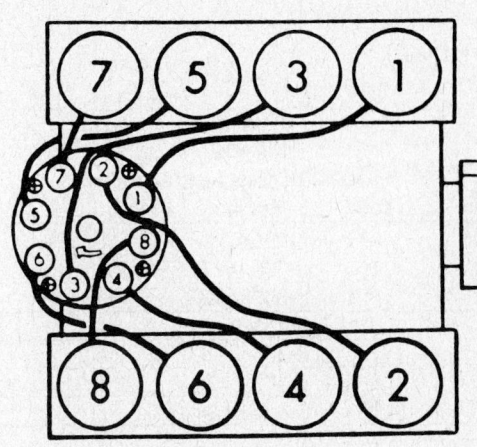

GM (Chevrolet) 305, 350 V8 engines
Firing order: 1–8–4–3–6–5–7–2
Distributor rotation: clockwise

20–5

PONTIAC
BONNEVILLE · GRAND PRIX · SAFARI · PARISIENNE

VALVE SPECIFICATIONS

Year	Engine No. Cyl. Displacement (cu. in.)	Seat Angle (deg)	Face Angle (deg)	Spring Test Pressure (lbs. @ in.)	Spring Installed Height (in.)	Stem-to-Guide Clearance (in.) Intake	Stem-to-Guide Clearance (in.) Exhaust	Stem Diameter (in.) Intake	Stem Diameter (in.) Exhaust
'83–'87	6-231 Buick	45	45	168 @ 1.32	1.72	.0015–.0032	.0015–.0032	.3407	.3409
	V6-262 Chev.	46	45	206 @ 1.25	1.70	.0010–.0027	.0010–.0027	.3414	.3414
	8-305 Chev.	46	45	200 @ 1.25 ①	1.70 ②	.0010–.0027	.0010–.0027	.3414	.3414
	8-350 Olds. Diesel	45 ③	44 ④	205 @ 1.300	1.67	.0010–.0027	.0015–.0032	.3429	.3424

① VIN Y 180–194 lbs. @ 1.270 in.
② VIN Y 1.670 in.
③ Exhaust: 31°
④ Exhaust: 30°

CRANKSHAFT AND CONNECTING ROD SPECIFICATIONS
All measurements are given in inches

Year	Engine No. Cyl. Displacement (cu. in.)	Crankshaft Main Brg. Journal Dia.	Crankshaft Main Brg. Oil Clearance	Crankshaft Shaft End-Play	Crankshaft Thrust on No.	Connecting Rod Diameter Journal	Connecting Rod Clearance Oil	Connecting Rod Clearance Side
'83–'87	6-231 Buick	2.4995	.0004–.0015	.004–.008	2	2.2495–2.2487	.0005–.0026	.006–.027
	V6-262 Chev.	2.4484–2.4493 ⑤	.0008–.0020 ⑥	.002–.006	4	2.2487–2.2498	.0013–.0035	.006–.014
	8-305 Chev.	2.4484–2.4493 ⑤①	.0008–.0020 ⑥	.002–.006	5	2.0986–2.0998 ③	.0013–.0035 ④	.006–.014
	8-350 Olds. Diesel	2.9993–3.0003	.0005–.0021 ②	.0035–.0135	3	2.1238–2.1248	.0005–.0026	.006–.020

① VIN Y #2, 3, 4, 5—2.4985–2.4995 in.
   #1—2.4988–2.4998 in.
② No. 5—.0015–.0031 in.
③ VIN Y 2.1238–2.1248 in.
④ VIN Y—.0004–.0033 in.
⑤ Intermediate—2.4481–2.4490
   Rear—2.4479–2.4488
⑥ Intermediate—.0011–.0020
   Rear—.0017–.0032

PISTON AND RING SPECIFICATIONS
All measurements in Inches

Year	Engine	Ring Side Clearance Top Compression	Ring Side Clearance Bottom Compression	Ring Gap Top Compression	Ring Gap Bottom Compression	Piston-to-Bore Clearance (in.)
'83–'87	305	.0012–.0032	.0012–.0032	.010–.020	.010–.025	.0012
'83–'87	6-231	.0030–.0050	.0030–.0050	.013–.012	.013–.023	.0016–.0038
'83–'85	8-350 Diesel	.005–.007	.003–.005	.015–.025	.015–.025	.005–.006
'85–'87	V6-262	.0012–.0032	.0012–.0032	.010–.020	.010–.025	.0012

TORQUE SPECIFICATIONS
All readings in ft. lbs.

Year	Eng. V.I.N. Code	Engine No. Cyl. Displacement Cu. In.	Cylinder Head Bolts	Rod Bearing Bolts	Main Bearing Bolts	Crankshaft Bolt	Flywheel-to-Crankshaft Bolts	Manifold Intake	Manifold Exhaust
'83	A	6-231	80	40	100	225	60	45	25
	H	8-305	65	45	70	60	60	30	20
	N	8-350 Diesel	130 ①	42	120	200–310	60	40 ①	25
'84	A	6-231	80	40	100	225	60	45	25
	H	8-305	65	45	70	60	60	30	20
	G	8-305	65	45	70	60	60	30	20
	N	8-350 Diesel	130 ①	42	120	200–310	60	40 ①	25
'85	A	6-231	74	40	100	225	60	35	25
	Z	6-262	60–75	45	80	70	60	25–45	20
	H	8-305	60–75	45	80	70	60	25–45	20
	G	8-305	60–75	45	80	70	60	25–45	20
	N	8-350 Diesel	130 ①	42	120	200–310	60	40 ①	25

PONTIAC
BONNEVILLE · GRAND PRIX · SAFARI · PARISIENNE
SECTION 20

TORQUE SPECIFICATIONS
All readings in ft. lbs.

Year	Eng. V.I.N. Code	Engine No. Cyl. Displacement Cu. In.	Cylinder Head Bolts	Rod Bearing Bolts	Main Bearing Bolts	Crankshaft Bolt	Flywheel-to-Crankshaft Bolts	Manifold Intake	Manifold Exhaust
'86–'87	A	6-231	②	45	100	200	60	45	20
	Y	8-305	125 ①	42	80 ③	200–310	60	40 ①	25
	H	8-305	75	47	85	75	70	45	20 ④
	Z	6-262	75	47	85	75	70	45	20 ④

① Dip bolts in oil before tightening
② 1st step—Torque to 25 ft. lbs.
   2nd step—Tighten Bolts 90° (¼ turn)
   3rd step—Tighten Bolts another 90° (¼ turn)
   If 60 ft. lbs is reached before step 3 is completed, do not complete balance of second 90° turn.
③ Caps number 1, 2, 3 and 4—80 ft. lbs.
   Cap number 5—120 ft. lbs.
④ V8—Left side—two center bolts: 25 ft. lbs.
   V8—Right side—3rd 2nd 4th Bolts from Front: 25 ft. lbs.
   V6—Both sides—two center bolts: 25 ft. lbs.

WHEEL ALIGNMENT SPECIFICATIONS

Year	Model	Caster Range (deg)	Caster Pref. Setting (deg)	Camber Range (deg)	Camber Pref. Setting (deg)	Toe-in (in.)	Steering Axis inclin. (deg.)
'83	Gran Prix and Bonneville	2P–4P	3P	5/16N–15/16P	½P	1/8	8
'84	Gran Prix and Bonneville	3P–4P	3½P	5/16N–15/16P	½P	1/8	8
'85–'87	Gran Prix and Bonneville	2P–4P	3P	5/16N–15/16P	½P	1/8	8
'84–'87	Parisenne	2P–4P	3P	0–15/8P	13/16P	1/8	9¾

P Positive
N Negative

CAPACITIES

Year	Engine No. Cyl. (Cu. In.) Displacement	Engine Crankcase Add 1 Qt For New Filter	Transmission Pts-to-Refill After Draining Automatic •	Drive Axle (pts)	Gasoline Tank (gals)	Cooling System (qts) With Heater	Cooling System (qts) With A/C
'83	6-231	4	6.0	①	②	—	11¾
	8-305	4	6.0 ③	①	②	—	15½
	8-350 Diesel	6	6.0	①	②	—	18.3
'84–'87	6-231	4	6.0	①	②	—	11¾
	8-305, 350	4	6.0 ③	①	②	—	15½
	8-350 Diesel	6	6.0	①	②	—	18.3
'85–'87	V6-262	5	6.0	①	18.5	13.8	14.3

• Specifications do not include torque converter
  Add just enough fluid to fill the transmission to the proper level. It takes only one pint to raise the level from "ADD" to "FULL" with a hot transmission. Do not overfill.
—Not applicable
① 7.5" ring gear: 3.5 pts
   8.5" ring gear: 5.4 pts
   8.75" ring gear: 5.0 pts
② Gasoline coupe and sedan—25 gal;
   diesel—27 gal.
   All station wagons—22 gal.
③ Automatic Overdrive: 10 pts

SECTION 20

PONTIAC
BONNEVILLE • GRAND PRIX • SAFARI • PARISIENN™

ELECTRICAL SECTION

For Overhaul Procedures, Refer to the Unit Repair Section.

Charging System

ALTERNATOR

Removal and Installation

1. Disconnect the negative battery terminal.
2. Label and remove the alternator wires or connector.
3. Loosen the adjusting bolts.
4. Remove the V-belt and through-bolt.
5. Remove the alternator.
6. To install, reverse the removal procedure. Adjust the belt tension.

VOLTAGE REGULATOR

Removal and Installation

The voltage regulator is incorporated within the alternator assembly. There is no adjustment procedure. Should the regulator require service, the alternator must be disassembled.

Starting System

STARTER

Removal and Installation

1. Disconnect the negative battery terminal.
2. Raise the vehicle and support it safely.
3. Disconnect the brace. Remove the flywheel shield, as required.
4. Remove the mounting bolts and the starter motor with the cable and solenoid wires.
5. Remove the wires from the starter. Remove the starter from the vehicle.
6. To reinstall, reverse the procedure.

Ignition System

DISTRIBUTOR

Removal and Installation

1. Disconnect the ignition switch battery feed wire from the distributor cap. Disconnect the four wire connector.
2. Remove the distributor cap.
3. Crank the engine so that the rotor points to No.1 cylinder plug tower and the timing mark on the crankshaft pulley are indexed with the pointer.

NOTE: Observe the position of the rotor and make marks on the distributor housing and on the block that line up with tip of the rotor. Make sure these marks line up upon reassembly.

4. Remove the rotor.
5. Remove the distributor hold-down bolt and clamp. Do not disturb the engine after the distributor has been removed.
6. Lift the distributor out of its bore. Notice the slight rotation of the rotor as the distributor is removed from the block.
7. Installation procedure is the reverse of the removal procedure. However, before inserting the distributor into the block, the rotor should be moved slightly to one side. This is necessary because of the helical cut of the gears. As the distributor seats in its bore, the rotor will rotate slightly so that the reference marks will once again be in line. Re-time the engine with a timing light.

DRIVE BELT TENSIONING SPECIFICATIONS

Engine	VIN	Tensioning	Generator	Power Steering	Air Conditioning	A.I.R. Pump
\multicolumn{7}{c}{1983-84}
3.8L V-6	A	New	550N/125 lb.	600N/135 lb.	600N/135 lb.	350N/80 lb.
		Used	300N/70 lb.	350N/80 lb.	350N/80 lb.	250N/60 lb.
5.0L V-8	H & G	New	650N/145 lb.	650N/145 lb.	750N/165 lb.	650N/145 lb.
		Used	300N/70 lb.	300N/70 lb.	400N/90 lb.	300N/70 lb.
5.7L V-8 Diesel	N	New	650N/145 lb. ①	750N/165 lb.	750N/165 lb.	—
		Used	250N/60 lb.	400N/90 lb.	400N/90 lb.	—
5.7L V-8 Diesel	N	New	700N/155 lb. ②	750N/165 lb.	750N/165 lb.	—
		Used	350N/80 lb.	350N/80 lb.	400N/90 lb.	—
\multicolumn{7}{c}{1985-87}
3.8L V-6	A	New	650N/145 lb.	650N/145 lb.	750N/165 lb.	650N/145 lb.
		Used	300N/70 lb.	300N/70 lb.	400N/90 lb.	300N/70 lb.
4.3L V-6	Z	New	650N/145 lb.	650N/145 lb.	750N/165 lb.	650N/145 lb.
		Used	300N/70 lb.	300N/70 lb.	400N/90 lb.	300N/70 lb.
5.0L V-8	H & G, 6	New	650N/145 lb.	650N/145 lb.	750N/165 lb.	650N/145 lb.
		Used	300N/70 lb.	300N/70 lb.	400N/90 lb.	300N/70 lb.
5.7L V-8 Diesel	N	New	650N/145 lb. ft. ①	750N/165 lb. ft.	750N/165 lb. ft.	—
		Used	250N/60 lb. ft.	400N/90 lb. ft.	400N/90 lb. ft.	—
5.7L V-8 Diesel	N	New	700N/155 lb. ft. ②	750N/165 lb. ft.	750N/165 lb. ft.	—
		Used	350N/80 lb. ft.	350N/80 lb. ft.	400N/90 lb. ft.	—

① Cogged Belt
② Non-cogged Belt

8. If the engine has been cranked after the distributor was removed, the following procedure must be used.
9. With No.1 piston on the compression stroke, rotate the crankshaft until the pulley timing mark indexes with the stationary mark at TDC.
10. Replace the distributor to block gasket.
11. Install the distributor in the block. The rotor should point toward the contact in the cap for No.1 cylinder. Move the rotor slightly to the side because as the distributor is pressed into its bore it will rotate a small amount.
12. Install the distributor clamp and clamp bolt.
13. Install the rotor, cap, and coil wire.
14. Retime the engine with a timing light.

IGNITION TIMING

Adjustment

1. Refer to the vehicle control information label which is located on the radiator support panel, for the proper timing information.
2. If the engine timing requires adjustment, loosen the distributor hold down bolt and rotate the distributor slowly in either direction, to advance or retard the engine timing.
3. Tighten the hold down bolt and recheck the engine timing.
4. Some engines incorporate a magnetic timing probe hole which is used when setting the engine timing with special electronic equipment. Consult manufacturers instructions if using this form of timing equipment.

Electrical Controls

IGNITION LOCK CYLINDER

Removal and Installation

1. Disconnect the negative battery cable.
2. Remove the steering wheel.
3. Place the lock in the Run position.
4. Remove the lock plate, the turn signal switch and the buzzer switch.
5. Remove the lock retaining screw and remove the lock cylinder.
6. To install, hold the replacement cylinder and rotate the key clockwise.
7. Properly align the keyway in the cylinder with the housing and insert the lock cylinder into the lock column.
8. Install the retaining screw. Tighten the screw to 40 inch lbs. on regular columns and 22 inch lbs. on tilt columns.
9. Reverse the remainder of the removal procedure to install.

IGNITION SWITCH

Removal and Installation

1. Disconnect the negative battery terminal.
2. Loosen the toe pan screws on the steering column.
3. Remove the column to instrument panel trim plates and attaching nuts.
4. Lower the column and disconnect the switch wire connectors.

— CAUTION —
The steering column must be supported at all times to prevent damage.

5. Remove the switch attaching screws and remove the switch.
6. To replace, move the key lock to the LOCK position.
7. Move the actuator rod hole in the switch to the LOCK position.

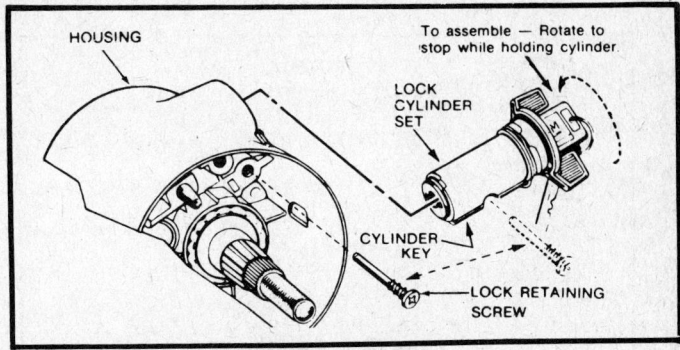

Lock cylinder installation details
(© General Motors Corporation)

8. Install the switch with the rod in the hole.
9. Position and reassemble the steering column in the reverse of the disassembly procedure.

Adjustment
STANDARD COLUMN

1. Place the switch in the OFF position.
2. Position the switch on the column, then move the slider to the extreme left (toward the wheel).
3. Move the slider back two positions to the right of ACCESSORY position.
4. Place the key in any run position and shift the transmission into any position but Park.
5. Position the lock toward ACCESSORY with a light finger pressure and secure the switch.

TILT COLUMN

1. Place the key in ACCESSORY position; leave the key in the lock.
2. Loosen the switch mounting screws.
3. Push the switch upward toward the wheel to make certain it is in ACCESSORY detent.
4. Hold the key in full counterclockwise Accessory position and tighten the switch mounting screws.
5. The switch is properly adjusted if: it will go into ACCESSORY position, the key can be removed when in lock, and the switch will go into START position.

NEUTRAL SAFETY/BACK-UP SWITCH

Removal and Installation
COLUMN MOUNTED SHIFTER

The neutral safety switch is incorporated into the steering column bowl, between the lock and the transmission selector and is non-adjustable.

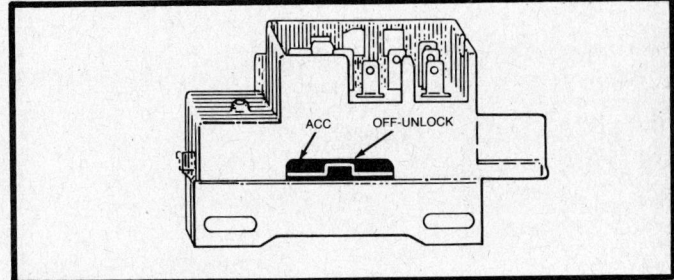

Positioning the ignition switch
(© General Motors Corporation)

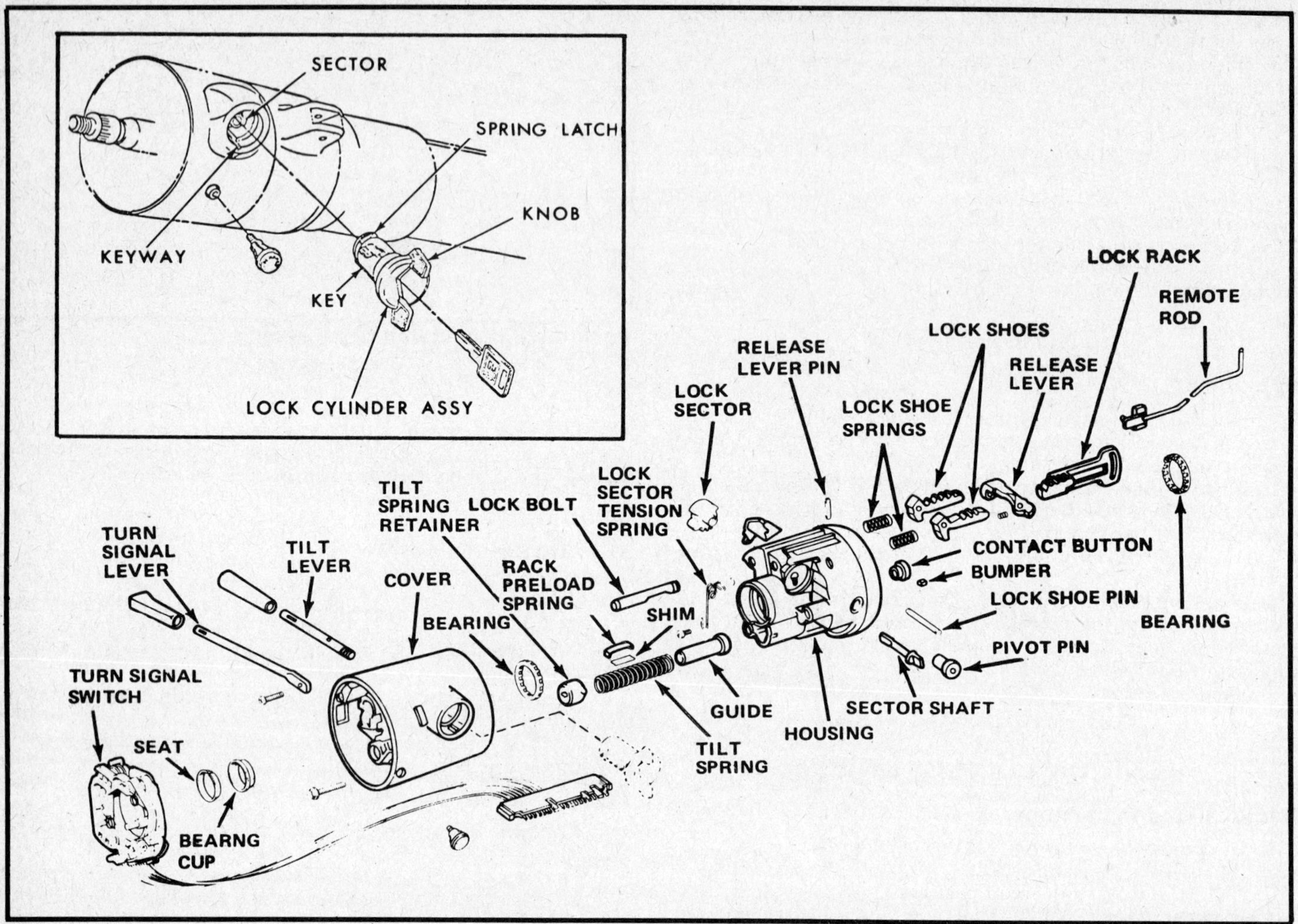

SECTION 20

PONTIAC
BONNEVILLE • GRAND PRIX • SAFARI • PARISIENNE

Exploded view of the ignition lock and upper steering column assembly (© General Motors Corporation)

The back-up light switch still remains on the steering column and looks similar to the previous switches except for the electrical terminals.

1. Remove wire connectors from the combination back-up and neutral safety switch.
2. Remove two screws attaching the switch to the steering column.
3. Installation is the reverse of removal. To adjust a new switch:
   a. Position the shift lever in neutral.
   b. Loosen the attaching screws. Install a 0.090 in. gauge pin into the outer hole in the switch cover.
   c. Rotate the switch until the pin goes into the alignment hole in the inner plastic slide.
   d. Tighten the switch to column attaching screws and remove the gauge pin. Torque the screws to 20 inch lbs. maximum.
3. Make sure that the engine starts only in the park and neutral positions.

FLOOR MOUNTED SHIFTER

1. Disconnect the negative battery cable.
2. Remove the floor console cover.
3. Disconnect all electrical connectors on the switch assembly.
4. Position the shift lever in the 'N' detent. Remove the screws securing the switch, and remove the unit from the vehicle.
5. Installation is the reverse of removal. Be sure that the new switch is installed with the selector level in the neutral position.
6. After installation move the selector from the 'N' position in order to shear the retaining pin.

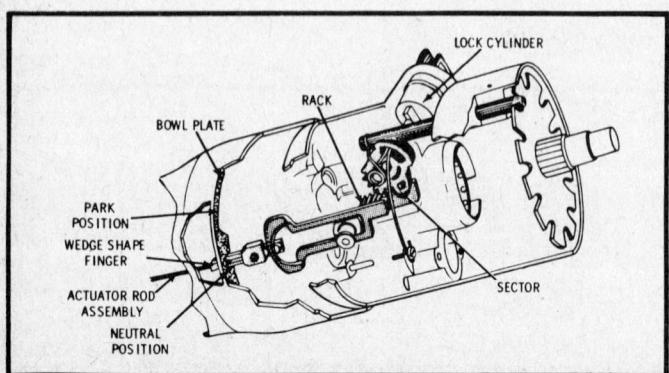

Mechanical neutral start system
(© General Motors Corporation)

HEADLIGHT SWITCH

Removal and Installation

1. Disconnect the negative battery terminal. Pull the knob all the way out. From under dash depress button on switch and remove knob and shaft.
2. Remove all the necessary trim panels in order to gain access to the switch retaining nut. Remove the retaining nut.
3. Remove the wire connector from the switch and remove the switch.
4. Reverse the procedure to install.

HORN SWITCH

Removal and Installation

1. Disconnect the negative battery cable.
2. Remove the horn pad. Remove the contract assembly and all other related components.
3. If the vehicle is equipped with tilt and telescopic steering column, remove the lock lever and plate.
4. Installation is the reverse of the removal procedure.

TURN SIGNAL SWITCH

Removal and Installation

1. Disconnect the negative battery cable.
2. Remove the steering wheel, using the proper wheel removal tool.
3. Pry the lockplate cover off, using a suitable tool.
4. Place a lockplate removal tool over the steering shaft and tighten the nut to depress the lockplate. Remove the snap ring retainer.
5. Remove the lockplate and the cancelling cam.
6. Remove the upper bearing preload spring. With the turn signal lever in the right turn position, remove the lever attaching screw and the lever. Remove the actuator arm screw and the arm. Remove the turn signal lever. Remove the three turn signal switch screws.
7. Push in the hazard switch knob and remove the retaining screw and the knob. On tilt columns, position the housing in the center position.
8. Remove the lower trim panel from the instrument panel and disconnect the turn signal connector from the wiring harness. Remove the connector.
9. Remove the bolts attaching the surrounding bracket assembly to the jacket. On some column shift automatics, it may be necessary to remove the shift indicator needle attaching screw and remove or disconnect the needle.
10. Hold the steering column in place and remove the two attaching nuts from below. Remove the bracket assembly and the wire protector. Loosely reinstall the nuts to hold the column in place.
11. Carefully remove the turn signal switch and the wiring.
12. To install, place the switch in the right turn position and push the switch in until it is properly seated. Torque the three attaching nuts to 35 inch lbs. Return the switch to the neutral position and reverse the removal procedure.

MULTI-FUNCTION SWITCH

Removal and Installation

1. Disconnect the negative battery cable. Remove the steering wheel. Remove the turn signal switch.
2. It may be necessary to loosen the two column mounting nuts and remove the four bracket-to-mast jacket screws, then separate the bracket from the mast jacket to allow the connector clip on the ignition switch to be pulled out of the column assembly.

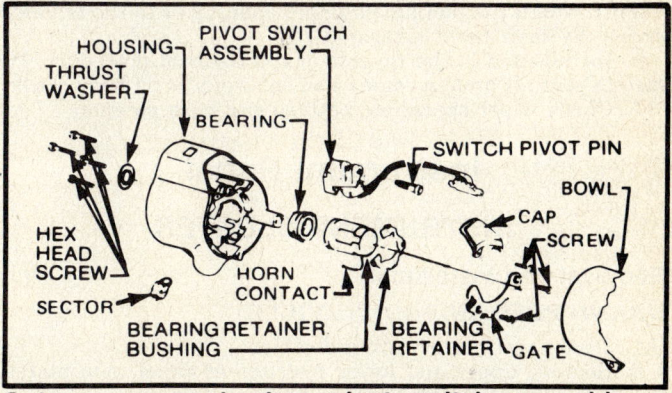

Column mounted wiper pivot switch assembly removal (© General Motors Corporation)

3. Disconnect the washer/wiper switch lower connector.
4. Remove the screws attaching the column housing to the mast jacket. Be sure to note the position of the dimmer switch actuator rod for reassembly in the same position. Remove the column housing and switch as an assembly.

NOTE: The tilt and travel columns have a removal plastic cover on the column housing. This provides access to the wiper switch without removing the entire column housing.

5. Turn upside down and use a drift to remove the pivot pin from the washer/wiper switch. Remove the switch.
6. Place the switch into position in the housing, then install the pivot pin.
7. Position the housing onto the mast jacket and attach by installing the screws. Install the dimmer switch actuator rod in the same position as noted earlier. Check switch operation.
8. Reconnect lower end of switch assembly.
9. Install remaining components in reverse order of removal. Be sure to attach column mounting bracket in original position.

WINDSHIELD WIPER MOTOR

Removal and Installation

1. Disconnect the negative battery cable.
2. Raise the hood and remove the cowl screen.
3. Loosen the transmission drive link to crank arm retaining bolts. Remove the drive link from the motor crank arm.
4. Disconnect the electrical wiring and the washer hoes from the motor assembly.
5. Remove the motor retaining screws. Remove the windshield wiper motor while guiding the crank arm through the hole.
6. Installation is the reverse of the removal procedure. The motor must be in the park position before assembling the crank arm to the drive link.

WIPER LINKAGE/TRANSMISSION

Removal and Installation

1. Disconnect the negative battery cable.
2. Raise the hood and remove the cowl vent screen. Remove both wiper arms and blade assemblies.
3. Loosen, but do not remove the retaining nuts securing the transmission drive link to the motor crank arm.
4. Disconnect the transmission drive link from the motor crank arm. Remove the transmission to body retaining screws.
5. Remove the transmission and linkage assembly by guid-

SECTION 20

PONTIAC
BONNEVILLE • GRAND PRIX • SAFARI • PARISIENNE

ing it through the plenum chamber opening or to the left side under the dash panel extension.

6. Installation is the reverse of the removal procedure. Be sure to seal all broken seams and cut welds with body caulk.
7. Check wiper operation, pattern and park position.

Instrument Panel

INSTRUMENT CLUSTER

Removal and Installation

GRAND PRIX AND BONNEVILLE

1. Disconnect battery ground cable.
2. Remove upper and lower instrument panel trim plates. Remove the cigar lighter retaining ring.
3. Remove instrument panel bezel attaching screws and bezel, if equipped.
4. On column mounted shift models, remove shift indicator cable.
5. Lower the steering column, as required.
6. Remove the cluster retaining screws, pull cluster outward and disconnect speedometer cable and printed circuit connector, if equipped.
7. Remove lower bezel anti-rattle clips, if equipped, then instrument cluster.
8. Reverse procedure to install.

PARISIENNE

1. Disconnect battery ground cable.
2. Remove four steering column lower cove screws and cover.
3. Disconnect shift indicator cable from steering column.
4. Remove two steering column to instrument panel screws and lower steering column.

NOTE: Use extreme care when lower steering to prevent damage to column assembly.

5. Remove six screws and three snap-in fasteners from perimeter of instrument cluster lens.
6. Remove two screws from upper surface of grey sheet metal trim plate.
7. Remove two stud nuts from lower corner of cluster.
8. Disconnect speedometer cable and pull cluster from instrument panel.
9. Disconnect electrical connectors from cluster and remove from vehicle.
10. Reverse procedure to install.

SPEEDOMETER

Removal and Installation

1. Disconnect the negative battery cable.
2. Remove the instrument cluster trim plate.
3. Remove the speedometer retaining screws. Pull the assembly forward in order to disconnect the speedometer cable. To gain slack it may be necessary to disconnect the cable at the cruise control transducer or the transmission.
4. Remove the speedometer assembly from the vehicle.
5. Installation is the same as the removal procedure.

Electrical Circuit Protectors

FUSE PANEL

The fuse panel is located on the left side of the vehicle, under the instrument panel assembly as a swing down unit, or on some models, may be found behind the glove box opening. Other models may have a swing down convenience center.

ELECTRONIC CONTROL MODULE

The electronic control module is located on the right side of the vehicle. It is positioned in front of the right hand kick panel. In order to gain access to the assembly, first remove the trim panel.

TURN SIGNAL FLASHER

The turn signal flasher is mounted on the fuse panel, located on the left side of the vehicle or behind the glove box opening. It may also be mounted on the convenience center swing down panel on certain models.

CONVENIENCE CENTER

The convenience center is a swing-down unit located on the underside of the instrument panel. The swing-down feature provides central location and easy access to buzzers, relays and flasher units. All units are serviced by plug-in replacements.

Cruise Control

OPERATION

1983

The main components of the Cruise Control System are the transducer assembly, resume solenoid valve, vacuum servo and linkage, engagement switch button, the OFF/ON/RESUME switch on the turnsignal lever and release switches, both vacuum and electrical.

If the engine is equipped with a vacuum pump, a check valve is used as part of the resume cruise control vacuum system.

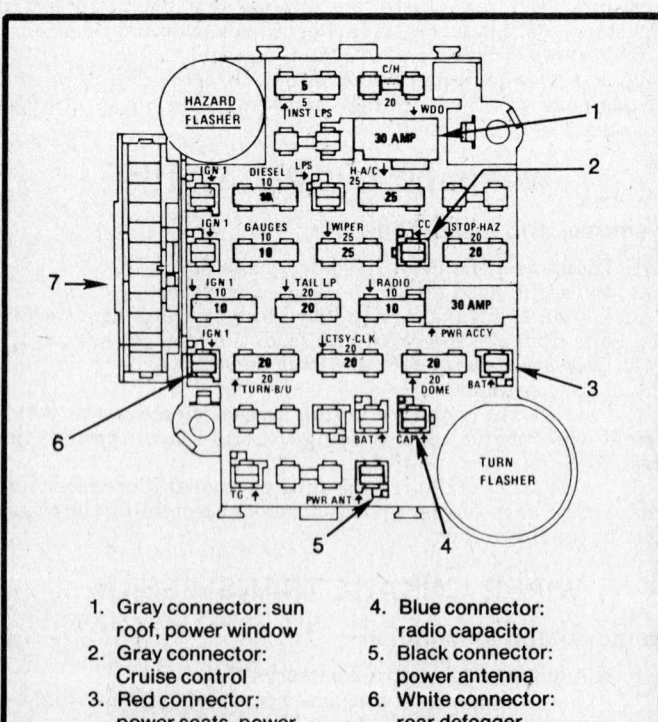

1. Gray connector: sun roof, power window
2. Gray connector: Cruise control
3. Red connector: power seats, power door locks, rear defogger
4. Blue connector: radio capacitor
5. Black connector: power antenna
6. White connector: rear defogger
7. Main body connector

Fuse block assembly—typical
(© General Motors Corporation)

PONTIAC
BONNEVILLE • GRAND PRIX • SAFARI • PARISIENNE
SECTION 20

CONTROL SWITCH CONTINUITY CHECK

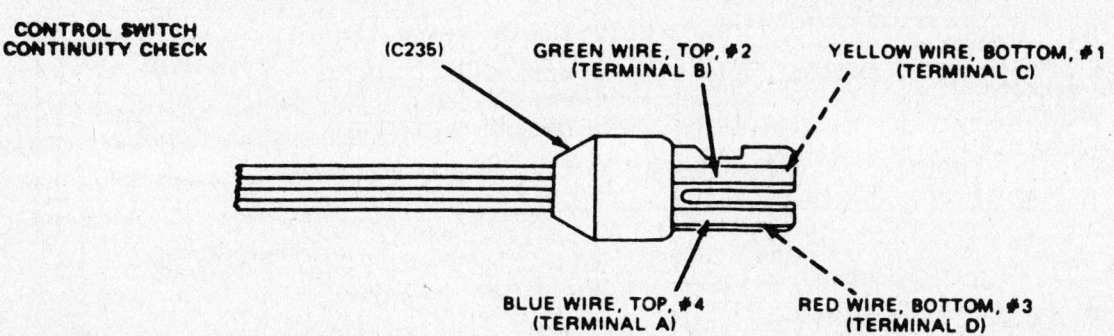

- (C235)
- GREEN WIRE, TOP, #2 (TERMINAL B)
- YELLOW WIRE, BOTTOM, #1 (TERMINAL C)
- BLUE WIRE, TOP, #4 (TERMINAL A)
- RED WIRE, BOTTOM, #3 (TERMINAL D)

C – CLOSED
O – OPEN

SET/COAST (S/C) SW	POSITION SLIDER	1-2	1-3	1-4	2-3	2-4	3-4
NORMAL	OFF	O	O	O	O	O	O
NORMAL	ON	O	O	O	O	C	O
NORMAL	R/A	C	O	C	O	C	O
DEPRESSED	OFF	O	O	O	C	O	O
DEPRESSED	ON	O	O	O	C	C	C
DEPRESSED	R/A	C	C	C	C	C	C

CRUISE CONTROLLER (MODULE) CHECKS AT CONNECTOR
- IGNITION ON
- CONTROLLER DISCONNECTED

PIN	FUNCTION	VOLTAGE TO GND	RESISTANCE	CONDITIONS
G	BRAKE INPUT	12 V / 0 V	–	BRAKE (AND CLUTCH) NOT DEPRESSED / BRAKE (AND/OR CLUTCH) DEPRESSED
L	SET/COAST INPUT	12 V / 0 V / 0 V	–	SLIDER SWITCH "ON" – SET/COAST DEPRESSED / SLIDER SWITCH "ON" – SET/COAST NORMAL / SLIDER SWITCH "OFF" – SET/COAST NORMAL
M	RESUME/ACCEL. INPUT	12 V / 0 V / 0 V	–	SLIDER SWITCH "R/A" POSITION / SLIDER SWITCH "ON" – SET/COAST DEPRESSED OR NORMAL / SLIDER SWITCH "OFF" – SET/COAST DEPRESSED OR NORMAL
J	GROUND	–	0 Ω	MEASURED TO VEHICLE GROUND
A	ON/OFF INPUT	12 V / 0 V	–	SLIDER SWITCH "ON" / SLIDER SWITCH "OFF" – SET/COAST DEPRESSED OR NORMAL
B	INDICATOR LAMP	12 V	–	CRUISE ARMED
F	SPS HIGH	–	20 - 30 Ω	MEASURED BETWEEN PINS F & H – SERVO CONNECTED
H	SPS LOW	–	0 Ω	MEASURED BETWEEN PINS F & H – SERVO DISCONNECTED
D	SPEED SIGNAL	→	→	SEE CHART (DIAGNOSTIC) ON SPEED SENDER TEST
K	VACUUM VALVE CONTROL	–	30 - 50 Ω / ∞ Ω	MEASURED TO GROUND – SERVO CONNECTED / MEASURED TO GROUND – SERVO NOT CONNECTED
C	VENT VALVE CONTROL	–	30 - 50 Ω / ∞ Ω	MEASURED TO GROUND – SERVO CONNECTED / MEASURED TO GROUND – SERVO NOT CONNECTED

SERVO CHECKS
- SERVO CONNECTOR DISCONNECTED
- MEASURE AT SERVO PINS

PIN	FUNCTION	RESISTANCE	CONDITIONS
D	SPS HIGH	20 - 30 Ω	MEASURED BETWEEN PINS D AND B
B	SPS LOW		(IF MEASURED RESISTANCE IS NOT STATED VALUE, REPLACE SERVO)
A	VENT VALVE	30 - 50 Ω	MEASURED BETWEEN PINS A AND C (IF MEASURED RESISTANCE IS NOT STATED VALUE, REPLACE SERVO)
E	VACUUM VALVE	30 - 50 Ω	MEASURED BETWEEN PINS E AND C (IF MEASURED RESISTANCE IS NOT STATED VALUE, REPLACE SERVO)

1984 and later Cruise Control controller, servo and control switch diagnosis

SECTION 20

PONTIAC
BONNEVILLE • GRAND PRIX • SAFARI • PARISIENNE

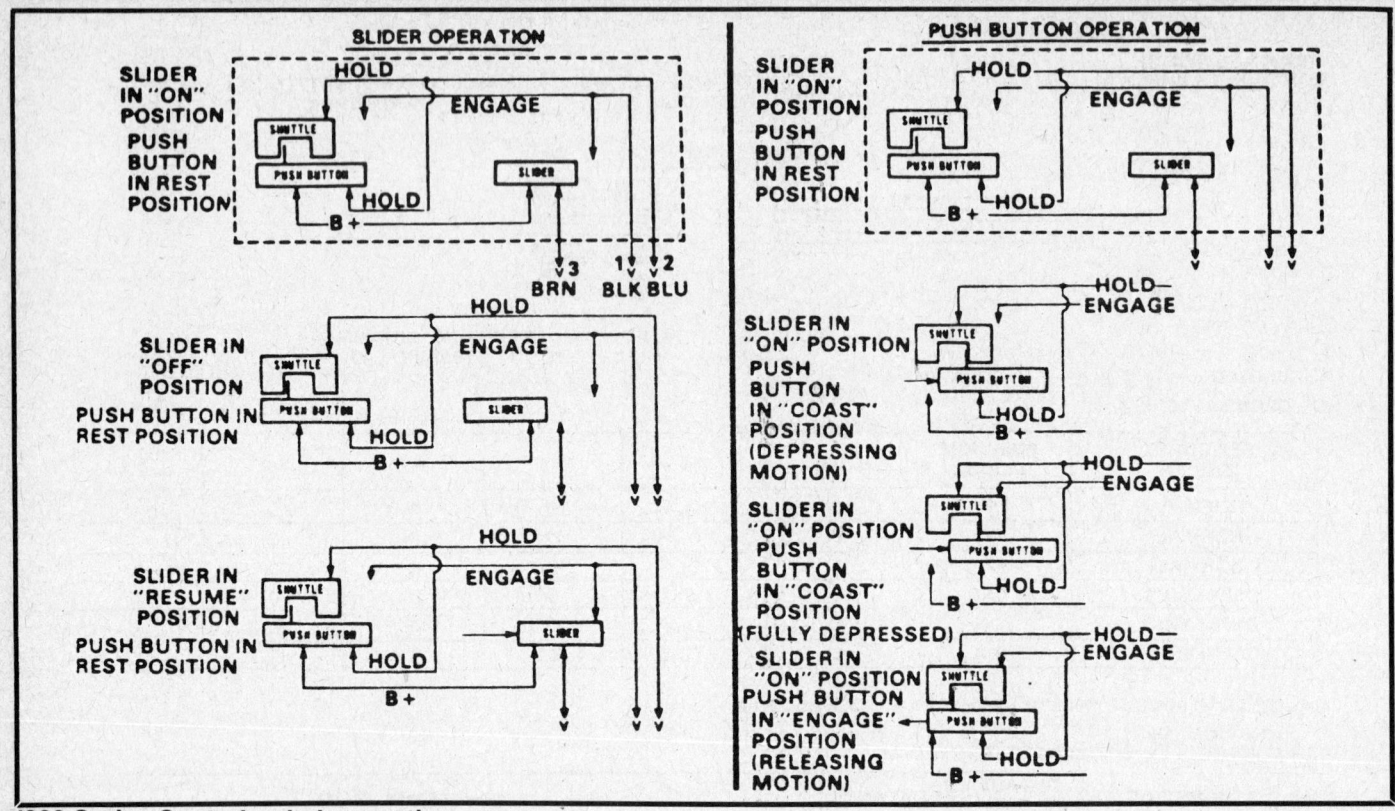

1983 Cruise Control switch operation

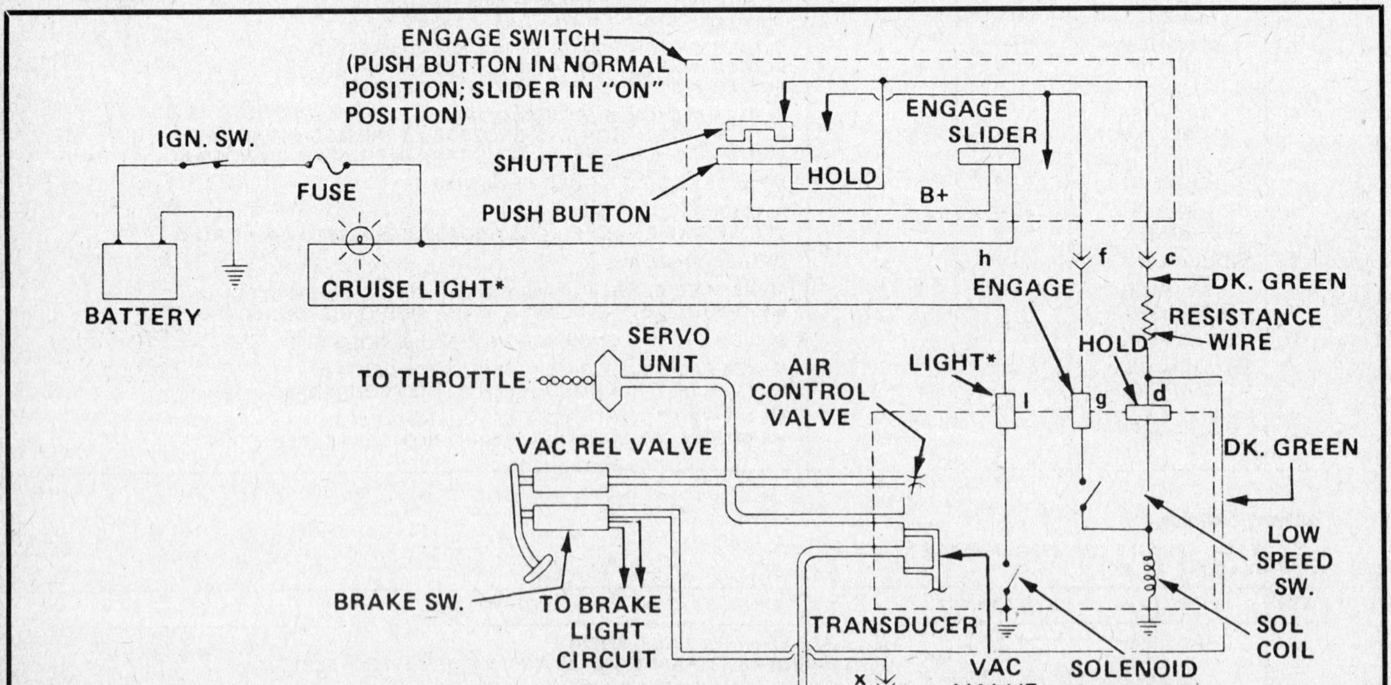

1983 Cruise Control electro-vacuum schematic

*Not on all models

20–14

The check valve selects the higher of the two available vacuum sources (manifold or vacuum pump) to allow maximum system performance under various driving conditions.

Transducer vacuum is sourced in parallel to the intake manifold and vacuum pump. Should the engine load require it, pump vacuum is used on all vacuum circuits.

Aspirator assisted vacuum is obtained from a connection at the air pump, which supplies a small amount of air through the aspirator to the atmosphere. Venturi action within the aspirator develops vacuum, which is used as an assistance when needed under high load cruise conditions.

1984 AND LATER

The main components of the Cruise Control System are the mode control switches, controller (electronic module), servo unit, speed sensor, vacuum supply, electrical and vacuum release switches and the electrical harness.

The electronic cruise control system has the capability to cruise, coast, resume speed, accelerate and "tap up" or "tap down" the speed.

The system uses vacuum to operate the throttle servo unit. The controller monitors vehicle speed, servo position and operates the vacuum. The servo vent valves maintain the correct speed through signals from the controller. The system is inoperative below approximately 25 mph.

The "Tap Up" switch (OFF/ON/RESUME/ACCEL SWITCH) controls speed increases in increments of one mph when quickly tapped. The "Tap Down" switch (SET/COAST) controls speed decrease in one mph increments when quickly tapped.

The vacuum supply comes from one of three supplies; manifold vacuum connected directly to the servo, manifold vacuum through a vacuum storage tank, or vacuum straight from a vacuum pump.

Adjustments

ROD TYPE

Screw rod into link with ignition "Off" and fast idle cam off and throttle closed. Hook the rod through tab on the servo assembly. Adjust the length so that rod assembles over the end of stud with approximately 0.0197 to 0.0397 in. (0.5–1.0 mm) clearance between the stud and the end of the rod channel Install the retainer.

DIESEL ENGINES

1. Adjustment is made with the engine not running.
2. Adjust the rod length to minimum slack with the pump on slow idle screw.

COOLING AND HEATER SECTION

WATER PUMP

Removal and Installation

NOTE: The following is a general procedure for all water pump removal and installation operations. The order of removal and installation can be tailored to the accessories mounted to the engine.

1. Disconnect the negative battery cable. Drain the cooling system. Remove the fan shroud, if required.
2. Remove all drive belts and other necessary components in order to gain access to the water pump assembly retaining bolts.
3. Remove the fan and pulley. Disconnect all hoses from the water pump.
4. Remove the water pump retaining bolts. Remove the water pump from the engine.
5. Installation is the reverse of the removal procedure. Be sure to clean the engine to water pump mating surface before installing the pump.
6. Use a new gasket when installing the pump assembly.
7. Refer to the belt tensioning guide for proper belt adjustment.

BLOWER MOTOR

Removal and Installation

1. Disconnect the negative battery cable.
2. Disconnect the electrical connections from the blower motor.
3. Remove the blower motor flange screws. Remove the blower motor assembly from the heater case.
4. Installation is the reverse of the removal procedure.

HEATER/AC CONTROL ASSEMBLY

Removal and Installation

NOTE: If the vehicle is equipped with touch climate control air conditioning, extreme care should be used when disconnecting the electrical connections from the unit. The removal and installation of the dash mounted temperature control unit is general in the vehicle models. The outlined Steps may not be in the correct order for a specific model. Re-arrange the Steps to relate to the vehicle being repaired.

1. Disconnect the negative battery cable.
2. Remove the necessary instrument panel trim.
3. Remove the radio and/or knobs, radio speaker, ash tray, cigar lighter, and the floor console trim plate, as required.
4. After exposing the control retaining screws, remove them and pull the control away from the dash. Disconnect the bowden cable, electrical and/or vacuum connections.
5. Remove the control unit.
6. The installation is the reverse of the removal procedure.

HEATER CORE

Removal and Installation

1. Drain the cooling system.
2. Remove the heater hoses from the core tubes.
3. Disconnect the electrical connections. Remove the right windshield arm, as required. As required, move the lower windshield trim molding out of the way.
4. Remove the front module cover screws, and remove the module assembly.
5. Remove the heater core from the module.
6. Reverse the procedure to install the heater core. Use a strip caulk type sealer when installing the module to the firewall.

SECTION 20
PONTIAC
BONNEVILLE • GRAND PRIX • SAFARI • PARISIENNE

FUEL SYSTEM

FUEL PUMP

Removal and Installation

EXCEPT DIESEL ENGINE AND FUEL INJECTED ENGINE

1. Disconnect the negative battery cable.
2. Disconnect the vapor return hose, if so equipped.
3. Remove all necessary components in order to gain access to the pump mounting bolts.
4. Disconnect and plug the fuel lines. Remove the bolts which hold the fuel pump and lift off the pump and gasket.
5. Reverse the procedure for installation.

DIESEL ENGINE

1. Disconnect the negative battery cable.
2. Remove the inlet and outlet fuel lines. Disconnect all electrical connectors from the pump assembly.
3. Remove the fuel pump retaining bolts. Remove the fuel pump from its mounting on the engine.
4. Installation is the reverse of the removal procedure. Be sure to torque the retaining bolts to 18 ft. lbs.

FUEL INJECTED ENGINE

1. Disconnect the negative battery cable.
2. Bleed off fuel pressure. Raise and support the vehicle safely.
3. Remove the fuel tank.
4. Remove fuel lever sending unit and pump assembly by turning cam lock ring counterclockwise. Lift assembly from fuel tank and remove fuel pump from fuel lever sending unit.
5. Pull fuel pump into attaching hose while pulling outward away from bottom support. Take care to prevent damage to rubber insulator and strainer during removal.
6. After pump assembly is clear of bottom support, pull pump assembly out of rubber connector for removal.
7. To install the fuel pump, reverse the removal procedure.

CARBURETOR

Removal and Installation

1. Remove air cleaner.
2. Disconnect accelerator linkage.
3. Disconnect transmission detent cable.
4. Disconnect cruise control, if equipped.
5. Disconnect all necessary electrical connectors.
6. Disconnect all necessary vacuum lines.
7. Disconnect fuel line at carburetor inlet.
8. Remove the carburetor retaining bolts and remove carburetor.
9. Reverse removal procedure to install.
10. Check idle speeds.

Adjustment

CHECKING CHOKE—HOT AIR TYPE

1. With parking brake applied, drive wheels blocked, transmission in park or neutral, start engine and allow engine to warm up, visually checking to be certain choke valve opens fully.
2. If choke valve fails to open fully, momentarily touch choke housing and hot air inlet pipe or hose to determine if sufficient heat is reaching the choke coil.

NOTE: The choke housing and hot air inlet pipe or hose are "hot" to the touch. Use care to prevent burning of hands.

3. If choke housing and/or heat inlet are cool to the touch, check for loss of vacuum to the housing, restricted heat inlet in the choke housing or choke heat pipe, collapsed or deteriorated heat inlet hose, or restricted passages in the manifold choke heat stove.
4. Replace or correct as necessary.

CHECKING CHOKE—ELECTRIC TYPE

NOTE: This test should be performed at approximately 70 degrees F. ambient temperature

1. Allow the engine to cool so that when the throttle is opened slightly, the choke blade fully closes.
2. Start the engine and determine a time for the choke blade to reach the full open position.
3. If the choke blade fails to open fully after 3–5 minutes, check the voltage at the choke heater connection.
4. If the voltage is approximately 12–15 volts, replace the electric choke unit.
5. If the voltage is low or zero, check all wires and connections. If any connections in the oil pressure switch circuitry are faulty, or if pressure switch is failed open, the oil warning light will be on with the engine running. Repair wires or connectors as required.

Computer Command Control System (CCC)

MIXTURE CONTROL

Adjustments

The computer command control system provides precise control of carburetor air/fuel mixtures during all ranges of engine operation. Because of this system control, the below listed mixture control adjustment procedures are to be used if required. The previously used propane enrichment or lean drop methods of idle mixture adjustment may not be used when adjusting carburetors used with this system because system control will change air/fuel mixtures to lean or rich as the mixture needles are adjusted rich or lean respectively.

The computer command control system is sensitive to any change in mixture control adjustment which, if improperly set,

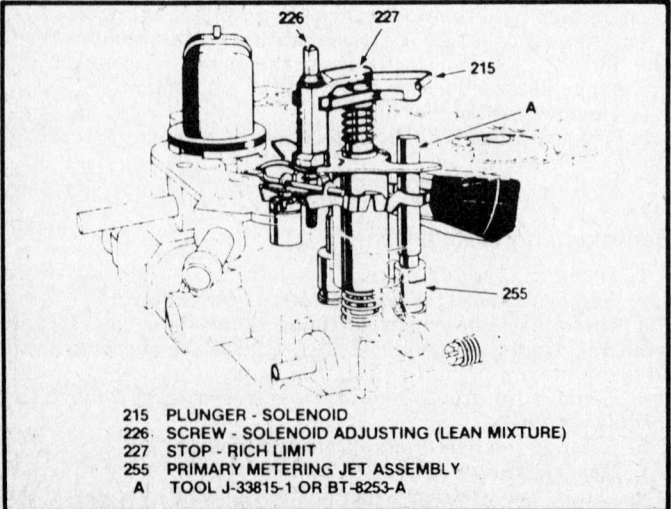

215 PLUNGER - SOLENOID
226 SCREW - SOLENOID ADJUSTING (LEAN MIXTURE)
227 STOP - RICH LIMIT
255 PRIMARY METERING JET ASSEMBLY
A TOOL J-33815-1 OR BT-8253-A

Installing mixture control solenoid gauging tool

PONTIAC
BONNEVILLE • GRAND PRIX • SAFARI • PARISIENNE
SECTION 20

can impair the ability of the system to maintain precise control of air/fuel mixtures. Plugs are installed in the carburetor air horn and over the idle mixture needles in the throttle body to seal the factory settings. For this reason, the mixture control adjustment points should never be changed from the original factory setting. However, if in diagnosis, the system indicates the carburetor to be the cause of a driver performance complaint, emissions failure or critical parts such as the air horn, float bowl, or throttle body are replaced, the plugs may then be removed and mixture control adjustments made, carefully following factory recommended procedures. After adjustment, replacement plugs (supplied in applicable service kits) must be installed.

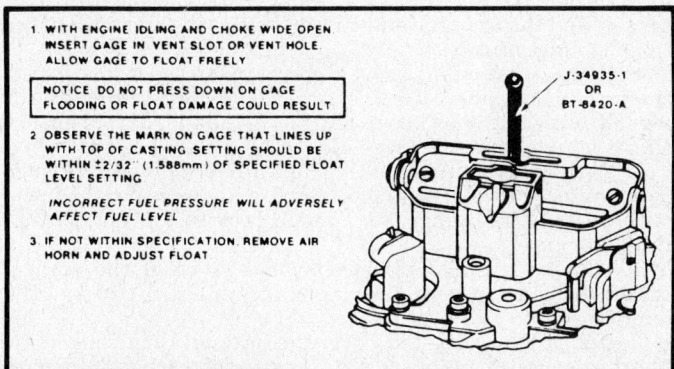

External float level check

Checking Mixture Control Solenoid Travel

Before proceeding, it will be necessary to modify float gauge J–9789–130, BT7720, or equivalent (used to externally check float level setting) by filing or grinding sufficient material off the gauge to allow insertion down the vertical vent ("D" shaped hole in the air horn casting next to the idle air bleed valve cover).

Check that gauge freely enters "D" vent hole and does not bind. The gauge will be used to determine total mixture control solenoid travel.

1. With engine off, air cleaner removed, measure mixture control solenoid travel as follows:
   a. Insert modified float gauge down "D" shaped vent hole. Press down on gauge and release, observing that gauge moves freely and does not bind. With gauge released (solenoid up position), reading at eye level record mark on gauge (in in.) that lines up with top of air horn casting (upper edge).
   b. Then, lightly press down on gauge until bottomed (solenoid down position). Record in in. mark on gauge that lines up with top of air horn casting.
   c. Subtract gauge up dimension (item "a") from gauge down position (item "b") and record difference (in in.). The difference in dimensions is total solenoid travel.
   d. If total solenoid travel (difference in item "c") is not within $2/32$–$6/32$ in., make mixture control solenoid adjustments as noted below. If difference is within the above specifications, proceed to idle air bleed valve adjustment.

Mixture Control Solenoid Adjustments

1. Remove air horn, mixture control solenoid plunger, air horn gasket and plastic filler block, using normal service procedures.
2. Remove throttle side metering rod. Install mixture control solenoid gauging tool J–33815–1 and BT–8253–A or equivalent, over throttle side metering jet rod guide and temporarily reinstall the solenoid plunger into the solenoid body.

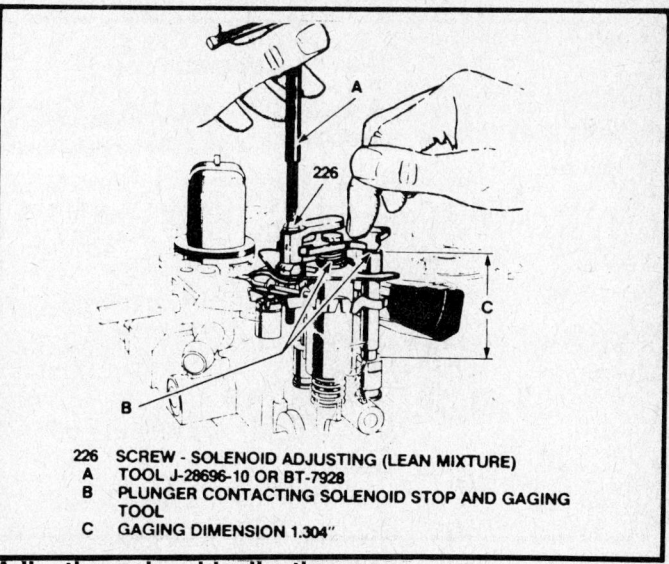

226 SCREW - SOLENOID ADJUSTING (LEAN MIXTURE)
A TOOL J–28696–10 OR BT–7928
B PLUNGER CONTACTING SOLENOID STOP AND GAGING TOOL
C GAGING DIMENSION 1.304"

Adjusting solenoid adjusting screw

3. Holding the solenoid plunger in the down position, use tool J–28696–10 and BT–7928 or equivalent, to turn lean mixture (solenoid) screw counterclockwise until the plunger breaks contact with the gauging tool. Turn slowly clockwise until the plunger just contacts the gauging tool. The adjustment is correct when the solenoid plunger is contacting both the solenoid stop and the gauging tool.

4. If the total difference in adjustment required less than $3/4$ turn of the lean mixture (solenoid) screw, the original setting was within the manufacturer's specifications.

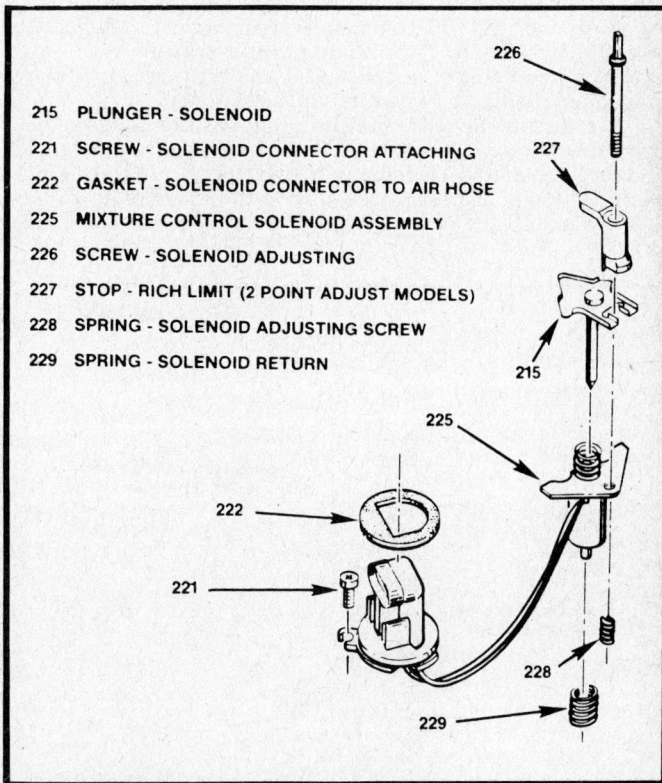

215 PLUNGER - SOLENOID
221 SCREW - SOLENOID CONNECTOR ATTACHING
222 GASKET - SOLENOID CONNECTOR TO AIR HOSE
225 MIXTURE CONTROL SOLENOID ASSEMBLY
226 SCREW - SOLENOID ADJUSTING
227 STOP - RICH LIMIT (2 POINT ADJUST MODELS)
228 SPRING - SOLENOID ADJUSTING SCREW
229 SPRING - SOLENOID RETURN

Mixture control solenoid assembly

PONTIAC
BONNEVILLE • GRAND PRIX • SAFARI • PARISIENNE

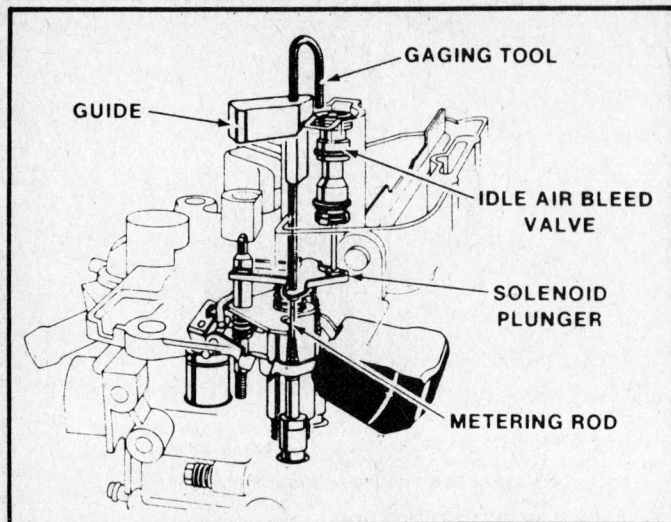

Installing air bleed valve assembly

5. Remove solenoid plunger and gauging tool, and reinstall metering rod and plastic filler block.
6. Invert air horn and remove rich mixture stop screw and (if used) the rich authority adjusting spring from bottom side of air horn, using tool J–28696–4 and BT–7967A or equivalent.
7. Remove lean mixture screw plug and the rich mixture stop screw plug from air horn, using a suitable sized punch.
8. Reinstall rich mixture stop screw and (if used) the rich authority adjusting spring in air horn and bottom lightly, then back screw out $1/4$ turn.
9. Reinstall air horn gasket, mixture control solenoid plunger and air horn to carburetor.
10. Insert external float gauge in vent hole and, with tool J–28696–10 and BT–7928, or equivalent, adjust rich mixture stop screw to obtain $4/32$ in. total plunger travel.
11. With solenoid plunger travel correctly set, install the plugs (supplied in service kits) in the air horn.
12. To install the lean mixture plug, position it hollow end down into the access hole of the lean mixture screw (solenoid), and use a suitably sized punch to drive plug into the air horn until the top of the plug is even with the lower plug.
13. To install the rich mixture stop screw, position it hollow end down, over the rich mixture stop screw access hole, and drive plug into place so that the top of the plug is $1/16$ in. below the surface of the air horn casting.

Idle Air Bleed Valve Adjustment

1. Position the parking brake and block the drive wheels. Disconnect and plug the hoses as directed on the vehicle emission control label.
2. Check and adjust ignition timing. Connect a dwell meter and a tachometer.
3. Start engine, and with transmission in park or neutral, run engine at idle until fully warm and a varying dwell is noted on the dwell meter. It is essential that the engine is operated for a sufficient length of time to ensure that the engine coolant sensor, and the oxygen sensor in the exhaust, are at full operational temperature.
4. Check engine idle speed and compare to specifications on the underhood label. If necessary, adjust curb idle speed. On models with idle speed control (ISC) or idle load compensator (ILC), no adjustment is possible.
5. With engine idling in drive (neutral for manual transmission), observe dwell reading on the 6 cylinder scale. If varying within the 10–50° range, adjustment is correct. If not, perform the following.
6. Remove the idle air bleed valve cover. If the cover is staked in place, pry it off using a suitable tool and an allen wrench.
7. If the cover is riveted, cover the internal bowl vents to the bleed valve with masking tape. Cover the carburetor air intakes with masking tape in order to prevent metal chips from entering the engine.
8. Cover carburetor air intakes with masking tape to prevent metal clips from entering carburetor and engine.
9. Carefully align a No. 35 (0.110 in.) drill bit on one of the steel rivet heads holding the idle air bleed valve cover in place. Drill only enough to remove rivet head. Drill the remaining rivet head located on the other side of the tower. Use a drift and small hammer to drive the remainder of the rivets out of the idle air bleed valve tower in the air horn casting. Use care in drill to prevent damage to the air horn casting.
10. Lift out cover over the idle air bleed valve and remove the rivet pieces from inside the idle air bleed valve tower.
11. Using shop air, carefully blow out any remaining clips from inside the tower. Discard cover after removal. A missing cover indicates that the idle air bleed valve setting has been changed from its original factory setting.
12. With cover removed, look for presence (or absence) of a letter identification on top of idle air bleed valve.
13. If an identifying letter appears on top of the valve proceed to the procedure outlined under type two. If an identifying letter does not appear on the top of the valve proceed to the procedure outlined under type one.

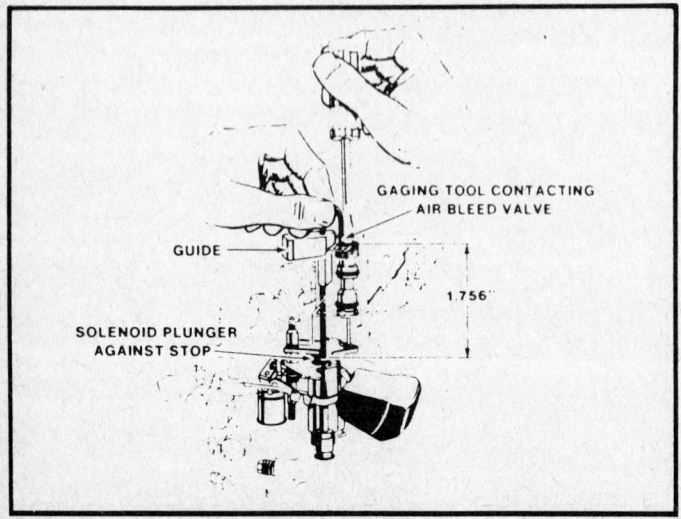

Adjusting air bleed valve assembly

TYPE ONE

1. Presetting the idle air bleed valve to a gauge dimension if the idle air bleed valve was serviced prior to on-vehicle adjustment.
   a. Install idle air bleed valve gauging tool J–33815–2, BT–8253–B, or equivalent, in throttle side "D" shaped vent hole in the air horn casting. The upper end of the tool should be positioned over the open cavity next to the idle air bleed valve.
   b. While holding the gauging tool down lightly, so that the solenoid plunger is against the solenoid stop, adjust the idle air bleed valve so that the gauging tool will pivot over and just contact the top of the valve. The valve is now preset for on-vehicle adjustment.
   c. Remove the gauging tool.

2. Adjusting the idle air bleed valve on the vehicle to obtain correct dwell reading.

   a. Start engine and allow it to reach normal operating temperature.

   b. While idling in drive (neutral for manual transmission), use a suitable tool to slowly turn valve counterclockwise or clockwise, until the dwell reading varies within the 25–35° range, attempting to be as close to 30° as possible. Perform this Step carefully. The air bleed valve is very sensitive and should be turned in 1/8 turn increments only.

   c. If, after performing Steps a and b above, the dwell reading does not vary and is not within the 25–35° range, it will be necessary to remove the plugs and to adjust the idle mixture needles.

3. Idle mixture needle plug removal, only if necessary.

   a. Remove the carburetor from the engine, following normal service procedures, to gain access to the plugs covering the idle mixture needles.

   b. Invert carburetor and drain fuel into a suitable container.

   c. Place carburetor on a suitable holding fixture, with manifold side up. Use care to avoid damaging linkage, tubes, and parts protruding from air horn.

   d. Make two parallel cuts in the throttle body, one on each side of the locator points beneath the idle mixture needle plug (manifold side), with a hacksaw.

   e. The cuts should reach down to the steel plug, but should not extend more than 1/8 in. beyond the locator points. The distance between the saw cuts depends on the size of the punch to be used.

   f. Place a flat punch near the ends of the saw marks in the throttle body. Hold the punch at a 45° angle and drive it into the throttle body until the casting breaks away, exposing the steel plug.

   g. The hardened plug will break, rather than remaining intact. It is not necessary to remove the plug in one piece, but remove the loose pieces.

   h. Repeat this procedure with the other mixture needle.

4. Setting the idle mixture needles (if necessary) where correct dwell reading could not be obtained with the idle air bleed valve adjustment.

   a. Using tool J-29030, BT-7610B or equivalent, turn both idle mixture needles clockwise until they are lightly seated, then turn each mixture needle counterclockwise the number of turns specified.

   b. Reinstall carburetor on engine using a new flange mounting gasket, but do not install air cleaner and gasket at this time.

5. Readjusting idle air bleed valve to finalize correct dwell reading.
(Only necessary if idle mixture needles required setting in Step 4, above.)

   a. Start engine and run until fully warm, and repeat "Adjusting the air bleed valve," Step 2, above.

   b. If unable to set dwell to 25–35°, and the dwell is below 25°, turn both mixture needles counterclockwise an additional turn. If dwell is above 35°, turn both mixture needles clockwise an additional turn. Readjust idle air bleed valve to obtain dwell limits.

   c. After adjustments are complete, seal the idle mixture needle openings in the throttle body, using silicone sealant, RTV rubber, or equivalent. The sealer is required to discourage unnecessary adjustment of the setting, and to prevent fuel vapor loss in that area.

   d. On vehicles WITHOUT a carburetor-mounted idle speed control or idle load compensator, adjust curb idle speed if necessary.

   e. Check and only if necessary adjust, fast idle speed as described on emission control information label.

TYPE TWO

1. Setting the idle air bleed valve to a gauge dimension;

   a. Install air bleed valve, gauging tool J-33815-2, BT-8253-B, or equivalent, in throttle side "D" shaped vent hole in the air horn casting. The upper end of the tool should be positioned over the open cavity next to the idle air bleed valve.

   b. While holding the gauging tool down lightly, so that the solenoid plunger is against the solenoid stop, adjust the idle air bleed valve so that the gauging tool will pivot over and just contact the top of the valve.

   c. The valve is now set properly. No further adjustment of the valve is necessary.

   d. Remove gauging tool.

2. Adjusting the idle mixture needles on the vehicle to obtain correct dwell readings.

   a. Remove idle mixture needle plugs, following instructions in the information given for type one.

   b. Using tool J-29030-B, BT-7610-B, or equivalent, turn each idle mixture needle clockwise until lightly seated, then turn each mixture needle counterclockwise three turns.

   c. Reinstall carburetor on engine, using a new flange mounting gasket, but do not install air cleaner or gasket at this time.

   d. Start engine and allow it to reach normal operating temperature.

   e. While idling in drive (neutral for manual transmission), adjust both mixture needles equally, in 1/8 turn increments, until dwell reading varies within the 25–35° range, attempting to be as close to 30° as possible. If reading is too low, turn mixture needles counterclockwise. If reading is too high, turn mixture needles clockwise. Allow time for dwell reading to stabilize after each adjustment.

   f. After adjustments are complete, seal the idle mixture needle openings in the throttle body, using silicone sealant, TRV rubber, or equivalent. The sealer is required to discourage unnecessary readjustment of the setting, and to prevent fuel vapor loss in that area.

   g. On vehicles without a carburetor-mounted idle speed control or idle load compensator, adjust curb idle speed if necessary.

   h. Check, and if necessary, adjust fast idle speed, as described on the emission control information label.

IDLE LOAD COMPENSATOR (ILC)

Adjustment

1. Prepare vehicle for adjustments–see emission label.
2. Connect tachometer (distributor side of TACH filter, if used).
3. Remove air cleaner and plug vacuum hose to thermal vacuum valve (TVV).
4. Disconnect and plug vacuum hose to EGR.
5. Disconnect and plug vacuum hose to canister purge port.
6. Disconnect and plug vacuum hose to ILC.

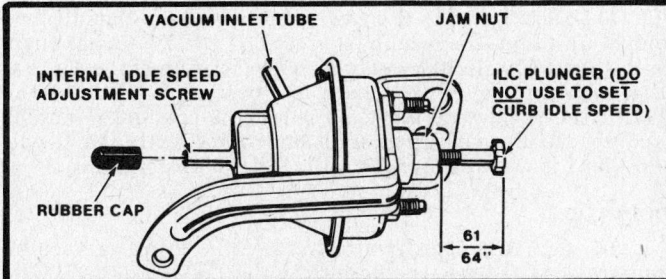

Preset adjustment—typical Idle Load Compensator (ILC) (© General Motors Corporation)

PONTIAC
BONNEVILLE • GRAND PRIX • SAFARI • PARISIENNE

7. Back out idle stop screw on carburetor 3 turns.
8. Turn A/C "OFF."

CAUTION
Before starting engine, place transmission in PARK, set parking brake and block drive wheels.

9. With engine running (engine warm, choke off), transmission in drive and ILC plunger fully extended (no vacuum applied), using tool J-29607, BT-8022, or equivalent, adjust plunger to obtain 750 rpm on E2MC carburetor models, 725 rpm on E4MC carburetor models. Jam nut on plunger must be held with wrench to prevent damage to guide tabs when tightening.
10. Remove plug from vacuum hose, reconnect hose to ILC and observe idle speed. Idle speed should be 500 rpm in drive.
11. If rpm in Step 10 is correct, proceed to Step 13. No further adjustment of the ILC is necessary.
12. If rpm in Step 10 is not correct:
   a. Stop engine and remove the ILC. Plug vacuum hose to ILC.
   b. With the ILC removed, remove the rubber cap from the center outlet tube and then remove the metal plug (IF USED) from this same tube.
   c. Install ILC on carburetor and re-attach throttle return spring and any other related parts removed during disassembly. Remove plug from vacuum hose and reconnect hose to ILC.
   d. Using a spare rubber cap with hole punched to accept a .090 in. (3/32 in.) hex key wrench, install cap on center outlet tube (to seal against vacuum loss) and insert wrench through cap to engage adjusting screw inside tube. Start engine and turn adjusting screw with wrench to obtain 550 rpm in drive. Turning the adjusting screw will change the idle speed approximately 75–100 rpm for each complete turn. Turning the screw counterclockwise will increase the engine speed.
   e. Remove wrench and cap (with hole) from center outlet tube and install new rubber cap.
   f. Engine running, transmission in drive, observe idle speed. If a final adjustment is required, it will be necessary to repeat Steps 12a through 12e.
13. After adjustment of the ILC plunger, measure distance from the jam nut to tip of the plunger, dimension must not exceed 25 mm (1 in.).
14. Disconnect and plug vacuum hose to ILC. Apply vacuum source, such as hand vacuum pump J-23768, BT-7517 or equivalent, to ILC vacuum inlet tube to fully retract the plunger.
15. Adjust the idle stop on the carburetor float bowl to obtain 500 rpm in drive.
16. Place transmission in PARK and stop engine.
17. Remove plug from vacuum hose and install hose on ILC vacuum inlet tube.
18. Remove plugs and reconnect all vacuum hoses.
19. Install air cleaner and gasket.
20. Remove block from drive wheels.

THROTTLE POSITIONER SENSOR (TPS)

Adjustment

1. The plug covering the TPS adjustment screw is used to provide a tamper-resistant design and retain the factory setting during vehicle operation.
2. Do not remove the plug unless diagnosis indicates the TPS Sensor is not adjusted correctly or it is necessary to replace the air horn assembly, float bowl, TPS sensor, to TPS adjustment screw. This is a critical adjustment that must be performed accurately and carefully to ensure proper vehicle performance and control of exhaust emissions.
3. If necessary to adjust the TPS sensor:
   a. Using a 5mm ($5/64$ in.) drill, drill hole in aluminum plug covering TPS adjustment screw, drilling only enough to start self-tapping screw (approximate drilling depth $1/16$–$1/8$ in.). Use care in drilling to prevent damage to adjustment screw head.
   b. Start a No. 8, $1/2$ in. long, self-tapping screw in drilled hole in plug, turning screw in only enough to ensure good thread engagement in hole.
   c. Placing a wide-blade section of screwdriver between screw head and air horn casting, pry against screw head to remove plug. Discard plug.
   d. Using tool J-28696, BT967A or equivalent, remove screw.
   e. Connect digital voltmeter (such as J-29125) or equivalent from TPS connector center terminal (B) to bottom terminal (C).

NOTE: *After TPS screw is adjusted, a new plug should be installed. If a new plug is not available, a locking type of sealer should be placed on the screw threads to prevent movement of the screw after installation.*

   f. With ignition on, engine stopped, reinstall TPS adjustment screw and with Tool J-28696, BT7967A, or equivalent turn screw to obtain specified voltage at specified throttle position with A/C off.
   g. After adjustment, install new plug (supplied in service kits) in air horn, driving plug in place until flush with raised pump lever boss on casting.

Differential Vacuum Delay Valve (DVDV) Adjustment

The DVDV is located in the vacuum line between the idle load control unit and the vacuum source. The DVDV acts as cushioning device by slightly delaying the operation of the ILC until a constant vacuum change has occurred. Without the DVDV, the ILC would react too quickly to changes in engine vacuum, causing a surging condition or if too restrictive to vacuum flow, it would cause a stalling or run-on condition.

Inspection

1. To check the operation of the DVDV, install a vacuum gauge with a "T" into the hose from the DVDV to the ILC.
2. Install a vacuum pump to port 1 of the DVDV and apply 17.8 in. Hg. while watching the other vacuum gauge, it should take six to nine seconds for the vacuum to rise to 16.9 in. Hg.

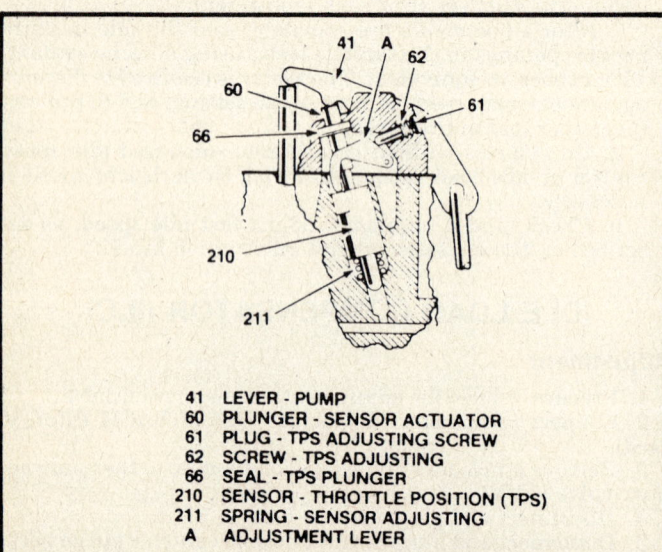

41	LEVER - PUMP
60	PLUNGER - SENSOR ACTUATOR
61	PLUG - TPS ADJUSTING SCREW
62	SCREW - TPS ADJUSTING
66	SEAL - TPS PLUNGER
210	SENSOR - THROTTLE POSITION (TPS)
211	SPRING - SENSOR ADJUSTING
A	ADJUSTMENT LEVER

Cross section of throttle positioner sensor assembly

3. Remove the vacuum gauge with "T", install the vacuum pump to port 2 and leave port 1 open. Air should flow through the valve after 5 in. Hg. is applied.

IDLE SPEED CONTROL (ISC)

Adjustment

The idle speed control (ISC) is controlled by the electronic control module (ECM), which has the desired idle speed programmed in its memory. The ECM compares the actual idle speed to the programmed idle speed in its memory and moves the plunger rod is in or out, automatically adjusting the throttle to hold the programmed idle rpm, independent of the engine loads.

An integral part of the ISC is the throttle contact switch. The position of the switch determines whether or not the ISC should control idle speed. When the throttle lever is resting against the ISC plunger, the switch contacts are closed, at which time the ECM moves the ISC to the programmed idle speed. When the throttle lever is not contacting the ISC plunger, the switch contacts are open; the ECM stops sending idle speed commands and the driver controls engine speed.

NOTE: Before starting engine, place transmission selector lever in park or neutral, set parking brake and block drive wheels.

When a new ISC assembly is installed, a base (minimum authority) and high (maximum authority) rpm speed check must be performed and adjustments made as required. These adjustments limit the low and high rpm speeds to the ECM. When making a low and high speed adjustment, the low speed adjustment is always made first. DO NOT use the ISC plunger to adjust curb idle speed as the idle speed is controlled by the ECM.

NOTE: Do not disconnect or connect ISC connector with ignition on as damage to the ECM may occur.

1. Connect tachometer (distributor side of tach filter, if used).
2. Connect dwell meter to mixture control (M/C) solenoid dwell lead. Remember to set dwell meter on the six cylinder scale, regardless of the engine being tested.
3. Turn A/C off.
4. Start engine and run until stabilized by entering "closed loop" (dwell meter needle starts to vary).
5. Turn ignition off.
6. Unplug connector from ISC motor.
7. Fully retract ISC plunger by applying 12 volts DC (battery voltage) to terminal "C" of the ISC motor connection and ground lead to terminal "D" of the ISC motor connection. It may be necessary to install jumper leads from the ISC motor in order to make proper connections.

NOTE: Do not apply battery voltage to motor longer than necessary to retract ISC plunger. Prolonged contact will damage motor. Also, never connect voltage source across terminals "A" and "B" as damage to the internal throttle contact switch will result.

8. Start engine and wait until dwell meter needle starts to vary, indicating "closed loop" operation.
9. With parking brake applied and drive wheels blocked, place transmission in Drive (Neutral, manual transmission models).
10. With ISC plunger fully retracted, adjust carburetor base (slow) idle stop screw to the specified rpm (see specifications). ISC plunger should not be left in full retracted position.
11. Place transmission in Park or Neutral and fully extend ISC plunger by applying 12 volts DC to terminal "D" of the ISC motor connection and ground lead to terminal "C" of the ISC motor connection.

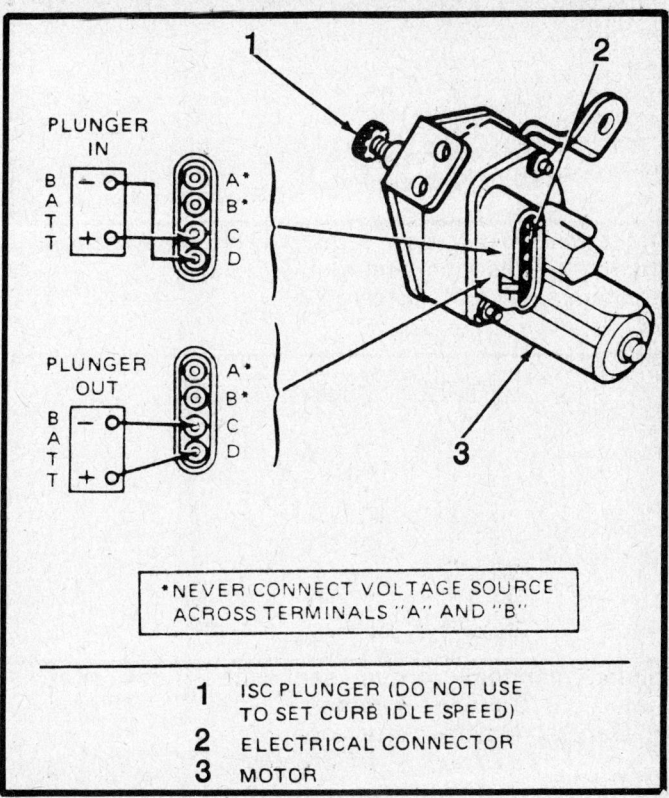

1. ISC PLUNGER (DO NOT USE TO SET CURB IDLE SPEED)
2. ELECTRICAL CONNECTOR
3. MOTOR

ISC unit and electrical connections

NOTE: Never connect voltage source across terminals "A" and "B" as damage to the internal throttle contact switch will result.

12. Adjustment procedure:
 a. With Transmission in park, using tool J–29607 or BT–8022 or equivalent, preset ISC plunger to obtain 1500 RPM.
 b. With parking brake set and drive wheels blocked, place transmission in drive. Using tool J–29607 or BT–8022 or equivalent, turn ISC Plunger to obtain ISC adjustment RPM (Maximum Authority).
13. Recheck ISC Maximum Authority, Adjustment RPM with voltage applied to motor. Motor will ratchet at full extension with power applied.
14. After adjustment of ISC plunger, measure distance from back side of plunger head to ISC nosepiece, Dimension "B." Dimension must not exceed that shown by plunger type as either identified by plunger length or letter identification.
15. Fully retract ISC Plunger. Place transmission in park or neutral and turn ignition "Off." Disconnect 12 volt power source, ground lead, tachometer and dwell meter. With ignition "OFF," reconnect four terminal harness connector to ISC motor. To prevent internal damage to ISC, apply finger pressure to ISC plunger while retracting.
16. Remove block from drive wheels.

INTAKE MANIFOLD

Removal and Installation

1. Disconnect the negative battery cable. Drain the radiator.
2. Remove the air cleaner assembly.
3. Disconnect the upper radiator hose and the heater hose at the manifold.
4. Disconnect the accelerator linkage at the carburetor and the linkage bracket at the manifold. Remove the cruise control chain or cable, if so equipped.

SECTION 20

PONTIAC
BONNEVILLE • GRAND PRIX • SAFARI • PARISIENNE

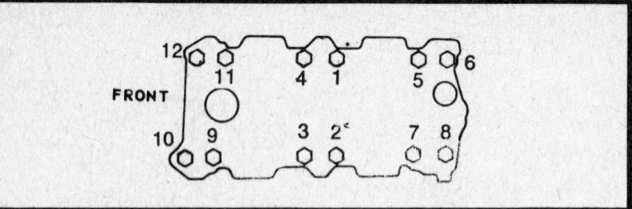

Intake manifold torque sequence—Chevrolet produced V8 gasoline engine
(© General Motors Corporation)

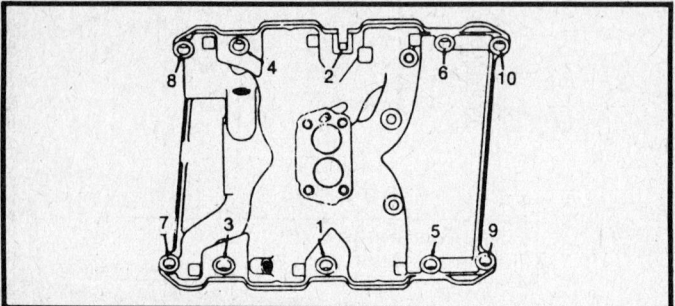

Intake manifold torque sequence—Buick produced V6 Gasoline engine
(© General Motors Corporation)

5. Remove the fuel line from the carburetor and the booster vacuum pipe from the manifold.
6. Disconnect and label the transmission vacuum modulator line, idle stop solenoid wire (if so equipped), distributor wires and the temperature sending unit wire.
7. Disconnect and mark the vacuum hoses at the distributor and the carburetor.
8. Disconnect the coolant bypass hose at the manifold. If required, remove the distributor.
9. On six cylinder models, it may be necessary to remove the distributor cap and wires to gain access to the Torx® head bolt. Remove the bolt.
10. Remove the throttle linkage springs.
11. Remove the A/C compressor top bracket, if so equipped.
12. Remove the manifold.
13. Installation is the reverse of the removal procedure.
14. Be sure to torque the manifold retaining bolts to specification.

EXHAUST MANIFOLD

Removal and Installation

1. Disconnect the negative battery cable.
2. Remove all the necessary components in order to gain access to the exhaust manifold retaining bolts.
3. Remove the exhaust manifold to exhaust flange retaining bolts. Remove the oxygen sensor wires, if equipped.
4. Remove the exhaust manifold to cylinder head retaining bolts.
5. Remove the exhaust manifold from the vehicle.
6. On some vehicles it may be necessary to raise the engine in order to gain clearance to remove the manifold.
7. Installation is the reverse of the removal procedure.

Fuel Injection System

For More Information on Fuel Injection System Refer to the Unit Repair Section

EMISSION CONTROL SECTION

1983 AND LATER

NOTE: The following emission systems are used on most gasoline engines, but all may not be used on the same engine. Refer to the Emission Identification and Specification label for emission applications.

GASOLINE ENGINES

Electronic control module
Fuel control system
Oxygen sensor
Mixture control solenoid
Coolant sensor
Throttle position sensor (TPS)
Idle speed control throttle switch
Early fuel evaporation (EFE)
Early fuel evaporation—thermal vacuum switch
Catalytic converter
Positive crankcase ventilation (PCV)
Barometric pressure sensor (BARO)
Manifold absolute pressure sensor (MAP)
E.G.R. control solenoid
Differential pressure sensor (DPS)
Thermostatic air cleaner (THERMAC)
Electronic spark timing (EST)
Electronic spark control (ESC)
Air injection reaction (AIR)
Air management valve
Deceleration valve
Canister purge valve check

DIESEL ENGINES

Exhaust gas recirculation (EGR)
Exhaust pressure regulator (EPR)
Vacuum pump
Flow control valve
EGR solenoid
EPR solenoid
VAcuum regulator valve

PONTIAC
BONNEVILLE • GRAND PRIX • SAFARI • PARISIENNE
SECTION 20

ENGINE SECTION

For Diesel Engine Services Refer to the Unit Repair Section.

ENGINE ASSEMBLY

Removal and Installation

V6 GASOLINE ENGINE

1. Scribe hinge locations and remove the hood.
2. Disconnect battery.
3. Drain coolant into a suitable container.
4. Remove air cleaner.
5. On vehicles equipped with air conditioning, disconnect compressor ground wire from the mounting bracket. Remove the electrical connector from the compressor clutch, remove the compressor to mounting bracket attaching bolts, and position the compressor out of the way.
6. Remove fan blade, pulleys, and belts.
7. Disconnect radiator and heater hoses from engine.
8. Remove fan shroud assembly.
9. Remove power steering pump to mounting bracket bolts and position pump assembly out of the way.
10. Disconnect fuel pump hoses and plug.
11. Disconnect battery ground cable from engine.
12. Disconnect the vacuum supply hose from carburetor to the vacuum manifold. On vehicles so equipped, the vacuum modulator, load leveler, and power brake vacuum hoses should all be disconnected at the engine.
13. Disconnect accelerator cable at carburetor.
14. Disconnect generator, oil and coolant sending unit switch connections at the engine. Remove the alternator.
15. Disconnect engine to body ground strap(s) at engine.
16. Raise the vehicle, disconnect the cable shield from the engine (if so equipped).
17. Disconnect exhaust pipes from exhaust manifolds.
18. Remove lower flywheel converter cover.
19. Remove flywheel to converter attaching bolts. Scribe chalk mark on the flywheel and converter for reassembly alignment.
20. Remove transmission in engine attaching bolts.
21. Remove motor mount through bolts and cruise control bracket if equipped.
22. Lower the vehicle and support the automatic transmission.
23. Attach a lifting device to the engine and raise the engine enough so mounting through-bolts can be removed. Make certain wiring harness, vacuum hoses, and other parts are free and clear before lifting engine out of the vehicle.
24. Raise engine far enough to clear engine mounts, raise transmission support accordingly and alternately until engine can be disengaged from the transmission and removed.
25. Installation is the reverse of the removal procedure.

V8 GASOLINE ENGINE

1. Drain cooling system.
2. Remove air cleaner and hot air pipe.
3. Mark hinge location and remove hood.
4. Disconnect battery negative cable at battery and ground wire at inner fender panel. Disconnect engine ground strap, right head to cowl.
5. Disconnect radiator hoses, automatic transmission cooler lines, heater hoses, vacuum hoses, power steering hose bracket from engine, air conditioning compressor with brackets and hoses attached, fuel hose from fuel line, wiring and throttle cable.
6. Remove upper radiator support and radiator.
7. Raise and support the vehicle.
8. Disconnect exhaust pipes at manifold.
9. Remove torque converter cover and the bolts holding converter to flywheel.
10. Remove engine mount bolts or nuts.
11. Remove three bolts, transmission to engine on the right side. Remove starter with with wires attached, then support the starter with the frame.
12. Lower the vehicle. Secure lift chain to engine.
13. Place board on top of jack and slightly raise transmission. Remove three left transmission to engine bolts. Remove engine.
14. Installation is the reverse of the removal procedure.

V8 DIESEL ENGINE

1. Drain cooling system.
2. Remove air cleaner and install cover screen J-26996 or equivalent.
3. Mark hood hinges and remove hood.
4. Disconnect negative battery cables at batteries and ground wires at inner fender panel. Disconnect engine ground strap, right head to cowl.
5. Disconnect radiator hoses, cooler lines, heater hoses, vacuum hoses, power steering pump hoses at power steering gear, air conditioning compressor with brackets and hoses attached, fuel hose from fuel pump and wiring.
6. Remove hairpin clip at bellcrank.
7. Remove throttle and T.V. cables from intake manifold brackets, then position cables away from engine.
8. Remove upper radiator support and radiator.
9. Raise the vehicle and support it safely.
10. Disconnect exhaust pipes at manifold.
11. Remove torque converter cover and three bolts holding converter to flywheel.
12. Remove engine mount bolts or nuts.
13. Remove the bolts, transmission to engine on the right side. Disconnect wires from starter and remove starter.
14. Lower the vehicle. Secure lift chain to engine.
15. Place board on top of jack and slightly raise transmission. Remove three left transmission to engine bolts. Remove engine.
16. Installation is the reverse of the removal procedure.

ENGINE MOUNTS

Removal and Installation

1. Disconnect the negative battery cable. Raise and support the vehicle safely.
2. Properly support the weight of the engine at the forward edge of the oil pan.
3. Remove the mount to engine block bolts. Raise the engine slightly and remove the mount to mount bracket bolt and nut. Remove the engine mount.
4. Installation is the reverse of the removal procedure.

VALVE SYSTEM

Valve Adjustment

Hydraulic valve lifters are used in all engines produced by General Motors Corporation. Certain engines have adjustable rocker arms, while others have no adjustment provisions, but rely upon a specific torque value. The following procedure applies to adjustable rocker arms.

1. Remove the valve covers.
2. By rotating the crankshaft and by positioning each valve on its base circle of the camshaft, remove the lash from each rocker arm and pushrod, one by one.

20-23

SECTION 20
PONTIAC
BONNEVILLE • GRAND PRIX • SAFARI • PARISIENNE

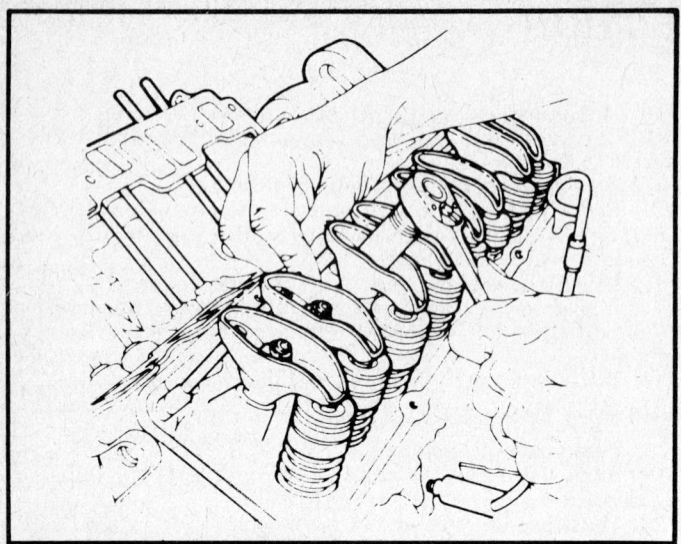

Adjusting valves—typical

3. To adjust the valves, crank the engine until the mark on the vibration damper lines up with the center or "O" mark on the timing tab fastened to the crankcase front cover. The engine will be either in the number one firing position or its opposite cylinder (No. 6 on V8 and No. 4 on V6 engines) firing position.

NOTE: The firing cylinder may be determined by placing your fingers on the number one cylinder valve rocker arms as the mark on the damper comes near the "O" mark on the crankcase front cover. If the valve rocker arms moves as the mark comes up to the timing tab, the engine is in the opposite cylinder (No. 6 on V8 and No. 4 on V6 engines) firing position and should be turned over one complete revolution to reach the number one cylinder firing position.

4. With the engine in the number one firing position, adjust the following valves.
    a. V8 engines—Exhaust—1, 3, 4, 8.
    b. V8 engine—Intake—1, 2, 5, 7.
    c. V6 engine—Exhaust—1, 5, 6.
    d. V6 engine—Intake—1, 2, 3.

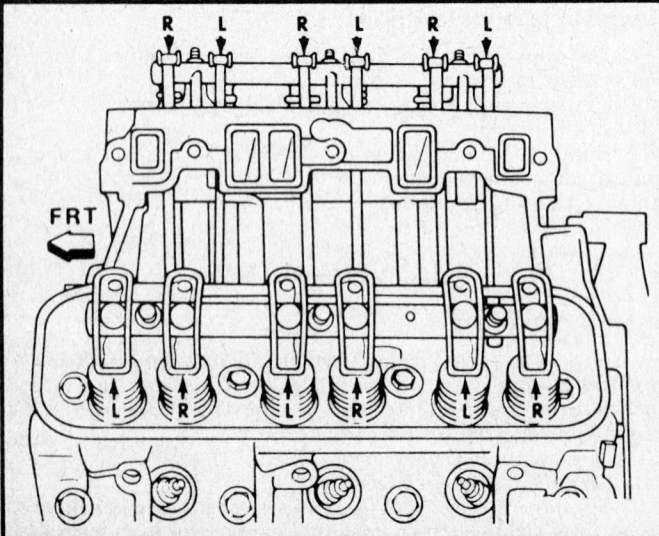

Positioning of rocker arms—3.8L V6 engine

5. Back out adjusting nut until lash is felt at the push rod, then turn in adjusting nut until all lash is removed. This can be determined by rotating push rod while turning adjusting nut. When play has been removed, turn adjusting nut in one full additional turn, which centers the lifter plunger.

6. Crank the engine one revolution until the pointer "O" mark and the vibration damper mark are again in alignment. This is the number six firing position.

7. With the engine in this position, adjust the following valves.
    a. V8 engine—Exhaust—2, 5, 6, 7.
    b. V8 engine—Intake—3, 4, 6, 8.
    c. V6 engine—Exhaust—2, 3, 4.
    d. V6 engine—Intake—4, 5, 6.

8. Install the rocker arm covers.
9. Start the engine and adjust the idle speed, as required.

VALVE LIFTERS

NOTE: Refer to the 4.3L and 5.7L Diesel Engine Section, Unit Repair for information and procedures on lifter bleed-down before starting the engine.

Removal and Installation

1. Disconnect the negative battery cable.
2. Remove the intake manifold assembly.

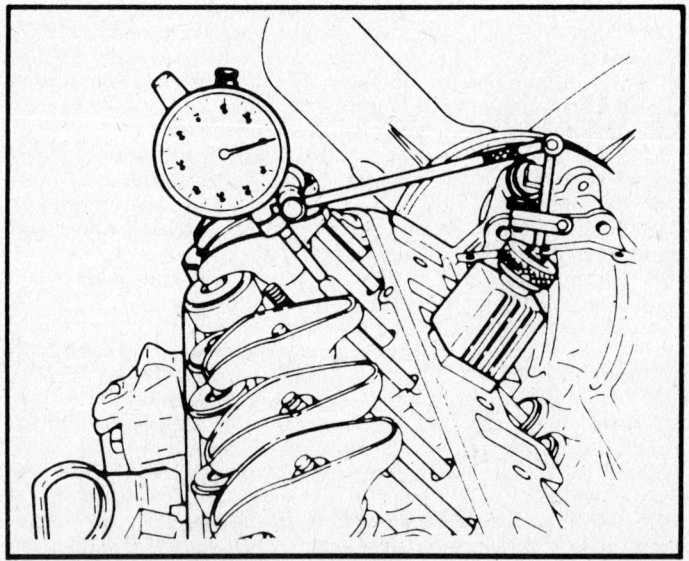

Measuring cam lobe lift—typical

3. Remove the rocker arm covers. Remove the rocker arm assembly. Remove the push rods. Be sure to keep them in order as they must be installed in the same bores as they were removed.
4. On diesel engines, remove the valve lifter guide retaining bolts. Remove the valve lifter guide.
5. Remove the valve lifters using the proper valve lifter removal tool.
6. Installation is the reverse of the removal procedure. Be sure to use new gaskets as required. Be sure to coat the lifter assemblies with clean engine oil prior to installation.

VALVE ROCKER ASSEMBLY

Removal and Installation

1. Disconnect the negative battery cable.
2. Remove all the necessary components in order to gain access to the rocker cover mounting bolts.
3. Remove the rocker cover bolts. Remove the rocker covers.

4. Remove the rocker arm assemblies. Be careful not to mix or lose the components.
5. Installation is the reverse of the removal procedure. Be sure to use new gaskets or RTV sealant as required.

VALVE TIMING

Adjustment

The manufacturer has no recommended procedure for valve timing. It is advisable to verify cam lobe lift and camshaft/crankshaft relationship through crankshaft pulley location and valve operation.

Goodwrench Engine Assembly

General Motors Parts released a 3.8L V6 Goodwrench engine (part number 25528795, replacing part number 25525217) for 1986 and prior year usage. Numerous differences exist and must be considered during its installation.

1. A thicker cylinder head gasket is used to improve cylinder head to block sealing.
2. To accommodate the new cylinder head gasket, the block deck height has been lowered approximately 0.038 in. To identify this Goodwrench engine block, a code of "6GW" is stamped next to the three digit julian date on the front of the engine block.
3. New cylinder head bolts are used to improve the clamping of the cylinder head to the block.
4. New, low tension piston ring expanders are used, reducing the internal engine friction.
5. Due to the engine changes in the cylinder head area, the Cylinder Head Service Label must be installed as per the instructions provided with the replacement engine. Failure to do so could result in the incorrect usage of parts or service procedures, should they become necessary at a later date.

CYLINDER HEAD

Removal and Installation

1. Disconnect the negative battery cable.
2. Remove the valve covers. Drain the cooling system.
3. Remove the necessary accessories and drive belts. Remove the intake manifold.
4. Remove the exhaust manifold retaining bolts.
5. Remove the rocker arm assemblies and push rods.
6. Remove the cylinder head retaining bolts. Remove the cylinder head from the engine.

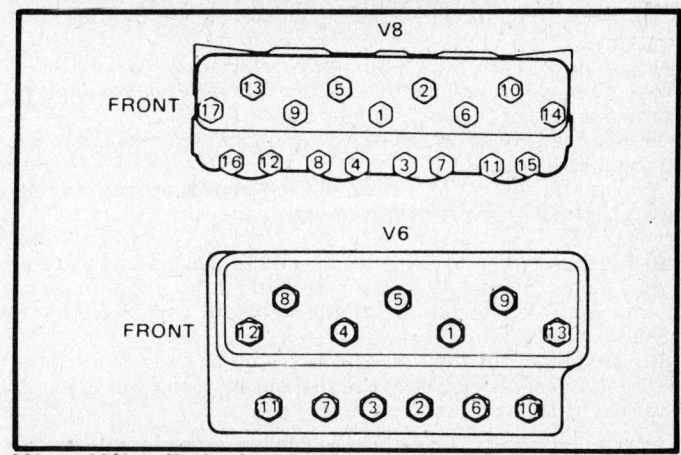

V6 and V8 cylinder head torque sequence—all except 3.8L (VIN A) and 5.0L (VIN Y) engines

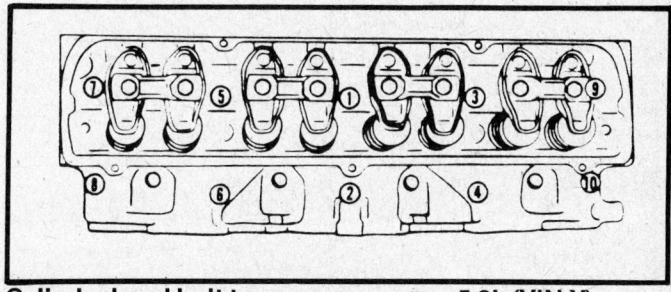

Cylinder head bolt torque sequence—5.0L (VIN Y) engine

7. Installation is the reverse of the removal procedure. Be sure to torque the cylinder head to specification.

CAMSHAFT

Removal and Installation

1. Disconnect the negative battery cable.
2. Remove the rocker covers. Drain the cooling system.
3. Remove the rocker arm assemblies and the pushrods.
4. Remove the intake manifold.
5. Remove the valve filters.
6. Remove the timing cover. Remove the camshaft gear and timing chain. Remove all the necessary components in order to remove the camshaft from the vehicle.
7. Slide the camshaft from the engine, being careful not to damage the camshaft bearings.
8. Installation is the reverse of the removal procedure.

TIMING CASE COVER/OIL SEAL

Removal and Installation

V6 GASOLINE ENGINE

1. Disconnect the negative battery cable. Drain the radiator.
2. Disconnect the radiator hoses and the heater return hose at the water pump.
3. Remove the fan assembly and pulleys. Remove the crankshaft vibration damper.
4. Remove the fuel pump. Remove the alternator.
5. Remove the distributor. If timing chain and sprockets are not going to be disturbed, note position of distributor rotor for reinstallation in same position.

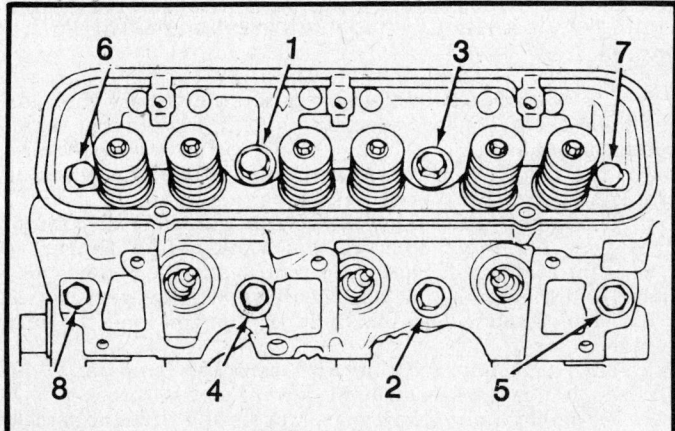

Cylinder head bolt torque sequence—3.8L (VIN A) engine

PONTIAC
BONNEVILLE • GRAND PRIX • SAFARI • PARISIENNE

6. Loosen and slide front clamp on thermostat by-pass hose rearward.
7. Remove bolts attaching timing chain cover to cylinder block. Remove two oil pan to timing chain cover bolts. Remove timing chain cover assembly and gasket.
8. Thoroughly clean the cover, taking care to avoid damage to the gasket surface.
9. Installation is the reverse of the removal procedure. Follow the following recommended procedures during the assembly.
10. Remove oil pump cover and pack the space around the oil pump gears completely full of petroleum jelly. There must be no air space left inside the pump. Reinstall cover using new gasket.
11. To replace the front oil seal, use a punch and drive out the old seal and shedder. Drive the seal out from the front toward the rear of the timing chain cover.
12. Coil new packing around opening so ends of packing are at top. Drive in shedder using suitable punch. Stake the shedder in place in at least three places.
13. Size the packing by rotating a hammer handle or similar tool around the packing until the balancer hub can be inserted through the opening.
14. Torque the front cover retaining bolts to 28 ft. lbs.

V8 GASOLINE ENGINES

1. Disconnect the negative battery cable.
2. Remove the vibration damper assembly.
3. Remove the water pump.
4. Remove the crankcase front cover retaining bolts. Remove the front cover and discard the gasket.
5. Installation is the reverse of the removal procedure.

TIMING GEARS

Removal and Installation
V6 GASOLINE ENGINE

1. Disconnect the negative battery cable.
2. Drain the cooling system. Remove the engine front cover.
3. With timing chain cover removed, temporarily install balancer bolt and washer in end of crankshaft. Turn crankshaft so that the timing marks on the sprockets are as close together as possible. Remove balancer bolt and washer.
4. Remove front crankshaft oil slinger. Remove the camshaft sprocket bolts.

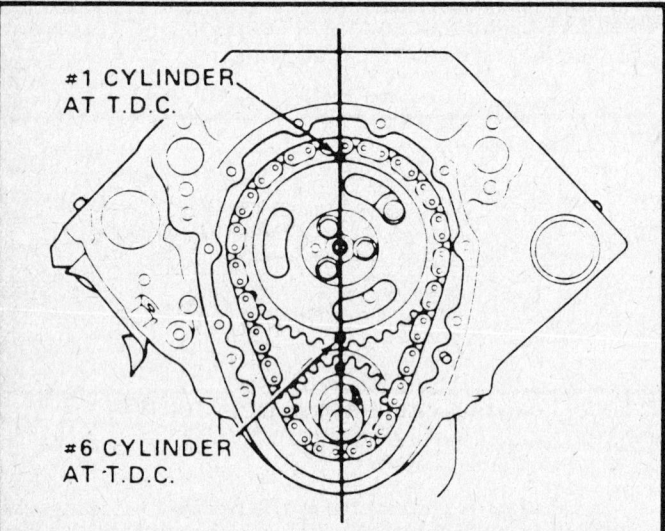

V8 engine timing gear marks in relation to cylinder in firing position

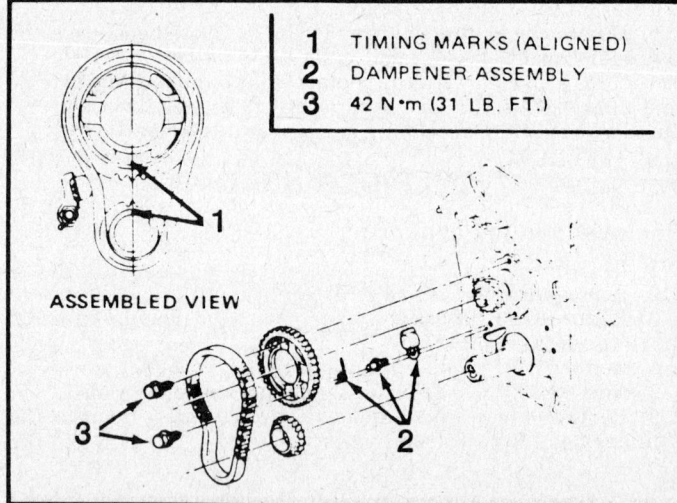

Timing chain assembly and mark locations—3.8L V6 engine

5. Use two large suitable tools to alternately pry the camshaft sprocket from the camshaft while prying the crankshaft sprocket forward until the camshaft sprocket is free, then remove the camshaft sprocket and chain and finish working crankshaft sprocket off crankshaft.
6. Thoroughly clean the timing chain, sprockets, distributor drive gear, fuel pump eccentric and crankshaft oil slinger.
7. If the crankshaft has not been turned in the engine, go to Step 10. If the crankshaft has been turned, start with Step 9.
8. Turn crankshaft so that number 1 piston is at top dead center.
9. Turn camshaft so that with sprocket temporarily installed, timing mark is straight down. Remove sprocket.
10. Assemble timing chain on sprockets and slide the sprocket and chain assembly on the shafts with the timing mark on the crankshaft gear at the twelve O'clock position and the camshaft gear in its six O'clock position.

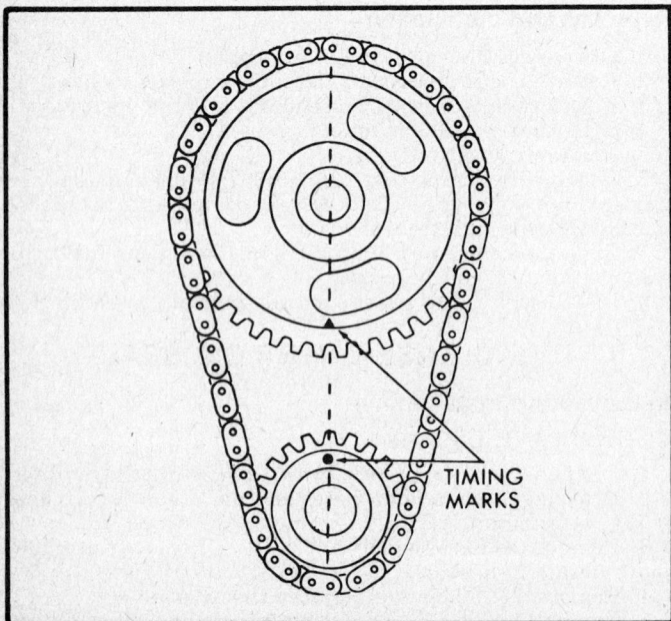

Timing mark alignment—Buick produced V6 gasoline engine (© General Motors Corporation)

PONTIAC
BONNEVILLE • GRAND PRIX • SAFARI • PARISIENNE
SECTION 20

NOTE: The timing marks should face each other and intersect an imaginary line drawn between the center of the camshaft and the center of the crankshaft.

11. Assemble slinger on crankshaft with large part of cone to front of engine.
12. Install camshaft sprocket bolts. Torque to specification.
13. Install camshaft thrust button and spring and timing chain dampers.
14. Install timing chain cover. Continue the installation in the reverse order of the removal procedure.

V8 GASOLINE ENGINE

1. Disconnect the negative battery cable.
2. Remove the engine front cover. Rotate the crankshaft and align the timing marks.
3. Remove the camshaft gear bolts. Remove the camshaft gear.

NOTE: Be sure the locating dowel is in place on the camshaft for the camshaft gear.

4. Remove the timing chain.
5. Remove the crankshaft gear sprocket, as required.
6. Installation is the reverse of the removal procedure. Position the number one/six cylinder pistons in the Top Dead Center Position. Assemble the gears and chain in the following manner.
7. Assemble timing chain on sprockets and slide the sprocket and chain assembly on the shafts with the timing mark on the crankshaft gear at the twelve O'clock position and the camshaft gear in its six O'clock position.

NOTE: The timing marks should face each other and intersect an imaginary line drawn between the center of the camshaft and the center of the crankshaft.

PISTON AND CONNECTING ROD POSITIONING

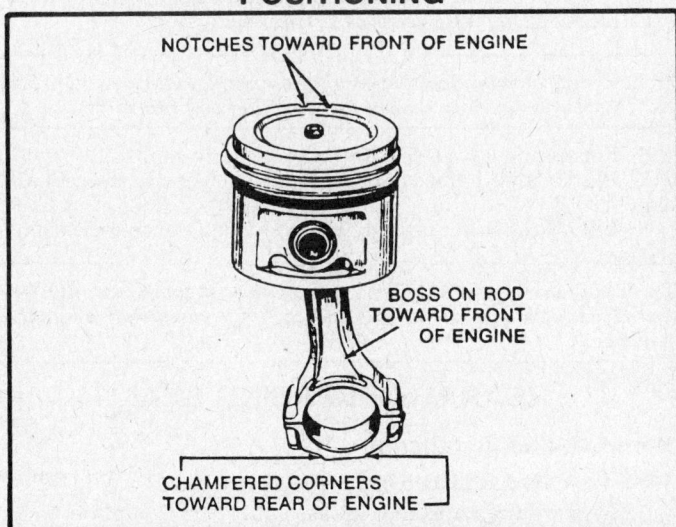

Piston assembly—**Buick** produced V6 gasoline engine (© General Motors Corporation)

Lubrication
OIL PAN

Removal and Installation

1. Disconnect the negative battery cable. Remove the air cleaner.

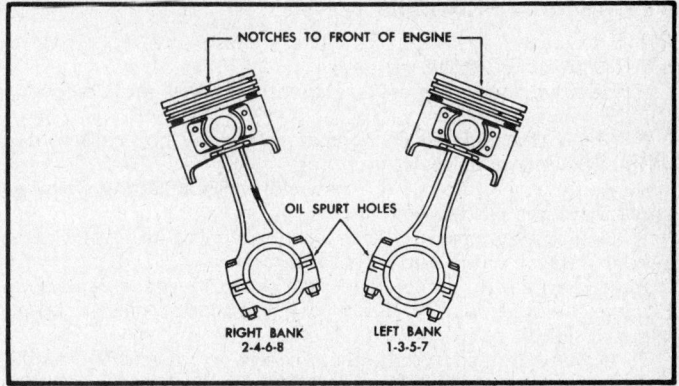

Piston assembly—**Chevrolet** produced V8 gasoline engine (© General Motors Corporation)

2. Remove the upper fan shroud. Raise the vehicle and drain the engine oil.
3. If equipped, disconnect the A.I.R. hose at the converter pipe and at the exhaust manifold.
4. Remove the exhaust crossover pipe at the manifold and converter.
5. Remove the starter. Remove the flywheel cover.
6. Disconnect the transmission oil cooler lines at the oil pan.
7. On V8 engines, remove the engine mount through bolts. On V6 engines, loosen the right bolt and remove the left bolt.
8. Remove oil pan bolts and lower oil pan. Check that forward crankshaft throw and/or counter balance weight are not extending downward so as to block oil pan removal. Turn crankshaft, as necessary, to put the crankshaft throw on a horizontal plane.
9. Raise the engine and remove the oil pan.
10. Installation is the reverse of the removal procedure.

OIL PUMP

Removal And Disassembly

V6 GASOLINE ENGINE

1. Disconnect the negative battery cable. Drain the engine oil. Remove the oil filter.
2. Unbolt the pump cover assembly from the timing chain cover.
3. Remove the cover assembly and slide out the pump gears.
4. Remove the oil pressure relief valve cap, spring, and valve. Do not remove the oil filter by-pass valve and spring.
5. Check that the relief valve spring isn't worn on its side or collapsed. Check that the relief valve is no more than an easy slip fit in its bore in the cover. If there is any perceptible sideplay, replace the valve. If there is still sideplay, replace the cover.
6. Check the filter by-pass valve for good condition.

Assembly And Installation

1. Lubricate and install the pressure relief valve and spring in the cover bore. Install the gasket and cap, torquing the cap to 35 ft. lbs.
2. Install the gears and check that gear-to-cover end clearance is between 0.002–0.006 in. If the clearance is less, check the timing cover gear pocket for wear.
3. Remove the gears and pack the gear pocket full of petroleum jelly. Don't use grease.
4. Install the gears. Install a new gasket and the cover. Torque the bolts evenly to 10 ft. lbs. Replace the filter.

20-27

PONTIAC
BONNEVILLE • GRAND PRIX • SAFARI • PARISIENNE

V8 GASOLINE ENGINE

1. Disconnect the negative battery cable. Drain the engine oil. Remove the engine oil pan.
2. Remove the pump cover attaching screws and the pump cover.
3. Mark the gear teeth so that they may be reassembled with the same gear teeth indexing.
4. Remove the idler gear and the drive gear, along with the shaft from the pump body.
5. Remove the pressure regulator valve retaining pin, pressure regulator valve and related parts.
6. If the pick-up screen and pipe assembly need replacing, remove the pipe from the pump with a soft jawed vise or clamping tool.
7. If a new pipe is installed, use sealer on the end of the pipe and press or tap the pipe end into the pump body, thus preventing air leaks, which could cause a loss of oil pressure.
8. Reinstall in reverse order. To ensure immediate oil pressure on start-up, the oil pump gear cavity should be packed with petroleum jelly.

REAR MAIN OIL SEAL

NOTE: The rear main bearing rope type oil seal replacement can be done with the crankshaft in the block and by one of two different methods.

1st Method Removal and Installation Procedure

ALL, EXCEPT 1985 ½ AND LATER 5.0L, VIN CODE H ENGINES

1. Remove the oil pan and pump where required. Remove the rear main bearing cap.
2. Pry the lower seal out of the bearing cap with a suitable tool, being careful not to gouge the cap surface.
3. Remove the upper seal by lightly tapping on one end with a brass pin punch until the other end can be grasped and pulled out with pliers.
4. Clean the bearing cap, cylinder block, and crankshaft mating surfaces with solvent. Inspect all these surfaces for gouges, nicks, and burrs.
5. Apply light engine oil on the seal lips and bead, but keep the seal ends clean.
6. Insert the tip of the installation tool between the crankshaft and the seal of the cylinder block. Place the seal between the tip of the tool and the crankshaft, so that the bead contacts the tip of the tool.

7. Be sure that the seal lip is facing the front of the engine, and work the seal around the crankshaft using the installation tool to protect the seal from the corner of the cylinder block.

NOTE: Do not remove the tool until the opposite end of the seal is flush with the cylinder block surface.

8. Remove the installation tool, being careful not to pull the seal out at the same time.
9. Using the same procedure, install the lower seal into the bearing cap. Use your finger and thumb to lever the seal into the cap.
10. Apply sealer to the cylinder block only where the cap mates to the surface. Do not apply sealer to the seal ends.
11. Install the rear cap and torque the bolts to specifications.

2nd Method Removal and Installation Method

ALL, EXCEPT 1985 ½ AND LATER 5.0L, VIN CODE H ENGINES

1. Remove the oil pan assembly and the rear main bearing cap, as previously described. Remove the old seal from the cap and save.
2. With a special tool, BT–6433, J–25282–2 or their equivalent, drive both sides of the old seal gently into the groove until it is packed tight.
3. Measure the distance the old seal was driven into the groove, add $1/16$ in. to the measurement and cut this amount from the old seal removed from the bearing cap.
4. Measure the distance on the opposite side that the seal was driven up into the groove and add $1/16$ in. to the measurement and cut this amount from the old seal that was removed from the bearing cap.

NOTE: Use the bearing cap as a holding fixture when cutting the seal ends.

5. Work the two cut pieces of seal into their respective groove sides. Using the packing tool, pack these short pieces into the groove until they are approximately flush with the engine block. Trim the excess seal from each side.

CAUTION

Place a piece of shim stock between the crankshaft and the seal to protect the bearing surface during the trimming procedure.

6. Form a new rope seal into the bearing cap.
7. Place a small amount of sealer on each end of the seal and cap.
8. Install the main bearing cap and torque to specifications.

CAUTION

Do not use the cap retaining bolts to pull the cap into place. Block or thread damage can result. Tap the cap into place with a suitable hammer.

REAR MAIN BEARING SEAL

Removal and Installation

1985 ½ AND LATER 5.0L, VIN NUMBER H ENGINE

1. Remove the transmission assembly and flex plate.
2. Using the notches provided in the seal retainer, remove the seal from the engine block, using a pry tool.
3. Lubricate the inside and outside of the new seal with engine oil.
4. Using seal installer tool number J–325621 or its equivalent, place the seal on the tool.
5. Install tool screws into the rear of the crankshaft and tighten securely. This will maintain the seal in a square position over the crankshaft while being installed.
6. Tighten the wing nut on the tool until it bottoms.
7. Remove the tool and screws from the crankshaft.
8. Install the transmission and complete the assembly.

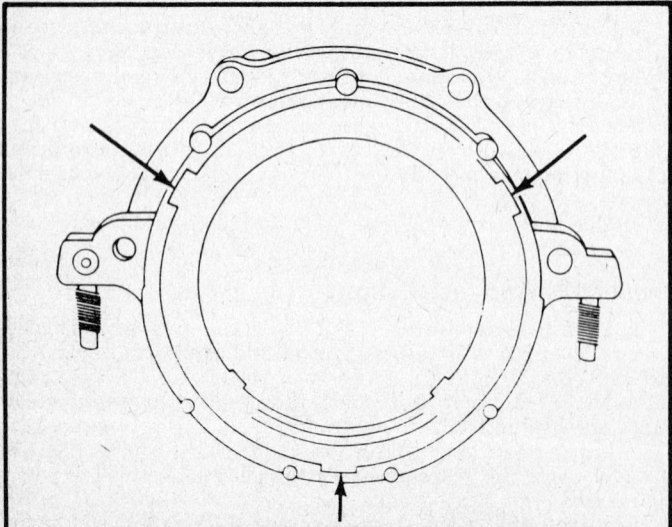

Seal and notch locations in the seal retainer

REAR MAIN SEAL RETAINER OR GASKET

Removal and Installation

1. Remove the transmission from the vehicle.
2. Remove the oil pan from the engine.

NOTE: When ever the retainer is removed, a new seal and gasket must be used during the installation.

3. Remove the retainer/seal assembly and the gasket. Remove the seal from the retainer.
4. Clean the seal and gasket area. Install a new gasket over the stud in the engine case.
5. Install the retainer to the case bolts and torque to 120–150 inch lbs. (13–16 Nm).
6. Install the oil pan assembly.
7. Install a new crankshaft oil seal as outline previously.
8. Install the transmission and complete the assembly.

FRONT SUSPENSION AND STEERING SECTION

For Front Suspension Services Refer to the Unit Repair Section. For Steering Gear Overhaul Refer to the Unit Repair Section.

STEERING GEAR

Removal and Installation

1. Remove or reposition flexible coupling shield.
2. Raise the vehicle and support safely.
3. Disconnect the hoses from the gear and cap the hose fittings.
4. Remove the pitman shaft nut, then disconnect the pitman arm from the pitman shaft.
5. Remove the three bolts attaching the gear to the frame side rail and remove the gear with the hoses attached.
6. Installation is the reverse of the removal procedure.

POWER STEERING PUMP

Removal and Installation

1. Disconnect the hoses at the pump. Plug the lines and the pump to prevent loss of fluid.
2. Remove all the drive belts. Remove all the necessary components in order to gain access to the power steering pump.
3. Loosen the bracket-to-pump mounting bolts.
4. Remove the bracket-to-pump mounting bolts and remove the pump.
5. Installation is the reverse of removal.

STEERING WHEEL

Removal and Installation

1. Disconnect the negative battery terminal.
2. On deluxe models, remove the screws holding the trim cover to the wheel or, if equipped with a horn button, lift the button off.
3. Remove the steering wheel snap ring and nut from the steering shaft.
4. Position the wheels in the straight-ahead position and make match marks on the steering shaft and steering wheel.
5. Using a puller, remove the steering wheel.

— CAUTION —
Don't pound on the steering wheel or the steering shaft. The collapsible column could be damaged enough to require replacement.

6. Disconnect the horn wire insulator by rotating the insulator counterclockwise to unlock position and then pull up.

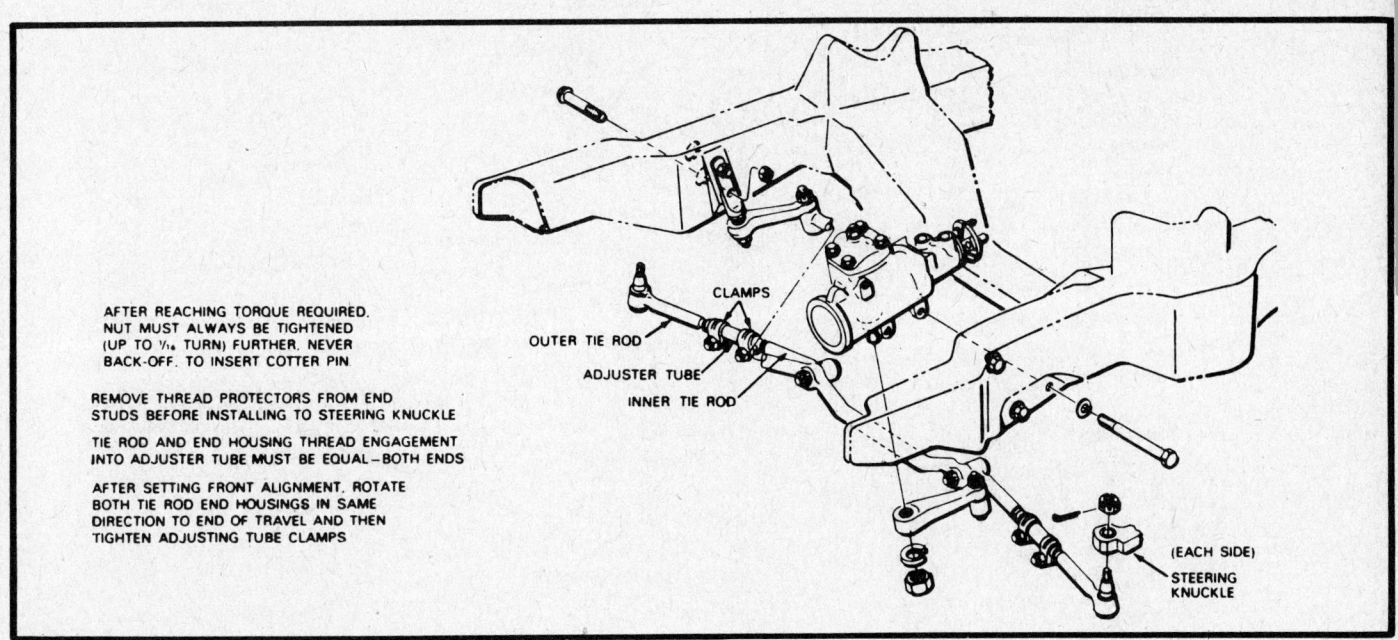

Typical steering linkage and steering gear mounting (© General Motors Corporation)

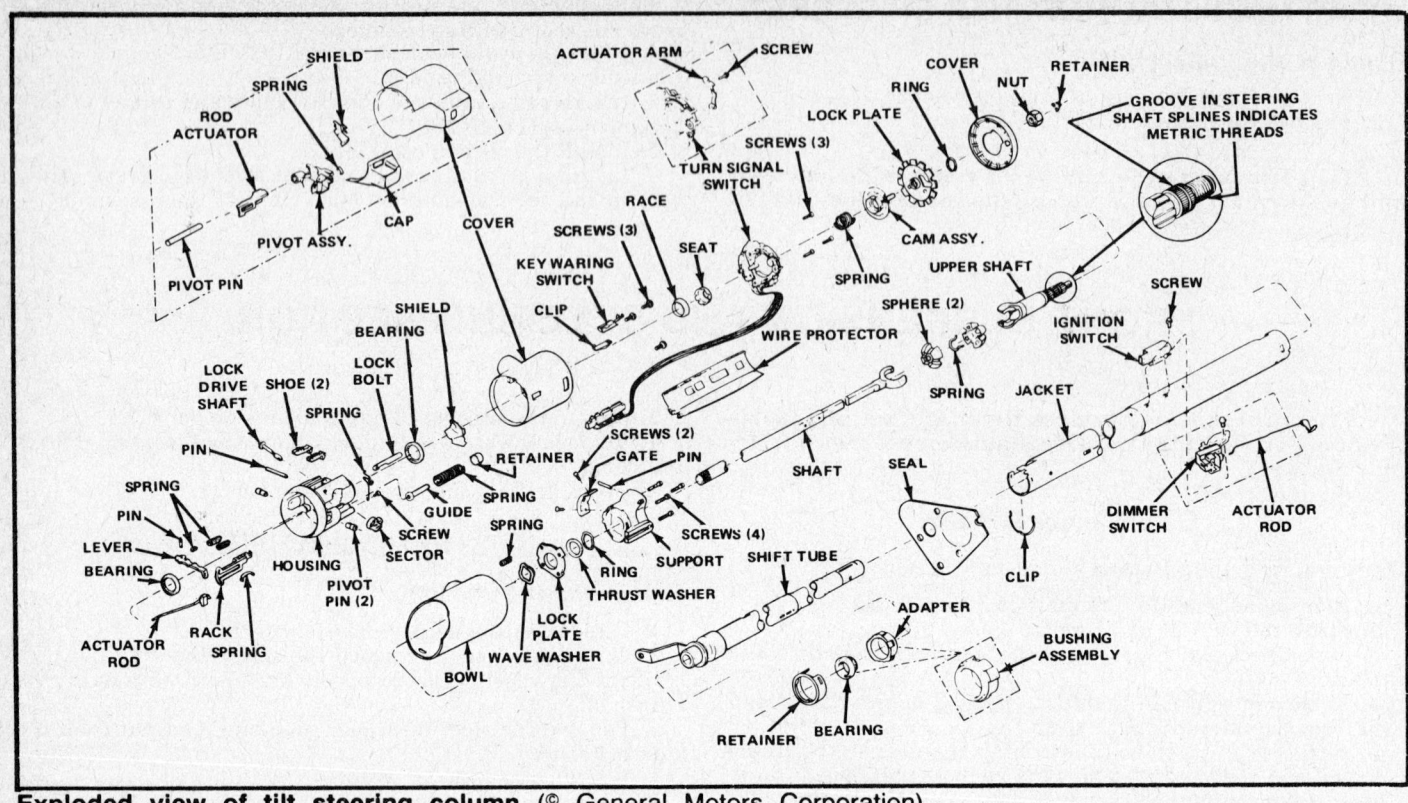

Exploded view of tilt steering column (© General Motors Corporation)

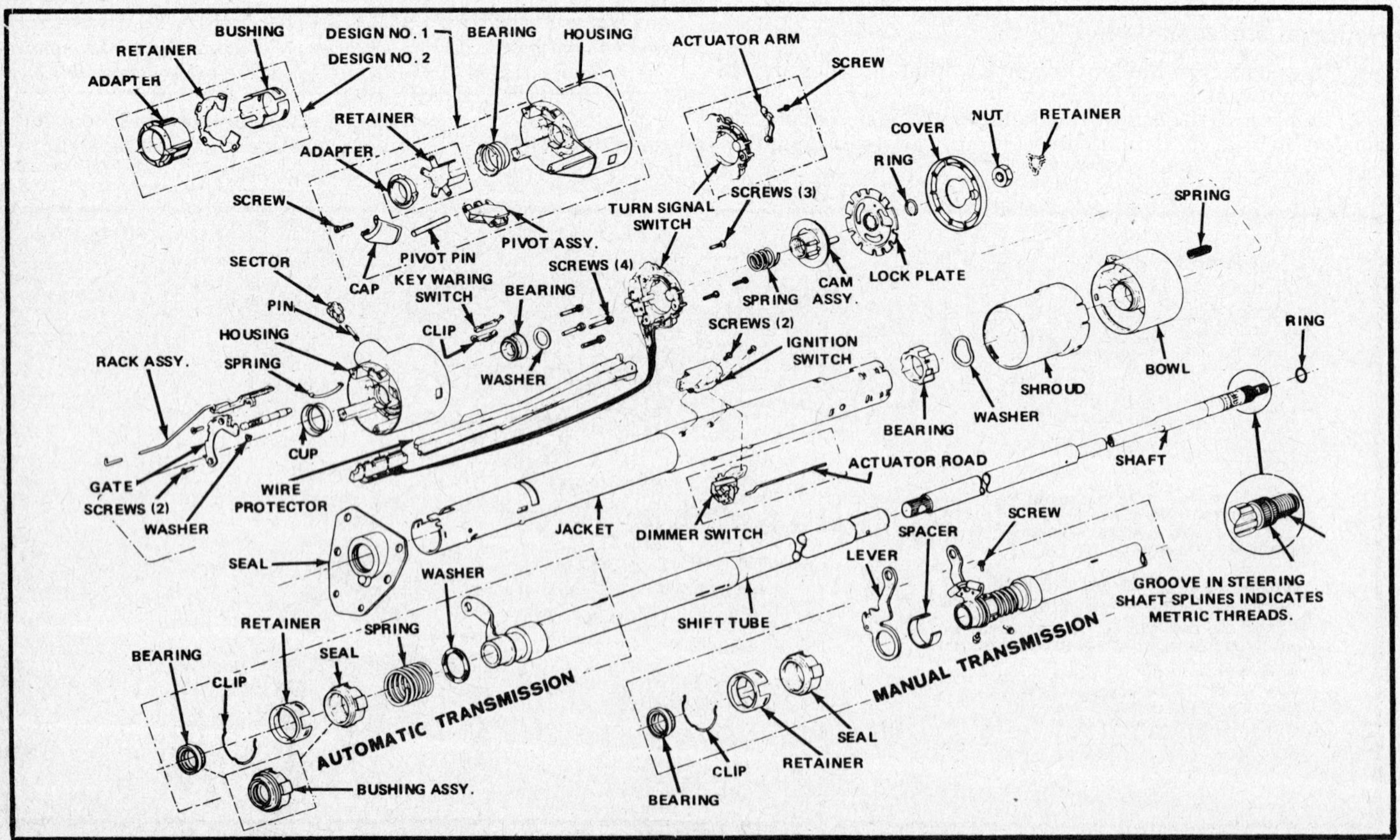

Exploded view of standard steering column (© General Motors Corporation)

7. Reverse the removal procedures to install. Make sure the match marks are lined up when installing the wheel. Tighten the nut to 35 ft. lbs.

STEERING COLUMN

Removal and Installation

NOTE: Handle the steering column very carefully. Rapping on the end of it or leaning on it could shear off the inserts which allow the column to collapse in a crash.

1. Disconnect battery.
2. Disconnect flexible coupling.
3. Remove cover and toe-pan attaching screws.
4. If necessary, remove instrument panel lower trim panel.
5. Disconnect shift linkages, wiring, etc.
6. Remove column mounts, and lower column.
7. When installing, check that flexible coupling alignment is correct.

NOTE: When installing use only the specified hardware. Over-length bolts could prevent the column from properly collapsing in a crash.

FRONT WHEEL BEARINGS

Adjustment

1. Raise the vehicle and support it safely.
2. Remove the dust cap from the hub.
3. Remove the cotter pin and discard it.
4. Tighten the spindle nut to 12 ft. lbs. while turning the wheel. Then back off the nut $1/4$–$1/2$ turn.
5. Retighten the nut by hand until it is finger-tight.
6. Loosen the nut no more than $1/6$ of a turn until the nearest hole in the spindle lines up with the slot in the spindle nut and insert a new cotter pin.
7. Feel the looseness in the hub assembly. There should be 0.001–0.005 in. endplay.
8. Replace the dust cover and lower the vehicle.

BRAKE SECTION

For Brake Service Refer to the Unit Repair Section.

MASTER CYLINDER

Removal and Installation

1. Disconnect hydraulic lines at master cylinder.
2. Remove the retaining nuts and lockwashers that hold cylinder to the brake booster.
3. Remove the master cylinder, gasket and rubber boot.
4. Install the cylinder on the booster.
5. Install nuts and lockwashers.
6. Install hydraulic lines then check brake pedal free play.
7. Bleed brakes.

POWER BRAKE UNIT

Removal and Installation

1. Unbolt the master cylinder from the power unit. Being careful not to kink or bend the brake lines, pull the master cylinder away from the power unit without disconnecting the brake lines.
2. Disconnect and plug the vacuum hose.
3. Disconnect the power brake pushrod from the brake pedal.
4. Unbolt the power brake unit from the firewall.
5. Remove the unit.
6. Mount the unit to the firewall.
7. Install the master cylinder to the power unit.
8. Connect the vacuum hose.
9. Connect the power brake pushrod to the brake pedal.

Vacuum Pumps

Vacuum pumps are used on selective engines to aid the engine in maintaining a proper level of vacuum for the power brake system.

ELECTRIC VACUUM PUMP

The vacuum pump is mounted under the battery tray on the left hand side of the car. The inlet hose is connected to the booster check valve and the outlet hose is connected to the intake manifold.

A low vacuum warning light switch is located in the inlet hose line operating a warning light on the instrument panel when the vacuum drops below a predetermined level.

Removal and Installation

1. Raise vehicle and remove splash shield, L.H. side of car.
2. Disconnect hoses at vacuum pump.
3. Disconnect electrical connector at vacuum pump.
4. Remove three nuts securing pump assembly to mounting bracket and remove pump.
5. Reverse procedure for installation of vacuum pump.

GEAR DRIVEN VACUUM PUMP

The gear driven vacuum pump is a diaphragm pump which requires no periodic maintenance. It is driven by a cam inside the drive assembly to which it mounts. The drive housing assembly has a drive gear on the lower end which meshes with the camshaft gear in the engine. This drive gear causes the cam in the drive housing to rotate. The drive gear also powers the engine oil lubricating pump.

Removal

1. Remove vacuum hose from vacuum pump inlet.
2. Remove bolt and clamp holding drive assembly to engine block.
3. Remove the vacuum pump from the engine. Place a protective cloth over the hole to prevent accidently dropping a foreign object into the engine.

Installation

1. Remove protective cloth from engine.
2. Insert pump and drive assembly in engine, making sure that the gears on the drive assembly mesh with the gears on the engine camshaft.
3. Rotate the pump into position so the bracket and bolt can be installed.
4. Install clamp and bolt.
5. Install vacuum hose to pump.

BELT DRIVEN VACUUM PUMP

The pump has a pulley attached and is driven by a belt. With

PONTIAC
BONNEVILLE • GRAND PRIX • SAFARI • PARISIENNE

the exception of the pulley, the vacuum pump is serviced as an assembly.

Removal and Installation

1. Loosen the retaining bolts for the vacuum pump and remove the drive belt.
2. Remove the retaining bolts and hoses/lines to the assembly and remove from the vehicle.
3. The installation is the reverse of the removal procedure.

HYDRO—BOOST POWER BRAKE UNIT

Removal and Installation

CAUTION

Power steering fluid and brake fluid are incompatible. If brake seals contact steering fluid or steering seals contact brake fluid, the seals will be ruined.

---

1. With the engine off, pump the brake pedal four or five times to empty the accumulator of pressurized fluid.
2. Disconnect the brake lines from the master cylinder and cap the lines. Remove the two master cylinder-to-booster attaching nuts and move the master cylinder away from the booster with the brake lines attached.
3. Remove and plug the three hydraulic lines from the booster. Remove the washer and retainer that secures the booster pedal rod to the brake pedal arm.

NOTE: To avoid booster damage, do not pry the pedal rod off the pedal arm.

4. Remove the four nuts holding the booster to the firewall.
5. Loosen the booster from the firewall and move the booster pedal rod inboard until it disconnects from the brake pedal arm. Remove the spring washer from the brake pedal arm and remove the booster.
6. To install, reverse the removal procedure. Tighten the booster mounting nuts to 30 ft. lbs. and the master cylinder to booster mounting to 20 ft. lbs. Bleed the system.

Power Master Brake System

If the vehicle is equipped with Power Master Brake System, refer to the Buick Rear Wheel Drive Section of this Manual.

PARKING BRAKE

Adjustment

Adjustment of the parking brake is necessary whenever the rear brake cables have been disconnected or the parking brake pedal can be depressed more than eight ratchet clicks under heavy foot pressure. The vehicle should first be raised on a lift.

1. Make sure that the service brakes are properly adjusted.
2. Depress the parking brake pedal two ratchet clicks on all models.
3. Loosen the jam nut on the equalizer adjusting nut. Tighten the adjusting nut until the left rear wheel can just be turned rearward by hand, but not forward.
4. Release the ratchet one click; the rear wheel should rotate rearward freely and forward with a slight drag.
5. Release the ratchet fully; the rear wheel should turn freely in either direction.

PARKING BRAKE CABLE

Removal and Installation

FRONT

1. Raise and support the vehicle safely.
2. Loosen adjuster nut and disconnect front cable from connector. Compress retainer fingers and loosen at frame.
3. Remove supports and lower car.
4. Remove lower rear bolt from wheelhouse panel and pull panel out to gain access to front cable.
5. Disconnect a cable from parking brake pedal assembly, compress retainer fingers and remove cable.
6. Install cable by reversing removal procedure. Make sure cable is routed properly and securely retained.
7. Adjust parking brake cable.

LEFT REAR

1. Raise and support the vehicle safely.
2. Loosen adjuster nut and compress retainer fingers at equalizer and loosen cable.
3. Disconnect cable from connector and remove from equalizer.
4. Mark relationship of wheel to axle flange and remove wheel and tire assembly.
5. Remove brake drum.
6. Remove primary shoe return spring and parking brake strut.
7. Compress retainer fingers and loosen cable from backing plate. Disconnect cable from parking brake lever and remove cable.
8. Installation is the reverse of the removal procedure.
9. Adjust the parking brake cable.

RIGHT REAR

1. Raise and support the vehicle safely.
2. Remove adjuster nut at equalizer and compress retainer fingers and loosen cable from retainers at frame and from axle housing clip.
3. Mark relationship of wheel to axle flange and remove wheel and tire assembly.
4. Remove brake drum.
5. Remove primary shoe return spring, parking brake strut, and secondary shoe hold down spring.
6. Compress retainer fingers and loosen cable from backing plate. Disconnect cable from parking brake lever and remove cable.
7. Install cable by reversing removal procedure. Make sure cable is routed properly and securely retained.
8. Adjust parking brake cable.

TRANSMISSION AND DRIVESHAFT SECTION

Automatic Transmission

MANUAL LINKAGE

Adjustment

1. Adjust the linkage so the shift lever positions correspond exactly to the transmission positions.
2. Some linkage arrangements have adjustment gauge pin holes. In these a free pin fit will insure proper adjustment.
3. After the linkage is adjusted, check operation of the neutral start switch and the backup lights.

CABLE DETENT

Adjustment

1. Disengage the snap lock and position the carburetor in the full open position.

2. Push the snap lock on the cable down until the top is flush with the cable.
3. Release the carburetor linkage.

AUTOMATIC TRANSMISSION

Removal and Installation

1. Disconnect the battery.
2. Disconnect detent cable (if so equipped) from accelerator lever or carburetor.
3. Remove, disconnect or relocate any of the following necessary for removal:
   a. Exhaust crossover pipe
   b. Drive shaft
   c. Oil cooler lines
   d. Transmission crossmember (support engine and transmission as needed)
   e. Speedometer cable
   f. Shift linkage
   g. Electrical connections
   h. Flywheel cover pan
4. Remove mounting bolts, and slide transmission back and out of vehicle.
5. Mark flywheel and converter for installation reference.

SHIFT QUADRANT POINTER

Adjustment

1. Disconnect the negative battery cable.
2. Remove the left hand instrument cluster bezel, from in front of the speedometer.
3. Loosen the shift indicator cable clip screw on the steering column.

NOTE: Make sure that the automatic transmission control linkage is properly adjusted before adjusting the shift quadrant indicator.

4. Position the shift lever in the detented neutral position.
5. Adjust the cable clip so that the indicator pointer is centered on the "N".
6. Secure the cable clip screw and move the transmission shift lever from park to low to check for full pointer travel from park to low.
7. Install the instrument cluster bezel and the negative battery cable.

Driveshaft

Removal and Installation

1. Mark the driveshaft rear yoke and the differential flange to assure correct alignment upon reassembly.
2. Remove the bolts and straps (or four bolts on double cardan U-joint) from the differential flange. If the bearing cups are loose, tape them together so the needle rollers don't fall out.
3. Remove the driveshaft assembly by first sliding the driveshaft forward to disengage the differential flange, then sliding the shaft downward and rearward to disengage the front splined yoke from the transmission output shaft.
4. Installation is the reverse of removal. Be sure to align the match mark made before disassembly.

Universal Joints

For U-joint service procedures, refer to the Unit Repair Section.

REAR AXLE AND SUSPENSION

For Overhaul Procedures Refer to the Unit Repair Section.

REAR AXLE ASSEMBLY

Removal and Installation

1. Raise the vehicle and support it safely. Be sure that the rear axle assembly is supported safely.
2. Disconnect shock absorbers from axle.
3. Mark drive shaft and pinion flange, then disconnect drive shaft and support out of the way.
4. Remove brake line junction bolt at axle housing, then disconnect brake lines at junction block or at wheel cylinder.
5. Disconnect upper control arms from axle housing.
6. Lower rear axle assembly on hoist and remove springs.
7. Remove rear wheels and drums.
8. Remove rear axle cover bolts and remove cover.
9. Remove axle.
10. Disconnect brake lines from axle housing clips.
11. Remove backing plates.
12. Disconnect lower control arms from axle housing.
13. Remove rear axle housing.
14. Installation is the reverse of the removal procedure.
15. Be sure to bleed the brake system, as required.

AXLE SHAFT

Removal and Installation

1. Raise vehicle and support it safely. Remove the tire and wheel assembly. Remove the brake drum.
2. Drain the fluid. Remove the rear carrier cover. Discard the gasket.
3. Remove the rear axle pinion shaft lock screw and the rear axle pinion shaft.
4. Push flanged end of axle shaft toward center of the vehicle and remove "C" lock from button end of shaft.
5. Remove axle shaft from housing, being careful not to damage oil seal.
6. Installation is the reverse of the removal procedure. Be sure to fill the rear assembly with the proper grade and type gear oil.

OIL SEAL/BEARING

Removal and Installation

1. Remove the axle shaft.
2. Remove seal from housing with a pry bar behind steel case of seal, being careful not to damage housing.
3. Insert tool J-23689 or equivalent into bore and position if behind bearing so that tangs on tool engage bearing outer race. Remove bearing, using slide hammer.
4. Lubricate the new bearing with gear lubricant and install bearing so that tool bottoms against shoulder in housing, using tool J-23690 or equivalent.
5. Lubricate seal lips with gear lubricant. Position seal on tool J-21128 or equivalent and position seal into housing bore. Tap seal into place so that it is flush with axle tube.

SECTION 21 ALTERNATORS

INDEX

Electrical Diagnosis
- Know your instruments 21-3

Alternators And Regulators
- Is it the alternator or the regulator? 21-3
- Alternator test plans 21-3
- Diagnosis 21-5

Bosch Alternator — With Internal Regulator
- Charging Circuit Resistance Test 21-14
- Current Output Test 21-16
- Voltage Regulator Test 21-17
- Disassembly of Unit 21-18
- Assembly of Unit 21-19

Bosch Alternator — With External Regulator
- Charging Circuit Resistance Test 21-19
- Current Output Test 21-20
- Voltage Regulator Test 21-21
- Disassembly of Unit 21-22
- Assembly of Unit 21-24

Bosch 40/90 And 40/100 Amp Alternator
- Charging Circuit Resistance Test 21-24
- Current Output Test 21-25
- Disassembly of Unit 21-26
- Assembly of Unit 21-26

Chrysler Isolated Field Alternator — With External Regulator
- Trouble Diagnosis .... 21-5 – 21-11
- Disassembly of Unit 21-7
- Bench Tests 21-9
- Assembly of Unit 21-10

Chrysler 40/90 Amp Alternator — With Regulator in Engine Electronics
- Operation 21-26
- Trouble Diagnosis 21-27
- Output Wire Resistance Test 21-28
- Current Output Test 21-29
- Regulator Test 21-30
- Charging System Fault Codes 21-30
- Disassembly of Unit 21-32
- Testing 21-32
- Assembly of Unit 21-33

Chrysler 60 and 78 Amp Alternator — With Regulator in Engine Electronics
- Operation 21-33
- Output Wire Resistance Test 21-33
- Current Output Test 21-34
- Regulator Rest 21-34
- Charging System Fault Codes 21-34
- Disassembly and Assembly 21-36

Ford Alternator — With External Regulator
- Trouble Diagnosis 21-52
- Charging System Operation 21-51
- Disassembly of Unit exc 65, 70 & 90 Amp 21-55
- Testing 21-56
- Assembly of Unit 21-58
- Disassembly of Unit 65, 70 & 90 Amp 21-58
- Assembly of Unit 65, 70 & 90 Amp 21-58

Ford Alternator — With Internal Regulator
- Operation 21-59
- Trouble Diagnosis 21-59
- Bench Tests 21-61
- Disassembly of Unit 21-62
- Assembly of Unit 21-62

Ford Side Terminal Alternator
- Operation 21-63
- Tests 21-63
- Disassembly and Assembly of Unit 21-64

GM Delcotron Alternator — With Internal Regulator
- GM Charging System Trouble Diagnosis ... 21-39 – 21-44
- Operation 21-36
- Trouble Diagnosis Tests 21-37
- Disassembly and Assembly of Unit 21-47

GM Delcotron Alternator — With Rear Vacuum Pump
- Description 21-47
- Disassembly of Unit 21-47
- Assembly of Unit 21-49

GM Delcotron CS-130 and CS-144 Alternator
- Description 21-49
- Trouble Diagnosis 21-50
- Bench Tests 21-51
- Disassembly and Assembly of Unit 21-51

Mitsubishi Alternator — With Electronic Voltage Regulator
- Description 21-12
- Voltage Regulator Test 21-12
- Current Output Test 21-13
- Disassembly of Unit 21-13
- Assembly of Unit 21-14

Alternators/ Regulators

ELECTRICAL DIAGNOSIS

To satisfy the growing trend toward organized engine diagnosis and tune-up, the following gauge and meter hook-ups, as well as diagnosis procedures are covered. The most sophisticated tune-up and diagnostic facilities are no more than a complex of the basic gauges and meters in common, everyday use. Therefore, to understand gauge and meter hook-ups, their applications and procedures, is to be equipped with the know-how to perform the most exacting diagnosis.

KNOW YOUR INSTRUMENTS

Ohmmeter

An ohmmeter is used to measure electrical resistance in a unit or circuit. The ohmmeter has a self contained power supply. In use, it is connected across (or in parallel with) the terminals of the unit being tested.

Ammeter

An ammeter is used to measure the amount of electricity flowing through a unit, or circuit. Ammeters are always connected in series with the unit or circuit being tested.

Voltmeter

A voltmeter is used to measure voltage pushing the current through a unit, or circuit. The meter is connected across the terminals of the unit being tested.

ALTERNATORS AND REGULATORS

Is it the alternator or the regulator

The first step in diagnosing troubles of the charging system, is to identify the source of failure. Does the fault lie in the alternator or the regulator? The next move depends upon preference or necessity, either repair or replace the offending unit.

It is just as easy to separate an alternator, electrically, from the AC regulator as it is to separate its counterpart, the DC generator from its regulator. AC generator output is controlled by the amount of current supplied to the field circuit of the system.

Unlike the DC generator, an AC generator is capable of producing substantial current at idle speed. Higher maximum output is also a possibility. This presents a potential danger when testing. As a precaution, a field rheostat should be used in the field circuit when making the following isolation test. The field rheostat permits positive control of the amount of current allowed to pass through the field circuit during the isolation test. Unregulated alternator capacity could ruin the unit.

Most manufacturers of precision gauges offer special test connectors, in sets, that will adapt to the leads and connections of any AC charging system.

ALTERNATOR TEST PLANS

The following is a procedure pattern for testing the various alternators and their control systems.

There are certain precautionary measures that apply to alternator tests in general. These items are listed in detail to avoid repetition when testing each make of alternator, and to encourage a habit of good test procedure.

1. Check alternator drive belt for condition and tension.
2. Disconnect the battery cables. Check physical, chemical, and electrical condition of battery.

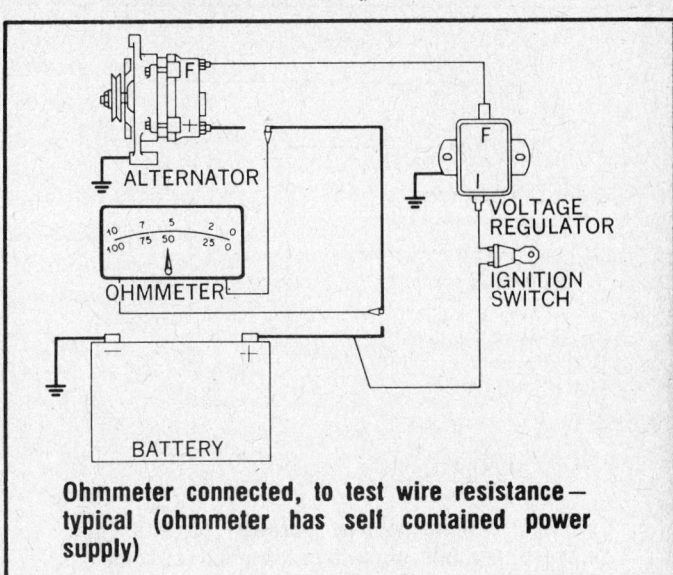

Ohmmeter connected, to test wire resistance — typical (ohmmeter has self contained power supply)

SECTION 21 ALTERNATORS
SYSTEM ELECTRICAL DIAGNOSIS

3. Be absolutely sure of polarity before connecting any battery in the circuit. Reversed polarity will ruin the diodes.
4. Never use a battery charger to start the engine.
5. Disconnect both battery cables when making a battery recharge hook-up.
6. Be sure of polarity hook-up when using a booster battery for starting.
7. Never ground the alternator output or battery terminal.
8. Never ground the field circuit between alternator and regulator.
9. Never run any alternator on an open circuit with the field energized.
10. Never try to polarize an alternator, unless directed by the manufacturer.
11. Do not attempt to motor an alternator.
12. The regulator cover must be in place when taking voltage limiter readings.
13. The ignition switch must be in off position when removing or installing the regulator cover.
14. Use insulated tools only to make adjustments to the regulator.
15. When making engine idle speed adjustments, always consider potential load factors that influence engine rpm. To com-

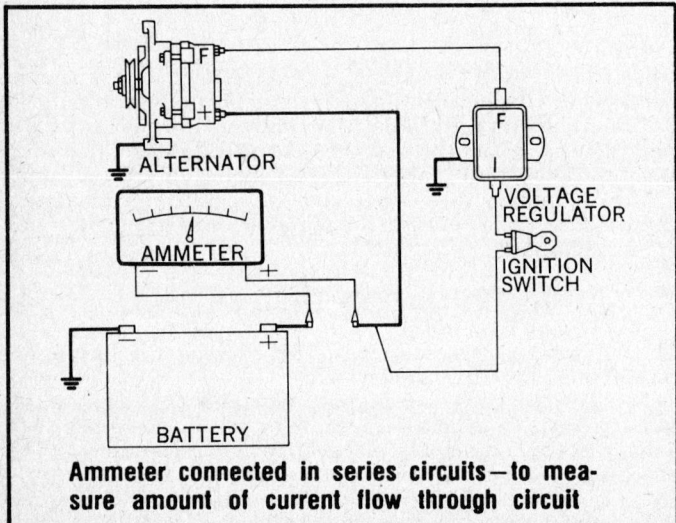

Ammeter connected in series circuits — to measure amount of current flow through circuit

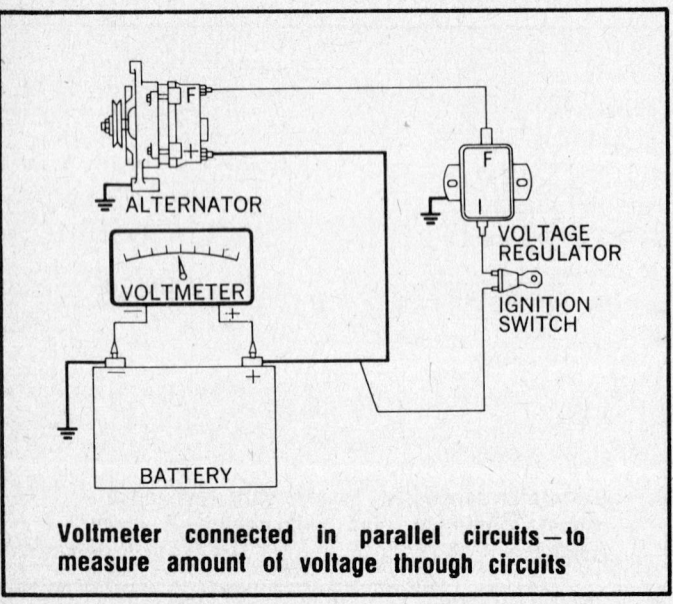

Voltmeter connected in parallel circuits — to measure amount of voltage through circuits

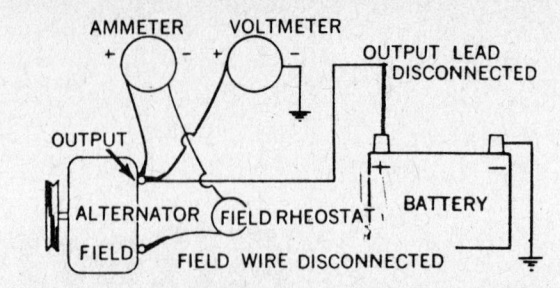

Checking field circuit current draw—As a precaution, a field rheostat should be used to control the amount of current allowed to pass throught the curcuit during isolation test

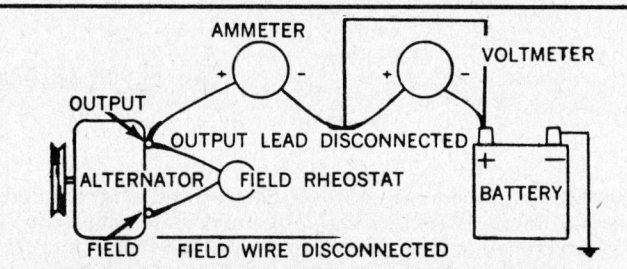

Checking charging system resistance to determine the amount of "voltage drop" between the alternator output terminal wire and the battery

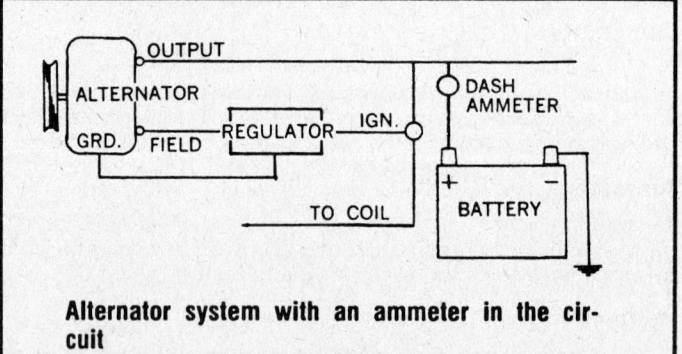

Alternator system with an ammeter in the circuit

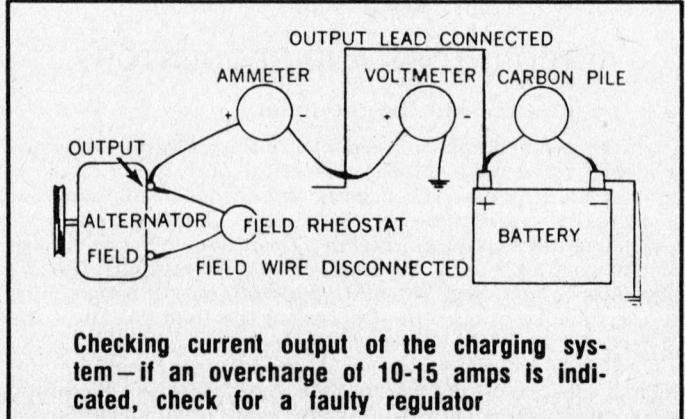

Checking current output of the charging system — if an overcharge of 10-15 amps is indicated, check for a faulty regulator

ALTERNATORS
SYSTEM ELECTRICAL DIAGNOSIS
SECTION 21

pensate for electrical load, switch on the lights, radio, heater, air conditioner, etc.

Diagnosis

LOW OR NO CHARGING

1. Blown fuse.
2. Broken or loose fan belt.
3. Voltage regulator not working.
4. Brushes sticking.
5. Slip ring dirty.
6. Open circuit.
7. Bad wiring connections.
8. Bad diode rectifier.
9. High resistance in charging circuit.
10. Voltage regulator needs adjusting.
11. Grounded stator.
12. May be open rectifiers (check all three phases).
13. If rectifiers are found blown or open, check capacitor.

NOISY UNIT

1. Damaged rotor bearings.
2. Poor alignment of unit.
3. Broken or loose belt.
4. Open diode rectifiers.

CHRYSLER ISOLATED FIELD ALTERNATOR (WITH EXTERNAL ELECTRONIC REGULATOR)

The Chrysler isolated field alternator derives its name from its construction. Both of the brushes are insulated from ground and there is no heat sink connection, thereby isolating the internal field.

TROUBLESHOOTING

Fusible Links

Chrysler Corporation vehicles have a single fusible link which is connected between the starter relay and the junction block. Failure of this link will cause all electrical systems to stop functioning.

Charging System Operation

NOTE: If the current indicator is to give an accurate reading, the battery cables must be of the same gauge and length as the original equipment.

1. With the engine running and all electrical systems off, place a current indicator over the positive battery cable.
2. If a charge of about 5 amps is recorded, the charging system is working. If a draw of about 5 amps is recorded the system is not working. The needle moves toward the battery when a charge condition is indicated and away from the battery when a draw condition is indicated. If a draw is indicated, proceed to the next testing procedure. If an overcharge of 10 to 15 amps is indicated, check for a faulty regulator.

Ignition Switch to Regulator Circuit Check

1. Disconnect the regulator wires at the regulator.
2. Turn the key on but do not start the engine.
3. Using a voltmeter or test light check for voltage across the I and F terminals. If there is current present the circuit is good. If there is no current check for bad connections, a bad ballast resistor, a bad ammeter, broken wires, or bad ground at the alternator or voltage regulator. Also, check for voltage

from the I wire to ground, current should be present. Check for voltage from the F terminal to ground, current should not be present.

Isolation Test

This test determines whether the regulator or alternator is bad if everything else in the circuit was ok.

1. Disconnect, at the alternator, the wire that runs between one of the alternator field connections and the voltage regulator.
2. Run a jumper wire from the disconnected alternator terminal to ground.
3. Connect a voltmeter to the battery. The positive voltmeter lead connects to the positive battery terminal, and the negative lead goes to the negative terminal. Record the reading.
4. Make sure that all electrical systems are turned off. Start the engine. Do not race the engine.
5. Gradually raise engine speed to 1500–2000 rpm. There should be an increase of one to two volts on the voltmeter. If this is true the alternator is good and the voltage regulator should be repaired. If there is no voltage increase the alternator is faulty.

Charging Circuit Resistance Test

The purpose of this test is to determine the amount of "voltage drop" between the alternator output terminal wire and the battery.

1. Disconnect the battery ground cable and the "BAT" lead at the alternator output terminal.
2. Connect an ammeter with a scale to 100 amps in series between the alternator "BAT" terminal and the disconnected "BAT" wire.
3. Connect the positive lead of a voltmeter to the disconnected "BAT" wire. Connect the negative lead of the voltmeter to the negative post of the battery.
4. Disconnect the green colored regulator field wire from the alternator. Connect a jumper lead from the alternator field terminal to ground.
5. Connect a tachometer to the engine and reconnect the battery ground cable.

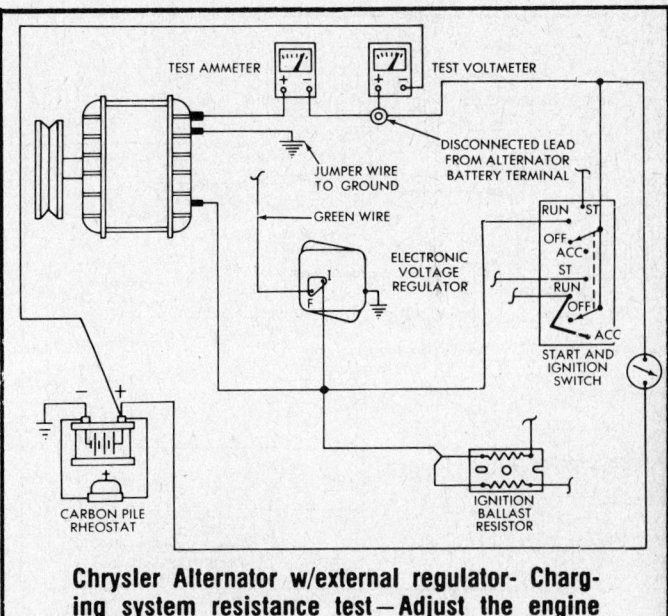

Chrysler Alternator w/external regulator- Charging system resistance test – Adjust the engine speed and carbon pile to maintain a flow of 20 amps in the circuit the voltmeter reading should not exceed 0.7 volts

Section 21 ALTERNATORS
CHRYSLER ISOLATED FIELD (W/EXTERNAL ELECTRONIC REGULATOR)

6. Connect a variable carbon pile rheostat to the battery cables. Be sure the carbon pile is in the "OPEN" or "OFF" position before connecting the leads to the battery terminals.

7. Start the engine and operate at an idle.

8. Adjust the engine speed and carbon pile to maintain a flow of 20 amperes in the circuit. Observe the voltmeter reading which should not exceed 0.7 volts.

9. If a higher voltage reading is indicated inspect, clean and tighten all connections in the charging system.

10. If necessary a voltage drop test can be done at each connection until the excessive resistance is located.

11. If the charging system resistance is within specifications reduce the engine speed, turn off the carbon pile rheostat and stop the engine. Remove battery ground cable.

12. Remove the test instruments from the electrical system and reconnect the charging system wiring. Reconnect the battery ground cable.

Current Output Test

This test determines if the alternator is capable of delivering its rated current output.

1. Disconnect the battery ground cable and the "BAT" lead wire at the alternator output terminal.

2. Connect an ammeter in series between the alternator output terminal and the disconnected "BAT" lead wire. The ammeter must have a scale of 100 amps.

3. Connect the positive lead of a voltmeter to the output terminal of the alternator and the negative lead to a good ground.

4. Disconnect the green colored wire at the voltage regulator and connect a jumper wire from the alternator field terminal to ground.

5. Connect a tachometer to the engine and reconnect the battery ground wire.

6. Connect a variable carbon pile rheostat between the positive and negative battery cables. Be sure the rheostat control is in the "OPEN" or "OFF" position before connecting the leads to the battery cables.

7. Start the engine and operate at idle. Adjust the carbon pile rheostat control and the engine speed in increments until the voltmeter reading is 15 volts (13 volts for the 114 and 117 amp alternators) and the engine speed is 1250 rpm (900 rpm for the 114 and 117 amp alternators). Do not allow the voltage to rise above 16 volts.

8. The ammeter readings must be within the following specifications.

Current Rating	Identification	Current Output
60 amp	Blue, natural or yellow	47 amps min.
78 amp	Brown tag	58 amps min.
114, 117 amp	Yellow	97 amps min.

NOTE: If measured at the battery, current output will be approximately 5 amperes lower than specified.

9. If the readings are less than specified, the alternator should be removed and checked during a bench test.

10. After the current output test is completed, reduce the engine speed, turn the carbon pile rheostat off and then stop the engine.

11. Disconnect the battery ground cable, remove the ammeter, voltmeter and carbon pile. Remove the jumper wire from the field terminal and reconnect the green colored wire to the alternator field terminal.

12. Reconnect the battery cable, if no further testing is to be done to the charging circuit.

Rotor Field Coil Draw Test

1. If on the vehicle remove the drive belt and wiring connections from the alternator.

2. Connect a jumper wire from the negative terminal of the battery to one of the field terminals of the alternator.

3. Connect the test ammeter positive lead to the other field terminal of the alternator and the negative ammeter lead to the positive battery terminal.

4. Connect a jumper wire between the alternator end shield and the battery negative terminal.

5. Slowly rotate the alternator pulley by hand and observe the ammeter reading.

6. The field coil draw should be 4.5 to 6.5 amperes at 12 volts. (4.75 to 6.0 amperes at 12 volts 114 and 117 amp alternators).

7. A low rotor coil draw is an indication of high resistance in

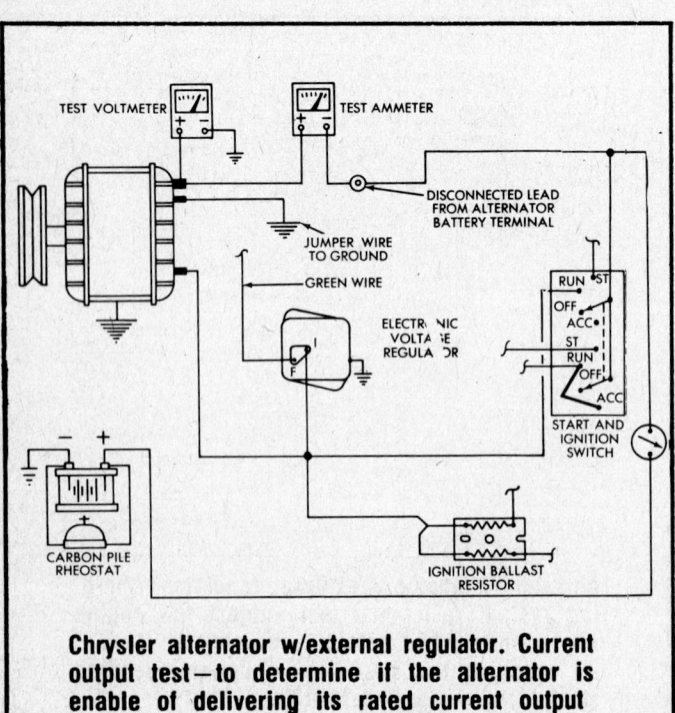

Chrysler alternator w/external regulator. Current output test—to determine if the alternator is enable of delivering its rated current output

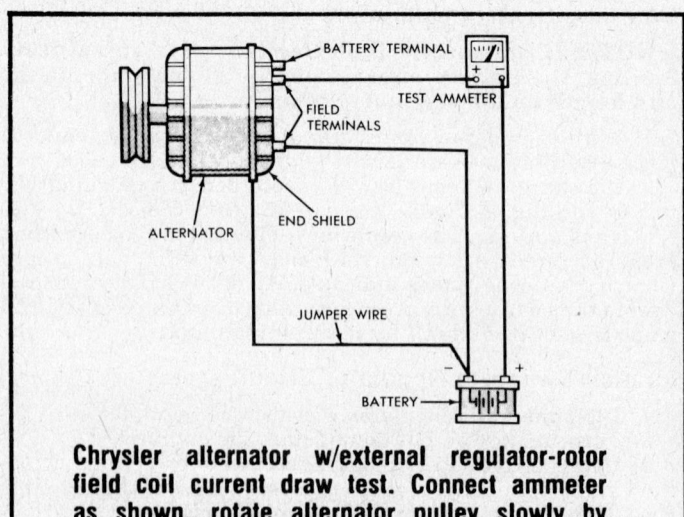

Chrysler alternator w/external regulator-rotor field coil current draw test. Connect ammeter as shown, rotate alternator pulley slowly by hand and observe the field coil draw reading

ALTERNATORS 21
CHRYSLER ISOLATED FIELD (W/EXTERNAL ELECTRONIC REGULATOR)

the field coil circuit (brushes, slip rings or rotor coil). A higher rotor coil draw indicates possible shorted rotor coil or grounded rotor. No reading indicates an open rotor or defective brushes.

8. Remove the test equipment and jumper leads.

Electronic Voltage Regulator Test

1. Make sure battery terminals are clean and battery is charged.
2. Connect the positive lead of a test voltmeter to ignition Terminal No. 1 of the ballast resistor.
3. Connect the negative voltmeter lead to a good body ground.
4. Start engine and allow it to idle at 1250 rpm, all lights and accessories turned off. Voltage should be as indicated.

Ambient Temp. 1/4 in. from Regulator	Voltage
−20°F.	14.9 to 15.9
80°F.	13.9 to 14.6
140°F.	13.3 to 13.9
Above 140°F.	Less Than 13.6

5. If the voltage is below specification check the following. Voltage regulator ground check voltage drop between regulator cover and ground. Harness wiring disconnect regulator plug (ignition switch off), then turn on ignition switch and check for battery voltage at the terminals having the red and green leads. Wiring harness must be disconnected from the regulator when checking individual leads. If no voltage is present in either lead the problem is in the wiring or alternator field.
6. If Step 5 tests showed no malfunctions install a new regulator and repeat Step 4.
7. If voltage is above specifications (Step 4), or fluctuates, check the following. Ground between regulator and body, and between body and engine. Ignition switch circuit between switch and regulator.
8. If voltage is still more than ½ volt above specifications install a new regulator and repeat Step 4.

Chrysler Alternator Overhaul and Internal Testing

Alternator disassembly, repair and assembly procedures are basically the same for all Chrysler alternators. Certain variations in design, or production modifications, could require slightly different procedures that should be obvious upon inspection of the unit being serviced.

Disassembly

To prevent damage to the brush assemblies (114 and 117 amp), they should be removed before proceeding with the disassembly of the alternator. The brushes are mounted in a plastic holder that positions the brushes vertically against the slip rings.

1. Remove the retaining screw, flat washer, nylon washer and field terminal and carefully lift the plastic holder containing the spring and brush assembly from the end housing.
2. The ground brush (60 amp) is positioned horizontally against the slip ring and is retained in the holder that is integral with the end housing. Remove the retaining screw and lift the clip, spring and brush assembly from the end housing. The stator is laminated so don't burr the stator or end housings.
3. Remove the through bolts and pry between the stator and drive end housing with a suitable tool. Carefully separate the drive end housing, pulley and rotor assembly from the stator and rectifier housing assembly.
4. The pulley is an interference fit on the rotor shaft. Remove with a puller and special adapters.

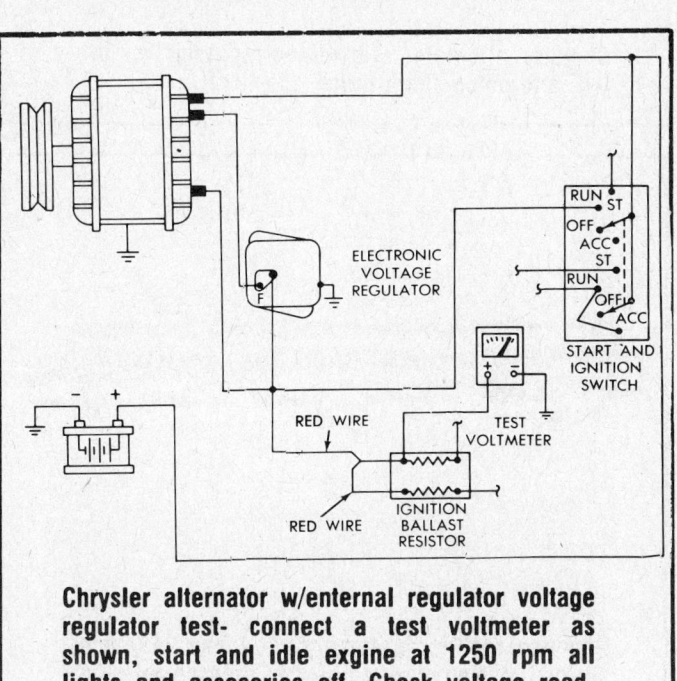

Chrysler alternator w/enternal regulator voltage regulator test- connect a test voltmeter as shown, start and idle exgine at 1250 rpm all lights and accesories off. Check voltage readings with those given in table

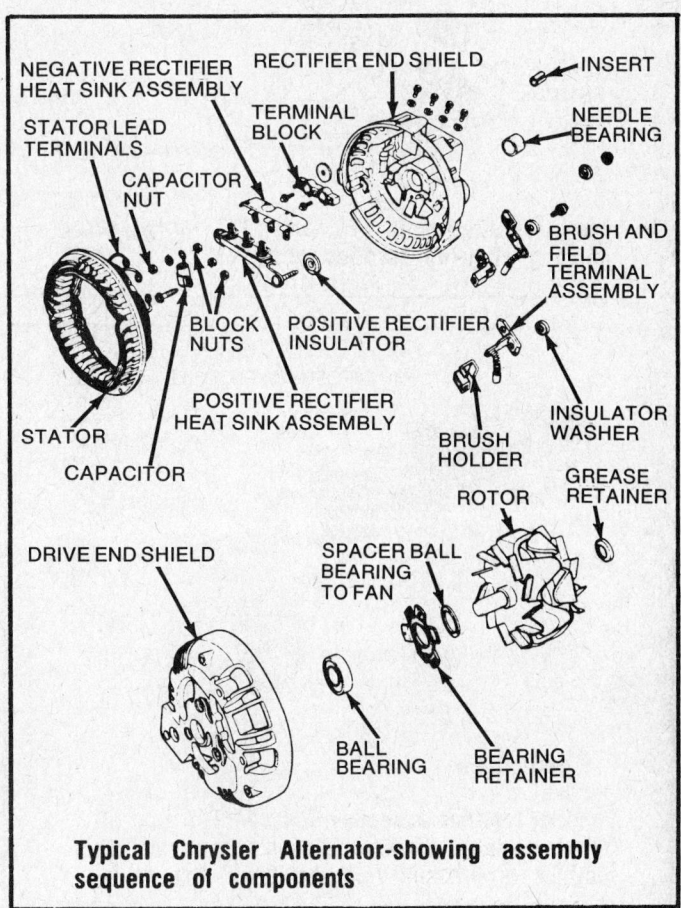

Typical Chrysler Alternator-showing assembly sequence of components

21-7

SECTION 21 ALTERNATORS
CHRYSLER ISOLATED FIELD (W/EXTERNAL ELECTRONIC REGULATOR)

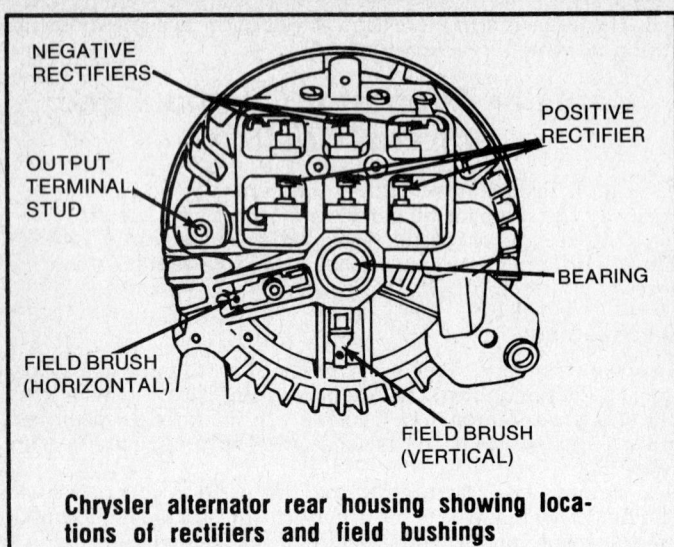

Chrysler alternator rear housing showing locations of rectifiers and field bushings

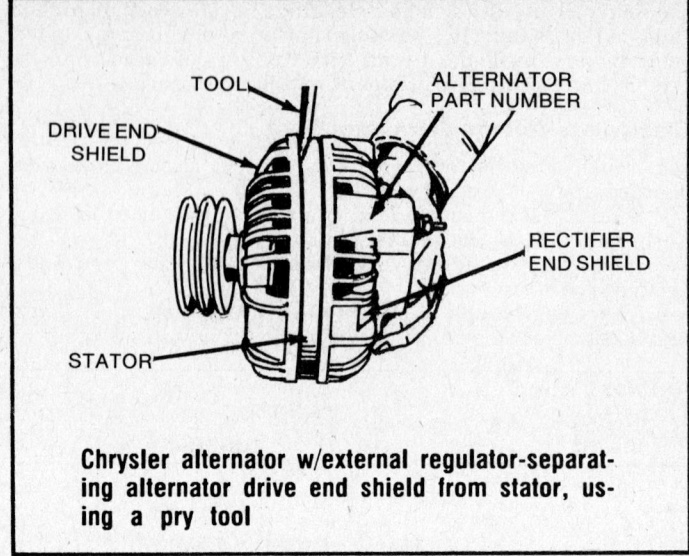

Chrysler alternator w/external regulator-separating alternator drive end shield from stator, using a pry tool

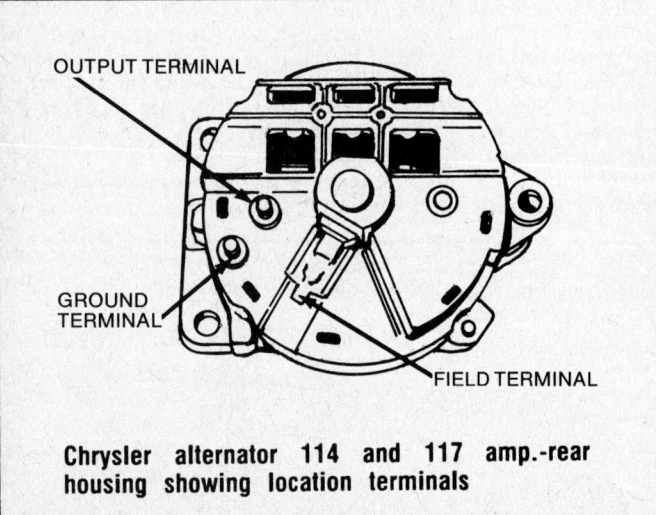

Chrysler alternator 114 and 117 amp.-rear housing showing location terminals

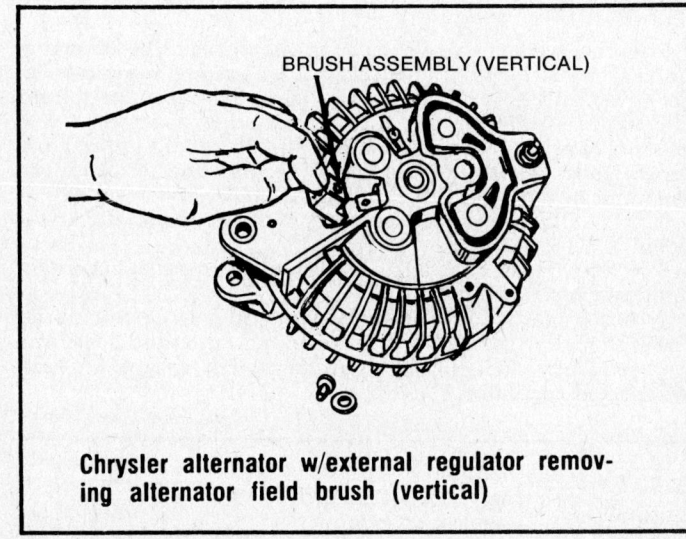

Chrysler alternator w/external regulator removing alternator field brush (vertical)

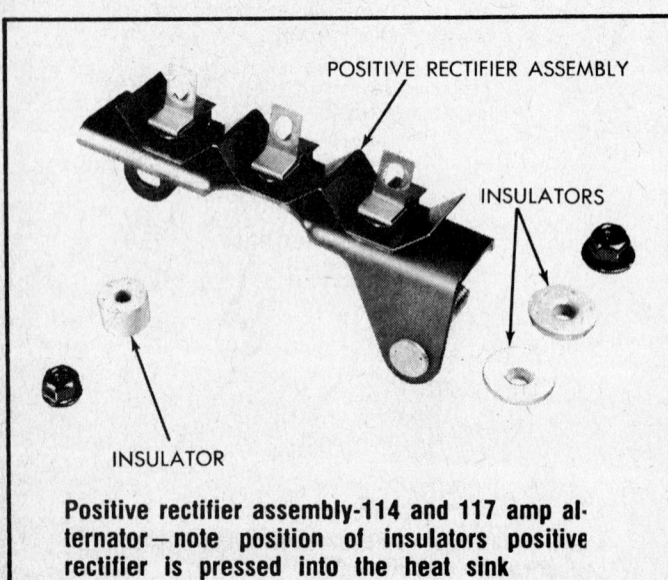

Positive rectifier assembly-114 and 117 amp alternator-note position of insulators positive rectifier is pressed into the heat sink

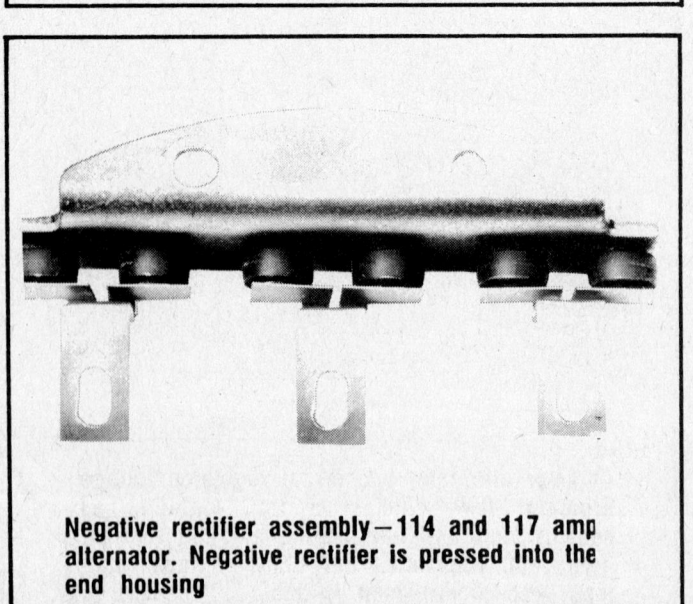

Negative rectifier assembly—114 and 117 amp alternator. Negative rectifier is pressed into the end housing

ALTERNATORS
CHRYSLER ISOLATED FIELD (W/EXTERNAL ELECTRONIC REGULATOR)

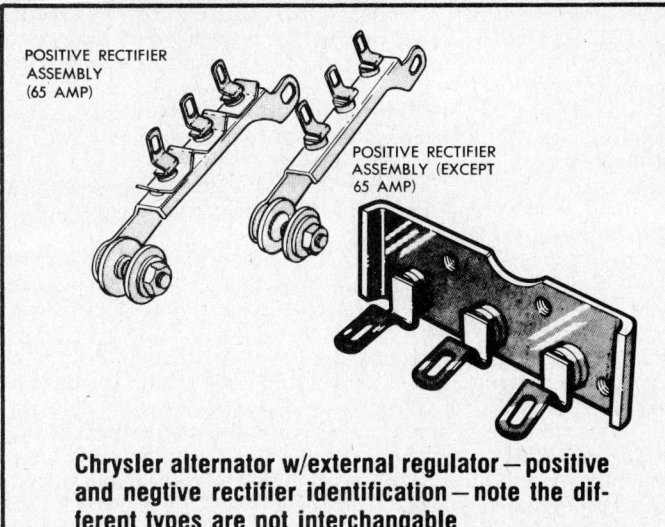

Chrysler alternator w/external regulator – positive and negtive rectifier identification – note the different types are not interchangable

5. Remove the three nuts and washers and, while supporting the end frame, tap the rotor shaft with a plastic hammer and separate the rotor and end housing.

6. The drive end ball bearing is an interference fit with the rotor shaft. Remove the bearing with puller and adapters.

NOTE: Further dismantling of the rotor is not advisable, as the remainder of the rotor assembly is not serviced separately.

7. Remove the DC output terminal nuts and washers and remove terminal screw and inside capacitor (on units so equipped).

8. Remove the insulator.

NOTE: Positive rectifiers are pressed into the heat sink and negative rectifiers in the end housing. When removing the rectifiers it is necessary to support the end housing and/or heat sink to prevent damage to these castings. Another caution is in order relative to the diode rectifiers. Don't subject them to unnecessary jolting. Heavy vibration or shock may ruin them. Cut rectifier wire at point of crimp. Support rectifier housing. The factory tool is cut away and slotted to fit over the wires and around the bosses in the housing. Be sue that the bore of the tool completely surrounds the rectifier, then press the rectifier out of the housing. The roller bearing in the rectifier end frame is a press fit. To protect the end housing it is necessary to support the housing with a tool when pressing out the bearing.

BENCH TESTS

Testing Silicon Diode Rectifiers With Ohmmeter

PREFERED METHOD RECTIFIERS OPEN IN ALL THREE PHASES

Disassemble the alternator and separate the wires at the Y-connection of the stator.

There are six diode rectifiers mounted in the back of the alternator (60 amp). Three of them are marked with a plus (+) and three are marked with a minus (-). These marks indicate diode case polarity. The 114 and 117 amp alternator has twelve silicone diodes. Six positive and six negative.

To test, set ohmmeter to its lowest range. If case is marked positive (+), place positive meter probe to case and negative probe to the diode lead. Meter should read between 4 and 10 ohms. Now, reverse leads of ohmmeter, connecting negative meter probe to positive case and positive meter probe to wire of rectifier. Set meter on a high range. Meter needle should move very little, if any (infinite reading). Do this to all positive diode rectifiers.

The diode rectifiers with minus (-) marks on their cases are checked the same way as above. Only now the negative ohmmeter probe is connected to the case for a reading of 4 to 10 ohms. Reverse leads as above for the other part to test. If a reading of 4 to 10 ohms is obtained in one direction and no reading (infinity) is read on the ohmmeter in the other direction, diode rectifiers are good. If either infinity or a low resistance is obtained in both directions on a rectifier it must be replaced. If meter reads more than 10 ohms when ohmmeter positive probe is connected to positive on diode and negative probe to negative diode, replace diode rectifier.

NOTE: With this test it is necessary to determine the polarity of the ohmmeter probes. This can be done by connecting the ohmmeter to a DC voltmeter. The voltmeter will read up scale when the positive probe of the ohmmeter is connected to the positive side of the voltmeter and the negative probe of the ohmmeter is connected to the negative side of the voltmeter.

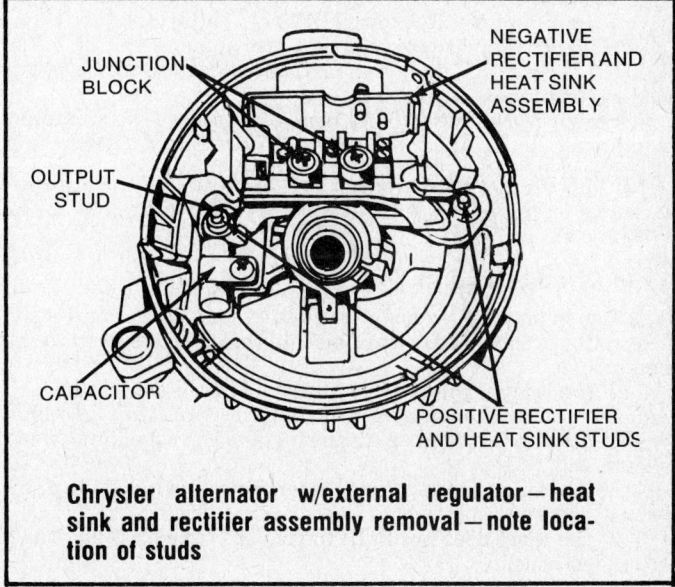

Chrysler alternator w/external regulator – heat sink and rectifier assembly removal – note location of studs

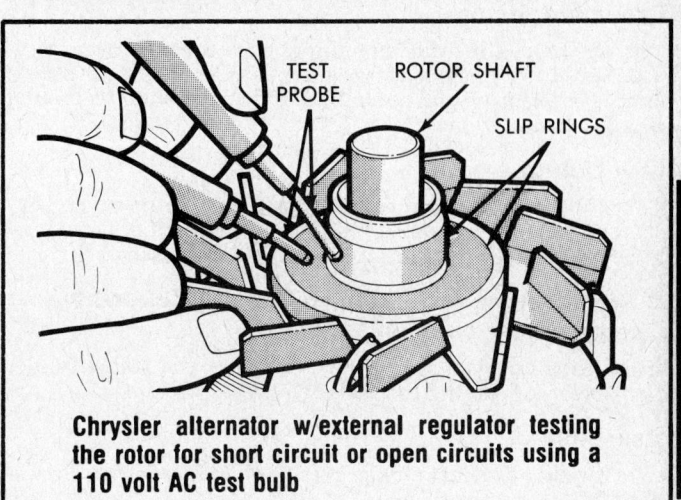

Chrysler alternator w/external regulator testing the rotor for short circuit or open circuits using a 110 volt AC test bulb

SECTION 21: ALTERNATORS
CHRYSLER ISOLATED FIELD (W/EXTERNAL ELECTRONIC REGULATOR)

ALTERNATE METHOD TEST LIGHT

Be sure that the lead from the center of the diode rectifiers is disconnected. To test rectifiers with plus (+) case, touch positive probe of tester to case and minus (-) probe to lead wire of rectifier. Bulb should light if rectifier is good. If bulb does not light, replace rectifier. Now reverse tester probe connections to rectifier. Bulb should not light. If bulb does light, replace rectifier. For testing minus (-) marked cases follow the above procedure except that now bulb should light with negative probe of tester touching rectifier case and positive probe touching lead wire. Rectifier is good if the bulb lights when tester probes are connected one way, and does not light when tester connections are reversed. Rectifier must be replaced if the bulb does not light either way. Also, replace rectifier if bulb lights both ways.

NOTE: The usual cause of an open or blown diode or rectifier is a defective capacitor or a battery that has been installed in reverse polarity. If the battery is installed properly and the diodes are open test the capacitor.

ALTERNATOR BENCH TESTS

Field Coil Draw

1. Connect a jumper between one FLD terminal and the positive terminal of a fully charged 12 volt battery.
2. Connect the positive lead of a test ammeter to the other field (FLD) terminal and the negative test lead to the negative battery terminal.
3. Slowly rotate the rotor by hand and observe the ammeter. The proper field coil draw is 2.3 to 2.7 amps at 12 volts.

NOTE: Field coil draw for the 114 and 117 ampere alternators should be 4.75 amperes to 6.0 amperes at 12 volts.

Field Circuit Ground Test

1. Touch one test lead of a 110 volt AC test bulb to one of the alternator brush (field) terminals and the other test lead to the end shield.
2. If the lamp lights, remove the field brush assemblies and separate the end housing by removing the three through bolts.
3. Place one test lead on a slip ring and the other on the end shield.
4. If the lamp lights the rotor assembly is grounded internally and must be replaced.
5. If the lamp does not light the cause of the problem was a grounded brush.

Grounded Stator

1. Disconnect the diode rectifiers from the stator leads.
2. Test from stator leads to stator core, using a 110 volt test lamp. Test lamp should not light. If it does the stator is grounded and must be replaced.

Low Output

About 50% output accompanied with a growl-hum caused by a shorted phase or a shorted rectifier. If the rectifiers are found to be within specifications replace the stator assembly.

Current Output Too High (No Control) Caused by Open Rectifier or Open Phase

If the rectifier tests satisfactorily, inspect the stator connections before replacing the stator.

Assembly

1. Support the heat sink or rectifier end housing on circular plate.
2. Check rectifier identification to be sure the correct rectifier is being used. The part numbers are stamped on the case of the rectifier. They are also marked red for positive and black for negative.
3. Start the new rectifier into the casting and press it in squarely. Do not start rectifier with a hammer or it will be ruined.
4. Crimp the new rectifier wire to the wires disconnected at removal or solder using a heat sink with rosin core solder.
5. Support the end housing on tool so that the notch in the support tool will clear the raised section of the heat sink, then press the bearing into position with tool SP-3381, or equivalent. New bearings are pre-lubricated, additional lubrication is not required.
6. Insert the drive end bearing in the drive end housing and install the bearing plate, washers and nuts to hold the bearing in place.
7. Position the bearing and drive end housing on the rotor shaft and, while supporting the base of the rotor shaft, press the bearing and housing in position on the rotor shaft with an arbor press and arbor tool. Be careful that there is no cocking of the bearing at installation; or damage will result. Press the bearing on the rotor shaft until the bearing contacts the shoulder on the rotor shaft.
8. Install pulley on rotor shaft. Shaft of rotor must be supported so that all pressing force is on the pulley hub and rotor shaft. Do not exceed 6800 lbs. pressure. Pulley hub should just contact bearing inner race.
9. Some alternators will be found to have the capacitor mounted internally. Be sure the heat sink insulator is in place.
10. Install the output terminal screw with the capacitor attached through the heat sink and end housing.
11. Install insulating washers, lockwashers and locknuts.
12. Make sure the heat sink and insulator are in place and tighten the locknut.
13. Position the stator on the rectifier end housing. Be sure that all of the rectifier connectors and phase leads are free of interference with the rotor fan blades and that the capacitor (internally mounted) lead has clearance.
14. Position the rotor assembly in the rectifier end housing. Align the through bolt holes in the stator with both end housings.
15. Enter stator shaft in the rectifier end housing baring, compress stator and both end housings manually and install through bolts, washers and nuts.
16. Install the insulated brush and terminal attaching screw.
17. Install the ground screw and attaching screw.
18. Rotate pulley slowly to be sure the rotor fan blades do not hit the rectifier and stator connectors.

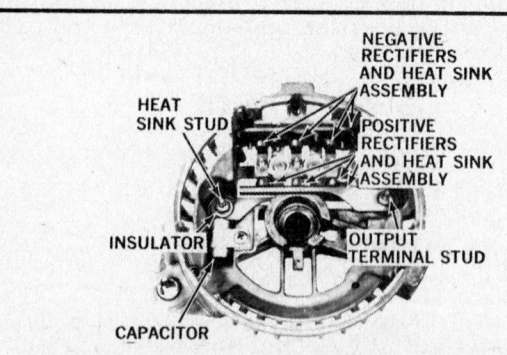

Chrysler alternator w/external regulator — location of negative and positive rectifiers check part number of rectifier to be sure correct rectifier is being used.

ALTERNATORS 21
CHRYSLER ISOLATED FIELD (W/EXTERNAL ELECTRONIC REGULATOR)

TROUBLESHOOTING
CHRYSLER ISOLATED FIELD ALTERNATOR
(WITH EXTERNAL ELECTRONIC REGULATOR)

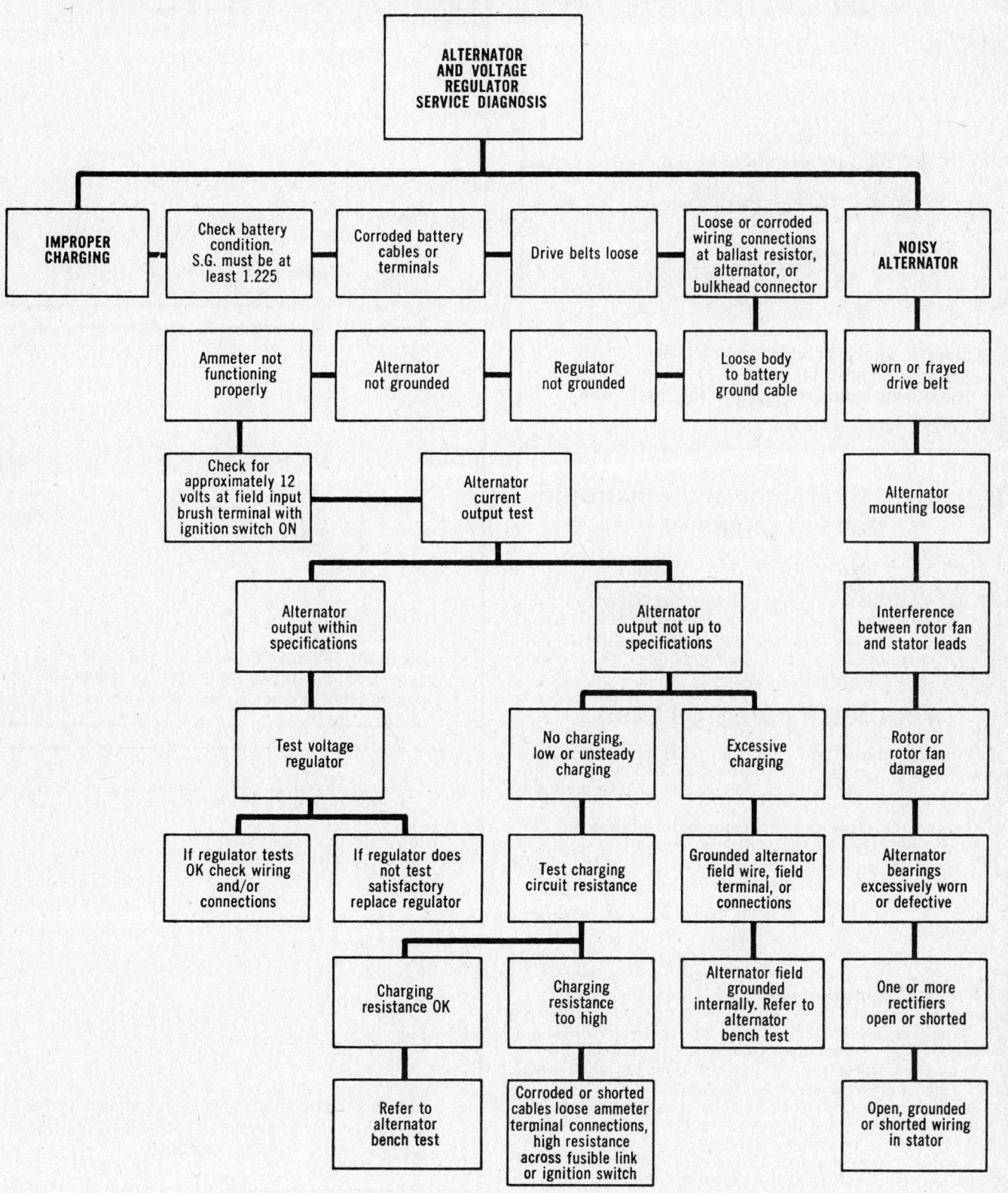

21-11

Section 21: ALTERNATORS
MITSUBISHI (W/INTERNAL REGULATOR)

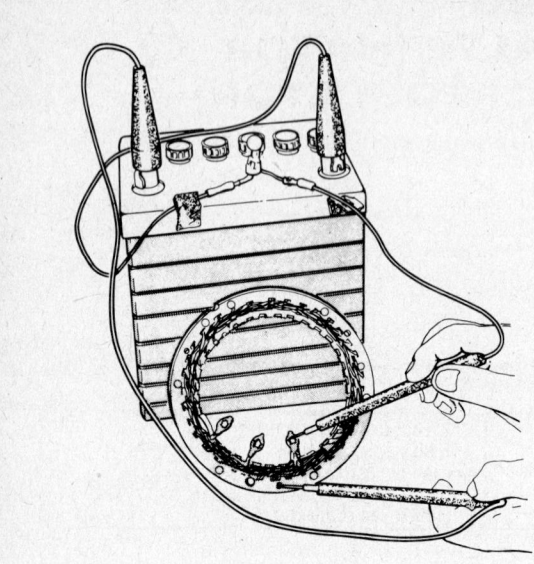

Chrysler Alternator w/external regulator — testing the stator for gounding using a 110 volt test lamp if lamp lights stator is grounded and must be replaced

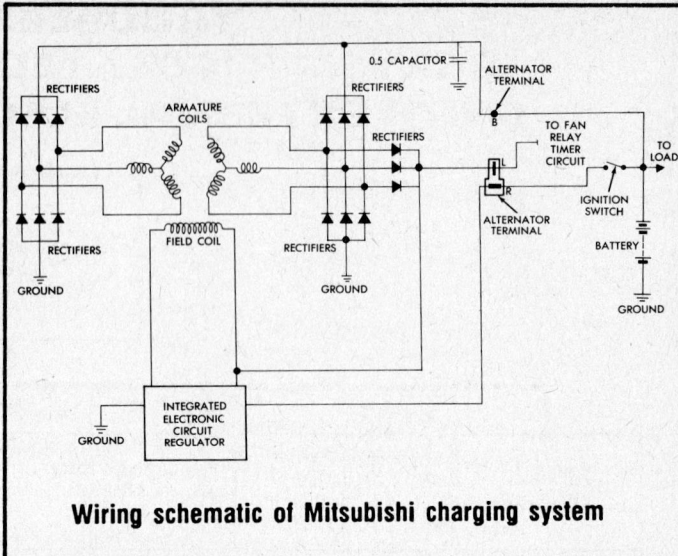

Wiring schematic of Mitsubishi charging system

Mitsubshi Alternator and Electronic voltage regulator

The alternator is the conventional type having a Wye wound stator, positive and negative rectifiers, along with an electronic voltage regulator with integrated circuits, mounted in the rear of the alternator housing. No adjustments are possible or required to the voltage regulator which has the capability of varying the regulated system voltage up or down as the ambient temperature changes.

VOLTAGE REGULATOR TEST

1. With the ignition switch in the "OFF" position, disconnect the positive cable from the battery and place a knife switch on the battery post and connect the cable to the knife switch.
2. Install the leads from an ammeter to the knife switch connectors and open the switch to battery current.
3. Connect the leads of a voltmeter between the "L" terminal of the alternator and a good ground.
4. The voltage reading should be "0" (zero) volts. Should voltage be present, a defective alternator or wiring is indicated.
5. If no voltage is present, turn the ignition switch to the "ON" position. The voltage present should be lower than battery voltage, by about one volt or less. If the voltage reading is higher or at battery voltage, a defective alternator is indicated.
6. Connect a tachometer to the engine and close the knife switch, mounted on the battery post. Start the engine. Do not apply any starting current through the ammeter when starting the engine. The ammeter can be ruined.
7. After the engine is operating, open the knife switch and increase the engine speed to approximately 2500 rpm and observe the ammeter reading.
8. If the ammeter reading is 5 amps or less, observe the voltage reading. This reading is the charging voltage.

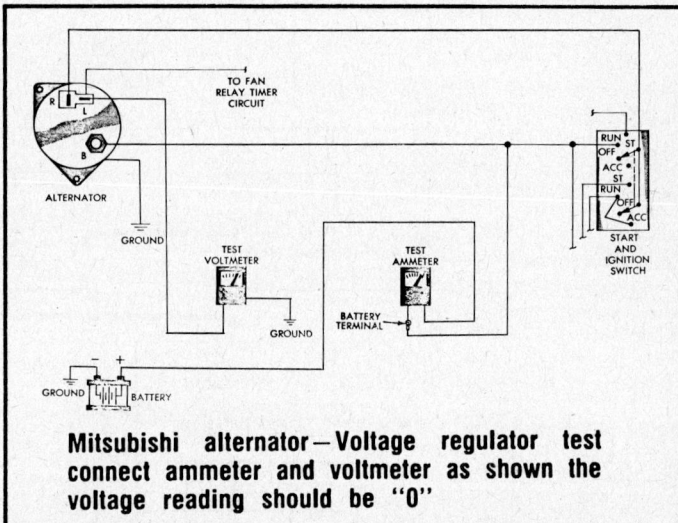

Mitsubishi alternator — Voltage regulator test connect ammeter and voltmeter as shown the voltage reading should be "0"

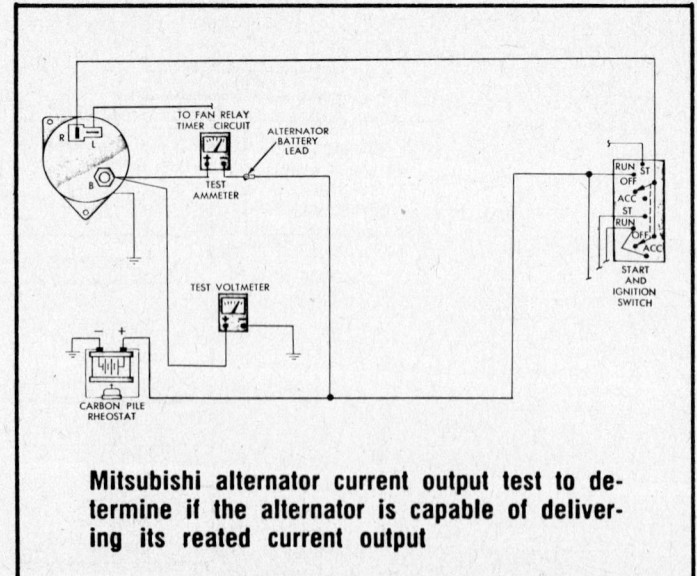

Mitsubishi alternator current output test to determine if the alternator is capable of delivering its reated current output

21-12

ALTERNATORS
MITSUBISHI (W/INTERNAL REGULATOR)

NOTE: The charging voltage varies with the ambient temperature. It is necessary to measure the temperature of the air around the rear of the alternator and correct the charging voltage reading as required.

9. If the ammeter reading is more than 5 amps, continue to charge the battery until the reading falls under 5 amps, or replace the battery with a fully charged one. An alternate method is to limit the charging circuit by connecting a ¼ ohm (25 watt) resistor in series with the battery.

10. Disconnect all test equipment, remove knife switch and re-install the battery positive cable.

CURRENT OUTPUT TEST

The purpose of this test is to determine the capability of the alternator to deliver its rated current output.

1. With the ignition switch in the "OFF" position, disconnect the battery ground cable.
2. Disconnect the "BAT" lead wire from the terminal of the alternator.
3. Connect a 0–100 scaled ammeter in series, between the "BAT" terminal and the "BAT" lead wire.
4. Connect the positive lead of a voltmeter to the "BAT" terminal of the alternator and ground the negative lead.
5. Disconnect the green field wire (to voltage regulator) at the alternator.
6. Connect a tachometer to the engine and reconnect the negative battery cable.
7. Connect a carbon pile rheostat between the battery terminals. Be sure the carbon pile is in the "OPEN" or "OFF" position before connecting the leads.
8. Start the engine and operate at idle.
9. Adjust the carbon pile and accelerate the engine to the specified speed and measure the output current. The current should be within specifications. Do not allow the voltage to increase over 16 volts.
10. The ammeter reading must be within the specified limits. If not the alternator should be removed and bench tested.
11. After the tests disconnect the test equipment from the components.

Output	12 Volts–75 Amps
Rotation	Clockwise As Viewed From Pulley End
Output Current	17-25 Amps at 13.5 Volts and 500 rpm
(Hot or Cold at Engine rpm)	63-70 Amps at 13.5 Volts and 1000 rpm
	74 Amps at 13.5 Volts and 2000 rpm
Regulated Voltage	14.1-14.7 Volts at 20°C (68°F)
Temperature Compensation Gradiant	−0.1 Volts at 10°C (50°F)

DISASSEMBLED ALTERNATOR TESTS

Rotor Assembly

1. Check the outside circumference of the slip ring for dirtiness and roughness. Clean or polish with fine sandpaper, if required. A badly roughened slip ring or a slip ring worn down beyond the service limit should be replaced.
2. Check for continuity between the field coil and slip ring. If there is no continuity, the field coil is defective. Replace the rotor assembly.
3. Check for continuity between the slip ring and shaft (or core). If there is continuity, it means that the coil or slip ring is grounded. Replace the rotor assembly.

Stator Assembly

Check for continuity between the leads of the stator coil. If there is no continuity the stator coil is defective. Replace the starter assembly.

Rectifier Assembly

POSITIVE (+) HEAT SINK ASSEMBLY

Check for continuity between the positive (+) heat sink and stator coil lead connection terminal with a continuity tester. If there is continuity in both directions the diode is short circuited. Replace the rectifier assembly.

NEGATIVE (-) HEAT SINK ASSEMBLY

Check for continuity between the negative (-) heat sink and stator coil lead connection terminal. If there is continuity in both directions the diode is short circuited. Replace the rectifier assembly.

Rectifier Trio Test

Using a circuit tester check the three diodes for continuity in both directions. If there is either continuity or an open circuit in both directions the diode is defective. Replace the rectifier assembly.

Disassembly

1. Place the alternator in a vise or similar holding fixture, mark the body components and remove the three through body bolts.
2. Pry between the stator and the drive end shield and carefully separate the drive end plate, the pulley and the rotor assembly from the stator and rectifier end shield assembly.
3. Carefully clamp the rotor and remove the pulley nut from the end of the shaft. Remove the pulley, the pulley fan, the pulley fan spacer and the alternator drive end shield from the rotor shaft.
4. The front bearing can be removed from the front drive housing by the removal of the dust seals, front and rear, the three bearing retainer screws, the retainer, exposing the bearing so that it can be tapped from the drive housing.

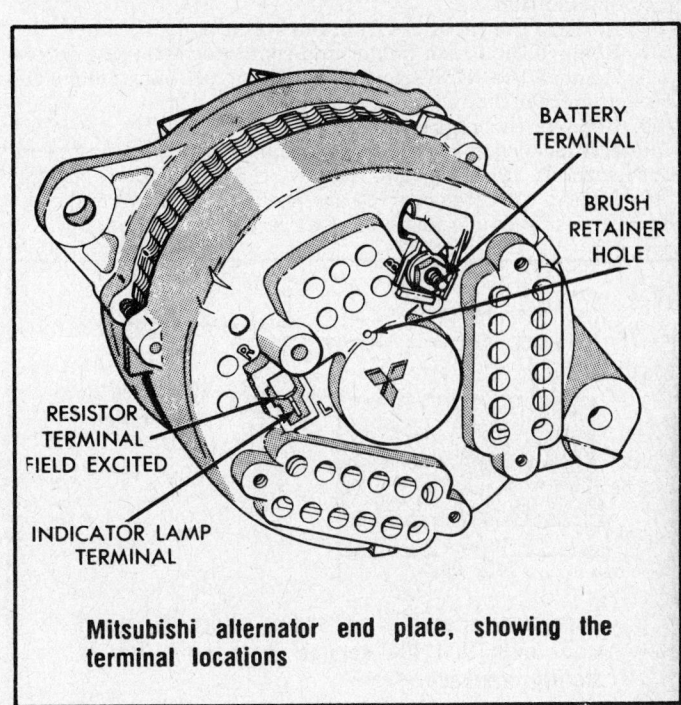

Mitsubishi alternator end plate, showing the terminal locations

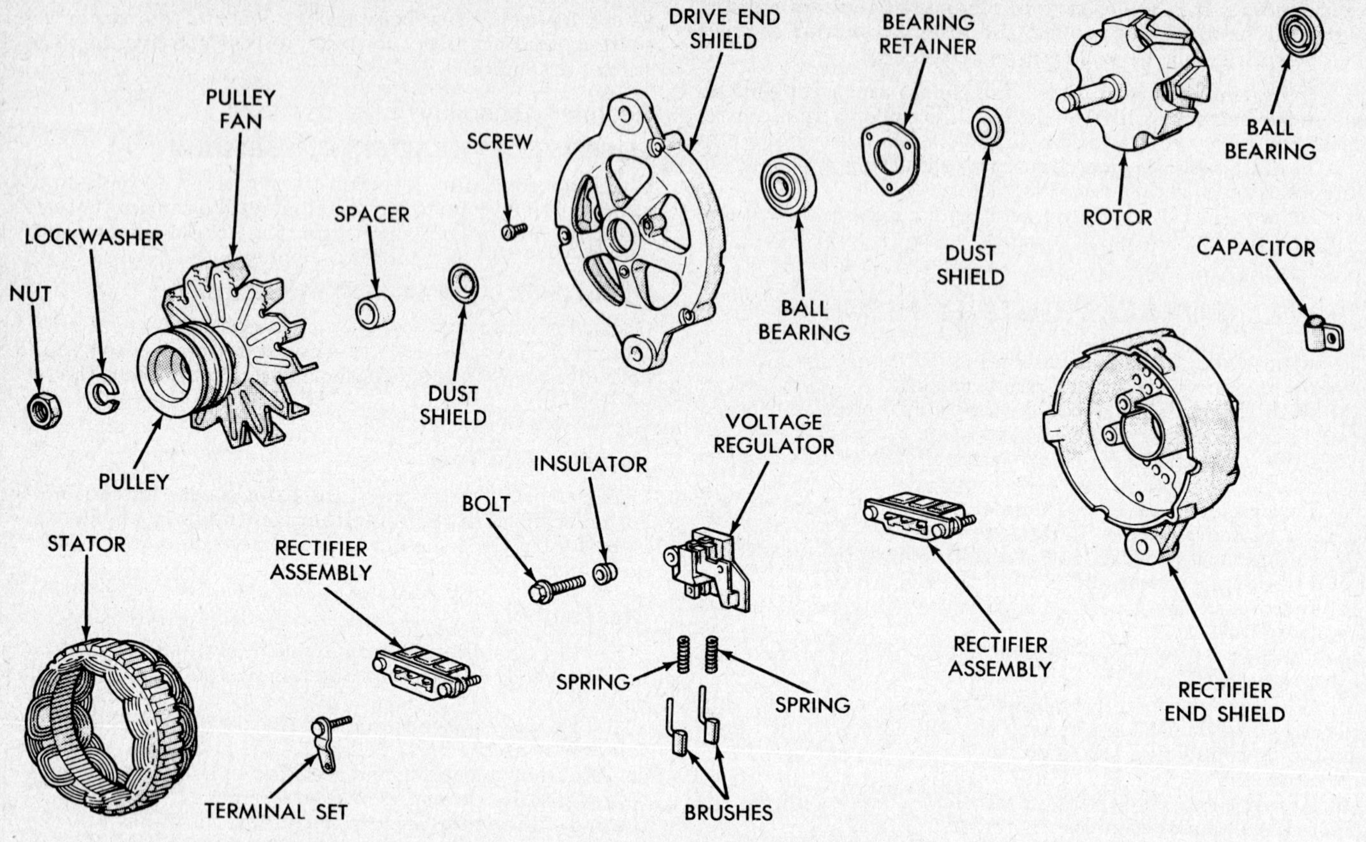

Section 21 ALTERNATORS
MITSUBISHI (W/INTERNAL REGULATOR)

Exploded view of Mitsubishi alternator showing assembly sequence fo components

5. To remove the stator assembly. The six stator leads must be unsoldered from the rectifiers, as per the manufacturer's recommendation.
6. Remove the rectifiers from the stator end shield housing.
7. Remove the brush holder and regulator retaining screw.
8. Remove the "B" Terminal retaining nut and remove the capacitor from the terminal.
9. Remove the regulator and rectifier assembly. Unsolder one rectifier to regulator assembly and remove the other rectifier assembly by sliding the battery stud out of the regulator.
10. Inspect the rotor bearing surface for scores and make the necessary off-vehicle test on the electrical components.

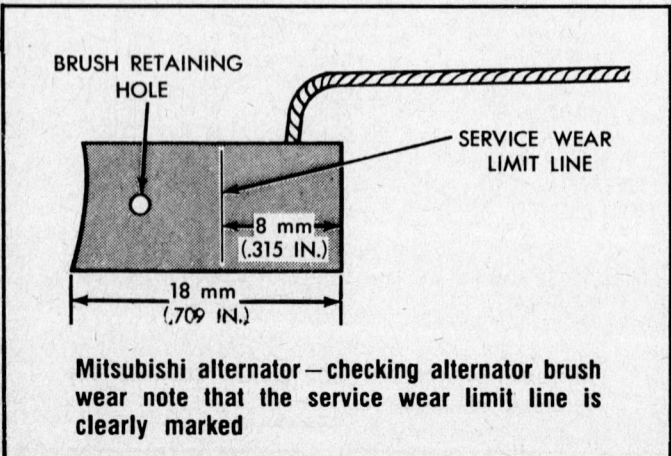

Mitsubishi alternator — checking alternator brush wear note that the service wear limit line is clearly marked

Assembly

1. The assembly of the alternator is the reverse of the removal procedure. Certain steps must be performed as the alternator is assembled.
2. Install the seals in the front and in the rear of the front bearing with the angled lip away from the bearing.
3. Push the brushes into the brush holder and insert a wire to hold them in the raised position. Install the rotor and remove the holding wire.

Bosch Alternator with Internal Regulator

CHARGING CIRCUIT RESISTANCE TEST

1. Make sure that the battery is fully charged.
2. Disconnect negative battery cable.
3. Disconnect "Bat" lead at alternator output terminal.
4. Connect a 0 to 100 ampere scale D.C. ammeter in series between alternator "Bat" terminal and disconnected "Bat" lead wire. Connect ammeter positive lead to "Bat" terminal and negative lead to disconnected "Bat" lead.
5. Connect the positive lead of a test voltmeter to disconnected "Bat" lead wire. Connect negative lead of test voltmeter to battery positive post.
6. Connect an engine tachometer and reconnect the negative battery cable.
7. Connect a variable carbon pile rheostat to battery termi-

ALTERNATORS
BOSCH (W/INTERNAL REGULATOR)

SECTION 21

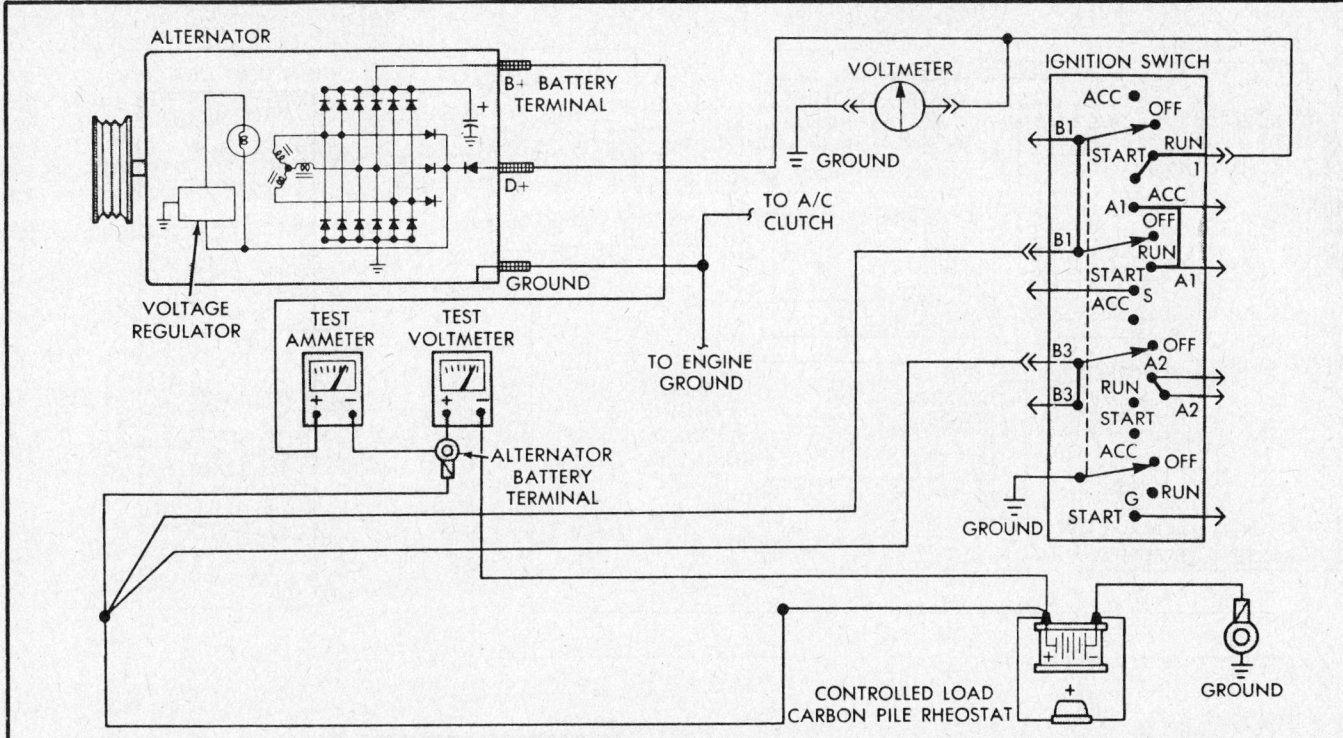

Bosch alternator with internal regulator — charging system resistance test — adjust engine speed and carbon pile to maintanin 20 amps, voltmeter reading should not exceed 0.5 volts

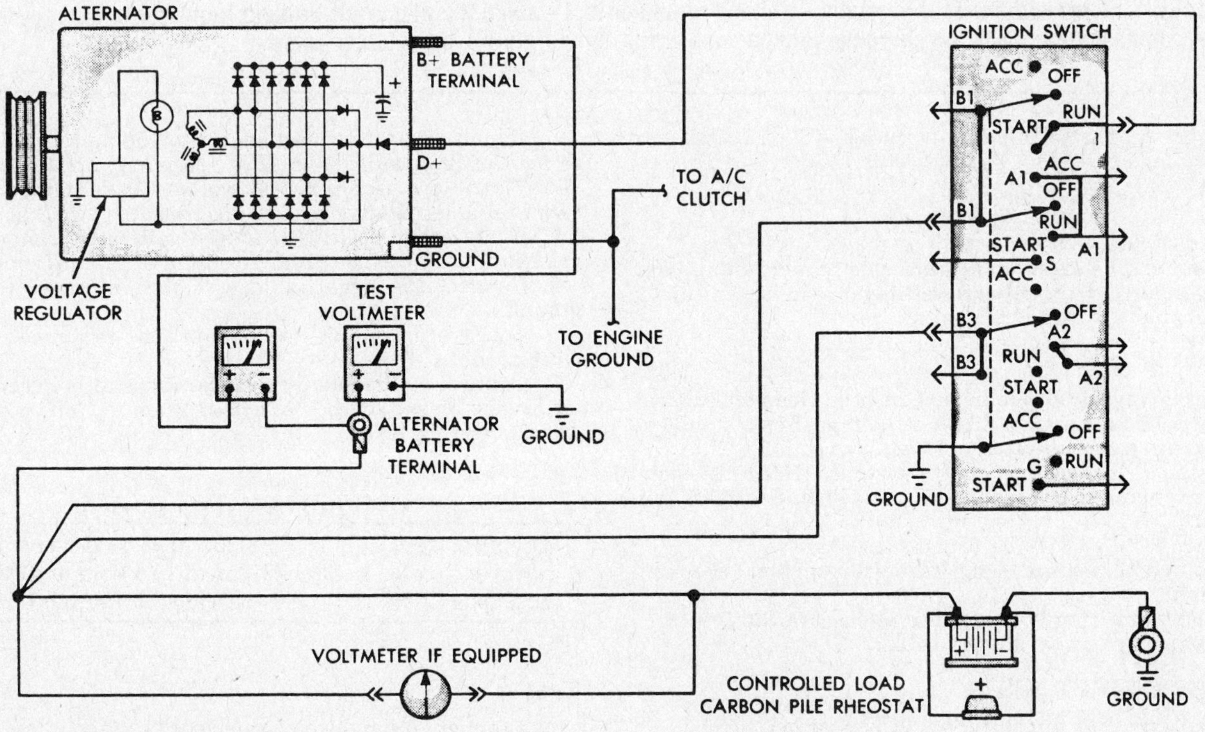

Bosch alternator with internal regulator — current output test — adjust carbon pile and engine speed and check output current, it should read close to specification in chart

21–15

SECTION 21 ALTERNATORS
BOSCH (W/INTERNAL REGULATOR)

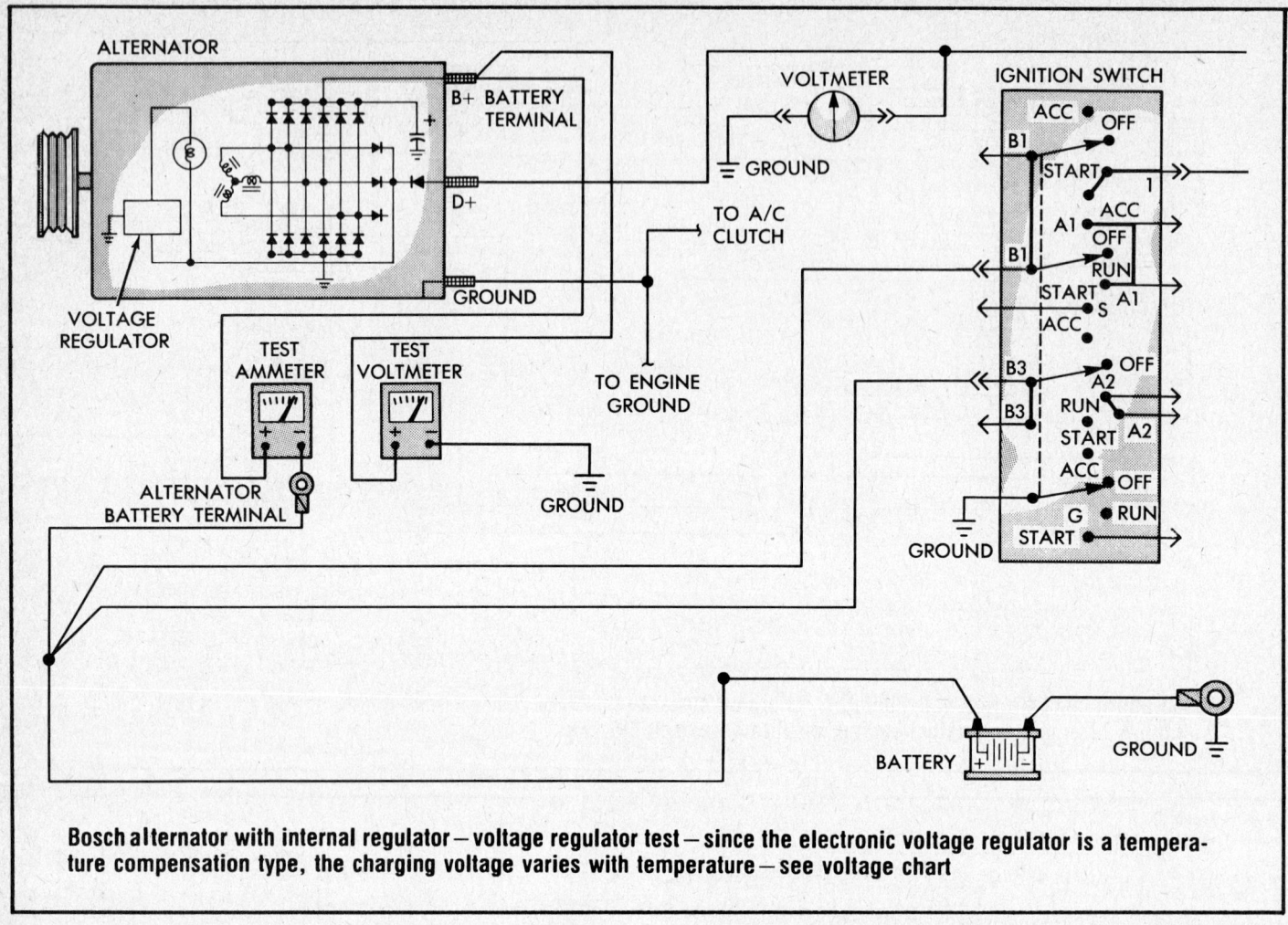

Bosch alternator with internal regulator — voltage regulator test — since the electronic voltage regulator is a temperature compensation type, the charging voltage varies with temperature — see voltage chart

nals. Be sure the carbon pile is in "open" or "off" position before connecting leads.

Test
1. Start engine.
2. Adjust engine speed and carbon pile to maintain 20 amperes flowing in circuit. Observe voltmeter reading. Voltmeter reading should not exceed 0.5 volts.

Results
If a higher voltage drop is indicated, inspect, clean and tighten all connections in charging circuit. A voltage drop test may be performed at each connection to locate connection with excessive resistance. If charging circuit resistance tested satisfactorily reduce engine speed, turn off carbon pile and turn off ignition switch.
1. Disconnect negative battery cable.
2. Remove test ammeter, voltmeter carbon pile, and tachometer.
3. Reconnect wiring "Bat" lead to alternator "Bat" post.
4. Reconnect negative battery cable.

CURRENT OUTPUT TEST
1. Make sure that the battery is fully charged.
2. Turn off the ignition switch.
3. Disconnect the negative battery cable.
4. Disconnect the battery lead wire at the alternator output terminal.

5. Connect an ammeter (range 0 to 100 amps minimum) in series between alternator "Bat" terminal and disconnected "Bat" lead wire. Connect positive lead to disconnected "Bat" terminal and negative lead to disconnected "Bat" lead.
6. Connect the positive lead of a voltmeter (range 0 to 18 volts minimum) to the "Bat" terminal of the alternator.
7. Connect the negative lead of the voltmeter to a good ground.
8. Connect an engine tachometer and reconnect negative battery cable.
9. Connect a variable carbon pile rheostat between battery terminals. Be sure carbon pile is in "open" or "off" position before connecting leads.

CURRENT OUTPUT CHART

Output current	28-35A at 13.5 Volts and 500 RPM
(Hot or Cold)	75-85A at 13.5 Volts and 1000 RPM
at engine RPM	89A at 13.5 Volts and 2000 RPM

Test
1. Start engine reduce engine speed to idle.
2. Adjust carbon pile and engine speed to specified speed and check output current. Output current should read close to specification. Do not allow voltage meter to read above 16 volts.

ALTERNATORS
BOSCH (W/INTERNAL REGULATOR)
SECTION 21

Results

1. The ammeter reading must be within the required limits.
2. If the reading is less than specified the alternator should be removed from vehicle and bench tested.
3. After current output test is completed reduce engine speed, turn off carbon pile and turn off ignition switch.
4. Disconnect negative battery cable.
5. Remove test ammeter, voltmeter, tachometer and carbon pile.
6. Reconnect "Bat" lead to alternator output terminal.
7. Reconnect negative battery cable.

INTERNAL VOLTAGE REGULATOR TEST

1. Make sure that the battery is fully charged.
2. Clean battery terminals.
3. Turn ignition switch off.
4. Disconnect "Bat" lead wire at alternator output terminal.
5. Connect an ammeter (range 0 to 100 amps minimum) in series between alternator "Bat B+" terminal and disconnected "Bat" lead wire. Connect positive lead to disconnected "Bat" terminal and negative lead to disconnected "Bat" lead.
6. Connect positive lead of a voltmeter (range 0 to 18 volts minimum) to "Bat B=" terminal of alternator. Connect negative lead of voltmeter to a good ground.

Test

1. Check to ensure that voltmeter is "0" (zero). If pointer of voltmeter deflects (a voltage is present), a defective alternator is suspected.
2. Set ignition switch to on but do not start engine. Voltmeter reading should be within one half volt of battery voltage, about 12 volts.
3. Connect a tachometer to engine.
4. With test ammeter terminals short-circuited start the engine. Make sure that when the engine is started, no starting current is applied to the ammeter.
5. Remove the short circuit across the test ammeter terminals and increase the engine speed immediately to about 2000–3000 rpm. Record ammeter reading.

Results

1. If the test ammeter reading is 10 amps or less, take the voltmeter reading without changing the engine speed (2000–3000 rpm). The reading is the charging voltage. Since the electronic voltage regulator is a temperature compensation type, the charging voltage varies with temperature. Therefore, the temperature around the rear bracket of the alternator must be measured and the charging voltage corrected to the temperature.

VOLTAGE CHART

Charging voltage	14.1	+0.1V at 25°C(77°F) −.25V
Temperature compensation gradient		−.055 to .09V For each 10°C or (18°F)

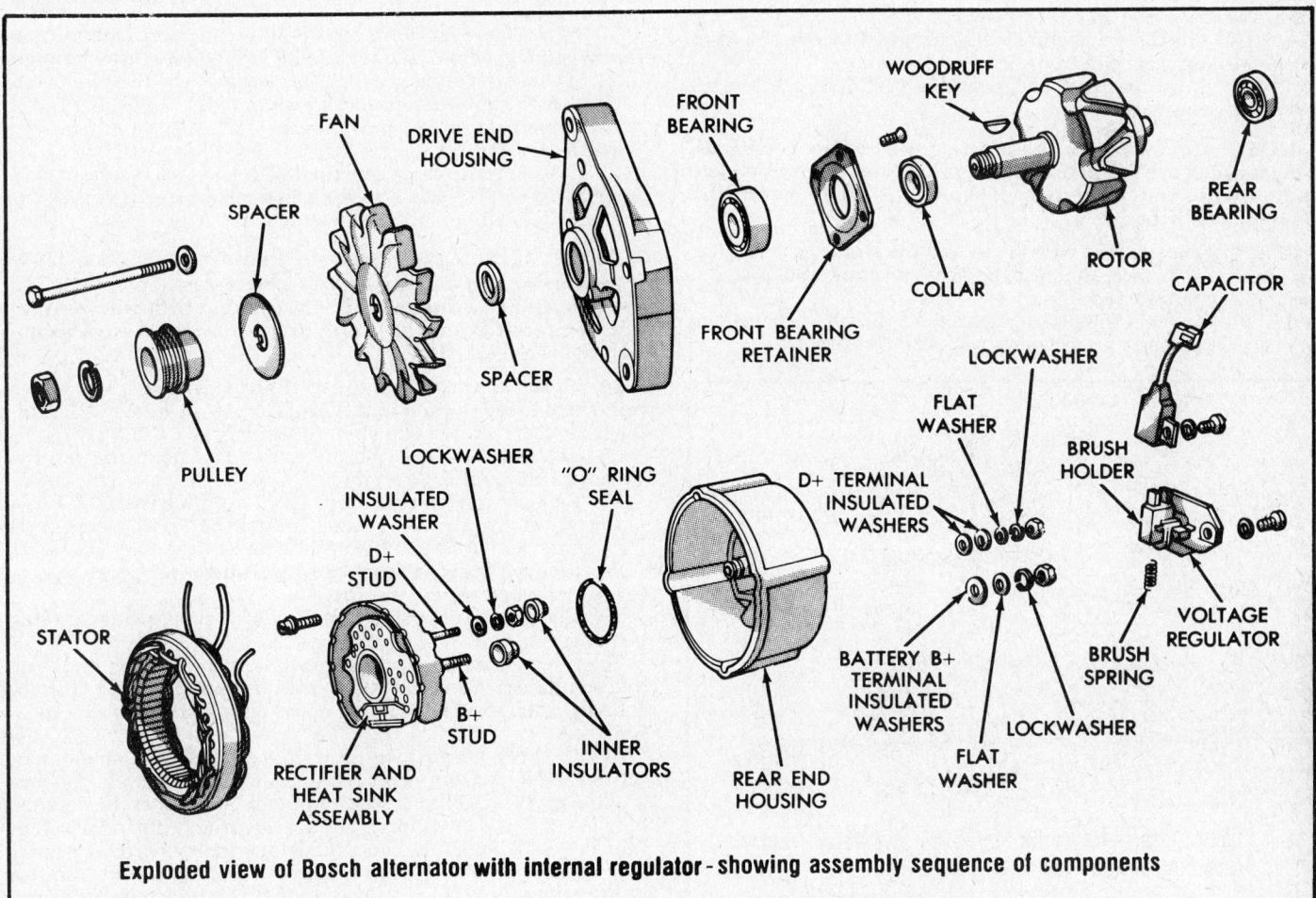

Exploded view of Bosch alternator with internal regulator - showing assembly sequence of components

21–17

SECTION 21 ALTERNATORS
BOSCH (W/INTERNAL REGULATOR)

2. If the ammeter reading is more than 10 Amps, continue to charge the battery until the reading falls to less than 10 Amps or replace the battery with a fully charged one. An alternative method is to limit the charging current by connecting a ¼Ω (25W) resistor in series with the battery. Disconnect all test equipment and connect battery cable.

Disassembly

1. Remove the alternator from the vehicle.
2. Position the unit in a suitable holding fixture.
3. Remove the pulley nut, lock washer and pulley.
4. Remove the fan spacer and the pulley fan from the alternator shaft.
5. Remove the woodruff key from the rotor shaft.
6. From the rear of the alternator disconnect the capacitor terminal and remove the capacitor mounting screw. Remove the capacitor from the alternator.
7. Remove the voltage regulator and brush holder mounting screw. Remove the holder.
8. Remove the D+ stud nut, lock washer, stud washer and stud insulators.
9. Remove the battery (B+) stud nut, lock washer, stud flat washer and the stud insulator.
10. Remove the four alternator through bolts.
11. Pry between the stator and the drive end shield with a suitable tool. Carefully separate the drive end shield, pulley and rotor assembly away from the stator and rectifier end shield assembly.
12. Press the rotor out of the drive end shield and remove the spacer. Remove the alternator pulley fan spacer.
13. Remove the four alternator drive end bearing screws. Remove the drive end shield bearing retainer.
14. Press out the drive end shield bearing. Remove the front drive bearing from the front drive end shield.
15. To test the positive and negative rectifiers use tool C-3929-A or equivalent.

NOTE: Do not break the plastic cases of the rectifiers. These cases are for protection against corrosion. Be sure they always touch the test probe to the metal pin of the nearest rectifier.

16. Position the rear end shield and the stator assembly on an insulated surface. Connect the test lead clip to the alternator battery output terminal.
17. Plug in tool C-3829-A or equivalent. Touch the metal pin of each of the positive rectifiers with the test probe.

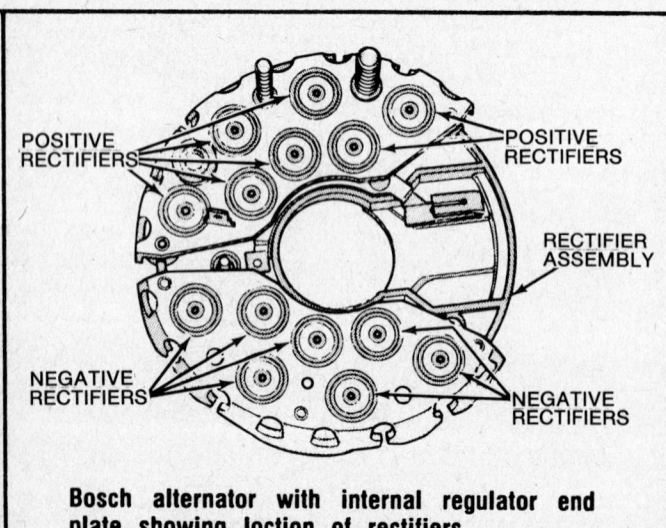

Bosch alternator with internal regulator end plate showing loction of rectifiers

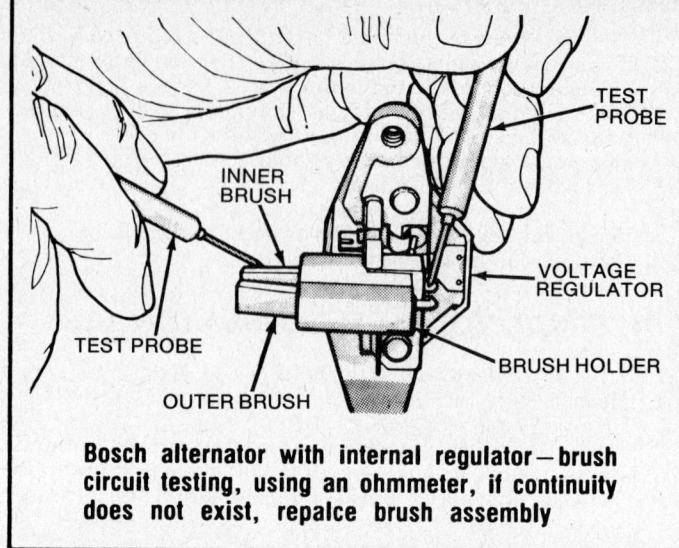

Bosch alternator with internal regulator—brush circuit testing, using an ohmmeter, if continuity does not exist, repalce brush assembly

18. Reading for satisfactory rectifiers will be 1¾ amperes or more. Reading should be approximately the same and meter needle must move in same direction for all three rectifiers.
19. When some rectifiers are good and one is shorted reading taken at good rectifiers will be low and reading taken at shorted rectifiers will be zero. Disconnect stator lead to rectifiers reading zero and retest. Reading of good rectifiers will now be within satisfactory range.
20. When one rectifier is open it will read approximately one ampere and good rectifiers will read within satisfactory range.
21. To test the negative rectifiers connect the test clip of tool C-3829-A to the rectifier end housing.
22. Touch the metal pin of each of the negative rectifiers with the test probe.
23. Test specifications are the same and test results will be approximately the same as for positive case rectifiers, except meter will read on opposite side of scale.

NOTE: If a negative rectifier shows shorted remove stator from rectifier assembly and retest. It is possible that a stator winding could be grounded to stator laminations or rectifier end shield which would indicate a shorted negative rectifier.

24. Unsolder the stator to rectifier leads. Mark the stator coil frame to aid in reinstallation of the stator. Remove the stator from the rectifier end shield assembly.
25. Remove the three rectifier assembly mounting screws. Remove the rectifier assembly.
26. Remove the inner battery (B+) stud insulator.
27. Remove the D+ stud insulator, stud nut, stud flatwasher and stud insulating washer.
28. Remove the rear bearing oil and dust seal. Check the rotor bearing surface for scoring.
29. Using puller C-4068 or equivalent, remove the rear rotor bearing.
30. Check outside circumference of slip ring for dirtiness and roughness. Clean or polish with fine sandpaper, required. A badly roughened slip ring or a worn down slip ring should be replaced.
31. To check for an open rotor field coil, connect an ohmmeter to slip rings. Ohmmeter reading should be between 1.5 and 2 ohms on rotor coils at room ambient conditions. Resistance between 2.5 and 3.0 ohms would result from alternator rotors that have been operated on vehicle at higher engine compartment temperatures. Reading above 3.5 ohms would indicate high resistance rotor coils and further testing or replacement may be required.

ALTERNATORS
BOSCH (W/EXTERNAL REGULATOR)
SECTION 21

32. To check for a shorted field coil, connect an ohmmeter to slip rings. If reading is below 1.5 ohms, field coil is shorted.

33. To check for a grounded rotor field coil; connect an ohmmeter from each slip ring to rotor shaft.

NOTE: Ohmmeter should be set for "infinite" reading when probes are apart and zero when probes are shorted. The ohmmeter should read "infinite". If reading is zero or higher, rotor is grounded.

34. Check for continuity between leads of stator coil. Press test probe firmly to each of three phase (stator) lead terminals one at a time. If there is no continuity stator coil is defective. Replace stator assembly.

35. To test the stator for ground, check for continuity between the stator coil leads and the stator coil frame. If there is no continuity the stator is grounded and must be replaced.

36. To test the inner and outer brush circuit, use an ohmmeter and touch one test probe to the inner brush and the other test probe to the brush terminal. If continuity does not exist replace the brush assembly. Repeat the same procedure for the outer brush.

Assembly

1. To assemble the alternator reverse the disassembly procedure.
2. Be sure to check all parts for wear. Replace defective components as required.
3. Push the brushes into the brush holder and insert a wire to hold them in the raised position. Install the rotor and remove the holding wire.

Bosch Alternator with External Regulator

CHARGING CIRCUIT RESISTANCE TEST

1. Be sure that the battery is fully charged.
2. Turn off ignition switch.
3. Disconnect negative battery cable.
4. Disconnect "Bat" terminal wire from alternator output "Bat" terminal post.
5. Connect a 0 to 100 amps minimum range scale D.C. test ammeter in series between alternator "Bat" terminal and disconnected "Bat" terminal wire. Connect ammeter positive lead wire to alternator "Bat" terminal and negative ammeter lead to disconnected alternator "Bat" terminal wire.
6. Connect a 0 to 18 volt minimum range scale test Voltmeter between disconnected alternator "Bat" terminal wire and positive battery cable. Connect voltmeter positive lead to disconnected alternator "Bat" terminal wire and negative voltmeter lead to battery positive cable.
7. Disconnect wiring harness connector from electronic voltage regulator on vehicle.
8. Connect a jumper wire from wiring harness connector green wire (outside terminal) to ground. Do not connect blue J2 lead of wiring connector to ground.
9. Connect an engine tachometer and reconnect negative battery cable. Connect a variable carbon pile rheostat to battery terminals. Be sure carbon pile is in open or off position be-

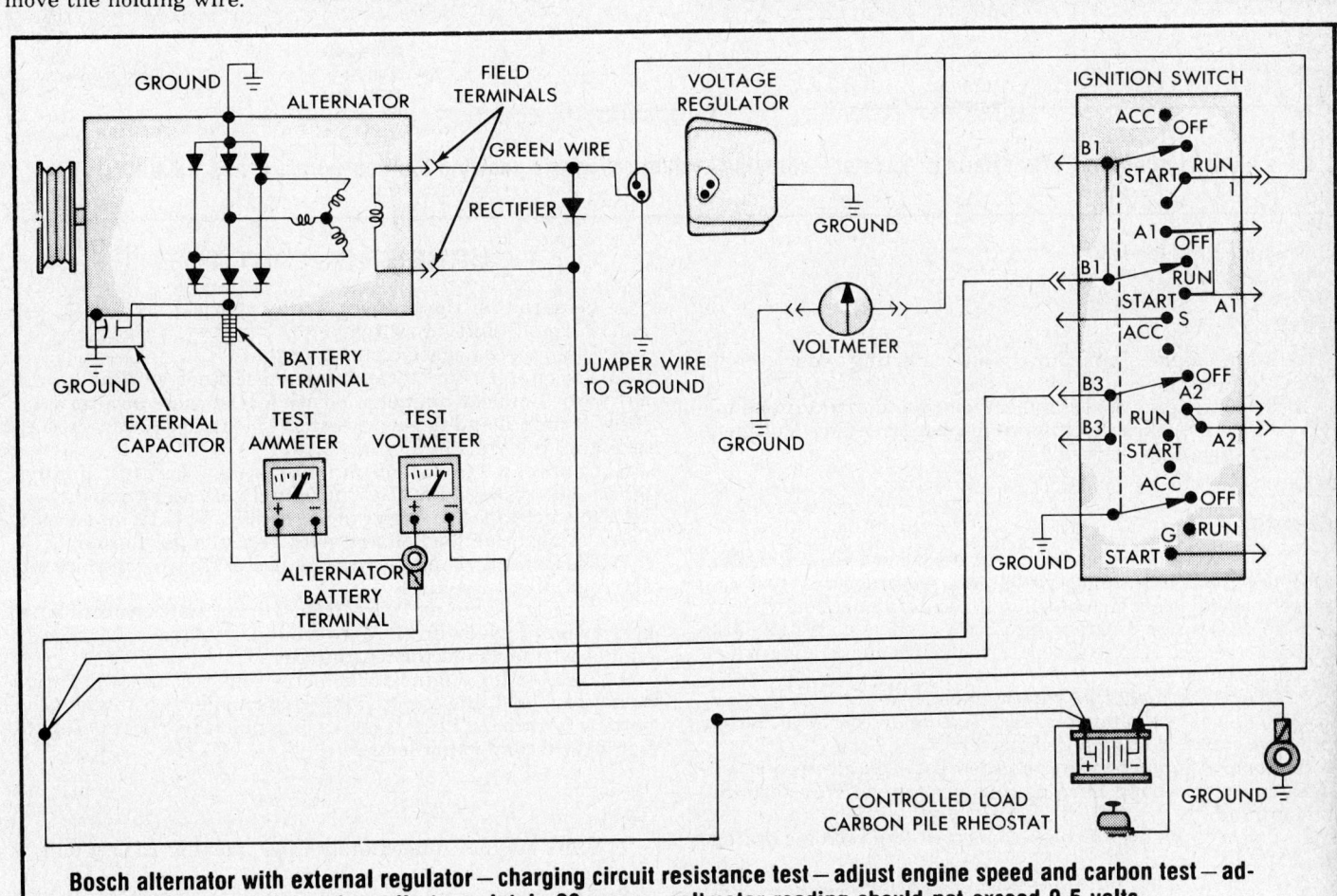

Bosch alternator with external regulator—charging circuit resistance test—adjust engine speed and carbon test—adjust engine speed and carbon pile to maintain 20 amps., voltmeter reading should not exceed 0.5 volts

21-19

SECTION 21 ALTERNATORS
BOSCH (W/EXTERNAL REGULATOR)

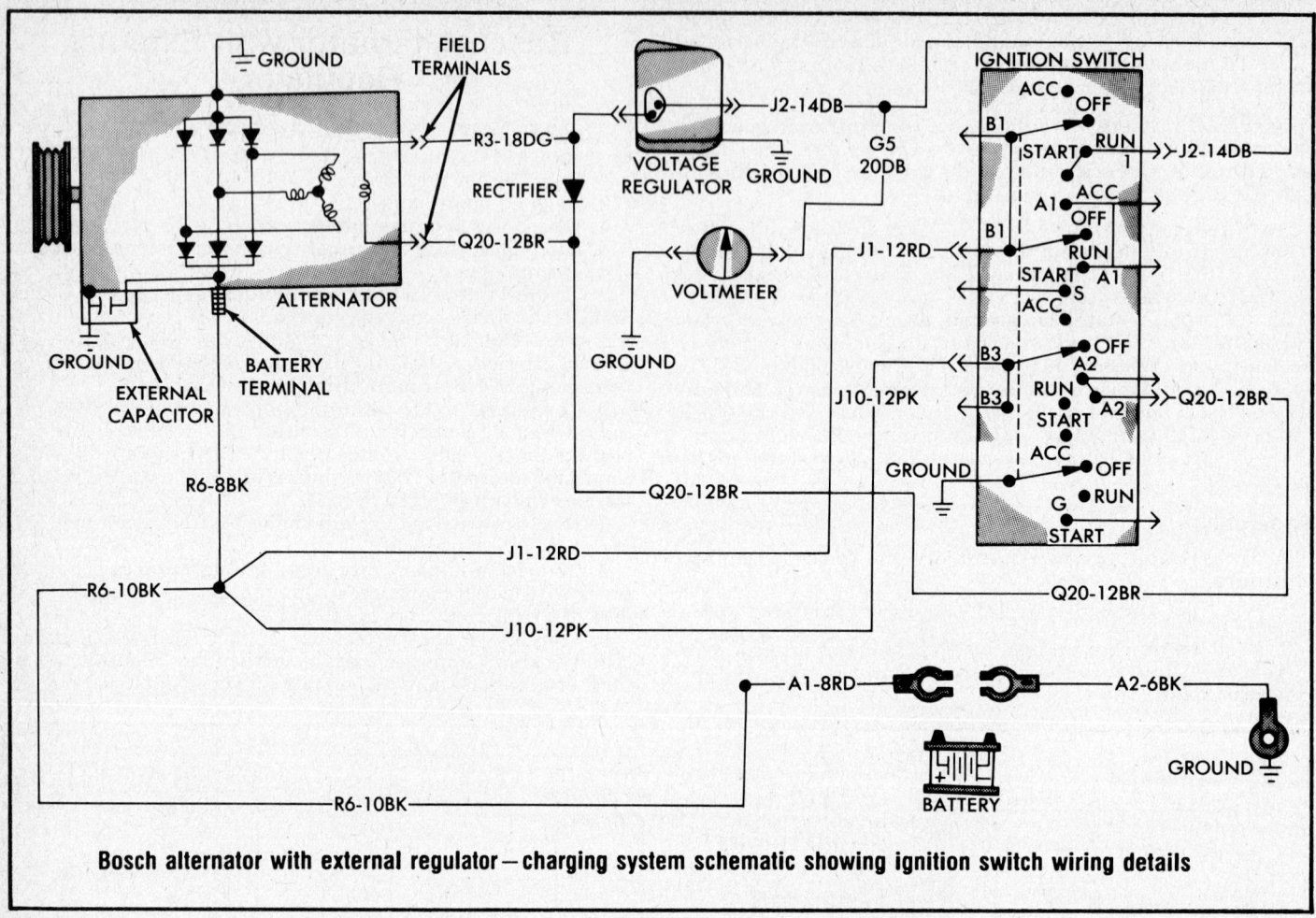

Bosch alternator with external regulator—charging system schematic showing ignition switch wiring details

fore connecting leads.

Test

1. Start engine. Immediately after starting reduce engine speed to idle.
2. Adjust engine speed and carbon pile to maintain 20 amperes flowing in circuit. Observe voltmeter reading. Voltmeter reading should not exceed 0.5 volts.

Results

If a higher voltage drop is indicated, inspect, clean, and tighten all connections in the charging circuit. A voltage drop test may be performed at each connection to locate connection with excessive resistance. If charging circuit resistance tested satisfactorily, reduce engine speed, turn off carbon pile and turn off ignition switch.

1. Disconnect negative battery cable.
2. Remove test ammeter, test voltmeter, variable carbon pile rheostat and engine tachometer.
3. Remove jumper wire connected between electronic voltage regulator wiring harness connector green wire terminal and ground.
4. Connect wiring harness connector to electronic voltage regulator.
5. Connect "Bat" terminal wire to alternator output "Bat" terminal.
6. Connect negative battery cable.

CURRENT OUTPUT TEST

1. Be sure that the battery is fully charged.
2. Turn off ignition switch.
3. Disconnect negative battery cable.
4. Disconnect "Bat" terminal and disconnected "Bat" terminal wire. Connect ammeter positive lead wire to alternator "Bat" terminal and negative ammeter lead to disconnected alternator "Bat" terminal wire.
6. Connect a 0 to 18 volt minimum range scale test Voltmeter between alternator "Bat" terminal post and ground. Connect voltmeter positive lead to alternator "Bat" terminal post. Connect negative lead of test voltmeter to a good ground.
7. Disconnect wiring harness connector from electronic voltage regulator on vehicle.
8. Connect a jumper wire from wiring harness connector green wire (outside terminal) to ground. Do not connect blue J2 lead of wiring connector to ground.
9. Connect an engine tachometer and reconnect negative battery cable. Connect a variable carbon pile rheostat between battery terminals. Be sure the carbon pile is in open or off position before connecting leads.

Test

1. Start engine. Immediately after starting reduce engine sped to idle.
2. Adjust carbon pile and engine speed in increments until a speed of 1250 rpm and voltmeter reading of 15 volts is obtained. Do not allow voltage meter to read above 16 volts.

ALTERNATORS
BOSCH (W/EXTERNAL REGULATOR)

SECTION 21

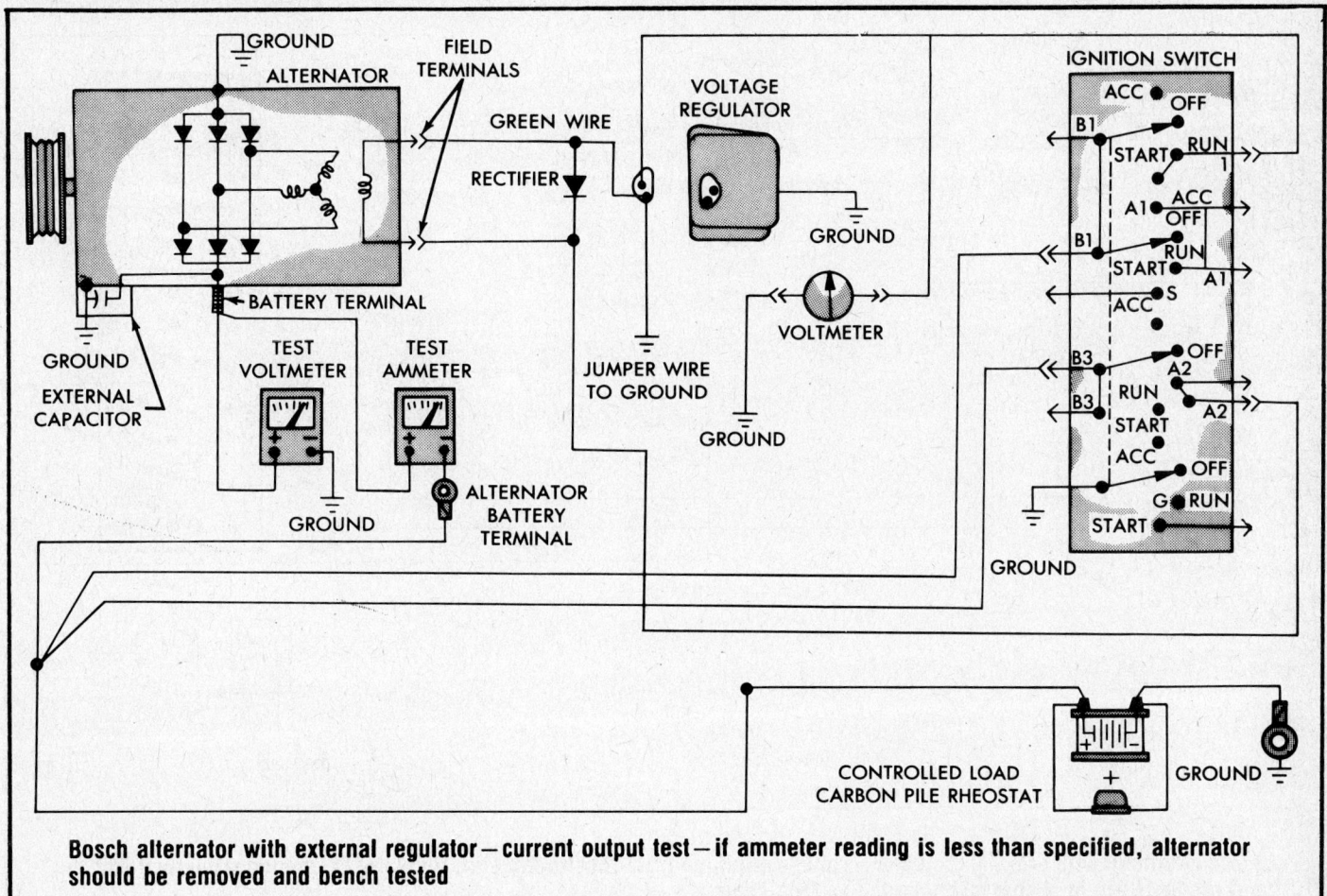

Bosch alternator with external regulator—current output test—if ammeter reading is less than specified, alternator should be removed and bench tested

Results

1. Ammeter reading must be within the proper limits. If reading is less than specified alternator should be removed from vehicle and bench tested.
2. After current output test is completed reduce engine speed, turn off carbon pile and turn off ignition switch.
3. Disconnect negative battery cable.
4. Remove test ammeter, test voltmeter, tachometer and variable carbon pile rheostat.
5. Remove jumper wire connected between electronic voltage regulator wiring harness connector green wire terminal and ground.
6. Connect wiring harness connector to electronic voltage regulator.
7. Connect "Bat" terminal wire to alternator output "Bat" terminal.
8. Connect negative battery cable.

VOLTAGE REGULATOR TEST

1. Be sure that the battery is fully charged.
2. Turn off ignition switch.
3. Connect a 0 to 18 volts minimum range scale test voltmeter between vehicle battery and ground. Connect positive lead of voltmeter to positive battery cable terminal. Connect negative lead of voltmeter to a good vehicle body ground.
4. Connect a tachometer to engine.

Test

1. Start engine and adjust engine speed to 1250 with all lights and accessories turned off.

Results

1. Check voltmeter, regulator is working properly if voltage readings are in accordance with the voltage chart.
2. If voltage is below limits or is fluctuating, proceed as follows. Check for a good voltage regulator ground. Voltage regulator ground is obtained through regulator case to mounting screws and to sheet metal of vehicle. This is ground circuit that is to be checked for opens.
3. Turn off ignition switch and disconnect voltage regulator wiring harness connector. Be sure terminals of connector have not spread open to cause an open or intermittant connection.
4. Do not start engine or distort terminals with voltmeter probe: turn on ignition switch and check for battery voltage at

VOLTAGE CHART

AMBIENT TEMPERATURE NEAR VOLTAGE REGULATOR	VOLTAGE RANGE
−30°C −20°F	14.9 to 15.8
27°C 80°F	13.9 to 14.4
60°C 140°F	13.0 to 13.7
Above 60°C Above 140°F	Less than 13.60

21-21

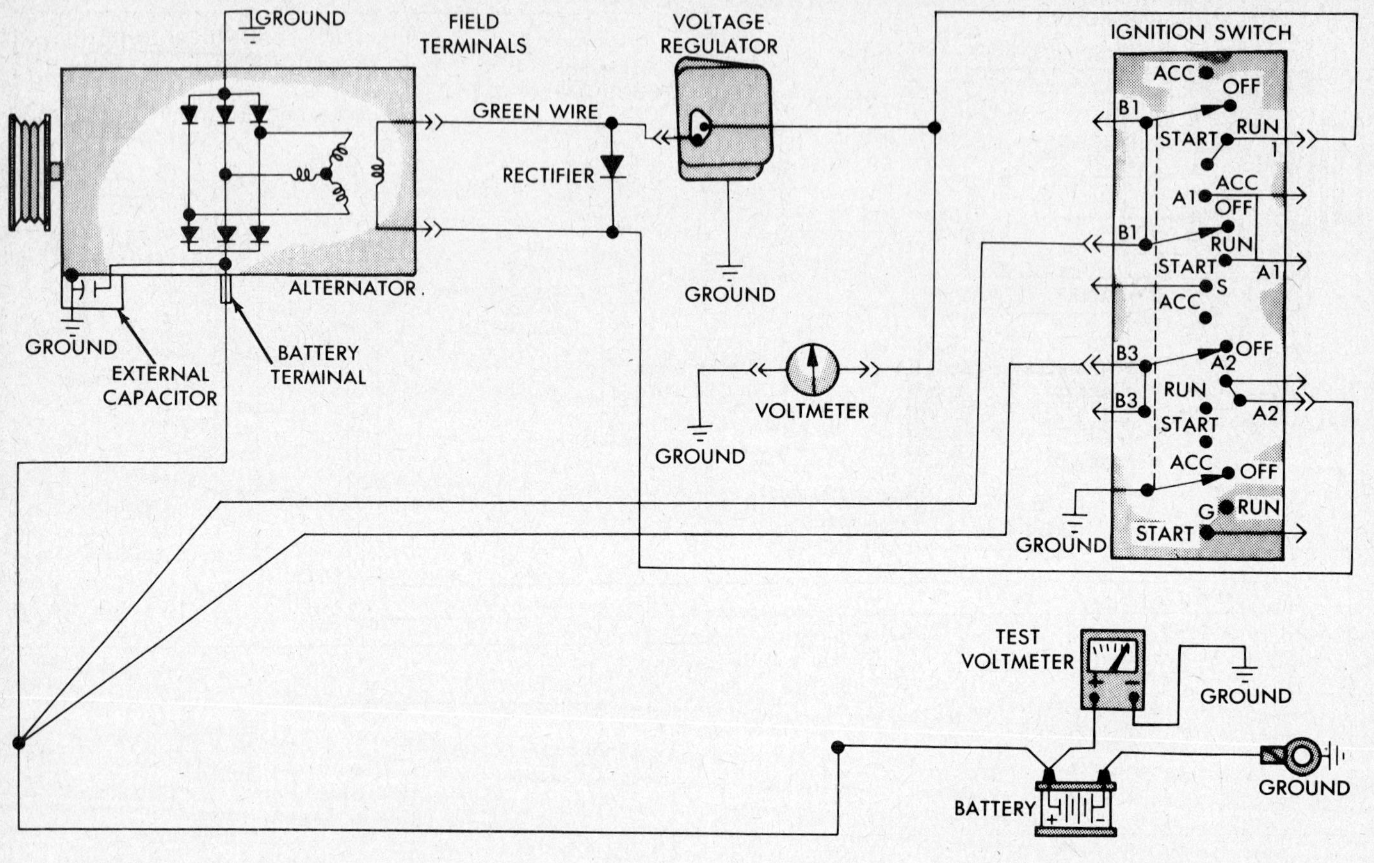

Section 21 ALTERNATORS
BOSCH (W/EXTERNAL REGULATOR)

Bosch alternator with external regulator — voltage regulator test. Check voltmeter, regulator is working properly if voltage readings are in accordance with the voltage chart

voltage regulator wiring harness connector terminals. Both blue and green terminals should read battery voltage. Turn off ignition switch.

5. If satisfactory then replace regulator and repeat test.

6. If the voltage is above limits specification proceed as follows. Turn off ignition switch and disconnect voltage regulator wiring harness connector. Be sure terminals in connector have not spread open.

8. Do not start engine or distort terminals with voltmeter probe. Turn on ignition switch and check for battery voltage at voltage regulator wiring harness connector terminals. Both blue and green terminals should read battery voltage. Turn off ignition switch.

9. If satisfactory, then replace regulator and repeat test. Remove test voltmeter and tachometer.

Disassembly

1. Remove the alternator from the vehicle. Mount the unit in a suitable holding fixture.
2. Hold the alternator pulley and remove the pulley retaining nut.
3. Remove the pulley lockwasher, pulley fan spacer, and pulley from the alternator assembly.
4. Remove the woodruff key from the rotor shaft.
5. From the rear of the alternator remove the brush holder retaining screws. Remove the brush holder.
6. To test the inner and outer brush circuits, use an ohmmeter and touch one test probe to the inner brush and the other test probe to the brush terminal. If continuity does not exist re-

place the brush assembly. Repeat the same test for the outer brush circuit.

7. Disconnect the capacitor electrical connection and remove the capacitor retaining screw. Remove the capacitor from its mounting on the alternator.

8. Remove the ground stud nut and stud washer.

9. Remove the four alternator through bolts that retain the

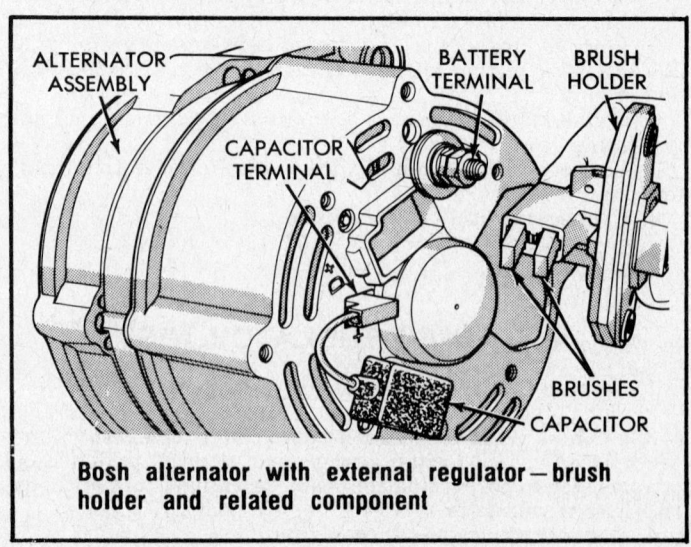

Bosh alternator with external regulator — brush holder and related component

ALTERNATORS
BOSCH (W/EXTERNAL REGULATOR)

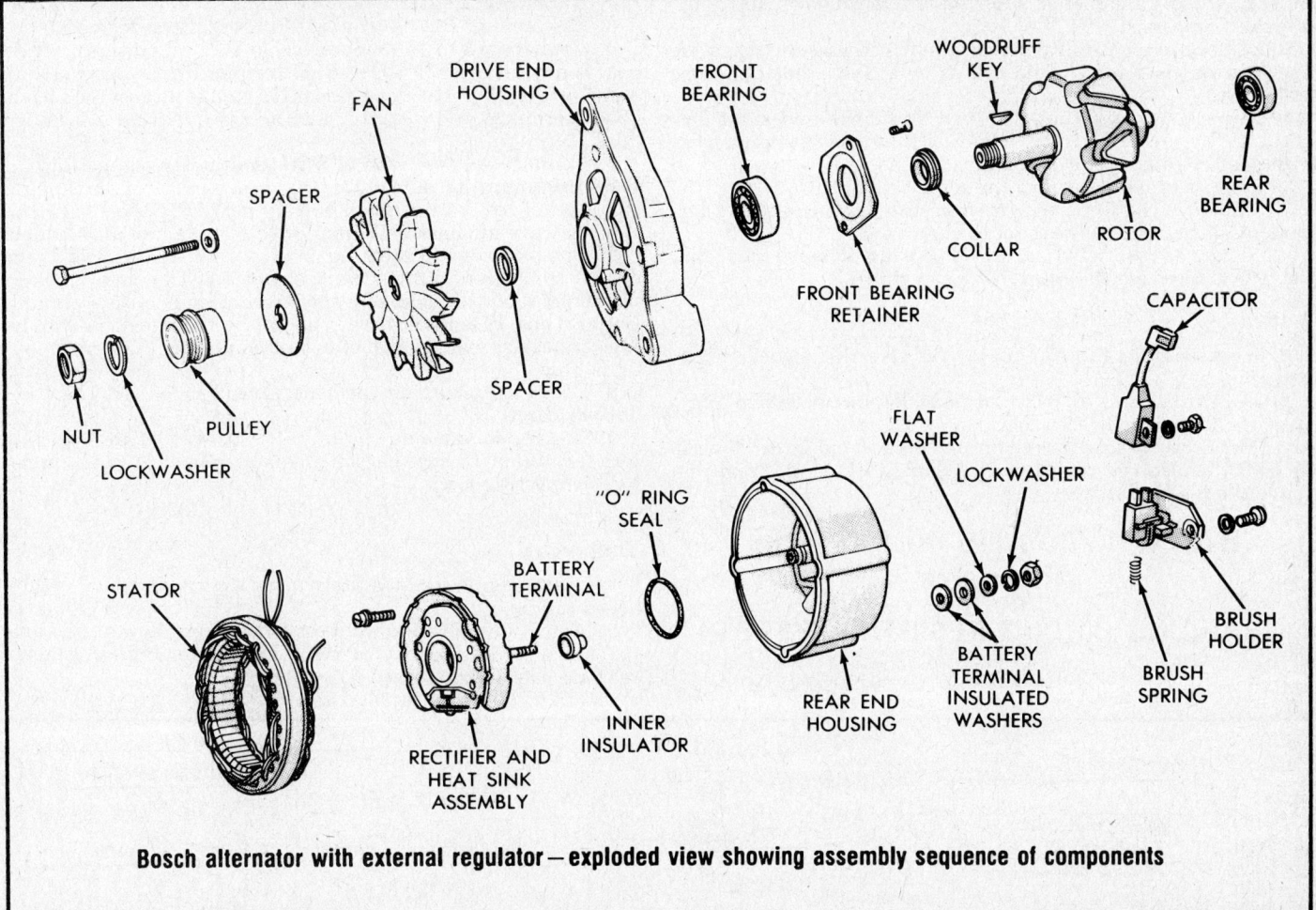

Bosch alternator with external regulator — exploded view showing assembly sequence of components

unit together.

10. Using the proper tool, separate the stator and the drive end shield.

11. To test the positive and negative rectifiers use tool C-3929-A or equivalent.

NOTE: Do not break the plastic cases of the rectifiers. These cases are for protection against corrosion. Be sure to always touch the test probe to the metal pin of the nearest rectifier.

12. Position the rear end shield and the stator assembly on an insulated surface. Connect the test lead clip to the alternator battery output terminal.

13. Plug in tool C-3829-A or equivalent. Touch the metal pin of each of the positive rectifiers with the test probe.

14. Reading for satisfactory rectifiers will be 1¾ amperes or more. Reading should be approximately the same and meter needle must move in the same direction for all three rectifiers.

15. When some rectifiers are good and one is shorted the reading taken at good rectifiers will be low and reading at shorted rectifiers will be zero. Disconnect stator lead to rectifiers reading zero and retest. Reading of good rectifiers will now be within satisfactory range.

16. When one rectifiers is open it will read approximately one ampere and good rectifiers will read within satisfactory range.

17. To test the negative rectifiers connect the test clip of tool C-3829-A to the rectifier end housing.

18. Touch the metal pin of each of the negative rectifiers with the test probe.

19. Test specifications are the same and test results will be approximately same as for positive case rectifiers except that the meter will read on opposite side of scale.

NOTE: If a negative rectifier shows shorted remove stator from rectifier assembly and retest. It is possible that a stator winding could be grounded to stator laminations or rectifier end shield which would indicate a shorted negative rectifier.

20. Remove the battery (B+) stud nut, stud lockwasher, stud flatwasher and stud insulator.

21. Remove the rectifier assembly retaining screws. Remove the stator assembly along with the rectifier unit. Unsolder the stator to rectifier leads.

22. Check for continuity between stator coil leads. Press test probe firmly to each of three phase (stator) lead terminals one at a time. If there is no continuity, stator coil is defective. Replace stator assembly.

23. To test stator for ground. Check for continuity between stator coil leads and stator coil frame. If there is continuity stator is grounded. Replace stator assembly.

24. Remove the rear bearing oil and dust seal. Check the rotor bearing surface for wear and scoring. Replace as required.

25. Remove the inner battery (B+) stud insulator.

26. Press the rotor out of the drive end shield and remove the spacer.

27. Check outside circumference of slip ring for dirtiness and roughness. Clean or polish with fine sandpaper, if re-

SECTION 21

ALTERNATORS
BOSCH (W/EXTERNAL REGULATOR)

quired. A badly roughened slip ring or a worn down slip ring should be replaced.

28. Check for continuity between field coil and slip rings. If there is no continuity, field coil is defective. Replace rotor assembly.

29. Check for continuity between slip rings and shaft (or core). If there is continuity, it means that coil or slip ring is grounded. Replace rotor assembly.

30. Using a puller remove the rotor bearing.

31. Remove the front bearing from the drive end shield by removing the front bearing retaining screws.

32. Press out the drive end shield bearing. Remove the front drive bearing from the front drive end shield.

Assembly

1. To assemble the alternator reverse the disassembly procedure.

2. Be sure to check all parts for wear. Replace defective components as required.

3. Push the brushes into the brush holder and insert a wire to hold them in the raised position. Install the rotor and remove the holding wire.

Bosch 40/90 AND 40/100 Amp Alternator

CHARGING CIRCUIT RESISTANCE TEST

1. Be sure that the battery is fully charged.

2. Disconnect negative battery cable.

3. Disconnect "Bat" lead at alternator output terminal.

4. Connect a 0 to 150 ampere scale D.C. ammeter in series between alternator output "Bat" terminal and disconnected "Bat" terminal wire. Connect positive lead to alternator output "Bat" terminal and negative lead to disconnected alternator "Bat" terminal.

5. Connect positive lead of a test voltmeter (range 0 to 18 volts minimum) to alternator "Bat" terminal. Connect negative lead of test voltmeter to battery positive post.

6. Remove air hose between power module and air cleaner.

7. Connect one end of a jumper wire to ground and with other end probe green R3 lead wire of Black 8 Way connector. Do not connect blue J2 lead of 8 way Wiring connector to ground. Both R3 and J2 leads are green on alternator side of 8 way wiring connector. At dash end of 8 way connector R3 is green and J2 is blue.

8. Connect an engine tachometer and reconnect negative battery cable.

9. Connect a variable carbon pile rheostat (C3950) to battery terminals. Be sure carbon pile is in open or off position before connecting leads.

Test

1. Start engine. Immediately after starting, reduce engine speed to idle.

2. Adjust engine speed and carbon pile to maintain 20 amperes flowing in circuit. Observe voltmeter reading. Voltmeter reading should not exceed 0.5 volts.

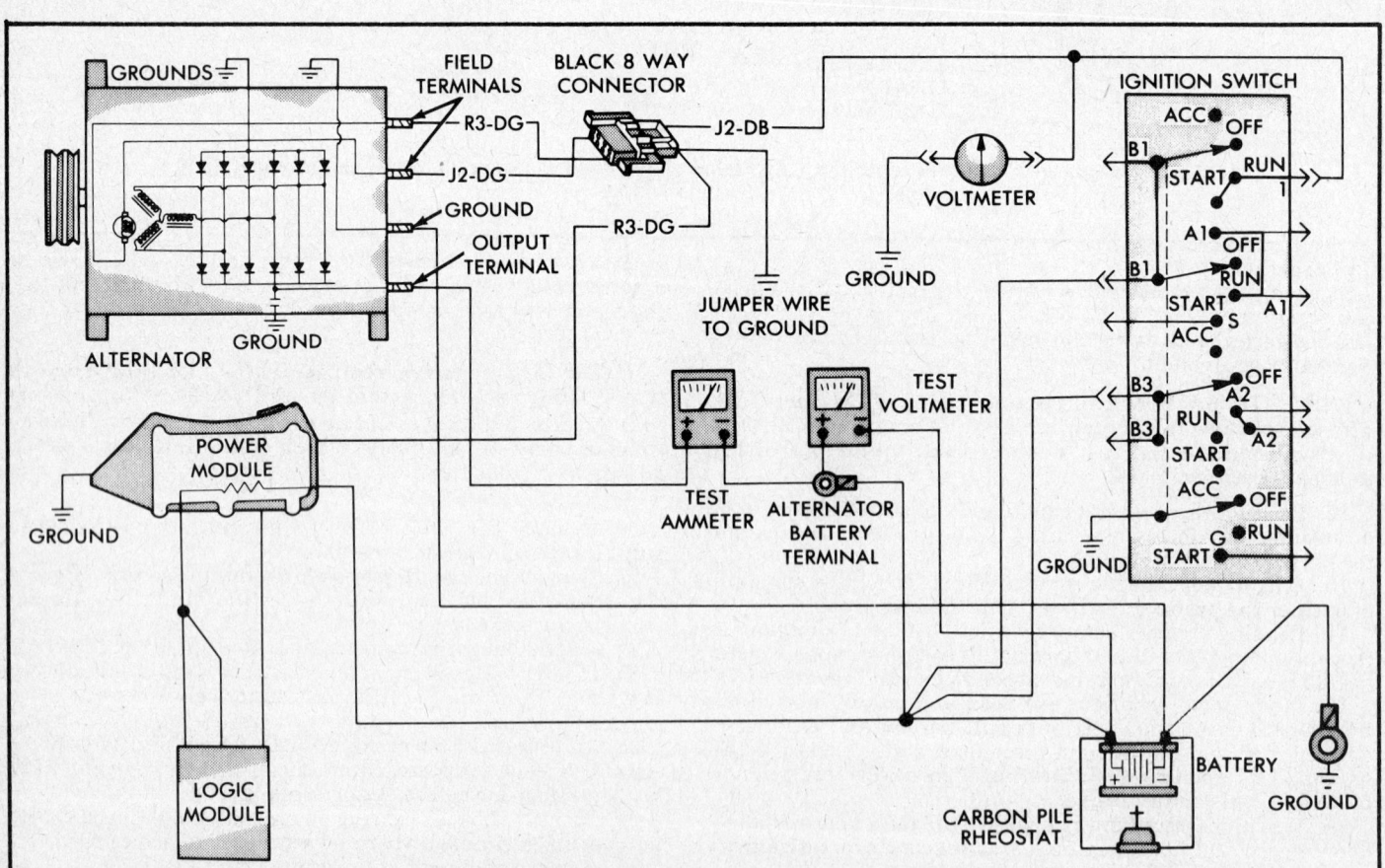

Bosch 40/90 amp alternator — charging resistance test — adjust engine speed and carbon pile to maintain 20 amps flowing in circuit. Voltmeter reading should not exceed 0.5 volts

ALTERNATORS
BOSCH 40/90 AMP.

Results

If a higher voltage drop is indicated, inspect, clean and tighten all connections in charging circuit. A voltage drop test may be performed at each connection to locate connection with excessive resistance. If charging circuit resistance tested satisfactorily, reduce engine speed, turn off carbon pile and turn off ignition switch.

1. Disconnect negative battery cable.
2. Remove test ammeter, voltmeter, carbon pile, and tachometer.
3. Remove jumper wire between 8 way black connector and ground.
4. Connect "Bat" lead to alternator output "Bat" terminal post.
5. Reconnect negative battery cable.
6. Reconnect hose between power module and air cleaner.

CURRENT OUTPUT TEST

1. Be sure that the battery is fully charged.
2. Disconnect negative battery cable.
3. Disconnect the "Bat" lead wire at the alternator output terminal.
4. Connect a 0 to 150 ampere scale D.C. ammeter in series between alternator output "Bat" terminal and disconnected "Bat" terminal and negative lead to disconnected "Bat" terminal.
5. Connect positive lead of a test voltmeter (range 0 to 18 volts minimum) to alternator output "Bat" terminal.
6. Connect negative lead of test voltmeter to a good ground.
7. Connect an engine tachometer and reconnect negative battery cable.
8. Connect a variable carbon pile rheostat (C3950) between battery terminals. Be sure carbon pile is in open or off position before connecting leads.
9. Remove air hose between power module and air cleaner.
10. Connect one end of a jumper wire to ground and with other end probe green R3 lead wire of Black 8 Way connector. Do not connect blue J2 lead of 8 way Wiring connector to ground. Both R3 and J2 leads are green on alternator side of 8 way wiring connector. At dash end of 8 way connector R3 is green and J2 is blue.

Test

1. Start engine. Immediately after starting reduce engine speed to idle.
2. Adjust carbon pile and engine speed in increments until a speed of 1250 rpm and voltmeter reading of 15 volts is obtained. Do not allow voltage meter to read above 16 volts.
3. The ammeter reading must be within the proper limits.

Results

1. If reading is less than specified alternator should be removed from vehicle and bench tested.
2. After current output is completed reduce engine speed, turn off carbon pile and turn off ignition switch.
3. Disconnect negative battery cable.
4. Remove test ammeter, voltmeter, tachometer and carbon pile.

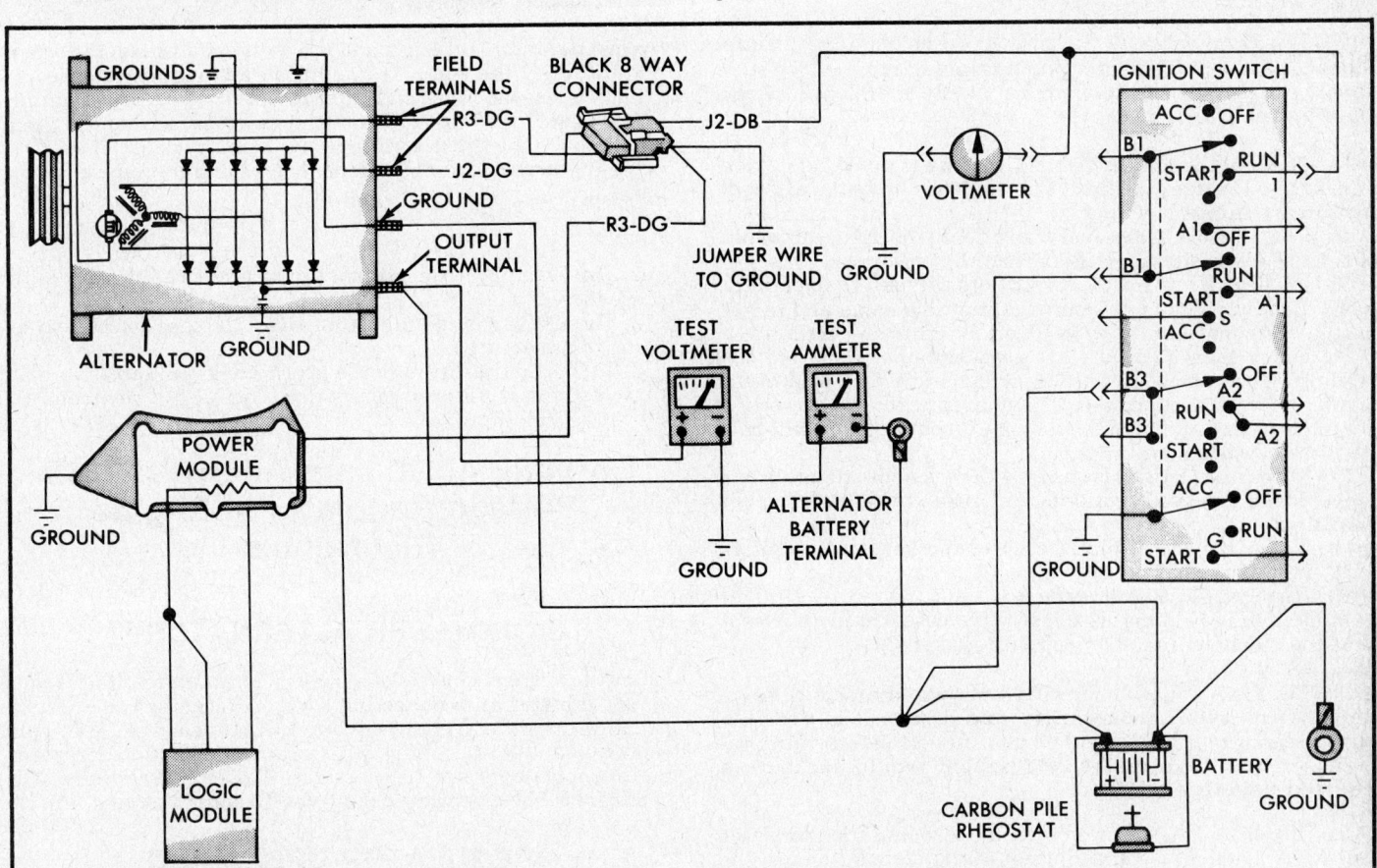

Bosch 40/90 amp. alternator—current output test—adjust carbon pile and engine speed untill a speed of 1250 rpm and voltmeter reading of 15 volts is obtained. The ammeter reading must be within proper limits

SECTION 21

ALTERNATORS
BOSCH 40/90 AMP.

5. Remove jumper wire between 8 way black connector and ground.
6. Connect "Bat" lead to alternator output "Bat" terminal post.
7. Reconnect negative battery cable.
8. Reconnect hose between power module and air cleaner.

Disassembly

1. Remove the alternator from the vehicle. Position the unit in a suitable holding fixture.
2. Remove the pulley nut and lockwasher. Remove the alternator pulley.
3. Remove the pulley to fan spacer and pulley fan.
4. Remove the woodruff key from the rotor shaft.
5. From the rear of the alternator disconnect the electrical terminal from the capacitor. Remove the capacitor retaining screw and the capacitor.
6. Remove the brush holder retaining screw and remove the brush holder from its mounting on the rear of the alternator.
7. Remove the alternator through bolts. Using a suitable tool pry between the stator and the drive end shield and carefully separate the assembly.
8. Press the rotor out of the drive end shield and remove the spacer. Remove the pulley fan spacer.
9. Remove the front alternator drive end bearing screws.
10. Remove the drive end shield bearing retainer and press out the drive end shield bearing.
11. Remove the front drive bearing from the front of the drive end shield.
12. To test the positive and negative rectifiers use tool C-3929-A or equivalent.

NOTE: Do not break the plastic cases of the rectifiers. These cases are for protection against corrosion. Be sure to always touch the test probe to the metal pin of the nearest rectifier.

13. Position the rear end shield and the stator assembly on an insulated surface. Connect the test lead clip to the alternator battery output terminal.
14. Plug in tool C-3829-A or equivalent. Touch the metal pin of each of the positive rectifiers with the test probe.
15. Reading for satisfactory rectifiers will be 1¾ amperes or more. Reading should be approximately the same and meter needle must move in same direction for all three rectifiers.
16. When some rectifiers are good and one is shorted the reading taken at good rectifiers will be low and reading at shorted rectifiers will be zero. Disconnect stator lead to rectifiers reading zero and retest. Reading of good rectifiers will now be within satisfactory range.
17. When one rectifier is open it will read approximately one ampere and the good rectifiers will read within satisfactory range.
18. Touch the metal pin of each of the negative rectifiers with the test probe.
20. Test specifications are the same, and the test results will be approximately same as for positive case rectifiers except that the meter will read on opposite side of scale.

NOTE: If a negative rectifier shows shorted remove stator from rectifier assembly and retest. It is possible that a stator winding could be grounded to stator laminations or rectifiers end shield which would indicate a shorted negative rectifier.

21. Unsolder the stator to rectifier leads. Mark the stator coil frame, to aid in reinstallation of the stator. Remove the stator from the rectifier end shield assembly.
22. Remove the threes rectifier assembly mounting screws. Remove the rectifier assembly.
23. Remove the inner battery (B+) stud insulator.
24. Remove the D+ stud insulator, stud nut, stud flatwasher and stud insulating washer.
25. Remove the rear bearing oil and dust seal. Check the rotor bearing surface for scoring.
26. Using puller C-4068 or equivalent, remove the rear rotor bearing.
27. Check outside circumference of slip ring for dirtiness and roughness. Clean or polish with fine sandpaper, required. A badly roughened slip ring or a worn down slip ring should be replaced.
28. To check for an open rotor field coil, connect an ohmmeter to slip rings. Ohmmeter reading should be between 1.5 and 2 ohms on rotor coils at room ambient conditions. Resistance between 2.5 and 3.0 ohms would result from alternator rotors that have been operated on vehicle at higher engine compartment temperatures. Readings above 3.5 ohms would indicate high resistance rotor coils and further testing or replacement may be required.
29. To check for a shorted field coil connect an ohmmeter to slip rings. If reading is below 1.5 ohms field coil is shorted.
30. To check for a grounded rotor field coil connect an ohmmeter from each slip ring to rotor shaft.

NOTE: Ohmmeter should be set for "infinite" reading when probes are apart and zero when probes are shorted. The ohmmeter should read "infinite". If reading is zero or higher, rotor is grounded.

31. Check for continuity between leads of stator coil. Press test probe firmly to each of three phase (stator) lead terminals one at a time. If there is no continuity, stator coil is defective. Replace stator assembly.
32. To test the stator for ground check for continuity between the stator coil leads and the stator coil frame. If there is no continuity the stator is grounded and must be replaced.
33. To test the inner and outer brush circuit, use an ohmmeter and touch one test probe to the inner brush and the other test probe to the brush terminal. If continuity does not exist replace the brush assembly. Repeat the same procedure for the outer brush.

Assembly

1. To assemble the alternator reverse the disassembly procedure.
2. Be sure to check all parts for wear. Replace defective components as required.
3. Push the brushes into the brush holder and insert a wire to hold them in the raised position. Install the rotor and remove the holding wire.

Chrysler 40/90 amp Alternator with Voltage Regulator in Engine Electronics

CHRYLSER ALTERNATOR

Charging system consists of a battery alternator voltage regulator voltmeter and connecting wires. Alternator has six built in silicon rectifiers, that convert A.C. current into D.C. current. Current at alternator battery terminal is D.C. Alternator main components are rotor, stator, capacitor, rectifiers, end shields, brushes, bearings, Poly-Vee Drive pulley and fan.

REGULATOR OPERATION

The electronic voltage regulator is contained within engine electronics Power Module and Logic Module. It is a device that regulates vehicle electrical system voltage by limiting output

ALTERNATORS
CHRYSLER 40/90 AMP. (REGULATOR IN ENGINE ELECTRONICS)

SECTION 21

Alternator Diagnosis Chart — Chrysler 40/90 amp with Electronic Engine Electronics

IMPROPER CHARGING → CHECK BATTERY CONDITION SEE BATTERY SECTION FOR DETAILS → CORRODED BATTERY CABLES OR TERMINALS → DRIVE BELTS LOOSE → LOOSE OR CORRODED WIRING CONNECTIONS AT ALTERNATOR → **NOISY ALTERNATOR**

LOOSE OR CORRODED WIRING CONNECTIONS AT TERMINAL BLOCK → WORN OR FRAYED DRIVE BELT

CHECK FOR APPROXIMATELY 12 VOLTS AT FIELD INPUT BRUSH TERMINAL WITH IGNITION SWITCH "ON" ← LOOSE OR CORRODED WIRING CONNECTIONS AT BULKHEAD DISCONNECT

LOOSE CHASSIS TO BATTERY GROUND CABLE → ALTERNATOR MOUNTING LOOSE

LOOSE ALTERNATOR GROUND WIRE → INTERFERENCE BETWEEN ROTOR AND STATOR LEADS

ALTERNATOR CURRENT OUTPUT TEST * → FAN, PULLEY, OR ROTOR DAMAGED

ALTERNATOR OUTPUT WITHIN SPECIFICATIONS / **ALTERNATOR OUTPUT NOT UP TO SPECIFICATIONS**

REFER TO ONBOARD DIAGNOSTIC FAULT CODES

UNSTEADY OR LOW CHARGING

EXCESSIVE CHARGING → GROUNDED ALTERNATOR FIELD WIRE, FIELD TERMINAL, OR CONNECTIONS → ALTERNATOR FIELD GROUNDED INTERNALLY. REFER TO ALTERNATOR BENCH TEST

ALTERNATOR BEARINGS EXCESSIVELY WORN OR DEFECTIVE

TEST ALTERNATOR OUTPUT WIRE RESISTANCE*

ONE OR MORE RECTIFIERS OPEN OR SHORTED

CHARGING RESISTANCE TOO HIGH

OPEN, GROUNDED OR SHORTED WIRING IN STATOR

CORRODED OR SHORTED CABLES OR HIGH RESISTANCE ACROSS FUSIBLE LINK

REFER TO ALTERNATOR BENCH TEST ← RESISTANCE O.K.

21-27

SECTION 21 ALTERNATORS
CHRYSLER 40/90 AMP. (REGULATOR IN ENGINE ELECTRONICS)

voltage that is generated by the alternator. This is accomplished by controlling amount of current that is allowed to pass through alternator field winding. The alternator field is turned on by a driver in power module which is controlled by a pre-driver in the logic module. The logic module looks at battery temperature to determine control voltage. The field is then driven at a duty cycle proportional to the difference between battery voltage and desired control voltage. One important feature of the electronic regulator is the ability of its control circuit to vary regulated system voltage up or down as temperature changes. This provides varying charging conditions for battery throughout seasons of the year.

ALTERNATOR OUTPUT WIRE RESISTANCE TEST

Alternator output wire resistance test will show amount of "Voltage Drop" across alternator output wire between alternator "Bat" terminal and positive "Battery" post.

1. Before starting test, make sure vehicle has a fully charged battery.
2. Turn off ignition switch.
3. Disconnect negative battery cable.
4. Disconnect alternator output wire from alternator output "Battery" terminal.
5. Connect a 0 to 150 ampere scale D.C. ammeter in series between alternator "Bat" terminal and disconnected alternator output wire. Connect positive lead to alternator "Bat" terminal and negative lead to disconnected alternator output wire.
6. Connect positive lead of a test voltmeter (Range 0 to 18 volts minimum) to disconnected alternator output wire. Connect negative lead of test voltmeter to positive battery cable at positive post.
7. Remove air hose between power and module and air cleaner.
8. Connect one end of a "Jumper Wire" to ground and with other end probe green R3 lead wire on dash side of Black 8 Way connector.

NOTE: Do not connect the blue J2 lead of the eight way connector to ground. Both R3 and J2 leads are green on the alternator side of the eight way connector. At the dash end of the connector, R3 is green and J2 is blue.

9. Connect an engine tachometer and reconnect negative battery cable.
10. Connect a variable carbon pile rheostat between battery terminals. Be sure carbon pile is in "Open" or "Off" position before connecting leads.
11. Start engine. Immediately after staring, reduce engine speed to idle. Adjust engine speed and carbon pile to maintain 20 amperes flowing in circuit. Observe voltmeter reading. Voltmeter reading should not exceed 0.5 volts.
12. If a higher voltage drop is indicated, inspect, clean and tighten all connections between alternator "Bat" terminal and "Positive" battery post.
13. A voltage drop test may be performed at each connection

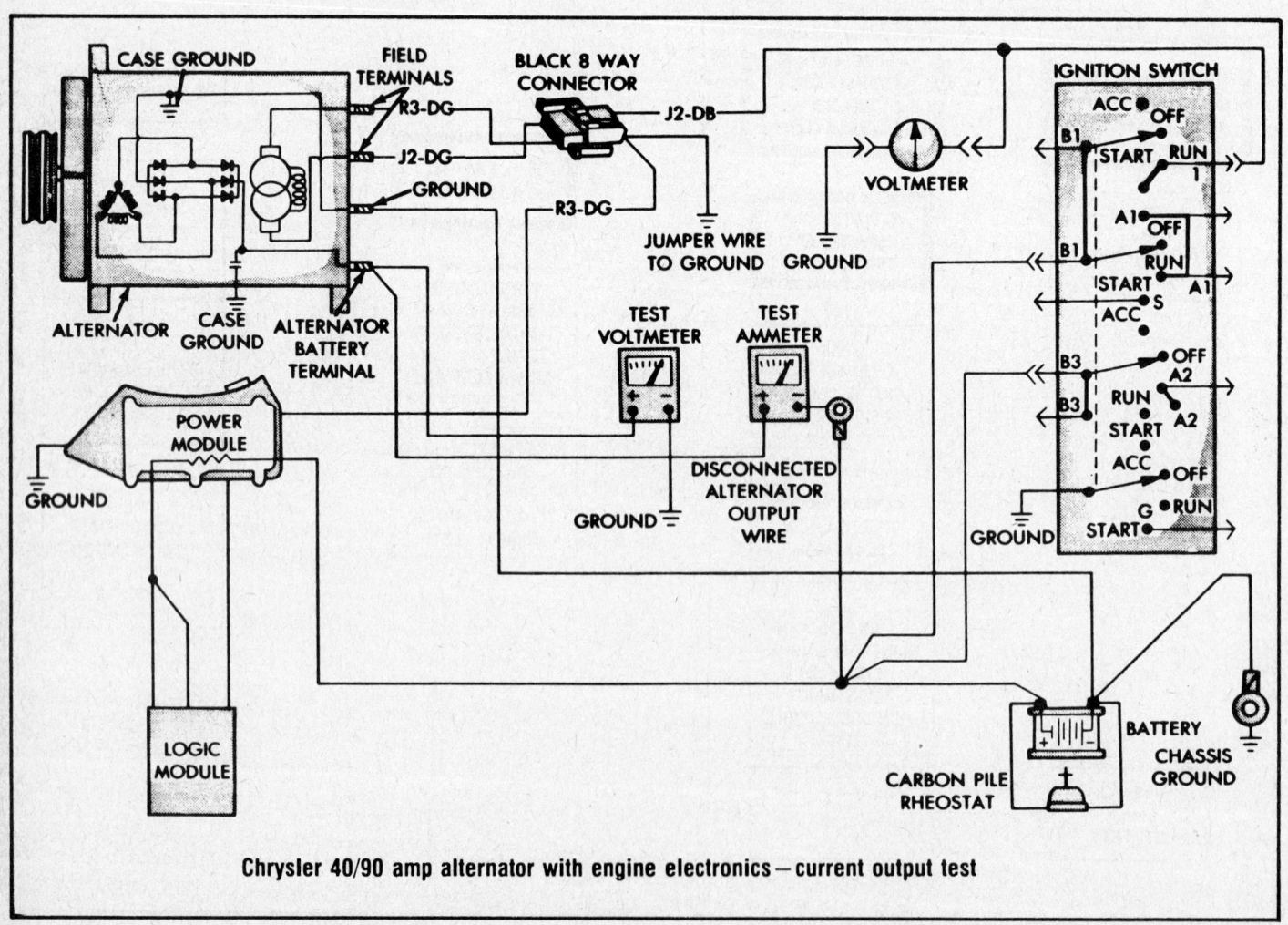

Chrysler 40/90 amp alternator with engine electronics—current output test

ALTERNATORS 21
CHRYSLER 40/90 AMP. (REGULATOR IN ENGINE ELECTRONICS)

to locate connection with excessive resistance. If resistance tested satisfactorily, reduce engine speed, turn off carbon pile and turn off ignition switch.

14. Disconnect negative battery cable. Remove test ammeter, voltmeter, carbon pile and tachometer. Remove "Jumper Wire" between 8 way black connector and ground.
15. Connect alternator output wire to alternator "Bat" terminal post. Tighten 45 to 75 inch lbs. Reconnect negative battery cable. Reconnect hose between power module and air cleaner.

CURRENT OUTPUT TEST

Current output test determines whether or not alternator is capable of delivering its rated current output.

1. Before starting any tests, make sure vehicle has a fully charged battery.
2. Disconnect negative battery cable.
3. Disconnect alternator output wire at the alternator battery terminal.
4. Connect a 0 to 150 ampere scale D.C. ammeter in series between alternator "Bat" terminal and disconnected alternator output wire. Connect positive lead to alternator "Bat" terminal and negative lead to disconnected alternator output wire.
5. Connect positive lead of a test voltmeter (range 0 to 18 volts minimum) to alternator "Bat" terminal.
6. Connect negative lead of test voltmeter to a good ground.
7. Connect an engine tachometer and reconnect negative battery cable.
8. Connect a variable carbon pile rheostate between battery terminals. Be sure carbon pile is in "Open" or "Off" position before connecting leads.
9. Remove air hose between power module and air cleaner.
10. Connect one end of a "Jumper Wire" to ground and with other end probe green R3 lead wire on dash side of Black 8 Way connector.

NOTE: Do not connect the blue J2 lead of the eight way connector to ground. Both R3 and J2 leads are green on the alternator side of the eight way connector. At the dash end of the connector, R3 is green and J2 is blue.

11. Start engine. Adjust carbon pile and engine speed in increments until a speed of 1250 rpm and voltmeter reading of 15 volts is obtained. Do not allow the voltage meter to read above 16 volts.
12. The ammeter reading must be within the proper limits.
13. If reading is less than specified and alternator output wire resistance is not excessive alternator should be removed from vehicle and "bench tested".
14. After current output test is completed, reduce engine speed, turn off carbon pile and ignition switch. Disconnect negative battery cable.
15. Remove test ammeter, voltmeter, tachometer and carbon pile. Remove "Jumper Wire" between 8 way black connector and ground. Disconnect alternator output wire to alternator "Bat" terminal post.
16. Reconnect negative battery cable. Reconnect air hose between power module and air cleaner.

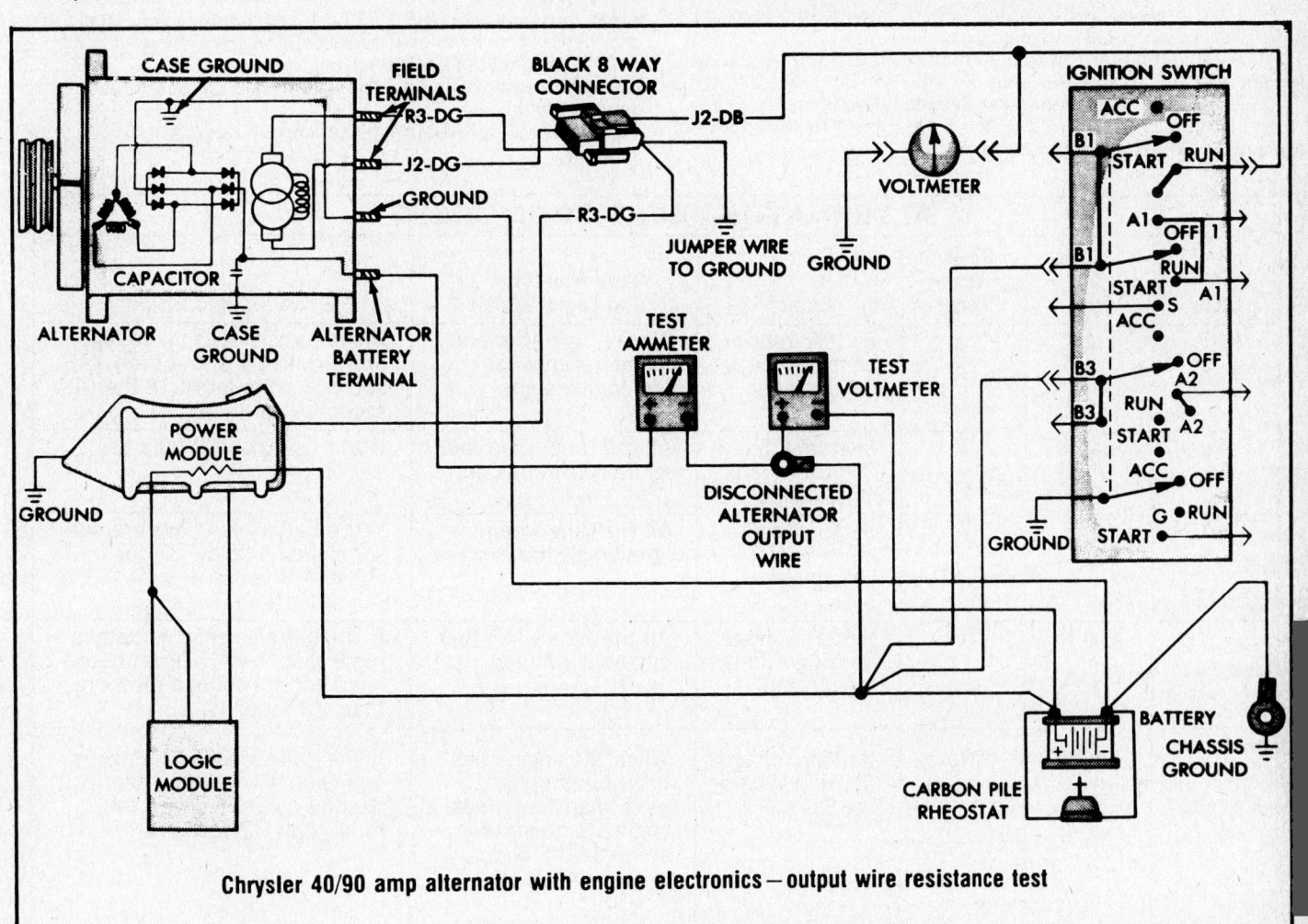

Chrysler 40/90 amp alternator with engine electronics—output wire resistance test

SECTION 21 ALTERNATORS
CHRYSLER 40/90 AMP. (REGULATOR IN ENGINE ELECTRONICS)

VOLTAGE REGULATOR TEST USING ON BOARD DIAGNOSTICS SYSTEM FAULT CODES

On-Board diagnostic fault codes play a major role in case of a charging system failure.

FAULT CODES

Fault codes are two digit numbers that identify which circuit is bad. In most cases, they do not identify which component in a circuit is bad. Therefore, a fault code is only a "result", not necessarily a "reason" for the problem. It is important that the test procedure be followed in order to understand what the fault codes of the on-board diagnostic system are trying to sell.

HOW TO USE DIAGNOSTIC READOUT BOX

The diagnostic readout box is used to put the on-board diagnostic system in three different modes of testing as called for in the driveability test procedure, only one of which is used in charging system diagnosis.

Diagnostic Mode

1. Connect diagnostic readout box C-4805 to the mating connector located in the wiring harness by right front shock tower.
2. Place read/hold switch on readout box in read position.
3. Turn ignition switch on-off, on-off, on within 5 seconds.
4. Record all codes, displaying of codes may be stopped by moving read/hold button to hold button. Returning to read position will continue displaying of codes.
5. If for some reason diagnostic readout box is not available, logic module can show fault codes by means of flashing power loss lamp on instrument cluster.

HOW TO USE POWER LOSS OR POWER LIMIT LAMP FOR CODES

To activate this function, turn ignition key on-off-on-off-on within five seconds. The power loss lamp will then come on for two seconds as a bulb check. Immediately following this it will display a fault code by flashing on and off. There is a short pause between flashes and a longer pause between digits. All codes displayed are two digit numbers with a four second pause between codes. An example of a code is as follows.
1. Lamp on for two seconds then turns off.
2. Lamp flashes four times then pauses and then flashes once.
3. Lamp pauses for four seconds, flashes four times, pauses and then flashes seven times.
4. The two codes are 41 and 47. Any number of codes can be displayed as long as they are in memory. The lamp will flash until all of them are displayed.

CHARGING SYSTEM FAULT CODES

Perform test procedure categories using the following guide lines.
1. Each category is made up of many tests. Always start at test one of category. Starting at any other test will only give incorrect results.
2. Each test may have many steps. Only perform steps indicated under action required. It is not necessary to perform all steps in a test. If you do, the problem will not be found. Some steps may have reminders. These are to inform you that previous instructions are still required.
3. At the end of each test (not step) reconnect all wires and turn the engine off, and reinstall any components that were removed for testing.
4. The vehicle being tested must have a fully charged battery.

ALTERNATOR FAULT CODE CHART

Code	Type	Power Loss Lamp	Circuit	When Monitored By The Logic Module	When Put Into Memory
16	Fault	Yes	Battery Voltage Sensing (Charging System)	All the time after one minute from when the engine starts.	If the battery sensing voltage drops below 4 or between 7½ and 8½ volts for more than 20 seconds.
41	Fault	No	Alternator Field Control (Charging System)	All the time when the ignition switch is on.	If the field control fails to switch properly.
44	Fault	No	Battery Temperature Sensor (Charging System)	All the time when the ignition switch is on.	If the battery temperature sensor signal is below .04 or above 4.9 volts.
46	Fault	Yes	Battery Voltage Sensing (Charging System)	All the time when the engine is running.	If the battery sense voltage is more than 1 volt above the desired control voltage for more than 20 seconds.
47	Fault	No	Battery Voltage Sensing (Charging System)	When the engine has been running for more than 6 minutes. engine temperature above 160°F and engine rpm above 1,500 rpm.	If the battery sense voltage is less than 1 volt below the desired control voltage for more than 20 seconds.

ALTERNATORS
CHRYSLER 40/90 AMP. (REGULATOR IN ENGINE ELECTRONICS)
SECTION 21

TEST 1 STEP A (CHECKING BATTERY SENSING CIRCUIT CODE 16)

This test will check for direct battery feed to logic module. Circuit is also memory feed to logic module. Code 16 with lower battery voltage will turn on Power Loss lamp.
1. Turn the ignition switch off.
2. Disconnect the (black EFI blue turbo) connector from the logic module.
3. Connect a voltmeter to cavity No. 22 of logic module connector and ground.
4. Voltmeter should read within one volt of battery voltage. Voltage okay, replace logic module. Before replacing logic module, make sure the terminal in cavity No. 22 is not crushed so that it cannot touch logic module pin.
5. 0 volts, repair wire of cavity No. 22 for an open circuit to the wiring harness splice.

TEST 2 STEP A (CHECKING CHARGING SYSTEM FAULT CODES 41,46 or 46)

1. Disconnect the power module 10 way connector.
2. Connect a voltmeter between cavity No. 8 of 10 way connector and ground.
3. Turn ignition switch to run position.
4. Voltmeter should read within one volt of battery voltage. Not within 0 to 1 volts, repair alternator field circuit for short to ground. Voltage okay, perform Step B.

STEP B (CHECKING POWER MODULE CIRCUIT)

1. Turn the ignition switch off.
2. Reconnect the power module 10 way connector.
3. Disconnect the power module 12 way connector.
4. Connect a voltmeter between F2 terminal on alternator and ground.
5. Turn the ignition switch to the run position.
6. Voltage should read within one volt of battery voltage. Not within 0 to 1 volt, replace power module. Voltage okay, perform Step C.

STEP C (CHECKING CONTROL WIRE TO POWER MODULE)

1. Turn the ignition switch off.
2. With power module 12 way connector disconnected.
3. Disconnect the logic module (white EFI, red Turbo) connector.
4. Connect an ohmmeter between cavity No. 11 of power module 12 way connector and ground.
5. Ommeter should not show continuity. No continuity, replace logic module. Continuity repair wire of cavity no. 11 for short circuit to ground.

TEST 3 STEP A (CHECKING CHARGING SYSTEM CODES 41,47 OR 47)

1. Conenct a voltmeter between battery positive and ground.
2. Connect one end of jumper wire to a good engine ground.
3. Start the engine and note reading of voltmeter.
4. Very quickly touch other end of jumper wire to F2 terminal on alternator and watch voltmeter.
5. Voltmeter should show an increase in voltage. Voltage increases, this indicates alternator is operating correctly. Move on to Step B, for field circuit check. Voltage does not increase, this indicates alternator is not operating and you should immediately perform Step "E" which checks for voltage to alternator field.

STEP B (CHECKING CHARGING SYSTEM FIELD CIRCUIT)

1. Connect a voltmeter between cavity No. 2 of logic module (black E.F.I. blue turbo) connector and ground.
2. Connect one end of a jumper wire to cavity No. 5 of the logic module white connector.
3. Very quickly touch other end of jumper wire to logic module mounting stud and watch voltmeter.
4. Voltmeter should show an increase in voltage. If voltage increases, this indicates all components of system, except logic module, are operating correctly.
5. Before replacing the logic module be sure that the terminal in cavity NO 5 is not crushed so that it cannot touch the logic module pin. If terminal in cavity five is not damaged, replace logic module. If no increase is indicated, move on to Step C.

STEP C (CHECKING CONTROL WIRE TO POWER MODULE)

1. Turn the engine off.
2. Disconnect logic module (white EFI red turbo) connector.
3. Connect a voltmeter between cavity No. 5 of logic module connector and ground.
4. Turn the ignition switch to run position. Voltmeter should read within one volt of battery voltage. 0 volts, disconnect power module 12 way and connect an ohmmeter between cavity 5 of logic module (white EFI, red turbo) connector and cavity 11 of power module. If open repair wire or connector. If meter shows continuity replace power module. If voltage shown is within one volt of battery voltage, go on to Step D.

STEP D (CHECKING POWER MODULE CIRCUIT)

1. Turn ignition switch off.
2. Disconnect 10 way connector from power module.
3. Connect a voltmeter between cavity No. 8 of 10 way connect and ground.
4. Turn ignition switch to run position. Voltmeter should read within one volt of battery voltage. If voltage shown is within one volt of battery voltage, replace power module.
5. 0 volts, turn ignition switch off and place an ohmmeter between cavity 8 of power module 10 way connector and F2 terminal of alternator. If open, repair wire or connector. If meter shows continuity, proceed to Step E.

STEP E (CHECKING FOR VOLTAGE TO ATLERNATOR FIELD)

1. Turn ignition switch to off position.
2. Connect a voltmeter between F1 terminal of alternator and ground.
3. Turn ignition switch to run position.
4. Voltmeter should read within one volt of battery voltage. If voltage shown is within one volt of battery voltage, alternator is not functioning properly and must be removed form vehicle and repaired.
5. If no voltage is shown, this indicates an "open" and wire from the F1 terminal to ignition switch must be repaired.

SECTION 21
ALTERNATORS
CHRYSLER 40/90 AMP. (REGULATOR IN ENGINE ELECTRONICS)

TEST 4 STEP A (CHECKING BATTERY TEMPERATURE CIRCUIT FAULT CODE 44)

1. Turn the ignition switch off.
2. Disconnect the logic module (black connector EFI, blue connector turbo).
3. Connect an ohmmeter between cavity No. 20 of logic module (black EFI blue turbo) connector and ground.
4. Ohmmeter should show resistance, amount of resistance should be between 8000 and 29000 thousand ohms. Correct resistance, replace logic module. 0 resistance, perform Step B. Open circuit, perform Step C.

STEP B (CHECKING BATTERY TEMPERATURE SENSOR FOR SHORTS)

1. Ohmmter connected between cavity No. 20 of logic module (black EFI, blue turbo) connector and ground.
2. Disconnect power module 12 way connector.
3. Ohmmeter should show an open circuit. Open circuit, replace power module. 0 resistance, repair wire of cavity No. 20 and cavity No. 3 of power module 12 way connector.

STEP C (CHECKING BATTERY TEMPERATURE FOR OPENS)

1. Disconnect power module 12 way connector.
2. Connect an ohmmeter between pin 3 of power module 12 way and ground.
3. Ohmmeter should show resistance, amount of resistance should be between 8000 and 29000 thousand ohms.
4. Correct resistance, repair wire in cavity No. 20 of logic module (black EFI blue turbo) and cavity No. 3 of power module 12 way connector. Open circuit, replace power module.

Disassembly

1. Remove the dust cover mounting nut. Remove the dust cover.
2. Remove the two brush holder assembly mounting screws. Remove the brush holder assembly.
3. Remove the three stator to rectifier mounting screws. Remove the two stator to rectifier assembly mounting screws. Remove the rectifier insulator. Remove the capacitor mounting screw. Remove the rectifier assembly.
4. Remove the four through bolts. Carefully pry between the stator and the drive end shield, using a suitable tool, and separate the end shields. The stator is laminated, do not burr the stator or the end shield.
5. Position the drive end of the alternator over the bosses of the holding fixture. Do not position the rotor plastic termination plate over the fixture boss or damage to the assembly will result.
6. Bolt the drive end of the assembly to shield fixture. Loosen the pulley mounting nut. Remove the pulley mounting nut. Remove the pulley washer.
7. Remove the poly-vee pulley. Remove the fan. Remove the front bearing spacer. Press the rotor assembly out of the drive end shield.
8. Remove the inner bearing spacer. Position the alternator bearing puller tool under the rear rotor bearing. Tighten the right puller bolt one half turn. Tighten the left puller bolt one half turn. Continue tightening the tool one half turn on each bolt until the rear rotor bearing is free. Remove the rear rotor bearing assembly from the rotor.
9. Position the rotor assembly in the holding fixture. Position the rear rotor bearing onto the rotor shaft.
10. Drive the rear rotor bearing onto the rotor until it bottoms. The rear rotor position is critical and must be installed using special tools C-4885 and C-4894.
11. Remove the four front bearing retaining screws. Press the front bearing out of the drive end shield.
12. Carefully remove the stator from the rectifier end shield.

Testing Disassembled Alternator

ROTOR ASSEMBLY TEST

Checking Slip Rings

Checking outside circumference of slip ring for dirtiness and roughness. Clean or polish with fine sandpaper, if required. A badly roughened slip ring or a worn down slip ring should be replaced.

REPLACING SLIP RINGS

Slip rings are not serviced as a separate item. They are serviced with the rotor assembly.

TESTING ROTOR FIELD COILS FOR OPENS AND SHORTS

To check for an "open" rotor field coil connect an ohmmeter between slip rings. Ohmmeter readings should be between 1.5 and 2 ohms on rotor field coils at room ambient conditions. Resistance between 2.5 and 3.0 ohms would result from alternator rotor field coils that have been operated on vehicle at higher engine compartment temperatures. Readings about 3.5 ohms would indicate high resistance rotor field coils and further testing or replacement may be required.

To check for a "shorted" rotor field coil, connect an ohmmeter between the two slip rings. If the reading is below 1.5 ohms, rotor field coil is shorted.

TESTING ROTOR FIELD COIL FOR GROUND

To check for a "grounded" rotor field coil, connect an ohmmeter from each slip ring to rotor shaft. Ohmmeter should be set for "infinite" reading when probes are apart and zero when probes are shortened. The ohmmeter should read "infinite". If the reading is zero or low in value, rotor is grounded.

STATOR ASSEMBLY TEST

Testing Stator Coil for ground

1. Remove varnish from a spot on a stator frame.
2. Press one ohmmeter test probe firmly onto cleaned spot on frame. Be sure varnish has been removed from stator so that spot is bare.
3. Press other ohmmeter test probe firmly to each of the three phase (stator) lead terminals one at a time. If ohmmeter reads zero or low in value stator lead is "grounded".
4. Replace stator if stator tested grounded.

Testing Stator for Open or Short Circuit

The stator windings are Delta Wound. Therefore, they cannot be tested for opens or shorts with an ohmmeter. They can only be tested for these items with test equipment not common to automotive service test equipment. If stator is not grounded, and all other electrical circuits and components of alternator test okay, it can be suspected that stator could possibly be open or shorted and must be replaced.

TESTING RECTIFIER ASSEMBLIES

When testing rectifiers with an ohmmeter, disconnect three

ALTERNATORS
CHRYSLER 60/70 AMP. (REGULATOR IN ENGINE ELECTRONICS)

SECTION 21

phase stator lead terminals from rectifier assembly. Pry stator lead terminals away from rectifier assembly.

POSITIVE RECTIFIER TEST

With an ohmmeter check for continuity between each positive (+) rectifier strap and positive (+) heat sink. Reverse test probes and retest. There should be continuity in one direction only. If there is continuity in both directions, rectifier is short circuited. If there is no continuity in either direction, rectifier is open. If rectifier is shorted or open, replace rectifier assembly.

NEGATIVE RECTIFIER TEST

With an ohmmeter, check for continuity between each negative (-) rectifier strap and negative (-) sink. Reverse test probes and retest. There should be continuity in one direction only. If there is continuity in both directions, rectifier is short circuited. If there is no continuity in either direction, rectifier is open. If rectifier is shorted or open, replace rectifier assembly. When installing a new rectifier assembly, apply three dabs (0.1 grams each) of heat sink compound to bottom of negative rectifier prior to mounting rectifier assembly to rectifier end shield.

TESTING BRUSHES AND BRUSH SPRINGS FOR CONTINUITY

When testing brushes an brush springs make sure that brushes move smoothly in brush holder. Sticking brushes require replacement of brush holder assembly.

TESTING INNER BRUSH CIRCUIT

With an ohmmeter, touch one test probe to inner brush, and another probe to field terminal. If there is no continuity, replace the brush assembly.

TESTING OUTER BRUSH CIRCUIT

With an ohmmeter, touch one test probe to outer brush and other probe to field terminal. If there is no continuity, replace brush assembly.

CLEANING ALTERNATOR PARTS

Do not immerse stator field coil assembly, rotor assembly or rectifier assembly in cleaning solvent, as solvent will damage these parts.

Assembly

1. Assembly is the reverse of the disassembly procedure. Be sure to repair or replace defective components as required.

Chrysler 60 and 78 amp Alternator with Voltage Regulator in Engine Electronics

CHRYLSER ALTERNATOR

Charging system consists of a battery alternator voltage regulator voltmeter and connecting wires. Alternator has six built in silicon rectifiers, that convert A.C. current into D.C. current. Current at alternator battery terminal is D.C. Alternator main components are rotor, stator, capacitor, rectifiers, end shields, brushes, bearings, Poly-Vee Drive pulley and fan.

REGULATOR OPERATION

The electronic voltage regulator is contained within engine electronics Power Module and Logic Module. It is a device that regulates vehicle electrical system voltage by limiting output voltage that is generated by the alternator. This is accomplished by controlling amount of current that is allowed to pass through alternator field winding. The alternator field is turned on by a driver in power module which is controlled by a pre-driver in the logic module. The logic module looks at battery temperature to determine control voltage. The field is then driven at a duty cycle proportional to the difference between battery voltage and desired control voltage. One important feature of the electronic regulator is the ability of its control circuit to vary regulated system voltage up or down as temperature changes. This provides varying charging conditions for battery throughout seasons of the year.

ALTERNATOR OUTPUT WIRE RESISTANCE TEST

Alternator output wire resistance test will show amount of "Voltage Drop" across alternator output wire between alternator "Bat" terminal and positive "Battery" post.

1. Before starting test, make sure vehicle has a fully charged battery.
2. Turn off ignition switch.
3. Disconnect negative battery cable.
4. Disconnect alternator output wire from alternator output "Battery" terminal.
5. Connect a 0 to 150 ampere scale D.C. ammeter in series between alternator "Bat" terminal and disconnected alternator output wire. Connect positive lead to alternator "Bat" terminal and negative lead to disconnected alternator output wire.
6. Connect positive lead of a test voltmeter (Range 0 to 18 volts minimum) to disconnected alternator output wire. Connect negative lead of test voltmeter to positive battery cable at positive post.
7. Remove air hose between power and module and air cleaner.
8. Connect one end of a "Jumper Wire" to ground and with other end probe green R3 lead wire on dash side of Black 8 Way connector.

NOTE: Do not connect the blue J2 lead of the eight way connector to ground. Both R3 and J2 leads are green on the alternator side of the eight way connector. At the dash end of the connector, R3 is green and J2 is blue.

9. Connect an engine tachometer and reconnect negative battery cable.
10. Connect a variable carbon pile rheostat between battery terminals. Be sure carbon pile is in "Open" or "Off" position before connecting leads.
11. Start engine. Immediately after staring, reduce engine speed to idle. Adjust engine speed and carbon pile to maintain 20 amperes flowing in circuit. Observe voltmeter reading. Voltmeter reading should not exceed 0.5 volts.
12. If a higher voltage drop is indicated, inspect, clean and tighten all connections between alternator "Bat" terminal and "Positive" battery post.
13. A voltage drop test may be performed at each connection to locate connection with excessive resistance. If resistance tested satisfactorily, reduce engine speed, turn off carbon pile and turn off ignition switch.
14. Disconnect negative battery cable. Remove test ammeter, voltmeter, carbon pile and tachometer. Remove "Jumper Wire" between 8 way black connector and ground.
15. Connect alternator output wire to alternator "Bat" termi-

21-33

SECTION 21 ALTERNATORS
CHRYSLER 60/70 AMP. (REGULATOR IN ENGINE ELECTRONICS)

nal post. Tighten 45 to 75 inch lbs. Reconnect negative battery cable. Reconnect hose between power module and air cleaner.

CURRENT OUTPUT TEST

Current output test determines whether or not alternator is capable of delivering its rated current output.
 1. Before starting any tests, make sure vehicle has a fully charged battery.
 2. Disconnect negative battery cable.
 3. Disconnect alternator output wire at the alternator battery terminal.
 4. Connect a 0 to 150 ampere scale D.C. ammeter in series between alternator "Bat" terminal and disconnected alternator output wire. Connect positive lead to alternator "Bat" terminal and negative lead to disconnected alternator output wire.
 5. Connect positive lead of a test voltmeter (range 0 to 18 volts minimum) to alternator "Bat" terminal.
 6. Connect negative lead of test voltmeter to a good ground.
 7. Connect an engine tachometer and reconnect negative battery cable.
 8. Connect a variable carbon pile rheostate between battery terminals. Be sure carbon pile is in "Open" or "Off" position before connecting leads.
 9. Remove air hose between power module and air cleaner.
 10. Connect one end of a "Jumper Wire" to ground and with other end probe green R3 lead wire on dash side of Black 8 Way connector.

NOTE: Do not connect the blue J2 lead of the eight way connector to ground. Both R3 and J2 leads are green on the alternator side of the eight way connector. At the dash end of the connector, R3 is green and J2 is blue.

 11. Start engine. Adjust carbon pile and engine speed in increments until a speed of 1250 rpm and voltmeter reading of 15 volts is obtained. Do not allow the voltage meter to read above 16 volts.
 12. The ammeter reading must be within the proper limits.
 13. If reading is less than specified and alternator output wire resistance is not excessive alternator should be removed from vehicle and "bench tested".
 14. After current output test is completed, reduce engine speed, turn off carbon pile and ignition switch. Disconnect negative battery cable.
 15. Remove test ammeter, voltmeter, tachometer and carbon pile. Remove "Jumper Wire" between 8 way black connector and ground. Disconnect alternator output wire to alternator "Bat" terminal post.
 16. Reconnect negative battery cable. Reconnect air hose between power module and air cleaner.

VOLTAGE REGULATOR TEST USING ON BOARD DIAGNOSTICS SYSTEM FAULT CODES

On-Board diagnostic fault codes play a major role in case of a charging system failure.

FAULT CODES

Fault codes are two digit numbers that identify which circuit is bad. In most cases, they do not identify which component in a circuit is bad. Therefore, a fault code is only a "result", not necessarily a "reason" for the problem. It is important that the test procedure be followed in order to understand what the fault codes of the on-board diagnostic system are trying to sell.

HOW TO USE DIAGNOSTIC READOUT BOX

The diagnostic readout box is used to put the on-board diagnostic system in three different modes of testing as called for in the driveability test procedure, only one of which is used in charging system diagnosis.

Diagnostic Mode

 1. Connect diagnostic readout box C-4805 to the mating connector located in the wiring harness by right front shock tower.
 2. Place read/hold switch on readout box in read position.
 3. Turn ignition switch on-off, on-off, on within 5 seconds.
 4. Record all codes, displaying of codes may be stopped by moving read/hold button to hold button. Returning to read position will continue displaying of codes.
 5. If for some reason diagnostic readout box is not available, logic module can show fault codes by means of flashing power loss lamp on instrument cluster.

HOW TO USE POWER LOSS OR POWER LIMIT LAMP FOR CODES

To activate this function, turn ignition key on-off-on-off-on within five seconds. The power loss lamp will then come on for two seconds as a bulb check. Immediately following this it will display a fault code by flashing on and off. There is a short pause between flashes and a longer pause between digits. All codes displayed are two digit numbers with a four second pause between codes. An example of a code is as follows.
 1. Lamp on for two seconds then turns off.
 2. Lamp flashes four times then pauses and then flashes once.
 3. Lamp pauses for four seconds, flashes four times, pauses and then flashes seven times.
 4. The two codes are 41 and 47. Any number of codes can be displayed as long as they are in memory. The lamp will flash until all of them are displayed.

CHARGING SYSTEM FAULT CODES

Perform test procedure categories using the following guide lines.
 1. Each category is made up of many tests. Always start at test one of category. Starting at any other test will only give incorrect results.
 2. Each test may have many steps. Only perform steps indicated under action required. It is not necessary to perform all steps in a test. If you do, the problem will not be found. Some steps may have reminders. These are to inform you that previous instructions are still required.
 3. At the end of each test (not step) reconnect all wires and turn the engine off, and reinstall any components that were removed for testing.
 4. The vehicle being tested must have a fully charged battery.

TEST I STEP A (CHECKING BATTERY SENSING CIRCUIT CODE 16)

This test will check for direct battery feed to logic module. Circuit is also memory feed to logic module. Code 16 with lower battery voltage will turn on Power Loss lamp.
 1. Turn the ignition switch off.
 2. Disconnect the (black EFI blue turbo) connector from the logic module.
 3. Connect a voltmeter to cavity No. 22 of logic module connector and ground.
 4. Voltmeter should read within one volt of battery voltage.

ALTERNATORS 21

CHRYSLER 60/70 AMP. (REGULATOR IN ENGINE ELECTRONICS)

Voltage okay, replace logic module. Before replacing logic module, make sure the terminal in cavity No. 22 is not crushed so that it cannot touch logic module pin.

5. 0 volts, repair wire of cavity No. 22 for an open circuit to the wiring harness splice.

TEST 2 STEP A (CHECKING CHARGING SYSTEM FAULT CODES 41,46 or 46)

1. Disconnect the power module 10 way connector.
2. Connect a voltmeter between cavity No. 8 of 10 way connector and ground.
3. Turn ignition switch to run position.
4. Voltmeter should read within one volt of battery voltage. Not within 0 to 1 volts, repair alternator field circuit for short to ground. Voltage okay, perform Step B.

STEP B (CHECKING POWER MODULE CIRCUIT)

1. Turn the ignition switch off.
2. Reconnect the power module 10 way connector.
3. Disconnect the power module 12 way connector.
4. Connect a voltmeter between F2 terminal on alternator and ground.
5. Turn the ignition switch to the run position.
6. Voltage should read within one volt of battery voltage. Not within 0 to 1 volt, replace power module. Voltage okay, perform Step C.

STEP C (CHECKING CONTROL WIRE TO POWER MODULE)

1. Turn the ignition switch off.
2. With power module 12 way connector disconnected.
3. Disconnect the logic module (white EFI, red Turbo) connector.
4. Connect an ohmmeter between cavity No. 11 of power module 12 way connector and ground.
5. Ommeter should not show continuity. No continuity, replace logic module. Continuity repair wire of cavity no. 11 for short circuit to ground.

TEST 3 STEP A (CHECKING CHARGING SYSTEM CODES 41,47 OR 47)

1. Conenct a voltmeter between battery positive and ground.
2. Connect one end of jumper wire to a good engine ground.
3. Start the engine and note reading of voltmeter.
4. Very quickly touch other end of jumper wire to F2 terminal on alternator and watch voltmeter.
5. Voltmeter should show an increase in voltage. Voltage increases, this indicates alternator is operating correctly. Move on to Step B, for field circuit check. Voltage does not increase, this indicates alternator is not operating and you should immediately perform Step "E" which checks for voltage to alternator field.

STEP B (CHECKING CHARGING SYSTEM FIELD CIRCUIT)

1. Connect a voltmeter between cavity No. 2 of logic module (black E.F.I. blue turbo) connector and ground.
2. Connect one end of a jumper wire to cavity No. 5 of the logic module white connector.

3. Very quickly touch other end of jumper wire to logic module mounting stud and watch voltmeter.
4. Voltmeter should show an increase in voltage. If voltage increases, this indicates all components of system, except logic module, are operating correctly.
5. Before replacing the logic module be sure that the terminal in cavity NO 5 is not crushed so that it cannot touch the logic module pin. If terminal in cavity five is not damaged, replace logic module. If no increase is indicated, move on to Step C.

STEP C (CHECKING CONTROL WIRE TO POWER MODULE)

1. Turn the engine off.
2. Disconnect logic module (white EFI red turbo) connector.
3. Connect a voltmeter between cavity No. 5 of logic module connector and ground.
4. Turn the ignition switch to run position. Voltmeter should read within one volt of battery voltage. 0 volts, disconnect power module 12 way and connect an ohmmeter between cavity 5 of logic module (white EFI, red turbo) connector and cavity 11 of power module. If open repair wire or connector. If meter shows continuity replace power module. If voltage shown is within one volt of battery voltage, go on to Step D.

STEP D (CHECKING POWER MODULE CIRCUIT)

1. Turn ignition switch off.
2. Disconnect 10 way connector from power module.
3. Connect a voltmeter between cavity No. 8 of 10 way connect and ground.
4. Turn ignition switch to run position. Voltmeter should read within one volt of battery voltage. If voltage shown is within one volt of battery voltage, replace power module.
5. 0 volts, turn ignition switch off and place an ohmmeter between cavity 8 of power module 10 way connector and F2 terminal of alternator. If open, repair wire or connector. If meter shows continuity, proceed to Step E.

STEP E (CHECKING FOR VOLTAGE TO ATLERNATOR FIELD)

1. Turn ignition switch to off position.
2. Connect a voltmeter between F1 terminal of alternator and ground.
3. Turn ignition switch to run position.
4. Voltmeter should read within one volt of battery voltage. If voltage shown is within one volt of battery voltage, alternator is not functioning properly and must be removed form vehicle and repaired.
5. If no voltage is shown, this indicates an "open" and wire from the F1 terminal to ignition switch must be repaired.

TEST 4 STEP A (CHECKING BATTERY TEMPERATURE CIRCUIT FAULT CODE 44)

1. Turn the ignition switch off.
2. Disconnect the logic module (black connector EFI, blue connector turbo).
3. Connect an ohmmeter between cavity No. 20 of logic module (black EFI blue turbo) connector and ground.
4. Ohmmeter should show resistance, amount of resistance should be between 8000 and 29000 thousand ohms. Correct resistance, replace logic module. 0 resistance, perform Step B. Open circuit, perform Step C.

SECTION 21 ALTERNATORS
CHRYSLER 60/70 AMP. (REGULATOR IN ENGINE ELECTRONICS)

STEP B (CHECKING BATTERY TEMPERATURE SENSOR FOR SHORTS)

1. Ohmmter connected between cavity No. 20 of logic module (black EFI, blue turbo) connector and ground.
2. Disconnect power module 12 way connector.
3. Ohmmeter should show an open circuit. Open circuit, replace power module. 0 resistance, repair wire of cavity No. 20 and cavity No. 3 of power module 12 way connector.

STEP C (CHECKING BATTERY TEMPERATURE FOR OPENS)

1. Disconnect power module 12 way connector.
2. Connect an ohmmeter between pin 3 of power module 12 way and ground.
3. Ohmmeter should show resistance, amount of resistance should be between 8000 and 29000 thousand ohms.
4. Correct resistance, repair wire in cavity No. 20 of logic module (black EFI blue turbo) and cavity No. 3 of power module 12 way connector. Open circuit, replace power module.

Disassembly and Assembly

At the time of publication disassembly and assembly procedures were not available from the manufacturer.

Delcotron Alternator

Delcotron alternators are available with different idle outputs and rated amp outputs.

All models incorporate a solid state voltage regulator which is mounted inside the alternator. The construction and operation of each alternator is basically the same. The Delcotron alternator consists of two end frame assemblies, a rotor, a stator, brushes, slip rings and diodes. The rotor is supported in the drive end frame by ball bearings and in the slip ring end frame by roller bearings. The bearings do not require periodic lubrication.

There are two brushes which carry current through the slip rings to the field coil. The field coil is mounted on the rotor. The stator windings are assembled on the inside of a laminated core that is part of the alternator frame. The rectifier bridge which is connected to the stator windings contains six diodes, three of which are negative and three of which are positive. The positive and negative diodes are moulded into the assembly. The rectifier bridge changes stator AC voltage into DC voltage which appears at the output "Bat" terminal.

The blocking action of the diodes prevents the battery from discharging, back through the alternator. The need for a cutout relay is eliminated because of this blocking action. The alternator field current is supplied through a diode trio, which is connected to the stator windings. A capacitor is mounted in the end frame to protect the rectifier bridge and the six diodes from high voltage and radio interference. Periodic alternator adjustment or maintenance is not required. The voltage regulator is preset and needs no adjustment.

Delcotron Alternator Availability Chart

Alternator Type	Rated Amp Output
10SI	37, 42, 63
12SI	56, 66, 78, 94
15SI	70, 85
17SI	—
27SI	65, 80, 100

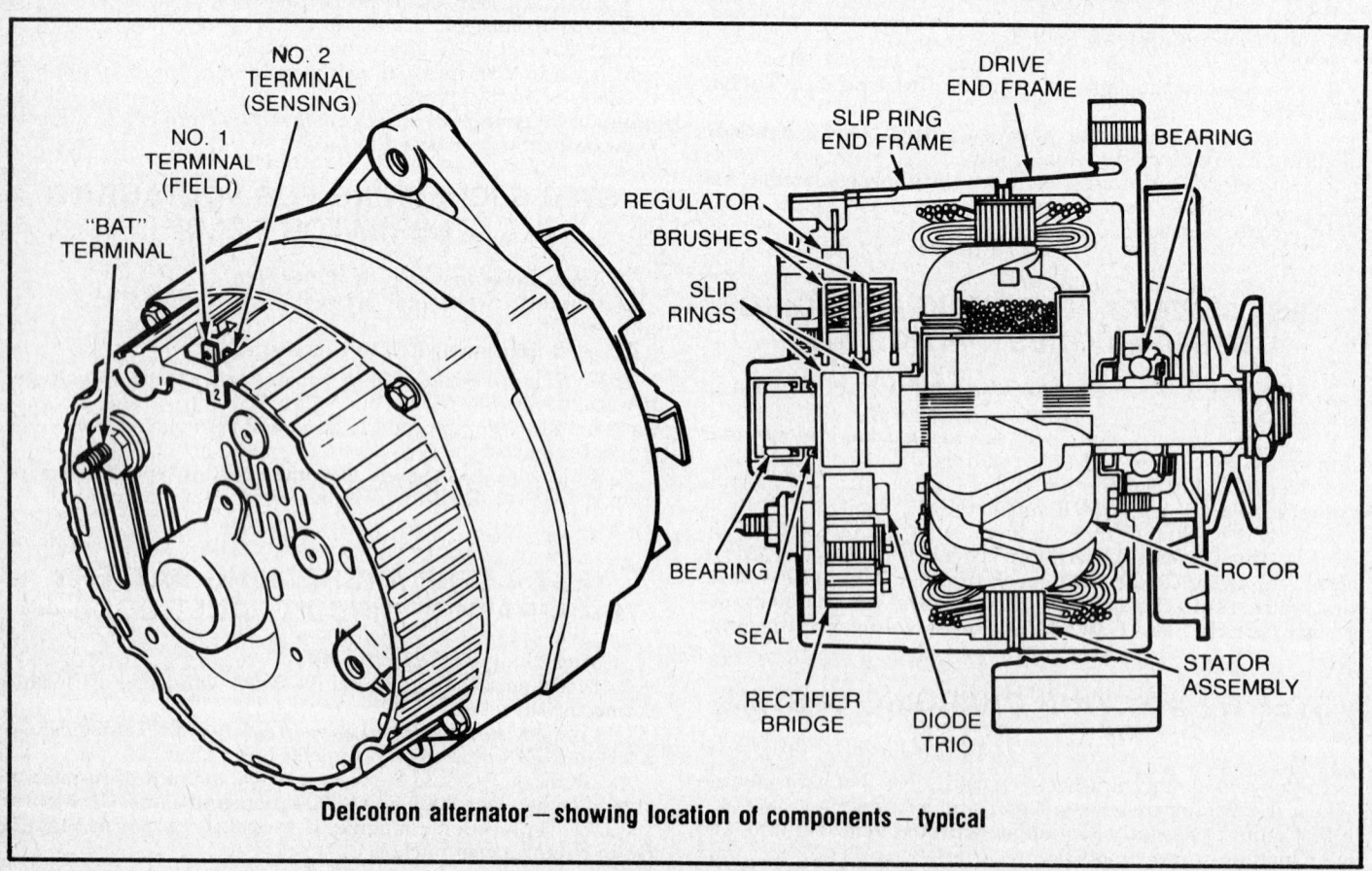

Delcotron alternator—showing location of components—typical

ALTERNATORS
GM DELCOTRON (W/INTERNAL REGULATOR)
Section 21

DIAGNOSTIC TESTING

Indicator Lamp Operation Test

1. Check the indicator lamp for normal operation. If the indicator lamp operates properly refer to the undercharged battery test. If the indicator lamp does not operate properly, proceed accordingly.
2. Switch off, lamp on. Unplug the connector from the generator No. 1 and No. 2 terminals. If the lamp stays on, there is a short between these two leads. If the lamp goes out, replace the rectifier bridge.
3. Switch on, lamp off, engine stopped. This condition can be caused by the defects listed above or by an open in the circuit. To determine where an open exists proceed as follows. Check for a blown fuse, or fusible link, a burned out bulb, defective bulb socket, or an open in No. 1 lead circuit between generator and ignition switch. If no defects have been found proceed to undercharged battery test.
4. Switch on, lamp on, engine running. Check for a blown fuse, (where used), between indicator lamp and switch, and also in A/C circuit.

Undercharged Battery Test

1. Be sure that the undercharged battery condition has not been caused by accessories that have been left on for an extended period of time.
2. Check the alternator belt for proper belt tension. Inspect the battery for physical defects replace as required.
3. Inspect the wiring for defects. Check all connections for proper contact and cleanliness, including the slip connectors at the generator and baulkhead connections.
4. With ignition switch "on" and all wiring harness leads connected, connect a voltmeter from the generator "Bat" terminal to ground, from the generator No. 1 terminal to ground and from the generator No. 2 terminal to ground. A zero reading indicates an open between voltmeter connection and battery.
5. Delcotron alternators have a built in feature which prevents overcharge and accessory damage by preventing the alternator from turning on if there is an open in the wiring harness connected to the No. 2 alternator terminal.
6. If Steps 1 through 5 check out okay, check the alternator as follows. Disconnect negative battery cable. Connect an ammeter or alternator tester in the circuit at the "Bat" terminal of the alternator. Reconnect negative battery cable.
7. Turn on radio, windshield wipers, lights high beam and blower motor on high speed. Connect a carbon pile across the battery (or use alternator tester). Operate engine about 2000 rpm, and adjust carbon pile as required, to obtain maximum current output. If ampere output is within 10 amperes of rated output as stamped on generator frame, alternator is not defective. Recheck Steps 1 through 5.
8. If ampere output is not within 10 percent of rated output, determine if test hole is accessible. Ground the field winding by inserting a suitable tool into the test hole. Tab is within ¾ inch of casting surface. Do not force suitable tool deeper than one inch into end frame to avoid damaging alternator.

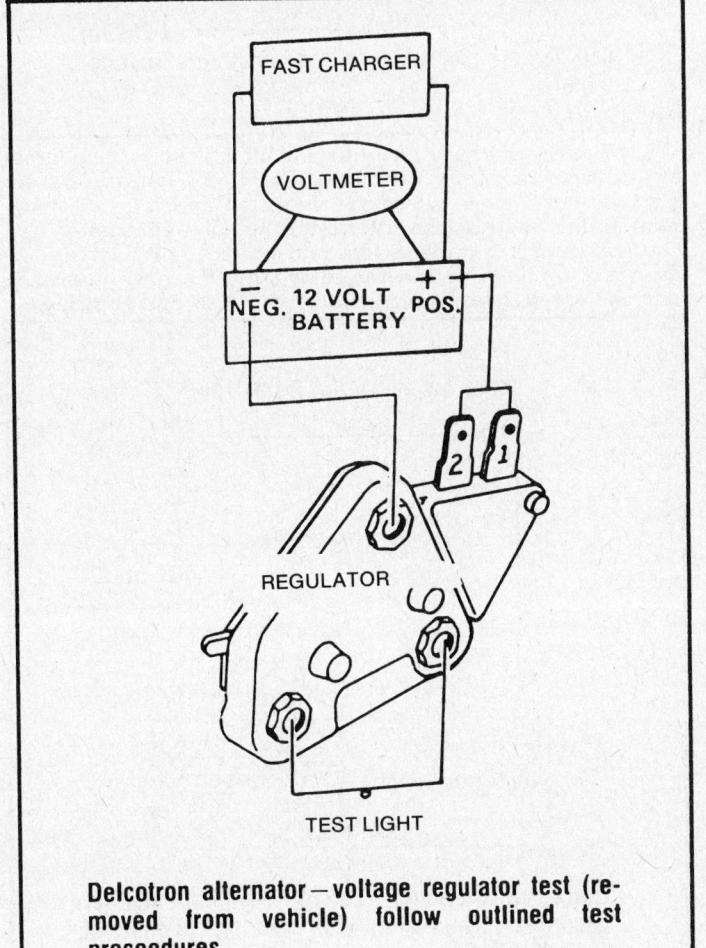

Delcotron alternator — voltage regulator test (removed from vehicle) follow outlined test proceedures

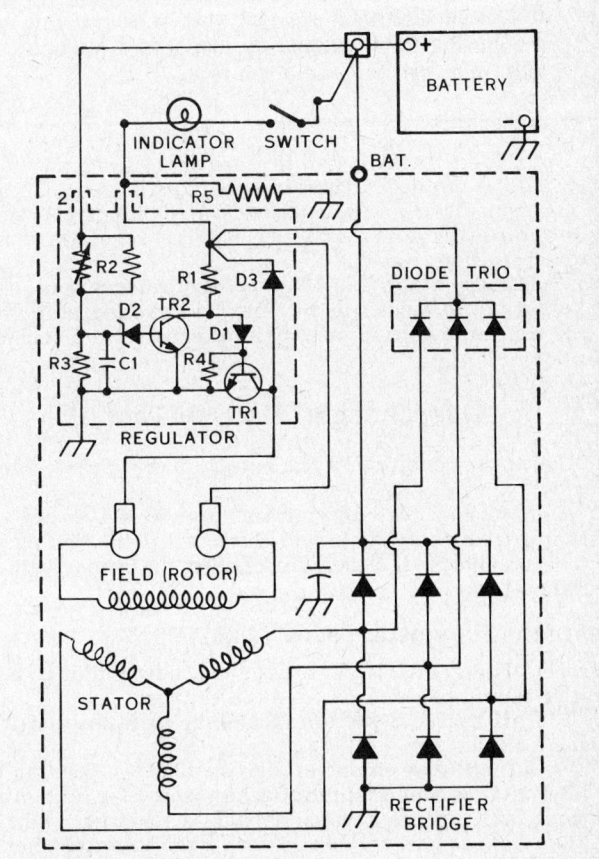

Typical Delcotron charging system wiring schematic

21-37

SECTION 21 ALTERNATORS
GM DELCOTRON (W/INTERNAL REGULATOR)

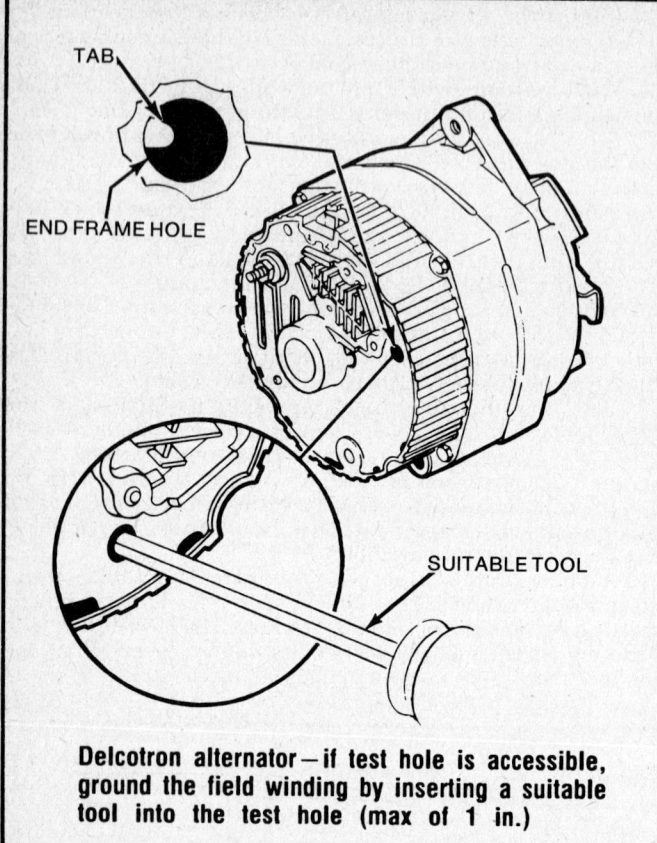

Delcotron alternator—if test hole is accessible, ground the field winding by inserting a suitable tool into the test hole (max of 1 in.)

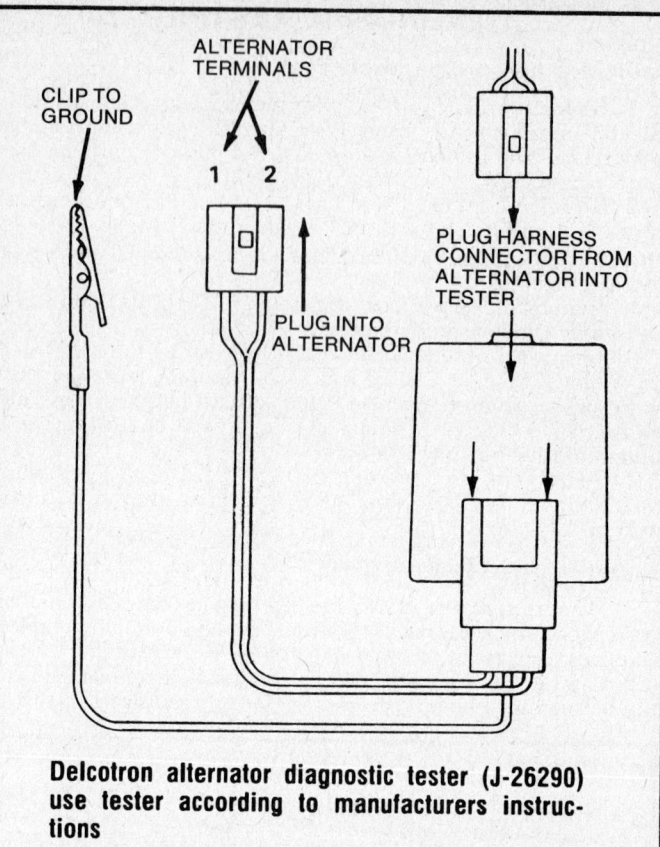

Delcotron alternator diagnostic tester (J-26290) use tester according to manufacturers instructions

9. Operate engine at moderate speed as required, and adjust carbon pile as required to obtain maximum current output.

10. If output is within 10 amperes of rated output, check field winding, diode trio, and rectifier bridge. Test regulator with an approved regulator tested.

11. If output is not within 10 amperes of rated output, check the field winding, diode trio, rectifier bridge, and stator. If test hole is not accessible, disassemble alternator and repair as required.

Overcharged Battery Test

1. Check the condition of the battery before any testing is done.
2. If an obvious overcharging condition exists, remove the alternator from the vehicle and check the field windings for grounds or shorts. If defective, replace the rotor. Test the regulator.

Alternator Diagnostic Tester (J-26290)

This special diagnostic tester is designed to determine if the alternator should be removed from the vehicle.

1. Install tester J-26290 according to manufacturers instructions.
2. With the engine off and all lights and accessories off, test the alternator as follows. Light flashes, go to Step 3. Light on, indicates fault in tester which should be replaced. Light off, pull plug from generator. One flashing light, indicates that the alternator should be removed and the rectifier bridge replaced. Light off, indicates faulty tester or no voltage to tester. Check for 12 volts at #2 terminal of harness connector. Repair wiring or terminals if 12 volts is not available. Replace tester if 12 volts is available.

3. With the engine at fast idle and all accessories and lights off, test the alternator as follows. Light off--charging system good, do not remove alternator. Light on--indicates a component failure within the alternator. Remove alternator and check diode trio, rectifier bridge and stator. Light flashing--indicates a problem within the alternator. Remove alternator and check regulator, rotor field coil, brushes and slip rings.

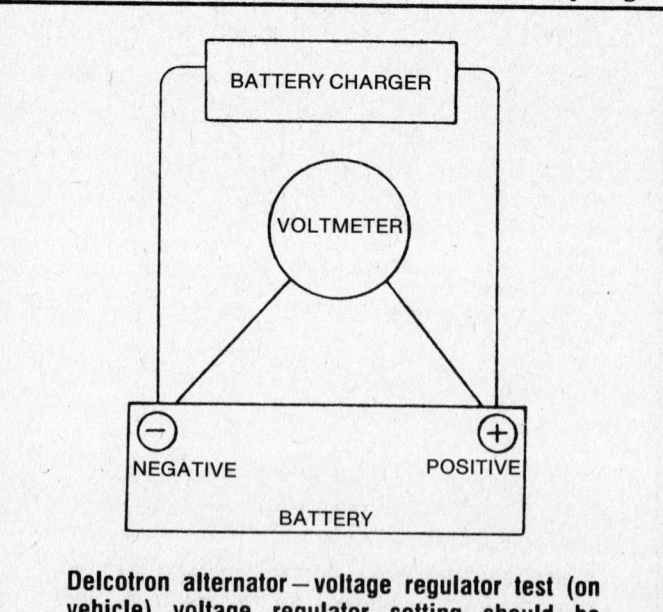

Delcotron alternator—voltage regulator test (on vehicle) voltage regulator setting should be 13.5-16.0 volts

21-38

ALTERNATORS
SYSTEM ELECTRICAL DIAGNOSIS
SECTION 21

GM CHARGING SYSTEM TROUBLE DIAGNOSIS

 Graphic Mode Diagnosis & Repair Chart

Problem: Generator Light "ON" – Engine Running

21-39

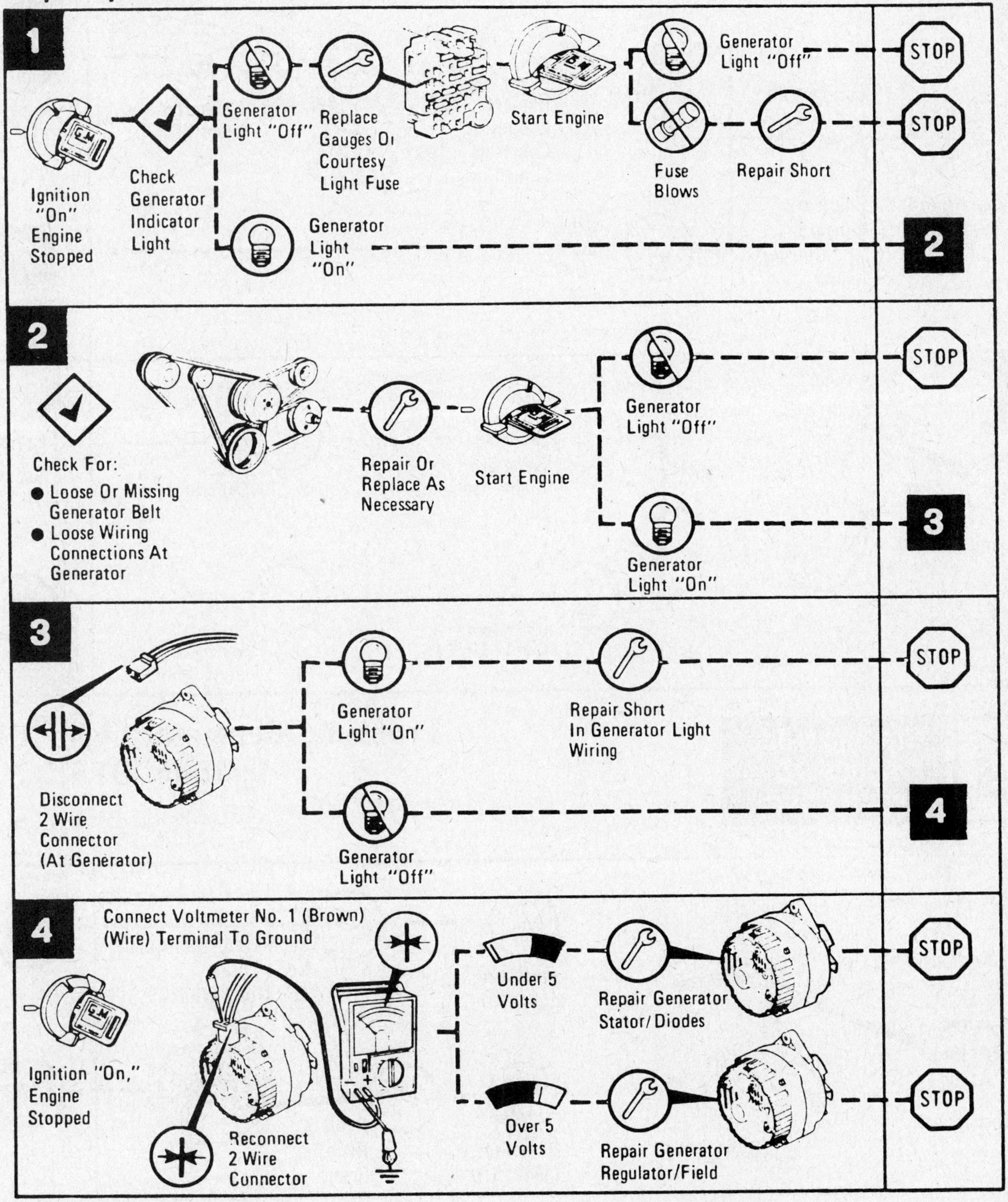

SECTION 21 ALTERNATORS
SYSTEM ELECTRICAL DIAGNOSIS

Graphic Mode Diagnosis & Repair Chart

Problem: Generator Light "OFF," Ignition "ON," Engine Not Running

Step/Sequence — Result

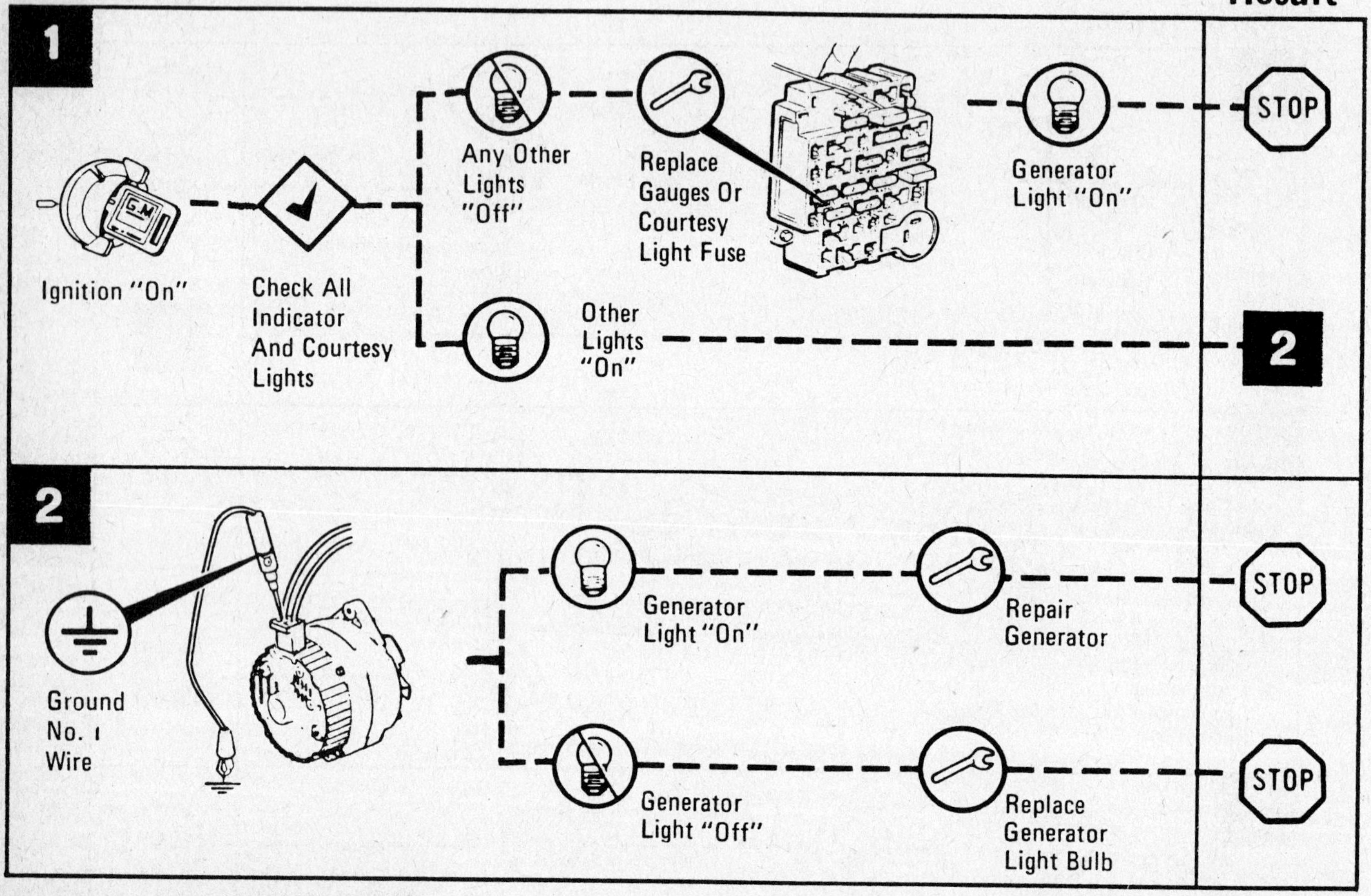

1. Ignition "On" → Check All Indicator And Courtesy Lights
- Any Other Lights "Off" → Replace Gauges Or Courtesy Light Fuse → Generator Light "On" → STOP
- Other Lights "On" → 2

2. Ground No. 1 Wire
- Generator Light "On" → Repair Generator → STOP
- Generator Light "Off" → Replace Generator Light Bulb → STOP

Graphic Mode Diagnosis & Repair Chart

Problem: Generator Light "ON," Ignition "OFF"

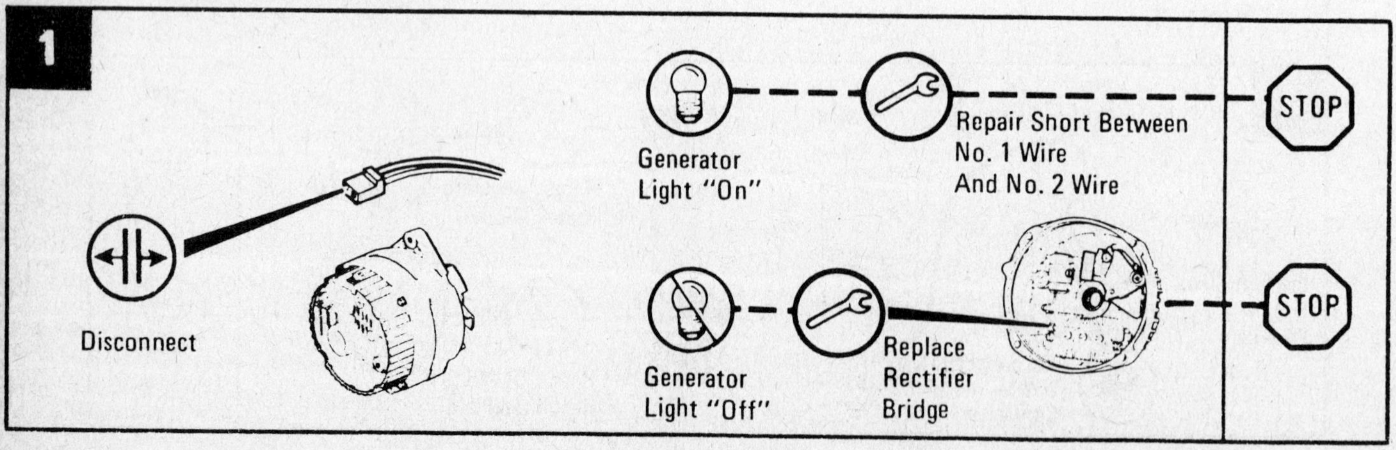

1. Disconnect
- Generator Light "On" → Repair Short Between No. 1 Wire And No. 2 Wire → STOP
- Generator Light "Off" → Replace Rectifier Bridge → STOP

21-40

ALTERNATORS
SYSTEM ELECTRICAL DIAGNOSIS — SECTION 21

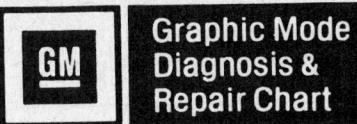
Graphic Mode Diagnosis & Repair Chart

Problem: Battery Does Not Stay Charged (Generator Indicator Light OK)

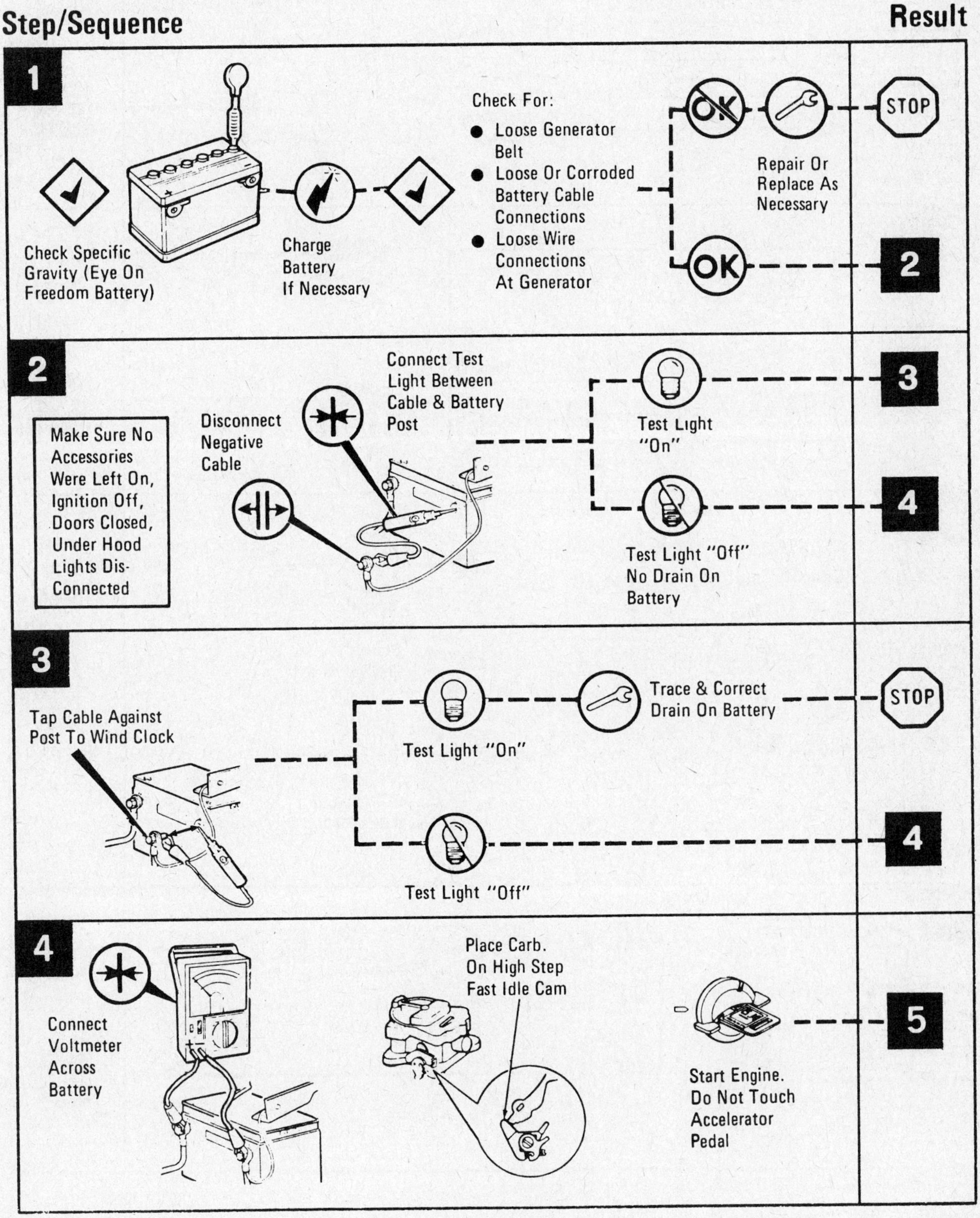

Step/Sequence — **Result**

1
- Check Specific Gravity (Eye On Freedom Battery)
- Charge Battery If Necessary
- Check For:
  - Loose Generator Belt
  - Loose Or Corroded Battery Cable Connections
  - Loose Wire Connections At Generator
- OK → Repair Or Replace As Necessary → STOP
- OK → **2**

2
Make Sure No Accessories Were Left On, Ignition Off, Doors Closed, Under Hood Lights Disconnected
- Disconnect Negative Cable
- Connect Test Light Between Cable & Battery Post
- Test Light "On" → **3**
- Test Light "Off" No Drain On Battery → **4**

3
Tap Cable Against Post To Wind Clock
- Test Light "On" → Trace & Correct Drain On Battery → STOP
- Test Light "Off" → **4**

4
- Connect Voltmeter Across Battery
- Place Carb. On High Step Fast Idle Cam
- Start Engine. Do Not Touch Accelerator Pedal → **5**

21-41

SECTION 21 ALTERNATORS
SYSTEM ELECTRICAL DIAGNOSIS

Step/Sequence — **Result**

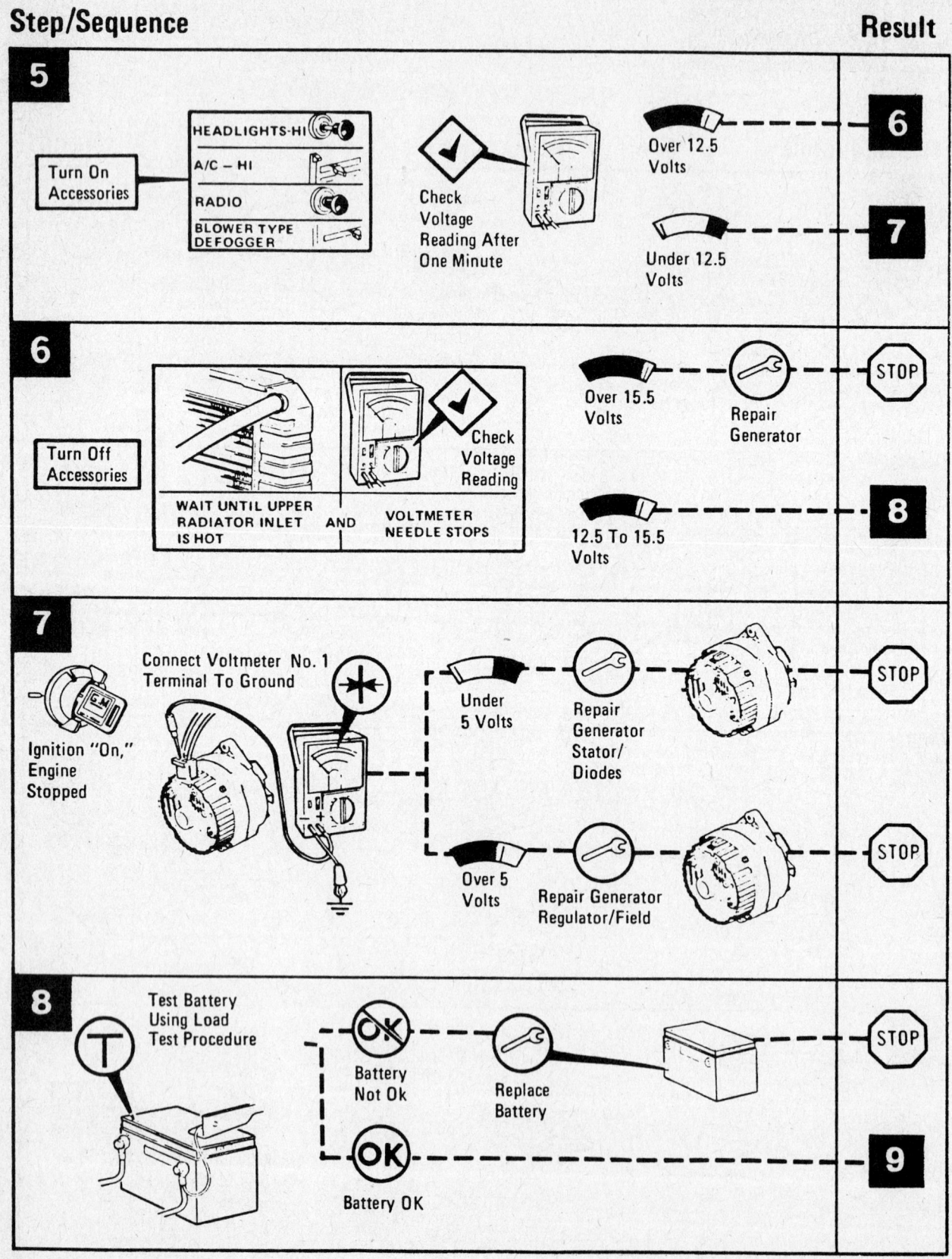

21-42

ALTERNATORS
SYSTEM ELECTRICAL DIAGNOSIS
SECTION 21

Step/Sequence — **Result**

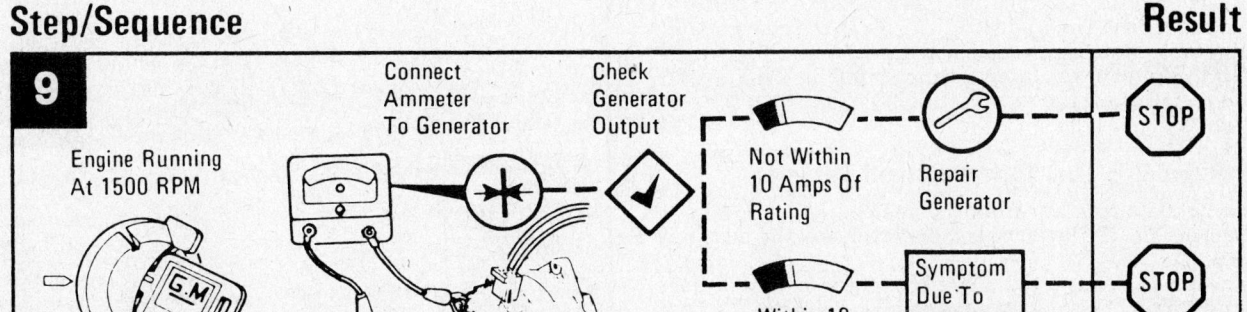

 **Graphic Mode Diagnosis & Repair Chart**

Problem: Battery Overcharged (uses too much water)

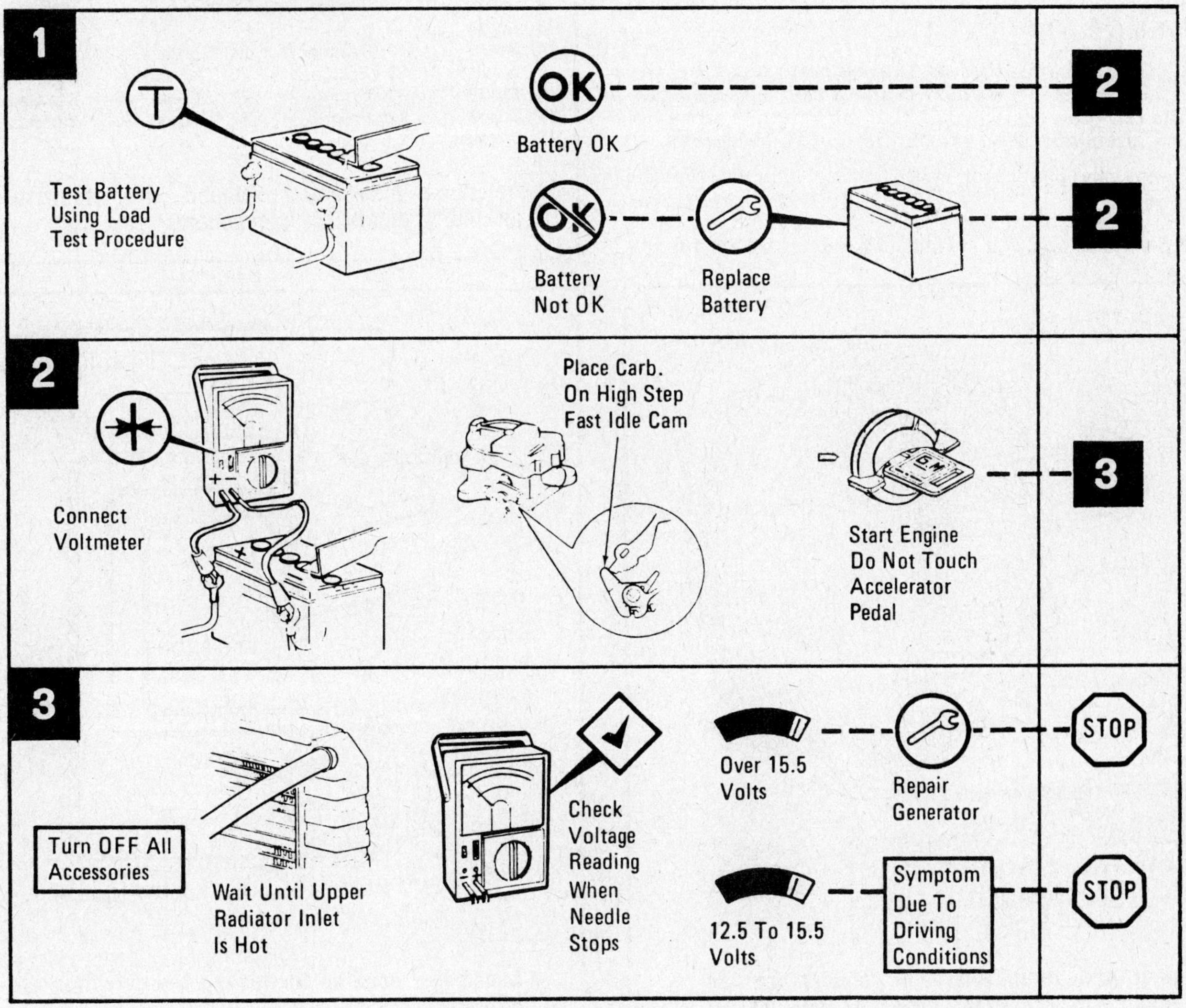

Step 1: Test Battery Using Load Test Procedure
- Battery OK → 2
- Battery Not OK → Replace Battery → 2

Step 2: Connect Voltmeter. Place Carb. On High Step Fast Idle Cam. Start Engine Do Not Touch Accelerator Pedal → 3

Step 3: Turn OFF All Accessories. Wait Until Upper Radiator Inlet Is Hot. Check Voltage Reading When Needle Stops.
- Over 15.5 Volts → Repair Generator → STOP
- 12.5 To 15.5 Volts → Symptom Due To Driving Conditions → STOP

21-43

SECTION 21 ALTERNATORS
GM DELCOTRON (W/INTERNAL REGULATOR)

Voltage Regulator Test (Alternator on Vehicle)

1. Connect a battery charger and a voltmeter to the battery.
2. Turn the ignition on and slowly increase the charge rate. The alternator light in the vehicle will dim at the voltage regulator setting. Voltage regulator setting should be 13.5 to 16.0 volts. This test works if the rotor setting is good, even if the stator rectifier bridge or diode trio is bad.

Voltage Regulator Test (Alternator off Vehicle)

1. Remove the alternator from the vehicle.
2. Disassemble the alternator and remove the voltage regulator.
3. Connect a voltmeter and a fast charger to a 12 volt battery. Connect a test light to the regulator and observe the battery polarity.
4. The test light should light.
5. Turn on the fast charger and slowly increase the charge rate. Observe the voltmeter, the light should go out at the voltage regualtor setting. The voltage regulator setting specification is 13.5 to 16.0 volts.

Alternator Bench Test

1. Remove the alternator from the vehicle. Position the unit in a suitable test stand.
2. Connect the alternator in series, but leave the carbon pile disconnected.

NOTE: Ground polarity of the battery must be the same as the alternator. Be sure to use a fully charged battery and a ten ohm resistor rated at six watts or more between the alternator No. 1 terminal and the battery.

3. Increase the alternator speed slowly and observe the voltage.
4. If the voltage is uncontrolled with speed and increases above 15.5 volts on a 12 volt system, or 31 volts on a 24 volt sys-

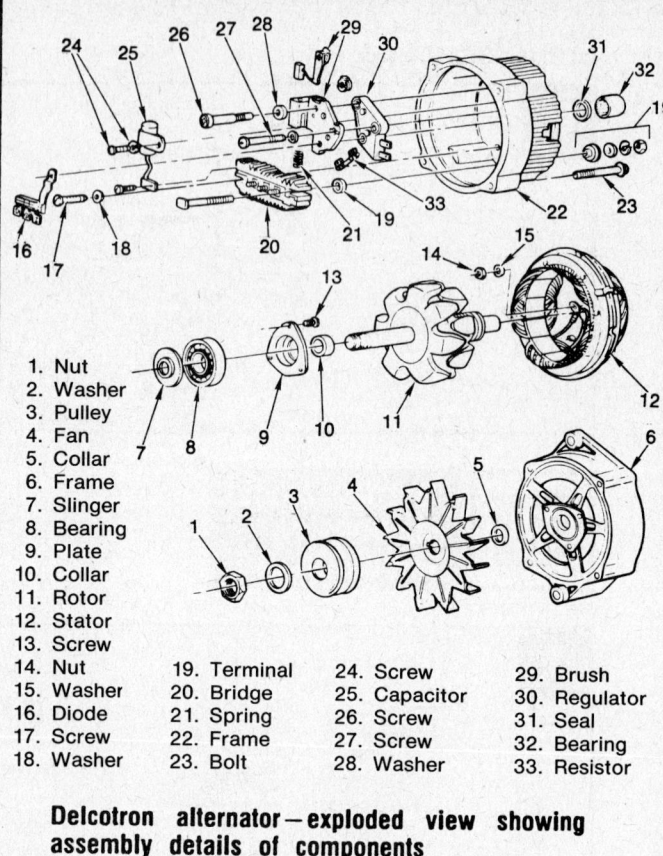

1. Nut
2. Washer
3. Pulley
4. Fan
5. Collar
6. Frame
7. Slinger
8. Bearing
9. Plate
10. Collar
11. Rotor
12. Stator
13. Screw
14. Nut
15. Washer
16. Diode
17. Screw
18. Washer
19. Terminal
20. Bridge
21. Spring
22. Frame
23. Bolt
24. Screw
25. Capacitor
26. Screw
27. Screw
28. Washer
29. Brush
30. Regulator
31. Seal
32. Bearing
33. Resistor

Delcotron alternator—exploded view showing assembly details of components

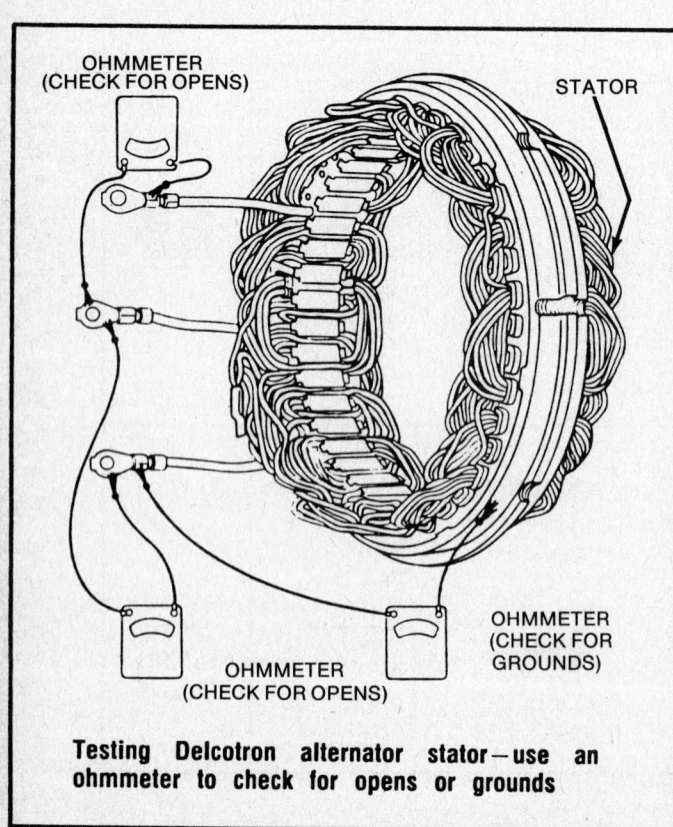

Testing Delcotron alternator stator—use an ohmmeter to check for opens or grounds

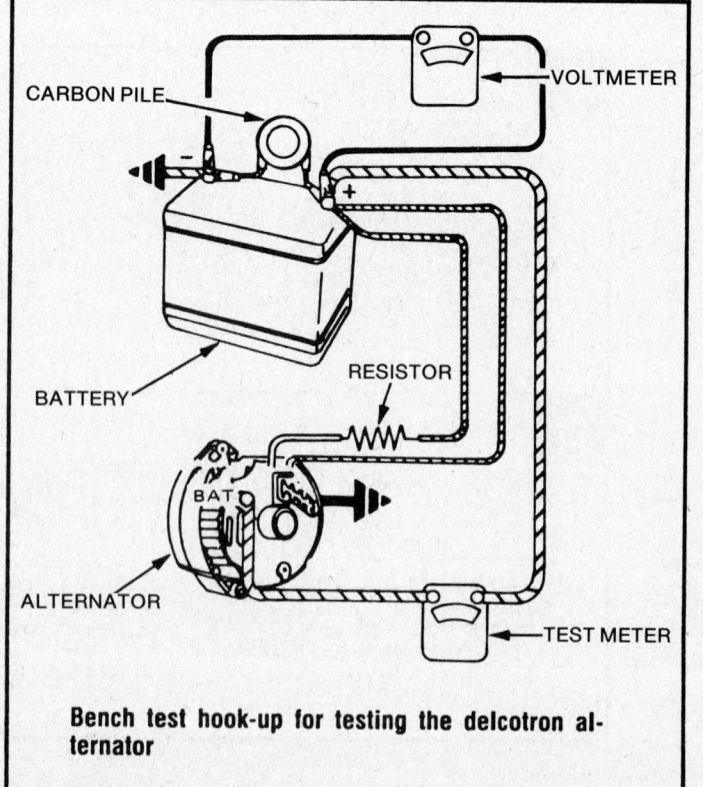

Bench test hook-up for testing the delcotron alternator

ALTERNATORS
GM DELCOTRON (W/INTERNAL REGULATOR)
SECTION 21

tem, test regulator with an approved regulator tester, and check field winding. If voltage is below 15.5 volts on a 12 volt system, or 31 volts on a 24 volt system, connect the carbon pile.

5. Operate the alternator at moderate speed as required and adjust the carbon pile as required to obtain maximum current output.

6. If output is within 10 amperes of rated output as stamped on alternator frame, alternator is good. If output is not within 10 amperes of rated output, keep battery loaded with carbon pile, and ground alternator field.

7. Operate alternator at moderate speed and adjust carbon pile as required to obtain maximum output. If output is within 10 amperes of rated output, test regulator with an approved regulator tester, and check field winding.

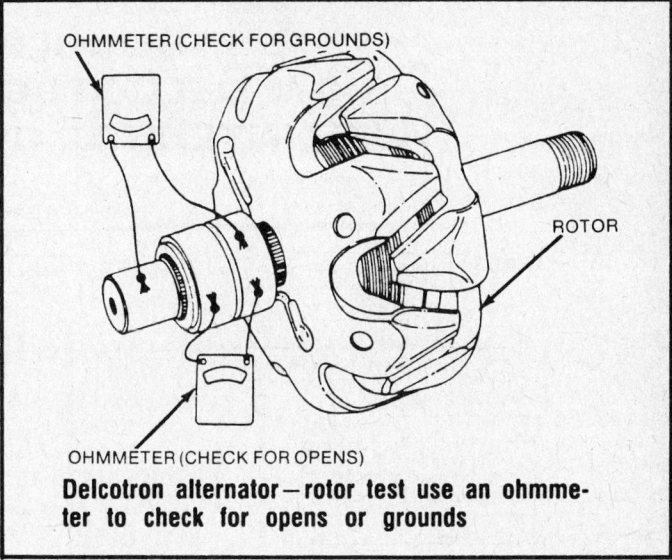

Delcotron alternator—rotor test use an ohmmeter to check for opens or grounds

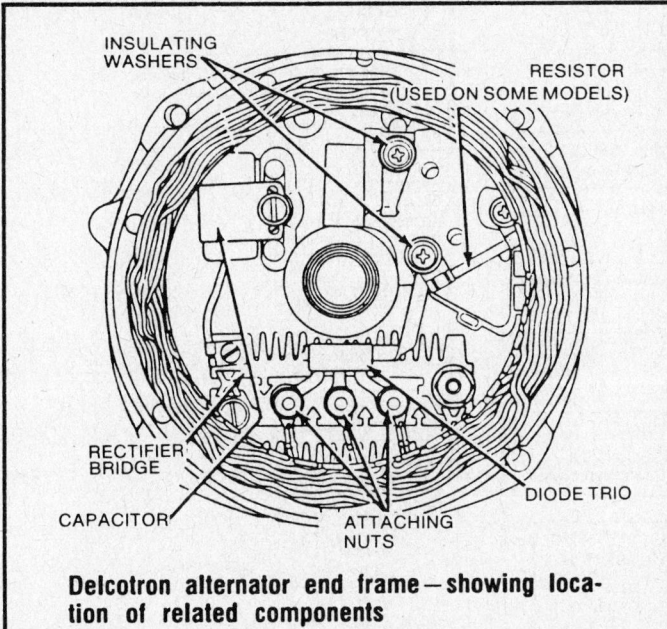

Delcotron alternator end frame—showing location of related components

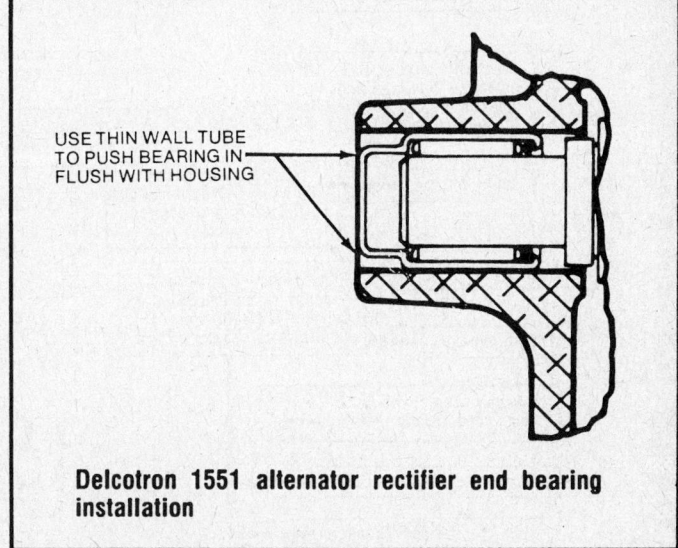

Delcotron 1551 alternator rectifier end bearing installation

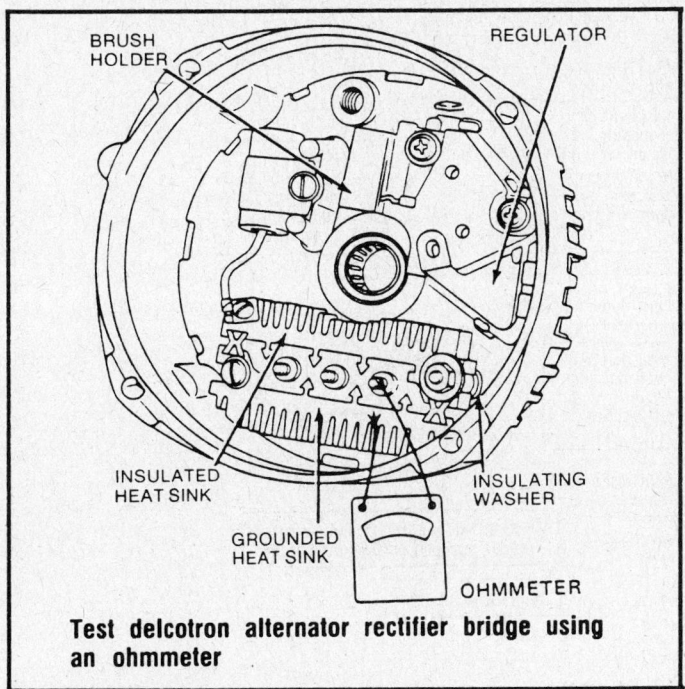

Test delcotron alternator rectifier bridge using an ohmmeter

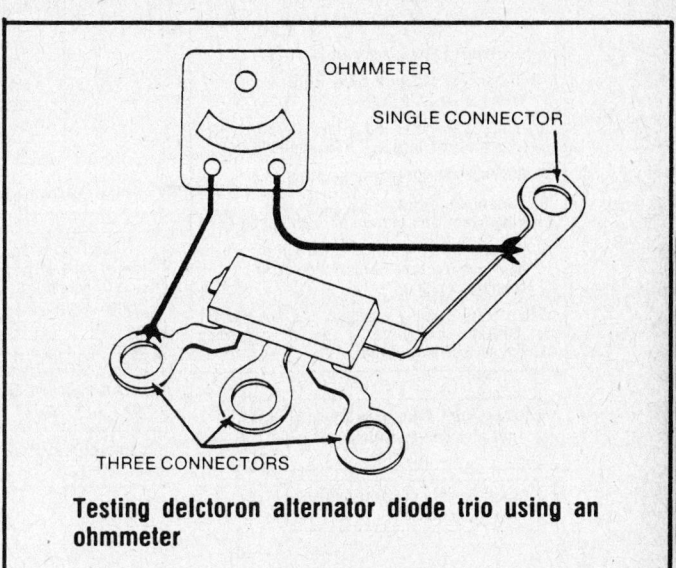

Testing delctoron alternator diode trio using an ohmmeter

21–45

SECTION 21 ALTERNATORS
GM DELCOTRON (W/INTERNAL REGULATOR)

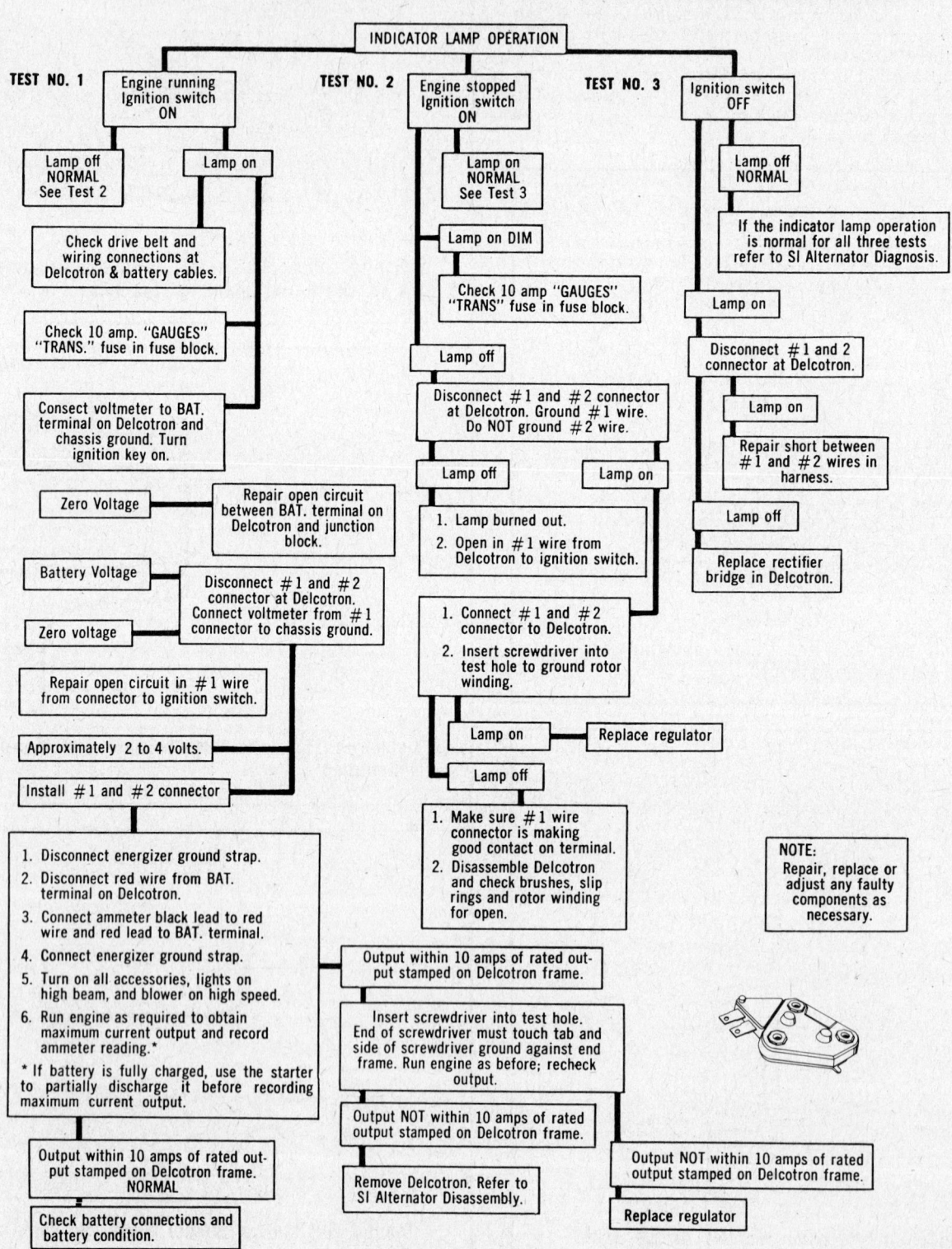

TROUBLESHOOTING GM DELCOTRON ALTERNATOR (WITH INTERNAL CONTROL REGULATOR)

21-46

ALTERNATORS
DELCOTRON (W/INTERNAL REGULATOR)
SECTION 21

9. If output is not within 10 amperes of rated output, check the field winding, diode trio, rectifier bridge, and stator.

Disassembly and Assembly

1. Remove the alternator from the vehicle. Position the assembly in a suitable holding fixture.
2. Make scribe marks on the alternator case end frames to aid in reassembly.
3. Remove the four through bolts that retain the assembly together. Separate the drive end frame assembly from the rectifier end frame assembly.
4. Remove the three rectifier attaching nuts and the three regulator attaching screws from the end frame assembly.
5. Separate the stator, diode trio and voltage regulator from the end frame assembly.
6. On the 10SI alternator, check the stator for opens using an ohmmeter. If high readings are obtained replace the stator.
7. Check the stator for grounds using an ohmmeter. If readings are low replace the stator.
8. Using an ohmmeter check the rotor for grounds. The ohmmeter reading should be very high if not replace the rotor.
9. Using an ohmmeter, check the rotor for opens. If the ohmmeter reading is not 2.4 to 3.5 ohms replace the rotor.
10. To check the diode trio connect the ohmmeter to the diode trio and then reverse the lead connections. The ohmmeter should read high and low if not replace the diode trio. Repeat the same test between the single connector and each of the other connectors.
11. Check rectifier bridge with ohmmeter connected from grounded heat sink to flat metal on terminal. Reverse leads. If both readings are the same replace rectifier bridge.
12. Repeat test between grounded heat sink and other two flat metal clips.
13. Repeat test between insulated heat sink and three flat metal clips.

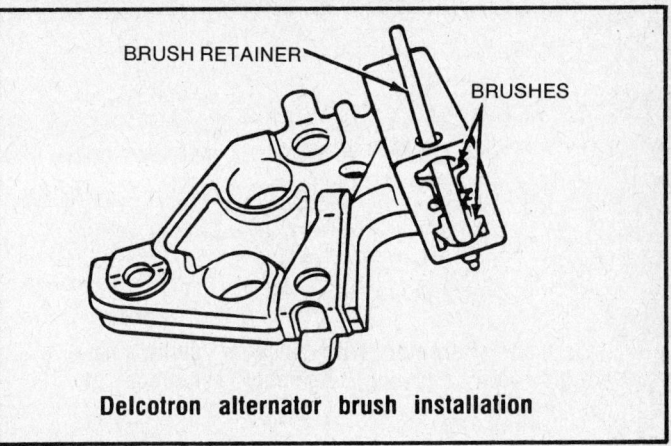

Delcotron alternator brush installation

14. Clean or replace the alternator brushes as required. Position the brushes in the brush holder and retain them in place using the brush retainer wire or equivalent.
15. To remove the rotor and drive end bearing, remove the shaft nut, washer and pulley, fan and collar. Push the rotor from the housing.
16. Remove the retainer plate from inside the drive end frame. Push the bearing out. Clean or replace parts as required.
17. Press against the outer bearing race to push the bearing in. On early production alternators it will be necessary to fill the bearing cavity with lubricant. Late production alternators use a sealed bearing and lubricant is not required for assembly.
18. Press rotor into end frame. Assemble collar, fan, pulley, washer, and nut. Torque shaft nut 40 to 60 ft. lbs.
19. Push slip ring end bearing out from outside toward inside of end frame.
20. On 10SI and 15SI, place flat plate over new bearing and press from outside toward inside until bearing is flush with end frame.
21. On 15SI alternators use the thin wall tube in the space between the grease cup and the housing to push the bearing in flush with the housing.
22. Assemble brush holder, regulator, resistor, diode trio, rectifier bridge and stator to slip ring end frame.
23. Assemble end frames together with through bolts. Remove brush retainer wire.

Delcotron Alternator with Rear Vacuum Pump

The Delcotron alternator with rear vacuum pump, which is manufactured by Mitsubishi, is basically the same as the Delcotron alternator with the exception of a rear vacuum pump which is mounted on the back of the alternator assembly. The vacuum pump is driven by the alternator shaft and is used to provide vacuum to various control systems throughout the vehicle that this alternator is used on.

Disassembly

1. Remove the alternator from the vehicle. Position the unit in a suitable holding fixture.
2. Remove the vacuum pump retaining bolts. Remove the vacuum pump from the rear of the alternator while holding the center plate.
3. Remove the brush cover retaining bolts and brushes. Wrap the pump drive shaft spline with tape in order to protect the rear seal from damage.

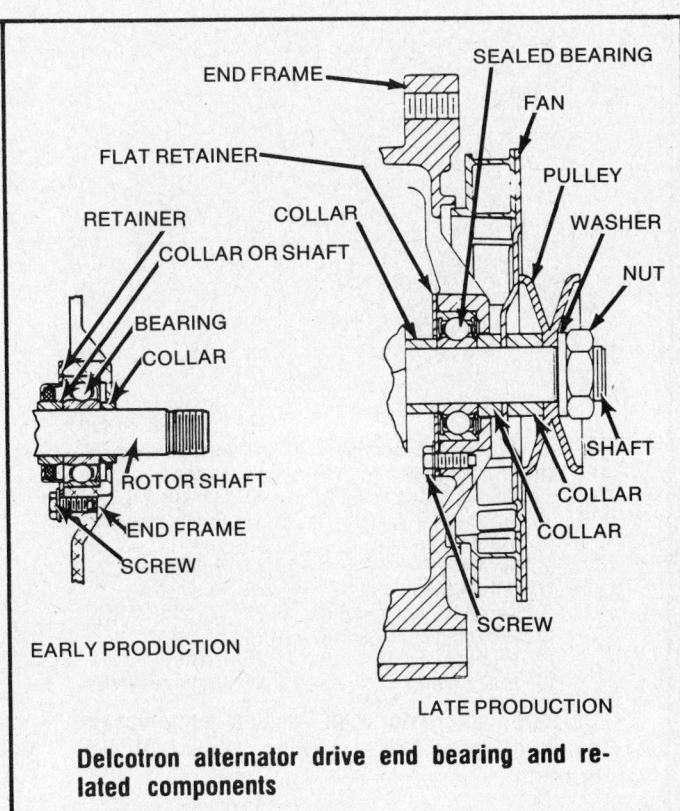

Delcotron alternator drive end bearing and related components

SECTION 21 ALTERNATORS
GM DELCOTRON (W/VACUUM PUMP)

Delcotron alternator with vacuum pump—exploded view showing assembly sequence of components

4. Inspect the vacuum pump for wear and damage, replace defective components as required. Measure the length of the vanes, replace if not within specification (0.511 to 0.531 in.) Measure the inside diameter of the housing and replace if not within specification (2.440 to 2.441 in.).
5. Examine the check valve for damage. Apply light pressure to the valve and make sure that the valve operates properly. Replace as required.
6. Check the inner face of the rear cover on the vacuum pump for oil leakage. Check the inner face of the oil seal for wear and damage. Replace the oil seal in the rear end housing of the vacuum pump as required.
7. Remove the alternator through bolts which hold the unit together. Match mark the assembly to aid in reassembly. Separate the front end housing from the stator and rear end housing.
8. Remove the pulley nut, fan and front end housing from the rotor.
9. Remove the front bearing retainer screws. Remove the front bearing retainer and the bearing from the front end housing.
10. Remove the bolt and nuts retaining the stator, diodes and brush holder to the rear end housing. Note the position of the insulating washers for reassembly.
11. Separate the rear end housing from the stator and diode assembly.
12. Remove the diodes from the stator by melting the solder from the terminals. Be sure to protect the diodes while melting the solder.
13. Remove the solder from the voltage regulator holder plate terminal. Remove the voltage regulator.
14. Check the slip ring surfaces of the rotor for wear and damage, repair or replace as required.
15. Measure the outside diameter of the rotor slip rings. If ring diameter is not 1.18 to 1.24 in., replace the rotor.
16. Connect the ohmmeter test leads to each slip ring. Resistance should be 4.2 ohms at 68°F. If continuity does not exist the coil is open and the rotor must be replaced.
17. Connect the ohmmeter to either slip ring and the rotor core. If continuity exists the coil is grounded and the rotor must be replaced.
18. Check the front and rear rotor bearings for wear and damage. Replace defective parts as required.
19. Check for continuity across the stator coils. If continuity does not exist in any one stator coil replace the stator assembly.
20. Check for continuity across any of the stator coils and the stator core. If continuity exists one of the stator coils is grounded and the stator must be replaced.
21. Coil resistance should be 0.05 ohms at 68°F, and should be measured from the coil lead to terminal "N".
22. Inspect the alternator brush assembly for wear and damage. Replace defective components as required.
23. Check for continuity of positive diodes between each stator coil terminal and "Bat" terminal of rectifier assembly. Reverse ohmmeter leads and recheck for continuity.
24. If continuity exists in both polarity directions or does not exist in both directions diode is defective and must be replaced.
25. Check for continuity of negative diodes between each stator lead and "E" terminal or rectifier assembly. Reverse ohmmeter leads and recheck for continuity. Continuity should exist in one direction only.
26. Assemble a test circuit using the following components: One 10 ohm 3 watt resistor (R_1) one 0 to 300 ohm 3 watt variable resistor (R_2), two 12 volt batteries (BAT_1 and BAT_2) and one 0 to 30 volt DC voltmeter.
27. Adjust variable resistor (R_2) until voltage at V_4 reads the same as voltage at V_3 (this should be all the way to one end of travel or zero ohms).
28. Connect the test circuit to the integrated circuit regulator terminals. Measure voltage at V_1 and V_2. Voltage should measure 10 to 13 volts at V_1 and 0 to 2 volts at V_2.
29. Disconnect terminal "S" from circuit and measure voltage at V_3. Voltage at V_3 should be 20 to 26 volts. Reconnect terminal "S".
30. Measure voltage at V_4 while increasing resistance at R_2 from 0 ohms. V_4 voltmeter reading should increase from 2 volts to 10 to 13 volts. Stop increasing R_2 when voltage reaches 10 to 13 volts.
31. If increase at V_4 is interrupted at any point up to 10 to 13 volts, while increasing resistance at R_2, regulator is defective.

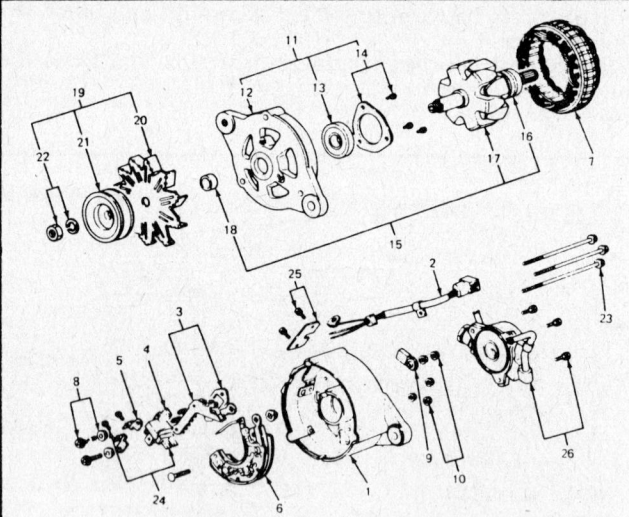

1. Rear cover
2. Lead wire
3. Regulator assembly
4. Brush holder
5. Holder plate
6. Diode
7. Stator
8. Screw
9. Condenser
10. Terminal bolt and nut
11. Front cover assembly
12. Front cover
13. Ball bearing
14. Bearing retainer
15. Rotor assembly
16. Ball bearing
17. Rotor
18. Spacer
19. Pulley assembly
20. Fan
21. Pulley
22. Pulley nut
23. Through bolt
24. Brush
25. Cover
26. Vacuum pump

Delcotron alternator with vacuum pump-vacuum pump disassembled—showing related of components

ALTERNATORS
GM DELCOTRON (W/VACUUM PUMP)

32. Measure voltage at V_4 with R_2 at same setting as previous step that produced 10 to 13 volt reading at V_2. If V_4 not within 14 to 14.6 volts, regulator is defective.

33. Disconnect wire at terminal "S". Connect it to terminal "B". Repeat Step 30. If V_2 does not vary or V_4 is not within 14.5 to 16.6 volts, regulator is defective.

Assembly

1. To assemble the alternator reverse the disassembly procedure.
2. Be sure to check all parts for wear and damage. Replace defective components as required.
3. Insert the brushes into the brush holder and insert a wire to retain them in place. Install the rotor and remove the retaining wire.

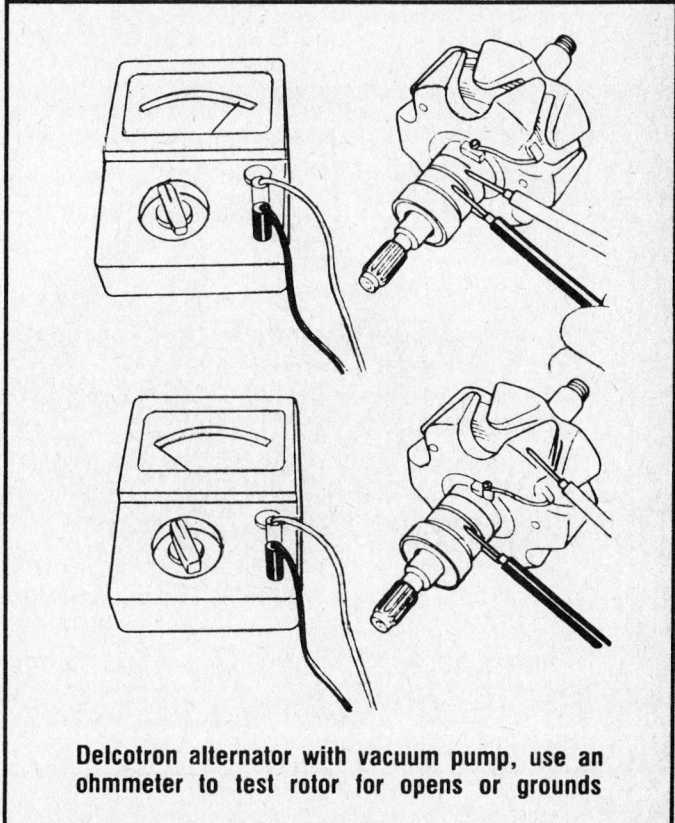

Delcotron alternator with vacuum pump, use an ohmmeter to test rotor for opens or grounds

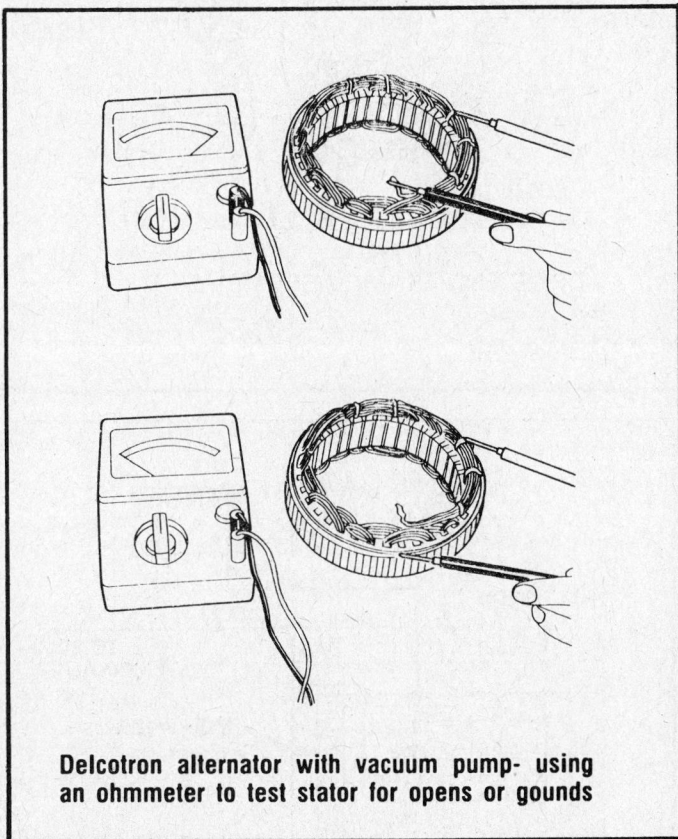

Delcotron alternator with vacuum pump- using an ohmmeter to test stator for opens or gounds

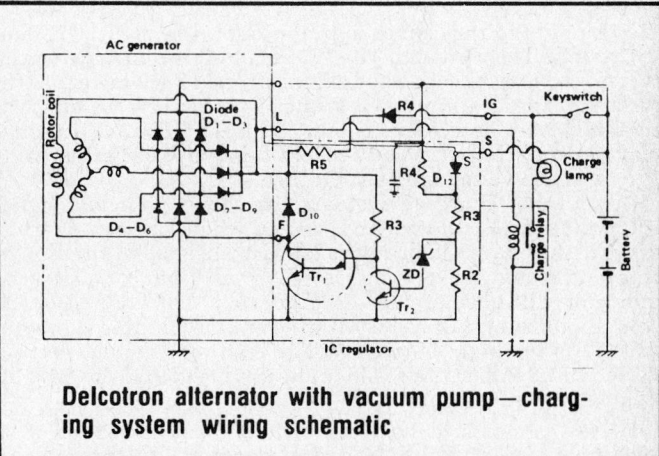

Delcotron alternator with vacuum pump – charging system wiring schematic

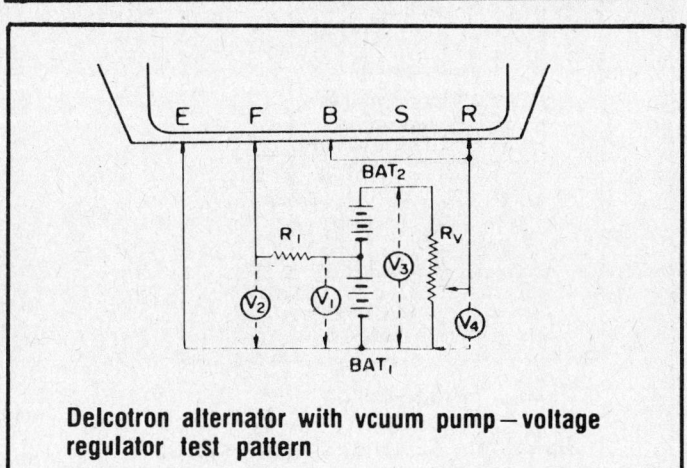

Delcotron alternator with vcuum pump – voltage regulator test pattern

Delcotron CS-130 and CS-144 Alternator
CS CHARGING SYSTEM

Another type of charging system is the CS Charging System. Two sizes are available, CS-130 and CS-144, denoting the OD in mm of the stator laminations. CS generators use a new type regulator an diode trio is not used. A delta stator, rectifier bridge, and rotor with slip rings and brushes are electrically similar to earlier generators. A regular pulley and fan is used and, on the CS-130, an internal fan cools the slip ring end frame, rectifier bridge and regulator.

SECTION 21 ALTERNATORS
GM DELCOTRON (W/VACUUM PUMP)

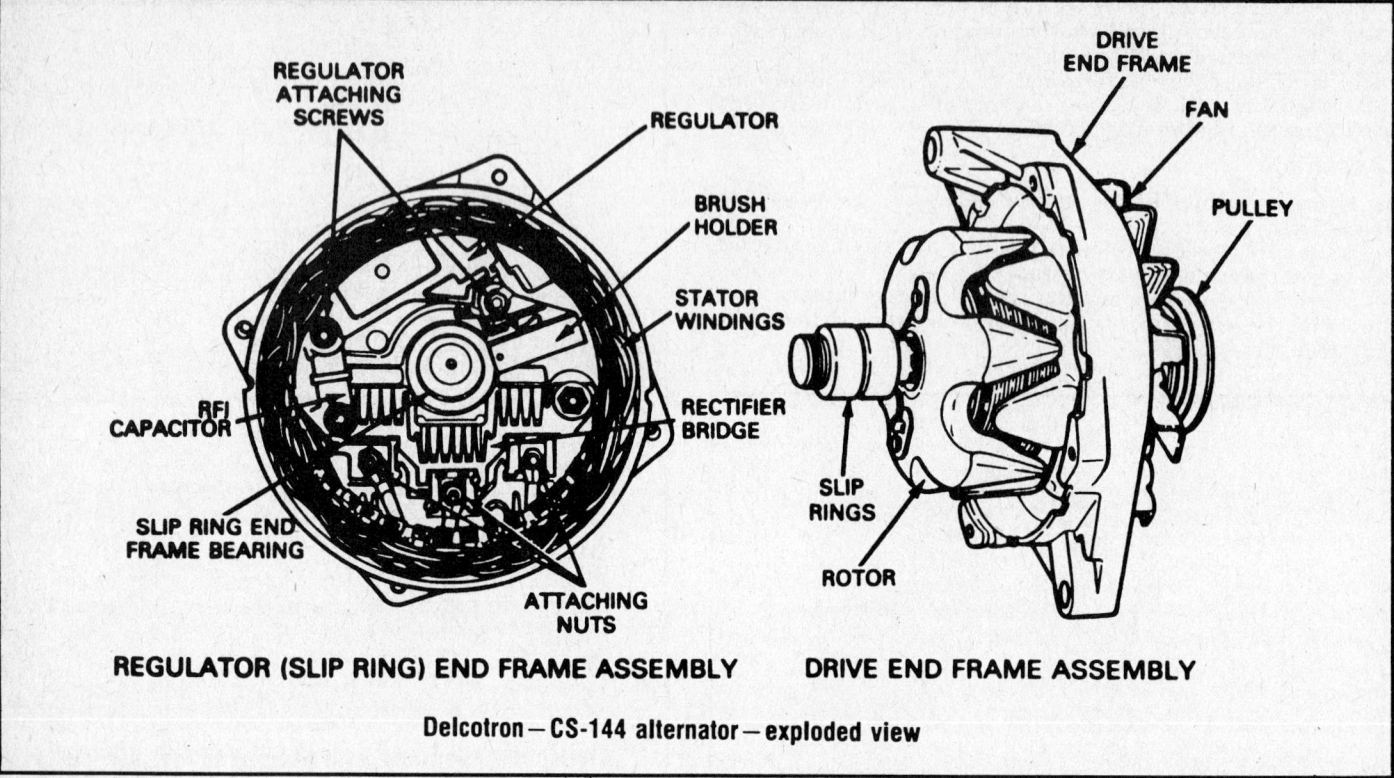

Delcotron—CS-144 alternator—exploded view

Unlike three-wire generators, the CS-130 and CS-144 may be used with only two connections the battery positive and an "L" terminal to the charge indicator bulb. Use of "P", "F" and "S" terminals is optional. The "P" terminal is connected to the stator, and may be connected externally to a tachometer or other device. The "F" terminal is connected internally to field positive, and may be used as a fault indicator. The "S" terminal may be connected externally to a voltage, such as battery voltage, to sense voltage to be controlled.

As on other charging systems, the charge indicator lights when the switch is closed, and goes out when the engine is running. If the charge indicator is on with the engine running, a charging system defect is indicated. For all kinds of defects, the indicator will glow at full brilliance, not "half lit". Also, the charge indicator will be on with the engine running if system voltage is too high or too low. The regulator voltage setting varies with temperature, and limits system voltage by controlling rotor field current.

This regulator switches rotor field current on and off at a fixed frequency of about 400 cycles per second. By varying the on-off time, correct average field current for proper system voltage control is obtained. At high speeds, the on-time may be 10% and the off time 90%. At low speeds, with high electrical loads, on-off time may be 90% and 10% respectively. No periodic maintenance on the generator is required.

CS TYPE ALTERNATOR DIAGNOSIS

When operating normally, the indicator lamp will come on when the ignition switch is turned on and go out when the engine starts. If the lamp operates abnormally, or if an undercharged or overcharged battery condition occurs, the following procedure may be used to diagnose the charging system. Remember that an undercharged battery is often caused by acces-

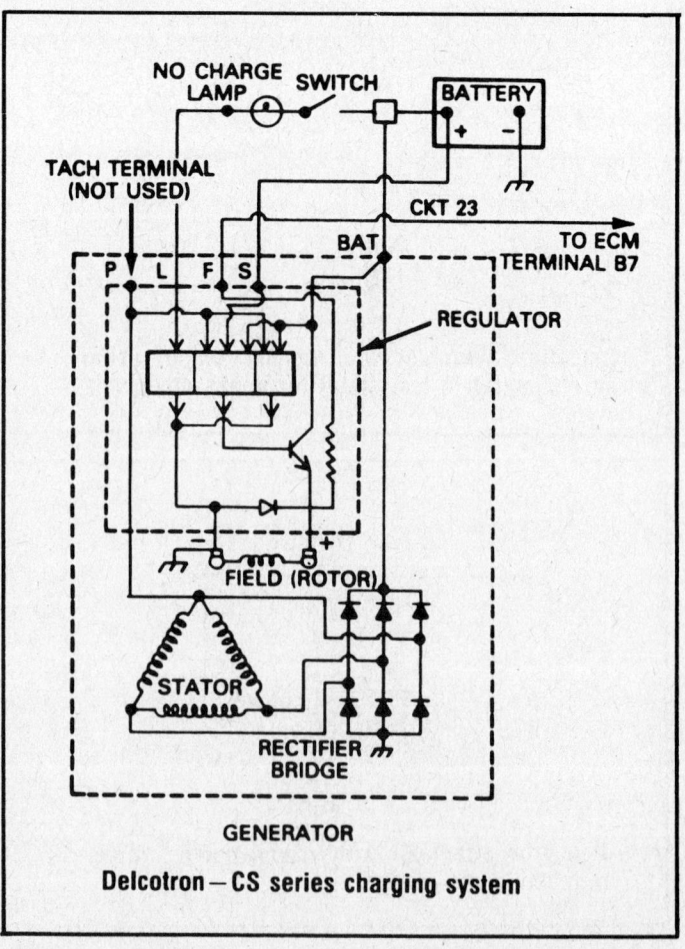

Delcotron—CS series charging system

21-50

ALERTNATORS
GM CS-130 AND CS-144 TYPE
SECTION 21

sories being left on overnight or by a faulty switch which allows a lamp, such as a trunk or glove box lamp, to stay on. Also, this generator does not have a test hole.

To diagnose the CS-130 and CS-144 charging systems, use the following procedure.

1. Visually check belt and wiring.
2. For vehicles without charge indicator lamp, go to Step 5.
3. With switch on, engine stopped, lamp should be on. If not, detach harness at generator, and ground "L" terminal. If the lamp lights, repair or replace the generator. If the lamp does not light locate open circuit between grounding lead and ignition switch. Lamp may be open.
4. With switch on, engine running at moderate speed, lamp should be off. If not, detach wiring harness at generator. If the lamp goes off, replace or repair generator. If the lamp stays on, check for grounded "L" terminal wire in harness.
5. Battery undercharged or overcharged. Detach wiring harness connector from generator. With switch on, engine not running, connect voltmeter from ground to "L" terminal. Zero reading indicates open circuit between terminal and battery. Correct as required. Reconnect harness connector to generator, run engine at moderate speed. Measure voltage across battery. If above 16 V, replace or repair generator.
6. Turn on accessories, load battery with carbon pile to obtain maximum amperage. Maintain voltage at 13 V or above. If within 15 amperes of rated output, generator is fine. If not within 15 amperes of rated output, repair or replace the generator.

CS GENERATOR BENCH CHECK

To check generator in a test stand, proceed as follows.

1. Make the proper connections and except leave the carbon pile disconnected. The ground polarity of generator and battery must be the same. The battery must be fully charged. Use a 30 to 500 OHM resistor between battery and "L" terminal.
2. Slowly increase generator speed and observe voltage.
3. If the voltage is uncontrolled and increase above 16.0 volts, the rotor field is shortened, the regulator is defective or both. A shorted rotor field coil can cause the regulator to become defective. The battery must be fully charged when making this test.
4. If voltage is below 16.0 volts, increase speed and adjust carbon pile to obtain maximum amperage output. Maintain voltage above 13.0 volts.
5. If output is within 15 amperes of rated output, generator is good.
6. If output is not within 15 amperes of rated output, generator if faulty and requires repair or replacement.

DISASSEMBLY AND ASSEMBLY

NOTE: The following procedures are given for the CS144 alternator at the time of publication. Disassembly and assembly procedures were not available for the CS 130 alternator.

1. Remove the alternator from the vehicle. Scribe marks on the end frames to facilitate assembly.
2. Remove the through bolts and separate the end frames.
3. Check the rotor for grounds using an ohmmeter. The reading should be infinite, if not, replace the rotor.
4. Check the rotor for shorts and opens. Replace the rotor as required.
5. Remove the three attaching nuts and remove the stator from the end frame.
6. Check the stator for grounds using an ohmmeter. If the reading is low replace the stator.

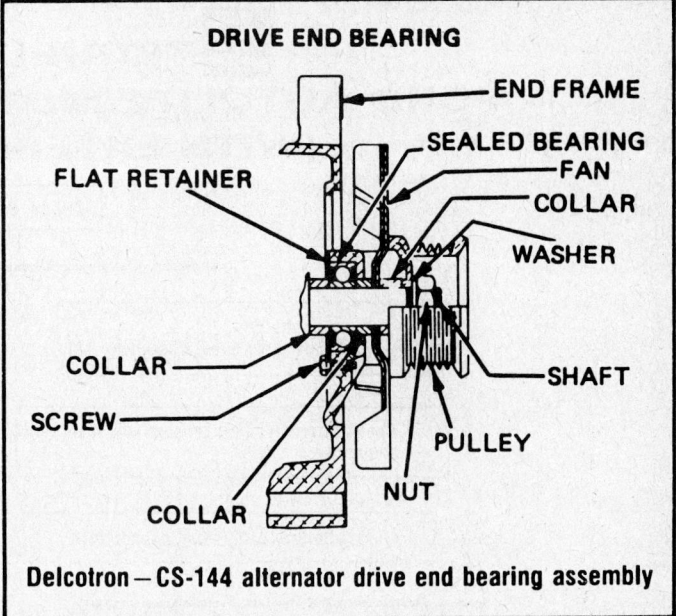

Delcotron—CS-144 alternator drive end bearing assembly

7. Unsolder the connections, remove the retaining screws and connector from the end frame. Separate the regulator and the brush holder from the end frame.
8. Check the rectifier bridge using an ohmmeter. Replace as required.
9. Check the heat sink, using an ohmmeter. Replace as required.
10. Clean the brushes. Replace them as required.
11. To remove the rotor and drive end bearing, Hold the rotor using a hex wrench in the shaft end while removing the nut. Push the rotor from the housing. Remove the plate and push the bearing out.
12. Assembly is the reverse of the disassembly procedure. Repair or replace defective components as required.

Ford Alternator with External Regulator

The Ford charging system is a negative ground system. It includes an alternator, electronic regulator, a charge indicator or an ammeter and a storage battery.

TROUBLESHOOTING

NOTE: See the "Alternator Test Plans" section before proceeding further.

Fusible Links

1. Check the fusible link located between the starter relay and the alternator. Replace the link if it is burned or open.

CHARGING SYSTEM OPERATION

NOTE: If the current indicator is to give an accurate reading the battery cables must be of the same gauge and length as the original equipment.

1. With the engine running and all electrical systems turned off position a current indicator over the positive battery cable.
2. If a charge of about 5 amps is recorded the charging system is working. If a draw of about 5 amps is recorded the system is not working. The needle moves toward the battery when

21-51

SECTION 21 ALTERNATORS
FORD (W/EXTERNAL REGULATOR)

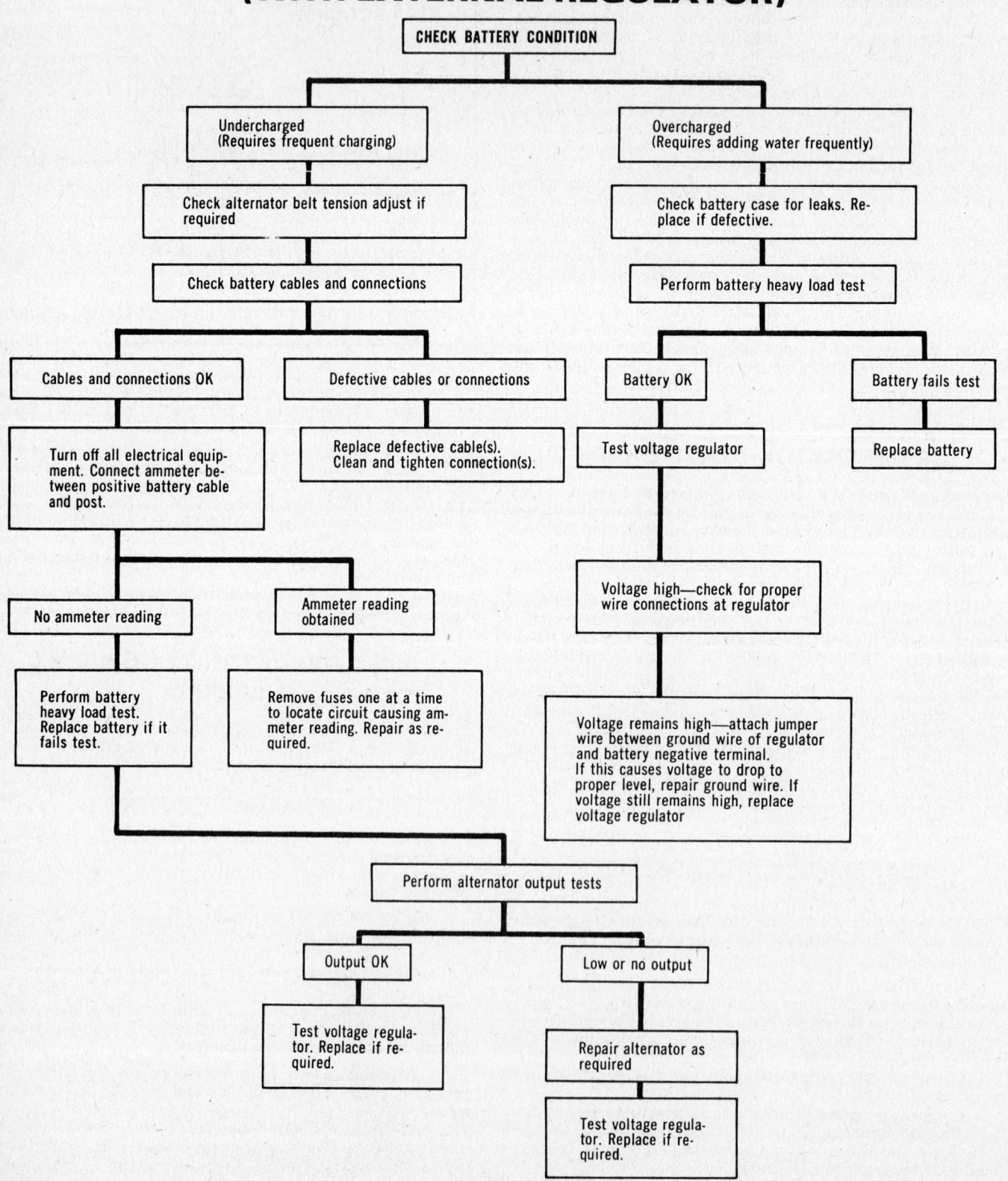

TROUBLESHOOTING FORD AUTOLITE/MOTORCRAFT ALTERNATOR (WITH EXTERNAL REGULATOR)

21-52

ALTERNATORS
FORD (W/EXTERNAL REGULATOR)
SECTION 21

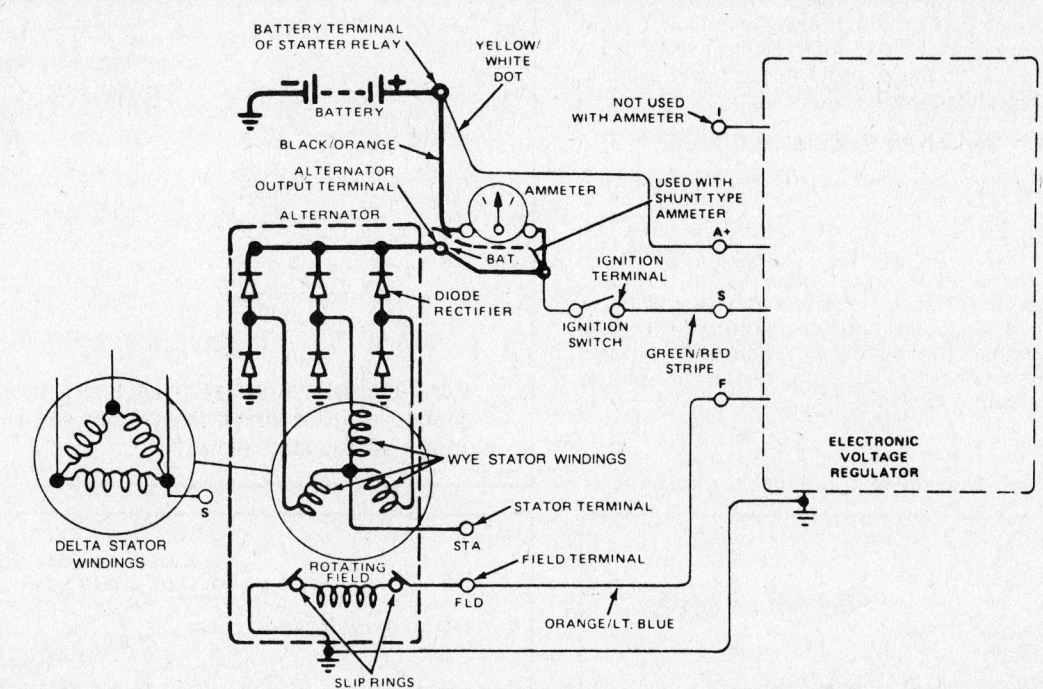

Ford alternator w/external reguatlor — rear terminal alternator charging system schematic with ammeter — typical of side terminal alternator. Wye stator windings on 40, 60 and 65 amp alternators. Delta stator windings on 70, 90 and 100 amp alternators

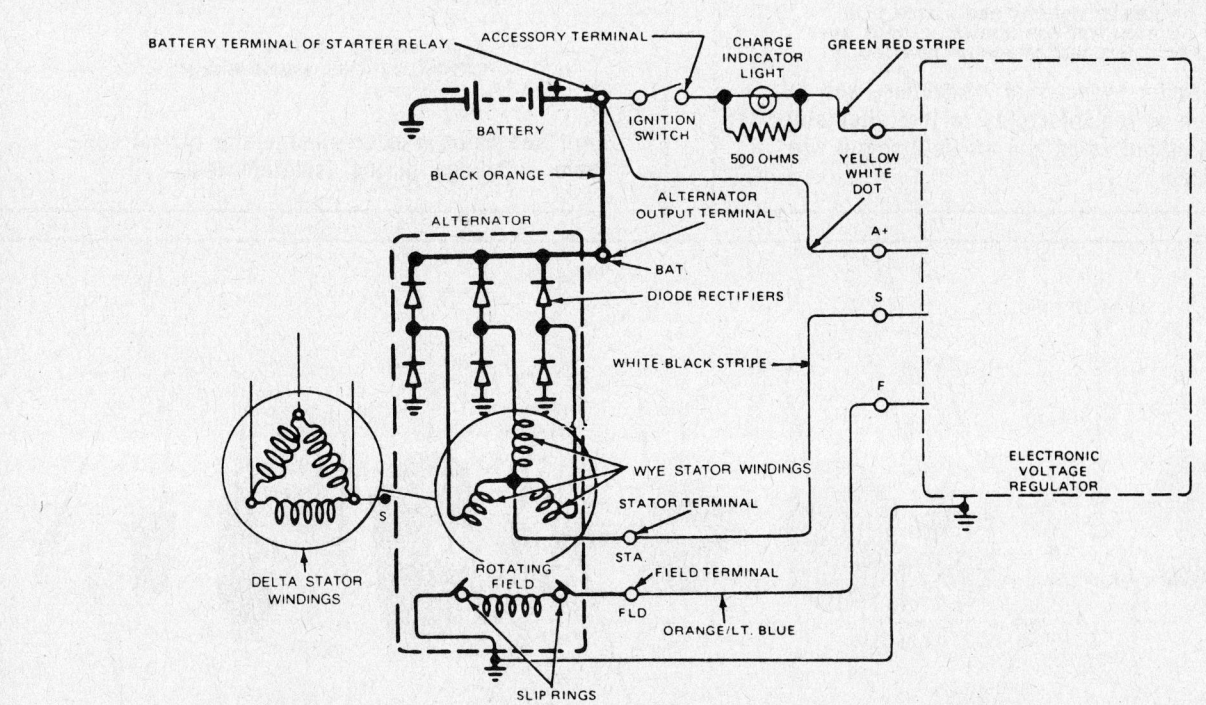

Ford alternator w/external regulator — rear terminal alternator charging system schematic with indicator light — typical of side terminal alternator. Wye stator windings on 40, 60, and 65 amp alternators. Delta stator windings on 70, 90 and 100 amp alternators

SECTION 21: ALTERNATORS
FORD (W/EXTERNAL REGULATOR)

a charge condition is indicated and away from the battery when a draw condition is indicated. If a draw is indicated continue to the next testing procedure. If an overcharge of 10 to 15 amps is indicated check for a faulty regulator or a bad ground at the regulator or the alternator.

Testing the Ignition Switch to Regulator Circuit

1. Disconnect the regulator wiring harness from the regulator.
2. Turn on the key. Using a test light or voltmeter check for voltage between the I wire and ground. Check for voltage between the A wire and ground. If voltage is present at this part of the system the circuit is OK. If there is no voltage at the I wire check for a burned out charge indicator bulb, a burned-out resistor, or a break or short in the wiring. If there is no voltage present at the A wire check for a bad connection at the starter relay or a break or short in the wire.

Isolation Test

This test determines whether the regulator or the alternator is

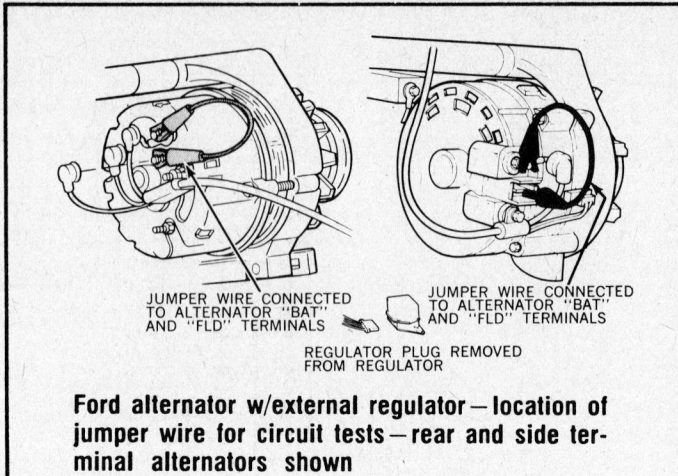

Ford alternator w/external regulator—location of jumper wire for circuit tests—rear and side terminal alternators shown

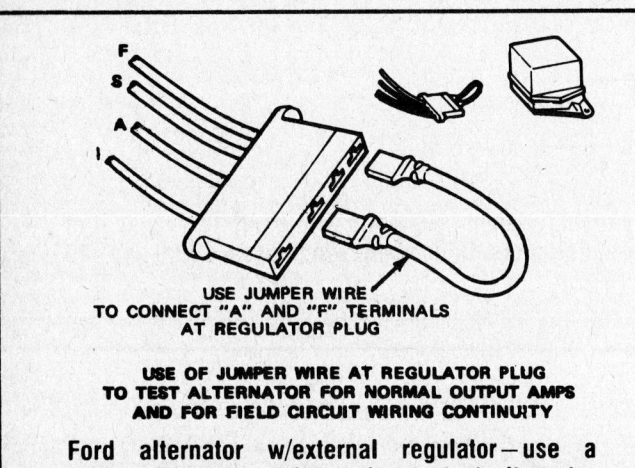

Ford alternator w/external regulator—use a jumper wire at regulator plug to test alternator for normal output amps and for field circuit wiring continuity

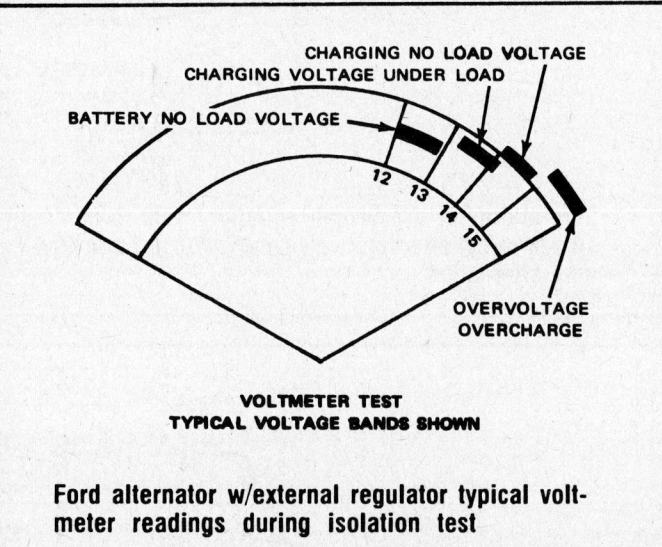

Ford alternator w/external regulator typical voltmeter readings during isolation test

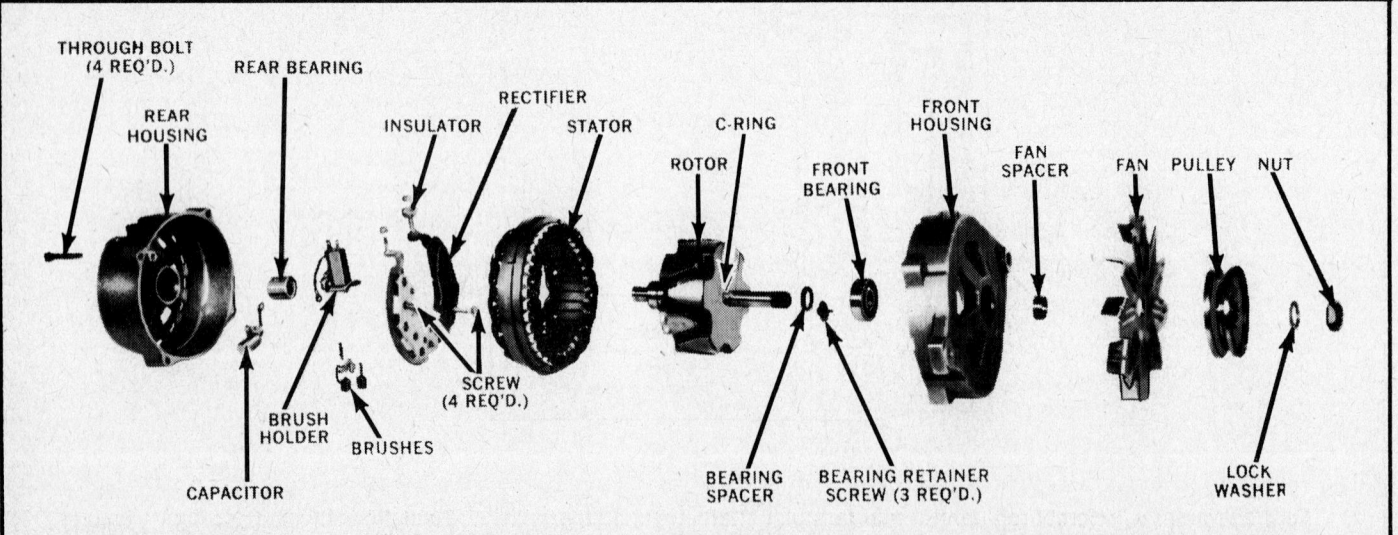

Ford alternator w/external regulator—exploded view showing assembly sequence of components (side terminal alternator).

21-54

ALTERNATORS
FORD (W/EXTERNAL REGULATOR)
SECTION 21

faulty after the rest of the circuit is found to be in good working order.

1. Disconnect the regulator wiring harness from the regulator.
2. Connect a jumper wire from the A wire to the F wire in the wiring harness plug.
3. Connect a voltmeter to the battery. The positive voltmeter lead goes to the positive terminal and the negative lead to the negative terminal. Record the reading on the voltmeter.
4. Turn off all of the electrical systems and start the engine. Do not race the engine.
5. Gradually increase engine speed 1500 to 2000 rpm. The voltmeter reading should increase above the previously recorded battery voltage reading by at least one to two volts. If there is no increase the alternator is not working correctly. If there is an increase the voltage regulator needs to be replaced.

Disassembly Except 65, 70, 90 Amp Alternators

1. Mark both end housings with a scribe mark for assembly.
2. Remove the three housing through bolts.
3. Separate the front housing and rotor from the stator and rear housing.
4. Remove the nuts from the rectifier to rear housing mounting studs and remove rear housing.

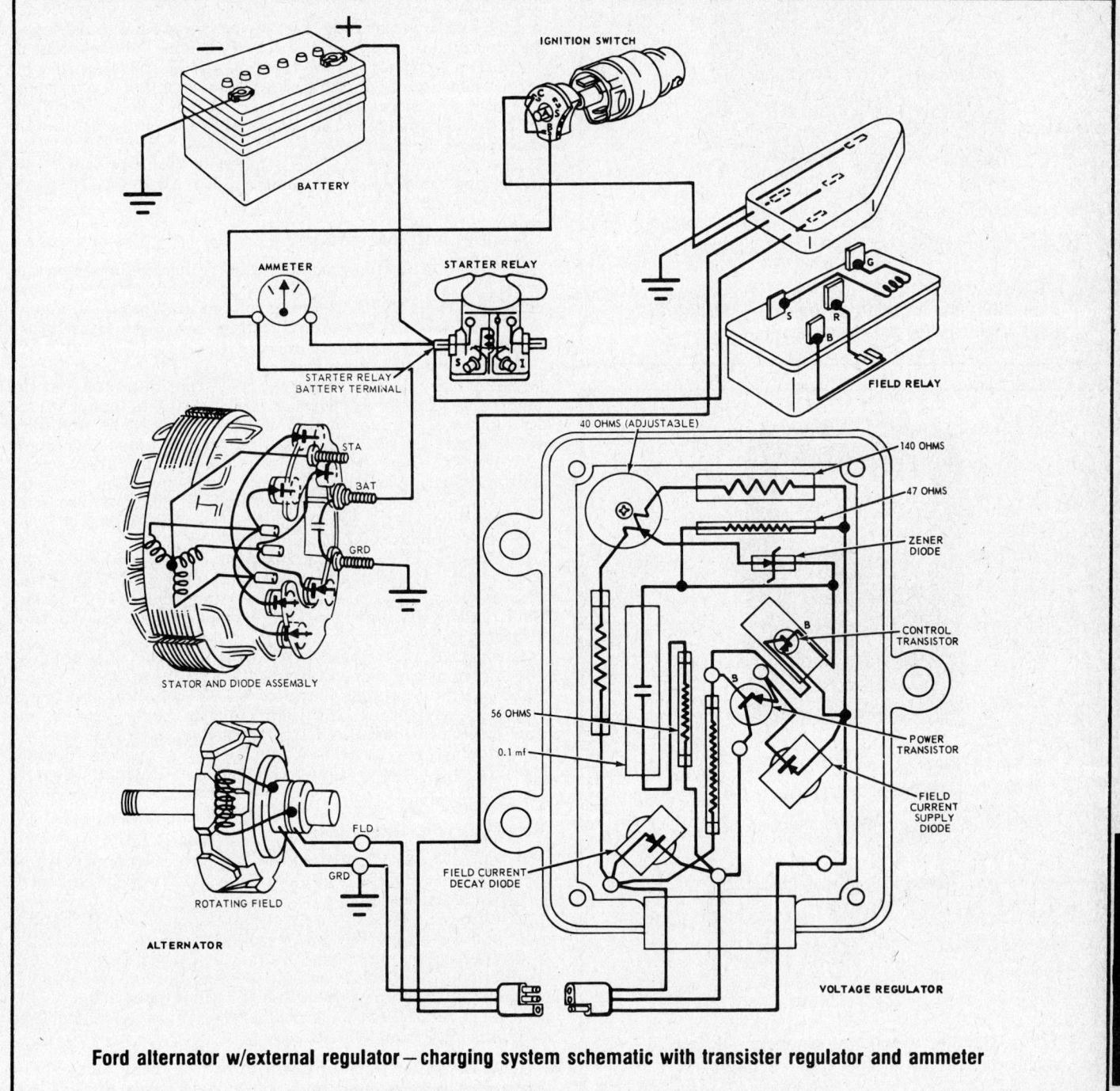

Ford alternator w/external regulator – charging system schematic with transister regulator and ammeter

21-55

SECTION 21: ALTERNATORS
FORD (W/EXTERNAL REGULATOR)

5. Remove the brush holder mounting screws and the holder, brushes, springs, insulator, and terminal.

6. If replacement is necessary press the bearing from the rear end housing while supporting the housing on the inner boss.

7. If rectifiers are to be replaced carefully unsolder the leads from the terminals. Use only a 100 watt soldering iron. Leave the soldering iron in contact with the diode terminals only long enough to remove the wires. Use pliers as temporary heat sinks in order to protect the diodes.

8. There are various types of rectifier assembly circuit boards installed in production. One type has the circuit board spaced away from the diode plates and the diodes are exposed. Another type consists of a single circuit board with integral diodes; and still another has integral diodes with an additional booster diode plate containing two diodes.

9. This last type is used only on the eight diode (61 amp) alternator. To disassemble use the following procedures. Exposed diodes remove the screws from the rectifier by rotating bolt heads ¼ turn clockwise to unlock, then unscrewing. Integral diodes press out the stator terminal screw, making sure not to twist it while doing this. Do not remove grounded screw. Booster diodes press out the stator terminal screw about ¼ inch, then remove the nut from the end of the screw and lift screw from circuit board. Be sure not to twist it as it comes out.

10. Remove the drive pulley and fan. On alternator pulleys with threaded holes in the outer end of the pulley use a standard puller for removal.

11. Remove the three screws that hold the front bearing retainer and remove the front housing. If the bearing is to be replaced press it from the housing.

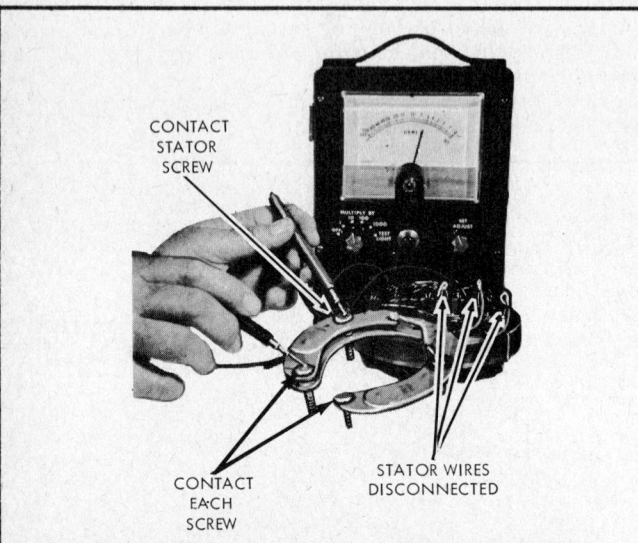

Ford alternator w/external regulator – testing diodes – typical fo flat type rectifiers

Cleaning and Inspection

1. The rotor, stator, diode rectifier assemblies, and bearings are not to be cleaned with solvent. These parts are to be wiped off with a clean cloth. Cleaning solvent may cause damage to the electrical parts or contaminate the bearing internal lubricant. Wash all other parts in solvent and dry them.

2. Rotate the front bearing on the drive shaft. Check for any scraping noise, looseness or roughness that indicates that the bearing is excessively worn. As the bearing is being rotated look for excessive lubricant leakage. If any of these conditions exist replace the bearing. Check rear bearing and rotor shaft.

3. Place the rear end housing on the slip ring end of the shaft and rotate the bearing on the shaft. Make a similar check for noise, looseness or roughness. Inspect the rollers and cage for damage. Replace the bearing if these conditions exist or if the lubricant is missing or contaminated.

4. Check both the front and rear housings for cracks.

5. Check all wire leads on both the stator and rotor assemblies for loose soldered connections and for burned insulation. Solder all poor connections. Replace parts that show burned insulation.

6. Check the slip rings for damaged insulation and runout. If the slip rings are more than 0.0005 inch out of round, take a light cut (minimum diameter limit 1.22 inch) from the face of the rings to true them. If the slip rings are badly damaged the entire rotor will have to be replaced as an assembly.

7. Replace any parts that are burned or cracked. Replace brushes that are worn to less than $5/16$ inch in length. Replace the brush spring if it had less than 7 to 12 oz. tension.

Field Current Draw Test

1. Remove the alternator from the vehicle. Connect a test ammeter between the alternator frame and the positive post of a 12 volt test battery.

2. Connect a jumper wire between the negative test battery post and the alternator field terminal.

3. Observe the ammeter. Little or no current flow indicates high brush resistance, open field windings, or high winding resistance. Current in excess of specifications (approximately 2.9 amps for most models) indicates shorted or grounded field windings, or brush leads touching.

NOTE: Sometimes the alternator produces current output at low engine speeds, but ceases to put out at high-

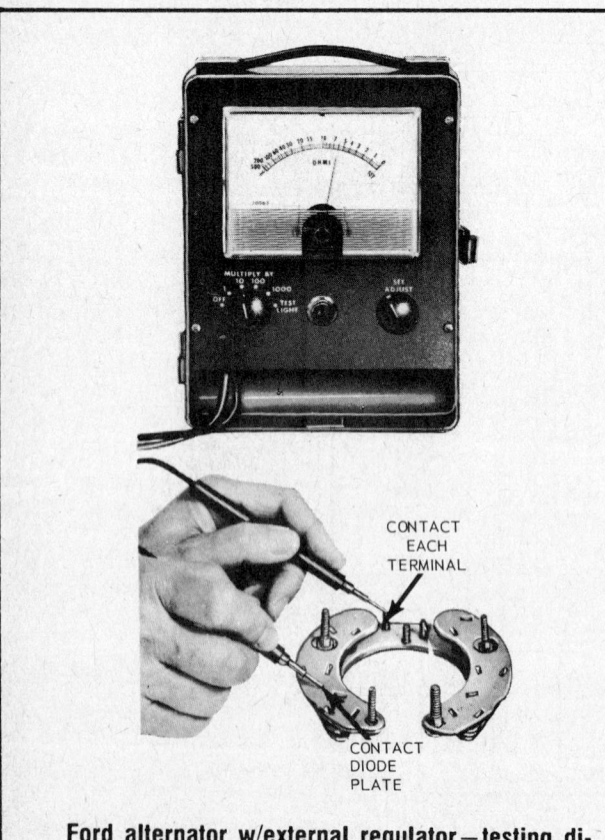

Ford alternator w/external regulator – testing diodes – typical of bridge type rectifiers

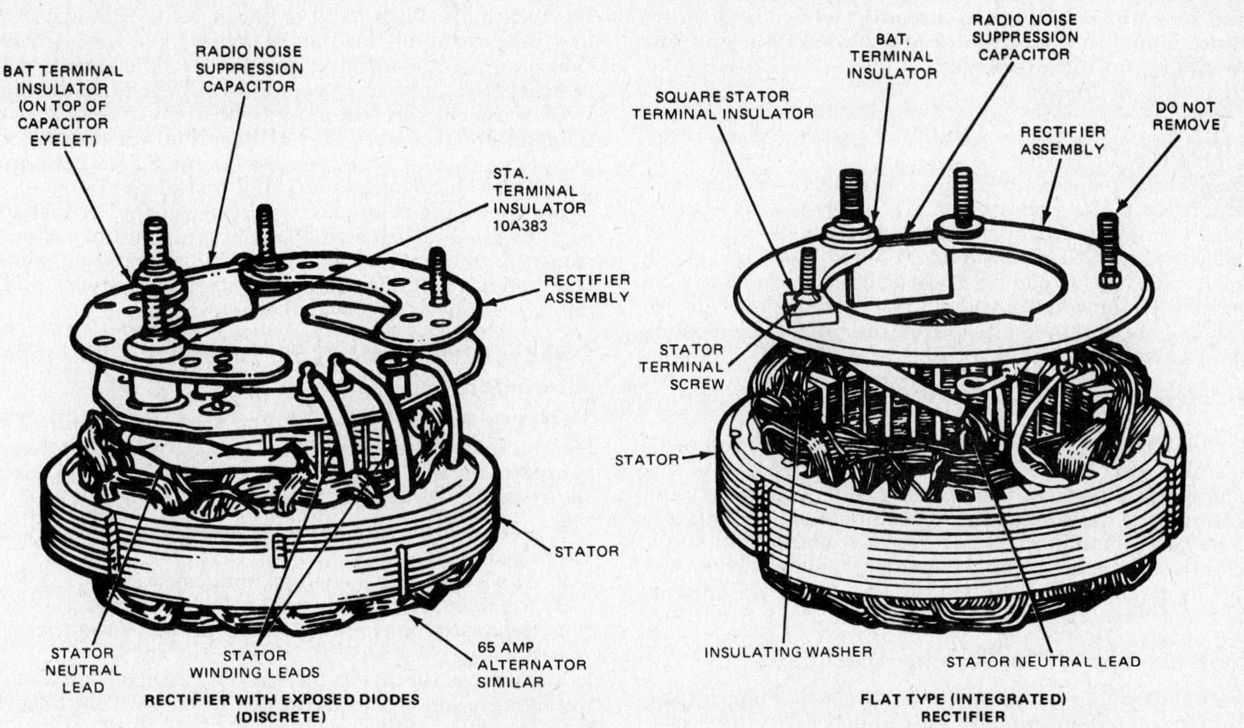

ALTERNATORS
FORD (W/EXTERNAL REGULATOR)
SECTION 21

Ford alternator w/external regulator — typical stator and rectifier assemblies and related terminals

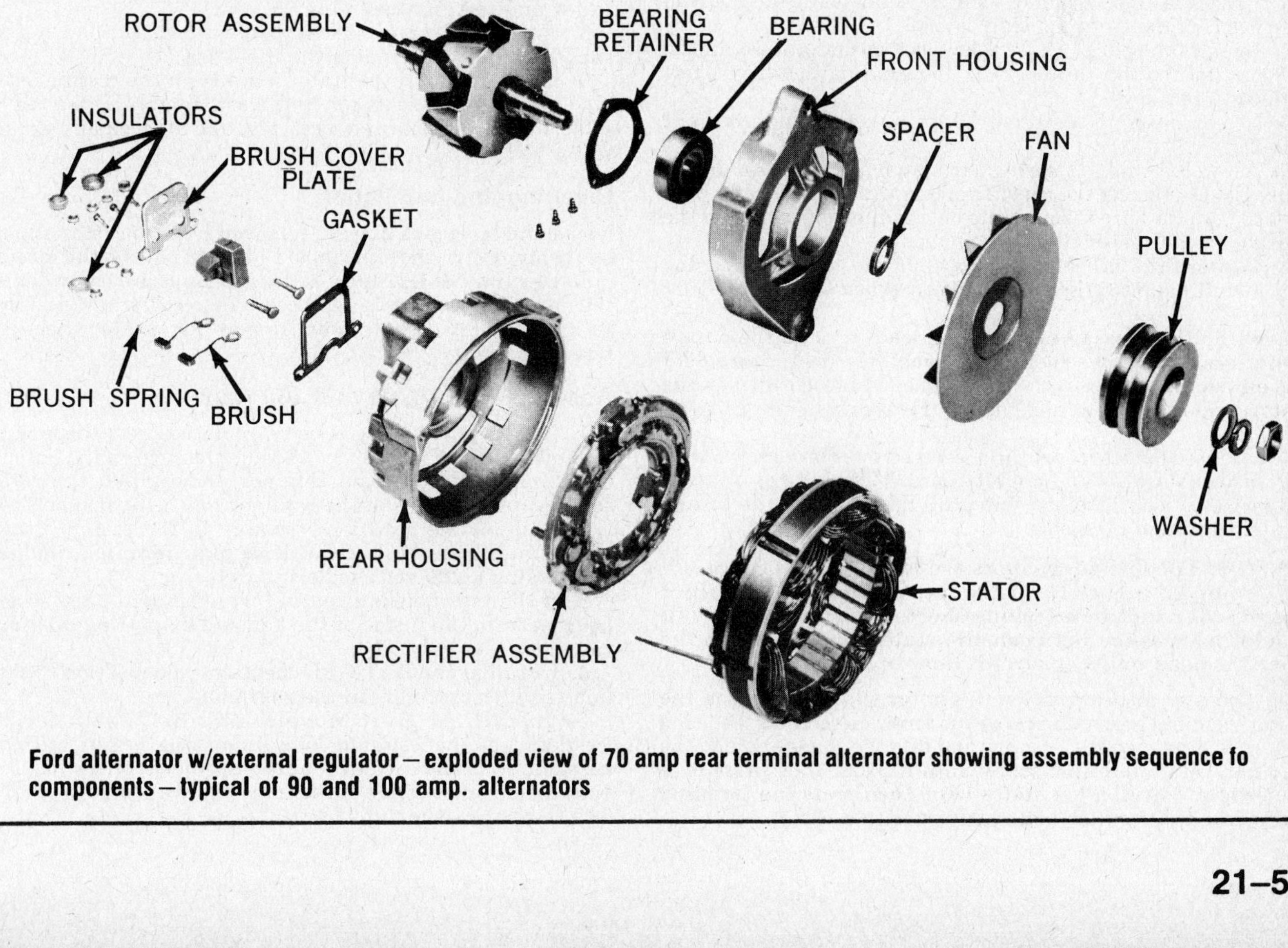

Left view (RECTIFIER WITH EXPOSED DIODES (DISCRETE), 65 AMP ALTERNATOR SIMILAR):
- BAT TERMINAL INSULATOR (ON TOP OF CAPACITOR EYELET)
- RADIO NOISE SUPPRESSION CAPACITOR
- STA. TERMINAL INSULATOR 10A383
- RECTIFIER ASSEMBLY
- STATOR
- STATOR WINDING LEADS
- STATOR NEUTRAL LEAD

Right view (FLAT TYPE (INTEGRATED) RECTIFIER):
- SQUARE STATOR TERMINAL INSULATOR
- BAT. TERMINAL INSULATOR
- RADIO NOISE SUPPRESSION CAPACITOR
- RECTIFIER ASSEMBLY
- DO NOT REMOVE
- STATOR TERMINAL SCREW
- STATOR
- INSULATING WASHER
- STATOR NEUTRAL LEAD

Ford alternator w/external regulator — exploded view of 70 amp rear terminal alternator showing assembly sequence for components — typical of 90 and 100 amp. alternators

Components: INSULATORS, BRUSH COVER PLATE, GASKET, BRUSH SPRING, BRUSH, REAR HOUSING, RECTIFIER ASSEMBLY, STATOR, ROTOR ASSEMBLY, BEARING RETAINER, BEARING, FRONT HOUSING, SPACER, FAN, PULLEY, WASHER

21-57

SECTION 21 ALTERNATORS
FORD (W/EXTERNAL REGULATOR)

er speeds. **This can be caused by centrifugal force expanding the rotor windings to the point where they short to ground. Place in a test stand and check field current draw while spinning alternator.**

Diode Tests

Disassemble the alternator. Disconnect diode assembly from stator and make tests. To test one set of diodes contact one ohmmeter probe to the diode plate and contact each of the three stator lead terminals with the other probe. Reverse the probes and repeat the test. All six tests (eight for 61 amp eight-diode models) should show a reading of about 60 ohms in one direction and infinite ohms in the other. If two high readings, or two low readings, are obtained after reversing probes the diode is faulty and must be replaced.

Stator Tests

Disassemble the stator from the alternator assembly and rectifiers. Connect test ohmmeter probes between each pair of stator leads. If the ohmmeter does not indicate equally between each pair of leads the stator coil is open and must be replaced.

Connect test ohmmeter probes between one of the stator leads and the stator core. The ohmmeter should not show any reading. If it does show continuity the stator winding is grounded and must be replaced.

Assembly Except 65, 70, 90 Amp Alternators

1. Press the front bearing into the front housing boss by putting pressure on outer race only. Install bearing retainer.
2. If the stop ring on the driveshaft was damaged install a new stop ring. Push the new ring onto the shaft and into the groove.
3. Position the front bearing spacer on the driveshaft against the stop ring.
4. Place the front housing over the shaft with the bearing positioned in the front housing cavity.
5. Install fan spacer, fan, pulley, lockwasher and retaining nut and tighten nut 60 to 100 ft. lbs. holding the drive shaft with an Allen key.
6. If rear bearing was removed, press a new one into rear housing.
7. Assemble brushes, springs, terminal and insulator in the brush holder, retract the brushes and insert a short length of 1/8 inch rod or stiff wire through the hole in the holder to hold the brushes in the retracted position.
8. Position the brush holder assembly in the rear housing and install mounting screws. Position brush leads to prevent shorting.
9. Wrap the three stator winding leads around the circuit board terminals and solder them using only rosin core solder and a solder iron. Position the stator neutral lead eyelet on the stator terminal screw and install the screw in the rectifier assembly.
10. Exposed diodes insert the special screws through the wire lug, dished washers and circuit board. Turn 1/4 turn counterclockwise to lock in place. Integral diodes insert the screws straight through the holes.

NOTE: The dished washers are to be used on the molded circuit boards only. Using these washers on a fiber board will result in a serious short circuit, as only a flat insulating washer between the stator terminal and the board is used on fiber circuit boards.

11. Booster diodes position the stator wire terminal on the stator terminal screw, then position screw on rectifier. Position square insulator over the screw and into the square hole in the rectifier, rotate terminal screw until it locks, then press it in fingertight. Position the stator wire, then press the terminal screw into the rectifier and insulator with a vise.

12. Place the radio noise suppression condenser on the rectifier terminals. With molded circuit board and install the STA and BAT terminal insulators. With fiber circuit board place the square stator terminal insulator in the square hole in the rectifier assembly, then position BAT terminal insulator.
13. Position the stator and rectifier assembly in the rear housing, making sure that all terminal insulators are seated properly in the recesses. Position STA, BAT and FLD insulators on terminal bolts and install the nuts.
14. Clean the rear bearing surface of the rotor shaft with a rag and then position rear housing and stator assembly over rotor. Align matchmarks made during disassembly and install the through bolts. Remove brush retracting wire and place a dab of silicone sealer over the hole.

Disassembly (Typical) 65, 70, 90 and 100 Ampere Alternators

NOTE: When disassembling the side terminal alternator the brush holder would be removed after the rectifier is removed. During the assembly the brush holder would be installed in the reverse order.

1. Remove the brush holder and cover assembly from the rear housing.
2. Mark both end housings and the stator.
3. Remove the three housing through bolts.
4. Separate the front housing and rotor from the stator and rear housing.
5. Remove the drive pulley nut, lockwasher, flat washer, pulley, fan, fan spacer and rotor from the front housing.
6. Remove the three screws that hold the front bring retainer and remove the retainer. If the bearing is damaged or has lost its lubricant, support the housing close to the bearing boss and press out the bearing.
7. Remove all the nut and washer assemblies and insulators from the rear housing and remove the rear housing from the stator and rectifier assembly.
8. If necessary press the rear bearing from the housing while supporting the housing on the inner boss.
9. Unsolder the three stator leads from the rectifier assembly and separate the stator from the assembly. Use a 200 watt soldering iron. Perform a diode test and an open and grounded stator coil test.

Cleaning and Inspection

Nicks and scratches may be removed from the rotor slip rings by turning down the slip rings. Do not go beyond the minimum diameter limit of 1.22 inch. If the slip rings are badly damaged the entire rotor must be replaced. The rectifier also is serviced as an assembly. See "Lower Ampere Alternator" Section for test procedures.

Assembly 65, 70, 90 and 100 Amp

1. If the front bearing is being replaced press the new bearing into the bearing boss by putting pressure on the outer race only. Install the bearing retainer and tighten the retainer screws until the tips of the retainer touch the housing.
2. Position the rectifier assembly to the stator, wrap the three stator leads around the diode plate terminals and solder them using a 200 watt soldering iron.
3. If the rear housing bearing was removed press in a new bearing from the inside of the housing by putting pressure on the other race only.
4. Install at the BAT-GRD insulator and position the stator and rectifier assembly in the rear housing.
5. Install the STA (purple) and BAT (red) terminal insulators on the terminal bolts and install the nut and washer assemblies. Make certain that the shoulders on all insulators, both inside and outside of the housing, are seated properly before tightening the nuts.

21-58

ALTERNATORS
FORD (W/EXTERNAL REGULATOR)
SECTION 21

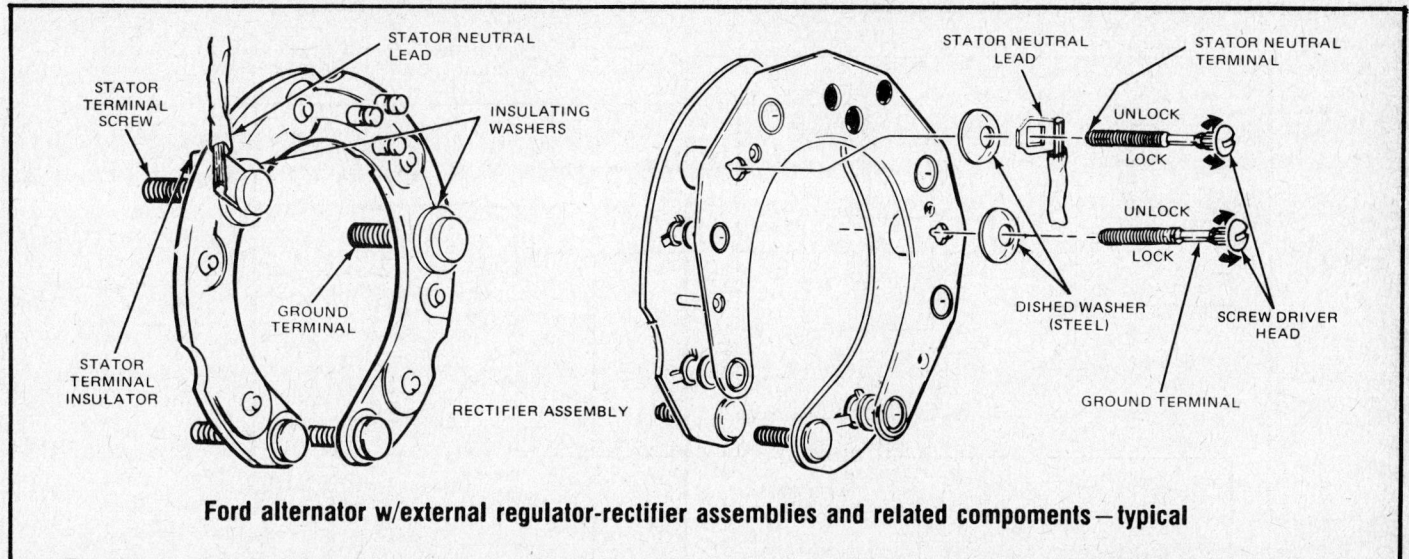

Ford alternator w/external regulator-rectifier assemblies and related compoments — typical

6. Position the front housing over the rotor and install the an spacer, fan, pulley, flat and lockwasher and nut on the rotor shaft.

7. Wipe the rear bearing surface of the rotor shaft with a clean rag.

8. Position the rotor with the front housing into the stator and rear housing assembly and align the matchmarks made during disassembly. Seat the machined portion of the stator core into the step in both housings and install the through bolts.

9. If the field brushes have worn to less than 3/8 inch, replace both brushes. Hold the brushes in position by inserting a stiff wire into the brush holder.

10. Position the brush holder assembly into the rear housing and install the three mounting screws. Remove the brush retracting wire and put a dab of silicone cement over the hole.

Brush Replacement 65, 70, 90 and 100 amp

1. Remove the brush holder and cover assembly from the rear housing.

2. Remove the terminal bolts from the brush holder and cover assembly. Then remove the brush assemblies.

3. Position the new brush terminals on the terminal bolts and assemble the terminals, bolts, brush holder washers and nuts. The insulating washer mounts under the FLD terminal nut. The entire brush and cover assembly also is available for service.

4. Depress the brush springs in the brush holder cavities and insert the brushes on top of the springs. Hold the brushes in position by inserting a stiff wire in the brush holder as shown. Position the brush leads as shown.

5. Install the brush holder and cover assembly into the rear housing. Remove the brush retracting wire and put a dab of silicone cement over the hole.

Ford Alternator with Internal Regulator

The Ford alternator with Internal Regulator is manufactured by Motorcraft, which is a division of the Ford Motor Company. The Field current is supplied from the alternator regulator which is mounted on the rear of the alternator, to the rotating field of the alternator through two brushes and two slip rings.

The alternator produces power in the form of alternating current. The alternating current is rectified to direct current by six diodes. The alternator regulator automatically adjusts the alternator field current to maintain the alternator output voltage within prescribed limits to correctly charge the battery. The alternator is self current limiting.

The regulator voltage control circuit is turned on when the ignition switch is On and voltage is applied to the regulator I terminal through a resistor in the I circuit. When the ignition switch is Off the control circuit is turned off and no field current flows to the alternator.

On warning lamp equipped vehicles, the warning lamp is connected across the terminals of a 500 ohm resistor at the instrument cluster. Current passes through the warning lamp when the ignition switch is in the Run position and there is no voltage at terminal S. When voltage at S rises to a preset value the regulator switching circuits stop the flow of current into terminal I and the lamp turns Off.

System voltage is "sensed" and alternator field current is drawn through terminal A. The regulator switching circuits will turn the warning lamp On, indicating a system fault, if terminal A voltage is excessively high or low, or if the terminal S voltage signal is abnormal. A fuse link in included in the charging system wiring on all models. The fuse link is used to prevent damage to the wiring harness and alternator if the wiring harness should become grounded, or if a booster battery is connected to the charging system with the wrong polarity.

DIAGNOSTIC TESTING

NOTE: The following diagnostic tests are made with the alternator installed in the vehicle. Be sure that the battery is fully charged before any testing is done.

Battery Voltage Test

1. Connect a voltmeter to the positive and negative battery terminals.

2. Record the battery voltage. If battery voltage is not within specification, correct as required.

Load Test

1. Be sure that the battery is fully charged before performing this test.

2. Connect the tachometer to the engine.

3. Start the engine. Turn the heater/A/C switch to the high blower position. Turn on the headlights with the high beams. Increase engine speed to 2000 rpm.

4. Voltmeter should indicate a minimum of a 0.5 volt in-

SECTION 21 ALTERNATORS
FORD (W/INTERNAL REGULATOR

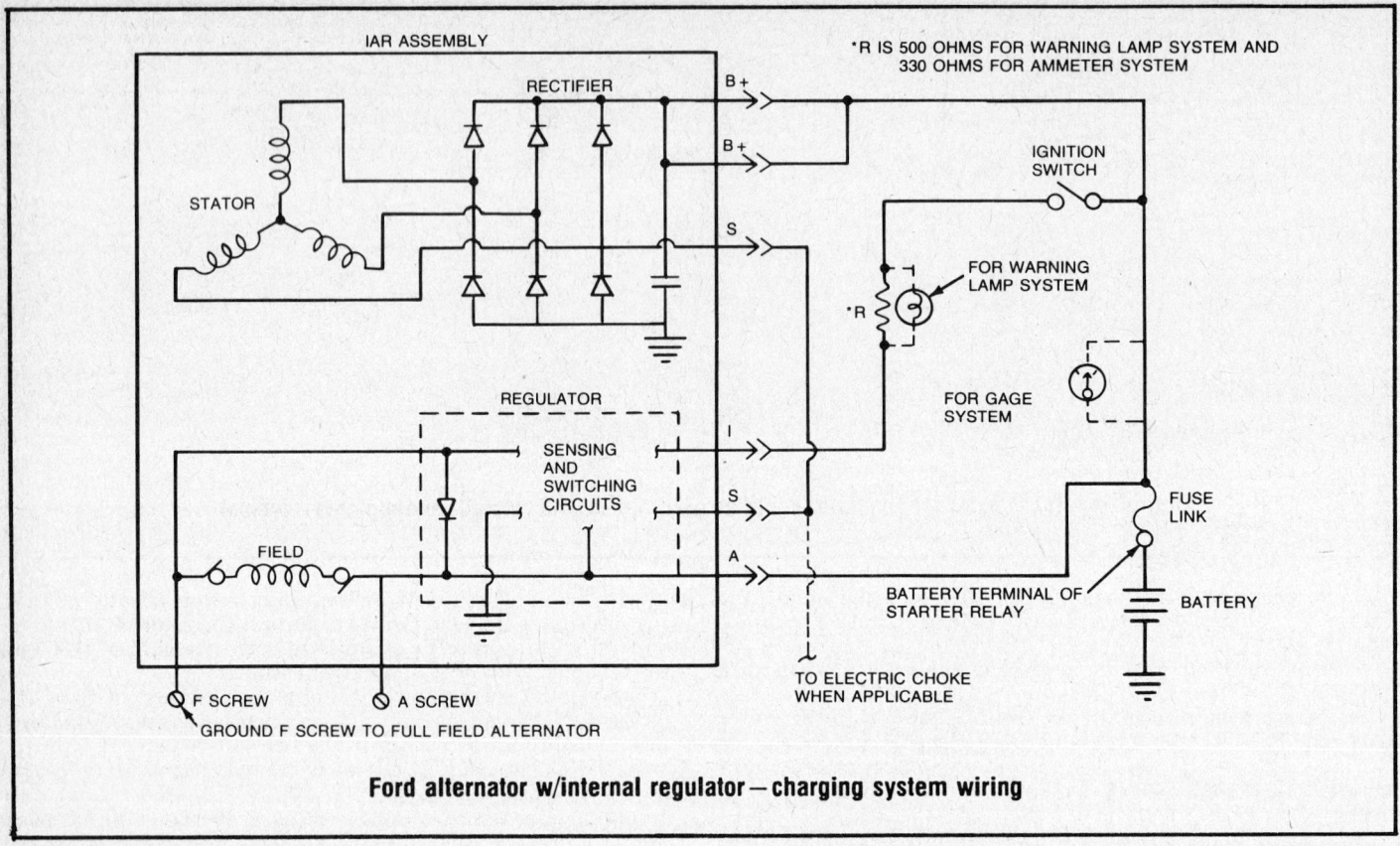

Ford alternator w/internal regulator – charging system wiring

crease over battery voltage.

5. If the system is working the above readings will be obtained. Be sure not to ground the "A" terminal of the voltage regulator.

No Load Test

1. Be sure that the battery is fully charged before performing this test.
2. Connect a tachometer to the engine. Start the engine and increase the engine speed to 1500 rpm with no electrical load.
3. The voltmeter reading should be taken when the voltmeter needle stops moving. The voltmeter reading should be 1 to 2 volts above the voltage of the battery.
4. If the voltage increased properly proceed with another test.

High Voltage Test

1. Be sure that the battery is fully charged before performing this test.
2. Turn the ignition switch to the "on" position. Connect the voltmeter negative lead to the rear of the alternator housing.
3. Connect voltmeter positive lead to alternator output terminal and record voltage. Connect voltmeter positive lead to the "A" terminal of regulator. Compare voltage difference recorded at alternator output terminal.
4. If voltage difference is greater than 0.5 volt, repair or replace wiring circuit to "A" terminal.
5. If high voltage condition still exists check ground connections at regulator to alternator, alternator to engine, firewall to engine and engine to battery.
6. If high voltage condition still exists connect voltmeter negative lead to rear of alternator housing. With ignition to off position connect voltmeter positive lead to "A" terminal of regulator and record reading. Connect voltmeter positive lead to "F" terminal of regulator.

7. Check if different voltage is present at "A" and "F" terminals. Different voltage readings indicate a defective regulator, grounded brush leads or grounded rotor coil.
8. If same voltage is present at both terminals and circuits tested in previous steps are good replace the regulator.

Low Voltage Test

1. Be sure that the battery is fully charged before performing this test.
2. Disconnect the wiring plug from the voltage regulator and install the ohmmeter between terminals "A" and "F."
3. The ohmmeter reading should indicate more than 2.2 ohms. If the reading is less than 2.2 ohms, replace the voltage regulator and check the alternator for a shorted rotor or open field circuit. Repeat the load test. Do not replace the voltage regulator before a shorted rotor coil or field circuit has been determined not to be the problem. If not damage to the new regulator could occur.
4. If the field circuit is okay, more than 2.2 ohms reconnect the voltage regulator wiring plug and connect the voltmeter negative lead to the rear of the alternator. Connect the positive lead of the voltmeter to terminal "A" of the voltage regulator. You should have battery voltage, if so go on. If not repair wiring in circuit "A".
5. With the ignition switch in the off position connect the positive lead of the voltmeter to the "F" terminal of the voltage regulator.
6. If battery voltage is present, go on. If not replace the voltage regulator. Repeat the load test.
7. Turn the ignition switch to the on position. The voltmeter should indicate 1.5 volts or less. If the reading is more than 1.5 volts perform the regulator "I" circuit test. Repair the voltage regulator as required. Repeat the load test.
8. If the voltmeter reading is 1.5 volts or less disconnect the alternator wiring plug and connect a twelve gauge jumper wire

ALTERNATORS
FORD (W/INTERNAL REGULATOR)
SECTION 21

between the alternator plug terminal and the wiring harness connector.

9. Connect the positive lead of the voltmeter to one of the "B+" terminals. Repeat the load test.

10. If the reading is 0.5 volt above battery voltage repair the wiring harness from the alternator to the starter relay.

11. If the voltmeter reading is less than 0.5 volt above battery voltage, connect a jumper wire from the rear of the alternator housing to terminal "F" of the voltage regulator.

12. Repeat the load test. If the voltmeter reading is more than 0.5 volt replace the voltage regulator. If the reading is less than 0.5 volt repair the alternator.

Voltage Regulator Circuit "I" Test

1. Disconnect the voltage regulator wiring plug harness.

2. Connect the voltmeter negative lead to the battery ground. Connect the voltmeter positive lead to the harness side of terminal "I."

3. With the ignition switch in the off position, voltage should not be present. If voltage is present repair the circuit as necessary.

4. With the ignition switch in the on position battery voltage should be present. If voltage is not present check the wiring for an open or grounded circuit. Repair as required.

5. If the voltage readings are within specification, check the resistance of the "I" circuit resistor. If the vehicle is equipped with an indicator light the resistance is 500 ohms. If the vehicle is equipped with a gauge the resistance is 300 ohms. If the specification obtained is not within plus or minus 50 ohms replace the resistor. Repeat the load test.

6. Disconnect the voltage regulator wiring plug, and remove the indicator light bulb, if equipped, before performing this test.

Field Circuit Drain Test

1. Connect the negative lead of the voltmeter to the rear of the alternator housing. Turn the ignition switch to the off position. Connect the positive lead of the voltmeter to the "F" terminal of the voltage regulator.

2. Battery voltage should be present. If no voltage is present, proceed.

3. If voltage is less than battery voltage, check "I" circuit. Disconnect regulator wiring harness. Connect voltmeter positive lead to "S" terminal of wiring plug. If voltage is present, proceed to Step 4. If no voltage is present replace regulator.

4. Disconnect wiring plug from alternator. Check "S" terminal for voltage. If no voltage is present replace alternator rectifier assembly. If voltage is still present replace or repair wiring between alternator and regulator plugs.

ALTERNATOR BENCH TESTS

NOTE: In performing the following tests digital meters cannot be used.

Stator Ground Test

1. Using an ohmmeter connect one test lead to the "B+" terminal and the other test lead to the "S" terminal.

2. Reverse the test leads and repeat the test. The ohmmeter should read about 6.5 ohms in one direction and infinity when the test probes are reversed.

3. A reading in both directions indicates a bad positive diode or a shorted radio suppression capacitor.

4. Perform the same test using the "S" terminal and the alternator rear housing.

5. Readings in both directions indicate a bad negative diode, grounded stator winding, grounded stator terminal or a shorted radio suppression capacitor.

6. If the ohmmeter needle does not move in one direction, or high resistance in the other direction exists, there is an open circuit in the rectifier assembly. Correct the problem as required.

Field Open or Short Circuit Test

1. Using an ohmmeter connect one test lead to terminal "A" on the voltage regulator. Connect the other test lead to terminal "F" of the voltage regulator. Spin the alternator pulley. Reverse the ohmmeter connections and repeat the test.

2. In one test the ohmmeter should read between 2.2 and 100 ohms. The reading may fluctuate while the pulley is spinning.

3. In the other test the ohmmeter should read between 2.2 and 9 ohms.

4. An infinite reading in one test and a 9 ohm reading in the other test indicates open brush lead, worn or stuck brushes, bad rotor assembly or loose voltage regulator to brush holder retaining screws.

5. A reading of less than 2.2 ohms in both tests indicates a shorted rotor or a bad voltage regulator.

6. A reading greater than 9 ohms in both tests indicates a defective voltage regulator or a loose "F" terminal screw.

7. Connect one ohmmeter test lead to the rear of the alternator. Connect the other test lead to terminal "A" of the voltage regulator and then to terminal "F" of the voltage regulator. The ohmmeter should read infinity at both points.

8. A test reading of less than infinity at both points indicates a grounded brush lead, grounded rotor or a bad voltage regulator.

Rectifier Assembly Test

1. Remove rectifier assembly from alternator. To test positive set of diodes contact one ohmmeter test lead to "B+" terminal and contact each of three stator lead terminals with other test lead.

2. Reverse the test leads and repeat test. All diodes should show readings of approximately 6.5 ohms in one direction and infinite readings with probes reversed.

3. Repeat test for negative set of diodes by connecting one test lead to rectifier assembly base plate and to other 3 terminals. If meter readings are not as specified replace rectifier assembly.

Radio Suppression Capacitor Test

NOTE: This is an open or shorted circuit test only and does not measure capacitance value.

1. Contact the ohmmeter test leads to the "B+" terminal and the rectifier base plate assembly. Reverse the test leads while observing the indicator needle.

2. If the needle jumps momentarily and then returns to previous position, capacitor is okay. If needle does not jump replace rectifier assembly. Radio suppression capacitor must be replaced as a complete rectifier assembly.

Stator Coil Ground Test

1. Remove the stator from the alternator.

2. Using an ohmmeter connect one test lead to one stator lead and the other test lead to the stator laminated core. The reading should be infinity.

3. If the meter needle moves then the stator winding is shorted to the core. Replace the stator. Repeat this test for each stator lead.

NOTE: Do not allow your hands to touch the metal test leads or the stator leads as an incorrect test reading will result.

Stator Coil Open Test

1. Disconnect the stator from the rectifier assembly.

21-61

SECTION 21 ALTERNATORS
FORD (W/INTERNAL REGULATOR)

2. Using an ohmmeter connect one test lead to a stator lead and the other test lead to another stator lead.

3. If the meter does not respond an open is present and the stator should be replaced. Repeat the test with the other wire combinations. A single phase cannot be detected on alternators using a "delta" connected stator.

Rotor Open Or Short Circuit Test

1. Remove the rotor assembly from the alternator.
2. Using an ohmmeter contact each test lead to a rotor slip ring. The ohmmeter should read 2.0 to 3.9 ohms.
3. If the readings are higher than specification it would indicate a damaged slip ring solder connection or a broken wire.
4. If the readings are lower than specification it would indicate a shorted wire or slip ring.
5. Replace the rotor if it is damaged. Connect one test lead of the ohmmeter to a rotor slip ring and the other test lead to the rotor shaft.
6. The ohmmeter reading should be infinity. If this is not the case the rotor is shorted to the shaft. Replace the rotor if the unit is shorted.

Disassembly

1. Remove the alternator from the vehicle. Position the unit in a suitable holding fixture.
2. Remove the voltage regulator and the brush holder from the rear of the alternator assembly.
3. Remove the two screws retaining the brush holder to the voltage regulator. Separate the two components.
4. Match mark the alternator end housings and stator frame to aid in reinstallation.
5. Remove the alternator through bolts. Separate the front housing and the rotor assembly from the stator and the rear housing.
6. Unsolder the three stator leads from the rectifier assembly. Be careful that the rectifiers are not in contact with the solder iron as overheating them will cause damage.
7. Remove the rectifier assembly from the rear of the alternator housing. Press the rear alternator housing bearing from the rear housing.
8. From the front housing of the alternator remove the drive pulley nut from the rotor shaft.
9. Remove the lockwasher, drive pulley, fan, and fan spacer from the rotor shaft.
10. Remove the rotor from the front housing. Remove the front bearing spacer from the rotor shaft. Do not remove the rotor stop ring unless it must be replaced.
11. Remove the front housing bearing retainer and bearing.

Assembly

1. Assembly of the alternator is the reverse of the disassembly procedure.

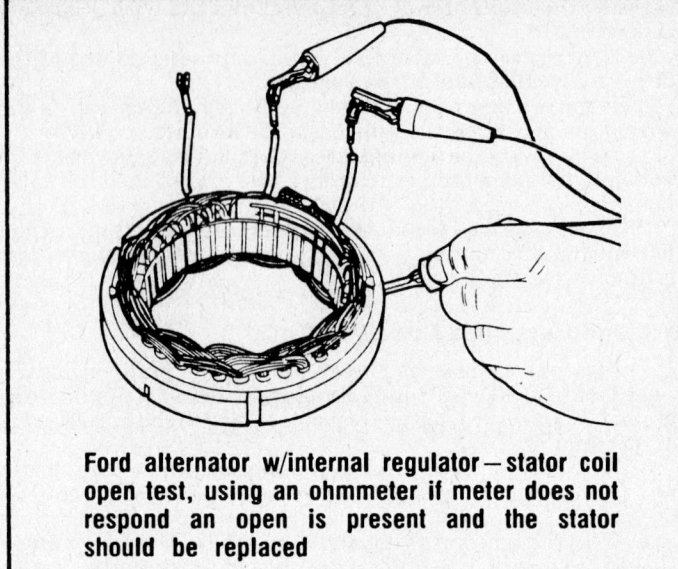

Ford alternator w/internal regulator—stator coil open test, using an ohmmeter if meter does not respond an open is present and the stator should be replaced

Ford alternator w/internal regulator—field open or short circuit test use an ohmmeter to contact each test lead to a rotor slip ring

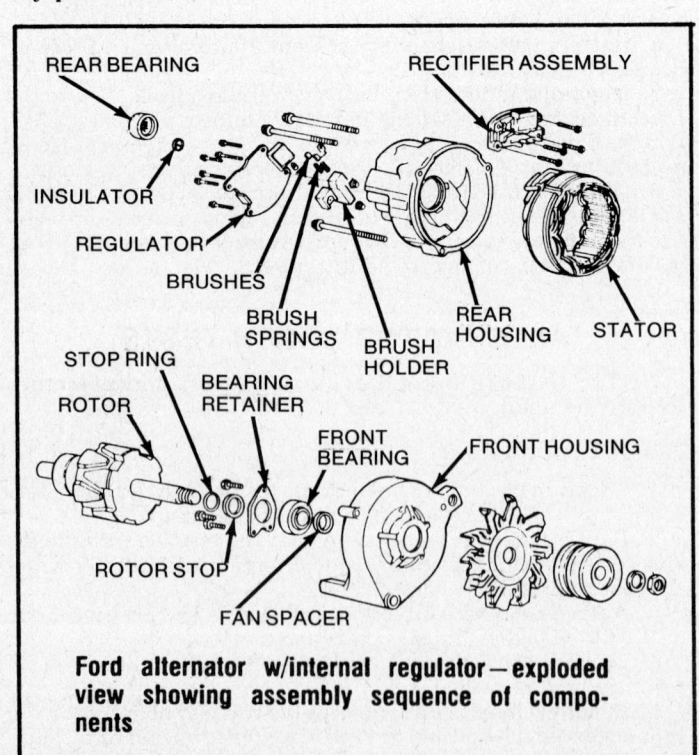

Ford alternator w/internal regulator—exploded view showing assembly sequence of components

ALTERNATORS
FORD (W/INTERNAL REGULATOR)

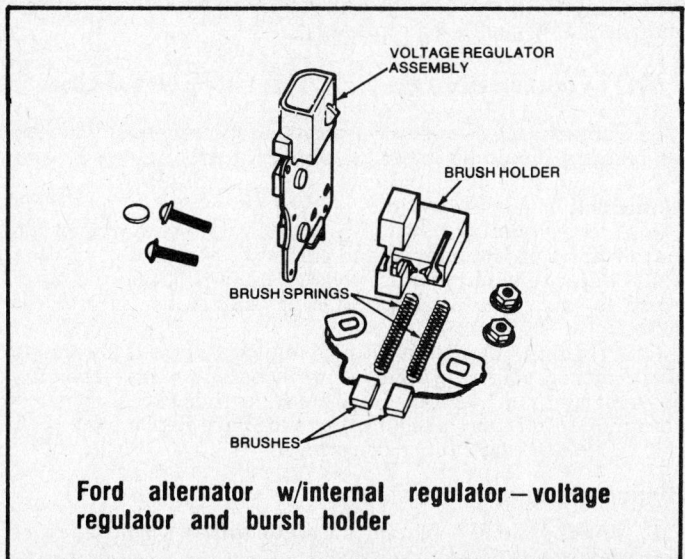

Ford alternator w/internal regulator—voltage regulator and brush holder

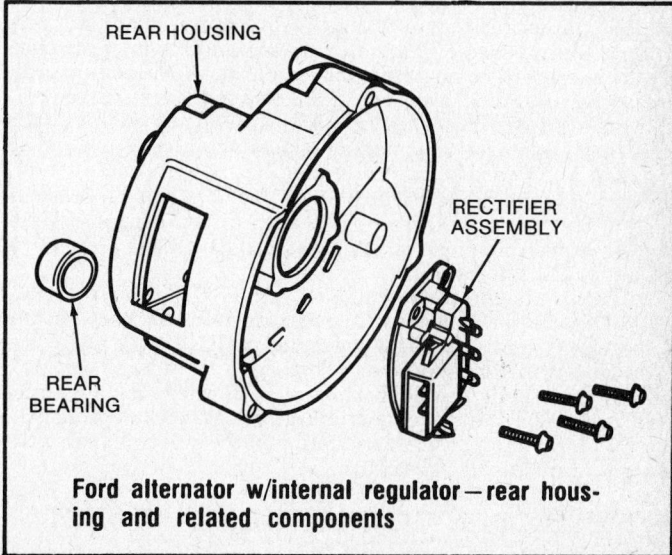

Ford alternator w/internal regulator—rear housing and related components

2. Be sure to clean and check all parts for wear and defects. Repair or replace defective components as required.

Ford Side Terminal Alternator

DESCRIPTION AND OPERATION

The alternator is belt driven from the engine. Current from the electronic voltage is supplied to the rotating field of the alternator through two brushes and two slip rings.

The alternator produces power in the form of alternating current. The alternating current is rectified to direct current by six diodes. The alternator regulator automatically adjusts the alternator field current to maintain the alternator output voltage within prescribed limits to correctly charge the battery. The alternator is self-current limiting.

The warning lamp control circuit passes current to the warning lamp when the ignition switch is in the RUN position and there is no alternator voltage at terminal S. When the voltage at terminal S rises to a preset value, current is cut off to the warning lamp. This circuit is not included in the regulator for vehicles equipped with an ammeter rather than a warning lamp.

A 500 ohm, ¼ watt resistor is connected across the terminals of the lamp at the instrument cluster in vehicles equipped with an indicator warning lamp. The regulator switching circuit receives voltage from the ignition switch through the warning lamp at terminal I on vehicles equipped with an indicator warning lamp or through terminal S on vehicles equipped with an ammeter. With an input voltage present, the switching circuit turns on the voltage control circuit which, in turn, adjusts field current to control alternator output voltage.

Fuse links are included in the charging system wiring on all models. This fuse link is used to prevent damage to the wiring harness and alternator if the wiring harness should become grounded or if a booster battery is connected to the charging system with the wrong polarity.

RECTIFIER SHORT GROUNDED AND STATOR GROUNDED TEST

NOTE: These tests are performed with an ohmmeter. Digital meters cannot be used to perform rectifier tests

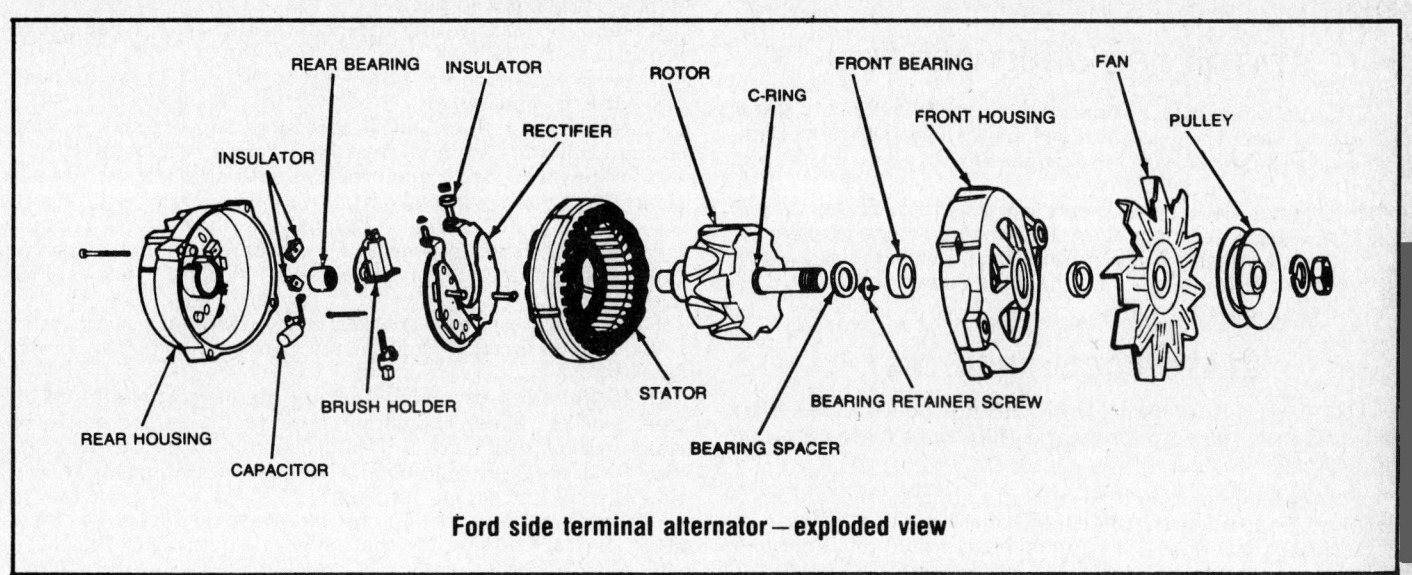

Ford side terminal alternator—exploded view

21-63

SECTION 21 ALTERNATORS
FORD (W/SIDE TERMINAL)

1. Connect one ohmmeter probe to alternator BAT terminal (red insulator) and other probe to STA terminal (rear blade terminal). Then reverse ohmmeter probes and repeat test. Normally, there will be no needle movement in one direction, indicating rectifier diodes are being checked in reverse current direction and are not shorted. A low reading with probes reversed indicates that rectifier positive diodes are being checked in forward current direction. Using referenced tester, low reading should be about 6 ohms, but may vary if another type of test is used. A reading in both directions indicates a damaged positive diode, a grounded positive diode plate, or a grounded BAT terminal.

2. Perform same test using STA and GND (ground) terminals of alternator. A reading in both directions indicates either a damaged negative diode, a grounded positive diode plate or a grounded BAT terminal.

3. If there is no needle movement with probes in one direction, and no needle movement or high resistance (significantly over 6 ohms) in opposite direction, a bad connection exists in stator circuit inside alternator.

FIELD OPEN OR SHORT CIRCUIT TEST

1. Using an ohmmeter, contact the alternator field terminal with one probe and ground terminal with other probe. Then, spin alternator pulley. Ohmmeter reading should be between 2.4 and 100 ohms and should fluctuate while pulley is turning.

2. An infinite reading (no meter movement) indicates a grounded brush lead, worn or stuck brushes or a worn or damaged rotor assembly.

3. An ohmmeter reading less than 2.4 ohms indicates a grounded brush assembly, a grounded field terminal or a worn or damaged rotor.

DIODE TEST

1. Remove the rectifier assembly from the alternator stator. To test one set of diodes, contact one probe to one terminal screw and contact each of three stator lead terminals with other probe. Reverse probes and repeat test. All diodes should show a low reading of about 6 ohms in one direction, and an infinite reading (no needle movement) with probes reversed. Low reading may vary with type of ohmmeter used.

2. Repeat preceding tests for other set of diodes by contacting other terminal screw and three stator lead terminals.

3. If meter readings are not as specified, replace rectifier assembly.

STATOR COIL GROUNDED TEST

1. Connect ohmmeter probes to one stator lead and to stator laminated core. Ensure that probe makes a good electrical connection with stator core. The meter should show an infinite reading (no meter movement).

2. If meter does not indicate an infinite reading (needle moves), stator winding is shorted to core and must be replaced.

3. Repeat this test for each stator lead. Do not touch the metal probes or stator leads with the hands. Such contact will result in an incorrect reading.

STATOR COIL OPEN TEST

NOTE: A single open phase will not be discovered by this test on a 100 amp alternator that has a delta connected stator.

1. Connect ohmmeter probe to a stator phase lead and touch other probe to another stator lead. Check meter reading.

2. Repeat this test with other two stator lead combinations. If no meter movement occurs (infinite resistance) on a lead paired with either of the other phase leads, that phase is open and the stator should be replaced.

ROTOR OPEN OR SHORT CIRCUIT TEST

1. Contact each ohmmeter probe to a rotor slip ring. The meter reading should be 2.3 to 2.5 ohms.

2. A higher reading indicates a damaged slip ring solder connection or a broken wire.

3. A lower reading indicates a shorted wire or slip ring. Replace rotor if it is damaged and cannot be serviced.

4. Contact one ohmmeter probe to a slip ring and the other probe to rotor shaft. Meter reading should be infinite (no deflection).

5. A reading other than infinite indicates rotor is shorted to shaft. Inspect slip ring soldered terminals to assure they are not bent and not touching rotor shaft, or that excess solder is not grounding rotor coil connections to shaft. Replace the rotor if it is shorted and cannot be serviced.

Disassembly and Assembly

1. Mark both end housings and stator with a scribe mark for assembly.

2. Remove four housings through bolts, and separate front housing and rotor from rear housing and stator. Slots are provided in front housing to aid in disassembly. Do not separate rear housing from stator at this time.

3. Remove drive pulley nut with Alternator Pulley Remover/Installer tool. Then, remove lockwasher, pulley, fan and fan spacer from rotor shaft.

4. Pull rotor and shaft from front housing and remove spacer from rotor shaft.

5. Remove three screws retaining bearing to front housing. If bearing is damaged or has lost lubricant, remove bearing from housing. To remove bearing, support housing close to bearing boss and press bearing from housing.

6. Unsolder and disengage three stator leads from rectifier. Work quickly to prevent overheating rectifier.

7. Lift stator from rear housing.

8. Unsolder and disengage brush holder lead from rectifier. Work quickly to prevent overheating rectifier.

9. Remove screw attaching capacitor lead to rectifier.

10. Remove four screws attaching rectifier to rear housing.

11. Remove two terminal nuts and insulator from outside housing. Remove rectifier from housing.

12. Remove two screws attaching brush holder to housing. Remove brushes and holder.

13. Remove any sealing compound from rear housing and brush holder.

14. Remove one screw attaching capacitor to rear housing and remove capacitor.

15. If bearing replacement is necessary, support rear housing close to bearing boss and press bearing out of housing.

16. Wipe rotor, stator and bearings with a clean cloth. Do not clean these parts with solvent.

17. Rotate front bearing on drive end of rotor shaft. Check for any scraping noise, looseness or roughness. Look for excessive lubricant leakage. If any of these conditions exist, replace bearing.

18. Inspect rotor shaft rear bearing surface for roughness or sever chatter marks. Replace rotor assembly if shaft is not smooth.

19. Place rear bearing on slip ring end of rotor shaft and rotate bearing. Make the same check for noise, looseness, or roughness as was made for front bearing. Inspect rollers and cage for damage. Replace bearing if these conditions exist, or if lubricant is lost or contaminated.

20. Check pulley and fan for excessive looseness on rotor shaft. Replace any pulley that is loose or bent out of shape.

21. Check both front and rear housing for cracks, particularly

ALTERNATORS
FORD (W/SIDE TERMINAL)

in webbed areas and at mounting ear. Replace damaged or cracked housing.

22. Check all wire leads on both stator and rotor assemblies for loose or broken soldered connections and for burned insulation. Resolder poor connections. Replace parts that show signs of burned insulation.

23. Check slip rings for nicks and surface roughness. Nicks and scratches may be removed by turning down slip rings. Do not go beyond minimum diameter of 1.22 in. If rings are badly damaged, replace rotor assembly.

24. Replace brushes if they are worn shorter than ¼ inch.

25. If front housing bearing is being replaced, press new bearing in housing. Apply pressure on bearing outer race only. Then, install bearing retaining screws and tighten to 25 to 40 inch lbs.

26. Place inner spacer on rotor shaft and insert rotor shaft into front housing and bearing.

27. Install fan spacer, fan, pulley, lockwasher and nut on rotor shaft. Use the proper tool to tighten pulley nut.

28. If rear bearing is being replaced, press a new bearing in from inside housing until rear bearing face is flush with boss outer surface.

29. Position brush terminal on brush holder. Install springs and brushes in brush holder and insert a piece of stiff wire to hold brushes in place.

30. Brushes and springs are serviced as part of brush holder assembly. Position brush holder in rear housing and install attaching screws. Brush retaining wire must stick out enough to be grabbed and pulled from housing assembly.

31. Waterproof glue sealer may have to be pushed out of pin hole in housing. Push brush holder toward brush holder attaching screws. Reseal crack between brush holder and brush cavity in rear housing with Caulking Cord or equivalent body sealer. Do not use silicone base sealer for this application.

32. Position capacitor to rear housing and install attaching screw. Place two rectifier insulators on bosses inside housing.

33. Place insulator on BAT (large) terminal of rectifier and position rectifier in rear housing. Place outside insulator on BAT terminal and install nuts on BAT AND GRD terminals fingertight. Install, but do not tighten, four rectifier attaching screws.

34. Tighten the BAT terminal nuts to 35 to 50 inch lbs. and GRD terminal nuts to 25 to 35 inch lbs. on outside of rear hous-

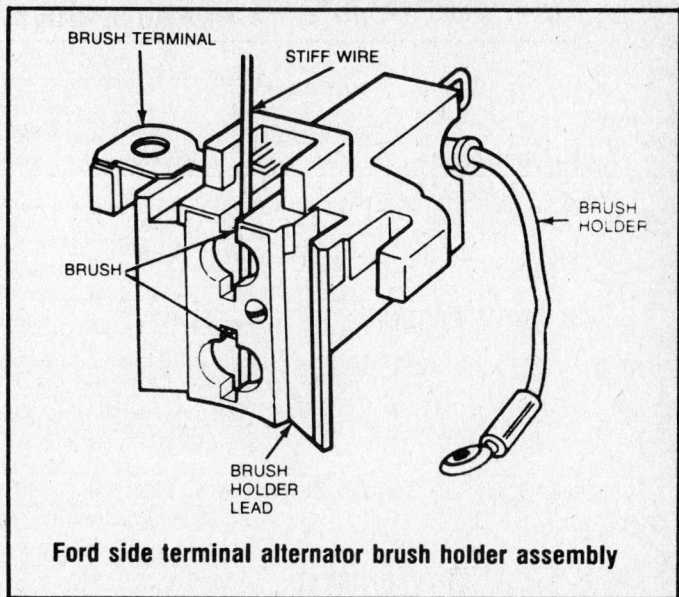

Ford side terminal alternator brush holder assembly

ing. Then, tighten four rectifier attaching screws to 40 to 50 inch lbs.

35. Position capacitor lead to rectifier and install attaching screw.

36. Press brush holder lead on rectifier pin and solder securely. Work quickly to prevent overheating of rectifier.

37. Position stator in rear housing and align scribe marks. Press three stator leads on rectifier pins and solder securely using resin core electrical solder. Work quickly to prevent overheating rectifier.

38. Position rotor and front housing into stator and rear housing. Align scribe marks and install four through bolts. Tighten two opposing bolts and then two remaining bolts.

39. Spin fan and pulley to be sure nothing is binding within alternator.

40. Remove brush retracting wire and place a daub of waterproof cement over hole to seal it. Do not use silicone sealer on hole.

SECTION 22
AIR CONDITIONING
MINOR SERVICE

REFRIGERANT CAPACITIES CHART

Auto Manufacturer	1980 Models	1980 Recharge Capacities (lbs.)①	1981 Models	1981 Recharge Capacities (lbs.)①	1982–87 Models	1982–87 Recharge Capacities (lbs.)①
AMERICAN MOTORS CORP.	Concord	2	Concord	2	All	2.00
	Pacer	2⅛	Spirit	2		
	Spirit	2	Eagle	2		
	Eagle	2				
BUICK MOTOR DIVISION	Skyhawk	2½	Skyhawk	2½	Electra, LeSabre	3.50
	Skylark	2¾	Skylark	2¾	Regal, Century, Skylark	2.75
	Electra, LeSabre	3¾	Electra, LeSabre	3¾		
	Century, Regal, Riviera	3½	Century, Regal, Riviera	3½	Riviera, Somerset Regal	3.25
					Skyhawk	2.50
CADILLAC MOTOR CAR DIVISION	Seville, Eldorado	3½	Seville, Eldorado	3½	Cimarron	1.87
	All others	3¾	All others	3¾	Seville	2.75
					All others	3.50
CHEVROLET MOTOR DIVISION	Monza, Nova	3½	Monza, Nova	3½	Corvette, Camaro	3.00
	Chevette	2¼	Chevette	2¼	Caprice, Impala	3.50
	Camaro	3¼	Camaro	3¼	Monte Carlo	3.25
	Corvette	3	Corvette	3	Malibu, Celebrity, Citation, Cavalier	2.75
	Citation	2¾	Citation	2¾		
	Malibu, Impala, Caprice	3¾	Malibu, Impala, Caprice	3¾	Chevette	2.25
CHRYSLER CORPORATION	All, except below	2⅝	All, except below	2⅝	Diplomat, Gran Fury, New Yorker, Mirada, Cordoba, Imperial	2.62
	Omni, Horizon	2⅛	Omni, Horizon, Aries, Reliant	2⅛		
					Aries, Reliant, LeBaron, E-Class, 400, 600	2.37 ③
					Omni, Horizon, 024, TC3, Charger, Turismo	2.12
FORD DIVISION	Pinto	2¼	Escort, EXP	2½	Thunderbird, Fairmont, Granada, Mustang, Escort, EXP	2.56
	All others②	3½	All others②	3½		
					LTD, Crown Victoria	3.25
LINCOLN-MERCURY DIVISION	Bobcat	2¼	Lynx, LN7	2½	Lincoln Continental, XR-7, Zephyr, Cougar, Capri, Lynx, LN7	2.56
	All others②	3½	All others②	3½		
					Lincoln, Mark VI	3.00
					Marquis, Grand Marquis	3.25
OLDSMOBILE DIVISION	Cutlass, 88, 98	3¾	Cutlass, 88, 98	3¾	88, 98	3.50
	Toronado	3½	Toronado	3½	Cutlass, Cutlass Ciera, Omega	2.75
	Starfire	2½	Starfire	2½		
	Omega	2¾	Omega	2¾	Toronado	3.25
					Firenza	2.50
PONTIAC MOTOR DIVISION	Catalina, Bonneville	3½	Catalina, Bonneville, Lemans, Gran Am	3½	Firebird	3.00
	Firebird	3¼	Firebird	3¼	Bonneville, Parisienne, Grand Am	3.30
	Sunbird	2½	Sunbird	2½		
	Phoenix	2¾	Phoenix	2¾	Grand Prix	3.30
					6000, Phoenix	2.75
					J-2000, Fiero, Sunbird	2.50
					T-1000	2.25

① All refrigerant charges listed are approximate and represent a minimal reserve with moderate head pressures. Check label on or near compressor for correct charge.

② Ford, Mercury and Lincoln vehicles using Frigidaire 6 cylinder compressor–4¼ lbs.

③ 1985 and later Aries, Reliant, LeBaron, E class, 400 & 600 recharge capacities are 2.12 lbs.

SECTION 22

Air Conditioning

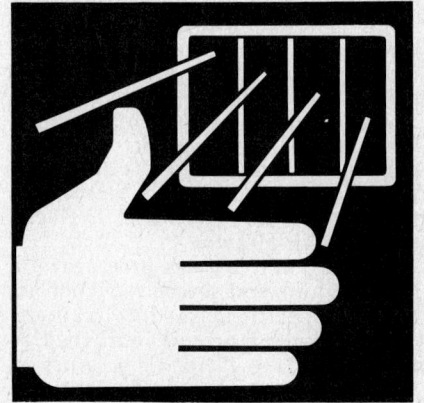

AIR CONDITIONING SYSTEMS

Automotive air conditioning systems are basic in design and operation, but many different components are used by the vehicle manufacturers to operate and control the systems to their specifications.

Basic System

The basic air conditioning system utilizes the compressor, condenser, evaporator, receiver-drier, expansion valve and a thermostatic or ambient type switch to control evaporator freeze-up. The controls are manually operated and the unit is basic in design. This system is usually installed as an add-on or after-market unit. A sight glass may be used in the system.

GENERAL SERVICING PROCEDURES

The most important aspect of air conditioning service is the maintenance of a pure and adequate charge of refrigerant in the system. A refrigeration system cannot function properly if a significant percentage of the charge is lost. Leaks are common because the severe vibration encountered in an automobile can easily cause a sufficient cracking or loosening of the air conditioning fittings; as a result, the extreme operating pressures of the system force refrigerant out.

The problem can be understood by considering what happens to the system as it is operated with a continuous leak. Because the expansion valve regulates the flow of refrigerant to the evaporator, the level of refrigerant there is fairly constant. The receiver-drier stores any excess of refrigerant, and so a loss will first appear there as a reduction in the level of liquid. As this level nears the bottom of the vessel, some refrigerant vapor bubbles will begin to appear in the stream of liquid supplied to the expansion valve. This vapor decreases the capacity of the expansion valve very little as the valve opens to compensate for

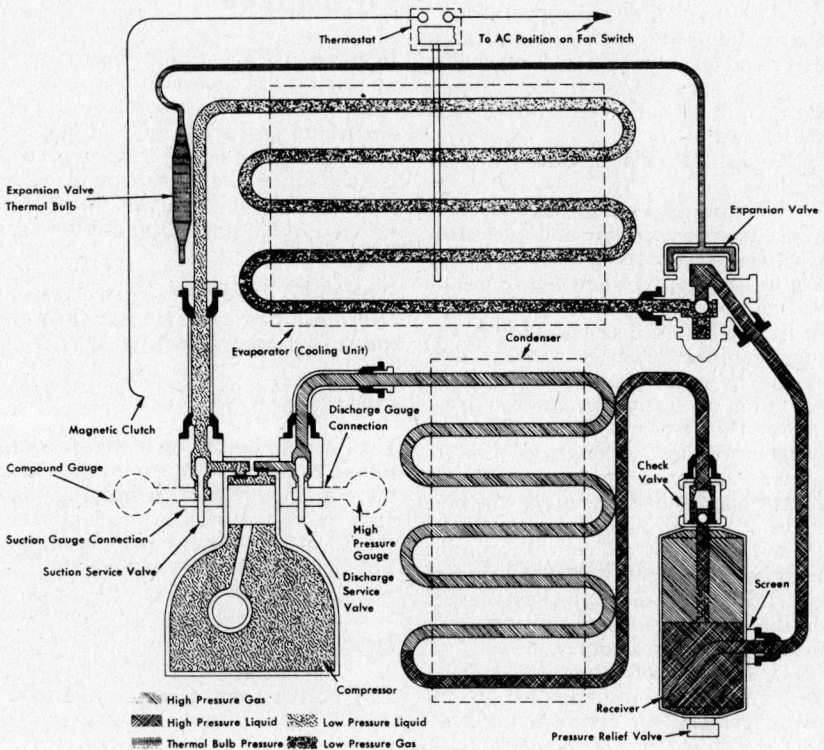

Basic air conditioning system

22-3

Section 22: Air Conditioning — Minor Service

its presence. As the quantity of liquid in the condenser decreases, the operating pressure will drop there and throughout the high side of the system. As the R-12 continues to be expelled, the pressure available to force the liquid through the expansion valve will continue to decrease, and, eventually, the valve's orifice will prove to be too much of a restriction for adequate flow even with the needle fully withdrawn.

At this point, low side pressure will start to drop, and severe reduction in cooling capacity, marked by freeze-up of the evaporator coil, will result. Eventually, the operating pressure of the evaporator will be lower than the pressure of the atmosphere surrounding it, and air will be drawn into the system wherever there are leaks in the low side.

Because all atmospheric air contains at least some moisture, water will enter the system and mix with the R-12 and the oil. Trace amounts of moisture will cause sludging of the oil, and corrosion of the system. Saturation and clogging of the filter-drier, and freezing of the expansion valve orifice will eventually result. As air fills the system to a greater and greater extent, it will interfere more and more with the normal flows of refrigerant and heat.

From this description, it should be obvious that much of the repairman's time will be spent detecting leaks, repairing them, and then restoring the purity and quantity of the refrigerant charge. A list of general precautions that should be observed while doing this follows:

1. Keep all tools as clean and dry as possible.
2. Thoroughly purge the service gauges and hoses of air and moisture before connecting them to the system. Keep them capped when not in use.
3. Thoroughly clean any refrigerant fitting before disconnecting it, in order to minimize the entrance of dirt into the system.
4. Plan any operation that requires opening the system beforehand, in order to minimize the length of time it will be exposed to open air. Cap or seal the open ends to minimize the entrance of foreign material.
5. When adding oil, pour it through an extremely clean and dry tube or funnel. Keep the oil capped whenever possible. Do not use oil that has not been kept tightly sealed.
6. Use only refrigerant 12. Purchase refrigerant intended for use in only automatic air conditioning systems. Avoid the use of refrigerant 12 that may be packaged for another use, such as cleaning, or powering a horn, as it is impure.
7. Completely evacuate any system that has been opened to replace a component, or that has leaked sufficiently to draw in moisture and air. This requires evacuating air and moisture with a good vacuum pump for at least one hour.
If a system has been open for a considerable length of time it may be advisable to evacuate the system for up to 12 hours (overnight).
8. Use a wrench on both halves of a fitting that is to be disconnected, so as to avoid placing torque on any of the refrigerant lines.
9. When overhauling a compressor, pour some of the oil into a clean glass and inspect it. If there is evidence of dirt or metal particles, or both, flush all refrigerant components with clean refrigerant before evacuating and recharging the system. In addition, if metal particles are present, the compressor should be replaced.
10. Schrader valves may leak only when under full operating pressure. Therefore, if leakage is suspected but cannot be located, operate the system with a full charge of refrigerant and look for leaks from all Schrader valves. Replace any faulty valves.

Additional Preventive Maintenance Checks

ANTIFREEZE

In order to prevent heater core freeze-up during A/C operation, it is necessary to maintain permanent type antifreeze protection of +15 degrees F, or lower. A reading of -15 degrees F is ideal since this protection also supplies sufficient corrosion inhibitors for the protection of the engine cooling system.

NOTE: The same antifreeze should not be used longer than the manufacturer specifies.

RADIATOR CAP

For efficient operation of an air conditioned car's cooling system, the radiator cap should have a holding pressure which meets manufacturer's specifications. A cap which fails to hold these pressures should be replaced.

CONDENSER

Any obstruction of or damage to the condenser configuration will restrict the air flow which is essential to its efficient operation. It is therefore a good rule to keep this unit clean and in proper physical shape.

NOTE: Bug screens are regarded as obstructions.

CONDENSATION DRAIN TUBE

This single molded drain tube expels the condensation, which accumulates on the bottom of the evaporator housing, into the engine compartment. If this tube is obstructed, the air conditioning performance can be restricted and condensation buildup can spill over onto the vehicle's floor.

Safety Precautions

Because of the importance of the necessary safety precautions that must be exercised when working with air conditioning systems and R-12 refrigerant, a recap of the safety precautions are outlined.

1. Avoid contact with a charged refrigeration system, even when working on another part of the air conditioning system or vehicle. If a heavy tool comes into contact with a section of copper tubing or a heat exchanger, it can easily cause the relatively soft material to rupture.
2. When it is necessary to apply force to a fitting which contains refrigerant, as when checking that all system couplings are securely tightened, use a wrench on both parts of the fitting involved, if possible. This will avoid putting torque on refrigerant tubing. (It is advisable, when possible, to use tube or line wrenches when tightening these flare nut fittings.)
3. Do not attempt to discharge the system by merely loosening a fitting, or removing the service valve caps and cracking these valves. Precise control is possible only when using the service gauges. Place a rag under the open end of the center charging hose while discharging the system to catch any drops of liquid that might escape. Wear protective gloves when connecting or disconnecting service gauge hoses.
4. Discharge the system only in a well ventilated area, as high concentrations of the gas can exclude oxygen and act as an anaesthetic. When leak testing or soldering, this is particularly important, as toxic gas is formed when R-12 contacts any flame.
5. Never start a system without first verifying that both service valves are back-seated, if equipped, and that all fittings throughout the system are snugly connected.
6. Avoid applying heat to any refrigerant line or storage vessel. Charging may be aided by using wa-

AIR CONDITIONING
MINOR SERVICE
SECTION 22

ter heated to less than 125° to warm the refrigerant container. Never allow a refrigerant storage container to sit out in the sun, or near any other source of heat, such as a radiator.

7. Always wear goggles when working on a system to protect the eyes. If refrigerant contacts the eyes, it is advisable in all cases to see a physician as soon as possible.

8. Frostbite from liquid refrigerant should be treated by first gradually warming the area with cool water, and then gently applying petroleum jelly. A physician should be consulted.

9. Always keep refrigerant drum fittings capped when not in use. Avoid sudden shock to the drum, which might occur from dropping it, or from banging a heavy tool against it. Never carry a drum in the passenger compartment of a car.

10. Always completely discharge the system before painting the vehicle (if the paint is to be baked on), or before welding anywhere near refrigerant lines.

AIR CONDITIONING TOOLS AND GAUGES

Test Gauges

Most of the service work performed in air conditioning requires the use of a set of two gauges, one for the high (head) pressure side of the system, the other for the low (suction) side.

The low side gauge records both pressure and vacuum. Vacuum readings are calibrated from 0 to 30 inches and the pressure graduations read from 0 to no less than 60 psi.

The high side gauge measures pressure from 0 to at least 600 psi. Both gauges are threaded into a manifold that contains two hand shut-off valves. Proper manipulation of these valves and the use of the attached test hoses allow the user to perform the following services:

1. Test high and low side pressures.
2. Remove air, moisture, and contaminated refrigerant.
3. Purge the system (of refrigerant).
4. Charge the system (with refrigerant).

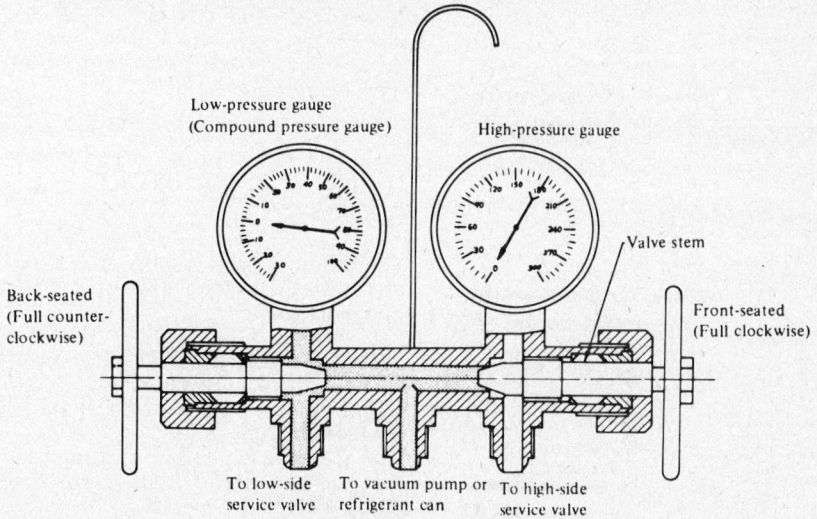

Typical manifold gauge set

NOTE: Chrysler Corp. requires the use of a third gauge on those units that have an evaporator pressure regulator (EPR) valve mounted on the suction side of the compressor.

The manifold valves are designed so they have no direct effect on gauge readings, but serve only to provide for, or cut off, flow of refrigerant through the manifold. During all testing and hook-up operations, the valves are kept in a closed position to avoid disturbing the refrigeration system. The valves are opened only to purge the system of refrigerant or to charge it.

When purging the system, the center hose is uncapped at the lower end, and both valves are cracked open slightly. This allows refrigerant pressure to force the entire contents of the system out through the center hose. During charging, the valve on the high side of the manifold is closed, and the valve on the low side is cracked open. Under these conditions, the low pressure in the evaporator will draw refrigerant from the relatively warm refrigerant storage container into the system.

Service Valves

For the user to diagnose an air conditioning system he or she must gain "entrance" to the system in order to observe the pressures. There are two types of terminals for this purpose, the hand shut off type and the familiar Schrader valve.

The Schrader valve is similar to a tire valve stem and the process of connecting the test hoses is the same as threading a hand pump outlet hose to a bicycle tire. As the test hose is threaded to the service port the valve core is depressed, allowing the refrigerant to enter the test hose outlet. Removal of the test hose automatically closes the system.

Extreme caution must be observed when removing test hoses from the Schrader valves as some refrigerant will normally escape, usually under high pressure. (Observe safety precautions.)

Some systems have hand shut-off valves (the stem can be rotated with a special ratcheting box wrench) that can be positioned in the following three ways:

1. FRONT SEATED—Rotated to full clockwise position.
   a. Refrigerant will not flow to

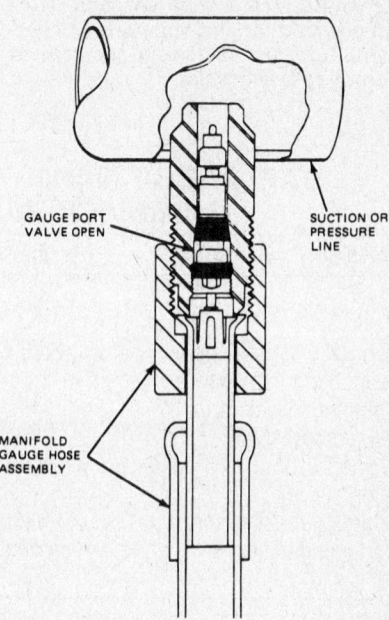

Manifold gauge hose connected to a Schraeder type service port

22-5

SECTION 22 AIR CONDITIONING
MINOR SERVICE

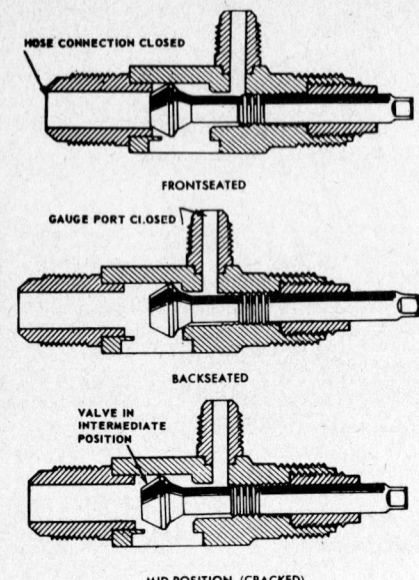

Manual service valve positions

3. MID-POSITION (CRACKED) — Refrigerant flows to entire system. Gauge port (with hose connected) open for testing.

USING THE MANIFOLD GAUGES

The following are step-by-step procedures to guide the user to correct gauge usage.
1. WEAR GOGGLES OR FACE SHIELD DURING ALL TESTING OPERATIONS. BACKSEAT HAND SHUT-OFF TYPE SERVICE VALVES.
2. Remove caps from high and low side service ports. Make sure both gauge valves are closed.
3. Connect low side test hose to service valve that leads to the evaporator (located between the evaporator outlet and the compressor).
4. Attach high side test hose to service valve that leads to the condenser.
5. Mid-position hand shutoff type service valves.
6. Start engine and allow for warm-up. All testing and charging of the system should be done after engine and system have reached normal operation temperatures (except when using certain charging stations).
7. Adjust air conditioner controls to maximum cold.
8. Observe gauge readings.

When the gauges are not being used it is a good idea to:
 a. Keep both hand valves in the closed position.
 b. Attach both ends of the high and low service hoses to the manifold, if extra outlets are present on the manifold, or plug them if not.

Also, keep the center charging hose attached to an empty refrigerant can. This extra precaution will reduce the possibility of moisture entering the gauges. If air and moisture have gotten into the gauges, purge the hoses by supplying refrigerant under pressure to the center hose with both gauge valves open and all openings unplugged.

DISCHARGING, EVACUATING AND CHARGING

Discharging the System

— CAUTION —
Perform operation in a well-ventilated area.

When it is necessary to remove (purge) the refrigerant pressurized in the system, follow this procedure:
1. Operate air conditioner for at least 10 minutes.
2. Attach gauges, shut off engine and air conditioner.
3. Place a container or rag at the outlet of the center charging hose on the gauge. The refrigerant will be discharged there and this precaution will avoid its uncontrolled exposure.
4. Open low side hand valve on gauge slightly.
5. Open high side hand valve slightly.

NOTE: Too rapid a purging process will be identified by the appearance of an oily foam. If this occurs, close the hand valves a little more until this condition stops.

6. Close both hand valves on the gauge set when the pressures read 0 and all the refrigerant has left the system.

Evacuating the System

Before charging any system it is necessary to purge the refrigerant and draw out the trapped moisture with a suitable vacuum pump. Failure to do so will result in ineffective charging and possible damage to the system.
Use this hook-up for the proper evacuation procedure:
1. Connect both service gauge hoses to the high and low service outlets.

compressor, but will reach test gauge port. COMPRESSOR WILL BE DAMAGED IF SYSTEM IS TURNED ON IN THIS POSITION.
 b. The compressor is now isolated and ready for service. However, care must be exercised when removing service valves from the compressor as a residue of refrigerant may still be present within the compressor. Therefore, remove service valves slowly observing all safety precautions.
2. BACK SEATED — Rotated to full counter clockwise position. Normal position for system while in operation. Refrigerant flows to compressor but not to test gauge.

BAR GAUGE MANIFOLD AND COMPRESSOR SERVICE VALVE SETTINGS

Condition	Manifold Valves	Compressor Valves
Testing System	Both fully closed	Both cracked off backseat
Depressurizing System	Both cracked open	Both at mid position
Evacuating the system	Both wide open	Both at mid position
Charging in gas form with compressor running	High pressure valve closed / Low pressure valve cracked	High pressure valve cracked off backseat / Low pressure valve at mid position
Charging in liquid form with compressor off	Low pressure valve closed / High pressure valve wide open	Both valves mid positioned

Note: A very small leak, causing system discharge about every two weeks, can be caused by a leaky Schrader type service valve. Check these valves with extra care when testing for a small leak.

AIR CONDITIONING
MINOR SERVICE
SECTION 22

2. Open high and low side hand valves on gauge manifold.

3. Open both service valves a slight amount (from back seated position), allow refrigerant to discharge from system.

4. Install center charging hose of gauge set to vacuum pump.

5. Operate vacuum pump for at least one hour. (If the system has been subjected to open conditions for a prolonged period of time it may be necessary to "pump the system down" overnight. Refer to "System Sweep" procedure.)

NOTE: If low pressure gauge does not show at least 28" hg. within 5 minutes, check the system for a leak or loose gauge connectors.

6. Close hand valves on gauge manifold.

7. Shut off pump.

8. Observe low pressure gauge to determine if vacuum is holding. A vacuum drop may indicate a leak.

System Sweep

An efficient vacuum pump can remove all the air contained in a contaminated air conditioning system very quickly, because of its vapor state. Moisture, however, is far more difficult to remove because the vacuum must force the liquid to evaporate before it will be able to remove it from the system. If a system has become severely contaminated, as, for example, it might become after all the charge was lost in conjunction with vehicle accident damage, moisture removal is extremely time consuming. A vacuum pump could remove all of the moisture only if it were operated for 12 hours or more.

Under these conditions, sweeping the system with refrigerant will speed the process of moisture removal considerably. To sweep, follow the following procedure:

1. Connect vacuum pump to gauges, operate it until vacuum ceases to increase, then continue operation for ten more minutes.

2. Charge system with 50% of its rated refrigerant capacity.

3. Operate system at fast idle for ten minutes.

4. Discharge the system.

5. Repeat twice the process of charging to 50% capacity, running the system for ten minutes, and discharging it, for a total of three sweeps.

6. Replace drier.

7. Pump system down as in Step 1.

8. Charge system.

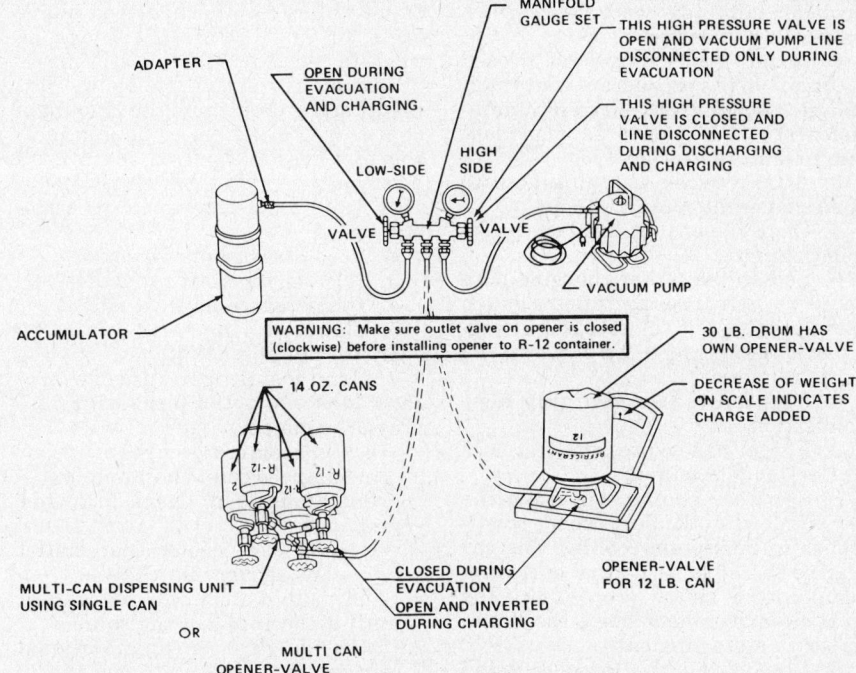

Typical gauge connections for discharge, evacuation and charging the system

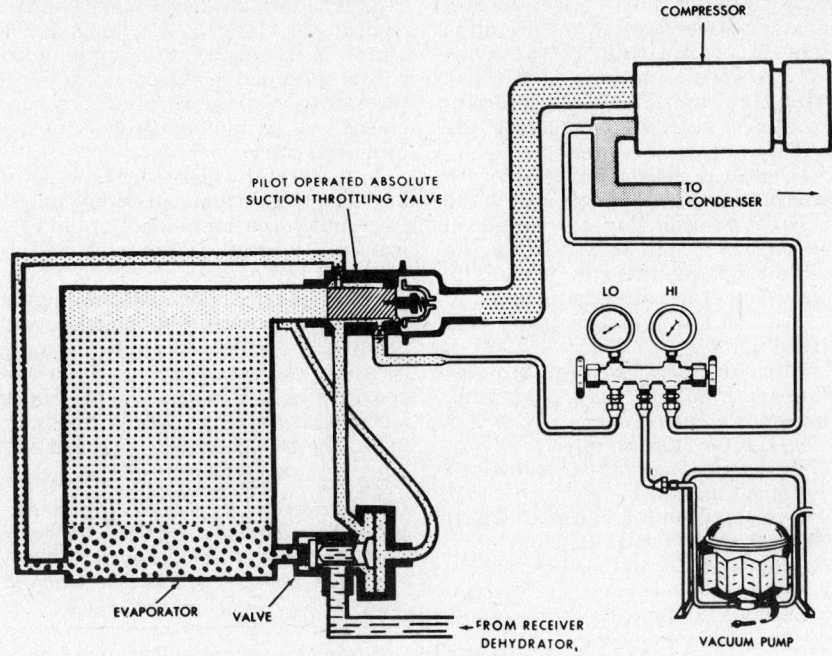

Schematic for evacuating the system

Charging the System

CAUTION

Never attempt to charge the system by opening the high pressure gauge control while the compressor is operating. The compressor accumulating pressure can burst the refrigerant container, causing sever personal injuries.

BASIC SYSTEM

In this procedure the refrigerant enters the suction side of the system as a vapor while the compressor is running. Before proceeding, the system should be in a partial vacuum after adequate evacuation. Both hand valves on the gauge manifold should be closed.

1. Attach both test hoses to their respective service valve ports. Mid-

22–7

SECTION 22 AIR CONDITIONING
MINOR SERVICE

position manually operated service valves, if present.

2. Install dispensing valve (closed position) on the refrigerant container. (Single and multiple refrigerant manifolds are available to accommodate one to four 15 oz. cans.)

3. Attach center charging hose to the refrigerant container valve.

4. Open dispensing valve on the refrigerant can.

5. Loosen the center charging hose coupler where it connects to the gauge manifold to allow the escaping refrigerant to purge the hose of contaminants.

6. Tighten center charging hose connection.

7. Purge the low pressure test hose at the gauge manifold.

8. Start car engine, roll down the car windows and adjust the air conditioner to maximum cooling. The car engine should be at normal operating temperature before proceeding. The heated environment helps the liquid vaporize more efficiently.

9. Crack open the low side hand valve on the manifold. Manipulate the valve so that the refrigerant that enters the system does not cause the low side pressure to exceed 40 psi. Too sudden a surge may permit the entrance of unwanted liquid to the compressor. Since liquids cannot be compressed, the compressor will suffer damage if compelled to attempt it. If the suction side of the system remains in a vacuum the system is blocked. Locate and correct the condition before proceeding any further.

NOTE: Placing the refrigerant can in a container of warm water (no hotter than 125°F) will speed the charging process. Slight agitation of the can is helpful too, but be careful not to turn the can upside down.

Some manufacturers allow for a partial charging of the A/C system in the form of a liquid (can inverted and compressor off) by opening the high side gauge valve only, and putting the high side compressor service valve in the middle position (if so equipped). The remainder of the refrigerant is then added in the form of a gas in the normal manner, through the suction side only.

SYSTEMS WITHOUT SIGHT GLASS, EXCEPT CCOT SYSTEM

The following procedure can be used to quickly determine whether or not an air conditioning system has the proper charge of refrigerant (providing ambient temperature is above 70°F, or 21°C). This check can be made in a manner of minutes, thus facilitating system diagnosis by pinpointing the problem to the amount of charge in the system or by eliminating this possibility from the overall checkout.

1. Engine must be warm (thermostat open).
2. Hood and body doors open.
3. Selector lever set at NORM.
4. Temperature lever at COLD.
5. Blower on HI.
6. Normal engine idle.
7. Hand-feel temperature of evaporator inlet and outlet pipes with compressor engaged.
   a. Both same temperature or some degree cooler than ambient—proper condition: check for other problems.
   b. Inlet pipe cooler than outlet pipe—low refrigerant charge.
   • Add a slight amount of refrigerant until both pipes feel the same.
   • Then add 15 oz. (1 can) additional refrigerant.
   c. Inlet pipe has frost accumulation—outlet pipe warmer: proceed as in Step b above.

If during the charging process the head pressure exceeds 200 psi, place an electric fan in front of the car and direct the turbulent air to the condenser. If no fan is available, repeatedly pour cool water over the top of the condenser. These cooling actions may be necessary on an extremely warm day to help dissipate the heat emitted by the engine during idle.

If this fails and pressure on the discharge side continues to rise, the system may be overcharged or the engine might be overheating. Never allow head pressure to go beyond 240 psi. during charging. If this condition occurs, stop engine, find and correct the problem.

8. Continue dispensing refrigerant until container is no longer cool to the touch. On a humid day, the outside of the container will frost. When the frost disappears the can is usually empty. To detach dispensing can:
   a. close low pressure test gauge hand valve.
   b. crack open low pressure test hose at manifold until remaining pressure escapes.
   c. tighten hose coupler.
   d. loosen hose coupler connected to refrigerant can.
   e. discard empty can and repeat Steps 2–8.
9. Continue to add refrigerant to the required capacity of the system. (Usually marked on the compressor).

--- **CAUTION** ---
DO NOT OVERCHARGE. This condition is usually indicated by an abnormally high side pressure reading and a noisy compressor resulting in ineffective cooling and damage to the system.

SYSTEMS WITH A SIGHT GLASS

The air conditioning systems that use a sight glass as a means to check the refrigerant level, should be carefully checked to avoid under or over charging. The gauge set should be attached to the system for verification of pressures.

To check the system with the sight glass, clean the glass and start the vehicle engine. Operate the air conditioning controls on maximum for approximately five minutes to stabilize the system. The room temperature should be above 70 degrees. Check the sight glass for one of the following conditions:

1. If the sight glass is clear, the compressor clutch is engaged, the compressor discharge line is warm and the compressor inlet line is cool, the system has a full charge of refrigerant.

2. If the sight glass is clear, the compressor clutch is engaged and there is no significant temperature difference between the compressor inlet and discharge lines, the system is empty or nearly empty. By having the gauge set attached to the system a measurement can be taken. If the gauge reads less than 25 psi, the low pressure cutoff protection switch has failed.

3. If the sight glass is clear and the compressor clutch is disengaged, the clutch is defective, or the clutch circuit is open, or the system is out of refrigerant. By-pass the low pressure cut-off switch momentarily to determine the cause.

4. If the sight glass shows foam or bubbles, the system can be low on refrigerant. Occasional foam or bubbles is normal when the room temperature is above 110 degrees or below 70 degrees. To verify, increase the engine speed to approximately 1500 rpm and block the airflow through the condenser to increase the compressor discharge pressure to 225–250 psi. If the sight glass still shows bubbles or foam, the refrigerant level is low.

--- **CAUTION** ---
Do not operate the vehicle engine any longer than necessary with the condenser airflow blocked. This blocking action also blocks the cooling system radiator and will cause the system to overheat rapidly.

When the system is low on refrigerant, a leak is present or the system

AIR CONDITIONING
MINOR SERVICE
SECTION 22

was not properly charged. Use a leak detector and locate the problem area and repair. If no leakage is found, charge the system to its capacity. (Refer to the refrigerant capacity chart at the end of this section.)

CAUTION
It is not advisable to add refrigerant to a system utilizing the suction throttling valve and a sight glass, because the amount of refrigerant required to remove the foam or bubbles will result in an overcharge and potentially damaged system components.

CCOT SYSTEM

When charging the CCOT system, attach only the low pressure line to the low pressure gauge port, located on the accumulator. Do not attach the high pressure line to any service port or allow it to remain attached to the vacuum pump after evacuation. Be sure both the high and the low pressure control valves are closed on the gauge set. To complete the charging of the system, follow the outline supplied.

1. Start the engine and allow to run at idle, with the cooling system at normal operating temperature.
2. Attach the center gauge hose to a single or multi-can dispenser.
3. With the multi-can dispenser inverted, allow one pound or the contents of one or two 14 oz. cans to enter the system through the low pressure side by opening the gauge low pressure control valve.
4. Close the low pressure gauge control valve and turn the A/C system on to engage the compressor. Place the blower motor in its high mode.
5. Open the low pressure gauge control valve and draw the remaining charge into the system. Refer to the capacity chart at the end of this section for the individual vehicle or system capacity.
6. Close the low pressure gauge control valve and the refrigerant source valve, on the multi-can dispenser. Remove the low pressure hose from the accumulator quickly to avoid loss of refrigerant through the Schrader valve.
7. Install the protective cap on the gauge port and check the system for leakage.
8. Test the system for proper operation.

Leak Testing the System

There are several methods of detecting leaks in an air conditioning system; among them, the two most popular are (1) halide leak-detection or the "open flame method," and (2) electronic leak-detection.

The halide leak detection is a torch like device which produces a yellow-green color when refrigerant is introduced into the flame at the burner. A purple or violet color indicates the presence of large amounts of refrigerant at the burner.

An electronic leak detector is a small portable electronic device with an extended probe. With the unit activated the probe is passed along those components of the system which contain refrigerant. If a leak is detected, the unit will sound an alarm signal or activate a display signal depending on the manufacturer's design. It is advisable to follow the manufacturer's instructions as the design and function of the detection may vary significantly.

CAUTION
Caution should be taken to operate either type of detector in well ventilated areas, so as to reduce the chance of personal injury, which may result from coming in contact with poisonous gases produced when R-12 is exposed to flame or electric spark.

Amount of refrigerant / Check item	Almost no refrigerant	Insufficient	Suitable	Too much refrigerant
Temperature of high pressure and low pressure lines.	Almost no difference between high pressure and low pressure side temperature.	High pressure side is warm and low pressure side is fairly cold.	High pressure side is hot and low pressure side is cold.	High pressure side is abnormally hot.
State in sight glass.	Bubbles flow continuously. **Bubbles will disappear and something like mist will flow when refrigerant is nearly gone.**	The bubbles are seen at intervals of 1 - 2 seconds.	Almost transparent. Bubbles may appear when engine speed is raised and lowered. **No clear difference exists between these two conditions.**	No bubbles can be seen.
Pressure of system.	High pressure side is abnormally low.	Both pressure on high and low pressure sides are slightly low.	Both pressures on high and low pressure sides are normal.	Both pressures on high and low pressure sides are abnormally high.
Repair.	**Stop compressor immediately and conduct an overall check.**	Check for gas leakage, repair as required, replenish and charge system.		Discharge refrigerant from service valve of low pressure side.

Using a sight glass to determine the relative refrigerant charge

22-9

SECTION 23: AUTOMATIC TRANSMISSIONS

INDEX

Transmission Identification by Pan Gasket 23–3
General Trouble Diagnosis 23–4

AUTOMATIC TRANSMISSIONS

AMC TORQUE COMMAND
Transmission & Converter Identification 23–5
Adjustment 23–5
Clutch & Band Applicators 23–8
On Car Services 23–8

CHRYSLER TORQUEFLITE A904, A998, A999
Transmission & Converter Identification 23–5
Adjustment 23–5
Clutch & Band Applications 23–8
On Car Services 23–8

FORD AUTOMATIC OVERDRIVE TRANSMISSION
Transmission & Converter Identification 23–11
Adjustment 23–11
Clutch & Band Applications 23–13
On Car Services 23–13

FORD C–3 TRANSMISSIONS
Transmission & Converter Indetification 23–13
Adjustments 23–14
Clutch & Band Applications 23–15
On Car Services 23–15

FORD C–5 TRANSMISSION
Transmission & Converter Identification 23–16
Adjustments 23–16
Clutch & Band Applications 23–19
On Car Services 23–18

ZF 4HP–22 TRANSMISSION
Transmission & Converter Identification 23–22
Adjustments 23–22
Clutch & Band Applications 23–26
On Car Services 23–25

GENERAL MOTORS TORQUE CONVERTER CLUTCH (T.C.C.)
Trouble Diagnosis 23–27

GM THM 180 C TRANSMISSION
Transmission & Converter Identification 23–33
Adjustments 23–33
Clutch & Band Applications 23–34
On Car Services 23–34

GM THM 200 C TRANSMISSION
Transmission & Converter Identification 23–35
Adjustments 23–36
Clutch & Band Applications 23–36
On Car Services 23–36

GM THM 200 4R TRANSMISSION
Transmission & Converter Identification 23–37
Adjustments 23–37
Clutch & Band Applications 23–39
On Car Services 23–38

GM THM 250C TRANSMISSION
Transmission & Converter Identification 23–39
Adjustments 23–45
Clutch & Band Applications 23–46
On Car Services 23–46

GM THM 400 TRANSMISSION
Transmission & Converter Identification 23–46
Adjustment 23–47
Clutch & Band Applications 23–48
On Car Services 23–47

GM THM 700 R4 TRANSMISSION
Transmission & Converter Identification 23–51
Adjustments 23–51
Clutch & Band Adjustments 23–53
On Car Services 23–52

AUTOMATIC TRANSAXLES

CHRYSLER A404, A413, A415, A470 TRANSAXLE
Transaxle & Converter Identification 23–9
Adjustments 23–9
Clutch & Band Applications 23–10
On Car Services 23–10

FORD ATX TRANSAXLE
Transaxle & Converter Identification 23–19
Adjustments 23–19
Clutch & Band Adjustments 23–21
On Car Services 23–21

FORD AXOD TRANSAXLE
Transaxle & Converter Identification 23–53
Adjustments 23–54
Clutch & Band Adjustments 23–57
On Car Services 23–56

GM THM 125 C TRANSAXLE
Transaxle & Converter Identification 23–31
Adjustments 23–31
Clutch & Band Applications 23–33
On Car Services 23–32

GM THM 325–4L TRANSAXLE
Transaxle & Converter Identification 23–42
Adjustments 23–42
Clutch & Band Applications 23–43
On Car Services 23–43

GM THM 440–T4 TRANSAXLE
Transaxle & Converter Identification 23–48
Adjustments 23–49
Clutch & Band Applications 23–51
On Car Services 23–49

A131L TRANSAXLE (1985½ AND LATER NOVA)
Transaxle & Converter Identification 23–58
Adjustments 23–58
Clutch & Band Applications 23–59
On Car Services 23–58

SECTION 23

Automatic Transmissions

TRANSMISSION IDENTIFICATION BY PAN GASKET

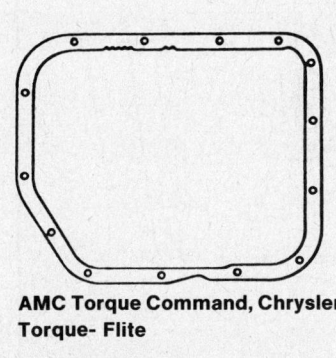

AMC Torque Command, Chrysler Torque-Flite

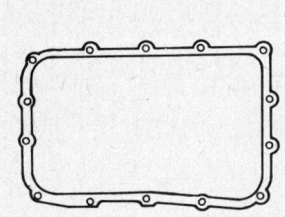

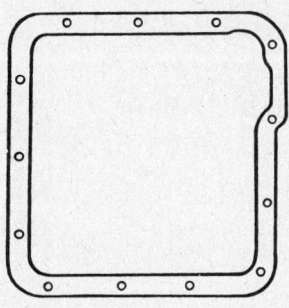

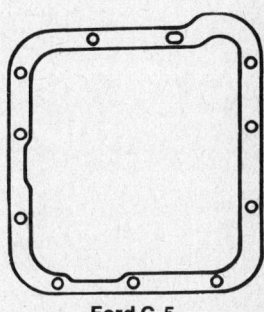

Ford C-5

ZF 4HP-22

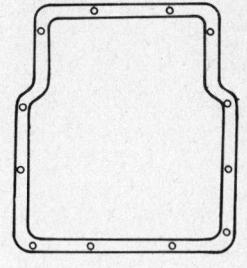

GM THM 180, 180C

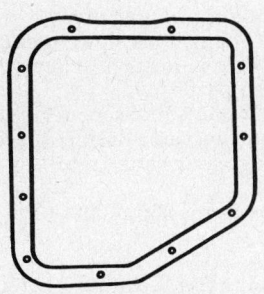

GM THM 200, 200C

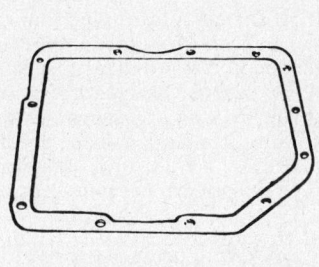

GM THM 250, 250C, 350, 350C

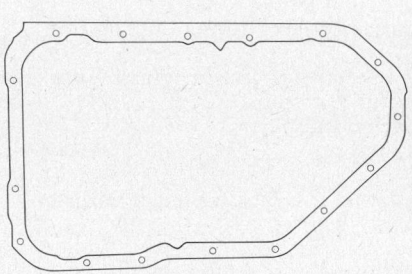

GM THM 200-4R

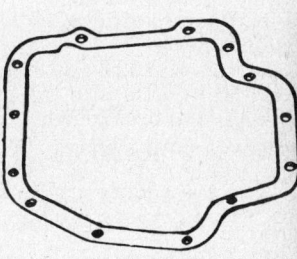

GM THM 400

23-3

SECTION 23 AUTOMATIC TRANSMISSIONS
TROUBLE DIAGNOSIS

TRANSMISSION IDENTIFICATION BY PAN GASKET

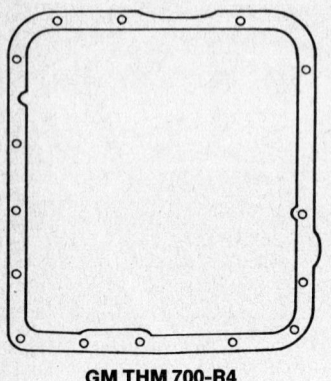
GM THM 700-R4

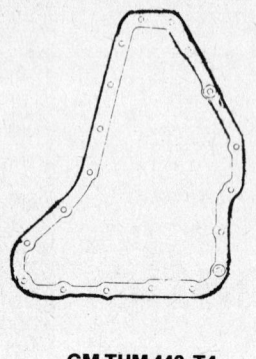
GM THM 440-T4

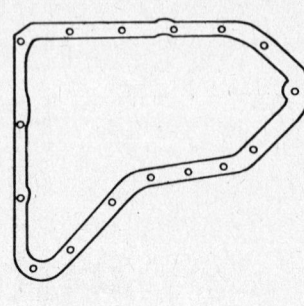
GM THM 125, 125C transaxle

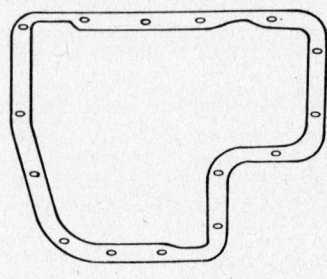
GM THM 325, 325-4L

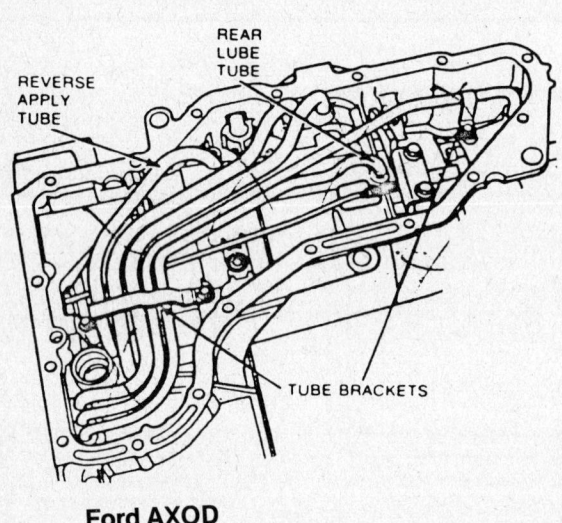
Ford AXOD

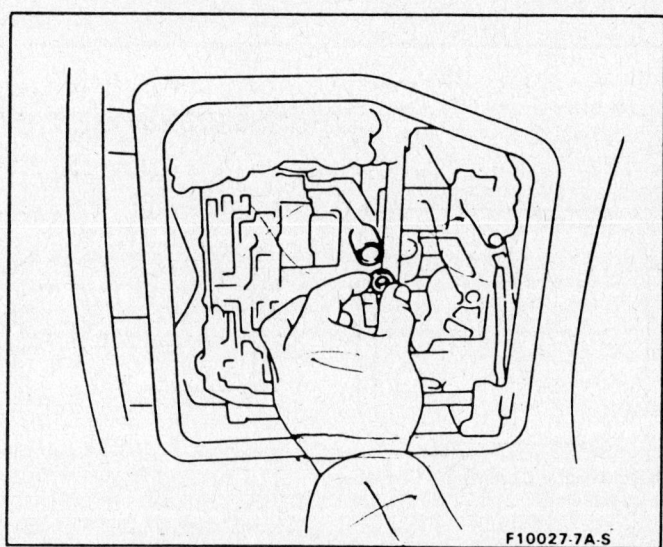
Figure 7A-28 Governor Oil Gaskets

A131L automatic transaxle

TROUBLE DIAGNOSIS GENERAL

Diagnosis Test

Automatic transmission problems caused by five general conditions: These are:
1. Poor engine performance (out of tune, improperly maintained).
2. Incorrect linkage, band or control pressure adjustments.
4. Malfunctions in the hydraulic system.
5. Actual breakdown of mechanical parts.

Testing Procedures

Two procedures can be followed in checking out a vehicle with transmission problems.

If the vehicle can be driven:
1. Check the level of the transmission fluid. Note the condition, color and appearance of the fluid. (Air bubbles, metal particles, burnt smell, etc.).
2. If the complaint was that the shifts were delayed, erratic or harsh, adjust the throttle and shift linkages before road testing. Check for obvious faults like broken linkage, etc.
3. If the complaint was that the acceleration is slow, or sluggish, or if an unusual amount of throttle is needed to keep up road speed, then a stall test should be performed.
4. Road test vehicle, preferably with the vehicle operator doing the driving. Observe for any malfunction, noting speed, load, any unusual noises or vibrations, gear range, etc.
5. Perform hydraulic pressure test.
6. Perform air pressure test of clutch and band operation.

If the vehicle cannot be driven:
1. Check the level of the transmission fluid. Note the condi-

AUTOMATIC TRANSMISSIONS
TROUBLE DIAGNOSIS
SECTION 23

tion, color and appearance of the fluid. (Air bubbles, metal particles, burnt smell, etc.).
2. Check for broken or disconnected throttle linkage.
3. Check for broken cooler lines, and loose or missing pressure port plugs, thus causing massive fluid loss.
4. Raise rear of car, start engine, shift into gear and check:
   a. If drive shaft turns but not the rear wheels, then the problem is in the differential or axle shaft, and not in the transmission.
   b. If drive shaft does not turn, and transmission is noisy, immediately stop engine, remove the pan and check for debris lying in the pan. If debris is not found, then the transmission must be removed. Check for broken drive plate, attaching bolts, broken converter hub shafts or oil pump.
   c. If drive shaft does not turn and transmission is not noisy, perform a hydraulic pressure test to determine if the problem is caused by a hydraulic or mechanical component.

AMC TORQUE COMMAND AND CHRYSLER TORQUEFLITE
A904, A998, and A999

Applications:
1983–87 American Motors Cars
1983–87 Chrysler Corp. Rear Wheel Drive Cars

Transmission and Torque Converter Identification

Transmission Identification

Three automatic transmission versions have been used. They are: Models 904, 998 and 999. Models 904, 998 and 999 are similar in size, appearance and operation, but have different internal components. Major differences are in the valve body and rear band. Model A904–LA (998/999) have a double wrap rear band while Model 904 has a single wrap. The Model A904–LA (998/999) also has reinforcing rib cast into place into the top of the rear servo boss.

Transmission models can also be determined by looking at the shape of the oil pan. The gasket outlines shown can be used in identifying a particular unit.

To further help with identification of transmissions, both AMC and Chrysler used a seven digit transmission part number stamped on the left side of the case just above the oil pan mating surface.

Various codes are used, after the transmission model numbers, to indicate internal transmission changes for specific engine/vehicle applications. Refer to the complete transmission model and identification numbers when ordering replacement parts.

TORQUE CONVERTER IDENTIFICATION

Torque Converters will vary with specific engine/transmission combinations. When ordering replacements, give diameter, engine size, and transmission code stamping numbers. Because the lock-up mechanism, used on some late models, is completely enclosed within the converter, and cannot be seen, look for lock-up converters to have an identifying decal attached to the front cover. The decal is circular in shape and states converter type and stall ratio such as "Lock-Up" and "LS" (Low Stall) or "HA" (High Stall).

--- CAUTION ---
Never attempt to interchange lock-up and conventional converters. The transmission input shaft and valve body required for the lock-up operation are very different

Fluid Specifications

When the automatic transmission fluid is replaced or topped off, only Dexron® or Dexron® II type fluid should be used.

Transmission code location - typical

Adjustments

THROTTLE LINKAGE

Throttle linkage is important to proper operation of this transmission. This adjustment positions a valve which controls shift speed, shift quality and downshift sensitivity at part throttle. If the setting is too short, early shifts and slippage between shifts may occur. If the linkage setting is too long, shifts may be delayed and part throttle downshifts may be very sensitive. This adjustment is to critical that the use of a throttle level holding spring is advised to remove slack in the linkage during adjustment.
1. Disconnect carburetor return spring at the carburetor.
2. Block the choke open and set the carburetor throttle off the fast idle cam.
3. Raise and safely support vehicle.
4. Use a spare carb return spring to hold the transmission throttle control lever fully forward against the stop. Do this by hooking one end of the spring on the throttle control lever and the other end at a convenient location, such as the bellcrank bracket on the converter housing.

NOTE: On some carburetors with a throttle operated solenoid valve, it will be necessary to turn the ignition to the ON position to energize the solenoid. Then open the throttle so that the solenoid can lock, and return the carb to the idle position.

5. Loosen the bolt on the throttle adjusting link. It is not necessary to remove it.

23-5

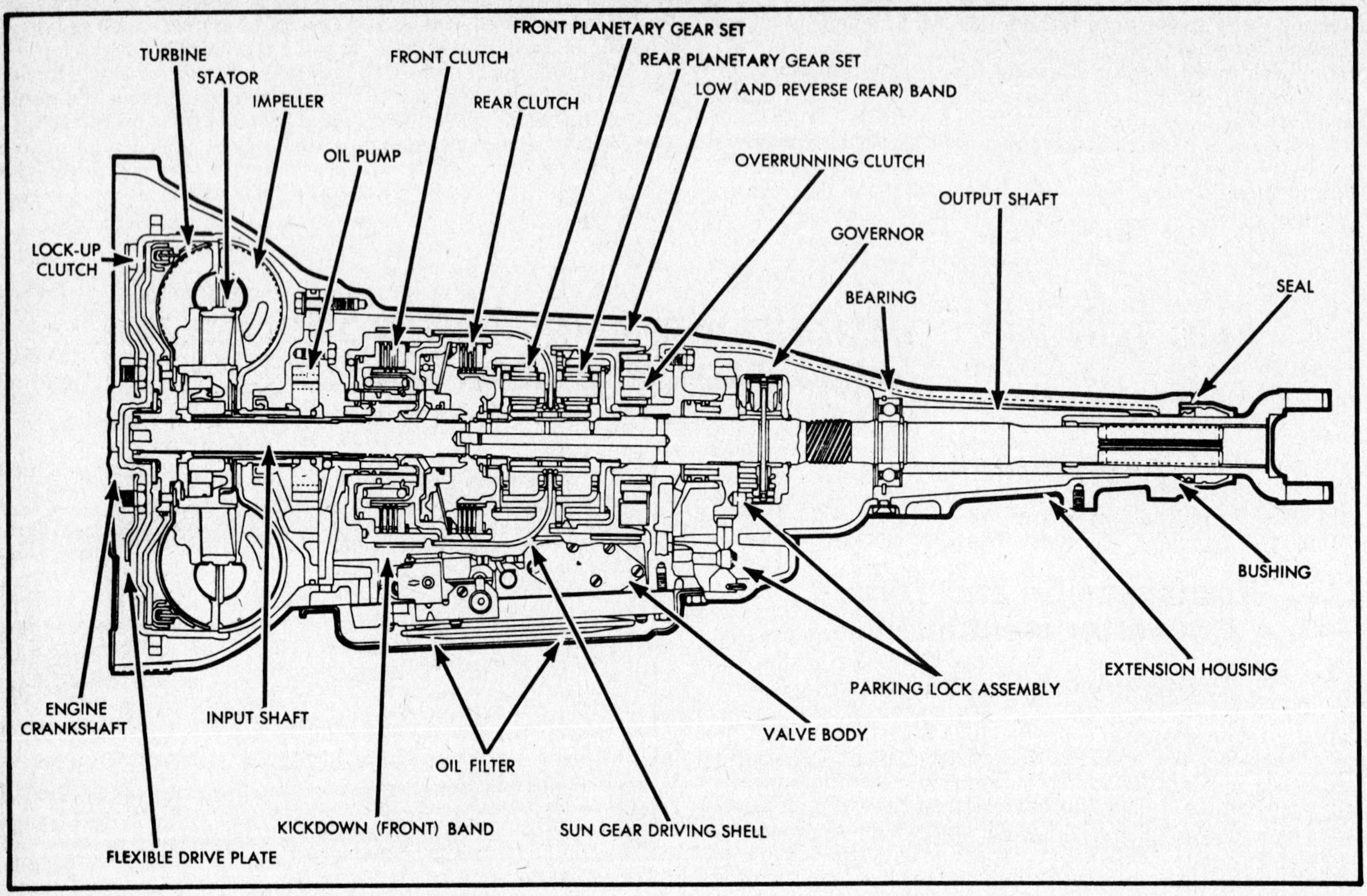

SECTION 23
AUTOMATIC TRANSMISSIONS
AMC TORQUE COMMAND/CHRYSLER TORQUEFLITE

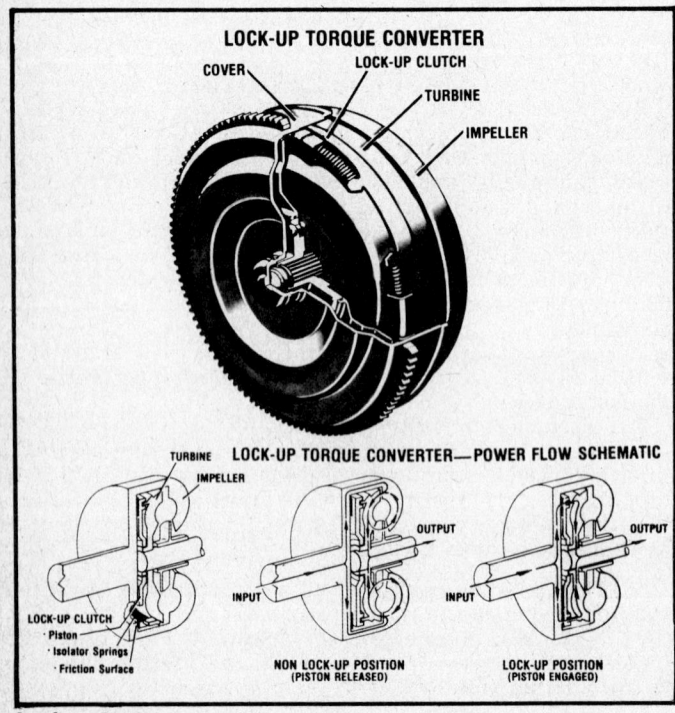

Cross section of Model A904 automatic transmission - typical

Lock-up torque converter

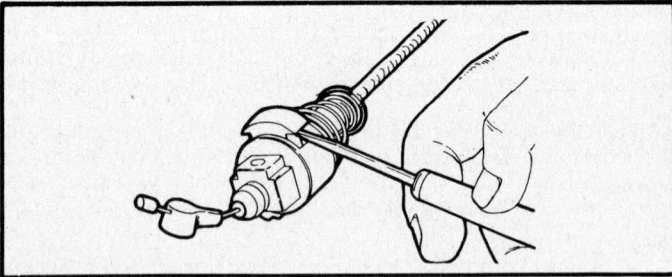

Releasing "T" shaped cable adjusting clamp - throttle cable, 4 cylinder engine

6. Pull on the end of the adjusting link to eliminate slack, then tighten retaining bolt.
7. Remove the spring put on the transmission throttle lever.

THROTTLE CABLE

4 CYLINDER ENGINE

1. Remove air cleaner.
2. Remove spark plus wire separator from throttle cable bracket and move separator and wires aside.
3. Raise automobile.
4. Remove strut rod bushing heat shield to gain access to transmission throttle control lever.

AUTOMATIC TRANSMISSIONS
AMC TORQUE COMMAND/CHRYSLER TORQUEFLITE

5. Hold throttle control lever rearward against its stop. Use spare spring to hold lever. Hook one end of spring to lever and hook opposite end of spring to convenient attachment point.
6. Lower automobile.
7. Block choke open and set carburetor linkage completely off fast idle cam.
8. On four-cylinder automobiles without air conditioning, turn ignition key to On position to energize throttle stop solenoid.
9. Unlock throttle control cable by releasing T-shaped cable adjuster clamp. Release clamp by lifting upward with small screwdriver.
10. Grasp cable outer sheath and move cable and sheath forward to remove any cable load on throttle cable bellcrank.

NOTE: The bellcrank is part of the carburetor throttle linkage.

11. Adjust cable by moving cable and sheath rearward until there is zero lash between plastic cable end and bellcrank ball.
12. When zero lash between cable end and bellcrank is achieved, lock cable by pressing T-shaped cable adjuster clamp downward until clamp snapes into place.
13. Turn ignition off. Install spark plus wires and separator, connect throttle stop solenoid on air conditioned automobiles and install air cleaner.
14. Raise automobile. Remove holding spring form transmission throttle control lever, install strut rod bushing heat shield and lower automobile.
15. Road test automobile and check transmission operation. Readjust throttle cable if necessary.

NOTE: Some V8 cars use a slightly different arrangement, in that the adjusting link is pushed instead of pulled to remove the slack. However, the end result should be the same, and no slack or lash should be permitted. Too, many Chrysler Corp. vehicles use a lower bellcrank with a short throttle rod and adjustable swivel to hook up to the transmission throttle lever. In these cases, make sure the swivel is free to slide along the throttle rod so the the small pre-load spring action is not impaired. If necessary, clean and lightly lubricate. Again, the throttle level must be held firmly forward against its internal stop. In this case, the linkage slack, or backlash was automatically removed by the small pre-load spring.

NEUTRAL SAFETY SWITCH

The neutral safety switch used on TorqueFlite transmission includes provision for the backup lamp switch function. The neutral start circuit is through the center pin on the three terminal switch. It provides a ground for the starter solenoid circuit through the center pin when the gear shift is in Park and Neutral positions only. The two outside terminals of the neutral switch are for the circuit feeding the backup lamps.

NOTE: When checking backup lamp circuit, continuity should exist between two outside pins of switch when transmission is in Reverse only. Continuity should not exist from either pin to the transmission case when in reverse. If the switch does not meet these tests, replace it.

BAND ADJUSTMENTS

Front Band

The front band adjustments is done from the outside of the transmission. While somewhat difficult to reach, it can nevertheless be adjusted while still in the vehicle. The front band adjusting screw is located on the left side of the transmission case just above the manual valve and throttle lever.

1. Raise and safely support car.

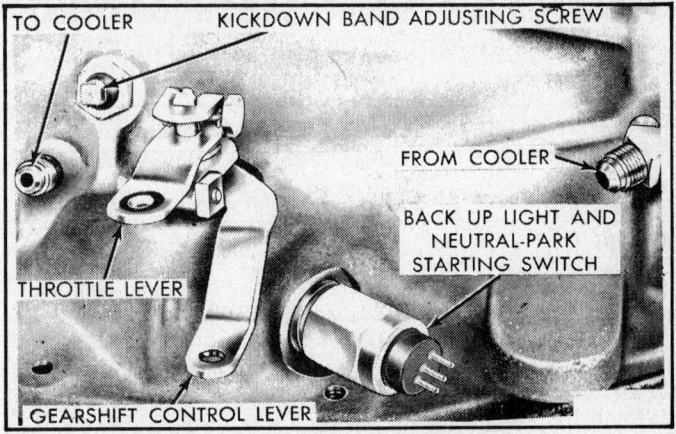
External control components - typical of models A904 and A727

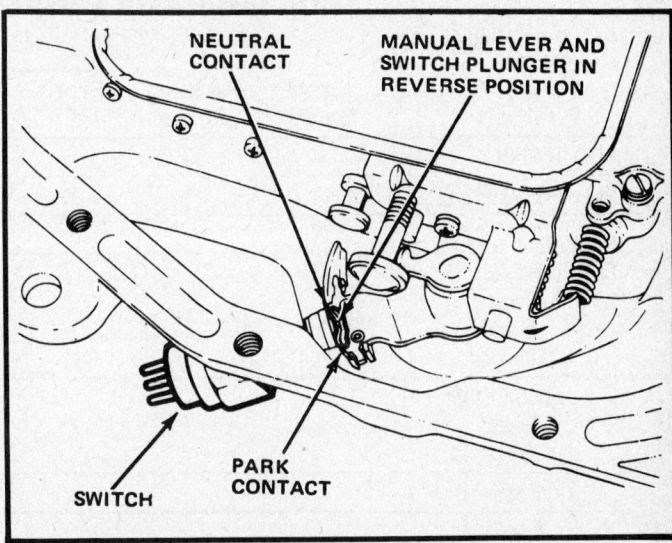
Neutral start and back-up light switch contact area on manual shift lever

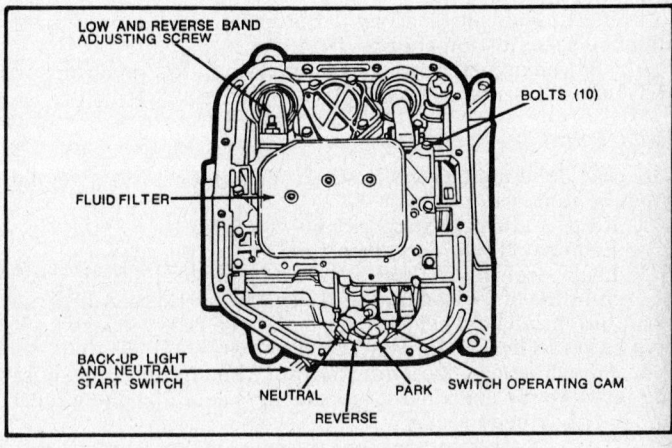
Low-reverse (rear) band adjustment location - typical

SECTION 23

AUTOMATIC TRANSMISSIONS
AMC TORQUE COMMAND/CHRYSLER TORQUEFLITE

BAND ADJUSTMENT SPECIFICATIONS
American Motors Corporation Torque Command

Engine and Transmission Models			
	2.5 L	258 CID	
	904	Std-904	998
'82-'86			
Front Band ①	2.5	2.5	2.5
Rear Band ①	7 ②	7	4

NOTE: Numbers represent back-off turns from specified torque Torque lock-nut to 35 ft. lbs when adjustment is completed.
① Backed off from 72 inch pounds
② Backed off from 41 inch pounds

BAND ADJUSTMENT SPECIFICATIONS
Chrysler Corporation TorqueFlite

Engine and Transmission Models		
A904		A904-LA
225	318	318
'82-'86		
Front Band ① 2.5 ③	2.5 ③	2.5
Rear Band ① 7 ②③	4 ③	2

① Backed off from 72 inch pounds torque
② Backed off from 41 inch pounds torque
③ With wide ratio gears

CLUTCH AND BAND APPLICATION
Torqueflite And Torque Command Transmissions

Lever Position	Start Safety	Parking Sprag	Clutches Front	Rear	Over-running	Lock-up	Bands (Kickdown) Front	(Low-Rev.) Rear
P — PARK	X	X						
R — REVERSE			X					X
N — NEUTRAL	X							
D — DRIVE								
First				X	X			
Second				X			X	
Direct			X	X		X		
2 — SECOND								
First				X	X			
Second				X			X	
— LOW (First)				X				X

X = Applied

2. Loosen adjusting screw locknut and back off locknut five turns.
3. Check that adjusting screw turns freely. Tighten adjusting screw to the specified torque, using a small torque wrench and a 5/16 square socket.
4. Back off adjusting screw to the specified amount of turns. Refer to specification chart.
5. Tighten adjuster screw locknut to 35 ft. lbs., making sure that adjuster screw setting does not change.

Rear Band

The rear band adjustment is an inside adjustment so the pan must be removed.
1. Raise and safely support car.
2. Remove oil pan and drain fluid.
3. Look carefully at fluid, filter and pan bottom for a heavy accumulation of friction material or metal particles. A little accumulation can be considered normal, but a heavy a heavy concentration indicates damages or worn parts.
4. Adjust band by loosening locknut, then tightening adjusting screw to the specified torque, using a small torque wrench and a 1/4 hex head socket.
5. Back off adjusting screw to the specified amount of turns. Refer to the specification chart.
6. Install locknut, tighten to 35 ft. lbs. (47 Nm) making sure adjusting screw does not turn.

NOTE: Install a new transmission filter. Torque the three screws to 35 inch lbs. (4 Nm).

7. Using a new gasket on the pan, install and torque bolts evenly to 150 inch lbs. (17 Nm).
8. Lower car and fill transmission with specified amount of Dexron® type fluid.

On-Car Services

OIL PAN

Removal and Installation
1. Raise and safely support vehicle.
2. Loosen oil pan bolts and gently pull one corner down so fluid will drain. If transmission is hot, be careful of spilling oil.
3. Remove oil pan bolts and pan.
4. Carefully inspect filter and pan bottom for a heavy accumulation of friction material or metal particles. A little accumulation can be considered normal, but a heavy concentration indicates damaged or worn parts.

NOTE: Filter replacement is recommended when a pan is removed. Also, read band can now be adjusted if necessary.

AUTOMATIC TRANSMISSIONS
AMC TORQUE COMMAND/CHRYSLER TORQUEFLITE

5. Check pan carefully for distortion, straightening the edges with a straight block of wood and a rubber mallet if necessary. Clean pan well.
6. Install new gasket on pan and install. Torque bolts to 150 inch lbs. (17 Nm).
7. Lower car, refill with Dexron®.

FLUID CHANGES AND CONVERTER DRAINING

NOTE: When refilling TorqueFlite transmissions, make sure only Dexron® type Automatic Transmission Fluid is used.

Drain and Refill

NOTE: The fluid cooler should be flushed during the fluid change operation.

1. Raise and safely support vehicle. Place a container with a large opening under the transmission oil pan.
2. Loosen, but do not remove all of the pan bolts and gently pull one corner down so fluid will drain. If transmission is hot, be careful of spilling oil.
3. Remove oil pan bolts and pan.
4. Perform any necessary band adjustments and/or filter change.
5. See cautions under "Oil Pan R & R" about debris accumulation and pan distortion.
6. Most converters no longer have drain plugs. If not is present, rotate until plug is at bottom so converter can be drained.

NOTE: If there is evidence of contamination or if trouble shooting indicates a problem in the converter, it must be replaced.

7. Install new gasket on pan and install torque bolts to 150 inch lbs. (17 Nm).
8. Lower car, refill with Dexron®.

CHRYSLER CORP. A-404, A-413, A-415 and A-470 TORQUEFLITE AUTOMATIC TRANSAXLE

Applications:

1983–87 Chrysler Corp. Front Wheel Drive Cars

Transaxle and Converter Identification

The Chrysler A-404, A-413, A-415 and A-470 TorqueFlite automatic transaxle combines a torque converter, a fully automatic three-speed transmission, final drive gearing and differential into a front drive system. The assembly is a metric design and some special tools will be required to service and overhaul the unit. The assembly is housed in an aluminum casting. Cooling is done in the usual oil-to-water cooler in the radiator, and fluid is filtered through a "Dacron Type" filter. The output torque is delivered through helical gears to the "transfer shaft" which carries the governor and parking sprag. The gear set is a factor in the final drive (axle) ratio. Venting of the transmission sump is accomplished through a hollow "dipstick", while the differential sump is vented by a spring-loaded cap on the "extension".

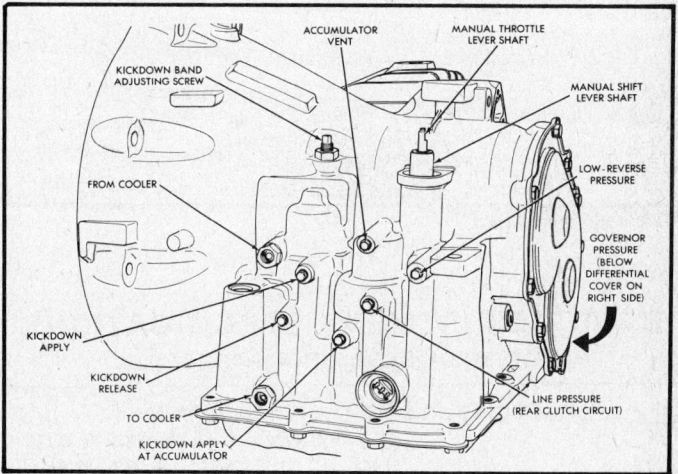
Exterior view of left side

Fluid Specification

Use only automatic transmission fluids of the type marked Dexron®, Dexron® II or its equivalent. Chrysler Corporation does not recommend the use of additives, other then the use of a dye to aid in the determination of fluid leaks.

Adjustments

THROTTLE CABLE

Bring engine to operating temperature and be sure the carburetor is off fast idle. Check idle speed with tachometer. Disconnect choke if necessary to keep carburetor off fast idle.
1. Loosen the adjustment bracket lock screw. The bracket must be free to slide on its slot. If necessary, disassemble and clean or repair. Lube with a good quality light grease.

2. Hold the transaxle throttle lever firmly rearward against its internal stop, and then tighten the adjusting lock screw to 105 inch lbs. (12 Nm). This automatically removes cable backlash.
3. Connect choke if it was disconnected. Test for freedom of movement by pushing the lever forward and slowly release it to confirm that it will return fully rearward.

BAND ADJUSTMENT

A–404

The kickdown (front) band has its adjusting screw located on the top front (left side) of the transaxle case. Adjustment is as follows:
1. Loosen the lock nut and back off about five turns.
2. Tighten the adjusting screw to 72 inch lbs. (8Nm).
3. Back off adjusting screw 3 turns for 1982 and later mod-

23–9

SECTION 23 AUTOMATIC TRANSMISSIONS
CHRYSLER TORQUEFLITE A404, A413, A415 AND A470

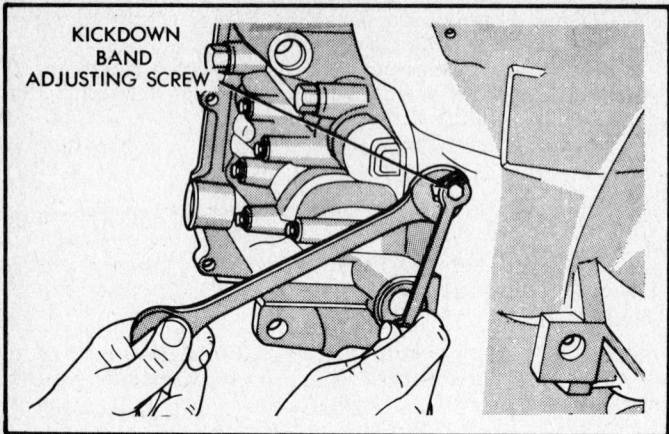
Kick down band adjustment location

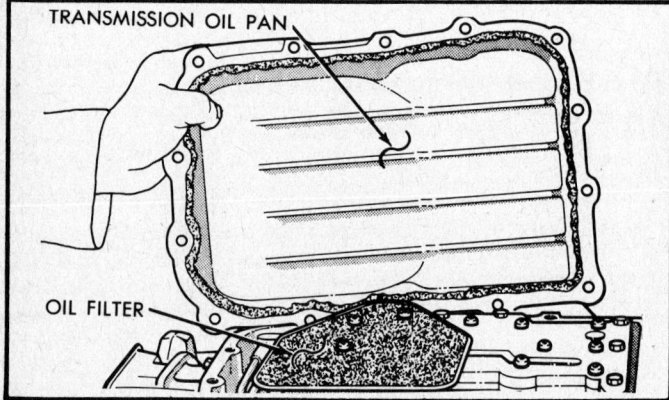
Transmission oil pan

1. Loosen the locknut and back off approximately five turns.
2. Tighten the band adjusting screw to 72 inch lbs. (8 Nm).
3. Back off the adjusting screw 2¾ turns.
4. Hold this position on the adjusting screw and tighten the lock nut to 35 ft. lbs. (47 Nm).

The Low-reverse band (rear) is adjustable with the bottom oil pan off. Before attempting the band adjustment, the low-reverse band should be checked for proper end gap as follows:
1. Remove the lower oil pan and pressurize the low-reverse servo with 30 psi shop air pressure.
2. Measure the gap between the band ends. If the gap is less than 0.080 in (2.0mm), the band is worn excessively and should be replaced.

To adjust the low-reverse band, proceed as follows:
1. Loosen the back off the locknut approximately 5 turns.
2. Tighten the adjusting screw to 41 inch lbs. (5 Nm) true torque.
3. Back off the adjusting screw 3 ½ turns, hold adjusting screw position and tighten the locknut to 10 ft. lbs. (14 Nm).
4. Reinstall oil pan and fill unit with correct type fluid.

NEUTRAL SAFETY SWITCH
The neutral safety switch used on this transaxle includes provision for the backup lamp switch function. The neutral start circuit is through the center pin on the three terminal/switch. It provides a ground for the starter solenoid circuit through the center pin when in Park or Neutral. The two outside terminals of the neutral switch are for the circuit feeding the backup lamps.

On-Car Services

OIL PAN R&R AND FLUID CHANGE
1. Raise vehicle on hoise and loosen, but do not remove the pan bolts. Gently pull one corner down so fluid will drain into a container with a large opening. If transmission is hot, be careful of the oil.
2. When drained, remove the bolts (14) and pan.
3. Carefully inspect the filter and pan bottom for a heavy concentration of friction material or metal particles. A little accumulation can be considered normal, but a heady build-up indicates damaged or worn parts.

NOTE: Filter replacement is recommended whenever oil pan is removed. A special Torx® drive bit will be required. Torque screws to 35 inch lbs. (47Nm).

4. Check pan carefully for distortion, straightening the

BAND ADJUSTMENT SPECIFICATIONS
Chrysler Corporation Transaxle

Engine and Transmission Models	A-404			A-413, A-470	
	1.7L	2.2L	2.6L	2.2L	2.6L
'82-'86 Front Band	3②	3.0②	3.0②	2.0②	2.0②
Rear Band	①	①	①	3.5③	3.5③

① Not adjustable
② Backed off from 72 inch pounds torque
③ Backed off from 41 inch pounds torque

els, from the 72 inch lbs. torque, then hold this position and tighten the lock nut to 35 foot lbs. (47Nm).

The low-reverse band (rear) band is not adjustable in this unit. The band lining itself needs to be inspected to determine the need for replacement. The grooves must be no less than 0.008 in (0.2mm) deep at any point to still be usable. With a 100 pound force applied to band around drum, the end gap must not be less than 0.020 in. (0.5mm).

A-413, A-415, A-470
The kickdown band (front) band has its adjusting screw located on the front left top of the transaxle case, in the same location as the A-404 transaxle. The adjustment is as follows:

CLUTCH AND BAND APPLICATION
A-404, A-413, A-415 and A-470 Transaxles

Lever Position	Clutches			Bands	
	Front	Rear	Over-running	(Kickdown) Front	(Low-Rev.) Rear
P—PARK					
R—REVERSE	X				X
N—NEUTRAL					
D—DRIVE					
First		X	X		
Second		X		X	
Direct	X	X			
2—SECOND					
First		X	X		
Second		X		X	
1—LOW (First)		X			X

23-10

AUTOMATIC TRANSMISSIONS
CHRYSLER TORQUEFLITE A404, A413, A415 AND A470

SECTION 23

edges with a block of wood and a mallet if necessary. Clean pan well.

5. Apply a bead of RTV sealant on pan and install. Torque bolts to 150 inch lbs. (16 Nm).

6. Refill with four quarts Dexron®. Idle engine for two minutes, moving selector through each position, ending in Park. Check fluid and add if necessary.

7. Make sure dipstick rubber seal is firmly seated to keep out water and dirt.

NOTE: The A404 Transaxle torque convertor does not have a drain plug.

FORD MOTOR CO. AUTOMATIC OVERDRIVE AUTOMATIC TRANSMISSION

Applications:

1983–87 Continental
  Lincoln Town Car
  Crown Victoria
  Cougar & XR7
  Ford & Mercury
  LTD & Marquis
  Thunderbird
  Mark VI
  Mark VII
  Mustang
  Capri

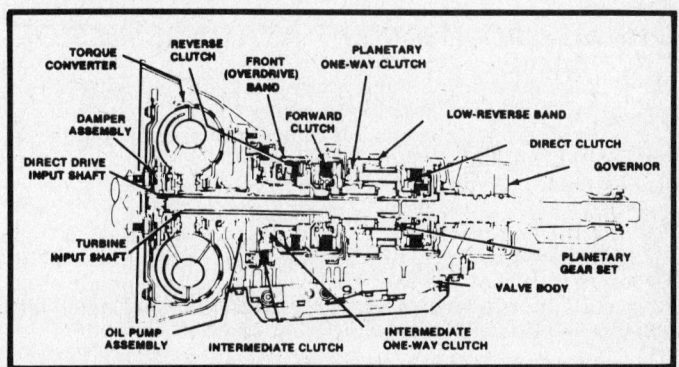

Cross section of Ford Motor Co Automatic Overdrive transmission

Transmission and Converter Identification

TRANSMISSION

The Vehicle Certification Label, which will identify the type of transmission used in the vehicle, will be found fastened to the left-side door lock pillar post. In the space marked "TRANS", the identification code for the A.O.T. will be stamped with the letter "T".

CONVERTER

The converter can be identified from the part number stamped on the converter cover. The converter is a welded unit and must be replaced as an assembly. If any internal problem exists within the converter, replacement of the unit is recommended.

Fluid Type Specifications

Use type CJ fluid or Dexron® II, Series D, which meets Ford specification ESP-M2C138-CJ in the Automatic Overdrive Transmission. This Ford specification number should appear on the fluid container.

The warranty will be void and damage to thee transmission could occur if incorrect fluid is used.

NOTE: Type CJ transmission fluid will appear amber when seen on the dipstick.

Adjustments

THROTTLE VALVE (TV) CONTROL LINKAGE SYSTEM

The throttle valve (TV) control linkage system consists of the linkage lever on the carburetor, the transmission control rod assembly and the external TV control lever on the transmission.

The TV control linkage is set to its proper length during initial assembly using the sliding trunnion block at the transmission end of the TV control rod assembly. Under normal circumstances, it should not be necessary to alter this adjustment. Any required adjustment of the TV control linkage can normally be accomplished using the adjustment screw on the linkage lever at the carburetor. Major linkage adjustment (sliding trunnion on rod) may only be required after maintenance involving the removal and/or replacement of the carburetor, TV control rod assembly or the transmission. Minor linkage adjustment (adjustment screw on linkage lever) may be required after idle speed adjustments greater than 50 rpm and to correct complaints of poor transmission shift quality.

When the linkage is properly adjusted, the TV control lever on the transmission will be at its internal idle stop position (lever up as far as it will travel) when the carburetor is at its hot idle stop with the engine off. There will be alight contact force between the throttle lever and end of the linkage lever adjustment screw. Due to flexibility in the linkage system, the linkage lever adjustment screw would have to be backed out approximately three turns before a gap between the screw and throttle lever could be detected.

At wide open throttle, the TV control lever on the transmission may or may not be at its wide open stop. The wide open throttle position must not be used as the reference point in adjusting the linkage.

LINKAGE ADJUSTMENT AT CARBURETOR

The TV control linkage may be adjusted at the carburetor using the following procedure.

1. De-cam the fast idle cam on the carburetor so that the throttle lever is at its idle stop. Place shift lever in Neutral and set parking brake. Engine off.

SECTION 23 AUTOMATIC TRANSMISSIONS
FORD OVERDRIVE (AOT)

2. Back out linkage lever adjusting screw all the way (scre end is flush with lever face).

3. Turn in adjusting screw until a thin shim (0.005 in. max.) or piece of writing paper fits snug between end of screw and throttle lever. To eliminate the effect of friction, push the linkage lever forward (tending to close gap.) Release it before checkink clearance between the end of the screw and the throttle lever. Do not apply any load on the levers with tools or hands while checking gap.

4. Turn in adjusting screw an additional three turns. (Three turns are preferred. One turn minimum is permissible if screw travel is limited,).

5. If it is not possible to turn in adjusting screw at least one additional turn or if there was insufficient screw adusting capacity to obtain in initial gap in Step Two, refer to "Linkage Adjustment at Transmission."

LINKAGE ADJUSTMENT AT TRANSMISSION

The linkage lever adjustment screw has a limited adjustment capability. If it is not possible to adjust the TV linkage using this screw, the length of the TV control rod assembly must be readusted using the following procedure. This procedure must also be followed whenever a new TV control rod assembly is installed.

1. Set the engine curb idle speed to specification.
2. With engine off, de-cam the fast idle cam on the carburetgor so that the throttle lever is against the idle stop. Place shift lefer in Neutral and set parking brake. Engine off.
3. Set the linkage lever adjustment screw at approximately mid-range.
4. If a new TV control rod assembly is being installed, connect the rod to the linkage lever at the carburetor.
5. Loosen the bolt on the sliding trunnion block on the TV control rod assembly. Remove any corrosion from the control rod and free-up the trunnion block so that it slides freely on the control rod.
6. Push up on the lower end of the control rod to insure that the linkage lever at carburetor is firmly against the throttle lever. Release force on rod. Rod must stay up.
7. Push the TV control lever on the transmission up against its internal stop with a firm force (approximately 5 pounds) and tighten the bolt on the trunnion block. Do no relax force on the lever until the bolt is tightened.

LINKAGE ADJUSTMENT USING TV CONTROL PRESSURE

NOTE: The following procedure may be used to check and/or adjust the TV control linkage using TV control pressure.

1. Place the shift selector lever in Neutral and disconnect the idle kicker solenoid. Set parking brake.
2. Attach a 0–100 psi pressure gauge to the TV port on the transmission.
3. Operate engine until normal operating temperature is reached and throttle lever is off fast idle.
4. Verify that the throttle lever is at its idle stop. Place a 0.063 gauge (use 1/16 in. or 1.6mm drill) between the linkage lever adjustment screw and the throttle lever. With engine operating at idle and in Neutral, TV pressure must be below 5 psi. If TV pressure is greater than 5 psi, the TV control linkage is set too long.
5. Place a 0.313 inch gauge (use 5/16 in. or 8mm drill) between the linkage lever adjustment screw and the throttle lever. With the engine operating at idle and in Neutral, the TV pressure must be at least 22 psi. A low reading indicates that the linkage is set short.

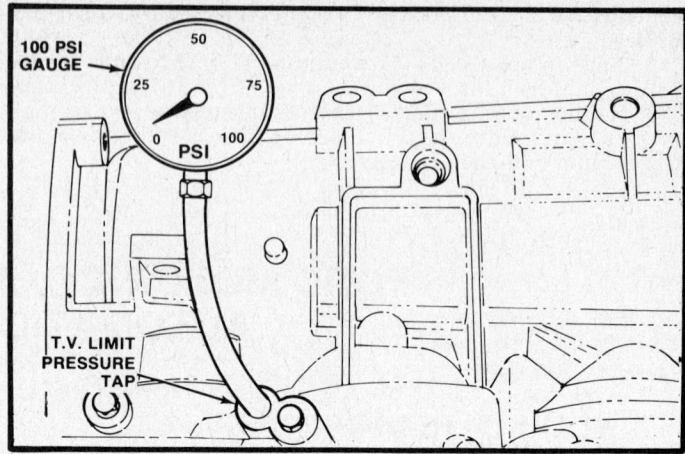
TV limit pressure gauge in place on transmission case

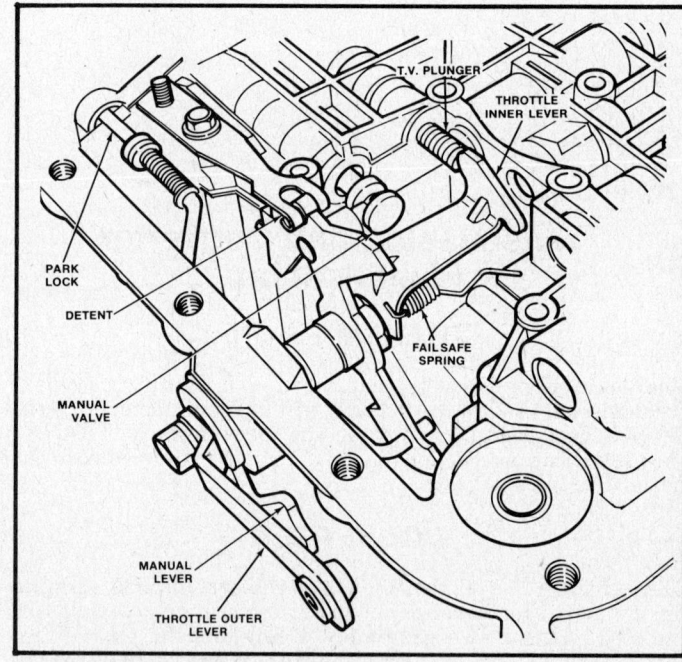
Manual valve and throttle valve components

6. Correct a long setting by backing out the linkage lever adjustment screw. Turn in the adjusting screw for a short rod condition. If insufficient adjusting capacity is available, the TV control rod length must be reset using the procedure described in "Linkage Adjustment Transmission".
7. If the limits specified cannot be obtained, diagnosis of the transmission control pressure system is required.

IDLE SPEED ADJUSTMENT

Whenever it is required to adjust idle speed by more than 50 rpm, the adjustment screw on the linkage lever at the carburetor should also be readjusted as shown in following chart.

After making any idle speed adjustments, always verify the linkage lever and throttle lever are in contact with the throttle lever at its idle stop and the shift lever is in Neutral.

NEUTRAL SAFETY SWITCH ADJUSTMENT

The neutral safety switch in the transmission is merely an on-

AUTOMATIC TRANSMISSIONS
FORD OVERDRIVE (AOT)
SECTION 23

off switch actuated by the manual linkage detent mechanism within he transmission. The switch is replaceable if defective, but is non-adustable.

On-Car Services

TRANSMISSION OIL PAN REMOVAL AND TRANSMISSION FLUID CHANGE

It is not necessary, under normal operating conditions, to periodically change the transmission fluid. Only under severe conditions (police or taxi) or in the case of a major overhaul is it recommended that the fluid be changed.

When the reason for a fluid change is internal transmission damage, it is necessary to also flush the transmission cooler and cooler lines to remove any traces of abrasive matter from the system.

CAUTION

When flushing torque converters, use only professional equipmennt designed for this purpose. Traces of solvent in the converter could cause severe transmission damage in the future.

---

1. Raise vehicle on hoise or jackstands.
2. Place drain pan under transmission.
3. Loosen transmission pan attaching bolts to drain fluid above pan level.
4. When the fluid has drained to the level of the pan mounting flange, remove the attaching bolts beginning at the rear of the pan. Gradually drop the pan and drain slowly.
5. After draining the fluid, remove and thoroughly clean the transmissions pan. Discard the filter, valve body to filter gasket, and transmission pan gasket.
6. Install new filter and filter to valve body gasket do not attempt to clean and re-use the old filter.
7. Using a new gasket, install the pan on the transmission.
8. Add three quarts of the specified fluid (see Fluid Type Specifications) through the fill tube.
9. Check and adjust the fluid level as necessary.

CLUTCH AND BAND APPLICATION CHART
FORD OVERDRIVE

	Intermediate Friction Clutch	Intermediate One-Way Clutch	Overdrive Band	Reverse Clutch	Forward Clutch	Planetary One-Way Clutch	Low-Reverse Band	Direct Clutch
1st gear, manual low					Applied	Holding	Applied	
2nd gear, manual low	Applied	Holding	Applied		Applied			
1st gear, O/D or 3					Applied	Holding		
2nd gear, O/D or 3	Applied	Holding			Applied			
3rd gear, O/D or 3	Applied				Applied			Applied
4th gear, O/D	Applied		Applied					Applied
Reverse				Applied			Applied	
Neutral								
Park							Applied	

FORD MOTOR COMPANY C-3 AUTOMATIC TRANSMISSION

Applications:

1983–87
Capri
Cougar & RX7
Fairmont
Granada
Mustang
Thunderbird
Zephyr
LTD & Marquis

Transmission and Converter Identification

TRANSMISSION TYPE

The C-3 automatic transmission can readily be identify by the location of the vacuum modulator valve assembly, mounted on the right center side of the transmission case.

The C-3 automatic transmission is identified by the letter "V" stamped under the heading "TRANS" on the Vehicle Certification Label, affixed to the left side door lock post.

CONVERTER

The C-3 automatic transmission converter assembly is identified by the part number stamped on the converter cover.

The converter is a welded unit and is not to be repaired. If internal problems exist, replacement of the converter is recommended.

Fluid Type Specifications

Only Type "F" automatic transmission fluids, meeting Ford Motor Comany's specifications, should be used in the C-3 automatic transmission.

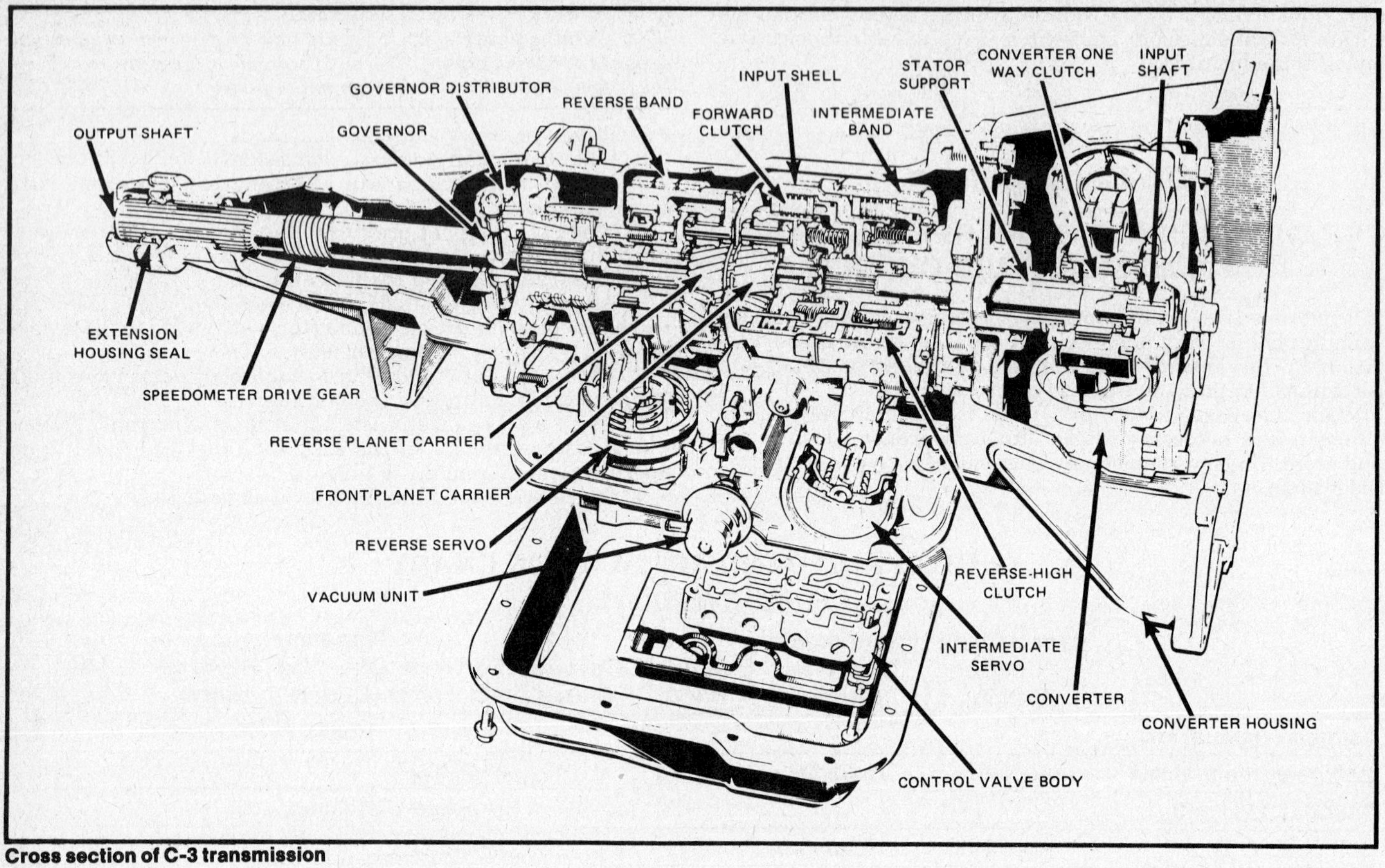

SECTION 23

AUTOMATIC TRANSMISSIONS
FORD C3

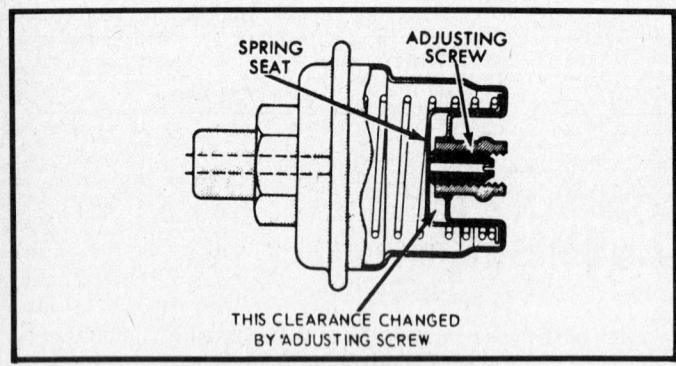

Cross section of C-3 transmission

Cross section of adjustable vacuum diaphragm

Adjustments

VACUUM DIAPHRAGM ADJUSTMENT

The vacuum diaphragms used in production are nonadjustable. Adjustable type units are available for installation in the transmission, allowing changes in the control pressures.

An adjusting screw is located in the vacuum nipple of the diaphragm and is accessible after removing the vacuum supply line from the diaphragm. Using a small screwdriver and turning the screw clockwise will increase the control pressure, while turning the screw counter-closkwise will decrease the control pressure. One complete turn of the adjusting screw will change the control pressure approximately 2–3 psi.

After adjustments are made, reinstall the vacuum supply line and make the pressure checks as outlined in the Troubl Diagnosis section.

— **CAUTION** —
The diaphragm should not be adjusted to provide pressures below the specified ranges to change shift engagement feel, as soft or slipping shift points could result and damage to the transmission could occur.

THROTTLE LINKAGE ADJUSTMENT

Throttle pressure control linkage is not used on the C–3 automatic transmission. A vacuum-operated diaphragm assembly is used to control and modulate the throttle pressure in proportion to the road spped, throttle opening and internal oil pressures.

A downshift control rod is used and is connected to the carburetor control linkage. Both linkages must be properly adjusted to actuage the downshift system.

Accelerator and Downshift Linkage Adjustment

1. With the engine off, fully depress the accelerator pedal and hold in place. Inspect the carburetor for wide open throttle plates and full accelerator linkage travel. Adjust as necessary.
2. With the accelerator fully depressed and adjusted, push the downshift control rod downward to its fully depressed position (downshift valve in the transmission full depressed).
3. A clearance of 0.010–0.080 in. between the tip of the kickdown adjusting screw and the throttle lever should exist. Adjust the screw as necessary.

AUTOMATIC TRANSMISSIONS
FORD C3
SECTION 23

CLUTCH AND BAND APPLICATION CHART
FORD C-3

Gear	Forward Clutch	Reverse High Clutch	Intermediate Band	Low Reverse Band	One-Way Clutch
1st ①	On	Off	Off	Off	Holding ②
2nd ①	On	Off	On	Off	Overrunning
3rd ①	On	On	Off	Off	Overrunning
Low	On	Off	Off	On	Holding ②
Reverse	Off	On	Off	On	Not Affected

① Transmission selector in "D" position
② Overrunning on coast

4. Release the accelerator linkage. The linkage and the downshift control rod must return to their closed position by return spring tension.

BAND ADJUST

The intermediate band is the only adjustment needed during normal operation. The reverse band is adjusted internally during assembly or at atimes of overhaul.

Intermediate Band Adjustment

1. Locate the adjusting screw on the left side of the transmission case, in front of the manual control lever.
2. Remove the downshift control rod from the downshift control lever to gain access to the adjusting screw and locknut.
3. Clean the dirt and foreign material from the locknut area. Loosen, remove and discard the locknut from the adjusting screw.
4. Install a new locknut on the adjusting screw.
5. Tighten the adjusting screw to 10 ft. lbs. of torque.

NOTE: A special wrench with a preset "click". "break" or "overrun", can be used to tighten the adjusting screw.

6. Back the adjusting screw off exactly 1 ½ turns.
7. Hold the adjustment and tighten the locknut to 35-45 ft. lbs. torque.
8. Install the downshift control rod to the downshift control lever.

NEUTRAL SAFETY SWITCH

The C-3 automatic transmission has a screw-type neutral start switch, located above the manual control lever on the transmission case. The internal shift operates the switch contacts to allow the engine to start in either Park or Neutral positions and to operate the back-up lights when the transmission is in the Reverse position.

On-Car Services
OIL PAN

Removal

1. Raise the vehicle and support safely.
2. Position a drain pan beneath the transmission pan and starting at the rear, loosen, but do not remove the pan bolts.

3. Loosen the pan from the transmission case and allow the fluid to drain gradually.
4. Remove all pan bolts except two at the front of the pan and allow the fluid to continue draining.
5. Remove the pan; clean the old gasket from the pan and transmission case.

Installation

1. Install a new gasket on the pan and install it to the transmission case.
2. Install all pan bolts and torque to 12-17 ft. lbs.
3. Install three quarts of transmission fluid type F, Ford Specification # ESW-M2C33-F into the filler tube (converter not drained).
4. Start the engine and operate the engine at idle speed for approximately two minutes. Then raise the engine speed to approximately 1200 rpm until the engine/transmission assembly reaches normal operating temperature.

---- CAUTION ----
Do not overspeed the engine during warm-up.

5. Check the fluid level after moving the gear selector through all ranges. Correct the fluid level as necessary

VACUUM DIAPHRAGM

Removal

1. Raise the vehicle and support safely. Disconnect the vacuum hose(s) from the diaphragm unit.
2. Remove the retaining bracket and bolt holding the diaphragm unit to the transmission case.

---- CAUTION ----
Do no pry or bend the retainer bracket.

3. Pull the vacuum diaphragm, the actuating pin the throttle valve from the transmission case. Remove the O-ring from the assembly.

Installation

1. Install a new O-ring on the diaphragm unit.
2. Install the throttle valve, the actuating pin and the vacuum diaphragm tubes towards the transmission case and install the assembly into the case.
3. Install the retaining bracket and bolt and torque to 15-23 inch lbs.

23-15

SECTION 23
AUTOMATIC TRANSMISSIONS
FORD C5

FORD MOTOR COMPANY C-5 AUTOMATIC TRANSMISSION

Applications:

1983–87
- Capri
- Mustang
- Fairmont
- Granada
- Cougar & RX7
- Zephyr
- LTD & Marquis
- Thunderbird

Transmission and Converter Identification

TRANSMISSION

The C-5 automatic transmission is identified by a tag located on the lower intermediate servo cover bolt. The tag contains the necessary information needed when replacement parts are required. A transmission code letter "C" is stamped on the vehicle certification lable, affixed to the left door lock post.

CONVERTER

The torque converter can be identified by letters stamped on the face of the converter. It should be noted that the converter is designed to centrifugally engage at various operating speeds, locking the engine to the rear wheels.

Fluid Specifications

The fluid used in the C-5 transmission is coded "H" and must meet Ford specifications: ESP–M2C166–H.

Adjustments

DOWNSHIFT LINKAGE ADJUSTMENT

1. Hold the throttle wide open against its stop.

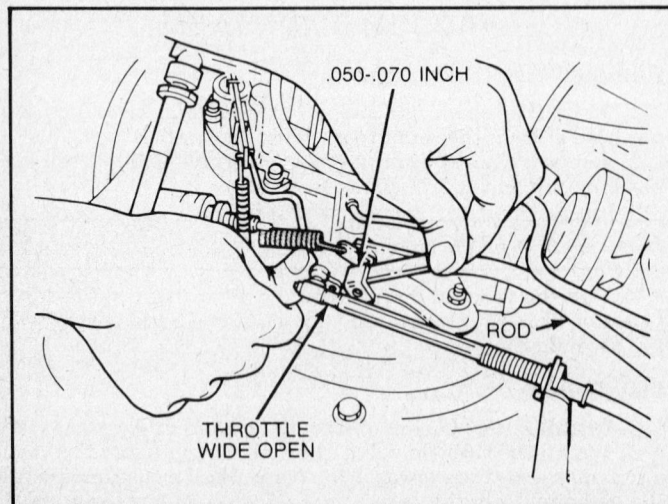
Adjustment of downshift rod

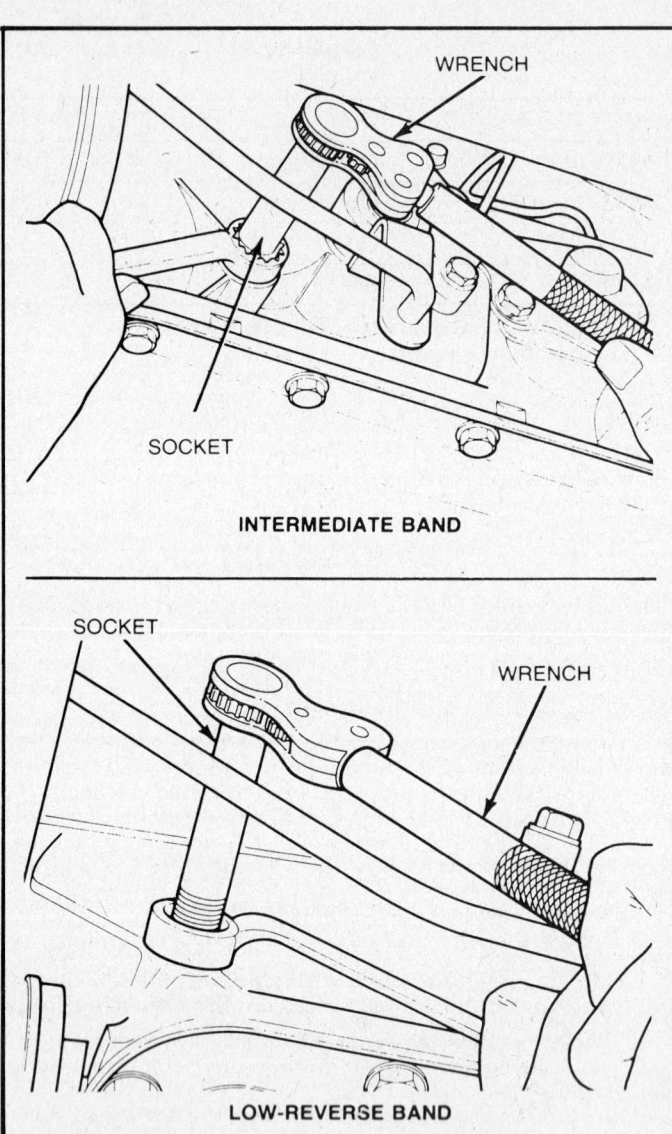
Band adjustments on intermediate and low/reverse bands

2. Push the rod down to force the downshift valve to bottom in the valve body.
3. Measure the clearance between the tip of the adjusting screw and the throttle lever. The clearance should be 0.050–0.070 in.
4. Turn the adjusting screw to obtain the proper clearance.

BAND ADJUSTMENTS (BOTH)

To adjust either band:
1. Remove the adjusting screw lock nut and discard.
2. Install a new lock nut on the adjusting screw, loosely.
3. Tighten the adjusting screw to 10 ft. lbs. torque, or until the adjusting tool over-runs and clicks.

AUTOMATIC TRANSMISSIONS
FORD C5

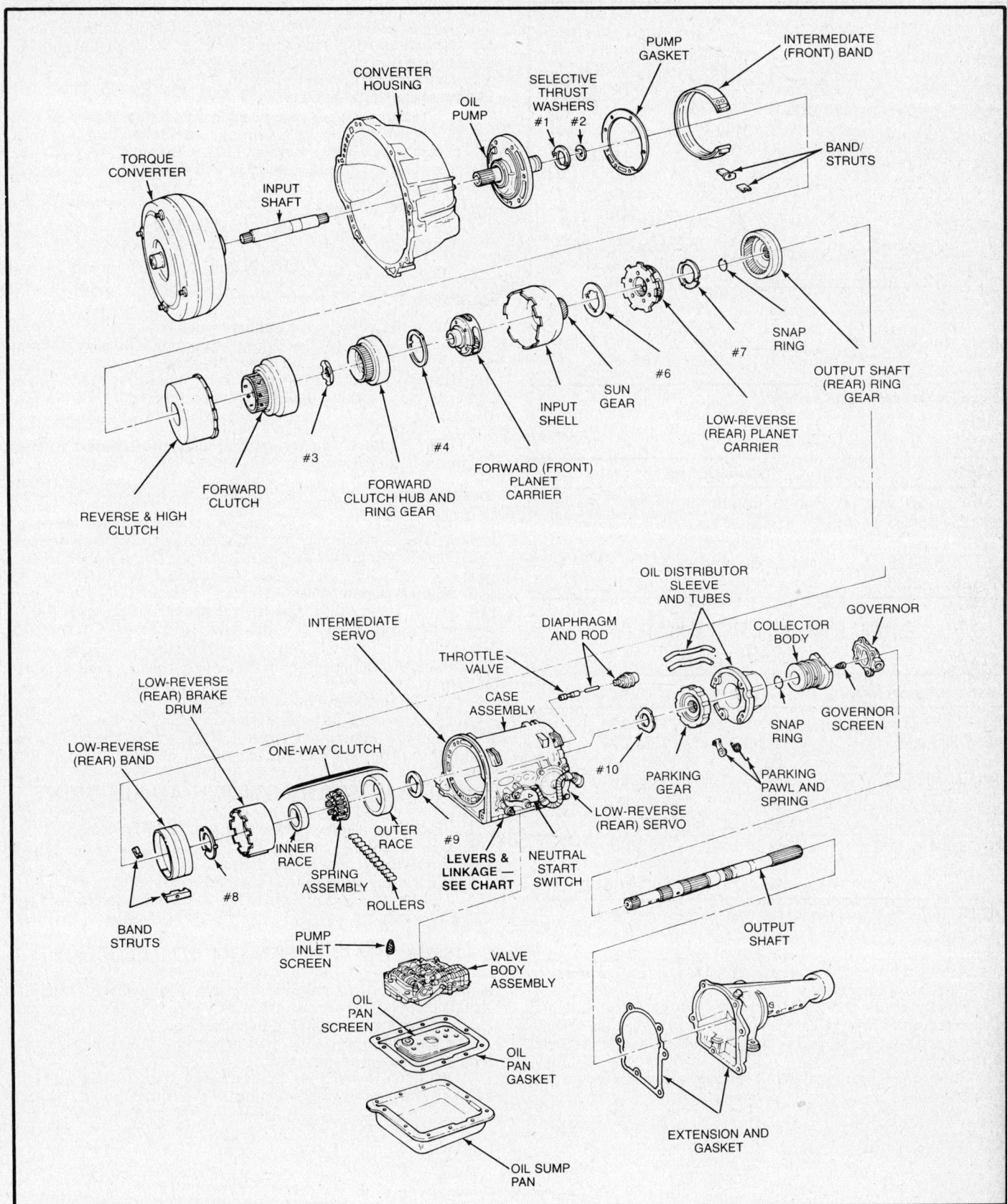

Exploded view of C-5 automatic transmission

SECTION 23

AUTOMATIC TRANSMISSIONS
FORD C5

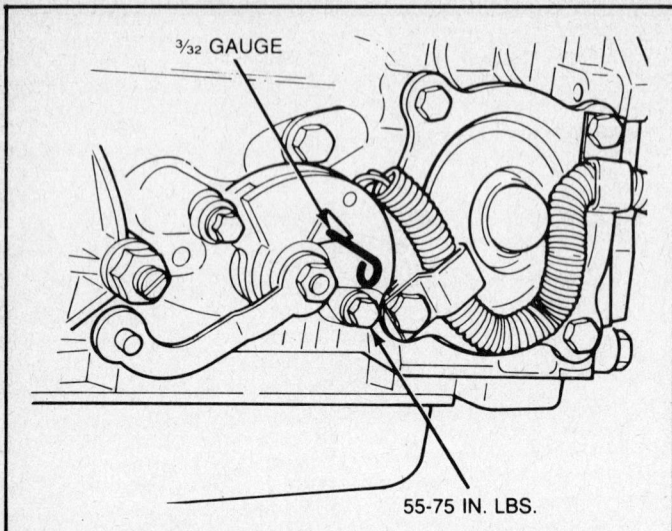

Adjustment of neutral start switch

Length	Color Code
1.5925-1.5875	Green
1.6075-1.6025	Blue
1.6225-1.6175	Orange
1.6375-1.6325	Black
1.6585-1.6535	Pink and White

LINE PRESSURE CHART
C-5

Transmission Model	Range	10" Vacuum
PEN-C, G, J, K	D	#90-101
PEM-AL, AM	2,1	123-136
	R	151-168
PEP-E, F, G, H, P, N	D	#87-97
	2,1	119-132
	R	145-162
PEP-B, D	D	#86-99
	2,1	120-132
	R	143-165

NOTE: Refer to the ID tag for the transmission model.

diaphragm unit.
3. Attach a hydraulic pressure gauge to the control pressure outlet on the transmission.
4. Firmly apply the parking brake. On vehicles equipped with a vacuum brake release, apply the service brakes. Otherwise the parking brake will release when the selector is moved to Drive.
5. Start the engine, allow it to reach normal operating temperature.
6. Set the engine idle speed to the specified rpm.
7. Adjust engine spped to 1000 rpm and apply 10 in. of vacuum to vacuum diaphragm unit. Read and record the control pressure in all selector positions.
8. Compare the pressure readings from Step 7 to the specified pressure in the line pressure chart and proceed as follows:
   a. Pressure within specification, no change required.
   b. Pressure below specification, use the next longest rod.
   c. Pressure above specification, use the next shortest rod.
If the length of the rod is not known, it should be measured with a micormeter.

On-Car Services

OIL PAN

Removal
1. Raise the vehicle and support safely.
2. Loosen the oil pan retaining bolts, removing only enough bolts to tilt the oil pan and drain the fluid.
3. Carefully remove the remaining bolts and the oil pan from the transmission. Pour out the remaining fluid from the oil pan.

NOTE: Discard the nylon shipping plug found in the bottom of the oil pan.

Installation
1. Thoroughly clean and remove all gasket material from the oil pan the pan mounting surface of the transmission case.
2. Install new gasket and mount the pan to the transmission case.
3. Install the pan retaining bolts and torque to 12–16 ft. lbs.
4. Lower the vehicle and fill the transmission with fluid. Start the engine and recheck the fluid level. Correct as required.
4. Back the adjusting screw off exactly the specified number of turns:
   a. Intermediate band 4 ¼ turns
   b. Low-reverse band 3 turns
5. Hold the adjustment screw at the specified back-off turns and tighten the new lock nuts to 35–45 ft. lbs.

NEUTRAL START SWITCH ADJUSTMENT

1. Place the selector in the "Neutral" position and hold.
2. Loosen the switch bolts and insert a ³⁄₃₂ in. gauge pin or drill through the hole in the switch.
3. Wiggle the switch until the drill seats in the case.
4. Tighten the switch bolts to 55–75 inch lbs. torque and remove the drill.

VACUUM DIAPHRAGM ADJUSTMENT

Adjustment of the vacuum diaphragm in controlled by the installation of longer or shorter throttle rods to obtain the proper line pressure. Five selective rods are used.
The following procedure will determine if a change in the length of the rod is required.
1. Attach a tachometer to the engine.
2. Attach a hand vacuum pump to the transmission vacuum

AUTOMATIC TRANSMISSIONS
FORD C5

CLUTCH AND BAND APPLICATION CHART
C-5

Gear	Forward Clutch	Reverse High Clutch	Intermediate Band	Low Reverse Band	One-Way Clutch
1st ①	On	Off	Off	Off	Holding ②
2nd ①	On	Off	On	Off	Overrunning
3rd ①	On	On	Off	Off	Overrunning
Low	On	Off	Off	On	Holding ②
Reverse	Off	On	Off	On	Not Affected

① Transmission selector in "D" position
② Overrunning on coast

FORD MOTOR COMPANY ATX AUTOMATIC TRANSAXLE

Applications

1983–87 Escort EXP Lynx, LN7, Tempo, Topaz

Transaxle and Converter Identification

TRANSAXLE

The ATX automatic transaxle can be identified by a plate attached to the case by a valve body cover retaining bolt. A vehicle certification label is attached to the left side door lock post and the transaxle code "B" is stamped in the space marked "TR".

CONVERTER

The torque converters are identified by letters or numbers stamped on the converter shell.

Fluid Type Specifications

Only Dexron® II type fluid, meeting Ford Motor Co. specifications, should be used in the ATX automatic transaxle.

Adjustments

THROTTLE LINKAGE ADJUSTMENT

Manual

The TV control linkage must be adjusted at the TV control rod assembly sliding trunnion block using the following procedure.
1. Set the engine curb idle speed to specification.
2. After the curb idle check, turn the engine off and insure that the carburetor throttle lever is against the hot engine curb idle stop. (The choke must be off.)

NOTE: The linkage cannot be properly set if the choke is allowed to cool and the throttle lever allowed to be on the choke fast idle cam.

3. Set the coupling lever adjustment screw at its approximate mid-range. Insure that the TV linkage shaft assembly is fully seated upward into the coupling lever.
4. Loosen the bolt on the sliding trunnion block on the TV control rod assembly one turn minimum.

─────────── **CAUTION** ───────────
The following steps inolve working in proximity to the EGR system. Allow the EGR system to cool before proceeding.
─────────────────────────────

5. Free-up the trunnion block so that it slides freely on the control rod.
6. Rotate the transaxle TV control lever up, using one finger and a light force, approximately 5 pounds, to insure that the TV control lever is against its internal idle stop. Without relaxing the force on the TV control lever, tighten the bolt on the trunnion block to specification.
7. Verify that the carburetor throttle lever is still against the hot engine curb idle stop.

Using Line Pressure

The following procedure may be used to check and/or adjust the TV control linkage using a line pressure gauge.
1. Place the shift selecor lever in the Park position.
2. Apply the emergency brake.
3. Attach a 300 psi pressure gauge to the line press port on the transaxle with sufficient flexible hose to make gauge accessible while operating engine.
4. Operate the engine until normal operating temperature is reached and the throttle lever is against the hot engine curb idle stop (with A/C off, if so equipped).
5. Verify that the coupling lever adjusting screw is in contsct with the TV linkage shaft assembly. If not, then the linkage must first be readjusted.
6. Verify that the carburetor throttle lever is against its hot engine curb idle stop. With the engine operating at idle and in Park, line pressure must be 43–59 psi. If line pressure is greater then 59 psi, the TV control linkage is set too long.
7. Place a 4 mm drill (a $5/32$ in. drill or 0.157 in. gauge pin) between the coupling lever adjustment screw and the TV linkage shaft. With the engine operating at idle and in Park, the line pressure must be 72–88 psi. A low reading indicates linkage is set short. A high reading indicates linkage is set too long.
8. Correct a long setting by backing out (CCW) the coupling

SECTION 23

AUTOMATIC TRANSMISSIONS
FORD ATX

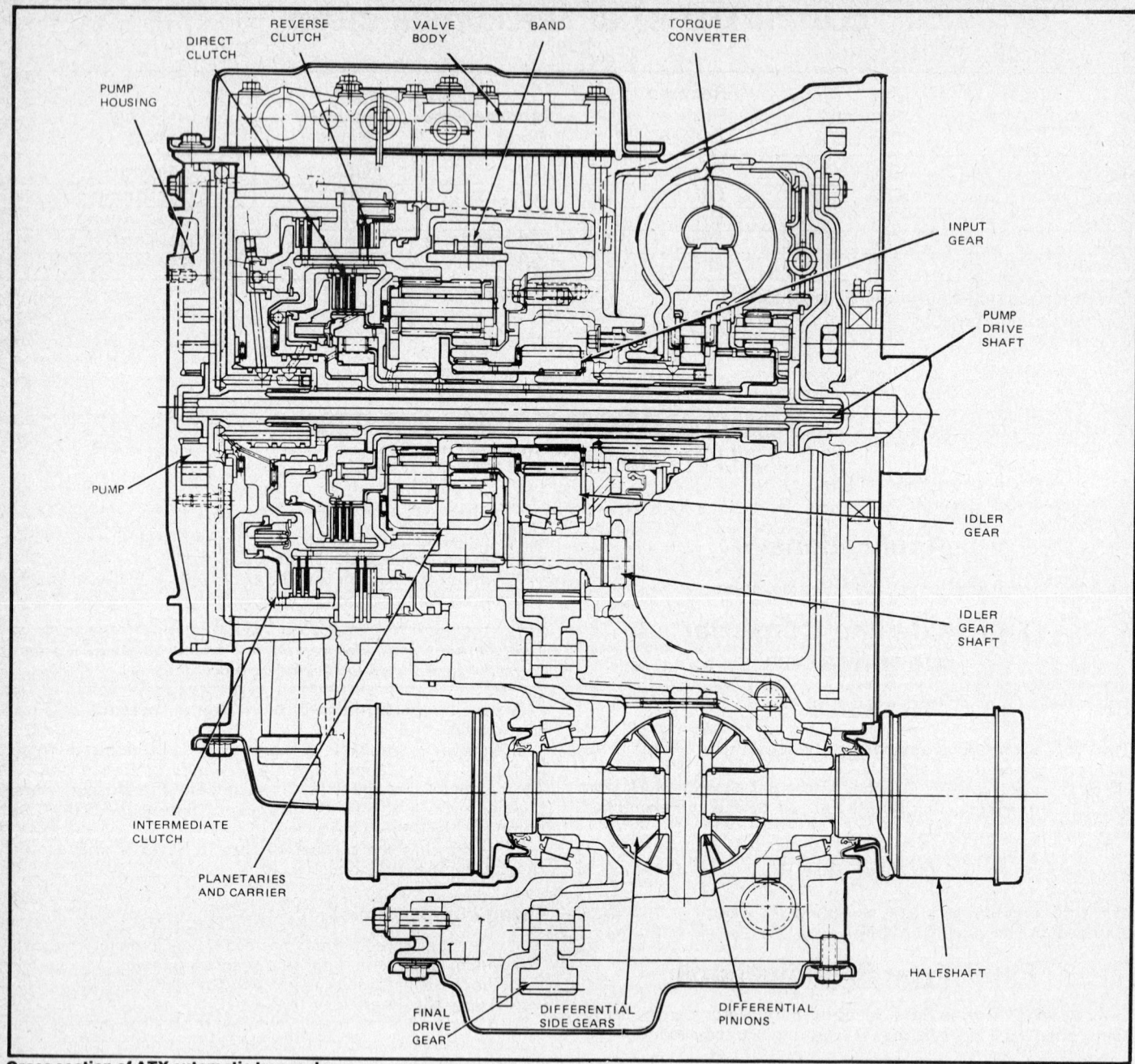

Cross section of ATX automatic transaxle

lever adjustment screw. Turn in (CW) the adjustment screw for a short rod condition. This adjusting screw will change line pressure by approximately 2 psi per turn. If insufficient adjusting capacity is available, the TV control rod length must be reset.

NEUTRAL SAFETY SWITCH ADJUSTMENT

1. Loosen the two swich retaining bolts and place the manual lever in the "Neutral" position.
2. Insert a $3/32$ in. drill bit through the hole in the neutral start switch.
3. Move the neutral start switch until the drill seats in the case.
4. Torque the neutral start switch retaining bolts to 7–9 ft. lbs.
5. Remove the drill from the switch

BAND ADJUSTMENT

The band adjustment is done during a transaxle overhaul with the use of special tools. Selective sized servo pistons are used to correctly position the band for its application.

AUTOMATIC TRANSMISSIONS
Ford ATX

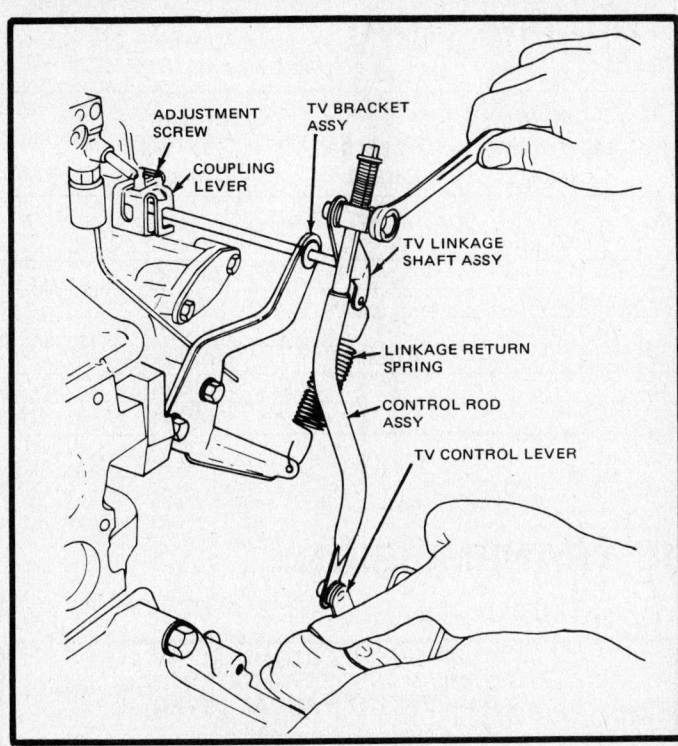

Adjustment of throttle linkage

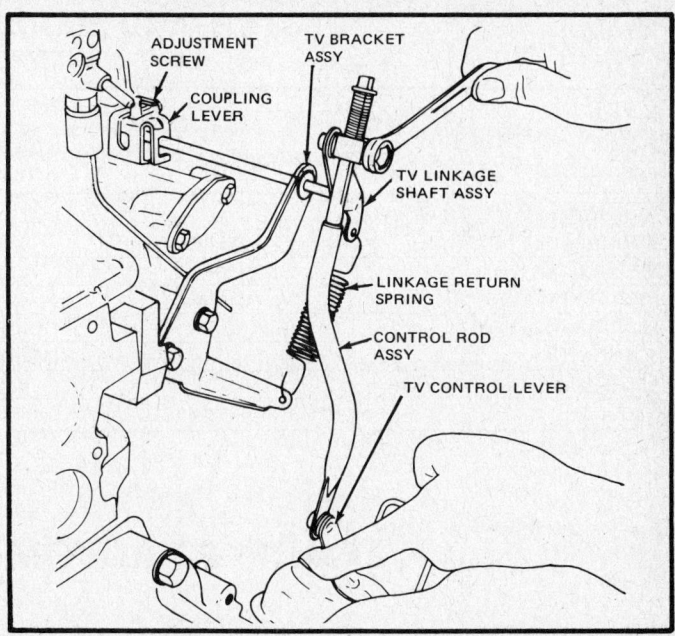

Adjustment procedure for T.V. linkage control (© Ford Motor Co.)

LINE PRESSURE ①

Range	Pressure (At Idle)	Pressure (WOT Stall)
D-2-1	43-58 psi	105-127 psi
R	70-105 psi	230-285 psi
P-N	43-58 psi	②

① Governor pressure is at zero (vehicle stationary).
  Transaxle is at operating temperature.
② Not available

On-Car Services

LOWER OIL PAN AND FILTER

Removal and Installation

1. Raise the vehicle on a hoist or jack stands.
2. Place a drain pan under the transaxle.
3. Loosen the pan attaching bolts and drain the fluid from the transaxle.
4. When fluid has drained to the level of the pan flange, remove the rest of the pan bolts. Work from the rear and both sides of the pan to allow it to drop and drain slowly.
5. When all fluid has drained from the transaxle, remove and thoroughly clean the pan. Discard the gasket.
6. Remove the three retaining bolts and remove the filter. Discard the seal.
7. Install new oil filter and seal. Tighten the bolts 7-9 ft. lbs.
8. Place a new gasket on the oil pan and install the oil pan on the transaxle case. Tighten the retaining bolts to 15-19 ft. lbs.
9. Fill the transaxle to the correct level with Dexron® II automatic transmission fluid.

Installation

1. Install the servo cover and snap ring using the servo installation tool (T81P-70027-A or equivalent).
2. Install the mount to case attaching bolt in the left frong (No. 1) mount.
3. Install the filler tube.
4. Install the filler tube to case attaching bolt.
5. Install the fan and fan shroud assembly.
6. Install the two fan shroud to radiator attaching units.
7. Connect the FM capacitor wiring, if so equipped.
8. Connect the fan motor and water temperature sending unit wiring.
9. Connect the battery.
10. Start the engine and cycle the transaxle through all ranges. Check the fluid level and fill if necessary, to the recommended level with the Motorcraft Dexron® II, series D or equivalent transmission fluid.
11. Check for fluid leaks.

CLUTCH AND BAND APPLICATION CHART
ATX Transaxle

	Band	Direct Clutch	Interm. Clutch	Reverse Clutch	Interm. One-Way Clutch
1st Gear Manual Low		Applied	Applied		Holding

SECTION 23 AUTOMATIC TRANSMISSIONS
FORD ATX

CLUTCH AND BAND APPLICATION CHART
ATX Transaxle

	Band	Direct Clutch	Interm. Clutch	Reverse Clutch	Interm. One-Way Clutch
2nd Gear Manual Low	Applied		Applied		
1st Gear (Drive)	Applied				Holding
2nd Gear (Drive)	Applied		Applied		
3rd Gear (Drive)		Applied	Applied		
Reverse (R)		Applied		Applied	Holding
Neutral (N)					Holding
Park (P)					Holding

ZF 4HP–22 AUTOMATIC TRANSMISSION

Application

1984½–85 Mark VII/Continental w/ Diesel Engines

Transmission and Converter Identification

The ZF 4HP–22 automatic transmission is a four speed transmission incorporating a lock-up clutch, located in the torque converter and is engaged only when the transmission is operating in the fourth gear range. The fourth gear is an overdrive ratio. This transmission is only available coupled to a diesel engine at the present time.

TRANSMISSION

The transmission identification tag is located adjacent to the manual lever on the left side of the unit. Both Volvo and Ford Motor Company have part numbers and model identifications stamped on the tag. The prefix and suffix of the part number is used as the model number for the Ford Motor Company's parts identification program.

CONVERTER

The torque converer is a 10 ¼ inch diameter unit with a 2.55:1 ratio at full stall speed. Identification numbers or symbols are either stamped into the cover or ink-stamped on the cover surface.

Fluid Capacities and Fluid Specifications

The fluid fill capacity with the transmission dry is 8 quarts (US) or 7.7 Liters. The fluid type to be used is Dextron® II or its equivalent.

Adjustments

KICKDOWN (T.V.) CABLE

Installation and Adjustment

NOTE: If a new cable is used, the reference bead will be loose on the cable. Proceed as follows:

ZF 4HP 22 AUTOMATIC TRANSMISSION IDENTIFICATION TAG (ADJACENT TO MANUAL LEVER)

22-XXX SERIAL NO.
1043 010 008 MODEL NO.
4HP-22
FORD ASSY. NO. E4LP-CA   ZF Getriebe GmbH Saarbrucken

PART NO. PREFIX AND SUFFIX ALSO USED AS MODEL NUMBER

ZF transmission identification tag (© Ford Motor Co.)

NEW CABLE

1. With cable reconnected at transmission and transmission bolted up to engine, follow steps B4–B5 and set adjusting nuts approximately in the center of the threaded barrel.
2. Pull the "T" head until you feel the wide-open throttle "full" stop, (about 6.4mm or 0.25 in. before maximum cable travel). Do not pull any father.
3. Slide the bead along the cable until there is a gap of 39–40mm (1.54–1.57 in.) between the end of the threaded barrel and the end of the bead closest to the barrel.
4. Crimp the bead to the braided cable core with a wire terminal crimper. Be careful to distort the bead as little as possible.
5. Remove the cable from the bracket.

WITH A USED CABLE, REFERENCE BEAD CRIMPED TIGHT TO CABLE

1. Rest the braided cable core wire on the split in the white plastic lever insert with "T" head on the trunnion side and pull it through.
2. Snap the "T" head into the insert trunnions.
3. Snap the insert into the lower rectangular hole in the in-

AUTOMATIC TRANSMISSIONS
ZF 4HP-22 MODEL

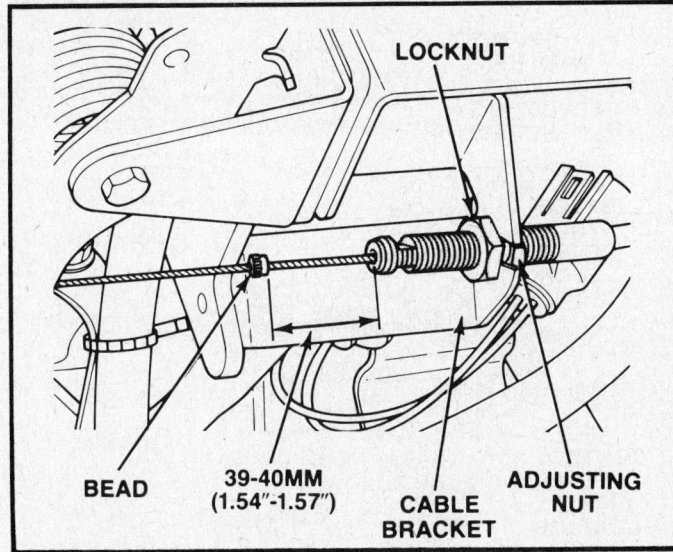

Kickdown (T.V.) cable adjustment (© Ford Motor Co.)

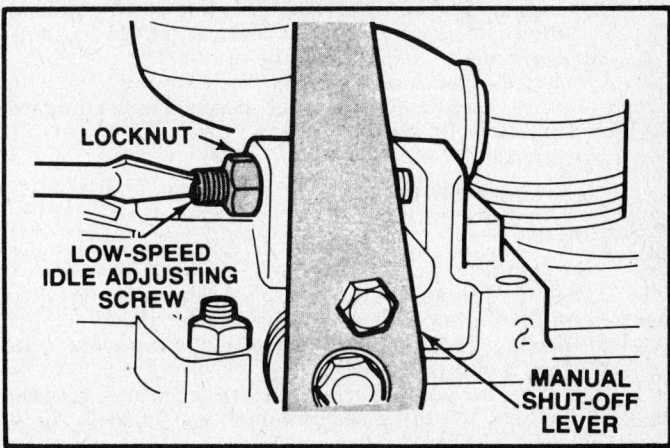

Low speed adjusting screw location (© Ford Motor Co.)

jector pump side lever after threading the braided cable core through the slot.

4. Spin the rearward adjusting nut back to end of the threaded barrel and place the threaded barrel through the slot in the cable bracket.

5. Pull the threaded barrel into the 10.2mm diameter hole in the bracket.

Cable Adjustment

6. Set the injector pump top lever at the full throttle position.

7. Tighten the rear adjusting nut on the threaded barrel until a gap of 1.54–1.57 in. (39–40mm) exists between the edge of the crimped bead on the cable closest to the barrel and the end of the threaded barrel.

8. Tighten the forward adjusting nut to lock the cable assembly to the bracket. Torque to 80–106 inch lbs. (9–12 Nm).

9. Recheck 1.54–1.57 in. (39–40mm) dimension and reset if necessary.

INJECTOR PUMP LINKAGE

Adjustment

Three adjustments affect the transmission performance and the transmission shift speeds: Low-Speed Idle Adjustment, High Engine "W.O.T."(Wide Open Throttle) Speed Adjustment and Injector Pump Operating Lever Linkage Setting. All these adjustments are performed on the injector pump. The Low-Speed Idle Adjustment and the High Engine "W.O.T." Speed Adjustment must be performed before the Injector Pump Operating Lever Linkage Setting. All three adjustments must be performed prior to adjusting the Kickdown (T.V.) Cable.

Before proceeding with any of these adjustments the following must be verified:

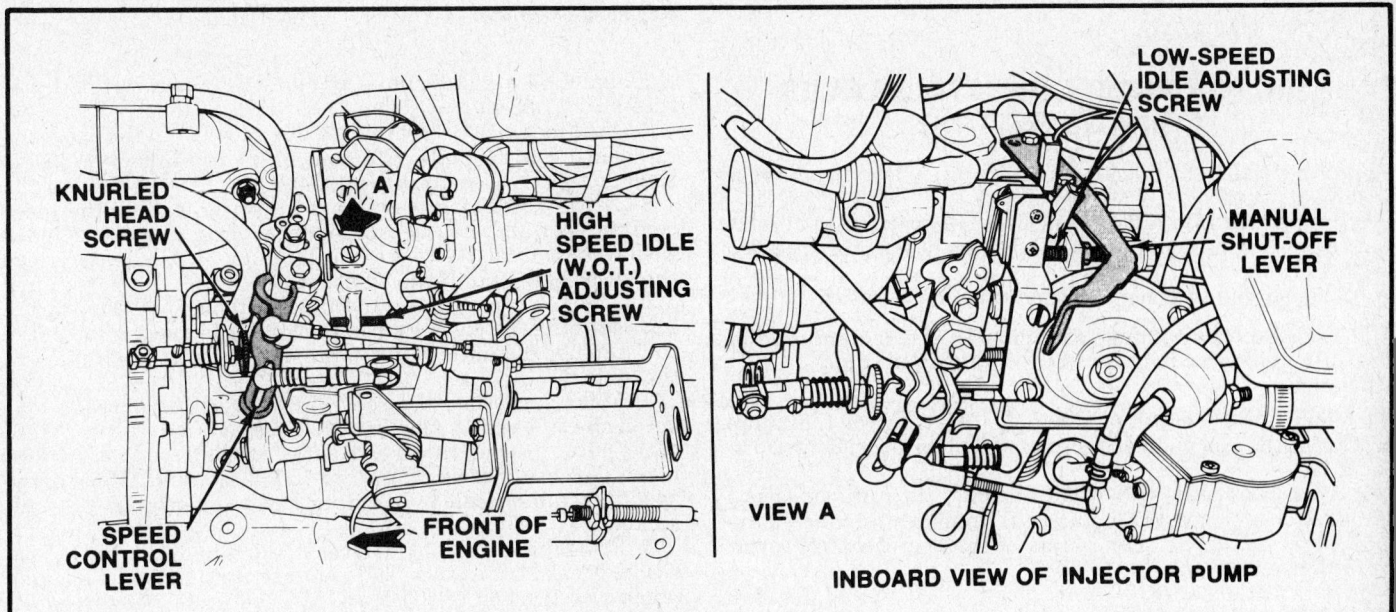

Speed controls on diesel engine injector pump (© Ford Motor Co.)

SECTION 23

AUTOMATIC TRANSMISSIONS
ZF 4HP-22 MODEL

1. The engine must be at normal operation temperature.
2. The valve clearance must be at the specified dimensions.
3. All electrical equipment must be in the OFF position.
4. A tachometer, such as the Diesel Tach/Timing Meter, Rotunda 78-0116 or equivalent, must be attached to the diagnostic plug connector of the diesel engine.

LOW-SPEED IDLE

Adjustment

1. Start engine.
2. Loosen the locknut on the low-speed idle adjusting screw (located on the top inboard side of the injector pump). Adjust the idle speed by turning the low-speed adjusting screw until 750–800 rpm is obtained.
3. Turn the knurled head screw until the clearance between the knurled head the the speed control lever is 0.020–0.040 in. (0.5–1.0mm).
4. Check, and if required, adjust the High Engine "W.O.T." Speed and the Injector Pump Operating Lever Setting.

HIGH ENGINE "W.O.T." (WIDE OPEN THROTTLE) SPEED

Adjustment

Before adjusting the High Engine "W.O.T." speed, make sure the engine is at normal operating temperature.
1. Start the engine.
2. Move the speed control lever to the full load or W.O.T. (Wide Open Throttle) position.
3. Loosen the locknut and turn the engine high idle speed (W.O.T.) adjusting screw (located on the outboard side of the injector pump) until 5350 ± 100 rpm is obtained.
4. Check the throttle cable so that the stop on the speed control lever rests on the engine high idle speed (W.O.T.) adjusting screw when the lever is in the full load or W.O.T. position.
5. Check to verify that the speed control lever is at the full load or W.O.T. position when the accelerator is depressed fully to the floor.

INJECTOR PUMP OPERATING LEVER LINKAGE SETTING

Prior to adjusting the injector pump operating lever, make sure of the following:
1. Low-Speed Idle Adjustment is at the specified setting.
2. High Engine W.O.T. Speed Adjustment is at the specified setting.
3. The engine is at normal operating termperature

NOTE: For the purpose of accuracy, it is recommended that the metric setting be used in taking all measurements.

4. Measure distance "A" from the front fact of the pump bracket to the rear radius of the speed control lever. Record distance "A".
5. Push the speed control lever against the full load or W.O.T. stop and measure distance "B" from the front face of the pump bracket to the rear radius of the speed control lever; record distance "B".
6. Subtract distance "B" from distance "A" to find distance "Y" ("A" – "B" = "Y"). For example: if distance "A" is 128mm (5.03 in.) and distance "B" is 81.0mm (3.18 in.), then by subtracting distance "B" from distance "A", distance "Y" is

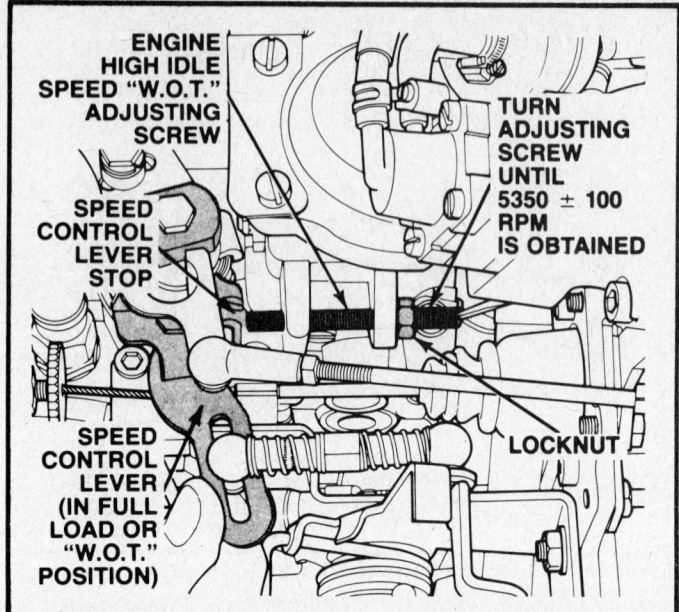

Wide open throttle (W.O.T.) speed adjustment (© Ford Motor Co.)

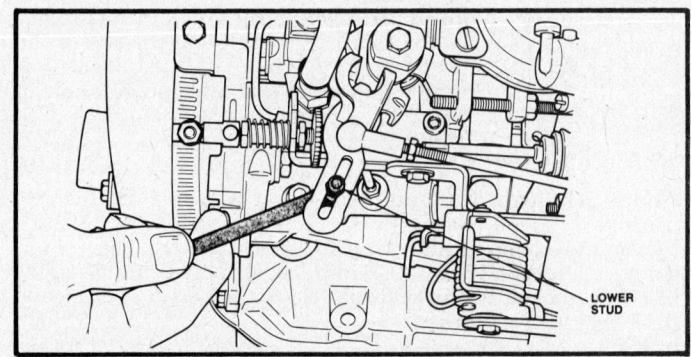

Adjusting dimension "C" (© Ford Motor Co.)

47.0mm (1.85 in.) (128mm – 81mm = 47.0mm or 5.03 in. – 3.18 in. = 1.85 in.).
7. Find distance "C" by finding distance "Y" in the appropriate chart. For example: if distance "Y" is 47.0mm (1.85 in.) then distance "C" is 67.0mm (2.64 in.).
8. Disconnect the linkage from the lower stud on the speed control lever and measure distance "C" from the centerline of the lever shaft (on top of the injector pump) to the centerline of the lower ball stud. If the measurement is not to the specified distance "C", adjust to the specified distance by loosening the nut retaining the lower stud to the lever and moving the nut to the specified distance. Tighten the nut. Connect the linkage to the stud.
9. Make sure the speed control lever rests against the low-speed idle stop screw. Meausre distance "X" from the front face of the pump bracket to the end of the rear ball stud socket. Distance "X" should be 68.0mm (2.68 in.). If required, adjust to the specified dimension by turning the nut between the ball sockets.
10. Place the speed control lever in the full load or W.O.T. position. Measure distance "Z" from the front face of thf pump bracket to the end of the rear ball stud socket. Distance "Z" must be 29.0 ± 0.5mm (1.14 ± 0.020 in.). If distance "Z" is not correct, repeat Steps 1–4 of this procedure.
11. Check, and if required, adjust the kickdown (T.V.) cable.

AUTOMATIC TRANSMISSIONS
ZF 4HP-22 MODEL
SECTION 23

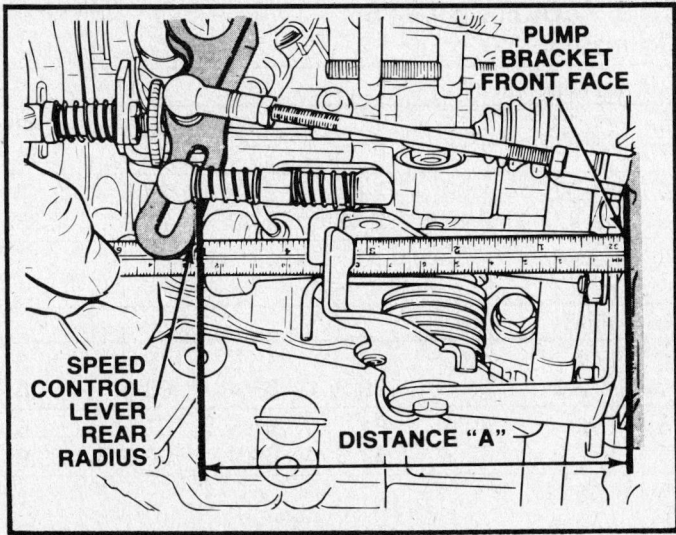

Measuring dimension "A" (© Ford Motor Co.)

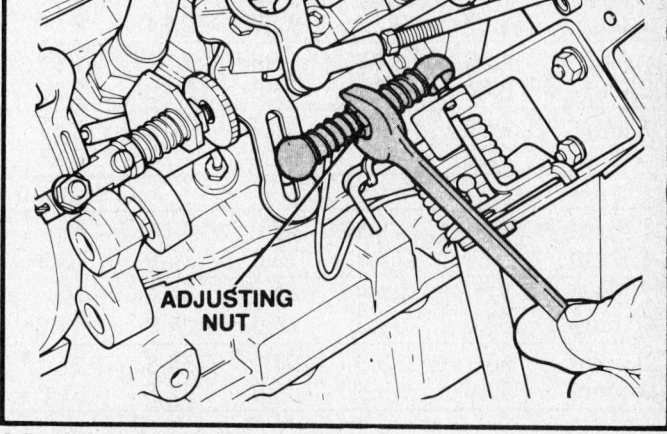

Adjusting dimension "X" (© Ford Motor Co.)

On-Car Services

FLUID CHANGE

1. Change fluid at 30,000 miles. Remove and clean oil pan.
2. Remove and inspect screen; replace if damaged or clogged.
3. Use only DEXRON® II fluid. Fill with approximately 3 or 4 quarts (does not include converter) and check fluid level (see Diagnosis section) with transmission hot.

OIL PAN AND SCREEN

Removal

1. Remove drain plug to drain out most of the fluid.
2. Remove the bolt attaching the filler stub tube to the converter housing.
3. Disconnect the stub tube from the oil pan.
4. Remove (6) bolts and clamps with 10mm socket.
5. Use Torx® bit 27 to remove three bolts attaching oil screen to valve body.

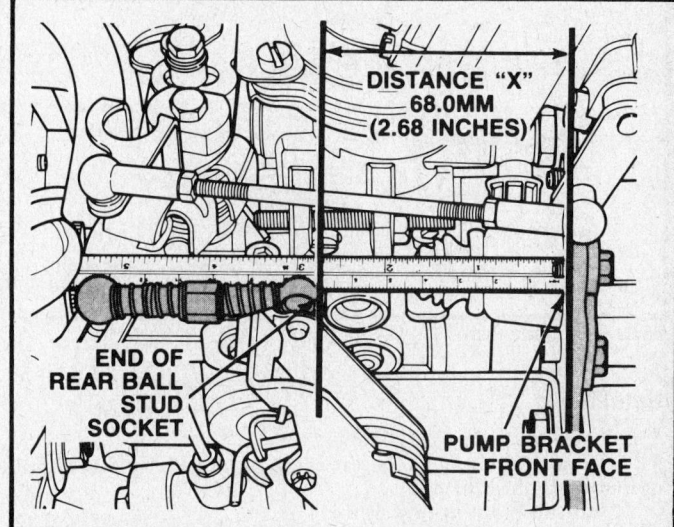

Measuring dimension "X" (© Ford Motor Co.)

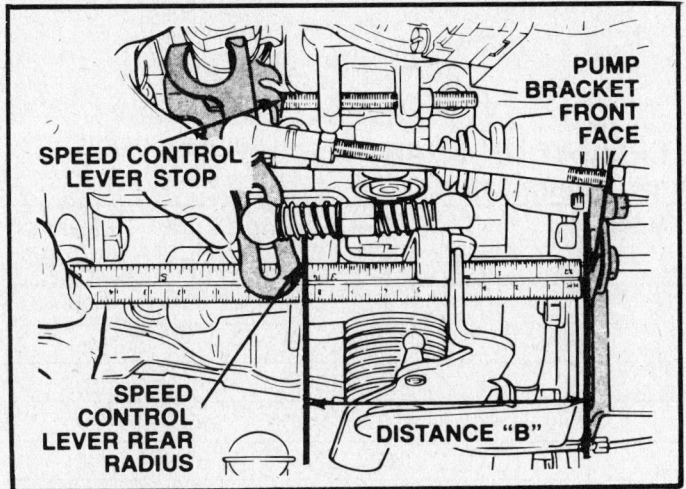

Measuring dimension "B" (© Ford Motor Co.)

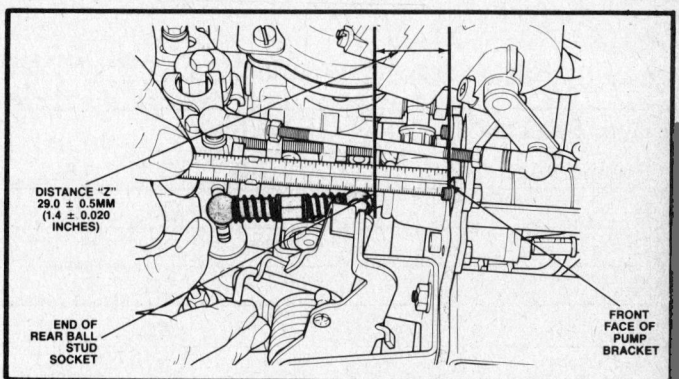

Checking dimension "Z" (© Ford Motor Co.)

23-25

SECTION 23
AUTOMATIC TRANSMISSIONS
ZF 4HP-22 MODEL

DISTANCE "C" ADJUSTING TABLE CHARTS
Ford Motor Company

Measurements in Inches

Y (in.)	1.61	1.63	1.65	1.67	1.69	1.71	1.73	1.75	1.77	1.79	1.81	1.83
C (in.)	3.07	3.03	3.00	2.94	2.90	2.87	2.83	2.79	2.76	2.73	2.70	2.66
Y (in.)	1.85	1.87	1.89	1.91	1.93	1.95	1.97	1.99	2.01	2.03	2.05	2.07
C (in.)	2.64	2.61	2.58	2.55	2.53	2.50	2.47	2.45	2.42	2.40	2.38	2.35
Y (in.)	2.09	2.11	2.13	2.15	2.17	2.19	2.20					
C (in.)	2.33	2.31	2.29	2.27	2.26	2.24	2.22					

Measurements in MM

Y (mm)	41	41.5	42	42.5	43	43.5	44	44.5	45	45.5	46	46.5
C (mm)	78.1	77.0	76.0	74.9	73.9	73.0	72.0	71.1	70.3	69.4	68.6	67.8
Y (mm)	47	47.5	48	48.5	49	49.5	50	50.5	51	51.5	52	52.5
C (mm)	67.0	66.3	65.6	64.9	64.2	63.5	62.9	62.3	61.6	61.0	60.5	59.9
Y (mm)	53	53.5	54	54.5	55	55.5	56					
C (mm)	59.4	58.8	58.3	57.8	57.3	56.8	56.4					

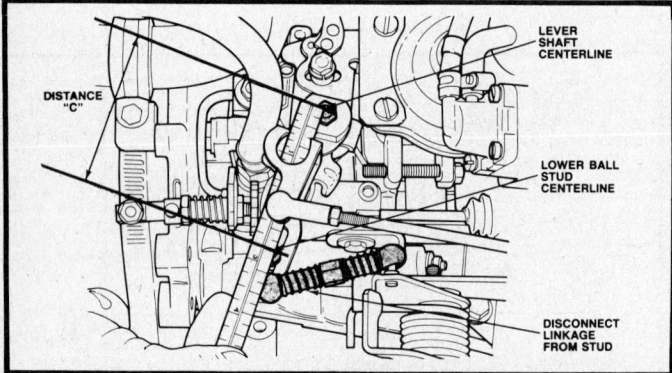

Measuring dimension "C" (© Ford Motor Co.)

Installation

1. Install new screen O-ring.
2. Pan gasket is reusable if it is not damaged. Gasket should be installed onto oil pan.
3. Tighten bolts at assembly:
4. Screen: 71 inch lbs. (8 Nm).
5. Pan: 71 inch lbs. (8 Nm).

NOTE: Two identical clamps without inner radius mount on sides of oil pan. Four long clamps with radius mount on corners. Corner clamps and bolts are to be installed first.

6. Connect the filler stub tube to the oil pan and the converter housing. Tighten the tube bracket bolt to 17 ft. lbs. (23Nm) and the pan nut to 78–45 ft. lbs. (100–110 Nm).

NEUTRAL START SWITCH

1. The switch is located just forward of the manual lever, near the cooler return line fitting.
2. There is no switch adjustment.

Replacement

Disconnect the electrical connector and remove the bolt, washer and retainer plate to remove the switch. Reverse the procedure to install it. Tighten the bolt to 88 inch lbs. (10Nm) torque.

CLUTCH AND BRAKE APPLICATION CHART
ZF 4HP22 Automatic Transmission

Gear Selector Position and Gear		Clutch			Brake				Overrunning Clutch			Parking Pawl
		C-1	C-2	C-3	B-1	B-2	B-3	B-4	F-1	F-2	F-3	
P				ON								ON
R			ON	ON			ON					
N				ON								
D	1st	ON		ON						ON		ON
	2nd	ON		ON	ON	ON			ON			ON
	3rd	ON	ON	ON		ON					ON	ON
	4th	ON	ON			ON		ON				

AUTOMATIC TRANSMISSIONS
ZF 4HP-22 MODEL
SECTION 23

CLUTCH AND BRAKE APPLICATION CHART
ZF 4HP22 Automatic Transmission

Gear Selector Position and Gear		Clutch			Brake				Overrunning Clutch			Parking Pawl
		C-1	C-2	C-3	B-1	B-2	B-3	B-4	F-1	F-2	F-3	
3	1st	ON		ON						ON	ON	
	2nd	ON		ON	ON	ON			ON		ON	
	3rd	ON	ON	ON		ON					ON	
2	1st	ON		ON						ON	ON	
	2nd	ON		ON	ON	ON			ON		ON	
1	1st	ON		ON			ON				ON ①	

① Only transfers power when engine is pulling

GENERAL MOTORS TORQUE CONVERTER CLUTCH (T.C.C.)

Troubleshooting Converter Clutch

G.M. TURBO HYDRAMATIC

Before diagnosing the TCC system as being at fault in the case of rough shifting or other malfunctions, make sure that the engine is in at least a reasonable state of tune. Also, the following points should be checked:

1. Check the transmission fluid level and correct as necessary.
2. Check the manual linkage adjustment and correct as necessary.
3. Road test the vehicle to verify the complaint. Make sure that the vehicle is at normal operating temperature.

Internal of External Problems

If it has been determinded that there is a problem with the TCC system, the next step is to determine if the problem is internal or external.The following procedure can be used:

1. Disconnect the electrical connector at the transmission case.
2. Raise and safely support vehicle.
3. Start engine and adjust the speed to 2000 rpm, gear selector in Neutral.
4. Test for 12 volts at the connector using a volt/ohm meter or a test light. If 12 volts are present, the problem is internal. If no voltage (or low voltage according to the meter) is present at the connecor, the problem is external.

If the problem is internal (12 volts at the connector) the following steps can be taken:

1. With the wire to the transmission case disconnected, take a 12 volt test light and connect it to the female connector and ground to the male transmission connector.
2. Start the engine and adjust the speed to 2000 rpm, gear selector in Park.
3. If the test light comes on, the governor switch or the internal wiring is shorted to ground. The oil pan will have to be removed, the wiring checked and/or the governor switch replaced.

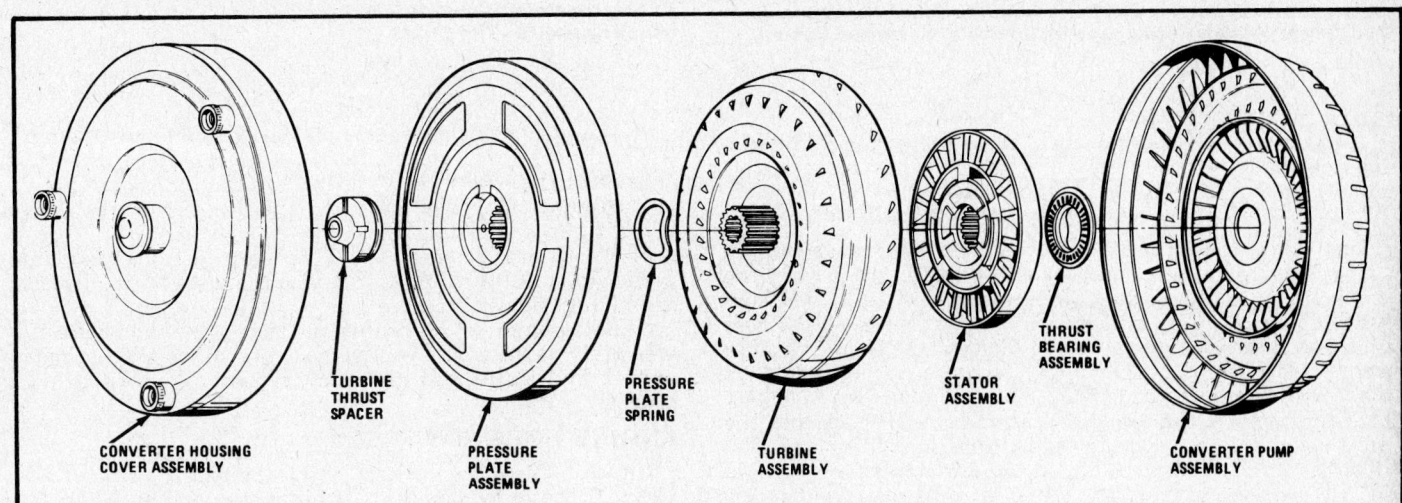

Exploded view of converter clutch assembly - typical

Section 23 AUTOMATIC TRANSMISSIONS
GM TORQUE CONVERTER CLUTCH (TCC)

4. If the test light does not light, make sure that the vehicle is off the ground, and run in Drive until the transmission shifts to 3rd gear. Keep the engine speed to 2000 rpm.

5. If the test light now comes on, the internal hydraulic/mechanical controls will have to be checked. Refer to the Hydraulic/Mechanical Controls section.

6. If the test light still does not light, there is a problem with the solenoid or governor switch.

Solenoid or Governor Switch Test

To test for solenoid or governor switch electrical malfunction, the following steps can be used:

1. Drain the transmission fluid and remove the oil pan.
2. Using an external 12 volt source, (self-powered test light or small lantern battery, etc.) connect a positive lead to the case connector. Remove the lead wire from the governor pressure switch and connect it to the ground lead of the external 12 volt source.

---- CAUTION ----

Do not reverse the leads or the solenoid diode will be destroyed by the reverse voltage. Do not use an automobile battery for this test. A self-powered test light is best for these tests.

3. If the solenoid clicks, it can be considered serviceable; replace the governor switch.

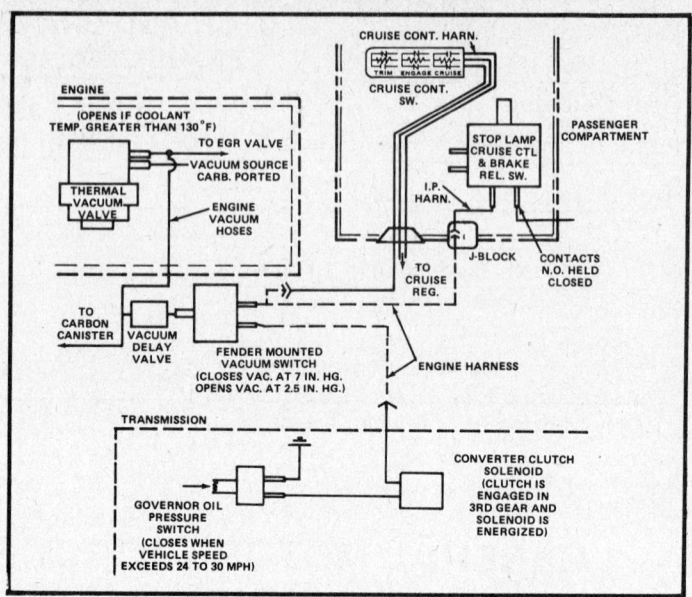
Converter clutch controls with gasoline engine usage - typical

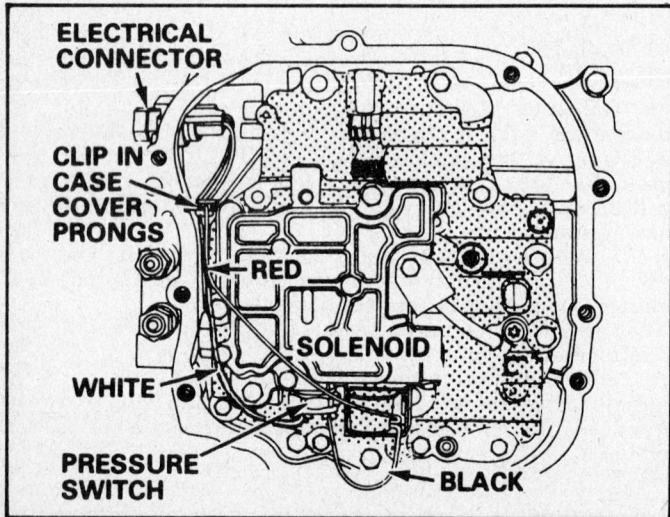
Auxiliary valve body - equipped with Computer Command Control

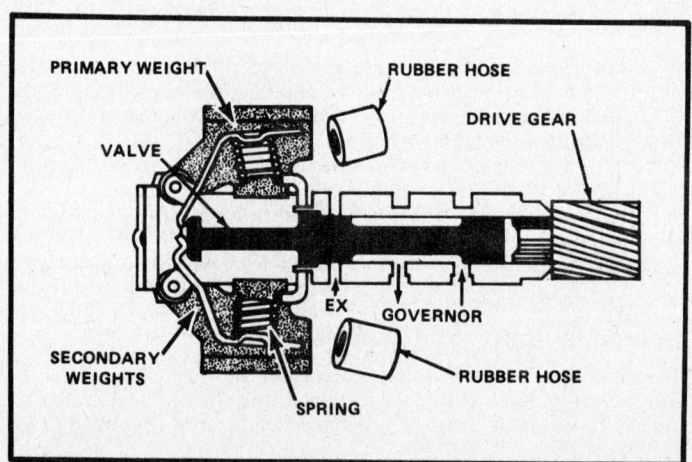
Rubber hose locations on governor assembly to test converter clutch operation - TH 250/350

4. If the solenoid does not click, check the wiring. If the wiring appears to be good, replace the solenoid and recheck.

Internal Hydraulic/Mechanical Controls Check

Since part of these checks involves the governor system, obtain, if possible, a test governor of the same type used in the transmission being serviced. Cut two pieces of 5/32 in O.D. rubber vacuum hose to 3/8 in long. Put one piece of the cut-off hose under each weight of the governor. Remove the engine vacuum switch electrical connector. The vacuum switch should be mounted on an inner fender wall. Using a jumper wire, connect both terminals of the connector together. As a check that the proper connection has been made, turn the ignition to ON, raise the vehicle and check for 12 volts at the transmission case female connector. There should be 12 volts on a volt meter. Then, proceed as follows:

1. Remove the transmission governor and replace with the test governor.

2. With the vehicle's wheels off the ground, apply the parking brake. The rear wheels must not be able to turn.
3. Start the engine, selector in Park, and allow to idle.
4. Step on the brake pedal. This will interrupt the flow of current to the transmission.
5. Place the selector in Drive. The transmission should automatically shift into 3rd gear because the test governor is causing high governor pressure.
6. Release the service brakes and the engine should stall immediately. If the engine stalls, the converter clutch and the internal hydraulic and mechanical controls ae operating properly.

ENGINE DOES NOT STALL

If the engine does not stall, check the following:
1. Missing or damaged O-ring at the end of the turbine shaft.
2. Missing check ball or O-ring at the solenoid.
3. Loose solenoid bolts.

23-28

AUTOMATIC TRANSMISSIONS
GM TORQUE CONVERTER CLUTCH (TCC)

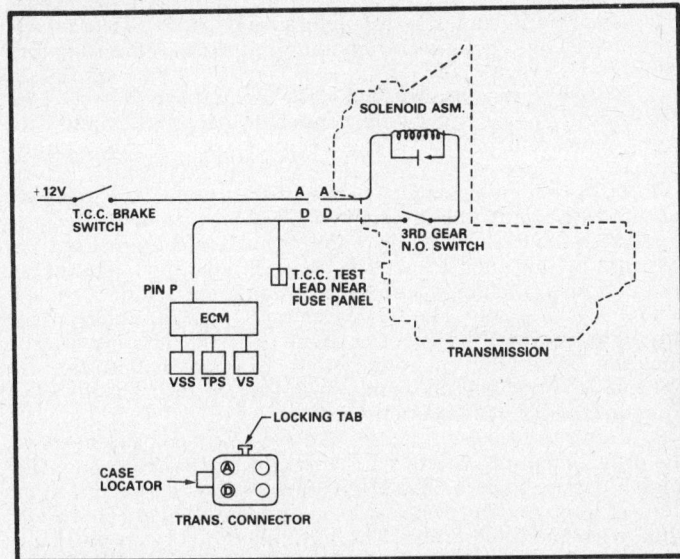

T.C.C. wiring schematic - equipped with Computer Command Control

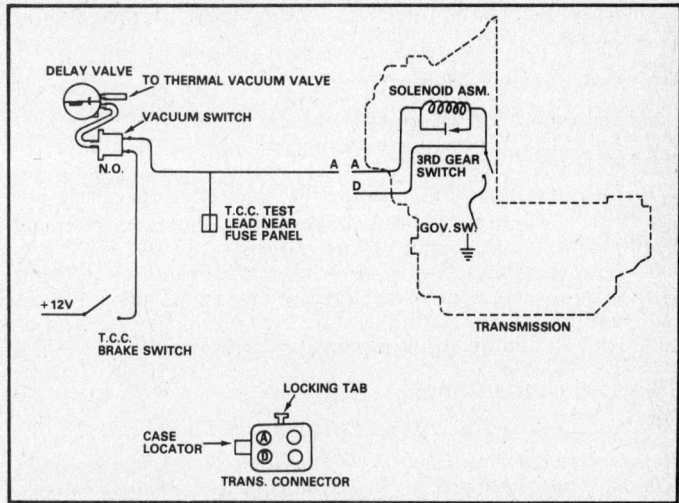

T.C.C. wiring schematic - except with Computer Command Control

4. Converter clutch apply passages in the pump blocked or restricted.
5. Defective converter.

NOTE: *After the test has been completed remove the test governor and replace it with the original governor. If the original governor was used for the test, remove the rubber bushings that were installed and be sure the weight springs are in the correct position before reinstalling.*

External Controls Check

1. Turn the ignition switch to the ON position.
2. Check the vacuum switch connector for 12 volts.
3. If no voltage is present at the vacuum switch, check the fuse block for a blown fuse, the brake switch and the wiring to the vacuum switch.
4. If there is a reading of 12 volts at the switch, reconnect the electrical connector to the vacuum switch. Using a hand vacuum pump with a gauge, apply 2.5-7 in. of vacuum to the vacuum switch.
5. With the ignition switch in the ON position, check for 12 volts at the female end of the transmission connector.
6. If no or low (as read on a voltmeter) voltage is present, look for a break in the wire between the vacuum switch and the transmission. Further vacuum switch checks are given below.

Vacuum Switch Check

1. Disconnect the vacuum hose and the electrical connector from the vacuum switch.
2. Attach one lead of a test light to either one of the terminals of the vacuum switch. Ground the other vacuum switch termina.
3. Apply 12 volts to the other test light lead.
4. Attach the hand vacuum pump and gauge to the vacuum switch port.
5. Turn the ignition switch to the ON position.
6. The test light should be off. Apply vacuum with the hand pump until the gauge reads between 2.45-7 in. of vacuum. The light should come on.
7. Bleed off some vacuum slowly. The light should remain on until the vacuum drops to between 1.5-2.5 in. of vacuum.
8. If the vacuum switch does not turn the test light on and off

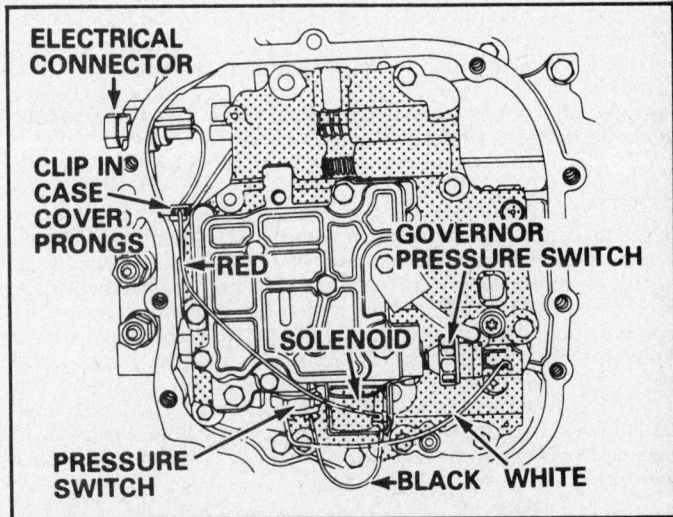

Auxiliary valve body - except with Computer Command Control

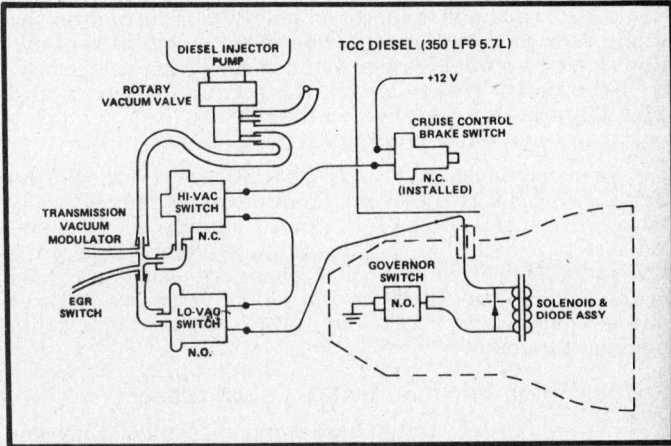

Converter clutch controls with diesel engine usage - typical

23-29

SECTION 23
AUTOMATIC TRANSMISSIONS
GM TORQUE CONVERTER CLUTCH (TCC)

at the specified vacuum readings, the switch is bad and should be replaced.

Thermal Vacuum Valve Check

1. Disconnect the vacuum hose at the vacuum switch and install a vacuum gauge to the hose.
2. Start the engine and check the vacuum reading, gear selector in Park. With the engine cold (coolant temperature below 130°F.), vacuum at idle should be zero. Adjust engine speed to 2000 rpm. The vacuum should still be zero.
3. With the engine warm, after about five minutes running at fast idle, the coolant temperature should be above 130°F. The vacuum at idle should still be zero while the vacuum at 2000 rpm should be 10 in. of vacuum minimum.

Solenoid Diode Check

CAUTION

Do not use an automotive battery for trouble-shooting solenoids. Solenoids must not be bench tested by touching the leads of an automotive battery. The internal diode will be destroyed when the leads are reversed, as they must be to check the diode.

Remember that the diode allows electricity to flow freely in one direction, and prevents or at least restricts the flow of current in the opposite direction.

To check the solenoid diode, an ohmmeter should be used. Use only a meter reading type of ohmmeter since electronic digital-type will often give a false indication. Use the X1 scale on the ohmmeter, and use the following procedure:

1. Verify that the ohmmeter is set to the X1 scale. Zero the meter.
2. Attach the positive solenoid lead (red) to the positive meter lead, and the negative solenoid lead (black) to the negative meter lead. The meter should read 20–40 ohms, depending on the solenoid temperature. If this reading is obtained, neither the coil or the diode is shorted and they should be considered useable. If the meter reads O ohms, then there is a short. The solenoid must be replaced. An open reading again indicates a bad coil in the solenoid, and it must be replaced.
3. Reverse the solenoid lead attachment. If the meter now reads lower (usually reads 2–15 ohms), the solenoid is good. If the reading is the same as before, the diode is bad and the solenoid will have to be replaced.

NOTE: On the Turbo-Hydra-Matic 250/350 transmissions, the solenoid is mounted on the valve body and the removal and replacement includes only R&R of the oil pan and the solenoid. However, on the Turbo Hydra-Matic 200 transmissions, the solenoid is mounted on the inside face of the oil pump. Therefore solenoid replacement for this model transmission will require the removal of the entire transmission, the torque converter and the oil pump. Be careful when diagnosing the solenoid so as not to burn out a good one.

4. Transmissions using the TCC system are also used in vehicles equipped with diesel engines. Due to the different vacuum characteristics of a diesel engine, a slightly different control system is used. Incorporated into the diesel system are a Low and a High Vacuum Switch. These are usually mounted on the engine, just above the right-hand valve cover. These switches can also be checked with a 12 volt test light and a hand vacuum pump.

Low and High Vacuum Switch Check Diesel

1. Disconnect the vacuum hose and the electrical connector from the switch. The test is run on both switches, but in this procedure, start with the Low Vacuum Switch. The Low Vacuum Switch should be the rearmost of the two, with the High Vacuum Switch to the front.
2. Attach one lead of a test light to eigher one of the terminals of the Low Vacuum Switch and ground the remaining terminal of the vacuum switch.
3. Attach the remaining lead of the test light to the hot (+12 volt) side of the vacuum switch connector. Attach the hand vacuum pump and gauge to the vacuum port of the vacuum switch.
4. Turn the ignition swith to the ON position. If using a self-powered test light, the ignition does not have to be turned on.
5. With the vacuum pump, apply 5.5 in. of vacuum. The Low Vacuum Switch should keep the text light off, and it should remain off until the gauge climbs to a reading of 5.5 in. Bleed off some vacuum slowly. The Low Vacuum Switch should keep the test light on until the vacuum drops to approximately 4 in of vacuum. If the Low Vacuum Switch does not turn on the test light at 5.5 on the gauge, and off at 4 in. of vacuum, the Low Vacuum Switch is malfunctioning.
6. Using the same electrical and vacuum hook-up, move to the other vacuum switch, which should be the front one, the High Vacuum Switch. The High Vacuum Switch should light the test lamp and keep the lamp on as vacuum begins to be applied with the hand pump. The light should stay on until the gauge reads approximately 12.5 in of vacuum, and then the lamp should go out. Bleed the vacuum slowly. The lamp should come back on at 12.5 in of vacuum. If the High Vacuum Switch does not turn on at 12.5 in ov vacuum and off as the vacuum goes higher, the High Vacuum Switch is malfunctioning.

High Vacuum Switch Adjustment Diesel

The High Vacuum Switch on the diesel engine must be adjusted anytime the throttle rod, transmission vacuum valve or high idle speed adjustments are altered. The following steps can be used for adjustment.

1. Disconnect the electrical connector from the High Vacuum Switch. This should be the front switch of the two. It has an adjustment port opposite the electrical connector.
2. Using a self-powered test light, connect one lead to either one of the terminals on the switch and connect the probe of the test light to the other switch terminal.
3. Start the engine and allow to run at high idle speed. To do this, actuate the fast idle solenoid. A pink and green wire connector goes to the coolant switch located on the left rear of the engine on the intake manifold, and this connector should be pulled off the coolant switch to produce the fast idle.
4. Remove the small dust cap from the back of the High Vacuum Switch.
5. The High Vacuum Switch must be closed before making the adjustment. This means that the test light should be on. If the test light is off, the contacts are open. Take a $5/64$ in. Allen wrench and turn the adjustment screw clockwise until the contacts close and the test light comes on.
6. Adjust the vacuum switch by turning the adjustment screw slowly counterclockwise until the switch contacts just open and the test light goes off. Turn the screw slowly so that the screw is not turned past this position.
7. Put the dust cap back on, reconnect the High Vacuum Switch electrical connector, and reconnect the coolant switch connector.

Brake Switch Check

1. Remove the electrical connector from the rear of the brake switch. These rear terminals are for the cruise control and converter clutch release. Turn the ignition switch to the ON position.
2. Ground one of the terminals of the brake release switch.
3. Connect one lead of the test light to the remaining brake release switch terminal. Attach the other lead of the test light to the brake connector wire. The test lamp should light.
4. Apply the brakes. The test light should go out. If the test light is off before applying the brakes or if it comes on during brake application, the switch is bad and should be replaced.

AUTOMATIC TRANSMISSIONS
GM TORQUE CONVERTER CLUTCH (TCC)

SECTION 23

GENERAL MOTORS CORP. TORQUE CONVERTER CLUTCH

Condition	Cause	Correction
Clutch applied in all ranges (engine stalls when put in gear)	a) Converter clutch valve stuck in apply position	a) R&R oil pump and clean valve (TH200)—R&R auxiliary valve body and clean valve (TH250/350)
Clutch does not apply: applies erratically or at wrong speeds	a) Electrical malfunction in most instances	a) Follow troubleshooting procedure to determine if problem is internal or external to isolate defect.
Clutch applies erratically; shudder and jerking felt	a) Vacuum hose leak b) Vacuum switch faulty c) Governor pressure switch malfunction d) Solenoid loose or damaged e) Converter malfunction; clutch plate warped	a) Repair hose as needed b) Replace switch c) Replace switch d) Service or replace e) Replace converter
Clutch applies at a very low or high 3rd gear	a) Governor switch shorted to ground b) Governor malfunction c) High line pressure d) Solenoid inoperative or shorted to case	a) Replace switch b) Service or replace governor c) Service pressure regulator d) Replace solenoid

CAUTION: When inspecting the stator and turbine of the torque converter clutch unit, a slight drag is normal when turned in the direction of freewheel rotation because of the pressure exerted by the waved spring washer, located between the turbine and the pressure plate.

GENERAL MOTORS CORP. THM 125C AUTOMATIC TRANSAXLE

Applications:

1983–87 Citation, Omega Phoenix, Skylark
1983–87 Cavalier, Cimarron, Firenza, 2000, Skyhawk
1983–87 Celebrity, Century, Cutlass Ciera, Pontiac 6000

Transaxle and Converter Identification

TRANSMISSION

The model identification code is located on the top of the transaxle, near the manual control lever shaft. The serial number is stamped on the oil pan flange pad, to the right of the dipstick.

CONVERTER

The THM 125C transaxle uses a converter with an electrical/hydraulically controlled pressure plate within the converter to mechanically engage the engine under certain operating conditions. The converter is stamped on the cover to provide proper usage.

Fluid Type Specification

Only automatic transmission fluid marked Dexron® II is to be used in the THM 125C transaxles.

Adjustment

THROTTLE LINKAGE ADJUSTMENT

The cable should be checked for freeness by pulling out on the upper end of the cable. The cable should travel a short distance with slight spring resistance. This light resistance is caused by the small coiled return spring on the T.V. lever and bracket that returns the lever to zero T.V., or closed throttle position. Pulling the cable farther out moves the lever to contact the T.V. plunger which compresses the T.V. cable, it should return to the zero T.V. position. This test checks the cable in its housing, the T.V. lever and bracket, and the throttle valve plunger in its bushing for freeness. To check on the adjustment and verify that it is correct, use the following procedure.

1. Install line pressure gauge. Adjust engine speed to 1000 rpm with the selector in Park, and check line pressure.
2. Check line pressure in Neutral at 1000 rpm. Presure should be in the same as or no more than 10 psi higher than in Park.
3. Adjust engine speed to 1400 rpm and make sure that there is an increase in line pressure.

Readjustment

If readjustment is necessary, the following procedure is suggested:

SECTION 23 AUTOMATIC TRANSMISSIONS
GM THM 125C

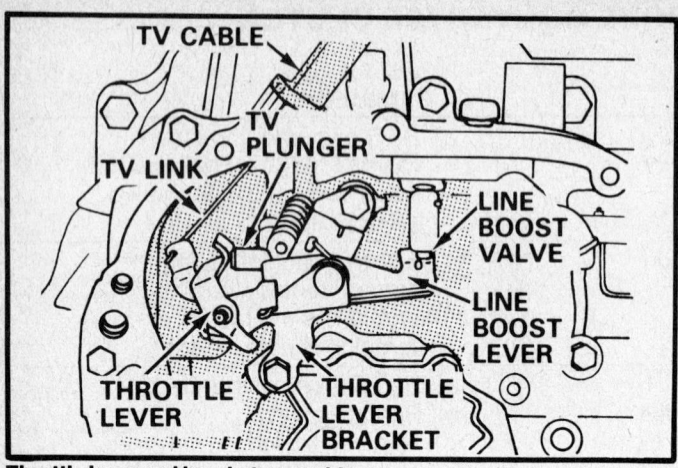
Throttle lever and bracket assembly

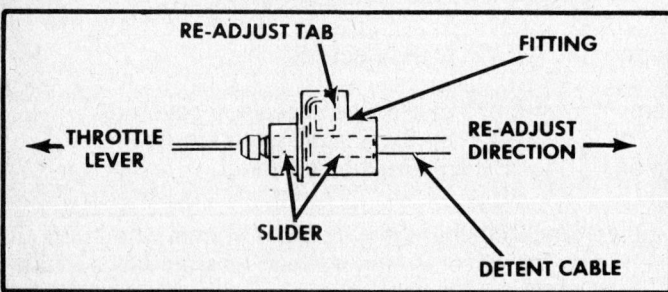
TV/Detent cable adjuster

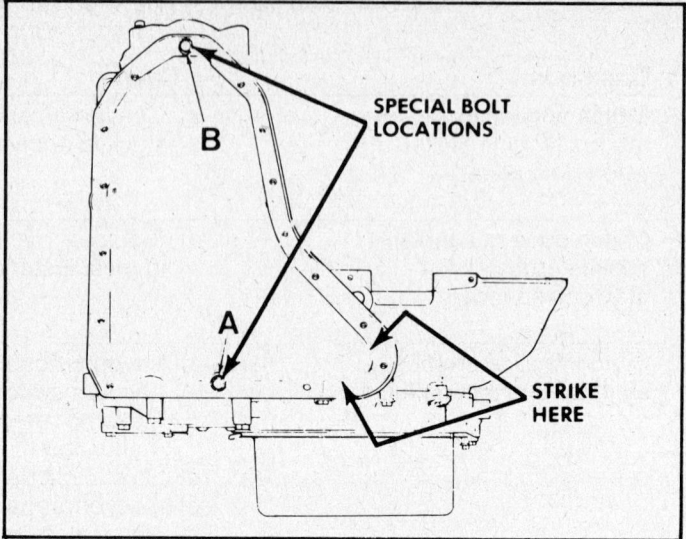
Oil pan removal when RTV silicone sealer is used

1. Depress and hold the metal lock tab that will be found on the cable adjuster by the idler lever.
2. Move the slider through the fitting away from the idler lever until the slider stops against the fitting.
3. Release the metal lock tab.
4. As a double check, repeat the adjustment.

INTERMEDIATE BAND

Selective sizes of the intermediate band apply pin are the only adjustment provided for the intermediate band. Special measuring tools are needed in conjunction with an inch pound torque wrench. To check for the proper intermediate band apply pin, the following procedure should be used.

1. Remove the lower cover pan and intermediate servo assembly as outlined in their respective sections.
2. Install the special indicator measuring tool and hold in place with two intermediate servo cover bolts.
3. Remove the band apply pin from the intermediate servo assembly and install the special measuring pin over the band apply pin.
4. Install the pin assembly into the previously attached indicator measuring gauge.
5. Apply 100 inch lbs. torque to the special indicator measuring tool to compress the band.
6. Should the indicator tool not register on its predetermined line, the apply pin would have to be changed and the procedure repeated.
7. Should the use of the selective pins not give the proper reading, the transaxle would have to be removed and disassembled and the band or components replaced.

OIL PANS

Removal When Gaskets Are Used

The side cover and the lower cover pans can be removed with the transaxle in the vehicle. Refer to the intermediate servo service procedure for the lower oil cover pan removal and to the valve body service procedure for the side cover pan removal.

OIL PAN

Removal When RTV Silicone Is Used

1. Raise the vehicle and support safely.
2. Fabricate a special bolt from an oil pan bolt by grinding down a section of the shank, directly under the bolt head, approximately 3/16 in.
3. Remove all the pan bolts except two, one at the top, which should be loosened four complete turns, and the center one at the bottom.
4. After all other bolts are out, remove the bottom center bolt and install the special fabricated bolt, finger tight, in its place.
5. Strike the bottom toe of the pan with a rubber mallet to loosen the pan from the transaxle case.

--- **CAUTION** ---

Do no try to pry the oil pan loose from the case as damage to the pan flange or case can occur.

6. Remove the special bolt and allow the oil to drain.
7. Remove the remaining bolt and the oil pan.

AUTOMATIC TRANSMISSIONS
GM THM 125C

CLUTCH AND BAND APPLICATIONS CHART
THM 125, 125C

Range	Gear	Direct Clutch	Intermediate Band	Forward Clutch	Roller Clutch	Low-Reverse Clutch
Park—Neut.	—	—	—	—	—	—
Drive	First	—	—	Applied	Holding	—
	Second	—	Applied	Applied	—	—
	Third	Applied	—	Applied	—	—
Int.	First	—	—	Applied	Holding	—
	Second	—	Applied	Applied	—	—
Low	First	—	—	Applied	Holding	Applied
	Second	—	Applied	Applied	—	—
Rev.	—	Applied	—	—	—	Applied

GENERAL MOTORS CORP. THM 180C AUTOMATIC TRANSMISSION

Applications:
1983–87 Chevette
1983–87 Pontiac 1000

Transmission and Converter Identification

TRANSMISSION

The transmission is identified from a model and serial number plate, located on the right side of the transmission case. When obtaining replacement parts, it is most important to refer to the model and serial numbers for correct parts application.

CONVERTER

No specific markings are given for quick identification of the converter. The model and serial number must be used when converter replacement is required.

Fluid Type Specifications

Only automatic transmission fluid marked Dexron® II is to be used in the THM 180C automatic transmission.

Adjustments

DETENT DOWNSHIFT CABLE

1. The detent cable runs from the right hand hook up on the transmission, through a support on the cam cover to the carburetor. A "snap-lock", device holds the cable to the support. To adjust the detent cable, first disengage the "snap-lock". The cable should be free to slide through this lock.
2. Move the carburetor lever to the wide open throttle position.

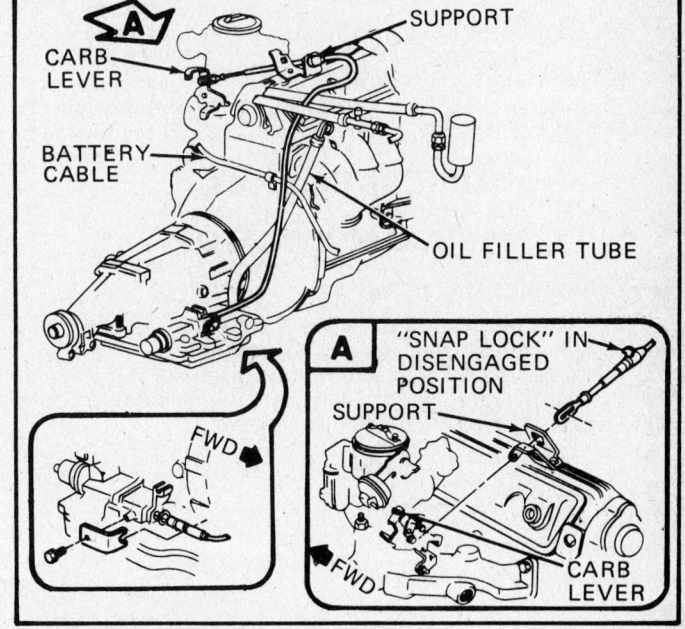

Throttle linkage (detent cable) adjustment

3. Push the "snap-lock" flush and return the carburetor to the closed position.

LOW BAND

1. Raise the vehicle and support safely.
2. Remove the oil pan and valve body from the transmission.
3. Loosen the locknut and tighten the servo adjusting bolt to forty in. lbs.
4. Back the adjusting bolt off exactly five turns and tighten

23-33

SECTION 23
AUTOMATIC TRANSMISSIONS
GM THM 180C

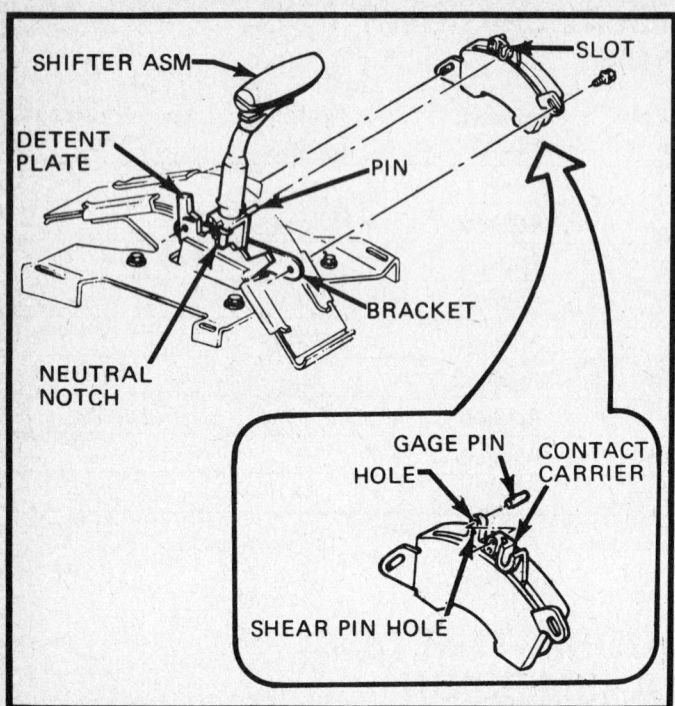

Neutral safety switch adjustment

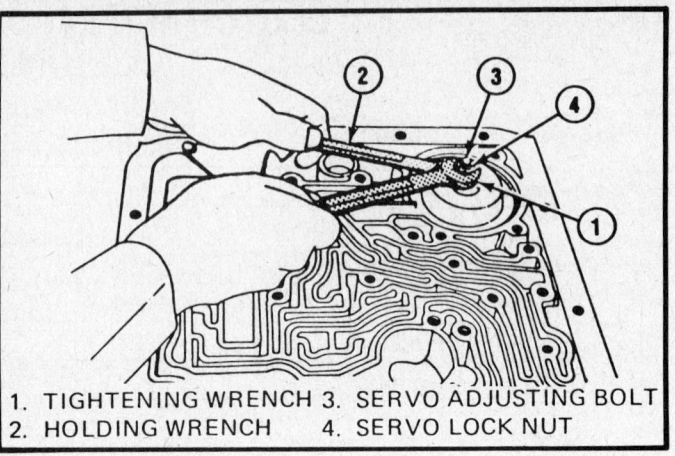

1. TIGHTENING WRENCH 3. SERVO ADJUSTING BOLT
2. HOLDING WRENCH 4. SERVO LOCK NUT

Adjusting the low band

the locknut while holding the adjusting bolt to prevent turning.

5. Reinstall the valve body and oil pan. Fill the transmission with fluid to specifications. Start the engine and recheck the level. Check for leakage. Lower the vehicle and roadtest.

On-Car Services

VACUUM MODULATOR

Removal and Installation

1. The vacuum modulator threads into the case from the rear, just above the transmission oil pan flange.
2. When removing the modulator, be careful of the plunger. Always install a new O-ring when changing modulators. Lube the O-ring with petroleum jelly or Dexron® II.
3. Due to the shape of the modulator, it will be difficult to use a torque wrench. However, torque should be 35–40 ft. lbs.

OIL PAN AND SCREEN

Removal and Installation

1. To remove the oil pan, first raise and safely support vehicle.
2. Remove the oil pan bolts from the front and side of the pan, allowing the oil to drain into a pan.
3. Remove the remaining bolts and tap pan loose.
4. Clean pan well. Debris in the pan should be investigated as part of transmission diagnosis.
5. Remove the bolts holding the screen to the valve body; remove the screen. Discard gasket and thoroughly clean the screen in solvent and dry with compressed air.
6. Install screen with new gasket and torque bolts to 13–15 ft. lbs.
7. Install pan with new gasket and torque bolts to 7–10 ft. lbs.
8. Lower car and refill with 3 quarts Dexron® II.
9. Allow engine to idle in Park, move selector through each range and end up in Park.
10. Add fluid if necessary.

NOTE: There is no provision for draining the converter.

CLUTCH APPLICATION CHART
GM—THM 180

Range	Reverse Clutch	Second Clutch	Third Clutch	Low Band	Sprag
Neutral and Park	Released	Released	Released	Released	Locked
Drive, 1st gear	Released	Released	Released	Applied	Locked
2nd gear	Released	Applied	Released	Applied	Overrunning
3rd gear	Released	Applied	Applied	Released	Locked
L1	Released	Released	Applied	Applied	Locked
L2	Released	Applied	Released	Applied	Overrunning
Reverse	Applied	Released	Applied	Released	Locked

AUTOMATIC TRANSMISSIONS
GM THM 200C
SECTION 23

GENERAL MOTORS CORP. THM 200C AUTOMATIC TRANSMISSION

Applications:

BUICK
1983–85
 Century Regal
LeSabre, Electra
1983–85
 Regal Diesel
CHEVROLET
1983–87
 Caprice & Impala
Malibu & Monte Carlo
Chevette & Chevette Diesel
Camaro

Transmission and Converter Identification

TRANSMISSION

The transmission may be identified by the use of a throttle pressure control cable. The transmission can also be identified by the word "METRIC" stamped on the bottom of the oil pan. The transmission model can be identified by the serial number, stamped on an identification plate, located on the right side of the transmission case.

The number contains a year built code, a two letter model code and the production serial number.

The 200C version, which is the lockup clutch version of the transmission, has the following differences. It has a governor pressure switch which screws into the case, a different oil pump, a different valve body and gasket assembly, a different forward clutch drum and few other control parts, depending on the vehicle application. Look for the elctrical connector on the left side. The solenoid is mounted on the back side of the pump, as opposed to the valve body mount used on the THM 350C.

CONVERTER

The torque converter is a welded unit and cannot be disassembled for service. Any internal malfunctions require the replacement of converter assembly. The replacement converter must be matched to the model transmission through parts identification. No specific identification is available for matching the converter to the transmission for the average repair shop.

Diesel Engines

Vehicles equipped with diesel engines use a different torque

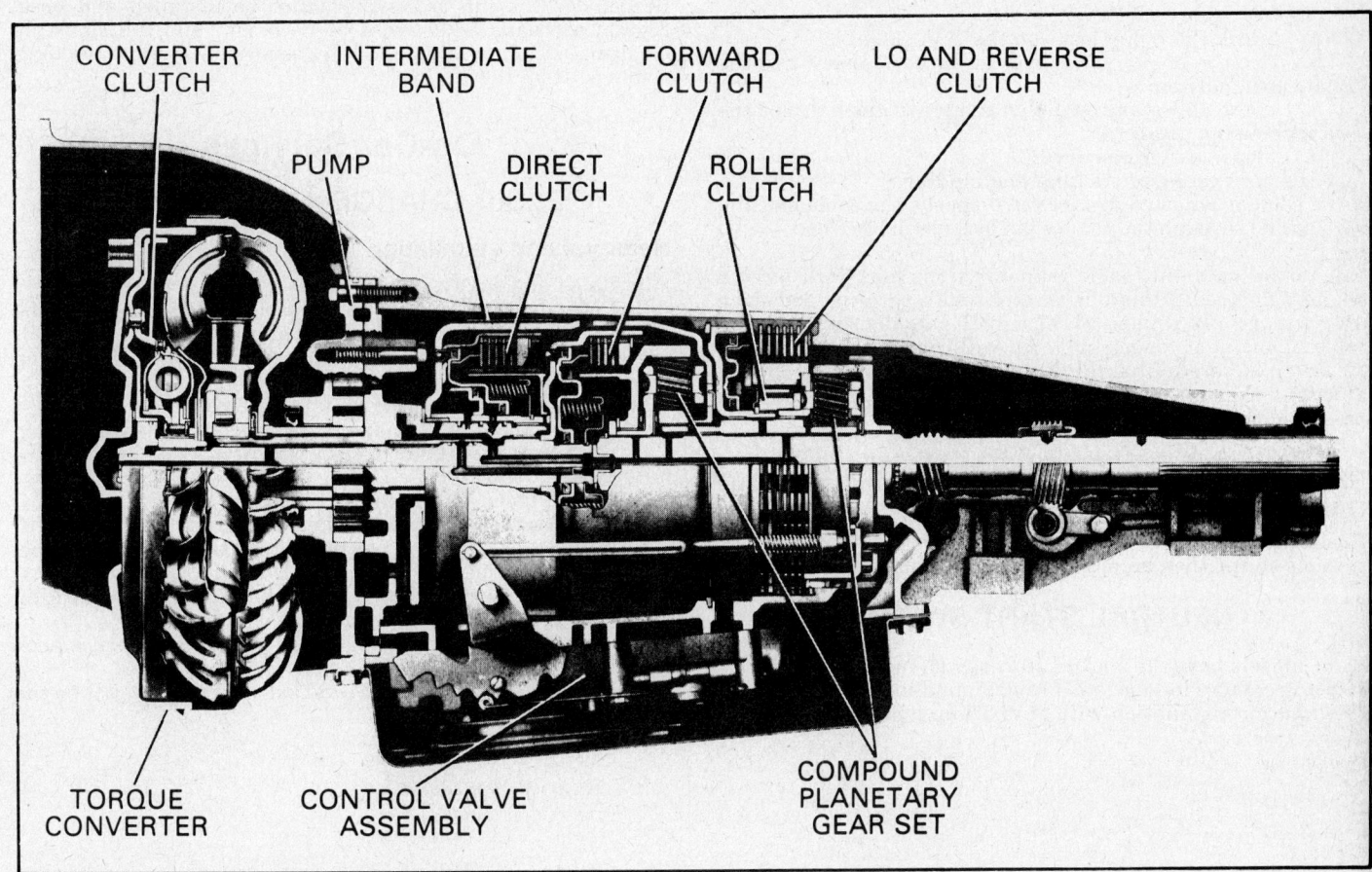

Cross section of the THM 200C, the THM 200 similar

23-35

SECTION 23

AUTOMATIC TRANSMISSIONS
GM THM 200C

converter. To identify these units, examine the weld nuts. Most gas engine converters have their weld nuts spot welded onto the converter housing, usually in two spots. The diesel converters have the weld nuts completely welded around their entire circumference.

Turbo-Charged V6 Engines

Vehicles equipped with turbocharged V6 engines use a different torque converter. These units have a high stall speed converter, allowing a stall speed of about 2800 rpm. These converters must not be replaced with a standard converter, otherwise performance will be sluggish and unsatisfactory. When ordering replacements for the turbo-charged units, make certain to specify that the vehicle has turbo-charging in order to obtain the proper replacement.

Fluid Specification

Use only Dexron® or Dexron® II automatic transmission fluid or its equivalent to fill, refill or correct the fluid level.

Adjustments

THROTTLE VALVE CABLE

1. Check transmission oil level and correct as required.
2. Make sure the engine is in a reasonable state of tuen.
3. If possible, doublecheck a parts catalog source to insure that the proper cable has been installed on the vehicle.
4. Check that the T.V. cable is connected at both ends.
5. Adjust cable as follows:
    a. Unlock the "snap lock" on the T.V. cable.
    b. With the engine off, move the carburetor lever to the wide open position.
    c. Hold the lever and push the "snap lock" flush to hold the cable housing securely.
    d. Release carburetor lever.
    e. Check cable for sticking and binding.

If the cable is adjusted and locked properly, the cable housing will extend through the cable snap lock assembly from $1/16$–$5/16$ in.

After adjustment, some transmissions may still have a slightly delayed minimum throttle shift pattern, and even drag out the 1–2 shift to 14–17 mph. Generally, tailoring the cable adjustment longer by $1/8$ in. will correct the complaint. However, be careful that the detent downshifts are still obtainable, and the transmission has not been forced into the high pressure mode.

NOTE: Check the throttle valve cable with the engine running in Neutral, not Park. Adjust the calbe with the engine off.

If, after cable adjustment, the shifts are delayed or are only full throttle shifts, then an oil pressure gauge should be installed.

NEUTRAL START SWITCH

Some models have the neutral start switch incorporated in the steering column linkage and are not found in the normal position and in combination with the backup lamp switch. A me-

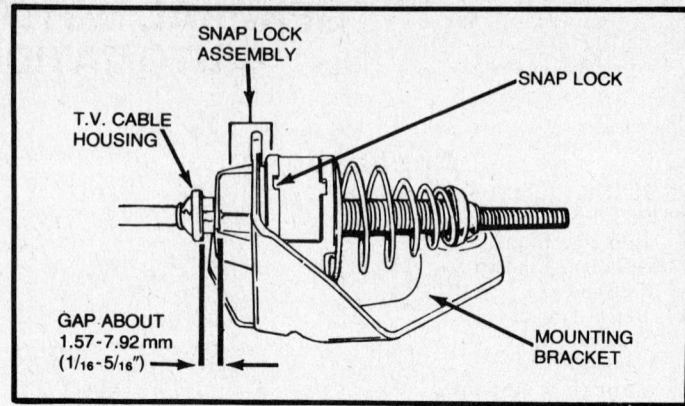
Throttle valve cable snap lock assembly

chanical block on the automatic transmission gear selector prevents the engine from starting except in the Neutral or Park positions.

INTERMEDIATE BAND

The intermediate band is adjusted by a selective intermediate servo apply pin. Because of possible inaccessiblity to the intermediate servo piston assembly on the transmission/vehicle application, due to the clearance restrictions, the special tools needed for the pin selection cannot be installed and used. Should the band adjustment be necessary and the adjusting clearance is not available, the transmission would have to be removed from the vehicle.

On-Car Services

FLUID CHANGE AND OIL PAN

Removal and Installation

1. Raise and safely support car.
2. Place drain pan under transmission oil pan. Remove the oil pan attaching bolts from the front and side of the pan.
3. Loosen, but do not remove the rear pan bolts, then bump the pan loose and allow fluid to drain.
4. Remove the remaining bolts and remove pan.
5. Clean pan in solvent and dry with compressed air.
6. Remove the two bolts holding the filter screen to the valve body. Discard gasket.
7. Clean screen in solvent and blow dry.
8. Install screen with new gasket; torque bolts to 6–10 ft. lbs.
9. Install new gasket on pan and torque bolts to 10–13 ft. lbs.
10. Lower car and add 3 quarts of Dexron® II.
11. With selector in Park start engine and idle. Apply parking brake. Do no race engine.
12. Move selector through all ranges and end in Park. Check fluid leve1.

Add if necessary to bring the level between the dimples on the dipstick.

AUTOMATIC TRANSMISSIONS
GM THM 200C
SECTION 23

CLUTCH AND BAND APPLICATION CHART
THM 200, 200C

Range	Gear	Direct Clutch	Int. Band	Forward Clutch	Roller Clutch	Low-Reverse Clutch
Park-Neut.		—	—	—	—	—
Drive	First	—	—	Applied	Holding	—
	Second	—	Applied	Applied	—	—
	Third	Applied	—	Applied	—	—
Int.	First	—	—	Applied	Holding	—
	Second	—	Applied	Applied	—	—
Low	First	—	—	Applied	Holding	Applied
Reverse		Applied	—	—	—	Applied

GENERAL MOTORS CORP. MODEL THM 200-4R AUTOMATIC TRANSMISSION

Applications:
BUICK
1983–86 Regal
LeSabre & Electra
LeSabre & Electra Diesel
CADILLAC
1983–87 DeVille & Brougham
DeVille & Brougham Diesel
OLDSMOBILE
1983–85 88 & 98
Hurst Olds
88 & 98 Diesel
PONTIAC
1983–85 Parisienne Diesel

Transmission and Converter Identification

TRANSMISSION
The transmission model and serial number identification tag is located on the right side of the transmission extension housing. The information from the identification tag must be used before the correct replacement parts can be obtained.

CONVERTER
The converter has no identifying letters or numbers for the average repair shop to recognize. Use the transmission identification model and serial numbers to correctly identify the converter unit.

Fluid Type Specifications
Use only Dexron® II automatic transmission or its equivalent to fill, refill or correct the fluid level.

Adjustments

T.V. CABLE

GASOLINE ENGINES WITH SELF-ADJUSTING CABLE

1. Be sure engine is stopped. Do not attempt to adjust with the engine running.
2. Depress the adjusting tab. Move the slider back through the fitting in the direction away from the throttle body until the slider stops against the fitting.
3. Release the adjusting tab.
4. Open the carburetor lever to the "full throttle stop" position to automatically adjust the cable. Release the carburetor lever.
5. Check the cable for binding and road test the vehicle. The adjustment is correct if the shifting is normal.
6. If the shift is delayed or only at full throttle, the oil pan will have to be removed and the internal linkage and valve body inspected for binding or distortion.

CABLES USED WITH DIESEL ENGINES

1. With the engine stopped, disconnect the cruise control rod, if equipped.
2. Disconnect the transmission T.V. or detent cable terminal from the throttel assembly.
3. Loosen the locknut on the pump rod and shorten by several turns.
4. Rotate the lever assembly to the full throttle position and hold.
5. Lenghten the pump rod until the injection pump lever contacts the full throttle stop.
6. Release the lever assembly and tighten the pump rod locknut.
7. Remove the pump rod from the lever assembly.
8. Reconnect the T.V. or detent cable terminal to the throttle assembly.
9. Depress and hold the metal re-adjustment tab on the cable upper end. Move the slider through the fitting in the direction away from the lever assembly until the slider stops against the fitting.

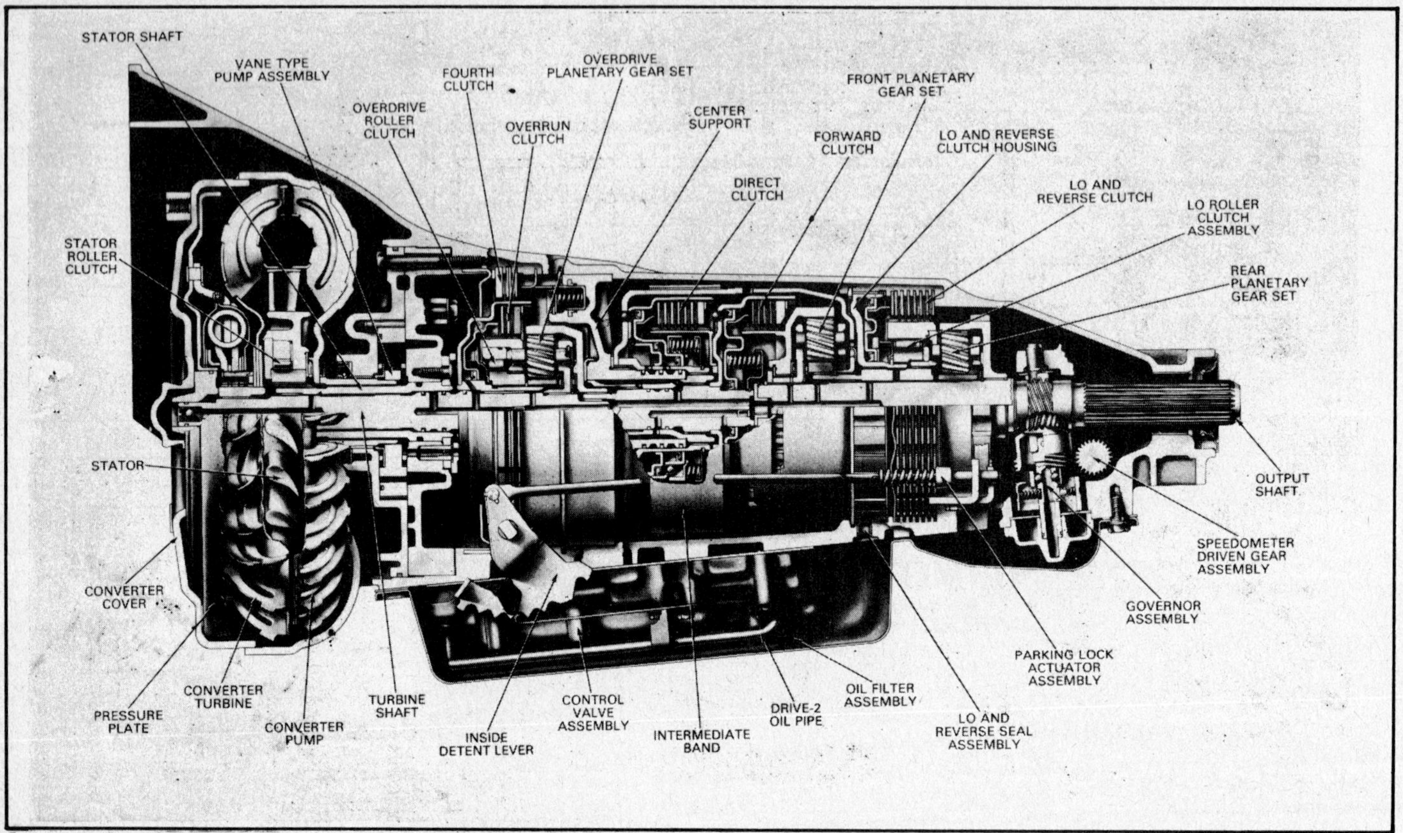

SECTION 23

AUTOMATIC TRANSMISSIONS
GM THM 200-4R

Cross section of THM 200-4R overdrive automatic transmission

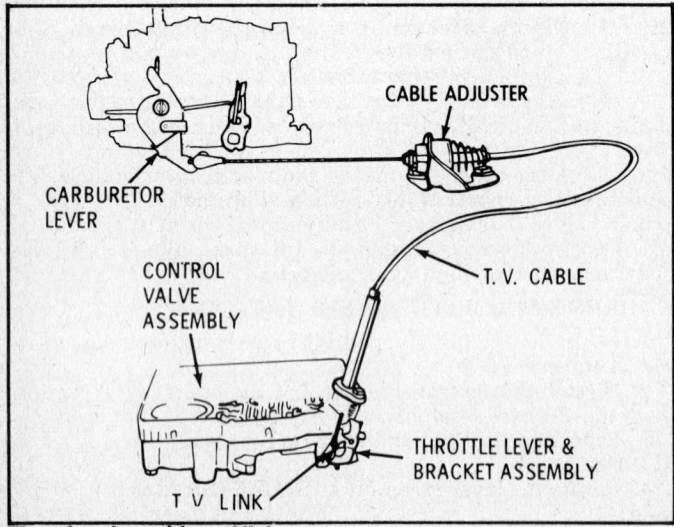

Throttle valve cable and linkage

10. Release the tab, rotate the lever assembly to the full throttle stop and release the lever assembly.
11. Reconnect the pump rod and cruise control rod, if equipped.
12. If equipped with cruise control, adjust the servo throttle rod to a minumum slack and put the clip in the first free hole nearest the bellcrank, but within the servo bail.

INTERMEDIATE BAND

The intermediate band is adjusted by selective sized apply pins, determined with the use of special measuring tools. This operation is normally accomplished during an overhaul.

On-Car Service

OIL PAN

Removal and Installation

1. Raise the vehicle and support safely.
2. With a drain pan under the oil pan, remove the retaining bolts from the front and sides of the oil pan.
3. Loosen the rear bolts approximately four turns and carefully pry the oil pan loose from the transmission case.
4. Allow the fluid to drain into the drain pan and remove the retaining bolts from the rear of the oil pan and remove the pan and gasket.

NOTE: Various transmission models may have RTV sealant used in place of gaskets.

5. Using either the RTV or gasket on a clean oil pan, install the pan to the transmission case and tighten the retaining bolts to 10–13 ft. lbs. torque.

CAUTION
Do no use the R.T.V. sealant on oil pans that have raised stiffening ribs on the pan flange.

---

6. Lower the vehicle and add the proper amount of fluid to the transmission. Start engine and correct the fluid level as necessary.

AUTOMATIC TRANSMISSIONS
GM THM 200-4R
SECTION 23

CLUTCH AND BAND APPLICATION CHART
Turbo Hydra-matic 200-4R

Selector	Converter Clutch	Overrun Clutch	Intermediate Band	Overdrive Roller Clutch	Direct Clutch	Low Reverse Clutch	Forward Clutch	Fourth Clutch	Low and Reverse Clutch
Park	Released	Released	Released	Holding	Released	Not Holding	Released	Released	Released
Neutral	Released	Released	Released	Holding	Released	Not Holding	Released	Released	Released
Drive (1st gear)	—	Holding	—	—	—	Holding	Applied	—	—
Drive (2nd gear)	Released	—	Applied	Holding	—	—	Applied	—	—
Drive (converter clutch applied)	Applied	—	Applied	Holding	—	—	Applied	—	—
Drive (3rd gear)	Applied	—	—	Holding	Applied	—	Applied	—	—
Drive (4th gear)	Applied	—	—	—	Applied	—	Applied	Applied	—
Reverse	—	—	—	Holding	Applied	Applied	—	—	—

GENERAL MOTORS CORP. THM 250C AUTOMATIC TRANSMISSION

Applications:
BUICK
1983 Regal, LeSabre
1984–85 Regal
CHEVROLET
1983–85 Impala, Caprice, Malibu
Monte Carlo
OLDSMOBILE
1983–85
Delta 88
Cutlass
PONTIAC
1982–83
Bonneville, Grand Prix, Parisienne
1984–85
Bonneville, Grand Pris

Transmission and Converter Identification

TRANSMISSION

A production day and shift built number, transmission model and model year are stamped on the governor cover, which is located on the middle rear left side of the transmission case. In addition, the vehicle identification number is stamped on the lower left side of the case, next to the manual shaft, on many late model units. Since the production day and model numbers furnish a key to the construction of the unit and interchangeability of parts in each transmission, they should be used in ordering replacement parts. Naturally, if the governor cover should become damaged and require replacement, it will be important to stamp the information found on the original cover on the new cover or otherwise record the information for future reference.

CONVERTER

The torque converter is of welded construction and if damaged or contaminated, it should be replaced.

Diesel Engines

Vehicles equipped with diesel engine use a different torque converter. To identify these units, examine the weld nuts. Most gas engine converters have their weld nuts spot welded onto the converter housing, usually in two spots. The diesel converters have the weld nuts completely welded around their entire circumference.

Turbo-Charged V6 Engines

Vehicles equipped with turbo-charged V6 engines use a different torque converter. These units have a high stall speed converter, allowing a stall speed of about 2800 rpm. These converters must not be replaced with a standard converter, otherwise performance will be sluggish and unsatisfactory. When ordering replacements for the turbo-charged units, make certain to specify that the vehicle has turbo-charging in order to obtain the proper replacement.

There are a number of differences between the standard version of this transmission and the lock-up torque converter ver-

23-39

SECTION 23 AUTOMATIC TRANSMISSIONS
GM THM 250C

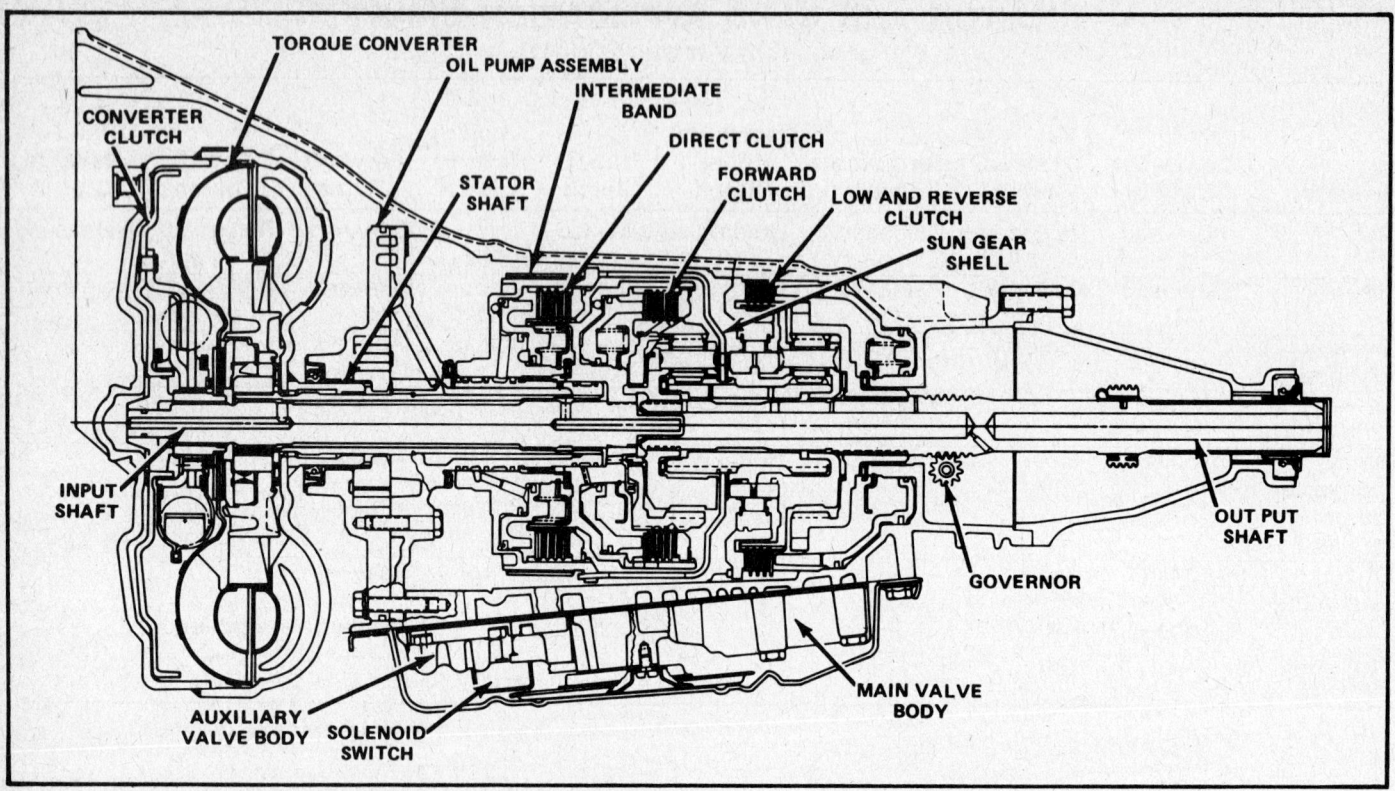

Cross section of the THM 250 C automatic transmission, THM 250 similar

sion. The lock-up converter versions use a different case, an additional (auxiliary) valve body, and electrical solenoid, a governor pressure switch, and a different pump assembly and gasket, as well as a different input shaft. There are a few other components added to control the system, depending on the vehicle.

Fluid Specifications

Use only automatic transmission fluids having the designations "Dexron® or Dexron® II".

Adjustments

THROTTLE LINKAGE (DETENT CONTROL CABLE)

1. With a small screwdriver, pry gently on the bottom of the snap-lock to release the detent cable.
2. Push the carburetor lever to the wide open throttle position (engine off) and hold. Push the snap-lock tab downward until flush with the cable.

BAND ADJUSTMENTS

The Turbo Hydra-Matic 250 is unique among the Hydra-Matic family in that it has an external band adjustment. The intermediate band adjustment should be performed every 60,000 miles along with a change of transmission fluid or sooner, if slippage is indicated. To adjust the band:

1. Place the gear selector in Neutral and raise vehicle.

2. Hold the adjusting screw by means of an allen socket and loosen the locknut.
3. With a torque wrench on the socket, tighten the adjuster screw to 30 inch lbs. (3.5 Nm) then back off three complete turns. Hold the adjuster in position and tighten the locknut to 15 ft. lbs. (20Nm).

NEUTRAL START SWITCH
FLOOR SHIFT MODELS

1. Remove the two screws that hold the console.
2. Disconnect the electrical plugs on the neutral switch. Place shifter in Neutral.
3. Remove the two screws holding the shift indication plate, two more holding the shift lever curved cover and the two others holding the neutral start switch.
4. The switch assembly may have to be tilted to the right as it is removed to disengage the actuator tang.
5. To install the new switch, take note that there is a plastic pin which aligns the switch. This will shear out of the way when the new switch is shifted the first time. Make sure the shift lever is in Neutral before installing the switch. Reverse the disassembly sequence, being careful not to over-tighten the screws.
6. Move the lever out of Neutral to shear the plastic locating pin. Check that the electrical connectors are firmly in place.
7. Apply brakes and check that vehicle will start in Park and Neutral only, and that the back-up lamps work properly.

If the switch is not being replaced, only adjusted, first obtain a piece of wire or other pin 0.090 in. in diameter. Then insert it in the service adjustment hole to hold the switch in Neutral. Tighten the screws, remove pin and assemble console.

AUTOMATIC TRANSMISSIONS
GM THM 250C
SECTION 23

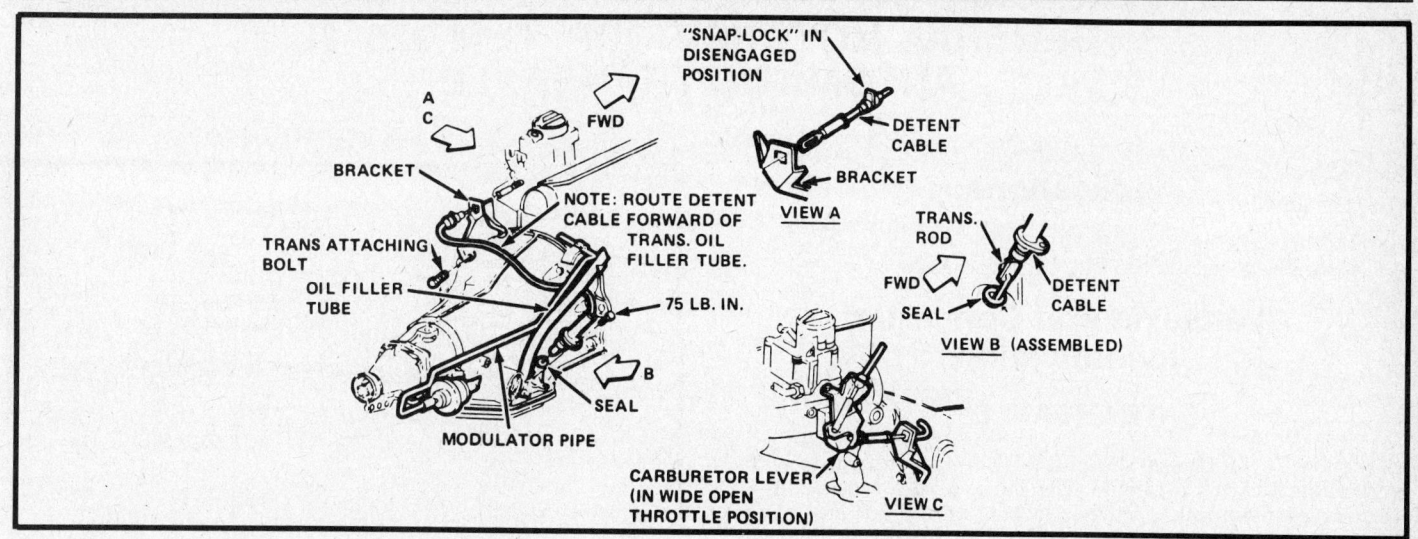

On-Car Services

VACUUM MODULATOR

Removal and Installation

1. Remove the vacuum hose from vacuum modulator. Inspect the hose for signs of transmission fluid that would indicate a leaky modulator.
2. Remove the modulator hold-down bolt and bracket.
3. Pull the modulator straight back from the case. If the modulator is to be reused, be sure to change the O-ring.
4. The modulator valve can be removed if necessary.
5. Installation is the reversal of the above sequence. Remember to renew the O-ring, coat it with petroleum jelly or Dexron® II. Check the vacuum hose for cracks and be sure to check and adjust the fluid level.

OIL PAN

Removal and Installation

1. Raise and safely support vehicle. On some vehicles, the transmission may have to be supported and the crossmember removed for access.
2. Place a large drain pan under the transmission and remove the front and side bolts on the pan.
3. Loosen but do not remove the rear pan bolts. Carefully bump the pan with a rubber mallet to free the pan. If the pan is pried loose instead, be very careful not to damage the gasket surfaces. Allow fluid to drain.
4. Remove the remaining screws, remove the pan and discard the gasket. Remove the two screws holding the strainer to the valve body, remove the strainer and its gasket.
5. Thoroughly clean the strainer with solvent and compressed air. If it cannot be cleaned well, replace it.
6. Make sure the pan is clean and that the gasket surfaces are clean and straight.
7. Using a new gasket, install the strainer and its two screws. Put a new gasket on the oil pan and carefully install the pan. Torque the pan bolts to 12 ft. lbs. (16 Nm).
8. Lower the vehicle and add approximately 5 pints of Dexron® II. With selector in Park, apply brakes, start engine and allow to idle. **Do not race engine.** Make sure carburetor comes off fast idle. Move the selector through each range, end in Park and check fluid level. Since the transmission is not yet to operating temperature, the proper level would be ¼ in. below "ADD". Do not overfill.

NOTE: There is no provision for draining the torque converter. In cases of transmission overhaul when the converter will be dry, approximately 20 pints will be required total. Do not overfill. Begin by adding 8 pints, and then continue to add while the engine is running, transmission in Park, until the proper level is reached.

CLUTCH AND BAND APPLICATION CHART
THM 250, 250C

Range	Gear	Int. Clutch	Direct Clutch	Forward Clutch	Low & Reverse Clutch	Int. Overrun Roller Clutch	Low & Reverse Roller Clutch	Int. Overrun Band
PARK-NEUT.		OFF	OFF	OFF	OFF	INEFFECTIVE	INEFFECTIVE	OFF
DRIVE	FIRST	OFF	OFF	ON	OFF	INEFFECTIVE	LOCKED UP	OFF
	SECOND	ON	OFF	ON	OFF	LOCKED UP	OVERRUNNING	OFF
	THIRD	ON	ON	ON	OFF	OVERRUNNING	OVERRUNNING	OFF
SUPER	FIRST	OFF	OFF	ON	OFF	INEFFECTIVE	LOCKED UP	OFF
	SECOND	ON	OFF	ON	OFF	LOCKED UP	OVERRUNNING	ON
LOW	FIRST	OFF	OFF	ON	ON	INEFFECTIVE	LOCKED UP	OFF
REV.		OFF	ON	OFF	ON	INEFFECTIVE	INEFFECTIVE	OFF

SECTION 23 — AUTOMATIC TRANSMISSIONS
GM THM 325-4L

GENERAL MOTORS CORP. THM 325–4L AUTOMATIC TRANSAXLE

Applications:
1983–85
Buick Riviera
Cadillac Eldorado & Seville, Olds Toronado

Transaxle and Converter Identification

TRANSAXLE

Since the Turbo Hydra-Matic 325–4L used is a transaxle design, identification is simple. The Turbo Hydra-Matic 325–4L transaxle unit number plate is located on the left side of the converter housing. Also, the vehicle identification number derivative is located on the vertical support pad on the left side of the transmission case.

CONVERTER

Torque converter usage differs with the type engine and the area in which the vehicle is to be operated. No specify physical markings are designated so that the repairman can identify the converter. It is most important to obtain the transmission model and serial number, know the specific operating area and the vehicle VIN number before replacement of the converter unit is attempted.

Fluid Specifications

Dexron® II automatic transmission fluid or its equivalent is thee only recommended automatic transmission fluid to be used in this unit.

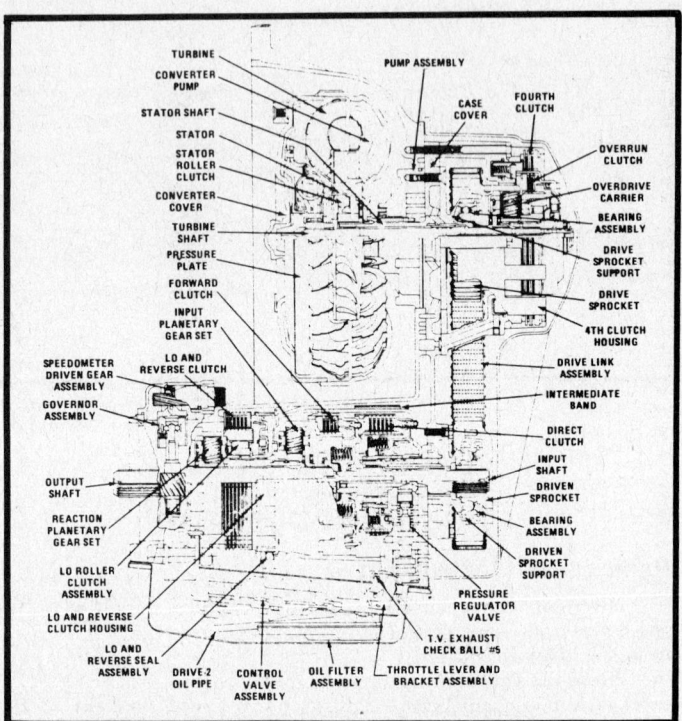

Cross section of THM 325-4L overdrive automatic transmission - THM 325 similar

Adjustments

THROTTLE VALVE LINKAGE

1. Check transmission oil level and correct as required.
2. Be sure engine is operating properly and brakes are not dragging.
3. Check for correct cable, according to the parts catalog source.
4. Check that the cable is connected at both ends.

ADJUSTING CABLE (DIESEL ENGINE ONLY)

1. Stop engine.
2. Remove cruise control rode (if so equipped).
3. Disconnect transmission detent cable terminal from throttle assembly.
4. Loosen locknut on pump rod and shorten several turns.
5. Rotate the lever assembly to the full throttle position and hold.
6. Lengthen pump rod until the injection pump lever contacts the full throttle stop.
7. Release the lever assembly and tighten pump rod locknut.
8. Remove the pump rod from the lever assembly.
9. Reconnect the transmission detent cable terminal to throttle assembly.
10. Depress and hold the metal re-adjust tab on the cable upper end. Move the slider through the fitting in the direction away from the lever assembly until the slider stops against the fitting.
11. Release the re-adjust tab, rotate the lever assembly to the full throttle stop and release the lever assembly.
12. Reconnect the pump rod (and cruise control throttle rod if so equipped).
13. If equipped with cruise control, adjust the servo throttle rod to minimum slack (engine off) then put clip in first free hole closest to the bellcrank but within the servo bail.

ADJUSTING SELF–ADJUSTING TYPE CABLE (GASOLINE ENGINE)

1. Stop engine.
2. Depress re-adjust tab. Move slider back through fitting in direction away from throttle body until slider stops against fitting.
3. Release re-adjust tab.
4. Open throttle valve lever to "full throttle stop" position to automatically adjust cable. Release throttle valve lever.
5. Check cable for sticking and binding.

BAND ADJUSTMENT

The THM 325-4L automatic transaxle uses an intermediate band and intermediate servo assembly with a selective band apply pin. The use of special tools are needed to select the proper length apply pin and because of the transaxle location in the vehicle body, only the servo cover and piston assembly removel should be attempted. Band apply pin measurements should be accomplished with the transaxle removed from the vehicle.

AUTOMATIC TRANSMISSIONS
GM THM 325-4L
SECTION 23

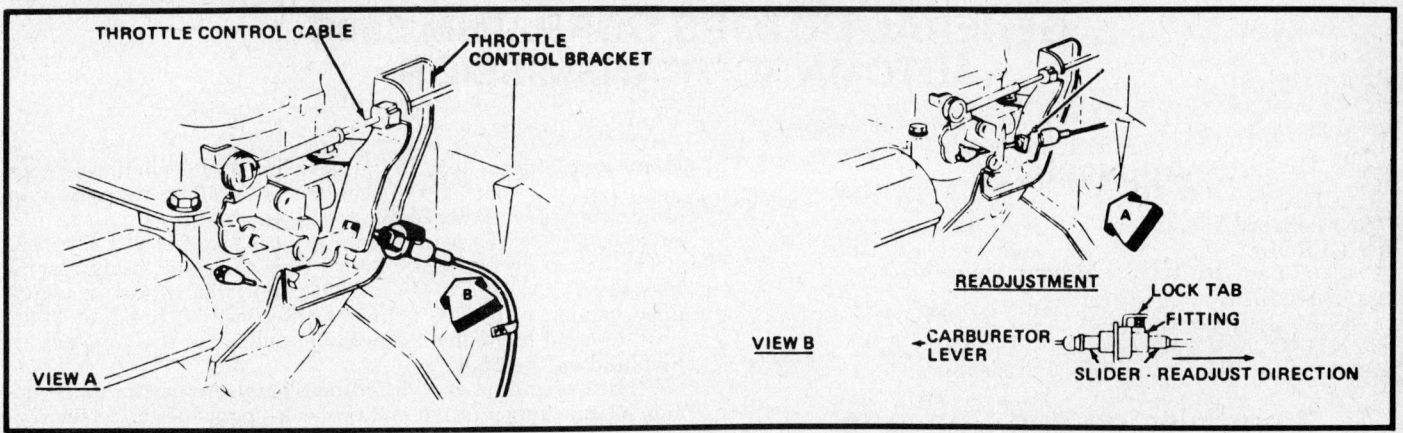

T.V. cable adjustment - typical

On-Car Services

OIL PAN

Removal

1. Remove the oil pan by first raising and safely supporting the vehicle.
2. Place a large drain pan under the transaxle and remove the bolts from just three sides and loosen the bolts on the fourth side just enough to allow the pan to hang down and drain.
3. Remove the remaining bolts and the pan. Discard the gasket.
4. The pan should be cleaned with solvent and blown dry with compressed air.
5. If the filter is to be services, remove it and discard the O-ring that makes the seal at the intake pipe.
6. Thoroughly clean the screen in solvent and blow dry with compressed air. If, for some reason, contaminates have made the screen too dirty to be easily cleaned, it should be replaced.

Installation

1. To reassemble, first install a new O-ring on the intake pipe and install the screen into the screen retainer.
2. Install a new gasket on the oil pan. Make sure that the gasket surface on the pan is clean and that the bolt holes are not distorted or dished-in from over-torqued bolts. Install the oil pan and tighten the screws evenly to a torque of 12 ft. lbs.
3. Lower the car and add approximately 5 quarts of Dexron® II automatic transmission fluid. Place the selector in Park and start the engine. Do not race the engine. Let the engine idle off fast idle, move the selector lever through the ranges and end up in Park. Check the fluid level and correct.

NOTE: There is no provision for draining the torque converter. If it is to be drained, the transaxle would have to be removed and the converter removed to drain through the hub. This would only be necessary during a rebuild. If the transaxle fails and metal particles and debris have been spread throughout the system, the converter should be replaced.

CLUTCH AND BAND APPLICATION CHART
THM 325 - 4L

Range/Gear	Lo-Reverse Clutch	Lo-Roller Clutch	Forward Clutch	Int. Band	Direct Clutch	4th Clutch	Overrun Clutch	Overdrive Roller Clutch
Park								
Reverse	Applied				Applied			Holding
Neutral								Holding
Drive 4								
1st		Holding	Applied					
2nd			Applied	Applied				Holding
3rd			Applied		Applied			Holding
4th			Applied		Applied	Applied		
Drive 3								
1st		Holding	Applied				Applied	
2nd			Applied	Applied			Applied	
3rd			Applied		Applied		Applied	
Drive 2								
1st		Holding	Applied				Applied	
2nd			Applied	Applied			Applied	
Lo								
1st	Applied		Applied				Applied	

SECTION 23
Automatic Transmissions
GM THM 350C

GENERAL MOTORS CORP. THM 350C AUTOMATIC TRANSMISSION

Applications:

BUICK
1983 LeSabre, Regal
CHEVROLET
1983–85 Caprice, Impala, Malibu, Monte Carlo
OLDSMOBILE
1983–85 Delta 88, Cutlass
PONTIAC
1983 Bonneville, Grand Prix, Parisienne

Transmission and Converter Identification

TRANSMISSION

A production day and shift built number, and a transmission model and model year are stamped on the governor cover. Since the production day and model numbers furnish a key to the construction of the unit and interchangeability of parts in each transmission, they should be used in ordering replacement parts, Naturally, if the governor cover should become damaged and require replacement, it will be important to stamp the information found on the original cover on the new cover or otherwise record the information for future reference.

The Turbo Hydra-Matic 350C, transmission closely resembles the Turbo Hydra-Matic 250C and it is, in fact, a heavy duty version of it. The primary difference is that that 350C unit does not have an external adjustment for the band as can be found on the 250C unit.

There are a number of differences between the standard version of this transmission and the lock-up torque converter version. The lock-up converter versions use a different case, an additional (auxiliary) valve body, an electrical solenoid, a governor pressure switch, and a different pump assembly and gasket, as well as a different input shaft. There are a few other components added to control the sytem, depending on the vehicle.

CONVERTER

The torque converter is of a welded construction and cannot be

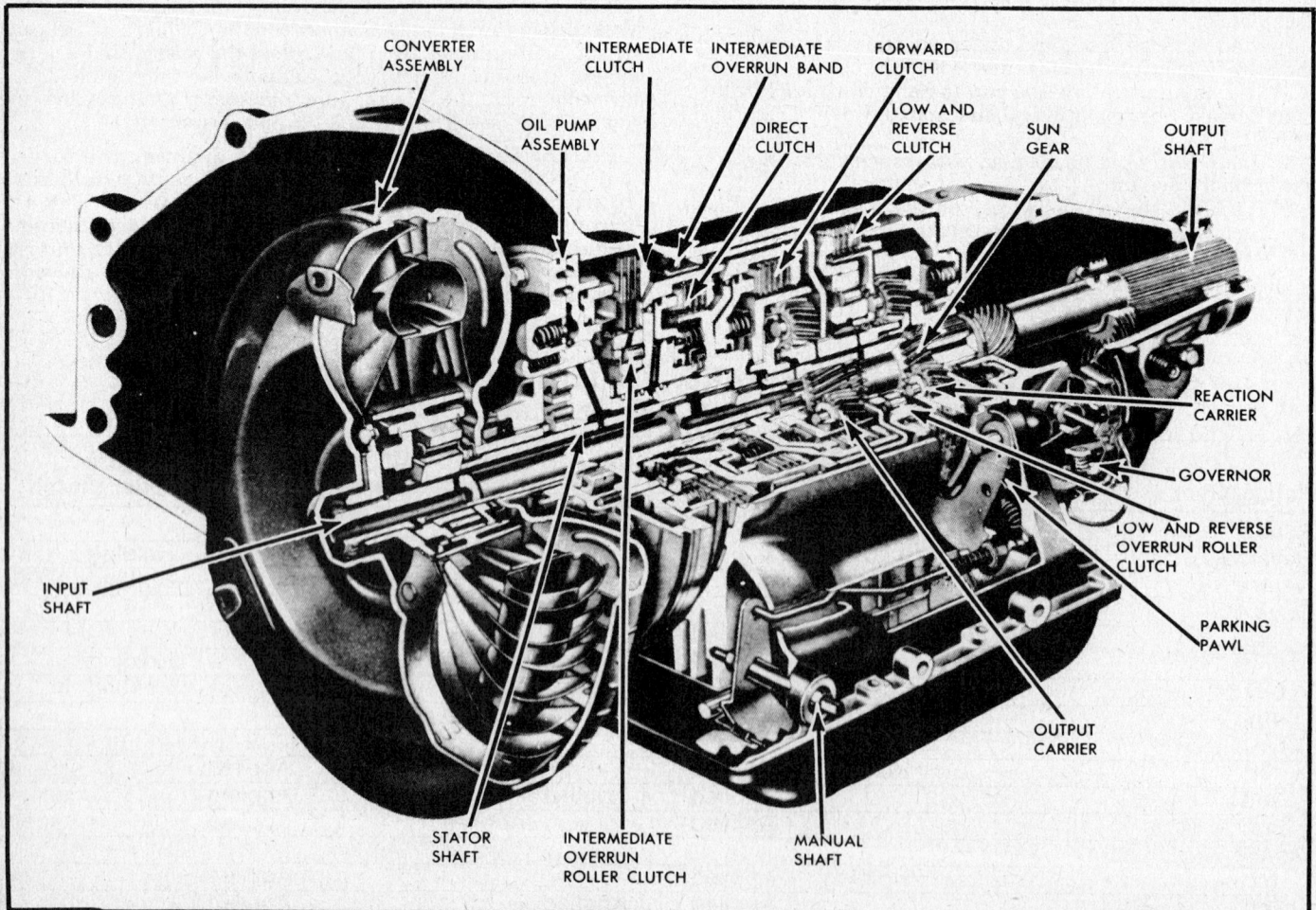

Sectional view of THM 350 automatic transmission – THM 350C similar

AUTOMATIC TRANSMISSIONS
GM THM 350C

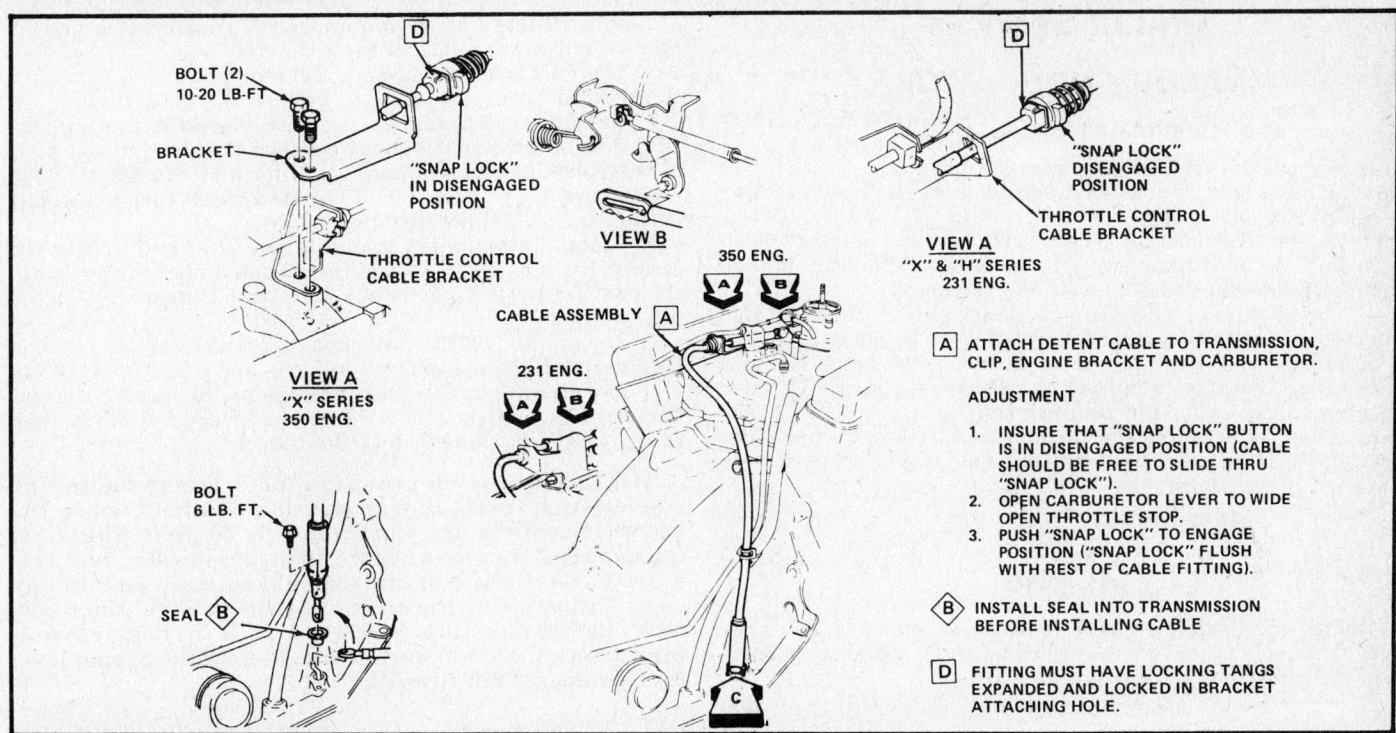

Detent cable adjustment - typical

disassembled for repairs. Any internal malfunctions require the replacement of the complete converter assembly. The diameter of the converters vary from 11–13 in., depending upon the engine application in the vehicle. Converter replacement should be confined to the converter matching the transmission model and engine size. Do no attempt to interchange converters by diameter size only, as poor vehicle speed or operation can result.

Diesel Engines

Vehicles equipped with diesel engines use a different torque converter. To identify these units, examine the weld nuts. Most gas engine converters have their weld nuts spot welded onto the converter housing, usually in two spots. The diesel converters have the weld nuts completely welded around their entire circumference.

Turbo-Charged V6 Engines

Vehicles eqipped with turbo-charged V6 engines use a different torque converter. These units have a high stall speed converter, allowing a stall speed of about 2800 rpm. These converters must not be replaced with a standard converter, otherwise performance will be sluggish and unsatisfactory. When ordering replacements for the turbo-charged units, make certain to specify that the vehicle has turbo-charging in order to obtain the proper replacement.

NOTE: Torrington bearings are used in various torque converter models in place of thrust spacers and should be considered when diagnosing bearing failure noises.

Converter clutch units are different for V6 or V8 engine applications and should not be interchanged. Poor engine and/or transmission operation will occur.

Fluid Specifications

Use only Dexron® II automatic transmission fluid or its equivalent.

THROTTLE LINKAGE ADJUSTMENT

If the shift linkage and related parts do not appear to be at fault or out of adjustment, then the Detent Control Cable should be checked. The following procedure is suggested.
1. With a small screwdriver, pry gently on the snap-lock retainer to release the detent cable.
2. Push the carburetor lever to the wide open throttle position (engine off) and hold.
3. Push the snap-lock downward until flush with the cable. If none of the adjustments have cured the problem, and assuming that the engine is in at least a reasonable state of tune, then improper adjustment and incorrect fluid level can be ruled out. This leaves only hydraulic malfunctions or mechanical malfunctions. Therefore, to help pinpoint the problem, an oil pressure check should be made.

BAND ADJUSTMENT

The intermediate overrun band has no external adjusting provision. A selective pin is used to control the servo piston travel during the application of the band. The valve body must be removed for this operation and a special pin selection tool must be used to determine the length pin needed.

MECHANICAL NEUTRAL START SYSTEM

This system relies on a mechanical block, rather than the starter safety switch to prevent starting the engine in other than "P" (Park) or "N" (Neutral).

The mechanical block is achieved by a cast in finger added to the switch actuator rack, which interferes with the bowl plate in all shift positions except "N" (Neutral) or "P" (Park). This interference prevents rotation of the lock cylinder into the "START" position.

In either "P" or "N", this finger passes through the bowl plate slots, allowing the lock cylinder full rotational travel into the "Start" position.

SECTION 23
AUTOMATIC TRANSMISSIONS
GM THM 350C

On-Car Services

VACUUM MODULATOR

Removal and Installation

1. Remove the vacuum hose from the modulator. Inspect the hose for signs of transmission fluid that would indicate a leaky modulator.
2. Remove the modulator hold-down bolt and bracket.
3. Pull the modulator straight back from the case. If the modulator is to be reused, be sure to change the O-ring seal.
4. The modulator valve can be removed from the case for cleaning or inspection is necessary.
5. Installation is the reverse of the above sequence. Renew the O-ring, coat it with petroleum jelly or Dexron® II. The attaching bolt is torqued to 130 inch lbs.
6. When re-installing the vacuum hose be sure to check for cracks. The transmission fluid level should also be checked and adjusted if necessary.

OIL PAN

1. Raise and safely support vehicle. On some vehicles, the transmission may have to be jacked up slightly and supported and the crossmember removed for access.
2. Place a large drain pan under the transmission and remove the front and side bolts on the pan.
3. Loosen but do not remove the rear pan bolts. Allow the fluid to drain.
4. Remove the remaining screws, remove the pan and discard the gasket. Remove the two screws that hold the oil filter to the valve body and discard the filter and its gasket.
5. Thoroughly clean the oil pan and check that the gasket surface is flat and not distorted.
6. Using a new gasket, install a new filter and tighten the screws. Place a new gasket on the oil pan and carefully install the pan. Torque the pan bolts to 13 ft. lbs., being careful not to over-tighten.
7. Lower the vehicle and add approximately 6 pints of Dexron® II. With the selector in Park, apply brakes, start engine and allow to idle. Do not race engine. Make sure the carburetor comes off fast idle. Move the selector through each range, end in Park and check fluid level.

NOTE: There is no provision for draining the torque converter. In cases of transmission overhaul, when the converter will be dry approximately 20 pints will be required total. In cases where just the pan has been removed and drained, 6 pints should be sufficient. In any case, always check the dipstick rather than rely on a specific number of pints of fluid. Add while the engine is running, transmission in Park, and add until the proper level is reached. Do not overfill.

CLUTCH AND BAND APPLICATION CHART
THM 350C

Range	Gear	Int. Clutch	Direct Clutch	Forward Clutch	Low & Reverse Clutch	Int. Overrun Roller Clutch	Low & Reverse Roller Clutch	Int. Overrun Band
PARK-NEUT.		—	—	—	—	—	—	—
DRIVE	FIRST	—	—	Applied	—	—	Holding	—
DRIVE	SECOND	Applied	—	Applied	—	Holding	—	—
DRIVE	THIRD	Applied	Applied	Applied	—	—	—	—
INT.	FIRST	—	—	Applied	—	—	Holding	—
INT.	SECOND	Applied	—	Applied	—	Holding	—	Applied
LOW	FIRST	—	—	Applied	Applied	—	Holding	—
LOW	SECOND	Applied	—	Applied	—	Holding	—	Applied
REV.		—	Applied	—	Applied	—	—	—

GENERAL MOTORS CORP. THM 400 AUTOMATIC TRANSMISSION

Transmission and Converter Identification

TRANSMISSION

An identification tag is attached to the transmission bearing two code letters as well as the serial number of the unit. These letters identify the transmission, the car series in which it was originally installed and the engine size and type to which it was originally installed. This plate is located on the right side of the transmission case on the 400 units.

CONVERTER

The torque converter application is determined by the diameter of the unit, as well as the year and size of the engine to which it is mated. The transmission code letters will be helpful

AUTOMATIC TRANSMISSIONS
GM THM 400

to dealership parts personnel when replacement torque converters may be needed.

Fluid Specifications

Use only automatic transmission fluids having the designations Dexron® or Dexron® II.

Adjustments

VACUUM MODULATOR

Original equipment type modulators are not usually adjustable except on some older vehicles. Aftermarket type units often have a set screw that can be adjusted to "fine tune" the shift speeds of the transmission. In practice, most rebuilders change the modulator with each unit that they rebuild since the modulator is sealed and it is difficult to determine a good one from a marginal one.

BAND ADJUSTMENT

There is no external band adjustment on this unit. Band adjustment is only possible after the unit has been disassembled. General Motor has a special tool for checking the pin length of the servo apply pin. These pins are changed if any adjustment is required. Generally, the band apply pins will not have to be changed unless the case is replaced.

NEUTRAL SAFETY SWITCH

Some General Motors vehicles have a mechanical neutral start device enclosed in the steering column. This works in conjunction with the steering lock. This system does not affect transmission operation and will normally not concern the transmission technician.

On-Car Services

OIL PAN

Removal

1. Raise and safely support vehicle. On some vehicles, the transmission may have to be supported and the crossmember removed for access.
2. Place a large drain pan under the transmission and remove the front and side bolts from the pan.
3. Loosen but do not remove the rear pan bolts. Carefully bump the pan with a rubber mallet to free the pan. If the pan is pried loose instead be very careful not to damage the gasket surfaces. Allow the fluid to drain.
4. Remove the remaining screws. Remove the pan and discard the gasket. Remove the attaching screw from the filter and remove the filter and pipe assembly.
5. Remove the pump intake pipe from the filter and discard the filter.
6. Remove and discard the intake pipe O-ring.

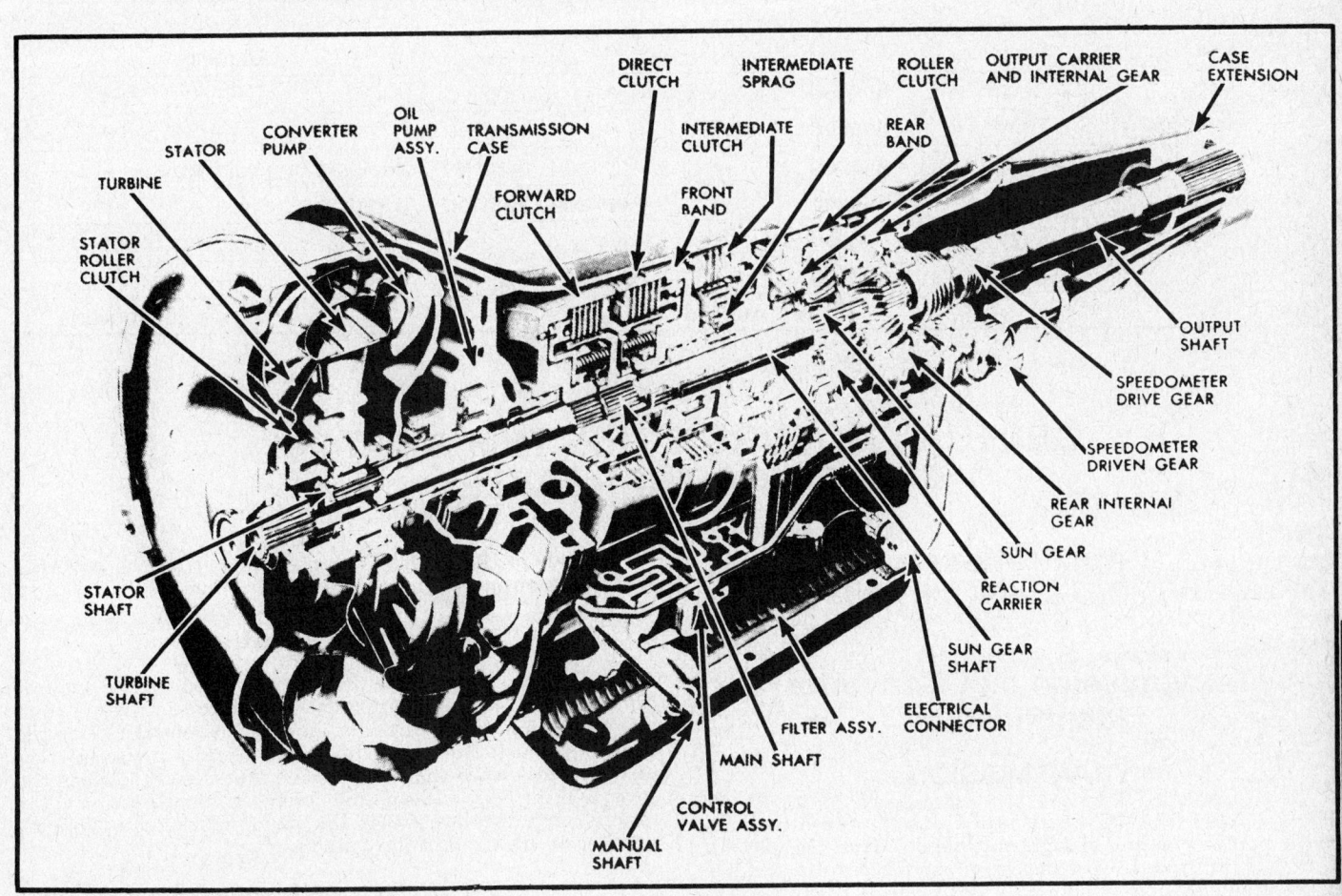

Cross section of THM 400 automatic transmission

23-47

SECTION 23
AUTOMATIC TRANSMISSIONS
GM THM 400

CLEANING THE OIL PAN
Thoroughly clean the oil pan and dry with compressed air. Make sure that all traces of the old gasket have been removed. Check the gasket surfaces of the pan for distortion, particularly around the bolt holes which are often dished in due to overtorque. If distorted, they can be straighten with a mallet and a clock of wood.

Installation
1. Install a new O-ring onto the intake pipe and install the pipe into the filter.
2. Install the filter and pipe assembly into the transmission and install the retaining bolt.
3. Install a new gasket on the oil pan, making sure that all traces of the old gasket have been removed. Torque the pan bolts evenly to a torque of 12 ft. lbs.
4. Lower the vehicle and refill the transmission with approximately four quarts of Dexron® II since the filter has been replaced. If only the pan had been removed and the filter assembly was not disturbed, then less fluid will be required; usually approximately two to three quarts will fill it depending on the model of the transmission.

VACUUM MODULATOR
Removal
1. Raise and safely support vehicle.
2. Locate and remove the modulator retaining bolt. Disconnect the vacuum line.
3. Pull the modulator straight back from the case.
4. Discard the O-ring. The modulator valve can be removed from the case for cleaning if desired.

Installation
1. Install a new O-ring on the modulator body. Lube with petroleum jelly or transmission fluid.
2. Install the modulator valve if it was removed. Install the vacuum unit into the case.
3. Install the retainer and bolt. Torque to 20 ft. lbs. Connect the vacuum line.

CLUTCH AND BAND APPLICATION CHART
THM 400

Range	Gear	Forward Clutch	Direct Clutch	Front Band	Int. Clutch	Int. Roller Clutch	Low Roller Clutch	Rear Band
Park-Neut.		—	—	—	—	—	—	—
Drive	First	Applied	—	—	—	—	Holding	—
	Second	Applied	—	—	Applied	Holding	—	—
	Third	Applied	Applied	—	Applied	—	—	—
Int.	First	Applied	—	Applied	Applied	Holding	Holding	—
	Second	Applied	—	Applied	Applied	Holding	—	—
Low	First	Applied	—	—	—	—	Holding	Applied
	Second	Applied	—	Applied	Applied	Holding	—	—
Rev.		—	Applied	—	—	—	—	Applied

GENERAL MOTORS CORP. THM 440-T4 AUTOMATIC TRANSAXLE

Applications:
1984 ½ and later General Motors "C" Cars

Transmission and Converter Identification

TRANSMISSION
The THM 440-T4 (ME9) automatic transaxle is a fully automatic unit, consisting of four multiple disc clutches, a roller clutch, a sprag and two bands, requiring hydraulic and mechanical applications to obtain the desired gear ratios from the compound planetary gears. The transaxle identification can be located on one of three areas of the unit. An identification plate on the side of the case, a stamped number on the governor housing or an ink stamp on the bell housing.

CONVERTER
Two types of converters are used in the varied vehicle applications. The first type is the three element torque converter combined with a lock-up converter clutch. The second type is the three element torque converter combined with a viscous lock-up converter clutch that has silicone fluid sealed between the cover and the body of the clutch assembly. Identification of the torque converters are either ink stamp marks or a stamped number on the shell of the converter.

Fluid Specifications
Dexron® II automatic transmission fluid or its equivalent is

AUTOMATIC TRANSMISSIONS
GM THM 440-T4
SECTION 23

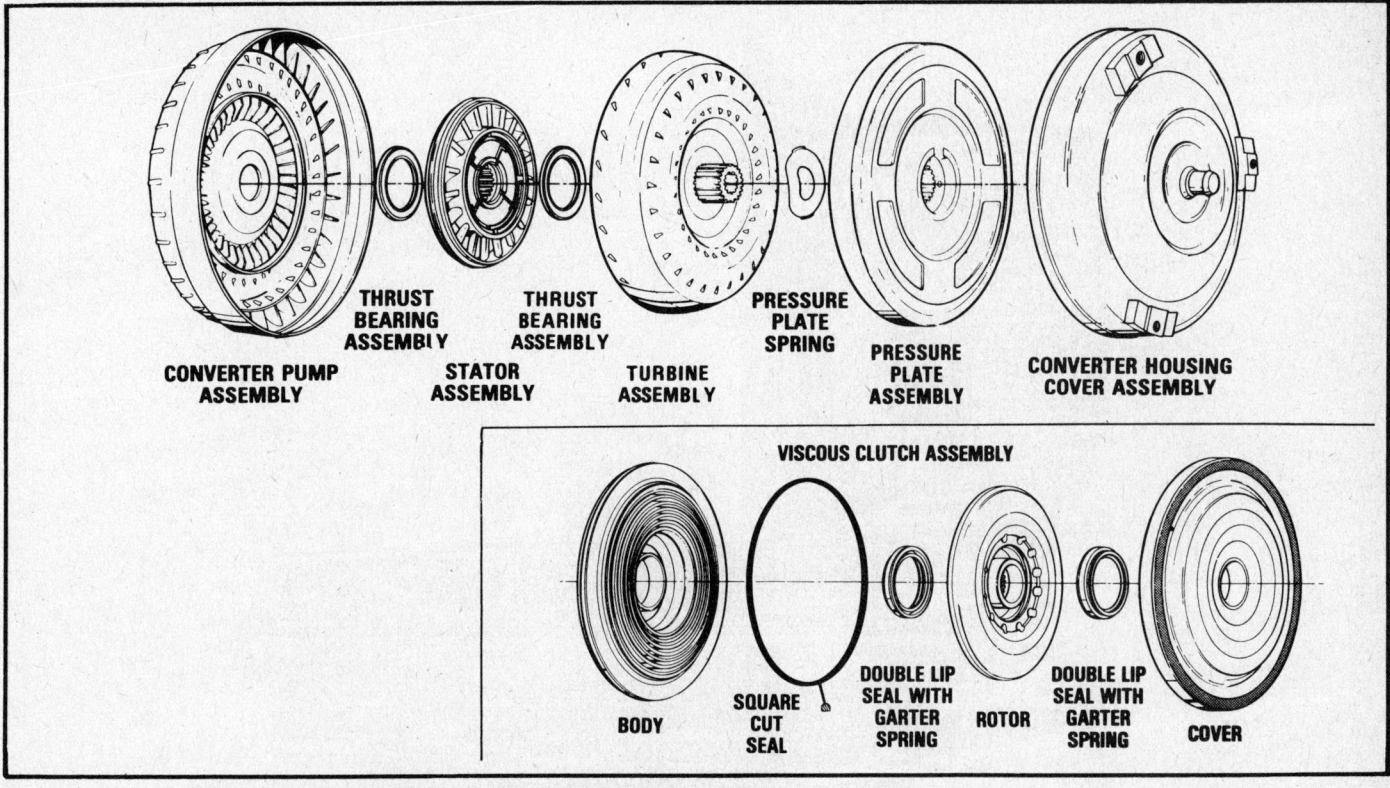

Two types of converters used with the THM 440-T4 transaxle (© General Motors Corp.)

the only recommended automatic transmission fluid to be used in this unit. Make certain that only good quality, clean fluid is used when servicing this transmission. The use of any other grade of fluid can lead to unsatisfactory performance or complete unit failure.

Adjustments

BAND ADJUSTMENT

The Reverse and 1–2 bands are adjusted by selective sized apply pins, determined with the use of special tools. This operation is accomplished during major overhaul procedures, due to space limitations within the vehicle's body.

T.V. CABLE

Adjustment

1. After the installation of the cable to the transaxle, engine bracket and cable actuating lever, be sure the cable slider is in its "zero" of fully re-adusted position.
2. Rotate the cable actuating lever to its full travel position.
3. The slider must move (or rachet) towards the lever when the lever is in its rotated position.

Re-adjustment

1. Be sure the engine is stopped.
2. Depress and hold the metal re-adjust tab at the engine end of the T.V. cable.
3. Move the slider until it stops against the fitting.
4. Release the re-adjustment tab.
5. Check to be sure the cable moves freely. The cable may

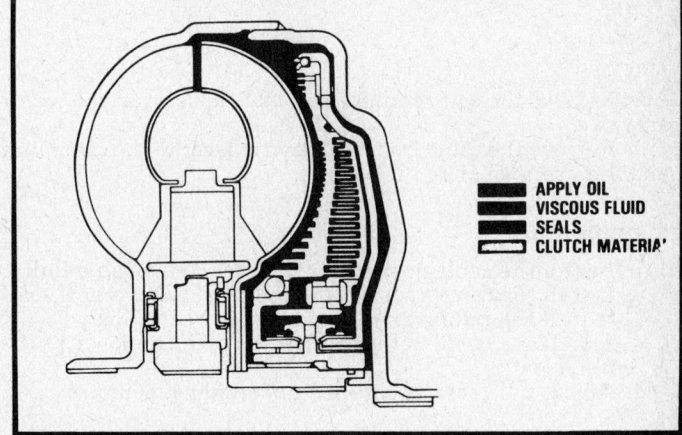

Viscous converter clutch applied (© General Motors Corp.)

appear to function properly with the engine stopped and cold. Re-check after the vehicle has warmed to normal operating temperature.

On-Car Service

T.V. CABLE OR SEAL

Removal

1. Remove the cable from the bracket and throttle lever at the carburetor.

SECTION 23

AUTOMATIC TRANSMISSIONS
GM THM 440-T4

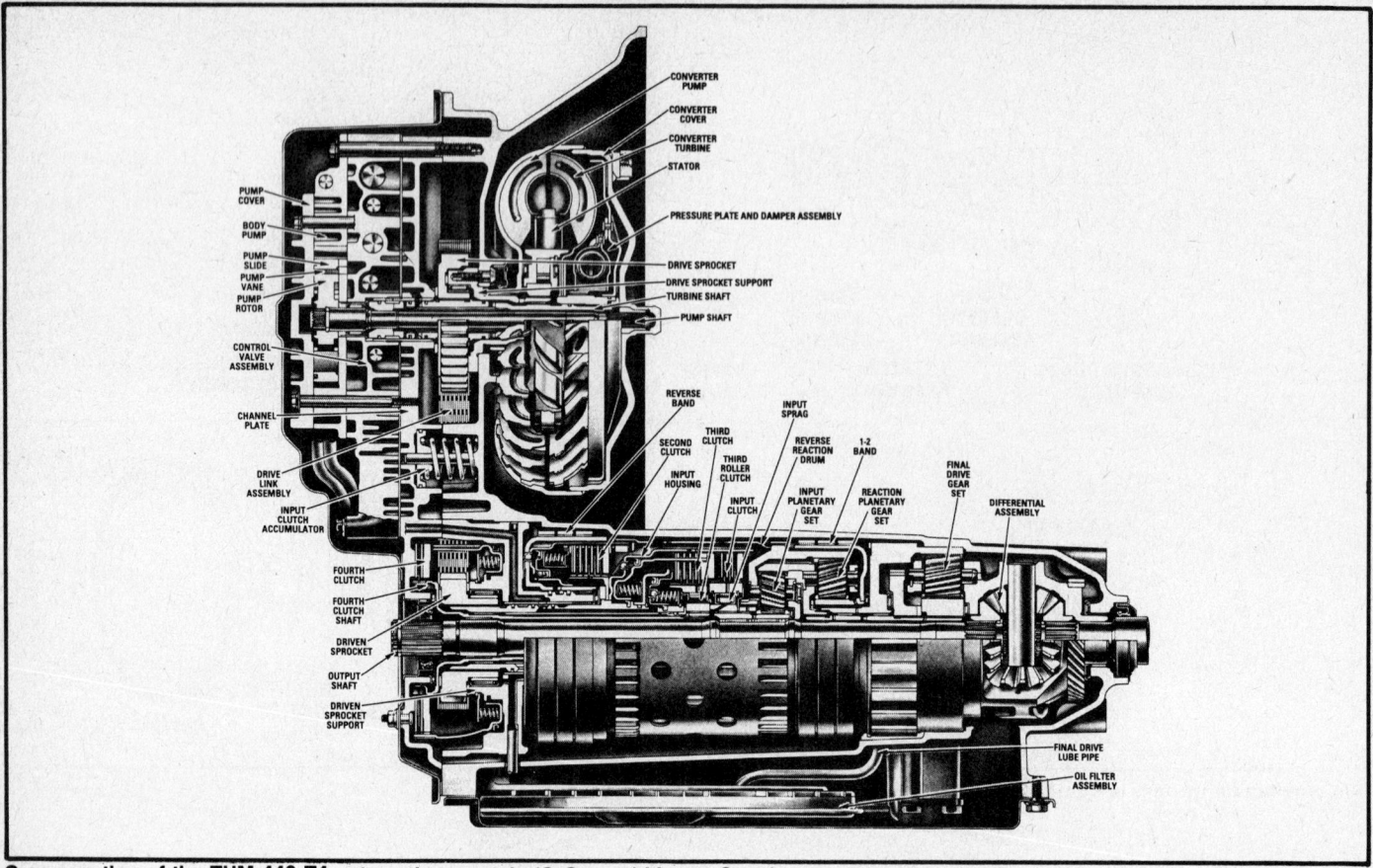

Cross section of the THM 440-T4 automatic transaxle (© General Motors Corp.)

2. Remove the bolt retaining the cable housing at the transaxle case.
3. Remove the cable from the throttle lever to the cable link and remove the cable.

Installation

1. Install the cable at the throttle lever to the cable link.
2. Install the cable housing into the case, using a new seal.
3. Install the retaining bolt and torque to 7 ft. lbs.
4. Install the cable to the bracket and throttle lever at the carburetor.
5. Adjust the cable as outlined under adjustments.

OIL PAN AND/OR GASKET

Removal

1. Raise the vehicle and support safely.
2. Loosen the oil pan bolts and drain the fluid carefully to avoid personal injury.
3. Remove the oil pan bolts and remove the oil pan and gasket.
4. Remove the gasket from the oil pan.

Installation

1. Install the oil pan and gasket.
2. Install the oil pan retaining bolts and torque to 10 ft. lbs.
3. Fill the transaxle with specified automatic transmission fluid, start the engine and recheck fluid level.

VACUUM MODULATOR

Removal

1. Depending upon vehicle model, either raise and support safely or work from the top of the engine compartment, and remove the vacuum line at the modulator.
2. Remove the modulator retaining screw and clamp at the base of the unit.
3. Remove the modulator and O-ring from the transaxle assembly.

Installation

1. Carefully install the modulator into the transaxle case. Do not damage the modulator valve.
2. Install the clamp and screw to hold the modulator to the case. Torque to 20 ft. lbs.
3. Install the vacuum hose to the modulator and complete assembly as required.

AUTOMATIC TRANSMISSIONS
GM THM 440-T4

CLUTCH AND BAND APPLICATION CHART
THM 440-T4 Automatic Transaxle

Range		4th Clutch	Reverse Band	2nd Clutch	3rd Clutch	3rd Roller Clutch	Input Sprag	Input Clutch	1-2 Band
Neutral Park							①	①	
Drive	1						Hold	On	On
	2			On			Over-Running	①	On
	3			On	On	Hold			
	4	On		On	①	Over-Running			
Manual	3			On	On	Hold	Hold	On	
	2			On			Over-Running	①	On
	1			On	Hold	Hold	On	On	
Reverse			On				Hold	On	

① Applied but not effective

GENERAL MOTORS CORP. THM 700-R4 AUTOMATIC TRANSMISSION

Applications:

CHEVROLET
1983–86 Corvette
Caprice & Impala
1983–86 Camaro
PONTIAC
1983–86 Firebird

Transmission and Converter Identification

TRANSMISSION

The transmission identification number is located on the left side of the transmission case, above the oil pan flange, on certain units, while other units will have the transmission identification numbers located on the right front and/or the right rear of the case. Refer to the identification numbers when replacement parts are required.

CONVERTER

The torque converter is matched to the transmission and is obtained by reference to the transmission identification numbers.

Fluid Specidications

Use only automatic transmission fluid having the designation of Dexron® II or its equivalent.

Adjustments

T.V. CABLE

GASOLINE ENGINES WITH SELF-ADJUSTING CABLE

1. Be sure engine is stopped. Do no attempt to adjust with the engine running.
2. Depress the adjusting tab. Move the slider back through the fitting in the direction away from the throttle body until the slider stops against the fitting.
3. Release the adjusting tab.
4. Open the carburetor lever to the "full throttle stop" position to automatically adjust the cable. Release the carburetor lever.
5. Check the cable for binding and road test the vehicle. The adjustment is correct if the shifting is normal.
6. If the shift is delayed or only at full throttle, the oil pan will have to be removed and the internal linkage and valve body inspected for binding or distortion.

CABLES USED WITH DIESEL ENGINES

1. With the engine stopped, disconnect the cruise control rod, if equpped.
2. Disconnect the transmission T.V. or detent cable terminal from the throttle assembly.
3. Loosen the locknut on the pump rod and shorten by several turns.
4. Rotate the lever assembly to the full throttle position and hold.
5. Lengthen the pump rod until the injection pump lever contacts the full throttle stop.
6. Release the lever assembly and tighten the pump rod locknut.
7. Remove the pump rod from the lever assembly.
8. Reconnect the T.V. or detent cable terminal to the throttle assembly.

SECTION 23 Automatic Transmissions
GM THM 700-R4

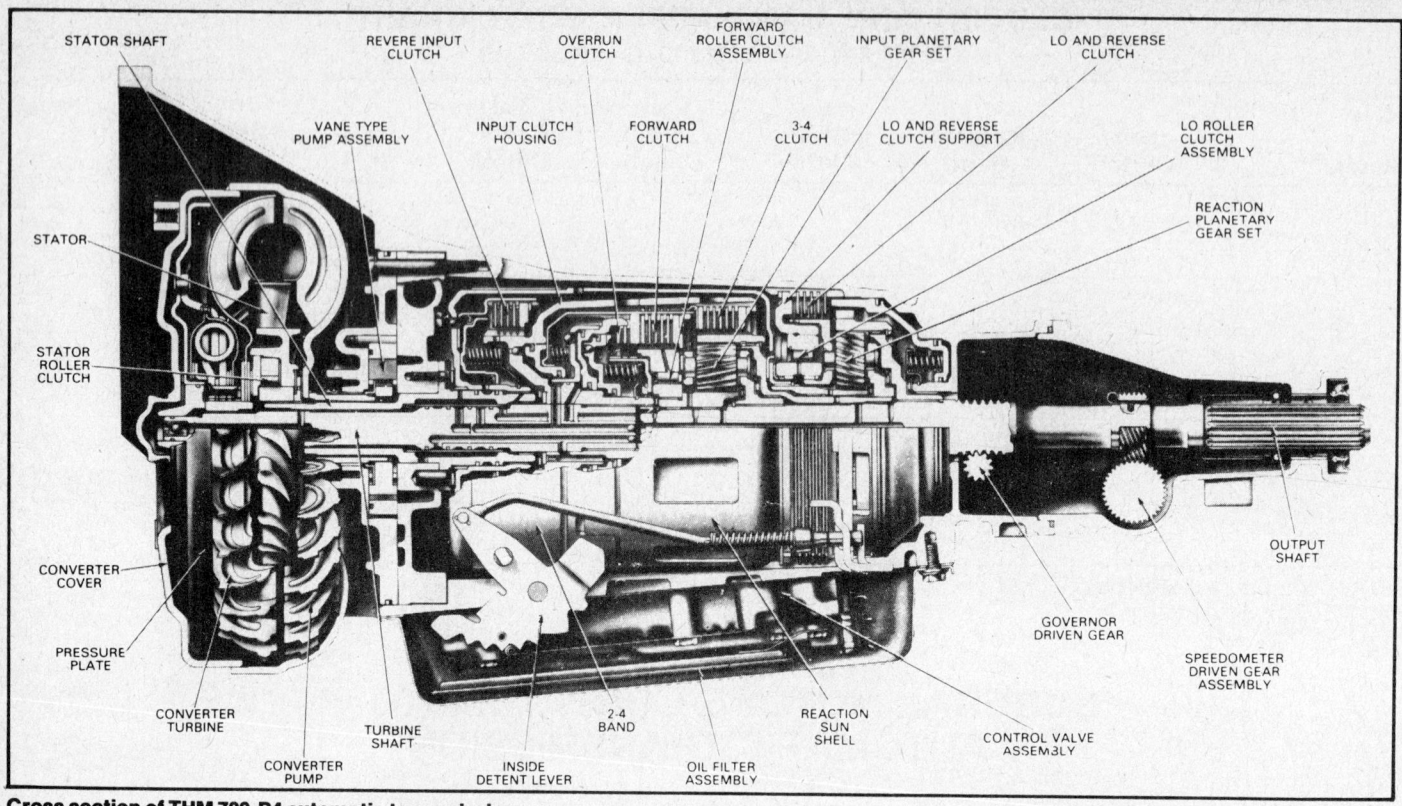

Cross section of THM 700-R4 automatic transmission

9. Depress and hold the metal re-adjustment tab on the cable upper end. Move the slider through the fitting in the direction away from the lever assembly until the slider stops against the fitting.
10. Release the tab, rotate the lever assembly to the full throttle stop and release the lever assembly.
11. Reconnect the pump rod and cruise control rod, if equipped.
12. If equipped with cruise control, adjust the servo throttle rod to a minumum slack and put the clip in the first free hole neares the bellcrank, but with the servo bail.

2–4 BAND

The 2–4 band is adjusted by selective sized apply pins, determined with the use of special measuring tools. This operation is normally accomplished during an overhaul.

On-Car Service

OIL PAN

Removal and Installation
1. Raise the vehicle and support safely.
2. With a drain pan under the oil pan, remove the retaining bolts from the front and sides of the oil pan.
3. Loosen the rear bolts approximately four turns and carefully pry the oil pan loose from the transmission case.
4. Allow the fluid to drain into the drain pan and remove the retaining bolts from the rear of the oil pan and remove the pan and gasket.

NOTE: Various transmission models may have RTV sealant used in place of gaskets.

5. Using either the RTV or gasket on a clean oil pan, install the pan to the transmission case and tighten the retaining bolts to 10–13 ft. lbs. torque.

--- **CAUTION** ---
Do not use the R.T.V. sealant on oil pans that have raised stiffening ribs on the pan flange.

6. Lower the vehicle and add the proper amount of fluid to the transmission. Start engine and correct the fluid level as necessary.

AUTOMATIC TRANSMISSIONS
GM THM 700-R4

CLUTCH AND BAND APPLICATION CHART
THM 700-R4

Gear Range	2-4 Band	Rev Input Clutch	Overrun Clutch	Forward Clutch	Forward Roller Clutch	3-4 Clutch	Lo Roller Clutch	Lo-Rev. Clutch
1st Dr$_4$				On	On		On	
2nd Dr$_4$	On			On	On			
3rd Dr$_4$				On	On	On		
4th Dr$_4$	On				On	On		
3rd Dr$_3$			On	On	On	On		
2nd Dr$_2$	On		On	On	On			
1st Lo			On	On	On		On	On
Rev.		On						On

FORD AXOD TRANSAXLE

Application

1986 And Later Ford Taurus/Mercury Sable

Transaxle and Converter Identification

TRANSAXLE

The transaxle identification tag is located on the top of the converter housing. The tag contains the transaxle assembly number, the mirror image print model and number, the build date and the serial number.

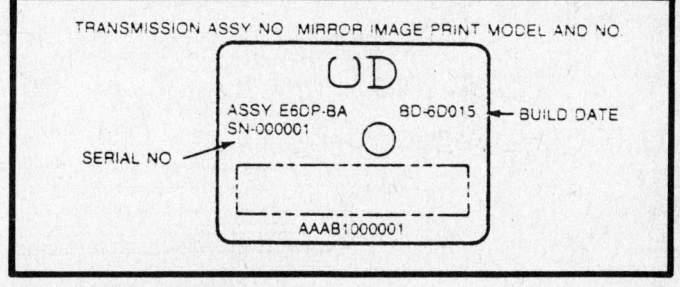
Typical identification tag

CONVERTER

A lock-up converter is used and is controlled through the electronic control, which is integral in the on-board EEC-IV system. These controls, along with the hydraulic controls in the valve body, operate the piston plate clutch in the converter unit.

The identification numbers are stamped or printed on the converter shell to identify the units.

Fluid Specifications

The fluid used in the AXOD transaxle unit must be Motorcraft Type H, XT-4-H or equivalent.

Checking Fluid Level

NOTE: Transaxle at Operating Temperature = 65°C. – 82°C. (150°F. – 180°F.).

1. With transaxle in PARK, engine at curb idle rpm, foot brakes applied and vehicle on level surface, move the transaxle selector lever through each range. Allow time in each range to engage transaxle, return to PARK, and apply parking brake. Do not turn off the engine during the fluid level check.

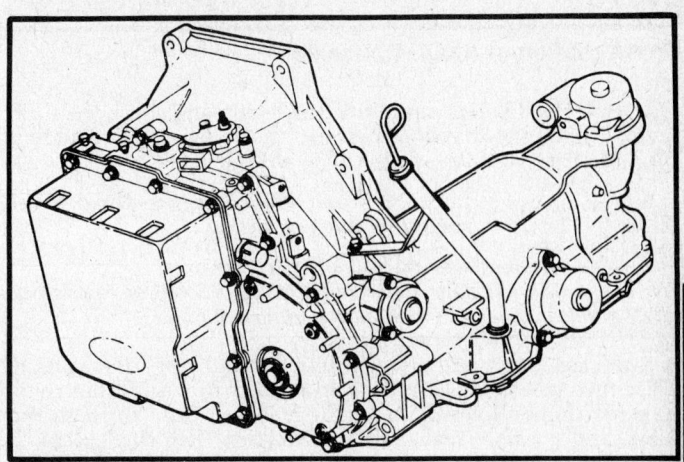
Exterior view of AXOD transaxle

2. Clean all dirt from the transaxle fluid dipstick cap before removing the dipstick from the filler tube.
3. Push the dipstick out of the tube, wipe it clean, and push all the way back into the tube. Be sure it is fully seated.

23-53

SECTION 23

AUTOMATIC TRANSMISSIONS
FORD AXOD

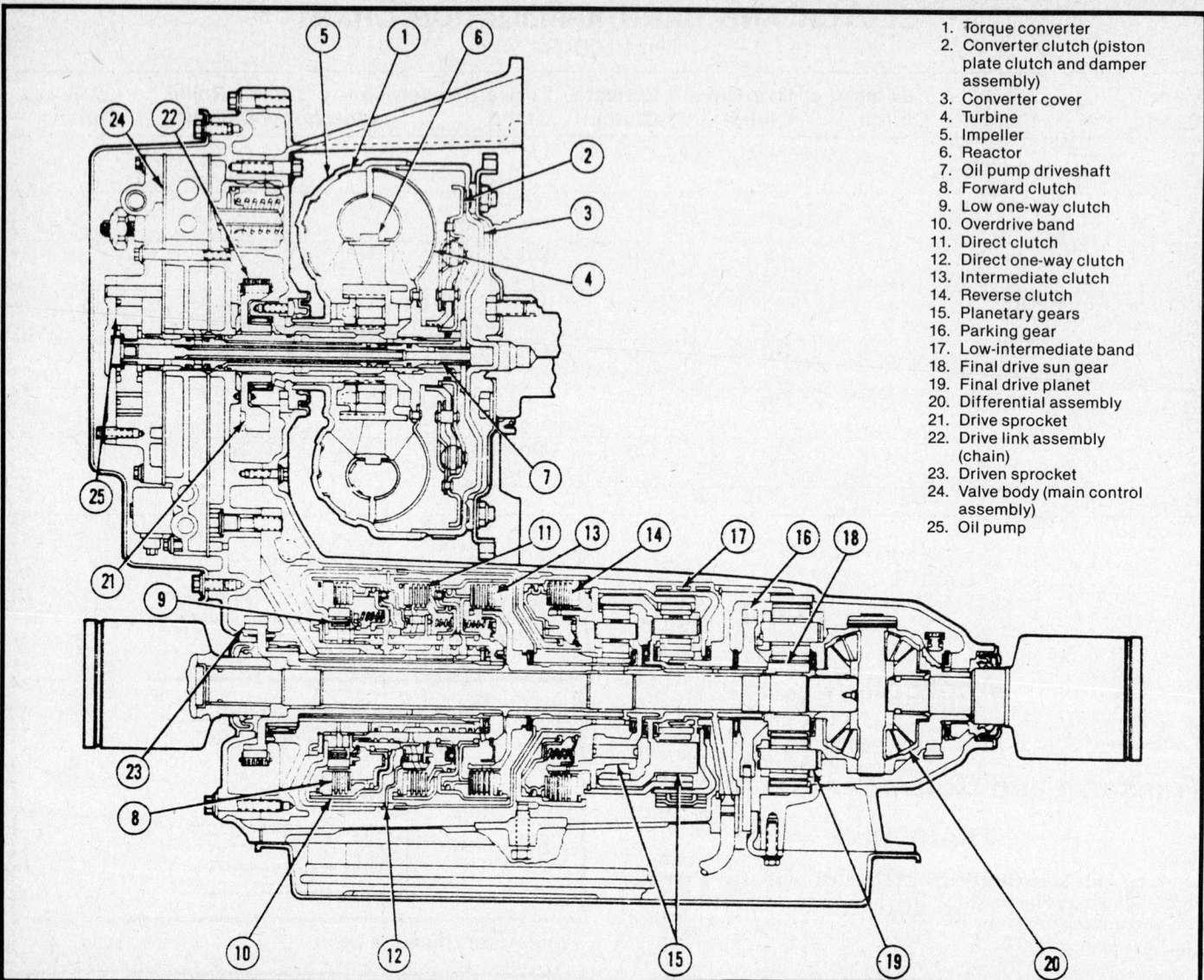

1. Torque converter
2. Converter clutch (piston plate clutch and damper assembly)
3. Converter cover
4. Turbine
5. Impeller
6. Reactor
7. Oil pump driveshaft
8. Forward clutch
9. Low one-way clutch
10. Overdrive band
11. Direct clutch
12. Direct one-way clutch
13. Intermediate clutch
14. Reverse clutch
15. Planetary gears
16. Parking gear
17. Low-intermediate band
18. Final drive sun gear
19. Final drive planet
20. Differential assembly
21. Drive sprocket
22. Drive link assembly (chain)
23. Driven sprocket
24. Valve body (main control assembly)
25. Oil pump

Cross section of AXOD transaxle

4. Pull the dipstick out of the tube again and check the fluid level. Fluid level should be between the arrows. Before adding fluid, be sure that the correct type will be used.

NOTE: Approximately 8 oz. will raise the fluid level from the bottom arrow to the top arrow.

CAUTION

Use of a fluid other than Motorcraft Type H, XT-4-H or equivalent, could result in transaxle malfunction and/or failure.

---

5. If necessary, add enough fluid through the filler tube to raise the level to the correct position. Do not overfill the transaxle, as this will result in foaming, loss of fluid through the vent, and possible transaxle malfunction. Remove excess, if overfilled.
6. Install the dipstick, making sure it is fully seated in the tube.

HIGH OR LOW FLUID LEVEL

A fluid level that is too high will cause the fluid to become aerated. Aerated fluid will cause low control pressure, and the aerated fluid may be forced out the vent.

A fluid level that is too low can affect the operation of the transaxle. Low level may indicate fluid leaks that could cause transaxle damage.

Adjustments

THROTTLE VALVE (TV) CABLE

The throttle valve (TV) cable normally does not need adjustment. The only time the cable should be adjusted is if one of the following components are replaced:

1. Main control assembly.
2. Throttle valve cable.
3. Throttle valve cable engine mounting bracket.
4. Throttle control lever link or lever assembly.
5. Engine throttle body.
6. Transaxle assembly.

AUTOMATIC TRANSMISSIONS
FORD AXOD
SECTION 23

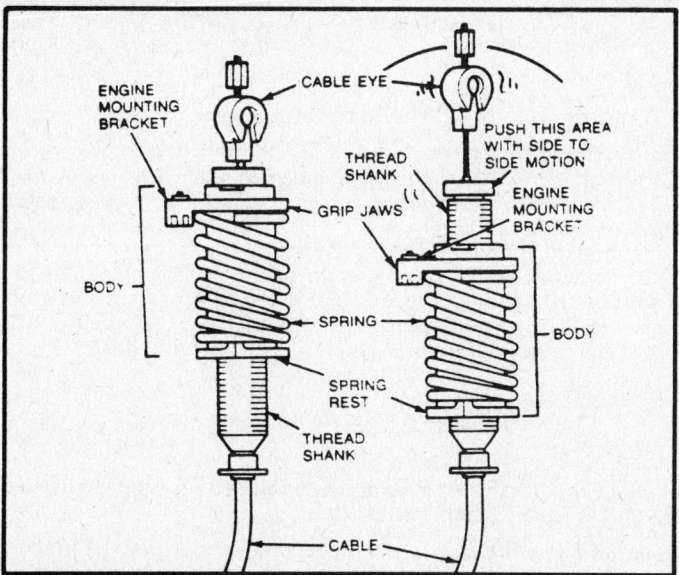

Adjustment of TV cable

Adjustment

1. Connect TV cable eye to throttle control lever link and attach cable boot to chain cover.
2. With TV cable mounted in engine bracket, make sure threaded shank is fully retracted. To retract shank, hold spring rest and wiggle top of thread shank while pressing shank toward spring.
3. Attach end of TV cable to throttle body.
4. Rotate throttle lever to WOT position and release.

NOTE: Threaded shank must show movement or "ratchet" out of grip jaws. If no movement is observed, inspect TV cable system for broken or disconnected components and repeat procedure.

FLOOR OR COLUMN SHIFT

Adjustment

1. Position selector lever in OVERDRIVE position against rearward stop. The shift lever must be held in the rearward position while linkage is being adjusted.
2. Loosen manual lever to control cable retaining nut.
3. Move transaxle manual lever to OVERDRIVE position, second detent from most rearward position.
4. Tighten attaching nut to 10-15 ft. lbs. (14-20 Nm).
5. Check operation of transaxle in each selector lever position. Make sure that park and neutral start switch are functioning properly.

NEUTRAL START SWITCH

Adjustment

1. With the manual shaft in the neutral detent, align the switch, using a No. 43 (0.089 in.) drill bit or equivalent.
2. Tighten the retaining bolts to 7–9 ft. lbs. (9–12 Nm).

NOTE: The neutral Start switch is located on the side of the transaxle assembly.

Band Adjustments

Both the overdrive band and the low/intermediate band has special measurements that must be taken with special measuring tools that measure the servo travel.

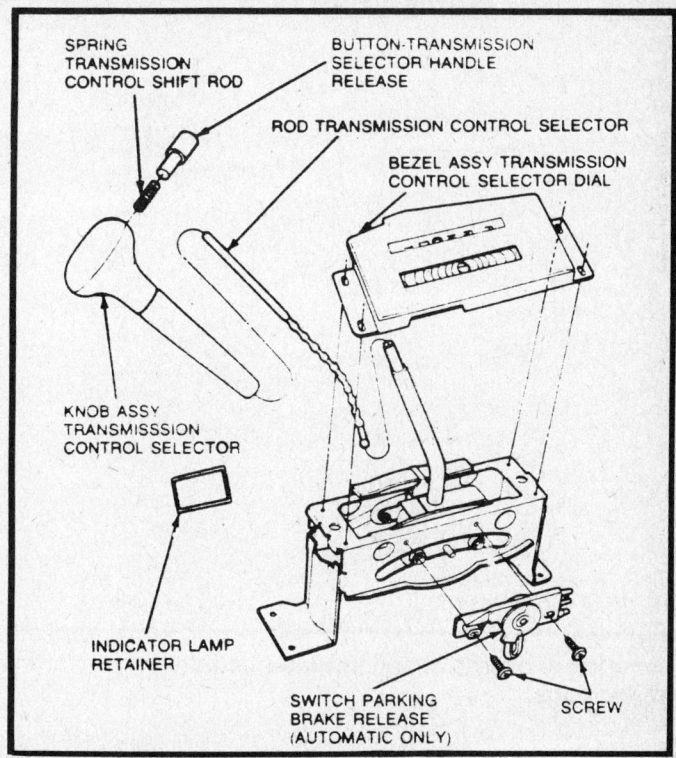

Exploded view of floor shift mechanism

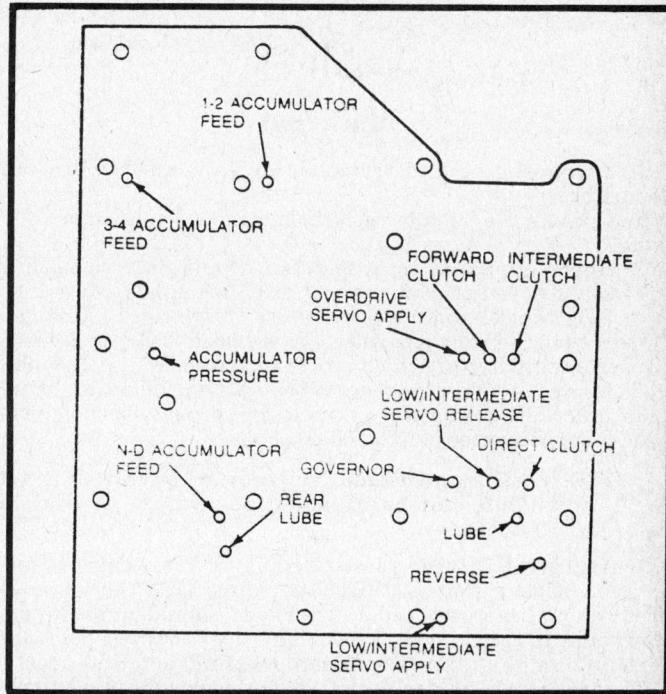

Airtest plate to be used during air pressure check of transaxle fluid circuits

Overdrive Servo Management
0.070 – 0.149 in. (1.8 – 3.8mm).

Low/Intermediate Servo Measurement
0.216 – 0.255 in. (5.5 – 6/5mm)

23-55

SECTION 23 AUTOMATIC TRANSMISSIONS
FORD AXOD

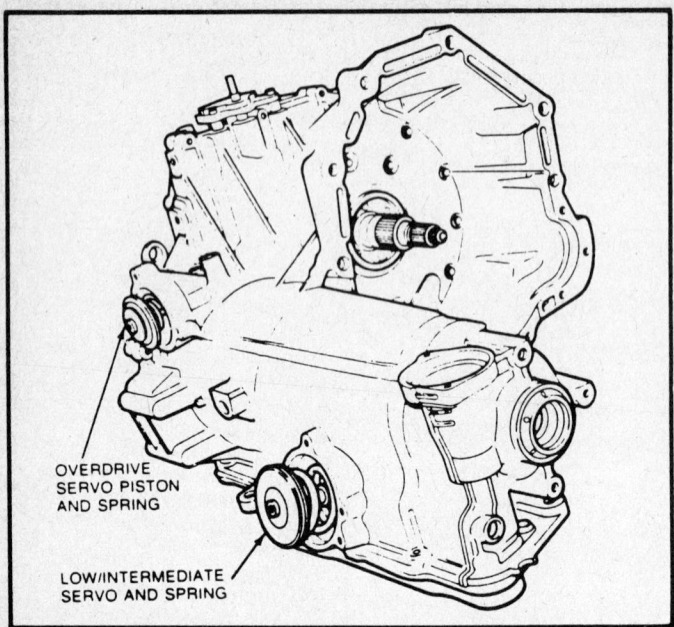

Location of overdrive and low/intermediate servo pistons and springs

NOTE: If a new low/intermediate band is installed, the reading should be 0.196–0.236 in. (5–6 mm).

Diagnosis

Road Test

1. Bring engine and transaxle up to normal operating temperature.
2. Operate the vehicle with the transmission selector in D range.
3. Apply minimum throttle pressure and observe upshift speeds and speed at which converter clutch applies.
4. Stop vehicle and move transmission selector to D range. Repeat Step 3. Transaxle will make all upshift except 3-4 and converter clutch apply should occur above 46 Km/H (27 mph).
5. Depress accelerator pedal to floor (WOT). Transxle should shift from third to second, or third to first depending on vehicle speed and converter clutch should release.

NOTE: With transmission selector in D range, a 4-3 WOT downshift can be obtained regardless of vehicle speed.

6. With vehicle speed above 48 Km/h (30 mph), move transmission selector from D range to 1 range (LOW) and remove foot from accelerator pedal. Transaxle should immediately downshift to second gear. When vehicle speed drops below 32 Km/H (20 mph), transaxle should downshift into first gear.
7. If transaxle fails to upshift and/or downshift as outlined, refer to Diagnosis for Governor Pressure and Shift Control Valves.

In-Shop Test

The following items can be checked during an in-shop shift test:
1. Governor circuits.
2. Shift delay pressures.
3. Throttle boost.

Test

1. Raise front of vehicle so that front wheels clear the floor.

CAUTION

Do not exceed 97 Km/h (60 mph) indicated speedometer speed. Indicated speed is one-half of actual tire speed. Do not exceed recommended tire speed rating.

---

2. To check shift valves and governor circuit, place selector lever in D range. Apply minimum throttle pressure and observe upshift speeds and speeds at which converter locks up.
3. The transaxle should shift in the following order:
   a. 1-2.
   b. 2-3.
   c. Converter lockup.
   d. 3-4.

NOTE: Converter will remain locked up when transaxle shifts into fourth gear.

4. At the shift points, the speedometer needle will make a momentary surge, a slight driveline bump may be felt and engine speed will drop without releasing accelerator pedal. If shift speeds are not within specification, perform Governor Check as outlined. If shift points are too low, the shift modulator valves may be the possible cause.
5. To check downshift valve operations, turn engine off and disconnect throttle lever and pull out to maximum travel. Do not crimp or kink cable. Start engine and place selector lever in D. Apply minimum throttle pressure and observe speed at which 1-2 upshift occurs.

SERVICE CODES

1. The following lists are service codes that may appear during the EEC-IV system self-test and that would affect the operation of the transaxle.
   a. 39 – Transaxle converter by-pass clutch not operating properly.
   b. 59 – 4/3 pressure switch circuit failed open.
   c. 62 – 4/3 and/or 3/2 pressure switch circuit failed closed. If code appears in Key On, Engine Off test, 3/2 circuit failed. If code appears in Engine Running test, 4/3 circuit failed. If code appears in both tests, both circuits must be checked.
   d. 69 – 3/2 circuit failed open.
   e. 89 – Transaxle converter by-pass clutch solenoid failed always open or always closed.
2. The following service codes are not transaxle related, but can affect converter clutch by-pass operation. Service these components before servicing the transaxle codes:
   a. 21 – Engine coolant temperature (ECT) sensor out of range.
   b. 22 – Manifold absolute pressure (MAP) sensor out of range.
   c. 23 – Throttle position (TP) sensor out of range.
   d. 24 – Air charge temperature (ACT – sensor out of range.
   e. 29 – Vehicle speed sensor (VSS) not functioning.
   f. 74 – Brake On/Off (BOO) switch always open or brake not applied during Engine Running On-demand self-test.
   g. 75 – Brake On/Off (BOO) switch always closed.
3. The following service code is for a transaxle component that may cause faulty engine idle speed control if not working properly:
   a. 57 – Neutral pressure (NPS) switch failed in NEUTRAL (open). The NPS is a normally open switch that closes with hydraulic pressure. Failure of the transaxle to engage in D or R would result in service code 57. Check for proper hydraulic function before testing electrical components.

AUTOMATIC TRANSMISSIONS
FORD AXOD

AIR PRESSURE CHECKS

A NO DRIVE condition can exist, even with correct transaxle fluid pressure, because of inoperative clutches or bands. A erratic shift can be located through a series of checks by substituting air pressure for fluid pressure to determine the location of the malfunction.

When the selector lever is in a forward gear range (D, D, 1) a NO DRIVE condition may be caused by an inoperative forward clutch, low/intermediate one-way or low/intermediate band. No manual low (1) coast could be caused by an inoperative direct clutch or direct one-way clutch.

Failure to drive in R (REVERSE) could be caused by a malfunction of the reverse clutch, forward clutch or low/intermediate one-way clutch.

1. Drain transaxle fluid and remove oil pan.
2. Remove main control cover. Then remove oil pump and main control assembly.
3. Install air pressure test plate with main control assembly-to-chain cover gasket.
4. The inoperative clutches or bands can be located by introducing air pressure into the various test plate passages as follows:

FORWARD CLUTCH

Apply air pressure to forward clutch test port. A dull thud can be heard, or movement of piston felt when clutch piston is applied. If clutch seal(s) are leaking, a hissing sound will be heard.

GOVERNOR

Apply air pressure to governor test port and listen for a sharp clicking or whistling noise. The noise indicates proper governor movement.

OVERDRIVE SERVO

Apply air pressure to overdrive servo apply test port. Operation of servo is indicted by a tightening of overdrive band around overdrive drum. Because of the cushioning effect of the servo release spring, application of band may not be heard or felt. The servo should hold air pressure without leakage and a dull thud should be heard when air pressure is removed, allowing servo piston to return to release position.

DIRECT CLUTCH

Apply air pressure to direct clutch test port. A dull thud can be heard, or movement of piston felt on case as clutch piston is applied. If clutch seal(s) are leaking, a hissing sound will be heard.

IINTERMEDIATE CLUTCH

Apply air pressure to intermediate clutch test port. A dull thud can be heard, or movement of piston can be felt on case as clutch piston is applied. If clutch seal(s) are leaking, a hissing should will be heard.

LOW – INTERMEDIATE CLUTCH

Apply air pressure at low-intermediate servo feed test port. The low-intermediate band should tighten around sun gear of rear planetary gear set. Because of the cushioning effect of the servo release spring, application of band may not be hard or felt. The servo should hold air pressure without leakage and a dull thud should be heard when air pressure is removed, allowing servo piston to return to release position. Apply air pressure to low-intermediate servo release test port while continuing to pressurize the apply port. Servo piston should return to the release position. The band should loosen and a dull thud should be heard. Release the feed test port. The release test port should hold pressure without leakage. Any leakage or failure of piston movement requires servo service.

LUBE AND REAR LUBE

Apply air pressure to lube and rear lube test ports. These passages can only be checked for blockage. If either passage holds air pressure, remove service tool plate and check for an obstruction or damage.

1-2, 3-4 AND N-D ACCUMULATORS

Apply air pressure to each accumulator feed port. Accumulator should apply. Because of the cushioning effect of the accumulator release spring, application of accumulator may not be felt or heard. The accumulator should hold air pressure without leakage and a dull thud should be heard when air pressure is removed, allowing accumulator to return to release position.

CLUTCH AND BAND APPLICATION CHART
Ford AXOD

Gear	Lo-Int Band	Overdrive Band	Forward Clutch	Intermediate Clutch	Direct Clutch	Reverse Clutch	Low One-Way Clutch	Direct One-Way Clutch
1st Gear Manual Low	Applied		Applied		Applied		Applied	Applied
1st Gear (Drive)	Applied		Applied				Applied	
2nd Gear (Drive)	Applied		Applied	Applied			Holding	
3rd Gear (Drive)			Applied	Applied	Applied			
4th Gear (Overdrive)		Applied		Applied	Applied			Holding
Reverse (R)			Applied			Applied	Holding	
Neutral (N)								
Park (P)								

SECTION 23 AUTOMATIC TRANSMISSIONS
NOVA A131L

A131L AUTOMATIC TRANSAXLE

Application

1985 ½ AND LATER NOVA

Transaxle and Converter Identification

TRANSAXLE

The transaxle identification number is located on the top of the transaxle case. It contains the manufacturing year, the manufacturing month and the production digit number

CONVERTER

The converter is equipped with a hydraulically controlled lockup converter. Identification numbers or letters are stamped or printed on the converter shell. If the converter I.D. is missing, refer to the transaxle I.D. number plate when parts ordering becomes necessary.

Fluid Specifications

The drain and refill capacity is 2.4 U.S. quarts and the dry fill capacity is 5.8 U.S. quarts. The correct fluid specification is the use of Dexron II automatic transmission fluid, or its equivalent.

CHECKING FLUID LEVELS

The transaxle dipstick is marked with hot and cool indicator nicks. With the transaxle at normal operating temperature, the fluid level should register between the two nick marks on the stick at the HOT indicator level. If the level is low or overfull, it must be adjusted by draining or filling to its proper level.

Adjustments

THROTTLE CABLE

Adjustment

1. Depress the accelerator pedal completely and check that the throttle valve opens fully. If the throttle valve does not open fully, adjust the accelerator link
2. Fully depress the accelerator
3. Loosen the adjustment nuts.
4. Adjust the throttle cable housing so that the distance between the end of the boot and the stopper on the cable is correct. The distance must be 0.04 in. (0.1mm).
5. Tighten the adjusting nuts and recheck the adjustment.

TRANSAXLE SHIFT CONTROL

Adjustment

1. Loosen the swivel nut on the lever.
2. Push the manual lever fully towards the right side of the vehicle.
3. Return the lever two notches to the "N" position.
4. Set the shift lever in the "N" position.
5. While holding the lever lightly towards the "R" position, tighten the swivel nut.

NEUTRAL START SWITCH

Adjustment

NOTE: If the engine will start with the shift selector in any range other than "N" or "P" positions, adjustment is required.

1. Loosen the neutral start switch bolts and set the shift lever in the "N" position.
2. Disconnect the neutral start switch connector.
3. Connect an ohmmeter between the terminals.
4. Adjust the switch to the point where there is continuity between terminals.
5. Connect the neutral switch connector.
6. Torque the switch bolts to 48 in. lbs. (5.4 Nm).
7. Recheck the switch operation.

On-Vehicle Service

OIL PAN AND GASKET

Remove and Replace

1. Raise the vehicle and support safely. Drain the transaxle fluid

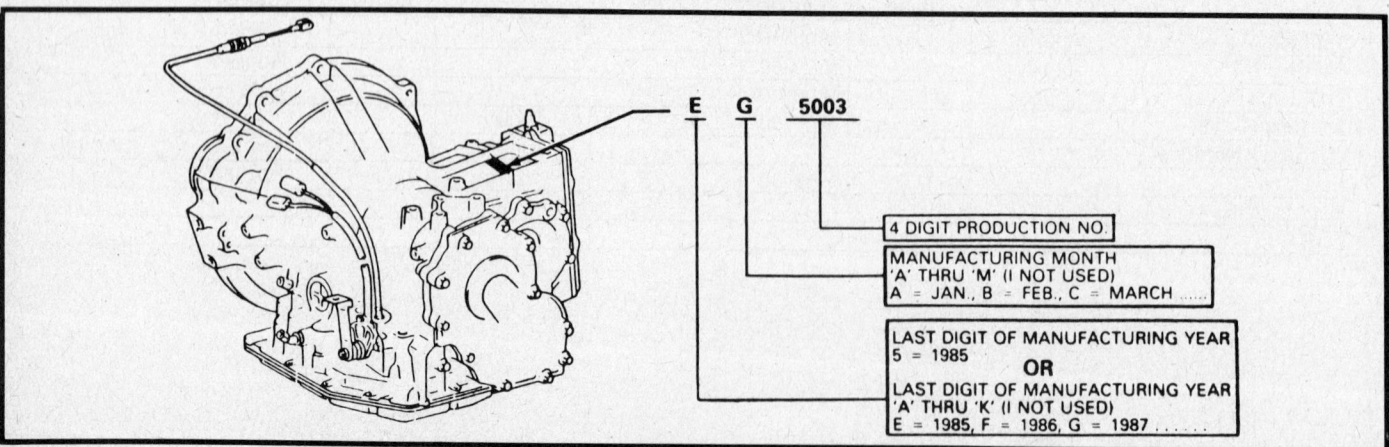

A131L automatic transaxle identification number location

AUTOMATIC TRANSMISSIONS
NOVA A131L

CLUTCH AND BAND APPLICATION CHART
A131L Automatic Transaxle

Shift lever position	Gear position	C_1	C_2	B_1	B_2	B_3	F_1	F_2
P	Parking							
R	Reverse		On			On		
N	Neutral							
D	1st	On						On
D	2nd	On			On		On	
D	3rd	On	On		On			
2	1st	On						On
2	2nd	On		On	On		On	
L	1st	On				On		On
L	*2nd	On		On	On		On	

B_1 —No. 1 brake, second coast brake
B_2 —No. 2 brake, second brake
B_3 —No. 3 brake, first and reverse brake
C_1 —Front clutch, forward clutch
C_2 —Rear clutch, direct clutch
F_1 —No. 1 one-way clutch
F_2 —No. 2 one-way clutch
*Downshift only in "L" range, 2nd gear—no upshift.

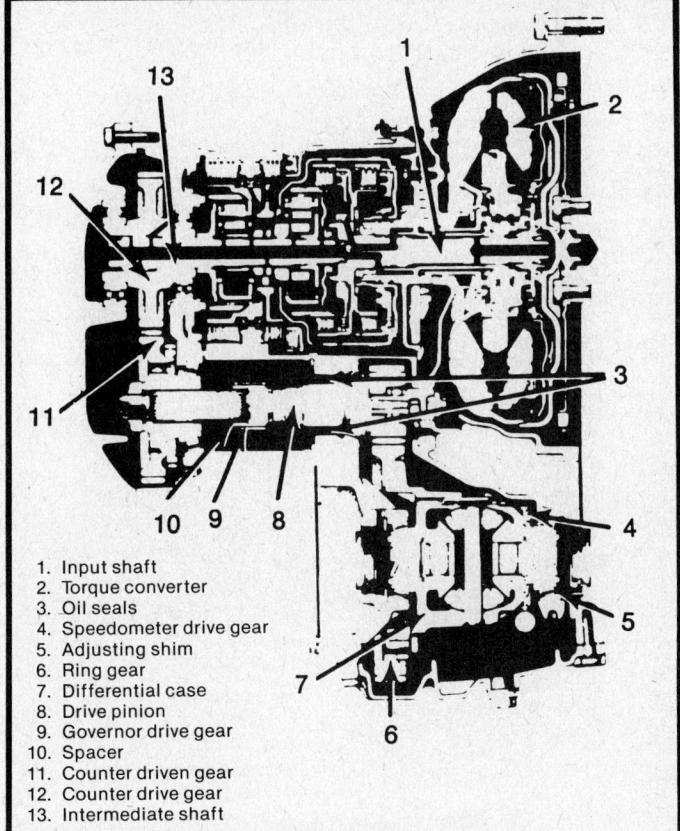

1. Input shaft
2. Torque converter
3. Oil seals
4. Speedometer drive gear
5. Adjusting shim
6. Ring gear
7. Differential case
8. Drive pinion
9. Governor drive gear
10. Spacer
11. Counter driven gear
12. Counter drive gear
13. Intermediate shaft

Cross section of A131L automatic transaxle

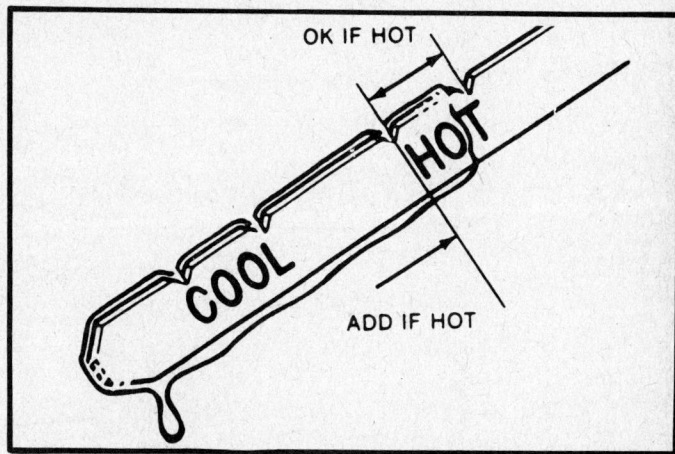

Fluid level indication on dipstick

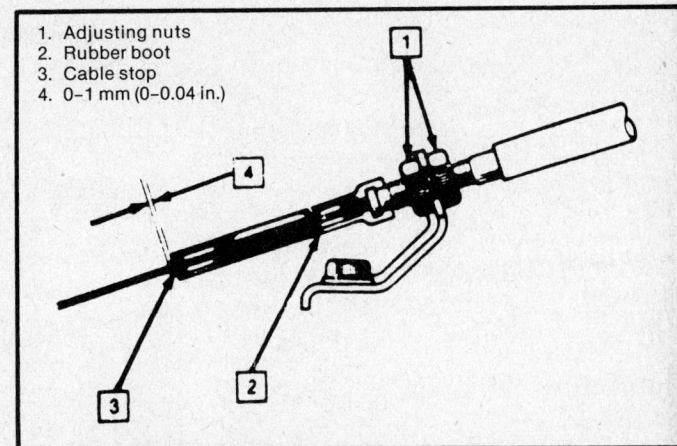

1. Adjusting nuts
2. Rubber boot
3. Cable stop
4. 0–1 mm (0–0.04 in.)

Throttle cable adjustment location

2. Remove the oil pan retaining bolts, tap the oil pan lightly to remove.
3. Remove the oil pan gasket material and clean the surfaces thoroughly.
4. When installing the oil pan, be sure a new gasket is used.
5. Install a new filter or pick-up screen and replace the magnet into the oil cleaner.
6. Install the oil pan and fill the transaxle with the correct type of fluid and to the proper level.

NOTE: The differential unit can be drained and refilled by removing the necessary plugs. Add new oil (ATF Dexron II or its equivilant) until it runs from the fill hole. The capacity is 1.5 U.S. quarts.

Section 23 Automatic Transmissions
NOVA A131L

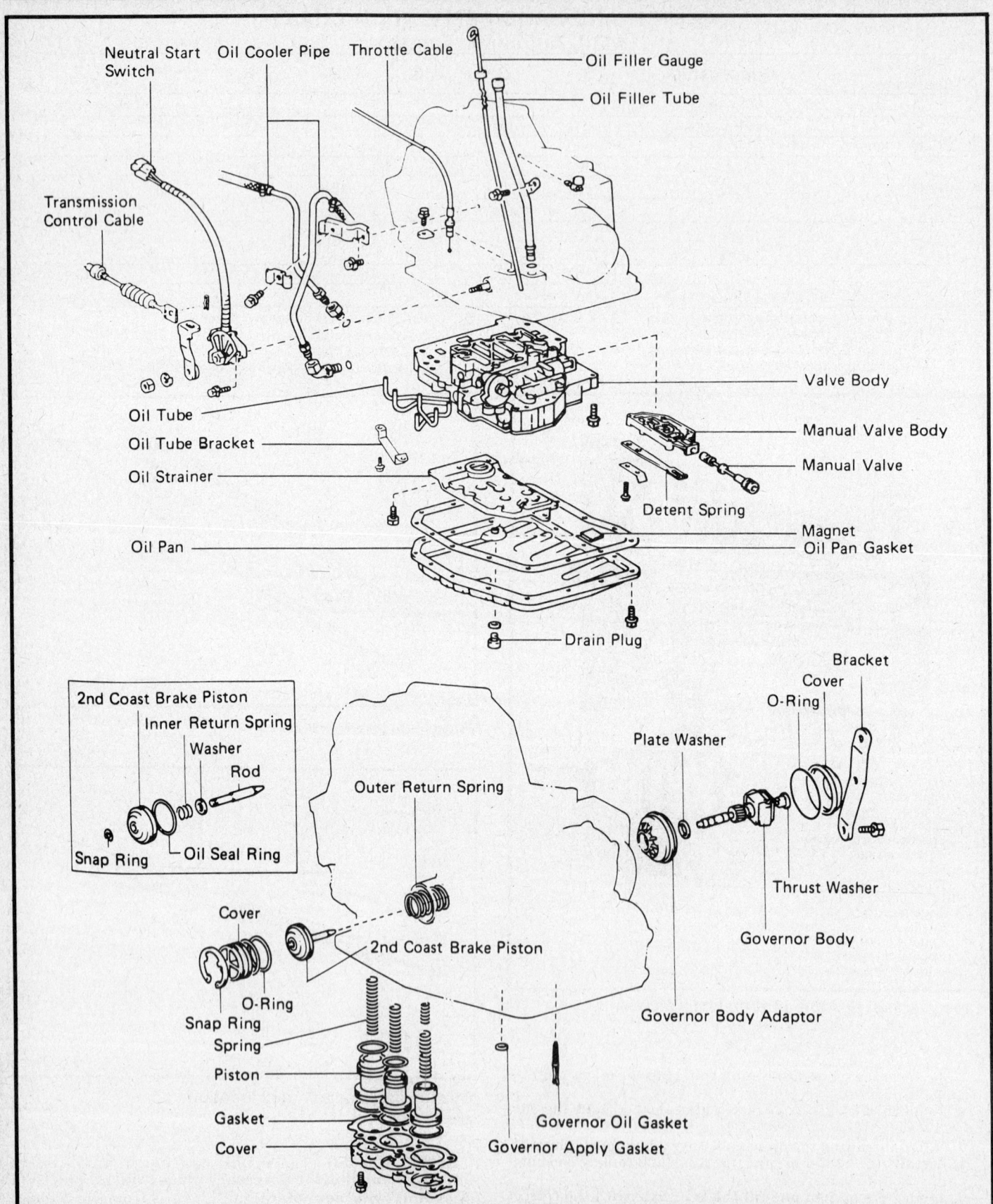

Location of external and internal components that may be serviced with the unit in the vehicle

AUTOMATIC TRANSMISSIONS
NOVA A131L

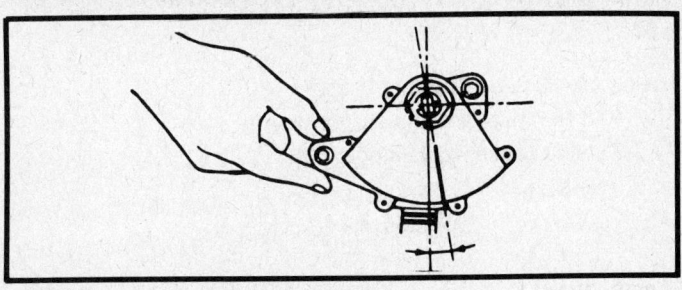

Neutral start switch adjustment

SECOND BRAKE SERVO

Adjustment

NOTE: Special tools are needed to properly determine if the piston stroke is longer than specifications. A procedure follows.

1. With the cover, piston and outer spring removed from the transaxle housing, reinstall the piston without the outer spring.

NOTE: A compressing tool will be needed to remove the cover and snap ring.

2. Install the snap ring back into its groove.
3. Install Kent Moore tool Number J-35679, observe the groove on the plunger of the tool Firmly push on the bottom of the tool, which pushes the brake apply rod into the case. If the groove is visible, the piston rod and stroke is to specifications. 0.059 – 0.118 in. (1.5 – 3.0mm).
4. If the stroke is more than specified, replace the piston rod with a longer one. The available lengths are 2.870 in. (72.9mm) and 2.811 in. (71.4mm).
5. Remeasure the stroke. If it is still more than specified, replace the brake band.
6. Remove the snap ring, install the outer spring and piston and install the cover and snapring.

SECTION 24 BRAKES

INDEX

HYDRAULIC BRAKE COMPONENT SERVICE

General Information	24–3

SERVICING MASTER CYLINDER
Conventional Tandem Cylinder	24–4
Quick Take-Up Cylinder	24–4
Master Cylinder Push Rod	24–6

SERVICING DISC BRAKE CALIPERS
Single Bore	24–7
Four Bore	24–8
Sliding or Floating Caliper	24–9
Fixed Caliper	24–9

WHEEL CYLINDERS
Overhaul	24–10

HYDRAULIC CONTROL VALVES
Pressure Differential Valve	24–11
Metering Valve	24–11
Proportioning Valve	24–11
Combination Valve	24–11

BLEEDING BRAKES
Bleeding Sequence Chart	24–12
Manual Bleeding	24–12
Pressure Bleeding	24–12
Flushing System	24–15
Bench Bleeding Master Cylinder	24–15
Quick Take-Up System Bleeding	24–15

FRONT DISC BRAKES

Application Chart & Specifications	24–13
Trouble Diagnosis	24–21
Rotors	24–19
Caliper & Pad	24–20

Type 1 – Kelsey Hayes or Bendix (Single Piston)
Pad Removal and Installation	24–22

Type 2 – Delco Floating Caliper (Single Piston)
Pad Removal and Installation	24–22

Type 3 – Kelsey Hayes Chrylser (Sliding Caliper)
Pad Removal and Installation	24–22

Type 4 – Chevette and T-1000 Disc Brakes
Pad Removal and Installation	24–23

Type 5 – Ford Front Drive Disc Brake
Pad Removal and Installation	24–23

Type 6 – Kelsey Hays (Floating Caliper)
Pad Removal and Installation	24–24

Type 7 – ATE Floating Caliper
Pad Removal and Installation	24–24

Type 8 – Ford Floating Caliper
Pad Removal and Installation	24–24

REAR DISC BRAKES

Type 9 – Delco Fixed Caliper (Four Piston)
Pad Removal and Installation	24–32

Type 10 – GM Rear Disc Brake
Pad Removal and Installation	24–32
Caliper Parking Brake Mechanism	24–34

Type 11 – GM Delco Floating Caliper
Pad Removal and Installation	24–34

Type 12 – Girlock Floating Caliper
Pad Removal and Installation	2–435
Parking Brake Adjustment	24–36

DRUM BRAKES

Specifications	24–36
Trouble Diagnosis	24–39
Applications	24–40
Brake Drums – Resurfacing	24–36

DUO-SERVO BRAKE
Adjustment	24–40
Testing Adjuster	24–40
Brake Shoes Removal and Installation	24–41

FORD NON-SERVO BRAKE
Adjustment	24–42
Brake Shoes Removal and Installation	24–44

CHRYSLER NON-SERVO BRAKE
Adjustment	24–44
Brakes Shoes Removal and Installation	24–44

POWER BRAKES

VACUUM OPERATED BOOSTER
Trouble Diagnosis	24–45
Service	24–47

VACUUM PUMP (GM)
Removal and Installation	24–47
Controller Removal and Installation	24–47
Piston Assembly Removal and Installation	24–48

HYDRO-BOOST, HYDRO-BOOST II (FORD)
System Checks	24–48
Trouble Diagnosis	24–50
Bleeding System	24–49
Overhaul	24–51
Spool Valve Removal and Installation	24–53
Tandem Diaphragm Brake Booster Overhaul	24–53

POWER MASTER POWER BRAKE UNIT
Description	24–15
Depressurizing System	24–15
Brake Unit R&R	24–16
Electro Hydraulic Pump R&R	24–17
Pressure Switch R&R	24–17
Accumulator Switch R&R	24–17
Power Unit Overhaul	24–17
Power Master Trouble Diagnosis	24–18

ANTI-LOCK BRAKE SYSTEMS

FORD MOTOR COMPANY
Description	24–26
System Service	24–28

GENERAL MOTORS CORPORATION
Description	24–53
System Service	24–55

Brakes

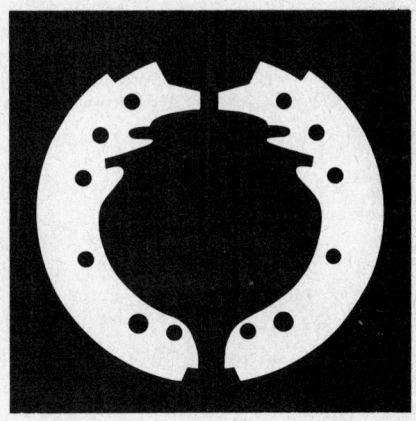

HYDRAULIC BRAKE SERVICE

Federal law requires cars to be equipped with two separate brake systems, so that if one system should fail, the other will provide enough braking power to safely stop the car. The standard approach has been to use a tandem master cylinder and separate hydraulic circuits for the front and rear brakes, or a diagonally split system separating opposite front and rear wheels. A tandem master cylinder actually uses two piston-and-seal assemblies in-line in a single bore. The dual system includes a red warning lamp on the instrument panel and, to activate it, a "Pressure Differential" valve which is connected to both sides of the system. The valve is sensitive to any loss of hydraulic pressure which results from a braking failure on either side of the system and alerts the driver by switching on the lamp. The lamp is connected to the ignition switch. With the switch in "start" position, the lamp is lit, furnishing a bulb check, but in "running" position, it will light only if a brake failure occurs. Although usual stops occur at moderate hydraulic pressures, during a "panic stop" the master cylinder develops pressure higher than 800 psi (pounds per square inch). Caliper disc brakes, being nonenergized, require more applying force than comparable energized-shoe/drum brakes. Caliper pistons, comparatively, are quite large and generally a higher pressure range is provided by power braking. Front disc-rear

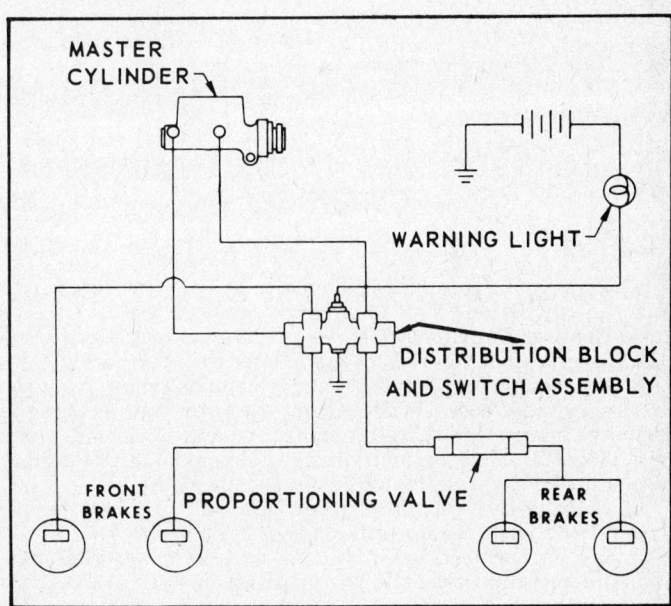

Brake system schematic

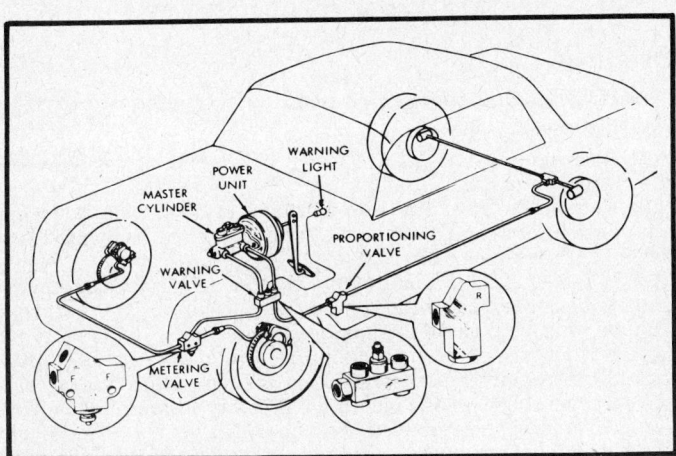

Typical dual system disc brake

drum brake vehicles are provided with pressure regulating units. Pressure-regulating units refine the braking balance, by changing the ratio of front-to-rear pressure, regulating it for moderate or severe stops as required to lessen skidding and diving. The "pressure metering" valve inhibits pressure to front disc brakes during easy, rolling stops. The "proportioning" valve reduces pressure to rear drum brakes in severe stops. One or both types of valves are found in various systems.

NOTE: All brake valving should be considered as nonrepairable. Replacement should be an exact duplicate of the unit that was designed for the car.

The dual master cylinder has two pistons, located one behind the other. The primary piston is actuated directly by mechanical linkage from the brake pedal. The secondary piston is actuated by fluid trapped between the two pistons. If a leak develops in front of the secondary piston, it moves forward until it

SECTION 24 BRAKES
HYDRAULIC BRAKES COMPONENT SERVICE

light switch incorporated in the master cylinder body. The piston is accessible by removing the large plug at the front of the master cylinder body. Only remove the plug when overhauling the cylinder, as brake fluid will escape.

Overhaul procedures on these new type master cylinders are basically the same as those on conventional master cylinder. bottoms against the front of the master cylinder. The fluid trapped between the pistons will operate one side of the split system. If the other side of the system develops a leak, the primary piston will move forward until direct contact with the secondary piston takes place, and it will force the secondary piston to actuate the other side of the split system. In either case the brake pedal drops closer to the floor board and less braking power is available.

HYDRAULIC BRAKE ACTUATING SYSTEM

Master Cylinders

The master cylinder unit is a highly calibrated unit specifically designed for the car it is on. Although the cylinders may look alike there are many differences in calibration. If replacement is necessary, make sure the replacement unit is the one specified for the car.

Some 1983 and later G.M. cars are equipped with "Quick Take-Up" master cylinders which provide a large volume of fluid to the wheel brakes at low pressure when the brake pedal is initially applied. This large volume of fluid is needed because of the new self retracting piston seals at the front disc brake calipers which pull the pistons into the calipers after the brakes are released, thereby preventing the brake pads from causing a drag on the rotors.

The master cylinder used on G.M. "X", "A" and "J" body front wheel drive cars has a hydraulically operated brake warning

CONVENTIONAL TANDEM MASTER CYLINDER

Overhaul

1. Remove the secondary piston stop bolt from the bottom or inside the reservoir if so equipped.
2. Depress the primary piston and remove snap ring from retaining groove at the rear of the master cylinder bore.
3. Remove push rod and primary piston assembly from the master cylinder bore. Do not remove the screw that secures the primary return spring retainer, return spring, primary cup and protector on the primary piston. This assembly is factory pre-adjusted and should not be disassembled.
4. Remove the secondary piston assembly. Do not remove the outlet tube seats from the master cylinder body.
5. Inspect the parts for chipping, excessive wear or damage. When using a master cylinder repair kit, install all the parts supplied.
6. Be sure that all recesses, openings and internal passages are open and clean.
7. Inspect the master cylinder bore for signs of etching, pitting, scoring or rust. If necessary to hone the master cylinder bore to repair damage, do not exceed allowable home specifications, .003 thousands.
8. To assemble: dip all parts except the master cylinder body in clean brake fluid.
9. Carefully insert the complete secondary piston and return spring assembly in the master cylinder bore.
10. Install the primary piston assembly in the master cylinder bore.
11. Depress the primary piston and install the snap ring in the cylinder bore groove.
12. Install the push rod, boot and retainer on the push rod, if so equipped. Install the push rod assembly into the primary piston. Make sure the retainer is properly seated and holding the push rod securely.
13. Position the inner end of the push rod boot (if so equipped) in the master cylinder body retaining groove.

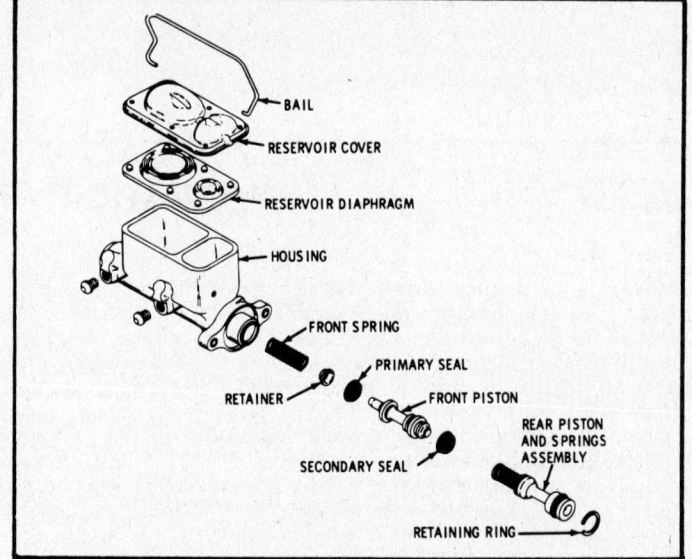

General Motors diesel engine type master cylinder

14. Install the secondary piston stop bolt, if used, with an O-ring if screw is on bottom outside of master cylinder casting. Pre-bleed the master cylinder before reinstalling in the car.
15. Install the cover and gasket on the master cylinder and secure the cover into position with the retainer.

QUICK TAKE UP & DIAGONAL SPLIT MASTER CYLINDER

Overhaul

NOTE: Plastic reservoirs need to be removed only for the following reasons.

1. Reservoir is damaged or the rubber grommet(s) between the reservoir and bore is leaking.
2. Removal of stop pin from Chrysler style plastic reservoir master cylinder to allow removal of pistons. Pin is located underneath front reservoir nipple.
3. If the G.M. quick take-up valve is defective, the entire master cylinder body must be replaced. The plastic reservoir may be reused on the new master cylinder body. The reservoir should be removed by first clamping the cylinder flange in a vise. Next remove the reservoir for the Chrysler style. Grasp the reservoir base on one end and pull away from the body. GM reservoirs must be removed by prying between the reservoir and casting with a pry bar. Grommets can be reused if they are in good condition. Whether or not the reservoir is removed, it and the cover or caps should be thoroughly cleaned.

BRAKES
HYDRAULIC BRAKES COMPONENT SERVICE
SECTION 24

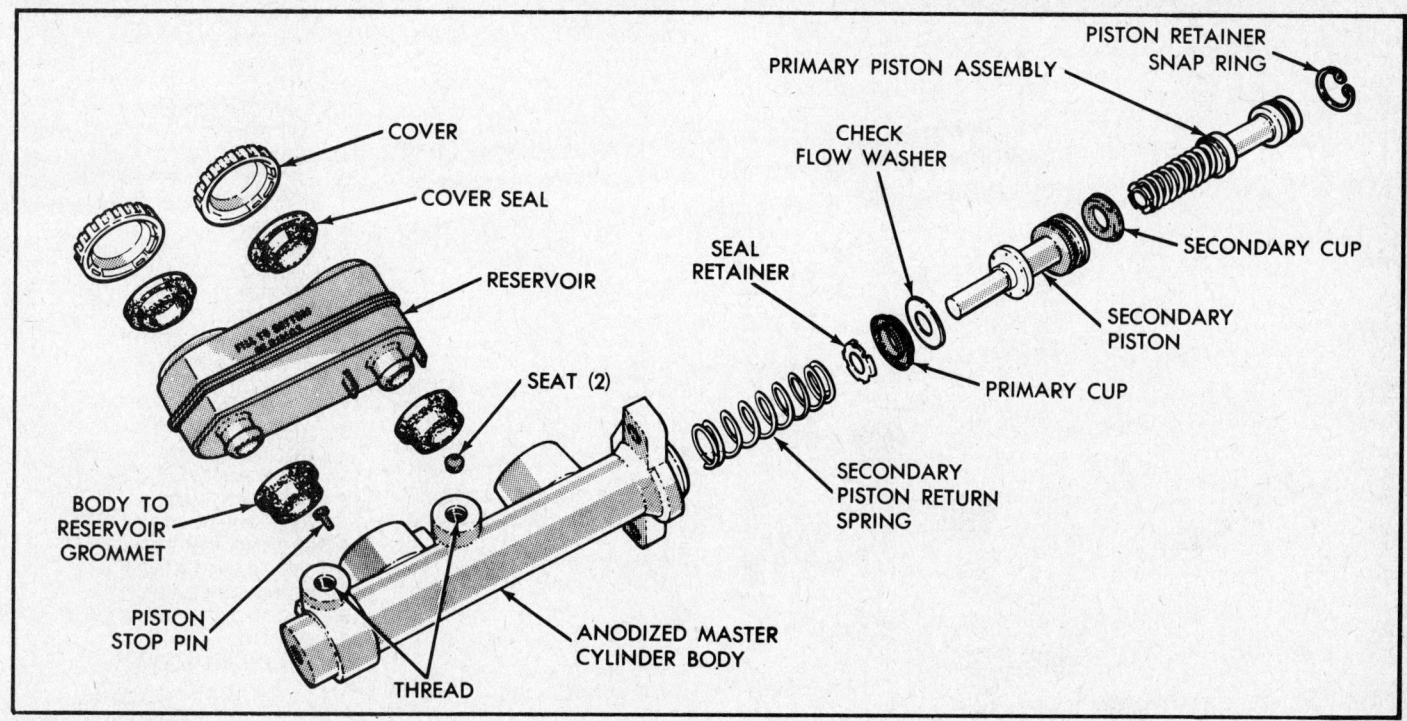

Chrysler Aluminum master cylinder—Exploded view

4. Remove the cylinder from the car and drain the brake fluid.
5. Mount the cylinder in a vise so that the outlets are up and remove the seal from the hub.
6. Remove the stop pin or screw from the bottom of the front reservoir, if present.
7. Remove the snap-ring from the front of the bore and remove the primary piston assembly.
8. Remove the secondary piston assembly using compressed air or a piece of wire.
9. Clan metal parts in brake fluid and discard rubber parts. Inspect the bore for damage or wear, and check pistons for damage and proper clearance in the bore. Aluminum cylinder bores cannot be honed. The cylinder must be replaced if the bore is scored.
10. If the bore is only slightly scored or pitted it may be honed. Always use hones that are in good condition and completely clean the cylinder with brake fluid when honing is completed. If any sign of wear or corrosion is apparent on "Quick Take-Up" master cylinder bores, the master cylinder must be replaced; it cannot be honed. If any evidence of contamination exists in the master cylinder the entire hydraulic system should be flushed and refilled with clean brake fluid. Blow out passages with compressed air.
11. Install new secondary seals in the two grooves in the flat end of the front piston. The lips of the seals will be facing away from each other.
12. Install a new primary seal and the seal protector on opposite end of the front piston with the lips of the seal facing outward.
13. Coat the seals with brake fluid. Install the spring on the front piston with the spring retainer in the primary seal.
14. Insert the piston assembly, spring end first, into the bore and use a wooden rod to seat it.
15. Coat the rear piston seals with brake fluid and install them into the piston grooves with the lips facing the spring end.
16. Assemble the spring onto the piston and install the as-

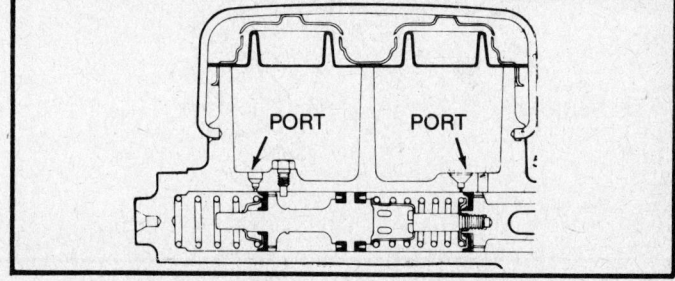

Feed and return ports

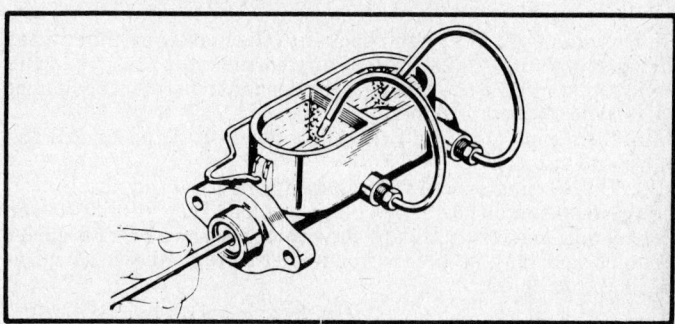

Pre-bleeding master cylinder

sembly into the bore spring first. Install the snapring.
17. Hold the piston at the bottom of the bore and install the stop screw.
18. On G.M. models with the hydraulic brake warning light switch, (Quick Take-Up Units) remove the allen head plug and remove the switch assembly with needle nose pliers. Remove the O-rings and retainers from the piston. Install new O-rings

24-5

SECTION 24
BRAKES
HYDRAULIC BRAKES COMPONENT SERVICE

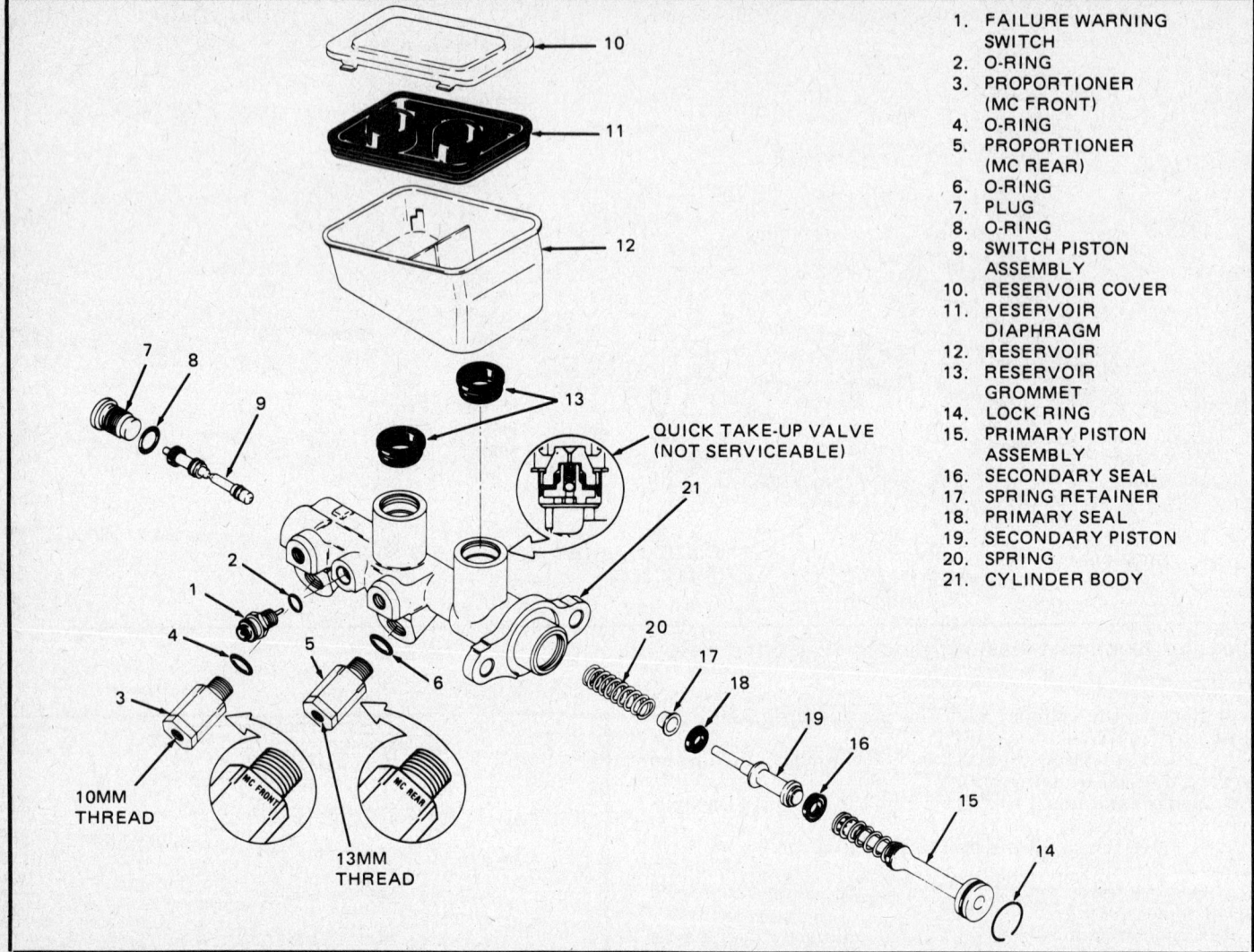

1. FAILURE WARNING SWITCH
2. O-RING
3. PROPORTIONER (MC FRONT)
4. O-RING
5. PROPORTIONER (MC REAR)
6. O-RING
7. PLUG
8. O-RING
9. SWITCH PISTON ASSEMBLY
10. RESERVOIR COVER
11. RESERVOIR DIAPHRAGM
12. RESERVOIR
13. RESERVOIR GROMMET
14. LOCK RING
15. PRIMARY PISTON ASSEMBLY
16. SECONDARY SEAL
17. SPRING RETAINER
18. PRIMARY SEAL
19. SECONDARY PISTON
20. SPRING
21. CYLINDER BODY

Typical diagonal split master cylinder

and retainers, fit the piston back into the master cylinder after lubricating with brake fluid. If any corrosion is present in the switch piston bore the master cylinder must be replaced; do not attempt to hone the bore.

19. Fit a new O-ring on the allen head plug and install the plug and tighten.

20. On all master cylinder, install a new seal in the hub, if equipped, then either bench bleed or bleed the cylinder on the car. Some master cylinders have bleed screws on the outlet flanges and may be bled without disturbing the wheel cylinders and calipers.

MASTER CYLINDER PUSH ROD

Adjustable

After assembly of the master cylinder to the power section or firewall, the piston cup in the hydraulic cylinder should just clear the compensating port hole when the brake pedal is fully released. If the push rod is too long, it will hold the piston over the port.

A push rod that is too short, will give too much loose travel (excessive pedal play). Apply the brakes and release the pedal all the way observing the brake fluid flow back into the master cylinder.

A full flow indicates the piston is coming back far enough to release the fluid. A slow return of the fluid indicates the piston is not coming back far enough to clear the ports. The push rod adjustment is too tight, and should be adjusted.

Non Adjustable

When installing a non-adjustable type push rod, make sure that the push rod is fully seated in the master cylinder.

Disc Brake Calipers

Caliper disc brakes can be dived into three types: the four-piston, fixed-caliper type; the single-piston, floating-caliper type, and the single-piston sliding-caliper type. Refer to the Brake Specifications Chart for applications.

In the four piston type (two in each side of the caliper) braking effect is achieved by hydraulically pushing both shoes against the disc sides. With the single piston floating-caliper type, the inboard shoe is pushed hydraulically into contact with the disc, while the reaction force thus generated is used to

BRAKES
HYDRAULIC BRAKES COMPONENT SERVICE
SECTION 24

pull the outboard shoe into frictional contact (made possible by letting the caliper move slightly along the axle centerline).

In the sliding caliper (single piston) type, the caliper assembly slides along the machined surfaces of the anchor plate. A steel key located between the machined surfaces of the caliper and the machined surfaces of the anchor plate is held in place with either a retaining screw or two cotter pins. The caliper is held in place against the anchor plate with one or two support springs.

SINGLE BORE

Overhaul

1. Raise the vehicle and safely support it. Remove the front wheels.
2. Working on one side at a time only, disconnect the hydraulic inlet line from the caliper and plug the end. Remove the caliper mounting bolts or pins, and shims (if used) and slide the caliper off the disc.
3. Remove the disc pads from the caliper or mounting adapter. If the old ones are to be reused, mark them so that they can be reinstalled in their original positions.
4. Open the caliper bleed screw and drain the fluid. Clean the outside of the caliper and mount it in a vise with padded jaws.

NOTE: When cleaning any brake components, use only brake fluid or denatured (Isopropyl) alcohol. Never use a mineral-based solvent, such as gasoline or paint thinner, since it will swell and quickly deteriorate rubber parts.

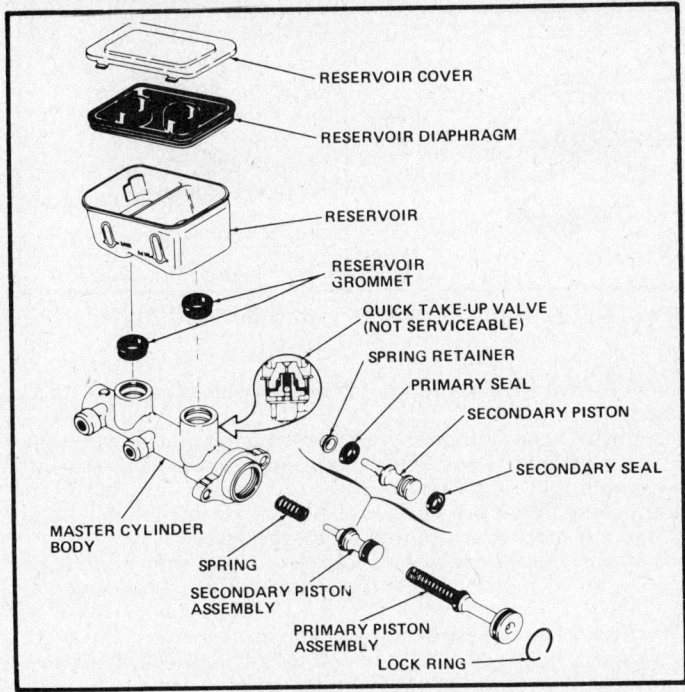

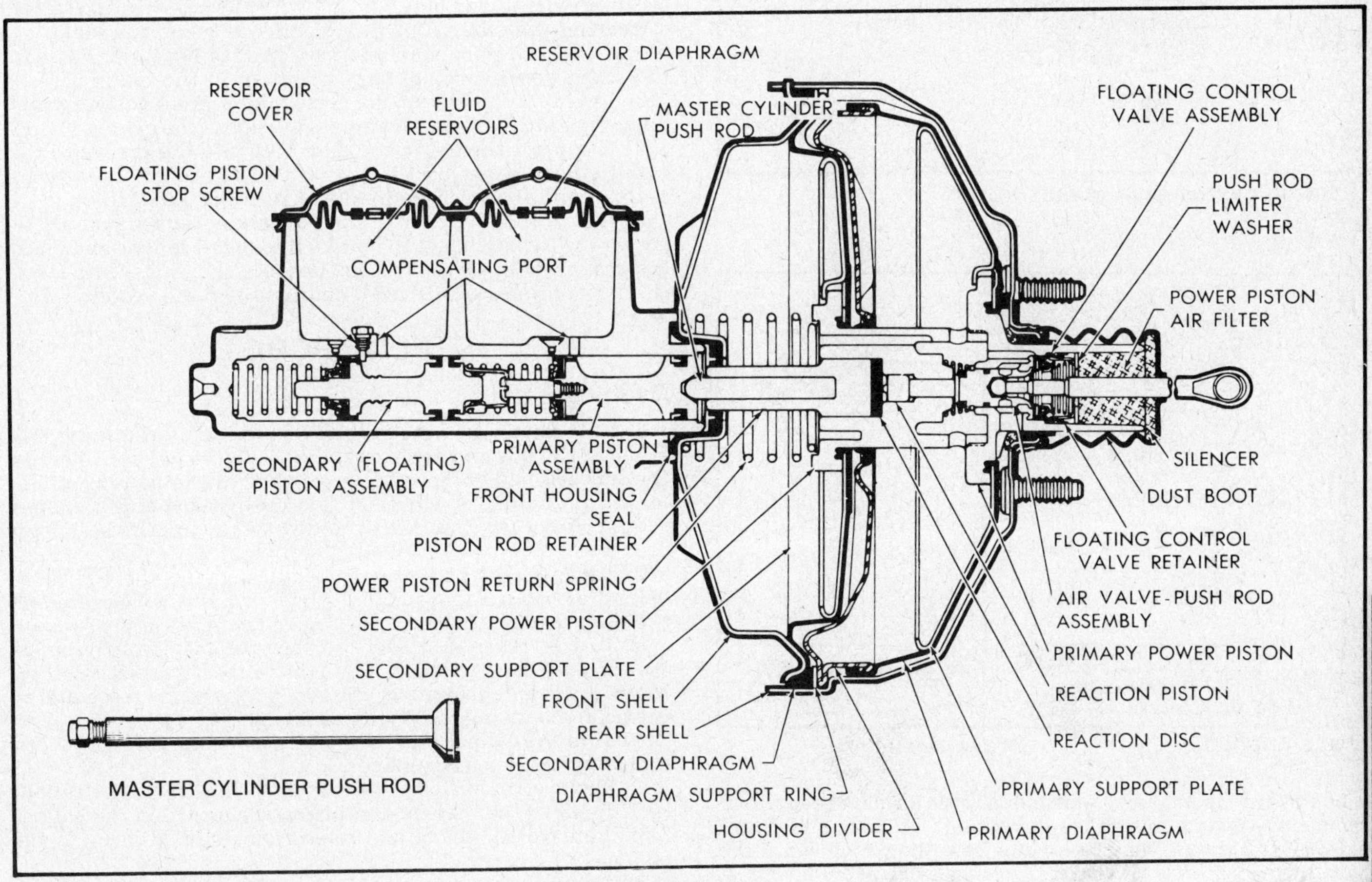

1981 and later General Motors Quick Take-Up master cylinder (not used on diesel engines)

Typical Power brake booster and master cylinder installation

24-7

SECTION 24 Brakes
HYDRAULIC BRAKES COMPONENT SERVICE

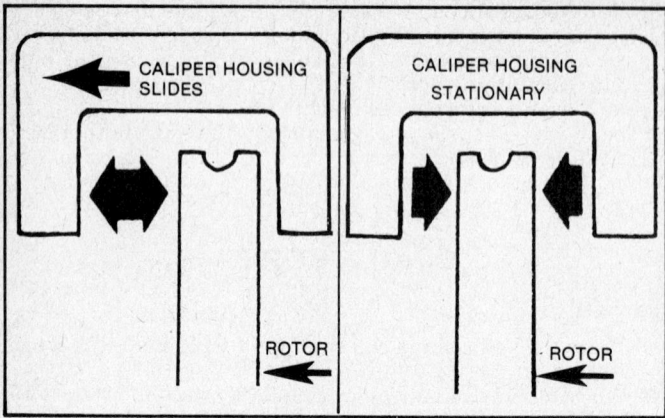

Floating (or sliding) caliper type   Fixed caliper type

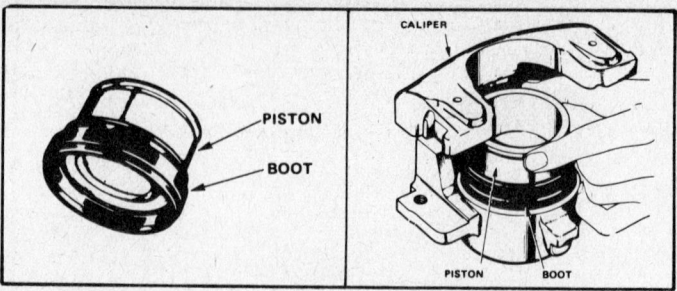

Assembling boot on piston   Installing piston

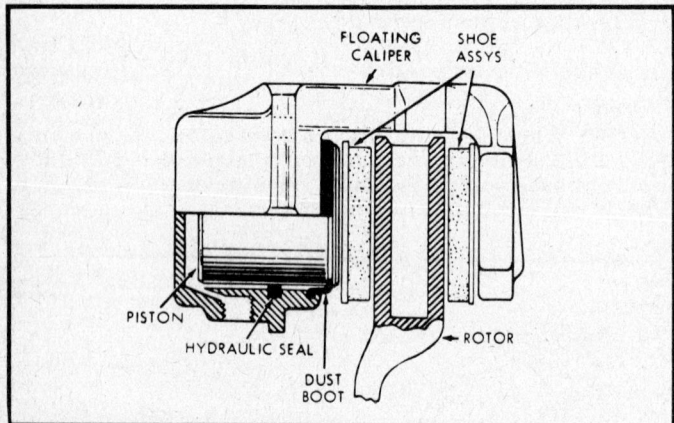

Floating caliper disc brake

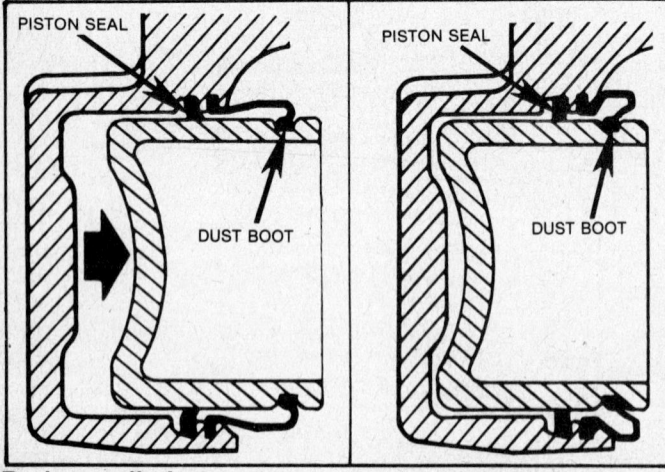

Brake applied   Brake released

5. Pry the lip on (each) piston dust boot from its groove and remove the piston assemblies and spring from the bore. If necessary, air pressure may be used to force the piston out of the bore, using care to prevent the piston from popping out of control.

6. Remove the boot and seal from the piston and clean the piston in brake fluid. Blow out the caliper passages with an air hose.

7. Inspect the cylinder bore for scoring, pitting, or corrosion. Corrosion is a pitted or rough condition not to be confused with staining. Light rough spots may be removed by rotating crocus cloth, using finger pressure, in the bores. Do not polish with an in and out motion or use any other abrasive.

8. If the pistons are pitted, scored, or worn, they must be replaced. A corroded or deeply scored caliper should also be replaced.

9. Check the clearance of the piston in the bores using a feeler gauge. Clearance should be 0.002 to 0.006 inch. If there is excessive clearance the caliper must be replaced.

10. Replace all rubber parts and lubricate with brake fluid. Install the seals (or square cut rings) and boots in the grooves in each piston. The seal should be installed in the groove closest to the closed end of the piston with the seal lips facing the closed end. The lip on the boot should be facing the seal.

11. Lubricate the piston and bore with brake fluid. Position the piston return spring, large coil first, in the piston bore.

12. Install the piston in the bore, taking great care to avoid damaging the seal lip as it passes the edge of the cylinder bore.

13. Compress the lip on the dust boot into the groove in the caliper. Be sure the boot is fully seated in the groove, as poor sealing will allow contaminants to ruin the bore.

14. Install the disc pads in the caliper and remount the caliper on the hub. Connect the brake line to the caliper and bleed the brakes. Replace the wheels. Recheck the brake fluid level, check the brake pedal travel, and road test the vehicle.

FOUR BORE

Overhaul

1. Pull cotter pin from end of shoe assembly retaining pin. Remove the pin and shoe assembly from the caliper. Identify the inboard and outboard shoes if they are to be reused. Remove the end of brake hose at bracket by removing U-shaped retainer from the hose fitting and withdrawing the hose from bracket.

2. Separate the caliper halves by removing the two large bolts. Remove the two small O-rings from the cavities around the fluid transfer holes in the two ends of the caliper halves.

3. To free the piston boots so that the pistons may be removed, push the piston down into the caliper as far as it will go. Insert a suitable tool under the inner edge of the steel ring in the boot, and using the piston as a fulcrum, pry the boot from its seat in the caliper half. Use care not to puncture seal when removing pistons from caliper.

4. Remove the pistons and piston springs from the caliper half. Remove the pistons and piston springs from the caliper half. Remove the boots and seals from their grooves in the piston.

NOTE: Always use clean brake fluid to clean caliper parts. Never use mineral-base cleaning solvents such as

BRAKES
HYDRAULIC BRAKES COMPONENT SERVICE
SECTION 24

gasoline, kerosene, carbon-tetrachloride, acetone, paint thinner or units of like nature as these solvents deteriorate rubber parts, causing them to become soft and swollen in an extremely short time.

5. To install, clean all metal parts using clean brake fluid. Remove all traces of dirt and grease. After cleaning, wipe all fluid from boot counter bore in caliper and from boot groove in piston. These surfaces must be clean and dry at assembly to permit RTV to properly adhere.

6. Using an air hose, blow out all fluid passages in the caliper halves, making sure that there is no dirt or foreign material blocking any of these passages.

7. Discard all rubber parts. Boots, seals, and O-rings should be replaced with new service kit parts.

8. Carefully inspect the piston bores in the caliper halves. They must be frees of scores and pits. A scored or otherwise damaged bore will cause leaks and unsatisfactory brake operation. The bore surface should be restored by polishing with a very fine crocus cloth. If the bore surface cannot be restored using a very fine crocus cloth, it may be lightly honed. Replace the caliper half if either bore is damaged to the extent that light honing will not restore it.

9. Check the fit of the piston in the bore using a feeler gauge. Clearance should be, 0.0045 to 0.010 inch for the 1⅛ inch bore and 0.0035 to .009 inch for the 1⅜ inch bore. If the bore is not damaged, and the clearance exceeds either of the upper limits, a new piston that does meet the clearance specified will be required.

10. Assemble the seal in the groove in the piston which is closest to the flat end of the piston. The lip on the seal must face toward the large end of the piston.

11. Install the piston assembly in the bore using Piston Ring Compressor Tool J-22629 or J-22639 or equivalent. Use care not to damage the seal lip as piston is pressed past the edge of the bore.

12. The boot groove on the piston is the groove closest to the concave end of the piston. Insert a bead of silastic sealant GM1052366 or equivalent into the boot groove in the piston and assemble the boot in the groove. The fold in the boot must face toward the end of the piston with the seal on it.

13. Depress the pistons and check that they slide smoothly into the bore until the end of the piston is flush with the end of the bore. If not, recheck piston assembly and location of the piston spring and the seal.

14. Position Boot Seal Installer Tool J-22628 or J-22638 or equivalent over the piston and seat the steel boot retaining ring evenly in the counterbore as shown. The boot retaining ring must be flush or below the machined face of the caliper. Any distortion of uneven seating could allow contaminating and corrosive elements to enter the bore.

15. Depress pistons and while holding in a depressed position place a bead of silastic sealant GM1052366 or equivalent on outer diameter of the boot retaining ring forming a seal between the boot retainer ring and the housing.

16. Position the O-rings in the small cavities around the brake fluid transfer hole in both ends of the outboard caliper halves. Lubricate the hex head bolts with Delco Brake Lube (or equivalent) or dip in clean brake fluid. Fit caliper halves together and secure with bolts.

17. Carefully mount the assembled caliper over the edge of the disc. Use two screwdrivers to depress pistons so that the caliper can be lowered into position on the disc. Use care to prevent damage to boots on the edge of the disc as the caliper is mounted.

18. Secure the caliper to the mounting bracket with two hex head bolts. Refer to torque specifications in rear of manual for correct torque values. If replacing old shoe assemblies, be sure to install the shoes in the same position from which they were removed.

19. Install the shoe and lining assemblies as outlined in this section.

20. Place a new copper gasket on the male end of the front wheel brake hose. Install brake hose in the calipers. With the wheels straight ahead, pass the female end of the brake hose through the support bracket.

21. Make sure the tube seat is clean and connect the brake line tube nut to the caliper. Tighten securely.

22. Allowing the hose to seek a normal position without twist, insert hex of the hose fitting into the hole in the support bracket and secure it in place with the U-shaped retainer (maximum allowed twist is ±1 notch). Turn the steering geometry from lock to lock while observing the hose. Check that the hose does not touch other parts at any time during suspension or geometry travel. If contact does occur, remove the U-shaped retainer and rotate the end of the hose in the support bracket in a direction which will eliminate hose contact. Reinstall the retainer and recheck for hose contact. If it is satisfactory, place the steel tube connector in the hose fitting and tighten securely.

23. If rear brake caliper is being serviced, connect brake line to caliper.

24. Bleed brakes as outlined in this section.

25. Install wheels and lower vehicle. Do not move car until a firm pedal is obtained.

SLIDING OR FLOATING CALIPER, FROZEN CALIPER PISTON

Hydraulic Removal

1. Remove the caliper assembly from the rotor.
2. Remove brake pads and dust seal. With brake flexible line connected and bleed screw closed apply enough pedal pressure to move the piston most of the way out of the bore (brake fluid will begin to ooze past the piston inner seal).

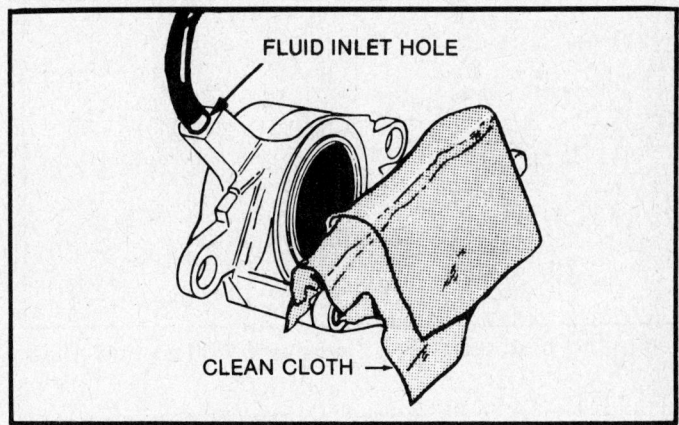

Removing piston hydraulically

Pneumatic Removal

1. Remove the caliper from the car.
2. With the bleed screw closed apply air pressure to force the piston out. Hydraulic and pneumatic methods of piston removal should be done carefully to prevent personal injury or piston damage.

FIXED CALIPER, FROZEN CALIPER PISTONS

NOTE: The hydraulic or pneumatic methods which apply to the single piston type caliper will not work on the multiple piston type brake caliper.

SECTION 24 Brakes
HYDRAULIC BRAKES COMPONENT SERVICE

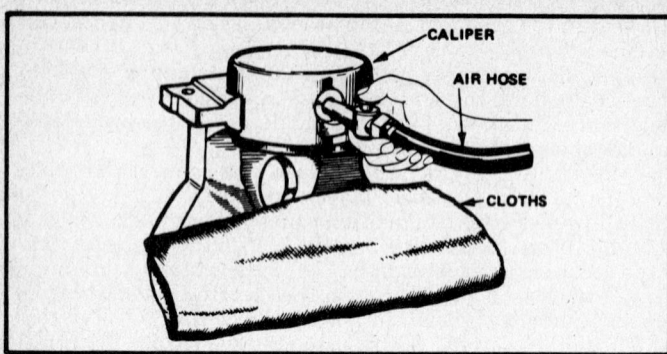
Removing piston pneumatically

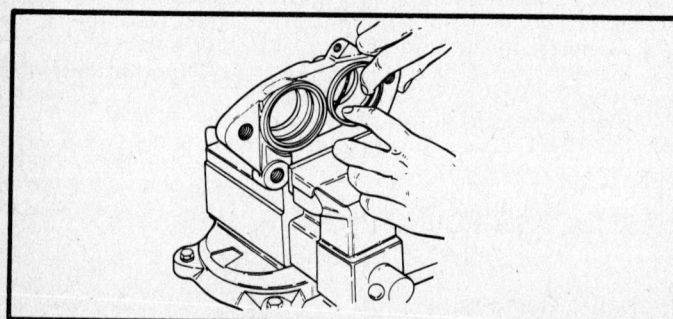
Installing fixed position rectangular ring seal (seal lip toward pressure slide)

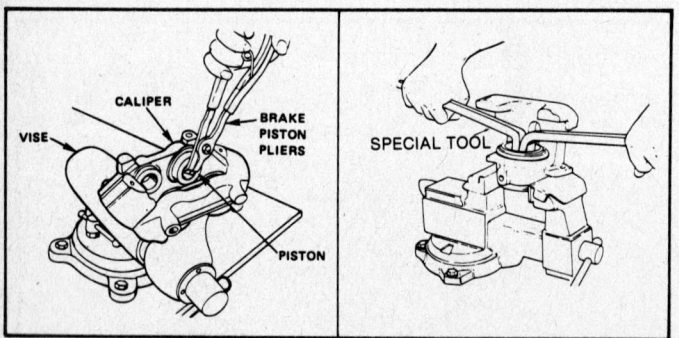
Removing pistons   Removing hollow and piston

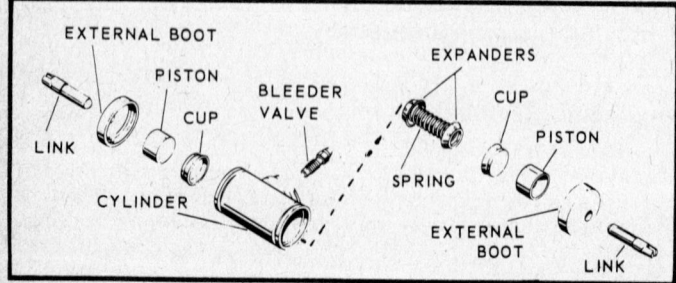
Wheel cylinder components

1. Remove the caliper from the car with the two halves separated.
2. Mount in a vise and use a piston puller (many types available) to remove the pistons.

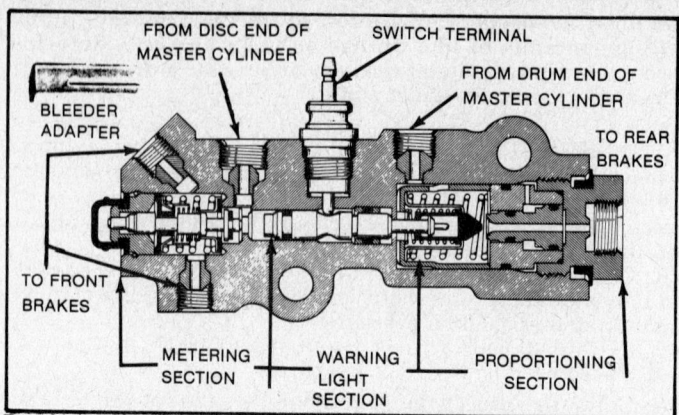
Push valve in when pressure bleeding — not necessary when using pedal bleed method

CALIPER CLEANING AND HONING

Castings may be cleaned with any type cleaning fluid after all rubber seals have been removed. It is important that all traces of cleaning fluid be completely removed from the caliper casting. Rubber components are compatible with alcohol and/or brake fluid.

Use a lint free wiping cloth to clean the caliper and parts. Black stains on pistons or walls, caused by the seals, will not do harm; however, extreme cleanliness is essential. Blow out passages with compressed air. A fine grade of crocus cloth may be used to correct minor imperfections in the cylinder bore. Slide crocus cloth with finger pressure in a circular rather than a lengthwise motion. Do not use any form of abrasive on a plated piston. Discard a piston which is pitted or has signs of plating wear.

If a fine stone honing of a caliper bore is necessary it should be done with skill and caution. Some cars can develop 800 psi. hydraulic pressure on severe application so the honing must never exceed .003 in. Also the dust seal groove must be free of rush or nicks so that a perfect mating surface is possible on piston and casting.

Wheel Cylinder

Overhaul

1. Raise the car and support it safely. Remove the wheel and drum from the side to be serviced.
2. Remove the brake shoes and clean the backing plate and wheel cylinder. Rebuilding can be done on the car, depending on the design of the brake backing plate. If the backing plate is recessed to the point that it is impossible to get a hone into the cylinder, the cylinder has to be removed.
3. To remove the cylinder: disconnect the brake line from the rear of the cylinder, remove the mounting bolts or retainers and remove the cylinder.

NOTE: On some models, in order to remove the rear wheel cylinders you must remove the wheel cylinder retainer. Insert two awls into the access slots and bend both tabs at the same time thereby releasing the cylinder. You must use a new retainer when reinstalling the wheel cylinder. The new retainer can be driven on using an 1 1/8 inch socket with an extension bar.

4. Remove the rubber boots (dust covers) from the ends of the cylinder. Remove the pistons, piston cups (expanders, if

BRAKES
HYDRAULIC BRAKES COMPONENT SERVICE

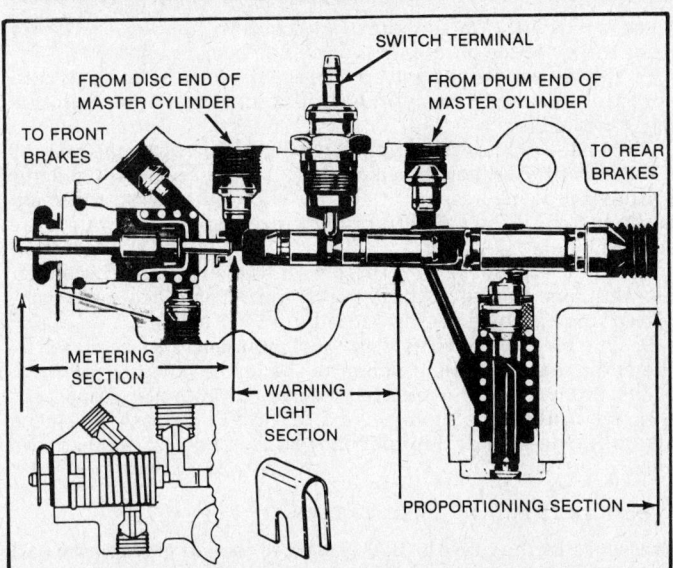

Hold valve out .060 in pressure bleed only—not necessary when using pedal bleed method

equipped) and spring from the inside of the cylinder. Remove the bleeder screw and make sure it is not clogged.

5. Discard all of the parts that the rebuilding kit will replace.

6. Examine the inside of the cylinder. If it is severely rusted, pitted or scratched install a new or rebuilt cylinder.

7. If the condition of the cylinder indicates that it can be rebuilt, hone the bore. Light honing will provide a new surface on the inside of the cylinder which promotes better cup sealing.

8. Wash out the cylinder with brake fluid after honing. Reassemble the cylinder using the new parts provided in the kit. When assembling the cylinder dip all parts in brake fluid.

9. Install the cylinder on the car. Reinstall the brakes, drum and wheel. Bleed the brake system.

Hydraulic Control Valves

PRESSURE DIFFERENTIAL VALVE

The pressure differential valve activates a dash panel warning light if pressure loss in the brake system occurs. If pressure loss occurs in one half of the split system the other system's normal pressure causes the piston in the switch to compress a spring until it touches an electrical contact. This turns the warning lamp on the dash panel to light, thus warning the driver of possible brake failure.

On some cars the spring balance piston automatically recenters as the brake pedal is released warning the driver only upon brake application. On other cars, the light remains on until manually cancelled. Valves may be located separately or as part of a combination valve. On GM front wheel drive cars, the valve and switch are usually incorporated into the master cylinder.

Resetting Valves

On some cars, the valve piston(s) remain off-center after failure until necessary repairs are made. The valve will automatically reset itself (after repairs) when pressure is equal on both sides of the system.

If the light does not go out, bleed the brake system that is opposite the failed system. If front brakes failed, bleed the rear brakes; this should force the light control piston toward center. If this fails, remove the terminal switch. If brake fluid is present in the electrical area, the seals are gone, replace the complete valve assembly.

METERING VALVE

The metering valve's function is to improve braking balance between the front disc and rear drum brakes, especially during light brake application. The metering valve prevents application of the front disc brakes until the rear brakes overcome the return spring pressure. Thus, when the front disc pads contact the rotor, the rear shoes will contact the brake drum at the same time.

Inspect the metering valve each time the brakes are serviced. A slight amount of moisture inside the boot does not indicate a defective valve, however, fluid leakage indicates a damaged or worn valve. If fluid leakage is present the valve must be replaced.

The metering valve can be checked very simply. With the car stopped, gently apply the brakes. At about an inch of travel a very small change in pedal effort (like a small bump) will be felt if the valve is operating properly. Metering valves are not serviceable, and must be replaced if defective.

PROPORTIONING VALVE

The proportioning (pressure control) valve is used, on some cars, to reduce the hydraulic pressure to the rear wheels to prevent skid during heavy brake application and to provide better brake balance. It is usually mounted in line to the rear wheels.

Whenever the brakes are serviced the valve should be inspected for leakage. Premature rear brake application during light braking can mean a bad proportioning valve. Repair is by replacement of the valve. Make sure the valve port marked "R" is connected toward the rear wheels.

On GM Quick Take-Up master cylinders, the proportioning valve(s) are screwed into the master cylinder. Since these cars have a diagonally split brake system, two valves are required. One rear brake line screws into each valve. The early type valves (GM front wheel drive) were steel and silver colored, an occasional "clunking" noise was encountered on some early models, but does not affect brake efficiency. Replacement valves are now made of aluminum. Never mix an aluminum valve with a steel valve, always use two aluminum valves.

COMBINATION VALVE

The combination valve may perform two or three functions. They are: metering, proportioning and brake failure warning. Variations of the two-way combination valve are: proportioning and brake failure warning or metering and brake failure warning. A three-way combination valve directs the brake fluid to the appropriate wheel, performs necessary valving and contains a brake failure warning. The combination valve is usually mounted under the hood close to the master cylinder, where the brake lines can easily be connected and routed to the front or rear wheels. The combination valve is non-serviceable and must be replaced if malfunctioning.

Brake Bleeding

The hydraulic brake system must be free of air to operate properly. Air can enter the system when hydraulic parts are disconnected for servicing or replacement, or when the fluid level in the master cylinder reservoirs is very low. Air in the system will give the brake pedal a spongy feeling upon application.

The quickest and easiest of the two ways for system bleeding is the pressure method, but special equipment is needed to ex-

SECTION 24 BRAKES
HYDRAULIC BRAKES COMPONENT SERVICE

ternally pressurize the hydraulic system. The other, more commonly used method of brake bleeding is done manually.

Bleeding Sequence

Bleeding may be required at only one or two wheels or at the master cylinder, depending upon what point the system was opened to air. If after bleeding the cylinder/caliper that was rebuilt or replaced and the pedal still has a spongy feeling upon application, it will be necessary to bleed the entire system.

Procedure

1. Master Cylinder: If the cylinder is not equipped with bleeder screws, open the brake line(s) to the wheels slightly while pressure is applied to the brake pedal. Be sure to tighten the line before the brake pedal is released. The procedure for bench bleeding the master cylinder is in the following section.
2. Power Brake Booster: If the unit is equipped with bleeder screws, it should be bled after the master cylinder. The car engine should be off and the brake pedal applied several times to exhaust any vacuum in the booster. If the unit is equipped with two bleeder screws, always bleed the higher located one first.
3. Combination Valve: If equipped with a bleeder screw.
4. Front/Back Split Systems: Start with the wheel farthest away from the master cylinder, usually the right rear wheel. Bleed the other rear wheel then the left front and right front.

NOTE: If you are unsuccessful in bleeding the front wheels, it may be necessary to deactivate the metering valve. This is accomplished by either pushing in, or pulling out a button or stem on the valve. The valve may be held by hand, with a special tool or taped; it should remain deactivated while the front brakes are bled.

5. Diagonally Split System: Start with the right rear then the left front. The left rear then the right front (refer to the following "GM Quick Take-Up Master Cylinder" section.
6. Rear Disc Brakes: If the car is equipped with rear disc brakes and the calipers have two bleeder screws, bleed the inner first then the outer. Do not allow brake fluid to spill on the car's finish, it will remove the paint. Flush the area with water.

Manual Bleeding

1. Clean the bleed screw at each wheel.
2. Start with the wheel farthest from the master cylinder (right rear).
3. Attach a small rubber hose to the bleed screw and place the end in a clear container of brake fluid.
4. Fill the master cylinder with brake fluid. (Check often during bleeding). Have an assistant slowly pump up the brake pedal and hold pressure.
5. Open the bleed screw about one-quarter turn, press the brake pedal to the floor, close the bleed screw and slowly release the pedal. Continue until no more air bubbles are forced from the cylinder on application of the brake pedal.
6. Repeat procedure on remaining wheel cylinders and calipers still working from cylinder/caliper farthest away from the master cylinder.
7. Master cylinders equipped with bleed screws may be bled independently. When bleeding the Bendix-type dual master cylinder it is necessary to solidly cap one reservoir section while bleeding the other to prevent pressure loss through the cap vent hole.
8. The disc should be rotated to make sure that the piston has returned to the unapplied position when bleeding is completed and the bleed screw closed.
9. The bleeder valve at the wheel cylinder must be closed at the end of each stroke, and before the brake pedal is released, to insure that no air can enter the system. It is also important that the brake pedal be returned to the full up position so the piston in the master cylinder moves back enough to clear the bypass outlets.

Pressure Bleeding Disc Brakes

Pressure bleeding disc brakes will close the metering valve and the front brakes will not bleed. For this reason it is necessary to manually hold the metering valve open during pressure bleeding. Never use a block or clamp to hold the valve open, and never force the valve stem beyond its normal position. Two different types of valves are used. The most common type requires the valve stem to be held in while bleeding the brakes, while the second type requires the valve stem to be held out (0.060 inch minimum travel). Determine the type of visual inspection.

Special adapters are required when pressure bleeding cylinders with plastic reservoirs. Pressure bleeding equipment should be diaphragm type; placing a diaphragm between the pressurized air supply and the brake fluid. This prevents moisture and other contaminants from entering the hydraulic system.

Front disc/rear drum equipped vehicles use a metering valve which closes off pressure to the front brakes under certain conditions. These systems contain manual release actuators which must be engaged to pressure bleed the front brakes.

1. Connect the tank hydraulic hose and adapter to the master cylinder.
2. Close hydraulic valve on the bleeder equipment.
3. Apply air pressure to the bleeder equipment. Follow equipment manufacturer's recommendations for correct air pressure.
4. Open the valve to bleed air out of the pressure hose to the master cylinder. Never bleed this system using the secondary piston stopscrew on the bottom of many master cylinders.
5. Open the hydraulic valve and bleed each wheel cylinder and caliper. Bleed rear brake system first when bleeding both front and rear systems.

BRAKES BLEEDING SEQUENCE CHART

Make	Model	System Split	Special Procedures	Bleeding Sequence
AMC	All except Alliance	Front-to-Rear	①	1. Passenger rear 2. Driver rear 3. Passenger front 4. Driver front
Chrysler	All	Front-to-Rear And Diagonal	①	1. Passenger rear 2. Driver rear 3. Passenger front 4. Driver front

BRAKES
HYDRAULIC BRAKES COMPONENT SERVICE
SECTION 24

BRAKES BLEEDING SEQUENCE CHART

Make	Model	System Split	Special Procedures	Bleeding Sequence
General Motors	Rear Drive and E,K Body ⑤	Front-to-rear	①	1. Passenger rear 2. Driver rear 3. Passenger front 4. Driver front
	Front Drive Except E,K Body ⑤	Diagonal	②③	1. Passenger rear 2. Drive front 3. Driver rear 4. Passenger front
Corvette		Front-to-Rear	①④	1. Driver rear-inner 2. Driver rear-outer 3. Passenger rear-inner 4. Passenger rear-outer 5. Driver front 6. Passenger front
Ford	Rear Drive-Front-to-Rear		①	1. Passenger rear 2. Driver rear 3. Passenger front 4. Driver front
	Front Drive	Diagonal		1. Passenger rear 2. Driver front 3. Driver rear 4. Passenger front

① It may be necessary to push on or pull out a button or rod on the metering valve to bleed front disc brakes, particularly when pressure bleeding.
② Use SLOW strokes only when manually bleeding the quick take-up system.
③ Always bleed the master cylinder first in the quick take-up system. Bleed the left front caliper fitting first and then the right hand fitting.
④ Raise the front of the vehicle slightly when bleeding the rear brakes.
⑤ E = Riviera, Eldorado and Toronado
   K = Seville

DISC BRAKE APPLICATION CHART & SPECIFICATIONS

Make/Model	Text Reference Type	Caliper Style	Manufacturer	Anchor Bolt (ft lbs)	Bridge, Pin or Key Bolts (ft lbs)	Wheel Lugs (ft lbs)	Minimum Thickness Normal Standard	Minimum Thickness Machine To	Minimum Thickness Discard At	Rotor Parallel Variation	Max. Run-out
American Motors Eagle	1	Sliding	Bendix	100	30	75	.880	.815	.810	.0005	.003
Concord, Spirit	1	Sliding	Bendix	85	30	75	.880	.815	.810	.0005	.003
Chrysler Corporation (Front Wheel Drive) Aries, Reliant LeBaron, Dodge 400, 600-H.D. Brakes	6	Floating	K/H	70-100	18-22	80	9.35	.912	.882	.0005	.004
WO/H.D. Brakes	7	Floating	ATE	70-100	18-22	80	9.35	.912	.882	.0005	.004
E Class, New Yorker, Town & Country, Lazer	6	Floating	ATE or K/H	70-100	ATE 18-22 K/H 25-35	80	.935	.912	.882	.0005	.004
Omni, Horizon, Charger, Turismo	6	Floating	K/H	70-100	25-40	80	.500	.461	.431	.0005	.004
Aries, Reliant, LeBaron, Dodge 400	7	Floating	ATE	70-100	18-22	85	.935	.912	.882	.0005	.004
Omni, Horizon	6	Floating	K/H	70-100	25-40	85	.500	.461	.431	.0005	.004
Chrysler Corporation (Rear Wheel Drive) Cordoba, Diplomat Gran Fury, Mirada, New Yorker, Imperial	3	Sliding	Chrysler	95-125	15-20	85	1.010	.955	.940	.0005	.004

SECTION 24 BRAKES
HYDRAULIC BRAKES COMPONENT SERVICE

DISC BRAKE APPLICATION CHART & SPECIFICATIONS

Make/Model	Text Reference Type	Caliper Style	Manufacturer	Anchor Bolt (ft lbs)	Bridge, Pin or Key Bolts (ft lbs)	Wheel Lugs (ft lbs)	Minimum Thickness Normal Standard	Minimum Thickness Machine To	Minimum Thickness Discard At	Rotor Parallel Variation	Max. Run-out
Ford Motor Company (Front Wheel Drive) Escort, Lynx, LN7 EXP, Tempo, Topaz	5	Sliding	Ford	—	18–25	80–105	.945	—	.882	.0005	.003
Ford Motor Company (Rear Wheel Drive) Linc, Continental, Mark VII-Front	8	Sliding	Ford	—	40–60	80–105	1.030	—	.972	.0005	.003
Rear	6	Sliding	K/H	85–115	15–20	80–105	.945	—	.895	.0004	.004
Linc, Town Car, Crown Victoria, Grand Marquis	8	Sliding	Ford	—	40–60	80–105	1.030	—	.972	.0005	.003
Ford, Mercury-Front	8	Sliding	Ford	—	40–60	80–105	1.030	—	.972	.0005	.003
All models exc. noted	8	Sliding	Ford	—	30–40	80–105	.870	—	.810	.0005	.003
LTD, Cougar, XR7, Country Squire	1	Sliding	K/H	90–120	12–16	80–105	1.180	—	1.120	.0005	.003
Disc Brakes-Rear	6	Sliding	K/H	81–115	15–20	80–105	.945	—	.895	.0004	.0003
General Motors—Buick Electra Limited, Park Ave (Front Whl Drive)	2	Floating	Delco	—	35	70	1.043	.972	.957	.0005	.002
Electra, Estate Wagon (Rear Whl. Drive)	2	Floating	Delco	—	35	80 ①	1.037	.980	.965	.0005	.002
Riviera Front	2	Floating	Delco	—	35	100	1.037	.980	.965	.0005	.004
Rear	10	Floating	Delco	35	30	100	—	.980	.965	.0005	.004
Century W/H.D.	2	Floating	Delco	—	28	100	—	.972	.957	.0005	.002
Exc. H.D.	2	Floating	Delco	—	28	100	—	.830	.815	.0005	.002
Skyhawk-W/Vented Disc.	2	Floating	Delco	—	28	100	—	.830	.815	.0005	.002
W/Solid Disc.	2	Floating	Delco	—	28	100	—	.444	.429	.0005	.002
Regal, LeSabre	2	Floating	Delco	—	35	70–80	—	.980	.965	.0005	.004
Skylark	2	Floating	Delco	—	21–35	102	.885	.830	.815	.0005	.003
Century, Regal, LeSabre	2	Floating	Delco	—	35	80	—	.980	.965	.0005	.004
General Motors—Cadillac Cimarron	2	Floating	Delco	—	28	100	.885	.830	.815	.0005	.004
DeVille, Fleetwood (Rear Whl. Drive) Front	2	Floating	Delco	—	30	100	1.037	.980	.965	.0005	.004
Rear	10	Floating	Delco	35	30	100	.974	.910	.905	.0005	.003
CC Limousine	2	Floating	Delco	—	30	100	1.250	1.230	1.215	.0005	.004
Eldorado, Seville Front	2	Floating	Delco	—	28	100	1.000	.980	.965	.0005	.004
Rear	10	Floating	Delco	35	30	100	.974	.910	.905	.0005	.004
General Motors—Chevrolet Caprice, Impala	2	Floating	Delco	—	35	80 ②	1.030	.980	.965	.0005	.004
Malibu, Monte Carlo	2	Floating	Delco	—	35	80 ③	1.030	.980	.965	.0005	.004
Camaro-Front	2	Floating	Delco	—	21–35	80	1.030	.980	.965	.0005	.004
Rear	2	Floating	Delco	—	30–45	80	1.030	.980	.965	.0005	.004
Corvette-Front	9	Fixed	Delco	70	130	70 ④	1.285	1.230	1.215	.0005	.004
Rear	9	Fixed	Delco	70	60	70 ④	1.285	1.230	1.215	.0005	.004
Corvette-Front	12	Floating	Girlock	70	24	100	—	.724	—	.0005	.006
Rear	12	Floating	Girlock	44	24	100	—	.724	—	.0005	.006
Celebrity, Cavalier	2	Floating	Delco	—	28	100	Vented .885 / Solid .490	Vented .830 / Solid .444	Vented .815 / Solid .429	.0005	.004

24-14

BRAKES
HYDRAULIC BRAKES COMPONENT SERVICE
SECTION 24

DISC BRAKE APPLICATION CHART & SPECIFICATIONS

Make/Model	Text Reference Type	Caliper Style	Manufacturer	Anchor Bolt (ft lbs)	Bridge, Pin or Key Bolts (ft lbs)	Wheel Lugs (ft lbs)	Minimum Thickness Normal Standard	Minimum Thickness Machine To	Minimum Thickness Discard At	Rotor Parallel Variation	Max. Run-out
Citation	2	Floating	Delco	—	28	102	.885	.830	.815	.0005	.003
Chevette	4	Floating	Delco	70	28	70	.440	.390	.374	.0005	.005
	2	Floating	Girlock	—	21–25	70	—	.390	.374	.0005	.005
General Motors—Oldsmobile 98, Regency, Brougham (Front Whl. Drive)	2	Floating	Delco	—	35	70	1.043	.972	.957	.0005	.002
Full Size	2	Floating	Delco	—	35	80 ①	1.040	.980	.965	.0005	.004
Toronado—Front	2	Floating	Delco	—	35	100	1.000	.980	.965	.0005	.004
Rear	10	Floating	Delco	32	30	100	1.000	.980	.965	.0005	.004
Cutlass, Cutlass Supreme	2	Floating	Delco	—	35	80	1.040	.980	.965	.0005	.004

Flushing Hydraulic Brake Systems

Hydraulic brake systems must be totally flushed if the fluid becomes contaminated with water, dirt or other corrosive chemicals. To flush, simply bleed the entire system until all fluid has been replaced with the correct type of new fluid.

Bench Bleeding Master Cylinder

1. Connect two short pieces of brake line to the outlet fittings, bend them until the free end is below the fluid level in the master cylinder reservoirs.
2. Fill the reservoirs with fresh brake fluid. Pump the piston until no more air bubbles appear in the reservoir(s).
3. Disconnect the two short lines, refill the master cylinder and securely install the cylinder cap(s).
4. Install the master cylinder on the car. Attach the lines but do not completely tighten them. Force any air that might have been trapped in the connection by slowly depressing the brake pedal. Tighten the lines before releasing the brake pedal.

GM Quick Take Up System Bleeding

Bleed the master cylinder as follows. Disconnect the left front brake line at the master cylinder. Fill the cylinder with fluid until it flows from the opened port. Connect the line and tighten the fitting. Apply the brake pedal slowly one time and keep it applied. Loosen the same brake line fitting to allow any air to escape. Retighten the fitting and release the brake pedal slowly. Wait 15 seconds and repeat the procedure until all of the air is expelled. Bleed the right front connection in the same manner. Bleed the cylinders and calipers after you are sure all the air is out of the master cylinder. Rapid pumping will move the secondary piston down the bore and make it difficult to bleed the system. Always apply slow pedal pressure.

Powermaster Power Brake Unit

DESCRIPTION

The Powermaster unit is a complete, integral power brake apply system, consisting of an electro-hydraulic pump, fluid accumulator, pressure switch, fluid reservoir and a hydraulic booster, with an integral dual master cylinder. The nitrogen charged accumulator stores fluid at 510-675 psi for the hydraulic booster operation. The electro-hydraulic operates between pressure limits with the ignition switch on. When the pressure switch senses accumulator pressure is below 510 psi, the 12 volt pump operates to increase the accumulator fluid pressure to 675 psi. When the brake pedal is depressed, fluid from the accumulator acts on the booster power piston to apply the master cylinder which functions in the same manner as the conventional dual master cylinder.

Because of the excessively high hydraulic pressure, the system must be depressurized before any service operations are performed on the system. Failure to depressurize could result in personal injury and/or damage to the vehicle's painted surfaces.

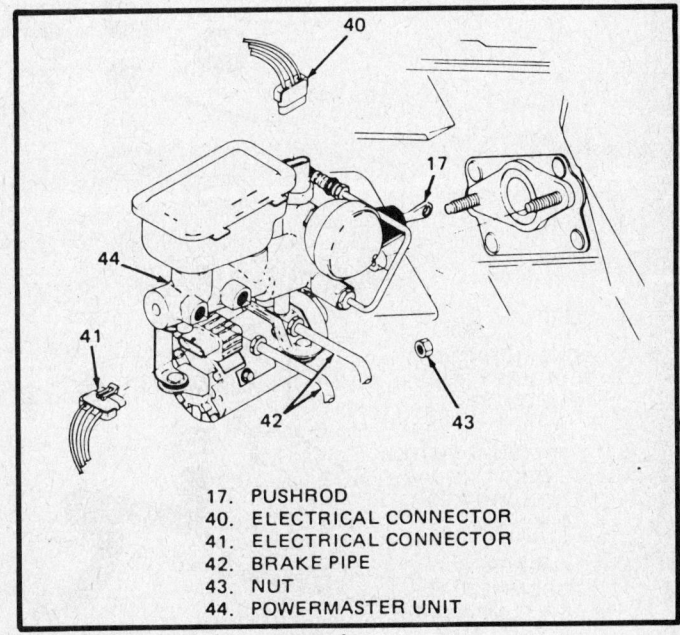

17. PUSHROD
40. ELECTRICAL CONNECTOR
41. ELECTRICAL CONNECTOR
42. BRAKE PIPE
43. NUT
44. POWERMASTER UNIT

Powermaster unit removal

DEPRESSURIZING THE POWERMASTER SYSTEM

1. With the ignition switch in the OFF position, apply and release the brake pedal a minimum of ten (10) times, using approximately 50 pounds of force on the brake pedal.

SECTION 24

BRAKES
HYDRAULIC BRAKES COMPONENT SERVICE

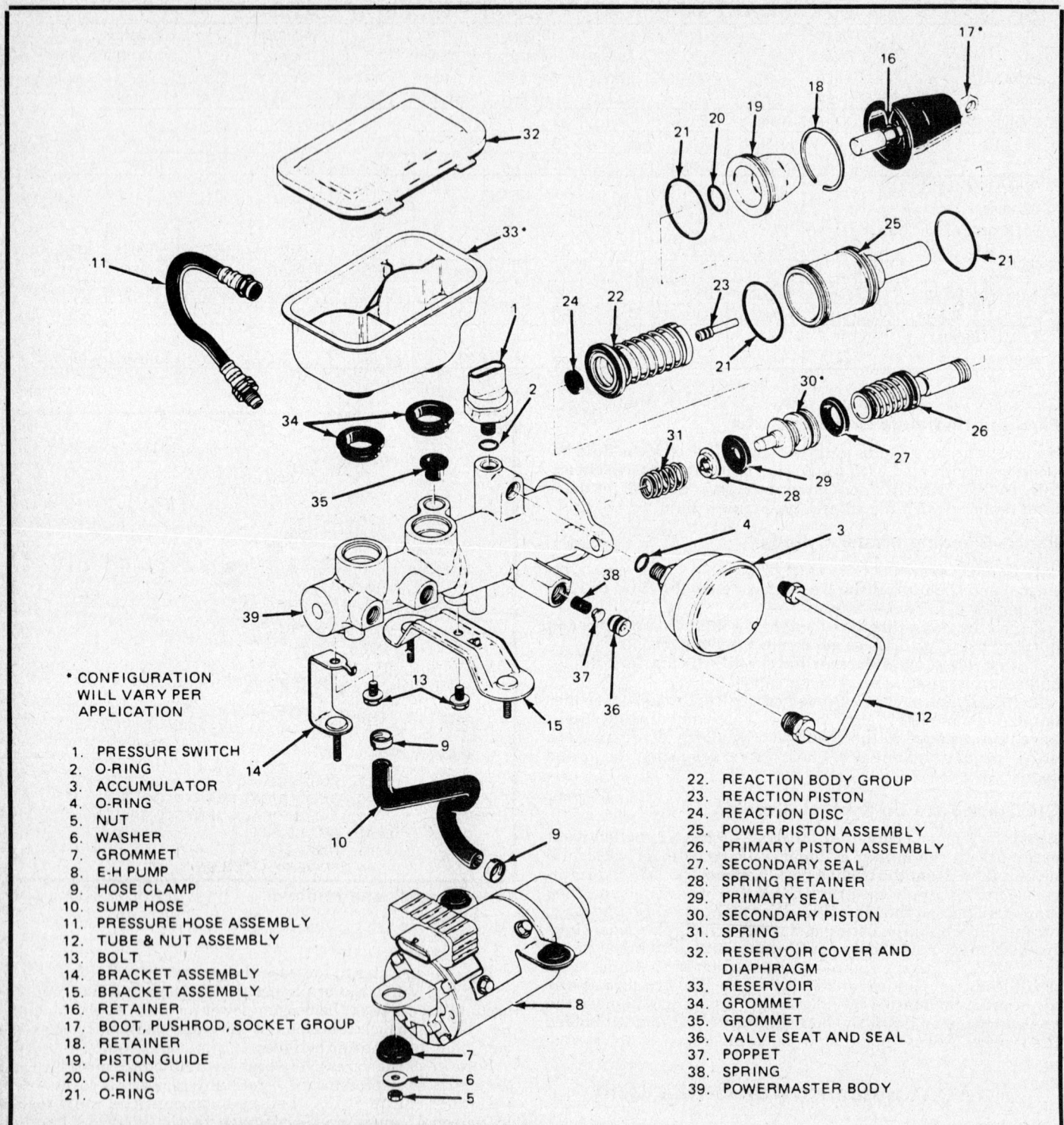

* CONFIGURATION WILL VARY PER APPLICATION

1. PRESSURE SWITCH
2. O-RING
3. ACCUMULATOR
4. O-RING
5. NUT
6. WASHER
7. GROMMET
8. E-H PUMP
9. HOSE CLAMP
10. SUMP HOSE
11. PRESSURE HOSE ASSEMBLY
12. TUBE & NUT ASSEMBLY
13. BOLT
14. BRACKET ASSEMBLY
15. BRACKET ASSEMBLY
16. RETAINER
17. BOOT, PUSHROD, SOCKET GROUP
18. RETAINER
19. PISTON GUIDE
20. O-RING
21. O-RING
22. REACTION BODY GROUP
23. REACTION PISTON
24. REACTION DISC
25. POWER PISTON ASSEMBLY
26. PRIMARY PISTON ASSEMBLY
27. SECONDARY SEAL
28. SPRING RETAINER
29. PRIMARY SEAL
30. SECONDARY PISTON
31. SPRING
32. RESERVOIR COVER AND DIAPHRAGM
33. RESERVOIR
34. GROMMET
35. GROMMET
36. VALVE SEAT AND SEAL
37. POPPET
38. SPRING
39. POWERMASTER BODY

Exploded view of the powermaster power brake assembly

2. When loosening hoses or pipe fittings, wrap shop towels close to the fittings to prevent spraying of residual pressurized fluid.

Removal

1. Disconnect the power lead from the pressure switch.
2. Disconnect the electrical connector from the electro-hydraulic pump.
3. Disconnect the brake tubing fittings from the Powermaster unit.
4. Remove the two retaining nuts for the unit to dash panel.
5. Remove the brake pedal pushrod.

BRAKES
HYDRAULIC BRAKES COMPONENT SERVICE
SECTION 24

6. Remove the Powermaster unit from the vehicle.

Installation

1. Install the Powermaster unit, the brake pedal pushrod and install the two retaining nuts. Torque 22 to 30 ft. lbs.
2. Install the brake pipes to the unit.
3. Install the electrical connections to the unit.

BLEEDING OF UNIT

The brake system is bled in the conventional manner, either manually or by pressure. It must be remembered not to have the ignition switch on during the bleeding operation.

Powermaster Fluid Filling

1. Fill both sides of reservoir to the full marks on the inside of the reservoir. Use only clean new brake fluid meeting DOT specifications shown on reservoir cover.
2. Turn ignition "On". With the pump running, the brake fluid level in the booster side of the reservoir should decrease as brake fluid is moved to the accumulator.
3. If the booster side of the reservoir begins to run dry, add brake fluid to just cover the reservoir pump port until the pump stops.

NOTE: Pump must be shut off within 20 seconds. Turn ignition off after 20 seconds have elapsed. Check for leaks or flow back into reservoir from booster return port.

4. Properly install reservoir cover assembly to reservoir.
5. Turn ignition "OFF" and apply and release brake pedal 10 times, Remove reservoir cover and adjust booster fluid level to full mark.
6. Turn ignition "On". Pump will run and refill accumulator. Make sure that pump does not run longer than 20 seconds and that fluid level remains above pump sump port in reservoir.
7. Properly install reservoir cover. With ignition on, apply and release brake pedal to cycle pump on and off 10 to 15 cycles and remove air from booster section. Do not allow pump to run more than 20 seconds for each cycle.
8. Recheck high and low reservoir fluid levels per Steps 4 and 5. Check power master diagnosis if fluid levels do not stabilize high and low levels or if pump runs more than 20 seconds. Pump should not cycle without brake applications.

ELECTRO HYDRAULIC PUMP

Removal and Installation

1. Relieve the pressure from the powermaster unit and remove the reservoir cover and diaphragm.
2. Remove the end of the sump hose connected to the electro-hydraulic pump and drain the reservoir sump pump.
3. Disconnect the electrical connector from the pump and disconnect the pressure hose assembly from the tube and nut assembly.
4. Disconnect the other end of the hose assembly from the pump.
5. Remove the three pump retaining bolts and remove the pump.
6. Installation is the reverse order of the removal procedure. Torque the pump retaining bolts to 23 to 35 ft. lbs. and the pressure hose assembly to 10 to 15 ft. lbs.

PRESSURE SWITCH

Removal and Installation

1. Relieve the pressure from the power master as previously outlined.

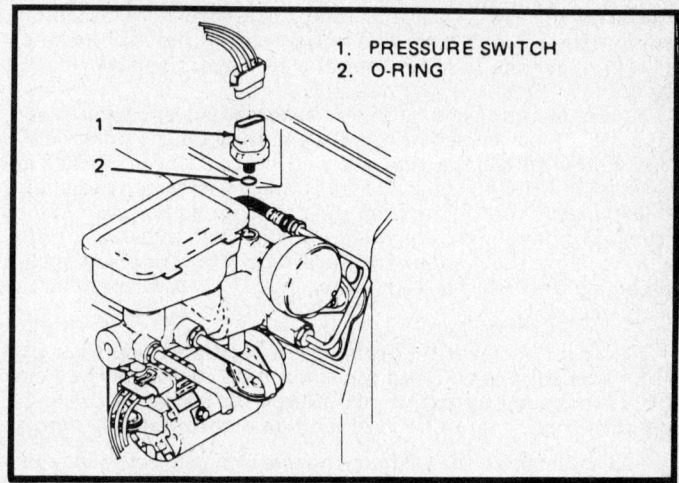
Pressure switch removal

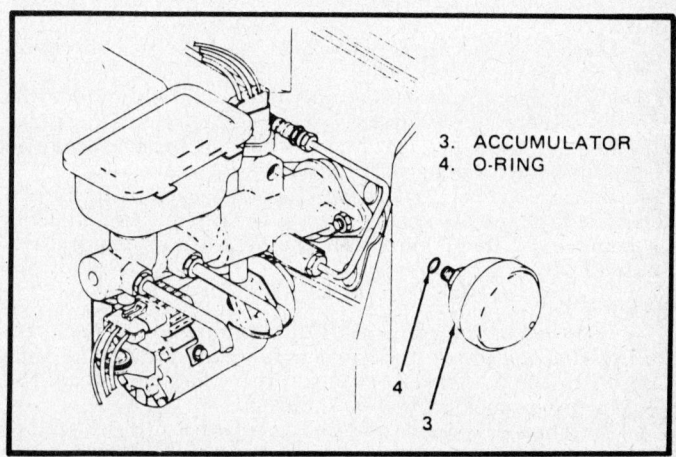
Accumulator removal

2. Disconnect the electrical connector from the pressure switch and remove the pressure switch with the O-ring.
3. Installation is the reverse order of the removal procedure. Be sure to use a new O-ring on the pressure switch and torque the pressure switch to 15 to 20 ft. lbs.

ACCUMULATOR

Removal and Installation

1. Relieve the pressure from the powermaster and remove the accumulator by unscrewing it from the powermaster unit.
2. Installation is the reverse order of the removal procedure. Be sure to install a new O-ring on the accumulator and torque the accumulator to 15 to 20 ft. lbs.

POWERMASTER OVERHAUL

Disassembly

1. Remove the powermaster from the vehicle as previously outlined.
2. Remove the reservoir cover with the diaphragm and empty the brake fluid from the reservoir.
3. Remove the following components, pressure switch, accu-

SECTION 24
BRAKES
HYDRAULIC BRAKES COMPONENT SERVICE

mulator, electro-hydraulic pump, pressure hose assembly, sump hose, clamps, tube and nut assembly and all brackets.

4. Remove the retainer from the groove in the powermaster body.
5. Remove the boot, retainer, pushrod, power piston group, remove the power piston group by pulling on the pushrod.
6. Disassemble the retainer and boot, pushrod, socket assembly and the piston guide from the power piston assembly.
7. Remove the O-ring from the piston guide and the O-rings from the power piston assembly and piston guide.
8. Remove the reaction body assembly from the power piston assembly and the reaction piston and disc from the reaction body assembly.

NOTE: The reaction body assembly and the power piston assembly have been disassembled as far as they can be. If there is any major problem with either of these assemblies, they must be replaced as a complete assembly.

9. Disassemble the primary piston from the secondary piston assembly, by blowing a small amount of compressed air into an outlet port at the blind end of the body (the other outlet port is plugged).
10. Remove the secondary seal, spring retainer and primary seal from the secondary piston. Remove the spring from the body core.
11. Place the powermaster body in a vise, be sure not to clamp across the powermaster body.
12. Using a small pry bar or equivalent remove the reservoir and the reservoir grommets.
13. Remove the valve seat and seal (do not reuse). It may be necessary to use an easy out to remove the valve seat.
14. Remove the poppet and spring and discard them. Before re-assembling the powermaster unit, be sure to clean all parts in denatured alcohol, except for the pressure switch and the electro-hydraulic pump.

Assembly

1. Use the clean fresh brake fluid to lubricate all parts before assembling the unit. Be sure to lubricate the new O-rings also. With the powermaster body still in the vise, install the new spring, poppet, valve seat and seal.
2. Bottom out the valve seat and seal by threading the nut of the tube and nut assembly in the powermaster body port.
3. Remove the powermaster body from the vise and install the grommets and the reservoir.
4. Install the spring into the powermaster body, along with the secondary seal, primary seal and spring retainer on the secondary piston.
5. Install the secondary piston assembly into the powermaster body.
6. Install the primary piston assembly into the powermaster body.
7. Assemble the reaction piston and disc into the reaction body assembly.
8. Install the two O-rings on the power piston assembly and install the reaction body assembly into the power piston assembly.
9. Install the power piston assembly into the powermaster body.
10. Install the O-ring on the piston guide and the O-ring in the piston guide.
11. Install the piston guide over the power piston in the powermaster body.
12. While depressing the piston guide install the retainer and the power piston.
13. Install the boot, pushrod, socket assembly, socket into the end of the power piston assembly and secure it with the retainer.
14. Install the brackets, sump hose, clamps, tube and nut assembly, electro-hydraulic pump and pressure hose assembly, accumulator and pressure switch.

15. Install the reservoir cover and diaphragm on the reservoir, and bench bleed the powermaster unit.
16. Install the powermaster unit on the vehicle and bleed the system as previously outlined. Also follow the instruction previously outlined on how to fill the powermaster unit with brake fluid.

Powermaster Diagnostic Procedure

PRELIMINARY PROCEDURE

1. Complete the fluid filling and bleeding procedures per powermaster bleed and fill instructions. Assure that pump cycle time and reservoir fluid levels are maintained within prescribed limits. Brake fluid temperature at 60 degrees to 80 degrees F. Warm fluid to 60 degrees F minimum by cycling pump.
2. Fully discharge accumulator by making 10 medium brake applications with ignition off.
3. Inspect for fluid leakage at brake pedal push rod, reservoir cover, hose and pipe connections, reservoir attaching points, pressure switch and accumulator.
4. Remove pressure switch from powermaster and install J-35126 test gauge adapter or equivalent. Reinstall pressure switch in test adapter. Attach pressure switch electrical connector. Close bleed valve.

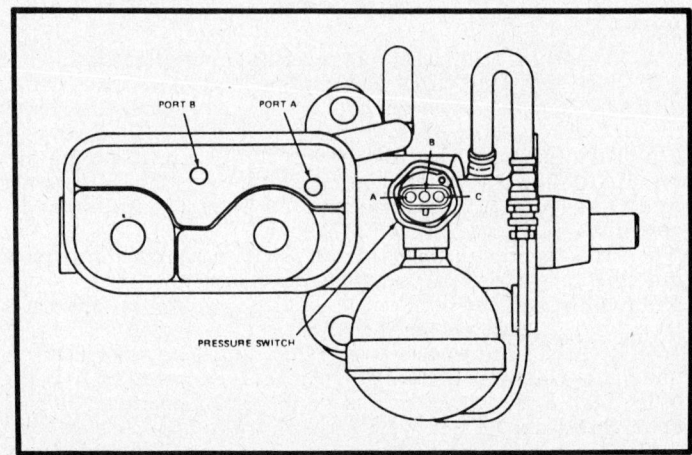

Powermaster vacuum ports and electrical terminals

FUNCTIONAL CHECK SEQUENCE

Test

1. Turn the ignition on. The electro-hydraulic pump will run and then shut off. Do not allow pump to run more than 20 seconds.
2. Observe the pump stops at 635 to 735 psi reading on the test gauge.
3. Slowly bleed off accumulator pressure with bleed valve return fluid to pump reservoir. Observe that the pump turns on again at 490 to 530 psi.
4. Have an assistant slowly apply brake pedal, reservoir cover off, and hold at steady medium force. Observe pressure gauge for indication of continuous pressure drop. Pressure drop rate should not cause pump to recycle within 30 seconds of first apply.
5. Turn the ignition off and remove the pressure switch electrical connector. With ohmmeter connected to the switch terminals B and C, and ignition off, slowly bleed off accumulator

BRAKES
DISC BRAKE SERVICE
SECTION 24

pressure. Terminals B and C should close at 355 to 435 psi. This is the low pressure warning signal.

6. Continue to bleed off accumulator pressure and note sudden drop off in gauge pressure reading at 200 to 330 psi. This sudden drop is at the accumulator pre-charge pressure.

7. Assure that pump sump fluid level is at the full mark on the inside of the reservoir when accumulator is fully depressurized.

8. Turn ignition on and cycle the pump several times to remove air by opening and closing bleed valve. Pump on time should now be less than 10 seconds each cycle.

9. During pump on/off cycles, note sump reservoir fluid level. It normally will be just covering the sump hose port when pump is off and 1/2 full when pump comes on.

FINAL EVALUATIONS

1. Depressurize accumulator and remove J-35126 or equivalent test gauge adapter. Reinstall pressure switch and electrical connector and the reservoir cover.

2. With powermaster functioning normally, apply the brake pedal and note pedal travel. Pedal should not creep at steady pressure. Brake warning light should not indicate pressure differential between pressure circuits.

3. Observe running motor and pump sound from driver's seat. Compare to a good unit.

4. Consult the powermaster diagnosis for conditions and performance values which differ from normal.

POWERMASTER DIAGNOSIS

1. Symptom brake warning light on after engine start.
2. Parking brake applied. Temporarily release parking brake observe light. Reapply if light remains on.
3. Partial failure in brake hydraulic pressure circuit. Evaluate for excessive brake pedal travel. Evaluate for hard brake pedal force to stop. Evaluate for excessive stopping distances and early wheel lock-up tendency. Repair as necessary.
4. Low pressure in powermaster accumulator. Electrical failure check ignition, 30 amp fuse, pressure switch A/C terminals motor relay, connectors, wiring. Low fluid in reservoir.
5. Faulty warning light pressure switch. Check warning switch actuation pressure at Terminals B and C.
6. Symptom pump motor will not run. Electrical failure check ignition, 30 amp fuse, pressure switch terminals A/C closed, connector terminals, motor/relay and wiring.
7. Symptom pump motor runs does not shut off in 20 seconds. Turn ignition off after 20 seconds. Check reservoir fluid level. Check reservoir port A for backflow then replace power piston.
8. Check pump pressure. If pressure is low, check pressure line for obstruction, then replace pump and motor. If pressure is high, replace switch if higher than normal. Replace pump if lower than normal cut-off.
9. Symptom pump self cycles without brake applied. Check for accumulator precharge pressure, replace accumulator if low. Recheck self cycle.
10. Symptom pump self cycles while applying steady brake pressure. Does not self cycle without brake pressure. Check for accumulator precharge pressure, replace accumulator if low then recheck self cycle. Check for fluid backflow at reservoir port and replace power piston.
11. Symptom fluid level in pump reservoir does not cycle between full and nearly empty when accumulator is fully charged and fully depressurized. Check for air in fluid cycle 5 to 10 pump cycles to remove the air. Check accumulator precharge pressure and replace if low.
12. Symptom fluid level in pump reservoir does not cycle between half full and nearly empty at pressure switch limits. Check for reservoir full at fully depressurized accumulator. Check for accumulator precharge pressure if reservoir level after pump cycle is not nearly empty.
13. Symptom pump and motor noisy. Check for grounded tube and motor. Check for reservoir fluid level. Replace motor mount grommets.
14. Symptom fluid leakage. Check pump reservoir for excess fluid fill with accumulator fully depressurized. Check for tight reservoir cover and diaphragm. Wipe dry and identify source of leakage, then overhaul as necessary.
15. Symptom pump cycle time at pressure switch limit exceeds 10 seconds. Check for air in system recycle 5 to 10 pump cycles to remove air. Check for normal pressure switch points. Check for obstructed pump inlet and outlet fluid circuits. Check for faulty pump.

FRONT DISC BRAKES

ROTORS

Resurfacing Rotors

Manufacturers differ widely on permissible runout, but too much can sometimes be felt as a pulsation at the brake pedal. A wobble pump effect is created when a rotor is not perfectly smooth and the pad hits the high spots forcing fluid back into the master cylinder. This alternating pressure causes a pulsating feeling which can be felt at the pedal when the brakes are applied. This excessive runout also causes the brakes to be out of adjustment because disc brakes are self-adjusting; they are designed so that the pads drag on the rotor at all times and therefore automatically compensate for wear.

To check the actual runout of the rotor, first tighten the wheel spindle nut to a snug bearing adjustment, end-play removed. Fasten a dial indicator on the suspension at a convenient place so that the indicator stylus contacts the rotor face approximately one inch from its outer edge. Set the dial at zero.

Check the total indicator reading while turning the rotor one full revolution. If the rotor is warped beyond the runout specification, it is unlikely that it can be successfully remachined.

Lateral Runout: A wobbly movement of the rotor from side to side as it rotates. Excessive lateral runout causes the rotor faces to knock back the disc pads and can result in chatter, excessive pedal travel, pumping or fighting pedal and vibration during the breaking action.

Parallelism (lack of): Refers to the amount of variation in the thickness of the rotor. Excessive variation can cause pedal vibration or fight, front end vibrations and possible "grab" during the braking action; a condition comparable to an "out-of-round brake drum." Check parallelism with a micrometer. "Mike" the thickness at eight or more equally spaced points, equally distant from the outer edge of the rotor, preferably at mid-points of the braking surface. Parallelism then is the amount of variation between maximum and minimum measurements.

Surface or Micro-inch finish, flatness, smoothness: Different from parallelism, these terms refer to the degree of perfection

SECTION 24
BRAKES
DISC BRAKE SERVICE

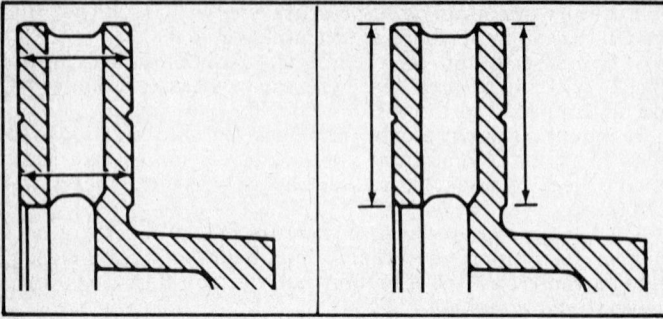

Taper variation not to exceed .003 in.

These surfaces to be flat and within .002 in.

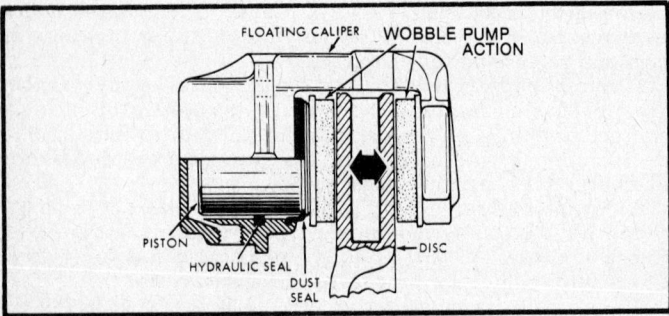

Wobble pump action

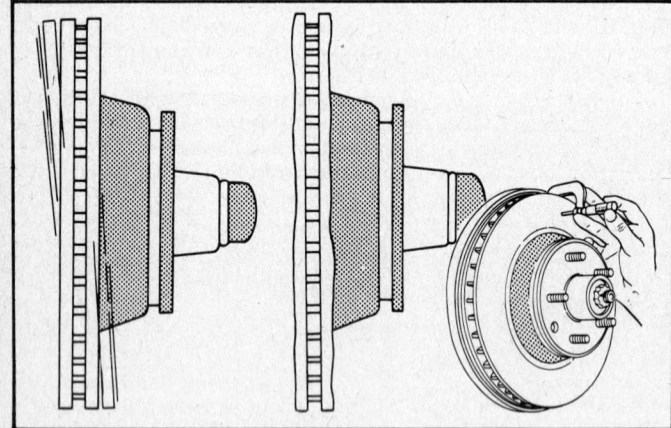

Excessive runout parallelism

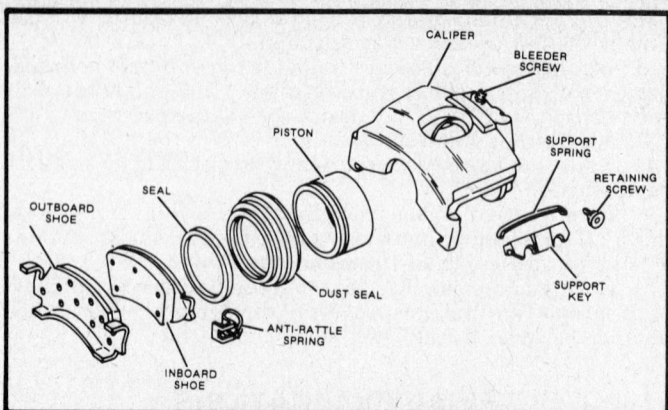

Type one Bendix caliper disc brakes (single piston)

Ideal rotor surface condition

of the flat surface on each side of the rotor; that is, the minute hills, valleys and swirls inherent in machining the surface. In a visual inspection, the remachined surface should have a fine ground polish with, at most, only a faint trace of non-directional swirls.

Removal and Installation

1. Raise the vehicle on a hoist or safely support on jackstands and remove the wheel.
2. Remove the caliper mounting bolts. Slide the caliper away from the disc and suspend it using a wire loop. On some cars, it is advisable to install a cardboard spacer between the pads to prevent the piston from coming out of its cylinder.
3. Remove the wheel bearing nut from the spindle and remove the outer wheel bearing roller assembly from the hub.
4. On Ford sliding caliper brakes, remove the wheel bearing adjusting nut and pull the hub and disc assembly outward enough to loosen the washer and outer wheel bearing. Push the assembly back onto the spindle and remove the washer and outer wheel bearing from the spindle.
5. Remove the hub and disc assembly from the spindle. Installation of hub and disc is in reverse order of removal. The disc is removable from the hub on the El Dorado, Toronado, and Corvette (rear only).
6. To separate the rear disc and hub on a Corvette the three hub-to-disc attaching rivets must be drilled out. This can be done with the hub and rotor mounted on the car. It is not necessary to install new rivets when the disc is installed.

CALIPER AND PAD

Inspection

Disc pads (lining and shoe assemblies) should be replaced in axle sets (both wheels) when the lining on any pad is worn to 1/16 inch at any point. If lining is allowed to wear past 1/16 inch minimum thickness, severe damage to disc may result. State inspection specifications take precedence over these general recommendations.

Note that disc pads in floating caliper type brakes may wear at an angle, and measurement should be made at the narrow end of the taper. Tapered linings should be replaced if the taper

BRAKES
DISC BRAKE SERVICE
SECTION 24

TROUBLESHOOTING DISC BRAKES

CAUSE	Excessive Brake Pedal Travel	Brake Pedal Travel Gradually Increases	Excessive Brake Pedal Effort	Excessive Braking Action	Brakes Slow to Respond	Brakes Slow to Release	Brakes Drag	Uneven Braking Action (Side to Side)	Uneven Braking Action (Front to Rear)	Scraping Noise from Brakes	Brakes Squeak During Application	Brakes Squeak During Stop	Brakes Chatter (Roughness)	Brakes Groan at End of Stop	Brakes Tell-Tale Glows
Leaking Brake Line or Connection	X	XX	X						X						XX
Leaking Wheel Cylinder or Piston Seal	X	XX	X	X				X							X
Leaking Master Cylinder	X	XX	X												X
Air in Brake System	XX		X						X						XX
Contaminated or Improper Brake Fluid	X				X	X	X								X
Leaking Vacuum System			XX	X											
Restricted Air Passage in Power Head		X	X		XX	X									
Damaged Power Head			X	X	X	X	XX								
Worn Out Brake Lining			X	X				X	X	X	X	X		X	
Uneven Brake Lining Wear - Replace	X			X				X	X	X	X	XX		X	X
Glazed Brake Lining - Sand			XX		X			X	X		X	X			
Incorrect Lining Material - Replace			X	X				X	X			X		X	
Contaminated Brake Lining - Replace				XX				XX	XX	X	X	X		X	
Linings Damaged by Abusive Use - Replace			X	XX				X	X	X	X	X		X	
Excessive Brake Lining Dust - Remove with Air			X	XX				XX	XX		X	XX		X	
Heat Spotted or Scored Brake Drums or Discs				X				X	X		X	X	XX	X	
Out-of-Round or Vibrating Brake Drums												X	XX		
Out-of-Parallel Brake Discs	X												XX		
Excessive Disc Run-Out	X												X		
Faulty Automatic Adjusters	X					X	X	X							X
Incorrect Wheel Cylinder Sizes			X	X				X	X						
Weak or Incorrect Brake Shoe Retention Springs				X		X	XX	X	X	XX	X	XX			
Brake Assembly Attachments - Missing or Loose	X						X	X	X	X		X	X	X	
Insufficient Brake Shoe Guide Lubricant							X	X	X	XX	XX				
Restricted Brake Fluid Passage or Sticking Wheel Cylinder Piston		X	X		X	X	X	X							X
Improperly adjusted Stoplight Switch or Cruise Control Vacuum Dump								X							
Faulty Metering Valve	X		X	X	X	X	X		X						X
Faulty Proportioning Valve			X	X	X	X	X		X						
Brake Pedal Linkage Interference or Binding			X		X	XX	XX								
Improperly Adjusted Parking Brake							X								
Improperly Adjusted Master Cylinder Push Rod	X					X	XX								X
Incorrect Front End Alignment								XX							
Incorrect Tire Pressure								X	X						
Incorrect Wheel Bearing Adjustment	X										X		X		
Loose Front Suspension Attachments								X	X		XX		X	X	
Out-of-Balance Wheel Assemblies													XX		
Incorrect Body Mount Torque													X		
Need to Slightly Increase or Decrease Pedal Effort														XX	
Operator Riding Brake Pedal			X				X	X						X	
Sticking Caliper or Wheel Cylinder Pistons							XX								

XX – Indicates more probable cause(s)
X – Indicates other causes

SECTION 24 BRAKES
DISC BRAKE SERVICE

exceeds 1/8 inch from end to end (the difference between the thickest and thinnest points).

To prevent costly paint damage, remove some brake fluid (don't re-use) from the reservoir and install the reservoir cover before replacing the disc pads. When replacing the pads, the piston is depressed and fluid is forced back through the lines to squirt out of the fluid reservoir.

When the caliper is unbolted from the hub do not let it dangle by the brake hose, it can be rested on a suspension member or wired onto the frame. All disc brake systems are self-adjusting and have no provision for manual adjustment.

Type One

KELSEY HAYES OR BENDIX SLIDING CALIPER DISC BRAKES (SINGLE PISTON)

Pad Removal

1. Remove half of the brake fluid from the master cylinder.
2. Remove the retaining screw holding the caliper support key.
3. Use a hammer and drift to drive the caliper retaining key and support spring out of the anchor plate.
4. Lift the caliper off of the rotor.
5. Support caliper so it doesn't hang by the brake hose.
6. Use a large C-clamp to force the piston back into its bore, being careful not to scratch the piston or bore, and being careful not to cut or tear the dust boot.
7. Remove the inboard pad and anti-rattle spring from the caliper support adapter.
8. Remove the outboard pad from the caliper. Check the condition of the rotor. If rotor run out exceeds manufacturer's specifications or has deep scratches, re-machine the rotor.
9. Clean all sliding surfaces on the adapter and caliper.

Pad Installation

1. Position the inboard brake pad and anti-rattle spring in the caliper support adapter.
2. Position the outboard brake pad in the caliper. Bend ears if necessary to provide slight interference fit in caliper.
3. Position the caliper over the rotor, take care not to damage the caliper piston dust boot.
4. Position the caliper support spring and support key into the slot and drive them into the opening between the lower end of the caliper and the lower anchor plate abutment.
5. Install and tighten the key retaining screw.
6. Fill the master cylinder with brake fluid. Bleed the system if necessary.

Type Two

DELCO FLOATING CALIPER (SINGLE PISTON)

Pad Removal

1. Remove half of the brake fluid from the master cylinder.
2. Position a large C-clamp over the caliper with the screw end against the outboard brake pad. Tighten the clamp until the caliper is pushed out enough to bottom the piston.
3. Remove the C-clamp. Remove the two caliper guide pin mounts and lift the caliper off of the rotor.
4. Support the caliper so there is no strain on the brake hose.
5. Press the inboard pad outward, then lift from the caliper.
6. Press the inboard pad outward, then lift from the caliper.
7. Remove and discard the four O-ring bushings and steel

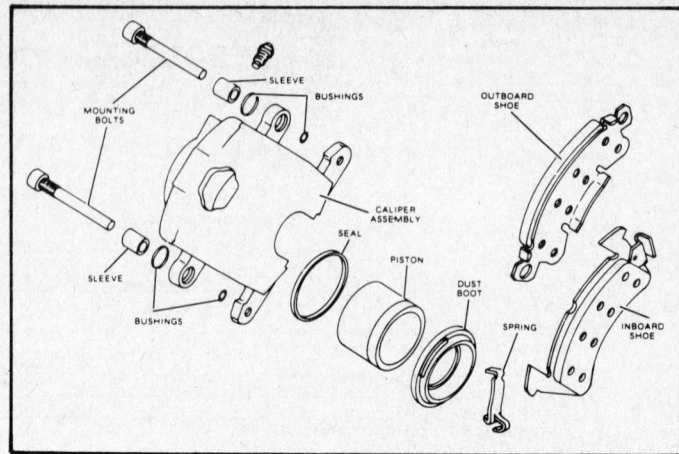

Type two Delco flating disc brakes (single piston)

sleeves if new ones are to be installed. Check the condition of the rotor. If rotor run out exceeds manufacturer's specifications or has deep scratches, re-machine the rotor.

Pad Installation

1. Lubricate and install the four O-ring bushings, install the sleeves pressing them through the O-rings until the sleeve end on the pad side is flush with caliper ear. Position the inboard pad so the pad contacts the piston and the two support spring ends. Note that the inboard and outboard pads are similar but not interchangeable.
2. Press down on the ears at the top of the inboard pad until the pad lies flat and the spring ends are just inside the lower edge of the pad.
3. Position the outboard pad with the ears toward the positioning pin holes and the tab on the inner edge of the pad resting in the notch in the edge of the caliper. Bend ears if necessary to provide slight interference fit in caliper.
4. Press the outboard pad tightly into position and use a pair of pliers to clinch the ears of the outboard pad over the outboard caliper half.
5. Position the caliper over the rotor.
6. Install the caliper mounting bolts and tighten to specification.
7. Fill the master cylinder with brake fluid.

Type Three

KELSEY HAYES CHRYSLER SLIDING CALIPER

Pad Removal

1. Remove half of the brake fluid from the master cylinder.
2. Remove caliper retaining clips and anti-rattle springs.
3. Lift the caliper off of the rotor.
4. Support the caliper so there is no strain on the brake hose.
5. Use a large C-clamp to force the piston back into its bore, being careful not to scratch the piston or bore, and being careful not to cut or tear the dust boot.
6. Pry the outboard pad from caliper.
7. Remove inboard pad from the adapter.
8. Check the condition of the rotor. If rotor run out exceeds manufacturer's specifications or has deep scratches, re-machine the rotor.

BRAKES
DISC BRAKE SERVICE
SECTION 24

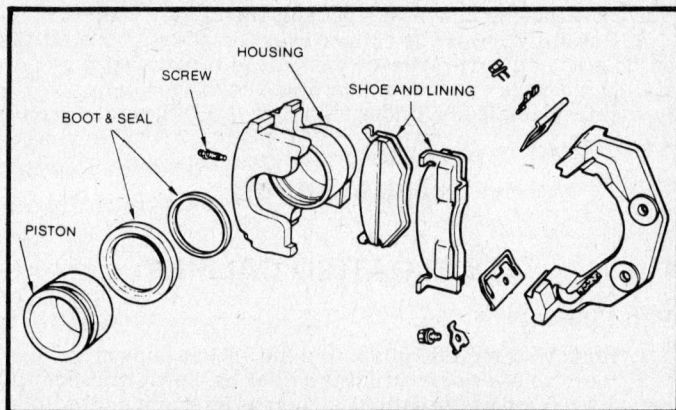

Type three—Kelsey Hayes sliding caliper

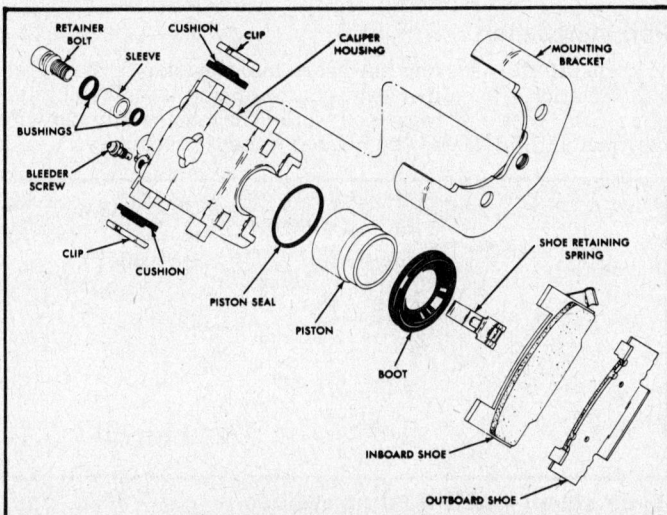

Type four—Chevette, T1000 disc brake

Pad Installation

1. Adjust ears of outboard pad to provide tight fit and install pad in caliper recess.
2. Install inboard pad with flanges inserted in adapter "ways."
3. Position the caliper on the rotor with the caliper engaging the adapter "ways."
4. Install anti-rattle springs and caliper retaining clips and torque retaining screws to 180 inch lbs.
5. Fill the master cylinder with brake fluid.

Type Four

CHEVETTE, T1000 DISC BRAKE

Pad Removal

1. Remove half of the brake fluid from the master cylinder.
2. Use a large C-clamp to force the piston back into its bore, being careful not to scratch the piston or bore, and being careful not to cut or tear the dust boot.
3. Remove the two hex head bolts that attach the caliper mounting bracket to the steering knuckle.

4. Support the caliper so there is no strain on the brake hose. Do not remove the socket head retainer bolt.
5. Remove the old shoe and lining assemblies. If the retaining spring does not come out with the inboard shoe, remove the spring from the piston.
6. Check the condition of the rotor. If rotor run out exceeds manufacturer's specifications or has deep scratches, re-machine the rotor.

Pad Installation

1. Before installing the inboard shoe, make sure that the shoe retaining spring is properly installed. Push the tab on the single-leg end of the spring down into the shoe hole, then snap the other two legs over the edge of the shoe notch.
2. Position the caliper over the rotor, lining up the bracket mounting holes. Install the mounting bolts.
3. Clinch the outboard shoe to the caliper. After clinching, radial and end play of the outboard shoe should be 0 to 0.005 inch.

Type Five

FORD FRONT DRIVE DISC BRAKE

Pad Removal

1. Remove master cylinder cap and check fluid level in reservoirs. Remove brake fluid until each reservoir is half full. Discard the removed fluid.

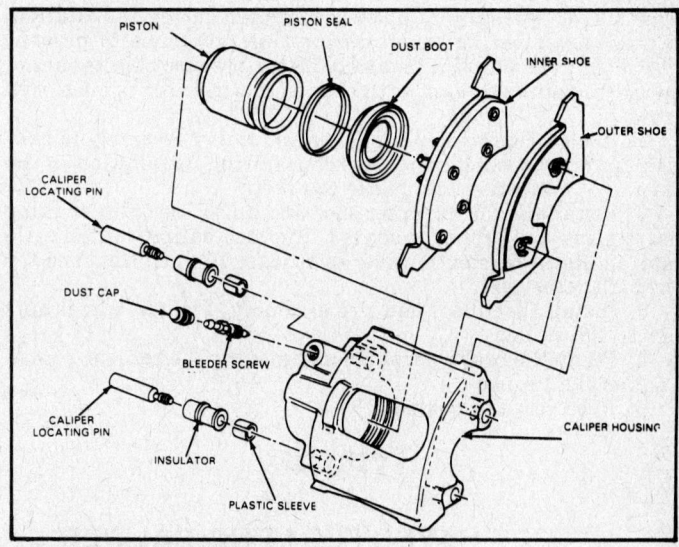

Type five—Ford front drive caliper

2. Remove wheel and tire assembly from rotor mounting face. Use care to avoid damage or interference with the caliper splash shield or bleeder screw fitting.
3. Remove brake caliper anti-rattle spring by applying upward pressure to center portion of spring until the spring tabs are free of the caliper holes.
4. Back out the caliper locating pins. Do not remove pins completely unless new bushings are to be installed. Reinstalling pins after complete removal can be difficult.
5. Lift caliper assembly from integral knuckle and anchor plate and rotor. Remove outer shoe and lining assembly from caliper assembly.
6. Remove inner shoe and lining assembly and inspect both

24-23

SECTION 24 BRAKES
DISC BRAKE SERVICE

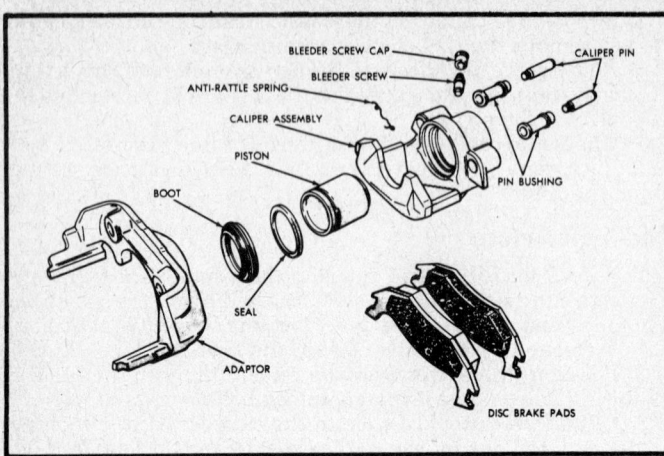

Type six—Kelsey Hayes floating caliper

rotor braking surfaces. Minor scoring or build-up of lining material does not require machining or replacement of the rotor.

7. Suspend caliper inside the fender housing. Use care not to damage caliper or stretch the brake hose.

Pad Installation

1. Use a 4 inch C-clamp and a block of wood 2 3/4 in. x 1 in. and approximately 3/4 inch thick to seat the caliper hydraulic piston in its bore. This must be done to provide clearance for the caliper assembly to fit over the rotor during installation. Extra care must be taken during this procedure to prevent damage to the aluminum piston. Metal or sharp objects cannot come into direct contact with the piston surface or damage will result.
2. Install the correct inner shoe and lining assembly in caliper piston(s). Do not bend shoe clips during installation in the piston or distortion and rattle can occur.
3. Install the correct outer shoe and lining assembly making sure clips are properly seated. Replace caliper anti-rattle spring. Refill master cylinder to at least 1/4 inch from the top in both reservoirs.
4. Install the wheel and tire assembly. Tighten wheel nuts 80 to 105 ft. lbs.
5. Pump the brake pedal prior to moving the vehicle to position brake linings.
6. Road test the vehicle.

Type Six

KELSEY-HAYES FLOATING CALIPER

Pad Removal

1. Remove half of the brake fluid from each master cylinder reservoir.
2. Remove the caliper guide pins, positioners and anti-rattle spring.
3. Lift the caliper from the rotor and support to prevent strain on the brake hose.
4. Pry the caliper piston back into the bore. Use a C-clamp if necessary.
5. Remove the brake pads from the caliper adaptor. Remove and discard the four bushings if they are to be replaced.

Pad Installation

1. Clean and lubricate the caliper guide pins and guide mounting surfaces. Install new guide bushings.
2. Position the new brake pads in the caliper adaptor.
3. Carefully lower the caliper over the adaptor. Install the guide pins and anti-rattle spring. The anti-rattle spring is installed with the end loop inboard on the caliper lug.
4. Fill the master cylinder with new fluid. Bleed the brakes if necessary.

Type Seven

ATE FLOATING CALIPER

Pad Removal

1. Remove the guide pin(s) and anti-rattle clips or springs.
2. Remove the caliper from the rotor by slowly sliding it up and away. Support the caliper so there is no strain on the brake hose. Late model calipers may be pivoted on the anchor bolt.
3. Remove the pads from the adaptor or caliper. In some cases the rotor must be removed to replace the inboard pad.
4. Push the caliper piston back into its bore.

Pad Installation

1. Install the pads and hardware into the adaptor or caliper.
2. Position the caliper over the rotor and install the guide pin(s), anti-rattle springs or clips. Fill the master cylinder with new brake fluid. Bleed the brake system if necessary.

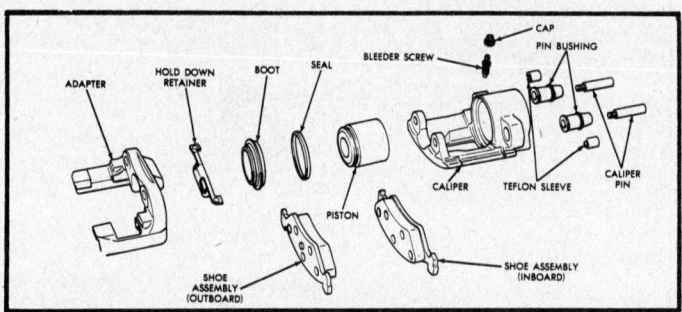

Type seven—ATE floating caliper

Type Eight

FORD FLOATING CALIPER

Pad Removal
EXCEPT MARK VII CONTINENTAL

1. Remove half of the brake fluid from the master cylinder reservoirs.
2. Remove the caliper guide pins.
3. Lift the caliper assembly from the rotor. Support the caliper so there is no strain on the brake hose.
4. Remove the outboard pad from the caliper. Remove the inboard pad from the piston. Step six can now be accomplished by using a C-clamp against the inboard pad.
5. Remove the insulators and inserts from the guide pin holes if they are to be replaced.
6. Push the caliper piston back into its bore.

Pad Installation
EXCEPT MARK VII CONTINENTAL

1. Install new guide bushings and insulators if they are to be replaced.
2. Install the inboard pad into the piston. Install the out-

24-24

BRAKES
DISC BRAKE SERVICE
SECTION 24

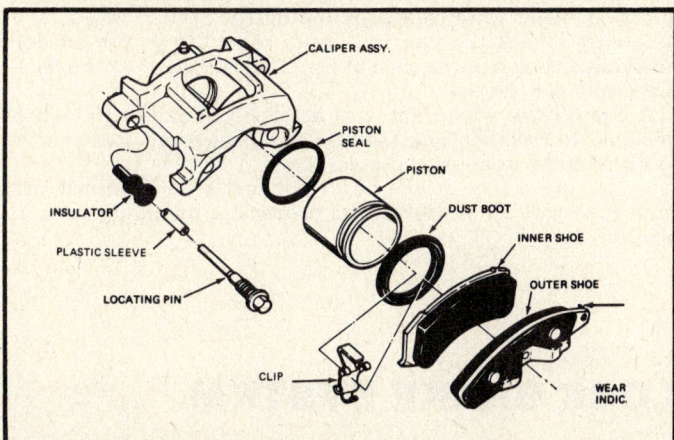

Type eight—Ford floating caliper

board making sure the buttons are seated into the caliper body. The wear indicator faces toward the front of the car.

3. Lower the caliper assembly onto the anchor plate and slide the guide pins through the holes in the caliper. When the guide pins reach the rubber insulators, they will require more pressure. After the pins bottom thread them into the hole. Take care not cross thread the guide pins.

4. Refill the master cylinder with new brake fluid. Bleed the brake system if necessary.

Pad Removal
MARK VII CONTINENTAL AND MUSTANG SVO

1. Raise the vehicle, and install safety stands. Block both front wheels.
2. Remove the wheel assemblies.
3. Disconnect the parking brake cable from the lever and bracket. Use care to avoid kinking or cutting the cable or return spring.
4. Remove the caliper locating pins.
5. Lift the caliper assembly away from the anchor plate by pushing the caliper upward toward the anchor plate, and then rotate the lower end out of the anchor plate.
6. If insufficient clearance between the caliper and shoe and lining assemblies prevents removal of the caliper, it is necessary to loosen the caliper end retainer 1/2 turn, maximum, to allow the piston to be forced back into its bore. To loosen the end retainer, remove the parking brake lever, then mark or scribe the end retainer and caliper housing to be sure that the end retainer is not loosened more than 1/2 turn. Force the piston back in its bore, and then remove the caliper.
7. If the retainer must be loosened more than 1/2 turn, the seal between the thrust screw and the housing may be broken, and brake fluid may leak into the parking brake mechanism chamber. In this case, the end retainer must be removed, and the internal parts cleaned and lubricated.
8. Remove the outer shoe and lining assembly from the anchor plate. Remove the two rotor retainer nuts and the rotor from the axle shaft.
9. Remove the inner brake shoe and lining assembly from the anchor plate. Remove the anti-rattle clip from anchor plate. If no further service than pad replacement is required, brake hose removal is not necessary. Do not support the caliper by the brake hose.
10. Remove the flexible hose from the caliper by removing the hollow retaining bolt that connects the hose fitting to the caliper.
11. Clean the caliper, anchor plate, and rotor assemblies and inspect for signs of brake fluid leakage, excessive wear, or damage. The caliper must be inspected for leakage both in the piston boot area and at the operating shaft seal area.
12. Lightly and or wire brush any rust or corrosion from the caliper and anchor plate sliding surfaces as well as the outer and inner brake shoe abutment surfaces. Inspect the brake shoes for wear. If either lining is worn to within 1/8 in. of the shoe surface, both shoe and lining assemblies must be replaced using the shoe and lining removal procedures.

Pad Installation
MARK VII CONTINENTAL AND MUSTANG SVO

1. If the end retainer has been loosened only 1/2 turn, reinstall the caliper in the anchor plate without shoe and lining assemblies. Tighten the end retainer 75 to 96 ft. lbs.
2. Install the parking brake lever on its keyed spline. The lever arm must point down and rearward. The parking brake cable will then pass freely under the axle. Tighten the retainer screw 16 to 22 ft. lbs. The parking brake lever must rotate freely after tightening the retainer screw. Remove the caliper from the anchor plate.
3. If new shoe and lining assemblies are to be installed, the piston must be screwed back into the caliper bore, using Tool T75P-2588-B or equivalent to provide installation clearance. Remove the rotor, and install the caliper, less shoe and lining assemblies, in the anchor plate. While holding the shaft, rotate the tool handle counterclockwise until the tool is seated firmly against the piston.
4. Now, loosen the handle about 1/4 turn. While holding the handle, rotate the tool shaft clockwise until the piston is fully bottomed in its bore; the piston will continue to turn even after it becomes bottomed. When there is no further inward movement of the piston and the tool handle is rotated until there is firm seating force, the piston is bottomed. Remove the tool and the caliper from the anchor plate.
5. Lubricate anchor plate sliding ways with D7AE-019590-A or equivalent grease. Use only specified grease because a lower temperature type of lubricant may melt and contaminate the brake pads. Use care to prevent any lubricant from getting on the braking surface. Install the anti-rattle clip on the lower rail of the anchor plate.
6. Install inner brake shoe and lining assembly on the anchor plate with the lining toward the rotor. Be sure shoes are installed in their original positions as marked for identification before removal. Install rotor and two retainer nuts.
7. Install the correct hand outer brake shoe and lining assembly on the anchor plate with the lining toward the rotor and wear indicator toward the upper portion of the brake.
8. Install the flexible hose by placing a new washer on each side of the fitting outlet and inserting the attaching bolt through the washers and fitting. Tighten 20 to 30 ft. lbs.
9. Rotate the caliper housing until it is completely over the rotor. Use care so that the piston dust boot is not damaged.
10. Piston Position Adjustment: Pull the caliper outboard until the inner shoe and lining is firmly seated against the rotor, and measure the clearance between the outer shoe and caliper. The clearance must be 1/32 to 3/32 inch. If it is not, remove the caliper, then readjust the piston to obtain required gap. Follow the procedure given in Step 3, and rotate the shaft counterclockwise to narrow gap and clockwise to widen gap (1/4 turn of the piston moves it approximately 1/16 inch.
11. A clearance greater than 3/32 inch may allow the adjuster to be pulled out of the piston when the service brake is applied. This will cause the parking brake mechanism to fail to adjust. It is then necessary to replace the piston/adjuster assembly.
12. Lubricate locating pins and inside of insulator with D7AZ-19A331-A or equivalent silicone grease. Add one drop of Loctite EOAC-19554-A or equivalent to locating pin threads.
13. Install the locating pins through caliper insulators and into the anchor plate; the pins must be hand inserted and hand started. Tighten to 29-37 ft. lbs.

SECTION 24 BRAKES
DISC BRAKE SERVICE

14. Connect the parking brake cable to the bracket and the lever on the caliper.
15. Bleed the brake system. Replace rubber bleed screw cap after bleeding. Fill master cylinder as required to within 1/8 inch of the top of the reservoir.
16. Caliper Adjustment: With the engine running, pump the service brake lightly (approximately 14 lbs. pedal effort) about 40 times. Allow at least one second between pedal applications. As an alternative, with the engine Off, pump the service brake lightly (approximately 87 lbs. pedal effort) about 30 times. Now check the parking brake for excessive travel or very light effort. In either case, repeat pumping the service brake, or if necessary, check the parking brake cable for proper tension. The caliper levers must turn to the Off position when the parking brake is released.
17. Install the wheel and tire assembly. Tighten the wheel lug nuts to specification. Install the wheel cover. Remove the safety stands, and lower the vehicle.
18. Be sure a firm brake pedal application is obtained, and then road test for proper brake operation, including parking brakes.

FORD FOUR WHEEL ANTI-LOCK BRAKE SYSTEM

General Description

The 1985 Mark VII and Continental models powered by the 5.0 liter V8 engine, are now equipped with an electronic anti-lock brake system. This new brake system is designed to prevent braking-induced wheel lock on any road surface and on high traction surfaces such as dry pavement, the system is seldom activated. On a surface where the traction is reduced such as ice on the road, the system will operate to provide the best braking possible, and will help to retain the driver's ability to steer the vehicle around a potential accident situation while maintaining the maximum braking power. The anti-lock system contains four sensors, one in each wheel hub. The function of each sensor is to constantly send signals to the central microprocessor which compares the speeds of all four wheels. There are three hydraulic brake circuits being employed in this system, one is for the left front wheel, one is for the right front wheel and the other one controls both rear wheel brakes simultaneously as an axle set. During a braking situation, if one wheel slows down faster than the other three, this would indicate imminent wheel lock (as in a skidding situation) and the microprocessor would signal the appropriate hydraulic braking circuit to pulse the braking pressure to that wheel or axle set. To aid the four wheel sensors, twin microprocessors are used in the system. Each computer checks itself against the other. If the computers do not agree with one another, the anti-lock feature of the brakes will be bypassed and braking will go back to the normal mode. A big difference between the systems with and without the anti-lock system is the power source for the brakes. The conventional hydro-boost actuation system for the Mark VII and the Continental is powered from the power steering pump. On the electronic anti-lock system, the power assist for brakes is generated as required, on demand, by an electric pump charging a nitrogen filled accumulator. There will be no noticeable difference between the two systems in the braking feel or efficiency during normal stopping.

MASTER CYLINDER AND HYDRAULIC BOOSTER

The master cylinder and the brake booster are arranged in the basic fore and aft position with the booster behind the master cylinder. The booster control valve is located in a parallel bore above the master cylinder centerline and is operated by a lever connected to the brake pedal pushrod.

ELECTRIC PUMP AND ACCUMULATOR

The electric pump is a high pressure pump design that runs at frequent intervals for a short period to charge the hydraulic accumulator that supplies the brake system. The accumulator is

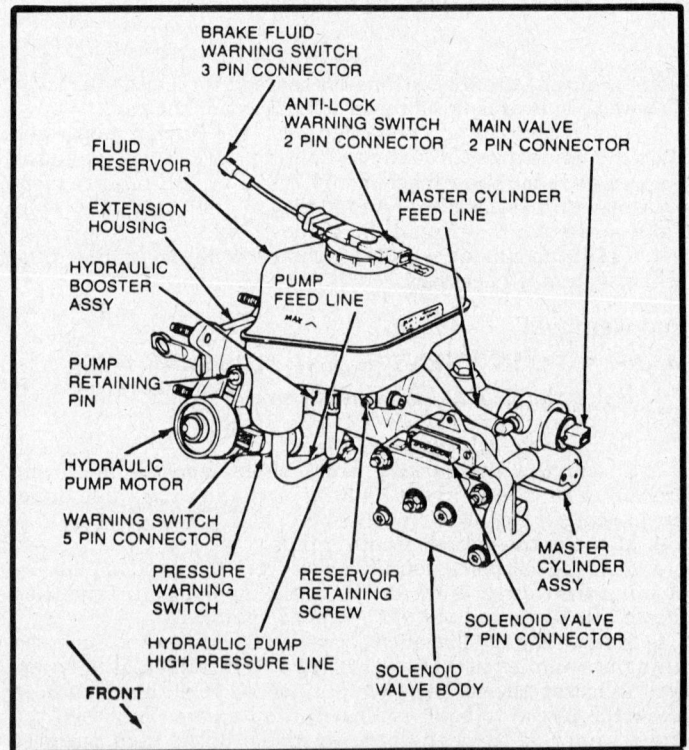

Master cylinder and booster assembly

a gas filled pressure chamber that is part of the pump and motor assembly. The electric motor, pump and accumulator assembly is shock mounted to the master cylinder/booster assembly.

VALVE BODY ASSEMBLY

The valve body assembly incorporates three pairs of solenoid valves, one pair for each front wheel, and a third pair for both the rear wheels combined. These solenoid valves are inlet-outlet valves with the inlet valve normally open and the outlet valve normally closed. The valve body itself is bolted to the inboard side of the master cylinder/booster assembly.

FLUID LEVEL WARNING SWITCHES

These two integral fluid level switches are incorporated in the

BRAKES
FORD ANTI-LOCK SYSTEM
SECTION 24

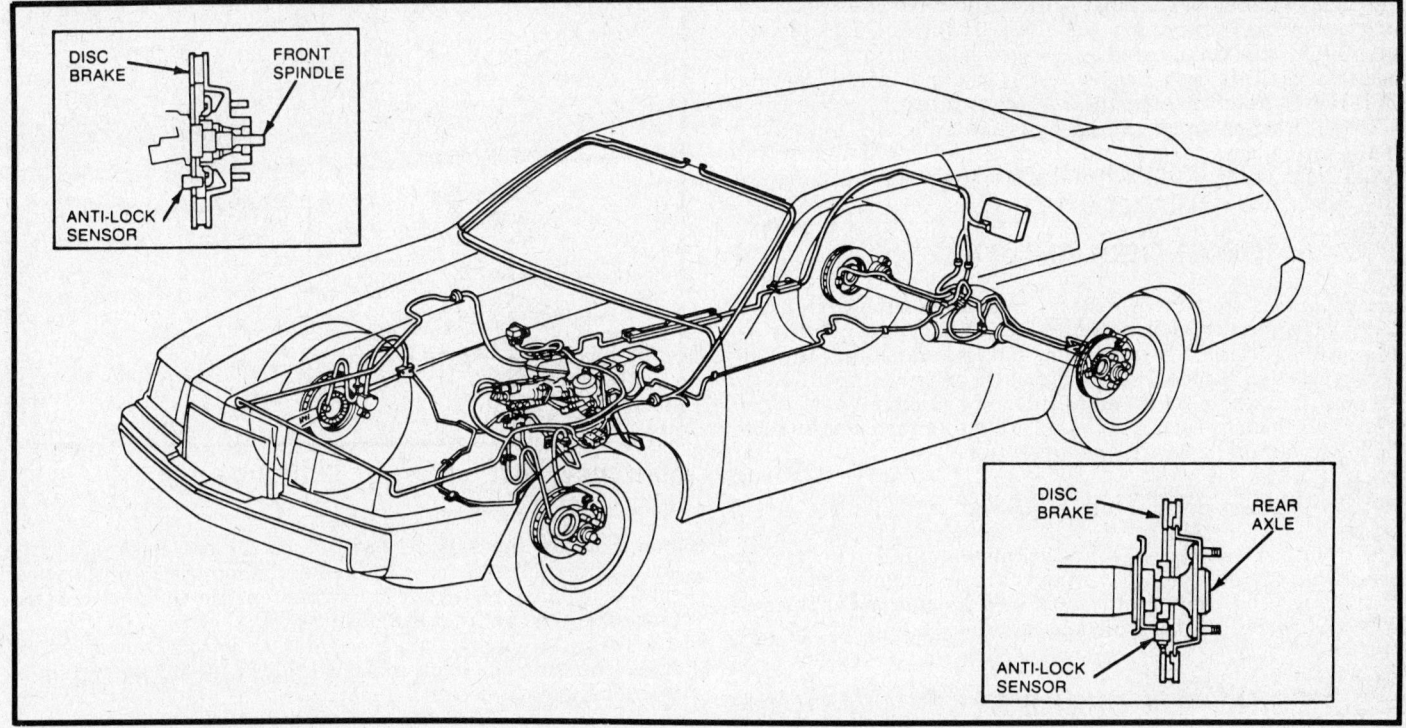
Ford anti-lock brake system

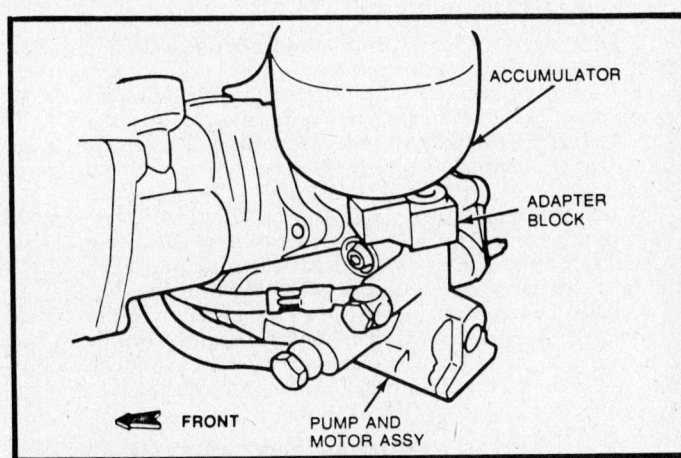
Accumulator and pump assembly

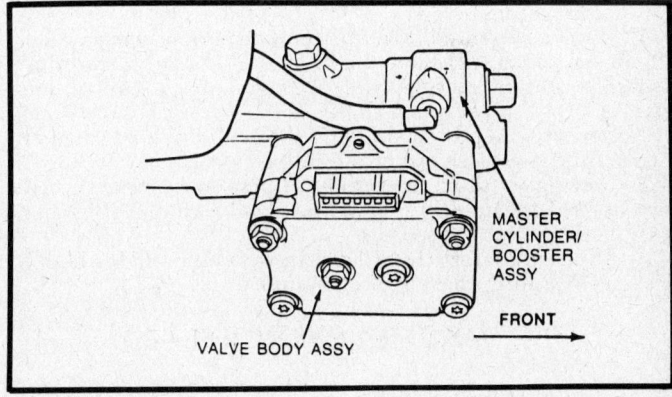
Valve body assembly

brake fluid reservoir cap assembly with two electrical connectors, one for each end of the cap, for wire harness connections.

WHEEL SENSORS

The sensors are four variable reluctance electronic sensor assemblies, each with a 104 tooth ring in the anti-lock system. The sensors are connected to an electronic controller through a wiring harness. The front sensors are bolted to brackets which are bolted to the front spindles. The front toothed sensor rings are pressed onto the inside of the front rotors. The rear sensors are bolted to brackets, that in turn are bolted to the rear disc brake axle adapters. The toothed rear sensor rings are pressed to the axle shafts, inboard of the axle shaft flange.

ELECTRONIC CONTROLLER

The controller is a self-contained non-serviceable unit, which consists of two microprocessors and the necessary circuitry for their operation. The function of the controller is to monitor the system operations during normal driving and during anti-lock braking. Any malfunction of the anti-lock brake system will cause the controller to shut off and bypass the anti-lock brake system. When the anti-lock brake system is bypassed, the normal power assisted braking will still remain.

CHECK ANTI-LOCK BRAKE WARNING LIGHT

The four wheel anti-lock system is self-monitoring. When the

24-27

SECTION 24
BRAKES
FORD ANTI-LOCK SYSTEM

ignition switch is in the run position, the electronic controller will perform a preliminary self-check on the anti-lock electrical system, this is indicated by 3-4 second energizing of the amber "Check Anti-Lock Brakes" lamp in the overhead console. This light will go out after the 3-4 second interval, unless there is a malfunction in the anti-lock brake system. If there is a malfunction the "Check Anti-Lock Brake" light and/or the brake lamp will stay lit, and diagnostic tests will then pinpoint the exact component needing service.

DIAGNOSIS AND TESTING

The diagnosis procedures were not available at the time of this publication, but there is a partial self-diagnostic capability incorporated in the EEC-IV system, and total capability is in order for the future model years. Ford also has taken the EEC-IV diagnostic box and set up an adapter so equipment already on the market can be used. There is also a comprehensive diagnostic guide available by the manufacturer.

BLEEDING THE BRAKE SYSTEM

The front brakes can be bled in the conventional manner, with or without the accumulator being charged. When bleeding the rear brakes the accumulator must be fully charged or the system has to be pressure bled as previously outlined in this section.

BLEEDING THE BRAKE SYSTEM WITH A CHARGED ACCUMULATOR

Be careful when opening the rear caliper bleeder screws, due to the high pressure in the system from a fully charged accumulator at the bleeder screws.

1. With the accumulator fully charged, have someone hold the brake pedal in the applied position and place the ignition switch in the run position and open the rear brake caliper bleed screws for 10 seconds at a time.
2. Repeat this procedure until the air is cleared from the brake fluid and close the brake caliper bleed screws.
3. Do this to all of the brake calipers and after the bleed screws are closed, pump the brake pedal a couple of times to complete the bleed procedure.
4. Adjust the brake fluid level in the reservoir to the max level with a fully charged accumulator.

MASTER CYLINDER

Removal and Installation

NOTE: The hydraulic pressure must be discharged from the brake system before removing the master cylinder. To discharge the system, turn the ignition key to the off position and pump the brake pedal at least 20 times until an increase in pedal force is clearly felt.

1. Disconnect the negative battery cable and the electrical connectors from the master cylinder reservoir cap, main valve, solenoid valve body, pressure warning switch, the hydraulic pump motor, and ground connector from the master cylinder.
2. Disconnect the brake lines from the solenoid valve body and plug the line openings in the valve body to prevent fluid loss. Do not allow the brake fluid to leak or spill onto any of the electrical connectors.
3. From inside the vehicle, disconnect the hydraulic booster pushrod from the brake pedal in the following order. Disconnect the stop light switch wires at the connector on the brake pedal. Remove the hairpin clip at the stop light switch on the brake pedal and move the switch off of the pedal pin far enough for the switch outer hole to clear the pin. Using a twisting mo-

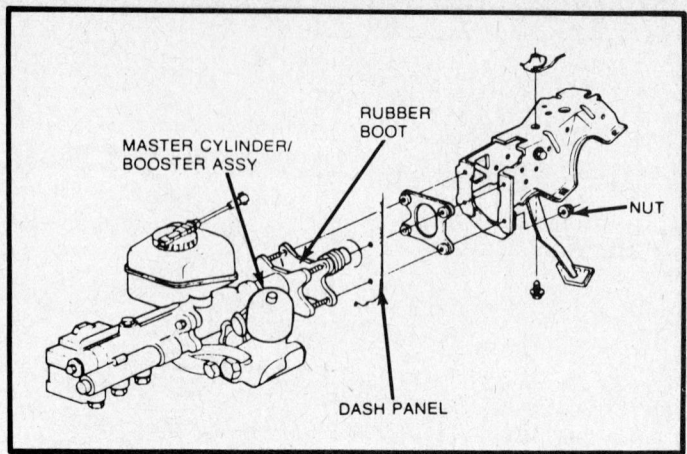

Master cylinder removal

tion, remove the switch, but be careful not to damage the switch during its removal. Remove the four retaining nuts at the dash panel and from inside the engine compartment remove the booster from the dash panel.

4. Installation is the reverse order of the removal procedure. After the unit has been installed, bleed the brake system as previously outlined in this section.

HYDRAULIC ACCUMULATOR

Removal and Installation

1. Discharge the pressure in the brake system and disconnect the electrical connection at the hydraulic pump motor.
2. Using an 8mm hex wrench or equivalent, unscrew the accumulator. Be sure that no dirt falls into the open port.
3. Using the same hex wrench or equivalent, remove the accumulator adapter block bolt and remove the block, if necessary.
4. Installation is the reverse order of the removal procedure, be sure to observe the following. Install new O-rings on the accumulator and adapter block. Torque the adapter block bolt 25 to 34 ft. lbs. and the accumulator 30 to 34 ft. lbs.
5. After installation, place the ignition switch in the on position and check to see if the "Check Anti-Lock Brake" light goes out after a maximum of one minute. Top off the master cylinder reservoir to the max mark with brake fluid.

HYDRAULIC PUMP MOTOR

Removal and Installation

1. Discharge the pressure in the brake system and disconnect the negative battery cable.
2. Disconnect the electrical connections at the hydraulic pump motor and pressure warning switch.
3. Remove the accumulator as previously outlined.
4. Remove the suction line between the reservoir and the pump at the reservoir by twisting the hose and pulling on it lightly. To prevent fluid loss, a large vacuum nipple can be slipped over the reservoir opening as the hose is removed.
5. Remove the retaining bolt on the pump high pressure line to the hydraulic booster housing at the housing. Make sure to save the two O-rings on both sides of the retaining bolt.
6. Remove the Allen head bolt that holds the pump and motor assembly to the extension housing located directly under the accumulator. Make sure to save the thick spacer between the extension housing and the shock mount.

BRAKES
FORD ANTI-LOCK SYSTEM
SECTION 24

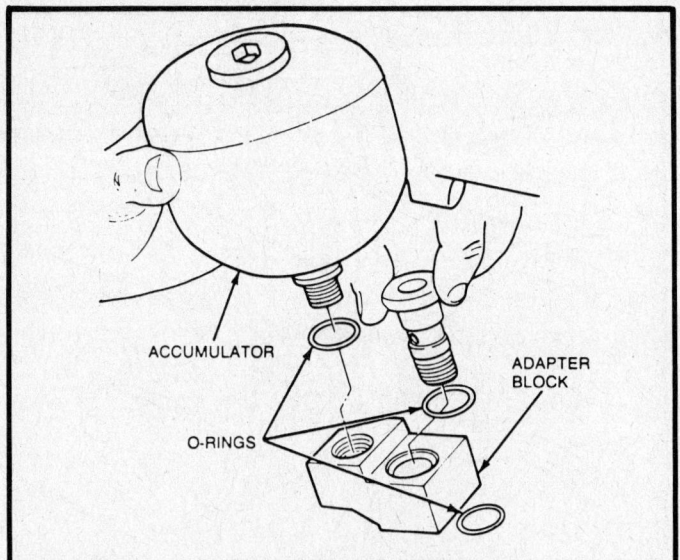

Accumulator removal and installation

Hydraulic pump motor connectors

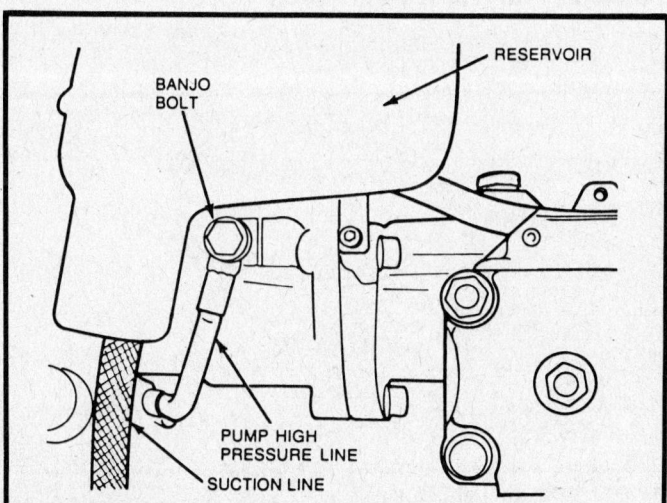

Hydraulic pump motor removal

Electronic controller location

7. Slide the pump assembly inboard to remove the assembly from the retainer pin located on the inboard side of the extension housing.

8. Installation is the reverse order of the removal procedure. Be sure to bleed the brake system and check to see if the "Check Anti-Lock Brake" light goes out after a maximum of one minute.

ELECTRONIC CONTROLLER

Removal and Installation

1. Disconnect the negative battery cable and the 35-pin connector from the electronic controller in the trunk of the vehicle in front of the forward trim panel.

2. Remove the three retaining screws holding the electronic controller to the seat back brace and remove the controller.

3. Installation is the reverse order of the removal procedure.

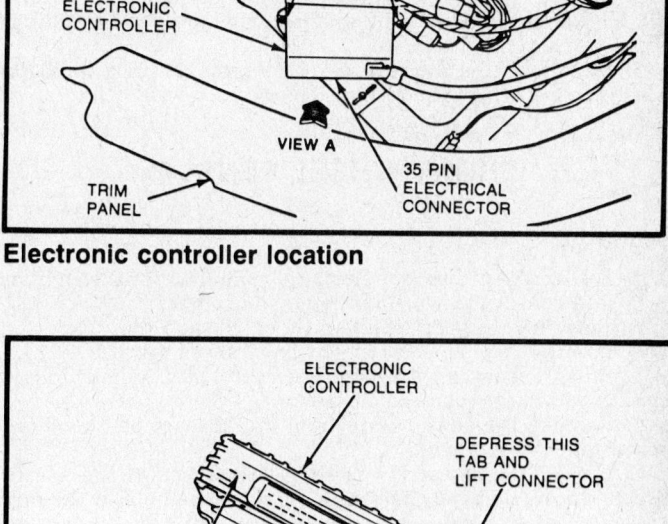

Electronic controller 35 pin connector

24–29

SECTION 24 BRAKES
FORD ANTI-LOCK SYSTEM

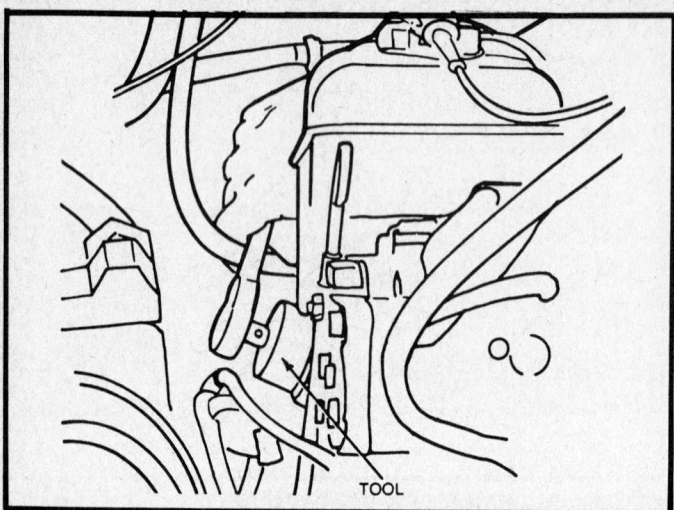

Removing or installing the pressure switch

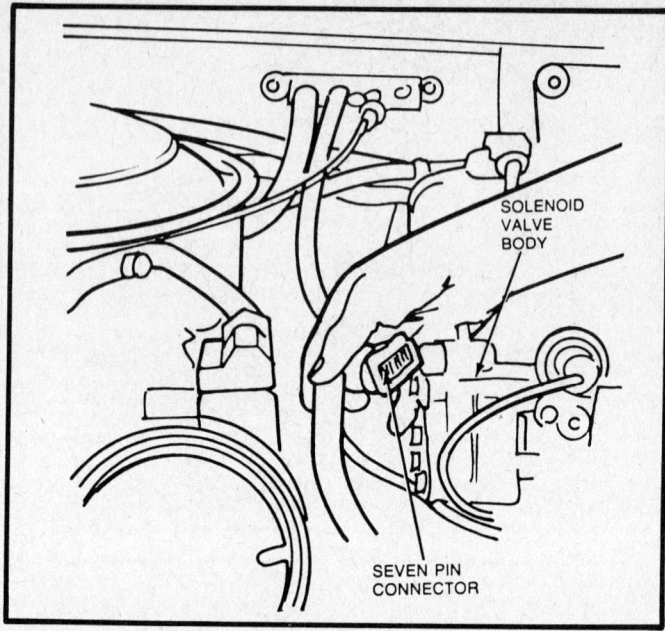

Location of the pressure switch

PRESSURE SWITCH

Removal and Installation

1. Discharge the pressure from the brake system and disconnect the negative battery cable.
2. Disconnect the solenoid valve body seven-pin connector and remove the pressure switch using special tool #T85P-20215-B or equivalent, a 1/2 to 3/8 inch adapter and a 3/8 inch drive ratchet.
3. Installation is the reverse of the removal procedure. Replace the O-ring on the switch. Torque the switch 15 to 25 ft. lbs.

FRONT WHEEL SENSOR

Removal

1. Disconnect the sensor electrical connector for the right or left front sensor from inside the engine compartment.
2. Raise and support the vehicle safely and disengage the wire grommet at the right or left hand shock tower.
3. Pull the sensor cable connector through the hole and be careful not to damage the connector.
4. Remove the sensor wire from the bracket on the shock tower and the side rail.
5. Loosen the set screw holding the sensor to the sensor bracket post. Remove the sensor through the hole in the disc splash shield.
6. Remove the sensor bracket or the sensor bracket post, if either has been damaged by removing the caliper, hub and rotor assembly (as previously outlined). Remove the two brake splash shield attaching bolts which hold the sensor bracket.

Installation

1. Install the sensor bracket and bracket post, if it has been removed. Torque the post retaining bolt 40 to 60 inch lbs. and the splash shield attaching bolts 10 to 15 ft. lbs. Install the hub and rotor assembly as previously outlined.

NOTE: If a sensor is going to be reused, the pole face must be cleaned of all dirt and grease and the pole face has to be scraped with a dull knife or equivalent so that the sensor slides freely on the post. Also glue a new front spacer paper (gasket) on the pole face.

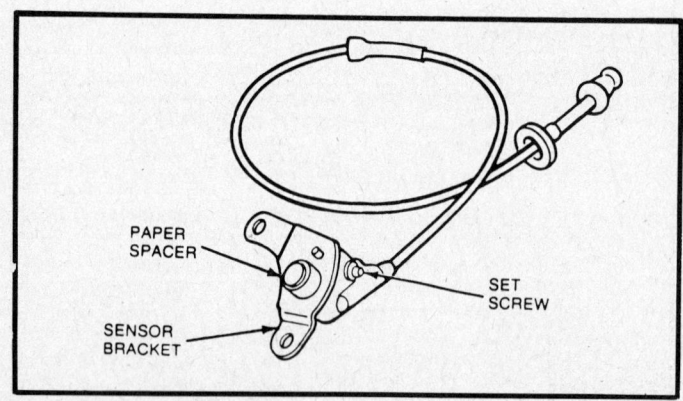

Paper spacer location

2. Install the sensor through the hole in the brake shield onto the sensor bracket post. Make sure the paper spacer does not come off during installation.
3. Push the sensor toward the toothed sensor ring until the new paper sensor contacts the ring. Hold the sensor against the sensor ring and torque the set screw to 21-26 inch lbs.
4. Insert the cable into the bracket on the shock strut, rail bracket and then through the inner fender apron to the engine compartment and the seat grommet.
5. Lower the vehicle and reconnect the sensor electrical connection.
6. Check the function of the sensor by road testing the vehicle and making sure the "Check Anti-Lock Brake" light does not stay on.

REAR WHEEL SENSOR

Removal

1. Disconnect the wheel sensor electrical connector located

BRAKES
FORD ANTI-LOCK SYSTEM
SECTION 24

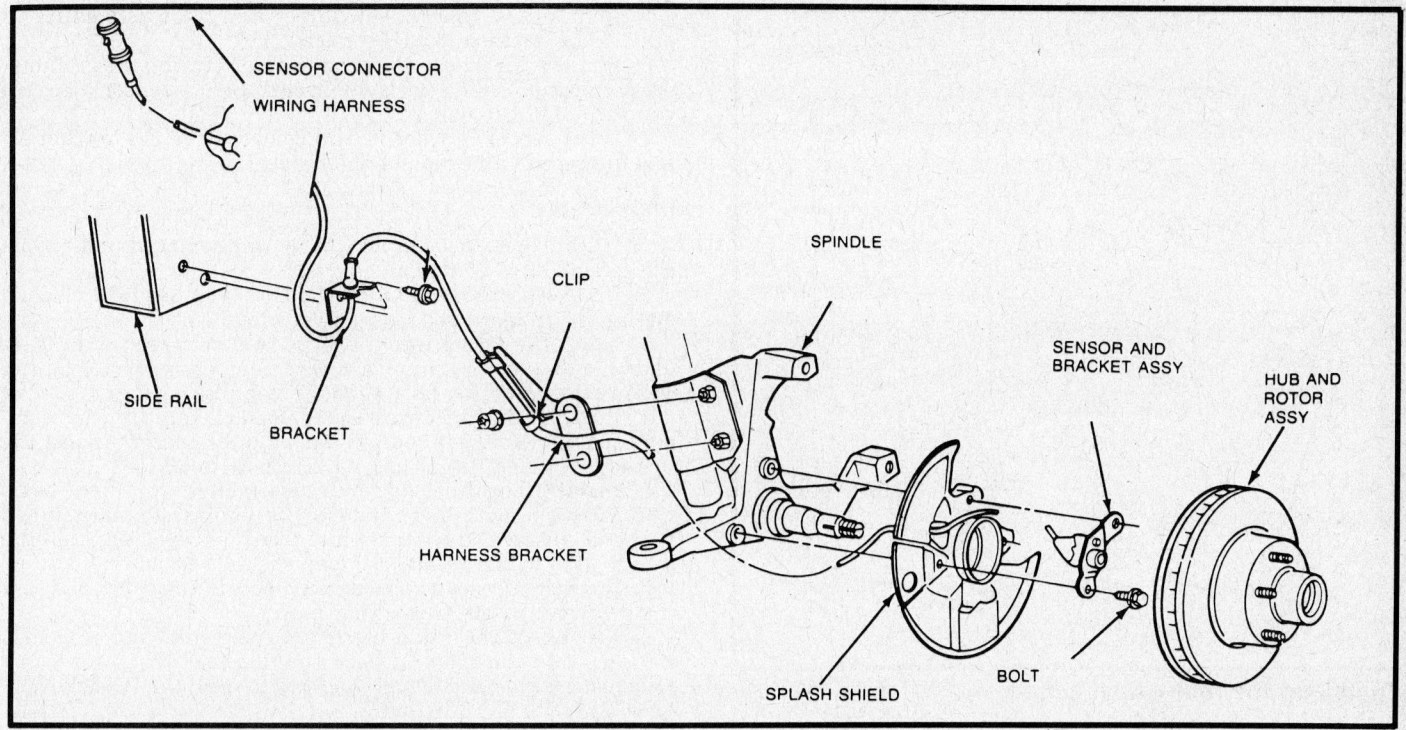

Removing the front wheel sensor

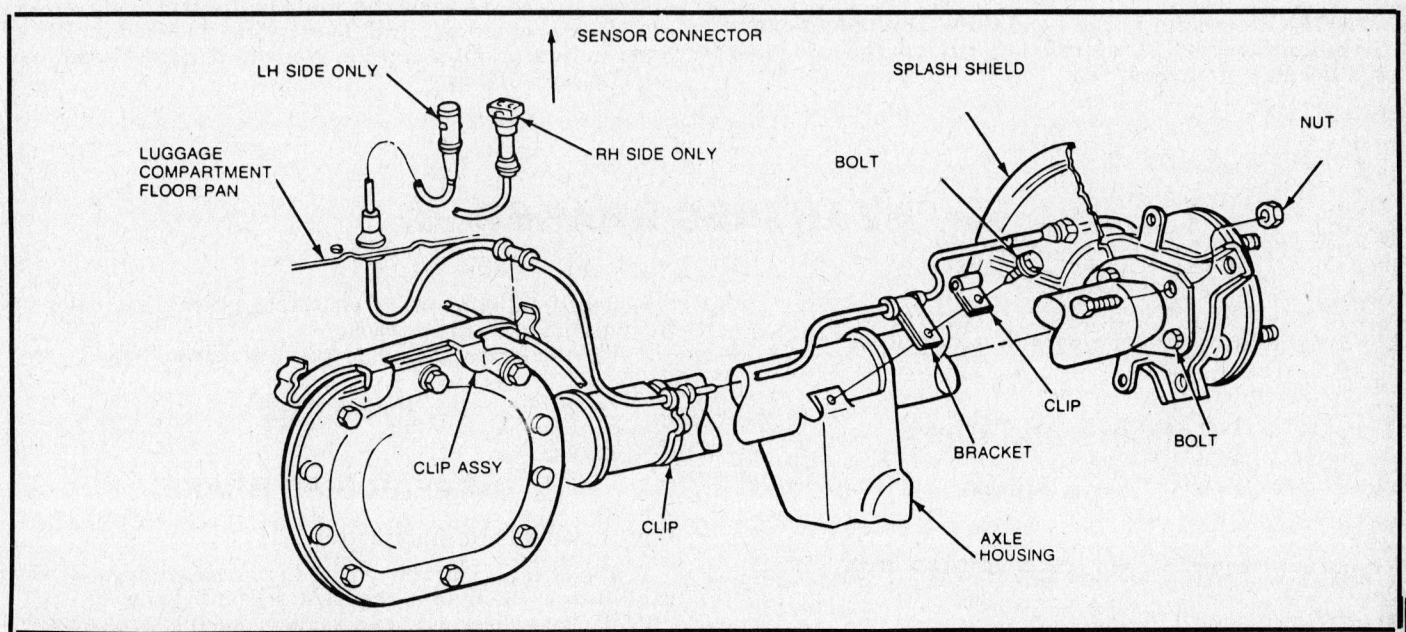

Removing the rear wheel sensor

behind the forward luggage compartment trim panel in the trunk.

2. Lift the carpet in the trunk and push the sensor wire grommet through the hole in the floor of the trunk.

3. Raise and support the vehicle safely and remove the appropriate wheel.

4. Remove the wheel sensor wiring from the axle shaft housing. The wiring harness has three different types of retainers, they are the following. The inboard retainer clip is located on the top of the differential housing. Just bend the clip far enough to remove the wiring harness. The second retainer clip is a C-clip and is located in the center of the axle shaft housing. Pull rearward on the clip to disengage the clip from the axle housing. The third clip is at the connection between the rear housing wheel brake tube and flexible hose. Remove the hold down bolt and open the clip to remove the wiring harness.

24-31

SECTION 24

BRAKES
FORD ANTI-LOCK SYSTEM

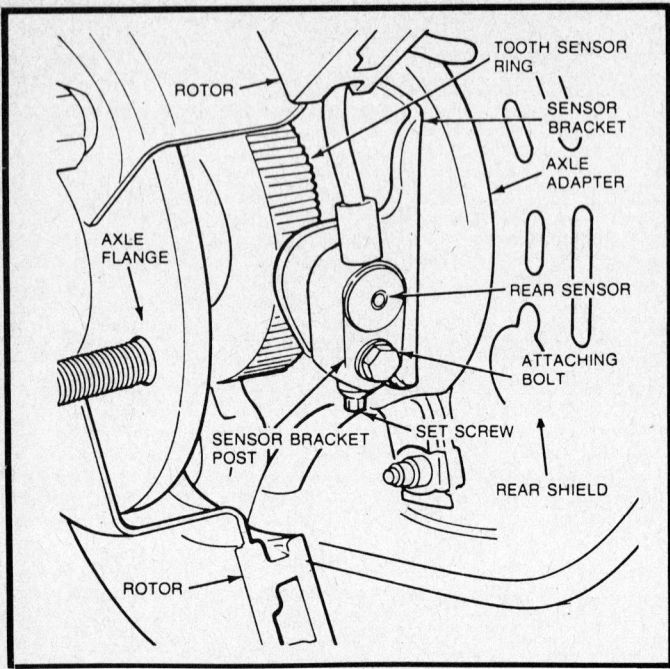

Installing the rear wheel sensor

NOTE: Be careful not to bend the C-clip open beyond the amount needed to remove the clip from the axle housing, because it could break.

5. Remove the rear wheel caliper and rotor assemblies as previously outlined in this section.
6. Remove the wheel sensor retaining bolt, slip the grommet out of the rear brake splash shield and pull the sensor wire outward through the hole.
7. If the sensor bracket is damaged, remove the bracket attaching screws and replace the bracket.

Installation

1. Install the sensor bracket if it was removed and torque the screws 11 to 15 ft. lbs.
2. If the sensor is going to be used again, it has to be cleaned just as the front wheel sensors were cleaned.
3. Insert the sensor into the large hole in the sensor bracket and install the retaining bolt into the sensor bracket post. Torque the retaining bolt 40 to 60 inch lbs.
4. Push the sensor toward the toothed ring until the new paper sensor touches the sensor ring, hold the sensor against the toothed ring and torque the set screw 21 to 26 inch lbs.
5. Install the caliper and rotor assemblies.
6. Push the wire and connector through the splash shield hole and engage the grommet into the shield eyelet. Install the sensor wire in the retainers along the axle housing.
7. Push the connector through the hole in the trunk and seat the grommet in the trunk floor pan.
8. Reconnect the cable electrical connector, and re-install the carpet in the trunk. Check the function of the sensor by road testing the vehicle and checking to see if the "Check Anti-Lock Brake" light goes out.

NOTE: If the toothed ring sensor is found to be malfunctioning on either the front or rear wheel, the rotor assembly has to be removed and the toothed ring sensor has to be pressed out and the new one pressed in. Brake pad removal and installation is covered in the Ford Floating Caliper section.

REAR DISC BRAKES

Rotors

Refer to front rotors for removal, installation or service procedures.

Calipers and Pads

Type Nine

DELCO FIXED CALIPER (FOUR PISTONS)

Pad Removal and Installation

1. Remove half of the brake fluid from the master cylinder.
2. Remove the brake pad retaining pins.
3. Pry the pistons back into their bore (being careful to pry both pistons at once so as not to force one out of its bore) and lift out one pad by tipping it down at the rear and up at the front.
4. Hold the rear piston in and slide the rear end of the new pad into place, being careful not to force out the front piston.
5. Check the condition of the rotor. If rotor run out exceeds .003 thousands, or has deep scratches, re-machine the rotor.
6. Now push the front piston back in to its bore and slide the front of the new pad into position.
7. Change the other pad in the same manner.
8. Reinstall the retaining pin through the caliper holes and through the holes in the pads.
9. Fill the master cylinder with fresh brake fluid.

Type Ten

GM REAR DISC BRAKE

Pad Removal and Installation

1. The calipers must be removed to replace linings. Remove two-thirds of the fluid in the front master cylinder.
2. Remove wheel and tire assembly, and reinstall one wheel mounting nut, flat side toward rotor, to prevent rotor from falling when caliper is removed.
3. Loosen tension on the parking brake cable at equalizer, and remove the cable from the parking brake lever at the caliper.
4. Remove return spring, lock nut, lever, lever seal and anti-friction washer (lever must be held in place while removing nut).
5. Using a C-clamp with the solid end of the lever stop and the screw end of the back of the outboard lining assembly, tighten clamp until piston bottoms in the caliper. Do not position C-clamp on actuator screw.

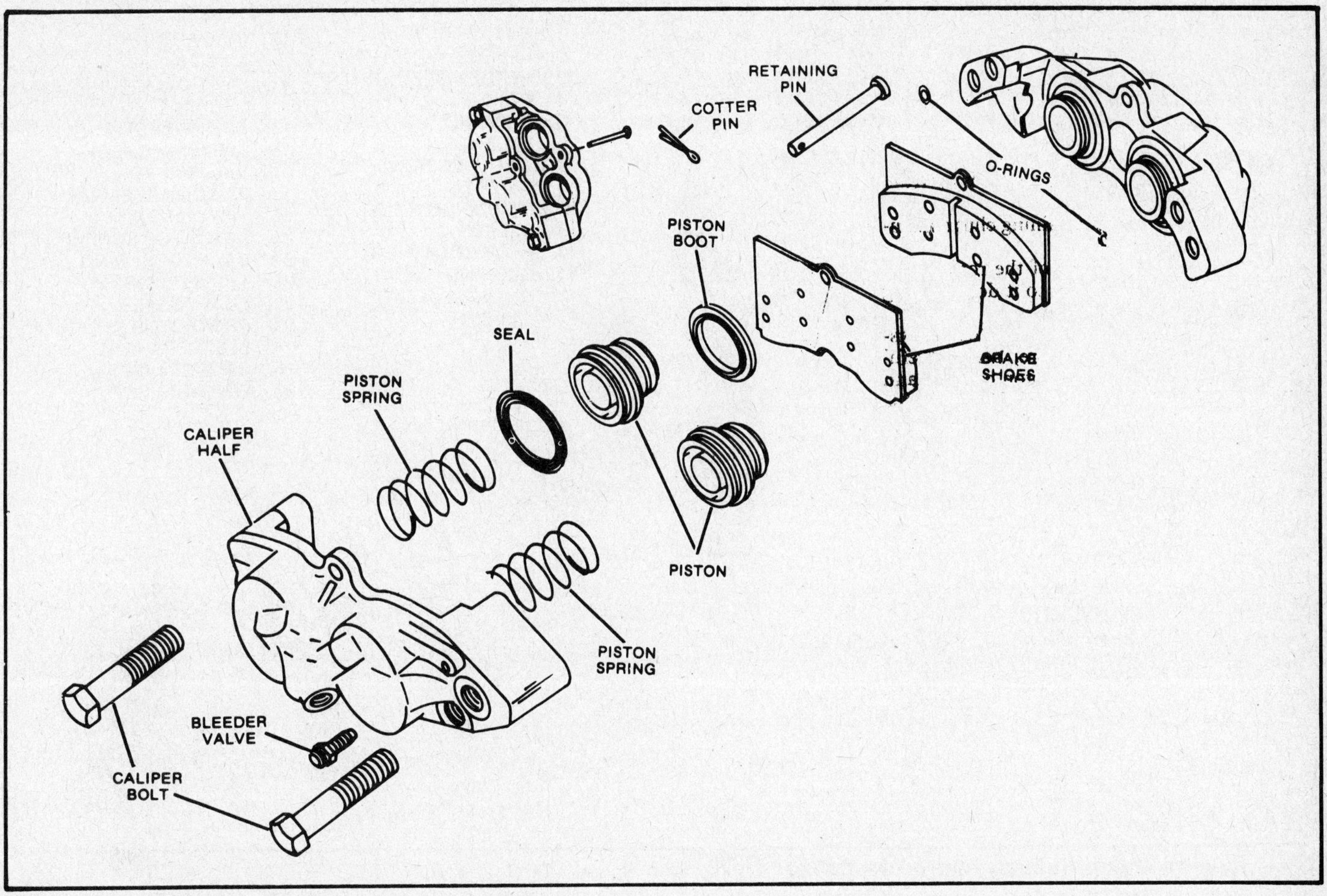

Brakes
Disc Brake Service
Section 24

Type nine—Delco fixed caliper (four pistons)

6. Before removing the clamp lube the caliper housing surface (under the lever seal) with silicone.
7. Install new anti-friction washer, new lever seal and lever. Be certain to install lever on hex with arm pointing downward.
8. Rotate lever toward front of car and while holding in this position install nut and torque to 25 ft. lbs. Rotate lever back to stop.
9. Install lever return spring, and remove C-clamp. Springs are color coded, red for right side caliper and black for left.
10. Remove brake line from caliper and plug openings to retain fluid. If brake line nut is seized, brass bolt and block on caliper can be removed with brake line attached by removing bolt and block copper washers after removing caliper mounting bolts.
11. Remove caliper mounting bolts and remove caliper and brake shoes.
12. Remove two caliper mounting sleeves and four bushings, and install new parts using a silicone lubricant. (Sleeves are installed in inner bushings.)
13. Position new inboard shoe assembly on piston. D shaped in the indentation provided in the piston.
14. Install new outboard shoe assembly.
15. To reinstall caliper replace any corroded caliper mounting bolts with new parts. Wire bushing or sanding will damage the bolt plating.
16. If brass bolt and block was removed with brass pipe, unplug fittings and install bolt and block using two new copper gaskets. Torque to 30 ft. lbs. Be sure that all sleeves, bushings

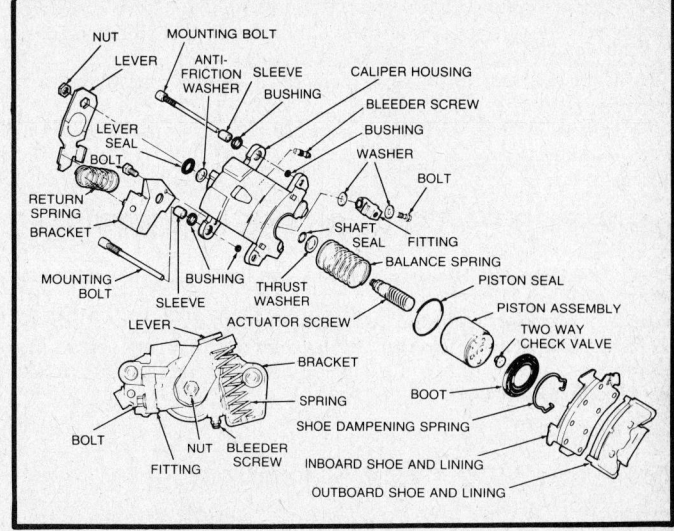

Type ten—General Motors rear disc and parking brake

and pins are well lubricated with silicone (mounting bolt should go under inboard shoe ears).

17. Install brake line tube nut into caliper and pump brake pedal to seat lining against rotor.

24-33

SECTION 24 BRAKES
DISC BRAKE SERVICE

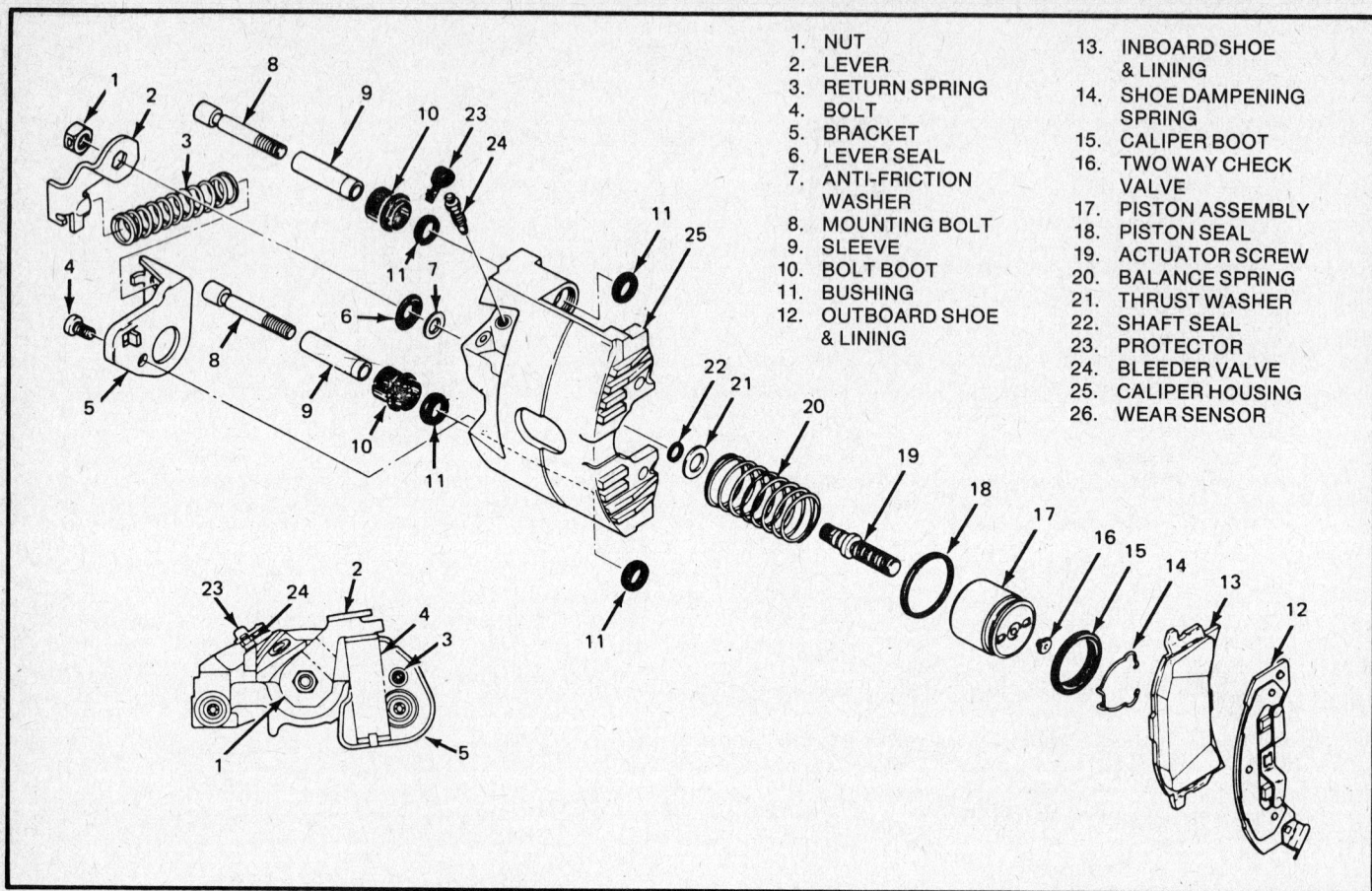

Type eleven—Delco floating rear brake caliper

1. NUT
2. LEVER
3. RETURN SPRING
4. BOLT
5. BRACKET
6. LEVER SEAL
7. ANTI-FRICTION WASHER
8. MOUNTING BOLT
9. SLEEVE
10. BOLT BOOT
11. BUSHING
12. OUTBOARD SHOE & LINING
13. INBOARD SHOE & LINING
14. SHOE DAMPENING SPRING
15. CALIPER BOOT
16. TWO WAY CHECK VALVE
17. PISTON ASSEMBLY
18. PISTON SEAL
19. ACTUATOR SCREW
20. BALANCE SPRING
21. THRUST WASHER
22. SHAFT SEAL
23. PROTECTOR
24. BLEEDER VALVE
25. CALIPER HOUSING
26. WEAR SENSOR

18. Clinch upper ear of outboard shoe by positioning pliers with one jaw on top of upper ear and other jaw in notch or bottom of shoe, opposite upper ear. After clinching there should be no radial clearance between the shoe ears and caliper housing. Repeat clinching procedure if necessary.
19. Connect and adjust parking rake cables and bleed rear brake system.
20. Install wheel and tire assembly. Torque steel mounting nuts to 130 ft. lbs.

CALIPER PARKING BRAKE MECHANISM

When the parking brake is applied, the lever turn the actuator screw which is threaded into a nut in the piston assembly. This causes the piston to move outward and the caliper to slide inward mechanically, forcing the linings against the rotor. The piston assembly contains a self-adjusting mechanism for the parking brake.

Type Eleven

DELCO FLATING REAR BRAKE CALIPER

Pad Removal

1. Remove 2/3 of the brake fluid from the master cylinder.
2. Loosen the rear wheel lugs. Raise and support the rear of the vehicle on jackstands.
3. Mark the wheel and axle lug for same reinstallment location and remove the wheel assemblies.
4. Reinstall two lug nuts to retain the brake rotor.
5. Loosen the tension on the parking brake cable by backing off the equalizer.
6. After cable tension has been released, remove the cable end from the apply lever at the caliper.
7. Hold the apply lever in position and remove the retaining nut.
8. Remove the lever, lever seal and anti-friction washer.

NOTE: If the parking brake levers are not disconnected from the caliper during pad removal and installation, damage to the piston assembly will occur when it is moved back in the caliper bore.

9. Position a C-clamp over the caliper and tighten until the piston bottoms in the caliper bore. Take care not to allow the C-clamp to contact the actuator screw on the caliper. Reinstall anti-friction washer, seal and lever.
10. If caliper service is required, disconnect the brake line. Plug all openings.
11. Remove the caliper mounting bolts using a 3/8 allen head socket or wrench.
12. Remove the caliper by lifting up and off the rotor. Do not permit the caliper to be suspended by the brake hose.
13. Remove the pads from the caliper. A suitable tool is required to pry the outboard pad from the caliper since it is retained by a spring button.
14. Remove the pin bushings and sleeves from the caliper ears.

BRAKES
DISC BRAKE SERVICE

Pad Installation

1. Install new sleeves and bushings after lubricating them. Insure that the sleeve is flush with the pad side of the caliper ear.
2. Install the inboard pad. Make sure that the D shaped retainer on the pad engages the D shaped slot in the caliper piston. Turn piston if necessary for correct alignment.
3. Be sure that the wear indicator is mounted on the leading edge of the pad for forward rotation of the wheel.
4. Slide the edge of the metal shoe under the ends of the dampening spring and snap the pad into position flat against the caliper piston.
5. Mount the outboard pad in position. Be sue it snaps into the caliper recess.
6. Install the caliper over the disc rotor in the reverse order of removal. Apply the brakes several times to seat the linings, after filing the master cylinder. Bleed brakes if necessary.

Type Twelve

GIRLOCK FLOATING FRONT AND REAR CALIPERS

Pad Removal

1. Remove 2/3 of the brake fluid from the master cylinder.
2. Loosen the rear wheel lugs. Raise and support the rear of the vehicle on jackstands.
3. Mark the wheel and axle lug for same reinstallment location and remove the wheel assemblies.
4. Reinstall two lug nuts to retain the brake rotor.
5. Loosen the tension on the parking brake cable by backing off the equalizer.
6. After cable tension has been released, remove the cable end from the apply lever at the caliper.
7. Hold the apply lever in position and remove the retaining nut.
8. Remove the lever, lever seal and anti-friction washer.

NOTE: If the parking brake levers are not disconnected from the caliper during pad removal and installation, damage to the piston assembly will occur when it is moved back in the caliper bore.

9. Position a C-clamp over the caliper and tighten until the piston bottoms in the caliper bore. Take care not to allow the C-clamp to contact the actuator screw on the caliper. Reinstall anti-friction washer, seal and lever.
10. If caliper service is required, disconnect the brake line. Plug all openings.
11. Remove the caliper mounting bolts using a 3/8 allen head socket or wrench.
12. Remove the caliper by lifting up and off the rotor. Do not permit the caliper to be suspended by the brake hose.
13. Remove the pads from the caliper. A suitable tool is required to pry the outboard pad from the caliper since it is retained by a spring button.
14. Remove the pin bushings and sleeves from the caliper ears.

Pad Installation

1. Install new sleeves and bushings after lubricating them. Insure that the sleeve is flush with the pad side of the caliper ear.
2. Install the inboard pad. Make sure that the D shaped retainer on the pad engages the D shaped slot in the caliper piston. Turn piston if necessary for correct alignment.
3. Be sure that the wear indicator is mounted on the leading edge of the pad for forward rotation of the wheel.

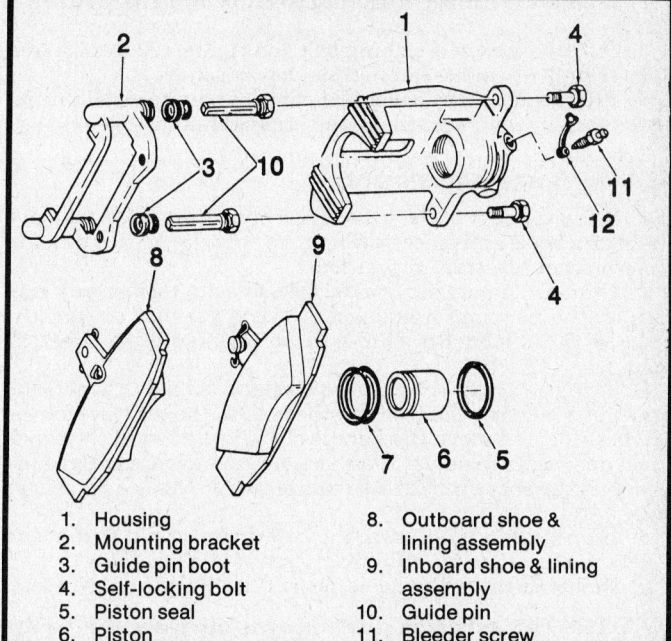

1. Housing
2. Mounting bracket
3. Guide pin boot
4. Self-locking bolt
5. Piston seal
6. Piston
7. Piston boot
8. Outboard shoe & lining assembly
9. Inboard shoe & lining assembly
10. Guide pin
11. Bleeder screw
12. Cap

Type twelve—Girlock front and rear brake caliper

4. Slide the edge of the metal shoe under the ends of the dampening spring and snap the pad into position flat against the caliper piston.
5. Mount the outboard pad in position. Be sure it snaps into the caliper recess.
6. Install the caliper over the disc rotor in the reverse order of removal. Apply the brakes several times to seat the linings, after filling the master cylinder. Bleed brakes if necessary.

Type Twelve

GIRLOCK FLOATING FRONT AND REAR CALIPERS

Pad Removal

1. Remove 2/3 of the brake fluid from the master cylinder.
2. Loosen the rear lugs and raise the rear of the vehicle. Support the vehicle on jackstands.
3. Remove the wheel assemblies. Install two lug nuts to hold the brake disc rotor in position.
4. Position a C-clamp over the caliper, one end on the outboard pad, the other on the inlet fitting bolt head.
5. Tighten the clamp to push the caliper piston until it bottoms in the bore.
6. Remove and discard the upper caliper self-locking bolt. Rotate the caliper on the lower bolt to expose the brake pads.
7. Remove the inner and outer pads from the caliper.
8. Clean the pad mounting frame on the caliper. Inspect the caliper for signs of fluid leakage. Remove and service caliper if necessary.

Pad Installation

1. Install the new inner and outer pad in position on the caliper.

24-35

SECTION 24 BRAKES
DISC BRAKE SERVICE

2. Rotate the caliper back into position over the disc brake rotor.
3. Install a new self-locking bolt and tighten 22 to 25 ft. lbs.
4. Install wheel assemblies and lower vehicle.
5. Fill the master cylinder and pump the brake pedal several times to seat the pads. Bleed the brakes if necessary.

Parking Brake Adjustment

1. Raise the rear of the vehicle and support it safely, remove the rear wheels and place two lug nuts opposite of each other to ensure proper disc/drum position.
2. Loosen the parking brake cable so as to release any tension on the parking brake shoes. Rotate the disc so that the hole in the disc/drum face will be aligned with the star adjuster.
3. Using a brake spoon or equivalent, adjust the parking brake by inserting the tool into the hole in the disc face on the drivers side and move the handle of the tool toward the top of the fender skirt to adjust the shoes out and toward the ground to adjust the shoes in. Reverse this procedure on the passenger side.
4. Adjust the shoes until the disc/drum won't rotate and back the star adjuster off 5 to 7 notches on both sides.
5. Reinstall the rear wheels, lower the vehicle and road test.

NOTE: The asbestos dust thrown off from the brake linings or disc pads may be dangerous to your health if inhaled, Never use compressed air or your own breath to blow the dust from the brake assembly. Use a damp rag or a well filtered vacuum cleaner. Dispose of the rag or cleaner bag properly.

Drums

Conditions and Resurfacing

The condition of the brake drum surface is just as important as the surface to the brake lining. All drum surfaces should be clean, smooth, free from hard spots, heat checks, score marks and foreign matter imbedded in the drum surface. They should not be out of round, bell-mouthed or barrel shaped. It is recommended that all drums be first checked with a drum micrometer to see if they are within over-size limits. If drum is within safe limits, even though the surface appears smooth, it should be turned not only to assure a true drum surface but also to remove any possible contamination in the surface from previous brake linings, road dusts, etc. Too much metal removed from a drum is unsafe and may result in the following.

1. Brake to fade due to the thin drum being unable to absorb the heat generated.
2. Poor and erratic brake due to distortion of drums.
3. Noise due to possible vibration caused by thin drums.
4. A cracked or broken drum on a severe or very hard brake application. Brake drum run-out should not exceed 0.005 inch Drums turned to more than 0.060 inch oversize are unsafe and should be replaced with new drums, except for some heavy ribbed drums which have an 0.080 inch limit. It is recommended that the diameters of the left and right drums on any one axle be within when replacing drums. It is always good to replace the drums on both wheels at the same time.
5. If the drums are true, smooth up any slight scores by polishing with fine emery cloth. If deep scores or grooves are present, which cannot be removed by this method, then the drum must be turned.

DRUM BRAKE SPECIFICATIONS

Vehicle Make and Model	Brake Shoe ① Minimum Lining Thickness	Brake Drum Diameter Standard Size	Brake Drum Diameter Machine To	Wheel Lugs or Nuts Torque (ft-lbs)
American Motors				
All exc. 6 cyl. Concord Wagon and Eagle	.030	9.000	9.060	75
6 cyl. Concord Wagon and Eagle	.030	10.000	10.060	75
Chrysler Corp.—Chrysler—Dodge—Plymouth				
Dodge 600, New Yorker	.030	8.661	—	85
Aries, Reliant, LeBaron Dodge 400	.030	7.870	7.900	85
Cordoba, Diplomat, Grand Fury, Mirada, New Yorker, Imperial				
w/10" rear brake	.030	10.000	10.060	85
w/11" rear brake	.030	11.000	11.060	85
Omni, Horizon	.030	7.870	7.900	85
Aries, Reliant	.030	7.870	7.900	85
Ford Motor Co.—Ford—Mercury—Lincoln				
Lincoln Continental				
Front	—	—	—	80-105
Rear	—	—	—	80-105
Thunderbird, XR-7				
w/9" rear brake	.030	9.000	9.060	80-105
w/10" rear brake	.030	10.000	10.060	80-105

BRAKES
DRUM BRAKE SERVICE

DRUM BRAKE SPECIFICATIONS

Vehicle Make and Model		Brake Shoe ① Minimum Lining Thickness	Brake Drum Diameter		Wheel Lugs or Nuts Torque (ft-lbs)
			Standard Size	Machine To	
'83	Cougar, Granada				
	w/9" rear brake	.030	9.000	9.060	80-105
	w/10" rear brake	.030	10.000	10.060	80-105
'82-'86	Escort, Lynx, EXP, LN7				
	w/7" rear brake	.030	7.000	7.060	80-105
	w/8" rear brake	.030	8.000	8.060	80-105
'83-'85	Mustang, Capri, Fairmount, Zephyr				
	w/9" rear brake	.030	9.000	9.060	80-105
	w/10" rear brake	.030	10.000	10.060	80-105
	Lincoln Town Car, Mark VI, LTD, Marquis				
	w/10" rear brakes	.030	10.000	10.060	80-105
	w/11" rear brakes	.030	11.030	11.090	80-105
General Motors Corp					
Buick					
	Century, Skyhawk	①	7.880	7.899	100
	Regal, LeSabre	①	9.500	9.560	80 ⑤
	Riviera				
	w/o rear disc brakes	①	9.500	9.560	100
	w/rear disc brakes	—	—	—	100
	Electra, Estate Wagon	①	11.000	11.060	100
	Skylark	①	7.880	7.899	103
Cadillac					
	Cimarron	.030	.880	7.899	100
	Fleetwood	.030	11.000	11.060	100
	Eldorado, Seville				
	Front	—	—	—	100
	Rear	—	—	—	100
	Fleetwood Limo, Commercial Chassis	①	12.000	12.060	100
Chevrolet					
	Celebrity, Cavalier	①	7.880	7.899	100
	Camaro				
	w/rear drum brakes	①	9.500	9.560	80†
	w/rear disc brakes	—	—	—	80†
	Malibu, Monte Carlo, El Camino	①	9.500	9.560	80†
	Citation	①	7.880	7.899	103
	Impala, Caprice				
	w/9½" rear brakes	①	9.500	9.560	80
	w/11" rear brakes	①	11.000	11.060	100
	Chevette	①	7.874	7.899	70
	Corvette				
	Front	—	—	—	70 ②
	Rear	—	—	—	70 ②
Oldsmobile					
	Ciera, Firenza	①	7.880	7.899	100
	Cutlass Supreme, 88	①	9.500	9.560	100 ③
'83-'84	Omega	①	7.880	7.899	103
	Toronado				
	w/o rear disc	①	9.500	9.560	100
	w/rear disc	—	—	—	100

24-37

SECTION 24 BRAKES
DRUM BRAKE SERVICE

DRUM BRAKE SPECIFICATIONS

Vehicle Make and Model		Brake Shoe ① Minimum Lining Thickness	Brake Drum Diameter		Wheel Lugs or Nuts Torque (ft-lbs)
			Standard Size	Machine To	
'83–'84	Custom Cruiser, 88 (w/403), 98				
	w/9.5″ rear brake	①	9.500	9.560	100
	w/11: rear brake	①	11.000	11.060	100
Pontiac					
	6000, J2000	①	7.880	7.899	100
	Firebird				
	w/rear drum brakes	①	9.500	9.560	80†
	w/rear disc brakes	—	—	—	80†
	T1000	①	7.874	7.899	70†
'83–'84	Phoenix (F.W.D.)	—	7.880	7.899	103
	Bonneville, Catalina, LeMans, Grand Prix, Grand Am, Safari				
	w/9.5″ rear brakes	①	9.500	9.560	80
	w/11″ rear brakes	①	11.000	11.060	80 ④

NOTE: State and local inspection regulations will take precedence over manufacturer's standards.
① .030 in. over rivet head, if bonded lining use .062 in.
② Aluminum whls; Corvette 80, Camaro 105, others 90.
③ 88 w/7/16 in. stud; 80 ft.-lbs.
④ 1/2 in. stud 100 ft.-lbs.
⑤ W/aluminum wheels, LeSabre 90 ft.-lbs., Regal 100 ft.-lbs.

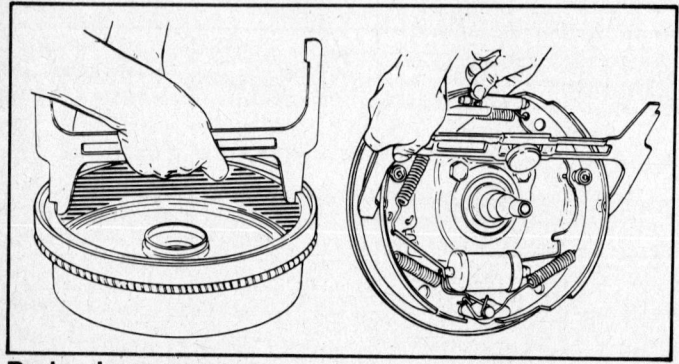

Brake drum gauge

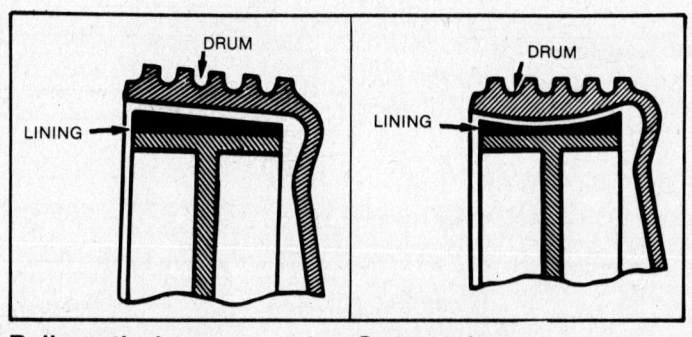

Bellmouth drum   Convex drum

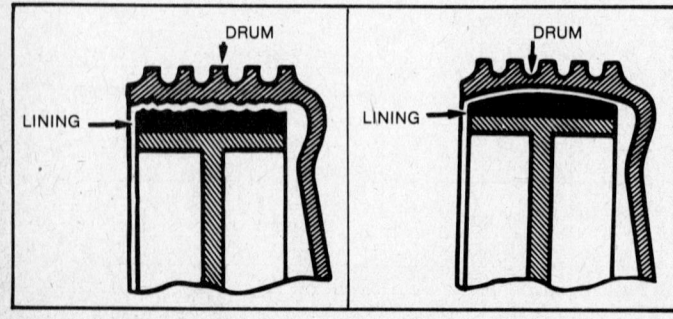

Scored drum surface   Concave drum

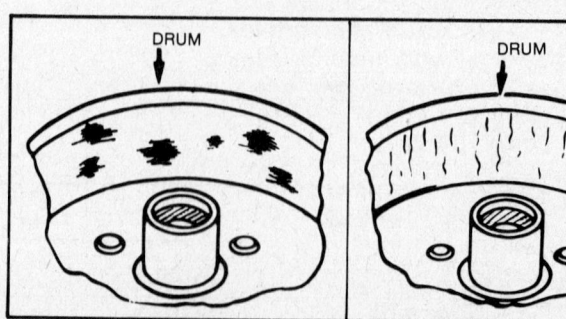

Hard or chill spots   Heat checks

BRAKES
DRUM BRAKE SERVICE — SECTION 24

DRUM BRAKES

 TROUBLESHOOTING DRUM BRAKES

Trouble Symptoms

Possible Causes of Trouble Symptoms	One Brake Drags	All Brakes Drag	Hard Pedal	Spongy Pedal	Car Pulls to One Side	One Wheel Locks	Brakes Chatter	Excessive Pedal Travel	Pedal Gradually Goes to Floor	Brakes Uneven	Shoe Click Release	Noisy or Grabbing Brakes	Brakes Do Not Apply
Mechanical Resistance at Pedal or Shoes Damaged Linkage		X	X										
Brake Line Restricted	X	X	X		X								
Leaks or Insufficient Fluid				X				X	X				X
Improper Tire Pressure					X					X			
Improperly Adjusted or Worn Wheel Bearing	X				X								
Distorted or Improperly Adjusted Brake Shoe	X	X	X		X	X		X			X		
Faulty Retracting Spring	X				X								
Drum Out of Round	X				X		X						
Linings Glazed or Worn				X	X	X	X	X				X	X
Oil or Grease In Lining				X	X	X	X			X		X	X
Loose Carrier Plate	X					X	X						
Loose Lining					X		X						
Scored Drum										X		X	
Dirt on Drum-Lining Surface												X	
Faulty Wheel Cylinder	X				X	X						X	
Dirty Brake Fluid	X	X								X			X
Faulty Master Cylinder		X						X	X				X
Air in Hydraulic System	X			X				X					X
Self Adjusters Not Operating					X			X			X		
Insufficient Shoe-to-Carrier Plate Lubrication	X										X		
Tire Tread Worn						X							
Poor Lining to Drum Contact							X						
Loose Front Suspension							X						
"Threads" Left by Drum Turning Tool Pull Shoes Sideways											X		
Cracked Drum								X					
Sticking Booster Control Valve		X										X	

SECTION 24 BRAKES
DRUM BRAKE SERVICE

DRUM BRAKE APPLICATION CHART

Car and Years	Brake Type	Self-Adjuster Type
American Motors	Duo-Servo	Star & Screw
Chrysler Corp. 1982-86 all models ①	Duo-Servo	Star & Screw
Ford Motor Co. 1982-86 all models except below	Duo-Servo	Star & Screw
1982-86 Escort, Lynx, EXP, LN7	Non-Servo	Star & Screw (8 in. brake) Strut & Pin (7 in. brake)
General Motors Corp. 1982-86 all models	Duo-Servo	Star & Screw

① The rear drum brakes on Chrysler front wheel drive cars through 1982, are not automatically adjusted.

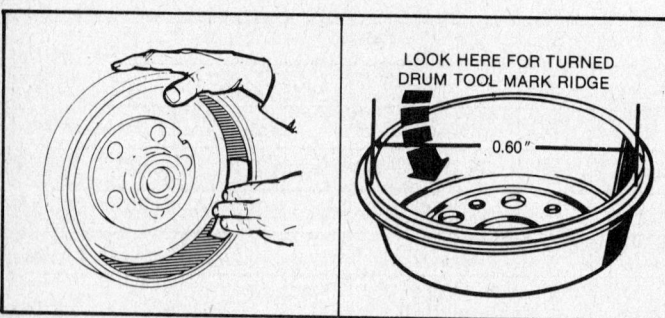

Sanding brake drums — Oversize drum

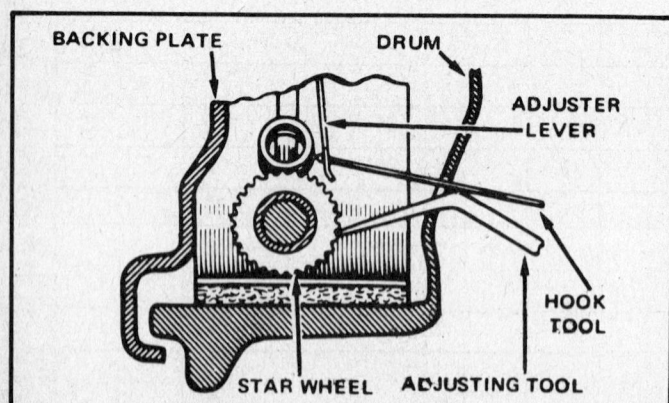

Release of adjusting lever with adjusting slot in brake drum

Duo-Servo Brake

Refer to the Drum Brake Application Chart for adjuster applications. In the Duo-Servo design, the force which the wheel cylinder applies to the shoes is supplemented by the tendency of the shoes to wrap or twist into the drum during braking. Thus two braking forces are applied at each drum every time the brakes are activated.

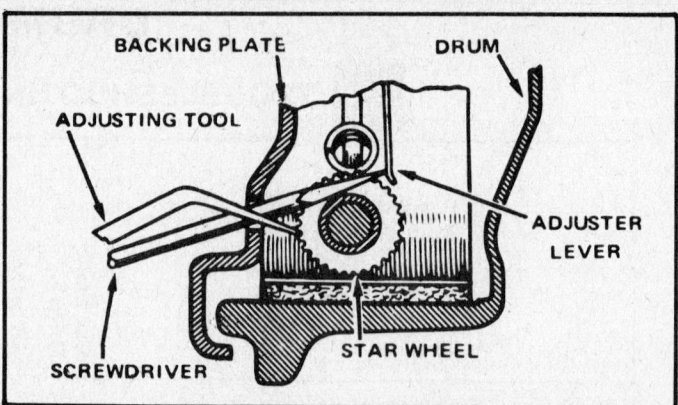

Release of adjusting lever with adjusting slot in backing plate

STAR AND SCREW ADJUSTER

The duo-servo brake, with star and screw type self-adjusters, is used on most late-model American cars. The same basic brake unit has been used on all cars. General Motors cars use a rod-operated lever to turn the star wheel, while all others use a cable-operated lever. This is the only difference, other than size, among units used on different models.

Brake Shoe Adjustment

The drum brakes used on today's cars are normally self-adjusting. They require manual adjustment only when the shoes have been replaced or when the star and screw adjuster has been disturbed.

NOTE: The drum brakes on most cars can be initially adjusted by removing the brake drum, measuring its internal diameter, then adjusting the shoes to that measurement and installing the drum. Use a vernier gauge to make the measurements. This method can be used on all models, and may be preferable to punching out the covering over the access hole in the backing plate or brake drum edge.

1. Remove the access slot plug from the backing plate or front of drum. On some cars, there is no access slot in the backing plate or in the front of the drums. Some have been filled in and must be punched out to gain access to the adjuster. Complete the adjustment and cover the hole with a plug to prevent entrance of dirt and water.
2. Using a brake adjusting spoon or screwdriver, pry downward on the end of the tool (starwheel teeth moving up) to tighten the brakes, or upward on the end of the tool (starwheel teeth moving down) to loosen the brakes.

NOTE: It may be necessary to use a small rod or suitable tool to hold the adjusting lever away from the star wheel. Be careful not to bend the adjusting lever.

3. When the brakes are tight almost to the point of being locked, back off on the starwheel until the wheel is able to rotate freely. The starwheel on each set of brakes (front or rear) must be backed off the same number of turns to prevent brake pull from side to side.
4. When all four brakes are adjusted, check brake pedal travel and then make several stops, while backing the car up, to equalize all the wheels.

Testing Adjuster

1. Raise the vehicle on a hoist, with a helper in the car, to apply the brakes.

BRAKES
DRUM BRAKE SERVICE
SECTION 24

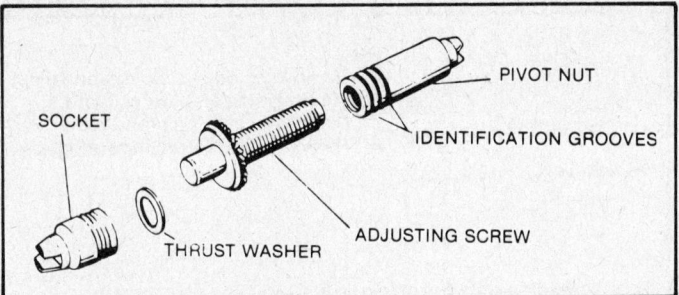

Adjusting screw assembly

2. On models with access plugs in the backing plate, loosen the brakes by holding the adjuster lever away from the starwheel and backing off the starwheel approximately 30 notches. On models without access plugs in the backing plate, remove wheel and drum, loosen the adjuster, then reinstall the drum and wheel.
3. Spin the wheel and brake drum in reverse and apply the brakes. The movement of the secondary shoe should pull the adjuster lever up, and when the brakes are released the lever should snap down and turn the starwheel.
4. If the automatic adjuster doesn't work, the drum must be removed and the adjuster components inspected carefully for breakage, wear, or improper installation.

BRAKE SHOES

Removal

1. Remove the brake drum.
2. Place the hollow end of a brake spring service tool on the brake shoe anchor pin and twist it to disengage one of the brake shoe retaining springs. Repeat this operation to remove the other spring. Be careful that the springs do not slip off the tool during removal, as the spring could break loose and cause personal injury.
3. Reach behind the brake backing plate and place a finger on the end of one of the brake holddown mounting pins. Using a pair of pliers, or special brake pin retainer tool, grasp the

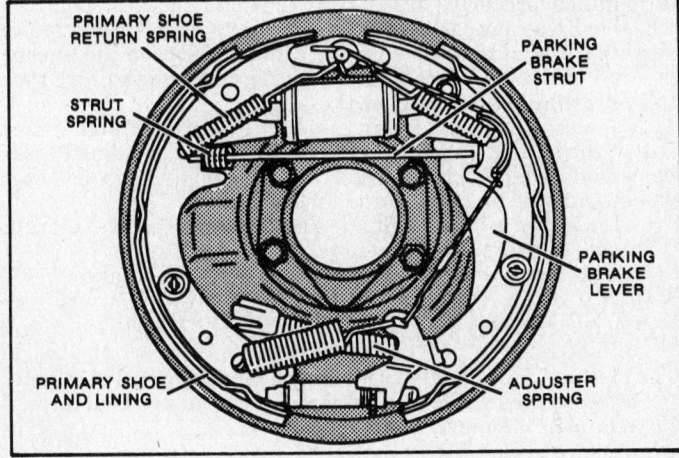

AMC, Ford type rear drum brake assembly

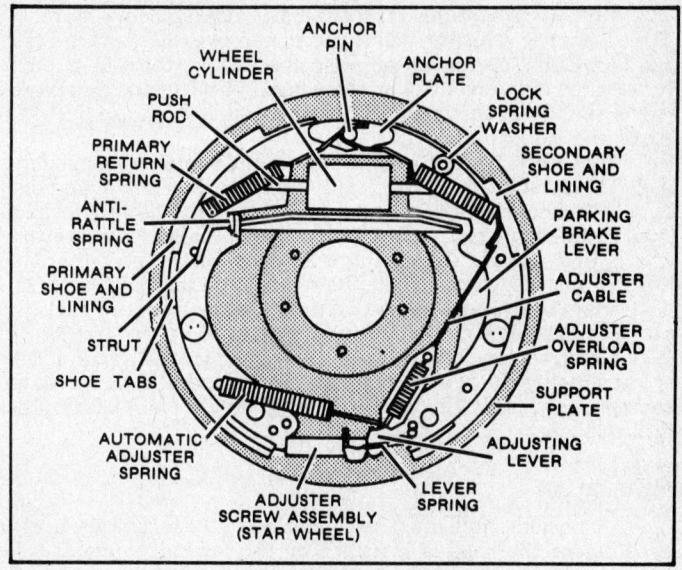

Chrsyler type rear drum brake assembly

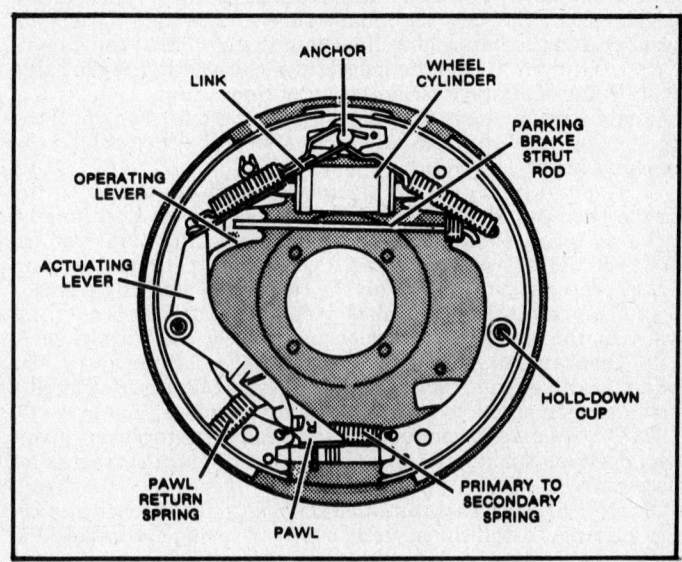

GM type rear drum brake assembly

washer on the top of the hold-down spring that corresponds to the pin that you are holding. Push down on the pliers and turn them 90° to align the slot in the washer with the head on the spring mounting pin. Remove the spring and washer and repeat this operation on the holddown spring of the other brake shoe.
4. On Ford and American Motors cars, place the tip of a suitable tool on the top of the brake adjusting screw and move the screwdriver upward to lift up on the brake adjusting lever. When there is enough slack in the automatic adjuster cable, disconnect the loop on the top of the cable from the anchor. Back off the adjusting screw while holding the adjustment lever away from the screw. Grasp the top of each brake shoe and move them outward to disengage from the wheel cylinder and parking brake link (if working on rear wheels). When the brake shoes are clear, lift them from the backing plate. Twist the shoes slightly and the automatic adjuster assembly will disassemble itself.

24-41

SECTION 24 BRAKES
DRUM BRAKE SERVICE

5. On GM cars, remove the automatic adjuster link. Remove the automatic adjuster lever, pivot, and override spring from the secondary spring as an assembly. Move the top of each brake shoe outward to clear the wheel cylinder pins and parking brake link (rear brakes). Lift the brakes from the backing plate and remove the adjusting screw.

6. On Chrysler cars, except some front wheel drive models, slide the automatic adjuster cable from the anchor pin and disengage it from the adjusting lever. Remove the cable, overload spring, and cable guide. Disconnect the automatic lever return spring and remove the spring and lever. Move the top of the brake shoes outward to clear the wheel cylinder pins and parking brake link (rear brakes). Lift the brakes from the backing plate and remove the adjusting screw.

7. Grasp the end of the brake cable spring with a pair of pliers and, using the brake lever as a fulcrum, pull the end of the spring away from the lever. Disengage the cable from the brake lever.

Installation

1. The brake cable must be connected to the secondary brake shoe before the shoe is installed on the backing plate. To do this, transfer the parking brake lever from the old secondary shoe to the new one. This is accomplished by spreading the bottom of the horseshoe clip and disengaging the lever. Position the lever on the new secondary shoe and install the spring washer and the horseshoe clip. Close the bottom of the clip after installing it. Grasp the metal tip of the parking brake cable with a pair of pliers. Position a pair of side cutters on the end of the cable coil spring and, using the pliers as a fulcrum, pull the coil spring back with the side cutters. Position the cable in the parking brake lever.

2. Apply a light coating of high-temperature grease to the brake shoe contact points on the backing plate. Position the primary brake shoe on the front of the backing plate and install the hold-down spring and washer over the mounting pin. Install the secondary shoe on the rear of the backing plate.

3. If working on rear brakes, install the parking brake link between the primary brake shoe and the secondary brake shoe.

4. On Ford and American Motors cars, install the automatic adjuster cable loop end on the anchor pin. Make sure that the crimped side of the loop faces the backing plate.

5. On GM cars, assemble the automatic adjuster lever, pivot, and override spring and install to the secondary spring as an assembly.

6. On Chrysler, install the automatic adjuster lever and return spring. Install the adjuster overload spring and cable. One end of the cable engages with the adjusting lever while the other slips over the anchor pin underneath the primary and secondary return springs.

7. Install the return spring in the primary brake shoe and, using the tapered end of a brake spring service tool, slide the top of the spring onto the anchor pin. Be careful to make sure that the spring does not slip off the tool during installation, as the spring could break loose and cause personal injury.

8. Install the automatic adjuster cable guide in the secondary brake shoe, making sure that the flared hole in the cable guide is inside the hole in the brake shoe. Fit the cable into the groove in the top of the cable guide.

9. Install the secondary shoe return spring through the hole in the cable guide and the brake shoe. Using the brake spring tool, slide the top of the spring onto the anchor pin.

10. Clean the threads on the adjusting screw and apply a light coating of high-temperature grease to the threads. Screw the adjuster closed, then open it one-half turn.

11. Install the adjusting screw between the brake shoes with the star wheel nearest to the secondary shoe. Make sure that the star wheel is in a position that is accessible from the adjusting slot in the backing plate.

12. Install the short, hooked end of the automatic adjuster

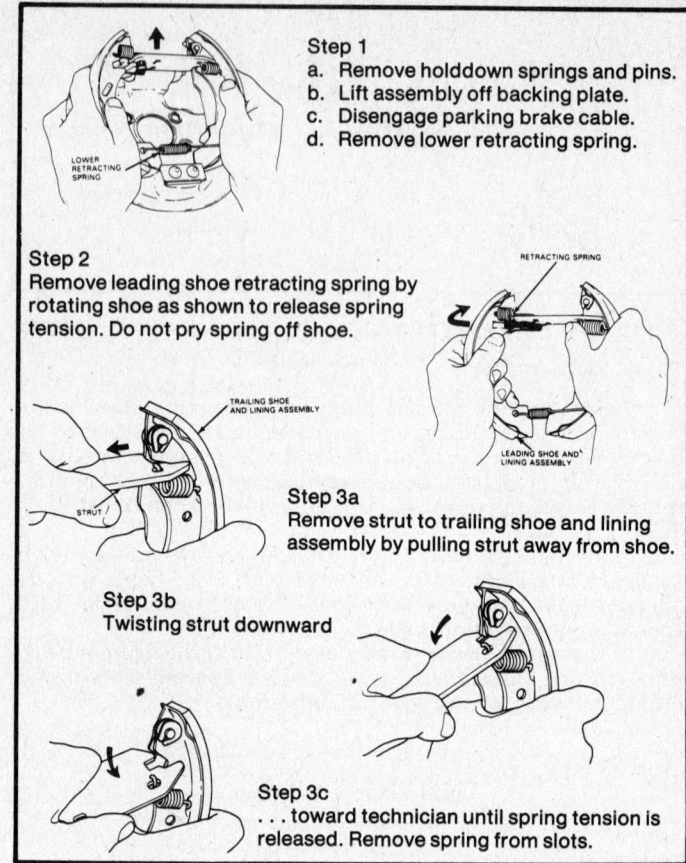

Step 1
a. Remove holddown springs and pins.
b. Lift assembly off backing plate.
c. Disengage parking brake cable.
d. Remove lower retracting spring.

Step 2
Remove leading shoe retracting spring by rotating shoe as shown to release spring tension. Do not pry spring off shoe.

Step 3a
Remove strut to trailing shoe and lining assembly by pulling strut away from shoe.

Step 3b
Twisting strut downward

Step 3c
...toward technician until spring tension is released. Remove spring from slots.

Non-servo—7 in. Ford rear brakes

spring in the proper hole in the primary brake shoe.

13. Connect the hooked end of the automatic adjuster cable and the free end of the automatic adjuster spring in the slot in the top of the automatic adjuster lever.

14. Pull the automatic adjuster lever (the lever will pull the cable and spring with it) downward and to the left, and engage the pivot hook of the lever in the hole in the secondary brake shoe.

15. Check the entire brake assembly to make sure everything is installed properly. Make sure that the shoes engage the wheel cylinder properly and are flush on the anchor pin. Make sure that the automatic adjuster cable is flush on the anchor pin and in the slot on the back of cable guide. Make sure that the adjusting lever rests on the adjusting screw star wheel. Pull upward on the adjusting cable until the adjusting lever is free of the star wheel, then release the cable. The adjusting lever should snap back into place on the adjusting screw star wheel and turn the wheel one tooth.

16. Expand the brake adjusting screw until the brake drum will just fit over the brake shoes.

17. Install the wheel and drum and adjust the brakes.

FORD NON-SERVO BRAKES

The star and screw adjuster is used on models with 8 in. diameter brake drums while the strut and pin adjuster is used on 7 inch diameter drums.

Adjustments

Normal shoe adjustments are automatic, however, when the

Brakes
Drum Brake Service
Section 24

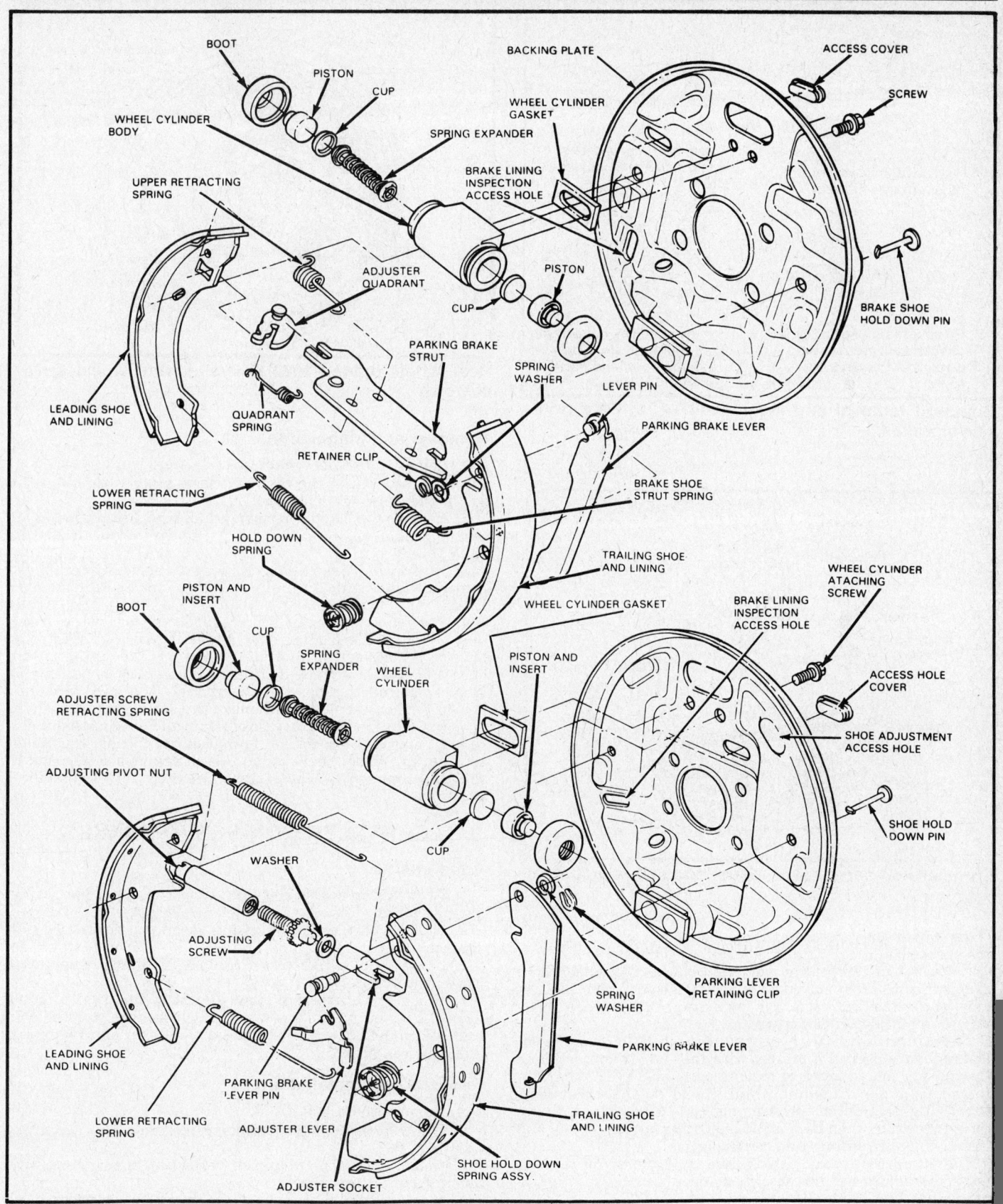

Rear brake assemblies, Ford front wheel drive. Upper—7 inch brake with strut and pin adjusters. Lower—8 inch brake with star and screw adjusters

24-43

SECTION 24 BRAKES
DRUM BRAKE SERVICE

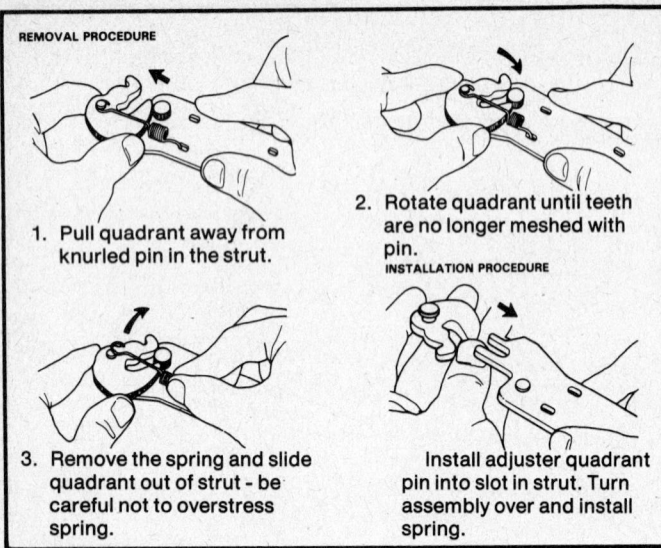

Quadrant removal and installation – 7 in. Ford non-servo brakes

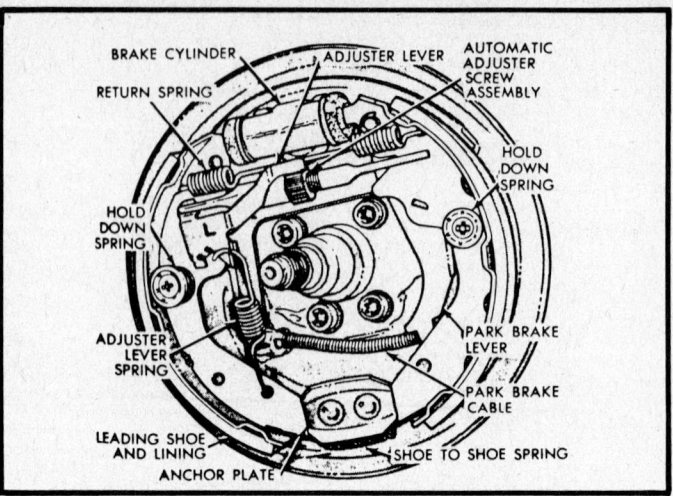

Rear wheel brake – 1983 Chrysler front wheel drive vehicles

Removal and Installation

1. Remove the wheel and hub. Adjusters can be backed off through the back of the brake backing plate with a suitable tool if the drum will not come off.
2. Remove the holddown springs and pins. Lift the assembly off the brake backing plate and disengage the parking brake cable.
3. On 7 inch drums, remove the lower retracting spring. On 8 inch drums, remove all retracting springs and the adjuster lever.
4. The following removal procedures are for 7 inch drums only. Remove the leading shoe retracting spring by rotating shoe to release spring tension. Do not pry the spring off the shoe. Remove the strut to trailing shoe assembly by pulling the strut away from the shoe and twisting the shoe downward until spring tension is released. Remove the spring from the slots.
5. Installation is the reverse of removal. See adjustment procedure, above, for special information on initial adjustment techniques. Wheel bearings on 8 inch drums are adjusted in the same manner as 7 inch drums. See Step 2 of "Adjustment" procedure.

CHRYSLER NON-SERVO BRAKES

Adjustments

1. Remove the access slot plug from the upper part of the backing plate.
2. Using a thin brake adjusting spoon pry downward (left side) or upward (right side) on the end of the tool (starwheel teeth moving up) to tighten the brakes. The opposite applies to loosen the brakes.
3. When the brakes are tight almost to the point of being locked, back off on the starwheel 10 clicks. The starwheel on each side must be backed off the same number of turns to provide for even braking.

Removal and Installation

1. Remove the brake drum.
2. Unhook the parking brake cable from the secondary (trailing) shoe.
3. Remove the shoe-to-anchor retracting spring(s) and the upper spring (if equipped).
4. Remove the shoe hold down springs; compress them slightly and slide them off of the hold down pins or push in and twist them from the mount pin.

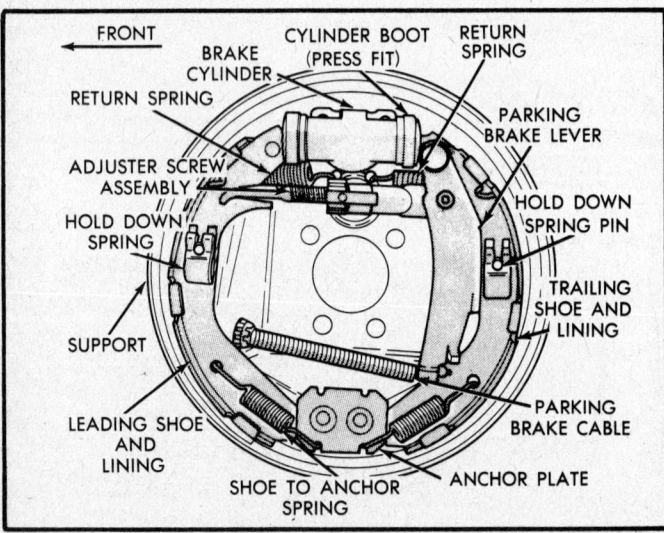

Chrysler non-servo rear brakes (non self adjusting)

shoes have been replaced or the adjuster has been disturbed, the shoes should be initially adjusted by hand.

1. Raise the rear of the car and remove the wheels and drums. Drums are removed by releasing the parking brake, removing the dust cap, cotter pin, adjusting nut and wheel bearing, then pulling off the drum.
2. On 7 inch drums with strut and pin adjuster, pivot the adjuster quadrant until it meshes with the knurled pin and is in the third or fourth notch of the outboard end of the quadrant. Install the brake drum and wheel and adjust the wheel bearings by tightening the adjusting nut to 17-15 ft. lbs. while rotating the drum, then back off the adjusting nut about 100° and install the nut retainer and cotter pin.
3. 8 inch drums are adjusted in the same manner as the star and screw adjuster drums described under "Duo-Servo" brakes, above. See that section for procedure.
4. Complete adjustment by applying the brakes several times.

BRAKES
DRUM BRAKE SERVICE
SECTION 24

5. Remove the adjuster screw assembly by spreading the shoes apart. Disconnect the adjuster spring from the trailing shoes on self-adjuster models. The adjuster nut must be fully backed off.
6. Raise the parking brake lever. Pull the secondary (trailing) shoe away from the backing plate so pull-back spring tension is released.
7. Remove the secondary (trailing) shoe and disengage the spring end from the backing plate.
8. Raise the primary (leading) shoe to release spring tension. Remove the shoe and disengage the spring end from the backing plate.
9. Inspect the brakes linings.
10. Lubricate the six shoe contact areas on the brake backing plate and the web end of the brake shoe which contacts the anchor plate. Use a multi-purpose lubricant or a high temperature brake grease made for the purpose.
11. Chrysler recommends that the rear wheel bearings be cleaned and repacked whenever the brakes are renewed. Be sure to install a new bearing seal.
12. With the leading shoe return spring in position on the shoe, install the shoe at the same time as you engage the return spring in the end support.
13. Position the end of the shoe under the anchor.
14. With the trailing shoe return spring in position, install the shoe at the same time as you engage the spring in the support (backing plate).
15. Position the end of the shoe under the anchor.
16. Spread the shoes and install the adjuster screw assembly making sure that the forked end that enters the shoe is curved down.
17. Insert the shoe hold down spring pins and install the hold down springs.
18. Install the shoe-to-anchor springs and adjuster spring (if equipped).
19. Install the parking brake cable onto the parking brake lever.
20. Replace the brake drum and tighten the nut 240 to 300 inch lbs. while rotating the wheel.
21. Back off the nut enough to release the bearing preload and position the locknut with one pair of slots aligned with the cotter pin hole.
22. Install the cotter pin. The end play should be 0.001 to 0.003 inch.
23. Install the grease cap.

POWER BRAKES

Vacuum Operated Booster

Power brakes operate just as standard brake systems except in the actuation of the master cylinder pistons. A vacuum diaphragm is located on the front of the master cylinder and assists the driver in applying the brakes, reducing both the effort and travel he must put into moving the brake pedal.

The vacuum diaphragm housing is connected to the intake manifold by a vacuum hose. A check valve is placed at the point where the hose enters the diaphragm housing, so that during periods of low manifold vacuum brake assist vacuum will not be lost.

Depressing the brake pedal closes off the vacuum source and allows atmospheric pressure to enter on one side of the diaphragm. This causes the master cylinder pistons to move and apply the brakes. When the brake pedal is released, vacuum is applied to both sides of the diaphragm, and return springs re-

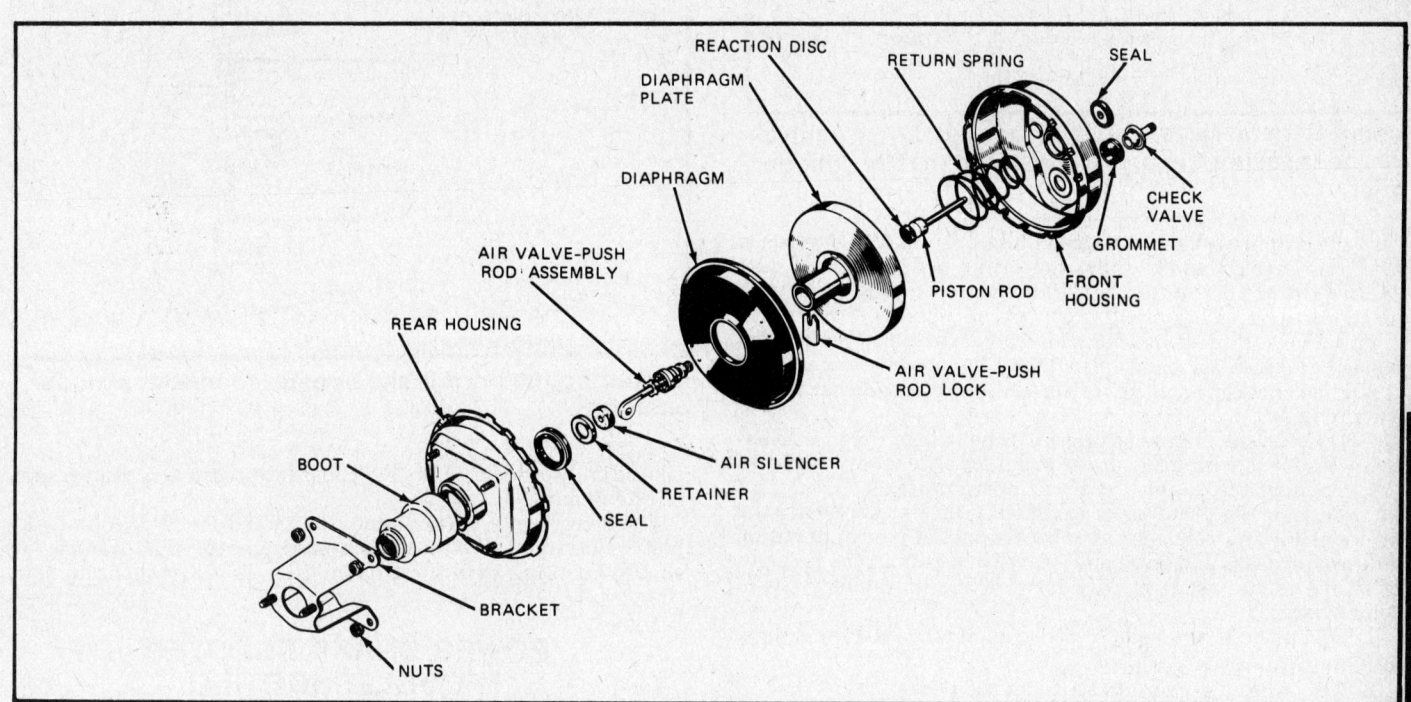

General Motors—Bendix—single diaphragm brake booster

24-45

SECTION 24 BRAKES
POWER BRAKE BOOSTERS

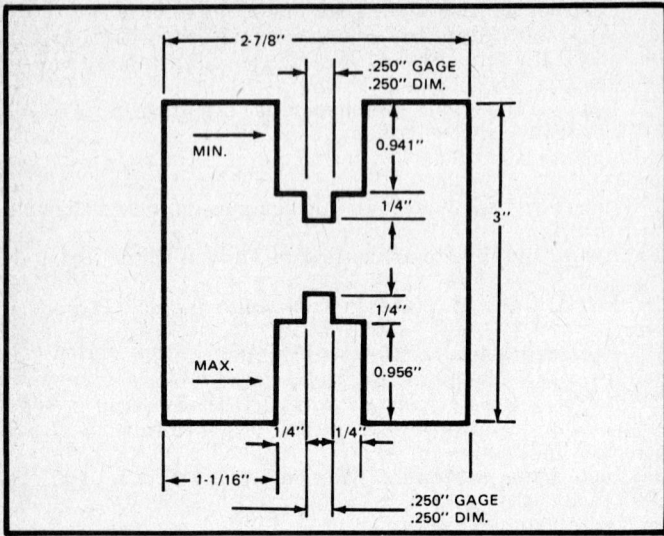

Ford brake booster to master cylinder push–rod gauge dimensions

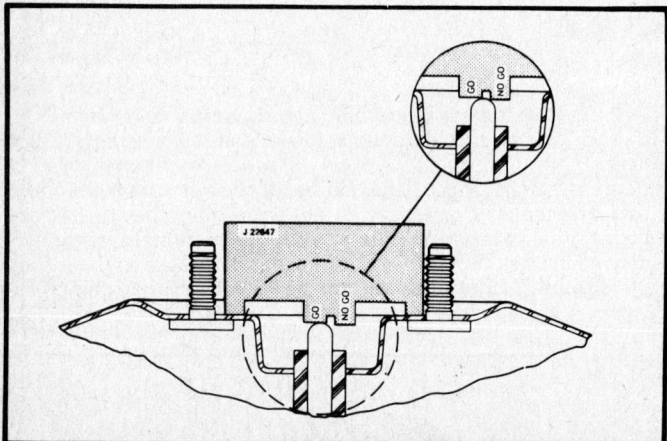

Using General Motors special tool J-22647 or equivalent to measure the brake booster to master cylinder push-rod

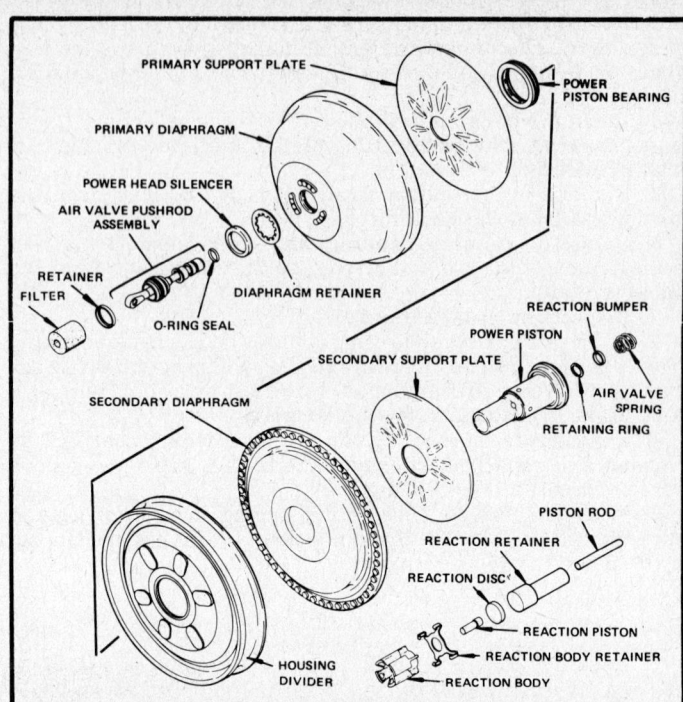

General Motors—Tandem brake booster, with an exploded view of the power piston group

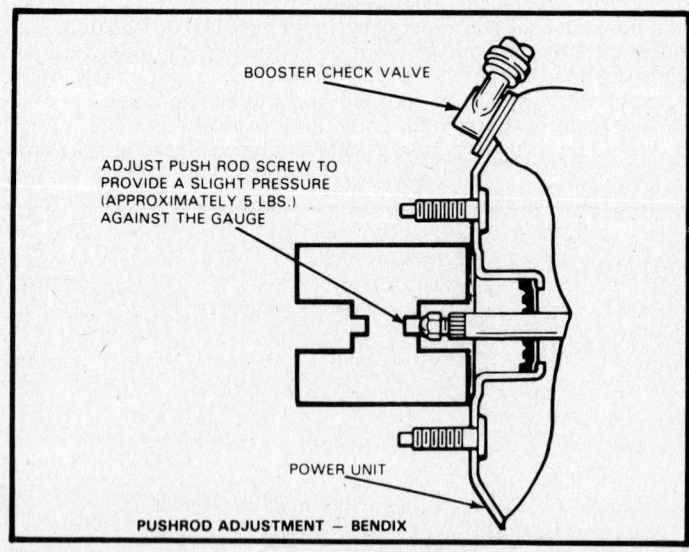

Measuring the Ford brake booster to master cylinder push-rod

turn the diaphragm and master cylinder pistons to the released position. If the vacuum fails, the brake pedal rod will butt against the end of the master cylinder actuating rod, and direct mechanical application will occur as the pedal is depressed.

The hydraulic and mechanical problems that apply to conventional brake systems also apply to power brakes, and should be checked or if the tests and chart below do not reveal the problem.

1. Operate the engine at idle with the transmission in Neutral without touching the brake pedal for at least one minute.
2. Turn off the engine, and wait one minute.
3. Test for the presence of assist vacuum by depressing the brake pedal and releasing it several times. Light application will produce less and less pedal travel, if vacuum was present. If there is no vacuum, air is leaking into the system somewhere.
4. Pump the brake pedal (with engine off) until the supply vacuum is entirely gone.
5. Put a light, steady pressure on the pedal.
6. Start the engine, and operate it at idle with the transmission in Neutral. If the system is operating, the brake pedal should fall toward the floor if constant pressure is maintained on the pedal.
7. Power brake systems may be tested for hydraulic leaks just as ordinary systems are tested, except that the engine should be idling with the transmission in Neutral throughout the test.

POWER BRAKE BOOSTER TROUBLESHOOTING

The following items are in addition to those listed in the General Troubleshooting Section. Check those items first.

BRAKES
POWER BRAKE BOOSTERS

HARD PEDAL

1. Faulty vacuum check valve.
2. Vacuum hose kinked, collapsed, plugged, leaky, or improperly connected.
3. Internal leak in unit.
4. Damaged vacuum cylinder.
5. Damaged valve plunger.
6. Broken or faulty springs.
7. Broken plunger stem.

GRABBING BRAKES

1. Damaged vacuum cylinder.
2. Faulty vacuum check valve.
3. Vacuum hose leaky or improperly connected.
4. Broken plunger stem.

PEDAL GOES TO FLOOR

Generally, when this problem occurs, it is not caused by the power brake booster. In rare cases, a broken plunger stem may be at fault.

Service and/or Overhaul

Most power brake boosters are serviced by replacement only. In many cases, repair parts are not available. A good many special tools are required for rebuilding these units. For these reasons, it would be most practical to replace a failed booster with a new or remanufactured unit.

AMC

If diagnosis indicates an internal malfunction in the power brake unit, service the unit as an assembly only. Do not attempt to disassemble, repair or adjust any power brake unit. If a unit must be replaced, use the master cylinder push rod supplied with the replacement unit. This push rod has been preset and gauged for use with the replacement unit.

CHRYSLER

Do not attempt to disassemble power brake unit as this booster is serviced as a complete assembly only. A properly installed power brake unit, with vacuum at the unit and pressure applied to the pedal, will vent the master cylinder (force a jet of fluid up through the front chamber vent port).

FORD

Adjustment of the pushrod and replacement of the check valve are the only services permitted on the brake booster. If any brake booster is damaged or inoperative, replace it with a new booster. The brake booster (excluding the check valve) is serviced only as an assembly.

GENERAL MOTORS

Use special tool number J22647 to gauge the power brake unit-to-master cylinder push rod length. The push rod length must fall within the go-no-go limits of the gauge.

Vacuum Pump

General Motors "J" body cars all use a vacuum pump designed to aid the 4 cylinder engine in maintaining a proper level of vacuum for the power brake system. The vacuum pump is equipped with an internal off-on switch in the controller. The switch will activate the pump when power brake vacuum falls

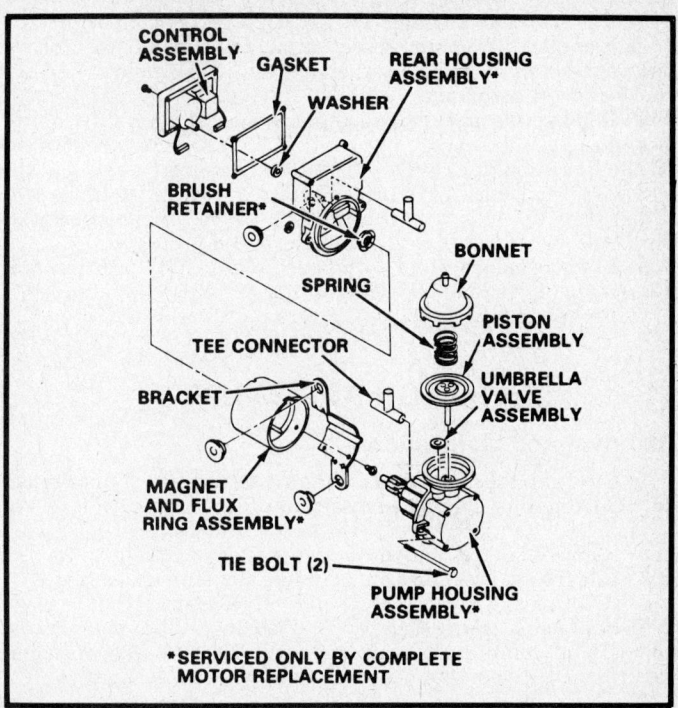

General Motors brake booster vacuum pump disassembled

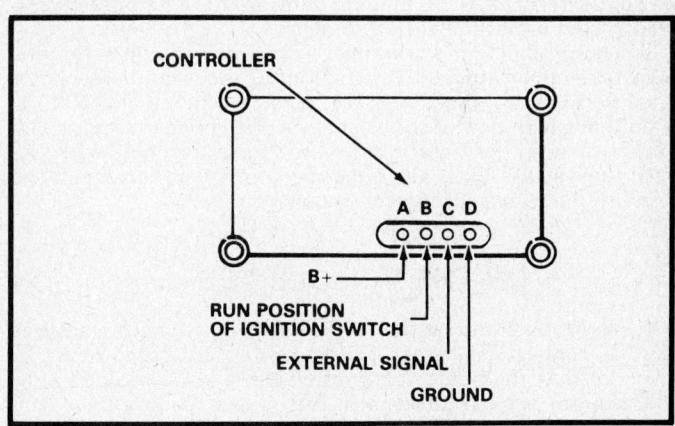

Brake booster vacuum pump electrical connector

below a designated level. The pump can only be activated by the controller when the ignition switch is in the run position.

Removal and Installation

1. Raise vehicle and remove splash shield from the driver's side of car.
2. Disconnect hoses at vacuum pump.
3. Disconnect electrical connector at vacuum pump.
4. Remove three nuts securing pump assembly to mounting bracket and remove pump.
5. Reverse procedure for installation or vacuum pump.

CONTROLLER

Removal and Installation

1. Remove tie bolts holding the body, pump housing, and rear housing together.

24-47

SECTION 24
BRAKES
POWER BRAKE BOOSTERS

2. Remove rear housing. Do not damage tee connector.

3. Remove self tapping screws attaching control assembly to the rear housing. Detach brushes from brush holder and remove control assembly.

4. Remove old gasket and replace control assembly, using new gasket and washer. Ensure that both brushes are located in the brush holder cavity of the rear housing.

5. Set brush springs in preload state by locking them in provided slots above spring access slots. Place brushes in brush channels, ensuring that shunts are routed properly.

6. Place brush retainer in proper preassembly position and return spring to load condition.

7. Complete reassembly by reversing Steps 1 and 2.

PISTON ASSEMBLY

Removal and Installation

1. Uncrimp tabs on bonnet. Pump housing and bonnet must be held together during disassembly, due to spring load on bonnet.

2. Remove bonnet and spring.

3. Lift piston assembly out of pump housing assembly.

4. Remove and replace umbrella valve assembly.

5. Replace piston assembly and spring. Place bonnet on spring and compress. Crimp tabs allowing no tolerance for movement between bonnet and pump housing assembly.

Testing

At no time during testing of the vacuum pump should the outlet nozzle by blocked. Permanent damage to the diaphragm can result from a blocked outlet nozzle.

The pump should not draw over 8 amps and should automatically turn off within 5 to 10 seconds after the vacuum reaches a level between 10 and 15 in. Hg. After the pump shuts off, it should not leak down more than 2 in. Hg. in one minute. The brake warning light will come on to indicate trouble with the vacuum system. The brake light may or may not come on if the vacuum pump is running continuously.

ON THE VEHICLE TESTS

1. With the pump on the vehicle attach a vacuum gauge to the "T" connector between the controller and pump housing. Observe that the pump turns off within 5 to 10 seconds after the vacuum reaches 10 to 15 in. Hg. Check for less than 2 in. per minute leakage after the pump turns off.

2. If the pump runs continuously and no vacuum leaks can be found, replace the controller.

OFF THE VEHICLE TESTING

1. Remove the pump from the vehicle. Remove the T-fitting connector from between the pump housing and the controller. Attach a hand operated vacuum pump to the controller inlet and apply 20 in. Hg. of vacuum to the controller. If the switch leaks more than 2 in. Hg. per minute, then replace the switch.

2. Attach a hand vacuum pump to the pump housing inlet fitting and draw 20 in. Hg. of vacuum. If the pump leaks down more than 2 in. Hg. per minute, then replace the umbrella valve.

3. Plug the pump housing vacuum inlet, attach a hand vacuum pump to pump outlet port, plug the pump housing inlet and draw 20 in. Hg. of vacuum. If the pump leaks down more than 2 in. Hg. of vacuum per minute, then replace the pump piston assembly. Make sure the bonnet is tight and not leaking, before condemning the piston assembly.

Hydro-Boost II

Hydro-Boost II differs from conventional power brake systems, in that it operates from power steering pump fluid pressure, rather than intake manifold vacuum. The Hydro-Boost II unit contains a spool valve with an open center which controls the strength of pump pressure when braking occurs. A lever assembly controls the valve's position. A boost piston provides the force necessary to operate the conventional master cylinder on the front of the booster.

A reserve of at least two assisted brake applications is supplied by an accumulator which is spring loaded on earlier models and pneumatic on later models. The brakes can be applied manually if the reserve system is depleted.

All vehicles with Hydro-Boost II, on which the accumulator is an integral part of the Hydro-Boost II unit. All system checks, tests and troubleshooting procedures are the same for the two systems.

HYDRO-BOOST II SYSTEM CHECKS

1. A defective Hydro-Boost cannot cause any of the following conditions. Noisy brakes, fading pedal or pulling brakes. If any of these occur, check elsewhere in the brake system.

2. Check the fluid level in the master cylinder. It should be within 1/4 in. of the top. If it isn't, add only DOT3 or DOT4 brake fluid until the correct level is reached.

3. Check the fluid level in the power steering pump. The engine should be at normal running temperature and stopped. The level should register on the pump dipstick. Add power steering fluid to bring the reservoir level up to the correct level. Low fluid level will result in both poor steering and stopping ability.

NOTE: The brake hydraulic system uses brake fluid only, while the power steering and Hydro-Boost systems use power steering fluid only. Don't mix the two.

4. Check the power steering pump belt tension, and inspect all of the power steering/Hydro-Boost hoses for kinks or leaks.

5. Check and adjust the engine idle speed, as necessary.

6. Check the power steering pump fluid for bubbles. If air bubbles are present in the fluid, bleed the system. Fill the power steering pump reservoir to specifications the engine at normal operating temperature. With the engine running rotate the steering wheel through its normal travel 3 or 4 times, without holding the wheel against the stops. Check the fluid level again.

7. If the problem still exists, go on the Hydro-Boost test sections and troubleshooting chart.

Functional Test

1. Check the brake system for leaks or low fluid level. Correct as necessary.

2. Place the transmission in Neutral and stop the engine. Apply the brakes 4 or 5 times to empty the accumulator.

3. Keep the pedal depressed with moderate (25 to 40 lbs.) pressure and start the engine.

4. The brake pedal should fall slightly and then push back up against your foot. If not movement is felt, the Hydro-Boost system is not working.

Accumulator Leak Test

1. Run the engine at normal idle. Turn the steering wheel against one of the stops, hold it there for no longer than 5 seconds. Center the steering wheel and stop the engine.

2. There should be a minimum of 2 power (1-Hydro-Boost II) assisted brake applications when pedal pressure of 20 to 25 lbs. is applied.

3. Start the engine and allow it to idle. Rotate the steering

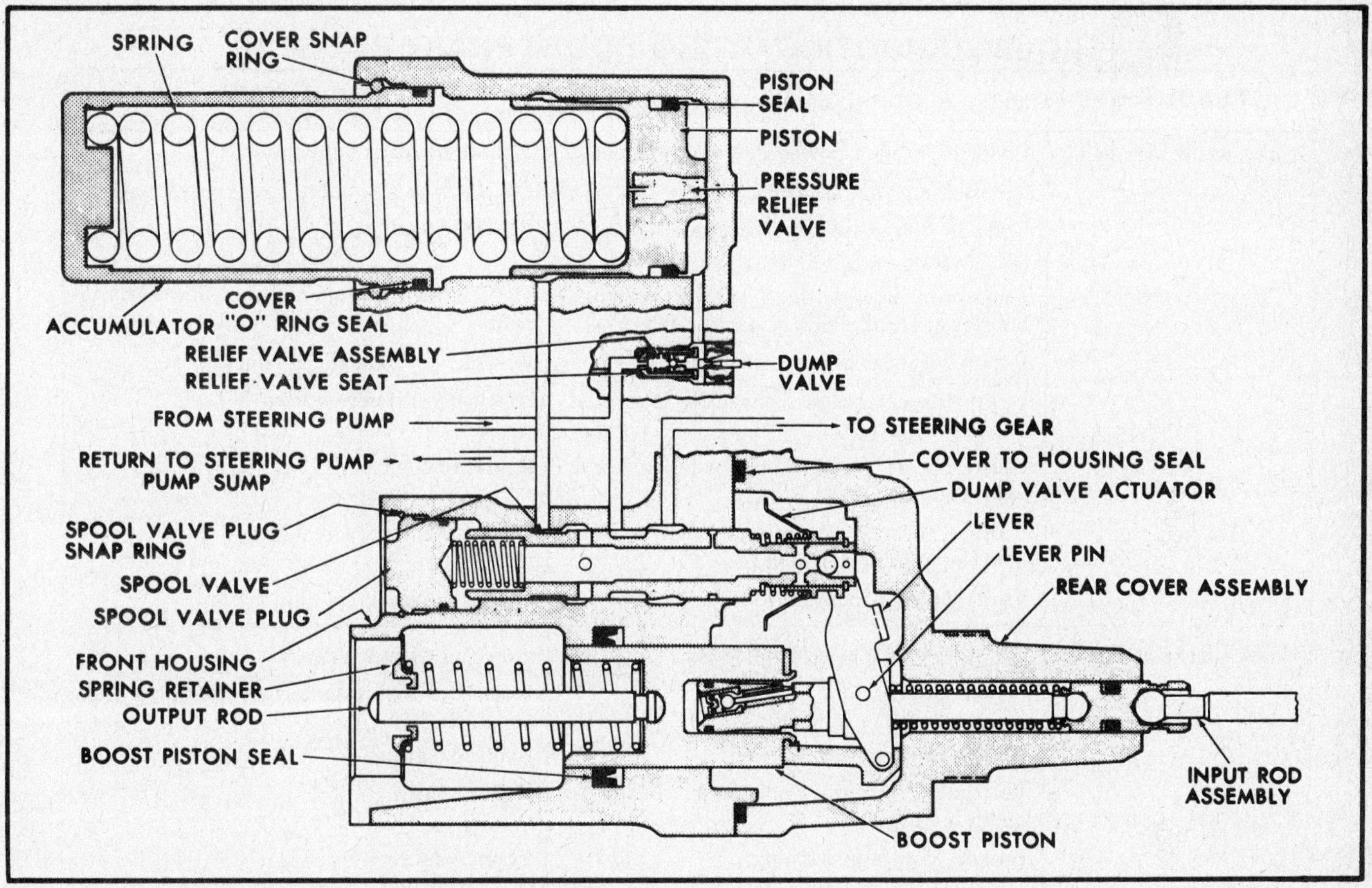

BRAKES
POWER BRAKE BOOSTERS

Bendix hydro-boost (spring accumulator type)

wheel against the stop. Listen for a light "hissing" sound, this is the accumulator being charged. Center the steering wheel and stop the engine.

4. Wait one hour and apply the brakes without starting the engine. As in Step 2, there should be at least 2 (1-Hydro-Boost II) stops with power assist. If not, the accumulator is defective and must be replaced.

Hydro-Boost System Bleeding

1. The system should be bled whenever the booster is removed and installed. Fill the power steering pump until the fluid level is at the base of the pump reservoir neck. Disconnect the battery lead from the distributor.

NOTE: On diesel engines remove the electrical lead to the fuel solenoid terminal on the injection pump before cranking the engine.

2. Jack up the front of the car, turn the wheels all the way to the left, and crank the engine for a few seconds.

3. Check steering pump fluid level. If necessary, add fluid to the "Add" mark on the dipstick.

4. Lower the car, connect the battery lead, and start the engine. Check fluid level and add fluid to the "Add" mark if necessary. With the engine running, turn the wheels from side to side to bleed air from the system. Make sure that the fluid level stays above the internal pump casting.

5. The Hydro-Boost system should now be fully bled. If the fluid is foaming after bleeding, stop the engine, let the system set for one hour, then repeat the second part of Step 4.

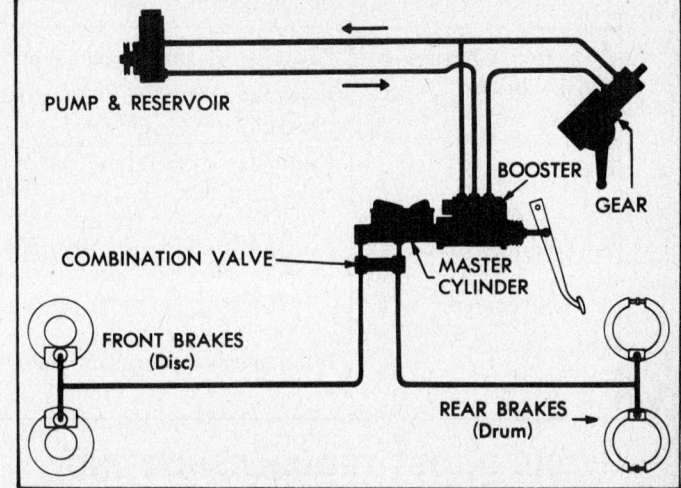

Schematic diagram of the hydro-boost system

6. The preceding procedures should be effective in removing excess air from the system, however sometimes air may still remain trapped. When this happens the booster may make a "gulping" noise when the brake is applied. Lightly pumping the brake pedal with the engine running should cause this noise to disappear. After the noise stops, check the pump fluid level and add as necessary.

SECTION 24
BRAKES
POWER BRAKE BOOSTERS

TROUBLESHOOTING HYDRO-BOOST BRAKE BOOSTER

CONDITION	CAUSE	CORRECTION
Excessive Brake Pedal Effort	Loose or broken power steering pump belt.	Tighten or replace the belt.
	No fluid in power steering reservoir.	Fill reservoir and check for external leaks.
	Leaks in power steering, booster or accumulator hoses.	Replace faulty parts.
	Leaks at tube fittings, power steering, booster or accumulator connections.	Tighten fittings or replace tube seats, if faulty.
	External leakage at accumulator.	Replace "O" ring and retainer.
	Faulty booster piston seal causing leakage at booster flange vent.	Overhaul with new seal kit.
	Faulty booster input rod seal with leakage at input rod end.	Replace booster.
	Faulty booster cover seal with leakage between housing and cover.	Overhaul with new seal kit.
	Faulty booster spool plug seal.	Overhaul with spool plug seal kit.
Slow Brake Pedal Return	Excessive seal friction in booster.	Overhaul with new seal kit.
	Faulty spool action.	Flush steering system while pumping brake pedal.
	Broken piston return spring.	Replace spring.
	Restriction in return line from booster to pump reservoir.	Replace line.
	Broken spool return spring.	Replace spring.
Grabby Brakes	Broken spool return spring.	Replace spring.
	Faulty spool action caused by contamination in system.	Flush steering system while pumping brake pedal.
Booster Chatters — Pedal Vibrates	Power steering pump belt slips.	Tighten belt.
	Low fluid level in power steering pump reservoir.	Fill reservoir and check for external leaks.
	Faulty spool operation caused by contamination in system.	Flush steering system while pumping brake pedal.
Accumulator Leak Down — System does not hold charge	Contamination in steering hydro-boost system	Flush steering system while pumping brake pedal.
	Internal leakage in accumulator system	Overhaul unit using accumulator rebuild kit and seal kit.

HYDRO-BOOST TROUBLESHOOTING

HIGH PEDAL AND STEERING EFFORT (IDLE)

1. Loose/broken power steering pump belt.
2. Low power steering fluid level.
3. Leaking hoses or fittings.
4. Low idle speed.
5. Hose restriction.
6. Defective power steering pump.

HIGH PEDAL EFFORT (IDLE)

1. Binding pedal/linkage.
2. Fluid contamination.
3. Defective Hydro-Boost unit.

POOR PEDAL RETURN

1. Binding pedal linkage.
2. Restricted booster return line.
3. Internal return system restriction.

BRAKES
POWER BRAKE BOOSTERS

SECTION 24

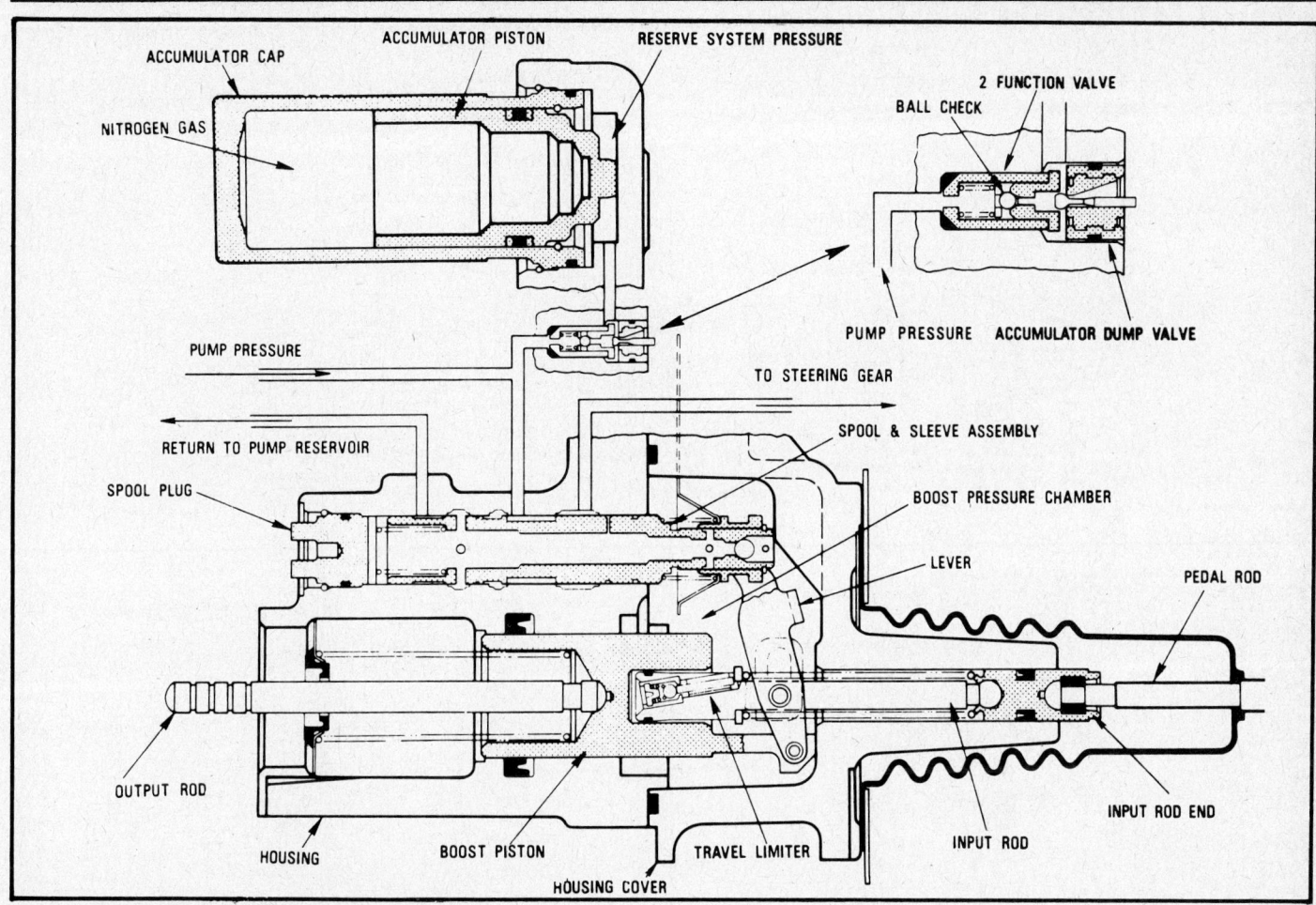

Bendix hydro-boost (nitrogen gas type)

PEDAL CHATTER/PULSATION

1. Power steering pump drivebelt slipping.
2. Low power steering fluid level.
3. Defective power steering pump.
4. Defective Hydro-Boost unit.

BRAKES OVERSENSITIVE

1. Binding pedal/linkage.
2. Defective Hydro-Boost unit.

NOISE

1. Low power steering fluid level.
2. Air in the power steering fluid.
3. Loose power steering pump drivebelt.

OVERHAUL

Ford Motor Company services the Hydro-Boost unit with a replacement new or rebuilt unit only. No provisions are made for overhaul of the unit. GM Hydro-Boost units may be overhauled. Do not attempt to interchange parts between Hydro-Boost units of different makes of cars, because of pressure differentials and differences of the tolerances of the internal parts. Pressure could exceed the normal accumulator release pressure of 1,400 psi, and injury or damage could result.

Disassembly

note: Have a drain pan ready to catch and discard leaking fluid during disassembly. Do not apply heat to the pneumatic accumulator. Do not attempt to repair an inoperative accumulator. Always replace with a new assembly. Before disposing of an inoperative accumulator drill a $1\frac{1}{16}$ inch diameter hole through the end of the accumulator pan. Do not drill through the piston end.

1. Remove the booster assembly from the car.
2. Secure the booster in a vise on a mounting bracket, if possible with the pedal rod down. Pump the pedal rod 4 to 5 times, assuring that accumulator pressure is depleted. Cut the strap securing the accumulator cap.
3. Depress the accumulator spring cap with a 12 in. C-clamp and unseat the retaining ring with a small punch and remove the ring.
4. Release the C-clamp slowly to relieve spring tension and remove the cap and spring.
5. To remove the piston, pressurize the booster thru the inlet port with air pressure, while the gear and return ports are plugged, and the piston will move out of its bore and can be removed.
6. If air is not available, form a hook from stiff wire and engage the piston in the piston fluid inlet hole. Wrap the wire around a suitable tool and pry against the housing to remove piston. Discard the piston.
7. Remove the accumulator plunger seat and guide assem-

SECTION 24 BRAKES
POWER BRAKE BOOSTERS

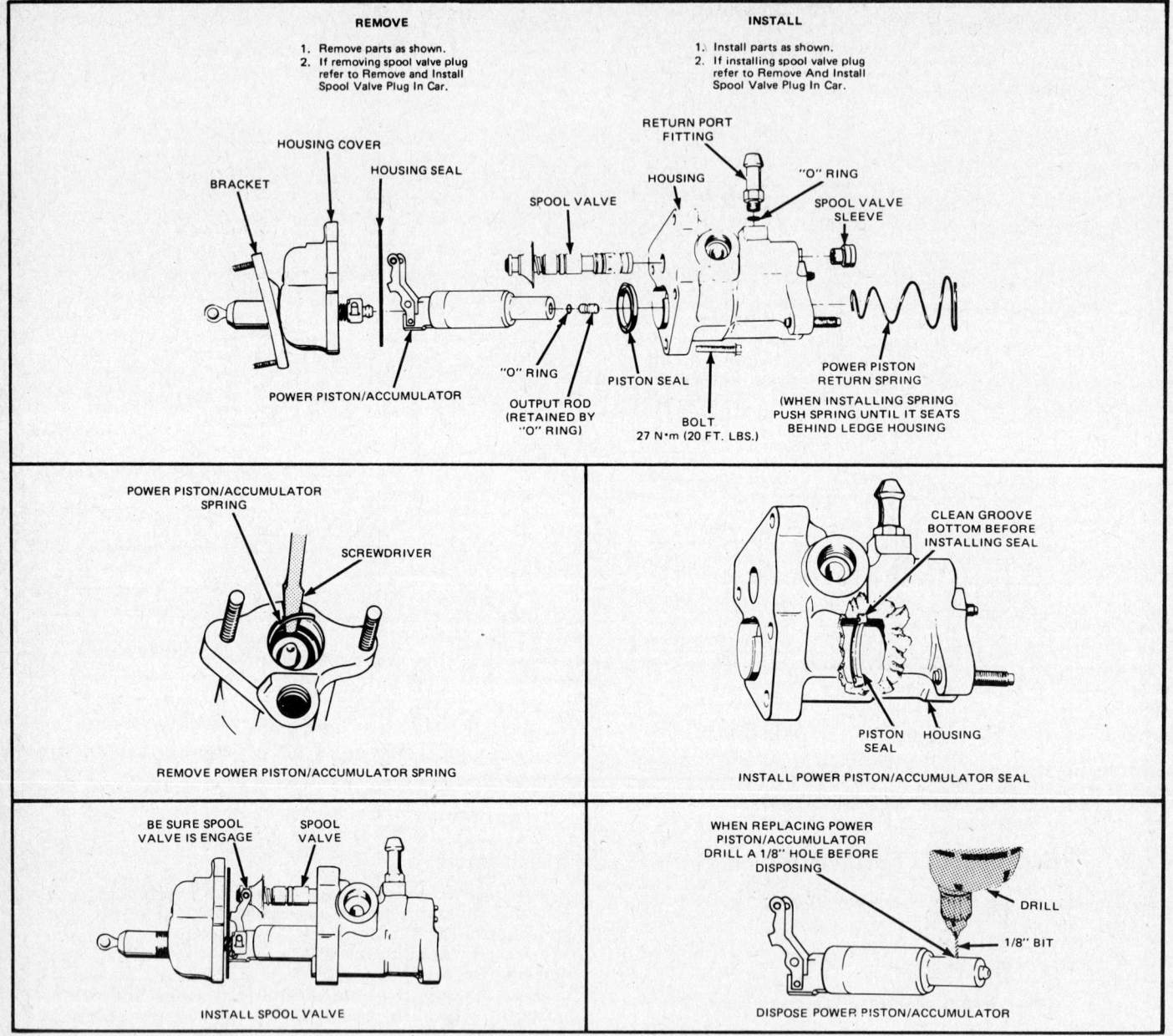

Remove and install spool valve, power piston/accumulator and seal

bly, and with a wire hook, remove the spacer-charging orifice and ball assembly and discard.

8. Loosen and remove five special bolts while holding the front housing and carefully lift off the front housing. A Torz® socket is required. The spool valve and power piston assembly will remain with the rear cover.

9. Remove the output rod and piston return spring from the power piston assembly and the spool valve spring from the valve. Remove the output rod retainer assembly from the housing.

10. Remove the spool valve and examine for scratches and wear marks. Reuse or replace as necessary.

11. Inspect the power piston for scratches and worn areas. Replace or reuse as necessary. If replacement of the power piston is necessary, snip off the staked end of the connecting pin and remove the pin with a small punch.

12. Clean and flush all parts with clean power steering fluid.

Assembly

1. Lower the new spacer-charging orifice and ball assembly into the accumulator valve bore on the front of the housing.

2. Mount a new O-ring onto the new accumulator plunger seat and guide the assembly and insert into the valve bore.

3. If a new power piston was needed, install a new pin in the hole to engage the piston connecting bracket to the small yoke in the lever and mushroom the end of the pin to avoid loss.

4. Install a new figure eight seal on the mating face of the rear housing and a new power piston seal in the front housing.

5. Insert the spool valve and spring into the bore while pulling up on the power piston and extending the lever to accept the sleeve on the spool valve. With the lever extended, put the

BRAKES
POWER BRAKE BOOSTERS
SECTION 24

front housing over the rear housing and slide the lever pins into the slot in the sleeve of the spool valve.

6. Lower the front housing down into the rear cover while centering the power piston in the bore. If a seal protector is not available, extreme care must be exercised in seating the piston to the seal so that the seal lip is not damaged.

7. Install the five special bolts and torque to 20 ft. lbs. A Torx® socket is required.

8. Install the output rod, spring and new spring retainer, securing the retainer by taping it into place with a 7/8 in. deep well socket and a hammer.

9. Install the new accumulator piston assembly and install the new O-ring to the accumulator cap. With the 12 inch C-clamp, depress the cap and spring and install the retaining clip in the bore of the front housing.

10. Install the new strap from the drip pan to the accumulator cap.

11. Install the unit on the car and bleed the system.

Tandem Diaphragm Power Brake Booster

OVERHAUL

Disassembly

1. Remove the power booster from the vehicle, remove the push rod boot, silencer, front housing seal, grommet and vacuum check valve.

2. Scribe a line on the front and rear housing for alignment purposes when reassembling the unit.

3. Install the front housing into a suitable holding fixture, on Cadillac models, press down on the holding tool and turn counterclockwise to unlock the housing.

4. On all other models place the special spanner wrench (J-9504) or equivalent over the rear housing studs, press down and turn counterclockwise to unlock the housing.

5. Remove the power piston group, power piston return spring, and power piston bearing.

6. Remove the piston rod, reaction retainer and power head silencer.

7. Hold the assembly at the outside edge of the divider and diaphragms. Holding the push rod down against a hard surface, apply a light impact to dislodge the diaphragm retainer.

8. Remove the primary diaphragm, primary support plate, secondary support plate and diaphragm and power piston assembly.

NOTE: Before reassembling the unit, be sure to clean all plastic, metal and rubber parts in denatured alcohol. Air dry all parts and do not reinstall any rubber parts with cuts, nicks or distortion.

Assembly

NOTE: Before installing any of the rubber, plastic, and metal friction parts, lubricate them with silicone lube.

1. Assembly is the reverse order of the disassembly procedure.

2. After the housing have been installed align the scribe marks and press down with the holding fixture handle on Cadillac models or the spanner wrench on the other models, clockwise to lock the two housing together. Stake the two housing tabs into sockets at two new locations 180° apart.

3. Install the assembly on the vehicle, bleed the brake system and road test the vehicle.

HYDRO-BOOST II SPOOL VALVE PLUG

Removal and Installation

1. Turn engine off and pump brake pedal 4 or 5 times to deplete accumulator.

2. Separate the master cylinder from the booster with brake lines attached.

3. Push the spool valve plug in and use a small screwdriver to remove retaining ring. Remove the spool valve plug and O-ring.

4. Install the reverse order of removal. Bleed the Hydro-Boost system.

ANTI-LOCK BRAKING SYSTEM (ABS)

OPERATION

The Anti-Lock Braking System (ABS) is essentially a brake system enhancement. The purpose of ABS is to increase the driver's control over a vehicle during braking--especially steering control. When a vehicle equipped with a conventional brake system must brake suddenly, one or more wheels may lock up offering little or no steering control to avoid hazards. ABS is designed to prevent braked wheels from locking. The advantages of the system are considerable. For instance, during a high-speed stop while entering a curve, ABS is designed to allow the driver to steer through the curve while decelerating. Additionally, ABS is designed to enhance the braking action of each front wheel independently and the two rear wheels independent of the front wheels. This allows controlled braking even if one or more wheels encounters a slippery surface. In this situation, ABS will automatically sense the initial loss of adhesion in any one wheel and reduce or prevent further hydraulic pressure on that wheel's brake caliper, or if the rear wheels (both calipers) until adhesion is regained.

COMPONENTS

ABS is essentially the familiar split circuit hydraulic four wheel disc brake system to which a sophisticated electronic and mechanical override system has been carefully mated. Wheel speed sensors, an electronic control unit and a hydraulic unit that incorporates solenoid operated brake line valves are the major components of the system. The sensors monitor the rotation speed of the wheels and provide data about wheel acceleration and deceleration over very small intervals of time. The signals from the sensors are transmitted to the control unit. The control unit monitors the signals and compares them to a contained program. If one of the sensors suddenly shows a deceleration rate that exceeds the threshold values of the programmed system, indicating that a wheel is about to lock and skid, the computer activates the hydraulic control unit to maintain the optimum brake pressure in that wheel, or both rear wheels to prevent lock-up. If, for any reason, the ABS should malfunction the brakes will operate as a normal system without ABS and a warning light will go on indicating service is required.

SECTION 24

BRAKES
ANTI-LOCK BRAKING SYSTEM (ABS)

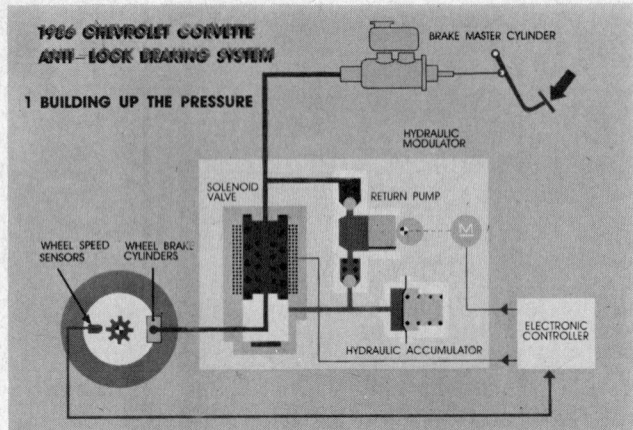

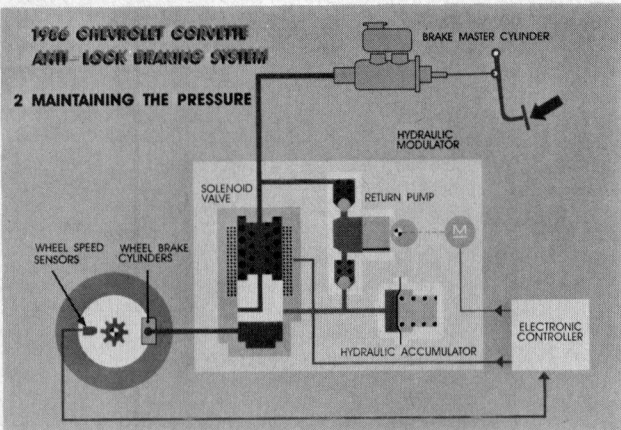

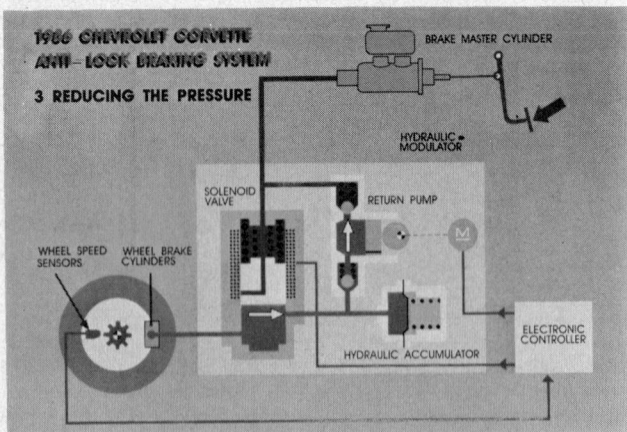

SYSTEMS

Ford and General Motors, with the exception of the Corvette use the Teves ABS system. Corvette is equipped with a Bosch ABS II system. Both systems achieve the same results to provide steering control during aggressive braking.

MASTER CYLINDER AND HYDRAULIC BOOSTER

The master cylinder and the brake booster are arranged in the basic fore and aft position with the booster behind the master cylinder. The booster control valve is located in a parallel bore above the master cylinder centerline and is operated by a lever connecting the brake pedal pushrod.

ELECTRIC PUMP AND ACCUMULATOR

The electric pump is a high pressure pump design that runs at frequent intervals for a short period to charge the hydraulic accumulator that supplies the brake system. The accumulator is a gas filled pressure chamber that is part of the pump and motor assembly. The electric motor, pump and accumulator assembly is shock mounted to the master cylinder booster assembly.

VALVE BODY ASSEMBLY

The valve body assembly incorporates three pairs of solenoid valves. One pair for each front wheel, and a third pair for both the rear wheels combined. These solenoid valves are inlet-outlet valves with inlet valve normally open and the outlet valve normally closed. The valve body itself is bolted to the inboard side of the master cylinder booster assembly.

FLUID LEVEL WARNING SWITCHES

These two integral fluid level switches are incorporated in the brake fluid reservoir cap assembly with two electrical connectors, one for each end of the cap, for wire harness connections.

WHEEL SENSORS

The sensors are four variable reluctance electronic sensor assemblies, each with a 104 tooth ring in the anti-lock system. The sensors are connected to the electronic controller through a wiring harness. The front sensors are bolted to brackets which are bolted to the front spindles. The front toothed sensor rings are pressed onto the inside of the front rotors. The rear sensors are bolted to brackets, that in turn are bolted to the rear disc brake axle adapters. The toothed rear sensor rings are pressed to the axle shafts, inboard of the axle shaft flange.

ELECTRONIC CONTROLLER

The controller is a self contained non-serviceable unit, which consists of two microprocessors and the necessary circuitry for their operation. The function of the controller is to monitor the system operations during normal driving and during anti-lock braking. Any malfunction of the anti-lock brake system will cause the controller to shut off and bypass the anti-lock brake system. When the anti-lock brake system is bypassed the normal power assisted braking will still remain.

CHECK ANTI-LOCK BRAKE WARNING LIGHT

The four wheel anti-lock system is self-monitoring. When the ignition switch is in the run position, the electronic controller will perform a preliminary self check on the anti-lock electrical system. This is indicated by a three to four second energizing of the amber. Check Anti-Lock Brakes lamp in the overhead console. This light will go out after the three to four second interval, unless there is a malfunction in the anti-lock brake system. If there is a malfunction the check anti-lock brake and/or the brake lamp will stay lit, and diagnostic tests will then pinpoint the exact component needing service.

BLEEDING THE BRAKE SYSTEM

The front brakes can be bled in the conventional manner, with

BRAKES
ANTI-LOCK BRAKING SYSTEM (ABS)
SECTION 24

or without the accumulator being changed. When bleeding the rear brakes the accumulator must be fully charged or the system has to be pressure bled as previously outlined in this section.

Bleeding The Brake System With a Charged Accumulator

NOTE: Be careful when opening the rear caliper bleeder screws, due to the high pressure in the system from a fully charged accumulator at the bleeder screws.

1. With the accumulator fully charged have someone hold the rake pedal in the applied position and place the ignition switch in the run position and open the rear brake caliper bleed screws for 10 seconds at a time.
2. Repeat this procedure until the air is cleared from the brake fluid and close the brake caliper bleed screws.
3. Do this to all of the brake calipers and after the bleed screws are closed. Pump the brake pedal a couple of times to complete the bleeding procedure.
4. Adjust the brake fluid level in the reservoir to the max level with a fully charged accumulator.

MASTER CYLINDER

Removal and Installation

NOTE: The hydraulic pressure must be discharged from the brake system before removing the master cylinder. To discharge the system, turn the ignition key to the off position and pump the brake pedal at least 20 times until an increase in pedal force is clearly felt.

1. Disconnect the negative battery cable and the electrical connectors from the master cylinder reservoir cap, main valve, solenoid valve body, pressure warning switch, the hydraulic pump motor, and ground connector from the master cylinder.
2. Disconnect the brake lines from the solenoid valve body and plug the line openings in the valve body to prevent fluid loss. Do not allow the brake fluid to leak or spill onto any of the electrical connectors.
3. From inside the vehicle, disconnect the hydraulic booster pushrod from the brake pedal in the following order: Disconnect the stop light switch wires at the connector on the brake pedal. Remove the hairpin clip at the stop light switch on the brake pedal and move the switch off of the pedal pin far enough for the switch outer hole to clear the pin. Using a twisting motion, remove the switch, but be careful not to damage the switch during its removal. Remove the four retaining nuts at the dash panel and from inside the engine compartment. Remove the booster from the dash panel.
4. Installation is the reverse order of the removal procedure. Also after the unit has been installed, bleed the brake system as previously outlined in this section.

HYDRAULIC ACCUMULATOR

Removal and Installation

1. Discharge the pressure in the brake system and disconnect the electrical connection at the hydraulic pump motor.
2. Using an 8 mm hex wrench or equivalent, unscrew the accumulator. Be sure that no dirt falls into the open port.
3. Using the same hex wrench or equivalent, remove the accumulator adapter block bolt and remove the block, if necessary.
4. Installation is the reverse order of the removal procedure and be sure to observe the following: Install new O-rings on the accumulator and adapter block. Torque the adapter block bolt to 25 to 34 ft. lbs. and the accumulator to 30 to 34 ft. lbs. After installation, place the ignition switch in the ON position and check to see if the check Anti-Lock Brake light goes out after a maximum of one minute. Top off the master cylinder reservoir to the max mark with brake fluid.

HYDRAULIC PUMP MOTOR

Removal and Installation

1. Discharge the pressure in the brake system and disconnect the negative battery cable.
2. Disconnect the electrical connections at the hydraulic pump motor and pressure warning switch.
3. Remove the accumulator.
4. Remove the suction line between the reservoir and the pump at the reservoir by twisting the hose and pulling on it lightly. To prevent fluid loss, a large vacuum nipple can be slipped over the reservoir opening as the hose is removed.
5. Remove the retaining bolt on the pump high pressure line to the hydraulic booster housing at the housing. Make sure to save the two O-rings, that are on both sides of the retaining bolt.
6. Remove the Allen head bolt that holds the pump and motor assembly to the extension housing located directly under the accumulator. Make sure to save the thick spacer between the extension housing and the shock mount.
7. Slide the pump assembly inboard to remove the assembly from the retainer pin located on the inboard side of the extension housing.
8. Installation is the reverse order of the removal procedure. Be sure to bleed the brake system and check to see if the Check Anti-Lock Brake light goes out after a maximum of one minute.

ELECTRONIC CONTROLLER

Removal and Installation

1. Disconnect the negative battery cable. Disconnect the 35 pin connector from the electronic controller, which is located in the trunk of the vehicle in front of the forward trim panel.
2. Remove the three retaining screws holding the electronic controller to the seat back brace and remove the controller.
3. Installation is the reverse order of the removal procedure.

PRESSURE SWITCH

Removal and Installation

1. Discharge the pressure from the brake system and disconnect the negative battery cable.
2. Disconnect the solenoid valve body seven pin connector and remove the pressure switch using special tool #T85P-20215-B or equivalent, a 1/2 inch to 3/8 inch adapter and a 3/8 inch drive ratchet.
3. Installation is the reverse of the removal procedure and replace the O-ring on the switch. Torque the switch to 15 to 25 ft. lbs.

FRONT WHEEL SENSOR

Removal and Installation

1. Disconnect the sensor electrical connector for the right or left front sensor from inside the engine compartment.
2. Raise and support vehicle safely and disengage the wire grommet at the right or left hand shock tower.
3. Pull the sensor cable connector through the hole and be careful not to damage the connector.
4. Remove the sensor wire from the bracket on the shock tower and the side rail.
5. Loosen the set screw holding the sensor to the sensor

SECTION 24 BRAKES
ANTI-LOCK BRAKING SYSTEM (ABS)

1986 FRONT-WHEEL-DRIVE DE VILLE AND FLEETWOOD AVAILABLE ELECTRONIC BRAKING SYSTEM

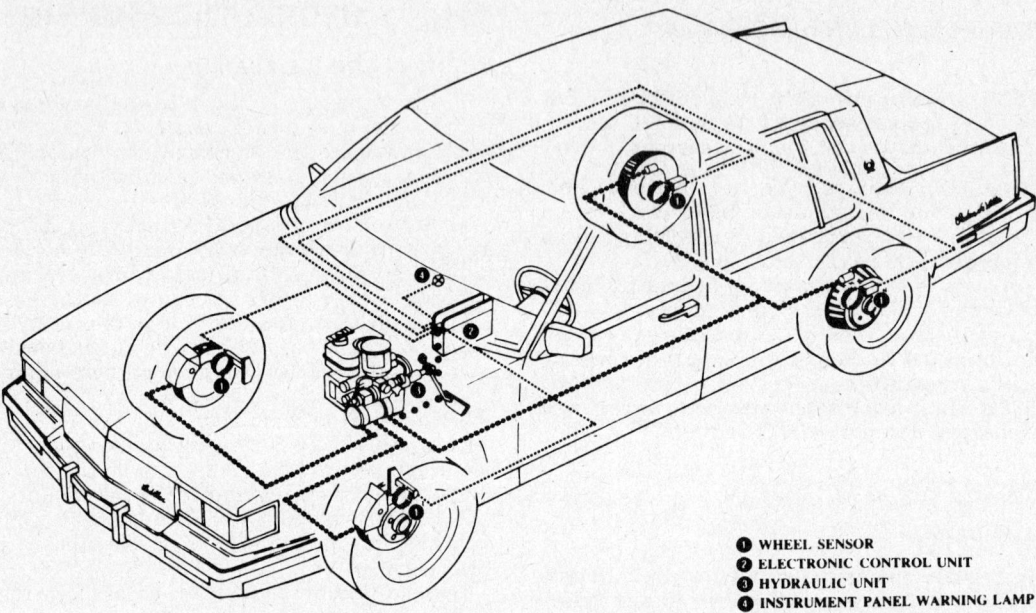

1. WHEEL SENSOR
2. ELECTRONIC CONTROL UNIT
3. HYDRAULIC UNIT
4. INSTRUMENT PANEL WARNING LAMP

bracket post. Remove the sensor through the hole in the disc brake splash shield.

6. Remove the sensor bracket or the sensor bracket post, if it has been damaged by removing the caliper, hub and rotor assembly (as previously outlined). Remove the two brake splash shield attaching bolts which hold the sensor bracket.

7. Install the sensor bracket with the sensor bracket post, if it has been removed. Torque the post retaining bolt 40 to 60 inch lbs. and the splash shield attaching bolts 10 to 15 ft. lbs. Install the hub and rotor assembly.

NOTE: If a sensor is going to be reused, the pole face must be cleaned of all dirt and grease and the pole face has to be scraped with a dull knife or equivalent so that the sensor slides freely on the post. Also glue a new front spacer paper on the pole face.

8. Install a new or old sensor through the hole in the brake shield onto the sensor bracket post. Make sure the paper spacer does not come off during installation.

9. Push the sensor toward the toothed sensor ring until the new paper sensor contacts the ring. Hold the sensor against the sensor ring and torque the set screw to 21 to 26 inch lbs.

10. Insert the cable into the bracket on the shock strut, rail bracket and then through the inner fender apron to engine compartment and the seat grommet.

11. Lower the vehicle and reconnect the sensor electrical connection.

12. Check the function of the sensor by road testing the vehicle and making sure the Check Anti-Lock Brake light does not stay on.

REAR WHEEL SENSOR

Removal and Installation

1. Disconnect the wheel sensor electrical connector located behind the forward luggage compartment trim panel in the trunk.

2. Lift the carpet in the trunk and push the sensor wire grommet through the hole in the floor of the trunk.

3. Raise and support the vehicle safely and remove the appropriate wheel.

4. Remove the wheel sensor wiring from the axle shaft housing. The wiring harness has three different types of retainers. They are the following: The inboard retainer clip is located on the top of the differential housing. Just bend the clip far enough to remove the wiring harness. The second retainer clip is a C-clip and is located in the center of the axle shaft housing. Pull rearward on the clip to disengage the clip from the axle housing. The third clip is at the connection between the rear housing wheel brake tube and flexible hose. Remove the holddown bolt and open the clip to remove the wiring harness.

NOTE: Be careful not to bend the C-clip open beyond the amount needed to remove the clip from the axle housing, because it could break.

5. Remove the rear wheel caliper and rotor assemblies as previously outlined in this section.

6. Remove the wheel sensor retaining bolt, slip the grommet out of the rear brake splash shield and pull the sensor wire outward through the hole.

7. If the sensor bracket is damaged, remove the bracket attaching screws and replace the bracket.

8. Install the sensor bracket, if it was removed and torque the screws 11 to 15 ft. lbs.

9. If the sensor is going to be used again it has to be cleaned just as the front wheel sensors were cleaned.

10. Insert the sensor into the large hole in the sensor bracket and install the retaining bolt into the sensor bracket and torque the retaining bolt 40 to 60 in. lbs.

11. Push the sensor toward the toothed ring until the new paper sensor touches the sensor ring, hold the sensor against the toothed ring and torque the set screw 21 to 26 in. lbs.

12. Install the caliper and rotor assemblies.

13. Push the wire and connector through the splash shield

BRAKES
ANTI-LOCK BRAKING SYSTEM (ABS)
SECTION 24

hole and engage the grommet into the shield eyelet. Install the sensor wire in the retainers along the axle housing.

14. Push the connector through the hole in the trunk and seat the grommet in the trunk floor pan.

15. Reconnect the cable electrical connector, and install the carpet back down in the trunk. Check the function of the sensor by road testing the vehicle and checking to see if the Check Anti-Lock Brakelight goes out.

16. If the toothed ring sensor is found to be malfunctioning on either the front wheel or rear wheel, the rotor assembly has to be removed and the toothed ring sensor has to be pressed out and the new one pressed in.

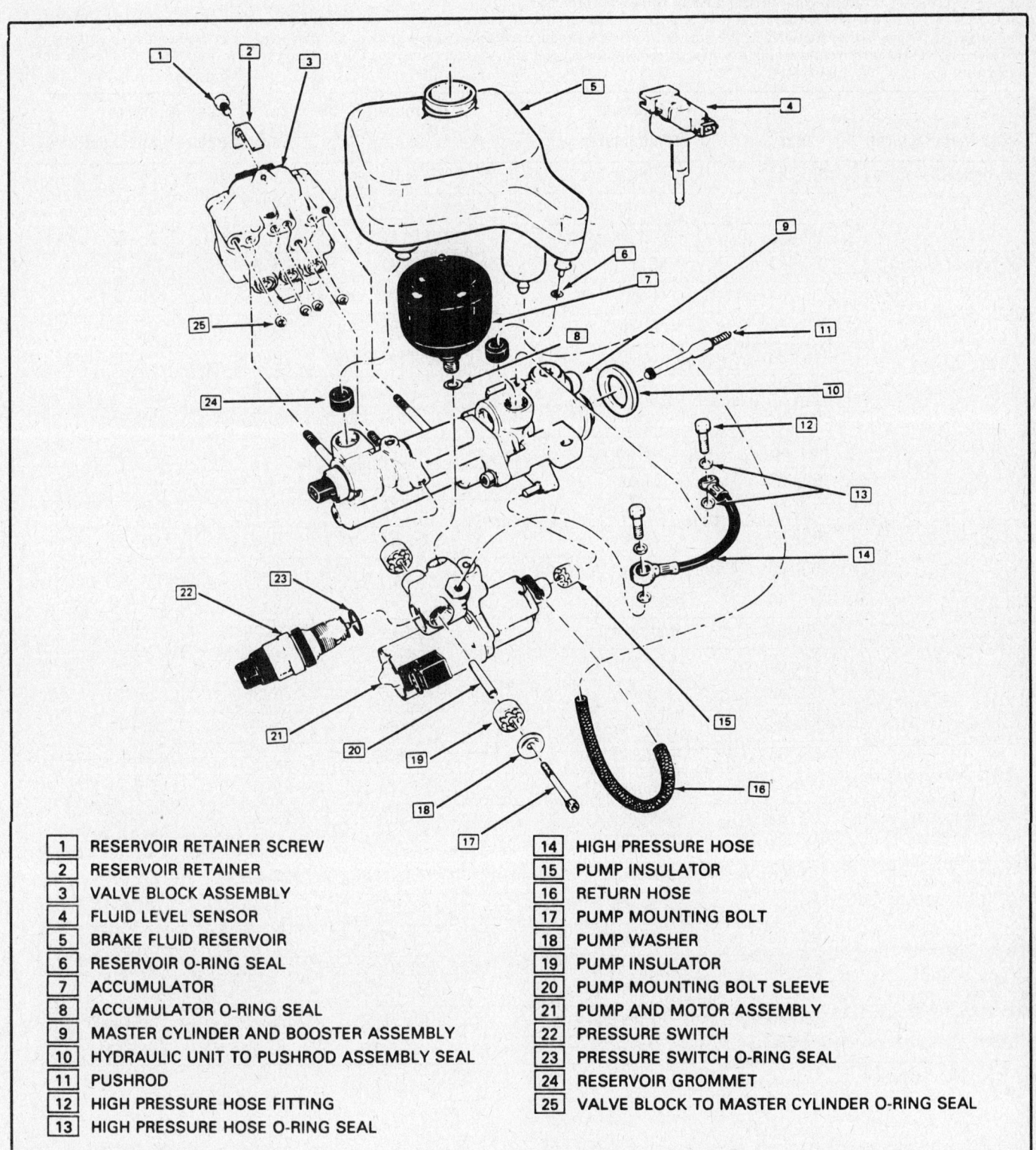

1 RESERVOIR RETAINER SCREW	14 HIGH PRESSURE HOSE
2 RESERVOIR RETAINER	15 PUMP INSULATOR
3 VALVE BLOCK ASSEMBLY	16 RETURN HOSE
4 FLUID LEVEL SENSOR	17 PUMP MOUNTING BOLT
5 BRAKE FLUID RESERVOIR	18 PUMP WASHER
6 RESERVOIR O-RING SEAL	19 PUMP INSULATOR
7 ACCUMULATOR	20 PUMP MOUNTING BOLT SLEEVE
8 ACCUMULATOR O-RING SEAL	21 PUMP AND MOTOR ASSEMBLY
9 MASTER CYLINDER AND BOOSTER ASSEMBLY	22 PRESSURE SWITCH
10 HYDRAULIC UNIT TO PUSHROD ASSEMBLY SEAL	23 PRESSURE SWITCH O-RING SEAL
11 PUSHROD	24 RESERVOIR GROMMET
12 HIGH PRESSURE HOSE FITTING	25 VALVE BLOCK TO MASTER CYLINDER O-RING SEAL
13 HIGH PRESSURE HOSE O-RING SEAL	

Antilock Brake Hydraulic Unit

SECTION 25 CARBURETORS

CARBURETOR APPLICATION CHART AND INDEX

The carburetor manufacturer and model and also the carburetor identification numbers which are listed in the specifications chart, appear either on a tag on the carburetor or stamped on the carburetor body.

NOTE: New model carburetor part numbers and specifications are not released by the manufacturers until well after the press date for this manual. These will be included in the next edition. New model carburetor part numbers are obtained from the most current factory sources, however, carburetors which are new or redesigned by the manufacturer during the production year and designated with new part numbers may not appear.

Car Manufacturer	Year	Carburetor Manufacturer	Carburetor Model	Page Numbers Adjustments	Page Numbers Specifications
American Motors	'80–'84	Carter	BBD	25–9	25–12
	'83–86	Carter	YF, YFA	25–12	25–15
	'80–'86	Rochester	2SE, E2SE	25–59	25–68
Chrysler Corp.	'80–'83	Carter	BBD	25–9	25–11
	'80–'84	Carter	TQ	25–16	25–18
	'80–'84	Holley	1945	25–35	25–37
	'85–'86	Holley	2280, 6280	25–44	25–46
	'80–'86	Holley	5220	25–51	25–52
	'81–'83	Holley	6145	25–54	25–56
	'81–86	Holley	6520	25–51	25–53
	'82–'85	Mikuni	NA	25–92	NA
	'85–'86	Rochester	Quadrajet	25–78	25–83
Ford Motor Co.	'80–'86	Carter	YF, YFA	25–12	25–15
	'80–'86	Ford, Autolite, Motorcraft	2100, 2150, 2150A	25–23	25–26
	'81–'86	Motorcarft	740	25–18	25–22
	'80–'81	Motorcraft	2700 VV	25–28	25–31
	'80–'86	Motorcraft	7200	25–34	25–34
	'80–'83	Holley	1946	25–38	25–40
	'84–'85	Holley	1949	25–40	25–44
	'83–'85	Holley	4180C	25–46	25–48
	'84	Holley	6149	25–40	25–44
	'80–'82	Holley	6500	25–56	25–58
	'80–'82	Holley	5200	25–31	25–33
General Motors	'80–'86	Holley	6510C	25–56	25–58
	'80–'86	Holley	5210C	25–49	25–51
	'80–'86	Rochester	2SE, E2SE	25–59	25–68
	'80–'86	Rochester	2MC, M2MC, M2ME, E2ME, E2MC	25–73	25–77
	'80–'86	Rochester	Quadrajet	25–78	25–83
	'85–'86	Nova	2bbl	25–97	25–97

NA — Not Available

Carburetors

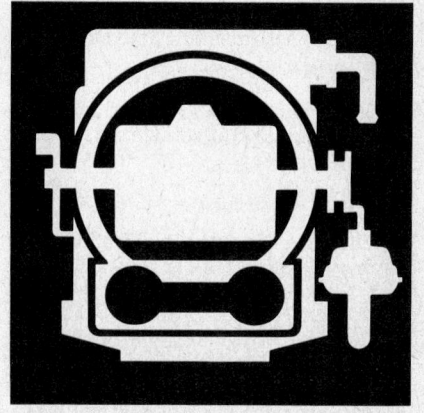

FUNCTIONS

Gasoline is the source of fuel for power in the automobile engine and the carburetor is the mechanism which automatically mixes liquid fuel with air in the correct proportions to provide the desired power output from the engine. The carburetor performs this function by metering, atomizing, and mixing fuel with air flowing through the engine. A carburetor also regulates the volume of air-to-fuel mixture which enters the engine. It is the carburetor's regulation of the mixture flow which gives the operator control of the engine speed.

Metering

The automotive internal combustion engine operates efficiently within a relatively small range of air-to-fuel ratios. It is the function of the carburetor to meter the fuel in exact proportions to the air flowing into the engine, so that the optimum ratio of air-to-fuel is maintained under all operating conditions. Regulations governing exhaust gas emissions have made the proper metering of fuel by the carburetor an increasingly important factor. Too rich a mixture will result in poor economy and increased emissions, while too lean a mixture will result in loss of power and generally poor performance. Carburetors are matched to engines so that metering can be accomplished by using carefully calibrated metering jets which allow fuel to enter the engine at a rate proportional to the engine's ability to draw air.

Atomization

The liquid fuel must be broken up into small particles so that it will more readily mix with air and vaporize. The more contact the fuel has with the air, the better the vaporization. Atomization can be accomplished in two ways; air may be drawn into a stream of fuel which will cause a turbulence and break the solid stream of fuel into smaller particles; or a nozzle can be positioned at the point of highest air velocity in the carburetor and the fuel will be torn into a fine spray as it enters the air stream.

Distribution

The carburetor is the primary device involved in the distribution of fuel to the engine. The more efficiently fuel and air are combined in the carburetor, the smoother the flow of vaporized mixture through the intake manifold to each combustion chamber. Hence, the importance of the carburetor in fuel distribution.

PRINCIPLES

Vacuum

All carburetors operate on the basic principle of pressure difference. Any pressure less than atmospheric pressure is considered vacuum or a low pressure area. In the engine, as the piston moves down on the intake stroke with the intake valve open, a partial vacuum is created in the intake manifold. The farther the piston travels downward, the greater the vacuum created in the manifold. As vacuum increases in the manifold, a difference in pressure occurs between the carburetor and cylinder. The carburetor is positioned in such a way that the high pressure above it, and the vacuum or low pressure above it, and the vacuum or low pressure beneath it, causes air to be drawn through it. Fuel and air always move from high to low pressure areas.

Venturi Principle

To obtain greater pressure drop at the tip of the fuel nozzle so that fuel will flow, the principle of increasing the air velocity to create a low pressure area is used. The device used to increase the velocity of the air flowing through the carburetor is called a venturi. A venturi is a specially designed restriction placed in the air flow. In order for the air to pass through the restriction, it must accelerate causing a pressure drop or vacuum as it passes.

CARBURETOR CIRCUITS

Float Circuit

The float circuit includes the float, float bowl, and a needle valve and seat. This circuit controls the amount of gas allowed to flow into the carburetor. As the fuel level rises, it causes the float to rise which pushes the needle valve into its seat. As soon as the valve and seat make contact, the flow of gas is cut off from the fuel inlet.

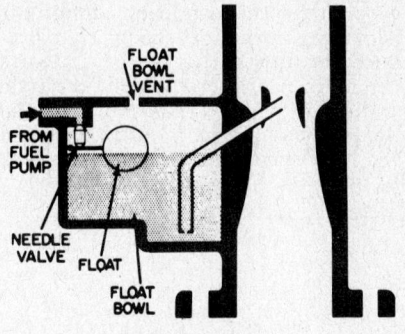

Float circuit

25-3

SECTION 25 CARBURETORS TROUBLESHOOTING

When the level of fuel drops, the float sinks and releases the needle valve from its seat which allows the gas to flow in. In actual operation, the fuel is maintained at practically a constant level. The float tend to hold the needle valve partly closed so that the incoming fuel just balances the fuel being withdrawn.

Idle and Low Speed Circuit

When the throttle is closed or only slightly opened, the air speed is low and practically no vacuum develops in the venturi. This means that the fuel nozzle will not feed. Thus, the carburetor must have another circuit to supply fuel during operation with a closed or slightly opened throttle. This circuit is called the idle and low speed circuit. It consists of passages in which air and gas can flow beneath the throttle plate. With the throttle plate closed, there is high vacuum from the intake manifold. Atmospheric pressure pushes the air/fuel mixture through the passages of the idle and low speed circuit and past the tapered point of the idle adjustment screw, which regulates engine idle mixture volume.

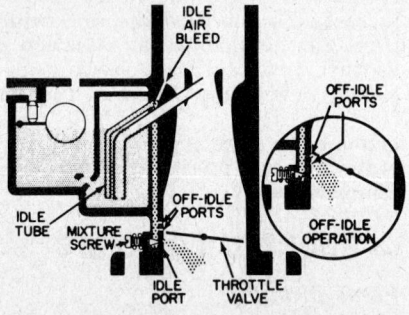

Idle and low speed circuit

High Speed Partial Load Circuit

When the throttle plate is opened sufficiently, there is little difference in vacuum between the upper and lower part of the air horn. Thus, little air/fuel mixture will discharge from the low speed and idle circuit. However, under this condition enough air is moving through the air horn to produce vacuum in the venturi to cause the main nozzle or high speed nozzle to discharge fuel. The circuit from the float bowl to the main nozzle is called the high speed partial load circuit. A

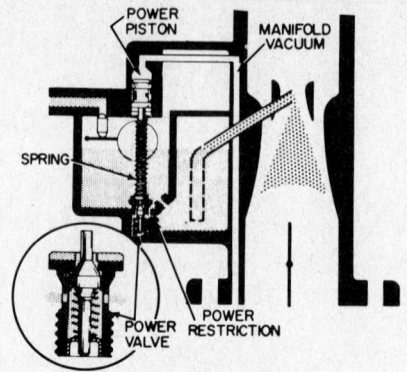

Power circuit

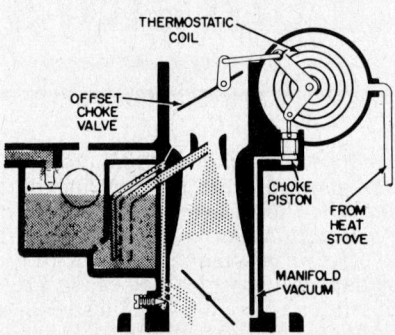

Choke system

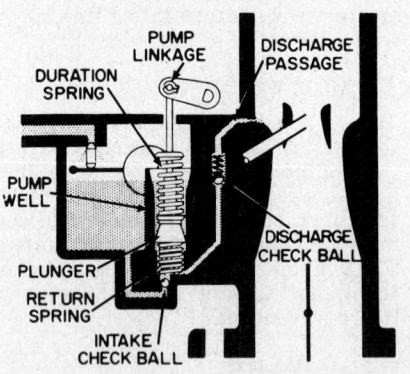

Accelerator pump circuit

nearly constant air/fuel ratio is maintained by this circuit from part to full-throttle.

High Speed Full Power Circuit

For high-speed, full-power, wide open throttle operation, the air/fuel mixture must be enriched; this is done either mechanically or by intake manifold vacuum.

Full Power Circuit (Mechanical)

This circuit includes a metering rod jet and a metering rod. The rod has two steps of different diameters and is attached to the throttle linkage. When the throttle is wide open, the metering rod is lifted bringing the smaller diameter of the rod into the jet. When the throttle is partly closed, the larger diameter of the metering rod is in the jet. This restricts fuel flow to the main nozzle but adequate amounts of fuel do flow for part-throttle operation.

Full Power Circuit (Vacuum)

This circuit is operated by intake manifold vacuum. It includes a vacuum diaphragm or piston linked to a valve. When the throttle is opened so that intake manifold vacuum is reduced, the spring raises the diaphragm or piston. This allows more fuel to flow in, either by lifting a metering rod or by opening a power valve.

Accelerator Pump Circuit

For acceleration, the carburetor must deliver additional fuel. A sudden inrush of air is caused by rapid acceleration or applying full throttle. When the throttle is opened, the pump lever pushes the plunger down and this forces fuel to flow through the accelerator pump circuit and out the pump jet. This fuel enters the air passage through the carburetor to supply additional fuel demands.

Choke

When starting an engine, it is necessary to increase the amount of fuel delivered to the intake manifold. This increase is controlled by the choke. The choke consists of a valve in the top of the air horn controlled mechanically by an automatic device. When the choke valve is closed, only a small amount of air can get past it.
When the engine is cranked, a fairly high vacuum develops in the air horn. This vacuum causes the main nozzle to discharge a heavy stream of fuel. The quantity delivered is sufficient to produce the correct air/fuel mixture needed for starting the engine. The choke is released either manually or by heat from the engine.

CARBURETORS
TROUBLESHOOTING

SECTION 25

TROUBLE SHOOTING

NOTE: Carburetor problems cannot be isolated effectively unless all other engine systems are functioning correctly and the engine is properly tuned.

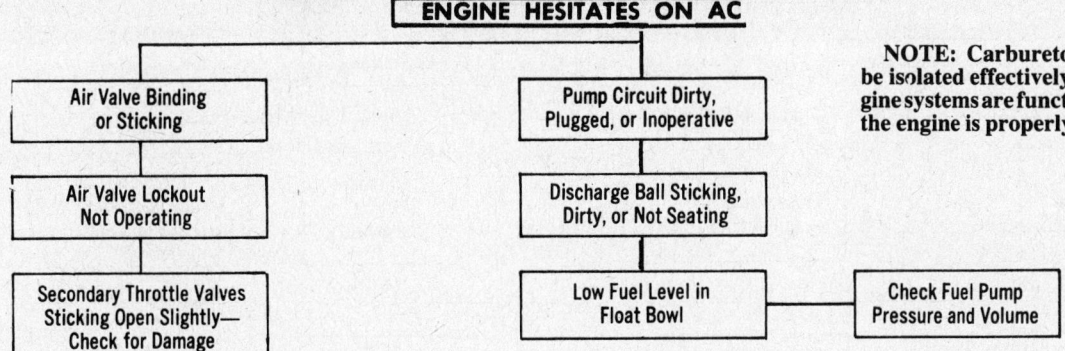

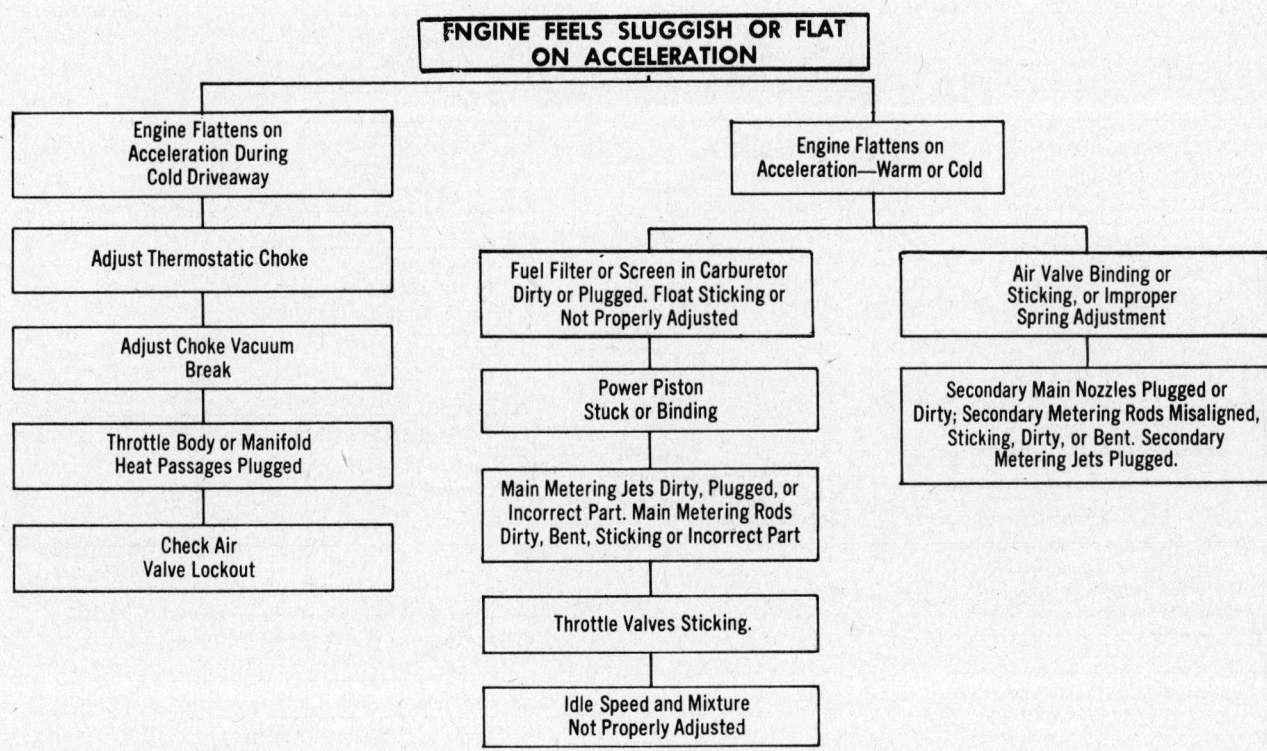

25-5

SECTION 25 CARBURETORS
TROUBLESHOOTING

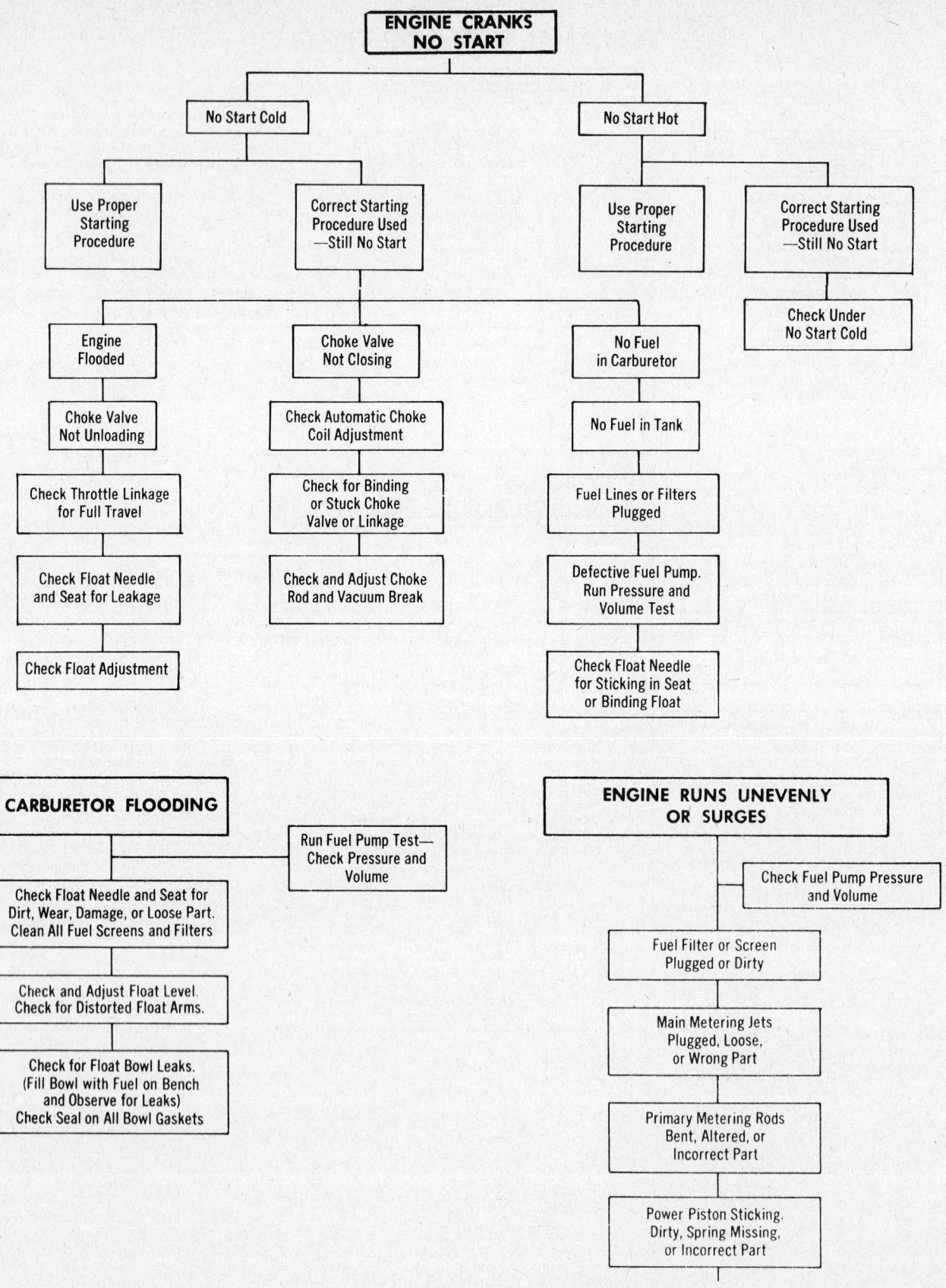

25-6

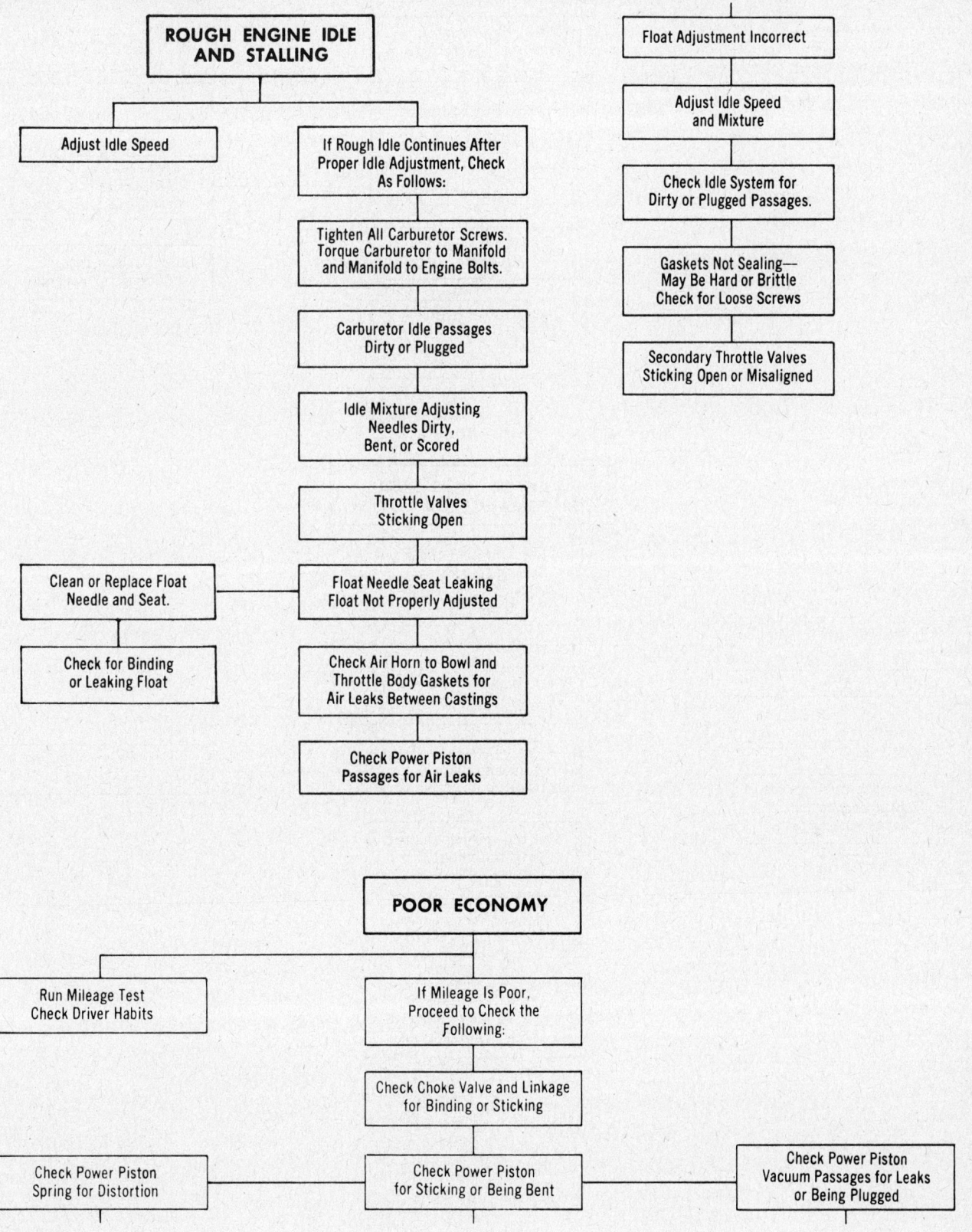

SECTION 25 CARBURETORS
TROUBLESHOOTING

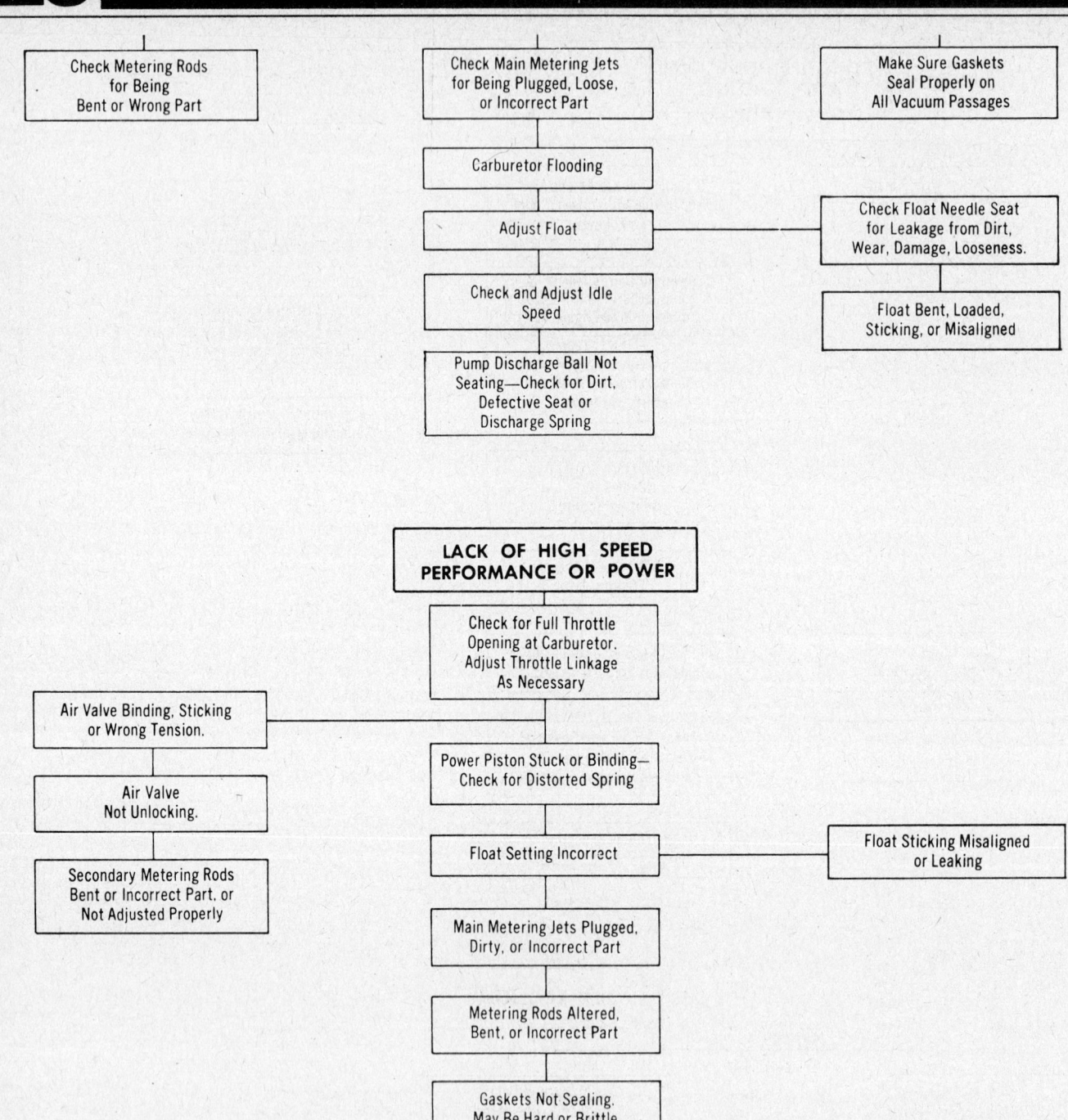

25-8

CARBURETORS
CARTER
SECTION 25

CARTER CARBURETORS
Model BBD

The BBD carburetor is a two barrel unit. It is equipped with a dashpot on some applications.

VACUUM STEP-UP PISTON ADJUSTMENT

1. Remove the dust cover.
2. Be sure not to disturb the adjusting screw on top of the piston. If it is disturbed, reset the gap at the top of the piston to 0.035–0.040 in.
3. Back off the curb idle adjustment until the throttle valves are completely closed. Count the number of turns so that the screw can later be returned to the original position. Then turn the idle screw in one full turn on AMC products only.
4. Fully depress the step-up piston while holding moderate pressure on the rod lifter tab and loosen and tighten the rod lifter lockscrew.
5. Release the piston and rod lifter; return the curb idle screw to its original position.
6. Replace the dust cover, unless the accelerator pump is to be adjusted.

ACCELERATOR PUMP STROKE ADJUSTMENT

1. Back off the idle adjusting screw.

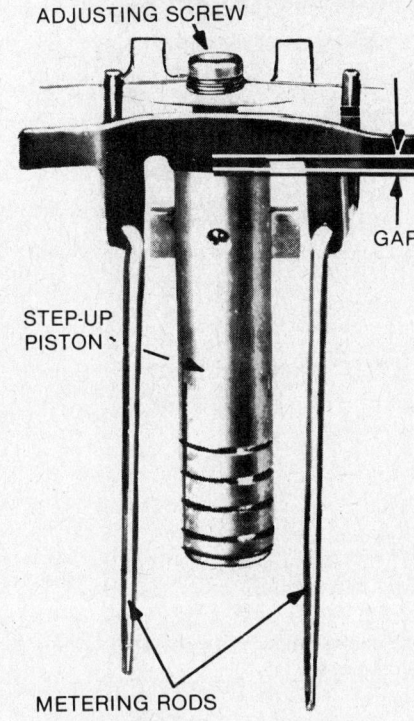

BBD vacuum step-up piston and metering rod assembly

Open the choke valve so that the fast idle cam allows the throttle valves to close. Be sure that the accelerator pump "S" link is in the outer hole of the pump arm if there are two holes.

2. Turn the idle adjusting screw in two complete turns after it contacts the stop.
3. Remove the dust cover. With the throttle valves closed tightly, measure the distance between the top of the air horn and the top of the pump plunger shaft. If the dimension is not as specified, loosen the pump arm adjusting lockscrew (near the plunger shaft) and rotate the sleeve to obtain the correct dimension.

FAST IDLE CAM POSITION ADJUSTMENT

1. With the fast idle speed adjusting screw contacting the second highest speed step on the fast idle cam, move the choke valve toward the closed position with light pressure on the choke shaft lever. On AMC, loosen the choke cover and turn 1/4 turn rich.
2. Insert the specified drill (refer to Specifications), between the top of the choke valve and the wall of the air horn. An adjustment will be neces-

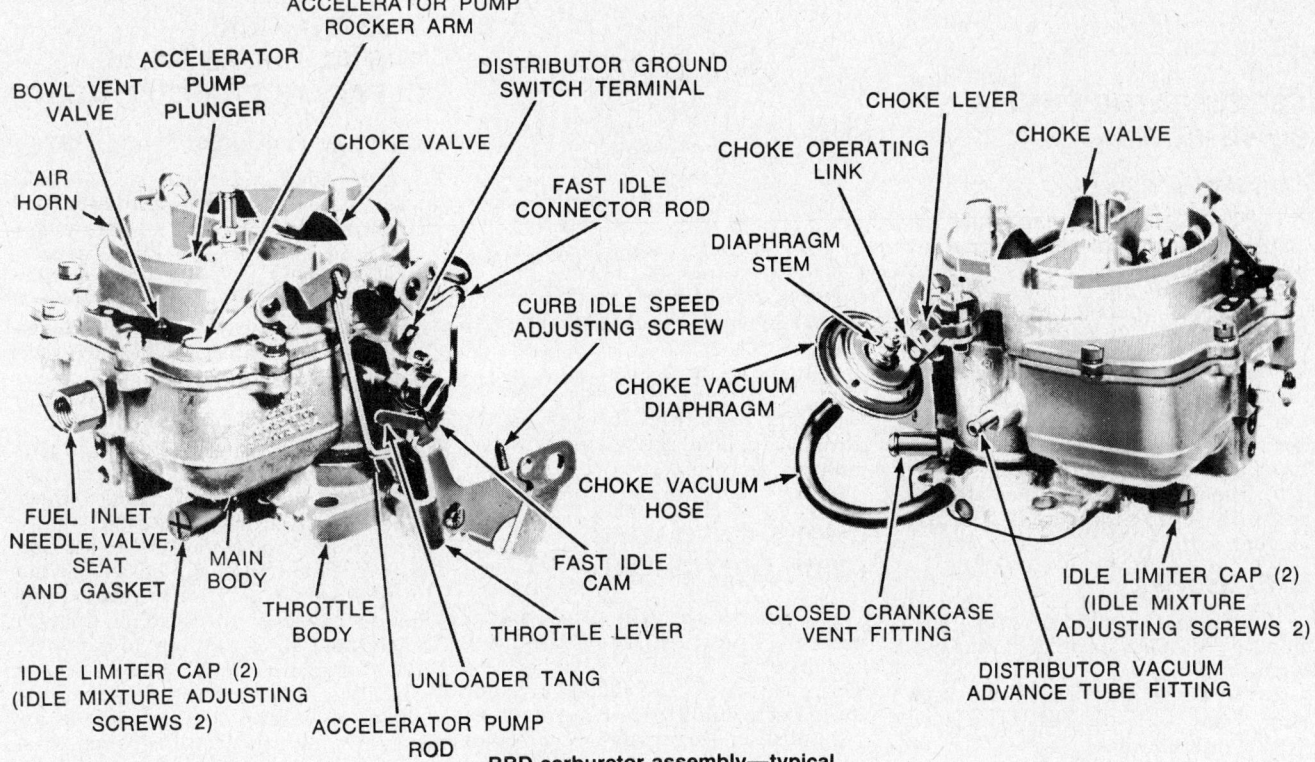

BBD carburetor assembly—typical

25-9

SECTION 25 CARBURETORS CARTER

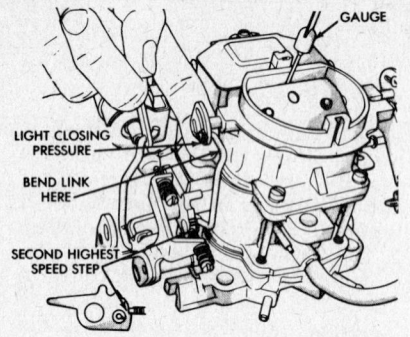

BBD fast idle cam position adjustment

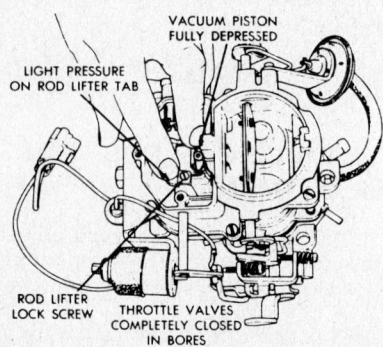

BBD vacuum step-up piston adjustment

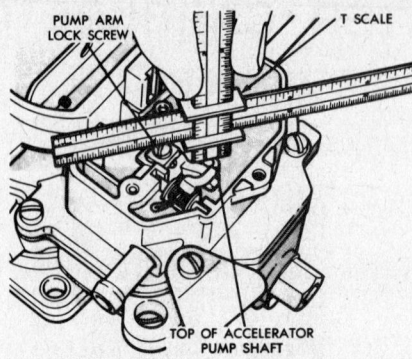

BBD accelerator pump stroke adjustment

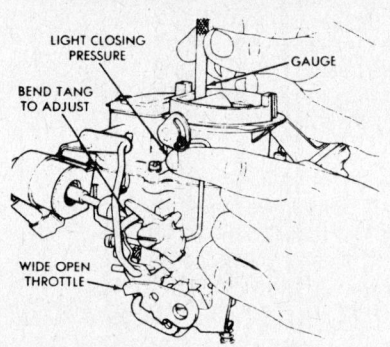

BBD choke unloader (wide open kick) adjustment

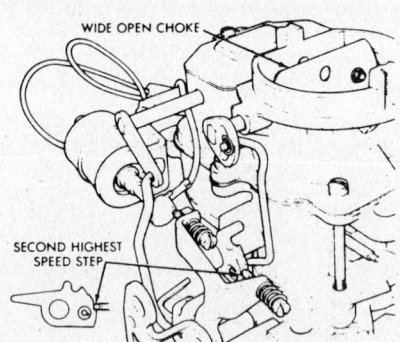

BBD on-car fast idle adjustment

sary if a slight drag is not obtained as the drill is being removed.
3. If an adjustment is required, bend the fast idle connector rod at the angle.
4. Reset the choke cover to specification.

ACCELERATOR PUMP & BOWL VENT

Chrysler Models

1. The accelerator pump stroke adjustment and the curb idle speed must be adjusted first.
2. Remove the air cleaner, step-up piston cover, and the gasket.
3. Insert the specified gauge (0.080 in.) between the top of the bowl vent valve and the seat.
4. If adjustment is needed, bend the bowl vent lever tab. Support the vent lever before bending the tab.
5. Install the gasket and step-up piston cover, and install the air cleaner.

AMC Models

1. Remove the rollover check valve from the air horn for access to the metering rod.
2. Place the throttle on the high step of the fast idle cam. The bowl vent should be closed.
3. Move the fast idle cam until the throttle screw drops to the second step. The vent should just start to open.
4. If the vent is not closed on the high, fourth and third steps of the cam, and beginning to open on the second step, bend the tab until the adjustment is correct.

CHOKE UNLOADER (WIDE OPEN KICK)

1. Hold the throttle valves in the wide open position. Insert the specified drill (see Specifications) between the upper edge of the choke valve and the inner wall of the air horn.
2. With a finger lightly pressing against the control lever, a slight drag should be felt as the drill is being withdrawn. If an adjustment is necessary, bend the unloader tang on the throttle lever until the correct opening has been obtained.

FAST IDLE SPEED (ON VEHICLE)

1. On Chrysler products, disconnect and plug the connections for the heated air control, EGR, and OSAC valve or distributor. On 1980-81 Chrysler products with ESA (Electronic Spark Advance), ground the idle switch. Do not disconnect the vacuum hose to the vacuum transducer. Disconnect the EGR and TCS solenoid on AMC cars through 1980. On 1981-84 AMC disconnect the EGR. With the engine off and the transmission in Park or Neutral position, open the throttle slightly.
2. Close the choke valve until the fast idle screw can be positioned on the second highest speed step of the fast idle cam.
3. Start the engine and let the idle stabilize. Turn the fast idle speed screw in or out to obtain the specified speed.
4. Stopping the engine between adjustments is not necessary. However, reposition the fast idle speed screw on the cam after each speed adjustment to provide the correct throttle closing torque.

VACUUM KICK (INITIAL CHOKE VALVE CLEARANCE) ADJUSTMENT

Chrysler Products

1. If the adjustment is to be made with the engine running, disconnect the fast idle linkage to allow the choke to close to the kick position with engine at curb idle. If an auxiliary vacuum source is to be used, as recommended, open the throttle valves (engine not running) and move the choke to the closed position. Release the throttle first, then release the choke.
2. When using an auxiliary vacuum source, disconnect the vacuum hose from the carburetor and connect it to the hose from the vacuum supply with a small length of tube to act as a fitting. Removal of the hose from the diaphragm may require sufficient force to damage the system. Apply a vacuum of 15 or more in. of mercury.
3. Insert the specified drill (refer to Specifications) between the top of the choke valve and the wall of the air horn. Apply sufficient closing pressure on the lever to which the choke

CARBURETORS
CARTER
SECTION 25

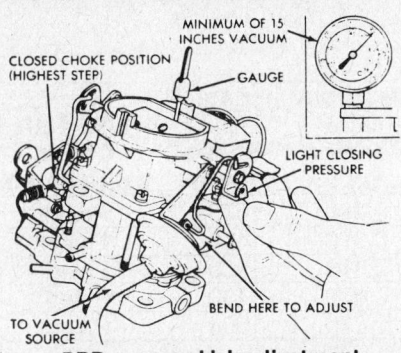

BBD vacuum kick adjustment

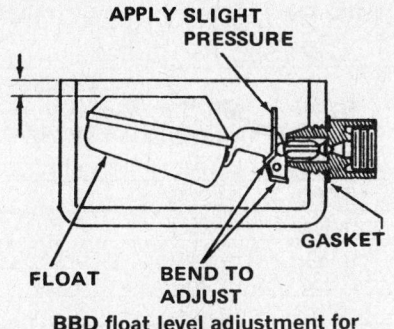

BBD float level adjustment for AMC products

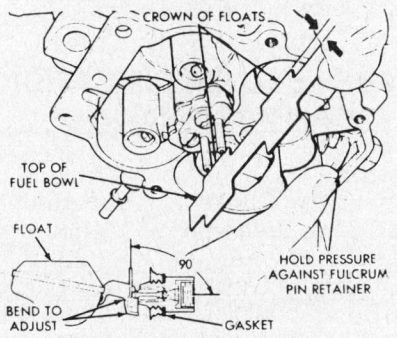

BBD float level adjustment

rod attaches to provide a minimum choke valve opening without distortion of the diaphragm link. Note that the cylindrical stem of the diaphragm will extend as the internal spring is compressed. This spring must be fully compressed for proper measurement of the vacuum kick adjustment.

4. An adjustment will be necessary if a slight drag is not obtained as the drill is being removed. Shorten or lengthen the diaphragm link to obtain the correct choke opening. Length changes should be made carefully by bending (opening or closing) the U-bend provided in the diaphragm link.

CAUTION
Do not apply twisting or bending force to the diaphragm.

5. Reinstall the vacuum hose on the correct carburetor fitting. Return the fast idle linkage to its original condition if it was disturbed, as suggested in Step 1.
6. Make the following check: with no vacuum applied to the diaphragm, the choke valve should move freely between the open and closed positions. If its movement is not free, examine the linkage for misalignment or interference caused by the bending operation. Repeat the adjustment if necessary to provide proper link operations.

AMC Models

This adjustment is called Initial Choke Valve Clearance Adjustment on AMC products.
1. Loosen the choke cover, turn ¼ turn rich, and tighten one cover screw.
2. Apply a vacuum of at least 19 in. Hg to pull the diaphragm in against the stop.
3. Open the throttle valve slightly to place the fast idle screw on the high step of the cam.
4. Measure the clearance between the choke plate upper edge and the air horn wall.
5. Adjust the clearance between the choke plate upper edge and the air horn wall.
5. Adjust the clearance by bending the diaphragm connector link at the angle. Reset the choke or replace the cover.

FLOAT LEVEL

Chrysler Models

1. Invert the carburetor so that the weight of the floats is the only force on the needle and seat.
2. Use a T-scale to check the float level. Measure from the surface of the fuel bowl to the crown of each float at center.
3. To adjust, hold the floats on the bottom of the bowl and bend the float lip to give the specified dimension.

AMC Models

1. Remove the air horn.
2. Hold the float lip gently against the needle to raise the float.
3. Place a straightedge across the float bowl to measure the float level at the top of the float.
4. To adjust, bend the float lip, being careful not to exert pressure on the synthetic needle tip.

DASHPOT ADJUSTMENT

Chrysler Models

The dashpot is used on manual transmission models only.
1. Make sure that the curb idle speed is correctly adjusted.
2. Start the engine. Position the throttle lever so that the actuating tab is just contacting the dashpot plunger stem. Let the engine speed stabilize for 30 seconds.
3. The speed should be 2500 rpm.
4. Adjust the setting by loosening the locknut and moving the dashpot.

CARTER BBD SPECIFICATIONS
Chrysler Products

Year	Model ②	Float Level (in.)	Accelerator Pump Travel (in.)	Bowl Vent (in.)	Choke Unloader (in.)	Choke Vacuum Kick (in.)	Fast Idle Cam Position (in.)	Fast Idle Speed (rpm)	Automatic Choke Adjustment
'80	8233S	¼	0.500 ①	0.080	0.280	0.130	0.070	1500	Fixed
	8235S	¼	0.500 ①	0.080	0.280	0.130	0.070	1700	Fixed
	8237S	¼	0.500 ①	0.080	0.280	0.110	0.070	1500	Fixed
	8239S	¼	0.500 ①	0.080	0.280	0.110	0.070	1500	Fixed
	8286S	¼	0.500 ①	0.080	0.280	0.100	0.070	1400	Fixed
'81–'82	8290S	¼	0.500 ①	0.080	0.280	0.100	0.070	1600	Fixed
	8291S	¼	0.500 ①	0.080	0.280	0.130	0.070	1400	Fixed
	8292S	¼	0.500 ①	0.080	0.280	0.130	0.070	1600 ③	Fixed

SECTION 25
CARBURETORS
CARTER

CARTER BBD SPECIFICATIONS
Chrysler Products

Year	Model ②	Float Level (in.)	Accelerator Pump Travel (in.)	Bowl Vent (in.)	Choke Unloader (in.)	Choke Vacuum Kick (in.)	Fast Idle Cam Position (in.)	Fast Idle Speed (rpm)	Automatic Choke Adjustment
'83	8290S	1/4	0.470 ①	0.080	0.280	0.100	0.070	1600	Fixed
	8291S	1/4	0.470 ①	0.080	0.280	0.130	0.070	1400	Fixed
	8369S	1/4	0.500 ①	0.080	0.280	0.130	0.070	1500	Fixed
'84	8385S	1/4	0.470 ①	0.080	0.280	0.130	0.070	1400	Fixed
	8369S	1/4	0.500	0.080	0.280	0.130	0.070	1500	Fixed

① At idle
② Models numbers located on tag or casting
③ 1982: 1500 rpm

CARTER BBD SPECIFICATIONS
American Motors

Year	Model ①	Float Level (in.)	Accelerator Pump Travel (in.)	Choke Unloader (in.)	Choke Vacuum Kick (in.)	Fast Idle Cam Position (in.)	Fast Idle Speed (rpm)	Automatic Choke Adjustment
'80	8216	1/4	0.520	0.280	0.140	0.090	1850	2 Rich
	8246	1/4	0.520	0.280	0.140	0.095	1850	2 Rich
	8247	1/4	0.520	0.280	0.150	0.095	1700	1 Rich
	8248	1/4	0.520	0.280	0.150	0.095	1700	1 Rich
	8253	1/4	0.470	0.280	0.128	0.095	1850	2 Rich
	8256	1/4	0.470	0.280	0.128	0.093	1850	2 Rich
	8278	1/4	0.542	0.280	0.140	0.093	1850	Index
'81	8310	1/4	0.525	0.280	0.140	0.095	1850	Index
	8302	1/4	0.500	0.280	0.128	0.095	1850	1 Rich
	8303	1/4	0.500	0.280	0.128	0.090	1700	1 Rich
	8306	1/4	0.500	0.280	0.128	0.090	1700	1 Rich
	8307	1/4	0.500	0.280	0.128	0.095	1850	1 Rich
	8308	1/4	0.500	0.280	0.128	0.095	1850	2 Rich
	8309	1/4	0.520	0.280	0.128	0.093	1700	2 Rich
'82	8338	1/4	0.520	0.280	0.140	0.095	1850	1 Rich
	8339	1/4	0.520	0.280	0.140	0.095	1850	1 Rich
'83	8360	1/4	0.520	0.280	0.140	0.095	1850	Fixed
	8364	1/4	0.520	0.280	0.140	0.095	1700	Fixed
	8367	1/4	0.520	0.280	0.140	0.095	1700	Fixed
	8362	1/4	0.520	0.280	0.140	0.095	1850	Fixed
'84–'85	8383	1/4	0.520	0.280	0.140	0.095	1850	1/2–1 1/2 Rich
	8384	1/4	0.520	0.280	0.140	0.095	1700	1/2–1 1/2 Rich

① Model numbers located on the tag or casting

Model YF, YFA

The YF carburetor is a single barrel downdraft carburetor with a diaphragm type accelerator pump and diaphragm operated metering rods.

FLOAT ADJUSTMENT

1. Invert the air horn assembly and check the clearance from the top of the float to the surface of the air horn with a T-scale. The air horn should be held at eye level when gauging and the float arm should be resting on the needle pin.

2. Do not exert pressure on the needle valve when measuring or adjusting the float. Bend the float arm as necessary to adjust the float level.

CAUTION
Do not bend the tab at the end of the float arm as it prevents the float from striking the bottom of the fuel bowl when empty and keep the needle in place.

METERING ROD ADJUSTMENT

1. Remove the air horn. Back out

CARBURETORS
CARTER

the idle speed adjusting screw until the throttle plate is seated fully in its bore.

2. Press down on the upper end of the diaphragm shaft until the diaphragm bottoms in the vacuum chamber.

3. The metering rod should contact the bottom of the metering rod well. The lifter link at the outer end nearest the springs and at the supporting link should be bottomed.

4. On models not equipped with an adjusting screw, adjust by bending the lip of the metering rod is attached.

5. On models with an adjusting screw, turn the screw until the metering rod just bottoms in the body casting. For final adjustment, turn the screw one additional turn clockwise.

FAST IDLE CAM ADJUSTMENT

1. Put the fast idle screw on the second highest step of the fast idle cam against the shoulder of the high step.

2. Adjust by bending the choke plate connecting rod to obtain the specified clearance between the lower edge of the choke plate and the air horn wall.

CHOKE UNLOADER ADJUSTMENT

With the throttle valve held wide open and the choke valve held in the closed position, bend the unloader tang on the throttle lever to obtain the specified clearance between the lower edge of the choke valve and the air horn wall.

AUTOMATIC CHOKE ADJUSTMENT

Loosen the choke cover retaining screws, then turn the choke cover so that the index mark on the cover lines up with the specified mark on the choke housing.

CHOKE PLATE PULLDOWN ADJUSTMENT

1983–84 Piston Type Choke

NOTE: This adjustment requires that the thermostatic spring housing and gasket (choke cap) are removed. Refer to the "Choke Cap" removal procedure below.

1. Remove the air cleaner assembly, then the choke cap.

2. Bend a 0.026 in. diameter wire gauge at a 90 degree angle approx-

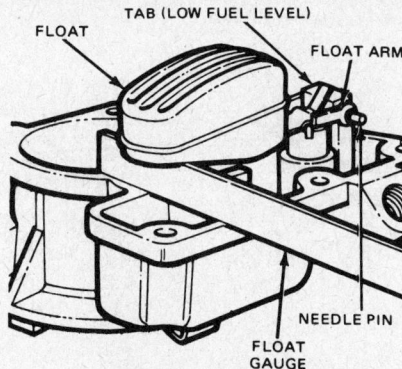

YFA float level adjustment

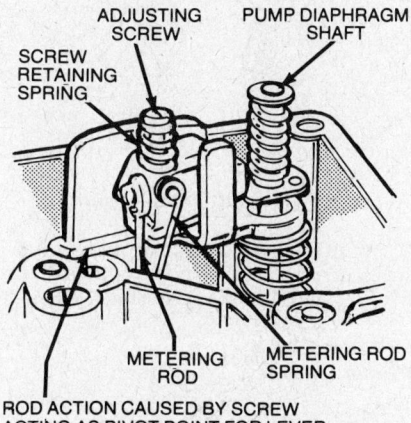

YFA metering rod adjustment

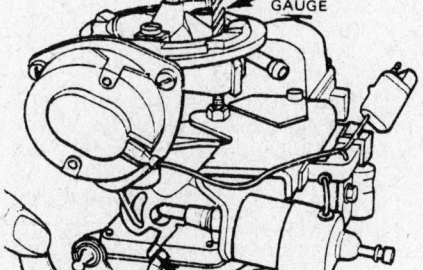

YFA choke unloader adjustment

imately 1/8 in. from one end. Insert the bent end of the gauge between the choke piston slot and the right hand slot in the choke housing. Rotate the choke piston lever counterclockwise until the gauge is shut in the piston slot.

3. Apply light pressure on the choke piston lever to hold the gauge in place, then measure the clearance between the lower edge of the choke plate and the carburetor bore using a drill with the diameter equal to the specified pulldown clearance.

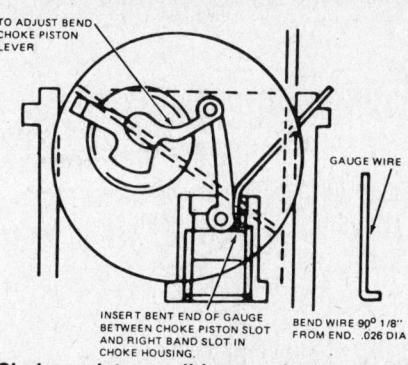

Choke plate pulldown—piston type choke—YFA

4. Bend the choke piston lever to obtain the proper clearance.
5. Install the choke cap.

Diaphragm Type Choke

1. Activate the pulldown motor by applying an external vacuum source.
2. Close the choke plate as far as possible without forcing it.
3. Using a drill of the specified size, measure the clearance between the lower edge of the choke plate and the air horn wall.
4. If adjustment is necessary bend the choke diaphragm link as required.

CHOKE CAP REMOVAL

1983–84

NOTE: The automatic choke has two rivets and a screw, retaining the choke cap in place. There is a locking and indexing plate to prevent misadjustment.

1. Remove the air cleaner assembly from the carburetor.

2. Check choke cap retaining ring rivets to determine if mandrel is well below the rivet head. If mandrel appears to be at or within the rivet head thickness, drive it down or out with a 1/16 inch diameter punch.

3. Use a 1/8 inch diameter or No. 32 drill (.128 inch diameter) for drilling the rivet heads. Drill into the rivet head until the rivet head comes loose from the rivet body.

4. After the rivet head is removed, drive the remaining portion of the rivet out of the hole with a 1/8 inch diameter punch.

NOTE: This procedure must be followed to retain the hole size.

5. Repeat Steps 1–4 for the remaining rivet.

6. Remove the screw in the conventional manner.

25-13

SECTION 25
CARBURETORS
CARTER

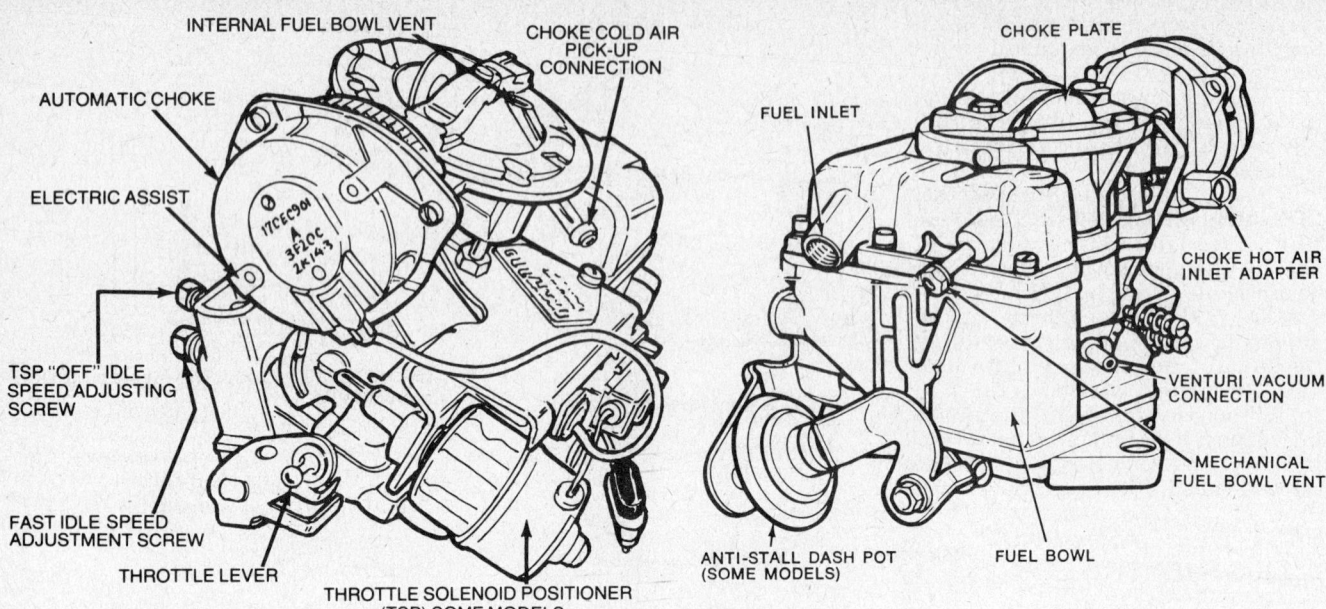

Carter YFA carburetor—typical

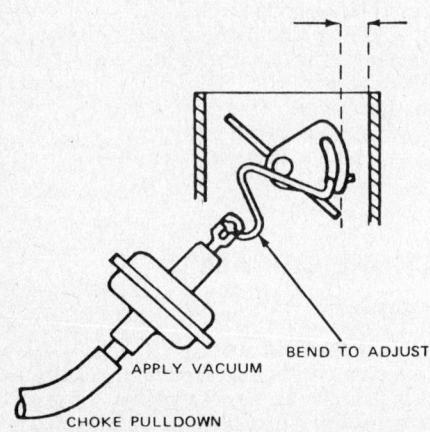

Choke plate pulldown—diaphragm type choke—YFA

ter passing through retaining clamp and pop rivet (mandrel breaks off).
8. Repeat this step for the remaining rivet.
9. Install screw in conventional manner. Tighten 17–20 inch lbs.

CHOKE CAP INSTALLATION

1. Install choke cap gasket.
2. Install the locking and indexing plate.
3. Install the notched gasket.
4. Install choke cap, making certain that bimetal loop is positioned around choke lever tang.
5. While holding cap in place, actuate choke plate to make certain bimetal loop is properly engaged with lever tang. Set retaining clamp over choke cap and orient clamp to match holes in casting (holes are not equally spaced). Make sure retaining clamp is not upside down.
6. Place rivet in rivet gun and trigger lightly to retain rivet ($\frac{1}{8}$ inch diameter x $\frac{1}{2}$ inch long x $\frac{1}{4}$ inch diameter head).
7. Press rivet fully into casting af-

CHOKER PLATE CLEARANCE (DECHOKE) ADJUSTMENT

1. Remove the air cleaner assembly.
2. Hold the throttle plate fully open and close the choke plate as far as possible without forcing it. Use a drill of the proper diameter to check the clearance between the choke plate and air horn.
3. If the clearance is not within specification, adjust by bending the arm on the choke lever of the throttle lever. Bending the arm downward will decrease the clearance, and bending it upward will increase the clearance. Always recheck the clearance after making any adjustment.

MECHANICAL FUEL BOWL VENT ADJUSTMENT

1. Start the engine and wait until it has reached normal operating temperature before proceeding.
2. Check engine idle rpm and set to specifications.
3. Check DC motor operation by opening throttle off idle. The DC motor should extend. Release the throttle, and the DC motor should retract

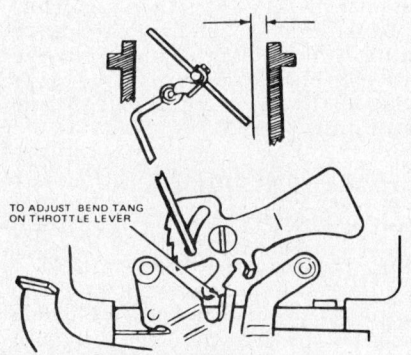

Dechoke adjustment—YFA

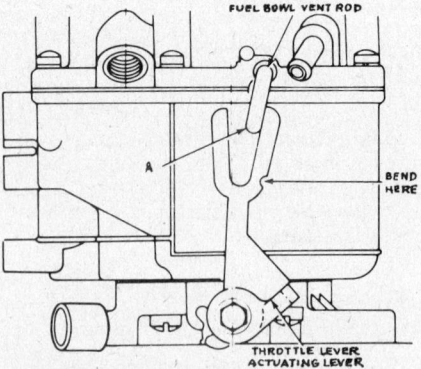

Mechanical fuel bowl vent adjustment—YFA

when in contact with the throttle lever.
4. Disconnect the idle speed motor in the idle position.
5. Turn engine OFF.
6. Open the throttle lever so that the throttle lever actuating lever does not touch the fuel bowl vent rod.
7. Close the throttle lever to the

25-14

CARBURETORS
CARTER

idle set position and measure the travel of the fuel bowl vent rod at point A. The distance measured represents the travel of the vent rod from where there is no contact with the actuating lever to where the actuating lever moves the vent rod to the idle set position. The travel of the vent rod at point A should be 0.100–0.150 in. (2.54–3.81mm).

8. If adjustment is required, bend the throttle actuating lever at notch shown.
9. Reconnect the idle speed control motor.

CARTER YF, YFA SPECIFICATIONS
American Motors

Year	Model ①	Float Level (in.)	Fast Idle Cam (in.)	Unloader (in.)	Choke
'83–'85	7700	0.600	0.175	0.370	Fixed
	7701	0.600	0.175	0.370	Fixed
	7702	0.600	0.175	0.370	Fixed
	7703	0.600	0.175	0.370	Fixed

① Model numbers located on the tag or casting

CARTER YF, YFA, YFA-FB SPECIFICATIONS
Ford Motor Co.

Year	Model ①	Float Level (in.)	Fast Idle Cam (in.)	Choke Plate Pulldown (in.)	Unloader (in.)	Dechoke (in.)	Choke
'80	DEDE-GA,HA EODE-JA,NA, LA,MA	25/32	0.140	—	0.250	—	2 Rich
'83	E3ZE-LA	0.650	0.140	0.260	—	0.220	—
	E3ZE-MA	0.650	0.140	0.260	—	0.220	—
	E3ZE-TB	0.650	0.140	0.240	—	0.220	—
	E3ZE-UA	0.650	0.140	0.240	—	0.220	—
	E3ZE-VA	0.650	0.140	0.260	—	0.220	—
	E3ZE-YA	0.650	0.140	0.260	—	0.220	—
	E3ZE-NB	0.650	0.160	0.260	—	0.220	—
	E3ZE-PB	0.650	0.160	0.260	—	0.220	—
	E3ZE-ASA	0.650	0.160	0.260	—	0.220	—
	E3ZE-APA	0.650	0.140	0.240	—	0.220	—
	E3ZE-ARA	0.650	0.140	0.240	—	0.220	—
	E3ZE-ADA	0.650	0.140	0.260	—	0.220	—
	E3ZE-AEA	0.650	0.140	0.260	—	0.220	—
	E3ZE-ACA	0.650	0.140	0.260	—	0.220	—
	E3ZE-ATA	0.650	0.160	0.260	—	0.220	—
	E3ZE-ABA	0.650	0.140	0.260	—	0.220	—
	E3ZE-UB	0.650	0.140	0.240	—	0.220	—
	E3ZE-TC	0.650	0.140	0.240	—	0.220	—
'84	E4ZE-HC,DB	0.650	0.140	0.260	—	0.270	—
	E4ZE-MA,NA	0.650	0.140	0.240	—	0.270	—
	E4ZE-PA,RA	0.650	0.140	0.260	—	0.270	—
'85	E5ZE-CA	0.650	0.140	0.260	—	0.270	—
	E5ZE-AA	0.650	0.140	0.260	—	0.270	—
'86	E5ZE-AA	0.650	0.140	0.260	—	0.270	—
	E5ZE-AB	0.650	0.140	0.260	—	0.270	—
	E5ZE-CA	0.650	0.140	0.260	—	0.270	—
	E5ZE-CB	0.650	0.140	0.260	—	0.270	—
	E6ZE-EA	0.650	0.140	0.260	—	0.270	—
	E6ZE-DA	0.650	0.140	0.260	—	0.270	—

① Model number located on the tag or casting

SECTION 25 CARBURETORS
CARTER

Model TQ

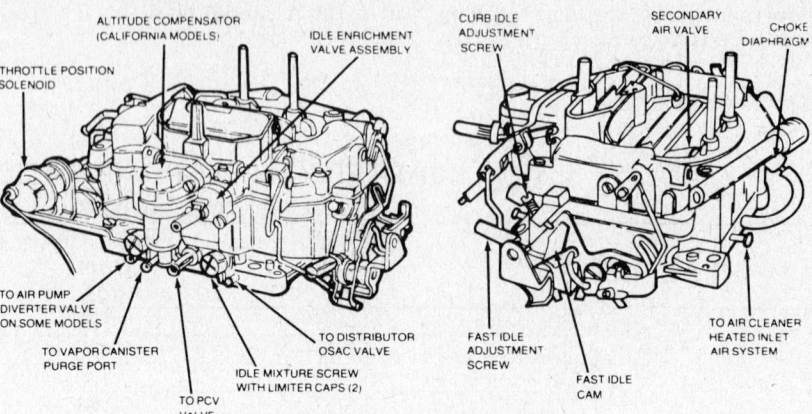

TQ carburetor assembly—typical

The TQ (Thermo-Quad) has a fuel bowl made of phenolic resin. This acts as a heat insulator. Fuel is kept 20 degrees cooler than in metal carburetors. It also has a suspended design metering system which aids in cooling. All the calibration points are in the upper aluminum casting or air horn and are in effect suspended in the cavities in the main body.

FLOAT ADJUSTMENT

1. With the bowl cover inverted, the gasket installed, and the floats resting on the seated needle, the dimension of each float from the bottom side of the float to the cover gasket should be as shown in the specifications chart.
2. To adjust, bend the float lever. Do not allow the float lever lip to be pressed against the needle during adjustment.

SECONDARY THROTTLE LINKAGE

1. Block the choke valve in the wide open position and invert the carburetor.
2. Slowly open the primary throttle valves until the secondary valves start to open. Measure between the lower edge of the primary valve and its bore. Open the throttle to the wide open position. The primary and secondary levers should contact the stops at the same time.
3. If it is necessary to adjust, bend the secondary throttle operating rod at the lower angle until the correct dimension is obtained.

SECONDARY AIR VALVE OPENING

1. With the air valve in the closed position, the opening along the air valve at its long side must be at its maximum and parallel with the air horn gasket surface.
2. With the air valve wide open, the opening of the air valve at the short side and the air horn must match the dimensions in the Specifications Charts. The corner of the air valve is notched for adjustment. Bend the corner with a pair of pliers to give proper opening.

ACCELERATOR PUMP STROKE ADJUSTMENT

1. Make sure the throttle connector

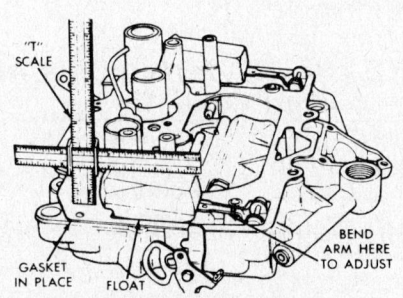

TQ float adjustment

TQ secondary throttle adjustment

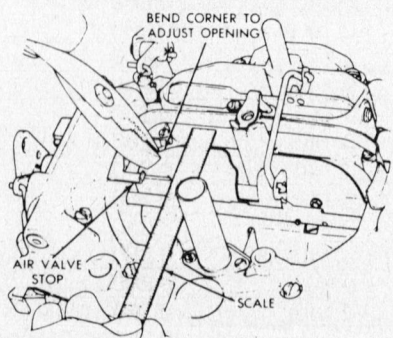

TQ secondary air valve adjustment

First Stage

1. Make sure the throttle connector rod is in the correct pump arm slot.

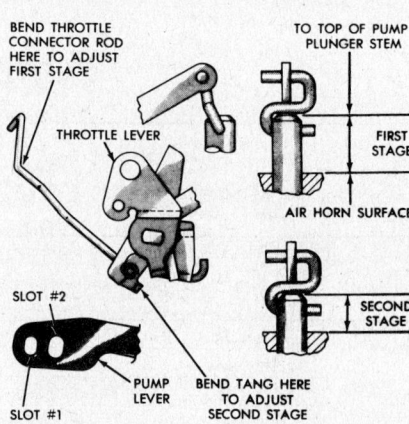

TQ accelerator pump stroke adjustment

rod is in the correct hole of the pump arm.
2. Measure the height of the accelerator pump plunger at curb idle. The ignition switch must be on if there is an idle stop solenoid.
3. Adjust plunger height by bending the throttle connector rod.

NOTE: Carburetors with staged pump systems require a second height measurement at the throttle position related to a secondary throttle lockout.

2. Use a scale to measure the height of the accelerator pump plunger stem at curb idle.
3. Adjust the pump plunger height by bending the throttle connector rod.

Second Stage

1. Open the choke then open the throttle until the secondary lockout is just applied. The plunger downward travel stops at that point.
2. Use a scale to measure the accelerator pump plunger height.
3. Adjust by bending the tang.

CARBURETORS
CARTER
SECTION 25

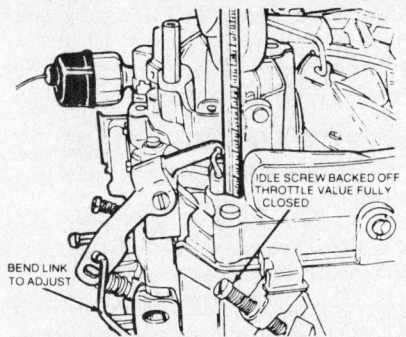
TQ accelerator pump adjustment

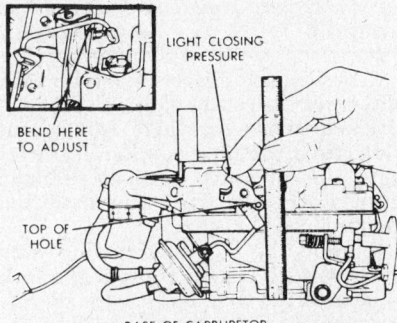
TQ choke control lever

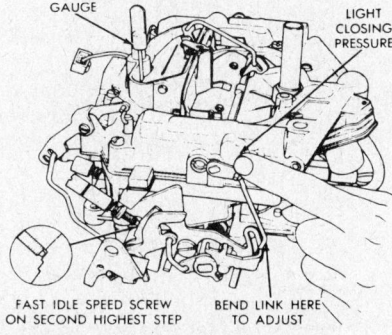
TQ vacuum kick adjustment

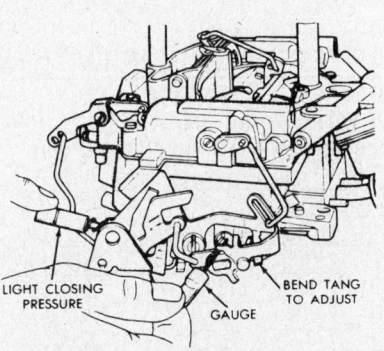
TQ fast idle cam linkage adjustment

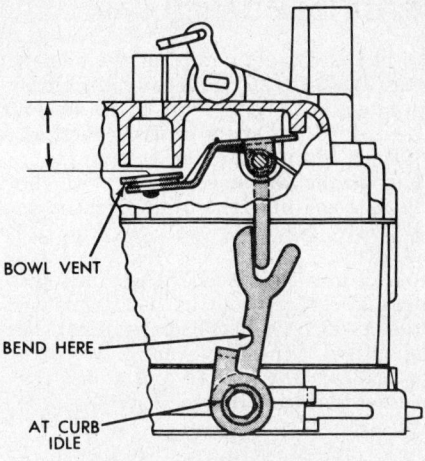
TQ bowl vent adjustment

TQ secondary throttle lockout adjustment

CHOKE CONTROL LEVER

1. Disconnect the diaphragm rod.
2. Close the choke by pushing on the choke lever with the throttle partly open.
3. Measure the vertical distance from the top of the rod hole in the control lever down to the carburetor base. The dimension should be as shown in the Specifications Chart.
4. To adjust, bend the link which connects the two choke shafts. If an adjustment is needed, the vacuum kick, fast idle cam, and choke unloader must be readjusted.

CHOKE VACUUM KICK ADJUSTMENT

NOTE: The test can be made on or off the vehicle.

1. If the adjustment is to be made with the engine running, back off the fast idle speed screw until the choke can be closed to the kick position with the engine at curb idle. Note the number of screw turns required so that the fast idle can be returned to the original adjustment.
2. If an auxiliary vacuum source is to be used, open the throttle valve (engine not running) and move the choke to the closed position. Release the throttle first, then release the choke. When using an auxiliary vacuum source, disconnect the vacuum hose from the carburetor and connect it to the hose from the vacuum supply with a small length of tube to act as a fitting. Removal of the hose from the diaphragm may require sufficient force to bend the bracket. Apply a vacuum of 15 or more inches of mercury.
3. Insert the specified drill between the long side, lower edge, of the choke valve and the air horn wall.
4. Apply sufficient pressure on the choke control lever to provide a minimum choke valve opening. The spring connecting the control lever to the adjustment lever must be fully extended for proper adjustment.
5. Bend the tang to change contact with the end of the diaphragm rod. Do not adjust the diaphragm rod. A slight drag should be felt as the drill is being removed.

FAST IDLE CAM LINKAGE

1. With the fast screw on the second fastest step of the cam against the shoulder of the first step, there should be 0.100 in. between the air horn wall and edge of the choke valve.
2. To adjust, bend the fast idle connector rod at the lower angle.

SECONDARY THROTTLE LOCKOUT

1. Move the choke control lever to the open choke position.
2. Measure the clearance between the lockout lever and the stop.
3. Bend the tang on the fast idle control lever to provide the proper clearance. Clearance should be 0.060–0.090 in.

BOWL VENT VALVE ADJUSTMENT

1. Remove the air cleaner. Disconnect the hose to the solenoid bowl vent diaphragm.
2. Connect an auxiliary vacuum source. With 15 in. Hg applied, the valve should move down. This can be observed down through the air horn vent tube.
3. Turn the ignition switch on and disconnect the auxiliary vacuum source. The valve should remain down. With the ignition off, the valve should move back up.
4. If the valve does not move down when vacuum is applied, the diaphragm is leaking and must be replaced. If the valve does not stay down with the ignition on and the vacuum removed, the solenoid or the wiring is defective.

25-17

SECTION 25 CARBURETORS
CARTER

FAST IDLE SPEED CAM

1. Disconnect and plug the heated air, EGR, OSAC valve, or distributor connections. With lean burn, do not disconnect the spark control computer hose. Use a jumper wire to ground the carburetor idle stop switch. With the engine off and the transmission in Park or Neutral, open the throttle slightly.
2. Close the choke valve until the fast idle screw can be positioned on the second step of the cam against the shoulder of the first step.
3. Start the engine and adjust the screw to obtain the specified fast idle speed.

CHOKE UNLOADER ADJUSTMENT

1. Hold the throttle valves in the wide open position and insert the specified drill between the bottom of the choke valve and inner wall of the air horn.
2. With a finger pressing lightly against the choke control lever, a slight drag should be felt as the drill is being withdrawn.
3. To adjust, bend the tang on the fast idle lever.

SECONDARY AIR VALVE SPRING TENSION

1. Loosen the air valve lock plug and allow the air valve to position itself in the wide open position.

—— **CAUTION** ——
Hold the adjustment plug with a screwdriver when loosening the lock plug. If you don't, the spring may snap out of position and require carburetor disassembly to retrieve it.

2. With a long screwdriver that will enter the center of tool C-4152 positioned on the air valve adjustment plug, turn the plug counterclockwise until the air valve contacts the stop lightly, then tighten the specified amount.
3. Hold the adjustment plug with the screwdriver and tighten the lock plug with the tool. Make sure the adjustment does not move and that the air valve moves freely.

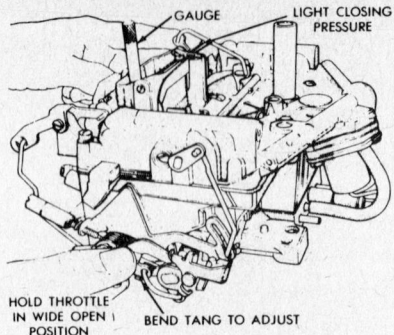
TQ choke unloader adjustment

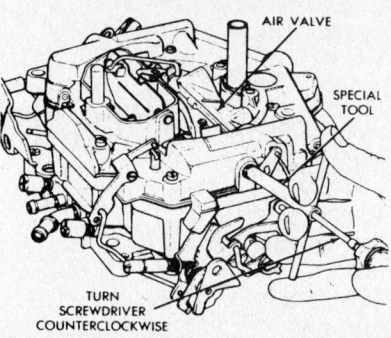
TQ air valve spring tension adjustment

CARTER TQ SPECIFICATIONS

Year	Model ①	Float Setting (in.)	Secondary Throttle Linkage (in.)	Secondary Air Valve Opening (in.)	Secondary Air Valve Spring (turns)	Accelerator Pump (in.)	Choke Control Lever (in.)	Choke Unloader (in.)	Vacuum Kick (in.)	Fast Idle Speed (rpm)
'80	9235S	29/32	②	1/2	3	11/32 ③	3 3/8	0.310	0.100	1600
	9243S	29/32	②	1/2	2 5/8	11/32 ④	3 3/8	0.310	0.100	1600
	9244S	29/32	②	1/2	2 1/2	11/32 ④	3 3/8	0.310	0.100	1600
'81	9372S	29/32	②	13/32	1 3/4	33/64 ④	3 3/8	0.312	0.130	1400
	9373S	29/32	②	13/32	1 3/4	33/64 ④	3 3/8	0.312	0.130	1400
	9364S	29/32	②	13/32	1 7/8	33/64 ③	3 3/8	0.312	0.100	1500
'82	9372S	29/32	②	13/32	1 3/4	33/64 ④	3 3/8	0.310	0.130	1400
'83	9374S	29/32	②	13/32	1 3/4	⑤	3 3/8	0.310	0.130	1400
	9385S	29/32	②	13/32	1 3/4	33/64 ④	3 3/8	0.310	0.130	1400
'84	93895	29/32	②	13/32	1 3/4	⑤	—	0.310	0.130	1400

NOTE: All choke settings are fixed.
① Model numbers located on the tag or on the casting
② Adjust link so primary and secondary stops both contact at same time
③ Slot #1
④ Slot #2
⑤ First stage—33/64
  Second stage—25/64

FORD, AUTOLITE, MOTORCRAFT CARBURETORS
Model 740

The model 740 has five basic systems: choke system, idle system, main metering system, acceleration system and power enrichment system. The choke system is used for cold starting and features a bi-metallic spring and an electric heater for fast cold starts and improved warm-up. The idle system is a separate and adjustable system for the correct air/fuel mixture for both idle and low speed performance.
The main metering system provides the correct air/fuel mixture for normal cruising speeds. A main metering system is provided for both primary

CARBURETORS
AUTOLITE/FORD/MOTORCRAFT
SECTION 25

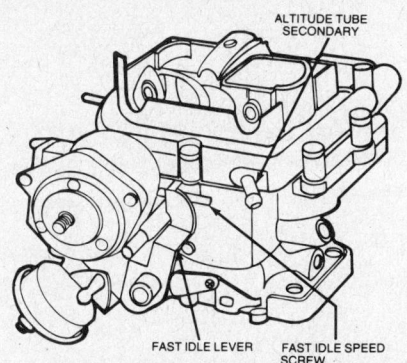

Model 740 carburetor—¾ front view

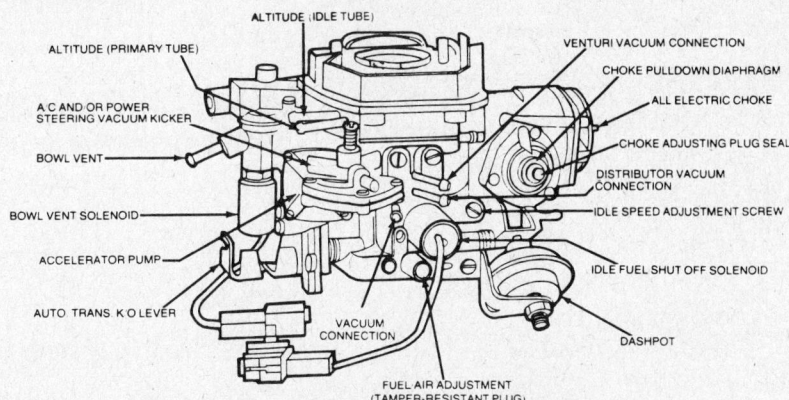

Model 740 carburetor—full rear

and secondary stage operation. The accelerating system is mechanically operated from the primary throttle linkage and provides fuel to the primary stage during acceleration. Fuel is provided by a diaphragm-type pump. The power enrichment system consists of a vacuum operated power valve and an airflow-regulated pull-over system in the secondary. This system is used along with the main metering system to provide satisfactory performance during moderate to heavy acceleration. Distributor and EGR vacuum ports are located in the primary venturi area of the carburetor.

FAST IDLE CAM

1. Set the fast idle screw on the kickdown step of the cam against the shoulder of the top step.
2. Manually close the primary choke plate, and measure the distance between the downstream side of the choke plate and the air horn wall.
3. Adjust the right fork of the choke bimetal shaft, which engages the fast idle cam, by bending the fork up and down to obtain the specified clearance.

FAST IDLE

1. Place the transmission in Neutral or Park.
2. Bring the engine to normal operating temperature.
3. Disconnect and plug the vacuum hose at the EGR and purge valves.
4. Identify the vacuum source to the air by-pass section of the air supply control valve. If a vacuum hose is connected to the carburetor, disconnect the hose and plug the hose at the air supply control valve.
5. Place the fast idle adjustment on the second step of the fast idle cam. Run the engine until the cooling fan comes on.
6. While the cooling fan is on,

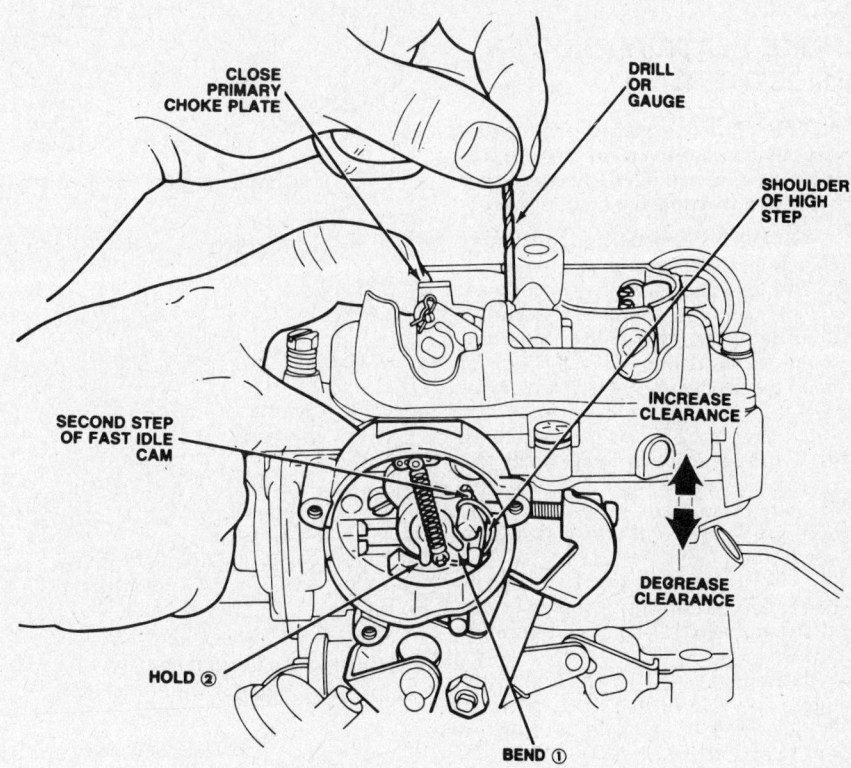

Fast idle cam adjustment – model 740

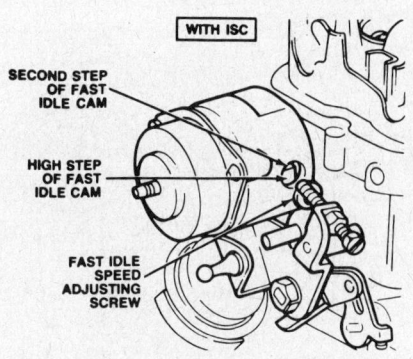

Fast idle speed adjusting screw and fast idle cam—model 740

check the fast idle rpm. If adjustment is necessary, loosen the locknut and adjust to specification on underhood decal.

7. Remove all plugs and reconnect hoses to their original position.

DASHPOT

With the throttle set at the curb idle position, fully depress the dashpot stem and measure the distance between the stem and the throttle lever. Adjust by loosening the locknut and turning the dashpot.

SECTION 25
CARBURETORS
AUTOLITE/FORD/MOTORCRAFT

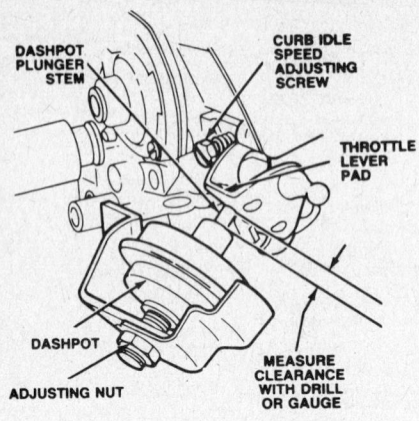

Dashpot assembly—model 740

CHOKE PLATE PULLDOWN ADJUSTMENT

NOTE: *The following procedure requires the removal of the carburetor and also the choke cap which is retained by two rivets.*

1. On 1981–83 models only, remove the carburetor from the engine.
2. Remove the choke cap as follows:
   a. Check the rivets to determine if mandrel is well below the rivet head. If mandrel is within the rivet head thickness, drive it down or out with a $1/16$ inch diameter tip punch.
   b. With a $1/8$ inch diameter drill, drill into the rivet head until the rivet head comes loose from the rivet body. Use light pressure on the drill bit or the rivet will just spin in the hole.
   c. After drilling off the rivet head, drive the remaining rivet out of the hole with a $1/8$ inch diameter punch.
   d. Repeat steps (a thru c) to remove the remaining rivet.
3. On 1981-83 models, connect a vacuum source to the vacuum passage adjacent to the primary throttle bore. On 1984 and later models connect a vacuum source to the vacuum tube on the choke pulldown cover.
4. Set the fast idle adjusting screw on the high step of the fast idle cam by temporarily opening the throttle lever and rotating the choke bimetal shaft lever counterclockwise until the choke plates are in the fully closed position.
5. While applying the external vacuum, lightly force the choke thermostat actuating lever counterclockwise.
6. Using the drill diameter specified in the carburetor specifications table at the end of this section, measure the clearance between the downstream side of the choke plate and the air horn wall.

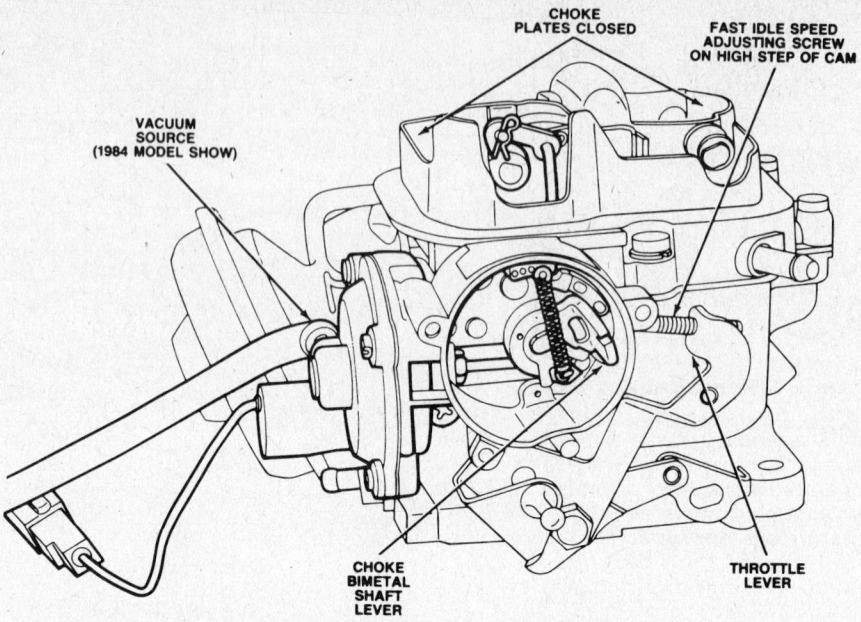

Connecting the vacuum source on 1984 and later 740 models

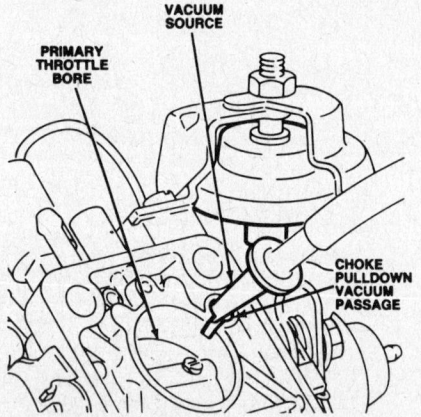

Connecting the vacuum source on 1981–83 740 models

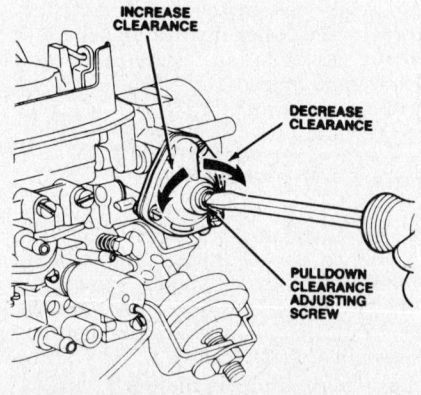

Adjusting choke plate pulldown clearance on 1981–83 740 models

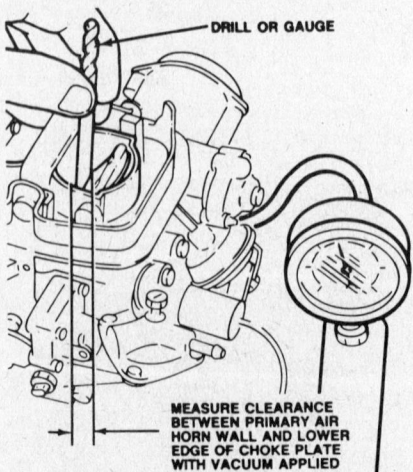

Measuring choke plate pulldown clearance on 1981–83 740 models

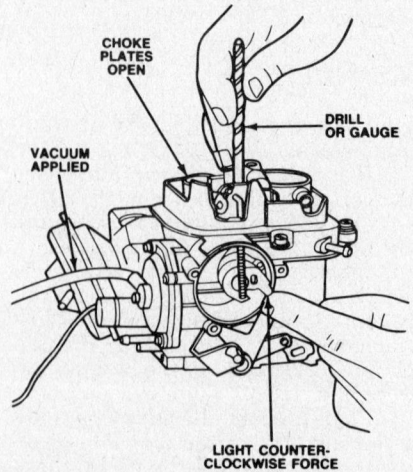

Measuring choke plate pulldown clearance on 1984 and later 740 models

CARBURETORS
Autolite/Ford/Motorcraft

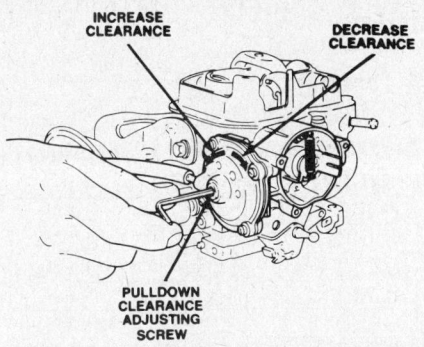

Adjusting choke plate pulldown clearance on 1984 and later 740 models

7. If an adjustment is necessary, turn the vacuum diaphragm adjusting screw in or out as required.

NOTE: On 1984 and later models the choke pulldown adjustment screw is sealed with a limiting plug. Refer to the procedure which follows for removal.

Choke Pulldown Limiting Plug Removal

1984 and Later Models Only

1. Remove the choke pulldown diaphragm cover.
2. Using pliers, grasp the back of the adjustment screw and turn out of the cover.
3. Drive the plugs out of the cover, using a punch and a hammer.

---- CAUTION ----

Wear eye protection when driving out plugs.

DRY FLOAT ADJUSTMENT

1. Place the air horn assembly upside down and at a 45 degree angle with the air horn gasket in place. The float tang should rest lightly on the inlet needle.
2. Measure the clearance with a suitable gauge at the extreme end or toe of the float.
3. Remove float and adjust to specification by bending the float level adjusting tang up or down.

NOTE: Care must be taken not to scratch or damage the float tang while adjusting.

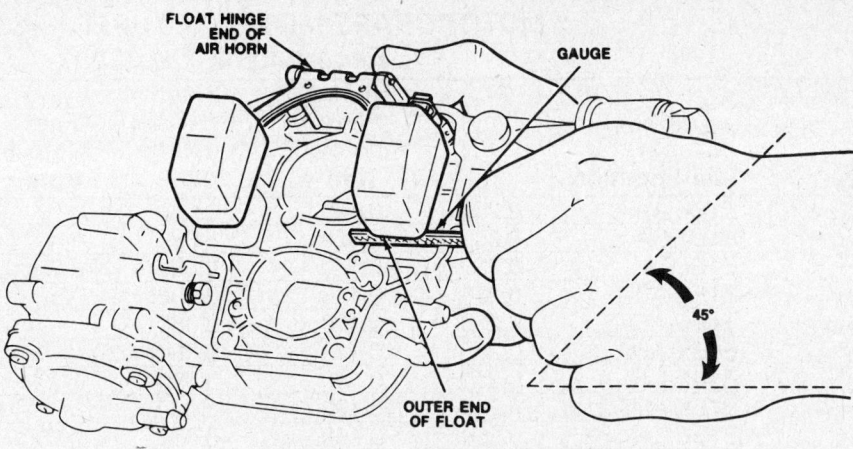

Measuring float clearance—model 740

FLOAT DROP ADJUSTMENT

1. Suspend air horn assembly in normal position with air horn gasket in position.
2. The distance from the air horn gasket to the bottom of the float should be 1.69 ± 0.31 in. (43 ± 8mm).
3. Remove float and adjust to specification by bending the float drop tang.

WIDE OPEN THROTTLE (WOT) A/C CUT-OUT SWITCH

A visual inspection is required to ensure adequate pin and actuating arm overlap with the carburetor linkage in the WOT position.

Adjustments to the switch position are made by bending its support bracket outboard. A 0.120 in. (3mm)

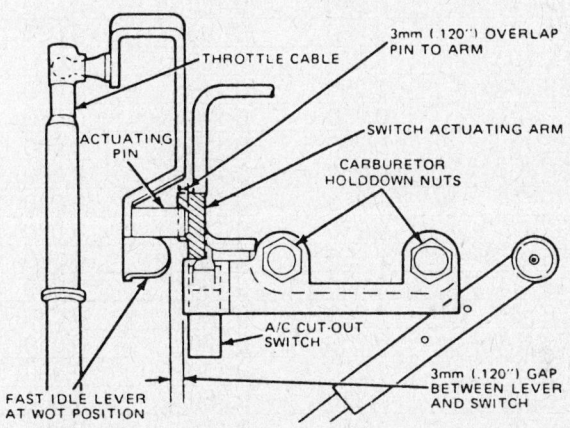

(WOT) A/C cut-off switch adjustment—Model 740

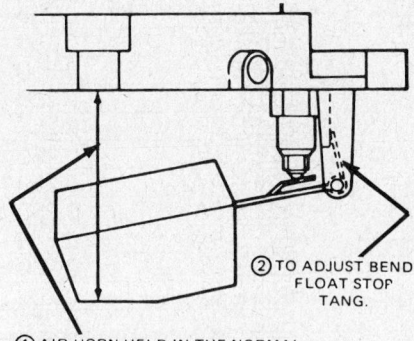

Float drop adjustment—Model 740

minimum overlap is desired. Precaution is required to ensure adequate clearance between the tip of the carburetor fast idle lever and switch housing.

25-21

SECTION 25
CARBURETORS
AUTOLITE/FORD/MOTORCRAFT

MOTORCRAFT MODEL 740 SPECIFICATIONS
Escort, Lynx, Exp, Lynx

Year	(9510)* Carburetor Identification	Dry Float Level (in.)	Choke Plate Pulldown (in.)	Fast Idle Cam Linkage (in.)	Fast Idle (rpm)	Dechoke (in.)	Choke Setting	Dashpot (in.)
'81	E1EE-AAA	0.250	0.120	0.080	①	0.140	Index	0.140
	E1EE-SA	0.250	0.120	0.080	①	0.140	Index	0.140
	E1EE-TA	0.250	0.120	0.080	①	0.140	Index	0.140
	E1EE-AEA	0.250	0.120	0.080	①	0.140	Index	0.140
	E1EE-AFA	0.250	0.120	0.080	①	0.140	Index	0.140
	E1EE-ADA	0.250	0.120	0.080	①	0.140	Index	0.140
	E1EE-LA	0.250	0.120	0.080	①	0.140	Index	0.140
	E1EE-AHA	0.250	0.100	0.080	①	0.140	Index	0.160
	E1EE-ZA	0.250	0.160	0.080	①	0.140	1 Lean	0.160
	E1EE-MA	0.250	0.160	0.080	①	0.140	1 Lean	0.160
	E1EE-NA	0.250	0.160	0.080	①	0.140	1 Lean	0.160
	E1EE-PA	0.250	0.160	0.080	①	0.140	1 Lean	0.160
	E1EE-ACA	0.250	0.160	0.080	①	0.140	1 Lean	0.160
	E1EE-RA	0.250	0.160	0.080	①	0.140	1 Lean	0.160
	E1EE-ARA	0.250	0.118	0.080	①	0.140	Index	0.140
	E1EE-ASA	0.250	0.118	0.080	①	0.140	Index	0.140
	E1EE-AVA	0.250	0.118	0.080	①	0.140	Index	0.140
	E1EE-ATA	0.250	0.118	0.080	①	0.140	Index	0.140
'82	E1GE-CA	0.250	0.120	0.080	2400	0.140	Index	0.140
	E1GE-DA	0.250	0.120	0.080	2400	0.140	Index	0.140
	E1EE-ALA	0.250	0.160	0.080	2400	0.140	1 Lean	0.160
	E1GE-GA	0.250	0.160	0.080	2400	0.140	1 Lean	0.160
	E1EE-APA	0.250	0.160	0.080	2400	0.140	1 Lean	0.160
	E1EE-NA	0.250	0.160	0.080	2400	0.140	1 Lean	0.160
	E1GE-EA	0.250	0.160	0.080	2400	0.140	1 Lean	0.160
	E1EE-ZA	0.250	0.160	0.080	2400	0.140	1 Lean	0.160
	E2EE-JA	0.250	0.138	0.080	2400	0.140	Index	0.060
	E2EE-GA	0.250	0.138	0.080	2200	0.140	Index	0.060
	E2EE-GC	0.250	0.138	0.080	2200	0.140	Index	0.140
	E2EE-EA	0.250	0.138	0.080	2400	0.140	Index	0.160
	E2EE-SA	0.250	0.138	0.080	2400	0.140	Index	0.060
	E2EE-LC	0.250	0.177	0.080	①	0.140	Index	0.160
	E2EE-LA	0.250	0.138	0.080	2400	0.140	Index	0.160
	E2EE-ZA	0.250	0.138	0.080	2400	0.140	2 Rich	0.160
	E2EE-NA	0.250	0.138	0.080	2400	0.140	Index	0.160
	E2EE-AAA	0.250	0.138	0.080	2400	0.140	2 Rich	0.160
	E2EE-PA	0.250	0.138	0.080	2400	0.140	Index	0.160
	E2EE-PC	0.250	0.177	0.080	2200	0.140	Index	0.160
	E2EE-NC	0.250	0.177	0.080	2200	0.140	Index	Dashpot
	E2EE-VA	0.250	0.138	0.080	2400	0.140	1 Lean	0.160
	E2EE-YA	0.250	0.138	0.080	2400	0.140	1 Lean	0.160
	E2EE-MC	0.250	0.177	0.080	2200	0.140	Index	0.160
	E2EE-MA	0.250	0.138	0.080	2400	0.140	Index	0.160
'83	E3EE-CA	0.300	0.320	0.080	①	0.140	NA	0.140
	E3EE-EA	0.300	0.320	0.080	①	0.140	NA	0.140
	E3EE-DA	0.300	0.340	0.080	①	0.140	NA	0.140
	E3EE-AA	0.300	0.140	0.080	①	0.140	NA	0.140
	E3EE-JA	0.300	0.140	0.080	①	0.140	NA	0.140
	E3EE-BA	0.300	0.140	0.080	①	0.140	NA	0.140
	E3EE-KA	0.300	0.140	0.080	①	0.140	NA	0.140
	E3EE-GB	0.300	0.312	0.080	①	0.140	NA	0.095
	E3EE-NA	0.300	0.140	0.080	①	0.140	NA	—
	E3EE-PA	0.300	0.140	0.080	①	0.140	NA	0.140
	E3GE-DA	0.300	0.170	0.080	①	0.140	NA	0.140

CARBURETORS
AUTOLITE/FORD/MOTORCRAFT

MOTORCRAFT MODEL 740 SPECIFICATIONS
Escort, Lynx, Exp, Lynx

Year	(9510)* Carburetor Identification	Dry Float Level (in.)	Choke Plate Pulldown (in.)	Fast Idle Cam Linkage (in.)	Fast Idle (rpm)	Dechoke (in.)	Choke Setting	Dashpot (in.)
'83	E3GE-HA	0.300	0.170	0.080	①	0.140	NA	0.140
	E3GE-FA	0.300	0.170	0.080	①	0.140	NA	0.140
	E3GE-JA	0.300	0.170	0.080	①	0.140	NA	0.160
	E3GE-PA	0.300	0.260	0.080	①	0.140	NA	0.140
	E3GE-SA	0.300	0.260	0.080	①	0.140	NA	0.140
	E3GE-RA	0.300	0.260	0.080	①	0.140	NA	0.140
	E3GE-MA	0.300	0.280	0.093	①	0.140	NA	0.160
	E3GE-UA	0.300	0.280	0.093	①	0.140	NA	0.160
	E3GE-NA	0.300	0.140	0.093	①	0.140	NA	0.160
	E3GE-KB	0.300	0.300	0.080	①	0.140	NA	0.160
	E3GE-KD	0.300	0.300	0.080	①	0.140	NA	0.160
	E3GE-LA	0.300	0.300	0.080	①	0.140	NA	0.160
	E3GE-LC	0.300	0.300	0.080	①	0.140	NA	0.160
	E3GE-DC	0.300	0.170	0.080	①	0.140	NA	—
	E3GE-FC	0.300	0.170	0.080	①	0.140	NA	—
	E3GE-JC	0.300	0.170	0.080	①	0.140	NA	—
'84–'85	E4EE-YA	0.300	0.320	0.110	①	0.140	NA	0.095
	E4EE-ACA	0.300	0.320	0.080	①	0.140	NA	0.080
	E4EE-ADA	0.300	0.260	0.080	①	0.140	NA	0.140
	E4EE-ABA	0.300	0.320	0.110	①	0.140	NA	0.095
	E4EE-AAA	0.300	0.320	0.095	①	0.140	NA	0.095
	E4EE-AFA	0.300	0.218	0.080	①	0.140	NA	—
	E4GE-LA	0.300	0.300	0.080	①	0.140	NA	0.160
	E4GE-KA	0.300	0.300	0.080	①	0.140	NA	0.160
	E4GE-SA	0.300	0.280	0.100	①	0.140	NA	0.160
	E4GE-MA	0.300	0.300	0.180	①	0.140	NA	0.160
	E4GE-UA	0.300	0.325	0.080	①	0.140	NA	—
	E4GE-TA	0.300	0.300	0.125	①	0.140	NA	—
	E4GE-RA	0.300	0.325	0.130	①	0.140	NA	—
	E4GE-ACA	0.300	0.140	0.080	①	0.140	NA	0.080
	E4GE-ZA	0.300	0.250	0.108	①	0.140	NA	—
'86	E5GE-AAA	0.300	0.300	0.110	①	0.140	NA	0.060
	E5GE-ADA	0.300	0.300	0.100	①	0.140	NA	0.020
	E5GE-ACA	0.300	0.300	0.100	①	0.140	NA	0.020
	E5GE-AEC	0.300	0.280	0.080	①	0.140	NA	0.080
	E5GE-AFC	0.300	0.280	0.080	①	0.140	NA	0.060

*Basic carburetor number for Ford Carburetors
NA—Not available
① See underhood decal.

Models 2100, 2150

The Model 2100 and 2150 two barrel carburetor are basically the same in construction. Adjustments are performed in the same manner for both carburetors.

FLOAT LEVEL (DRY)

The dry float level measurement is a preliminary check and must be followed by a wet float level measurement with the carburetor mounted on the engine.

1. With the air horn removed gently raise the float to seat the inlet needle by applying light finger pressure at the float tab. Lower the float by reducing finger pressure until a light step is felt. Measure the distance between the main body gasket surface (gasket removed) and the top of the float. This measurement should be taken near the center of the float at a point 1/8 in. from the free-end of the float.

NOTE: 1983 and later carburetors are equipped with a spring loaded fuel inlet needle and the ball must not be depressed when the fuel level check is being made.

2. If necessary, bend the float tab to obtain the correct level.

SECTION 25 CARBURETORS
Autolite/Ford/Motorcraft

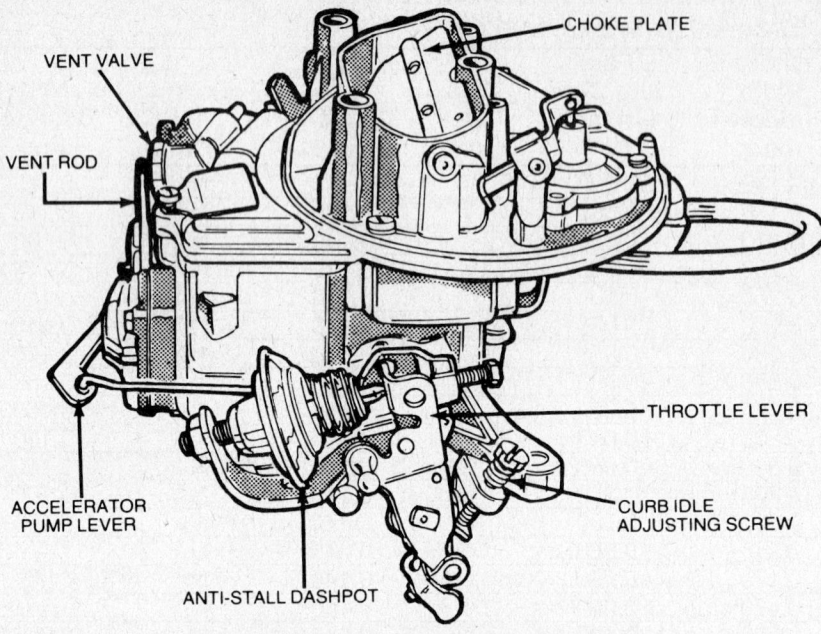

Model 2100 two barrel carburetor

FLOAT LEVEL (WET)

1. Remove the screws that hold the air horn to the main body and break the seal between the air horn and main body. Leave the air horn and gasket loosely in place on top of the main body.
2. Start the engine and allow it to idle for at least three minutes.
3. After the engine has idled long enough to stabilize the fuel level, remove the air horn assembly.
4. With the engine idling, use a T-scale to measure the distance from the top of the fuel bowl machined surface to the surface of the fuel. The scale must be held at least ¼ in. away from any vertical surface to ensure proper measurement.
5. If any adjustment is required, stop the engine to avoid a fire from fuel spraying on the engine.
6. Bend the float tab upward to raise the level and downward to lower the level.

CAUTION
Be sure to hold the fuel inlet needle off its seat when bending the float tab so as not to damage the Viton® tip.

7. Each time the float level is changed, the air horn must be temporarily positioned and the engine started to stabilize the fuel level before again checking it.

CHOKE PLATE PULLDOWN

Model 2100

1. Loosen the screws on the choke

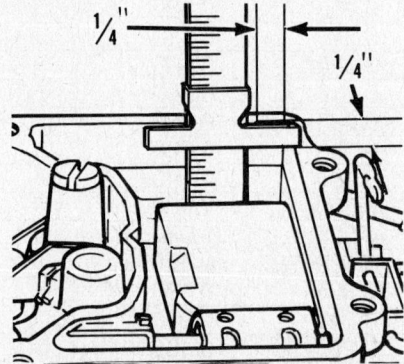

Fuel level measurement (wet)

cover and rotate the cover ¼ turn counterclockwise (rich), then tighten the screws.
2. Operate the throttle to allow full closing of the choke plate.
3. Press down on the choke modulator arm until the choke modulator diaphragm is bottomed and then measure the distance from the lower edge of the choke plate to the inside air horn wall.
4. Adjustment is achieve by turning the diaphragm stop screw on the underside of the air horn.
5. Turn the screw clockwise to decrease clearance and counterclockwise to increase clearance.

NOTE: Do not reset the choke cover until the fast idle cam adjustment is made.

Model 2150

1. Remove the air cleaner assembly.
2. Set the throttle on the top step of the fast idle cam.
3. Noting the position of the choke housing cap, loosen the retaining screws and rotate the cap 90 degrees in the rich (closing) direction.
4. Activate the pull-down motor by manually forcing the pull-down control diaphragm link in the direction of applied vacuum or by applying vacuum to the external vacuum tube.
5. Using a drill gauge of the specified diameter, measure the clearance between the choke plate and the center of the air horn wall nearest the fuel bowl.
6. To adjust, reset the diaphragm stop on the end of the choke pull-down diaphragm.

NOTE: Loctite® was applied to the adjusting screw during manufacture and this will have to be loosened before the adjustment can be made. Heat the area around the screw with an electric soldering gun until the Loctite® softens enough to permit the screw to turn freely.

7. After adjusting, check and adjust the fast idle cam. Check and reset fast idle speed, if necessary. Install the air cleaner.

FAST IDLE CAM

1. The choke setting should still be 90° rich, as in Step 1 of the "Pulldown" procedure. Press and release the throttle to set the fast idle cam.
2. Activate the choke pulldown mechanism as in step 4 of the pulldown procedure.
3. Press and release the throttle to set the fast idle cam. It should drop to the kickdown step, and the fast idle speed screw should be opposite the V notch in the cam.
4. To adjust, turn the hex head screw on the plastic fast idle cam lever. After adjustment, allow the choke plate to close and check that it closes tightly. Reset the choke cover and connect the vacuum hose if removed.

CHOKE UNLOADER (DECHOKE)

1. With the throttle held completely open, move the choke plate to the closed position.
2. Measure the distance between the lower edge of the choke plate and the air horn wall.
3. Adjust by bending the tang on the fast idle speed lever which is located on the throttle shaft.

CARBURETORS
Autolite/Ford/Motorcraft
SECTION 25

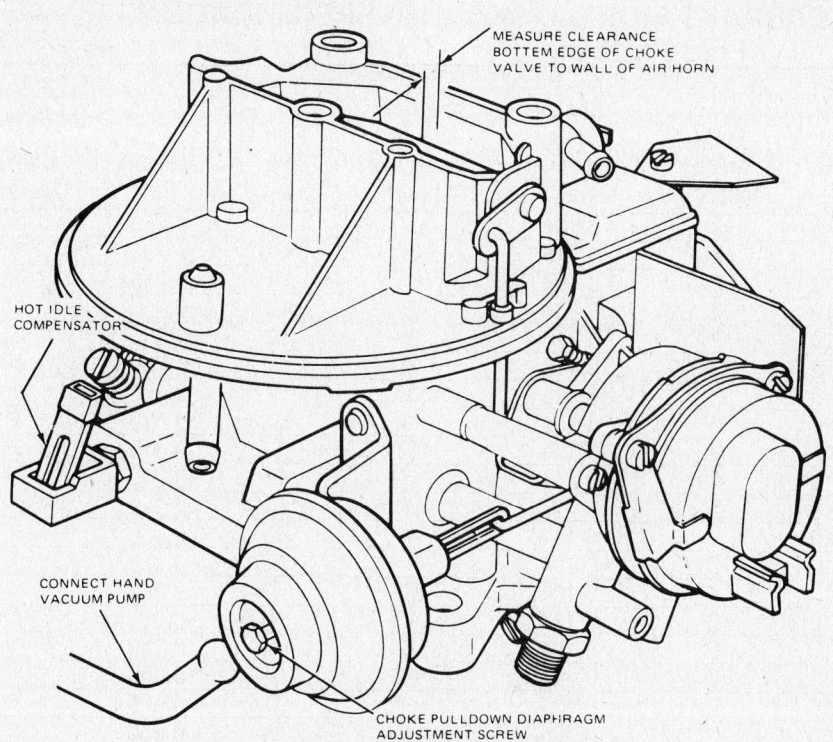

Adjusting choke plate pulldown

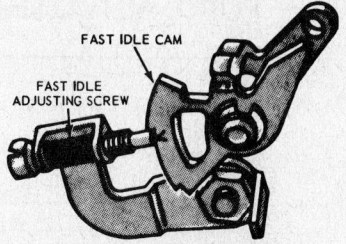

CONVENTIONAL ONE - PIECE FAST IDLE LEVER

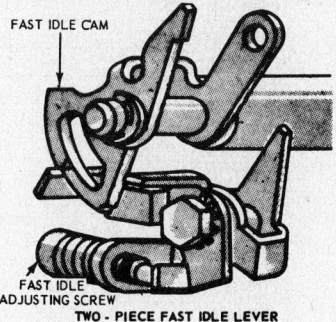

TWO - PIECE FAST IDLE LEVER FOR 351-C ENGINE

Fast idle adjustment

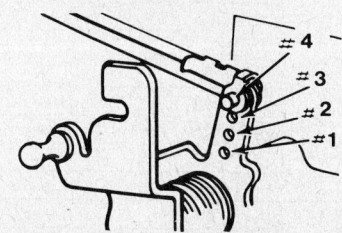

Accelerator pump stroke adjustment

NOTE: Final unloader adjustment must be performed on the car and the throttle should be opened by using the accelerator pedal of the car. This is to be sure that full throttle operation is achieved.

ACCELERATOR PUMP

The accelerator pump operating rod must be positioned in the proper holes of the accelerator pump lever and the throttle over-travel lever to assure correct pump travel. If adjusting is required, additional holes are provided in the throttle over-travel lever.

DASHPOT ADJUSTMENT

With the throttle set at the curb idle position, fully depress the dashpot stem and measure the distance between the stem and the throttle lever. Adjust by loosening the locknut and turning the dashpot.

FAST IDLE

Adjust the fast idle with the engine at

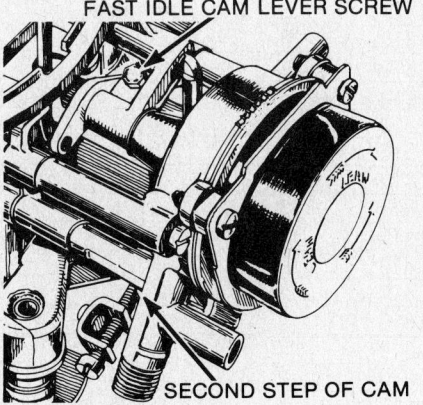

2100, 2150 fast idle cam linkage adjustment

normal operating temperature. On AMC cars, plug the spark port on the carburetor, and remove the EGR vacuum line at the valve and plug it. On Ford cars, if the engine is equipped with a spark delay valve, remove it and reroute the partial throttle vacuum signal line directly to the advance side of the distributor. If the distributor is a dual diaphragm type, leave the manifold vacuum line connected to the retard side of the distributor, and remove and plug the line to the advance side.

If an EGR/PVS valve or cold weather modulator is located in the vacuum hose routing, disconnect and plug the hose at the EGR valve. If the engine does not have a cold weather modulator or an EGR/PVC valve, leave the EGR hose attaching. Trace the thermactor (air pump) dump valve vacuum hose from the dump valve to the carburetor; disconnect the dump valve vacuum hose nearest the carburetor, plug the original vacuum source and connect the dump valve directly to manifold vacuum. The fast idle screw should be resting against the second step of the fast idle cam on all models except Fords with the 302 engine, which have the screw set on the high step of the cam. Adjust the fast idle speed by turning the fast idle screw.

SECTION 25
CARBURETORS
AUTOLITE/FORD/MOTORCRAFT

FORD, AUTOLITE, MOTORCRAFT MODELS 2100, 2150 SPECIFICATIONS
Ford Products

Year	(9510)* Carburetor Identification	Dry Float Level (in.)	Wet Float Level (in.)	Pump Setting Hole # ①	Choke Plate Pulldown (in.)	Fast Idle Cam Linkage Clearance (in.)	Fast Idle (rmp)	Dechoke (in)	Choke Setting
'80	E04E-PA, RA	—	0.810	2	0.104	②	③	0.250	③
	E0BE-AUA	—	0.810	3	0.116	②	③	0.250	③
	E0DE-SA, TA	—	0.810	2	0.104	②	③	0.250	③
	E0KE-CA, DA	—	0.810	3	0.116	②	③	0.250	③
	E0KE-GA, HA	—	0.810	3	0.116	②	③	0.250	③
	E0KE-JA, KA	—	0.810	3	0.116	②	③	0.250	③
	D84E-TA, UA	—	0.810	2	0.125	②	③	0.250	③
	E04E-ADA, AEA	—	0.810	2	0.104	②	③	0.810	③
	E04E-CA	—	0.810	2	0.104	②	③	0.810	③
	E04E-EA, FA	—	0.810	2	0.104	②	③	0.250	③
	E04E-JA, KA	—	0.810	2	0.137	②	③	0.250	③
	E04E-SA, TA	—	0.810	2	0.104	②	③	0.250	③
	E04E-VA, YA	—	0.810	2	0.104	②	③	0.250	③
	E0DE-TA, VA	—	0.810	2	0.104	②	③	0.250	③
	E0SE-GA, HA	—	0.810	2	0.104	②	③	0.250	③
	E0SE-LA, MA	—	0.810	2	0.104	②	③	0.250	③
	E0SE-NA	—	0.810	2	0.104	②	③	0.250	③
	E0SE-PA	—	0.810	2	0.137	②	③	0.250	③
	E0VE-FA	—	0.810	2	0.104	②	③	0.250	⑨
	E0WE-BA, CA	—	0.810	2	0.137	②	③	0.250	③
	D9AE-ANA, APA	—	0.810	3	0.129	②	③	0.250	③
	D9AE-AVA, AYA	—	0.810	3	0.129	②	③	0.250	③
	E0AE-AGA	—	0.810	3	0.159	②	③	0.250	③
'81	E1KE-CA	7/16	0.810	3	0.124	②	③	0.250	④
	E1KE-EA	7/16	0.810	3	0.124	②	③	0.250	④
	E1KE-DA	7/16	0.810	3	0.124	②	③	0.250	④
	E1KE-FA	7/16	0.810	3	0.124	②	③	0.250	④
	E1KE-GA	7/16	0.810	3	0.124	②	③	0.250	④
	E1KE-SA	7/16	0.810	3	0.124	②	③	0.250	④
	E1KE-RA	7/16	0.810	3	0.120	②	③	0.250	④
	E1KE-HA	7/16	0.810	3	0.120	②	③	0.250	④
	E1WE-FA	7/16	0.810	2	0.120	②	③	0.250	④
	E1WE-EA	7/16	0.810	2	0.120	②	③	0.250	④
	E1WE-CA	7/16	0.810	2	0.120	②	③	0.250	④
	E1WE-DA	7/16	0.810	2	0.120	②	③	0.250	④
	E1AE-AKA	7/16	0.810	3	0.124	②	③	0.250	④
	E1AE-AJA	7/16	0.810	3	0.124	②	③	0.250	④
	E1AE-YA	7/16	0.810	3	0.124	②	③	0.250	④
	E1AE-ZA	7/16	0.810	3	0.124	②	③	0.250	④
	E1AE-ADA	7/16	0.810	3	0.124	②	③	0.250	④
	E1AE-AEA	7/16	0.810	3	0.124	②	③	0.250	④
	E1AE-TA	—	0.810	3	0.104	②	③	0.250	④
	E1AE-UA	—	0.810	2	0.104	②	③	0.250	④
	E1DE-LA	7/16	0.810	2	0.120	②	③	0.250	④
	E1DE-KA	7/16	0.810	2	0.120	②	③	0.250	④
	E1DE-JA	7/16	0.810	2	0.120	②	③	0.250	④
	E1DE-HA	7/16	0.810	2	0.120	②	③	0.250	④
'82	E2BE-UA	7/16	0.810	2	0.110	②	2200	0.250	④
	E2BE-AAA	7/16	0.810	2	0.110	②	2200	0.250	④
	E2BE-VA	7/16	0.810	2	0.113	②	2200	0.250	④
	E2BE-ABA	7/16	0.810	2	0.113	②	2200	0.250	④
	E2BE-AGA	7/16	0.810	2	0.113 ⑤	②	2200	0.250	④
	E2BE-AHA	7/16	0.810	2	0.113	②	2200	0.250	④

CARBURETORS
AUTOLITE/FORD/MOTORCRAFT
SECTION 25

FORD, AUTOLITE, MOTORCRAFT MODELS 2100, 2150 SPECIFICATIONS
Ford Products

Year	(9510)* Carburetor Identification	Dry Float Level (in.)	Wet Float Level (in.)	Pump Setting Hole # ①	Choke Plate Pulldown (in.)	Fast Idle Cam Linkage Clearance (in.)	Fast Idle (rpm)	Dechoke (in)	Choke Setting
'82	E2VE-CA	7/16	0.810	2	0.113	②	2200	0.250	④
	E24E-CA	7/16	0.810	2	0.110	②	1200	0.250	④
	E24E-DA	7/16	0.810	2	0.110	②	1200	0.250	④
	E24E-AA	7/16	0.810	2	0.110	②	2100	0.250	④
	E24E-BA	7/16	0.810	2	0.110	②	2100	0.250	④
	E24E-EA	7/16	0.810	2	0.110	②	③	0.250	④
	E24E-FA	7/16	0.810	2	0.110	②	③	0.250	④
	E2KE-AA	7/16	0.810	2	0.140	②	1500	0.250	④
	E2KE-BA	7/16	0.810	2	0.140	②	1500	0.250	④
	E2WE-EA	7/16	0.810	2	0.137	②	1500	0.250	④
	E2WE-FA	7/16	0.810	2	0.137	②	1500	0.250	④
	E2DE-JA	7/16	0.810	2	0.137	②	1600	0.250	④
	E2DE-KA	7/16	0.810	2	0.137	②	1600	0.250	④
	E2DE-LA	7/16	0.810	2	0.137	②	1700	0.250	④
	E2DE-MA	7/16	0.810	2	0.137	②	1700	0.250	④
	E25E-DA	7/16	0.810	2	0.144	②	1500	0.250	④
	E2AE-SA	7/16	0.810	2	0.172	②	1550	0.250	④
	E25E-CA	7/16	0.810	2	0.137	②	1700	0.250	④
	E2ZE-BAA	13/32	0.780	2	0.172 ⑤	②	1400	0.250	④
	E2ZE-BBA	13/32	0.780	2	0.172 ⑤	②	1400	0.250	④
	E3CE-LA	7/16	0.810	3	0.103	②	2200	0.250	④
	E3CE-MA	7/16	0.810	3	0.103	②	2200	0.250	④
	E3CE-JA	7/16	0.810	3	0.103	②	2200	0.250	④
	E3CE-KA	7/16	0.810	3	0.103	②	2200	0.250	④
	E3CE-NA	7/16	0.810	3	0.120	②	2100	0.250	④
	E3CE-PA	7/16	0.810	3	0.120	②	2100	0.250	④
'83	E3CE-AA	7/16	0.810	3	0.103	②	2200	0.250	④
	E3CE-BA	7/16	0.810	3	0.103	②	2200	0.250	④
	E3CE-GA	7/16	0.810	3	0.103	②	2200	0.250	④
	E3CE-HA	7/16	0.810	3	0.103	②	2200	0.250	④
	E3CE-EA	7/16	0.810	3	0.113	②	2100	0.250	④
	E3CE-FA	7/16	0.810	3	0.113	②	2100	0.250	④
	E3SE-ATA	7/16	0.810	3	0.113	②	2200	0.250	④
	E3SE-AUA	7/16	0.810	3	0.113	②	2200	0.250	④
	E3SE-ALA	7/16	0.810	3	0.107	②	2200	0.250	④
	E3SE-AMA	7/16	0.810	3	0.107	②	2200	0.250	④
	E3SE-BDA	7/16	0.810	3	0.107	②	2200	0.250	④
	E3SE-BEA	7/16	0.810	3	0.107	②	2200	0.250	④
	E3SE-ANA	7/16	0.810	3	0.101	②	2200	0.250	④
	E3SE-APA	7/16	0.810	3	0.101	②	2200	0.250	④
	E3SE-AJA								
	E3SE-BFA	7/16	0.810	3	0.107	②	2200	0.250	④
	E3SE-BGA	7/16	0.810	3	0.107	②	2200	0.250	④
	E3SE-EA	7/16	0.810	3	0.113	②	2200	0.250	④
	E3SE-FA	7/16	0.810	3	0.113	②	2200	0.250	④
	E3SE-LA	7/16	0.810	3	0.107	②	2200	0.250	④
	E3SE-MA	7/16	0.810	3	0.107	②	2200	0.250	④
	E3SE-JA	7/16	0.810	3	0.101	②	2200	0.250	④
	E3SE-KA	7/16	0.810	3	0.101	②	2200	0.250	④
	E3SE-NA	7/16	0.810	3	0.107	②	2200	0.250	④
	E3SE-PA	7/16	0.810	3	0.107	②	2200	0.250	④
	E3SE-GA	7/16	0.810	3	0.120	②	2100	0.250	④
	E3SE-HA	7/16	0.810	3	0.120	②	2100	0.250	④

SECTION 25

CARBURETORS
AUTOLITE/FORD/MOTORCRAFT

FORD, AUTOLITE, MOTORCRAFT MODELS 2100, 2150 SPECIFICATIONS
Ford Products

Year	(9510)* Carburetor Identification	Dry Float Level (in.)	Wet Float Level (in.)	Pump Setting Hole # ①	Choke Plate Pulldown (in.)	Fast Idle Cam Linkage Clearance (in.)	Fast Idle (rmp)	Dechoke (in)	Choke Setting
'83	E3AE-TA	7/16	0.810	3	0.103	②	2200	0.250	④
	E3AE-ADA	7/16	0.810	3	0.103	②	2200	0.250	④
	E3AE-UA	7/16	0.810	3	0.103	②	2200	0.250	④
	E3AE-AEA	7/16	0.810	3	0.103	②	2200	0.250	④
	E3AE-TA	7/16	0.810	3	0.103	②	2200	0.250	④
	E3AE-UA	7/16	0.810	3	0.103	②	2200	0.250	④
	E3AE-RA	7/16	0.810	3	0.103	②	2200	0.250	④
	E3AE-SA	7/16	0.810	3	0.103	②	2200	0.250	④
	E3AE-EA	7/16	0.810	2	—	②	1550	0.250	④
'84	E3EA-EA	7/16	0.810	2	—	②	1550	0.250	④
	E4CE-AA	7/16	0.810	3	0.103	②	2200	0.250	2NR
	E4CE-BA	7/16	0.810	3	0.103	②	2200	0.250	2NR
	E4SE-CA	7/16	0.810	3	0.103	②	2200	0.250	④
	E4SE-DA	7/16	0.810	3	0.103	②	2200	0.250	④
'85	E4SE-CA	3/32	0.810	3	0.103	—	③	0.250	4NR
	E4SE-DA	3/32	0.810	3	0.103	—	③	0.250	4NR
	E5SE-CA E3AE-EA(Alt)	7/16	0.810	2	—	④	③	0.250	④

*Basic carburetor number for Ford products
① With link in inboard hole of pump lever
② Opposite "V" notch; see text
③ See underhood decal
④ V-notch
⑤ ± .010"

Model 2700 VV

Since the design of the 2700 VV (variable venturi) carburetor differs considerably from the other carburetors in the Ford lineup, an explanation in the theory and operation is presented here.

In exterior appearance, the variable venturi carburetor is similar to conventional carburetors and, like a conventional carburetor, it uses a normal float and fuel bowl system. However, the similarity ends there. In place of a normal choke plate and fixed area venturis, the 2700VV carburetor has a pair of small oblong castings in the top of the upper carburetor body where you would normally expect to see the choke plate. These castings slide back and forth across the top of the carburetor in response to fuel-air demands. Their movement is controlled by a spring-loaded diaphragm valve regulated by a vacuum signal taken below the venturis in the throttle bores. As the throttle is opened, the strength of the vacuum signal increases, opening the venturis and allowing more air to enter the carburetor.

Fuel is admitted into the venturi area by means of tapered metering rods that fit into the main jets. These rods are attached to the venturis, and, and the venturis open or close in response to air demand, the fuel needed to maintain the proper mixture increases or decreases as the metering rods slide in the jets. In comparison to a conventional carburetor with fixed venturis and a variable air supply, this system provides much more precise control of the fuel-air supply during all modes of operation. Because of the variable venturi principle, there are fewer fuel metering systems and fuel passages. The only auxiliary fuel metering systems required are an idle trim, accelerator pump (similar to a conventional carburetor), starting enrichment, and cold running enrichment.

NOTE: Adjustment, assembly and disassembly of this carburetor require special tools for some of the operations. These tools are available (see the Tools and Equipment Section). Do not attempt any operations on this carburetor without first checking to see if you need the special tools for that particular operation. The adjustment and repair procedures given here mention when and if you will need the special tools.

Some 1980–81 models equipped with the 2700 VV carburetor experienced engine stalling, stumbling and poor performance. According to a Ford Motor Company service bulletin No. 81-9-10 issued in May of 1981, this condition may be caused by fluids trapped in the venturi valve diaphragm cavity which eventually deteriorate the diaphragm, resulting in a leak. A quick check to verify if the above condition exists is to visually observe the venturi valve action while running the engine. Throttle movement from idle to just above idle should show a corresponding movement of the venturi valves. If no venturi valve action is observed and the valves are not sticking, there may be a leak in the diaphragm (stalls may be encountered while performing this

CARBURETORS
Autolite/Ford/Motorcraft

check). If the above condition is suspected, it is advised that the car be serviced at a Ford or Mercury dealer using the procedure stated in the service bulletin.

FLOAT LEVEL ADJUSTMENT

1. Remove and invert the upper part of the carburetor, with the gasket in place.
2. Measure the vertical distance between the carburetor body, outside the gasket, and the bottom of the float.
3. To adjust, bend the float operating lever that contacts the needle valve. Make sure that the float remains parallel to the gasket surface.

FLOAT DROP ADJUSTMENT

1. Remove and hold upright the upper part of the carburetor.
2. Measure the vertical distance between the carburetor body, outside the gasket, and the bottom of the float.
3. Adjust by bending the stop tab on the float lever that contacts the hinge pin.

FAST IDLE SPEED ADJUSTMENT

1. With the engine warmed up and idling, place the fast idle lever on the step of the fast idle cam specified on the engine compartment sticker or in the specifications chart. Disconnect and plug the EGR vacuum line.
2. Make sure the high speed cam positioner lever is disengaged.
3. Turn the fast idle speed screw to adjust to the specified speed.

FAST IDLE CAM ADJUSTMENT

You will need a special tool for this job; Ford calls it a stator cap (No. T77L-9848-A). It fits over the choke thermostatic lever when the choke cap is removed.

1. Remove the choke coil cap. On 1980 California model and all 1981 and later models, the choke cap is riveted in plate. The top rivets will have to be drilled out; the bottom rivet will have to be driven out from the rear. New rivets must be used upon installation.
2. Place the fast idle lever in the corner of the specified step of the fast idle cam (the highest step is first) with the high speed cam positioner retracted.
3. If the adjustment is being made

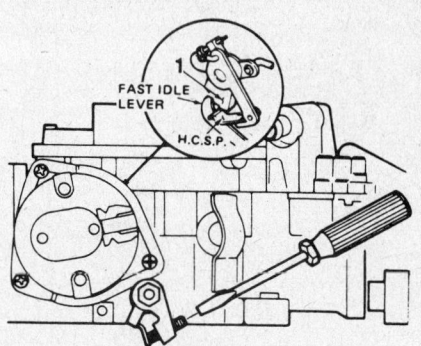

2700 VV fast idle speed adjustment

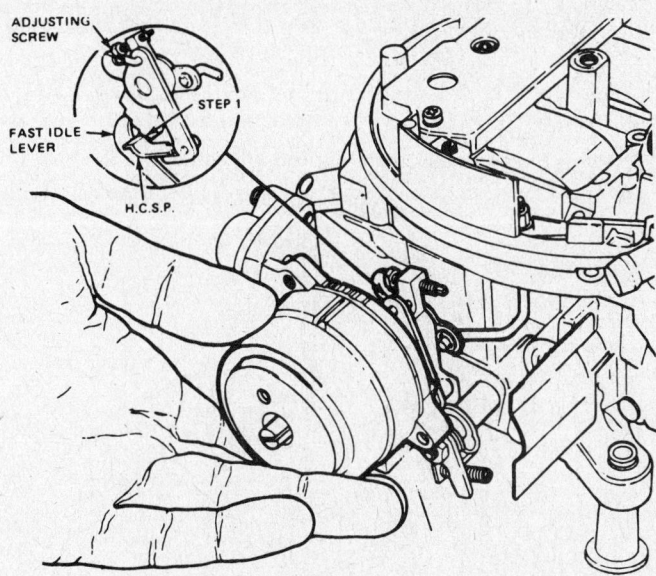

2700 VV fast idle cam adjustment

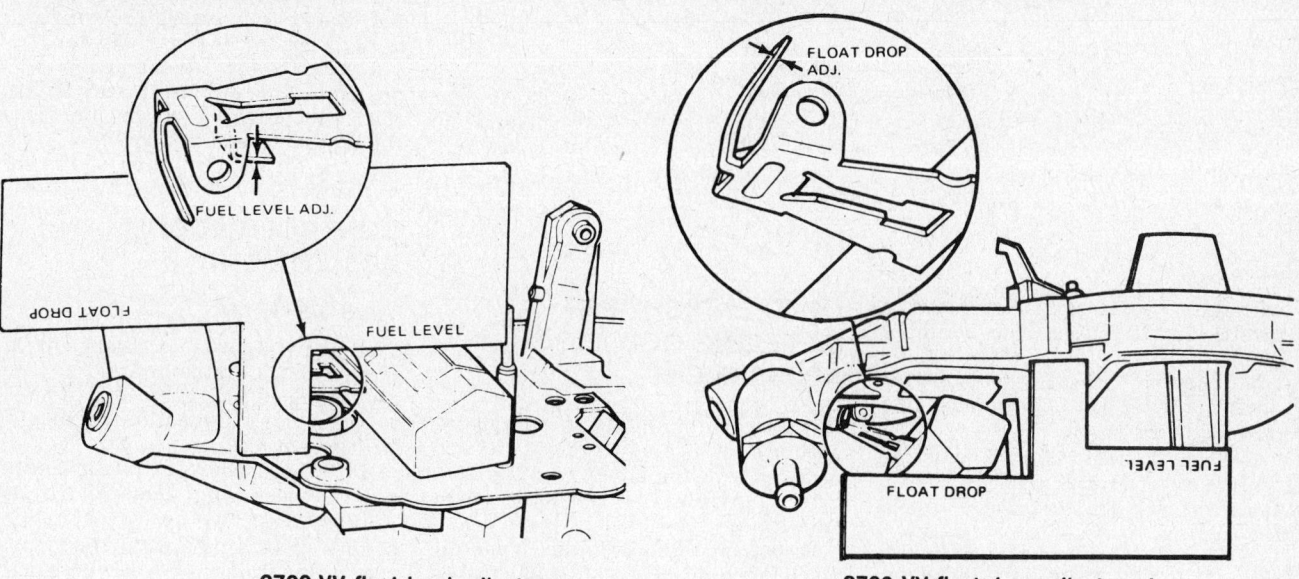

2700 VV float level adjustment

2700 VV float drop adjustment

SECTION 25: CARBURETORS
Autolite/Ford/Motorcraft

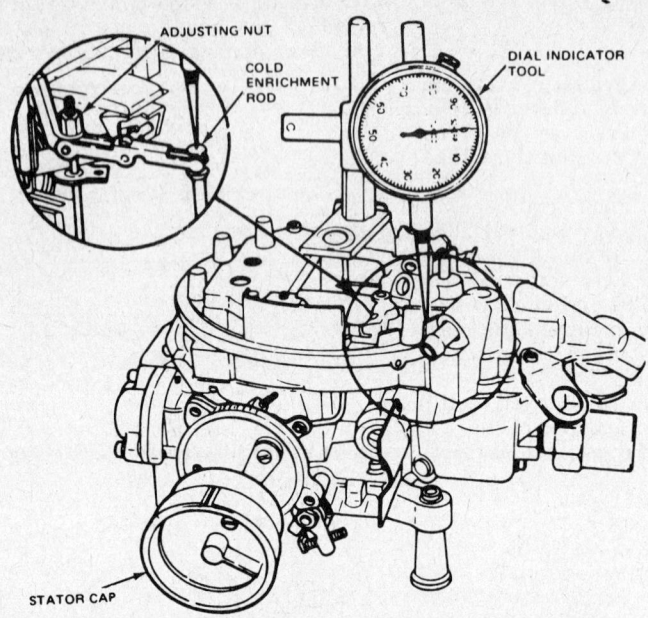

2700 VV cold enrichment metering rod adjustment

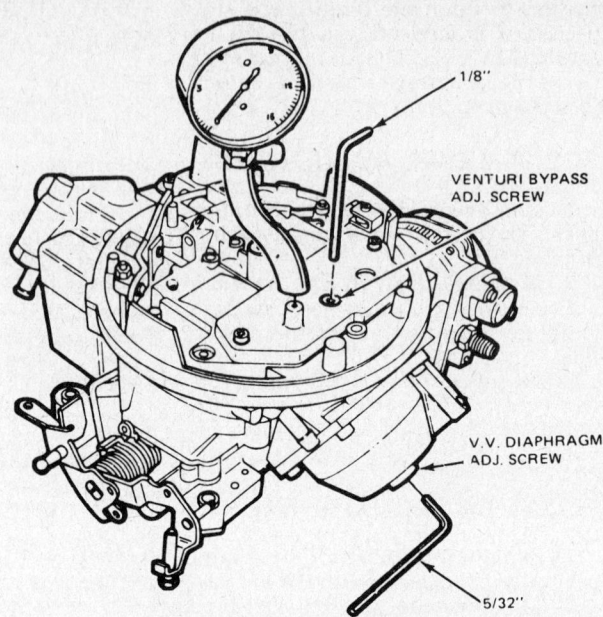

2700 VV control vacuum adjustment

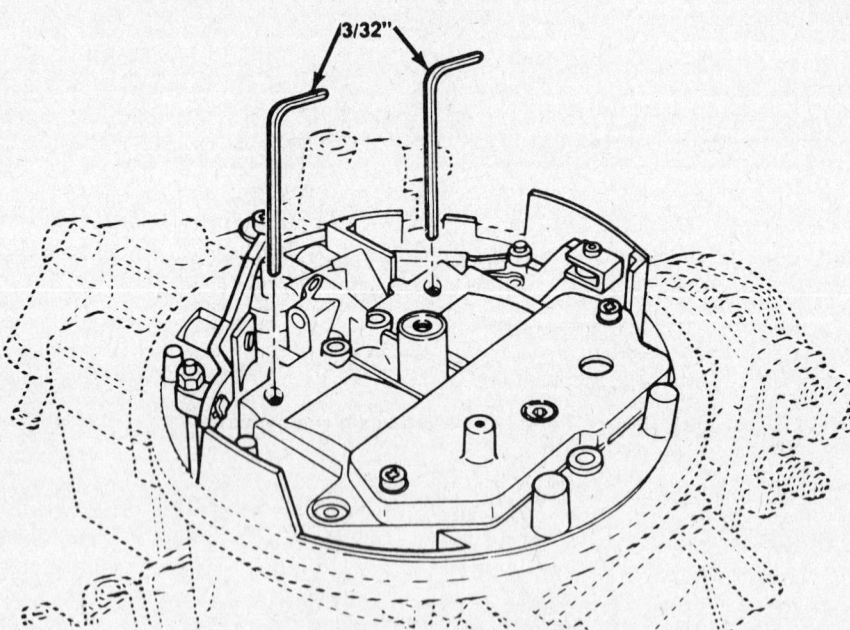

2700 VV idle mixture adjustment

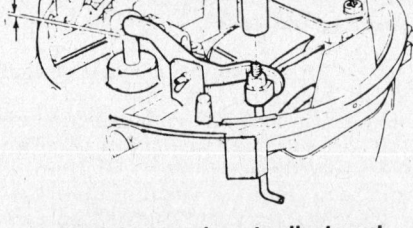

2700 VV internal vent adjustment

with the carburetor removed, hold the throttle lightly closed with a rubber band.

4. Turn the stator cap clockwise until the lever contacts the fast idle cam adjusting screw.

5. Turn the fast idle cam adjusting screw until the index mark on the cap lines up with the specified mark on the casting.

6. Remove the stator cap. Install the choke coil cap and set to the specified housing mark.

COLD ENRICHMENT METERING ROD ADJUSTMENT

A dial indicator and the stator cap are required for this adjustment.

1. Remove the choke coil cap. See Step 1 of the "Fast Idle Cam Adjustment".

2. Attach a weight to the choke coil mechanism to seat the cold enrichment rod.

3. Install and zero a dial indicator with the tip on top of the enrichment rod. Raise and release the weight to verify zero on the dial indicator.

4. With the stator cap at the index position, the dial indicator should read the specified dimension. Turn the adjusting nut to correct.

5. Install the choke cap at the correct setting.

CONTROL VACUUM ADJUSTMENT

1980–82 Only

This adjustment is necessary only on non-feedback systems.

1. Remove the carburetor. Remove the venturi valve diaphragm plug with a centerpunch.

2. If the carburetor has a venturi valve bypass plug, remove it by removing the two cover retaining screws; invert and remove the by-pass screw plug from the cover with a drift. Install the cover.

25–30

CARBURETORS
AUTOLITE/FORD/MOTORCRAFT

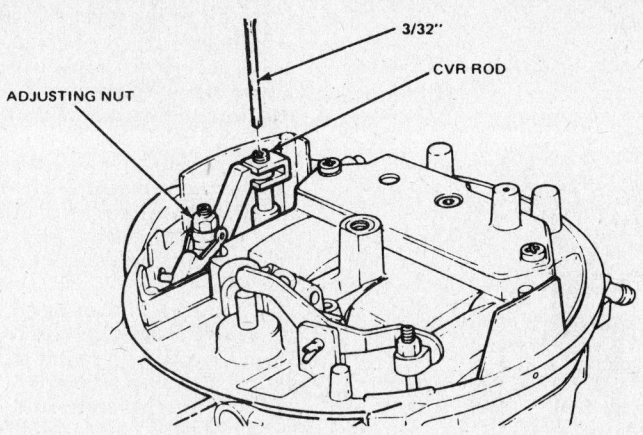

2700 VV control vacuum regulator adjustment

3. Install the carburetor. Start the engine and allow it to reach normal operating temperature. Connect a vacuum gauge to the venturi valve cover. Set the idle speed to 500 rpm with the transmission in Drive.
4. Push and hold the venturi valve closed. Adjust the bypass screw to obtain a reading of 8 in. H_2O on the vacuum gauge. Make sure the idle speed remains constant. Open and close the throttle and check the idle speed.
5. With the engine idling, adjust the venturi valve diaphragm screw to obtain a reading of 6 in. H_2O. Set the curb idle to specification. Install new venturi valve bypass and diaphragm plugs.

VENTURI VALVE LIMITER ADJUSTMENT

1. Remove the carburetor. Take off the venturi valve cover and the two rollers.
2. Use a center punch to loosen the expansion plug at the rear of the carburetor main body on the throttle side. Remove it.
3. Use an Allen wrench to remove the venturi valve wide open stop screw.
4. Hold the throttle wide open.
5. Apply a light closing pressure on the venturi valve and check the gap between the valve and the air horn wall. To adjust, move the venturi valve to the wide open position and insert an Allen wrench into the stop screw hole. Turn clockwise to increase the gap. Remove the wrench and check the gap again.
6. Replace the wide open stop screw and turn it clockwise until it contacts the valve.
7. Push the venturi valve wide open and check the gap. Turn the stop screw to bring the gap to specifications.
8. Reassemble the carburetor with a new expansion plug.

CONTROL VACUUM REGULATOR (CVR) ADJUSTMENT

The cold enrichment metering rod adjustment must be checked and set before making this adjustment.
1. After adjusting the cold enrichment metering rod, leave the dial indicator in place but remove the stator cap. Do not re-zero the dial indicator.
2. Press down on the CVR rod until it bottoms on its seat. Measure this amount of travel with the dial indicator.
3. If the adjustment is incorrect, hold the $3/8$ in. CVR adjusting nut with a box wrench to prevent it from turning. Use a $3/32$ in. Allen wrench to turn the CVR rod; turning counterclockwise will increase the travel, and vice versa.

MOTORCRAFT MODEL 2700 VV SPECIFICATIONS
Ford Products

Year	Model	Float Level (in.)	Float Drop (in.)	Fast Idle Cam Setting (notches)	Cold Enrichment Metering Rod (in.)	Control Vacuum (in. H_2O)	Venturi Valve Limiter (in.)	Choke Cap Setting (notches)	Control Vacuum Regulator Setting (in.)
'80	All	$1^{3/64}$	$1^{15/32}$	1 Rich/4th step	.125	①	②	③	.075
'81	E1AE-AAA	1.010–1.070	1.430–1.490	1 Rich/4th step	④	①	②	Index	—
	D9AE-AZA	1.015–1.065	1.435–1.485	1 Rich/4th step	.125	①	②	Index	—

① See text
② Opening gap: 0.99–1.01
   Closing gap: 0.94–0.98
③ See underhood decal
④ 0°F—0.490 @ starting position
   75°F—0.475 @ starting position

Model 5200

The 5200 carburetor is a two-stage, two-venturi carburetor in which the secondary venturi is the larger. The secondary system is mechanically operated.

FAST IDLE CAM
1980–82

1. Place the fast idle screw on the second step of the fast idle cam against the shoulder of the top step.
2. Apply light pressure (downward) on the choke lever tang, and, using the proper size drill, measure the clearance between the lower edge of

SECTION 25

CARBURETORS
AUTOLITE/FORD/MOTORCRAFT

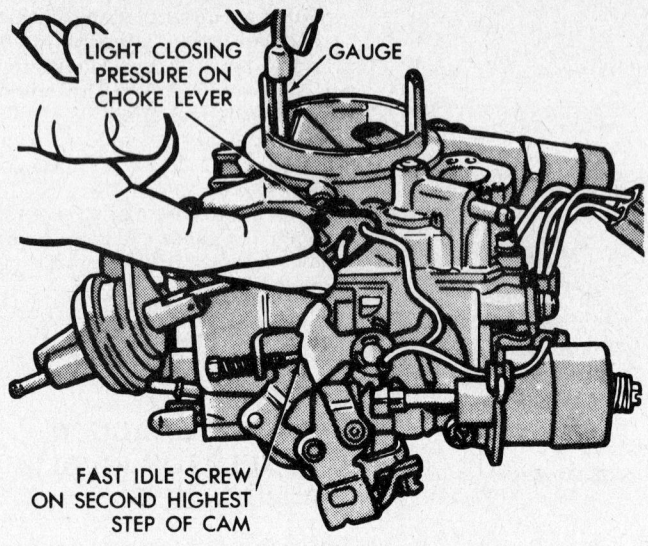

Fast idle cam adjustment—Holley 1945

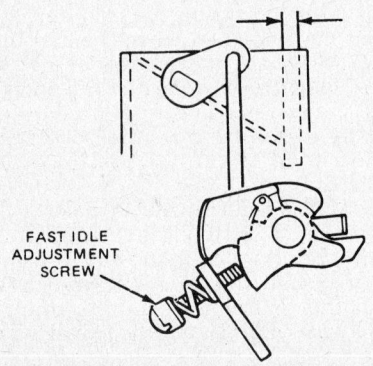

1980 and later fast idle cam adjustment—measure the clearance between the lower edge of the choke plate and the air horn wall

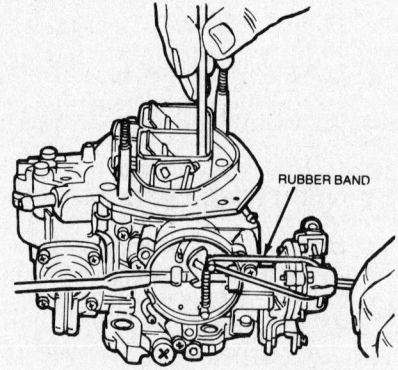

Choke plate pulldown adjustment

the choke plate and the air horn wall.

3. Bend the choke lever tang down to increase clearance and up to decrease the clearance.

NOTE: On 1982 and later models Ford recommends that if an adjustment is necessary, the choke lever should be replaced since the lever tang is hardened. This may also be necessary for 1980–81 models.

CHOKE PLATE PULLDOWN

1980

1. Remove the choke thermostatic spring cover.
2. Pull the water cover and the thermostatic spring cover assembly or the electric choke assist assembly out of the way.
3. Set the fast idle cam on the second step.
4. Push the diaphragm stem against its stop and insert the specified gauge between the lower edge of the choke valve and the air horn wall.
5. Apply sufficient pressure to the upper edge of the choke valve to take up any slack in the choke linkage.
6. Turn the adjusting screw in or out to adjust the choke plate-to-air horn clearance.

1981–82

NOTE: The following procedure requires the removal of the carburetor and also the choke cap which is retained by two rivets.

1. Remove the carburetor from the engine.
2. Remove the choke cap as follows:
   a. Check the rivets to determine if mandrel is well below the rivet head. If mandrel is within the rivet head thickness, drive it down or out with a $1/16$ inch diameter tip punch.
   b. With a $1/8$ inch diameter drill, drill into the rivet head until the rivet head comes loose from the rivet body. Use light pressure on the drill bit or the rivet will just spin in the hole.
   c. After drilling off the rivet head, drive the remaining rivet out of the hole with a $1/8$ inch diameter punch.
   d. Repeat steps (a thru c) to remove the remaining rivet.
3. Remove the plastic dust cover.
4. Place the fast idle adjusting screw on the high step of the fast idle cam.
5. Attach a rubber band to remove the slack from the choke linkage. Push the diaphragm stem back against the stop screw.
6. Using the specified diameter drill check the clearance between the lower edge of the choke plate and the air horn wall.
7. If adjustment is necessary, obtain a replacement kit containing a new choke pulldown diaphragm cover, adjusting screw and cup plug.
8. After installing the adjusting screw in the cover, adjust the pulldown by turning the screw clockwise to decrease and counterclockwise to increase the setting.
9. After making the adjustment, install a new plug in the choke pulldown adjustment access opening.
10. Remove the rubber band and re-install the choke cap using rivets ($1/8$ inch diameter x $1/2$ inch long with a $1/4$ inch diameter head).

DECHOKE (UNLOADER) ADJUSTMENT

Dechoke clearance adjustment is controlled by the fast idle cam adjustment. The figures in the specification chart refer to choke plate clearance between the plate and the air horn wall. Clearance can be measured as follows:

1. Hold the throttle wide open. Remove any slack from the choke linkage by applying pressure to the upper edge of the choke valve.
2. Measure the distance between the lower edge of the choke plate and the air horn wall.
3. Adjust by bending the tab on the fast idle lever where it touches the cam.

FAST IDLE SPEED

Set the fast idle speed with the fast idle screw positioned on the second step of the fast idle cam and with the engine at operating temperature. Remove the EGR line at the valve and plug it. If the car is equipped with a spark delay valve, remove the valve and route the distributor advance

CARBURETORS
Autolite/Ford/Motorcraft
SECTION 25

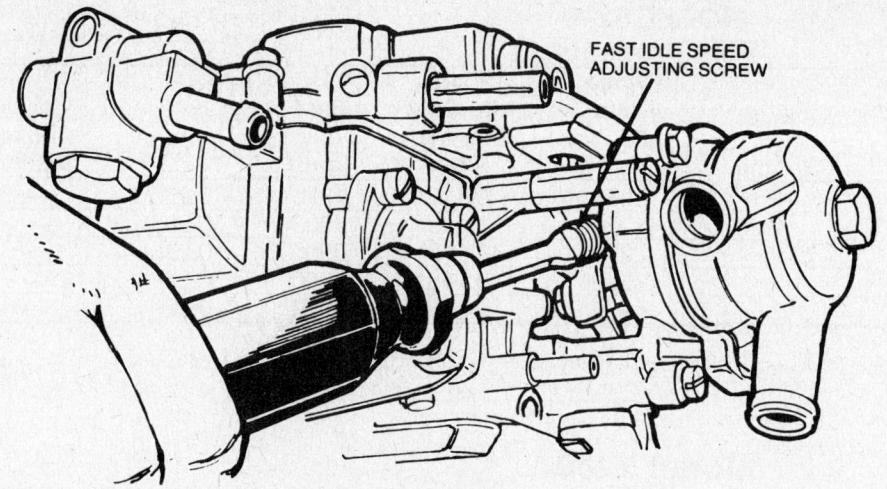

Fast idle adjustment

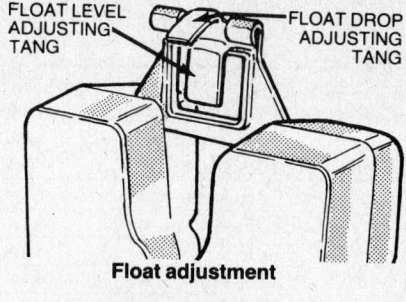

Float adjustment

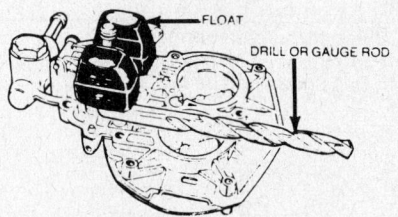

Checking the float level

vacuum signal directly to the distributor advance diaphragm. On all manual transmission models, remove and plug the vacuum line to the distributor. If the distributor also has a retard diaphragm, leave the hose connected to it alone. If the engine has a deceleration valve, remove this hose at the carburetor and plug it. Finally, if the car has air conditioning it must be off before adjusting the fast idle.

FLOAT LEVEL ADJUSTMENT

With the bowl cover held upside down and the float tang resting lightly on the spring loaded fuel inlet needle, measure the clearance between the edge of the float and the bowl cover. To adjust the level, bend the float tang up or down as required. Adjust both floats equally.

SECONDARY THROTTLE STOP SCREW

1. Turn the secondary throttle stop screw counterclockwise until the secondary throttle plate seats in its bore.
2. Turn the screw clockwise until it touches the tab on the secondary throttle lever.
3. Add $\frac{1}{4}$ turn clockwise for four cylinder engines.

MODEL 5200
Ford Products

Year	(9510)* Carburetor Identification ①	Dry Float Level (in.)	Pump Hole Setting	Choke Plate Pulldown (in.)	Fast Idle Cam Linkage (in.)	Fast Idle (rpm)	Dechoke (in.)	Choke Setting
'80	D9EE-APA, ANA	0.460	2	0.236	0.118	②	0.236	1 Rich
	EOEE-GA, RA	0.460	2	0.196	0.078	②	0.196	②
	EOEE-JA, TA	0.460	2	0.196	0.078	②	0.196	②
	EOEE-JC, TC	0.460	—	0.196	0.078	②	0.196	②
	EOEE-JD, TD	0.460	2	0.177	0.078	②	0.196	②
	EOEE-AEA, AFA	0.460	2	0.196	0.078	②	0.196	②
	EOZE-ACB	0.460	—	0.275	0.157	②	0.236	②
	EOZE-AZA	0.460	2	0.275	0.157	②	0.393	②
	EOZE-AAA	0.460	3	0.275	0.157	②	0.236	②
	EOZE-ACA	0.460	2	0.275	0.157	②	0.236	②
	EOZE-ATA	0.460	2	0.275	0.118	②	0.236	②
'81	E1ZE-YA	.41–.51	2	0.200	.080	②	0.200	②
	EOEE-RB	.41–.51	2	0.200	.080	②	0.200	②
	E1ZE-VA	.41–.51	2	0.200	.080	②	0.200	②
	D9EE-ANA	.41–.51	2	0.200	.080	②	0.200	②
	D9EE-APA	.41–.51	2	0.240	0.720	②	0.200	②
'82	E1ZE-ADB	.41–.51	2	0.240	0.120	②	0.200	②
	E1ZE-ACA	.41–.51	3	0.275	0.240	1600	0.393	—
	E1BE-RA, GA	.41–.51	2	0.200	.080	1800	0.196	—
	E1ZE-YA	.41–.51	2	0.200	.080	2000	0.196	—
	E1ZE-VA	.41–.51	2	0.200	.080	2000	0.196	—

SECTION 25
CARBURETORS
AUTOLITE/FORD/MOTORCRAFT

MODEL 5200
Ford Products

Year	(9510)* Carburetor Identification ①	Dry Float Level (in.)	Pump Hole Setting	Choke Plate Pulldown (in.)	Fast Idle Cam Linkage (in.)	Fast Idle (rpm)	Dechoke (in.)	Choke Setting
'82	E2ZE-AFA	.41–.51	2	0.236	0.118	1800	0.236	—
	E2ZE-AHA	.41–.51	2	0.236	0.118	2000	0.236	—
	E2ZE-ABA	.41–.51	2	0.236	0.118	2000	0.236	—
	E2ZE-AGA	.41–.51	2	0.236	0.118	2000	0.236	—
	E2ZE-AAA	.41–.51	2	0.236	0.118	2000	0.236	—

*Basic carburetor number
① Figure given is for all manual transmissions; for automatic trans. the figures are: (49 states) 2000 RPM; (Calif.) 1800 RPM.
② See underhood decal

Model 7200

The Motorcraft model 7200 variable venturi (VV) carburetor shares most of its design features with the model 2700 VV. The major difference between the two is that the 7200 is designed to work with Ford's EEC (electronic engine control) feedback system. The feedback system precisely controls the air/fuel ratio by varying signals to the feedback control monitor located on the carburetor, which opens or closes the metering valve in response. This expands or reduces the amount of control vacuum above the fuel bowl, leaning or richening the mixture accordingly.

For further information on feedback carburetors, please refer to Chilton's Guide To Fuel Injection And Feedback Carburetors.

FLOAT LEVEL, FLOAT DROP, FAST IDLE SPEED ADJUSTMENTS

These adjustments are performed in the same manner as for the 2700 VV. See that section for procedures.

FAST IDLE CAM ADJUSTMENT

This procedure is the same as for the 2700 VV. Use the procedure in that section. The 7200 VV used on California models has a choke cover held on with rivets. The carburetor must be removed to remove the rivets. With the carburetor removed, the top two rivets can be drilled out with a 1/8 in. drill bit. Drill only through the rivet head. The bottom rivet is located in a blind hole and must be removed by lightly tapping the backside of the retainer ring with a punch. The cover must be installed with replacement rivets, Ford part No. 388575, or the equivalent.

COLD ENRICHMENT METERING ROD ADJUSTMENT

This adjustment is made in the same manner as for the 2700 VV. See the paragraph under "Fast Idle Cam Adjustment," concerning the riveted choke cover used on California models.

INTERNAL VENT, VENTURI VALVE LIMITER ADJUSTMENTS

These adjustments are the same as for the 2700 VV. See that section for details.

CONTROL VACUUM REGULATOR (CVR) ADJUSTMENT

Use the procedure in the 2700 VV section. Note that the control vacuum is not adjustable on any 7200 carburetor; only the regulator is adjustable.

HIGH SPEED CAM POSITIONER, IDLE MIXTURE ADJUSTMENTS

Procedures are the same as for the 2700 VV. See that section for details. Like the 2700 VV, the 7200 idle trim is preset at the factory and non-adjustable.

MOTORCRAFT MODEL 7200 VV SPECIFICATIONS

Year	Model	Float Level (in.)	Float Drop (in.)	Fast Idle Cam Setting (notches)	Cold Enrichment Metering Rod (in.)	Control Vacuum (in. H₂O)	Venturi Valve Limiter (in.)	Choke Cap Setting (notches)
'80	All	1 3/64	1 15/32	1 Rich/3rd step	.125	②	③	④
'81	D9AE-AZA	1.015–1.065	1.435–1.485	1 Rich/3rd step	.125	②	⑤	Index
	EIAE-LA	1.015–1.065	1.435–1.485	0.360/2nd step	⑦	②	⑥	1 Rich
	EIAE-SA	1.015–1.065	1.435–1.485	0.360/2nd step	⑦	②	⑥	1 Rich
	EIAE-KA	1.010–1.070	1.430–1.490	0.360/2nd step	⑩	②	⑭	Index
	EIDE-AA	1.010–1.070	1.430–1.490	0.360/2nd step	⑩	②	⑭	Index
	EIVE-AA	1.015–1.065	1.435–1.485	0.360/2nd step	⑦	②	③	Index

CARBURETORS
Autolite/Ford/Motorcraft
SECTION 25

MOTORCRAFT MODEL 7200 VV SPECIFICATIONS

Year	Model	Float Level (in.)	Float Drop (in.)	Fast Idle Cam Setting (notches)	Cold Enrichment Metering Rod (in.)	Control Vacuum (in. H₂O)	Venturi Valve Limiter (in.)	Choke Cap Setting (notches)
'82	E2AE-LB	1.010–1.070	1.430–1.490	0.360/2nd step	⑧	②	⑨	Index
	E2DE-NA	1.010–1.070	1.430–1.490	0.360/2nd step	⑧	②	⑨	Index
	E2AE-LC	1.010–1.070	1.430–1.490	0.360/2nd step	⑧	②	⑨	Index
	E25E-FA	1.010–1.070	1.430–1.490	0.360/2nd step	⑧	②	⑨	Index
	E25E-GB	1.010–1.070	1.430–1.490	0.360/2nd step	⑧	②	⑨	Index
	E2SE-GA	1.010–1.070	1.430–1.490	0.360/2nd step	⑧	②	⑨	Index
	E2AE-RA	1.010–1.070	1.430–1.490	0.360/2nd step	⑩	②	⑨	Index
	E1AE-ACA	1.010–1.070	1.430–1.490	0.360/2nd step	⑩	②	⑨	Index
	E2SE-DB	1.010–1.070	1.430–1.490	0.360/2nd step	⑪	②	⑨	Index
	E2SE-DA	1.010–1.070	1.430–1.490	0.360/2nd step	⑪	②	⑨	Index
	E1AE-SA	1.010–1.070	1.430–1.490	0.360/2nd step	⑫	②	⑬	1 Rich
	E2AE-MA	1.010–1.070	1.430–1.490	0.360/2nd step	⑫	②	⑬	1 Rich
	E2AE-MB	1.010–1.070	1.430–1.490	0.360/2nd step	⑫	②	⑬	1 Rich
	E2AE-TA	1.010–1.070	1.430–1.490	0.360/2nd step	⑫	②	⑬	Index
	E2AE-TB	1.010–1.070	1.430–1.490	0.360/2nd step	⑫	②	⑬	Index
	E25E-AC	1.010–1.070	1.430–1.490	0.360/2nd step	⑪	②	⑨	Index
	E1AE-AGA	1.010–1.070	1.430–1.490	0.360/2nd step	⑫	②	⑨	Index
	E2AE-NA	1.010–1.070	1.430–1.490	0.360/2nd step	⑫	②	⑨	Index
'83	E2AE-NA	1.010–1.070	1.430–1.490	0.360/2nd step	⑫	②	⑨	Index
	E2AE-AJA	1.010–1.070	1.430–1.490	0.360/2nd step	⑫	②	⑨	Index
	E2AE-APA	1.010–1.070	1.430–1.490	0.360/2nd step	⑫	②	⑨	Index
'84–'86	E2AE-AJA	1.010–1.070	1.430–1.490	0.360/2nd step	⑫	②	⑨	Index
	E2AE-APA	1.010–1.070	1.430–1.490	0.360/2nd step	⑫	②	⑨	Index

① Not used
② See text
③ Opening gap: 0.99–1.01
   Closing gap: 0.39–0.41
④ See underhood decal
⑤ Maximum opening: .99/1.01
   Wide open on throttle: .94/.98
⑥ Maximum opening: .99/1.01
   Wide open on throttle: .74/.76
⑦ 0°F—0.490 @ starting position
   75°F—0.475 @ starting position
⑧ 0°F—0.525 @ starting position
   75°F—0.445 @ starting position
⑨ Maximum opening: .99/1.01
   Wide open on throttle: .39/.41
⑩ 0°F—0.490 @ starting position
   75°F—0.445 @ starting position
⑪ 0°F—0.525 @ starting position
   75°F—0.475 @ starting position
⑫ 0°F—0.490 @ starting position
   75°F—0.460 @ starting position
⑬ Maximum opening: .99/1.01
   Wide open on throttle: .74/.76
⑭ Maximum opening: .99/1.01
   Wide open on throttle: .48/.52

HOLLEY CARBURETORS

Model 1945

The model 1945 carburetor is a concentric downdraft single barrel carburetor with an internal float bowl which completely surrounds the venturi. The unit uses dual nitrophyl floats which permit operation at extreme angles. It is used on Chrysler Corporation six cylinder engines.

FLOAT ADJUSTMENT

1. Remove the float bowl cover and invert the bowl. Hold the retaining spring in place.
2. Place a straight-edge across the surface of the bowl. The gasket should be in place. The straight-edge should just clear the toes of the floats by the specified measurement.
3. If the adjustment is necessary, bend the float tang to obtain the correct adjustment.

FAST IDLE ADJUSTMENT

1. Remove the air cleaner and disconnect the vacuum lines to the heated air control and the OSAC (Orifice Spark Advance Control) valve. If there is no OSAC valve, disconnect the hose to the distributor and the EGR hose. Cap all carburetor vacuum fittings.
2. With the engine off, transmission in Neutral and the parking brake set, open the throttle and close the choke.
3. Close the throttle. This will place the fast idle speed screw on the highest step.
4. Move the fast idle cam until the screw drops to the second highest speed step.
5. Start the engine and stabilize the engine speed. Rotate the fast idle speed screw to obtain the specified setting. See Specifications Chart.

FAST IDLE CAM ADJUSTMENT

1. Place the fast idle speed adjust-

SECTION 25: CARBURETORS
HOLLEY

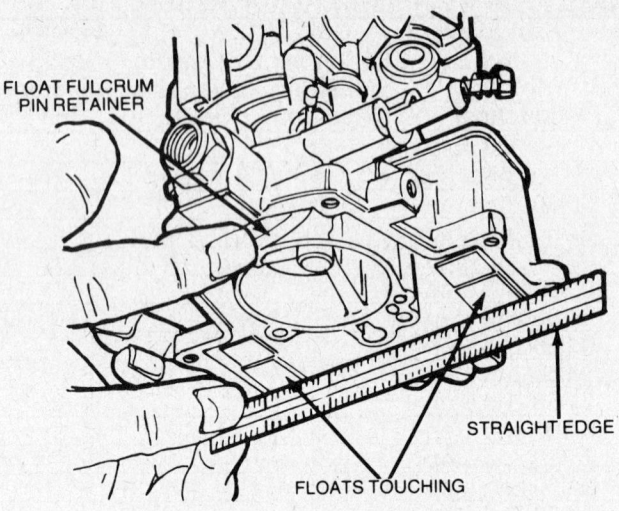

Checking the float adjustment—Holley 1945

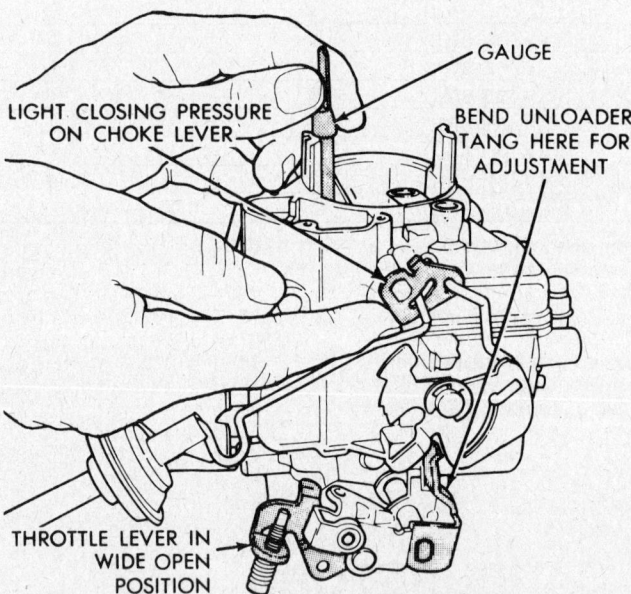

Choke unloader adjustment—Holley 1945

ing screw on the second highest step of the fast idle cam.

2. Place light pressure on the choke shaft lever to move the choke valve towards the close position.

3. Insert the specified gauge between the top of the choke and the air horn wall at the choke lever side.

4. To adjust bend the fast idle connector rod at angle until the correct valve opening is obtained.

CHOKE UNLOADER ADJUSTMENT

1. Hold the throttle valves wide-open and insert the specified gauge between the upper edge of the choke valve and the inner wall of the air horn.

2. Place slight pressure against the control lever and attempt to remove the gauge. There should be a slight drag as the gauge is being withdrawn. If adjustment is necessary, bend the unloader tang on the throttle lever until the correct opening has been obtained.

CHOKE VACUUM KICK ADJUSTMENT

1. With the engine not running, open the throttle and move the choke to the closed position. Release the throttle first and then the choke.

2. If an auxiliary vacuum source is used, disconnect the vacuum hose from the carburetor and connect it to the hose from the vacuum supply with an extra length of tube. Apply a vacuum of 15 or more in. Hg.

3. Insert the correct gauge (see Specifications chart) between the choke valve upper edge and the wall of the air horn. Close and hold the choke rod lever with light pressure. The cylindrical stem of the diaphragm will extend as the internal spring is compressed. This spring must be fully compressed for proper measurement of the vacuum kick.

4. If adjustment is necessary, shorten or lengthen the diaphragm link to obtain the correct opening on models through 1981. On 1982 and later models insert a $5/64$ inch Allen wrench into the vacuum diaphragm and turn to adjust.

—— **CAUTION** ——
Do not twist or bend the diaphragm.

5. Install the vacuum hose on the correct carburetor fitting and connect the fast idle linkage.

6. Check the operation in the following manner. With vacuum applied to the diaphragm, the choke valve should move freely between the open and closed positions. If there is binding, examine the linkage for misalignment or interference caused by bending.

ACCELERATOR PUMP ADJUSTMENT

1. With the throttle in the curb idle position, measure the distance between the pump link pivot and the link connection to the throttle lever. 1980 models have two holes in the throttle lever. Make sure the link is in the correct hole or slot.

2. If the measurement is incorrect, the link may be bent at the "U" to adjust.

NOTE: *If the pump link is adjusted, the "Bowl Vent Adjustment" must be checked and, if necessary, reset.*

BOWL VENT ADJUSTMENT

1. With the throttle set at curb idle speed, measure the distance from the cover support surface down to the flat on the bowl vent leer.

2. If adjustment is necessary, turn the bowl vent lever adjusting screw with a screwdriver.

3. Install the bowl vent spring and cover plate.

CARBURETORS
HOLLEY
SECTION 25

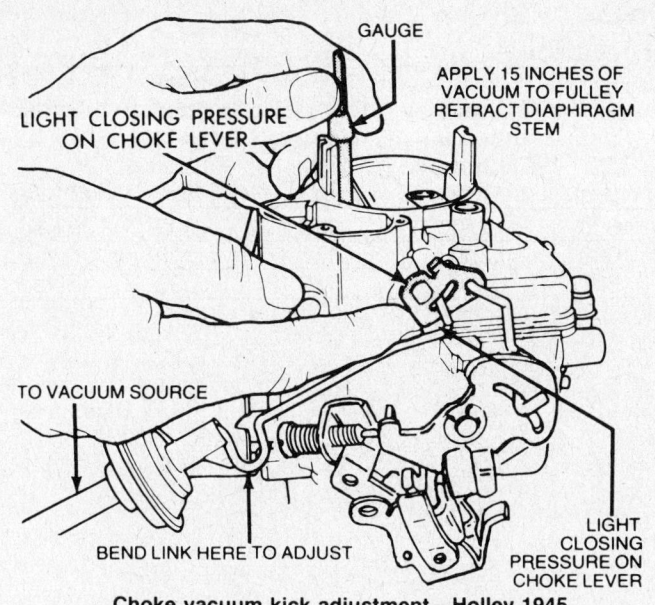

Choke vacuum kick adjustment—Holley 1945

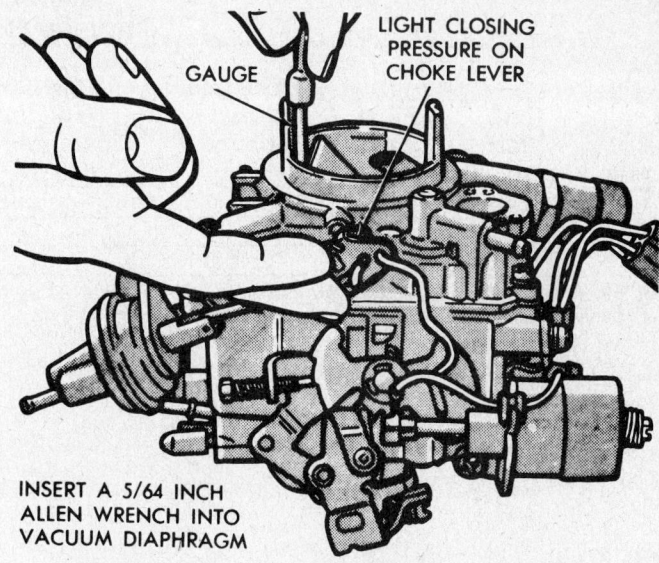

Choke vacuum kick adjustment, 1982—Holley 1945

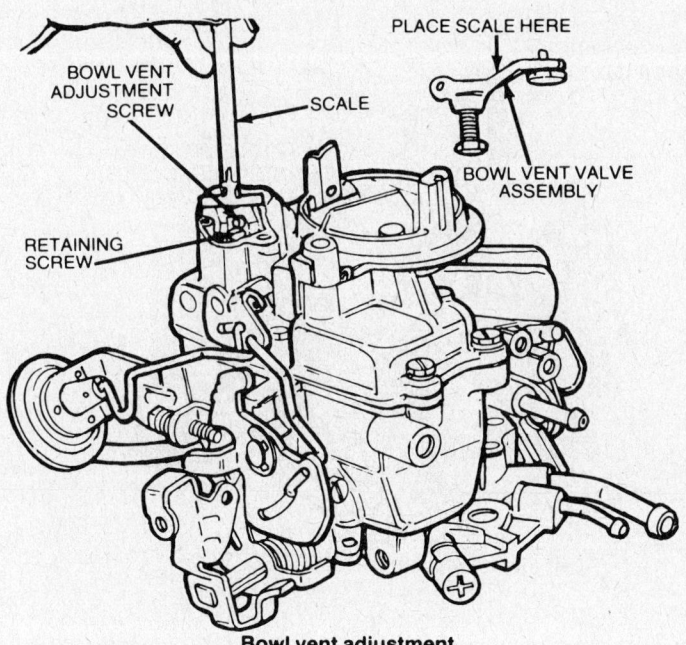

Bowl vent adjustment

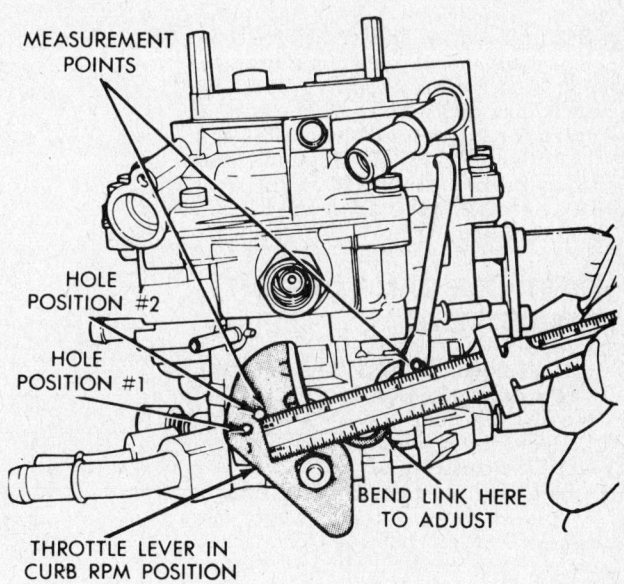

Accelerator pump adjustment

MODEL 1945
Chrysler Corporation

Year	Carb. Part No. ②	Float Level (in.)	Accelerator Pump Adjustment (in.)	Bowl Vent Clearance (in.)	Fast Idle (rpm)	Choke Unloader Clearance (in.)	Vacuum Kick (in.)	Fast Idle Cam Position (in.)	Choke
'80	R-8718-A	①	1.70 ③	1/16	1400	.250	.150	.090	Fixed
	R-8831-A	①	1.615 ④	1/16	1600	.250	.140	.090	Fixed
	R-8832-A	①	1.70 ③	1/16	1400	.250	.110	.090	Fixed
	R-8833-A	①	1.615 ④	1/16	1600	.250	.110	.090	Fixed

25-37

SECTION 25 CARBURETORS
HOLLEY

MODEL 1945
Chrysler Corporation

Year	Carb. Part No. ②	Float Level (in.)	Accelerator Pump Adjustment (in.)	Bowl Vent Clearance (in.)	Fast Idle (rpm)	Choke Unloader Clearance (in.)	Vacuum Kick (in.)	Fast Idle Cam Position (in.)	Choke
'81	R-9253-A	⑤	1.615 ④	—	1600	.250	.150	.090	Fixed
'82	R-9627A	⑤	1.615 ④	—	1600	.250	.150	.090	Fixed
	R-9628A	⑤	1.615 ④	—	1800	.250	.150	.090	Fixed

① Flush with the top of the bowl cover gasket, plus or minus 1/32
② Located on a tag attached to the carburetor.
③ Position #1
④ Position #2
⑤ Flush with the top of the main body casting to 0.050" above

Model 1946

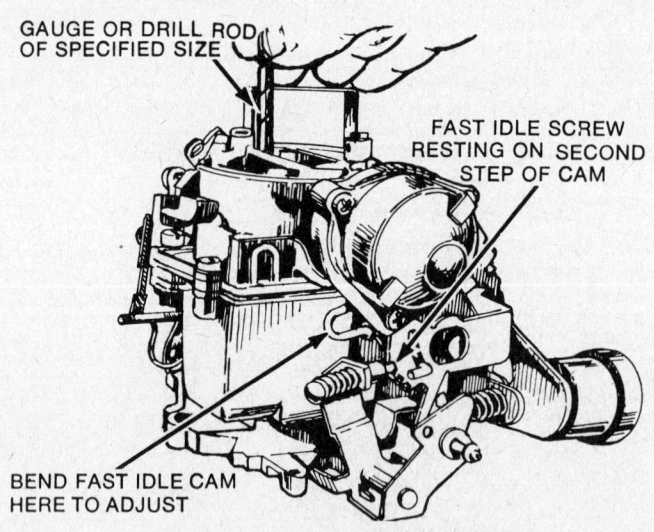

Fast idle cam position adjustment

This unit is a one barrel, altitude compensating model used on Fairmont, Fairmont Futura, Zephyr, Mustang, and Capri cars with the 200 cu. in., 6 cylinder engine and the 1981–82 Thunderbird, XR-7, Granada and Cougar cars with the 200 cu. in. 6 cylinder engine and automatic transmission.

FAST IDLE CAM POSITION ADJUSTMENT

1. Position the fast idle adjusting screw on the second highest step of the fast idle cam.
2. Lightly move the choke plate toward the closed position.
3. Check the fast idle cam setting by placing the correct gauge (see specifications) between the upper edge of the choke plate and the air horn wall.
4. If the setting is not as specified, bend the fast idle cam link.

FAST IDLE ADJUSTMENT

1. Remove the spark delay valve, if so equipped, and route the distributor vacuum hose directly to the advance side of the distributor.
2. Trace the EGR signal vacuum hose from the EGR valve to the carburetor. If an EGR/PVS valve or cold weather modulator is located in the hose, disconnect the EGR hose at the EGR valve and plug the hose. If not equipped with EGR/PVS or a cold weather modulator, do not detach the hose except on 1980 models; disconnect and plug the EGR hose on all 1980 models. On all 1981 and later models disconnect and plug the vacuum hoses at the EGR and purge valves.
3. Run the engine to normal operating temperature. With the choke plate fully open and the transmission in Park, place the fast idle screw on the next to the highest step of the fast idle cam. Allow the engine speed to stabilize and adjust the speed to the fast idle speed specification found on the underhood sticker.
4. Run the engine at 2500 rpm for about 15 seconds and recheck the fast idle speed.
5. When the speed is properly adjusted, turn off the engine and reroute the vacuum lines.

ACCELERATOR PUMP STROKE

The accelerator pump stroke is preset at the factory and should not be adjusted to improve driveability.

DECHOKE ADJUSTMENT

1. With the engine OFF, hold the throttle in the wide open position.
2. Insert the specified gauge between the upper edge of the choke plate and the wall of the air horn.
3. With a slight pressure against the choke shaft a slight drag should be felt when the gauge is withdrawn.
4. To adjust, bend the unloader tab

CARBURETORS
HOLLEY
SECTION 25

5. Activate the pulldown diaphragm by applying vacuum to the external tube.
6. Make sure that the pulldown diaphragm is fully retracted.

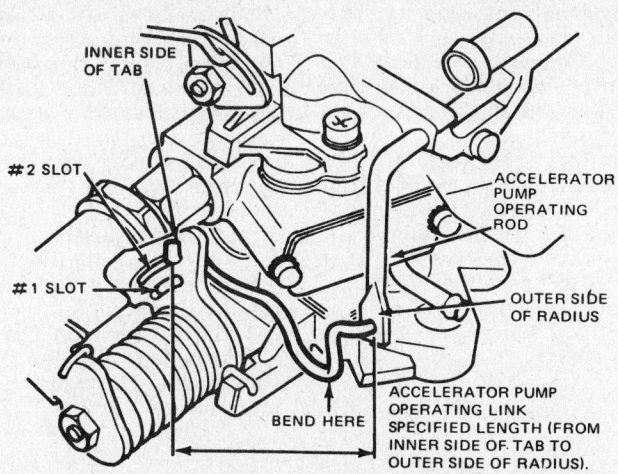

Accelerator pump adjustment

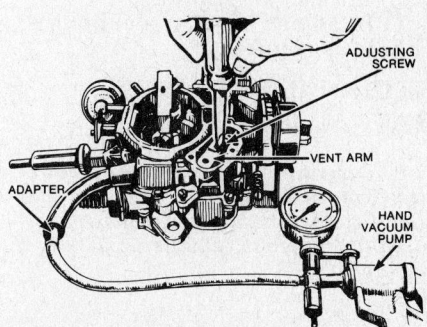

External fuel bowl vent adjustment

on the throttle lever until the correct opening is obtained.

CHOKE PULLDOWN 1980

NOTE: On 1981 and later models this adjustment is preset at the factory and protected by a tamper resistant plug.

1. Set the fast idle screw on the highest step of the fast idle cam.
2. Cool the choke housing until the plate is fully closed.
3. Mark the choke setting for later resetting.

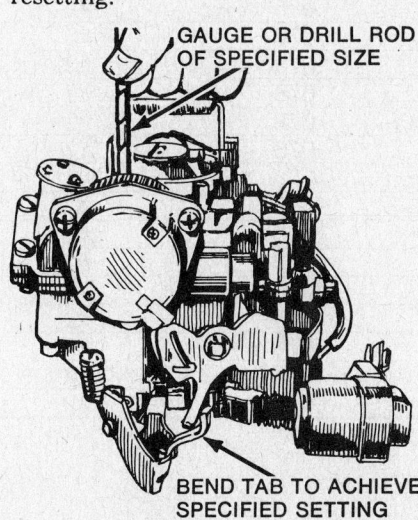

Dechoke adjustment

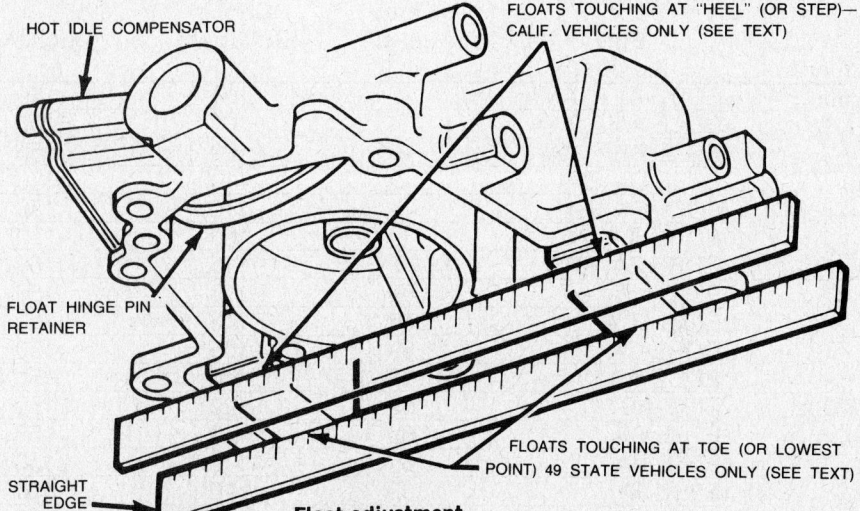

Float adjustment

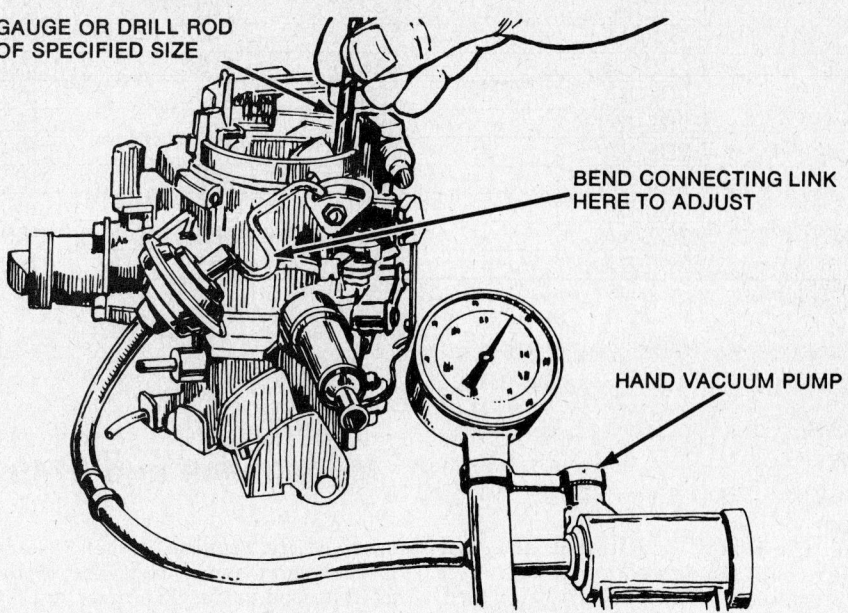

Choke pulldown adjustment

4. On 1980 California models, removes the choke thermostat housing, retaining ring and screws. Temporarily remove the index spacer. Reinstall the housing, retainer, and screws. Then, on all models, loosen the choke housing screws and rotate the choke cap 90° in the rich (closed) direction. Tighten the screws.

25-39

SECTION 25

CARBURETORS
HOLLEY

7. If the motor does not fully retract with vacuum, test it for leakage. Replace it if it leaks.
8. Insert the specified gauge between the upper edge of the choke plate and the air horn wall.
9. To adjust, bend the pulldown linkage as required.

EXTERNAL FUEL BOWL VENT ADJUSTMENT

1. Disconnect the canister vent hose from the fuel bowl vent.
2. Attach a hand operated vacuum pump to the vent tube using a 3/8 in. adapter.
3. Remove the vent cover and gasket and vent spring.
4. The adjusting screw is located on the nylon arm. Turn it clockwise until no more than 1/8 in. of threads is visible above the vent arm.
5. Operate the hand vacuum pump and turn the screw 1/8 turn at a time counterclockwise, until vacuum is registered on the gauge. Release the vacuum and turn the screw 1/2 turn clockwise. Disconnect the pump and replace the vent cover.

FLOAT LEVEL

1. Remove the air horn, place a finger over the hinge pin retainer and catch the accelerator pump ball when the main body is inverted.
2. Lay a straight edge across the housing under the floats. The lowest point of the floats should just touch the straight edge for 49 states models through 1981. For California Models, through 1981 and all 1982 models the straight edge should just contact the step (or heel) of the float.
3. If necessary, bend the tang on the float arm.
4. Turn the main body back and check the float alignment. No binding should exist through the float movement range.

MODEL 1946
Ford Motor Co.

Year	Part Number	Float Level (in.)	Choke Pulldown (in.)	Dechoke (in.)	Fast Idle Cam (in.)	Accelerator Pump Stroke Slot
'80	EOBE-ALA, AMA	①	.100	.150	.070	#2
	EOEE-ANA, APA	①	.100	.150	.070	#2
	EOZE-BBA, BAA	①	.120	.150	.086	#2
	EOZE-DA, EA	①	.110	.150	.070	#2
	EOZE-FA, GA	①	.110	.150	.070	#2
	EOBE-AA, CA	①	.100	.150	.070	#2
	EOBE-ZA, AAA	①	.115	.150	.090	#1
'81	EIBE-AFA	.69	.113	.150	.082	#2
	EIBE-AKA	.69	.113	.150	.082	#2
	EOBE-CA	.69	.100	.150	.070	#2
	EOBE-AA	.69	.100	.150	.070	#2
'82	EIBE-AGA	.69	.120	.150	.086	#2
	E2BE-CA	.69	.110	.150	.078	#2
	E2BE-BA	.69	.110	.150	.078	#2
	E2BE-JA	.69	.110	.150	.078	#2
	E2BE-HA	.69	.110	.150	.078	#2
	E2BE-TA	.69	.110	.150	.078	#2
	E2BE-SA	.69	.110	.150	.078	#2
'83	E2BE-CA	.69	.110	.150	.078	#2
	E2BE-BA	.69	.110	.150	.078	#2
	E2BE-TA	.69	.110	.150	.078	#2
	E2BE-SA	.69	.110	.150	.078	#2
	E3SE-CA	.69	.105	.150	.078	#2
	E3SE-DA	.69	.105	.150	.078	#2
	E3SE-AA	.69	.095	.150	.078	#2
	E3SE-BA	.69	.095	.150	.078	#2

① See text

Model 1949 and 6149

The Holley Models 1949 and 6149 are both single venturi booster style carburetors. The Model 6149 is a feedback carburetor. Both carburetors are used on the 2.3 liter High Swirl Combustion (HSC) engine, in the 1984 and later Tempo and Topaz. The Model 6149 is used in the USA and the 1949 in Canada. Both models are used with either manual or automatic transaxles. The Model 6149 carburetor uses twelve basic systems. The Model 1949 carburetor uses thirteen systems. Ten systems are common to both carburetors.

CARBURETORS
HOLLEY

DRY FLOAT LEVEL ADJUSTMENT

1. Remove the carburetor air horn.
2. With the air horn assembly removed, place a finger over float hinge pin retainer, and invert the main body. Catch the accelerator pump check ball and weight.
3. Using a straight edge, check the position of the floats. The correct dry float setting is that both pontoons at the extreme outboard edge by flush with the surface of the main body casting (without gasket). If adjustment is required, bend the float tabs to raise or lower the float level.
4. Once adjustment is correct, turn main body right side up, and check the float alignment. The float should move freely throughout its range without contacting the fuel bowl walls. If the float pontoons are misaligned, straighten by bending the float arms. Recheck the float level adjustment.
5. During assembly, insert the check ball first and then the weight.

AUXILIARY MAIN JET/ PULLOVER VALVE ADJUSTMENT

The length of the auxiliary main jet/pullover valve adjustment screw which protrudes through the back side (side opposite the adjustment screw head) of the throttle pick-up lever must be 0.345 ± 0.010 in. (8.76mm). To adjust, turn screw in or out as required.

MECHANICAL FUEL BOWL VENT ADJUSTMENT (LEVER CLEARANCE)

Off Vehicle Adjustment

1. Secure the choke plate in the wide-open position.
2. Set the throttle at the TSP Off position.
3. Turn the TSP Off idle adjustment screw counterclockwise until the throttle plate is closed in the throttle bore.
4. Fuel bowl vent clearance: Dimension A should be within 0.120 ± 0.010 in. (3.05mm).
5. If out of specification, bend the bowl vent actuator lever at the adjustment point to obtain the required clearance.

— **CAUTION** —
Do not bend fuel bowl vent arm and/or adjacent portion of the actuator lever.

NOTE: TSP Off rpm must be set after carburetor installation.

On Vehicle Adjustment

NOTE: This adjustment must be performed after curb idle speed has been set to specification.

1. Secure the choke plate in the wide open position.
2. Turn ignition key to the On position to activate the TSP (engine not running). Open throttle so that the TSP plunger extends.
3. Verify that the throttle is in the idle set position (contacting the TSP plunger). Measure the clearance of the fuel bowl vent arm to the bowl vent actuating lever.
4. Fuel bowl vent clearance: Dimension A should be within 0.020–0.040 in.

NOTE: There is a difference in the on vehicle and off vehicle specification.

5. If out of specification, bend the bowl vent actuator lever at the adjustment point to obtain the required clearance.

— **CAUTION** —
Do not bend fuel bowl vent arm and/or adjacent portion of the actuating lever.

ACCELERATOR PUMP STROKE ADJUSTMENT

1. Check the length of the accelerator pump operating link from its inside edge at the accelerator pump operating rod to its inside edge at the throttle lever hole. The dimension should be 2.15 ± .010 in. (54.61 ± .25 mm).
2. Adjust to proper length by bending loop in operating link.

CHOKE PLATE PULLDOWN ADJUSTMENT

NOTE: This adjustment is pre-set at the factory and protected by a tamper resistant plug.

FAST IDLE CAM INDEX ADJUSTMENT

1. With the engine cool, position the fast idle screw on the high step of the fast idle cam.
2. Activate the pulldown motor by applying an external vacuum source of 15–20 inches Hg.
3. Apply light pressure to the upper edge of the choke plate in the closing direction to remove clearance between the pulldown motor clevis and the modulator stem.
4. Open the throttle slightly and allow the fast idle cam to drop.
5. Close the throttle and measure

Accelerator pump stroke adjustment— Models 1949 and 6149

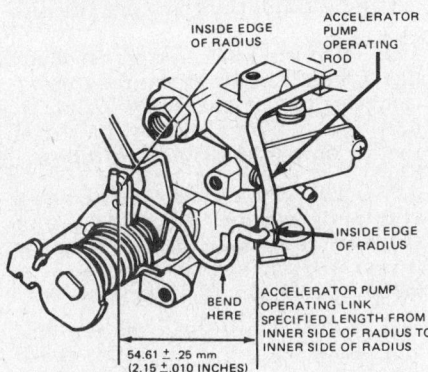

Auxiliary main jet/Pullover valve (timing adjustment)—Models 1949 and 6149

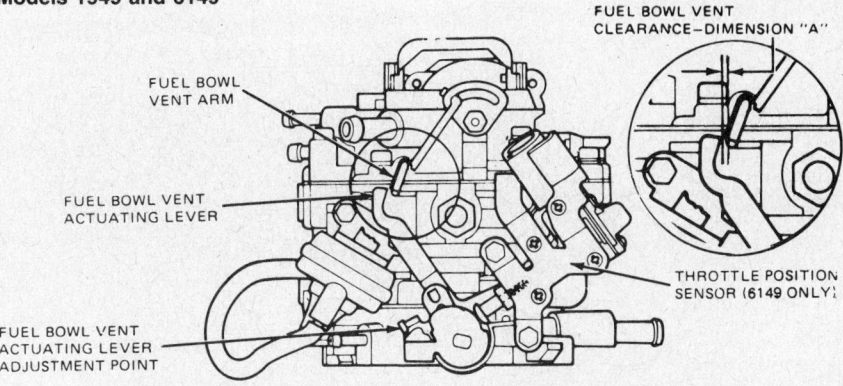

Mechanical fuel bowl vent adjustment—Models 1949 and 6149

SECTION 25
CARBURETORS
HOLLEY

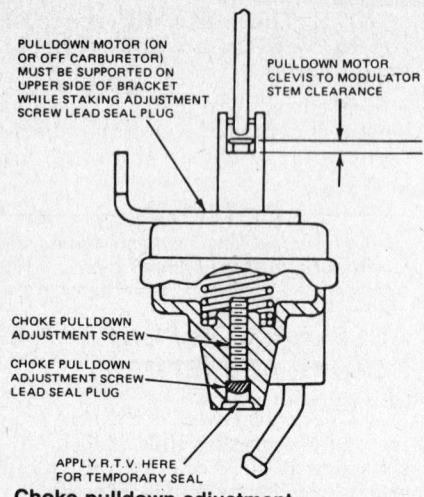

Choke pulldown adjustment—Models 1949 and 6149

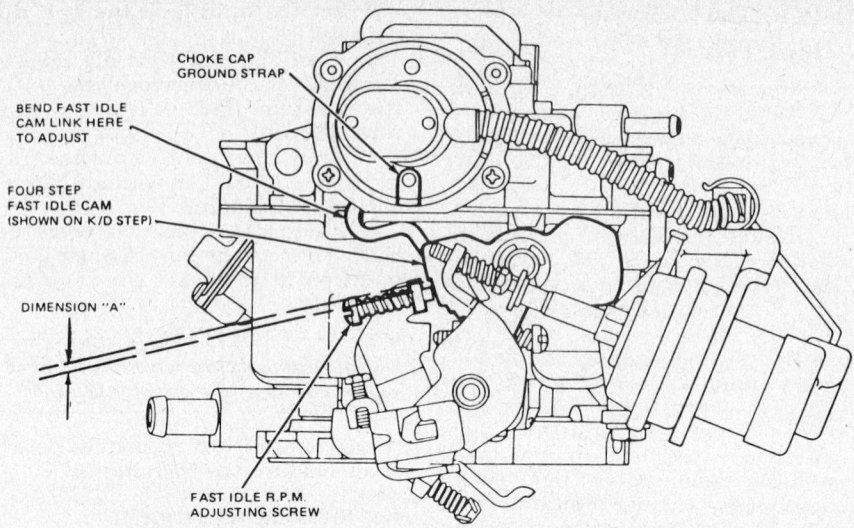

Fast idle cam index adjustment—Models 1949 and 6149

the clearance between the top edge of the fast idle rpm adjusting screw and the shoulder of the fast idle cam high step (dimension A is the fast idle cam index shown in the illustration). Refer to the specifications table.

6. Remove the light closing pressure from the upper edge of the choke plate.

7. Open the throttle to the wide open position and return slowly.

8. The fast idle adjustment screw must contact the lower end of the fast idle cam kickdown step by at least half of its diameter four carburetors with four step cams or must contact the third step by at least half of its diameter without contacting the second or fourth steps for carburetors with five step cams.

9. If Steps 5 and 8 are okay, the fast idle cam index is within specification. If adjustment is necessary bend the fast idle cam link at the loop to obtain the correct specification at Dimension A (see the specifications table).

DECHOKE ADJUSTMENT

1. With the engine off and cool, hold the throttle in the wide open position.

2. Use a drill of the specified size and measure the clearance between the upper edge of the choke plate and the air horn wall.

3. With slight pressure against the choke shaft, a slight drag should be felt when the gauge is withdrawn.

4. To adjust, bend the tang on the throttle lever as required.

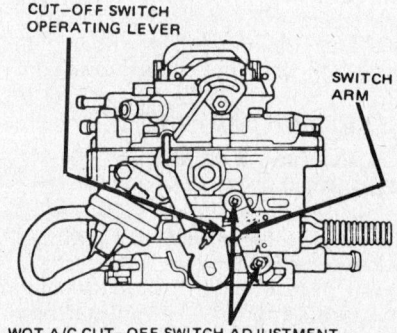

WOT A/C cut-off switch adjustment screws—Model 1949

FEEDBACK SYSTEM DIAPHRAGM ADJUSTMENT

Model 6149

1. Remove the main system feedback diaphragm adjustment screw lead sealing disc from the air horn screw boss by drilling a $\frac{3}{32}$ inch diameter hole through the disc, then inserting a small punch to pry the disc out.

2. Turn the main system feedback adjustment screw as required to position the top of the screw 0.180 ± 0.010 in. (4.57mm) below the top of the air horn adjustment screw boss.

NOTE: For carburetors stamped with an "S" on the top of the air horn adjustment screw boss, adjust screw position to 0.250 ± 0.010 in. (6.35mm).

3. Install a new lead sealing disc and stake with a $\frac{1}{4}$ inch flat-ended punch.

4. Apply an external vacuum source (hand vacuum pump, 10 in. Hg

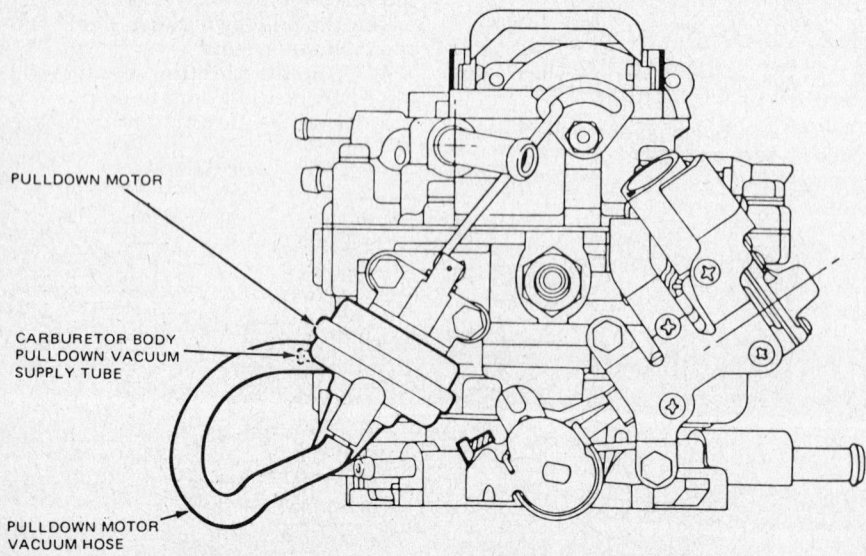

Choke plate pulldown motor—Models 1949 and 6149

CARBURETORS
HOLLEY
SECTION 25

maximum) and check for leaks, diaphragm should hold vacuum.

WOT A/C CUT-OFF SWITCH ADJUSTMENT

Model 1949

The WOT A/C cut-off switch is a normally closed switch (allowing current to flow at any throttle position other than wide-open throttle).

1. Disconnect the wiring harness at the switch connector.
2. Connect a 12 volt DC power supply and test lamp. With the throttle at curb idle, TSP off idle or fast idle position, the test light must be ON. If the test lamp does not light, replace the switch assembly.
3. Rotate the throttle to the wide-open position. The test lamp must go OFF, indicating an open circuit.
4. If the lamp remains ON, insert a 0.165 in. drill or gauge between the throttle lever WOT stop and the WOT stop boss on the carburetor main body casting. Hold the throttle open as far as possible against the gauge. Loosen

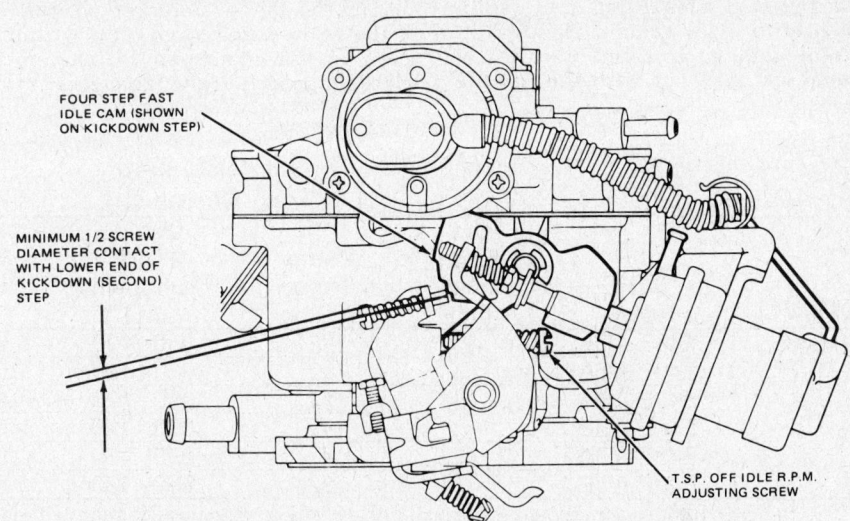
Fast idle cam index (four step idle cams)—Models 1949 and 6149

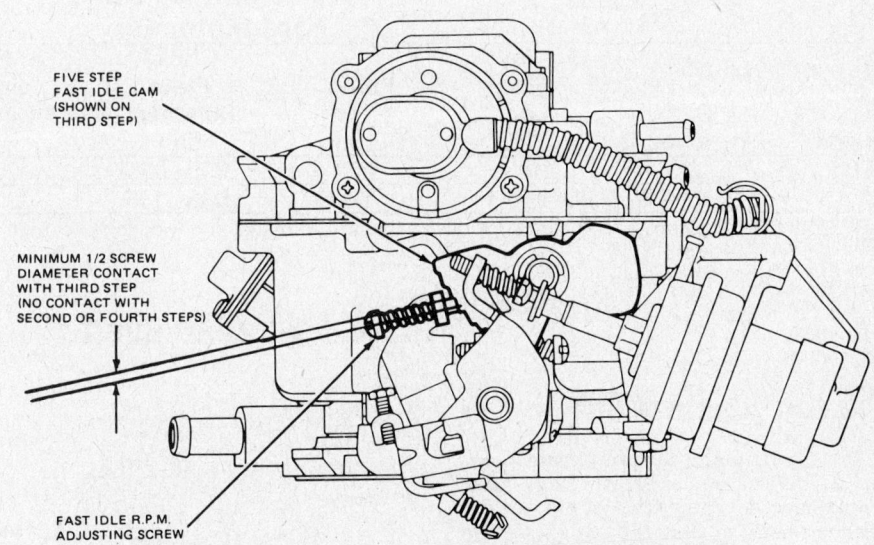
Fast idle cam index (five step cams)—Models 1949 and 6149

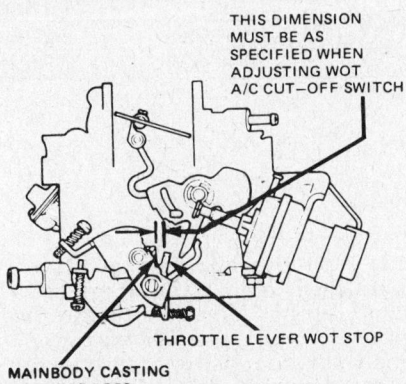
WOT A/C cut-off switch adjustment (clearance)—Model 1949

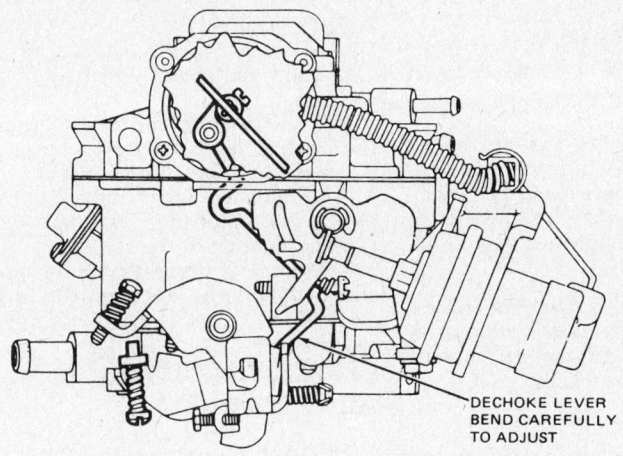
Dechoke adjustment—Models 1949 and 6149

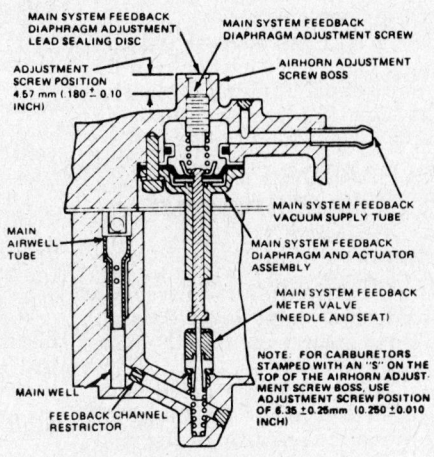
Diaphragm adjustment—Model 6149

25-43

SECTION 25 CARBURETORS
HOLLEY

the two switch mounting screws sufficiently to allow the switch to pivot. Rotate the switch assembly so the test lamp just goes out with the throttle held in the above referenced position. If the lamp does not go OFF within the allowable adjustment rotation, replace the switch. If the lamp goes out, tighten the two switch bracket-to-carburetor screws to 45 inch lbs. (5 Nm) and remove drill or gauge and repeat Step 3.

MODEL 1949
Ford Motor Co.

Year	Carb. Iden.	Dry Float Level (in.)	Pump Hole Setting	Choke Plate Pulldown (in.)	Fast Idle Cam Linkage (in.)	Dechoke (in.)	Choke Setting
'84–'85	E43E-ADA	①	#2	.080–.120	.020–.030	.180–.220	2 Rich
	E43E-AEA	①	#2	.080–.120	.020–.030	.180–.220	2 Rich
	E43E-ABA	①	#2	.090–.120	.020–.030	.180–.220	1 Rich
	E43E-ABB	①	#2	.090–.120	.020–.030	.180–.220	1 Rich
	E43E-ACA	①	#2	.090–.130	.020–.030	.180–.220	1 Rich
	E43E-ACB	①	#2	.090–.130	.020–.030	.180–.220	1 Rich

① Both float pontoons at outboard edge flush with surface of main body casting (without gasket).

MODEL 6149-FB
Ford Motor Co.

Year	Carb. Iden.	Dry Float Level (in.)	Pump Hole Setting	Choke Plate Pulldown (in.)	Fast Idle Cam Linkage (in.)	Dechoke (in.)	Choke Setting
'84	E43E-VA	①	#2	.095–.135	.020–.030	.180–.220	2 Rich
	E43E-ZA	①	#2	.095–.135	.020–.030	.180–.220	2 Rich

① Both float pontoons at outboard edge flush with surface of main body casting (without gasket).

Model 2280/6280

FLOAT ADJUSTMENT

1. Remove the carburetor air horn.
2. Invert the carburetor body, taking care to catch the pump intake check ball, so that the weight of the floats only is forcing the needle against the seat. Hold a finger against the hinge pin retainer to fully seat the float in the float pin cradle.
3. Lay a straight edge across the float bowl. The toe of each float should be as per specifications from the straight-edge. If necessary, bend the float tang to adjust.

ACCELERATOR PUMP STROKE MEASUREMENT

2280 Models

1. Remove the bowl vent cover plate and vent valve lever spring. Take care to avoid loosening the vent valve retainer.
2. Make sure that the accelerator pump connector rod is in the inner hole of the pump operating lever and the throttle is at curb idle.
3. Place a straight edge on the bowl vent cover surface of the air horn, over the accelerator pump lever.
4. The lever surface should be flush with the air horn. If not, adjust it by bending the pump connector rod at the 90 degree bend.

NOTE: If this adjustment is changed, both the bowl vent and the mechanical power valve adjustments must be reset.

6280 Models

1. Remove the bowl vent cover plate and gasket.

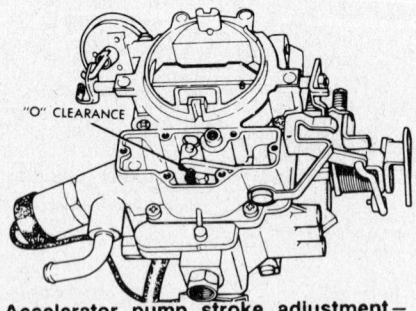

Accelerator pump stroke adjustment—model 6280

2. With all pump links and levers installaed, adjust the accelerator pump cap nut for zero clearance between the pump lever and the cap nut. Check that the wide open throttle can be reached without binding.
3. Install the gasket and the bowl vent cover plate.

CHOKE UNLOADER ADJUSTMENT

1. Hold the throttle valves in the wide open position.
2. Lightly press a finger against the control lever to move the choke valve toward the closed position.
3. Insert the specified gauge between the top of the choke valve and the air horn wall.
4. Adjust, if necessary, by bending the tang on the accelerator pump lever.

CHOKE VACUUM KICK ADJUSTMENT

1. Open the throttle, close the choke, then close the throttle to trap

CARBURETORS
HOLLEY
SECTION 25

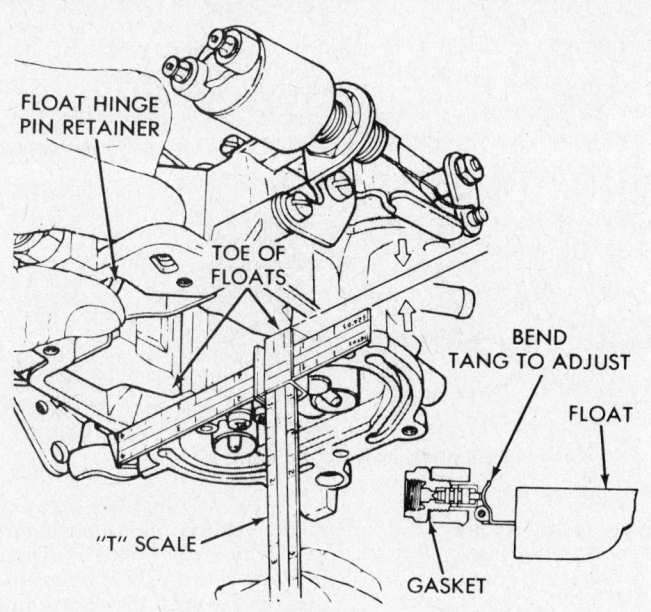

Float adjustment

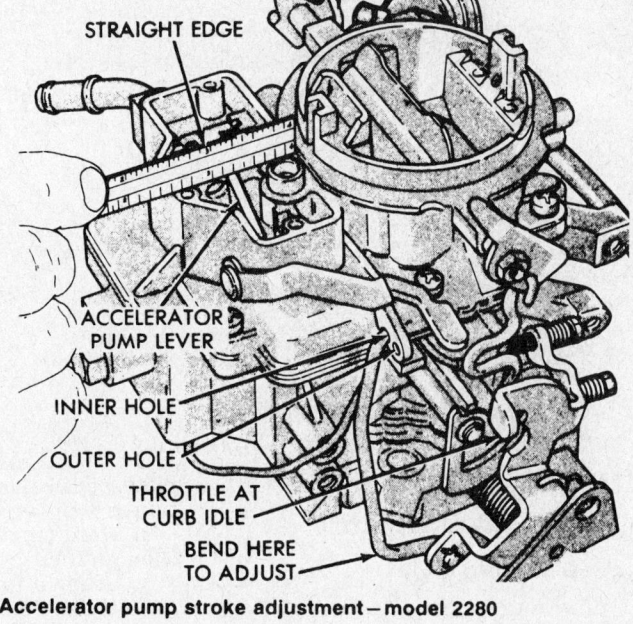

Accelerator pump stroke adjustment—model 2280

the fast idle cam at the closed choke position.

2. Disconnect the vacuum hose from the carburetor and connect it to an auxiliary vacuum source with a length of hose. Apply at least 15 in. Hg.

3. Completely compress the choke lever spring in the diaphragm stem without distorting the linkage.

4. Insert the specified gauge between the top of the choke valve and the air horn wall.

5. Adjust by bending the diaphragm link. Check for free movement. Replace the vacuum hose.

FAST IDLE CAM POSITION ADJUSTMENT

1. Position the adjusting screw on the second highest step of the fast idle cam.

2. Move the choke towards the closed position with light finger pressure.

3. Insert the specified gauge between the choke valve and the air horn wall.

4. Adjust by opening or closing the U-bend in the fast idle connector link.

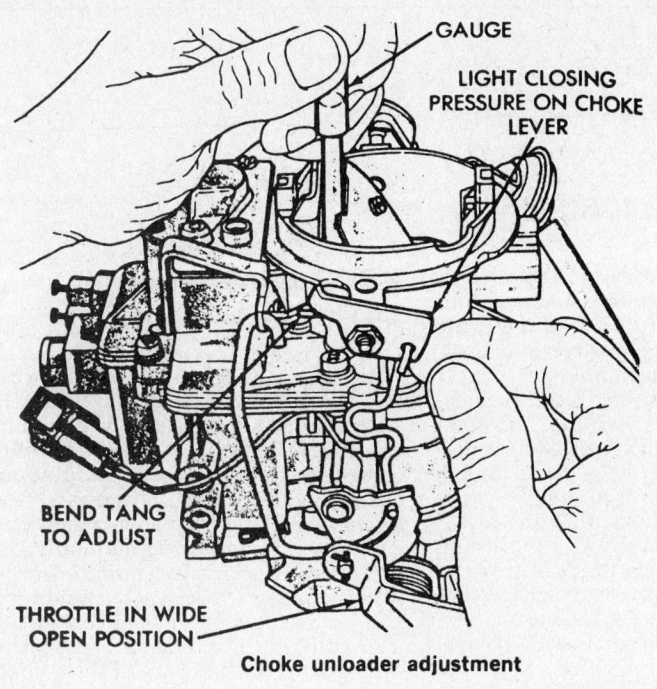

Choke unloader adjustment

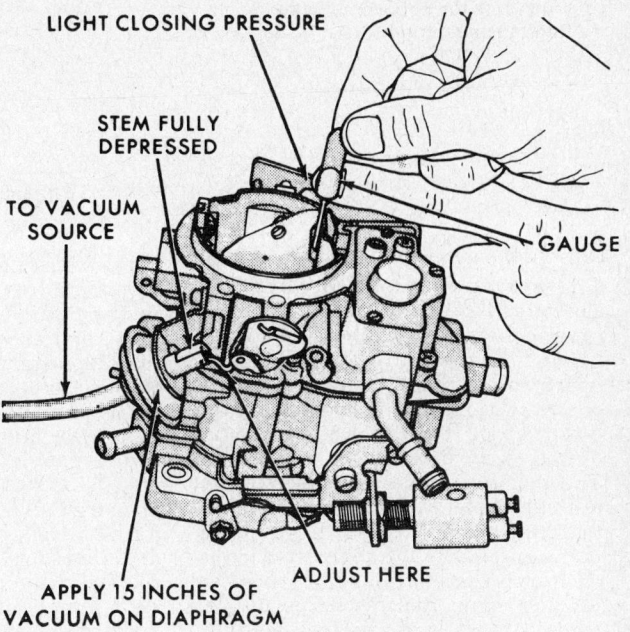

Choke vacuum kick adjustment

25-45

SECTION 25 CARBURETORS
HOLLEY

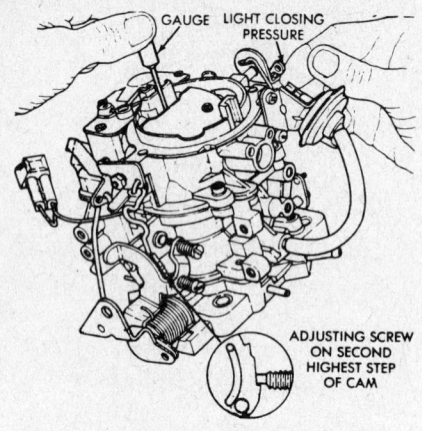

Fast idle cam position adjustment

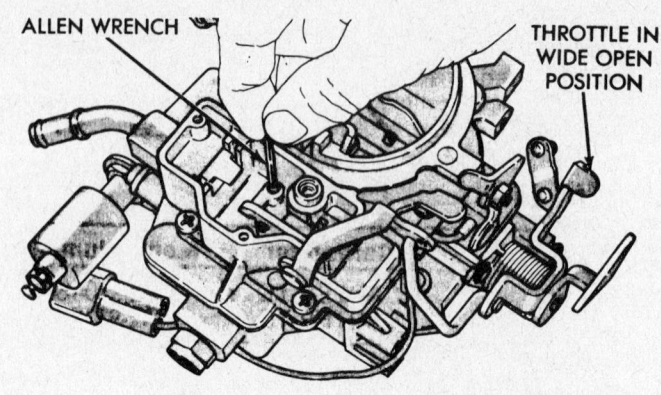

Mechanical power valve adjustment

MECHANICAL POWER VALVE ADJUSTMENT

2280 Models Only

1. Remove the bowl vent cover plate, vent valve lever, spring and retainer. Remove the lever pivot pin.
2. Hold the throttle in the wide open position.
3. Using a ⁵⁄₆₄ in. Allen wrench, press the mechanical power valve adjustment screw down, and release it to determine if clearance exists. Turn the screw clockwise until clear is zero.
4. Adjust by turning the screw one turn counterclockwise.
5. Install all parts.

MODEL 2280/6280
Chrysler Corporation

Year	Carb. Part No.	Float Level (in.)	Accelerator Pump Adjustment (in.)	Fast Idle (rpm)	Choke Unloader Clearance (in.)	Vacuum Kick (in.)	Fast Idle Cam Position (in.)	Choke
'85	R-40121-A	9/32	①	1700	.280	.130	.060	Fixed
	R-40157-A	9/32	①	1600	.200	.140	.052	Fixed
'86	R-40276A	9/32	①	②	.280	.130	.060	Fixed
	R-40245A	9/32	①	②	.200	.140	.052	Fixed

① Flush with top of bowl vent casting
② Refer to underhood sticker

Model 4180-C

The Holley 4180-C 4 bbl carburetor is a downdraft, two-stage carburetor, It can be considered as two dual carburetors; one supply a fuel/air mixture throughout the entire range of engine operating (primary stage), and the other functioning only when a greater quantity of fuel/air mixture is required (secondary stage).

The primary stage (front section of the carburetor contains a fuel bowl, metering block, and an accelerating pump assembly. The primary barrels each contain a primary and booster venturi, main fuel discharge nozzle, throttle plate, and idle fuel passage. The Model 4180-C uses an electric choke with hot air assist. The secondary stage, (rear section) of the carburetor contains a fuel bowl, metering body, and secondary throttle operating diaphragm assembly.

Each secondary barrel contains a primary and booster venturi, idle fuel passages, main secondary fuel discharge nozzle, throttle plate, and a transfer system fuel passage from the primary fuel bowl. A fuel inlet system for both the primary and the secondary stages for the carburetor provides the fuel metering systems with a constant supply of fuel. The 4180-C carburetor is used on the 1983 Ford Mustang with the 302 V8 engine.

ACCELERATING PUMP LEVER ADJUSTMENT

1. Using a feeler gauge and with the throttle plates (primary throttle plates) in the wide open position, there should be the specified clearance between the accelerating pump operating lever adjustment screw head and the pump arm when the pump arm is depressed manually.
2. If adjustment is required, loosen and then hold the lock screw and turn the adjusting nut in to increase the clearance and out to decrease the clearance. One half turn of the adjust-

CARBURETORS
HOLLEY

ing nut is equal to approximately 0.015 in. (0.381mm). When the proper adjustment has been obtained hold the adjustment in position with a wrench and tighten the nut.

DRY FUEL LEVEL FLOAT ADJUSTMENT

The dry float adjustment is a preliminary fuel level adjustment only. The final adjustment ("Wet Fuel Level Adjustment") must be performed after the carburetor is installed on the engine. With the fuel bowls and float assemblies removed, adjust the floats so that the floats are parallel to the fuel bowls, with the top of the fuel bowls inverted.

WET FUEL LEVEL ADJUSTMENT

The fuel pump pressure and volume must be to specifications prior to performing the following adjustments.

1. Operate the engine to normalize engine temperatures and place the vehicle on a flat surface, as near level as possible. Remove the air cleaner, if it was not previously removed.
2. Run engine at 1000 rpm for about 30 seconds to stabilize fuel level.
3. Stop engine and remove sight plug on side of primary carburetor bowl.
4. Check fuel level. It should be at bottom of sight plug hole. If fuel spills out when sight plug is removed, lower fuel level. If fuel level is below sight plug hole, raise fuel level.

CAUTION
Do not loosen lock screw or nut or attempt to adjust fuel level with sight plug removed or engine running because fuel may spray out creating a fire hazard.

5. Adjust the front level as necessary by loosening the lock screw, and turning the adjusting nut clockwise to lower fuel level or counterclockwise to raise fuel level ($1/16$ turn adjusting nut will change fuel level approximately $1/32$ inch). Tighten lock screw and install sight plug, using old gasket. Start engine and run at 1000 rpm for about 30 seconds to stabilize fuel level.
6. Stop engine, remove sight plug and check fuel level. Repeat Step 5 until fuel level is at bottom of sight plug hole. When fuel level is at bottom of sight plug hole, install sight plug using new adjusting plug gasket.
7. Repeat Steps 3–6 for secondary fuel bowl.

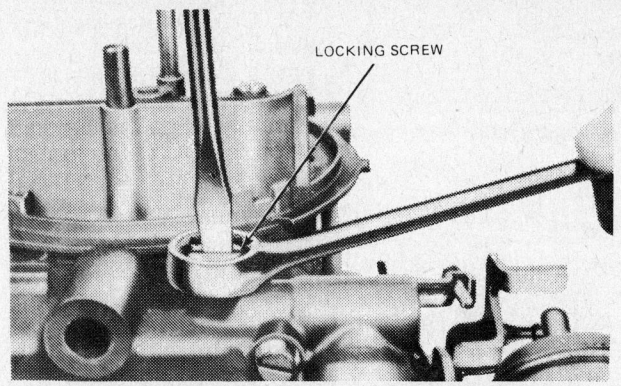
Fuel level adjustment—wet—Holley 4180C

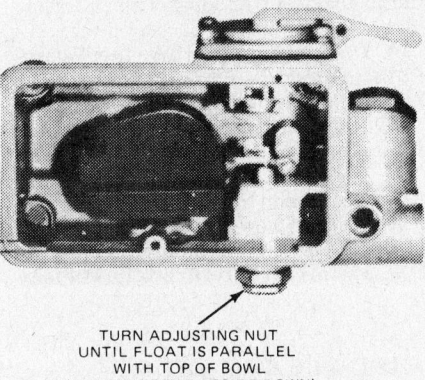
Dry float adjustment—Holley 4180C

NOTE: The secondary throttle must be used to stabilize the fuel level in the secondary fuel bowl.

SECONDARY THROTTLE PLATE ADJUSTMENT

1. With carburetor off the engine, hold the secondary throttle plates closed.
2. Turn the secondary throttle shaft lever adjusting screw (stop screw) out (counterclockwise) until the secondary throttle plates seat in the throttle bores.
3. Turn the screw in clockwise until the screw JUST contacts the secondary lever, then turn screw in (clockwise) $1/4$ turn.

CHOKE PULLDOWN ADJUSTMENT

1. Remove the choke thermostat housing, gasket and retainer. See the choke cap removal and installation proccedure below.
2. Insert a piece of wire into the choke piston bore to move the piston down against the stop screw. Main-

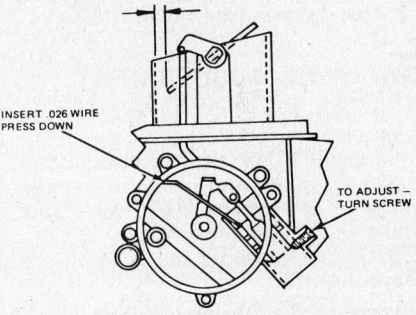
Choke pulldown adjustment—Holley 4180C

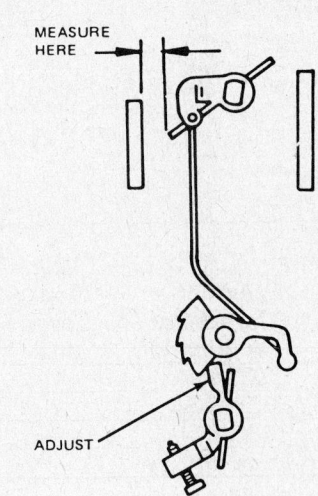
Dechoke adjustment—Holley 4180C

tain light closing pressure on the choke plate and measure the gap between the lower edge of the choke plate and the air horn wall.

3. To adjust, remove the putty covering the adjustment screw and turn the screw clockwise to decrease or counter-clockwise to increase the gap setting. Take care to close the choke plate during screw adjustment. Screw may be turned into side of piston, resulting in damage to piston.
4. Reinstall the choke thermostatic housing, gasket, and retainer.

SECTION 25 CARBURETORS
HOLLEY

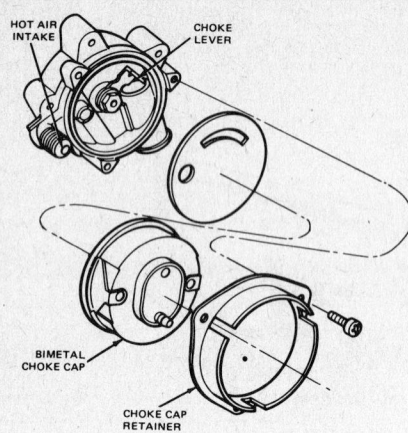

Automatic choke—Holley 4180C

DECHOKE ADJUSTMENT

1. Hold the throttle in the wide open position.
2. Apply light closing pressure to the choke plate and measure the gap between the lower edge of the choke plate and the air horn wall.
3. To adjust, bend the pawl on the fast idle lever.

CHOKE THERMOSTATIC SPRING HOUSING (CHOKE CAP)

Removal

1. Remove the carburetor from vehicle.
2. Using a hacksaw carefully cut a slot in the head of the breakaway screw. Using a proper sized straight blade screw driver, remove the breakaway screw in the conventional manner.
3. Repeat Step 2 for the remaining breakaway screw.
4. Remove the remaining standard screw. Remove the retaining ring, choke cap and gasket.

Installation

1. Install the choke cap gasket. Install the choke cap by engaging the bimetal loop on the choke thermostatic lever.
2. Install the retaining ring. Loosely install two new breakaway screws and one standard screw.
3. Align the choke cap to the proper index mark.
4. Tighten the breakaway screws until the heads break off. Tighten the remaining screw to 16–18 inch lbs. (1.8–2.0 Nm).
5. Install carburetor on the vehicle.

FAST IDLE CAM SET

1. Rotate the choke cap 45 degrees counterclockwise (rich) to close the choke plate. Tighten the attaching screw at the time.

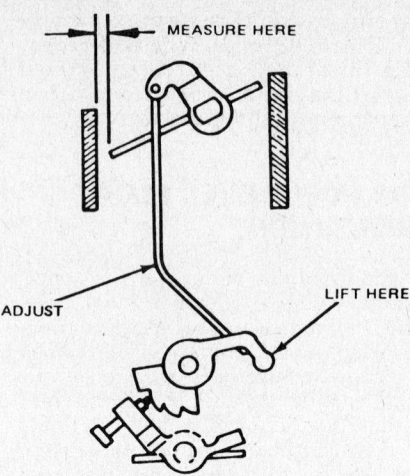

Fast idle cam set—Holley 4180C

2. Open and close the throttle to place the fast idle screw on the top step of the cam.
3. Place a pulldown gauge between the lower edge of the choke plate and the air horn wall, then open and close the throttle to allow the fast idle cam to drop.
4. Press upward on the fast idle cam. There should be little or no movement indicating that the fast idle screw is on the kickdown (2nd) step of the cam, against the first step.

MODEL 4180C
Ford Motor Company

Year	(9510)* Carburetor Identification	Dry Float Level (in.)	Wet Float Level (in.)	Pump Setting Hole	Choke Plate Pulldown (in.)	Fast Idle Cam Linkage Clearance (in.)	Fast Idle (rpm)	Dechoke (in)	Choke Setting
'83	E3ZE-AUA	②	①	#1	.195–.215	NA	③	.300	3 Rich
	E3ZE-BGA	②	①	#1	.195–.215	NA	③	.300	3 Rich
'84	E4ZE-SA	②	①	#1	.195–.215	NA	③	.300	1 Lean
'85	E5ZE-GA	—	①	#1	.168–.188	—	③	.300	2 Lean

NA—not available
① Bottom of sight plug
② See text
③ See Underhood sticker

CARBURETORS
HOLLEY
Section 25

Model 5210-C

The Holley 5210-C is a progressive two barrel carburetor with an automatic choke system which is activated by a water heated thermostatic coil. An electrically heated choke is used on most later models. It also has an exhaust gas recirculation system with the valve located in the intake manifold. It is used on 1980 Chevettes (USA). 1980–86 Chevettes (Canada).

FLOAT LEVEL

1. With the carburetor air horn inverted, and the float tang resting lightly on the inlet needle, insert the specified gauge between the air horn and the float.
2. Bend the float tang if an adjustment is needed.

FAST IDLE CAM ADJUSTMENT

1. Place the fast idle screw on the second step of the fast idle cam and against the shoulder of the high step.
2. Place the specified drill or gauge on the down side of the choke plate.
3. To adjust, bend the choke lever tang.

CHOKE PLATE PULLDOWN (VACUUM BREAK) ADJUSTMENT

1980–86 Models

1. Attach a hand vacuum pump to the vacuum break diaphragm; apply vacuum and seat the diaphragm.
2. Push the fast idle cam lever down to close the choke plate.
3. Take any slack out of the linkage in the open choke position.
4. Insert the specified gauge between the lower edge of the choke plate and the air horn wall.
5. If the clearance is incorrect, turn the vacuum break adjusting screw, located in the break housing, to adjust.

CHOKE UNLOADER ADJUSTMENT

1. Position the throttle lever at the wide open position.
2. Insert a gauge of the size specified in the chart between the lower edge of the choke valve and the air horn wall.
3. Bend the unloader tang for adjustment.

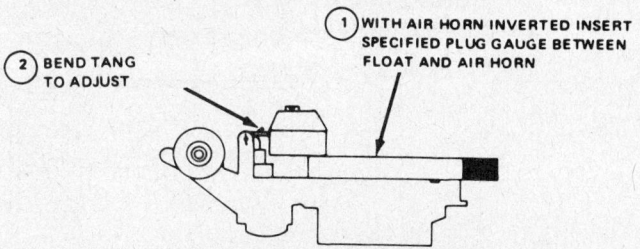

5210-C Float level adjustment

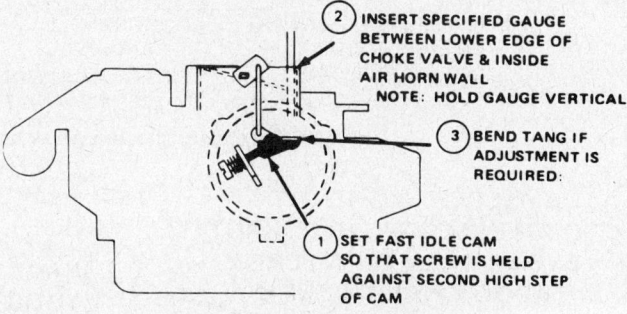

5210-C Fast idle cam adjustment

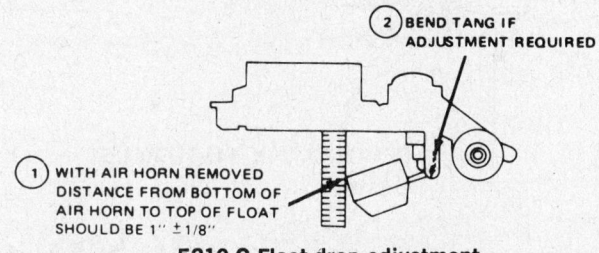

5210-C Float drop adjustment

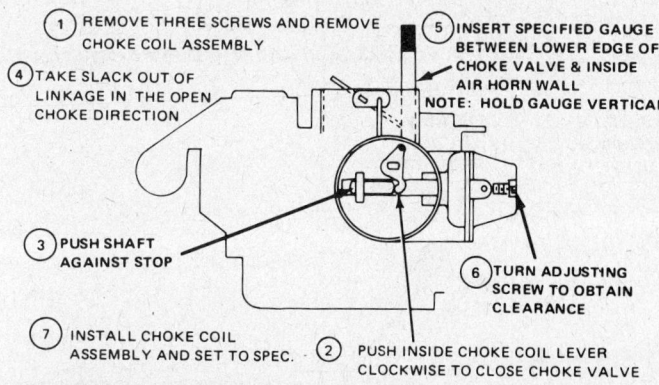

5210-C Vacuum break (choke plate pulldown) adjustment

FAST IDLE SPEED ADJUSTMENT

1. The engine must be at normal operating temperature with the air cleaner off.
2. With the engine running, position the fast idle screw on the high step of the cam for GM cars, or on the second step against the shoulder of the high step for AMC cars. Plug the EGR Port on the carburetor.
3. Adjust the speed by turning the fast idle screw.

SECTION 25 CARBURETORS
HOLLEY

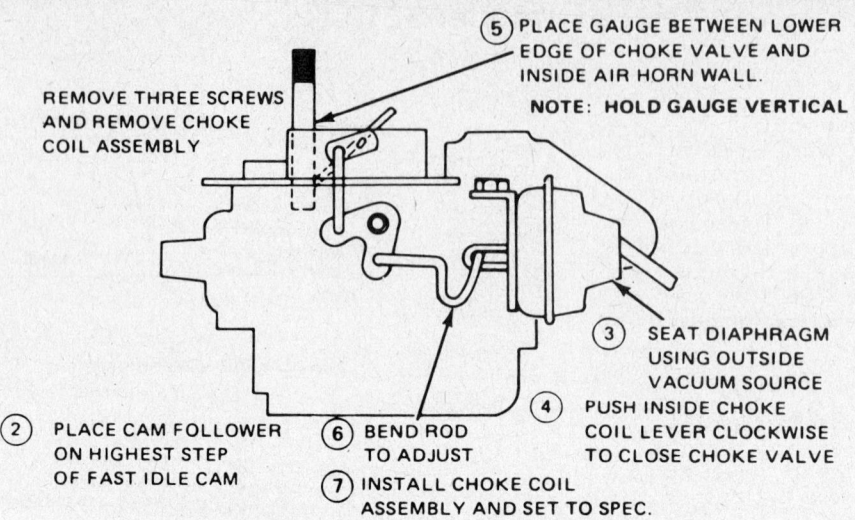

5210-C Secondary vacuum break adjustment

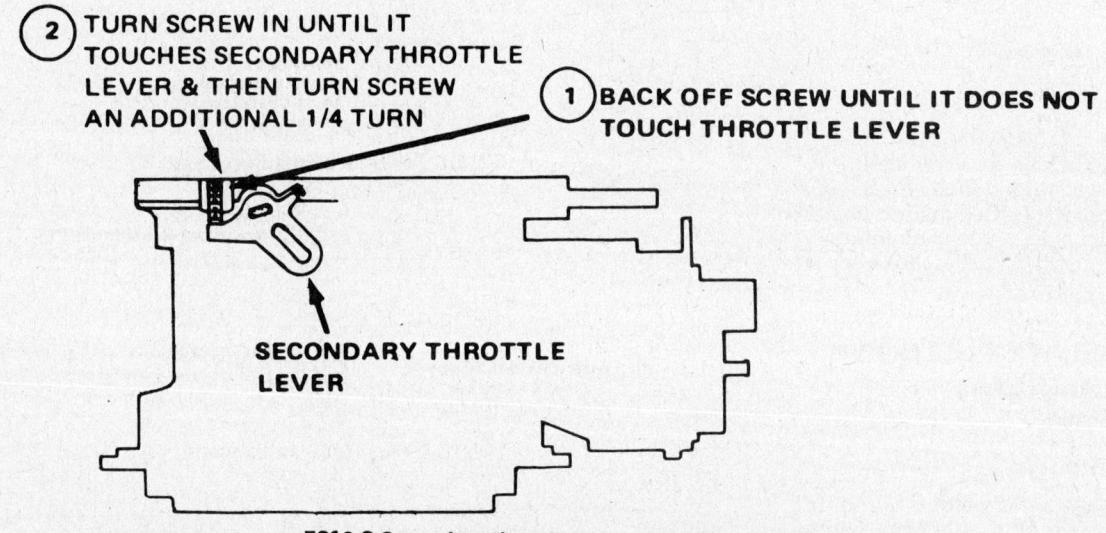

5210-C Secondary throttle stop screw adjustment

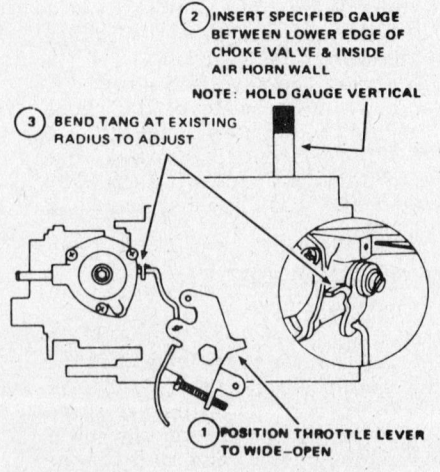

5210-C Fast idle speed adjustment

5210-C Choke unloader adjustment

25-50

CARBURETORS
HOLLEY

MODEL 5210-C
Chevrolet Chevette

Year	Carb. Part No. ① ②	Float Level (Dry) (in.)	Fast Idle Cam (in.)	Secondary Vacuum Break (in.)	Fast Idle Setting (rpm)	Choke Unloader (in.)	Choke Setting
'80	All	0.50	0.110	0.120	2500	0.350	Fixed
'81	14032301	0.50	0.110	0.120	2500	0.350	Fixed
	14032302	0.50	0.110	0.120	2500	0.275	Fixed
'82	14043392	0.50	0.110	0.120	2500	0.275	Fixed
	14043393	0.50	0.110	0.120	2500	0.350	Fixed
'83 (Canada)	All	0.50	0.090	③	④	0.275	Fixed
'84–'85 (Canada)	14076317	0.50	0.110	⑤	④	0.350	Fixed
	14076318	0.50	0.110	⑤	④	0.300	Fixed
	14076319	0.50	0.120	⑥	④	0.350	Fixed
'86 (Canada)	14076393	0.50	0.100	⑤	④	0.325	Fixed
	14076394	0.50	0.090	⑤	④	0.275	Fixed

① Located on tag attached to the carburetor, or on the casting or choke plate
② GM identification numbers are used in place of the Holley numbers
③ Hot: 0.280 Cold: 0.100
④ See underhood sticker
⑤ Hot: 0.250 Cold: 0.100
⑥ Hot: 0.290 Cold: 0.110

Model 5220, 6520

Both these models are staged dual venturi carburetors. The model 6520 has the electronic feedback system. On the 6520 always check the condition of hoses and related wiring before making carburetor adjustments.

For further information on feedback carburetors, please refer to *Chilton's Guide To Fuel Injection And Feedback Carburetors.*

FLOAT SETTING AND FLOAT DROP ADJUSTMENT

1. Remove and invert the air horn.
2. Insert a 0.480 inch gauge between the air horn and float.
3. If necessary, bend the tang on the float arm to adjust.
4. Turn the air horn right side up and allow the float to hang freely. Measure the float drop from the bottom of the air horn to the bottom of the float. It should be exactly $1\frac{7}{8}$ in. Correct by bending the float tang.

VACUUM KICK ADJUSTMENT

1. Open the throttle, close the choke, then close the throttle to trap the fast idle system at the closed choke position.
2. Disconnect the vacuum hose to the carburetor and connect it to an auxiliary vacuum source.
3. Apply at least 15 in. Hg vacuum to the unit.
4. Apply sufficient force to close the choke valve without distorting the linkage.
5. Insert a gauge (see Specification Chart) between the top of the choke plate and the air horn wall.
6. Adjust by rotating the Allen screw in the center diaphragm housing.

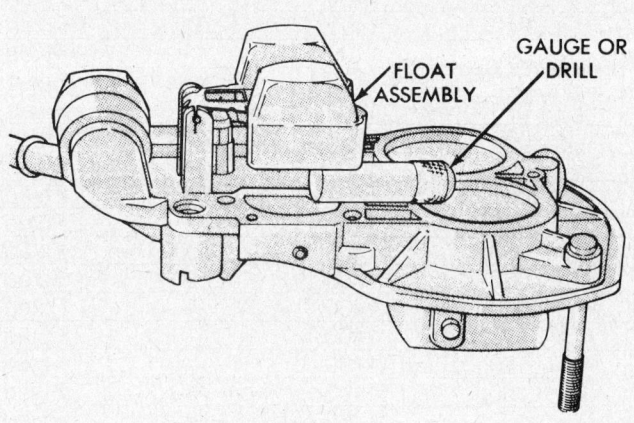

Float setting adjustment

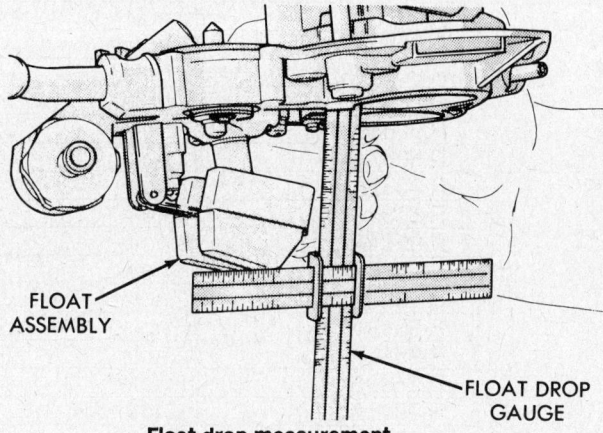

Float drop measurement

SECTION 25
CARBURETORS
HOLLEY

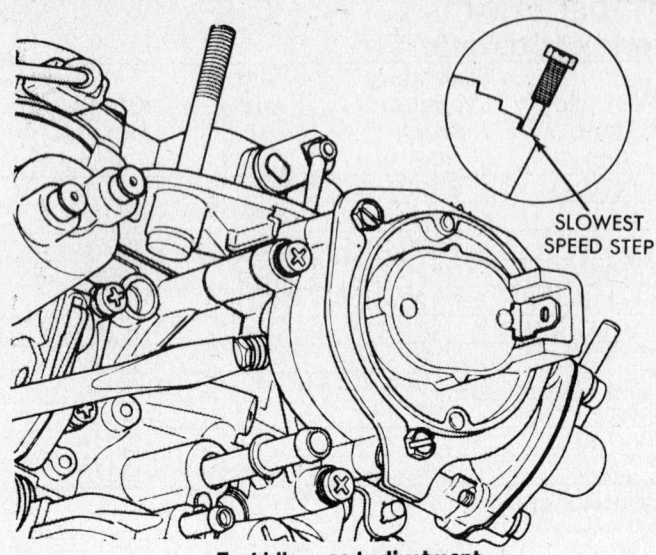

Fast idle speed adjustment

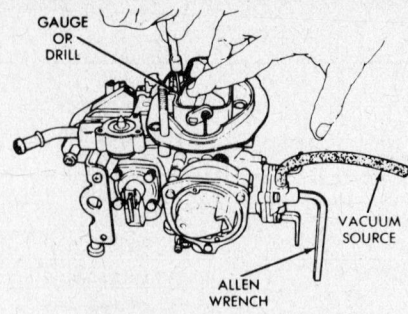

Vacuum kick adjustment

7. Replace the vacuum hose.

FAST IDLE SPEED ADJUSTMENT

1. Remove the air cleaner, disconnect and plug the EGR line, but do not disconnect the spark control computer vacuum line. Turn the air conditioning off.
2. Disconnect the radiator fan electrical connector and use a jumper wire to complete the circuit at the fan. Do not short to ground, as this will damage the system.
3. With the parking brake set and the transmission in Neutral (engine still off), open the throttle and place the fast idle screw on the slowest step of the cam.
4. Start the engine and check the idle speed. If it continues to rise slowly, the idle stop switch is not grounded properly.
5. Adjust the fast idle with the screw, moving the screw off the cam each time to adjust. Allow the screw to fall back against the cam and the speed to stabilize between each adjustment.

MODEL 5220
Chrysler Corporation

Year	Carb. Part No.	Accelerator Pump	Dry Float Level (in.)	Vacuum Kick (in.)	Fast Idle RPM (w/fan)	Throttle Stop Speed RPM	Choke
'80	R8838A, 8839A, 9110A, 9111A, 9325A, 9327A	#2 hole	.480	.040	1700	700	Fixed
	R8726A, 8727A, 8837A, 9108A, 9321A, 9323A	#2 hole	.480	.070	1400	700	Fixed
	R9109A	#2 hole	.480	.100	1400	700	Fixed
'81	R-9056A	#2 hole	.480	.070	1400	700	Fixed
	R-9057A	#2 hole	.480	.070	1400	—	Fixed
	R-9058A	#2 hole	.480	.040	1400	700	Fixed
	R-9059A	#2 hole	.480	.040	1400	—	Fixed
	R-9064A	#2 hole	.480	.070	1300	—	Fixed
	R-9065A	#2 hole	.480	.070	1300	—	Fixed
	R-9066A	#2 hole	.480	.060	1300	700	Fixed
	R-9067A	#2 hole	.480	.060	1300	—	Fixed
'82	R-9582A	#3 hole	.480	.060	1200	700	Fixed
	R-8583A	#3 hole	.480	.060	1200	—	Fixed
	R-9584A	#3 hole	.480	.060	1500	700	Fixed
	R-9585A	#3 hole	.480	.060	1500	700	Fixed
	R-9820A	#2 hole	.480	.080	1400	—	Fixed
	R-9513A	#2 hole	.480	.120	1400	—	Fixed
	R-9514A	#2 hole	.480	.120	1400	—	Fixed
	R-9499A	#2 hole	.480	.130	1400	700	Fixed
	R-9511A	#3 hole	.480	.130	1400	700	Fixed
	R-9512A	#2 hole	.480	.130	1400	—	Fixed

CARBURETORS
HOLLEY
SECTION 25

MODEL 5220
Chrysler Corporation

Year	Carb. Part No.	Accelerator Pump	Dry Float Level (in.)	Vacuum Kick (in.)	Fast Idle RPM (w/fan)	Throttle Stop Speed RPM	Choke
'83	R-40020A	#3 hole	.480	.055	1500	—	Fixed
	R-40022A	#3 hole	.480	.055	1500	—	Fixed
	R-40023A	#2 hole	.480	.070	1400	700	Fixed
	R-40024A	#2 hole	.480	.070	1400	700	Fixed
	R-40025A	#2 hole	.480	.070	1400	700	Fixed
	R-40026A	#7 hole	.480	.070	1400	700	Fixed
'84	R-400601A	#2 hole	.480	.055	1200	—	Fixed
	R-400851A	#2 hole	.480	.040	1500	—	Fixed
	R-40170A	#3 hole	.480	.060	1650	—	Fixed
	R-40171A	#3 hole	.480	.060	1700	—	Fixed
	R-400671A	#3 hole	.480	.070	1500	—	Fixed
	R-400681A	#3 hole	.480	.070	1700	—	Fixed
	R-400581A	#2 hole	.480	.070	1400	—	Fixed
	R-401071A	#2 hole	.480	.070	1600	—	Fixed
'85	R-40060-A	#2 hole	.480	.050	①	—	Fixed
	R-40116-A	#3 hole	.480	.095	①	—	Fixed
	R-40117-A	#3 hole	.480	.095	①	—	Fixed
'86	R-40060-2A	—	.480	.055	①	—	Fixed
	R-40116-A	—	.480	.095	①	—	Fixed
	R-40117-A	—	.480	.095	①	—	Fixed

① See underhood sticker

MODEL 6520
Chrysler Corporation

Year	Carb. Part No. ①	Accelerator Pump	Dry Float Level (in.)	Float Drop (in.)	Vacuum Kick (in.)	Fast Idle RPM
'81	R-9052A	#2 hole	.480	1.875	.070	1400 ②
	R-9053A	#2 hole	.480	1.875	.070	1400 ②
	R-9054A	#2 hole	.480	1.875	.040	1400 ②
	R-9055A	#2 hole	.480	1.875	.040	1400 ②
	R-9060A	#2 hole	.480	1.875	.030	1100 ②
	R-9061A	#2 hole	.480	1.875	.030	1100 ②
	R-9602A	#2 hole	.480	1.875	.035	1500 ②
	R-9603A	#2 hole	.480	1.875	.035	1500 ②
	R-9125A	#2 hole	.480	1.875	.030	1200 ②
	R-9126A	#2 hole	.480	1.875	.030	1200 ②
	R-9604A	#2 hole	.480	1.875	.035	1600 ②
	R-9605A	#2 hole	.480	1.875	.035	1600 ②
'82	R-9822A	#2 hole	.480	1.875	.080	1400
	R-9823A	#2 hole	.480	1.875	.080	1400
	R-9824A	#2 hole	.480	1.875	.065	1400
	R-9503A	#3 hole	.480	1.875	.085	1300
	R-9504A	#3 hole	.480	1.875	.085	1300
	R-9505A	#3 hole	.480	1.875	.100	1600
	R-9506A	#3 hole	.480	1.875	.100	1600
	R-9750A	#3 hole	.480	1.875	.085	1300
	R-9751A	#3 hole	.480	1.875	.085	1300
	R-9509A	#3 hole	.480	1.875	.085	1600
	R-9510A	#3 hole	.480	1.875	.085	1600

SECTION 25
CARBURETORS
HOLLEY

MODEL 6520
Chrysler Corporation

Year	Carb. Part No. ①	Accelerator Pump	Dry Float Level (in.)	Float Drop (in.)	Vacuum Kick (in.)	Fast Idle RPM
'82	R-9752A	#3 hole	.480	1.875	.100	1600
	R-9753A	#3 hole	.480	1.875	.100	1600
	R-9507A	#3 hole	.480	1.875	.085	1300
	R-9508A	#3 hole	.480	1.875	.085	1300
'83	R-40003A	#3 hole	.480	1.875	.070	1400
	R-40004A	#3 hole	.480	1.875	.080	1500
	R-40005A	#3 hole	.480	1.875	.080	1350
	R-40006A	#3 hole	.480	1.875	.080	1275
	R-40007A	#3 hole	.480	1.875	.070	1400
	R-40008A	#3 hole	.480	1.875	.070	1600
	R-40010A	#3 hole	.480	1.875	.080	1500
	R-40012A	#3 hole	.480	1.875	.070	1600
	R-40014A	#3 hole	.480	1.875	.080	1275
	R-40080A	#2 hole	.480	1.875	.045	1400
	R-40081A	#3 hole	.480	1.875	.045	1400
'84	R-400641A	#3 hole	.480	1.875	.080	1500
	R-400651A	#3 hole	.480	1.875	.080	1600
	R-400811A	#2 hole	.480	1.875	.080	1500
	R-400821A	#2 hole	.480	1.875	.080	1600
	R-40071A	#3 hole	.480	1.875	.080	1500
	R-40122A	#2 hole	.480	1.875	.080	1500
'85	R-40058A	#2 hole	.480	1.875	.070	1400
	R-40134A	#3 hole	.480	1.875	.075	1700
	R-40135A	#3 hole	.480	1.875	.075	1850
	R-40138A	#3 hole	.480	1.875	.075	1700
	R-40139A	#3 hole	.480	1.875	.075	1850
'86	R-40058-1A	—	.480	1.875	.070	③
	R-40134-A	—	.480	1.875	.075	③
	R-40135-1A	—	.480	1.875	.075	③
	R-40138-1A	—	.480	1.875	.075	③
	R-40139-1A	—	.480	1.875	.075	③

① Located on tag attached to the carburetor
② With radiator fan running
③ Refer to underhood sticker

Model 6145

FLOAT ADJUSTMENT

1. With the gasket in place invert the bowl and place a straight edge across the gasket surface. The portion of the floats, farthest from the fuel inlet, should just touch the straight edge.
2. If adjustment is necessary, bend the float tang.

CHOKE VACUUM KICK ADJUSTMENT

1. Open the throttle, close choke then close throttle so that the fast idle cam is at the closed position.
2. Disconnect the vacuum hose from the carburetor and connect to a hose of an auxiliary vacuum source with an extra length of tube. Apply a vacuum of 15 or more inches of mercury.
3. Apply light pressure on the choke lever to close the choke and measure the distance between the choke valve and the air horn wall on the throttle lever side with the specified gauge.
4. On 1981 models bend the diaphragm link at the U-bend to adjust on 1982–83 models insert a 5/64 in. Allen wrench into the choke diaphragm and turn to adjust the choke vacuum kick.
5. Reconnect the vacuum hose after adjustment.

FAST IDLE CAM ADJUSTMENT

1. Position the fast idle speed adjusting screw on the second highest step of the fast idle cam.
2. Using light pressure on the choke shaft lever, move the choke towards the closed position.
3. Insert the specified gauge between the top of the choke valve and the air horn wall at the throttle lever side.
4. If an adjustment is necessary, bend the fast idle connecting rod at the angle until the correct valve opening is obtained.

CARBURETORS
HOLLEY
SECTION 25

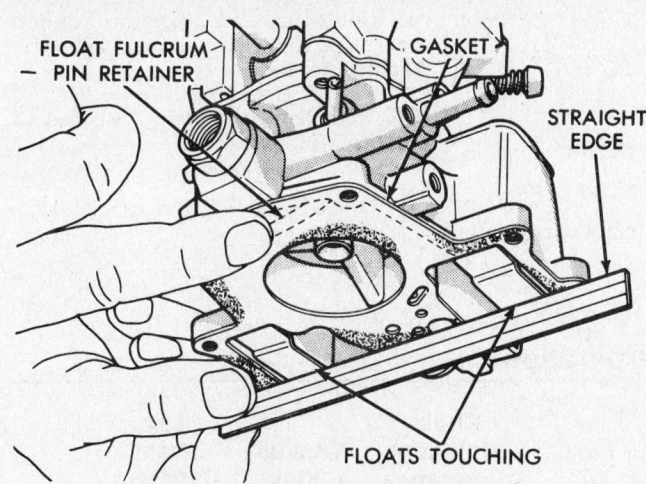
Float level adjustment—Holley 6145

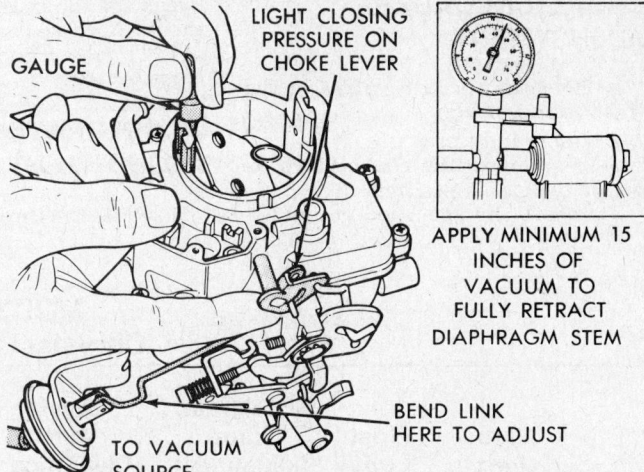
Choke vacuum kick adjustment, 1981—Holley 6145

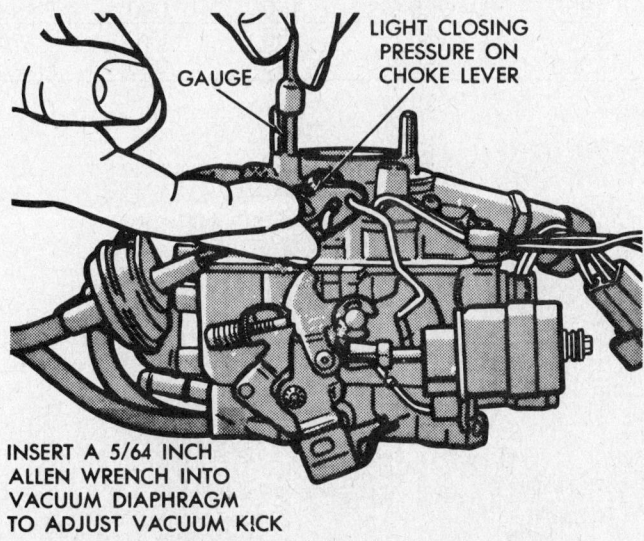
Choke vacuum kick adjustment, 1982–83—Holley 6145

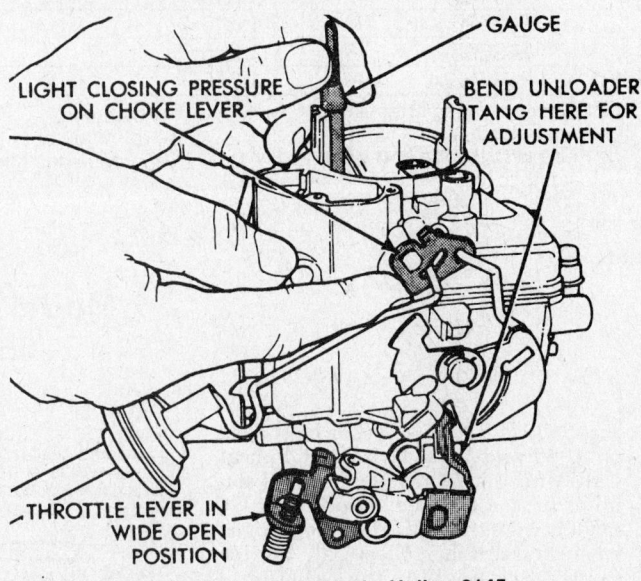
Choke unloader adjustment, typical—Holley 6145

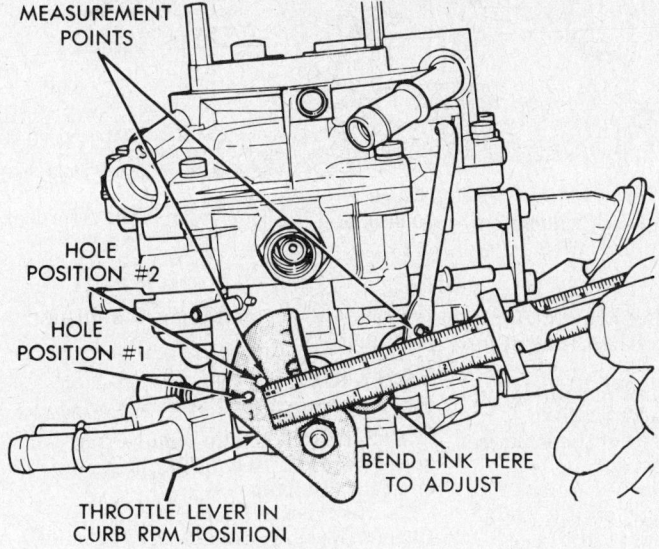
Accelerator pump adjustment, typical—Holley 6145

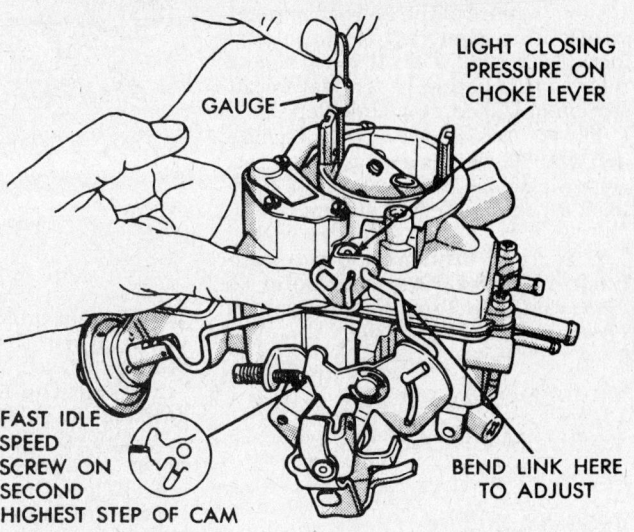
Fast idle cam adjustment, typical—Holley 6145

25–55

SECTION 25 CARBURETORS
HOLLEY

CHOKE UNLOADER ADJUSTMENT

1. Hold the throttle valves in the wide open position.
2. Using light pressure on the control lever, move the choke valve towards the closed position.
3. Insert the specified gauge between the top of the choke valve and the air horn wall.
4. To adjust bend the tang on the throttle lever.

ACCELERATOR PUMP ADJUSTMENT

1. Place the throttle in the curb idle position with the accelerator pump operating link in the proper slot in the throttle lever.
2. Measure the pump operating link and bend the link if needed to specifications.

MODEL 6145
Chrysler Corporation

Year	Carb. Part No. ①	Float Level (in.)	Accelerator Pump Adjustment (in.)	Bowl Vent Clearance (in.)	Fast Idle (rpm)	Choke Unloader Clearance (in.)	Vacuum Kick (in.)	Fast Idle Cam Position (in.)	Choke
'81	R-9129A	②	1.615 ③	④	2000	.250	.150	.090	Fixed
'82	R-9936A	②	1.616 ③	④	1950	.250	.150	.090	Fixed
	R-9695A	②	1.615 ③	④	1950 ⑤	.250	.150	.090	Fixed
'83	R-40042A	②	1.615 ③	④	2000	.250	.150	.090	Fixed

① Located on a tag attached to the carburetor
② Flush with the top of the main body casting to .050" above
③ Position #2
④ Not Adjustable
⑤ Cordoba and Mirada—2000 rpm

Model 6500 and 6510-C

The 6500 is a Holley-Weber Unit used on 1980 and later Pinto and Bobcat California models with the 2.3L engine. It is also used on all 1981–82 models with the 2.3L engine equipped with the Feedback Electronic Engine Control System. With the exception of an externally variable fuel metering system in place of the fuel enrichment valve, it is identical to the model Motorcraft 5200. For all adjustments, refer to this listing in the Motorcraft section of Carburetor Unit Repair.

The 6510-C is used on the Chevette and T-1000. This is a staged, two barrel unit which incorporates a feedback air/fuel metering system.

For further information on feedback carburetors, please refer to Chilton's Guide To Fuel Injection And Feedback Carburetors.

Vacuum break adjustment, 1980 and later—Holley 6510C

VACUUM BREAK ADJUSTMENT

1980–83 Models

1. Attach a hand vacuum pump to the vacuum break diaphragm. Apply vacuum until the diaphragm is seated.
2. Push the fast idle cam lever down to close the choke plate.
3. Take the slack out of the linkage in the open choke position.
4. Insert the specified gauge between the lower edge of the choke plate and the air horn wall.
5. If the clearance is incorrect, turn the screw in the end of the diaphragm to adjust.

FAST IDLE CAM ADJUSTMENT

1. Set the fast idle cam so that the screw is on the second highest step of the fast idle cam.
2. Insert the specified gauge between the lower edge of the choke valve and the air horn wall.

CARBURETORS
HOLLEY

SECTION 25

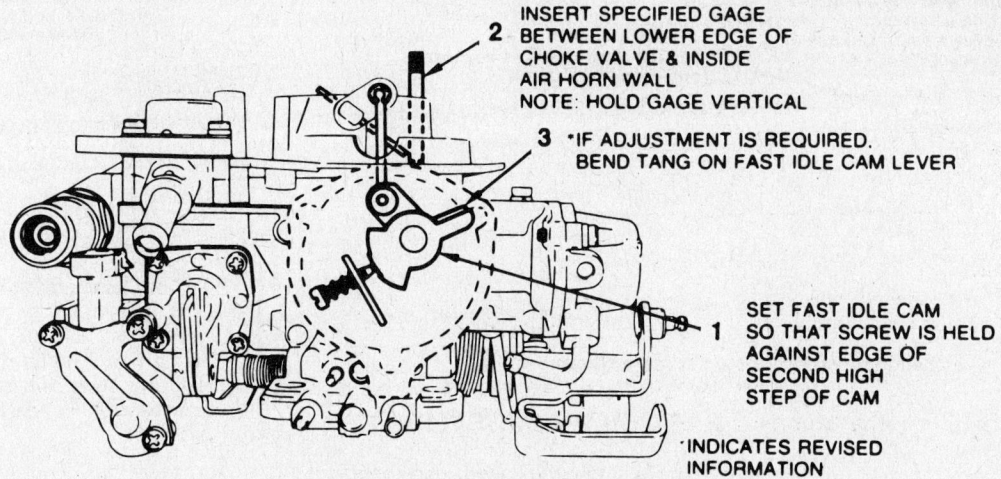

Fast idle cam adjustment—Holley 6510C

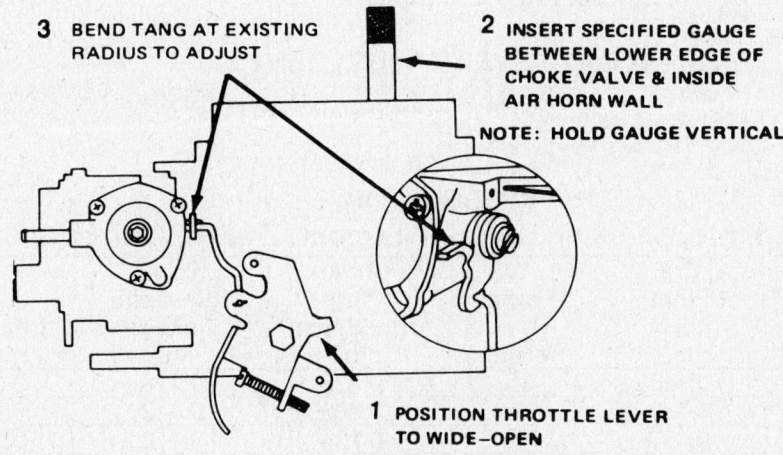

Choke unloader adjustment

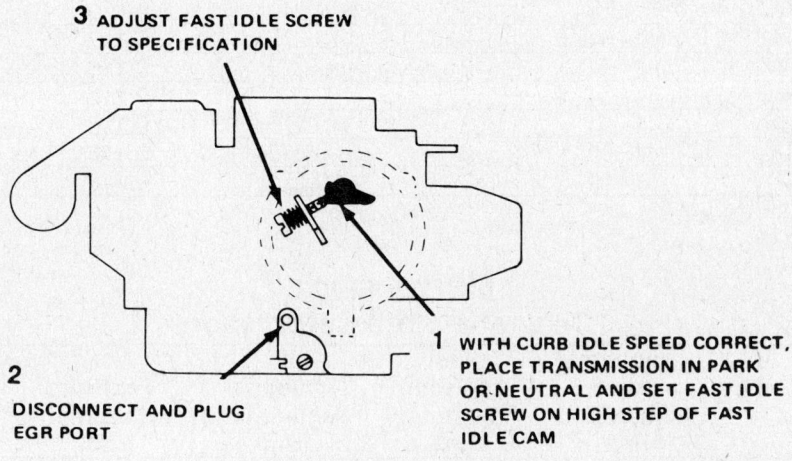

Fast idle speed adjustment

25-57

SECTION 25: CARBURETORS
HOLLEY

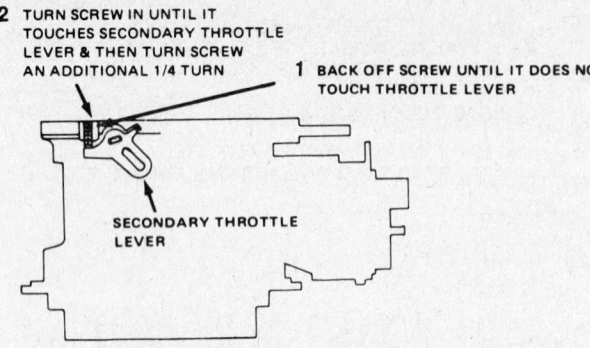

Secondary throttle stop screw adjustment

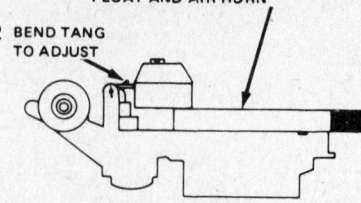

Float level adjustment

3. Bend the tang on the arm to adjust.

UNLOADER ADJUSTMENT

1. Place the throttle in the wide open position.
2. Insert a 0.350 inch gauge between the lower edge of the choke valve and the air horn wall.
3. Bend the tang on the choke arm to adjust.

FAST IDLE ADJUSTMENT

With the curb idle speed correct, place the fast idle screw on the highest cam step and adjust to the specified rpm.

NOTE: The EGR line must be disconnected and plugged.

FLOAT LEVEL ADJUSTMENT

1. Remove and invert the air horn.
2. Place the specified gauge between the air horn and the float.
3. If necessary, bend the float arm tang to adjust.

SECONDARY THROTTLE STOP SCREW ADJUSTMENT

1. Back off the screw until it does not touch the lever.
2. Turn the screw in until it touches the lever, then turn it an additional ¼ turn.

MODEL 6500
Ford Bobcat, Pinto, Mustang, Capri, Fairmont, Zephyr, Granada, Cougar

Year	Carburetor Identification	Dry Float Level (in.)	Pump Hole Setting	Choke Plate Pulldown (in.)	Fast Idle Cam Linkage (in.)	Dechoke (in.)	Choke Setting
'80	EOEE-NA, VA	0.460	2	0.236	0.118	0.393	①
	EOEE-NC, NV	0.460	2	0.236	0.118	0.157	①
	EOEE-ND, VD	0.460	2	0.236	0.118	0.393	①
	EOZE-AFA, SA	0.460	2	0.236	0.118	0.393	①
	EOZE-AFC, SC	0.460	—	0.236	0.118	0.393	①
'81	EIZE-RA	0.460	3	0.240	0.120	0.400	—
	EIZE-SA	0.460	3	0.240	0.120	0.400	—
	EIDE-DA	0.460	3	0.240	0.120	0.400	—
	EIDE-EA	0.460	3	0.240	0.120	0.400	—
'82	E2ZE-ARA	.41–.51	2	0.275	0.118	0.393	—
	E2ZE-APA	.41–.51	2	0.275	0.118	0.393	—
	E2ZE-VA	.41–.51	3	0.275	0.118	0.393	—
	E2ZE-ADA	.41–.51	3	0.275	0.118	0.393	—
	E2ZE-ACA	.41–.51	3	0.275	0.118	0.393	—
	E2ZE-UA	.41–.51	3	0.275	0.118	0.393	—

① See underhood decal

MODEL 6510-C
General Motors Corporation

Year	Part Number	Vacuum Break Adjustment (in.)	Fast Idle Cam Adjustment (in.)	Unloader Adjustment (in.)	Fast Idle Adjustment (rpm)	Float Level Adjustment (in.)	Choke Setting
'80	All w/manual	.275	.130	.350	2600	.500	Fixed
	All w/automatic	.300	.130	.350	2500	.500	Fixed

CARBURETORS
ROCHESTER
SECTION 25

MODEL 6510-C
General Motors Corporation

Year	Part Number	Vacuum Break Adjustment (in.)	Fast Idle Cam Adjustment (in.)	Unloader Adjustment (in.)	Fast Idle Adjustment (rpm)	Float Level Adjustment (in.)	Choke Setting
'81	14004768	.300	.130	.350	①	.500	Fixed
	14004769	.300	.130	.350	①	.500	Fixed
	14004770	.300	.130	.350	①	.500	Fixed
	14004771	.300	.130	.350	①	.500	Fixed
	14004777	.300	.130	.350	①	.500	Fixed
'82	14032364	.270	.080	.350	①	.500	Fixed
	14032365	.270	.080	.350	①	.500	Fixed
	14032366	.270	.080	.350	①	.500	Fixed
	14032367	.270	.080	.350	①	.500	Fixed
	14032368	.270	.080	.350	①	.500	Fixed
	14032369	.270	.080	.350	①	.500	Fixed
	14032370	.270	.080	.350	①	.500	Fixed
	14032371	.270	.080	.350	①	.500	Fixed
	14033392	.270	.080	.350	①	.500	Fixed
	14033393	.270	.080	.350	①	.500	Fixed
	14047072	.270	.080	.350	①	.500	Fixed
'83	14048827	.270	.080	.350	①	.500	Fixed
	14048828	.300	.080	.350	①	.500	Fixed
	14048829	.270	.080	.350	①	.500	Fixed
'84–'86	14068690	.270	.080	.350	①	.500	Fixed
	14068691	.270	.080	.350	①	.500	Fixed
	14068692	.300	.080	.350	①	.500	Fixed
	14076363	.300	.080	.350	①	.500	Fixed

① See underhood decal

ROCHESTER CARBURETORS

Angle Degree Tool

An angle degree tool is recommended by Rochester Products Division, for use to confirm adjustments to the choke valve and related linkages on their late model two and four barrel carburetors, in place of the plug type gauges. Decimal and degree conversion charts are provided for use by technicians who have access to an angle gauge and not plug gauges. It must be remembered that the relationship between the decimal and the angle readings are not exact, due to manufacturers tolerances.

To use the angle gauge, rotate the degree scale until zero (0) is opposite the pointer. With the choke valve completely closed, place the gauge magnet squarely on top of the choke valve and rotate the bubble until it is centered. Make the necessary adjustments to have the choke valve at the specified degree angle opening as read from the degree angle tool.

NOTE: The carburetor may be off the engine for adjustments. Be sure the carburetor is held firmly during the use of the angle gauge.

Model Identification

General Motors Rochester carburetors are identified by their model number. The first number indicates the number of barrels, while one of the last letters indicates the type of choke used. These are V for the manifold mounted choke coil, C for the choke coil mounted on the carburetor, and E for electric choke, also mounted on the carburetor. Model numbers ending in A indicate an altitude-compensating carburetor.

Models 2SE and E2SE

The Rochester 2SE and E2SE Varajet II carburetors are two barrel, two stage downdraft units. Most carburetor components are aluminum, although a zinc choke housing is used on four cylinder engines installed in 1980 models. The E2SE is used both in conventional installations and in the Computer Controlled Catalytic Converter System. In that installation the E2SE is equipped with an electrically operated mixture control solenoid, controlled by the Electronic Control Module. The 2SE and E2SE are also used on the AMC four cylinder in 1980–83.

For further information on feedback carburetors, please refer to *Chilton's Guide To Fuel Injection And Feedback Carburetors*.

FLOAT ADJUSTMENT

1. Remove the air horn from the throttle body.
2. Use your fingers to hold the retainer in place, and to push the float down into light contact with the needle.
3. Measure the distance from the toe of the float (furtherest from the hinge) to the top of the carburetor (gasket removed).

25-59

SECTION 25 CARBURETORS
ROCHESTER

ANGLE DEGREE TO DECIMAL CONVERSION
Model 4MV Carburetor

Angle Degrees	Decimal Equiv. Top of Valve	Angle Degrees	Decimal Equiv. Top of Valve
5	.019	33	.158
6	.022	34	.164
7	.026	35	.171
8	.030	36	.178
9	.034	37	.184
10	.038	38	.190
11	.042	39	.197
12	.047	40	.204
13	.051	41	.211
14	.056	42	.217
15	.060	43	.225
16	.065	44	.231
17	.070	45	.239
18	.075	46	.246
19	.080	47	.253
20	.085	48	.260
21	.090	49	.268
22	.095	50	.275
23	.101	51	.283
24	.106	52	.291
25	.112	53	.299
26	.117	54	.306
27	.123	55	.314
28	.128	56	.322
29	.134	57	.329
30	.140	58	.337
31	.146	59	.345
32	.152	60	.353

PLUGGING AIR BLEED HOLES

- PUMP CUP OR VALVE STEM SEAL
- TAPE HOLE IN TUBE
- TAPE END OF COVER

Vacuum break information—E2SE

4. To adjust, remove the float and gently bend the arm to specification. After adjustment, check the float alignment in the chamber.

NOTE: Some models have a float stabilizer spring. If used, remove the spring with float. Use care when removing.

PUMP ADJUSTMENT

1. With the throttle closed and the fast idle screw off the steps of the fast idle cam, measure the distance from the air horn casting to the top of the pump stem.

2. To adjust, remove the retaining screw and washer and remove the pump lever. Bend the end of the lever to correct the stem height. Do not twist the lever or bend it sideways.

3. Install the lever, washer and screw and check the adjustment. When correct, open and close the throttle a few times to check the linkage movement and alignment.

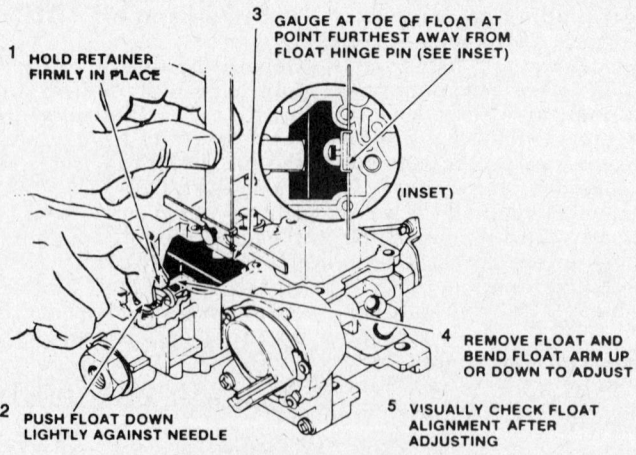

1. HOLD RETAINER FIRMLY IN PLACE
2. PUSH FLOAT DOWN LIGHTLY AGAINST NEEDLE
3. GAUGE AT TOE OF FLOAT AT POINT FURTHEST AWAY FROM FLOAT HINGE PIN (SEE INSET)
4. REMOVE FLOAT AND BEND FLOAT ARM UP OR DOWN TO ADJUST
5. VISUALLY CHECK FLOAT ALIGNMENT AFTER ADJUSTING

2SE, E2SE float adjustment

NOTE: No pump adjustment is required on 1981 and later models.

CARBURETORS
ROCHESTER

ANGLE DEGREE TO DECIMAL CONVERSION
Model M2MC, M2ME and M4MC Carburetor

Angle Degrees	Decimal Equiv. Top of Valve	Angle Degrees	Decimal Equiv. Top of Valve
5	.023	33	.203
6	.028	34	.211
7	.033	35	.220
8	.038	36	.227
9	.043	37	.234
10	.049	38	.243
11	.054	39	.251
12	.060	40	.260
13	.066	41	.269
14	.071	42	.277
15	.077	43	.287
16	.083	44	.295
17	.090	45	.304
18	.096	46	.314
19	.103	47	.322
20	.110	48	.332
21	.117	49	.341
22	.123	50	.350
23	.129	51	.360
24	.136	52	.370
25	.142	53	.379
26	.149	54	.388
27	.157	55	.400
28	.164	56	.408
29	.171	57	.418
30	.179	58	.428
31	.187	59	.439
32	.195	60	.449

NOTE: ON MODELS USING A CLIP TO RETAIN PUMP ROD IN PUMP LEVER, NO PUMP ADJUSTMENT IS REQUIRED. ON MODELS USING THE "CLIPLESS" PUMP ROD, THE PUMP ADJUSTMENT SHOULD NOT BE CHANGED FROM ORIGINAL FACTORY SETTING UNLESS GAUGING SHOWS OUT OF SPECIFICATION. THE PUMP LEVER IS MADE FROM HEAVY DUTY, HARDENED STEEL MAKING BENDING DIFFICULT. DO NOT REMOVE PUMP LEVER FOR BENDING UNLESS ABSOLUTELY NECESSARY.

1 THROTTLE VALVES COMPLETELY CLOSED. MAKE SURE FAST IDLE SCREW IS OFF STEPS OF FAST IDLE CAM.

3 IF NECESSARY TO ADJUST, REMOVE PUMP LEVER RETAINING SCREW AND WASHER AND REMOVE PUMP LEVER BY ROTATING LEVER TO REMOVE FROM PUMP ROD. PLACE LEVER IN A VISE, PROTECTING LEVER FROM DAMAGE, AND BEND END OF LEVER (NEAREST NECKED DOWN SECTION).

NOTE: DO NOT BEND LEVER IN A SIDEWAYS OR TWISTING MOTION.

2 GAUGE FROM AIR HORN CASTING SURFACE TO TOP OF PUMP STEM. DIMENSION SHOULD BE AS SPECIFIED.

5 OPEN AND CLOSE THROTTLE VALVES CHECKING LINKAGE FOR FREEDOM OF MOVEMENT AND OBSERVING PUMP LEVER ALIGNMENT.

4 REINSTALL PUMP LEVER, WASHER AND RETAINING SCREW. RECHECK PUMP ADJUSTMENT ① AND ②. TIGHTEN RETAINING SCREW SECURELY AFTER THE PUMP ADJUSTMENT IS CORRECT.

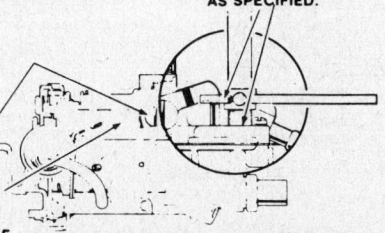

2SE, E2SE pump adjustment

FAST IDLE ADJUSTMENT

1. Set the ignition timing and curb idle speed, and disconnect and plug hoses as directed on the emission control decal.
2. Place the fast idle screw on the highest step of the cam.
3. Start the engine and adjust the engine speed to specification with the fast idle screw.

NOTE: On models using a clip to retain pump rod in pump lever, no pump adjustment is required. On models using the "CLIPLESS" pump rod, the pump rod adjustment should not be changed from the origional factory setting unless gauging shows out of specification. The pump lever is made from heavy duty, hardened steel making bending difficult. Do not remove pump lever for bendsing unless absolutely necessary.

CHOKE COIL LEVER ADJUSTMENT

1. Remove the three retaining screws and remove the choke cover and coil. On models with a riveted choke cover, drill out the three rivets and remove the cover and choke coil.

NOTE: A choke stat cover retainer kit is required for reassembly.

2. Place the fast idle screw on the high step of the cam.
3. Close the choke by pushing in on the intermediate choke lever. On front wheel drive models, the intermediate choke lever is behind the choke vacuum diaphragm.
4. Insert a drill or gauge of the specified size into the hole in the choke housing. The choke lever in the housing should be up against the side of the gauge.
5. If the lever does not just touch the gauge, bend the intermediate choke rod to adjust.

FAST IDLE CAM (CHOKE ROD) ADJUSTMENT

1980–82 Models

NOTE: A special angle gauge should be used.

1. Adjust the choke coil lever and fast idle first.
2. Rotate the degree scale until it is zeroed.
3. Close the choke and install the

SECTION 25
CARBURETORS
ROCHESTER

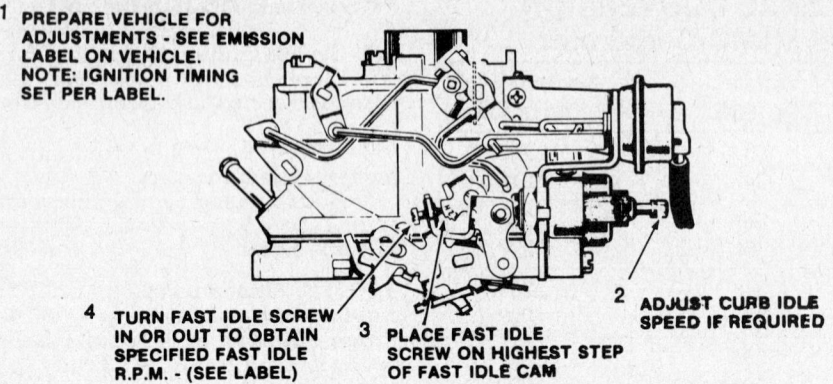

1. PREPARE VEHICLE FOR ADJUSTMENTS - SEE EMISSION LABEL ON VEHICLE. NOTE: IGNITION TIMING SET PER LABEL.
2. ADJUST CURB IDLE SPEED IF REQUIRED
3. PLACE FAST IDLE SCREW ON HIGHEST STEP OF FAST IDLE CAM
4. TURN FAST IDLE SCREW IN OR OUT TO OBTAIN SPECIFIED FAST IDLE R.P.M. - (SEE LABEL)

2SE, E2SE fast idle adjustment

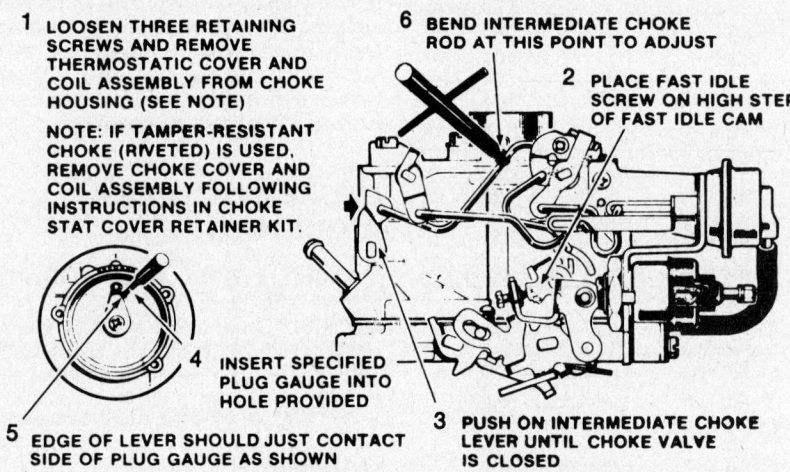

1. LOOSEN THREE RETAINING SCREWS AND REMOVE THERMOSTATIC COVER AND COIL ASSEMBLY FROM CHOKE HOUSING (SEE NOTE)

   NOTE: IF TAMPER-RESISTANT CHOKE (RIVETED) IS USED, REMOVE CHOKE COVER AND COIL ASSEMBLY FOLLOWING INSTRUCTIONS IN CHOKE STAT COVER RETAINER KIT.

2. PLACE FAST IDLE SCREW ON HIGH STEP OF FAST IDLE CAM
3. PUSH ON INTERMEDIATE CHOKE LEVER UNTIL CHOKE VALVE IS CLOSED
4. INSERT SPECIFIED PLUG GAUGE INTO HOLE PROVIDED
5. EDGE OF LEVER SHOULD JUST CONTACT SIDE OF PLUG GAUGE AS SHOWN
6. BEND INTERMEDIATE CHOKE ROD AT THIS POINT TO ADJUST

2SE, E2SE choke coil lever adjustment

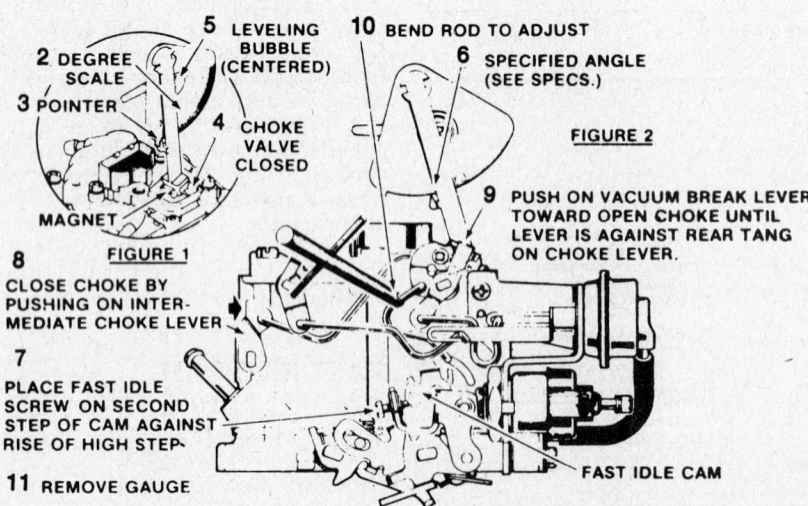

1. (see instructions)
2. DEGREE SCALE
3. POINTER
4. CHOKE VALVE CLOSED
5. LEVELING BUBBLE (CENTERED)
6. SPECIFIED ANGLE (SEE SPECS.)
7. PLACE FAST IDLE SCREW ON SECOND STEP OF CAM AGAINST RISE OF HIGH STEP
8. CLOSE CHOKE BY PUSHING ON INTERMEDIATE CHOKE LEVER
9. PUSH ON VACUUM BREAK LEVER TOWARD OPEN CHOKE UNTIL LEVER IS AGAINST REAR TANG ON CHOKE LEVER.
10. BEND ROD TO ADJUST
11. REMOVE GAUGE

MAGNET — FIGURE 1 — FIGURE 2 — FAST IDLE CAM

2SE, E2SE fast idle cam adjustment—models through 1982

degree scale onto the choke plate. Center the leveling bubble.

4. Rotate the scale so that the specified degree is opposite the scale pointer.

5. Place the fast idle screw on the second step of the cam (against the high step). Close the choke by pushing in the intermediate lever.

6. Push on the vacuum break lever

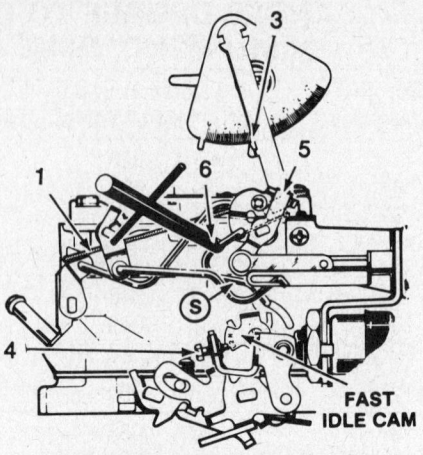

FAST IDLE CAM

1. ATTACH RUBBER BAND TO INTERMEDIATE CHOKE LEVER.
2. OPEN THROTTLE TO ALLOW CHOKE VALVE TO CLOSE.
3. SET UP ANGLE GAGE AND SET ANGLE TO SPECIFICATIONS.
4. PLACE FAST IDLE SCREW ON SECOND STEP OF CAM AGAINST RISE OF HIGH STEP.
5. PUSH ON CHOKE SHAFT LEVER TO OPEN CHOKE VALVE AND TO MAKE CONTACT WITH BLACK CLOSING TANG.
6. SUPPORT AT "S" AND ADJUST BY BENDING FAST IDLE CAM ROD UNTIL BUBBLE IS CENTERED.

E2SE fast idle cam (choke rod) adjustment—1983 and later

in the direction of opening choke until the lever is against the rear tang on the choke lever.

7. Bend the fast idle cam rod at the U to adjust angle to specifications.

1983–84 Models

Refer to the illustration for adjustment procedure on these models.

AIR VALVE ROD ADJUSTMENT

1980 Models

1. Seat the vacuum diaphragm with an outside vacuum source. Tape over the purge bleed hole if present.
2. Close the air valve.
3. Insert the specified gauge between the rod and the end of the slot in the plunger on fours, or between the rod and the end of the slot in the air valve on V6s.
4. Bend the rod to adjust the clearance.

1981–82 Models

1. Align the zero degree mark with the pointer on an angle gauge.

25-62

CARBURETORS
ROCHESTER

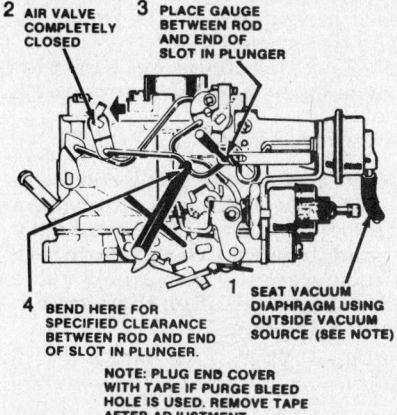

2SE and E2SE air valve rod adjustment—1980 G.M. models, 1980–82 American Motors

2. Close the air valve and place a magnet on top of it.
3. Rotate the bubble until it is centered.
4. Rotate the degree scale until the specified degree mark is aligned with the pointer.
5. Seat the vacuum diaphragm using an external vacuum source.
6. On four cylinder models plug the end cover. Unplug after adjustment.
7. Apply light pressure to the air valve shaft in the direction to open the air valve until all the slack is removed between the air link and plunger slot. 8. Bend the air valve link until the bubble is centered.

1983–84 Models

Refer to the illustration for the adjustment procedure on these models.

PRIMARY SIDE VACUUM BREAK ADJUSTMENT

1980 GM Models and 1980–83 AMC Models

1. Follow Steps 1–4 of the "Fast Idle Cam Adjustment" procedure.
2. Seat the choke vacuum diaphragm with an outside vacuum source.
3. Push in on the intermediate choke lever to close the choke valve, and hold closed during adjustment.
4. Adjust by bending the vacuum break rod until the bubble is centered.

1981–82 GM Models

NOTE: Prior to adjustment, remove the vacuum break from the carburetor. Place the bracket in a vise and using the proper safety precautions, grind off the adjustment screw cap then reinstall the vacuum break.

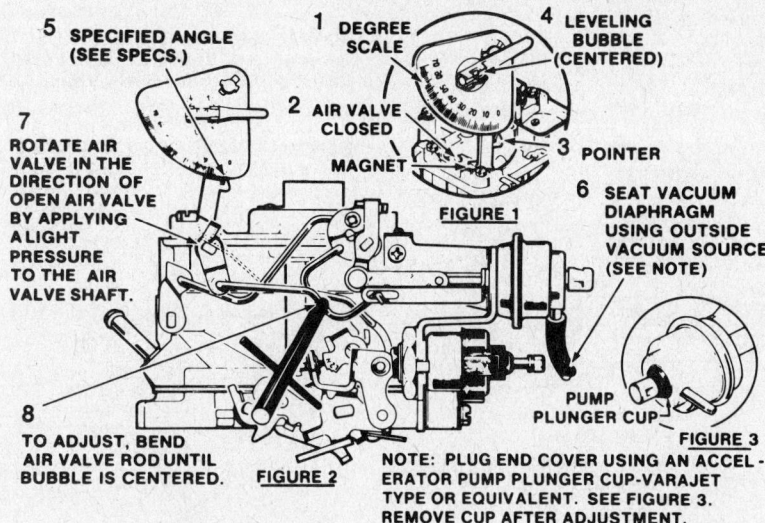

E2SE air valve adjustment—1981–82 4 cyl. except G.M. "J" series

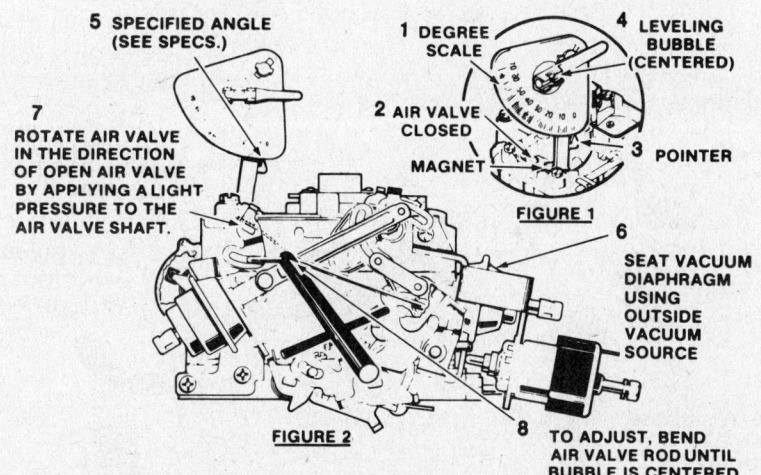

E2SE air valve adjustment—1981–82 V6 engine

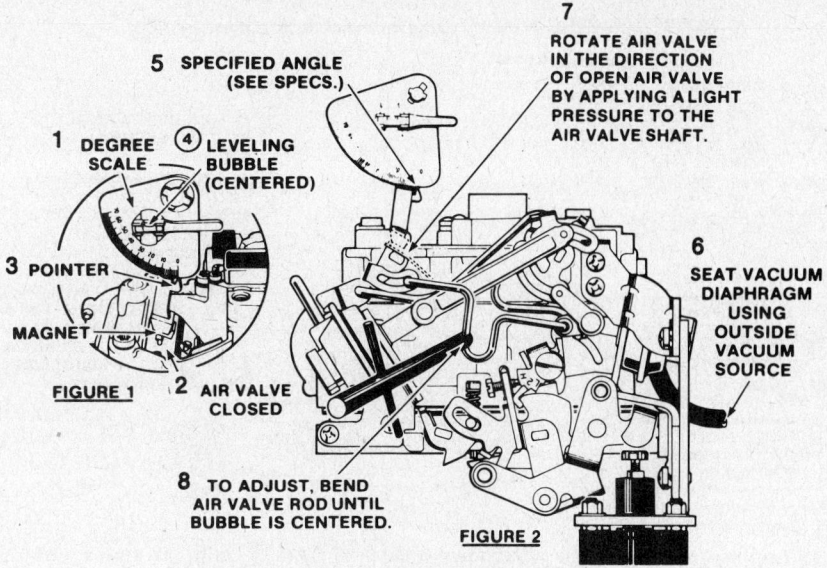

E2SE air valve adjustment—1982 G.M. J series

SECTION 25 CARBURETORS
ROCHESTER

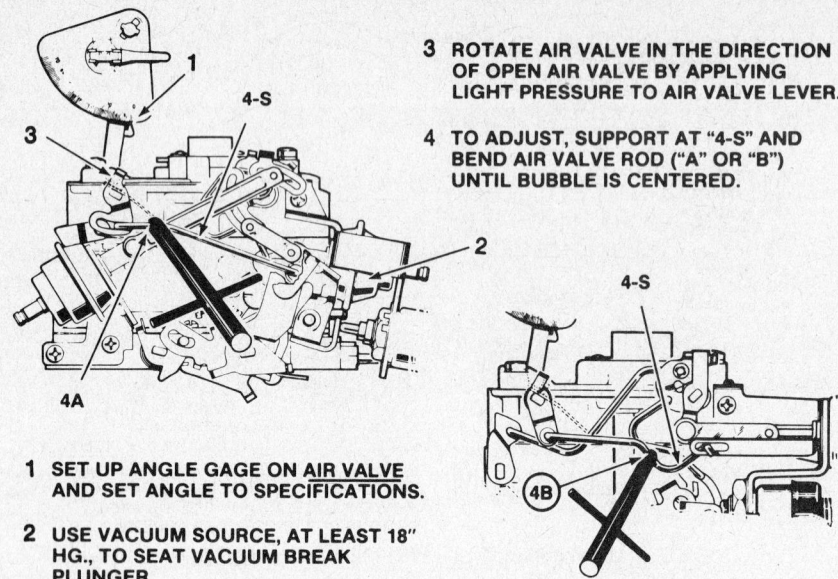

E2SE air valve rod adjustment—1983 and later

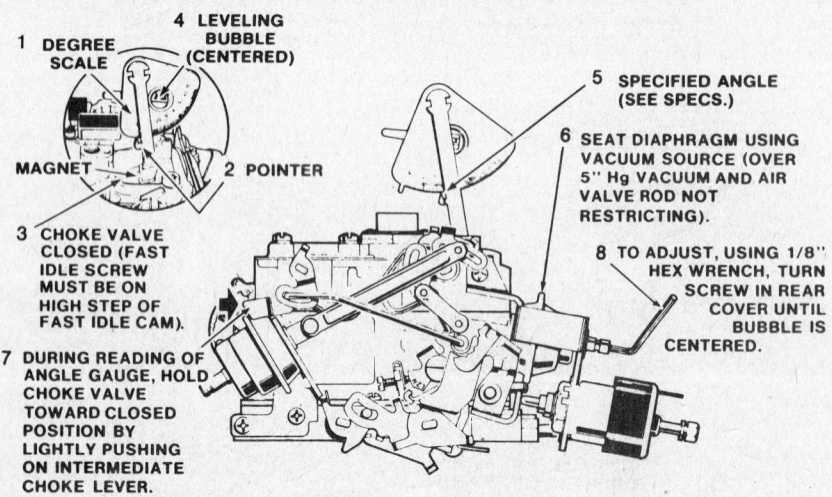

V6 2SE and E2SE primary vacuum break adjustment—1980

E2SE primary vacuum break adjustment—1981–82 G.M. "A" and "X" series with V6 engine

1. Rotate the degree scale on the measuring gauge until the zero is opposite the pointer.
2. Seat the choke vacuum diaphragm by applying an external vacuum source of over 5 in. Hg vacuum to the vacuum brake.

NOTE: If the air valve rod is restricting the vacuum diaphragm from seating it may be necessary to bend the air valve rod slightly to gain clearance. Make an air valve rod adjustment after the vacuum break adjustment.

3. Read the angle gauge while lightly pushing on the intermediate choke lever so that the choke valve is toward the close position.
4. Use a 1/8 in. hex wrench and turn the screw in the rear cover until the bubble is centered. Apply a silicone sealant over the screw head to seal the setting.

1983–84 GM Models
Refer to the illustration for the adjustment procedure on these models.

ELECTRIC CHOKE SETTING

This procedure is only for those carburetors with choke covers retained by screws. Riveted choke covers are preset and nonadjustable.
1. Loosen the three retaining screws.
2. Place the fast idle screw on the high step of the cam.
3. Rotate the choke cover to align the cover mark with the specified housing mark.

NOTE: The specification "index" which appears in the specification table refers to the mark between "1 notch lean" and "1 notch rich".

SECONDARY VACUUM BREAK ADJUSTMENT

1980 Models
This procedure is for V6 installations in front wheel drive models only.
1. Follow Steps 1–4 of the "Fast Idle Cam Adjustment" procedure.
2. Seat the choke vacuum diaphragm with an outside vacuum source.
3. Push in on the intermediate choke lever to close the choke valve, and hold closed during adjustment. Make sure the plunger spring is compressed and seated, if present.
4. Bend the vacuum break rod at the U next to the diaphragm until the bubble is centered.

CARBURETORS
ROCHESTER

NOTE: Prior to adjustment, remove the vacuum break from the carburetor. Place the bracket in the vise and using the proper safety precautions, grind off the adjustment screw cap then reinstall the vacuum break.

1981–82 GM Models

NOTE: Plug the end cover using an accelerator pump plunger cup or equivalent. Remove the cup after the adjustment (A and X series only).

1. Rotate the degree scale on the measuring gauge until the zero is opposite the pointer.

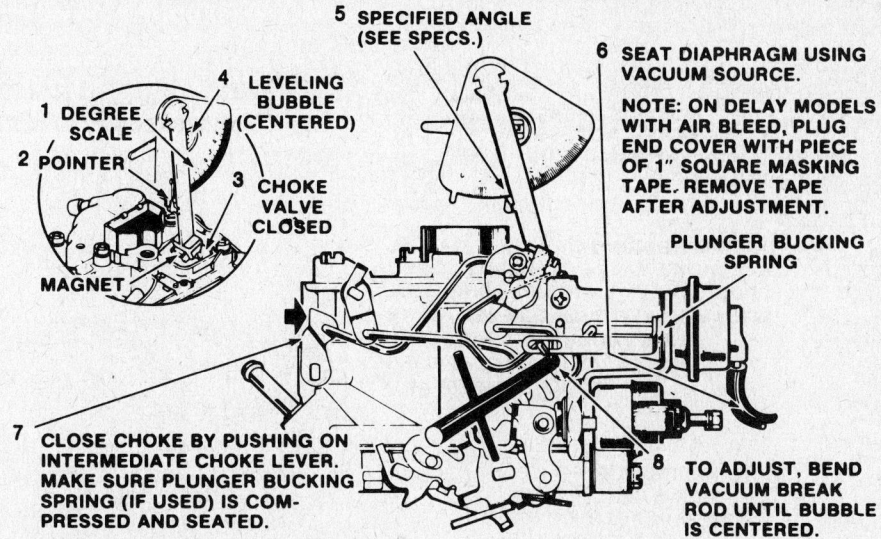

2SE, E2SE primary vacuum break adjustment—1980 G.M. and 1980–83 American Motors with 4 cyl. engines

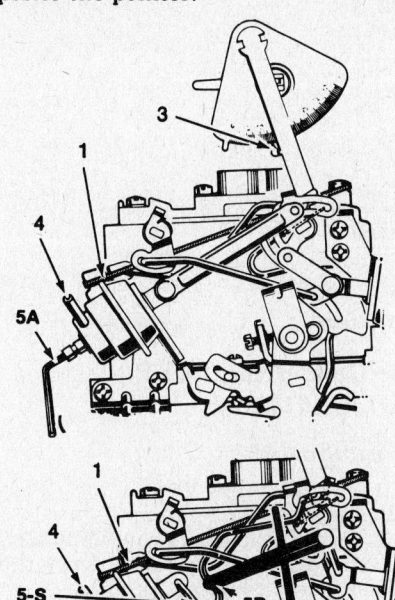

1. ATTACH RUBBER BAND TO INTERMEDIATE CHOKE LEVER.
2. OPEN THROTTLE TO ALLOW CHOKE VALVE TO CLOSE.
3. SET UP ANGLE GAGE AND SET ANGLE TO SPECIFICATION.
4. RETRACT VACUUM BREAK PLUNGER USING VACUUM SOURCE, AT LEAST 18" HG. PLUG AIR BLEED HOLES WHERE APPLICABLE.
   WHERE APPLICABLE, PLUNGER STEM MUST BE EXTENDED FULLY TO COMPRESS PLUNGER BUCKING SPRING.
5. TO CENTER BUBBLE, EITHER:
   A. ADJUST WITH 1/8" (3.175 mm) HEX WRENCH (VACUUM STILL APPLIED)
   -OR-
   B. SUPPORT AT "5-S", BEND WIRE-FORM VACUUM BREAK ROD (VACUUM STILL APPLIED)

E2SE secondary vacuum break adjustment—1983 and later

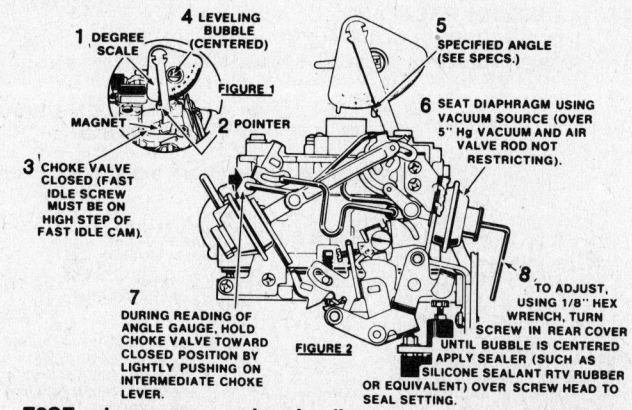

E2SE primary vacuum break adjustment—4 cyl.—1982 G.M. J series

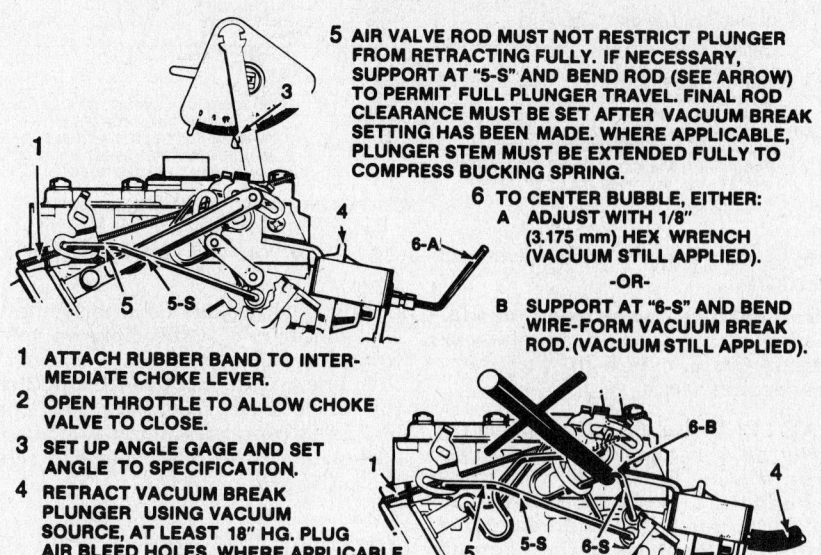

1. ATTACH RUBBER BAND TO INTERMEDIATE CHOKE LEVER.
2. OPEN THROTTLE TO ALLOW CHOKE VALVE TO CLOSE.
3. SET UP ANGLE GAGE AND SET ANGLE TO SPECIFICATION.
4. RETRACT VACUUM BREAK PLUNGER USING VACUUM SOURCE, AT LEAST 18" HG. PLUG AIR BLEED HOLES WHERE APPLICABLE.
5. AIR VALVE ROD MUST NOT RESTRICT PLUNGER FROM RETRACTING FULLY. IF NECESSARY, SUPPORT AT "5-S" AND BEND ROD (SEE ARROW) TO PERMIT FULL ROD PLUNGER TRAVEL. ROD CLEARANCE MUST BE SET AFTER VACUUM BREAK SETTING HAS BEEN MADE. WHERE APPLICABLE, PLUNGER STEM MUST BE EXTENDED FULLY TO COMPRESS BUCKING SPRING.
6. TO CENTER BUBBLE, EITHER:
   A. ADJUST WITH 1/8" (3.175 mm) HEX WRENCH (VACUUM STILL APPLIED).
   -OR-
   B. SUPPORT AT "6-S" AND BEND WIRE-FORM VACUUM BREAK ROD. (VACUUM STILL APPLIED).

E2SE primary vacuum break adjustment—1983 and later

SECTION 25: CARBURETORS — ROCHESTER

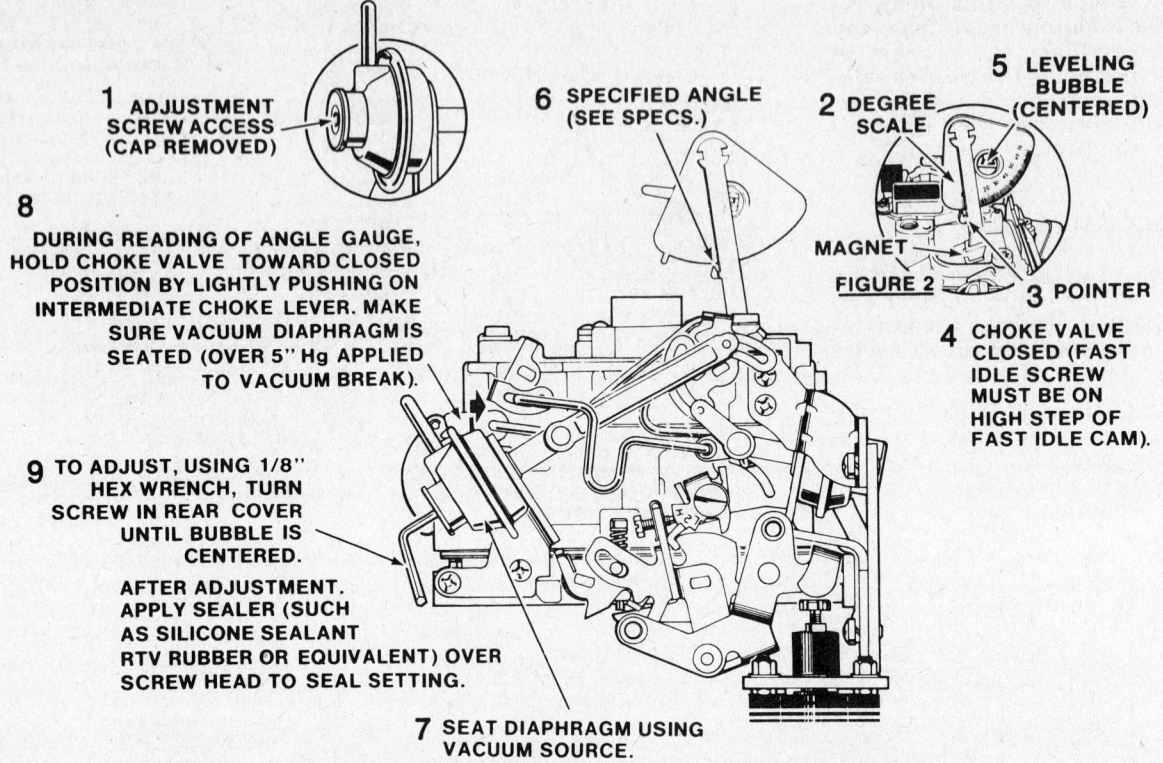

E2SE secondary vacuum break adjustment—1982 G.M. J series

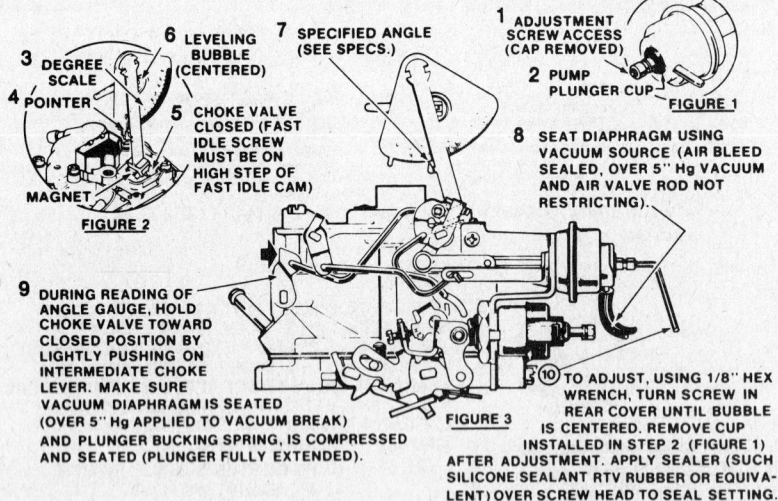

E2SE primary vacuum break adjustment—1981-82 G.M. "A" and "X" series with 4 cyl engine

2. Seat the choke vacuum diaphragm by applying an external vacuum source of over 5 in. vacuum to the vacuum break.

NOTE: If the air valve rod is restricting the vacuum diaphragm from seating it may be necessary to bend the air valve rod slightly to gain clearance. Make an air valve rod adjustment after the vacuum break adjustment.

3. Read the angle gauge while lightly pushing on the intermediate choke lever so that the choke valve is toward the close position.

4. Use a 1/8 in. hex wrench and turn the screw in the rear cover until the bubble is centered. Apply a silicone sealant over the screw head to seal the setting.

1983–84 GM Models

Refer to the illustration for the adjustment procedure on these models.

CHOKE UNLOADER ADJUSTMENT

Through 1982

1. Follow Steps 1–4 of the "Fast Idle Cam Adjustment" procedure.
2. Install the choke cover and coil, if removed, aligning the marks on the housing and cover as specified.
3. Hold the primary throttle wide open.
4. If the engine is warm, close the choke valve by pushing in on the intermediate choke lever.
5. Bend the unloader tang until the bubble is centered.

1983–84 Models

Refer to the illustration for the adjustment procedure on these models.

SECONDARY LOCKOUT ADJUSTMENT

1. Pull the choke wide open by pushing out on the intermediate choke lever.
2. Open the throttle until the end of the secondary actuating lever is opposite the toe of the lockout lever.
3. Gauge clearance between the lockout lever and secondary lever should be as specified.◊
4. To adjust, bend the lockout lever where it contacts the fast idle cam.

CARBURETORS
ROCHESTER

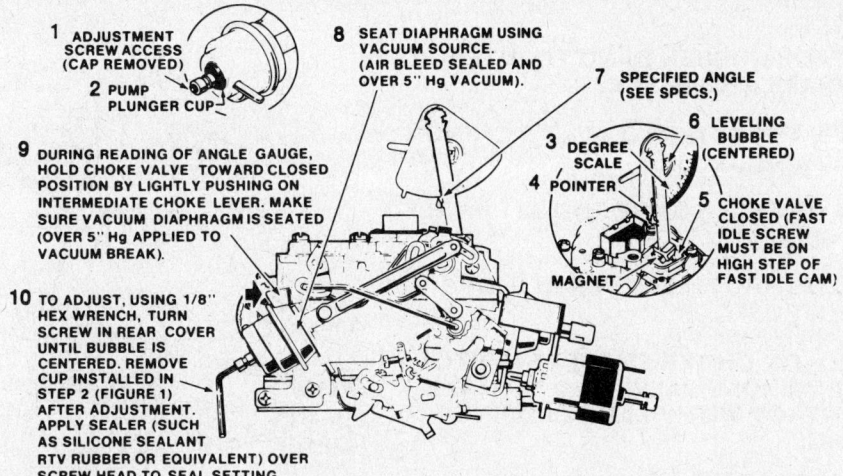

E2SE secondary vacuum break adjustment—1981 and later G.M. A and X series

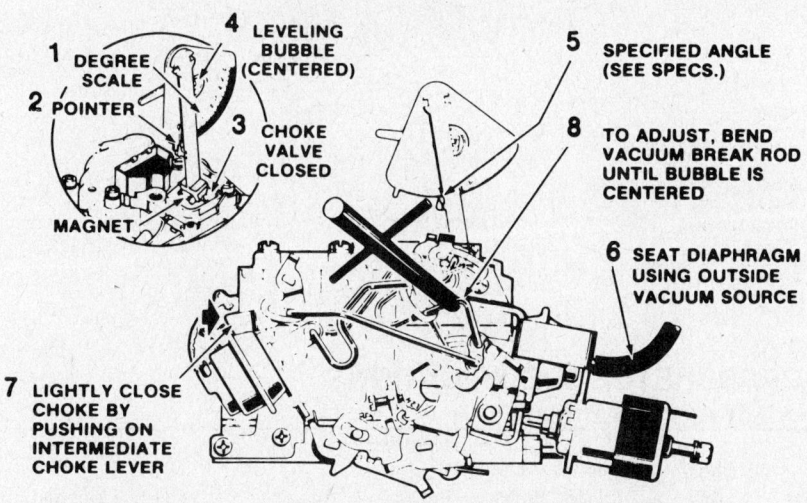

E2SE secondary vacuum break adjustment—1980 models

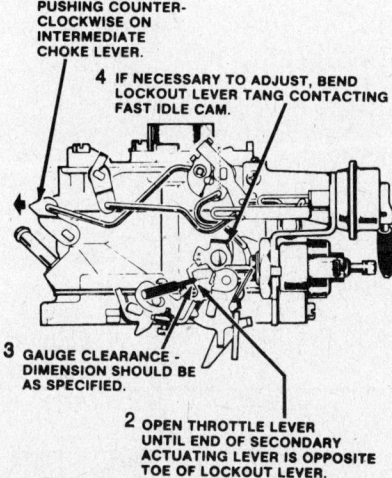

2SE and E2SE secondary lockout adjustment—typical

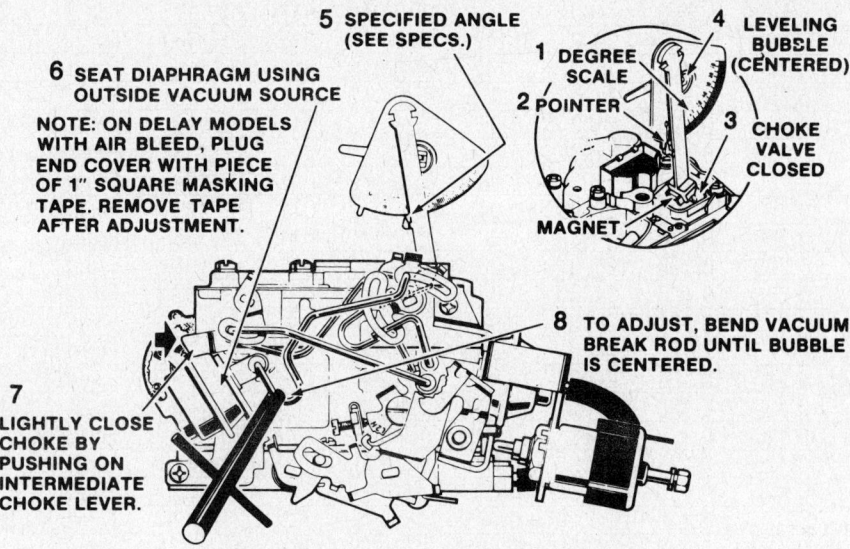

E2SE choke unloader adjuster—typical

SECTION 25

CARBURETORS
ROCHESTER

1. ATTACH RUBBER BAND TO INTERMEDIATE CHOKE LEVER.
2. OPEN THROTTLE TO ALLOW CHOKE VALVE TO CLOSE.
3. SET UP ANGLE GAGE AND SET ANGLE TO SPECIFICATIONS.
4. HOLD THROTTLE LEVER IN WIDE OPEN POSITION.
5. PUSH ON CHOKE SHAFT LEVER TO OPEN CHOKE VALVE AND TO MAKE CONTACT WITH BLACK CLOSING TANG.
6. ADJUST BY BENDING TANG UNTIL BUBBLE IS CENTERED.

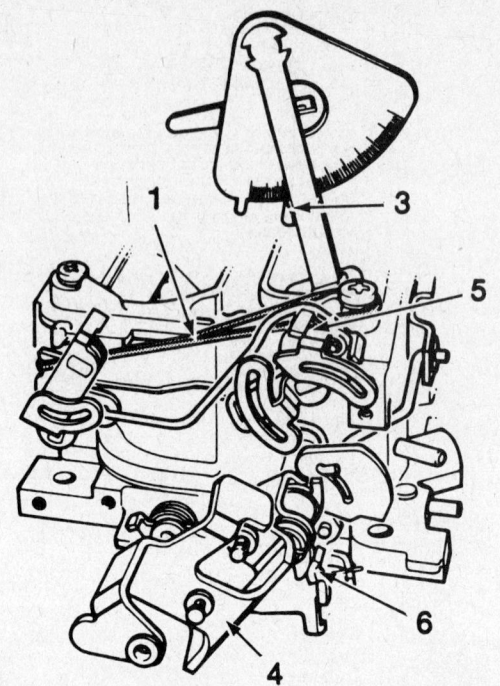

E2SE choke unloader adjustment—1983 and later

2SE, E2SE CARBURETOR SPECIFICATIONS
American Motors

Year	Carburetor Identification	Float Level (in.)	Pump Rod (in.)	Fast Idle (rpm)	Choke Coil Lever (in.)	Fast Idle Cam (deg./in.)	Air Valve Rod (in.)	Primary Vacuum Break (deg./in.)	Choke Setting (notches)	Choke Unloader (deg./in.)	Secondary Lockout (in.)
'80	17080681	3/16	17/32	2400	.142	18/0.096	.018	20/.110	Fixed	32/.195	N.A.
	17080683	3/16	1/2	2400	.142	18/0.096	.018	20/.110	Fixed	32/.195	N.A.
	17080686	3/16	1/2	2600	.142	18/0.096	.018	20/.110	Fixed	32/.195	N.A.
	17080688	3/16	1/2	2600	.142	18/0.096	.018	20/.110	Fixed	32/.195	N.A.
'81	17081790	0.256	0.128	2600	0.085	25/0.142	.011	19/.103	Fixed	32/.195	0.065
	17081791	0.256	0.128	2400	0.085	25/0.142	.011	19/.103	Fixed	32/.195	0.065
	17081792	0.256	0.128	2400	0.085	25/0.142	.011	19/.103	Fixed	32/.195	0.065
	17081794	0.256	0.128	2600	0.085	25/0.142	.011	19/.103	Fixed	32/.195	0.065
	17081795	0.256	0.128	2600	0.085	25/0.142	.011	19/.103	Fixed	32/.195	0.065
	17081796	0.208	0.128	2400	0.065	25/0.142	.011	19/.103	Fixed	32/.195	0.065
	17081797	0.208	0.128	2600	0.085	25/0.142	.011	19/.103	Fixed	32/.195	0.085
	17081793	0.256	0.128	2400	0.085	25/0.142	.011	19/.103	Fixed	32/.195	0.065
'82	17082385	0.256	0.128	2400	0.085	18/096	2①	21/117	Fixed	34/.211	0.065
	17082383	0.256	0.128	2400	0.085	18/096	2①	21/117	Fixed	34/.211	0.065
	17082380	0.216	0.128	2400	0.085	18/096	2①	21/117	Fixed	34/.211	0.065
	17082386	0.125	0.128	2400	0.065	18/096	2①	19/103	Fixed	34/.211	0.065
	17082387	0.125	0.128	2600	0.085	18/096	2①	19/103	Fixed	34/.211	0.065
	17082388	0.125	0.128	2500	0.085	18/096	2①	19/103	Fixed	34/.211	0.065
	17082389	0.125	0.128	2500	0.085	18/096	2①	19/103	Fixed	34/.211	0.065
'83–'84	1982380	0.216②	0.128	2500③	0.085	18/096	2①	21/117	Fixed	34/.211	0.065
	1983384	0.138	0.128	2700	0.085	18/096	2①	19/103	Fixed	34/.211	0.065
	1983385	0.138	0.128	2700	0.085	18/096	②①	19/103	Fixed	34/.211	0.065

CARBURETORS
ROCHESTER

2SE, E2SE CARBURETOR SPECIFICATIONS
American Motors

Year	Carburetor Identification	Float Level (in.)	Pump Rod (in.)	Fast Idle (rpm)	Choke Coil Lever (in.)	Fast Idle Cam (deg./in.)	Air Valve Rod (in.)	Primary Vacuum Break (deg./in.)	Choke Setting (notches)	Choke Unloader (deg./in.)	Secondary Lockout (in.)
'85–'86	17085006	4/32	0.128	④	0.085	22/.123	1①	21/.117	Fixed	40/.260	0.025
	17085380	5/32	0.128	④	0.085	22/.123	1①	26/.149	Fixed	40/.260	0.025
	17085381	5/32	0.128	④	0.085	22/.123	1①	26/.149	Fixed	40/.260	0.025
	17085382	5/32	0.128	④	0.085	22/.123	1①	26/.149	Fixed	40/.260	0.025
	17085383	5/32	0.128	④	0.085	22/.123	1①	26/.149	Fixed	40/.260	0.025
	17085385	5/32	0.128	④	0.085	22/.123	1①	26/.149	Fixed	40/.260	0.025
	17085388	4/32	0.128	④	0.085	22/.123	1①	21/.117	Fixed	30/.179	0.025
	17086081	4/32	0.128	④	0.085	22/.123	1①	25/.142	Fixed	30/.179	0.025

N.A.: Not Available
① Degrees—see procedure
② Auto. trans.—.138
③ Auto. trans.—2700
④ See underhood decal

2SE, E2SE CARBURETOR SPECIFICATIONS
General Motors—U.S.A.

Year	Carburetor Identification	Float Level (in.)	Pump Rod (in.)	Fast Idle (rpm)	Choke Coil Lever (in.)	Fast Idle Cam (deg./in.)	Air Valve Rod (in.)	Primary Vacuum Break (deg./in.)	Choke Setting (notches)	Secondary Vacuum Break (deg./in.)	Choke Unloader (deg./in.)	Secondary Lockout (in.)
'80	17059614	3/16	1/2	2600	.085	18/.096	.025	17/.090	Fixed	—	36/.227	.120
	17059615	3/16	5/32	2600	.085	18/.096	.025	19/.103	Fixed	—	36/.227	.120
	17059616	3/16	1/2	2600	.085	18/.096	.025	17/.090	Fixed	—	36/.227	.120
	17059617	3/16	5/32	2600	.085	18/.096	.025	19/.103	Fixed	—	36/.227	.120
	17059618	3/16	1/2	2600	.085	18/.096	.025	17/.090	Fixed	—	36/.227	.120
	17059619	3/16	5/32	2600	.085	18/.096	.025	19/.103	Fixed	—	36/.227	.120
	17059620	3/16	1/2	2600	.085	18/.096	.025	17/.090	Fixed	—	36/.227	.120
	17059621	3/16	5/32	2600	.085	18/.096	.025	19/.103	Fixed	—	36/.227	.120
	17059650	3/16	3/32	2600	.085	27/.157	.025	30/.179	Fixed	38/.243	30/.179	.120
	17059651	3/16	3/32	1900	.085	27/.157	.025	22/.123	Fixed	23/.120	30/.179	.120
	17059652	3/16	3/32	2000	.085	27/.157	.025	30/.179	Fixed	38/.243	30/.179	.120
	17059653	3/16	3/32	1900	.085	27/.157	.025	22/.123	Fixed	23/.120	30/.179	.120
	17059714	11/16	5/32	2600	.085	18/.096	.025	23/.129	Fixed	—	32/.195	.120
	17059715	11/16	3/32	2200	.085	18/.096	.025	25/.142	Fixed	—	32/.195	.120
	17059716	11/16	5/32	2600	.085	18/.096	.025	23/.129	Fixed	—	32/.195	.120
	17059717	11/16	3/32	2200	.085	18/.096	.025	25/.142	Fixed	—	32/.195	.120
	17059760	1/8	5/64	2000	.085	17.5/.093	.025	20/.110	Fixed	33/.203	35/.220	.120
	17059762	1/8	5/64	2000	.085	17.5/.093	.025	20/.110	Fixed	33/.203	35/.220	.120
	17059763	1/8	5/64	2000	.085	17.5/.093	.025	20/.110	Fixed	33/.203	35/.220	.120
	17059774	5/32	1/2	①	.085	18/0.096	.018	19/.103	Fixed	—	32/.195	.012
	17059775	5/32	17/32	①	.085	18/0.096	.018	21/.117	Fixed	—	32/.195	.012
	17059776	5/32	1/2	①	.085	18/0.096	.018	19/.103	Fixed	—	32/.195	.012
	17059777	5/32	17/32	①	.085	18/0.096	.018	21/.117	Fixed	—	32/.195	.012
	17080674	3/16	1/2	①	.085	18/0.096	.018	19/.103	Fixed	—	32/.195	.012
	17080675	3/16	1/2	①	.085	18/0.096	.018	21/.117	Fixed	—	32/.195	.012
	17080676	3/16	1/2	①	.085	18/0.096	.018	19/.103	Fixed	—	32/.195	.012
	17080677	3/16	1/2	①	.085	18/0.096	.018	21/.117	Fixed	—	32/.195	.012
'81	17081650	1/4	Fixed	2600	.085	17/.090	1②	25/.142	Fixed	34/.211	35/.220	.012
	17081651	1/4	Fixed	2400	.085	17/.090	1②	29/.171	Fixed	35/.220	35/.220	.012
	17081652	1/4	Fixed	2600	.085	17/.090	1②	25/.142	Fixed	34/.211	35/.220	.012
	17081653	1/4	Fixed	2600	.085	17/.090	1②	29/.171	Fixed	35/.220	35/.220	.012
	17081670	5/32	Fixed	2600	.085	18/.096	1②	19/.103	Fixed	—	32/.195	.012
	17081671	5/32	Fixed	2600	.085	33.5/.207	1②	21/.117	Fixed	—	32/.195	.012

CARBURETORS
ROCHESTER

2SE, E2SE CARBURETOR SPECIFICATIONS
General Motors—U.S.A.

Year	Carburetor Identification	Float Lever (in.)	Pump Rod (in.)	Fast Idle (rpm)	Choke Coil Lever (in.)	Fast Idle Cam (deg./in.)	Air Valve Rod (in.)	Primary Vacuum Break (deg./in.)	Choke Setting (notches)	Secondary Vacuum Break (deg./in.)	Choke Unloader (deg./in.)	Secondary Lockout (in.)
'81	17081672	5/32	Fixed	2600	.085	18/.096	1 ②	19/.103	Fixed	—	32/.195	.012
	17081673	5/32	Fixed	2600	.085	33.4/.207	1 ②	21/.117	Fixed	—	32/.195	.012
	17081740	1/4	Fixed	2400	.085	17/.090	1 ②	25/.142	Fixed	35/.220	35/.220	.012
	17081742	1/4	Fixed	2400	.085	17/.090	1 ②	25/.142	Fixed	35/.220	35/.220	.012
'82	17081600	5/16	Fixed	①	③	24/.136	1 ②	20/.110	Fixed	27/.157	35/.220	③
	17081601	5/16	Fixed	①	③	24/1.36	1 ②	20/.110	Fixed	27/.157	35/.220	③
	17081607	5/16	Fixed	①	③	24/.136	1 ②	20/.110	Fixed	27/.157	35/.220	③
	17081700	5/16	Fixed	①	③	24/.136	1 ②	20/.110	Fixed	27/.157	35/.220	③
	17081701	5/16	Fixed	①	③	24/.136	1 ②	20/.110	Fixed	27/.157	35/.220	③
	17082196	5/16	Fixed	①	.085	18/.096	1 ②	21/.117	Fixed	19/.103	27/.157	③
	17082316	1/4	Fixed	2600	.085	17/.090	1 ②	30/.179	Fixed	34/.211	45/.304	③
	17082317	1/4	Fixed	2600	.085	17/.090	1 ②	30/.179	Fixed	35/.220	45/.304	③
	17082320	1/4	Fixed	2800	.085	25/.142	1 ②	30/.179	Fixed	35/.220	45/.304	③
	17082321	1/4	Fixed	2600	.085	25/.142	1 ②	30/.179	Fixed	35/.220	45/.304	③
	17082390	13/32	Fixed	2500	.085	17/.090	1 ②	26/.149	Fixed	34/.211	35/.220	.011-.040
	17082391	13/32	Fixed	2600	.085	25/.142	1 ②	29/.171	Fixed	35/.220	35/.220	.011-.040
	17082490	13/32	Fixed	2500	.085	17/.090	1 ②	26/.149	Fixed	34/.211	35/.220	.011-.040
	17082491	13/32	Fixed	2600	.085	25/.142	1 ②	29/.171	Fixed	35/.220	35/.220	.011-.040
	17082640	1/4	Fixed	2600	.085	17/.090	1 ②	30/.179	Fixed	34/.211	45/.304	③
	17082641	1/4	Fixed	2400	.085	17/.090	1 ②	30/.179	Fixed	35/.220	45/.304	③
	17082642	1/4	Fixed	2800	.085	25/.142	1 ②	30/.179	Fixed	35/.220	45/.304	③
'83	17083356	13/32	Fixed	①	.085	22/.123	1 ②	25/.142	Fixed	35/.220	30/.179	.025
	17083357	13/32	Fixed	①	.085	22/.123	1 ②	25/.142	Fixed	35/.220	30/.179	.025
	17083358	13/32	Fixed	①	.085	22/.123	1 ②	25/.142	Fixed	35/.220	30/.179	.025
	17083359	13/32	Fixed	①	.085	22/.123	1 ②	25/.142	Fixed	35/.220	30/.179	.025
	17083368	13/32	Fixed	①	.085	22/.123	1 ②	25/.142	Fixed	35/.220	30/.179	.025
	17083369	13/32	Fixed	①	.085	22/.123	1 ②	25/.142	Fixed	35/.220	30/.179	.025
	17083370	13/32	Fixed	①	.085	22/.123	1 ②	25/.142	Fixed	35/.220	30/.179	.025
	17083391	13/32	Fixed	①	.085	28/.164	1 ②	30/.179	Fixed	35/.220	38/.243	.025
	17083392	13/32	Fixed	①	.085	28/.164	1 ②	30/.179	Fixed	35/.220	38/.243	.025
	17083393	13/32	Fixed	①	.085	28/.164	1 ②	30/.179	Fixed	35/.220	38/.243	.025
	17083394	13/32	Fixed	①	.085	28/.164	1 ②	30/.179	Fixed	35/.220	38/.243	.025
	17083395	13/32	Fixed	①	.085	28/.164	1 ②	30/.179	Fixed	35/.220	38/.243	.025
	17083396	13/32	Fixed	①	.085	28/.164	1 ②	30/.179	Fixed	35/.220	38/.243	.025
	17083397	13/32	Fixed	①	.085	28/.164	1 ②	30/.179	Fixed	35/.220	38/.243	.025
	17083450	1/4	Fixed	①	.085	28/.164	1 ②	27/.157	Fixed	35/.220	45/.304	.025
	17083451	1/4	Fixed	①	.085	28/.164	1 ②	27/.157	Fixed	35/.220	45/.304	.025
	17083452	1/4	Fixed	①	.085	28/.164	1 ②	27/.157	Fixed	35/.220	45/.304	.025
	17083453	1/4	Fixed	①	.085	28/.164	1 ②	27/.157	Fixed	35/.220	45/.304	.025
	17083454	1/4	Fixed	①	.085	28/.164	1 ②	27/.157	Fixed	35/.220	45/.304	.025
	17083455	1/4	Fixed	①	.085	28/.164	1 ②	27/.157	Fixed	35/.220	45/.304	.025
	17083456	1/4	Fixed	①	.085	28/.164	1 ②	27/.157	Fixed	35/.220	45/.304	.025
	17083630	1/4	Fixed	①	.085	28/.164	1 ②	27/.157	Fixed	35/.220	45/.304	.025
	17083631	1/4	Fixed	①	.085	28/.164	1 ②	27/.157	Fixed	35/.220	45/.304	.025
	17083632	1/4	Fixed	①	.085	28/.164	1 ②	27/.157	Fixed	35/.220	45/.304	.025
	17083633	1/4	Fixed	①	.085	28/.164	1 ②	27/.157	Fixed	35/.220	45/.304	.025
	17083634	1/4	Fixed	①	.085	28/.164	1 ②	27/.157	Fixed	35/.220	45/.304	.025
	17083635	1/4	Fixed	①	.085	28/.164	1 ②	27/.157	Fixed	35/.220	45/.304	.025
	17083636	1/4	Fixed	①	.085	28/.164	1 ②	27/.157	Fixed	35/.220	45/.304	.025
'84	17072683	9/32	Fixed	①	.085	28/.164	1 ②	25/.142	Fixed	35/.220	45/.304	.025
	17074812	9/32	Fixed	①	.085	28/.164	1 ②	25/.142	Fixed	35/.220	45/.304	.025
	17084356	9/32	Fixed	①	.085	22/.123	1 ②	25/.142	Fixed	30/.179	30/.179	.025
	17084357	9/32	Fixed	①	.085	22/.123	1 ②	25/.142	Fixed	30/.179	30/.179	.025
	17084358	9/32	Fixed	①	.085	22/.123	1 ②	25/.142	Fixed	30/.179	30/.179	.025

CARBURETORS
ROCHESTER

2SE, E2SE CARBURETOR SPECIFICATIONS
General Motors—U.S.A.

Year	Carburetor Identification	Float Lever (in.)	Pump Rod (in.)	Fast Idle (rpm)	Choke Coil Lever (in.)	Fast Idle Cam (deg./in.)	Air Valve Rod (in.)	Primary Vacuum Break (deg./in.)	Choke Setting (notches)	Secondary Vacuum Break (deg./in.)	Choke Unloader (deg./in.)	Secondary Lockout (in.)
'84	17084359	9/32	Fixed	①	.085	22/.123	1 ②	25/.142	Fixed	30/.179	30/.179	.025
	17084368	1/8	Fixed	①	.085	22/.123	1 ②	25/.142	Fixed	30/.179	30/.179	.025
	17084370	1/8	Fixed	①	.085	22/.123	1 ②	25/.142	Fixed	30/.179	30/.179	.025
	17084430	11/32	Fixed	①	.085	15/.077	1 ②	26/.149	Fixed	30/.179	30/.179	.025
	17084431	11/32	Fixed	①	.085	15/.077	1 ②	26/.149	Fixed	38/.243	42/.277	.025
	17084434	11/32	Fixed	①	.085	15/.077	1 ②	26/.149	Fixed	38/.243	42/.277	.025
	17084435	11/32	Fixed	①	.085	15/.077	1 ②	26/.149	Fixed	38/.243	42/.277	.025
	17084452	5/32	Fixed	①	.085	28/.164	1 ②	25/.142	Fixed	38/.243	42/.377	.025
	17084453	5/32	Fixed	①	.085	28/.164	1 ②	25/.142	Fixed	35/.220	45/.304	.025
	17084455	5/32	Fixed	①	.085	28/.164	1 ②	25/.142	Fixed	35/.220	45/.304	.025
	17084456	5/32	Fixed	①	.085	28/.164	1 ②	25/.142	Fixed	35/.220	45/.304	.025
	17084458	5/32	Fixed	①	.085	28/.164	1 ②	25/.142	Fixed	35/.220	45/.304	.025
	17084532	5/32	Fixed	①	.085	28/.164	1 ②	25/.142	Fixed	35/.220	45/.304	.025
	17084534	5/32	Fixed	①	.085	28/.164	1 ②	25/.142	Fixed	35/.220	45/.304	.025
	17084535	5/32	Fixed	①	.085	28/.164	1 ②	25/.142	Fixed	35/.220	45/.304	.025
	17084537	5/32	Fixed	①	.085	28/.164	1 ②	25/.142	Fixed	35/.220	45/.304	.025
	17084538	5/32	Fixed	①	.085	28/.164	1 ②	25/.142	Fixed	35/.220	45/.304	.025
	17084540	5/32	Fixed	①	.085	28/.164	1 ②	25/.142	Fixed	35/.220	45/.304	.025
	17084542	1/8	Fixed	①	.085	28/.164	1 ②	25/.142	Fixed	35/.220	45/.304	.025
	17084632	9/32	Fixed	①	.085	28/.164	1 ②	25/.142	Fixed	35/.220	45/.304	.025
	17084633	9/32	Fixed	①	.085	28/.164	1 ②	25/.142	Fixed	35/.220	45/.304	.025
	17084635	9/32	Fixed	①	.085	28/.164	1 ②	25/.142	Fixed	35/.220	45/.304	.025
	17084636	9/32	Fixed	①	.085	28/.164	1 ②	25/.142	Fixed	35/.220	45/.304	.025
'85	17084534	5/32	Fixed	①	.085	28/.164	1 ②	25/.142	Fixed	35/.220	45/.304	—
	17084535	5/32	Fixed	①	.085	28/.164	1 ②	25/.142	Fixed	35/.220	45/.304	—
	17084540	5/32	Fixed	①	.085	28/.164	1 ②	25/.142	Fixed	35/.220	45/.304	—
	17084542	4/32	Fixed	①	.085	28/.164	1 ②	25/.142	Fixed	35/.220	45/.304	—
	17085356	9/32	Fixed	①	.085	22/.123	1 ②	25/.142	Fixed	30/.179	30/.179	—
	17085357	9/32	Fixed	①	.085	22/.123	1 ②	25/.142	Fixed	30/.179	30/.179	—
	17085358	9/32	Fixed	①	.085	22/.123	1 ②	25/.142	Fixed	30/.179	30/.179	—
	17085359	9/32	Fixed	①	.085	22/.123	1 ②	25/.142	Fixed	30/.179	30/.179	—
	17085368	4/32	Fixed	①	.085	22/.123	1 ②	25/.142	Fixed	30/.179	30/.179	—
	17085369	9/32	Fixed	①	.085	22/.123	1 ②	25/.142	Fixed	30/.179	30/.179	—
	17085370	4/32	Fixed	①	.085	22/.123	1 ②	25/.142	Fixed	30/.179	30/.179	—
	17085371	9/32	Fixed	①	.085	22/.123	1 ②	25/.142	Fixed	30/.179	30/.179	—
	17085452	5/32	Fixed	①	.085	28/.164	1 ②	25/.142	Fixed	35/.220	45/.304	—
	17085453	5/32	Fixed	①	.085	28/.164	1 ②	25/.142	Fixed	35/.220	45/.304	—
	17085458	5/32	Fixed	①	.085	28/.164	1 ②	25/.142	Fixed	35/.220	45/.304	—
'86	17084534	5/32	Fixed	①	.085	28/.164	1 ②	25/.142	Fixed	35/.220	45/.304	—
	17084535	5/32	Fixed	①	.085	28/.164	1 ②	25/.142	Fixed	35/.220	45/.304	—
	17084540	5/32	Fixed	①	.085	28/.164	1 ②	25/.142	Fixed	35/.220	45/.304	—
	17084542	5/32	Fixed	①	.085	28/.164	1 ②	25/.142	Fixed	35/.220	45/.304	—

① See underhood decal
② Measurement in degrees
③ Not available

SECTION 25 CARBURETORS
ROCHESTER

2SE, E2SE CARBURETOR SPECIFICATIONS
General Motors—Canada

Year	Carburetor Identification	Float Lever (in.)	Pump Rod (in.)	Fast Idle (rpm)	Choke Coil Lever (in.)	Fast Idle Cam (deg./in.)	Air Valve Rod (in.)	Primary Vacuum Break (deg./in.)	Choke Setting (notches)	Secondary Vacuum Break (deg./in.)	Choke Unloader (deg./in.)	Secondary Lockout (in.)
'81	17059660	1/4	17/32	①	.085	24/.136	1	30/.179	Fixed	32/.195	30/.179	②
	17059662	1/4	17/32	①	.085	24/.136	1	30/.179	Fixed	37/.195	30/.179	②
	17059651	1/4	17/32	①	.085	24/.136	1	30/.179	Fixed	32/.195	30/.179	②
	17059666	1/4	17/32	①	.085	24/.136	1	26/.149	Fixed	32/.195	30/.179	②
	17059667	1/4	17/32	①	.085	24/.136	1	26/.149	Fixed	32/.195	30/.179	②
	17059622	5/32	17/32	①	.085	18/.096	1	17/.090	Fixed	—	36/.227	②
	17059623	5/32	17/32	①	.085	18/.096	1	19/.103	Fixed	—	36/.227	②
	17059624	5/32	17/32	①	.085	18/.096	1	17/.090	Fixed	—	36/.227	②
'82	17082440	1/4	19/32	①	.085	24/.136	1	30/.179	Fixed	32/.195	45/.304	②
	17082441	1/4	19/32	①	.085	24/.136	1	30/.179	Fixed	32/.195	45/.304	②
	17082443	1/4	19/32	①	.085	24/.136	1	30/.179	Fixed	32/.195	45/.304	②
	17082460	1/4	19/32	①	.085	18/.096	1	21/.117	Fixed	—	36/.227	②
	17082461	1/4	19/32	①	.085	18/.096	1	21/.117	Fixed	—	36/.227	②
	17082462	1/4	19/32	①	.085	18/.096	1	21/.117	Fixed	—	36/.227	②
	17082464	1/8	19/32	①	.085	18/.096	1	21/.117	Fixed	—	36/.227	②
	17082465	1/8	19/32	①	.085	18/.096	1	21/.117	Fixed	—	36/.227	②
	17082466	1/8	19/32	①	.085	18/.096	1	21/.117	Fixed	—	36/.227	②
	17082620	7/16	19/32	①	.085	24/.136	1	30/.179	Fixed	32/.195	45/.304	②
	17082621	7/16	19/32	①	.085	24/.136	1	30/.179	Fixed	32/.195	45/.304	②
	17082622	7/16	19/32	①	.085	24/.136	1	30/.179	Fixed	32/.195	45/.304	②
	17082623	7/16	19/32	①	.085	24/.136	1	30/.179	Fixed	32/.195	45/.304	②
'83	17083311	5/16	Fixed	①	.085	24/.136	1	18/.096	Fixed	20/.110	35/.220	.025
	17083314	5/16	Fixed	①	.085	24/.136	1	16/.083	Fixed	20/.110	35/.220	.025
	17083401	5/16	Fixed	①	.085	24/.136	1	18/.096	Fixed	20/.110	35/.220	.025
	17083440	1/4	19/32	①	.085	24/.136	1	28/.164	Fixed	32/.195	40/.260	.025
	17083441	1/4	19/32	①	.085	24/.136	1	28/.164	Fixed	32/.195	40/.260	.025
	17083442	1/4	19/32	①	.085	24/.136	1	28/.164	Fixed	32/.195	40/.260	.025
	17083443	1/4	19/32	①	.085	24/.136	1	28/.164	Fixed	32/.195	40/.260	.025
	17083444	1/4	19/32	①	.085	24/.136	1	28/.164	Fixed	32/.195	40/.260	.025
	17083445	1/4	19/32	①	.085	24/.136	1	28/.164	Fixed	32/.195	40/.260	.025
	17083460	1/4	19/32	①	.085	18/.096	1	19/.103	Fixed	—	36/.227	.025
	17083461	1/4	19/32	①	.085	18/.096	1	18/.096	Fixed	—	36/.227	.025
	17083462	1/4	19/32	①	.085	18/.096	1	19/.103	Fixed	—	36/.227	.025
	17083464	1/8	19/32	①	.085	18/.096	1	19/.103	Fixed	—	36/.227	.025
	17083465	1/8	19/32	①	.085	18/.096	1	20/.110	Fixed	—	36/.227	.025
	17083466	1/8	19/32	①	.085	18/.096	1	19/.103	Fixed	—	36/.227	.025
	17083620	7/16	19/32	①	.085	24/.136	1	28/.164	Fixed	32/.195	40/.260	.025
	17083621	7/16	19/32	①	.085	24/.136	1	28/.164	Fixed	32/.195	40/.260	.025
	17083622	7/16	19/32	①	.085	24/.136	1	28/.164	Fixed	34/.195	40/.260	.025
	17083623	7/16	19/32	①	.085	24/.136	1	28/.164	Fixed	32/.195	40/.260	.025
'84	17084312	5/16	Fixed	①	.085	24/.136	1	18/.096	Fixed	20/.110	35/.220	.025
	17084314	5/16	Fixed	①	.085	29/.171	1	16/.083	Fixed	20/.110	30/.179	.025
	17084480	1/4	Fixed	①	.085	24/.136	1	28/.164	Fixed	32/.195	45/.304	.025
	17084481	1/4	Fixed	①	.085	24/.136	1	28/.164	Fixed	32/.195	45/.304	.025
	17084482	1/4	Fixed	①	.085	24/.136	1	28/.164	Fixed	32/.195	45/.304	.025
	17084483	1/4	Fixed	①	.085	24/.136	1	28/.164	Fixed	32/.195	45/.304	.025
	17084484	1/4	Fixed	①	.085	24/.136	1	28/.164	Fixed	32/.195	45/.304	.025
	17084485	1/4	Fixed	①	.085	24/.136	1	28/.164	Fixed	32/.195	45/.304	.025
	17084486	1/4	Fixed	①	.085	24/.136	1	28/.164	Fixed	32/.195	45/.304	.025
	17084487	1/4	Fixed	①	.085	24/.136	1	28/.164	Fixed	32/.195	45/.304	.025
	17084620	7/16	Fixed	①	.085	24/.136	1	26/.149	Fixed	32/.195	45/.304	.025
	17084621	7/16	Fixed	①	.085	24/.136	1	26/.149	Fixed	32/.195	45/.304	.025
	17084622	7/16	Fixed	①	.085	24/.136	1	26/.149	Fixed	32/.195	45/.304	.025
	17084623	7/16	Fixed	①	.085	24/.136	1	26/.149	Fixed	32/.195	45/.304	.025

CARBURETORS
ROCHESTER

2SE, E2SE CARBURETOR SPECIFICATIONS
General Motors—Canada

Year	Carburetor Identification	Float Lever (in.)	Pump Rod (in.)	Fast Idle (rpm)	Choke Coil Lever (in.)	Fast Idle Cam (deg./in.)	Air Valve Rod (in.)	Primary Vacuum Break (deg./in.)	Choke Setting (notches)	Secondary Vacuum Break (deg./in.)	Choke Unloader (deg./in.)	Secondary Lockout (in.)
'85	17084312	5/16	Fixed	①	.085	—	1	18/.096	Fixed	20/.110	35/.220	—
	17084314	5/16	Fixed	①	.085	—	1	16/.083	Fixed	20/.110	30/.179	—
	17085484	12/32	Fixed	①	.085	—	1	28/.164	Fixed	32/.195	45/.304	—
	17085485	12/32	Fixed	①	.085	—	1	28/.164	Fixed	32/.195	45/.304	—
	17085482	12/32	Fixed	①	.085	—	1	28/.164	Fixed	32/.195	45/.304	—
	17085483	12/32	Fixed	①	.085	—	1	28/.164	Fixed	32/.195	45/.304	—
	17085484	12/32	Fixed	①	.085	—	1	28/.164	Fixed	32/.195	45/.304	—
	17085485	12/32	Fixed	①	.085	—	1	28/.164	Fixed	32/.195	45/.304	—
	17085486	12/32	Fixed	①	.085	—	1	28/.164	Fixed	32/.195	45/.304	—
	17085487	12/32	Fixed	①	.085	—	1	28/.164	Fixed	32/.195	45/.304	—
'86	17086484	12/32	Fixed	①	.085	—	1	28/.164	Fixed	32/.195	45/.304	—
	17086485	12/32	Fixed	①	.085	—	1	28/.164	Fixed	32/.195	45/.304	—
	17086486	4/32	Fixed	①	.085	—	1	28/.164	Fixed	32/.195	45/.304	—
	17086487	4/32	Fixed	①	.085	—	1	28/.164	Fixed	32/.195	45/.304	—

① See underhood decal
② Not available

Models 2MC, M2MC, M2ME and E2ME

The Rochester model 2MC carburetor is a two-barrel single stage carburetor which incorporates the design features of the primary side of the Rochester Quadrajet four-barrel carburetor. It is used on small displacement V8s. The M2MC version with front and rear vacuum brake diaphragms, was introduced on the 301 V8.

The Dualjet E2ME Model 210 is a variation of the M2ME, modified for use with the Electronic Fuel Control System (also called the Computer Controlled Catalytic Converter, or C-4, System). An electrically operated mixture control solenoid is mounted in the float bowl. Mixture is thus controlled by the Electronic Control Module, in response to signals from the oxygen sensor mounted in the exhaust system upstream of the catalytic converter.

For further information on feedback carburetors, please refer to *Chilton's Guide To Fuel Injection And Feedback Carburetors*.

FLOAT LEVEL ADJUSTMENT

See the illustration for float level adjustment for all carburetors. The E2ME procedure is the same except for adjustment (step 4 in the figure). For the E2ME only, if the float level is too high, hold the retainer firmly in place and push down on the center of the float to adjust.

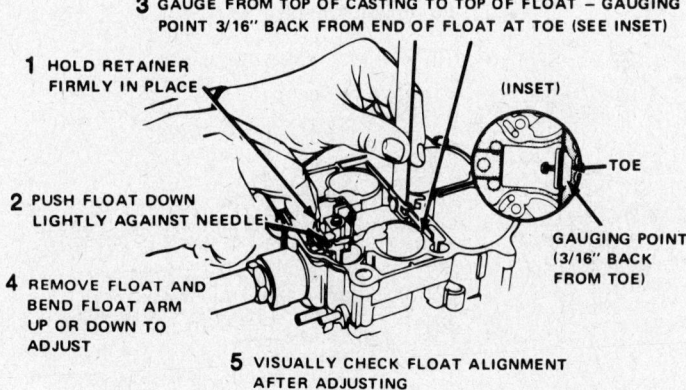

2MC, M2MC, M2ME, E2ME float level adjustment—typical

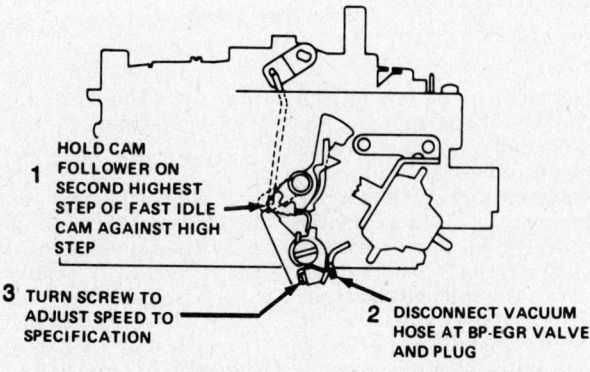

M2MC and E2ME fast idle speed adjustment—typical

SECTION 25
CARBURETORS
ROCHESTER

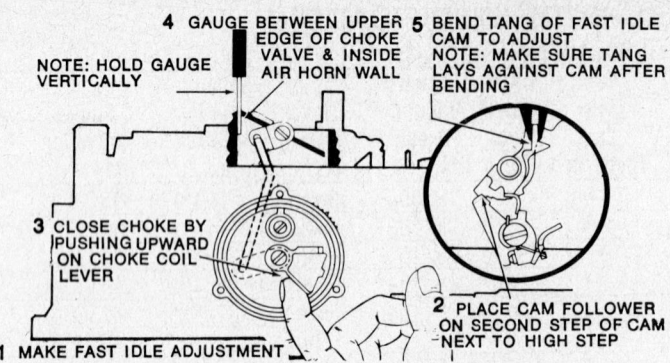

2MC, M2MC, M2ME, E2ME fast idle cam adjustment—typical

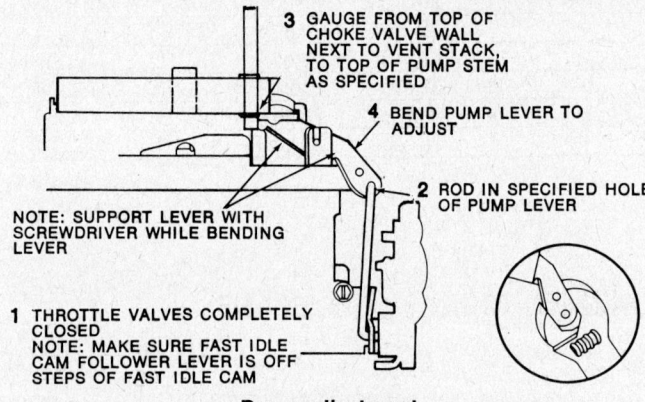

Pump adjustment

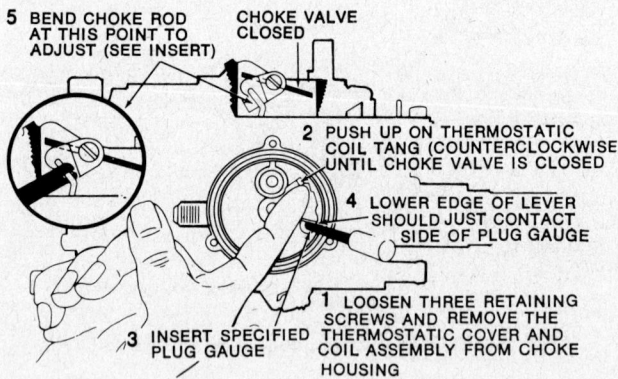

2MC, M2MC, M2ME, E2MC choke coil lever adjustment—typical

FAST IDLE CAM (CHOKE ROD) ADJUSTMENT

1. Adjust the fast idle speed.
2. Place the cam follower lever on the second step of the fast idle cam, holding it firmly against the rise of the high step.
3. Close the choke valve by pushing upward on the choke coil lever inside the choke housing, or by pushing up on the vacuum break lever tang.
4. Gauge between the upper edge of the choke valve and the inside of the air horn wall.
5. Bend the tang on the fast idle cam to adjust.

PUMP ADJUSTMENT

This adjustment is not required on E2ME carburetors used in conjunction with the computer controlled systems.

1. With the fast idle cam follower off the steps of the fast idle cam, back out the idle speed screw until the throttle valves are completely closed.
2. Place the pump rod in the proper hole of the lever.
3. Measure from the top of the choke valve wall, next to the vent stack, to the top of the pump stem.
4. Bend the pump lever to adjust.

CHOKE COIL LEVER ADJUSTMENT

1. Remove the choke cover and thermostatic coil from the choke housing. On models with a fixed choke cover, drill out the rivets and remove the cover. A stat cover kit will be required for assembly.
2. Push up on the coil tang (counterclockwise) until the choke valve is closed. The top of the choke rod should be at the bottom of the slot in the choke valve lever. Place the fast idle cam follower on the high step of the cam.
3. Insert a 0.120 in. plug gauge in the hole in the choke housing.
4. The lower edge of the choke coil lever should just contact the side of the plug gauge.
5. Bend the choke rod to adjust.

2MC LEAN/RICH VACUUM BRAKE ADJUSTMENT

1. Place the cam follower on the highest step of the fast idle cam.
2. Seat the vacuum break diaphragm by using an outside vacuum source. Tape over the bleed hole, if any, under the rubber cover on the diaphragm.
3. Remove the choke cover and

If the float level is too low on the E2ME, lift out the metering rods. Remove the solenoid connector screws. Turn the lean mixture solenoid screw in clockwise, counting the exact number of turns until the screw is lightly bottomed in the bowl. Then turn the screw out counterclockwise and remove it. Lift out the solenoid and connector. Remove the float and bend the arm up to adjust. Install the parts, installing the mixture solenoid screw in until it is lightly bottomed, then turning it out the exact number of turns counted earlier.

FAST IDLE SPEED

1. Place the fast idle lever on the high step of the fast idle cam.
2. Turn the fast idle screw out until the throttle valves are closed.
3. Turn the screw in to contact the lever, then turn it in the number of turns listed in the specifications. Check this preliminary setting against the sticker figure.

CARBURETORS
ROCHESTER
SECTION 25

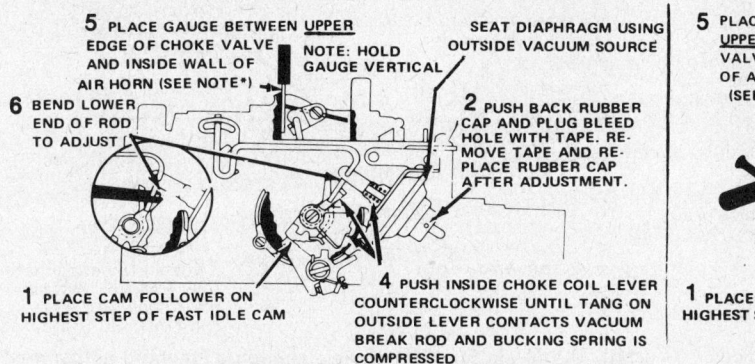

2MC rich vacuum break setting

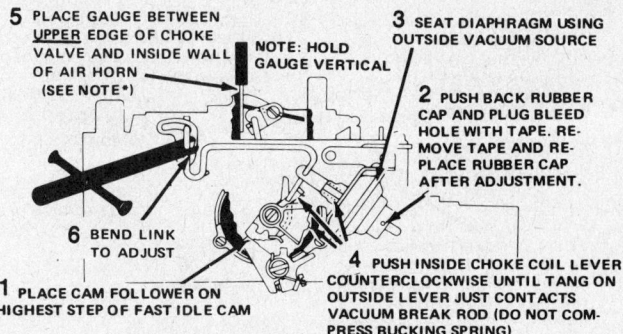

2MC lean vacuum break setting

thermostatic coil and push up on the coil lever inside the choke housing until the tang on the vacuum break lever contacts the tang on the vacuum break plunger stem. Do not compress the bucking spring for lean adjustment. Compress the bucking spring for rich adjustment.

4. With the choke rod in the bottom of the slot in the choke lever, gauge between the upper edge of the choke valve and the inside wall of the air horn.

5. Bend the link rod at the vacuum break plunger stem to adjust the rich setting. Bend the link rod at the opposite end from the diaphragm to adjust the lean setting.

FRONT/REAR VACUUM BRAKE ADJUSTMENT
M2MC, M2ME and E2ME (1980)

1. Sat the front diaphragm, using an outside vacuum source. If there is an air bleed hole on the diaphragm, tape it over.

2. Remove the choke cover and coil. Rotate the inside coil lever counterclockwise. On models with a fixed choke cover (riveted), push up on the vacuum break lever tang and hold it in position with a rubber band.

3. Check that the specified gap is present between the top of the choke valve and the air horn wall.

4. Turn the front vacuum break adjusting screw to adjust.

5. To adjust the rear vacuum break diaphragm, perform Steps 1–3 on the rear diaphragm, but make sure that the plunger bucking spring is compressed and seated in Step 2. Adjust by bending the link at the bend nearest the diaphragm.

1981–84 Models

On these models a choke valve measuring gauge J-26701 or equivalent is used to measure angle (degrees instead of inches). See illustration for procedure.

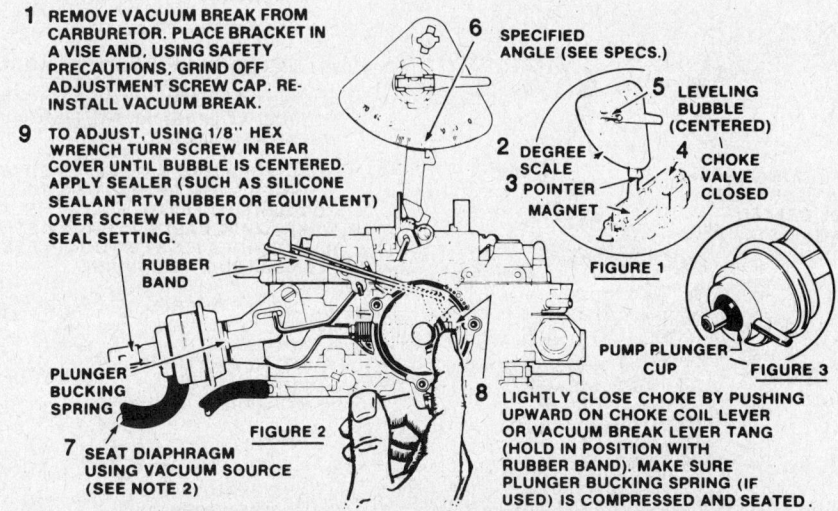

E2ME rear vacuum break adjustment—1981–82

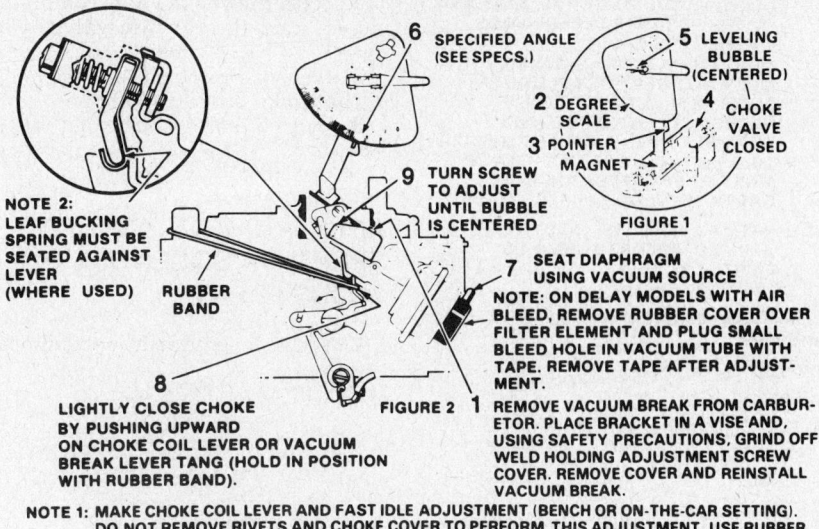

E2ME front vacuum break adjustment—1981–82

25-75

SECTION 25 CARBURETORS
ROCHESTER

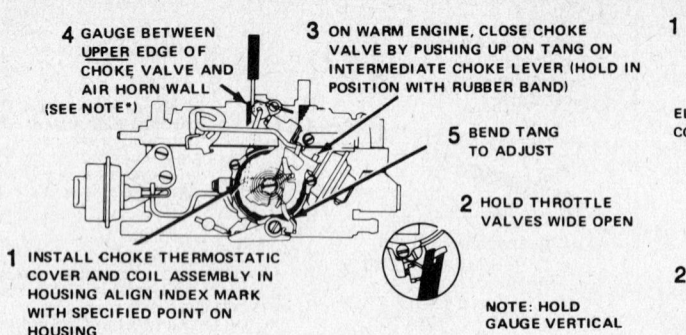

2MC, M2MC, M2ME, E2ME unloader adjustment—typical

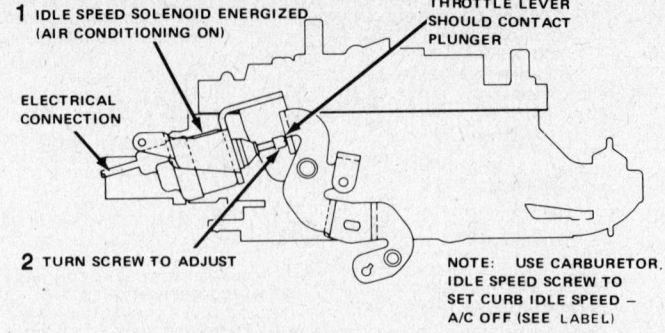

2MC, M2MC air conditioning idle speed-up solenoid adjustment

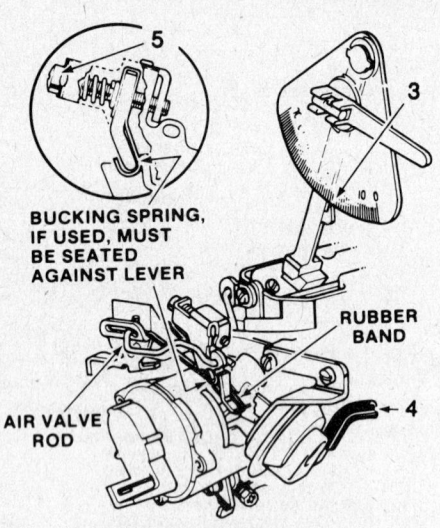

1. ATTACH RUBBER BAND TO GREEN TANG OF INTERMEDIATE CHOKE SHAFT.
2. OPEN THROTTLE TO ALLOW CHOKE VALVE TO CLOSE.
3. SET UP ANGLE GAGE AND SET ANGLE TO SPECIFICATION.
4. RETRACT VACUUM BREAK PLUNGER, USING VACUUM SOURCE, AT LEAST 18" HG. PLUG AIR BLEED HOLES WHERE APPLICABLE.
4A. ON QUADRAJETS, AIR VALVE ROD MUST NOT RESTRICT PLUNGER FROM RETRACTING FULLY. IF NECESSARY, BEND ROD HERE TO PERMIT FULL PLUNGER TRAVEL. WHERE APPLICABLE, PLUNGER STEM MUST BE EXTENDED FULLY TO COMPRESS PLUNGER BUCKING SPRING.
5. TO CENTER BUBBLE, EITHER:
   A. ADJUST WITH 1/8" HEX WRENCH (VACUUM STILL APPLIED)
   -OR-
   B. SUPPORT AT "S" AND BEND VACUUM BREAK ROD (VACUUM STILL APPLIED)

1. ATTACH RUBBER BAND TO GREEN TANG OF INTERMEDIATE CHOKE SHAFT
2. OPEN THROTTLE TO ALLOW CHOKE VALVE TO CLOSE
3. SET UP ANGLE GAGE AND SET TO SPECIFICATION
4. RETRACT VACUUM BREAK PLUNGER USING VACUUM SOURCE, AT LEAST 18" HG. PLUG AIR BLEED HOLES WHERE APPLICABLE ON QUADRAJETS, AIR VALVE ROD MUST NOT RESTRICT PLUNGER FROM RETRACTING FULLY. IF NECESSARY, BEND ROD (SEE ARROW) TO PERMIT FULL PLUNGER TRAVEL. FINAL ROD CLEARANCE MUST BE SET AFTER VACUUM BREAK SETTING HAS BEEN MADE.
5. WITH AT LEAST 18" HG STILL APPLIED, ADJUST SCREW TO CENTER BUBBLE

E2ME front vacuum break adjstment—1983 and later

E2ME rear vacuum break adjustment— 1983 and later

UNLOADER ADJUSTMENT

1. With the choke valve completely closed, hold the throttle valves wide open.
2. Measure between the upper edge of the choke valve and air horn wall.
3. Bend the tang on the fast idle lever to obtain the proper measurement.

AIR CONDITIONING IDLE SPEED-UP SOLENOID ADJUSTMENT

1. With the engine at normal operating temperature and the air conditioning turned on but the compressor clutch lead disconnected, the solenoid should be electrically energized (plunger stem extended). Open the throttle slightly to allow the solenoid plunger to fully extend.
2. Adjust the plunger screw to obtain the specified idle speed.
3. Turn off the air conditioner. The solenoid plunger should move away from the tang on the throttle lever.
4. Adjust the curb idle speed with the idle speed screw, if necessary.

NOTE: Do not adjust if carburetor is computer controlled.

CARBURETORS
ROCHESTER
SECTION 25

2MC, M2MC, M2ME, E2ME CARBURETOR SPECIFICATIONS
General Motors—U.S.A.

Year	Carburetor Identification ①	Flat Level (in.)	Choke Rod (in.)	Choke Unloader (in.)	Vacuum Break Lean or Front (deg./in.)	Vacuum Break Rich or Rear (deg./in.)	Pump Rod (in.)	Choke Coil Lever (in.)	Automatic Choke (notches)
'80	17080108, 110 17080130, 131	3/8	.243	.243	.142	—	5/16 ②	.120	Fixed
	17080132, 133, 147, 148, 149	5/16	.243	.243	.142	—	5/16 ②	.120	Fixed
	17080138, 140	3/8	.243	.243	.142	—	5/16 ②	.120	Fixed
	17080150, 152, 153	3/8	.071	.220	.243	.157	11/32 ③	.120	Fixed
	17080160	5/16	.110	.243	.168	.207	1/4 ②	.120	Fixed
	17080190, 192	9/32	.074	.243	.123	.110	1/4 ②	.120	Fixed
	17080191	11/32	.139	.243	.096	.096	1/4 ②	.120	Fixed
	17080195, 197	9/32	.139	.243	.103	.071	1/4 ②	.120	Fixed
	17080490, 492	5/16	.139	.243	.117	.203	1/4 ②	.120	Fixed
	17080491	5/16	.139	.243	.117	.220	1/4 ②	.120	Fixed
	17080493, 495	5/16	.139	.243	.117	.179	3/8	.120	Fixed
	17080494	5/16	.139	.243	.117	.179	1/4 ②	.120	Fixed
	17080496, 498	5/16	.139	.243	.117	.203	Fixed	.120	Fixed
'81	17080185, 187	9/32	.139	.243	19/.103	14/.071	1/4 ②	.120	Fixed
	17080191	11/32	.139	.243	18/.096	18/.096	1/4 ②	.120	Fixed
	17081130, 131, 132, 133	11/32	.110	.243	25/.142	—	Fixed	.120	Fixed
	17081138, 140	11/32	.110	.260	25/.142	—	Fixed	.120	Fixed
	17081150, 152	13/32	.071	.220	24/.136	36/.227	Fixed	.120	Fixed
	17081160	11/32	.074	.220	24/.136	37/.234	④	.120	Fixed
	17081196	5/16	.139	.243	28/.164	24/.136	④	.120	Fixed
	17081190, 193	5/16	.139	.243	21/.117	31/.187	Fixed	.120	Fixed
	17081191, 194	5/16	.139	.243	28/.164	24/.136	④	.120	Fixed
	17081198	3/8	.139	.243	28/.164	24/.136	④	.120	Fixed
	17081192, 197	5/16	.139	.243	21/.117	30/.179	④	.120	Fixed
	17081199	3/8	.096	.243	18/.096	24/.136	Fixed	.120	Fixed
'82	17082130, 132, 138, 140	3/8	.110	.164	27/.157	—	④	④	Fixed
	17082150	13/32	.071	.220	24/.136	38/.243 ⑤	④	④	Fixed
	17082182, 184	5/16	.096	.195	28/.164	24/.136	④	④	Fixed
	17082192, 194	5/16	.096	.195	28/.164	24/.136	④	④	Fixed
	17082196	5/16	.096	.157	21/.117	19/.103	④	④	Fixed
	17082497	5/16	.113	.195	28/.164	24/.136	④	.120	Fixed
'83	17082130, 132	3/8	.110	.243	27/.157	—	④	.120	Fixed
	17083190, 192	5/16	.096	.195	28/.164	24/.136	④	.120	Fixed
	17083193	5/16	.090	.157	23/.129	28/.164	④	.120	Fixed
	17083194	5/16	.090	.220	27/.157	25/.142	④	.120	Fixed
'84	17082130	3/8	.110	.243	27/.157	None	④	.120	Fixed
	17082132	3/8	.110	.243	27/.157	None	④	.120	Fixed
	17084191	5/16	.096	.195	28/.164	24/.136	④	.120	Fixed
	17084193	5/16	.090	.220	27/.157	25/.142	④	.120	Fixed
	17084194	5/16	.090	.220	27/.157	25/.142	④	.120	Fixed
	17084195	5/16	.090	.220	27/.157	25/.142	④	.120	Fixed
'85	17085190	10/32	.096	.195	28/.164	24/.136	④	.120	Fixed
	17085192	11/32	.090	.220	27/.157	25/.142	④	.120	Fixed
	17085194	11/32	.090	.220	27/.157	25/.142	④	.120	Fixed
'86	17086190	10/32	.096	.195	28/.164	24/.136	④	.120	Fixed

① The carburetor identification number is stamped on the float bowl, next to the fuel inlet nut.
② Inner hole
③ Outer hole
④ Not Adjustable
⑤ High altitude—0.206

CARBURETORS
ROCHESTER

2MC, M2MC, M2ME, E2ME CARBURETOR SPECIFICATIONS
General Motors—Canada

Year	Carburetor Identification ①	Float Level (in.)	Choke Rod (in.)	Choke Unloader (in.)	Vacuum Break Lean or Front (deg./in.)	Vacuum Break Rich or Rear (deg./in.)	Pump Rod (in.)	Choke Coil Lever (in.)	Automatic Choke (notches)
'81	17080191	11/32	.139	.243	18/.096	18/.096	1/4 ②	.120	Fixed
	17081492	9/32	.139	.243	17/.090	19/.103	1/4 ②	.120	Fixed
	17081493	9/32	.139	.243	17/.090	19/.103	1/4 ②	.120	Fixed
	17081170	13/32	.110	.243	25/.142	—	1/4 ②	.120	Fixed
	17081171	13/32	.110	.243	25/.142	—	1/4 ②	.120	Fixed
	17081174	9/32	.110	.243	25/.142	—	1/4 ②	.120	Fixed
	17081175	9/32	.110	.243	25/.142	—	1/4 ②	.120	Fixed
'82	17082174	9/32	.110	.243	25/.142	—	5/16 ②	.120	Fixed
	17082175	9/32	.110	.243	25/.142	—	5/16 ②	.120	Fixed
	17082492	9/32	.139	.243	17/.090	19/.103	1/4 ②	.120	Fixed
	17082172	9/32	.110	.243	25/.142	—	5/16 ②	.120	Fixed
	17082173	9/32	.110	.243	25/.142	—	5/16 ②	.120	Fixed
'83–'84	17083172	9/32	.139	.243	17/.090	19/.103	1/4 ②	.120	Fixed
'85	17085170	9/32	.139	.243	17/.090	19/.103	9/32 ②	.120	Fixed
'86	17086170	9/32	.139	.243	17/.090	19/.103	9/32 ②	.120	Fixed

① The carburetor identification number is stamped on the float bowl, next to the fuel inlet nut.
② Inner hole

Quadrajet

The Rochester Quadrajet carburetor is a two stage, four-barrel downdraft carburetor. It has been built in many variations designated as 4MC, 4MV, M4MC, M4MCA, M4ME, M4MEA, E4MC, and E4ME. See the beginning of the Rochester section for an explanation of these designations.

The primary side of the carburetor is equipped with two primary bores and a triple venturi with plain tube nozzles. During off idle and part throttle operation, the fuel is metered through tapered metering rods operating in specially designed jets positioned by a manifold vacuum responsive piston.

The secondary side of the carburetor contains two secondary bores. An air valve is used on the secondary side for metering control and supplements the primary bore. The secondary air valve operates tapered metering rods which regulate the fuel in constant proportion to the air being supplied.

FAST IDLE SPEED

1. Position the fast idle lever on the high step of the fast idle cam.
2. Be sure that the choke is wide open and the engine warm. Plug the EGR vacuum hose. Disconnect the vacuum hose to the front vacuum break unit, if there are two.
3. Make a preliminary adjustment by turning the fast idle screw out un-

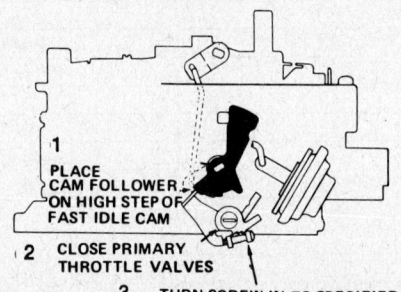

1 PLACE CAM FOLLOWER ON HIGH STEP OF FAST IDLE CAM
2 CLOSE PRIMARY THROTTLE VALVES
3 TURN SCREW IN TO SPECIFIED FAST IDLE RPM TO ADJUST

Quadrajet fast idle adjustment

til the throttle valves are closed, then screwing it in the specified number of turns after it contacts the lever (see the carburetor specifications).

4. Use the fast idle screw to adjust the fast idle to the speed, and under the conditions, specified on the engine compartment sticker or in the specifications chart.

CHOKE ROD (FAST IDLE CAM)

1. Adjust the fast idle and place the cam follower on the second step of the fast idle cam against the shoulder of the high step.
2. Close the choke valve by exerting counter-clockwise pressure on the external choke lever. Remove the coil assembly from the choke housing and push upon the choke coil lever. On models with a fixed (riveted) choke cover, push up on the vacuum brake lever tang and hold in position with a rubber band.
3. Insert a gauge of the proper size between the upper edge of the choke valve and the inside air horn wall.
4. To adjust, bend the tang on the fast idle cam. Be sure that the tang rests against the cam after bending.

PRIMARY (FRONT) VACUUM BREAK ADJUSTMENT

1980–81 Models

1. Seat the front vacuum diaphragm using an outside vacuum source. If there is a diaphragm unit bleed hole, tape it over.
2. Push up on the inside choke coil lever until the tang on the vacuum brake lever contacts the tang on the vacuum break plunger. On models with a fixed choke coil cover, push up on the vacuum brake lever tang.
3. Place the proper size gauge between the upper edge of the choke valve and the inside of the air horn wall.
4. To adjust, turn the adjustment screw on the vacuum break plunger lever.
5. Install the vacuum hose to the vacuum brake unit.

CARBURETORS
ROCHESTER
SECTION 25

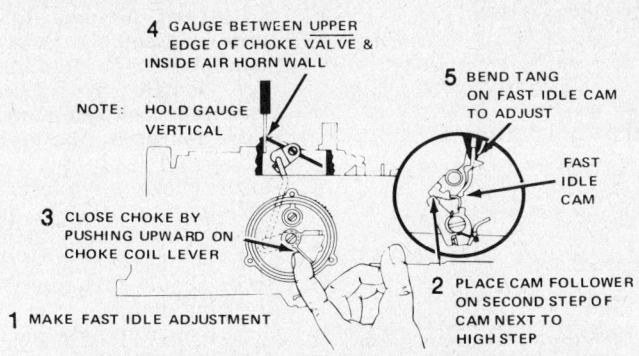

Quadrajet choke rod (fast idle cam) adjustment—typical

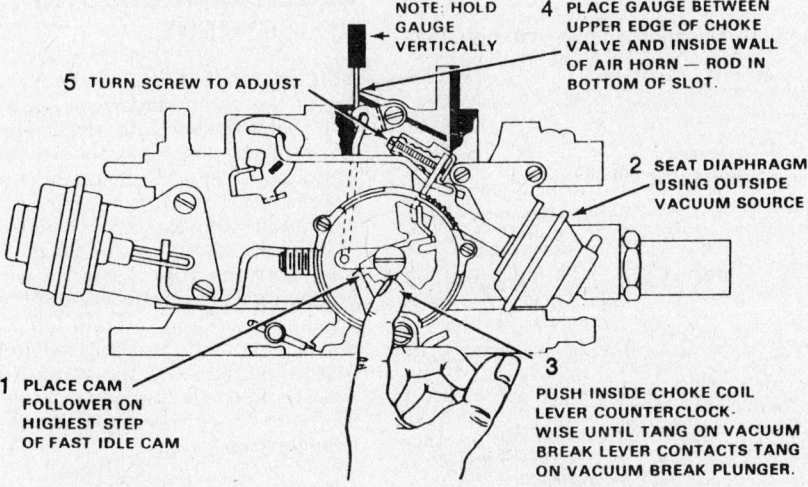

Quadrajet front vacuum break adjustment—typical through 1981

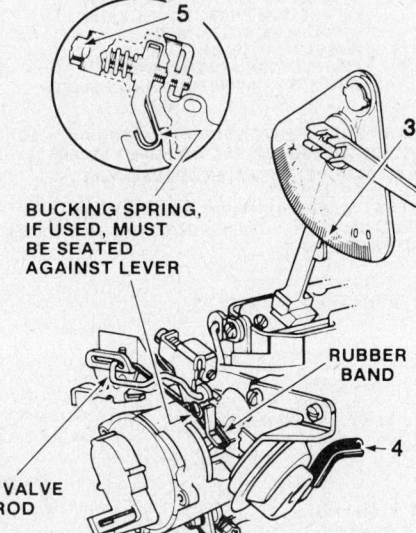

Quadrajet front vacuum break adjustment—1982 and later

1982–84 Models

On these models a choke valve measuring gauge J-26701 or equivalent is used to measure angle (degrees instead of inches). See illustration for procedure.

rear vacuum break diaphragm and seat the diaphragm using an outside vacuum source. Make sure the diaphragm plunger bucking spring, if any, is compressed. On delay models (1980), plug the end cover with a pump plunger cup or equivalent and remove after adjustment.

2. Close the choke by pushing up on the choke coil lever inside the choke housing. On models with a fixed choke coil cover, push up on the vacuum break lever tang and use a rubber band to hold in place.

3. With the choke rod in the bottom of the slot in the choke lever, measure between the upper edge of the choke valve and the air horn wall with a wire-type gauge.

4. To adjust, bend the vacuum brake rod at the first bend near the diaphragm except on 1980 models with a screw at the rear of the diaphragm; on those models, turn the screw to adjust.

5. Remove the tape covering the bleed hole of the diaphragm and connect the vacuum hose.

1981–84 Models

On these models a choke valve measuring gauge J-26701 or equivalent is used to measure angle (degrees instead of inches). See illustration for procedure.

CHOKE UNLOADER

1. Push up on the vacuum break lever to close the choke valve, and fully open the throttle valves.
2. Measure the distance from the upper edge of the choke valve to the air horn wall.
3. To adjust, bend the tang on the fast idle lever.

4MV CHOKE COIL ROD

1. Close the choke valve by rotating the choke coil lever counterclockwise.
2. Disconnect the thermostatic coil rod from the upper lever.
3. Push down on the rod until it contacts the bracket of the coil.
4. The rod must fit in the notch of the upper lever.
5. If it does not, it must be bent on the curved portion just below the upper lever.

MC, ME CHOKE COIL LEVER ADJUSTMENT

1. Remove the choke cover and thermostatic coil from the choke housing. On models with a fixed (rivet) choke cover, the rivets must be

SECONDARY (REAR) VACUUM BRAKE ADJUSTMENT

1980 Models

1. Tape over the bleed hole in the

25-79

SECTION 25 CARBURETORS
ROCHESTER

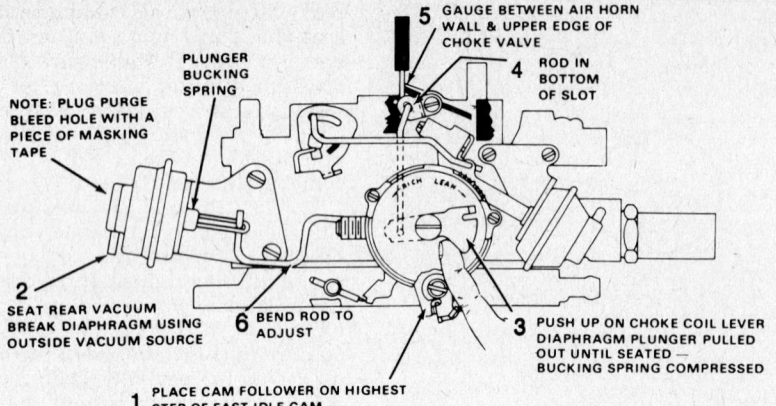

Quadrajet rear vacuum break adjustment (without adjusting screw)—through 1980

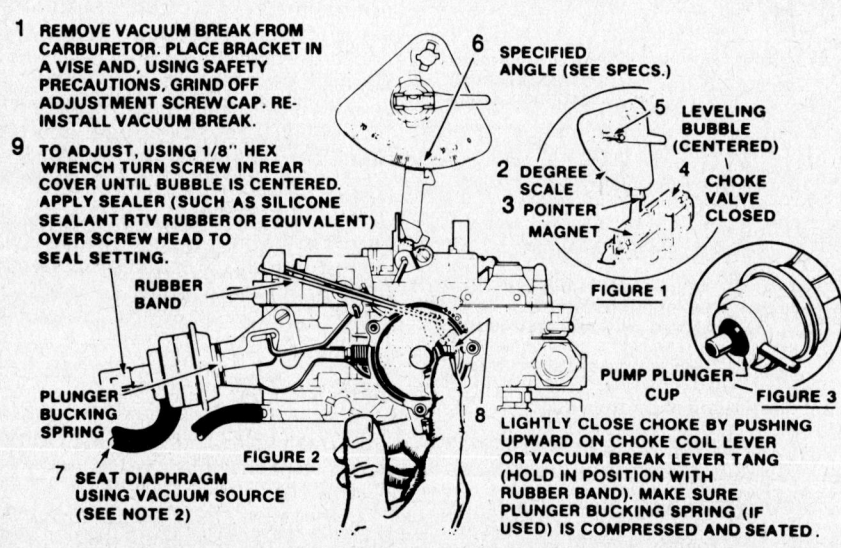

Quadrajet rear vacuum break adjustment—1981-82

drilled out. A choke stat kit is necessary for assembly. Place the fast idle cam follower on the high step.

2. Push up on the coil tang (counter-clockwise) until the choke valve is closed. The top of the choke rod should be at the bottom of the slot in the choke valve lever.

3. Insert a 0.120 in. drill bit in the hole in the choke housing.

4. The lower edge of the choke coil lever should just contact the side of the plug gauge.

5. Bend the choke rod at the top angle to adjust.

SECONDARY CLOSING ADJUSTMENT

This adjustment assures proper closing of the secondary throttle plates.

1. Set the slow idle as per instructions in the appropriate car section. Make sure that the fast idle cam follower is not resting on the fast idle cam and the choke valve is wide open.

2. There should be 0.020 in. clearance between the secondary throttle actuating rod and the front of the slot on the secondary throttle lever with the closing tang on the throttle lever resting against the actuating lever.

3. Bend the secondary closing tang on the primary throttle actuating rod or lever to adjust.

SECONDARY OPENING ADJUSTMENT

1. Open the primary throttle valves until the actuating link contacts the upper tang on the secondary lever.

2. With two point linkage, the bottom of the link should be in the center of the secondary lever slot.

3. With three point linkage, there should be 0.070 in. clearance between the link and the middle tang.

4. Bend the upper tang on the secondary lever to adjust as necessary.

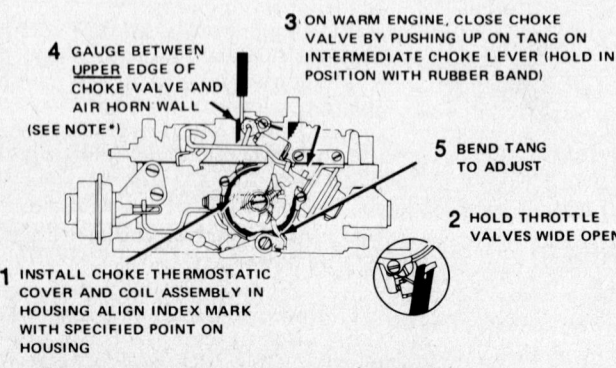

Quadrajet unloader adjustment—typical

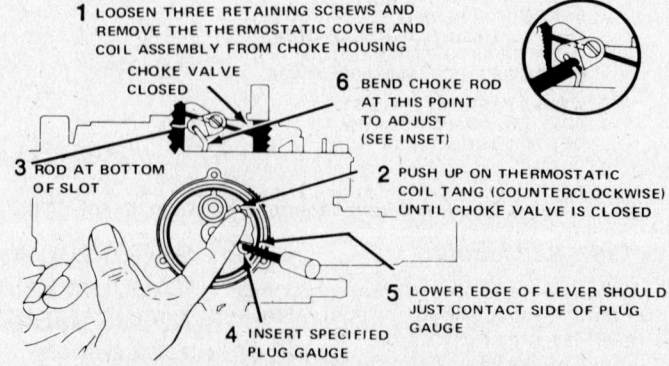

Quadrajet choke coil lever adjustment—typical

CARBURETORS
ROCHESTER
SECTION 25

1. ATTACH RUBBER BAND TO GREEN TANG OF INTERMEDIATE CHOKE SHAFT.
2. OPEN THROTTLE TO ALLOW CHOKE VALVE TO CLOSE.
3. SET UP ANGLE GAGE AND SET ANGLE TO SPECIFICATION.
   RETRACT VACUUM BREAK PLUNGER, USING VACUUM SOURCE, AT LEAST 18" HG. PLUG AIR BLEED HOLES WHERE APPLICABLE.
4A. ON QUADRAJETS, AIR VALVE ROD MUST NOT RESTRICT PLUNGER FROM RETRACTING FULLY. IF NECESSARY, BEND ROD HERE TO PERMIT FULL PLUNGER TRAVEL. WHERE APPLICABLE, PLUNGER STEM MUST BE EXTENDED FULLY TO COMPRESS PLUNGER BUCKING SPRING.
5. TO CENTER BUBBLE, EITHER:
   A. ADJUST WITH 1/8" HEX WRENCH (VACUUM STILL APPLIED)
   -OR-
   B. SUPPORT AT "S" AND BEND VACUUM BREAK ROD (VACUUM STILL APPLIED)

Quadrajet rear vacuum break adjustment—typical 1983 and later

and connector. Remove the float and bend the arm up to adjust. Install the parts, turning the mixture solenoid screw in until it is lightly bottomed, then unscrewing it the exact number of turns counted earlier.

ACCELERATOR PUMP

The accelerator pump is not adjust-

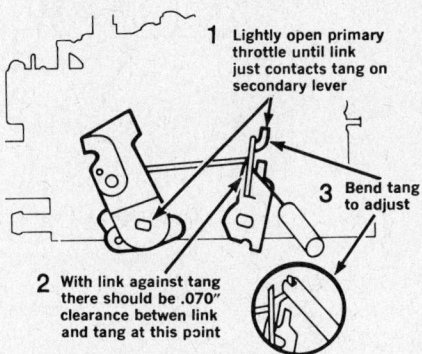

Secondary opening adjustment—three point linkage

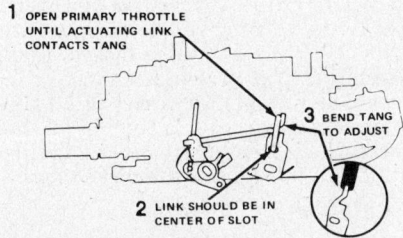

Quadrajet secondary opening adjustment, two point linkage

FLOAT LEVEL

With the air horn assembly removed, measure the distance from the air horn gasket surface (gasket removed) to the top of the float at the toe (3/16 in. back from the toe).

NOTE: Make sure the retaining pin is firmly held in place and that the tang of the float is lightly held against the needle and seat assembly.

Remove the float and bend the float arm to adjust except on carburetors used with the computer controlled systems (E4MC and E4ME). For those carburetors, if the float level is too high, hold the retainer firmly in place and push down on the center of the float to adjust. If the float level is too low on models with the computer controlled system, lift out the metering rods. Remove the solenoid connector screw. Turn the lean mixture solenoid screw in clockwise, counting and recording the exact number of turns until the screw is lightly bottomed in the bowl. Then turn the screw out clockwise and remove. Lift out the solenoid

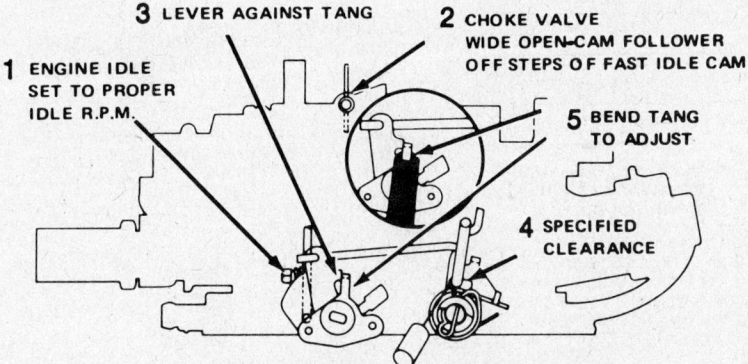

Quadrajet Secondary Closing Adjustment

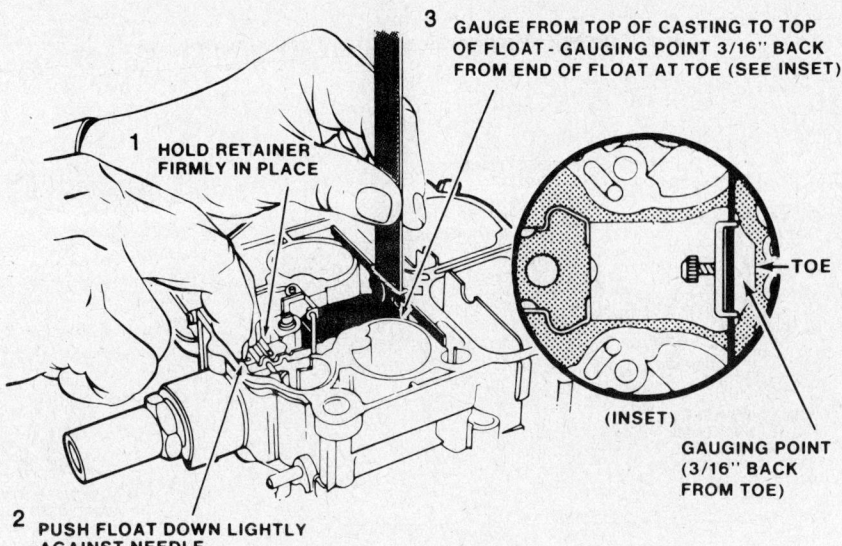

Quadrajet float level adjustment—typical

SECTION 25 CARBURETORS
ROCHESTER

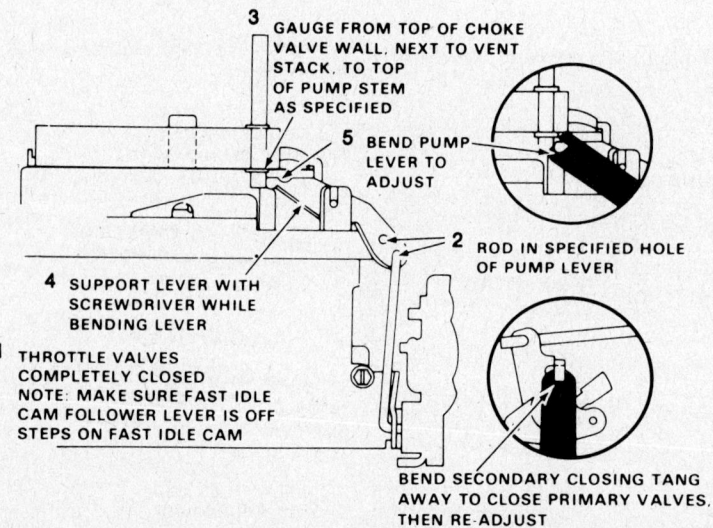

Quadrajet air valve spring setting—typical

able on computer controlled carburetors (E4MC and E4ME).

1. Close the primary throttle valves by backing out the slow idle screw and making sure that the fast idle cam follower is off the steps of the fast idle cam.
2. Bend the secondary throttle closing tang away from the primary throttle lever, if necessary, to insure that the primary throttle valves are fully closed.
3. With the pump in the appropriate hole in the pump lever, measure from the top of the choke valve wall to the top of the pump stem.
4. To adjust, bend the pump lever.
5. After adjusting, readjust the secondary throttle tang and the slow idle screw.

AIR VALVE SPRING ADJUSTMENT

To adjust the air valve spring windup, loosen the Allen head lockscrew and turn the adjusting screw counterclockwise to remove all spring tension. With the air valve closed, turn the adjusting screw clockwise the specified number of turns after the torsion spring contacts the pin on the shaft. Hold the adjusting screw in this position and tighten the lockscrew.

Quadrajet accelerator pump rod adjustment

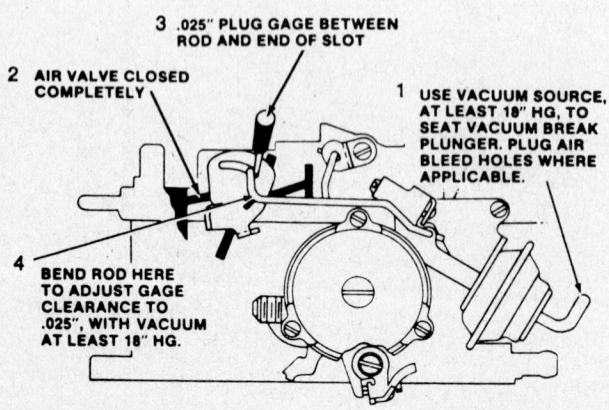

Air valve rod adjustment, Front—E4ME, E4MC

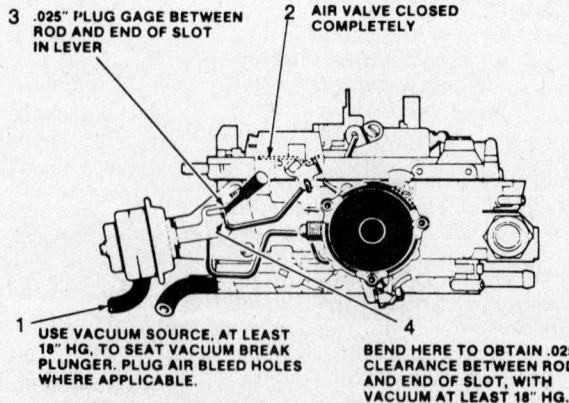

Air valve rod adjustment, Rear—E4ME, E4MC

CARBURETORS
ROCHESTER
SECTION 25

QUADRAJET CARBURETOR SPECIFICATIONS
Chrysler Products

Year	Carburetor Identification ①	Float Level (in.)	Air Valve Spring (turn)	Pump Rod (in.)	Primary Vacuum Break (in./deg.)	Secondary Vacuum Break (in./deg.)	Secondary Opening (in.)	Choke Rod (in.)	Choke Unloader (in.)	Fast Idle Speed ④ (rpm)
'85	17085407	14/32	7/8	—	.193/25°	—	—	—	.250	1450
'86	17085433	14/32	7/8	—	.140/25	—	—	.120	.179	①

① Refer to the underhood sticker

QUADRAJET CARBURETOR SPECIFICATIONS
Cadillac

Year	Carburetor Identification ①	Float Level (in.)	Air Valve Spring (turn)	Pump Rod (in.)	Primary Vacuum Break (in./deg.)	Secondary Vacuum Break (in./deg.)	Secondary Opening (in.)	Choke Rod (in.)	Choke Unloader (in.)	Fast Idle Speed (rpm)
'80	17080230	7/16	1/2	9/32 ②	0.149	0.136	③	0.083	0.220	1450
	17080530	17/32	1/2	Fixed	0.142	0.400	③	0.083	0.260	1350
'81	17081248	3/8	5/8	Fixed	0.164	0.136	③	0.139	0.243	④
	17081289	13/32	5/8	Fixed	0.164	0.136	③	0.139	0.243	④
'82	17082246	3/8	5/8	Fixed	0.149/26	0.149/26	③	0.139	0.195	④
	17082247	13/32	5/8	Fixed	0.164/28	0.136/24	③	0.139	0.243	④
'83	17082266	3/8	5/8	Fixed	0.149/26	0.149/26	③	0.071	0.195	④
	17082267	3/8	5/8	Fixed	0.149/26	0.149/26	③	0.071	0.195	④

① The carburetor identification number is stamped on the float bowl, near the secondary throttle lever.
② Inner hole
③ No measurement necessary on two point linkage; see text.
④ See underhood decal.

QUADRAJET CARBURETOR SPECIFICATIONS
Buick

Year	Carburetor Identification ①	Float Level (in.)	Air Valve Spring (turn)	Pump Rod (in.)	Primary Vacuum Break (in./deg.)	Secondary Vacuum Break (in./deg.)	Secondary Opening (in.)	Choke Rod (in.)	Choke Unloader (in/degrees)	Fast Idle Speed ④ (rpm)
'80	17080240	3/16	9/16	9/32 ③	0.083	0.083	②	0.074	0.179	⑥
	17080241	7/16	3/4	9/32 ③	0.129	0.114	②	0.096	0.243	⑥
	17080242	13/32	9/16	9/32 ③	0.077	0.096	②	0.074	0.220	⑥
	17080243	3/16	9/16	9/32 ③	0.083	0.083	②	0.074	0.179	⑥
	17080244	5/16	5/8	9/32 ③	0.096	0.071	②	0.139	0.243	⑥
	17080249	7/16	3/4	9/32 ③	0.129	0.114	②	0.096	0.243	⑥
	17080253	13/32	1/2	9/32 ③	0.149	0.211	②	0.090	0.220	⑥
	17080259	13/32	1/2	9/32 ③	0.149	0.211	②	0.090	0.220	⑥
	17080270	15/32	5/8	3/8 ⑦	0.149	0.211	②	0.074	0.220	⑥
	17080271	15/32	5/8	3/8 ⑦	0.142	0.211	②	0.110	0.203	⑥
	17080272	15/32	5/8	3/8 ⑦	0.129	0.175	②	0.074	0.203	⑥
	17080502	1/2	7/8	Fixed	0.136	0.179	②	0.110	0.243	⑥
	17080504	1/2	7/8	Fixed	0.136	0.179	②	0.110	0.243	⑥
	17080540	3/8	9/16	Fixed	0.103	0.129	②	0.074	0.243	⑥
	17080542	3/8	9/16	Fixed	0.103	0.066	②	0.074	0.243	⑥
	17080543	3/8	9/16	Fixed	0.103	0.129	②	0.074	0.243	⑥
	17080553	15/32	1/2	Fixed	0.142	0.220	②	0.090	0.220	⑥
	17080554	15/32	1/2	Fixed	0.142	0.211	②	0.090	0.220	⑥
'81	17081202 204	11/32	7/8	Fixed	0.157 ⑧	—	②	0.110	0.243	⑩

25-83

CARBURETORS
ROCHESTER

QUADRAJET CARBURETOR SPECIFICATIONS
Buick

Year	Carburetor Identification ①	Float Level (in.)	Air Valve Spring (turn)	Pump Rod (in.)	Primary Vacuum Break (in./deg.)	Secondary Vacuum Break (in./deg.)	Secondary Opening (in.)	Choke Rod (in.)	Choke Unloader (in/degrees)	Fast Idle Speed ④ (rpm)
'81	17081203 207	11/32	7/8	Fixed	0.157 ⑧	—	②	0.110	0.243	⑩
	17081216 218	11/32	7/8	Fixed	0.157 ⑧	—	②	0.110	0.243	⑩
	17081242	3/8	9/16	Fixed	0.090 ⑧	0.077 ⑨	②	0.139	0.243	⑩
	17081243	5/16	9/16	Fixed	0.103 ⑧	0.090 ⑨	②	0.139	0.243	⑩
	17081245	3/8	5/8	Fixed	0.164 ⑧	0.136 ⑨	②	0.139	0.243	⑩
	17081247	3/8	5/8	Fixed	0.164 ⑧	0.136 ⑨	②	0.139	0.243	⑩
	17081248 249	3/8	5/8	Fixed	0.164 ⑧	0.136 ⑨	②	0.139	0.243	⑩
	17081253 254	15/32	1/2	Fixed	0.142 ⑧	0.227 ⑨	②	0.071	0.220	⑩
	17081270	7/16	5/8	Fixed	0.136 ⑧	0.211 ⑨	②	0.074	0.220	⑩
	17081272	5/8	5/8	Fixed	0.136 ⑧	0.260 ⑨	②	0.074	0.220	⑩
	17081274	5/8	5/8	Fixed	0.136 ⑧	0.220 ⑨	②	0.083	0.220	⑩
	17081289	5/8	5/8	Fixed	0.164 ⑧	0.136 ⑨	②	0.139	0.243	⑩
'82	17082202	11/32	7/8	Fixed	0.110/20	—	②	0.110	0.243	⑤
	17082204	11/32	3/8	Fixed	0.110/20	—	②	0.110	0.243	⑤
	17082244	7/16	9/16	Fixed	0.117/21	0.083/16	②	0.139	0.195	⑤
	17082245	3/8	5/8	Fixed	0.149/26	0.149/26	②	0.139	0.195	⑤
	17082246	3/8	5/8	Fixed	0.149/26	0.149/26	②	0.139	0.195	⑤
	17082247	13/32	5/8	Fixed	0.164/28	0.136/24	②	0.139	0.243	⑤
	17082248	13/32	5/8	Fixed	0.164/28	0.136/24	②	0.139	0.243	⑤
	17082251	15/32	1/2	Fixed	0.142/25	0.304/45	②	0.071	0.220	⑤
	17082253	15/32	1/2	Fixed	0.142/25	0.227/36	②	0.071	0.220	⑤
	17082264	7/16	9/16	Fixed	0.117/20	0.083/16	②	0.139	0.195	⑤
	17082265	3/8	5/8	Fixed	0.149/26	0.149/26	②	0.139	0.195	⑤
	17082266	3/8	5/8	Fixed	0.149/26	0.149/26	②	0.139	0.195	⑤
	17082267	3/8	5/8	Fixed	0.164/28	0.136/24	②	0.139	0.243	⑤
	17082268	13/32	5/8	Fixed	0.164/28	0.136/24	②	0.139	0.243	⑤
'83	17082265	3/8	5/8	Fixed	0.149/26	0.149/26	②	0.139	0.195	⑪
	17082266	3/8	5/8	Fixed	0.149/26	0.149/26	②	0.139	0.195	⑪
	17082267	3/8	5/8	Fixed	0.149/26	0.149/26	②	0.096	0.195	⑪
	17082268	3/8	5/8	Fixed	0.149/26	0.149/26	②	0.096	0.195	⑪
	17083242	9/32	9/16	Fixed	0.110/20	—	②	0.139	0.243	⑪
	17083244	1/4	9/16	Fixed	0.117/21	0.083/16	②	0.139	0.195	⑪
	17083248	3/8	5/8	Fixed	0.149/26	0.149/26	②	0.139	0.195	⑪
	17083250	7/16	1/2	Fixed	0.157/27	0.271/42	②	0.071	0.220	⑪
	17083253	7/16	1/2	Fixed	0.157/27	0.269/41	②	0.071	0.220	⑪
	17083553	7/16	1/2	Fixed	0.157/27	0.269/41	②	0.071	0.220	⑪
'84	17084201	11/32	7/8	Fixed	0.157/27	—	②	0.110	0.243	⑪
	17084205	11/32	7/8	Fixed	0.157/27	—	②	0.243	0.243	⑪
	17084208	11/32	7/8	Fixed	0.157/27	—	②	0.110	0.243	⑪
	17084209	11/32	7/8	Fixed	0.157/27	—	②	0.243	0.243	⑪
	17084210	11/32	7/8	Fixed	0.157/27	—	②	0.110	0.243	⑪
	17084240	5/16	1	Fixed	0.136/24	—	②	—	0.195	⑪
	17084244	5/16	1	Fixed	0.136/24	—	②	—	0.195	⑪
	17084246	5/16	1	Fixed	0.123/22	0.136/24	②	—	0.195	⑪
	17084248	5/16	1	Fixed	0.136/24	—	②	—	0.195	⑪
	17084252	7/16	1/2	Fixed	0.157/27	0.269/41	②	—	0.220	⑪
	17084254	7/16	1/2	Fixed	0.157/27	0.269/41	②	—	0.220	⑪

CARBURETORS
ROCHESTER

QUADRAJET CARBURETOR SPECIFICATIONS
Buick

Year	Carburetor Identification ①	Float Level (in.)	Air Valve Spring (turn)	Pump Rod (in.)	Primary Vacuum Break (in./deg.)	Secondary Vacuum Break (in./deg.)	Secondary Opening (in.)	Choke Rod (in.)	Choke Unloader (in/degrees)	Fast Idle Speed ④ (rpm)
'85	17085202	11/32	7/8	Fixed	0.157/27	—	②	—	38°	⑪
	17085203	11/32	7/8	Fixed	0.157/27	—	②	—	38°	⑪
	17085204	11/32	7/8	Fixed	0.157/27	—	②	—	38°	⑪
	17085208	11/32	7/8	Fixed	0.157/27	—	②	—	38°	⑪
	17085218	11/32	7/8	Fixed	0.157/27	—	②	—	38°	⑪
	17085282	11/32	1/2	Fixed	0.142/25	0.273/43	②	—	35°	⑪
	17085502	14/32	7/8	Fixed	0.149/26	0.227/36	②	—	39°	⑪
	17085503	14/32	7/8	Fixed	0.149/26	0.227/36	②	—	39°	⑪
	17085506	14/32	1	Fixed	0.157/27	0.227/36	②	—	36°	⑪
	17085508	14/32	1	Fixed	0.157/27	0.227/36	②	—	36°	⑪
	17085524	14/32	1	Fixed	0.142/25	0.227/36	②	—	36°	⑪
	17085526	14/32	1	Fixed	0.142/25	0.227/36	②	—	36°	⑪
	17085554	14/32	1/2	Fixed	0.157/27	0.269/41	②	—	35°	⑪

① The carburetor identification number is stamped on the float bowl, near the secondary throttle lever.
② No measurement necessary on two point linkage; see text
③ Inner hole
④ On high step of cam, automatic in Park
⑤ 3 turns after contacting lever for preliminary setting
⑥ 2 turns after contacting lever for preliminary setting
⑦ Outer hole
⑧ Front
⑨ Rear
⑩ 4½ turns after contacting lever for preliminary setting
⑪ See underhood decal

QUADRAJET CARBURETOR SPECIFICATIONS
Chevrolet

Year	Carburetor Identification ①	Float Level (in.)	Air Valve Spring (turn)	Pump Rod (in.)	Primary Vacuum (deg./in.)	Secondary Vacuum (deg./in.)	Secondary Opening (in.)	Choke Rod (in.)	Choke Unloader (in.)	Fast Idle Speed ④ (rpm)
'80	17080202	7/16	7/8	1/4 ⑧	0.157	—	⑤	0.110	0.243	⑩
	17080204	7/16	7/8	1/4 ⑧	0.157	—	⑤	0.110	0.243	⑩
	17080207	7/16	7/8	1/4 ⑧	0.157	—	⑤	0.110	0.243	⑩
	17080228	7/16	7/8	9/32 ⑧	0.179	—	⑤	0.110	0.243	⑩
	17080243	3/16	9/16	9/32 ⑧	0.016	0.083	⑤	0.074	0.179	⑩
	17080274	15/32	5/8	5/16 ⑨	0.110	0.164	⑤	0.083	0.203	⑩
	17080282	7/16	7/8	11/32 ⑨	0.142	—	⑤	0.110	0.243	⑩
	17080284	7/16	7/8	11/32 ⑨	0.142	—	⑤	0.110	0.243	⑩
	17080502	1/2	7/8	Fixed	0.136	0.179	⑤	0.110	0.243	⑩
	17080504	1/2	7/8	Fixed	0.136	0.179	⑤	0.110	0.243	⑩
	17080542	3/8	9/16	Fixed	0.103	0.066	⑤	0.074	0.243	⑩
	17080543	3/8	9/16	Fixed	0.103	0.129	⑤	0.074	0.243	⑩
'81	17081202	11/32	7/8	Fixed	0.149	—	⑤	0.110	0.243	⑪
	17081203	11/32	7/8	Fixed	0.149	—	⑤	0.110	0.243	⑪
	17081204	11/32	7/8	Fixed	0.149	—	⑤	0.110	0.243	⑪
	17081207	11/32	7/8	Fixed	0.149	—	⑤	0.110	0.243	⑪
	17081216	11/32	7/8	Fixed	0.149	—	⑤	0.110	0.243	⑪
	17081217	11/32	7/8	Fixed	0.149	—	⑤	0.110	0.243	⑪
	17081218	11/32	7/8	Fixed	0.149	—	⑤	0.110	0.243	⑪
	17081242	5/16	9/16	Fixed	0.090	0.077	⑤	0.139	0.243	⑪
	17081243	1/4	9/16	Fixed	0.103	0.090	⑤	0.139	0.243	⑪
'82	17082202	11/32	7/8	Fixed	0.157	—	⑤	0.110	0.243	⑫
	17082204	11/32	7/8	Fixed	0.157	—	⑤	0.110	0.243	⑫
	17082203	11/32	7/8	Fixed	0.157	—	⑤	0.243	0.243	⑫
	17082207	11/32	7/8	Fixed	0.157	—	⑤	0.243	0.243	⑫

CARBURETORS
ROCHESTER

QUADRAJET CARBURETOR SPECIFICATIONS
Chevrolet

Year	Carburetor Identification ①	Float Level (in.)	Air Valve Spring (turn)	Pump Rod (in.)	Primary Vacuum (deg./in.)	Secondary Vacuum (deg./in.)	Secondary Opening (in.)	Choke Rod (in.)	Choke Unloader (in.)	Fast Idle Speed ④ (rpm)
'83	17083202	11/32	7/8	Fixed	—	27/.157	⑤	0.110	0.243	⑬
	17083203	11/32	7/8	Fixed	—	27/.157	⑤	0.243	0.243	⑬
	17083204	11/32	7/8	Fixed	—	27/.157	⑤	0.110	0.243	⑬
	17083207	11/32	7/8	Fixed	—	27/.157	⑤	0.243	0.243	⑬
	17083216	11/32	7/8	Fixed	—	27/.157	⑤	0.110	0.243	⑬
	17083218	11/32	7/8	Fixed	—	27/.157	⑤	0.110	0.243	⑬
	17083236	11/32	7/8	Fixed	—	27/.157	⑤	0.110	0.243	⑬
	17083506	7/16	7/8	Fixed	27/.157	36/.227	⑤	0.110	0.227	⑬
	17083508	7/16	7/8	Fixed	27/.157	36/.227	⑤	0.110	0.227	⑬
	17083524	7/16	7/8	Fixed	25/.142	36/.227	⑤	0.110	0.227	⑬
	17083526	7/16	7/8	Fixed	25/.142	36/.227	⑤	0.110	0.227	⑬
'84	17084201	11/32	7/8	Fixed	.157/27	—	⑤	0.110	0.243	⑬
	17084205	11/32	7/8	Fixed	.157/27	—	⑤	0.243	0.243	⑬
	17084208	11/32	7/8	Fixed	.157/27	—	⑤	0.110	0.243	⑬
	17084209	11/32	7/8	Fixed	.157/27	—	⑤	0.243	0.243	⑬
	17084210	11/32	7/8	Fixed	.157/27	—	⑤	0.110	0.243	⑬
	17084507	7/16	1	Fixed	.157/27	.227/36	⑤	0.110	0.227	⑬
	17084509	7/16	1	Fixed	.157/27	.227/36	⑤	0.110	0.227	⑬
	17084525	7/16	1	Fixed	.142/25	.227/36	⑤	0.110	0.227	⑬
	17084527	7/16	1	Fixed	.142/25	.227/36	⑤	0.110	0.227	⑬
'85	17085202	11/32	7/8	Fixed	0.157/27	—	②	0.110	0.243/38°	⑪
	17085203	11/32	7/8	Fixed	0.157/27	—	②	⑭	0.243/38°	⑪
	17085204	11/32	7/8	Fixed	0.157/27	—	②	0.110	0.243/38°	⑪
	17085207	11/32	7/8	Fixed	0.157/27	—	②	0.243	0.243/38°	⑪
	17085218	11/32	7/8	Fixed	0.157/27	—	②	0.110	0.243/38°	⑪
	17085282	11/32	1/2	Fixed	0.142/25	0.273/43	②	0.110	0.220/35°	⑪
	17085502	14/32	7/8	Fixed	0.149/26	0.227/36	②	0.110	0.251/39°	⑪
	17085503	14/32	7/8	Fixed	0.149/26	0.227/36	②	0.110	0.251/39°	⑪
	17085506	14/32	1	Fixed	0.157/27	0.227/36	②	0.110	0.227/36°	⑪
	17085508	14/32	1	Fixed	0.157/27	0.227/36	②	0.110	0.227/36°	⑪
	17085524	14/32	1	Fixed	0.142/25	0.227/36	②	0.110	0.227/36°	⑪
	17085526	14/32	1	Fixed	0.142/25	0.227/36	②	0.110	0.227/36°	⑪
	17085554	14/32	1/2	Fixed	0.157/27	0.269/41	②	0.071	0.220/35°	⑪
'86	17086003	11/32	7/8	Fixed	0.157/27	—	②	—	0.243/38°	⑪
	17086004	11/32	7/8	Fixed	0.157/27	—	②	—	0.243/38°	⑪
	17086005	11/32	7/8	Fixed	0.157/27	—	②	—	0.243/38°	⑪
	17086006	11/32	7/8	Fixed	0.157/27	—	②	—	0.243/38°	⑪

① The carburetor identification number is stamped on the float bowl, near the secondary throttle lever.
② Without vacuum advance.
③ With automatic transmission; vacuum advance connected and EGR disconnected and the throttle positioned on the high step of cam.
④ With manual transmission; without vacuum advance and the throttle positioned on the high step of cam.
⑤ No measurement necessary on two point linkage; see text.
⑥ 3 turns after contacting lever for preliminary setting.
⑦ 2 turns after contacting lever for preliminary setting.
⑧ Inner hole
⑨ Outer hole
⑩ 4 turns after contacting lever for preliminary setting.
⑪ 4½ turns after contacting lever for preliminary setting
⑫ 3⅛ turns after contacting lever for preliminary setting
⑬ See underhood sticker
⑭ 3 step cam: 0.110, 2 step cam: 0.243

CARBURETORS
ROCHESTER
SECTION 25

QUADRAJET CARBURETOR SPECIFICATIONS
Oldsmobile

Year	Carburetor Identification ①	Float Level (in.)	Air Valve Spring (turn)	Pump Rod (in.)	Primary Vacuum Break (in./deg.)	Secondary Vacuum Break (in./deg.)	Secondary Opening (in.)	Choke Rod (in.)	Choke Unloader (in.)	Fast Idle Speed ④ (rpm)
'80	17080202	7/16	7/8	1/4 ⑦	0.157	—	④	0.110	0.243	⑤
	17080204	7/16	7/8	1/4 ⑦	0.157	—	④	0.110	0.243	⑤
	17080250	13/32	1/2	9/32 ⑦	0.149	0.211	④	0.090	0.220	⑤
	17080251	13/32	1/2	9/32 ⑦	0.149	0.211	④	0.090	0.220	⑤
	17080252	13/32	1/2	9/32 ⑦	0.149	0.211	④	0.090	0.220	⑤
	17080253	13/32	1/2	9/32 ⑦	0.149	0.211	④	0.090	0.220	⑤
	17080259	13/32	1/2	9/32 ⑦	0.149	0.211	④	0.090	0.220	⑤
	17080260	13/32	1/2	9/32 ⑦	0.149	0.211	④	0.090	0.220	⑤
	17080504	1/2	7/8	⑧	0.136	0.179	④	0.110	0.243	⑤
	17080553	15/32	1/2	⑧	0.142	0.220	④	0.090	0.220	⑤
	17080554	15/32	1/2	⑧	0.142	0.211	④	0.090	0.220	⑤
'81	17081250	13/32	1/2	9/32 ⑦	0.149 ⑨	0.211 ⑩	④	0.090	0.220	⑤
	17081253	15/32	1/2	⑧	0.142 ⑨	0.227 ⑩	④	0.071	0.220	⑤
	17081254	15/32	1/2	⑧	0.142 ⑨	0.227 ⑩	④	0.071	0.220	⑤
	17081248	3/8	—	⑧	0.164 ⑨	0.136 ⑩	④	0.139	0.243	⑤
	17081289	13/32	—	⑧	0.164 ⑨	0.136 ⑩	④	0.139	0.243	⑤
'82	17082202	11/32	7/8	Fixed	0.110/20	—	④	0.110	0.243	⑤
	17082204	11/32	3/8	Fixed	0.110/20	—	④	0.110	0.243	⑤
	17082244	7/16	9/16	Fixed	0.117/21	0.083/16	④	0.139	0.195	⑤
	17082245	3/8	5/8	Fixed	0.149/26	0.149/26	④	0.139	0.195	⑤
	17082246	3/8	5/8	Fixed	0.149/26	0.149/26	④	0.139	0.195	⑤
	17082247	13/32	5/8	Fixed	0.164/28	0.136/24	④	0.139	0.243	⑤
	17082248	13/32	5/8	Fixed	0.164/28	0.136/24	④	0.139	0.243	⑤
	17082251	15/32	1/2	Fixed	0.142/25	0.304/45	④	0.071	0.220	⑤
	17082253	15/32	1/2	Fixed	0.142/25	0.227/36	④	0.071	0.220	⑤
	17082264	7/16	9/16	Fixed	0.117/20	0.083/16	④	0.139	0.195	⑤
	17082265	3/8	5/8	Fixed	0.149/26	0.149/26	④	0.139	0.195	⑤
	17082266	3/8	5/8	Fixed	0.149/26	0.149/26	④	0.139	0.195	⑤
	17082267	3/8	5/8	Fixed	0.164/28	0.136/24	④	0.139	0.243	⑤
	17082268	13/32	5/8	Fixed	0.164/28	0.136/24	④	0.139	0.243	⑤
'83	17082265	3/8	5/8	Fixed	0.149/26	0.149/26	②	0.139	0.195	⑪
	17082266	3/8	5/8	Fixed	0.149/26	0.149/26	②	0.139	0.195	⑪
	17082267	3/8	5/8	Fixed	0.149/26	0.149/26	②	0.096	0.195	⑪
	17082268	3/8	5/8	Fixed	0.149/26	0.149/26	②	0.096	0.195	⑪
	17083242	9/32	9/16	Fixed	0.110/20	—	②	0.139	0.243	⑪
	17083244	1/4	9/16	Fixed	0.117/21	0.083/16	②	0.139	0.195	⑪
	17083248	3/8	5/8	Fixed	0.149/26	0.149/26	②	0.139	0.195	⑪
	17083250	7/16	1/2	Fixed	0.157/27	0.271/42	②	0.071	0.220	⑪
	17083253	7/16	1/2	Fixed	0.157/27	0.269/41	②	0.071	0.220	⑪
	17083553	7/16	1/2	Fixed	0.157/27	0.269/41	②	0.071	0.220	⑪
'84	17084201	11/32	7/8	Fixed	0.157/27	—	②	0.110	0.243	⑪
	17084205	11/32	7/8	Fixed	0.157/27	—	②	0.243	0.243	⑪
	17084208	11/32	7/8	Fixed	0.157/27	—	②	0.110	0.243	⑪
	17084209	11/32	7/8	Fixed	0.157/27	—	②	0.243	0.243	⑪
	17084210	11/32	7/8	Fixed	0.157/27	—	②	0.110	0.243	⑪
	17084240	5/16	1	Fixed	0.136/24	—	②	—	0.195	⑪
	17084244	5/16	1	Fixed	0.136/24	—	②	—	0.195	⑪
	17084246	5/16	1	Fixed	0.123/22	0.136/24	②	—	0.195	⑪
	17084248	5/16	1	Fixed	0.136/24	—	②	—	0.195	⑪
	17084252	7/16	1/2	Fixed	0.157/27	0.269/41	②	—	0.220	⑪
	17084254	7/16	1/2	Fixed	0.157/27	0.269/41	②	—	0.220	⑪

CARBURETORS
ROCHESTER

QUADRAJET CARBURETOR SPECIFICATIONS
Oldsmobile

Year	Carburetor Identification ①	Float Level (in.)	Air Valve Spring (turn)	Pump Rod (in.)	Primary Vacuum Break (in./deg.)	Secondary Vacuum Break (in./deg.)	Secondary Opening (in.)	Choke Rod (in.)	Choke Unloader (in.)	Fast Idle Speed ④ (rpm)
'85	17084282	11/32	1/2	9/32	0.142/25	0.278/43	④	0.110	0.220	⑤
	17085554	14/32	1/2	9/32	0.157/27	0.269/41	④	0.110	0.220	⑤
'86	17086008	11/32	1/2	Fixed	0.142/25	0.287/43	④	0.171	0.220	⑤
	17086009	14/32	1/2	Fixed	0.142/25	0.287/43	④	0.171	0.220	⑤

① The carburetor identification number is stamped on the float bowl, next to the secondary throttle lever.
② 1800 rpm on Omega and 400 cu. in. engines with the cam follower on the highest step of the fast idle cam; 900 rpm on all others with the fast idle cam follower on the lowest step of the fast idle cam.
④ No measurement necessary on two point linkage; see text.
⑤ 3 turns after contacting lever for preliminary setting.
⑥ 2 turns after contacting lever for preliminary setting.
⑦ Inner hole
⑧ Not Adjustable
⑨ Front
⑩ Rear
⑪ See underhood sticker

QUADRAJET CARBURETOR SPECIFICATIONS
Pontiac

Year	Carburetor Identification ①	Float Level (in.)	Air Valve Spring (turn)	Pump Rod (in.)	Primary Vacuum Break (in./deg.)	Secondary Vacuum Break (in./deg.)	Secondary Opening (in.)	Choke Rod (in.)	Choke Unloader (in./deg.)	Fast Idle Speed ② (rpm)
'80	17080249	7/16	3/4	9/32 ⑥	0.129	0.114	④	0.096	0.243	③
	17080270	15/32	5/8	3/8 ⑦	0.149	0.211	④	0.074	0.220	③
	17080272	15/32	5/8	3/8 ⑦	0.129	0.175	④	0.074	0.203	③
	17080274	15/32	5/8	5/16 ⑥	0.110	0.164	④	0.083	0.203	③
	17080502	1/2	7/8	⑧	0.136	0.179	④	0.110	0.243	③
	17080504	1/2	7/8	⑧	0.136	0.179	④	0.110	0.243	③
	17080553	15/32	1/2	⑧	0.142	0.220	④	0.090	0.220	③
'81	17081202, 204	11/32	7/8	⑧	0.157 ⑩	—	④	0.110	0.243	⑨
	17081203, 207	11/32	7/8	⑧	0.157 ⑩	—	④	0.110	0.243	⑨
	17081216, 217, 218	11/32	7/8	⑧	0.157 ⑩	—	④	0.110	0.243	⑨
	17081242	3/8	9/16	⑧	0.090 ⑩	0.077	④	0.139	0.243	⑨
	17081243	5/16	9/16	⑧	0.103 ⑩	0.090	④	0.139	0.243	⑨
	17081245	3/8	5/8	⑧	0.164 ⑩	0.136	④	0.139	0.243	⑨
	17081247	3/8	5/8	⑧	0.164 ⑩	0.136	④	0.139	0.243	⑨
	17081248, 249	3/8	5/8	⑧	0.164 ⑩	0.136	④	0.139	0.243	⑨
	17081253, 254	15/32	1/2	⑧	0.142 ⑩	0.227	④	0.071	0.220	⑨
	17081270	7/16	5/8	⑧	0.136 ⑩	0.211	④	0.074	0.220	⑨
	17081272	7/16	5/8	⑧	0.136 ⑩	0.260	④	0.074	0.220	⑨
	17081274	7/16	5/8	⑧	0.136 ⑩	0.220	④	0.083	0.220	⑨
	17081289	13/36	5/8	⑧	0.164 ⑩	0.136	④	0.139	0.243	⑨
'82	17082202	11/32	7/8	Fixed	0.110/20 ⑭	—	④	0.110	0.243	⑫ ⑮
	17082204	11/32	3/8 ⑬	Fixed	0.110/20 ⑭	—	④	0.110	0.243	⑫ ⑮
	17082203	11/32	7/8	Fixed	0.157/27	—	④	0.243	0.243	⑮
	17082207	11/32	7/8	Fixed	0.157/27	—	④	0.243	0.243	⑮
	17082244	7/16	9/16	Fixed	0.117/21	0.083/16	④	0.139	0.195	⑫
	17082245	3/8	5/8	Fixed	0.149/26	0.149/26	④	0.139	0.195	⑫
	17082246	3/8	5/8	Fixed	0.149/26	0.149/26	④	0.139	0.195	⑫
	17082247	13/32	5/8	Fixed	0.164/28	0.136/24	④	0.139	0.243	⑫
	17082248	13/32	5/8	Fixed	0.164/28	0.136/24	④	0.139	0.243	⑫
	17082251	15/32	1/2	Fixed	0.142/25	0.304/45	④	0.071	0.220	⑫
	17082253	15/32	1/2	Fixed	0.142/25	0.227/36	④	0.071	0.220	⑫

CARBURETORS
ROCHESTER
SECTION 25

QUADRAJET CARBURETOR SPECIFICATIONS
Pontiac

Year	Carburetor Identification ①	Float Level (in.)	Air Valve Spring (turn)	Pump Rod (in.)	Primary Vacuum Break (in./deg.)	Secondary Vacuum Break (in./deg.)	Secondary Opening (in.)	Choke Rod (in.)	Choke Unloader (in./deg.)	Fast Idle Speed ② (rpm)
'82	17082264	7/16	9/16	Fixed	0.117/20	0.083/16	④	0.139	0.195	⑫
	17082265	3/8	5/8	Fixed	0.149/26	0.149/26	④	0.139	0.195	⑫
	17082266	3/8	5/8	Fixed	0.149/26	0.149/26	④	0.139	0.195	⑫
	17082267	3/8	5/8	Fixed	0.164/28	0.136/24	④	0.139	0.243	⑫
	17082268	13/32	5/8	Fixed	0.164/28	0.136/24	④	0.139	0.243	⑫
'83	17082265	3/8	5/8	Fixed	0.149/26	0.149/26	②	0.139	0.195	⑯
	17082266	3/8	5/8	Fixed	0.149/26	0.149/26	②	0.139	0.195	⑯
	17082267	3/8	5/8	Fixed	0.149/26	0.149/26	②	0.096	0.195	⑯
	17082268	3/8	5/8	Fixed	0.149/26	0.149/26	②	0.096	0.195	⑯
	17083242	9/32	9/16	Fixed	0.110/20	—	②	0.139	0.243	⑯
	17083244	1/4	9/16	Fixed	0.117/21	0.083/16	②	0.139	0.195	⑯
	17083248	3/8	5/8	Fixed	0.149/26	0.149/26	②	0.139	0.195	⑯
	17083250	7/16	1/2	Fixed	0.157/27	0.271/42	②	0.071	0.220	⑯
	17083253	7/16	1/2	Fixed	0.157/27	0.269/41	②	0.071	0.220	⑯
	17083553	7/16	1/2	Fixed	0.157/27	0.269/41	②	0.071	0.220	⑯
'84	17084201	11/32	7/8	Fixed	0.157/27	—	②	0.110	0.243	⑯
	17084205	11/32	7/8	Fixed	0.157/27	—	②	0.243	0.243	⑯
	17084208	11/32	7/8	Fixed	0.157/27	—	②	0.110	0.243	⑯
	17084209	11/32	7/8	Fixed	0.157/27	—	②	0.243	0.243	⑯
	17084210	11/32	7/8	Fixed	0.157/27	—	②	0.110	0.243	⑯
	17084240	5/16	1	Fixed	0.136/24	—	②	—	0.195	⑯
	17084244	5/16	1	Fixed	0.136/24	—	②	—	0.195	⑯
	17084246	5/16	1	Fixed	0.123/22	0.136/24	②	—	0.195	⑯
	17084248	5/16	1	Fixed	0.136/24	—	②	—	0.195	⑯
	17084252	7/16	1/2	Fixed	0.157/27	0.269/41	②	—	0.220	⑯
	17084254	7/16	1/2	Fixed	0.157/27	0.269/41	②	—	0.220	⑯
'85	17085202	11/32	7/8	Fixed	0.157/27	—	②	0.110	0.243/38	⑯
	17085203	11/32	7/8	Fixed	0.157/27	—	②	⑰	0.243/38	⑯
	17085204	11/32	7/8	Fixed	0.157/27	—	②	0.110	0.243/38	⑯
	17085207	11/32	7/8	Fixed	0.157/27	—	②	0.243	0.243/38	⑯
	17085218	11/32	7/8	Fixed	0.157/27	—	②	0.110	0.243/38	⑯
	17085282	11/32	1/2	Fixed	0.142/25	0.273/43	②	0.110	0.220/35	⑯
	17085502	14/32	7/8	Fixed	0.149/26	0.227/36	②	0.110	0.251/39	⑯
	17085503	14/32	7/8	Fixed	0.149/26	0.227/36	②	0.110	0.251/39	⑯
	17085506	14/32	1	Fixed	0.157/27	0.227/36	②	0.110	0.227/36	⑯
	17085508	14/32	1	Fixed	0.157/27	0.227/36	②	0.110	0.227/36	⑯
	17085524	14/32	1	Fixed	0.142/25	0.227/36	②	0.110	0.227/36	⑯
	17085526	14/32	1	Fixed	0.142/25	0.227/36	②	0.110	0.227/36	⑯
	17085554	14/32	1/2	Fixed	0.157/27	0.269/41	②	0.071	0.220/35	⑯
'86	17086003	11/32	7/8	Fixed	0.157/27	—	②	0.110	0.243/38	⑯
	17086004	11/32	7/8	Fixed	0.157/27	—	②	0.110	0.243/38	⑯
	17086005	11/32	7/8	Fixed	0.157/27	—	②	0.243	0.243/38	⑯
	17086006	11/32	7/8	Fixed	0.157/27	—	②	0.110	0.243/38	⑯
	17086007	11/32	1/2	Fixed	0.142/25	0.287/43	②	0.071	0.220/35	⑯
	17086008	11/32	1/2	Fixed	0.142/25	0.287/43	②	0.071	0.220/35	⑯
	17086040	11/32	7/8	Fixed	0.157/27	—	②	0.110	0.243/38	⑯

① The carburetor identification number is stamped on the float bowl, near the secondary throttle lever.
② On highest step.
③ 1½ turns after contacting lever for preliminary setting
④ No measurement necessary on two point linkage; see text.
⑤ 2 turns after contacting lever for preliminary setting.
⑥ Inner hole
⑦ Outer hole
⑧ Not Adjustable
⑨ 4½ turns after contacting lever for preliminary setting
⑩ Front
⑪ Rear
⑫ 3 turns after contacting lever for preliminary setting
⑬ Firebird—7/8
⑭ Firebird—0.157 in./27°
⑮ Firebird—3⅛ turns after contacting lever for preliminary setting
⑯ See underhood sticker
⑰ 3 step cam: 0.110, 2 step cam: 0.243

25–89

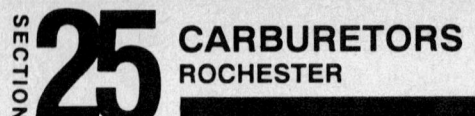

QUADRAJET CARBURETOR SPECIFICATIONS
All Canadian Models

Year	Carburetor Identification ①	Float Level (in.)	Air Valve Spring (turn)	Pump Rod (in.)	Primary Vacuum Break (deg./in.)	Secondary Vacuum Break (deg./in.)	Secondary Opening (in.)	Choke Rod (in.)	Choke Unloader (deg./in.)	Fast Idle Speed ② (rpm)
'81	17080201	15/32	7/8	9/32 ②	—	23/0.129	④	0.314	0.277	⑤
	17080205	15/32	7/8	9/32 ②	—	23/0.129	④	0.314	0.277	⑤
	17080206	15/32	7/8	9/32 ②	—	23/0.129	④	0.314	0.277	⑤
	17080290	15/32	7/8	9/32 ②	—	26/0.149	④	0.314	0.277	⑤
	17080291	15/32	7/8	9/32 ②	—	26/0.149	④	0.314	0.277	⑤
	17080292	15/32	7/8	9/32 ②	—	26/0.149	④	0.314	0.277	⑤
	17080213	3/8	1	9/32 ②	23/0.129	30/0.179	④	0.234	0.260	⑤
	17080215	3/8	1	9/32 ②	23/0.129	30/0.179	④	0.234	0.260	⑤
	17080298	3/8	1	9/32 ②	23/0.129	30/0.179	④	0.234	0.260	⑤
	17080507	3/8	1	9/32 ②	23/0.129	30/0.179	④	0.234	0.260	⑤
	17080513	3/8	1	9/32 ②	23/0.129	30/0.179	④	0.234	0.260	⑤
	17081250	13/32	1/2	9/32 ②	26/0.149	34/0.211	④	0.090	0.220	⑤
	17080260	13/32	1/2	9/32 ②	26/0.149	34/0.211	④	0.090	0.220	⑤
	17081276	15/32	5/8	5/16 ②	20/0.110	28/0.164	④	0.083	0.203	⑤
	17081286	13/32	1/2	9/32 ②	18/0.096	34/0.211	④	0.077	0.220	⑤
	17081287	13/32	1/2	9/32 ②	18/0.096	34/0.211	④	0.077	0.220	⑤
	17081282	3/8	5/8	9/32 ②	20/0.110	—	④	0.110	0.243	⑤
	17081283	3/8	7/8	9/32 ②	20/0.110	—	④	0.110	0.243	⑤
	17081284	1/2	7/8	9/32 ②	20/0.110	—	④	0.110	0.243	⑤
	17081285	1/2	7/8	9/32 ②	20/0.110	—	④	0.110	0.243	⑤
	17080243	3/16	9/16	9/32 ②	14.5/0.075	16/0.083	④	0.075	0.179	⑤
	17081295	13/32	9/16	9/32 ②	14.5/0.075	13/0.066	④	0.075	0.220	⑤
	17081294	5/16	5/8	9/32 ②	24.5/0.139	14/0.071	④	0.139	0.243	⑤
	17081290	13/32	7/8	9/32 ②	46/0.314	24/0.136	④	0.314	0.277	⑤
	17081291	13/32	7/8	9/32 ②	46/0.314	24/0.136	④	0.314	0.277	⑤
	17081292	13/32	7/8	9/32 ②	46/0.314	24/0.136	④	0.314	0.277	⑤
	17081506	13/32	7/8	9/32 ②	46/0.314	36/0.227	④	0.314	0.277	⑤
	17081508	13/32	7/8	9/32 ②	46/0.314	36/0.227	④	0.314	0.277	⑤
	17080202	7/16	7/8	1/4 ②	20/0.110	—	④	0.110	0.243	⑤
	17080204	7/16	7/8	1/4 ②	20/0.110	—	④	0.110	0.243	⑤
	17080207	7/16	7/8	1/4 ②	20/0.110	—	④	0.110	0.243	⑤
'82	17082280	3/8	7/8	9/32 ②	25/0.142	—	④	0.110	0.243	⑤
	17082281	3/8	7/8	9/32 ②	25/0.142	—	④	0.110	0.243	⑤
	17082282	3/8	7/8	9/32 ②	25/0.142	—	④	0.110	0.243	⑤
	17082283	3/8	7/8	9/32 ②	25/0.142	—	④	0.110	0.243	⑤
	17082286	13/32	1/2	9/32 ②	22/0.123	34/0.211	④	0.077	0.243	⑤
	17082287	13/32	1/2	9/32 ②	22/0.123	34/0.211	④	0.077	0.243	⑤
	17082288	3/8	7/8	9/32 ②	25/0.142	—	④	0.110	0.243	⑤
	17082289	3/8	7/8	9/32 ②	25/0.142	—	④	0.110	0.243	⑤
	17082296	1/2	7/8	9/32 ②	25/0.142	—	④	0.110	0.243	⑤
	17082297	1/2	7/8	9/32 ②	25/0.142	—	④	0.110	0.243	⑤
'83	17080213	3/8	1	9/32	23/.129	30/.179	④	0.234	0.260	⑤
	17082213	9/32	1	9/32	23/.129	30/.179	④	0.234	0.260	⑤
	17082282	3/8	7/8	9/32	25/.142	—	④	0.110	0.243	⑤
	17082283	3/8	7/8	9/32	25/.142	—	④	0.110	0.243	⑤
	17082286	13/32	1/2	9/32	23/.129	34/.211	④	0.107	0.220	⑤
	17082287	13/32	1/2	9/32	23/.129	34/.211	④	0.107	0.220	⑤
	17082296	1/2	7/8	9/32	25/.142	—	④	0.110	0.243	⑤
	17082297	1/2	7/8	9/32	25/.142	—	④	0.110	0.243	⑤
	17083280	3/8	7/8	9/32	25/.142	—	④	0.110	0.243	⑤
	17083281	3/8	7/8	9/32	25/.142	—	④	0.110	0.243	⑤
	17083282	3/8	7/8	9/32	25/.142	—	④	0.110	0.243	⑤
	17083283	3/8	7/8	9/32	25/.142	—	④	0.110	0.243	⑤
	17083290	13/32	7/8	9/32	—	24/.136	④	0.314	0.251	⑤

CARBURETORS
ROCHESTER
SECTION 25

QUADRAJET CARBURETOR SPECIFICATIONS
All Canadian Models

Year	Carburetor Identification [1]	Float Level (in.)	Air Valve Spring (turn)	Pump Rod (in.)	Primary Vacuum Break (deg./in.)	Secondary Vacuum Break (deg./in.)	Secondary Opening (in.)	Choke Rod (in.)	Choke Unloader (deg./in.)	Fast Idle Speed [2] (rpm)
'83	17083292	13/32	7/8	9/32	—	24/.136	[4]	0.314	0.251	[5]
	17083298	3/8	1	9/32	23/.129	30/.179	[4]	0.234	0.260	[5]
'84	17084280	3/8	7/8	9/32 [2]	23/.129	—	[4]	0.110	0.243	[5]
	17084281	3/8	7/8	9/32 [2]	23/.129	—	[4]	0.110	0.243	[5]
	17084282	3/8	7/8	9/32 [2]	23/.129	—	[4]	0.110	0.243	[5]
	17084283	3/8	7/8	9/32 [2]	23/.129	—	[4]	0.110	0.243	[5]
	17084284	3/8	7/8	9/32 [2]	23/.129	—	[4]	0.110	0.243	[5]
	17084285	3/8	7/8	9/32 [2]	23/.129	—	[4]	0.110	0.243	[5]
	17084286	13/32	1/2	9/32 [2]	23/.129	34/.211	[4]	0.107	0.220	[5]
	17084287	13/32	1/2	9/32 [2]	23/.129	34/.211	[4]	0.107	0.220	[5]
	17084288	3/8	7/8	9/32 [2]	23/.129	—	[4]	0.110	0.243	[5]
	17084289	3/8	7/8	9/32 [2]	23/.129	—	[4]	0.110	0.243	[5]
	17084296	1/2	7/8	9/32 [2]	23/.129	—	[4]	0.110	0.243	[5]
	17084297	1/2	7/8	9/32 [2]	23/.129	—	[4]	0.110	0.243	[5]
'85	17080213	3/8	1	9/32 [2]	23/.129	30/0.179	[4]	0.234	40/0.260	[5]
	17080298	3/8	1	9/32 [2]	23/.129	30/0.179	[4]	0.234	40/0.260	[5]
	17082213	3/8	1	9/32 [2]	23/.129	30/0.179	[4]	0.234	40/0.260	[5]
	17083298	3/8	1	9/32 [2]	23/.129	30/0.179	[4]	0.234	40/0.260	[5]
	17085247	13/32	7/8	9/32 [2]	20/0.110	—	[4]	0.096	30/0.179	[5]
	17085246	13/32	7/8	9/32 [2]	20/0.110	—	[4]	0.096	30/0.179	[5]
	17085249	13/32	7/8	9/32 [2]	20/0.110	—	[4]	0.096	30/0.179	[5]
	17085248	13/32	7/8	9/32 [2]	20/0.110	—	[4]	0.096	30/0.179	[5]
	17085580	3/8	7/8	9/32 [2]	21/0.117	—	[4]	0.077	30/0.179	[5]
	17085582	3/8	7/8	9/32 [2]	21/0.117	—	[4]	0.077	30/0.179	[5]
	17085581	3/8	7/8	9/32 [2]	21/0.117	—	[4]	0.077	30/0.179	[5]
	17085583	3/8	7/8	9/32 [2]	21/0.117	—	[4]	0.077	30/0.179	[5]
	17085584	3/8	7/8	9/32 [2]	21/0.117	—	[4]	0.077	30/0.179	[5]
	17085586	3/8	7/8	9/32 [2]	21/0.117	—	[4]	0.077	30/0.179	[5]
	17085592	13/32	1/2	9/32 [2]	21/0.117	34/.211	[4]	0.077	35/0.220	[5]
	17085594	13/32	1/2	9/32 [2]	21/0.117	34/.211	[4]	0.077	28/0.164	[5]
	17085588	3/8	7/8	9/32 [2]	21/0.117	—	[4]	0.077	30/0.179	[5]
	17085590	3/8	7/8	9/32 [2]	21/0.117	—	[4]	0.077	30/0.179	[5]
	17085596	1/2	7/8	9/32 [2]	23/0.129	—	[4]	0.077	38/0.243	[5]
	17085598	1/2	7/8	9/32 [2]	23/0.129	—	[4]	0.077	38/0.243	[5]
'86	17086246	13/32	7/8	9/32 [2]	20/0.110	—	[4]	0.096	30/0.179	[5]
	17086247	13/32	7/8	9/32 [2]	20/0.110	—	[4]	0.096	30/0.179	[5]
	17086248	13/32	7/8	9/32 [2]	20/0.110	—	[4]	0.096	30/0.179	[5]
	17086249	13/32	7/8	9/32 [2]	20/0.110	—	[4]	0.096	30/0.179	[5]
	17086580	12/32	7/8	9/32 [2]	21/0.117	—	[4]	0.077	30/0.179	[5]
	17086581	12/32	7/8	9/32 [2]	21/0.117	—	[4]	0.077	30/0.179	[5]
	17086582	12/32	7/8	9/32 [2]	21/0.117	—	[4]	0.077	30/0.179	[5]
	17086583	12/32	7/8	9/32 [2]	21/0.117	—	[4]	0.077	30/0.179	[5]
	17086584	12/32	7/8	9/32 [2]	21/0.117	—	[4]	0.077	30/0.179	[5]
	17086586	12/32	7/8	9/32 [2]	21/0.117	—	[4]	0.077	30/0.179	[5]
	17086588	12/32	7/8	9/32 [2]	21/0.117	—	[4]	0.077	30/0.179	[5]
	17086590	12/32	7/8	9/32 [2]	21/0.117	—	[4]	0.077	30/0.179	[5]
	17086596	16/32	7/8	9/32 [2]	21/0.117	—	[4]	0.077	30/0.179	[5]
	17086598	16/32	7/8	9/32 [2]	21/0.117	—	[4]	0.077	30/0.179	[5]

[1] The carburetor identification number is stamped on the float bowl, near the secondary throttle lever.
[2] Inner hole
[3] Outer hole
[4] No measurement necessary on two point linkage; see text.
[5] See underhood decal

SECTION 25 CARBURETORS
MIKUNI

MIKUNI CARBURETORS

2.6L Feedback Carburetor

All Federal and California 2.6L Mitsubishi engines are equipped with a two barrel downdraft carburetor designed for electronic fuel control and closed loop operation. With the closed loop system of mixture control, this carburetor includes the special feature to provide optimum air-fuel control during all ranges of engine operation. Fuel metering is accomplished through the use of three solenoid valves which reduce or add fuel to the engine.

There are eight basic systems in the feedback carburetor: fuel inlet, primary metering, secondary metering, accelerator pump, choke, jet mixture, enrichment, and fuel cut-off. The first five systems are basically the same between standard and feedback carburetors. The remaining three are unique to feedback carburetors. The enrichment system consist of an enrichment solenoid and a metering jet.

This system is used to provide additional fuel to the main metering system. Activation of the enrichment valve is controlled by the length of time that current is supplied by the solenoid valve. The jet mixture system supplies fuel to the engine through the jet mixture jet and passages. This system is calibrated by the jet mixture solenoid valve, which responds to a signal from the ECU.

The closed loop system provides the capability to perform closed loop fuel control in response to various sensor signals. The throttle position sensor (TPS) provides angle information to the ECU. The (TPS) is mounted on the carburetor. The idle position switch is installed on the carburetor and is "ON" when the throttle plate is at the closed or idle position. It provides information to the ECU and is used to adjust idle speed.

Standard Carburetor

All front wheel drive models (USA and Canadian), with the 2.6 liter (156 cubic inch) Mitsubishi engine are equipped with a conventional downdraft two barrel compound type carburetor. The automatic choke is a thermowax type which is controlled by engine coolant temperature. This carburetor also features a diaphragm type accelerator pump, bowl vent, fuel cut-off solenoid, air switching valve (ASV), sub EGR valve, coasting air valve (CAV), jet air control valve (JACV) and a high altitude compensation (HAC) system (California only). The air switching valve system is activated by ported carburetor vacuum and supplies additional air to the low speed passage by cutting off fuel flow to the bypass holes and pilot outlet.

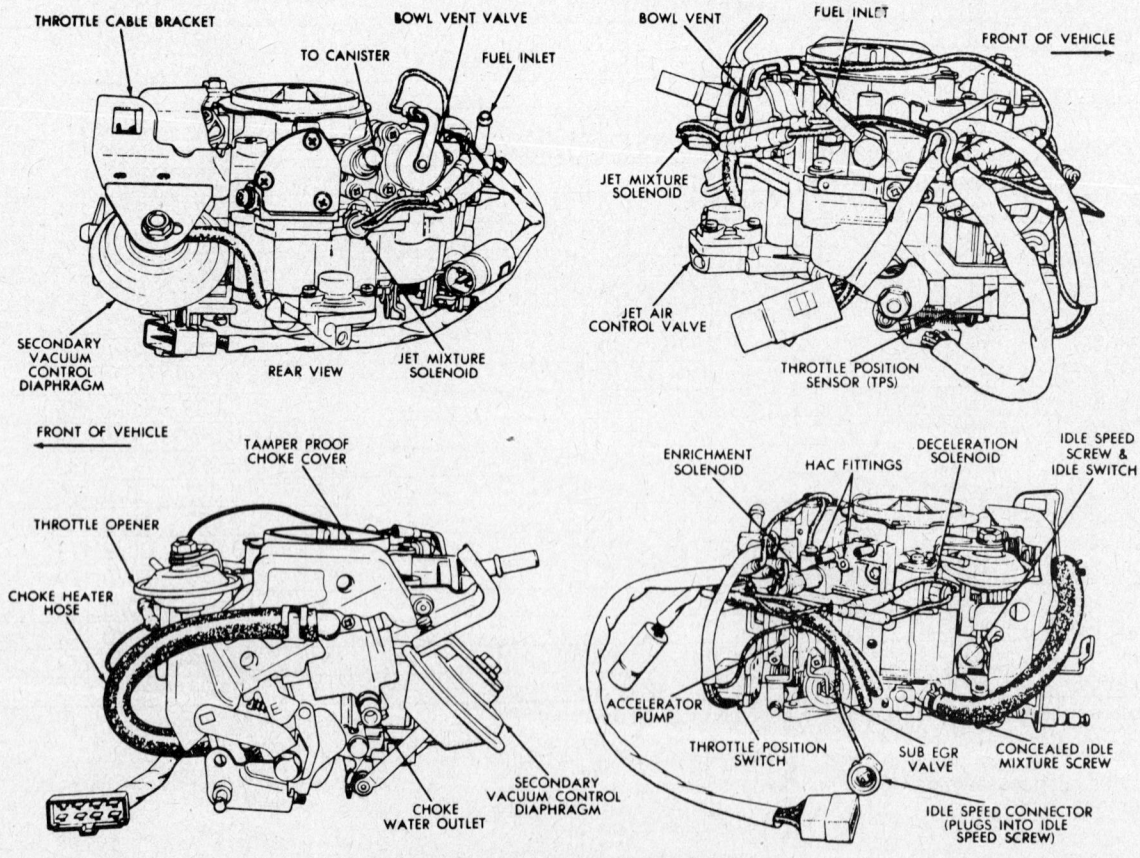

Mikuni feedback carburetor assembly

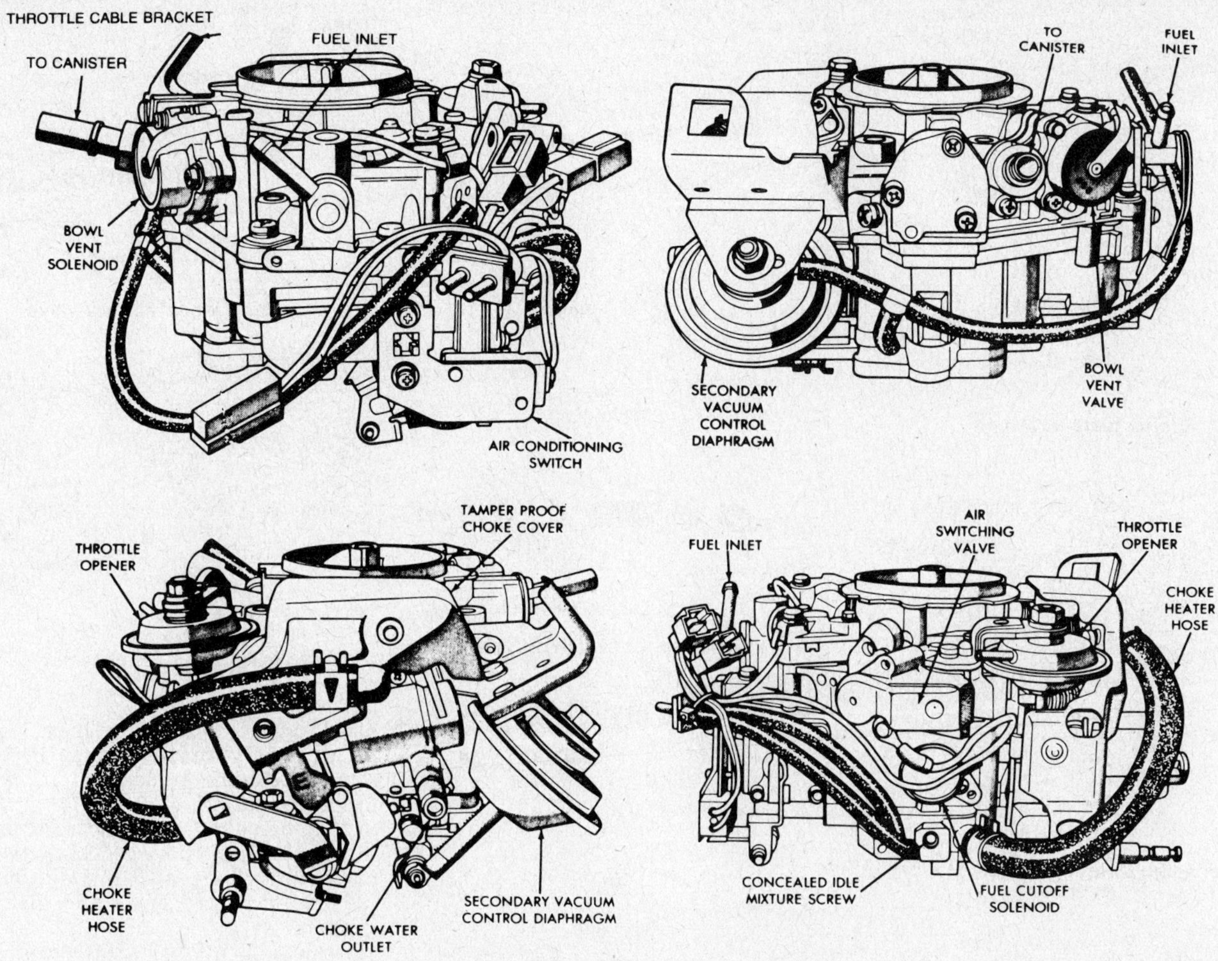

CARBURETORS
MIKUNI
SECTION 25

Mikuni non—feedback carburetor assembly

DISASSEMBLY

1. Compress clamps and remove water hose from choke assembly.
2. Drill out staked portions of staked covered screws.
3. Using a small hammer and a pointed punch, gently tap the edge of the remaining screw counterclockwise until the screw is removed. Remove the choke cover.
4. Note the relationship between the punched mark and the scribed line on the choke pinion plate. During reassembly the line and punch mark must be aligned to this position.
5. Remove "E" clip from throttle opener link. Remove throttle opener screws and set opener aside.
6. Remove ground wire from fuel cut-off solenoid (if equipped), then remove the mounting screw and set solenoid aside.
7. Remove throttle return spring and damper spring.
8. Remove "E" clips and choke unloader link from carburetor.

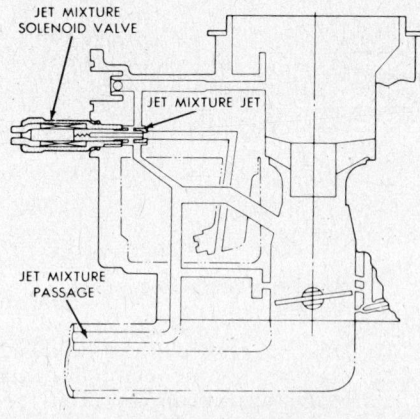

Jet mixture system

9. Disconnect vacuum hose and link from vacuum chamber, remove mounting screws and set chamber aside.
10. On feedback models, remove screws securing throttle position sensor and set sensor aside. Remove vacuum connector hoses from carburetor on all models.

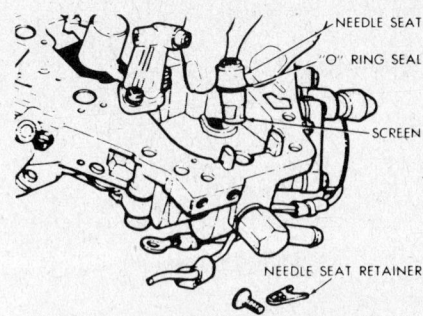

Servicing needle seat assembly

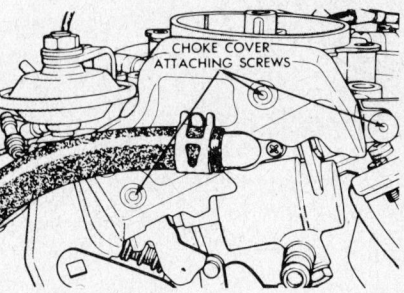

Feedback model choke cover screws

25-93

Section 25 CARBURETORS
ROCHESTER

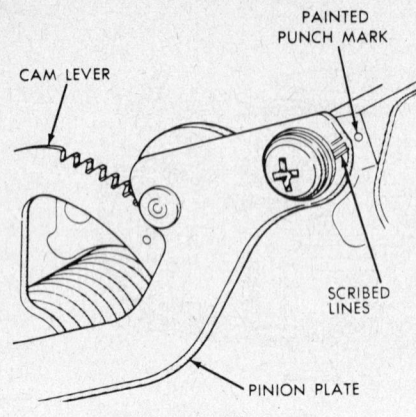
Pinion plate alignment

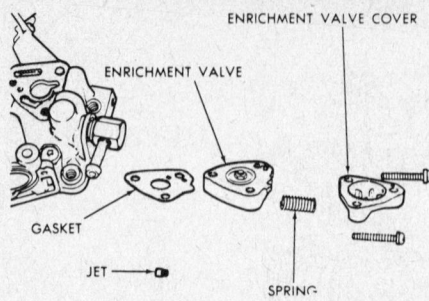
Servicing enrichment jet

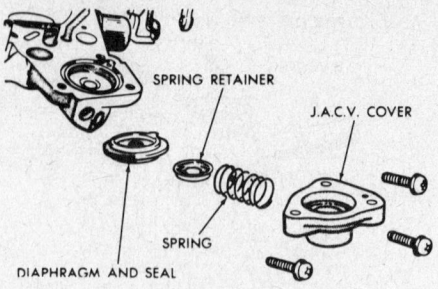
Servicing jet air control valve

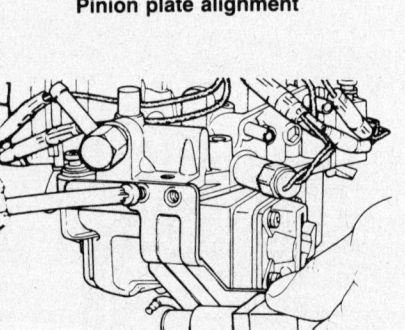
Servicing throttle position sensor

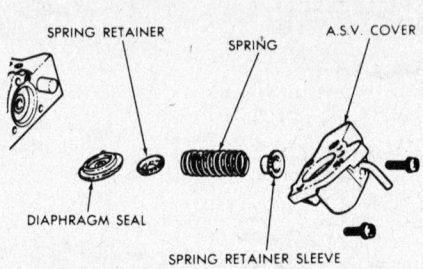
Servicing air switching valve

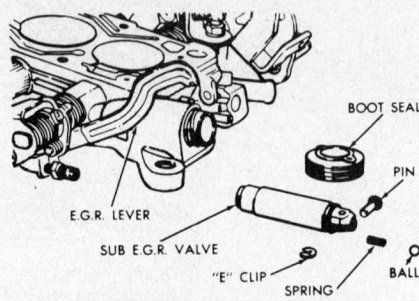
Servicing sub EGR assembly

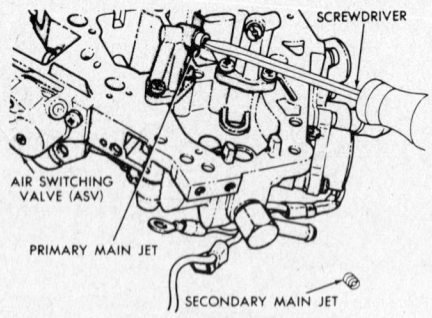
Servicing main jets

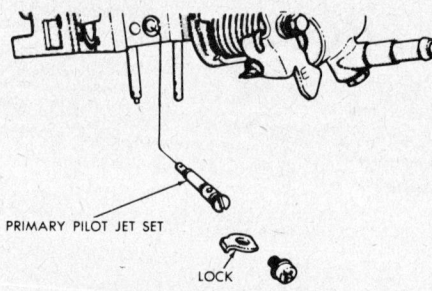
Servicing primary jet set

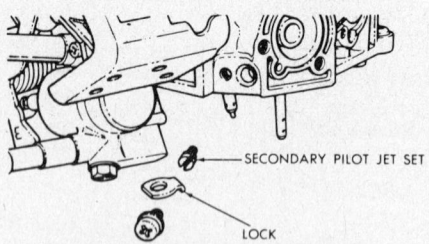
Servicing secondary jet set

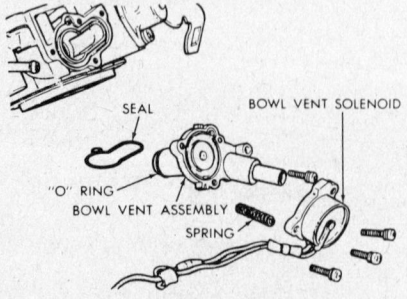
Servicing bowl vent

11. Disconnect accelerator linkage.
12. Remove six airhorn mounting screws and seperate air horn from carburetor body.
13. Slide out float pivot pin and remove float assembly.
14. Unscrew retainer and remove needle seat and screen assembly. Do not lose shim from under needle seat assembly.
15. On feedback models, disconnect solenoid wiring and unscrew solenoid from air horn.
16. Remove venturi retainers and both venturi. Discard O-rings. Mark both primary and secondary venturi so they can be reinstalled in their proper positions.
17. Remove primary and secondary main jets from their pedestals. Note jet numbers for proper installation.
18. Remove pedestals and discard gaskets.
19. Remove bowl vent solenoid mounting screws, seperate bowl vent from air horn, and discard O-ring and seal.
20. Remove enrichment valve screws and seperate valve from air horn. Remove jet.
21. On non feedback models, remove air switching valve screws and seperate valve from air horn.
22. Remove screw, lock and primary jet set.
23. Remove screw, lock, and secondary jet set.
24. Remove primary and secondary air bleed jets from top of air horn. Note sizes for proper reinstallation.
25. Invert air horn carefully and drop out pump weight, check ball and hex nut.
26. Remove accelerator pump screws and seperate pump from air horn.
27. Remove jet air control valve screws and seperate valve from throttle body.
28. Remove "E" clip from sub EGR lever. Carefully slide pin from lever and sub EGR valve. The lever will be under spring tension caused by a steel ball and spring in the sub EGR valve and the lever. Be careful not to lose

CARBURETORS
ROCHESTER
SECTION 25

the ball and spring when removing lever. Remove valve from throttle boby. Reverse procedure to Assemble the carburetor.

CAUTION
Priming a carburetor by pouring gasoline into the air horn is dangerous and should be avoided. Cranking the engine, and then depressing the accelerator several times is the recommended way to prime the carburetor.

FLOAT LEVEL ADJUSTMENT

1. Invert the air horn assembly without a gasket.
2. With a gauge, measure the distance from the bottom of the float to the surface of the air horn. The distance should be 0.0787–0.779 in. (17.8–20.8mm).
3. If the reading is not within this range the shim under the needle seat must be changed. Shim kits are available which have three shims: 0.0118 in. (0.3mm), 0.0157 in. (0.4mm), 0.0196 in. (0.5mm). Adding or removing a shim will change the float level by three times the thickness of the shim.

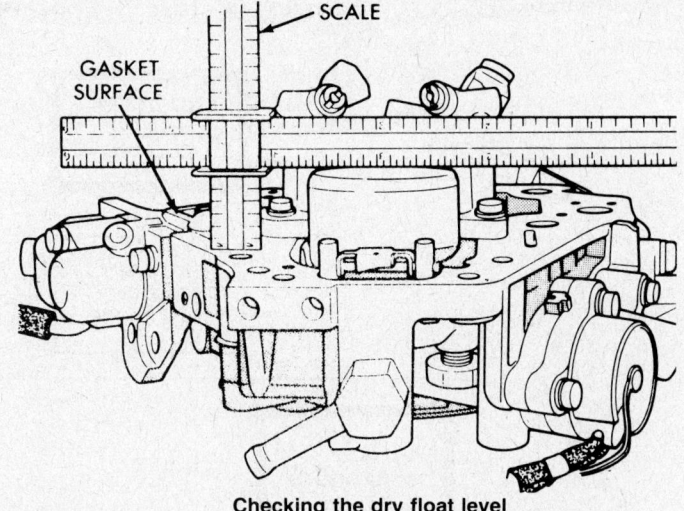
Checking the dry float level

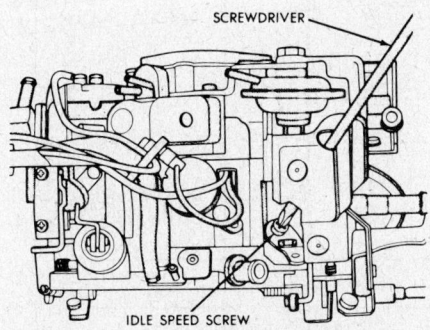
Idle speed adjustment

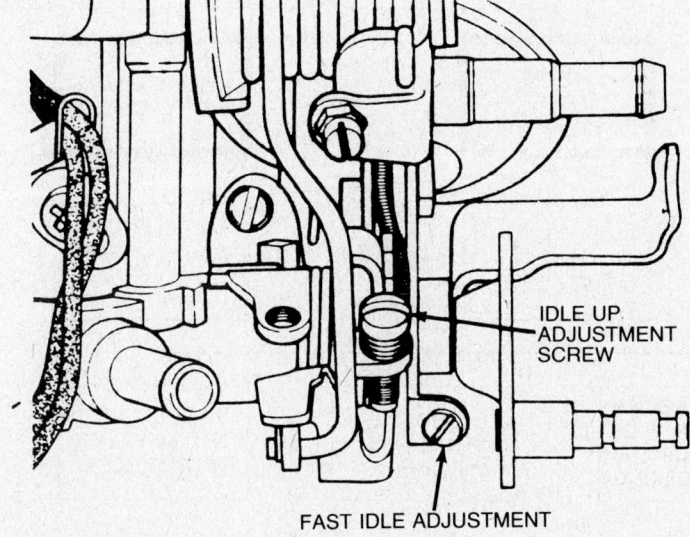
Idle up adjustment

CAM LEVER ALIGNMENT

Refer to illustration for adjustment.

IDLE SPEED ADJUSTMENT

Before adjusting idle speed, check ignition timing and adjust if necessary.
1. Set the parking brake and place the car in neutral. Turn off all lights and accessories. Disconnect the radiator fan. Connect tachometer to engine.
2. Start and run engine until it reaches normal operating temperature.
3. Open throttle and raise engine rpm to 2500 for ten seconds, then return engine to idle.
4. Wait two minutes and rpm indicated on the tachometer. If rpm is different from that specified on the underhood sticker, turn adjusting screw until correct rpm is obtained. On feedback models, the idle switch

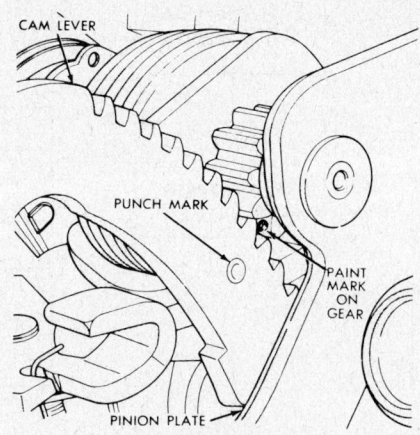
Cam lever alignment

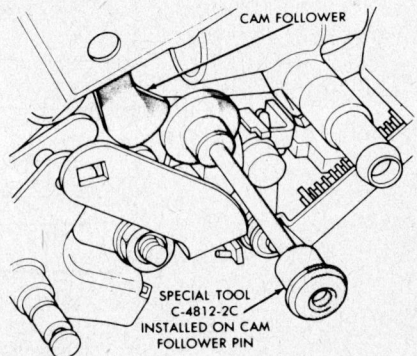
Tool C—4812—2C installed on feedback models

connector must be removed before making this adjustment. On air conditioned models, set temperation control lever to coldest position and turn A/C on. With air compressor running,

25-95

SECTION 25 CARBUROTORS
MIKUNI

FUEL SYSTEM DIAGNOSIS

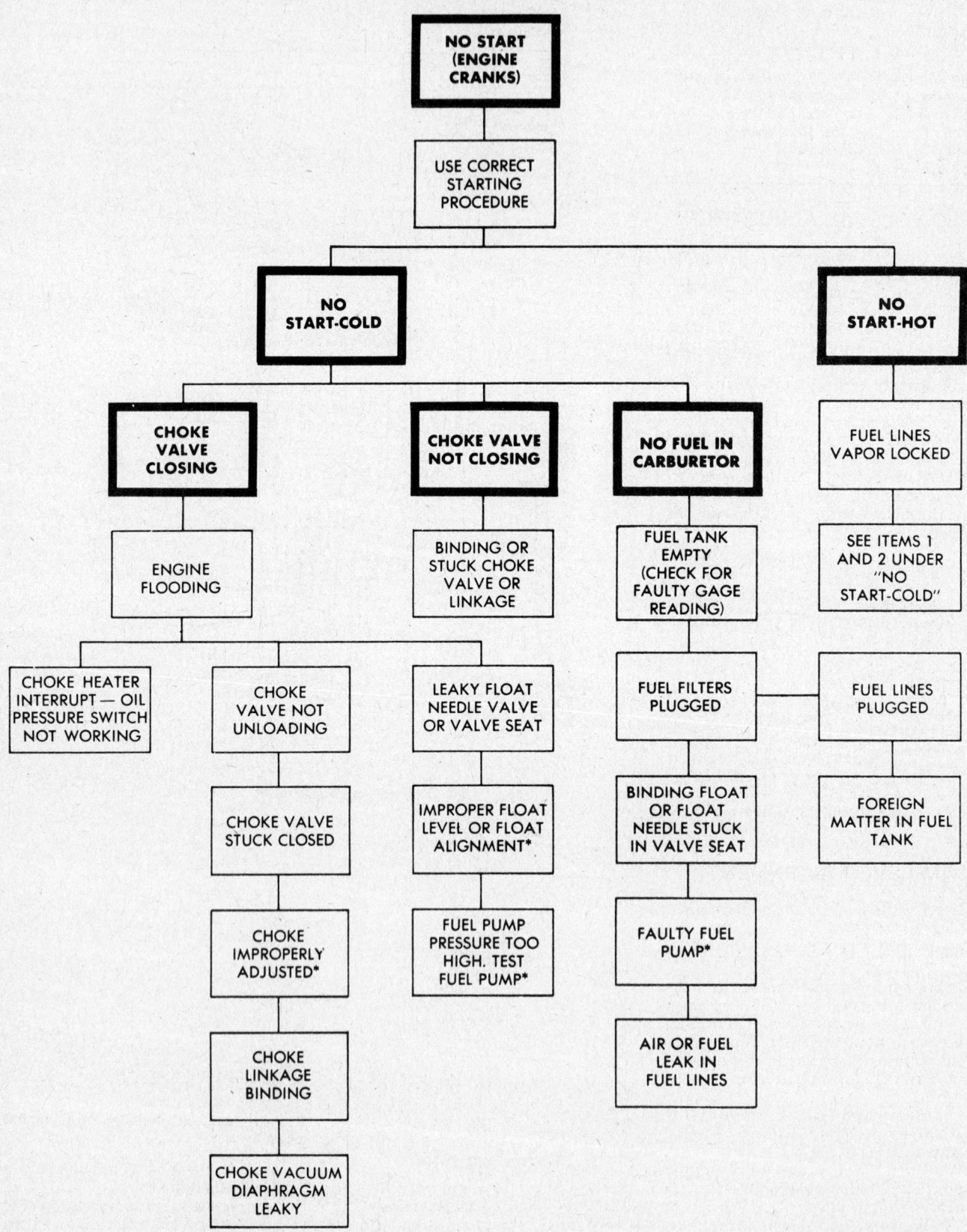

25-96

CARBURETORS
MIKUNI
SECTION 25

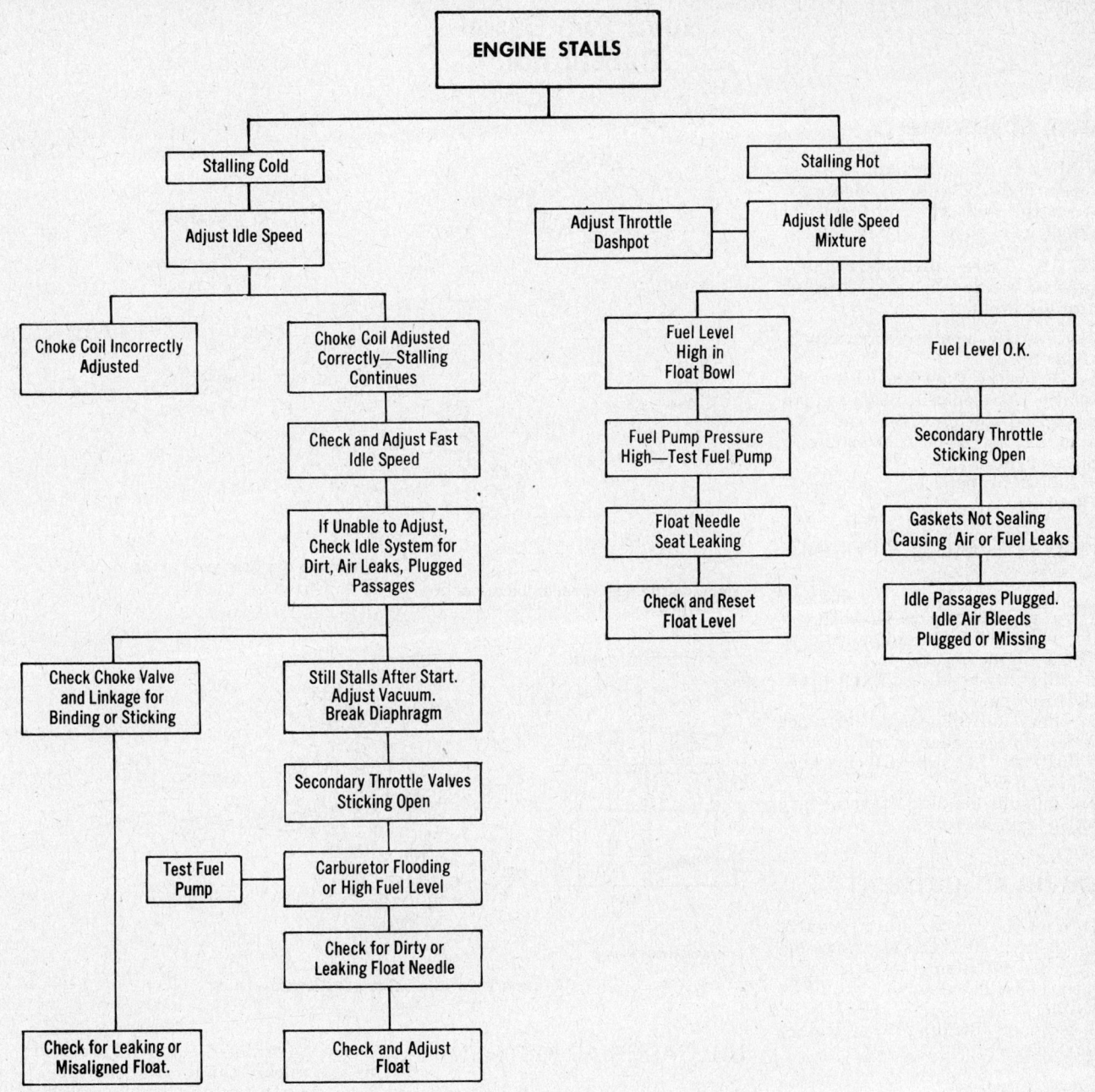

set engine speed to 900 rpm with idle up screw.

5. Turn off engine, reconnect fan, disconnect tachometer, and reconnect idle switch connector.

FAST IDLE SPEED ADJUSTMENT

1. Set the parking brake and place the car in Neutral. Turn off all lights and accessories. Disconnect the radiator fan. Connect tachometer to engine.

2. Start and run engine until it reaches normal operating temperature.

3. Disconnect and plug vacuum advance hose at distributor. Disconnect radiator fan.

4. Open throttle slightly and install tool C-4812-2C on choke cam follower pin.

5. Release throttle lever and adjust fast idle speed to specification on the underhood sticker.

6. Remove tool, turn off engine, reconnect fan, unplug and reconnect vacuum advance hose, and remove tachometer.

25-97

SECTION 25 CARBURETORS
NOVA—2BBL

Nova Two Barrel Carburetor

FLOAT ADJUSTMENT

1. Allow the float the hang down by its own weight. Check the clearance between the float tip and air horn. The float level should be 0.075 in.

NOTE: This measurement should be made without a gasket on the air horn.

2. Adjust by bending a portion of the float lip.
3. Lift up the float and check the clearance between the needle valve plunger and the float lip. The float level in the lowered position should be 0.0657–0.0783 in.
4. Adjust by bending a portion of the float lip.

THROTTLE VALVE OPENING

1. Check the full opening angle of the primary throttle valve, with a T scale. The standard angle should be 90° from the horizontal plane.
2. Adjust by bending the 1st throttle lever stopper.
3. Check the full opening clearance between the secondary throttle valve and the body. The standard clearance should be 0.500 in.
4. Adjust by bending the secondary throttle lever stopper.

KICK-UP ADJUSTMENT

1. With the primary throttle valve fully opened, check the clearance between the secondary throttle valve and the body. The clearance should be 0.006 in.
2. Adjust by bending the secondary throttle lever.

SECONDARY TOUCH ADJUSTMENT

1. Check the primary throttle valve opening clearance at the same time the 1st kick lever just touches the 2nd kick lever. The clearance should be 1985: 0.170 in., 1986: 0.230 in.
2. Adjust by bending the 1st kick lever.

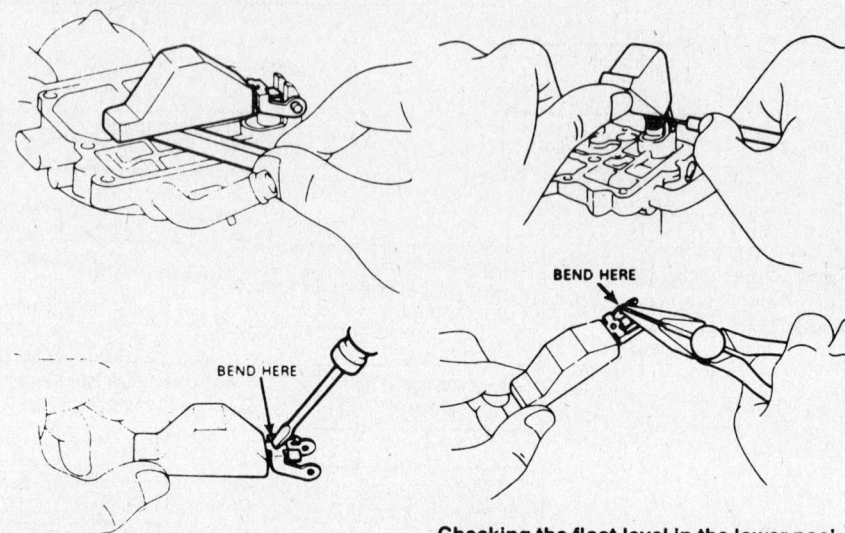

Checking the float level in the upper position—Nova

Checking the float level in the lower position—Nova

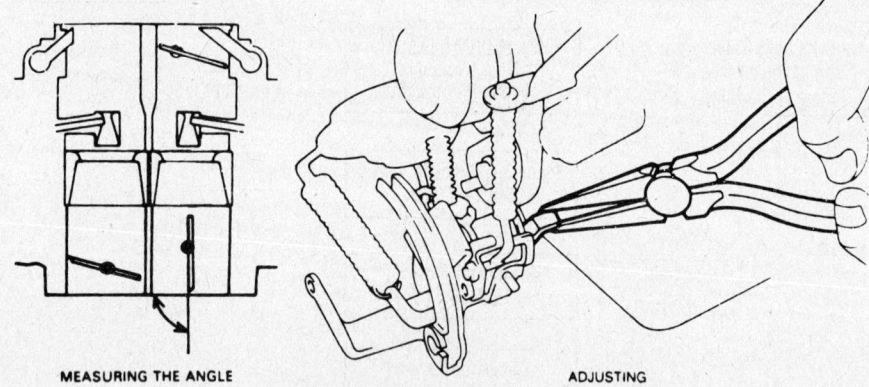

MEASURING THE ANGLE   ADJUSTING

Primary throttle valve adjustment—Nova

UNLOADER ADJUSTMENT

1. With the primary throttle valve fully opened, check that the choke valve clearance is 0.120 in.
2. Adjust by bending the fast idle lever.

CHOKE BREAKER ADJUSTMENT

1. Set the idle cam. While holding the throttle slightly open, push the choke valve closed, and hold it closed as you release the throttle valve.
2. Apply vacuum to the choke breaker 1st diaphragm.
3. Check the choke valve clearance. It should be 0.095 in.
4. Adjust by bending the relief lever.
5. Apply vacuum to choke diaphragms 1st and 2nd.
6. Check the choke valve clearance. It should be 0.245 in.
7. Adjust by turning the diaphragm adjusting screw.

CARBURETORS
NOVA — 2BBL

SECTION 25

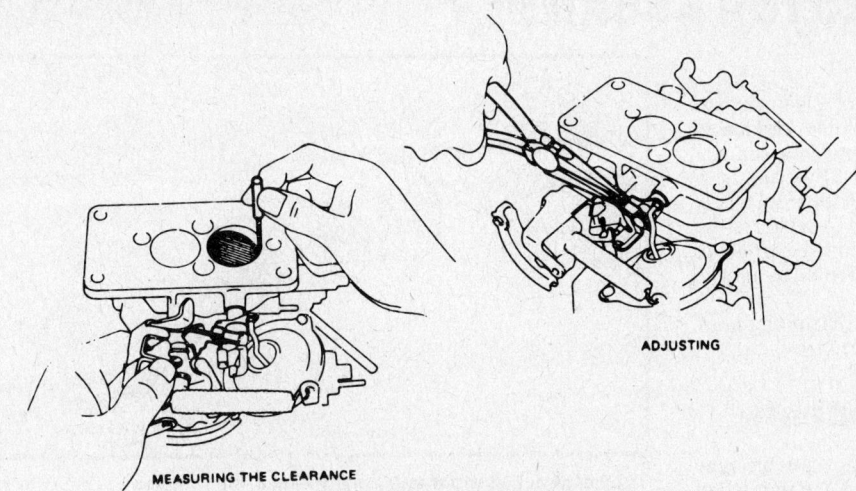
Kick-up adjustment — Nova

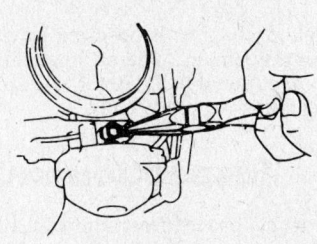
Choke breaker 1st diaphragm adjustment — Nova

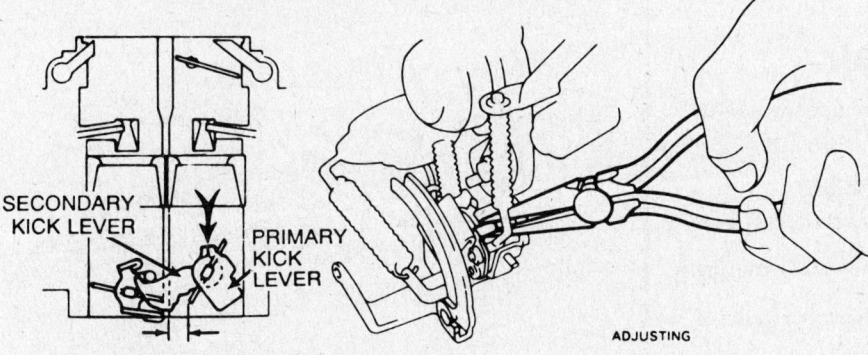
Secondary touch adjustment — Nova

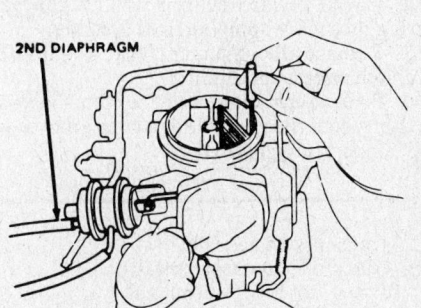

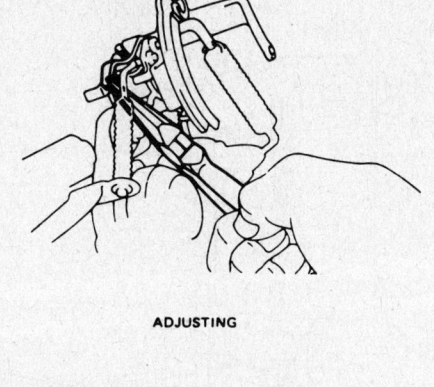
Unloader adjustment — Nova

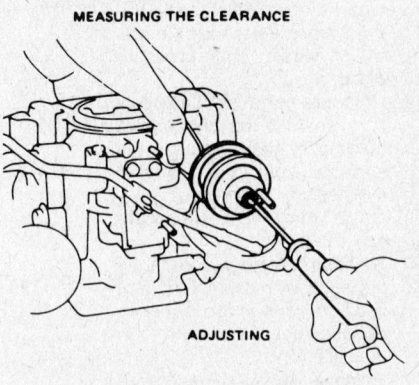
Choke breaker 1st and 2nd diaphragm adjustment — Nova

PUMP STROKE ADJUSTMENT

1. With the choke fully opened, measure the length of the stroke. 1985: 0.157 in., 1986: 0.079 in.
2. Adjust the pump stroke by bending the connecting link.

25-99

SECTION 26 CLUTCH SERVICE

CLUTCH ASSEMBLY

Removal and Installation Procedures

The introduction of the front wheel drive cars has caused a change in the removal and installation procedures of the clutch assembly. Where it is possible to remove the drive line components and the transmission from underneath the conventional rear drive cars, it is now necessary to work from both the top and bottom of the front wheel cars, in order to disconnect the front drive axles and to separate the engine/transaxle assembly, exposing the clutch assembly. After the clutch assembly is exposed, it is removed and replaced in the conventional manner.

The respective vehicle section should be consulted for the engine—transmission/transaxle removal and installation procedures.

Clutch Operating Components

The clutch mechanism is operated by either a solid or a cable type linkage arrangement. The adjustments are either accomplished manually or automatically. Refer to the individual vehicle sections for the proper adjusting procedures.

Inspection and Repair

The following procedures apply to all clutch components with exceptions as indicated.

CLUTCH RELEASE MECHANISM

1. Check release fork and ball stud for wear, distortion, cracks or other damage.
2. Check release bearing for roughness or noise by rotating bearing race while spplying light pressure.
3. Replace all components that would affect proper operation of the clutch release mechanism.
4. Prior to installation of the clutch release bearing and support assembly, coat the inside and outside grooves with a small quantity of high temperature grease.

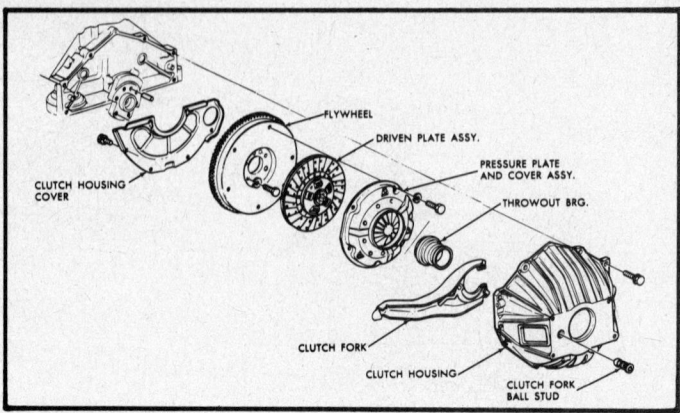
Typical clutch components, rear wheel drive vehicles

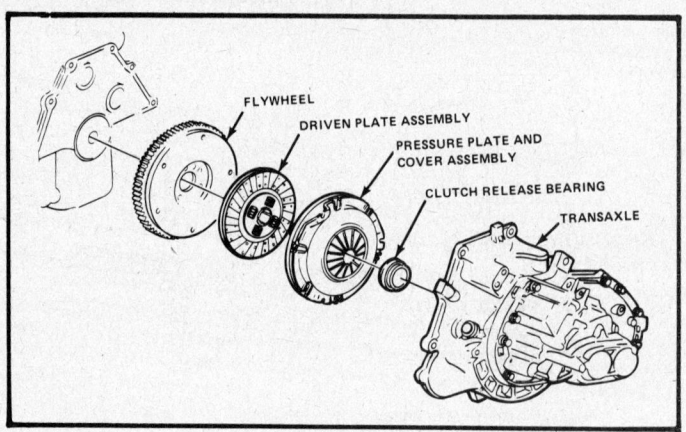
Front wheel drive clutch components - typical

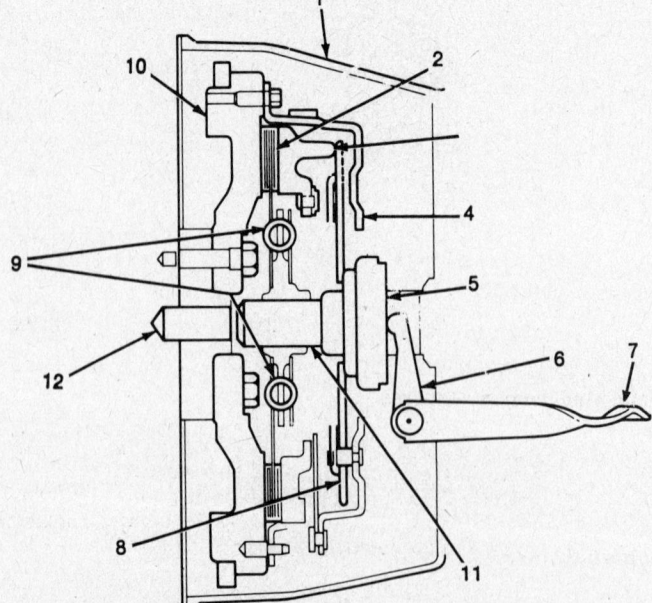

1. Transmission housing
2. Clutch disc: an assembly attached to the transmission shaft with a splined hub. The disc has friction material on both sides where it contacts the flywheel and pressure plate.
3. Pressure plate: applies pressure against the clutch disc holding it tight against the surface of the engine flywheel.
4. Cover: part of pressure plate assembly.
5. Release bearing: constantly engaged with release fingers provide connection between release fingers and fork.
6. Release fork.
7. Release lever: release fork and release lever impart pedal motion to release bearing lever is connected to clutch cable.
8. Release fingers: part of the belleville load spring. Movement toward flywheel removes clamp load from clutch disc.
9. Damper springs: part of the disc assembly. Aid in isolating engine pulses from power train.
10. Engine flywheel: bolted to engine crankshaft and rotates with the crankshaft. It is machined to provide a friction or face which meets with the friction surface of the clutch disc when the clutch is engaged. This forms a continuous system by which engine power is connected to the transmission.
11. Transmission input shaft.
12. Engine crankshaft.

Clutch component operation - typical

CLUTCH SERVICE
SECTION 26

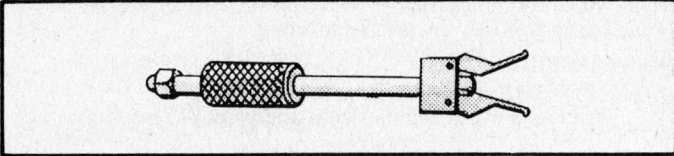

Pilot bearing/bushing puller tool, typical

PILOT BUSHING

The pilot bushing, which is pressed into crankshaft is an oil impregnated type bronze bearing. This bushing requires attention only when the clutch is removed from the vehicle, at which time it should be cleaned and inspected for excessive wear or damage and should be replaced if necessary.

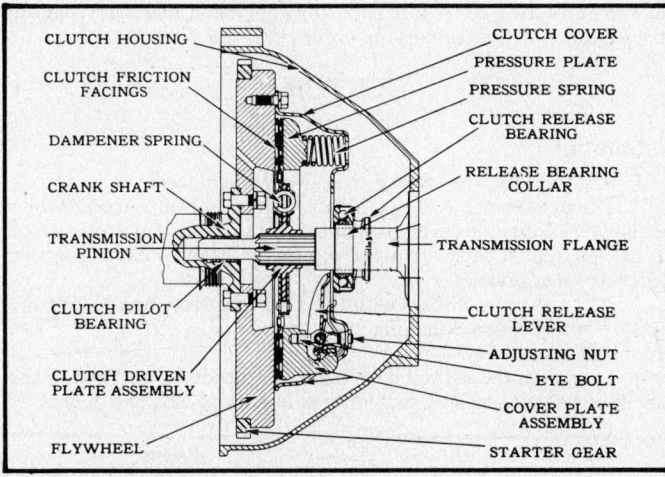

Cross section of typical clutch assembly

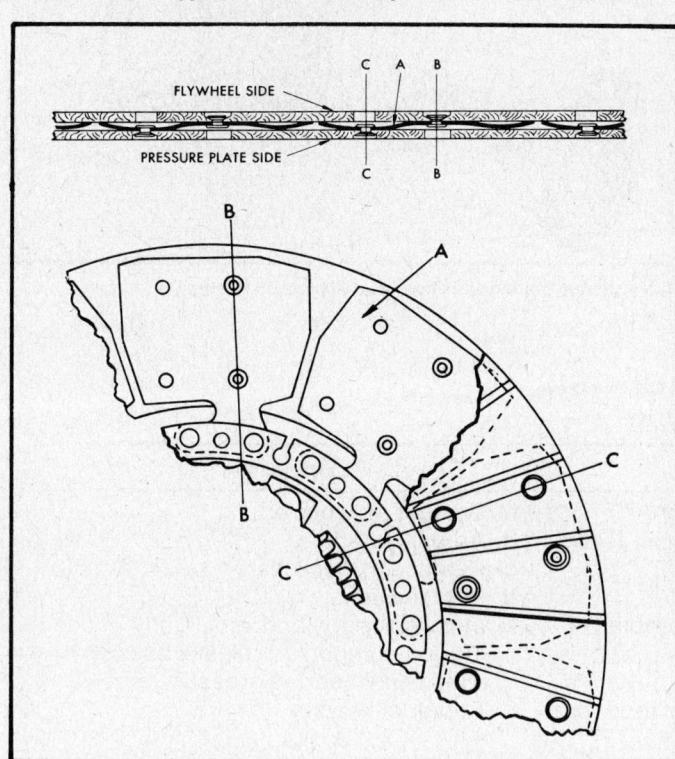

Clutch driven plate inner construction

Removal

To remove bushing type pilot bearing, install a special puller or a universal type slide hammer knocker with expanding jaws, to pull bushing.

Installation

It is important that the new bushing be driven in with a tool that protects the bushing during installation. Special driving tools are available.

NOTE: Certain engines are not equipped with pilot bushings or bearings in the crankshaft. Do not attempt to install one where it is not needed.

PILOT BEARING

Roughness or noise can be detected by rotating the bearing race while applying light pressure. Replace bearing if it rough, noisy, or damaged.

Removal

Remove clutch pilot bearing from engine, using slide hammer. With fingers on puller closed, insert fingers through bearing inner race as far as they will go, then tighten thumb screw to spread fingers. Slide weight sharply against stop on puller shaft to remove bearing.

Installation

1. Pack clutch pilot bearing with small quantity of high temperature lubricant.
2. With shielded side of bearing toward the rear, drive pilot bearing into position using a suitable driver. Bearing should be seated firmly.

FLYWHEEL

Inspect flywheel surface which is contacted by the clutch facing. This surface must be smooth and should not be grooved or show deep heat checks. Replace flywheel if the above conditions are evident.

DRIVEN DISC

Inspect driven disc assembly for worn, loose, and grease or oil-soaked facings. Check for broken springs, loose rivets, or cracks in the driven disc hub. Examine splines in hub for wear and make sure they slide freely on splines of the main drive gear. If any wear or damage is evident, replace with a new driven disc assembly.

DRIVEN PLATE

Reconditioning

No reconditioning of the driven plate other than replacing the friction facings is recommended. Facing replacement requires extreme care and use of proper tools and riveting equipment, usually found at an auto machine shop.

CLUTCH RELEASE BEARING

The ball-type clutch release bearing is prelubricated and requires no lubrication other than the lubricant that is sealed in the unit. This bearing can not be washed in cleaning solvent of any kind. The solvent will enter the bearing and destroy the lubricant.

NOTE: On certain clutch applications, the release bearing is in constant contact with the pressure plate assembly.

Removal From Sleeve

Examine condition of bearing. If noisy, rough or dry, under light thrust load, remove bearing from sleeve.
  Support bearing in a vise or press and carefully press out sleeve.
  Clean sleeve in solvent and remove all old lubricant.

SECTION 26 CLUTCH SERVICE

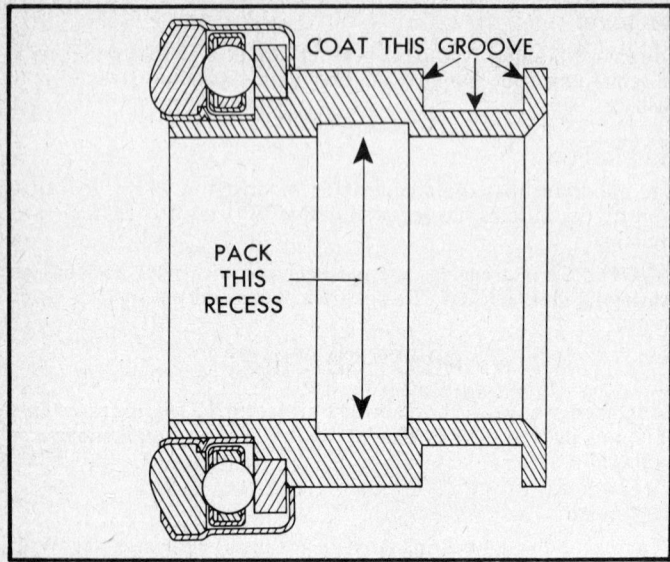

Clutch release bearing lubrication points, typical

Installation On Sleeve

CAUTION

Exercise care when installing a new clutch release bearing to avoid damaging the bearing race. Never drive the bearing on the sleeve with a hammer. Use either of the following two methods.

VISE METHOD

1. Position new bearing on sleeve and place old bearing against face of new bearing.
2. Support parts in a vise and carefully press new bearing on sleeve. **Make certain bearing is seated on shoulder of bearing sleeve. Rotate bearings as they are pressed together.**

PRESS METHOD

1. Support sleeve on press bed.
2. Position new bearing on sleeve and place old bearing on new one.
3. Bring press ram into contact with old bearing and apply sufficient pressure to **seat new bearing on shoulder of sleeve. Rotate bearings as they are pressed together.**

FLYWHEEL HOUSING ALIGNMENT

Inspection and/or alignment of the flywheel housing is indicated when symptoms exist of excessive transmission gear wear, transmission jumping out of gear, driveline vibration, clutch pedal vibration or scrubby pedal feel, pilot bearing noise, release bearing noise, or excessive clutch spin time. Common complaint areas should always be checked and corrected prior to checking alignment, to be sure that the basic system is in proper working order.

CLUTCH

Installation

1. Install the clutch release lever if it was removed.
2. Place the clutch disc, and pressure plate assembly in position on the flywheel. Start the cover attaching bolts to hold the pieces in place but do not tighten them. **Avoid dropping the parts or contaminating them with oil or grease.**
3. Align the clutch disc with the alignment tool and torque the pressure plate cover attaching bolts evenly to specification. Then remove the tool.
4. Complete the assembly as per the procedures outlined in the individual vehicle sections, including linkage or cable adjustments.

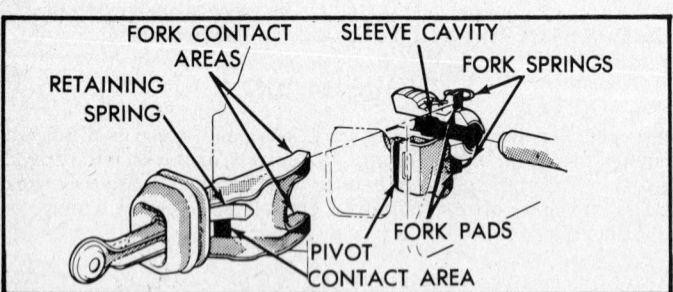

Typical clutch release bearing fork

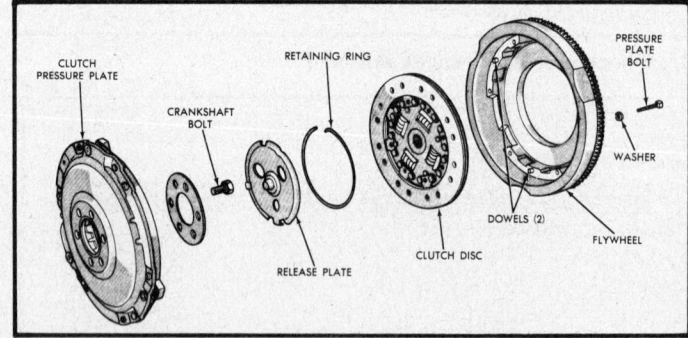

Clutch assembly, Dodge Omni and Plymouth Horizon

CLUTCH DIAGNOSIS
Cable Type

Condition	Probable Cause	Correction
Fails to release (pedal pressed to floor-shift lever does not move freely in and out of reverse gear without gear clash	a. Improper linkage operation. b. Improper pedal travel. c. Loose linkage. d. Faulty driven disc. e. Fork and bearing not assembled properly. f. Clutch disc hub binding on input shaft splines. g. Clutch disc warped or bent.	a. Correct as required. b. Adjust linkage. c. Replace as necessary. d. Replace disc. e. Install properly and very lightly lubricate fingers at release bearing with wheel bearing grease. f. Repair or replace. g. Replace disc.

CLUTCH SERVICE — SECTION 26

CLUTCH DIAGNOSIS
Cable Type

Condition	Probable Cause	Correction
Slipping	a. Improper linkage adjustment. b. Improper operation. c. Oil soaked driven disc. d. Worn facing or facing torn from disc. e. Warped pressure plate or flywheel. f. Weak diaphragm spring. g. Driven plate not seated in. h. Driven plate overheated.	a. Adjust linkage. b. Correct as required. c. Install new disc and correct leak at its source. d. Replace disc. e. Replace pressure plate or flywheel. f. Replace pressure plate. g. Make 30 to 40 normal starts. CAUTION: Do not overheat h. Allow to cool.
Grabbing (chattering)	a. Oil on facing. Burned or glazed facings. b. Worn splines on input shaft. c. Loose engine mountings. d. Warped pressure plate or flywheel. e. Burned or smeared resin on flywheel or pressure plate.	a. Install new disc and correct leak to engine or transaxle. b. Replace input shaft. c. Tighten or replace mountings. d. Replace pressure plate or flywheel. e. Sand off if superficial, replace burned or heat checked parts.
Rattling-transmission click	a. Release fork loose. b. Oil in driven plate damper. c. Driven plate damper spring failure.	a. Install properly. b. Replace driven disc. c. Replace driven disc.
Release bearing noise with clutch fully engaged	a. Improper operation. b. Release bearing binding. c. Fork shaft improperly installed. d. Weak linkage return spring. e. Faulty bearing.	a. Correct as required. b. Clean, relubricate, check for burrs, nicks, etc. c. Install properly. d. Replace spring in detent. e. Replace bearing.
Noisy	a. Worn release bearing. b. Fork shaft improperly installed.	a. Replace bearing. b. Install properly and lubricate fork fingers at bearing.
Pedal stays on floor	a. Bind in linkage or release bearing. b. Adjusting mechanism failed. c. Cable dis-engaged from detent or transaxle lever. d. Cable broken. e. High friction in cable. f. Fork shaft binds in housing.	a. Lubricate and free up linkage and release bearing. b. Replace detent, pawl and spring. c. Connect cable. d. Replace cable. e. Replace cable. f. Free up shaft and lubricate.
Hard pedal effort	a. Bind in linkage. b. Driven plate worn. c. Cable friction high. d. Fork shaft binds in housing.	a. Lubricate and free up linkage. b. Replace driven plate. c. Replace cable. d. Free up shaft and lubricate.

SECTION 27: DIESEL ENGINES

INDEX

FORD 2.0 L 4 CYL DIESEL ENGINE

Specifications
- General Engine 27-3
- Engine Tune-Up 27-3
- Valves 27-3
- Crankshaft & Connecting Rods 27-3
- Piston & Rings 27-4
- Bolt Torque Specifications 27-4

Tune-Up
- Compression Test 27-5
- Valve Adjustment 27-5
- Injection Timing, Adjust 27-5
- Idle Speed, Adjust 27-6
- Timing Belt R&R 27-7

On Car Service
- Timing Belt (Front) R&R 27-10
- Water Pump R&R 27-10
- Intake Manifold R&R 27-11
- Exhaust Manifold R&R 27-12
- Cylinder Head R&R 27-12

Fuel System
- Injection Pump R&R 27-13
- Injection Nozzles R&R 27-13
- Fuel Cut-Off Solenoid R&R 27-14
- Oil Cooling Jets R&R 27-14

FORD 2.4 L 6 CYL TURBO DIESEL ENGINE

Specifications
- General Engine 27-16
- Engine Tune-Up 27-16
- Valves 27-16
- Crankshaft & Connecting Rods 27-17
- Piston & Rings 27-17
- Bolt Torque Specifications 27-17

Tune-Up
- Compression Test 27-18
- Valve Adjustment 27-19
- Injection Timing, Adjust 27-19
- Idle Speed, Adjust 27-21
- Turbocharger 27-23

On Car Service
- Rocker Arm Cover or Gasket R&R 27-23
- Camshaft Drive Belt R&R 27-23
- Vacuum Pump R&R 27-25
- Rocker Arms R&R 27-26
- Camshaft R&R 27-26
- Engine Front Cover R&R 27-26
- Cylinder Head R&R 27-27
- Water Pump 27-29

Fuel System
- Injection Pump R&R 27-29
- Turbocharger R&R 27-31
- Fuel-Shut Off Valve R&R 27-31
- Injection Nozzles R&R 27-32
- Intake Manifold R&R 27-32
- Exhaust Mainfold R&R 27-32

GM 4.3L V6 DIESEL ENGINE

Specifications
- Engine Tune-Up 27-33
- Engine Firing Order 27-33
- Valves 27-34
- Crankshaft & Connecting Rods 27-24
- Pistons & Rings 27-35
- Bolt Torque Specifications 27-35

Tune-Up
- Compression Test 27-36
- Valve Adjustment 27-36
- Injection Timing, Adjust 27-37
- Idle Speed, Adjust 27-40
- Vacuum Regulator Valve, Adjust 27-40

Fuel System
- Fuel Pump R&R 27-41
- Injection Pump R&R 27-42
- Injectiors R&R 27-43
- Shut Down Problems 27-43
- Water in Fuel System 27-43

GM 5.7L V8 DIESEL ENGINE

Specifications
- General Engine 27-44
- Engine Tune-Up 27-44
- Engine Firing Order 27-45
- Crankshaft & Connecting Rods 27-45
- Valves 27-45
- Pistons & Rings 27-45
- Bolt Torque Specifications 27-46

Tune-Up
- Compression Test 27-47
- Valve Adjustment 27-47
- Injection Timing, adjust 27-47
- Idle Speed, Adjust 27-56
- Detent Cable, Adjust 27-52
- Glow Plugs R&R 27-52

Fuel System
- Fuel Pump R&R 27-52
- Injection Pump 27-53
- Injectors R&R 27-54
- Shut Down Problems 27-54
- Water in Fuel System 27-55

ISUZU 1.8L 4 CYL DIESEL ENGINE

Specifications
- General Engine 27-55
- Engine Tune-Up 27-55
- Engine Firing Order 27-55
- Valves 27-56
- Crankshaft & Connecting Rods 27-56
- Pistons & Rings 27-56
- Bolt Torque Specifications 27-56

On Car Service
- Compression Test 27-57
- Valve Adjustment 27-57
- Injection Timing, Adjust 27-57
- Governor, Adjust 27-58
- Idle Speed, Adjust 27-58
- Glow Plug System 27-58
- Fuel Filter R&R 27-59
- Water Separator 27-59
- Injection Pump & Timing Belt R&R 27-61

Diesel Maintenance

FORD 2.0L 4 CYL DIESEL ENGINE

GENERAL ENGINE SPECIFICATIONS

Year	Eng V.I.N. Code	Engine No. Cyl. Displacement (cc)	Eng Mfg	Engine Type	Horsepower @ rpm ■	Torque @ rpm (ft. lbs.) ■	Bore × Stroke (mm)	Compression Ratio	Oil Pressure @ 2000 rpm
'84 and Later	H	4-2000	Toyo Kogyo	Diesel	53 @ 4000	82.2 @ 2750	86.0 × 86.0 ①	22.7:1	②

① 3.39 × 3.39 inch
② Greater than 42.7 psi @ 3000 RPM
  Oil Temp. 80°C

TUNE-UP SPECIFICATIONS

Year	Engine No. Cyl. Displacement (cu. in.)	Injection Timing (deg) Auto. Trans.	Compression (psi)	Valves Intake Opens (deg)	Fuel Pump Pressure (psi)	Idle Speed (rpm) Man. Trans.	Idle Speed (rpm) Auto. Trans.
'84 and Later	4-121.92	TDC Hot	390-435 @ 200 RPM	13° BTC	—	725 + 50	725 + 50

VALVE SPECIFICATIONS

VIN Code	Engine (cc)	Seat Angle (deg)	Face Angle (deg)	Valve Clearance (Cold—inch)	Spring Installed Height (in.)	Stem-to-Guide Clearance (in.) Intake	Stem-to-Guide Clearance (in.) Exhaust	Stem Diameter (in.) Intake	Stem Diameter (in.) Exhaust
H	4-2000	45°	45°	In. 0.010 Ex. 0.014	1.7760	0.0016-0.0029	0.0018-0.0031	0.3138-0.3144	0.3138-0.3142

CRANKSHAFT AND CONNECTING ROD SPECIFICATIONS

(All measurements are given in inches.)

Year	Engine No. Cyl. Displacement (cc)	Crankshaft Main Brg. Journal Dia	Crankshaft Main Brg. Oil Clearance	Crankshaft Shaft End-Play	Crankshaft Thrust on No.	Connecting Rod Journal Diameter	Connecting Rod Oil Clearance	Connecting Rod Side Clearance
'84 and Later	4-2000	2.3598-2.3605	0.0012-0.0020	0.0016	—	2.0055-2.0061	0.0031	0.0043-0.0103

SECTION 27

DIESEL ENGINES
FORD 2.0L FOUR CYLINDER

PISTON AND RING SPECIFICATIONS
(All measurements are given in inches.)

Year	Engine Displacement (cc)	Piston Clearance	Ring Gap			Ring Side Clearance		
			Top Compression	Bottom Compression	Oil Control	Top Compression	Bottom Compression	Oil Control
'84 and Later	4-2000	0.0013-0.0020	0.0079-0.0157	0.0079-0.0157	0.0079-0.0157	0.0020-0.0035	0.0016-0.0031	—

TORQUE SPECIFICATIONS

Description	N·m	Lb-Ft
Camshaft Pulley (Front)	56-82	40.5-59.3
Camshaft Pulley (Rear)	56-82	40.5-59.3
Camshaft Caps	20-27	14.5-19.5
Connecting Rod Caps	70-75	50.6-54.2
Crankshaft Pulley	160-170	115.7-123.0
Cylinder Head Cover	7-10	5.1-7.2
Exhaust Manifold	22-27	15.9-19.5
Flywheel	180-190	130.2-137.4
Glow Plugs	15-20	10.8-14.5
Injection Nozzles	60-70	43.4-50.6
Injection Pump Pulley	60-70	43.4-50.6
Injection Pump Bracket (Nuts)	32-47	23.1-34.0
Injection Pump Bracket (Bolt)	16-23	11.6-16.6
Injection Pump Body (Nuts)	16-23	11.6-16.6
Injection Pump Body (Bolt)	32-47	23.1-34.0
Intake Manifold	16-23	11.6-16.6
Main Bearing Caps	84-90	60.8-65.1
Oil Jets	32-47	23.1-34.0
Oil Pan	7-10	5.1-7.2
Oil Pump Body	32-47	23.1-34.0
Oil Pump Gear Cover (Screw)	7-10	5.1-7.2
Oil Strainer	16-23	11.6-16.6
Thermostat Casing (Bolt)	16-23	11.6-16.6
Thermostat Cover (Bolt)	7-10	5.1-7.2
Water Pump	32-47	23.1-34.0

TUNE-UP

VEHICLE APPLICATION

Tempo/Topaz, Escort/Lynx

DESCRIPTION

The 2.0L diesel is an inline four cylinder engine with an overhead camshaft.

The engine is a lightweight, compact design, displacing 1998 cc (122 CID). The crankshaft uses piston cooling jets, which direct oil onto the under side of the piston. This helps to cool the piston during engine operation.

The crankshaft is a five main bearing unit, with fore and aft thrust controlled at the No. 3 main bearing.

The camshaft is supported by five machined bearing bores in the cylinder head. The No. 1 and No. 5 bearing caps are different designs and easily recognizable from each other. The No. 2, 3 and 4 camshaft bearing caps are identical and numbered. The bearing caps have arrows casting their top surfaces. The bearing caps must be installed with the arrows to the front of the engine and in the correct order. Camshaft thrust is controlled by a flange on the camshaft located under the No. 1 bearing cap.

The valves are adjusted by changing valve shims located on top of the cam followers.

A cogged drive belt at the front of the engine is used t drive the water pump and camshaft. Another cogged drive belt is driven off the rear of the camshaft to drive the injection pump.

DIESEL ENGINES
FORD 2.0L FOUR CYLINDER
SECTION 27

COMPRESSION TEST

1. Check starting system and battery to determine if required cranking speed can be achieved. Charge battery if necessary.
2. Run the engine until operating temperature is reached.
3. Remove glow plugs and disconnect the fuel cutoff solenoid on the injection pump.

---- CAUTION ----
Disconnect the glow plug harness (blue/red stripe) from engine wiring harness to prevent shorting of terminal leads when ignition is turned on.

4. Install Glow Plug Adapter into No. 1 cylinder.
5. Connect Diesel Engine Compartment Tester to the adapter.
6. Crank engine at least six compression cycles and take a gauge reading. Record results. Vent the gauge and repeat to check readings.

---- CAUTION ----
Do not attempt to add oil to cylinders in any attempt to qualify rings or valves as extensive damage may result.

7. Repeat test for each cylinder.

Test Conclusion

Compression pressures should average approximately 3000 kPa (427 psi) with a minimum of 2700 kPa (384 psi) at 200 rpm and should not vary ore than 300 kPa (42.7 psi) between cylinders.

If compression pressures are not within limits, disassemble and repair engine as necessary.

VALVE ADJUSTMENT

1. Disconnect breather hose from the intake manifold and remove camshaft cover.
2. Rotate crankshaft until No. 1 piston is at TDC on the compression stroke.
3. Using a Go-No-Go feeler gauge, check the valve shim to cam lobe clearance for No. 1 and No. 2 intake valves, and No. 1 and No. 3 exhaust valves.
   a. Intake Valves: 0.008–0.011 in. (0.2–0.3mm).
   b. Exhaust Valves: 0.011–0.015 in. (0.3–0.4mm).
4. Rotate crankshaft one complete revolution. Measure valve clearance for No. 3 and No. 4 intake valves, and No. 2 and No. 4 exhaust valves.
5. If valve is out of specification, adjust as follows:
   a. Rotate crankshaft until lobe of the valve to be adjusted is down.
   b. Install cam follower retainer.
   c. Rotate crankshaft until the cam lobe is on the base circle.
   d. Using O-ring pick tool, pry the valve adjusting shim out of the cam follower.
   e. Valve shims are available in thickness ranging from 3.40mm–4.60mm.
   f. If the valve was too tight, install a new shim of the appropriate size.
   g. If the valve was too loose, install a new shim of the appropriate size.

NOTE: Shim thickness is stamped on valve shim. Install new shim with numbers down, to avoid wearing the numbers off the shim. If numbers have been worn off, use a micrometer to measure shim thickness.

6. Rotate crankshaft until cam lobe is down and remove cam follower retainer.
7. Recheck valve clearance.
8. Repeat Steps 4, 5 and 6 for each valve to be adjusted.
9. Make sure the camshaft cover gasket is fully seated in the camshaft cover and install valve cover. Tighten bolts to 5–7 ft. lbs. (7–10 Nm).
10. Connect breather hose.

INJECTION TIMING

Adjustment

NOTE: Engine coolant temperature must be above 80°C (176°F) before injection timing can be checked and/or adjusted.

1. Disconnect battery ground cable from battery, located in luggage compartment.
2. Remove injection pump distributor head plug bolt and sealing washer.
3. Install Static Timing Gauge Adapter with Metric Dial Indicator, so that the indicator pointer is in contact with injection pump plunger.
4. Remove timing mark cover from transmission housing. Align timing mark (TDC) with pointer on rear engine cover plate.
5. Rotate crankshaft pulley slowly, counterclockwise until dial indicator pointer stops moving approximately 40°BTDC.
6. Adjust dial indictor to Zero.

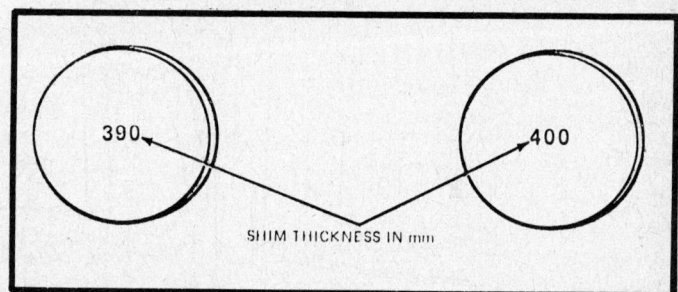

Valve shim sizes

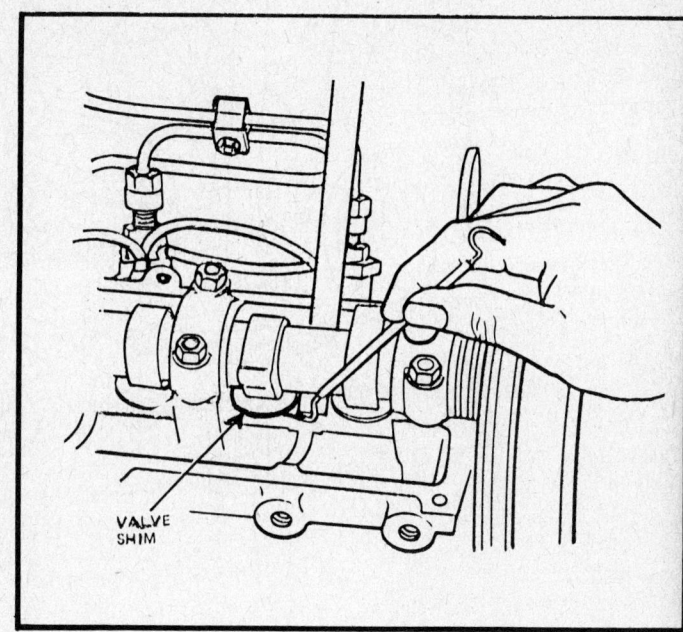

Shim removal adjustment

SECTION 27 Diesel Engines
FORD 2.0L FOUR CYLINDER

NOTE: Confirm that dial indicator pointer does not move from Zero by slightly rotating crankshaft left and right.

7. Turn crankshaft clockwise until crankshaft timing mark aligns with indicator pin. Dial indicator should read 0.039 in. (1.0mm). If reading is not within specifications, adjust as follows:

   a. Loosen injection pump attaching bolts and nuts.
   b. Rotate injection pump toward the engine to advance timing and away from the engine to retard timing. Rotate injection pump until dial indicator reads to specification.
   c. Tighten injection pump attaching nuts and bolts to 13–20 ft. lbs. (18–27 Nm).
   d. Repeat Steps 5, 6 and 7 to check that timing is adjusted correctly.

8. Remove dial indicator and adapter and install injection pump distributor head plug and tighten to 10–14.5 ft. lbs. (13.5–19.5 Nm).
9. Connect battery ground cable to battery.
10. Run engine and check and adjust idle arm rpm, if necessary. Check for fuel leaks.

IDLE SPEED

Curb Idle Speed Adjustment

1. Place transmission in Neutral.
2. Bring engine up to normal operating temperature. Stop engine.
3. Remove timing hole cover. Clean flywheel surface and install reflective tape.
4. Idle speed is measured with manual transmission in Neutral.

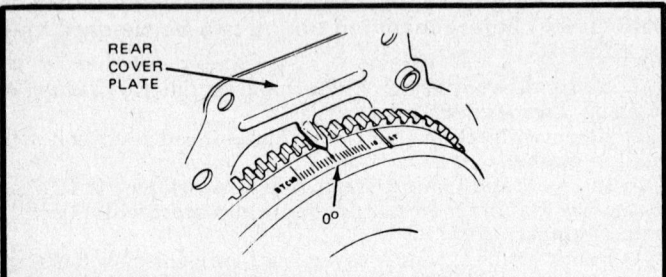

Flywheel timing mark

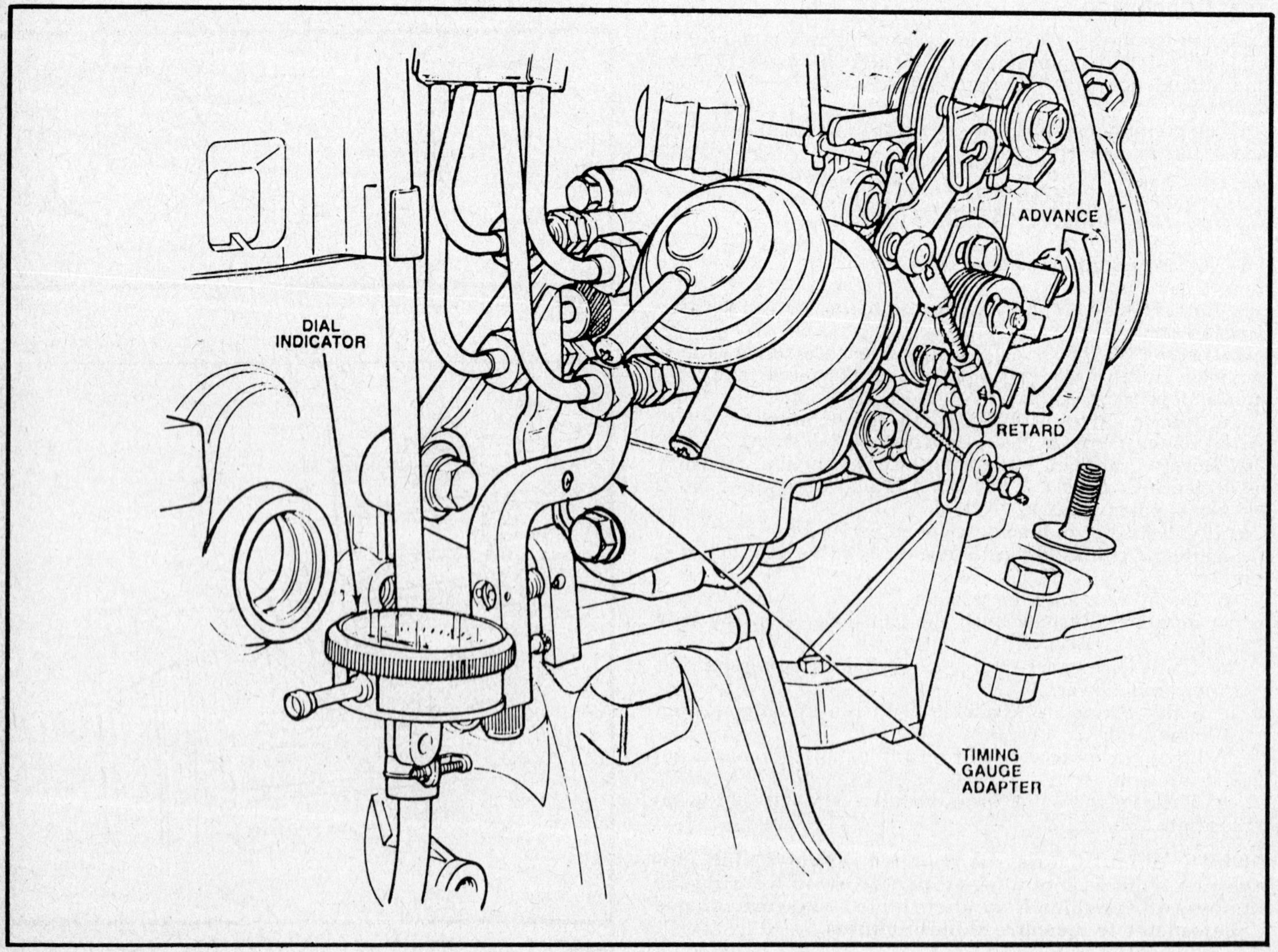

Installing timing gauge

DIESEL ENGINES
FORD 2.0L FOUR CYLINDER
SECTION 27

5. Check curb idle speed. Curb idle speed is specified on the Vehicle Emissions Control Information decal (VECI). Adjust to specification by loosening lock nut on the idle speed bolt. Turn idle speed adjusting bolt clockwise to increase, or counterclockwise to decrease engine idle speed. Tighten lock nut.
6. Place transmission in Neutral. Rev Engine momentarily and recheck curb idle RPM. Readjust if necessary.
7. Turn A/C On. Check idle speed. Adjust to specification by loosening nut on A/C throttle kicker and rotating screw.

ADJUSTMENTS

Timing Belt—Front

1. Remove the flywheel timing mark cover.
2. Remove the front timing belt upper cover.
3. Remove the belt tension spring from the storage pocket in the front cover.
4. Install the tensioner spring in the belt tensioner lever and over the stud mounted on the front of the crankcase.
5. Loosen the tensioner pulley lockbolt.
6. Rotate the crankshaft pulley two revolutions clockwise until the flywheel TDC timing mark aligns with the pointer on the rear cover plate.
7. Check the front camshaft sprocket to see that it is aligned with its timing mark.
8. Tighten the tensioner lockbolt to 23–34 ft. lbs. (32–47 Nm).
9. Check the belt tension. Belt tension should be 3–44 lbs. (147–196 Nm).
10. Remove the tensioner spring and install it in the storage pocket in the front cover.
11. Install the front cover and tighten the attaching bolts to 5–7 ft. lbs. (7–10 Nm).
12. Install the flywheel timing mark cover.

Timing Belt—Rear

1. Remove flywheel timing mark cover.
2. Remove rear timing belt cover.
3. Loosen tensioner pulley locknut.
4. Rotate crankshaft two revolutions until the flywheel TDC timing mark aligns with the pointer on the rear cover plate.
5. Check that the camshaft sprocket and injection pump sprocket are aligned with their timing marks.
6. Tighten tensioner locknuts to 15–20 ft. lbs. (20–27 Nm).
7. Check belt tension. Belt tension should be 22–33 lbs. (98–147 Nm).
8. Install rear timing belt cover. Tighten the 6mm bolts to 7–12 Nm and the 8mm bolt to 12–16 ft. lbs. (16–23 Nm).
9. Install flywheel timing mark cover.

OUT-OF-VEHICLE

NOTE: Use this procedure for front timing belt replacement, or if the engine is being overhauled.

Removal

1. With engine removed from the vehicle and installed on an engine stand, remove front timing belt upper cover.
2. Install flywheel holding tool.
3. Remove six bolts attaching the crankshaft pulley to the crankshaft sprocket.
4. Install crankshaft pulley remover and remove crankshaft pulley.
5. Remove front timing belt lower cover.
6. Loosen tensioning pulley and remove the timing belt.

Installation

1. Align camshaft sprocket with the timing mark.

NOTE: Check crankshaft sprocket to see that the timing marks are aligned.

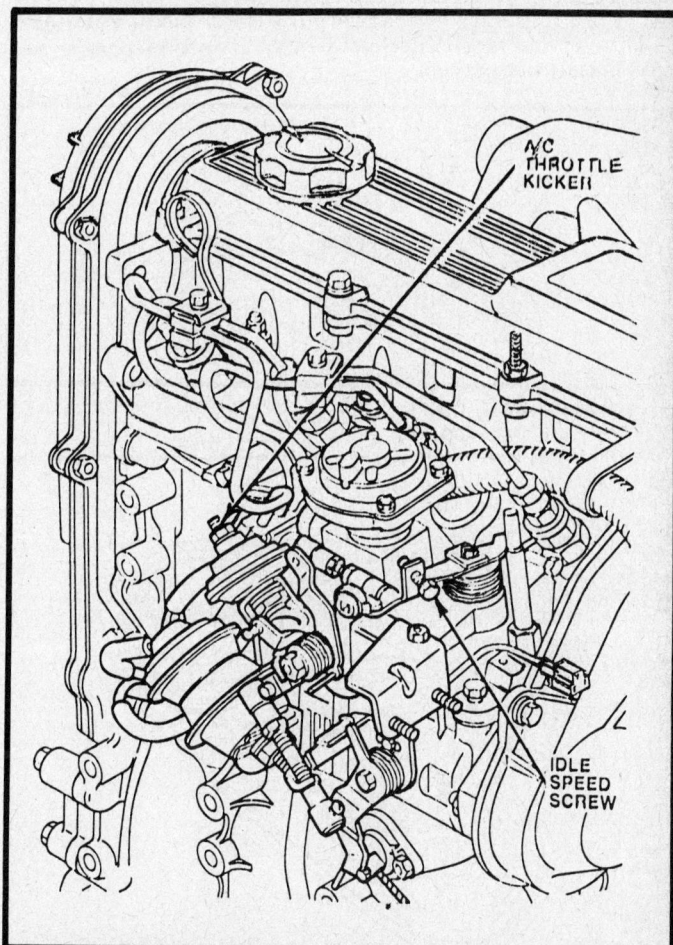

Adjusting idle speed

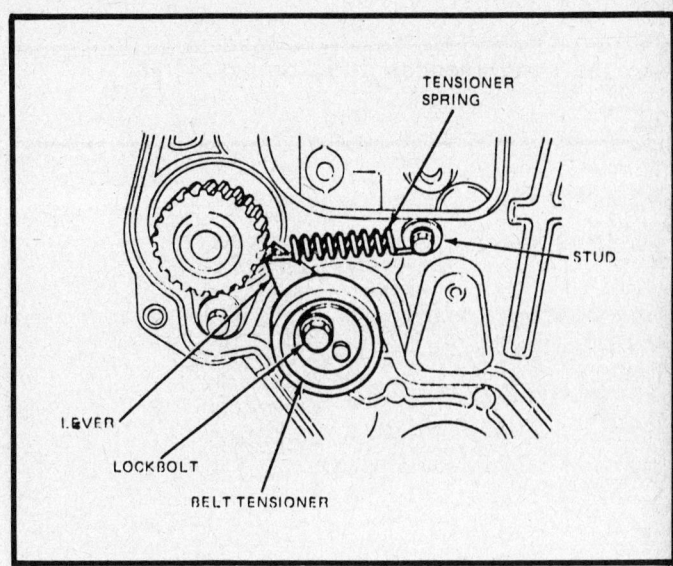

Front timing belt tensioner spring installation

27-7

SECTION 27

DIESEL ENGINES
FORD 2.0L FOUR CYLINDER

2. Remove tensioner spring from the pocket in the front timing belt upper cover and install it in the slot in the tensioner lever and over the stud in the crankcase.
3. Push tensioner lever toward the water pump as far as it will travel and tighten lockbolt snug.
4. Install timing belt.
5. Adjust timing belt tension.
6. Install front timing belt lower cover and tighten bolts to 5–7 ft. lbs. (7–10 Nm).
7. Install crankshaft pulley and tighten bolts to 17–24 ft. lbs. (17–24 Nm).
8. Install front timing belt upper cover and tighten bolts to 5–7 ft. lbs. (7–10 Nm).

REAR TIMING BELT

Removal and Installation

OUT-OF-VEHICLE

1. Remove rear timing belt cover.
2. Remove flywheel timing mark cover from clutch housing.
3. Rotate crankshaft until the flywheel timing mark is at TDC on No. 1 cylinder.
4. Check that the injection pump and camshaft sprocket timing marks are aligned.
5. Loosen tensioner locknut. With a screwdriver, or equivalent tool, inserted in the slot provided, rotate the tensioner clockwise to relieve belt tension. Tighten locknut snug.

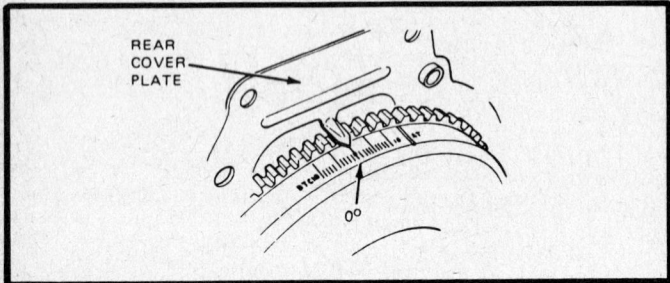
Flywheel timing mark

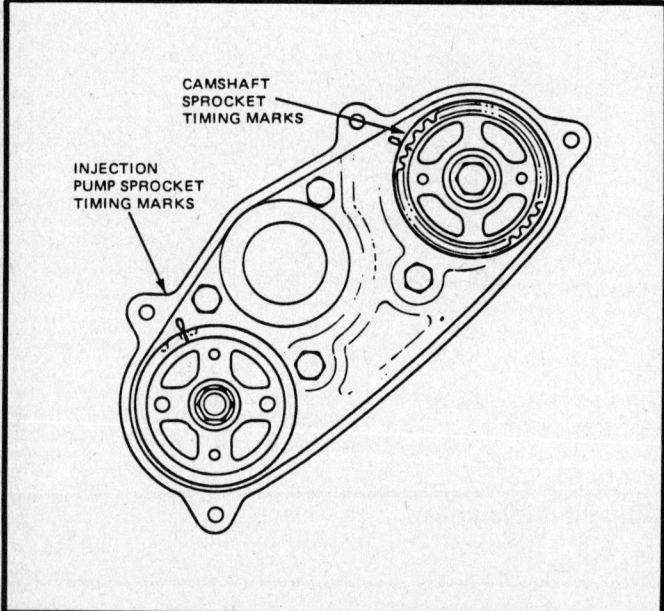
Camshaft and injection pump timing marks

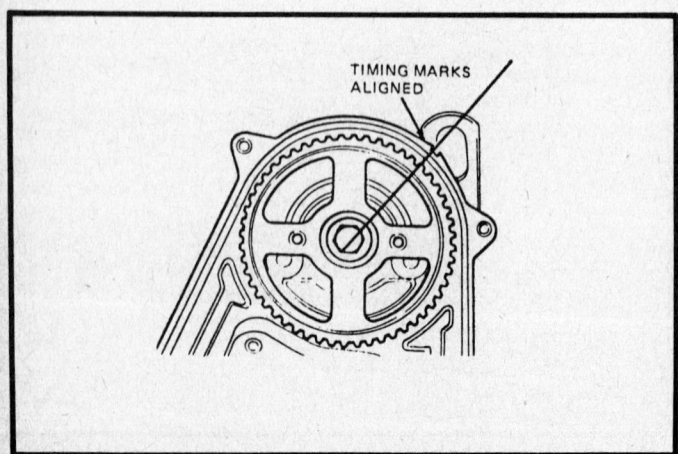
Camshaft timing mark

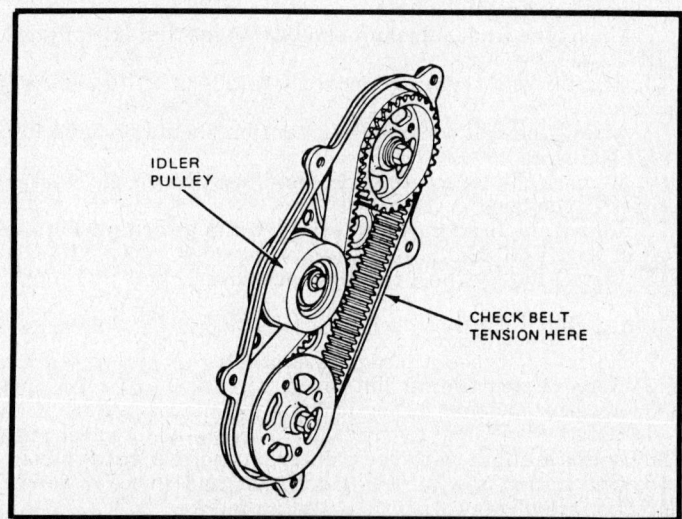
Timing belt tensioner – rear

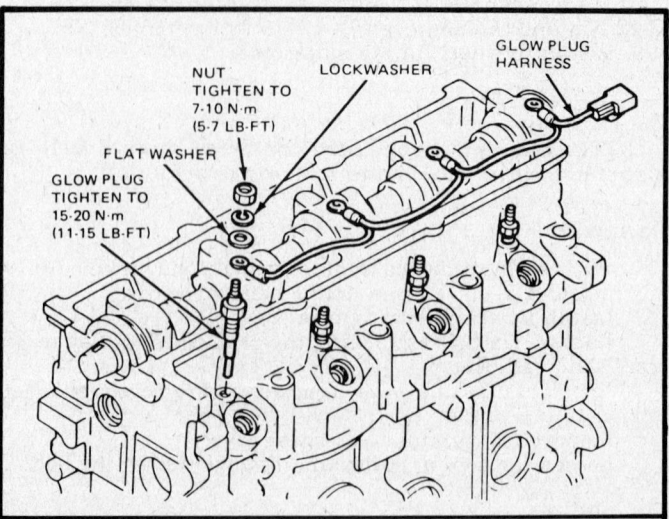
Glow plugs

DIESEL ENGINES
FORD 2.0L FOUR CYLINDER

6. Remove timing belt.
7. Install belt.
8. Loosen tensioner locknut and adjust timing belt.
9. Install rear timing belt cover and tighten bolts to 5–7 ft. lbs. (7–10 Nm).

GLOW PLUGS

Removal

1. Disconnect battery ground cable from the battery, located in the luggage compartment.
2. Disconnect glow plug harness from the glow plugs.
3. Using a 12mm deepwell socket, remove the glow plugs.

Installation

1. Install glow plugs, using a 12mm deepwell socket. Tighten the glow plugs to 11–15 ft. lbs. (15–20 Nm).
2. Connect the glow plug harness to the glow plugs. Tighten the nuts to 5–7 ft. lbs. (7–10 Nm).
3. Connect battery ground cable to the battery located in the luggage compartment.
4. Check the glow plug system operation.

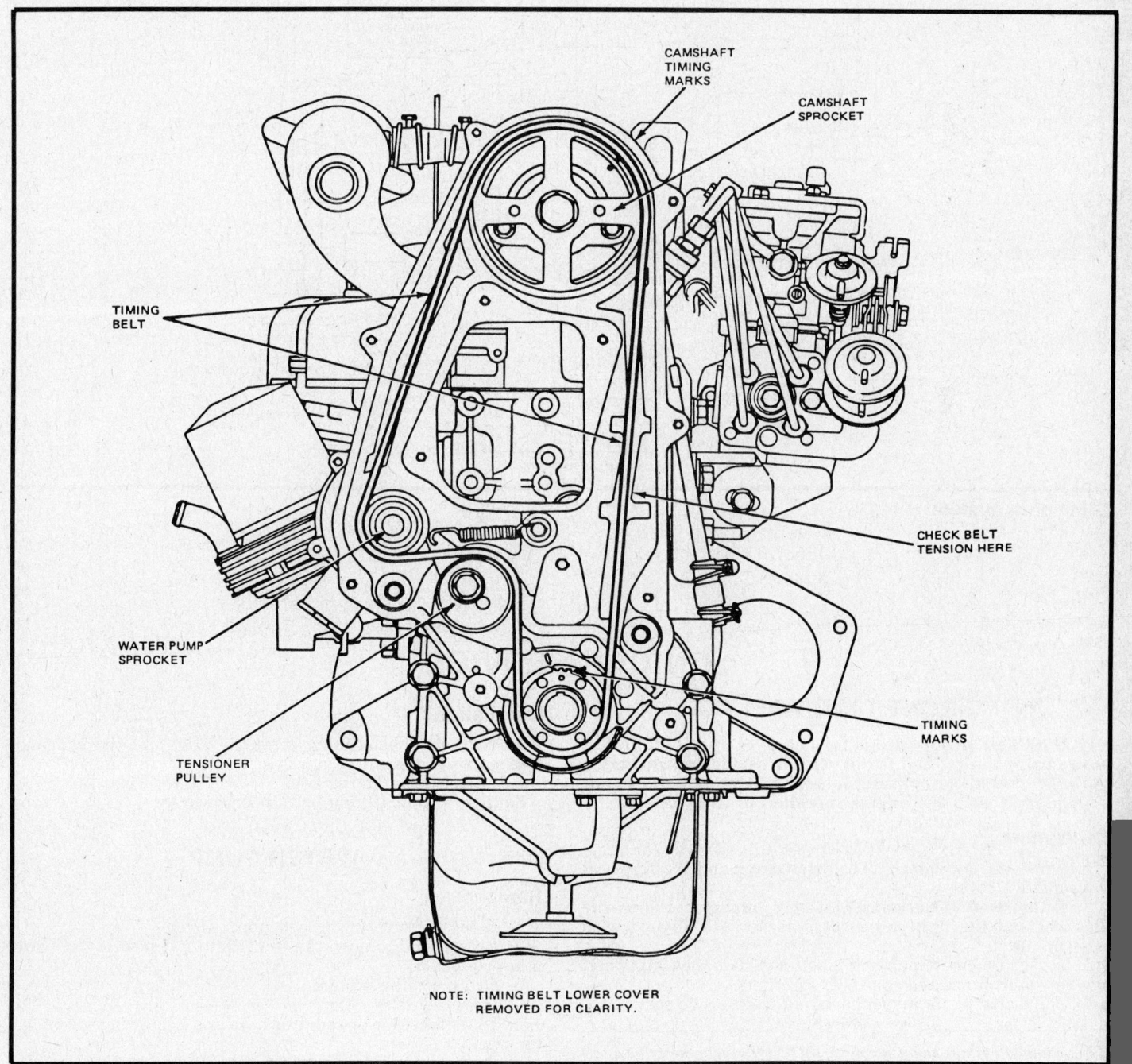

Front timing belt installation

SECTION 27

DIESEL ENGINES
FORD 2.0L FOUR CYLINDER

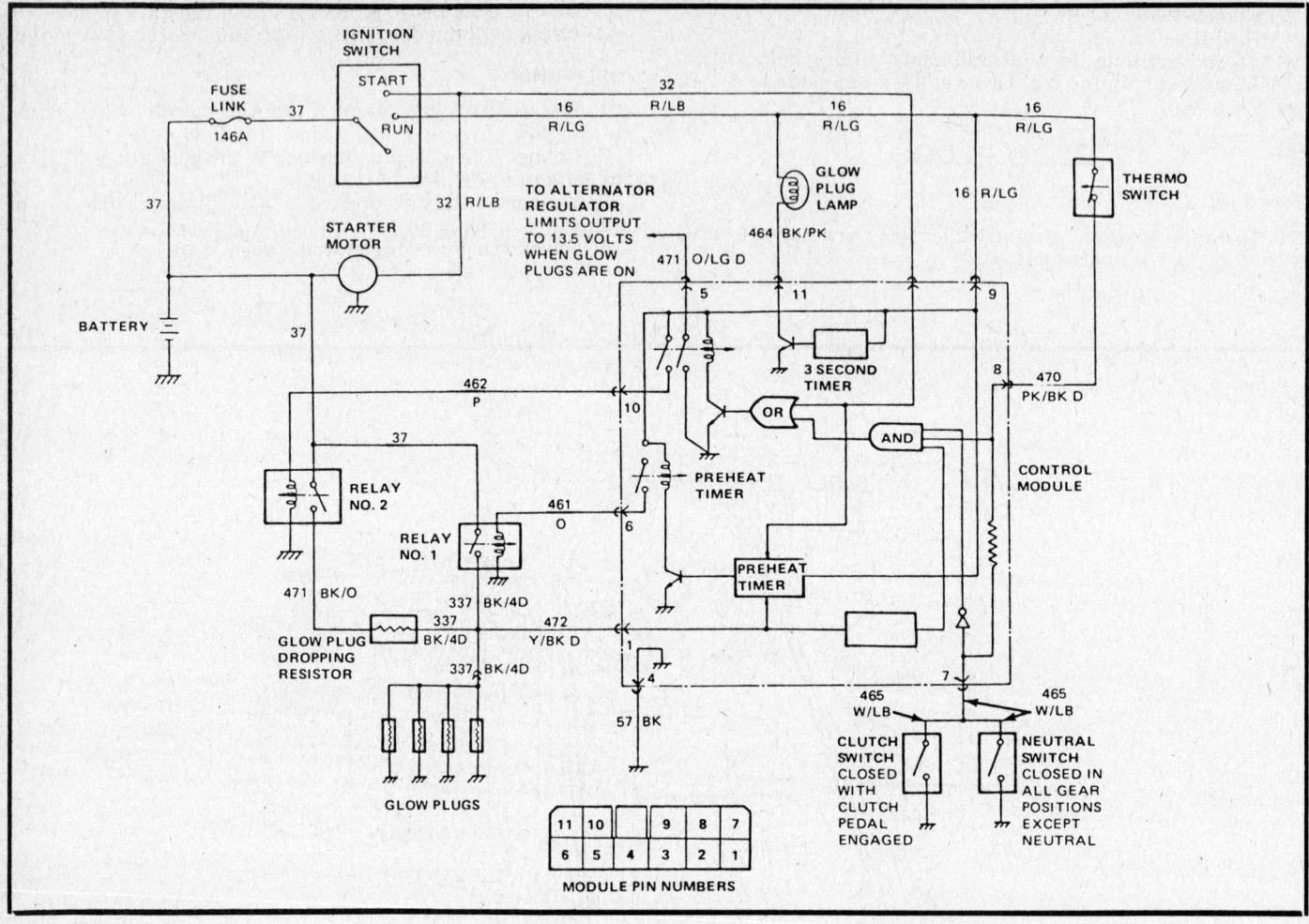

Glow plug system

ON CAR SERVICE

FRONT TIMING BELT

NOTE: This procedure is for removal and installation of the front timing belt for in vehicle service of the water pump, camshaft or cylinder head. The timing belt cannot be replaced with the engine installed in the vehicle.

Removal

1. Remove front timing belt upper cover and the flywheel timing mark cover.
2. Rotate engine clockwise until the timing marks on the flywheel and the front camshaft sprocket are aligned with their pointers.
3. Loosen tensioner pulley lockbolt and slide the timing belt off the water pump and camshaft sprockets.
4. The water pump and/or camshaft can now be serviced.

CAUTION
If the camshaft is not being removed, DO NOT rotate the crankshaft with the front timing belt removed.

Installation

1. With flywheel timing mark at TDC and the camshaft aligned with its timing mark. Install front timing belt.
2. Adjust front timing belt.
3. Install front timing belt upper cover.

WATER PUMP

Removal

1. Remove front timing belt upper cover.
2. Loosen and remove the front timing belt from the water pump sprocket.
3. Drain cooling system.
4. Raise vehicle.
5. Disconnect lower radiator hose and heater hose from water pump.
6. Disconnect coolant tube from the thermostat housing and discard gasket.

DIESEL ENGINES
FORD 2.0L FOUR CYLINDER

7. Remove the three bolts attaching the water pump to the crankcase and remove water pump. Discard gasket.

Installation

1. Clean water pump and crankshaft gasket mating surfaces.
2. Install water pump, using a new gasket. Tighten bolts to 23–34 ft. lbs. (32–47 Nm).
3. Connect coolant tube from thermostat housing to the water pump using a new gasket. Tighten bolts to 5–7 ft. lbs. (7–10 Nm).
4. Connect heater hose and lower radiator hose to water pump.
5. Lower vehicle.
6. Fill and bleed the cooling system.
7. Install and adjust the front timing belt.
8. Run engine and check for coolant leaks.
9. Install front timing belt upper cover.

INTAKE MANIFOLD

Removal

1. Disconnect air inlet duct from the intake manifold and install a protective cap in the intake manifold.

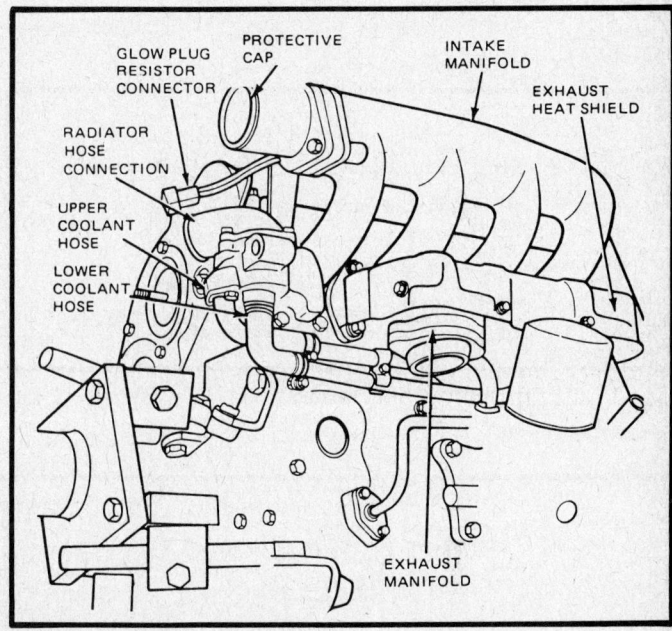
Intake manifold removal

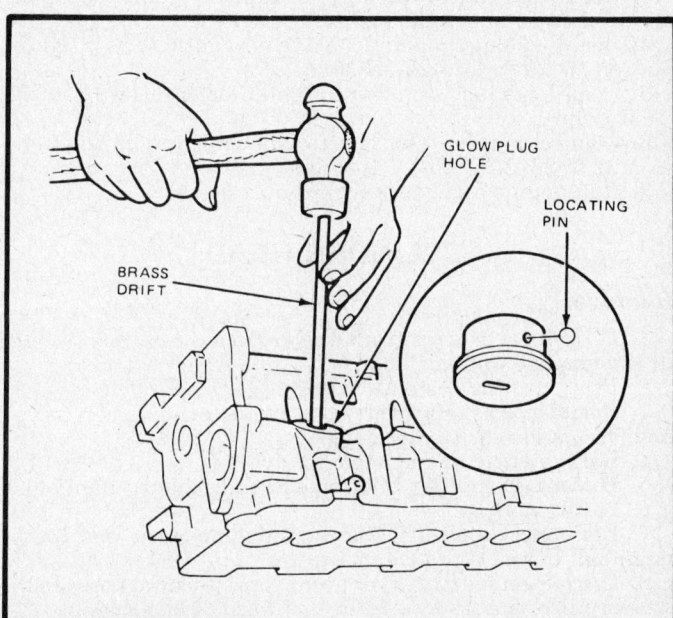
Pre-chamber removal

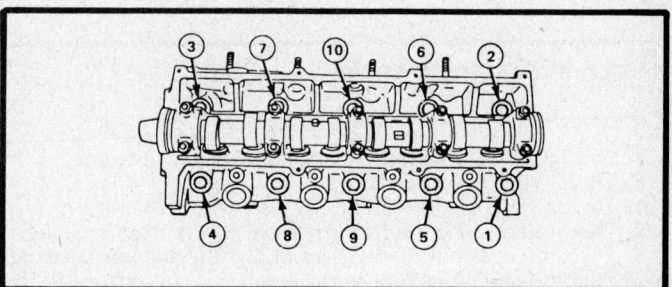
Cylinder head bolt removal

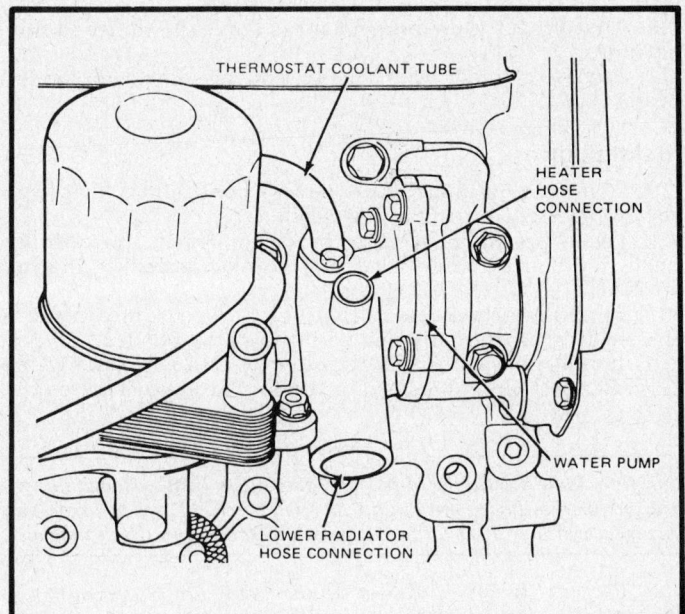
Water pump installation

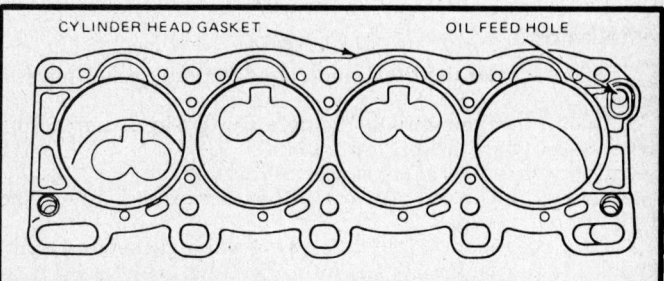
Head gasket installation

27-11

SECTION 27
DIESEL ENGINES
FORD 2.0L FOUR CYLINDER

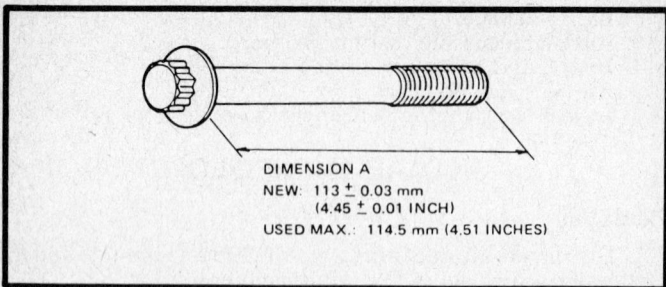

Head bolt dimension

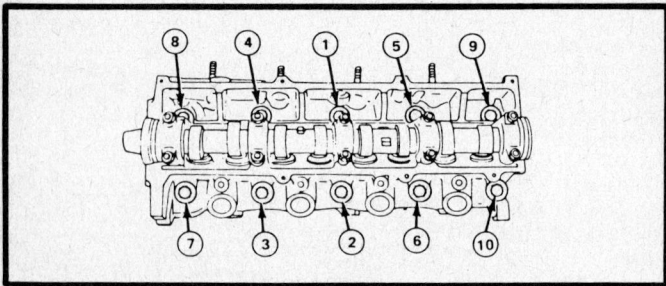

Head bolt tightening sequence

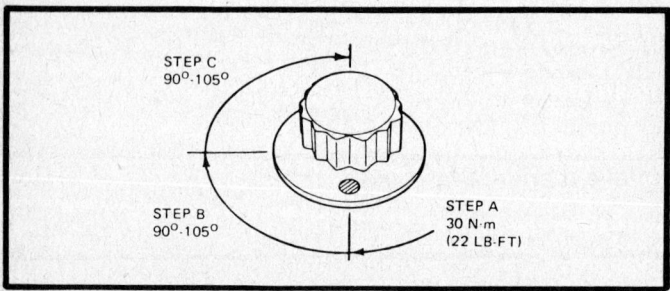

Head bolt tightening steps

2. Disconnect glow plug resistor electrical connector.
3. Disconnect breather hose.
4. Drain the cooling system.
5. Disconnect upper radiator hose at thermostat housing.
6. Disconnect two coolant hoses at the thermostat housing.
7. Disconnect connectors to the temperature sensors in the thermostat housing.
8. Remove bolts attaching the intake manifold to the cylinder head and remove the intake manifold.

Installation

1. Clean intake manifold and cylinder head gasket mating surfaces.
2. Install intake manifold, using a new gasket, and tighten the bolts to 12–16 ft. lbs. (16–23 Nm).
3. Connect temperature sensor connectors.
4. Connect lower coolant hose at the thermostat housing and tighten hose clamp.
5. Connect upper coolant tube, using a new gasket and tighten bolts to 5–7 ft. lbs. (7–10 Nm).
6. Connect upper radiator hose to thermostat housing.
7. Connect breather hose.
8. Connect glow plug resistor electrical connector.

9. Remove protective cap and install air inlet duct.
10. Fill and bleed the cooling system.
11. Run engine and check for intake air leaks and coolant leaks.

EXHAUST MANIFOLD
Removal and Installation

1. Remove nuts attaching the muffler inlet pipe to the exhaust manifold.
2. Remove bolts attaching the heat shield to the exhaust manifold.
3. Remove the nuts attaching the exhaust manifold to cylinder head and remove the exhaust manifold.
4. Install exhaust manifold, using new gaskets, and tighten nuts to 16–20 ft. lbs. (22–27 Nm).
5. Install exhaust shield and tighten bolts to 12–16 ft. lbs. (16–23 Nm).
6. Connect muffler inlet pipe to exhaust manifold and tighten nuts to 23–35 ft. lbs. (34–47 Nm).
7. Run engine and check for exhaust leaks.

CYLINDER HEAD
Removal

1. Disconnect battery ground cable from the battery, located in the luggage compartment.
2. Drain cooling system.
3. Remove camshaft cover, front and rear timing belt covers, and front and rear timing belts.
4. Raise vehicle and support safely.
5. Disconnect muffler inlet pipe at the exhaust manifold.
6. Lower vehicle.
7. Disconnect air inlet duct at the air cleaner and intake manifold. Install a protective cap.
8. Disconnect electrical connectors and vacuum hoses to the temperature sensors located in the thermostat housing.
9. Disconnect upper and lower coolant hoses, and the upper radiator hose at the thermostat housing.
10. Disconnect and remove the injection lines at the injection pump and nozzles. Cap all lines and fittings.
11. Disconnect glow plug harness from the main engine harness.
12. Remove cylinder head bolts in sequence. Remove cylinder head.

Installation

1. Remove glow plugs. Then, remove pre-chamber cups from the cylinder head using a brass drift.
2. Clean pre-chamber cups, pre-chambers in the cylinder head and the cylinder head and crankcase gasket mating surfaces.
3. Install pre-chambers in the cylinder heads, making sure the locating pins are aligned with the slots provided.
4. Install glow plugs and tighten to 11–15 ft. lbs. (15–20 Nm). Connect glow plug harness to the glow plugs. Tighten the nuts to 5–7 ft. lbs. (7–10 Nm).

CAUTION
Carefully blow out the head bolt threads in the crankcase with compressed air. Failure to thoroughly clean the thread bores can result in incorrect cylinder head torque or possible cracking of the crankcase.

---

5. Position a new cylinder head gasket on the crankcase making sure the cylinder head oil feed hole is not blocked.
6. Measure each cylinder head bolt dimension A. If the measurement is more than 4.51 in. (114.5mm), replace the head bolt.

DIESEL ENGINES
FORD 2.0L FOUR CYLINDER
SECTION 27

CAUTION

Rotate the camshaft in the cylinder head until the cam lobes for No. 1 cylinder are at the base circle (both valves closed). Then, rotate the crankshaft clockwise until No. 1 piston is halfway up in the cylinder bore toward TDC. This is to prevent contact between the pistons and valves.

---

7. Install cylinder head on the crankcase.

NOTE: Before installing the cylinder head bolts, paint a white reference dot on each one, and apply a light coat of engine oil on the bolt threads.

8. Tighten head bolts as follows:
   a. Tighten bolts to 22 ft. lbs. (30 Nm) in sequence.
   b. Using the painted reference marks, tighten each bolt in sequence, 90–105 degrees.
   c. Repeat Step b turning the bolts another 90–105 degrees.
9. Connect glow plug harness to main engine harness.
10. Remove protective caps and install injection lines to injection pump and nozzles. Tighten capnuts to 18–22 ft. lbs. (25–29 Nm).
11. Air bleed the system as outlined.
12. Connect upper (with a new gasket) and lower coolant hoses, and the upper radiator hose to the thermostat housing. Tighten upper coolant hose bolts to 5–7 ft. lbs. (7–10 Nm).
13. Connect electrical connectors and vacuum hoses to the temperature sensors in the thermostat housing.
14. Remove protective cap and install the air inlet duct to the intake manifold and air cleaner.
15. Raise vehicle and connect the muffler inlet pipe to the exhaust manifold. Tighten nuts to 25–35 ft. lbs. (34–47 Nm).
16. Lower vehicle.
17. Install and adjust the front timing belt.
18. Install and adjust the rear timing belt.
19. Install front upper timing belt cover and rear timing belt cover. Tighten the bolts to 5–7 ft. lbs. (7–10 Nm).
20. Check and adjust the valves as outlined. Install the valve cover and tighten the bolts to 5–7 ft. lbs. (7–10 Nm).
21. Fill and bleed the cooling system.
22. Check and adjust the injection pump timing.
23. Connect battery ground cable to battery.
24. Run engine and check for oil, fuel and coolant leaks.

FUEL SYSTEM

INJECTION PUMP

Removal

1. Disconnect battery ground cable from the battery, located in the luggage compartment.
2. Disconnect the air inlet duct from the air cleaner and intake manifold. Install protective cap in intake manifold.
3. Remove rear timing belt cover and flywheel timing mark cover.
4. Remove rear timing belt as outlined.
5. Disconnect throttle cable and speed cable, if so equipped.
6. Disconnect vacuum hoses at the altitude compensator and cold start diaphragm.
7. Disconnect fuel cut-off solenoid connector.
8. Disconnect fuel supply and fuel return hoses at injection pump.
9. Remove injection lines at the injection pump and nozzles. Cap all lines and fittings.
10. Rotate injection pump sprocket until timing marks are aligned. Install two bolts in the holes to hold the injection pump sprocket. Remove sprocket retaining nut.
11. Remove injection pump sprocket using Gear Puller and Adapter, using two bolts installed in the threaded holes in the sprocket.
12. Remove bolt attaching the injection pump to the pump front bracket.
13. Remove the two attaching the injection pump to the pump rear bracket and remove the pump.

Installation

1. Install injection pump in position on the pump brackets.
2. Install two nuts attaching the pump to the rear bracket and tighten to 23–34 ft. lbs. (32–47 Nm).
3. Install bolt attaching the pup to the front bracket and tighten to 12–16 ft. lbs. (16–23 Nm).
4. Install injection pump sprocket. Hold the sprocket in place using the procedure described in Step 10, Removal. Install the sprocket retaining nut and tighten to 51–58 ft. lbs. (70–80 Nm).
5. Remove protective caps and install the fuel lines at the injection pump and nozzles. Tighten the fuel line capnuts to 18–22 ft. lbs. (25–29 Nm).

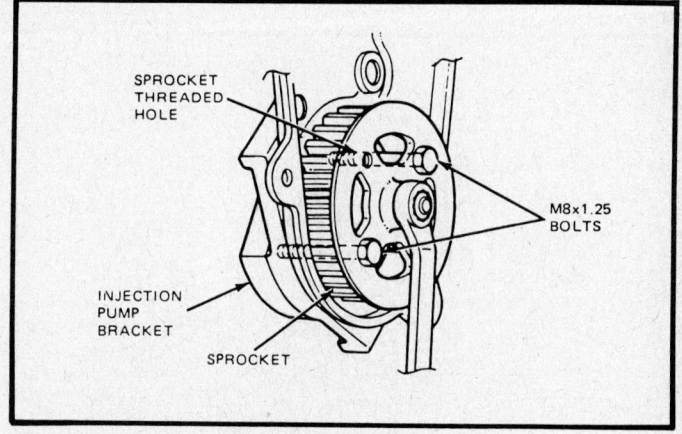

Injection pump sprocket removal

6. Connect fuel supply and fuel return hoses at the injection pump.
7. Connect fuel cut-off solenoid connector.
8. Connect vacuum lines to the cold start diaphragm and altitude compensator.
9. Connect throttle cable and speed control cable, if so equipped.
10. Install and adjust the rear timing belt.
11. Remove protective cap and install the air inlet duct to the intake manifold and air cleaner.
12. Connect battery ground cable to battery.
13. Air bleed fuel system.
14. Check and adjust the injection pump timing.
15. Run engine and check for fuel leaks.
16. Check and adjust engine idle.

INJECTION NOZZLES

Removal

1. Disconnect and remove injection lines from injection pump and nozzles. Cap all lines and fittings.

27-13

Section 27: DIESEL ENGINES
FORD 2.0L FOUR CYLINDER

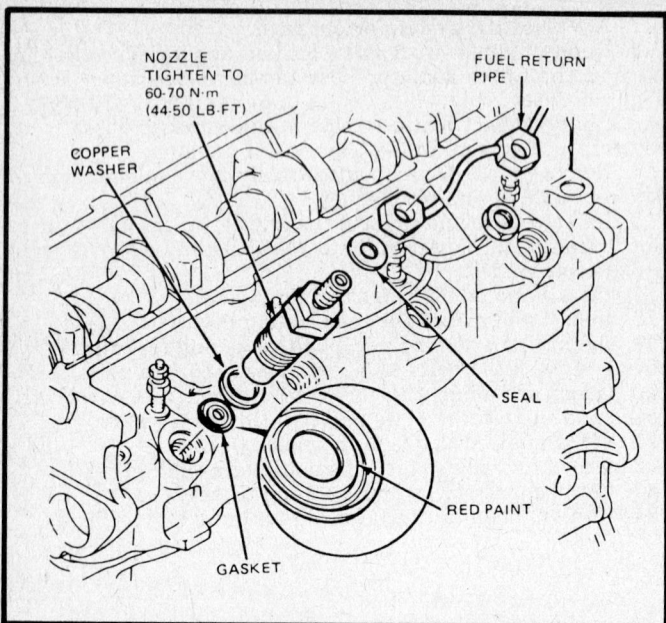

Injection nozzle installation

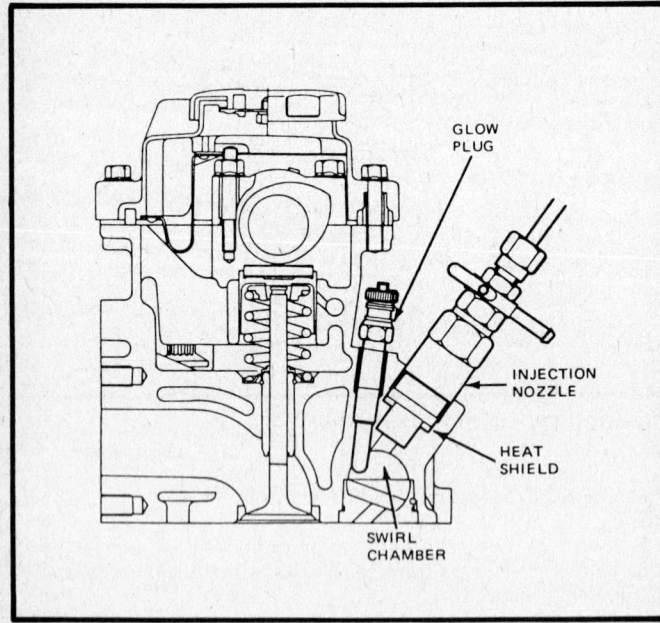

Injection nozzle and glow plug

NOTE: Install gasket with red painted surface facing up.

3. Position new copper washers in the nozzle bores.
4. Install nozzles and tighten to 44–51 ft. lbs. (60–70 Nm).
5. Position fuel return line on the nozzles, using new seals.
6. Install fuel return line retaining nuts and tighten to 10 ft. lbs. (14 Nm).
7. Install fuel lines on the injection pump and nozzles. Tighten capnuts to 18–22 ft. lbs. (25–29 Nm).
8. Air bleed fuel system.
9. Run engine and check for fuel leaks.

FUEL CUT-OFF SOLENOID
Removal and Installation

1. Disconnect battery ground cable from the battery located in the luggage compartment.
2. Remove connector from the fuel cut-off solenoid.
3. Remove fuel cut-off solenoid and discard the O-ring.
4. Install fuel cut-off solenoid using a new O-ring. Tighten to 30–33 ft. lbs. (40–45 Nm).
5. Connect electrical connector.
6. Connect battery ground cable.
7. Run engine and check for fuel leaks.

INJECTION NOZZLE ASSEMBLY
Disassembly and Cleaning

1. Prior to disassembly, wash complete assembly in a suitable solution to remove any excess oil and dirt.
2. Clamp nozzle assembly in a soft jawed vise and remove nozzle holder.

— CAUTION —
Do not cause damage to nozzle by overtightening vise.

3. Remove internal parts and lay on a clean surface for inspection.

— CAUTION —
Do not drop nozzle. Keep matched nozzle and needle valve together to prevent mixing with other parts and to prevent damage.

4. Clean all parts in a suitable cleaning solution. Wash nozzle and needle valve in a light oil. Remove carbon deposits using brass brush provided in Nozzle Cleaning Kit.

— CAUTION —
Do not use abrasive material to clean nozzle parts.

Inspection

1. Visually inspect all parts for wear and erosion.
2. Inspect valve seats for carbon deposits and damage.
3. Inspect injection orifices for wear.
4. Hold nozzle body vertically and lift needle valve up about $\frac{1}{3}$ of its entire length and release. The needle must slide to its seat by its own weight.

Assembly

1. Install needle valve and nozzle, spacer, push rod pressure, spring and adjusting shim and nozzle holder into retaining nut.
2. Clamp nozzle assembly in vise.
3. Tighten nozzle holder to specifications.

OIL COOLING JETS
Removal and Installation

1. Drain engine oil.

2. Remove nuts attaching the fuel return line to the nozzles, and remove return line and seals.
3. Remove nozzles using a deepwell socket.
4. Remove nozzle gaskets and washers from nozzle seat, using O-ring Pick Tool.

Installation

1. Clean the outside of the nozzle assemblies using Nozzle Cleaning Kit, and a suitable solvent. Dry thoroughly.
2. Position new sealing gaskets in the nozzle seats.

DIESEL ENGINES
FORD 2.0L FOUR CYLINDER
SECTION 27

2. Remove oil pan.
3. Remove bolt attaching oil cooling jet to crankcase.
4. Install oil cooling jet, using new sealing gaskets. Tighten the bolts to 23–34 ft. lbs. (32–47 Nm).

---- CAUTION ----
Be sure locating pin is installed in hole in crankcase before tightening bolts.

5. Install the oil pan.
6. Fill crankshaft with the specified quantity and quality of oil.
7. Run engine and check for oil leaks.

PRIMARY OIL FILTER, OIL COOLER AND OIL COOLER ADAPTER

NOTE: Perform only the portion(s) of this procedure necessary to remove the component being serviced.

Removal

1. Drain cooling system.
2. Raise vehicle.
3. Remove primary oil filter, if necessary.
4. Disconnect bypass oil filter lines.
5. Disconnect heater hose from the oil cooler.
6. Remove coolant line from the oil cooler.
7. Remove bolts attaching the oil cooler to the adapter.
8. Remove the two bolts attaching the adapter to the crankcase.

Installation

1. Install oil cooler, using new O-rings. Tighten bolts to 23–34 ft. lbs. (32–47 Nm).
2. Install coolant line on the oil cooler, using a new gasket. Tighten nuts to 5–7 ft. lbs. (7–10 Nm).
3. Connect heater hose to the oil cooler.
4. Connect bypass oil filter lines to the oil cooler, using new sealing gaskets. Tighten bolts to 10–12 ft. lbs. (14–16 Nm).
5. Install a new oil filter, if removed. Clean oil cooler sealing surface. Lightly coat filter gasket with engine oil and hand tighten the filter until the gasket touches the oil cooler. Tighten another ¾ turn, with a filter wrench if necessary.

6. Lower vehicle.
7. Fill and bleed the cooling system.

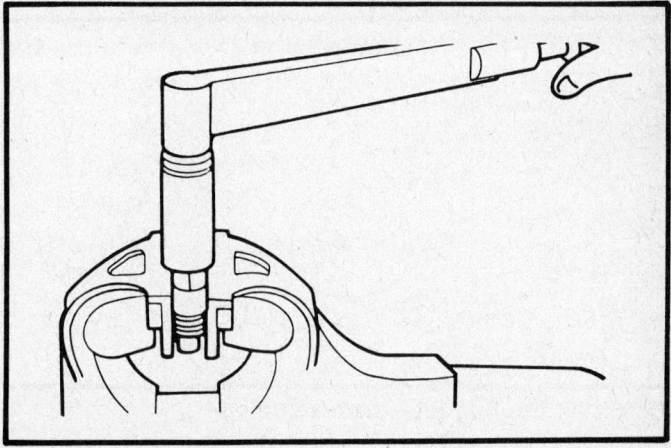
Nozzle holder removal

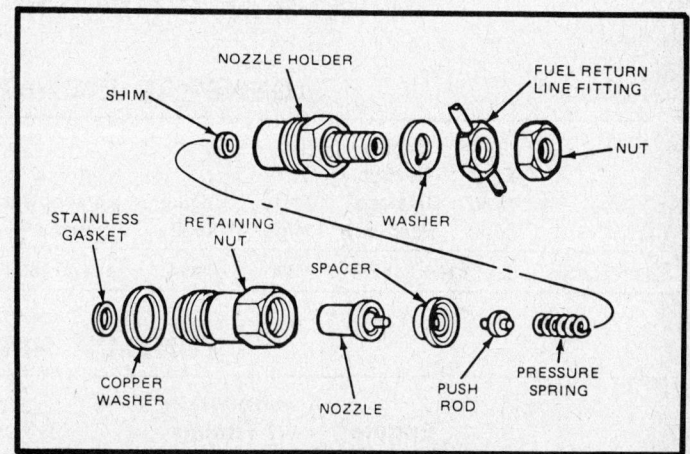
Injection nozzle components

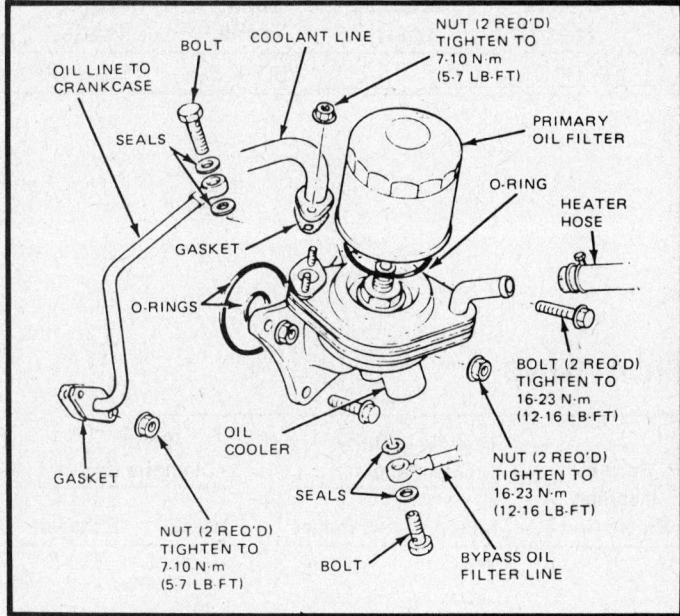
Primary oil cooler

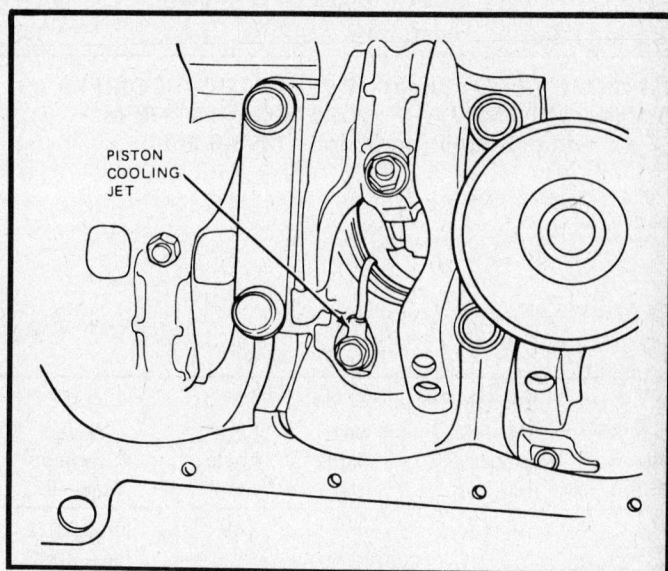
Piston oil cooling jet—installed

27-15

SECTION 27: DIESEL ENGINES
FORD 2.0L FOUR CYLINDER

8. Top off engine oil with specified quality of engine oil.
9. Run engine and check for coolant and oil leaks.

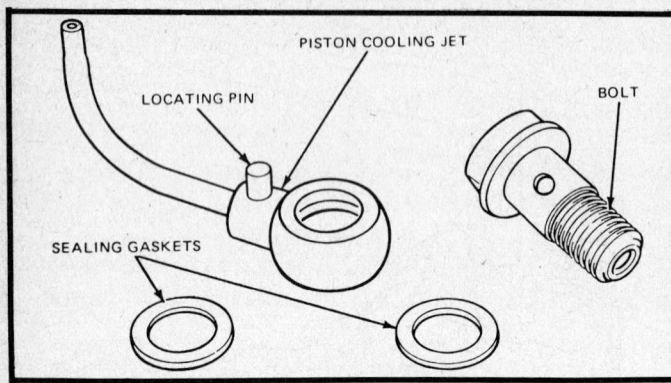

Piston oil cooling jet—disassembled

BYPASS OIL FILTER AND BRACKET

Removal
1. Raise vehicle.
2. Remove bypass oil filter, if necessary.
3. Disconnect inlet and outlet oil lines from adapter.
4. Remove bolts attaching adapter to side rail and remove adapter.

Installation
1. Install adapter on side rail and tighten bolts.
2. Connect inlet and outlet oil lines to adapter with new gaskets and tighten.
3. Install new bypass oil filter, if removed. Clean engine block mounting areas. Lightly coat gasket surface of new filter with engine oil and hand tighten until gasket touches base. Tighten another 1 ¼ turn, with filter wrench, if necessary.
4. Lower vehicle, and fill the engine with the specified quality of oil.
5. Run engine and check for oil leaks.

FORD 2.4L 6 CYL DIESEL TURBO ENGINE

GENERAL ENGINE SPECIFICATIONS

Year	Eng V.I.N. Code	Engine No. Cyl. Displacement (cc)	Eng Mfg	Engine Type	Horsepower @ rpm ■	Torque @ rpm (ft. lbs.) ■	Bore × Stroke (mm)	Compression Ratio	Oil Pressure @ 4800 rpm
'84 and Later	1	6-2442.9	BMW	Diesel	114 @ 4800	150 @ 2400	80 × 81	23:1	57-85

TUNE-UP SPECIFICATIONS

Year	Engine No. Cyl. Displacement (cu. in.)	Injection Timing (deg) Auto Trans.	Compression (psi)	Valves Intake Opens (deg)	Fuel Pump Pressure (psi)	Idle Speed (rpm) Man. Trans.	Idle Speed (rpm) Auto. Trans.
'84 and Later	6-149	1	348	6° BTDC	—	750 + 50	750 + 50

1 MODEL VE (49 states)—2.5° ± 1° BTDC @ 750 RPM
 Model VP (Calif)—6° ± 1.5° BTDC @ 2000 RPM
 Injection Firing Order—1-5-3-6-2-4

VALVE SPECIFICATIONS

VIN Code	Engine No. Cyl. Displacement (cu. in.)	Seat Angle (deg)	Face Angle (deg)	Valve Clearance Cold—in.	Spring Installed Height (in.)	Stem to Guide Clearance (in.) Intake	Stem to Guide Clearance (in.) Exhaust	Stem Diameter (in.) Intake	Stem Diameter (in.) Exhaust
1	6-149	45	45	Int.—0.012 Ex.—0.016	—	0.010 Max	0.010 Max	—	—

DIESEL ENGINES
FORD 2.4L SIX CYLINDER
SECTION 27

CRANKSHAFT AND CONNECTING ROD SPECIFICATIONS
(All measurements are given in inches.)

Year	Engine No. Cyl. Displacement (cu. in.)	Crankshaft Main Brg. Journal Dia	Main Brg. Oil Clearance	Shaft End-Play	Thrust on No.	Connecting Rod Journal Diameter	Oil Clearance	Side Clearance
'84 and Later	6-149	2.3610-2.3618	0.0008-0.0018	0.003-0.006	6	—	0.0008-0.002	—

PISTON AND RING SPECIFICATIONS
(All measurements are given in inches.)

Year	Engine No. Cyl. Displacement (cc)	Piston Clearance	Ring Gap Top Compression	Bottom Compression	Oil Control	Ring Side Clearance Top Compression	Bottom Compression	Oil Control
'84 and Later	6.2442.9	0.006 ① ②	0.008-0.016	0.008-0.016	0.010-0.020	0.0024-0.0055	0.0020-0.0031	0.0012-0.0024

① Alcan—0.0010-0.0021 in.
  KS—0.0016—0.0027 in.
  Mahle—0.0018—0.0029 in.
② Total Piston wear

TORQUE SPECIFICATIONS

Description	N·m	Lb-Ft
Main bearing caps	60-67	43-48
Engine support straps	39-47	28-34
Valve cover	8-10	6-7
Oil trap to valve cover	15-19	11-14
Cylinder head bolts		
Step 1	50-60	36-43
	wait 15 min.	
Step 2 (Torque Angle)	Turn in sequence 90°	
	Run engine 15-20 minutes	
	Turn in sequence another 90°	
Step 3 (torque angle)	Turn in sequence another 90°	
Oil spray bar to cylinder head	20-24	14-17
Oil drain plug	33-36	24-26
Oil pan to crankcase	9-10	6.5-7
Front/rear end covers to crankcase	w/Bolt M6X21—8-10	6-7
	w/Bolt M8X21—20-24	14-17
Flywheel to crankshaft (installed with Loctite No. 270)	98-112	71-81
Vibration damper hub to crankshaft	390-430	282-311
Pulley/vibration damper to vibration damper hub	22-24	16-17
Oil line from turbocharger to crankcase 22mm width across flats hollow bolt	40-50	29-36
Water pump to crankcase	20-24	14-17
Fan coupling to water pump nut with left-hand threads	50	36
Fan to fan coupling	8-10	6-7
Pulley to water pump	8-10	6-7
Thermostat housing	8-10	6-7
Bleeder screw	6-10	4-7
Temperature sensor/temperature switch	17-19	12-14
Intake manifold to cylinder head	20-24	14-17
Exhaust manifold to cylinder head (upper row of staybolts installed with Loctite 270)	20-24	14-17
Turbocharger to exhaust manifold	23-27	17-20
Exhaust to turbocharger	43-48	31-35
Vacuum pump	8-10	6-7
Pulse sensor to engine (holder)	8-10	6-7
Glow plugs	20-30	14-22

SECTION 27

DIESEL ENGINES
FORD 2.4L SIX CYLINDER

TORQUE SPECIFICATIONS

Description	N·m	Lb-Ft
Connecting rod bolts		
Step 1	20	14
Step 2 (torque angle)		70°
Sprocket to camshaft	55-65	40-47
Bearing cap of camshaft	w/Bolt M6X21—8-10	6-7
	w/Bolt M8X21—20-24	14-17
Tensioning roller holder to crankcase	20-24	14-17
Clamping bolt in rocker arm	7-9	5-6.5
Sprocket to auxiliary shaft	55-65	40-47
Oil pressure switch	30-40	22-29
Oil pump to crankcase	22-24	16-17
Oil pump cover	8-10	6-7
Oil filter housing to crankcase	20-24	14-17
Oil filter cover	21-25	15-18
Oil filter drain plug	10-13	7-9
Oil spray jet to crankcase	8-10	6-7
Oil cooler oil lines to oil filter housing	30-40	22-29
Oil lines to turbocharger	20-24	14-17

Description	N·m	Lb-Ft
Temperature switch to fuel filter housing	30	22
Wire to glow plug	4-5	3-4
Fuel filter housing to holder	43-48	31-35
Injection pump to holder, rear (nuts and bolts)	20-24	14-17
Injection pump to holder, front	20-24	14-17
Electric shut-off to injection pump	15-25	11-18
Electric valve for cold start accelerator to injection pump	15-20	11-14
Injection pump gear to injection pump	45-50	33-36
Tensioning torque for tensioning roller holder	45-50	33-36
Tensioning roller holder to engine (M8 nut and bolt)	25	18
Combination fuel injector in cylinder head	40-45	29-33
Injection line (coupling nut)	20-25	14-18
Nozzle holder to injection pump	45	33
Spill valve to injection pump (hollow bolt)	20-30	14-22

TUNE-UP

VEHICLE APPLICATION

Mark VII/Continental

DESCRIPTION

The 2.4L diesel engine is a four cycle, turbocharged, in-line six cylinder, with an overhead camshaft. Number one cylinder is located at the front of the engine.

The engine is a lightweight, compact design displacing 2,443cc (149 CID). The crankshaft uses piston cooling jets, which direct oil to a port on the underside of the piston. The port is connected to a circular chamber case into the top of the piston. The oil flowing through the chamber helps to cool the piston during engine operation.

The crankshaft is a seven main bearing unit with fore and at thrust controlled at the No. 6 main bearing.

A cogged drive belt s used to drive the camshaft, injection pump and intermediate shaft. The intermediate shaft is used to operate the oil pump.

The camshaft is supported by seven machined bearing bores in the cylinder head. The bearing caps are numbered, front to rear, and must be installed in the same position from which they were removed, with all the numbers facing the same way. Bearing inserts are not available for the camshaft. Camshaft thrust is controlled by a thrust washer located next to the No. 1 camshaft bearing.

The camshaft has an additional lobe, located between the intake and exhaust valve lobes for No. 5 cylinder. This lobe is used to operate the vacuum pump located on top of the camshaft. A replaceable, hardened steel sleeve is installed on this lobe.

The valves are adjusted by an eccentric located on the tip of the rocker arm, at the top of the valve stem.

The water pump and fan are driven by a separate, conventional V-belt, which also drives the alternator. A separate V-ribbed belt is used to drive the other accessories.

COMPRESSION TEST

1. Do not warm up the engine. The engine must be cold.
2. Stop the engine and remove all six glow plugs. Install the 2.4L adapter and the compression tester on the cylinder to be checked. Use the right adapter, so that the thread damage does not occur.
3. Disconnect the glow-plug circuit at the glow-plug module to prevent the glow-plug connectors from shorting to ground when the engine is cranked.

--- CAUTION ---

If the glow plug connectors are allowed to ground when the engine is cranked, severe damage to the glow-plug circuit and module may occur. For this reason, the glow-plug circuit must always be disconnected whenever the engine is cranked and the glow-plug terminals are not attached.

4. Disconnect the fuel cutoff solenoid valve wire on the fuel injection pump to de-activate the solenoid during testing. This will prevent fuel from getting to the engine and causing it to start.
5. Crank the engine and note the gauge indication when stabilized. Compression pressure must be a minimum of 348 psi (2400 kPa), and should not vary more than 50 psi (345 kPa) between cylinders.
    a. Check engine cranking speed if the compression is low-

DIESEL ENGINES
FORD 2.4L SIX CYLINDER
SECTION 27

er than normal.

b. If the cranking speed is normal, but compression pressure is lower than specifications, engine repair may be needed.

c. An abnormally high compression ratio in one or more cylinders may indicate heavy carbon deposits and the need for repairs.

CAUTION
When reinstalling the glow plugs, coat the threads with anti-seize compound.

VALVE CLEARANCE (COLD ENGINE)

Adjustment
ENGINE WARM

1. Remove valve cover.
2. Position camshaft so that base circle of the lobe of the valve to be adjusted is facing the rocker arm.
3. Loosen adjusting eccentric locknut using valve clearance adjusting wrench, and a 12mm open end wrench.
4. Rotate eccentric using a small punch until valve clearance is adjusted to specification: Intake 0.012 inch (0.3mm); Exhaust 0.016 inch (0.04mm). Engine cold-Intake 0.010 inch, Exhaust: 0.012 inch. Tighten eccentric locknut.
5. Repeat Steps 2, 3 and 4 for each valve.
6. Install valve cover as outlined.
7. Start engine and check for oil leaks.

INJECTION TIMING

The 49-state VE pump timing should be 2.5° ± 1.0°BTDC at 750 rpm. Dynamic timing check on California VP-20 pump should be 6° ± 1.5° BTDC at 2000 rpm. Refer to the vehicle emission label. Use the idle speed adjusting tool (D83T-9000-E or equivalent) to hold the engine at the specified rpm setting.

NOTE: Injection pump timing may retard slightly just off idle and then advance in a regular way. This is completely normal.

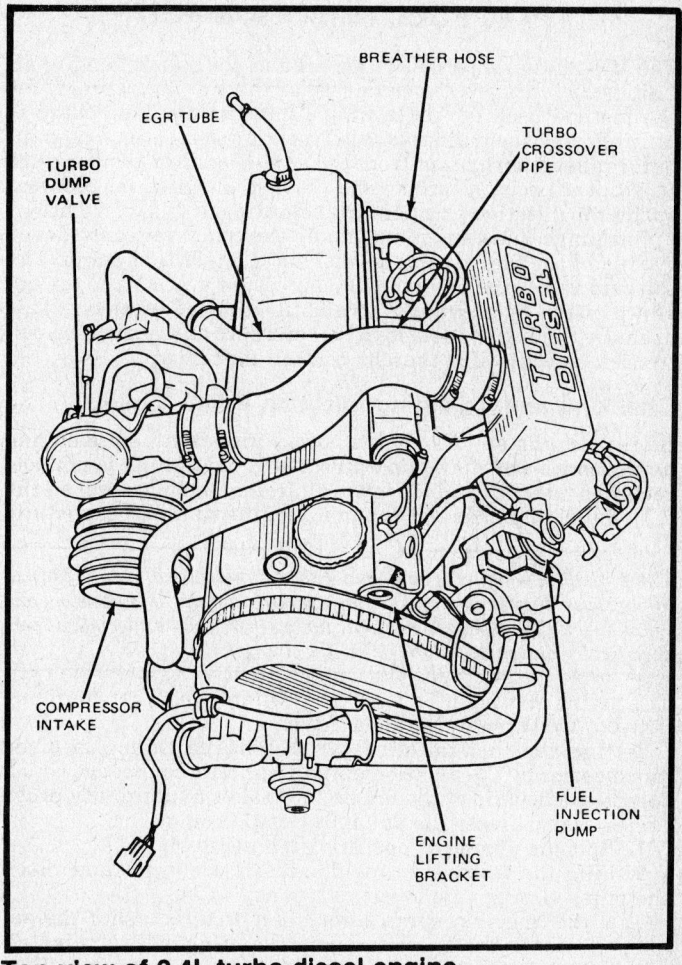

Top view of 2.4L turbo diesel engine

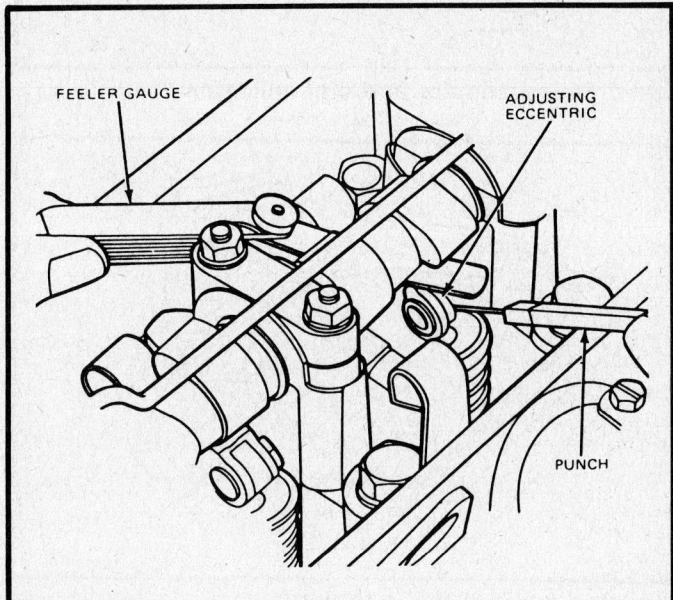

Valve adjustment

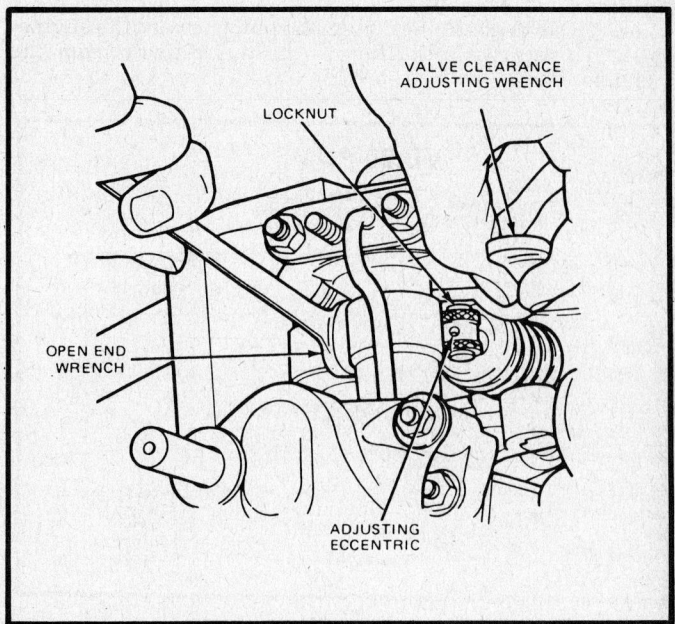

Eccentric locknut adjustment

27-19

Section 27: DIESEL ENGINES
FORD 2.4L SIX CYLINDER

VP-20 FUEL INJECTION PUMP

The VP-20 fuel injection pump used on 2.4L diesel engine in California functions the same way as the VE pump, except for the method used for controlling pump timing. This pump is controlled by the trunk mounted fuel flow computer. The computer takes information from the engine coolant temperature sensor, the position sensor, and the instrumented injector and varies the injection pump timing according to this information.

To change injection pump timing the computer controls the cycling of the fuel control solenoid in the injection pump. The solenoid varies the amount of fuel pressure available to the advance piston by providing an additional bleed whenever it is open. By cycling the solenoid, fuel pressure at the advance piston can be controlled thereby controlling timing.

Checking and Adjusting Injection Pump Timing

Setting timing on this engine is very important, since engine performance and emission will suffer if the timing is not correct. The method used for setting injection pump timing on the 2.4L diesel engine is the dynamic (engine running) procedure.

CAUTION

The 2.4L diesel engine is equipped with a diagnostic connector for use in checking engine rpm and setting dynamic timing. It is used in conjunction with the Rotunda dynamic timing meter and a special adapter specifically designed for the 2.4L diesel engine.

The meter and adapter are also available together (part no. 078-00116) through Rotunda Tools.

Setting the fuel injection pump dynamic timing is made much easier by the addition of the diagnostic connector, which speeds the hookup of the meter and makes a luminosity probe unnecessary. To set the dynamic pump timing.

1. Run the engine at operating temperature.
2. Plug the tester into the diagnostic connector and check the pump timing.
3. If the injection pump timing is not correct, shut the engine off, loosen the injection pump mounting bolts and install special tool T84P-9000-B and bracket, or equivalent, to turn the injection pump.
4. Restart the engine and turn the injection pump to correct the timing.
    a. To advance timing-Rotate the pump toward the engine.
    b. To retard timing-Rotate the pump away from the engine.
5. After setting the pump timing, retighten the mounting bolts and check to make sure that the timing did not change when the bolts were tightened.

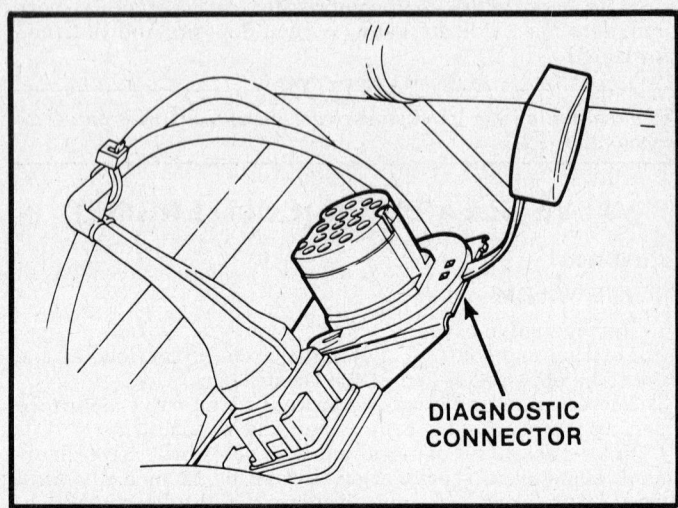
Diagnostic connector and cap

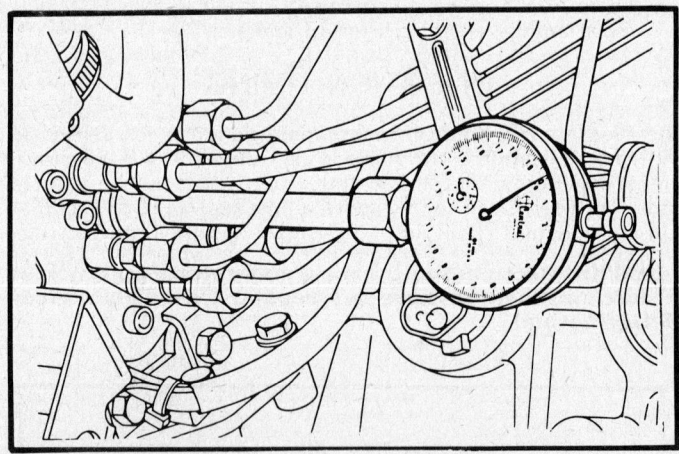
Static timing adapter and dial indicator

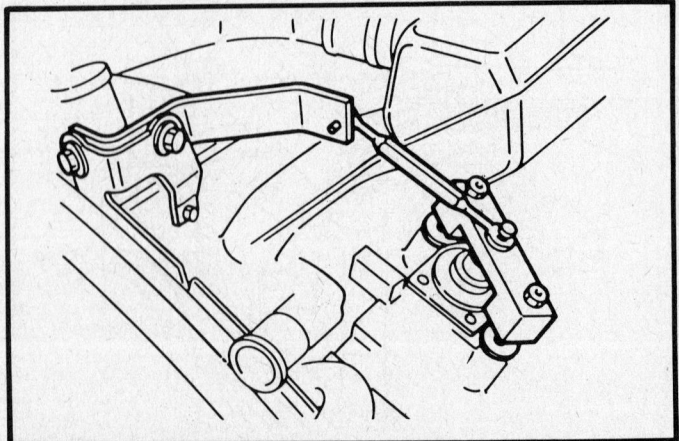
Injection pump rotating tool in place

Controlling of pump timing with additional components for California models

DIESEL ENGINES
FORD 2.4L SIX CYLINDER

SECTION 27

NOTE: Be sure to retighten the injection pump mounting bolts in the following order:

a. Tighten the nut on the front flange on the inside of the engine.
b. Tighten the nut on the front flange on the vehicle.
c. Tighten both rear bolts.

Static Timing Procedure

VP–20 PUMP

The static timing procedure is not needed under most circumstances. The only time which static timing is set is when a new fuel injection pump is installed; and this is only in California on the VP-20 pump. Use the following procedure to set the static timing.

1. Turn the engine to number 1 TDC.
2. Remove the timing plug in the injection pump head.
3. Install the adapter D84P-9000-D or equivalent into the injection pump. The plunger portion of the adapter must project into the pump so it can contact the fuel injection pump plunger. Mount the dial indicator into the adapter and make sure that there is at least 0.100 in (0.25mm) of preload on the dial indicator.
4. Turn the crankshaft in the direction of engine rotation until the dial gauge displays the lowest value.
5. Set the dial gauge to zero.
6. Continue turning the crankshaft in the direction of rotation until cylinder 1 is at TDC on the compression stroke. Hold the engine at number 1 TDC using special tool T84P-6400-A or equivalent. The measurement on the dial indicator should read:
   a. 0.0256 ± 0.0015 in. (0.65 ± 0.04mm) when the timing belt has more than 10,000 miles on it.
   b. 0.0248 ± 0.0015 in. (0.63 ± 0.04mm) when the timing belt has more than 10,000 miles on it.
7. If the measurement is not correct, the proper measurement can be attained by loosening the injection pump and turning it using special tool T84P-9000-B or equivalent, until the specified measurement is reached.
   a. Measurement too small-swing the pump toward the engine.
   b. Measurement too large-swing the pump away from the engine.
8. Tighten the injection pump mounting nuts in the specified order and remove special tools.
9. Turn the engine over twice and recheck the measurement with the engine at number 1 TDC. If the measurement is correct, remove the dial indicator and adapter and reinstall the plug in the injection pump. If the measurement is not correct, static timing will have to be reset by repeating Steps 1–9.
10. Dynamic timing should be checked on the 2.4L diesel after setting static timing to assure that the trunk mounted fuel flow computer is operating correctly.

NOTE: For information purposes only, the static timing readings on the VE pump are:

a. 0.0300 in. (0.76mm) when the timing belt has less than 10,000 miles on it.
b. 0.0291 in. (0.74mm) when the timing belt has more than 10,000 miles on it.

IDLE SPEED

Adjusting Engine Idle Speed and Maximum Speed

TO ADJUST THE WARM IDLE SPEED

1. Loosen the locknut on the adjusting screw and adjust the idle speed. The correct idle speed is 750–800 rpm.
2. Start the engine.
3. Tighten the locknut.
4. Check the knurled nut for play between the lever and knurled nut. Play should be 0.020–0.040 in. (0.5–1.0mm).
5. Check and, if necessary, correct linkage adjustment after adjusting idle speed.

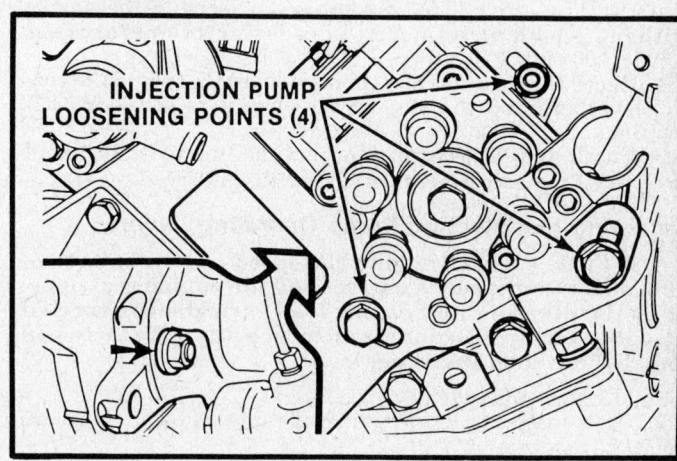

Injection pump bolts and nut locations

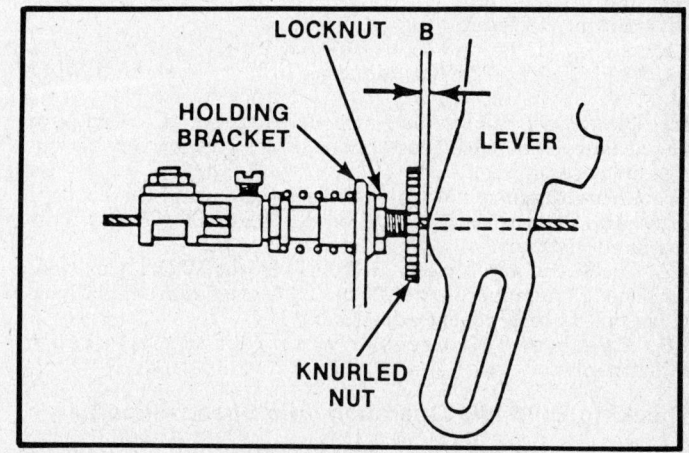

Idle speed adjustment with knurled nut

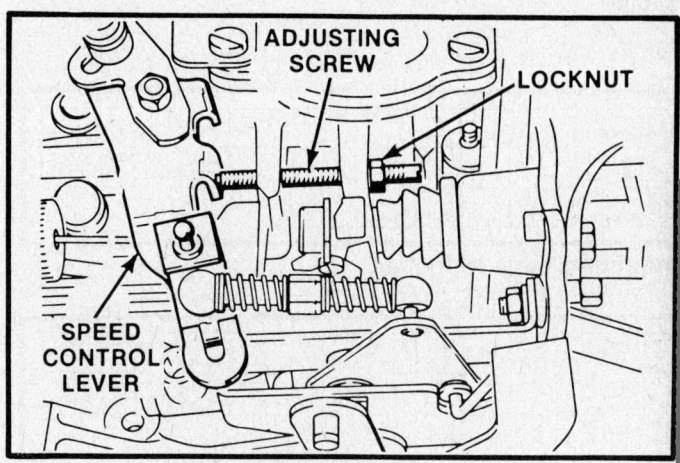

Maximum speed adjustment

SECTION 27 — DIESEL ENGINES
FORD 2.4L SIX CYLINDER

TO ADJUST THE MAXIMUM ENGINE SPEEDS.

1. Start the engine.
2. Move the speed control lever to the W.O.T. position.
3. Loosen the locknut and adjust the maximum speed with the adjusting screw. The maximum top speed of the engine without a load at its normal operating temperature is 5,350 ± 100 rpm.
4. Check the throttle cable adjustment so that the speed control lever rests on the stop screw when it is in the W.O.T. position.
5. Check and, if necessary, correct the linkage adjustment after finishing adjustments of the maximum speed.

Adjusting the Injection Pump Operating Lever

NOTE: Be sure the engine idle speed is correct, the engine maximum speed is correct and the engine is at operating temperature and partial load enrichment canceled or cable clamp disconnected to provide play between knurled nut and operating lever.

1. Measure and note distance "A".
2. Push operating lever against the full load stop. Measure and note distance "B".
3. Subtract distance "B" from distance "A".
A-B = Y
Example:
A = 3.6 in. (92.0mm)
B = 1.9 in. (48.5mm)
Y = 1.7 in. (43.5mm)
4. Find distance "C" for adjusting linkage in the following table.
5. Disconnect linkage and measure distance "C". Compare the measurement with those in the table, and correct the distance if necessary.
6. Check distance "X" in the idle position and correct it if necessary. The correct distance for "X" is 2.68 in. (68mm). This is a fixed distance.
7. Check the adjustment at W.O.T. In the W.O.T. position, distance "Z" must be 1.4 ± 0.20 in. (29.0 ± 0.5 mm). If distance "Z" is not correct, repeat adjustment 1–4.
8. Check and, if necessary, correct throttle cable adjustment.

Checking Cold Idle Operation (Idle Speed Boost)

1. Remove the rear thermostat housing.
2. Measure distance "A" between the locknut and holding bracket.
The measurement should be 0.216 ± 0.015 in. (5.5mm ± 0.4mm).

NOTE: During this measurement the lever should rest against the knurled nut.

---- CAUTION ----

This is a factory sealed adjustment which should not be tampered with. If the seal has been broken, and the adjustment tampered with use the following method to correct the adjustment.

3. Loosen both the front and rear clamps.
4. Adjust measurement "A" by moving the clamps. Tighten the rear clamp first.
5. Tighten the pinch screw on the front clamp.
6. Recheck the adjustment at point "A" and seal the nut on the rear clamp with yellow paint.

Adjusting the Knurled Nut

1. With the engine at normal operating temperature, the en-

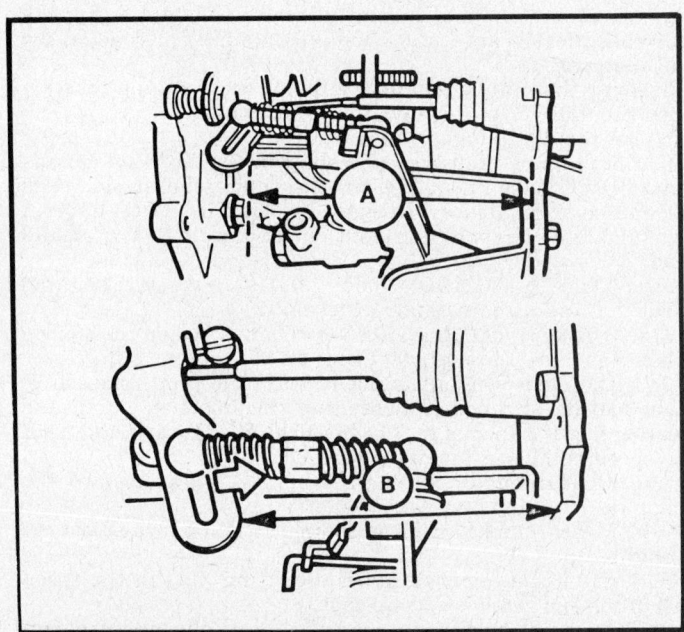

Locating distance A and B

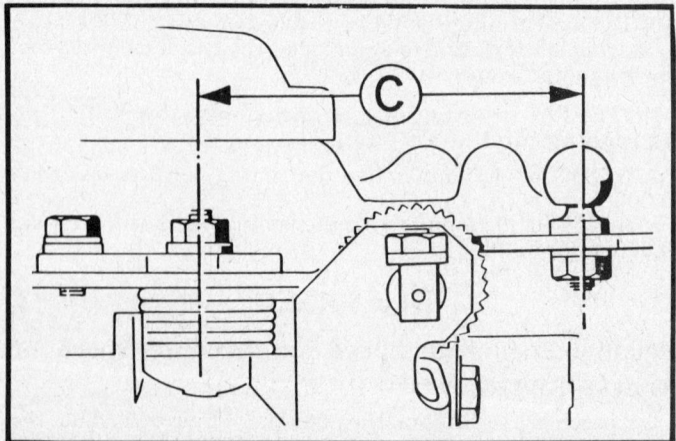

Finding distance C

Adjusting table in inches

Y (in.)	1.61	1.63	1.65	1.67	1.69	1.71	1.73	1.75	1.77	1.79	1.81	1.83
C (in.)	3.07	3.03	3.00	2.94	2.90	2.87	2.83	2.79	2.76	2.73	2.70	2.66
Y (in.)	1.85	1.87	1.89	1.91	1.93	1.95	1.97	1.99	2.01	2.03	2.05	2.07
C (in.)	2.64	2.61	2.58	2.55	2.53	2.50	2.47	2.45	2.42	2.40	2.38	2.35
Y (in.)	2.09	2.11	2.13	2.15	2.17	2.19	2.20					
C (in.)	2.33	2.31	2.29	2.27	2.26	2.24	2.22					

Adjusting table in metrics

Y (mm)	41	41.5	42	42.5	43	43.5	44	44.5	45	45.5	46	46.5
C (mm)	78.1	77.0	76.0	74.9	73.9	73.0	72.0	71.0	70.3	69.4	68.6	67.8
Y (mm)	47	47.5	48	48.5	49	49.5	50	50.5	51	51.5	52	52.5
C (mm)	67.0	66.3	65.6	64.9	64.2	63.5	62.9	62.3	61.6	61.0	60.5	59.9
Y (mm)	53	53.5	54	54.5	55	55.5	56					
C (mm)	59.4	58.8	58.3	57.8	57.3	56.8	56.4					

DIESEL ENGINES
FORD 2.4L SIX CYLINDER

gine idle to specifications, the locknut resting against the holding bracket and the lever resting against the idle speed stop, measures distance "B" between the lever and knurled nut. The measurement should be 0.020 ± 0.011 in. (0.5 ± 0.3mm).

2. To adjust "B" loosen the locknut and move the knurled nut to set the correct distance.

3. Tighten the locknut and recheck the adjustment.

GLOW PLUGS

Removal

1. Disconnect battery ground cable.
2. Unscrew glow plug electrical connection and remove wire.
3. Remove glow plug using a 12mm deepwell socket.

Installation

1. Coat glow plug threads with a copper based, antiseize compound.
2. Install glow plug into engine block using a 12mm deepwell socket.
3. Tighten glow plug to 15–22 ft. lbs. (20–30 Nm).
4. Connect electrical wire to glow plug with nut and tighten to 2–4 ft. lbs. (4.5 Nm).
5. Connect battery ground cable.

COLD START TIMING ADVANCE SYSTEM

The cold start timing advance system consists of a cold start advance solenoid, which is attached to the injection pump, and a cold start temperature switch located at the LH rear of the cylinder head.

When engine coolant temperature is below 30°C (86°F) the cold start temperature switch is closed. With the ignition switch in Run, power flows through the cold start temperature switch, energizing the cold start advance solenoid. When the cold start advance solenoid is energized, the injection pump timing is advanced to provide a smoother running cold engine.

When the engine coolant temperature reaches 30°C (86°F), the cold start temperature switch opens and the cold start solenoid is de-energized, returning the injection timing back to normal.

TURBOCHARGER

The turbocharger turbine wheel is driven by exhaust gas flow from the engine. The turbine wheel is connected, by a shaft, to the compressor wheel. The compressor wheel takes in fresh air from the air cleaner, compresses and boosts the pressure and supplies it to the engine through the intake manifold. Once maximum turbo pressure is reached, a dump valve opens in the turbine side of the turbo, and dumps the excess pressure into the exhaust system, downstream from the turbo.

ON CAR SERVICE

ROCKER ARM COVER/OR GASKET

Removal

1. Loosen turbo crossover pipe boot clamps and remove pipe.
2. Disconnect vacuum pump hose.
3. Disconnect breather hose.
4. Remove oil trap.
5. Remove threaded sleeves attaching rocker arm cover to cylinder head and remove cover.

Installation

1. Inspect cover gasket and vacuum pump outlet O-ring. Replace if necessary.
2. Install valve cover on cylinder head and tighten bolts to 6–7 ft. lbs. (8–10 Nm).

--- CAUTION ---
Be sure half-moon on gasket is fully seated in cylinder head.

3. Install oil trap and tighten bolt to 11–14 ft. lbs. (15–19 Nm).
4. Connect breather hose.
5. Connect vacuum hose.
6. Install turbo crossover pipe.
7. Run engine and check for oil and intake air leaks.

CAMSHAFT DRIVE BELT

Removal

1. Disconnect battery ground cable.
2. Drain cooling system.

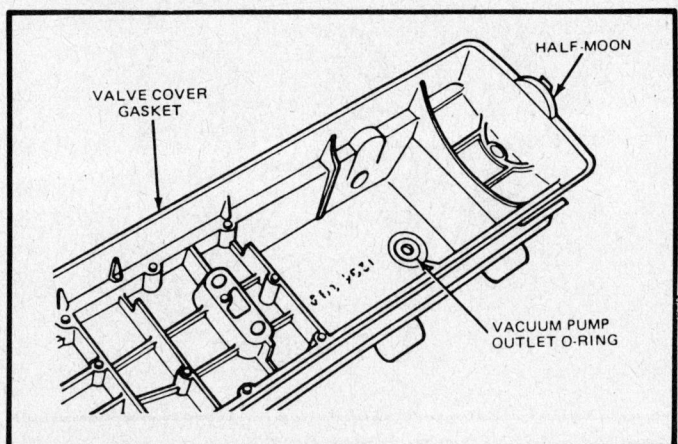

Valve cover gasket installation

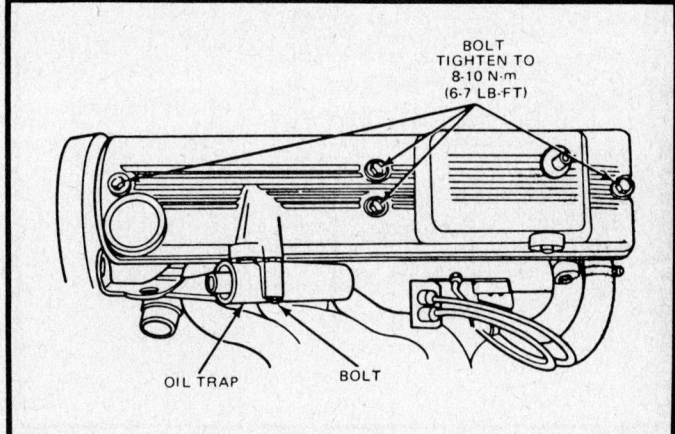

Valve cover bolt locations

Section 27: Diesel Engines
Ford 2.4L Six Cylinder

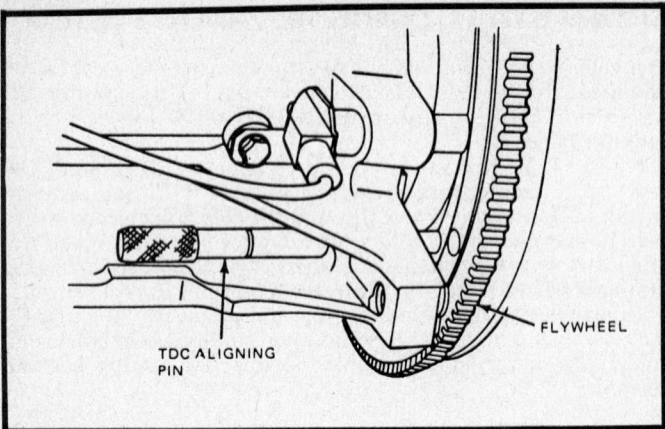
TDC aligning pin

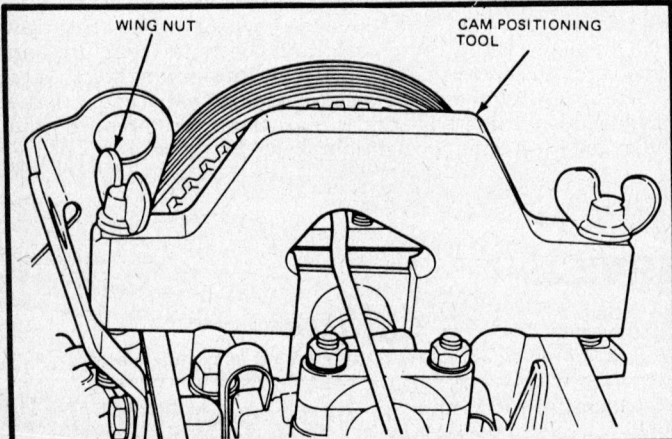
Cam positioning tool

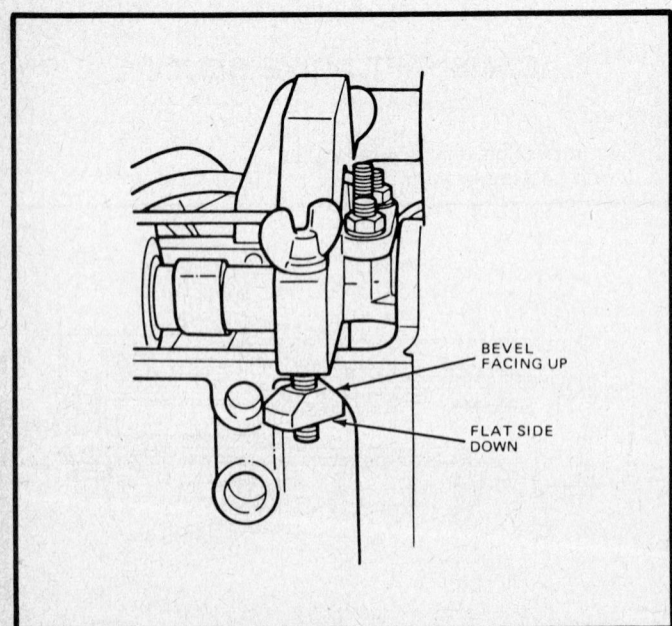
Cam positioning tool nut

3. Remove accessory drive belts.
4. Remove fan, clutch and water pump pulley assembly.
5. Remove vibration damper and pulley.
6. Disconnect heater hose from thermostat housing.
7. Remove four bolts attaching camshaft drive belt cover to crankcase, and remove cover.
8. Remove rocker cover.
9. Rotate engine until No. 1 cylinder is at TDC on compression stroke (intake and exhaust valves on base circle), and install TDC Aligning Pin through block flange and into the TDC hole in the flywheel.
10. Install Cam Positioning Tool on cylinder head.

NOTE: Flat side of nut or cam position tool should be facing down.

11. Loosen camshaft sprocket bolt.
12. Using a piece of chalk, or similar marker, mark direction of engine rotation on drive belt, if it is to be reinstalled.
13. Loosen two bolts on belt tensioner.
14. Remove camshaft drive belt.

Installation

1. Insert a 0.098 inch (2.5mm) thick feeler gauge blade between Cam Positioning Tool and the right front corner of the gasket mating surface of the cylinder head if using a new drive belt or a drive belt used with less than 16,000 km (10,000 miles).
2. Install Injection Pump Aligning Pin, through injection pump sprocket.
3. Rotate cam sprocket clockwise against pin.
4. Install camshaft drive belt. Starting at crankshaft, route belt around intermediate shaft sprocket, injection pump sprocket, camshaft sprocket and then tension roller, keeping slack to a minimum.

--- **CAUTION** ---
Used drive belts must be installed in same direction of engine rotation as removed.

5. Hand tighten belt with belt tensioner until all slack is gone.

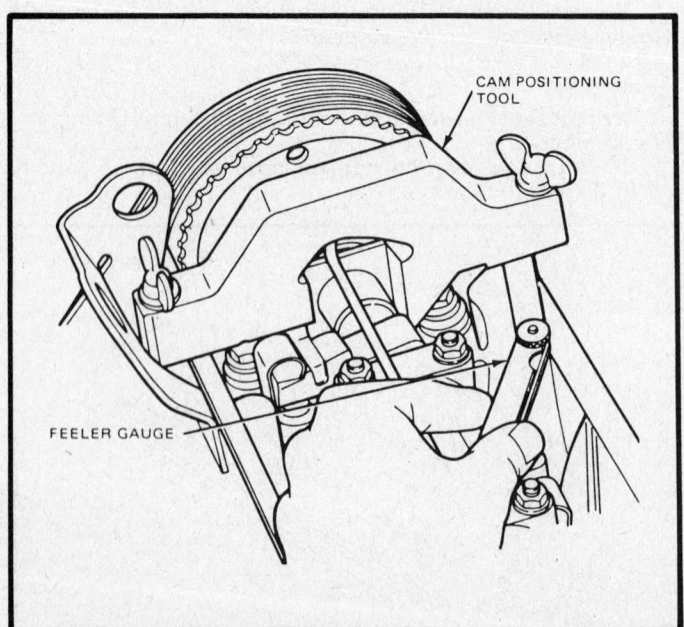
Cam positioning with feeler gauge

DIESEL ENGINES
FORD 2.4L SIX CYLINDER

6. Remove Injection Pump Aligning Pin from injection pump sprocket.

7. Adjust belt tension by tightening belt tensioner. Tighten belt tensioner to 34–36 ft. lbs. (45–50 Nm). On belts with less than 16,000 km (10,000 miles) and 23–25 ft. lbs. (30–35 Nm) for belts with more than 16,000 km (10,000 miles).

NOTE: Use only a dial type torque wrench.

8. Tighten two belt tensioner holding bolts to 15–18 ft. lbs. (20–24 Nm).
9. Tighten camshaft sprocket to 41–47 ft. lbs. (55–65 Nm).
10. Remove Cam Positioning Tool and TDC Aligning Pin.

CAUTION
Do not start engine with Cam Positioning Tool or TDC Aligning Pin in place. Engine and Tool damage can result.

11. Install camshaft drive belt cover and tighten bolts to 6–7 ft. lbs. (8–10 Nm).
12. Connect heater hose to thermostat housing.
13. Install vibration damper.
14. Install fan, clutch and water pump pulley assembly.
15. Install and adjust accessory drive belts.
16. Fill and bleed cooling system.
17. Connect battery ground cable.
18. Run engine and check for oil and coolant leaks.
19. Check injection pump timing and adjust as required.

VACUUM PUMP

Removal and Installation

1. Remove valve cover.

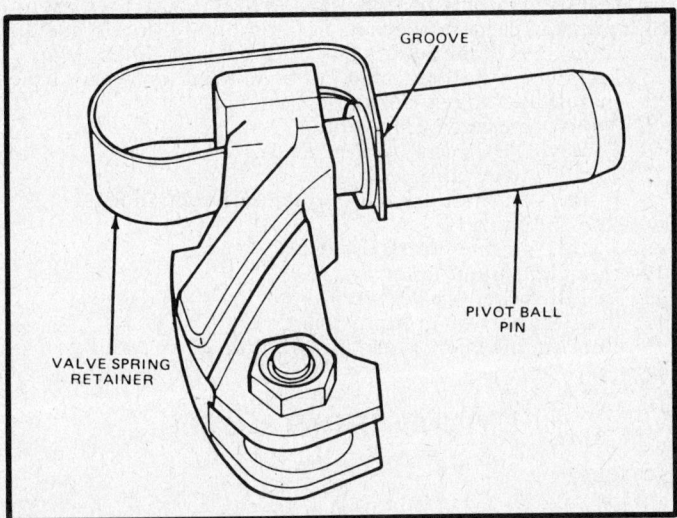

Rocker arm assembly

Injection pump aligning pin

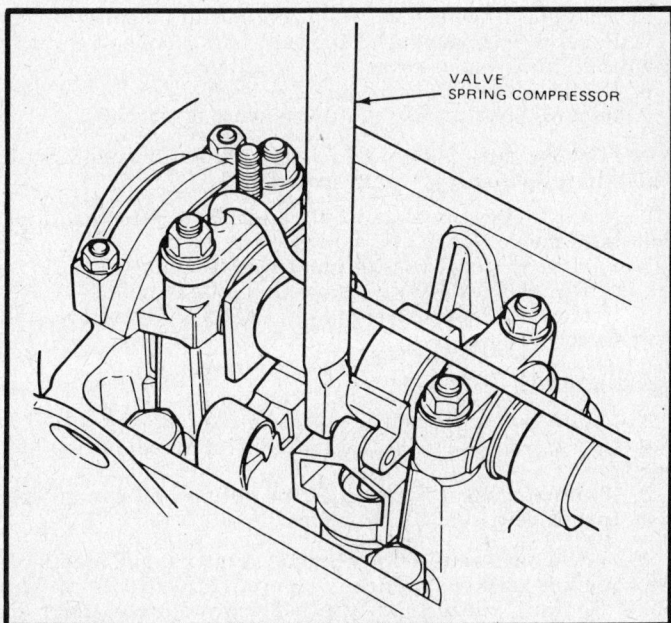

Using valve spring compressor tool

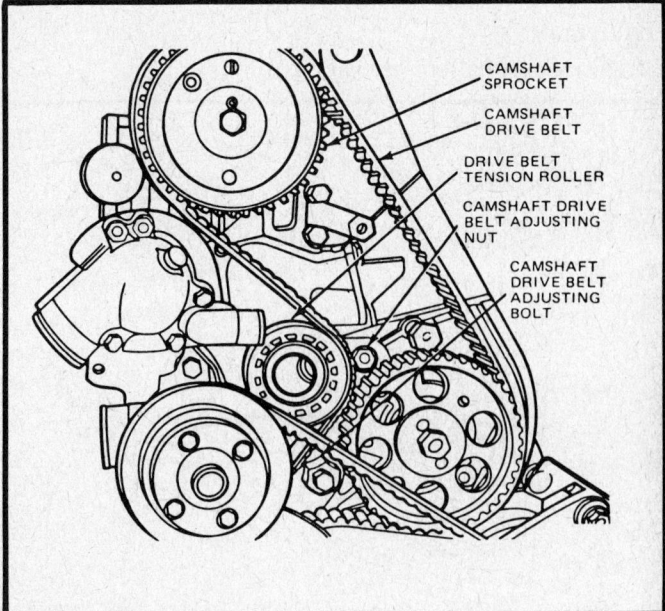

Camshaft drive belt installation

SECTION 27

DIESEL ENGINES
FORD 2.4L SIX CYLINDER

2. Rotate engine until vacuum pump eccentric is on low side of camshaft.
3. Remove bolts attaching vacuum pump to cylinder head, and remove pump.
4. Install vacuum pump on cylinder head and evenly tighten bolts to 6–7 ft. lbs. (8–10 Nm).
5. Inspect vacuum pump outlet port O-ring in valve cover. Replace if necessary.
6. Install valve cover.
7. Run engine and check for oil leaks.

ROCKER ARMS

Removal

1. Remove valve cover and vacuum pump.
2. Rotate engine until cam lobe for cylinder of rocker arm to be removed is on base circle.
3. Remove rocker arm retaining clip.
4. Compress spring assembly using Valve Spring Compressor Tool, and remove rocker arm.

CAUTION
Be sure that the valve spring retainers remain locked in the valve stem.
---

5. Remove rocker arm pivot ball pin, if necessary.

Installation

1. Install rocker arm pivot ball pin.

NOTE: Coat barrel of pivot ball pin with Loctite® 270 or equivalent before installation.

2. Compress spring assembly using valve spring compressor tool, and install rocker arm, making sure rocker arm is seated on pivot ball pin.
3. Install rocker arm retaining clip, making sure clip is engaged in groove on pivot ball pin.
4. Adjust valve clearance.
5. Install vacuum pump and valve cover.
6. Start engine and check for oil and intake air leaks.

CAMSHAFT

Removal

1. Disconnect battery ground cable.

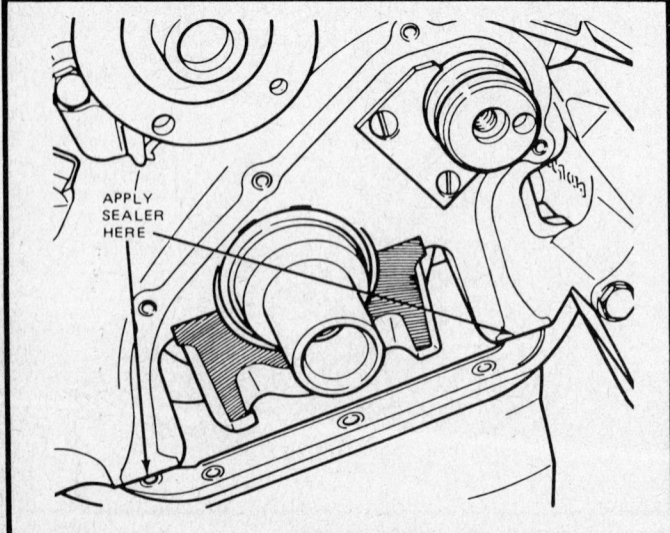

Front cover gasket sealing area

2. Remove valve cover.
3. Remove vacuum pump.
4. Remove fan and clutch assembly.
5. Remove camshaft drive belt cover.
6. Remove rocker arms.
7. Rotate engine until No. 1 cylinder is at TDC of compression stroke. Install TDC aligning pin.
8. Loosen camshaft sprocket bolt.
9. Loosen drive belt tension roller nut and bolt.
10. Remove camshaft sprocket.
11. Remove camshaft bearing caps and mark the caps so that they can be installed in their original position, and remove camshaft.

Installation

1. Install camshaft in position on cylinder head.
2. Install camshaft bearing caps, making sure they are installed in the correct position. Tighten 6mm nuts 6–7 ft. lbs. (8–10 Nm) and 8mm nuts to 14–17 ft. lbs. (20–24 Nm).
3. Install camshaft sprocket but do not tighten at this time.
4. Install and adjust camshaft drive belt.
5. Adjust cam and pump timing.
6. Remove TDC Aligning Pin Tool.
7. Install rocker arm.
8. Install camshaft drive belt cover and tighten bolts to 6–7 ft. lbs. (8–10 Nm).
9. Install fan and clutch assembly.
10. Install vacuum pump.
11. Install rocker arm cover.
12. Connect battery ground cable.
13. Run engine and check for oil, intake air, and coolant leaks.

ENGINE FRONT COVER

Removal

1. Disconnect battery ground cable.
2. Drain cooling system.
3. Loosen and remove accessory drive belts.
4. Remove engine cooling fan and clutch assembly.
5. Remove vibration damper.
6. Disconnect heater hose from thermostat housing.
7. Remove four bolts attaching camshaft drive belt cover to crankcase and remove cover.
8. Remove camshaft drive belt.
9. Remove bolts attaching intermediate shaft sprocket.

NOTE: Be sure Allen head screws are aligned with holes in intermediate shaft sprocket.

10. Remove vibration damper flange and sprocket retaining bolt and remove flange and sprocket.
11. Remove three oil pan-to-front cover attaching bolts. Loosen, but DO NOT REMOVE, remaining oil pan bolts.
12. Remove six bolts attaching front cover to crankcase, and remove cover.

Installation

1. Clean front cover and crankcase gasket mating surfaces.
2. Inspect and replace crankshaft and intermediate shaft oil seals.
3. If oil pan gasket is damaged, install new oil pan gasket.
4. Install new front cover gasket.

NOTE: Coat areas where front cover gasket meets oil pan gasket with a $\frac{1}{4}$ inch (6.35mm) RTV Sealant. The RTV Sealant should be applied immediately prior to front cover installation. When applying RTV Sealant always use the bead size specified and join the components within 15 minutes of application. After this amount of

DIESEL ENGINES
FORD 2.4L SIX CYLINDER
SECTION 27

time the sealant begins to "setup" and its sealing effectiveness may be reduced.

5. Position front engine cover on crankcase and tighten 6mm bolts to 6–7 ft. lbs. (8–10 Nm) and 8mm bolts to 14–17 ft. lbs. (20–24 Nm).
6. Install three oil pan-to-front cover attaching bolts. Tighten oil pan bolts to 6.5–7 ft. lbs. (9–10 Nm).
7. Position vibration damper flange and sprocket on crankshaft, with shoulder toward front of vehicle.
8. Position intermediate shaft sprocket on intermediate shaft, guiding locating pin into bore.
9. Install Holding Tool. Align Allen head screws in tool with holes in intermediate shaft.
10. Install and tighten vibration damper flange and sprocket bolt to 282–311 ft. lbs. (390–430 Nm).
11. Install and tighten intermediate shaft sprocket bolt to 40–47 ft. lbs. (55–65 Nm). Remove the Holding Tool.
12. Install and adjust camshaft drive belt.
13. Install camshaft drive belt cover and tighten bolts to 6–7 ft. lbs. (8–10 Nm).
14. Connect heater hose to thermostat housing.
15. Install vibration damper and pulley and tighten to 16–17 ft. lbs. (22–24 Nm).
16. Install fan and clutch assembly.
17. Install and adjust accessory drive belts.
18. Connect battery ground cable.
19. Start and idle engine. Check for oil leaks.

CYLINDER HEAD

Removal

1. Disconnect battery ground cable.
2. Drain cooling system.
3. Disconnect heater hose.
4. Loosen and remove accessory drive belts.
5. Remove valve cover.
6. Disconnect diagnostic connectors.
7. Disconnect coolant temperature switch and glow plug connector.
8. Disconnect breather hose and bracket.
9. Remove clamp attaching oil dipstick tube to intake manifold and position dipstick out of the way.
10. Disconnect boost pressure switch connector.

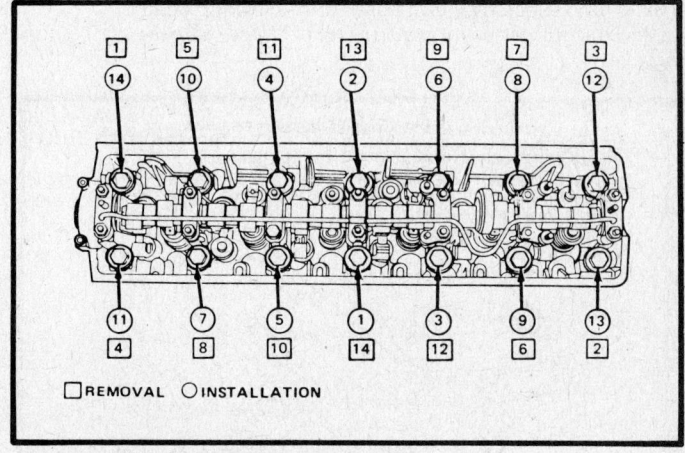
Cylinder head bolt removal order

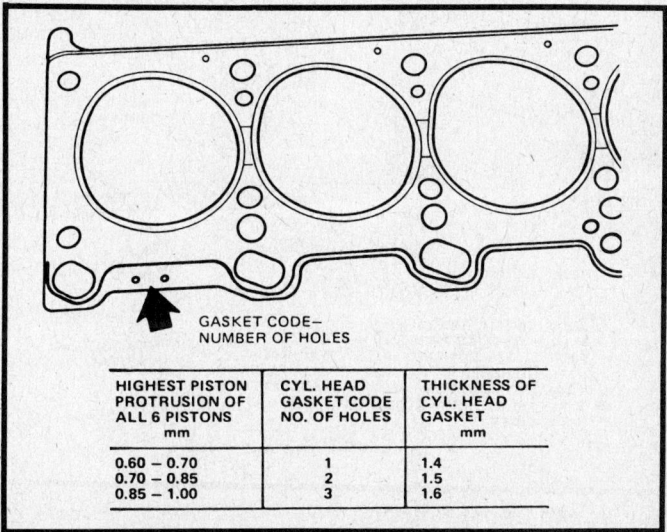
Selecting proper cylinder head gasket

HIGHEST PISTON PROTRUSION OF ALL 6 PISTONS mm	CYL. HEAD GASKET CODE NO. OF HOLES	THICKNESS OF CYL. HEAD GASKET mm
0.60 – 0.70	1	1.4
0.70 – 0.85	2	1.5
0.85 – 1.00	3	1.6

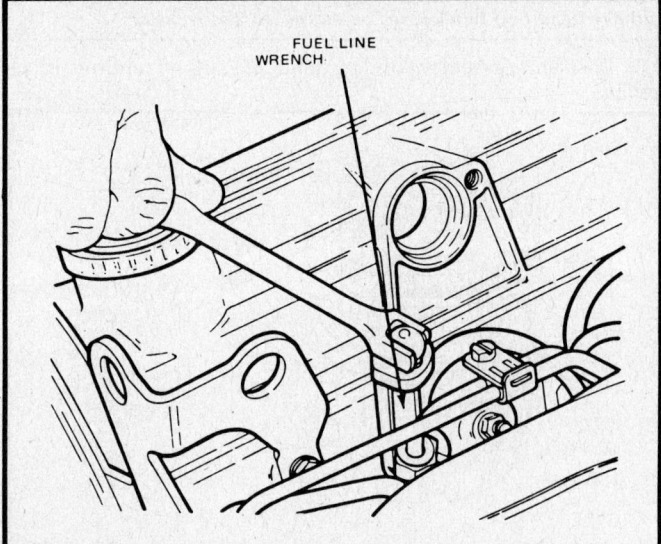
Injection pump nozzle high pressure line removal

Mounting dial indicator

SECTION 27

DIESEL ENGINES
FORD 2.4L SIX CYLINDER

11. Disconnect radiator hose from cylinder head.
12. Disconnect temperature controlled idle boost coolant hose.
13. Remove vacuum pump from cylinder head.
14. Disconnect No. 1 nozzle to injection pump leak hose.
15. Disconnect injection lines from nozzles and injection pump.
16. Disconnect turbocharger oil lines.
17. Rotate crankshaft until No. 1 cylinder is at TDC of compression stroke (intake and exhaust valves on base circle). Install TDC Aligning Pin.

CAUTION

Do not rotate engine with Aligning Pin in Position.

18. Loosen camshaft drive sprocket retaining bolt.
19. Loosen camshaft drive belt tensioning roller nut and bolt, and remove drive belt.
20. Loosen cylinder head bolts in order shown in the squares, and remove cylinder head.

Installation

1. Clean gasket sealing surfaces on cylinder had and crankcase. Check for warpage.

CAUTION

Use care when cleaning gasket surfaces. Slight scoring of these surfaces can cause leakage due to high compression pressures.

2. Clean top of each piston.
3. Using dial indicator and piston height gauge, measure the amount the piston top extends above crankcase surface as follows:
   a. Mount dial indicator and bracket with dial indictor tip on engine block surface and zero dial indicator tip on the engine block surface.
   b. Rotate crankshaft, if necessary, to position at TDC.
   c. Move tip to front of piston. Record measurement.
   d. Move tip to rear of piston. Record measurement.
   e. Repeat this procedure for each cylinder.
   f. Average the two readings for each cylinder.
   g. Using measurement of highest piston, select correct cylinder head gasket.
4. Clean carbon and oil deposits from cylinder head bolts.

CAUTION

Keep all antifreeze from entering cylinder head bolt holes. If either enters bolt holes, carefully blow out with compressed air. The presence of oil and/or antifreeze in bolt holes could result in insufficient cylinder head bolt tightening, or a cracked crankcase.

5. Position correct cylinder head gasket on engine block surface.

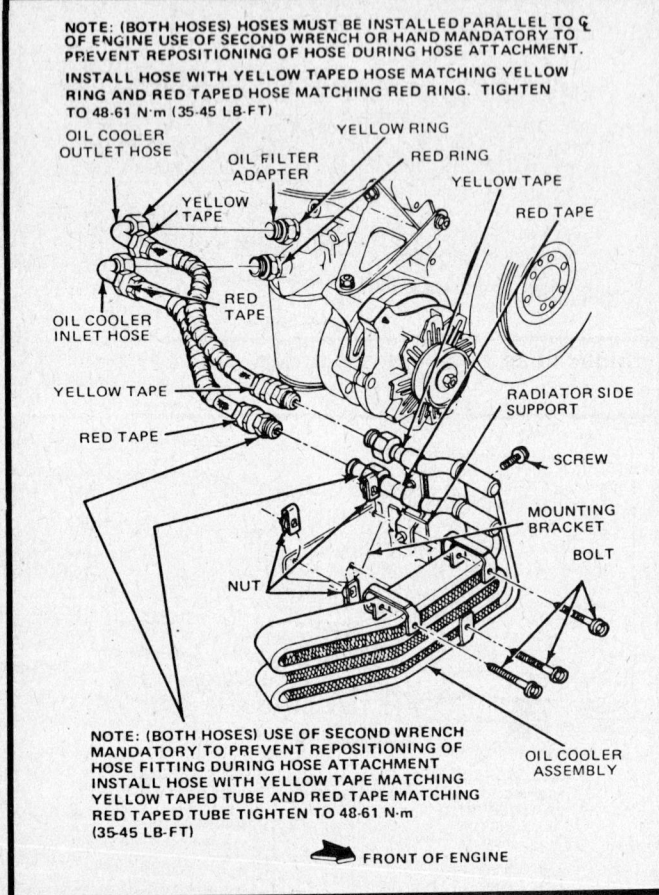

Idle speed boost housing

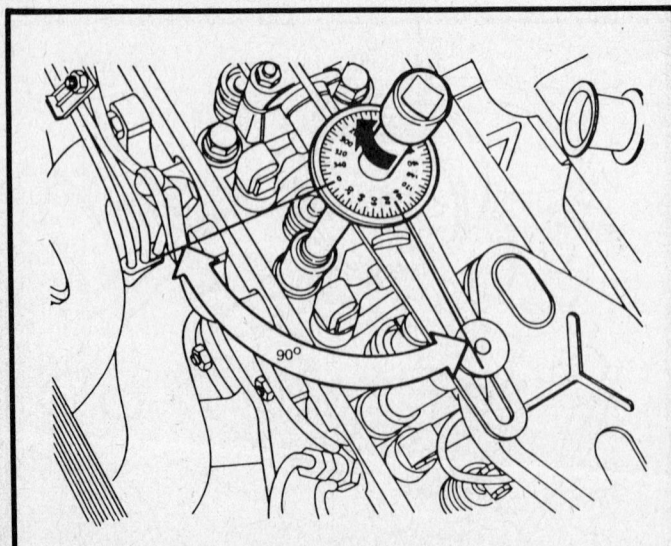

Cylinder head bolt tightening

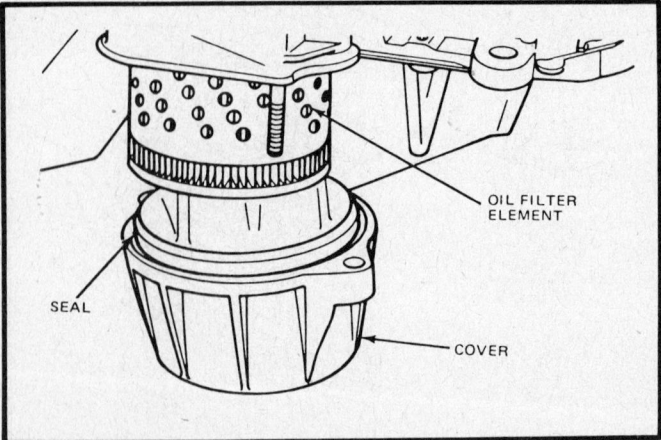

Oil filter installation

27-28

DIESEL ENGINES
FORD 2.4L SIX CYLINDER
SECTION 27

6. Carefully lower cylinder head onto crankcase, using care not to damage gasket.
7. Install and tighten cylinder head bolts, in sequence to 36–43 ft. lbs. (50–60 Nm). Wait 15 minutes and tighten bolts, in sequence, to 90°. Run the engine for 15–20 minutes and turn the bolts in sequence another 90°.
8. Install and adjust drive belt.
9. Connect turbocharger oil lines and tighten to 14–17 ft. lbs. (20–24 Nm).
10. Connect nozzle high pressure lines to nozzles and injection pump. Tighten to 14–18 ft. lbs. (20–25 Nm), using fuel line wrench.
11. Connect No. 1 nozzle to injection pump leak hose.
12. Install vacuum pump on cylinder head and tighten to 6–7 ft. lbs. (8–10 Nm).
13. Connect temperature controlled, idle boost coolant hose.
14. Connect temperature controlled, idle boost coolant hose.
15. Connect oil pressure switch connector.
16. Install oil dipstick tube.
17. Install breather hose and bracket.
18. Connect coolant temperature switch and glow plug connectors.
19. Connect diagnostic connectors.
20. Install valve cover, as outlined.
21. Install and adjust accessory drive belts.
22. Connect heater hose.
23. Fill and bleed coolant system.
24. Connect battery ground cable.
25. Start engine and idle for 15 minutes. Check for fuel, coolant and oil leaks.

WATER PUMP

Removal
1. Drain cooling system.
2. Loosen and remove accessory drive belts.
3. Remove fan and clutch assembly.
4. Remove water pump pulley.
5. Disconnect heater hose from thermostat housing.
6. Remove camshaft drive belt cover.
7. Remove three bolts attaching water pump to crankcase and remove water pump.

NOTE: Do not loosen cam belt.

Installation
1. Clean gasket mating surfaces of water pump and crankcase.
2. Install water pump with new gasket, on crankcase and tighten bolts to 14–17 ft. lbs. (20–24 Nm).
3. Install camshaft drive belt cover and tighten bolts to 6–7 ft. lbs. (8–10 Nm).
4. Connect heater hose to thermostat housing.
5. Install water pump pulley and tighten bolts to 6–7 ft. lbs. (8–10 Nm).
6. Install fan and clutch assembly.
7. Install and adjust accessory drive belts.
8. Fill and bleed cooling system.
9. Run engine and check for coolant leaks.

OIL FILTER

Removal and Installation
1. Raise vehicle and support safely.
2. Remove oil filter drain plug and drain oil from filter.
3. Remove nuts attaching oil filter cover and remove cover and filter element.
4. Clean oil filter cover using a suitable solvent.
5. Install new gasket on oil filter cover.
6. Install oil filter element and cover. Tighten bolts to 15–18 ft. lbs. (21–25 Nm).
7. Install oil filter drain plug and tighten to 7–9 ft. lbs. (10–13 Nm).
8. Lower vehicle and fill crankcase with specified quantity and quality of oil.
9. Run engine and check for oil leaks

OIL COOLER

Removal
1. Drain oil from crankcase.
2. Remove and cap oil cooler lines at oil cooler.
3. Remove three bolts retaining oil cooler to mounting bracket.
4. Remove one oil cooler-to-radiator side support retaining screw.
5. Remove oil cooler assembly from vehicle.

Installation
1. Position oil cooler assembly to vehicle and install four bolts to attach to mounting bracket.
2. Install one oil cooler-to-radiator side support retaining screw.
3. Remove caps from oil cooler lines and attach oil cooler lines to oil cooler.
4. Fill crankcase with specified quantity and quality of oil.
5. Run engine and check for oil leaks.

NOTE: Oil will not flow through the oil cooler until the oil temperature reaches at least 95°C (203°F).

FUEL SYSTEM

INJECTION PUMP

Removal
1. Disconnect battery ground cable.
2. Drain cooling system.
3. Remove accessory drive belts.
4. Remove fan and clutch assembly.
5. Remove camshaft drive belt as outlines.
6. Install Injection Pump Sprocket Aligning Pin, and remove nut and washer attaching sprocket to injection pump.
7. Install puller and remove sprocket.
8. Remove woodruff key from pump shaft.
9. Disconnect clamp attaching oil dipstick tube to intake manifold, and position out of the way.
10. Disconnect turbo pressure indicator switch connector.
11. Remove diagnostic plug bracket and position out of the way.
12. Loosen clamp attaching turbo crossover pipe boot to intake manifold.
13. Remove nuts attaching intake manifold to cylinder head, and remove cylinder head.

27-29

SECTION 27 DIESEL ENGINES
FORD 2.4L SIX CYLINDER

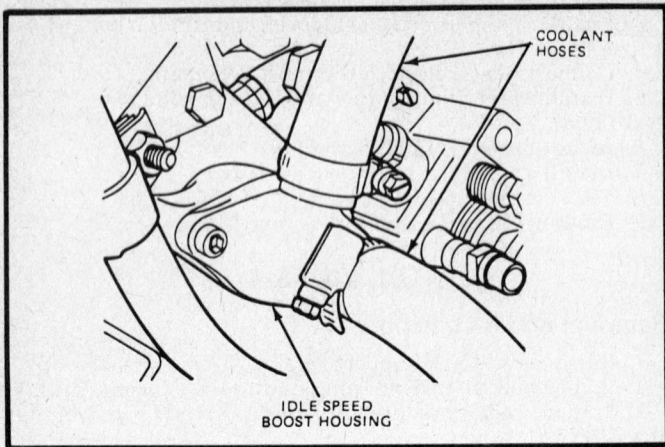

Oil cooler installation

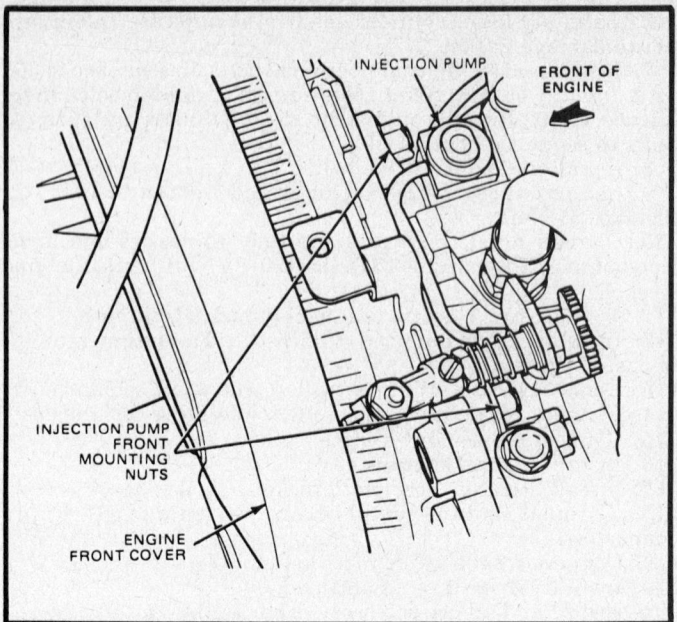

Injection pump—front mounting bolts

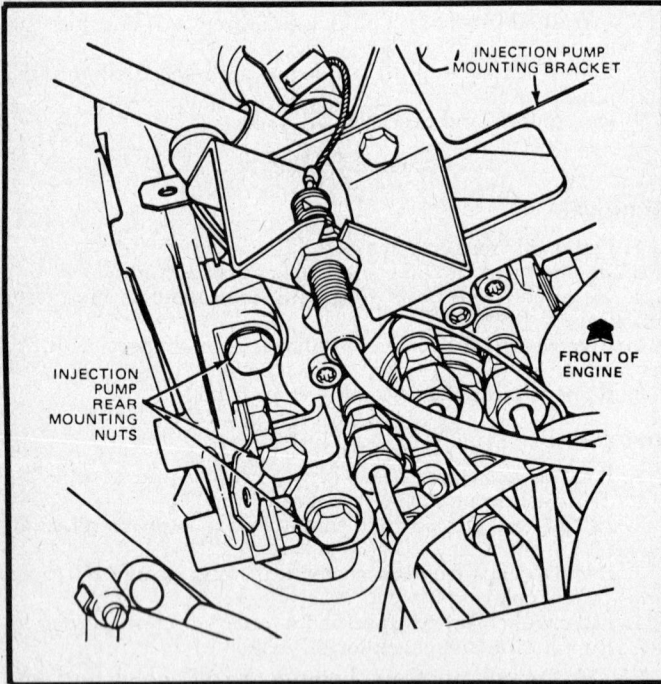

Injection pump—rear mounting bolts

NOTE: To prevent fuel system contamination, cap all fuel lines and fittings.

14. Disconnect and cap nozzle fuel lines at nozzles.
15. Remove injection nozzle lines from injection pump using Fuel Line Nut Wrench. Install caps on each end of each fuel line and pump fittings as it is removed and identify each fuel line accordingly.
16. Disconnect coolant hoses from the idle speed boost housing.
17. Disconnect electrical connectors to the fuel shut-off and cold start accelerator valves, micro-switch and fuel pressure switch.
18. Disconnect nozzle return line at injection pump.
19. Disconnect fuel return hose from fuel return line on left fender apron.
20. Disconnect fuel inlet hose from fuel inlet line on left fender apron.
21. Disconnect vacuum hoses at altitude compensation valve. Note position of hoses, so they may be returned to the original position.
22. Disconnect throttle cable and speed control cable, if so equipped, from injection pump.
23. Remove three nuts attaching injection pump to bracket.
24. Remove two nuts attaching injection pump to engine front cover, and remove injection pump.

Installation

1. Install pump in position. Line up mark on front cover with the mark on the injection pump mounting boss. Install attaching nuts and bolts, and tighten to 14–17 ft. lbs. (20–24 Nm).
2. Connect throttle cable, and speed control cable, if so equipped.
3. Remove protective caps and install fuel inlet hose to fuel inlet line on left fender apron.
4. Connect fuel return hose to fuel return line on the left fender apron.
5. Connect vacuum hoses to altitude compensation valve. Refer to VECI decal.
6. Connect nozzle return line to injection pump.
7. Connect electrical connectors to fuel pressure sensor, microswitch, cold start accelerator valve and fuel shut-off valve.
8. Connect coolant hoses to idle speed boost housing.
9. Install fuel lines on injection pump, and tighten to 14–17 ft. lbs. (20–25 Nm).
10. Connect fuel lines to nozzles and tighten to 14–17 ft. lbs. (20–25 Nm).
11. Clean intake manifold and cylinder head gasket mating surfaces.
12. Position new intake manifold gasket on cylinder head, and install intake manifold. Be sure intake manifold inlet port is inserted into turbo crossover pipe boot. Tighten attaching bolts to 14–17 ft. lbs. (20–25 Nm). Tighten clamp at crossover pipe boot.
13. Install diagnostic plug bracket on cylinder head and tighten to 14–17 ft. lbs. (20–25 Nm).
14. Connect turbo pressure indicator switch connector.
15. Position oil dipstick tube to intake manifold and install

DIESEL ENGINES
FORD 2.4L SIX CYLINDER
SECTION 27

clamp.

16. Install woodruff key in injection pump shaft.
17. Install sprocket on injection pump. Install Injection Pump Aligning Pin in sprocket. Install sprocket attaching washer and nut and tighten to 33–36 ft. lbs. (45–50 Nm).
18. Install and adjust camshaft drive belt.
19. Install camshaft drive belt cover and tighten to 6–7 ft. lbs. (8–10 Nm).
20. Install fan and clutch assembly.
21. Install and adjust accessory drive belts.
22. Fill and bleed cooling system.
23. Air bleed fuel system.
24. Adjust injection pump timing.
26. Start engine and check for fuel, coolant and oil leaks.
27. Adjust curb idle, fast idle and injection pump timing.

TURBOCHARGER

Removal

1. Remove two bolts attaching exhaust pipe to turbocharger.
2. Remove EGR tube and clamps.
3. Loosen four hose clamps on crossover tube and remove tube.
4. Remove air cleaner assembly and bellows. Cap turbocharger openings using protective caps.
5. Remove two oil supply line bolts on top of turbocharger center housing.
6. Remove clamp and oil lines.
7. Remove oil return line.
8. Remove bolt and sealing washers attaching oil supply line to oil filter housing.
9. Disconnect and remove EGR valve.
10. Remove four bolts attaching turbocharger to exhaust manifold and remove turbocharger.

Installation

1. Clean mating surfaces of turbocharger and exhaust manifold.
2. Position turbocharger on exhaust manifold and install four mounting bolts. Tighten to 17–20 ft. lbs. (23–27 Nm).
3. Install EGR valve. Tighten to 18 ft. lbs. (25 Nm).
4. Install oil supply line using new seals. Tighten bolt to 26–33 ft. lbs. (33–45 Nm).

CAUTION
Do not overtighten bolt. Oil leaks may occur if overtightened.

---

5. Install clamp retaining oil lines.
6. Install oil supply line bolts to turbocharger housing and tighten to 15–18 ft. lbs. (20–24 Nm).
7. Remove protective caps from turbocharger and install air cleaner assembly and bellows.
8. Install crossover tube. Tighten hose clamps snug.
9. Install EGR tube clamp.
10. Install two bolts attaching exhaust pipe to turbocharger and tighten to 17–20 ft. lbs. (23–27 Nm).
11. Run engine and check for oil and air leaks.

FUEL SHUT-OFF VALVE

Removal

1. Disconnect battery ground cable.
2. Remove nut attaching electrical connector to shut-off valve and remove connector.
3. Remove shut-off valve.

CAUTION
Piston and spring may fall out when removing valves.

SPECIFICATIONS

Description	Ft. lbs. (In. lbs.)	N·m
EGR Valve	18	25
Hose Clamps	(15–22)	1.7–2.5
Oil Supply Line To Turbo	15–18	20–24
To Engine Block	26–33	35–45
Oil Return Line—To Turbo	15–18	20–24
Turbocharger-to-Exhaust Manifold	17–20	23–27
Turbocharger-to-Exhaust Pipe	17–20	23–27

Installation

1. Replace O-ring and valve, and install valve on injection pump. Tighten valve to 11–18 ft. lbs. (15–25 Nm).

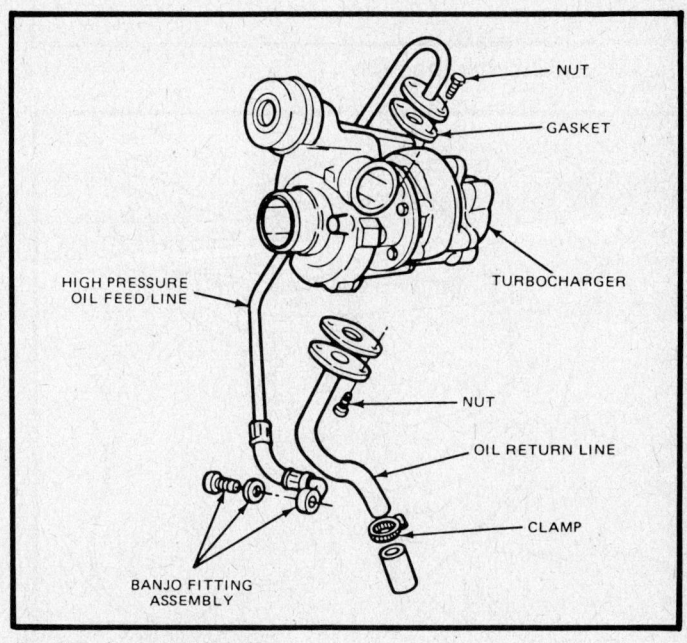

Turbocharger details

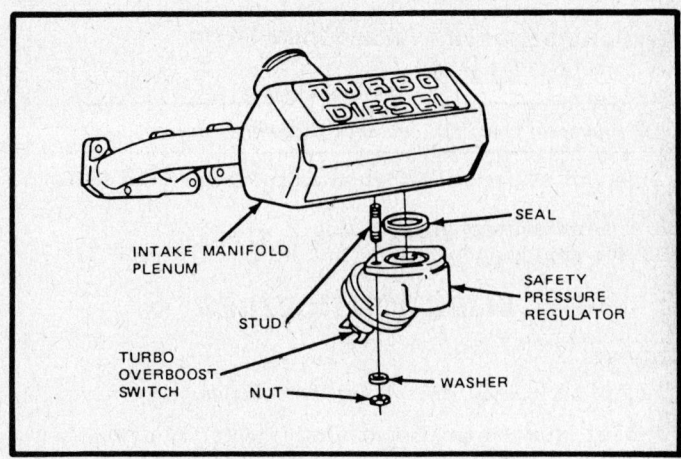

Safety pressure regulator valve mounting

SECTION 27
DIESEL ENGINES
FORD 2.4L SIX CYLINDER

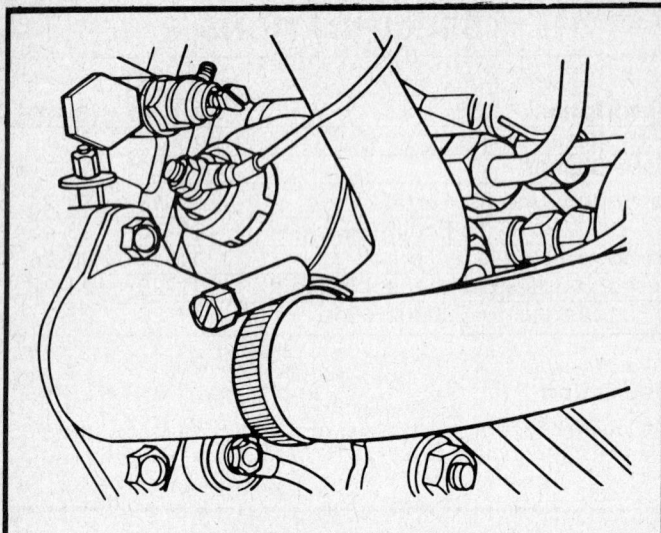

Fuel shut off valve location

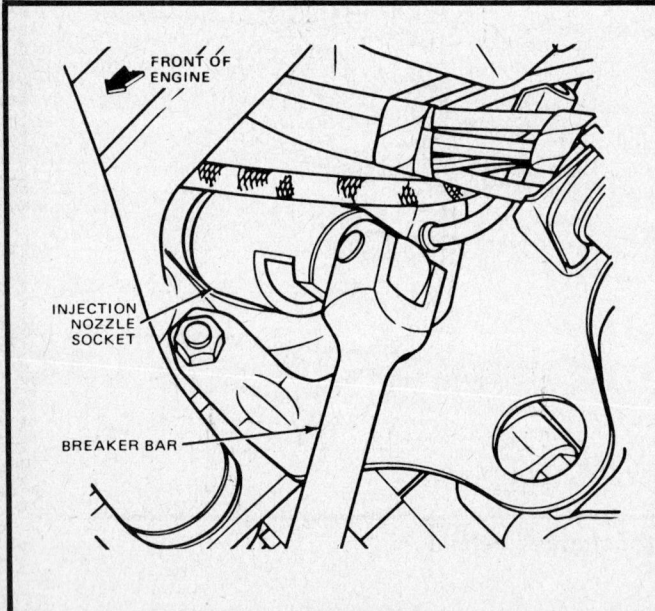

Injection nozzle removal and installation

CAUTION
Piston and spring may fall out when installing valves.

---

2. Install connector on shut-off valve. Tighten nut to 3–3.5 ft. lbs. (4–5 Nm).
3. Connect battery ground cable.
4. Run engine and check for fuel leaks.

INJECTION NOZZLES

Removal

1. Pull off leak oil lines on injector nozzles.

NOTE: Make sure area around injector is clean.

2. Remove fuel lines at injectors and at fuel injection pump with Fuel Line Wrench. Cap all fuel lines and openings with Protective Cap Set as fuel lines are removed.

3. Unscrew fuel injectors with Injector Nozzle Socket. Note injector order for installation.

NOTE: On injectors with sensors, disconnect sensor plug wires and guide sensor wires through Injector Nozzle Socket while installing tool on injector.

4. Plug cylinder block injector nozzle opening.

Installation

1. Clean injector nozzle opening in cylinder block.
2. Install new heat shields into injection nozzle openings.
3. Apply copper based, anti-seize compound to injector nozzle threads. Remove protective plug in cylinder block and install injector nozzles in original positions with Injector Nozzle socket, and tighten to 30–33 ft. lbs. (40–45 Nm).

NOTE: On injectors with sensors, guide sensor plug wire through socket before installing injector nozzle. Reconnect sensor wire after nozzle installation.

4. Remove protective caps from fuel lines, injector pump and injector nozzles and install fuel lines using Fuel Line Wrench. Tighten to 15–18 ft. lbs. (20–25 Nm).

INTAKE MANIFOLD

Removal

1. Disconnect battery ground cable.
2. Remove diagnostic plug bracket and position out of the way.
3. Disconnect turbo boost pressure indicator connector.
4. Disconnect oil dipstick tube clamp from intake manifold and position dipstick out of the way.
5. Loosen clamp at turbo crossover pipe boot.
6. Remove bolts attaching intake manifold to cylinder head and remove intake.

Installation

1. Clean intake manifold and cylinder head gasket mating surfaces.
2. Install intake manifold on cylinder head, with new gasket, making sure inlet port is installed in turbo crossover pipe boot.
3. Tighten intake manifold bolts to 14–17 ft. lbs. (20–24 Nm), and tighten crossover pipe boot clamp.
4. Connect turbo boost pressure indicator switch connector.
5. Install diagnostic plug bracket and tighten bolts to 14–17 ft. lbs. (20–24 Nm).
6. Connect battery ground cable.
7. Start engine and check for intake leaks.

EXHAUST MANIFOLD

Remove

1. Disconnect battery ground cable.
2. Disconnect muffler inlet pipe at turbo outlet an cap.
3. Disconnect EGR valve vacuum line.
4. Disconnect inlet duct at turbo can cap turbo inlet.
5. Loosen clamp at turbo crossover pipe boot.
6. Remove clamp attaching turbo oil feed tube to oil return tube.
7. Remove bolts attaching oil feed tube to turbo.

CAUTION
Cap oil feel and oil feed inlet port on turbo to prevent contamination of turbo oiling system.

---

8. Disconnect oil return line from turbo oil drain port.

DIESEL ENGINES
FORD 2.4L SIX CYLINDER
SECTION 27

9. Remove bolts attaching exhaust manifold to cylinder head and remove exhaust manifold and turbo as an assembly. Cap turbo outlet to crossover pipe.

Installation

1. Clean exhaust manifold and cylinder head gasket mating surfaces.
2. Install exhaust manifold, with new gasket, making sure turbo outlet is installed in crossover pipe boot. Tighten bolts to 14–17 ft. lbs. (20–24 Nm), and tighten crossover pipe boot clamp.
3. Remove caps and install oil feed line, with new gasket, on turbo oil inlet port. Tighten bolts to 14–17 ft. lbs. (20–24 Nm).
4. Remove caps and connect oil return line to turbo oil return port. Tighten fitting to 29–36 ft. lbs. (40–50 Nm).
5. Install oil feed tube to exhaust manifold clamp and tighten to 6.5–7 ft. lbs. (8–10 Nm).
6. Remove cap and connect inlet duct to turbo inlet.
7. Remove cap and connect muffler inlet pipe to turbo exhaust outlet. Tighten bolts to 31–35 ft. lbs. (43–48 Nm).
8. Connect EGR valve vacuum line.
9. Connect battery ground cable.
10. Run engine and check for intake, exhaust and oil leaks.

G.M. DIESEL ENGINE 4.3 LITER, 262 CU.IN. V6

ENGINE SPECIFICATIONS

Engine VIN Code	Engine	Engine Mfg.	Tax H.P.	Horsepower @ rpm	Torque @ rpm (ft. lbs.)	Bore & Stroke (in.)	Comp. Ratio	Oil Capacity W/Filter Change	Fuel Pump Press. (psi)	Oil Press. @ 2000 rpm
V	262.5 (4.3L) V6	Olds.	39.2	NA	NA	4.057 × 3.385	21.6:1	6 qts.	5–6	30–45
T	262.5 (4.3L) V6	Olds.	39.2	NA	NA	4.057 × 3.385	21.6:1	6 qts.	5–6	30–45

TUNE-UP SPECIFICATIONS

Year	Engine No. Cyl. Displacement (cu. in.)	Injection Timing (deg) Auto. Trans.	Compression (psi)	Valves Intake Opens (deg)	Fuel Pump Pressure (psi)	Idle Speed (rpm) Man. Trans.	Idle Speed (rpm) Auto. Trans.
'83–'87	(262.5) 4.3L V6	6°A ①	②	—	5.8–8.7	—	650

A—After top dead center
① At 1300 rpm in park
② The lowest reading should not be less than 70% of the highest and no cylinder should be less than 275 psi

FIRING ORDERS

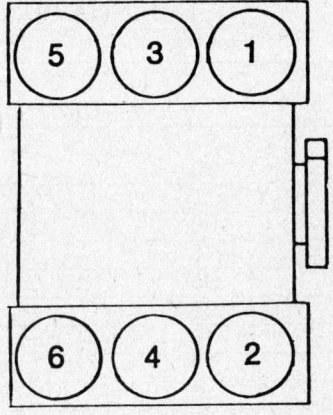

Engine firing order: 1-6-5-4-3-2

SECTION 27: DIESEL ENGINES
GM 4.3L, 262 CU. IN. V6

VALVE SPECIFICATIONS

VIN Code	Engine	Seat Angle (deg)	Face Angle (deg)	Spring Test Pressure (lbs. @ in.)	Spring Installed Height (in.)	Stem to Guide Intake	Stem to Guide Exhaust	Stem Intake	Stem Exhaust
V	262.5 (4.3L) V6	①	②	④	③	.0010-.0027	.0015-.0027	.3425-.3432	.3420-.3427
T	262.5 (3.4L) V6	①	②	④	③	.0010-.0027	.0015-.0035	.3425-.3432	.3420-.3427

① Intake 45°, exhaust 31°
② Intake 44°, exhaust 30°
③ Very critical, special tool (gauge) #B76428 or J-25289. If this measurement is less than .127 mm (.005 in.), a new valve should be installed. There must be a minimum of .762 mm (.030 in.) clearance between valve rotator and gauge. Failure to maintain this clearance will cause rocker arm and valve rotator interference.
④ Closed—88-95 lbs. @ 1.670 in.
   Open—203-217 lbs. @ 1.220 in.

CRANKSHAFT AND CONNECTING ROD SPECIFICATIONS

VIN Code	Engine	Engine Mounting	Bearing Number	Crankshaft Main Brg. Journal Diam.	Crankshaft Main Brg. Oil Clearance	Shaft End-Play	Thrust on No.	Connecting Rod Journal Diameter	Connecting Rod Oil Clearance	Connecting Rod Side Clearance
V	262.5 (4.3L) V6	Longitudinal	1,2 4,5	2.9993-3.0003	①	.0030-.0135	3	2.2490-2.2510	.0005-.0026	.006-.020
			3	1.1985-1.2015	①					
T	262.5 (4.3L) V6	Transverse	1,2 4,5	2.9993-3.0003	①	.0035-.0135	3	2.2490-2.2510	.0005-.0026	.006-.020
			3	1.1985-1.2015	①					

① Main bearing clearance: no. 1, 2, and 3: .013-.053 mm (.0005-.0021 in.)
   no. 4 (rear): .051-.086 mm (.0020-.0034 in.)
Bearing shell width: no. 1 and 2: 24.638-892 mm (.970-.980 in.)
   no. 3: 30.302-30.353 mm (1.193-1.195 in.)
   no. 4: 32.26 mm (1.27 in.)

ENGINE TORQUE SPECIFICATIONS

Application	262.5 (4.3L) V6 VIN V LONGITUDINAL Ft. Lbs.	N·m	262.5 (4.3L) V6 VIN T TRANSVERSE Ft. Lbs.	N·m
Fuel Pump				
Fuel pump-to-block bolt and nut	Electric		Electric	
Engine				
Controller (glow plug)	20	27	NA	NA
Cylinder head bolts	② ③		③	
Crankshaft pulley or damper bolt	160	217	160	217
Injection pump attaching nuts	18	24		
Injection line nut-to-pump	35	48	35	48
Injection pump adapter bolts	22	30		
Injection line nut-to-nozzle	18	24	18	24
Injection pump fuel filter inlet line	20	27	20	17
Injection pump fuel filter outlet line	10	14	10	14
Injection pump fuel inlet line	20	27	20	27
Injection nozzle	25	34		

DIESEL ENGINES
GM 4.3L, 262 CU. IN. V6
SECTION 27

ENGINE TORQUE SPECIFICATIONS

Application	262.5 (4.3L) V6 VIN V LONGITUDINAL		262.5 (4.3L) V6 VIN T TRANSVERSE	
	Ft. Lbs.	N·m	Ft. Lbs.	N·m
Manifold (intake)	41	55	41	55
(Exhaust)	—	—	—	—
Main bearing nuts	107	145	107	145
Glow plug	15	21		
Flywheel-to-converter	35	47	35	47
Flywheel-to-crankshaft	48	65	48	65
Oil pump-to-bearing cap bolts	18	24	18	24
Oil pump cover-to-pump bolts	8	11	8	11
Rocker arm pivot bolt-to-head	28	37		
Rod bearing nuts	42	57	42	57
Oil pan bolts	10	14	10	14
Oil pan drain plug	26	36	26	36
Crankshaft balancer-to-crankshaft bolt	60-350	217-475	160-350	217-475
Oil filter element-to-base	④	④	④	④
Oil filter assembly-to-cylinder block bolts	29	40	29	40
Oil cooler lines-to-oil filter base	29	40	29	40
Oil cooler lines-to-radiator	25	34	25	34
Front cover-to-cylinder block	41	55		
Fan driven pulley-to-hub bolts	20	27	20	27
Fan driving pulley-to-balancer bolts	20	27	20	27
Water pump-to-front cover bolts ②	21	28	NA	NA
Water outlet-to-manifold bolts	18	24	NA	NA
Engine mount-to-cylinder block bolts	37	50	37	50
Engine mount-to-frame mount	38	52	38	52
Starter-to-cylinder block bolts	20	27	20	27
Starter brace-to-cylinder block bolts	29	40	29	40
Starter brace-to-starter bolt	13	17	13	17
Vacuum pump clamp-to-cylinder block bolt	18	Belt Driven	—	Electric
Camshaft sprocket bolt	64	87	64	87

① Clean and dip bolt in engine oil before tightening to obtain a correct torque reading.
② Cylinder head bolts: Torque all bolts 5, 6, 11, 12, 13 and 14 to 142 ft. lbs. (193 N·m).
  Torque bolts 5, 6, 11, 12, 13 and 14 to 59 ft. lbs. (80 N·m).
③ Use sealer on threads.
④ ⅔ turn after gasket contact

PISTON AND RING SPECIFICATIONS
All measurements are given in inches

Year	Engine No. Cyl. Displacement (cu. in.)	Ring Gap			Ring Side Clearance			Piston Clearance
		Top Compression	Bottom Compression	Oil Control	Top Compression	Bottom Compression	Oil Control	
'83–'87	262.5	.015–.025	.015–.025	.015–.055	.005–.007	.003–.005	.001–.005	.003–.004

SECTION 27 — DIESEL ENGINES
GM 4.3L, 262 CU. IN. V6

HEAD BOLT TORQUE SEQUENCE

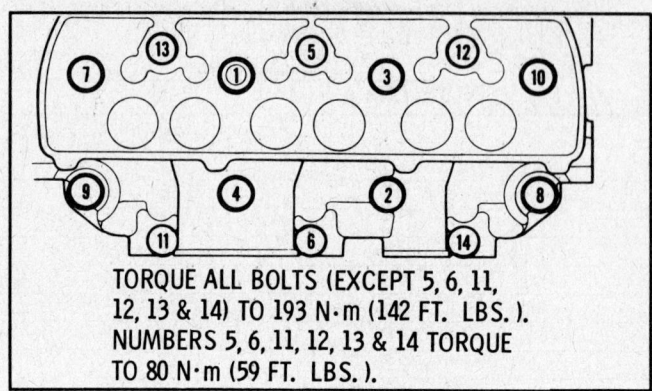

V6 engine cylinder head torque sequence

TUNE-UP

COMPRESSION TEST

When checking the compression, always make sure that the batteries are at or near full charge. The total reading for any given cylinder is not as important as the difference between all cylinders. The cylinder with the lowest reading should not be less than 70% of the one with the highest reading and no cylinder should be less than 275 psi.

1. Remove the air cleaner and cover the air crossover.
2. Disconnect the wire from the fuel solenoid terminal on the injection pump.
3. Tag and disconnect all glow plug wiring and then remove the glow plugs.
4. Screw a compression gauge into the hole of the cylinder that is being checked.
5. Crank the engine. Six "puffs" per cylinder should be enough for an accurate reading. Normal compression will build up quickly and evenly if the cylinder is OK.

NOTE: Never add oil to any cylinder during a compression test, as extensive damage may result.

6. Install all parts removed during the testing procedure.

VALVE LIFTERS

Roller hydraulic lifters are used to reduce the amount of friction between the valve lifter and the camshaft lobe. Guides keep the lifters from rotating on the camshaft lobes.

Valve Lifter Bleed Down

If the intake manifold has been removed and if any rocker arms have been loosened or removed; it will be necessary to remove those valve lifters, disassemble, drain then reassemble the filters.

If the intake manifold has not been removed but rocker arms have been loosened or removed, valve lifters can be bled down by the following procedure:

1. Before installing any removed rocker arms, rotate the engine crankshaft to a position of number 1 cylinder being 32° before top dead center. This is 2 in. (50mm) counter-clockwise from the 0° pointer. If only the right valve cover was removed, remove No. 1 cylinder's glow plug to determine if the position of the piston is the correct one. The compression pressure will tell you that you are in the right position.

If the left valve cover was removed, rotate the crankshaft until the number 5 cylinder intake valve push rod ball is 0.28 in. (20mm) above the number 5 cylinder exhaust valve push rod ball.

NOTE: Use only hand wrenches to torque the rocker arm pivot nuts or bolts to avoid engine damage.

2. If removed, install the No. 5 cylinder pivot and rocker arms. Torque the nuts or bolts alternately between the intake and exhaust valves until the intake valve begins to open, then stop.
3. Install remaining rocker arms except No. 3 exhaust valve. (If this rocker arm was removed).
4. If removed, install but do not torque No. 3 valve pivots beyond the point that the valve would be fully open. This is indicated by a strong resistance while still turning the pivot retaining nuts or bolts. Going beyond this would bend the push rod. Torque the nuts or bolts slowly allowing the lifter to bleed down.
5. Finish torquing No. 5 cylinder rocker arm pivot nut or bolt slowly. Do not go beyond the point that the valve would be fully open. This is indicated by strong resistance while still turning the pivot retaining nuts or bolts. Going beyond this would bend the push rod.
6. Do not turn the engine crankshaft for at least 45 minutes.
7. Finish reassembling the engine as the lifters are being bled.

— CAUTION —
Do not rotate the engine until the valve lifters have been bled down, or damage to the engine will occur.

VALVE ADJUSTMENT

This engine uses hydraulic valve lifter; no adjustment is necessary or possible.

DIESEL ENGINES
GM 4.3L, 262 CU. IN. V6
SECTION 27

INJECTION TIMING

Checking Injection Timing

The timing meter J–33075 or equivalent picks up the engine speed and crankshaft position from the crankshaft balancer. It uses a luminosity signal through a glow plug probe to determine combustion timing. Certain engine malfunctions may cause incorrect timing readings. Engine malfunctions should be corrected before a timing adjustment is made. The marks on the pump and adapter flange will normally be aligned within 0.050 in. (1.27mm).

NOTE: Alignment of timing marks may be used in emergency situations (i.e. timing meter not available). However for optimum engine operation, the timing should be adjusted with the timing meter as soon as possible.

1. Place transmission selector lever in park, apply parking brake and block drive wheels.
2. Start the engine and let it run at idle until fully warmed up. Then shut off the engine.

NOTE: Failure to have the engine fully warmed up will result in incorrect timing reading and adjustments.

3. Remove air cleaner assembly and install cover J–26996–1 or equivalent. The EGR valve hose must be disconnected.
4. Clean any dirt from the engine probe holder (rpm counter) and crankshaft balancer rim.
5. Clean the lens on both ends of the glow plug probe and clean the lens in the photo-electric pick-up. Use a dulled toothpick to scrape the carbon from the combustion chamber side of the glow plug probe. Look through the probe to be sure it's clean. Retarded readings will result if the probe is not clean.
6. Install the rpm probe into the crankshaft rpm counter (probe holder).
7. Remove the glow plug from No. 1 cylinder. Install the glow plug probe in the glow plug opening. Torque the probe to 9 ft. lbs. (12 Nm).
8. Set the timing meter offset selector to the 6 cylinder setting.
9. Connect the battery leads; red to positive, black to negative. Disconnect the alternator two lead wire connector.
10. Start the engine and adjust the rpm to the speed specified on the "Vehicle Emission Control Information Label".
11. Observe the timing reading during a two minute interval. When the readings stabilize over the 2 minute interval, compare the reading to the one specified on the "Vehicle Emission Control Information Label". The timing reading, when set to specification will be "Negative" (after top dead center).
12. Disconnect the timing meter. Connect the alternator two lead wire connector.
13. Lubricate only the threads of the removed glow plug with anti-seize lubricant 9985462 or equivalent.

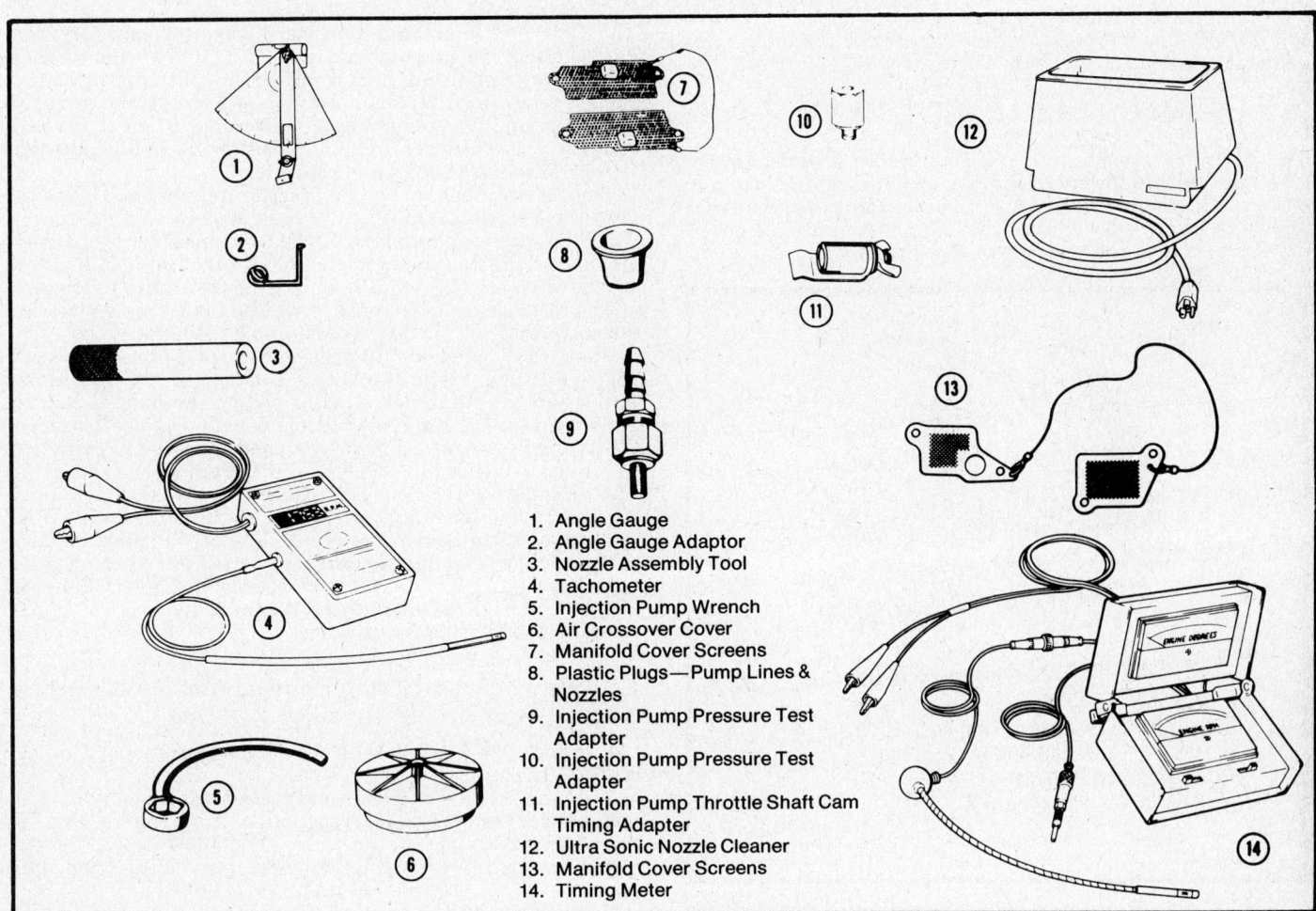

1. Angle Gauge
2. Angle Gauge Adaptor
3. Nozzle Assembly Tool
4. Tachometer
5. Injection Pump Wrench
6. Air Crossover Cover
7. Manifold Cover Screens
8. Plastic Plugs—Pump Lines & Nozzles
9. Injection Pump Pressure Test Adapter
10. Injection Pump Pressure Test Adapter
11. Injection Pump Throttle Shaft Cam Timing Adapter
12. Ultra Sonic Nozzle Cleaner
13. Manifold Cover Screens
14. Timing Meter

Diesel service and tune-up tools

SECTION 27
DIESEL ENGINES
GM 4.3L, 262 CU. IN. V6

NOTE: Failure to apply the correct lubricant can cause engine damage.

14. Install the removed glow plug. Torque the glow plug to 15 ft. lbs. (21 Nm).
15. Install the air cleaner being certain to reconnect the EGR valve hose.

Adjusting Injection Timing

1. Shut off the engine.
2. Note the relative position of the marks on the pump flange and pump intermediate adapter.
3. Loosen the bolts holding the pump to the adapter to a point where the pump can be rotated. Use a one in, open end wrench. Tool J–25304 has the proper offset on the handle to clear the fuel return line.
4. Rotate the pump to the left to advance the timing and to the right to retard the timing. The width of the mark on the intermediate adapter is about $2/3$ degree. Move the pump the amount that is needed and tighten the pump retaining bolts to 35 ft. lbs. (47 Nm).
5. Start the engine and recheck the timing reading as outlined previously. Reset and recheck the timing if needed.
6. Reset the fast and curb idle speeds. Both procedures are in this section.

Please note the following:
1. Sooty, dirty probes will result in retarded readings.
2. The luminosity probe will soot up very fast when used in a cold engine.
3. Wild needle fluctuations on the timing meter indicate a cylinder not firing properly. Correction of this condition must be made prior to adjusting the timing.

MECHANICAL GOVERNOR

The governor serves the purpose of maintaining the desired engine speed within the operating range under varying load conditions. The limits of throttle travel are set by throttle linkage screws for proper slow idle and maximum high idle. The governor operates automatically and is not adjustable.

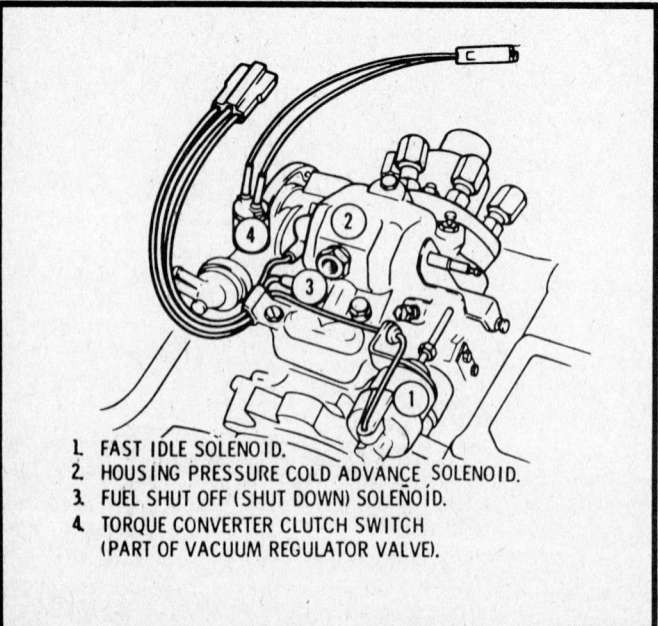

1. FAST IDLE SOLENOID.
2. HOUSING PRESSURE COLD ADVANCE SOLENOID.
3. FUEL SHUT OFF (SHUT DOWN) SOLENOID.
4. TORQUE CONVERTER CLUTCH SWITCH (PART OF VACUUM REGULATOR VALVE).

Location of injection pump solenoids and connectors, typical

HOUSING PRESSURE COLD ADVANCE (HPCA)

The HPCA Feature is designed to advance the injection timing about 4° during cold operation. This circuit is actuated by the EGR-TVS switch. The switch is calibrated to open the circuit at about 41°C (105°F). Below the switching point, housing pressure is decreased from 62–82.7 kPa (9–11 psi) to zero which advances the timing about 4°. Above about 41°C (105°F) the switch opens, de-energizing the solenoid and the housing pressure is returned to 9–12 psi. The fast idle solenoid is energized by the same switch. The switch again closes when the temperature falls below 95°F.

Its Advantages Are:

1. Emission Control device.
2. Better cold starts.
3. Improves idle, reduces white smoke and noise when cold.

When changing the fuel filter or injection pump, or when the car has run out of fuel, disconnect the connector from the temperature switch and jumper connector terminals. This will aid in purging air from the pump by allowing more fuel to pass to the return. (This procedure is necessary only on a hot engine, as the circuit will always be closed when the engine is cold.).

HOUSING PRESSURE ALTITUDE ADVANCE (HPAA)

The 1984 and later diesel engine must meet emission standards at both low and high altitudes. Altitude compensation is achieved by timing and EGR modification controlled by an altitude-sensitive switch on non-Calif. cars. Two systems are used: a low-altitude system, and a high-altitude system. A low-altitude car at low altitude, or a high-altitude car at high altitude, has a minimum of activated controls.

Timing is controlled by two pressure regulators. One is the Housing Pressure cold Advance (HPCA) located in the pump. The other pressure regulator is the Housing Pressure Altitude Advance (HPAA) located in the fuel return line, (EGR is controlled with an additional solenoid and a vacuum reducer.

The altitude control switch, with the appropriate electrical circuitry controls HPCA, HPAA, and EGR trim.

The HPCA solenoid will regulate housing pressure according to altitude. When the HPAA solenoid is "ON," the glass check ball is seated, and it will regulate pressure at its calibrated value. When HPAA solenoid is "OFF," the ball is moved off its seat, the return line is open, and there is no regulation. So, it is possible to have both the HPCA (OFF) and the HPAA (ON) regulating the housing Pressure at the same time. It is also possible to have just the HPCA (OFF) or just the HPAA (ON) regulating housing pressure. The HPCA must be energized (plunger extended holding the housing pressure regulating check ball off its seat), and not regulating to allow the HPAA solenoid to regulate at its calibrated value. Higher housing pressures retard timing.

Checking Injection Pump Housing fuel Pressure—Engine Warm

1. Check the operation of the temperature switch on the EGR-TVS.
2. Remove the air cleaner and install screened cover.
3. Disconnect the fuel return line from the return line connector.
4. Remove the return line connector from the injection pump cover.
5. Push the HPCA solenoid plunger into the solenoid.
6. Remove the electrical connector from the housing pressure cold advance terminal.

DIESEL ENGINES
GM 4.3L, 262 CU. IN. V6

7. With a jumper lead, apply 12V to the HPCA terminal. The HPCA solenoid plunger should fully extend. If not, remove the pump cover and repair or replace the HPCA solenoid.
8. Install adapter J–34151 or equivalent in the pump cover.
9. Install the return line into adapter J–34151 or equivalent.
10. Attach a low pressure gauge to adapter.
11. Install magnetic pick-up tachometer J–26925 or equivalent.
12. Check the pressure with the engine running at 1000 rpm, transmission in Park, parking brake on, drive wheels blocked. The pressure should be 62–82.7 kPa (9–11 psi) with not more than 6.895 kPa (1) psi fluctuation, because pressure will change depending on the system (package) and altitude car is checked at.
13. If the pressure is low, replace the fuel return line connector assembly.
14. If the pressure is too high, the fuel return system or the HPAA may be restricted. Remove the return line at the adapter pump. Install a fitting and short piece of hose to allow the return flow to empty into a small container.
If the fuel return line connector assembly is replaced, check and if necessary, reset pump timing.
15. If the pressure is lower than before, correct the restriction in the fuel line.
16. If still too high, replace the fuel return line connector assembly.
17. If it remains too high, remove the injection pump for repair.
18. Remove the tachometer, pressure gauge, and adapter.
19. Using a new O-ring, install the fuel return line connector into the pump cover.
20. Connect the fuel return line to the return line connector.
21. Start the engine and check for leaks.
22. Remove screened covers, then install air crossover.

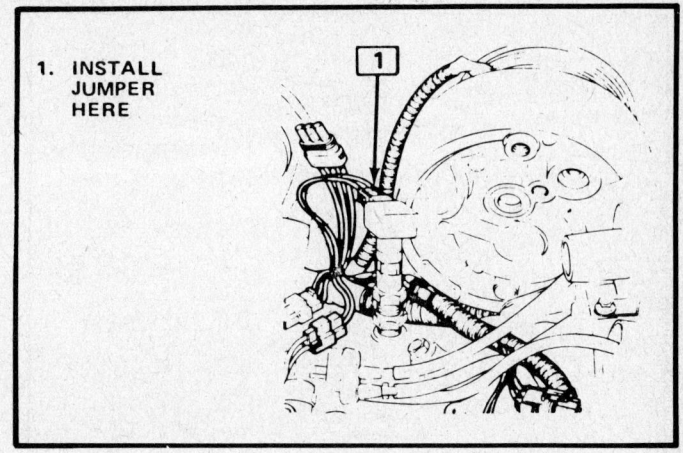

EGR-TVS switch jumper location, GM V6 diesel engine

REDUCING CRANKING TIME

When replacing a fuel filter or injection pump the Housing Pressure Cold Advance should be activated manuals if the engine temperature is above 41°C (105°F). Activating the HPCA will reduce cranking time.

To activate the HPCA solenoid, disconnect the two lead connectors at the EGR-TVS switch and bridge the connector with a jumper. After the engine is running, remove the jumper and reconnect the connector to the engine temperature switch.

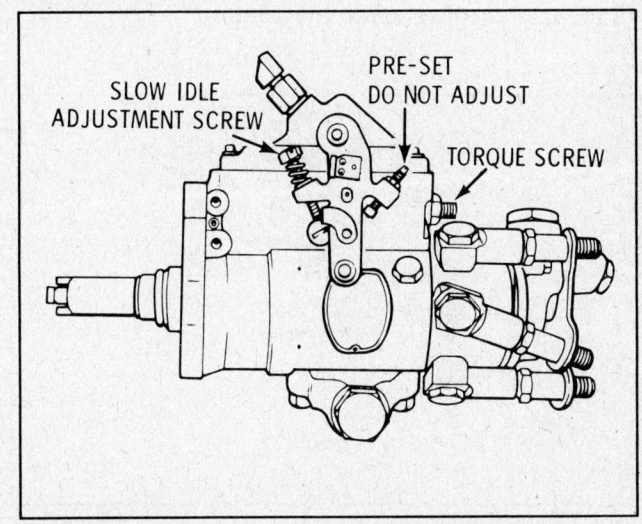

CAV injection pump slow idle adjustment screw

INJECTION PUMP TIMING CONTROL
V-6 and V-8 Engines

Condition Altitude	Coolant	HPCA	HPAA	Nominal Housing Pressure kPa (psi)
FEDERAL PACKAGE				
BELOW 1219m (4000 FT.)	COLD	ON	OFF	0
BELOW 1219m (4000 FT.)	HOT	OFF	OFF	68.9 (10)
ABOVE 1219m (4000 FT.)	COLD	ON	OFF	0
ABOVE 1219m (4000 FT.)	HOT	ON	ON	48.3 (7)
ALTITUDE PACKAGE				
ABOVE 1219m (4000 FT.)	COLD	ON	OFF	0
ABOVE 1219m (4000 FT.)	HOT	OFF	OFF	68.9 (10)
BELOW 1219m (4000 FT.)	COLD	ON	OFF	0
BELOW 1219m (4000 FT.)	HOT	OFF	ON	89.6 (13)

HPCA = HOUSING PRESSURE COLD ADV.   HPAA = HOUSING PRESSURE ALTITUDE ADV.
TIMING RETARDS WITH HIGHER HOUSING PRESSURE

SECTION 27 DIESEL ENGINES
GM 4.3L, 262 CU. IN. V6

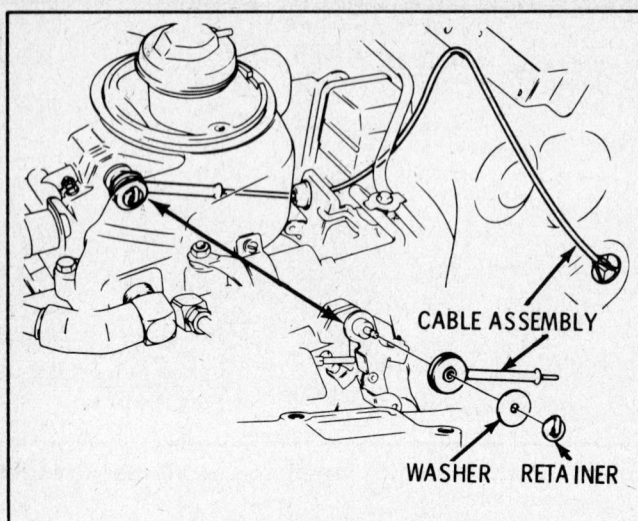

V6 diesel—throttle cable installation

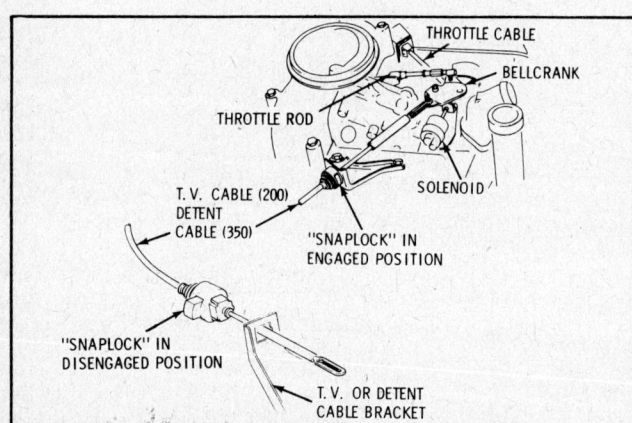

V6 diesel—detent of T.V. cable adjustment

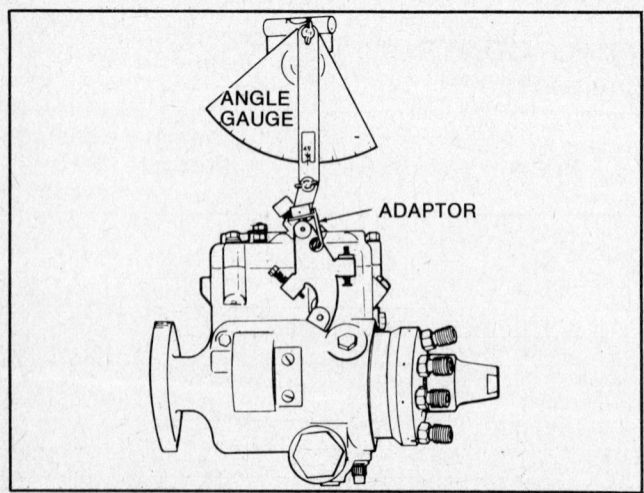

Using an angle gauge to adjust the vacuum regulator valve

IDLE SPEED

Slow Idle and Fast Idle Solenoid Adjustment

1. Run the engine until it reaches normal operating temperature.
2. Insert the probe of a magnetic pickup tachometer into the timing indicator hole.
3. Set the parking brake and block the drive wheels.
4. Place the transmission in Drive and turn the A/C off (if so equipped). Disconnect the two lead connector at the alternator.
5. Turn the slow idle adjustment screw on the injection pump to obtain the idle speed specified on the emission control label.
6. Set the parking brake and block the drive wheels.
7. Run the engine until it reaches normal operating temperature.
8. Place the transmission in Drive and disconnect the compressor clutch wire.
9. Unplug the connector from the EGR-TVS and install a jumper between the connector terminals.
10. Adjust the fast idle solenoid plunger to obtain the specified rpm.
11. Complete installation of removed components.

NOTE: If equipped with cruise control, adjust the servo throttle rod to minimum slack, then put clip in first Free hole closest to the bellcrank or throttle lever, but within the servo bail.

THROTTLE CABLE

Adjustment

NOTE: The V6 throttle cable is not adjustable.

DETENT CABLE

Adjustment

1. Depress and hold the metal lock tab on the cable upper end.
2. Move the slider through the fitting, away from the lever assembly, until it stops against the metal fitting.
3. Release the metal tab, rotate the lever assembly to the full throttle stop and then release it.
4. Reconnect the pump rod and the cruise control rod if necessary.

VACUUM REGULATOR VALVE

Adjustment

1. Remove the air crossover, install the screened covers in the intake manifold openings, disconnect the throttle rod from the throttle lever and loosen the vacuum regulator valve injection pump bolts.
2. Place the carburetor angle gauge adapter on the injection pump throttle lever. Place the angle gauge on the adapter.

NOTE: It may be necessary to rework the adapter by filing, in order to fit the V-6 pump's thicker throttle lever.

3. Rotate the throttle lever to wide open throttle and set the angle gauge to zero degrees. Center the bubble in the level and reset the angle gauge to 49 degrees.
4. Rotate the throttle lever to center the bubble. Apply an outside vacuum source of 18–22 inches to the inboard port of the vacuum valve. Rotate the valve clockwise to obtain 10.6 inches of vacuum.
5. Tighten vacuum valve bolts. Remove gauge and/or pump.
6. Connect throttle cable and T.V. cable to the pump throttle.

DIESEL ENGINES
GM 4.3L, 262 CU. IN. V6
SECTION 27

7. Remove the screen covers and install the air crossover.

GLOW PLUGS

Six glow plugs are used to heat the pre-chamber to aid in starting. They are essentially small heaters that turn on when the ignition switch is turned to the "RUN" position prior to starting the engine. They remain on for a short time after starting and then automatically shut off.

There are two types of glow plugs used on GM diesels; the "fast-glow" type and the "slow-glow" type. The fast-glow type use pulsing current applied to 6 volt glow plugs, while the slow-glow type use a continuous current applied to 12 volt glow plugs.

An easy way to tell the plugs apart is that the fast-glow (6V) plugs have a $\frac{5}{16}$ in. wide electrical connector plug, while the slow-glow (12V) connector is $\frac{1}{4}$ in. wide. Do not attempt to interchange any parts of these two glow plug systems.

Removal and Installation

NOTE: Use extreme care when removing a glow plug as the tip may break off; requiring cylinder head removal.

1. Tag and disconnect the electrical connectors.
2. Using the large hex nut, loosen the glow plug and carefully lift it out of the cylinder head.
3. Installation is in the reverse order.
4. Torque the glow plugs to 15 ft. lbs. (21 Nm).

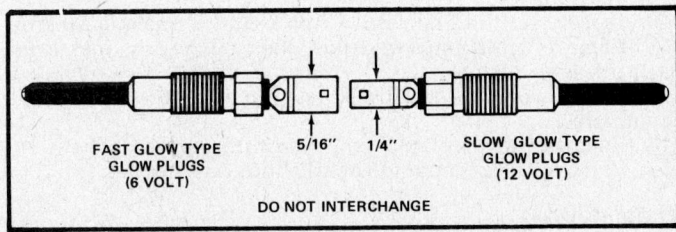

Diesel Engine Glow Plug Identification

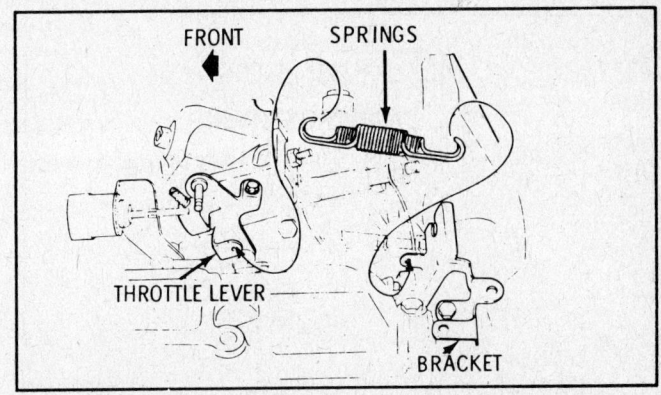

Installation of the V6 diesel throttle return spring

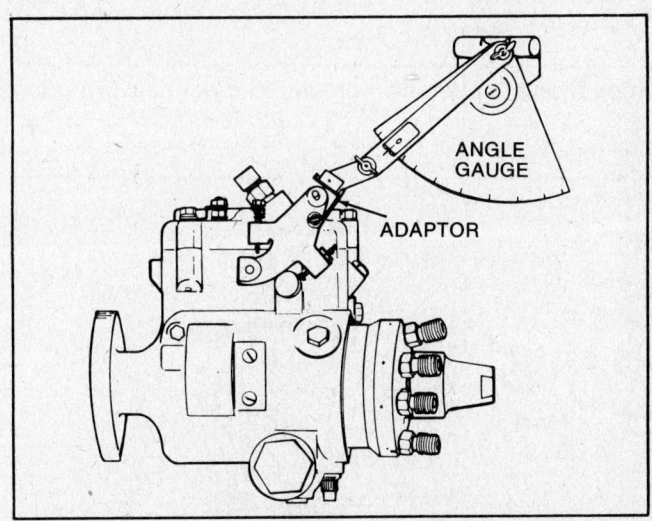

Vacuum valve adjustment at wide open throttle position—engine not running

FUEL SUPPLY

Fuel Supply Pump

The 4.3L–V6 engines use an electric fuel pump mounted on the engine.

Removal

1. Remove the air cleaner.
2. Disconnect the electrical wiring connections.
3. Disconnect and plug the two fuel lines.
4. Remove the pump bracket mounting bolt.
5. Remove the pump and gasket.

Installation

1. Install the pump and tighten the mounting bracket bolts to 18 ft. lbs. (24 Nm).
2. Install both fuel lines and torque to 19 ft. lbs. (26 Nm). Install the electrical wire connectors.
3. Bleed the fuel system, start the engine and check for fuel leakage.

BLEEDING THE FUEL SYSTEM

After the pump is installed, disconnect the fuel line at the fuel filter and turn the ignition switch to the "ON" position, in order to prime and bleed the lines. Use a container to collect the diesel fuel during the bleeding and priming operation. If, after torquing the the fuel line, the pump runs with a click-like sound or air bubbles appear in the fuel, check for leaks in the lines. Also, check all connections to see that they are dry and no fuel is leaking. When the click-like sound diminishes, tighten the fuel line at the filter.

Fuel Filter

Removal and Installation

The fuel filter is a square assembly located at the back of the engine, between the fuel pump and the injection pump and above the intake manifold. Disconnect the fuel lines, remove the mounting bolt and remove the filter. Install a new filter in the reverse.

27-41

SECTION 27 — DIESEL ENGINES
GM 4.3L, 262 CU. IN. V6

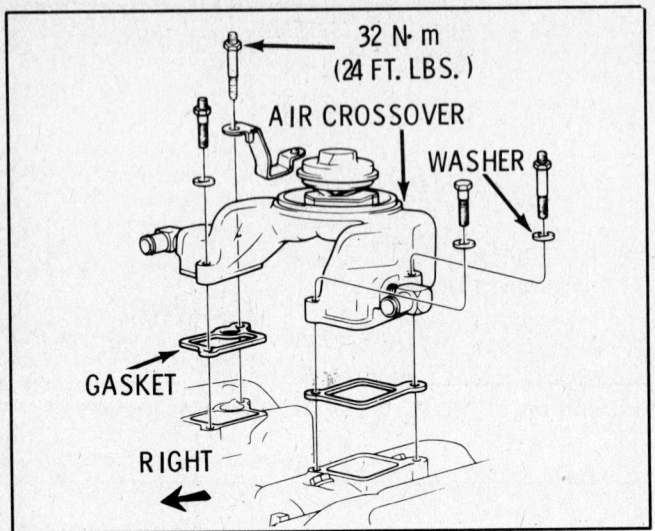

Removal and installation of the V6 diesel air crossover

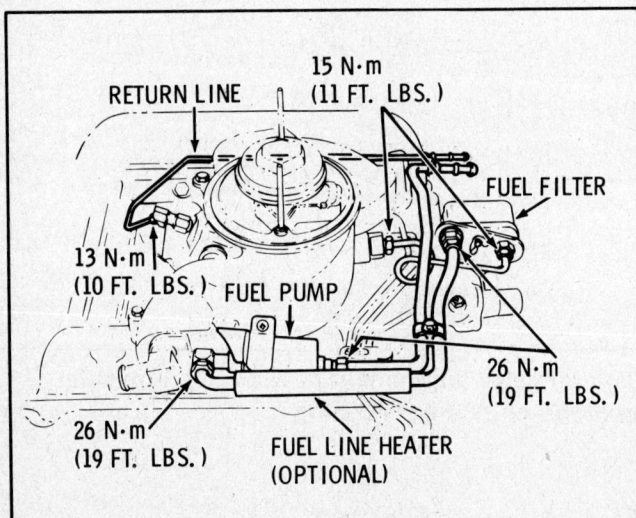

V6 diesel fuel filter, pump and lines

Injection Pump

Removal

1. Remove the air cleaner.
2. Remove the filter and pipes from the valve covers and air crossover.
3. Remove the air crossover and cap the intake manifold with screened covers. Disconnect and/or remove the fuel lines and the fuel pump.
4. Remove fuel line heater, if equipped. If equipped, remove throttle rod and return spring. Remove bellcrank, if necessary.
5. Remove the throttle and detent cables from the intake manifold brackets.
6. Disconnect the fuel lines from the filter and remove the filter.
7. Disconnect the fuel inlet line at the pump.
8. Remove the rear A/C compressor brace (if so equipped) and remove the fuel line.

— **CAUTION** —
When removing the injection pump and lines on transverse mount V6 diesel engines, it may be necessary to raise the rear side of the engine to obtain working clearance. Failure to disconnect the intermediate shaft from the rack and pinion stub shaft, before raising the engine, can result in damage to the steering gear and/or intermediate shaft. This damage can cause loss of steering control.

9. Transverse mount V6:
   a. Remove the engine support strut.
   b. Place a floor jack under the front crossmember of the cradle and raise the jack until the jack just starts to raise the car.
   c. Remove the front two body mounts (No. 1 and No. 3) bolts with the lower cushions and retainers. Remove the cushions from the bolts.
   d. Thread the body mount bolts with retainers a minimum of three (3) turns into the cage nuts so that the bolts restrain cradle movement.
   e. Release the floor jack slowly until the crossmember contacts the body mount bolt retainers. As the jack is being lowered watch and correct any interference with hose, lines, pipes and cables.

— **CAUTION** —
Do not lower the cradle without it being restrained as possible damage can occur to the body and underhood items.

   f. Reverse the above steps after completion of injection pump replacement. Torque the intermediate steering shaft clamp bolt to 46 ft. lbs. (62 Nm). Torque the body mount bolts to 77 ft. lbs. (105 Nm).
10. Disconnect the fuel return line from the injection pump.
11. Remove the clamps and pull the fuel return lines from each injection nozzle.
12. Using two wrenches, disconnect the high pressure lines at the nozzles.
13. Remove the injection pump retaining nuts or bolts.
14. Remove the pump and cap all lines and nozzles.

Installation

1. Remove the protective caps from all lines and nozzles. Place the engine on TDC for the No. 1 cylinder. The mark on the hamonic balancer on the crankshaft will be aligned with the zero mark on the timing tab, and both valves for No. 1 cylinder will be closed. The index mark on the injection pump driven gear should be offset to the right when No. 1 is at TDC. Check that all of these conditions are met before continuing.
2. Line up the offset tang on the pump driveshaft with the pump driven gear and install the pump with new pump to adapter O-ring.
3. Install, but do not tighten the pump retaining nuts.
4. Connect the high pressure lines at the nozzles.
5. Using two wrenches, torque the high pressure line nuts to 25 ft. lbs.
6. Connect the fuel return lines to the nozzles and pump.
7. Align the timing mark on the injection pump with the line on the pump adapter and torque the mounting nuts to 38 ft. lbs.

NOTE: A one in. open end wrench on the boss at the front of the injection pump will aid in rotating the pump to align the marks.

8. Adjust the throttle rod.
9. Install the fuel inlet line between the transfer pump and the filter.
10. Install the rear A/C compressor brace (if so equipped).
11. Install the bellcrank and clip, if equipped.
12. Connect the throttle rod and return spring, if equipped.
13. Adjust the transmission cable.

14. Bleed the fuel system, start the engine and check for fuel leaks.
15. Remove the screened covers and install the air crossover.
16. Install the tubes in the airflow control valve in the air crossover and install the ventilation filters in the valve covers.
17. Install the air cleaner.
18. Start the engine and allow it to run for two minutes. Stop the engine, let it stand for two minutes, then restart. This permits the air to bleed off within the pump.
19. Check and if necessary reset the pump timing.
20. Adjust the vacuum regulator valve only if the valve's original position is disturbed or a replacement injection pump is installed.
21. Adjust the idle speeds.

Injectors

Removal

When the lines are disconnected, use a back-up wrench on the upper injection nozzle hex.

1. Remove nozzle by applying torque to the largest nozzle hex.

   NOTE: Always cap the nozzle and lines to prevent damage or contamination.

2. When working on the rear (right) bank, it may be necessary to perform the following:

   a. Rotate the intermediate steering shaft so that the steering gear stub shaft clamp bolt is in the up position and remove the clamp bolt. Disconnect the intermediate shaft from the stub shaft.

   — CAUTION —
   Failure to disconnect the intermediate shaft from the rack and pinion stub shaft can result in damage to the steering gear and/or intermediate shaft. This damage can cause loss of steering control which could result in a vehicle crash with possible bodily injury.

   b. Remove the engine support strut.
   c. Place a floor jack under the front crossmember of the cradle and raise the jack until the jack just starts to raise the car.
   d. Remove the front two body mount (#1 and #3) bolts with the lower cushions and retainers. Remove the cushions from the bolts.
   e. Thread the body mount bolts with retainers a minimum of three (3) turns into the cable nuts so that the bolts restrain cradle movement.
   f. Release the floor jack slowly until the crossmember contacts the body mount bolt retainers. As the jack is being lowered watch and correct any interference with hose, lines, pipes and cables.

   NOTE: Do not lower the cradle without it being restrained as possible damage can occur to the body and underhood items.

3. Remove copper nozzle gasket from the cylinder head if the gasket did not remain on the nozzle.

Installation

1. Apply lubricant Part No. 1052771 or equivalent to the threads of the nozzle.

   NOTE: Failure to apply the correct lubricant can cause engine damage.

2. Remove protective caps from nozzles (if installed after testing).
3. Make sure copper nozzle gasket is installed on the nozzle.
4. Install the nozzle and torque to 25 ft. lbs. (34 Nm). Torque must be applied to the largest nozzle hex.
5. Attach the lines using a back-up wrench on the upper injection nozzle hex. Torque the line nut to 25 ft. lbs. (34 Nm).
6. If a rear nozzle was removed, reverse Steps 2A through 2F. Torque the intermediate steering shaft clamp bolt to 46 ft. lbs. (62 Nm), and the body mount bolts to 77 ft. lbs. (105 Nm).

NOTE: The V6 nozzle uses a red color band, for identification. In case the band is lost, a part number, 403, is used as a back-up identification.

Shut Down Problems

ENGINE CONTINUES TO RUN WITH IGNITION OFF

1. With engine turned off, and engine still running, disconnect connector at diode unit on the firewall. If engine stops, diode C is shorted. Replace the diode unit.
2. If engine continues to run, disconnect pink wire connector at fuel solenoid in fuel injection pump. If engine still continues to run, stop engine by crimping flexible fuel return line near fuel supply pump (lower right front of engine). The repair or replace fuel solenoid.

Water In Fuel (WIF) System

The WIF system consists of a revised fuel tank sending unit and a warning lamp on the dash panel which lights when there

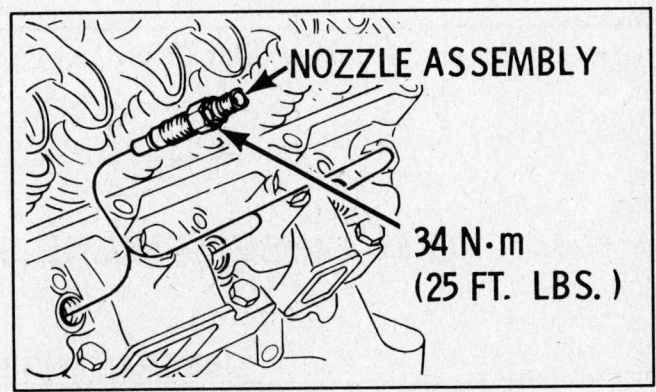

Installation of the V6 engine — injection nozzle

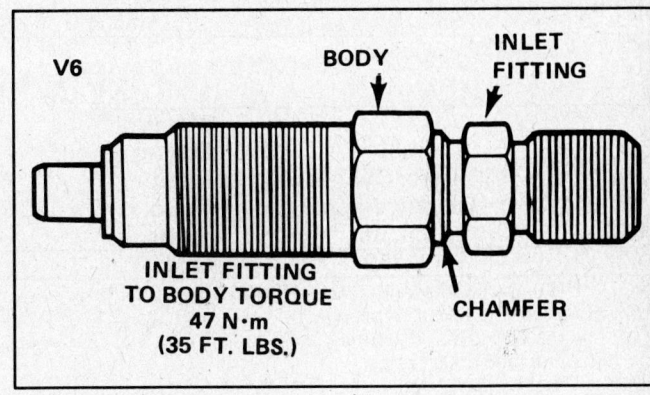

Chamfer on V6 injection nozzle distinguishes it from the V8 nozzle

SECTION 27 DIESEL ENGINES
GM 4.3L, 262 CU. IN. V6

is water in the fuel tank. The sending unit consists of the following:
1. An electronic water detector mounted close to the bottom of the fuel tank.
2. A water separator filter.
3. A rubber hose extension on the fuel return line that allows fuel tank draining without removing the tank.
4. A new fuel tank wiring harness.

Draining WIF—Equipped Fuel Tanks
1. Connect a siphon pump to the ¼ in. fuel return hose located above the rear axle or at the fuel pump under the hood. Continue siphoning until pure diesel begins to drain.

CAUTION
Remove the fuel filler cap before draining the tank.

Bench Testing the WIF Unit
1. Submerge the water sensing probe into a container of water and connect to a 12 volt source. Be sure to ground the water.
2. Connect a 12 volt, 2 candle power bulb into the positive wire. The bulb should light until the probe is removed from the water.

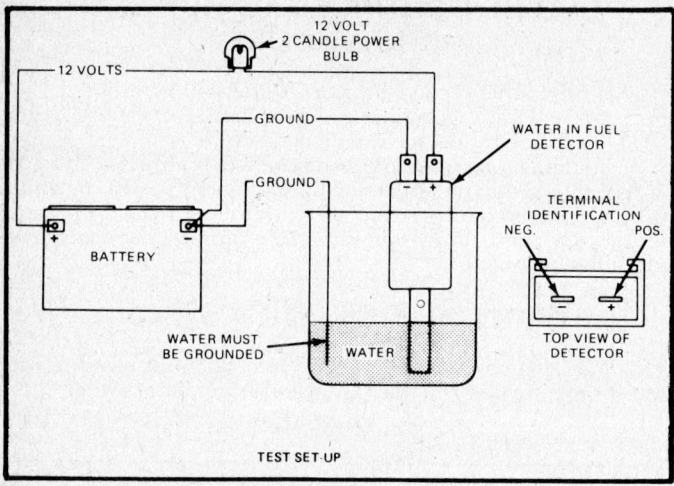

Diagram of the water-in fuel detector circuit

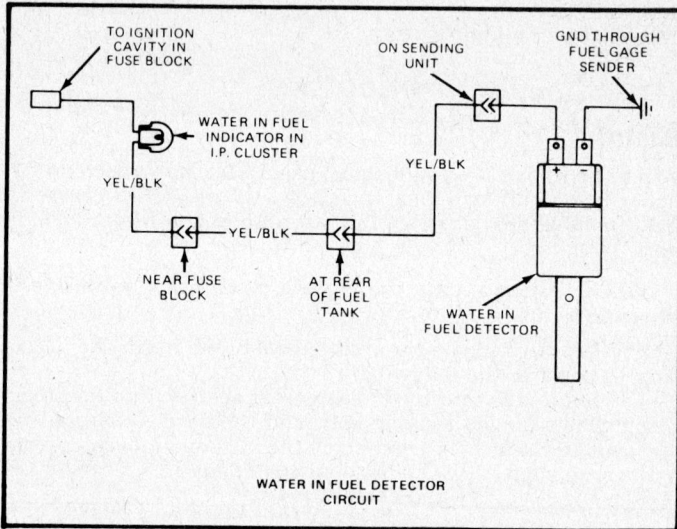

Testing the water-in fuel detector unit

G.M. DIESEL ENGINE 5.7 LITER, 350 CU. IN. V8

GENERAL ENGINE SPECIFICATIONS

Year	Engine No. Cyl. Displacement (cu. in.)	Engine Type	Horsepower @ rpm	Torque @ rpm (ft. lbs.)	Bore × Stroke (in.)	Compression Ratio	Oil Pressure @ 2000 rpm
'83–'87	8-350	Diesel	125 @ 3600	225 @ 1600	4.057 × 3.385	22.5:1	40

TUNE-UP SPECIFICATIONS

Year	Engine No. Cyl. Displacement (cu. in.)	Injector Timing (deg) Auto. Trans.	Minimum Compression (lbs)	Valves Intake Opens (deg)	Fuel Pump Pressure (psi)②	Idle Speed (rpm)① Auto. Trans.
'83–'87	8-350	4ATDC	275	16	5.5–6.5	600

NOTE: The underhood specifications sticker often reflects tune-up specification changes made in production. Sticker figures must be used if they disagree with those in this chart.
① Align the timing marks on the injection pump and drive flange
② Fuel transfer pump pressure given—Injection pump = 8-12 PSI @ 1000 rpm (take the reading at the injection pump pressure tap—injector opening can be as high as 1225 psi)

DIESEL ENGINES
GM 5.7L, 350 CU. IN. V8

SECTION 27

FIRING ORDERS

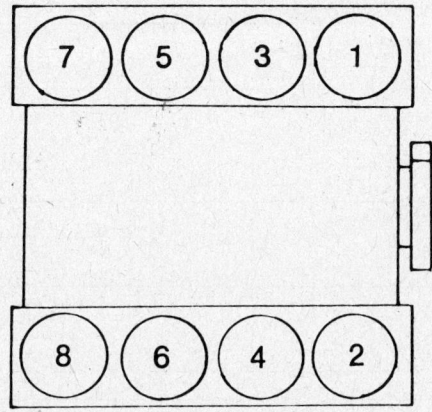

Engine firing order: 1-8-4-3-6-5-7-2

CRANKSHAFT AND CONNECTING ROD SPECIFICATIONS

All measurements are given in inches.

Year	Engine No. Cyl. Displacement (cu. in.)	Crankshaft				Connecting Rod		
		Main Brg. Journal Dia	Main Brg. Oil Clearance	Shaft End-Play	Thrust on No.	Journal Diameter	Oil Clearance	Side Clearance
'83-'87	8-350	2.9993-3.0003	.0005-.0021 ①	.0035-.0135	3	2.1238-2.1248	.0005-.0026	.006-.020

① #5: .0015-.0031

VALVE SPECIFICATIONS

Year	Engine No. Cyl. Displacement (cu. in.)	Seat Angle (deg)	Face Angle (deg)	Spring Test Pressure ③ (lbs @ in.)	Spring Installed Height (in.)	Stem-to-Guide Clearance (in.)		Stem Diameter (in.)	
						Intake	Exhaust	Intake	Exhaust
'83-'87	8-350	45 ①	44 ②	205 @ 1.300	1⁴³⁄₆₄	.0010-.0027	.0015-.0032	.3425-.3432	.3420-.3427

① Figure is for intake valve; for exhaust—31°
② Figure is for intake valve; for exhaust—30°
③ Valve open

PISTON AND RING SPECIFICATIONS

All measurements are given in inches

Year	Engine No. Cyl. Displacement (cu. in.)	Ring Gap			Ring Side Clearance			Piston Clearance
		Top Compression	Bottom Compression	Oil Control	Top Compression	Bottom Compression	Oil Control	
'83-'87	8-350	.015-.025	.015-.025	.015-.055	.005-.007	.0018-.0038	.001-.005	.005-.006

DIESEL ENGINES
GM 5.7L, 350 CU. IN. V8

ENGINE TORQUE SPECIFICATIONS

Application	350 (5.7L) V8 VIN N Ft. Lbs.	N·m
Fuel Pump	25	34
Fuel pump to block bolt and nut		
Engine	20	27
Controller (glow plug)		
Cylinder head bolts	130 ①	176
Crankshaft bolts	200-310	270-420
Injection pump attaching nuts	18	24
Injection line nut to pump	25	34
Injection pump adapter bolts	25	34
Injection line nut to nozzle	25	34
Injection pump fuel filter inlet line	20	27
Injection pump fuel filter outlet line	18	24
Injection pump fuel inlet line	20	27
Injection nozzle	25	34
Glow plug	12	16
Flywheel to converter	40	54
Flywheel to crankshaft	60	81
Main bearing bolts	120	162
Manifold bolts (Intake)	40 ①	54
(Exhaust)	25	33
Oil pump to bearing cap bolts	35	47
Oil pump cover to pump bolts	8	11
Rocker arm pivot bolt to head	28	38
Oil pan bolts	10	14
Oil pan drain plug	30	41
Crankshaft balancer to crankshaft bolt	200-310	271-420
Oil filter element to base	20	27
Oil filter assembly to cylinder block bolts	35	47
Oil cooler lines to oil filter base	12	16
Oil cooler lines to radiator	25	34
Front cover to cylinder block	35	47
Fan driven pulley to hub bolts	20	27
Fan driving pulley to balancer bolts	20	27
Water pump to front cover bolts ①	13	18
Water outlet to manifold bolts	20	27
Engine mount to cylinder block bolts	75	102
Engine mount to frame mount	50	68
Starter to cylinder block bolts	35	47
Starter brace to cylinder block bolts	25	34
Starter brace to starter bolt	15	20
Vacuum pump clamp to cylinder block bolt	17	23
Camshaft sprocket bolt	65	88

① Clean and dip entire bolt in engine oil before tightening to obtain a correct torque reading.
   Dip bolts in sealer

DIESEL ENGINES
GM 5.7L, 350 CU. IN. V8
SECTION 27

HEAD BOLT TORQUE SEQUENCE

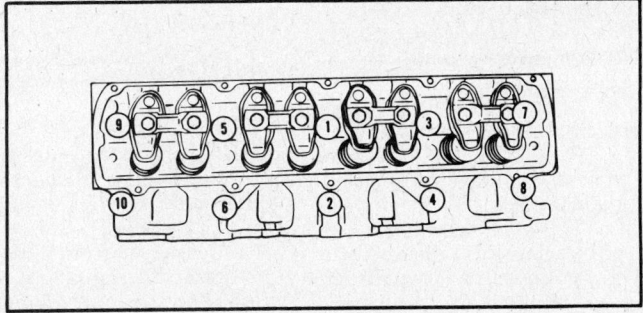

V8 engine cylinder head bolt torque sequence

TUNE-UP

COMPRESSION TEST

When checking the compression, always make sure that the batteries are at or near full charge. The total reading for any given cylinder is not as important as the difference between all cylinders. The cylinder with the lowest reading should not be less than 70% of the one with the highest reading and no cylinder should be less than 275 psi.

1. Remove the air cleaner and cover the air crossover.
2. Disconnect the wire from the fuel solenoid terminal on the injection pump.
3. Tag and disconnect all glow plug wiring and then remove the glow plugs.
4. Screw a compression gauge into the hole of the cylinder that is being checked.
5. Crank the engine. Six "puffs" per cylinder should be enough for an accurate reading. Normal compression will build up quickly and evenly if the cylinder is OK.

NOTE: Never add oil to any cylinder during a compression test, as extensive damage may result.

6. Installation is in the reverse order.

VALVE ADJUSTMENT

This engine uses hydraulic valve lifters; no adjustment is necessary or possible.

INJECTION TIMING

Checking Injection Timing

1983 AND LATER

The timing meter J-33075 or equivalent picks up the engine speed and crankshaft position from the crankshaft balancer. It uses a luminosity signal through a glow plug probe to determine combustion timing. Certain engine malfunctions may cause incorrect timing readings. Engine malfunctions should be corrected before a timing adjustment is made. The marks on the pump and adapter flange will normally be aligned within 0.030 in. (762mm).

NOTE: Alignment of timing marks may be used in emergency situations (i.e. timing meter not available).

However for optimum engine operation, the timing should be adjusted with the timing meter as soon as possible.

1. Place the transmission selector lever in park, apply parking brake and block drive wheels.
2. Start the engine and let it run at idle until fully warmed up. Then shut off the engine.

NOTE: Failure to have the engine fully warmed up will result in incorrect timing reading and adjustments.

3. Remove air cleaner assembly and install cover J-26996-2 or equivalent. The EGR valve hose must be disconnected.
4. Clean any dirt from the engine probe holder (rpm counter) and crankshaft balance rim.
5. Clean the lens on both ends of the glow plug probe and clean the lens in the photo-electric pick-up. Use a dulled tooth-

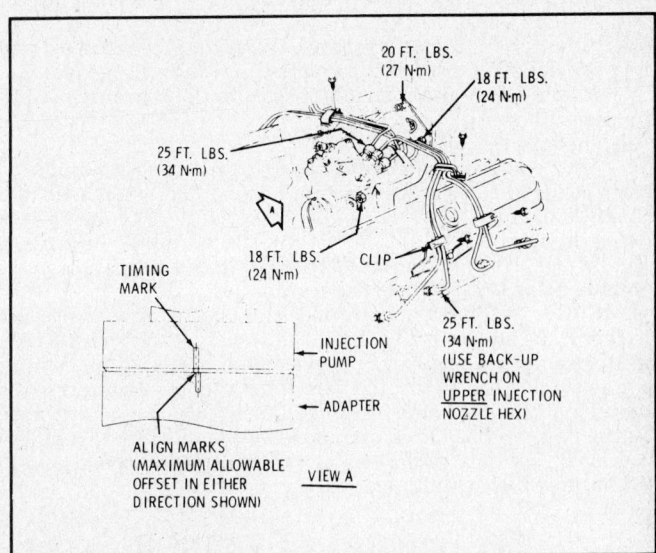

Adaptor flange-to-injection pump timing mark alignment

27-47

SECTION 27
DIESEL ENGINES
GM 5.7L, 350 CU. IN. V8

pick to scrape the carbon from the combustion chamber side of the glow plug probe. Look through the probe to be sure it's clean. Retarded readings will result if the probe is not clean.

6. Install the rpm probe into the crankshaft rpm counter (probe holder).
7. Remove the glow plug from No. 1 cylinder. Install the glow plug probe in the glow plug opening. Torque the probe to 8 ft. lbs. (11 Nm).
8. Set the timing meter offset selector to the 8 cylinder setting.
9. Connect the battery leads; red to positive, black to negative. Disconnect the alternator two lead connector.
10. Start the engine and adjust the RPM to the speed specified on the "Vehicle Emission Control Information Label".
11. Observe the timing reading then at 2 minute intervals, again observe the reading. When the readings stabilize over the 2 minute interval, compare that reading to the one specified on the "Vehicle Emission Control Information Label.". The timing reading, when set to specification will be "Negative" (after top dead center).
12. Disconnect the timing meter.
13. Lubricate only the threads of the removed glow plug with lubricant 9985462 or equivalent.

NOTE: Failure to apply the correct lubricant can cause engine damage.

14. Install the removed glow plug. Torque the glow plug to 12 ft. lbs. (16 Nm). Connect the alternator two lead connector.
15. Install the air cleaner being certain to reconnect the EGR valve hose.

Adjusting Injection Timing

1. Shut off the engine.
2. Note the relative position of the marks on the pump flange and pump adapter.
3. Loosen the bolts holding the pump to the adapter to a point where the pump can be rotated. Use a 1" open end wrench. (Tool J–25304 has the proper offset on the handle to clear the fuel return line).
4. Rotate the pump to the left to advance the timing and to the right to retard the timing. The width of the mark on the intermediate adapter is equal to one degree. Move the pump the amount that is needed and tighten the pump retaining bolt to 18 ft. lbs. (24 Nm).
5. Start the engine and recheck the timing reading as outlined previously. Reset and recheck the timing if needed.
6. Reset the fast and curb idle speeds. Both procedures are in this section.

Please note the following:
1. Sooty or dirty probes will result in retarded readings.
2. The luminosity probe will soot up very fast when used in a cold engine.
3. Wild needle fluctuations on the timing meter indicate a cylinder not firing properly. Correction of this condition must be made prior to adjusting the timing.
4. If after resetting the timing, the timing marks are far apart and the engine still exhibits a problem, the dynamic timing still could be incorrect. It is possible that a malfunctioning cylinder will result in incorrect timing. Whenever this occurs it is essential that timing be checked in the "alternate" cylinder. Timing can be checked in cylinders 2 or 3 on a V8. If a difference it timing exists between cylinders, try both positions to determine which timing works best.

MECHANICAL GOVERNOR

The governor serves the purpose of maintaining the desired engine speed within the operating range under varying load conditions. The limits of throttle travel are set by throttle travel are set by throttle linkage screws for proper slow idle and maximum high idle. The governor operates automatically and is not adjustable. The maximum high idle is factory set and should not be adjusted at any time. The slow and A/C fast idle settings are adjustable.

HOUSING PRESSURE COLD ADVANCE (HPCA)

The HPCA Feature is designed to advance the injection timing about 4° during cold operation. This circuit is actuated by the EGR-TVS switch. The switch is calibrated to open the circuit at about 41°C (105°F). Below the switching point, housing pressure is decreased from 62–82.7 kPa (9–11 psi) to zero which advances the timing about 4°. Above about 41°C (105°F) the switch opens, de-energizing the solenoid, and the housing pressure is returned to 9–12 psi. The fast idle solenoid is energized by the same switch. The switch again closes when the temperature falls below 95°F.

Its advantages are:
1. Emission Control device.
2. Better cold starts.
3. Improves idle, reduces white smoke and noise when cold.

When changing the fuel filter or injection pump, or when the car has run out of fuel, disconnect the connector from the temperature switch and jumper connector terminals. This will aid in purging air from the pump by allowing more fuel to pass to the return (this procedure is necessary only on a hot engine, as the circuit will always be closed when the engine is cold.).

HOUSING PRESSURE ALTITUDE ADVANCE (HPAA)

The 1984 and later diesel engine must meet emission standards at both low altitudes. Altitude compensation is achieved by timing and EGR modification controlled by an altitude-sensitive switch on non-Calif. cars. Two systems are used: a low-altitude system, and a high-altitude system. A low altitude car at low altitude, or a high-altitude car at high altitude, has a minimum of activated controls.

Timing is controlled by two pressure regulators. One is the Housing Pressure Cold Advance (HPCA) located in the pump. The other pressure regulator is the Housing Pressure Altitude Advance (HPAA) located in the fuel return line, (EGR is controlled with an additional solenoid and a vacuum reducer.

The altitude control switch, with the appropriate electrical circuitry controls HPCA, HPAA, and EGR trim.

The HPAA solenoid will regulate housing pressure according to altitude. When the HPAA solenoid is "ON," the glass check ball is seated, and it will regulate pressure at its calibrated value. When HPAA solenoid is "OFF," the ball is moved off its seat, the return line is open, and there is no regulation. So, it is possible to have both the HPCA (OFF) and the HPAA (ON) regulating the housing pressure at the same time. It is also possible to have just the HPCA (OFF) or just the HPAA (ON) regulating housing pressure. The HPCA must be energized (plunger extended holding the housing pressure regulating check ball off its seat), and not regulating to allow the HPAA solenoid to regulate at its calibrated value. Higher housing pressures retard timing.

Checking Injection Pump Housing Fuel/Pressure—Engine Warm

1. Check the operation of the temperature switch on the EGR-TVS.
2. Remove the air cleaner and install screened cover.
3. Disconnect the fuel return line from the return line connector.
4. Remove the return line connector from the injection pump cover.

5. Push the HPCA solenoid plunger into the solenoid.
6. Remove the electrical connector from the housing pressure cold advance terminal.
7. With a jumper lead, apply 12V to the HPCA terminal. The HPCA solenoid plunger should fully extend. If not, remove the pump cover and repair or replace the HPCA solenoid.
8. Install adapter J–34151 or equivalent in the pump cover.
9. Install the return line into adapter J–34151 or equivalent.
10. Attach a low pressure gauge to adapter.
11. Install magnetic pick-up tachometer J–26925 or equivalent.
12. Check the pressure with the engine running at 1000 rpm, transmission in Park, parking brake on, drive wheels blocked. The pressure should be 62–82.7 kPa (9–11 psi) with not more than 6.895 kPa (1 psi) fluctuation, because pressure will change depending on the system (package) and altitude car is checked at.
13. If the pressure is low, replace the fuel line connector assembly.
14. If the pressure is too high, the fuel return system or the HPAA may be restricted. Remove the return line at the adapter pump. Install a fitting and short piece of hose to allow the return flow to empty into a small container.
If the fuel return line connector assembly is replaced, check and if necessary, reset pump timing.
15. If the pressure is lower than before, correct the restriction in the fuel line.
16. If still too high, replace the fuel return connect assembly.
17. If it remains too high, remove the injection pump for repair.
18. Remove the tachometer, pressure gauge and adapter.
19. Using a new O-ring, install the fuel return line connector into the pump cover.
20. Connect the fuel return line to the return line connector.
21. Start the engine and check for leaks.
22. Remove screened covers, then install air crossover.

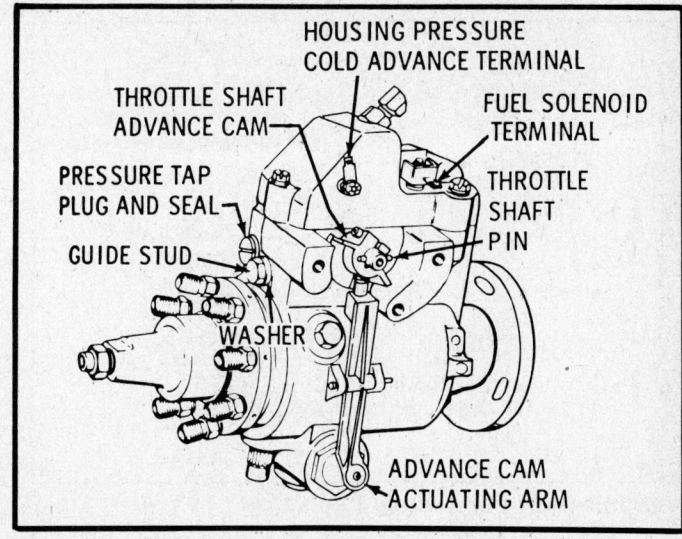

Housing pressure cold advance solenoid, GM V8 diesel engine

REDUCING CRANKING TIME

When replacing a fuel filter or injection pump the Housing Pressure Cold Advance should be activated manually if the engine temperature is above 41°C (105°F). Activating the HPCA will reduce cranking time.

To activate the HPCA solenoid, disconnect the two lead connectors at the EGR-TVS switch and bridge the connector with a jumper. After the engine is running, remove the jumper and reconnect the connector to the engine temperature switch.

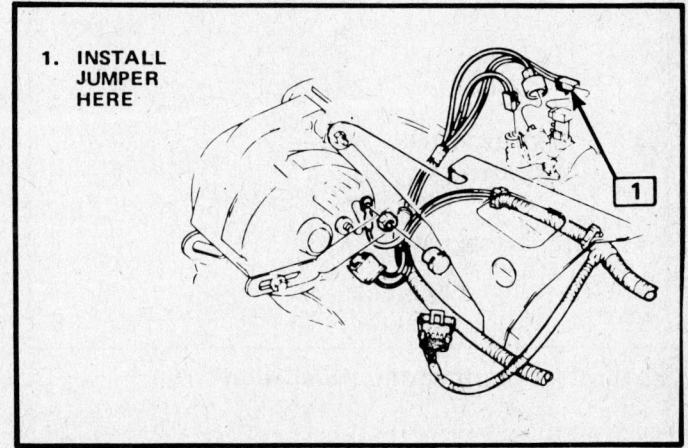

EGR-TVS switch jumper location, typical, GM V8 diesel engine

INJECTION PUMP TIMING CONTROL
V-6 and V-8 Engines

Condition Altitude	Coolant	HPCA	HPAA	Nominal Housing Pressure kPa (psi)
FEDERAL PACKAGE				
BELOW 1219m (4000 FT.)	COLD	ON	OFF	0
BELOW 1219m (4000 FT.)	HOT	OFF	OFF	68.9 (10)
ABOVE 1219m (4000 FT.)	COLD	ON	OFF	0
ABOVE 1219m (4000 FT.)	HOT	ON	ON	48.3 (7)
ALTITUDE PACKAGE				
ABOVE 1219m (4000 FT.)	COLD	ON	OFF	0
ABOVE 1219m (4000 FT.)	HOT	OFF	OFF	68.9 (10)
BELOW 1219m (4000 FT.)	COLD	ON	OFF	0
BELOW 1219m (4000 FT.)	HOT	OFF	ON	89.6 (13)

HPCA = HOUSING PRESSURE COLD ADV. HPAA = HOUSING PRESSURE ALTITUDE ADV.
TIMING RETARDS WITH HIGHER HOUSING PRESSURE

SECTION 27

DIESEL ENGINES
GM 5.7L, 350 CU. IN. V8

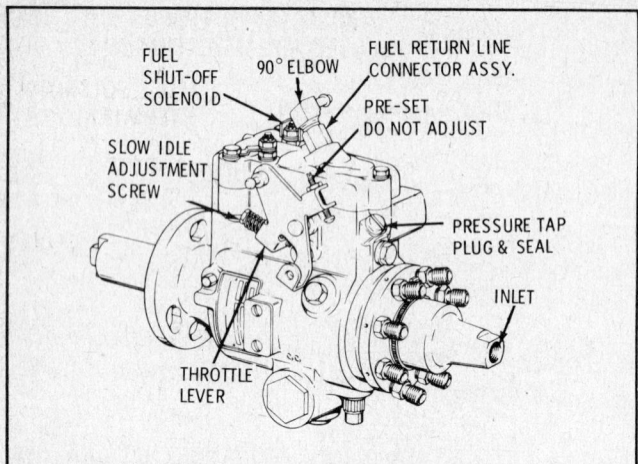

V8 injection pump slow idle screw

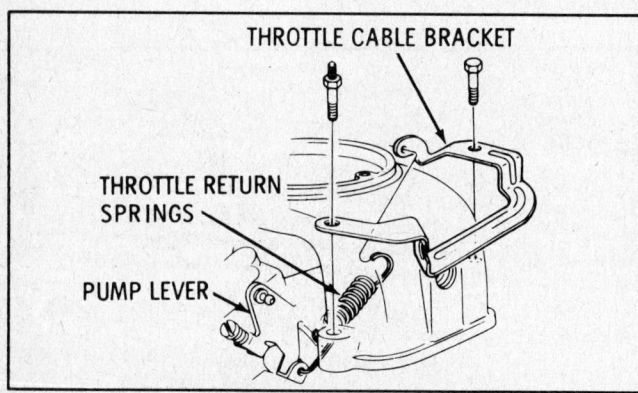

V8 throttle return spring installation

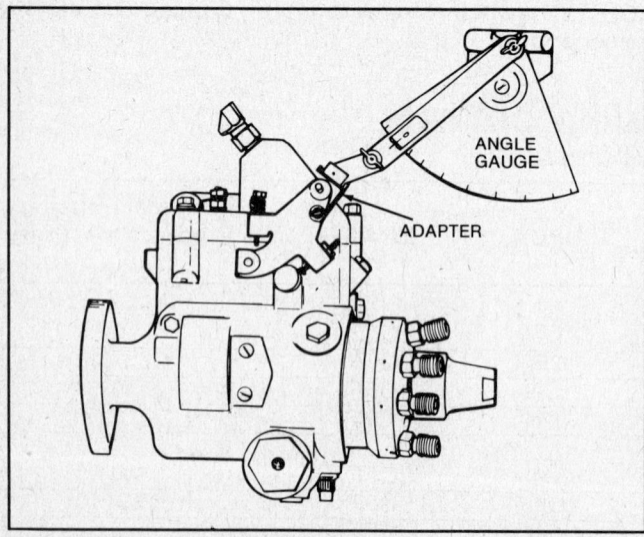

Vacuum valve adjustment at wide open throttle position — engine not running

IDLE SPEED

NOTE: **Perform throttle rod adjustment first, if required.**

Slow Idle Adjustment

1. Run the engine until it reaches normal operating temperature.
2. Insert the probe of a magnetic pickup tachometer into the timing indictor hole.
3. Set the parking brake and block the drive wheels.
4. Place the transmission in Drive and turn the A/C off (if so equipped).
5. Turn the slow idle adjustment screw on the injection pump to obtain the idle speed specification on the emission control label.

Fast Idle Solenoid Adjustment

1. Set the parking brake and block the drive wheels.
2. Run the engine until it reaches normal operating temperature.
3. Place the transmission in Drive and disconnect the two lead connectors at the alternator.
4. Disconnect the connector from the EGR-TVS and install a jumper between the terminal of the connector.
5. Adjust the fast idle solenoid plunger to obtain the specified rpm.
6. Complete assembly and re-connect wiring connectors.

THROTTLE ROD

Adjustment

1. Check timing.
2. Remove the clip from the cruise control rod (if so equipped) and disconnect the rod from the throttle lever assembly.
3. Disconnect the detent cable from the throttle assembly.
4. Loosen the lock nut on the pump rod and shorten it several turns.
5. Rotate the lever assembly to the full throttle position and hold it there.
6. Lengthen the pump rod until the injection pump lever just contacts the full throttle stop.
7. Release the lever assembly and tighten the pump rod lock nut.
8. Remove the pump rod from the lever assembly and reconnect the detent cable.

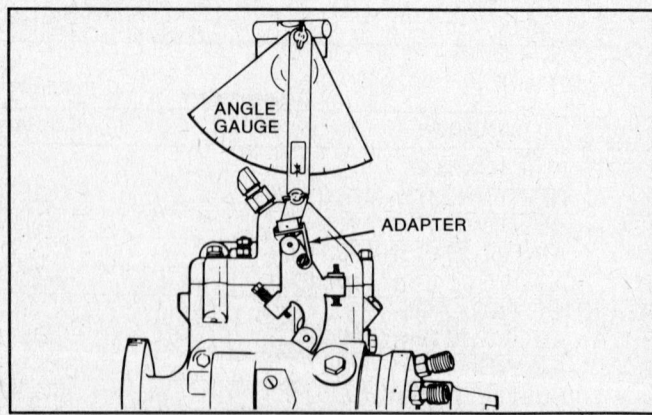

Using an angle gauge to adjust the vacuum regulator valve

27-50

DIESEL ENGINES
GM 5.7L, 350 CU. IN. V8
SECTION 27

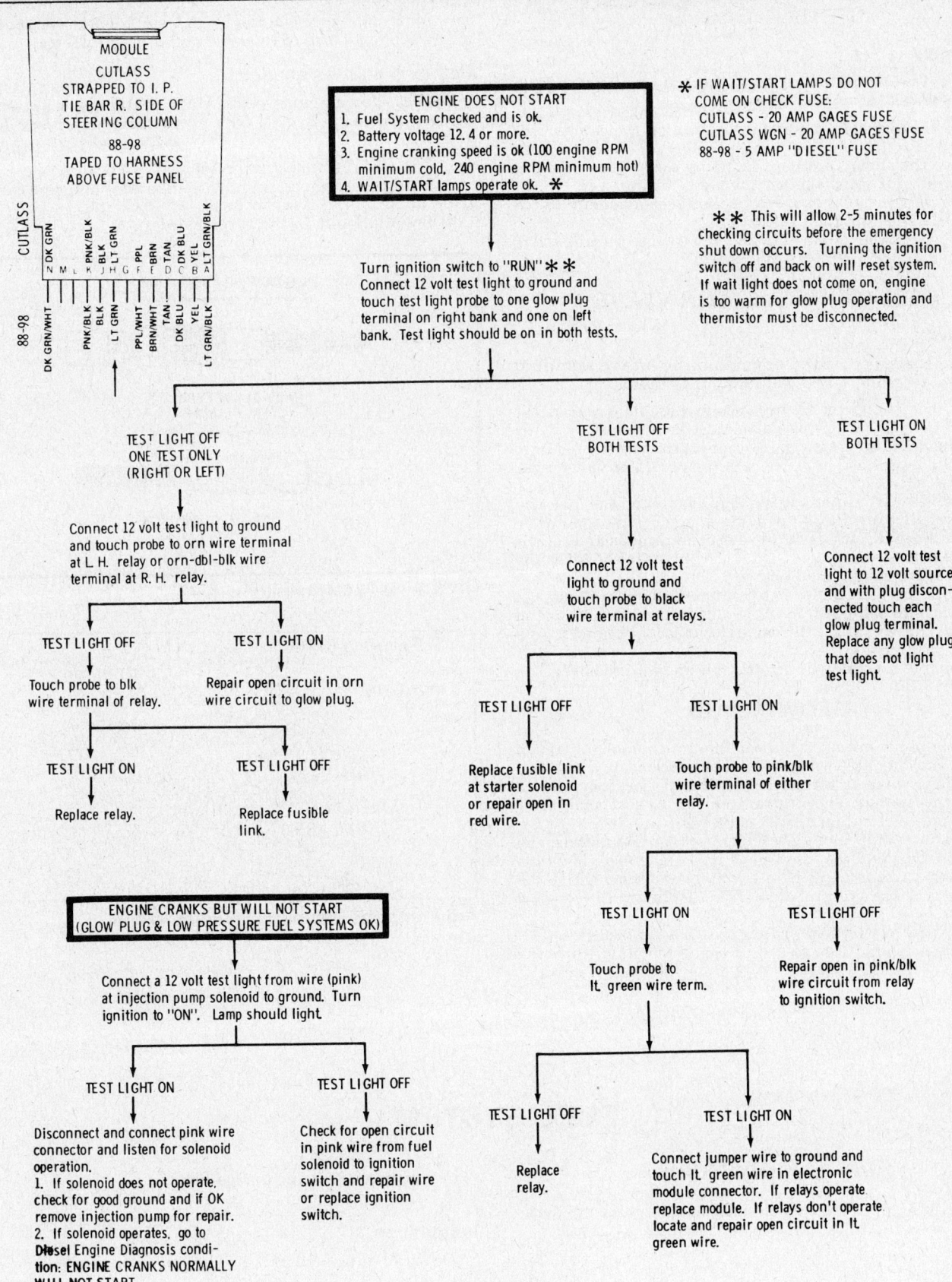

12 volt diesel glow plug diagnostic chart

27-51

SECTION 27: DIESEL ENGINES
GM 5.7L, 350 CU. IN. V8

DETENT CABLE

Adjustment

NOTE: The throttle rod must be adjusted before adjusting the detent cable.

1. Depress and hold the metal lock tab on the cable upper end.
2. Move the slider through the fitting away from the lever assembly until it stops against the metal fitting.
3. Release the metal tab, rotate the lever assembly to the full throttle stop and then release it.
4. Reconnect the pump rod and the cruise control rod if necessary.

VACUUM REGULATOR VALVE

Adjustment

NOTE: Install screened covers on the intake manifold openings. Remove when adjustment is done.

1. Note the location of the two vacuum hoses and remove the valve. (When installing, the valve must be adjusted).
2. Remove the air crossover, disconnect the throttle rod from the throttle lever and loosen the vacuum regulator valve injection pump bolts.
3. Place the carburetor angle gauge adapter on the injection pump throttle lever. Place the angle gauge on the adapter.
4. Rotate the throttle lever to wide open throttle and set the angle gauge to zero degrees. Center the bubble in the level and reset the angle gauge to 58 degrees.
5. Rotate the throttle lever to center the bubble. Apply an outside vacuum source of 18–22 inches to the inboard port of the vacuum valve. Rotate the valve clockwise to obtain 10.6 ± 3 inches of vacuum.
6. Complete assembly of throttle rod and air crossover.

GLOW PLUGS

Eight glow plugs are used to heat the pre-chamber to aid in starting. They are essentially small heaters that turn on when the ignition switch is turned to the "RUN" position prior to starting the engine. They remain on for a short time after starting and then automatically shut off.

There are two types of glow plugs used on GM diesels; the "fast-glow" type and the "slow-glow" type. The fast-glow type use pulsing current applied to 6 volt glow plugs, while the slow-glow type use a continuous current applied to 12 volt glow plugs.

An easy way to tell the plugs apart is that the fast-glow (6V) plugs have a 5/16 in. wide electrical connector plug, while the slow glow (12V) connector is 1/4 in. wide. Do not attempt to interchange any parts of these two glow plug systems.

Removal and Installation

NOTE: Use extreme care when removing a glow plug as the tip may break off; requiring cylinder head removal.

1. Tag and disconnect the electrical connectors.
2. Using the large hex nut, loosen the glow plug and carefully lift it out of the cylinder head.
3. Installation is in the reverse order.

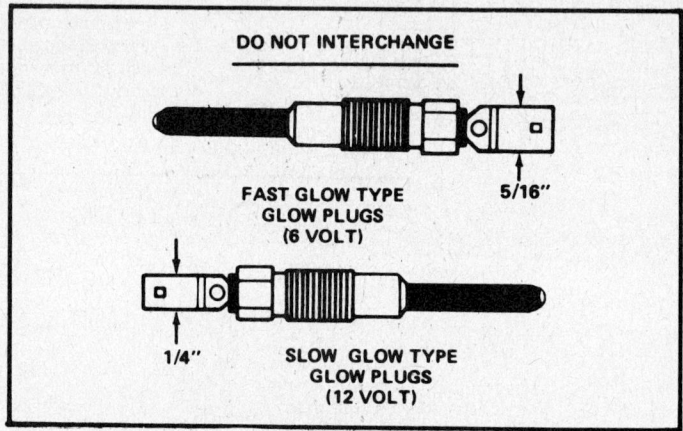

Glow plug system identification

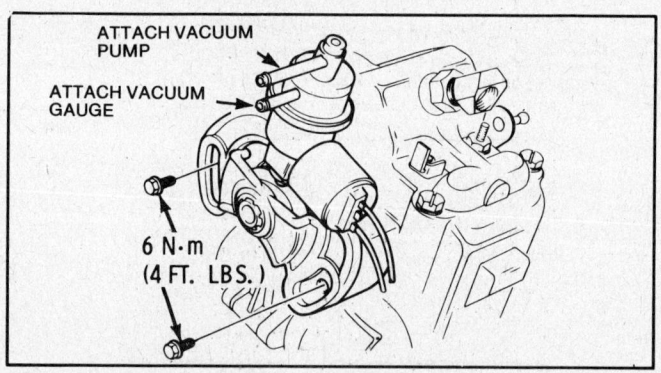

Adjusting the vacuum regulator valve

FUEL SYSTEM

Fuel Supply Pump

The 350 (V8) engines use a small, mechanical fuel pump to deliver fuel from the lines to the injection pump.

Removal

1. Disconnect and plug the two fuel lines. Disconnect the vapor return hose (if so equipped).
2. Remove the two mounting bolts.
3. Remove the pump and gasket.

Installation

1. Install pump and gasket. Tighten mounting bolts to 27 ft. lbs.
2. Install both fuel lines and the vapor return hose.
3. Start engine and check for leaks.

DIESEL ENGINES
GM 5.7L, 350 CU. IN. V8
SECTION 27

Fuel Filter

Removal and Installation

The fuel filter is a square assembly located at the back of the engine, above the intake manifold. Disconnect the fuel lines, remove the mounting bolt and remove the filter. Install a new filter in the reverse.

Injection Pump

Removal

1. Remove the air cleaner.
2. Remove the filters and pipes from the valve covers and air crossover.
3. Remove the air crossover and cap the intake manifold with screened covers.
4. Disconnect the throttle rod and return spring.
5. Remove the bellcrank. Remove the crankcase depression regulator valve.
6. Remove the throttle and detent cables from the intake manifold brackets.
7. Disconnect the fuel lines from the filter and remove the filter.
8. Disconnect the fuel inlet line at the pump.
9. Remove the fuel line retaining clips.
10. Disconnect the fuel return line from the injection pump.
11. Remove the clamps and pull the fuel return lines from each injection nozzle.
12. Using two wrenches, disconnect the high pressure lines at the nozzles.
13. Remove the three injection pump retaining nuts.
14. Remove the pump and cap all lines and nozzle.

Installation

1. Remove the protective caps from all lines and nozzles. Place the engine on TDC for the No. 1 cylinder. The mark on the harmonic balancer on the crankshaft will be aligned with the zero mark on the timing tab, and both valves for No. 1 cylinder will be closed. The index mark on the injection pump driven gear should be offset to the right when No. 1 is at TDC. Check that all of these conditions are met before continuing.
2. Line up the offset tang on the pump driveshaft with the pump driven gear and install the pump, using a new O-ring.
3. Install, but do not tighten the pump retaining nuts.
4. Connect the high pressure lines at the nozzles.
5. Using two wrenches, torque the high pressure line nuts to 25 ft. lbs.
6. Connect the fuel return lines to the nozzle and pump.
7. Align the timing mark on the injection pump with the line on the pump adaptor and torque the mounting nuts to 18 ft. lbs. (24 Nm).

NOTE: A one in. open end wrench on the boss at the front of the injection pump will aid in rotating the pump to align the marks.

8. Adjust the throttle rod.
9. Install the fuel inlet line between the transfer pump and the filter.
10. Install the crankcase depression regulator valve.
11. Install the bellcrank and clip.
12. Connect the throttle rod and return spring.
13. Adjust the transmission cable.
14. Start the engine and check for fuel leaks.
15. Remove the screened covers and install the air crossover.
16. Install the tubes in the airflow control valve in the air crossover and install the ventilation filters in the valve covers.
17. Install the air cleaner.
18. Start the engine and allow it to run for two minutes. Stop the engine, let it stand for two minutes, then restart. This permits the air to bleed of within the pump.

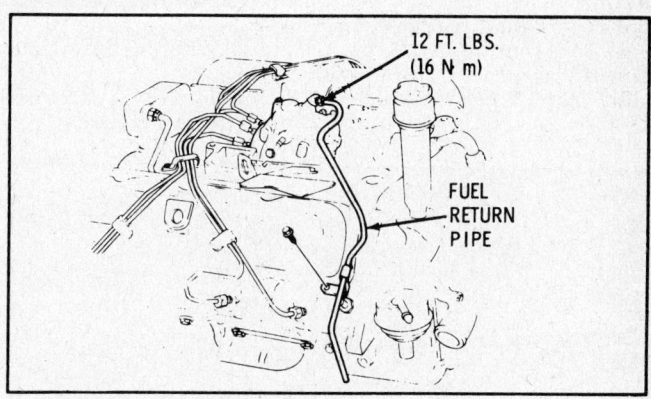

V8 engine—fuel return line

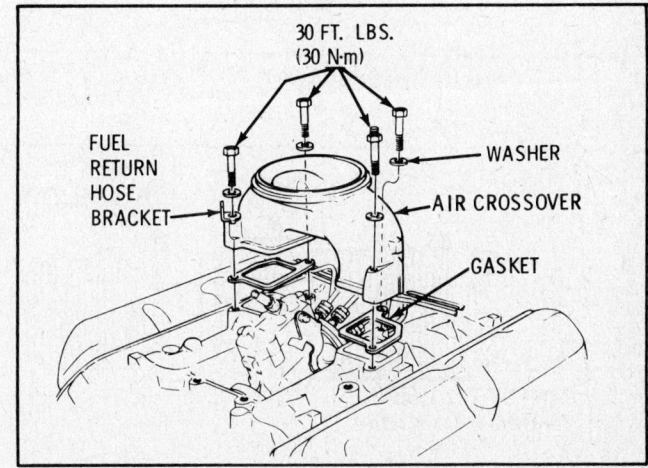

V8 engine—air crossover removal and installation

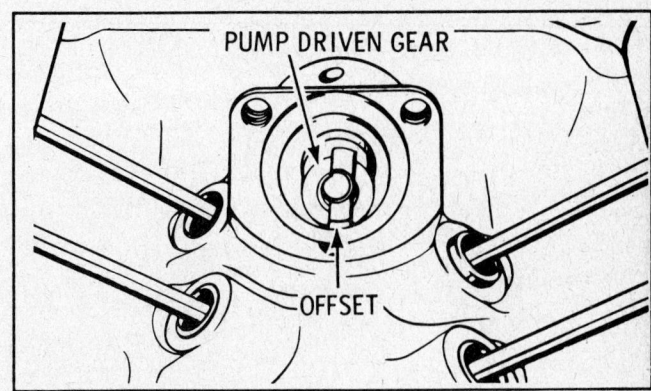

Align offset on the pump drive shaft with the offset on the pump driven gear

27-53

SECTION 27

DIESEL ENGINES
GM 5.7L, 350 CU. IN. V8

Injectors

Removal and Installation

The injectors on these engines are simply unscrewed from the cylinder head, after the fuel lines have been removed, much like a spark plug. Be careful not to damage the injector tip and make sure that the copper gasket is removed from the cylinder head if it does not come off with the injector.

1. Clean the carbon build-up from the tip of the injector with a soft brass wire brush. Installation is in the reverse.

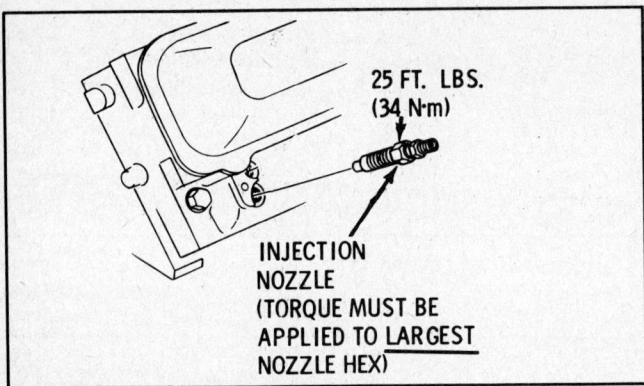

V8 engine — nozzle installation

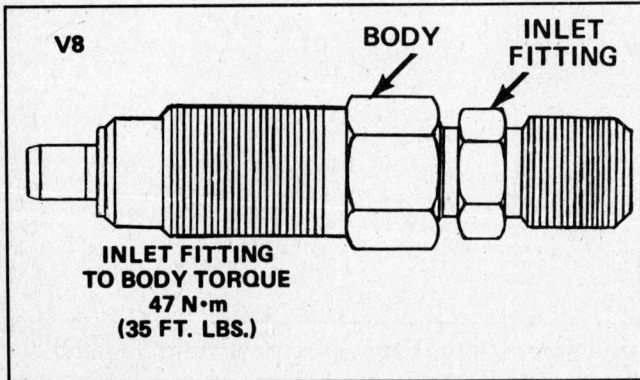

V8 diesel injection nozzle

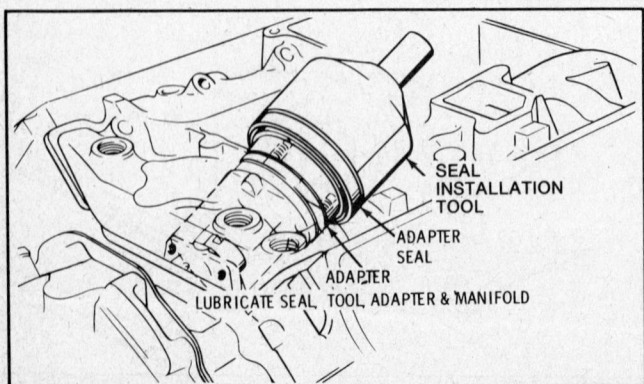

Using special tool to install the adaptor-to-manifold seal

2. Torque injectors to 25 ft. lbs. (34 Nm).
3. To identify the V8 injectors, a blue color band is used. To verify, a part number 404 is also used.

Injection Pump Fuel Lines

When any fuel lines are to be removed, clean all the fittings before loosening. Immediately cap all lines, nozzles and fittings to maintain system cleanliness.

Removal and Installation

All lines may be removed without removing the injection pump. No back-up wrench is necessary when removing a line from the pump fitting.

1. Remove the air cleaner.
2. Disconnect and remove all filters and pipes from the valve covers and the air crossover.
3. Remove the air crossover and cap the openings with screened covers or tape.
4. Remove the injection pump line clamps. Cap all open lines, nozzles or fittings. Use a back-up wrench on the upper hex nut of the injector to prevent a fuel leak.
5. Loosely install the new fuel lines. Check that routing is correct and then tighten the pump end to 35 ft. lbs., and the nozzle end to 25 ft. lbs. Use a back-up wrench on the upper hex nut of the injector to prevent nozzle damage.

NOTE: If more than one line is being replaced, always start with the bottom line.

6. Install the clamps. Installation of remaining components is the reverse.
7. Start the engine and check for leaks.

Shut Down Problems

ENGINE CONTINUES TO RUN WITH IGNITION OFF

1. With ignition turned off, and engine still running, disconnect connector at diode unit on the firewall. If engine stops, diode C is shorted. Replace the diode unit.
2. If engine continues to run, disconnect pink wire connector at fuel solenoid in fuel injection pump. If engine still continues

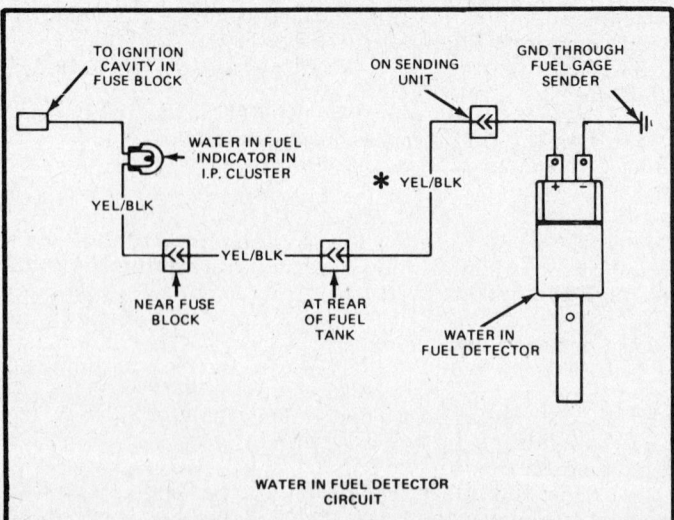

Diagram of water-in-fuel detector circuit

27-54

DIESEL ENGINES
GM 5.7L, 350 CU. IN. V8
SECTION 27

to run, stop engine by crimping flexible fuel return line near fuel supply pump (lower right front of engine). Then repair or replace fuel solenoid.

Water In Fuel (WIF) System

The WIF system consists of a revised fuel tank sending unit and a warning lamp on the dash panel which lights when there is water in the fuel tank. The sending unit consists of the following.
1. An electronic water detector mounted close to the bottom of the fuel tank.
2. A water separator filter.
3. A rubber hose extension on the fuel return line that allows fuel tank draining without removing the tank.
4. A new fuel tank wiring harness.

Draining WIF—Equipped Fuel Tanks

1. Connect a siphon pump to the ¼ in. fuel return hose located above the rear axle or at the fuel pump under the hood. Continue siphoning until pure diesel fuel begins to drain.

CAUTION
Remove the fuel filler cap before draining the tank.

Bench Testing the WIF Unit

1. Submerge the water sensing probe into a container of water and connect to a 12 volt source. Be sure to ground the water.
2. Connect a 12 volt, 2 candle power bulb into the positive wire. The bulb should light until the probe is removed from the water.

ISUZU DIESEL ENGINE (CHEVETTE) 4 CYLINDER — 111 CU. IN. — 1.8 LITRE

GENERAL ENGINE SPECIFICATIONS

Year	Eng. V.I.N. Code	Engine No. Cyl. Displacement liters (cu. in.)	Mfg.	Carburetor Type	Horsepower @ rmp ①	Torque @ rpm (ft. lbs.) ①	Bore × Stroke (in.)	Compression Ratio	Oil Pressure @ 2000 rpm
'83–'87	D	4–1.8(111)	Isuzu	Fuel Injection	51 @ 5000	72 @ 2000	3.310 × 3.230	22.0:1	64 ②

① Horsepower and torque are SAE net figures. They are measured at the rear of the transmission with all accessories installed and operating. Since the figures vary when a given engine is installed in different models, some are representative rather than exact.
② @ 5000

DIESEL TUNE-UP SPECIFICATIONS

Year	Engine No. Cyl. Displacement (liters)	Static Injection Timing	Fuel Injection Order	Compression (lbs.)	Injection Nozzle Opening Pressure (psi)	Intake Valve Opens (deg)	Idle Speed ① (rpm) Man.	Auto.
'83–'87	L4(1.8)	11°B	1-3-4-2	441 ②	1707	32	625	720

NOTE: The underhood specifications sticker often reflects changes made in production. Sticker figures must be used if they disagree with those in the above chart.
① See underhood sticker for fast idle speed.
② At 200 rpm

ENGINE FIRING ORDER

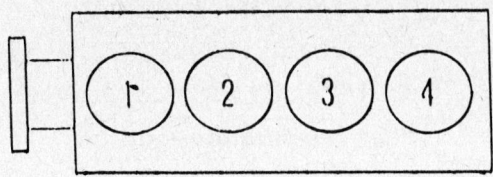

Engine firing order: 1-3-4-2

SECTION 27 — DIESEL ENGINES
ISUZU 1.8L, 111 CU. IN. FOUR CYLINDER

VALVE SPECIFICATIONS

Year	Engine No. Cyl. Displacement (liters)	Seat Angle (deg)	Face Angle (deg)	Spring Test Pressure (lbs. @ in.)	Spring Installed Height (in.)	Stem-to-Guide Clearance (in.)		Stem Diameter (in.)	
						Intake	Exhaust	Intake	Exhaust
'83–'87	4-1.8 Diesel	45	45	108 @ 1.24 ①	1.61	.0015–.0028	.0018–.0030	.3128–.3134	.3126–.3132

① Exhaust 112 @ 1.22; inner spring test pressures—intake 58 @ 1.14 exhaust 60 @ 1.12

CRANKSHAFT AND CONNECTING ROD SPECIFICATIONS
All measurements are given in inches

Year	Engine No. Cyl. Displacement (liters)	Crankshaft				Connecting Rod		
		Main Brg. Journal Dia	Main Brg. Oil Clearance	Shaft End-Play	Thrust on No.	Journal Diameter	Oil Clearance	Side Clearance
'83–'87	4-1.8 Diesel	2.2010–2.2020	.0015–.0027	.0024–.0094	3	1.927–1.928	.0016–.0032	N.A.

N.A.—Not Applicable

PISTON AND RING SPECIFICATIONS
All measurements are given in inches

Year	Engine Type/Disp. (liters)	Piston-to-Bore Clearance	Ring Gap			Ring Side Clearance		
			Top Compression	Bottom Compression	Oil Control	Top Compression	Bottom Compression	Oil Control
'83–'87	4-1.8 Diesel	.0002–.0017	.0078–.0157	.0078–.0157	.0078–.0157	.0035–.0049	.0019–.0033	.0012–.0028

TORQUE SPECIFICATIONS
All readings in ft. lbs.

Year	Engine No. Cyl. Displacement (liters)	Cylinder Head Bolts	Rod Bearing Bolts	Main Bearing Bolts	Crankshaft Pulley Bolt	Flywheel-to-Crankshaft Bolts	Manifold	
							Intake	Exhaust
'83–'87	4-1.8 Diesel	①	65	75	N/A	N/A	30	N/A

N/A Not available
① First tighten to 21–36 ft. lbs. then retighten to 83–98 (new bolt), 90–105 (reused bolt)

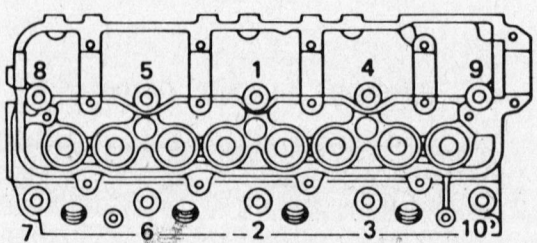

Head bolt torque sequence

DIESEL ENGINES
ISUZU 1.8L, 111 CU. IN. FOUR CYLINDER
SECTION 27

On Vehicle Service

COMPRESSION TEST

1. Start the engine and bring engine to operating temperature (75°–80°C).
2. Remove the sensing resistor, the glow plug connector, 4 glow plugs and the fuel cut solenoid connector.
3. Install special tool adaptor J–26999–20 and J–26–999 or equivalent compression test equipment.
4. Crank the engine and take the compression reading. The standard compression reading should be 441.0 psi (31.0 kg.cm) and the lower limit of not less than 370 psi (26.9 kg.cm.).

VALVE ADJUSTMENT

1. Check the rocker arm shaft bracket bolts and nuts for looseness and torque to 20 ft. lbs. (27.0 Nm) before adjusting valves.
2. Rotate crankshaft until No. 1 or No. 4 cylinder piston is at TDC on the compression stroke.
3. For each valve, insert a feeler gauge of the specified thickness into the clearance between the valve stem end and the rocker arm; adjust as required.
4. Rotate the crankshaft one revolution (360°) and adjust the remaining valves.

INJECTION TIMING

1. Bring the No. 1 piston to TDC of the compression stroke.
2. With the upper timing belt cover removed, check for proper timing belt tension and valve timing mark alignment.
3. With the cam cover removed, check that the fixing plate fits smoothly into the slot at the rear of the camshaft, then remove the fixing plate.
4. With the injection lines removed, remove the distributor head screw and washer.
5. Install the static timing gauge, set left approximately 0.04 in. (1mm) from the plunger.
6. Bring the piston in cylinder to a point 45°–60° before TDC by turning the crankshaft, then calibrate the dial indicator to zero.

NOTE: The damper pulley is provided with notched lines. The damper pulley is provided with a total of 11 notch lines, (4 lines at one side 7 lines at another area). The 4 lines are used for static timing.

7. Turn the crankshaft until the line (18°) on the damper pulley is brought into alignment with the pointer, then take reading of the dial indicator. Standard reading 0.5mm (0.02 in.). Turn the crankshaft in normal direction of rotation.
8. If the reading of the dial indicator deviates from the specified range, hold the crankshaft in position 18° before TDC and loosen two nuts on injection pump flange. Move the injection pump to a point where the dial indicator gives reading of 0.02 in. (0.5mm), then tighten pump flange nuts.

CYLINDER NO.	1		2		3		4	
VALVES	I	E	I	E	I	E	I	E
STEP. 1	○	○	○			○		
STEP. 2				◎	◎		◎	◎

I : INTAKE VALVE
E : EXHAUST VALVE

Valve adjustment chart

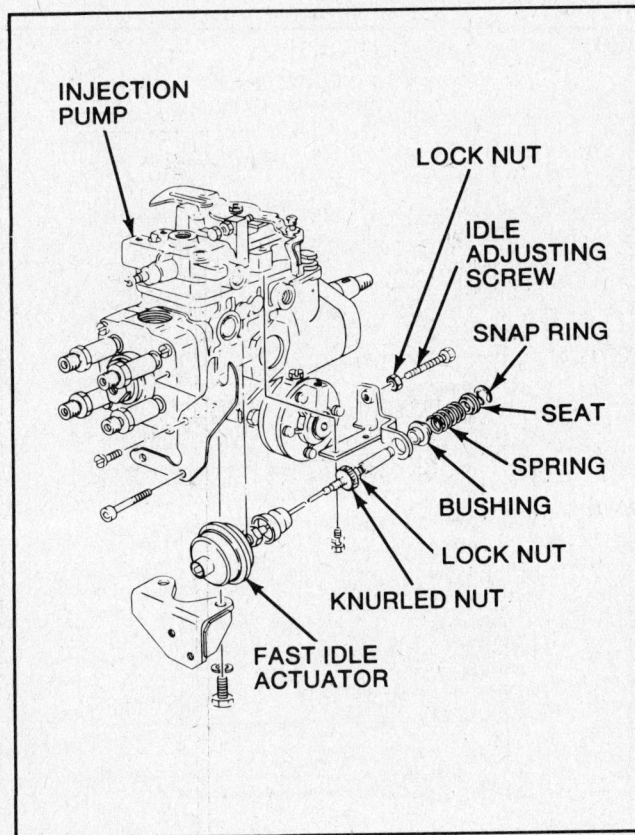

Base idle screw and fast idle adjuster (knurled nut)

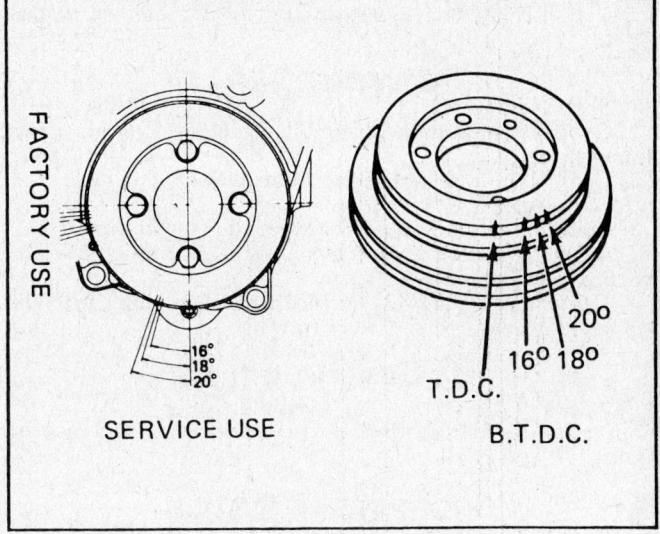

Factory use and service damper pulley timing notches

SECTION 27: DIESEL ENGINES
ISUZU 1.8L, 111 CU. IN. FOUR CYLINDER

9. Recheck dial indicator reading and readjust as necessary.
10. Install the distributor screw and washer into injection pump.
11. Install cam cover.

GOVERNOR ADJUSTMENT

The governor on Isuzu-Kiki injector pumps automatically controls engine speed and is not adjustable.

IDLE SPEEDS

Base Idle Adjustment

NOTE: Adjust idle speeds with engine at normal operating temperature and air cleaner installed.

1. Set parking brake and block drive wheels.
2. Place transmission in neutral.
3. Connect tachometer.
4. Start engine and allow to run until it reaches normal operating temperature.
5. Loosen lock nut on idle speed adjusting screw.
6. Turn adjusting to obtain speed specification on emission label.
7. Tighten lock nut.
8. Stop engine and disconnect tach.

Fast Idle Adjustment

1. Set parking brake and block drive wheels.
2. Place transmission in neutral.
3. Connect a tachometer.
4. Start the engine and allow it to run until it reaches normal operating temperature.
5. Apply vacuum to the fast idle actuator.
6. Loosen the lock nut on the fast idle adjusting screw.
7. Adjust the knurled nut to obtain the rpm specified on emission label.
8. Tighten the lock nut.
9. Stop the engine and disconnect the tachometer.

Glow Plug System

The Quick On System (QOS) provides electronically controlled cold starting, and the electronic module monitors and corrects combustion chamber temperature during the preheat mode.

CONTROLLER

1. Controls rapid preheat circuit up to 900°C of glow plug temperature.
2. Controls glow plug preheat indicator lamp during preheat cycle (3.5 sec.).
3. Monitors the difference between the sensing resistance and glow plug resistance as a means of determining glow plug heating requirements.
4. Control glow plug relay according to changing the engine coolant temperature.

GLOW PLUG RELAY

Main relay for rapid preheat cycle and stabilized heating circuit.

DROPPING RESISTOR

Fixed value resistor used to drop (lower) the voltage of the glow plugs during stabilized heating.

SENSING RESISTOR

Shunt type resistance used in series with the glow plugs causing a small voltage drop which is monitored by the controller.

GLOW PLUGS

Fast glow type (fast warm up).

THERMO SWITCH

The thermo switch should close at engine coolant temperature above 122°F (50°C) and provide ground to the controller circuitry.

GLOW PLUG RELAYS

The 2 glow plug relays provide stabilizing heating during diesel engine starting.

FUSIBLE LINKS

Two fusible links protect the glow plug circuit wiring from electrical overloads.

The glow plug system is designed to provide a fast chamber preheat if the temperature at the thermo switch is less than 122°F (50°C). Under these conditions, relay No. 1 is energized and the glow plugs indicator lamp is illuminated for a period of 3.5 seconds or more, after which time the indicator lamp goes out. Chamber preheat temperatures are a a level which permits starting the engine. At temperatures above 122°F (50°C), relay No. 1 is inoperative and relay No. 2 turns on and provides stabilizing heat during starting.

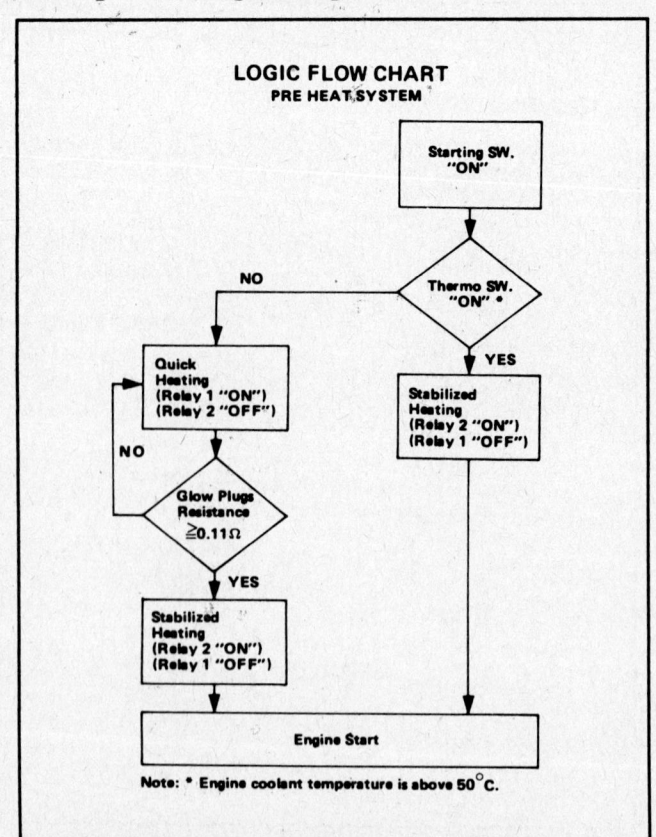

QOS glow plug system operational diagram

DIESEL ENGINES
ISUZU 1.8L, 111 CU. IN. FOUR CYLINDER
SECTION 27

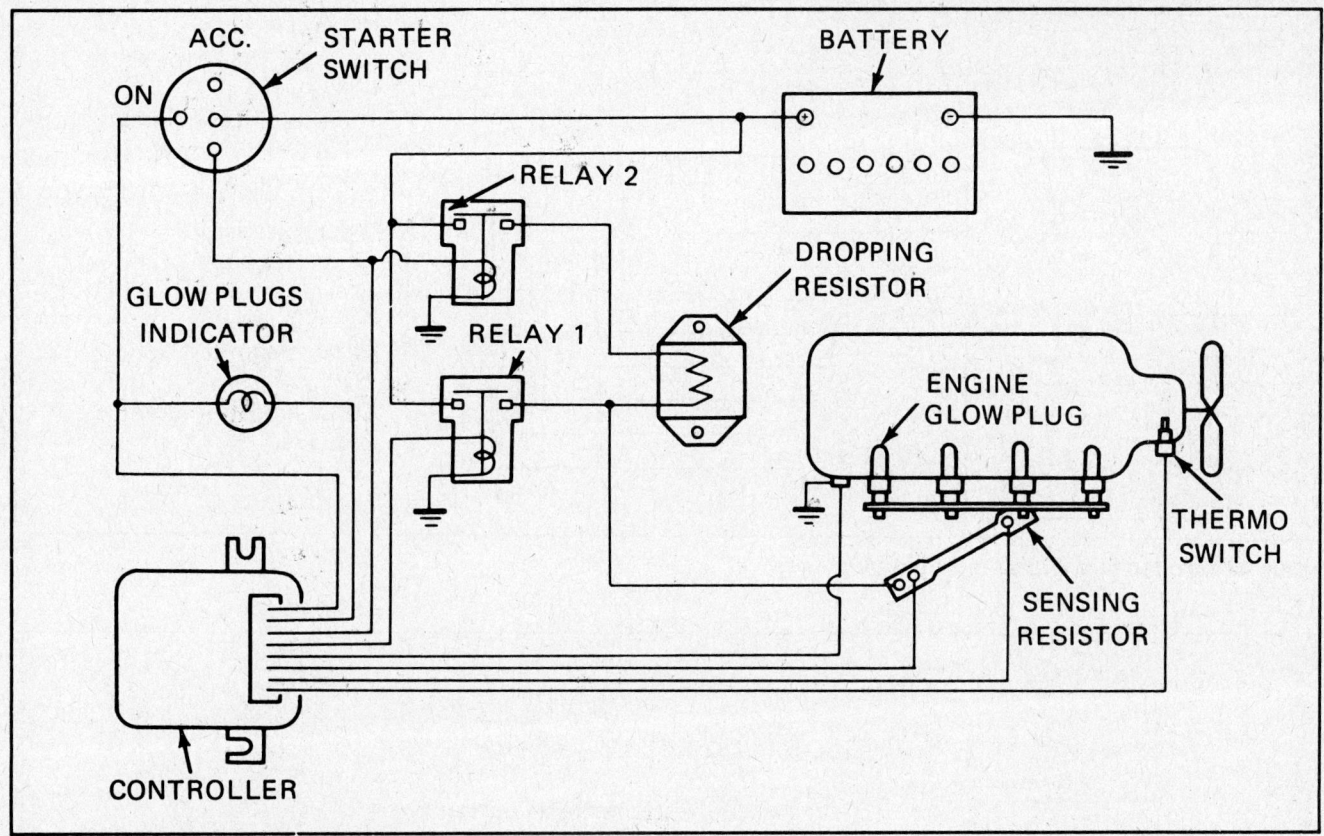

QOS glow system electrical diagram

Diagnosis

Check the system with the ignition "ON" and the engine cold (below 122°F).

1. Disconnect the thermo switch connector from the thermo switch on the thermostat outlet pipe.
2. If glow plug relay No. 1 makes a clicking noise within 5–9 seconds after the starter switch is turned on, normal operation of the quick on system is indicated.
3. With the ignition switch on, measure the glow terminal voltage from the glow plug to ground.

NOTE: The voltage at the ground plugs must read between 8 and 9 volts.

FUEL FILTER ELEMENT

Replacement

1. Disconnect the negative battery cable.
2. Disconnect the water sensor wiring at connector.
3. Disconnect the water sensor to main body hose.
4. Remove the filter element by turning clockwise, using filter wrench J–22700 or equivalent, being careful not to spill fuel from element.
5. Drain the fuel from filter element into a suitable container.
6. Remove the water sensor from bottom of old filter element.
7. Apply a thin film of diesel fuel to the water sensor "O" ring.
8. Install the water sensor on bottom of new filter and tighten.
9. Wipe the filter body sealing surface clean.
10. Apply a thin film of diesel fuel to gasket on new filter element.
11. Install the filter element and turn clockwise until gasket on element contacts sealing surface on main body.
12. Continue turning an additional $\frac{2}{3}$ of a turn after the element contacts sealing surface.
13. Connect the water sensor wiring.
14. Disconnect the fuel outlet hose from injector pump and place in a suitable container.
15. Fill the filter with fuel by operating the priming pump handle several times.
16. Reconnect fuel outlet hose to injector pump.
17. Start engine and check for leaks.

WATER SEPARATOR

Draining

1. Place a 2 liter (4 pint) container at the end of the vinyl hose beneath the drain plug on the water separator.
2. Open the drain plug approximately 4 turns.
3. Operate the priming pump handle up and down about ten times or until all water is drained.
4. Close drain plug and again operate pump handle up and down several times.
5. Start the engine and check for fuel leaks and that "Water in Fuel" indicator light has turned off.

Purging Fuel Tank

1. Remove fuel tank cap.
2. Disconnect fuel return hose from injector pump.
3. Connect a pump or siphon hose at the fuel return hose.

27-59

SECTION 27
DIESEL ENGINES
ISUZU 1.8L, 111 CU. IN. FOUR CYLINDER

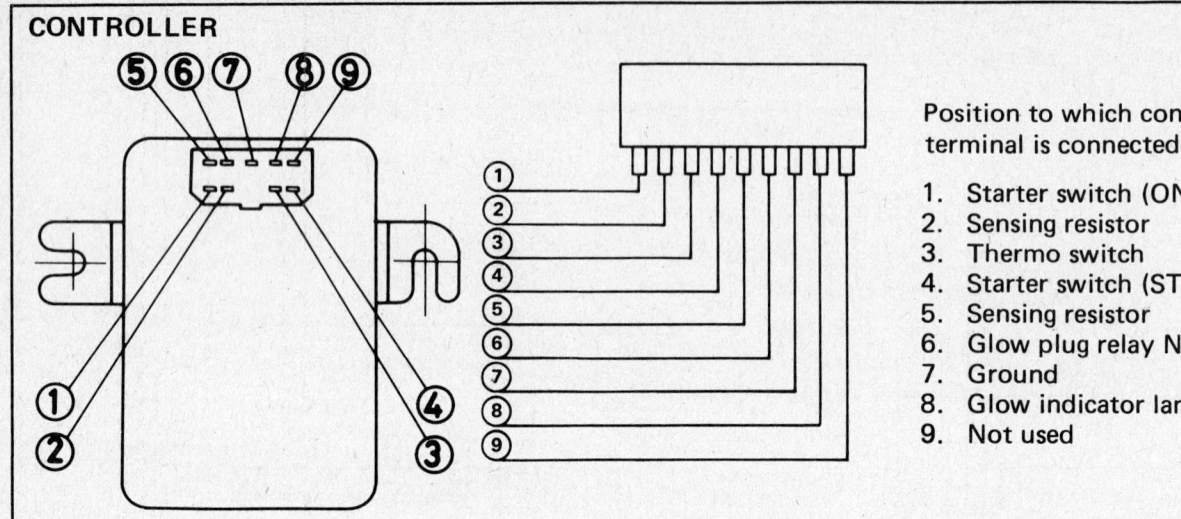

CONTROLLER

Position to which connector terminal is connected

1. Starter switch (ON position)
2. Sensing resistor
3. Thermo switch
4. Starter switch (ST position)
5. Sensing resistor
6. Glow plug relay No. 1
7. Ground
8. Glow indicator lamp
9. Not used

Basic controller terminals — all systems

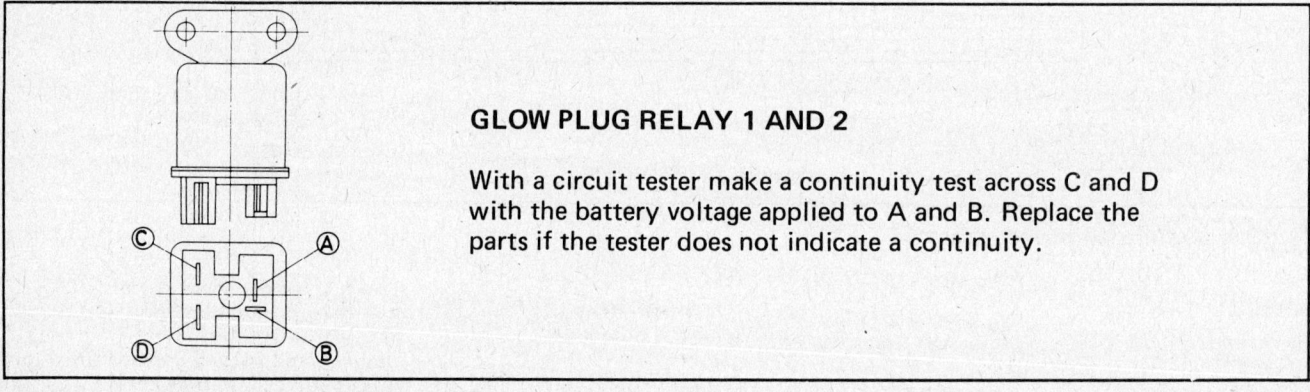

GLOW PLUG RELAY 1 AND 2

With a circuit tester make a continuity test across C and D with the battery voltage applied to A and B. Replace the parts if the tester does not indicate a continuity.

Glow plug relays — all systems

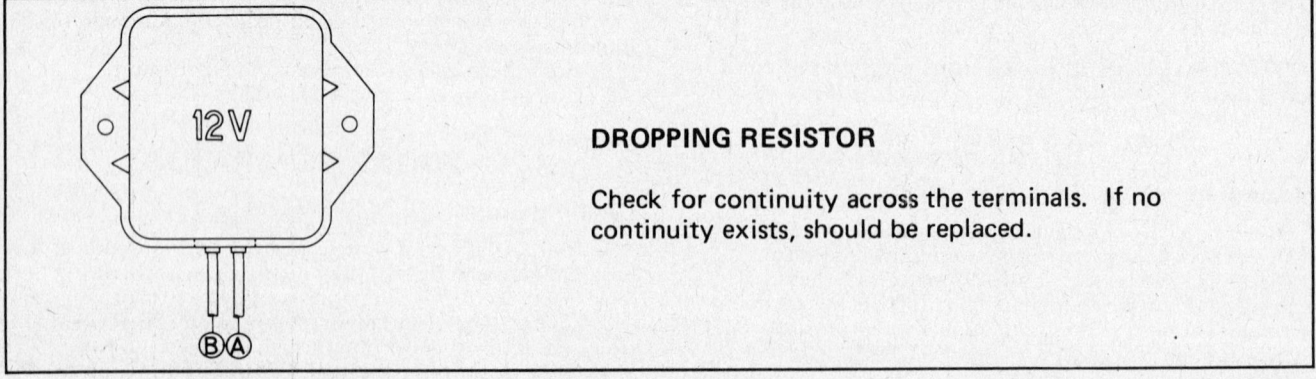

DROPPING RESISTOR

Check for continuity across the terminals. If no continuity exists, should be replaced.

Dropping resister — all systems

27-60

DIESEL ENGINES
ISUZU 1.8L, 111 CU. IN. FOUR CYLINDER
SECTION 27

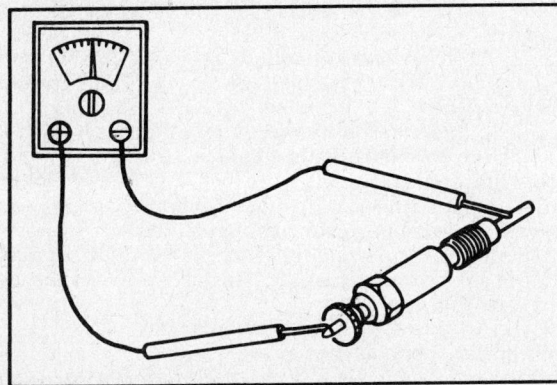

GLOW PLUG

Check for continuity across the plug terminals and body. If no continuity exists, the heater wire is broken and should be replaced.

Glow plug testing—all systems

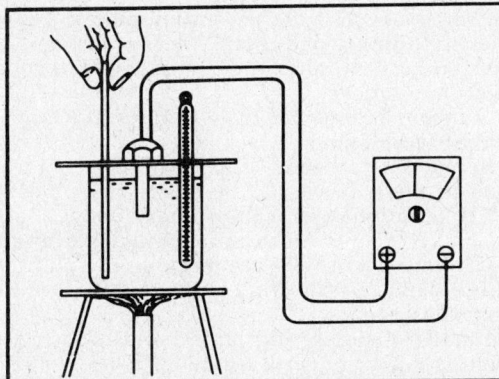

THERMO SWITCH

Submerge the end of the thermo switch in water and raise the temperature of water gradually and make a continuity test across the terminal and body using a circuit tester.

Thermo switch testing—all systems

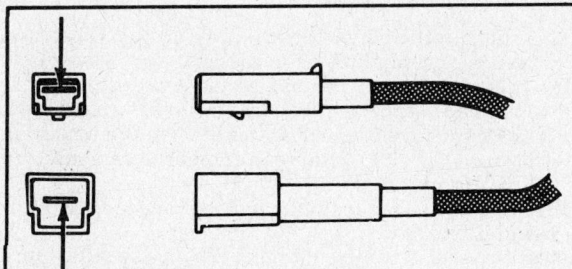

FUSIBLE LINK

Make a continuity test across the fusible link terminals. If the tester does not indicate a continuity, the fusible link has been fused out and should be replaced with a new one.

Fusible link testing—all systems

4. Operate pump or siphon until all water is removed from the fuel tank.
5. Remove pump or siphon and reinstall fuel return hose.
6. Replace fuel tank cap.

INJECTION PUMP AND TIMING BELT
Removal

1. Disconnect battery negative cable.
2. Drain cooling system.
3. Remove fan shroud.
4. Remove radiator.
5. Remove coolant recover bottle.
6. Remove upper dust cover.
7. Loosen tension pulley and plate bolt. Remove tension spring.
8. Remove the nut attaching the pump gear.
9. Remove injection pump gear using tool J–22888.
10. Disconnect necessary wires, hoses and cables. Use care so as not to spill fuel within the fuel hoses.
11. Remove fuel filter at bracket.
12. Remove injector lines at pump and nozzles and remove injector lines.

SECTION 27
DIESEL ENGINES
ISUZU 1.8L, 111 CU. IN. Four Cylinder

13. Remove 4 bolts attaching the pump rear bracket and remove the rear brackets.
14. Remove the nuts attaching the injection pump flange and remove the injection pump together with the fast idle device and return spring.

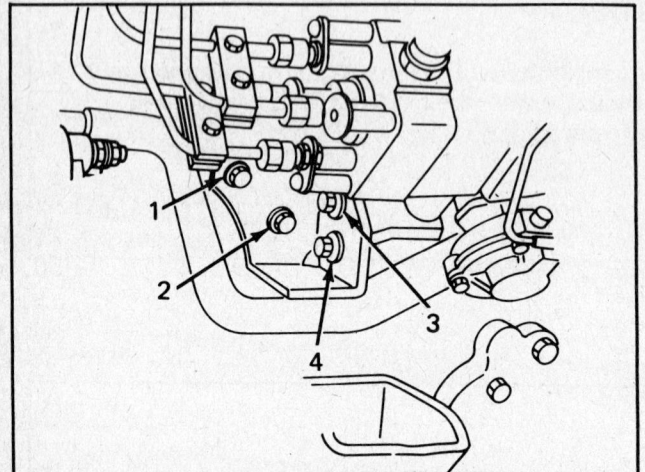

Installation sequence for injection pump rear bracket bolts

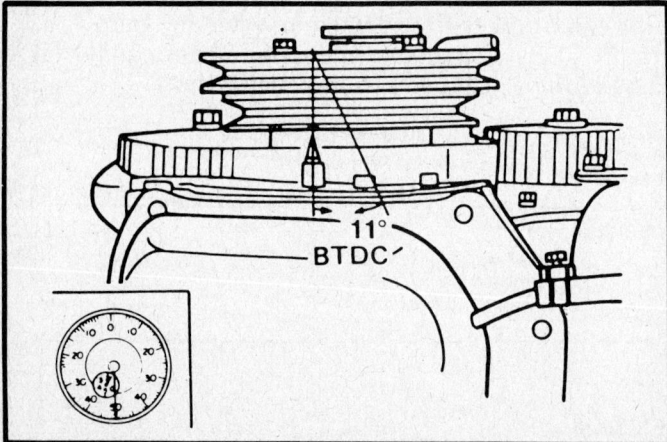

Static timing setting

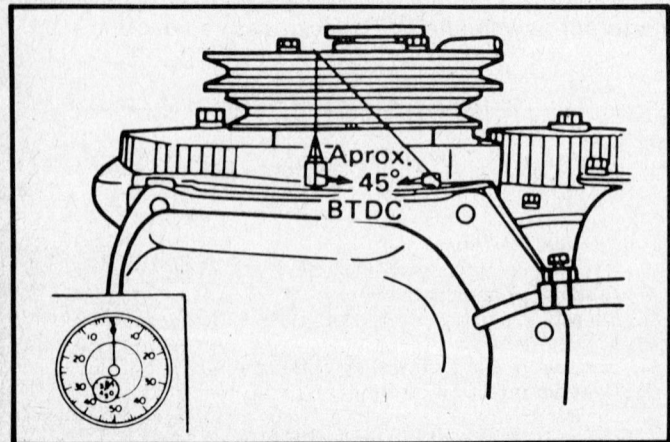

Calibrating the dial inidcator

Installation of Timing Belt

1. Install the injection pump.
2. Tighten the 4 rear bracket bolts in sequence. No clearance should be provided between the rear bracket and injection pump bracket.
3. Install the injection pump pulley by aligning it with the key groove. Align the mark on the gear with the mark on the front plate. Tighten the nut using the lock bolt to prevent turning of pulley, torque nut to 45 ft. lbs. (60 Nm).
4. Remove cam cover as previously outlined.
5. With piston in No. 1 piston TDC, install J-29761 fixing plate to slot in the rear of camshaft. This is to prevent the camshaft from rotating.
6. Remove the bolt attaching camshaft gear.
7. Using puller, remove cam gar.
8. Reinstall cam gear loosely so the gear can be turned smoothly by hand.
9. Install the timing belt with the following noted:
    a. Belt should be properly tensioned between pulleys.
    b. Cogs on belt and pulley should be engaged properly.
    c. Crankshaft should not be turned.
    d. Concentrate belt looseness on tension pulley. Depress tension pulley with finger and install tension spring.
10. Semi-tighten bolts in numerical sequence to prevent movement of tension pulley.
11. Tighten camshaft pulley bolt to 45 ft. lbs. (60 Nm).
12. Remove injection pump gear lock bolt.
13. Remove fixing plate on end of camshaft.
14. Check that piston is in No. 1 TDC position. Do not turn the crankshaft in an attempt to make an adjustment.
15. Check to make certain that the mark on the injection pump pulley is in alignment with the mark on the plate.
16. Fixing plate should fit smoothly into slot at rear of camshaft, then remove the fixing plate.
17. Loosen tensioner pulley and plate bolts. Concentrate looseness of belt on tensioner, then tighten bolts in numerical sequence as shown.
18. Belt tension should be checked at a point between the camshaft gear and the injection pump gear.

Injection Timing Procedure

1. Bring the number 1 piston to TDC or the compression stroke by turning crankshaft as necessary.
2. With the upper cover removed, check the timing belt is properly tensioned and that the timing marks are aligned.
3. With the cam cover removed, check that the fixing plate fits smoothly into the slot at the rear end of the camshaft, then remove the fixing plate.
4. With the injection lines removed, remove the distributor head screw and washer.
5. Install the static timing gauge J-29763, set lift approximately 0.04 in. (1mm) from the plunger.
6. Bring the piston in number 1 cylinder to a point 45-60 degrees before TDC by turning the crankshaft, then calibrate the dial indicator to zero. The damper pulley is provided with notched lines.
The damper pulley is provided wit a total of 11 notch lines, (4 lines at one side 7 lines at another area).The 4 lines re used for static timing.
7. Turn the crankshaft until the line (18°) on the damper pulley is brought into alignment with the pointer, then take reading of the dial indicator. Standard reading 0.02 in. (5mm). Turn the crankshaft in normal direction of rotation.
8. If the reading of the dial indicator deviates from the specified range, hold the crankshaft in position 18° before TDC and loosen two nuts on injection pump flange. Move the injection pump to a point where the dial indicator gives reading of 0.02 in. (5mm), then tighten pump flange nuts.
9. Recheck dial indicator reading and readjust as necessary.

DIESEL ENGINES
ISUZU 1.8L, 111 CU. IN. FOUR CYLINDER
SECTION 27

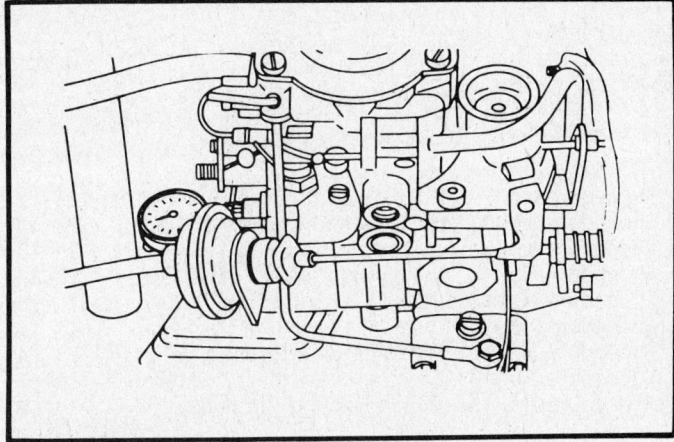

Installation of static timing gauge

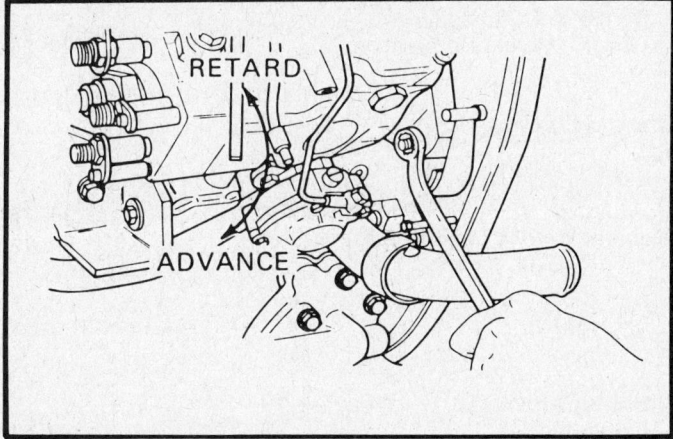

Adjustment of injection pump

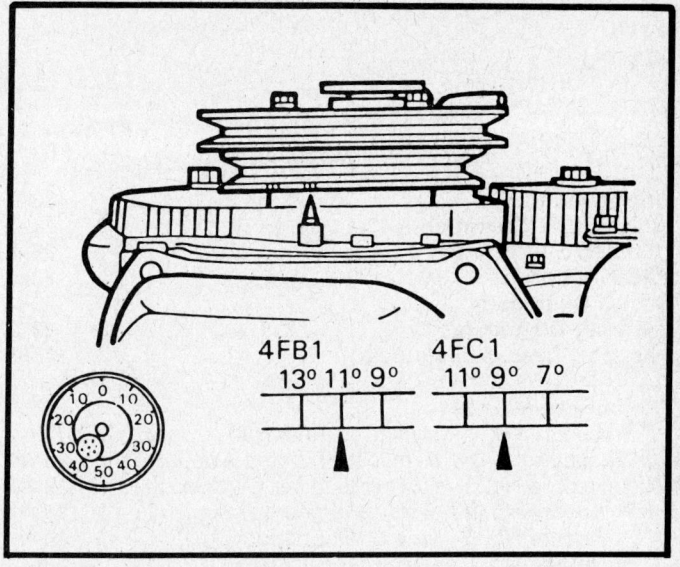

Damper pulley notches for two engine models

10. Install the distributor screw and washer into injection pump.
11. Install cam cover.
12. Install injection lines.
13. Install fuel filter.
14. Connect necessary wires and hoses.
15. Install the upper dust cover.
16. Install coolant recovery bottle.
17. Install radiator.
18. Install fan shroud.
19. Refill coolant.
20. Adjust engine idle speed and fast idle speed as described, and TV cable adjustment.

27-63

SECTION 28 DRIVE AXLES

INDEX

REAR AXLES

Introduction 28–3	Procedure No. 7 – R&R Flanged Axle & Bearing.... 28–11
Differential Operation 28–3	Procedure No. 8 – R&R Pressed On Axle Bearing .. 28–13
Limited Slip Operation 28–3	Procedure No. 9 – Adjust Axle End Play 28–13
Gear Ratios 28–3	Procedure No. 10 – Install Side Gear Seal 28–13
Noise Diagnosis 28–3	Procedure No. 11 – Install Pinion Oil Seal 28–13
Bearing Diagnosis 28–3	Procedure No. 12 – Install Oil Seal In Retainer 28–14
General Trouble Diagnosis 28–8	Procedure No. 13 – Setting Pinion Depth 28–14
	Procedure No. 14 – Ring Gear Backlash, Adjust... 28–17
Repair Procedures	Procedure No. 15 – Pinion Bearing Preload 28–18
Procedure No. 1 – Replacing Rear Hub............. 28–9	
Procedure No. 2 – Remvoing Tapered Axle & Bearing 28–10	**Rear Axle Specifications**
Procedure No. 3 – R&R Axle Outer Oil Seal........ 28–10	American Motors 28–19
Procedure No. 4 – R&R Axle Inner Oil Seal 28–11	Chrysler Corporation 28–23
Procedure No. 5 – Axle Shaft End Play Adjust...... 28–11	Ford Motor Company 28–25
Procedure No. 6 – Pinion Oil Seal R&R............. 28–11	General Motors Corporation........................ 28–28

LIMITED SLIP DIFFERENTIALS

Trouble Diagnosis 28–19	Ford Motor Company Traction-Lok 28–38
American Motors Twin-Grip 28–34	General Motors Limited Slip 28–45
Chrysler Corporation Sure-Grip 28–36	

UNIVERSAL JOINTS

Rear Wheel Drive	**Front Wheel Drive**
Introduction 28–54	Introduction 28–57
Cross and Yoke Type Overhaul 28–55	Attachment of Drive Shaft To Transaxle 28–58
Constant Velocity Type Overhaul 28–56	Boot Replacement 28–60
Noise Diagnosis Chart 28–63	

Drive Axles
U-Joint/CV-Joint

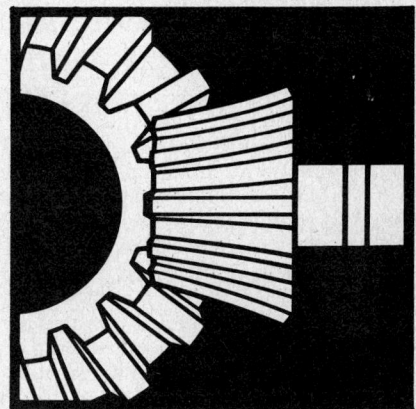

REAR AXLES

Introduction

OPERATION

The drive pinion, which is turned by the driveshaft, turns the ring gear. The ring gear, which is bolted to the differential case, rotates the case. The differential pinion forces the pinion gears against the side gears. In cases where both wheels have equal traction, the pinion gears do not rotate on the pinion shaft, because the input force of the pinion gear is divided equally between the two side gears. Consequently the pinion gears revolve with the pinion shaft, although they do not revolve on the pinion shaft itself. The side gears, which are splined to the axle shafts, and meshed with the pinion gears, rotate the axle shafts.

LIMITED-SLIP DIFFERENTIAL OPERATION

Limited-slip differential provide driving force to the wheel with the best traction before the other wheel begins to spin. This is accomplished through clutch plates or cones. The clutch plates or cones are located between the side gears and inner wall of the differential case. When they are squeezed together through spring tension and outward force from the side gears, three reactions occur. Resistance on the side gears causes more torque to be exerted on the clutch packs or clutch cones. Rapid one-wheel spin cannot occur, because the side gear is forced to turn at the same speed as the case. Most important, with the side gear and the differential case turning at the same speed, the other wheel is forced to rotate in the same direction and at the same speed as the differential case. Thus driving force is applied to the wheel with the better traction.

GEAR RATIOS

The drive axle of a vehicle is said to have a certain axle ratio. This number (usually a whole number and a decimal fraction) is actually a comparison of the number of gear teeth on the ring gear and the pinion gear. For example, a 4.11 rear means that theoretically, there are 4.11 teeth on the ring gear and one tooth on the pinion. Actually, on a 4.11 rear, there are 37 teeth on the ring gear and nine teeth on the pinion gear. By dividing the number of teeth on the pinion gear into the number of teeth on the ring gear, the numerical axle ratio (4.11) is obtained. This also provides a good method of ascertaining exactly with axle ratio one is dealing with.

NOISE DIAGNOSIS

Any gear driven unit will produce a certain amount of noise, therefore, a specific diagnosis for each individual unit is the best practice. Acceptable or normal noise can be classified as a slight noise heard only at certain speeds or unusual conditions. This noise tends to reach a peak at 40–60 mph, depending on the road condition, load, gear ratio and tire size. Frequently, other noises are mistakenly diagnosed as coming from the rear axle. Vehicle noises from tires, transmission, driveshaft, U-joints and front and rear wheel bearings will often be mistaken as emanating from the rear axle. Raising the tire pressure to eliminate tire noise (although this will not silence mud or snow treads), listening for noise at varying speeds and road conditions and listening for noise at drive and coast conditions will aid in diagnosing rear axle noises.

EXTERNAL NOISE ELIMINATION

It is advisable to make a thorough road test to determine whether the noise originates in the rear axle or whether it originates from the tires, engine, transmission, wheel bearings or road surface.

FRONT WHEEL BEARING NOISE

Front wheel bearing noises, sometimes confused with rear axle noises, will not change when comparing drive and coast conditions. While holding the car speed steady, lightly apply the footbrake. This will often cause the wheel bearing noise the lessen, as some of the weight is taken off the bearing. Front wheel bearings are easily checked by jacking up the wheels. Shaking the wheels will also determine if the wheel bearings are excessively loose.

SECTION 28 DRIVE AXLES
TROUBLE DIAGNOSIS

REAR AXLE NOISES

If a logical test of the vehicle shows that the noise is not caused by external items, it can be assumed that the noise originates from the rear axle. The rear axle should be tested on a smooth level road to avoid road noise. It is not advisable to test the axle by jacking up the rear wheels and running the car.

True rear axle noises generally fall into two classes; gear noise and bearing noises, and can be caused by a faulty driveshaft, faulty wheel bearings, worn differential or pinion shaft bearings, U-joint misalignment, worn differential side gears and pinions, or mismatched, improperly adjusted, or scored ring and pinion gears.

REAR WHEEL BEARING NOISE

A rough rear wheel bearing causes a vibration or growl which will continue with the car coasting or in neutral. A brinelled rear wheel bearing will also cause a knock or click approximately every two revolutions of the rear wheel, due to the fact that the bearing rollers do not travel at the same speed as the rear wheel and axle. Jack up the rear wheels and spin the wheel slowly, listening for signs of a rough or brinelled wheel bearing.

DIFFERENTIAL SIDE GEAR AND PINION NOISE

Differential side gears and pinion seldom cause noise, since their movement is relatively slight on straight ahead driving. Noise produced by these gears will be more noticeable on turns.

PINION BEARING NOISE

Pinion bearing failures can be distinguished by their speed of rotation, which is higher than side bearings or axle bearings. Rough or brinelled pinion bearings cause a continuous low pitch whirring or scraping noise beginning at low speeds.

SIDE BEARING NOISE

Side bearings produce a constant rough noise, which is slower than the pinion bearing noise. Side bearing noise may also fluctuate in the above rear wheel bearing test.

GEAR NOISE

Two basic types of gear noise exist. First is the type produced by bent or broken gear teeth which have been forcibly damaged. The noise from this type of damage is audible over the entire speed range. Scoring or damage to the hypoid gear teeth generally results from insufficient lubricant, improper lubricant, improper breakin, insufficient gear backlash, improper ring and pinion gear alignment or loss of torque on the drive pinion nut. If corrected, the scoring will lead to eventual erosion or fracture of the gear teeth. Hypoid gear tooth fracture can also be caused by extended overloading of the gear set (fatigue fracture) or by shock overloading (sudden failure). Differential and side gears rarely give trouble, but common causes of differential failure are shock loading, extended overloading and differential pinion seizure at the cross-shaft, resulting from excessive wheel spin and consequent lubricant breakdown.

The second type of gear noise pertains to the mesh pattern between the ring and pinion gears. This type of abnormal gear noise can be recognized as a cycling pitch or whine audible in either drive, float or coast conditions. Gear noises can be recognized as they tend to peak out in a narrow speed range and remain constant in pitch.

Bearing Diagnosis

This section will help on the diagnosis of bearing failure and the causes. Bearing diagnosis can be very helpful in determining the cause of rear axle failure. The illustrations will help to take some of the guess-work out of determining when to reuse a bearing and when to replace a bearing with a new one.

When disassembling a rear axle, the general condition of all bearings should be noted and classified where possible. Proper recognition of the cause will help in correcting the problem and avoiding a repetition of the failure.

Some of the common causes of bearing failure are:
1. Abuse during assembly or disassembly.
2. Improper assembly methods.
3. Improper or inadequate lubrication.
4. Bearing contact with dirt or water.
5. Wear caused by dirt or metal chips.
6. Corrosion or rust.
7. Seizing to overloading.
8. Overheating.
9. Frettage of the bearing seats.
10. Brinelling from impact or shock loading.
11. Manufacture defects.
12. Pitting due to fatigue.

To avoid damage to the bearing from improper handling, it is best to treat a used bearing the same as a new bearing. Always work in a clean area with clean tools. Remove all outside dirt from the housing before exposing a bearing and clean all bearing seats before installing a bearing.

TAPERED WHEEL BEARING DIAGNOSIS

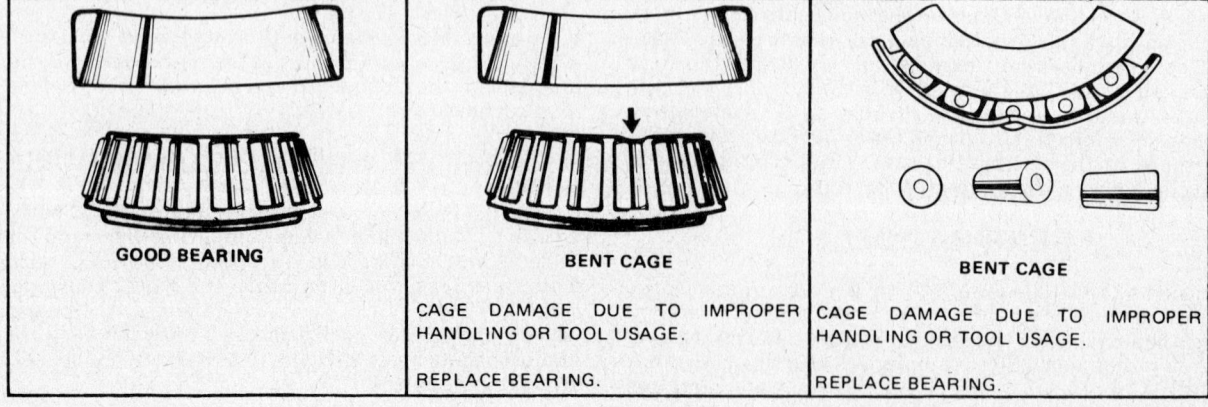

GOOD BEARING

BENT CAGE
CAGE DAMAGE DUE TO IMPROPER HANDLING OR TOOL USAGE.
REPLACE BEARING.

BENT CAGE
CAGE DAMAGE DUE TO IMPROPER HANDLING OR TOOL USAGE.
REPLACE BEARING.

DRIVE AXLES
TROUBLE DIAGNOSIS
SECTION 28

TAPERED WHEEL BEARING DIAGNOSIS

GALLING

METAL SMEARS ON ROLLER ENDS DUE TO OVERHEAT, LUBRICANT FAILURE OR OVERLOAD.

REPLACE BEARING – CHECK SEALS AND CHECK FOR PROPER LUBRICATION.

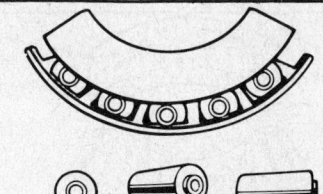

ABRASIVE STEP WEAR

PATTERN ON ROLLER ENDS CAUSED BY FINE ABRASIVES.

CLEAN ALL PARTS AND HOUSINGS, CHECK SEALS AND BEARINGS AND REPLACE IF LEAKING, ROUGH OR NOISY.

ETCHING

BEARING SURFACES APPEAR GRAY OR GRAYISH BLACK IN COLOR WITH RELATED ETCHING AWAY OF MATERIAL USUALLY AT ROLLER SPACING.

REPLACE BEARINGS – CHECK SEALS AND CHECK FOR PROPER LUBRICATION.

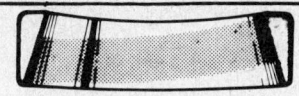

MISALIGNMENT

OUTER RACE MISALIGNMENT DUE TO FOREIGN OBJECT.

CLEAN RELATED PARTS AND REPLACE BEARING. MAKE SURE RACES ARE PROPERLY SEATED.

INDENTATIONS

SURFACE DEPRESSIONS ON RACE AND ROLLERS CAUSED BY HARD PARTICLES OF FOREIGN MATERIAL.

CLEAN ALL PARTS AND HOUSINGS, CHECK SEALS AND REPLACE BEARINGS IF ROUGH OR NOISY.

FATIGUE SPALLING

FLAKING OF SURFACE METAL RESULTING FROM FATIGUE.

REPLACE BEARING – CLEAN ALL RELATED PARTS.

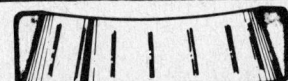

BRINELLING

SURFACE INDENTATIONS IN RACEWAY CAUSED BY ROLLERS EITHER UNDER IMPACT LOADING OR VIBRATION WHILE THE BEARING IS NOT ROTATING.

REPLACE BEARING IF ROUGH OR NOISY.

CAGE WEAR

WEAR AROUND OUTSIDE DIAMETER OF CAGE AND ROLLER POCKETS CAUSED BY ABRASIVE MATERIAL AND INEFFICIENT LUBRICATION. CHECK SEALS AND REPLACE BEARINGS.

ABRASIVE ROLLER WEAR

PATTERN ON RACES AND ROLLERS CAUSED BY FINE ABRASIVES.

CLEAN ALL PARTS AND HOUSINGS, CHECK SEALS AND BEARINGS AND REPLACE IF LEAKING, ROUGH OR NOISY.

SECTION 28 DRIVE AXLES
TROUBLE DIAGNOSIS

TAPERED WHEEL BEARING DIAGNOSIS

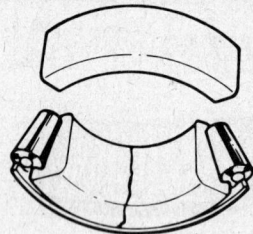

CRACKED INNER RACE

RACE CRACKED DUE TO IMPROPER FIT, COCKING, OR POOR BEARING SEATS.

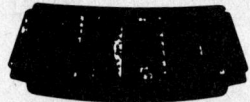

HEAT DISCOLORATION

HEAT DISCOLORATION CAN RANGE FROM FAINT YELLOW TO DARK BLUE RESULTING FROM OVERLOAD OR INCORRECT LUBRICANT.

EXCESSIVE HEAT CAN CAUSE SOFTENING OF RACES OR ROLLERS.

TO CHECK FOR LOSS OF TEMPER ON RACES OR ROLLERS A SIMPLE FILE TEST MAY BE MADE. A FILE DRAWN OVER A TEMPERED PART WILL GRAB AND CUT META, WHEREAS, A FILE DRAWN OVER A HARD PART WILL GLIDE READILY WITH NO METAL CUTTING.

REPLACE BEARINGS IF OVER HEATING DAMAGE IS INDICATED. CHECK SEALS AND OTHER PARTS.

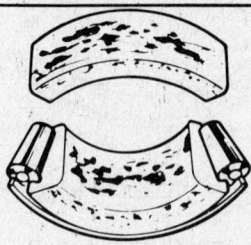

SMEARS

SMEARING OF METAL DUE TO SLIPPAGE. SLIPPAGE CAN BE CAUSED BY POOR FITS, LUBRICATION, OVERHEATING, OVERLOADS OR HANDLING DAMAGE.

REPLACE BEARINGS, CLEAN RELATED PARTS AND CHECK FOR PROPER FIT AND LUBRICATION.

REPLACE SHAFT IF DAMAGED.

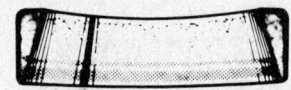

STAIN DISCOLORATION

DISCOLORATION CAN RANGE FROM LIGHT BROWN TO BLACK CAUSED BY INCORRECT LUBRICANT OR MOISTURE.

RE-USE BEARINGS IF STAINS CAN BE REMOVED BY LIGHT POLISHING OR IF NO EVIDENCE OF OVERHEATING IS OBSERVED.

CHECK SEALS AND RELATED PARTS FOR DAMAGE.

FRETTAGE

CORROSION SET UP BY SMALL RELATIVE MOVEMENT OF PARTS WITH NO LUBRICATION.

REPLACE BEARING. CLEAN RELATED PARTS. CHECK SEALS AND CHECK FOR PROPER LUBRICATION.

DRIVE AXLES
TROUBLE DIAGNOSIS
SECTION 28

ROLLER WHEEL BEARING DIAGNOSIS

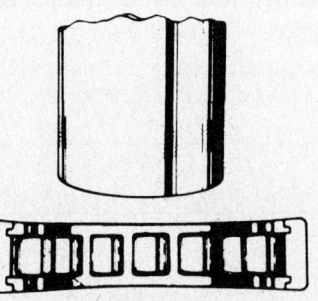

WEAR (MINOR)

LIGHT PATTERN ON RACES AND ROLLERS CAUSED BY FINE ABRASIVES.

CLEAN ALL PARTS AND HOUSINGS. CHECK SEALS AND REPLACE BEARINGS IF ROUGH OR NOISY.

REPLACE SHAFT IF DAMAGED

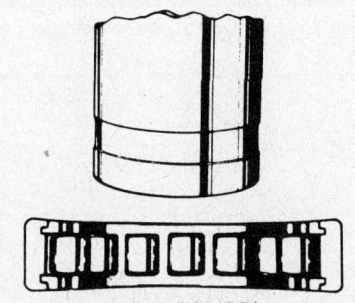

WEAR (MAJOR)

HEAVY PATTERN ON RACES AND ROLLERS CAUSED BY FINE ABRASIVES.

CLEAN ALL PARTS AND HOUSINGS. CHECK SEALS AND REPLACE BEARINGS IF ROUGH OR NOISY.

REPLACE SHAFT IF DAMAGED

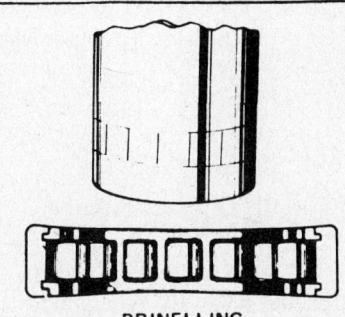

BRINELLING

SURFACE INDENTATIONS IN RACEWAY CAUSED BY ROLL EITHER UNDER IMPACT LOADING OR VIBRATION WHILE THE BEARING IS NOT ROTATING.

REPLACE BEARING IF ROUGH OR NOISY.

REPLACE SHAFT IF DAMAGED

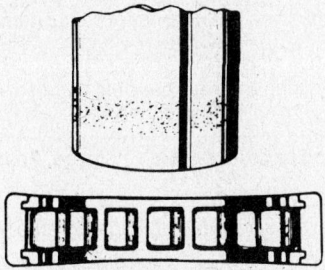

INDENTATIONS

SURFACE DEPRESSIONS ON RACE AND ROLLERS CAUSED BY HARD PARTICLES OF FOREIGN MATERIAL.

CLEAN ALL PARTS AND HOUSINGS. CHECK SEALS AND REPLACE BEARINGS IF ROUGH OR NOISY.

REPLACE SHAFT IF DAMAGED

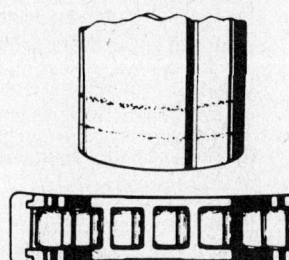

SINGLE EDGE PITTING

FLAKING OF SURFACE METAL RESULTING FROM FATIGUE, USUALLY AT ONE EDGE OF RACE AND ROLLERS.

REPLACE BEARING — CLEAN ALL RELATED PARTS.

REPLACE SHAFT IF DAMAGED

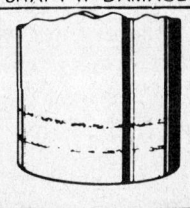

DOUBLE EDGE PITTING

FLAKING OF SURFACE METAL RESULTING FROM FATIGUE, USUALLY AT BOTH EDGES OF RACE AND ROLLERS.

REPLACE BEARING — CLEAN ALL RELATED PARTS.

REPLACE SHAFT IF DAMAGED

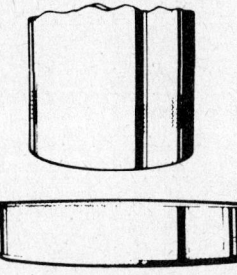

MISALIGNMENT

REPLACE BEARING AND MAKE SURE RACES ARE PROPERLY SEATED.

REPLACE SHAFT IF BEARING OPERATING SURFACE DAMAGED.

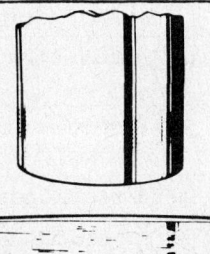

FRETTAGE

CORROSION SET UP BY SMALL RELATIVE MOVEMENT OF PARTS WITH NO LUBRICATION.

REPLACE BEARING. CLEAN RELATED PARTS. CHECK SEALS AND CHECK FOR PROPER FIT AND LUBRICATION.

REPLACE SHAFT IF DAMAGED.

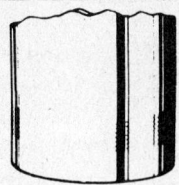

SMEARS

SMEARING OF METAL DUE TO SLIPPAGE. SLIPPAGE CAN BE CAUSED BY POOR FITS. LUBRICATION, OVERHEATING, OVERLOADS OR HANDLING DAMAGE.

REPLACE BEARINGS, CLEAN RELATED PARTS AND CHECK FOR PROPER FITS AND LUBRICATION.

SECTION 28 DRIVE AXLES TROUBLE DIAGNOSIS

GENERAL DRIVE AXLE DIAGNOSTIC GUIDE

Condition	Possible Cause	Correction
Rear Wheel Noise	(a) Loose Wheel.	(a) Tighten loose wheel nuts.
	(b) Spalled wheel bearing cup or cone.	(b) Check rear wheel bearings. If spalled or worn, replace.
	(c) Defective or brinelled wheel bearing.	(c) Defective or brinelled bearings must be replaced. Check rear axle shaft endplay.
	(d) Excessive axle shaft endplay.	(d) Readjust axle shaft endplay.
	(e) Bent or sprung axle shaft flange.	(e) Replace bent or sprung axle shaft.
Scoring of Differential Gears and Pinions	(a) Insufficient lubrication.	(a) Replace scored gears. Scoring marks on the pressure face of gear teeth or in the bore are caused by instantaneous fusing of the mating surfaces. Scored gears should be replaced. Fill rear axle to required capacity with proper lubricant.
	(b) Improper grade of lubricant.	(b) Replace scored gears. Inspect all gears and bearings for possible damage. Clean and refill axle to required capacity with proper lubricant.
	(c) Excessive spinning of one wheel.	(c) Replace scored gears. Inspect all gears, pinion bores and shaft for scoring, or bearings for possible damage.
Tooth Breakage (Ring Gear and Pinion)	(a) Overloading.	(a) Replace gears. Examine other gears and bearings for possible damage. Avoid future overloading.
	(b) Erratic clutch operation.	(b) Replace gears, and examine remaining parts for possible damage. Avoid erratic clutch operation.
	(c) Ice-spotted pavements.	(c) Replace gears. Examine remaining parts for possible damage. Replace parts as required.
	(d) Improper adjustment.	(d) Replace gears. Examine other parts for possible damage. Be sure ring gear and pinion backlash is correct.
Rear Axle Noise	(a) Insufficient lubricant.	(a) Refill rear axle with correct amount of the proper lubricant. Also check for leaks and correct as necessary.
	(b) Improper ring gear and pinion adjustment.	(b) Check ring gear and pinion tooth contact.
	(c) Unmatched ring gear and pinion.	(c) Remove unmatched ring gear and pinion. Replace with a new matched gear and pinion set.
	(d) Worn teeth on ring gear or pinion.	(d) Check teeth on ring gear and pinion for contact. If necessary, replace with new matched set.
	(e) End-play in drive pinion bearings.	(e) Adjust drive pinion bearing preload.
	(f) Side play in differential bearings.	(f) Adjust differential bearing preload.
	(g) Incorrect drive gear lash.	(g) Correct drive gear lash.
	(h) Limited-Slip differential—moan and chatter.	(h) Drain and flush lubricant. Refill with proper lubricant.
Loss of Lubricant	(a) Lubricant level too high.	(a) Drain excess lubricant.
	(b) Worn axle shaft oil seals.	(b) Replace worn oil seals with new ones. Prepare new seals before replacement.
	(c) Cracked rear axle housing.	(c) Repair or replace housing as required.
	(d) Worn drive pinion oil seal.	(d) Replace worn drive pinion oil seal with a new one.
	(e) Scored and worn companion flange.	(e) Replace worn or scored companion flange and oil seal.

28–8

DRIVE AXLES
TROUBLE DIAGNOSIS
SECTION 28

GENERAL DRIVE AXLE DIAGNOSTIC GUIDE

CONDITION	POSSIBLE CAUSE	CORRECTION
Loss of Lubricant	(f) Clogged vent.	(f) Remove obstructions.
	(g) Loose carrier housing bolts or housing cover screws.	(g) Tighten bolts or cover screws to specifications and fill to correct level with proper lubricant.
Overheating of Unit	(a) Lubricant level too low.	(a) Refill rear axle.
	(b) Incorrect grade of lubricant.	(b) Drain, flush and refill rear axle with correct amount of the proper lubricant.
	(c) Bearings adjusted too tightly.	(c) Readjust bearings.
	(d) Excessive wear in gears.	(d) Check gears for excessive wear or scoring. Replace as necessary.
	(e) Insufficient ring gear-to-pinion clearance.	(e) Readjust ring gear and pinion backlash and check gears for possible scoring.

REPAIR PROCEDURES INDEX

Manufacturer and Ring Gear Size	R&R Rear Hub	R&R Pressed-on Bearing From Axle	R&R Axle and Bearing	Install Outer Oil Seal ⓑ	Install Inner Oil Seal ⓑ	Axle Shaft Endplay Adj.	Install Pinion Oil Seal	Install Side Gear Seal	Set Pinion Depth	Ring Gear Backlash Adjustment	Pinion Bearing Preload
AMERICAN MOTORS (AMC)											
7-9/16	1	8	2	3	4	5	6	None	13	14	15
CHRYSLER CORPORATION											
7-1/4	Ⓐ	8	7	12	4	9	6	None	13	14	15
8-1/4	Ⓐ	8	7	12	4	9	6	None	13	14	15
FORD MOTOR COMPANY											
6-3/4	Ⓐ	8	7	12	4	9	6	None	13	14	15
7.5	Ⓐ	8	7	12	4	9	6	None	13	14	15
8.5, 8.8	Ⓐ	8	7	12	4	9	6	None	13	14	15
GENERAL MOTORS CORPORATION											
7-1/2	Ⓐ	8	7	12	4	9	6①	None	13	14	15
8-1/2	Ⓐ	8	7	12	4	9	6	None	13	14	15
8-3/4	Ⓐ	8	7	12	4	9	6	None	13	14	15
7-1/2 Corvette	Ⓐ			See Car Chapter				10	13	14	15

① See Procedure No. 11 for Chevette
Ⓐ Hub is not separate, but part of the Axle Shaft Assembly.
Ⓑ Certain models use seal within axle bearing and is replaced as an assembly.

CAUTION
Never spin a bearing with compressed air, as this will lead to almost certain bearing

PROCEDURE NO. 1

Removing and Replacing Rear Hub
AMC ONLY

1. With the weight of the car on the wheels, remove the axle shaft nut, and loosen each lug nut ¼ turn.
2. Raise and safely support the car so the wheels are clear of the floor.
3. Remove the lug nuts, wheel, and brake drum.
4. Attach a hub puller and remove the hub.

CAUTION
Do not use the type of puller that screws into the end of the axle and provides a surfaces for striking. The heavy blows necessary with this type of puller may damage the rear wheel bearings and the differential thrust block. A screw-type or wedge-type puller must be used.

REPLACEMENT

1. If the same hub is being put back on, reverse the removal procedure and tighten the axle shaft nut to 250 ft. lbs. torque. Install a cotter key if the holes line up. If not, tighten the nut to the next slot and install the cotter key. Do not loosen the nut to align the holes.
2. If a new hub is being installed, it must be pressed onto the axle shaft to form the serrations. The hub is pressed on by using two thrust washers under the nut, greased with chassis

SECTION 28 Drive Axles
REPAIR PROCEDURES

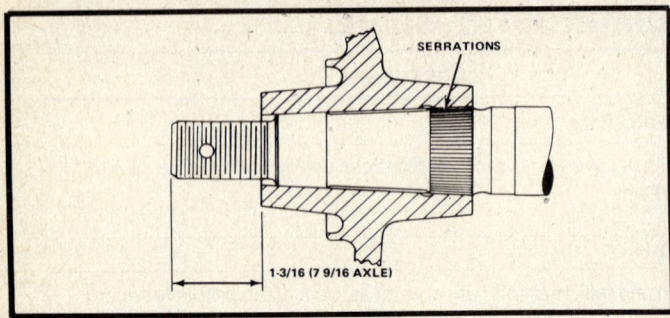
Hub installation measurement

grease. With the wheel, hub, and drum installed, the parking brake should be firmly applied and the car weight on the wheels. Tighten the nut to the following measurement, from the end of axle to the end of the hub.

$7 \frac{9}{16}$ in. axle = $1 \frac{3}{16}$ in.

NOTE: The $7 \frac{9}{16}$ in. axle is stamped with the letters E, F, G, H, K, R, S, T, U, or V on the side of the differential housing.

3. Remove the axle shaft nut and one thrust washer, then re-install the nut and tighten it to 250 ft. lbs. Install a cotter key if the holes line up. It not, tighten the nut to the next slot and install the cotter key.

PROCEDURE NO. 2

Removing Tapered Axle and Bearing
AMC ONLY

1. Remove wheel, drum, and hub.
2. Disconnect brake line at wheel cylinder.
3. Remove bolts and nuts from housing flange and remove brake backing plate, oil, seal, and retainer. Remove shims if left side shaft is being removed.

NOTE: Axle shaft end play shims are installed on the left side of the axle only.

4. Use a screw-type puller or slide hammer to pull the axle shaft and bearing out of the housing.

---- **CAUTION** ----
On cars equipped with a self-locking differential, do not rotate the other shaft while one shaft is removed. The side gear splines may misalign if the differential is rotated, preventing insertion of the replacement shaft.

To install the axle, reverse the removal procedure. On $7 \frac{9}{16}$ in. axles, the outer oil seal and retainer is installed between the housing flange and the brake backing plate.

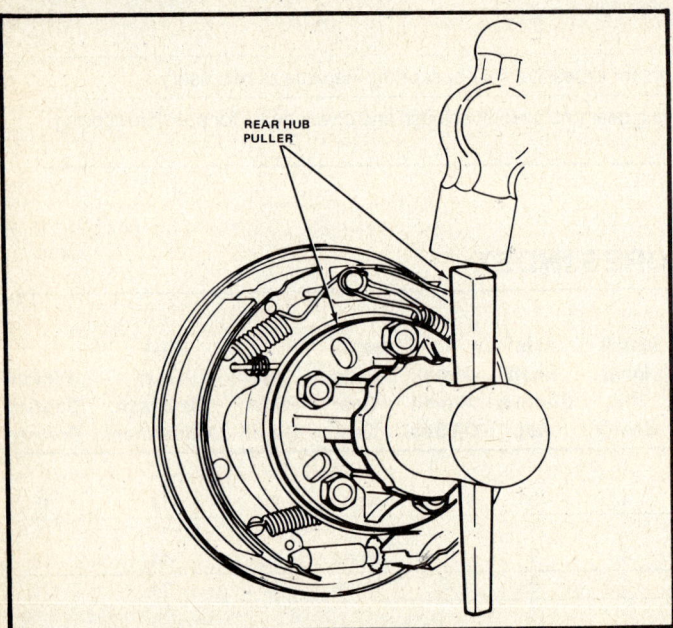
Removing axle

PROCEDURE NO. 3

R & R Axle Outer Oil Seal
AMC ONLY

1. Remove wheel, drum, and hub.
2. Disconnect brake line at wheel cylinder.
3. Remove bolts and nuts from housing flange and remove brake backing plate, oil seal, and retainer. If left side is being removed, make note of any shims next to the backing plate.

To install a new seal, reverse the removal procedure, replacing shims in the original position. On $7 \frac{9}{16}$ in. axles, the outer seal and retainer is installed between the housing flange ad the brake backing plate.

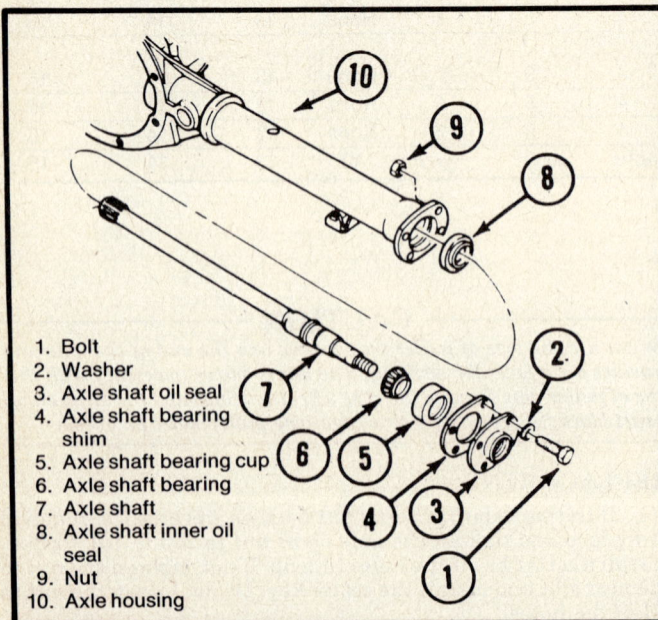
1. Bolt
2. Washer
3. Axle shaft oil seal
4. Axle shaft bearing shim
5. Axle shaft bearing cup
6. Axle shaft bearing
7. Axle shaft
8. Axle shaft inner oil seal
9. Nut
10. Axle housing

Exploded view of AMC axle, bearing assembly, inner and outer oil seal assembly
(© American Motors Corp.)

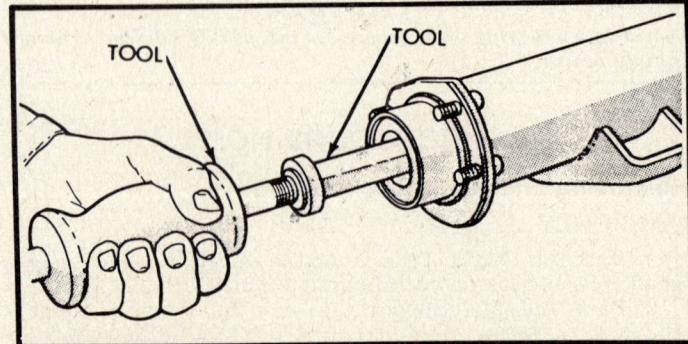
Removing inner seal from axle tube, typical
(© Chrysler Corp.)

DRIVE AXLES
REPAIR PROCEDURES
SECTION 28

PROCEDURE NO. 4

R & R Axle Inner Oil Seal
ALL CARS

NOTE: Some cars do not use an inner seal.

1. Remove the axle according to the correct procedure.
2. Use a slide hammer puller that will hook onto the seal and pull it out of the axle housing. Or use the end of the axle to pry the seal out, being careful not to gourge or damage the housing, In the same designs, it may be necessary to remove the bearing, also, because the puller will not grab the seal alone. Clean the inside of the housing to remove old sealer.
3. To install a new seal, coat the lip of the seal with rear axle lubricant. Coat the outer metal part of the seal with nonhardening sealer.
4. Use a driver that fits the seal and drive the seal into the axle housing to the same depth as the old seal, with the lip pointing inward.
5. Replace the axle and the other parts, using the correct procedure.

PROCEDURE NO. 5

Axle Shaft End Play Adjustment
AMC ONLY

1. Remove the drum and hub by the correct procedure under the axle shaft removal.
2. Strike the end of each axle shaft with a lead hammer to seat the bearing cups against the support plates.
3. Attach a large flat 18 in. bar with a hole in the middle to the end of the axle. The bar will be used as a handle to move the axle in and out while checking end play.
4. Attach a dial indicator to the axle housing backing plate so it will read the in and out movement of the axle.
5. Pull and push on the bar so the axle moves in and out to the limit of its end play. Correct end play is 0.006 in. Allowable end play is 0.004–0.008 in.
6. Correct the end play with shims on the left side of the axle only. Adding shims will increase end play. Removing shims will decrease end play.
7. The outer oil seal housing acts as a bearing retainer. To be effective, shims must be installed inboard from the oil seal. Any other parts that install inboard from the bearing retainer will affect the end play of the axle. On those axles that the shims are inboard from the brake backing plate, the backing plate must be removed to take out the shims.
8. Install the hub and drum by the correct procedure under axle shaft removal.

PROCEDURE NO. 6

Pinion Oil Seal Replacement
ALL CARS

1. Raise and safely support the car. Remove the rear wheels and brake drums.
2. Mark the driveshaft and rear yoke for correct reassembly, then disconnect the driveshaft from the yoke.
3. Rotate the pinion several revolutions, then use an inch lbs. torque wrench to measure the amount of inch lbs. required to turn the pinion. If a torque wrench is not available, scribe a line on a nut and pinion shaft, and count the number of exposed threads to establish the position of the nut.
4. Remove the pinion nut. Mark the position of the yoke of the pinion, and remove the yoke. Some lubricant will drain out when the yoke is removed.
5. Check seal surface of yoke. If the surface is damaged or grooved, replace the yoke.

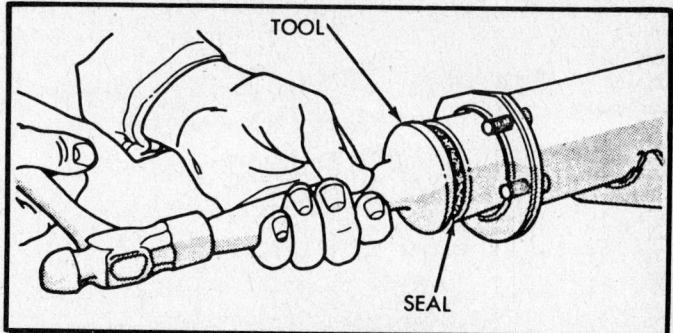
Installing the axle shaft seal, typical
(© Chrysler Corp.)

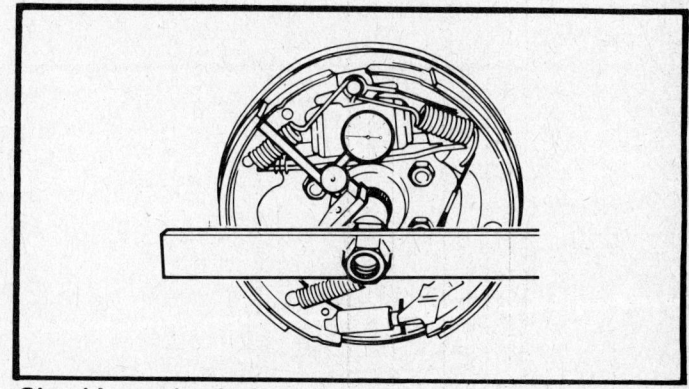
Checking axle shaft end play

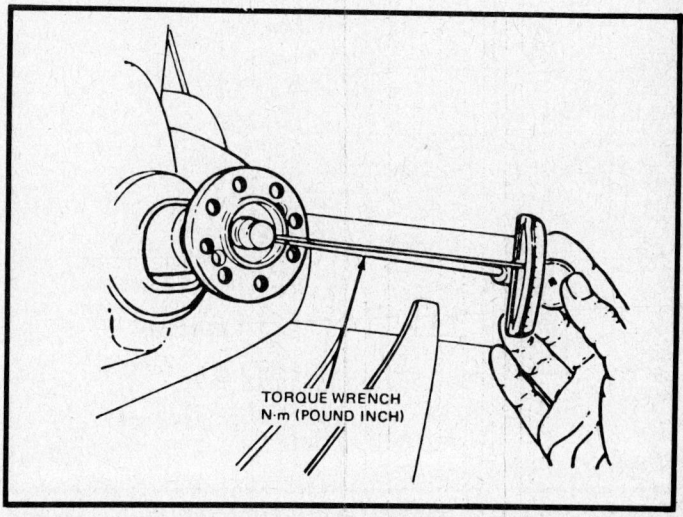
Use of torque wrench to check pinion bearing preload
(© Ford Motor Co.)

6. Remove the pinion seal using a tool that threads into the inner diameter of the seal, or equivalent.
7. To replace the seal, coat the lip with rear axle lubricant, and drive the seal into position with the lip pointing inward.
8. Install the yoke, aligning the reference marks, and snug the nut, but do not tighten. AMC recommends using a new nut.
9. Use the torque wrench to measure the inch lbs. required to turn the pinion. Turn the pinion several revolutions to insure an accurate reading.
10. Tighten the pinion nut very slightly and measure the rotation torque again. continue to tighten and measure until the torque is 1–5 inch lbs. more than it was before disassembly. Do

28–11

SECTION 28
Drive Axles
Repair Procedures

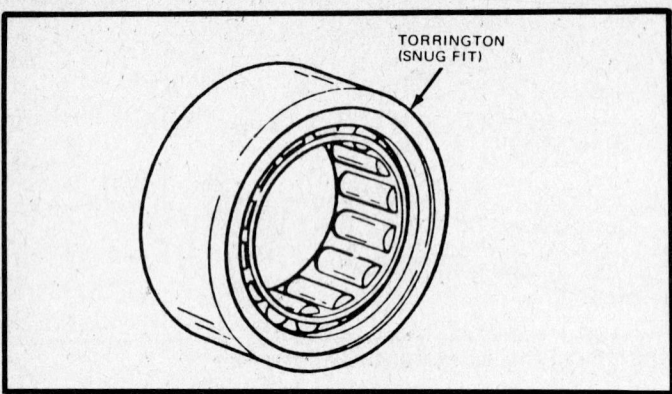

Typical axle tube bearing assembly
(© Ford Motor Co.)

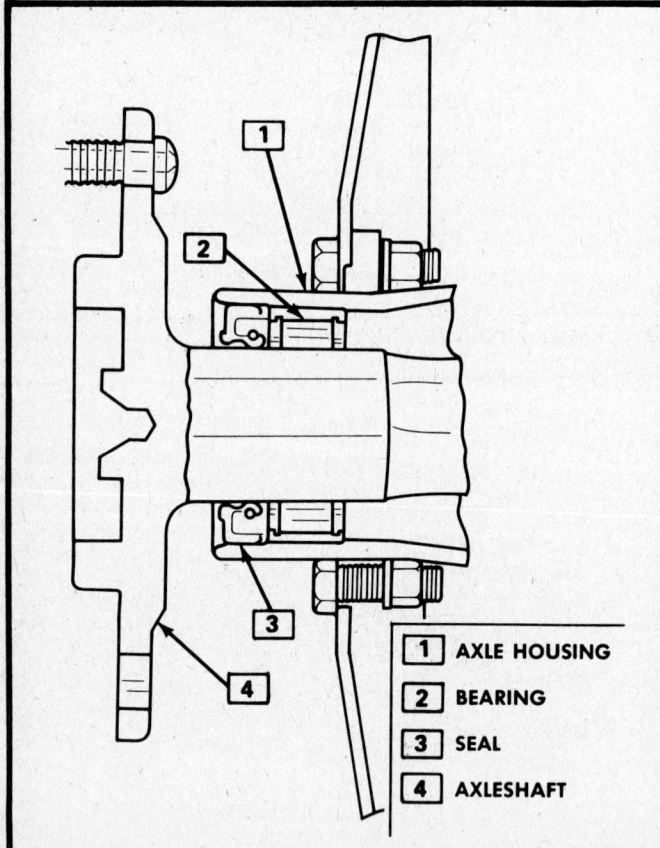

Cross section of bearing and seal used with C-type axles, typical (© General Mtors Corp.)

not exceed 5 inch lbs. If a torque wrench is not available, tighten the nut until the scribe marks line up then tighten 1/16–1/8 in. more.

---- **CAUTION** ----

Do not overtighten, or loosen and retighten the pinion nut. If the correct torque is exceeded, or the nut is tightened or loosened, the nut and collapsible spacer must be replaced and the pinion bearing preload reset.

11. Complete the installation by reversing the removal procedure.

PROCEDURE NO. 7

R & R Flanged Axle and Bearing

NOTE: Two different axle shaft designs are used. The "C" type axles are retained in the housing by "C" locks at the inner ends. To remove the axles, the differential housing cover must be removed. The other type of axle is retained in the housing by a retainer plate held by the same bolts that hold the brake backing plate. On the retainer plate type, all the work of removing the axle shafts is done at the wheel ends of the axle housing.

The easiest way to find out which type is on any car is to remove a rear wheel and drum. Inspect the area behind the axle flange. If the axle is a retainer type, the retainer can be seen. On "C" types, the housing sticks out more, and there is no retainer plate.

RETAINER PLATE TYPE

1. Raise and safely support the car. Remove the wheel and brake drum.
2. Remove the nuts holding the retainer plate to the backing plate, using a socket and extension through the hole in the axle flange.
3. Use a slide hammer puller to pull the axle and bearing loose from the axle housing. Once the bearing is free, support the axle while removing it. Dragging the axle out may damage the inner seal, if one is used.
4. Clean the retainer plate mounting area before replacing the axle. Make sure that the backing plate is seated flat against any dirt caught between the flanges.
5. Reverse the removal procedure to complete the installation.

NOTE: The retainer plate gasket is usually not available. It is common practice to replace the plate without a gasket, or to use the old gasket.

"C" TYPE

1. Raise and safely support the car. Remove the wheel and brake drum.
2. Remove the differential cover and catch the lubricant in a pan.
3. Remove the pinion shaft lock bolt and the pinion shaft.
4. Push the axle shaft inward to permit removal of the "C" remove the "C" lock and lock, then pull the axle out of the housing.
5. The axle shaft bearing is a press fit in the housing. It can be removed with a slide hammer puller. When the bearing is removed, the seal will come out with it.

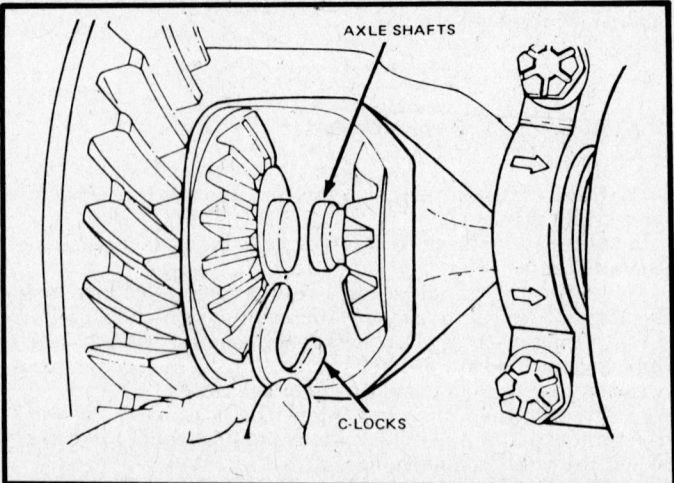

Removal or installation of "C" locks
(© Ford Motor Co.)

28-12

DRIVE AXLES
REPAIR PROCEDURES

6. Drive a new bearing into the housing to the same depth as the old one. A new seal should be driven into the end of the housing.

7. To complete the procedure, reverse the removal, being sure to avoid any gasket leaks at the differential cover, and refilling the differential with the correct lubricant.

PROCEDURE NO. 8

Removing Pressed-On Bearing From Axle

NOTE: A hydraulic or mechanical press is necessary. The press should be one that is recommended for axle bearing work.

1. Remove the axle and bearing assembly from the car, following the correct procedure.
2. The retainer ring that is pressed against the bearing (not on AMC with tapered axle) must be V-grooved with a chisel and heavy hammer to relieve the pressure, so it can be slipped off the shaft. Do not attempt to split the ring, because the chisel might damage the shaft. Several deep V-grooves will usually loosen the ring enough that it can be removed by hand.
3. Use a safe press setup, with press blocks that fit the bearing, and a cage or bearing cap that will contain the bearing pieces in case it factures.
4. Press the bearing from the shaft.
5. Knock the old seal out of the retainer plate (not used on AMC) and install a new seal, with the lip facing in. Slip the retainer plate over the axle, with the seal lip facing in. On some makes, the retainer plate does not contain a seal.
6. Press a new bearing onto the axle, following the same precautions as in removing the old bearing. Then press a new retaining ring up against the bearing.

PROCEDURE NO. 9

Adjust Axle End Play

There is no end play adjustment on these axles. If the end play is excessive, it means the bearing is worn, and must be replaced.

PROCEDURE NO. 10

Install Side Gear Seal

CORVETTE ONLY

1. Remove axle by the correct procedure. Remove differential housing cover.
2. Remove snap ring and remove side yoke.
3. Remove seal with slide hammer puller or prybar.
4. Drive new seal into bore to same distance as old, with lip of seal pointing inward.
5. Replace yoke, snap ring, and axle. Re-install cover and fill assembly with lubricant.

NOTE: Snap rings come in three sizes and colors, to control yoke shaft end play.

1. Yellow — 0.060 in.
2. Green — 0.065 in.
3. Orange — 0.070 in.
4. End Play — 0.0005–0.0085 in.

PROCEDURE NO. 11

Install Pinion Oil Seal

CHEVETTE, T1000, 1000

1. Raise and safely support the car. Disconnect the driveshaft at the rear U-joint, then remove the shaft by pulling the slip joint out of the transmission.

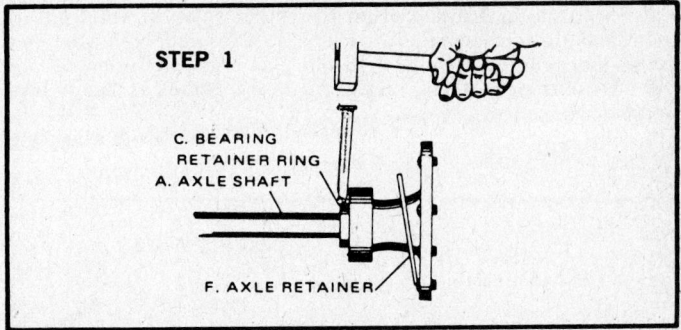

1. Mount axle shaft (A) in vise. Remove the bearing retainer ring

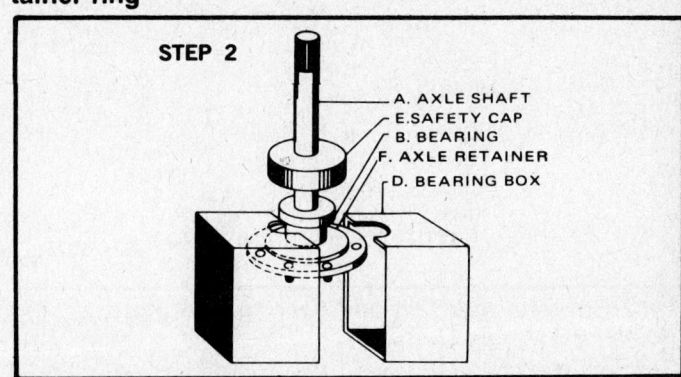

2. At the press table, insert the axle flange and retainer (F) within the removal box (D). Both sections of the box should rest against the axle under the bearing (B). Place safety cap (E) over the shaft on top of the bearing. Press against shaft end to remove bearing. If it does not easily break loose, tap shaft with a ballpean hammer.

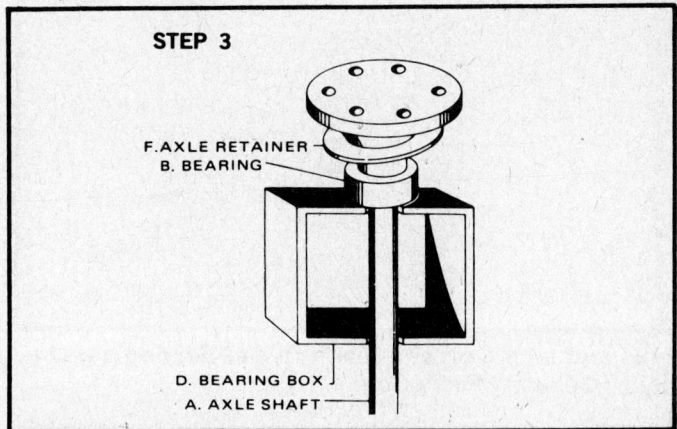

3. Clean shaft and reatainer (F) and replace retainer against axle flange. Slip new bearing (B) over the shaft. Be sure a sealed bearing faces the proper directions. Locate axle shaft (A) in the removal box (D) and press the bearng to its seat on the shaft. Also press a new retaining ring (C) against the bearng ends. To remove the axles, the differential housing cover must be removed. The other type of axle is retained in the housing by a retainer plate held by the same bolts that hold the brake backing plate. On the retainer plate type, all the work of removing the axle shafts is done at the wheel ends of the axle housing

SECTION 28
DRIVE AXLES
REPAIR PROCEDURES

2. Put an axle stand or other firm support under the front of the rear axle carrier housing. Place another support under the extension housing to hold it in place as it is disconnected.
3. Disconnect the center support bracket from the underbody.
4. Disconnect the extension housing flange from the axle carrier housing.

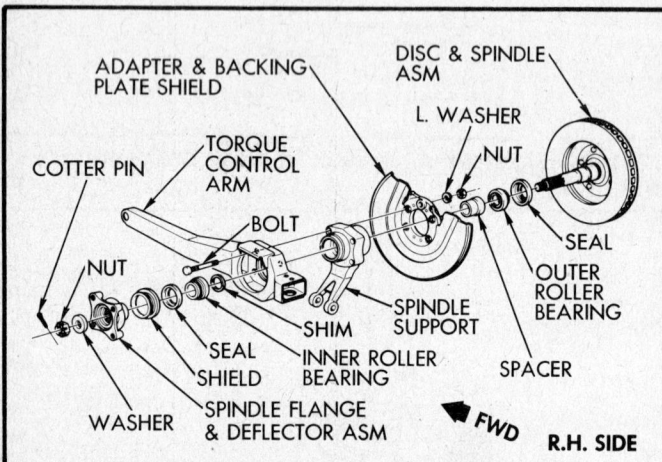

1982 Corvette rear hub and bearing assembly
(© General Motors Corp.)

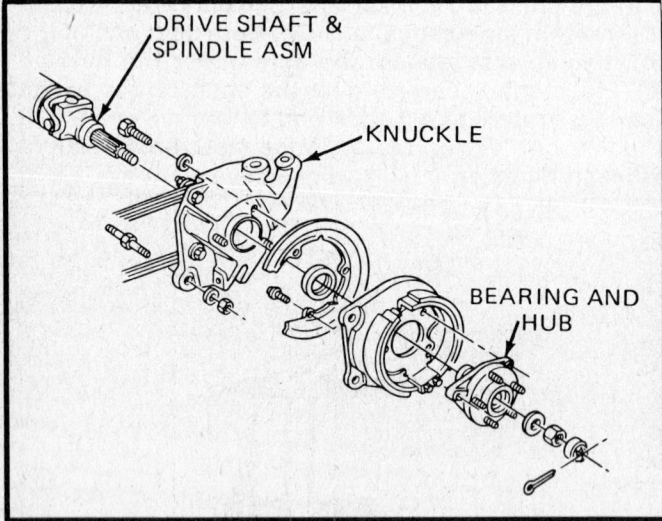

1984 and later Corvette rear hub and bearing assembly (© General Motors Corp.)

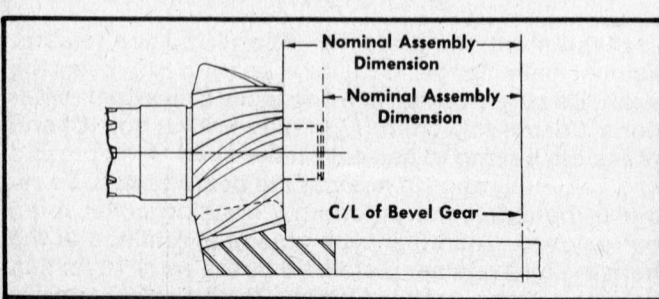

Nominal assembly dimension
(© General Motors Corp.)

5. Remove the extension housing carefully. If necessary, use a screwdriver to pry the extension housing away from the carrier housing.
6. Use a slide hammer puller or pry bar to pull the seal from the front of the carrier housing.

--- CAUTION ---
Do not damage the splines on the drive coupling.

7. Drive a new seal into the housing to the same depth as the old one, with the lip facing to the rear. Reassembly the extension housing by reversing the removal procedure.

PROCEDURE NO. 12

Installing Outer Oil Seal in Retainer Flange

NOTE: Some cars do not use a seal in the retainer flange.

1. Follow the correct procedure for removing the axle.
2. Follow the correct procedure for removing the pressed-on bearing from the axle.
3. Remove the retainer from the axle and install a new seal in the retainer.
4. Replace the retainer and bearing on the axle, and the axle in the housing, following the correct procedure.

PROCEDURE NO. 13

Setting Pinion Depth

If the original pinion and bearings are to be re-installed, the original shims can be reused to provide the correct shim thickness, providing the ring and pinion gear teeth wear pattern is acceptable.

Methods of adjusting pinions to obtain the proper depths will vary from axle types and the manufacturers' recommenda-

Markings etched on pinion illustrating metric and standard measurement digits (© Ford Motor Co.)

28-14

DRIVE AXLES
REPAIR PROCEDURES
SECTION 28

tions. Pinion depth settings and gear teeth contact may be determined by the use of pinion setting gauges or by the use of marking dye on the gear teeth and observing the meshing pattern.

When using the gauge method, back lash is established after the pinion has been properly set. With the dye method, backlash is established first, then the proper pinion tooth contact is established

Terms Used

Certain dimensions must be determined when using the pinion setting gauge:

1. NOMINAL ASSEMBLY DIMENSION. (standard pinion depth) This dimension (varying with axle model) is the distance between the center line of the drive gear (or differential carrier bore) and the end of the drive pinion. This dimension may be marked on the pinion or listed on the Nominal Assembly Dimension and Adapter Disc chart.

2. INDIVIDUAL VARIATION DISTANCE, (pinion depth variance) This dimension is a plus or minus variation of the NOMINAL ASSEMBLY DIMENSION on each individual pinion which may be caused by manufacturing variations.

3. CORRECTED NOMINAL DIMENSION (desired pinion depth) This dimension is the NOMINAL ASSEMBLY DIMENSION plus or minus the INDIVIDUAL VARIATION DISTANCE.

4. CORRECTED MICROMETER DISTANCE IS THE CORRECTED NOMINAL DIMENSION less the thickness of the gauge set step plate (0.400 in.) mounted on end of pinion.

5. INITIAL MICROMETER READING is the dimension taken by micrometer to the gauge step plate.

6. SHIM PACK CORRECTION is determined by the difference between the CORRECTED MICROMETER DISTANCE and the INITIAL MICROMETER READING, and represents the amount of shim pack to be added or removed as later explained.

7. MEASURED PINION DEPTH. This measurement is the distance between the axle center line and the top of the pinion gear. If a step plate or other type gauge tool is used, this measurement is included in the total.

Markings on the Pinion and Drive Gears

Drive gears and pinions are tested at the time of manufacture to detect machining variances and to obtain desirable tooth contact and quietness. When the correct setting is achieved, the gears are considered matched and a set of numbers, along with other identifying marks are etched on the gear set.

A + (plus) or - (minus) sign a used, followed by a digit to represent the factory setting where to tooth contact and quietness were the best. This is called the PINION DEPTH VARIANCE or INDIVIDUAL VARIATION DISTANCE.

If the pinion is marked +5 for example, this means the distance from the pinion gear rear face to the axle shaft center line is 0.005 in. more than the standard setting, and if the pinion gear is marked -5, this means that the distance is 0.005 in. less than the standard setting. To move the pinion to the standard setting, compensating for the variation, shims must be either added or subtracted from the total shim pack, located under the rear pinion bearing cup, between the pinion cage and the differential carrier, or under the rear pinion bearing, depending upon the differential model being serviced.

As a rule of thumb on the addition or removal of shims for the pinion depth adjustment, draw a diagram as shown and determine which way the pinion must be moved to obtain the desired pinion depth.

NOTE: When a pinion is found to have a plus or minus reading, the reading is etched on the head of the pinion gear, along with other pertinent information. The plus or minus reading can be expressed in either metric or standard inch measurement. The metric measurement will have a letter "M" after the measurement digit.

Pinion Gauge Method

The pinion gauge method can be a direct reading micrometer, mounted on or through an arbor bar, set in adaptor discs and located in the side carrier bearing cup locations on the differential housing and held in place by the bearing cup caps. The arbor bar coincides and represents the center line of the axle shafts. A reading is taken by the mounted micrometer, from the arbor bar to the head of the pinion, to determine the need to add or subtract shims from the shim pack total, in order to adjust the pinion to the proper nominal assembly dimension or standard pinion depth.

Another method, using the arbor bar and discs, is the use of a gauge block with a spring loaded plunger and thumb screw to lock the plunger upon expansion. A micrometer is used to measure the gauge block after the plunger has been allowed to expand between the arbor bar and the pinion head. As in the mounted micrometer procedure, the shim pack thickness is determined by the reading obtained.

A third method is the use of a gauge block tool, installed in the differential housing in place of the pinion gear, and a large arbor bar placed in the axle housing differential bearing seats and tightened securely. A measurement is taken between the arbor bar and the pinion tool by either a dial indicator unit, feeler gauge blades or the use of individual shims from the shim pack. This measurement would represent the shim pack needed for a zero marked pinion. Should the pinion be marked either plus or minus, the shim pack would be adjusted accordingly.

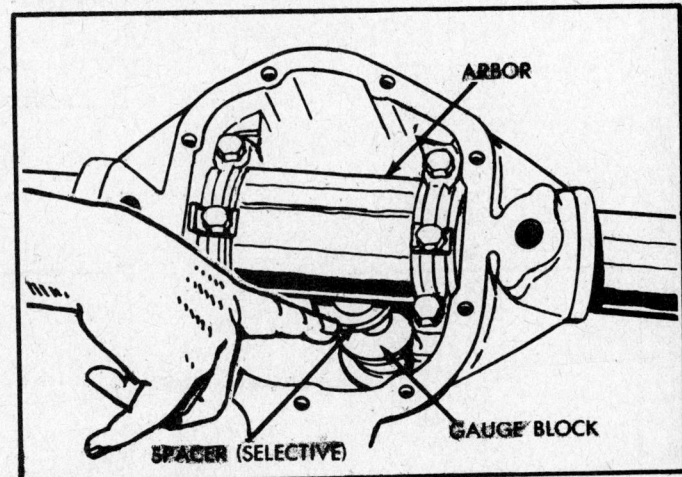

Movement of pinion to obtain desired pinion depth
(© Ford Motor Co.)

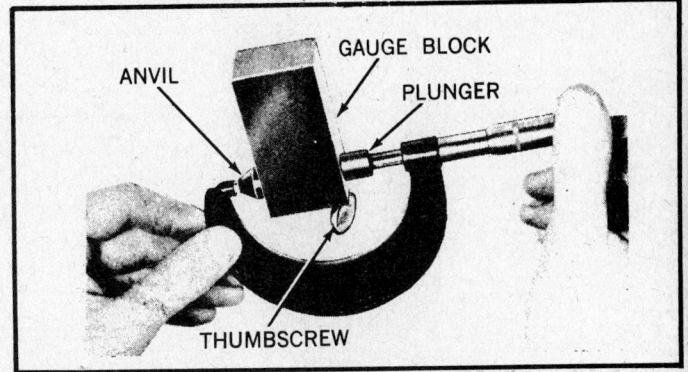

Use of typical pinion depth gauge assemlby

28-15

SECTION 28: DRIVE AXLES — REPAIR PROCEDURES

Setting New Pinion Without Gauge

Whenever a pinion gauge is not available, measure the thickness of the pinion shim pack at the rear pinion bearing cup or between the pinion rear bearing and pinion gear head. Change the sign of the marking (individual variation distance) on the NEW pinion (plus to minus or minus to plus), then add or subtract the variation on the old pinion (sign unchanged) which will determine the amount the original shim pack must be changed when installing the new pinion.

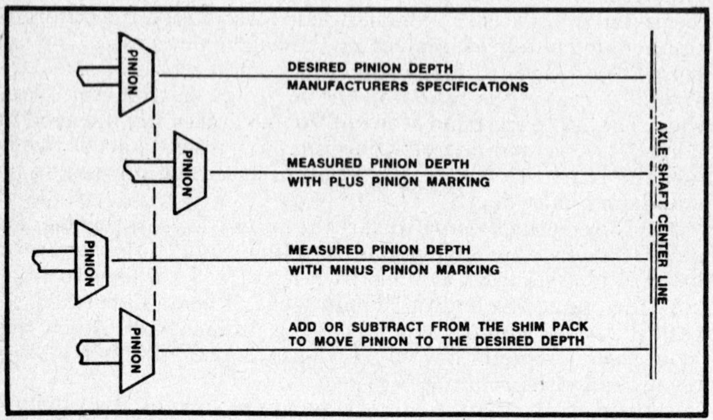

Movement of pinion to obtain desired pinion depth (© Ford Motor Co.)

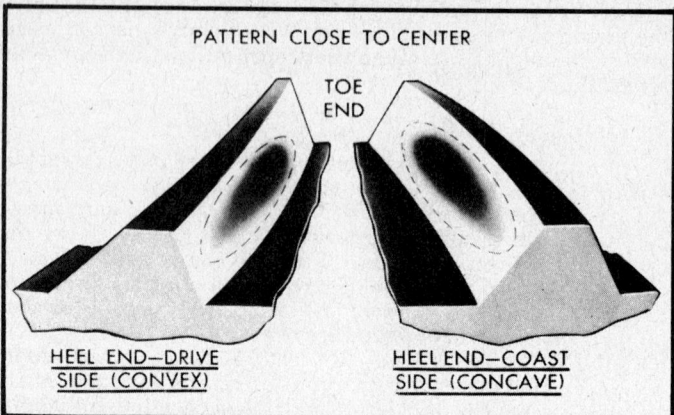

Desired tooth contact (© Chrysler Corp.)

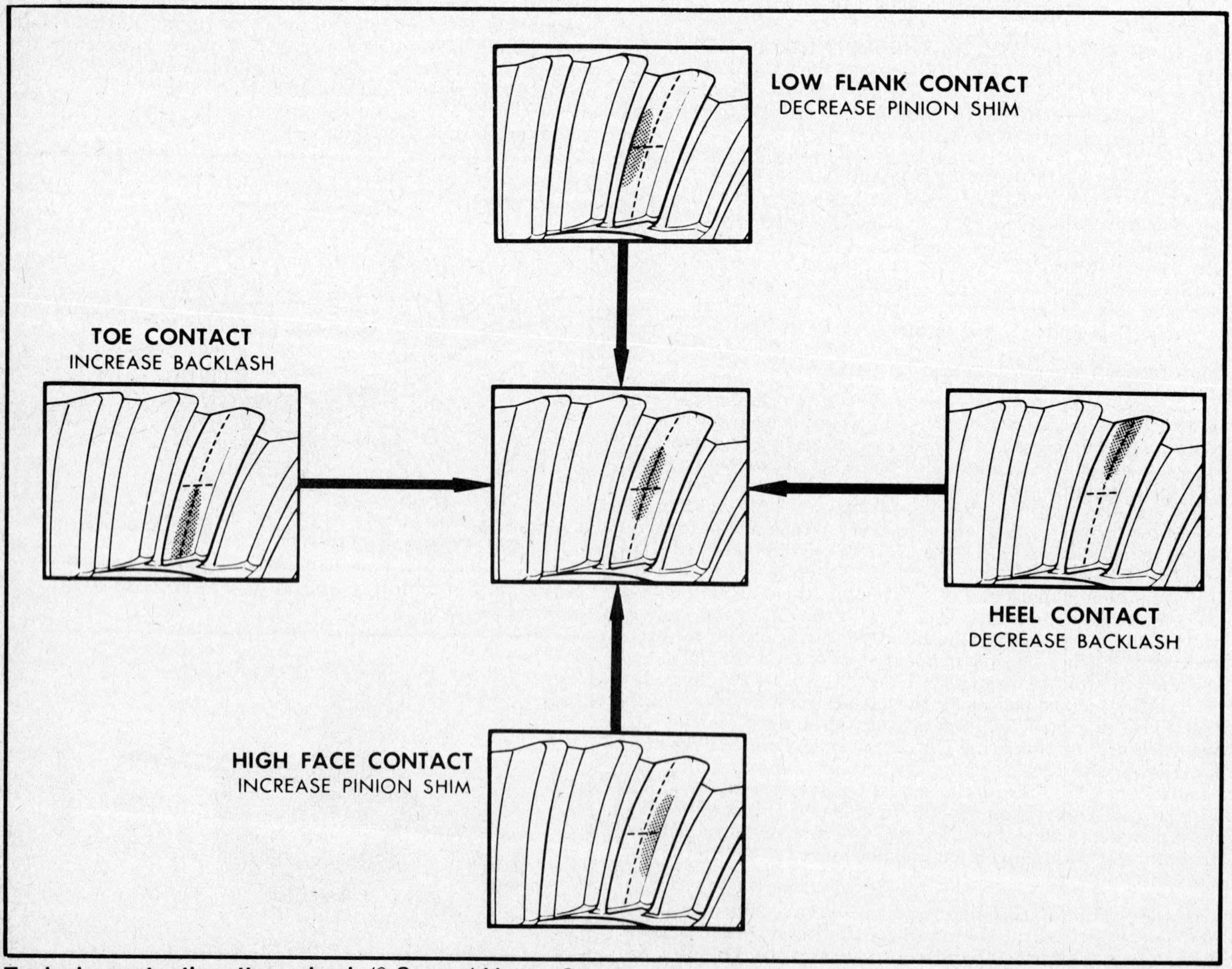

Typical gear tooth pattern check (© General Motors Corp.)

- LOW FLANK CONTACT — DECREASE PINION SHIM
- TOE CONTACT — INCREASE BACKLASH
- HEEL CONTACT — DECREASE BACKLASH
- HIGH FACE CONTACT — INCREASE PINION SHIM

DRIVE AXLES
REPAIR PROCEDURES
SECTION 28

On the type of differential units where the shims are located between the pinion cage and differential carrier, change the sign of the marking (individual variation distance) on the pinion (plus to minus or minus to plus), then add the variation of the new pinion (sign unchanged) which will determine how much the original shim pack must be altered when installing a new pinion.

When the approximate thickness of shim pack has been determined, final check of the tooth contact must be made by using the dye method.

CAUTION
Do not put the differential unit in service until the tooth contact pattern is satisfactory.

Marking Dye Method

Extra time is needed when using the marking dye method, due to the numerous times the ring and pinion components may have to be assembled and disassembled, in search of the correct shim pack thickness to give the proper tooth contact pattern between the teeth of the ring and pinion gears. Usually, the only time this method is used, is when special tools or rebuilding specifications are not available for a specific unit.

PROCEDURE NO. 14

Ring Gear Backlash Adjustment

Operating clearance is needed between the ring gear and the pinion gear. This clearance is known as backlash and is measured in either the standard inch or metric measurements. Two major adjustment procedures are used to control the backlash tolerance, either adjusting rings or shim packs. The differential bearing preload must be considered when making the backlash adjustment and is usually accomplished after the backlash measurement is made.

Backlash is increased by moving the ring gear away from the pinion gear or can be decreased by moving the ring gear closer to the pinion gear.

Adjusting Ring Method

With the differential carrier assembly set in place on the differential housing, position the left and right threaded adjusting rings at zero preload against the side carrier bearing cups. With the use of a dial indicator, determine the backlash between the ring gear and the pinion gear. Move the differential carrier closer to or away from the pinion gear by moving the adapter rings. When one ring is tightened, the opposite ring must be loosened an equal amount to maintain the previously established zero bearing preload. When the proper backlash is obtained, a preload must be placed on the side carrier bearings. This is accomplished by tightening each adjusting ring a specific torque or a predetermined distance, usually one opening

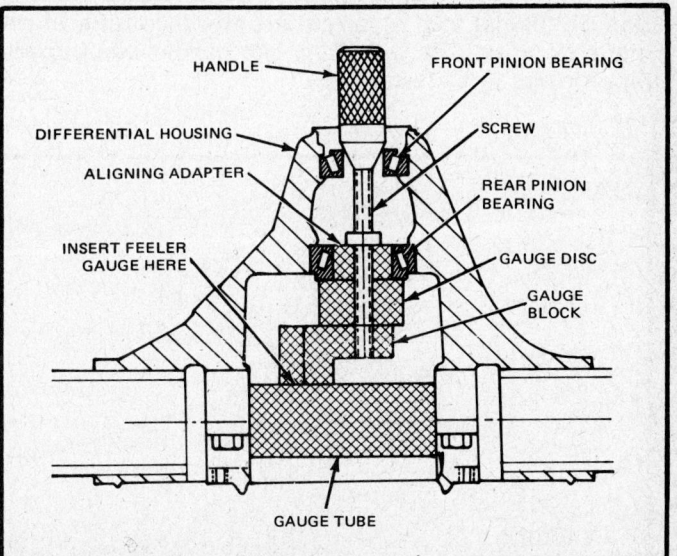

Use of typical pinion depth gauge assembly
(© Ford Motor Co.)

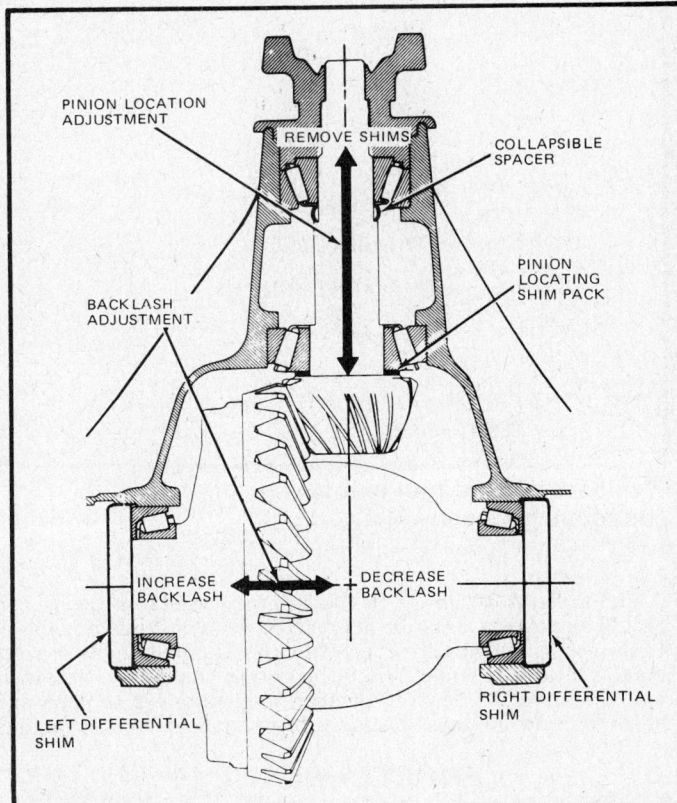

Typical pinion and ring gear tooth contact used with integral carrier axles (© Ford Motor Co.)

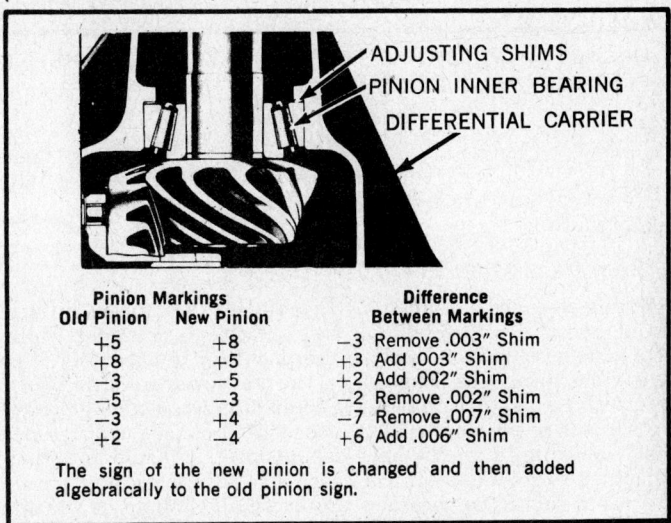

Pinion Markings		Difference
Old Pinion	New Pinion	Between Markings
+5	+8	−3 Remove .003" Shim
+8	+5	+3 Add .003" Shim
−3	−5	+2 Add .002" Shim
−5	−3	−2 Remove .002" Shim
−3	+4	−7 Remove .007" Shim
+2	−4	+6 Add .006" Shim

The sign of the new pinion is changed and then added algebraically to the old pinion sign.

Determining pinion shim pack thickness when shim pack is located at rear pinion bearing cup
(© General Motors Corp.)

28-17

SECTION 28 DRIVE AXLES
REPAIR PROCEDURES

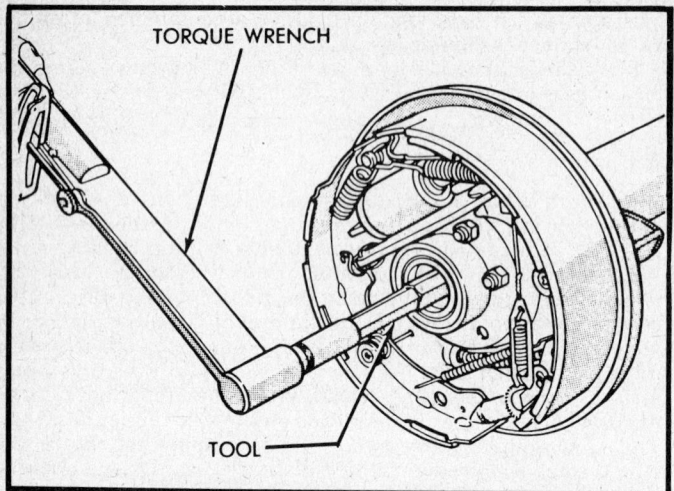

Use of special tool inserted into the axle tube to remove or adjust the threaded side carrier bearing adjuster rings (© Chrysler Corp.)

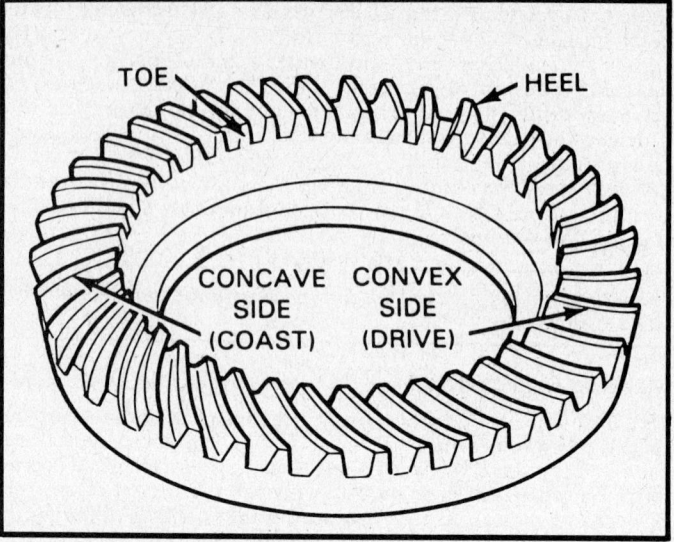

Ring gear tooth nomenclature (© General Motors Corp.)

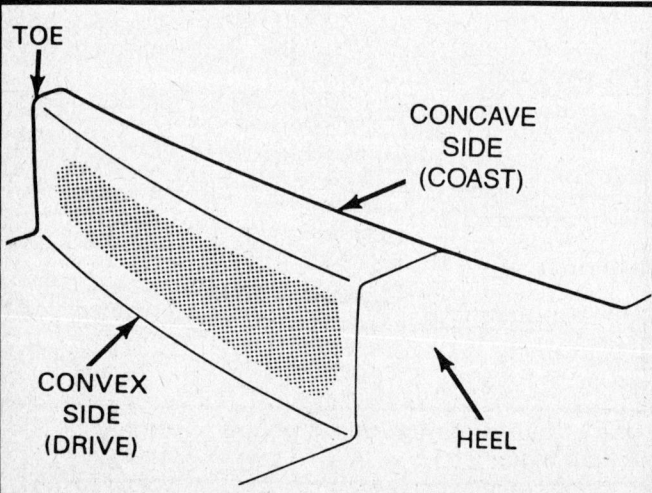

Desired ring gear tooth contact under light load (© General Motors Corp.)

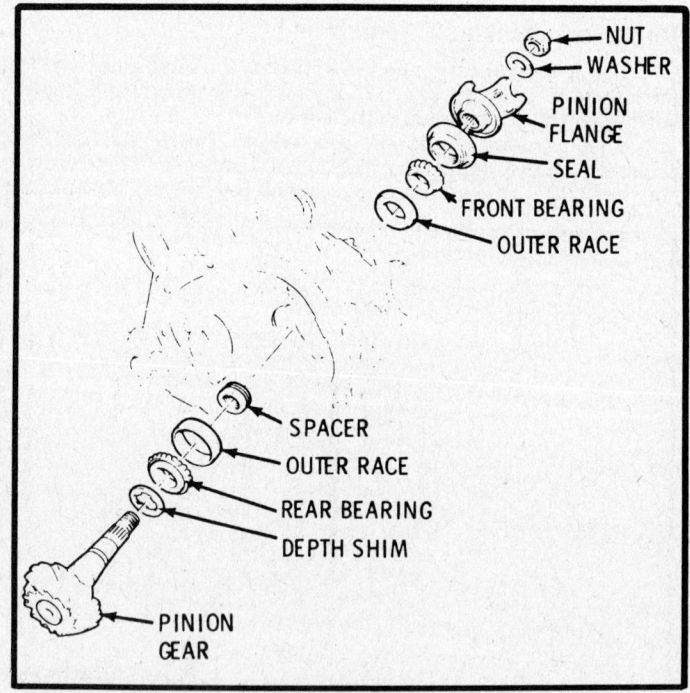

Typical standard rear axle using shims for pinion adjustment (© General Motors Corp.)

for the ring locking lug from the zero bearing preload. When specifications are available, refer to them for the correct procedure.

Shim Pack Method

Shims are used to control the backlash in numerous differential assemblies. Special tools are available to be used in finding zero bearing preload before the backlash is obtained. If the original shim pack is available, the measurements can be used to arrive at a starting point to determine zero bearing preload. As a rule of thumb, 0.004 in. is used to preload the differential side bearings after the backlash has been adjusted and, therefore, subtract 0.002 in. from each side shim pack and the zero preload should be obtained or only small changes in the shim packs would be needed to obtain the zero bearing preload. Measure the gear backlash and again adjust the left and right shim packs to move the ring gear closer to or away from the pinion gear until the correct backlash is obtained.

The amount of change in the shim thickness needed to correct the backlash must be subtracted from one side and added to the other, keeping the total shim thickness (left side + right side = total) the same. When the proper backlash is obtained, add the specified bearing preload measurement to each side shim pack. Recheck the backlash and the tooth contact pattern.

PROCEDURE NO. 15

Pinion Bearing Preload

As with other bearing applications, the pinion bearings must

DRIVE AXLES
REPAIR PROCEDURES
SECTION 28

be preloaded after the pinion depth has been corrected. Shims or crushable sleeves are used to provide the necessary preload adjustments.

The preload is usually determined from a rotating torque reading of the pinion, less the pinion oil seal, by the use of a torque wrench. When using shims, the pinion nut, yoke and front pinion bearing are required to be removed when adjusting the shim pack thickness. When the crushable spacer is used, the pinion nut is tightened, less pinion oil seal, until the correct turning torque is obtained.

CAUTION

Should the turning torque be loose due to the spacer being crushed too far, a new spacer must be used and the procedure repeated. Never back the nut off to obtain a torque reading.

LIMITED SLIP DIFFERENTIALS

Limited-Slip Differential Diagnosis

LUBRICATION

The use of proper lubricant is very important in limited-slip type drive axles. The forces applied when cornering tend to apply the clutch pack or clutch cones. The use of the wrong lubricant can cause the clutch surfaces to grap and chatter while turning. Always follow the manufacturer's recommendations regarding drive axle lubrication. When chatter is encountered, the differential lubricant should be drained and refilled with the specified lubricant.

TESTING

The clutch operation on all limited-slip type axles can be tested as follows:

American Motors "Twin-Grip"

1. With the engine off and the transmission in neutral, jack up one rear wheel.
2. Block the other wheel to prevent it from moving.
3. With a socket and a torque wrench on the axle shaft nut, turn the raised wheel forward.
4. The torque required to move the wheel should be 80–120 ft. lbs. for 7 9/16 in. axles.
5. A breakaway torque which is less than the specified figure, indicates a need for repair or replacement.

NOTE: When service is required on the unloading cone-type Twin Grip differential, the complete Twin Grip unit must be replaced.

Cadillac Controlled Differential

This unit should not be serviced. If a malfunction exists that cannot be cured by changing the fluid, remove the unit and install a new one.

AMERICAN MOTORS AXLE SPECIFICATIONS
REAR AXLE

Operation	USA	Metric
Axle Hub Installation Dimension	1-3/16 inch	30.16 mm
Differential Side Gear to Case Clearance	.000-.007 inches	.0-.17 mm

FRONT AXLE

	USA	Metric
7-9/16 in. Ring Gear		
Axle Shaft End Play	0.003	0.088
Differential Bearing Preload	0.15 in	0.38 mm
Differential Side Gear-to Case Clearance	.000-.006 inn	0.000-0.15 mm
Ring Gear Backlash	0.005-0.010	0.12-0.25 mm
Pinion Bearing Break-Away Preload		
Original Bearings	15-25 in-lbs	2-3 N·m
New Bearings	20-40 in-lbs	2-5 N·m
Pinion Depth		
Standard Setting	2.250	57.1 mm
Lubricant Capacity	2.5 pts.*	1.2 liters
Lubricant Type	SAE 85W-90**	SAE 85W-90**

* add 5 ounces (148 ml) to front axle shift housing
** use SAE 80W-140 lubricant during prolonged trailer towing

SECTION 28 DRIVE AXLES
REPAIR PROCEDURES

AMERICAN MOTORS AXLE SPECIFICATIONS
REAR AXLE

Operation	USA	Metric
7-9/16 in. Ring Gear		
Lubricant Capacity	3 pts.	1.41 liters
Pinion Depth Standard Setting	2.095 inch	53.21 mm
Pinion Bearing Preload	15-25 in-lbs	2.3 N·m
Ring and Pinion Backlash	.005-.009 in. (.008 preferred)	.13-.23 mm (.20 preferred)
Differential Bearing Preload	.008 inch	.20 mm
Differential Case Face Runout	.002 inch	.05 mm
Axle Shaft End Play	.004-.008 in. (.006 preferred)	.10-.20 mm (.15 preferred)

AMERICAN MOTORS AXLE TORQUE SPECIFICATIONS

(Service Set-To Torques should be used when assembling components. Service In-Use Recheck Torques should be used for checking a pre-tightened item.)

Rear Axle Differential Torque Specifications

	USA (ft-lbs)		Metric (N·m)	
	Service Set-To Torque	In-Use Recheck Torque	Service Set-To Torque	In-Use Recheck Torque
Brake Tubing-to-Rear Wheel Brake Cylinder	97 in-lb	90-105 in-lb	11	10-12
Differential Bearing Cap Bolt	57	52-67	77	71-91
Drive Gear-to-Case Bolt	52	42-65	71	57-88
Rear Brake Support Plate Screw Nut	32	25-40	43	34-54
Rear Wheel Hub-to-Axle Shaft Nut	250 min.	250 min.	339 min.	339 min.
Axle Cover Screw	15	10-18	20	14-27
Clamp Strap Bolt	14	10-18	19	14-24

Front Axle Differential Torque Specifications

	Service Set-To Torque	In-Use Recheck Torque	Service Set-To Torque	In-Use Recheck Torque
Axle Housing Cover Bolts	20	15-25	27	20-34
Axle Housing to left Engine Mounting Bracket	33	27-38	45	36-51
Axle Tube to right Engine Mounting Bracket Bolt and Nut	33	27-38	45	36-51
Differential Bearing Cap Bolts	40	35-50	54	47-68
Front Axle Support-to-Engine and Axle Housing Bolts	33	27-38	45	36-51
Pinion Nut	210	200-220	271	285-298
Propeller Shaft Flange Bolt Four-Cylinder Engine	15	12-18	20	16-24
Ring Gear-to-Case Bolts	55	45-65	75	61-88
Universal Joint Clamp Strap Bolts	17	15-20	23	20-27

All Torque values given in foot-pounds and newton-meters with dry fits unless otherwise specified.

DRIVE AXLES
REPAIR PROCEDURES
SECTION 28

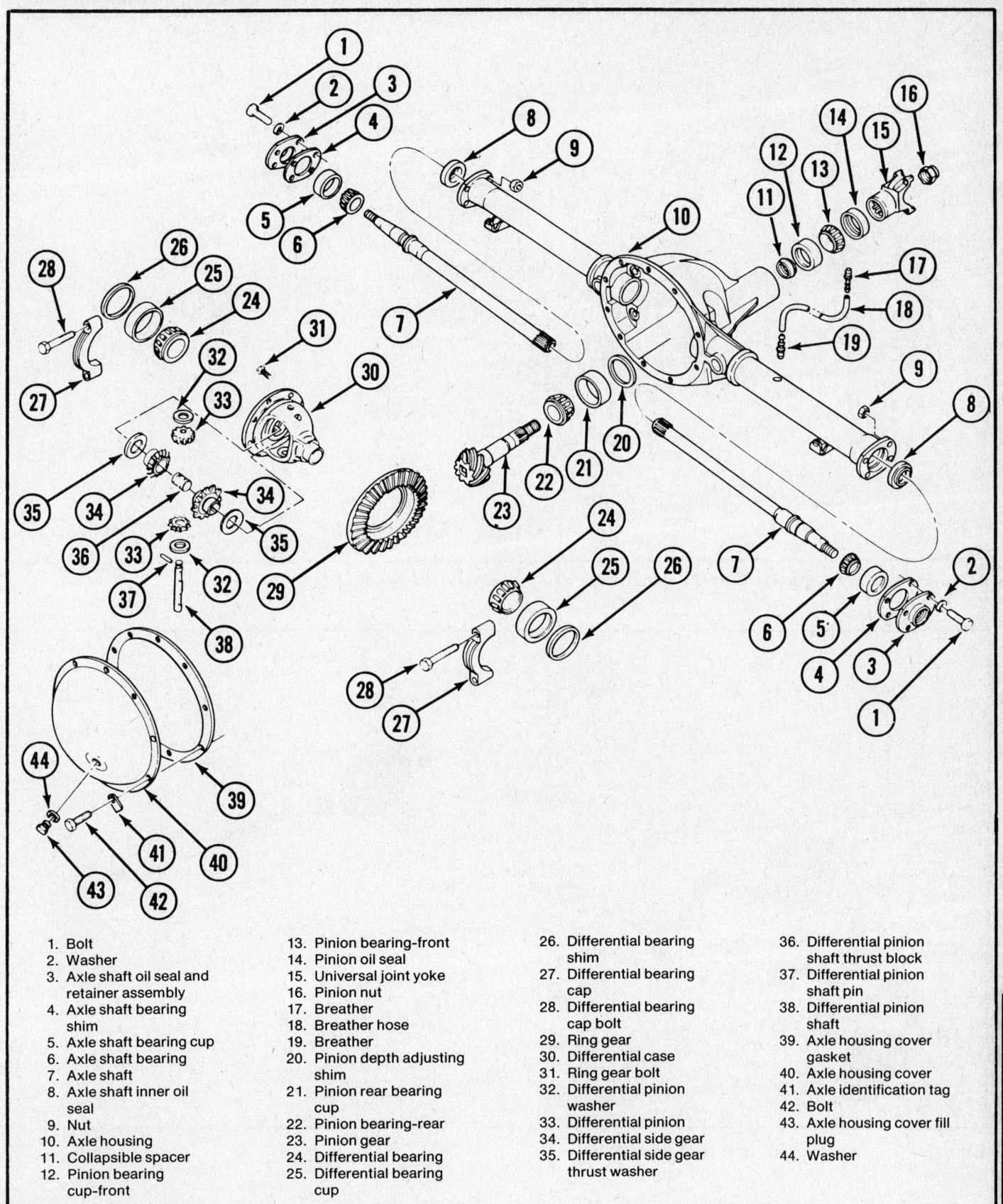

1. Bolt
2. Washer
3. Axle shaft oil seal and retainer assembly
4. Axle shaft bearing shim
5. Axle shaft bearing cup
6. Axle shaft bearing
7. Axle shaft
8. Axle shaft inner oil seal
9. Nut
10. Axle housing
11. Collapsible spacer
12. Pinion bearing cup-front
13. Pinion bearing-front
14. Pinion oil seal
15. Universal joint yoke
16. Pinion nut
17. Breather
18. Breather hose
19. Breather
20. Pinion depth adjusting shim
21. Pinion rear bearing cup
22. Pinion bearing-rear
23. Pinion gear
24. Differential bearing
25. Differential bearing cup
26. Differential bearing shim
27. Differential bearing cap
28. Differential bearing cap bolt
29. Ring gear
30. Differential case
31. Ring gear bolt
32. Differential pinion washer
33. Differential pinion
34. Differential side gear
35. Differential side gear thrust washer
36. Differential pinion shaft thrust block
37. Differential pinion shaft pin
38. Differential pinion shaft
39. Axle housing cover gasket
40. Axle housing cover
41. Axle identification tag
42. Bolt
43. Axle housing cover fill plug
44. Washer

Exploded view of AMC 7⁹/₁₆ in. rear axle with standard differential (© American Motors Corp.)

SECTION 28: DRIVE AXLES
REPAIR PROCEDURES

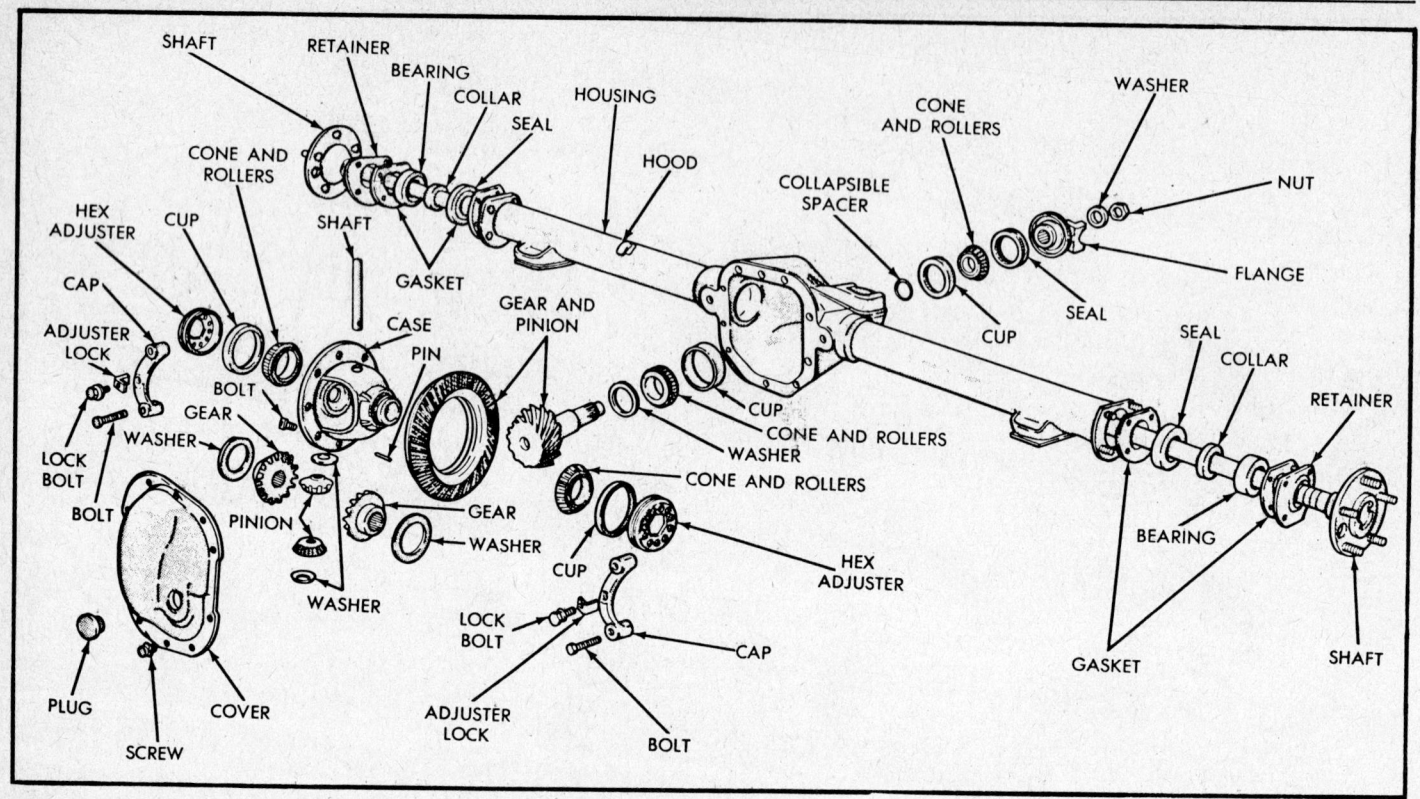

Exploded view of Chrysler Corp 7 7/4 inch rear axle assembly (© Chrysler Corp.)

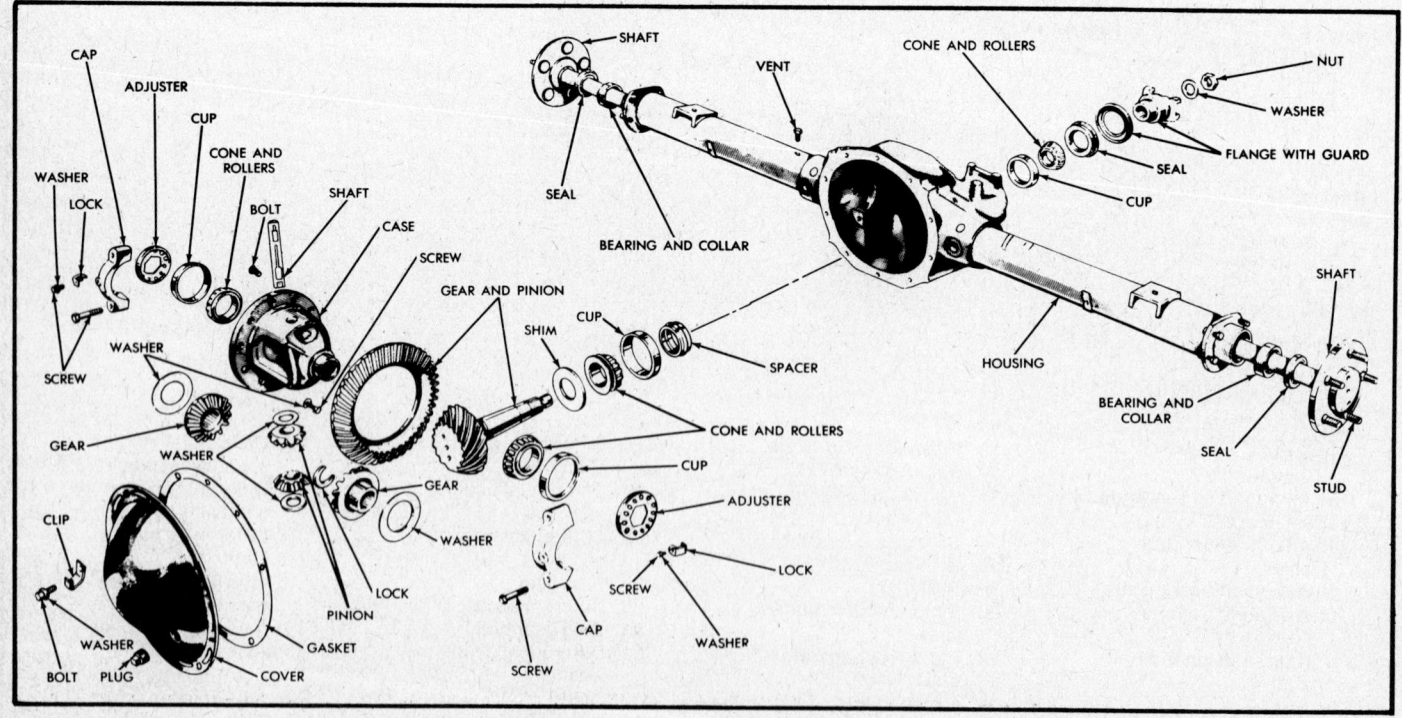

Chrysler 8 1/4 in. ring gear rear axle assembly

DRIVE AXLES
REPAIR PROCEDURES
SECTION 28

CHRYSLER REAR AXLE SPECIFICATIONS

7-1/4" Axle

TYPE	Semi-Floating Hypoid
Ring Gear Diameter	7.250"
Number of Teeth	
Drive Gear	43
Pinion	19
Ratio to 1	2.26
DIFFERENTIAL BEARINGS	
Adjustment by	Threaded Adjustment
PINION AND DRIVE GEAR BACK LASH	.004-.006" at point of minimum back lash
PINION BEARING PRELOAD ADJUSTMENT BY	Collapsible Spacer
PINION BEARING DRAG TORQUE	15-25 inch-pounds
PINION DEPTH OF MESH ADJUSTMENT BY	Selected Shims
	.020-.038 inch in .001 inch graduations
RUNOUT-CASE AND DRIVE GEAR	.005 inch Maximum
WHEEL BEARING TYPE	Single Row Sealed Ball
LUBRICATION	
Capacity	2.5 Pints (2 Imperial) 1.18 litres
Type	Multi-Purpose Gear Lubricant

CHRYSLER REAR AXLE SPECIFICATIONS

8-1/4" Axle

TYPE	Semi-Floating Hypoid
Ring Gear Diameter	8.250"
Number of Teeth	
Drive Gear	47
Pinion	21
Ratio to 1	2.24
PINION BEARINGS	
Type	Taper Roller
Number Used	Two
Adjustment	Collapsible Spacer
Pinion Bearing Preload New Bearings	20-35 Inch-Pounds
Used Rear And New Front	10-25 Inch-Pounds
DIFFERENTIAL	Conventional or Sure-Grip
Bearings (Type)	Taper Roller
Number Used	Two
Preload Adjustment	Threaded Adjustment
RING GEAR AND PINION	Hypoid
Serviced In	Matched Sets
Pinion Depth Of Mesh Adjustment	Select Shims
Pinion and Ring Gear Backlash	.006-.008" At Point
	Of Minimum Backlash
Runout-Differential Case 0.003 in. max.,	and Ring Gear Backface 0.005 in. Max.
WHEEL BEARINGS	
Type	Straight Roller
Adjustment	None
End Play	Built-In
Lubrication	Rear Axle Lubricant
LUBRICATION	
Capacity	4.4 PTS. (3-1/2 Imperial) 2.08 litres
Type	Multi-Purpose Gear Lubricant. In Sure-Grip Differentials 4 ounces (.1183 litres) of MOPAR Hypoid Gear Oil Additive Friction Modifier, Part No. 4057100 or equivalent must be included with every refill.

SECTION 28
Drive Axles
REPAIR PROCEDURES

CHRYSLER REAR AXLE
TORQUE SPECIFICATIONS

Components	Ft. lbs.	Inch lbs.	Nm
7-1/4 inch Axle			
Differential Bearing Cap Bolts	45		61
Ring Gear to Differential Case Bolts (Left Hand Thread)	70		95
Drive Pinion Flange Nut	210 (Min.)		285
Carrier Cover Bolts		250	28
Axle Shaft Retainer Nuts	35		47
Propeller Shaft Bolts (Rear)		170-200	19-23
Spring Clip (U Bolt) Nuts	45 (Max.)		61
Wheel Stud Nuts	85		115
Shock Absorber Stud Nuts (Lower)	50		68
8-1/4 inch Axle			
Differential Bearing Cap Bolts	100		136
Ring Gear to Differential Case Bolts	70		95
Drive Pinion Flange Nut	210 (Min.)		285
Carrier Cover Bolts		250	28

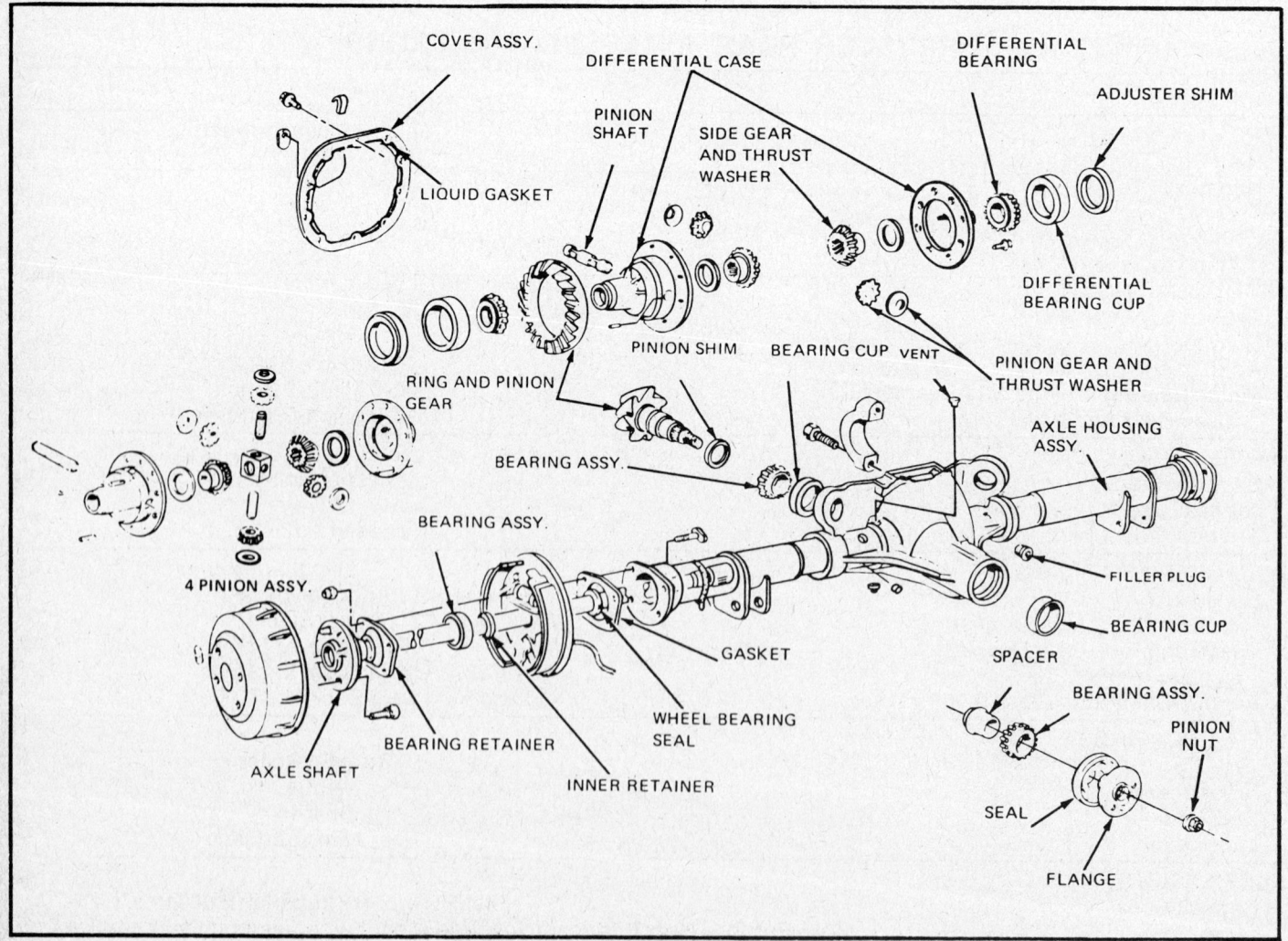

Exploded view of Ford Motor Co. 6³/₄ in. rear axle assembly

28-24

DRIVE AXLES
REPAIR PROCEDURES
SECTION 28

CHRYSLER REAR AXLE
TORQUE SPECIFICATIONS

Components	Ft. lbs.	Inch lbs.	Nm
Brake Support Plate Retainer Nuts	35		47
Propeller Shaft Bolts (Rear)		170-200	19-23
Spring Clip (U Bolt) Nuts	45		61
Wheel Stud Nuts	85		115
Shock Absorber Stud Nuts	50		68

FORD REAR AXLE SPECIFICATIONS
Integral Carrier—6-3/4 Inch Ring Gear (1982)

ADJUSTMENT TORQUE SPECIFICATIONS (INTEGRAL CARRIER)—CONVENTIONAL

Description	Nm	Torque (inch lbs.)	NM	Torque (ft. lbs.)
Minimum torque required to tighten pinion flange nut to obtain correct pinion bearing preload	—	—	189	(140)①
Pinion Bearing Preload— (Collapsible Spacer) Original Bearings—171.45 (6-3/4 inch)②	.9-1.6	(8-14)	—	—
New Bearings—171.45 (6-3/4 inch)	1.8-3.2	(16-29)	—	—

① If pinion bearing preload exceeds specifications before this torque is obtained, install a new spacer.
② With Oil Seal.

CLEARANCE, TOLERANCE AND ADJUSTMENTS (INTEGRAL CARRIER)—CONVENTIONAL

Description	mm	Inches	Description	mm	Inches
Maximum Runout of Backface of Ring Gear	.010	0.004	Available Pinion Gear Shims in Steps of: .0254mm (0.001 inch) 171.45mm (6-3/4 inch)	.533-.94	0.021-0.037
Differential Side Gear Thrust Washer Thickness	.762-.812	0.030-0.032	Backlash Between Ring Gear & Pinion Teeth	.203-.4	0.008-0.015
Differential Side Pinion Thrust Washer Thickness	.762-.812	0.030-0.032	Maximum Backlash Variation Between Teeth	.010	0.004
Differential Bearing (Case spread across Case)	0.41	0.016	Maximum Radial Runout of U-joint Flange in Assembly	.30 T.I.R.	0.012 T.I.R.
Nominal Pinion Locating Shim	.762	0.030			

ATTACHING TORQUE SPECIFICATIONS (INTEGRAL CARRIER)—CONVENTIONAL

Description	Torque Nm	ft. lbs.	Description	Torque Nm	ft. lbs.
Differential Bearing Cap Bolt—6-3/4 inch	95-115	70-85	Oil Filter Plug	20-41	15-30
Ring Gear Attaching Bolts—6-3/4 inch①	61-81	45-60	Rear Axle Shaft Bearing Retainer Nuts	27-54	20-40
Rear Cover Screw and Washer Assy's.	34-47	25-35			

① Using Loctite.

SECTION 28 — DRIVE AXLES REPAIR PROCEDURES

FORD REAR AXLE SPECIFICATIONS
Integral Carrier—7-1/2 Inch Ring Gear

CLEARANCE, TOLERANCE AND ADJUSTMENTS

Description	mm	Inches	Description	mm	Inches
Maximum Runout of Backface of Ring Gear	.010	.004	Backlash Between Ring Gear and Pinion Teeth	.203-.4	.008-.015
Differential Side Gear Thrust Washer Thickness	.762-.812	.030-.032	Maximum Backlash Variation Between Teeth	.10	.004
Differential Pinion Gear Thrust Washer Thickness	.762-.812	.030-.032	Maximum Radial Runout of Companion Flange in Assembly	.25 TIR	.010 TIR
Differential Carrier Spread	.041	.016	Available Pinion Gear Shims in Steps of: .0254mm (0.001 inch)		
Nominal Pinion Locating Shim	.762	.030	191mm (7.5 inch)	.533-.94	.021-.037

LUBRICANT CAPACITIES AND CHECKING PROCEDURES (INTEGRAL CARRIER)—CONVENTIONAL

Vehicle	Engine	Axle	U.S. Measure Capacity (Pints) ①	Imperial Capacity (Pints) ①
Mustang/Capri, Fairmont/Zephyr	2.3L	171.45mm (6-3/4 inch) Ring Gear	2.50 ②	2.08

① All conventional axles use ESP-M2C154-A (E0AZ-19580-A, B, C) lubricant or equivalent.
② Approximate refill capacity—actual lubricant capacities are determined by filling to the bottom of the filler plug hole.

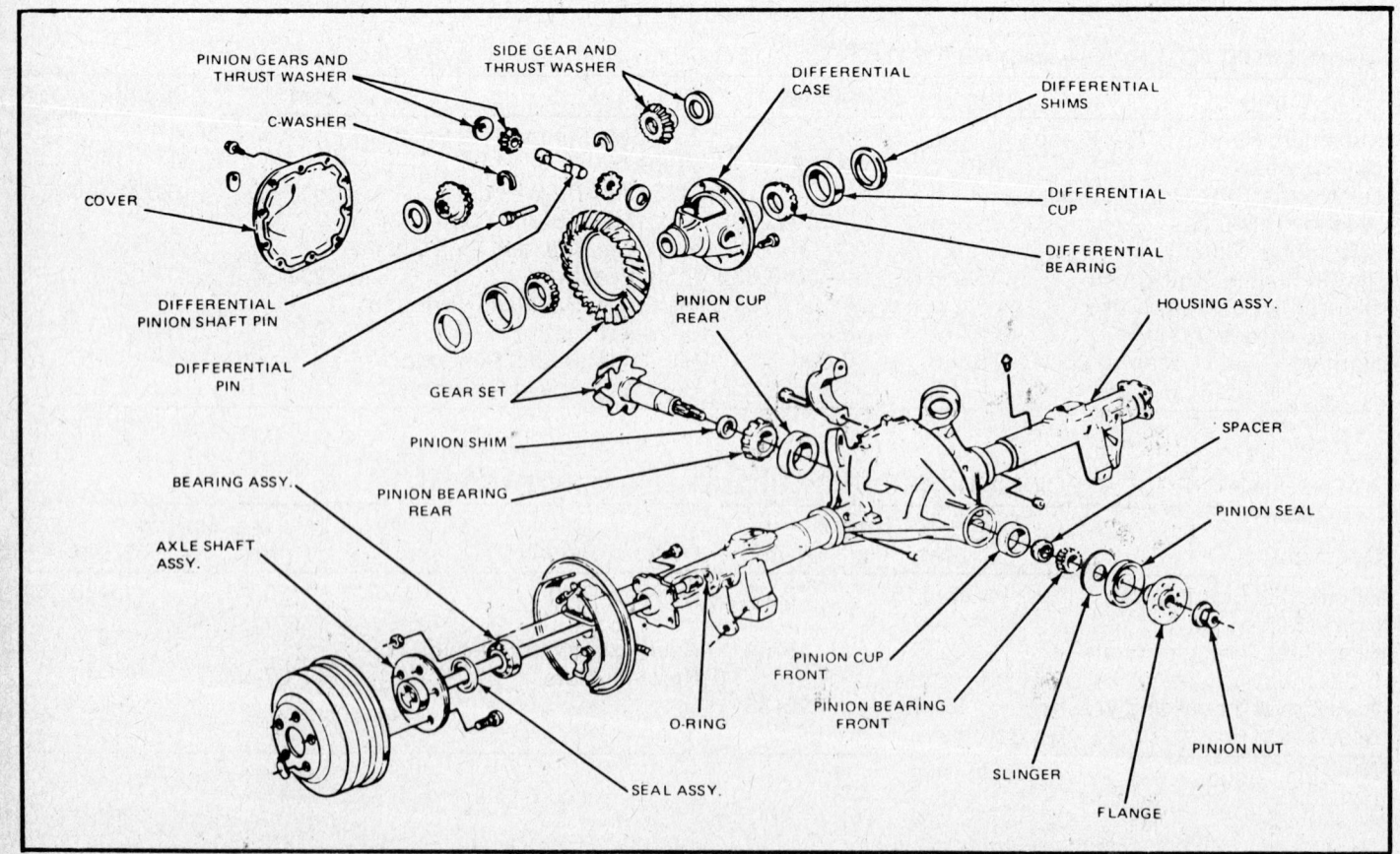

Exploded view of Ford Motor Co. 8.5 and 8.8 in. rear axle assembly (© Ford Motor Co.)

DRIVE AXLES
REPAIR PROCEDURES

SECTION 28

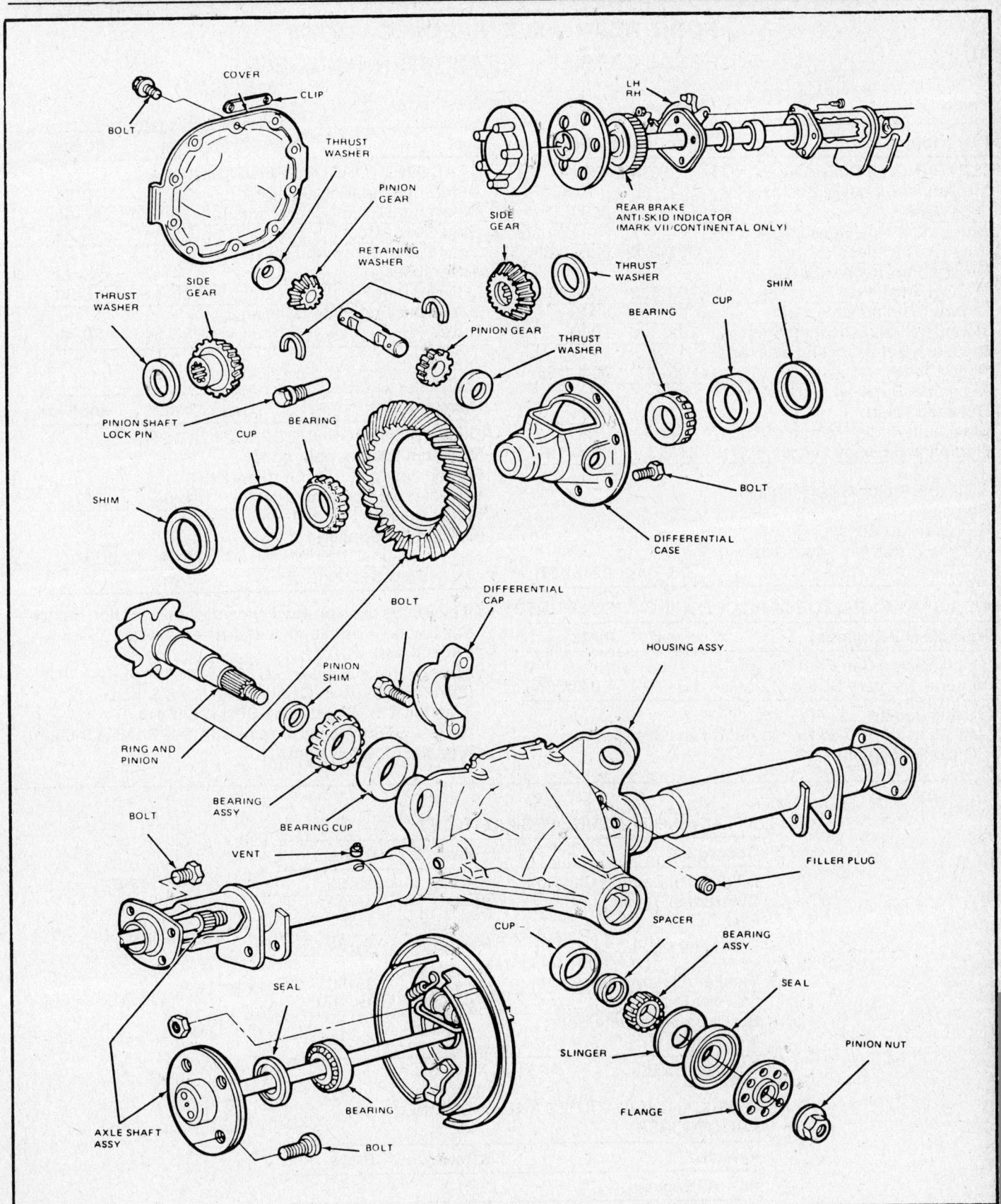

Exploded view of Ford Motor Co. 7½ in. rear axle assembly (© Ford Motor Co.)

SECTION 28 — DRIVE AXLES REPAIR PROCEDURES

FORD REAR AXLE SPECIFICATIONS
INTEGRAL CARRIER—8.5 AND 8.8 IN. RING GEAR

Description	mm	Inches
CLEARANCE, TOLERANCE AND ADJUSTMENTS		
Maximum Runout of Backface of Ring Gear	.0762	.004
Differential Side Gear Thrust Washer Thickness	.762-.812	.030-.032
Differential Pinion Gear Thrust Washer Thickness	.762-812	.030-.032
Differential Carrier Spread	.041	0.016
Nominal Pinion Locating Shim	.762	0.030
Backlash Between Ring Gear and Pinion Teeth	.203-.4	.008-.015
Maximum Backlash Variation Between Teeth	.1016	0.004
Maximum Radial Runout of Companion Flange in Assembly	.25 TIR	0.010 TIR
Available Pinion Gear Shims in Steps of: .0254mm (.001 inch) 224mm (8.8 inch) and 191mm (7.5 inch)	.533-.94	.021-.037

LUBRICANT CAPACITIES AND CHECKING PROCEDURES		
Vehicle (All Engines)	Liters	Pints
Lincoln Town Car, Ford Crown Victoria/Mercury Grand Marquis	1.9	4.0/3.75 ⑤

① Using Loctite
② 15-25 ft. lbs. (20-33 Nm) at Ratio Tag Location (Two O'clock Position).

Description	Nm	ft. lbs.
ATTACHING TORQUE SPECIFICATIONS		
Differential Bearing Cap Bolt	95-115	70-85
Differential Pinion Shaft Lock Bolt	20-41	15-30
Ring Gear Attaching Bolt ①	95-115	70-85
Rear Cover Screw and Washer Assemblies ②	34-47	25-35
Oil Filler Plug	20-41	15-30
Brake Backing Plate Bolts and Nuts	27-54	20-40

Description	Nm	inch lbs.
ADJUSTMENT TORQUE SPECIFICATIONS		
Minimum torque required to tighten pinion flange nut to obtain correct pinion bearing preload.	190 ③	140 (lb-ft)
Pinion Bearing Preload—(Collapsible Spacer)		
Original Bearings ④	11-19	8-14
New Bearings	23-37	16-29

③ If pinion bearing preload exceeds specification before this torque is obtained, install a new spacer.
④ With oil seal.
⑤ All conventional axles use ESP-M2C154-A (E0AZ-19580-A, B, C) lubricant. For 8.8 inch Traction-Lok Axles: Use ESP-M2C154-A (E0AZ-19580-A) plus 4 oz. of C8AZ-19B546-A friction modifier (or equivalent).

ATTACHING TORQUE SPECIFICATIONS

Description	Nm	ft. lbs.
Differential Bearing Cap Bolt	95-115	70-85
Differential Pinion Shaft Lock Bolt	20-41	15-30
Ring Gear Attaching Bolts ①	95-115	70-85
Rear Cover Screw and Washer Assemblies	34-47	25-35
Oil Filler Plug	20-41	15-30
Brake Backing Plate Bolts and Nuts	27-54	20-40

① Using Loctite

LUBRICANT CAPACITIES AND CHECKING PROCEDURES

Vehicles	Liters	Pints
All—All Engines	① 1.5	3.5

① All conventional axles use ESP-M2C154-A (E0AZ-19580-A, B, C) lubricant or equivalent.

DRIVE AXLES
REPAIR PROCEDURES

ADJUSTMENT TORQUE SPECIFICATIONS

Description	Nm	inch lbs.
Minimum torque required to tighten pinion flange nut to obtain correct pinion bearing preload.	① 230	170 (lb-ft)
Pinion Bearing Preload—(Collapsible Spacer)②		
Original Bearings	.9-1.6	8-14
New Bearings	1.8-3.2	16-29

① If pinion bearing preload exceeds specification before this torque is obtained, install a new spacer.
② With oil seal.

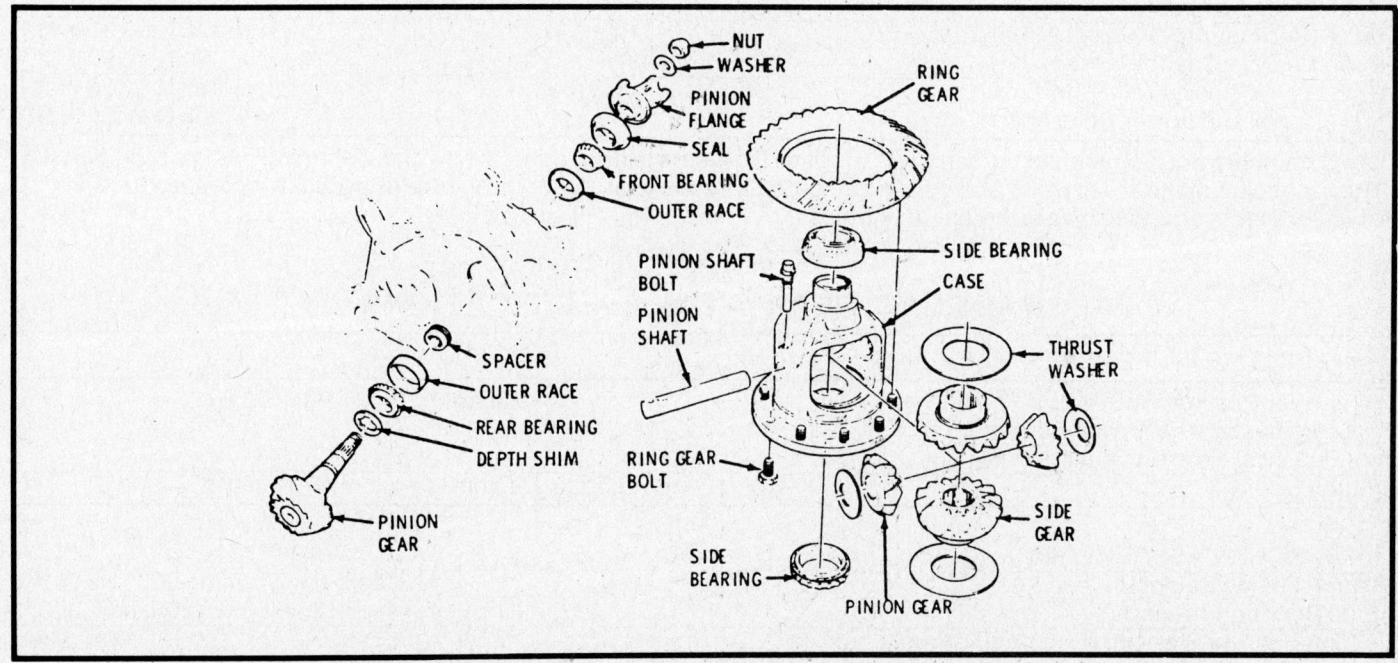

Exploded view of typical General Motors standard rear axle, used with all models (© General Motors Corp.)

BUICK REAR AXLE SPECIFICATIONS

Rear Axle Type Drive and Torque (All)	Semi-Floating Hypoid Through 4 Arms
Rear Axle Oil Capacity -	
7-1/2 in. Ring Gear Axle	1.66 Liters, 3.5 Pints
8-1/2 in. Ring Gear Axle	2.0 Liters, 4.25 Pints
8-3/4 in. Ring Gear Axle	2.0 Liters, 4.25 Pints
Ring and Pinion Gear Set Type	Hypoid
Differential Lubricant (All Axles)	GM 1052271 or Equivalent

LIMITS FOR FITTING AND ADJUSTMENTS

Pinion Bearing Pre-Load (Measured at Pinion Flange Nut) New Bearings	2.26 - 2.82 N·m (20-25 Lb. In.) Rotating Torque With New Seal
Reused Bearings - All	1.69 N·m (10-15 Lb. In.) Rotating Torque With New Seal

28-29

SECTION 28 DRIVE AXLES REPAIR PROCEDURES

BUICK REAR AXLE SPECIFICATIONS

Total Assembly Preload (Measured at Pinion Flange Nut)	
New Bearings	3.95 - 4.52 N·m (35-40 Lb. In.) Rotating Torque W/New Seal-Ring Gear
Reused Bearings	2.26 - 2.82 N·m (20-25 Lb. In.) Rotating Torque W/New Seal-Ring Gear
Ring Gear Position	.006"-.008" Backlash

BUICK REAR AXLE TORQUE SPECIFICATIONS

Bolt - Rear Universal Joint to Pinion Flange	
Strap or U-Bolt - All	20 N·m (15 lb.ft.)
Bolt - Rear Axle Housing Cover to Carrier	41 N·m (30 lb.ft.)
Nut - Brake Assembly to Rear Axle Housing	48 N·m (35 lb.ft.)
Bolt - Ring Gear to Differential Tail Case	120 N·m (90 lb.ft.)
Bolt - Bearing Cap to Carrier	81 N·m (60 lb.ft.)
Nut - Rear Wheel to Axle Shaft	108 N·m (80 lb.ft.)
Nut - Upper and Lower Control Arm	108 N·m (80 lb.ft.)

Use a reliable torque wrench to tighten the parts listed to insure proper tightening without staining or distorting parts. These specifications are to clean and lightly-lubricated threads only; dry or dirty threads produce increased friction which prevents accurate measurement of tightness.

CADILLAC REAR AXLE SPECIFICATIONS

8-1/2 INCH MEASUREMENTS

Ring Gear Position Backlash	.13-.23mm	.005-.009 in.
Lash must not vary over .05mm (.002 in) around ring gear		
Pinion Depth	.50 to 1.27mm	.020-.050 in.

8-7/8 INCH MEASUREMENTS

Pinion Flange Radial Runout	Zero to .076 mm (.000" to .003")
Side Bearing Pre-load	Slip Fit Plus .203 mm (.008")
Pinion Bearing Pre-load (Rotating Torque)	
New Bearings	2.7 to 3.6 N·m (24-32 in. lbs.)
Used Bearings	1.0 to 1.4 N·m (8-12 in. lbs.)
Ring Gear to Pinion Backlash	
New Gears	.127 to .228 mm (.005" to .009")
Used Gears (More than 3,000 mi.)	Original "Pre-checked" reading
Lubricant Capacity	2 Liters (4-1/4 Pints)

CADILLAC REAR AXLE TORQUE SPECIFICATIONS

8-1/2 INCH TORQUE SPECIFICATIONS

Bearing Cap Bolts	75 N·m	55 ft. lbs.
Carrier Cover Bolts	27 N·m	20 ft. lbs.
Pinion Shaft Lock Screw	27 N·m	20 ft. lbs.
Strap Bolts	21 N·m	16 ft. lbs.
Pinion Bearing Pre-Load		
New Bearings	2.26-2.82 N·m	20-25 in. lbs.
Used Bearings	1.13-1.69 N·m	10-15 in. lbs.
Total Assembly Pre-Load (measured at pinion flange nut)		
*New Bearings	3.95-4.52 N·m	35-40 in. lbs.
*Reused Bearings	2.26-2.82 N·m	20-25 in. lbs.

DRIVE AXLES
REPAIR PROCEDURES
SECTION 28

CADILLAC REAR AXLE TORQUE SPECIFICATIONS

8-1/2 INCH TORQUE SPECIFICATIONS

Pinion Depth Measurement Gage Plate Assembly Nut	1.6-2.2 N·m	15-25 in. lbs.
*Rotating Torque With New Seal - Ring Gear		

8-7/8 INCH TORQUE SPECIFICATIONS

Bearing Cap Bolts	90 N·m	65 ft. lbs.
Ring Gear-to-Gear Case Bolts	120 N·m	90 ft. lbs.
Housing Rear Cover Screws	27 N·m	20 ft. lbs.
Wheel Mounting Nuts	125 N·m	90 ft. lbs.
Pinion Cross Shaft Lock Screw	27 N·m	20 ft. lbs.
Pinion Flange to Driveshaft Screws	90 N·m	65 ft. lbs.
Differential Filler Plug	27 N·m	20 ft. lbs.
Lower Shock Absorber Bolts	90 N·m	65 ft. lbs.

CHEVROLET REAR AXLE SPECIFICATIONS

Ring Gear to Pinion Backlash		.005''-.008''
Pinion Bearing Preload—Inch/Pounds of Rotating	New	15-30
Torque	Used	10-10

CHEVROLET REAR AXLE TORQUE SPECIFICATIONS

B-G-F CARLINE

BOLT TORQUES—FOOT/POUNDS	7-1/2''	8-1/2''	8-3/4''	LUBRICANT CAPACITIES Complete Drain and Refill	
Carrier Cover	15-25	15-25	20-30		
Filler Plug	15-25	15-25	20-30	7-1/2'' Ring Gear	3.5 pints
Pinion Lock Screw	15-25	15-25	15-25	8-1/2'' Ring Gear	4.25 pints
Bearing Caps	46-65	45-65	60-75	8-3/4'' Ring Gear	5.4 pints
Ring Gear Bolts	80-95	70-90	70-90		

T CARLINE

Rear Cover-to-Axle Housing	30 N·m	22 Ft. Lbs.
Bearing Caps	75 N·m	55 Ft. Lbs.
Ring Gear-to-Case	65 N·m	48 Ft. Lbs.
Pinion Bearing Rotational Torque		10-20 in. lbs. (NDH) 5-15 in. lbs.
New Bearings	1.2-22 N·m (NDH) .6-1.6 N·m (Timken)	(Timken)
Used Bearings	0.56-1.13 N·m	5-10 in. lbs.
Lubricant Capacity	0.8 litres	(28 oz.)
Axle Shaft End-Play	0.5 mm	(.020 in.)

OLDSMOBILE REAR AXLE SPECIFICATIONS

Capacity	
7-1/2'' Ring Gear	1-3/4L (3-1/2 Pts.) approx.
8-1/2'' Ring Gear	2L (4-1/4 Pts.) approx.
8-3/4'' Ring Gear	2L (4-1/4 Pts.) approx.

SECTION 28 DRIVE AXLES REPAIR PROCEDURES

OLDSMOBILE REAR AXLE SPECIFICATIONS

Replenish (Conventional)	Lubricant No. SAE 80W GL-5, SAE 80W-90 GL-5, 1052271, or equivalent
Replenish (Limited Slip)	Special Lubricant No. 1052271, 1052272 or equivalent
	On 8-1/2" and 8-3/4" Axle Add 4 Ounces Lubricant Additive 1052358
Adjustments	
Backlash	.13-.23mm (.005"-.009")
Drive Pinion Bearing Pre-Load	
New Bearings	2.7 to 3.6 N·m (24 to 32 in. lbs.)
Old Bearings	1.0 to 1.4 N·m (8 to 12 in. lbs.)

OLDSMOBILE REAR AXLE TORQUE SPECIFICATIONS

Application	N·m	Ft. Lbs.
Cover to Carrier	30	20
Ring Gear Bolts	120	90
Side Bearing Cap Bolts	75	55
Pinion Gear Shaft Retaining Bolt	27	20

PONTIAC REAR AXLE SPECIFICATIONS

Rear Axle Type	Semi-Floating Hypoid
Drive and Torque (All)	Through 4 Arms
Rear Axle Oil Capacity -	
7-1/2" Ring Gear	3.50 Pints
8-1/2" Ring Gear	4.25 Pints
8-3/4" Ring Gear	5.40 Pints
Ring and Pinion Gear Set Type	Hypoid
Differential Lubricant (All Axles)	GM 1052271 or Equivalent

LIMITS FOR FITTING AND ADJUSTMENTS

Pinion Bearing Pre-Load (Measured at Pinion Flange Nut)	
New Bearings	15-30 inch lbs. Rotating Torque With New Seal
Reused Bearings - All	10-10 inch lbs. Rotating Torque With New Seal
Total Assembly Preload (Measured at Pinion Flange Nut)	
New Bearings	3.95 - 4.52 N·m (35-40 Lb. In.) Rotating Torque W/New Seal-Ring Gear
Reused Bearings	2.26 - 2.82 N·m (20-25 Lb. In.) Rotating Torque W/New Seal-Ring Gear
Ring Gear Backlash	.005 in.-.008 in. Backlash

PONTIAC REAR AXLE TORQUE SPECIFICATIONS

Bolt - Rear Universal Joint to Pinion Flange	
Strap or U-Bolt - All	20 N·m (15 lb.ft.)
Bolt - Rear Axle Housing Cover to Carrier	41 N·m (30 lb.ft.)
Nut - Brake Assembly to Rear Axle Housing	48 N·m (35 lb.ft.)
Bolt - Ring Gear to Differential Tail Case	120 N·m (90 lb.ft.)
Bolt - Bearing Cap to Carrier	81 N·m (60 lb.ft.)
Nut - Rear Wheel to Axle Shaft	108 N·m (80 lb.ft.)
Nut - Upper and Lower Control Arm	108 N·m (80 lb.ft.)

Use a reliable torque wrench to tighten the parts listed to insure proper tightening without staining or distorting parts. These specifications are to clean and lightly-lubricated threads only; dry or dirty threads produce increased friction which prevents accurate measurement of tightness.

DRIVE AXLES
REPAIR PROCEDURES
SECTION 28

CHEVROLET REAR AXLE TORQUE SPECIFICATIONS
1986 and Later B-G Carlines

Ring Gear (in.)	Carrier Cover	Filler Plug	Case Lock Screw		Bearing Caps	Ring Gear Bolts	Lubricant* Capacities (pints)
			Std. Slip	Ltd. Slip			
7½	15-25	15-25	15-25	23-30	45-65	80-95	3.5
7⅝	15-25	15-25	15-25	23-30	45-65	80-95	3.5
8½	15-25	15-25	15-25	23-30	45-65	70-90	4.25

Ring Gear to Pinion Backlash . . . . .005"-.008"
Pinion Bearing Preload (inch lbs. of
   rotating torque New 15-30
                        Used. 10-10

*Complete drain and refill

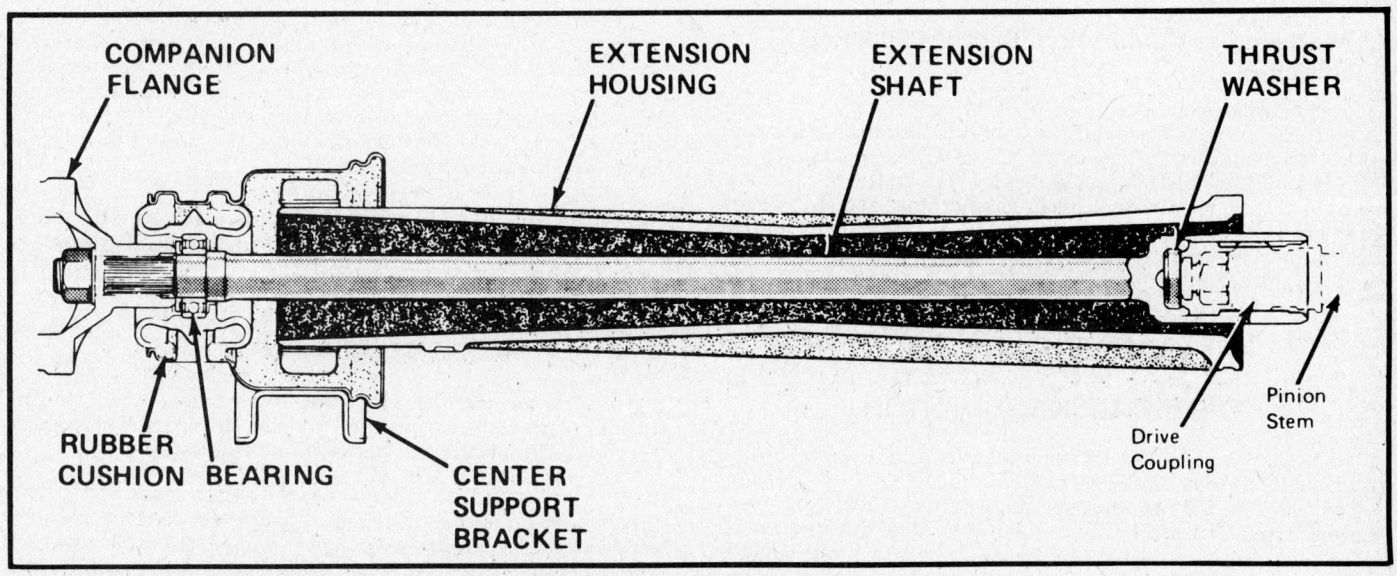

Chevette and 1000 models rear extension assembly (© General Motors Corp.)

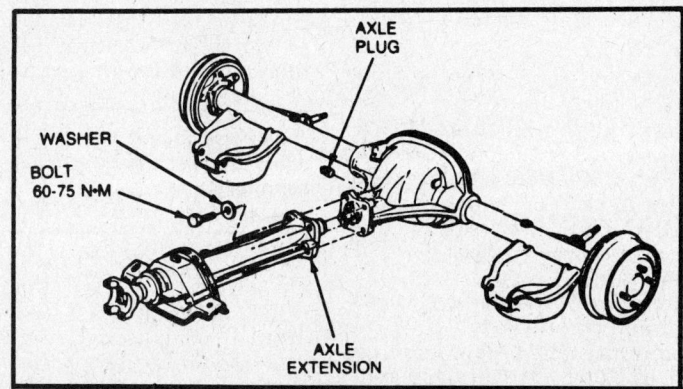

Mounting of rear axle extension on rear axle assembly — Chevette and 1000 models (General Motors Corp.)

28-33

SECTION 28
DRIVE AXLES
REPAIR PROCEDURES

Chrysler Corporation Sure-Grip

1. Place the vehicle on a hoist with the engine off and the automatic transmission in low gear.
2. Attempt to rotate the wheel by hand, by gripping the tire.
3. If it is extremely difficult, if not impossible, to rotate either wheel the Sure-Grip differential can be assumed to be performing satisfactorily.
4. If it is relatively easy to continuously turn either rear wheel, the unit should be removed and replaced.

CAUTION

The Sure-Grip differential is serviced as a unit only. Under no circumstances should the unit be disassembled and reinstalled.

Ford Motor Company Traction-Lok

Follow the procedure for the Ford Motor Company Equa-Lok rear. The minimum torque to continuously rotate the wheel (disregarding the breakaway torque) should be at least 40 ft. lbs.

General Motors Corporation (Except Cadillac) Positraction

1. Place the transmission in neutral.
2. Raise one rear wheel off the floor and block the other rear wheel (front and rear) to prevent the car from moving.
3. Install a torque wrench and extension on the lug nut and note the torque required to continuously rotate one rear wheel. Disregard the breakaway torque figure, as this may be a great deal higher.
4. The minimum torque to continuously rotate the rear wheel should be at least 35 ft. lbs. If it is not, the rear axle is in need of service.

General Diagnosis

Improper operation of a limited-slip type rear axle is generally indicated by clutch slippage or grabbing, which will sometimes produce a whirring or chatter sound. Occasionally, this condition is induced by improper lubrication. Check the unit for the wrong type of lubricant or lubricant which has broken down or become contaminated. Replace the lubricant with the type specified by the manufacturer.

During normal operation, i.e., straight-ahead driving, both wheels are rotating at equal speeds, and the driving force is distributed equally between both wheels. When cornering, the inside wheel delivers extra driving force, causing slippage in both clutch packs. Therefore, if the wheel rotation of both rear wheels is not equal, the unit will constantly be functioning as if the car were cornering. This will cause constant slippage and lead to eventual failure of the unit. It is important that there be no excessive differences in wheel and tire size, wear pattern, or tire pressures between both rear wheels. Swerving on acceleration is an indication of one or more of the above conditions. Before attempting an overhaul or replacement operation, check both rear wheels for identical tire sizes, tire pressure, tire tread depth, and wear pattern.

NOTE: Refer to General Drive Axle Diagnostic Guide at front of section, to determine possible conditions.

AMERICAN MOTORS TWIN-GRIP DIFFERENTIAL

GENERAL INFORMATION

A Twin-Grip limited-slip differential is available as an option in all AMC automobiles except Eagle models.

The 7 $9/16$ in. axle is equipped with an unloading cone type-limited slip differential. The conventional type differential divides available torque equally between both driving wheels, causing the wheel with the least traction to slip first. Twin-Grip provides many times the torque of the slipping wheel to the driving wheel however the unit is not a positive-lock type design and will release before excessive driving force can be directed to one rear wheel.

Twin-Grip Operation

Locking action is accomplished through unloading clutch cones. The cones are spring loaded to allow adequate driving force at the high traction wheel yet not interfere with steering characteristics or normal differential action. The locking action is produced by spring load which is automatically increased by differential pinion reaction when wheel traction increases.

Under extremely unbalanced traction conditions, such as with one wheel on dry pavement and the other on ice, wheel spin can occur if overacceleration is attempted. This spinning produces a whirring sound caused by clutch overrun. This spinning condition or sound does not indicate failure of the unit.

The spring load is calibrated to be rendered ineffective by variable torque; that is, when turning corners, the torque created by wheel travel differential will overcome the spring load.

TWIN-GRIP SERVICE

The unloading cone-type Twin-Grip differential is **serviced as an assembly only.**

When replacement is required, follow the removal and installation procedures outlined in the Standard Differential Overhaul section. Do not disassemble this differential.

CAUTION

After installing a Twin-Grip unit in the axle housing, do not attempt to rotate one axle shaft until both are in position. Rotating one axle shaft without the other axle shaft being installed will result in misalignment of the side gear hub and side gear splines and prevent installation of the second axle shaft.

Always fill a Twin-Grip axle with AMC Rear Axle Lubricant or equivalent lubricant marked SAE85W–90 only. Do not use lubricants containing sulfur at any time.

CAUTION

Do not use on-automobile type wheel balancers on the rear wheels of automobiles equipped with a Twin-Grip differential unless the wheel opposite the wheel being balanced is removed and the rear end of the automobile is raised.

SERVICE CHECK

The following procedure for checking the effectiveness of the unit should be performed before attempting repairs. This is necessary to avoid unnecessary disassembly or replacement.

1. Shift transmission into neutral.
2. Stop engine.
3. Raise one rear wheel only.
4. Rotate axle shaft in forward direction using socket and torque wrench installed on axle shaft nut. If necessary, bend cotter pin to allow installation of socket.
5. Torque required to rotate axle shaft should be 80–120 ft. lbs. (108–163 Nm).

LIMITED SLIP DIFFERENTIALS
AMERICAN MOTORS

28 SECTION

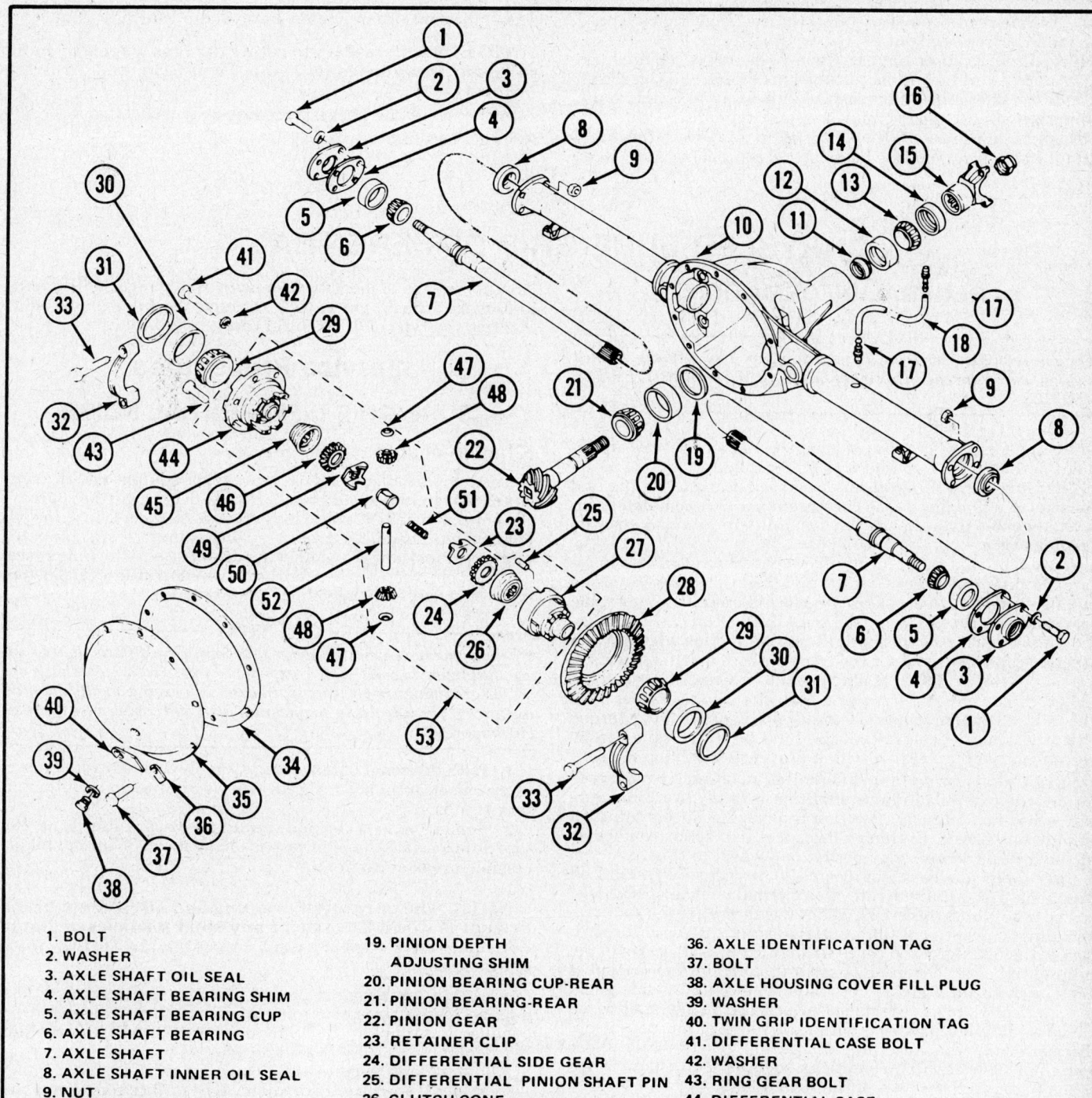

1. BOLT
2. WASHER
3. AXLE SHAFT OIL SEAL
4. AXLE SHAFT BEARING SHIM
5. AXLE SHAFT BEARING CUP
6. AXLE SHAFT BEARING
7. AXLE SHAFT
8. AXLE SHAFT INNER OIL SEAL
9. NUT
10. AXLE HOUSING
11. COLLAPSIBLE SPACER
12. PINION BEARING CUP-FRONT
13. PINION BEARING-FRONT
14. PINION OIL SEAL
15. UNIVERSAL JOINT YOKE
16. PINION NUT
17. BREATHER
18. BREATHER HOSE
19. PINION DEPTH ADJUSTING SHIM
20. PINION BEARING CUP-REAR
21. PINION BEARING-REAR
22. PINION GEAR
23. RETAINER CLIP
24. DIFFERENTIAL SIDE GEAR
25. DIFFERENTIAL PINION SHAFT PIN
26. CLUTCH CONE
27. DIFFERENTIAL CASE
28. RING GEAR
29. DIFFERENTIAL BEARING
30. DIFFERENTIAL BEARING CUP
31. DIFFERENTIAL BEARING SHIM
32. DIFFERENTIAL BEARING CAP
33. DIFFERENTIAL BEARING CAP BOLT
34. AXLE HOUSING COVER GASKET
35. AXLE HOUSING COVER
36. AXLE IDENTIFICATION TAG
37. BOLT
38. AXLE HOUSING COVER FILL PLUG
39. WASHER
40. TWIN GRIP IDENTIFICATION TAG
41. AXLE CASE BOLT
42. WASHER
43. RING GEAR BOLT
44. DIFFERENTIAL CASE
45. CLUTCH CONE
46. DIFFERENTIAL SIDE GEAR
47. DIFFERENTIAL PINION THRUST WASHER
48. DIFFERENTIAL PINION
49. RETAINER CLIP
50. DIFFERENTIAL PINION SHAFT THRUST BLOCK
51. SPRING
52. DIFFERENTIAL PINION SHAFT
53. DIFFERENTIAL SERVICED AS ASSEMBLY ONLY.

AMC Twin-Grip differential—exploded view (© Ford Motor Co.)

28–35

SECTION 28
LIMITED SLIP DIFFERENTIALS
AMERICAN MOTORS

6. Torque readings not within specified range indicate need for repair or replacement.

If repair or replacement of a Twin-Grip unit is required, remove and install the unit as outlined in Differential Overhaul-Standard Differential. Replace the unit as an assembly only. Do not attempt to disassemble or repair the unit.

To eliminate chatter from a Twin-Grip unit, drain the original lubricant from the axle housing and refill using AMC Rear Axle lubricant or equivalent limited slip gear lubricant.

NOTE: It is necessary to rotate the rear wheels by hand to cause the lubricant in the Twin-Grip unit to drain properly.

In the event the above procedure is not effective after 200 miles of operation, it will be necessary to remove and service the unit.

CHRYSLER SURE-GRIP DIFFERENTIAL

GENERAL INFORMATION

─────── **CAUTION** ───────

Anytime rear axle servicing is necessary, or axle is being rotated through use of the engine or other means, ELEVATE BOTH REAR WHEELS.

The **Sure-Grip** differential is being offered as a special equipment option in 8 1/4 in. and 9 1/4 in. rear axles.

The **Sure-Grip** differential design is basic and simple and consists of a two piece case construction and is completely interchangeable with the conventional differential and also the previous type.

A conventional differential allows the driving wheels to rotate at different speeds while dividing the driving torque equally between them. This function is ordinarily desirable and satisfactory. However, the total driving torque can be no more than double the torque at the lower-traction wheel. When traction conditions are not the same for both driving wheels, a portion of the available traction cannot be used.

The **Sure-Grip** differential allows the driving wheel with the better traction condition to develop more driving torque than the other wheel, so that the total driving torque can be significantly greater than with a conventional differential.

Sure-Grip is not locking differential. In normal driving conditions the controlled internal friction is easily overcome during cornering and turning so that the driving wheels can turn at different speeds. Extreme differences in traction conditions at the driving wheels may permit one wheel to spin.

Sure-Grip has been engineered to perform its specialized functions with minimum effect on normal vehicle operations.

The cone clutch **Sure-Grip** differentials are similar to corresponding conventional differentials except for the incorporation of the helix-grooved cones that clutch the side gears to the differential case. The grooves assure maximum lubrication of the clutch surface during operation. The cones an side gears are statically spring preloaded to provide an internal resistance to differential action within the differential case itself. This internal resistance provides pulling power while under extremely low tractive conditions such as mud, snow or ice when encountered at one of the rear wheels.

During torque application to the axle, the initial spring loading of the cones is supplemented by the gear separating forces between the side gears and differential pinions which progressively increases the friction in the differential. It should be remembered that this differential is not a positive locking type and will release before excessive driving force can be applied to one wheel.

SURE-GRIP DIFFERENTIAL IDENTIFICATION

Identification of **Sure-Grip** differential assembly can easily be made by lifting both rear wheels off the ground and turning them. If both rear wheels turn in the same direction simultaneously, the vehicle is equipped with a **Sure-Grip** differential.

Another means of identification is by removing the filler plug and using a flashlight to look through the filler plug hole to identify the type of differential case.

Service Procedures

SURE-GRIP DIFFERENTIAL NOISE

(Chatter-Moan)

Noise complaints related to rear axles equipped with cone-clutch **Sure-Grip** should be checked to determine the source of the noise. If a vehicle ride check produces the noise in turns but not straight ahead, the probable cause is incorrect ordissipated rear axle lubricant. The following draining and flushing procedure has been established for the **Sure-Grip** differential before it is removed from the vehicle and replaced.

─────── **CAUTION** ───────

When servicing vehicles equipped with Sure-Grip differentials do not use the engine to rotate axle components unless both rear wheels are off the ground. Sure-Grip equipped axles can exert a significant driving force if one wheel is in contact with floor and could cause the vehicle to move

1. With lubricant of rear axle assembly at operating temperature raise car on hoist so rear wheels are free to turn. Install jack stands.
2. Remove axle cover and drain and discard lubricant. Rotate differential so hole in case is facing down. Wipe out all accessible areas of carrier.

NOTE: The purpose of draining and discarding this lubricant is to rid the axle of any solid particles or liquid contaminants that may be contributing to the noise condition.

3. Scrape any gasket material from housing cover and thoroughly clean surface with mineral spirits or equivalent and dry completely. Apply a 1/16–3/32 in. bead of MOPAR Silicone Rubber Sealant.

Allow sealant to cure while cleaning carrier gasket flange with mineral spirits or equivalent. Dry surface completely. Install cover on axle and torque cover screws to 250 inch lbs. (28 Nm). Beneath one of the cover screws, install the ratio identification tag.

If for any reason cover is not installed within 20 minutes after applying sealant, old sealand should be removed and a new bead installed.

4. Remove jack stands. Raise or lower hoist until vehicle is in a level position.
5. Remove filler plug. Install 4 ounces (0.1183 litres) of MOPAR Hypoid Gear Oil Additive Friction Modifier, Part No. 4057100 or equivalent in the axle. Refill axle to proper level with MOPOR Hypoid Lubricant, Part No. 3744994 or equivalent.
6. Install filler plug. Lower vehicle.

28-36

LIMITED SLIP DIFFERENTIALS
CHRYSLER CORPORATION
SECTION 28

TESTING SURE-GRIP DIFFERENTIAL

The **Sure-Grip** differential can be checked to determine if its performance is satisfactory without removing the differential and carrier assembly from the vehicle.

1. Position vehicle on a hoist with engine off and the transmission selector lever in park if automatic or in low gear if manual.
2. Attempt to rotate wheel by applying turning force with hands gripping tire tread area.
3. If you find it extremely difficult, if not impossible to manually turn either wheel, you can consider the **Sure-Grip** differential to be performing satisfactorily. If you find it relatively easy to continuously turn either wheel the differential is not performing properly and should be removed and replaced. The **Sure-Grip** differential and internal parts are serviced as a complete assembly only. **Under no circumstances should the differential be removed, disassembled, assembled and reinstalled.**

SURE-GRIP DIFFERENTIAL

CAUTION

During removal and installation of axle shafts, DO NOT rotate an axle shaft unless both are in positon. Rotation of one axle shaft without the other in place may result in misaligment of the two spline segments with which the axle shaft spline engages, and will necessitate difficult realignment procedures when shaft is installed.

Removal
Follow the same procedure outlined under conventional differential removal.

Cleaning and Inspection

1. Clean the **Sure-Grip** differential assembly in a fast evaporating mineral spirits or a dry cleaning solvent and with exception of bearings, dry with compressed air.

Testing sure grip differential effectiveness (© Chrysler Corp.)

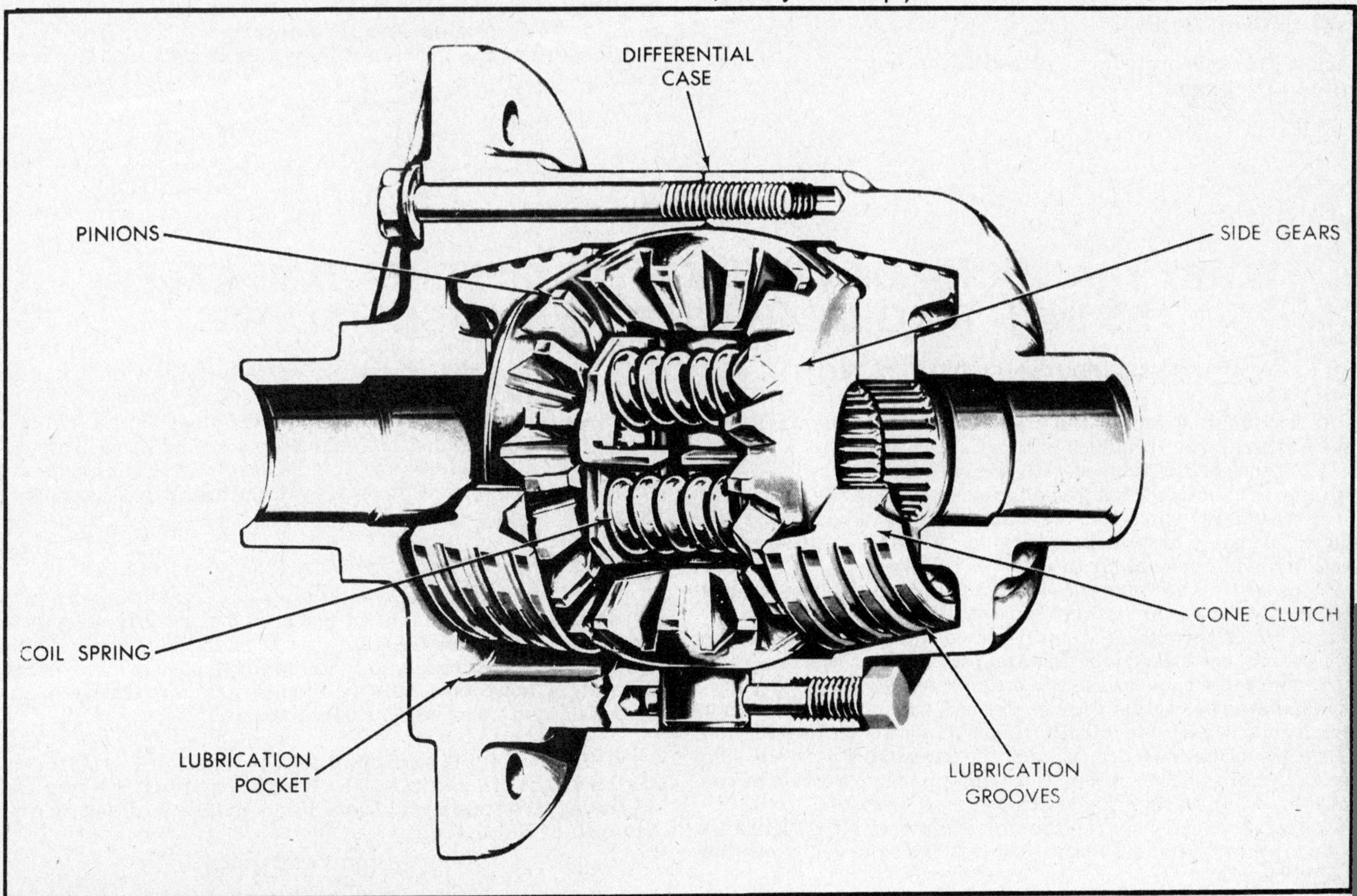

Sure-grip differential (schematic) (© Chrysler Corp.)

28-37

SECTION 28
LIMITED SLIP DIFFERENTIALS
CHRYSLER CORPORATION

2. Inspect differential bearing cones, cups and rollers for pitting, spalling or other visible damage. If replacement is necessary, remove bearing cones from differential case using procedure outlined in conventional axle section of this group.

3. Visually inspect differential case for cracks or other visible damage which might render it unfit for further service.

Assembly

1. If during cleaning and inspection the differential bearings were found to be unfit for further use and were removed follow procedure outlined in conventional axle section of this group.

2. On axles requiring ring gear to be installed on differential case, relieve the sharp edge of the chamfer on the inside diameter of the ring gear using an Arkansas stone. This is very important, otherwise during the installation of ring gear on differential case, the sharp edge will remove metal from the pilot diameter of case, which can get imbedded between differential case flange and gear; causing ring gear not to seat properly.

3. Heat the ring gear with a heat lamp or by immersing the gear in a hot fluid (water or oil). The temperature should not exceed 300°F (149.0°C). DO NOT USE A TORCH. It is advantageous to use pilot studs equally spaced in three positions to align the gear to the case.

4. Using new drive gear screws (left hand threads) insert through case flange and into drive gear.

5. Position unit between brass jaws of a vise and alternately tighten each screw to 70 ft. lbs. (95 Nm) on all axles.

6. Follow procedure outlined in conventional axle assembly for setting drive pinion depth of mesh, drive gear backlash adjustment and bearing preload adjustment.

Installation

Follow the same procedure outlined under conventional differential installation.

LUBRICATION

Multi-Purpose Gear Lubricant, as defined by MIL-L-2105-B (APIGL-5) should be used in all rear axles with conventional differentials; MOPAR Hypoid Lubricant, Part No. 3744994 is an oil of this type and is recommended or equivalent.

In Sure-Grip Differentials 4 ounces (0.1183 litres) or MOPAR Hypoid Gear Oil Additive Friction Modifier, Part No. 4057100 or equivalent must be included with this fill.

Fluid Level Check

For normal passenger car service, periodic fluid level checks are not required. At each engie oil change however, the exterior surfaces of the axle assembly should be inspected for evidence of gear oil leakage. Perform a fluid level check to confirm and suspectted leakage. When this check is made with the car in a level position, supported by the suspension, on an Axle or Wheel Type Hoist or on the ground, the fluid levels listed should be located as follows:

8 ¼ in. axle—at bottom of filler hole.

NOTE: When the fluid level check is made with the vehicle on a frame contact type hoist, with the axle hanging free, the fluid level should not be lower than the bottom of the filler plug opening.

Confirmed leakage should be repaired as soon as possible!

NOTE: Should the rear axle become submerged in water, the lubricant must be changed immediately to avoid the possibility of early axle failure resulting from contamination of the lubricant by water drawn into the vent hole.

FORD TRACTION-LOK LIMITED SLIP DIFFERENTIAL AXLE— 7.5 INCH RING GEAR WITH TWO CASE HALVES

DESCRIPTION AND OPERATION

The frictional surface of the brake cones, consists of a coarse spiral thread that provides lubrication passages.

The cones are pre-loaded with five springs mounted between spring thrust plates that press against the side gear and brake cone assembly, which sets in cavities in both halves of the differential case. These springs provide resistance to differential action during normal operation.

The pressure between the side gear and brake cones, created by the five pre-load springs, opposes differential action at all times. Since the side gears are splined to the axle shafts, the axle shafts are locked together and rotate with the case. When the vehicle turns a corner, the brake cones slip, allowing normal differential action to take place. Under adverse weather conditions, where one or both wheels may be on a low-traction surface such as snow, ice, or mud, the friction between the side gear and brake cone assemblies will transfer a portion of the usable torque to the wheel with the most traction.

Never raise one wheel and run the engine with the transmission in gear. The wheel on the floor will drive the vehicle off the stand or jack.

The driving force to the wheel on the floor or ground will cause the vehicle to move.

Do not use On-the-Car type wheel balancers on the rear wheels, unless **both** wheels are off the floor.

The case assembly of this locking differential is a non-serviceable item and must be replaced as a complete case assembly. Service procedures for this locking differential case are presented for information only, or in the event that cleaning of component parts should be necessary.

Noise Acceptability

A gear driven unit especially an automotive drive axle, will produce a certain amount of noise. Some noise is acceptable and may be audible at certain speeds or under various driving conditions, for example, as on a newly paved blacktop road. The slight noise is in no way detrimental to operation of the rear axle and must be considered normal.

NOTE: Vehicles equipped with a traction-lok differential, a slight stick-slip noise on tight turns after extended highway driving is considered acceptable and has no detrimental effect.

ADJUSTMENTS

No in-vehicle adjustment are possible on this unit.

LIMITED SLIP DIFFERENTIALS
FORD MOTOR COMPANY

TESTING

Bench Check

With the locker Tool T59L–4204–A or equivalent, check the torque required to rotate one side gear while the other is held stationary. The initial break-away torque should be no less than 41 Nm (30 ft. lbs.).

In-Vehicle Check

A traction-lok differential can be checked for proper operation without removing the differential from the axle housing.

Jack up on rear wheel and remove the wheel cover.

Install Tool T59L–4204–A or equivalent, on the axle shaft flange studs.

Using a torque wrench of at least 271 Nm (200 ft. lbs.) capacity, rotate the axle shaft. Be sure that the transmission is in Neutral, one rear wheel is on the floor, and the other rear wheel is raised off the floor. The break-away torque required to start rotation should be at least 41 Nm (30 ft. lbs.). The initial break-away torque may be higher than the continuous turning torque, but this is normal.

The axle shaft should turn with even pressure throughout the check without slipping or binding. If the torque reading is less than specification, replace the differential assembly.

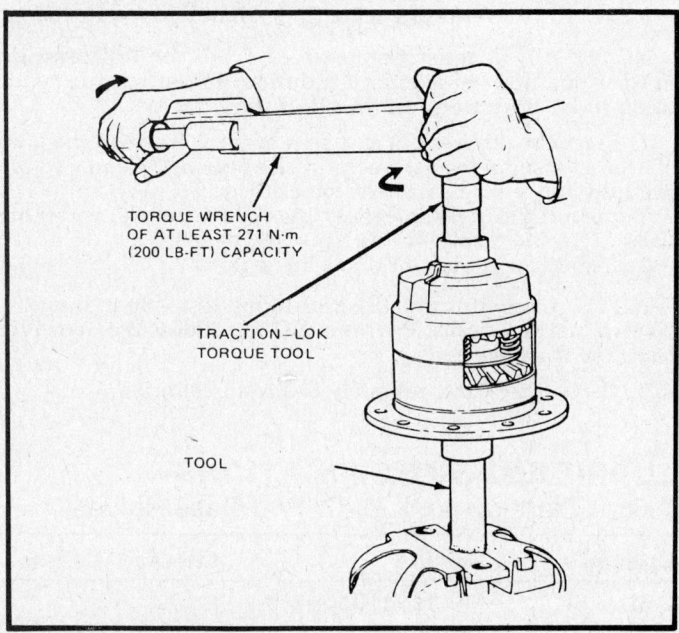

Bench torque check (© Ford Motor Co.)

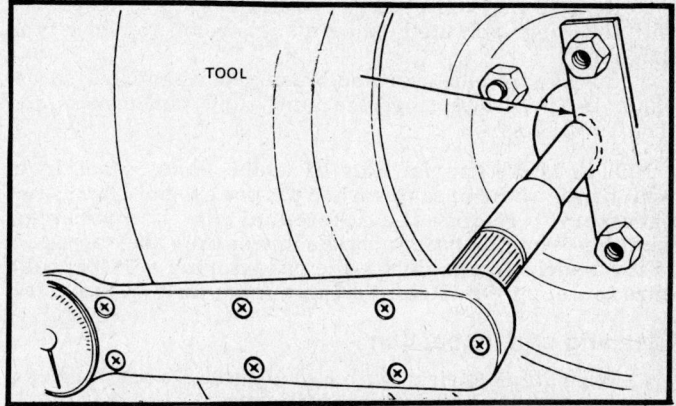

Traction-lok differential check (© Ford Motor Co.)

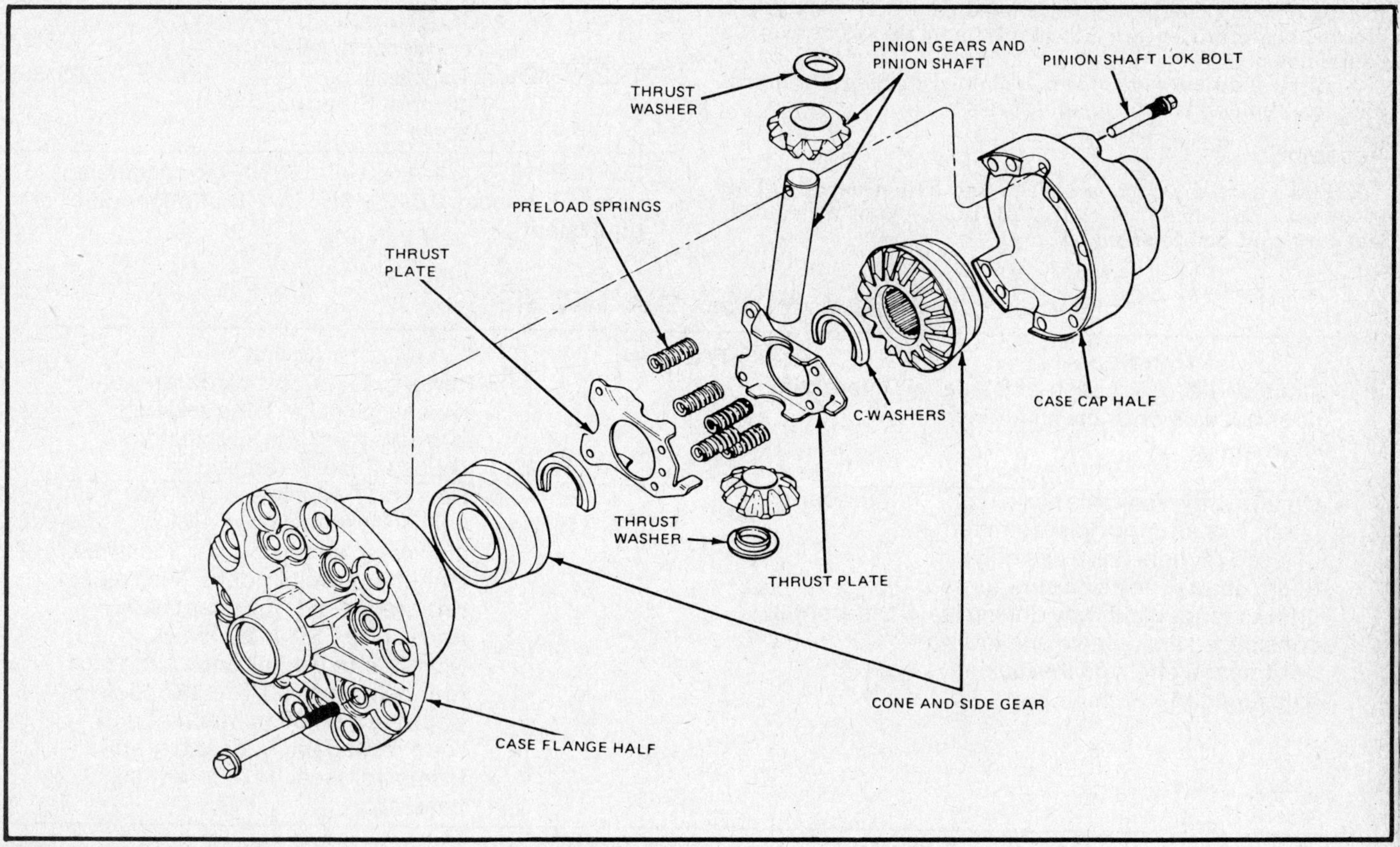

Differential assembly – sectional view (© Ford Motor Co.)

SECTION 28
LIMITED SLIP DIFFERENTIALS
FORD MOTOR COMPANY

A vehicle equipped with a traction-lok differential will always have both wheels driving. If while the vehicle is being serviced, only one wheel is raised off the floor and the rear axle is driven by the engine, the wheel on the floor could drive the vehicle off the stand or jack.

DISASSEMBLY AND ASSEMBLY

Disassembly

1. Place the differential case in a press, or between the jaws of a large vise, to load the case at the bearing journals so the pre-load of the springs is overcome. Then, loosen the eight capscrews that hold the case together until 3 or 4 threads remain engaged. Loosen the press or vise loads slightly, but do not remove the case at this time, and tap the flange-half of the case with a soft hammer, to spring it loose.
2. Remove the case assembly from the press or large vise with the flange-half up. Remove all capscrews, and lift off the flange-half.
3. Remove the side gear and brake cone assemblies, thrust plates, five pre-load springs, the pinion shaft, pinion gears, and thrust washers.

NOTE: Make special note of which cone comes from which half of the case to assure proper assembly. It is not necessary to remove the differential cone and roller assemblies from the case journals unless they are damaged. If the bearings remain on the case during service, take care to keep them clean and free from foreign material.

Cleaning and Inspection

1. Wipe all parts clean with a shop towel. Do not use cleaners or solvents on this locking differential.
2. Inspect all mating parts for surface condition. Excessive scoring or wear should not be accepted (However, very slight grooves or scratches are acceptable, and the parts can be reassembled.)
3. Any condition worse than explained in Step 2 requires complete replacement of the unit.

Assembly

1. Make sure the parts are clean and free of burrs. Oil all parts with ESP–M2C154–A (EOAZ–19580–A) or an equivalent lubricant before assembly.
2. Place the cap half of the differential case in a vise with the inside of the case half facing upward.
3. Install the proper cone in the case and seat it in position.
4. Assemble in proper order the remaining parts including the thrust plates, pre-load springs, pinion gears, thrust washers and pinion shaft. Finally, install the second cone assembly.
5. Install the flange-half of the case over the cone in position.
6. Install two retaining bolts fingertight at opposite sides.

NOTE: All oil must be removed from the bolt and its mating surface before installation or a false torque reading will be obtained and the bolt may break.

7. Place the differential case in a press or between the jaws of a large vise, to load the case at the bearing journals so the pre-load of the springs is overcome.
8. Install and tighten evenly the balance of the retaining bolts to 34–39 ft. lbs. (45–53 Nm).
9. Install the pinion lock bolt fingertight.

NOTE: Lock bolt must be tightened to 15–30 ft. lbs. (20–30 Nm) using Loctite Part No. EOAZ–19554–B or equivalent, for final assembly.

10. Bench check the assembly before installation.

LUBRICANT SPECIFICATIONS
7.5 in. Traction-LOK With Two Case Halves

Engine	Vehicle	Liters①	Pints
2.3L, 3.8L (140 CID 232 CID)	Mustang/Capri, Fairmont Futura/ Zephyr, LTD/Marquis, Thunderbird/XR-7		
3.3L (200 CID)	LTD/Marquis, Fairmont Futura/ Zephyr	1.5/1.6	3.25/3.50

① Use ESP-M2C154-A (E0AZ-19580-A) or equivalent, plus four ounces C8AZ-19B546-A friction modifier or equivalent.

AXLE NOISE DIAGNOSIS

Condition	Possible Source	Action
Limited-Slip or Traction-Lok axle does not work in snow, mud or on ice.	Differential	Perform Traction-Lok differential in-vehicle check. If the rotating torque is less than specification, replace the differential.
On turns, the rear axle has a high pitched chattering noise (Limited Slip or Traction-Lok axles only). Slight chatter noise on slow turns after extended highway driving is considered acceptable and has no detrimental effect on the locking axle function.	Lubricant Differential	Road test vehicle—drive the vehicle in tight circles—5 clockwise and 5 counterclockwise. If chatter is still evident, flush and replace the axle lubricant with Ford Lube ESP-M2C154-A (E0AZ-19580-A) or equivalent plus four ounces of C8AZ-19B546-A (or equivalent) friction modifier and road test again ①. If chatter still exists, replace the differential assembly.

① The locking axle may continue to chatter for approximately 20 miles after lubricant replacement.

LIMITED SLIP DIFFERENTIALS
FORD MOTOR COMPANY

TORQUE SPECIFICATIONS

Description		N·m	Lb-Ft
Differential case half attaching bolts		45-53	34-39
Pinion shaft lock bolt		20-30	15-30
Rotating torque required during bench check or in Vehicle with one wheel on the ground	Original Cones	41	30
	New Cones	54	40

FORD TRACTION-LOK LIMITED SLIP DIFFERENTIAL AXLE – 7.5, 8.5 AND 8.8 IN. RING GEAR

DESCRIPTION

The traction-lok axle assembly, except for the differential case and its internal components, is identical to the conventional axle.

The traction-lok differential employs two sets of multiple disc clutches to control differential action. The side gear mounting distance is controlled by nine plates; five steel, four friction, and one steel shim by select size to control side gear position.

The plates are stacked on the side gear hub and are housed in the differential case. Also located in the differential case, between the side gears, is a one-piece pre-load spring, which applies an initial force to the clutch packs. Additional clutch capacity is delivered from the side gears thrust loads. The four friction plates are splined to the side gear hub which, in turn, is splined to the left and right axle shafts. The geared steel plates are dogged to the case, thus, the clutch packs are always engaged.

OPERATION

The pressure between clutch plates opposes differential action at all times. When the vehicle turns a corner the clutch slips allowing normal differential action to take place. Under adverse weather conditions, where one or both wheels may be on a low-traction surface such as snow, ice or mud, the friction between the clutch plates will transfer a portion of the usable torque to the wheel with the most traction. Thus, the wheel that is on ice or snow will have a tendency to operate with the opposite wheel in a combined driving effort.

— CAUTION —
Never drive a vehicle equipped with a traction-lok rear axle and the new mini-spare tire. The two different size tires cause differentiation in the unit and will cause excessive damage to the clutches.

Noise Acceptability

A gear driven unit especially automotive drive axles, will produce a certain amount of noise. Some noise is acceptable and may be heard at certain speeds or under various driving conditions. For example as on a newly paved blacktop road. The slight noise is in no way detrimental to operation of the rear axle and **must** be considered normal.

NOTE: *On vehicles equipped with a traction-lok differential, a slight stick-slip noise on tight turns after extended highway driving is considered acceptable and has no detrimental effect.*

TESTING

Operation Check

A traction-lok differential can be checked for proper operation without removing the differential from the axle housing.

Raise one rear wheel and remove the wheel cover. Install Tool T59L–4204–A or equivalent on the axle shaft flange studs.

Using a torque wrench of at least 200 ft. lbs. (271 Nm) capacity, rotate the axle shaft. Be sure that the transmission is in Neutral, one rear wheel is on the floor, and the other rear wheel is raised off the floor. The break-away torque required to start rotation should be at least 30 ft. lbs. (41 Nm). The initial break-away torque may be higher than the continuous turning torque, but this is normal. The axle shaft should turn with even pressure throughout the check without slipping or binding. If the torque reading is less than specified, check the differential for proper assembly.

— CAUTION —
A vehicle equipped with a traction-lok differential will always have both wheels driving. If, while the vehicle is being serviced, only one wheel is raised off the floor and the rear axle is driven by the engine, the wheel on the floor could drive the vehicle off the stand or jack.

ADJUSTMENTS

In-vehicle adjustment are possible on this unit without removing the differential case from the axle assembly. If the testing check was not to specification, the following procedure can be used to correct the condition:

Removal

1. Raise the vehicle on a hoist and install safety stands. Remove rear wheels and brake drums.
2. Remove the cover from the carrier casting rear face and drain the lubricant.
3. Perform the inspection before disassembly.
4. Working through the cover opening, remove the pinion shaft lock bolt and remove the pinion shaft.
5. Push the axle shaft inward until the C-locks at the button end of the shafts are clear of the side gear recess.
6. Remove the C-locks and pull the axle shafts out of the housing.

SECTION 28 — LIMITED SLIP DIFFERENTIALS
FORD MOTOR COMPANY

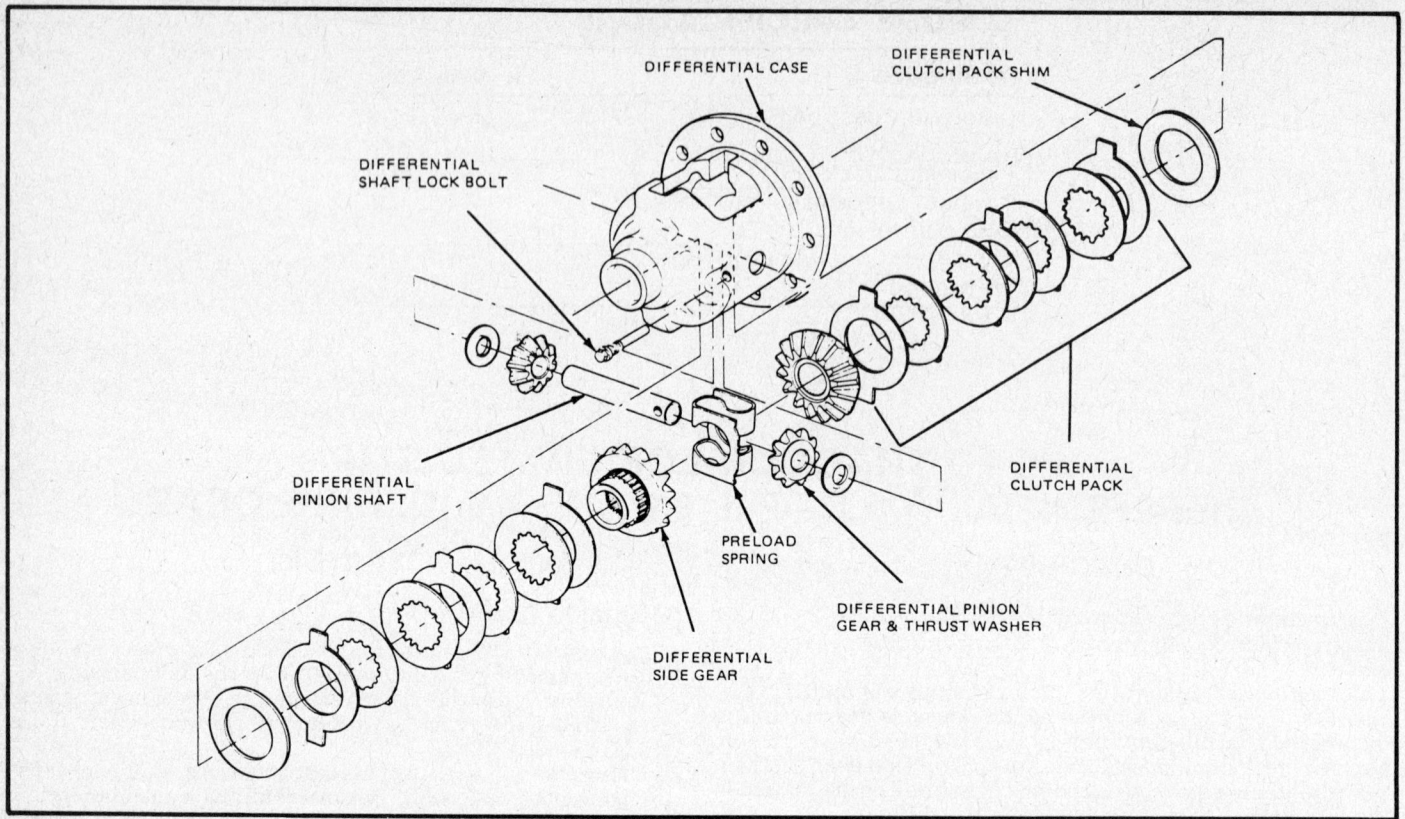

Differential assembly components (© Ford Motor Co.)

CAUTION

Care should be taken not to damage the wheel seals when removing the axle shaft from the axle housing. In addition, the axle shafts must be completely removed from the axle housing.

7. With a suitable drift, drive the S-shaped preload spring half-way out of the differential case. Rotate the differential case 180°.
8. Hold the S-shaped preload spring with a pair of pliers and tap the spring until it is removed from the differential.

CAUTION

Care must be used when removing the preload spring due to the spring tension.

9. Using Tool T80P–4205–A or equivalent, rotate the pinion gears until the gears can be removed from the differential.

NOTE: A 12 in. extension is required to remove the pinion gears.

10. Remove the right and left side gear and clutch pack with the shim and tag them "right and left side."
11. Inspect the clutch packs for wear and replace parts as necessary.

NOTE: Do not use cleaning solution on clutch plate surfaces. Wipe clean only.

12. Install Tool T80P–4946–A or equivalent on each of the side gear clutch packs without the shim. Tighten to 40 inch lbs. (4.5 Nm).

Using a feeler blade, select the thickest blade that will enter between the tool and the clutch pack. This reading will be the thickness of the new shim.

NOTE: Be sure to lubricate friction plates with the proper hypoid gear lubricant prior to reassembly.

Installation

1. Install the left side-gear, clutch pack and new shim into the cavity in the differential case. Repeat this step for the right side.
2. Place the pinion gears and thrust washers 180° apart on the side gears.
3. Install Tool T80P–4205–A or equivalent.

NOTE: A 12 in. extension is required to install the pinion gears.

4. Rotate the tool until pinion gears are aligned with the pinion shaft hole. Remove the tool from the differential case.
5. Hold the S-shaped preload spring up to the differential case window and with a soft-faced hammer, hammer the spring into position.

NOTE: Inspect the pre-load spring for damage.

6. Install the axle shafts and C-locks into position. Push the axle shaft outboard as far as possible.
7. Install the pinion shaft and pinion shaft lock bolt and tighten the bolt to 15–30 ft. lbs. (20–40 Nm).

NOTE: Lock bolt must be tightened to specification using EOAZ–19554–B or equivalent.

8. Install the rear brake drums and wheels. Perform the traction-lok operational check to insure that the unit is within specification.
9. Using slicone sealant No. D6AZ–19562–B or equivalent, install the rear cover assembly and bolts and tighten to 25–35 ft. lbs. (34–47 Nm).

LIMITED SLIP DIFFERENTIALS
FORD MOTOR COMPANY
SECTION 28

10. Fill with lubricant to the bottom of the fill hole with the axle in the running position. The axle capacity is 1.9 liters (4 pints). Install the oil filler plug and tighten to 15–30 ft. lbs. (20–40 Nm).

DIFFERENTIAL CASE

Removal and Installation

This differential is removed and installed in the same manner as a conventional differential.

NOTE: It is not necessary to remove the differential cone and roller assemblies from the case journals unless they are damaged. If the bearings remain on the case during service, take care to keep them clean and free from foreign material.

Disassembly

1. Remove and discard the ten bolts securing the ring gear to the differential case assembly.
2. Remove the ring gear by tapping the gear with a soft hammer or press the gear from the case.
3. Remove the differential pinion shaft lock bolt and remove the pinion shaft.
4. With a suitable drift, drive out the S-shaped preload spring.

— **CAUTION** —

Care must be used when removing the preload spring due to the spring tension.

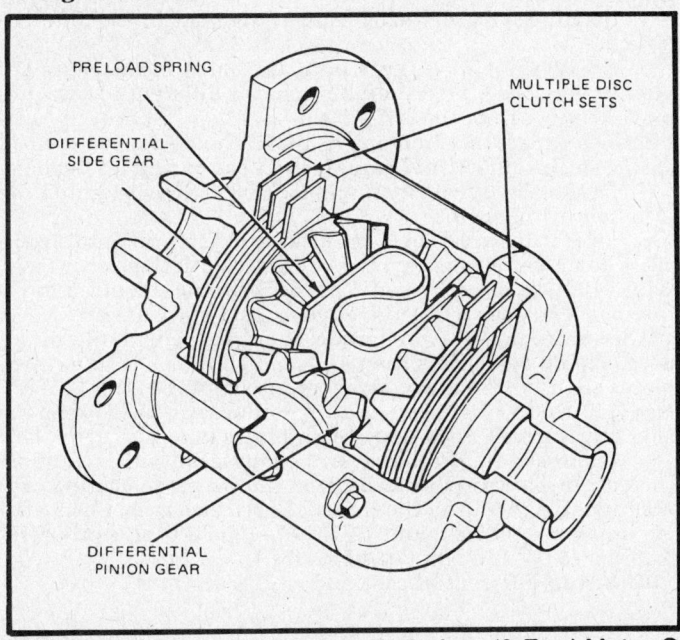

Differential assembly—exploded view (© Ford Motor Co.)

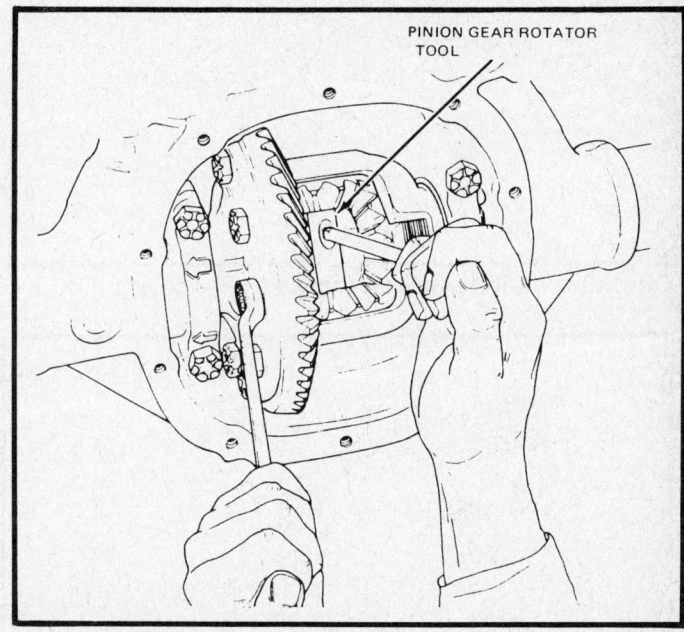

Differential pinion gears and thrust washers removal or installation (© Ford Motor Co.)

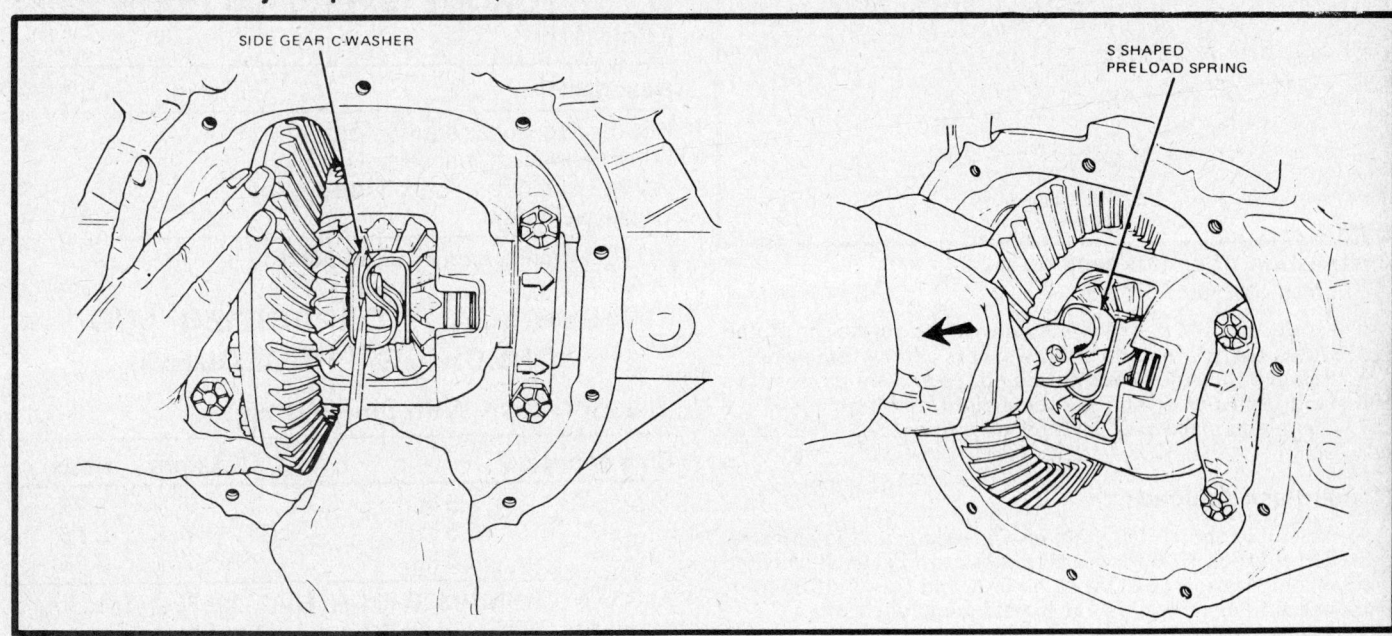

Side gear C-washer and S shaped pre-load spring removal or installation (© Ford Motor Co.)

28–43

SECTION 28
LIMITED SLIP DIFFERENTIALS
Ford Motor Company

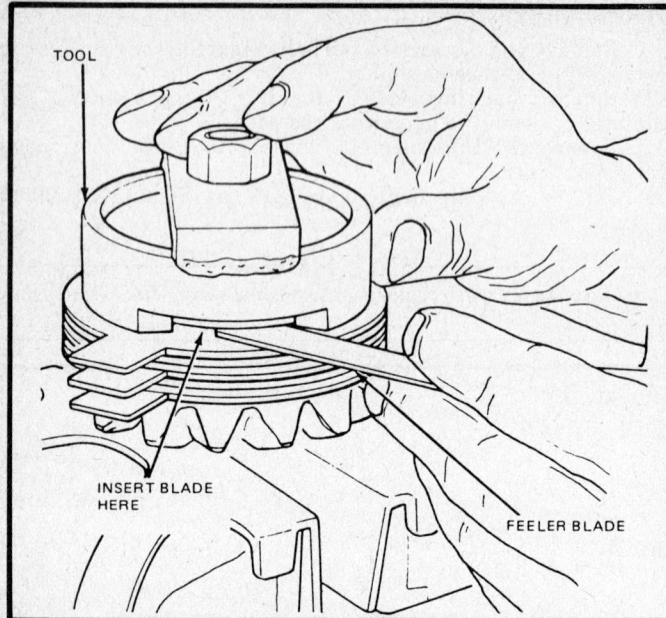

Checking clutch pack clearance (© Ford Motor Co.)

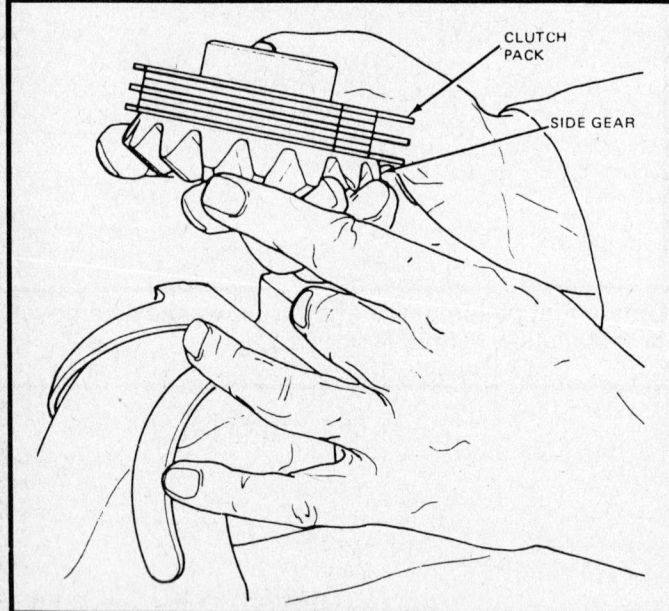

Installation of clutch pack on side gear
(© Ford Motor Co.)

5. Using Tool T80P–4205–A or equivalent, rotate the pinion gears until the gears and thrust washers can be removed.
6. Remove the side gears, clutch plates and shims from the right and left cavities and tag them right and left.
7. Clean and inspect all parts for wear or damage, replace as necessary.

Clutch Pack Preload

1. Assemble the clutch pack on the side gear (no shim required at this point). However all plates must be pre-lubricated with a combination of EOAZ–19580–A and C8AZ–19B546–A friction modifier or equivalent hypoid gear lubricant.
2. Assemble Tool T80P–4946–A or equivalent on side gear clutch pack.
3. Using a feeler gauge tool, select the thickest feeler blade that will enter between the tool and the clutch pack.
4. Note the thickness; this will be the shim required for that clutch pack.

NOTE: Do not mix the clutches or shims.

5. Repeat Steps 1–4 for the opposite clutch pack.

Assembly

1. Lubricate all parts with EOAZ–19580–D or equivalent lubricant prior to assembly.
2. Mount the differential case in a soft jaw vise and place the clutch packs and side gears in their proper cavities in the differential case.
3. Place the pinion gears and thrust washers on the side gears.
4. Install Tool T80P–4205–A or equivalent in the differential case.
5. Rotate the pinion gears until the bores in the gears are aligned with the pinion shaft holes in the differential case. Remove the tool from the differential case.
6. With a soft faced hammer, install the S-shaped preload spring in the differential case. Inspect the spring for damage.
7. Install the pinion shaft and lock bolt. Do not tighten the lock bolt at this point.
8. Prior to installation of the locking differential into a vehicle, a bench torque check must be made. With the locker tools, T59L–4204–A or equivalent check the torque required to rotate one side gear while the other is held stationary.
The initial break-away torque, if original clutch plates are used, should be not less than 41 Nm (30 ft. lbs.). If new clutch plates are used, the break-away torque should be from 135–338 Nm (150–250 ft. lbs.). The rotating torque required to keep the side gear turning with new clutch plates may fluctuate.
9. Clean the tapped holes in the ring gear with a suitable solvent. If the new bolts to be used show a green coating over approximately ½ in. of the threaded area, use as is. If not coated, apply a small amount of EOAZ–19554–B or equivalent. Tighten to 95–115 Nm (70–85 ft. lbs.).
10. Install differential case and ring gear.

TORQUE SPECIFICATIONS
Minimum

Description	N·m	Lb-Ft
Rotating torques required during bench check after assembly or in vehicle with one wheel on the ground.		
Clutch Plates	41	30

NOTE: Rotating torque may fluctuate.

LUBRICANT CAPACITIES AND CHECKING PROCEDURES

Traction-LOK With Single Case

Ring gear size	Liters	Pints
7.5 in.	1.7	3.75
8.5 in.	1.7	3.75
8.8 in.	1.7	3.75

All Axles use ESP-M2C154-A (E0AZ-19580-A) plus four ounces of C8AZ-19546-A Friction Modifier (or equivalent).

LIMITED SLIP DIFFERENTIALS
GENERAL MOTORS

GENERAL MOTORS LIMITED SLIP REAR AXLE

Disc Type

DESCRIPTION

The conventional rear axle divides the driving force equally to both rear wheels. The driving force is limited by the wheel which has the least amount of traction; therefore, if one wheel is on snow or mud, the wheel will spin and the driving force is lost.

The Limited Slip rear axle through the use of clutch plates directs the driving force to the wheel with the best traction thus improving the ability of the car to pull out of mud or snow.

— **CAUTION** —
On cars equipped with limited slip rear axles, do not run engine with one rear wheel off the ground and transmission in gear. Also, "on the car" type wheel balancers should not be used on the rear wheels unless both rear wheels are off the floor. Leaving one wheel on floor may cause car to move forward, and possibly cause property damage or personal injury.

OPERATION

The Limited Slip rear axle transmits torque from the drive pinion gear to the ring gear and to the case in the same manner as the conventional rear axle. In addition, the Limited Slip rear axle incorporates the use of clutch plates which tend to lock the axle shafts to the case, or in effect, to each other.

As driving torque is developed at the rear wheels, side gear separating loads are developed which load the rear axle clutch packs. This induced clutch torque capacity resists relative motion between the side gears and the rear axle case. Therefore, if one wheel is on slippery pavement, such as ice or snow, the other wheel must develop considerably more torque before the case assembly will differentiate and allow wheel spin.

The axle shaft torques developed when turning a corner will overcome the clutch capacities and allow differentiation.

LIMITED SLIP CONVERSION INFORMATION

The case assembly (less ring gear and side bearings) is available for converting a conventional rear axle to Limited Slip. The ring gear and side bearings of the conventional rear axle, if in good condition, can be used with the Limited Slip case assembly.

NOTE: Four disc types are used.

1. "G" type – (GM) plates on both differential side gears.
2. "P" type – (Eaton) plates on one differential side gear, locked with pre-load springs.
3. Corvette type – (Dana) plates on one differential side gear, tensioned by one disked washer in clutch pack.
4. Eaton type with governor – plates on both differential side gears, using governor and latching bracket.

DISASSEMBLY

"G" Type

1. If side bearings are to be removed, they can be removed as outlined in the CONVENTIONAL REAR AXLE section.
2. If the ring gear or rear axle case is to be replaced, remove ring gear from case.
3. Remove pinion shaft lock screw and then remove pinion shaft from case.
4. Drive the pre-load spring from the case.
5. Rotate side gears until the pinions are in the open area of the case, Remove the pinion gears and thrust washers.
6. Remove a side gear, clutch pack and shims from the case, noting its location in the case to aid in reassembly. Remove the side gear clutch pack and shims from the opposite side.
7. Remove the shims and clutch plates from the side gears. Keep the clutch plates in their original location in the clutch pack.

DISASSEMBLY

"P" Type

1. If necessary to remove ring gear and side bearings, follow the procedures established for the conventional rear axle unit.
2. Drive the pro-load spring retainer and springs through the observation hole in case only far enough to secure a C-clamp. The install ¼ in. bolts through retainers and secure enough to remove retainer and spring pack.

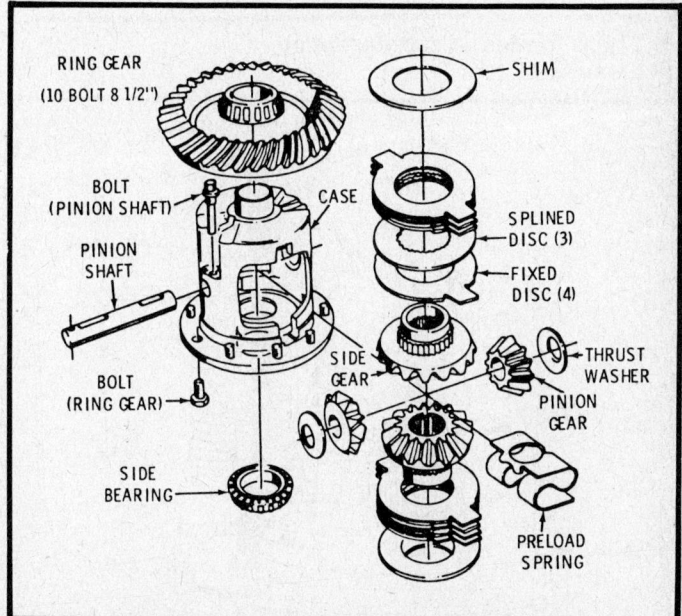

"G" type limited slip differential exploded veiw
(© General Motors Corp.)

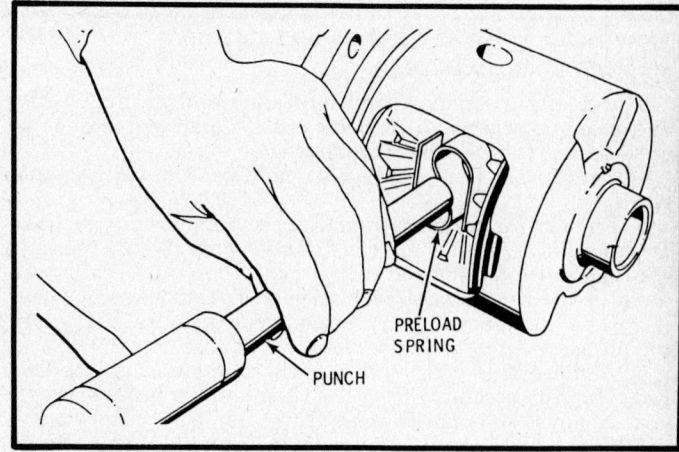

Removing pre-load spring (© General Motors Corp.)

SECTION 28
LIMITED SLIP DIFFERENTIALS
GENERAL MOTORS

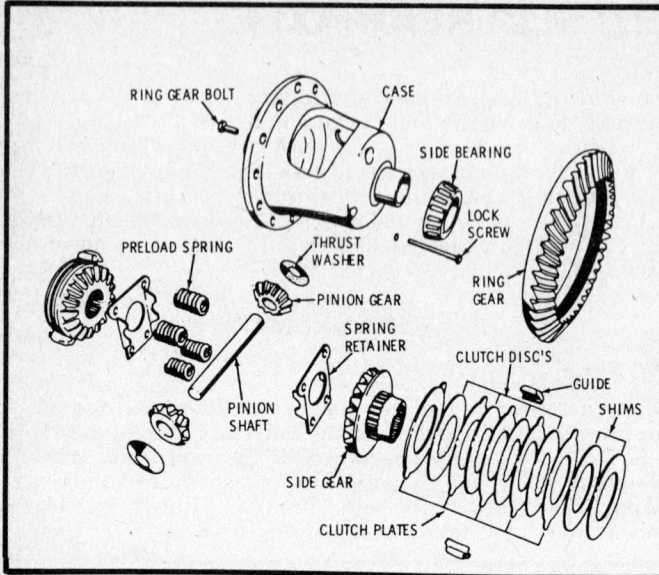

"P" type limited slip differential
(© General Motors Corp.)

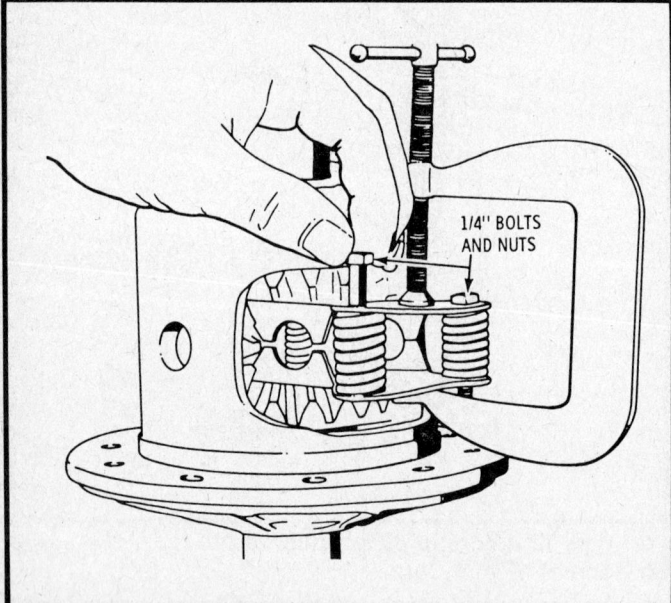

Removing pre-load springs and retainers
(© General Motors Corp.)

3. If necessary to disassemble retainer and spring, position in a vise and remove ¼ in. bolts and C-clamp and loosen vise until spring compression is relieved.
4. Remove the pinion thrust washer from behind the pinion gears.
5. Remove pinion gears from the case-pinion gears can be removed by rotating them in one direction only. Rotate rear axle case clockwise to remove the first gear, then rotate case counterclockwise to remove the second gear. To remove second gear, it may be necessary to assist pinion gear upon its seat by prying on gear through observation hole in case.
6. Remove side gear, clutch pack, shims and guides from case. Tap the assembly from the case, using a brass drift. Repeat removal on opposite gear.
7. Separate clutch pack assembly from side gear. Retain clutch pack assembly with original side gear.

CORVETTE TYPE (DANA)
Disassembly

1. Reposition the differential case onto the axle shaft. Remove the two snap rings from the cross pin. Use two screwdrivers and push the ring free from the cross pin. Place a shop towel behind the case to prevent the snap rings from flying out of the case.
2. Remove the cross pin. Use a hammer and a punch to remove the cross pin from the case.
3. Assemble the adapter plate from tool J-34174 or equivalent, into the bottom side gear.
4. Install threaded adapter plate into top side gear. Thread the forcing screws into the threaded adapter until it becomes centered into the bottom adapter plate.
5. Torque the forcing screw until it becomes slightly tight. This will collapse the dished spacers and allow a loose condition between the side gears and pinion gears.
6. Remove both pinion gear spherical washers. Use a shim stock of 0.020 in. (0.51mm) thickness or an equivalent tool to push out the spherical washers.
7. Relieve the tension of the dished spacers by loosening the forcing screw. It might be necessary to adjust the forcing screw slightly to allow the case to rotate.
8. Assemble turning adapter J-34174-3 onto J-8592 or their equivalents. Insert the small O.D. end of the adapter into the cross pin hole of the case. Pull on the bar and rotate the case until the pinion gears can be removed. Remove gears.
9. Hold the top clutch pack with one hand and remove the tools.
10. Remove the top side gear and clutch pack. Keep the stack of plates and discs intact in exactly the same position while they are being removed.
11. Remove the case from the axle shaft. Turn the case with the flange or ring gear side up and allow the adapter plate, side gear and clutch pack to be removed from the case. Remove the retainer clips from both clutch packs to allow separation of the plates and discs. Keep the stack of plates and discs exactly as they were removed.

Assembly

1. Prelubricate the trust face of the side gears, and the plates and discs.
2. Assemble the plates and discs in exactly the same position as they were removed, regardless of whether they are new parts of the original parts. Be sure the lubricant that is used is of the specified type.
3. Assemble the retainer clips to the ears of the plates. Make sure both clips are completely assembled or seated onto the ears of the plates. Assemble the clutch pack and side gear into the top side gear splines, and that the retainer clips are completely seated into the pockets of the case. To prevent pack from falling out of the case, it will be necessary to hold them in place by hand while repositioning the case on bench.
4. Position the adapter plate into the side gear.
5. Assemble the other clutch pack and side gear. Make sure the clutch pack stays assembled to the side gear splines, and that the retainer clips are completely seated into the pockets of the case.
6. Hold the clutch pack in position and insert tool J-34174 or equivalent. tighten the forcing screw into the bottom adapter. This will hold both clutch packs in position. With tools assembled into the case, position case into the axle shaft by aligning the splines of the side gear with those of the shaft.
7. Tighten the forcing screw to compress clutch packs in order to provide clearance for pinion gears. Insert pinion gears.
8. While holding the clutch pack in place, insert the adapter in the cross pin hole in the case. Pull on the bar and rotate the case allowing the gears to turn. Make sure that the holes of the pi-

LIMITED SLIP DIFFERENTIALS
General Motors

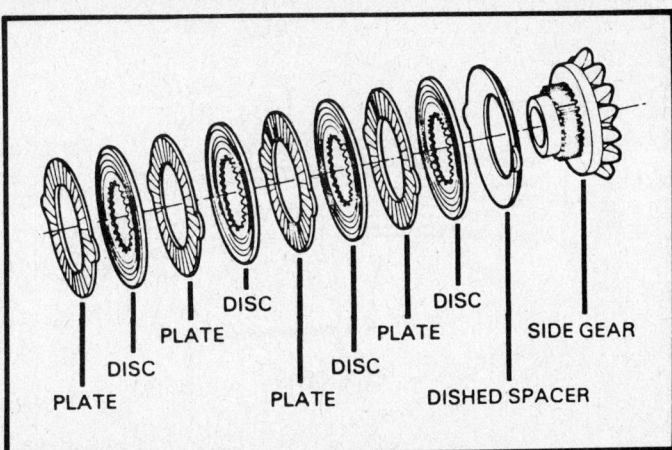

Arrangement of clutch pack in Corvette type rear axle (© General Motors Corp.)

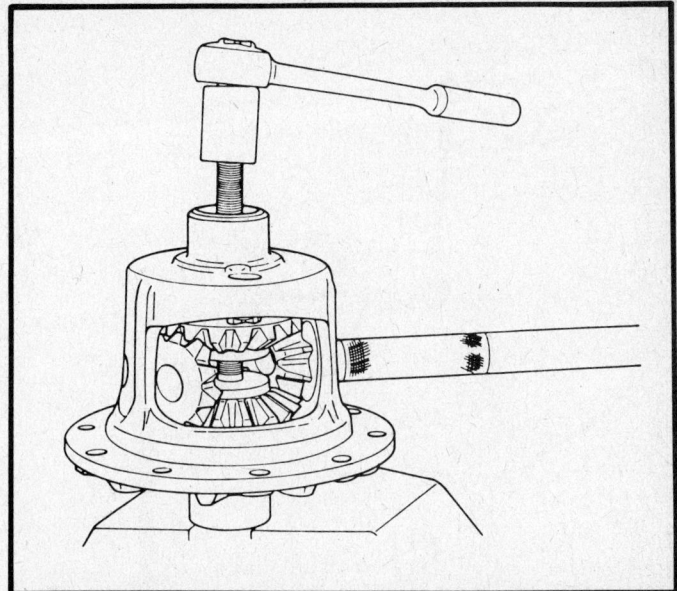

Removing or installing side and pinion gears with special tools, Corvette type (© General Motors Corp.)

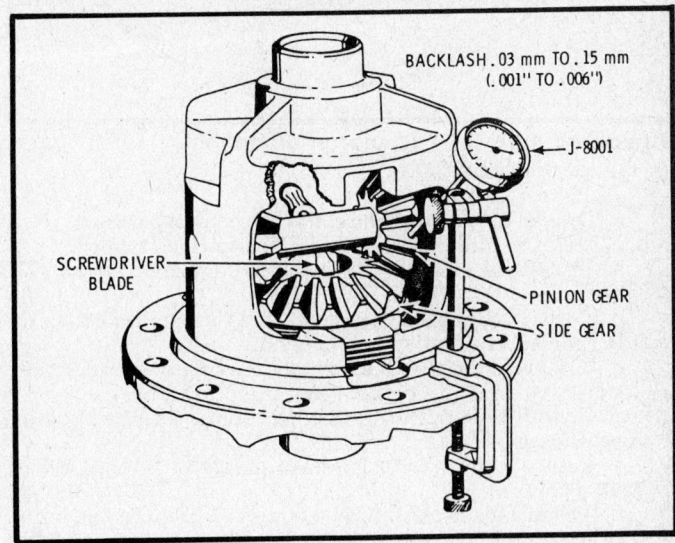

Removing clutch pack (© General Motors Corp.)

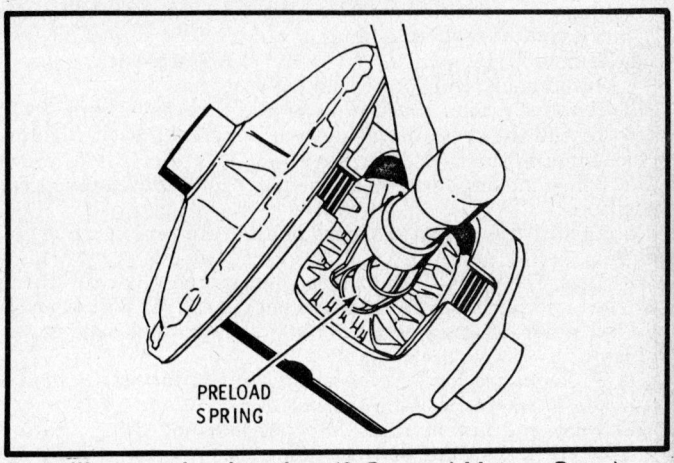

Installing pre-load spring (© General Motors Corp.)

non gears are in alignment with holes of the case. It may be necessary to adjust the tension on the forcing screw to rotate the case.

9. Prelubricate the spherical washers. Assemble the spherical washers into case. Use a small screwdriver to push the washers into place. Remove the tools.

10. Position the cross pin shaft in the case and drive in with a hammer. Be sure the snap ring grooves of the cross pin shaft are exposed to allow assembly of the snap rings. Install the snap rings.

Cleaning and Inspection of Case

1. Clean side bearings thoroughly in clean solvent (do not use a brush). Examine bearings visually and by feel. Bearings should feel smooth when oiled and rotated while applying as much hand pressure as possible.

Minute scratches and pits that appear on rollers and races at low mileage are due to the initial pre-load, and bearings having these marks should not be rejected.

2. Examine the ring gear and drive pinion teeth for nicks, burrs or scoring. Any of these conditions will require replacement of the gear set.

3. Inspect pinion shaft, pinion gears and side gears. Replace if parts are excessively scored, pitted or worn.

4. Check the press fit of the side bearing inner race on the rear axle case. Side bearings must be a tight press fit on the hub.

5. Inspection clutch plates for scored, worn, cracked or a distorted condition. If any of these conditions exist, new clutch plates must be installed.

Rear Axle Case Assembly

"G" TYPE

1. If side bearings were removed, lubricate the bearings with lubricant No. 1052271 or equivalent and install on case hubs.

2. Apply lubricant No. 1052271 or equivalent to the clutch plates.

3. Assemble the clutch pack as follows:
   a. Alternately position 7 clutch plates on the side gear, STARTING and ENDING with a clutch plate having external lugs.
   b. Next, place the spacer against the plate having external lugs, position the shims last. Be careful to install the same spacer and shims or an equal amount on the clutch pack for a starting point.

28–47

SECTION 28
LIMITED SLIP DIFFERENTIALS
GENERAL MOTORS

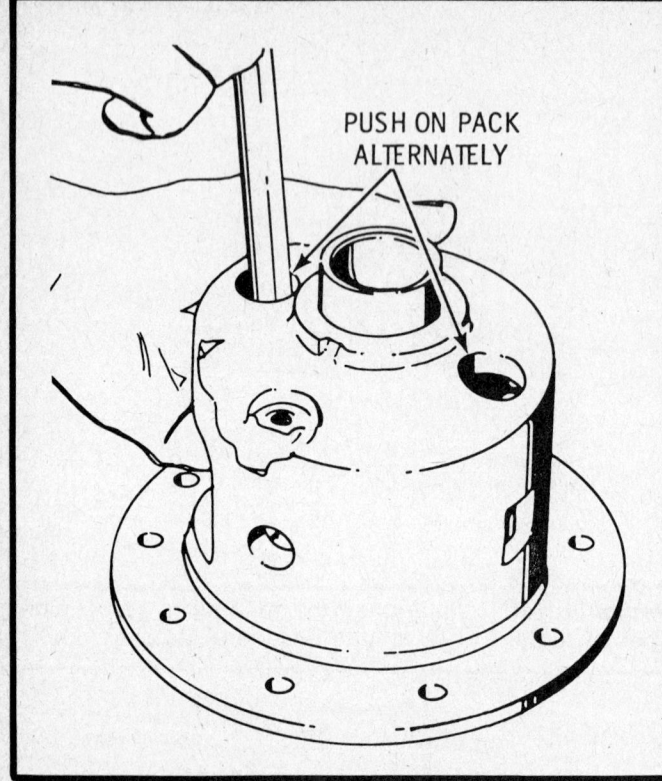

Checking side gear to pinion backlash
(© General Motors Corp.)

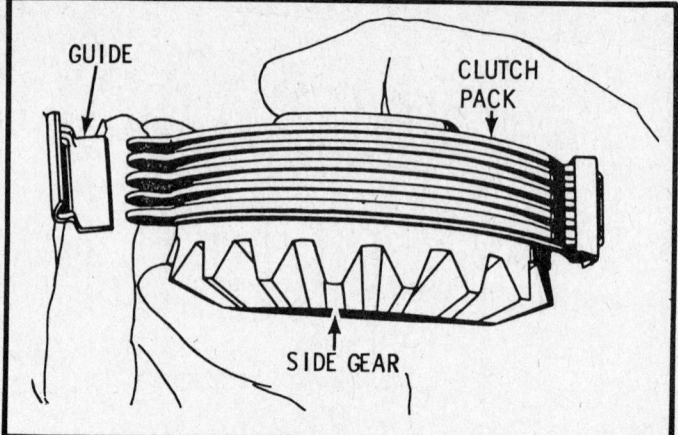

Installing clutch pack guides
(© General Motors Corp.)

   c. Repeat Steps a and b on the other clutch pack.
  4. Check the pinion to side gear clearance as follows:
   a. Install one side gear with clutch pack and shims in the case.
   b. Position the two pinion gears and thrust washers on the side gear and install the pinion shaft.
   c. Compress the clutch stack by inserting a screwdriver or wedge between the side gear and pinion shaft.
   d. Install dial indicator with the contact button against the pinion gear.
   e. Rotate pinion gear. Clearance should be 0.001–0.006 in. (0.03–0.15mm).
   f. If clearance is more than 0.006 in. (0.15mm), add shims between clutch pack and case. If clearance is less than 0.001 in. (0.03mm), remove shims. A 0.002 in. (0.05mm) shim will change clearance approximately 0.001 in. (0.03mm). Recheck clearance after adding or subtracting shims.
   g. Remove side gear and repeat procedure with opposite clutch pack, on opposite side of case.
  5. Remove pinion shaft, pinions and thrust washers.
  6. Install the remaining side gear and clutch pack with correct shims in the case.
  7. Place the pinion gears on the gears and rotate into correct position.
  8. Install the thrust washers behind the pinion gears and align.
  9. Insert the pinion shaft into the case, through the thrust washer and part way into the pinion gear. This will keep the pinion gears aligned while driving the pre-load spring into place.
  10. Position pre-load spring as shown in illustration next to the side gears and drive into place.
  11. Push the pinion shaft into position and align the lock screw hole in the shaft with the hole in the case. Install the pinion shaft lock screw and torque to 20 ft. lbs. (27 Nm).

  12. If the ring gear was removed, position the gear on the case flange and install NEW attaching bolts. Tighten the attaching bolts evenly and alternately across the diameter in progressive stages. Torque to 90 ft. lbs. (120 Nm).

Assembly
"P" TYPE
  1. Lubricate clutch plates and discs with lubricant No. 1052271 or equivalent.
  2. Alternately position clutch plate and clutch disc on side gear, beginning and ending with clutch plate, until assembly to clutch pack is complete.
  3. Install clutch pack guides on the clutch plate lugs. Make sure that the clutch disc lugs engage with side gear teeth.
  4. Select shims of equal thickness as those removed from the case, or if old shims are suitable, reinstall them over the side gear hub.
  5. Lubricate and assembly opposite side gear as above.
  6. Install one side gear, clutch pack assembly and shim(s) in the rear axle case.
  7. Position pinion gears and thrust washers on side gears, install pinion shaft through case and gears.
  8. Install dial indicator on case so that contact button rests against pinion gear.
  9. Compress clutch pack, using a suitable pry bar. Move the pinion gear to obtain tooth clearance.
  10. Tooth clearance should be 0.001–0.006 in. (0.03–0.15mm), if required change shims to obtain proper tooth clearance.
  11. Remove side gear assembly and repeat tooth clearance procedure for gear on opposite side of case.
  12. Remove pinion shaft, gears and thrust washers.
  13. Install remaining side gear, clutch pack assembly and shims in case.
  14. Install pinion gears and thrust washers. Installation of pinion gears can be performed by reversing the pinion gear removal procedure.
  15. Assemble springs in spring retainer and clamp assembly in vise. Install C-clamp and bar stock on spring retainer then install a ¼ in. bolt and nut in each front spring.
  16. Position spring pack between side gears and remove bar stock and C-clamp.
  17. Drive spring pack into side gear sufficiently to retain front springs, then remove ¼ in. bolts from springs. Drive spring pack into position.
  18. Check alignment of spring retainer with side gears. Slight movement of the spring pack can be made if necessary.
  19. Install side bearings and ring gear to case, if removed, using procedure outlined for the conventional rear axle.

LIMITED SLIP DIFFERENTIALS
GENERAL MOTORS

EATON TYPE WITH GOVERNOR

Disassembly

1. Note position of governor and latching bracket assembly. Remove ring gear and side bearings following procedures established for the standard differential.

2. Using bushing puller tool J–26252, remove governor assembly and latching bracket by pulling the retaining bushings. Pull the lathing bracket spring out of the way while pulling the governor assembly to prevent damage.

3. Remove lock screw and pinion shaft, and roll out differential pinion gears and pinion thrust washers. Discard lock screw.

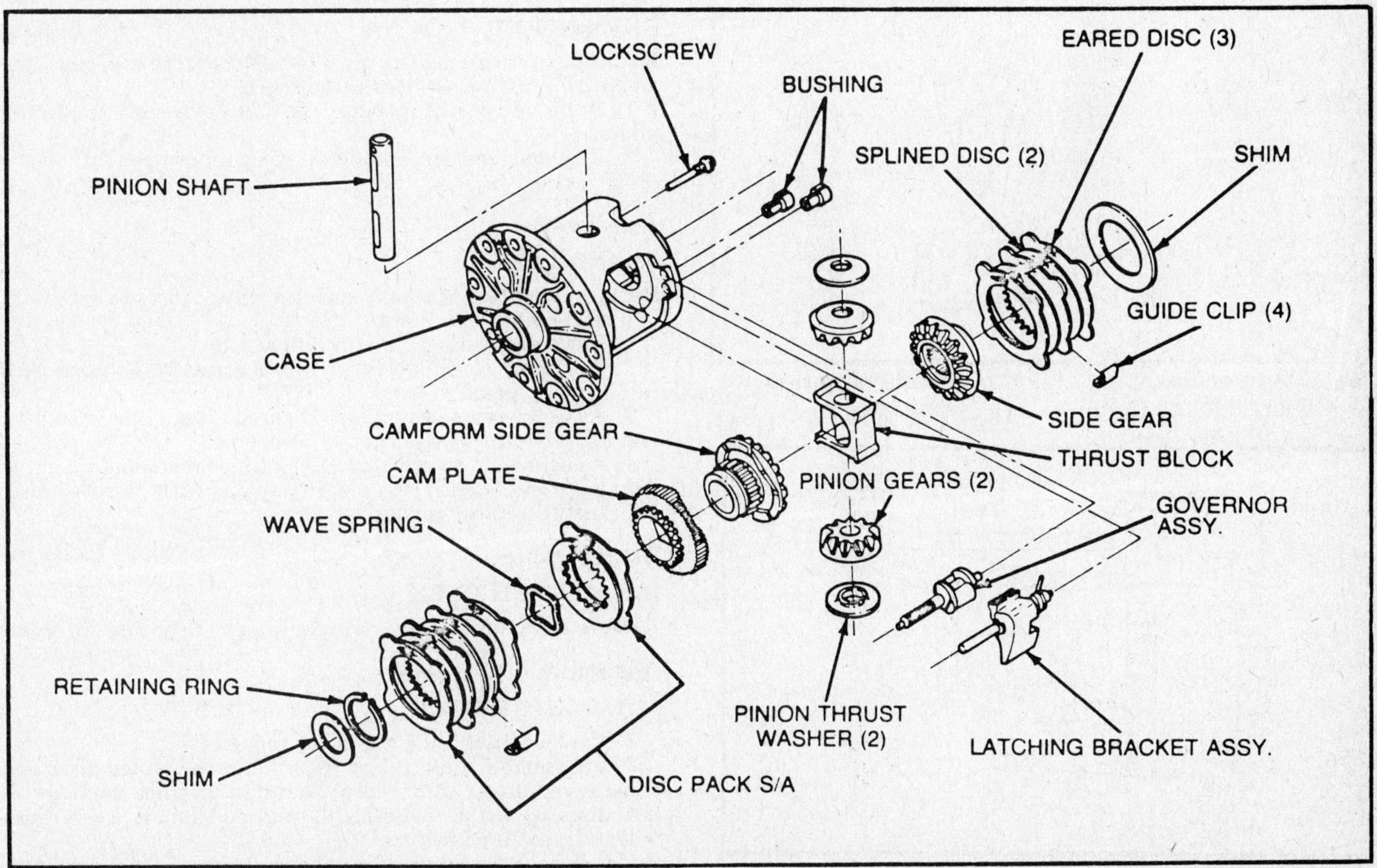

Exploded view of Eaton locking type differential, using governor and latching bracket (© General Motors Corp.)

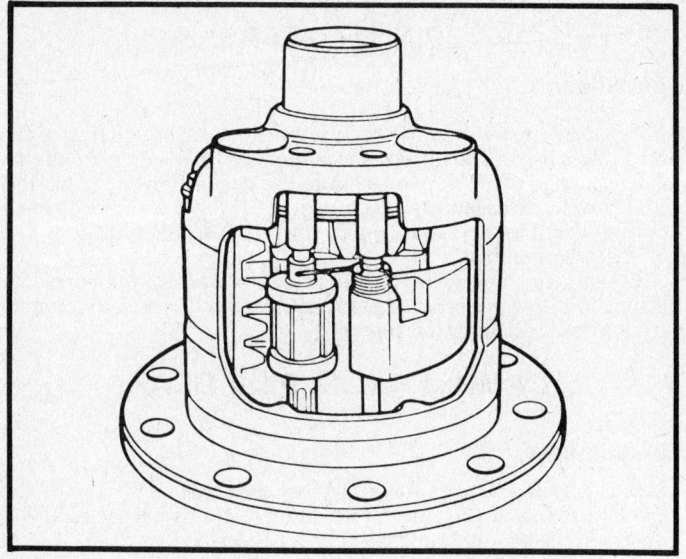

Positioning of governor and latching bracket (© General Motors Corp.)

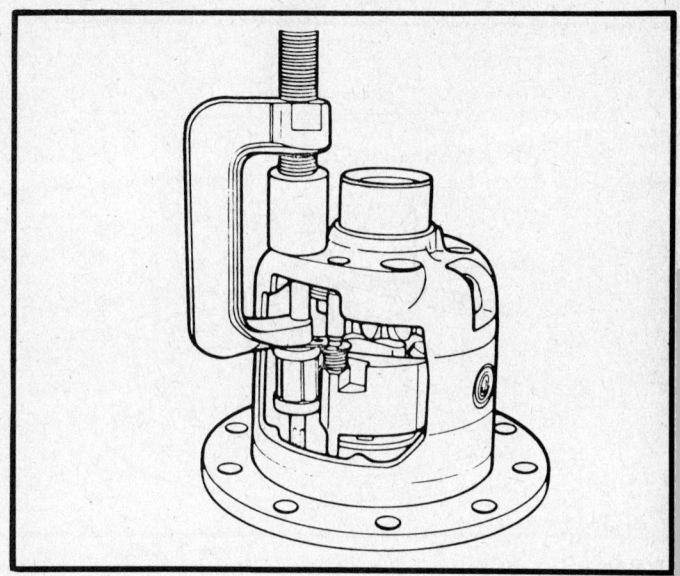

Removal of governor shaft (© General Motors Corp.)

28–49

SECTION 28 LIMITED SLIP DIFFERENTIALS
GENERAL MOTORS

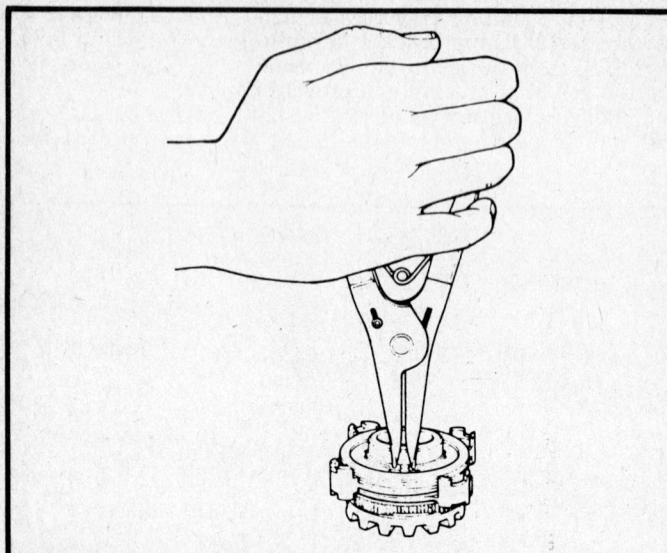

Removing or installing clutch plate retaining ring
(© General Motors Corp.)

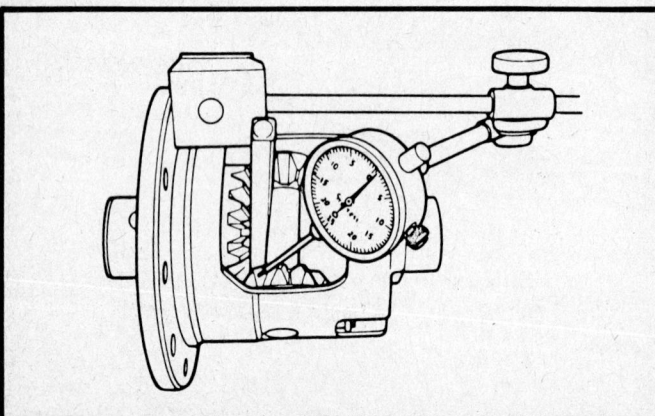

Measuring cam gear backlash
(© General Motors Corp.)

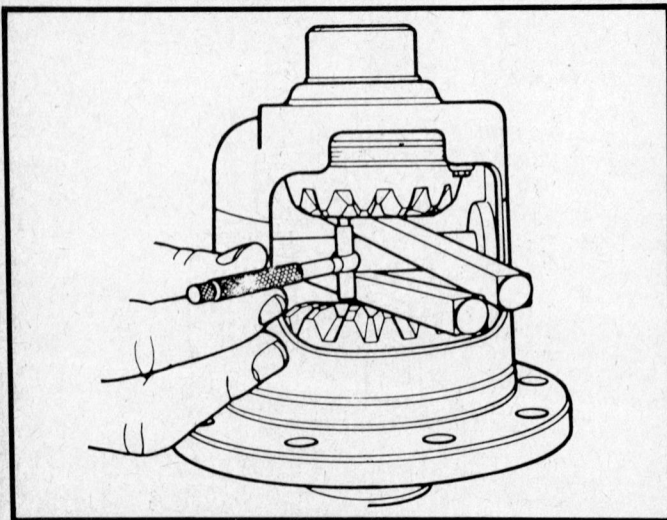

Measuring side gear spread
(© General Motors Corp.)

4. Remove thrust block.
5. Remove cam gear, disc pack assembly and shim.
6. Remove R.H. disc pack assembly and shim.

CAM/CLUTCH SERVICE

Disassembly
FLANGE END

If cam plate or clutch discs must be replaced, the cam gear subassembly must be serviced as follows:
 1. Remove retaining ring (use 0.06 external snap ring pliers).
 2. Remove discs and camplate. Keep all components in the proper order.

Assembly
FLANGE END

Replace cam plate and wave spring or clutch discs as necessary and reassemble as follows:
 1. Place gear on bench with hub end up.
 2. Assembly cam plate with cam form down to mate with cam form on gear.
 3. Assemble onto cam plate: (2) eared discs, (1) splined disc, and (1) wave spring alternately as shown.
 4. Assemble on to gear hub (2) sliplined discs and (3) eared discs alternately as shown. Begin and end with an eared disc.
 5. Install retaining ring.

Disassembly
R.H. CLUTCH PACK

Remove disc pack and shim from side gear. Keep discs in order.

Assembly
R.H. CLUTCH PACK

 1. Replace discs and/or clips, as required.
 2. Reassemble material on gear hub (two splined discs and three eared discs) alternately. Maintain original sequence, if new discs are not used. Reinstall original shim, or a new shim with original thickness.

If gear hubs scored, rough or abnormal wear, check condition of bores in case. If they are damaged or oversize, the entire unit must be replaced.

PINION GEARS

Installation

If it is necessary to replace the pinion gears due to pitting of the teeth, scoring of the pinion shaft bearing surface, or breakage, it will be necessary to disassemble the unit following Steps 1–3 under case disassembly. Install new pinion gears and pinion thrust washers, and reassembly unit as described in Steps 4–9 of case reassembly.

If camgear, side gear, or pinion gears are broken, check for other damage and replace parts as needed. If case is damaged, the entire unit must be replaced.

CAMGEAR (L.H. SIDE GEAR)

Installation

If it is necessary to replace the camgear due to pitting of the teeth, scoring of the hub, or breakage, it will be necessary to disassemble the unit completely as described in Steps 1–6 of case disassembly and in Steps 1–2 of cam/clutch service. When replacing the camgear, it will be necessary to adjust (by select-

LIMITED SLIP DIFFERENTIALS
GENERAL MOTORS

ing the correct shim) the camgear to pinion gear backlash using the following procedure:

1. Install the new camgear and disc pack sub assembly, using the original shim, into the flange end of the case. Place pinion gears and pinion thrust washers into their respective locations in the case, manually depress the camgear into its bore and slide the pinion shaft through the case and both pinion gears.

If installation of the pinion shaft is prevented by the pinion gears, it will be necessary to replace the original shim with one of less thickness.

2. Once the pinion shaft is installed, with lockscrew in place, index one tooth of the pinion gear nearest the pinion shaft lockscrew so that it points downward, perpendicular to the case flange. Use a large tapered screwdriver or similar shaped tool and firmly wedge it between the camgear and pinion shaft.

3. Using a dial indictor mounted to the case flange check pinion to camgear backlash by pulling the pinion gear firmly into its seat and rotate back and forth while reading the gage, note reading. Repeat the above procedure of indexing and checking backlash of the pinion gear opposite the pinion shaft lockscrew, and not reading. If backlash is not between 0.010 and 0.018, change shim size and repeat backlash procedure until the correct backlash is obtained. The thinner the shim used, the greater the backlash reading will be.

When camgear and/or side gear is replaced, thrust block replacement and clearance procedure must be followed during reassembly of the unit. Failure to do so may disturb critical clearances and could result in differential complaints.

SIDE GEAR (R.H.)

Installation

If it is necessary to replace the R.H., side gear due to pitting of the teeth, scoring of the hub, or breakage, it will be necessary to disassemble the unit as described in Steps 1–6 of case disassembly. When replacing the side gear, it will be necessary to adjust (by selecting the correct shim) the side to pinion gear backlash using a similar procedure as described in the camgear replacement section. However, backlash for the side gear should be adjusted to within 0.002–0.010, with R.H. side gear wedged against case.

THRUST BLOCK

Installation

If it is necessary to replace the thrust block only, replace it with a new one of identical thickness. If the thrust block is broken, check for other damage and replace parts as necessary. If case is damaged, replace the entire unit.

If camgear and/or side gear is replaced, it will be necessary to check the side gear spread dimension and adjust block clearance as follows:

1. Install camgear and disc pack with camgear shim into the flange end of the case.
2. Install side gear and disc pack with shim into the bell end of the case.
3. Install pinion shaft and a new lockscrew into case. Firmly wedge a large tapered screwdriver similar shaped tool between the pinion shaft and camgear. Wedge another tapered tool between the pinion shaft and side gear.
4. Using a 1–2 in. telescoping gage, measure the distance between the camgear face and side gear face (side gear spread). Make sure telescoping gage ends rest on the gear face, not on the gear teeth. Measure the telescoping gage with a 1–2 in. micrometer and note reading.
5. Measure the thickness of the original thrust block at outer corner, and note reading.
6. If the thrust block thickness is not within a range of .000–.006 in. less than the side gear spread, adjust clearance with one of the following procedures:
   a. Reshim R.H. clutch disc pack.

NOTE: Backlash of 0.002–0.010 MUST still be maintained.

   b. Select a new thrust block of the correct size to obtain 0.000–0.006 clearance.
1. Install (4) clutch pack guide clips on the ears of the cam gear clutch pack using grease for retention.
2. Install cam gear assembly and original shim in flange end of case. If a new cam gear is installed, refer to differential gear replacement.
3. Lock an axle shaft in vise, in a vertical position. Mount the differential case over the end of the axle shaft engaging the spline of the side gear with the shaft.

Assemble on to bell and gear hub (2) splined discs and (3) eared discs alternately as shown. Begin and end with an eared disc. Install (4) small clutch pack guide clips on the ears of the bell end clutch pack using grease of retention. Install in case with shim. If a new R.H. side gear is installed, refer to differential gear replacement. Install thrust washers onto back surface of pinion gears. Use a small amount of grease to adhere washers to gears.

4. Insert one pinion gear through the small window opening in the case while at the same time inserting the reaction block and other pinion gear through the large window opening. Rotate the two pinion gears and thrust block 90° so as to position the reaction block with the open side towards the small window opening in the case. Be sure the two pinion gears and thrust washers are in their proper location.

NOTE: Thrust block thickness is critical to proper differential function. If new side gear or thrust block is installed, refer to thrust block or side gear replacement for adjustment procedures.

5. Install pinion shaft and a new lock screw.
6. Insert pinion governor assembly and latching bracket into case. Place straight end of latching bracket spring over and to the outside of the engagement shaft to preload the latching bracket against the governor assembly. Press bushing for governor assembly into case to give 0.004–0.020 shaft end play. A $\frac{3}{8}$ in. diameter plug or socket will aid in pressing the bushings into the housing. Press latching bracket assembly bushing into the case to provide 0.000–0.003 shaft end play.

For the latching bracket, use bushing with the tapered hole. The bushing for the governor assembly has a straight hole.

7. Installing gear an side bearing using the procedure outlined of standard differentials.
8. Place differential unit in carrier and adjust ring gear and pinion backlash and gear tooth pattern.
9. Check axle operation.

NOTE: Use only the rear axle lubricant recommended. The usage of any other lubricant or any additive may result in damage to the differential.

Locking Differential, Cone Type (Borg Warner)

GENERAL DESCRIPTION

The Limited Slip rear axle can be identified by a tag attached to the lower right section of axle cover. It is designed to direct the major driving force to the wheel with greater traction, thereby reducing the possibility of the car becoming stuck while driving under adverse conditions.

All rear axle parts of cars equipped with the Limited Slip

SECTION 28: LIMITED SLIP DIFFERENTIALS
GENERAL MOTORS

rear axle are interchangeable with those equipped with the conventional rear axle, except for the case assembly. It is similar in all respects to the conventional case assembly, with the addition of cone clutches splined to each side gear.

SERVICE PROCEDURES

Rear axle service procedures are the same for the Limited Slip as for the conventional rear axle, except for servicing the case assembly.

If the case, clutch cone/side gears, or pinion gears are damaged, it is necessary to replace case assembly.

CAUTION

Never raise one wheel and run the engine with the transmission in gear. The driving force to the wheel on the floor will cause the car to move. Do not use "on the car" type wheel balancers on the rear wheels, unless both wheels are off the floor. Leaving one wheel on floor may cause car to move forward, and possibly cause property damage or personal injury.

REAR AXLE CASE

Disassembly

1. Before disassembling rear axle case, inspect rear axle side bearings for visible damage of rollers and outer races.
2. Place one outer race onto its matched inner race and roller assembly and turn slowly, applying hand load.
3. If bearing outer race turns smoothly and no visible damage is found, bearing can be reused.
4. Repeat above operation with outher race and matched bearing and check for smoothness.

Both side bearings and their outer races are matched parts. If either bearing is to be replaced, its matching outer race must also be replaced.

5. Inspect fit of inner races on case hubs by prying against shoulders at puller recesses. Bearing inner races must be tight on case hubs. If either bearing is loose on case, entire case must be replaced.
6. If bearing inspection indicates that bearngs should be replaced, remove side bearings using proper tools.
7. If removing ring gear, clamp case in vise so jaws are 90° to pinion shaft holes and remove ring gear retaining bolts.
8. Partially install two bolts on opposite sides of ring gear.
9. Remove ring gear from case by alternately tapping on bolts. Do not pry between case and ring gear.

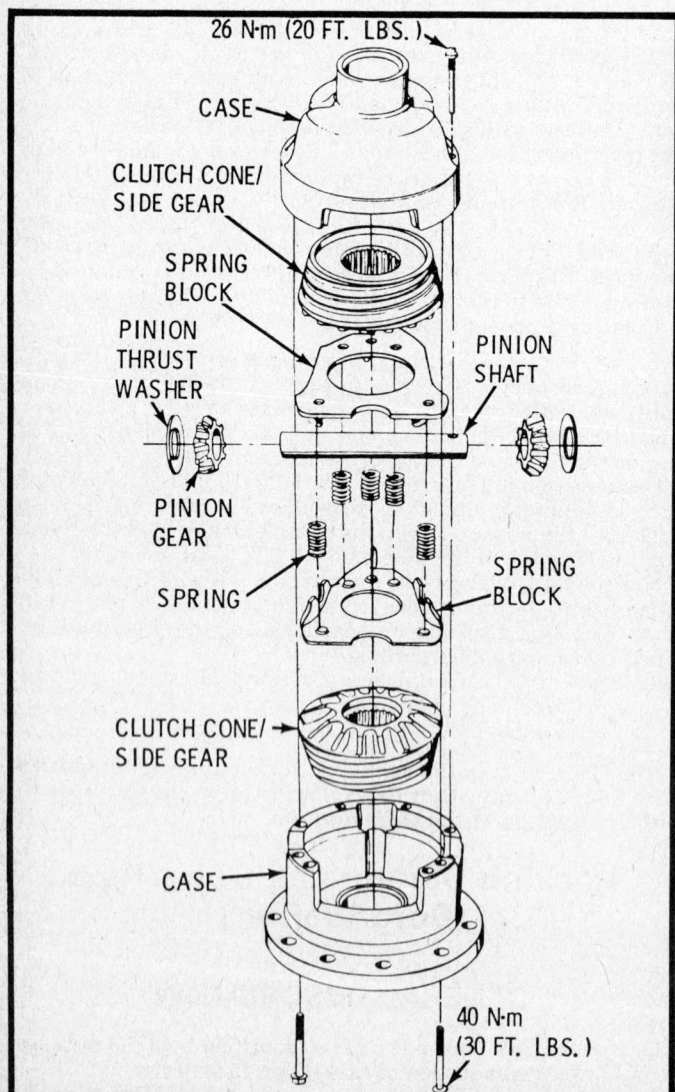

Limited slip differential (cone type) – exploded view (© General Motors Corp.)

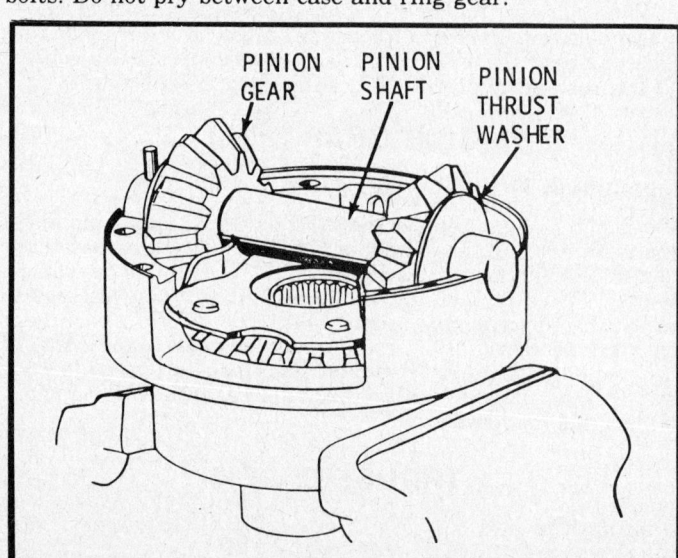

Installing parts in case half (© General Motors Corp.)

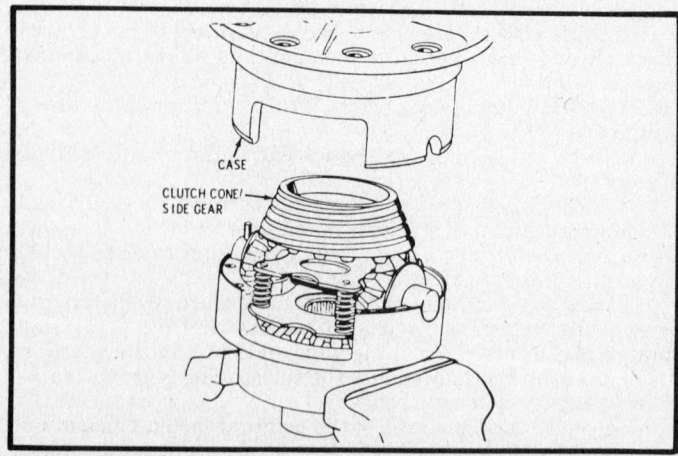

Case flange installation (© General Motors Corp.)

LIMITED SLIP DIFFERENTIALS
GENERAL MOTORS
SECTION 28

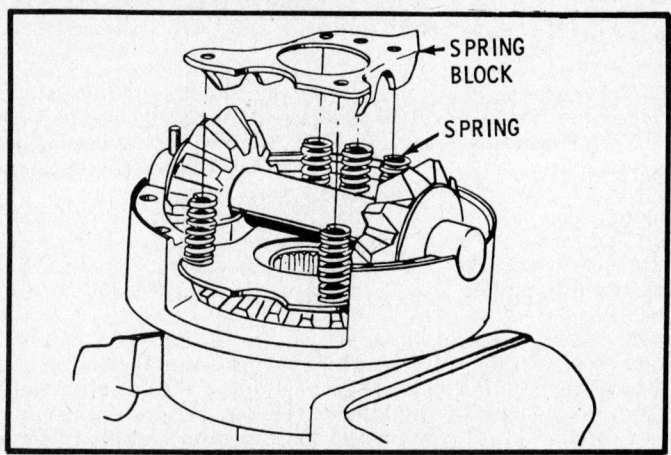

Installation of spring block (© General Motors Corp.)

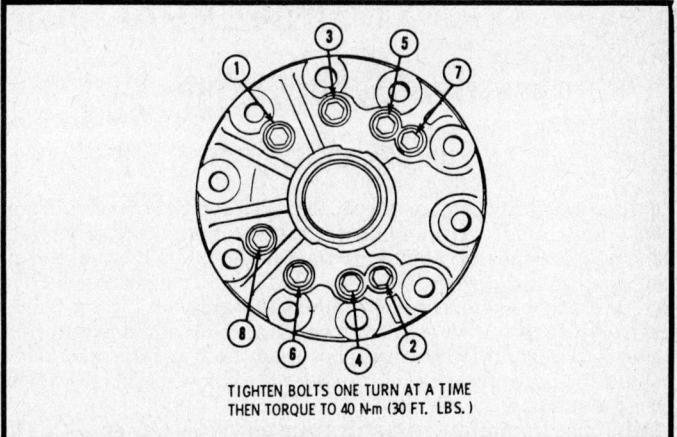

TIGHTEN BOLTS ONE TURN AT A TIME
THEN TORQUE TO 40 N·m (30 FT. LBS.)

Case bolt tightening sequence (© General Motors Corp.)

2. Inspection pinion shaft, pinion an side gears, brake cone surfaces and corresponding cone seats in case. The cone seats in case should be smooth and free of any excessive scoring. Slight grooves or scratches, indicating passage of foreign material, are permissible and normal. The land surface on the heavy spirals of male cones will duplicate case surface condition. If case or clutch cone/side gear are damaged, it is necessary to replace case assembly. All other parts are serviceable.

Assembly

1. Install proper cone/gear assembly, seating it into position in cap half of case. Be certain that each cone/gear is installed in proper case half, since tapers and surfaces become matched and their positions should not be changed.
2. Place one spring block inposition over gear face, in alignment with pinion gear shaft grooves. Install pinion shaft, pinion gears and thrust washers into cap half of case in such a manner that pinion shaft retaining dowel can be inserted through pinion gear shaft into case. This prevents pinion shaft from sliding out and causing damage to carrier. Be certain that pinion gears are installed in their original locations.
3. Insert five springs into springs block that is already installed into case, then place second spring block over springs.
4. Install second cone/gear assembly face down on spring block so that gear will mesh with pinion gears.
5. Install flange half of rear axle case over cone, insert case bolts finger tight.
6. Tighten bolts one turn at a time in sequence. Then torque case bolts to 30 ft. lbs., (40 Nm).
7. If side bearings were removed, lubricate outer bearing surfaces and press on bearings.
8. After making sure that matching surfaces are clean and free of burrs, position ring gear on case so holes are in line.
9. Lubricate NEW attaching bolts with clean engine oil and install.
10. Pull ring gear onto case by alternately tightening bolts around case. When all bolts are snug, tighten bolts evenly and alternately across diameter to 90 ft. lbs. (120 Nm) torque. Do not use hammer to force ring gear on case.
11. Install unit into axle carrier following instructions given for Standard Rear Axle.

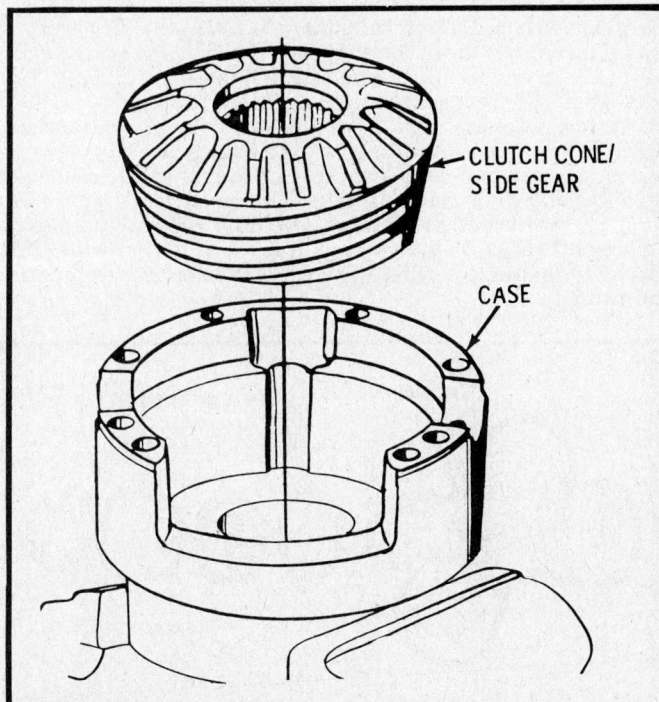

Installing clutch cone/side gear
(© General Motors Corp.)

10. Remove case half attaching bolts.
11. Lift cap half of case form flange half. Remove clutch cone/side gears, spring blocks, preload springs, pinion gears and shaft.

Be certain that each clutch cone/side gear and pinion gear are marked so they can be installed in their original location.

Cleaning and Inspection

1. Make certain all parts are absolutely clean and dry.

28-53

SECTION 28
UNIVERSAL JOINTS SERVICE

UNIVERSAL JOINTS, DRIVE SHAFTS

Rear Wheel Drive

INTRODUCTION

Universal joints provide flexibility between the driveshaft and axle housing to accommodate changes in the angle between them. (Changes of length are accommodated by the sliding splined yoke between the driveshaft and transmission.) The engine and transmission are mounted rigidly on the car frame, while the driving wheels are free to move up and down in relation to the frame. The angles between the transmission, driveshaft and axle change constantly as the car responds to various road conditions.

To give flexibility and still transmit power as smoothly as possible, several types of universal joints are used.

The most common type of universal joint is the cross and yoke type. Yokes are used on the ends of the driveshaft with the yoke arms opposite each other. Another yoke is used opposite the driveshaft and when placed together, both yokes engage a center member, or cross, with four arms spaced 90° apart. (The U-joint cross is alternately referred to as a spider, and the arms are called trunnions.) A bearing cup (or cap) is used on each arm of the cross to accommodate movement as the driveshaft rotates. The bearings used are invariably needle bearings.

The second type of universal joint is the ball and trunnion universal, a T-shaped shaft which is enclosed in the body of the joint. The trunnion ends are each equipped with a ball mounted in needle bearings and move freely in grooves in the outer body of the joint, in effect creating a slip-joint. This type of joint is always enclosed. On american cars, it is only used on front wheel drive axles (Toronado, Eldorado, etc.), and because of the complexities of service will not be considered here.

A conventional universal joint will cause the dirveshaft to speed up an slow down through each revolution an cause a corresponding change in the velocity of the driven shaft. This change in speed causes natural vibrations to occur through the driveline, necessitating a third type of universal joint: the constant velocity joint. A rolling ball moves in a curved groove, located between two yoke-and-cross universal joints, connected to each other by a coupling yoke. The result is a uniform motion as the driveshaft rotates, avoiding the fluctuations in driveshaft speed. This type of joint is found in cars with sharp driveline angles, or where the extra measure of isolation is desirable.

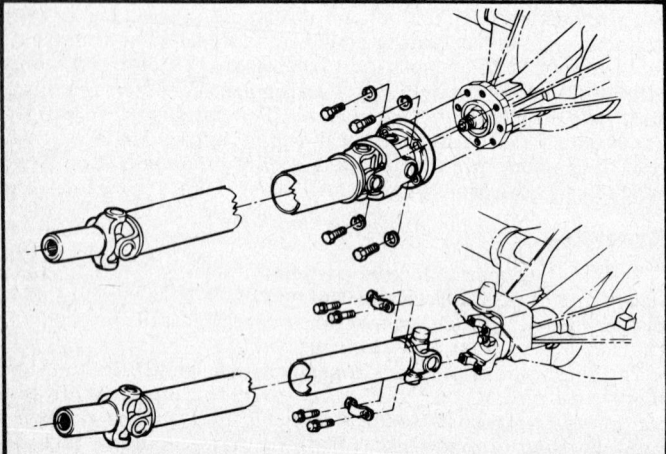

The driveshaft may be retained to the differential pinion by a flange (top or by U-bolts or straps (bottom)
(© Pontiac Div. G.M. Corp.)

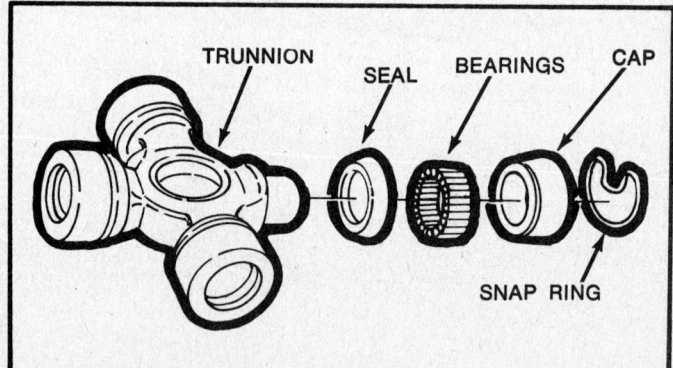

Snap ring type universal joint

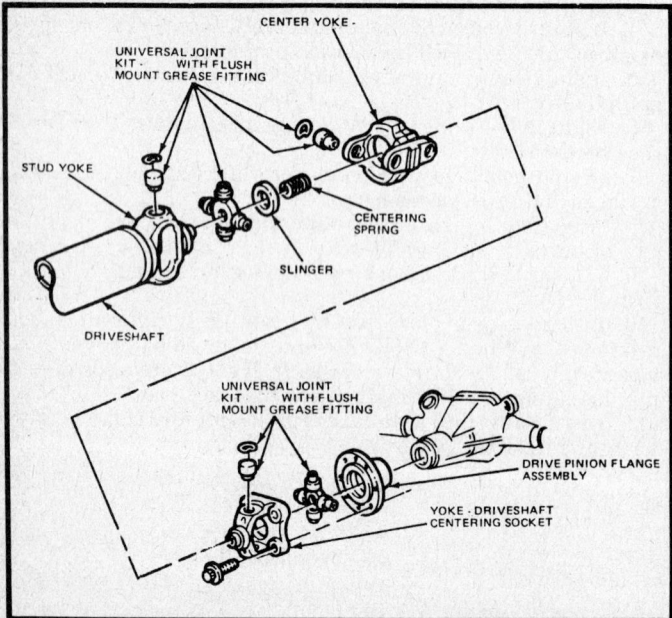

Typical driveshaft with constant velocity joints
(© Ford Motor Co.)

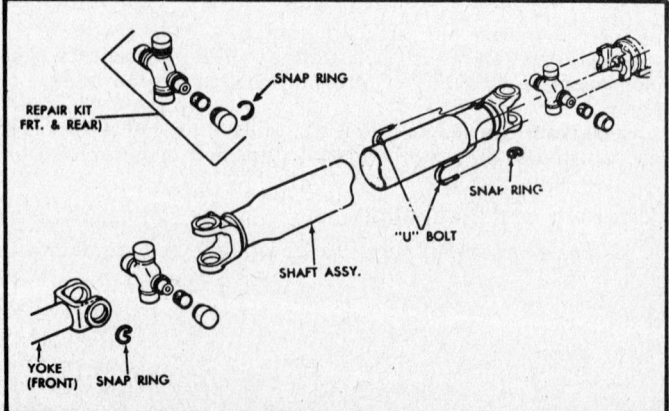

Typical driveshaft and U-joints
(© Oldsmobile Div. G.M. Corp.)

UNIVERSAL JOINTS SERVICE

Cross and Yoke U-Joint Overhaul

There are two types of cross and yoke U-joints. One type retains the cross within the yoke with C-shaped snap rings. This type is found on all American Motors, Chrysler, and Ford cars. GM cars generally use the second type of joint, which is held together by injection molded plastic (delrin) rings. The second type cannot be reassembled with the same parts, once disassembled. However, repair kits are available.

Snap-Ring Type

1. Remove the driveshaft. For the correct procedure, see the car section for the model you are working on.
2. If the front yoke is to be disassembled, matchmark the driveshaft and sliding splined yoke (transmission yoke) so that driveline balance is preserved upon reassembly. Remove the snap rings which retain the bearing caps.
3. Select two sockets, one small enough to pass through the yoke holes for the bearing caps, the other large enough to receive the bearing cap.
4. Use a vise or a press, position the small and large sockets on either side of the U-joint. Press in on the smaller socket so that it presses the opposite bearing cap out of the yoke and into the larger socket. If the cap does not come all the way out, grasp it with a pair of pliers and work it out.
5. Reverse the position of the sockets so that the smaller socket presses on the cross. Press the other bearing cap out of the yoke.
6. Repeat the procedure on the other bearings.
7. To install, grease the bearing caps and needles thoroughly if they are not pregreased. Start a new bearing cap into one side of the yoke. Position the cross in the yoke.
8. Select two sockets small enough to pass through the yoke holes. Put the sockets against the cross and the cap, and press the bearing cap 1/4 in. below the surface of the yoke. If there is a sudden increase in the force needed to press the cap into place, or if the cross starts to bind, the bearings are cocked. They must be removed and restarted in the yoke. Failure to do so will greatly reduce the life of the bearing.
9. Install a new snap-ring.
10. Start a new bearing into the opposite side. Place a socket on it and press in until the opposite bearing contacts the snap ring.
11. Install a new snap ring. It may be necessary to grind the facing surface of the snap ring slightly to permit easier installation.
12. Install the other bearings in the same manner.
13. Check the joint for free movement. If binding exists, smack the yoke ears with a brass or plastic faced hammer to seat the bearing needles. Do not strike the bearings, and support the shaft firmly. Do not install the driveshaft until free movement exists at all joints.

Plastic Retainer Type

Remove and install the bearing caps and trunnion (cross) as described for the snap-ring type universal joints. On an original universal joint, however, the bearing caps will be secured in the yokes with injected plastic. The plastic will shear when the bearing caps are pressed. Service snap-rings are installed in the groove on the inside (of yoke) of the installed caps.

NOTE: The plastic which retains the bearing will be sheared when the bearing cup is pressed out. Be sure to remove the remains of the plastic retainer from the ears of the yoke. It is easier to remove the remains if a small pin or punch is first driven through the injection holes in the yoke. Failure to remove all of the plastic remains may prevent the bearing cups from being pressed into place and the bearing retainers from being properly seated.

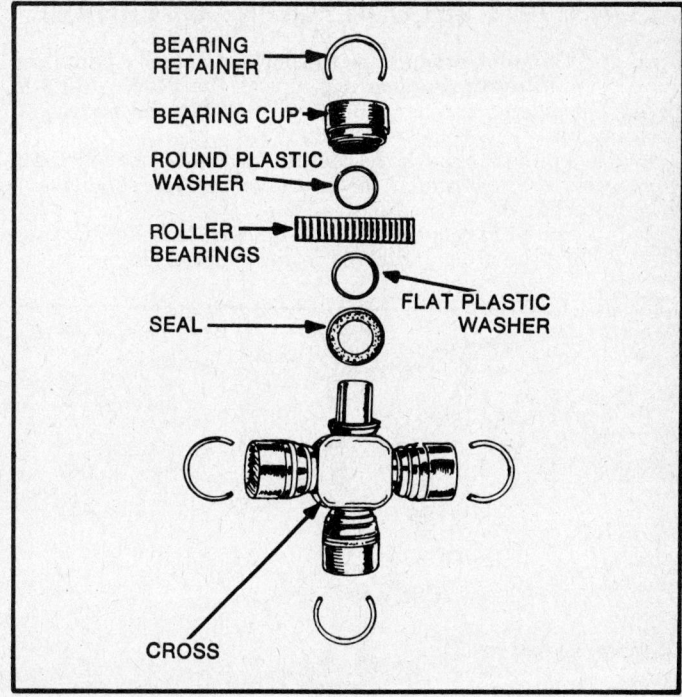

Plastic retainer U-joint repair kit components

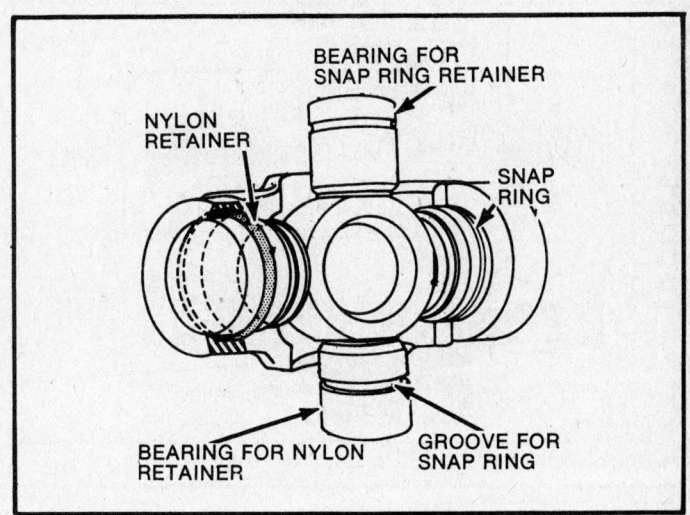

U-joint locking methods (© Pontiac Div. G.M. Corp.)

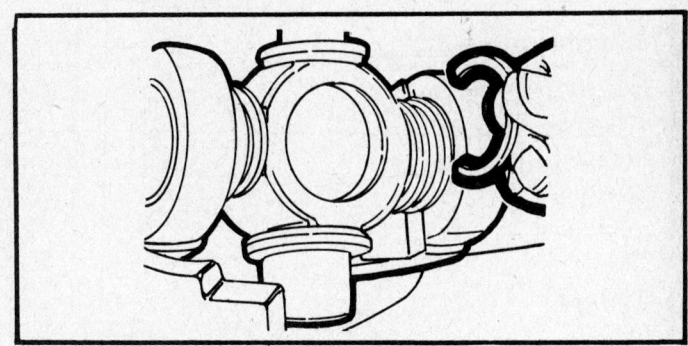

Service snap rings are installed

SECTION 28 UNIVERSAL JOINTS SERVICE

CONSTANT VELOCITY JOINT OVERHAUL

Ford and Chrysler products with constant velocity joints use snap rings to retain the bearing cups in the jokes. Most GM cars have plastic retainers. Be sure to obtain the correct rebuilding kit.

1. Use a punch to mark the coupling yoke and the adjoining yokes before disassembly, to ensure proper reassembly and driveline balance.
2. It is easiest to remove the bearings from the coupling yoke first. Follow the order indicated in the illustration.

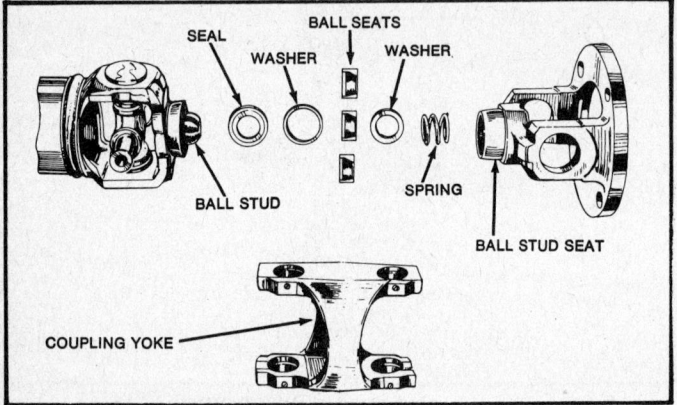

Constant velocity joint

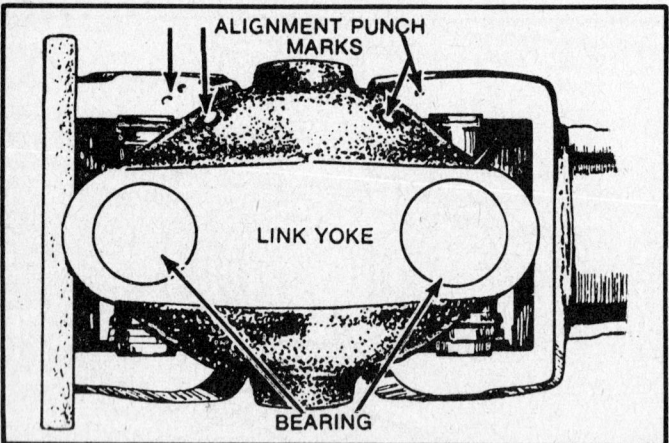

Match marks for double cardan joint

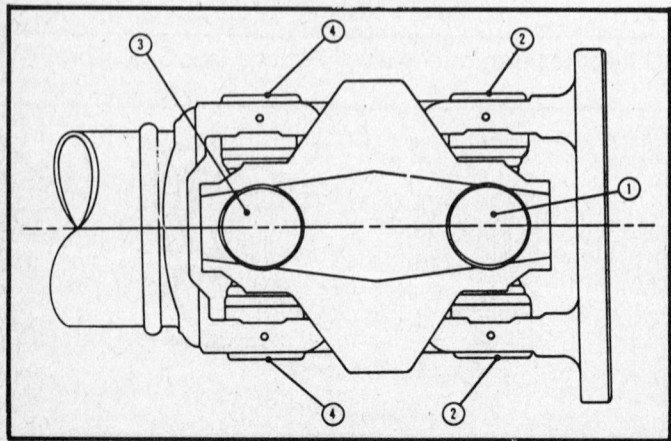

C.V. joint disasemlby sequence

3. Support the driveshaft horizontally on a press stand, or on the workbench if a vise is being used.
4. If snap rings are used to retain the bearings cups, remove them. Place the rear ear of the coupling yoke over a socket large enough to receive the cup. Place a smaller socket, or a cross press make for the purpose, over the opposite cup. Press the bearing cup out of the coupling yoke ear. If the cup is not completely removed, insert a spacer and complete the operation, or grasp the cup with a pair of slip joint pliers and work it out. If the cups are retained by plastic, this will shear the retainers. Remove any bits of plastic.
5. Rotate the driveshaft and repeat the operation on the opposite cup.
6. Disengage the trunnions of the spider, still attached to the flanged yoke, from the coupling yoke, and pull the flanged yoke an spider from the center ball on the ball support tube yoke.

NOTE: The joint between the shaft and coupling yoke can be serviced without disassembly of the joint between the coupling yoke and flanged yoke.

7. Pry the seal from the ball cavity, remove the washers, spring and three seats. Examine the ball stud seat and the ball stud for scores or wear. Worn parts can be replaced with a kit. Clean the ball seat cavity and fill it with grease. Install the spring, washer, ball seats, and spacer (washer) over the ball.
8. To assemble, insert one bearing cup part way into one ear of the ball support tube yoke and turn this cup to the bottom.
9. Insert the spider (cross) into the tube yoke so that the trunnion (arm) seats freely in the cup.
10. Install the opposite cup part way, making sure that both cups are straight.
11. Press the cups into position, making sure that both cups squarely engage the spider. Back off if there is a sudden increase in resistance, indicating that a cup is cocked or a needle bearing is out of place.
12. As soon as one bearing retainer groove clears the yoke, stop and install the retainer (plastic retainer models). On models with snap rings, press the cups into place, then install the snap rings over the cups.
13. If difficulty is encountered installing the plastic retainers or snap rings, smack the yoke sharply with a hammer to spring the ears slightly.
14. Install one bearing cup part way into the ear of the cupling yoke. Make sure that the alignment marks are matched, than engage the coupling yoke over the spider and press in the cups, installing the retainers or snap rings as before.
15. Install the cups and spider into the flanged yoke as with the previous yoke.

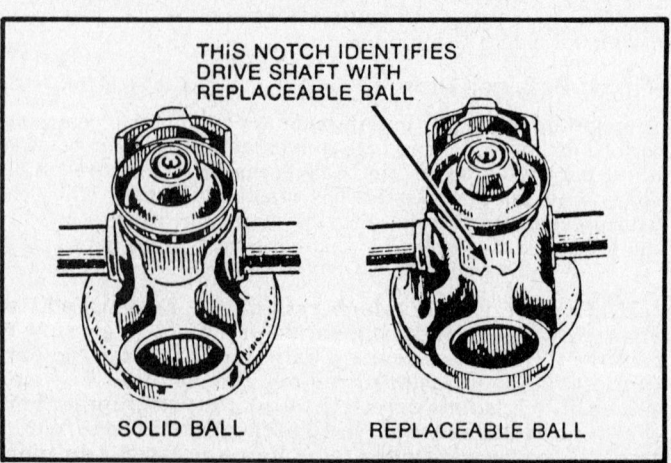

Solid and replaceable U-joint balls

UNIVERSAL JOINTS SERVICE
SECTION 28

NOTE: The flange yoke should snap over center to the right or left and up or down by the pressure of the ball seat spring.

Front Wheel Drive

INTRODUCTION

Natural drive line vibrations are created by the fluctuations in the speed of the drive shaft as the drive line angle is changed during a single revolution of the shaft. With the increased use of the front drive transaxles, the drive shafts and universal joints must transfer the driving power to the front wheels and at the same time, compensate for steering action on turns. Special universal joints were developed, one a constant velocity (CV) or double offset type, and a second type known as the tri-pod joint. The constant velocity joint uses rolling balls in curved grooves to obtain uniform motion. As the joint rotates in the driving or steering motion, the balls, which are in driving contact between the two halves of the joint coupling, remain in a plane which bisects the angle between the two shafts, thus cancelling out the fluctuations of speed in the drive shaft.

The tri-pod type uses a three legged spider, with needle bearing and balls incased in a three grooved housing. With the spider attached to the drive shaft, the joint assembly is free to roll back and forth in the housing grooves as the shaft length varies in normal drive line operation.

The front drive shafts are normally of two different lengths from the transaxle to the drive wheels, due to the location of the engine/transaxle mounting in the vehicle. Care should be excercised when removing or replacing the drive shafts, as to their locations (mark if necessary), removal procedures and handling so as not to damage the boots covering the universal joints, or if equipped, with boots covering the transaxle drive shaft opening. Should the boots become torn or otherwise damaged, premature failure of the universal joint would result due to loss of lubricant and entrance of contaminates.

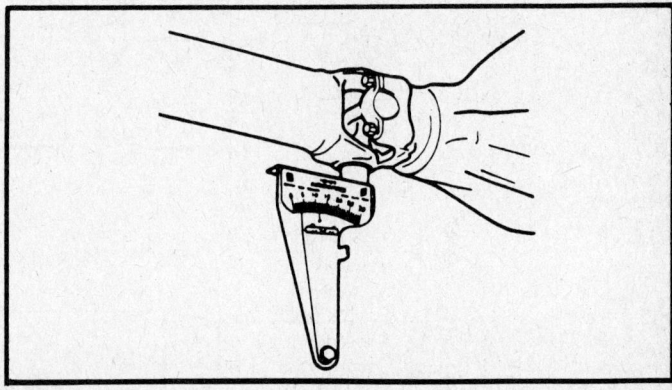

Typical measuring of universal joint angle at rear propeller shaft bearing cap

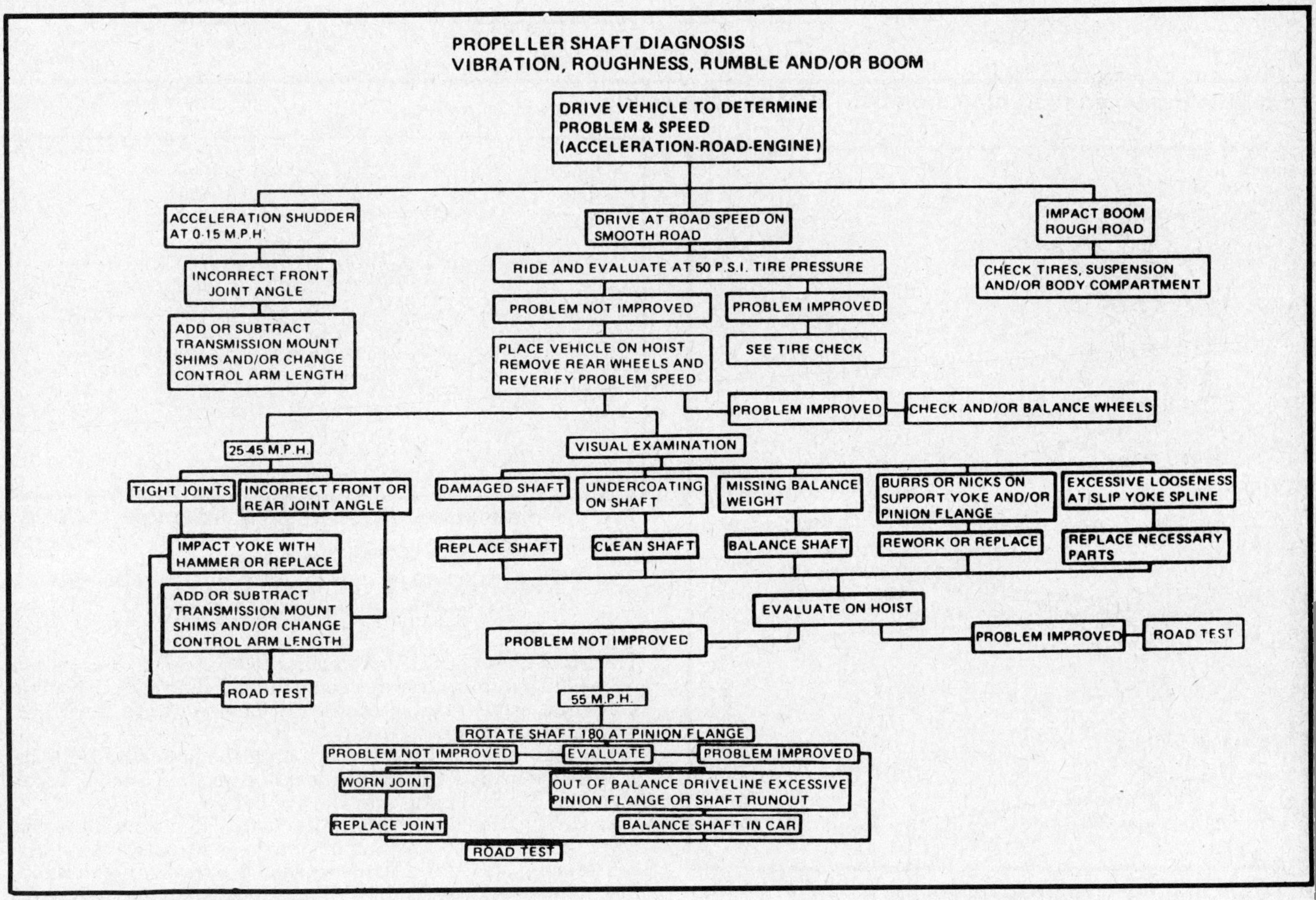

Propeller shaft diagnosis

28-57

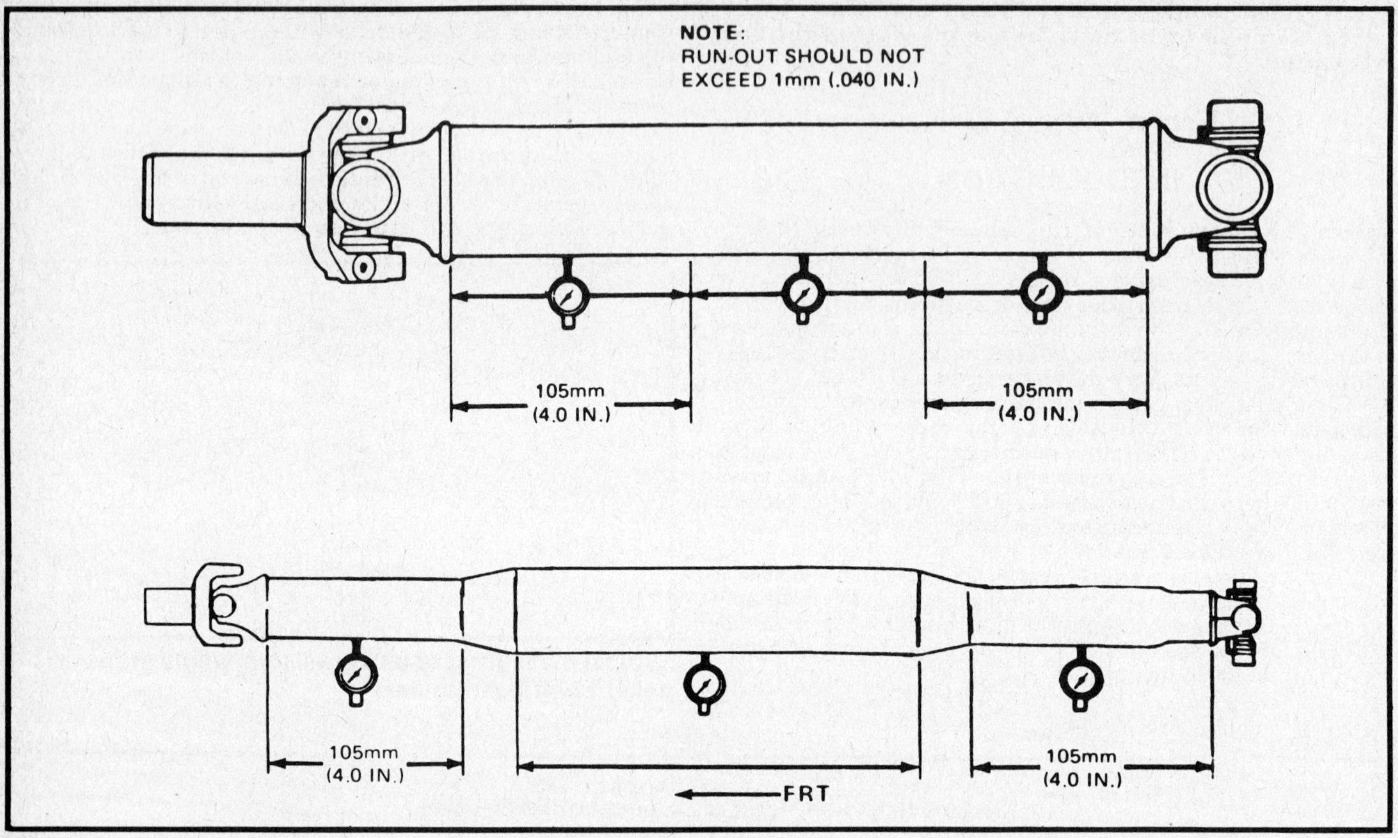

SECTION 28 UNIVERSAL JOINTS SERVICE

Allowable propeller shaft runout on two different type shafts

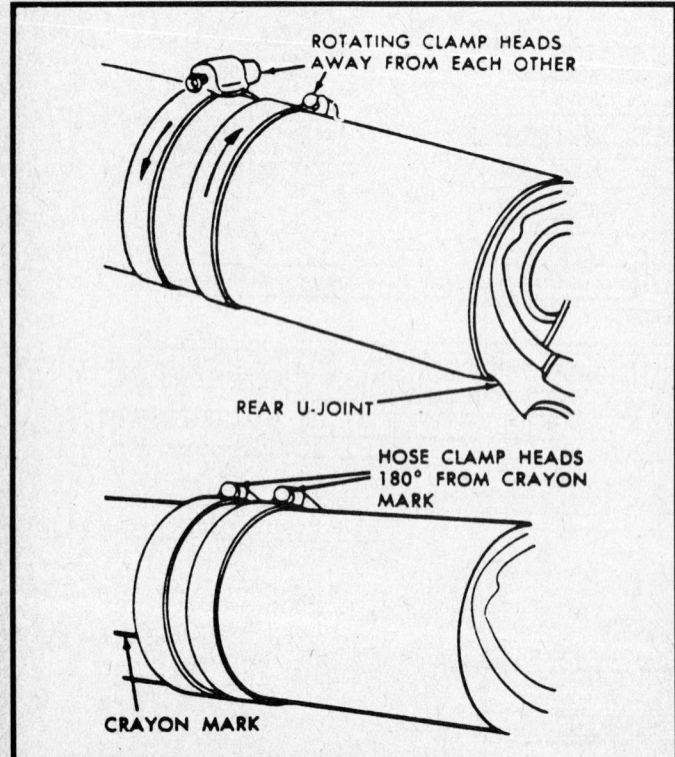

Rotation of hose clamps to balance a propeller shaft. A third clamp may be needed, but the shaft should be replaced if balancing cannot be accomplished

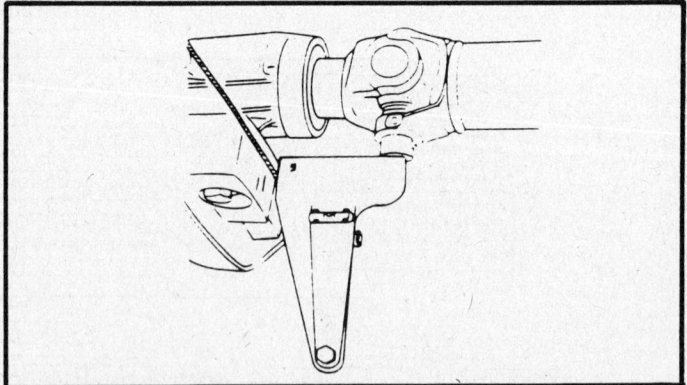

Typical measuring of universal joint angle at front propeller shaft bearing cap

ATTACHMENT OF THE DRIVE SHAFT TO THE TRANSAXLE

The attachment of the drive shafts to the transaxle is accomplished in a number of ways and if not familiar with the particular shaft attachment, do not pry or hammer until the correct procedure is known.

The shafts can be attached by one of the following methods:
1. Drive shaft flange to transaxle stub shaft flange, bolted together. Mark flanges and remove bolts.
2. Circlips inside differential housing. Remove differential cover, compress circlips and push axle shaft outward.
3. Spring loaded circlip mounted in groove on axle shaft and mating with a groove in the differential gear splines. Is usually pryed or tapped from differential gear with care.

UNIVERSAL JOINTS SERVICE 28

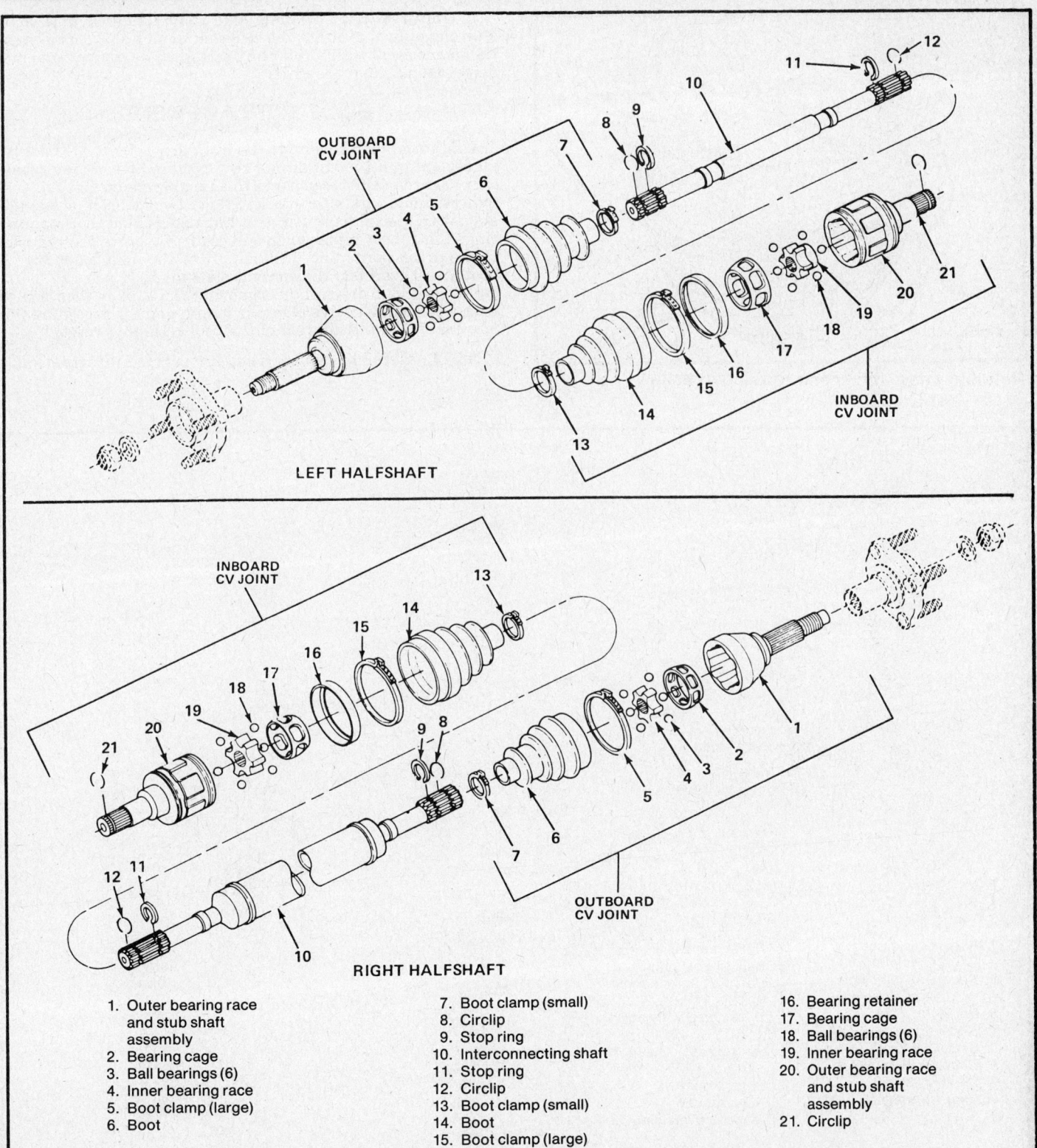

1. Outer bearing race and stub shaft assembly
2. Bearing cage
3. Ball bearings (6)
4. Inner bearing race
5. Boot clamp (large)
6. Boot
7. Boot clamp (small)
8. Circlip
9. Stop ring
10. Interconnecting shaft
11. Stop ring
12. Circlip
13. Boot clamp (small)
14. Boot
15. Boot clamp (large)
16. Bearing retainer
17. Bearing cage
18. Ball bearings (6)
19. Inner bearing race
20. Outer bearing race and stub shaft assembly
21. Circlip

Exploded view of left and right half-shafts, typical of Ford Motor Co. front wheel drive models (© Ford Motor Co.)

28-59

SECTION 28: UNIVERSAL JOINTS SERVICE

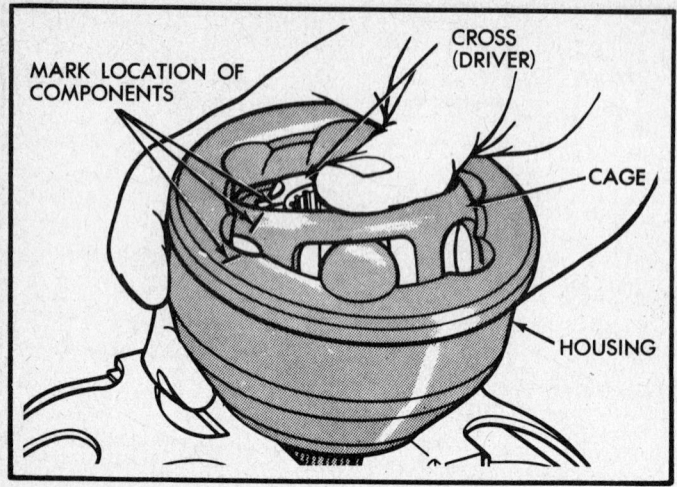

Rotating cage and cross to remove balls
(© Chrysler Corp.)

4. Universal joint housing, axle shaft flange or axle shaft stub end pinned to either the differential stub shaft of differential gear flange with a roll pin. Mark the two components and drive the pin from the units.

BOOT REPLACEMENT

The most common repairs to the front drive shafts are boot replacement and boot retaining ring replacement. Many repair shops are requested to perform this type of repairs for their customers. EOM and after-market replacement boots are available, with special tools used to crimp and tighten the retaining rings. Most boot replacement procedures require the removal of the drive shafts and disassembly of the joint assembly. A boot kit is available that provides a split boot that can be installed without drive shaft removal. The boot is then sealed with a special adhesive along its length and the procedure finished with the installation of the boot retaining rings.

NOTE: Refer to car sections for service information.

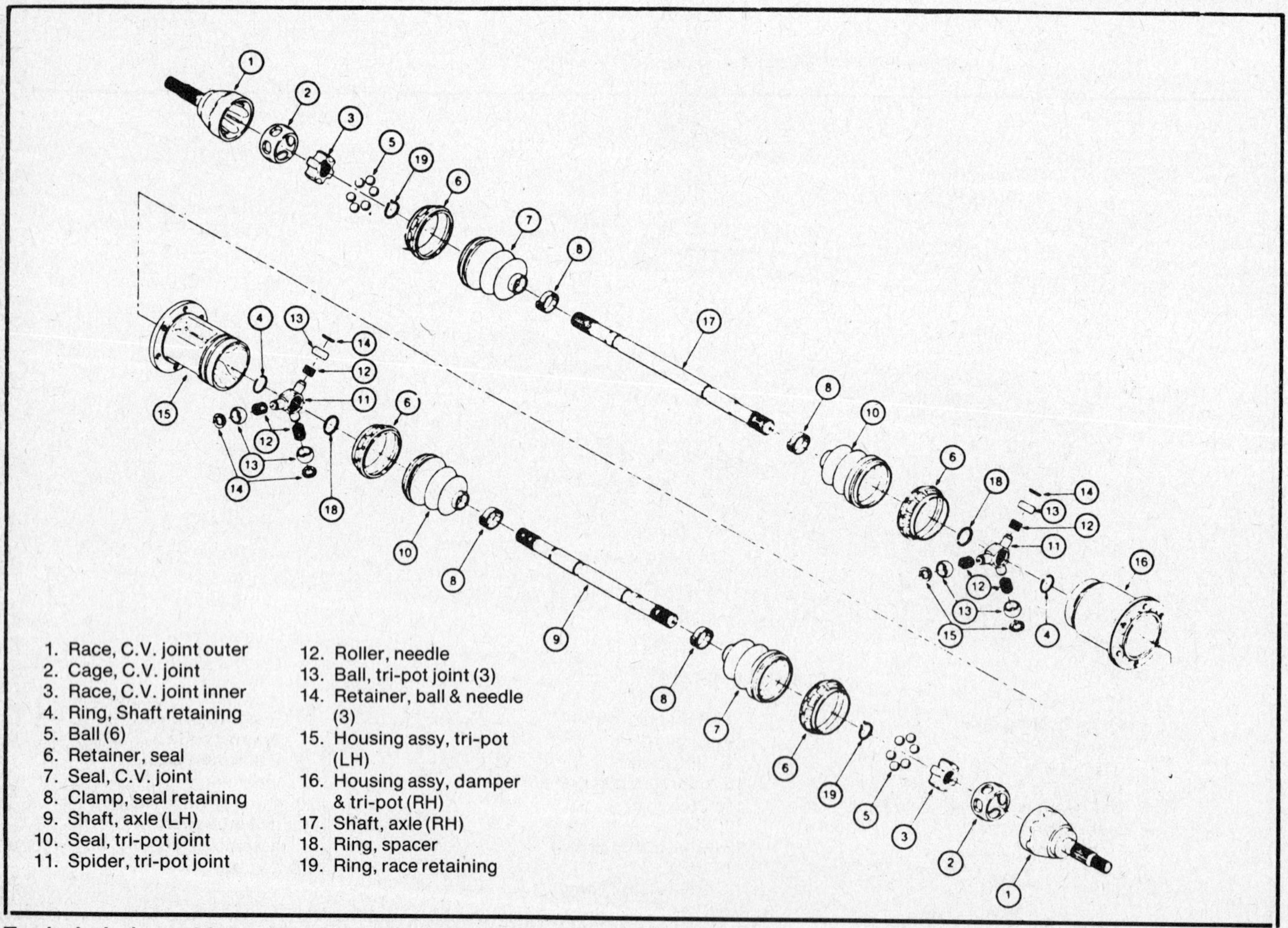

1. Race, C.V. joint outer
2. Cage, C.V. joint
3. Race, C.V. joint inner
4. Ring, Shaft retaining
5. Ball (6)
6. Retainer, seal
7. Seal, C.V. joint
8. Clamp, seal retaining
9. Shaft, axle (LH)
10. Seal, tri-pot joint
11. Spider, tri-pot joint
12. Roller, needle
13. Ball, tri-pot joint (3)
14. Retainer, ball & needle (3)
15. Housing assy, tri-pot (LH)
16. Housing assy, damper & tri-pot (RH)
17. Shaft, axle (RH)
18. Ring, spacer
19. Ring, race retaining

Exploded view of left and right half-shafts, typical of General Motors Corp. (© General Motors Corp.)

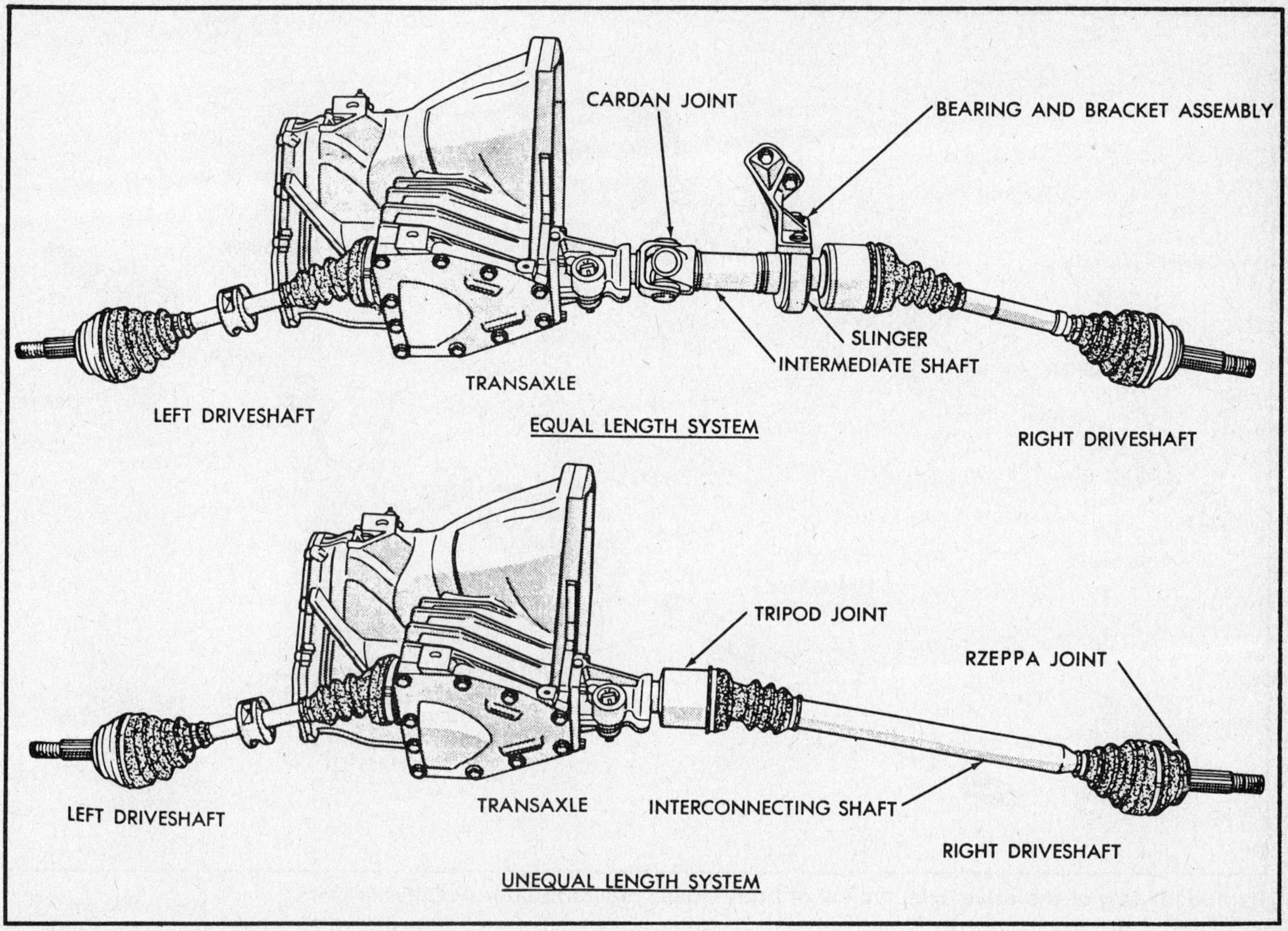

UNIVERSAL JOINTS
SERVICE
SECTION 28

Typical front wheel drive shaft system (© Chrysler Corp.)

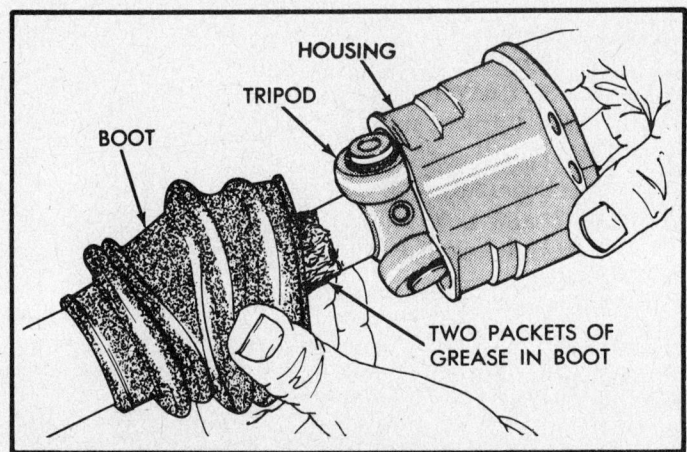

Reassembly to Tri-pod joint into housing (© Chrysler Corp.)

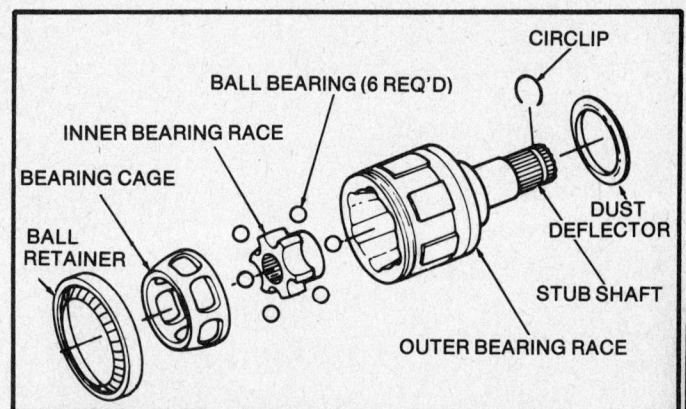

Exploded view of inboard CV joint—typical (© Ford Motor Co.)

28-61

SECTION 28: UNIVERSAL JOINTS SERVICE

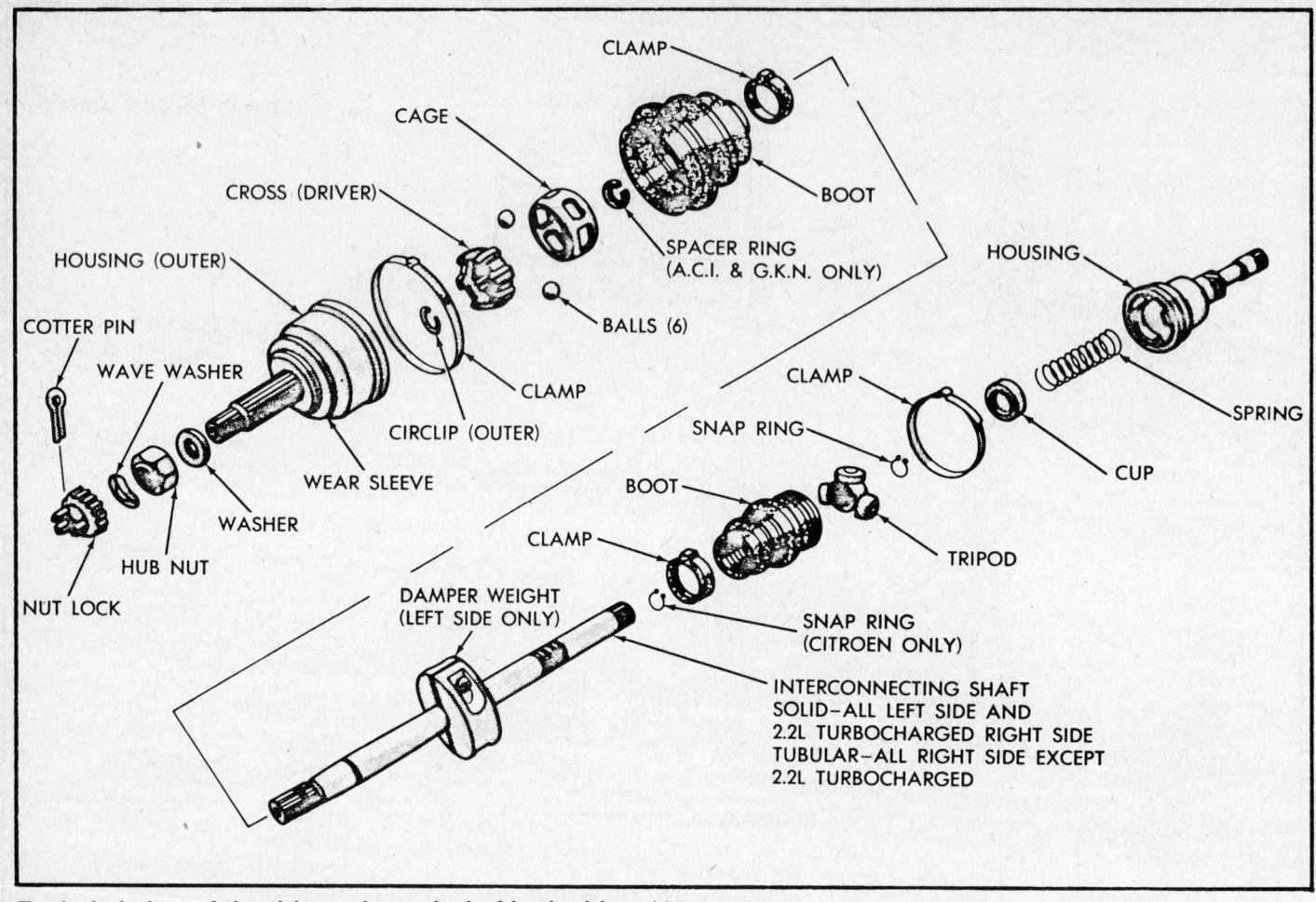

Exploded view of the drive axle, typical of both sides, 1984 and later (© Chrysler Corp.)

UNIVERSAL JOINTS SERVICE — SECTION 28

NOISE DIAGNOSIS CHART

PROBLEM	CAUSE
1. Identical noise in Drive or Coast conditions	1. Road noise Tire noise Front wheel bearing noise
2. Noise changes on a different type of road	2. Road noise Tire noise
3. Noise tone lowers as car speed is lowered	3. Tire noise
4. Similar noise is produced with car standing and driving	4. Engine noise Transmission noise
5. Vibration	5. Rough rear wheel bearing Unbalanced or damaged driveshaft Unbalanced tire Worn universal joint in driveshaft Misaligned drive shaft at companion flange Excessive companion flange runout
6. A knock or click approximately every two revolutions of rear wheel	6. Brinelled rear wheel bearing

NOISE DIAGNOSIS CHART

PROBLEM	CAUSE
7. Noise most pronounced on turns	7. Differential side gear and pinion wear or damage
8. A continuous low pitch whirring or scraping noise starting at relatively low speed	8. Damaged or worn pinion bearing
9. Drive noise, coast noise or float noise	9. Damaged or worn ring and pinion gear
10. Clunk on acceleration or deceleration	10. Worn differential cross-shaft in case
11. Clunk on stops	11. Insufficient grease in driveshaft slip yoke
12. Groan in Forward or Reverse	12. Improper differential lubricant
13. Chatter on turns	13. Improper differential lubricant. Worn clutch plates
14. Clunk or knock during operation on rough roads	14. Excessive end-play of axle shafts to differential cross-shaft

28-63

SECTION 29
ENGINE CONTROLS

INDEX

AMERICAN MOTORS

COMPUTERIZED ENGINE CONTROL SYSTEM (CEC)
6 cylinder
General Information	29-3
System Operation	29-4
Data Sensors	29-7
Preliminary Tests	29-8
Diagnostic Tests	29-8

4 cylinder
System Operation	29-8
Diagnostic Tests	29-11 29-13
Preliminary Checks	29-12
Switch Calibrations	29-14
Testing Procedures	29-13
Component Replacement	29-14

COMPUTER COMMAND CONTROL SYSTEM (C-4)
Components	29-15
Electronic Control Module	29-15
Diagnostic Procedures	29-16
Data Sensors	29-15
Calibration Unit (Prom)	29-17
Test and Troube Codes	29-17

CADILLAC

ELECTRONIC CONTROL MODULE (ECM)
General Information	29-17
Body Comptuer Moduel	29-18
ECM Functions	29-18
Diagnostic Display	29-19
Switch Test	29-19
Intermittent Codes	29-20

CHRYSLER CORPORATION

ELECTRONIC FEEDBACK CARBURETOR
Description	29-23
Troubleshooting	29-23
Electrical Connections	29-24
Hose Connections	29-26
Air Switching System	29-28
Sensor Tests	29-27
Driveability Diagnosis	29-29

ELECTRONIC CONTROL SYSTEM
Components	29-29
On Board Diagnostics	29-31
System Tests	29-32

GENERAL MOTORS

COMPUTER CONTROLLED CATALYTIC CONVERTER (C-4)
Introduction	29-33
System Operation	29-33

COMPUTER COMMAND CONTROL (CCC)
System Operation	29-34
Basic Troubleshooting	29-35
Remote Lamp Driver	29-37
Self Diagnostic System	29-38
Trouble Code Identification	29-39
Trouble Code Clearing Procedures	29-41
Explanation of Trouble Codes	29-43

ELECTRONIC TIMING CONTROLS (ETC)
Generarl Information	29-44

ELECTRONIC MODULE RETARD SYSTEM (EMR)
General Information	29-45

ELECTRONIC SPARK CONTROL SYSTEM (ESC)
General Information	29-45
Testing	29-46

ELECTRONIC SPARK TIMING (EST)
General Information	29-47
System Operation	29-47
Components R&R	29-48
Trouble Diagnosis	29-49

ELECTRONIC WASTEGATE CONTROLS (EWC)
General Information	29-54
Testing	29-55

TRANSMISSIONS CONVERTER CLUTCH (TCC)
General Information	29-55
Componenets R&R	29-55
Trouble Diagnosis	29-57

IDLE SPEED CONTROL (ISC)
General Information	29-59
Removal & Installation	29-60
On Car Adjustments	29-60

FORD MOTOR COMPANY

FEEDBACK CARBURETOR SYSTEM
System Operation	29-62
Operating Modes	29-62
System Components	29-63

THERMACTOR AIR SYSTEM
General Information	29-64
Ignition System	29-64
Fuel System	29-66
Trouble Diagnosis	29-65

ELECTRONIC ENGINE CONTROLS (ECCIII)
Generarl Information	29-67
Trouble Diagnosis	29-67
Self Test Features	29-67
System Description & Operation	29-71
System Components	29-72

DURA SPARK II & III IGNITION SYSTEM
General Information	29-76
Ignition Module	29-77
Vacuum Spark Control Mech.	29-77
Rotor Alignment	29-77

THICK FILM INTEGRATED SYSTEM (TFI-IV)
General Information	29-78
Octane Adjustments	29-79
Engine Control System (EEC-IV)	
General Informaiton	29-79
Monitoring System	29-79
Components	29-82
Carburetor Feedback Systems	29-83
Fuel Injection Systems	29-84
Quick Tests & Service Codes	29-87

AMERICAN MOTORS CORPORATION

Computerized Emission Control System Six Cylinder Engines 1983 and Later

GENERAL INFORMATION

On all four and six cylinder models the computerized emission control system (CEC) is being used to control the air-fuel ratio, the pulse air injection, idle speed control and ignition system. The main job of the CEC system is to maintain an air-fuel ratio of 14.7:1 (14.7 lbs. of air to 1 lb. of fuel) under all operating conditions. By maintaining the proper air-fuel ratio, the catalytic converter can effectively control nitric oxide, hydro-carbons and carbon monoxide emissions.

The CEC system is made up of several sub systems, fuel control, microcomputer control unit (MCU) data sensors, catalytic converter, idle speed control, pulse air injection control, and ignition advance control. All models are equipped with feedback carburetors, which contain an electronically operated mixture control (MC) solenoid on the four cylinder models and a stepper motor on the six cylinder models.

The job of the MC solenoid is to provide the proper air-fuel ratio by controlling the amount of air allowed to mix with the fuel. During the open loop operation air supplied by the MC solenoid is pre-programmed by the MCU. During the closed loop operation, the MC solenoid relies on the MCU data sensor operating conditions. The stepper motor controls the metering pins which vary the size of the idle and main bleed orifices in the carburetor body. The stepper motor moves the pins in and out of the orifices in steps, in response to signals received from the MCU.

The motor has a range of 100 steps, but normally operates in the middle of its range. When the metering pins are strepped into the orifices, the air-fuel mixture becomes richer. When the

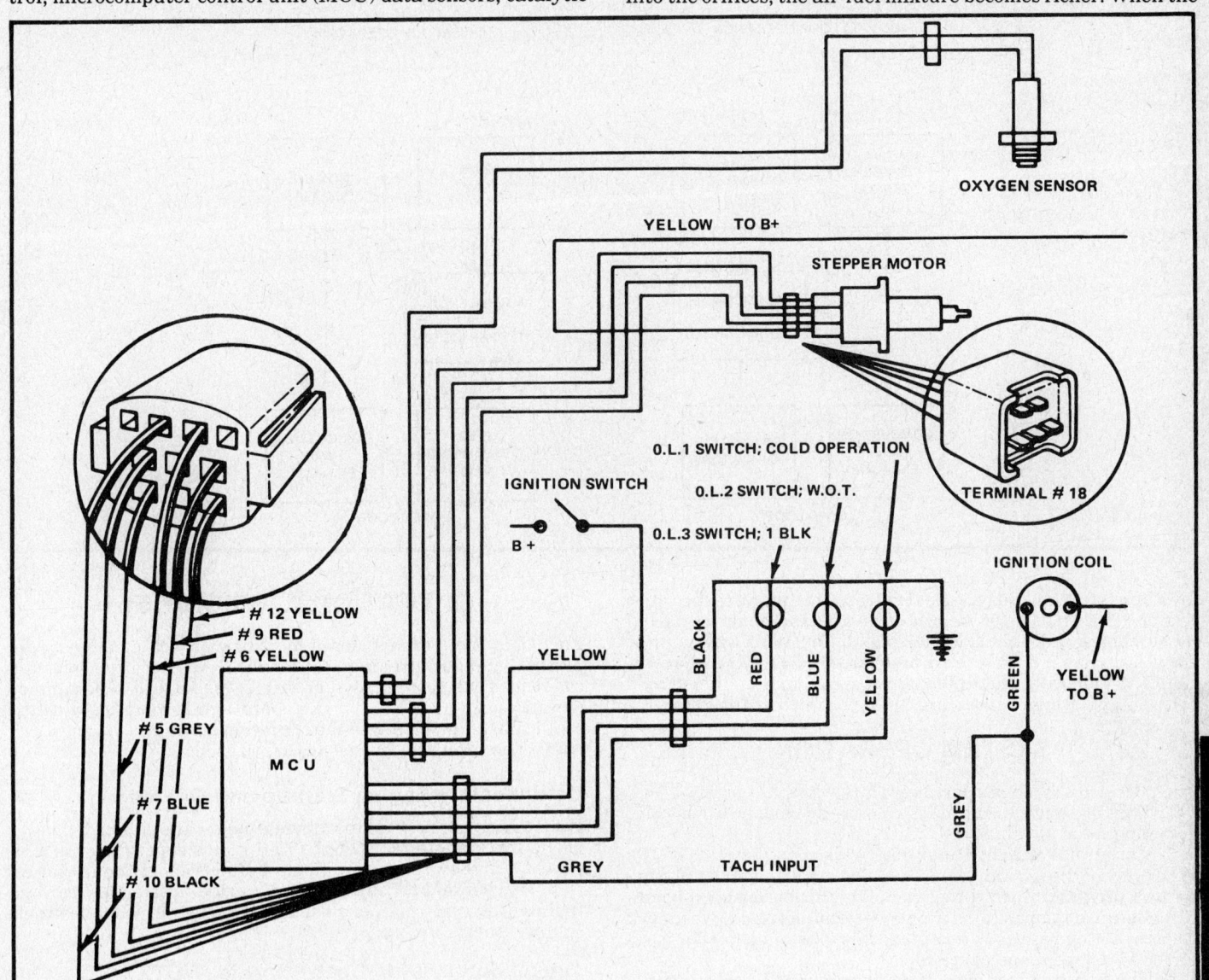

Computerized emission control (CEC) wiring diagram

SECTION 29
ENGINE CONTROLS
AMERICAN MOTORS

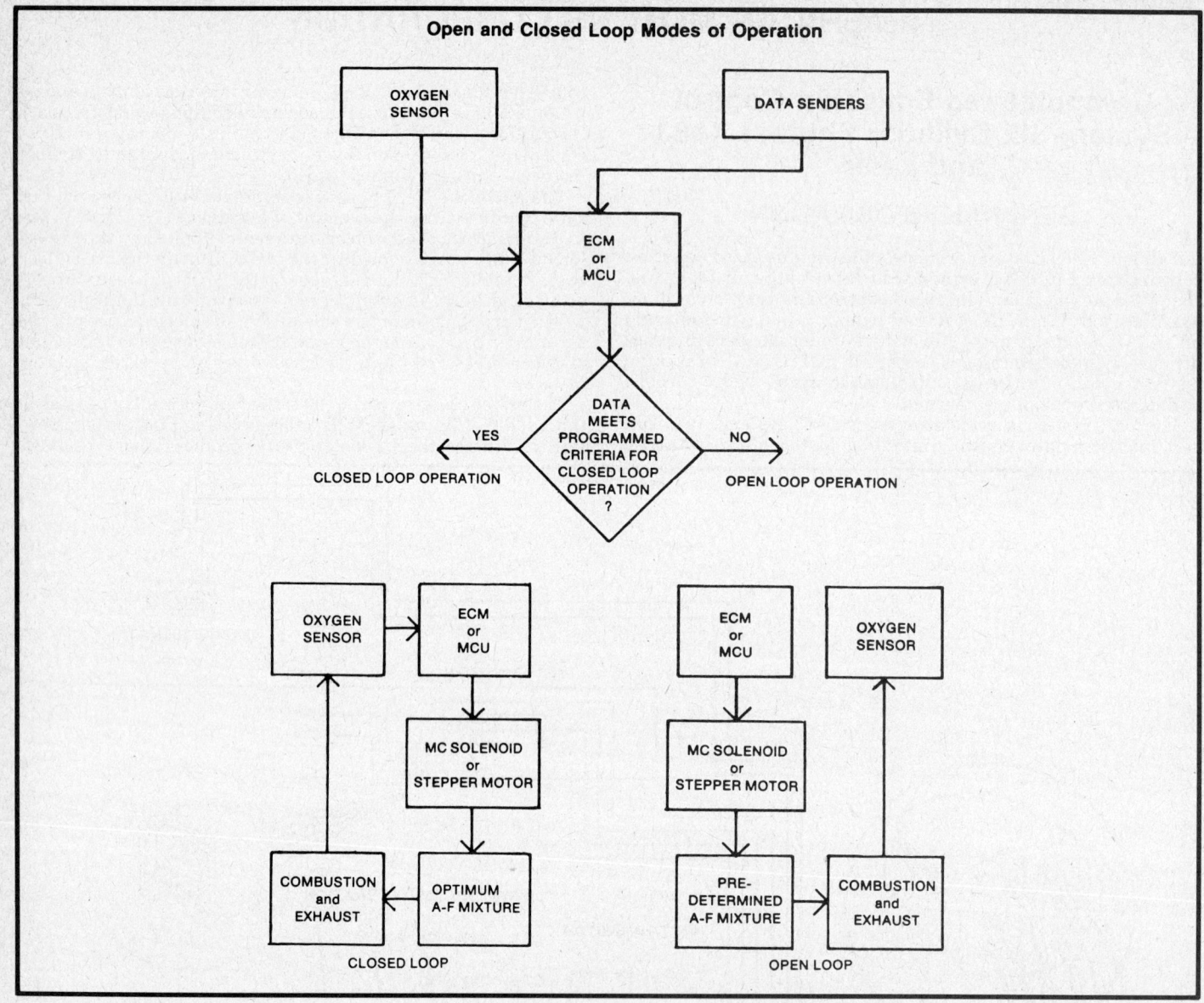

Open and Closed Loop Modes of Operation

pins are stepped out of the orifices, the mixture becomes leaner. The MCU unit is located in the passenger compartment, behind the right side kick panel. The MCU will monitor the CEC, system data sensors and based on the mode of operation, will generate an output control signal to the MC solenoid or the stepper motor, both are mounted in the carburetor.

SYSTEM OPERATION

The open loop mode of opertion occurs when:
1. Starting engine, engine is cold or air cleaner air is cold.
2. Engine is at idle speed.
3. Carburetor is either at or near wide open throttle (WOT). When any of these conditions occur, the metering pins are driven to a predetermined (programmed) position for each condition. Because the positions are predetermined and no feedback relative to the results is accepted, this type of operation is referred to as open loop operation.
4. The five open loop operations are characterized by the metering pins being driven to a position where they are stopped and remain stationary.

OPERATIONAL PRIORITIES

Each operation (except closed loop) has a specific metering pin position and because more than one of the operation selection conditions can be present at one time, the MCU is programmed with a priority ranking for the operation. It complies with the conditions that pertain to the operation having the highest priority. The priorities are as described below.

Cold Weather Engine Start-up and Operation

If the air cleaner air temperature is below the calibrated value of the thermal electric switch (TES), the stepper motor is positioned a predetermined number of steps rich of the initialization position and air injection is diverted upstream. Lean air/fuel mixtures are not permitted for a preset period following a cold weather start-up.

Open Loop 2, Wide Open Throttle (WOT)

Open loop 2 is selected whenever the air cleaner air temperature is above the calibrated value of the thermal electric switch

29-4

ENGINE CONTROLS
AMERICAN MOTORS
SECTION 29

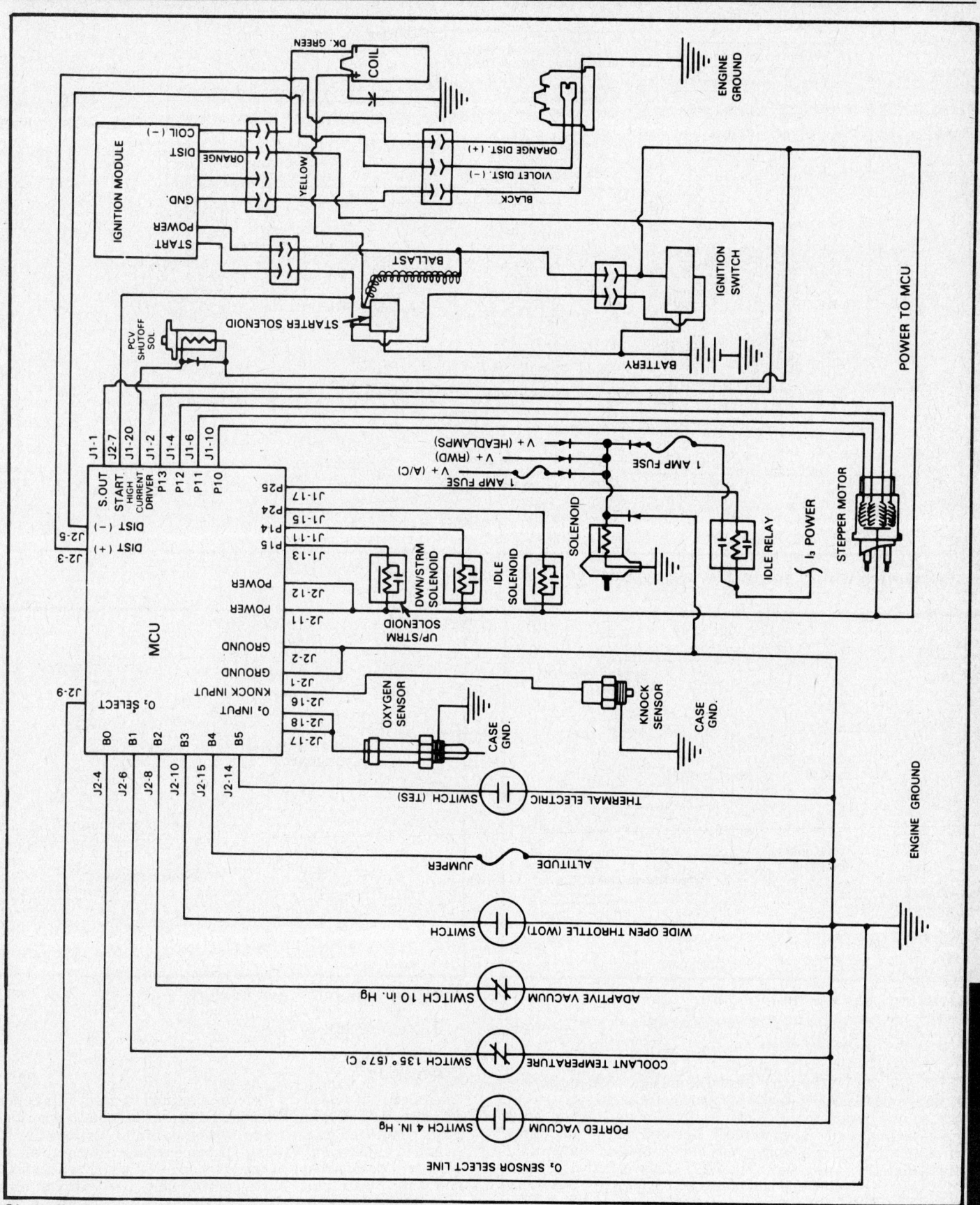

Six cylinder engine CEC system wiring schematic

29-5

SECTION 29

ENGINE CONTROLS
AMERICAN MOTORS

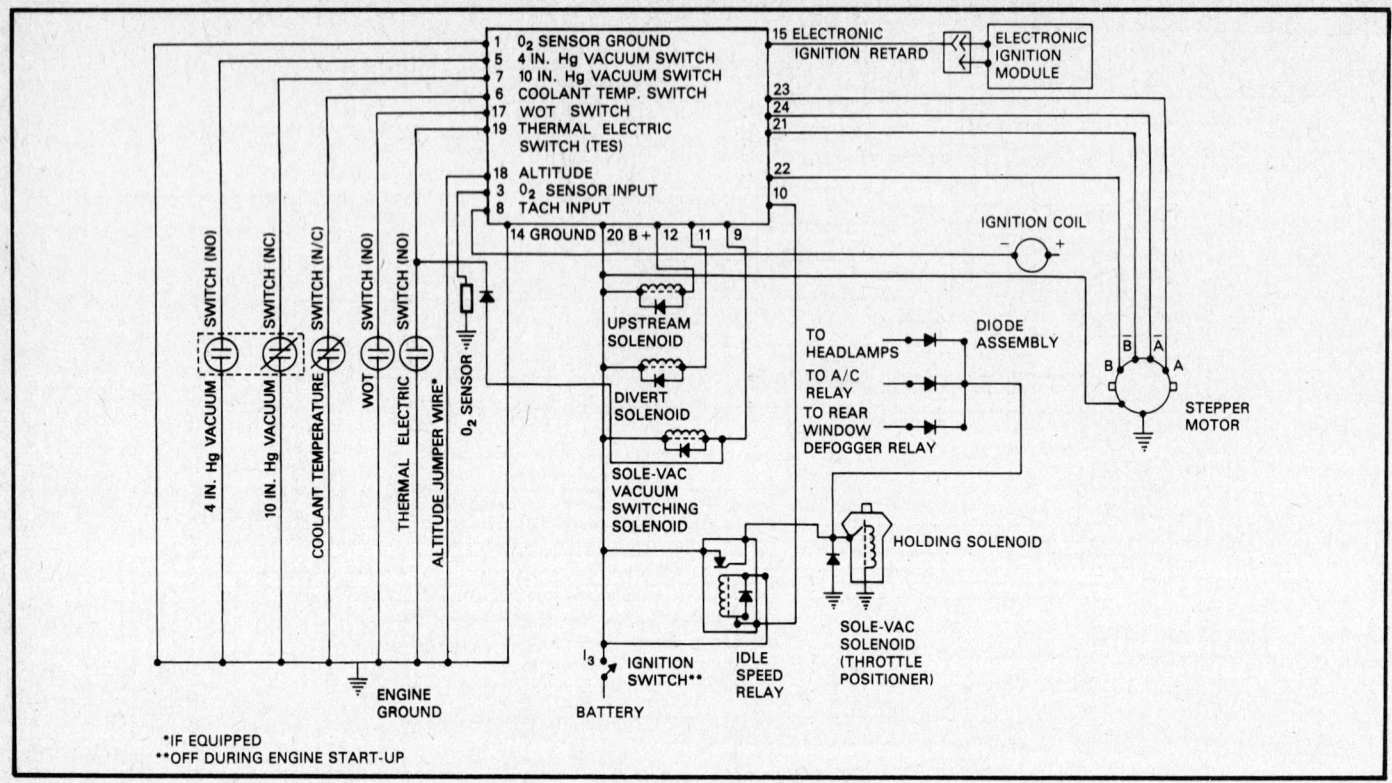

CEC system wiring schematic, six cylinder engines, 1982 and later

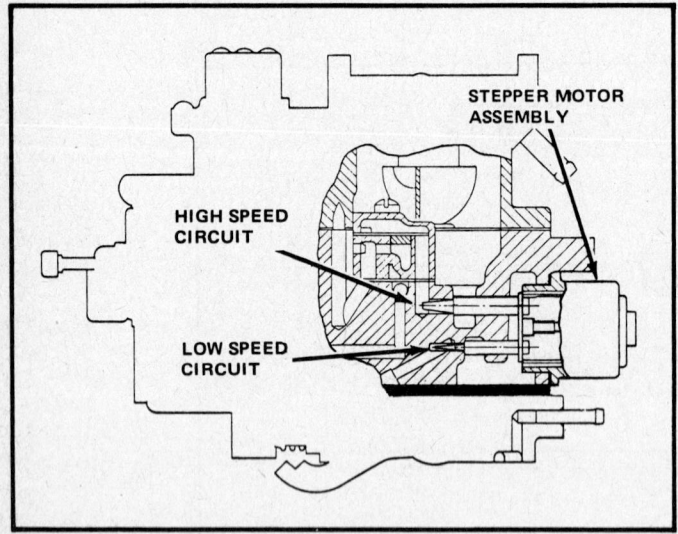

Metering pins in - rich mixture

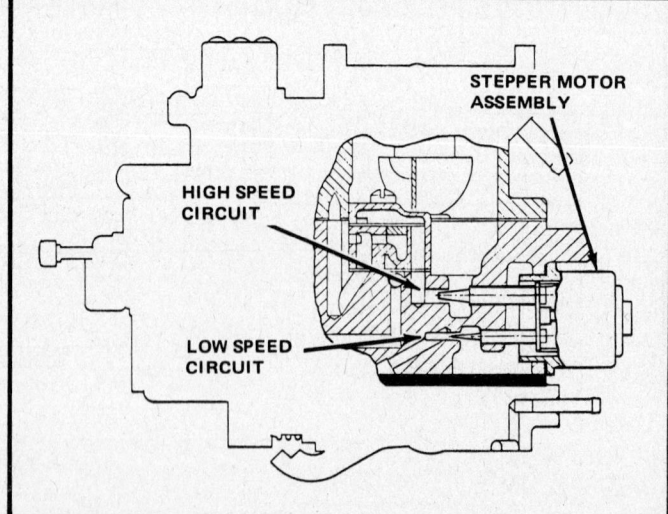

Metering pins out - lean mixture

(TES) and the WOT switch has been engaged. When the Open Loop 2 mode is selected, the stepper motor is driven to a calibrated number of steps rich of initialization and the air control valve switches air "downstream". However, if the "lean limit" circuit (with altitude jumper wire) is being used, the air is instead directed "upstream". The WOT timer is activated whenever OL2 is selected and it remains active for a preset period of time. The WOT timer remains inoperative if the "lean limit" circuit is being used.

Open Loop 4

Open Loop 4 is selected whenever manifold vacuum falls below a predetermined level. During OL4 operation, the stepper motor is positioned at the initialization position. Air injection is switched "upstream" during OL4 operation. However, air is switched "downstream" if the extended OL4 timer is activated and if the "lean limit" circuit is not being used (without altitude jumper wire). Air is also switched "downstream" if the WOT timer is activated.

ENGINE CONTROLS
AMERICAN MOTORS
SECTION 29

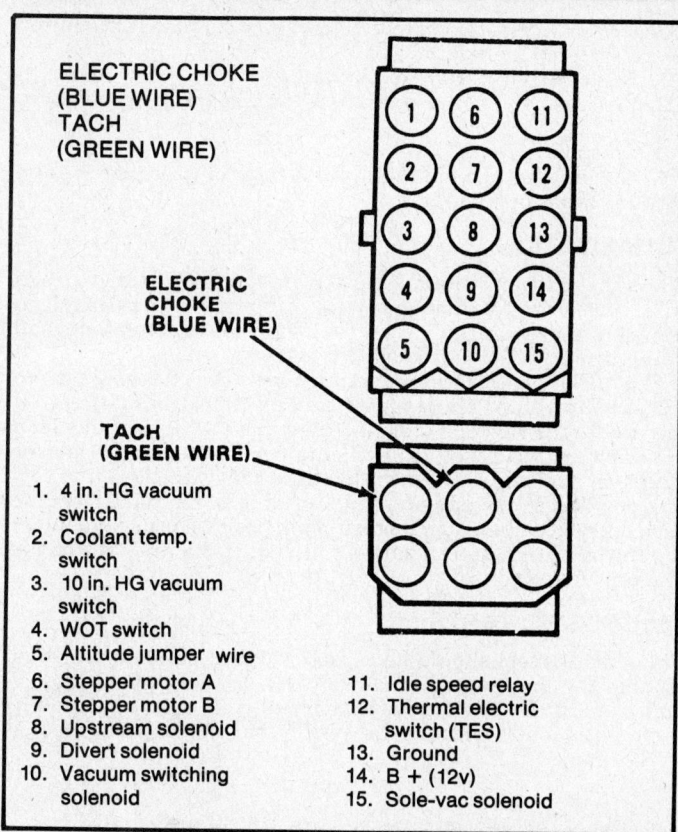

Diagnostic connector, CEC system, six cylinder engines, 1982 and later

Open Loop 3

Open Loop 3 is selected when the ignition advance vacuum level falls below a predetermined level. When the OL3 mode is selected, the engine rpm is also determined. If the rpm (tach) voltage is greater than the calibrated value, an engine deceleration condition is assumed to exist. If the rpm (tach) voltage is less than the calibrated value, an engine idle speed condition is assumed to exist.

Open Loop 1

Open Loop 1 will be selected if the air cleaner air temperature is above a calibrated value and open loop 2, 3 or 4 is not selected, and if the engine coolant temperature is below the calibrated value. The OL1 mode operates in lieu of normal closed-loop operation during a cold engine operating condition. If OL1 operation is selected, one of two predetermined stepper motor positions are chosen, dependent if the altitude circuit (lean limit) jumper wire is installed. With each engine start-up, a start-up timer is activated. During this interval, if the engine operating condition would otherwise trigger normal closed loop operation, OL1 operation is selected.

Closed Loop

Closed loop operation is selected after either OL1, OL2, OL3 or OL4 modes have been selected and the start-up timer has timed out. Air injection is routed "downstream" during closed loop operation. The predetermined "lean" air/fuel mixture ceiling is selected for a preset length of time at the onset of closed loop operation.

OPEN LOOP OPERATION PREDETERMINED POSITION VARIATION

An additional function of the MCU is to correct for a change in ambient conditions (e.g., high altitude). During closed loop operation the MCU stores the number of steps and direction that the metering pins are driven to correct the oxygen content of the exhaust. If the movements are consistently to the same position, the MCU will vary all open loop operate predetermined metering pin positions a corresponding amount. This function allows the open loop air/fuel mixture ratios to be "tailored" to the existing ambient condition during each uninterrupted use of the system. This optimizes emission control and engine performance.

CLOSED LOOP OPERATION

The CEC system controls the air/fuel ratio with movable air metering pins, visible from the top of the carburetor air horn, that are driven by the stepper motor. The stepper motor moves the metering pins in increments or small steps via electrical impulses generated by the MCU. The MCU causes the stepper motor to drive the metering pins to a "richer" or "leaner" position in reaction to the voltage input from the oxygen sensor located in the exhaust manifold.

The oxygen sensor voltage varies in reaction to changes in oxygen content present in the exhaust gas. Because of the content of oxygen in the exhaust gas indicates the completeness of the combustion process, it is a reliable indicator of the air/fuel mixture that is entering the combustion chamber. Because the oxygen sensor only reacts to oxygen, any air leak or malfunction between the carburetor and sensor may cause the sensor to provide an erroneous voltage output. This could be caused by a manifold air leak or malfunctioning secondary air check value.

The engine operation characteristics never quite permit the MCU to compute a single metering pin position that constantly provides the optimum air/fuel mixture. Therefore, closed loop operation is characterized by constant movement of the metering pins because the MCU is forced constantly to make small corrections in the air/fuel mixture in an attempt to create an optimum air/fuel mixture ratio.

DATA SENSORS

Oxygen Sensor

The oxygen sensor is located in the exhaust manifold and is used to measure the oxygen content in the exhaust gases. When a lean mixture is indicated an electrical signal generated by the sensor drops in voltage. When a rich mixture is indicated it causes the sensor to increase the voltage signal output.

Thermal Electric Switch

This switch is located inside the air cleaner and is used to provide either a ground for the MCU, which will indicate a cold weather engine start up air temperature below 50°F, or it will act as an open circuit to indicate a normal start up air temperature above 50°F.

Coolant Temperature Switch

The switch is controlled by the coolant temperature and is normally open in a cold engine and when the switch closes it indicates the engine temperature is higher than 135°F. The switch is located at the rear of the intake manifold.

Four Inch Hg Vacuum Switch

This vacuum switch is controlled by ported vacuum from the carburetor and has a normally open electrical switch, which indicates a closed throttle position. The switch is closed when 4

29-7

SECTION 29: ENGINE CONTROLS — American Motors

inch Hg of ported vacuum is reached. The switch is located in a bracket attached to the right inner fender.

Ten Inch Hg Vacuum Switch

This switch is green in color and is located on the same bracket as the 4 inch Hg vacuum switch. The switch is operated by manifold vacuum and when open, will signal the computer a throttle position that is above partial throttle, but below idle open throttle. This vacuum switch is normally in the closed position.

Wide Open Throttle Switch

The WOT switch is a mechanically operated electrical switch, that is located on the carburetor and is controlled by the throttle position to indicate a wide open throttle condition, this switch is normally in the open position.

Closed Throttle Switch
FOUR CYLINDER ENGINE ONLY

This switch indicates a closed throttle condition to the MCU whenever the throttle is in the closed position. The switch is also a part of the sole-vac throttle positioner.

Knock Sensor

The knock sensor is a finely tuned piezoelectric crystal transducer, which is located in the cylinder head. The crystal inside the sensor picks up the vibration caused by an engine knock, as the crystal vibrates it produces an electrical signal which is sent to the MCU. The MCU will then retard the timing of one cylinder or multiple cylinders to eliminate the engine knock.

Idle Speed Control

The ISC system is controlled by vacuum signals and signals from the MCU. The idle speed system raises and or maintains the engine idle at high engine loads. The system is comprised of a sole-vac throttle positioner, an idle vacuum switching solenoid and an idle speed relay. The sole-vac actuator is energized if the headlamps (six cylinder) or accessories such as air conditioning or rear window defogger are in operation.

It is also energized during vehicle deceleration or if the power steering is turned to the full stop position on power steering equipped vehicles (four cylinders only). The ISC system is interrelated with the CEC system and must be diagnosed in conjunction with the CEC system. Refer to the diagnostic tests 9, 10, and 11, if a malfunction occurs.

Air Injection Control

The pulse air injection system is switched from upstream to downstream injection by the MCU. There are two electrically controlled vacuum valves the supply operating vacuum to the upstream air injection valve and the downstream air injection valve. This will allow the MCU to control the catalyst operation and in turn reduce exhaust emissions.

ELECTRONIC IGNITION RETARD

The electronic ignition retard function of the ignition control module is interrelated with the CEC System and must be diagnosed in conjunction with the CEC System.

NOTE: For more elaborate test procedures on the AMC Computerized Engine Controls refer to the Chilton Electronic Engine Controls Manual #7545.

PRELIMINARY TESTS

Before performing the Diagnostic Tests, other engine associated systems that can affect air/fuel mixture, combustion efficiency or exhaust gas composition should be tested for faults. These systems include:
1. Basic carburetor adjustments.
2. Mechanical engine operation (i.e., spark plugs, valves, rings).
3. Ignition system.
4. Gaskets (intake manifold, carburetor or base plate); loose vacuum hoses or fittings.

INITIALIZATION

When the ignition system is turned off, the MCU is also turned off. It has no long term memory circuit for prior operation. As a result, it has an initialization function that is activated when the ignition switch is turned On.

The MCU initialization function moves the metering pins to the predetermined starting position by first driving them all the way to the rich end stop and then driving them in the lean direction by a predetermined number of steps. No matter where they were before initialization, they will be at the correct position at the end of every initialization period. Because each open loop operation metering pin position is dependent on the initialization function, this function is the first test in the diagnostic procedure.

DIAGNOSTIC TESTS

The CEC System should be considered as a possible source of trouble for engine performance, fuel economy and exhaust emission complaints only after normal tests that would apply to an automobile without the system have been performed.

Computerized Emission Control System Four Cylinder Engines 1983 and Later

SYSTEM OPERATION

The open loop mode of operation occurs when:
1. Starting engine, engine is cold or air cleaner air is cold.
2. Engine is at idle speed, accelerating to partial throttle or decelerating from partial throttle to idle speed.
3. Carburetor is either at or near wide open throttle (WOT), predetermined air/fuel mixture ratio for each condition. Because the air/fuel ratios are predetermined and no feedback relative to the results is accepted, this type of operation is referred to as open loop operation. All open loop operations are characterized by predetermined air/fuel mixture ratios.

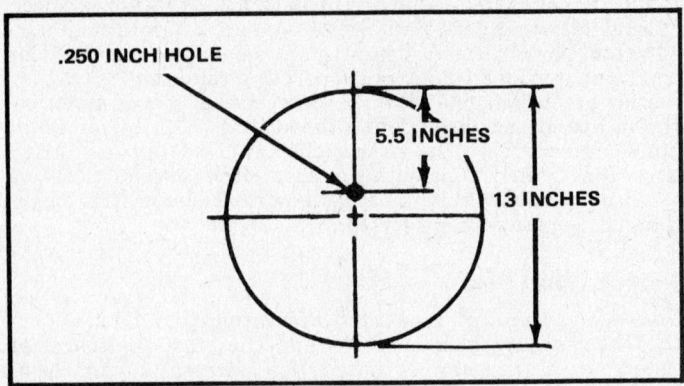

Air cleaner cover

ENGINE CONTROLS
AMERICAN MOTORS
SECTION 29

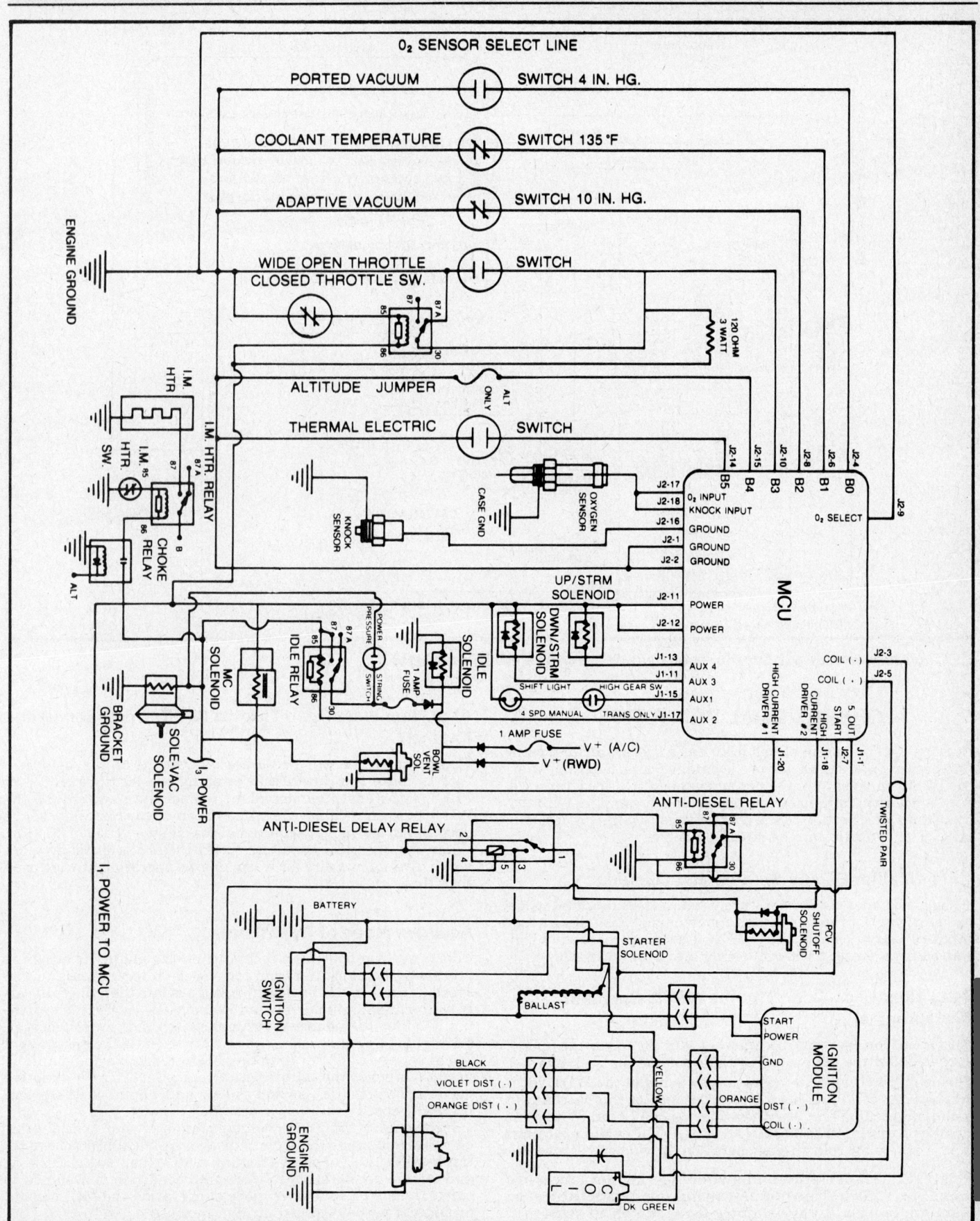

Four cylinder engine CEC system wiring schematic

29-9

SECTION 29
ENGINE CONTROLS
AMERICAN MOTORS

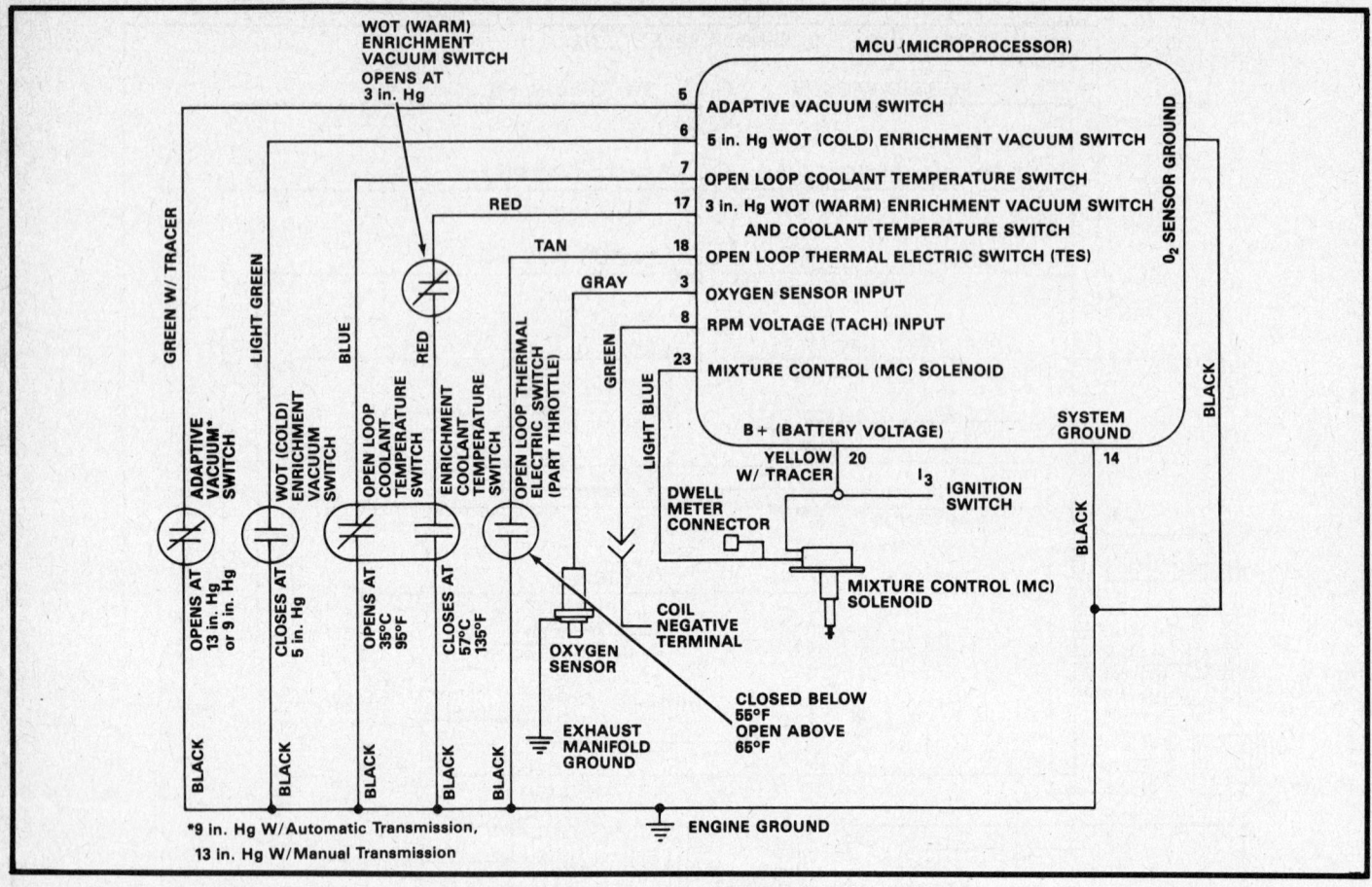

CEC system wiring schematic, four cylinder engines, 1982 and later

OPERATIONAL PRIORITIES

Each operation (except closed loop) has a specific air/fuel ratio and because more than one of the engine operational selection conditions can be present at one time, the MCU is programmed with a priority ranking for the operations. It complies with the conditions that pertain to the operation having the highest priority. The priorities are as described below.

Cold Weather Engine Start-up and Operation

If the air cleaner air temperature is below the calibrated value (55°F or 13°C) of the thermal electric switch (TES), the air/fuel mixture is at a "rich" ratio. Lean air/fuel mixtures are not permitted for a preset period following a cold weather start-up.

At or Near Wide Open Throttle (WOT) Operation (Cold Engine)

This open loop operation occurs whenever the coolant temperature is below the calibrated switching value (95°F or 35°C) of the open loop coolant temperature switch and the WOT vacuum switch (cold) has been closed because of the decrease in manifold vacuum (i.e., less than 5 in. Hg or 17 kPa). When this open loop condition occurs the MC solenoid provides a rich air/fuel mixture for cold engine operation at wide open throttle.

NOTE: Temperature and switching vacuum levels are nominal values. The actual switching temperature or vacuum level will vary slightly from switch to switch.

At or Near Wide Open Throttle (WOT) Operation (Warm Engine)

This open lop operation occurs whenever the coolant temperature is above the calibrated switching temperature (135°F or 57°C) of the enrichment coolant temperature switch and the WOT vacuum switch (warm) has been opened because of the decrease in manifold vacuum (i.e., less than 3 in. Hg or 10 kPa). When this open loop condition occurs the MC solenoid provides a rich air/fuel mixture for warm engine operation at wide open throttle.

Adaptive Mode of Operation

This open loop operation occurs when the engine is either at idle speed, accelerating from idle speed or decelerating to idle speed. If the engine rpm (tach) voltage is less than the calibrated value and manifold vacuum is above the calibrated switching level for the adaptive vacuum switch (i.e., switch closed), an engine idle condition is assumed to exist. If the engine rpm (tach) voltage s greater than the calibrated value and manifold vacuum is below the calibrated switching level for the adaptive vacuum switch (i.e., switch open), and engine-acceleration-from-idle speed condition is assumed to exist.

If the engine rpm (tach) voltage is greater than the calibrated value and manifold vacuum is above the calibrated switching level of the adaptive vacuum switch (i.e., switch closed), and engine-deceleration-to-idle speed condition is assumed to exist. During the adaptive mode of operation the MC solenoid provides a predetermined air/fuel mixture.

ENGINE CONTROLS
AMERICAN MOTORS
SECTION 29

 DIAGNOSTIC TEST CEC SYSTEM

IF THE RESULTS OF THE DIAGNOSTIC TESTS INDICATE THAT THE CEC SYSTEM IS FUNCTIONING NORMALLY AND ENGINE PERFORMANCE REMAINS INADEQUATE, PERFORM THE FOLLOWING TEST.

DETERMINE WHICH DIRECTION, RICH OR LEAN, THAT STEPPER MOTOR METERING PINS CONSISTENTLY MOVE TOWARD.

RICH?
- NO → (go to LEAN?)
- YES →
  - INSPECT FOR AIR LEAKS AT INTAKE MANIFOLD AND CARBURETOR GASKETS. INSPECT FOR FAULTY VACUUM HOSES OR FITTINGS. REPAIR SOURCE OF AIR LEAKS AND RETEST.
  - CHECK FOR EXHAUST LEAKS AT OR NEAR O_2 SENSOR. REPAIR AND RETEST.

LEAN?
- NO → IF METERING PINS VARY CONSISTENTLY WITHIN MIDRANGE, OPERATION IS NORMAL. TEST COMPLETE.
- YES → CHECK FOR FAULTY SPARK PLUG(S); MISADJUSTED IGNITION TIMING; AND MALFUNCTIONING IGNITION ADVANCE MECHANISMS. REFER TO GENERAL SERVICE AND DIAGNOSIS SECTION.

OK?
- YES → (continue below)
- NO → ADJUST AND/OR REPLACE COMPONENTS AS NECESSARY. RETEST.

- CHECK CARBURETOR IDLE SPEED ADJUSTMENT AND CHOKE ADJUSTMENT. CHECK OPERATION OF CHOKE LINKAGE. ENSURE HOSES AND WIRES ARE NOT INTERFERRING WITH OR RESTRICTING CARBURETOR LINKAGE. REPAIR AS NECESSARY AND RETEST.
- INSPECT HEATED AIR TUBE FOR PROPER CONNECTION AT AIR CLEANER AND EXHAUST MANIFOLD HEAT STOVE. REPAIR AS NECESSARY AND RETEST.
- INSPECT EGR VALVE FOR CORRECT INSTALLATION AND PROPER OPERATION. REPAIR AS NECESSARY AND RETEST.
- INSPECT PCV VALVE FOR PROPER OPERATION. REPAIR AS NECESSARY AND RETEST.
- INSPECT VAPOR CANISTER FOR PROPER "PURGE" OPERATION AND CONDITION OF HOSES. REPAIR AS NECESSARY AND RETEST.

Basic engine diagnostic test

SECTION 29: ENGINE CONTROLS — AMERICAN MOTORS

Closed Loop

Closed loop operation occurs whenever none of the open loop engine operating conditions exist. The MCU causes the MC solenoid to vary the air/fuel mixture in reaction to the voltage input from the oxygen sensor located in the exhaust manifold. The oxygen sensor voltage varies in reaction to changes in oxygen content present in the exhaust gas. Because the content of oxygen in the exhaust gas indicates the completeness of the combustion process, it is a reliable indicator of the air/fuel mixture that is entering the combustion chamber.

Because the oxygen sensor only reacts to oxygen, manifold air leak or malfunction between the carburetor and sensor may cause the sensor to provide an erroneous voltage output.

The engine operation characteristics never quite permit the MCU to compute a single air/fuel mixture ratio that constantly provides the optimum air/fuel mixture. Therefore, closed loop operation is characterized by constant variation of the air/fuel mixture because the MCU is forced constantly to make small corrections in an attempt to create an optimum air/fuel mixture ratio.

DIAGNOSTIC TESTS

The CEC System should be considered as a possible source of trouble for engine performance, fuel economy and exhaust emission complaints only after normal tests and inspections that would apply to an automobile without the system have been performed.

The steps in each test will provide a systematic evaluation of each component that could cause an operational malfunction. Refer to the Switch Calibrations chart during tests. To determine if fault exists with the system, a system operational test is necessary. This test should be performed when the CEC System is suspected because no other reason can be determined for a specific complaint. A dwell meter, digital volt-ohmmeter, tachometer, vacuum gauge and jumper wires are required to diagnose system problems. Although most dwell meters should be acceptable, if one causes a change in engine operation when it is connected to the mixture control (MC) solenoid dwell pigtail wire test connector, it should not be used.

The dwell meter, set for the six-cylinder engine scale and connected to a pigtail wire test connector leading from the mixture control (MC) solenoid, is used to determine the air/fuel mixture dwell. When the dwell meter is connected, do not allow the connector terminal to contact any engine component that is connected to engine ground. This includes hoses because they may be electrically conductive. With a normally operating engine, the dwell at both idle speed and partial throttle will be between 10 degrees and 50 degrees and will be varying. Varying means the pointer continually moves back and forth across the scale. The amount it varies is not important, only the fact that it does vary.

This indicates closed loop operation, indicating he mixture is being varied according to the input voltage to the MCU from the oxygen sensor. With wide open throttle (WOT) and/or cold engine operation, the air/fuel mixture ratio will be predetermined and the pointer will only vary slightly. This is open loop operation, indicating the oxygen sensor output has no effect on the air/fuel mixture. If there is a question whether or not the system is in closed loop operation, richening or leaning the air/fuel mixture will cause the dwell to vary more if the system is in closed loop operation.

TEST EQUIPMENT

The equipment required to perform the checks and tests includes a tachometer, a hand vacuum pump and a digital volt-ohmmeter (DVOM) with a minimum ohms per volt of 10 meg-ohms.

---- CAUTION ----

The use of a voltmeter with less than 10 meg-ohms per volt input independence can destroy the oxygen sensor. Since it is necessary to look inside the carburetor with the engine running, observe the following precautions:

1. Shape a sheet of clear acrylic plastic at least .250 in. thick and 15 x 15 inches.
2. Secure the acrylic sheet with an air cleaner wing nut after the top of the air cleaner has been removed.
3. Wear eye protection whenever performing checks and tests.
4. When engine is operating, keep hands and arms clear of fan, drive pulleys and belts. Do not wear loose clothing. Do not stand in line with fan blades.
5. Do not stand in front of running car.

PRELIMINARY CHECKS 1983

Check A: Initialization (Start-up)

1. Remove air cleaner cover. Install plastic air cleaner cover in its place.

NOTE: Metering pins operate in tandem. Only the upper pin is visible.

2. While observing metering pins by looking down into carburetor, have a helper turn ignition switch to "ON" position without starting the engine.
3. Metering pins should move fully toward front of automobile, then reverse direction and move partially back toward rear. They will then stop and remain stationary for approximately 40 seconds, and then move in either direction.
4. If okay, continue with Step 7.
5. If not okay and pins do not move at all, perform Test 1.
6. If not okay and pins do not move at the end of 40 seconds, perform Test 2 starting with Step 3.
7. Turn ignition off.
8. Continue with Check B.

Check B: Open Loop 1 Cold Start and Operation

This check should be performed with the coolant temperature below 100°F (38°C) to ensure the CTO diverts vacuum to the yellow vacuum switch. If the coolant temperature is above 100°F (38°C), cold operation may be simulated by removing the vacuum hose from the yellow vacuum switch and applying (and maintaining) a vacuum of 5 to 10 in. Hg to the switch.

1. Start engine and maintain engine rpm at 1,500.
2. At the end of initialization period (approximately 40 seconds if cold, but may vary if hot), metering pins should not move. Release vacuum applied to yellow vacuum switch (disconnect vacuum hose or vacuum pump, if used). The metering pins should move.
3. If okay, perform Check C.
4. If not okay, perform Test 2.

Check C: Open Loop 2 Wide Open Throttle (WOT)

1. While observing metering pins with engine at idle below 800 rpm and no vacuum applied to yellow vacuum switch, disconnect vacuum hose connected to blue vacuum switch.
2. Metering pins should move toward front of automobile, stop and remain stationary.
3. If okay, continue with Step 5.
4. If not okay, continue with Step 7.
5. Reconnect vacuum hose to blue vacuum switch.
6. Continue with Check D.
7. Reconnect vacuum hose to blue vacuum switch.
8. Continue with Test 3.

ENGINE CONTROLS
AMERICAN MOTORS

Check D: Open Loop 3 Idle

1. Turn engine off. Have a helper restart and idle engine below 800 rpm.
2. Observe metering pins during initialization function.
3. At the end of initialization period, metering pins should move forward, stop and remain stationary.
4. If okay, perform Check E.
5. If not okay, perform Test 4.

Check E: Closed Loop Warm Mid-Range

1. With no vacuum applied to yellow vacuum switch, increase engine speed slowly to 2,000 rpm while observing metering pins. Maintain 2,000 rpm and determine if metering pins start moving and continue in incremental steps.
2. If okay, CEC system is functioning normally. Continue with Step 5.
3. If not okay and metering pins do not move, perform Test 4.
4. If not okay and metering pins move fully to either stop and remain stationary, perform Test 5.
5. Turn engine off.
6. Install carpet pulled down during test procedures, if required.
7. Connect all vacuum hoses.
8. Install air cleaner cover.

TESTING PROCEDURE

Test 1: Failure to Initialize

1. Pull down forward edge of carpeting that extends up dash panel on passenger side to expose MCU and harness connectors.
2. Disconnect six-wire connector.
3. With voltmeter, check terminal 12 to determine if battery voltage is present at harness side of connector.
4. If okay, continue with Step 6.
5. If not okay, repair circuit and perform Check A.
6. Turn ignition off.
7. With ohmmeter, check terminal 10 for electrical continuity to ground.
8. If okay, continue with Step 10.
9. If not okay, repair ground circuit and perform Check A.
10. Disconnect four-wire connector.
11. Check electrical continuity between harness side connector terminal 12 of six-wire connector and each of four harness-side terminals of four-wire connector. All four indications should be nearly equal and between 50 and 95 ohms.
12. If okay, continue with Step 17.
13. If not okay, continue with Step 14.
14. Disconnect the five-wire connector on stepper motor and check electrical continuity between terminal 18 and motor housing and between other four terminals on stepper motor. Resistance to housing should be infinite. Resistance to all four terminals should be nearly equal and between 53 an d85 ohms.
15. If okay, repair wiring defect in harness between stepper motor and MCU, then perform Check A.
16. If not okay, replace stepper motor and perform Check A.
17. Turn ignition on.
18. With voltmeter, check for presence of battery voltage on terminal 18, harness side of connector.
19. If okay, continue with Step 21.
20. If not okay, repair voltage supply circuit to stepper motor and perform Check A.
21. Turn ignition off.
22. Remove stepper motor, push metering pins further into motor. Install motor.
23. Connect the connector disconnected in Step 14.
24. While observing metering pins, have ignition turned on and check for metering rod movement. Pins should move.
25. If okay, replace stepper motor and perform Check A.
26. If not okay, replace MCU and perform Check A.

Test 2: Loop 1 Cold Start and Operation

NOTE: If an alternate vacuum source was used for Check B, start with step 4.

1. With the coolant temperature less than 100°F (38°C), check vacuum hose to yellow vacuum switch for vacuum. A vacuum of 5 in. Hg or more should be indicated.
2. If okay, continue with Step 4.
3. If not okay, repair vacuum leak or replace CTO valve and return to Check B.
4. Turn ignition off.
5. Pull down forward edge of carpeting extending up dash panel on passenger side to expose MCU and harness connectors.
6. Disconnect six-wire connector.
7. Check terminal 6 on harness connector for electrical continuity to ground. There should be no continuity (infinite resistance).
8. If okay, continue with Step 13.
9. If not okay, continue with Step 10.
10. Disconnect vacuum switch from harness and check feed wire (terminal 6) for electrical continuity to ground. There should be no continuity (infinite resistance).
11. If okay, repair short in harness and return to Check B.
12. If not okay, replace vacuum switch and return to Check B.
13. Apply and hold vacuum of 5–10 in. Hg to yellow vacuum switch.
14. Repeat check for electrical continuity to ground from terminal 6 of harness connector. There should be continuity.
15. If okay, replace MCU and return to Check B.
16. If not okay, continue with Step 17.
17. With vacuum still applied, check yellow wire at vacuum switch harness connector (switch side) for electrical continuity to ground. There should be continuity.
18. If okay, reconnect six-wire connector. Repair open circuit in harness and return to Check B.
19. If not okay, reconnect six-wire connector and replace vacuum switch. Return to Check B.

Test 3: Open Loop 2 Wide Open Throttle (WOT)

1. Pull down forward edge of carpeting extending up dash panel on passenger side to expose MCU and harness connector.
2. Disconnect six-wire connector.
3. Using ohmmeter with engine still at idle, test for electrical continuity to ground from terminal 7 on harness side of connector. There should be no continuity to ground (infinite resistance).
4. If okay, continue with Step 9.
5. If not okay, continue with Step 6.
6. Disconnect vacuum switches from engine compartment harness and test blue wire for electrical continuity to ground. There should be no continuity (infinite resistance).
7. If okay, repair short in harness and return to Check C.
8. If not okay, continue with Step 15.
9. Disconnect and plug vacuum hose to blue vacuum switch and retest terminal 7 for continuity to ground. There should be continuity.
10. If okay, replace MCU and return to Check C.
11. If not okay, continue with Step 12.
12. Disconnect blue vacuum switch from engine compartment harness and test blue wire for continuity to ground. There should be continuity.
13. If okay, repair open circuit in harness and return to Check C.
14. If not okay, replace switch and return to Check C.
15. Disconnect vacuum hose to blue vacuum switch and check

29-13

SECTION 29
ENGINE CONTROLS
AMERICAN MOTORS

SWITCH CALIBRATIONS—CEC SYSTEM
Four Cylinder Engines

Component	Opens At	Closes At
Open Loop Coolant Temperature Switch	95°F	
Enrichment Coolant Temperature Switch		135°F
Thermal Electric Switch (TES)	65°F	55°F
Adaptive Vacuum Switch ①	13 in Hg or 9 in. Hg	
5 in. Hg WOT (Cold) Vacuum Switch		5 in. Hg
3 in. Hg WOT (Warm) Vacuum Switch	3 in. Hg	

① 9 in. Hg for automatic transmission equipped automobiles
13 in. Hg for manual transmission equipped automobiles

for vacuum in hose. With engine still at idle, there should be vacuum.
16. If okay, replace blue vacuum switch. Reconnect harness and vacuum hose and return to Check C.
17. If not okay, repair vacuum leak. Reconnect harness and vacuum hose and return to Check C.

Test 4: Open Loop 3 Idle and Closed Loop Switch-In

1. Pull down forward edge of carpeting extending up dash panel on passenger side to expose MCU and harness connector.
2. Disconnect six-wire connector.
3. Check voltage at terminal 5 on harness side of connector. Voltage should be 7 volts ± 2 volts.
4. If okay, continue with Step 6.
5. If not okay, repair harness wiring to coil and return to Check D.
6. Check for electrical continuity to ground from terminal 9 on harness side of connector with engine at idle. There should be continuity.
7. If okay, continue with Step 15.
8. If not okay, continue with Step 9.
9. Check for vacuum at pink vacuum switch. There should be no vacuum at idle.
10. If okay, continue with Step 12.
11. If not okay, correct vacuum line routing or carburetor idle speed setting. Return to Check D.
12. Disconnect vacuum switch harness connector and check pink wire for electrical continuity to ground with no vacuum applied. There should be continuity.
13. If okay, repair open circuit in harness wiring and reconnect. Return to Check D.
14. If not okay, replace switch and reconnect harness. Return to Check D.
15. Increase engine speed to 1,500 rpm and recheck continuity. There should be no continuity.
16. If okay, return engine to idle. Replace MCU and return to Check D.
17. If not okay, continue with Step 18.
18. With engine still at 1,500 rpm, check vacuum hose at pink vacuum switch for vacuum. There should be more than 5 in. Hg.
19. If okay, continue with Step 21.
20. If not okay, return engine to idle. Repair vacuum hose routing and return to Check D.
21. Reconnect vacuum hose to pink switch.
22. Disconnect harness connection to vacuum switches.
23. With engine at 1,500 rpm, check pink wire for electrical continuity to ground at switch. There should be no continuity (infinite resistance).
24. If okay, repair short circuit in harness wiring and reconnect. Return to Check D.
25. If not okay, replace switch and reconnect harness. Return to Check D.

Test 5: Closed Loop Operation

—————— CAUTION ——————
The use of a voltmeter with less than 10 meg-ohms per volt input independence in this test will destroy the oxygen sensor. A digital volt-ohm meter must be used.

1. Turn engine off.
2. Remove air cleaner assembly and plug vacuum hoses.
3. Turn ignition to on for four seconds. Then turn off.
4. Disconnect stepper motor connector.
5. Disconnect oxygen sensor connector.
6. Using voltmeter with minimum of 10 meg-ohms per volt, connect positive (+) lead to pin 2 on oxygen sensor connector and negative (-) lead to pin 4. Set meter on 1–volt scale.
7. Start engine and warm up for four minutes.
8. Increase engine speed to 1,200 rpm and hold while closing choke butterfly valve. Keep valve closed for one minute, while observing voltmeter. Turn engine off.
9. While choke was closed, voltmeter should have indicated minimum of 0.6 volts. Turn ignition switch off.
10. If okay, replace MCU and continue with Step 19.
11. If not okay, continue with Step 12.
12. Disconnect and plug hose leading to exhaust manifold air distribution check valve at manifold.
13. Start engine and warm up for one minute.
14. Close choke valve with engine at 1,200 rpm and observe voltmeter. Turn engine off.
15. While choke was closed, voltmeter should have indicated 0.6 volts or more.
16. If okay, replace air distribution check valve and continue with Step 18.
17. If not okay, replace oxygen sensor and continue with Step 18.
18. Unplug and reconnect hose to air distribution check valve.
19. Connect oxygen sensor to harness.
20. Connect stepper motor connector.
21. Install air cleaner (without cover) and vacuum hoses.
22. Start engine and return to Check E.

NOTE: If, after completing Test 5 and returning to Check E, the problem persists, it is not in the CEC system. Any other engine associated system that can affect mixture, combustion efficiency or exhaust gas composition can be at fault. These systems include the following.

1. Basic carburetor adjustments.
2. Mechanical engine operation (plugs, valves and rings).
3. Ignition.
4. Gaskets (intake manifold, carburetor or base plate).
5. Loosen vacuum hoses or fittings.

Component Replacement
OXYGEN SENSOR

1. Disconnect two-wire plug.

ENGINE CONTROLS
AMERICAN MOTORS
SECTION 29

2. Remove sensor from exhaust pipe.
3. Clean threads in pipe.
4. Coat replacement sensor threads with antiseize compound.
5. Tighten sensor to 31 ft.lbs. (42 Nm) torque.

───── CAUTION ─────
Ensure that wire terminal ends are properly seated in plug prior to connecting plug.

NOTE: Do not push rubber boot down on sensor body beyond 1/2 inch above base. Oxygen sensor pigtail wires cannot be spliced or soldered. If broken, replace sensor.

VACUUM SWITCHES

NOTE: The vacuum switches are not serviced individually. The complete assembly must be replaced as a unit.

1. Remove vacuum switch and bracket assembly from left inside fender panel.
2. Install replacement vacuum switch and bracket.
3. Connect electrical plug and vacuum hoses.

COMPUTER

The computer unit is located in the passenger compartment beneath the dash panel on the right-hand side. Replace complete unit.

NOTE: The ECM bracket is insulated from automobile ground. Do not ground bracket.

───── CAUTION ─────
Ensure that the terminal ends are not forced out of position when connecting plug.

STEPPER MOTOR (CARBURETOR)

───── CAUTION ─────
Avoid dropping metering pins and spring when removing motor.

1. Remove retaining screw and unit from carburetor.
2. Install replacement motor on carburetor with retaining screw. Tighten to 25 inch lbs. (2.8 Nm) torque.
3. Connect wire plug.
4. Install air cleaner.

COOLANT TEMPERATURE SWITCH

1. Disconnect electrical connector.
2. Remove switch.
3. Install replacement switch. Tighten to 72 inch lbs. (7 Nm) torque.

Computer Command Control System (C-4)

The C-4 system incorporates a self-diagnostic feature that enables quicker determination of system malfunctions. This system is used with selected four cylinder engines, depending upon the emission requirements.

ELECTRONIC CONTROL MODULE (ECM)

The ECM (microprocessor) is the "brains" of the C4 System. It is programmed to determine the correct air/fuel mixture necessary for each engine operating mode. This is accomplished via the several data inputs and the standard data stored in the "read only memory" (ROM) circuit. The ECM also contains a "programmable read only memory" (PROM) circuit (calibration unit) that has stored data unique to the automobile.

OXYGEN SENSOR

This component of the system provides a variable voltage (100 to 900 mv) for the microprocessor (ECM) that is actually a voltage analog for the oxygen content in the exhaust gas. As the oxygen content increases (lean mixture), the voltage output from the sensor decreases proportionally and as the oxygen content decreases (rich mixture), the voltage output increases proportionally. The microprocessor uses the voltage data to control the mixture control (MC) solenoid in the model E2SE carburetor and maintain an optimum air/fuel mixture.

C4 SYSTEM DATA SENDERS

In addition to the oxygen sensor, the following data senders are used with the C4 System.
1. Vacuum Switch Closed during engine idle and partial throttle (Adaptive Mode of Operation).
2. Wide Open Throttle (WOT) Switch. When a wide open throttle condition occurs, the decreased manifold vacuum (at 5 in. Hg) closes the WOT switch, which results in the mixture control solenoid being regulated to provide the rich air/fuel mixture necessary for the increased air flow (WOT Mode of Operation).
3. Engine rpm Voltage from Distributor to The Mixture Control Solenoid is de-energized until the voltage is equivalent to 200 rpm. The result is a rich air/fuel mixture for engine starting (Inhibit or Starting Mode of Operation).
4. Coolant Temperature Sensor During engine warmup, below 150°F (66°C), the electrical impedance of the Coolant Temperature Sensor is high. The result is the C4 Computer does not accept the Oxygen Sensor voltage output and a fixed air/fuel mixture is maintained (Open Loop Mode of Operation).

In addition to the above data input to the C4 Computer, the computer also determines the temperature of the Oxygen Sensor by sensing its electrical impedance. Until the Oxygen Sensor is heated to a temperature of 600°F (320°C), a fixed air/fuel mixture is maintained (Open Loop Mode of Operation).

ELECTRONIC CONTROL MODULE (ECM)

The ECM is the "brains" of the C4 System. It is programmed to determine the correct air/fuel mixture necessary for each engine operating mode. This is accomplished via the several data inputs and the standard data stored in memory (ROM).
The ECM also contains a Programmable Read Only Memory (PROM) that has stored data unique to each automobile (i.e., axle ratio, body style, etc.)

MIXTURE CONTROL SOLENOID

The MC Solenoid is an electro-mechanical device integral with the carburetor that regulates the air/fuel mixture according to "commands" from the ECM. One terminal of the MC Solenoid is connected to 12v (battery voltage) and the other is connected to the ECM. The ECM functions as a switch that provides either a ground for current flow to energize the MC Solenoid or an open circuit to de-energize the MC Solenoid. The ECM switches the MC Solenoid ON and OFF ten times a second.

When the MC Solenoid is energized the needle is inserted into the jet and the result is a lean air/fuel mixture. When the solenoid is de-energized the needle is withdrawn from the jet and the result is a rich air/fuel mixture. The average or effective air/fuel mixture is determined by the length of time the solenoid is either energized or de-energized (period of dwell) during each ON OFF cycle.

SECTION 29: ENGINE CONTROLS — AMERICAN MOTORS

C4 SYSTEM MALFUNCTION INDICATOR

The C4 System utilizes an instrument panel mounted indicator lamp that will inform the driver of the need for service. If a malfunction occurs, the lamp will be illuminated and display CHECK ENGINE. The ECM also incorporates a diagnostic program that will flash a code identifying the malfunction when this function is activated.

DIAGNOSTIC PROCEDURES FOR C4 SYSTEM

The C4 System should be considered as a possible source of trouble for engine performance, fuel economy and exhaust emission complaints only after normal tests and inspections that would apply to an automobile without the C4 system have been performed. An integral self-diagnostic system within the ECM detects the problems that are most likely to occur.

The diagnostic system will illuminate a test bulb (to be installed by service technician) if a fault exists. If the trouble code test pigtail wire (located under the dash) is manually connected to ground, the system will flash a trouble code if a fault has been detected.

As a routine system test, the test bulb will also be illuminated when the ignition switch is first turned on and the engine not started. If the test wire is grounded, the system will flash code 12, which indicates that the diagnostic system is functioning normal (i.e., no engine rpm voltage to the ECM). This consists of one flash followed by a pause and then two flashes. After a longer pause, the code will be repeated two more times. The cycle will repeat itself until the engine is either started or the ignition switch turned off. When the engine is started, the bulb will remain illuminated for a few seconds.

If the test wire is grounded with the engine operating and a fault has been detected by the system, the trouble code will be flashed three times. If more than one fault has been detected, the second trouble code will be flashed three times after the first code is flashed. The series of code flashes will then be repeated.

A trouble code indicates a problem within a specific circuit, for example, code 14 indicates a problem in the coolant temperature sensor circuit. This includes the coolant temperature sensor, wire harness, and Electronic Control Module (ECM). The procedure for determining which of the three is at fault is located in the Trouble Code 14 chart. For other trouble codes, refer to the applicable charts.

Because the self-diagnostic subsystem does not detect all possible faults, the absence of a flashed code does not always indicate that there is no problem with the system. To determine this, a system operational test is necessary. This test should be performed when the test bulb does not flash a trouble code but the C4 System is suspected because no other reason can be determined for a specific complaint. In addition to the test bulb, a dwell meter, test lamp, digital voltohmmeter, tachometer, vacuum gauge and jumper wires are required to diagnose system problems.

A test lamp rather than a voltmeter should be used when so instructed. Although most dwell meters should be acceptable, if one causes a change in engine operation when it is connected to the mixture control (MC) solenoid dwell pigtail wire connector, it should not be used. The dwell meter, set for the six-cylinder engine scale and connected to a pigtail wire connector leading from the mixture control (MC) solenoid at the carburetor, is used to determine the air/fuel mixture dwell. When the dwell meter is connected, do not allow the terminal to contact any engine component that is connected to engine ground. This includes hoses because the may be electrically conductive.

With a normally operating engine, the dwell at both idle speed and partial throttle will be between 10 degrees and 50 degrees and will be varying. Varying means the pointer continually moves back and forth across the scale. The amount it varies is not important, only the fact that it does vary. This indicates closed loop operation, meaning the mixture is being varied according to the input voltage to the ECM from the oxygen sensor. With a wide open throttle (WOT) condition or cold engine operation, the air/fuel mixture ratio will be fixed and the pointer will not vary.

This is open loop operation, meaning the oxygen sensor output has no effect on the air/fuel mixture. If there is a question whether or not the system is in closed loop operation, richening or leaning the mixture will cause the dwell to vary if the system is in closed loop operation.

NOTE: Normally, system tests should be performed with the engine warm (upper radiator hose hot).

Trouble Code Memory

When a fault is detected in the system, the test bulb will be illuminated and a trouble code will be set in the memory of the ECM. However, if the fault is intermittent, the test bulb will be extinguished when the fault no longer exists, but the trouble code will remain in the ECM memory.

Long Term Memory

The ECM, with most C4 Systems, has a long term memory. With this provision, trouble codes are not lost when the ignition switch is turned off. Certain troubles may not appear until the engine has been operated 5–18 minutes at partial throttle. For this reason, and for intermittent troubles, a long term memory is desirable. To clear the long term memory, disconnect and connect the battery negative cable.

NOTE: Long term memory causes approximately a 13 ma battery drain with the ignition switch off.

Trouble Codes

The test bulb will only be illuminated under the conditions listed below when a malfunction exists. If the malfunction is eliminated, the bulb will be extinguished and the trouble code will be reset, except for one fault, trouble code 12. If the bulb is illuminated intermittently, but not trouble code is flashed, refer to this symptom within Drive Complaint.

1. Trouble Code 12 No rpm (tach) voltage to the ECM.
2. Trouble Code 13 Oxygen sensor circuit. The engine has to operate for approximately five minutes at partial throttle before this code will be flashed.
3. Trouble Code 14 Short circuit within coolant temperature sensor circuit. The engine has to operate two minutes before this code will be flashed.
4. Trouble Code 15 Open circuit within coolant temperature sensor circuit. The engine has to operate for approximately five minutes at partial throttle before this code will be flashed.
5. Trouble Code 21 and 22 (at same time) WOT switch circuit has short circuit to ground.
6. Trouble Code 22 Adaptive vacuum or WOT switch circuit has short circuit to ground.
7. Trouble Code 23 Carburetor MC solenoid circuit has short circuit to ground or open circuit exists.
8. Trouble Code 44 Voltage input to ECM from oxygen sensor indicates continuous "lean" mixture. MC solenoid is regulated to produce continuous "rich" mixture. The engine has to operate approximately five minutes at partial throttle with a torque load and the C4 System in closed loop operation before this code will be flashed.
9. Trouble Codes 44 and 45 (at same time) Faulty Oxygen Sensor.
10. Trouble Code 45 Voltage input to ECM from oxygen sensor indicates continuous "rich" mixture. MC solenoid is regulated to produce continuous "lean" mixture. The engine has to operate approximately five minutes at partial throttle with a

ENGINE CONTROLS
AMERICAN MOTORS
SECTION 29

torque load and the C4 System in closed loop operation before this code will be flashed.

11. Trouble Code 51 Faulty calibration unit (PROM) or installation.
12. Trouble Codes 52 and 53 Test bulb off, intermittent ECM problem. Test bulb on, faulty ECM.
13. Trouble Code 54 Faulty MC Solenoid and/or ECM.
14. Trouble Code 55 Faulty oxygen sensor circuit or ECM.

When the test bulb is not illuminated with the engine operating, but a trouble code can be obtained, the situation must be evaluated to determine if the fault is intermittent or because of engine operating conditions.

For all malfunctions, except those represented by trouble codes 13, 44, and 45, the test bulb should be illuminated with the engine rpm below 800 after five minutes of operation.

If trouble codes other than 13, 44, and 45 can be obtained when the test bulb is not illuminated, the diagnostic charts cannot be used because the system is operating normally. All that can be performed is a physical inspection of the circuit indicated by the trouble code. The circuit should be inspected for faulty wire connections, frayed wires, etc., then the System Operational Test should be performed.

Trouble codes 13, 44, and 45 require engine operation at partial throttle with an engine torque load for an extended period of time before a code will be flashed. Trouble code 15 requires five minutes of engine operation before it will be flashed. The diagnostic chart should be used if these codes are flashed even though the test bulb is not illuminated with the engine at idle speed.

CALIBRATION UNIT (PROM)

The microprocessor (ECM) has a calibration unit called a PROM that is programmed with specific instructions for the engine. It is not a replaceable assembly. Trouble code 51 indicates the PROM has been installed improperly or is defective. When code 51 is flashed the ECM (microprocessor) should be replaced.

CAUTION

If trouble code 51 was caused by the PROM (calibration unit) being installed backwards, replace the ECM with another unit. Whenever the calibration unit is installed backwards and the ignition switch is turned on, the unit is destroyed.

C4 SYSTEM TESTS AND TROUBLE CODE DIAGNOSIS

The self-diagnostic system does not detect all possible faults. The absence of a trouble code does not indicate there is not a malfunction with the system. To determine whether or not a system problem exists, an operational test is necessary.

NOTE: The System Operational Test should also be performed after all repairs on the C4 System have been completed.

CADILLAC ELECTRONIC CONTROL MODULE

GENERAL INFORMATION

The Electronic Control Module, (ECM) or computer provides all computation and controls for the DEFI system. Sensor inputs are fed into the computer from the various sensors. They are processed to produce the appropriate pulse duration for the injectors, the correct idle speed for the particular operating condition and the proper spark advance.

Analog inputs from the sensors are converted to digital signals before processing. The computer assembly is mounted under the instrument panel and consists of various printed circuit boards mounted in a protective metal box. The computer receives power from the vehicle battery. When the ignition is set to the "ON" or "CRANK" position, the following information is received from the sensors.

1. Engine coolant temperature.
2. Intake manifold air temperature.
3. Intake manifold absolute pressure.
4. Barometric pressure.
5. Engine speed.
6. Throttle position

NOTE: The following commands are transmitted by the ECM.

1. Electric fuel pump activation.
2. Idle speed control.
3. Spark advance control.
4. Injection valve activation.
5. EGR solenoid activation.

The desired air-fuel mixture for various driving and atmospheric conditions are programmed into the computer. As signals are received from the sensors, the computer processes the signals and computes the engine's fuel requirements. The computer issues commands to the injection valves to open for a specific time duration. The duration of the command pulses varies as the operating conditions change.

The digital electronic fuel injection system is activated when the ignition switch is turned to the "ON" position. The following events occur at this moment.

1. The computer receives the ignition "ON" signal.
2. The fuel pump is activate by the ECM. The pump will operate for approximately one second only, unless the engine is cranking or running.
3. All engine sensors are activated and begin transmitting signals to the computer.
4. The EGR solenoid is activated to block the vacuum signal to the EGR valve at coolant temperatures below 110°F.
5. The "CHECK ENGINE" and "COOLANT" lights are illuminated as a functional check of the bulb and circuit.
6. Operation of the fuel economy lamps begins.

NOTE: The following events occur when the engine is started.

1. The fuel pump is activated for continuous operation.
2. The idle speed control motor will begin controlling idle speed, including fast idle speed, if the throttle switch is closed.
3. The spark advance shifts from base (bypass) timing to the computer programmed spark curve.
4. The fuel pressure regulator maintains the fuel pressure at 10.5 psi by returning excess fuel to the fuel tank.
5. The following sensor signals are continuously received and processed by the computer.
   a. Engine coolant temperature.
   b. Intake manifold air temperature.
   c. Barometric pressure.
   d. Intake manifold absolute air pressure.
   e. Engine speed.
   f. Throttle position changes.

29—17

SECTION 29
ENGINE CONTROLS
CADILLAC ELECTRONIC CONTROL MODULE

6. The computer alternately grounds each injector, precisely controlling the opening and closing time (pulse width) to deliver fuel to the engine.

BODY COMPUTER MODULE (BCM)
1985 and Later Cadillac

At the heart of the 1985 Cadillac self-diagnosis system is the body computer module (BCM). The BCM is located behind the glove box opening and has an internal microprocessor which is used to control the various vehicle functions based upon the monitored sensor and switch inputs. Cadillac models equipped with HT4100 digital fuel injection have in addition to the BCM the electronic control module (ECM) which provides microprocessor control for the various engine and emission related functions.

The ECM on these models are located to the right side of the instrument panel. On the models equipped with both the BCM and the ECM, a communication process has been incorporated which allows the two modules to share information and use this information for additional control capability. The module's internal circuitry rapidly switches a circuit between 0 and 5 volts. This process is used to convert information into a series of pulses which represent coded data messages, which is understood by the other component. One of these data messages frequently transferred from the BCM is a request for specific ECM diagnostic action.

This action could affect one of the ECM controlled outputs or require the ECM to transfer some information back to the BCM. When the data message transfer occurs it gives the BCM control over the ECM's self-diagnostic capabilities in addition to its own. In order to access and control the self-diagnostic features available tot he BCM, there have been two additional electronic components added to the system to be utilized by the service technician. Located to the right of the steering column is the climate control panel (CCP). Located to the left of the steering column will be either the fuel data center (FDC) which is used with the DFI engines or the diesel data center (DDC) used with the diesel engines.

These new components provide displays and keyboard switches used on several BCM controlled sub-systems. The display and keyboard information is then transferred over a single wire data circuits which carry the coded data messages back and forth between the BCM and the display panels. By pushing the correct buttons on the electronic climate control panel (ECC), the data messages can be sent to the BCM requesting the specific diagnostic feature required.

ECM FUNCTIONS

Fuel Delivery System

The computer's control of fuel delivery can be considered in three basic modes: cranking, part throttle and wide open throttle. If the engine is determined to be in the cranking mode by the presence of a voltage in the cranking signal wire from the ignition switch, the starting fuel delivery consists of one long "prime" pulse from both injectors followed by a series of "starting" pulses until the cranking mode signal is no longer present. In addition, there is a "clear flood" condition in which smaller alternating fuel pulses are delivered if the throttle is held wide open and cranking exceeds five seconds.

Once the engine is running, injector pulse width is then adjusted to account for operating conditions such as idle, part throttle, acceleration, deceleration and altitude. For wide open throttle conditions, which are sensed by matching the manifold absolute pressure and barometric pressure sensor inputs, additional enrichment is provided.

Spark System

Engine ignition timing is controlled by the computer. The two basic operating modes are cranking (or bypass) and normal engine operation. When the engine is in the cranking/bypass mode, ignition timing occurs at a reference setting (distributor timing set point) regardless of other engine operating parameters. Under all other normal operating conditions, basic engine ignition timing is controlled by the computer and modified or added to, depending on particular conditions such as altitude and/or engine loading.

Idle Speed Control System

The idle speed control system is controlled by the computer. The system acts to control engine idle speed in three ways; as a normal idle (rpm) control, as a fast idle device and as a "dashpot" on decelerations and throttle closing.

The normal engine idle speed is programmed into the computer and no adjustments are possible. Under normal engine operating conditions, idle speed is maintained by monitoring idle speed in a closed loop fashion. To accomplish this loop, the computer periodically senses the engine idle speed and issues commands to the idle speed control to move the throttle stop to maintain the correct speed.

For engine starting, the throttle is either held open by the idle speed control for a longer (cold) or a shorter (hot) period to provide adequate engine warm-up prior to normal operation. When the engine is shut off, the throttle is opened by fully extending the idle speed control actuator to get ready for the next start.

Signal inputs for transmission gear, air conditioning compressor clutch (engaged or not engaged) and throttle (open or closed) are used to either increase or decrease throttle angle in response to these particular engine loadings.

Electronic Spark Timing (EST)

The EST type HEI distributor receives all spark timing information from the computer when the engine is running. The computer provides spark plug firing pulses based upon the various engine operating parameters. The electronic components for the electronic spark control system are integral with the computer.

Idle Speed Control System (ISC)

Vehicle idle speed is controlled by an electrically driven actuator (idle speed control) which changes the throttle angle by acting as a movable idle stop. Inputs to the ISC actuator motor come from the ECM and are determined by the idle speed required for the particular operating condition. The electronic components for the ISC system are integral with the ECM. An integral part of the ISC is the throttle switch.

The position of the switch determines whether the ISC should control idle speed or not. When the switch is closed, as determined by the throttle lever resting upon the end of the ISC actuator, the ECM will issue the appropriate commands to move the idle speed control to provide the programmed idle speed. When the throttle lever moves off the idle speed control actuator from idle, the throttle switch is opened. The computer then extends the actuator and stops sending idle speed commands and the driver controls the engine speed.

DIAGNOSTIC LIGHT

An amber dash-mounted "CHECK ENGINE" light, in the right-hand information center, is used to inform the driver of certain computer detected DEFI system malfunctions or abnormalities. These malfunctions may be related to the various sensors or to the computer itself. The light resets automatically when the fault clears. However, the computer stores the trouble code associated with the detected failure until the diagnostic system is cleared.

ENGINE CONTROLS
CADILLAC ELECTRONIC CONTROL MODULE
SECTION 29

DIAGNOSTIC DISPLAY

The dash-mounted digital display panel normally used for the Electronic Climate Control (ECC) system, is used to display trouble codes stored in the computer when desired. Any codes that may be stored can be called up and/or cleared by properly exercising the ECC controls.

OPERATION WITH SYSTEM FAILURES

In the event the computer detects a system malfunction, the "CHECK ENGINE" light will be activated, the corresponding trouble code stored and substitute values to replace missing data may be made available for computations by the computer. This can be thought of as a "Fail-Safe" operation. In this mode, driveability of the car may be poor under certain conditions and the diagnostic procedures should be exercised.

HOW TO ENTER DIAGNOSTIC MODE

To enter diagnostics, proceed as follows.
1. Turn ignition "ON".
2. Depress "OFF" and "WARMER" buttons on the ECC panel simultaneously and hold until ".." appears. "88" will then be displayed, which indicates the beginning of the diagnostic readout.
3. Trouble codes will be displayed on the digital ECC panel beginning with the lowest numbered code. Note that the test panel does not display when the system is in the diagnostic mode.

TROUBLE CODE DISPLAY

After the displays end the segment check, any trouble code stored in the computer memory will be displayed on the "DATA CENTER". These trouble codes will appear prefixed with an "E" or "F" to designate which computer detected the malfunction (the ECM or BCM). After all codes have been displayed or if no trouble codes are stored, ".7.0" will appear on the "DATA CENTER" display.

HOW TO CLEAR TROUBLE CODES

The trouble codes stored in the memory of the ECM, can be erased (cleared) by entering the diagnostic mode and then depressing the Off and Hi buttons on the electronic climate control panel simultaneously until the E.O.O. appears. The trouble codes stored in the memory of the BCM can be cleared by depressing the Off and Lo buttons simultaneously until F.O.O. appears. After the E.O.O. and the F.O.O. are displayed the .7.0 will appear. When the .7.0 is displayed turn the ignition off for at least ten seconds before re-entering the diagnostic mode.

HOW TO EXIT DIAGNOSTIC MODE

To get out of the diagnostic mode, depress any of the ECC function keys (Auto, Econ, etc. except Rear Defog) or turn ignition switch off for 10 seconds. Trouble codes are not erased when this is done.

System Diagnosis

Illumination of the "CHECK ENGINE" light indicates that a malfunction has occurred for which a trouble code has been stored and can be displayed on the ECC control panel. The malfunction may or may not result in abnormal engine operation. To determine which system(s) has malfunctioned, proceed as follows.
1. Turn ignition switch "ON" for 5 seconds.
2. Depress the "OFF" and "WARMER" buttons on the electronic climate control panel simultaneously and hold until ".." appears.
3. Numerals "88" should then appear. The purpose of the "88" display is to check that all segments of the display are working. Diagnosis should not be attempted unless the entire "88" appears, as this could lead to misdiagnosis (Code 31 could be Code 34 with two segments of the display inoperative, etc.).
4. Trouble codes will then be displayed on the digital test panel as follows.
   a. The lowest numbered code will be displayed for approximately three seconds.
   b. Progressively higher codes, if present, will be displayed consecutively for three second intervals until the highest code present has been displayed.
   c. "88" is again displayed.
   d. Displays from steps a, b and c will be repeated a second time.
   e. Displays from steps a and b will be repeated a third time.
   f. Code 70 will then be displayed, which signals the beginning of the "switch tests" section.
5. Switch tests require some action on the part of the technician. This action is analyzed by the computer for proper operation.

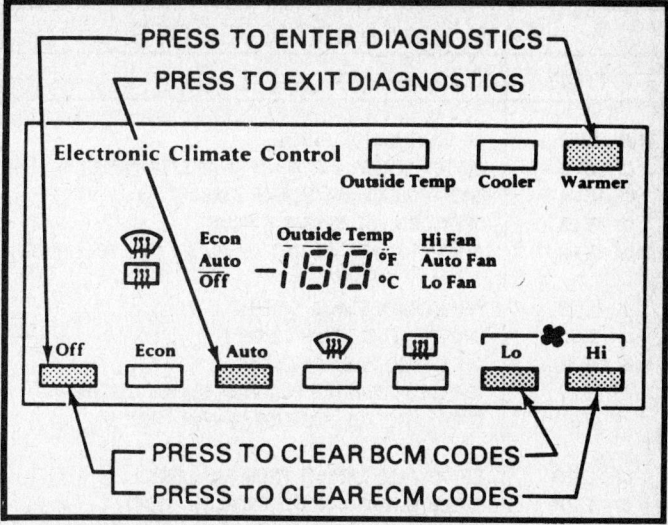

Typical Cadillac climate control panel

SWITCH TEST PROCEDURE

When all stored trouble codes have been displayed for the third time, the computer will automatically begin the switch tests. To perform these checks, proceed as follows.
1. Display of trouble Code 70 signals the beginning of this section. This code will continue to be displayed until the proper test action is taken. When ready to begin tests, depress service brake pedal. This begins the test sequence by displaying Code 71.
2. With Code 71 displayed, depress the service brake pedal again to test the brake light circuit. When this check is completed, the test program will automatically sequence to Code 72. If the test action is not performed within 10 seconds, the test program will automatically sequence to "72" and Code 71 will be stored in the computer memory as "not passed".
3. With Code 72 displayed, depress the throttle from idle to wide open throttle and release. This action allows the computer to analyze the operation of the throttle switch. When this check is completed, the test program will automatically sequence to

SECTION 29

ENGINE CONTROLS
CADILLAC ELECTRONIC CONTROL MODULE

ECM DIAGNOSTIC CODES

CODE	MALFUNCTION
■■ E12	NO DISTRIBUTOR SIGNAL
☐ E13	OXYGEN SENSOR NOT READY (CANISTER PURGE)
☐ E14	SHORTED COOLANT SENSOR CIRCUIT
☐ E15	OPEN COOLANT SENSOR CIRCUIT
■■ E16	GENERATOR VOLTAGE OUT OF RANGE (ALL SOLENOIDS)
☐ E18	OPEN CRANK SIGNAL CIRCUIT
☐ E19	SHORTED FUEL PUMP CIRCUIT
■■ E20	OPEN FUEL PUMP CIRCUIT
☐ E21	SHORTED THROTTLE POSITION SENSOR CIRCUIT
☐ E22	OPEN THROTTLE POSITION SENSOR CIRCUIT
☐ E23	EST/BYPASS CIRCUIT PROBLEM (AIR)
☐ E24	SPEED SENSOR CIRCUIT PROBLEM (VCC)
☐ E26	SHORTED THROTTLE SWITCH CIRCUIT
☐ E27	OPEN THROTTLE SWITCH CIRCUIT
☐ E28	OPEN THIRD OR FOURTH GEAR CIRCUIT
☐ E30	ISC CIRCUIT PROBLEM
■■ E31	SHORTED MAP SENSOR CIRCUIT (AIR)
■■ E32	OPEN MAP SENSOR CIRCUIT (AIR)
■■ E34	MAP SENSOR SIGNAL TOO HIGH (AIR)
☐ E37	SHORTED MAT SENSOR CIRCUIT
☐ E38	OPEN MAT SENSOR CIRCUIT
☐ E39	VCC ENGAGEMENT PROBLEM
☐ E40	OPEN POWER STEERING PRESSURE CIRCUIT
■■ E44	LEAN EXHAUST SIGNAL (AIR & CL & CANISTER PURGE)
■■ E45	RICH EXHAUST SIGNAL (AIR & CL & CANISTER PURGE)
☐ E47	BCM - ECM DATA PROBLEM
■■ E51	ECM PROM ERROR
▼ E52	ECM MEMORY RESET INDICATOR
▼ E53	DISTRIBUTOR SIGNAL INTERRUPT
▼ E59	VCC TEMPERATURE SENSOR CIRCUIT
▼ E60	TRANSMISSION NOT IN DRIVE
▼ E63	CAR SPEED AND SET SPEED DIFFERENCE TOO HIGH
▼ E64	CAR ACCELERATION TOO HIGH
▼ E65	COOLANT TEMPERATURE TOO HIGH
▼ E66	ENGINE RPM TOO HIGH
▼ E67	CRUISE SWITCH SHORTED DURING ENABLE

ECM AND CRUISE CONTROL COMMENTS:

■■	TURNS ON "SERVICE NOW" LIGHT
☐	TURNS ON "SERVICE SOON" LIGHT
▼	DOES NOT TURN ON ANY TELLTALE LIGHT
( )	FUNCTIONS WITHIN BRACKETS ARE DISENGAGED WHILE SPECIFIED MALFUNCTION REMAINS CURRENT (HARD)

E16 & E24 DISABLE VCC FOR ENTIRE IGNITION CYCLE
E24 & E67 DISABLE CRUISE FOR ENTIRE IGNITION CYCLE
CRUISE IS DISENGAGED WITH CODE(S) E16, E51 OR E60 - E67

Diagnostic codes for the Digital Fuel Injected Cadillac

Code 73. Again, if action is not taken within 10 seconds, a Code 72 will be stored as "not passed".

4. With Code 73 displayed, shift the transmission lever to Drive and then to Neutral. When this check is completed, the test program will automatically sequence to Code 74. This action must be taken within 10 seconds or a Code 73 will be set.

5. With Code 74 displayed, shift the transmission lever to Reverse and then to Park. Shift transmission within 10 seconds or a Code 74 will be set. When this check is completed, the test program will automatically sequence to Code 78.

NOTE: On vehicles not equipped with cruise control, the codes 75, 76 and 77 will be displayed but cannot be performed during the switch test. When these codes appear during the switch tests, allow each code to reach its ten second time out. After this time out has passed, the display will advance to the next code. Since the 75, 76 and 77 codes will be recorded as failures in the switch tests sequence, a display of 00 will never be displayed at the completion of the tests. To be sure that the proper operations of the remaining switch, code 78 must be observed as having advanced within the ten second time out. If the code cannot be advanced within its time out, it should be considered a failed test.

6. With code 75 displayed, switch the cruise control instrument panel switch from on to off and back to on to check the operation of the switch.

7. With code 76 displayed and with the cruise control instrument panel switch in the on position, depress and release the set/coast button to check the operation of the switch.

8. With code 77 displayed and with the cruise control instrument panel switch in the on position depress and release the resume/acceleration switch to check the operation of this switch.

9. With code 78 displayed and the engine running, turn the wheels from straight ahead to the full right position and the full left position and then return the wheels to the straight ahead position. While performing this test the ECM checks the power steering pressure switch for proper operation.

10. With the switch test completed, the ECM will now go back and display the switch codes that did not properly operate during the switch testing.

11. All the codes that did not pass will be displayed beginning with the lowest number. These codes will continue to be displayed until the affected switch circuit has been repaired or retested.

12. After the switch tests are completed and all the circuits passed, the ECC panel will display 00 and then return to code 70. The code 00 indicates that all of the switch circuits are operating properly.

"INTERMITTENT" CODES VS. "HARD FAILURE" CODES

Trouble codes stored in the ECM's memory at any time can be either of the following:

1. A code for malfunctions which are occurring now ("HARD FAILURE"). This malfunction will cause illumination of the "CHECK ENGINE" light.

2. A code for any intermittent malfunctions which have occurred within the last 20 ignition switch cycles. These codes will not cause the "CHECK ENGINE" light to be on now.

3. Intermittent codes should be diagnosed by inspecting the connectors. During any diagnostic interrogation which displays more than one diagnostic code, it is necessary to determine which code is for the "HARD FAILURE" and which is the "INTERMITTENT". To make this determination, proceed as follows:

   a. Enter diagnostics, read and record stored trouble codes.

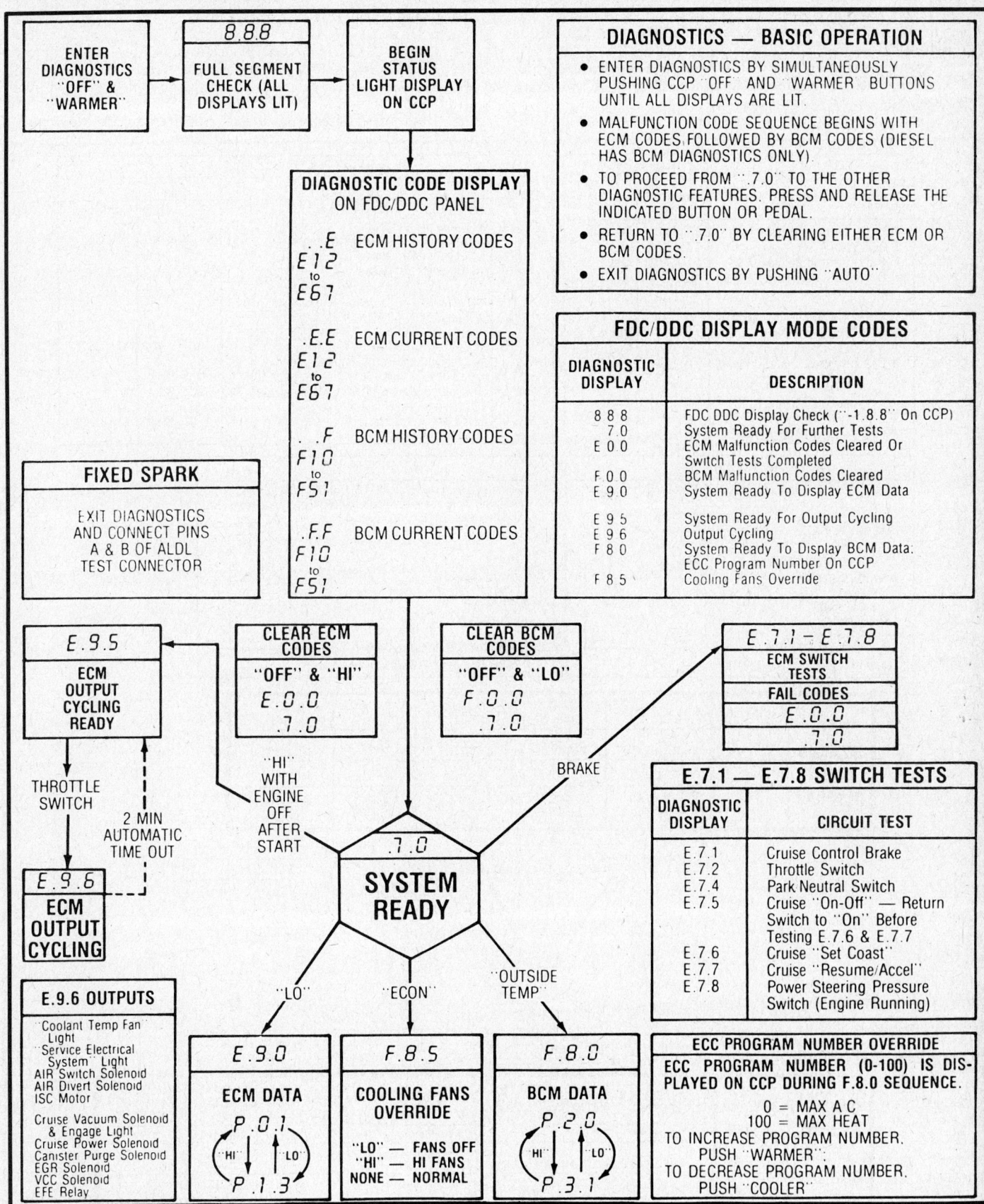

Cadillac diagnostic flow chart

SECTION 29
ENGINE CONTROLS
CADILLAC ELECTRONIC CONTROL MODULE

b. Clear trouble codes.

c. Exit diagnostics by turning the ignition switch off for ten seconds.

d. Turn ignition on and wait 5 seconds, then start engine.

e. Accelerate the engine (to approximately 2000 rpm) for a few seconds.

f. Return to idle.

g. Shift transmission into Drive.

h. Shift to Park.

4. If the "CHECK ENGINE" light comes on, enter diagnostics. Read and record trouble codes. This will reveal only "HARD FAILURE" codes. If the light does not come on, then all stored codes are "INTERMITTENTS".

5. Begin diagnosis with lowest numbered code displayed.

E.9.0 ENGINE DATA DISPLAY

PARAMETER NUMBER	PARAMETER	PARAMETER RANGE	DISPLAY UNITS
P.0.1	Throttle Position	-10 - 90	Degrees
P.0.2	MAP	14 - 109	kPa
P.0.3	Computed BARO	61 - 103	kPa
P.0.4	Coolant Temperature	-40 - 151	°C
P.0.5	MAT	-40 - 151	°C
P.0.6	Injector Pulse Width	0 - 99.9	ms
P.0.7	Oxygen Sensor Voltage	0 - 1.14	Volts
P.0.8	Spark Advance	0 - 52	Degrees
P.0.9	Ignition Cycle Counter	0 - 50	Key Cycles
P.1.0	Battery Voltage	0 - 25.5	Volts
P.1.1	Engine RPM	0 - 6370	RPM ÷ 10
P.1.2	Car Speed	0 - 255	MPH
P.1.3	ECM PROM I.D.	0 - 255	Code

F.8.0 BCM DATA DISPLAY

PARAMETER NUMBER	PARAMETER	PARAMETER RANGE	DISPLAY UNITS
P.2.0	Commanded Blower Voltage	-3.3 - 18.0	Volts
P.2.1	Coolant Temperature	-40 - 215	°C
P.2.2	Commanded Air Mix Door Position	0 - 100	%
P.2.3	Actual Air Mix Door Position	0 - 100	%
P.2.4	Air Delivery Mode 0 = Max A/C 4 = Off 1 = A/C 5 = Normal Purge 2 = Intermediate 6 = Cold Purge 3 = Heater 7 = Front Defog	0 - 7	Code
P.2.5	In-Car Temperature	-40 - 102	°C
P.2.6	Actual Outside Temperature	-40 - 93	°C
P.2.7	High Side Temperature (Condenser Out)	-40 - 215	°C
P.2.8	Low Side Temperature (Evaporator In)	-40 - 93	°C
P.2.9	Actual Fuel Level	0 - 19.0	Gallons
P.3.0	Ignition Cycle Counter	0 - 99	Key Cycles
P.3.1	BCM PROM I.D.	0 - 255	Code

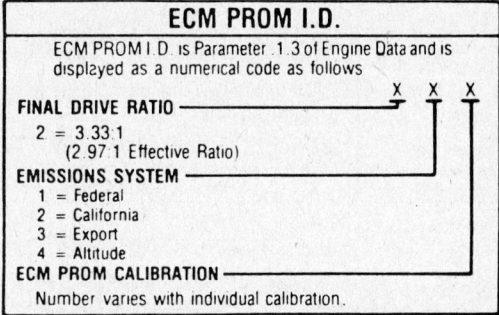

ECM PROM I.D.

ECM PROM I.D. is Parameter .1.3 of Engine Data and is displayed as a numerical code as follows:

```
                                    X X X
FINAL DRIVE RATIO ──────────────────┘ | |
   2 = 3.33:1                         | |
   (2.97:1 Effective Ratio)           | |
EMISSIONS SYSTEM ─────────────────────┘ |
   1 = Federal                          |
   2 = California                       |
   3 = Export                           |
   4 = Altitude                         |
ECM PROM CALIBRATION ───────────────────┘
Number varies with individual calibration.
```

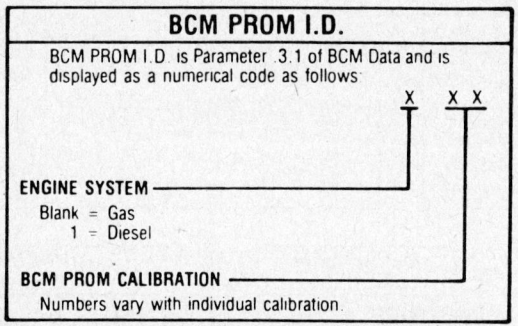

BCM PROM I.D.

BCM PROM I.D. is Parameter .3.1 of BCM Data and is displayed as a numerical code as follows:

```
                                    X X X
ENGINE SYSTEM ──────────────────────┘ | |
   Blank = Gas                        | |
   1 = Diesel                         | |
BCM PROM CALIBRATION ─────────────────┘ (etc.)
Numbers vary with individual calibration.
```

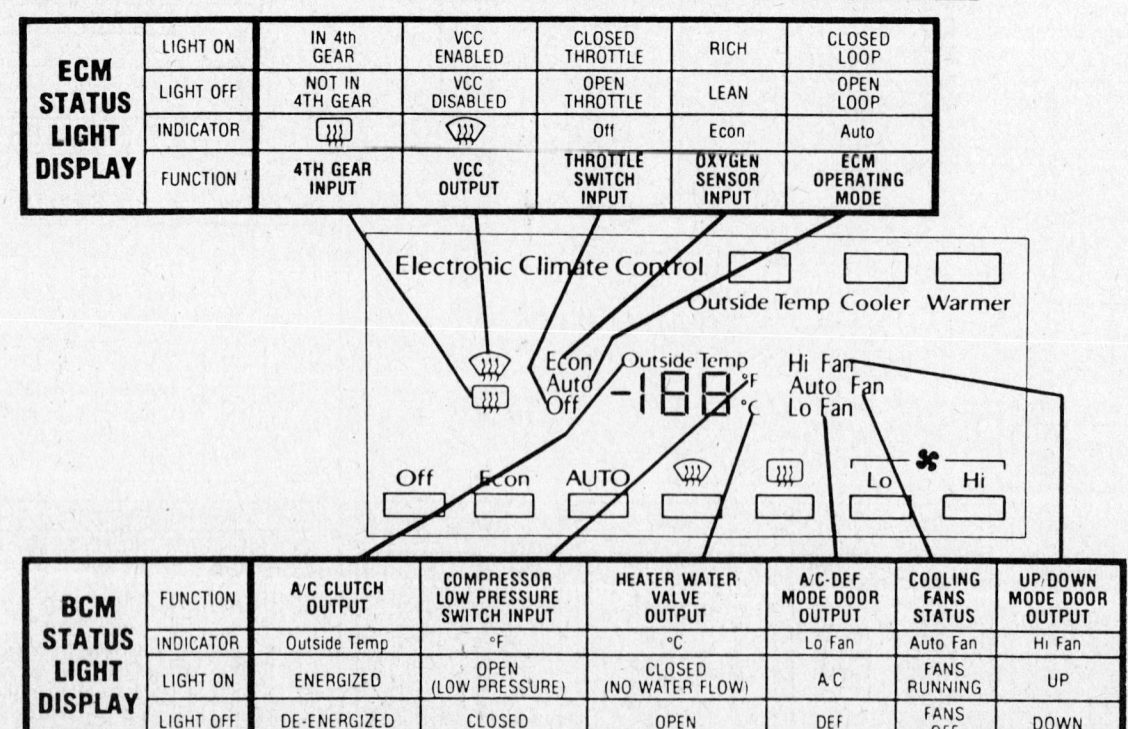

ECM STATUS LIGHT DISPLAY						
	LIGHT ON	IN 4th GEAR	VCC ENABLED	CLOSED THROTTLE	RICH	CLOSED LOOP
	LIGHT OFF	NOT IN 4TH GEAR	VCC DISABLED	OPEN THROTTLE	LEAN	OPEN LOOP
	INDICATOR	🟰	🟰	Off	Econ	Auto
	FUNCTION	4TH GEAR INPUT	VCC OUTPUT	THROTTLE SWITCH INPUT	OXYGEN SENSOR INPUT	ECM OPERATING MODE

BCM STATUS LIGHT DISPLAY						
	FUNCTION	A/C CLUTCH OUTPUT	COMPRESSOR LOW PRESSURE SWITCH INPUT	HEATER WATER VALVE OUTPUT	A/C-DEF MODE DOOR OUTPUT	COOLING FANS STATUS	UP/DOWN MODE DOOR OUTPUT
	INDICATOR	Outside Temp	°F	°C	Lo Fan	Auto Fan	Hi Fan
	LIGHT ON	ENERGIZED	OPEN (LOW PRESSURE)	CLOSED (NO WATER FLOW)	A/C	FANS RUNNING	UP
	LIGHT OFF	DE-ENERGIZED	CLOSED	OPEN	DEF	FANS OFF	DOWN

Cadillac diagnostic flow chart—(cont.)

ENGINE CONTROLS
CHRYSLER ELECTRONIC FEEDBACK CARBURETOR

CHRYSLER ELECTRONIC FEEDBACK CARBURETOR

The Chrysler Electronic Feedback Carburetor (EFC) system was introduced in mid-1979 on Volares and Aspens sold in California with the six cylinder engine. The system is a conventional one, incorporating an oxygen sensor, a three-way catalytic converter, an oxidizing catalytic converter, a feedback carburetor, a solenoid-operated vacuum regulator valve, and a Combustion Computer. Also incorporated into the system are Chrysler's Electronic Spark Control, and a mileage counter which illuminates a light on the instrument panel at 15,000 mile, (now 30,000 mile) intervals, signaling the need for oxygen sensor replacement.

In Chrysler's system, "Combustion Computer" is a collective term for the Feedback Carburetor Controller and the Electronic Spark Control computer, which are housed together in a case located on the air cleaner. The feedback carburetor controller is the information processing component of the system, monitoring oxygen sensor voltage (low voltage/lean mixture, high voltage/rich mixture), engine coolant temperature, manifold vacuum, engine speed, and engine operating mode (starting or running). The controller examines the incoming information and then sends a signal to the solenoid-operated vacuum regulator valve (also located in the Combustion Computer housing), which then sends the proper rich or lean signal to the carburetor.

The 1 bb1 Holley R-8286A carburetor is equipped with two diaphragms, controlling the idle system and the main metering system. The diaphragms move tapered rods, which vary the size of the orifices in the idle system air bleed and the main metering system fuel flow. A "lean" command from the controller to the vacuum regulator results in increased vacuum to both diaphragms, which simultaneously raise both the idle air bleed rod (increasing idle air bleed) and the main metering rod (reducing fuel flow). A "rich" command reduces vacuum level, causing the spring-loaded rods to move in the other direction, enriching the mixture.

Both closed loop and open loop operation are possible in the EFC system. Open loop operation occurs under any one of the following conditions: coolant temperature under 150°F; oxygen sensor temperature under 660°F, low manifold vacuum (less than 4.5 in. Hg. engine cold, or less than 3.0 in. Hg. engine hot); oxygen sensor failure; or hot engine starting. Closed loop operation begins when engine temperature reaches 150°F.

Air injection is supplied by an air pump. At cold engine temperature, air is injected into the exhaust manifold upstream of both catalytic converters. At operating temperature, an air switching valve diverts air from the exhaust to an injection point downstream from the three-way catalyst, but upstream of the conventional oxidizing catalyst.

The 1980 and later system is used with Electronic Spark Advance (ESA). Differences lie in the deletion of some components within the combustion computer. The start timer, vacuum transducer count-up clock and memory throttle transducer, and ambient air temperature sensor are not used.

The feedback system for the six cylinder engines is essentially unchanged. The four and eight cylinder systems differ from the six mainly in the method used to control the carburetor mixture. Instead of having vacuum-controlled diaphragms to raise or lower the mixture rods, the carburetors are equipped with an electric solenoid valve, which is part of the carburetor.

Other differences between the systems are minor. On the four cylinder, the ignition sensor is the Hall Effect distributor, but it functions in the same manner as the six cylinder pick-up coil. The eight cylinder uses two pick-up coils (a Start pick-up and a Run pick-up); troubleshooting is included in the "Lean Burn/Electronic Spark Control" section. The four and six cylinder engines use a 150°F coolant switch; the eight cylinder uses a 150°F switch with Combustion Computer 4145003, and a

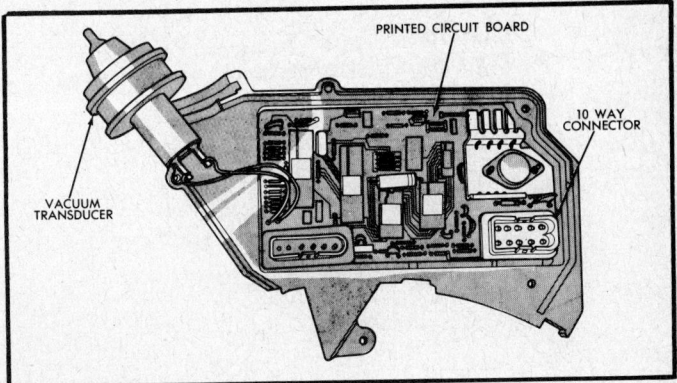
Combustion computer

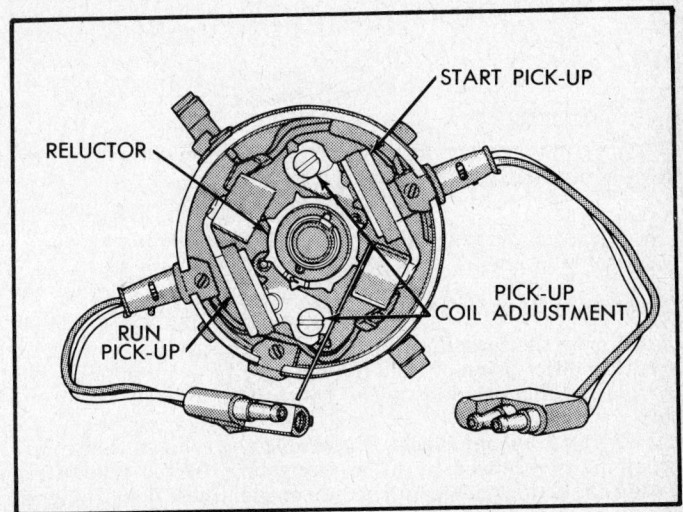
Dual pick-up distributor

98°F switch with Computer 4145088. The eight cylinder engine has a detonation sensor (see the "Lean Burn/Electronic Spark Control" section), and the six and eight cylinder engines have a charge temperature switch to monitor intake charge temperature. Below approximately 60°F, the switch prevents EGR timer function and EGR valve operation; additionally, on eight cylinder engines, air injection is routed upstream of the exhaust manifolds.

Finally, the replacement interval for the oxygen sensor has been doubled, from 15,000 to 30,000 miles. Replacement procedures and odometer resetting are the same as for the 1979 six cylinder system.

TROUBLESHOOTING

Equipment Needed

1. Volt/ohm meter.
2. Jumper wires.
3. Auxiliary vacuum supply (hand held vacuum pump).
4. Fuel pressure gauge.
5. Tachometer.
6. Timing light.
7. Oscilloscope.

SECTION 29 ENGINE CONTROLS
CHRYSLER ELECTRONIC FEEDBACK CARBURETOR

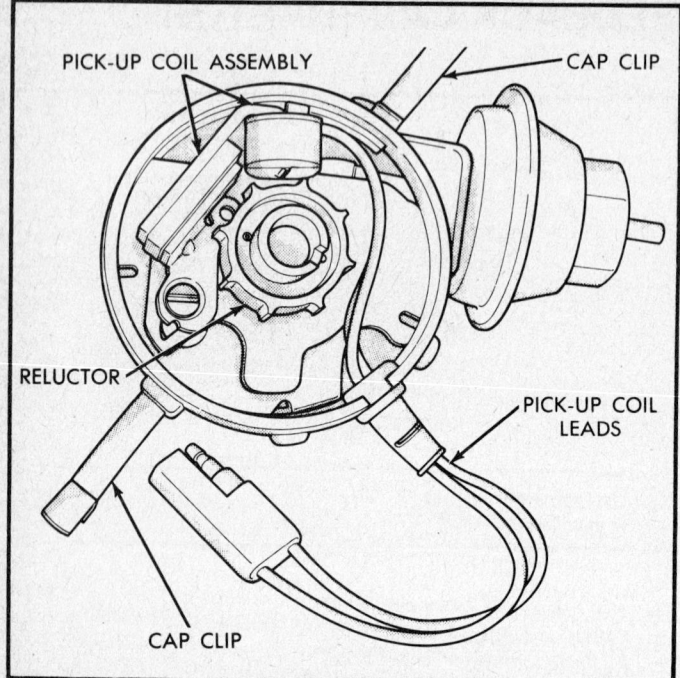

Single pick-up distributor

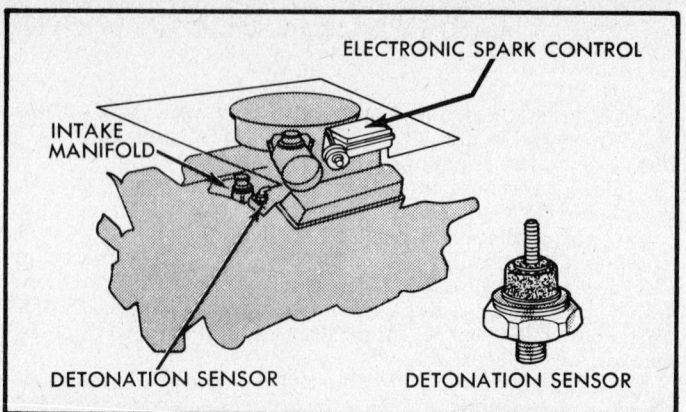

Detonation sensor

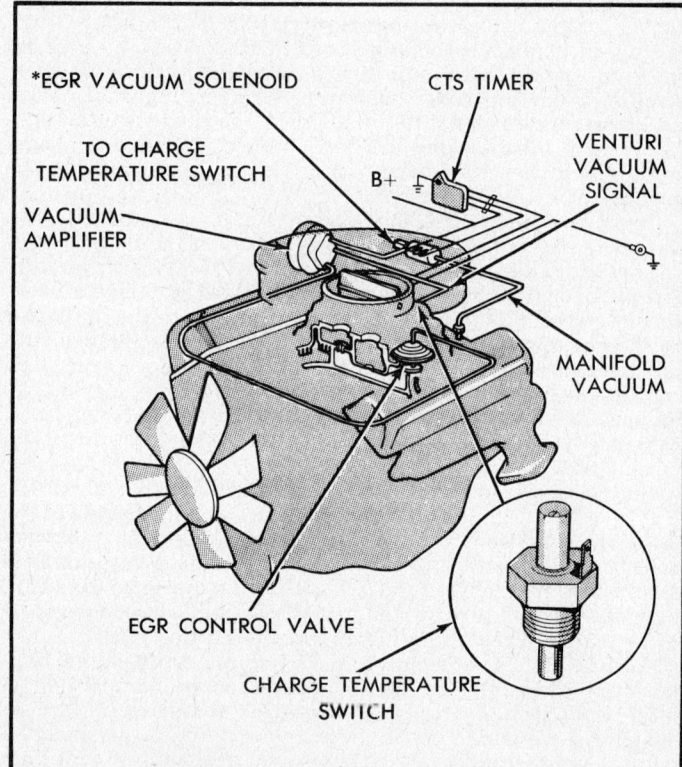

Charge temperature switch

8. Vacuum gauge.
9. Propane kit

Diagnosis Sequence

1. Verify the complaint. It is very important that you get an accurate description of the problem. Verify when possible the complaint. Road testing is the only recommended way to do this.
2. Perform visual checks. Experience has shown that many problems are caused by loose connectors, frayed insulation, loose hose clamps, leaks in vacuum or fuel lines. A short visual check will help you spot these most common faults and save a lot of unnecessary test and diagnostic time. If there are no obvious faults that can be identified visually, proceed with the test sequence.
3. Perform test procedure. The procedure is broken down into four categories: Visual Inspection, No Start, Cold Driveability, and Warm Driveability. The customer complaint will tell you which one to use. Only use that procedure. There is no need to go through the No Start Test when the complaint is Warm Driveability.

PROBLEMS

Vacuum leaks will cause the system to operate richer than normal and the owner may complain about poor fuel economy. This may be indicated in the warm driveability procedure with a variable voltmeter reading of 4–14 volts.
Because of a stock-up of tolerances, some engines may have good driveability but an 02 solenoid voltage of 9–13 volts. Do not attempt to make any repairs.
Fuel contamination of the crankcase will cause the oxygen feedback system to operate the engine leaner than normal. The owner complaint will be a surging condition. The warm driveability procedure should be followed after the visual inspection. If test 12 indicates a voltmeter reading between 0–5 volts, then fuel contamination of the crankcase can be suspected and/or extremely rich carburetion. High altitude areas may see lower closed loop voltage specifications.

VISUAL INSPECTION

In order for the ignition and fuel systems to function properly, all electrical, vacuum, or air hose connections must be complete and tight. Before proceeding with the test procedure, the following must be checked.

ELECTRICAL CONNECTIONS

Terminal in connectors must lock together. Look for connectors that are not fully plugged into each other or terminals that are not fully plugged into the insulator.

Ignition System Components

1. Connectors at SCC.

ENGINE CONTROLS
CHRYSLER ELECTRONIC FEEDBACK CARBURETOR

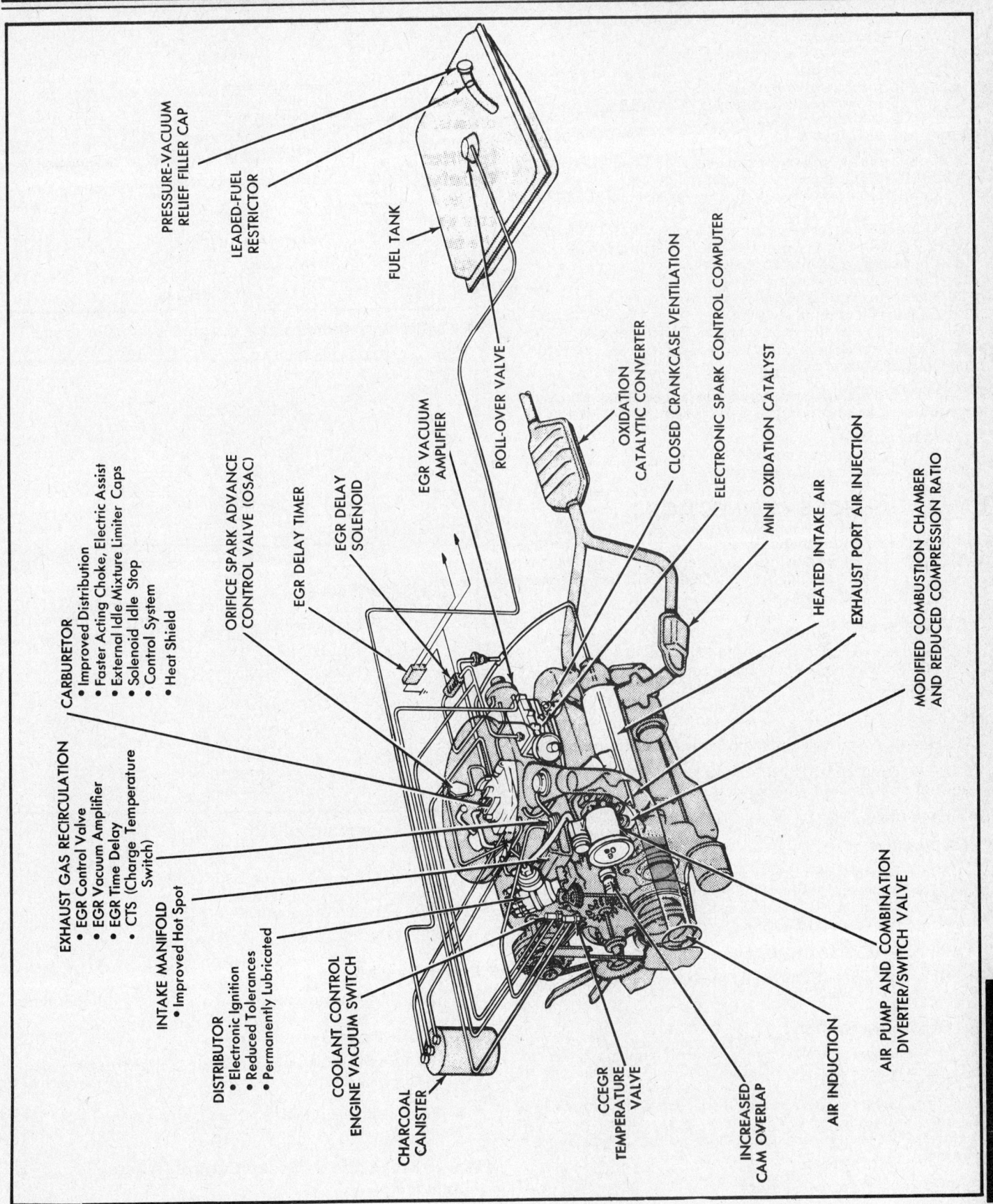

Chrysler combustion computer system

SECTION 29 ENGINE CONTROLS
CHRYSLER ELECTRONIC FEEDBACK CARBURETOR

2. Start and run pick-up coil connectors at distributor.
3. Spark plug wires.
4. Coil wire (cap and coil connections).
5. Connectors at coil.
6. Connectors at starter relay.
7. Connector at detonation sensor (5.2L-4BBL).

Fuel Control System

1. Connector at engine coolant sensor (3.7L–5.2L-4BBL) located in the front of the intake manifold.
2. Connect at charge temperature sensor (5.2L-2BBL) located in the rear of the intake manifold.
3. Connector at charge temperature switch (3.7L–5.2L-4BBL) located in the rear of the intake manifold.
4. Connector at oil pressure switch.
5. Connector and choke control.
6. Connectors at carburetor harness.
7. Carburetor ground switch.
8. Connectors at air switching and EGR solenoids.
9. Engine harness to main harness sensor connectors.
10. Oxygen sensor connections.

NOTE: On 5.2L there is a jumper harness used between oxygen sensor and computer harness.

11. Battery cables.
12. Battery ground on engine.
13. Engine to firewall ground strap.

HOSE CONNECTIONS

All hoses must be fully and firmly fitted at their connections. Also, they cannot be pinched anywhere along their routing. Look for hoses that are not fully plugged on, or are pinched and cut.

PCV System

1. Hose between carburetor and PCV valve.
2. PCV valve plugged into valve cover grommet.
3. Correct PCV valve. White in color.

SCC

1. Hose between vacuum transducer and carburetor.

NOTE: On 5.2L-2BBL this hose has a CVSCC (coolant vacuum switch cold closed) in it.

2. Air intake hose.

EGR System

1. Hose between carburetor and EGR amplifier.
2. Hose between intake manifold and EGR amplifier.
3. Hose between EGR amplifier and EGR solenoid.
4. Hose between EGR solenoid and EGR valve.

NOTE: Some 5.2L-4BBL have a delay valve in this hose.

5. Hose between EGR amplifier and vacuum reservoir (3.7L only).

Air Switching System

1. Hose between intake manifold and air switching solenoid.
2. Hose between air switching solenoid and air switching/relief valve.
3. Hose between air switching/relief valve and plumbing to exhaust manifolds.
4. Hose between air switching/relief valve and plumbing to catalyst.

Evaporative Control System

1. Hose between carburetor bowl vent and canister.

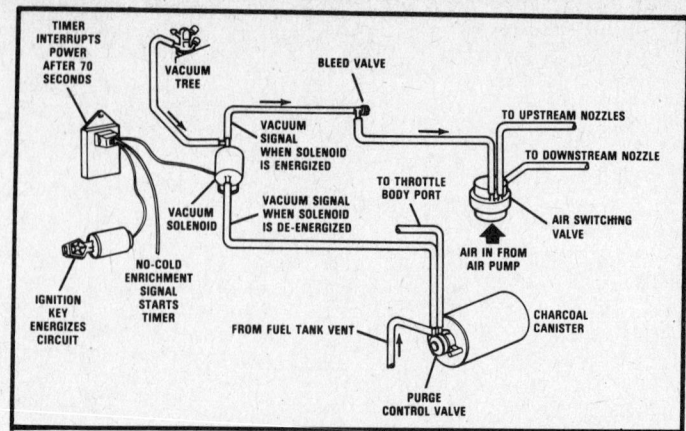

Air switching and canister purging control circuits

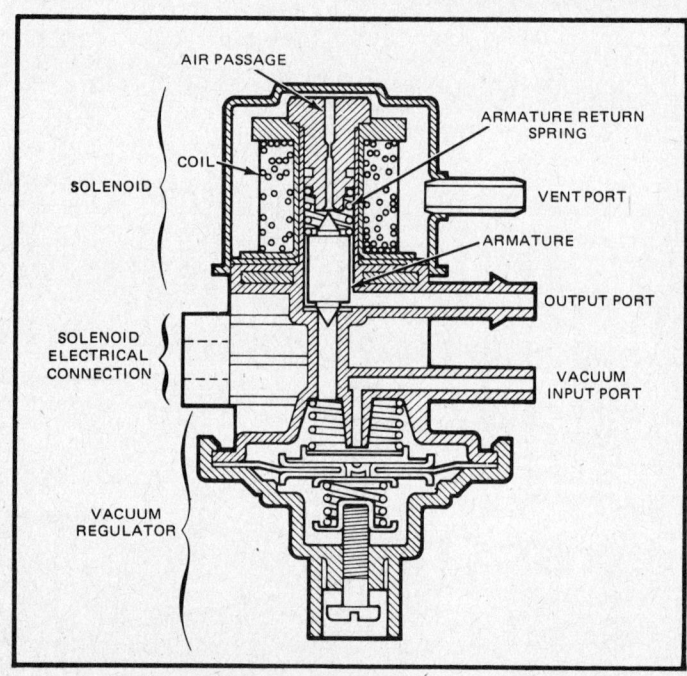

Vacuum solenoid/regulator

2. Hose between canister and air cleaner.
3. Hoses between canister and air pump.
4. Hose between canister and fuel tank line.

NOTE: This hose has a shut off valve in it.

Choke System

1. Hose between carburetor and vacuum kick diaphragm.

Heated Air Door System

1. Hose between carburetor and air temperature sensor.
2. Hose between air temperature sensor and door diaphragm.
3. Hose between air cleaner and exhaust manifold heat stove.

Power Brake and/or Speed Control (Where Applicable)

1. Hose between carburetor and power brake booster.

ENGINE CONTROLS
CHRYSLER ELECTRONIC FEEDBACK CARBURETOR
SECTION 29

NOTE: This hose has a charcoal canister in it.

2. Hose between power brake booster and speed control servo.

Heater/AC System

1. Vacuum hose at water valve.
2. Vacuum supply hose to instrument panel control.

Operational Diagnosis

Prior to starting test sequence, check all vacuum hose connections. Refer to the vacuum hose routing diagram in the engine compartment for the correct hose routing. Check the resistance in all related wiring, giving specific attention to the connectors at the output devices and at the fuel control computer. Connect an auxiliary vacuum source to the vacuum transducer. Apply 16 inches of vacuum. Set the parking brake. Start the engine and let it warm up until normal operating temperature is reached. After any hot start, maintain 1,500 rpm for at least two minutes before proceeding. Do not ground the carburetor switch.

AIR SWITCHING SYSTEM DIAGNOSIS

Vacuum Supply System

1. Remove vacuum hose for air switching/diverter valve and connect a vacuum gauge to hose.
2. Set the parking brake. Start engine and observe gauge reading.

ENGINE COLD

Engine vacuum should be present on gauge until engine coolant temperature and the charge temperature switch reach their normal operating conditions. When the temperature and time delay have been reached, vacuum should drop to zero. If no vacuum is present on gauge, check the vacuum supply, air switching solenoid, coolant switch, and charge temperature switch (CTS) and wiring and connections to computer. If they are okay, then it is possible that the computer is bad, preventing air switching to occur.

ENGINE WARM

Vacuum should be present for the specified period of time after the engine starts, and then should drop to zero. If there is no vacuum, check vacuum supply, air switching solenoid, engine temperature and charge temperature switch (CTS) and wiring and connections to computer. If they are okay, then it is possible that the computer is bad, preventing air switching to occur. Connect a voltmeter to the light green wire on the air switching solenoid. With the engine at normal operating temperature and the engine off, start the engine. Voltage should be less than one volt. Allow the O2 feedback air switching schedule to time out. This will permit the catalyst to reach normal operating temperature before the electronics begin fuel control operation. When the warmup schedule is completed, the solenoid will de-energize and the voltmeter will read charging system voltage. If not, replace the solenoid and repeat the procedure. If the voltmeter indicates charging system voltage before the warmup schedule is complete, replace the computer.

AIR SWITCHING VALVE

1. Remove air supply hose from valve.
2. Remove vacuum hose from valve and install an auxiliary vacuum supply.
3. Start engine, air should be blowing out of side port. Apply vacuum to valve. Air should now be blowing out of bottom port.

ENGINE TEMPERATURE SENSOR TESTS

Engine Temperature Switch (Charge Temperature and Coolant)

1. Turn ignition OFF and disconnect wire from temperature switch.
2. Connect one lead of ohmmeter to a good ground on engine, or in the case of the charge temperature switch to its ground terminal.
3. Connect other lead of ohmmeter to center terminal of coolant switch.
4. Check for continuity using the following ohmmeter readings.
   a. For Cold Engine: Continuity should be present with a resistance less than 100 ohms. If not replace the switch. The charge temperature switch must be cooler than 60°F (15°C) in order to achieve this reading.
   b. For Hot Engine At Normal Operating Temperature: Terminal reading should show no continuity, if it does, replace coolant switch.

Coolant Sensor

1. Connect the leads of ohmmeter to the terminals of the sensor.
2. With the engine cold and the ambient temperature less than 90°F (32°C) the resistance should be between 500 and 1,000 ohms.

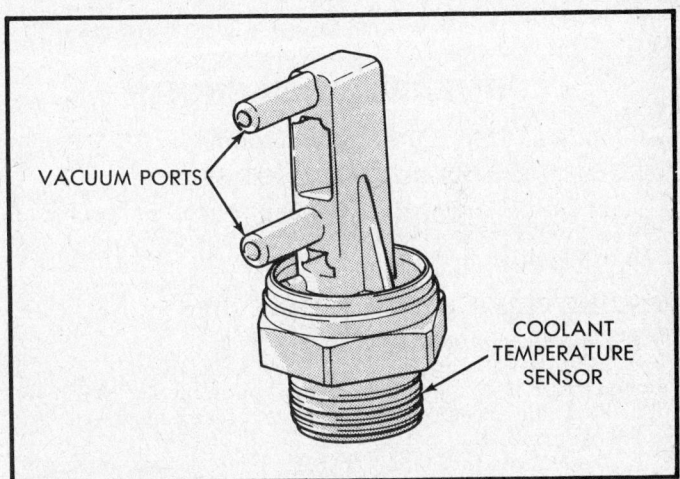

Coolant switch

Carburetor Regulator Test

Using a tachometer, maintain an engine speed of 1,500 rpm. Disconnect the regulator solenoid connector from the solenoid. Average engine speed should increase a minimum of 50 rpm. Reconnect the regulator solenoid connector. The engine speed should slowly return to 1,500 rpm. Disconnect the twelve pin connector at the fuel control computer. Connect a ground to harness connector pin 15. Engine speed should decrease a minimum of 50 rpm. If the engine speed does not change accordingly, service the carburetor (check for air leaks).

Electronic Fuel Control Computer Test

With the engine at normal operating temperature, make certain the carburetor switch is not grounded. Using a tachometer, maintain an engine speed of 1,500 rpm. Connect a voltmeter to the solenoid output wire going to the carburetor (green). Do not separate the connector from the wiring harness. Separate the connector at the oxygen sensor and connect a jumper wire to the harness end.

29-27

SECTION 29

ENGINE CONTROLS
CHRYSLER ELECTRONIC FEEDBACK CARBURETOR

1. Connect the other end of the jumper wire to a good ground. An increase in engine speed should be observed (minimum of 50 rpm). Voltmeter should indicate more than 9 volts.
2. Hold the wire with one hand and with the other touch the battery positive terminal. Engine speed should decrease (minimum of 50 rpm). Voltmeter should now indicate less than 3 volts. If the computer fails both tests replace it. Reconnect the oxygen sensor wire.

Leave voltmeter connected to carburetor regulator solenoid.

Oxygen Sensor Test

The feedback electronics must be working properly for this test.
1. Set the parking brake. Run the engine at 1,500 rpm (carburetor switch not grounded).
2. Using the voltmeter connected to the solenoid output wire going to the carburetor (green).
3. Full Rich Test: Hold the choke blade(s) closed. During the next ten seconds the voltage should decrease to three volts or less and maintain that level. If engine does not respond, go to Step 4.
4. Full Lean Test: Disconnect the PCV system. During the next ten seconds, the voltage should increase to nine volts and maintain that level. The voltage will remain at this level until the vacuum hoses are reconnected.
5. If the sensor fails both tests 3 and 4, replace it. Reconnect all hoses and wires. Steps 2 and 3 should not be performed for longer than 90 seconds.

DRIVEABILITY DIAGNOSIS

All Models (Cold Starting Symptom)

ENGINE CRANKS BUT WILL NOT START

1. Choke not closing check binding or interferences hot and cold and with accessories on.
2. No ignition firing.

ENGINE FIRES, RUNS UP, THEN DIES

1. Choke vacuum kick setting too wide.
2. EGR system on at start check CCEGR valve or CTS switch timer, and solenoid for proper operation also EGR valve.
3. Fast idle speed set too low or cam index incorrect.
4. Vacuum leak.
5. Inadequate fuel pump output.
6. Low fuel level in carb reset floats.

ENGINE DIES ON KICKDOWN AFTER START

1. Check vacuum kick, cam index, hot fast idle speed mis-set.

ENGINE FIRES, RUNS UP, THEN IDLES SLOWLY WITH BLACK SMOKE

1. Choke vacuum diaphragm leaks or is not receiving vacuum signal.
2. Choke vacuum kick setting too tight.
3. Cam index and/or hot fast idle mis-set too low.
4. EGR system on during warmup check CCEGR or CTS and timer.

ENGINE FIRES, BUT DOES NOT RUN UP AND DIES WHEN KEY IS RELEASED

1. Choke vacuum diaphragm leaks or is not receiving vacuum signal.
2. Choke linkage binding preventing proper closing or breathing of blade.
3. Timing mis-set.

Cold Engine Driveability Symptom

ENGINE STALLS WHEN TRANSMISSION IS PLACED IN GEAR

1. Improper choke vacuum kick setting.
2. Fast idle speed or cam index mis-set.
3. Ignition timing vacuum advance OSAC.

ENGINE STALLS, HESITATES OR SAGS DURING ACCELERATION TIP-INS DURING FIRST MILE

1. Choke vacuum kick setting.
2. Exhaust Manifold Heat Control Valve stuck open.
3. Choke control switch in high heat at low ambients.
4. Incorrect float heights low fuel level.
5. EGR on during warm-up defective CCEGR or CTS.
6. Weak or low output, carburetor accelerator pump.
7. Secondary lockout mis-set 4 bbl. carb.
8. Defective OSAC no vacuum advance.

ENGINE HESITATES OR SAGS, STALLS AFTER FIRST MILE OF WARMUP

1. Choke control switch in high heat at lower ambients.
2. Exhaust Manifold Heat Control Valve stuck open.
3. Weak or poor output accelerator pump.
4. Incorrect float heights low fuel level.
5. EGR on during warmup defective CCEGR or CTS (Low ambients).
6. Ignition system PSAC, vacuum advance, etc.
7. Heated air inlet in cold position (Icing).

Warmed Up Driveability Symptom

HESITATION SAG, STUMBLE (WITH SLIGHT ACCELERATOR PEDAL MOVEMENT)

1. Vacuum leak hose off or misrouted or split.
2. Mis-set timing or defective distributor governor or vacuum advance.
3. Weak or defective accelerator pump in carburetor-output to only one bore results in backfire on 2- or 4-bbl. carburetor.
4. Incorrect float height in carb low fuel level.
5. Sticking or binding carburetor power valve (Holley) or metering rod carrier binding or sticking (Carter).
6. Heated inlet air stuck in either full hot or cold position, due to binding door hinge or faulty sensor.
7. Carburetor transfer or idle system plugged or obstructed.
8. Plugged or restricted OSAC giving little or no vacuum advance.
9. Binding, bent or defective EGR valve or control system, resulting in excessive EGR rates.

HESITATION, SAG, STUMBLE (WITH HEAVY ACCELERATOR PEDAL MOVEMENT)

1. Weak or defective accelerator pump.
2. Major vacuum leak.
3. Sticking or binding carburetor power valve or step-up rods.
4. Mis-set basic timing or distributor governor advance faulty.
5. Mis-set carburetor float levels low fuel.
6. Faulty fuel pump obstructed lines or filter.
7. Binding or bent carburetor float arms inadequate fuel.
8. Mis-set air valve spring tension on 4-bbl. carburetors causing premature opening.

Surge at constant speed

LOW SPEED

1. Vacuum leak hoses off.
2. Mis-set timing failed vacuum advance.

ENGINE CONTROLS
CHRYSLER ELECTRONIC FEEDBACK CARBURETOR
SECTION 29

3. Defective ASAC plugged or restricted giving no vacuum advance.
4. Partially plugged idle or transfer system in carb including mis-set idle.
5. Incorrect float setting low fuel level.
6. Defective PCV stuck in high flow position.
7. Heated air system stuck in cold position at low ambient.

HIGH SPEED

1. Incorrect spark advance defective distributor or ASAC valve plugged.
2. Major vacuum leak.
3. Defective or sticking gradient power valve (Holley Carb).
4. Incorrect float setting low fuel level.
5. Restricted fuel supply.

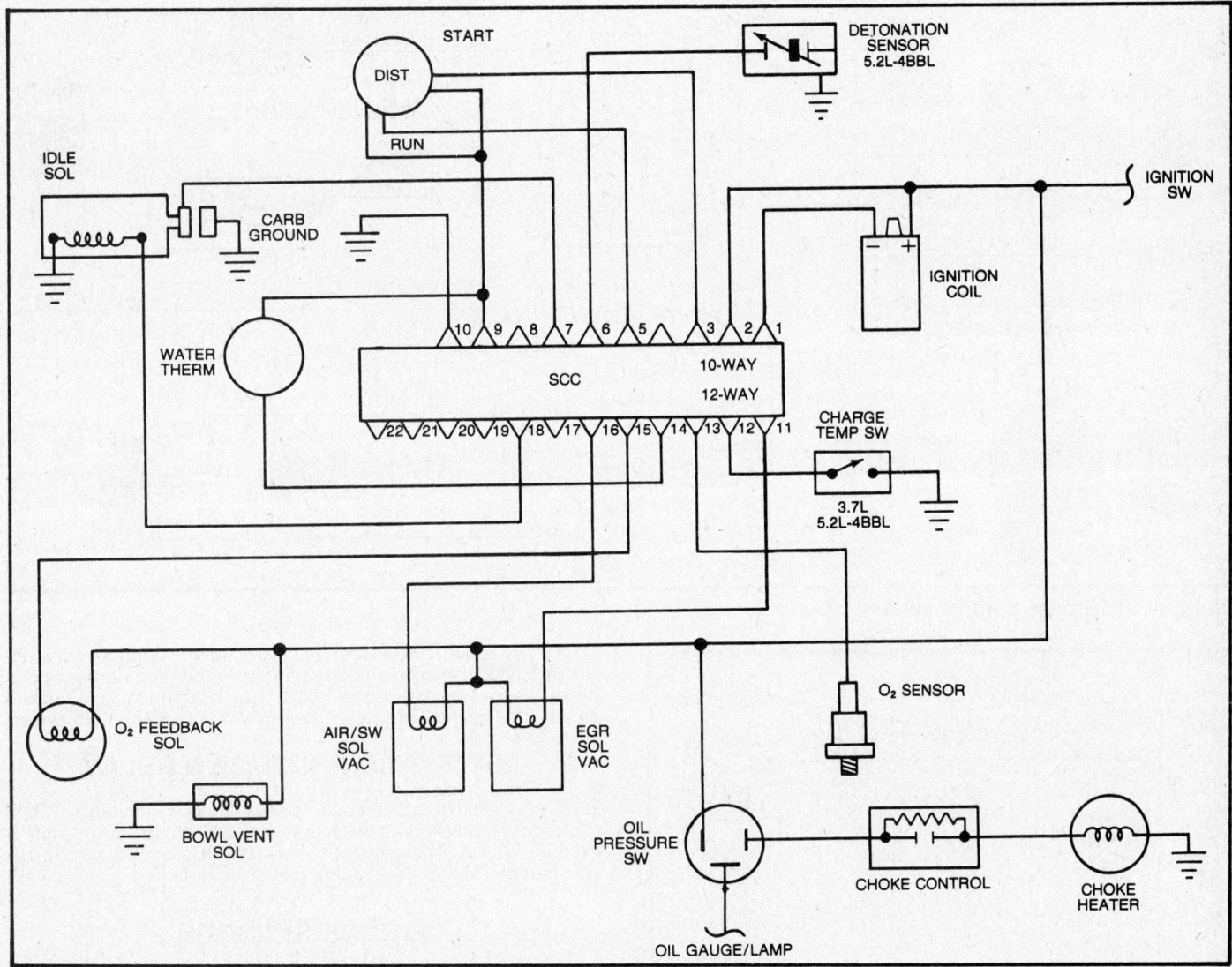

Schematic of the Chrysler electronic feedback carburetor system on the 3.7 snf 5.2 liter engines

CHRYSLER ELECTRONIC CONTROL SYSTEM

Components

POWER MODULE

The power module circuits power the ignition coil and the fuel injector. The power module also supplies the power to the Logic module and the Automatic Shutdown (ASD) Relay which in turn activates the fuel pump, ignition coil and the power module itself. The power module also receives a signal from the distributor, and in case there is no signal from the distributor, the ASD relay will not be activated and the power to the fuel pump and ignition coil will be shut off.

LOGIC MODULE

The logic module is a digital computer containing a microproc-

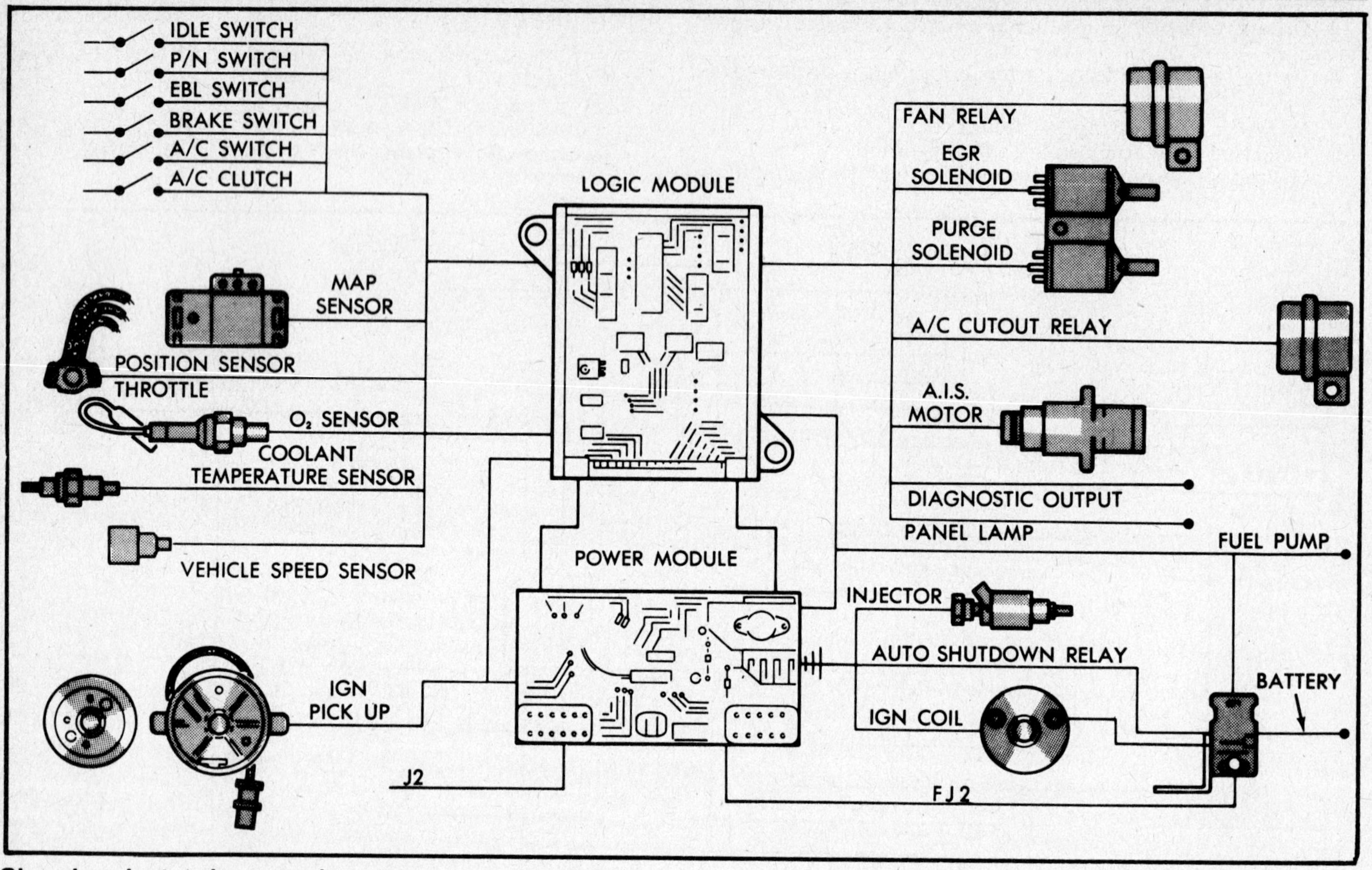

SECTION 29
ENGINE CONTROLS
CHRYSLER ELECTRONIC CONTROL SYSTEM

Chrysler electronic control system

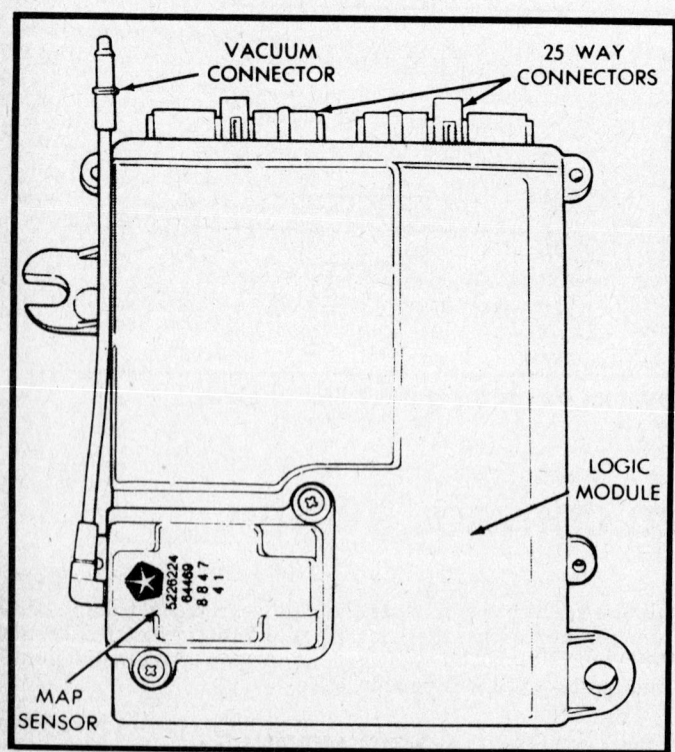

Exploded view of the logic module

essor. The module receives electrical input signals from various switches, sensors and components. The module then computes the fuel injector pulse width, spark advance, ignition coil dwell, idle speed and purge, and EGR control solenoid cycles.

AUTOMATIC SHUTDOWN RELAY

This relay is powered and operated by the power module. When the module receives a distributor signal during cranking, it grounds, the ASD closing its contacts. This completes the circuit for the electric fuel pump, power module and ignition coil.

ENGINE SENSORS

Manifold Absolute Pressure (MAP) Sensor

The manifold absolute pressure (MAP) sensor is a device which monitors manifold vacuum. It is mounted in the right side passenger compartment and is connected to a vacuum nipple on the throttle body and, electrically to the logic module. The sensor transmits information on manifold vacuum conditions and barometric pressure to the logic module. The MAP sensor data on engine load is used with data from other sensors to determine the correct air-fuel mixture.

Oxygen Sensor

The oxygen sensor (O_2 sensor) is a device which produces an electrical voltage when exposed to the oxygen present in the exhaust gases. The sensor is mounted in the exhaust manifold and must be heated by the exhaust gases before producing the voltage. When there is a large amount of oxygen present (lean mixture), the sensor produces a low voltage. When there is a

29-30

ENGINE CONTROLS
CHRYSLER ELECTRONIC CONTROL SYSTEM

lesser amount present (rich mixture) it produces a higher voltage. By monitoring the oxygen content and converting it to electrical voltage, the sensor acts as a rich-lean switch. The voltage is transmitted to the logic module. The logic module signals the power module to trigger the fuel injector. The injector changes the mixture.

Coolant Temperature Sensor

The coolant temperature sensor is mounted in the thermostat housing. This sensor provides data on engine operating temperature to the logic module. This data long with data provided by the charge temperature switch allows the logic module to demand slightly richer air-fuel mixtures and higher idle speeds until normal operating temperatures are reached. The coolant temperature sensor allows the logic module to act as an automatic choke.

Charge Temperature Sensor

The charge temperature sensor is a device mounted in the intake manifold which measures the temperature of the air-fuel mixture. This information is used by the logic module to determine engine operating temperature and engine warm-up cycles in the event of a coolant temperature sensor failure.

Switch Input

Various switches provide information to the logic module. These include the idle, neutral safety, electric backlite, air conditioning, air conditioning clutch, and brake light switches. If one or more of these switches is sensed as being in the on position, the logic module signals the automatic idle speed motor to increase idle speed to a scheduled rpm.

With the air conditioning on and the throttle blade above a specific angle, the wide open throttle cut-out relay prevents the air conditioning clutch from engaging until the throttle blade is below this angle.

Power Loss Lamp

The power loss lamp comes on each time the ignition key is turned on and stays on for a few seconds as a bulb test. If the logic module receives an incorrect signal or no signal from either the coolant temperature sensor, manifold absolute pressure sensor, or the throttle position sensor, the power loss lamp on the instrument panel is illuminated. This is a warning that the logic module has gone into limp in mode in an attempt to keep the system operational.

Limp in mode is the attempt by the logic module to compensate for the failure of certain components by substituting information from other sources. If the logic module senses incorrect data or no data at all from the MAP sensor, throttle position sensor or coolant temperature sensor, the system is placed into Limp in Mode and the power loss lamp on the instrument panel is activated.

Throttle Position Sensor (TPS)

The throttle position sensor (TPS) is an electric resistor which is activated by the movement of the throttle-shaft. It is mounted on the throttle body and senses the angle of the throttle blade opening. The voltage that the sensor produces increases or decreases according to the throttle blade opening. This voltage is transmitted to the logic module where it is used along with data from other sensors to adjust the air-fuel ratio to varying conditions and during acceleration, deceleration, idle, and wide open throttle operations.

Automatic Idle Speed (AIS) Motor

The automatic idle speed motor (AIS) is operated by the logic module. Data from the throttle position sensor, speed sensor, coolant temperature sensor, and various switch operations, (electric backlite, air conditioning safety/neutral, brake) are used by the logic module to adjust engine idle to an optimum during all idle conditions. The AIS adjusts the air portion of the air/fuel mixture through an air bypass on the back of the throttle body. Basic (no load) idle is determined by the minimum air flow through the throttle body.

The AIS opens or closes off the air bypass as an increase or decrease is needed due to engine loads or ambient conditions. The logic module senses an air/fuel change and increases or decreases fuel proportionally to change engine idle. Deceleration die out is also prevented by increasing engine idle when the throttle is closed quickly after a driving (speed) condition.

ON BOARD DIAGNOSTICS

The logic module has been programmed to monitor several different circuits of the fuel injection system. This monitoring is called On Board Diagnosis. If a problem is sensed with a monitored circuit, often enough to indicate an actual problem, its fault code is stored in the logic module for eventual display to the service technician. If the problem is repaired or ceases to exist, the logic module cancels the fault code after 30 ignition key on/off cycles.

Fault Codes

When a fault code appears (either by flashes of the light emitting diode or by watching the diagnostic readout -- Tool C-4805 or equivalent, it indicates that the logic module has recognized an abnormal signal in the system. Fault codes indicate the results of a failure but do not always identify the failed component.

CODE 11 – means a problem in the distributor circuit. This code appears when the logic module has not seen a distributor signal since the battery was reconnected.

CODE 12 – indicates a problem in the stand-by memory circuit. This code appears if direct battery feed to the logic module is interrupted.

CODE 13 – means a problem exists in the MAP sensor pneumatic system. This code appears if the MAP sensor vacuum level does not change between start and start/run transfer speed (500–600 rpm).

CODE 14 – means a problem exists in the MAP sensor electrical system. This code appears if the MAP sensor signal is either too low (below .02 volts) or too high (above 4.9 volts).

CODE 15 – means a problem exists in the vehicle Speed Sensor circuit. This code appears if engine speed is above 1468 rpm and speed sensor indicates less than 2 mph. This code is valid only if it is sensed while vehicle is moving.

CODE 16 – means a battery voltage sense. This will happen when the sensing voltage drops below four volts or the battery voltage is between 7.5 to 8.0 volts for more than twenty seconds.

CODE 17 – means the engine is running too cool. This code wiil appear when the engine temperature does not reach 160°F within twenty minutes, after the engine is started.

CODE 21 – indicates a problem in the O2 sensor circuit. This code appears if there has been no O2 signal for more than 5 seconds.

CODE 22 – means a problem exists in the coolant temperature sensorcircuit. This code appears if the temperature sensor circuit indicates an incorrect temperature or a temperature that changes too fast to be real.

CODE 23 – means a problem withthe charge temperature sensor. This will occur when the charge temperature sensor voltage is below .06 volt or above 4.98 volts.

CODE 24 – means a problem exists in the throttle position sensor circuit. This code appears if the sensor signal is either below 0.16 volts or above 4.7 volts.

CODE 25 – means a problem in the automatic idle speed (AIS) control circuit. This code appears if the proper voltage

29-31

SECTION 29
ENGINE CONTROLS
CHRYSLER ELECTRONIC CONTROL SYSTEM

from the AIS system is not present. An open harness or motor will not activate code.

CODE 26 – means there is a problem with the fuel injector driver on the non-turbo models only. On the Turbo models code 26 means there is a problem with fuel injectors one and two firing improperly during cranking.

CODE 27 – means a problem with fuel injectors three and four firing improperly during cranking on the turbo charged models only.

CODE 31 – means a problem in the canister purge solenoid circuit. This code appears when the proper voltage at the purge solenoid is not present (open or shorted system).

CODE 32 – means a problem in the power loss lamp circuit. This code appears when proper voltage to the power loss lamp circuit is not present (open or shorted system).

CODE 33 – means a problem in the air conditioning wide open throttle cut out relay circuit. This code appears if the proper voltage at the air conditioning wide open throttle relay circuit is not present (open or shorted).

CODE 34 – means a problem in the EGR solenoid circuit. This code appears if proper voltage at the EGR solenoid circuit is not present (open or shorted system).

CODE 35 – indicates a problem in the fan relay circuit. This code appears if the radiator fan is either not operating or operating at wrong time.

CODE 36 – means a problem with the wastegate solenoid circuit on the turbocharged models only.

CODE 37 – means a problem with the barometric read solenoid circuit on the turbo charged models. On the non-turbocharged models code 37 means a problem with the shift indicator lamp circuit (manual transmissions only).

CODE 41 – means a problem in the charging system. This code appears if battery voltage from the automatic shut down relay is below 11.75 volts.

CODE 42 – means a problem in the automatic shut down relay (ASD) circuit. This code appears if during cranking, battery voltage from ASD relay is not present for at least 1/3 second after first distributor pulse or after engine stall, battery voltage is not off within 3 seconds after last distributor pulse.

CODE 43 – means a problem in the interface circuit. This code appears if the anti-dwell or injector control signal is not present between the logic module and power module.

CODE 44 – means a problem in the logic module. This code appears if an internal failure exists in the logic module.

CODE 45 – means a problem with the overboost shut-off circuit on the turbo charged models only. This code will appear if the MAP sensor signal exceeds a predetermined amount of boost indication.

CODE 46 – means a problem of the battery voltage being too high. This code will appear when the battery sense voltage is more then 1 volt above the desired control voltage for more than 20 seconds.

CODE 47 – means a problem of the battery voltage being too low. This code will appear when the battery sense voltage is less then 1 volt below the desired control voltage for more than 20 seconds. This usuallu occurs when the engine temperature is above 160°F and the the engine speed is above 1500 rpm.

CODE 51 – indicates a problem in the closed loop fuel system. This code appears if during closed loop conditions, the O2 signal is either low or high for more than 2 minutes.

CODE 52 – means a problem in the logic module. This code appears if an internal failure exists in the logic module.

CODE 53 – means a problem in the logic module. This code appears if an internal failure exists in the logic module.

CODE 54 – means a problem in the logic module. This code appears if an internal failure exists in the logic module.

CODE 55 – means "end of message". This code appears as the final code after all other fault codes have been displayed and means "end of message".

CODE 88 – means start of message. This code only appears on the diagnostic readout Tool C–4805 or equivalent, and means start of message.

SYSTEMS TEST

Obtaining Fault Codes

1. Connect diagnostic readout box tool C–4805 or equivalent, to the diagnostic connector located in the engine compartment near the passenger side strut tower.
2. Start the engine if possible, cycle the transmission selector and the A/C switch if applicable. Shut off the engine.
3. Turn the ignition switch on, off, on, off, on. Within 5 seconds record all the diagnostic codes shown on the diagnostic readout box tool, observe the power loss lamp on the instrument panel the lamp should light for 2 seconds then go out (bulb check).

Switch Test

After all codes have been shown and has indicated Code 55 end of message, actuate the following component switches. The digital display must change its numbers when the switch is activated and released:
Brake pedal.
Gear shift selector park, reverse, park.
A/C switch (if applicable).
Electric backlite switch (if applicable).

Actuator Test Mode (ATM)

1. Remove coil wire from cap and place 1/4 in. from a ground.

--- **CAUTION** ---

Coil wire must be 1/4 in. or less from ground or power module damage may result.

2. Remove air cleaner hose from throttle body.
3. Press the ATM button on the diagnostic readout box tool and observe the following:
3 sparks from the coil wire to ground.
2 AIS motor movements (1 open, 1 close) you must listen carefully for AIS operation.
1 fuel pulse from the injector into the throttle body
4. The ATM capability is cancelled 5 minutes after the ignition switch is turned on. To reinstate this capability cycle the ignition ON and OFF three times ending in the ON position.
5. When the ATM button is pressed, fault code 42 is generated because the ASD relay is bypassed. Do not use this code for diagnostics after ATM operation.
6. The ATM test will check 3 categories of operation:

When coil fires three times:
    a. Coil operational.
    b. Logic module portion operational.
    c. Power module portion operational.
    d. Interface between power module and logic module is working.
    AIS is operational
    Injector fuel pulse into Throttle Body:
    a. Fuel injector operational.
    b. Fuel pump operational.
    c. Fuel lines intact.
7. The electronic fuel injection system must be evaluated using all the information found in the systems test:
Start/no start
Fault codes
Loss of power lamp on or off (limp in)
ATM results:
    a. Spark yes/no.
    b. Fuel yes/no.

ENGINE CONTROLS
CHRYSLER ELECTRONIC CONTROL SYSTEM
SECTION 29

c. AIS movement yes/no.

Once this information is found, it will be easier to determine what circuit to look at for further testing.

NOTE: For more detailed information on Chrysler engine controls refer to the Chrysler Fuel Injection section located in the fuel injection unit repair section of this manual.

GENERAL MOTORS COMPUTER CONTROLLED CATALYTIC CONVERTER (C–4) SYSTEM, AND COMPUTER COMMAND CONTROL (CCC) SYSTEM

INTRODUCTION

The GM designed Computer Controlled Catalytic Converter System (C-4 System), is a revised version of the 1978–79 Electronic Fuel Control System (although parts are not interchangeable between the systems). The C-4 System primarily maintains the ideal air/fuel ratio at which the catalytic converter is most effective. Some versions of the system also control ignition timing of the distributor.

The CCC System monitors up to fifteen engine/vehicle operating conditions which it uses to control up to nine engine and emission control systems. In addition to maintaining the ideal air/fuel ratio for the catalytic converter and adjusting ignition timing, the CCC System also controls the Air Management System so that the Catalytic converter can operate at the highest efficiency possible.

The system also controls the lockup on the transmission torque converter clutch (certain automatic transmission models only), adjusts idle speed over a wide range of conditions, purges the evaporative emissions charcoal canister, controls the EGR valve operation and operates the early fuel evaporative (EFE) system. Not all engines use all of the above subsystems.

There are two operation modes for both the C-4 System and the CCC System; closed loop and open loop fuel control. Closed loop fuel control means the oxygen sensor is controlling the carburetor's air/fuel mixture ratio. Under open loop fuel control operating conditions (wide open throttle, engine and/or oxygen sensor cold), the oxygen sensor has no effect on the air/fuel mixture.

NOTE: On some engines, the oxygen sensor will cool off while the engine is idling, putting the system into open loop operation. To restore closed loop operation, run the engine at part throttle and accelerate from idle to part throttle a few times.

Computer Controlled Catalytic Converter (C–4) System Operation

Major components of the system include an Electronic Control Module (ECM), an oxygen sensor, and electronically controlled variable-mixture carburetor, and a three-way oxidation-reduction catalytic converter.

The oxygen sensor generates a voltage which varies with exhaust gas oxygen content. Lean mixtures (more oxygen) reduce voltage; rich mixtures (less oxygen) increase voltage. Voltage output is sent to the ECM.

An engine temperature sensor installed in the engine coolant outlet monitors coolant temperatures. Vacuum control switches and throttle position sensors also monitor engine conditions and supply signals to the ECM.

The Electronic Control Module (ECM) monitors the voltage input of the oxygen sensor along with information from other input signals. It processes these signals and generates a control signal sent to the carburetor. The control signal cycles between ON (lean command) and OFF (rich command). The amount of ON and OFF time is a function of the input voltage sent to the ECM by the oxygen sensor.

The ECM has a calibration unit called a PROM (Programmable Read Only Memory) which contains the specific instructions for a given engine application. In other words, the PROM unit is specifically programmed or "tailor made" for the system in which it is installed. The PROM assembly is a replaceable component which plugs into a socket on the ECM and requires a special tool for removal and installation.

On some 231 cu. in. V6 engines, the ECM controls the Electronic Spark Timing System (EST), AIR control system and on the Turbocharged 231 cu. in. C-4 System it controls the early fuel evaporative system (EFE) and the EGR valve control (on some models). On some 350 V8 engines, the ECM controls the electronic module retard (EMR) system, which retards the engine timing 10 degrees during certain engine operations to reduce the exhaust emissions.

NOTE: Electronic Spark Timing (EST) allows continuous spark timing adjustments to be made by the ECM. Engines with EST can easily be identified by the absence of vacuum and mechanical spark advance mechanisms on the distributor. Engines with EMR systems may be recognized by the presence of five connectors, instead of the HEI module's usual four.

To maintain good idle and driveability under all conditions, other input signals are used to modify the ECM output signal. Besides the sensors and switches already mentioned, these input signals include the manifold absolute pressure (MAP) or vacuum sensors, and the barometric pressure (BARO) sensor.

The MAP or vacuum sensors sense changes in manifold vacuum, while the BARO sensor senses changes in barometric pressure. One important function of the BARO sensor is the maintenance of good engine performance at various altitudes.

These sensors act as throttle position sensors on some engines. See the following paragraph for description. A Rochester Dualjet carburetor is used with the C-4 System. It may be an E2SE, E2ME, E4MC or E4ME model, depending on engine application. An electronically operated mixture control solenoid is installed in the carburetor float bowl. The solenoid controls the air/fuel mixture metered to the idle and main metering systems. Air metering to the idle system is controlled by an idle air bleed valve.

It follows the movement of the mixture solenoid to control the amount of air bled into the idle system, enriching or leaning out the mixture as appropriate. Air/fuel mixture enrichment occurs when the fuel valve is open and the air bleed is closed. All cycling of this system, which occurs ten times per second, is controlled by the ECM. A throttle position switch informs the ECM of open or closed throttle operation. A number of different switches are used, varying with application. The four cylinder engine (151 cu. in.) uses two vacuum switches to sense open throttle and closed throttle operation.

29-33

SECTION 29 ENGINE CONTROLS
GM—COMPUTER COMMAND CONTROL SYSTEM

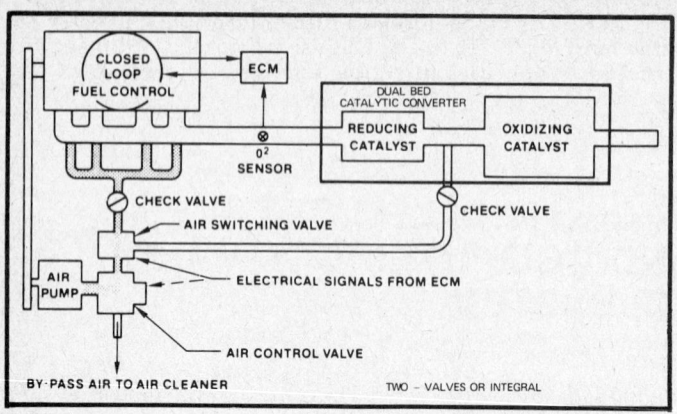

Air management system operation, cold engine mode

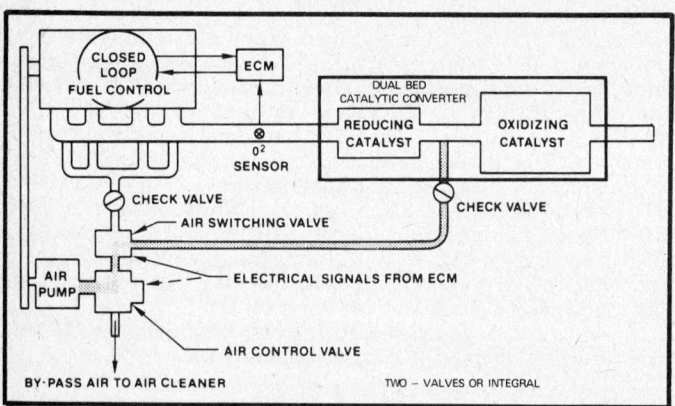

Air management system operation, warm engine mode

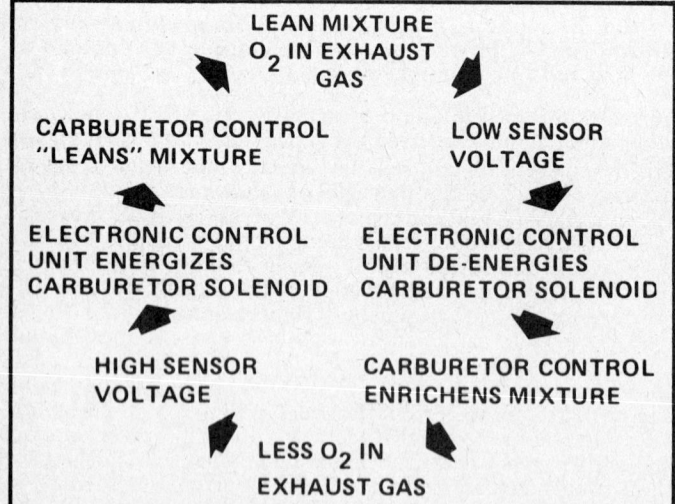

Basic cycle of operation

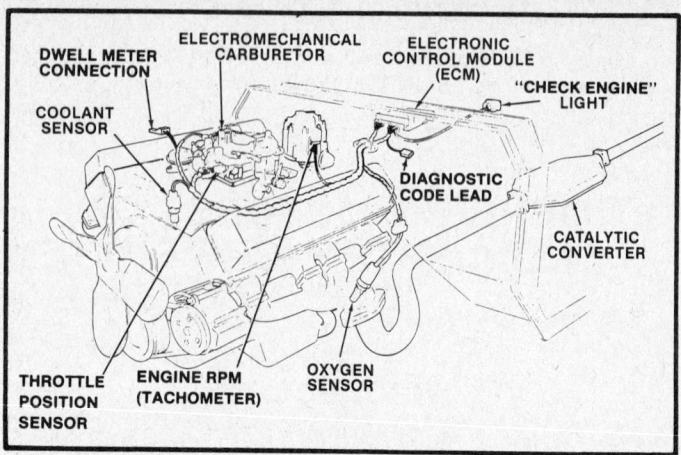

C-4 system air-fuel metering control

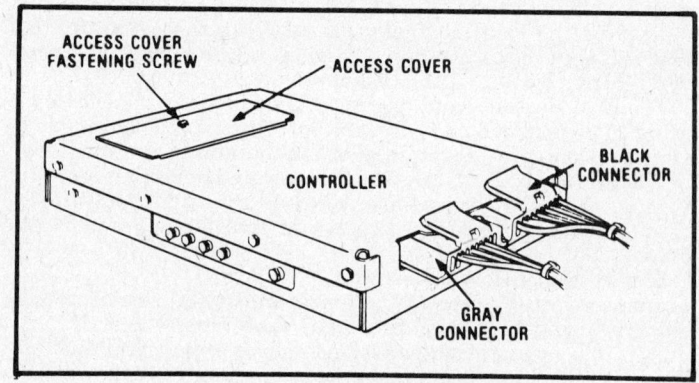

Electronic control module (computer)

ory for the last set of operating conditions that resulted in an ideal air/fuel ratio, and shifts to that set of conditions. The memory is continually updated during normal operation. Some 173 cu. in. V6 engines are equipped with a Pulsair control solenoid which is operated by the ECM. Likewise, many C–4 equipped engines with AIR systems (Air Injection Reaction systems) have an AIR system diverter solenoid controlled by the ECM.

These systems are similar in function to the AIR Management system used in the CCC System. See below for information. Most C–4 Systems include a maintenance reminder flag connected to the odometer which becomes visible in the instrument cluster at regular intervals, signaling the need for oxygen sensor replacement.

Computer Command Control (CCC) System Operation

The CCC has many components in common with the C–4 system (although they should probably not be interchanged between systems). These include the Electronic Control Module (ECM), which is capable of monitoring and adjusting more sensors and components than the ECM used on the C–4 System, an oxygen sensor, an electronically controlled variable-mixture carburetor, a three way catalytic converter, throttle position and coolant sensors, a barometric pressure (BARO) sensor, a manifold absolute pressure (MAP) sensor, a "check engine" light on the instrument cluster, and an Electronic Spark Timing (EST) distributor, which on some engines (turbocharged) is equipped with an Electronic Spark Control (ESC) which retards ignition spark under some conditions (detonation, etc.).

The V6 engines (except the 231 cu. in. turbo V6) use two pressure sensors MAP (Manifold Absolute Pressure) and BARO (Barometric Pressure) as well as a throttle-actuated wide open throttle switch mounted in a bracket on the side of the float bowl. The 231 cu. in. turbo V6, and V8 engines, use a throttle position sensor mounted in the carburetor bowl cover under the accelerator pump arm.

When the ECM receives a signal from the throttle switch, indicating a change of position, it immediately searches its mem-

ENGINE CONTROLS
GM—COMPUTER COMMAND CONTROL SYSTEM
SECTION 29

Components used almost exclusively by the CCC System include the Air Injection Reaction (AIR) Management System, charcoal canister purge solenoid, EGR valve control, vehicle speed sensor (located in the instrument cluster), transmission torque converter clutch solenoid (automatic transmission models only), idle speed control, and early fuel evaporative (EFE) system. See the operation descriptions under C–4 System for those components (except the ECM) the CCC System shares with the C–4 System.

The CCC System ECM, in addition to monitoring sensors and sending a control signal to the carburetor, also controls the following components or sub-systems: charcoal canister purge, AIR Management System, idle speed control, automatic transmission converter lockup, distributor ignition timing, EGR valve control, EFE control, and the air conditioner compressor clutch operation. The CCCECM is equipped with a PROM assembly similar to the one used in the C–4 ECM. See above for description.

The AIR Management System is an emission control which provides additional oxygen either to the catalyst or the cylinder head ports (in some cases exhaust manifold). An AIR Management System, composed of an air switching valve and/or an air control valve, controls the air pump flow and is itself controlled by the ECM. A complete description of the AIR system is given elsewhere in this unit repair section. The major difference between the CCC AIR System and the systems used on other cars is that the flow of air from the air pump is controlled electrically by the ECM, rather than by vacuum signal.

The charcoal canister purge control is an electrically operated solenoid valve controlled by the ECM. When energized, the purge control solenoid blocks vacuum reaching the canister purge valve. When the ECM de-energizes the purge control solenoid, vacuum is allowed to reach the canister and operate the purge valve. This releases the fuel vapors collected in the canister into the induction system.

The EGR valve control solenoid is activated by the ECM in similar fashion to the canister purge solenoid. When the engine is cold, the ECM energizes the solenoid, which blocks the vacuum signal to the EGR valve. When the engine is warm, the ECM de-energizes the solenoid and the vacuum signal is allowed to reach and activate the EGR valve.

The Transmission Converter Clutch (TCC) lock is controlled by the ECM through an electrical solenoid in the automatic transmission. When the vehicle speed sensor in the instrument panel signals the ECM that the vehicle has reached the correct speed, the ECM energizes the solenoid which allows the torque converter to mechanically couple the engine to the transmission. When the brake pedal is pushed or during deceleration, passing, etc., the ECM returns the transmission to fluid drive.

The idle speed control adjusts the idle speed to load conditions, and will lower the idle speed under no-load or low-load conditions to conserve gasoline.

The Early Fuel Evaporative (EFE) system is used on some engines to provide rapid heat to the engine induction system to promote smooth start-up and operation. There are two types of system: vacuum servo and electrically heated. They use different means to achieve the same end, which is to pre-heat the incoming air/fuel mixture. They are controlled by the ECM.

NOTE: The following explains how to activate the Trouble Code signal light in the instrument cluster and gives an explanation of what each code means. This is not a full C–4 or CCC System troubleshooting and isolation procedure.

Before suspecting the C–4 or CCC System or any of its components as faulty, check the ignition system including distributor, timing, spark plugs and wires. Check the engine compression, air cleaner, and emission control components not controlled by the ECM. Also check the intake manifold, vacuum hoses and hose connectors for leaks and the carburetor bolts for

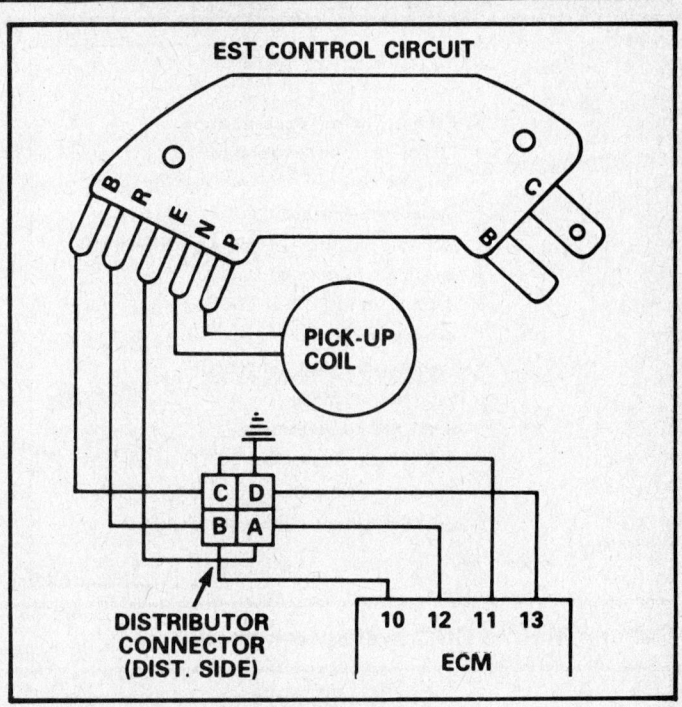

Computer controlled distributor

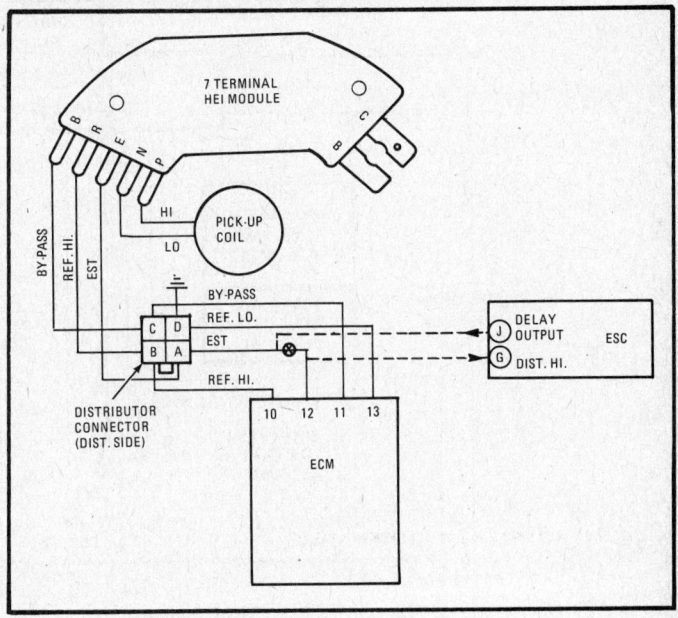

EST control circuit

tightness. The following symptoms could indicate a possible problem with the C–4 or CCC System.
1. Detonation.
2. Stalls or rough idle - cold.
3. Stalls or rough idle - hot.
4. Missing.
5. Hesitation.
6. Surges.
7. Poor gasoline mileage.
8. Sluggish or spongy performance.
9. Hard starting - cold.
10. Hard starting - hot.
11. Objectionable exhaust odors.
12. Cuts out

29-35

SECTION 29 ENGINE CONTROLS
GM — COMPUTER COMMAND CONTROL SYSTEM

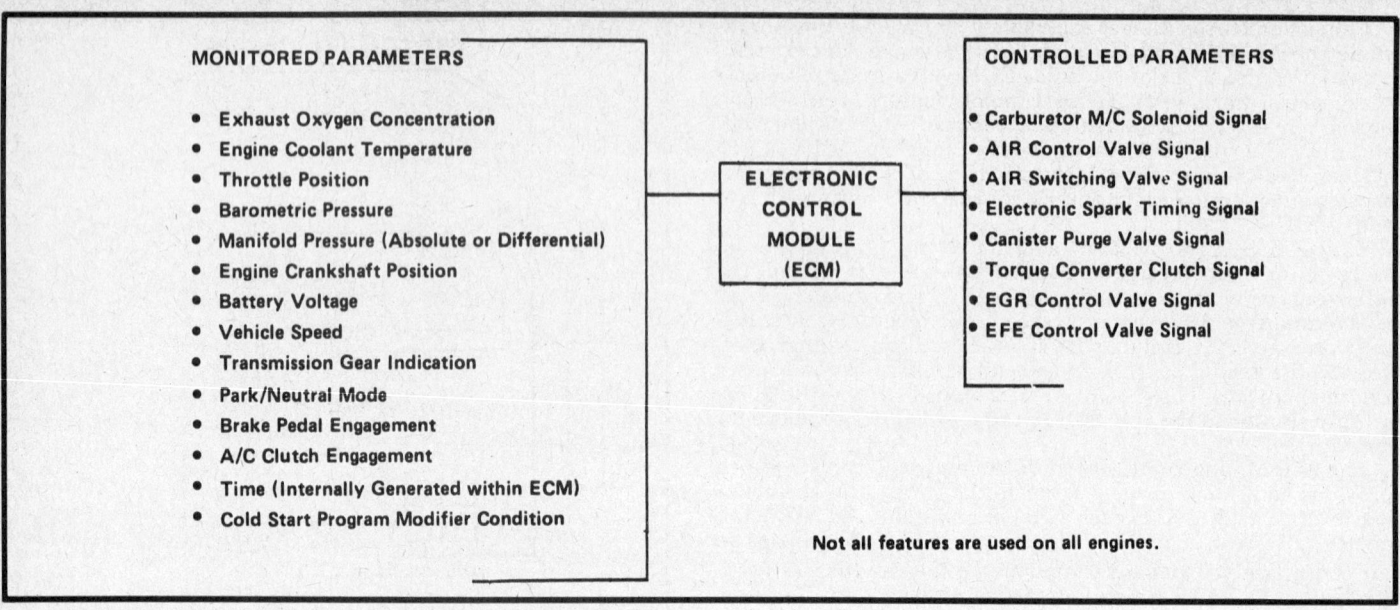

General Motors CCC system schematic

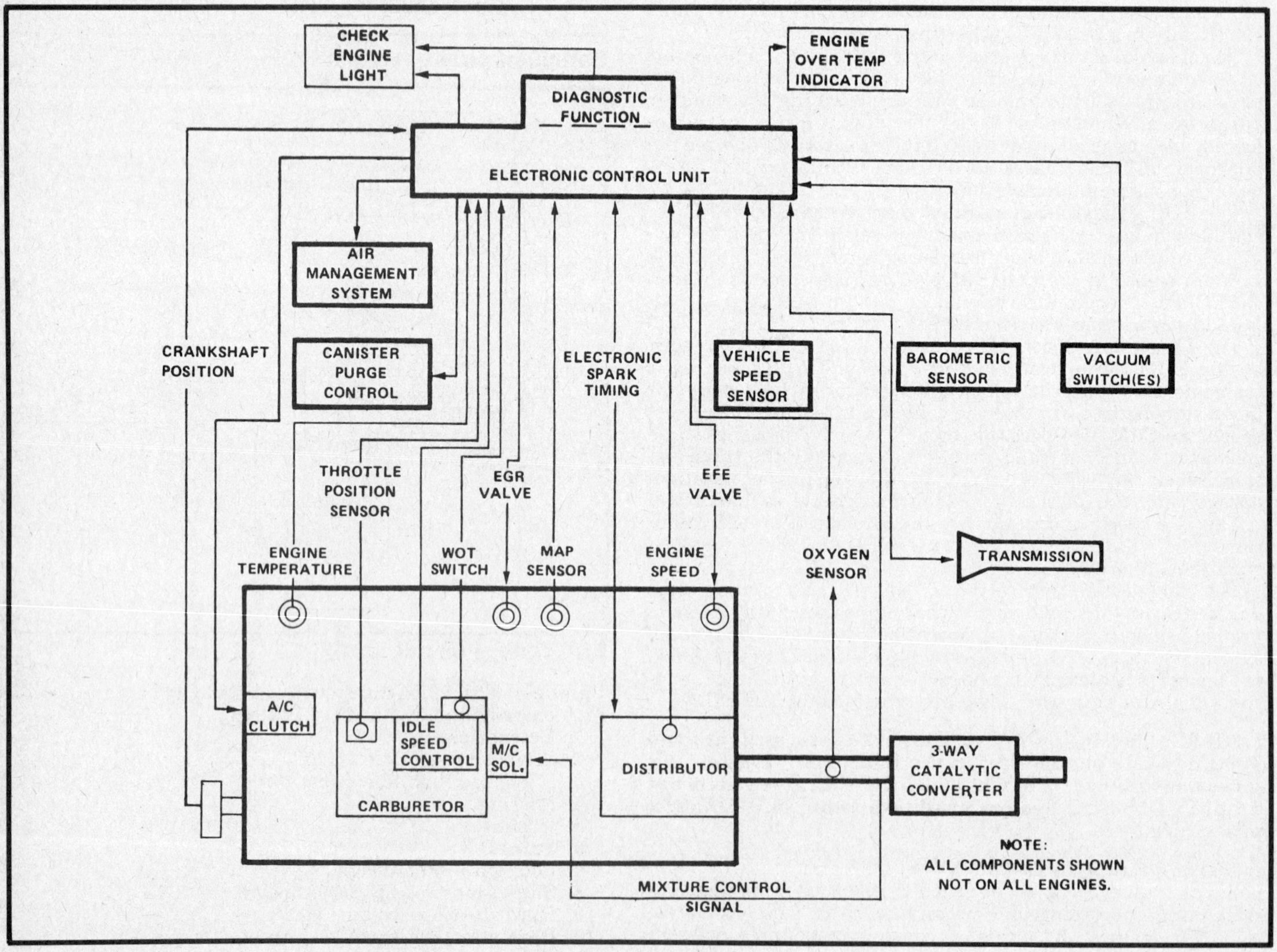

Computer command control system schematic

29-36

ENGINE CONTROLS
GM—COMPUTER COMMAND CONTROL SYSTEM
SECTION 29

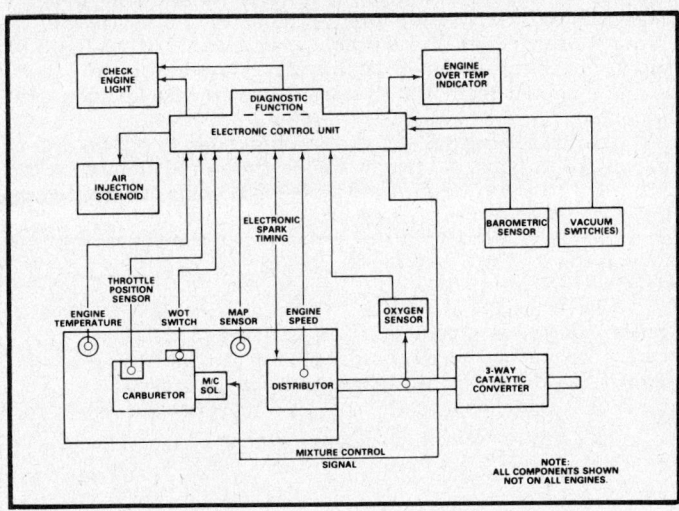

C-4 system schematic

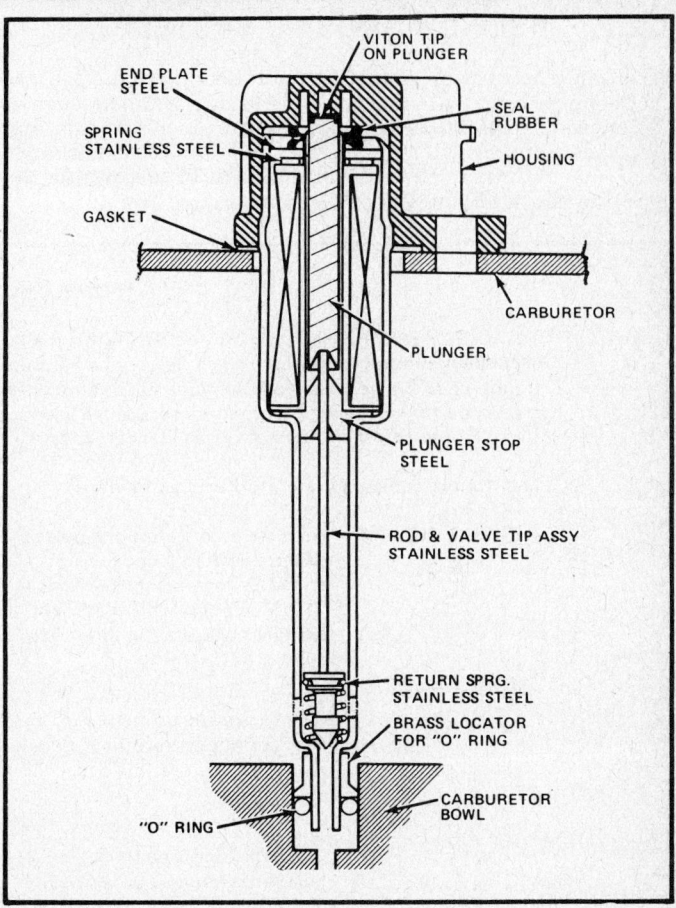

Computer controlled carburetor - plunger pulses ten times per second

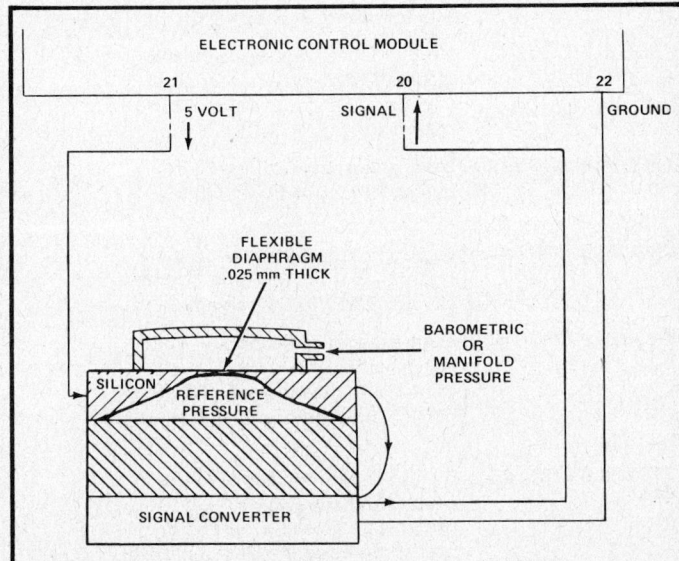

Typical pressure sensor

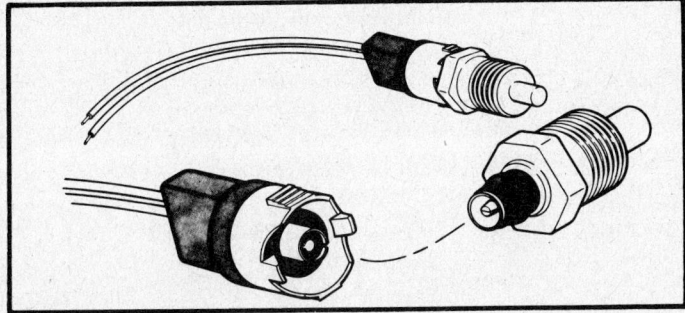

Coolant sensor assembly

REMOTE LAMP DRIVER

This small circuit board, which is located under the right side of the instrument panel, remote from the electronic control module, is put in the system to turn on the check engine light under malfunction conditions.

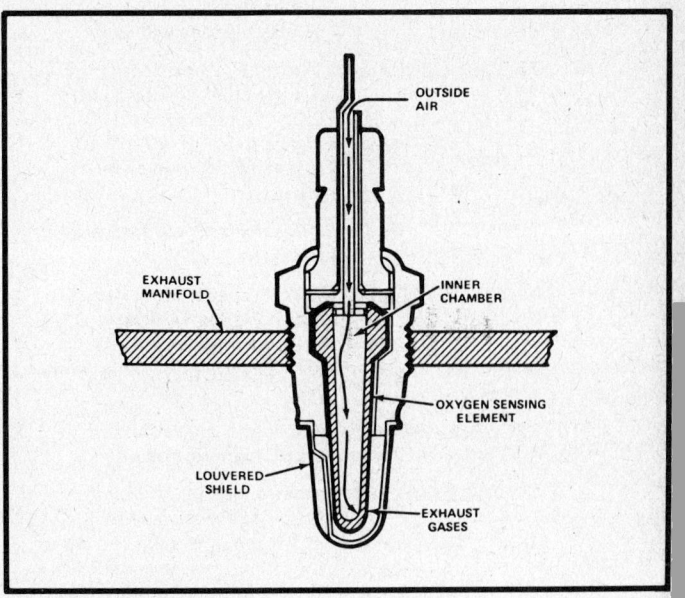

Exhaust exygen sensor

29-37

SECTION 29
ENGINE CONTROLS
GM—COMPUTER COMMAND CONTROL SYSTEM

SELF-DIAGNOSTIC SYSTEM

When an electrical or electronic malfunction is detected the check engine light will come on. When an input circuit, such as the engine temperature is supplying unreasonable information, the computer will substitute a fixed value so that the vehicle can continue to be driven. If this type of substitution occurs, the check engine light will come on and the numerical code will be stored in the computer memory to indicate why the light was turned on. If the problem was intermittent the light will go out, but the trouble code will be stored until the battery is disconnected from the system (20 amp fuse momentarily removed).

To minimize accumulation of trouble codes stored for one-of-a-kind events, such as stray voltages, the stored memory is programmed to erase itself after a preset number of ignition cy-

TROUBLE CODE IDENTIFICATION

The "CHECK ENGINE" light will only be "ON" if the malfunction exists under the conditions listed below. It takes up to five seconds minimum for the light to come on when a problem occurs. If the malfunction clears, the light will go out and a trouble code will be set in the ECM. Code 12 does not store in memory. If the light comes "on" intermittently, but no code is stored, go to the "Driver Comments" section. Any codes stored will be erased if no problem reoccurs within 50 engine starts. A specific engine may not use all available codes.

The trouble codes indicate problems as follows:

TROUBLE CODE 12	No distributor reference pulses to the ECM. This code is not stored in memory and will only flash while the fault is present. Normal code with ignition "on," engine not running.
TROUBLE CODE 13	Oxygen Sensor Circuit — The engine must run up to four minutes at part throttle, under road load, before this code will set.
TROUBLE CODE 14	Shorted coolant sensor circuit — The engine must run two minutes before this code will set.
TROUBLE CODE 15	Open coolant sensor circuit — The engine must run five minutes before this code will set.
TROUBLE CODE 21	Throttle Position Sensor (TPS) circuit voltage high (open circuit or misadjusted TPS). The engine must run 10 seconds, at specified curb idle speed, before this code will set.
TROUBLE CODE 22	Throttle Position Sensor (TPS) circuit voltage low (grounded circuit or misadjusted TPS). Engine must run 20 seconds at specified curb idle speed, to set code.
TROUBLE CODE 23	M/C solenoid circuit open or grounded.
TROUBLE CODE 24	Vehicle speed sensor (VSS) circuit — The vehicle must operate up to two minutes, at road speed, before this code will set.
TROUBLE CODE 32	Barometric pressure sensor (BARO) circuit low.
TROUBLE CODE 34	Vacuum sensor or Manifold Absolute Pressure (MAP) circuit — The engine must run up to two minutes, at specified curb idle, before this code will set.
TROUBLE CODE 35	Idle speed control (ISC) switch circuit shorted. (Up to 70% TPS for over 5 seconds.)
TROUBLE CODE 41	No distributor reference pulses to the ECM at specified engine vacuum. This code will store in memory.
TROUBLE CODE 42	Electronic spark timing (EST) bypass circuit or EST circuit grounded or open.
TROUBLE CODE 43	Electronic Spark Control (ESC) retard signal for too long a time; causes retard in EST signal.
TROUBLE CODE 44	Lean exhaust indication — The engine must run two minutes, in closed loop and at part throttle, before this code will set.
TROUBLE CODE 45	Rich exhaust indication — The engine must run two minutes, in closed loop and at part throttle, before this code will set.
TROUBLE CODE 51	Faulty or improperly installed calibration unit (PROM). It takes up to 30 seconds before this code will set.
TROUBLE CODE 53	Exhaust Gas Recirculation (EGR) valve vacuum sensor has seen improper EGR vacuum.
TROUBLE CODE 54	Shorted M/C solenoid circuit and/or faulty ECM.
TROUBLE CODE 55	Grounded Vref (terminal "21"), high voltage on oxygen sensor circuit or ECM.

ENGINE CONTROLS
GM—COMPUTER COMMAND CONTROL SYSTEM
SECTION 29

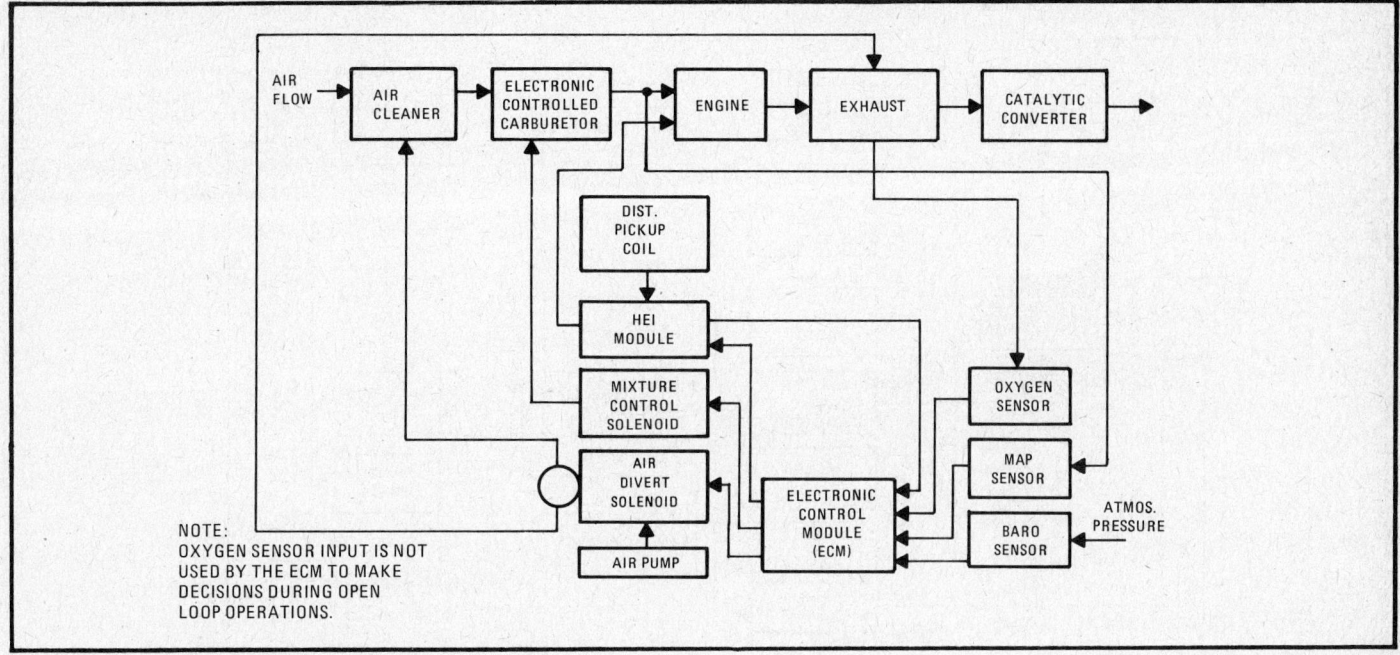

Non-turbocharged functional block diagram

cles. The check engine light comes on each time the ignition is turned on with the engine stopped. The light remains on for approximately two seconds after the engine is started. If the light comes on while driving, it will stay on for a minimum of two seconds, even for a momentary intermittent condition.

TROUBLE CODES

The trouble code 12 basically means that no tachometer signal is being received at the ECM. If this code is displayed while the engine is running, it means that there is a problem that needs to be isolated and corrected. However, with the ignition on and the engine stopped, no tach signals are generated and a code 12 should be displayed. This proves that the self diagnostic system is operating and should not be taken to mean that there is a problem in the tach circuit. If the check engine light does not flash a code 12 under these conditions, then refer to the trouble codes explanation chart.

The trouble code will flash three times, if the test lead is grounded, the engine is running and the problem is occurring. If more than one fault is occurring, each additional code will be flashed three times, after the first code. The codes will come up in numerical order and then the pattern will repeat itself.

Each possible trouble code that may come up will have a correspondingly numbered diagnostic chart. For instance, a trouble code 14 indicates a problem in the temperature sensor circuit. A series of systematic checks found in the trouble code identification chart, will isolate the problem, either by direct test or by elimination. These charts apply to faults that are actually occurring at the time of testing.

If a trouble code was recorded for an intermittent condition the charts cannot be used. All that can be done for the intermittent fault is to physically check the system. Look for bad connections, bent or corroded connector terminals and pinched or broken wires. If the check engine light can be made to come on by manipulating a wire or connector, the actual fault has been recreated and the probable location of the fault has been discovered.

NOTE: There has been some new trouble codes added to this system. They are as follows:

1. CODE 24B – means a problem in the Park/Neutral circuit.
2. CODE 25 – means the Manifold Air Temperature Sensor signal voltage is low.
3. CODE 31 (Turbo Models) – means a problem with the Wastegate solenoid
4. CODE 33 – means the Mass Airflow Sensor voltage is too high or on fuel injected models the Mass Airflow Sensor frequency is too high.

ACTIVATING THE TROUBLE CODE

The trouble code test lead terminal is mounted in a 12 terminal connector located under the left side of the dash below the steering column. This is the connector used at the assembly plant when the vehicle is assembled to evaluate the system.

This connector is known as the Assembly Line Diagnostic Link (ALDL). With the ignition in the on position run a jumper wire from the test lead terminal to the ground terminal. When the test lead terminal is grounded the terminal signals the ECM to flash any trouble codes stored in memory. With the test lead terminal grounded, the ignition on and the engine stopped, the ECM will do the following:

1. Display a code "12" by flashing the "SERVICE ENGINE SOON" light (this will indicate the system is working). A code "12" consists of one flash followed by a short pause and then two quick flashes in succession. This code will be flashed three times. If no other codes are stored., code "12" will continue to flash until the diagnostic terminal is ungrounded.
2. On a carbureted engine, the engine should not be started with the diagnostic terminal grounded, because it may continue to flash a code "12" with the engine running. Also a carbureted engine if the test terminal is grounded after the engine is running, any stored codes will falsh , but code 12 will flash only if there is a problem with the distributor reference signal.
3. On a fuel injected engine, the codes can be only be obtained with the engine stopped. Grounding the diagnostic terminal with the engine running gives the "field service mode".
4. Display any stored trouble codes by grounding the diag-

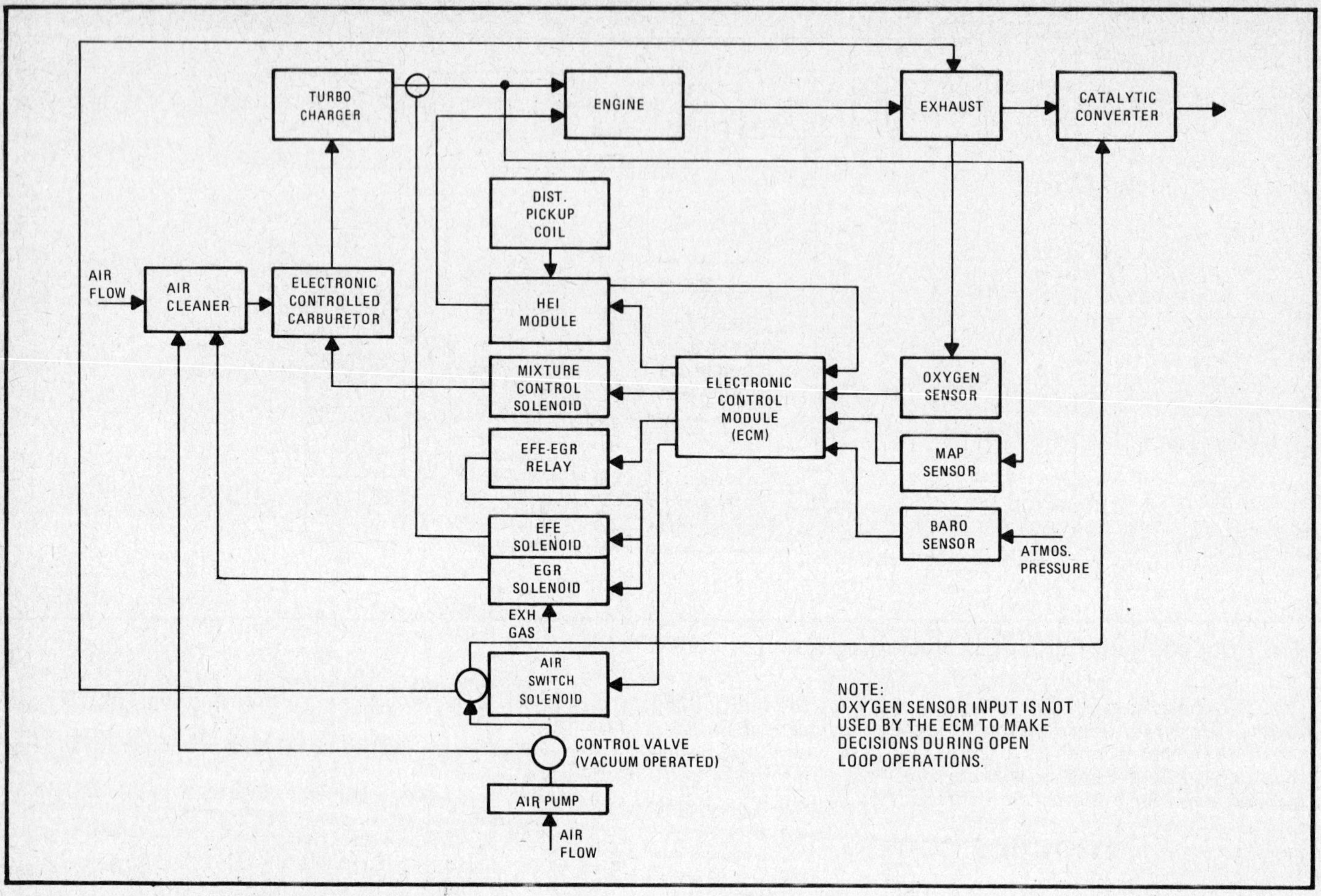

SECTION 29
ENGINE CONTROLS
GM—COMPUTER COMMAND CONTROL SYSTEM

Turbocharged functional block diagram

NOTE:
OXYGEN SENSOR INPUT IS NOT USED BY THE ECM TO MAKE DECISIONS DURING OPEN LOOP OPERATIONS.

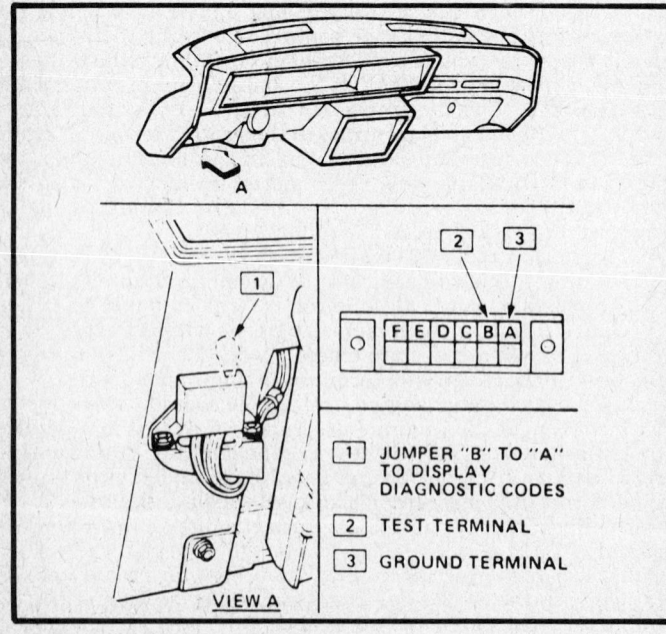

ALDC connector location

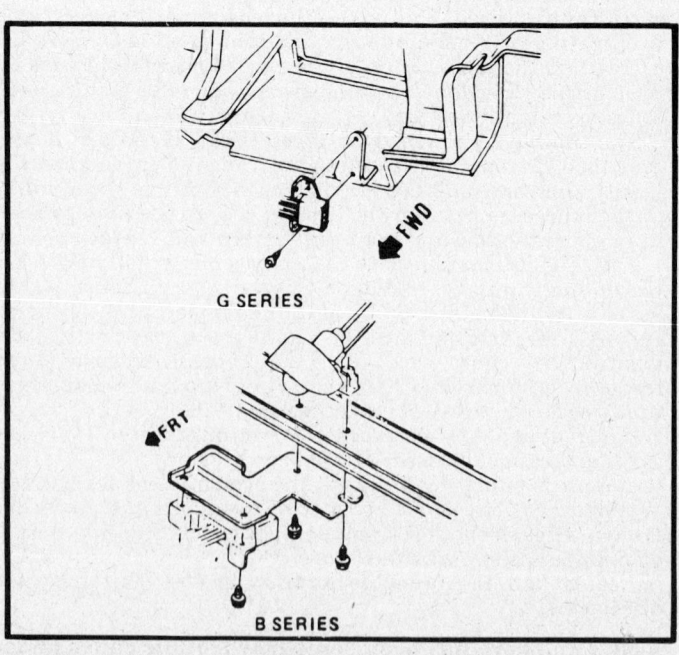

ALDC connector location on G & B series

ENGINE CONTROLS
GM—COMPUTER COMMAND CONTROL SYSTEM

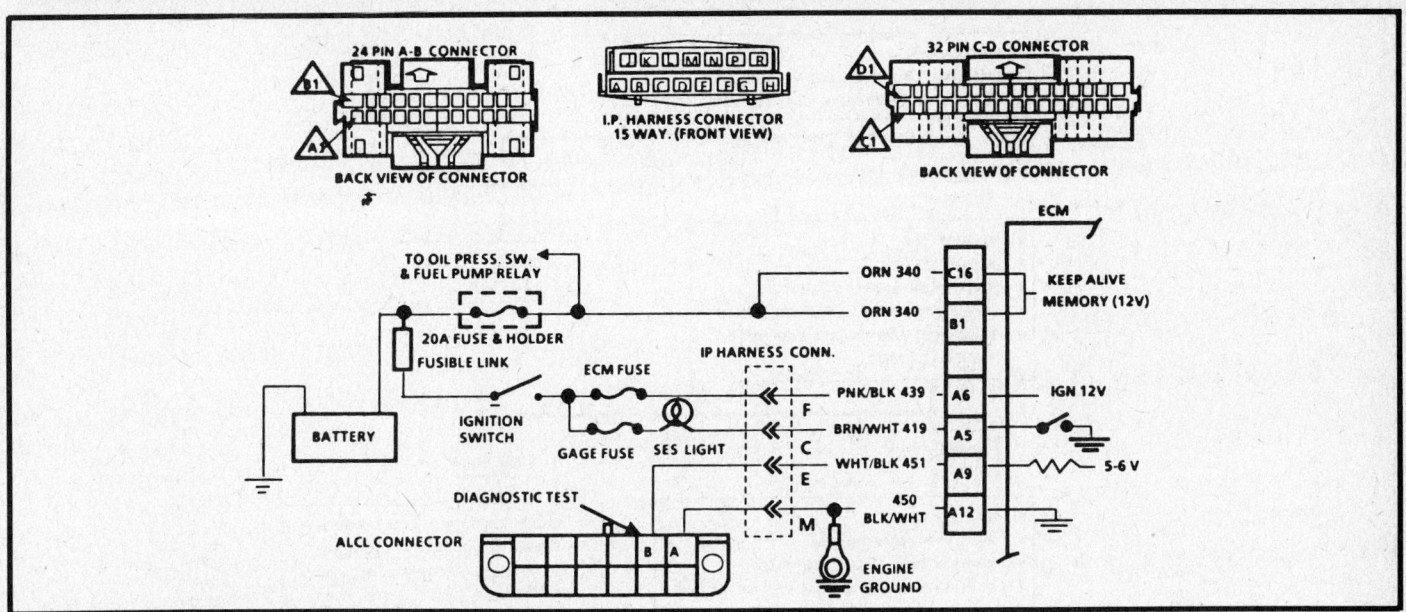

"SERVICE ENGINE SOON" wiring schematic

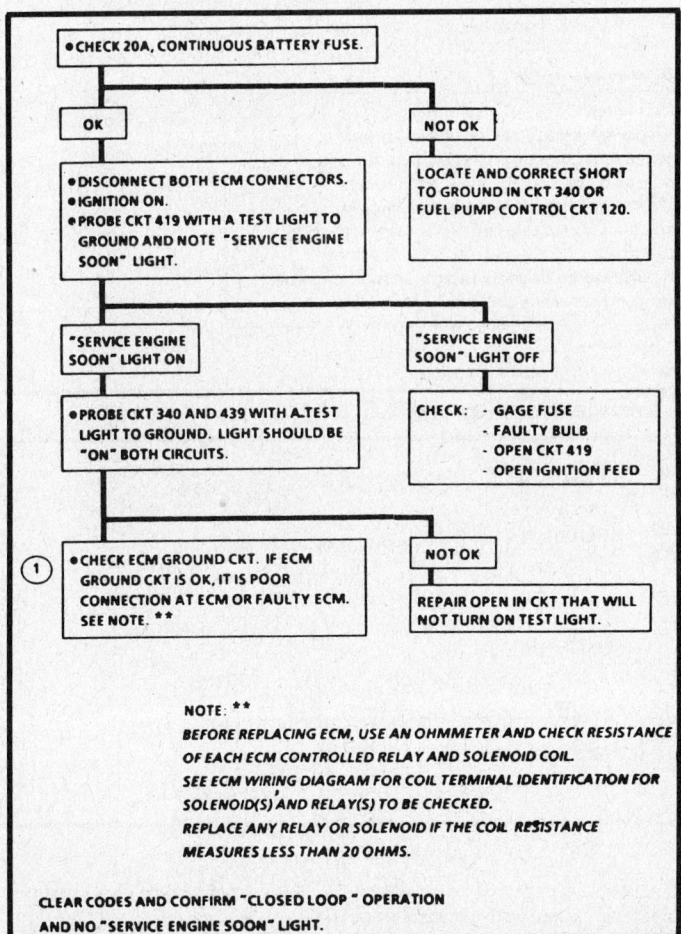

"SERVICE ENGINE SOON" lamp will not light—troubleshooting chart

5. The ECM will also send a 30" dwell signal to the M/C solenoid and energize all ECM controlled solenoids.
6. Pulse the idle speed motor in and out (if used). On fuel injected engines the idle air control valve will move back and forth or is fully extended depending on the engine family.
7. With the test lead terminal grounded and the engine running, the ECM will do the following:
   a. Will not flash any trouble codes if none are stored.
   b. Cause the EST to be set at a fixed spark advance.
   c. Take out the open loop timer, start-up enrichment, and blended enrichment.
   d. Send a 30" dwell to the M/C solenoid whenever the system is in open loop if not in the enrichment mode.

FIELD SERVICE MODE (FUEL INJECTED ENGINES)

If the diagnostic terminal is grounded with the engine running, the system will enter into the "field service mode". In this mode the "SERVICE ENGINE SOON" light will indicate whether the system is in Open or Closed Loop.
In Open loop the "SEVICE ENGINE SOON" light will flash two and one-half times per second. In the Closed loop the light will stay flash once per second. Also in Closed loop the light will stay OUT most of the time if the system is too lean and will stay On most of the time if the system is too rich.
In either case the "field service mode" check, which is a part of the diagnostic circuit check, will lead to the proper diagnosis. While the system is in the "field service mode" the ECm will be in the following mode:
1. The distributor will have a fixed spark advance.
2. New trouble codes can not be stored in the ECM.
3. The closed loop timer is bypassed.

CLEARING TROUBLE CODES

In order to clear the trouble codes from the ECM memory the battery voltage to the ECM has to be removed. The battery voltage to the ECM can be removed by disconnecting the ECM harness form the positive battery pigtail, ECM fuse or the ECM connector for at least ten seconds, with the ignition off.

nostic terminal and flashing the "SERVICE ENGINE SOON" light. Each trouble code will be flashed three times and then code "12" will be flashed again.

29-41

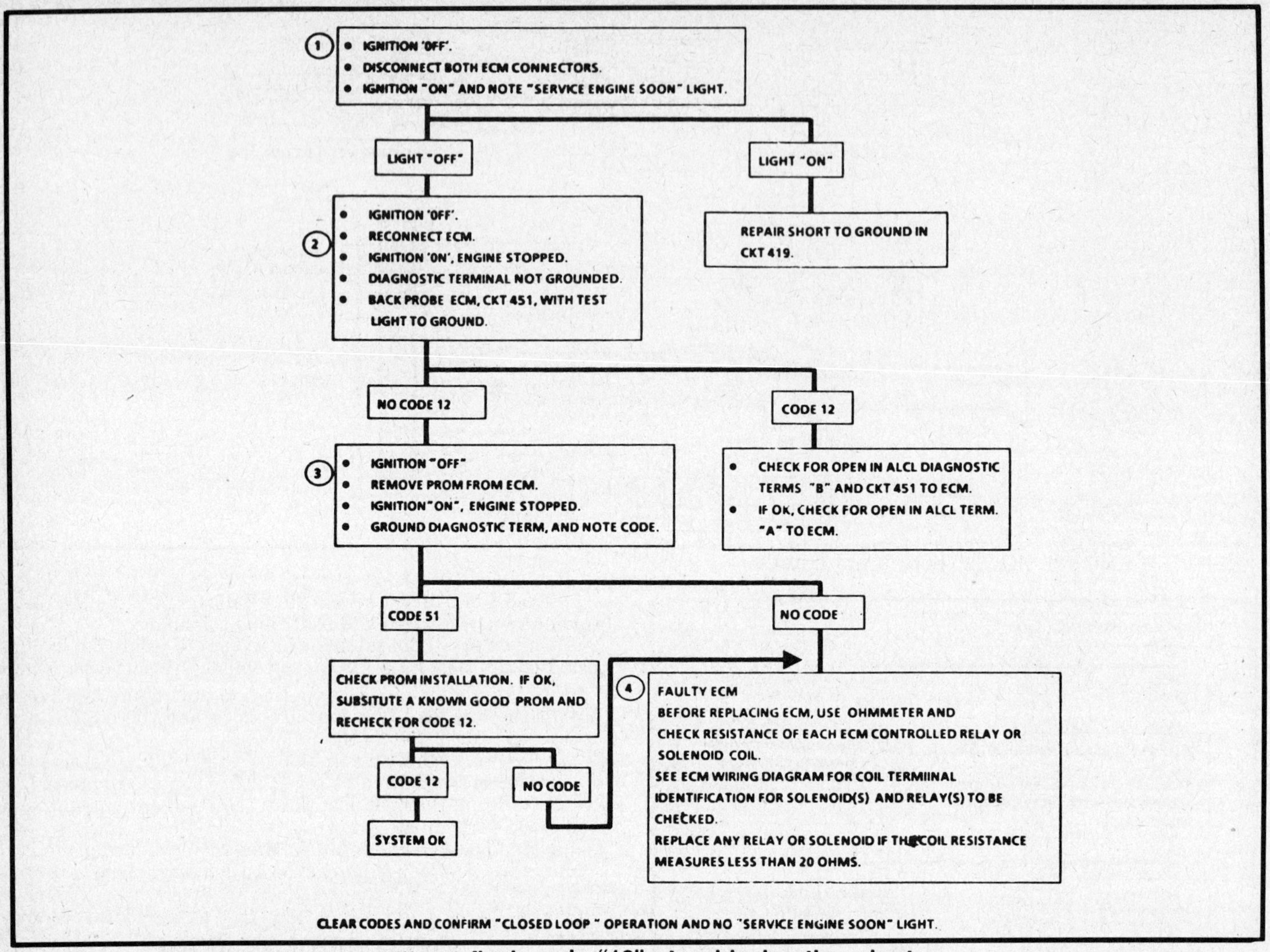

SECTION 29
ENGINE CONTROLS
GM—COMPUTER COMMAND CONTROL SYSTEM

"SERVICE ENGINE SOON" lamp will not flash code "12"—troubleshooting chart

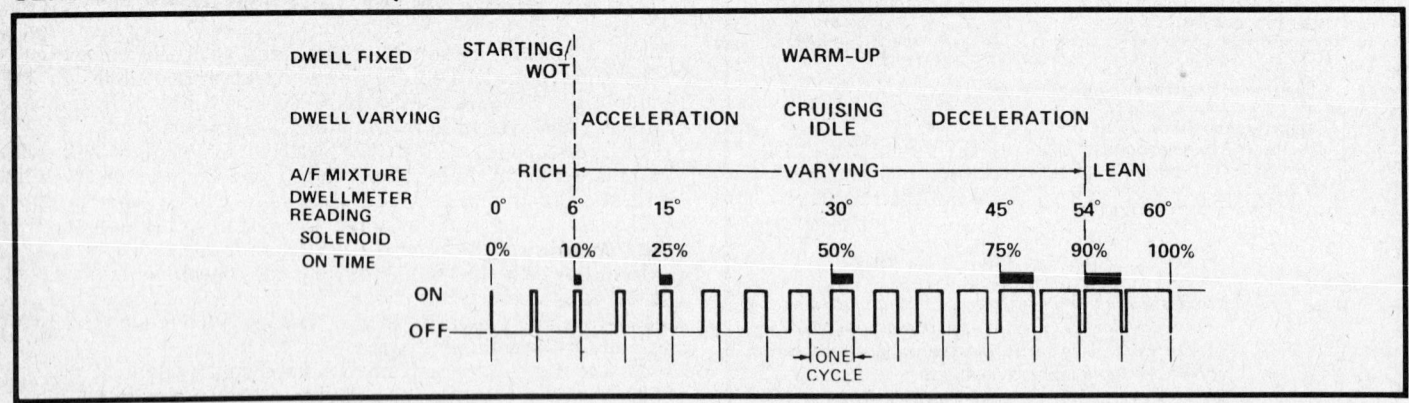

Analyzing dwellmeter readings

Trouble codes should be cleared after repairs have been completed on a problem.

Code Clearing Procedure
1983 DEFI AND DFI ENGINES

Use of an improper code clearing procedure following repairs may result in recurrence of the trouble code and illumination of the tell-tale indicator even though the problem has been corrected. To prevent misdiagnosis, the correct code clearing procedure must be followed exactly.

1. Enter the diagnostic mode by depressing the OFF and WARMER buttons on the ECC panel simultaneously until "..." appears.
2. Depress the OFF and HI buttons simultaneously. Hold until "0.0" or "00" appears.
3. When the ECC control panel displays "7. 0" or "70", turn the

29-42

ENGINE CONTROLS
GM—COMPUTER COMMAND CONTROL SYSTEM

SECTION 29

ignition off for at least 10 seconds before re-entering the diagnostic mode.

NOTE: Unnecessary ECM replacements may result if the above procedure is not followed exactly.

EXPLANATION OF TROUBLE CODES
GM C-4 AND CCC SYSTEMS
(Ground test lead or terminal AFTER engine is running.)

Trouble Code	Applicable System	Notes	Possible Problem Area
12	C-4, CCC		No tachometer or reference signal to computer (ECM). This code will only be present while a fault exists, and will not be stored if the problem is intermittent.
13	C-4, CCC		Oxygen sensor circuit. The engine must run for about five minutes (eighteen on C-4 equipped 231 cu in. V6) at part throttle (and under road load—CCC equipped cars) before this code will show.
13 & 14 (at same time)	C-4	Except Cadillac and 171 cu in. V6	See code 43.
13 & 43 (at same time)	C-4	Cadillac and 171 cu in. V6	See code 43.
14	C-4, CCC		Shorted coolant sensor circuit. The engine has to run 2 minutes before this code will show.
15	C-4, CCC		Open coolant sensor circuit. The engine has to operate for about five minutes (18 minutes for C-4 equipped 231 cu in. V6) at part throttle (some models) before this code will show.
21	C-4		Shorted wide open throttle switch and/or open closed-throttle switch circuit (when used).
	C-4, CCC		Throttle position sensor circuit. The engine must be run up to 10 seconds (25 seconds—CCC System) below 800 rpm before this code will show.
21 & 22 (at same time)	C-4		Grounded wide open throttle switch circuit (231 cu in. V6, 151 cu in. 4 cylinder).
22	C-4		Grounded closed throttle or wide open throttle switch circuit (231 cu in. V6, 151 cu in. 4 cylinder).
23	C-4, CCC		Open or grounded carburetor mixture control (M/C) solenoid circuit.
24	CCC		Vehicle speed sensor (VSS) circuit. The car must operate up to five minutes at road speed before this code will show.
32	C-4, CCC		Barometric pressure sensor (BARO) circuit output low.
32 & 55 (at same time)	C-4		Grounded +8V terminal or V(REF) terminal for barometric pressure sensor (BARO), or faulty ECM computer.
34	C-4	Except 1980 260 cu in. Cutlass	Manifold absolute pressure (MAP) sensor output high (after ten seconds and below 800 rpm).
34	CCC	Including 1980 260 cu in. Cutlass	Manifold absolute pressure (MAP) sensor circuit or vacuum sensor circuit. The engine must run up to five minutes below 800 RPM before this code will set.
35	CCC		Idle speed control (ISC) switch circuit shorted (over ½ throttle for over two seconds).
41	CCC		No distributor reference pulses to the ECM at specified engine vacuum. This code will store in memory.

29-43

SECTION 29: ENGINE CONTROLS
GM—COMPUTER COMMAND CONTROL SYSTEM

EXPLANATION OF TROUBLE CODES
GM C-4 AND CCC SYSTEMS
(Ground test lead or terminal AFTER engine is running.)

Trouble Code	Applicable System	Notes	Possible Problem Area
42	CCC		Electronic spark timing (EST) bypass circuit grounded.
43	C-4		Throttle position sensor adjustment (on some models, engine must run at part throttle up to ten seconds before this code will set).
44	C-4, CCC		Lean oxygen sensor indication. The engine must run up to five minutes in closed loop (oxygen sensor adjusting carburetor mixture), at part throttle and under road load (drive car) before this code will set.
44 & 55 (at same time)	C-4, CCC		Faulty oxygen sensor circuit.
45	C-4, CCC	Restricted air cleaner can cause code 45	Rich oxygen sensor system indication. The engine must run up to five minutes in closed loop (oxygen sensor adjusting carburetor mixture), at part throttle under road load before this code will set.
51	C-4, CCC		Faulty calibration unit (PROM) or improper PROM installation in electronic control module (ECM). It takes up to thirty seconds for this code to set.
52 & 53	C-4		"Check Engine" light off: Intermittent ECM computer problem. "Check Engine" light on: Faulty ECM computer (replace).
52	C-4, CCC		Faulty ECM computer.
53	CCC	Including 1980 260 cu in. Cutlass	Faulty ECM computer.
54	C-4, CCC		Faulty mixture control solenoid circuit and/or faulty ECM computer.
55	C-4	Except 1980 260 cu. in. Cutlass	Faulty oxygen sensor, open manifold absolute pressure sensor or faulty ECM computer (231 cu in. V6). Faulty throttle position sensor or ECM computer (except 231 cu. in. V6). Faulty ECM computer (151 cu in. 4 cylinder)
55	CCC	Including 1980 260 cu in. Cutlass	Grounded +8 volt supply (terminal 19 of ECM computer connector), grounded 5 volt reference (terminal 21 of ECM computer connector), faulty oxygen sensor circuit or faulty ECM computer.

ELECTRONIC TIMING CONTROLS

General Information

Before the development of computerized engine control systems, ignition timing advance has been regulated by mechanical weights which centrifugally varied the timing with engine speed (rpm), or vacuum advance devices which varied the timing according to throttle position (manifold vacuum). The electronic spark timing distributor replaces both the centrifugal and vacuum advance devices with an electronic control module which controls the ignition timing much more reliably and exactly. By monitoring engine operating conditions (such as rpm, load and temperature), the on-board computer is able to adjust the spark timing once each crankshaft revolution to the programmed setting for those instantaneous values and insure that the engine operates with peak efficiency at all times.

Under normal operating conditions, the on-board computer will control the spark advance. However, under certain operating conditions such as cranking or setting base timing, the dis-

ENGINE CONTROLS
GM—COMPUTER COMMAND CONTROL SYSTEM

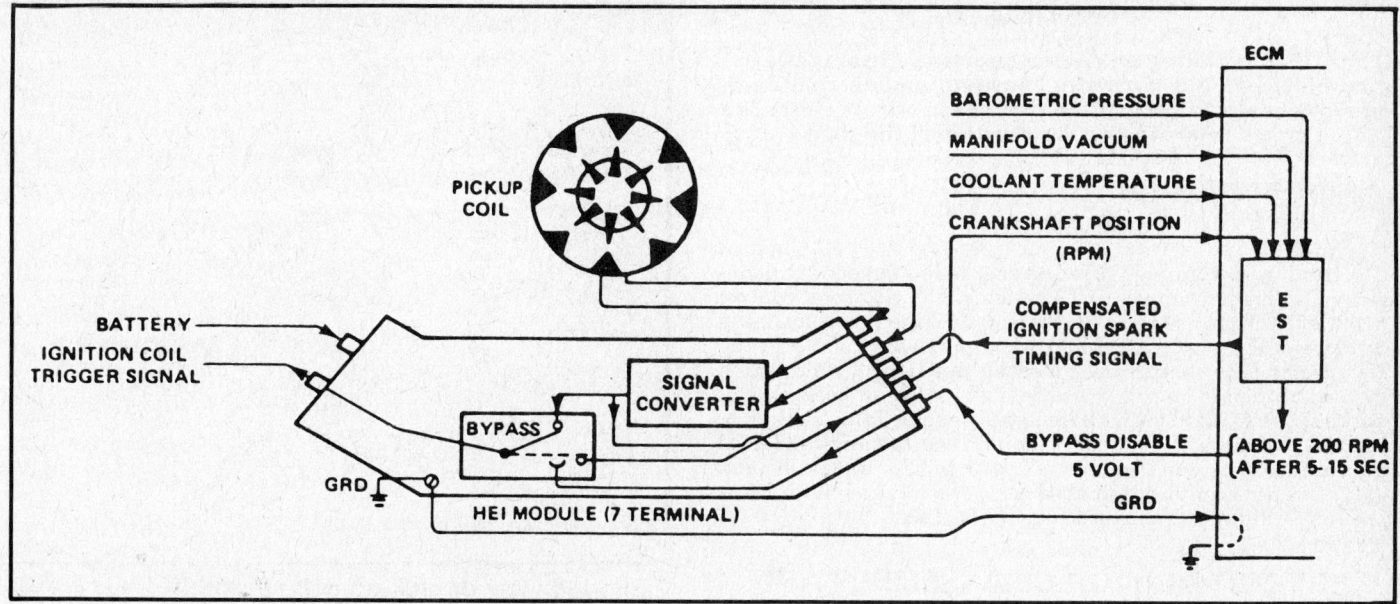

EST control circuit - 7 terminal module shown

tributor will operate in a bypass mode and timing will be maintained at a fixed, preset value programmed into the distributor module to aid engine starting. Some systems are programmed to advance or retard the spark timing according to engine temperature to meet different emission requirements for cold operation and some on-board computers incorporate a "limp home" mode that will allow the vehicle to be driven reasonably short distances should the timing control circuit fail.

Electronic spark timing has existed in different forms for a number of years, but all are part of some form of electronic ignition system. Distributors with electronic spark controls can be identified by their lack of vacuum connections and the absence of centrifugal flyweights. Since some early and late distributor control modules are similar in appearance, it is very important to carefully identify exactly which engine control system is being serviced in order to correctly diagnose problems and order replacement parts. The original General Motors HEI spark control module, for example, has a four terminal connector, while the later distributor modules have five or seven terminals. In addition to different calibrations, some spark control systems incorporate different functions and capabilities than earlier models, such as detonation sensors to retard the spark advance during periods of engine operation when detonation occurs. This is particularly critical for turbocharged engines where detonation under boost can cause serious engine damage.

GM Electronic Module Retard (EMR) System

This system is used on 1981 Chevrolet (engine code K) models. EMR is a spark control system which uses an HEI module with five terminals. The ignition timing is electronically retarded when the HEI module is grounded through the EMR vacuum switch on all except California models. On California engines, the EMR module is controlled by the C4 system electronic control module (ECM). EMR retards the timing about 10 degrees during engine warm-up (coolant below 120 degrees F), but operates like a standard HEI module the rest of the time.

On California models, the timing is retarded only when the coolant is between 66–130 degrees F, with the throttle open position below 45% and the engine speed above 400 rpm. When the retard circuit is open, there is no delay and the distributor fires the spark plugs as controlled by engine speed and vacuum. If the EMR-HEI module is removed and/or replaced for any reason, the ignition timing must be checked and set to specifications.

GM Electronic Spark Control (ESC) System

This modified spark control system is used on turbocharged engines to control engine detonation by automatically retarding ignition timing during periods of engine operation when detonation occurs. 1983 Chevrolet and Buick V6 and Pontiac V8 turbo engines use an HEI/EST/ESC system. The ESC system consists of a detonation sensor, controller and HEI distributor.

The intake manifold transmits the vibrations caused by detonation to the sensor mounting location. The sensor detects the presence and intensity of detonation and feeds this information to the controller which evaluates the sensor signal and sends a command signal to the distributor to adjust timing. The HEI distributor has a modified electronic module which responds to signals from the controller and will retard timing up to 15 degrees to minimize detonation levels, if necessary.

Loss of the ESC knock sensor signal or loss of the ground at the ESC module terminal D would cause the ECM to control the ESC as if no detonation were occurring; no timing retard would occur and spark knock would become severe under heavy engine load conditions. Loss of the ESC signal to the ECM would cause the ECM to constantly retard the spark timing, resulting in sluggish performance and causing a trouble code 43 to be set in the ECM memory. Code 43 indicates that the ECM terminal 4 (white connector) is receiving less than 6 volts for a 4 second period with the engine running. This is circuit 485, which normally provides a 6–16 volt signal from the ESC module to the ECM. When no code 43 is present, but the ESC is suspect as a cause of excessive spark knock, perform the ESC test procedures to check the system function.

NOTE: A slight amount of engine knock is normal on vehicles equipped with this system.

SECTION 29

ENGINE CONTROLS
GM—COMPUTER COMMAND CONTROL SYSTEM

TESTING

NOTE: Simulating an engine knock by tapping the engine block should normally cause an engine rpm drop due to retarded timing. If the rpm doesn't drop, either the timing is not retarding or is retarded all the time.

GM Electronic Spark Timing (EST) System

Electronic spark timing is used on engines equipped with Computer Command Control (CCC) systems. The electronic control module (ECM) is used to advance or retard the ignition timing in place of the mechanical and vacuum advance units in the distributor. The system uses a seven pin HEI module which converts the pick-up coil signal into a crankshaft position signal that the ECM modifies to advance or retard the spark timing. Early Computer Command Control engines and 1982 CCC minimum function systems do not use EST. For all testing and diagnosis procedures not covered here, or for more information, see the Computer Command Control Section.

EST DISTRIBUTOR DISASSEMBLY AND TEST

1. A 6 cyl. EST distributor with coil-in-cap is illustrated.
2. Detach the wiring connector from the cap, as shown.
3. Turn four latches and remove the cap and coil assembly from the lower housing.
4. Connect the ohmmeter, Test 1.
5. The reading should be zero or nearly zero. If not, replace the coil, Step 8.
6. Connect the ohmmeter both ways, Test 2. Use the high scale. Replace the coil only if both readings are infinite, Step 8.
7. If the coil is good, go to Step 13.
8. Remove the ignition coil attaching screws and lift the coil with the leads from the cap.
9. Remove the ignition coil arc seal.
10. Clean with a soft cloth and inspect the cap for defects. Replace, if needed.
11. Assemble the new coil and cover to cap.
12. On all distributors, remove the rotor and pickup coil leads form the module.
13. Connect the ohmmeter Test 1 and then Test 2.
14. If the vacuum unit is used, connect the vacuum source to the vacuum unit. Replace the unit if inoperative. Observe the ohmmeter throughout the vacuum range. Flex the leads by hand without vacuum to check for intermittent opens.
15. Test 1 should read infinite at all times. Test 2 should read steady at one value within 500–1,500 ohm range.

NOTE: The ohmmeter may deflect if the operating vacuum unit causes the teeth to align. This is not a defect.

16. If the pickup coil is defective, go to Step 18. If okay, go to Step 23.
17. Mark the distributor shaft and gear so they can be reassembled in the same position.
18. Drive out the roll pin.
19. Remove the gear and pull the shaft assembly from the distributor.
20. Remove the three attaching screws and remove the magnetic shield.
21. Remove the retaining ring. Remove the pickup coil magnet and pole piece.
22. Remove the two module attaching screws and the capacitor attaching screw. Lift the module, capacitor and harness assembly from the base.
23. Disconnect the wiring harness from the module.

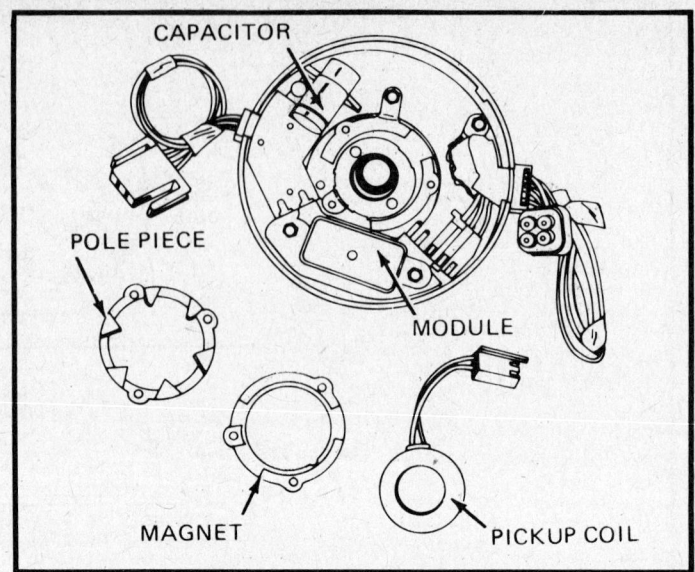

Exploded view of pick-up coil assembly

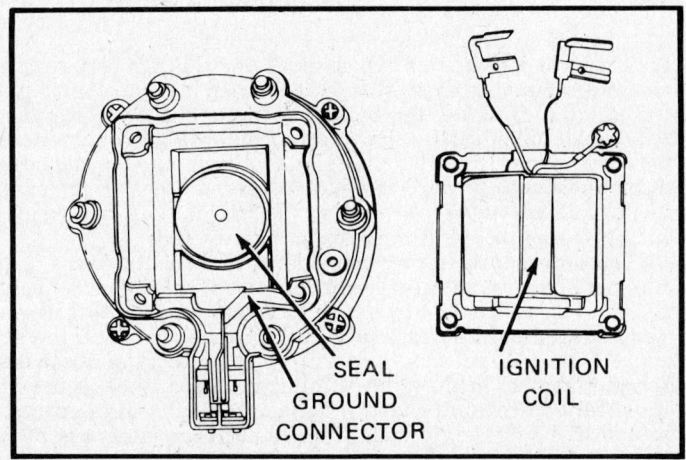

Ignition coil separation from distribution cap on HEI system

24. Check the module with an approved module tester.
25. Install the module, wiring harness and capacitor assembly. Use silicone lubricant on the housing under the module.
26. Install the pickup coil assembly, shaft and gear.
27. Spin the shaft and, if used, operate the vacuum unit to insure that the teeth do not touch. To eliminate contact, loosen the three pickup screws. Then retighten and check for contact.
28. Assemble the rotor, cap assembly and attach wiring harness to cap.

Component R&R

DISTRIBUTOR

Removal and Replacement

1. Disconnect the ignition switch battery feed wire and the tachometer lead (if equipped) from the distributor cap. Also release the coil connectors from the cap. (Do not use a screwdriver or tool to release the locking tabs.)
2. Remove the distributor cap by turning the four latches counterclockwise. Move the cap out of the way. If necessary to remove the secondary wires from the cap, release the wire har-

ENGINE CONTROLS
GM—COMPUTER COMMAND CONTROL SYSTEM

ness latches and remove the wiring harness retainer. The spark plug wire numbers are indicated on the retainer.

3. Remove the distributor clamp screw and hold-down clamp.

4. Note the position of the rotor. Then pull the distributor up until the rotor just stops turning counterclockwise. Again note the position of the rotor. To insure correct timing of the distributor, the distributor must be installed with the rotor correctly positioned.

MODULE

NOTE: It is not necessary to remove the distributor from car.

Removal and Installation

1. Remove the distributor cap and rotor.
2. Disconnect the two pick-up leads from the module. (Observe the color code on the leads, as these cannot be interchanged.)
3. Remove the two module attaching screws.
4. Remove the module from the distributor base and remove the two wire connectors. Do not wipe grease from the module of distributor base if the same module is to be replaced. If a new module is to be installed, a package of silicone lubricant will be included with it. Spread the lubricant on the metal face of the module and on the distributor base where the module seats. This lubricant is important as it aids heat transfer for module cooling.
5. Installation is the reverse of removal.

PICK-UP COIL

Removal and Installation

1. Remove the distributor from the car.
2. Drive out the roll pin and remove the gear.
3. Remove the distributor shaft with rotor.
4. Remove the thin C-washer on top of the pickup coil assembly. Remove the pickup coil leads from the module and remove the pickup coil assembly. (Do not remove the three screws.)
5. Installation is the reverse of removal.

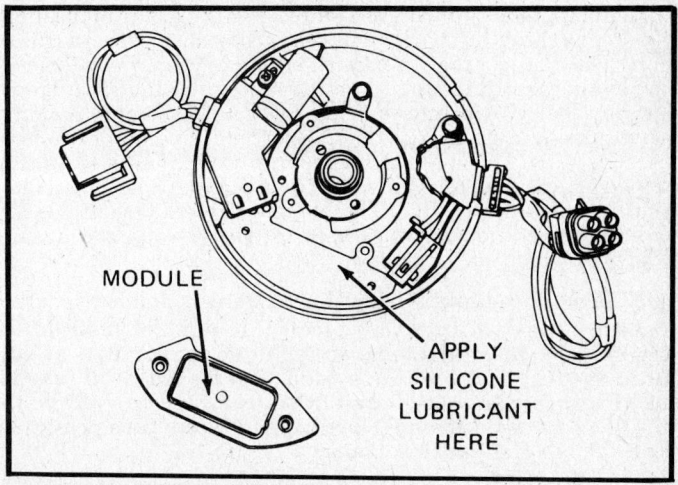

Installing module into HEI distributor - typical

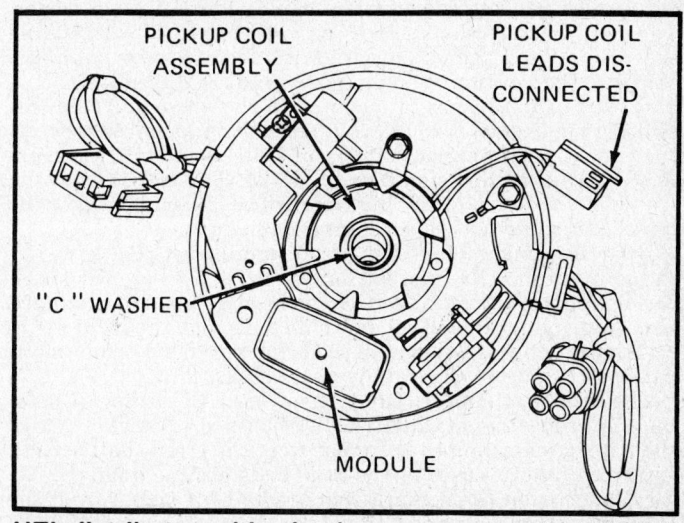

HEI distributor with aluminum non-magnetic shield removed

GM COMPUTER CONTROLLED COIL IGNITION (C3I) SYSTEM

GENERAL INFORMATION

The C3I system eliminates the need for a distributor to control the flow of current between the battery and spark plugs. In its place, an electromagnetic sensor consisting of a Hall effect switch, magnet and interruptor ring. The gear on the shaft of this sensor is connected directly to the camshaft gear. At the heart of this system is an electronic coil module that replaces the distributor and coil used on previous electronic ignition systems. A microprocessor within the module receives and processes signals from the crankshaft and camshaft and, by way of three interconnecting coils, distributes high voltage current to the spark plugs.

Electromagnetic sensors take position readings from the crankshaft and camshaft, then transmit these readings to the electronics package. Using the information relayed from the electronic control module, the microprocessor then selects and sequentially triggers each of the three interconnecting coils to fire the spark plugs at the proper crankshaft position. An electronic spark control (ESC) is incorporated into the system to adjust the spark timing according to engine load and operating conditions. This closed loop system includes a piezoelectronic sensor which transforms engine detonation vibrations into an electrical signal which is then fed to the electronic control module.

The ECM uses this and other information on engine speed (rpm), intake air mass, coolant temperature and converter clutch operation to adjust the spark advance for the most efficient performance with the lowest emissions. Because of this feature, there is no timing adjustment or regular maintenance required aside from periodic replacement of the spark plugs.

System Operation

The C3I system uses a waste spark method of spark distribu-

SECTION 29 — ENGINE CONTROLS
GM — COMPUTER CONTROLLED COIL IGNITION SYSTEM (C3I SYSTEM)

tion. Companion cylinders are paired (1–4, 5–2, 3–6 on the 3.8L V6 engine) and the spark occurs simultaneously in both cylinders. The cylinder on the exhaust stroke requires very little of the available voltage to arc, so the remaining high voltage is used by the cylinder in the firing position (TDC/compression). This same process is repeated when the companion cylinders reverse roles. There are three separate coils combined in the sealed coil/module assembly on the V6 engine. Spark distribution is synchronized by a signal from the crankshaft sensor which the ignition modules uses to trigger each coil at the proper time.

NOTE: The signal from the camshaft sensor is also used by the fuel injection electronic control module to trigger the fuel injectors, so a failed sensor can affect both the fuel and ignition system. A 7.5 amp ECM fuse is used to provide a low current source for the voltage to the sensors and internal circuitry; a 10 amp fuse provides voltage for the ignition coils.

This system also incorporates an electronic spark timing (EST) system similar to other Delco distributor ignition systems. All connectors are lettered to make circuit identification easier. Terminal C (crankshaft sensor) provides the ECM with engine speed (rpm) and crankshaft position information by passing a signal to the ignition module and then to ECM terminal B5. A plate with three vanes is mounted to the harmonic balancer and the vanes pass through slots in the crankshaft sensor. As the vanes pass through the slots, the Hall effect switch triggers and sends a voltage signal to the ECM. The signal from the Hall effect switch is either high or low and is used to trigger the ignition module for proper engine timing.

Both the camshaft and crankshaft signal must be received by the ignition module in order for the ECM to take over spark timing control from the ignition module. An open or grounded circuit (terminal B) will set a trouble code 42 in the ECM memory and the engine will run in the bypass or "limp home" mode with the timing fixed at 10 degrees BTDC.

The EST terminal A circuit triggers the HEI module by passing a reference signal which the ECM uses to advance or retard the timing according to the input from the crankshaft sensor. Cam terminal E is used by the ECM to determine when the No. 1 cylinder is on the compression stroke by a signal from the Hall effect camshaft position sensor. A loss of the cam signal will store a trouble code 41 if the engine is running and a loss of sensor signal during cranking will prevent the engine from starting.

The electronic control module uses information from the coolant sensor and mass air flow sensor in addition to engine speed to calculate the spark advance to allow more spark advance when the engine is cold or under minimum load. The ECM will retard the timing when the engine is hot or under a heavy load. When the system is running on the HEI module, it grounds the electronic spark timing signal. If the ECM detects voltage in the bypass circuit through a loss of ground for the EST signal, it sets a trouble code 42 and will not switch into the EST mode. When the engine reaches 400 rpm, the ECM applies 5 volts to the bypass circuit and the EST voltage will vary. If the bypass circuit is open, the ECM will store a trouble code 42.

IGNITION COIL
Removal and Installation

1. Disconnect the negative battery cable.
2. Remove the spark plug wires.
3. Remove the Torx screws holding the coil to the ignition module.
4. Tilt the coil assembly to the rear and remove the coil to module connectors.
5. Remove the coil assembly.
6. Installation is the reverse of removal.

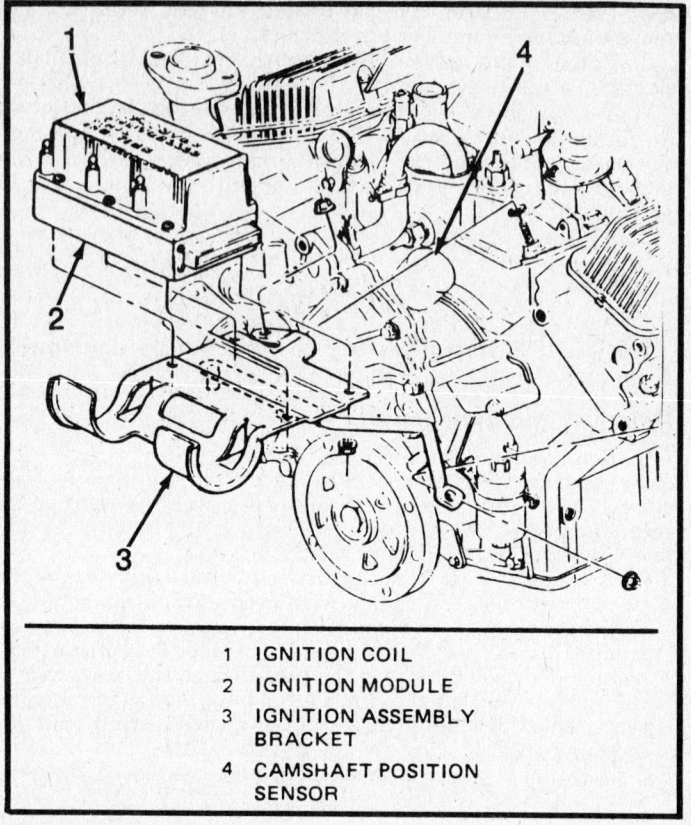

1 IGNITION COIL
2 IGNITION MODULE
3 IGNITION ASSEMBLY BRACKET
4 CAMSHAFT POSITION SENSOR

C3I Ignition coil

IGNITION MODULE
Removal and Installation

1. Disconnect the negative battery cable.
2. Disconnect the 14-pin connector at the ignition module.
3. Remove the spark plug wires at the coil assembly.
4. Remove the nuts and washers securing the ignition module assembly to the mounting bracket.
5. Remove the Torx screws securing the ignition module to the coil.
6. Tilt the coil and disconnect the coil to module connectors.
7. Separate the coil and module.
8. Installation is the reverse of removal.

CRANKSHAFT SENSOR
Removal and Installation

NOTE: It is not necessary to remove the sensor bracket.

1. Disconnect the negative battery cable.
2. Disconnect the sensor 3-way connector.
3. Raise the vehicle and support it safely.
4. Rotate the harmonic balancer so the slot in the disc is aligned with the sensor.
5. Loosen the sensor training bolt.
6. Slide the sensor outboard and remove through the notch in the sensor housing.
7. Install the new sensor in the housing and rotate the harmonic balancer so that the disc is positioned in the sensor.
8. Adjust the sensor so that there is an equal distance on each side of the disc. There should be approximately 0.030 in. (0.76 mm) clearance between the disc and the sensor.

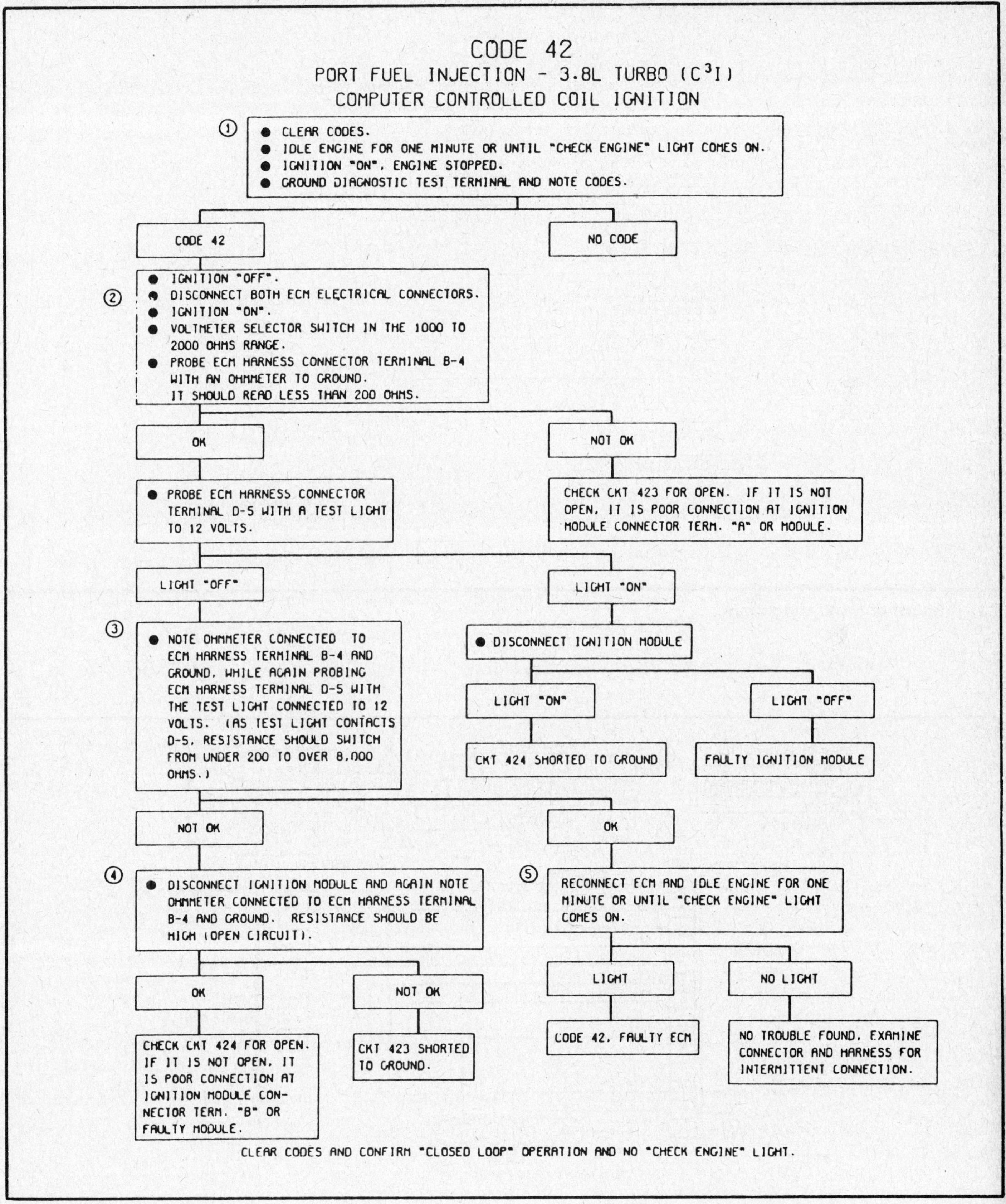

ENGINE CONTROLS
GM – COMPUTER CONTROLLED COIL IGNITION SYSTEM (C3I SYSTEM)

SECTION 29

CODE 42
PORT FUEL INJECTION – 3.8L TURBO (C³I)
COMPUTER CONTROLLED COIL IGNITION

①
- CLEAR CODES.
- IDLE ENGINE FOR ONE MINUTE OR UNTIL "CHECK ENGINE" LIGHT COMES ON.
- IGNITION "ON", ENGINE STOPPED.
- GROUND DIAGNOSTIC TEST TERMINAL AND NOTE CODES.

CODE 42 →

②
- IGNITION "OFF".
- DISCONNECT BOTH ECM ELECTRICAL CONNECTORS.
- IGNITION "ON".
- VOLTMETER SELECTOR SWITCH IN THE 1000 TO 2000 OHMS RANGE.
- PROBE ECM HARNESS CONNECTOR TERMINAL B-4 WITH AN OHMMETER TO GROUND. IT SHOULD READ LESS THAN 200 OHMS.

OK:
- PROBE ECM HARNESS CONNECTOR TERMINAL D-5 WITH A TEST LIGHT TO 12 VOLTS.

NOT OK:
- CHECK CKT 423 FOR OPEN. IF IT IS NOT OPEN, IT IS POOR CONNECTION AT IGNITION MODULE CONNECTOR TERM. "A" OR MODULE.

LIGHT "OFF":

③
- NOTE OHMMETER CONNECTED TO ECM HARNESS TERMINAL B-4 AND GROUND, WHILE AGAIN PROBING ECM HARNESS TERMINAL D-5 WITH THE TEST LIGHT CONNECTED TO 12 VOLTS. (AS TEST LIGHT CONTACTS D-5, RESISTANCE SHOULD SWITCH FROM UNDER 200 TO OVER 8,000 OHMS.)

LIGHT "ON":
- DISCONNECT IGNITION MODULE

 - **LIGHT "ON":** CKT 424 SHORTED TO GROUND
 - **LIGHT "OFF":** FAULTY IGNITION MODULE

NOT OK:

④
- DISCONNECT IGNITION MODULE AND AGAIN NOTE OHMMETER CONNECTED TO ECM HARNESS TERMINAL B-4 AND GROUND. RESISTANCE SHOULD BE HIGH (OPEN CIRCUIT).

 - **OK:** CHECK CKT 424 FOR OPEN. IF IT IS NOT OPEN, IT IS POOR CONNECTION AT IGNITION MODULE CONNECTOR TERM. "B" OR FAULTY MODULE.
 - **NOT OK:** CKT 423 SHORTED TO GROUND.

OK:

⑤ RECONNECT ECM AND IDLE ENGINE FOR ONE MINUTE OR UNTIL "CHECK ENGINE" LIGHT COMES ON.

 - **LIGHT:** CODE 42, FAULTY ECM
 - **NO LIGHT:** NO TROUBLE FOUND, EXAMINE CONNECTOR AND HARNESS FOR INTERMITTENT CONNECTION.

NO CODE (from step 1)

CLEAR CODES AND CONFIRM "CLOSED LOOP" OPERATION AND NO "CHECK ENGINE" LIGHT.

C3I Ignition code 42 diagnosis

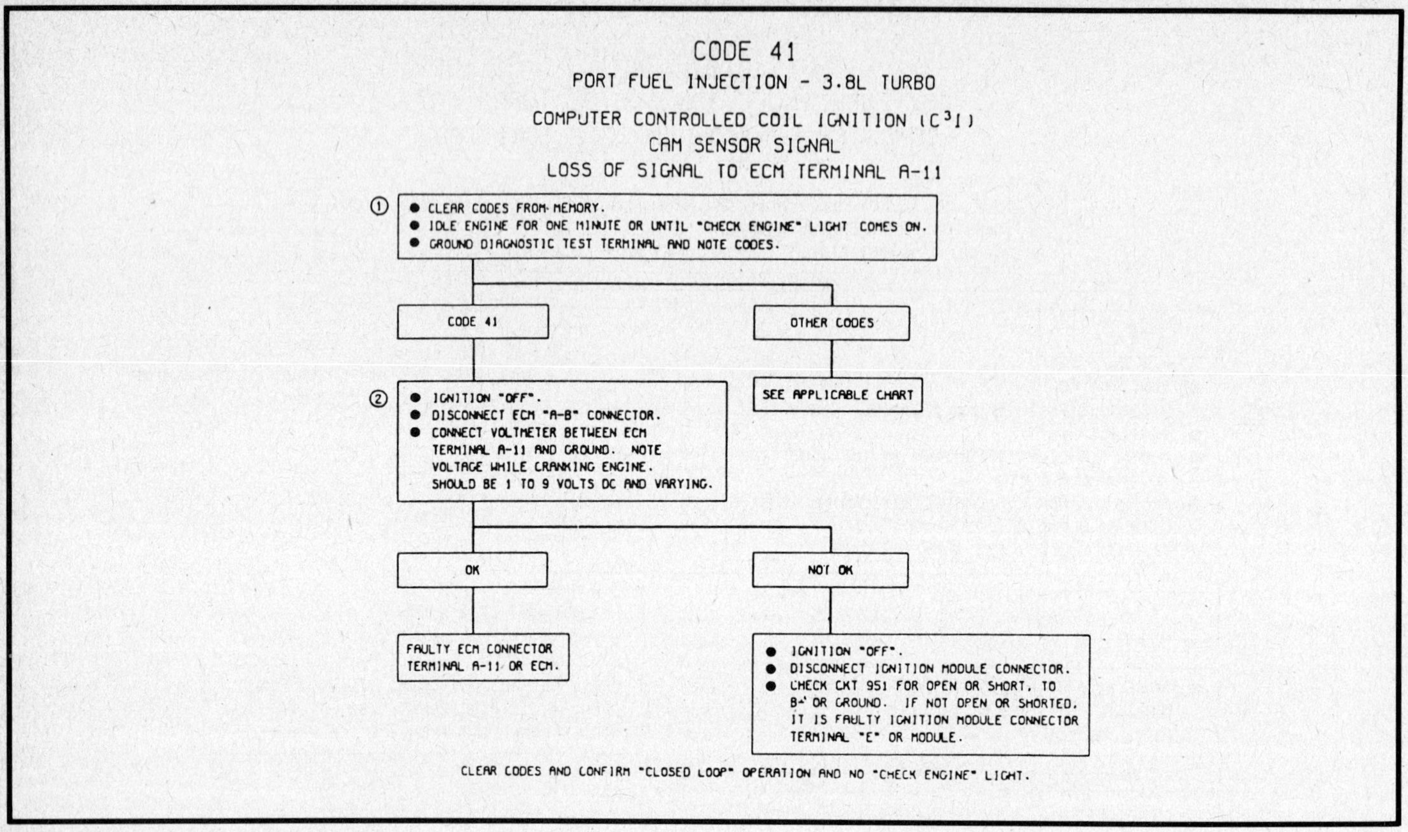

SECTION 29
ENGINE CONTROLS
GM—COMPUTER CONTROLLED COIL IGNITION SYSTEM (C3I SYSTEM)

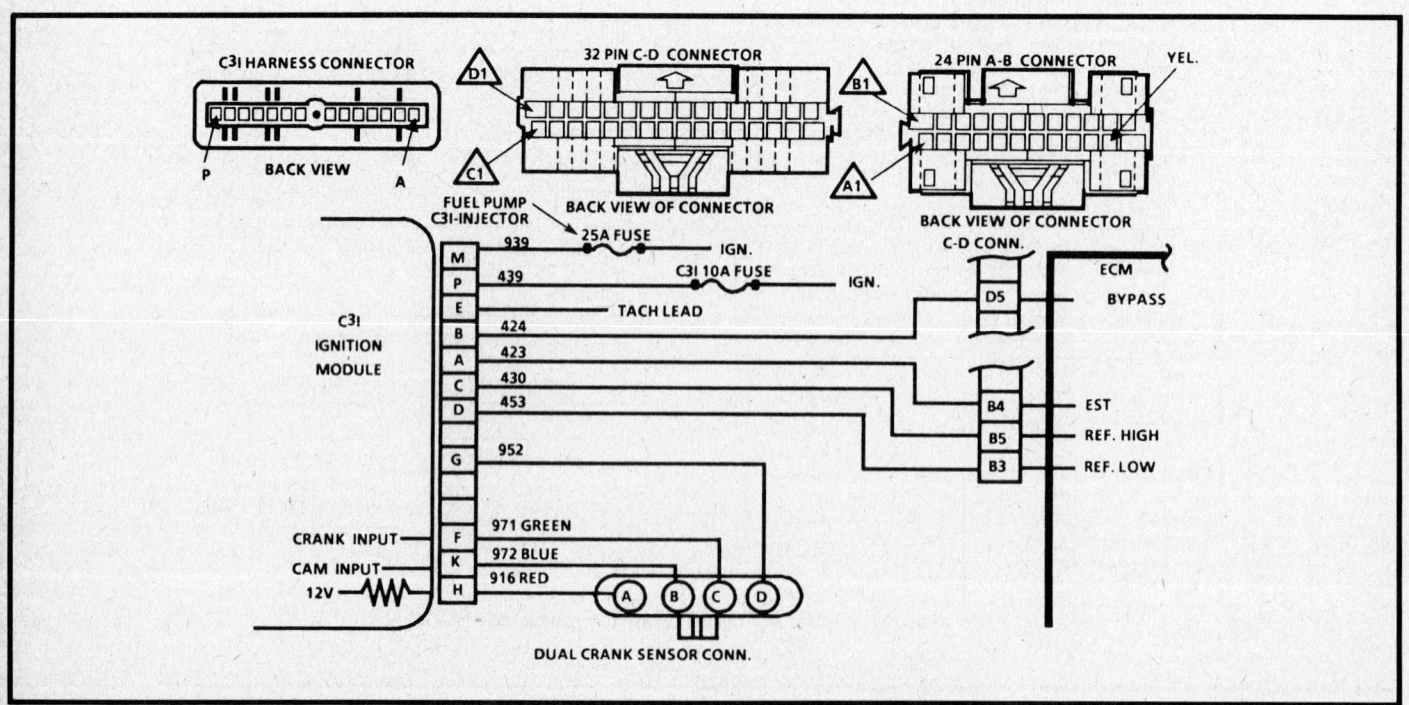

C31 Ignition code 41 diagnosis

C31 Ignition code 42 wiring diagram

ENGINE CONTROLS
GM—COMPUTER CONTROLLED COIL IGNITION SYSTEM (C3I SYSTEM)

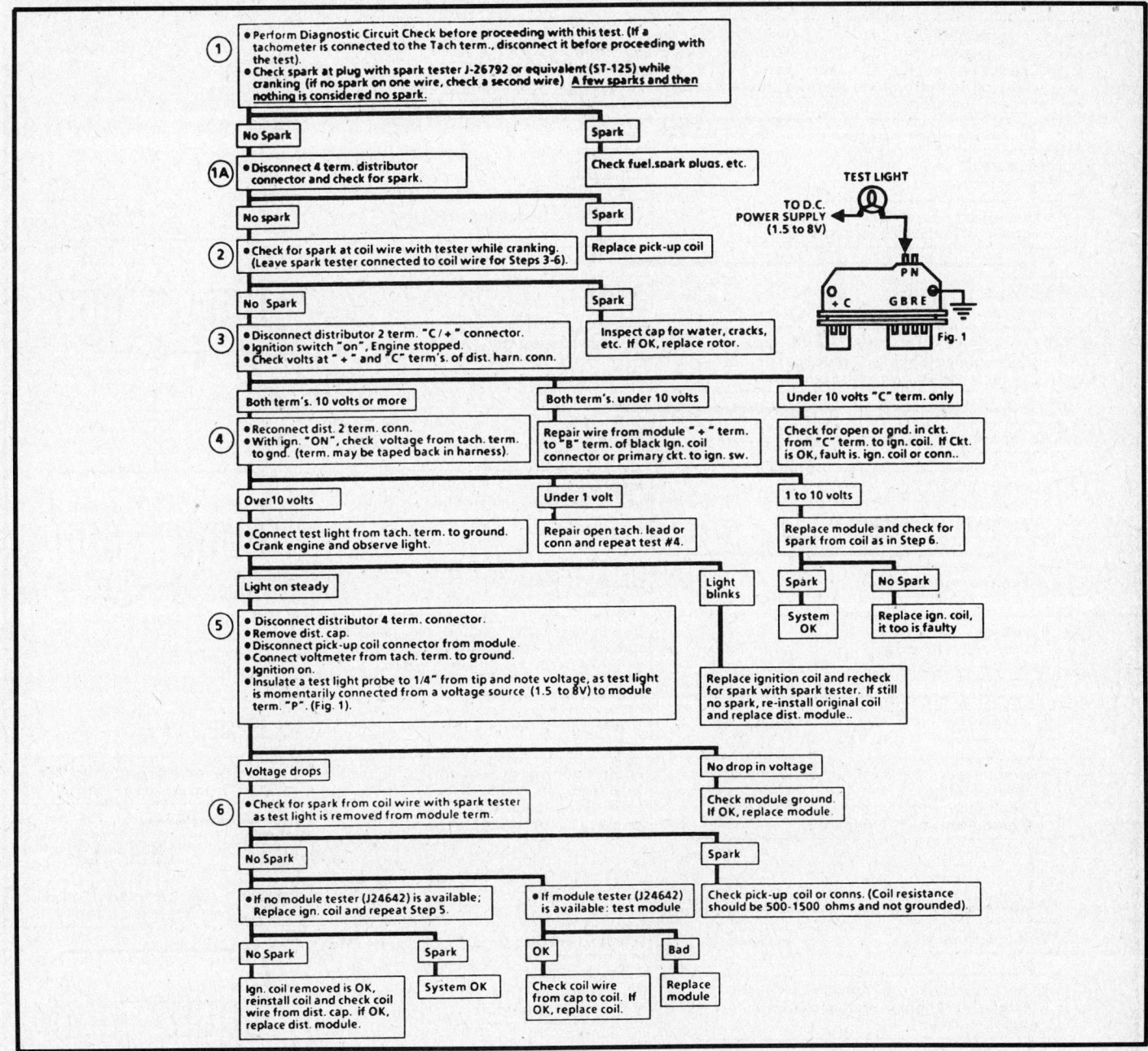

Ignition system check (remote coil/sealed module connector distributor) 2.0L and 2.5L TBI engines

9. Tighten the retaining bolt and recheck the clearance.
10. Install remaining components in the reverse order of removal.

CAMSHAFT POSITION SENSOR

Removal and Installation

NOTE: If only the camshaft sensor is being replaced, it is not necessary to remove the entire assembly. The sensor is replaceable separately.

1. Disconnect the negative battery cable.
2. Disconnect the ignition module 14-pin connector.
3. Remove the spark plug wires at the coil assembly.
4. Remove the ignition module bracket assembly.

5. Disconnect the sensor 3-way connector.
6. Remove the sensor mounting screws, then remove the sensor.
7. Installation is the reverse of removal.

CAMSHAFT POSITION SENSOR DRIVE ASSEMBLY

Removal and Installation

1. Follow steps 1-6 of the cam sensor removal procedure. Note the position of the slot in the rotating vane.
2. Remove the bolt securing the drive assembly to the engine.
3. Remove the drive assembly.

SECTION 29
ENGINE CONTROLS
GM – COMPUTER CONTROLLED COIL IGNITION SYSTEM (C3I SYSTEM)

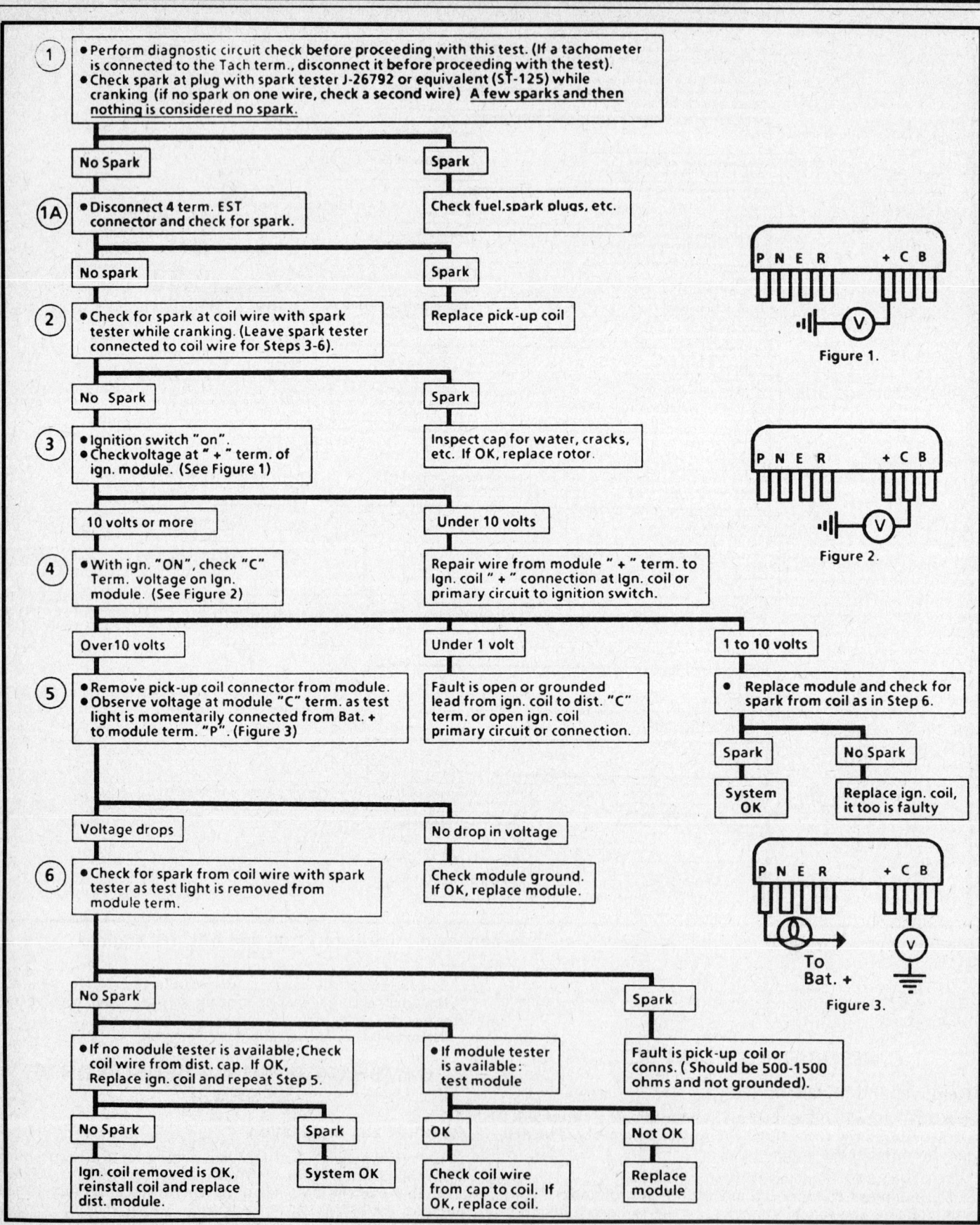

Ignition system check (remote coil) 1.8L TBI engine

ENGINE CONTROLS 29
GM—COMPUTER CONTROLLED COIL IGNITION SYSTEM (C3I SYSTEM)

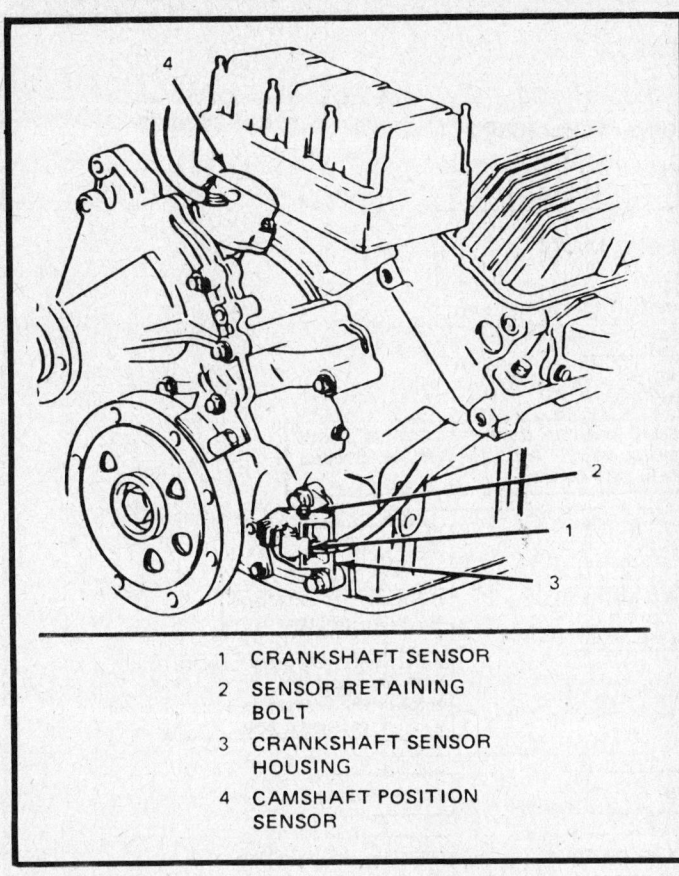

1. CRANKSHAFT SENSOR
2. SENSOR RETAINING BOLT
3. CRANKSHAFT SENSOR HOUSING
4. CAMSHAFT POSITION SENSOR

C3I crankshaft sensor location (3.8L Turbo)

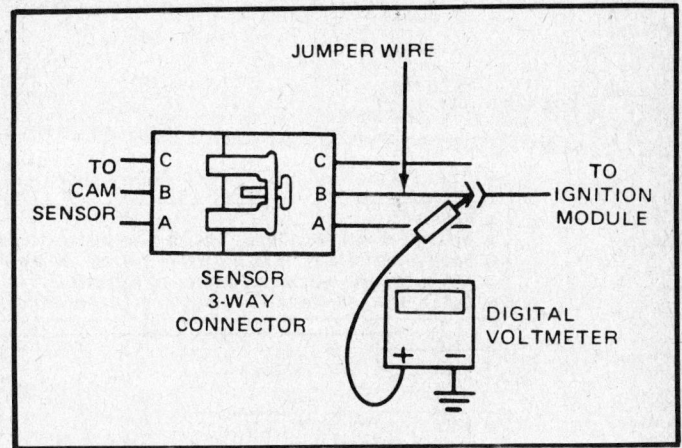

Adjusting the crankshaft sensor

4. Install the drive assembly with the slot in the vane. Install mounting bolt.
5. Install the camshaft sensor.
6. Rotate the engine to set the No. 1 cylinder at TDC/compression.
7. Mark the harmonic balancer and rotate the engine to 25 degrees after top dead center.
8. Remove the plug wires from the coil assembly.
9. Using weatherpack removal tool J–28742–A, or equivalent, remove terminal B of the sensor 3–way connector on the module side.
10. Probe terminal B by installing a jumper and reconnecting the wire removed to the jumper wire.
11. Connect a voltmeter between the jumper wire and ground.

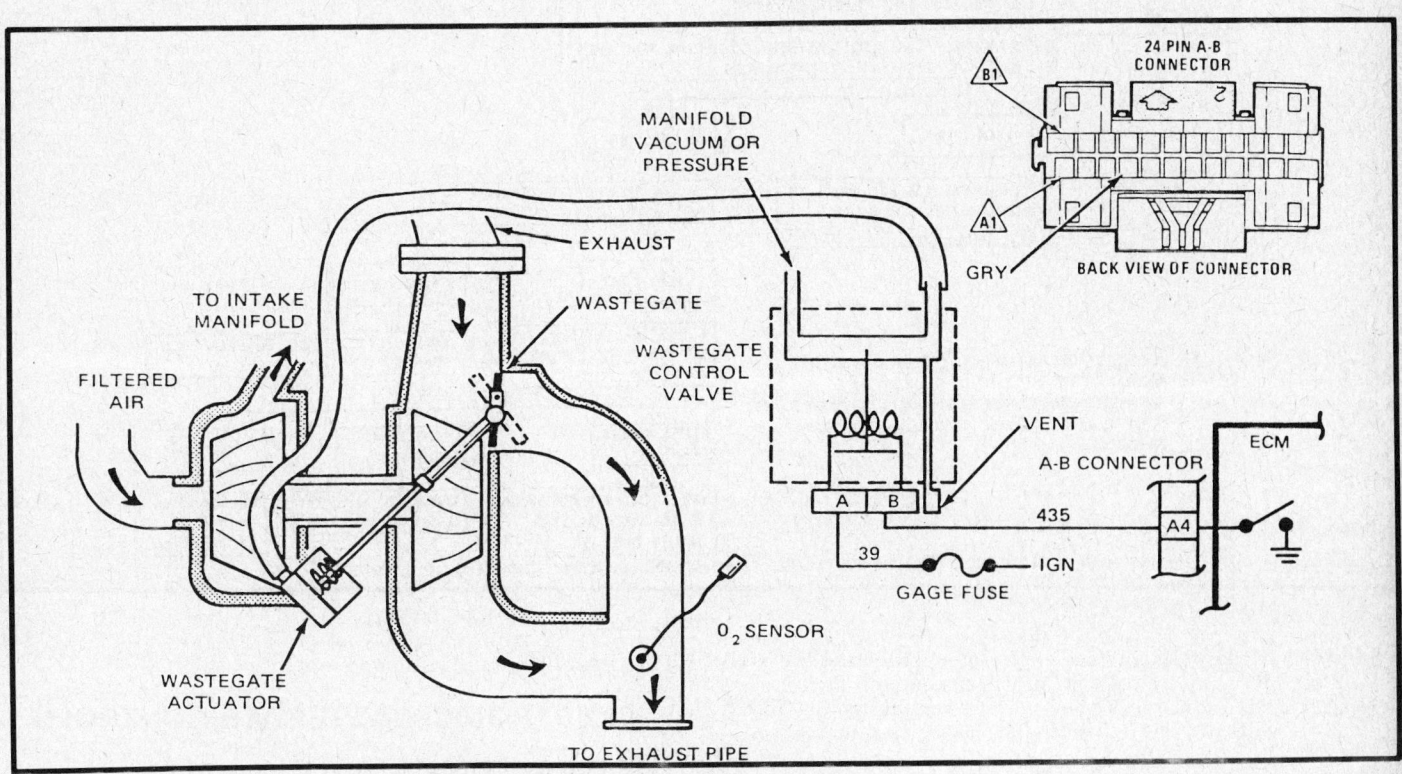

Wiring diagram of electronic wastegate system - 1.8L engine shown

29-53

SECTION 29: ENGINE CONTROLS
GM—COMPUTER CONTROLLED COIL IGNITION SYSTEM (C3I SYSTEM)

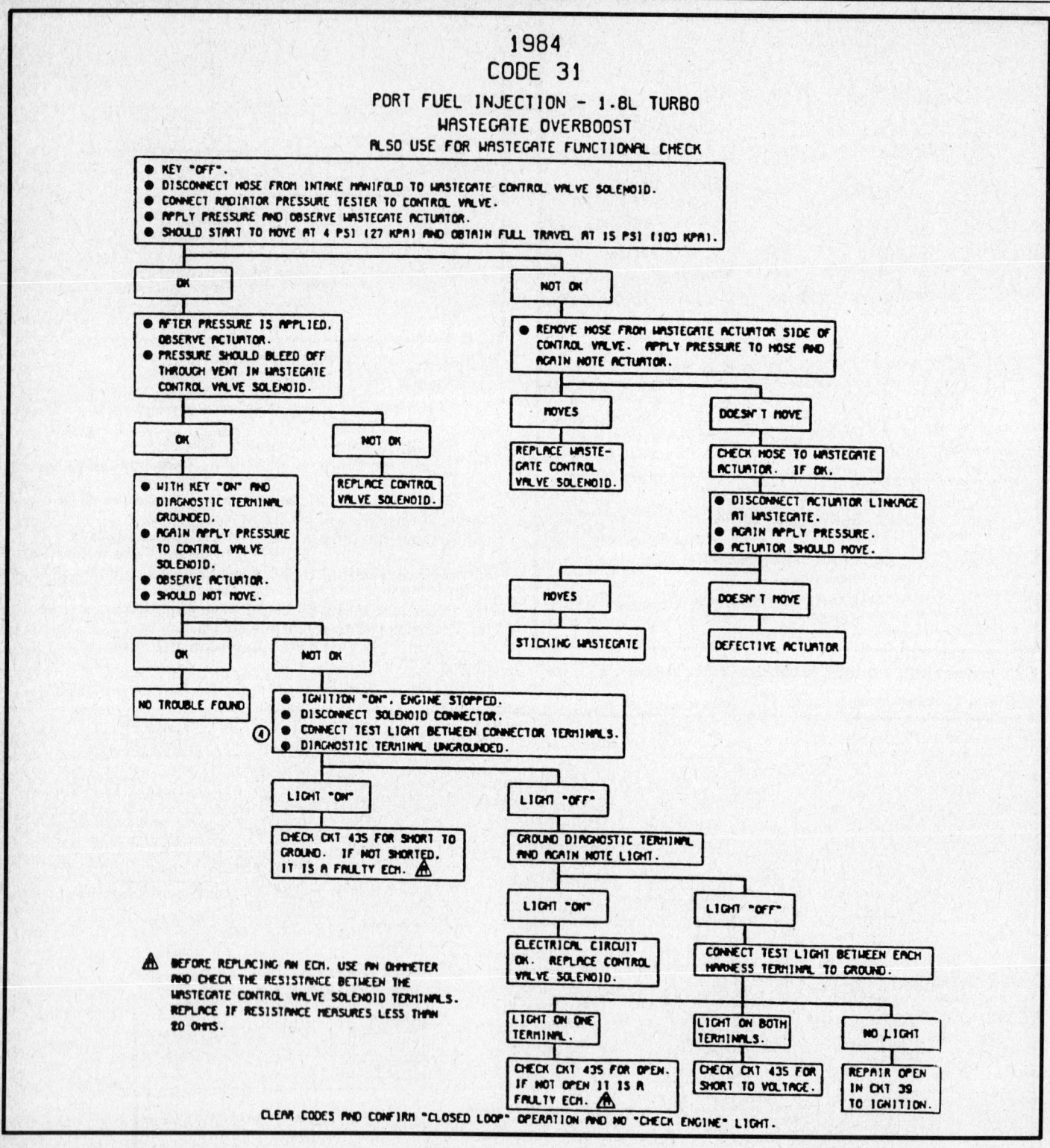

12. With the key ON and the engine stopped, rotate the camshaft sensor counterclockwise until the sensor switch just closes. This is indicated by the voltage reading going from a high 5–12 volts to a low 0–2 volts. The low voltage indicates the switch is closed.

13. Tighten the retaining bolt and reinstall the wire into terminal B.

14. Install remaining components.

ELECTRONIC WASTEGATE CONTROLS

1984 and Later Models

The wastegate is used on turbocharged engines and is normally closed, but opens to bleed off exhaust gases to prevent an overboost condition. The wastegate will open when pressure is applied to the actuator and is controlled by a wastegate control solenoid valve that is pulsed on and off by the ECM. Under normal driving conditions, the control solenoid is energized all of the time and closes off the manifold to the wastegate actuator. This allows for rapid increase in boost pressure.

As boost increases, the increase in pressure is detected by the MAP sensor and the ECM will read the signal and pulse the wastegate control valve, causing the wastegate to open and bleed off the excess boost pressure to prevent possible engine damage. As the boost pressure decreases, the ECM closes the control valve and the wastegate actuator pressure bleeds off through the vent in the control valve.

NOTE: If the MAP sensor detects an overboost condition, the ECM will reduce fuel delivery to prevent engine damage.

A code 31 will be set when the manifold pressure exceeds about 15 psi of boost as determined by the MAP sensor for two seconds and a code 33 has not previously been set. A trouble code 31 will illuminate the SERVICE ENGINE SOON light for as long as the overboost condition exists and for ten seconds after the condition disappears. The trouble code will be stored in the memory if the condition exists long enough to illuminate the SERVICE ENGINE SOON light.

TESTING

An overboost condition could be caused by the actuator circuit shorted to ground, a sticking wastegate actuator or wastegate, control valve stuck in the closed position, cut or pinched hose or a defective ECM. An underboost condition can be caused by the wastegate actuator sticking open, wastegate sticking open, control valve sticking open, no ignition signal to the control valve or an open circuit to the ECM, or a defective ECM.

1. With the key OFF, the control valve solenoid is open and should allow pressure to be applied to the wastegate actuator.
2. When 15 psi is applied to the valve and then removed, the actuator should slowly move back and close the wastegate. If the pressure does not bleed off, the vent in the control valve solenoid could be plugged.
3. With the ignition ON and the diagnostic terminal grounded, the control valve solenoid should be energized, closing off the manifold to the wastegate actuator.
4. Check the electrical control portion of the system with the ignition ON and the engine off. The solenoid should not be energized. With the key ON and the diagnostic terminal grounded, the solenoid should be energized.

TRANSMISSION CONVERTER CLUTCH (TCC)

GENERAL INFORMATION

This system has an electrical solenoid mounted in the automatic transmission, which is controlled by the ECM. When the vehicle reaches a certain speed the ECM will then energize the solenoid which in turn allows the torque converter to mechanically couple the engine to the transmission. When the transmission (during deceleration and passing) the ECM then de-energizes the solenoid. The transmission is also returned to the normal operating mode when the brake pedal is depressed. The TCC system is made up of the following switches and sensors: Vehicle speed sensor (VSS), park/neutral switch (P/N), stop light switch, coolant temperature sensor, throttle position sensor, third gear switch (125C transmission only) and auxiliary control valve assembly (125C transmission only).

VEHICLE SPEED SENSOR (VSS)

The VSS provides the ECM with a series of electrical pulses, which the ECM uses to determine the vehicle speed. This sensor is located behind the speedometer mounted in the instrument cluster.

PARK/NEUTRAL SWITCH (PN)

The park and neutral switch affects the operation of the converter clutch and the idle speed control. When the shift lever is in the park or neutral position the switch is in the closed position and as soon as the shift lever is put into gear the switch is opened. The switch is located and connected to the shift selector.

STOP LIGHT SWITCH

The stop light switch is used in this system to de-energize the TCC solenoid when the brake pedal is depressed. This switch is located above the brake pedal.

COOLANT TEMPERATURE SENSOR

This sensor lets the ECM know, by electrical pulses, when the engine is at normal operating temperature. The engine must be at operating temperature before the torque converter clutch can be applied.

THROTTLE POSITION SENSOR (TPS)

Once the torque converter clutch is applied, the ECM takes the information from the TPS and uses it to release the clutch when the vehicle accelerates or decelerates at a specific rate.

THIRD GEAR SWITCH (125C TRANSMISSION ONLY)

This switch is closed when the transmission is in third gear to complete electrical circuit of the TCC solenoid to the ECM.

AUXILIARY CONTROL VALVE ASSEMBLY (125C TRANSMISSION ONLY)

This valve assembly contains the TCC apply and regulator valves. The apply controls the amount of transmission fluid feed to the torque converter assembly in order to enable or disable the clutch mechanism.

TORQUE CONVERTER CLUTCH SOLENOID

Removal

1. Remove the negative battery cable and set it aside.
2. Raise and support vehicle safety and drain the ATF.
3. Remove the transaxle case side cover pan.
4. Remove the TCC solenoid retaining screws and then remove the electrical connector, solenoid and check ball.

SECTION 29 ENGINE CONTROLS
TRANSMISSION CONVERTER CLUTCH (TCC)

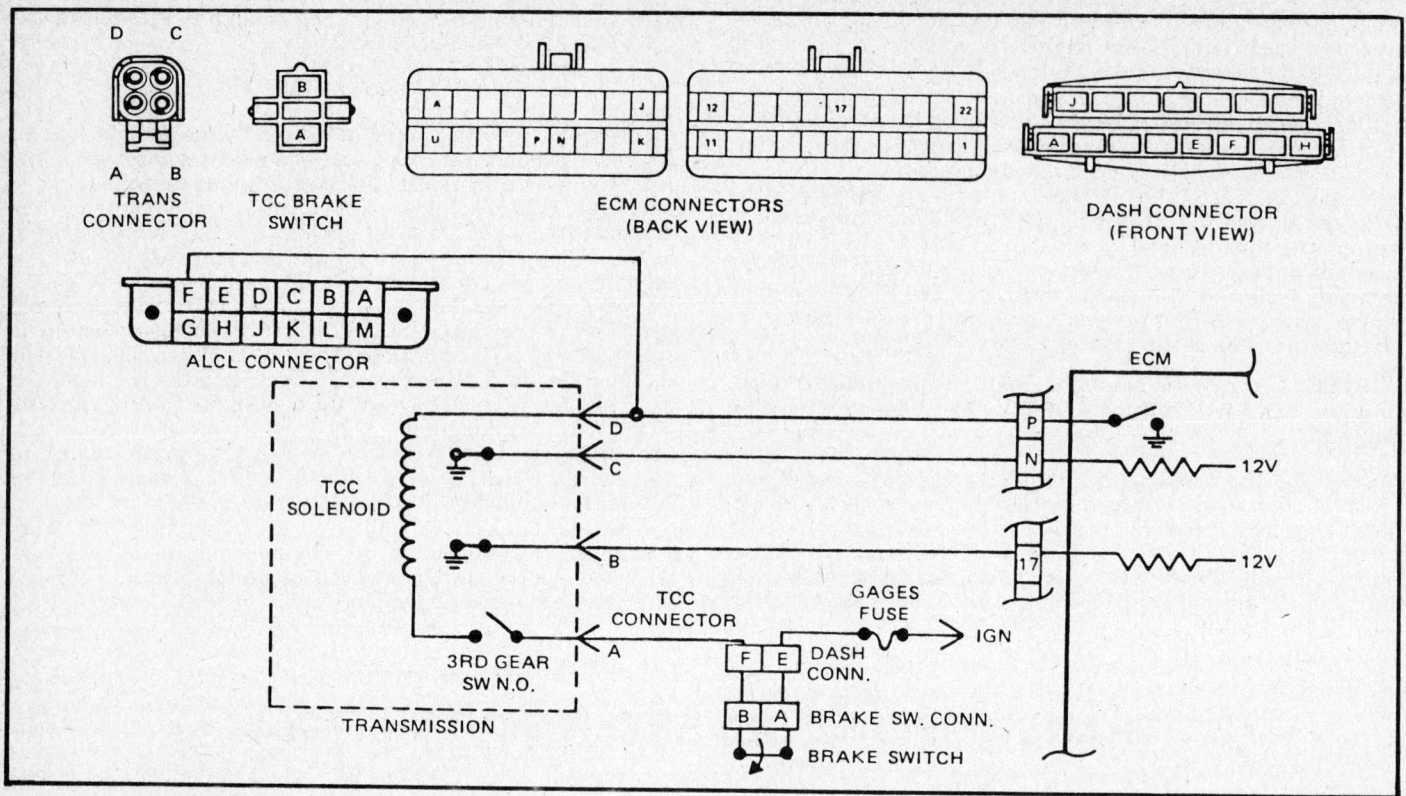

TCC wiring diagram

Installation

1. Install the check ball, TCC solenoid and electrical connector.
2. Install the solenoid retaining screws and torque them to 10 ft.lbs. (14 Nm).
3. Install transaxle case side cover pan with new gasket and torque the mounting bolts to 10 ft.lbs. (14 Nm).
4. Lower the vehicle and reconnect the negative battery cable. Refill transaxle to the proper level.

NOTE: The Removal and Installation procedure is basically the same for the automatic transmission; just remove the oil pan and remove the solenoid from the transmission.

VEHICLE SPEED SENSOR (VSS)

Removal and Installation

1. Remove the instrument cluster from the dash board.
2. Remove the 2 screws on the back side of the instrument cluster, one in the optic head and one in the buffer amplifier.
3. Disconnect the electrical connection from the foil to the buffer amplifier.
4. Remove the vehicle speed sensor. Installation is the reverse order of the removal procedure.

NOTE: If the vehicle is equipped with a digital cluster, just pull the cluster out far enough from the dash so that the optic head can be disconnected. Then remove the left side sound insulator and reach up to the instrument panel harness and disconnect the buffer amplifier connection.

STOP LIGHT SWITCH

Testing

1. Using an ohmmeter place the test leads from the ohmmeter on each of the blade terminals at the rear of the brake switch.
2. With the plunger on the brake switch fully extended, resistance on the ohmmeter should be infinite.
3. With the plunger pushed in the resistance should be zero.
4. If the brake switch fails either one of these tests then the switch should be removed and replaced. The switch can be removed by removing the electrical connectors and backing off the adjusting nut.

Adjustments

Adjust the brake switch so that the plunger just makes contact with the brake pedal lever when the brake pedal is released. If the switch is not adjusted correctly, the contacts that complete the circuit to the TCC will open when the brakes are not being used. This could cause the engine to stall when the vehicle is at idle speed.

COOLANT TEMPERATURE SENSOR

Removal and Installation

The coolant sensor will be located on the intake manifold water jacket and may be near the thermostat housing.

1. Disconnect the electrical connector from the terminals of the sensor.
2. Remove the threaded temperature sensor from the engine.

ENGINE CONTROLS
TRANSMISSION CONVERTER CLUTCH (TCC)
SECTION 29

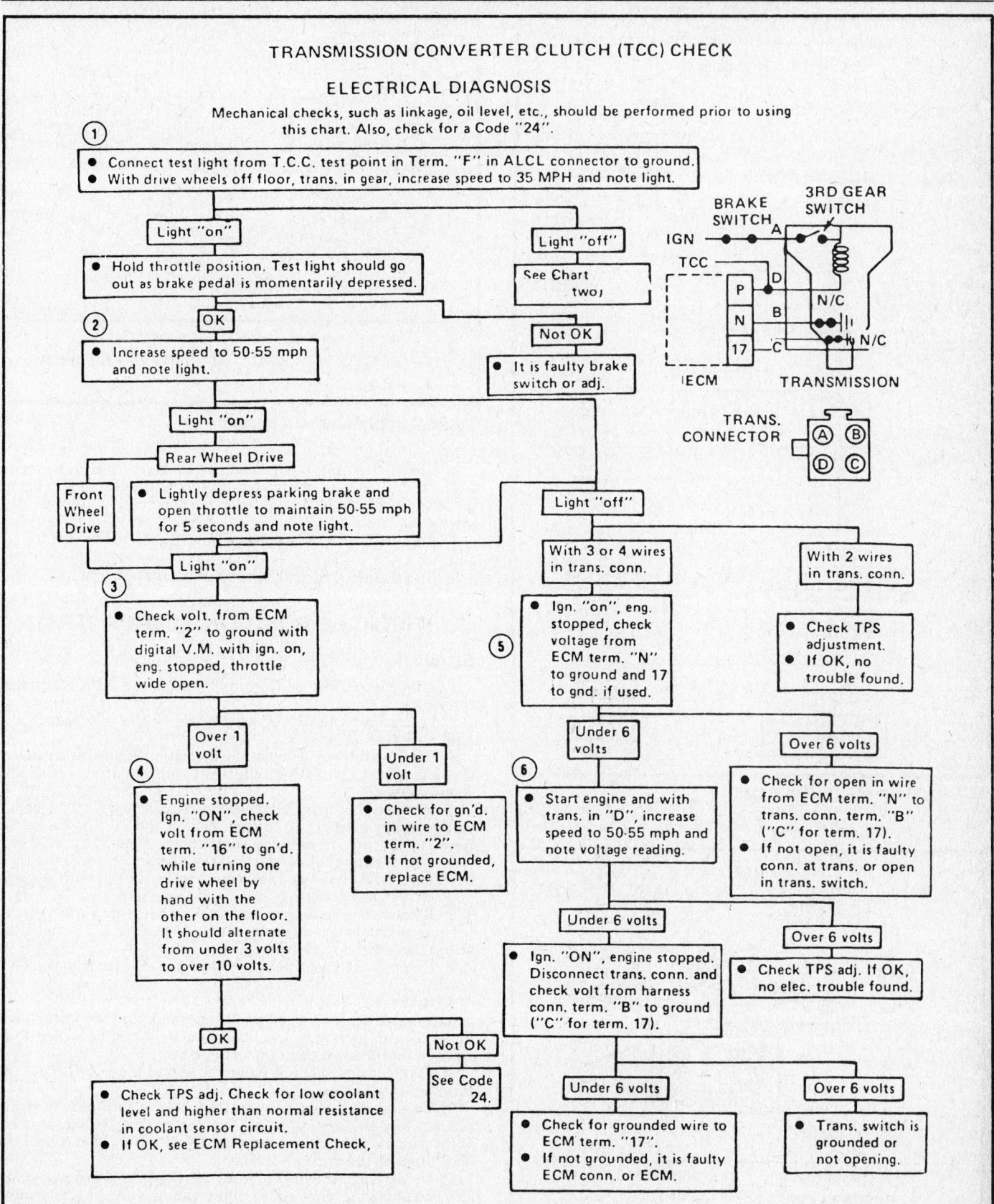

TCC system diagnosis

29-57

SECTION 29 ENGINE CONTROLS
TRANSMISSION CONVERTER CLUTCH (TCC)

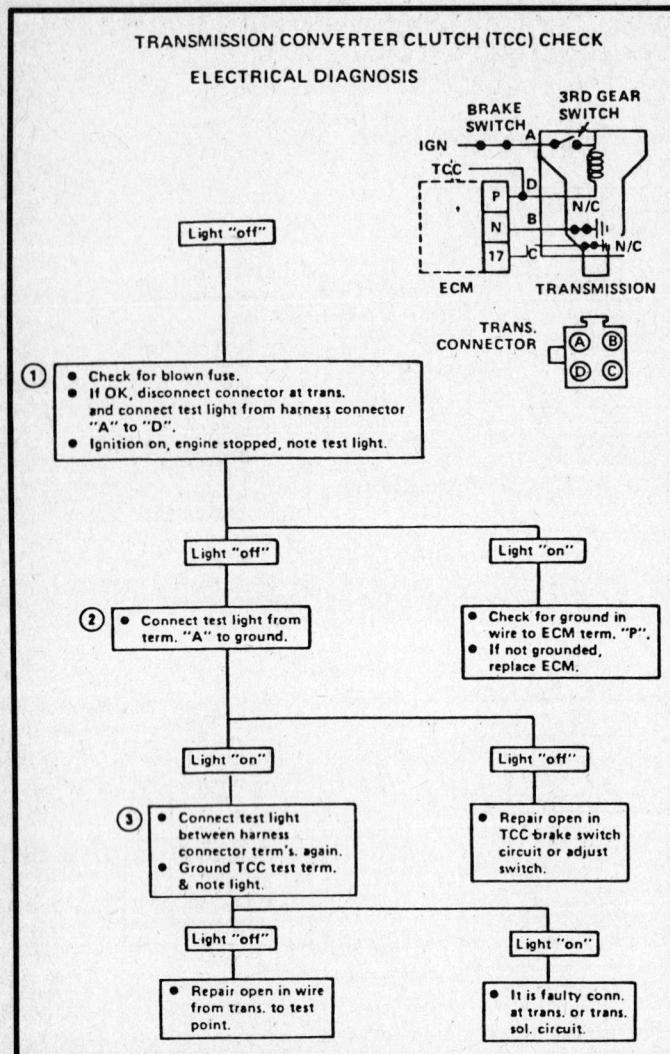

TCC system diagnosis (cont.)

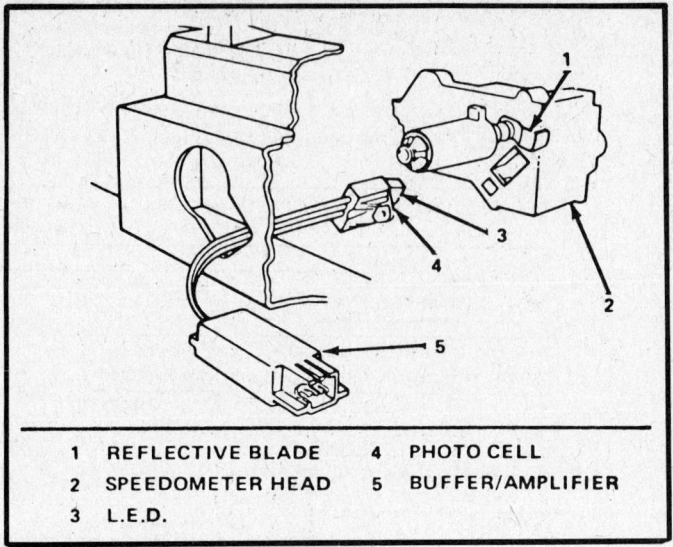

1. REFLECTIVE BLADE 4 PHOTO CELL
2. SPEEDOMETER HEAD 5 BUFFER/AMPLIFIER
3. L.E.D.

Typical vehicle speed sensor

3. Check the sensor with coolant tip immersed in water at 59°F (15°C). The resistance across the terminals should check to 4114–4743 ohms. If not within specification, replace the sensor.
4. Install the threaded sensor and tighten it to 6 ft.lbs. (7 Nm).
5. Install the electrical connector on the sensor.

THROTTLE POSITION SENSOR (TPS)

Removal

1. Disconnect the M/C solenoid and the TPS electrical connector.
2. Disconnect the idle speed control or the idle speed solenoid electrical connector.
3. On the air horn, remove the attaching screws and remove the idle speed control or, idle load compensator or the idle speed solenoid.
4. Remove the upper choke lever from the end of the choke shaft by removing the retaining screw, then remove choke rod from the slot in the lever by rotating the upper choke lever.
5. Remove the choke rod from the lower level inside the float bowl casting by holding the lower level outward with a small screwdriver and twisting the rod counterclockwise.
6. Remove the retainer clip from the pump link and remove the pump link from the pump lever. Be sure not to remove the pump lever from the air horn.
7. Remove the vacuum break hose from the tube on the float bowl.
8. Remove the air horn-to-bowl screws, then remove the two countersunk attaching screws located next to the venturi. Remove the air horn from the float bowl by lifting it straight up, remove and discard the air horn gasket.
9. Remove the solenoid-metering rod plunger by lifting the plunger straight up.
10. To remove the TPS lay a flat tool or a flat piece of metal across the bowl casting to protect the gasket sealing surface. With a small screwdriver depress the TPS lightly and hold the TPS against the spring tension.
11. Using a small chisel or equivalent pry upward to remove the bowl staking, be sure to apply the upward pressure on to the flat metal surface not the gasket surface.
12. Pushing upward from the bottom on the electrical connector, remove the TPS and connector assembly from the bowl.

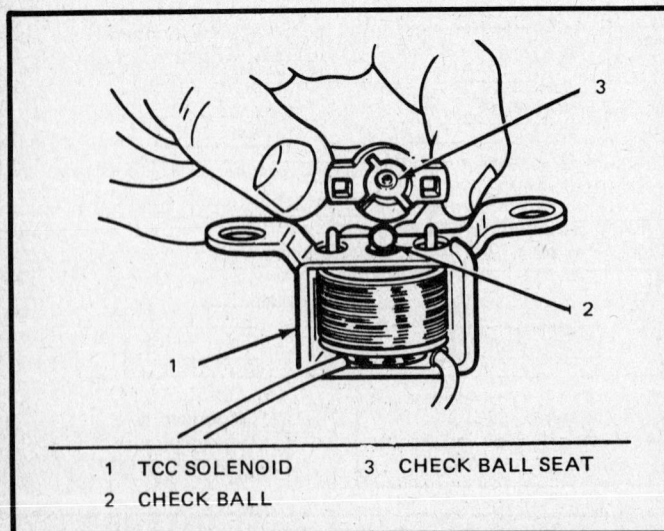

1. TCC SOLENOID 3. CHECK BALL SEAT
2. CHECK BALL

Typical TCC solenoid

ENGINE CONTROLS
TRANSMISSION CONVERTER CLUTCH (TCC)
SECTION 29

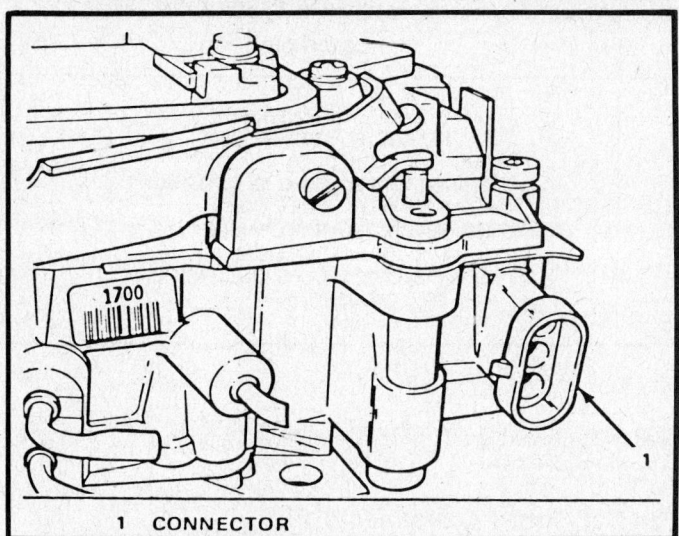

Throttle position sensor

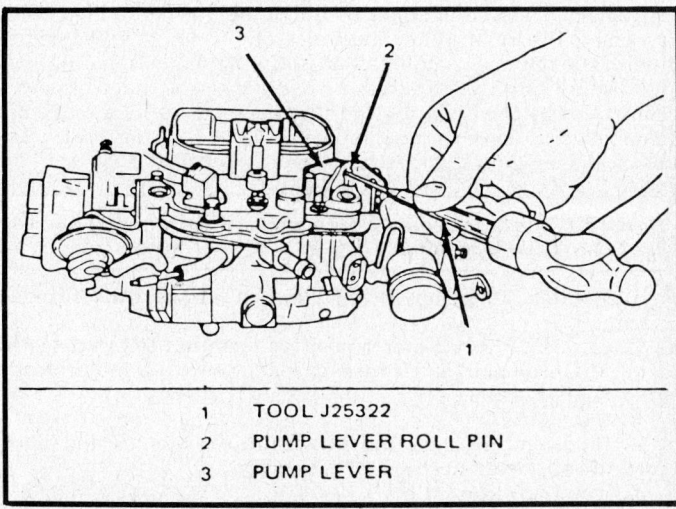

1. TOOL J25322
2. PUMP LEVER ROLL PIN
3. PUMP LEVER

Removing the pump lever

Installation

1. Install the TPS and connector assembly into the float bowl by aligning the groove in the electrical connector with the slot provided in the float bowl casting. Push downward on the TPS assembly so that the connector and wires are located below the bowl casting surface.

NOTE: Make sure that the green TPS actuator plunger is in place in the air horn.

2. Install the air horn with a new gasket by holding down on the pump plunger assembly and aligning the pump plunger stem with the hole in the gasket. Then align the holes in the gasket over the TPS plunger, solenoid plunger return spring, metering rods, solenoid attaching screw and electrical connector.
3. Install the solenoid-metering rod plunger by holding down on the air horn gasket and pump plunger assembly, and align the slot in the end of the plunger with the solenoid attaching screw.
4. Lower the air horn assembly onto the float bowl while positioning the TPS adjustment lever over the TPS sensor, and also guide the pump plunger stem through the seal in the air horn casting.
5. Install the air horn screws and lockwashers, and the two countersunk screws located next to the carburetor venturi area. Tighten all screws evenly and securely.
6. Using the two attaching screws, install the vacuum break and bracket assembly onto the air horn, and attach the pump link to the pump lever with the link retainer.
7. Install choke rod into the lower choke lever inside the float bowl cavity. Place the choke rod in the slot in the upper choke lever, and position the lever on the end of the choke shaft being sure that the flats on the end of the shaft align with the flats in the lever.
8. Install the attaching screw and tighten securely, when the choke rod is properly installed the lever will point to the rear of the carburetor, and the number on the lever will be facing outward.
9. Install the idle speed control motor, M/C solenoid, TPS and idle speed control or idle speed solenoid electrical connectors.
10. Clear the trouble code from the ECM memory after replacement and adjust the throttle position sensor.

THROTTLE POSITION SENSOR ADJUSTMENT

Adjustment

The plug covering the TPS adjustment screw is used to provide a tamper-resistant design and retain the factory setting during vehicle operation. DO NOT REMOVE the plug unless, in diagnosis, the System Performance Check indicates the TPS sensor is not adjusted correctly or it is necessary to replace the air horn assembly, float bowl, TPS sensor, or TPS adjustment screw. This is a critical adjustment that must be performed accurately and carefully to ensure proper vehicle performance and control of emissions. If necessary to adjust the TPS sensor, proceed as follows:

1. Using a .078 (5/64) drill, drill a hole in the steel plug covering the TPS adjustment screw. Use care in drilling to prevent damage to adjustment screw head.
2. Using a small hammer or equivalent, remove steel plug from air horn.
3. Disconnect the TPS connector and jump all three terminals. (Jumpers can be made up using terminals 12014836 and 12014837.) Make jumpers up with #16, #18 or #20 wire approximately 6" long.
4. Connect digital voltmeter (such as J-29125-A) from TPS connector center terminal (B) to bottom terminal (C).
5. With ignition on, engine stopped, turn the TPS screw with flat bladed screwdriver or equivalent to obtain .26 volts at curb idle throttle position with A/C OFF and ISC fully retracted.
6. After adjustment, install new plug (supplied in service kits) in air horn, driving plug in place until flush with raised pump lever boss on casting.

NOTE: Plug must be installed to retain tamper-resistant design. If plug is not available, the TPS screw hole should be sealed with silicone sealant, RTV rubber or equivalent.

Idle Speed Control (ISC)

1983 AND LATER

Before making the ISC adjustment, check the ISC adjustment plunger for an identification number. If there is not a letter on the plunger, then using special tool J-29607, BT-8022 or equivalent, remove the plunger from the ISC unit. Once the plunger is removed, measure the length of the plunger from

29-59

SECTION 29

ENGINE CONTROLS
TRANSMISSION CONVERTER CLUTCH (TCC)

ENGINE	VOLTAGE SETTING	CONDITION
1.6L L-4 (VIN C) FULL SYSTEM	.40 VOLTS	CURB IDLE
1.6L L-4 (VIN C) MIN SYSTEM	.92 VOLTS	HIGH STEP OF FAST IDLE CAM
1.8L L-4 (VIN G)	.26 VOLTS	I.S.C. RETRACTED AT SLOW IDLE
2.5L L-4 EFI (VINS R & 2)	.525 ± .075 VOLTS	THROTTLE CLOSED
2.8L V-6 (VINS B, X, Z & 1)	.26 VOLTS	ENGINE STOPPED, CURB IDLE POSITION
3.8L V-6 (VIN A)	.77 VOLTS	HIGH STEP OF FAST IDLE CAM
3.8L V-6 (VIN K)	.51 VOLTS	I.S.C. RETRACTED AT SLOW IDLE
4.1L V-8 (VIN 4)	.97 VOLTS	HIGH STEP OF FAST IDLE CAM
5.0L V-8 (VIN H)	.51 VOLTS	ENGINE STOPPED, CURB IDLE POSITION
5.0L V-8 CFI (VIN 7)	.525 ± .075 VOLTS	THROTTLE CLOSED
5.7L V-8 CFI (VIN 8)	.525 ± .075 VOLTS	THROTTLE CLOSED

1982 and later TPS specifications

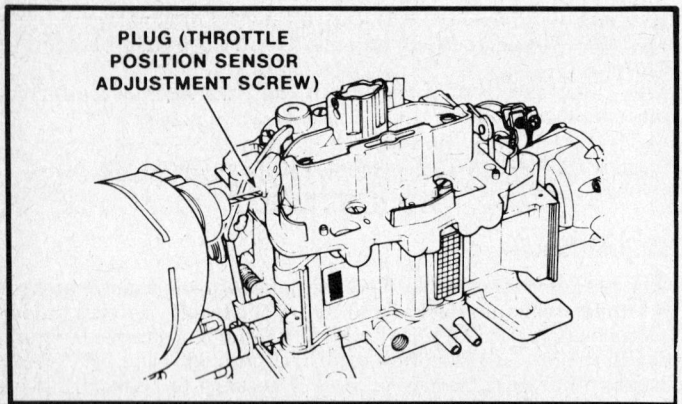

Removing the TPS adjustment screw plug

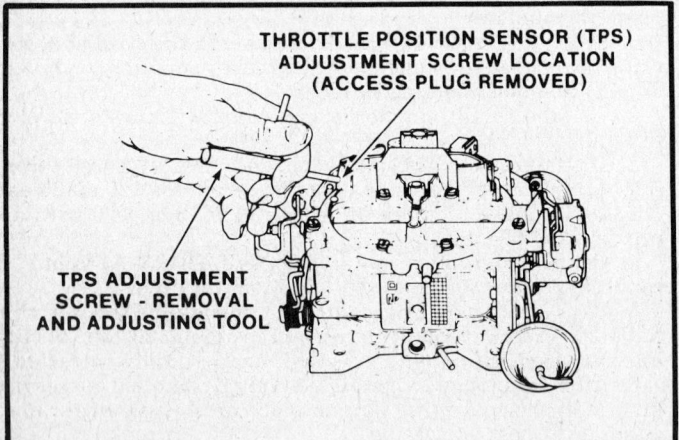

TPS adjustment tool

the backside of the plunger head to the end of the plunger screw (dimension A). Be sure to record this measurement, because it will be needed for Step 13. Reinstall the plunger screw into the ISC unit, turning the plunger into a preset position so that the distance measured from the backside of the plunger head to the ISC nosepiece is less than dimension B.

Replacement

1. With ignition OFF, disconnect wiring from ISC motor and remove (2) screws that attach the ISC bracket to the carburetor and remove ISC and bracket assembly.
2. Install new Idle Speed Control (ISC) assembly to carburetor and reattach throttle return spring and any other related parts removed during disassembly. Perform the ON-CAR speed adjustments.

On-Car Speed Adjustments

When a new Idle Speed Control (ISC) assembly is installed, a base (minimum authority) and high (maximum authority) RPM speed check must be performed and adjustments made as required. These adjustments limit the low and high RPM speeds to the ECM. When making a low and high speed adjustment, the low speed adjustment is always made first. DO NOT use the ISC plunger to adjust curb idle speed as the idle speed is controlled by the ECM. Before starting engine, place transmission selector lever in park or neutral, set parking brake, and block drive wheels.

--- CAUTION ---
Do not disconnect or connect ISC connector with ignition ON as damage to the ECM may occur.

1. Connect tachometer (distributor side of tach filter, if used).
2. Connect a dwell meter positive terminal to mixture control (M/C) solenoid dwell (green) lead. Set dwell meter on the six cylinder scale.
3. Turn A/C OFF.
4. Start engine and run until stabilized by entering closed loop (dwell meter needle starts to vary).
5. Turn ignition OFF.
6. Unplug connector from ISC motor.
7. Fully retract ISC plunger by applying 12 volts to terminal C of the ISC motor connection and ground lead to terminal D of the ISC motor connection.
It may be necessary to install jumper leads from the ISC motor in order to make proper connections.

NOTE: DO NOT leave battery voltage applied to motor longer than necessary to retract ISC plunger. Prolonged contact will damage motor. Also, NEVER connect voltage source across terminals A and B as damage to the internal throttle contact switch will result.

8. Start engine and wait until dwell meter needle starts to vary, indicating closed loop operation.
9. With parking brake applied and drive wheels blocked, place transmission in Drive (Neutral-manual transmission models).
10. With ISC plunger fully retracted, adjust carburetor base (slow) idle stop screw to the specified RPM (see Adjustment Specifications at rear of this section). ISC plunger should not be left in full retracted position.
11. Place transmission in Park or Neutral and fully extend ISC plunger by applying 12 volts to terminal D of the ISC motor connection and ground lead to terminal C of the ISC motor connection. Never connect voltage source across terminals A

ENGINE CONTROLS
TRANSMISSION CONVERTER CLUTCH (TCC)

IDLE SPEED CONTROL PLUNGER		
IDENTIFICATION LETTER	PLUNGER LENGTH DIMENSION A	AFTER ADJUSTMENT DISTANCE AT DIMENSION "B" MUST NOT EXCEED
NONE	14.1 mm (9/16")	5.6 mm (7/32")
NONE	16.3 mm (41/64")	8.0 mm (5/16")
X	18.5 mm (47/64")	10.0 mm (25/64")
A	19.3 mm (49/64")	10.8 mm (27/64")
Y	20.5 mm (51/64")	12.0 mm (15/32")
S	21.2 mm (27/32")	12.7 mm (1/2")
Z	22.5 mm (7/8")	14.0 mm (35/64")
G	23.2 mm (29/32")	14.7 mm (37/64")
E	25.6 mm (1")	17.1 mm (43/64")
L	27.5 mm (1 3/32")	19.0 mm (3/4")
J	30.0 mm (1 3/16")	21.5 mm (27/32")
N	32.0 mm (1 17/64")	23.5 mm (59/64")
T	34.0 mm (1 11/32")	25.5 mm (1")

Typical ISC assembly

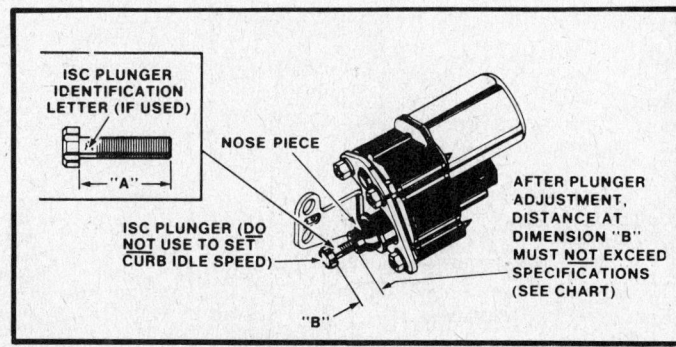

Making plunger adjustment

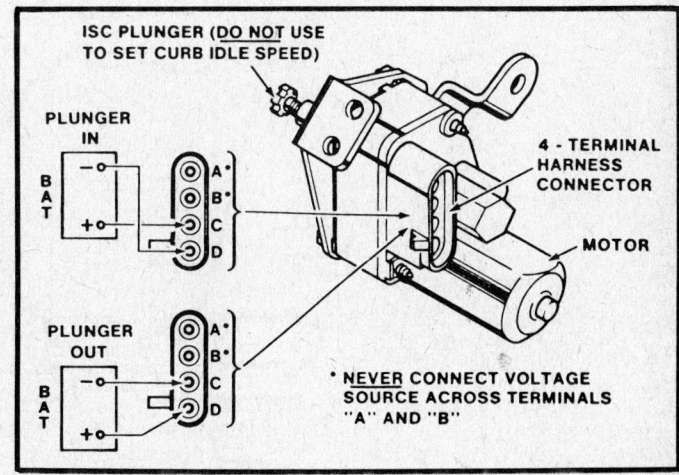

Typical ISC assembly

and B as damage to the internal throttle contact switch will result.

12. With ISC plunger fully extended, using Tool J-29831 or equivalent, turn ISC plunger to obtain ISC adjustment rpm. This adjustment must be made within 8 seconds. After 8 seconds, the rpm will increase and correct adjustment cannot be made. Verify ISC adjustment rpm with voltage applied to motor; motor will ratchet in and out.

13. When the ISC plunger adjustment has been made, measure the distance from the back side of the plunger head to the ISC nosepiece (dimension B). The dimension must not exceed the specified plunger adjustment.

NOTE: Use the plunger measurement recorded earlier.

14. Place the transmission in Park or Neutral and turn the ignition off. Disconnect the 12 volt DC power source, jumper leads, ground lead, tachometer, and dwell meter. Reconnect the four terminal harness connector to the ISC motor.

15. Tricking the ISC motor as described will cause the Check Engine light to come on and the ISC motor trouble code to be set. By restoring the system to normal operation, the light will go out but the trouble code will continue to be stored as an intermittent problem. In this case, it is necessary to clear this diagnosis trouble code. To clear the code momentarily disconnect the pigtail lead at the positive battery terminal.

SECTION 29
ENGINE CONTROLS
FORD FEEDBACK CARBURETORS

FORD FEEDBACK CARBURETOR

SYSTEM OPERATION

The system is equipped to supply input signals to the microprocessor control unit module (MCU). These inputs originate from the exhaust gas oxygen sensor, cold temperature vacuum switch, idle tracking switch and the rpm tach input from the coil.

The MCU module continuously monitors the input signals and computes the correct operating mode for a given condition. Output signals from the MCU module are applied to control the vacuum solenoid regulator, thermactor bypass control solenoid and the thermactor diverter control solenoid (manual transmission only).

The primary function of the 2.3L MCU module is to control the vacuum regulator solenoid. The MCU module sends ten signals per second to the vacuum regulator solenoid in a timed duty cycle. By varying the "ON" time to the "OFF" time of the cycle, the MCU module is able to maintain or change the air-fuel mixture. The MCU module does not control ignition timing. The system uses a conventional distributor and coil.

OPERATING MODES

The MCU system has three operating modes. These modes are system initialization (start-up), open loop and closed loop.

System Initialization (Start-Up)

The MCU module will initialize when battery power is applied to the computer prior to engine cranking and again immediately with engine starting. During initialization, the duty cycle to the vacuum regulator solenoid is maintained at 50%. After starting, initialization lasts for only a fraction of a second. Then, the MCU system goes into the open or closed loop.

Open Loop

The system is in the open loop mode when either the cold temperature vacuum switch or idle tracking switch is activated. In the open loop mode, the MCU module will control the duty cycle with "ON" time signals to the vacuum regulator solenoid. These will provide a calibrated air-fuel mixture.

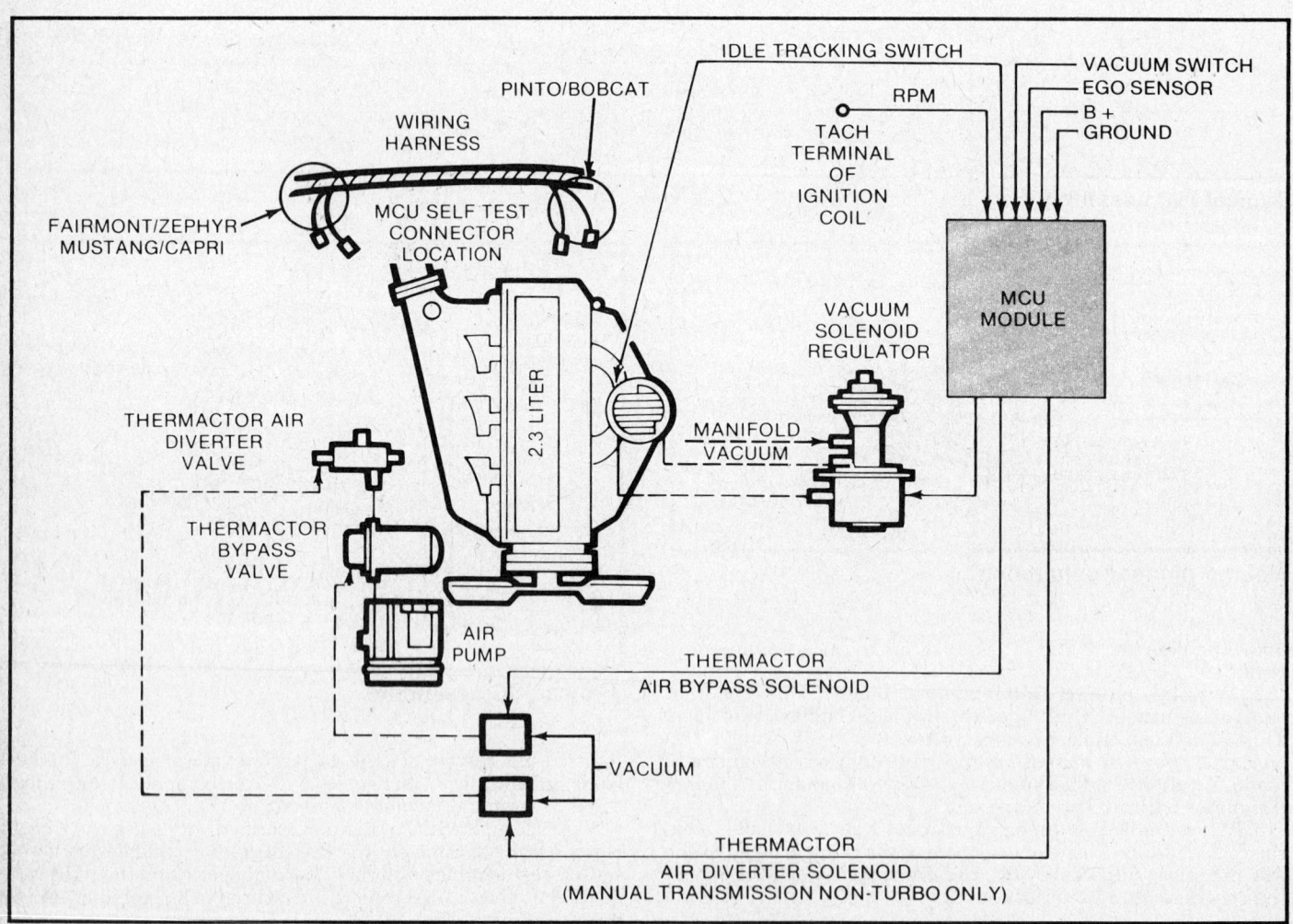

System components

29-62

ENGINE CONTROLS
FORD FEEDBACK CARBURETORS
SECTION 29

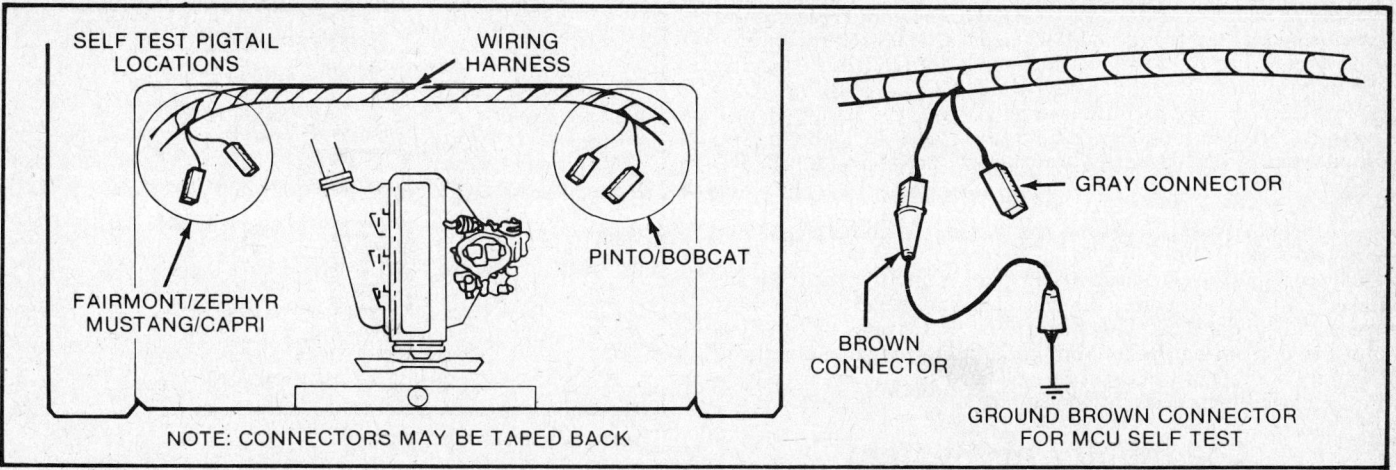

MCU self-test connectors

Closed Loop

With the proper signals from the idle tracking switch and the cold temperature switch, the MCU module changes to the closed loop mode for close range monitoring and control of the air-fuel ratio. The exhaust gas oxygen sensor monitors the exhaust gas to determine if the engine is running rich or lean.

This information is used by the MCU module to adjust the carburetor to the air-fuel ratio desired for the operating condition. Signals from the MCU module, which produce carburetor adjustments, are calibrated. This provides a damping effect to minimize over-correction and abrupt changes.

System Components

MCU MODULE

The MCU is the brain of the system. It is a solid-state, programmed micro-computer. It takes the information inputs and uses its program to provide output control signals to the control solenoids. The MCU module receives its power from the battery through the ignition switch.

The module is located either in the engine compartment or under the instrument panel to the left of the steering column. It appears similar to an ignition switch module, but differences in the wiring connectors prevent interchangeability.

With the engine cold or at idle, the air-fuel ratio is at a preset level. When the engine is warm and off idle, the air-fuel mixture is adjusted by a signal from the exhaust gas oxygen sensor. These adjustments are made by an "ON-OFF" control signal from the module. For example, when the sensor signals a rich mixture, control "ON" time is increased, while "ON" time is decreased for a lean mixture.

COLD TEMPERATURE VACUUM SWITCH

The cold temperature switch is a normally closed switch, with vacuum controlled through a ported vacuum switch (PVS). The MCU system will enter a closed loop mode when the cold temperature switch is activated, provided the vehicle is operating at part throttle.

When the engine is cold, the PVS valve blocks vacuum from the cold temperature vacuum switch. The switch position provides a ground path as a signal to the control unit. When the engine is above 95°F, the PVS valve opens to allow ported vacuum to activate the normally closed switch. With the contacts opened, the ground path signal to the control unit is interrupted.

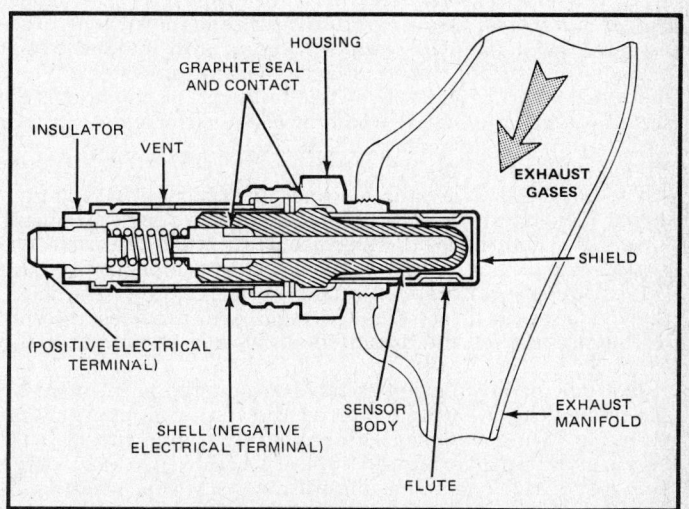

Exhaust gas oxygen sensor

IDLE TRACKING SWITCH

The idle tracking switch is a limit switch used to detect the throttle in the idle position. It is normally closed but opens at closed throttle, sending the MCU system into an open loop mode. The idle tracking switch is mounted on the rear of the carburetor.

EXHAUST GAS OXYGEN SENSOR

The exhaust gas oxygen sensor is threaded into the exhaust manifold, directly in the path of the exhaust gas stream. The sensor provides information to the computer about the air-fuel ratio, indicated by the oxygen concentration in the exhaust gases.

When it senses a rich mixture, the sensor generates a high voltage signal to the computer. A low voltage is generated when a lean mixture (high oxygen level in the exhaust) is sensed. The voltage signal is used by the MCU module for adjustment of the duty cycle during the closed loop mode of operation.

VACUUM SOLENOID REGULATOR

The vacuum solenoid regulator controls manifold vacuum

SECTION 29
ENGINE CONTROLS
FORD FEEDBACK CARBURETORS

which has been regulated to 5 in. Hg. This solenoid receives ten signals per second from the MCU module. The vacuum applied to the metering rod of the carburetor is controlled by varying the duty cycle ("ON-OFF" ratio of the MCU signal). At 100% duty cycle, 5 in. Hg. vacuum is applied to the metering rod, producing a full lean condition. At 0% duty cycle, the metering rod diaphragm is vented to the atmosphere, producing a full rich condition.

RPM INPUT TO THE MCU MODULE

The rpm signal to the computer is taken from the "tach" terminal of the ignition coil. This circuit is identified by the dark green-yellow dot wire. This negative signal is used by the computer to determine the amount of damping to use in changing the duty signals to the carburetor. These signals are used only in the closed loop mode of operation.

Thermactor Air System

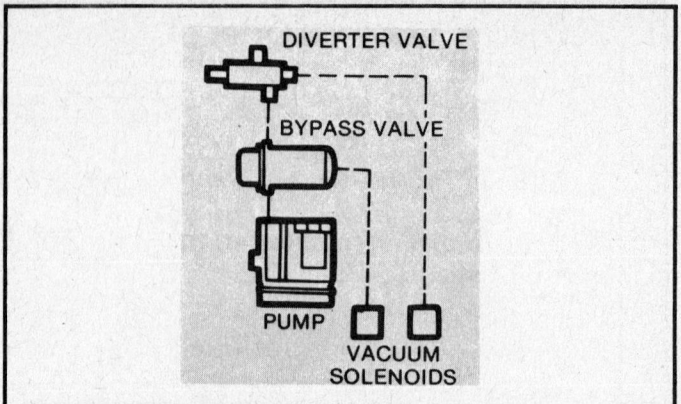
Thermactor air system

The thermactor air system is used to operate the three-way catalytic converter system. The thermactor air system consists of the air pump, bypass and diverter valves and the air control solenoids. The 2.3L MCU-equipped engine with manual transmission (non-turbo) has a managed thermactor system. When the thermactor air is not bypassed to the atmosphere, it is directed upstream or downstream by the diverter valve. In this application, the diverter valve is controlled by a MCU-controlled solenoid.

The automatic transmission and turbocharged 2.3L engine do not have an air diverter solenoid or a managed thermactor air system. Routing for the thermactor air is determined by engine performance, mode and operating temperature. The valves are pre-calibrated. During normal engine operation, thermactor air is directed downstream. This provides fresh air to the catalyst for the oxidation of HC and CO gases in the exhaust.

Thermactor air venting to the atmosphere is controlled by the idle tracking switch to protect the vehicle from over temperature during extended idling. Venting begins after 2–2 1/2 minutes of uninterrupted idle. To reduce the excessive amounts of HC and CO during warm-up, thermactor air is directed upstream during this period. The thermactor air valves are located at the right front of the engine.

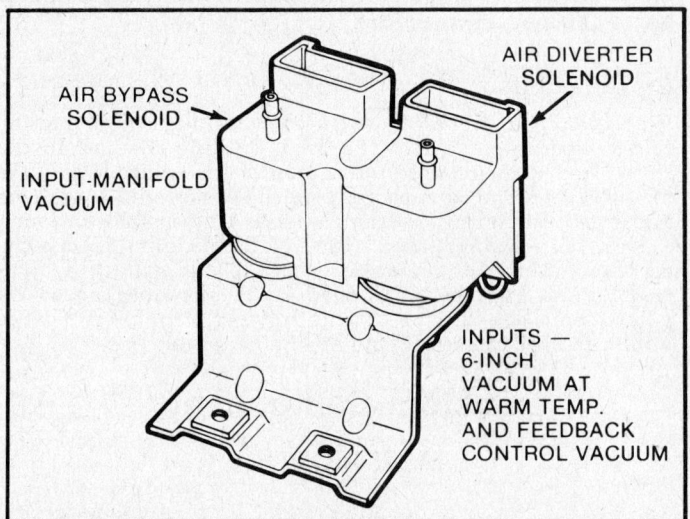
Thermactor air control solenoids

THERMACTOR AIR PUMP

The air pump is an impeller-type centrifugal air filter fan. Heavier than air contaminants are thrown from the air intake by centrifugal force. This type of air pump does not have a pressure relief valve because this function is controlled by the thermactor bypass valve.

THERMACTOR BYPASS SOLENOID AND DIVERTER SOLENOID

The bypass valve operation and diverter valve operation for non-turbocharged engines with manual transmissions are controlled by the thermactor air control solenoids. The solenoids route vacuum in three possible directions: bypass, upstream or downstream.

In the bypass mode, air is vented to the atmosphere. In the upstream mode, air is injected into the exhaust manifold. In the downstream mode, air is directed into the three-way catalyst between the two catalyst stages.

IGNITION SYSTEM

A conventional ignition system is used with the MCU-equipped 2.3L engine. The ignition system includes the

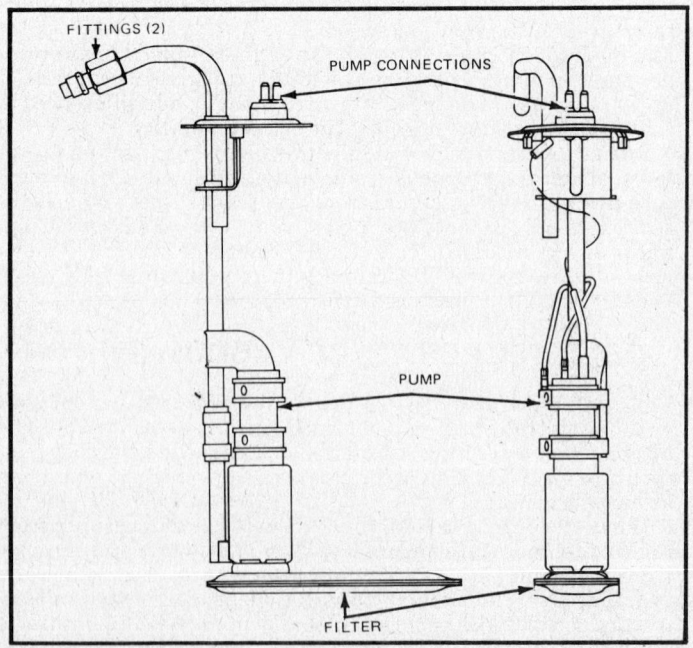
Electric fuel pump

29-64

ENGINE CONTROLS
FORD FEEDBACK CARBURETORS
SECTION 29

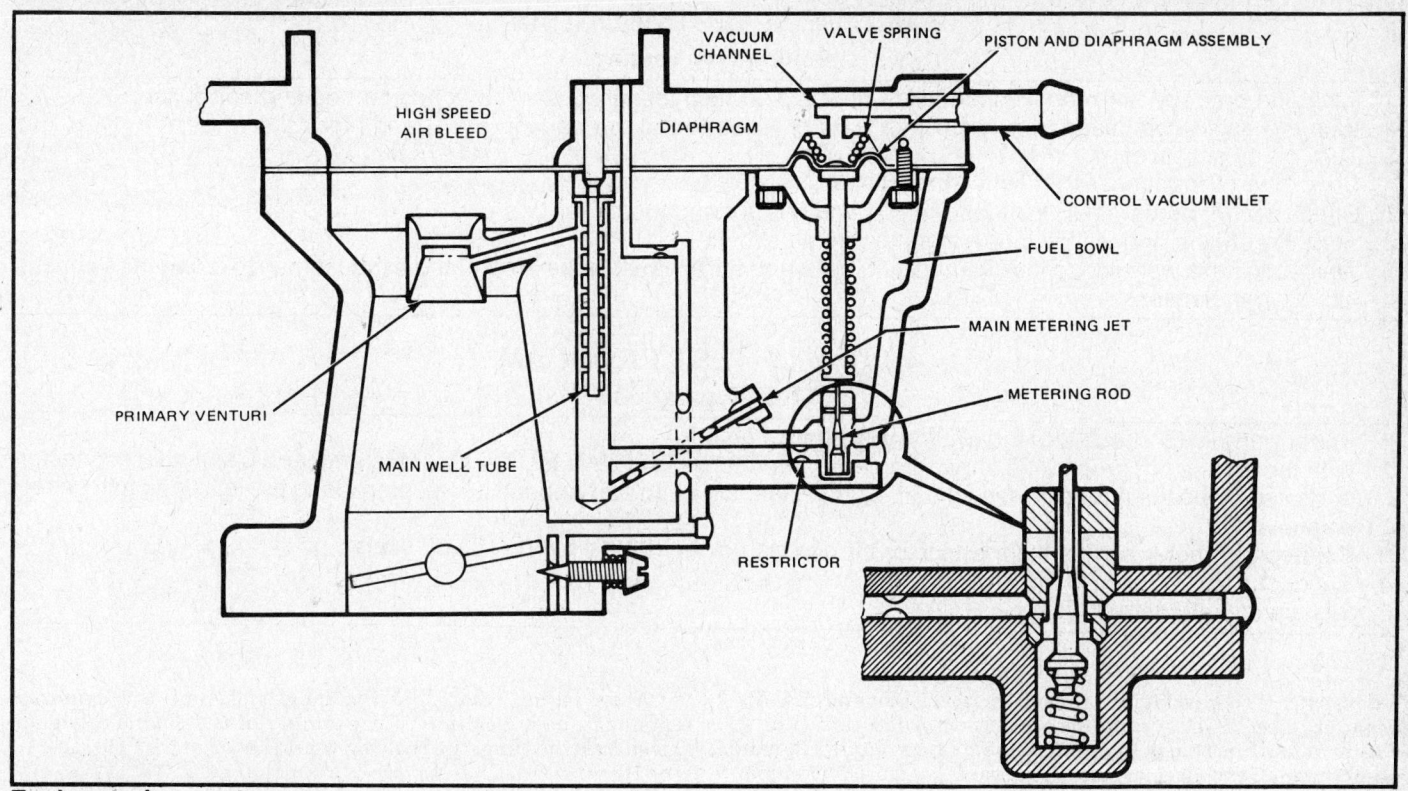

Fuel metering system

MICROPROCESSOR SYSTEM DIAGNOSTIC TESTS
DIAGNOSING NO START CONDITION

Procedure	Result	Action
Battery Voltage Check Ignition key off.	a. 10-16 volts b. Less than 10, more than 16 volts	a. Battery good, go to the next step. b. Service the charging system.
Harness Check Disconnect ignition coil connector and ignition module. Check circuit 11 (dark green with yellow dot) tach terminal for short to ground.	a. No short b. Short to ground	a. Reconnect ignition coil connector and ignition modules. Check for fuel to carburetor and spark to spark plugs. b. Go to next step.
MCU Module Check Disconnect the MCU module and check circuit 11 for short to ground.	a. No short b. Short to ground	a. Replace module and retest. b. Repair harness.

DIAGNOSING COLD ENGINE CONDITION
If condition occurs only when engine is cold, perform this test first

Procedure	Result	Action
Ported Vacuum Switch (PVS) (PVS) Check This test must be performed without starting the engine and with the PVS temperature below 80°F. Disconnect the hose from the cold temperature switch and leave disconnected. Remove the vacuum hose from the carburetor port. Apply vacuum to the hose.	a. Vacuum is held b. Vacuum is not held	a. PVS is good. b. Check for leaks. If there are no leaks, replace PVS and repeat vacuum test.

29-65

SECTION 29
ENGINE CONTROLS
FORD FEEDBACK CARBURETORS

MCU SELF-TEST PROGRAM
Preliminary Testing

1. A routine pre-test can produce immediate results and help identify a service condition needing correction.
2. With the engine off, place transmission in Park or Neutral. Set the parking brake and block the wheels.
3. Turn off all accessories.
4. Check the vacuum hoses for tight connections.
5. Check the wiring harness, tach lead to coil and MCU components for bad connections and physical damage.
6. Start the engine and warm to operating temperature.
7. While engine is warming, check for vacuum leaks and for exhaust leaks around the exhaust manifold and the exhaust gas oxygen sensor.

MCU SELF-TEST PROGRAM
Test Preparations

1. Perform the PVS check and the preliminary checks first.
2. With the engine off, ground the brown single-pin connector. On Fairmont, Zephyr, Mustang, and Capri, this connector is located along the right side dash panel, engine side. On Pinto and Bobcat, it is located along the left side dash panel, engine side.
3. Connect voltmeter across the thermactor air bypass solenoid. Use the 0–15 volt scale.
4. Connect a tachometer to the engine.
5. System is now ready to test.

Duraspark II coil and ignition module, and a conventional distributor. The MCU system does not control ignition timing. The primary function of the MCU system is the monitoring and adjustment of the air-fuel ratio. The two separate systems complement each other to produce performance in a wide range of operating conditions.

Fuel System

CARBURETOR CONTROL

Controlled vacuum from the vacuum regulator solenoid is channeled to the cavity above the metering rod diaphragm. With no vacuum present, the valve spring causes the valve to move to its lowest (richest) position, where maximum fuel can pass through the orifice. As vacuum is applied to the diaphragm, spring pressure is overcome and the metering rod rises, making the mixture leaner.

VACUUM SOLENOID/REGULATOR

The component that supplies the vacuum signal to the carburetor feedback valve is the vacuum solenoid/regulator. When current from the control module is applied to the solenoid coil, the armature moves upward until it rests on its upper seat. This blocks the atmospheric pressure passage and opens the vacuum passage to the output port. The output vacuum will now reach a constant 5 in. Hg.

When current is removed from the coil, the armature moves downward until it rests against its lower seat. This opens the atmospheric passage and closes the vacuum passage, causing the output vacuum to drop to zero. In operation, the armature actually cycles up and down ten times per second, according to the signal received from the module. The output vacuum is an average value, related to the length of time the armature spends in each position. For example, if the solenoid is energized half the time, the reading would be 1/2 of 5 in. Hg. or 2 1/2 in. Hg.

The metering valve is calibrated so that the maximum vacuum signal supplied to the diaphragm by the regulator/solenoid (5 in. Hg.) raises the rod to its highest (leanest) position.

Solenoid Test With Engine Running

1. Connect a voltmeter to the vacuum solenoid at the regulator input lead.
2. Start the engine and observe the voltmeter reading. Increase engine rpm until the reading jumps to approximately 12 volts. Hold it at that rpm.
3. Slowly reduce engine rpm and check to see if the voltmeter pulsates. This proves that the solenoid is getting signals from the module.

Feedback Fuel Valve Piston and Diaphragm Assembly

If the feedback fuel valve piston and diaphragm assembly is removed for any reason during servicing of the Holley Model 6500 carburetor, it is essential that this procedure is followed during reassembly to insure proper operation.

1. Apply one drop of Loctite or equivalent to the threads in each of the three tapped retaining screw holes.
2. Position the feedback fuel diaphragm and piston assembly over the spring so that the attaching screw holes align with the tapped holes in the upper body (air horn). Make sure the diaphragm is properly installed. One end of the spring should be over the end of the adjustment screw, the other end centered within the cupped washer of the diaphragm and piston assembly.
3. Install and tighten the three retaining screws.

ENGINE CONTROLS
FORD ELECTRONIC ENGINE CONTROLS (EEC III)

Section 29

FORD ELECTRONIC ENGINE CONTROLS III

Introduction

This section is designed to serve as a guide in understanding, testing and servicing the vehicles equipped with the electronic engine control III (EEC III) feedback carburetor and electronic fuel injection (EFI) system. Self-test is a diagnostic feature built into the electronic control assembly. When triggered, the ECA checks the EEC III system and if a problem is found, the technician is given a diagnostic code indicating the problem area.

This chapter covers description of the system and its components, operation of the system, and diagnosis of the system and its components.

Diagnosis

VISUAL INSPECTION

Before attempting any repairs or extensive diagnosis, visually examine the vehicle for obvious faults.

1. Remove air cleaner assembly. Check for dirt, foreign matter or other contamination in and around filter element.
2. Examine vacuum hose for proper routing and connection. Also check for broken, cracked or pinched hoses or fittings.
3. Examine each portion of the EEC III wiring harness. Check for the following at each location.
   a. Proper connection to sensors and solenoids.
   b. Loose or disconnected connectors.
   c. Broken or disconnected wires.
   d. Partially seated connectors.
   e. Broken or frayed wires.
   f. Shorting between wires.
   g. Corrosion.
4. Inspect sensor for obvious physical damage.
5. Operate engine and inspect exhaust manifold and exhaust gas oxygen sensor for leaks.
6. Repair faults as necessary. Reinstall air cleaner. If the problem has not been corrected, proceed to self-test.

SELF-TEST FEATURE

The EEC III system is equipped with a self-test feature to aid in diagnosing possible problems. The self-test is a set of instructions programmed in the computer memory of the calibration assembly. When the program is activated, the computer performs a system test. This verifies the proper connection and operation of the various sensors and actuators. The self-test program controls vehicle operation during the test sequence. Basically, the self-test program does the following.

1. Sends commands to the solenoids and checks for proper response.
2. Checks for reasonable readings from the sensors.
3. Produces numbered codes that inform the technician of a trouble area or of "all okay" operation.

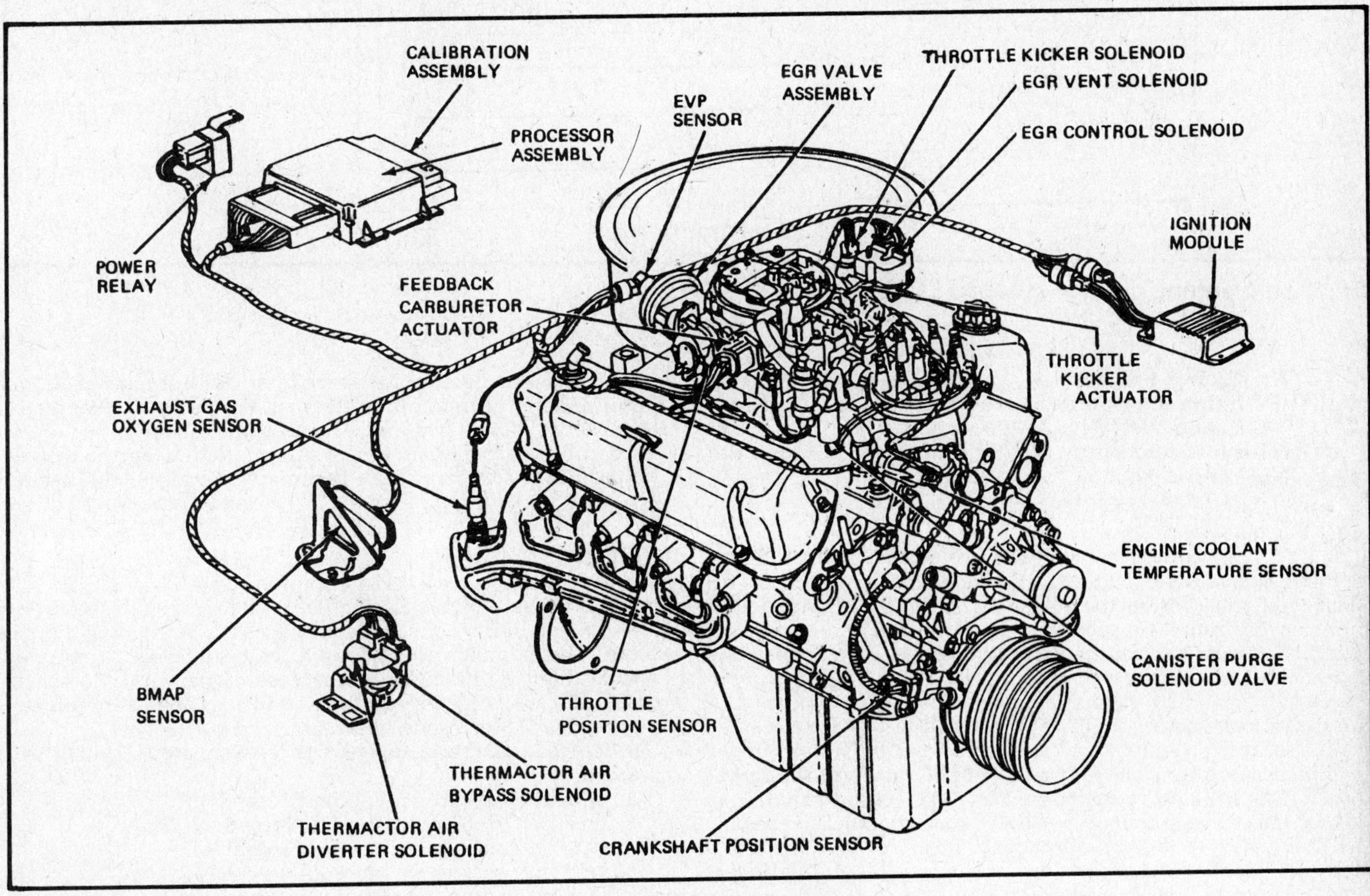

Electronic engine control (EEC III) system - with feedback carburetor

SECTION 29

ENGINE CONTROLS
FORD ELECTRONIC ENGINE CONTROLS (EEC III)

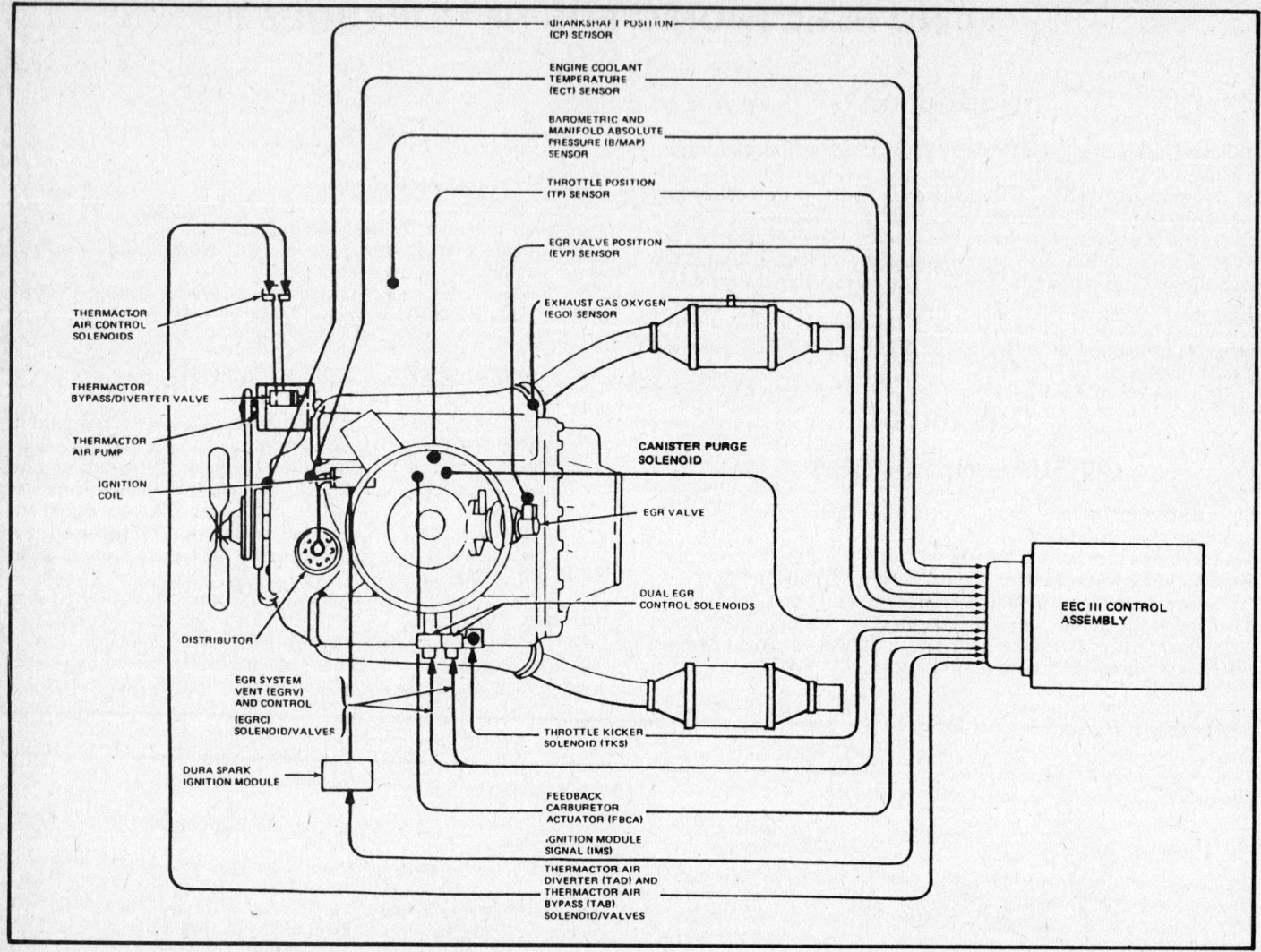

Electronic engine control system (EEC III)

NOTE: During the self-test the TAB and TAD "NO" and "UP" lights may blink alternately with the TAB and TAD "YES" and "DOWN" lights. Ignore the "YES" and "DOWN" lights and count only the number of times the TAB "NO" and TAD "UP" lights blink.

Self-Test Operation

The EEC diagnostic tester includes provisions for the self-test feature. In this case, the technician monitors the test panel for flashes of the thermactor solenoids operation. The series of light flashes represent a service code. The test can also be accomplished using a vacuum pump and gauges. In this case, the technician must actually monitor the solenoids for pulses or observe corresponding vacuum signals caused by the pulses. In all cases, the starting method for the self-test is the same.

The technician should activate the self-test only after proper engine preparation. The engine should be run until the radiator hose is hot and pressurized. With the engine running at idle, connect a vacuum pump to the barometric sensor vent outlet. Pump down the sensor vacuum to 20 in. Hg. and hold for 5 seconds. This low reading is below any possible normal barometric pressure and it triggers the self-test to start.

At first, the program pulses the throttle kicker solenoid and then holds it on during the entire test. The test lasts about one minute. After completion of the test, the program deactivates the throttle kicker solenoid. Any malfunctions recorded are indicated by thermactor solenoid pulses. Following the completion of all the service codes, the canister purge solenoid is energized for about fifteen seconds.

Service Codes

The service codes are a series of pulses on both thermactor solenoids at the same time. Each pulse is on for one-half second and off for one-half second. This sequence represents the number "one". The solenoids are off for a full second before starting the second digit of the code. In the case of the multiple service codes, the solenoids are off for five full seconds between two-digit codes. An example follows.

Service code 23 throttle position sensor, would follow this pattern.

1. One-half second on; one-half second off.
2. One-half second on; one full second off (2).
3. One-half second on; one-half second off.
4. One-half second on; one-half second off.
5. One-half second on; five full seconds off (3).

The vehicle remains in self-test for 15 seconds after completing

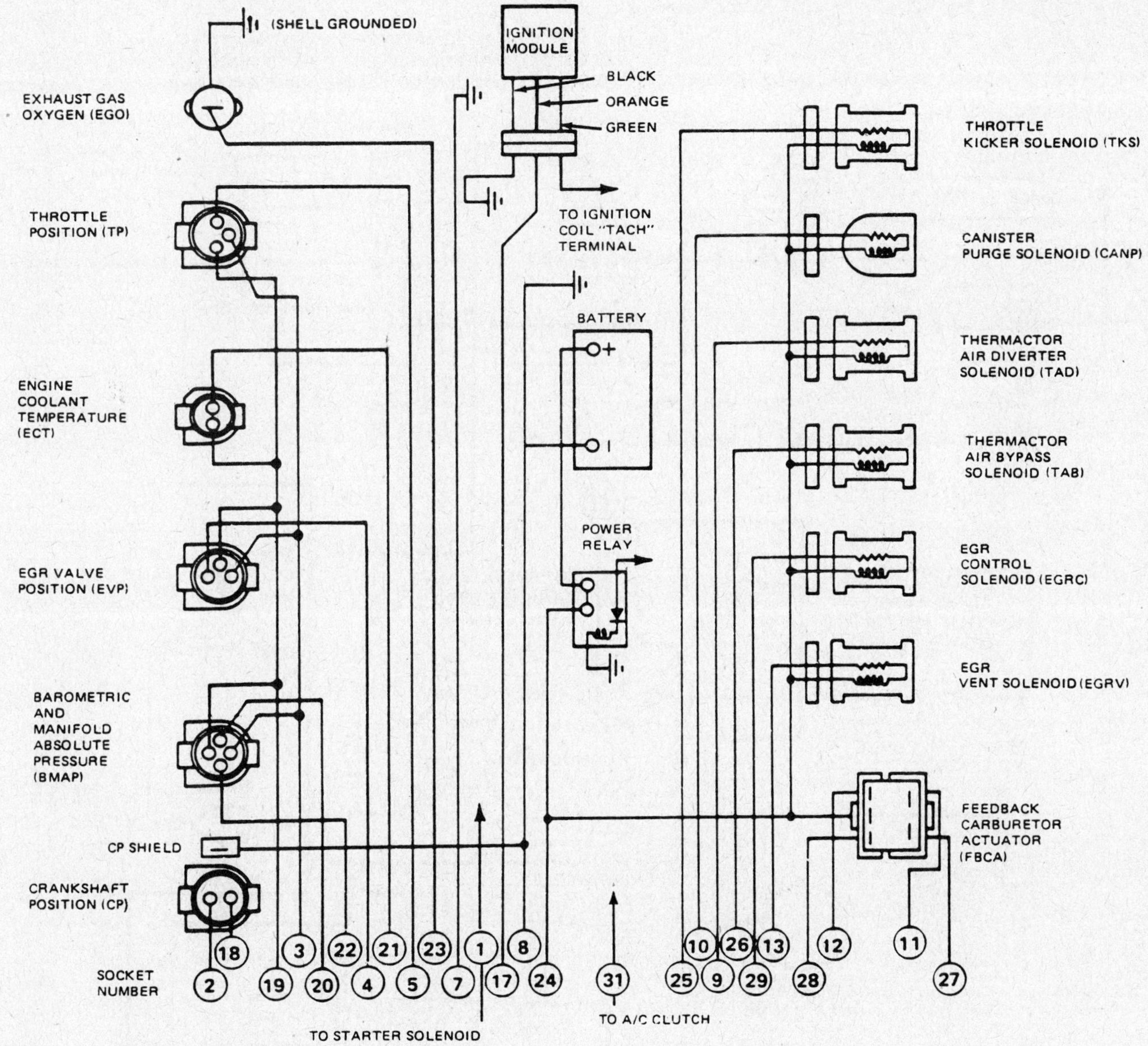

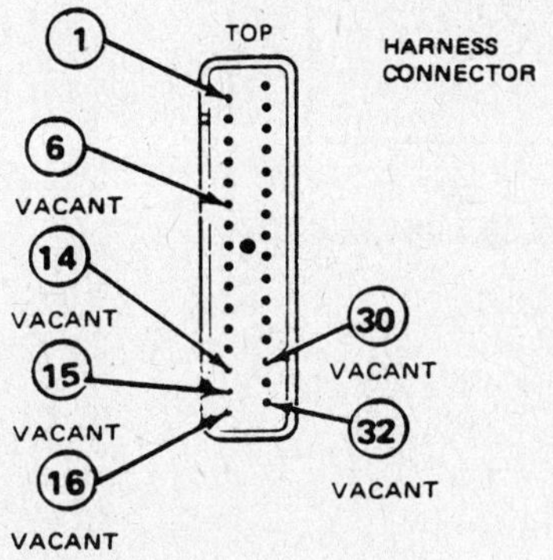

ENGINE CONTROLS
FORD ELECTRONIC ENGINE CONTROLS (EEC III)

29-69

SECTION 29

ENGINE CONTROLS
FORD ELECTRONIC ENGINE CONTROLS (EEC III)

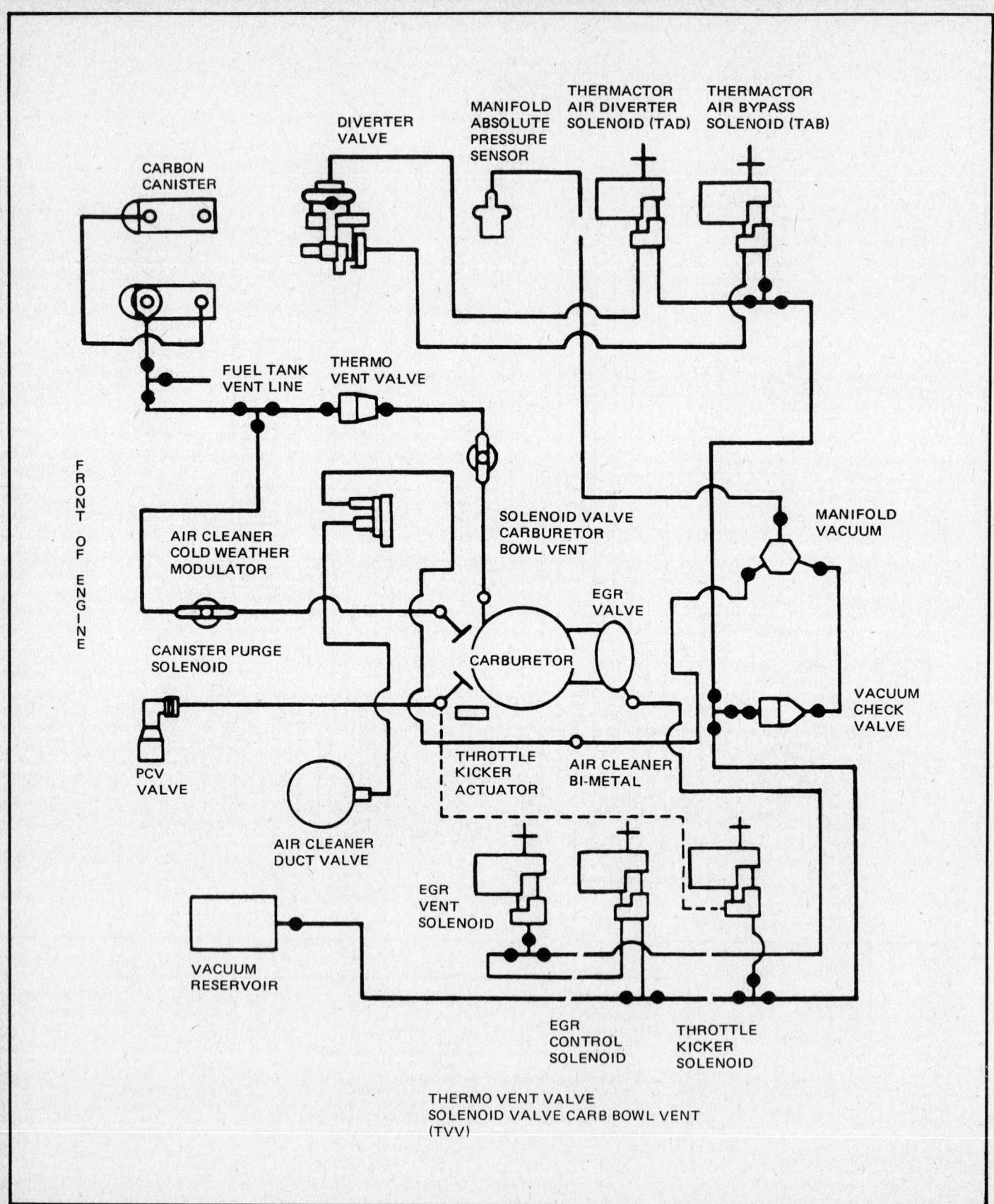

Electronic engine control system (EEC III) vacuum schematic

ENGINE CONTROLS
FORD ELECTRONIC ENGINE CONTROLS (EEC III)

SECTION 29

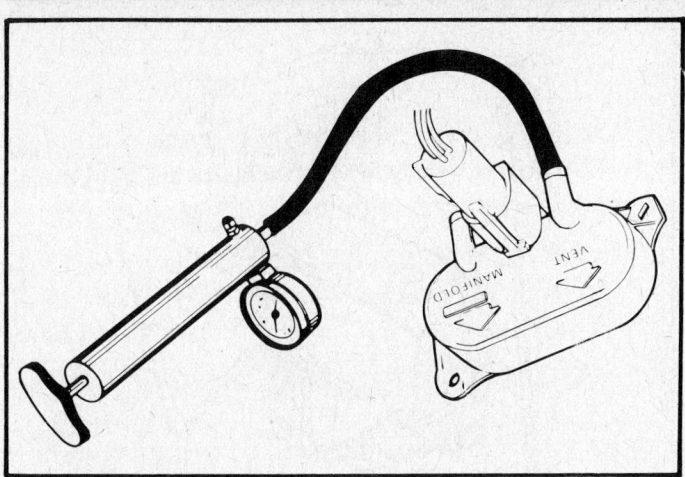

Trigger self-test

Code Number	Malfunction
11	EEC system okay
12	Engine rpm is out of specifications
21	Engine coolant temperature sensor (ECT) fault
22	Manifold absolute pressure sensor (MAP) fault
23	Throttle position sensor (TP) fault

Code Number	Malfunction
31	EGR position sensor (EVP) fails to open
32	EGR position sensor (EVP) fails to close
41	Fuel control lean
42	Fuel control rich
43	Engine temperature reading below 120 deg. F
44	Thermactor air system (TAB and TAD) fault

the last code. It then returns to normal operation. When beginning diagnosis, consider the final code first. In the above case of 23 then 41, begin with diagnosis of code 41–fuel control lean, and then continue with code 23–throttle position sensor.

Explanation of Code

Service codes are a series of pulses on both the thermactor air lights (TAB and TAD). The pulses form two-digit numbers. Each pulse is on for 1/2 second then off for 1/2 second for each count. A full second pause separates the digits, a 5–second pause separates service code numbers.

System Description

EMISSION CONTROL SYSTEMS

The emission control system regulates specific emission control functions. Based on sensor voltage inputs, the computer calculates appropriate voltages to energize engine control solenoids or trigger the Dura Spark ignition module. The solenoids cause desired vacuum or air flow and the module controls the spark advance timing curve. As engine operating conditions vary, sensor voltages change and the computer recalculates input data into output voltages.

In this manner, the computer directs the engine emission control systems to continuously control exhaust emission performance. The EEC III system consists of two types of emission control systems, feedback carburetor and electronic throttle body fuel injection. Basically the two systems differ in the method of controlling air-fuel ratio.

The feedback carburetor contains an electronically controlled actuator which varies fuel mixture and uses a conventional fuel pump. The electronic fuel injection is an electric fuel pump which supplies high pressure fuel to a fuel charging assembly consisting of a throttle body and two electronically controlled fuel injectors.

Both systems include several engine sensors, an electronic control assembly, several control solenoids and a vacuum operated thermactor air system and exhaust gas recirculation (EGR). A four-lobe crankshaft pulse ring and crankshaft position sensor provide engine speed and location measurements. The distributor has no advance or retard mechanism.

The control assembly determines timing depending on the engine operation conditions and individual vehicle calibration. A calibration assembly attached to the electronic control assembly contains specific calibration values for "tailored" engine performance. A power relay attached to the control assembly bracket, supplies system electrical power.

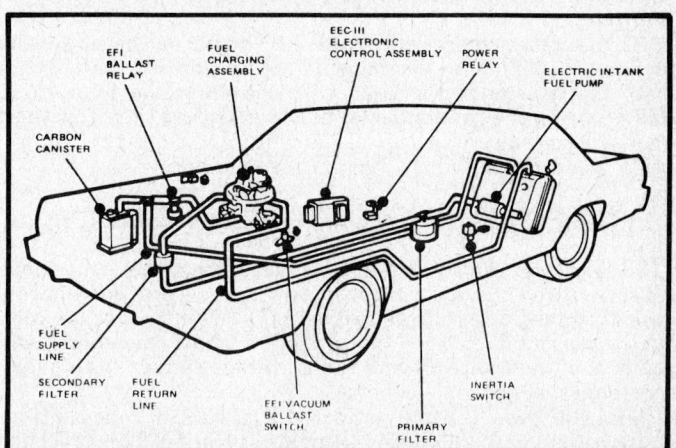

Electronic fuel injection (EFI) system - with throttle body injection

System Operation

The EEC III system uses the following sensors.
1. Throttle position sensor.
2. Barometric pressure and manifold absolute pressure sensors, contained in a single housing.
3. Engine coolant temperature sensor.
4. Crankshaft position sensor.
5. EGR valve position sensor.
6. Exhaust gas oxygen sensor.
7. Manifold charging temperature sensor, electronic fuel injection only. During engine starting and operation, the electronic control assembly constantly monitors these sensors to determine required timing advance, EGR flow rate, thermactor air mode and air-fuel ratio for any given instant of vehicle operation.
8. The electronic control assembly then sends output commands to the following.
   a. Ignition module, for spark timing.
   b. Throttle kicker solenoid, if equipped.
   c. EGR control solenoids, to control EGR flow rate.
   d. Canister purge solenoid.
   e. Feedback carburetor actuator or fuel injectors, to adjust air-fuel mixture.

SECTION 29

ENGINE CONTROLS
FORD ELECTRONIC ENGINE CONTROLS (EEC 111)

f. Thermactor solenoids, to direct thermactor air flow. The continuous control and adjustment of ignition timing, EGR flow rate and air-fuel ratio results in optimum engine performance under all vehicle operating modes.

LOS MODE (FAIL SAFE)

If for some reason there is a failure in the electronic control assembly, the system goes into what's called the limited operational strategy (LOS) mode. In this mode, the electronic control assembly output commands are cut off, and the engine operates with a fixed 10° BTDC spark advance only, regardless of sensor input signals. The engine can be operated until repairs are made, but poor performance may be experienced as long as the system is in the limited operational strategy (LOS) mode.

System Components

SENSOR AND SOLENOID CONNECTORS

All other sensor and solenoid connectors in the EEC III system are the "pull apart" type that feature a release tab attached to the male side of the connector. This assures that proper contact between the sockets and pins in the connector will be maintained.

To disconnect these connectors, lift the tab on the side of the connector slightly to decrease its holding pressure and separate the two connector halves. To reconnect the connectors, simply align the two connector halves and press them together. The holding tab on the side of the connector is designed to provide pressure to hold the two halves together.

ELECTRONIC CONTROL ASSEMBLY

The electronic control assembly controls the various functions of the entire emission control system. A separate relay powers the assembly. The control unit delivers 8.1–9.9 reference volts to the sensors. It collects the voltage data from the sensors, calculates output voltages and sends voltage signals to the various emission control solenoids.

The electronic control performs all of its functions continuously throughout all phases of engine operation. This precision enables engine operation with extremely good control of unde-

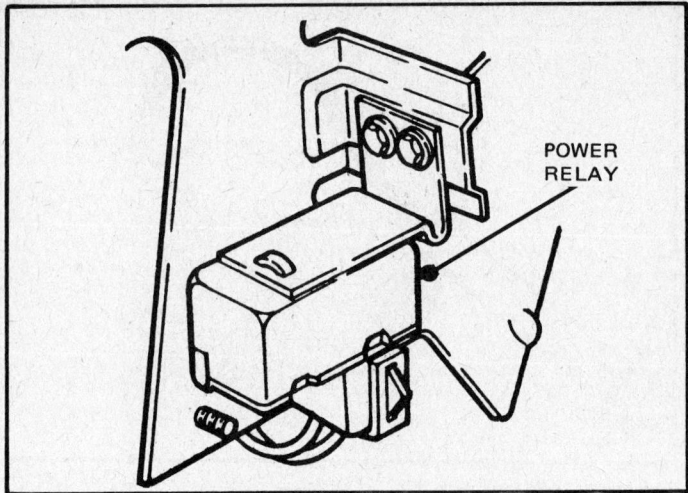
Electronic control assembly power relay

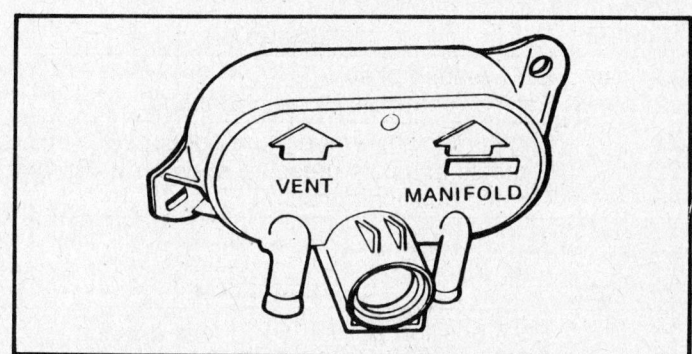
Barometric and manifold absolute pressure sensor

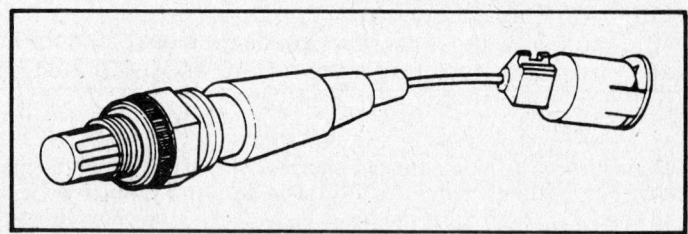
Exhaust gas oxygen sensor

sirable exhaust emission gases, while maintaining good driveability and fuel economy.

Processor Assembly

The processor assembly contains several groups of electronic devices that each perform specific functions. The processor performs five functions.
1. Analyzes sensor input voltages.
2. Converts voltages to input for computer calculations.
3. Selects operating strategy.
4. Calculates spark, EGR flow, air-fuel ratio, canister purge, throttle kicker and other output voltage values.
5. Dispatches voltage signals to the various emission control solenoids and ignition module to cause emissions control functions.

Calibration Assembly

The calibration assembly is a memory storage device and is at-

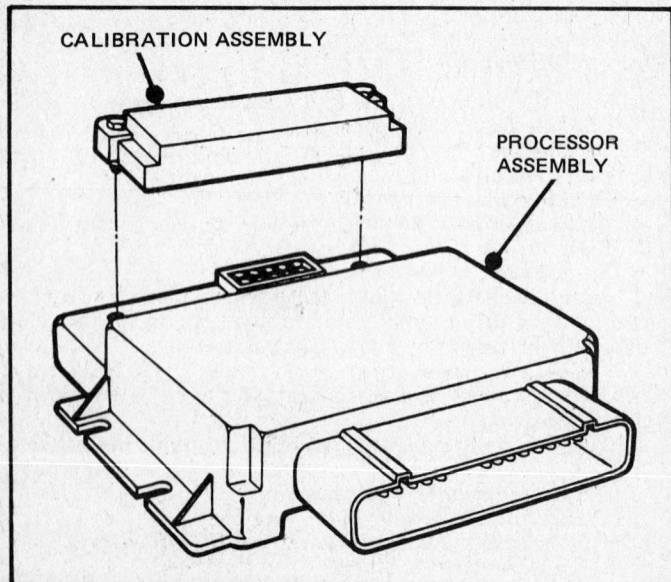
Electronic control assembly

ENGINE CONTROLS
FORD ELECTRONIC ENGINE CONTROLS (EEC III)

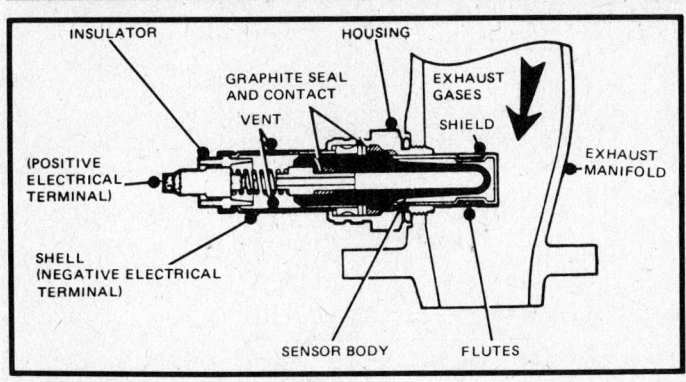

Exhaust gas oxygen sensor

tached to top side of processor assembly. It performs two functions.
1. Provides calibration information unique to the vehicle for use by processor assembly.
2. Recalls appropriate data from memory bank, when required.

Power Relay

A separate electrical relay provides the source of EEC III current. From a common battery positive terminal, a fusible link carries voltage to one relay terminal. The relay is normally open. With the ignition switch in the "RUN" position, current travels through a single relay diode to the pull-in coil and grounds through the relay case attached to the steering column. The relay connects battery or system voltage to the computer.

In the event of reversed polarity, which would damage electronic components in the control assembly, the relay diode prevents reversed flow and immediately releases the relay pull-in field.

MONITORING SYSTEM

The monitoring system measures key engine operating conditions.
1. Barometric and manifold absolute pressure sensor.
2. Engine coolant temperature sensor.
3. Throttle position sensor.
4. Crankshaft position sensor.
5. EGR valve pintle position sensor.
6. Exhaust gas oxygen sensor.
7. Manifold charging temperature sensor, electronic fuel injection only.

Each of these components senses a mechanical condition. It then converts it to an electrical voltage signal. The sensors provide the monitoring necessary to control the engine combustion process. The sensors react mechanically to pressure, temperature and position variations. They constantly adjust voltage signals to the electronic control assembly.

Barometric and Manifold Absolute Pressure Sensor

The barometric pressure and manifold absolute pressure sensor assembly contains two sensors. Each sensor converts a pressure into an electrical voltage. The assembly is mounted on the right fender apron.

The barometric pressure sensor reacts to normal atmospheric pressure. The computer uses this voltage to determine EGR flow requirements depending on the altitude at which the vehicles operate. The manifold absolute pressure sensor converts the manifold vacuum signal to an electrical voltage. The computer reads the voltages which indicate changes in engine load an atmospheric pressure. It reacts to control distributor spark advance at part throttle. It also controls EGR valve flow and air-fuel ratio.

Exhaust Gas Oxygen Sensor

The exhaust gas oxygen sensor monitors the overall effectiveness of the engine exhaust emission control system. It does this by measuring the presence of oxygen in the exhaust gas. Unlike the other sensors in the monitoring system which provide computer input about operating conditions, the exhaust gas oxygen sensor provides voltage data about engine operation output.

Engine Coolant Temperature Sensor

The engine coolant temperature sensor measures coolant temperature for the computer. The sensor threads into the heater water outlet at the front of the intake manifold.

Crankshaft Pulse Ring

The pulse ring position establishes reference timing for the engine. The lobes positioned on the crankshaft align with the sensors at 10° in advance of TDC. This sets timing at 10° BTDC.

The crankshaft pulse ring is located on the crankshaft vibration damper inside hub. It is installed during manufacturing and cannot be removed or adjusted. The ring contains four lobes equally spaced at 90°. Since the crankshaft rotates twice for each distributor revolution, four lobes suffice for 8 cylinder operation.

Crankshaft Sensor

The crankshaft sensor mounts immediately in front of the cylinder block aligned with the crankshaft pulse ring. The sensor identifies the actual position of the crankshaft. It produces a

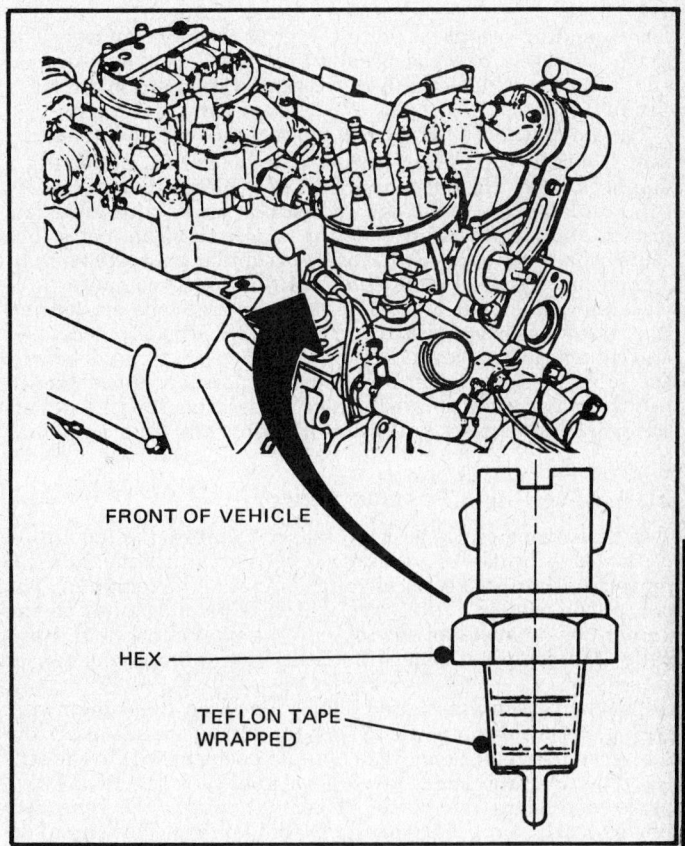

Engine coolant temperature sensor

SECTION 29

ENGINE CONTROLS
FORD ELECTRONIC ENGINE CONTROLS (EEC 111)

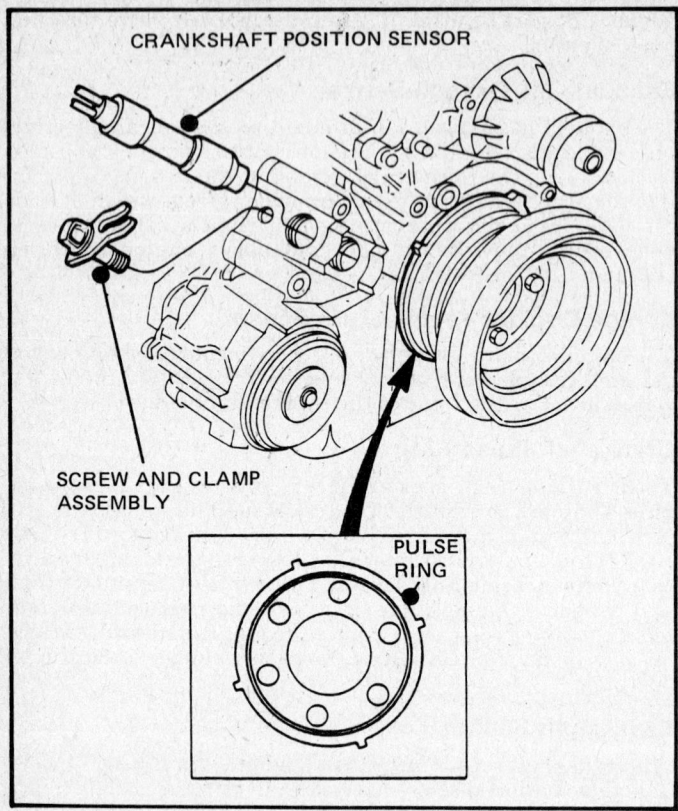

Crankshaft position sensor

corresponding electrical voltage signal to the computer. The sensor operates like the breakerless distributor pick-up coil and reluctor which make and break the ignition primary circuit.

The tip contains a permanent magnet and wire coil. The current from the computer passes through the coil, producing a magnetic field. The output wire carries voltage to the ECA. As the crankshaft rotates, the individual pulse ring lobes approach and finally align with the sensor tip. The metal lobe "cuts" the magnetic field. This interruption generates a voltage output signal of crankshaft position to the computer.

As the crankshaft rotates and a pulse ring lobe approaches the sensor, sensor voltage increases then sharply decreases and returns to base level. This occurs once each time a lobe cuts the sensor magnetic field. Crankshaft position sensor identifies the correct ignition firing. An inoperative sensor, connector or wiring harness will prevent engine starting.

EGR Valve Pintle Position Sensor

The EGR valve pintle position sensor monitors the amount of EGR valve pintle movement. It converts this mechanical movement into an electrical voltage input to the computer. The computer reads the voltage which is proportional to the amount of exhaust gas flowing into the intake manifold. Basically, the computer measures EGR flow through the sensor signals.

The valve contains a completely enclosed diaphragm and spring. It reveals no pintle movement during operation. As the diaphragm and pintle move, a plunger operates within the sensor. The computer sends a reference voltage to the EGR valve position sensor. The pintle movement causes the sensor to move, which changes the sensor output voltage. This signal returns to the computer where EGR flow is calculated. Depending on the voltage input from the EGR valve and other sensors,

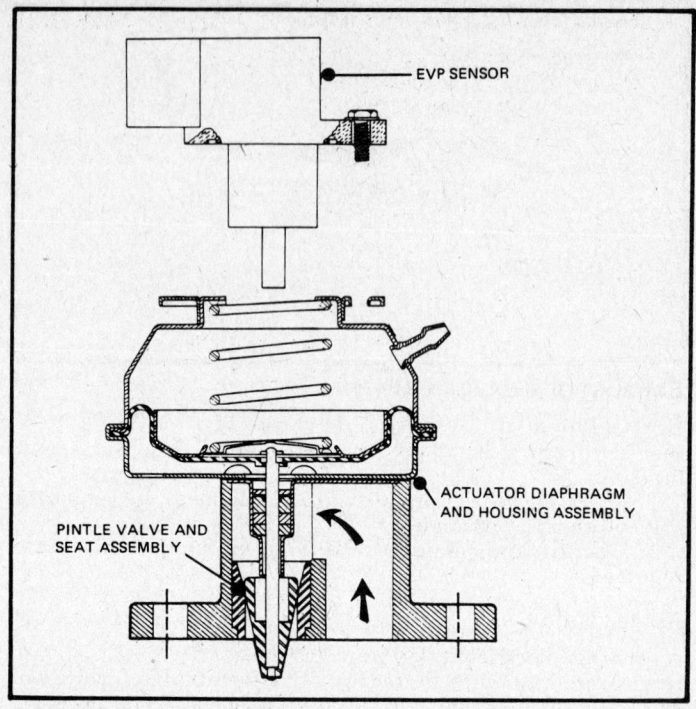

EGR valve

the computer can change the amount of EGR flow by controlling electrical voltage signals to the EGR valve vacuum solenoids.

The EGR valve position sensor does not move or control the EGR valve. The valve pintle, as always, operates by vacuum applied to the diaphragm. The sensor produces an electrical signal that describes the position of the EGR valve to the computer. The computer controls the solenoids which actually control EGR flow. The sensor only monitors valve position.

Throttle Position Sensor

The throttle position sensor indicates driver demand through use of a potentiometer. A potentiometer is a variable resistor control. As the driver operates the accelerator and throttle shaft, the sensor delivers voltage signals depending on electrical resistance.

Three operating modes are sensed. They are closed throttle (idle or deceleration), part throttle (normal operation) and wide open throttle (maximum acceleration). The computer applies a set voltage to the sensor as a reference. It then classifies the output which depends on the resistance caused by one of the three modes. The ECA identifies driver demand and reacts to control spark advance, EGR flow, air-fuel ratio and thermactor air flow.

The throttle position sensor is mounted on a slotted bracket that provides proper adjustment if replaced. The sensor must be correctly positioned or the ECA will read erroneous information.

Throttle Sensor Adjustment

1. Key on, engine off.
2. Verify throttle is off fast idle cam.
3. Remove vacuum hose from throttle kicker actuator.
4. Adjust sensor until voltmeter reads between 1.8 and 2.4 volts.

CATALYTIC CONVERTER

The EEC III system contains a three-way catalyst for final pro-

ENGINE CONTROLS
FORD ELECTRONIC ENGINE CONTROLS (EEC III)

SECTION 29

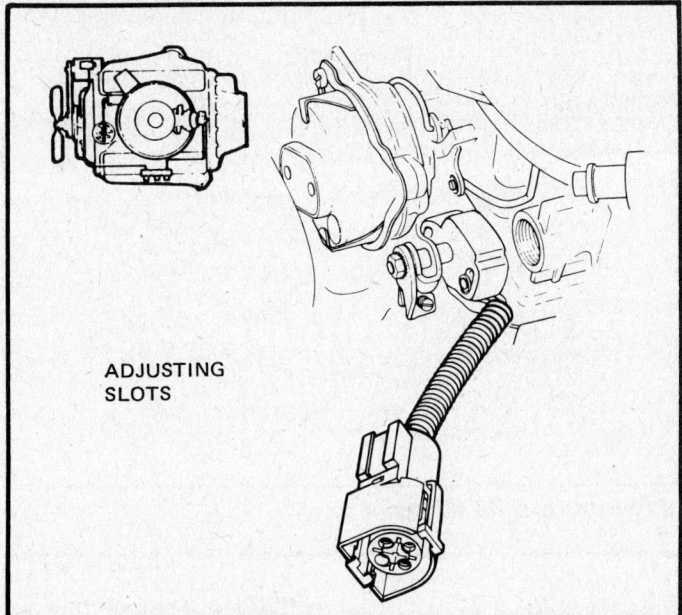

Throttle position sensor

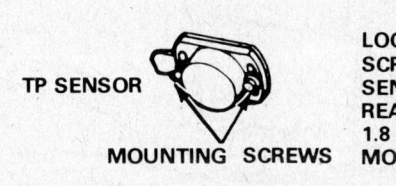

Throttle sensor adjustment

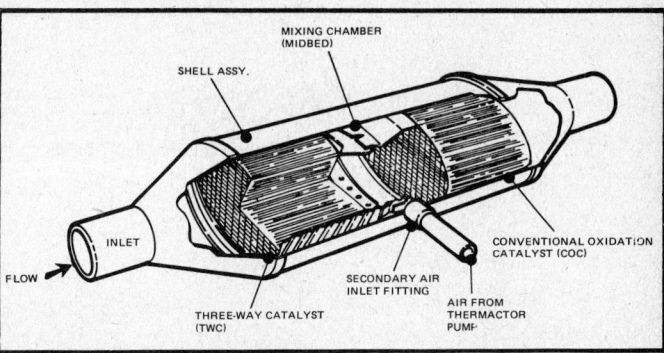

Dual catalytic converter

Operation

Exhaust gases enter the converter and flow first through the three-way catalyst. They pass through a "midbed" of air injected from the thermactor air pump and into the oxidizing catalyst. The combined effect of the chemical reactions and mixing with air results in acceptable reduction of pollutants and exhaust air quality which complies with emission regulations.

Under some conditions when rich mixtures (such as cold enrichment and wide open throttle) could enter the converter, the thermactor air might result in overreaction and converter overheating. In these cases, thermactor air is redirected to treat exhaust gases at the manifold ports or bypassed to the atmosphere.

The exhaust gas oxygen sensor plays a key role in monitoring exhaust air quality. Combined with the computer control voltages, the complete system effectively controls undesirable pollutants under all engine operating conditions.

Feedback Carburetor

FEEDBACK CARBURETOR ACTUATOR

The feedback carburetor actuator consists of a solenoid stepper motor which controls a metering rod position. The metering rod varies the vacuum level applied to the carburetor fuel reservoir. The degree of pressure acting on the fuel affects how easily fuel leaves the main discharge tube. Control of this function then controls carburetor air-fuel ratio.

The computer sends a voltage signal that actuates the feedback motor. Based on voltage inputs from the exhaust gas oxygen sensor, barometric pressure and manifold absolute pressure sensors, etc., the electronic control assembly computes an output timed voltage to the feedback actuator. This achieves the desired air-fuel ratio.

The actuator stepper motor is mounted on the carburetor's right side. It contains 120 steps in a total linear travel range of 0.400 in. The computer sequentially energizes four separate armature windings to obtain the necessary vacuum metering rod position. The motor varies the position of this metering valve to achieve the desired effect. The extended position provides a rich air-fuel mixture. Admitting vacuum to the fuel chamber lowers the pressure above the fuel and results in a leaner air-fuel mixture.

During cranking and immediately after starting, the computer sets the feedback actuator to initial position, depending on calibration. As engine operation continues, the computer modulates the actuator, based on sensor voltage inputs.

THROTTLE KICKER

A throttle kicker is used to control engine idle speed for different engine operations. The assembly includes a solenoid valve

---

cessing of undesirable exhaust emission gases. The control assembly provides the precise control that enables use of the three-way catalyst. Without it, the lean mixtures required would not be possible and converter efficiency would drop.

The EEC III converter contains two catalysts. Each is a porous honeycomb construction coated with a catalytic material. The honeycomb shape maximizes available surface area to improve converter efficiency. The forward element is coated with a rhodium/platinum catalyst designed to "reduce" oxides of nitrogen (NOx), unburned hydrocarbons (HC), and carbon monoxide (CO). The front element is called a three-way catalyst. The rear converter is coated with a platinum/paladium catalyst and is called a conventional oxidation catalyst.

Catalyst

A catalyst is a substance that initiates a chemical reaction that would otherwise not occur. It also enables the reaction to proceed under milder conditions than otherwise possible. In the case of engine exhaust gases, the engine emission control systems minimize the output of undesirable pollutants.

These "engine-out" emissions would be too high to comply with current emission standards. Once in the exhaust system, both temperature and additional air for oxidation are too low to complete the processing of pollutants into less harmful gases. The catalysts, rhodium/platinum and platinum/paladium, enable the gases to continue oxiding with available air.

The result is a conversion of NOx into nitrogen dioxide and HC and CO into carbon dioxide and water. Some other gases also result in small concentrations.

29-75

SECTION 29

ENGINE CONTROLS
FORD ELECTRONIC ENGINE CONTROLS (EEC 111)

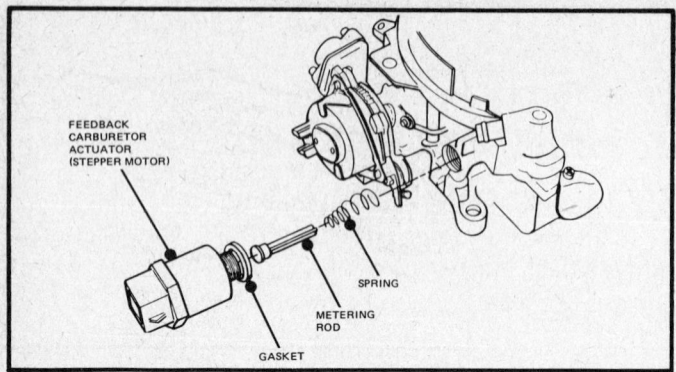
Feedback carburetor actuator

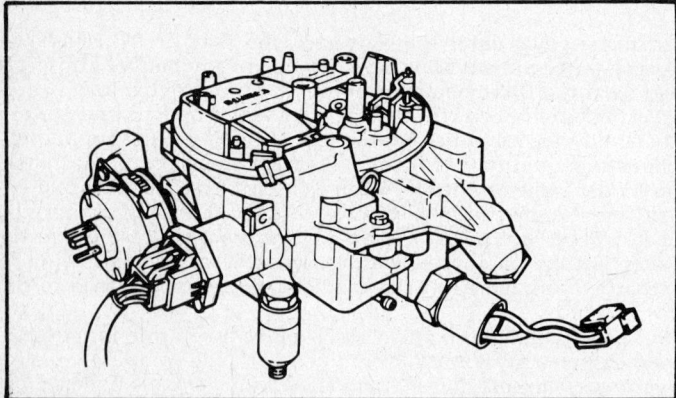
Feedback carburetor

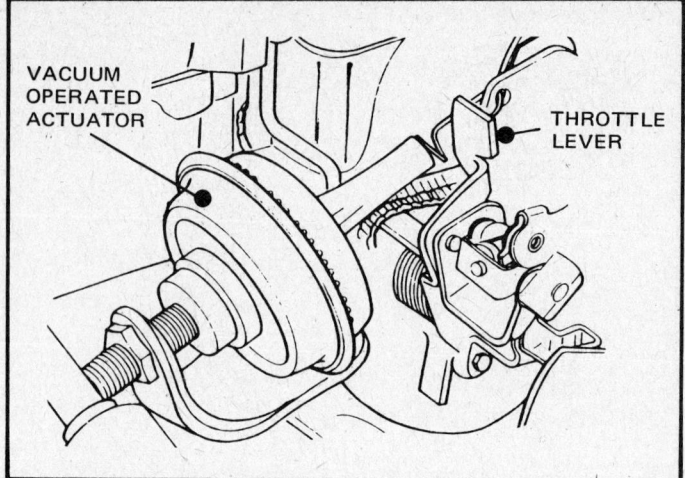
Vacuum throttle kicker

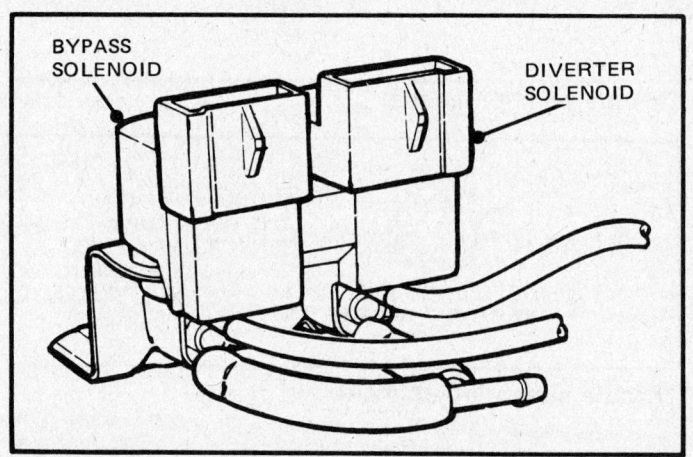
Thermactor air bypass and diverter solenoids

which controls the vacuum signal to a vacuum actuator. The computer provides the output voltage signal to operate the throttle kicker solenoid. When energized, the actuator diaphragm extends a carburetor throttle stop to increase engine idle speed. The computer operates the solenoid for the following conditions.

1. Below specified temperature to improve warm-up idle performance.
2. Above a specified temperature to increase engine cooling as needed.
3. With the air conditioning unit on to improve idle quality while under additional compressor load.
4. Above a specified altitude to improve idle quality.

The thermactor bypass-diverter valve contains three outlet passages: downstream to the catalytic converter, upstream to the exhaust manifold and bypass to the atmosphere. During normal engine temperature, thermactor air is directed downstream to the catalyst. The computer controls the desired routing based on coolant temperature for a calibrated time and other sensor inputs.

The ECA energizes the bypass solenoid when time at closed throttle exceeds a calibrated time value. If time between the EGO lean/rich sensor exceeds a set time value, it also bypasses. These two calibrated functions are intended to protect the catalytic converter from damage and/or for vehicle safety. The computer also energizes the bypass solenoid during wide open throttle.

Canister purge occurs above a calibrated cold temperature and below a set overheat temperature, with engine rpm above a calibrated speed and after a set delay period following engine starting. The canister does not purge with the engine at closed throttle. Also, once the canister purge solenoid activates or deactivates, a slight delay may occur in the change of purge operation.

DURA-SPARK II IGNITION SYSTEM

The Dura-Spark II system is a solid state ignition system consisting of an electronically controlled (breakerless) distributor, ignition coil, battery, electronic control module (ECM), ignition switch, ignition wires and different wiring harnesses. The Dura-Spark II system operates when the distributor sends an electronic signal to the electronic control module. The distributor receives this signal as the armature which is attached to the distributor shaft, rotates past the stator assembly (pick-up coil). The rotating armature causes fluctuations in a magnetic field produced by the stator assembly magnet.

These fluctuations produce a voltage in the stator assembly pick-up coil. Once the distributor sends the electronic signal to the electronic control module, the module then controls the timing of the spark at the spark plugs.

DURA-SPARK III IGNITION SYSTEM

This system is basically the same as the Dura-Spark II system, only the distributor on the Dura-Spark III system uses an Electronic Engine Control system. The EEC system controls the spark advance in response to different engine sensors.

This includes a crankshaft position sensor which replaces the stator assembly and armature normally positioned in the distributor assembly. Due to these engine sensors the distribu-

ENGINE CONTROLS
FORD ELECTRONIC ENGINE CONTROLS (EEC III)

SECTION 29

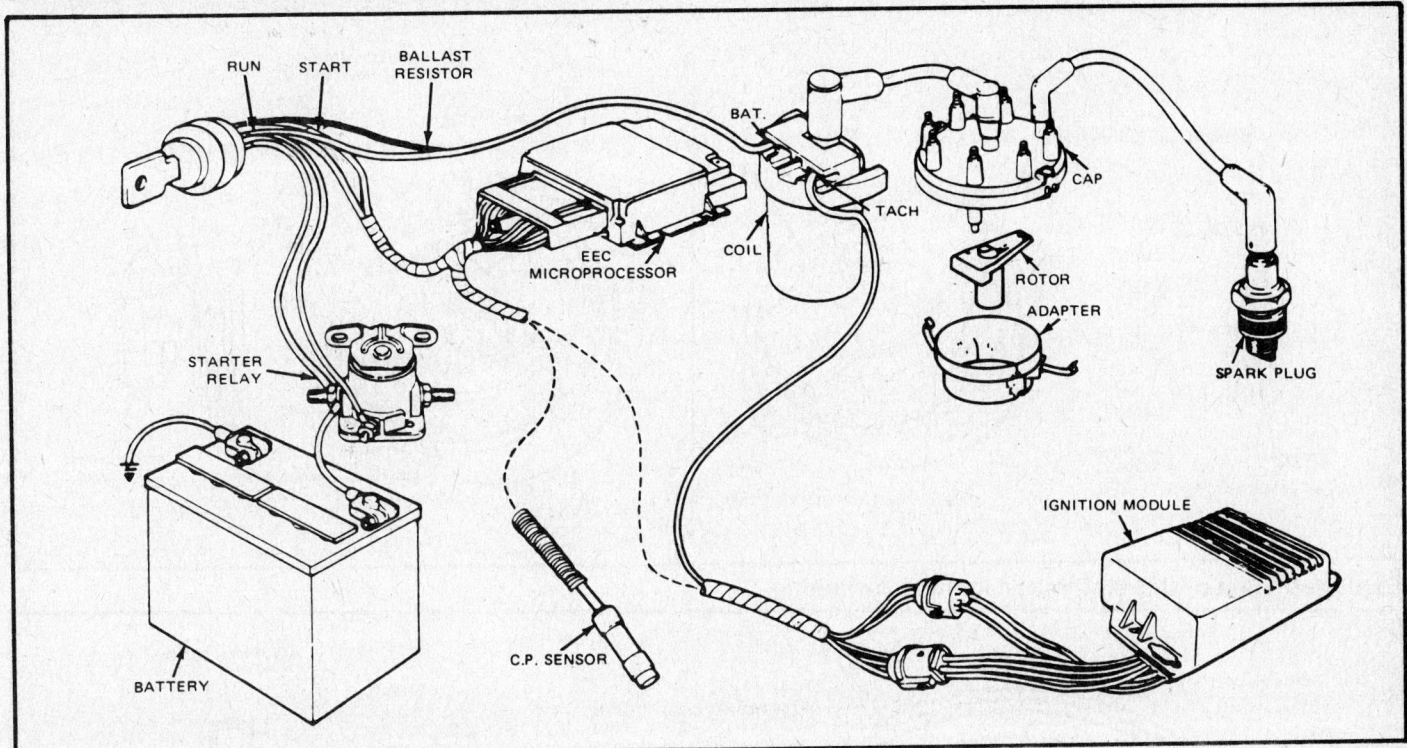

Typical Dura Spark III Ignition System

tor for the Dura-Spark III system serves only to distribute the high voltage generated by the ignition coil. Because the position of the distributor rotor to cap is important for proper high voltage distribution, the distributor is mounted to the engine and the rotor position is adjustable.

UNIVERSAL IGNITION MODULE (UIM)

Some of the Ford models have an added electronic control module with an extra connector with three wires. This extra connector is connected to a switch, which can be used as either a distributor vacuum modulator valve or an ignition barometric pressure switch.

VACUUM SPARK CONTROL MECHANISM

The vacuum spark control mechanism can provide spark advance if a single diaphragm is used or spark advance and retard if a dual diaphragm assembly is used. The diaphragm used depends on the engine calibration. Vacuum applied to the single diaphragm assembly causes the diaphragm and the attached diaphragm to move compressing the advance spring, which controls the rate of spark advance. The diaphragm rod is attached to the stator assembly, so when the diaphragm rod moves the stator assembly moves in relation to the armature.

When vacuum is applied to the dual diaphragm it causes the advance diaphragm and the diaphragm rod to move, all other action is the same as the single diaphragm.

DURA-SPARK III ROTOR ALIGNMENT

Procedure

1. Bring the engine up until number one piston is on compression stroke.
2. Remove the distributor cap, and position the cap and wires to one side. Now remove the rotor.

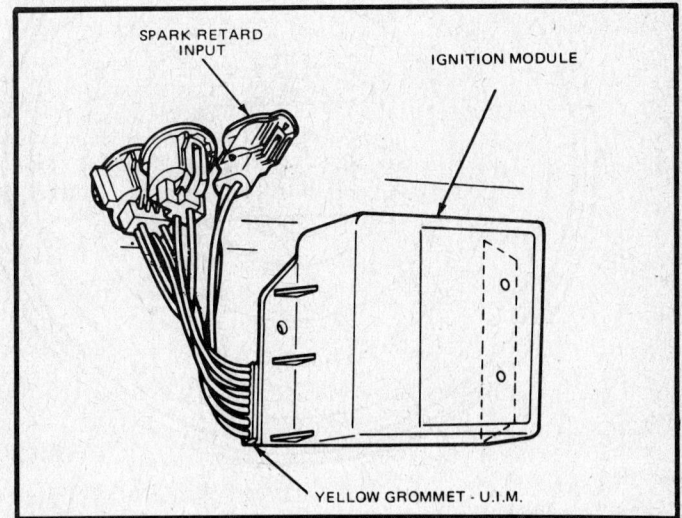

Typical UIM module

3. Check the rotor alignment by slowly rotating the engine until the rotor alignment tool T79P-12200-A or equivalent can be inserted in the alignment slots provided in the distributor.
4. Read the timing mark on the damper, if the timing mark is 0° ± 4° the rotor alignment is within specifications.

Adjusting the Rotor

1. With engine up on number one piston at compression stroke, rotate the engine until the timing pointer is on the 0° timing mark.
2. Remove the distributor cap and rotor and loosen the two sleeve assembly adjustment screws.

29-77

SECTION 29 ENGINE CONTROLS
FORD ELECTRONIC ENGINE CONTROLS (EEC 111)

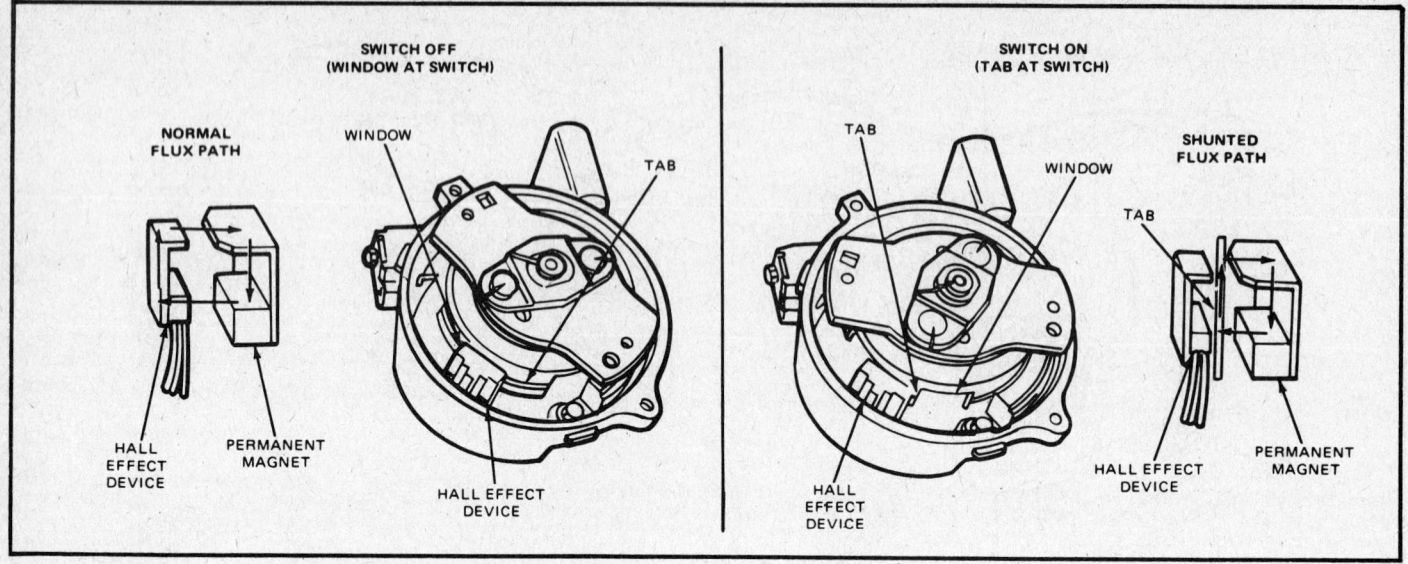

Exploded view of the distributor ignition switching

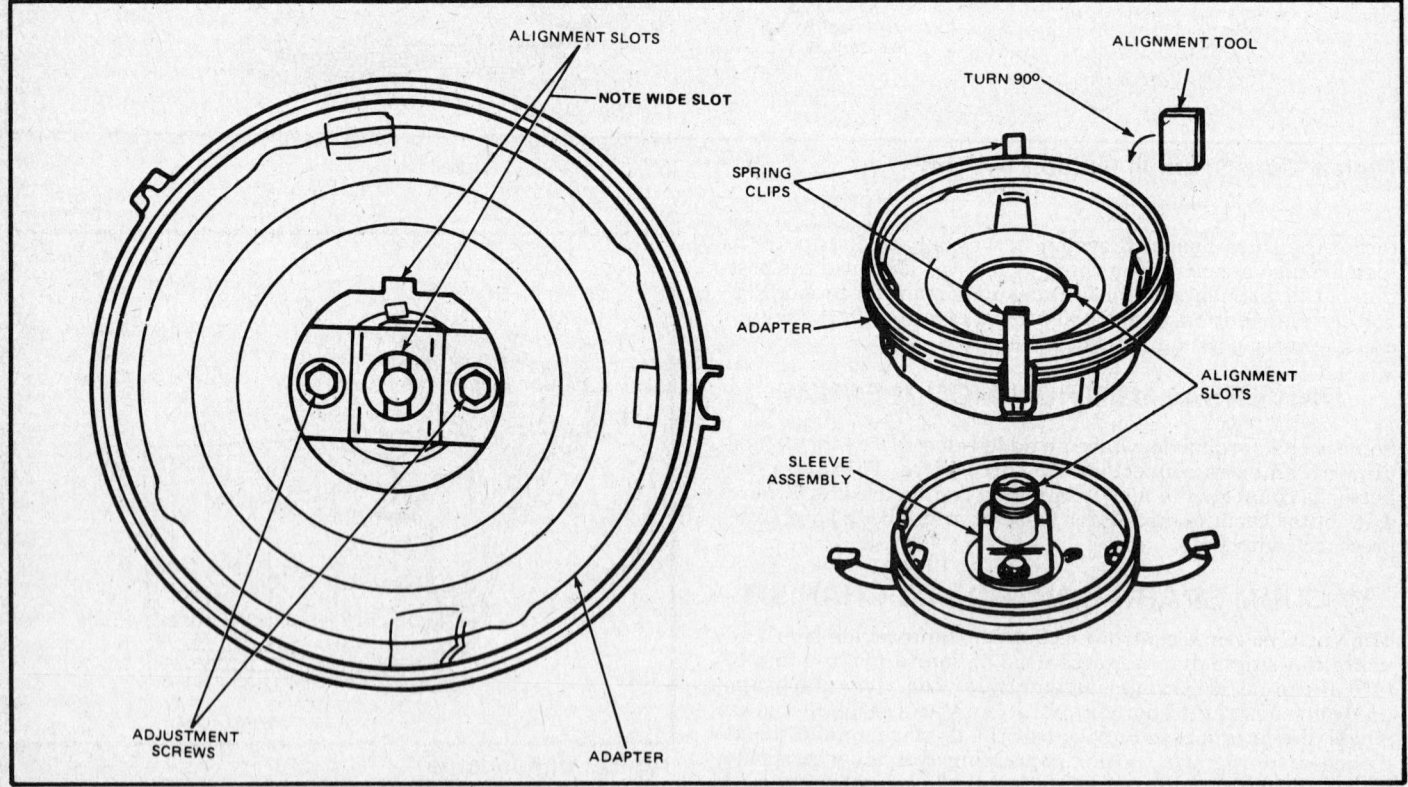

Rotor alignment for the dura spark III system

3. Insert the rotor alignment tool T79P–122000–A or its equivalent into the slots provided in the distributor.
4. Torque the two sleeve assembly adjustment screws to 25–35 inch lbs.
5. Reinstall the rotor, distributor cap and ignition wires.

THICK FILM INTEGRATED IV IGNITION SYSTEM (TFI-IV)

The TFI-IV module is made of a thermo plastic and is mounted to the base of the distributor. This module supplies voltage to the profile ignition pick-up (PIP) sensor, which sends the crankshaft position information to the TFI module.

The TFI module then sends this information to the EEC-IV module, which determines the spark timing and sends an electronic signal to the TFI ignition module to turn off the coil and produce a spark to fire the spark plug. The TFI-IV Ignition system is used on the 1.6 EFI and the 2.3 liter engines.

This ignition system also uses a universal distributor, which is cam gear driven and uses centrifugal or vacuum advance. This distributor also has a "Hall Effect" vane switch stator as-

ENGINE CONTROLS
FORD ELECTRONIC ENGINE CONTROLS (EEC 111)
SECTION 29

sembly, and provision for a fixed octane adjustment. The Hall Effect vane switch stator assembly consists of a Hall Effect device on one side and a magnet on the other, the rotary cup has windows and vanes in it.

When the rotary cup rotates it passes through the space between the Hall Effect device and the magnet. So when a window is between the Hall Effect device and the magnet the switch is in the off position and the Hall Effect device will send no signals. When a vane passes between the device and the magnet the switch is turned on and the Hall Effect Drive will start sending signals. The voltage pulse is used by the EEC-IV system for sensing the crankshaft position and computing the spark advance based on engine demand and calibrations.

NOTE: The timing set on the TFI ignition system is not recognized as a normal adjustment.

OCTANE ADJUSTMENTS

The octane adjustment is done by taking the standard 0° rod which is located in the bowl of the distributor bowl with either a 3° or a 6° retard rod.

FORD EEC IV ENGINE CONTROL SYSTEM

System Description

The EEC IV system is similar to other Ford engine control systems in that the center of the system is a microprocessor called an Electronic Control Assembly (ECA). The ECA receives data from sensors, switches, relays and other electronic components an issues commands (output signals) to control engine functions. The ECA is calibrated to optimize emissions, fuel economy and driveability.

The ECA in the EEC IV system is a microprocessor like other EEC systems, but the calibration modules are located within the ECA assembly instead of being attached to the outside, as in previous models. The harness connectors are edge-card type connectors, providing a more positive connection and allowing probing from the rear while connected. The ECA is usually mounted in the passenger compartment under the front section of the center console.

NOTE: The EEC IV system does not control the pulse air injection (Thermactor air pump) or the upshift lamp.

The EEC IV system electronically controls the fuel injectors for air/fuel ratio control, spark timing, deceleration fuel cut-off, EGR function (on or off), curb and fast idle speed, evaporative emissions purge, A/C cut-off during wide open throttle, cold engine start and enrichment, electric fuel pump and self-test engine diagnostics.

EEC-IV Monitoring System

THROTTLE POSITION SENSOR (TPS)

This sensor is mounted on the throttle body and provides the ECA with a signal in relationship to the opening angle of the throttle plate. This sensor output signal uses the operating voltage of 5 volts. On the EEC-IV system with electronic fuel injection the TPS signal to the ECA is used only to change the spark timing during the wide open throttle mode. When the throttle plate moves from closed to the wide open position, the voltage output signal from the TPS is changed from 1.0 volts to a high voltage of 5 volts.

NOTE: The throttle position sensor used on the 1.6 liter EFI-EEC-IV system is not adjustable and should be replaced if it is out of specifications.

ENGINE COOLANT TEMPERATURE SENSOR (ECT)

This sensor is located in the heater supply tube, which is located at the rear of the engine. The ECT sensor measures the engine coolant temperature and sends a corresponding signal to

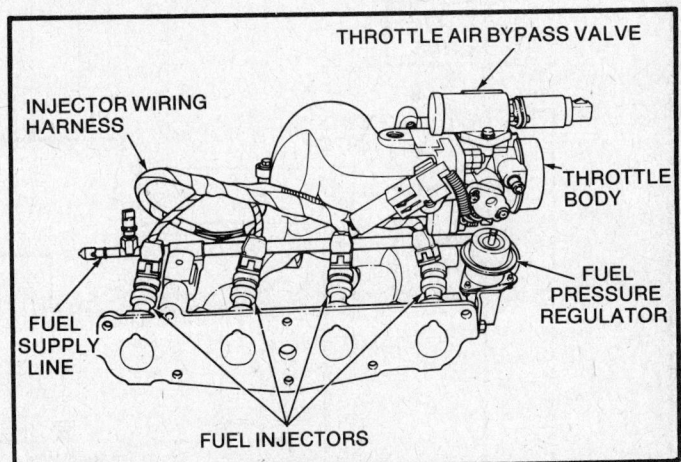
Fuel charging manifold assembly

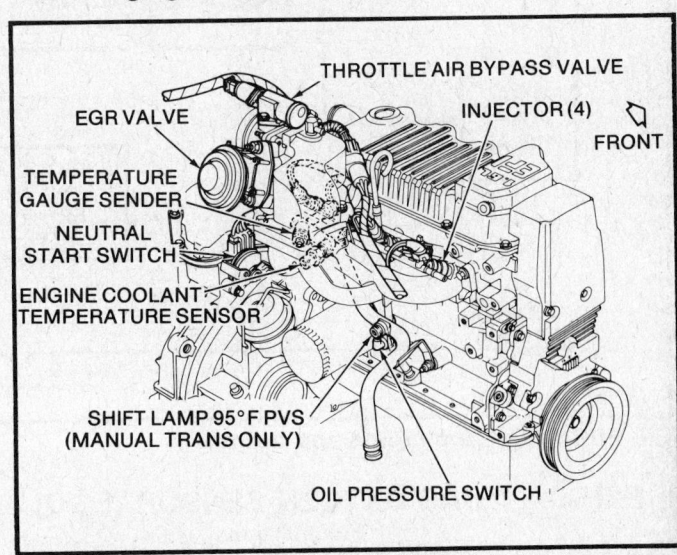
1.6L EFI-EEC IV Engine - front view

the ECA. The ECT sensor output signal also uses the operating voltage of 5 volts. When the ECA receives the signal from the ECT sensor, the ECA will alter the following as a function of engine coolant temperature, air-fuel ratio, idle speed, spark, and EGR and canister purge control. When the engine coolant is cold the ECT sensor will signal the ECA to provide enrichment to the air-fuel ratio for good cold drive-away.

SECTION 29: ENGINE CONTROLS
FORD EEC IV ENGINE CONTROL SYSTEM

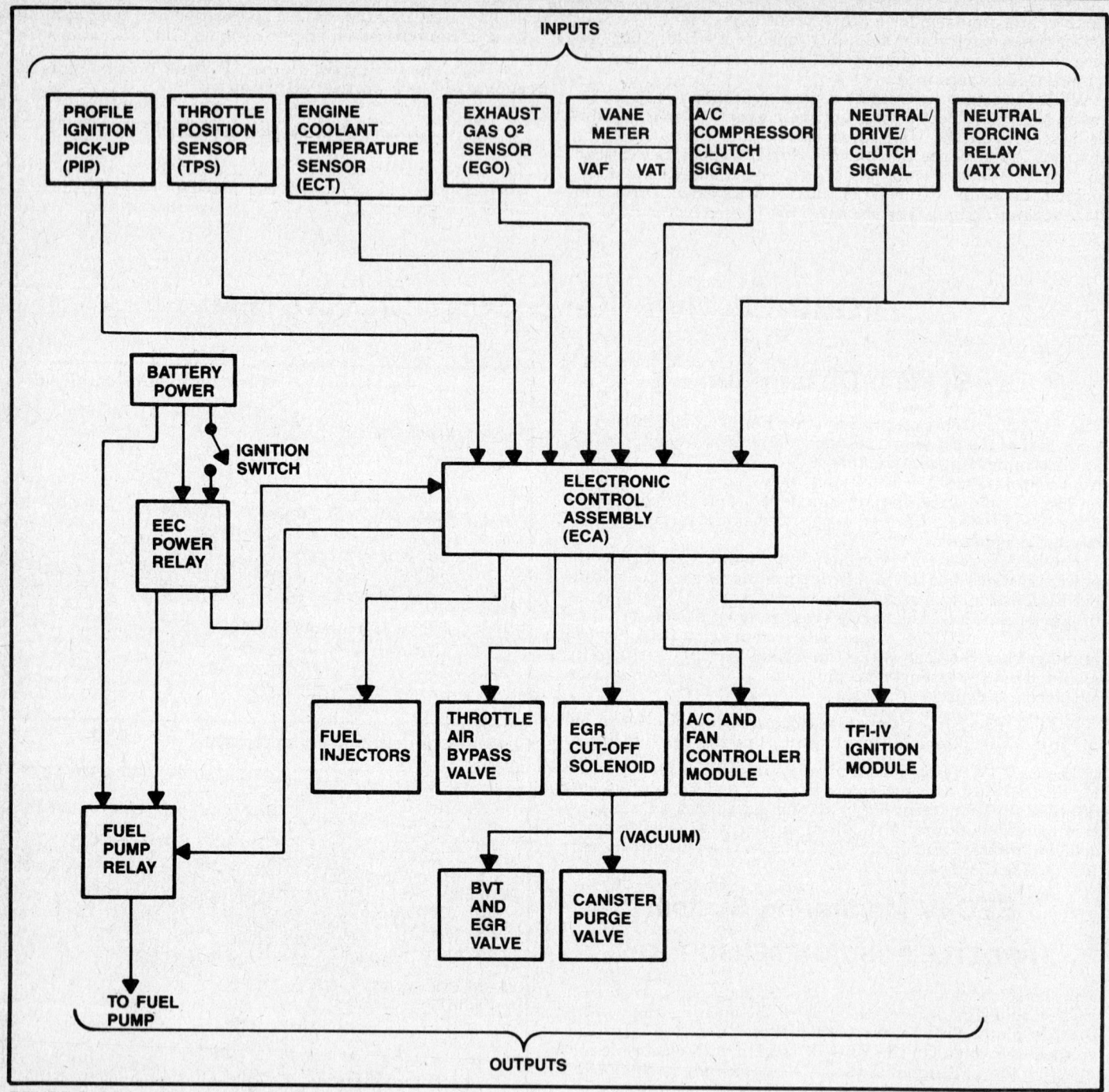

EFI-EEC IV System inputs and outputs

EXHAUST GAS OXYGEN SENSOR (EGO)

This newly designed EGO sensor is mounted in its own mounting boss, which is located between the two downstream tubes in the header near the divided Y pipes. This sensor works with an operating voltage between zero and one volt output. The voltage all depends on the presence (lean) or absence (rich) of oxygen in the exhaust gas. A voltage reading more than 0.6 volt indicates a rich air-fuel ratio, while a reading of less than 0.4 volt indicates a lean ratio. The new design is that the rubber protective cap used on top of the sensor on other modules has been replaced with a metal cap.

NOTE: Voltage must never be directly applied to the EGO sensor, because it could damage the calibration of the sensor. This includes the use of an ohmmeter. When using a volt meter, be sure that it has a high input impedance of at least 10 megohms and is set on the proper voltage range.

VANE METER

The vane meter is made up of two sensors packaged in one assembly, the Vane Airflow Sensor (VAF) and the Vane Air Temperature Sensor (VAT). The vane meter is used to measure the

ENGINE CONTROLS
FORD EEC IV ENGINE CONTROL SYSTEM
SECTION 29

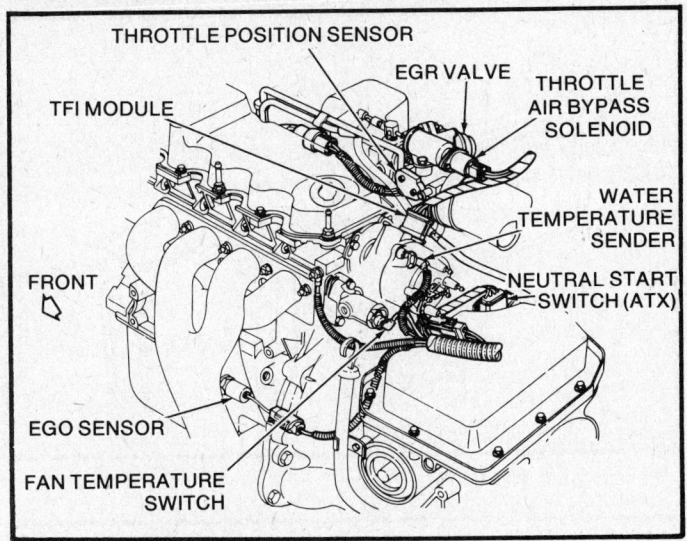

1.6L EFI-EEC IV Engine - rear view

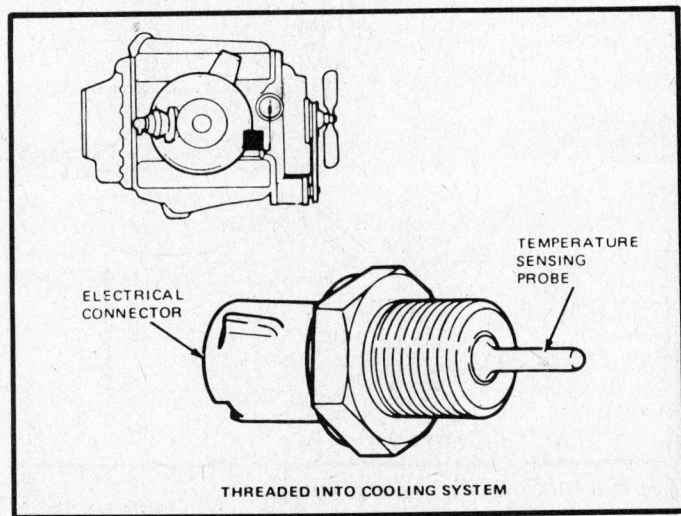

Typical engine coolant temperature sensor

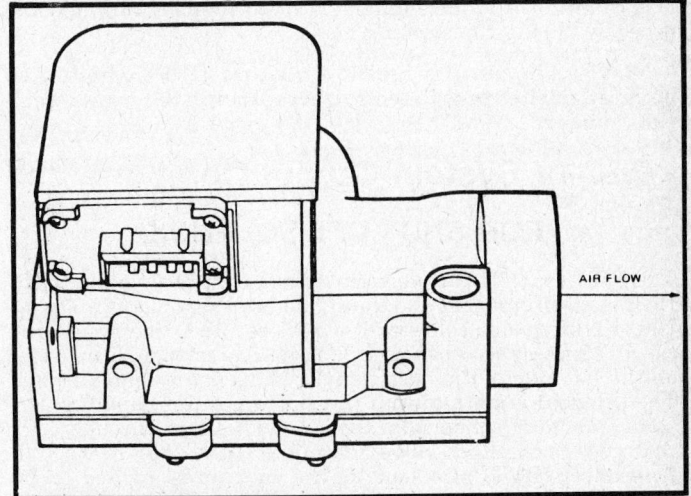

Typical Vane air flow meter

A/C CLUTCH COMPRESSOR SIGNAL (ACC)

At the same time that battery voltage is applied to the A/C clutch it is also supplied to the ECA. This allows the ECA to maintain the engine idle speed using the Throttle Air Bypass Valve control solenoid to counterbalance the added load put on the engine by the operation of the A/C clutch. When the ECA is using the throttle air bypass valve it will maintain the engine idle speed at 850 rpm for automatic transmissions and 950 rpm for the manual transmissions.

NEUTRAL START SWITCH

Manual Transmission

The manual transmission uses two switches to indicate to the ECA the load or no-load condition of the transmission. The Clutch Engaged Switch operates in two positions, when the clutch pedal is depressed the switch is closed and the switch is open when the pedal is in the upright position. The switch is mounted on the clutch pedal lever. The other switch is called the Transmission Neutral Switch, this switch is mounted on the clutch shift linkage and is closed only when the transmission is in the neutral position.

Automatic Transmission

The neutral start switch is mounted on the transmission and sends a signal tot he ECA to let the ECA know if the transmission is in gear or out of gear. The operating voltage between the switch and the ECA is 5 volts. When the 5 volt signal is sent the switch is open and the transmission is in drive or reverse. When the signal is one volt or less the switch is closed and indicates to the ECA that the transmission is in park or neutral.

NEUTRAL FORCING RELAY (AUTOMATIC TRANSMISSION ONLY)

This relay is located in the wiring harness that runs parallel to the left front headlight connector. It is energized when the engine is in the start mode, the job of this relay is to bring the neutral start switch voltage down to less than one volt. When this happens it is telling the ECA that the engine is in a no-load condition so it maintains the engine fast idle speed. This fast idle speed used during the starting mode, improves the cold starting performance of the engine. Without the relay the ECA would take the signal from the neutral start switch as a

air flow to the engine and the temperature of the air stream. The vane meter is located between the air cleaner and the throttle body and is mounted to a bracket near the left side shock tower. There is a vane mounted on a pivet pin inside the vane meter body, the airflow going through the body moves the vane.

The more air going through the vane meter body the further the vane rotates around the pivet point. The pivet pin in the vane assembly is connected to a variable sensor and like the other sensors in the EEC-IV system, the vane meter output signal also uses the operating voltage of 5 volts. The output signal from this sensor will vary from zero to 5 volts depending on how much air is going through the vane meter at the time the signal is sent out. The more air the vane meter receives the higher the voltage output will be. The VAT is mounted in the front of the vane meter to measure the incoming air temperature.

The ECA then picks up the signal from the VAT and uses it with a pre-programmed pressure value to convert the VAP signal into a mass airflow value. This converted value is used to calculate the fuel flow for the proper air-fuel ratio. The VAT also affects timing as a function of air temperature.

29-81

SECTION 29
ENGINE CONTROLS
FORD EEC IV ENGINE CONTROL SYSTEM

load condition and the engine idle speed would not be adjusted properly during the starting mode.

NOTE: The profile ignition pick-up (PIP) which was covered earlier in this section is replacing the crank position sensor.

EEC-IV System Output Components

EGR SHUT-OFF SOLENOID

The ECA controls the electrical signal that is supplied to the EGR shut-off solenoid and the signal is either on or off. The solenoid is off during cold starts or at closed and wide open throttle positions, at all other times it is on. The solenoid is mounted on the left side of the dash panel in the engine compartment. The solenoid is normally in the closed position, and the controlled vacuum taken from the solenoid is sent through a tee that goes to the EGR valve and to the back pressure variable transducer (BVT) also some of the vacuum is applied to the canister purge valve.

BACK PRESSURE VARIABLE TRANSDUCER (BVT ON EFI SYSTEM)

The BVT valve operates as a bleed valve and is mounted on the right side of the dash panel in the engine compartment. The BVT valve is connected to the exhaust system collector and is on the control pressure and back pressure side of the exhaust collector.

The position of the bleed valve and how much of the vacuum is bled off from the input vacuum to the EGR valve is determined by the ratio of the control pressure and back pressure. When the ratio of the back pressure is increased to the control pressure in the BVT valve, the BVT valve will increase the vacuum to the EGR valve. The BVT valve operates as a type of control valve to determine how far the EGR valve should be open.

CANISTER PURGE VALVE

This valve is controlled by the vacuum from the EGR solenoid and is the standard type valve that operates the same as the purge valve in the previous system.

IGNITION TIMING MODULE

The EFI-EEC-IV system uses the Thick Film Integrated ignition system (TFI) and is very similar to the TFI module used in the 1983 models except the new module has six connector pins, instead of three like the 1982 module.

THROTTLE AIR BYPASS VALVE

This valve is electronically controlled by the ECA and controls both cold and warm idle airflow. This valve operates by controlling a variable amount of air around the throttle plate. The valve has an air inlet which is located in front of the throttle plate and the air outlet is behind the throttle plate. With the air inlet and outlet positioned where they are, more air can be added to the mixture without having to move the throttle plate. This valve also replaces the other throttle position modulators that have been used on the previous systems. The other function of this valve is to counterbalance the added load put on the engine by the operation of the A/C clutch.

A/C AND COOLING FAN CONTROLLER MODULE

This module is used on engines equipped with electronic fuel

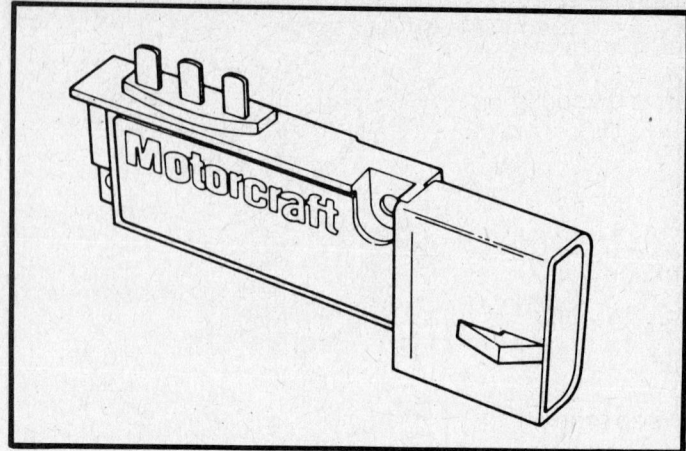
TFI ignition module

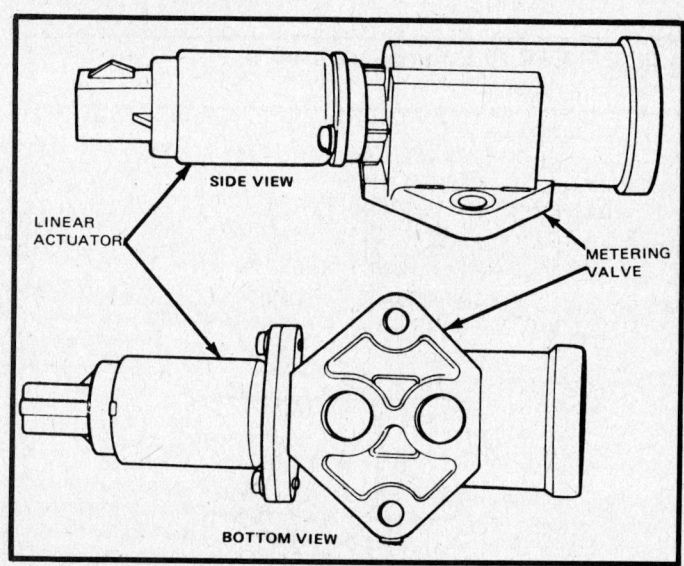
Typical throttle air bypass valve

injection and is used to control the operation of the A/C compressor and the engine cooling fan. It is located under the instrument panel on the right side and receives input signals from the coolant temperature switch, the stop light switch and the ECA.

When the engine temperature is less than 221°F the ECA will deenergize the cooling fan motor as soon as the temperature goes over 221°F the coolant temperature switch sends a signal to the controller module which overrides the ECA signal and prevents the cooling fan from shutting off. When the brakes are applied a disabling signal is sent to the A/C compressor and the engine cooling fan for 3-5 seconds.

KNOCK SENSOR

This sensor is a piezoelectric accelerometer designed to produce frequency excitation at approximately the same frequency as the engine frequency (5-6 KHz range) and then provide this information to the ECA. The sensor is made up of a thin circular piezoelectric (dielectric crystal) ceramic disk which is bonded to a metal diaphragm. The electrical connections are made through a two pin integral connector.

ENGINE CONTROLS
FORD EEC IV ENGINE CONTROL SYSTEM
SECTION 29

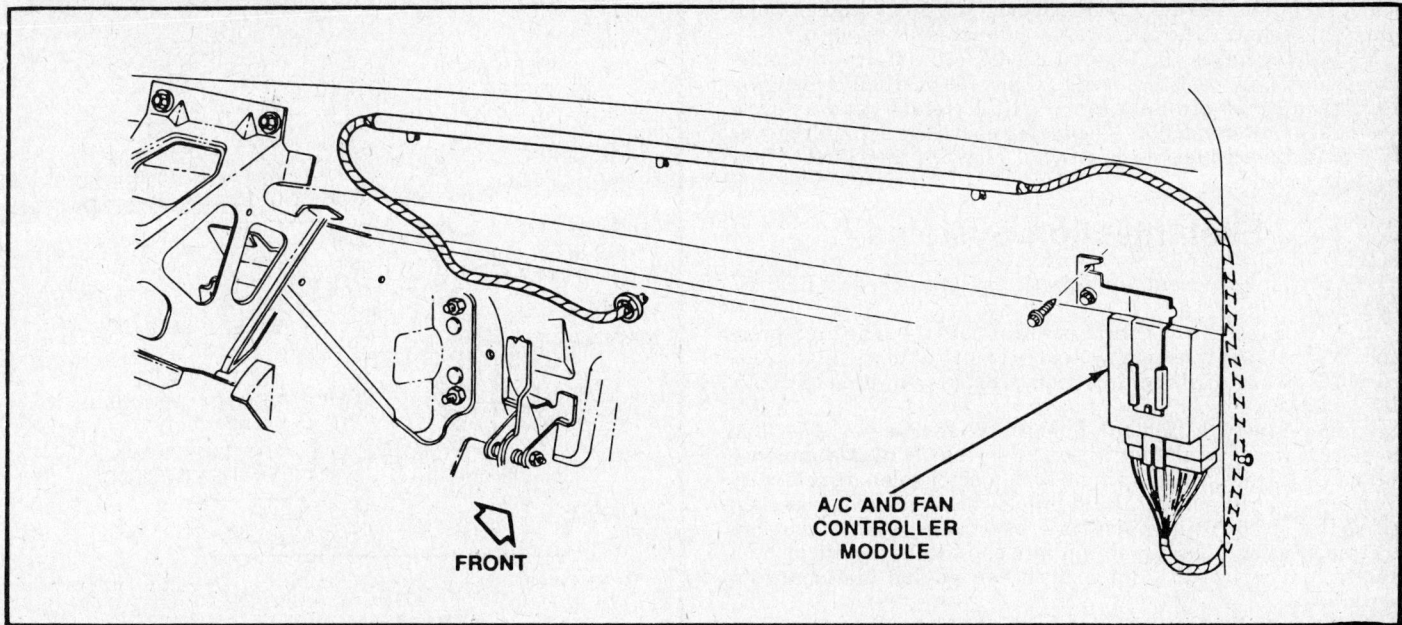

A/C & fan controller module location

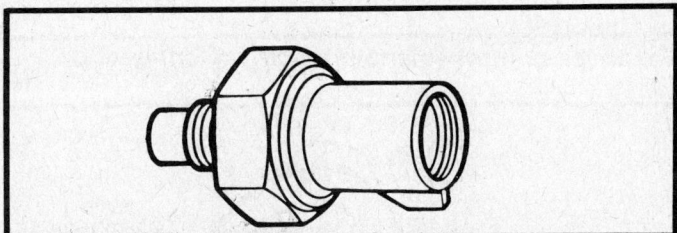

Typical knock sensor

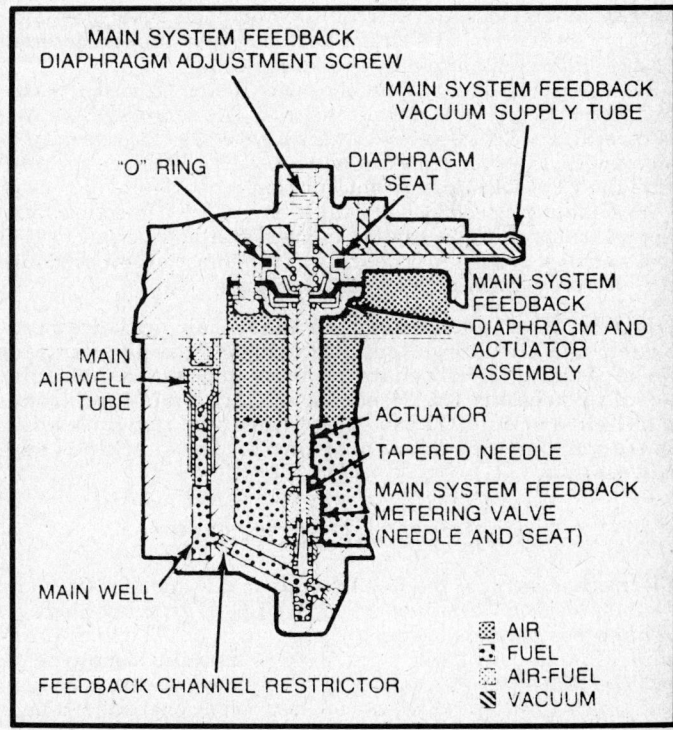

Feedback control solenoid in main metering mode

Carburetor Feedback Systems

There are two different types of feedback control systems used on EEC-IV vehicles: the feedback control solenoid and the duty cycle solenoid.

1. The feedback control solenoid is a pulsing solenoid that introduces fresh air from the air cleaner into the idle and main system vacuum passages. An electrical signal from the ECA activates the solenoid.

The amount of air the solenoid allows to enter depends on its duty cycle. A zero percent duty cycle closes the solenoid (no voltage) and the carburetor will go to a maximum rich condition. A 100 percent duty cycle (voltage applied) fully opens the solenoid and the carburetor will go to a maximum lean condition. The two feedback control solenoids used look different and mount differently on the carburetors, but they operate in the same manner.

2. The remote mounted duty cycle solenoid regulates idle, off idle, and main system air/fuel ratios.

A separate channel in the air horn of the carburetor conveys the idle feedback regulated bleed air into the idle fuel mixture. This channel has an external port connected to the duty cycle solenoid by a 7/32 inch I.D. rubber hose. The air channel intersects the idle channel at the same point as the fixed idle air bleed. As the amount of air bleed into the system increases, the air/fuel ratio becomes leaner. Thus, the duty cycle solenoid regulates the idle air/fuel ratio.

For main system control, the duty cycle solenoid regulates a vacuum to a fuel control valve assembly. The valve assembly consists of a diaphragm and actuator in the air horn and a metering valve (needle and seat) in the main body. The regulated vacuum above the diaphragm moves the actuator which, in turn, positions a tapered needle in the valve seat, allowing additional fuel to flow through the feedback channel restrictor into the main well. This regulates the fuel flow into the main system, thus controlling the off idle and part throttle air/fuel ratios. When the ECA recognizes the need for a leaner air/fuel

29-83

SECTION 29
ENGINE CONTROLS
FORD EEC IV ENGINE CONTROL SYSTEM

ratio, it signals the duty cycle solenoid to supply higher vacuum, which moves the diaphragm and actuator upward.

The spring below the tapered needle forces it upward to decrease fuel flow past the needle. Conversely, when the engine requires a richer air/fuel ratio, the ECA signals the duty cycle solenoid to lower vacuum. The spring above the actuator moves it and the tapered needle downward, allowing more fuel to flow past the needle.

Fuel Injection Systems

There are four different fuel injection systems used on EEC-IV vehicles.

1. High-Pressure Central Fuel Injection — — The high-pressure central fuel injection system is identical to the high pressure (39 psi) central fuel injection (CFI) system used on EEC-III vehicles.
2. Low-Pressure Central Fuel Injection System — — The low-pressure central fuel injection system is also commonly called CFI, since it had a single fuel injector solenoid centrally located on the engine intake manifold. This system is also classified as a single point, pulse time, modulated injection system. In this system, fuel is metered into the intake manifold by a single fuel injector mounted inside an engine fuel charging assembly.
3. Mass Airflow Multi-Point Fuel Injection System — — The mass airflow multi-point fuel injection system has its injectors located in the intake manifold above each cylinder's intake valve.

This system is classified as a multi-point, pulse time, mass airflow air measurement system. In this system fuel is metered into the intake manifold by the fuel injectors.

In a mass airflow system the vane meter is used. As explained earlier, a vane meter consists of two sensors: Vane Air Temperature (VAT), and Vane Airflow (VAF). These sensors, along with a Barometric Absolute Pressure (BAP) sensor, provide the ECA with airflow information.

4. Adaptive Speed/Density Multi-Point Fuel Injection System -- This system is similar in operation and design to the mass airflow system just described. The major difference is in the electronic control of the fuel injectors.

NOTE: In an adaptive speed/density air measurement system the air charge temperature (ACT) sensor is used for measuring the air charge temperature and a manifold absolute pressure (MAP) sensor is used to monitor intake manifold vacuum. These sensors provide the ECA with the necessary airflow information for fuel delivery calculation.

ELECTRONIC CONTROL

Electronic control of the fuel injectors is the same for the four systems used on EEC-IV as it was on EEC-III vehicles. There is a difference in how the fuel injectors operated. The high-pressure CFI and both multi-point systems used the same type of injector that EEC-III vehicles did. The low-pressure CFI system uses a new type of injector. When this is energized, a ball moves inward off the seat to allow fuel to flow. It does not use a pintle as the other injectors do.

TEMPERATURE COMPENSATED ACCELERATOR PUMP (TCP) SYSTEM

The temperature compensation accelerator pump (TCP) system was developed to provide better control over "cold" engine and "warm" engine accelerator pump discharge volume delivery requirements. The temperature compensated (rate-sensitive) pump allows delivery of a large pump capacity to facilitate cold engine requirements and a smaller pump capacity

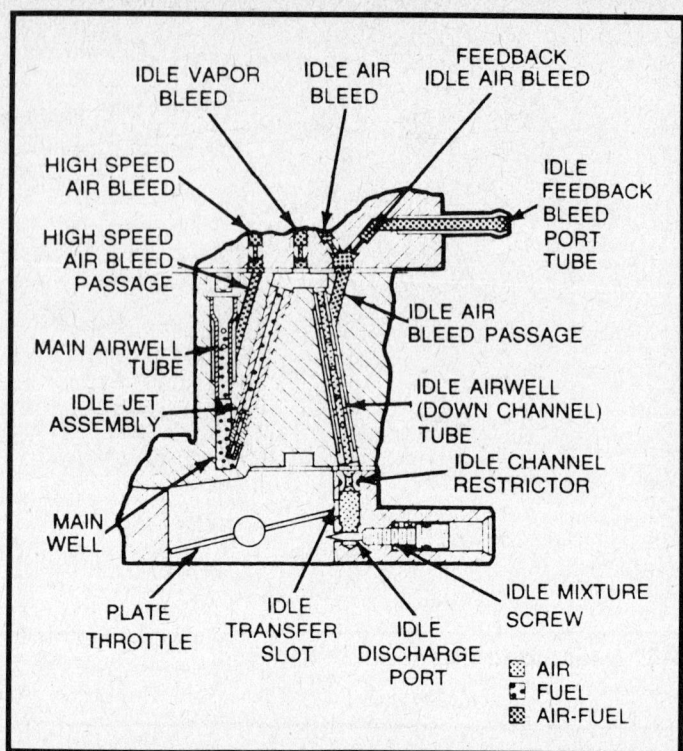
Feedback control solenoid in idle metering mode

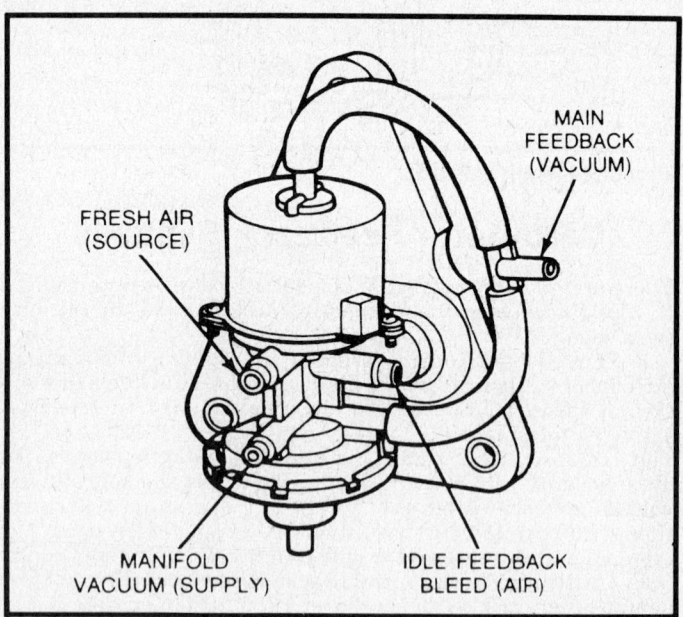
Duty cycle solenoid

during warm engine operation. The amount of fuel delivered during warm engine operation is a function of the rate at which the accelerator pedal is opened (fast opening-low capacity; slow opening-higher capacity).

The design incorporates a bypass bleed controlled by a vacuum operated solenoid. The position of this valve is controlled by an electric solenoid vacuum valve, which is in turn controlled by the EEC-IV system. The vacuum-operated valve is normally closed when no vacuum is applied, allowing full pump capacity during cold operation. With vacuum applied, the pump

ENGINE CONTROLS
FORD EEC IV ENGINE CONTROL SYSTEM

SECTION 29

functions as a rate-sensitive valve, controlling the amount of fuel bypassed back to the fuel bowl and not delivered to the intake air stream.

System Operation

The EFI-EEC-IV system can be divided into three subsystems:
1. Fuel System.
2. Air System.
3. Electronic Engine Controls:

The fuel sub-system consists of a high-pressure electric fuel pump to deliver fuel from the fuel tank, a fuel filter to remove contaminants from the fuel, a Fuel Charging Manifold Assembly, a fuel pressure regulator, and solid and flexible fuel supply and return lines. The Fuel Charging Manifold Assembly incorporates four electronically controlled fuel injectors. One injector is mounted directly above each intake port in the lower intake manifold. All injectors are energized simultaneously and fire once every crankshaft revolution.

The injectors spray a predetermined quantity of fuel into the intake airstream. A constant pressure drop is maintained across the injector nozzles through a pressure regulator which

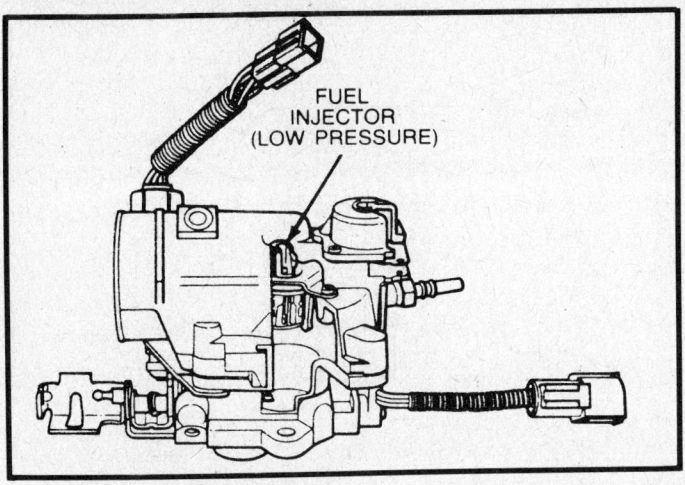

Low pressure CFI system

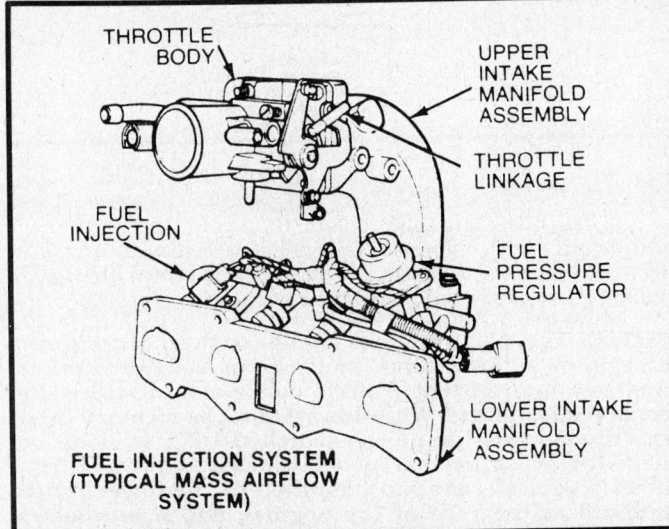

Mass airflow Fuel Injection System

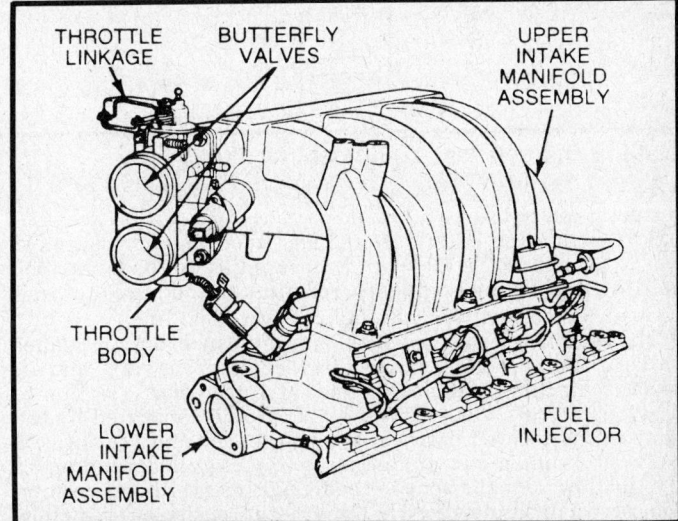

Adaptive Speed/Density Fuel Injection System

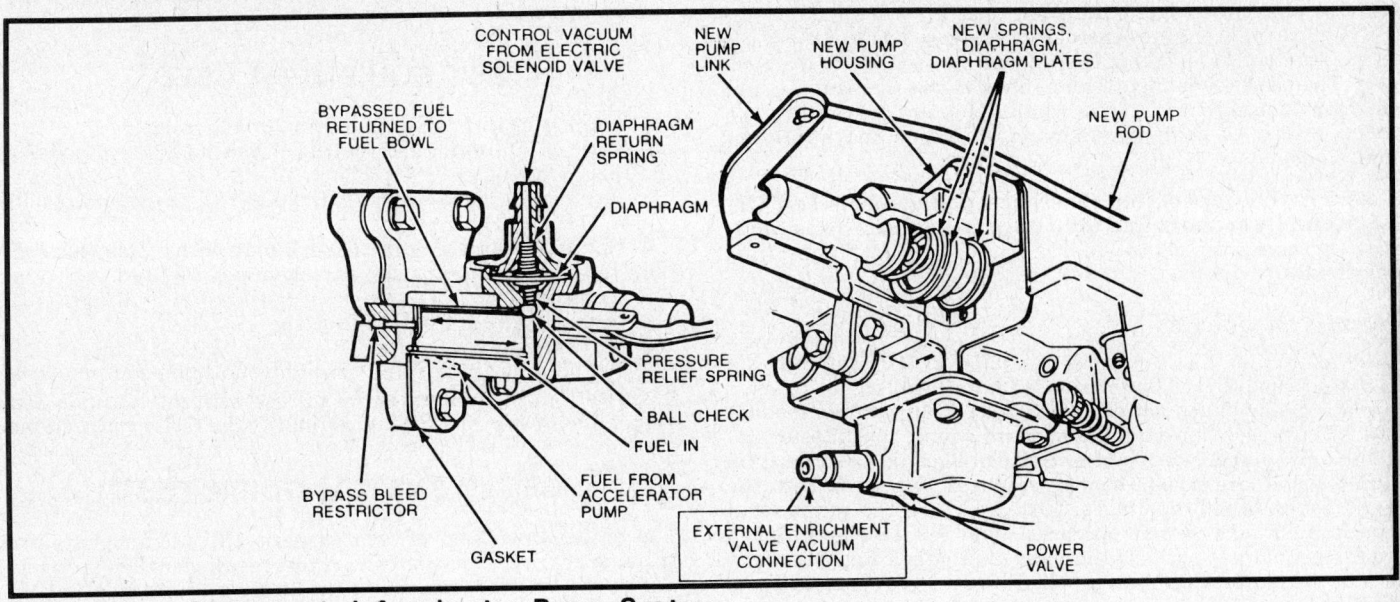

Temperature Compensated Accelerator Pump System

29-85

SECTION 29

ENGINE CONTROLS
FORD EEC IV ENGINE CONTROL SYSTEM

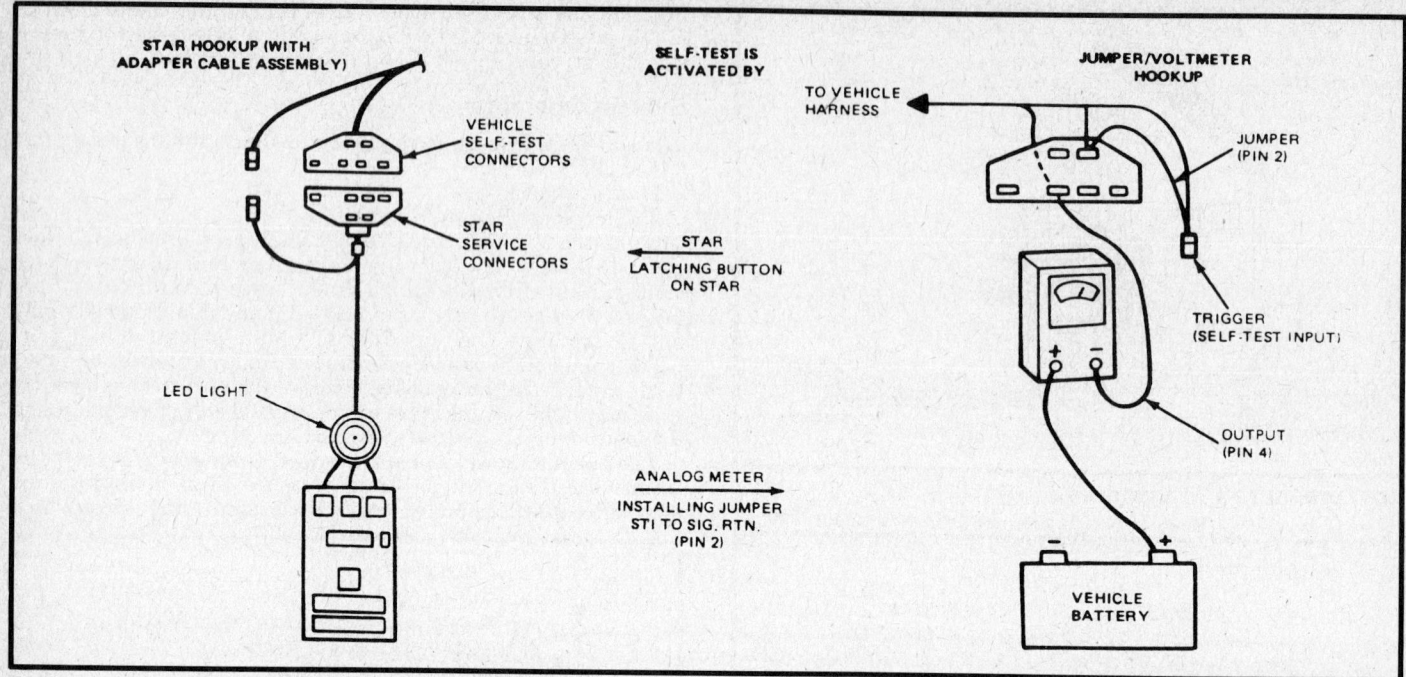

Making the self test equipment hookups

is referenced to intake manifold pressure (vacuum). The regulator is connected parallel to the fuel injectors and positioned on the far end of the fuel rail. Fuel supplied by the pump, but not required by the engine, passes through the regulator and returns to the fuel tank through a fuel return line.

The air subsystem consists of an air cleaner, an air cleaner valve assembly, a vane meter, throttle air bypass valve and associated air tubes. Air cleaner and valve operation is similar to previous models. Air entering the engine is measured by the vane meter located between the air cleaner and the throttle body. The vane meter produces a voltage signal depending on the air flow which is sent to the ECA to assist in determining the correct air/fuel ratio. The vane meter consists of an airflow sensor and an air temperature sensor. The throttle air bypass valve regulates the amount of air which flows around the throttle plate to control engine idle speed.

The electronic engine control subsystem consists of the Electronic Control Assembly (ECA) and various sensors and actuators. The ECA reads inputs from the sensors to control the fuel injector opening time (pulse width), thereby controlling the air/fuel ratio to achieve maximum efficiency and minimum emissions.

NOTE: The operating reference voltage between the ECA and its sensors and actuators is 5 volts. This is to allow the components to work during cranking when battery voltage drops.

System Diagnosis

Like all earlier EEC systems, the EFI-EEC-IV system has a self-test capability. The primary tools needed for the self-test are an analog voltmeter or Ford Self-Test Automatic Readout (STAR) tester, a timing light, vacuum gauge, spark tester, tachometer, jumper wire, fuel pressure gauge and hand vacuum pump. There are three testing procedures, the Quick Test, the Self Test and the Pinpoint Test. The Quick Test is a functional check of EEC-IV system operation. The Self Test is equipped with a set of instructions programmed into the computer memory of the calibration system. The Pinpoint Test is an individual component check. Perform the Quick Test first and then the Self Test to isolate the problem; then perform the Pinpoint Test to verify any component failure before replacing any part. After all tests and services are completed, repeat the entire Quick Test to make sure the system is working properly.

NOTE: The 2.3L system is similar to the 1.6L, with the addition of a "keep alive" memory in the ECA that retains any intermittent trouble codes stored within the last 20 engine starts. With this system, the memory is not erased when the ignition is switched OFF. In addition, the 2.3L EEC-IV system incorporates a knock sensor to detect engine detonation (mounted in the lower intake manifold at the rear of the engine), and a barometric pressure sensor to compensate for altitude variations. The barometric pressure sensor is mounted on the right fender apron.

TEST EQUIPMENT USED

1. Analog Voltmeter with a 0 to 20 volt range.
2. Digital Volt-Ohmmeter with a minimim input impedance of 10 mega-ohms.
3. A Vacuum gauge with a 0 to 30 in.Hg. range and resolution in the 1 in.Hg. range.
4. Spark Tester: a modified spark plug with a side electrode removed and a alligator clip attached may be used.
5. Tachometer.
6. Jumper wire a least 15 in. long.
7. Vacuum pump.
8. An optional Star cable assembly Rotunda Part Number 07-0010 from the manufacturer for use with the Rotunda Star Tester 07-0004 or equivalent to simplify the tester connections.

EEC IV SYSTEM QUICK TEST

The proper operation of related non—EEC components and systems are necessary for correct test results for the quick test. Before starting the test or hooking up any equipment check the following.

ENGINE CONTROLS
FORD EEC IV ENGINE CONTROL SYSTEM
SECTION 29

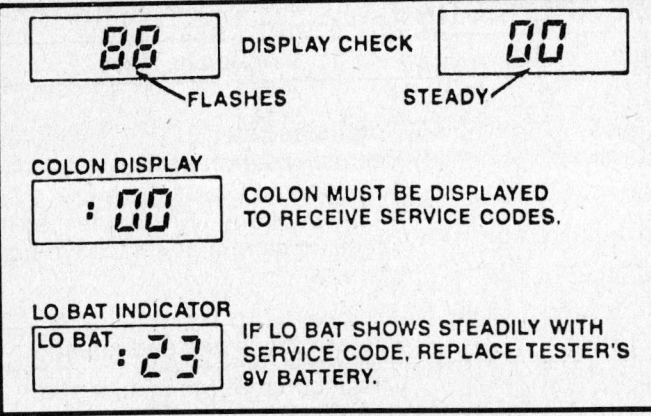

Self test output code format (Star Tester)

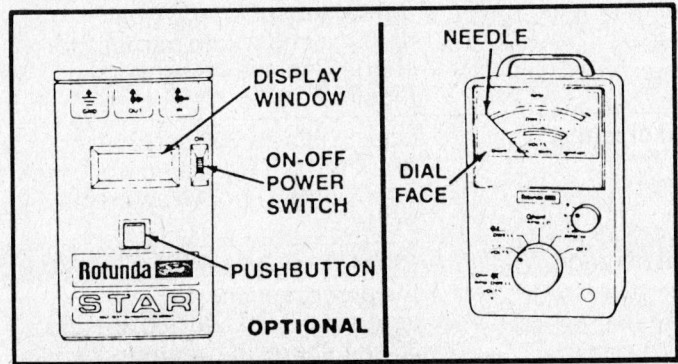

Analog voltmeter and the Star Tester

1. Check the air cleaner and ducting.
2. Check all vacuum hoses for proper routing, tight connections and breaks or damage.
3. Check the EEC system wiring harness connections for looseness, corrosion, broken or frayed wires, shorted connections, proper routing and tight connections. Shake or wiggle wires to check connections while performing continuity tests.
4. Check control module, sensors and actuators for physical damage.
5. Turn OFF all electrical accessories and make sure all doors are closed when taking readings.
6. Start and warm up the engine before testing any further.

Performing The Quick Test

1. Place the transmission in park, apply the parking brake and block the drive wheels.
2. Make sure that the vacuum lines are connected to the air cleaner and turn off all accessories.
3. Using a analog voltmeter check to see if there is power going to the choke, with the engine running.
4. Let the engine run until it reaches normal operating temperature and then turn the ignition switch to the "OFF" position.
5. Locate the self test connector which is usually located in the wiring harness under the hood on the passenger side of the vehicle.
6. If using the analog voltmeter, connect a jumper wire from the self test circuit 201 to ground circuit 60 on the slef test connector. Then connect the analog voltmeter from the positive post on the battery to the self test output on the self test connector.
7. Now set the voltmeter to read from 0 to 15 VDC on the DC volt range.
8. On the 2.3L engine wioth a vacuum purge valve, disable the canister purge system during the quick test.
9. Make sure the carburetor throttle linkage is off the high cam and the choke is open.

NOTE: If the star tester is being used for the quick test, connect the black lead to the negative terminal on the battery and the red lead to the self test output terminal on the self test connector, then hook up the white lead to the self test trigger. Now follow the manufacturers instructions on the back of the start tester.

SELF TEST OPERATION

The ECA stores the self-test program in its permanent memory. When activated, it checks the EEC IV system by testing its memory integrity and processing capability, and it verifies that various sensors and actuators are connected and operating properly. The self-test is divided into three categories: Key ON/Engine OFF, Engine Running, and Continuous Testing.

NOTE: Engine ID and Fast Codes are issued at the beginning of the engine running and self-test modes. Some meters in service may detect these codes as a short burst (meter deflection) but they serve no purpose in the field.

With the Key ON/Engine OFF and Engine Running tests, the EEC IV system components are checked by applying voltage with the engine at rest and running. A fault must be present in the system at the time of testing to be detected and registered as a trouble code. The Continuous Self-Test has the ability to store a service code indicating a suspected problem. The information from this test must be retrieved prior to turning the key off as the codes are erased each time the ignition switch is turned off. In the continuous test mode, the technician is able to monitor the self-test output while operating the engine.

NOTE: The Key ON/Engine OFF and Engine Running tests are intended to detect hard failures only. Intermittent faults are detected by Continuous Testing.

Before connecting any equipment to diagnose the EEC system, make the following checks:
1. Check the air cleaner and ducting.
2. Check all vacuum hoses for proper routing, tight connections and breaks or damage.
3. Check the EEC system wiring harness connections for

QUICK TEST DIAGNOSIS AND TESTING

Test Step	Result	Action to Take
1. **Vehicle Voltage Test** Turn off all accessories and operate the engine at 2000 RPM for 2 minutes. Battery voltage has to be between 14.2–14.7 volts.	Battery within specifications	Continue to step 2
	Battery not in specifications	Recharge the battery, check the charging system and do step 1 again.

SECTION 29
ENGINE CONTROLS
FORD EEC IV ENGINE CONTROL SYSTEM

QUICK TEST DIAGNOSIS AND TESTING

Test Step	Result	Action to Take
2. Key On-Engine Off-Self Test a. With the transmission in Park and the AC control off, put the key in run position. Now record the service codes as they come up on the voltmeter. (Refer to the output code format as previously outlined.)	Code 11—System Pass No service codes Meter always high Meter always low	Continue to step 3 Recheck the non-EEC components Check the MCU module and the TFI module also check the continuity in the wiring harness.
b. Read Only Memory Test Failed	Code 15—Memory Check	Replace processor and retest.
c. Engine Coolant Temperature Failed	Code 21—ECT Check	Check temperature sensor and connections, repair as necessary or replace the ECT sensor.
d. Throttle Position Sensor Failed	Code 23—TPS out of range	Check sensor for physical damage and wiring harness for shorts Replace TP sensor if required.
e. Manifold Charge Temperature Failed	Code 24—VAT out of range	Check circuits 357 and 359 for any shorts, if these circuits check out OK, then remove and replace the VAT.
f. Manifold Absolute Pressure Failed	Code 26—VAF out of range	Check for air leaks, vacuum leaks, the processor and harnesscircuits 190, 280, 351 and 359 for shorts. If everything works out, then remove and replace the VAF.
g. Neutral Drive Switch Failed	Code 67—Engine won't start	Check the processor the N/D switch neutral forcing relay and harness circuits 150, 347, 359 and 69. On manual transmissions, check the gear clutch linkage and the gear clutch switch. If everything works out remove and replace the neutral drive switch.

NOTE: When more than one service code is received, always start with the first code received. If a suspended vehicle condition is present, continue on with the continuous testing.

QUICK TEST DIAGNOSIS AND TESTING

Test Step	Result	Action to Take
3. Engine Running Test a. Disconnect the self-test trigger, start engine and bring the rpm's up above 2000 rpm for 2 minutes.	No service codes or voltmeter always reads above 10V	Recheck the non-EEC components check the spark timing and the MCU module. Also check the TFI module and the continuity in the wiring harness.
b. With the engine off reconnect the self-test trigger, now restart the engine and let it idle. Two identification pulses will occur followed by the service codes. Record the codes and refer to the output code format as previously outlined.	Code 11—System Pass	Any other trouble go on to step 4, otherwise the testing is complete and the EEC system is OK.

NOTE: Testing is completed when the codes have been outputted twice.

ENGINE CONTROLS
FORD EEC IV ENGINE CONTROL SYSTEM
SECTION 29

QUICK TEST DIAGNOSIS AND TESTING

Test Step	Result	Action to Take

4. Continuous Testing
This test utilizes the system's ability to indicate sensor and circuit failure at the moment the interrupt occurs. It also remembers the service code of the affected sensor.

Implementing Continuous Test
Key in OFF Position
Disconnect the self-test trigger and connect an analog voltmeter negative lead to the self test output pin, and the positive lead to the positive battery post.

Key in the Run Position
Wiggle, move, twist, the vehicle wiring harness; tap, shake, or otherwise exercise the sensors. Watch the voltmeter while doing the above, a deflection at any time indicates an intermittent short has occured in a sensor circuit.

NOTE: The sensor circuit could be in the harness, sensor or processor. Once the intermitten fault has been found and induced, the appropriate service code has been stored. Do not turn the key off because the codes will be erased.

Initiate Self-Test. (Install jumper and observe the service code[s].)
Vehicle could be prepared as above and driven in an attempt to link a drive complaint with the meter indication of an EEC intermittent fault at which time, again, the Service Code would be observed and followed in an attempt to isolate the intermittent fault.
If the indicated Service Code from Continuous Testing does not make the repair obvious (damaged sensor, pinched harness, etc.) contact your District Office for additional assistance.

---

looseness, corrosion, broken or frayed wires, shorted connections, proper routing and tight connections. Shake or wiggle wires to check connections while performing continuity tests.
  4. Check control module, sensors and actuators for physical damage.
  5. Turn OFF all electrical accessories and make sure all doors are closed when taking readings.
  6. Start and warm up the engine before testing any further.

Analog Voltmeter Hookup

  1. Turn ignition key OFF.
  2. Connect a jumper wire from the self test input (STI) pin to pin 2 signal return on self-test connector.
  3. Set analog voltmeter on a DC voltage range to read from 0–15 volts DC. Connect voltmeter from battery (+) to pin 4 self-test output in the self-test connector.
  4. Connect a timing light according to manufacturer's instructions.

NOTE: If a STAR tester is available, be sure to follow the manufacturer's instructions when connecting it to the system. The STAR tester will give a digital trouble code readout.

Star Tester Hookup

  1. Turn the ignition key off. Connect the color-coded adapter cable leads to the Star tester.
  2. Connect the adapter cable's two service connectors to the vehicle's appropiate Self Test connectors.
  3. Connect a timing light.

READING THE SERVICE CODES DURING THE SELF TEST

Analog Voltmeter Method

When using the analog voltmeter to perform a function test, the service codes will present themselves as a sweeping or pulsing movement of the voltmetere's needle across the dial face of the voltmeter. The service code is represented by a two digit number, such as 2-3. To get the service code number, the number of voltmeter needle pulses must be counted. If the number is a single digit number of three it will be represented bt three needle pulses on the voltmeter.
The self test's service code of 2-3 will appear on the voltmeter as two needle pulses; then after a two second pause, the needle will pulse three times. The continuous testing codes are separated from functional codes by a six second delay and a single ½ second sweep and another six second delay. They are produced on the voltmeter in the same manner as the functional codes.

Rotunda Star Tester Method

In order to use the start tester, the star tester cable assembly (Rotunda 07-0010) must be attached to the vehicle self test connector. After hooking up the star tester put the power switch to the on position. When the power switch is on the tester will run a display check and the numerals 88 wiil flash in the display window.
When the tester is ready to recieve the service codes a steady 00 will appear in the display window. For the tester to receive the service codes, the pushbutton on the front of the tester must be pressed in, so a colon will appear in the display window in front of the :00 numerals.

NOTE: The colon must be displayed in order to receive the service codes.

The only way to clear the display window, is to turn off the engine and press down the pushbuttons on the fron tof the tester to clear the display window. When the star tester is turned off, the Low Battery Indicator (LO BAT) will show up briefly in the upper left corner of the display window. If the LO BAT indicator comes on steadily during any other self test operation, turn the power switch off and replace the 9 volt battery in the tester.

SERVICE CODES

The service codes are transmitted in the form of timed pulses

29–89

SECTION 29

ENGINE CONTROLS
Ford EEC IV Engine Control System

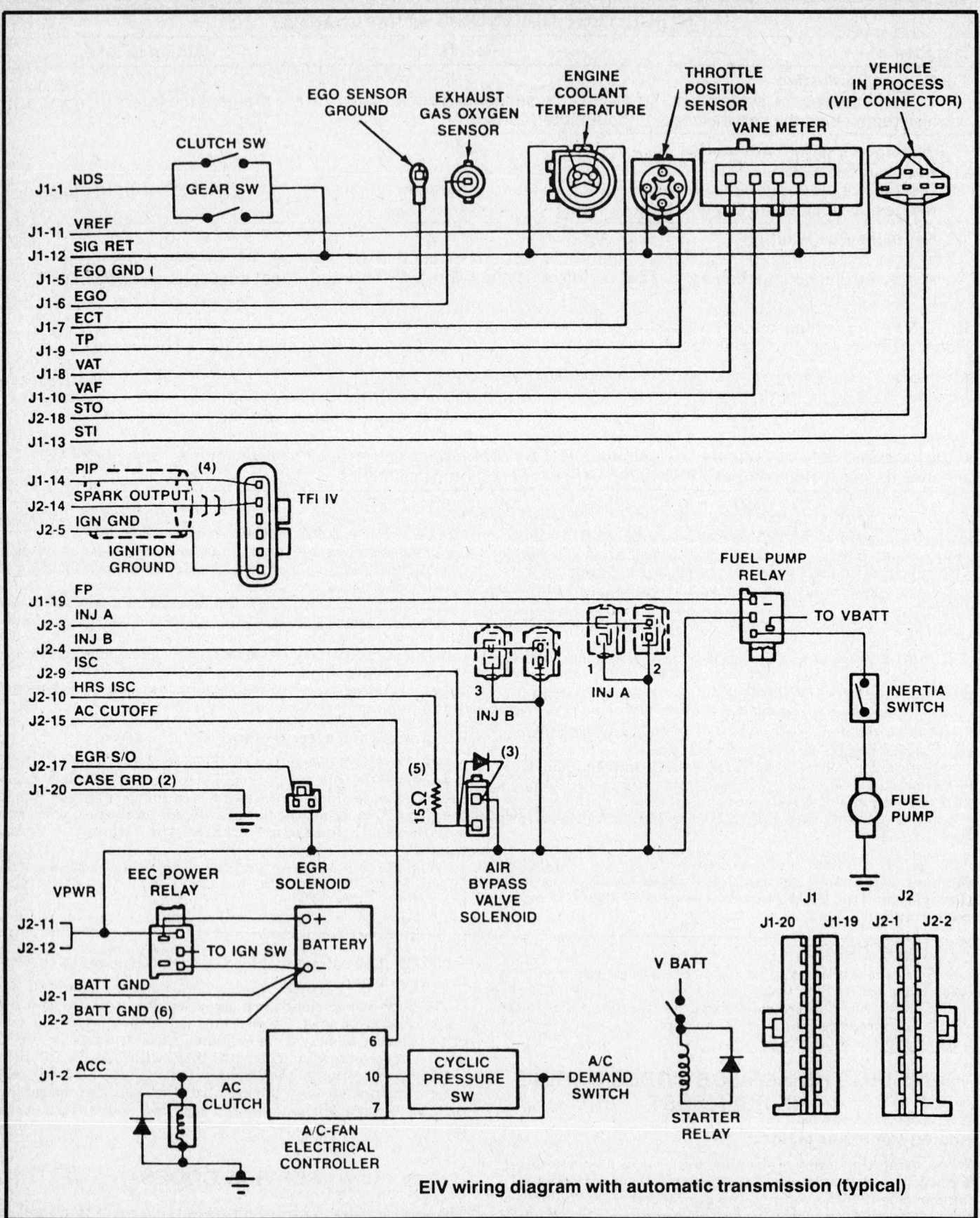

EIV wiring diagram with automatic transmission (typical)

29-90

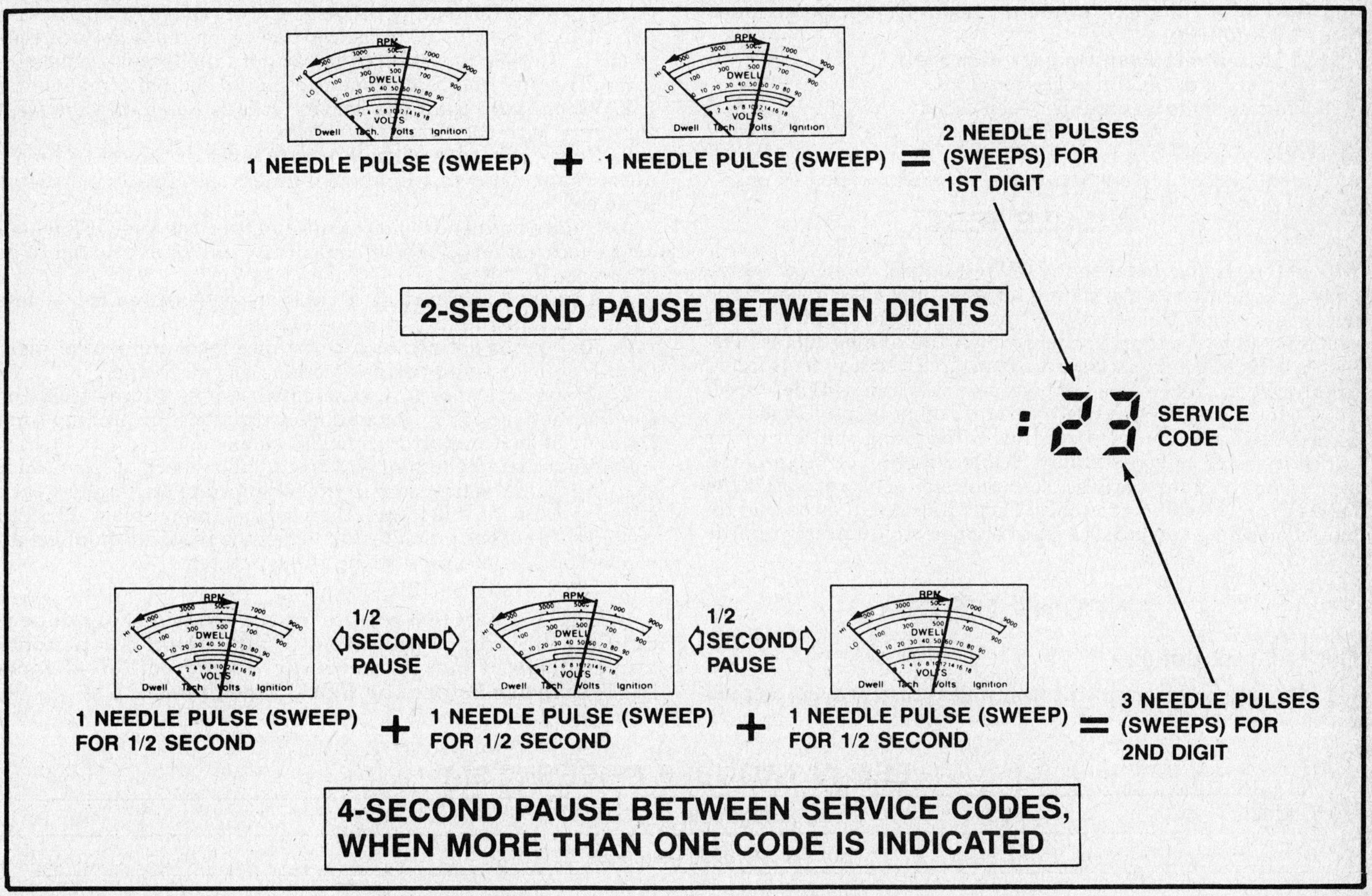

ENGINE CONTROLS
FORD EEC IV ENGINE CONTROL SYSTEM
SECTION 29

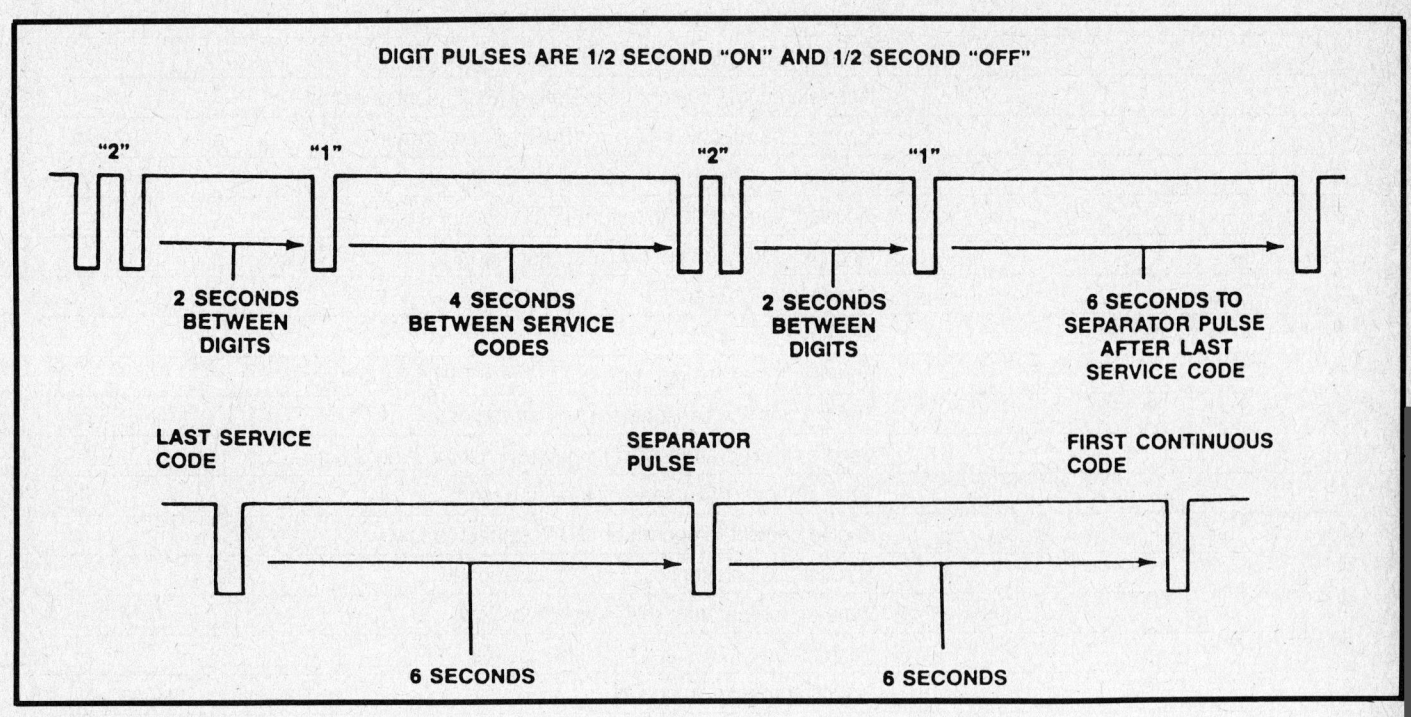

Reading service code on analog voltmeter

Self test service code digit pulses

29-91

ENGINE CONTROLS
FORD EEC IV ENGINE CONTROL SYSTEM

and read on a voltmeter or a start tester, the pulse arrangement is as follows:
1. A half of second on time for each digit.
2. Two seconds off time between digits.
3. Four seconds off time between codes.
4. Six seconds off time before and after the half of second separator pulse.

All testing is complete when codes have been repeated once.

WIGGLE TEST

Attach the analog meter to the self test output connector which is usually located in the wiring harness under the hood on the passenger side of the vehicle. While wiggling or tapping on the system and the wiring harness watch the analog meter. The meter will deflect every time an open circuit or a short is found in the system. When this happens a service code will be stored. To retrieve the service code a self test must be performed.

This same test can be performed while using the star tester and star tester cable assembly. While wiggling or tapping the system or the wire harness, connectors or sensors, watch the led light on the cable assembly. The led light will go on and remain on as long as there is a short or open circuit present in the system.

PINPOINT TESTS

General Instructions

1. Do not run any pinpoint tests unless instructed to do so in the quick test. Each pinpoint test assumes that a failure has occurred in a specific system that has triggered a service code readout. Testing a system that has not failed may produce incorrect results and replacement of non-defective components.
2. When more than one service code is noted, always start servicing with the first code received.
3. Do not measure voltage or resistance at the control module or connect any test lights to it unless specifically instructed to do so.
4. Isolate both ends of a circuit and turn the key OFF whenever checking for shorts or continuity, unless instructed to do otherwise.
5. A short is defined as a resistance measurement of less than 10K ohms to any other conductor.
6. An open is defined as a resistance measurement of more than 5 ohms as read across a conductor end to end.
7. Connectors shown in schematics are as viewed from the front of the connector. Take all measurements by probing from the rear of the connector (harness side).
8. When using the pinpoint tests, follow each step in order starting from the first step in the appropriate test. Follow each step until the fault is found, then correct the problem. Proceed to step three of the quick test to verify the repair. Reconnect all connections before conducting the quick test.

NOTE: Correct test results for the quick test are dependent on the proper operation of all related components and systems. It may be necessary to correct any defects in these areas before the EEC IV will pass.

EEC IV TROUBLE CODES (2.3L)

Code	Diagnosis
11	Normal operation (no codes stored)
12	Incorrect high idle rpm value
13	Incorrect curb idle rpm value
14	Erratic Profile Ignition Pickup (PIP) signal
15	Read Only Memory (ROM) failure
21	Incorrect engine coolant temperature (ECT) sensor signal
22	Incorrect barometric pressure (BAP) sensor signal
23	Incorrect throttle position sensor (TPS) signal
24	Incorrect vane air temperature (VAT) sensor signal
26	Incorrect vane air flow (VAF) sensor signal
41	System always lean
42	System always rich
51	Engine coolant temperature (ECT) sensor signal too high
53	Throttle position sensor (TPS) signal too high
54	Vane air temperature (VAT) sensor signal too high
56	Vane air flow (VAF) sensor signal too high
61	Engine coolant temperature (ECT) signal too low
63	Throttle position sensor (TPS) signal too low
64	Vane air temperature (VAT) signal too low
66	Vane air flow (VAF) sensor signal too low
67	A/C compressor clutch ON
73	No vane air temperature (VAT) signal change when engine speed is increased

ENGINE CONTROLS
FORD EEC IV ENGINE CONTROL SYSTEM

EEC IV TROUBLE CODES (2.3L)

Code	Diagnosis
76	No vane air flow (VAF) signal change when engine speed is increased
77	Engine speed not increased to check VAT and VAF signal change

NOTE: Incorrect sensor signals could be out of range or not being received by the control unit. Perform wiring harness and sensor checks to determine the cause, or check for additional codes to indicate high or low reading

EEC IV TROUBLE CODES (1.6L)

Code	Diagnosis
11	Normal operation (no codes stored)
12	Incorrect high idle rpm value
13	Incorrect curb idle rpm value
15	Read Only Memory (ROM) failure
21	Incorrect engine coolant temperature (ECT) sensor signal
23	Incorrect throttle position sensor (TPS) signal
24	Incorrect vane air temperature (VAT) sensor signal
26	Incorrect vane air flow (VAF) sensor signal
41	System always lean
42	System always rich
67	Neutral/Drive switch in Neutral

NOTE: Incorrect rpm values could be high or low and an incorrect sensor signal could be caused by a defective sensor or a wiring harness problem. Use the trouble codes to isolate the circuit, then continue diagnosis to determine the exact cause of the problem

SECTION 30: ELECTRONIC IGNITION

INDEX

AMERICAN MOTORS

GENERAL INFORMATION
- General Service Procedures 30–3
- Quick Check Chart 30–4

AMERICAN MOTORS SOLID STATE (SSI) SYSTEM
- General Information 30–4
- Control Unit & Sensor Test 30–6
- Ignition Feed To Control Unit Test 30–6
- Rotor Test 30–7
- Secondary Coil Test 30–5
- Troubleshooting 30–5

AMERICAN MOTORS HIGH ENERGY (HEI) SYSTEM
- Component Replacement
  - Control Module 30–8
  - Distributor R&R 30–8
  - External Ignition Coil 30–8
  - Internal Ignition Coil 30–8
  - Rotor 30–8
- General Information 30–7

CHRYSLER CORPORATION

CHRYSLER ELECTRONIC IGNITION
- Acceleration Spark Advance System 30–9
- General Information 30–9
- Servicing
  - Air Gap Adjust 30–10
  - Distributor Overhaul 30–11
  - Pick–Up Coil R&R 30–10
- Testing 30–9
- Troubleshooting 30–11

CHRYSLER ELECTRONIC IGNITION (EIS) SYSTEM
- Distributor R&R 30–13
- Distributor Overhaul 30–15
- General Information 30–13
- Testing 30–13
- Troubleshooting 30–13

CHRYSLER HALL EFFECT ELECTRONIC IGNITION SYSTEM
- General Information 30–15
- Pick-Up R&R 30–16
- Testing 30–16

CHRYSLER LEAN BURN ELECTRONIC SPARK CONTROL SYSTEM
- Components R&R 30–24
- General Information 30–17
- Operation 30–18
- Pick-Up Gaps 30–24
- Testing
  - Coolant Switch 30–24
  - Detonation Sensor 30–24
  - Primary Circuit 30–24
  - Start Timer 30–25
  - Vacuum Advance 30–24

FORD MOTOR COMPAMY

FORD SOLID STATE IGNITION DURA SPARK II & III, TFI (THICK FILM INTEGRATED) SYSTEMS
- Components 30–31
- Crankshaft Sensor 30–33
- Distributor Pick–Up 30–33
- Solid State Ignition
  - Check Timing 30–37
  - Dual Mode Function Test 30–38
  - General Information 30–33
  - Operation 30–34
  - Preliminary Checks 30–34
  - Plug Wire Resistance 30–34
  - Run Mode Spark Check 30–35
  - Start Mode Spark Check 30–36
  - Testing 30–37
  - Troubleshooting 30–34
- Special Controls Modules 30–30
- TFI System Testing
  - Ignition Coil Voltage 30–39
  - Stator & Module 30–39
  - Stator R&R 30–42
  - TFI Module R&R 30–43
  - Wire Harness 30–39

FORD EEC-IV IGNITION SYSTEM
- General Information 30–43
- System Service 30–39

GENERAL MOTORS

DELCO-REMY HIGH ENERGY (HEI) SYSTEM
- General Infromation 30–44
- Repair Procedures
  - Coil R&R 30–46
  - Distributor Cap R&R 30–46
  - Distributor R&R 30–47
  - Module R&R 30–47
  - Rotor R&R 30–46
  - Vacuum Advance R&R 30–46
- Testing
  - Hall Effect Switch 30–46
  - Ignition Module 30–46
  - Module Draw Test 30–46
  - Secondary Circuit 30–44
- Troubleshooting 30–48

GM COMPUTER CONTROLLED COIL IGNITION (C3I) SYSTEM
- Component Replacement
  - Camshaft Sensor 30–51
  - Coil 30–51
  - Crankshaft Sensor 30–51
  - Module 30–51
- General Information 30–50
- Operation 30–50
- Troubleshooting 30–53

GM SOLID STATE IGNITION SYSTEM— NOVA 1985 AND LATER
- Distributor Overhaul 30–56
- Distributor R&R 30–56
- General Information 30–55
- Ignition Coil Test 30–57
- Troubleshooting 30–58

Electronic Ignition Systems

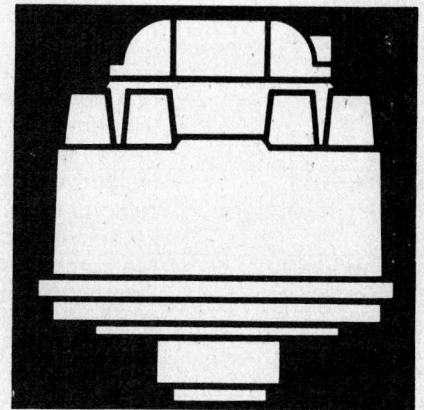

ELECTRONIC IGNITION SYSTEMS

General Information

The solid state electronic ignition system has replaced the breaker point distributor on all current production automotive gasoline engines. By eliminating the breaker points, electronic ignition systems have become almost maintenance-free and performance does not deteriorate with mileage. In a typical system, the distributor contains an electronic control unit or module which replaces the breaker plate. Within the distributor body is a permanent magnet and a variable reluctance pick-up (or Hall Effect pick-up and rotating shutter). The electronic control module receives signals from the pick-up coil and in turn charges and fires the secondary ignition coil. A rotor then distributes the high voltage current to the proper spark plug through the distributor cap and wires. The only exception to this general description is the GM Computer Controlled Coil Ignition (C3I) system which eliminates the distributor altogether.

All solid state ignition systems can be checked for proper operation by performing simple resistance tests, however some computer-based electronic ignition systems can be damaged by the use of incorrect test equipment. Before testing any primary ignition components, a secondary system inspection should be done to eliminate obvious problems such as loose or corroded connections, broken or shorted wires and damaged components.

CAUTION

Due to the dangerously high voltage levels present in any electronic ignition system, DO NOT touch any secondary ignition system components while the engine is running or the starter is being cranked. Use insulated tools to hold coil or spark plug wires when testing.

Intermittent problems can be caused by extremely high or low temperature operating conditions and any damage to the trigger wheel or Hall Effect pick-up (cracks, chips, etc.) will degrade ignition system performance. Service of solid state ignition systems involves testing and fault diagnosis of electronic components and circuits, using a volt/ohmmeter or digital multimeter. The control units, magnetic pick-ups and other solid state components are replaced as a unit so accurate troubleshooting is essential to avoid the needless replacement of expensive parts.

General Service Precautions

- Always turn the ignition switch OFF when disconnecting or connecting any electrical connectors or components.
- Never reverse the battery polarity or disconnect the battery with the engine running.
- Do not pierce spark plug or wiring harness wires with test probes for any reason. Due to their more pliable construction, it is important to route spark plug wires properly to avoid chafing or cutting.
- Disconnect the ignition switch feed wire at the distributor when making compression tests to avoid arcing that may damage components, especially on computer-based ignition systems.
- Do not remove grease or dielectric compound from components or connectors when installing. Some manufacturers use grease to prevent corrosion and dielectric compound to dissipate heat generated during normal module operation.
- Check all replacement part numbers carefully. Installing the wrong components for a specific application can damage the system.
- All manufacturers instructions included with any testing equipment must be read carefully to insure proper capability and test results. Inaccurate readings and/or damage to ignition system components may result due to the use of improper test equipment.

SECTION 30: ELECTRONIC IGNITION
AMC SOLID STATE IGNITION (SSI) SYSTEM

ELECTRONIC IGNITION QUICK CHECK CHART
(Non-computer controlled systems only)

Condition	Possible Cause	Correction
Abrupt backfire	Control unit or ignition module malfunction. Incorrect timing. Bad cap or rotor	Check ignition timing. Replace control unit or module. Replace cap or rotor
Intermittent running	Magnetic pick-up or stator malfunction. Bad trigger wheel, reluctor or armature. Control unit or ignition module failure	Replace defective components after testing as described under appropriate system in this unit repair section
Does not fire on one or more cylinders	Defective pick-up, stator, trigger wheel, reluctor or armature. Bad spark plugs or ignition wires	Replace components as necessary
Cuts off suddenly	Malfunction in control unit of module. Damaged pick-up or stator	Check operation of pick-up and stator. Replace control unit or module
Won't start	Control unit or module failure. Defective cap, rotor, pick-up or stator ①	Replace control unit or module after testing. Replace distributor components as necessary
Poor performance, no power under load	Defective pick-up, stator, or ignition coil. Worn or fouled spark plugs. Bad plug wires	Check distributor components for signs of wear or damage. Replace spark plugs and wires
Arcing or excessive burning on rotor or distributor cap	Worn or fouled spark plugs. Bad plug wires	Replace spark plugs and wires

NOTE: This chart assumes the described conditions are problems in the electronic ignition system and not the result of another malfunction. Always perform basic checks for fuel, spark and compression first. See the individual system sections for all test procedures.
① Check ballast resistor on Chrysler models

AMC SOLID STATE IGNITION (SSI) SYSTEM

General Information

American Motors Solid State Ignition (SSI) is standard equipment on all 1983 and later 6 cylinder engines and 4 cylinder 150 CID engines. The 4 cylinder 151 CID engine manufactured by General Motors, is equipped with the Delco-Remy High Energy Ignition (HEI) system.

The system consists of a sensor and toothed trigger wheel inside the distributor, and a permanently sealed electronic control unit which determines dwell, in addition to the coil, ignition wires, and spark plugs.

The trigger wheel rotates on the distributor shaft. As one of its teeth nears the sensor magnet, the magnetic field shifts toward the tooth. When the tooth and sensor are aligned, the magnetic field is shifted to its maximum, signaling the electronic control unit to switch off the coil primary current. This starts an electronic timer inside the control unit, which allows the primary current to remain off only long enough for the spark plug to fire. The timer adjusts the amount of time primary current is off according to conditions, thus automatically adjusting dwell. There is also a special circuit within the control unit to detect and ignore spurious signals. Spark timing is adjusted by both mechanical (centrifugal) and vacuum advance.

A wire of 1.35 ohms resistance is spliced into the ignition feed to reduce voltage to the coil during running conditions. The resistance wire is by-passed when the engine is being started so that full battery voltage may be supplied to the coil. Bypass is accomplished by the I-terminal on the solenoid.

The remainder of the system includes a pointless distributor, standard construction ignition coil, ignition switch, resistance wire and bypass, secondary spark plug wires and spark plugs.

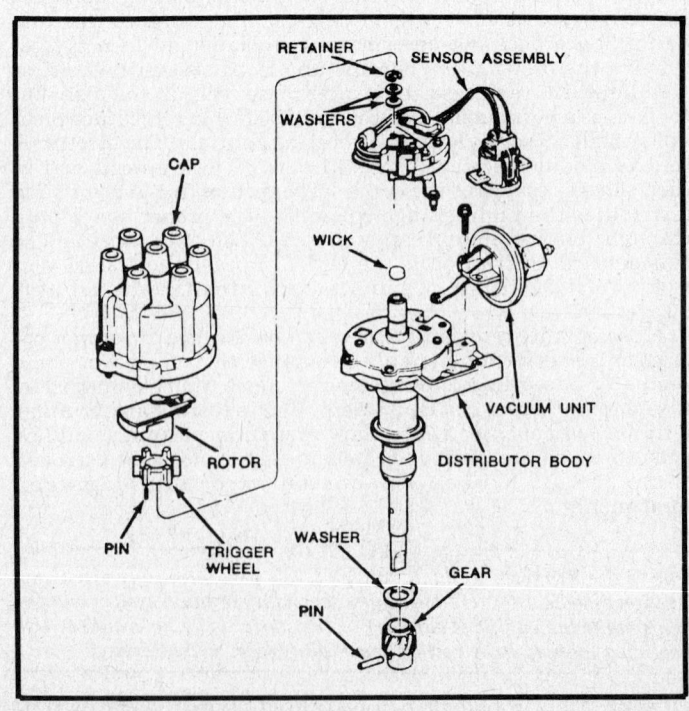

Six cylinder SSI distributor (© American Motors Corp.)

ELECTRONIC IGNITION
AMC SOLID STATE IGNITION (SSI) SYSTEM

The electronic control unit (module) is a solid state, nonserviceable, sealed unit. This unit has reverse polarity and voltage surge circuit protection built in. Two weatherproof connectors attach the control unit to the ignition circuit.

NOTE: All system electrical connectors use lock tabs that must be released to disconnect the various components.

Troubleshooting

SECONDARY CIRCUIT TEST

1. Disconnect the coil wire from the center of the distributor cap.

NOTE: Twist the rubber boot slightly in either direction, then grasp the boot and pull straight up. Do not pull on the wire, and do not use pliers.

Hold the wire ½ in. from a ground with a pair of insulated pliers and a heavy glove. As the engine is cranked, watch for a spark.

2. If a spark appears, reconnect the coil wire. Remove the wire from one spark plug, and test for a spark as above.

CAUTION

Do not remove the spark plug wires from cylinder 1 or 5 (1983 and later) on a 6 cylinder engine, or cylinders 3 or 4 of a V8 when performing this test, as sensor damage could occur.

If a spark occurs, the problem is in the fuel system or ignition timing. If no spark occurs, check for a defective rotor, cap, or spark plug wires.

3. If no spark occurs from the coil wire in Step 2, test the coil wire resistance with an ohmmeter. It must not exceed 10,000 ohms.

COIL PRIMARY CIRCUIT TEST

1. Turn the ignition On. Connect a voltmeter to the coil positive (+) terminal and a ground. If the voltage is 5.5–6.5 volts, go to Step 2. If above 7 volts, go to Step 4. If below 5.5 volts, disconnect the condenser lead and measure. If the voltage is now 5.5–6.5 volts, replace the condenser. If not, go to Step 6.

2. With the voltmeter connected as in Step 1, read the voltage with the engine cranking. If battery voltage is indicated, the circuit is okay. If not, go to Step 3.

3. Check for a short or open in the starter solenoid I-terminal wire. Check the solenoid for proper operation.

4. Disconnect the wire from the starter solenoid I-terminal, with the ignition On and the voltmeter connected as in Step 1. If the voltage drops to 5.5–6.5 volts, replace the solenoid. If not, connect a jumper between the coil negative (-) terminal and a ground. If the voltage drops to 5.5–6.5 volts, go to Step 5. If not, repair the resistance wire.

5. Check for continuity between the coil (-) terminal and D4, and D1 to ground. If the continuity is okay, replace the control unit. If not, check for an open wire and go back to Step 2.

6. Turn ignition Off. Connect an ohmmeter between the + coil terminal and dash connector AV. If above 1.40 ohms, repair the resistance wire.

7. With the ignition Off, connect the ohmmeter between connector AV and ignition switch terminal 11. If less than 0.1 ohm, replace the ignition switch or repair the wire, whichever is the cause. If above 0.1 ohm, check connections, and check for defective wiring.

COIL TEST

1. Check the coil for cracks, carbon tracks, etc., and replace as necessary.

2. Connect an ohmmeter across the coil (+) and (-) terminals, with the coil connector removed. If 1.13–1.23 ohms/75°F, go to Step 3. If not, replace the coil.

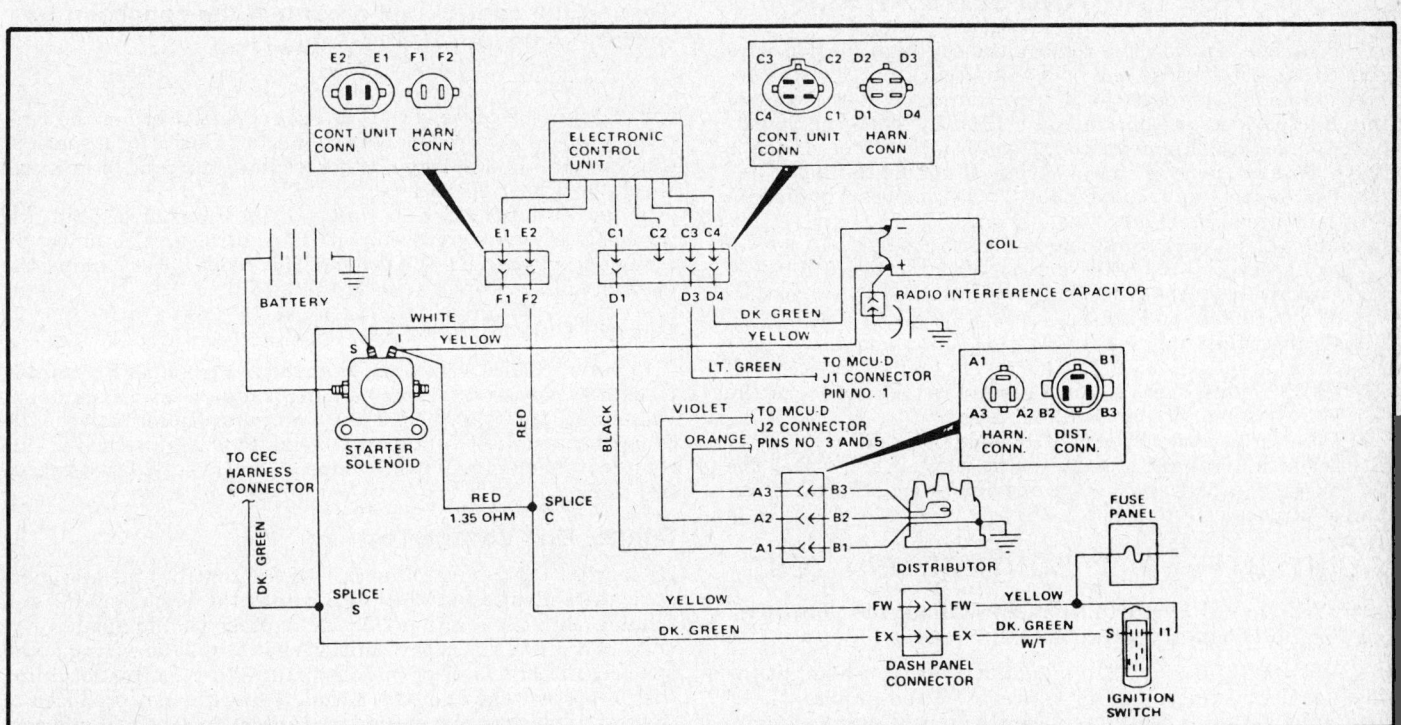

SSI system schematic (© American Motors Corp.)

SECTION 30

ELECTRONIC IGNITION
AMC SOLID STATE IGNITION (SSI) SYSTEM

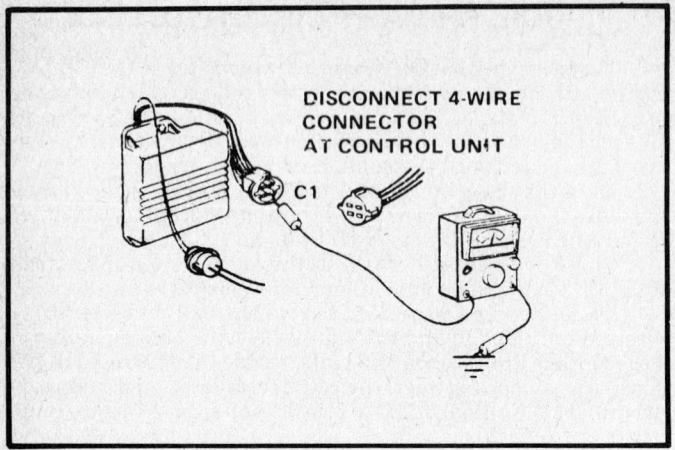

Step 3 of the ignition feed to control unit test
(© American Motors Corp.)

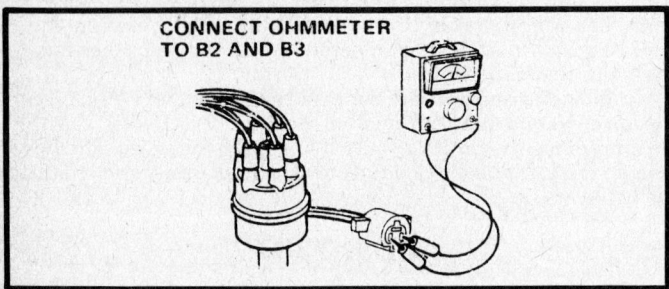

Step 4 of the control unit and sensor test
(© American Motors Corp.)

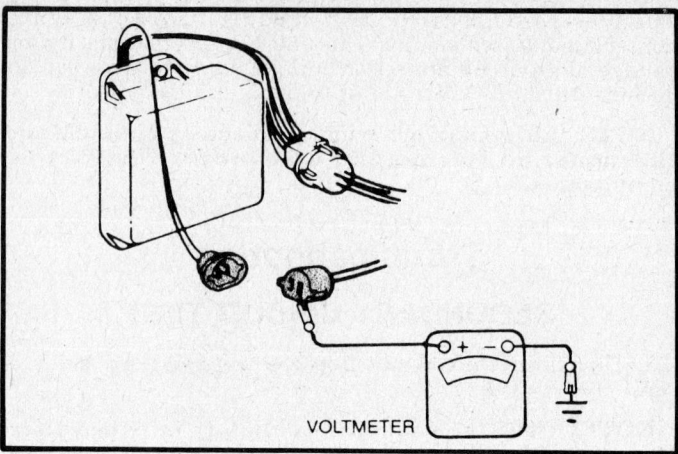

Control unit voltage test (© American Motors Corp.)

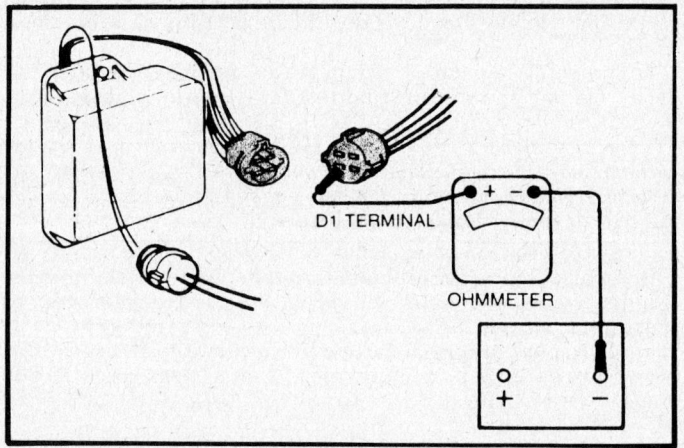

Testing the control unit ground at the connector terminal (© American Motors Corp.)

3. Measure the resistance across the coil center tower and either the + or - terminal. If 7700–9300 ohms at 75°F, the coil is okay. If not, replace.

CONTROL UNIT AND SENSOR TEST

1. With the ignition On, remove the coil high tension wire from the distributor cap and hold ½ in. from ground with insulated pliers. Disconnect the 4 wire connector at the control unit. If a spark occurs (normal), go to Step 2. If not, go to Step 5.
2. Connect an ohmmeter to D2 and D3. If the resistance is 400–800 ohms (normal), go to Step 6. If not, go to Step 3.
3. Disconnect and reconnect the 3 wire connector at distributor. If the reading is now 400–800 ohms, go to Step 6. If not, disconnect the 3 wire connector and go to Step 4.
4. Connect the ohmmeter across B2 and B3. If 400–800 ohms, repair the harness between the 3 wire and 4 wire connectors. If not, replace the sensor.
5. Connect the ohmmeter between D1 and the battery negative terminal. If the reading is 0 (0.002 or less), go to Step 2. If above 0.002 ohms, there is a bad ground in the cable or at the distributor. Repair the ground and retest.
6. Connect a voltmeter across D2 and D3. Crank the engine. If the needle fluctuates, the system is okay. If not, either the trigger wheel is defective, or the distributor is not turning. Repair or replace as required.

IGNITION FEED TO CONTROL UNIT TEST

NOTE: Do not perform this test without first performing the Coil Primary Circuit Test.

1. With the ignition ON, unplug the 2 wire connector at the module. Connect a voltmeter between F2 and ground. If the reading is battery voltage, replace the control unit and go to Step 3. If not, go to Step 2.

2. Repair the cause of the voltage reduction: either the ignition switch or a corroded dash connector. Check for a spark at the coil wire. If okay, stop. If not, replace the control unit and check for proper operation.
3. Reconnect the 2 wire connector at the control unit, and unplug the 4 wire connector at the control unit. Connect an ammeter between C1 and ground. If it reads 0.9–1.1 amps, the system is okay. If not, replace the module.

Control Unit Current Draw Test

If 11 volts or more were present at the connector's F2 terminal, measure the current draw of control unit with an ammeter. Disconnect 4-wire connector and connect ammeter between the connector terminal C1 and ground. With the ignition ON, current draw should be 0.9–1.1 amps; if it is not, replace the control unit.

Control Unit Voltage Test

Disconnect the 2-wire connector at the control unit and measure the voltage between the connector terminal F2 and ground, with the ignition ON. The voltage should be above 11 volts. If it is not, check the ignition switch and the wiring for an open circuit, or a loose or corroded connector. If, after obtaining the proper voltage at F2 terminal, a spark is not produced at the coil wire when the engine is cranked and the coil and sensor check are OK, replace the control unit.

ELECTRONIC IGNITION
AMC SOLID STATE IGNITION (SSI) SYSTEM
SECTION 30

Sensor Tests

1. Connect an ohmmeter (R x 100 scale) to D2 and D3 connector terminals. The resistance should be 400–800 ohms.

2. If the resistance is not within 400–800 ohms, check the voltage output of the sensor. Connect a voltmeter, 2–3 volt scale, to D2 and D3 connector terminals. Crank the engine and observe the voltmeter. A fluctuating voltmeter indicates proper sensor and trigger wheel operation. If not fluctuations are noted, check for a defective trigger wheel, distributor not turning, or a missing trigger wheel pin.

3. If the resistance in Step 1 was not 400–800 ohms, disconnect and reconnect 3–wire connector at the distributor. If the resistance is now 400–800 ohms, check sensor voltage output, Step 2.

4. If the sensor circuit resistance is still not within specification, disconnect 3–wire connector at the distributor and connect an ohmmeter to B2 and B3 terminals. If the resistance is 400–800 ohms, repair or replace the harness between 3–wire and 4–wire connector. If the resistance is still incorrect, replace the sensor.

Rotor Test

The rotor has silicone dielectric compound applied to the blade to reduce the radio interference. After a few thousand miles, the dielectric compound will become charred by the high voltage, which is normal. Do not scrape the residue off. When installing a new rotor, apply a thin coat (0.03–0.12 in.) of Silicone Dielectric Compound to the rotor blade.

AMC HIGH ENERGY IGNITION (HEI)

General Information

COMPONENTS AND OPERATION

The Delco-Remy High Energy Ignition (HEI) system is a breakerless, pulse triggered, transistor controlled inductive discharge ignition system used on all 4–151 engines as standard equipment. The ignition coil is located externally on the engine block or is integral with the cap.

The magnetic pick-up assembly, located inside the distributor, contains a permanent magnet, a pole piece with internal teeth and a pick-up coil. When the teeth of the rotating timer core align with the pole piece, an induced voltage in the pickup signals the electronic module to open the coil primary circuit. As the primary voltage decreases, a high voltage is induced in the secondary windings of the ignition coil, directing a spark through the rotor and high voltage leads, to fire the spark plugs. The dwell period is automatically controlled by the electronic module and is increased with increasing engine rpm. The HEI system features a longer spark duration which is instrumental in firing lean/diluted fuel and air mixtures. The condenser located within the distributor provides noise suppression only and is not a regularly replaced ignition system component.

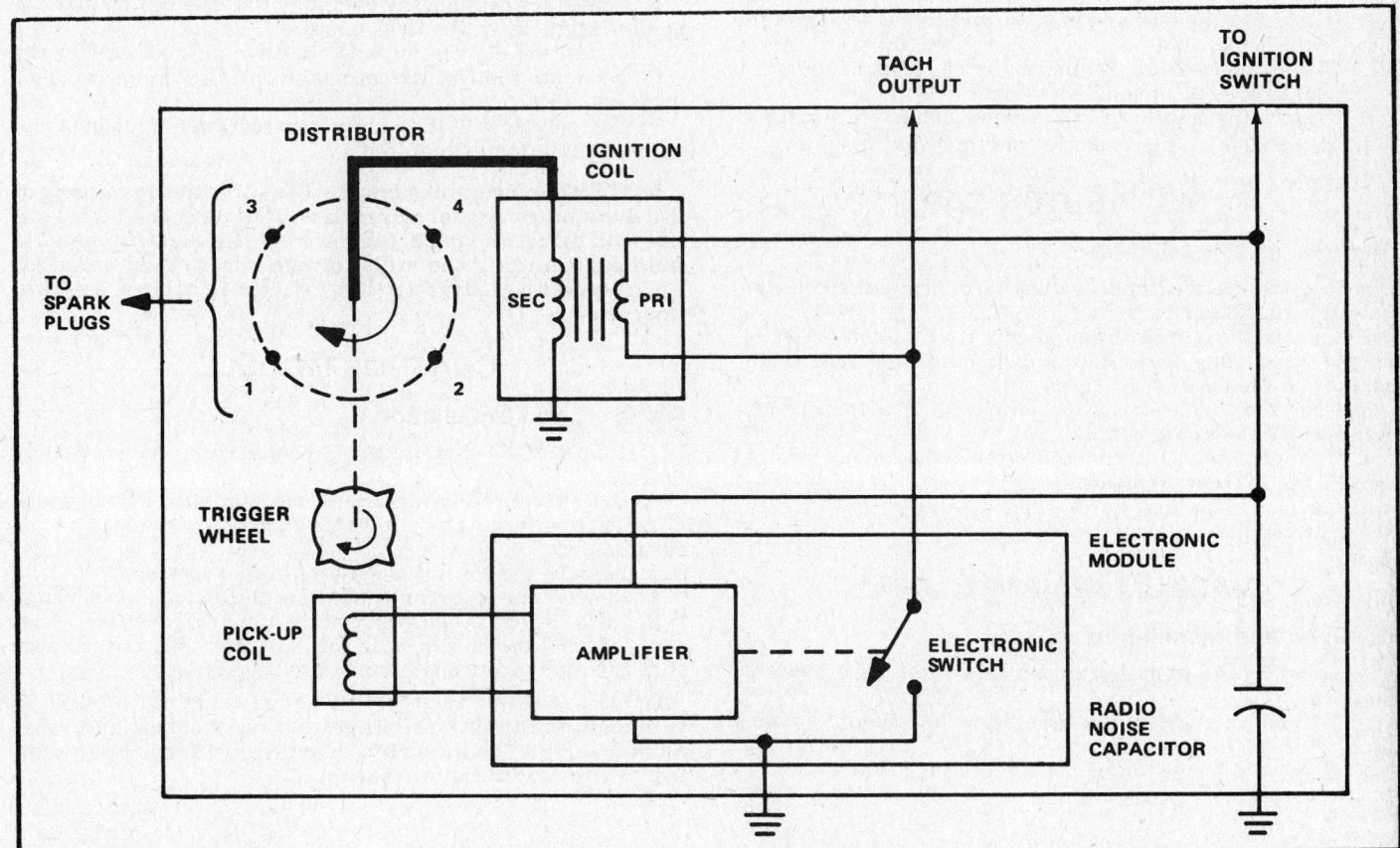

Heisystem schematic (© American Motors Corp.)

SECTION 30
ELECTRONIC IGNITION
AMC HIGH ENERGY IGNITION (HEI) SYSTEM

Component Replacement (Distributor in Engine)

INTERNAL IGNITION COIL

Removal and Installation

1. Disconnect the feed and module wire terminal connectors from the distributor cap.
2. Remove the ignition wire set retainer.
3. Remove the coil cover-to-distributor cap screws and the coil cover.
4. Remove the coil-to-distributor cap screws.
5. Using a suitable tool, press the coil wire spade terminals up out of the distributor cap.
6. Lift the coil up out of the distributor cap.
7. Remove and clean the coil spring, rubber seal washer and coil cavity of the distributor cap.
8. Installation is the reverse of the removal procedure.

EXTERNAL IGNITION COIL

Removal and Installation

1. Remove the ignition switch-to-coil lead from the coil.
2. Unfasten the distributor leads from the coil.
3. Remove the screws which hold the coil to the engine and remove it.
4. Installation is the reverse of the removal procedure.

ROTOR

Removal and Installation

1. Disconnect the feed and module wire connectors from the distributor housing.
2. Depress and release the distributor cap to housing retainers. Remove the cap assembly.
3. Remove the rotor attaching screws. Remove the rotor.
4. Installation is the reverse of the removal procedure.

DISTRIBUTOR CAP

Removal and Installation

1. Remove the feed and module wire terminal connectors from the distributor cap.
2. Remove the retainer from the cap. Tag for installation later, the spark plug wires at the distributor and remove the wires from the cap.
3. Depress and release the distributor cap-to-housing retainers. Remove the cap assembly.
4. If the cap has an internal coil, remove the coil from the old cap. Install into the new cap.
5. Using a new distributor cap, install by reversing the above procedures.

VACUUM ADVANCE UNIT

Removal and Installation

1. Remove the distributor cap and rotor as previously described.
2. Disconnect the vacuum hose from the vacuum advance unit.
3. Remove the vacuum advance retaining screws.
4. Pull the vacuum advance unit outward, rotate and disengage the operating rod from its tang.
5. Installation is the reverse of the removal procedure.

DISTRIBUTOR

Removal

1. Remove the distributor cap, mark the position of the rotor relative to the distributor body and mark the body relative to the block. Remove the carburetor air cleaner if necessary, the distributor primary wire and the distributor vacuum lines. Tag any disconnected wires or hoses for installation as required.
2. Remove the hold-down bolt and pull the distributor up and out of the block.

The rotor and body are marked so that they can be returned to the position from which they were removed. Do not turn the engine after distributor removal.

Installation

ENGINE NOT DISTURBED TIMING RETAINED

Install the distributor in the reverse order of removal. Be sure that the rotor and distributor are installed with the marks, which were made during removal, in alignment. Adjust the timing as required.

ENGINE DISTURBED TIMING LOST

If the rotor position was not noted during removal, or if the engine was cranked with the distributor out, install it as follows:

1. Remove the spark plug from the No. 1 cylinder and position a compression gauge or a thumb over the spark plug hole.
2. Slowly crank the engine, until compression pressure starts to build up.
3. Continue cranking the engine so that the timing mark or pointer aligns with the TDC mark.
4. Install the distributor with its drive meshed, so that the rotor points to the No. 1 terminal on the distributor cap with engine at TDC.
5. Complete installation in the reverse order of removal and adjust the timing as required.

NOTE: Some engines may be sensitive to the routing of the distributor sensor wires. If routed near the high-voltage coil wire or spark plug wires, the electromagnetic field surrounding the high-voltage wires could generate an occasional disruption of the ignition system operation.

CONTROL MODULE

Removal and Installation

1. Remove the distributor cap and rotor as previously described.
2. Disconnect the harness connector and pick-up coil spade connectors from the module (tag their positions for reassembly).
3. Remove the control module retaining screws.
4. Remove the control module from the distributor housing.
5. Installation is the reverse of the removal procedure. Coat the bottom of the new module with silicone lubricant. Be sure that the electrical leads are installed correctly.

NOTE: If a five terminal or seven terminal module is replaced, the ignition timing must be checked and reset as necessary. The lubricant is necessary for proper cooling of the module in operation.

ELECTRONIC IGNITION
CHRYSLER TYPE
SECTION 30

CHRYSLER ELECTRONIC IGNITION SYSTEM

General Information

The system consists of a special pulse sending distributor, an electronic control unit, a two element ballast resister, and a special ignition coil. The distributor does not contain breaker points or a condenser, these parts are replaced by a distributor reluctor and a pick-up unit.

For better timing control and fuel economy, 1983 and later models use a dual pick-up system. Vehicles using this system use a Start pick-up, a Run pick-up and a dual pick-up start run relay. In the Run model, the operation of the dual pick-up system is the same as that of a single pick-up system. During engine cranking, the dual pick-up start-run relay is energized (through the starter solenoid circuit), which allows the start pick-up to adjust the timing for starting purposes only. As soon as the starter solenoid is de-energized, the start-run relay switches the sensing function back to the run pick-up.

The ignition primary circuit is connected from the battery, through the ignition switch, through the primary side of the ignition coil, to the control unit where it is grounded. The secondary circuit is the same as in conventional system. The magnetic pulse distributor is also connected to the control unit. As the distributor shaft rotates, the distributor reluctor turns past the pick-up unit. As the reluctor turns past the pick-up unit, each of the teeth on the reluctor pass near the pick-up unit once during each distributor revolution. As the reluctor teeth move close to the pick-up unit, the magnetic reluctor induces voltage into the magnetic pick-up unit. This voltage pulse is sent to the ignition control unit from the magnetic pick-up unit. When the pulse enters the control unit, it signals the control unit to interrupt the ignition primary circuit. This causes the primary circuit to collapse and begins the induction of the magnetic lines of force from the primary side of the coil into the secondary side of the coil. This induction provides the voltage necessary to fire the spark plugs.

DECELERATION SPARK ADVANCE SYSTEM

During deceleration the ignition timing is advanced by the deceleration spark advance system. The reason for the advance in the ignition timing during deceleration is to reduce the hydrocarbons emissions during deceleration.

The deceleration spark advance system is made up of two major components, the solenoid valve and the engine speed sensor. While the vehicle is decelerating, the ignition timing is advanced by intake manifold vacuum which works on the vacuum diaphragm of the distributor through the solenoid valve. If the speed sensor detects engines speed at or below specifications, it sends a signal to the solenoid and the solenoid changes from the intake manifold vacuum to the carburetor ported vacuum to keep the vehicle in smooth operation.

Testing Ignition

ALL EXCEPT 2.6L ENGINE

To properly test the Electronic Ignition System, special testers should be used. But in the event they are not available, the system may be tested using a voltmeter with a 20,000 ohm/volt rating and an ohmmeter which uses a 1 1/2 volt battery for its operation. Both meters should be in calibration. When Ignition System problems are suspected, the following procedure should be followed:

1. Visually inspect all secondary cables at the coil, distributor and spark plugs for cracks and tightness.
2. To check wiring harness and connections, check primary wire at the ignition coil and ballast resistor for tightness. If the above checks do not determine the problem, the following steps will determine if a component is faulty.
3. Check and note battery voltage reading using voltmeter. Battery voltage should be at least 12 volts.
4. Remove the multi-wiring connector from the control unit.

— **CAUTION** —
Whenever removing or installing the wiring harness connector to the control unit, the ignition switch must be in the OFF position.

5. Turn the ignition switch On.
6. Connect the negative lead of a voltmeter to a good ground.
7. Connect the positive lead of the voltmeter to the wiring harness connector cavity No. 1. Available voltage at cavity No.

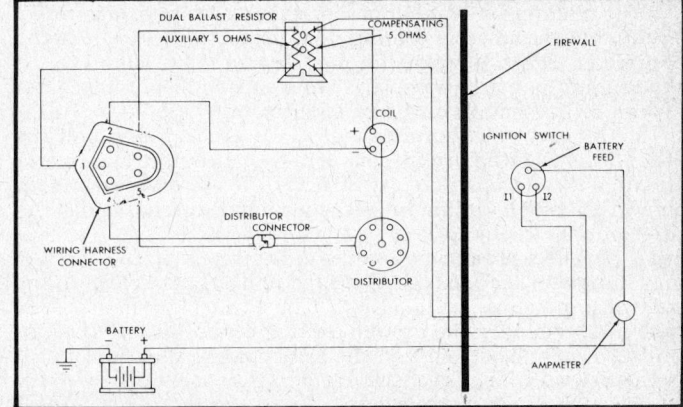

Electronic Ignition system schematic

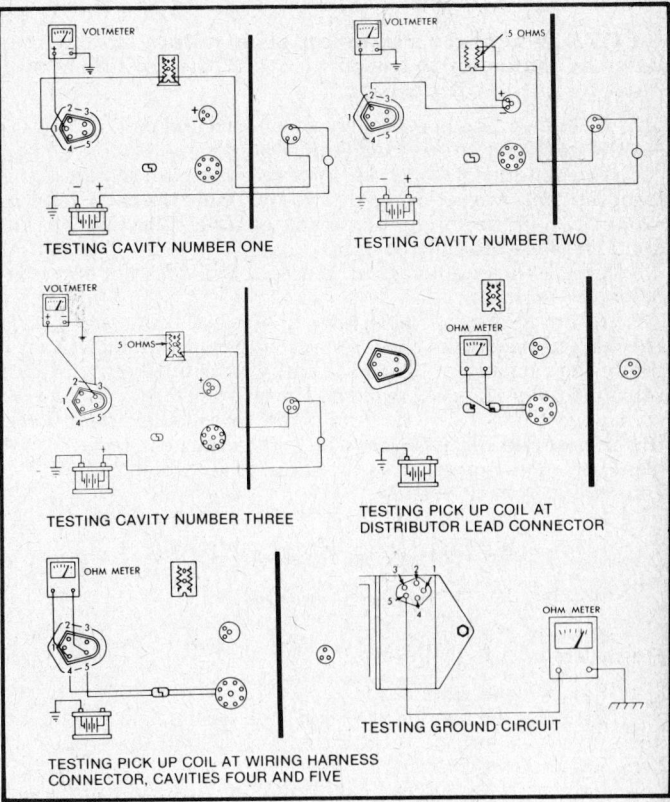

Testing the Electronic Ignition system

30-9

SECTION 30
ELECTRONIC IGNITION
CHRYSLER TYPE

1 should be within 1 volt of battery voltage with all accessories off. If there is more than a 1 volt difference, the circuit must be checked between the battery and the connector.

8. Connect the positive lead of the voltmeter to the wiring harness connector cavity No. 2. Available voltage at cavity No. 2 should be within 1 volt of battery voltage with all accessories off. If there is more than a 1 volt difference, the circuit must be checked back to the battery.

9. Connect the positive lead of the voltmeter to the wiring harness connector cavity No. 3. Available voltage at cavity No. 3 should be within 1 volt of battery voltage with all accessories off. If there is more than a 1 volt difference, the circuit must be checked back to the battery.

10. Turn ignition switch Off.

11. To check distributor pickup coil connect an ohmmeter to wiring harness connector cavity No. 4 and No. 5. The ohmmeter resistance should be 150–900 ohms.

If the readings are higher or lower than specified, disconnect the dual lead connector coming from the distributor. Using the ohmmeter, check the resistance at the dual lead connector. If the reading is not between the resistance values, replace the pickup coil assembly in the distributor.

12. Connect one ohmmeter lead to a good ground and the other lead to either connector of the distributor. Ohmmeter should show an open circuit (infinity). If the ohmmeter does show a reading less than infinity the pick up coil in the distributor must be replaced.

13. To check electronic control unit ground circuit, connect one ohmmeter lead to a good ground and the other lead to the control unit connector pin No. 5. The ohmmeter should show continuity between the ground and the connector pin. If continuity does not exist, tighten the bolts holding the control unit to the fire wall. Then recheck. If continuity does still not exist, control unit must be replaced.

14. Reconnect wiring harness at control unit and distributor.

NOTE: Whenever removing or installing the wiring harness connector to the control unit, the ignition switch must be in the Off position.

15. Check air gap between reluctor tooth and pick up coil. To set the gap refer to Air Gap Adjustment.

16. Check ignition secondary; remove the high voltage cable from the center tower of the distributor. Hold the cable approximately 3/16 in. from engine. Crank engine. If arcing does not occur, replace the control unit.

17. Crank the engine again. If arcing still does not occur, replace the ignition coil.

18. If a problem does not show up when making the voltage checks, coil resistance checks, or ground continuity checks it is likely the control unit or coil is faulty. It is unlikely that both units would fail simultaneously. However, before replacing the control unit make sure no foreign matter is lodged in or blocking the female terminal cavities in the harness connector. If clear, try replacing control unit or coil to see which one restores secondary ignition voltage.

Servicing Procedures

PICK-UP COIL

Removal and Installation

1. Remove the distributor.
2. Remove the two screws and lockwashers attaching the vacuum control unit to the distributor housing. Disconnect the arm and remove the vacuum unit.
3. Remove the reluctor by pulling it off with your fingers, or use two small screwdrivers to pry it off. Be careful not to distort or damage the teeth on the reluctor.
4. Remove the two screws and lockwashers attaching the lower plate to the housing and lift out the lower plate, upper plate, and pick-up coil as an assembly.
5. Remove the upper plate and pick-up coil assembly from the lower plate by depressing the retaining clip and moving it away from the mounting stud.
6. Remove the upper plate and pick-up coil assembly. The pick-up coil is not removable from the upper plate, and is serviced as an assembly. On early models, the coil was removable from the plate.
7. To install the pick-up coil assembly, put a little distributor cam lube on the upper plate pivot pin and lower plate support pins.
8. Position the upper plate pivot pin through the smallest hole in the lower plate.
9. Install the retaining clip. The upper plate must ride on the three support pins on the lower plate.
10. Install the lower plate, upper plate, and pickup coil assembly into the distributor and install screws.
11. Attach the vacuum advance arm to the pick-up plate, then install the vacuum unit attaching screws and washers.
12. Position the reluctor keeper pin in place on the reluctor sleeve, then slide the reluctor down the sleeve and press firmly into place.

Air Gap Adjustment

1. Align one reluctor tooth with the pick-up coil tooth.
2. Loosen the pick-up coil hold-down screw.
3. Insert a 0.008 in. nonmagnetic feeler gauge between the reluctor tooth and the pick-up coil tooth.
4. Adjust the air gap so that contact is made between the reluctor tooth, the feeler gauge, and the pick-up coil tooth.
5. Tighten the hold-down screw.
6. Remove the feeler gauge.

NOTE: No force should be required in removing the feeler gauge.

7. A 0.010 in. feeler gauge should not fit into the air gap. Do not force the feeler gauge.

---- CAUTION ----
A 0.010 in. feeler gauge can be forced into the air gap. DO NOT FORCE THE FEELER GAUGE INTO THE AIR GAP.

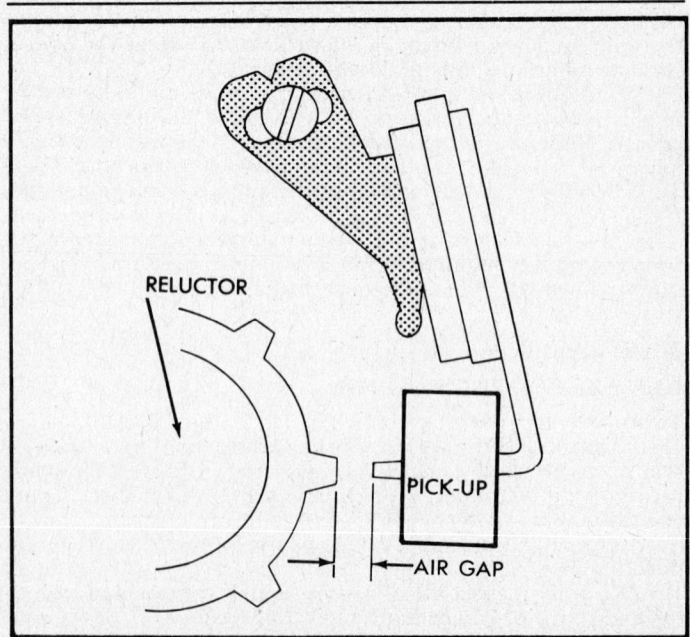

Air adjustment (© Chrysler Corp.)

ELECTRONIC IGNITION
CHRYSLER TYPE
SECTION 30

8. Apply vacuum to the vacuum unit and rotate the governor shaft. The pick-up pole should not hit the reluctor teeth. The gap is not properly adjusted if any hitting occurs. If hitting occurs on only one side of the reluctor, the distributor shaft is probably bent, and the governor and shaft assembly should be replaced.

Shaft and Bushing Wear Test

1. Remove distributor and rotor.
2. Clamp distributor in a vise equipped with soft jaws and apply only enough pressure to restrict any movement of the distributor during the test.
3. Attach a dial indicator to distributor housing so indicator plunger arm rests against reluctor.
4. Wiggle the shaft and read the total movement of the dial indicator plunger. If the movement exceeds 0.006 in. replace the housing or shaft.

DISTRIBUTOR OVERHAUL

1. Remove distributor rotor.
2. Remove the two screws and lockwashers attaching the vacuum control unit to distributor housing, disconnect the vacuum control arm from upper plate, and remove control.

TROUBLESHOOTING
CHRYSLER TYPE IGNITION

Condition	Possible Cause	Correction
ENGINE WILL NOT START (Fuel and Carburetion Known to be OK)	a) Dual Ballast	a) Check resistance of each section: Compensating resistance: .50-.60 ohms @ 70°-80°F Auxiliary Ballast: 4.75-5.75 ohms Replace if faulty. Check wire positions.
	b) Faulty Ignition Coil	b) Check for carbonized tower. Check primary and secondary resistances: Primary: 1.41-1.79 ohms @ 70°-80°F Secondary: 9,200-11,700 ohms @ 70°-80°F Check in coil tester.
	c) Faulty Pickup or Improper Pickup Air Gap	c) Check pickup coil resistance: 400-600 ohms Check pickup gap. .010 in. feeler gauge should not slip between pickup coil core and aligned reluctor blade. No evidence of pickup core striking reluctor blades should be visible. To reset gap, tighten pickup adjustment screw with a .008 in. feeler gauge held between pickup core and an aligned reluctor blade. After resetting gap, run distributor on test stand and apply vacuum advance, making sure that the pickup core does not strike the reluctor blades.
	d) Faulty Wiring	d) Visually inspect wiring for brittle insulation. Inspect connectors. Molded connectors should be inspected for rubber inside female terminals.
	e) Faulty Control Unit	e) Replace if all of the above checks are negative. Whenever the control unit or dual ballast is replaced, make sure the dual ballast wires are correctly inserted in the keyed molded connector.
ENGINE SURGES SEVERELY (Not Lean Carburetor)	a) Wiring	a) Inspect for loose connection and/or broken conductors in harness.
	b) Faulty Pickup Leads	b) Disconnect vacuum advance. If surging stops, replace pickup.
	c) Ignition Coil	c) Check for intermittent primary.
ENGINE MISSES (Carburetion OK)	a) Spark Plugs	a) Check plugs. Clean and regap if necessary.
	b) Secondary Cable	b) Check cables with an ohmmeter, or observe secondary circuit performance with an oscilloscope.
	c) Ignition Coil	c) Check for carbonized tower. Check in coil tester.
	d) Wiring	d) Check for loose or dirty connections.
	e) Faulty Pickup Lead	e) Disconnect vacuum advance. If miss stops, replace pickup.
	f) Control Unit	f) Replace if the above checks are negative.

30-11

SECTION 30: ELECTRONIC IGNITION
CHRYSLER TYPE

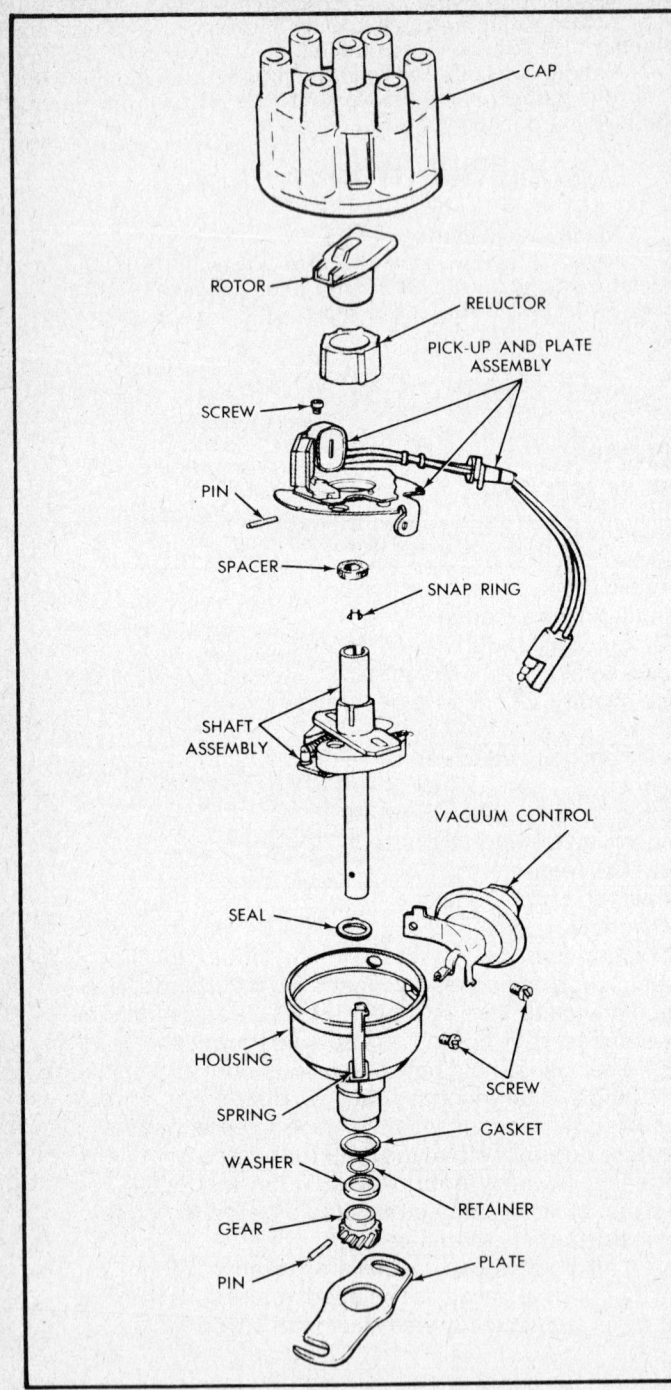

Chrysler electronic distributor (© Chrysler Corp.)

3. Remove reluctor by prying up from the bottom of the reluctor with two screwdrivers. Be careful not to distort or damage the teeth on the reluctor.

4. Remove two screws and lockwashers attaching the lower plate to the housing and lift out the lower plate, upper plate, and pick-up coil as an assembly. Distributor cap clamp springs are held in place by peened metal around the openings and should not be removed.

5. If the side play exceeds 0.006 in. in "Shaft and Bushing Wear Test", replace distributor housing assembly or shaft and governor assembly as follows: Remove distributor drive gear retaining pin and slide gear off end of shaft.

--- CAUTION ---

Support hub of gear in a manner that pin can be driven out of gear and shaft without damaging gear teeth.

Use a file to clean burrs from around pin hole in the shaft and remove the lower thrust washer. Push shaft up and remove shaft through top of distributor body.

6. If gear is worn or damaged, replace as follows: Install lower thrust washer and old gear on lower end of shaft and temporarily install rollpin. Scribe a line on the end of the shaft from center to edge, so line is centered between two gear teeth as shown. Do not Scribe completely across the shaft. Remove rollpin and gear. Use a fine file to clean burrs from around pin hole. Install new gear with thrust washer in place. Drill hole in gear and shaft approximately 90° from old hole in shaft and with scribed line centered between the two gear teeth as shown. Before drilling through shaft and gear, place a 0.007 in. feeler gauge between gear and thrust washer and after again observing that the centerline between two of the gear teeth is in line with centerline of rotor electrode drill a 0.124–0.129 in. hole and install the rollpin.

--- CAUTION ---

Support hub of gear when installing rollpin so that gear teeth will not be damaged.

7. Test operation of governor weights and inspect weight springs for distortion.
8. Lubricate governor weights.
9. Inspect all bearing surfaces and pivot pins for roughness, binding or excessive looseness.
10. Lubricate and install upper thrust washer (or washers) on the shaft and slide the shaft into the distributor body.
11. Install lower plate, upper plate and pick-up coil assembly and install attaching screws.
12. Slide shaft into distributor body, then align scribe marks and install gear and rollpin.
13. Attach vacuum advance unit arm to the pick-up plate.
14. Install vacuum unit attaching screws and washers.
15. Position reluctor keeper pin into place on reluctor sleeve.
16. Slide reluctor down reluctor sleeve and press firmly into place.
17. Lubricate the felt pad in top of reluctor sleeve with 1 drop of light engine oil and install the rotor.

ELECTRONIC IGNITION
CHRYSLER (EIS) SYSTEM

CHRYSLER ELECTRONIC IGNITION (EIS) SYSTEM

General Information

2.6L ENGINE ONLY

This system consists of the battery, ignition coil, IC igniter (electronic control unit) which is built into the distributor, spark plugs and primary and secondary wiring. Primary current to the coil is switched on and off by the IC igniter in response to timing signals produced by a distributor magnetic pick-up.

The distributor is composed of a power distributing section, IC igniter, advance mechanism, drive section and the signal generator. The signal generator, which houses a small magneto, produces a signal for driving the IC igniter. The signal is produced in exact synchronism with distributor shaft rotation. It is produced at equal intervals four times distributor shaft rotation. The distributor uses this signal as an ignition timing signal during its operation. The distributor is equipped with vacuum and centrifugal advance mechanisms.

The centrifugal advance mechanism is located below the rotor assembly. It is equipped with governor weights that move outward and inward depending on engine speed. As engine speed increases, the weights move outward which causes the reluctor to rotate ahead of the distributor shaft. This causes the ignition timing to advance.

The vacuum advance incorporates a spring loaded diaphragm which is connected to the breaker assembly. The diaphragm moves against the spring pressure by carburetor vacuum pressure. When the vacuum increases, the diaphragm causes the movable breaker assembly to pivot in direction opposite to distributor rotation. This action advances the ignition timing.

Troubleshooting

COIL SPARK

Test

1. Remove the coil wire from the center of the distributor cap.
2. Using heavy gloves and insulated pliers, hold the end of the wire $3/16 - 3/8$ in. away from a good engine ground and crank the engine.

NOTE: Make sure there are no fuel leaks before performing this test.

3. If there is a spark at the coil wire, it must be bright blue in color and fire consistently. If it is, continue to crank the engine while slowly moving the coil wire away from ground. Look for arcing at the coil tower. If arcing occurs, replace coil. If there is no spark, or spark is weak or not consistent, proceed to the next step.
If a good spark is present, check the condition of the distributor cap, rotor, plug wires and spark plugs. If these check out, the ignition system is working; check the fuel system and engine mechanical systems.
4. With the ignition on, measure the voltage at the negative coil terminal. It should be the same as battery voltage. If it is 3 volts or less, the IC distributor is defective. If there is no voltage, check for an open circuit in the coil or wiring.
5. With the ignition on, hold the coil wire as instructed in Step 2 and, using a jumper wire, momentarily connect the negative coil terminal to ground. There should be a spark at the coil wire.
6. If there is no spark, check for voltage at the positive coil terminal with the key on. Voltage should be at least 9 volts. If proper voltage is obtained, the coil is defective and should be replaced. If proper voltage is not obtained, check the wiring and connections.

CENTRIFUGAL ADVANCE

Test

Run the engine at idle and remove the vacuum hose (non-stripped hose) from the vacuum controller. Slowly accelerate the engine to check for advance. Excessive advance indicates a damaged governor spring (a broken spring will result in abrupt advance). Insufficient advance is usually caused by a broken governor weight or a malfunction in cam operation. Correct as needed.

VACUUM ADVANCE

Test

Set engine speed at 2500 rpm. Check for advance by disconnecting and then reconnecting the vacuum hose at the distributor. For a more accurate determination of whether the vacuum advance mechanism is operating properly, remove the vacuum hose from the distributor and connect a hand vacuum pump. Run the engine at idle and slowly apply vacuum pressure to check for advance. Excessive advance, look for a deteriorated vacuum controller spring. Insufficient advance or no advance may be caused by linkages problems or a ruptured vacuum diaphragm. Correct as necessary.

IGNITION COIL

Test

Clean the ignition coil. Check the coil terminals for cleanliness and exterior of body for cracks. Replace if necessary. Check for carbon deposit or corrosion in the high tension cable inserting hole. Repair or replace if necessary. Measure the resistance of the primary coil, secondary coil and external resistor. If the reading is not within 1.3–1.8 ohms on the primary coil and 9000–12000 ohms on the secondary coil windings, replace the coil.

IGNITION WIRE RESISTANCE

Test

— **CAUTION** —
When removing the high voltage cable coming off the ignition coil, grasp the cable rubber cap. Twist and pull slowly. Do not bend the cable. This could result in breaking the conductor.

Check the cable terminals. A corroded terminal should be cleaned or replaced. A broken or severely distorted cable should also be replaced. Check the resistance of each cable between both ends. If it exceeds 22 kilo-ohms, replace the wire. Use silicone lubricant when installing wires on spark plugs.

DISTRIBUTOR

Removal

1. Disconnect the negative battery cable.
2. Disconnect the wiring harness from the distributor and the wires from the distributor cap. Note or label their location for ease of reassembly.

SECTION 30

ELECTRONIC IGNITION
CHRYSLER (EIS) SYSTEM

3. Disconnect the vacuum hose from the vacuum advance unit.

4. Rotate the engine crankshaft (in the direction of normal rotation) until the number one cylinder is at top dead center (TDC) on the compression stroke. Make a mark on the block where the rotor points to act as a reference for installation.

5. Remove the distributor hold-down nut and lift the distributor assembly away from the engine.

Installation

ENGINE DISTURBED

1. If the engine has been cranked over while the distributor was removed, rotate the crankshaft until the No. 1 piston is at TDC on the compression stroke. Align the timing marks on the crankshaft to TDC mark on the timing plate.

2. Align the mating mark on the distributor housing with the mating mark on the distributor driven gear.

3. Lower the distributor into the engine. Tighten the hold-down nut and connect the wires.

4. Check and if necessary, adjust the ignition timing.

ENGINE NOT DISTURBED

1. If the engine was not disturbed while the distributor was out, lower the distributor into the engine.

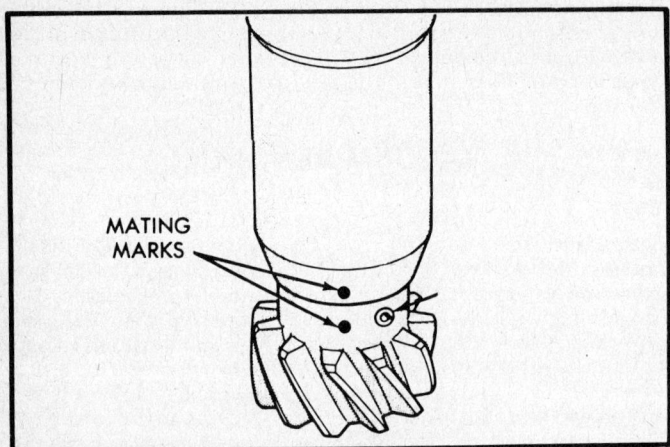

Timing mating marks (© Chrysler Corp.)

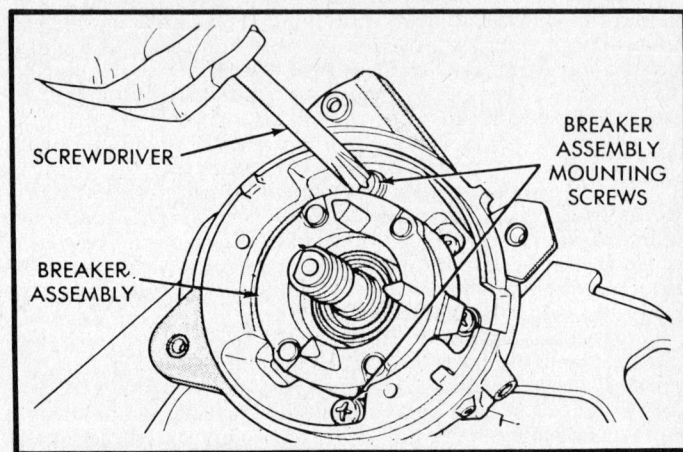

Removing the centrifugal governor assembly

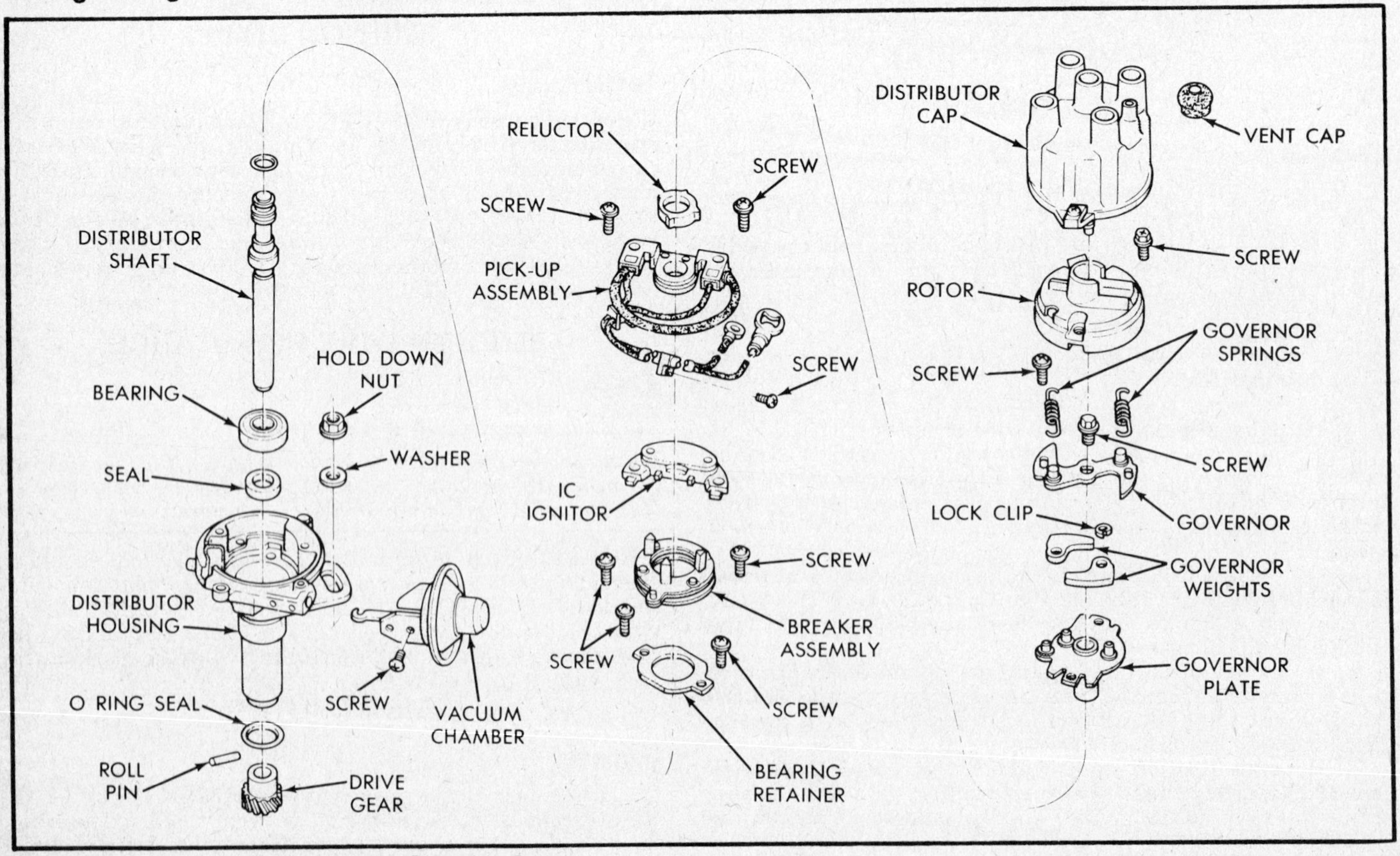

Exploded view of distributor (© Chrysler Corp.)

30-14

ELECTRONIC IGNITION
CHRYSLER (EIS) SYSTEM

2. Make sure that the distributor gears are properly engaged with the engine.
3. Tighten the hold-down nut and connect the wires.
4. Check the ignition timing. Adjust if necessary.

DISTRIBUTOR

Overhaul

1. Remove the distributor cap mounting screws. Remove the distributor cap.
2. Remove the rotor screws. Remove the rotor assembly.
3. Remove the governor assembly bolt. Remove the governor.

NOTE: Since the bolt is very tight, it is recommended that a box or socket wrench be used to loosen the governor mounting bolt. The two springs on the governor are built to different specifications, so each must be installed in its original position. Mark the springs accordingly if the governor flyweights are being disassembled.

4. Remove the wire clamp screws and remove the clamp.
5. Remove the pick-up screws and the IC igniter mounting screws.
6. Remove the pick-up coil and the IC igniter as an assembly.
7. Remove the vacuum advance diaphragm screws and remove the vacuum advance assembly.
8. Remove the breaker assembly mounting screws. Remove the breaker assembly. Do not allow iron filings or other metallic debris to contaminate the breaker assembly while removed.

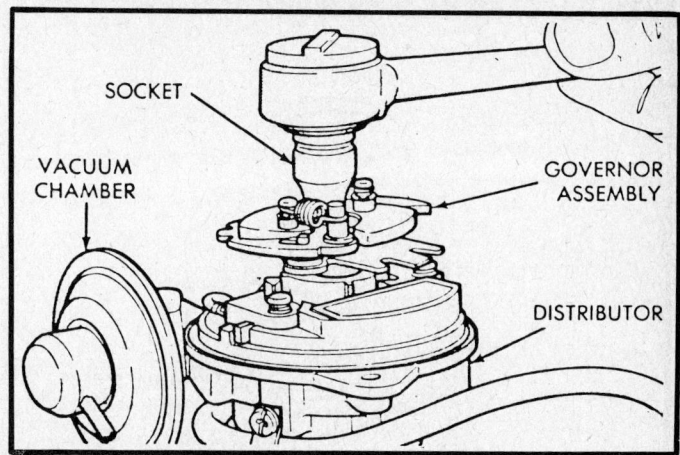

Removing the breaker assembly (© Chrysler Corp.)

9. Remove the bearing retaining plate screws and remove the bearing retainer.
10. Scribe alignment marks on the drive gear and distributor shaft for reassembly, then drive out the gear roll pin using a suitable punch and remove the drive gear.
11. Remove the distributor shaft and bearing assembly, then remove the housing seal.
12. Reassemble the distributor in the reverse order of disassembly.

CHRYSLER CORPORATION HALL EFFECT ELECTRONIC IGNITION

General Information

EXCEPT 2.6L ENGINE

The Hall Effect electronic ignition is used in conjunction with the Chrysler Lean Burn Electronic Spark Control System. It consists of a sealed Spark Control Computer, five engine sensors (vacuum transducer, coolant switch, Hall Effect pickup assembly, throttle position transducer, and carburetor switch), coil, spark plugs, ballast resistor, and the various wires needed to connect the components. Only four of the five engine sensors are used on 1983 and later models not equipped with the Feed Back carburetor; the throttle position transducer is no longer used. On models with Feed Back carburetor, an oxygen sensor in the exhaust manifold is included.

The distributor contains the Hall Effect pickup assembly which replaces the breaker points assembly in conventional systems. The pickup assembly supplies the computer with information on engine speed and crankshaft position, and is only one of signals which the computer uses as input to determine ignition timing. The Hall Effect is a shift in magnetic field, caused, in this installation, when one of the rotor blades passes between the two arms of the sensor.

There are essentially two modes of operation of the Spark Control computer: the start mode and the run mode. The start mode is only used during engine cranking. During cranking only the Hall Effect pickup signals the computer. These signals are interpreted to provide a fixed number of degrees of spark advance. The computer shuts off coil primary current in accordance with the pickup signals. As in conventional ignition systems, primary current shutdown causes secondary field collapse, and the high voltage is sent from the coil to the distributor, which then sends it to the spark plug.

After the engine starts, and during normal engine operation, the computer functions in the run mode. In this mode the Hall Effect pickup serves as only one of the signals to the computer. It is a reference signal of maximum possible spark advance. The computer then determines, from information provided by the other engine sensors, how much of this advance is necessary, and shuts down the primary current accordingly to fire the spark plug at the exact moment when this advance (crankshaft position) is reached.

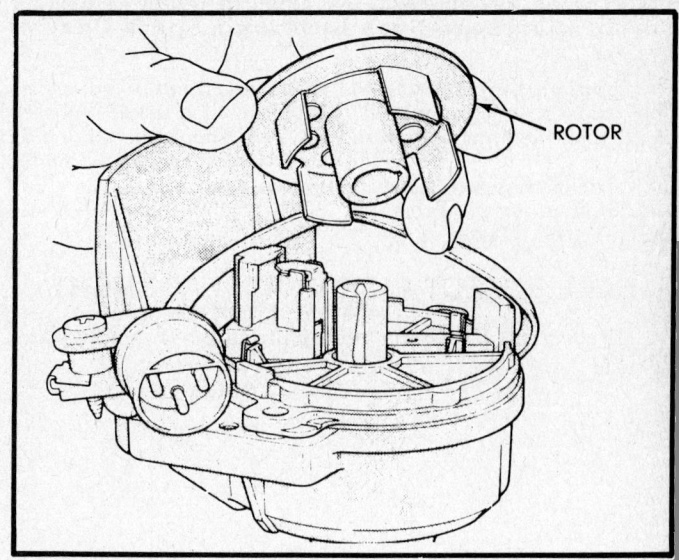

Hall Effect rotor removal (© Chrysler Corp.)

SECTION 30
ELECTRONIC IGNITION
CHRYSLER HALL EFFECT SYSTEM

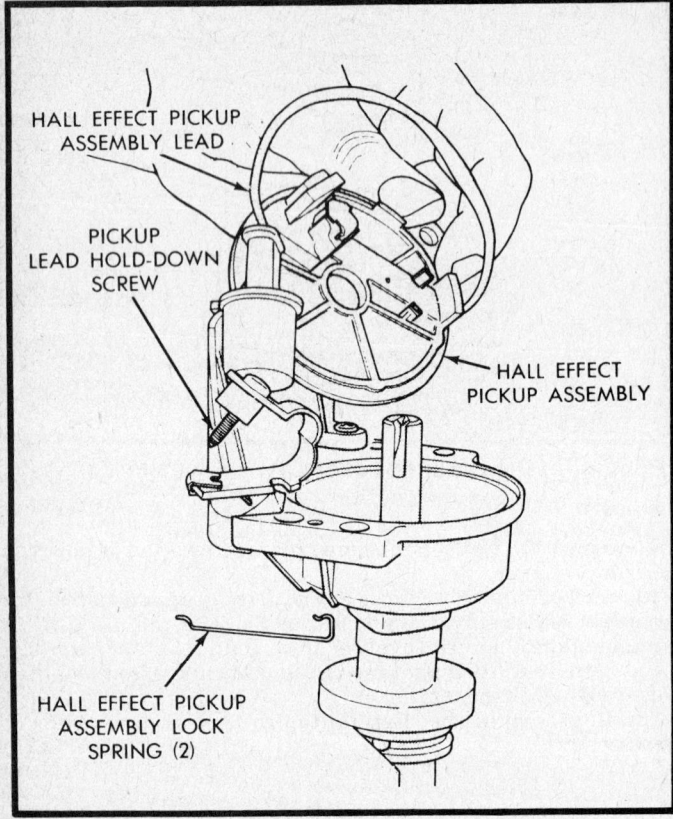

Hall Effect pickup installation (© Chrysler Corp.)

There is a third mode of operation which only becomes functional when the computer fails. This is the limp-in mode. This mode functions on signals from the pickup only, and results in very poor engine performance. However, it does allow the car to be driven to a repair shop. If a failure occurs in the pickup assembly or the start mode of the computer, the engine will neither start nor run.

SYSTEM TESTS

NOTE: All system tests are covered under "Chrysler Corporation Lean Burn Electronic Spark Control System".

The ignition coil can be tested on a conventional coil tester. The ballast resistor, mounted on the firewall, must be included in all tests. Primary resistance at 70°F should be 1.60–1.79 ohms for the Chrysler Prestolite coil, and 1.41–1.62 ohms for the Chrysler Essex coil. Secondary resistance should be 9400–11,700 ohms for the Prestolite, 9000–12,200 ohms (1983 and later) for the Essex.

HALL EFFECT PICKUP REPLACEMENT

1. Loosen the distributor cap retaining screws and remove the cap.

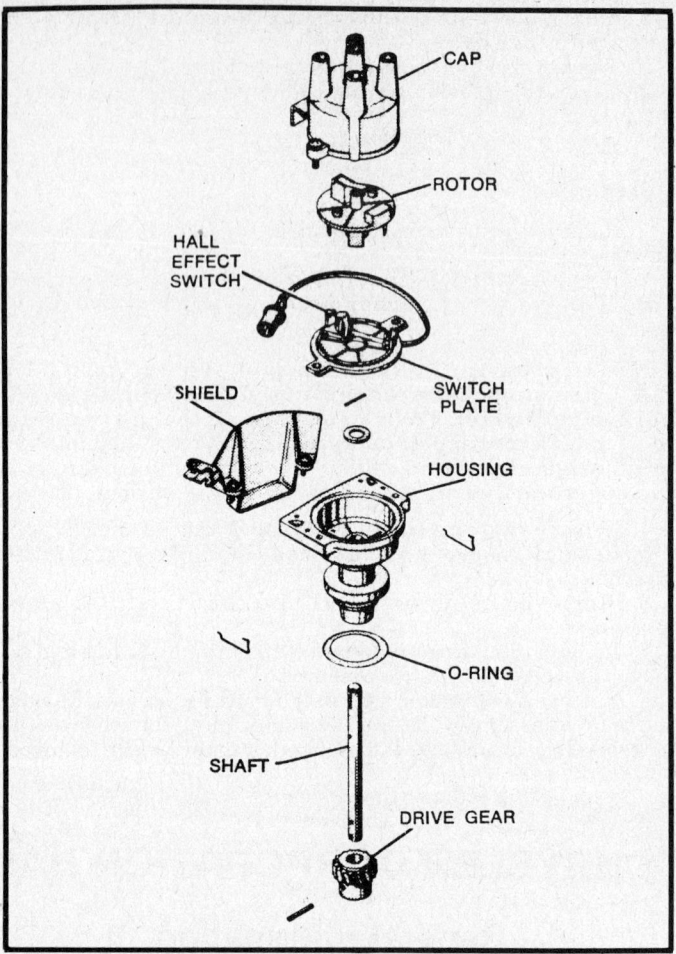

Hall Effect distributor—exploded view (© Chrysler Corp.)

2. Pull straight up on the rotor and remove it from the shaft.
3. Disconnect the pickup assembly lead.
4. Remove the pickup lead hold down screw.
5. Remove the pickup assembly lock springs and lift off the pickup.
6. Install the new pickup assembly onto the distributor housing and fasten it into place with the lock springs.
7. Fasten the pickup lead to the housing with the hold down screw.
8. Reconnect the lead to the harness.
9. Press the rotor back into place on the shaft. Do not wipe off the silicone grease on the metal portion of the rotor.
10. Replace the distributor cap and tighten the retaining screws.

--- **CAUTION** ---
Care must be exercised during pick-up installation. The Hall Effect pick-up assembly leads may be damaged if not properly installed. Make sure that the lead retainer is properly seated in the locating hole before attaching the distributor cap.

ELECTRONIC IGNITION
CHRYSLER LEAN BURN SYSTEM
30 SECTION

CHRYSLER CORPORATION LEAN BURN ELECTRONIC SPARK CONTROL SYSTEM

This system was introduced as the Lean Burn System and was renamed Electronic Spark Control later. It is based on the principle that lower NOx emissions would occur if the air/fuel ratio inside the cylinder area was raised from its current point (15.5:1) to a much leaner point (18:1). In order to make the engine workable, a solution to the problems of carburetion and timing had to be found, since a lean running engine is not the most efficient in terms of driveability. Chrysler adapted a conventional Thermo-Quad carburetor, and later a two barrel unit, to handle the added air coming in, but the real advance of the system is the Spark Control Computer. Since a lean burning engine demands precise ignition timing, additional spark control was needed for the distributor. The computer supplies this control by providing an infinitely variable advance curve. Input data is fed instantaneously to the computer by a series of sensors located in the engine compartment which monitor timing, water temperature, air temperature, idle/off-idle operation, and intake manifold vacuum. The program schedule module of the Spark Control Computer receives the information from the sensors, processes it, and then directs the ignition control module to advance or retard the timing as necessary. This whole process is going on continuously as the engine is running, taking only a thousandth of a second to complete a circuit from sensor to distributor. The components of the system are a modified carburetor and Spark Control Computer, which is responsible for translating input data, and which transmits data to the distributor to advance or retard the timing.

The start pick-up sensor, located inside the distributor, supplies a signal to the computer providing a fixed timing point that is only used for starting the car. It also has a back-up function of taking over engine timing in case the run pick-up fails.

Since the timing in this pick-up is fixed at one point, the car will be able to run but not very well. The run pick-up sensor, also located in the distributor, provides timing data to the computer once the engine is running. It also monitors engine speed, and helps the computer decide when the piston is reaching the top of its compression stroke. On 1983 and later models, the system is simplified to use only one distributor pick-up. This pick-up provides the basic timing signal to the computer for both the start and the run models.

NOTE: The two systems will not operate at the same time.

The coolant temperature sensor, located in the thermostat housing (4 cyl.), in the head 6 cyl.) or in the intake manifold (V8), informs the computer when the coolant temperature reaches normal operating levels.

The carburetor switch sensor, located on the end of the idle stop solenoid, tells the computer if the engine is at idle or off-idle.

The vacuum transducer, located on the computer, monitors the amount of intake manifold vacuum; the more vacuum, the more spark advance to the distributor. In order to obtain this spark advance in the distributor, the carburetor switch sensor has to remain open for a specified amount of time, during which time the advance will slowly build up to the amount indicated as necessary by the vacuum transducer. If the carburetor switch should close during that time, the advance to the distributor will be cancelled. From here the computer will start with an advance countdown if the carburetor switch is re-opened within a certain amount of time. The advance will con-

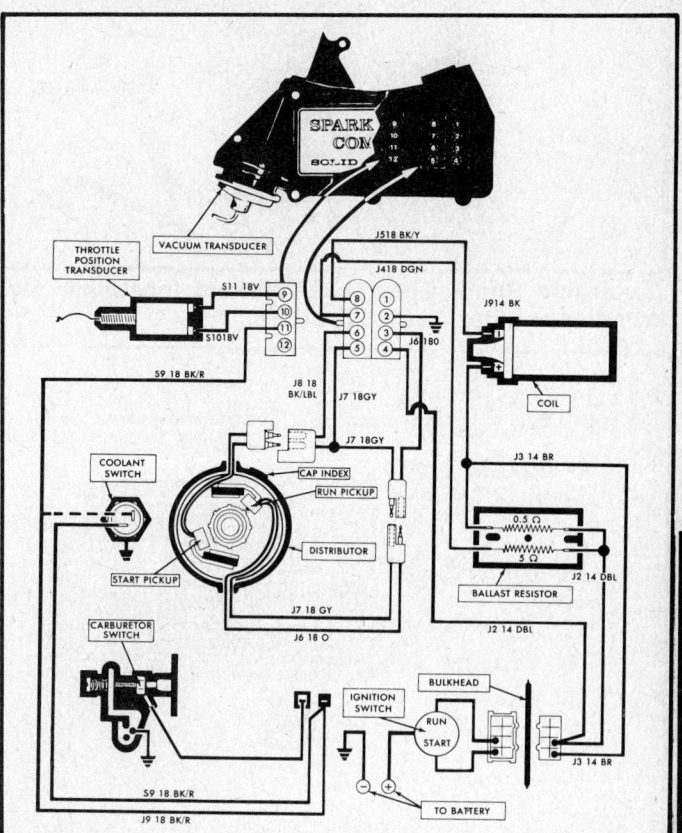

Single pick-up type electronic ignition (© Chrysler Corp.)

Dual pick-up type electronic ignition (© Chrysler Corp.)

30–17

Section 30: ELECTRONIC IGNITION
CHRYSLER LEAN BURN SYSTEM

tinue from a point decided by the computer. If the switch is reopened after the computer has counted down to "no advance," the vacuum advance process must start over again.

Some 1983 and later models have a detonation sensor mounted on the intake manifold. The sensor is tuned to the frequency characteristic of engine knocking. When detonation (knocking) occurs, the sensor sends a low voltage signal to the computer, which retards ignition timing in proportion to the strength and frequency of the signal. The maximum amount of retard is 11°. When the detonation has ceased, the computer advances timing to the original value.

1983 and later models (except Omni, Horizon Aries, and Reliant) are equipped with an Electronic Throttle Control (ETC) system which is incorporated within the spark control computer. A solenoid mounted on the carburetor is energized whenever the air conditioning (A/C) or electronic timers (some models) are activated. The solenoid acts to control idle under varying engine loads.

The 1983 and later models, the EGR value is controlled by the spark control computer.

Operation

When you turn the ignition key on, the start pick-up sends its signal to the computer, which relays back information for more spark advance during cranking. As soon as the engine starts, the run pick-up takes over, and receives more advance for about one minute. This advance is slowly eliminated during the one minute warm up period. While the engine is cold, (coolant temperature below 150° as monitored by the coolant temperature sensor), no more advance will be given to the distributor until it reaches normal operation temperature. At this point, normal operation of the system will begin.

In normal operation, the basic timing information is related by the run pick-up to the computer along with input signals from all the other sensors. From this data, the computer determines the maximum allowable advance or retard to be sent to the distributor for any situation.

In either the run pick-up or the computer should fail, the back up system of the start pick-up takes over. This supplies a fixed timing signal to the distributor which allows the car to be driven until it can be repaired. In this mode, very poor fuel economy and performance will be experienced. If the start pick-up or the ignition control module section of the computer should fail, the car will not start or run.

NOTE: Some of the procedures in this section refer to an adjustable timing light. This is also known as a spark advance tester, i.e., a device that will measure how much spark advance is present going from one point, a base figure, to another. Since precise timing is very important to the system, do not attempt to perform any of the tests calling for an adjustable timing light without one. Refer to appropriate car section for specifications.

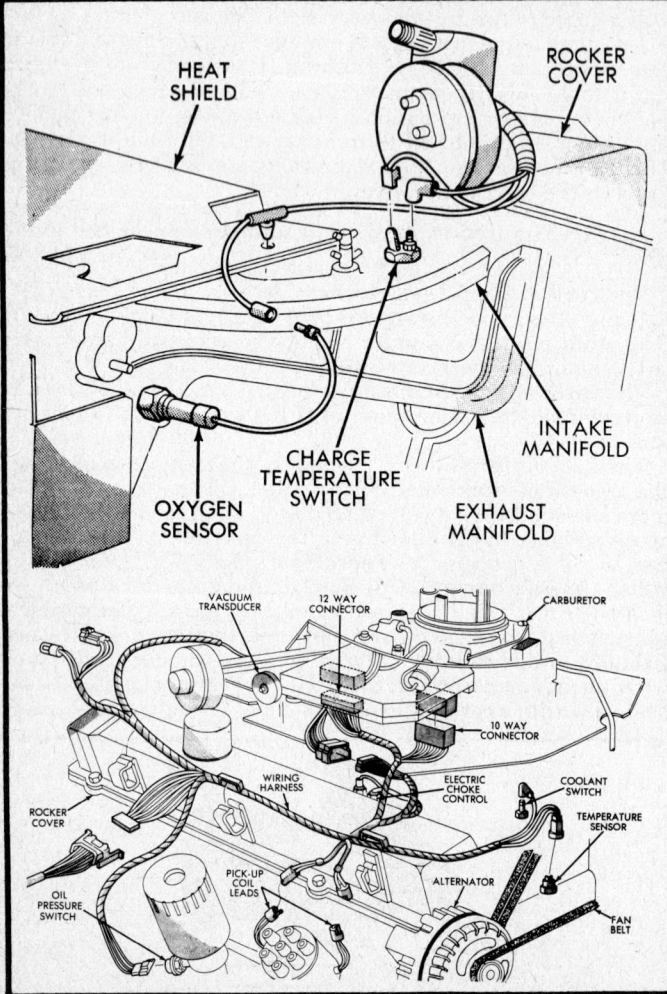

Electronic Spark Control component locations, six cylinder engines (© Chrysler Corp.)

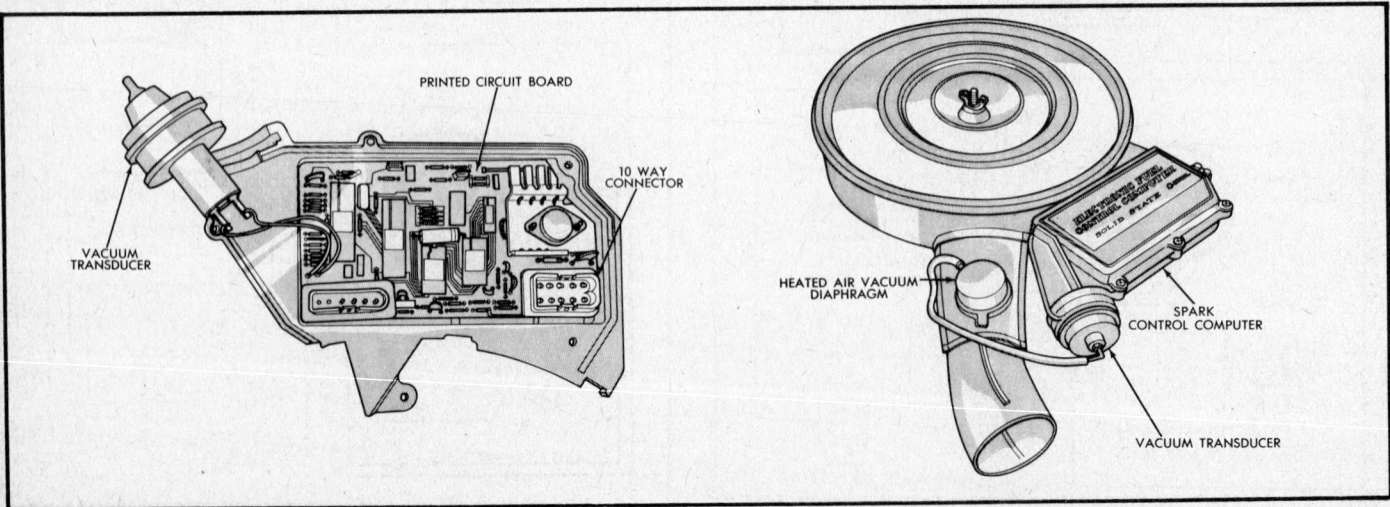

Combustion Computer assembly – typical (© Chrysler Corp.)

Electronic Ignition
CHRYSLER LEAN BURN SYSTEM
Section 30

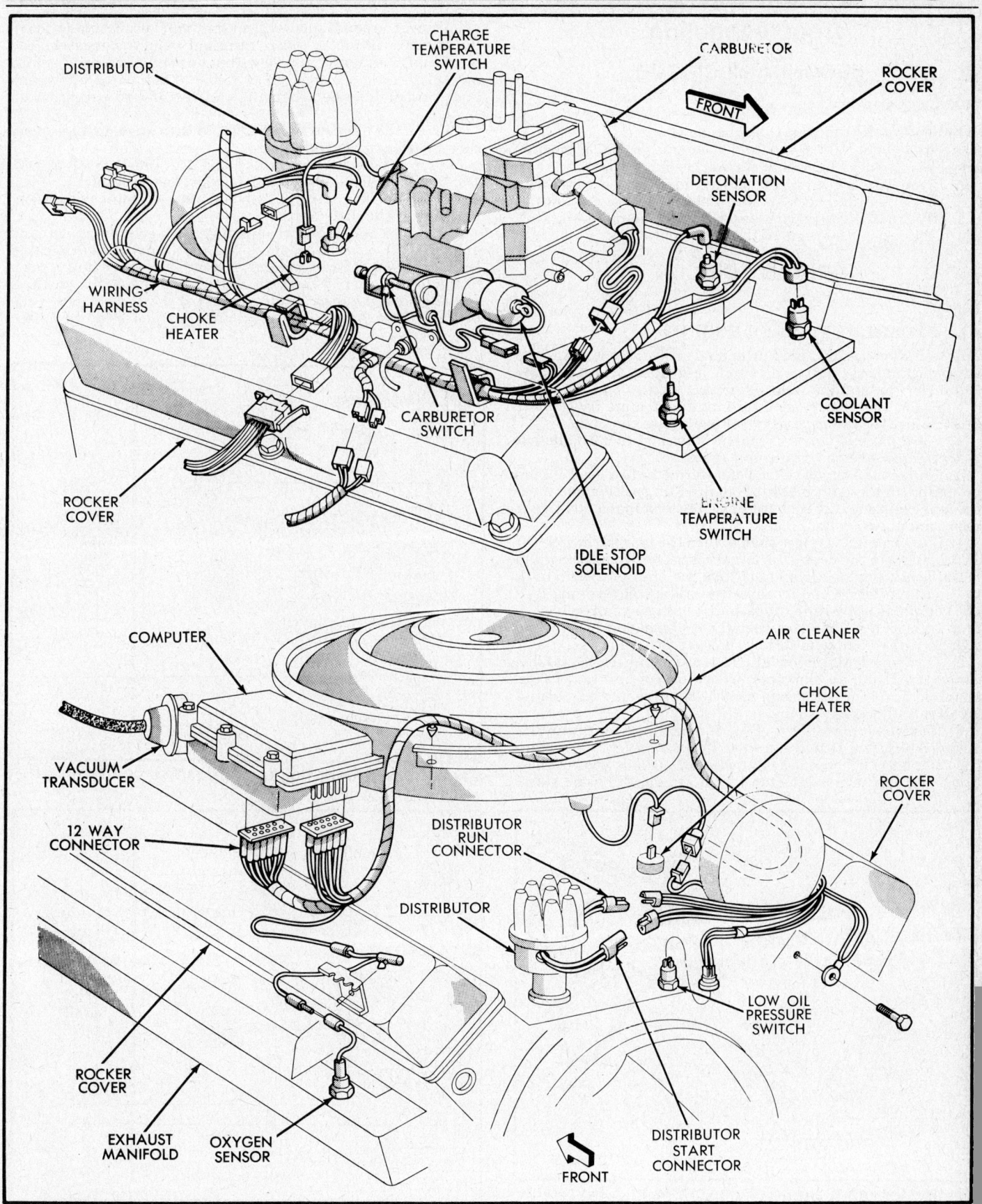

Electronic Spark Control component locations, V8 engines

SECTION 30

Electronic Ignition
CHRYSLER LEAN BURN SYSTEM

Troubleshooting

SECONDARY CIRCUIT

Test

1. Remove the coil wire from the distributor cap and hold it cautiously about ¼ in. away from an engine ground, then have someone crank the engine while you check for spark.
2. If you have a good spark, slowly move the coil wire away from the engine and check for arcing at the coil while cranking.
3. If you have good spark and it is not arcing at the coil, check the rest of the parts of the ignition system.

PRIMARY CIRCUIT

Test

ALL EXCEPT 4 CYLINDER ENGINES

This test is for the start pick-up in dual pick-up models, and the entire pick-up assembly in all single pick-up models except the Omni/Horizon and the Aries/Reliant.

1. Check the battery specific gravity; it must be at least 1.220 to deliver the necessary voltage to fire the plugs.
2. Put a piece of paper or plastic between the curb idle adjusting screw and the carburetor switch.
3. Connect the negative lead of a voltmeter to a good engine ground, turn the ignition switch to the Run position and measure the voltage at the carburetor switch terminal. If voltage is approximately 5 volts, proceed to Step 8.
4. If the voltage was less than 5, turn the ignition switch Off and disconnect the double terminal connector from the bottom of the Spark Control Computer. Turn the ignition switch back to the Run position and measure the voltage at terminal 2. If the voltage is not within 1 volt of the voltage you received in Step 1, check the wiring between the terminal and the ignition switch. If the voltage is correct, proceed to Step 5.
5. Turn the ignition switch Off and disconnect the double connector. Using an ohmmeter, check for continuity between terminal 7 and the carburetor switch. There should be continuity. If not, check the wiring.
6. If there is continuity in Step 5, next check for continuity between terminal 10 and a ground. If continuity exists, replace the computer. If not, check the wire for open or poor connections, and only proceed to Step 7 if the engine still won't start.
7. Turn the ignition switch to the "run" position and touch the positive voltmeter lead to terminal 1 and the negative lead to ground. Voltage should be within one volt of battery voltage measured in Step 1. If so, go to Step 8. If not, check the wiring and connections between the connector and the ignition switch.
8. Turn the ignition switch Off and with an ohmmeter, measure resistance between terminals 5 and 9. Dual pick-up coil models, test between terminals 5 and 9 for the run pick-up coil, and between terminals 3 and 9 for the start pick-up coil. If you do not receive a reading of 150–900 ohms disconnect the pick-up leads at the distributor.
9. Connect one lead of an ohmmeter to a good engine ground and with the other lead, check the continuity of both pick-up leads going into the distributor. If there is not continuity, go on to the next step. If you do get a reading, replace the pickup.
10. Remove the distributor cap and check the air gap of the pick-up coil(s). Adjust if necessary and proceed to the next step.

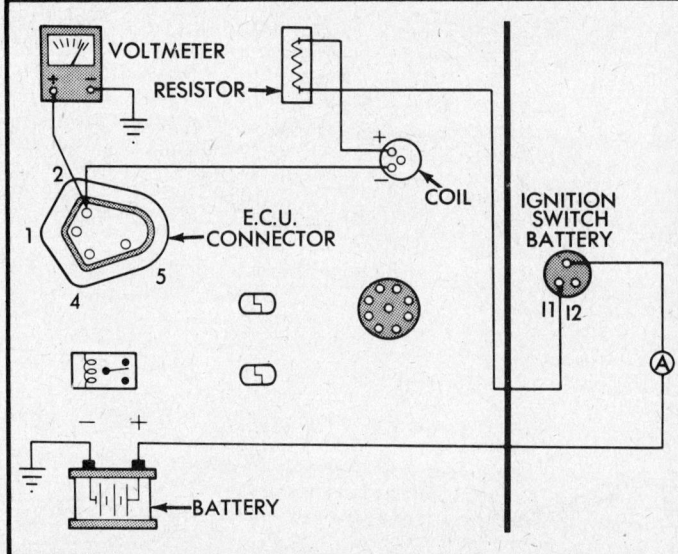

Testing for battery boltage at positive coil terminal
(© Chrysler Corp.)

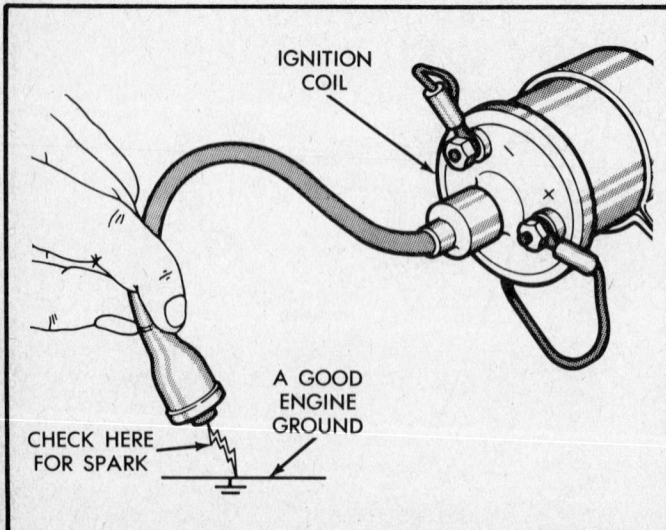

Testing for spark during engine cranking. Use insulated pliers and heavy gloves to handle coil wire
(© Chrysler Corp.)

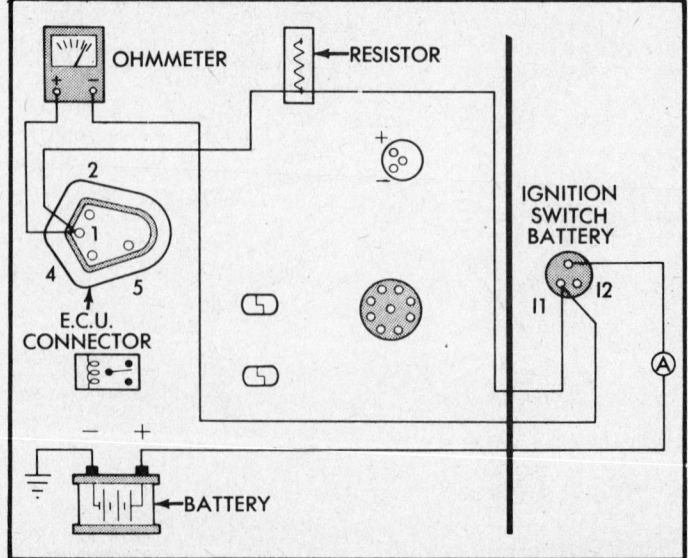

Checking continuity between cavity "1" and the ignition switch (© Chrysler Corp.)

ELECTRONIC IGNITION
CHRYSLER LEAN BURN SYSTEM

11. Replace the distributor cap, and start the engine. If it still will not start, replace the Spark Control Computer. If the engine still does not work, put the old one back and retrace your steps paying close attention to any wiring which may be shorted.

4 CYLINDER ENGINES

1. Perform the "Troubleshooting" test before proceeding with the following. Make sure the battery is fully charged, then measure and record the battery voltage.
2. Remove the coil secondary wire from the distributor cap.
3. With the key on, use the special jumper wire and momentarily connect the negative terminal of the ignition coil to ground while holding the coil secondary wire (using insulated pliers and heavy gloves) about ¼ in. from a good ground. A spark should fire.
4. If spark was obtained, go to Step 9.
5. If no spark was obtained, turn off the ignition and disconnect the 10–wire harness going into the Spark Control Computer. Do not remove the grease from the connector.
6. With the ignition key on, use the special jumper wire and momentarily connect the negative terminal of the ignition coil to ground while holding the coil wire ¼ in. from a good engine ground. A spark should fire.
7. If a spark is present, the computer output is shorted; replace the computer.
8. If no spark is obtained, measure the voltage at the coil positive terminal. It should be within 1 volt of battery voltage. If voltage is present but no spark is available when shorting negative terminal, replace the coil. If no voltage is present, replace the coil or check the primary wiring.
9. If voltage was obtained but the engine will not start, hold the carburetor switch open with a thin cardboard insulator and measure the voltage at the switch. It should be at least 5 volts. If voltage is present, go to Step 16.
10. If no voltage is present, turn the ignition switch off and disconnect the 10–wire harness going into the computer.

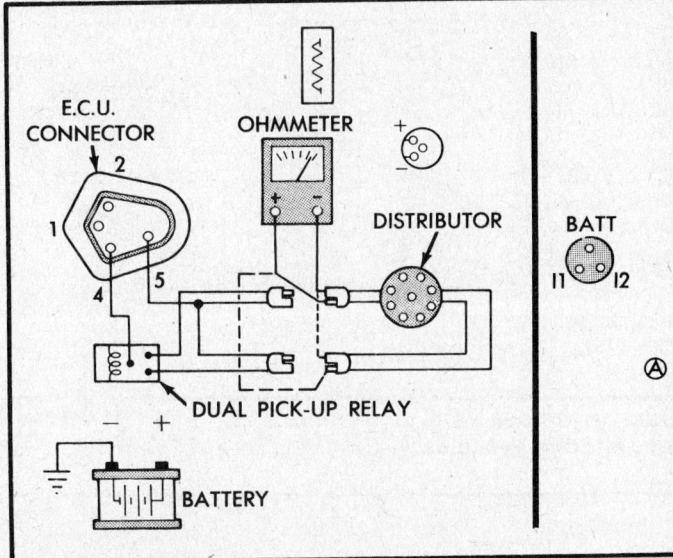

Testing resistance at both pick-up coils
(© Chrysler Corp.)

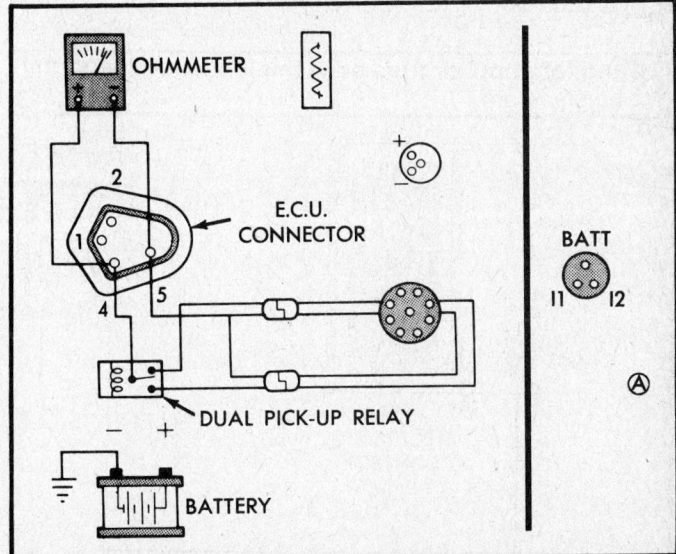

Checking resistance between cavities "4" and "5"

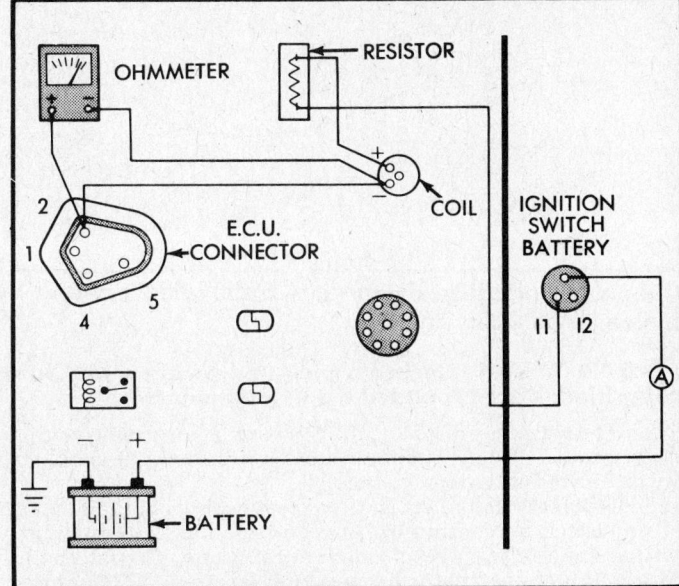

Checking continuity between cavity "2" and the negative coil terminal (© Chrysler Corp.)

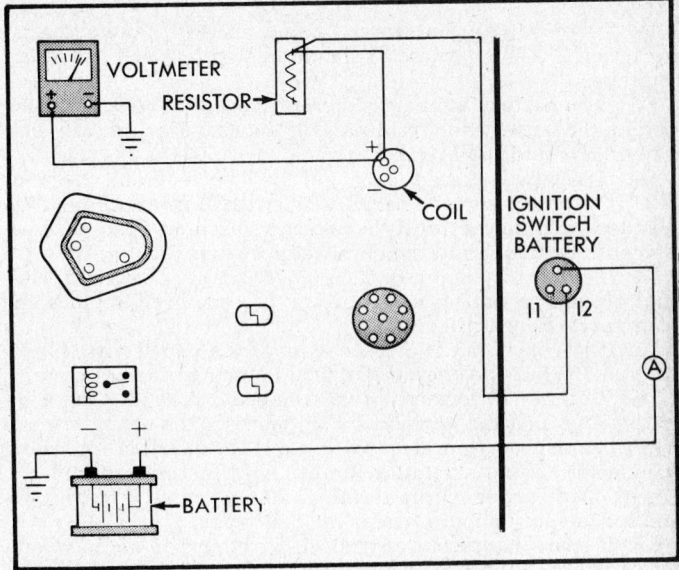

Testing for battery voltage at positive coil terminal

SECTION 30 ELECTRONIC IGNITION
CHRYSLER LEAN BURN SYSTEM

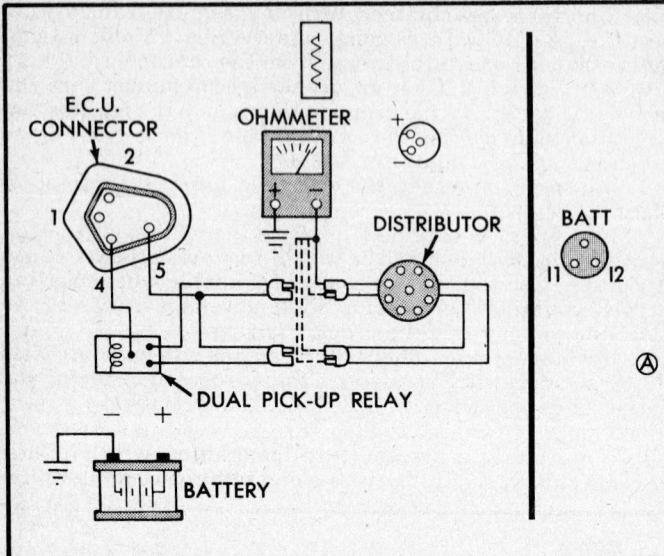

Testing for short circuits at each pick-up coil terminal (© Chrysler Corp.)

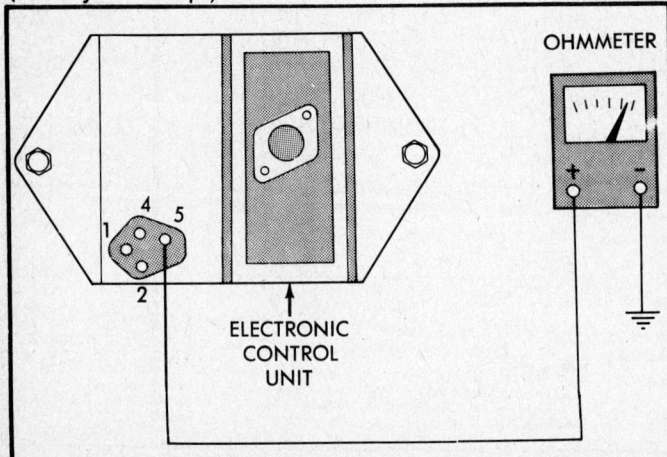

Testing electronic control unit pin "5" for ground

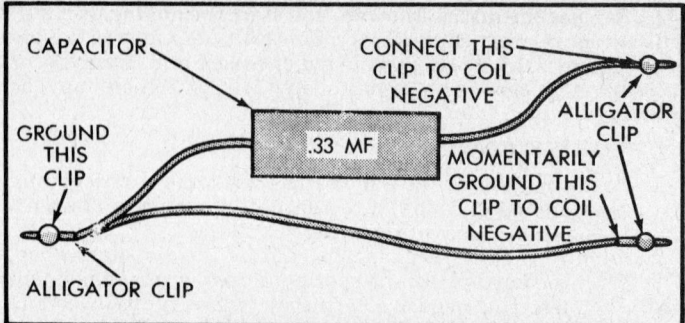

Special jumper wire from coil negative terminal to ground — front wheel drive vehicles. (© Chrysler Corp.)

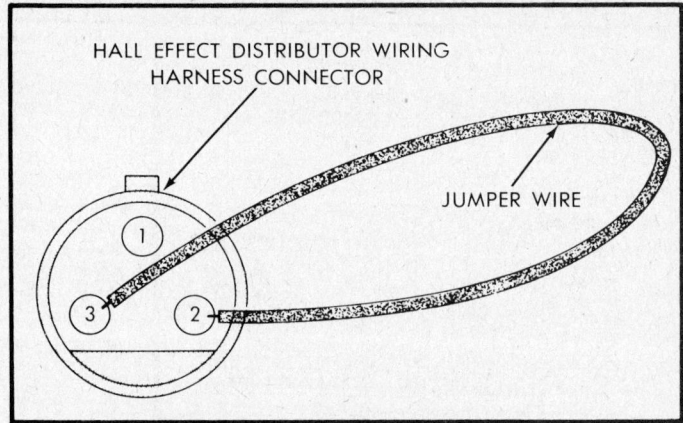

Use of jumper wire at terminals "2" and "3" — front wheel drive vehicles (© Chrysler Corp.)

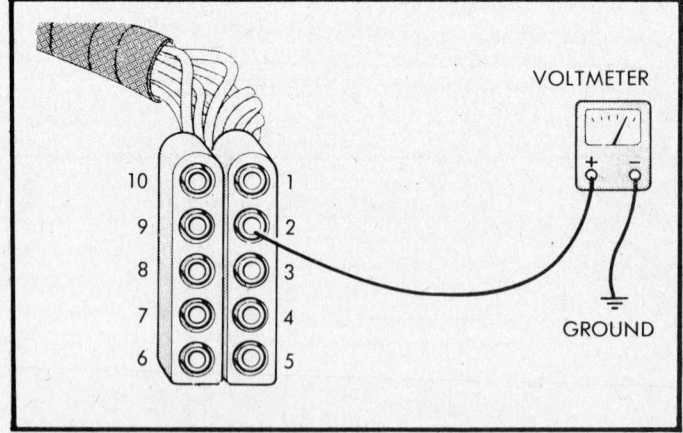

Checking voltage at cavity "2" — front wheel drive vehicles (© Chrysler Corp.)

11. Turn the ignition switch on and measure the voltage at terminal 2 of the harness. It should be within 1 volt of battery voltage.

12. If no battery voltage is present, check for continuity between the battery and terminal 2 of the harness. If no continuity, repair fault and repeat Step 11.

13. If voltage is present turn ignition switch off and check for continuity between the carburetor switch and terminal 7 on connector. If no continuity is present, check for open wire between terminal 7 and the carburetor switch.

14. If continuity is present, check continuity between terminal 10 and ground. If continuity is present here, replace the computer. Repeat Step 9.

15. If no continuity is present, check for an open wire. If wiring is OK, but the engine still won't start, go to next step.

16. Plug the 10 terminal dual connector back into the computer and turn the ignition switch on, hold the secondary coil wire near a good ground and disconnect the distributor harness connector. Using a regular jumper wire (not the special one mentioned earlier), jump terminal 2 to terminal 3 of the connector; a spark should fire at the coil wire.

17. If spark is present at the coil wire but the engine won't start, replace the Hall Effect pick-up and check the rotor for cracks or burning. Replace as necessary.

NOTE: When replacing a pick-up, always make sure rotor blades are grounded using an ohmmeter.

18. If no spark is present at the coil wire, measure the voltage at terminal 1 of the distributor harness connector; it should be within 1 volt of battery voltage.

19. If correct, disconnect the dual connector from the computer and check for continuity between terminal 2 of distributor harness and terminal 9 of the dual connector. Repeat test on terminal 3 of distributor harness and terminal 5 of dual connector. If no continuity, repair the harness. If continuity is present, replace the computer and repeat Step 16.

ELECTRONIC IGNITION
CHRYSLER LEAN BURN SYSTEM
SECTION 30

20. If no battery voltage is present in Step 18, turn off the ignition switch, disconnect the 10 terminal dual connector from the computer and check for continuity between terminal 1 of distributor harness and terminal 3 of dual connector. If no continuity, repair wire and repeat Step 16.

21. If continuity is present, turn the ignition switch on and check for battery voltage between terminal 2 and terminal 10 of the dual connector. If voltage is present, replace the computer and repeat Step 16. If no battery voltage is present, the computer is not grounded. Check and repair the ground wire and repeat Step 16.

Start Timer Advance Test

1. Connect an adjustable timing light.
2. Connect a jumper wire from the carburetor switch to a ground.
3. Start the engine and immediately adjust the timing light so that the basic timing light is seen on the timing plate of the engine. Refer to the emission control decal in the engine compartment for the proper specification. Continue to observe the mark for 90 seconds, adjusting the light as necessary. The additional advance will slowly decrease to the basic timing signal over a period of about one minute. If not, replace the Spark Control Computer and recheck. If it is okay, go on to the next test.

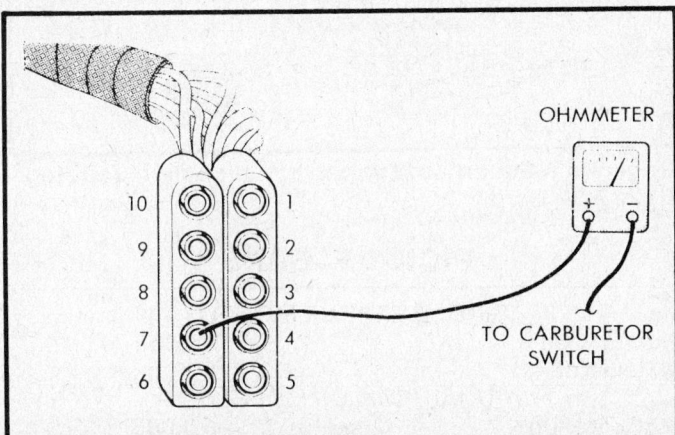

Checking continuity at cavity "7"—front wheel drive vehicles (© Chrysler Corp.)

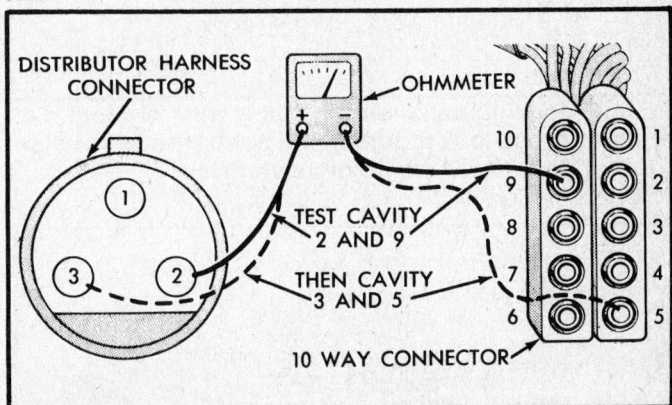

Testing cavities "2" and "9" and then cavities "3" and "5" for continuity—front wheel drive vehicles

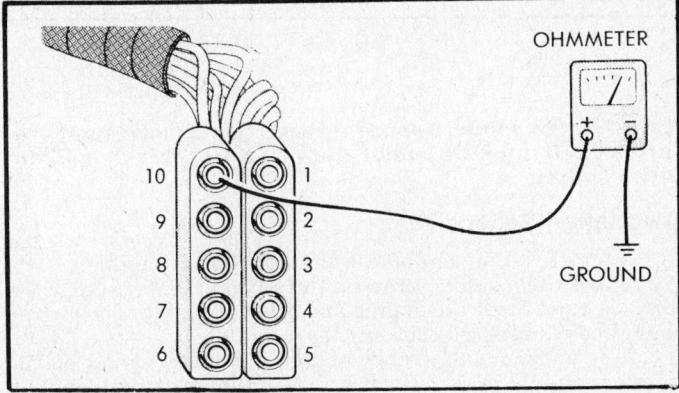

Checking continuity at cavity "10"—front wheel drive vehicles (© Chrysler Corp.)

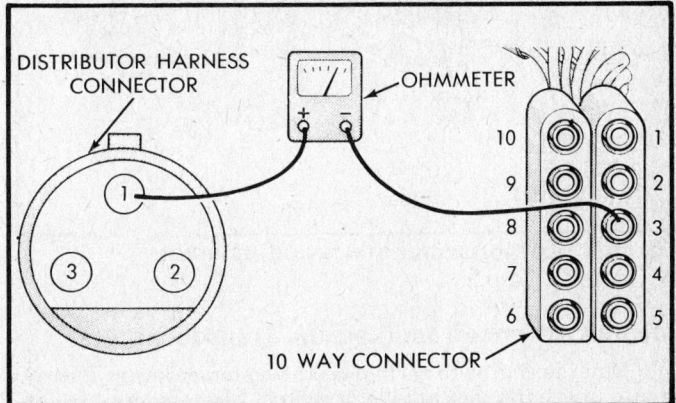

Testing for continuity between cavities "1" and "3"—front wheel drive vehicles (© Chrysler Corp.)

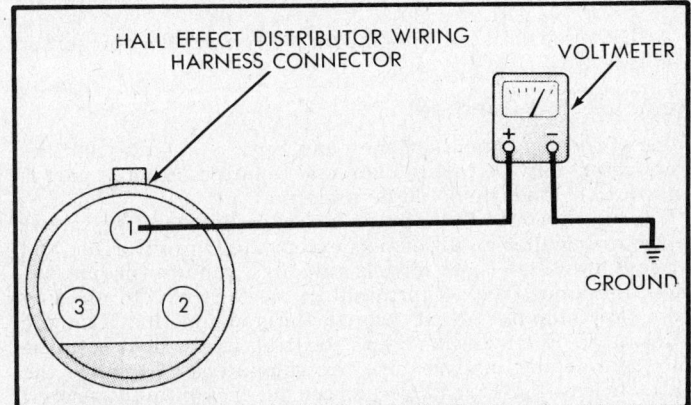

Checking voltage at distributor harness cavity "1"—front wheel drive vehicles (© Chrysler Corp.)

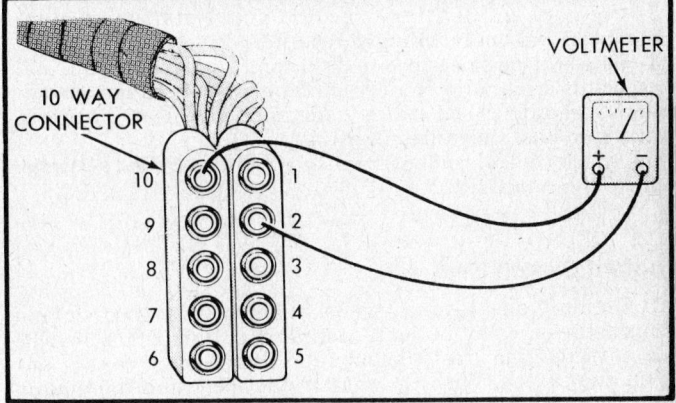

Testing for voltage between cavities "2" and "10"—front wheel drive vehicles (© Chrysler Corp.)

30-23

SECTION 30

ELECTRONIC IGNITION
CHRYSLER LEAN BURN SYSTEM

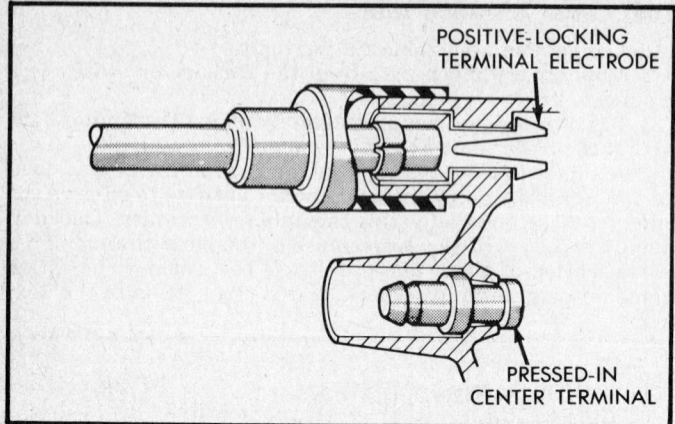

Positive locking secondary ignition wire terminal. To remove, press lock together and push wire out of distributor cap—front wheel drive vehicles
(© Chrysler Corp.)

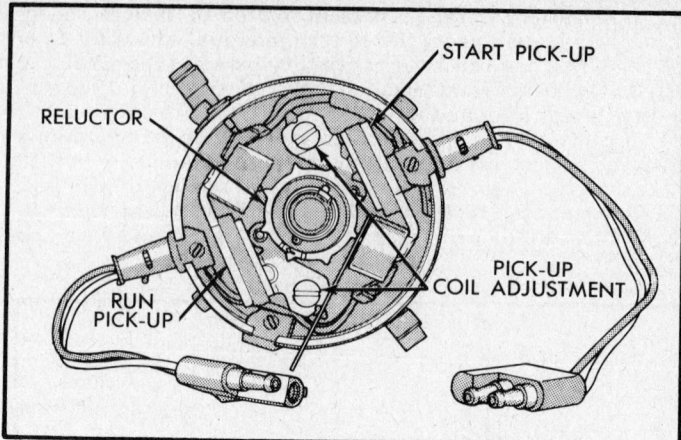

Air gap adjustment locations, dual pick-up illustrated
(© Chrysler Corp.)

PICK-UP GAPS

	SINGLE PICK-UP MODELS	
Pick-up Coil to Reluctor		0.006
	DUAL PICK-UP MODELS	
Start Pick-up	(set to)	0.006
	(check)	0.008
Run Pick-up	(set to)	0.012
	(check)	0.014

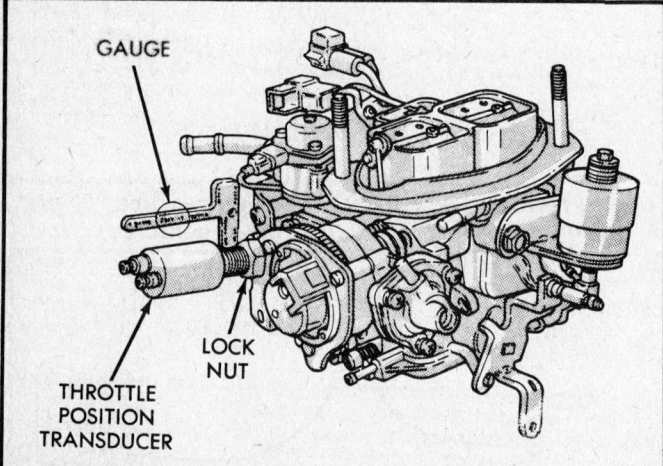

Throttle positioner transducer adjustment
(© Chrysler Corp.)

NOTE: On models so equipped, the charge temperature switch must be cooler than 60°F to achieve cold engine reading.

Detonation Sensor Test

1. Connect an adjustable timing light to the engine.
2. Place the fast idle screw on the second highest step of the fast idle cam. Start the engine and allow it to idle. The engine should be running at 1200 rpm or more.
3. Use an open end wrench or the like to tap lightly on the intake manifold next to the detonation sensor. As you do this, watch the timing marks; a decrease in timing advance should be seen. The amount of decrease should be directly proportional to the strength and frequency of tapping. Maximum retard is 11°.
4. If the sensor is not working correctly, install a new sensor and retest.

Vacuum Advance Test (Vacuum Transducer)

1. Run the engine to normal operating temperature. Disconnect or unground the carburetor switch. The temperature sensor should remain connected.
2. Remove the plug vacuum hose at the vacuum transducer on the spark control computer.
3. Connect an auxiliary vacuum supply to the vacuum transducer and apply 16 in. of vacuum.
4. Raise the engine speed to 2000 rpm, wait one minute and (or specified accumulator clock-up time) and check the specifications (see underhood sticker). Advance specifications are in addition to basic advance specifications.
If the spark control computer fails to obtain specified settings, replace the computer.

Removal and Overhaul

None of the components of the Lean Burn System (except the carburetor) may be taken apart and repaired. When a part is known to be bad, it should be replaced.

The Spark Control Computer is held on by mounting screws in the air cleaner on all models except the Omni/Horizon and Aries/Reliant. On those models only, first remove the battery, then disconnect the 10 terminal connector and the air duct from the computer. Next remove the vacuum line from the transducer. Remove the screws securing the computer to the left front fender, and remove the computer. To remove the Throttle Position Transducer, loosen the locknut and unscrew it from the mounting bracket, then unsnap the core from the carburetor linkage.

Coolant Switch Test

1. Connect one lead of the ohmmeter to a good engine ground, the other to the center terminal of the coolant switch.
2. If the engine is cold (below 150°) there should be continuity in the switch. With the thermostat open, and the engine warmed up, there should be no continuity. If either of the conditions in this step are not met, replace the switch.

ELECTRONIC IGNITION
CHRYSLER LEAN BURN SYSTEM
SECTION 30

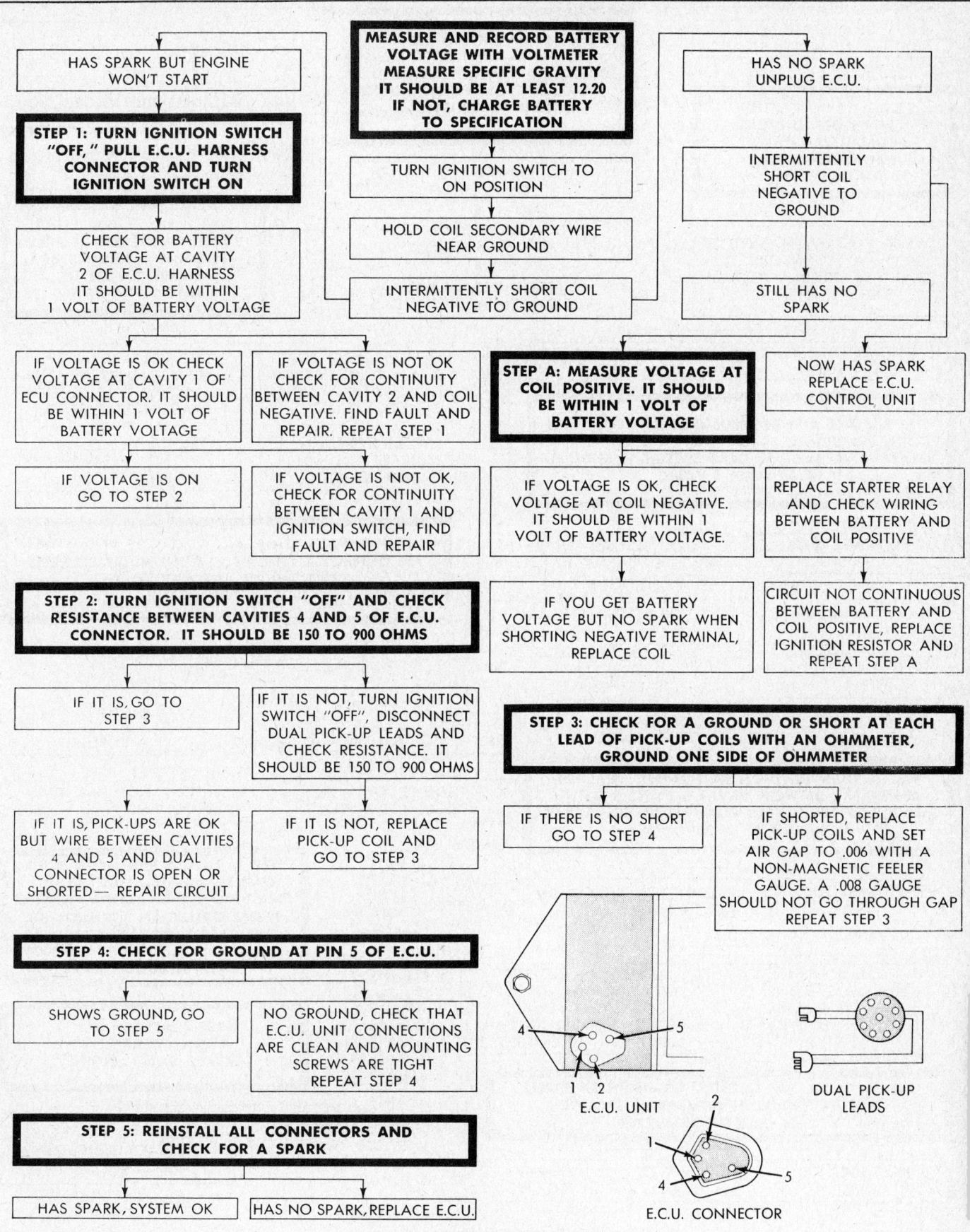

Electronic Ignition system diagnosis

30-25

SECTION 30
ELECTRONIC IGNITION
CHRYSLER LEAN BURN SYSTEM

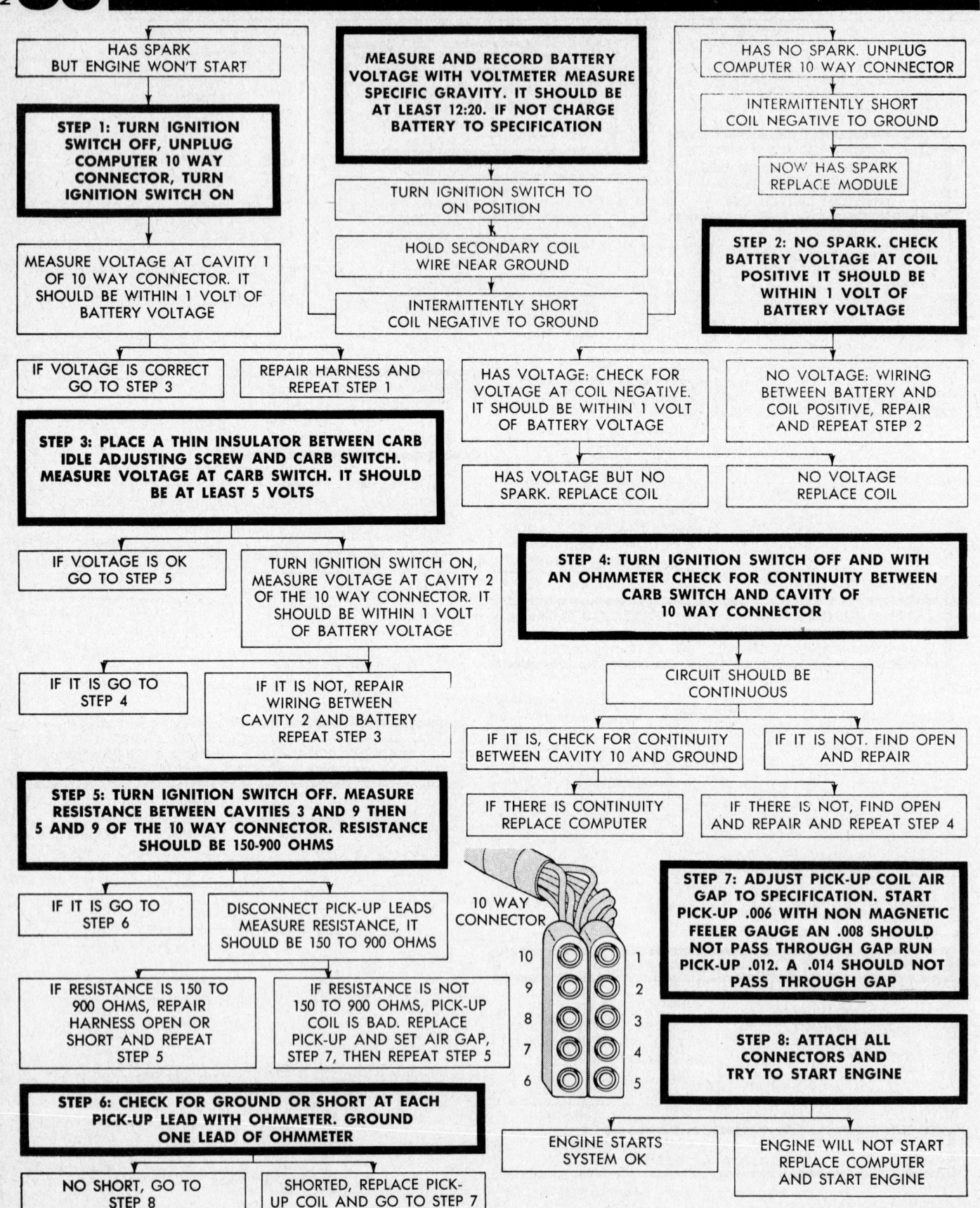

Electronic Spark Control system diagnosis

ELECTRONIC IGNITION
CHRYSLER LEAN BURN SYSTEM
SECTION 30

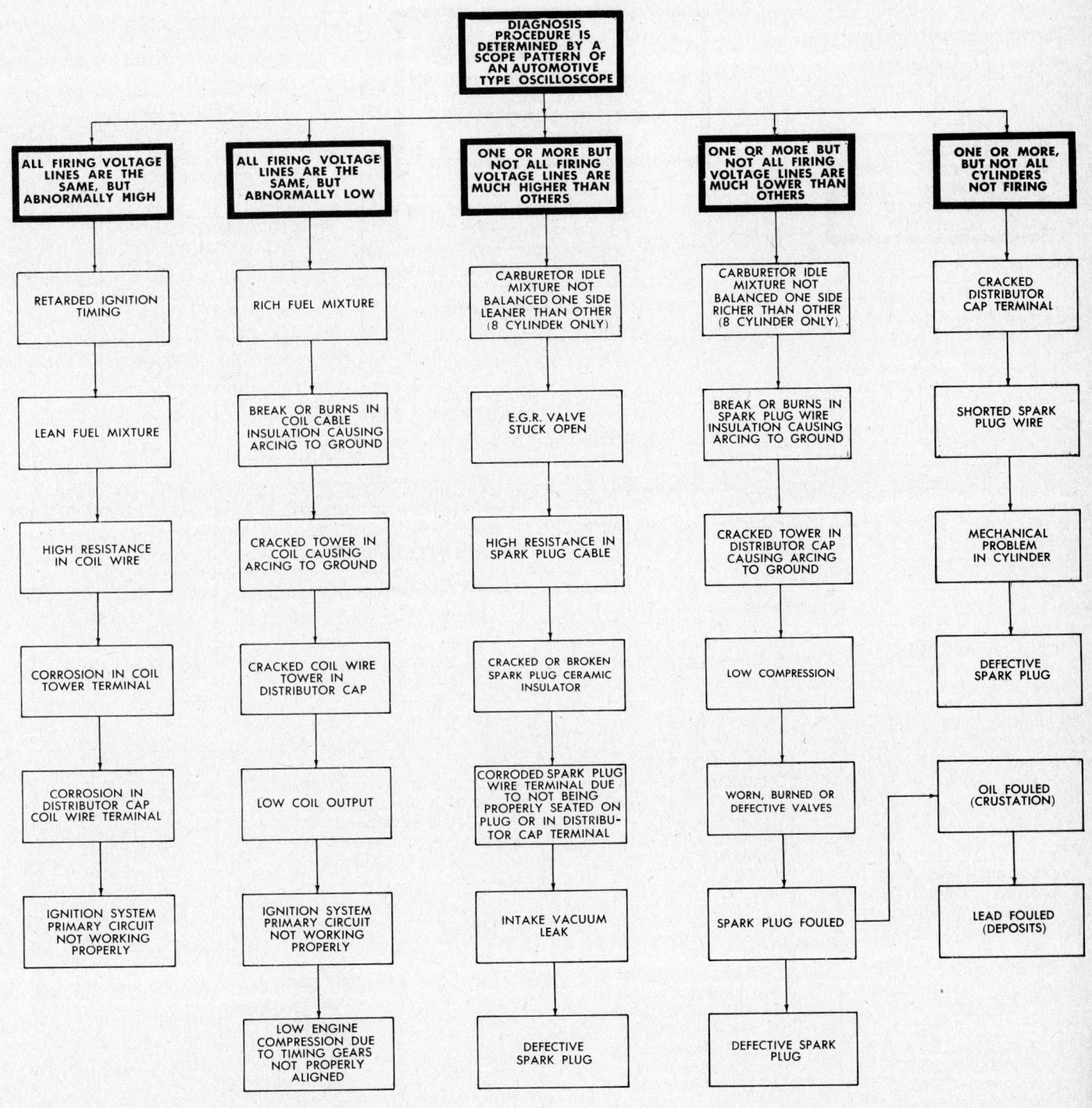

Electronic Ignition system secondary circuit diagnosis

30-27

SECTION 30: ELECTRONIC IGNITION
CHRYSLER LEAN BURN SYSTEM

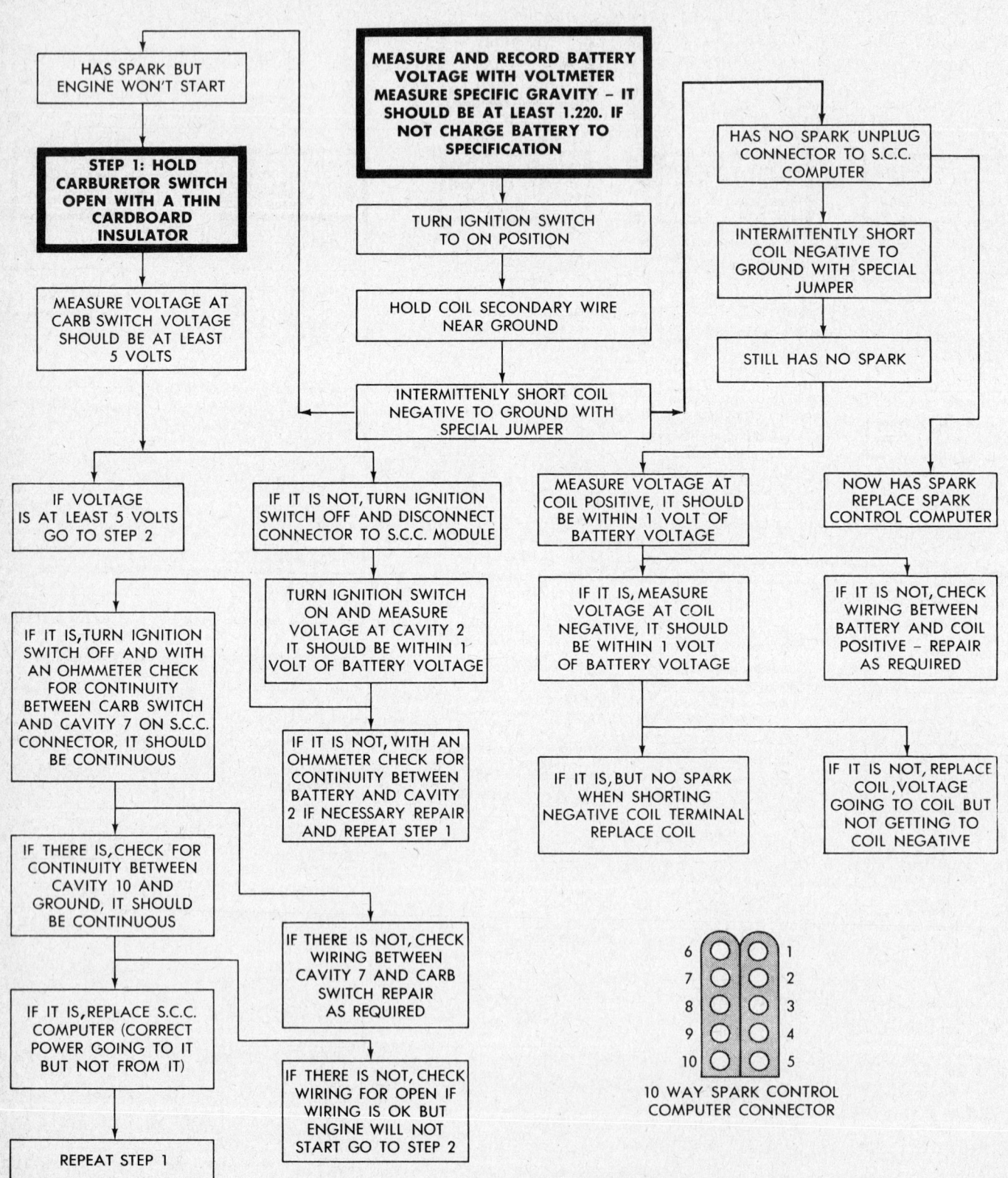

Hall-Effect electronic spark advance system diagnosis

ELECTRONIC IGNITION
CHRYSLER LEAN BURN SYSTEM
SECTION 30

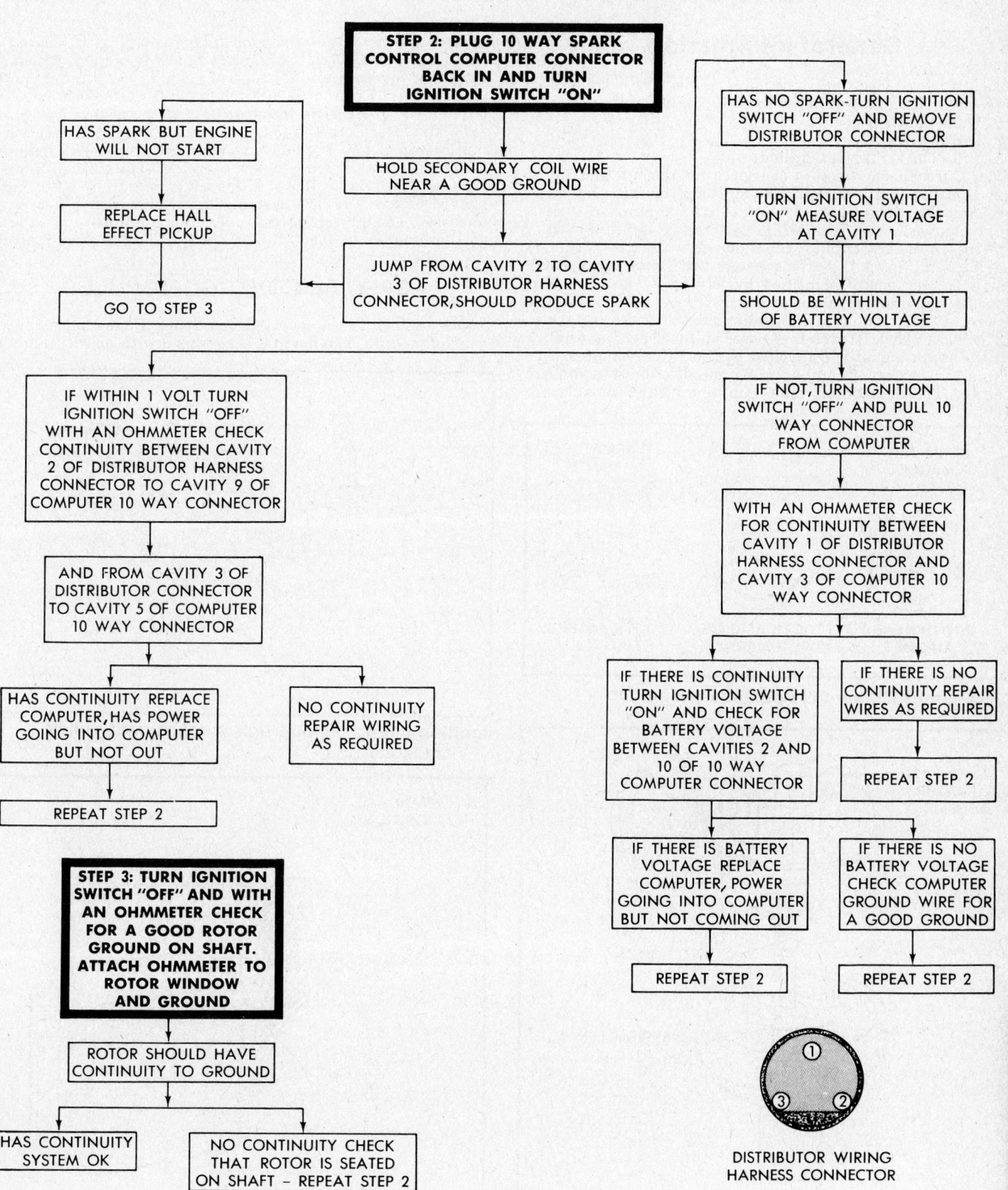

Hall-Effect electronic spark advance system diagnosis

SECTION 30
ELECTRONIC IGNITION
FORD SOLID STATE SYSTEM

FORD SOLID STATE IGNITION SYSTEMS

General Information

Basically, three electronic ignition systems have been used in Ford Motor Company vehicles from 1983 and later.
1. Dura Spark II
2. Dura Spark III
3. TFI (Thick Film Integrated)

The Dura Spark II coil is energized for the full amount of time that the ignition switch is On. Keep this in mind when servicing the Dura Spark II system, as the ignition system could inadvertently "fire" while performing ignition system services (such as distributor cap removal) while the ignition is ON. All Dura Spark II systems (except the Escort, Lynx, EXP, and LN7) are easily identified by having a two-piece, flat topped distributor cap. Escort, Lynx, EXP, and LN7 models use a conventional, one-piece distributor cap.

The Dura Spark III system is based on the previous systems, but the input signal is controlled by the EEC system, rather than as a function of engine timing and distributor armature position. The distributor, rotor, cap, and control module are unique to this system: the spark plugs and plug wires are the same as those used with the Dura Spark II system. Although the Dura Spark II and III control modules are similar in appearance, they cannot be interchanged between systems.

The TFI (Thick Film Integrated) ignition system is used on 1983 and later Escort, Lynx, EXP, and LN7 models with automatic transaxles. Previous models, and those with manual transaxles, use the Dura Spark II system. The main difference between Dura Spark II and TFI is not in operation, but in component usage. The TFI system uses a new distributor base-mounted, TFI ignition module, which is contained in a moulded thermo-plastic. Also, this system uses an E-Core ignition coil in lieu of the Dura Spark coil.

SPECIAL CONTROL MODULES

Some engines use a special Dura Spark Dual Mode ignition control module. The module is equipped with an altitude sen-

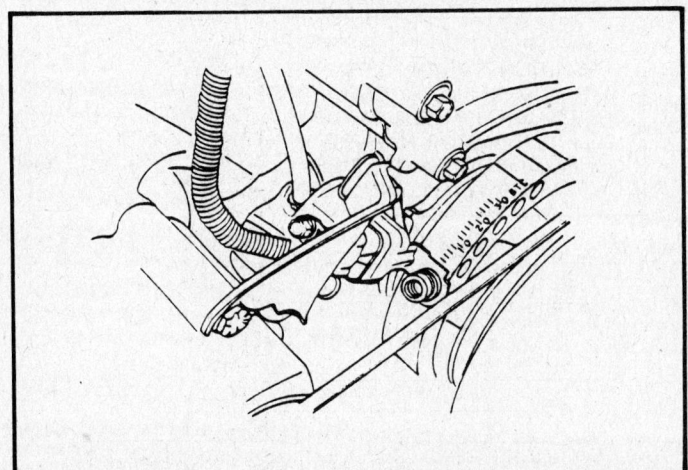

Ignition timing pick-up unit at crankshaft pulley (© Ford Motor Co.)

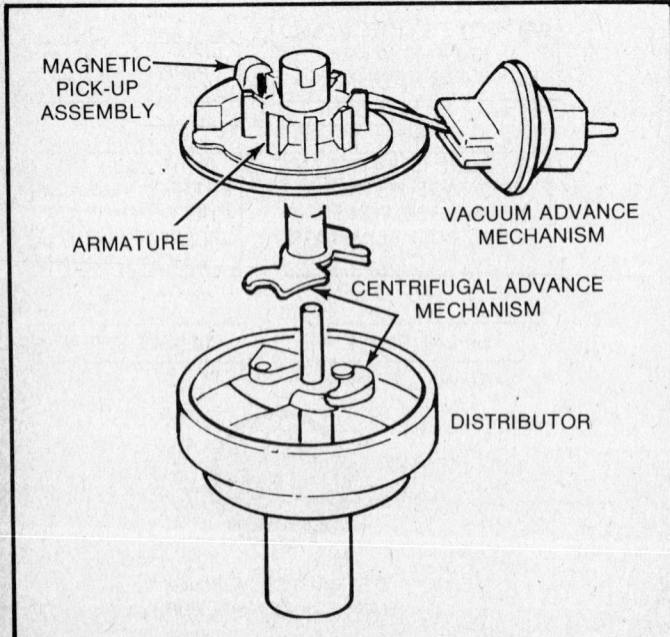

Distributor pick-up coil operation (© Ford Motor Co.)

Typical distributor plate and advance mechanism, Duraspark II system (© Ford Motor Co.)

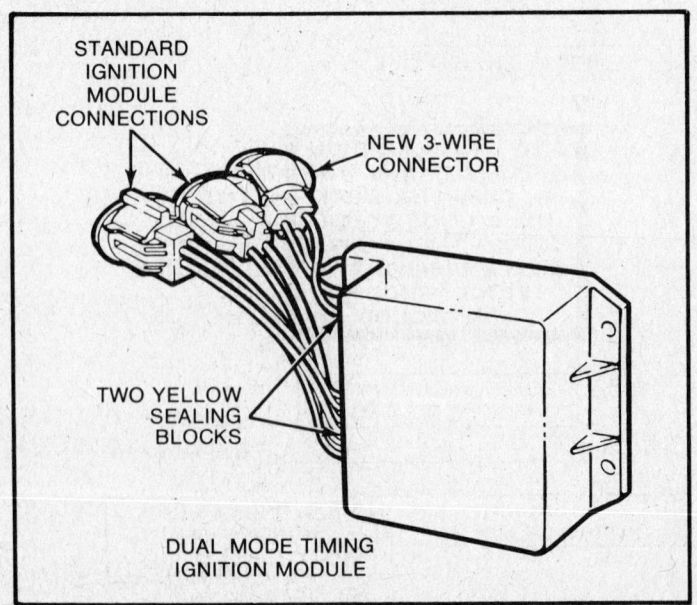

Dual mode electronic module (© Ford Motor Co.)

ELECTRONIC IGNITION
FORD SOLID STATE SYSTEM
SECTION 30

sor, an economy modulator, or pressure switches (turbocharged engines only). This module, when combined with the additional switches and sensor, varies the base engine timing according to altitude and engine load conditions. Dura Spark Dual Mode ignition control modules have three wiring harness from the module.

Some 1983 and later Dura Spark II systems used with some 255 and 302 cu. in. engines are equipped with a Universal Ignition Module (UIM) which includes a run-retard function. The operation of the module is basically the same as the Dura Spark Dual Mode module.

NOTE: When replacing the ignition control module, always use the old module as a reference to identify the wiring, connectors, and type of the new module.

Components

All solid state magnetic inductance ignition systems operate on the same basic principle. A magnetic field is provided by a permanent magnet which is part of the pick-up assembly. As an armature tooth approaches the pole piece, it reduces the reluctance of the magnetic circuit, thus increasing the field

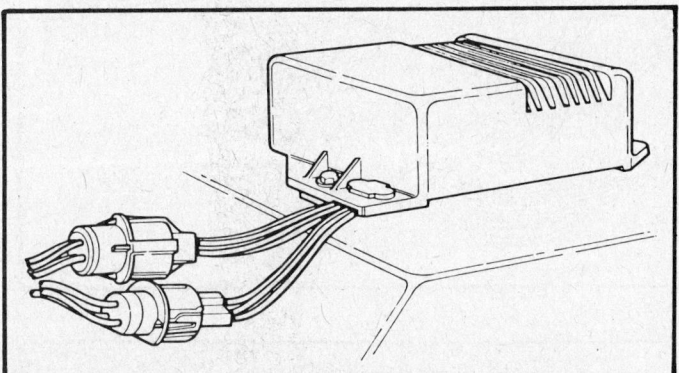

Typical ignition module, numerous types used
(© Ford Motor Co.)

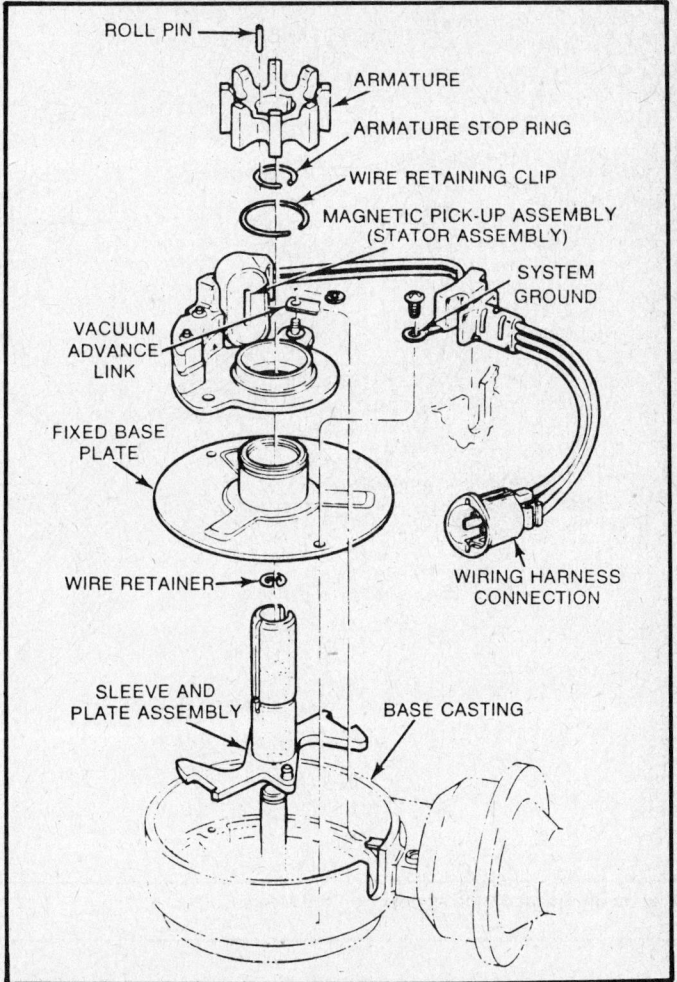

Exploded veiw of typical electronic distributor
(© Ford Motor Co.)

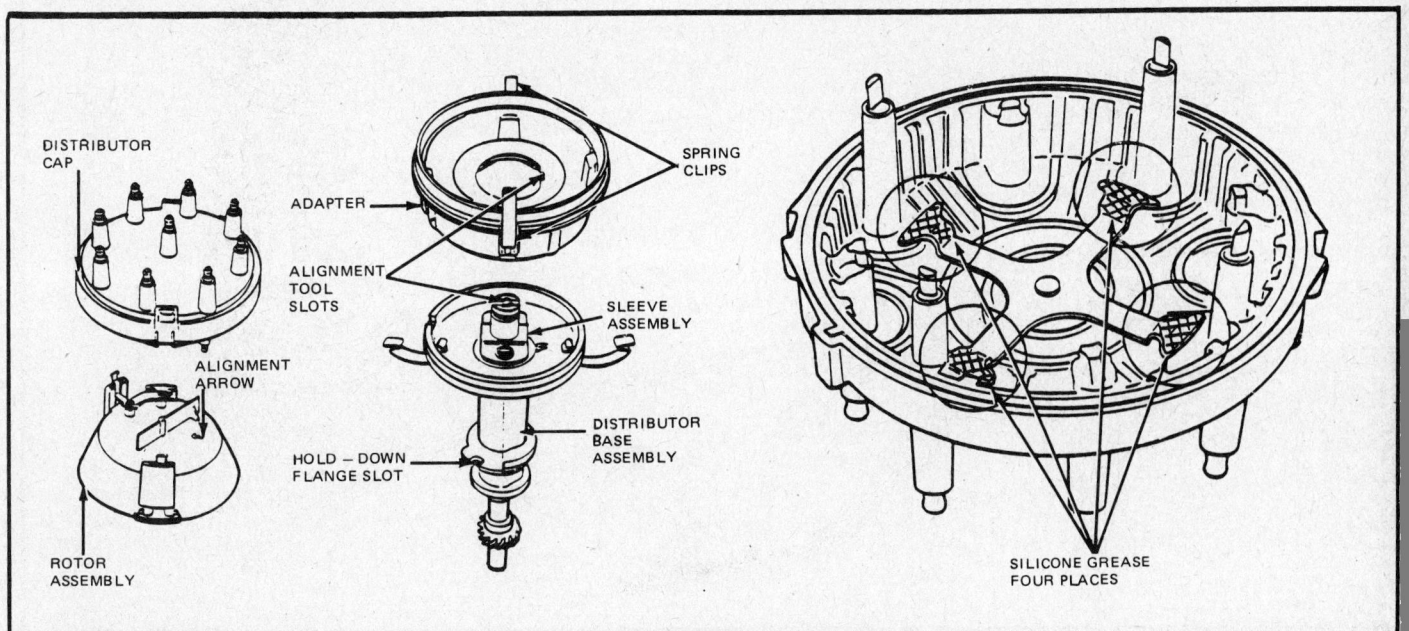

bi-level rotor and distributor cap used with the EEC 111 System (© Ford Motor Co.)

30-31

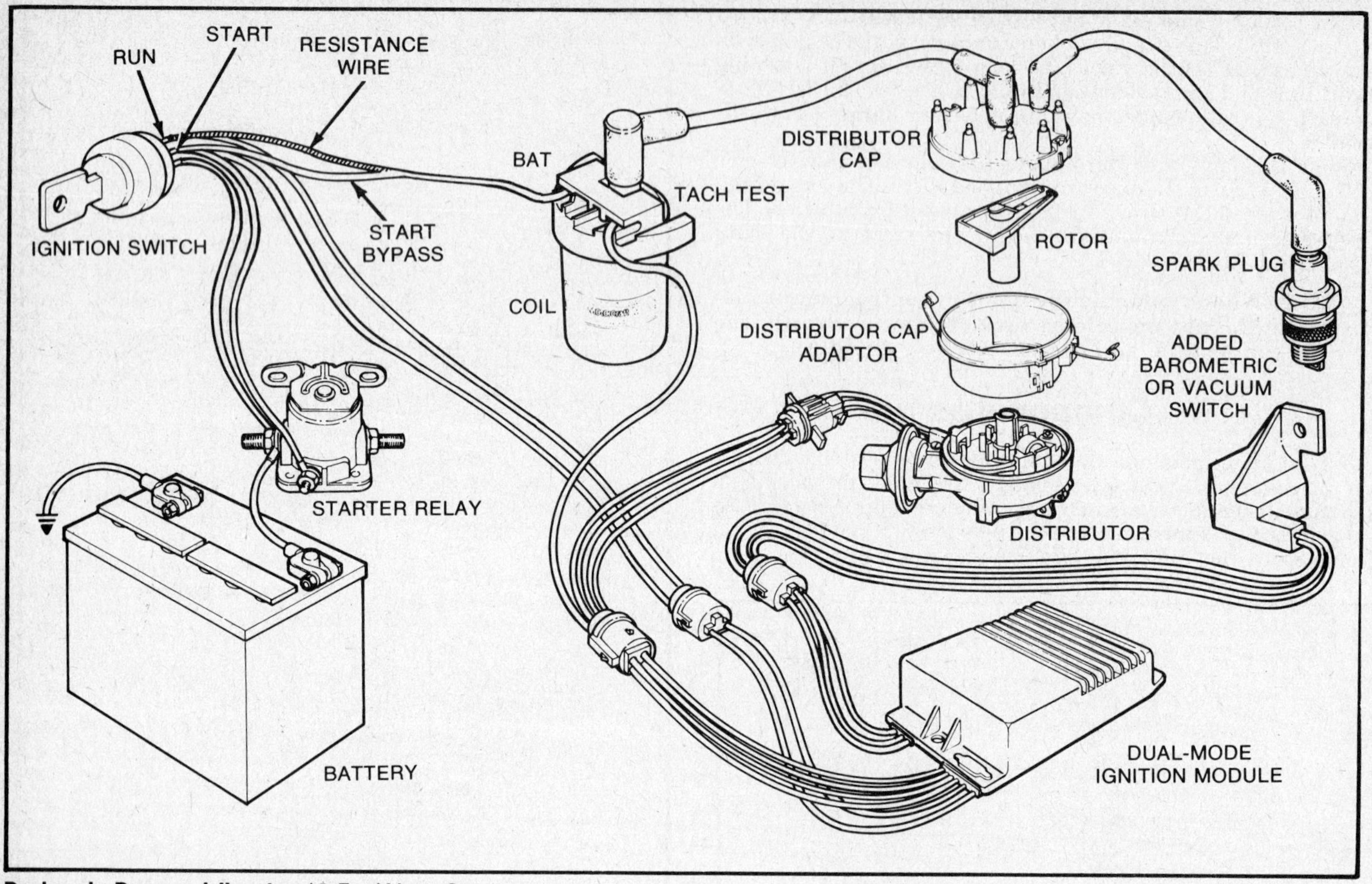

SECTION 30: ELECTRONIC IGNITION
FORD SOLID STATE SYSTEM

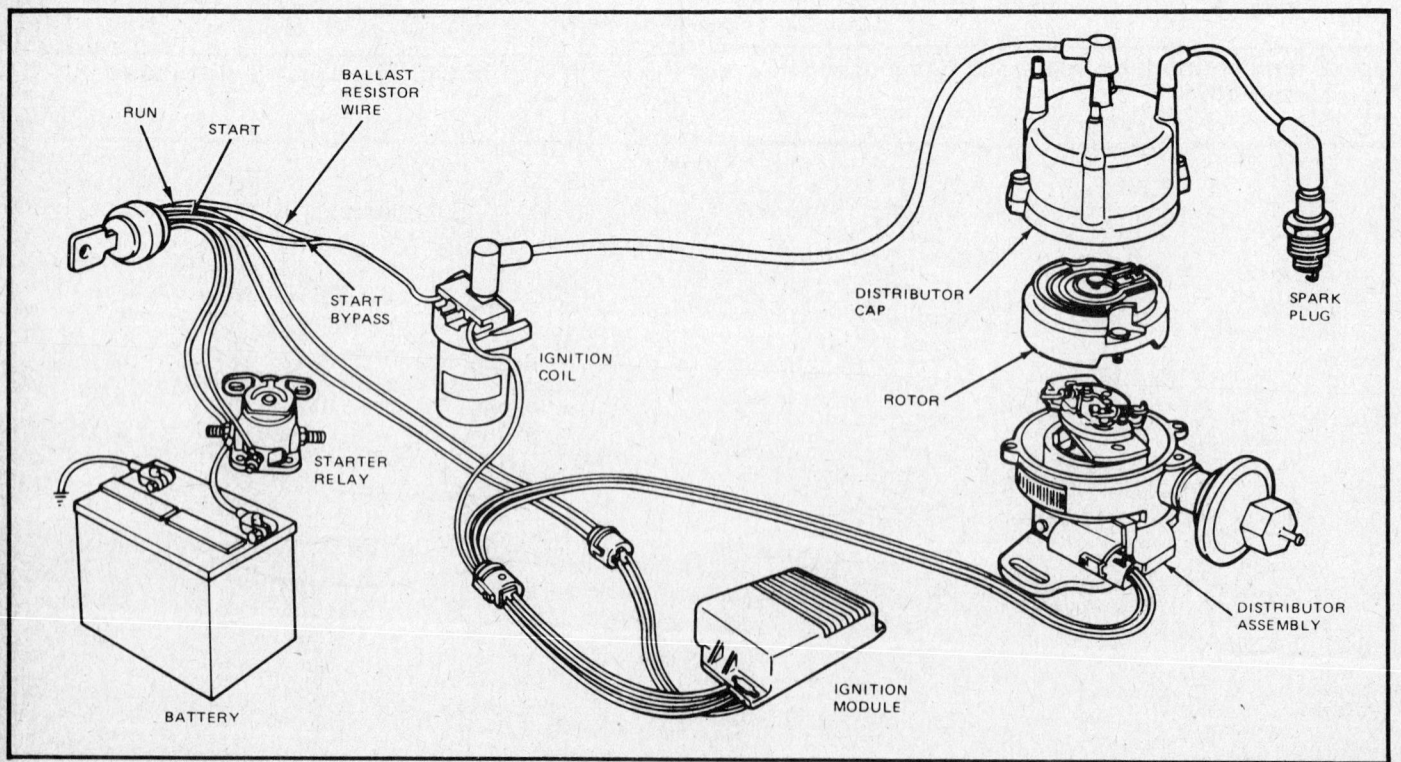

Dual mode, Duraspark II system (© Ford Motor Co.)

Escort, EXP, Lynx and LN7 ignition system—Dura Spark II (© Ford Motor Co.)

ELECTRONIC IGNITION
FORD SOLID STATE SYSTEM
SECTION 30

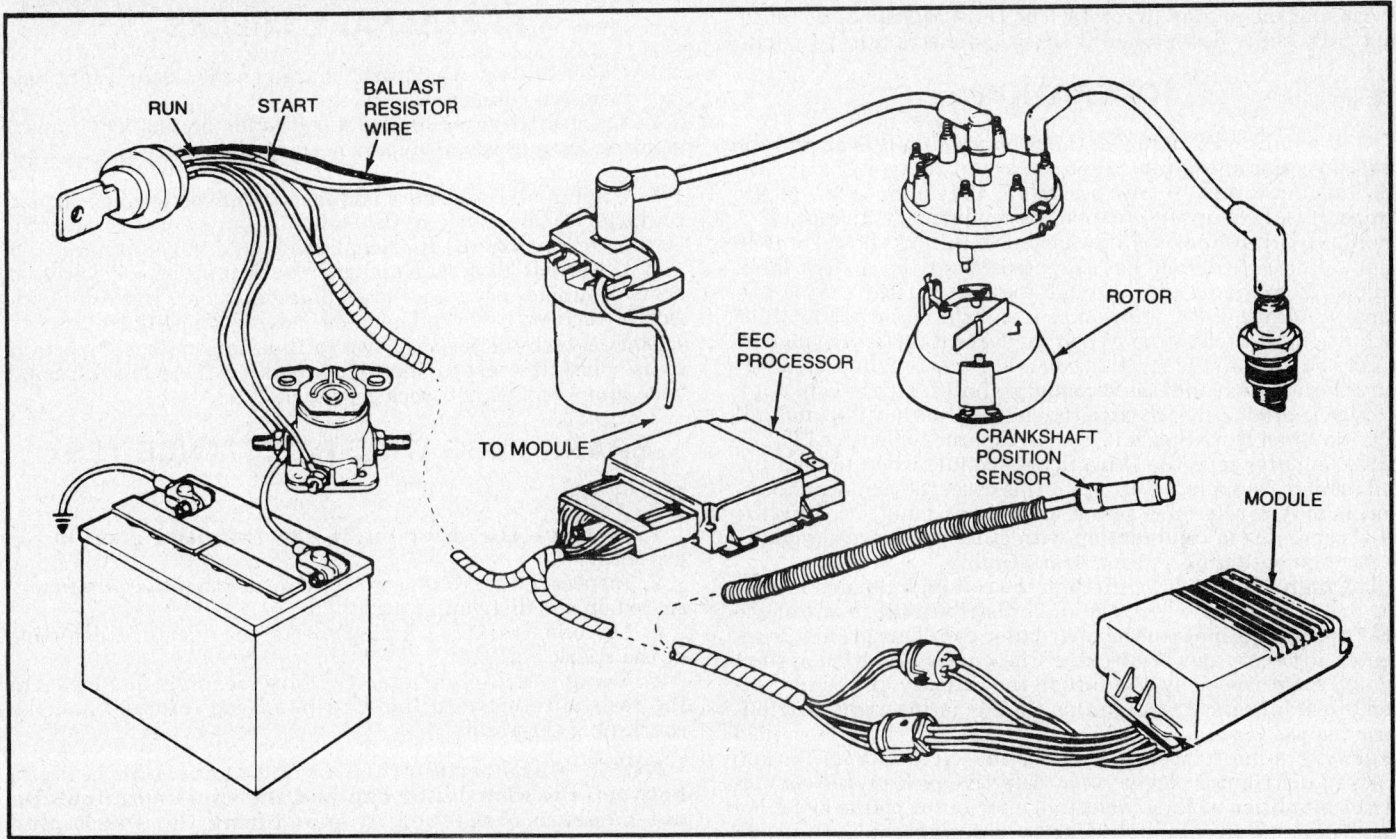

Typical Dura Spark III ignition system (© Ford Motor Co.)

strength. The resultant alternating voltage is applied to the ignition module at a rate proportional to the engine speed. The signal-generating systems vary in detail but generally follow the pattern of a gear-shaped iron rotor or armature, driven by the distributor shaft, which rotates past the stationary pole piece.

DISTRIBUTOR MOUNTED PICK−UP

Spark advance is controlled by a centrifugal advance mechanism which varies armature position and by a vacuum advance diaphragm which varies the pick-up coil position exactly as in prior conventional distributors where the cam and breaker points were repositioned respectively.

CRANKSHAFT SENSOR

The sensor operates like the breakerless distributor pick-up coil and reluctor which make and break the ignition primary circuit. The tip contains a permanent magnet and wire coil. The current from the computer passes through the coil producing a magnetic field. The output wire carries voltage to the module. As the crankshaft rotates, the individual pulse ring lobes approach and finally align with the sensor tip. The metal lobe "cuts" the magnetic field. This interruption generates a voltage output signal of crankshaft position to the computer. This chapter describes the basic solid state ignition systems and the changes in the system.

IGNITION MODULE

The ignition module is simply an electronic switching circuit which turns the primary circuit off and on in response to volt-

age pulses received from the magnetic pulse-signal generator. The ignition module shuts off the primary circuit each time it receives a pulse from the magnetic pick-up. Timing circuity in the module leaves this circuit Off just long enough for the coil to discharge into the secondary circuit, and then turns the primary ON again. (The time intervals for this switching are on the order of milliseconds.) Maximum time is allowed for the coil to charge. Internal resistance of coil windings prevents excessive current flow and overheating.

NOTE: Different ignition modules are used on different vehicle models. Many do not interchange.

SOLID STATE IGNITION SYSTEM

1983 49−State 2.3 liter four cylinder engines with automatic transmission have a Dual Mode Crank Retard ignition module, which has the same function as a Dura Spark II module plus an ignition timing retard function which is operational during engine cranking. The spark timing retard enhances engine starting, but allows normal timing advance once the engine is running. The module can be identified by the presence of a white connector shell on the four pin connector at the module. Certain models equipped with either the 255 or 302 cu. in. engines are equipped with a Universal Ignition Module (UIM) which includes a run-retard function. This module basically performs the same functions as the Dual Mode Timing module. Theses include altitude and economy timing calibrations and engine knock control.

It is important to note that the amplifier module and coil on the Dura Spark II system are on when the ignition switch is on, and will generate a spark when the key is turned off. Certain service actions, such as removing the distributor cap with the ignition switch on, could cause the system to fire, inadvertent-

30−33

SECTION 30: ELECTRONIC IGNITION
FORD SOLID STATE SYSTEM

ly causing the engine to rotate. The Dura Spark system automatically shuts down when it senses no distributor rotation.

OPERATION

With the ignition switch On, the primary circuit is on and the ignition coil is energized. When the armature spokes approach the magnetic pickup coil assembly, they induce a voltage which tells the amplifier to turn the coil primary current off. A timing circuit in the amplifier module will turn the current on again after the coil field has collapsed. When the current is on, it flows from the battery through the ignition switch, the primary windings of the ignition coil, and through the amplifier module circuits to ground. When the current is off, the magnetic field built up in the ignition coil is allowed to collapse, inducing a high voltage into the secondary windings of the coil. High voltage is produced each time the field is thus built up and collapsed. When Dura Spark is used in conjunction with EEC, the EEC computer tells the Dura Spark module when to turn the coil primary current off or on. In this case, the armature position is only a reference signal of engine timing, used by the EEC computer in combination with other reference signals to determine optimum ignition spark timing.

The high voltage flows through the coil high tension lead to the distributor cap where the rotor distributes it to one of the spark plug terminals in the distributor cap. This process is repeated for every power stroke of the engine. Ignition system troubles are caused by a failure in the primary and/or the secondary circuit; incorrect ignition timing; or incorrect distributor advance. Circuit failures may be caused by shorts, corroded or dirty terminals, loose connections, defective wire insulation, cracked distributor cap or rotor, defective pick-up coil assembly or amplifier module, defective distributor points or fouled spark plugs. If an engine starting or operating trouble is attributed to the ignition system, start the engine and verify the complaint. On engines that will not start, be sure that there is gasoline in the fuel tank and that fuel is reaching the carburetor or fuel injectors.

Troubleshooting

Many times a quick check can locate the cause of a problem without going into full system checkout. Included are checks which may isolate the cause of the problem. Just as with a conventional breaker point ignition system, the first step is to verify that the problem exists and then to make some preliminary checks to find out whether the problem is in the ignition system or somewhere else. The following procedures are intended to provide quick checks to identify and locate some of the more frequently encountered problems.

There is also the possibility that there is an intermittent problem in the module or the magnetic pick-up. Some intermittent problem checks are included at the end of these quick checks.

PRELIMINARY CHECKS

1. Check battery for state of charge and for clean, tight battery terminal connections.
2. Inspect all wires and connectors for breaks, cuts, abrasions or burned spots. Repair or replace as necessary. Make sure all wires are connected correctly.
3. Unplug all connectors and inspect for corroded or burned contacts. Repair as necessary and plug connectors back together. Do not remove the lubricant compound in connectors.
4. Check for loose or damaged spark plug or coil wires. If boots or nipples are removed on 8mm ignition wires, reline inside of each with new silicone-di-electric compound.

Make a test jumper as shown in illustration. It is important to use only this test jumper when making these checks. Solid wire jumpers will not work for quick checks.

SPARK PLUG WIRE RESISTANCE TEST

Procedure

1. Remove the distributor cap from the distributor assembly.
2. Inspect the spark plug wires to insure that they are firmly seated on the distributor cap.
3. Disconnect the spark plug wire(s) thought to be defective at the spark plug.
4. Using a volt-ohmmeter (VOM) or equivalent, measure the resistance between the distributor cap terminal and the spark plug terminal.

NOTE: Make certain that a good connection is made between the distributor cap and the spark terminal. Do not measure resistance by puncturing the spark plug wire.

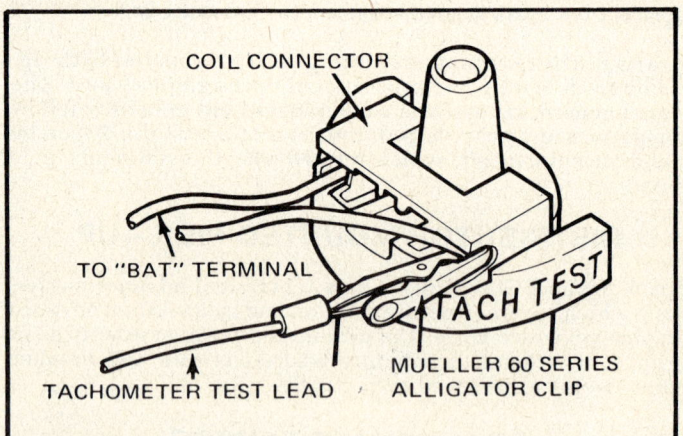

Special test jumper (© Ford Motor Co.)

FORD MOTOR COMPANY ELECTRONIC IGNITION

Year	Models	
	DURA SPARK II	
1983–86	All models except:	Lincoln and Mark VI and VII with the 302 cubic inch engine. Police models with the 351 cubic inch engine. Escort, Lynx, EXP and LN7 with automatic transaxles.
	DURA SPARK II	
1983–86	Lincoln and Mark VI and VII with the 302 cubic inch engine. Police models with 351 cubic inch engines.	
	THICK FILM INTEGRATED (TFI)	
1983–86	Escort, Lynx, EXP and LN7 with automatic transaxles.	

ELECTRONIC IGNITION
FORD SOLID STATE SYSTEM

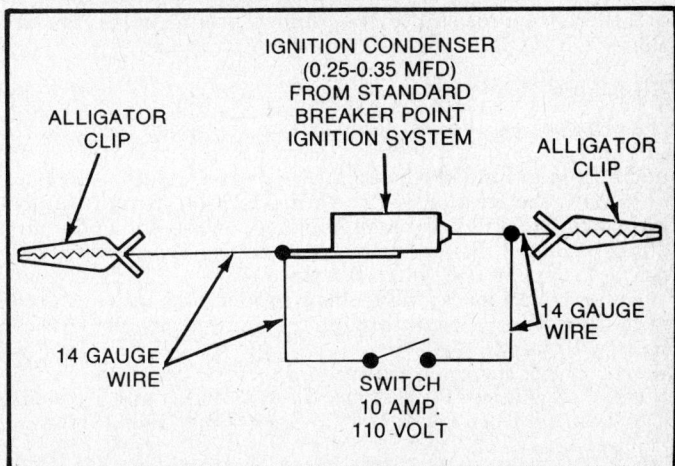

Special test jumper schematic (© Ford Motor Co.)

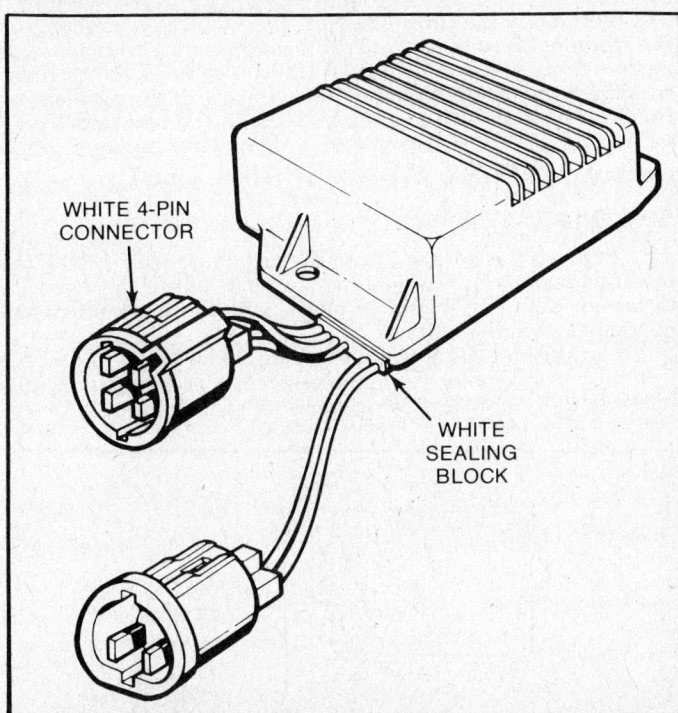

Cranking retard module, identified by white connector shell—typical (© Ford Motor Co.)

5. If the measured resistance is less than 5000 ohms per in. of wire, the wire is good. If the measured resistance is greater than 5000 ohms per in., the wire is defective and should be replaced.

RUN MODE SPARK CHECK

Step One

1. Remove distributor cap and rotor from distributor.
2. Crank engine to align one tooth of armature with magnet in pick-up coil (ignition Off).
3. Remove coil wire from distributor cap, install a modified spark plug (side electrode removed) in the coil wire terminal and, using insulated pliers, hold the spark plug shell against the engine block.
4. Turn the ignition switch to Run and tap the distributor body with a screwdriver handle. There should be a spark at the spark plug or coil wire terminal.

If there is a spark, the primary circuit is okay in the run mode. Check for a problem in the secondary circuit and/or perform the start mode spark test. If there is no spark, perform Step 2.

Step Two

1. Unplug the module connector(s) which contain(s) the green and black module leads.
2. To the harness side of the connector(s), connect the special test jumper between the leads which connects to the green and black leads of the module pigtails. Use paper clips in connector socket holes to make contact.
3. With the ignition switch turned to Run, close the test jumper switch. Leave it closed for approximately one second, then open. Repeat this several times. There should be a spark each time this switch is opened.

If there is no spark, the problem is most probably in the primary circuit through the ignition switch, coil, green lead, black lead or ground connection in the distributor. Perform Step 3.

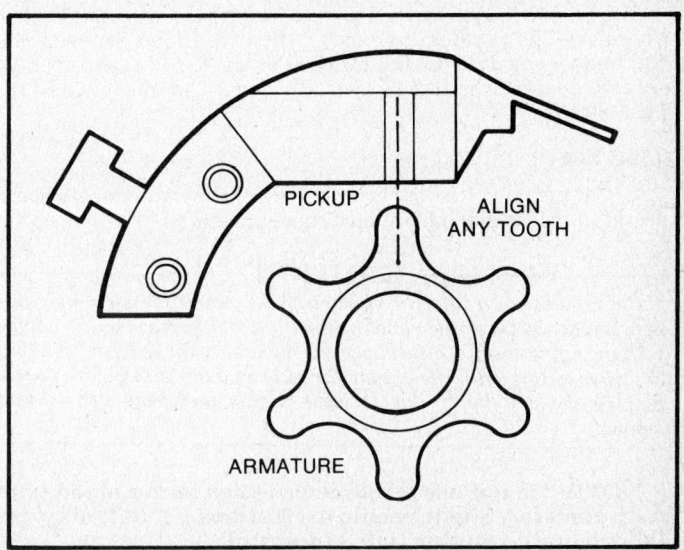

Distributor armature to pick-up alignment (© Ford Motor Co.)

If there is a spark, the primary circuit wiring and coil are probably okay. The problem is most probably in the distributor pick-up, the module bias power feed (red wire) or the module. Perform Step 6.

Step Three

1. Disconnect the test jumper lead from the black lead and connect to a good ground on the engine. Turn the test jumper switch On and Off several times as in Step 2.
2. If there is no spark, the problem is most probably in the green lead, the coil or the coil feed circuit. Perform Step 5.
If there is a spark, the problem is most probably in the black lead or the ground connection in the distributor. Perform Step 4.

Step Four

1. Connect an ohmmeter between the black lead and a good ground on the engine. With the meter on its lowest scale, there should be no measurable resistance in the circuit.
2. If there is resistance, check the ground connection in the distributor and the black lead from the module. Repair or replace as necessary. Remove the meter, plug in all the connectors and repeat Step 1.

SECTION 30: ELECTRONIC IGNITION
FORD SOLID STATE SYSTEM

If there is no resistance, the primary ground wiring is okay. Perform Step 6.

Step Five

1. Disconnect the test jumper from the green lead and the ground and connect it between the tach-test terminal of the coil and a good ground on the engine.

2. With the ignition switch turned to Run, turn the jumper switch on. Hold it on for approximately one second and turn it off as in Step 2. Repeat this several times. There should be a spark each time the switch is turned off.

If there is no spark, the problem is most probably in the coil or in the primary circuit through the ignition switch to the coil battery terminal.

   a. Check the coil for internal shorts or opens and for primary resistance (Dura Spark II – 1.17 ohms) and secondary resistance (Dura Spark II – 7.7–9.3 k ohms). Replace the coil if necessary.

   b. Check the coil power circuit for opens, shorts or high resistance. Repair as necessary. Remove test jumper, plug in connectors and recheck Step 1.

If there is a spark, the coil and its feed circuit are most probably okay. The problem may be in the green lead between the coil and the module. Check for open or short and repair as necessary. Remove the test jumper. Plug in all connectors and repeat Step 1.

Step Six

1. Connect a voltmeter between the orange and purple leads on the harness side of the module connectors.

---- **CAUTION** ----

If the vehicle has a catalytic converter, disconnect the air supply line between the by-pass valve and the manifold before turning the engine with the ignition off. This will prevent damage to the catalytic converter. After testing, run the engine for at least 3 minutes before reconnecting the air supply line to clear excess fuel from the exhaust system.

NOTE: Do not use a voltmeter which is combined with a dwellmeter. Slight needle oscillations (½ volt) may not be detectable on this type of test unit.

2. Set the meter on its lowest scale and crank the engine. The meter needle should oscillate slightly (approximately ½ volt).

If the meter needle does not oscillate, check the circuit through magnetic pick-up (in the distributor) for open, shorts, shorts to ground and resistance. Resistance between the orange and purple leads should be 400–1000 ohms and between each lead and the ground should be more than 80 k ohms. Repair as necessary. Plug in all connectors and recheck Step 1.

If the meter oscillates, the problem is most probably in the power feed to the module (red wire) or in the module itself. Perform Step 7.

Step Seven

1. Remove all meters and jumpers. Plug in all connectors.
2. Turn the ignition switch to Run and measure voltage to engine ground at the following:
   a. Battery positive terminal, reading should be at least 12 volts.
   b. The red lead of the module. Use a straight pin to pierce the insulation of the lead and connect the voltmeter to the pin.
3. These two readings should be within 1 volt of each other.

If readings are not within one volt, check the circuit feeding power to the red lead for shorts, open, or high resistance. Repair as necessary and repeat Step 1.

If readings are within one volt, the problem is probably in the module. Disconnect the module and connect a known-good module in its place. Repeat Step 1. If this corrects the problem, reconnect the original module and recheck. If the problem returns, remove the old module and install the new one.

START MODE SPARK TEST

Step One

1. Remove the coil wire from the distributor cap, install the modified spark plug (side electrode removed) in the coil wire terminal. Using an insulated pliers, hold the spark plug shell against the engine block.
2. Crank the engine (from the ignition switch).
3. If there is a good spark, the problem is probably in the distributor cap, rotor, ignition cable(s) or spark plug(s).

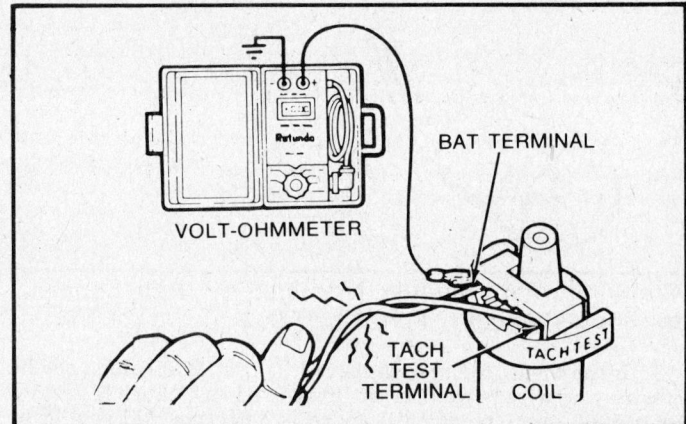

Testing coil primary wiring for intermittent current flow (© Ford Motor Co.)

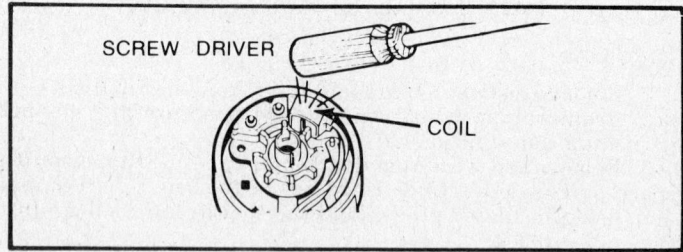

Tapping pick-up coil (© Ford Motor Co.)

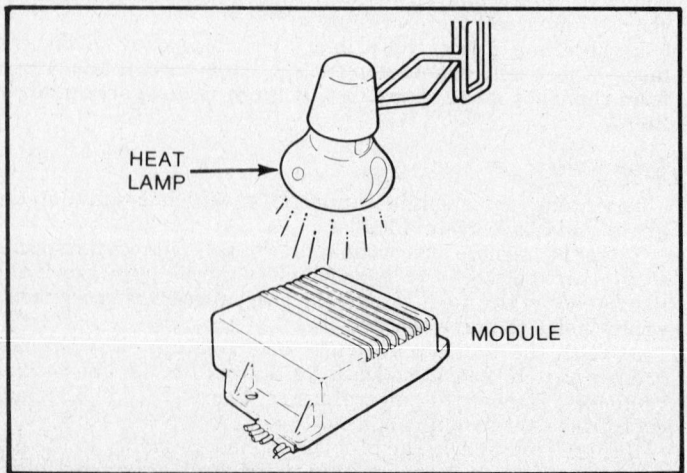

Heat test of module (© Ford Motor Co.)

ELECTRONIC IGNITION
FORD SOLID STATE SYSTEM
SECTION 30

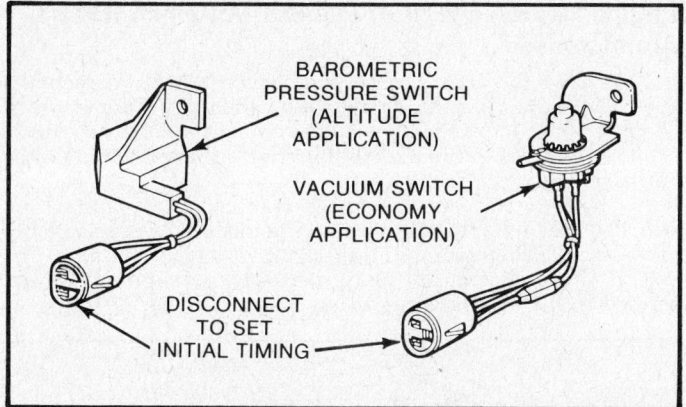

Disconnect barometric and vacuum switches to set ignition timing (© Ford Motor Co.)

4. If there is no spark, proceed to Step 2.

Step Two

1. Measure battery voltage and voltage at the white wire of the module (use a straight pin to pierce the wire) while cranking the engine.
2. These two readings should be within 1 volt of each other. If readings are not within one volt, check and repair the feed through the ignition switch to the white wire. Recheck for spark (Step 1). If readings are within one volt, or if there is still no spark after the power feed to white wire is repaired, proceed to Step 3.

Step Three

1. Measure coil battery terminal voltage while cranking the engine (see catalytic converter caution).
2. The reading should be within 1 volt of battery voltage. If the reading is not within one volt, check and repair the feed through the ignition switch to the coil. Recheck for spark (Step 1). If the reading is within one volt, the problem is probably in the ignition module. Plug in a known-good module and recheck for spark (Step 1).

NOTE: *If all the above steps check out okay, checks should be made of the fuel system and of the engine itself.*

TESTING FOR INTERMITTENT CONDITIONS

If the ignition system becomes operative in the course of performing these procedures and you have not made a repair, it is likely an intermittent connection or an intermittent ignition component has become functional. The following suggestions are offered.

With the engine running, attempt to recreate the problem by wiggling the wires at the coil, module, distributor and other harness connectors. Start first with the connections you might have already disturbed. Also check the ground connection in the distributor. Disconnecting and reconnecting connectors may also be helpful.

--- CAUTION ---
Do not clean lubricant compound from connectors as it is required to prevent terminal corrosion.

Testing Pick-Up Coil

With the engine off, remove the distributor cap, rotor and adaptor if so equipped, and heat the stator pick-up coil by placing a 250 watt heat lamp approximately 1-2 in. from its top surface. Apply heat for 5-10 minutes while monitoring pick-up

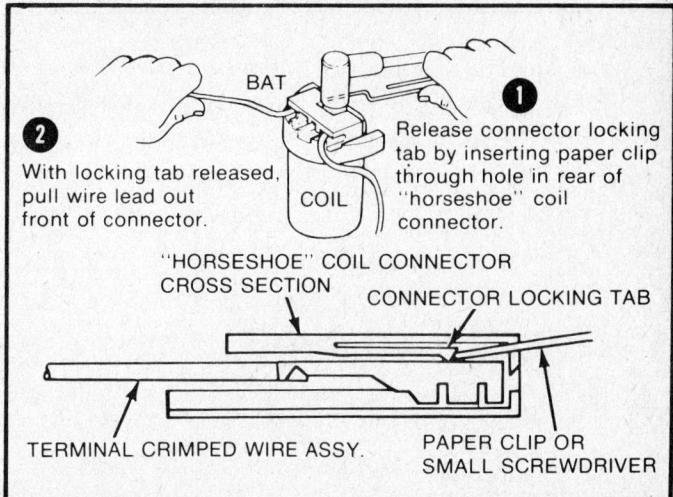

Proper primary wiring connector removal from coil (© Ford Motor Co.)

coil continuity between the parallel blades of the disconnected distributor connector. The resistance should be 400–1000 ohms. Tapping with a screwdriver handle may also be helpful. Reinstall the distributor cap. A reading less than 400 ohms would indicate a short, while an infinity reading would indicate an open.

Testing Ignition Module

With the engine running, heat module by placing a 250 watt heat lamp approximately 1-2 in. from the top surface of the module. Tapping may also be helpful.

--- CAUTION ---
The module temperature should not exceed 212°F (boiling). After the first 10 minutes of heating, check the temperature by applying a few drops of water to the module housing. Repeat this check every two minutes until the water droplets boil. Avoid tapping the module to the extent that the housing is distorted.

If this procedure results in ignition malfunction, substitute a known-good module. If the malfunction is corrected by the substitution validate that the original module is at fault by reconnecting it to the vehicle. A functional check of the original and known-good module can quickly be accomplished by using the run mode check.

CHECKING TIMING

NOTE: *The following points must be considered when checking timing on conventional type distributors. For vehicles equipped with the dual-mode ignition module using either the ignition barometric pressure switch assembly or the vacuum switch, disconnect the 3-pin switch assembly connector from the dual-mode timing ignition module. Failure to disconnect the switch will build in a 3–6° retard in the dual-mode ignition on V8 engines and more on 6 cylinder engines.*

1. Start the engine and allow the engine to warm up.
2. Set the timing idle speed to specification (per engine decal) to avoid centrifugal advance input.
3. Set initial timing to specifications using timing light. Use only the clamp-on type timing devices which have an inductive pick-up.
4. After adjusting the initial timing, check and if necessary, adjust curb idle and fast idle speeds.

SECTION 30: ELECTRONIC IGNITION
FORD SOLID STATE SYSTEM

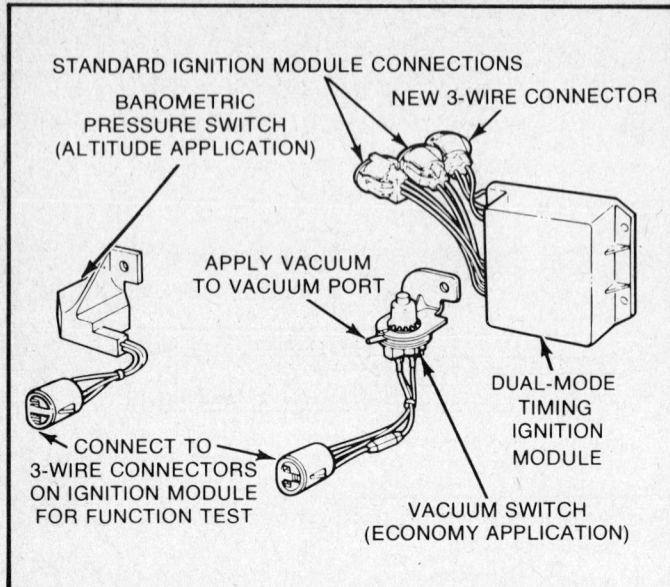

Barometric/vacuum modules (© Ford Motor Co.)

Applied Vacuum	Basic Timing
Greater than 10 in. Hg.	Per specification
Between 6 and 10 in. Hg.	Per specification or per specification less 3 – 6°
Less than 6 in. Hg. or 0	Per specification less 3 – 6°

Elevation	Basic Timing
Below 2400 ft.	Per specification less 3 – 6°
2400 ft. to 4300 ft.	Per specification or per specification less 3 – 6°
Over 4300 ft.	Per specification

CHECKING DUAL–MODE IGNITION SYSTEM (FUNCTIONAL TEST)

Perform the initial timing. Then reconnect the 3–pin switch assembly connector to the module.

1. Vacuum switch applications: disconnect the vacuum line to the switch. Using an external vacuum source, apply vacuum to the switch and compare basic timing to the requirements.
2. Barometric pressure switch applications:
3. If these requirements are not met, substitute a new vacuum switch or barometric pressure switch and recheck timing.
   a. If the timing is okay after the switch substitution, reconnect the original switch to validate failure. If the timing is not correct with the original switch, replace the switch.
   b. If the timing is outside specified limits after substituting the switch, reinstall the original switch and go on to the next step.
4. Substitute a new dual-mode ignition module and recheck the timing.
   a. If the timing is okay after the module substitution, reconnect the original module to validate the failure.
   b. If the timing is not okay with the original module, replace the module.

Engine Operates Well At Idle But Not When RPMs Are Increased

1. Remove the distributor cap and inspect for the presence of the roll pin holding the armature on the distributor shaft. If the roll pin is missing, the armature may have rotated out of position relative to the distributor shaft, causing timing to be out of phase.
2. Check for the correct connection of the orange and purple wires between the distributor and the module. If the wires are reversed, the distributor timing is 22 ½° out of phase.
3. If these checks are okay, perform further tests as described in the solid state ignition system.

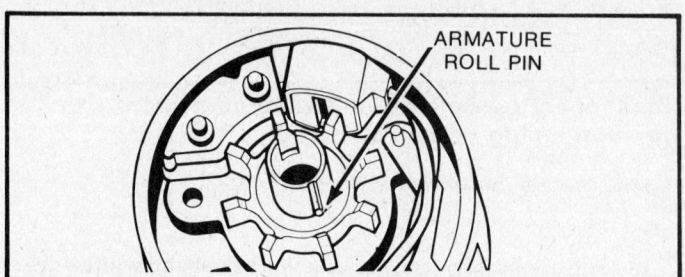

Loction of distributor armature roll pin (© Ford Motor Co.)

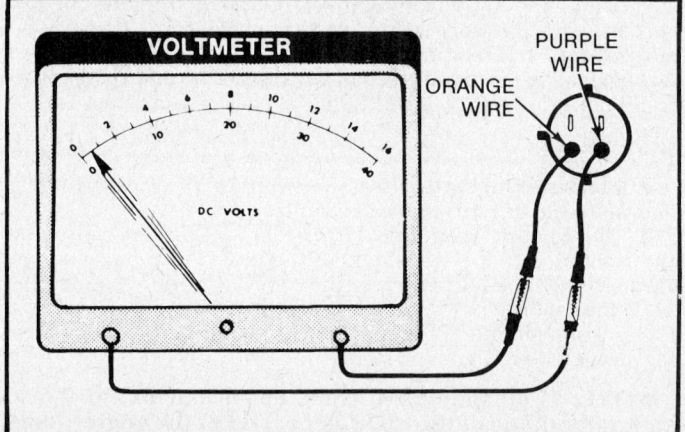

Voltmeter test of distributor pick-up connector, typical (© For Motor Co.)

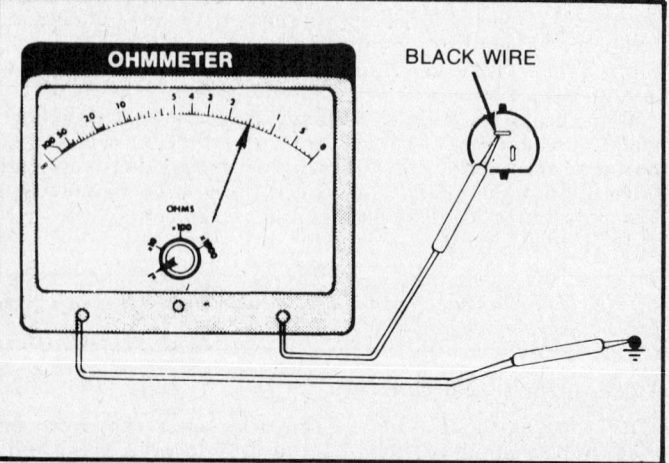

Ohmmeter test of distributor pick-up connector, typical (© Ford Motor Co.)

ELECTRONIC IGNITION
FORD SOLID STATE SYSTEM

Engine Starts and Runs Okay, But Quits As Normal Operating Temperature Is Reached

1. Run the engine until normal operating temperature is reached.
2. While cranking the engine, check the voltage between the orange and purple wires at the ignition module. With the voltmeter at the lowest range, only a slight meter movement should be noted (approximately ½ volt).
3. With the ignition switch off, check the resistance between the purple and orange wires at the distributor. Resistance should be 400–1000 ohms.
4. Again with the ignition switch off, check the resistance between the purple wire at the distributor and ground and between the orange wire and ground. In each case, the resistance should be over 70,000 ohms.

If any of these measurements are not within specification, replace the magnetic pick-up assembly.

Engine Quits Intermittently With Complete Loss of Ignition

1. Check the primary circuit ground resistance at the ignition module connector (black wire). The resistance should be 0 ohms.
2. If the resistant is not 0 ohms, remove the distributor cap and inspect the attaching screw at the rubber plug where the wires enter the distributor housing. A loose or cross-threaded screw or a dirty/corroded connection at this screw can cause an intermittent high-resistance ground or a complete loss of ground.

TFI SYSTEM TESTING

NOTE: *After performing any test which requires piercing a wire with a straight pin, remove the straight pin and seal the holes in the wire with silicone sealer.*

Ignition Coil Secondary Voltage

1. Disconnect the secondary (high voltage) coil wire from the distributor cap and install a spark tester between the coil wire and ground.
2. Crank the engine—a good, strong spark should be noted at the spark tester. If spark is noted, but the engine will not start, check the spark plugs, spark plug wiring, and fuel system. If there is no spark at the tester:
    a. Check the ignition coil secondary wire resistance; it should be no more than 5000 ohms per in.
    b. Inspect the ignition coil for damage and/or carbon tracking.
    c. With the distributor cap removed, verify that the distributor shaft turns with the engine; if it does not, repair the engine as required.
    d. If the fault was not found in Steps a, b, or c, proceed to the next test.

Ignition Coil Primary Circuit Switching

1. Insert a small straight pin in the wire which runs from the coil negative (-) terminal to the TFI module, about one inch from the module.

CAUTION

The pin must not touch ground.

---

2. Connect a 12 VDC test lamp between the straight pin and an engine ground.
3. Crank the engine, noting the operation of the test lamp. If the test lamp flashes, proceed to the next test. If the test lamp lights but does not flash, proceed to the Wiring Harness test. If the test lamp does not light at all, proceed to the Primary Circuit continuity test.

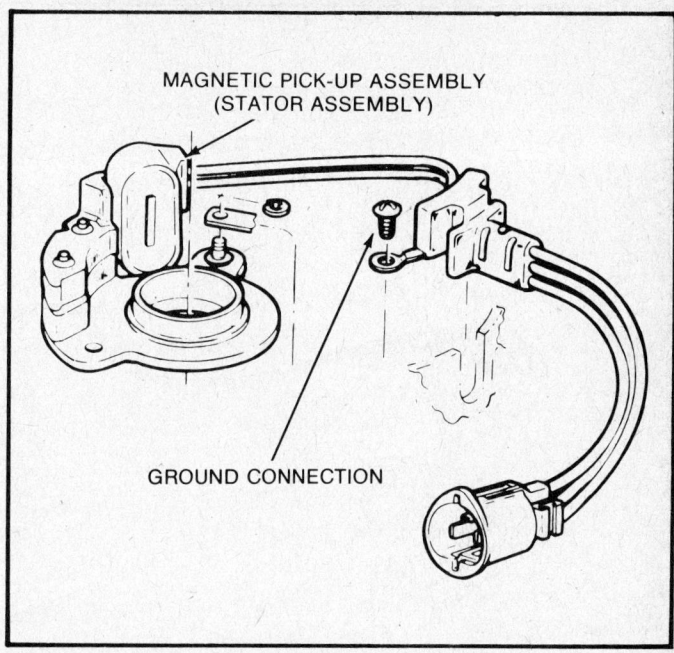

Magnetic pick-up assembly (© Ford Motor Co.)

Ignition Coil Resistance

Refer to the General Testing for an explanation of the resistance tests. Replace the ignition coil if the resistance is out of the specification range.

Wiring Harness

1. Disconnect the wiring harness connector from the TFI module; the connector tabs must be PUSHED to disengage the connector. Inspect the connector for damage, dirt, and corrosion.
2. Attach the negative lead of a voltmeter to the base of the distributor. Attach the other voltmeter lead to a small straight pin.
    a. With the ignition switch in the Run position, insert the straight pin into the No. 1 terminal of the TFI module connector. Note the voltage reading and proceed to Step.b.
    b. With the ignition switch in the Run position, move the straight pin to the No. 2 connector terminal. Again, note the voltage reading, then proceed to Step c.
    c. Move the straight pin to the No. 3 connector terminal, then turn the ignition switch to the Start position. Note the voltage reading then turn the ignition Off.
3. The voltage readings from Steps a, b, and c should all be at least 90% of the available battery voltage. If the readings are okay, proceed to the Stator Assembly and Module test. If any reading is less than 90% of the battery voltage, inspect the wiring, connectors, and/or ignition switch for defects. If voltage is low only at the No. 1 terminal, proceed to the ignition coil primary voltage test.

Stator Assembly and Module

1. Remove the distributor from the engine according to the procedure listed in the appropriate car section.
2. Remove the TFI module from the distributor as outlined under Component Replacement in this section.
3. Inspect the distributor terminals, ground screw, and stator wiring for damage. Repair as necessary.
4. Measure the resistance of the stator assembly, using an ohmmeter. If the ohmmeter reading is 800–975 ohms, the stator is okay, but the TFI module must be replaced. If the ohm-

SECTION 30
ELECTRONIC IGNITION
FORD SOLID STATE SYSTEM

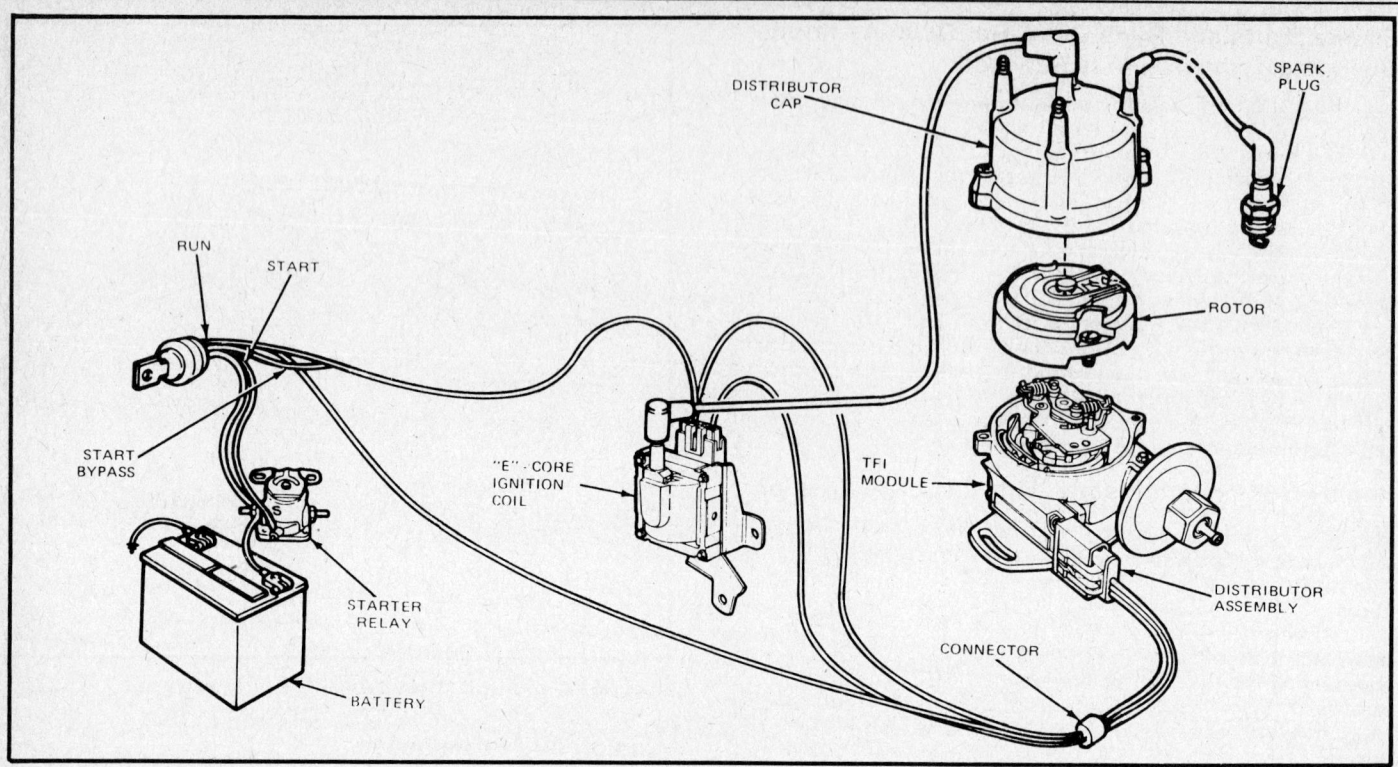

Thick Film Integrated (TFI) ignition system—basic wiring (© Ford Motor Co.)

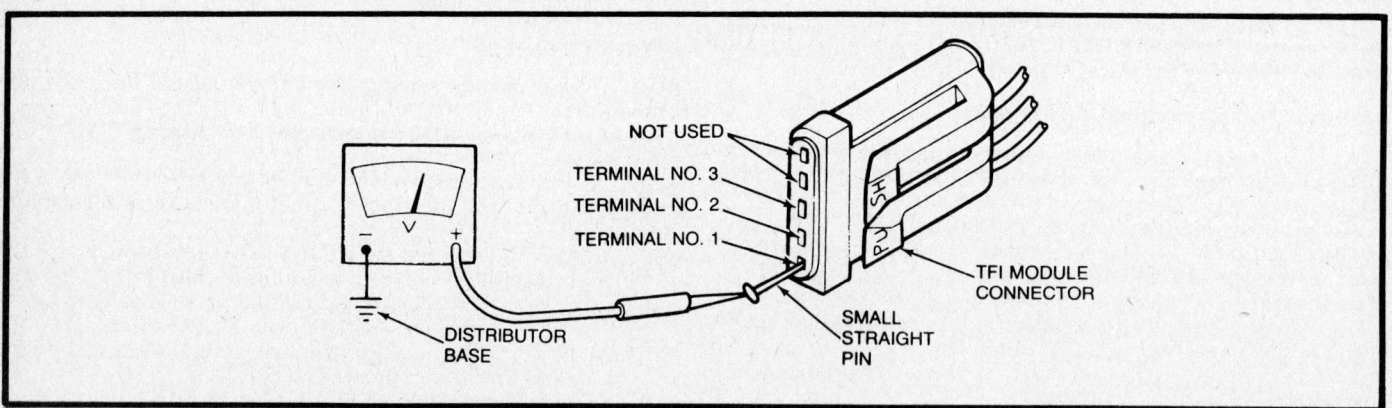

TFI ignition system—wiring harness test arrangement (© Ford Motor Co.)

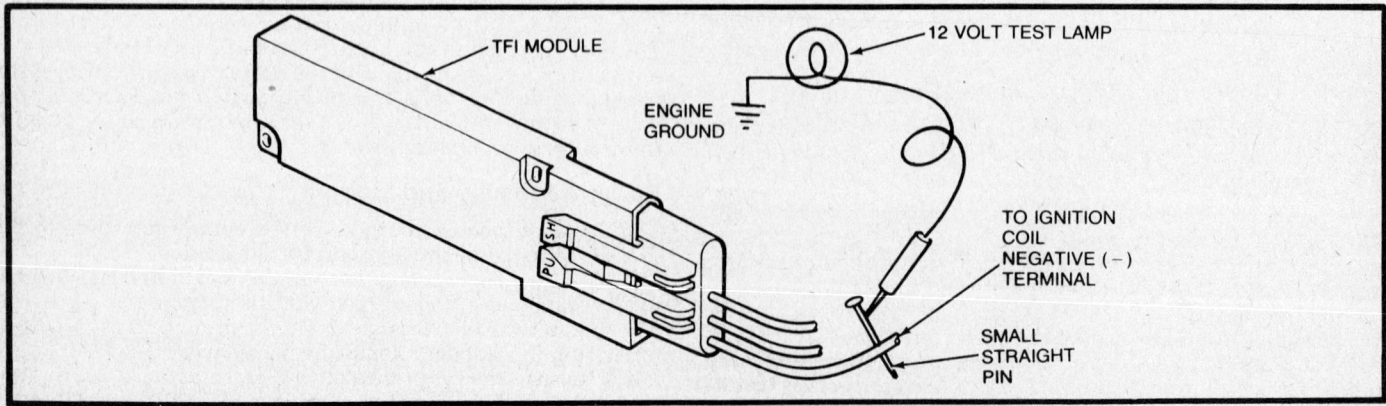

TFI ignition system—ignition coil primary circuit switching test arrangement (© Ford Motor Co.)

ELECTRONIC IGNITION
FORD SOLID STATE SYSTEM
SECTION 30

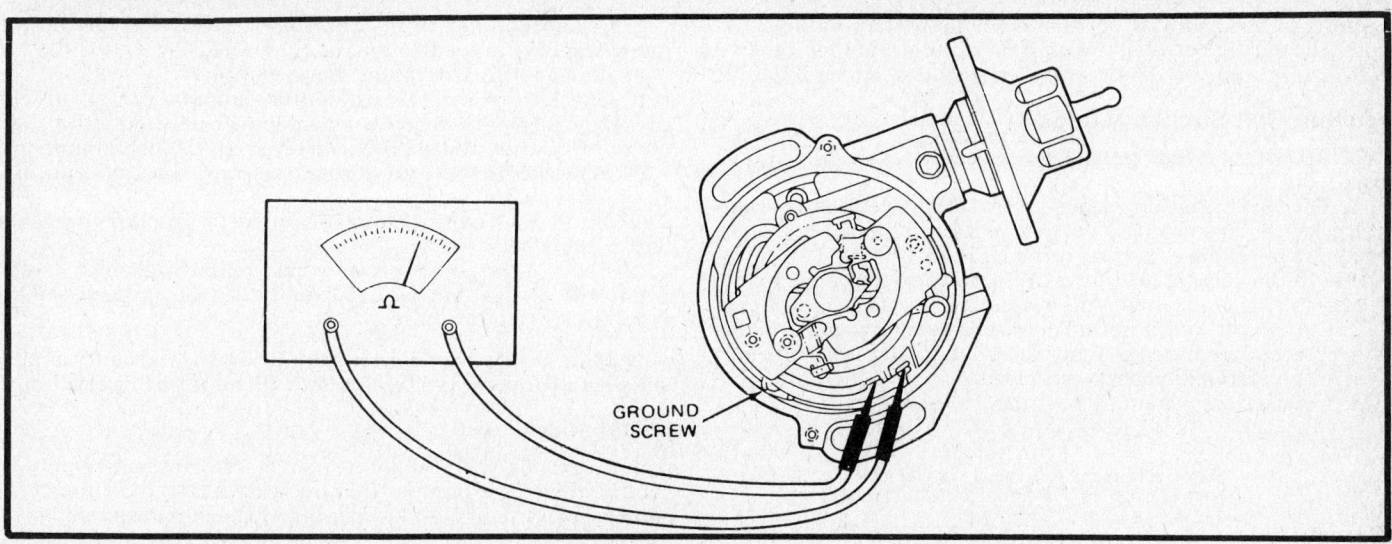

TFI ignition system—stator assembly and module test arrangement (© Ford Motor Co.)

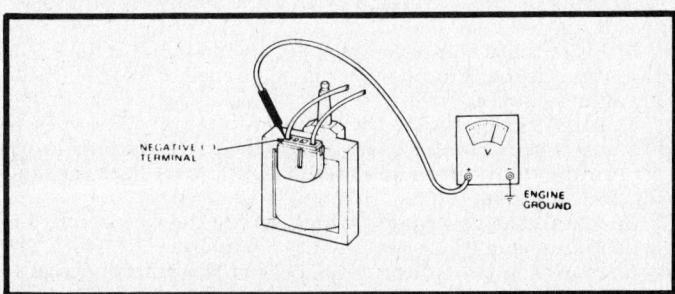

TFI ignition system—coil primary voltage test arrangement (© Ford Motor Co.)

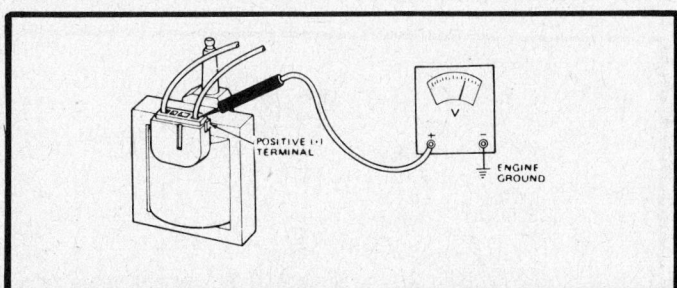

TFI ignition system—coil supply voltage test arrangement (© Ford Motor Co.)

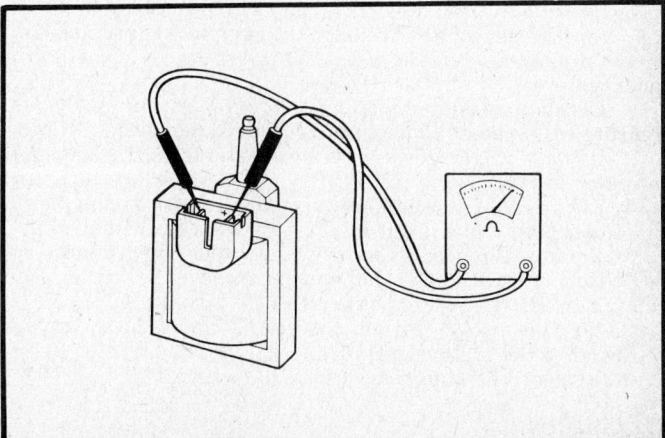

TFI ignition system—coil primary resistance test arrangement (© Ford Motor Co.)

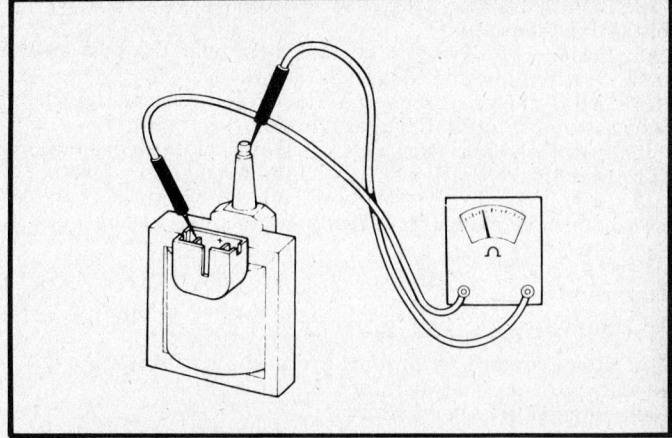

TFI ignition system—coil secondary resistance test arrangement (© Ford Motor Co.)

meter reading is less than 800 ohms or more than 975 ohms, the TFI module is okay, but the stator assembly must be replaced.

5. Reinstall the TFI module and the distributor according to the appropriate sections.

Primary Circuit Continuity

This test is performed in the same manner as the previous Wiring Harness test, but only the No. 1 terminal conductor is tested (ignition switch in Run position). If the voltage is less than 90% of the available battery voltage, proceed to the next test.

Ignition Coil Primary Voltage

1. Attach the negative lead of a voltmeter to the distributor base.

2. Turn the ignition switch On and connect the positive voltmeter lead to the negative (–) ignition coil terminal. Note the voltage reading and turn the ignition Off. If the voltmeter

30-41

Section 30: ELECTRONIC IGNITION
FORD SOLID STATE SYSTEM

reading is less than 90% of the available battery voltage, inspect the wiring between the ignition module and the negative (-) coil terminal, then proceed to the last test, which follows.

Ignition Coil Supply Voltage

1. Attach the negative lead of a voltmeter to the distributor base.
2. Turn the ignition switch ON and connect the positive voltmeter lead to the positive (+) ignition coil terminal. Note the voltage reading then turn the ignition Off.
   a. If the voltage reading is at least 90% of the battery voltage, yet the engine will still not run; first, check the ignition coil connector and terminals for corrosion, dirt, and/or damage; second, replace the ignition switch if the connectors and terminals are damaged or corroded.
3. Connect any remaining wiring.

STATOR ASSEMBLY

Removal

EXCEPT ESCORT, LYNX, EXP AND LN7

1. Remove the distributor cap and rotor. Disconnect the distributor harness plug. To remove the two piece Dura Spark distributor cap, take off the top, then the rotor, then the bottom adapter.
2. Using a small gear puller or equivalent, remove the armature from the advance plate sleeve. Remove the roll pin.
3. Remove the large wire retaining clip from the base plate annular groove.
4. Lift the vacuum advance arm off the post on the pick up assembly and move it out against the distributor housing.
5. Remove the ground screw which holds the ground strap.
6. Pull upward on the lead wires to remove the rubber grommet from the distributor base.
7. Remove the E-clip which retains the vacuum advance pull rod to the stator assembly.
8. Remove the stator assembly.

Installation

1. Place the new pick up assembly in position over the fixed base plate and slide the wiring into position through the slot in the side of the distributor housing.
2. Install the wire snap ring securing the pick up assembly to the fixed base plate.
3. Position the vacuum advance arm over the post on the pick up assembly and install the snap ring.
4. Install the grounding screw through the tab on the wiring harness and into the fixed base plate.
5. Install the armature on the advance plate sleeve making sure that the roll pin is engaged into the matching slots.
6. Install the distributor rotor cap.
7. Connect the distributor wiring plug to the vehicle harness.

Removal

ESCORT, LYNX, EXP AND LN7

1. Remove the distributor cap from the distributor, and set it aside (spark plug wires intact).
2. Remove the distributor.
3. Remove the rotor from the distributor.
4. Carefully remove the drive coupling spring, using a small screwdriver.
5. Blow the dirt and oil from the drive end of the distributor with compressed air.
6. Paint matchmarks on the drive coupling and the shaft to indicate their relationship for reassembly. Align the drive pin with the slot in the base.
7. Carefully support the distributor and drive out the roll pin using a 1/8 in. drift punch and hammer.
8. Remove the distributor drive coupling.
9. Check the end of the distributor shaft for burrs. If any are present, smooth them with emery paper and wipe the shaft clean. Withdraw the shaft assembly from the distributor.
10. Remove the two screws which retain the stator connector to the distributor bowl.
11. On TFI systems, remove the connector from the top of the TFI module.
12. Remove the three screws which retain the stator assembly to the distributor base. Carefully lift the stator assembly from the distributor base.

NOTE: While the distributor is disassembled, inspect all parts for damage, wear, and freedom of operation.

Installation

1. Assemble the stator retainer to the stator assembly by sliding the stator bumper into the groove in the bottom of the stator, with the horseshoe opening at the diaphragm rod pivot pin.
2. On TFI systems, place the connector on top of the module (with pins aligned). Press down on the connector to properly seat it.
3. Place the stator assembly over the distributor base bushing, with the diaphragm pivot pin positioned in front of the diaphragm mounting hole.
4. Align the holes in the stator retaining plate with the holes in the distributor base. Install the three stator retaining screws and torque the screws to 1.8–3.0 ft. lbs. Check the stator for free rotation.
5. Install the two screws which secure the connector to the base and torque the screws to 1.8–3.0 ft. lbs.
6. Place the two stator wires behind the wire guard of the connector. The wires must not be tangled or twisted.
7. Install the diaphragm assembly.
8. Apply a SMALL amount of Ford M2C162A (or its equivalent) lubricant to the distributor shaft below the armature.

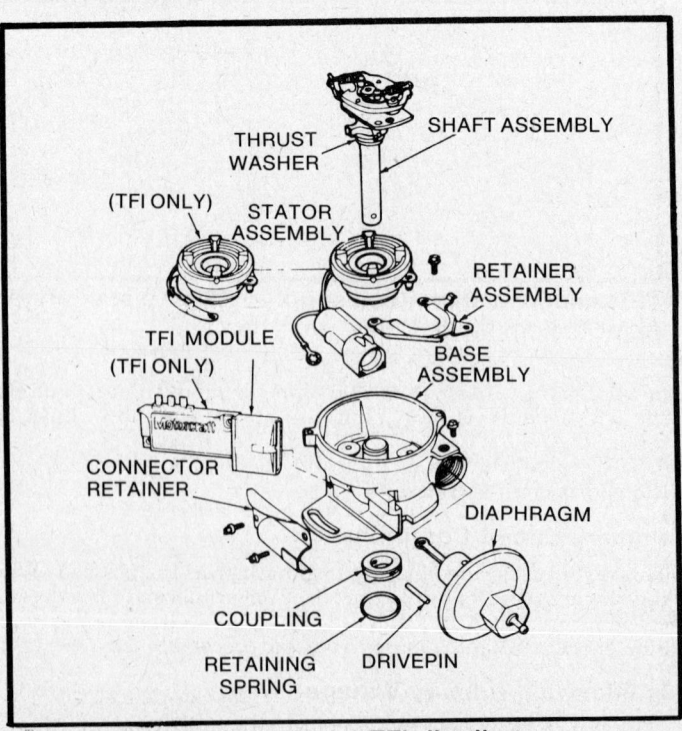

Exploded view of 4 cylinder TFI distributor
(© Ford Motor Co.)

ELECTRONIC IGNITION
FORD SOLID STATE SYSTEM

SECTION 30

9. Install the distributor shaft and the drive coupling, lining up the marks made during Step 6.
10. Support the distributor securely and drive the roll pin into place. The end of the pin should be flush with the step in the drive coupling. Check for free movement of the drive coupling and the distributor shaft.
11. Install the drive coupling retaining spring.
12. Install the distributor assembly, following the procedure listed in the appropriate car section.
13. Install the distributor cap and the rotor.

TFI MODULE

Removal and Installation

1. Remove the distributor cap from the distributor, and set it aside (spark plug wires intact). Do not remove the wires from the cap.
2. Disconnect the TFI harness connector.
3. Remove the distributor after matchmarking it to the engine with chalk, etc.
4. Remove the TFI module retaining screws.
5. To disengage the module terminals from the distributor base connector, pull the right side of the module down the distributor mounting flange and then back up. Carefully pull the module toward the flange and away from the distributor.

CAUTION
Step 5 must be followed exactly; failure to do so will result in damage to the distributor module connector pins.

TO INSTALL THE TFI MODULE

1. Coat the TFI module baseplate with a $1/32$ in. layer of silicone grease (Ford No. D7AX19A331–A or its equivalent).
2. Place the TFI module on the distributor base mounting flange. Position the module assembly toward the distributor bowl and carefully engage the distributor connector pins. Install and torque the TFI module retaining screws to 9–16 inch lbs.
3. Install the distributor assembly.
4. Install the distributor cap and check the engine timing.

NOTE: It is recommended to use a new roll pin in the armature groove position 180° away from the original groove.

FORD EEC–IV IGNITION SYSTEM

EEC-IV systems use the thick film integrated ignition-IV (TFI-IV) system. This system differs from Dura Spark III used on EEC-II and III.

The TFI-IV ignition system features a universal distributor design which is cam-gear driven and uses no centrifugal or vacuum advance. The distributor is conventionally mounted on the engine. It has a die cast base which incorporates an integrally mounted TFI-IV ignition module, a Hall effect vane switch stator assembly (PIP sensor), and provisions for fixed octane adjustment. No distributor calibration is required and

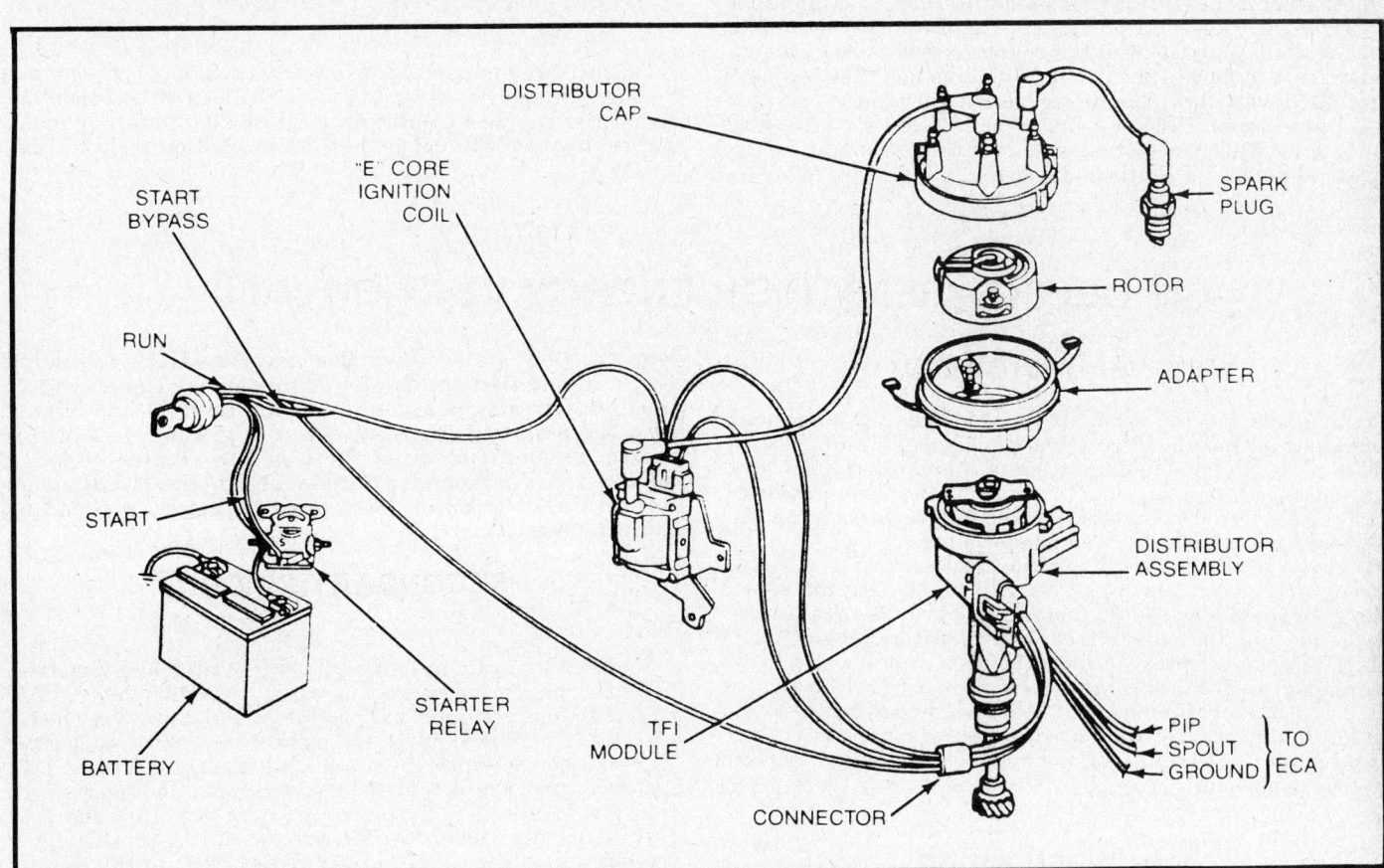

TFI-IV system (© Ford Motor Co.)

30–43

SECTION 30

ELECTRONIC IGNITION
FORD EEC-IV SYSTEM

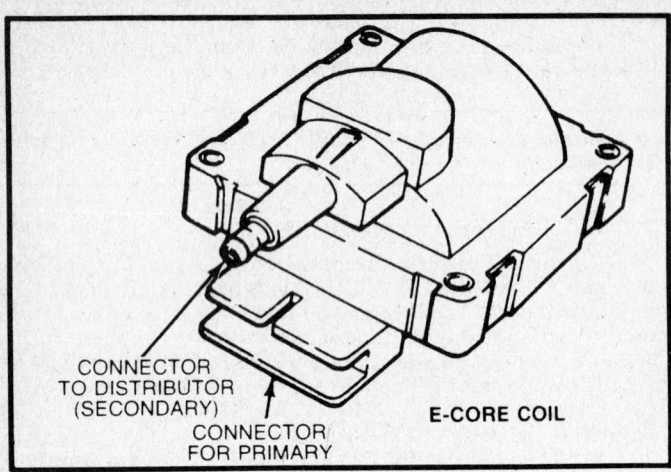

"E-Core" ignition coil (© Ford Motor Co.)

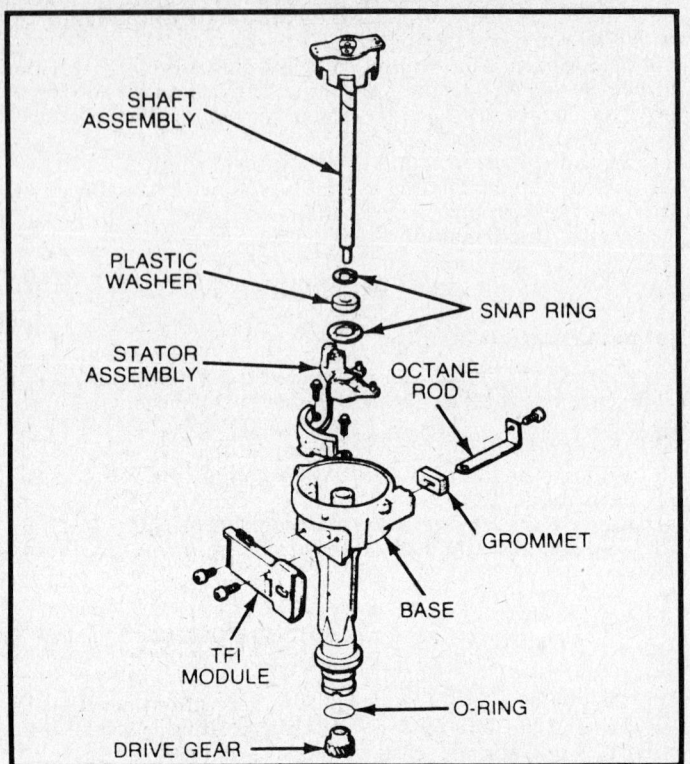

TFI-IV universal distributor (© Ford Motor Co.)

initial timing is not a normal adjustment. Provisions have been incorporated in the distributor to allow fixed adjustment capability for octane needs. The adjustment is accomplished by replacing the standard 0° rod located in the distributor bowl with a 3 or 6° retard rod which is released for service only.

NOTE: The timing is not intended to be changed by use of these octane rods without first having the proper authorization because federal emission requirements will be affected.

Vehicles equipped with TFI-IV use an "E-core" ignition coil which replaces the oil-filled coil used with Dura Spark ignition systems. The E-core coil provides the high voltage required to fire the spark plugs. The output voltage is generated by allowing current to flow in the primary winding and then to interrupt the current flow. The E-core has a higher energy transfer due to the laminations providing a closed magnetic path. Also the ignition coil connector allows a tachometer connection, using an alligator clip, without removing the coil connector.

The primary function of the universal distributor is to direct the high secondary voltage to the spark plugs. In addition, the distributor supplies crankshaft position and frequency information to the ECA using the profile ignition pickup (PIP) sensor.

GM DELCO–REMY HIGH ENERGY IGNITION (HEI)

General Information

The magnetic pick-up assembly located inside the distributor contains a permanent magnet, a pole piece with internal teeth, and a pick-up coil. When the teeth of the rotating timer core and pole piece align, an induced voltage in the pick-up coil signals the electronic module to open the coil primary circuit. As the primary current decreases, a high voltage is induced in the secondary windings of the ignition coil, directing a spark through the rotor and high voltage leads to fire the spark plugs. The dwell period is automatically controlled by the electronic module and is increased with increasing engine rpm. The HEI System features a longer spark duration which is instrumental in firing lean and EGR (Exhaust Gas Recirculation) diluted fuel/air mixtures. The condenser (capacitor) located within the HEI distributor is provided for noise (static) suppression purposes only and is not a regularly replaced ignition system component.

Troubleshooting

NOTE: An accurate diagnosis is the first step to problem solution and repair. For several of the following steps, a modified spark plug (side electrode removed) is needed. GM makes a modified plug (tool ST 125) which also has a spring clip to attach it to ground. Use of this tool is recommended, as there is less chance of being shocked. If a tachometer is connected to the TACH terminal on the distributor, disconnect it before proceeding with this test.

SECONDARY CIRCUIT

Test

1. Check for spark at the spark plugs by attaching the modified spark plug to one of the plug wires, grounding the modified plug shell on the engine and cranking the starter. Wear heavy gloves, use insulated pliers and make sure the ground is good. If no spark on one wire, check a second. If spark is present, HEI system is good. Check fuel system, plug wires, and spark plugs. If no spark (except EST), proceed to next step. If no spark on EST distributor, disconnect the 4 terminal EST connector and recheck for spark. If spark is present, EST system service check, as outlined under "Engine Controls," should be performed. If no spark, proceed to Step 2.

ELECTRONIC IGNITION
GM HIGH ENERGY IGNITION (HEI) SYSTEM

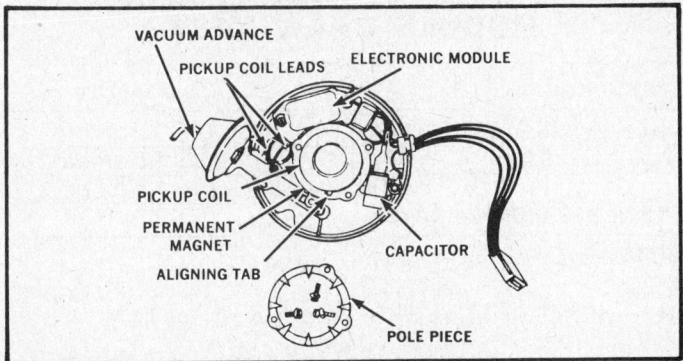

Pole piece removal (© General Motors Corp.)

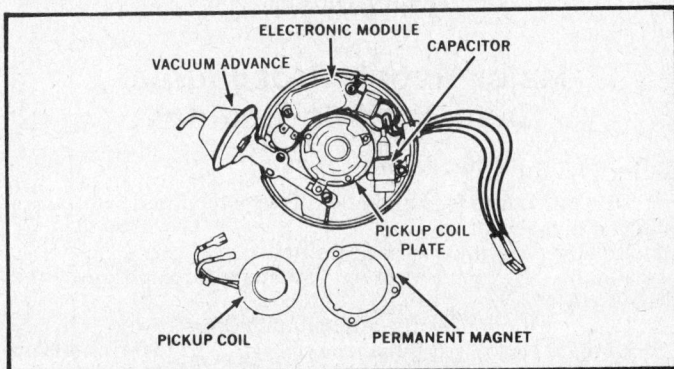

Coil and magnet removal (© General Motors Corp.)

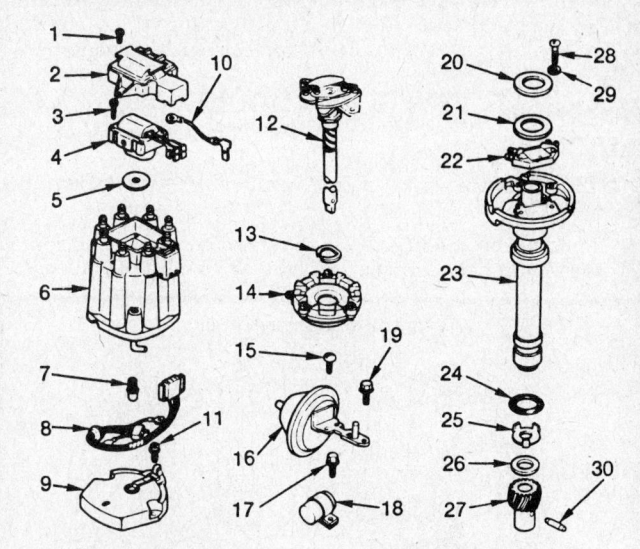

1. Cap cover attaching screw
2. Distributor cap cover
3. Coil attaching screw
4. Distributor coil
5. Coil to distributor cap seal
6. Distributor cap
7. Resistor brush
8. Module coil harness
9. Distributor rotor
10. Distributor ground lead
11. Rotor screw
12. Distributor mainshaft
13. Pole piece and plate retainer
14. Distributor pole piece and plate
15. Vacuum control attaching screw
16. Distributor vacuum control
17. Capacitor and attaching screw
18. Capacitor and attaching screw
19. Vacuum control attaching screw
20. Felt washer
21. Distributor housing seal
22. Module
23. Distributor housing
24. Housing stem washer
25. Shaft spacer washer
26. Shaft thrust washer
27. Distributor drive gear
28. Module attaching screw
29. Washer
30. Gear attaching pin

Exploded view of Hei distributor with integrated coil (© General Motors Corp.)

NOTE: Before making any circuit checks with test meters, be sure that all primary circuit connectors are properly installed and that spark plug cables are secure at the distributor and at the plugs. Also check that the distributor through-bolts are tight; loose bolts can cause radio interference and poor performance.

2. Check voltage at the BAT terminal of the distributor while cranking the engine. If under 7V, repair the primary circuit to the ignition switch. If over 7V, proceed to Step 3.

3. With the ignition switch on, check voltage at the TACH terminal of the distributor or coil (external). If under 1V, coil connection or coil are faulty. If over 10V, proceed to Step 4. If 1–10V, replace module and check for spark from coil. See Step 4.

4. On external coil models, disconnect the coil wire from the distributor, and connect to the grounded modified spark plug. On integral coils, remove the distributor cap from the distributor without removing its electrical connectors, remove the rotors, then modify a plug boot so that the modified plug can be connected directly to the center terminal of the distributor cap. Ground the shell of the modified plug to the engine block with a jumper wire. Make sure no wires, clothing, etc., are in the way of moving parts and crank the engine. On external coils, if no spark, check the secondary coil wire continuity and repair. If spark is present in either type of coil, inspect the distributor cap for moisture, cracks, etc. If cap is okay, install new rotor. If no spark, proceed to Step 5.

5. Remove the pick up coil leads from the module and check TACH terminal voltage with the ignition on. Watch the voltmeter and momentarily (not more than 5 seconds) connect a test light from the positive battery terminal to the appropriate module terminal: 4 terminal module, terminal "G" (small terminal); 5 terminal module (ESS or ESC), terminal "D"; 5 terminal module, (EMR) terminal "H"; 7 terminal module, terminal "P". If no drop in voltage is noted, test the module, check the module ground, and check for open wires between the cap and the distributor. If okay, replace the module. If voltage drops, proceed to the next step.

NOTE: 4 terminal modules may be tested with simple tools, according to the module test procedure which follows.

6. Reconnect the modified plug to the ignition coil as instructed in Step 4, and check for spark as the test light is removed from the appropriate module terminal (see Step 5 for module terminal). Do not connect the test light for more than 5 seconds. If spark is present, the problem is with the pick up coil or connections. Pick up coil resistance should be 500–1500 ohms and not grounded. If no spark, proceed to next step.

7. On integral coil distributors, check the coil ground by attaching a test light from the BAT terminal of the cap to the coil ground wire. If the light lights when the ignition is on, replace the ignition coil and repeat Step 6. If the light does not light, repair the ground. On external coil models, replace the ignition coil and repeat Step 6. On both integral and external coil dis-

SECTION 30
ELECTRONIC IGNITION
GM HIGH ENERGY IGNITION (HEI) SYSTEM

tributors, if no spark is present, replace the module and reinstall the original coil. Repeat Step 6 again. If no spark is present, replace the original ignition coil with a good one.

IGNITION MODULE

Test

NOTE: This test procedure applies only to 4 terminal HEI modules.

1. Remove the module from the distributor. Connect a 12 VDC test lamp between the "B" and "C" module terminals.

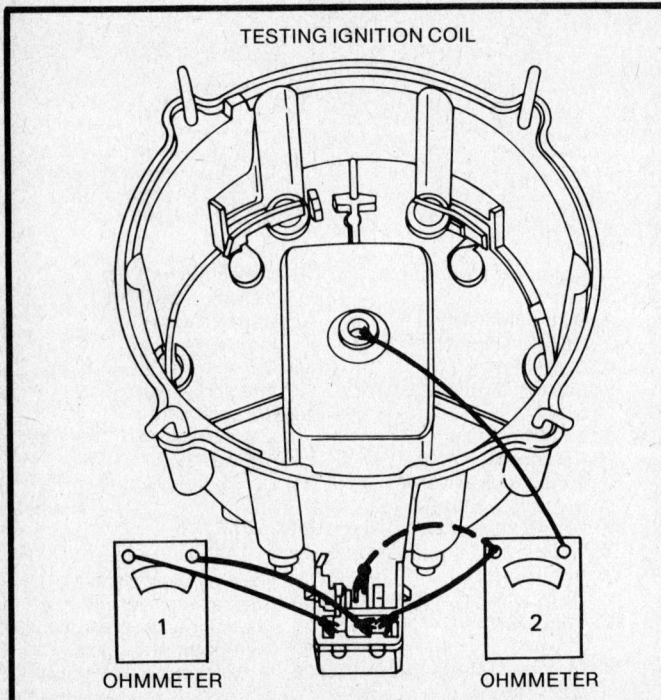

To test the Hei ignition coil on integral models, connect the ohmmeter as shown in test No. 1 The reading should be zero or nearly zero. Connect the ohmmeter both ways as shown in test No. 2 with the meter on the high scale. Replace the coil if both readings are infinite (© General Motors Corp.)

2. Connect a jumper wire from a 12 VDC source to the "B" module terminal.
3. Connect the module ground terminal to a good ground. If the test lamp lights, the module is defective and must be replaced.
4. Connect a jumper wire between the "B" and "G" module terminals. The test lamp will light if the module is okay.

HALL EFFECT SWITCH

Test

The Hall Effect Switch, when used, is installed in the HEI distributor. The purpose of the switch is to measure engine speed and send the information to the Electronic Control Module ECM. To remove the Hall Effect Switch, the distributor shaft must be removed from the distributor. The purpose of the switch is to measure engine speed and send the information to the Electronic Control Module ECM. To remove the Hall Effect Switch, the distributor shaft must be removed from the distributor.

1. Remove the switch connectors from the switch.
2. Connect a 12 volt battery and voltmeter to the switch.

MODULE DRAW TEST

Test Condition	Current Draw
Key on, ignition off	0.1-0.2 amp
Engine cranking	0.5-1.5 amps
Engine at idle	0.5-1.5 amps
Engine at 2,0000-2,500 rpm	1.0-2.8 amps

NOTE: Exact values may vary.

Note and follow the polarity markings as indicated in the illustration.

3. Without the knife blade inserted, the voltmeter should read less than 0.5 volts. If not, the switch is defective.
4. With the knife blade inserted, the voltmeter should read within 0.5 volts of battery voltage. If not, the switch is defective.

Major Repair Procedures (Distributor In Engine)

Ignition Coil Replacement

1. Disconnect the feed and module wire terminal connectors from the distributor cap.
2. Remove the ignition set retainer.
3. Remove the four coil cover-to-distributor cap screws and the coil cover.
4. Remove the four coil-to-distributor cap screws.
5. Using a blunt drift, press the coil wire spade terminals up out of distributor cap.
6. Lift the coil up out of the distributor cap.
7. Remove and clean the coil spring, rubber seal washer and coil cavity of the distributor cap.
8. Reverse the above procedures to install.

Distributor Cap Replacement

1. Remove the feed and module wire terminal connectors from the distributor cap.
2. Remove the retainer and spark plug wires from the cap.
3. Depress and release the four distributor cap-to-housing retainers and lift off the cap assembly.
4. Remove the four coil cover screws and cover.
5. Using a finger or a blunt drift, push the spade terminals up out of the distributor cap.
6. Remove all four coil screws and lift the coil, coil spring and rubber seal washer out of the cap coil cavity.
7. Using a new distributor cap, reverse the above procedures to assemble.

Rotor Replacement

1. Disconnect the feed and module wire connectors from the distributor.
2. Depress and release the four distributor cap to housing retainers and lift off the cap assembly.
3. Remove the two rotor attaching screws and rotor.
4. Reverse the above procedure to install.

Vacuum Advance Replacement

1. Remove the distributor cap and rotor as previously described.
2. Disconnect the vacuum hose from the vacuum advance unit.
3. Remove the two vacuum advance retaining screws, pull the advance unit outward, rotate and disengage the operating rod from its tang.
4. Reverse the above procedure to install.

Electronic Ignition
GM HIGH ENERGY IGNITION (HEI) SYSTEM

SECTION 30

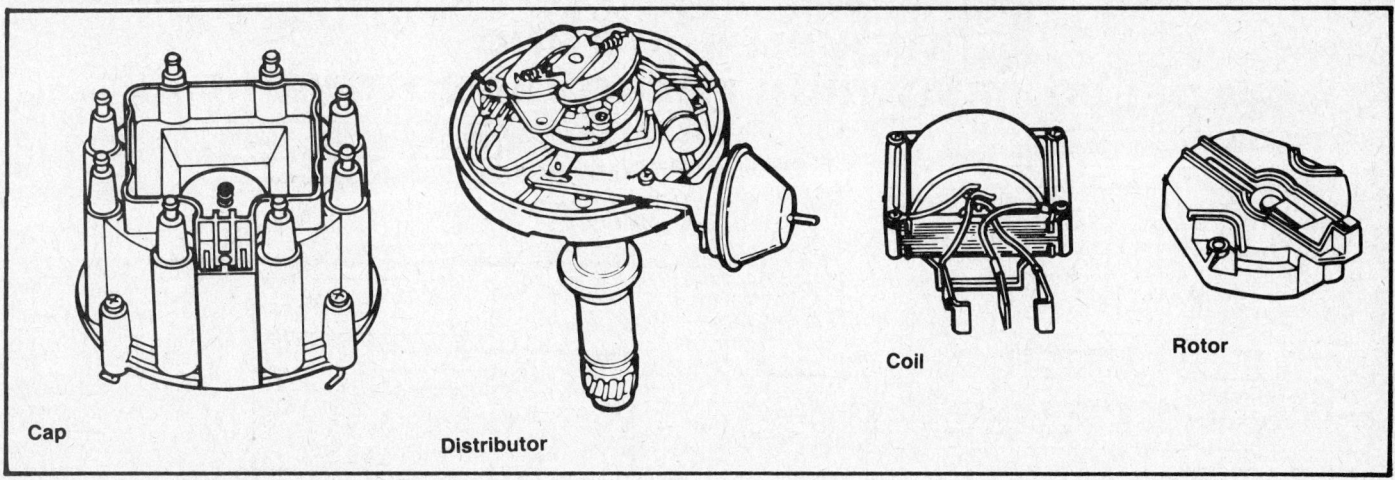

Delco-Remy High Energy (H.E.I.) Ignition

Module Replacement

1. Remove the distributor cap and rotor as previously described.
2. Disconnect the harness connector and pick-up coil spade connectors from the module.
3. Remove the two screws and module from the distributor housing.
4. Coat the bottom of the new module with dielectric lubricant. Reverse the above procedure to install.

DISTRIBUTOR

Removal

1. Disconnect the negative battery cable.
2. Disconnect the feed and module terminal connectors from the distributor cap.
3. Disconnect the hose at the vacuum advance.
4. Depress and release the four distributor cap-to-housing retainers and lift off the cap assembly.
5. Using crayon or chalk, make locating marks on the rotor and module and on the distributor housing and engine for installation purposes.
6. Loosen and remove the distributor clamp bolt and clamp, and lift distributor out of the engine. Noting the relative position of the rotor and module alignment marks, make a second mark on the rotor to align it with the one mark on the module.

Installation

1. With a new O-ring on the distributor housing and the second mark on the rotor aligned with the mark on the module, install the distributor, taking care to align the mark on the housing with the one on the engine. It may be necessary to lift the distributor and turn the rotor slightly to align the gears and the oil pump driveshaft.
2. With the respective marks aligned, install the clamp and bolt finger-tight.
3. Install and secure the distributor cap.
4. Connect the feed and module connectors to the distributor cap.
5. Connect a timing light to the engine and plug the vacuum hose.
6. Connect the ground cable to the battery.
7. Start the engine and set the timing.
8. Turn the engine off and tighten the distributor clamp bolt. Disconnect the timing light and unplug and connect the hose to the vacuum advance.

SERVICE PROCEDURES (DISTRIBUTOR REMOVED)

Driven Gear Replacement

1. With the distributor removed, use a 1/8 in. pin punch and tap out the driven gear roll pin.

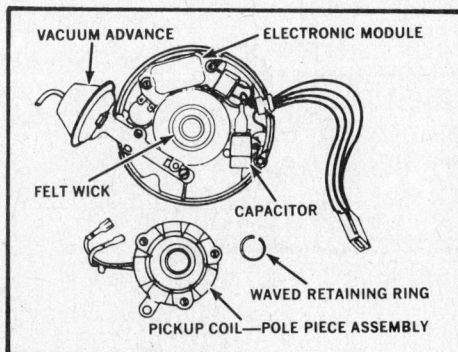

Pick-up coil removal

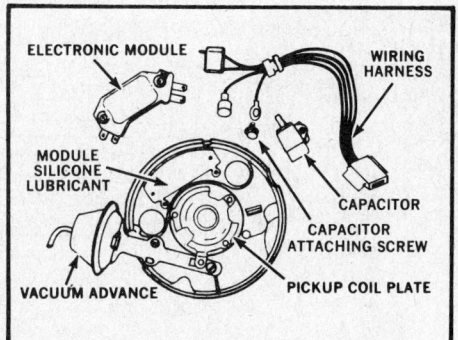

Module and harness removal

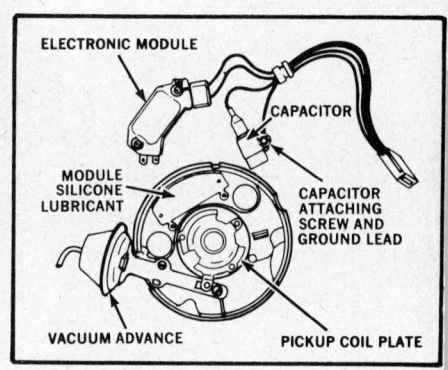

Module and harness installation

30-47

Section 30: Electronic Ignition
GM High Energy Ignition (HEI) System

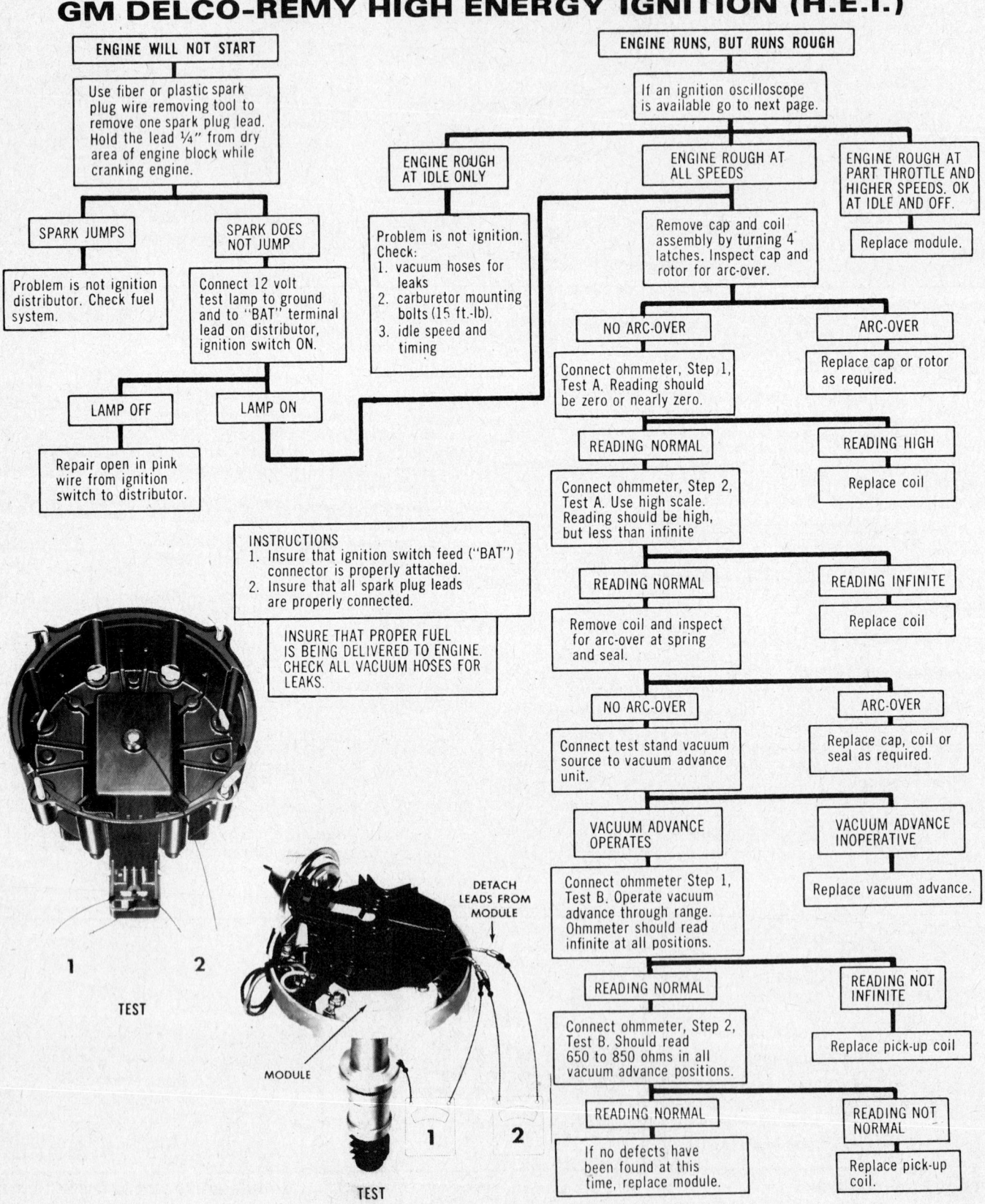

TROUBLESHOOTING — GM DELCO-REMY HIGH ENERGY IGNITION (H.E.I.)

30-48

Electronic Ignition
GM HIGH ENERGY IGNITION (HEI) SYSTEM

Section 30

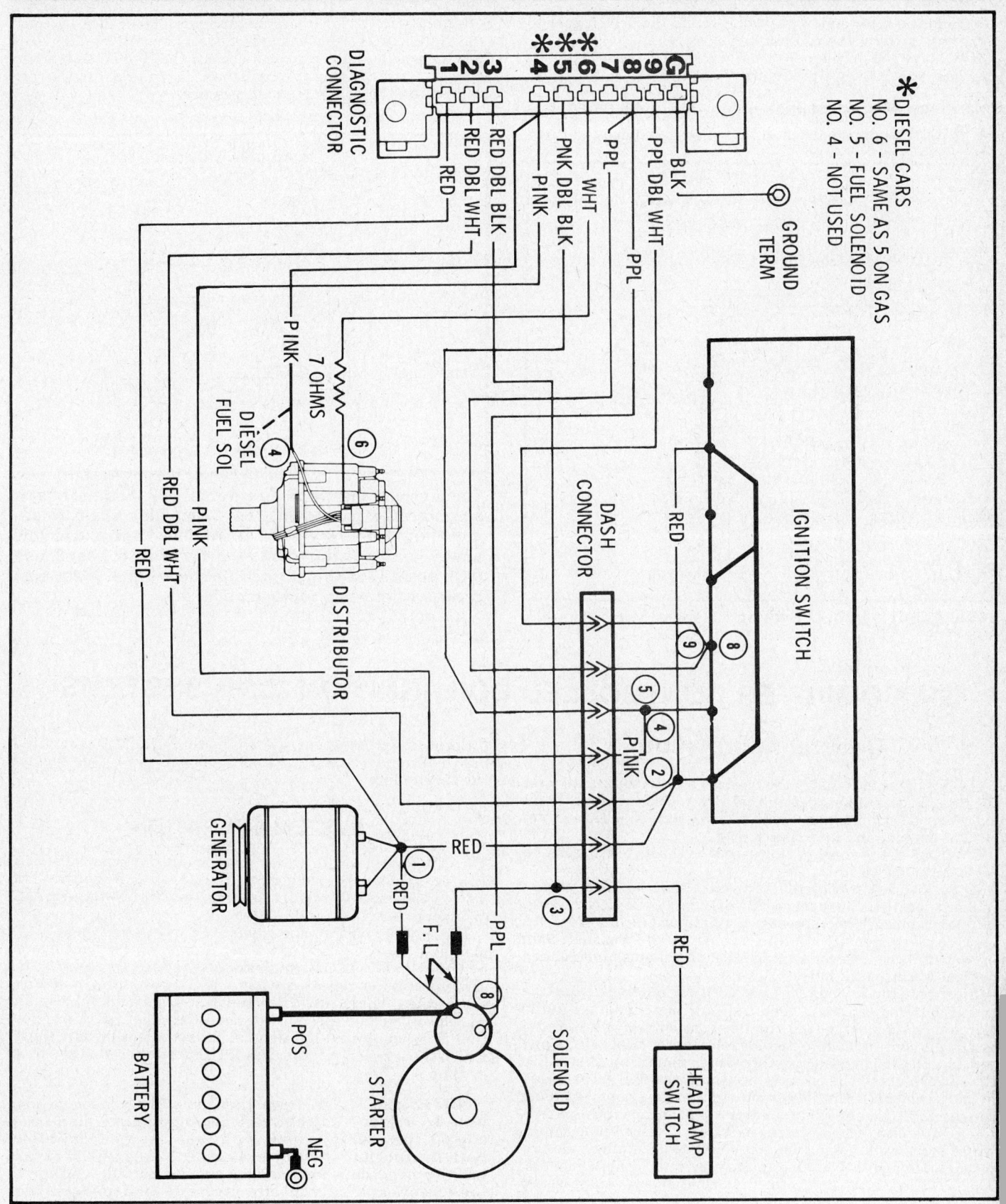

Engine electrical diagnostic connector, typical

30-49

SECTION 30
ELECTRONIC IGNITION
GM HIGH ENERGY IGNITION (HEI) SYSTEM

2. Hold the rotor end of shaft and rotate the driven gear to shear any burrs in the roll pin hole.
3. Remove the driven gear from the shaft.
4. Reverse the above procedure to install.

Pole Piece, Magnet or Pick—Up Coil Replacement

1. With the mainshaft out of its housing, remove the three retaining screws, pole piece and magnet and/or pick-up coil.
2. Reverse the removal procedure to install making sure that the pole piece teeth do not contact the timer core teeth by installing and rotating the mainshaft. Loosen the three screws and realign the pole piece as necessary.

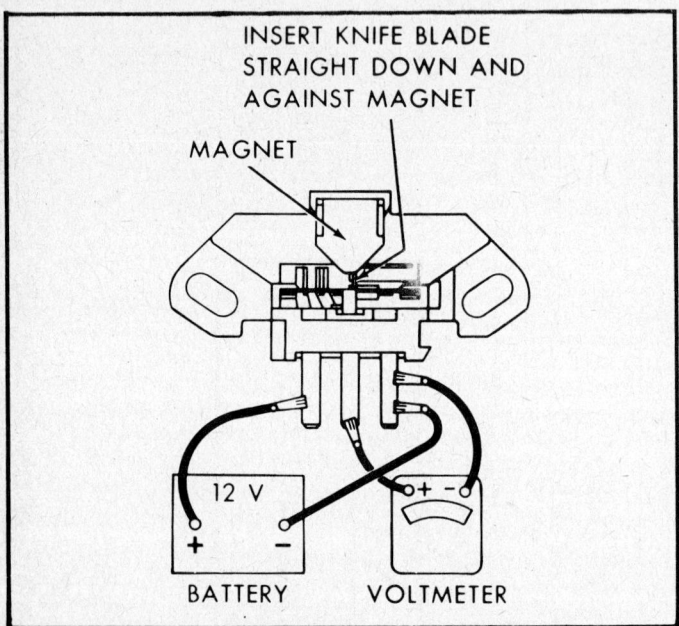

Testing the Hall Effect Switch (© General Motors Corp.)

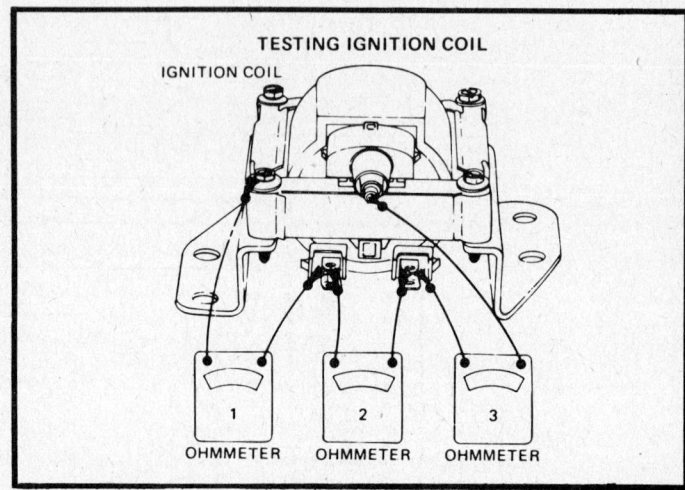

To test Hei ignition coil on external coil models, attach an ohmmeter as shown: Test 1, use high scale. Reading should be very high or infinite. Test 2, use low scale. Reading should be very low or zero. Test 3, use high scale. Reading should not be infinite. If any test proves otherwise, replace coil.
(© General Motors Corp.)

GM COMPUTER CONTROLLED COIL IGNITION (C3-I) SYSTEMS

General Information

The C3I system eliminates the need for a distributor to control the flow of current between the battery and spark plugs. In its place, an electromagnetic sensor consisting of a Hall effect switch, magnet and interruptor ring.

The gear of the shaft of this sensor is connected directly to the camshaft gear.

At the heart of this system is an electronic coil module that replaces the distributor and coil used on previous electronic ignition systems. A microprocessor within the module receives and processes signals from the crankshaft and camshaft and, by way of three interconnecting coils, distributes high voltage current to the spark plugs.

Electromagnetic sensors take position readings from the crankshaft and camshaft, then transmit these readings to the electronics package. Using the information relayed from the electronic control module, the microprocessor then selects and sequentially triggers each of three interconnecting coils to fire the spark plugs at the proper crankshaft position. An electronic spark control (ESC) is incorporated into the system to adjust the spark timing according to engine load and operating conditions. This closed loop system includes a piezoelectric sensor which transforms engine detonation vibrations into an electrical signal which is then fed to the electronic control module. The ECM uses this and other information on engine speed (rpm), intake air mass, coolant temperature and converter clutch operation to adjust the spark advance for the most efficient performance with the lowest emissions.

Because of this feature, there is no timing adjustment or regular maintenance required aside from periodic replacement of the spark plugs.

SYSTEM OPERATION

The C3I system uses a waste spark method of spark distribution. Companion cylinders are paired (1–4, 5–2, 3–6 on the 3.8L V6 engine) and the spark occurs simultaneously in both cylinders.

The cylinder on the exhaust stroke requires very little of the available voltage to arc, so the remaining high voltage is used by the cylinder in the firing position (TDC compression). This same process is repeated when the companion cylinders reverse roles. There are three separate coils combined in the sealed coil/module assembly on the V6 engine. Spark distribution is synchronized by a signal from the crankshaft sensor which the ignition module uses to trigger each coil at the proper time.

NOTE: The signal from the camshaft sensor is also used by the fuel injection electronic control module to trigger the fuel injectors, so a failed sensor can affect both the fuel and ignition system. A 7.5 amp ECM fuse is used to provide a low current source for the voltage to the sensors and internal circuitry; a 10 amp fuse provides voltage for the ignition coils.

This system also incorporates an electronic spark timing

ELECTRONIC IGNITION
GM COMPUTER CONTROLED IGNITION (C3I) SYSTEM
SECTION 30

(EST) system similar to other Delco distributor ignition systems. All connectors are lettered to make circuit identification easier. Terminal C (crankshaft sensor) provides the ECM with engine speed (rpm) and crankshaft position information by passing a signal to the ignition module and then to ECM terminal B5. A plate with three vanes is mounted to the harmonic balancer and the vanes pass through slots in the crankshaft sensor.

As the vanes pass through the slots, the Hall effect switch triggers and sends a voltage signal to the ECM. The signal from the Hall effect switch is either high or low and is used to trigger the ignition module for proper engine timing.

Both the camshaft and crankshaft signal must be received by the ignition module in order for the ECM to take over spark timing control from the ignition module. An open or grounded circuit (terminal B) will set a trouble code 42 in the ECM memory and the engine will run in the bypass or "limp home" mode with the timing fixed at 10° BTDC. The EST terminal A circuit triggers the HEI module by passing a reference signal which the ECM uses to advance or retard the timing according to the input from the crankshaft sensor. Cam terminal E is used by the ECM to determine when the No. 1 cylinder is on the compression stroke by a signal from the Hall effect camshaft position sensor. A loss of the cam signal will store a trouble code 41 if the engine is running and a loss of sensor signal during cranking will prevent the engine from starting.

The electronic control module uses information from the coolant sensor and mass air flow sensor in addition to engine speed to calculate the spark advance to allow more spark advance when the engine is cold or under minimum load. The ECM will retard the timing when the engine is hot or under a heavy load. When the system is running on the HEI module, it grounds the electronic spark timing signal. If the ECM detects voltage in the bypass circuit through a loss of ground for the EST signal, it sets a trouble code 42 and will not switch into the EST mode.

When the engine reaches 400 rpm, the ECM applies 5 volts to the bypass circuit and the EST voltage will vary. If the bypass circuit is open, the ECM will store a trouble code.

Component Replacement

IGNITION COIL

Removal and Installation

1. Disconnect the negative battery cable.
2. Remove the spark plug wires.
3. Remove the screws holding the coil to the ignition module.
4. Tilt the coil assembly to the rear and remove the coil to module connectors.
5. Remove the coil assembly.
6. Installation is the reverse of removal.

IGNITION MODULE

Removal and Installation

1. Disconnect the negative battery cable.
2. Disconnect the 14-pin connector at the ignition module.
3. Remove the spark plug wires at the coil assembly.
4. Remove the nuts and washers securing the ignition module assembly to the mounting bracket.
5. Remove the screws securing the ignition module to the coil.
6. Tilt the coil and disconnect the coil to module connectors.
7. Separate the coil and module.
8. Installation is the reverse of removal.

CRANKSHAFT SENSOR

Removal and Installation

NOTE: It is not necessary to remove the sensor bracket.

1. Disconnect the negative battery cable.
2. Disconnect the sensor 3-way connector.
3. Raise the vehicle and support it safely.
4. Rotate the harmonic balancer so the slot in the disc is aligned with the sensor.
5. Loosen the sensor retaining bolt.
6. Slide the sensor outboard and remove through the notch in the sensor housing.
7. Install the new sensor in the housing and rotate the harmonic balancer so that the disc is positioned in the sensor.
8. Adjust the sensor so that there is an equal distance on each side of the disc.

There should be approximately 0.030 in. (0.76mm) clearance between the disc and the sensor.

9. Tighten the retaining bolt and recheck the clearance.
10. Install remaining components in the reverse order of removal.

CAMSHAFT POSITION SENSOR

Removal and Installation

NOTE: If only the camshaft sensor is being replaced, it is not necessary to remove the entire assembly. The sensor is replaceable separately.

1. Disconnect the negative battery cable.
2. Disconnect the ignition module 14-pin connector.
3. Remove the spark plug wires at the coil assembly.
4. Remove the ignition module bracket assembly.
5. Disconnect the sensor 3-way connector.

1	CRANKSHAFT SENSOR
2	SENSOR RETAINING BOLT
3	CRANKSHAFT SENSOR HOUSING
4	CAMSHAFT POSITION SENSOR

Computer Controled Coil Ignition (C3I) System – V6 shown (© General Motors Corp.)

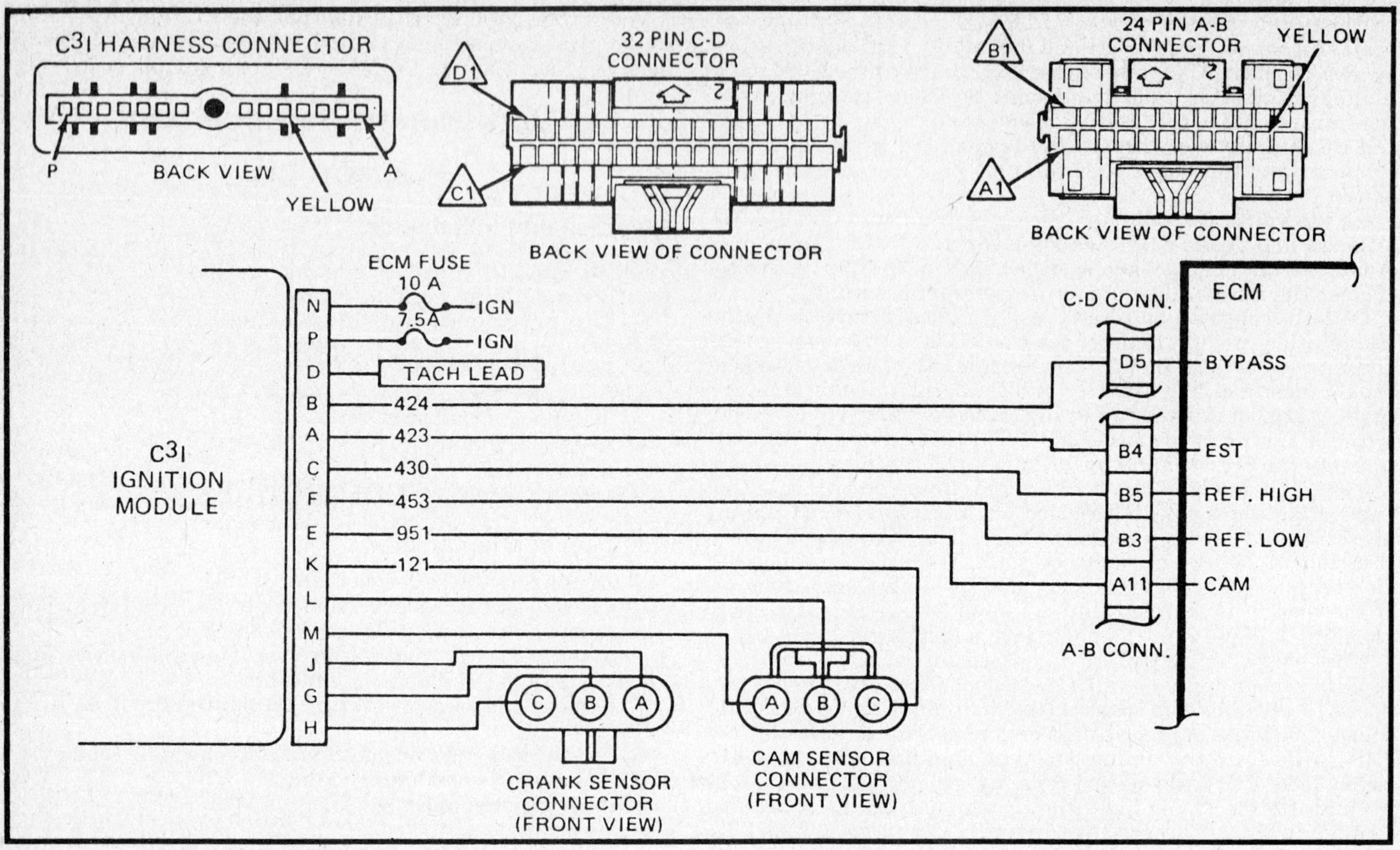

SECTION 30

ELECTRONIC IGNITION
GM COMPUTER CONTROLED IGNITION (C3I) SYSTEM

Computer Controlled Coil Ignition (C3I) System - schematic

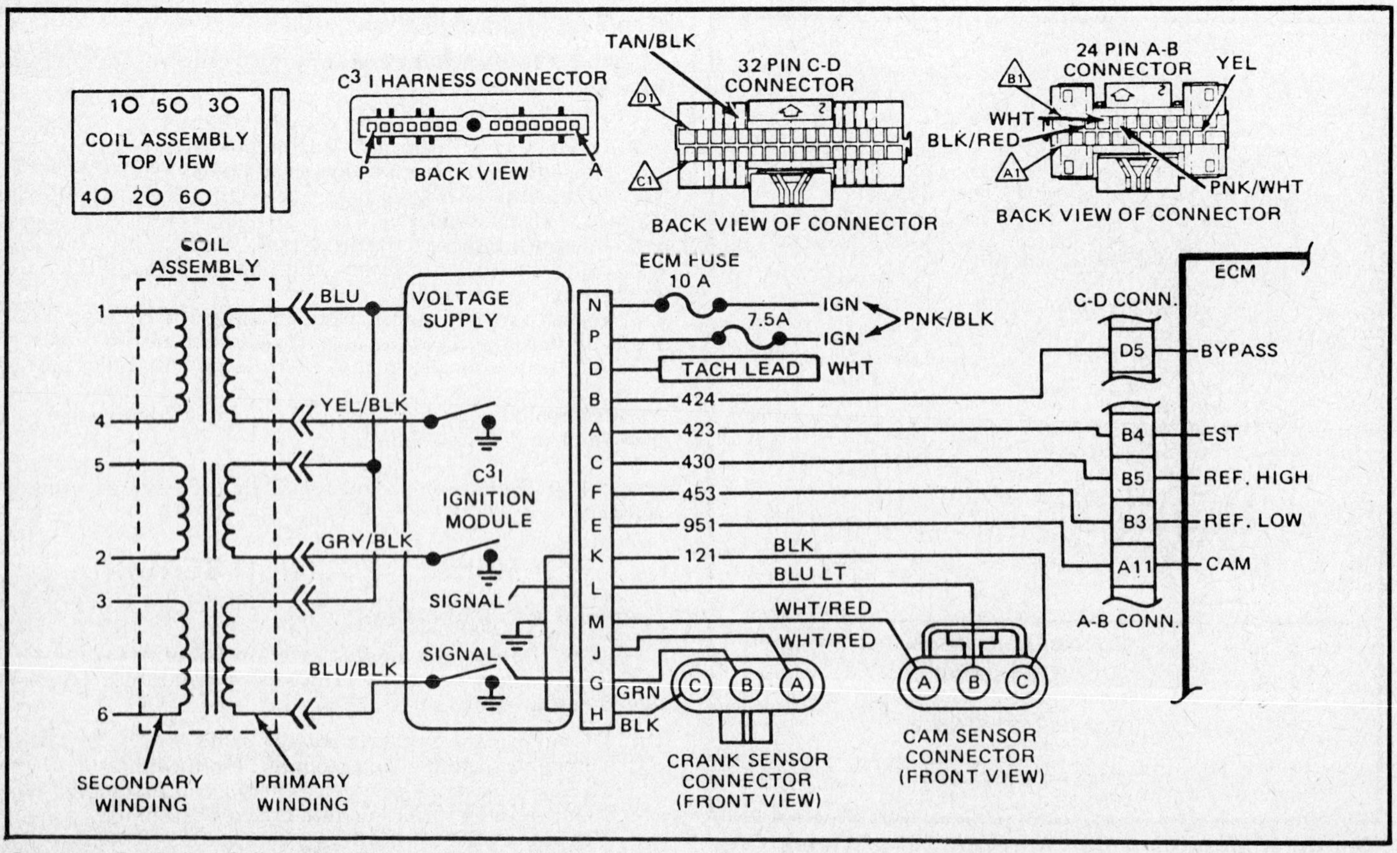

Computer Controlled Coil Ignition (C3I) - 3.8L turbo engine

30-52

ELECTRONIC IGNITION
GM COMPUTER CONTROLED IGNITION (C3I) SYSTEM

SECTION 30

PORT FUEL INJECTION – 3.8L TURBO
IGNITION SYSTEM CHECK (1 OF 2)

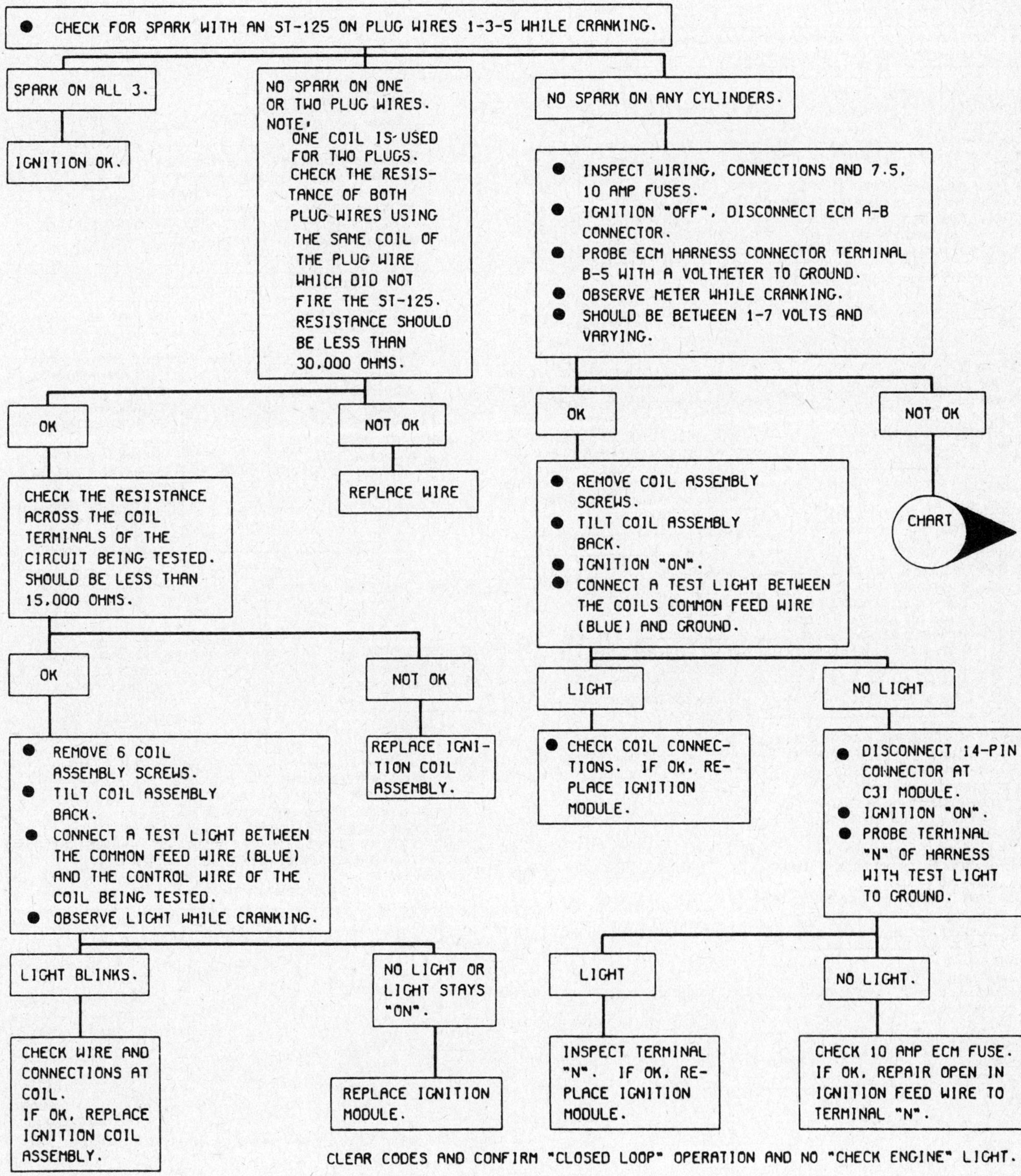

- CHECK FOR SPARK WITH AN ST-125 ON PLUG WIRES 1-3-5 WHILE CRANKING.

SPARK ON ALL 3.
→ IGNITION OK.

NO SPARK ON ONE OR TWO PLUG WIRES.
NOTE:
ONE COIL IS USED FOR TWO PLUGS. CHECK THE RESISTANCE OF BOTH PLUG WIRES USING THE SAME COIL OF THE PLUG WIRE WHICH DID NOT FIRE THE ST-125. RESISTANCE SHOULD BE LESS THAN 30,000 OHMS.

- **OK** → CHECK THE RESISTANCE ACROSS THE COIL TERMINALS OF THE CIRCUIT BEING TESTED. SHOULD BE LESS THAN 15,000 OHMS.
  - **OK** →
    - REMOVE 6 COIL ASSEMBLY SCREWS.
    - TILT COIL ASSEMBLY BACK.
    - CONNECT A TEST LIGHT BETWEEN THE COMMON FEED WIRE (BLUE) AND THE CONTROL WIRE OF THE COIL BEING TESTED.
    - OBSERVE LIGHT WHILE CRANKING.
    - **LIGHT BLINKS.** → CHECK WIRE AND CONNECTIONS AT COIL. IF OK, REPLACE IGNITION COIL ASSEMBLY.
    - **NO LIGHT OR LIGHT STAYS "ON".** → REPLACE IGNITION MODULE.
  - **NOT OK** → REPLACE IGNITION COIL ASSEMBLY.
- **NOT OK** → REPLACE WIRE.

NO SPARK ON ANY CYLINDERS.
- INSPECT WIRING, CONNECTIONS AND 7.5, 10 AMP FUSES.
- IGNITION "OFF", DISCONNECT ECM A-B CONNECTOR.
- PROBE ECM HARNESS CONNECTOR TERMINAL B-5 WITH A VOLTMETER TO GROUND.
- OBSERVE METER WHILE CRANKING.
- SHOULD BE BETWEEN 1-7 VOLTS AND VARYING.

- **OK** →
  - REMOVE COIL ASSEMBLY SCREWS.
  - TILT COIL ASSEMBLY BACK.
  - IGNITION "ON".
  - CONNECT A TEST LIGHT BETWEEN THE COILS COMMON FEED WIRE (BLUE) AND GROUND.
  - **LIGHT** → CHECK COIL CONNECTIONS. IF OK, REPLACE IGNITION MODULE.
  - **NO LIGHT** →
    - DISCONNECT 14-PIN CONNECTOR AT C3I MODULE.
    - IGNITION "ON".
    - PROBE TERMINAL "N" OF HARNESS WITH TEST LIGHT TO GROUND.
    - **LIGHT** → INSPECT TERMINAL "N". IF OK, REPLACE IGNITION MODULE.
    - **NO LIGHT** → CHECK 10 AMP ECM FUSE. IF OK, REPAIR OPEN IN IGNITION FEED WIRE TO TERMINAL "N".
- **NOT OK** → CHART ▶

CLEAR CODES AND CONFIRM "CLOSED LOOP" OPERATION AND NO "CHECK ENGINE" LIGHT.

30-53

Section 30: Electronic Ignition
GM COMPUTER CONTROLED IGNITION (C3I) SYSTEM

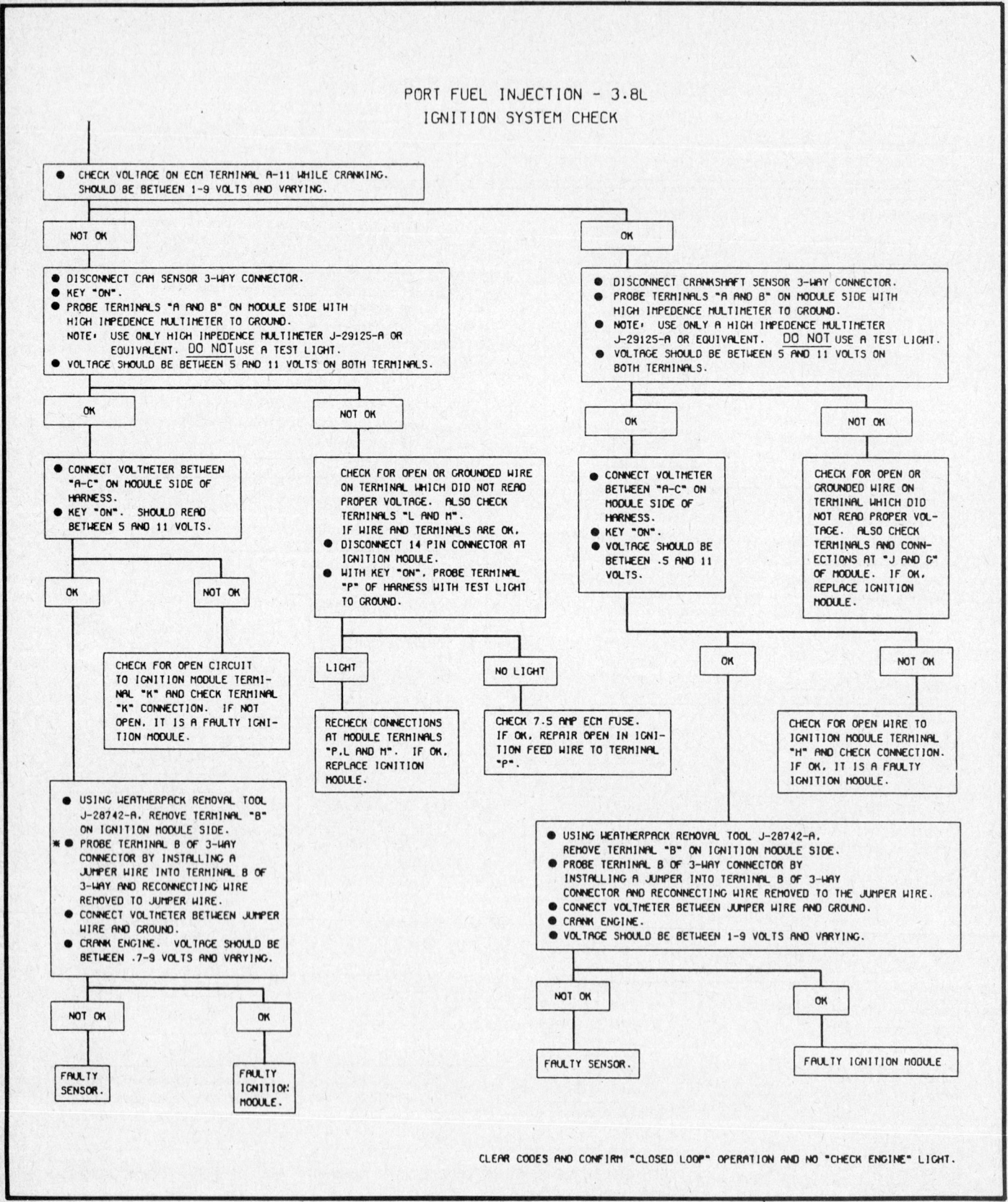

ELECTRONIC IGNITION
GM COMPUTER CONTROLLED IGNITION (C3I) SYSTEM

6. Remove the sensor mounting screws, then remove the sensor.
7. Installation is the reverse of removal.

CAMSHAFT POSITION SENSOR DRIVE ASSEMBLY

Removal and Installation

1. Follow Steps 1–6 of the cam sensor removal procedure. Note the position of the slot in the rotating vane.
2. Remove the bolt securing the drive assembly to the engine.
3. Remove the drive assembly.
4. Install the drive assembly with the slot in the vane. Install mounting bolt.
5. Install the camshaft sensor.
6. Rotate the engine to set the No. 1 cylinder at TDC compression.
7. Mark the harmonic balancer and rotate the engine to 25° after TDC.
8. Remove the plug wires from the coil assembly.
9. Using weatherpack removal tool J–28742–A, or equivalent, remove terminal B of the sensor 3–way connector on the module side.
10. Probe terminal B by installing a jumper and reconnecting the wire removed to the jumper wire.
11. Connect a voltmeter between the jumper wire and ground.
12. With the key On and the engine stopped, rotate the camshaft sensor counterclockwise until the sensor switch just closes. This is indicated by the voltage reading going from a high 5–12 volts to a low 0–2 volts. The low voltage indicates the switch is closed.
13. Tighten the retaining bolt and reinstall the wire into terminal B.
14. Install remaining components.

GM SOLID STATE IGNITION SYSTEM – 1985 AND LATER NOVA

General Information

The principal components of the ignition system are the ignition coil, spark plugs and distributor. The distributor has a rotor, pole piece, module, centrifugal advance and vacuum advance.

The signal generator (pick-up coil) is used to generate the ignition signal and consists of a signal rotor, signal generator and a magnet. The pole piece is attached to the distributor shaft and the magnet and the pick-up coil are attached to the pick-up coil base plate.

As the distributor shaft rotates, the magnetic flux passing through the pick-up coil varies due to the change of the air gap between the pick-up coil and the pole piece. Due to this action, the alternating current voltage is induced in the pick-up coil. The induced voltage turns the module on and off which in turn

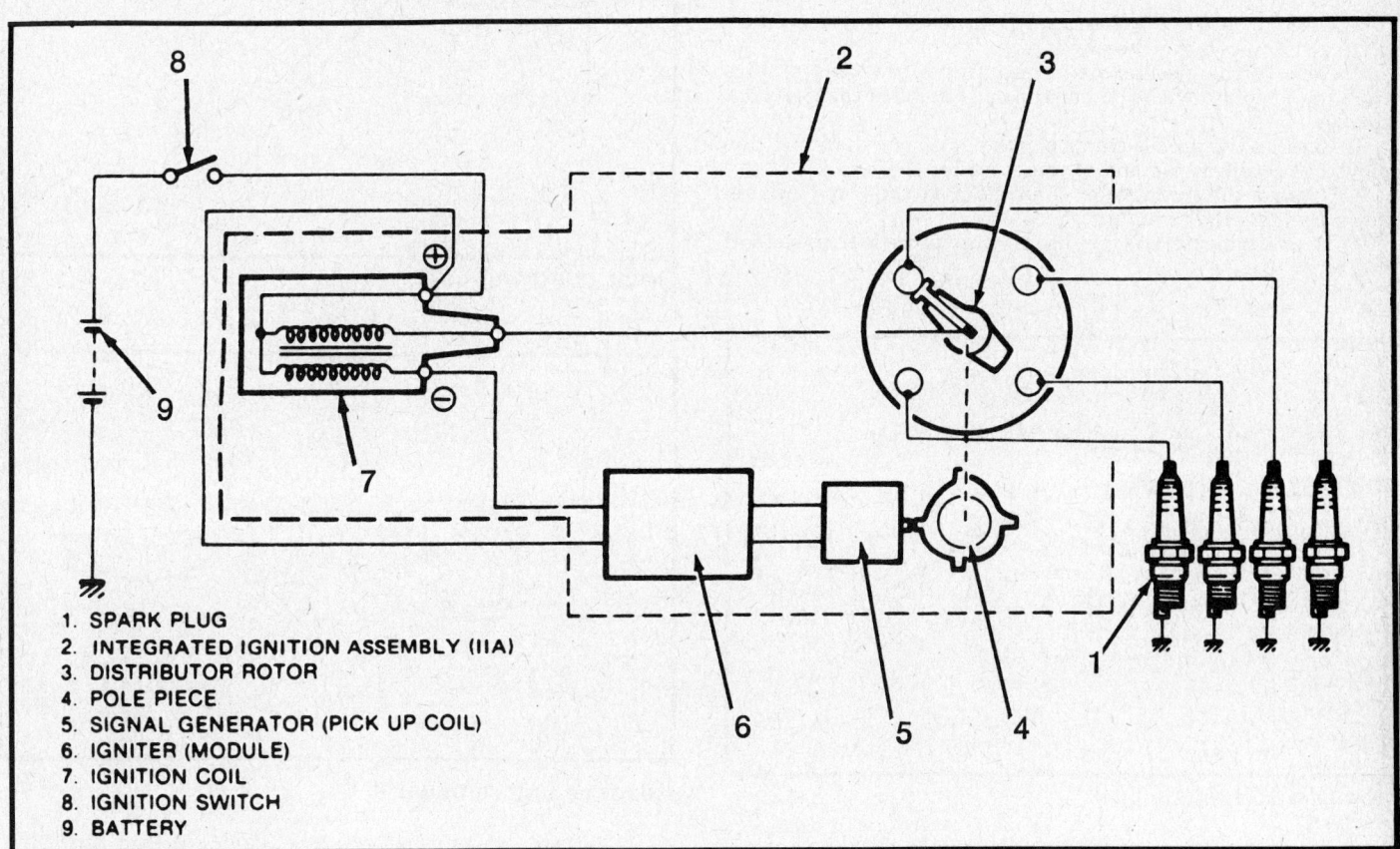

1. SPARK PLUG
2. INTEGRATED IGNITION ASSEMBLY (IIA)
3. DISTRIBUTOR ROTOR
4. POLE PIECE
5. SIGNAL GENERATOR (PICK UP COIL)
6. IGNITER (MODULE)
7. IGNITION COIL
8. IGNITION SWITCH
9. BATTERY

Ignition schematic

SECTION 30

ELECTRONIC IGNITION
GM SOLID STATE SYSTEM (NOVA)

switches off the ignition coil primary voltage. The high voltage is induced in the secondary winding of the ignition coil and ignition sparks are generated at the spark plugs.

DISTRIBUTOR

Removal and Installation

1. Disconnect the negative battery cable.
2. Tag and disconnect the terminal connectors from the distributor body.
3. Disconnect the hose at the vacuum advance.
4. Depress and release the distributor cap retainers, Remove the distributor cap.
5. Using crayon and chaulk, make locating marks on the rotor and module and on the distributor housing and engine for installation.
6. Remove the distributor hold down bolts.
7. Remove the distributor assembly.
8. Installation is the reverse of the removal procedure.

Disassembly

1. Remove the distributor cap packing and rotor.
2. Remove the dust cover, if equipped.
3. Disconnect the wires from the ignition coil terminals. Remove the ignition coil retaining nuts. Remove the ignition coil.
4. Remove the retaining nuts and disconnect the wire from the terminal of the igniter. Remove the igniter retaining screws and remove the igniter.
5. Remove the signal rotor and spring. Remove the vacuum advance screws.
6. Disconnect the advance unit link hole from the breaker plate pin and remove the advancer.
7. Remove the breaker plate retaining screws and remove the breaker plate with the pick-up coil. Remove the governor springs.
8. Remove the grease stopper in the governor shaft end. Remove the screw at the end of the governor shaft.
9. Remove the signal rotor shaft. Remove the C-clip and remove the governor weights.
10. To assemble, follow the disassembly procedure in reverse order.

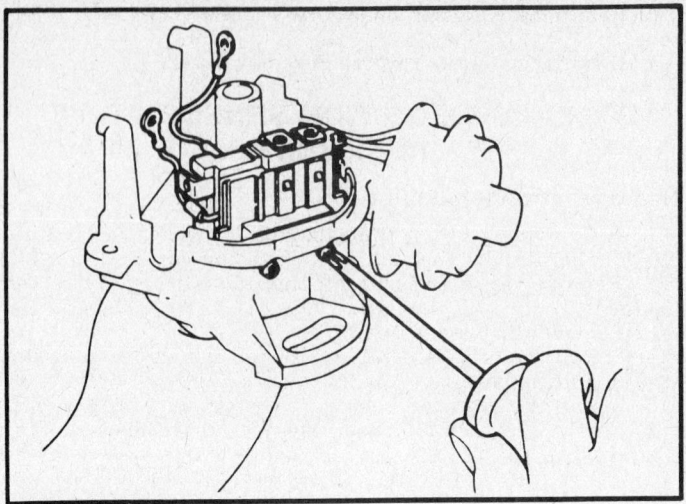
Ignitier removal

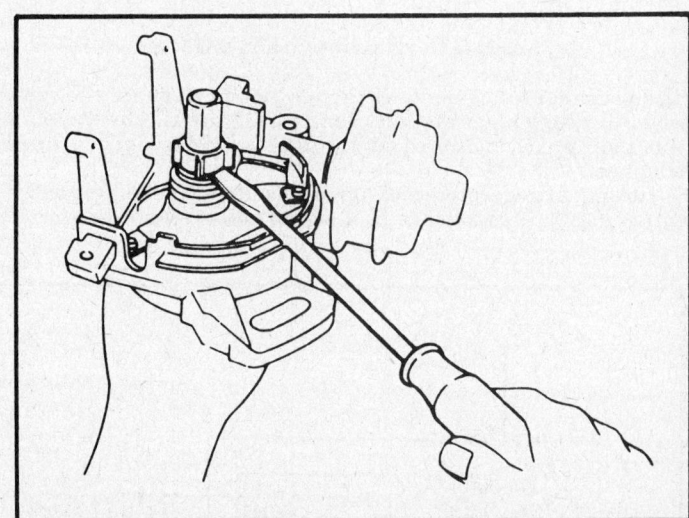
Rotor removal

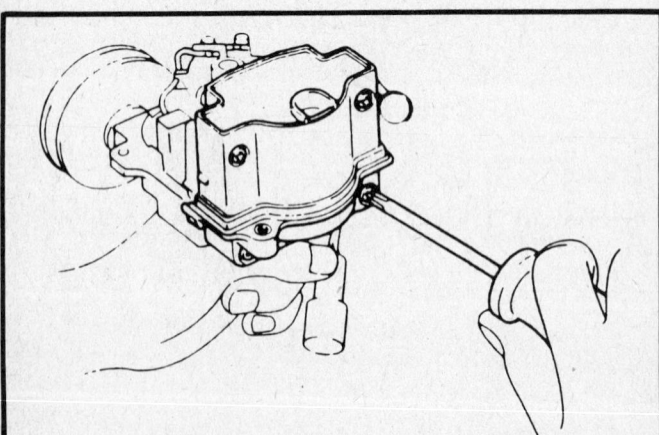
Ignition coil removal

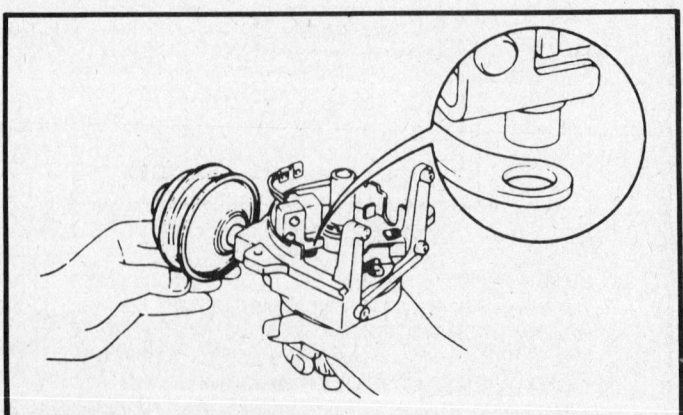
Advance unit removal

30-56

ELECTRONIC IGNITION
GM SOLID STATE SYSTEM (NOVA)

SECTION 30

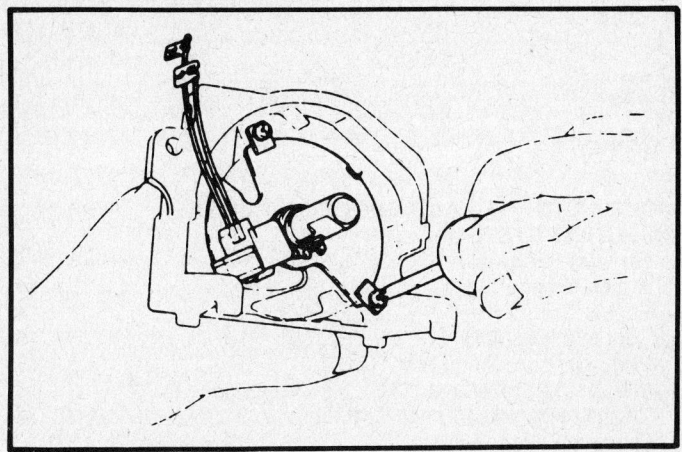
Breaker plate removal

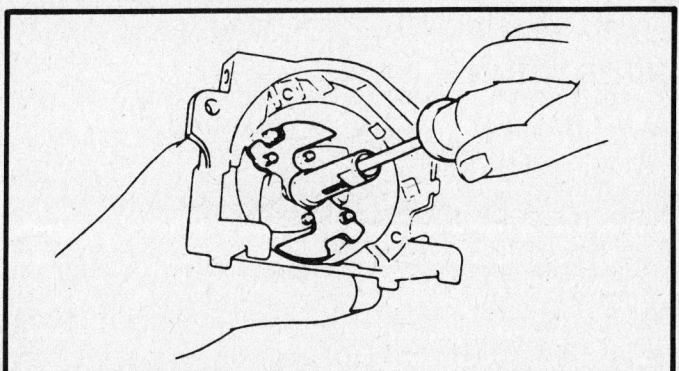
Governor shaft removal

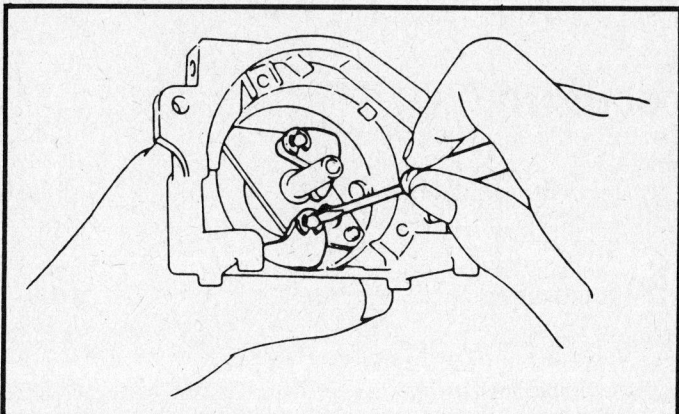
Governor weights

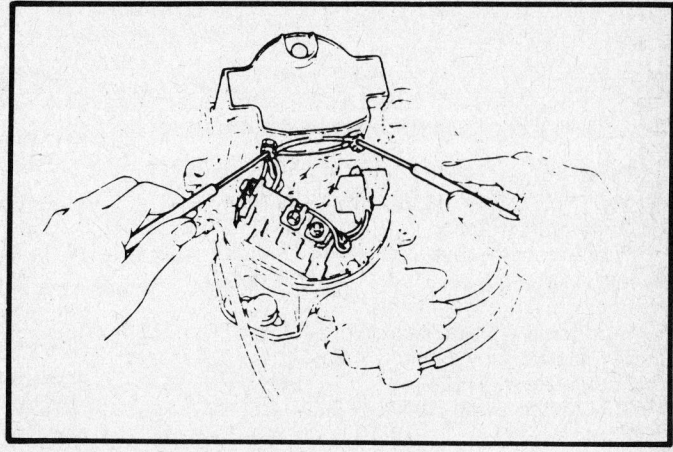
Measuring primary coil resistance

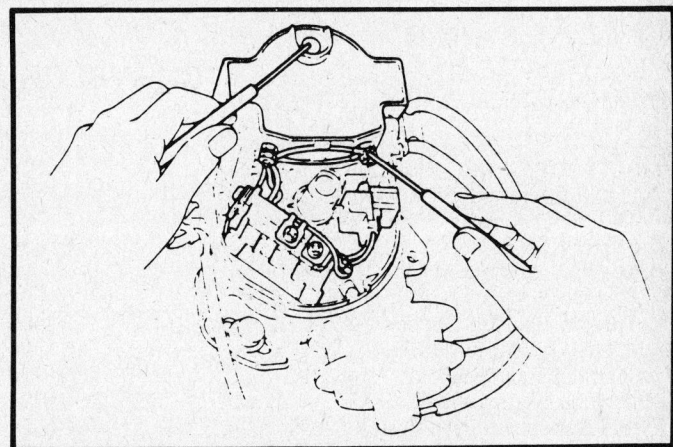
Measuring secondary coil resistance

IGNITION COIL

Testing

1. Disconnect the wiring, ignition coil and the high tension cable at the connector.
2. Measure the resistance between the positive and negative terminals. Primary coil resistance should be 0.4–0.5 ohms.
3. Measure the resistance between the positive terminal and the high tension terminal. Secondary coil resistance should be 7.5–10.4 kilo ohms.
4. If the measured resistance varies from the above specifications, replace defective components as necessary.

30-57

SECTION 31 — FUEL INJECTION

INDEX

GENERAL MOTORS

THROTTLE BODY INJECTION SYSTEM
- General Information 31-3
- Fuel Pressure Test 31-5
- Idle Air Control 31-5
- Fuel Pressure Regulator 31-5
- Curb Idle Air Rate, Adjust 31-6
- Throttle Position Sensor, Adjust 31-8
- Fuel Injectors R&R 31-9
- Fuel Meter, Body R&R 31-10
- Throttle Body 31-10

MULTI-PORT (MFI) AND SEQUENTIAL (SFI) INJECTION SYSTEM
- General Information 31-11
- Check Engine Light 31-14
- Fuel Pressure Test 31-14
- Fuel Injectors R&R 31-15
- Fuel Pressure Regulator R&R 31-15
- Idle Air Control Valve R&R 31-16
- Throttle Position Sensor R&R 31-16
- Oxygen Sensor R&R 31-16
- Idle Speed Adjust 31-17
- Electronic Control Module R&R 31-37

CHRYSLER CORPORATION

MULTI-PORT FUEL INJECTION SYSTEM
- General Information 31-20
- Trouble Diagnosis 31-24
- System Tests 31-25
- Mechanical Malfunctions 31-26
- Throttle Body 31-26
- Throttle Position Sensor 31-26
- Idle Speed Motor R&R 31-26
- Throttle Body R&R 31-27
- Oxygen Sensor R&R 31-27
- Idle Speed, Adjust 31-27
- Fuel Pressure Test 31-27
- Ignition Timing, Adjust 31-27

- Air Aspirator System 31-27

THROTTLE BODY INJECTION SYSTEM
- General Information 31-27
- Turbo Multi-Point System Schematic 31-30
- Trouble Diagnosi 31-31
- System Tests 31-32
- Mechanical Malfunctions 31-33
- Throttle Body R&R 31-33
- Pressure Regulator R&R 31-33
- Throttle Position Sensor R&R 31-34
- Idle Speed Motor R&R 31-34

FORD MOTOR COMPANY

THROTTLE BODY FUEL INJECTION SYSTEM
- Components
  - Fuel Charging Assembly 31-34
  - Fuel Pressure Regulator 31-34
  - Fuel Rail 31-34
  - Fuel Injectors 31-35
- Fuel Delivery System 31-35
  - Fuel Pump R&R 31-35
  - Fuel Filters 31-36
- Manifold Charging Temperature Sensor 31-36
- Trouble Diagnosis 31-38
- Wiring Diagram 31-37

EFI-EECIV PORT FUEL INJECTION SYSTEM
- General Information 31-38

- Components and Operation 31-38
- Fuel Injectors 31-38
- Air System 31-39
- Component Servicing 31-40
- Trouble Diagnosis 31-41

CENTRAL FUEL INJECITON (CFI) SYSTEM
- General Information 31-45
- Fuel Delivery System 31-47
- Electronic Control Ssytem 31-48
- Engine Sensors 31-48
- On-Car Services 31-49
- Component Removal and Installation 31-50
- Wiring Diagram 31-52

SECTION 31

Fuel Injection

GM THROTTLE BODY INJECTION

General Information

All 1982 and later USA cars equipped with the Pontiac 4-151, the 1.8L OHC or the 2.0L OHV engine use a single bore, throttle body fuel injection unit. All Canadian 4-151s retain the 2 bbl carburetors. The 1982 and later Corvette equipped with the V8 350 and the 1982 and later Camaro and Firebird equipped with the V8 305 engine use a pair of single bore throttle body injection units.

In this throttle body system, a single fuel injector mounted at the top of the throttle body sprays fuel down through the throttle valve and into the intake manifold. The throttle body resembles a carburetor in appearance but does away with much of the carburetor's complexity (choke system and linkage, power valves, accelerator pump, jets, fuel circuits, etc.), replacing these with the electrically operated fuel injector.

The injector is actually a solenoid which when activated lifts a pintle valve off its seat, allowing the pressurized (10 psi) fuel behind the valve to spray out. The nozzle of the injector is designed to atomize the fuel for complete air/fuel mixture.

The activating signal for the injector originates with the Electronic

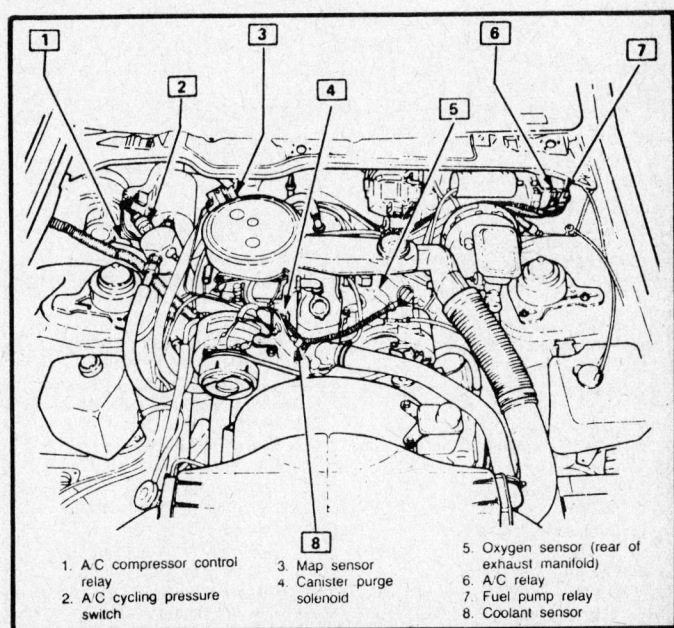

1. A/C compressor control relay
2. A/C cycling pressure switch
3. Map sensor
4. Canister purge solenoid
5. Oxygen sensor (rear of exhaust manifold)
6. A/C relay
7. Fuel pump relay
8. Coolant sensor

Engine component locations—4 cyl. 151 cu. in. engine

Control Module (ECM), which monitors engine temperature, throttle position, vehicle speed and several other engine-related conditions then continuously updates injector opening times in relation to the information given by these sensors.

The throttle body is also equipped with an idle air control motor. The idle air control motor operates a pintle valve at the side of the throttle body. When the valve opens it allows air to bypass the throttle, which provides the additional air required to idle at elevated speeds when the engine is cold. The idle air control motor also compensates for accessory loads and changing engine friction during break-in. The idle speed control motor is controlled by the ECM.

Fuel pressure for the system is provided by an in-tank fuel pump. The pump is a two-stage turbine designed powered by a DC motor. It is designed for smooth, quiet operation, high flow and fast priming. The design of the fuel inlet reduces the possibility of vapor lock under hot fuel conditions. The pump sends fuel forward through the fuel line to a stainless steel high-flow fuel filter mounted on the engine. From the filter the fuel moves to the throttle body. The fuel pump inlet is located in a reservoir in the fuel tank which insures a constant supply of fuel to the pump during hard cornering and on steep inclines. The

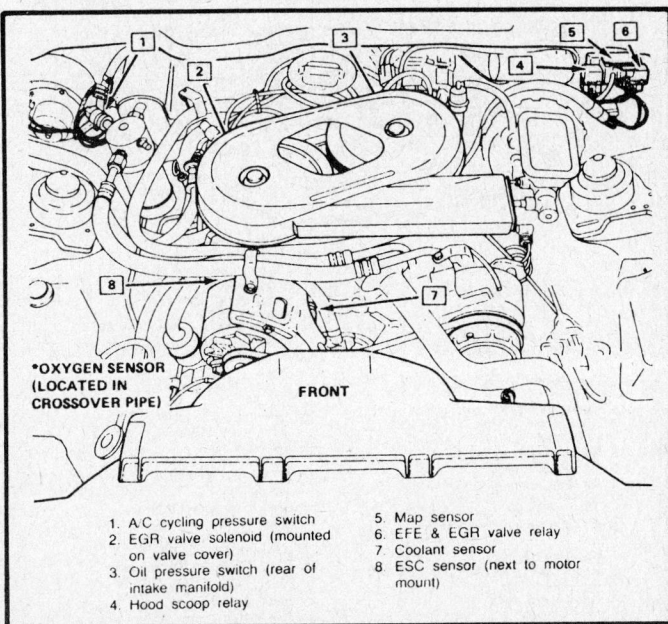

1. A/C cycling pressure switch
2. EGR valve solenoid (mounted on valve cover)
3. Oil pressure switch (rear of intake manifold)
4. Hood scoop relay
5. Map sensor
6. EFE & EGR valve relay
7. Coolant sensor
8. ESC sensor (next to motor mount)

Engine component locations—8 cyl. 305 cu. in. engine

31-3

SECTION 31: FUEL INJECTION
GM THROTTLE BODY INJECTION

system malfunctions occur, the diagnostic "check engine" light in the instrument panel will light, alerting the driver to the need for service.

Since both idle speed and mixture are controlled by the ECM on this system, no adjustments are necessary.

CROSS FIRE INJECTION

The 400 electronic fuel injection system is a computer controlled system that uses a pair of throttle body injection units, which are mounted on a single cover. The throttle body injection unit is the same unit as used in the other GM single TBI system. Each TBI unit feeds the cylinders on the opposite side of the engine and this is how the name cross fire injection came about. The sub-assemblies of the fuel system are the fuel supply system, throttle body injector units (TBI), idle air control system (IAC), electronic control module (ECM), data sensors and emission controls. The fuel is supplied to the engine through the electronically pulsed (timed) injector valves located in the throttle bodies. The ECM controls the amount of fuel metered through the injector vales, based on the engine demand and efficiency information.

NOTE: Most of the adjustments for the dual throttle body injection system are the same as the single throttle body injection system. They will just have to be performed twice.

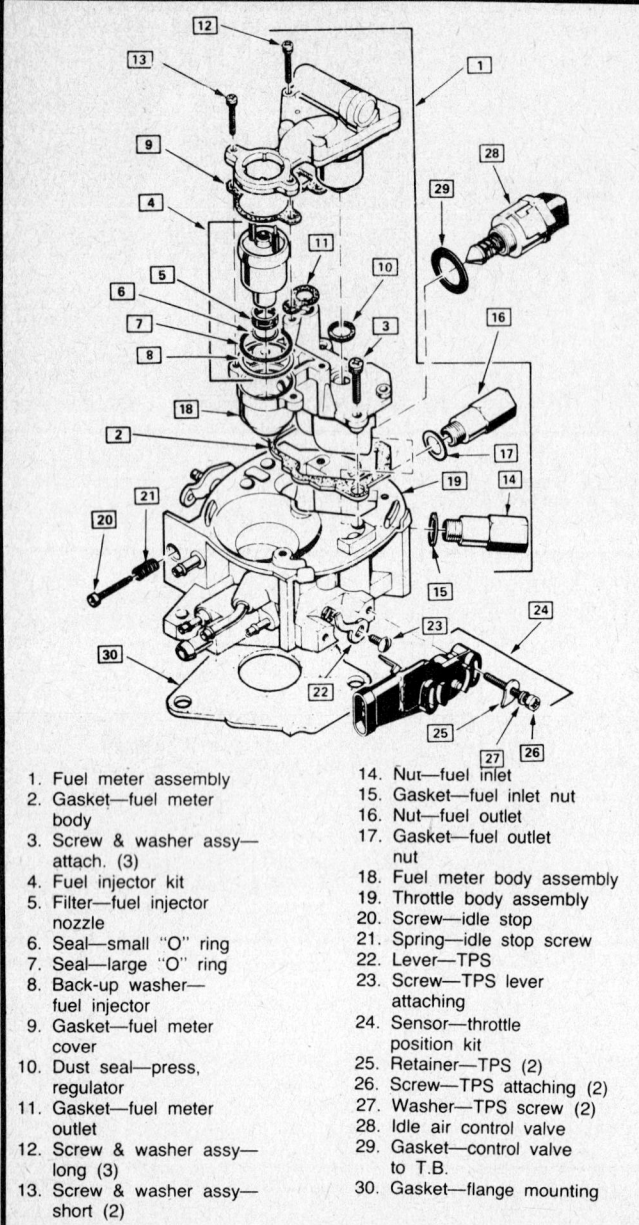

1. Fuel meter assembly
2. Gasket—fuel meter body
3. Screw & washer assy—attach. (3)
4. Fuel injector kit
5. Filter—fuel injector nozzle
6. Seal—small "O" ring
7. Seal—large "O" ring
8. Back-up washer—fuel injector
9. Gasket—fuel meter cover
10. Dust seal—press, regulator
11. Gasket—fuel meter outlet
12. Screw & washer assy—long (3)
13. Screw & washer assy—short (2)
14. Nut—fuel inlet
15. Gasket—fuel inlet nut
16. Nut—fuel outlet
17. Gasket—fuel outlet nut
18. Fuel meter body assembly
19. Throttle body assembly
20. Screw—idle stop
21. Spring—idle stop screw
22. Lever—TPS
23. Screw—TPS lever attaching
24. Sensor—throttle position kit
25. Retainer—TPS (2)
26. Screw—TPS attaching (2)
27. Washer—TPS screw (2)
28. Idle air control valve
29. Gasket—control valve to T.B.
30. Gasket—flange mounting

Exploded view of GM single throttle body injection unit.

fuel pump is controlled by a fuel pump relay, which in turn receives its signal from the ECM. A fuel pressure regulator inside the throttle body maintains fuel pressure at 10 psi and routes unused fuel back to the fuel tank through a fuel return line. On the dual throttle body system, a fuel pressure compensator is used on the second throttle body assembly to compensate for a momentary fuel pressure drop between the two units. This constant circulation of fuel through the throttle body prevents component overheating and vapor lock.

The electronic control module (ECM), also called a microcomputer, is the brain of the fuel injection system. After receiving inputs from various sensing elements in the system, the ECM commands the fuel injector, idle air control motor, EST distributor, torque converter clutch and other engine actuators to operate in a pre-programmed manner to improve driveability and fuel economy while controlling emissions. The sensing elements update the computer every tenth of a second for general information and every 12.5 milli-seconds for critical emissions and driveability information.

The ECM has limited system diagnostic capability. If certain

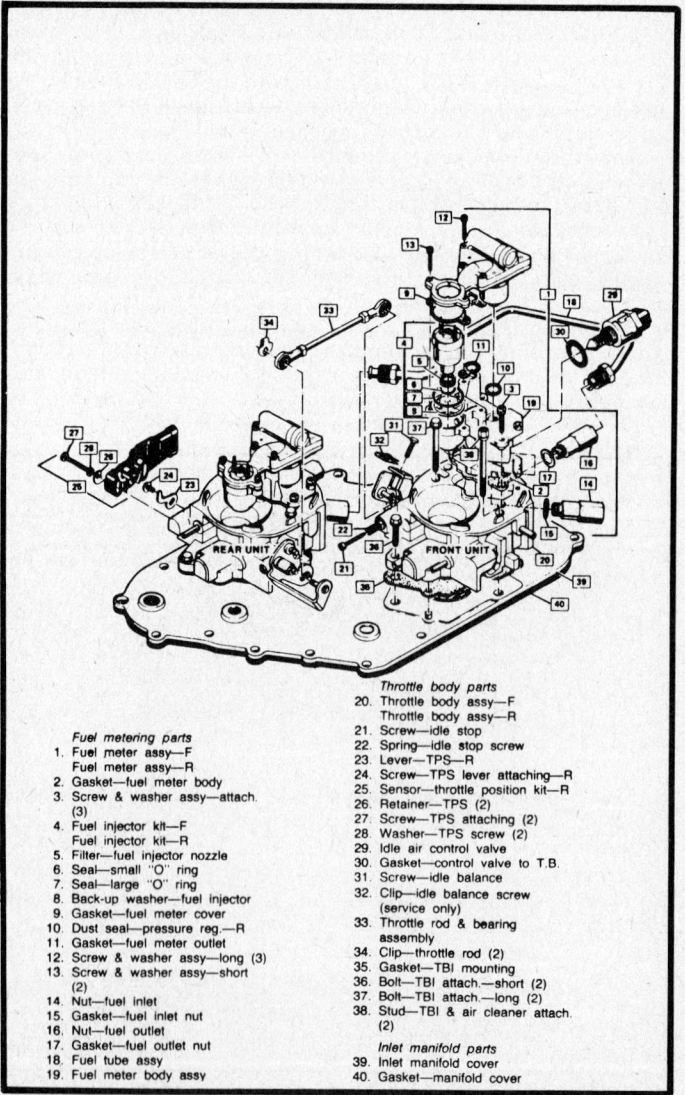

Fuel metering parts
1. Fuel meter assy—F
   Fuel meter assy—R
2. Gasket—fuel meter body
3. Screw & washer assy—attach. (3)
4. Fuel injector kit—F
   Fuel injector kit—R
5. Filter—fuel injector nozzle
6. Seal—small "O" ring
7. Seal—large "O" ring
8. Back-up washer—fuel injector
9. Gasket—fuel meter cover
10. Dust seal—pressure reg.—R
11. Gasket—fuel meter outlet
12. Screw & washer assy—long (3)
13. Screw & washer assy—short (2)
14. Nut—fuel inlet
15. Gasket—fuel inlet nut
16. Nut—fuel outlet
17. Gasket—fuel outlet nut
18. Fuel tube assy
19. Fuel meter body assy

Throttle body parts
20. Throttle body assy—F
    Throttle body assy—R
21. Screw—idle stop
22. Spring—idle stop screw
23. Lever—TPS—R
24. Screw—TPS lever attaching—R
25. Sensor—throttle position kit—R
26. Retainer—TPS (2)
27. Screw—TPS attaching (2)
28. Washer—TPS screw (2)
29. Idle air control valve
30. Gasket—control valve to T.B.
31. Screw—idle balance
32. Clip—idle balance screw (service only)
33. Throttle rod & bearing assembly
34. Clip—throttle rod (2)
35. Gasket—TBI mounting
36. Bolt—TBI attach.—short (2)
37. Bolt—TBI attach.—long (2)
38. Stud—TBI & air cleaner attach. (2)

Inlet manifold parts
39. Inlet manifold cover
40. Gasket—manifold cover

Exploded view of GM dual throttle body assembly

FUEL INJECTION
GM THROTTLE BODY INJECTION
SECTION 31

TOOLS

The system does not require special tools for diagnosis. A tachometer, test light, ohmmeter, digital voltmeter with 10 megohms impedance, vacuum pump, vacuum gauge and jumper wires are required for diagnosis. A test light or voltmeter must be used when specified in the procedures.

FUEL SYSTEM PRESSURE TEST

Primary Procedure

CAUTION

To reduce the risk of fire and personal injury, it is necessary to relieve the fuel system pressure before servicing fuel system components.

1. Remove the fuel pump fuse from the fuse block.
2. Crank the engine. The engine will run until it runs out of fuel. Crank the engine again for 3 seconds making sure it is out of fuel.
3. Turn the ignition off and replace the fuse.
4. Remove the air cleaner. Plug the thermal vacuum port on the throttle body.
5. Remove the fuel line between the throttle body and filter.
6. Install a fuel pressure gauge between the throttle body and fuel filter. The gauge should be able to register at least 15 psi.
7. Start the car. Observe the fuel pressure reading. It should be 9-13 psi.

NOTE: Before removing the fuel pressure gauge the fuel system must be depressurized.

8. Reinstall the parts in the reverse order of removal.

IDLE AIR CONTROL ASSEMBLY

Removal and Installation

1. Remove the air cleaner.
2. Disconnect the electrical connection from the idle air control assembly.
3. Using a 1¼ in. wrench, remove the idle air control assembly from the throttle body.

NOTE: Before installing a new assembly, measure the distance that the conical valve is extended. This measurement should be made from motor housing to end of cone. It should be greater than 1.259 in. If the cone is extended too far damage to the motor may result.

On cars with manual transmissions, idle speed will be controlled when operating temperature is reached. For automatic transmission cars, engage the transmission in drive after operating temperature is reached. This will allow the ECM to control idle speed.

FUEL PRESSURE REGULATOR/COMPENSATOR

Removal and Installation

1. Remove air cleaner.
2. Disconnect electrical connector to injector by squeezing on two tabs and pulling straight up.
3. Remove five screws securing fuel meter cover to fuel meter body. Notice location of two short screws during removal.

CAUTION

Do not remove the four screws securing the pressure regulator to the fuel meter cover. The fuel pressure regulator includes a large spring under heavy tension which, if accidentally released, could cause personal injury. The fuel meter cover is only serviced as a complete assembly and includes the fuel pressure regulator preset and plugged at the factory.

NOTE: DO NOT immerse the fuel meter cover (with pressure regulator) in any type of cleaner. Immersion in cleaner will damage the internal fuel pressure regulator diaphragms and gaskets.

4. Installation is the reverse of removal.

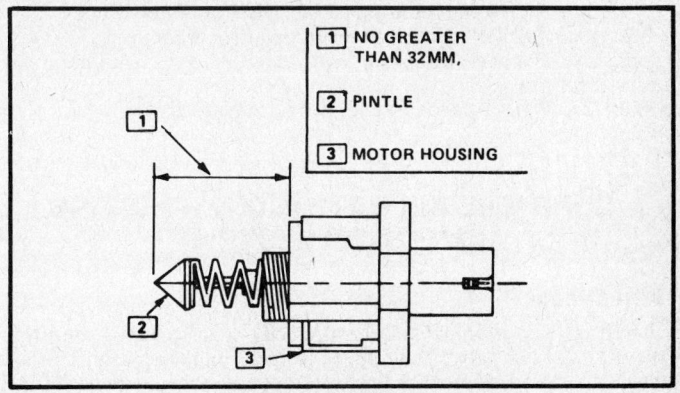
Idle air control valve installation check

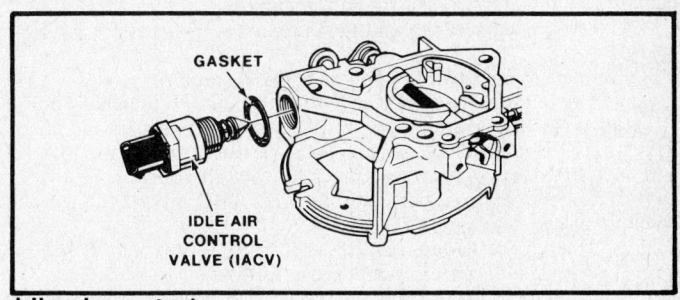
Idle air control

MINIMUM AIR RATE (2.5L ENGINE)

Adjustment

This adjustment should be performed only when the throttle body parts have been replaced or required to do so by the T.P.S. adjustment. Engine should be at normal operating temperature before making adjustment.

1. Remove air cleaner and air cleaner to TBI gasket. Plug vacuum port on TBI unit for THERMAC.

NOTE: On vehicles equipped with a tamper resistant plug covering the minimum air adjustment screw, the throttle body unit must be removed from the engine to remove the plug.

2. Remove T.V. cable from throttle control bracket to allow access to minimum air adjustment screw.
3. Connect a tachometer to engine.
4. Start engine, transmission in Park (Neutral on manual transmission) and allow engine RPM to stabilize.
5. Install tool J-33047, or equivalent, and idle air passage of throttle body. Be certain that tool seats fully in passage and no air leaks exist.
6. Using appropriate screwdriver, turn minimum air screw until engine RPM is 500 ± 25 in neutral with automatic transaxle, and 775 ± 25 in neutral with manual transaxle.

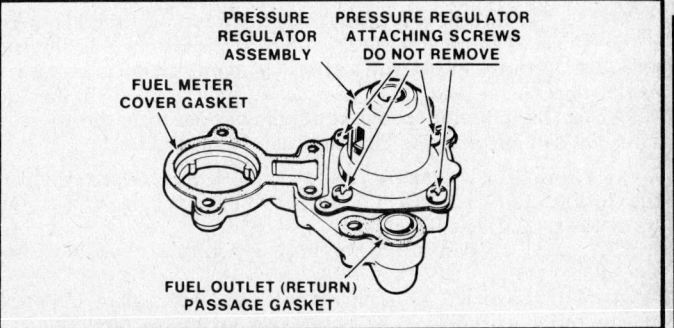
Fuel pressure regulator

31-5

SECTION 31: FUEL INJECTION
GM THROTTLE BODY INJECTION

7. Stop engine and remove tool J-33047 from throttle body.
8. Reinstall T.V. cable into throttle control bracket.
9. Use silicone sealant or equivalent to cover minimum air adjustment screw.
10. Install air cleaner gasket and air cleaner to engine.

CURB IDLE AIR RATE (5.0L CROSSFIRE INJECTION SYSTEM)

Adjustment

The throttle position of each throttle body must be balanced so that the throttle plates are synchronized to open simultaneously. This is a checking and adjustment procedure adjustment should be performed only when a throttle body has been replaced or when checking procedure indicates an adjustment is required.

1. Remove air cleaner and air cleaner to TBI unit for THERMAC.
2. Start engine and allow engine RPM to stabilize.
3. Plug idle air passages of each throttle body with plugs J-33047, or equivalent. Be certain plugs are fully seated in passages and no air leaks exist. Engine RPM should decrease to curb idle air rate. If engine RPM does not decrease, check for vacuum leak.
4. Remove cap from ported tube on rear TBI unit and connect the vacuum gauge.
5. Observe the gauge, reading should be approximately .45 in. Hg. If adjustment is required proceed as follows:
   a. Remove tamper resistant screw covering the minimum air adjustment screw if required.
   b. Adjust minimum air adjustment screw to obtain approximately .45 in. Hg.
   c. After adjustment, proceed to front TBI unit.
6. Remove gauge from rear TBI unit and re-install cap on ported tube.
7. Remove cap from ported tube on front TBI unit and connect vacuum gauge. Reading should also be approximately .45 in. Hg. If adjustment is required proceed as follows:
   a. Locate split lever screw on throttle linkage. If screw is welded for tamper resistance, break weld and install new screw with thread locking compound applied.
   b. Adjust split lever screw to obtain approximately .45 in. Hg.
8. Remove gauge from front TBI unit and re-install cap on ported tube.
9. If both readings are approximately .45 in. Hg., no adjustment is required; throttle plates are synchronized.
10. Stop engine and remove idle air passage plugs.
11. Check T.P.S. voltage and adjust if required.
12. Install air cleaner gaskets, connect vacuum line to TBI unit and install air cleaner.

IDLE SPEED ADJUSTMENT

1.8 and 2.5 Liter Engines

NOTE: The throttle stop screw that is used to adjust the idle speed of the vehicle, is adjusted to specifications at the factory. The throttle stop screw is then covered with a steel plug to prevent the unnecessary readjustment in the field. If it is necessary to gain access to the throttle stop screw, the following procedure will allow access to the throttle stop screw without removing the TBI unit from the manifold.

1. Using a small punch or equivalent mark over the center line of the throttle stop screw. Drill a 5/32 in. diameter hole through the casting to the hardened steel plug.
2. Using a 1/16 in. diameter punch or equivalent punch out the steel plug.
3. With the vehicle in the park position, the parking brake applied and the drive wheels blocked, remove the air cleaner and plug the thermac vacuum port.
4. Remove the transmission T.V. cable from the throttle control bracket in order to gain access to the minimum air adjustment screw (automatic transmission only).
5. Connect a tachometer to the engine and disconnect the idle air control motor connector.
6. Start the engine and let the engine reach normal operating temperature and the rpm to stabilize.
7. Install special tool J-3307 or equivalent in the idle air passage of the throttle body. Be sure to seat the tool in the air passage until it is bottomed out and no air leaks exist.
8. Using a #20 torx head bit or equivalent, turn the throttle stop screw until the rpm is 700 ± 25 rpm for the 1.8 liter and 500 ± 25 rpm for the 2.5 liter with an automatic transaxle, 800 ± 25 rpm for the 1.8 liter and 775 ± 25 rpm for the 2.5 liter with a manual transaxle.
9. Re-install the transmission T.V. cable into the throttle control bracket (automatic transmissions only).

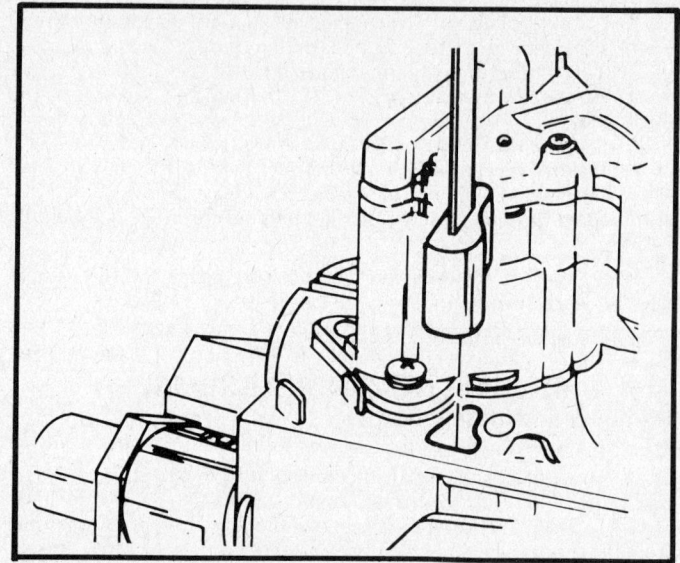

Special tool #J-33047 installation

10. Shut down the engine and remove the special tool or equivalent from the throttle body.
11. Reconnect the idle air control motor connector and seal the hole drilled through the throttle body housing with silicone sealant or equivalent.
12. Check the throttle position sensor voltage as outlined in this section and reinstall the air cleaner and thermac vacuum line.

2.0 Liter Engine

NOTE: The idle speed adjustment procedure for the 2.0 liter engine is basically the same as the 1.8 and 2.5 liter engine, with the exception of the following steps.

1. To install special tool J-33047 or equivalent, it may be necessary to remove the air cleaner isolator as follows:
   a. Remove the two isolator attaching bolts and isolator.
   b. Reinstall the bolts with .079 in. (2 mm) or thicker washers under each bolt head.
   c. After adjustment has been made, reinstall the isolator without the washers and torque the bolts to 17 ft. lbs. (23 N·m).
2. On vehicles equipped with automatic transaxles, place the selector in the drive position before making adjustment, the idle speed is 650 ± 25 rpm.

NOTE: The idle speed is controlled by the ECM and the idle adjustment is only necessary when the idle speed control or the throttle body has been replaced. Before adjusting the idle speed on the 4.1 liter engines, record, diagnosis and repair and clear all trouble codes in the ECM memory.

FUEL INJECTION
GM THROTTLE BODY INJECTION
SECTION 31

4.1 and 6.0 Liter Engines

1. With the engine at normal operating temperature and the A/C off, remove the air cleaner and check and adjust the engine timing as necessary.
2. Turn off all the electrical accessories and position the steering wheel to dead center and place the transmission selector lever in the park position.
3. With the idle speed control (ISC) plunger fully retracted and not touching the throttle lever, check the idle speed RPM. Idle speed for the 4.1L is 450 and the 6.0L is 375 rpm.
4. Disconnect the four wire connector at the distributor and check the throttle position sensor adjustment (as outlined in this section).
5. With the ISC motor fully retracted and the throttle against the stop screw, turn the ISC plunger adjusting screw to obtain a 0.060 in. (1.5 mm) gap between the throttle lever and the plunger. Disconnect all test equipment and reconnect all harness connectors.
6. This adjustment procedure could have recorded intermittent trouble codes in the DFI computer. So after the adjustment has been made and all the connectors reinstalled, the codes must be cleared.

4.3 Liter Engine

1. Leave the idle air control (IAC) valve connected and ground the diagnostic lead.
2. Turn the ignition switch to the on position, but do not start the engine. Wait for at least 30 seconds.
3. With the ignition switch still in the on position, disconnect the IAC electrical connector.
4. Remove the ground from the diagnostic lead and start the engine. Let the engine reach normal operating temperature.
5. Apply the parking brake and block the drive wheels. With the engine in the drive position adjust the idle set screw to obtain 550 ± 50 rpm.
6. Turn the ignition off and reconnect the IAC motor connector.
7. Adjust the throttle position sensor (as outlined in this section) to .525 ± .075 volts.
8. Recheck the adjustment settings, start the engine and check for proper idle operation.

5.7 Liter Engine (CFI)

1. Remove the air cleaner and gaskets, plug the thermal vacuum port on the rear of the throttle body. Remove the plugs covering both throttle stop screws, one for each throttle body.
2. With a small punch or equivalent mark over the center line of the throttle stop screw. Drill a 5/32 in. diameter hole through the casting to the hardened steel plug.
3. Using a 1/16 in. diameter punch or equivalent, punch out the steel plug.
4. With the vehicle in the park position, the parking brake applied and the drive wheels blocked, connect a tachometer and disconnect the idle air control (IAC) electrical connectors. Plug the idle air passages of each throttle body.
5. Before starting the engine make sure both throttle valves are slightly opened. Start the engine and let it run till it reaches normal operating temperature.
6. Place the transmission selector in the D position and check to see if the engine rpm decreases below the curb idle speed. If the rpm does not decrease check for vacuum leaks.
7. Remove the cap from the ported tube on the rear throttle body and connect a water manometer. Adjust the throttle stop screw on the rear throttle body to obtain approximately six inches of water on the manometer.
8. If six inches of water cannot be obtained on the manometer, check the throttle stop screw on the front unit and make sure it is not limiting the throttle rod movement. Remove the manometer and reinstalll the cap on the ported tube.
9. Remove the cap from the ported tube on the front throttle body and connect the manometer. The reading on the manometer should be six inches of water. If there is an adjustment required, locate the throttle synchronizing screw on the throttle linkage of the front unit.

10. If the screw is welded in place, grind the weld off of the screw collar and the throttle lever (be sure to block the throttle lever so it cannot move).
11. Remove the screw and collar and install the new screw, being sure to apply thread sealing compound or equivalent to the screw.
12. Adjust the screw to obtain six inches of water on the manometer. Remove the manometer and install the cap on the ported tube.
13. Adjust the throttle stop screw on the rear throttle body to set the idle speed (475 rpm) turn the ignition off and place the transmission selector in the park position.
14. Adjust the front throttle stop screw to obtain .005 in. (.13 mm) between the throttle stop screw and the throttle lever tang. Remove the idle air passage plugs and reconnect the idle air control electrical connectors.
15. Start the engine and wait for the engine rpm to decrease, the

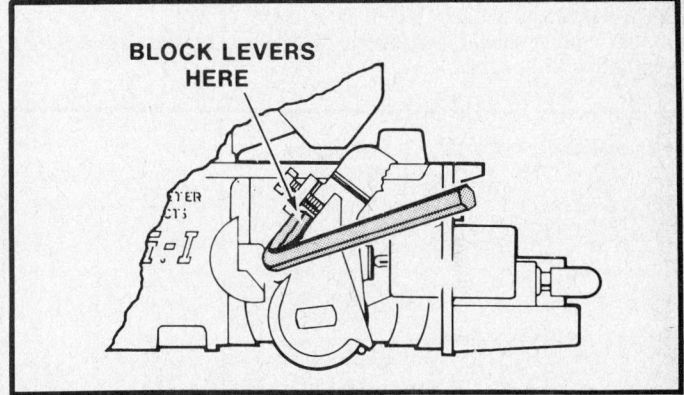

Throttle synchronizing collar removal

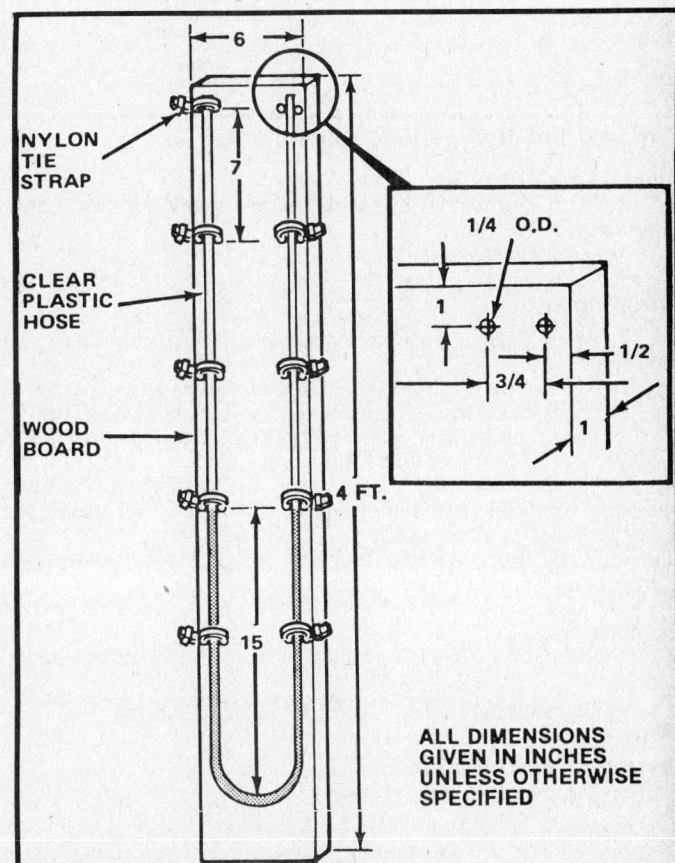

Typical fabricated manometer

SECTION 31: FUEL INJECTION
GM THROTTLE BODY INJECTION

rpm will decrease when the idle air control assembly closes the air passages. Check the throttle position sensor voltage.

16. Install the air cleaner gaskets, reconnect the vacuum line to the throttle body and install the air cleaner. Reset the IAC motors by driving the vehicle at 30 mph.

THROTTLE POSITION SENSOR (TPS)

Inspection

Throttle position sensor adjustment should be checked after minimum air adjustment is completed.
1. Remove air cleaner.
2. Disconnect T.P.S. harness from T.P.S.
3. Using three jumper wires connect T.P.S. harness to T.P.S.
4. With ignition ON, engine stopped, use a digital voltmeter to measure voltage between terminals B and C.
5. Voltage should read .525 ± .075 volts. 5.0L engine and .820 + .250 volts 2.5L engine.

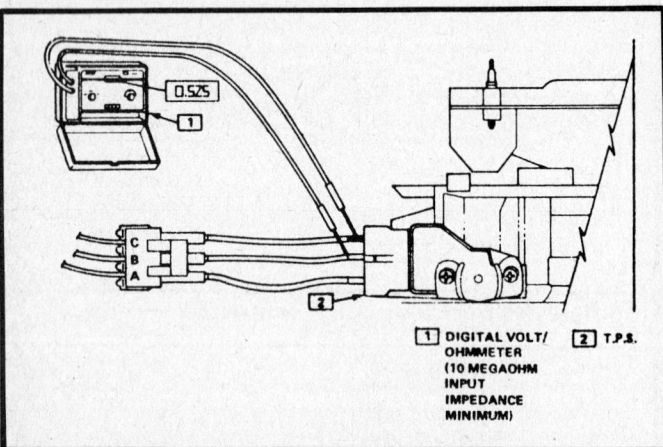

Throttle position sensor adjustment

6. Adjust T.P.S. if required.
7. With ignition OFF, remove jumpers and connect T.P.S. harness to T.P.S.
8. Install air cleaner.

Adjustment

1. After installing TPS to throttle body, install throttle body unit to engine.
2. Remove EGR valve and heat shield from engine.
3. Using three six inch jumpers, connect TPS harness to TPS.
4. With ignition ON, engine stopped, use a digital voltmeter to measure voltage between TPS terminals B and C.
5. Loosen two TPS attaching screws and rotate throttle position sensor to obtain a voltage reading of .525 ± .075 volts 5.0L engine and .820 ± .250 volts 2.5L engine.
6. With ignition OFF, remove jumpers and reconnect TPS harness to TPS.
7. Install EGR valve and heat shield to engine, using new gasket as necessary.
8. Install air cleaner gasket and air cleaner to throttle body unit.

THROTTLE POSITION SENSOR

Removal and Installation

The Throttle Position Sensor (TPS) is an electrical unit and must not be immersed in any type of liquid solvent or cleaner. The TPS is factory adjusted and the retaining screws are spot welded in place to retain the critical setting. With these considerations, it is possible to clean the throttle body assembly without removing the TPS if care is used. Should TPS replacement be required however, proceed using the following steps:

1. Invert throttle body and place on a clean, flat surface.
2. Using a 5/16 in. drill bit, drill completely through two (2) TPS screw access holes in base of throttle body to be sure of removing the spot welds holding TPS screws in place.
3. Remove the two TPS attaching screws, lockwashers, and retainers. Then, remove TPS sensor from throttle body. DISCARD SCREWS. New screws are supplied in service kits.
4. If necessary, remove screw holding Throttle Position Sensor actuator lever to end of throttle shaft.
5. Remove the Idle Air Control assembly and gasket from the throttle body.

NOTE: DO NOT immerse the Idle Air Control motor in any type of cleaner and it should always be removed before throttle body cleaning. Immersion in cleaner will damage the IAC assembly. It is replaced only as a complete assembly.

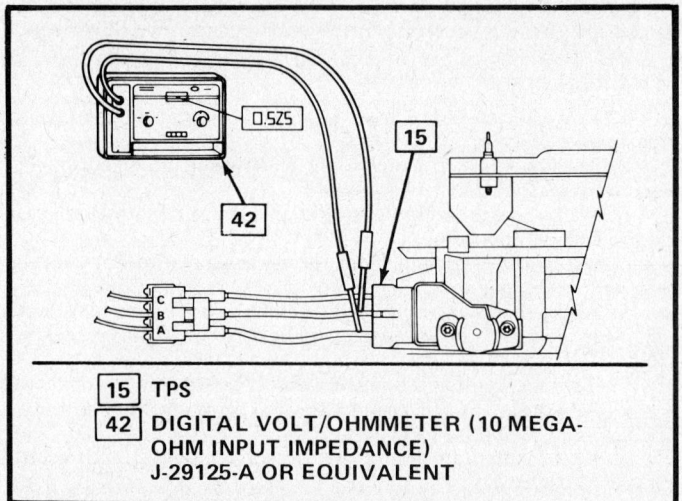

| 15 | TPS |
| 42 | DIGITAL VOLT/OHMMETER (10 MEGA-OHM INPUT IMPEDANCE) J-29125-A OR EQUIVALENT |

Checking the TPS adjustment

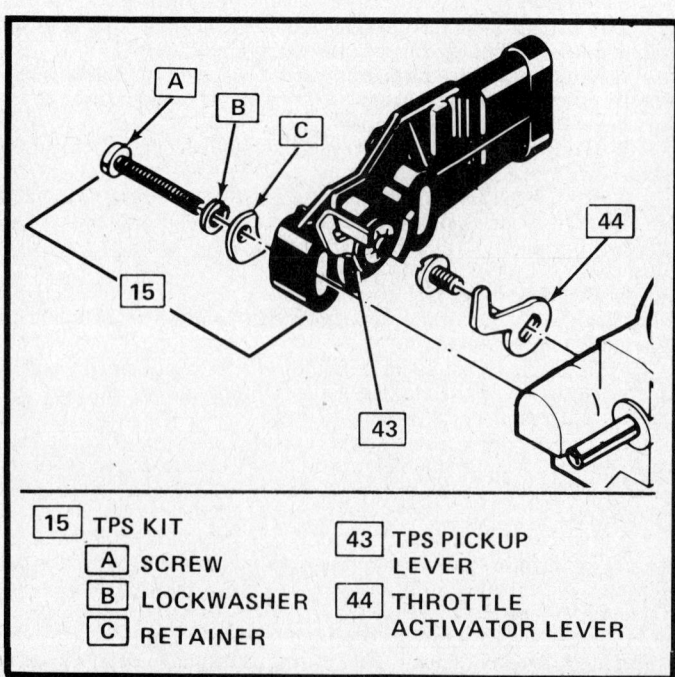

15	TPS KIT	43	TPS PICKUP LEVER
A	SCREW		
B	LOCKWASHER	44	THROTTLE ACTIVATOR LEVER
C	RETAINER		

Typical TPS sensor

31-8

FUEL INJECTION
GM THROTTLE BODY INJECTION
SECTION 31

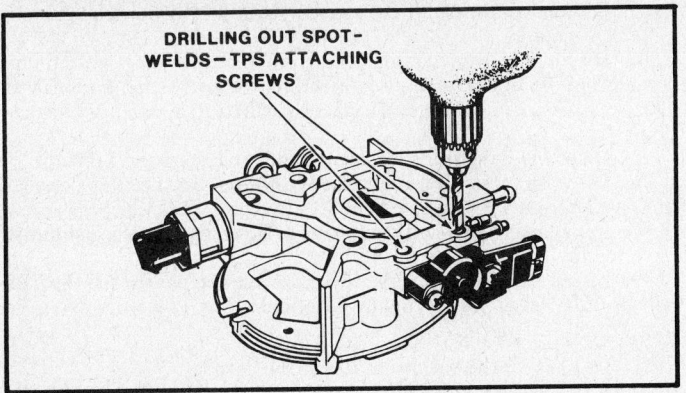

Spot weld removal

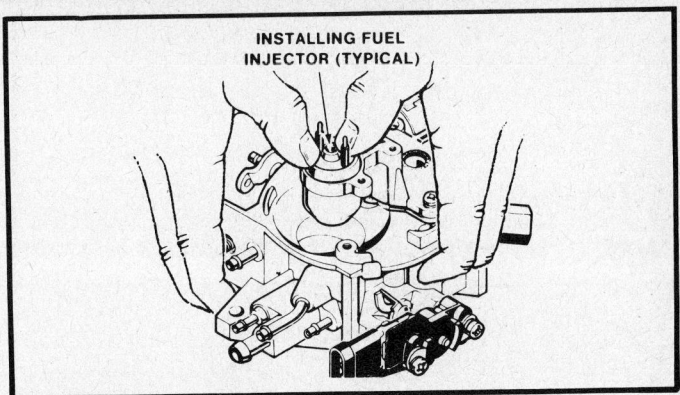

Fuel injector installation

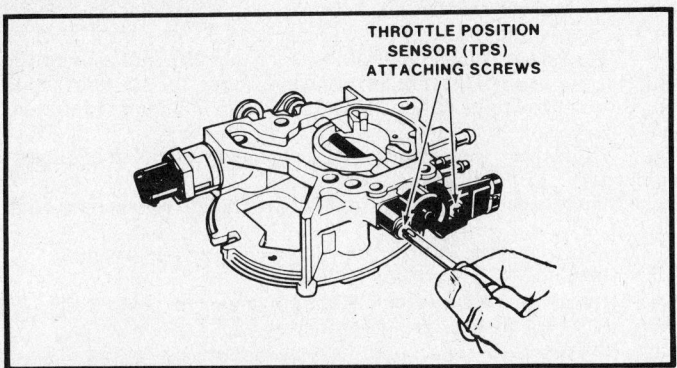

Removing TPS attaching screw

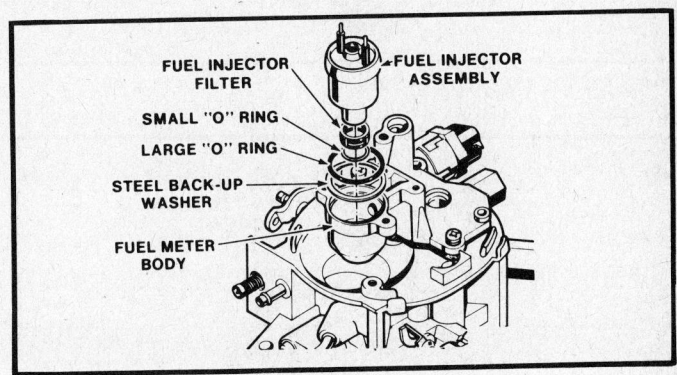

Fuel injector components

Further disassembly of the throttle body is not required for cleaning purposes. The throttle valve screws are permanently staked in place and should not be removed. The throttle body is serviced as a complete assembly.

Assembly

1. Place throttle body assembly on holding fixture to avoid damaging throttle valve.
2. Using a new sealing gasket, install Idle Air Control motor in throttle body. Tighten motor securely.

NOTE: DO NOT overtighten to prevent damage to valve.

3. If removed, install Throttle Position Sensor actuator lever by aligning flats on lever with flats on end of shaft. Install retaining screw and tighten securely.

NOTE: Install Throttle Position Sensor after completion of assembly of the throttle body unit. Use thread locking compound supplied in service kit on attaching screws.

FUEL INJECTOR

Removal and Installation

1. Remove the air cleaner.
2. Disconnect injector electrical connector by squeezing two tabs together and pulling straight up.

NOTE: Use care in removing to prevent damage to the electrical connector pins on top of the injector, injector fuel filter and nozzle. The fuel injector is only serviced as a complete assembly. Do not immerse it in any type of cleaner.

3. Remove the fuel meter cover.
4. Using a small awl, gently pry up on the injector evenly and carefully remove it.

5. Installation is the reverse of removal, with the following recommendations.

Use Dexron® II transmission fluid to lubricate all O-rings. Install the steel backup washer in the recess of the fuel meter body. Then, install the O-ring directly above backup washer, pressing the O-ring into the recess.

NOTE: Do not attempt to reverse this procedure and install backup washer and O-ring after injector is located in the cavity. To do so will prevent seating of the O-ring in the recess.

FUEL METER COVER

Removal and Installation

1. Remove the five fuel meter cover screws and lockwashers holding the cover on the fuel meter body.
2. Lift off fuel meter cover (with fuel pressure regulator assembly).
3. Remove the fuel meter cover gaskets.

CAUTION

Do not remove the four screws securing the pressure regulator to the fuel meter cover. The fuel pressure regulator includes a large spring under heavy tension which, if accidentally released, could cause personal injury. The fuel meter cover is only serviced as a complete assembly and includes the fuel pressure regulator preset and plugged at the factory.

NOTE: Do not immerse the fuel meter cover (with pressure regulator) in any type of cleaner. Immersion in cleaner will damage the internal fuel pressure regulator diaphragms and gaskets.

4. Remove the sealing ring (dust seal from the fuel meter body).
5. Installation is the reverse of removal.

31-9

SECTION 31: FUEL INJECTION
GM THROTTLE BODY INJECTION

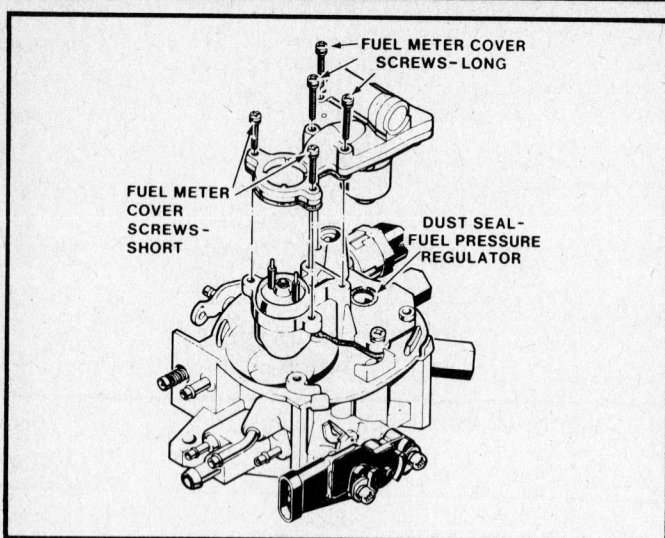

Fuel meter cover removal

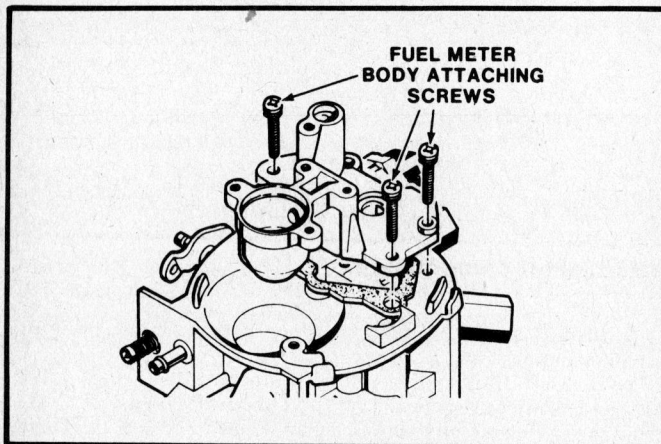

Removing fuel meter body assembly

FUEL METER BODY

Removal and Installation

1. Remove the fuel inlet and outlet nuts and gaskets from fuel meter body.
2. Remove three screws and lockwashers. Remove fuel meter body from throttle body assembly.

NOTE: The air cleaner stud must have been removed previously.

3. Remove fuel meter body insulator gasket.
4. Installation is the reverse of removal.

THROTTLE BODY

Removal and Installation

SINGLE UNIT—FOUR CYLINDER ENGINE
Refer to the "Rear Unit-V8 Engine" procedure which follows. Disregard Steps 6 and 7 of that procedure, instead, just disconnect the fuel feed and return lines.

FRONT UNIT—V8 ENGINE
1. Disconnect the battery cables at the battery.
2. Remove the air cleaner assembly, noting the connection points of the vacuum lines.
3. Disconnect the electrical connectors at the injector and the idle air control motor.
4. Disconnect the vacuum line from the TBI unit, noting the connection points. During installation, refer to the underhood emission control information decal for vacuum line routing information.
5. Disconnect the transmission detent cable from the TBI unit.
6. Disconnect the fuel inlet (feed) and fuel balance line connections at the front TBI unit.
7. Disconnect the throttle control rod between the two TBI units.
8. Unbolt and remove the TBI unit.
9. Installation is the reverse of the previous steps. Torque the TBI bolts to 120-168 in. lbs. during installation.

REAR UNIT—V8 ENGINE
1. Disconnect the battery cables at the battery.
2. Remove the air cleaner assembly, noting the connection points of the vacuum lines.
3. Disconnect the electrical connectors at the injector, idle air control motor, and throttle position sensor.
4. Disconnect the vacuum lines from the TBI unit, noting the connection points. During installation, refer to the underhood emission control information decal for vacuum line routing information.
5. Disconnect the throttle and cruise control (if so equipped) cables at the TBI unit.
6. Disconnect the fuel return and balance line connections from the rear TBI unit.
7. Disconnect the throttle control rod between the two units.
8. Unbolt and remove the TBI unit.
9. Installation is the reverse of the previous steps. Torque the TBI bolts to 120-168 in. lbs. during installation.

Disassembly
When servicing the single TBI unit on four cylinder engines, follow all steps except those specified "front unit." "Rear Unit" steps DO apply.

— CAUTION —
Use extreme care when handling the TBI unit to avoid damage to the swirl plates located beneath the throttle valve.

NOTE: If both TBI units are to be disassembled, DO NOT mix parts between either unit.

1. Remove the fuel meter cover assembly (five screws). Remove the gaskets after the cover has been removed. The fuel meter cover assembly is serviced only as a unit. If necessary, the entire unit must be replaced.

— CAUTION —
DO NOT remove the four screws which retain the pressure regulator (rear unit) or pressure compensator (front unit). There is a spring beneath the cover which is under great pressure. If the cover is accidentally released, personal injury could result.
Do not immerse the fuel meter cover in any type of cleaning solvent.

2. Remove the foam dust seal from the meter body of the rear unit.
3. Remove the fuel injector using a pair of small pliers as follows:
   a. Grasp the injector collar between the electrical terminals.
   b. Carefully pull the injector upward in a twisting motion.
   c. If the injectors are to be removed from both TBI units, mark them so that they may be installed in their original units.
4. Remove the filter from the base of the injector by rotating it back and forth.
5. Remove the O-ring and the steel washer from the top of the fuel meter body, then remove the small O-ring from the bottom of the injector cavity.
6. Remove the fuel inlet and outlet nuts (and gaskets) from the fuel meter body.
7. Remove the fuel meter body assembly and gasket from the throttle body assembly (three screws).
8. For the rear TBI unit only: Remove the throttle position sensor (TPS) from the throttle body (two screws). If necessary, remove the

FUEL INJECTION
GM THROTTLE BODY INJECTION
SECTION 31

screw which holds the TPS actuator lever to the end of the throttle shaft.

9. Remove the idle air control motor from the throttle body.

CAUTION

Because the TPS and idle air control motors are electrical units, they must not be immersed in any type of cleaning solvent.

Assembly

NOTE: During assembly, replace the gaskets, injector washer, O-rings, and pressure regulator dust seal with new parts.

1. Install the idle air control motor in the throttle body, using a new gasket. Torque the retaining screws to 13 ft. lbs.

NOTE: DO NOT overtighten the screws.

2. For the rear TBI unit only: If removed, install the TPS actuator lever by aligning the flats of the lever and the shaft. Install and tighten the retaining screw.

3. Install the fuel meter body on the throttle body, using a new gasket. Also, apply thread locking compound to the three fuel meter body screws according to the chemical manufacturers instructions. Torque the screws to 35 in. lbs.

4. Install the fuel inlet and outlet nuts, using new gaskets. Torque the nuts to 260 in. lbs.

5. Carefully twist the fuel filter onto the injector base.

6. Lubricate the new O-rings with Dexron II® transmission fluid.

7. Install the small O-ring onto the injector, pressing it up against the fuel filter.

8. Install the steel washer into the injector cavity recess of the fuel meter body. Install the large O-ring above the steel washer, in the cavity recess. The O-ring must be flush with the fuel meter body surface.

9. Using a pushing/twisting motion, carefully install the injector. Center the nozzle O-ring in the bottom of the injector cavity and align the raised lug on the injector base with the notch in the fuel meter body cavity. Make sure the injector is seated fully in the cavity. The electrical connections should be parallel to the throttle shaft of the throttle body.

10. For the rear TBI unit only: Install the new pressure regulator dust seal into the fuel meter body recess.

11. Install the new full meter cover and fuel outlet passage gaskets on the fuel meter cover.

12. Install the fuel meter cover assembly, using thread locking compound on the five retaining screws. Torque the screws to 28 in. lbs. Note that the two short screws must be installed alongside the fuel injector (one screw each side).

13. For the rear TBI unit only: With the throttle valve in the closed (idle) position, install the TPS but do not tighten the attaching screws. The TPS lever must be located ABOVE the tang on the throttle actuator lever.

14. Install the TBI unit(s) as previously outlined and adjust the throttle position sensor.

Cleaning and Inspection

The throttle body injection parts, except as noted below, should be cleaned in a cold immersion-type cleaner such as Carbon X (X-55) or its equivalent.

NOTE: The throttle position sensor, idle air control motor, fuel meter cover (with pressure regulator), fuel injector, fuel filter, rubber parts, diaphragms, etc., should NOT be immersed in cleaner as they will swell, harden or distort.

1. Thoroughly clean all metal parts and blow dry with shop air. Make sure all fuel passages are free of burrs and dirt.

2. Inspect casting mating surfaces for damage that could affect gasket sealing.

3. Check, repair or replace parts as required, if the following problems are encountered:
   a. Flooding
     (1) Inspect large and small fuel injector O-rings for damage such as cuts, distortion, etc. Check that the steel backup washer is located beneath the large (upper) O-ring. Use new O-rings when reinstalling injector.
     (2) Inspect fuel injector fuel filter for damage, cleanliness, etc. Clean or replace as necessary.
     (3) If the fuel injector continues to supply fuel with injector electrical connections removed, replace injector as required.
   b. Hesitation
     (1) Inspect fuel injector fuel filter for being plugged, dirty, etc. Clean or replace as necessary.
     (2) If improper fuel inlet and outlet pressure readings, are noted check for restricted passages or inoperative fuel pressure regulator. Repair or replace as required.

CAUTION

DO NOT remove the four screws securing the fuel pressure regulator to the fuel meter cover. The fuel pressure regulator includes a large spring under heavy tension, which if accidentally released, could cause personal injury. The fuel meter cover is only serviced as a complete assembly and includes the fuel pressure regulator preset and plugged at the factory.

---

   c. Hard Starting—Poor Cold Operation (See items listed under "Hesitation," above.)
   d. Rough Idle
     (1) Inspect large and small fuel injector O-rings for damage such as cuts, distortion, etc. Check that the steel backup washer is located beneath the large (upper) O-ring. Use new O-rings when reinstalling injector.
     (2) Inspect fuel injector fuel filter for damage, cleanliness, etc. Clean or replace as necessary.
     (3) If the fuel injector continues to supply fuel with injector electrical connections removed, replace injector as required.

GENERAL MOTORS MULTI-PORT (MFI) AND SEQUENTIAL (SFI) FUEL INJECTION SYSTEMS

General Information

On 1984 and later non-turbocharged models, a new multi-port fuel injection (MFI) system is available. The MFI system is controlled by an electronic control module (ECM) which monitors engine operations and generates output signals to provide the correct air/fuel mixture, ignition timing and engine idle speed control. Input to the control unit is provided by an oxygen sensor, coolant temperature sensor, detonation sensor, hot film air mass sensor and throttle position sensor. The ECM also receives information concerning engine rpm, road speed, transmission gear position, power steering and air conditioning.

On turbocharged models, a sequential port fuel injection system (SFI) is used for more precise fuel control. With SFI, metered fuel is timed and injected sequentially through six Bosch injectors into individual cylinder ports. Each cylinder receives one injection per working cycle (every two revolutions), just prior to the opening of the intake valve. The main difference between the two types of fuel injection systems is the manner in which fuel is injected. In the multiport system, all injectors work simultaneously, injecting half the fuel charge each engine revolution. The control units are different for SFI and MFI systems, but most other components are similar. In addition, the SFI system incorporates a new Computer Controlled Coil Ignition system that uses an electronic coil module that replaces

SECTION 31

FUEL INJECTION
GM MULTI-PORT (MFI) AND SEQUENTIAL (SFI) SYSTEMS

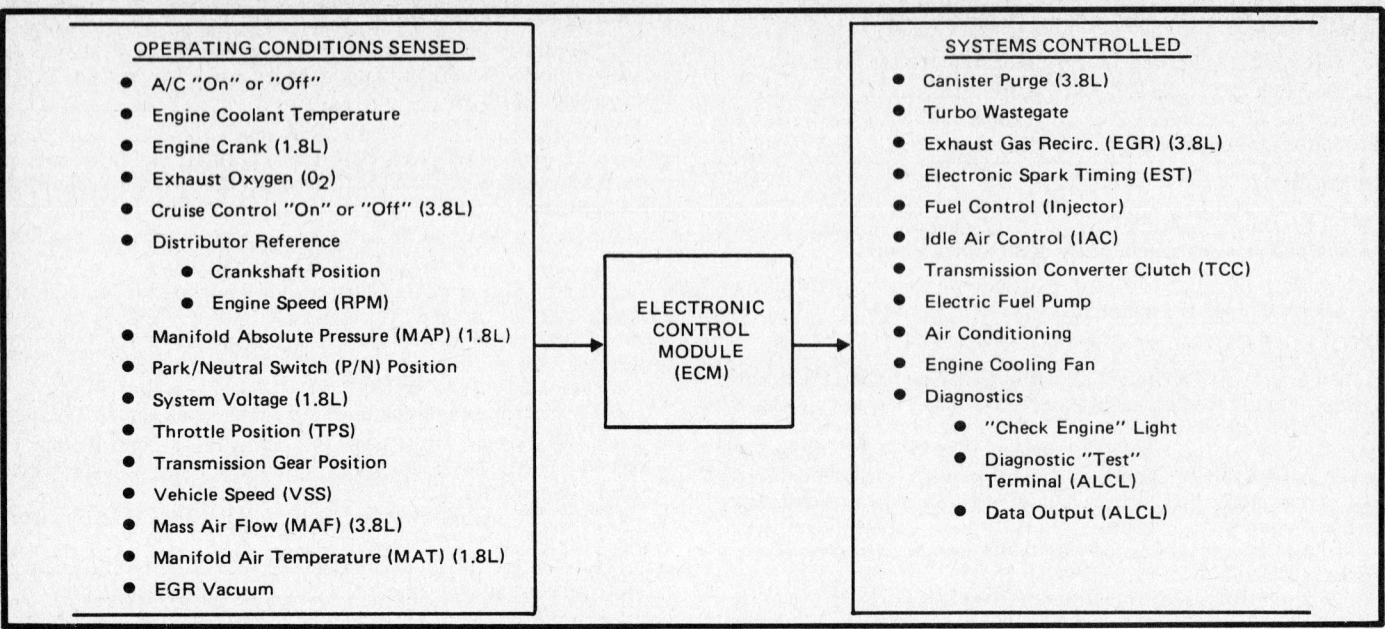

Schematic of GM MFI annd SFI injection system operation. Not all systems are used on all engines

the conventional distributor and coil used on most engines. An electronic spark control (ESC) is used to adjust the spark timing.

Both systems are Bosch injectors, one at each intake port, rather than the single injector found on the earlier throttle body system. The injectors are mounted on a fuel rail and are activated by a signal from the electronic control module. The injector is a solenoid-operated valve which remains open depending on the width of the electronic pulses (length of the signal) from the ECM; the longer the open time, the more fuel is injected. In this manner, the air/fuel mixture can be precisely controlled for maximum performance with minimum emissions.

Fuel is pumped from the tank by a high pressure fuel pump, located inside the fuel tank. It is a positive displacement roller vane pump. The impeller serves as a vapor separator and pre-charges the high pressure assembly. A pressure regulator maintains 28-36 psi (28-50 psi on turbocharged engines) in the fuel line to the injectors and the excess

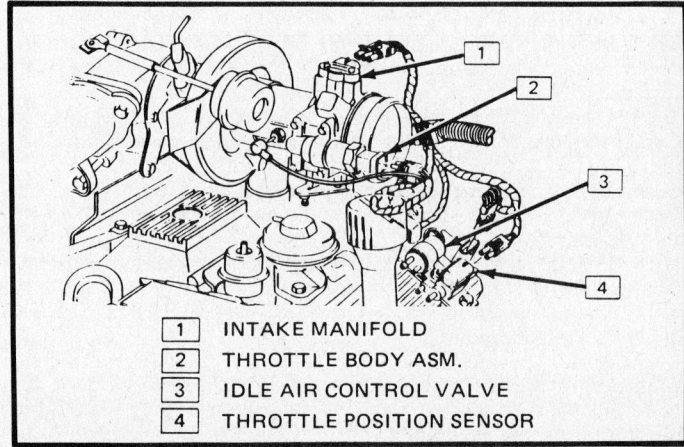

Throttle position sensor—1.8L engine

fuel is fed back to the tank. On MFI systems, a fuel accumulator is used to dampen the hydraulic line hammer in the system created when all injectors open simultaneously.

The Mass Air Flow Sensor is used to measure the mass of air that is drawn into the engine cylinders. It is located just ahead of the air throttle in the intake system and consists of a heated film which measures the mass of air, rather than just the volume. A resistor is used to measure the temperature of the incoming air and the air mass sensor maintains the temperature of the film at 75 degrees above ambient temperature. As the ambient (outside) air temperature rises, more energy is required to maintain the heated film at the higher temperature and the control unit uses this difference in required energy to calculate the mass of the incoming air. The control unit uses this information to determine the duration of fuel injection pulse, timing and EGR.

The throttle body incorporates an idle air control (IAC) that provides for a bypass channel through which air can flow. It consists of an orifice and pintle which is controlled by the ECM through a stepper motor. The IAC provides air flow for idle and allows additional air during cold start until the engine reaches operating temperature. As the engine temperature rises, the opening through which air passes is slowly closed.

The throttle position sensor (TPS) provides the control unit with information on throttle position, in order to determine injector pulse

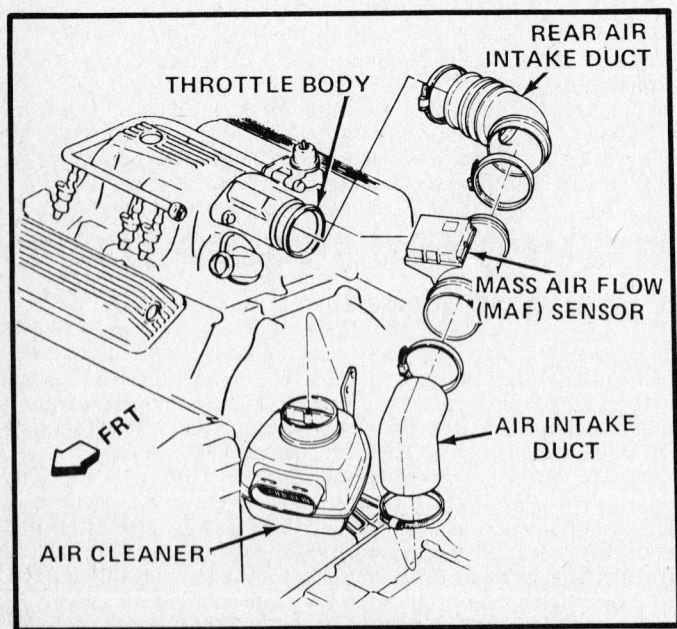

Mass air flow sensor installation—3.8L V6 shown

FUEL INJECTION
GM MULTI-PORT (MFI) AND SEQUENTIAL (SFI) SYSTEMS
SECTION 31

width and hence correct mixture. The TPS is connected to the throttle shaft on the throttle body and consists of a potentiometer with one end connected to a 5 volt source from the ECM and the other to ground. A third wire is connected to the ECM to measure the voltage output from the TPS which changes as the throttle valve angle is changed (accelerator pedal moves). At the closed throttle position, the output is low (approximately .4 volts); as the throttle valve opens, the output increases to a maximum 5 volts at wide open throttle (WOT). The TPS can be misadjusted open, shorted, or loose and if it is out of adjustment, the idle quality or WOT performance may be poor. A loose TPS can cause intermittent bursts of fuel from the injectors and an unstable idle because the ECM thinks the throttle is moving. This should cause a trouble code to be set. Once a trouble code is set, the ECM will use a preset value for TPS and some vehicle performance may return. A small amount of engine coolant is routed through the throttle assembly to prevent freezing inside the throttle bore during cold operation.

TUNED PORT INJECTION (TPI)

This system is new for 1985 and can be found in the Camaro/Firebird with the 5.0 liter V8 engine and the Corvette with the 5.7 liter V8 engine. The introduction of this new TPI system to these engines has improved the torque and power from both engines. The induction system for the TPI is made up of large forward mounted air cleaners, a new mass airflow sensor, a cast aluminum throttle body assembly with dual throttle blades, a large extended cast aluminum plenum, individual aluminum tuned runners and a protruding dual fuel rail assembly with computer controlled injectors. The base plate is cast aluminum and incorporates the crossover portion of the tuned runners. The base plate also serves as a mounting for the fuel injectors. The individual aluminum runners are designed to provide the best tuning or frequency of air pulses within the runners and for the optimum throttle response throughout the driving range, thus the name Tuned Port Injection. The runners are selected by length and size so as to take advantage of the air pulses set up by the opening and closing of the intake valves. The high pressure pulses result in denser air at each intake valve, and timing the pressure pulses to occur during the valve open period forces more air into the combustion chamber, which results in a more efficient cylinder charging and improved volumetric efficiency.

The eight fuel injectors fire at the same time, once each crankshaft revolution. During the first injection, fuel is sprayed at the base of the closed intake valve, during the second injection, fuel is sprayed into the air stream entering the combustion chamber. The fuel from the first injection vaporizes from the heat of the intake valve, and the fuel vapors are drawn into the combustion chamber along with the air when the valve opens to charge the cylinder. The regulated pressure of the fuel being injected in the 5.0 liter V8 engine is 44 psi and the 37 psi in the 5.7 liter V8 engine. This fuel pressure is regulated constantly, or, as the manifold vacuum changes, the regulator adjusts the fuel pressure to maintain a constant drop in pressure across the injectors.

When the signals are received by the computer from the mass airflow sensor and the engine coolant temperature sensor, the computer will search its pre-programmed information to determine the pulse width of the fuel injectors required to match the input signals. The computer now, based on the engine rpm, signals the injectors to release the required amount of fuel. The computer makes mass airflow sensor readings and fuel requirement calculations every 12.5 milliseconds.

The new mass airflow sensor and the individual fuel injectors are made by Bosch and supplied by General Motors. The new mass airflow sensor contains a hot-wire sensing unit, which is made up of an electronic balanced bridge network, and measures the mass of air entering the induction system. When ever current is supplied to the sensor, the bridge is energized and the sensing hot-wire is heated. When the air enters the mass airflow sensor it passes over and cools the hot wire. As the hot wire is cooled down its resistance is changed and additional current is then required, so as to maintain the resistance and keep the bridge network balanced. The increase in current is then

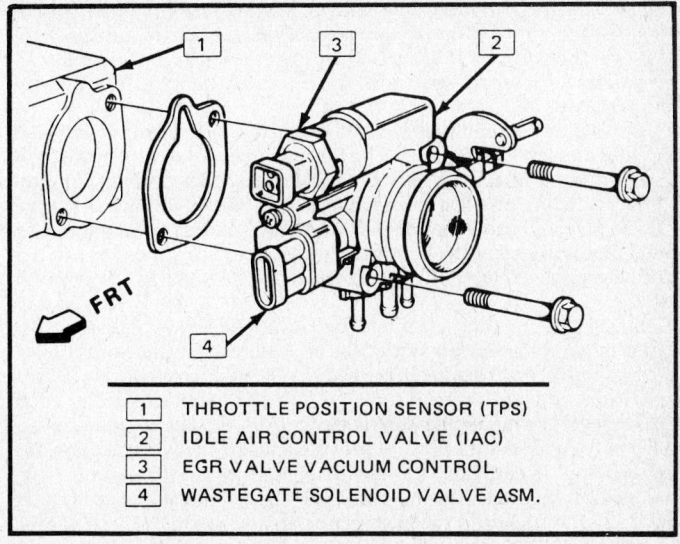

1. THROTTLE POSITION SENSOR (TPS)
2. IDLE AIR CONTROL VALVE (IAC)
3. EGR VALVE VACUUM CONTROL
4. WASTEGATE SOLENOID VALVE ASM.

Throttle position sensor—3.8L turbocharged engine

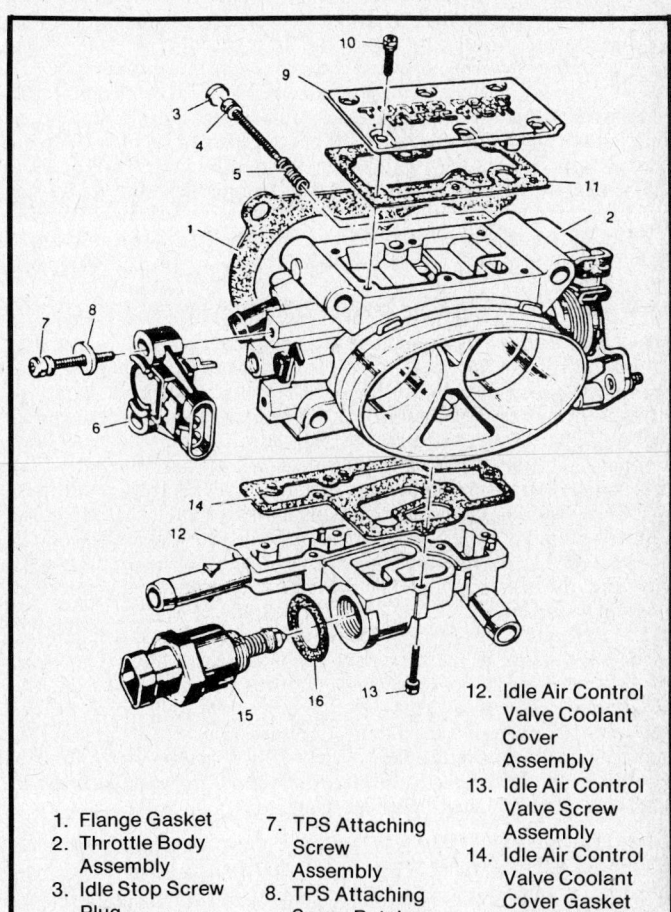

1. Flange Gasket
2. Throttle Body Assembly
3. Idle Stop Screw Plug
4. Idle Stop Screw Assembly
5. Idle Stop Screw Spring
6. Throttle Position Sensor (TPS)
7. TPS Attaching Screw Assembly
8. TPS Attaching Screw Retainer
9. Clean Air Cover
10. Clean Air Cover Screw Assembly
11. Clean Air Cover Gasket
12. Idle Air Control Valve Coolant Cover Assembly
13. Idle Air Control Valve Screw Assembly
14. Idle Air Control Valve Coolant Cover Gasket to Throttle Body
15. Idle Air Control Valve Assembly
16. Idle Air Control Valve Assembly Gasket

Exploded view of the TPI throttle body

FUEL INJECTION
GM MULTI-PORT (MFI) AND SEQUENTIAL (SFI) SYSTEMS

supplied to the computer as a voltage signal. The computer in turn converts the voltage signal into grams per second of airflow and because the system measures in grams of air, the changes in barometric pressure, altitude and humidity are automatically compensated.

The fuel rail assembly is located under the inlet plenum, between the right and left side runners. The fuel injectors (8) mount in the base plate and each injector is sealed with the use of an O-ring. The fuel injectors are mounted approximately 7/16 in. (110mm) from the intake valve and projects a cone-shaped spray with a 20° degree cone angle that is aimed at the base of the valve stem. The injectors are the pintle type, have electromagnetic solenoids, and operate on ignition voltage.

During cold starting, additional fuel is supplied by a cold start valve that is mounted in the left side of the base plate. The additional fuel is injected into a long passage in the base plate and fuel vapors are drawn out at low ambient temperatures (−20°F) through orifices to each intake port. During a cold starting situation, the engine requires an extremely rich air-fuel ratio to provide enough fuel vaporization for combustion. Because of the small amount of air drawn into the combustion chamber during cold starting cranking, the cold start valve supplies fuel into the base plate passage where only the vapors are drawn into the combustion chamber. This prevents flooding or fuel fouling the spark plugs that would occur if the fuel needed for a cold start situation was supplied only from the main injectors. This cold start valve is controlled by a type of coolant temperature sensor called the thermo-time switch, and also by the starter cranking circuit. When the ignition key is turned to crank the engine, the thermal-time switch will heat up until it reaches approximately 95°F at which time the switch will open and deenergize the cold start injector. The maximum time for the cold start injector to be energized is 12 seconds, with an engine temperature of −4°F or below. When the engine starts and the ignition key is released, the circuit is also de-energized. Except for the new mass airflow system, the new tuned runners and longer plenum assembly the rest of this TPI system is very similar to the multi-port fuel injection system.

CHECK ENGINE LIGHT

The "check engine" light on the instrument panel is used as a warning lamp to tell the driver that a problem has occurred in the electronic engine control system. When the self-diagnosis mode is activated by grounding the test terminal of the diagnostic connector, the check engine light will flash stored trouble codes to help isolate system problems. The electronic control module (ECM) has a memory that knows what certain engine sensors should be under certain conditions. If a sensor reading is not what the ECM thinks it should be, the control unit will illuminate the check engine light and store a trouble code in its memory. The trouble code incidates what circuit the problem is in, each circuit consisting of a sensor, the wiring harness and connectors to it and the ECM.

The Assembly Line Communications Link (ALCL) is a diagnostic connector located in the passenger compartment, usually under the left side of the instrument panel. It has terminals which are used in the assembly plant to check that the engine is operating properly before shipment. Terminal B is the diagnostic test terminal and Terminal A is the ground. By connecting the two terminals together with a jumper wire, the diagnostic mode is activated and the control unit will begin to flash trouble codes using the check engine light.

NOTE: Some models have a "Service Engine Soon" light instead of a "Check Engine" display.

When the test terminal is grounded with the key ON and the engine stopped, the ECM will display code 12 to show that the system is working. The ECM will usually display code 12 three times, then start to display any stored trouble codes. If no trouble codes are stored, the ECM will continue to display code 12 until the test terminal is disconnected. Each trouble code will be flashed three times, then code 12 will display again. The ECM will also energize all controlled relays and solenoids when in the diagnostic mode to check function.

When the test terminal is grounded with the engine running, it will cause the ECM to enter the Field Service Mode. In this mode, the service engine soon light will indicate whether the system is in Open or Closed Loop operation. In open loop, the light will flash 2½ times per second; in closed loop, the light will flash once per second. In closed loop, the light will stay out most of the time if the system is too lean and will stay on most of the time if the system is too rich.

NOTE: The vehicle may be driven in the Field Service mode and system evaluated at any steady road speed. This mode is useful in diagnosing driveability problems where the system is rich or lean too long.

Trouble codes should be cleared after service is completed. To clear the trouble code memory, disconnect the battery for at least 10 seconds. This may be accomplished by disconnecting the ECM harness from the positive battery pigtail or by removing the ECM fuse.

CAUTION
The ignition switch must be OFF when disconnecting or reconnecting power to the ECM. The vehicle should be driven after the ECM memory is cleared to allow the system to readjust itself. The vehicle should be driven at part throttle under moderate acceleration with the engine at normal operating temperature. A change in performance should be noted initially, but normal performance should return quickly.

GM PORT INJECTION TROUBLE CODES

Trouble Code	Circuit
12	Normal operation
13	Oxygen sensor
14	Coolant sensor (low voltage)
15	Coolant sensor (high voltage)
21	Throttle position sensor (high voltage)
22	Throttle position sensor (low voltage)
24	Speed sensor
32	EGR vacuum control
33	Mass air flow sensor
34	Mass air flow sensor
42	Electronic spark timing
43	Electronic spark control
44	Lean exhaust
45	Rich exhaust
51	PROM failure
52	CALPAK
55	ECM failure

Fuel System Pressure Test

When the ignition switch is turned ON, the in-tank fuel pump is energized for as long as the engine is cranking or running and the control unit is receiving signals from the HEI distributor. If there are no reference pulses, the control unit will shut off the fuel pump within two seconds. The pump will deliver fuel to the fuel rail and injectors, then the pressure regulator where the system pressure is controlled to maintain 26-46 psi.

1. Connect pressure gauge J-34370-1, or equivalent, to fuel pressure test point on the fuel rail. Wrap a rag around the pressure tap to absorb any leakage that may occur when installing the gauge.

2. Turn the ignition ON and check that pump pressure is 34-40 psi. This pressure is controlled by spring pressure within the regulator assembly.

3. Start the engine and allow it to idle. The fuel pressure should drop to 28-32 psi due to the lower manifold pressure.

NOTE: The idle pressure will vary somewhat depending on barometric pressure. Check for a drop in pressure indicating regulator control, rather than specific values.

4. On turbocharged models, use a low pressure air pump to apply

FUEL INJECTION
GM MULTI-PORT (MFI) AND SEQUENTIAL (SFI) SYSTEMS
SECTION 31

air pressure to the regulator to simulate turbocharger boost pressure. Boost pressure should increase fuel pressure one pound for every pound of boost. Again, look for changes rather than specific pressures. The maximum fuel pressure should not exceed 46 psi.

5. If the fuel pressure drops, check the operation of the check valve, the pump coupling connection, fuel pressure regulator valve and the injectors. A restricted fuel line or filter may also cause a pressure drop. To check the fuel pump output, restrict the fuel return line and run 12 volts to the pump. The fuel pressure should rise to approximately 75 psi with the return line restricted.

CAUTION
Before attempting to remove or service any fuel system component, it is necessary to relieve the fuel system pressure.

Relieving Fuel System Pressure

1. Remove the fuel pump fuse from the fuse block.
2. Start the engine. It should run and then stall when the fuel in the lines is exhausted. When the engine stops, crank the starter for about three seconds to make sure all pressure in the fuel lines is released.
3. Replace the fuel pump fuse.

FUEL INJECTORS

Removal and Installation

Use care in removing the fuel injectors to prevent damage to the electrical connector pins on the injector and the nozzle. The fuel injector is serviced as a complete assembly only and should not be immersed in any kind of cleaner.

1. Relieve fuel system pressure.
2. Remove the injector electrical connections.
3. Remove the fuel rail.
4. Separate the injector from the fuel rail.
5. Installation is the reverse of removal. Replace the O-rings when installing injectors into intake manifold.

FUEL PRESSURE REGULATOR

Removal and Installation

1. Relieve fuel system pressure.
2. Remove pressure regulator from fuel rail. Place a rag around the base of the regulator to catch any spilled fuel.
3. Installation is the reverse of removal.

COLD START VALVE (TPI)

Removal and Installation

1. Relieve the fuel system pressure as previously outlined.
2. Provide a clean container to catch any fuel, or wrap some clean rags around the electrical connections.

CAUTION
Be careful not to let any dirt enter the fuel system and take precautions to avoid the risk of fire.

---

3. Disconnect the electrical connector from the cold start valve and clean off any dirt or grease from the valve.
4. Remove the fuel line from the valve and be careful because the valve body is plastic. After removing the fuel hose from the valve, inspect the hose for cracks and/or leaks.
5. Remove the two fasteners holding the cold start valve in the base plate, remove the valve and discard the old O-ring or gasket.
6. Installation is the reverse order of the removal procedure. After installation make sure the system is tight and free from leaks and replace the rubber sealing ring, or gasket and hose clamp if necessary.

NOTE: The fuel injection systems are very susceptible to dirt in the system. Be sure that all components are clean and free from dirt and grease before reinstalling them.

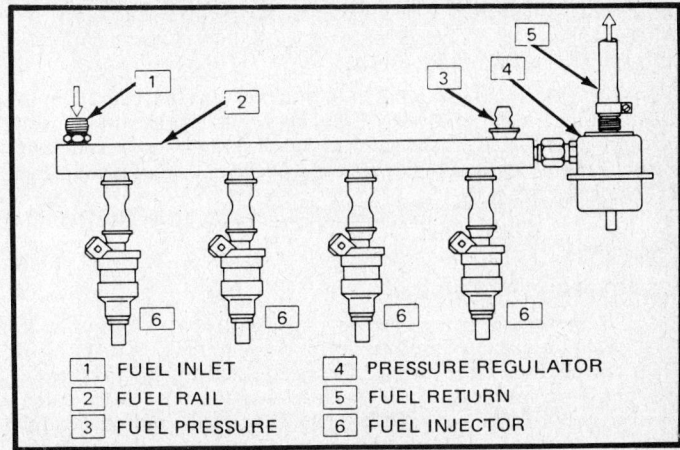

1	FUEL INLET	4	PRESSURE REGULATOR
2	FUEL RAIL	5	FUEL RETURN
3	FUEL PRESSURE	6	FUEL INJECTOR

Fuel rail assembly on 1.8L engine

Test

1. Remove the screws holding the valve in the intake manifold. DO NOT disconnect the fuel lines or electrical connector.
2. Place the cold start valve in a container to catch fuel. Wrap a clean rag around the mouth of the container.
3. Operate the starter and note the injection time. Valve should spray fuel for 1-12 seconds if the coolant temperature is lower than approximately 35°C (95°F). Above this temperature, no drip or spray should be noted.
4. If the cold start valve sprays continuously or drips, replace it.
5. If the cold start valve fails to function below 35°C (95°F), replace it.

NOTE: Perform this test as quickly as possible. Avoid energizing the injector for any length of time.

6. Disconnect the cold start valve and hook up a test light across its connector. Ground the No. 1 coil terminal and run the starter. The light should glow for several seconds and then go out. If not, replace

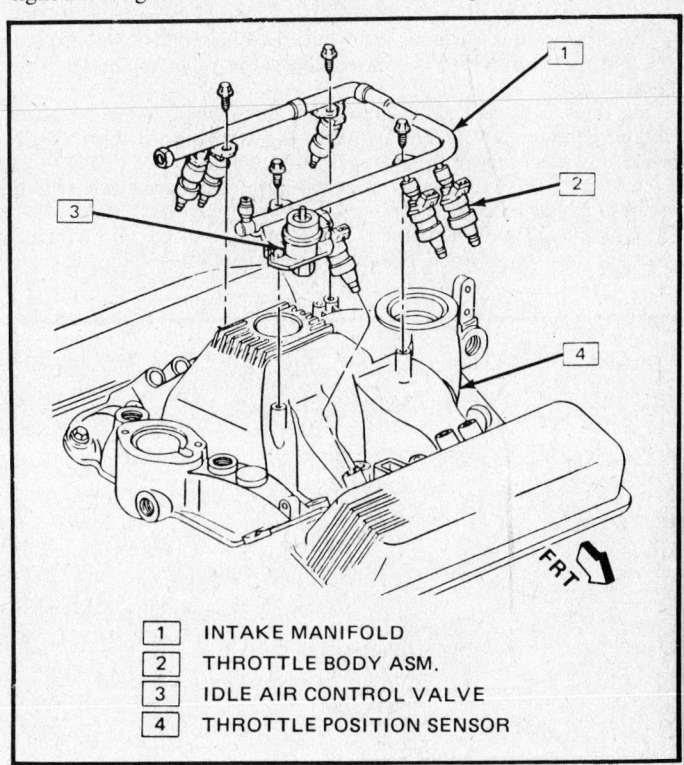

1	INTAKE MANIFOLD
2	THROTTLE BODY ASM.
3	IDLE AIR CONTROL VALVE
4	THROTTLE POSITION SENSOR

Fuel rail and injectors on 3.8L turbocharged engine

31-15

FUEL INJECTION
GM MULTI-PORT (MFI) AND SEQUENTIAL (SFI) SYSTEMS

the thermo-time switch. Measure the resistance of the cold start valve using an ohmmeter. Correct resistance is 3-5 ohms. Check continuity across the cold start valve terminals.

NOTE: No starts or poor cold starting can be caused by a malfunctioning cold start valve. Cranking a cold engine with the coil wire grounded should produce a cone-shaped spray from the cold start valve. Cranking a warm engine should produce no fuel; if the injector dribbles gas, replace it.

IDLE AIR CONTROL VALVE

Removal and Installation

1. Remove electrical connector from idle air control valve.
2. Remove the idle air control valve using a suitable wrench.
3. Installation is the reverse of removal. Before installing the idle air control valve, measure the distance that the valve is extended. Measurement should be made from the motor housing to the end of the cone. The distance should not exceed 1⅛ inches, or damage to the valve may occur when installed. Use a new gasket and turn the ignition on then off again to allow the ECM to reset the idle air control valve.

NOTE: Identify replacement IAC valve as being either Type 1 (with collar at electric terminal end) or Type 2 (without collar). If measuring distance is greater than specified above, proceed as follows:
Type 1: Press on valve firmly to retract it.
Type 2: Compress retaining spring from valve while turning valve in with a clockwise motion. Return spring to original position with straight portion of spring end aligned with flat surface of valve.

THROTTLE POSITION SENSOR

Removal and Installation

1. Disconnect the electrical connector from the sensor.
2. Remove the attaching screws, lockwashers and retainers.
3. Remove the throttle position sensor. If necessary, remove the screw holding the actuator to the end of the throttle shaft.
4. With the throttle valve in the normal closed idle position, install the throttle position sensor on the throttle body assembly, making sure the sensor pickup lever is located above the tang on the throttle actuator lever.
5. Install the retainers, screws and lockwashers using a thread locking compound. DO NOT tighten the screws until the throttle position switch is adjusted.
6. Install three jumper wires between the throttle position switch and the harness connector.
7. With the ignition switch ON, use a digital voltmeter connected to terminals B and C and adjust the switch to obtain .35-.45 volts.
8. Tighten the mounting screws, then recheck the reading to insure that the adjustment hasn't changed.
9. Turn ignition OFF, remove jumper wires, then reconnect harness to throttle position switch.

Adjustment
MULTI-PORT FUEL INJECTION

1. Install three jumper wires between the throttle position sensor (TPS) and harness connector.
2. With the ignition in the On position, connect a digital voltmeter to terminals B and C and adjust the TPS to reach 0.40 ± 0.05 volts.

NOTE: When adjusting the TPS, remove the screws and apply thread locking sealant, then reinstall the screws.

3. Tighten down the screws and recheck the reading to be sure the adjustment has not changed.
4. With the ignition in the off position, remove the jumper wires and connect the TPS harness.

TUNED PORT INJECTION

1. Install three jumper wires between the TPS harness and TPS connector.
2. With the ignition in the On position, connect a digital voltmeter to terminals A and B.
3. Adjust the TPS to reach 0.54 volts and torque the screws to 18 inch lbs. Re-check the adjustment to be sure it has not changed.
4. With the ignition in the off position, remove the jumper wires and connect the TPS harness.

OXYGEN SENSOR

Removal and Installation

NOTE: The oxygen sensor uses a permanently attached pigtail and connector. This pigtail should not be removed from the oxygen sensor. Damage or removal of the pigtail or connector could affect proper operation of the oxygen sensor.

The oxygen sensor is installed in the exhaust manifold and is removed in the same manner as a spark plug. The sensor may be difficult to remove when the engine temperature is below 120 deg. F (48 deg. C) and excessive force may damage threads in the exhaust manifold or exhaust pipe. Exercise care when handling the oxygen sensor; the electrical connector and louvered end must be kept free of grease, dirt, or other contaminants. Avoid using cleaning solvents of any kind and don't drop or roughly handle the sensor. A special anti-seize compound is used on the oxygen sensor threads when installing and care should be used NOT to get compound on the sensor itself. Disconnect the negative battery cable when servicing the oxygen sensor and torque to 30 ft. lbs. (41 Nm) when installing.

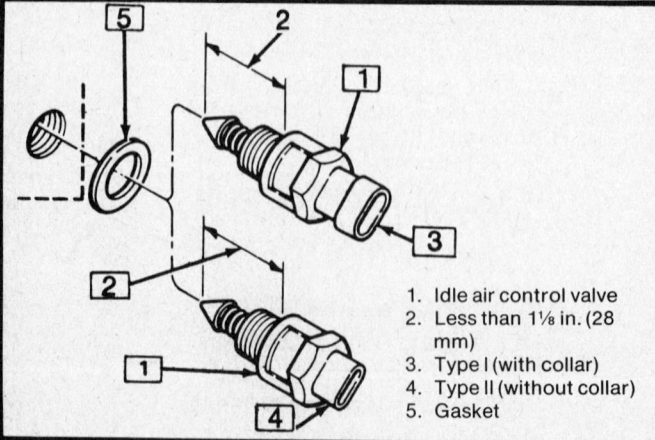

1. Idle air control valve
2. Less than 1⅛ in. (28 mm)
3. Type I (with collar)
4. Type II (without collar)
5. Gasket

Idle air control valve installation

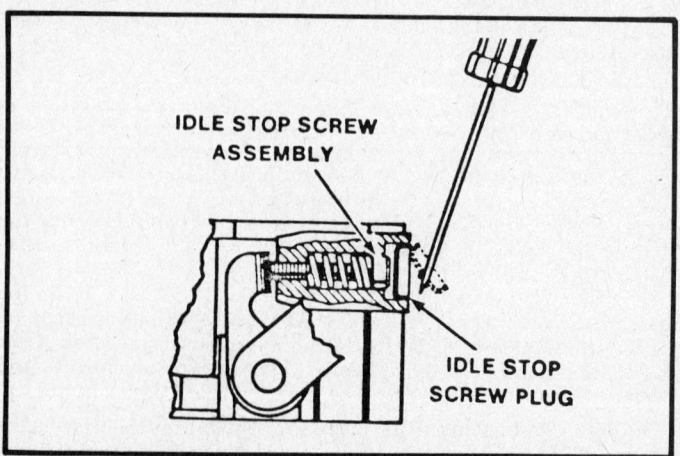

Idle stop screw plug removal

FUEL INJECTION
GM MULTI-PORT (MFI) AND SEQUENTIAL (SFI) SYSTEMS
SECTION 31

IDLE SPEED

Adjustment

TUNED PORT INJECTION

NOTE: The idle speed should only be adjusted if it is absolutely necessary.

1. Using an awl or equivalent pierce the idle stop plug and remove it.
2. Leave the idle air control motor connected and ground the diagnostic lead. Turn the ignition on but do not start the engine.
3. Wait for thirty seconds, and with the ignition switch still in the on position disconnect the idle air control connector.
4. Remove the ground from the diagnostic lead and start the engine.
5. Allow the engine to go into the closed loop mode and adjust the idle screw to specifications (5.0 and 5.7 liter engines automatic transmission is 400 rpm manual transmission is 450 rpm).
6. Turn the ignition off and reconnect the idle speed control connector.
7. Adjust the throttle position sensor, start the engine and check the engine for proper idle operation.

ELECTRONIC CONTROL MODULE (ECM)

Removal and Installation

The electronic control module (ECM) is located under the instrument panel. To allow one model of ECM to be used on different models, a device called a calibrator or PROM (Programmable Read Only Memory) is installed inside the ECM which contains information on the vehicle weight, engine, transmission, axle ratio, etc. The PROM is specific to the exact model and replacement part numbers must be checked carefully to make sure the correct PROM is being installed during service. Replacement ECM units (called Controllers) are supplied WITHOUT a PROM. The PROM from the old ECM must be carefully removed and installed in the replacement unit during service. Another device called a CALPAK is used to allow fuel delivery if other parts of the ECM are damaged (the "limp home" mode). The CALPAK is similar in appearance to the PROM and is located in the same place in the ECM, under an access cover. Like the PROM, the CALPAK must be removed and transferred to the new ECM unit being installed.

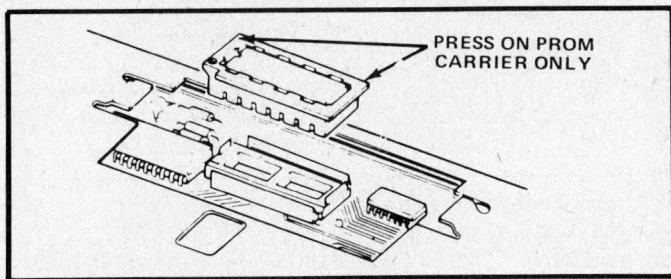

Do not press directly on the PROM when installing or it may be damaged

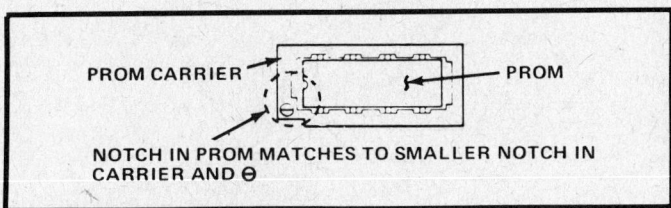

Be sure to install PROM correctly into carrier when replacing. Align notches as shown.

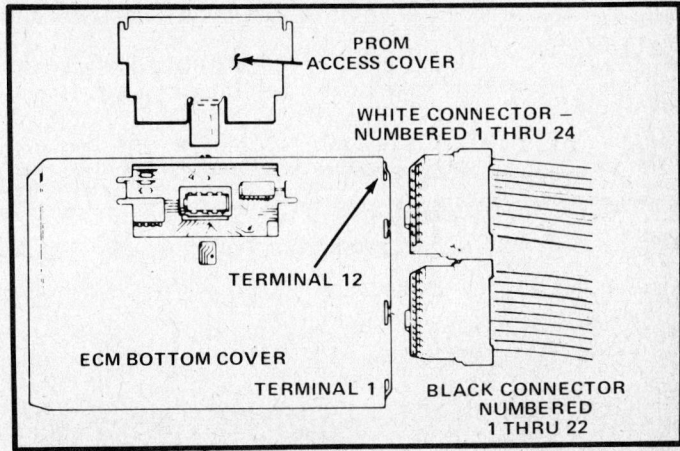

Typical General Motors ECM showing PROM access cover and harness connectors

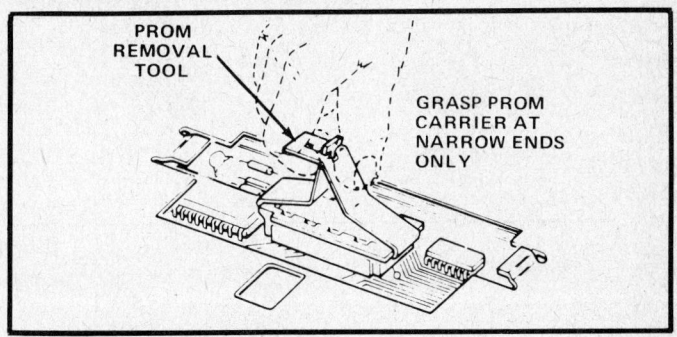

Using PROM removal tool

NOTE: If the diagnosis indicates a faulty ECM unit, the PROM should be checked to see if they are the correct parts. Trouble code 51 indicates that the PROM is installed incorrectly. When replacing the production ECM with a new part, it is important to transfer the Broadcast code and production ECM number to the new part label. Do not record on the ECM cover.

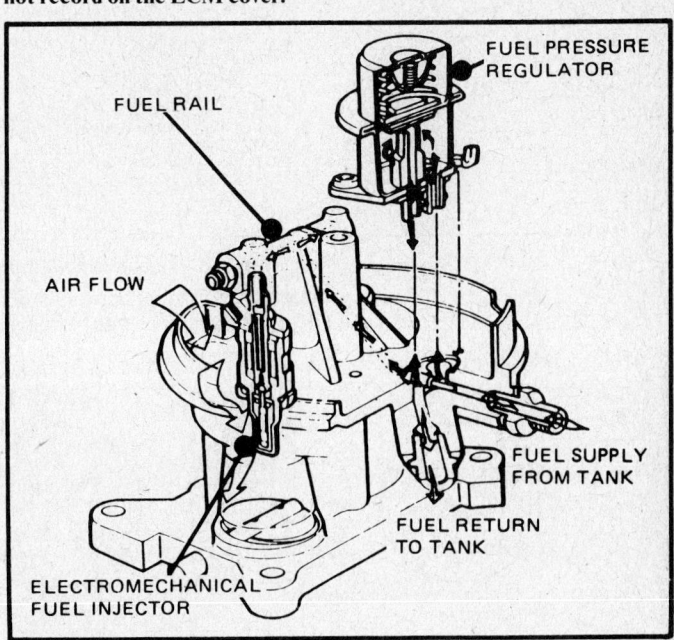

1985 and later Corvette mass airflow sensor code 34 diagnostic chart

SECTION 31: FUEL INJECTION
GM MULTI-PORT (MFI) AND SEQUENTIAL (SFI) SYSTEMS

1984

PORT FUEL INJECTION—INJECTOR BALANCE TEST

Before performing this test, the items listed below must be done.
- Check spark plugs and wires.
- Check compression.
- Check fuel injection harness for being open or shorted.

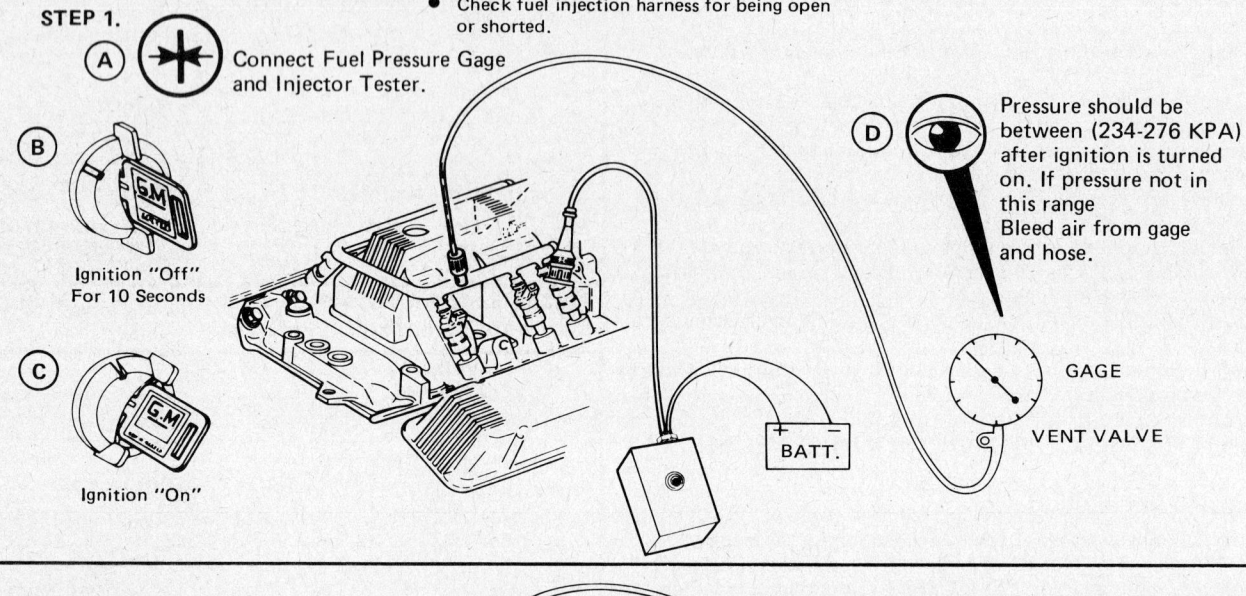

STEP 1.
- A. Connect Fuel Pressure Gage and Injector Tester.
- B. Ignition "Off" For 10 Seconds
- C. Ignition "On"
- D. Pressure should be between (234-276 KPA) after ignition is turned on. If pressure not in this range Bleed air from gage and hose.

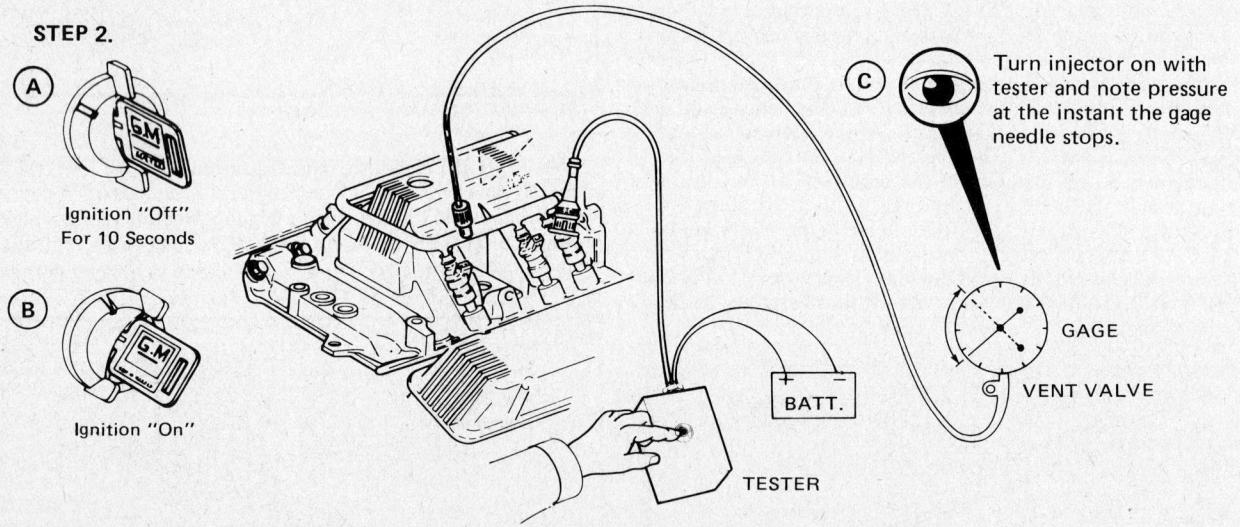

STEP 2.
- A. Ignition "Off" For 10 Seconds
- B. Ignition "On"
- C. Turn injector on with tester and note pressure at the instant the gage needle stops.

STEP 3. Repeat test as in step 2 on all injectors and record pressure drop on each.

Retest injectors that appear faulty. Replace any injectors that have a 10 KPA difference either (more or less) in pressure.

— EXAMPLE —

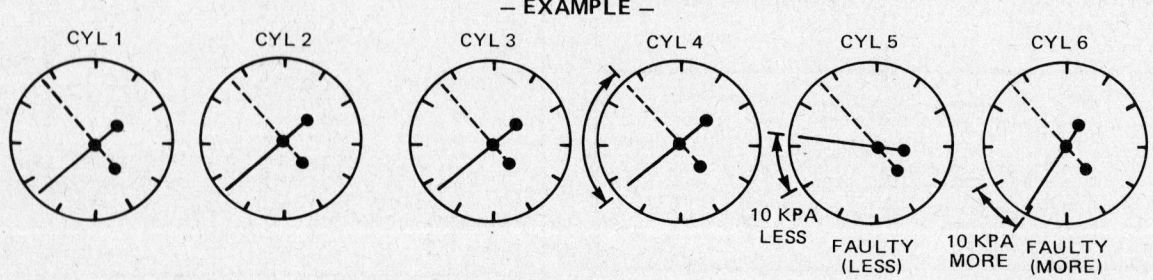

CYL 1, CYL 2, CYL 3, CYL 4, CYL 5 (10 KPA LESS — FAULTY (LESS)), CYL 6 (10 KPA MORE — FAULTY (MORE))

FUEL INJECTION
GM MULTI-PORT (MFI) AND SEQUENTIAL (SFI) SYSTEMS

SECTION 31

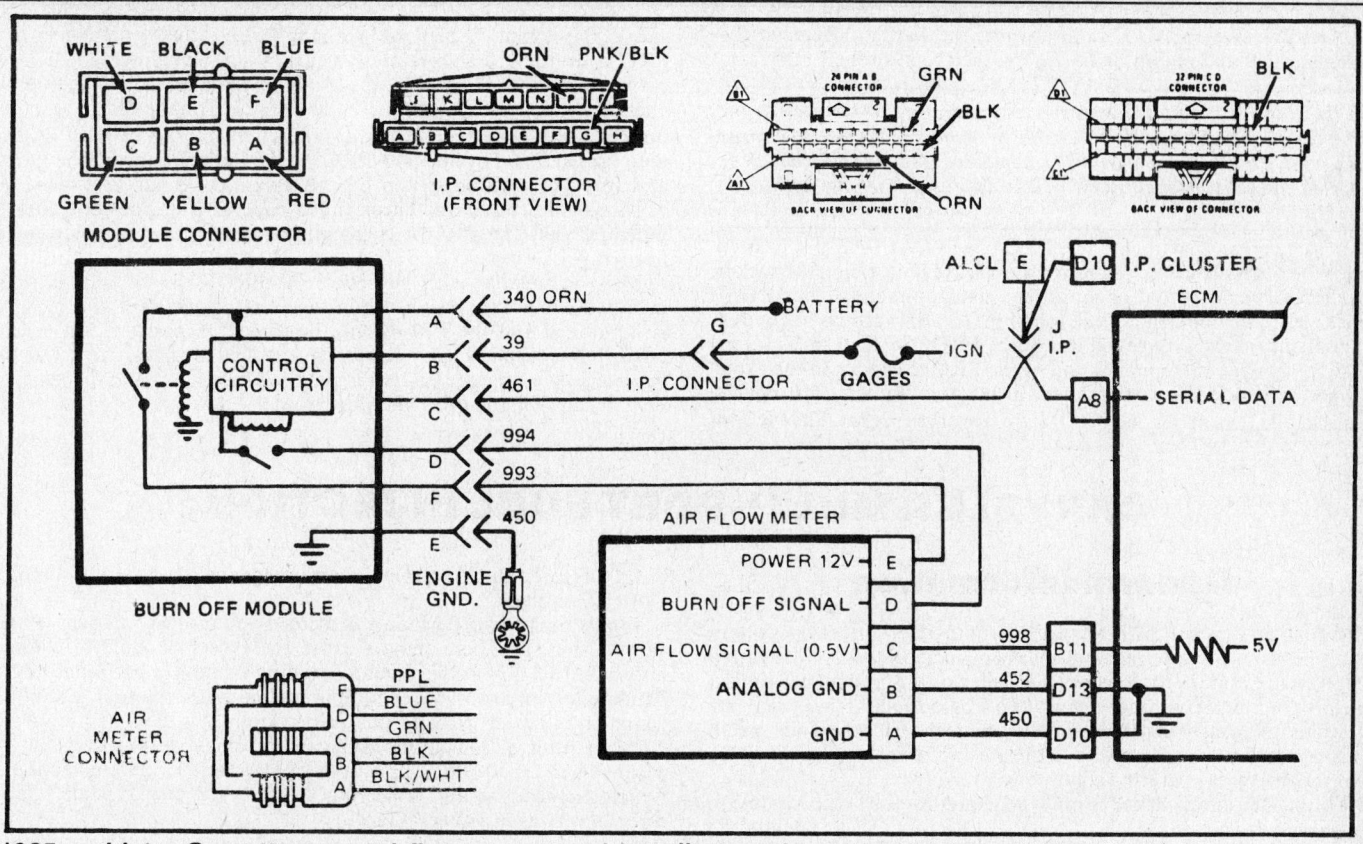

1985 and later Corvette mass airflow sensor—wiring diagram for code 33 high voltage signal

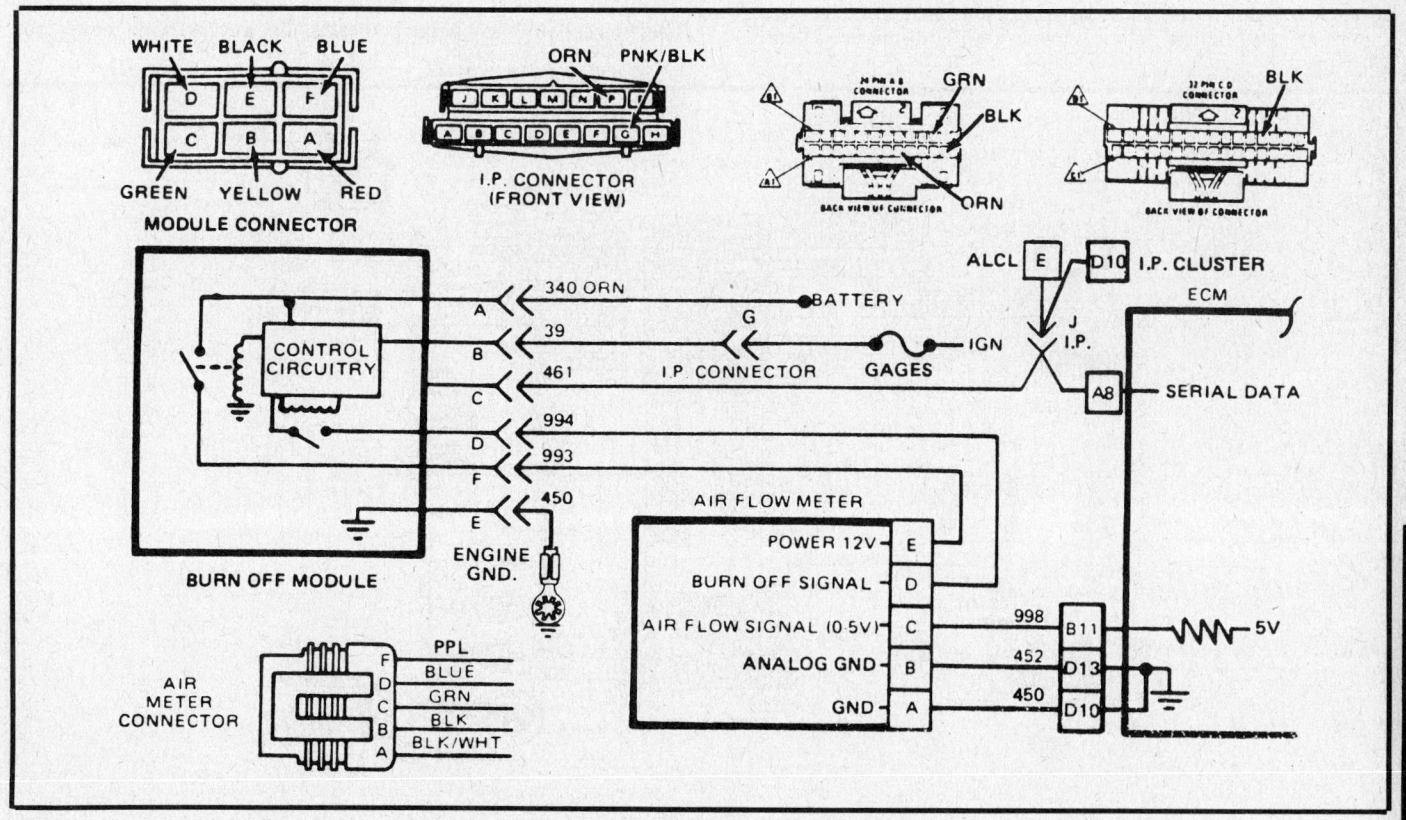

1985 and later Corvette mass airflow sensor—wiring diagram for code 34 low voltage signal

31-19

SECTION 31

FUEL INJECTION
GM MULTI-PORT (MFI) AND SEQUENTIAL (SFI) SYSTEMS

To remove the ECM, first disconnect the battery. Remove the wiring harness and mounting hardware, then remove the ECM from

— CAUTION —

The ignition must be OFF whenever disconnecting or connecting the ECM electrical harness. It is possible to install a PROM backwards during service. Exercise care when replacing the PROM that it is installed correctly, or the PROM will be destroyed when the ignition is switched ON.

the passenger compartment. The PROM and CALPAK are located under the access cover on the top of the control unit. Using the rocker type PROM removal tool, or equivalent, engage one end of the PROM carrier with the hook end of the tool. Press on the vertical bar end of the tool and rock the engaged end of the PROM carrier up as far as possible. Engage the opposite end of the PROM carrier in the same manner and rock this end up as far as possible. Repeat this process until the PROM carrier and PROM are free of the socket. The PROM carrier should only be removed with the removal tool or damage to the PROM or PROM socket may occur. When installing the PROM carrier in the PROM socket, the small notch of the carrier should be aligned with the small notch in the socket. Press on the PROM carrier until it is firmly seated in the socket. DO NOT press on the PROM; only the carrier. To check the PROM installation, reinstall the ECM and turn the ignition switch ON. Activate the diagnostic mode as previously described and check that a code 12 is displayed. Code 12 indicates that the PROM is installed correctly and is functioning normally. If trouble code 51 is displayed, or the "service engine soon" light is on steadily with no codes, the PROM is not fully seated, installed backwards, has bent pins, or is defective. Bent pins may be straightened and the PROM can be seated properly with a gentle push, but a PROM that has been installed backwards should be replaced. Any time the PROM is installed backwards and the ignition is switched ON, the PROM is destroyed.

CHRYSLER MULTI-PORT FUEL INJECTION

General Information

The turbocharged multi-point Electronic Fuel Injection system combines an electronic fuel and spark advance control system with a turbocharged intake system. At the center of this system is a digital pre-programmed computer known as a Logic Module that regulates ignition timing, air-fuel ratio, emission control devices and idle speed. This component has the ability to update and revise its programming to meet changing operating conditions.

Various sensors provide the input necessary for the Logic Module to correctly regulate fuel flow at the fuel injectors. These include the Manifold Absolute Pressure, Throttle Position, Oxygen Feedback, Coolant Temperature, Charge Temperature, and Vehicle Speed Sensors. In addition to the sensors, various switches also provide important information. These include the Transmission Neutral-Safety, Heated Backlite, Air Conditioning, and the Air Conditioning Clutch Switches.

Inputs to the Logic Module are converted into signals sent to the Power Module. These signals cause the Power Module to change either the fuel flow at the injector or ignition timing or both. The Logic Module tests many of its own input and output circuits. If a fault is found in a major circuit, this information is stored in the Logic Module. Information on this fault can be displayed to a technician by means of the instrument panel power loss lamp or by connecting a diagnostic readout and observing a numbered display code which directly relates to a general fault.

POWER MODULE

The Power Module contains the circuits necessary to power the

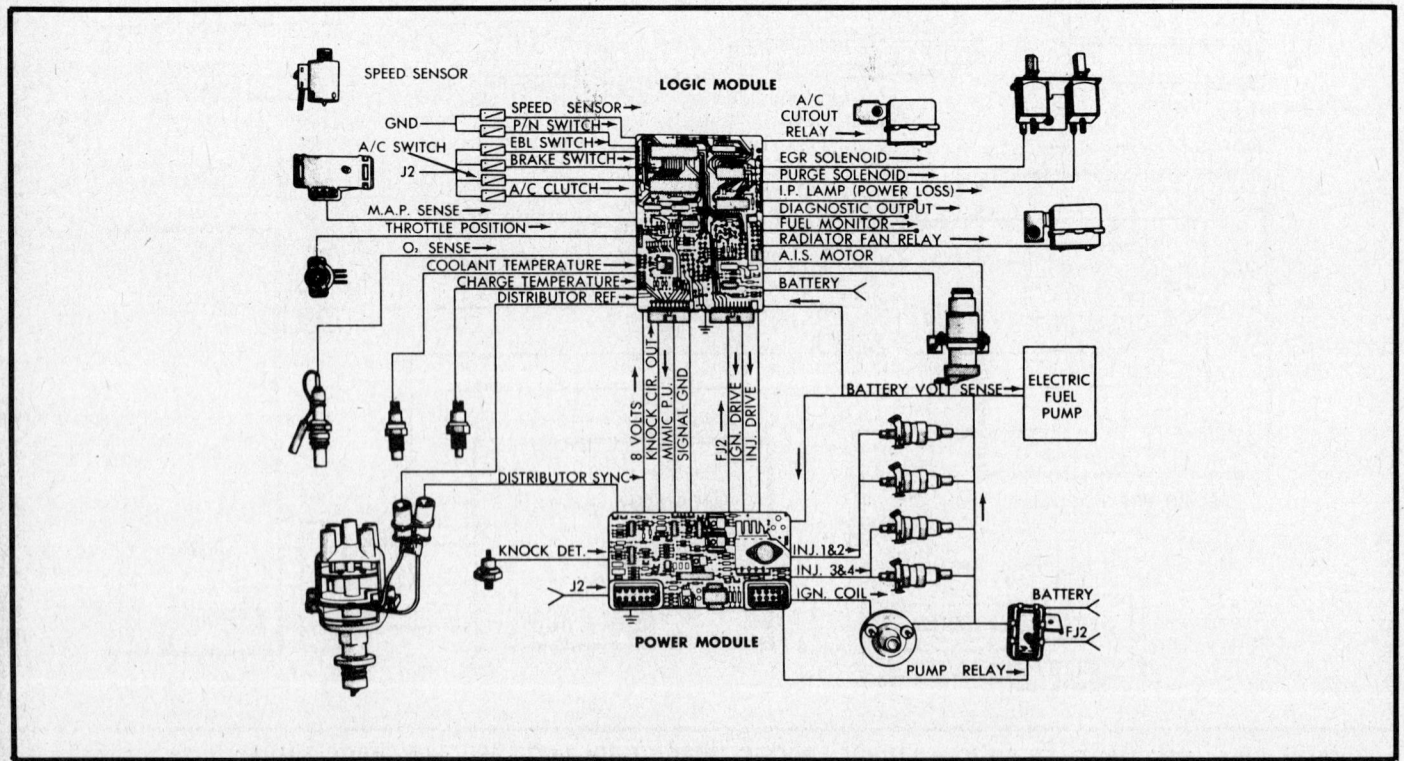

Chrysler multi-point fuel injection system schematic

FUEL INJECTION
CHRYSLER MULTI-PORT FUEL INJECTION
SECTION 31

ignition coil and the fuel injector. These are high current devices and their power supply has been isolated to minimize any "electrical noise" reaching the Logic Module. The Power Module also energizes the Automatic Shut Down (ASD) Relay which activates the fuel pump, ignition coil, and the Power Module itself. The module also receives a signal from the distributor. In the event of no distributor signal, the ASD relay is not activated and power is shut off from the fuel pump and ignition coil. The Power Module contains a voltage converter which reduces battery voltage to a regulated 8.0V output. This 8.0V output powers the distributor and also powers the Logic Module.

LOGIC MODULE

The logic module is a digital computer containing a microprocessor. The module receives input signals from various switches, sensors, and components. It then computes the fuel injector pulse width, spark advance, ignition coil dwell, idle speed, and purge and EGR solenoid cycles from this information. The Logic Module tests many of its own input and output circuits. If a fault is found in a major system, this information is stored in the Logic Module. Information on this fault can be displayed to a technician by means of flashing lamp on the instrument panel or by connecting a diagnostic readout tool and reading a numbered display code which relates to a general fault.

AUTOMATIC SHUTDOWN RELAY (ASD)

The Automatic Shutdown Relay (ASD) is powered and controlled through the Power Module. When the Power Module senses a distributor signal during cranking, it grounds the ASD closing its contacts. This completes the circuit for the electric fuel pump, Power Module, and ignition coil. If the distributor signal is lost for any reason the ASD interrupts this circuit in less than one second preventing fuel, spark, and engine operations.

MANIFOLD ABSOLUTE PRESSURE (MAP) SENSOR

The Manifold Absolute Pressure (MAP) sensor is a device which monitors manifold vacuum. It is mounted in the right side passenger compartment and is connected to a vacuum nipple on the throttle body and, electrically to the Logic Module. The sensor transmits information on manifold vacuum conditions and barometric pressure to the Logic Module. The MAP sensor data on engine load is used with data from other sensors to determine the correct air-fuel mixture.

OXYGEN SENSOR (O₂ SENSOR)

The Oxygen Sensor (O_2 Sensor) is a device which produces an electrical voltage when exposed to the oxygen present in the exhaust gasses. The sensor is mounted in the exhaust manifold and must be heated by the exhaust gasses before producing the voltage. When there is a large amount of oxygen present (lean mixture), the sensor produces a low voltage. When there is a lesser amount present (rich mixture) it produces a higher voltage. By monitoring the oxygen content and converting it to electrical voltage, the sensor acts as a rich-lean switch. The voltage is transmitted to the Logic Module. The Logic Module signals the Power Module to trigger the fuel injector. The injector changes the mixture.

CHARGE TEMPERATURE SENSOR

The Charge Temperature Sensor is a device mounted in the intake manifold which measures the temperature of the air-fuel mixture. This information is used by the Logic Module to determine engine operating temperature and engine warm-up cycles in the event of a Coolant Temperature Sensor failure.

COOLANT TEMPERATURE SENSOR

The Coolant Temperature Sensor is a device which monitors coolant

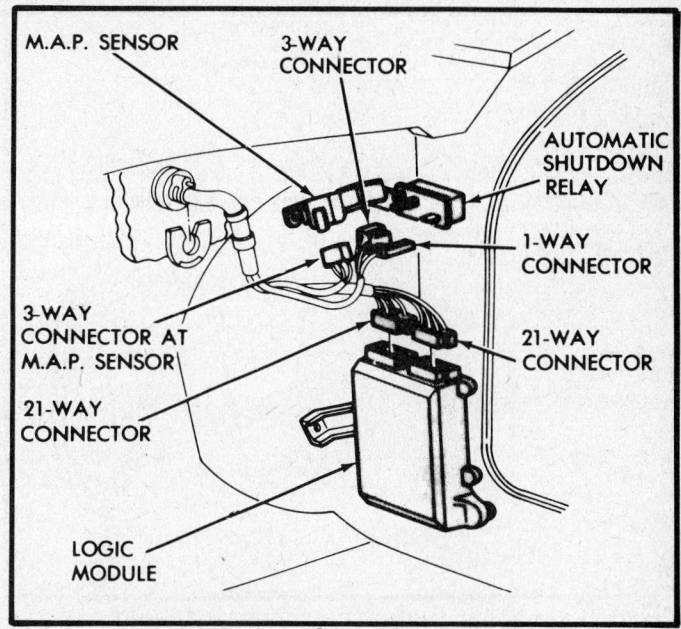

Location of logic module and components

temperature (which is the same as engine operating temperature). It is mounted in the thermostat housing. This sensor provides data on engine operating temperature to the Logic Module. This data along with data provided by the Charge Temperature Switch allows the Logic Module to demand slightly richer air-fuel mixtures and higher idle speeds until normal operating temperatures are reached. The sensor is a variable resistor with a range of $-60°F$ to $300°F$.

SWITCH INPUT

Various switches provide information to the Logic Module. These include the Neutral Safety, Air Conditioning Clutch, and Brake Light switches. If one or more of these switches is sensed as being in the on position, the Logic Module signals the Automatic Idle Speed Motor to increase idle speed to a scheduled rpm. With the air conditioning on and the throttle blade above a specific angle, the wide open throttle

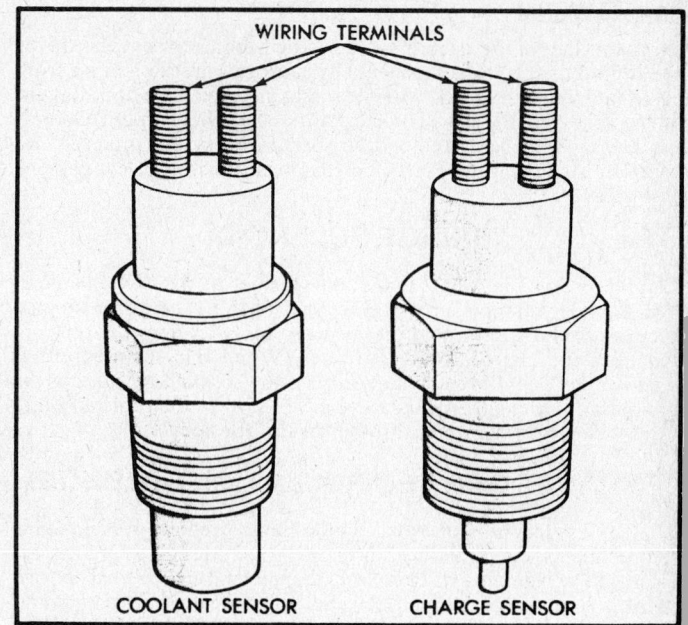

Typical temperature sensors

31–21

SECTION 31

FUEL INJECTION
CHRYSLER MULTI-PORT FUEL INJECTION

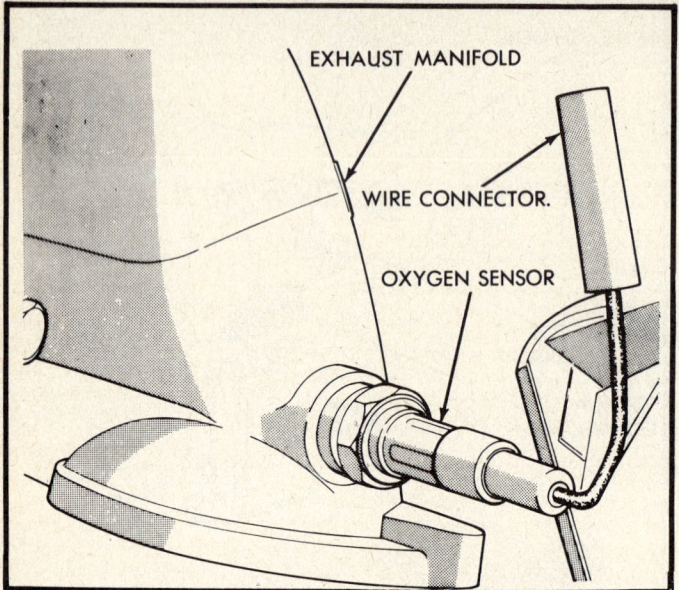

Oxygen sensor mounted in exhaust manifold

cut-out relay prevents the air conditioning clutch from engaging until the throttle blade is below this angle.

POWER LOSS LAMP

The Power Loss Lamp comes on each time the ignition key is turned on and stays on for a few seconds as a bulb test. If the Logic Module receives an incorrect signal or no signal from either the Coolant Temperature Sensor, Manifold Absolute Pressure Sensor, or the Throttle Position Sensor, the Power Loss Lamp on the instrument panel is illuminated. This is a warning that the Logic Module has gone into Limp in Mode in an attempt to keep the system operational. It signals an immediate need for service. The Power Loss can also be used to display fault codes. Cycle the ignition switch on, off, on, off, on within five seconds and any fault codes stored in the Logic Module will be displayed.

Limp In Mode

Limp In Mode is the attempt by the Logic Module to compensate for the failure of certain components by substituting information from other sources. If the Logic Module senses incorrect data or no data at all from the MAP Sensor, Throttle Position Sensor, Charge Temperature Sensor or Coolant Temperature Sensor, the system is placed into Limp In Mode and the Power Loss lamp on the instrument panel is activated.

PURGE SOLENOID

The Purge Solenoid works in the same fashion as the EGR solenoid. When engine temperature is below 61°C (145°F) the Logic Module grounds the Purge Solenoid energizing it. This prevents vacuum from reaching the charcoal canister valve. When this temperature is reached the Logic Module de-energizes the solenoid by turning the ground off. Once this occurs vacuum will flow to the canister purge valve and purge fuel vapors through the throttle body.

EXHAUST GAS RECIRCULATION SOLENOID

The EGR solenoid is operated by the Logic Module. When engine temperature is below 21°C (70°F), the Logic Module energizes the solenoid by grounding it. This closes the solenoid and prevents ported vacuum from reaching the EGR valve. When the prescribed temperature is reached, the logic module will turn off the ground for the solenoid de-energizing it. Once the solenoid is de-energized, ported vacuum from the throttle body will pass through to the EGR valve. At idle and wide open throttle the solenoid is energized which prevents EGR operation.

WASTEGATE CONTROL SOLENOID

On the turbocharged models the wastegate control solenoid by the logic module. The logic module adjusts the maximum boost to varying engine conditions by changing the duty cycle of the wastegate solenoid.

BAROMETRIC READ SOLENOID

This solenoid is also controlled by the logic module and is located in the MAP sensor vacuum line. The function of this solenoid is to measure the barometric pressure at closed throttle, once per throttle closure, but not more than once every thirty seconds and below a specified rpm. The barometric information is used mainly for boost control.

AIR CONDITIONING CUT OUT RELAY

The air conditioning cut out relay is electrically in series with the cycling clutch switch and low pressure cut out switch. This relay is in the normally closed (on) position during engine operation. When the Logic Module senses wide open throttle through the Throttle Position Sensor, it will energize the relay, open its contacts, and prevent air conditioning clutch engagement.

THROTTLE BODY

The throttle body assembly replaces a conventional carburetor air intake system and is connected to both the turbocharger and the intake manifold. The throttle body houses the Throttle Position Sensor and the Automatic Idle Speed Motor. Air flow through the throttle body is controlled by a cable operated throttle blade located in the base of the throttle body.

FUEL SUPPLY CIRCUIT

Fuel is pumped to the fuel rail by an electrical pump which is mounted in the fuel tank. The pump inlet is fitted with a filter to prevent water and other contaminants from entering the fuel supply circuit. Fuel pressure is controlled to a preset level above intake manifold pressure by a pressure regulator which is mounted near the fuel rail. The regulator uses intake manifold pressure at the vacuum tee as a reference.

FUEL INJECTORS AND FUEL RAIL ASSEMBLY

The four fuel injectors are retained in the fuel rail by lock rings. The rail and injector assembly is then bolted in position with the injectors inserted in the recessed holes in the intake manifold. The Fuel Injector is an electric solenoid powered by the Power Module but, controlled by

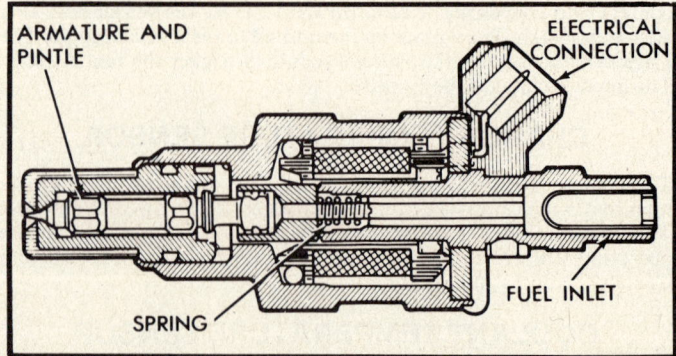

Cross section of solenoid-type fuel injector

FUEL INJECTION
CHRYSLER MULTI-PORT FUEL INJECTION
SECTION 31

the Logic Module. The Logic Module, based on ambient, mechanical, and sensor input, determines when and how long the Power Module should operate the injector. When an electric current is supplied to the injector, the armature and pintle move a short distance against a spring, opening a small orifice. Fuel is supplied to the inlet of the injector by the fuel pump, then passes through the injector, around the pintle, and out the orifice. Since the fuel is under high pressure a fine spray is developed in the shape of a hollow cone. The injector, through this spraying action, atomizes the fuel and distributes it into the air entering the combustion chamber.

FUEL PRESSURE REGULATOR

The pressure regulator is a mechanical device located downstream of the fuel injector on the throttle body. Its function is to maintain a constant 53 psi (380 kPa) across the fuel injector tip. The regulator uses a spring loaded rubber diaphragm to uncover a fuel return port. When the fuel pump becomes operational, fuel flows past the injector into the regulator, and is restricted from flowing any further by the blocked return port. When fuel pressure reaches 53 psi (380 kPa), it pushes on the diaphragm, compressing the spring, and uncovers the fuel return port. The diaphragm and spring will constantly move from an open to closed position to keep the fuel pressure constant. An assist to the spring loaded diaphragm comes from vacuum in the throttle body above the throttle blade. As venturi vacuum increases less pressure is required to supply the same amount of fuel into the air flow. The vacuum assists in opening the fuel port during high vacuum conditions. This fine tunes the fuel pressure for all operating conditions.

THROTTLE POSITION SENSOR (TPS)

The Throttle Position Sensor (TPS) is an electric resistor which is activated by the movement of the throttle shaft. It is mounted on the throttle body and senses the angle of the throttle blade opening. The voltage that the sensor produces increases or decreases according to the throttle blade opening. This voltage is transmitted to the Logic Module where it is used along with data from other sensors to adjust the air-fuel ratio to varying conditions and during acceleration, deceleration, idle, and wide open throttle operations.

AUTOMATIC IDLE SPEED (AIS) MOTOR

The Automatic Idle Speed Motor (AIS) is operated by the Logic Module. Data from the Throttle Position Sensor, Speed Sensor, Coolant Temperature Sensor, and various switch operations, (Electric Backlite, Air Conditionig, Safety/Neutral, Brake) are used by the Logic Module to adjust engine idle to an optimum during all idle conditions. The AIS adjusts the air portion of the air-fuel mixture through an air bypass on the back of the throttle body. Basic (no load) idle is determined by the minimum air flow through the throttle body. The AIS opens or closes off the air bypass as an increase or decrease is needed due to engine loads or ambient conditions. The Logic Module senses an air/fuel change and increases or decreases fuel proportionally to change engine idle. Deceleration die out is also prevented by increasing engine idle when the throttle is closed quickly after a driving (speed) condition.

In-tank fuel pump assembly

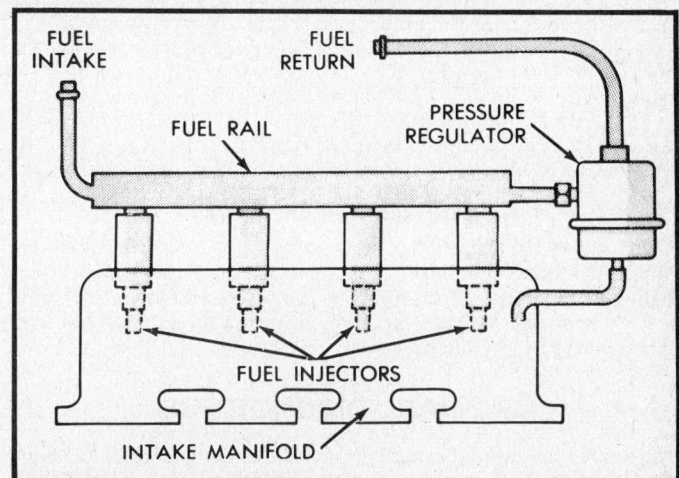
Multi-port fuel supply system

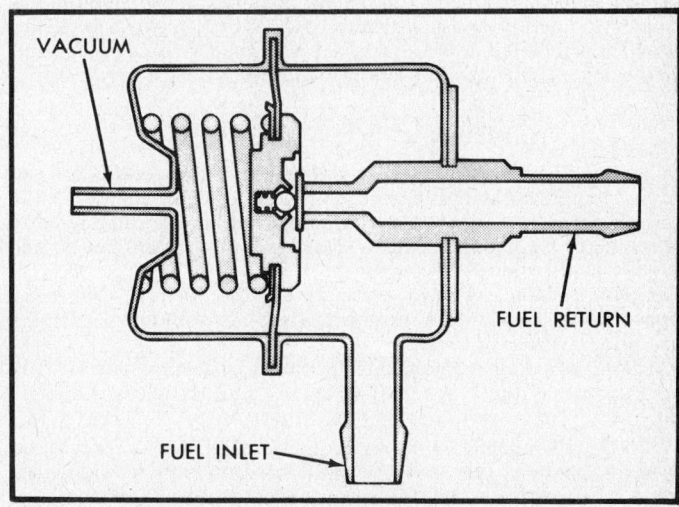
Cross section of typical fuel pressure regulator

FUEL PUMP

The fuel pump used in this system is a positive displacement, roller vane immersible pump with a permanent magnet electric motor. The fuel is drawn in through a filter sock and pushed through the electric motor to the outlet. The pump contains two check valves. One valve is used to relieve internal fuel pump pressure and regulate maximum pump output. The other check valve, located near the pump outlet, restricts fuel movement in either direction when the pump is not operational. Voltage to operate the pump is supplied through the Auto Shutdown Relay.

FUEL RESERVOIR

The fuel pump is mounted within a fuel reservoir in the fuel tank. The purpose of the reservoir is to provide fuel at the pump intake during all driving conditions, especially those when low fuel levels are present. The fuel return line directs fuel into a cup on the side of the reservoir. The stream of fuel coming into this cup creates a low pressure area and causes additional fuel from the main tank to flow into the reservoir. This combination of return fuel and fuel from the main tank keeps the reservoir full even when the fuel level is below the reservoir walls.

EXHAUST GAS RECIRCULATION (EGR)

The Exhaust Gas Recirculation system is a back pressure type and is controlled two ways. The Logic Module controls vacuum through the EGR solenoid, turning the vacuum circuit or or off. A back pressure

SECTION 31

FUEL INJECTION
CHRYSLER MULTI-PORT FUEL INJECTION

transducer measures the amount of exhaust back pressure on the exhaust side of the EGR valve and varies the strength of the vacuum signal applied to the EGR valve. The Logic Module will prevent EGR operation by turning the EGR solenoid off at idle, wide open throttle or when engine temperature falls below 70°F (21°C). The back pressure transducer adjusts the EGR signal to provide programmed amounts of Exhaust Gas Recirculation under all other conditions.

Troubleshooting

NOTE: Most complaints that may occur with turbocharged multi-point Electronic Fuel Injection can be traced to poor wiring or hose connections. A visual check will help spot these faults and save unnecessary test and diagnosis time.

ON BOARD DIAGNOSTICS

The Logic Module has been programmed to monitor several different circuits of the fuel injection system. This monitoring is called On Board Diagnosis. If a problem is sensed with a monitored circuit, often enough to indicate an actual problem, its Fault Code is stored in the Logic Module for eventual display to the service technician. If the problem is repaired or ceases to exist, the Logic Module cancels the Fault Code after 30 ignition key on/off cycles.

FAULT CODES—1982-84

When a fault code appears (either by flashes of the power loss lamp or by watching the diagnostic reading—Tool C-4805 or equivalent), it indicates that the Logic Module has recognized an abnormal signal in the system. Fault codes indicate the results of a failure but do not always identify the failed component.

CODE 11 indicates a problem in the distributor circuit. This code appears if the Logic Module has not sensed a distributor signal since the battery was reconnected.

CODE 12 indicates a problem in the stand-by memory circuit. This code appears if direct memory feed to the Logic Module is interrupted.

CODE 13 indicates a problem in the MAP sensor pneumatic system. This code appears if the MAP sensor vacuum level does not change between start and start/run transfer speed (500-600 rpm).

CODE 14 indicates a problem in the MAP sensor electrical system. This code appears if the map sensor signal is either too low (below .02 volts) or too high (above 4.9 volts).

CODE 15 indicates a problem in the vehicle Speed Sensor circuit. This code appears if engine speed is at idle and speed sensor indicates less than 2 mph. This code is valid only if it is sensed while moving.

CODE 21 indicates a problem in the O_2 feedback circuit. This code appears if engine temperature is above 170°F (77°C), engine speed is above 1500 rpm, and there has been no O_2 signal for more than 5 seconds.

CODE 22 indicates a problem in the coolant temperature circuit. This code appears if the temperature sensor indicates an improbable temperature or a temperature that changes too fast to be real.

CODE 23 indicates a problem in the charge temperature circuit. This code appears if the charge temperature is an improbable temperature or a temperature that changes too fast to be real.

CODE 24 indicates a problem in the Throttle Position Sensor circuit. This code appears if the sensor signal is either below .16 volts or above 4.7 volts.

CODE 25 indicates a problem in the Automatic Idle Speed system. This code appears if the proper voltage from the AIS system is not present. An open motor or harness will not activate this code.

CODE 31 indicates a problem in the Canister Purge Solenoid circuit. This code appears when the proper voltage at the purge solenoid is not present (open or shorted system).

CODE 32 indicates a problem in the Power Loss Lamp circuit. This code appears if proper voltage to the Power Loss Lamp is not present (open or shorted system).

CODE 33 indicates a problem in the Air Conditioning Wide Open Throttle Cut Out Relay circuit. This code appears if the proper voltage at the relay is not present (open or shorted).

CODE 34 indicates a problem in the EGR Solenoid circuit. This code appears if proper voltage at the EGR Solenoid is not present (open or shorted).

CODE 35 indicates a problem in the Fan Relay circuit. This code appears if the radiator fan is either not operating or operating at the wrong time.

CODE 41 indicates a problem in the Charging System. This code appears if battery voltage from the Automatic Shut Down Relay is below 11.75 volts.

CODE 42 indicates a problem in the Automatic Shut Down Relay (ASD) circuit. This code appears if during cranking, battery voltage from the ASD relay is not present for at least 1/3 second after the first distributor pulse or, after engine stall, battery voltage is not off within 3 seconds after last distributor pulse.

CODE 43 indicates a problem in the interface circuit. This code appears if the anti-dwell or injector control signal is not present between the Logic Module and Power Module.

CODE 44 indicates a problem in the Logic Module. This code appears if an incorrect PROM has been installed in the Logic Module.

CODE 45 indicates a problem in the Overboost Shut Off circuit. This code appears if MAP sensor electrical signal rises above 10 psi boost.

CODE 51 indicates a problem in the closed loop fuel system. This code appears if during closed loop conditions, the O_2 signal is either low or high for more than 2 minutes.

CODE 52 indicates a problem in the Logic Module. This code appears if an internal failure exists in the Logic Module.

CODE 53 indicates a problem in the Logic Module. This code appears if an internal failure exists in the Logic Module.

CODE 54 indicates a problem in the Synchronization pick-up circuit. This code appears, if at start/run transfer speed, the reference pick-up signal is present but the synchronization pick-up signal is missing at the Logic Module.

CODE 55 indicates message complete. This code appears after all fault codes are displayed.

CODE 88 indicates start of message. This code appears at start of fault code messages. This code only appears on Readout Tool C-4805 or equivalent, and may also be used for switch check.

FAULT CODES—1985 AND LATER

CODE 11 indicates engine has not been cranked since battery was disconnected.

CODE 12 indicates memory standby power was recently lost.

CODE 13 indicates a problem in the MAP sensor pneumatic circuit.

CODE 14 indicates a problem in the MAP sensor electrical circuit.

CODE 15 indicates a problem in the distance sensor circuit.

CODE 16 indicates a loss of battery voltage sense.

CODE 17 indicates a problem in the knock sensor circuit.

CODE 21 indicates a problem in the oxygen sensor circuit.

CODE 22 indicates a problem in the coolant temperature circuit.

CODE 23 indicates a problem in the charge temperature sensor code.

CODE 24 indicates a problem in the throttle position sensor circuit.

CODE 25 indicates a problem in the AIS motor driver circuit.

CODE 26 indicates a problem in injector one circuit.

CODE 27 indicates a problem in injector two circuit.

CODE 31 indicates a problem in the purge solenoid driver circuit.

CODE 32 indicates a problem in the power loss lamp driver circuit.

CODE 33 indicates a problem in the A/C cutout relay driver circuit.

CODE 34 indicates a problem in the EGR solenoid circuit.

CODE 35 indicates a problem in the fan control relay driver circuit.

CODE 36 indicates a problem in the wastegate solenoid circuit.

CODE 37 indicates a problem in the barometric read solenoid circuit.

CODE 41 indicates charging system excess or no field current.

CODE 42 indicates a problem with the ASD relay driver.

FUEL INJECTION
CHRYSLER MULTI-PORT FUEL INJECTION

CODE 43 indicates a problem in the spark interface circuit.
CODE 45 indicates a problem in the overboost shut-off system.
CODE 46 indicates battery voltage is too high.
CODE 47 indicates battery voltage is too low.
CODE 51 indicates oxygen feedback system is latched up.
CODE 52 indicates a problem in the battery temperature circuit.
CODE 53 indicates an internal logic module problem.
CODE 54 indicates a problem in the distributor synch circuit.
CODE 55 indicates end of message.

SYSTEM TESTS

Obtaining Fault Codes

1. Connect diagnostic readout box tool C-4805 or equivalent, to the diagnostic connector located in the engine compartment near the passenger side strut tower.
2. Start the engine if possible, cycle the transmission selector and the A/C switch if applicable. Shut off the engine.
3. Turn the ignition switch on, off, on, off, on. Within 5 seconds record all the diagnostic codes shown on the diagnostic readout box tool, observe the power loss lamp on the instrument panel, the lamp should light for 2 seconds then go out (bulb check).

Switch Test

After all codes have been shown and has indicated Code 55 end of message, actuate the following component switches. The digital display must change its numbers when the switch is activated and released:
- Brake Pedal
- Gear Shift Selector park, reverse, park.
- A/C Switch (if applicable).
- Electrical Backlite Switch (if applicable).

Actuator Test Mode (ATM)

1982-84

1. Remove coil wire from cap and place 1/4 in. from a ground.

--- **CAUTION** ---
Coil wire must be 1/4 in. or less from ground or power module damage may result.

2. Remove air cleaner hose from throttle body.
3. Press the **ATM** button on the diagnostic readout box tool and observe the following:
- 3 sparks from the coil wire to ground.
- 2 **AIS** motor movements (1 open 1 close) you must listen carefully for **AIS** operation.
- With the ATM button still depressed, install a jumper wire between pins 2 and 3 of the gray distributor synch. connector. Listen for the click which indicates one set of injectors has been activated. Remove jumper wire and second set of injectors will be activated. Reconnect distributor connector.

4. The **ATM** capability is cancelled 5 minutes after the ignition switch is turned on. To reinstate this capability cycle the ignition on and off three times ending in the on position.
5. When the **ATM** button is pressed, fault Code 42 is generated because the ASD relay is bypassed. Do not use this code for diagnostics after **ATM** operation.
6. The **ATM** test will check 3 categories of operation:
- When coil fires three times:
  a. Coil operational
  b. Logic Module portion operational
  c. Power Module portion operational
  d. Interface between Power Module and Logic Module is working.
- AIS is operational
- Injector fuel pulse into Throttle Body:
  a. Fuel injector operational
  b. Fuel pump operational
  c. Fuel lines intact

7. The Electronic Fuel Injection system must be evaluated using all the information found in the systems test:
- Start/No Start
- Fault Codes
- Loss of Power Lamp on or off (limp in)
- ATM Results:
  a. Spark yes/no
  b. Fuel yes/no
  c. AIS movement yes/no

Once this information is found, it will be easier to determine what circuit to look at for further testing.

1985 AND LATER

1. Put the system into the diagnostic test mode and wait for code 55 to appear on the display screen.
2. Press the ATM button on the diagnostic readout box to activate the display screen.
3. If a specific ATM test is desired, hold the ATM button down until the desired test code appears.
4. The computer will continue to turn the selected circuit on and off for as long as five minutes or until the ATM button is pressed again or if the ignition is turned off.
5. If the ATM button is not pressed again, the computer will continue cycling the selected circuit for five minutes and then shut the system off. The test mode can also be shut off by turning the ignition off.

ACTUATOR TEST DISPLAY CODES

Code	Description
01	Spark Activation
02	Injector Activation
03	AIS Activation
04	Radiator Fan Activation
05	A/C Cutout Relay Activation
06	ASD Relay Activation
07	Purge Solenoid Activation
08	EGR Solenoid Activation
09	Wastegate Solenoid Activation
10	Barometric Read Solenoid Activation

Relieving Fuel System Pressure

The E.F.I. fuel system is under a constant pressure of approximately 53 psi (380 kPa). Before servicing the fuel tank, fuel pump, fuel lines, fuel filter, or fuel components of the throttle body, the fuel pressure must be released as follows.

1. Loosen gas cap to release any in tank pressure.
2. Remove wiring harness connector from any injector.
3. Ground one injector terminal with a jumper.
4. Connect a jumper wire to second terminal and touch battery positive post for no longer than 10 seconds.
5. Remove jumper wires.
6. Continue fuel system service.

Fuel System Pressure Test

--- **CAUTION** ---
Fuel system pressure must be released each time a fuel hose is to be disconnected.

1. Remove fuel intake hose from throttle body and connect fuel system pressure testers C-3292, and C-4749 or equivalent, between fuel filter hose and throttle body.
2. Start engine. If gauge reads 380 kPa = 14 kPa (53 psi = 2 psi) pressure is correct and no further testing is required. Reinstall fuel hose using a new original equipment type clamp and torque to 10 in. lbs. (1 Nm).
3. If fuel pressure is **below** specifications, install tester between fuel filter hose and fuel line.

SECTION 31

FUEL INJECTION
CHRYSLER MULTI-PORT FUEL INJECTION

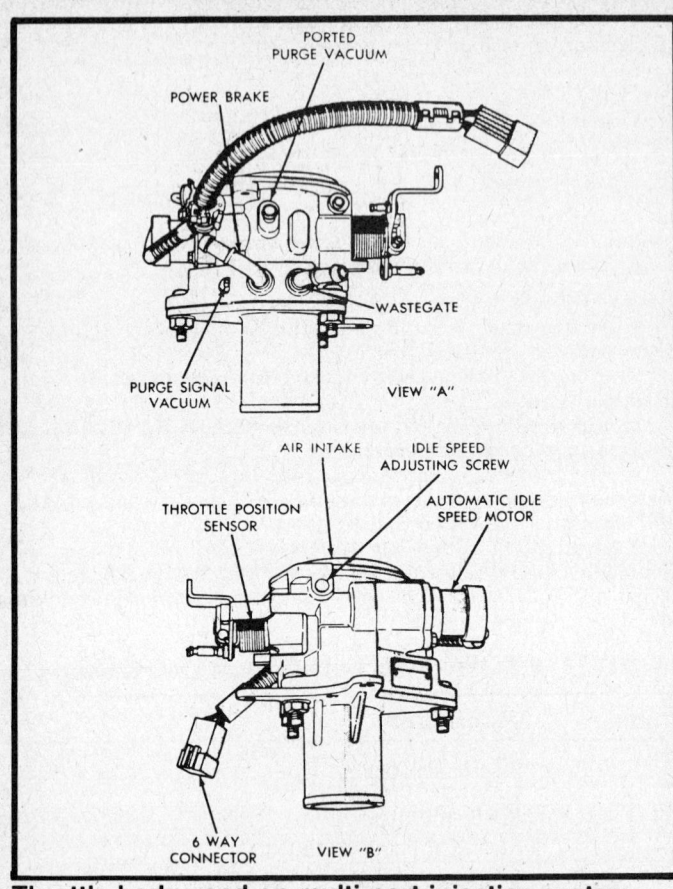

Throttle body used on multi-port injection system

4. Start engine. If pressure is now correct, replace fuel filter. If no change is observed, gently squeeze return hose. If pressure increases, replace pressure regulator. If no change is observed, problem is either a plugged pump filter sock or defective fuel pump.

5. If pressure is **above** specifications, remove fuel return hose from pressure regulator end. Connect a substitute hose and place other end of hose in clean container. Start engine. If pressure is now correct, check for restricted fuel return line. If no change is observed, replace fuel regulator.

MECHANICAL MALFUNCTIONS

Mechanical malfunctions are more difficult to diagnose with the EFI system. The Logic Module has been programmed to compensate for some mechanical malfunctions such as incorrect cam timing, vacuum leaks, etc. If engine performance problems are encountered and no fault codes are displayed, the problem may be mechanical rather than electronic.

THROTTLE BODY

When servicing the fuel portion of the throttle body it will be necessary to bleed fuel pressure before opening any hoses. Always reassemble throttle body components with new O-rings and seals where applicable. Never use lubricants on O-rings or seals, damage may result. If assembly of components is difficult use water to aid assembly. Use care when removing fuel hoses to prevent damage to hose or hose nipple. Always use new hose clamps of the correct type when reassembling and torque hose clamps to 10 in. lbs. (1 Nm). Do not use aviation-style clamps on this system or hose damage may result.

NOTE: It is not necessary to remove the throttle body from the intake manifold to perform component disassembly. If fuel system hoses are to be replaced, only hoses marked EFI/EFM may be used.

THROTTLE POSITION SENSOR

Removal and Installation

1. Disconnect negative battery cable and 6-way throttle body connector.
2. Remove 2 screws mounting throttle position sensor to throttle body.
3. Unclip wiring clip from convoluted tube and remove mounting bracket.
4. Lift throttle position sensor off throttle shaft and remove O-ring.
5. Pull the 3 wires of the throttle position sensor from the convoluted tubing.
6. Look inside the 6-way throttle body connector and lift a locking tab with a small screwdriver for each T.P.S. wire blade terminal. Remove each blade from connector. (Note wiring position for reassembly.)
7. Insert each wire blade terminal into throttle body connector. Make sure wires are inserted into correct locations.
8. Insert wires from throttle position sensor into convoluted tube.
9. Install throttle position sensor and new O-ring with mounting bracket to throttle body. Torque screws to 20 in. lbs. (2 Nm).
10. Install wiring clips to convoluted tube.
11. Connect 6-way connector and battery cable.

AUTOMATIC IDLE SPEED MOTOR

Removal and Installation

1. Disconnect negative battery cable and 6-way throttle body connector.
2. Remove 2 screws that mount the A.I.S. to its adaptor. (Do not remove the clamp on the A.I.S. or damage will result.)
3. Remove wiring clips and remove the two A.I.S. wires from the 6-way throttle body connector. Lift each locking tab with a small screwdriver and remove each blade terminal. (Note wiring position for reassembly.)
4. Lift A.I.S. from its adaptor.
5. Remove the 2 O-rings on the A.I.S. carefully.
6. Install 2 new O-rings on A.I.S.
7. Carefully work A.I.S. into its adaptor.
8. Install 2 mounting screws and torque to 20 in. lbs. (2 Nm).
9. Route A.I.S. wiring to 6-way connector and install each wire blade terminal into the connector. Make sure wires are inserted in correct locations.
10. Connect wiring clips, 6-way connector, and battery cable.

AUTOMATIC IDLE SPEED MOTOR ASSEMBLY

Removal and Installation

1. Disconnect negative battery cable and 6-way throttle body connector.
2. Remove 2 screws on back of throttle body from A.I.S. adaptor.
3. Remove wiring clips and remove the two A.I.S. wires from the 6-way throttle body connector. Lift each locking tab with a small screwdriver and remove each blade terminal. (Note wiring position for reassembly.)
4. Carefully pull the assembly from the rear of the throttle body. The O-ring at the top and seal at the bottom may fall off adaptor.
5. Remove O-ring and seal.
6. Place a new O-ring and seal on adaptor.
7. Carefully position assembly onto back of throttle body (make sure seals stay in place) insert screws and torque to 65 in. lbs. (7 Nm).
8. Route A.I.S. wiring to 6-way connector and install each wire blade terminal into the connector. Make sure wires are inserted in correct locations.
9. Connect wiring clips, 6-way connector, and battery cable.

FUEL INJECTION
CHRYSLER MULTI-PORT FUEL INJECTION
SECTION 31

THROTTLE BODY

Removal and Installation

1. Disconnect negative battery cable.
2. Remove air cleaner to throttle body screws, loosen hose clamp and remove air cleaner adaptor.
3. Remove accelerator, speed control, and transmission kickdown cables and return spring.
4. Remove throttle cable bracket from throttle body.
5. Disconnect 6-way connector.
6. Disconnect vacuum hoses from throttle body.
7. Loosen throttle body to turbocharger hose clamp.
8. Remove throttle body to intake manifold screws.
9. Remove throttle body.
10. Reverse the above procedure for installation.

OXYGEN SENSOR

Removal and Installation

Removing the oxygen sensor from the exhaust manifold may be difficult if the sensor was over-torqued during installation. Use Tool C-4589 or equivalent, to remove the sensor. The threads in the exhaust manifold must be cleaned with a 18 mm × 1.5 × 6E tap. If the same sensor is to be reinstalled, the threads must be coated with an anti-seize compound such as Loctite® 771-64 or equivalent. New sensors are packaged with anti-seize compound on the threads and no additional compound is required. Sensors must be torqued to 20 ft. lbs. (27 Nm).

IDLE SPEED

Adjustment

Before adjusting the idle on an electronic fuel injected vehicle the following items must be checked:
  a. AIS motor has been checked for operation.
  b. Engine has been checked for vacuum or EGR leaks.
  c. Engine timing has been checked and set to specifications.
  d. Coolant Temperature Sensor has been checked for operation.
1. Install a tachometer.
2. Warm up engine to normal operating temperature (accessories off).
3. Shut engine off and disconnect radiator fan.
4. Disconnect Throttle Body 6-way connector. Remove the brown with white tracer AI wire from the connector and reconnect connector.
5. Start engine with transaxle selector in park or neutral.
6. Apply 12 volts to AIS brown with white tracer wire. This will drive the AIS fully closed and the idle rpm should drop.
7. Disconnect then reconnect coolant temperature sensor.
8. With transaxle in neutral, idle speed should be 775 ± 25 rpm (700 ± 25 green engine).
9. If idle is not to specifications adjust idle air bypass screw.
10. If idle rpm will not adjust down, check for vacuum leaks, AIS motor damage, throttle body damage, or speed control cable adjustment.

FUEL SYSTEM PRESSURE TEST

Procedure

--- CAUTION ---
Fuel system pressure must be released each time a fuel hose is to be disconnected.

1. Remove fuel intake hose from throttle body and connect fuel system pressure testers C-3292, and C-4749, or equivalent, between fuel filter hose and throttle body.
2. Start engine. If gauge reads 380 kPa ± 14 kPa (53 psi ± 2 psi) pressure is correct and no further testing is required. Reinstall fuel hose using a new original equipment type clamp and torque to 10 in. lbs. (1 Nm).
3. If fuel pressure is **below** specifications, install tester between fuel filter hose and fuel line.
4. Start engine. If pressure is now correct, replace fuel filter. If no change is observed, gently squeeze return hose. If pressure increases, replace pressure regulator. If no change is observed, problem is either a plugged pump filter sock or defective fuel pump.
5. If pressure is **above** specifications, remove fuel return hose from pressure regulator end. Connect a substitute hose and place other end of hose in clean container. Start engine. If pressure is now correct, check for restricted fuel return line. If no change is observed, replace fuel regulator.

IGNITION TIMING

Adjustment

1. Connect a power timing light to the number one cylinder, or a magnetic timing unit to the engine. (Use a 10° offset when required.)
2. Connect a tachometer to the engine and turn selector to the proper cylinder position.
3. Start engine and run until operating temperature is reached.
4. Disconnect and reconnect the water temperature sensor connector on the thermostat housing. The loss of power lamp on the dash must come on and stay on. Engine rpm should be within emission label specifications.
5. Aim power timing light at timing hole in bell housing or read the magnetic timing unit.
6. Loosen distributor and adjust timing to emission label specifications if necessary.
7. Shut engine off, disconnect and reconnect positive battery quick disconnect. Start vehicle, the loss of power lamp should be off.
8. Shut engine off, then turn ignition on, off, on, off, on. Fault codes should be clear with 88-51-55 shown.

AIR ASPIRATOR SYSTEM

The air aspirator system uses exhaust pressure pulses to draw air into the exhaust system. This reduces carbon monoxide (CO) and hydrocarbon (HC) emissions. It draws fresh air from the clean side of the air cleaner past a one-way diaphragm in the aspirator valve. The diaphragm opens to allow fresh air to mix with exhaust gasses during negative pressure pulses. If pressure pulses are positive, the diaphragm closes, which prevents exhaust gasses from entering the air cleaner. The air aspirator is most effective at idle and slightly off idle where negative pressure pulses are greatest.

CHRYSLER THROTTLE BODY INJECTION SYSTEM

General Information

This Electronic Fuel Injection System is a computer regulated single point fuel injection system that provides precise air/fuel ratio for all driving conditions. At the center of this system is a digital pre-programmed computer known as a Logic Module that regulates ignition timing, air-fuel ratio, emission control devices and idle speed. This component has the ability to update and revise its programming to meet changing operating conditions.

Various sensors provide the input necessary for the Logic Module to correctly regulate the fuel flow at the fuel injector. These include the Manifold Absolute Pressure, Throttle Position, Oxygen Feedback, Coolant Temperature, Charge Temperature and Vehicle Speed sensors. In addition to the sensors, various switches also provide important information. These include the Neutral-safety, Heated Back Lite, Air Conditioning, Air Conditioning Clutch switches, and an Electronic Idle switch.

All inputs to the Logic Module are converted into signals sent to the

31-27

SECTION 31

FUEL INJECTION
CHRYSLER THROTTLE BODY FUEL INJECTION

Power Module. These signals cause the Power Module to change either the fuel flow at the injector or ignition timing or both.

The Logic Module tests many of its own input and output circuits. If a fault is found in a major system this information is stored in the Logic Module. Information on this fault can be displayed to a technician by means of a flashing light emitting diode (LED) or by connecting a diagnostic read out and reading a numbered display code which directly relates to a specific fault.

POWER MODULE

The Power Module contains the circuits necessary to power the ignition coil and the fuel injector. These are high current devices and their power supply has been isolated to minimize any "electrical noise" reaching the Logic Module. The Power Module also energizes the Automatic Shut Down (ASD) Relay which activates the fuel pump, ignition coil, and the Power Module itself. The module also receives a signal from the distributor and sends this signal to the Logic Module. In the event of no distributor signal, the ASD relay is not activated and power is shut off from the fuel pump and ignition coil. The Power Module contains a voltage converter which reduces battery voltage to a regulated 8.0V output. This 8.0V output powers the distributor and also powers the Logic Module.

LOGIC MODULE

The Logic Module is a digital computer containing a microprocessor. The module receives input signals from various switches, sensors, and components. It then computes the fuel injector pulse width, spark advance, ignition coil dwell, Automatic Idle Speed actuation, and purge, and EGR control solenoid cycles.

The Logic Module tests many of its own input and output circuits. If a fault is found in a major system, this information is stored in the Logic Module. Information on this fault can be displayed to a technician by means of a flashing, light emitting diode (LED) or by connecting a diagnostic read out and reading a numbered display code which directly relates to a specific fault.

When the power Module senses a distributor signal during cranking, it grounds the ASD closing its contacts. This completes the circuit for the electric fuel pump, Power Module, and ignition coil. If the distributor signal is lost for any reason the ASD interrupts this circuit in less than one second preventing fuel, spark, and engine operations. This fast shutdown serves as a safety feature in the event of an accident.

MANIFOLD ABSOLUTE PRESSURE (MAP) SENSOR

The Manifold Absolute Pressure (MAP) sensor is a device which monitors manifold vacuum. It is mounted in the right side passenger compartment and is connected to a vacuum nipple on the throttle body and, electrically to the Logic Module. The sensor transmits information on manifold vacuum conditions and barometric pressure to the Logic Module. The MAP sensor data on engine load is used with data from other sensors to determine the correct air-fuel mixture.

OXYGEN SENSOR (O_2 SENSOR)

The Oxygen Sensor (O_2 Sensor) is a device which produces an electrical voltage when exposed to the oxygen present in the exhaust gases. The sensor is mounted in the exhaust manifold and must be heated by the exhaust gases before producing the voltage. When there is a large amount of oxygen present (lean mixture), the sensor produces a low voltage. When there is a lesser amount present (rich mixture) it produces a higher voltage. By monitoring the oxygen content and converting it to electrical voltage, the sensor acts as a rich-lean switch. The voltage is transmitted to the Logic Module. The Logic Module signals the Power Module to trigger the fuel injector. The injector changes the mixture.

COOLANT TEMPERATURE SENSOR

The Coolant Temperature Sensor is mounted in the thermostat housing. This sensor provides data on engine operating temperature to the Logic Module. This data along with data provided by the Charge

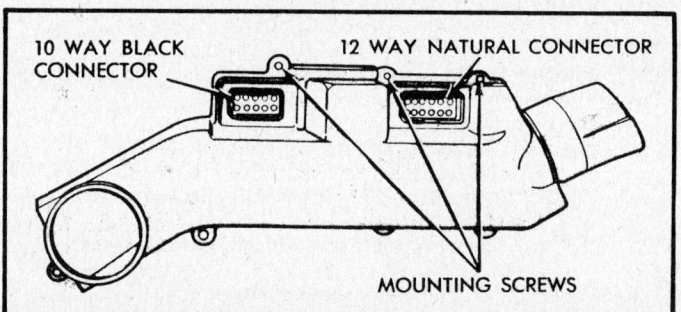

Power module showing connectors

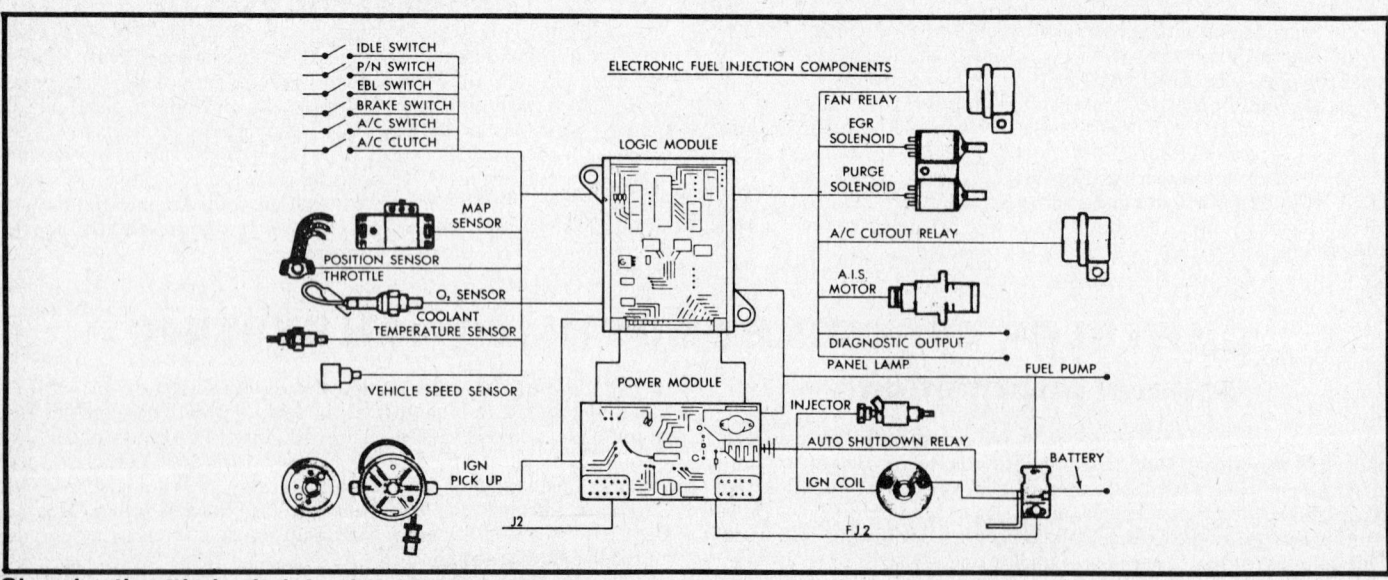

Chrysler throttle body injection system components

FUEL INJECTION
CHRYSLER THROTTLE BODY FUEL INJECTION

Temperature Switch allows the Logic Module to demand slightly richer air-fuel mixtures and higher idle speeds until normal operating temperatures are reached. The Coolant Temperature Sensor allows the Logic Module to act as an automatic choke.

CHARGE TEMPERATURE SENSOR

The Charge Temperature Sensor is a device mounted in the intake manifold which measures the temperature of the air-fuel mixture. This information is used by the Logic Module to determine engine operating temperature and engine warm-up cycles in the event of a Coolant Temperature Sensor failure.

SWITCH INPUT

Various switches provide information to the Logic Module. These include the Idle, Neutral Safety, Electric Backlite, Air Conditioning, Air Conditioning Clutch, and Brake Light switches. If one or more of these switches is sensed as being in the on position, the Logic Module signals the Automatic Idle Speed Motor to increase idle speed to a scheduled rpm.

With the air conditioning on and the throttle blade above a specific angle, the wide open throttle cut-out relay prevents the air conditioning clutch from engaging until the throttle blade is below this angle.

POWER LOSS LAMP

The Power Loss Lamp comes on each time the ignition key is turned on and stays on for a few seconds as a bulb test.

If the Logic Module receives an incorrect signal or no signal from either the Coolant Temperature Sensor, Manifold Absolute Pressure Sensor, or the Throttle Position Sensor, the Power Loss Lamp on the instrument panel is illuminated. This is a warning that the Logic Module has gone into Limp in Mode in an attempt to keep the system operational.

LIMP IN MODE

Limp In Mode is the attempt by the Logic Module to compensate for the failure of certain components by substituting information from other sources. If the Logic Module senses incorrect data or no data at all from the MAP Sensor, Throttle Position Sensor or Coolant Temperature Sensor, the system is placed into Limp In Mode and the Power Loss lamp on the instrument panel is activated.

PURGE SOLENOID

The purge solenoid is controlled by the logic module, the logic module will ground the purge solenoid energizing it, when the engine temperature is below 145°F (61°C). When the purge solenoid is energized, it prevents vacuum from reaching the charcoal canister valve. When the temperature reaches specifications the logic module will deenergize the solenoid by taking the ground off of it. This inturn allows the vacuum to flow to the canister purge valve and the purge fuel vapors through to the throttle body.

AIR CONDITIONING CUT OUT RELAY

The air conditioning cut out relay is electrically connected in series with the cycling clutch switch and the low pressure cut out switch. During engine operations this relay is in the normally (on) closed position. When the logic module senses wide open throttle through the throttle position sensor, it will energize the relay, open its contacts and prevent the air conditioning clutch from engaging.

THROTTLE BODY

The Throttle Body Assembly replaces a conventional carburetor and is mounted on top of the intake manifold. The throttle body houses the Fuel Injector, Pressure Regulator, Throttle Position Sensor, and Automatic Idle Speed Motor. Air flow through the throttle body is controlled by a cable operated throttle blade located in the base of the throttle body. The throttle body itself provides the chamber for metering atomizing and distributing fuel through out the air entering the engine.

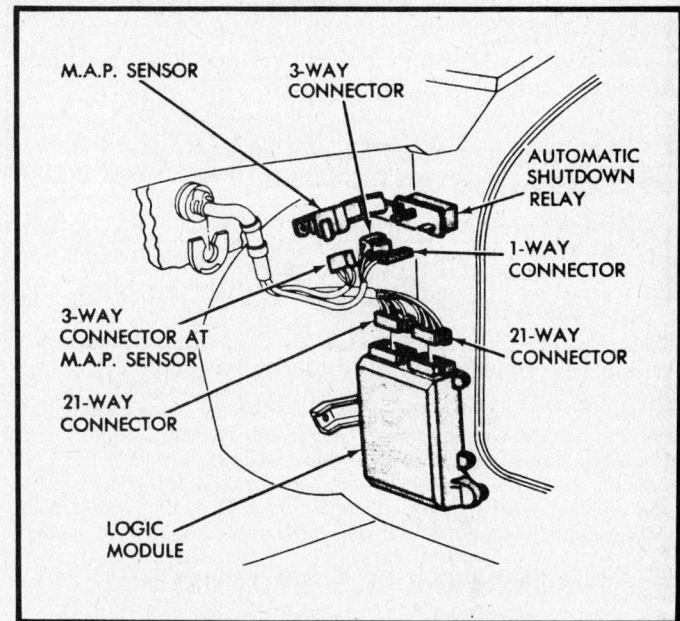

Location of logic module and components

FUEL INJECTOR

The Fuel Injector is an electric solenoid powered by the Power Module but, controlled by the Logic Module. The Logic Module, based on ambient, mechanical, and sensor input, determines when and how long the Power Module should operate the injector. When an electric current is supplied to the injector, the armature and pintle move a short distance against a spring, opening a small orifice. Fuel is supplied to the inlet of the injector by the fuel pump, then passes through the injector, around the pintle, and out the orifice. Since the fuel is under high pressure a fine spray is developed in the shape of a hollow cone. The injector, through this spraying action, atomizes the fuel and distributes it into the air entering the throttle body.

FUEL PRESSURE REGULATOR

The pressure regulator is a mechanical device located downstream of the fuel injector on the throttle body. Its function is to maintain a constant 250kPa (36PSI) across the fuel injector tip. The regulator uses a spring loaded rubber diaphragm to uncover a fuel return port. When the fuel pump becomes operational, fuel flows past the injector into the regulator, and is restricted from flowing any further by the blocked return port. When fuel pressure reaches 250kPa (36PSI) it pushes on the diaphragm, compressing the spring, and uncovers the fuel return port. The diaphragm and spring will constantly move from an open to closed position to keep the fuel pressure constant. An assist to the spring loaded diaphragm comes from vacuum in the throttle body above the throttle blade. As venturi vacuum increases less pressure is required to supply the same amount of fuel into the air flow. The vacuum assists in opening the fuel port during high vacuum conditions. This fine tunes the fuel pressure for all operating conditions.

THROTTLE POSITION SENSOR (TPS)

The Throttle Position Sensor (TPS) is an electric resistor which is activated by the movement of the throttle shaft. It is mounted on the

SECTION 31

FUEL INJECTION
CHRYSLER THROTTLE BODY FUEL INJECTION

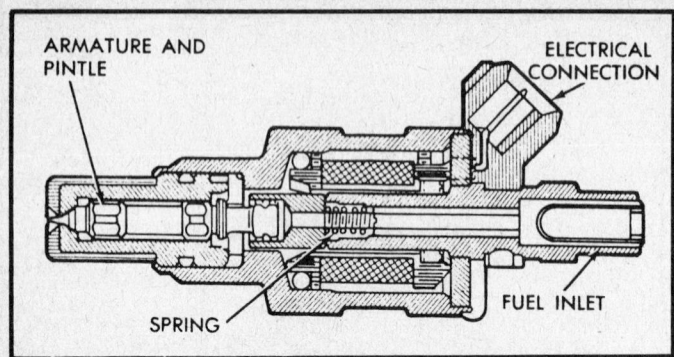

Cross section of solenoid-type fuel injector

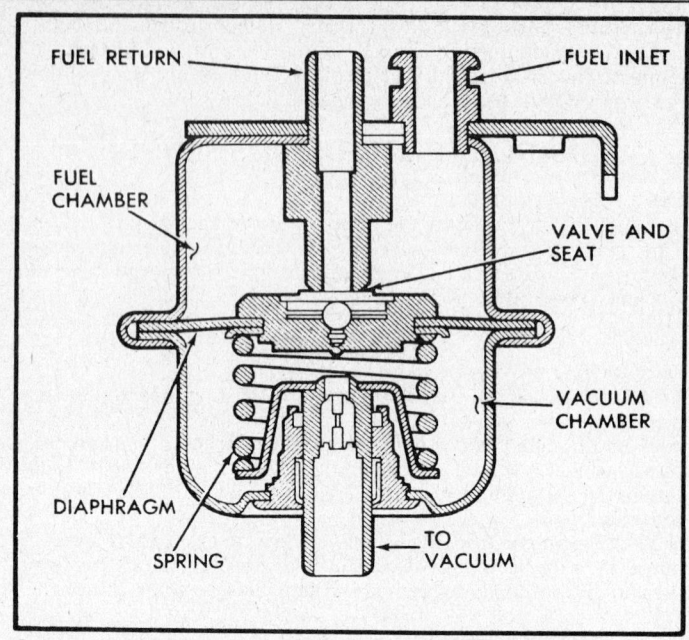

Cross section of typical fuel pressure regulator

throttle body and senses the angle of the throttle blade opening. The voltage that the sensor produces increases or decreases according to the throttle blade opening. This voltage is transmitted to the Logic Module where it is used along with data from other sensors to adjust the air-fuel ratio to varying conditions and during acceleration, deceleration, idle, and wide open throttle operations.

AUTOMATIC IDLE SPEED (AIS) MOTOR

The Automatic Idle Speed Motor (AIS) is operated by the Logic Module. Data from the Throttle Position Sensor, Speed Sensor,

TURBO MULTI-POINT FUEL INJECTION SYSTEM SCHEMATIC

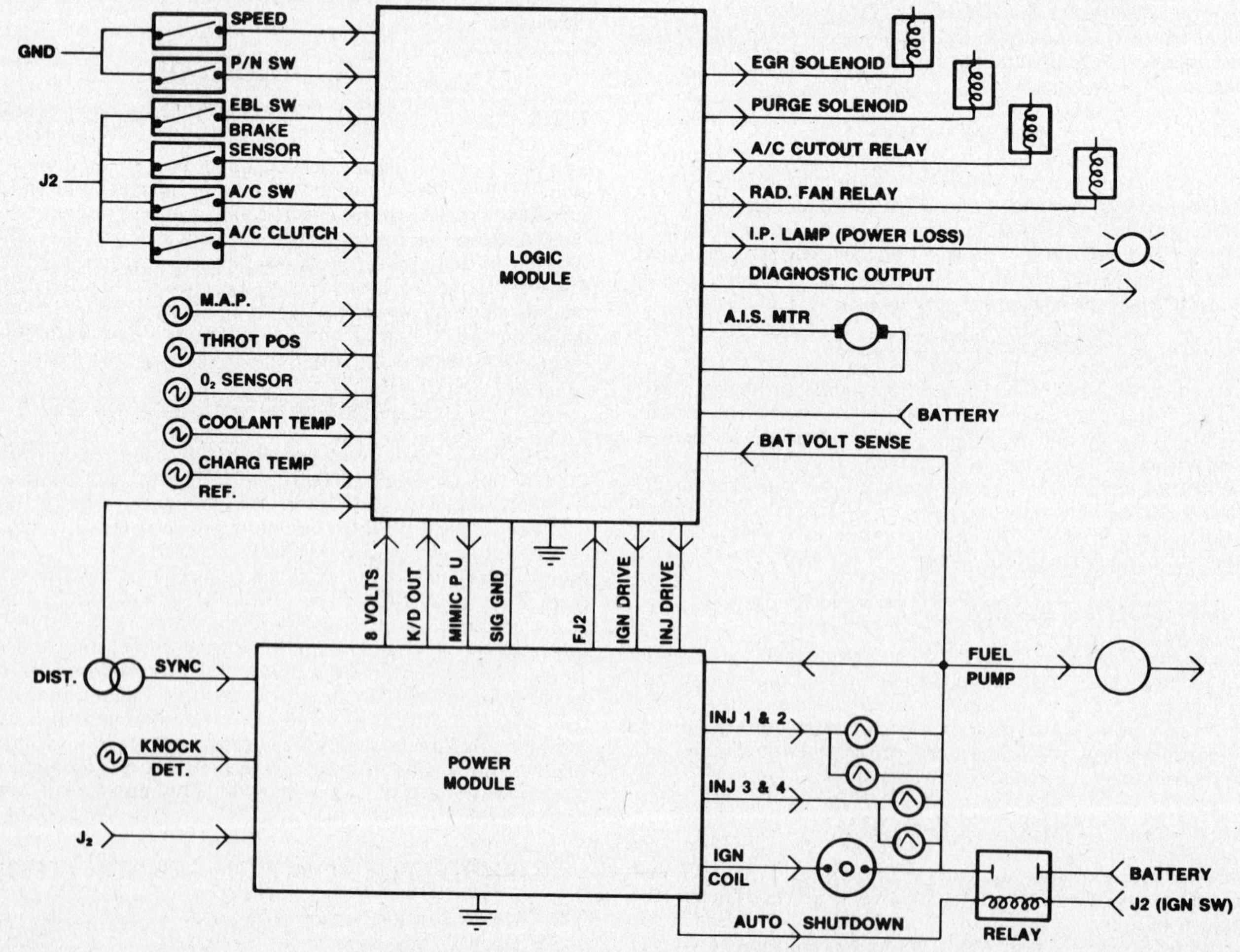

FUEL INJECTION
CHRYSLER THROTTLE BODY FUEL INJECTION
SECTION 31

Coolant Temperature Sensor, and various switch operations, (Electric Backlite, Air Conditioning, Safety/Neutral, Brake) are used by the Logic Module to adjust engine idle to an optimum during all idle conditions. The AIS adjusts the air portion of the air/fuel mixture through an air bypass on the back of the throttle body. Basic (no load) idle is determined by the minimum air flow through the throttle body. The AIS opens or closes off the air bypass as an increase or decrease is needed due to engine loads or ambient conditions. The Logic Module senses an air/fuel change and increases or decreases fuel proportionally to change engine idle. Deceleration die out is also prevented by increasing engine idle when the throttle is closed quickly after a driving (speed) condition.

FUEL PUMP

The fuel pump used in this system is a positive displacement, roller vane immersible pump with a permanent magnet electric motor. The fuel is drawn in through a filter sock and pushed through the electric motor to the outlet. The pump contains two check valves. One valve is used to relieve internal fuel pump pressure and regulate maximum pump output. The other check valve, located near the pump outlet, restricts fuel movement in either direction when the pump is not operational. Voltage to operate the pump is supplied through the Auto Shutdown Relay.

Troubleshooting

NOTE: Experience has shown that most complaints that may occur with EFI can be traced to poor wiring or hose connections. A visual check will help spot these most common faults and save unnecessary test and diagnosis time.

ON BOARD DIAGNOSTICS

The Logic Module has been programmed to monitor several different circuits of the fuel injection system. This monitoring is called On Board Diagnosis. If a problem is sensed with a monitored circuit, often enough to indicate an actual problem, its Fault Code is stored in the Logic Module for eventual display to the service technician. If the problem is repaired or ceases to exist, the Logic Module cancels the Fault Code after 30 ignition key on/off cycles.

FAULT CODE DESCRIPTION—1982-84

When a fault code appears (either by flashes of the light emitting diode or by watching the diagnostic readout—Tool C-4805 or equivalent), it indicates that the Logic Module has recognized an abnormal signal in the system. Fault codes indicate the results of a failure but do not always identify the failed component.

CODE 11 means a problem in the distributor circuit. This code appears when the Logic Module has not seen a distributor signal since the battery was reconnected.
CODE 12 indicates a problem in the stand-by memory circuit. This code appears if direct battery feed to the Logic Module is interrupted.
CODE 13 means a problem exists in the MAP sensor pneumatic system. This code appears if the MAP sensor vacuum level does not change between start and start/run transfer speed (500-600 rpm).
CODE 14 means a problem exists in the MAP sensor electrical system. This code appears if the MAP sensor signal is either too low (below .02 volts) or too high (above 4.9 volts).
CODE 15 means a problem exists in the vehicle Speed Sensor circuit. This code appears if engine speed is above 1468 rpm and speed sensor indicates less than 2 mph. This code is valid only if it is sensed while vehicle is moving.
CODE 21 indicates a problem in the O_2 sensor circuit. This code appears if there has been no O_2 signal for more than 5 seconds.
CODE 22 means problem exists in the Coolant Temperature Sensor circuit. This code appears if the temperature sensor circuit indicates an incorrect temperature or a temperature that changes too fast to be real.

CODE 24 means a problem exists in the Throttle Position Sensor circuit. This code appears if the sensor signal is either below .16 volts or above 4.7 volts.
CODE 25 means a problem in the Automaic Idle Speed (AIS) control circuit. This code appears if the proper voltage from the AIS system is not present. An open harness or motor will not activate code.
CODE 31 means a problem in the Canister Purge Solenoid circuit. This code appears when the proper voltage at the purge solenoid is not present (open or shorted system).
CODE 32 means a problem in the Power Loss Lamp circuit. This code appears when proper voltage to the Power Loss Lamp circuit is not present (open or shorted system).
CODE 33 means a problem in the Air Conditioning Wide Open Throttle Cut Out Relay circuit. This code appears if the proper voltage at the air conditioning wide open throttle relay circuit is not present (open or shorted).
CODE 34 means a problem in the EGR Solenoid circuit. This code appears if proper voltage at the EGR Solenoid circuit is not present (open or shorted system).
CODE 35 indicates a problem in the fan relay circuit. This code appears if the radiator fan is either not operating or operating at wrong time.
CODE 41 means a problem in the Charging System. This code appears if battery voltage from the automatic shut down relay is below 11.75 volts.
CODE 42 means a problem in the Automatic Shut Down Relay (ASD) circuit. This code appears if during cranking, battery voltage from ASD relay is not present for at least 1/3 second after first distributor pulse or after engine stall, battery voltage is not off within 3 seconds after last distributor pulse.
CODE 43 means a problem in the interface circuit. This code appears if the anti-dwell or injector control signal is not present between the Logic Module and Power Module.
CODE 44 means a problem in the Logic Module. This code appears if an internal failure exists in the Logic Module.
CODE 51 indicates a problem in the closed loop fuel system. This code appears if during closed loop conditions, the O_2 signal is either low or high for more than 2 minutes.
CODE 52 means a problem in the Logic Module. This code appears if an internal failure exists in the Logic Module.
CODE 53 means a problem in the Logic Module. This code appears if an internal failure exists in the Logic Module.
CODE 54 means a problem in the Logic Module. This code appears if an internal failure exists in the Logic Module.
CODE 55 means "end of message". This code appears as the final code after all other fault codes have been displayed and means "end of message".
CODE 88 means start of message. This code only appears on the diagnostic readout tool C-4805 or equivalent, and means start of message.

FAULT CODES—1985 AND LATER

CODE 11 indicates engine has not been cranked since battery was disconnected.
CODE 12 indicates memory standby power was recently lost.
CODE 13 indicates a problem in the MAP sensor pneumatic circuit.
CODE 14 indicates a problem in the MAP sensor electrical circuit.
CODE 15 indicates a problem in the distance sensor circuit.
CODE 16 indicates a loss of battery voltage sense.
CODE 17 indicates a problem in the knock sensor circuit.
CODE 21 indicates a problem in the oxygen sensor circuit.
CODE 22 indicates a problem in the coolant temperature circuit.
CODE 23 indicates a problem in the charge temperature sensor code.
CODE 24 indicates a problem in the throttle position sensor circuit.
CODE 25 indicates a problem in the AIS motor driver circuit.
CODE 26 indicates a problem in injector one circuit.
CODE 27 indicates a problem in injector two circuit.
CODE 31 indicates a problem in the purge solenoid driver circuit.
CODE 32 indicates a problem in the power loss lamp driver circuit.

31-31

FUEL INJECTION
CHRYSLER THROTTLE BODY FUEL INJECTION

CODE 33 indicates a problem in the A/C cutout relay driver circuit.
CODE 34 indicates a problem in the EGR solenoid circuit.
CODE 35 indicates a problem in the fan control relay driver circuit.
CODE 36 indicates a problem in the wastegate solenoid circuit.
CODE 37 indicates a problem in the barometric read solenoid circuit.
CODE 41 indicates charging system excess or no field current.
CODE 42 indicates a problem with the ASD relay driver.
CODE 43 indicates a problem in the spark interface circuit.
CODE 45 indicates a problem in the overboost shut-off system.
CODE 46 indicates battery voltage is too high.
CODE 47 indicates battery voltage is too low.
CODE 51 indicates oxygen feedback system is latched up.
CODE 52 indicates a problem in the battery temperature circuit.
CODE 53 indicates an internal logic module problem.
CODE 54 indicates a problem in the distributor synch circuit.

SYSTEMS TEST

Obtaining Fault Codes

1. Connect Diagnostic Readout Box Tool C-4805 or equivalent, to the diagnostic connector located in the engine compartment near the passenger side strut tower.
2. Start the engine if possible, cycle the transmission selector and the A/C switch if applicable. Shut off the engine.
3. Turn the ignitiion switch on, off, on, off, on. Within 5 seconds record all the diagnostic codes shown on the diagnostic readout box tool, observe the power loss lamp on the instrument panel the lamp should light for 2 seconds then go out (bulb check).

Switch Test

After all codes have been shown and has indicated Code 55 end of message, actuate the following component switches. The digital display must change its numbers when the switch is activated and released:
- Brake Pedal
- Gear Shift Selector park, reverse, park.
- A/C Switch (if applicable).
- Electric Backlite Switch (if applicable).

Actuator Test Mode (ATM)

1982-84

1. Remove coil wire from cap and place 1/4 in. from a ground.

---CAUTION---
Coil wire must be 1/4 in. or less from ground or power module damage may result.

2. Remove air cleaner hose from throttle body.
3. Press the **ATM** button on the diagnostic readout box tool, and observe the following:
- 3 sparks from the coil wire to ground.
- 2 **AIS** motor movement (1 open, 1 close) you must listen carefully for **AIS** operation.
- 1 fuel pulse from the injector into the throttle body.

4. The ATM capability is cancelled 5 minutes after the ignition switch is cancelled 5 minutes after the ignition switch is turned on. To reinstate this capability cycle the ignition ON and OFF three times ending in the ON position.
5. When the **ATM** button is pressed, fault Code 42 is generated because the ASD relay is bypassed. Do not use this code for diagnostics after **ATM** operation.
6. The **ATM** test will check 3 categories of operation:
- When coil fires three times:
  a. Coil operational
  b. Logic Module portion operational
  c. Power Module portion operational
  d. Interface between Power Module and Logic Module is working.
- AIS is operational
- Injector fuel pulse into Throttle Body:
  a. Fuel injector operational
  b. Fuel pump operational
  c. Fuel lines intact

7. The electronic fuel injection system must be evaluated using all the information found in the systems test:
- Start/No Start
- Fault Codes
- Loss of Power Lamp on or off (limp in)
- ATM Results:
  a. Spark yes/no
  b. Fuel yes/no
  c. AIS movement yes/no

Once this information is found, it will be easier to determine what circuit to look at for further testing.

1985 AND LATER

1. Put the system into the diagnostic test mode and wait for code 55 to appear on the display screen.
2. Press the ATM button on the diagnostic readout box to activate the display screen.
3. If a specific ATM test is desired, hold the ATM button down until the desired test code appears.
4. The computer will continue to turn the selected circuit on and off for as long as five minutes or until the ATM button is pressed again or if the ignition is turned off.
5. If the ATM button is not pressed again, the computer will continue cycling the selected circuit for five minutes and then shut the system off. The test mode can also be shut off by turning the ignition off.

ACTUATOR TEST DISPLAY CODES

Code	Description
01	Spark Activation
02	Injector Activation
03	AIS Activation
04	Radiator Fan Activation
05	A/C Cutout Relay Activation
06	ASD Relay Activation
07	Purge Solenoid Activation

Ignition Timing Adjustment

1. Connect a power timing light to the number one cylinder, or a magnetic timing unit to the engine. (Use a 10° offset when required).
2. Connect a tachometer to the engine and turn selector to the proper cylinder position.
3. Start engine and run until operating temperature is reached.
4. Disconnect and reconnect the water temperature sensor connector on the thermostat housing. The loss of power lamp on the dash must come on and stay on. Engine rpm should be within emission label specifications.
5. Aim power timing light at timing hole in bell housing or read the magnetic timing unit.
6. Loosen distributor and adjust timing to emission label specifications if necessary.
7. Shut engine off, disconnect and reconnect positive battery quick disconnect. Start vehicle, the loss of power lamp should be off.
8. Shut engine off, then turn ignition on, off, on, off, on. Fault codes should be clear with 88-51-55 shown.
9. Increase engine rpm to 2000.
10. Read timing, it should be approximately 40 degrees.
11. If timing advance does not reach specifications, replace logic module.

Idle Speed Adjustment

1. Before adjusting the idle on an Electronic Fuel Injected vehicle the following items must be checked.

FUEL INJECTION
CHRYSLER THROTTLE BODY FUEL INJECTION
SECTION 31

   a. AIS motor has been checked for operation.
   b. Engine has been checked for vacuum or EGR leaks.
   c. Engine timing has been checked and set to specifications.
   d. Coolant Temperature Sensor has been checked for operation.
2. Connect a tachometer and timing light to engine.
3. Disconnect throttle body 6 way connector. Remove brown with white tracer AIS wire from connector and rejoin connector.
4. Connect one end of a jumper wire to AIS wire and other end to battery positive post for 5 seconds.
5. Connect a jumper to radiator fan so that it will run continuously.
6. Start and run engine for 3 minutes to allow speed to stabilize.
7. Using tool C-4804, or equivalent, turn idle speed adjusting screw to obtain 800 ± 10 rpm (Manual) 725 ± 10 rpm (Automatic) with transaxle in neutral.

NOTE: *If idle will not adjust down, check for binding linkage, speed control servo cable adjustments, or throttle shaft binding.*

8. Check that timing is 18 ± 2° BTDC (Manual) 12 ± 2° BTDC (Automatic).
9. If timing is not to above specifications turn idle speed adjusting screw until correct idle speed and ignition timing are obtained.
10. Turn off engine, disconnect tachometer and timing light, reinstall AIS wire and remove jumper wire.

Relieving Fuel System Pressure

The E.F.I. fuel system is under a constant pressure of approximately 36 psi (250 kPa). Before servicing the fuel tank, fuel pump, fuel lines, fuel filter, or fuel components of the throttle body the fuel pressure must be released as follows.
1. Loosen gas cap to release any in tank pressure.
2. Remove wiring harness connector from injector.
3. Ground one injector terminal with a jumper.
4. Connect a jumper wire to second terminal and touch battery positive post for no longer than 10 seconds.
5. Remove jumper wires.
6. Continue fuel system service.

Fuel System Pressure Test

CAUTION
Fuel system pressure must be released each time a fuel hose is to be disconnected.

1. Remove fuel intake hose from throttle body and connect fuel system pressure testers C-3292, and C-4749, or equivalent, between fuel filter hose and throttle body.
2. Start engine. If gauge reads 250 kPa ± 14 kPa (36 psi ± 2 psi) pressure is correct and no further testing is required. Reinstall fuel hose using a new original equipment type clamp and torque to 10 in. lbs. (1 Nm).
3. If fuel pressure is **below** specifications, install tester between fuel filter hose and fuel line.
4. Start engine. If pressure is now correct, replace fuel filter. If no change is observed, gently squeeze return hose. If pressure increases, replace pressure regulator. If no change is observed, problem is either a plugged pump filter sock or defective fuel pump.
5. If pressure is **above** specifications, remove fuel return hose from throttle body. Connect a substitute hose and place other end of hose in clean container. Start engine. If pressure is now correct, check for restricted fuel return line. If no change is observed, replace fuel regulator.

MECHANICAL MALFUNCTIONS

Mechanical malfunctions are more difficult to diagnose with the EFI system. The Logic Module has been programmed to compensate for some mechanical malfunctions such as incorrect cam timing, vacuum leaks, etc. If engine performance problems are encountered, and no fault codes are displayed, the problem may be mechanical rather than electronic.

THROTTLE BODY

Removal and Installation

1. Release fuel system pressure.
2. Disconnect negative battery terminal.
3. Disconnect fuel injector wiring connector and throttle body 6-way connector.
4. Remove electrical ground wire from 6-way wiring connector.
5. Remove air cleaner hose.
6. Remove throttle cable and if so equipped, the speed control and transmission kickdown cables.
7. Remove return spring.
8. Remove vacuum hoses.
9. Loosen fuel intake and return hose clamps. Wrap a shop towel around each hose, twist and pull off each hose.
10. Remove throttle body mounting screws and lift throttle body from vehicle.
11. Installation is the reverse of removal. Using a new gasket, with tabs facing forward, install throttle body and torque mounting screws to 17 ft. lbs. (23 Nm).

Disassembly

When servicing the fuel portion of the throttle body it will be necessary to bleed fuel pressure before opening any hoses. Always reassemble throttle body components with new O-rings and seals where applicable. Never use lubricants with O-rings or seals, damage may result. If assembly of components is difficult use water to aid assembly. Use care when removing fuel hoses to prevent damage to hose or hose nipple. Always use new hose clamps of the correct type when reassembling and torque hose clamps to 10 inch lbs. (1 Nm). Do not use aviation-style clamps on this system or hose damage may result.

NOTE: *It is not necessary to remove the throttle body from the intake manifold to perform component disassembly. If fuel system hoses are to be replaced, only hoses marked EFI/EFM may be used.*

Injector Removal

1. Perform fuel system pressure release.
2. Disconnect negative battery cable.
3. Remove 4 Torx® screws holding fuel inlet chamber to throttle body.
4. Remove vacuum tube from pressure regulator to throttle body.

CAUTION
Place a shop towel around fuel inlet chamber to contain any fuel left in system.

5. Lift fuel inlet chamber and injector off throttle body.
6. Pull injector from fuel inlet chamber.
7. Remove upper and lower O-ring from fuel injector by peeling them off.
8. Remove snap ring that retains seal and washer on injector and remove seal and washer.
9. Installation is the reverse of removal. Place new O-ring, washer, and seal on injector and install snap ring.
10. Place assembly into throttle body, install 4 Torx® screws and torque these screws to 35 inch lbs. (4 Nm).

PRESSURE REGULATOR

Removal and Installation

1. Perform fuel system pressure release.
2. Disconnect negative battery cable.
3. Remove 3 Torx® screws mounting pressure regulator to fuel inlet chamber.

CAUTION
Place a shop towel around fuel inlet chamber to contain any fuel left in system.

4. Remove vacuum tube from pressure regulator to throttle body.

SECTION 31

FUEL INJECTION
CHRYSLER THROTTLE BODY FUEL INJECTION

5. Pull pressure regulator from throttle body.
6. Carefully peel O-ring off pressure regulator and remove flat seal.
7. Place new seal on pressure regulator and new O-ring.
8. Position pressure regulator on throttle body, press into place, install 3 Torx® screws and torque to 40 inch lbs. (5 Nm).
9. Install vacuum tube from pressure regulator to throttle body.
10. Connect battery, start vehicle, and check for any fuel leaks.

THROTTLE POSITION SENSOR

Removal and Installation

1. Disconnect negative battery cable and 6-way throttle body connector.
2. Remove 2 screws mounting throttle position sensor to throttle body.
3. Unclip wiring clip from convoluted tube and remove mounting bracket.
4. Lift throttle position sensor off throttle shaft and remove O-ring.
5. Pull the 3 wires of the throttle position sensor from the convoluted tubing.
6. Look inside the 6-way throttle body connector and lift a locking tab with a small screwdriver for each T.P.S. wire blade terminal. Remove each blade from connector. (Note wiring position for reassembly.)
7. Insert each wire blade terminal into throttle body connector. Make sure wires are inserted into correct locations.
8. Insert wires from throttle position sensor into convoluted tube.
9. Install throttle position sensor and new O-ring with mounting bracket to throttle body. Torque screws to 20 inch lbs. (2 Nm).
10. Install wiring clips to convoluted tube.
11. Connect 6 way connector and battery cable.

AUTOMATIC IDLE SPEED MOTOR

Removal and Installation

1. Disconnect negative battery cable and 6-way throttle body connector.
2. Remove screws that mount the A.I.S. to its adaptor. (Do not remove the clamp on the A.I.S. or damage will result.)
3. Remove wiring clips and remove the two A.I.S. wires from the 6-way throttle body connector. Lift each locking tab with a small screwdriver and remove each blade terminal (note wiring position for reassembly).
4. Lift A.I.S. from its adaptor.
5. Remove the O-rings on the A.I.S. carefully.
6. Install new O-rings on A.I.S.
7. Carefully work A.I.S. into its adaptor.
8. Install 2 mounting screws and torque to 20 inch lbs. (2 Nm).
9. Route A.I.S. wiring to 6-way connector and install each wire blade terminal into the connector. Make sure wires are inserted in correct locations.
10. Connect wiring clips, 6-way connector, and battery cable.

AUTOMATIC IDLE SPEED MOTOR ASSEMBLY

Removal and Installation

1. Disconnect negative battery cable and 6-way throttle body connector.
2. Remove 2 screws on back of throttle body from A.I.S. adaptor.
3. Remove wiring clips and remove the two A.I.S. wires from the 6-way throttle body connector. Lift each locking tab with a small screwdriver and remove each blade terminal. (Note wiring position for reassembly.)
4. Carefully pull the assembly from the rear of the throttle body. The O-ring at the top and seal at the bottom may fall off adaptor.
5. Remove O-ring and seal.
6. Place a new O-ring and seal on adaptor.
7. Carefully position assembly onto back of throttle body (make sure seals stay in place) insert screws and torque to 65 inch lbs. (20 Nm).
8. Route A.I.S. wiring to 6-way connector and install each wire blade terminal into the connector. Make sure wires are inserted in correct locations.
9. Connect wiring clips, 6-way connector, and battery cable.

FORD THROTTLE BODY FUEL INJECTION SYSTEM

COMPONENTS

1. In-tank (40 lbs. pressure) electric fuel pump
2. Upper body with two fuel injectors to meter air and fuel
3. Throttle body which houses the throttle, an electric bi-metal coil to control cold idle speed and an automatic kickdown motor
4. Primary and secondary fuel filters
5. Manifold charging temperature sensor
6. Necessary fuel supply and return lines

The electronic fuel injection system has several distinct advantages over conventional carburetion. It has improved fuel distribution, capability of fine tuning for altitude and temperature variations, fuel vapor formation and vapor lock largely eliminated due to high pressure in fuel system and reduced evaporative losses due to elimination of the fuel bowl. It also has eliminated engine run-on, since fuel flow immediately stops electrically with engine shut down and elimination of fuel starvation during hard driving maneuvers provided by constant high pressure injection. It provides the precise air-fuel control required for efficient three-way catalyst operation.

Fuel Charging Assembly

The fuel charging assembly controls air-fuel ratio. It consists of a typical carburetor throttle body. It has two bores without venturis. The throttle shaft and valves control engine air flow based on driver demand. The throttle body attaches to the intake manifold mounting pad.

A throttle position sensor is attached to the throttle shaft. It includes a potentiometer (or rheostat) that electrically senses throttle opening. A throttle kicker solenoid fastens opposite the throttle position sensor. During air conditioning operation, the solenoid extends to slightly increase engine idle speed.

Cold engine speed is controlled by an automatic kick-down vacuum motor. There is also an all-electric, bi-metal coil spring which controls cold idle speed. The bi-metal electric coil operates like a conventional carburetor choke coil, but the electronic fuel injection system uses no choke. Fuel enrichment for cold starts is controlled by the computer and injectors.

Fuel Pressure Regulator

The fuel pressure regulator controls critical injector fuel pressure. The regulator receives high pressure fuel from the electric fuel pump. It then adjusts the fuel to the desired pressure for uniform fuel injection. The regulator sets fuel pressure at 39 psi.

Fuel Rail

The fuel rail evenly distributes fuel to each injector. Its main purpose is to equalize the fuel flow. One end of the fuel rail contains a relief valve for testing fuel pressure during operation.

FUEL INJECTION
FORD THROTTLE BODY FUEL INJECTION
SECTION 31

Fuel Injectors

The two identical fuel injectors are electro-mechanical devices. The electrical solenoid operates a pintle valve which always travels the same distance from closed to open to closed. Injection is controlled by varying the length of time the pintle valve is open.

The delivery end of the injector is a precisely ground nozzle. The manufacturing and handling of this component is very important for proper operation. When closed, the valve must seal tightly to shut off fuel flow completely. It must seat itself repeatedly with the same precision. Any dirt particles from contaminated fuel can prevent the valve from seating.

The shape of the pintle valve and nozzle also determines the fuel spray pattern during injection. Since the injectors are atomizing fuel into droplets, this fuel mist pattern is important to fast vaporization and good combustion.

The computer, based on voltage inputs from the crank position sensor, operates the injector solenoids four (two per injector) times per engine revolution. When the injector pintle valve unseats, fuel is sprayed in a fine mist into the intake manifold.

The computer varies fuel enrichment based on voltage inputs from the exhaust gas oxygen sensor, barometric pressure sensor, manifold absolute pressure sensor, etc., by calculating how long to hold the injectors open. The longer the injectors remain open, the richer the mixture.

FUEL DELIVERY SYSTEM

An in-tank electric fuel pump is used on all vehicles equipped with Electronic Fuel Injected (EFI) engines. The fuel system is a recirculating system that delivers fuel to a pressure regulating valve in the throttle body and returns excess fuel from the throttle body regulator back to the fuel tank. The electrical system has two control relays, one controlled by a vacuum switch and the other controlled by an electronic engine control module. These provide for power to the fuel pump under various operating conditions.

With the ignition switch off, the vacuum switch controlled relay is closed and the EEC controlled relay is open. When the ignition switch is first turned to ignition "ON" position, the vacuum switch controlled relay remains closed and the EEC controlled relay also closes. This provides power to the fuel pump to pre-pressurize the fuel system. If the ignition switch is not turned to the "CRANK" position, the EEC module will open its relay after approximately two seconds and shut off power to the pump. When the ignition switch is turned to the "CRANK" position, both the vacuum switch controlled relay and the EEC controlled relay are closed. This provides full battery power to the pump. When the engine starts, manifold vacuum increases and causes the vacuum switch to close and the vacuum controlled relay to open. This provides reduced normal operating voltage to the fuel pump through the resistor which by-passes the vacuum controlled relay. Under heavy engine load conditions, manifold vacuum will reduce, causing the vacuum switch to open. This causes the vacuum controlled relay to close, thus providing the return of full battery power to the pump. The EEC module senses engine speed and shuts off the pump by opening the EEC controlled relay when the engine stops.

Fuel Pump Replacement (In-Tank Type)

CAUTION
The fuel supply lines will remain pressurized for long periods of time after the engine is turned off. A valve is provided on the throttle body for this purpose. Remove the air cleaner and relieve system pressure by depressing the pin in the relief valve cautiously. Fuel will be expelled into the throttle body.

REMOVAL
1. It is necessary to remove the fuel tank.
2. Depressurize the fuel system.
3. Remove fuel from the fuel tank by pumping out through the filter tube.
4. Disconnect the supply and return line fittings and the vent line.
5. Disconnect and remove the fuel filler tube.

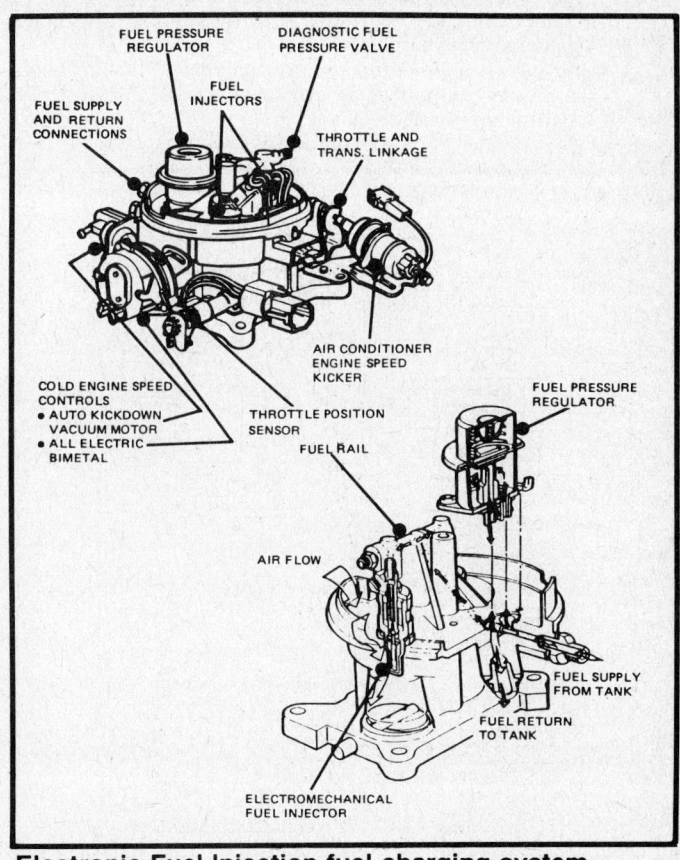
Electronic Fuel Injection fuel charging system

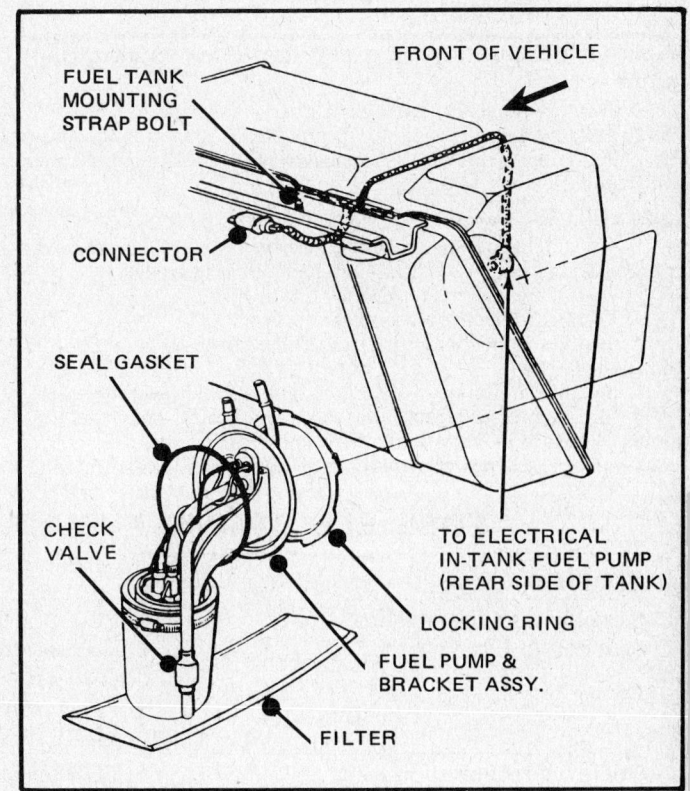
Electric fuel pump installation

31-35

SECTION 31: FUEL INJECTION
FORD THROTTLE BODY FUEL INJECTION

6. Disconnect the electrical connections to both the fuel sender and the fuel pump wiring harness.
7. Remove the fuel tank support straps and remove the fuel tank.
8. Turn the fuel pump locking ring counter-clockwise with the necessary tool and remove the locking ring.
9. Remove the fuel pump and bracket assembly.

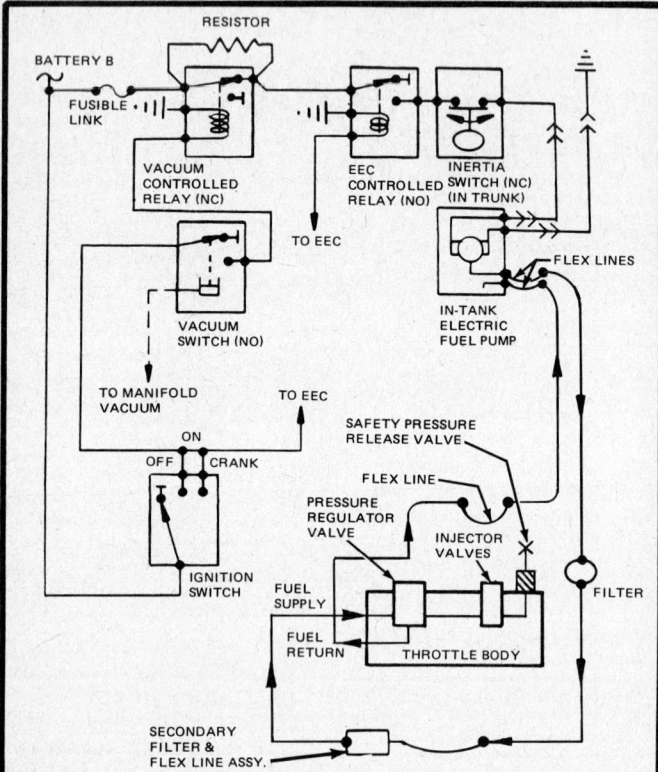

Electric fuel pump wiring and fuel lines routing diagram

10. Remove the seal gasket and discard.
11. Remove any dirt that has accumulated around the fuel pump attaching flange, to prevent it from entering the tank during removal and installation.

INSTALLATION

1. Put a light coating of heavy grease on a new seal ring to hold it in place during assembly. Install it in fuel tank ring groove.
2. Install the tank in the vehicle.
3. Install the electrical connector.
4. Install the fuel line fittings and tighten to 40-54 N·m (30-40 ft. lbs.).
5. Install a minimum of 10 gallons of fuel and inspect for leaks.
6. Install pressure gauge on valve on throttle body and turn ignition key to "ON" position for 3 seconds. Turn ignition key off and back on for 3 seconds repeatedly, 5-10 times, until pressure gauge

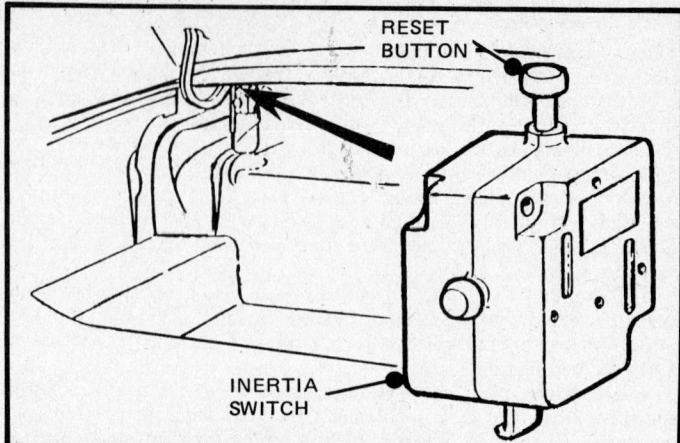

Electric fuel pump inertia switch

shows at least 35 psi. Reinspect for leaks at fittings.
7. Remove pressure gauge. Start engine and reinspect for leaks.

Inertia Switch

In the event of a collision impact, the inertia switch will open, shutting off the fuel pump even if the engine does not stop. The engine will stop moments after the pump is shut off and cannot be restarted until after the inertia switch is reset manually. The inertia switch, located in the luggage compartment, must not be manually reset until after the complete fuel system is thoroughly inspected for damage or leaks.

Fuel Lines

The fuel pump delivers filtered fuel to the pressure regulator. It passes to the fuel rail and on to the injectors. The capacity of the fuel pump exceeds the amount of fuel injection. Therefore, a fuel return line is provided to carry surplus fuel back to the fuel tank. Evaporative fuel vapors are routed from the tank to the charcoal canister by a third fuel line.

Fuel Filters

The close tolerances of the injector pintle valve and seat require extreme cleanliness in fuel handling. For this reason, two fuel filters are used. The primary filter is mounted at the rear of the vehicle. It includes an underbody stone shield to prevent hazard damage. The secondary filter is attached in the engine compartment also in the fuel supply line. Regularly scheduled maintenance of filters is essential for proper system operation.

Manifold Charging Temperature Sensor (MCT)

This sensor is similar in construction to the engine coolant temperature (ECT) sensor, except it is packaged to improve sensor response time. The sensor is threaded into a cylinder runner on the intake manifold and provides the electronic fuel injection (EFI) fuel metering system with fuel and air mixture temperature. The MCT is used both as a density corrector for air flow calculations and to proportion the cold enrichment fuel flow.

FORD ELECTRONIC FUEL INJECTION TROUBLESHOOTING

Symptom	Possible Problem Areas
Surging, backfire, misfire, runs rough	1. EEC distributor rotor registry ① 2. EGR solenoid(s) defective 3. Distributor, cap, body, rotor, ignition wires, plugs, coil defective 4. Pulse ring behind vibration damper misaligned or damaged 5. Spark plug fouling
Stalls on deceleration	1. EGR solenoid(s) or valve defective 2. EEC distributor rotor registry ①

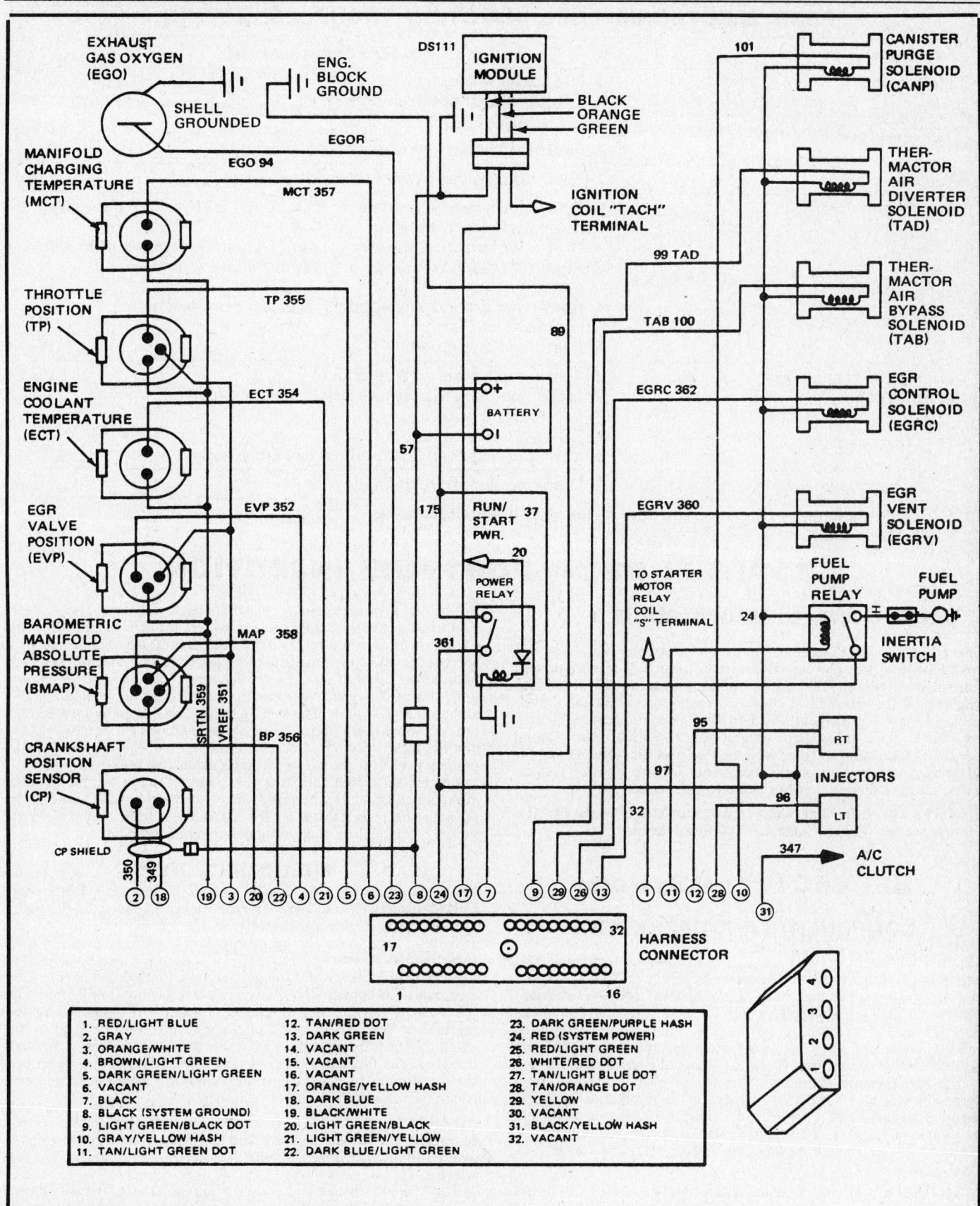

Electronic fuel injection wiring diagram

SECTION 31

FUEL INJECTION
FORD THROTTLE BODY FUEL INJECTION

FORD ELECTRONIC FUEL INJECTION TROUBLESHOOTING

Symptom	Possible Problem Areas
Stalls at idle	1. Idle speed wrong 2. Throttle kicker not working
Hesitates on acceleration	1. Acceleration enrichment system defective 2. Fuel pump ballast bypass relay not working
Fuel pump noisy	1. Fuel pump ballast bypass relay not working
Engine won't start	1. Fuel pump power relay defective, no spark, EGR system defective, no or low fuel pressure 2. Crankshaft position sensor not seated, clearance wrong, defective 3. Pulse ring behind vibration damper misaligned, sensor tabs damaged 4. Power and ground wires open or shorted, poor electrical connections 5. Inertia switch tripped
Engine starts and stalls or runs rough	1. Fuel pump ballast wire defective 2. Manifold absolute pressure (MAP) sensor circuit not working 3. Low fuel pressure 4. EGR system problem 5. Microprocessor and calibration assembly faulty
Starts hard when cold	1. Cranking signal circuit faulty

① See Ford Electronic Engine Control (EEC) for adjustment procedures.

FORD EFI-EEC IV PORT FUEL INJECTION

General Information

The EFI-EEC IV System combines an electronic engine control module with a port fuel injection system to provide a more precise control over the air/fuel ratio, spark timing, deceleration fuel shut-off, EGR, curb and fast idle speed, evaporative emission control, and cold engine enrichment. The EFI-EEC IV system can be divided into three basic subsystems—Fuel, Air and Electronic Engine Control. This section will deal with the Fuel and Air systems only; for all service information on the Electronic Engine Control system, please see the "Engine Controls" Unit Repair section.

NOTE: For wiring diagrams and diagnosis charts on the EEC IV System, see the "Engine Controls" Unit Repair section.

EFI-EEC IV Fuel System

COMPONENTS AND OPERATION

The fuel subsystem includes a high pressure electric fuel pump, fuel charging manifold, pressure regulator, fuel filter and both solid and flexible fuel lines. The fuel charging manifold includes four electronically controlled fuel injectors, each mounted directly above an intake port in the lower intake manifold. All injectors are energized simultaneously and spray once every crankshaft revolution, delivering a predetermined quantity of fuel into the intake airstream.

The fuel pressure regulator maintains a constant pressure drop across the injector nozzles. The regulator is referenced to intake manifold vacuum and is connected parallel to the fuel injectors and positioned on the far end of the fuel rail. Any excess fuel supplied by the pump passes through the regulator and is returned to the fuel tank via a return line.

NOTE: The pressure regulator reduces fuel pressure to 39-40 psi under normal operating conditions. At idle or high manifold vacuum condition, fuel pressure is reduced to about 30 psi.

The fuel pressure regulator is a diaphragm operated relief valve in which one side of the diaphragm senses fuel pressure and the other side senses manifold vacuum. Normal fuel pressure is established by a spring preload applied to the diaphragm. Control of the fuel system is maintained through the EEC power relay and the EEC IV control unit, although electrical power is routed through the fuel pump relay and an inertia switch. The fuel pump relay is normally located on a bracket somewhere above the Electronic Control Assembly (ECA) and the Inertia Switch is located in the left rear kick panel. The fuel pump is usually mounted on a bracket at the fuel tank.

The inertia switch opens the power circuit to the fuel pump in the event of a collision. Once tripped, the switch must be reset manually by pushing the reset button on the assembly. Check that the inertia switch is reset before diagnosing power supply problems.

FUEL INJECTORS

The fuel injectors used with the EFI-EEC IV system are electro-mechanical (solenoid) type designed to meter and atomize fuel delivered to the intake ports of the engine. The injectors are mounted in the lower intake manifold and positioned so that their spray nozzles direct the fuel charge in front of the intake valves. The injector body consists of a solenoid actuated pintle and needle valve assembly. The control unit sends an electrical impulse that activates the solenoid, causing the pintle to move inward off the seat and allow the fuel to flow. The amount of fuel delivered is controlled by the length of time the injector is energized since the fuel flow orifice is fixed and the fuel pressure drop across the injector tip is constant. Correct atomization is achieved by contouring the pintle at the point where the fuel enters the pintle chamber.

NOTE: Exercise care when handling fuel injectors during service. Be careful not to lose the pintle cap and replace damaged O-rings to assure a tight seal. Never apply direct battery voltage to test an EFI fuel injector.

The injectors receive high pressure fuel from the fuel manifold (fuel rail) assembly. The complete assembly includes a single, pre-formed tube with four injector connectors, mounting flange for the pressure

FUEL INJECTION
Ford EFI-EEC IV PORT FUEL INJECTION
SECTION 31

regulator, mounting attachments to locate the manifold and provide the fuel injector retainers and Schraeder quick disconnect fitting used to perform fuel pressure tests.

NOTE: The fuel manifold is normally removed with fuel injectors and pressure regulator attached. Fuel injector electrical connectors are plastic and have locking tabs that must be released when disconnecting.

EFI-EEC IV Air System

COMPONENTS AND OPERATION

The EFI-EEC IV air subsystem components include the air cleaner assembly, air flow (vane) meter, throttle air bypass valve and air ducts that connect the air system to the throttle body assembly. The throttle body regulates the air flow to the engine through a single butterfly-type throttle plate controlled by conventional accelerator linkage. The throttle body has an idle adjustment screw (throttle air bypass valve) to set the throttle plate position, a PCV fresh air source upstream of the throttle plate, individual vacuum taps for PCV and control signals and a throttle position sensor that provides a voltage signal for the EEC IV control unit.

NOTE: For information on diagnosis and testing of all EFI-EEC IV system sensors, see the Engine Controls Unit Repair section.

The hot air intake system uses a thermostatic flap valve assembly whose components and operation are similar to previous hot air intake systems. Intake air volume and temperature are measured by the vane meter assembly which is mounted between the air cleaner and throttle body. The vane meter consists of two separate devices; the vane airflow sensor (VAF) uses a counterbalanced L-shaped flap vallve mounted on a pivot pin and connected to a variable resistor (potentiometer). The control unit measures the amount of deflection of the flap vane by measuring the voltage signal from the potentiometer mounted on top of the meter body; larger air volume moves the vane further and produces a higher voltage signal. The vane air temperature (VAT) sensor is mounted in the middle of the air stream just before the flap valve. Since the mass (weight) of a specific volume of air varies with pressure and temperature, the control unit uses the voltage signal from the air temperature sensor to compensate for these variables and provide a more exact measurement of actual air mass that is necessary to calculate the fuel required to obtain the optimum air/fuel ratio under a wide range of operating conditions. On the EEC IV system, the VAT sensor affects spark timing as a function of air temperature.

NOTE: Make sure all air intake connections are tight before testing. Air leaking into the engine through a loose bellows connection can result in abnormal engine operation and affect the air/fuel mixture ratio.

THROTTLE AIR BYPASS VALVE

The throttle air bypass valve is an electro-mechanical (solenoid) device whose operation is controlled by the EEC IV control unit. A variable air metering valve controls both cold and warm idle airflow in response to commands from the control unit. The valve operates by bypassing a regulated amount of air around the throttle plate; the higher the voltage signal from the control unit, the more air is bypassed through the valve. In this manner, additional air can be added to the fuel mixture without moving the throttle plate. At curb idle, the valve provides smooth idle for various engine coolant temperatures, compensates for A/C load and compensates for transaxle load and no-load conditions. The valve also provides fast idle for start-up, replacing the fast idle cam, throttle kicker and anti-dieseling solenoid common to previous models.

NOTE: Curb and fast idle speeds are proportional to engine coolant temperature and controlled through the EEC IV control unit. Fast idle kick-down will occur when the throttle is depressed, or after approximately 15-25 seconds after coolant temperature reaches 160°F.

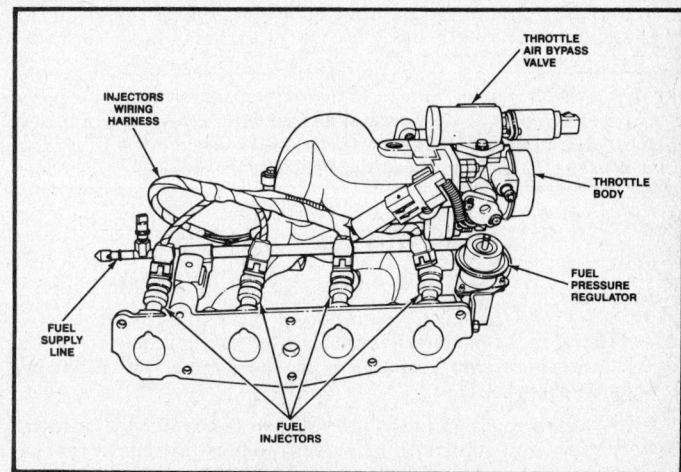
Components of EFI-EEC IV fuel system

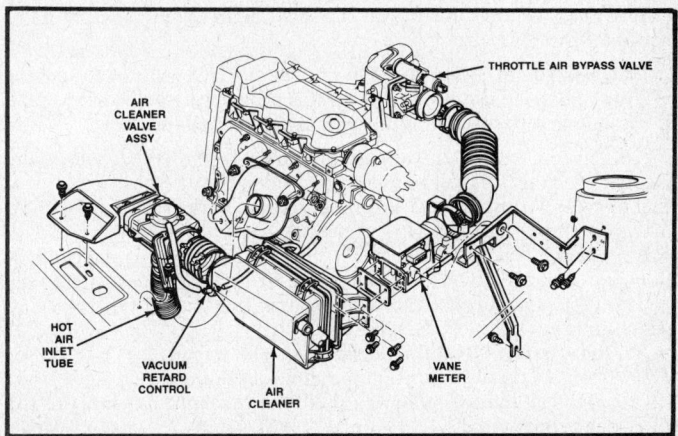
Components of EFI-EEC IV air intake system

EXHAUST GAS OXYGEN (EGO) SENSOR

The oxygen sensor used on the EFI-EEC IV system is a new design, located between the two downstream tubes in the header in its own mounting boss. The sensor works between zero and one volt output depending on the amount of oxygen in the exhaust gas. A voltage reading above 0.6 volt indicates a rich fuel mixture, while a reading below 0.4 volt indicates a lean fuel mixture. Operation of the oxygen sensor is the same as similar systems used on other EEC and MCU

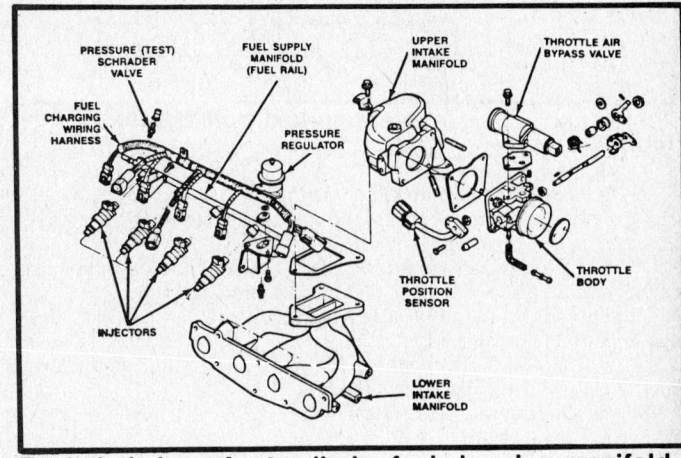
Exploded view of a 4 cylinder fuel charging manifold assembly

31-39

SECTION 31

FUEL INJECTION
FORD EFI-EEC IV PORT FUEL INJECTION

models. A new type oxygen sensor can be identified by the metal cap that replaces the rubber protective cover on earlier designs.

CAUTION
Applying direct battery voltage to the oxygen sensor will destroy the sensor's calibration. Even the use of an ohmmeter could cause damage. Before connecting and using a voltmeter, make sure it has a high-input impedence (at least 10 megohms) and is set on the correct voltage range.

FUEL CHARGING ASSEMBLY

Removal

NOTE: If the sub-assemblies are to be serviced or removed with the fuel charging assembly mounted on the engine, the following procedures should be used.

1. With the ignition in the off position, disconnect the negative battery cable, drain the coolant from the radiator and remove the fuel tank cap to relieve any fuel tank pressure.
2. Release the pressure from the fuel system at the fuel pressure relief valve, which is located on the fuel line in the upper right hand corner of the engine compartment.

NOTE: Not all of the assemblies can be serviced while on the engine and in some cases, the removal of the fuel charging assembly may make it possible to service some of the various sub-assemblies.

3. To remove the entire fuel charging assembly, disconnect the electrical connectors at the air bypass valve, throttle position sensor, fuel injector wiring harness, knock sensor, fan temperature sensor and coolant temperature sensor.
4. Disconnect the upper intake manifold vacuum fitting connections by disconnecting the vacuum line fitting at the cast tube, rear vacuum line to the dash panel tree, vacuum line to the EGR valve and vacuum line to the fuel pressure regulator.
5. Disconnect the throttle linkage and unbolt the accelerator cable from the bracket, position the cable out of the way.
6. Remove the two bolts that hold the cast tube assembly to the turbocharger assembly.

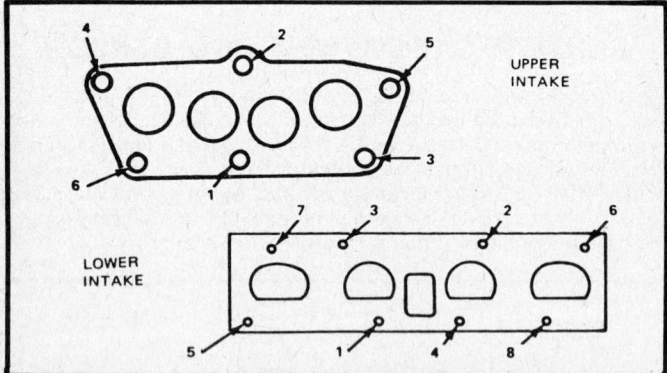

Upper and lower intake manifold bolt tightening sequence—Mustang SVO

7. Remove the four nuts that hold the air throttle body to the fuel charging assembly and separate the cast tube from the turbocharger assembly.
8. Remove and discard the gasket between the cast tube and turbocharger, also remove the throttle body and cast tube.
9. Disconnect the PCV hose from the fitting on the underside of the upper intake manifold.
10. Loosen the hose clamp on the water bypass line at the lower intake manifold and disconnect the hose.
11. Disconnect the EGR tube from the EGR valve by removing the flange nut.
12. Remove the fuel injector wiring harness bracket retaining nuts and remove the bracket.

NOTE: The dipstick bracket for the engine oil dipstick is bolted to the injector bracket. The Mustang SVO, has both brackets retained by one bolt.

13. Remove the two upper intake manifold retaining studs and two bolts. There are six bolts on the Mustang SVO.
14. Remove the upper intake manifold assembly, then disconnect the push connect fuel supply line, by removing the hairpin clip from the fitting.
15. Using special tool T82L-9500-AH or equivalent, disconnect the fuel return line from the fuel supply manifold.
16. Disconnect the electrical connectors from all the fuel injectors and move the harness aside, remove the two fuel supply manifold retaining bolts, carefully remove the fuel supply manifold.

NOTE: The fuel injectors can be removed at this time, by a slight twisting and pulling motion.

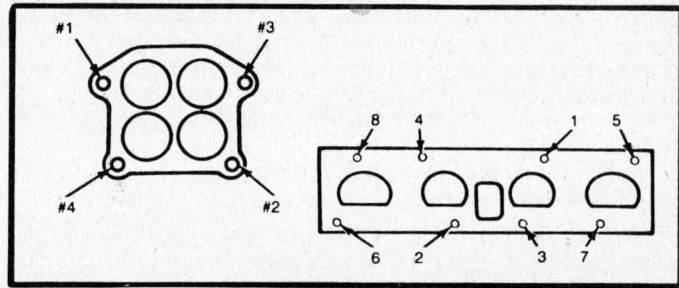

Upper and lower intake manifold bolt tightening sequence—except Mustang SVO

17. Remove the four bottom retaining bolts from the lower manifold.
18. Remove the four upper retaining bolts from the lower manifold, and remove the lower intake manifold assembly.

NOTE: The front two bolts are also used to hold an engine lift bracket.

Installation

NOTE: Before starting the installation procedure, clean and inspect the mounting surfaces of the fuel charging manifold assembly and the cylinder head. Both surfaces have to be clean and flat.

1. Clean and oil the manifold stud threads and install a new gasket.
2. Place the lower manifold assembly onto the cylinder head and install the engine lift bracket, also install the four upper manifold retaining nuts (fingertight).
3. Install the four remaining manifold nuts and torque all the nuts to 12-15 ft.lbs. (16-20 Nm). Follow the torque sequences provided in this section.
4. Install the fuel supply manifold with the two retaining bolts and torque the bolts to 12-15 ft. lbs. (16-20 Nm).
5. Connect the electrical connectors to the injectors.
6. Being sure that the gasket surfaces of the upper and lower intake manifolds are clean, install a new gasket on the lower intake manifold assembly and place the upper intake manifold in its proper position.
7. Install the retaining bolts and tighten them in sequence to a torque of 15-22 ft.lbs. (20-30 Nm).
8. Install the engine oil dipstick and injector wiring harness bracket. Torque the retaining nuts to 15-22 ft.lbs. (20-30 Nm).
9. Connect the fuel supply and fuel return lines, also connect the EGR tube to the upper intake manifold and torque the flange nut to 6-9 ft.lbs. (8-12 Nm).
10. Connect the water bypass line and torque the hose clamp to 12-20 ft.lbs. (17-20 Nm).
11. Connect the PCV hose to the fitting on the underside of the upper intake manifold.
12. Connect the upper intake manifold vacuum connection at the

FUEL INJECTION
FORD EFI-EEC IV PORT FUEL INJECTION
Section 31

rear vacuum line from the dash panel to the vacuum tee, EGR valve and the fuel pressure regulator.

13. Place the accelerator cable bracket in position on the upper manifold and install the retaining bolt, torque the bolt to 10-15 ft.lbs. (14-21 Nm).

14. Install the accelerator cable to the bracket.

15. Position cast tube gasket on the turbocharger and position a new gasket on the fuel charging assembly air throttle body mounting gasket.

16. Install the cast tube—air throttle body assembly on the turbocharger and install the two cast tube retaining bolts, torque the bolts to 14-21 ft.lbs. (19-29 Nm).

17. Install the air throttle—cast tube assembly to the fuel charging assembly. Install the four retaining nuts and torque them to 12-15 ft.lbs. (16-20 Nm).

18. Connect the accelerator cable, and all the electrical connectors to the air bypass valve, throttle position sensor, fuel injector wiring harness, knock sensor, fan temperature sensor and coolant temperature sensor.

19. Connect the negative battery cable and add the engine coolant.

20. Use the EEC self test connector to check for the proper EEC-IV system functioning.

NOTE: Diagnosis and testing of the EEC-IV system is covered in the end of this section and in the engine control section of this manual.

21. Start the engine and let it run until the engine cooling fan starts to operate. Check for engine coolant leaks and verify the correct engine idle.

NOTE: The following procedures are based on the fuel charging assembly having been removed from the vehicle.

AIR BYPASS ASSEMBLY

Removal and Installation

1. Disconnect the air bypass valve assembly connector from the wiring harness.
2. Remove the two air bypass valve retaining screws and remove the air bypass valve and gasket.
3. Installation is the reverse order of the removal procedure, and the torque for the two air bypass valve retaining screws is 6-8 inch lbs.

THROTTLE POSITION SENSOR

Removal

1. Disconnect the throttle position sensor from the wiring harness.
2. Make a scribe mark on the air throttle body and on the throttle position sensor for proper alignment during installation.
3. Remove the two throttle position sensor retaining screws and remove the sensor and gasket.

Installation

1. Install the throttle position sensor and new gasket, be sure during installation that the rotary tangs on the sensor are in proper alignment with the throttle shaft blade.

NOTE: In order to be sure the TPS is installed properly, slide the rotary tangs into position over the throttle shaft blade, then rotate the TPS to the installed position. If the sensor is installed incorrectly it could result in excessive idle speeds.

2. Align the scribe marks on the air throttle body and the TPS and install the two retaining screws, torque the screws to 14-16 inch lbs.
3. Secure the electrical connector with two retaining bolts, torque the bolts to 14-16 inch lbs.
4. Connect TPS electrical connector to the wiring harness and adjust the TPS to specifications.

NOTE: The throttle position sensor mounting holes are slotted to permit rotational adjustment. But on some 1983-84 models the only way to adjust the TPS is during installation as previously outlined.

Adjustment

1. With the engine off and the ignition in the run position, hook up a digital volt/ohmmeter to the TPS connector.
2. Check to see that the throttle is off the fast idle cam, and remove the vacuum hose from the throttle kicker actuator.
3. Loosen the TPS mounting screws and turn the sensor until the reading on the meter is between 1.6 and 2.4 volts and then tighten the TPS screws.

FUEL PRESSURE REGULATOR

Removal

1. Release the pressure in the fuel system as previously outlined, and remove the vacuum line at the pressure regulator.
2. Remove the three allen head retaining screws from the regulator housing.
3. Remove the fuel pressure regulator assembly, gasket and O-ring. Discard the old gasket and O-ring.

Installation

1. Lubricate the fuel pressure regulator O-ring with a light oil, do not use any form of silicone grease, because it will clog the fuel injectors.
2. Install the new gasket and new O-ring on the regulator and be sure the regulator mating surfaces are clean.
3. Install the fuel pressure regulator on the injector manifold and torque the three allen head screws to 27-40 inch lbs.

DIAGNOSIS AND TESTING THE EEC-IV SYSTEM

Visual Inspection

Before attempting any repairs or extensive diagnosis, visually examine the vehicle for obvious faults.

1. Remove air cleaner assembly. Check for dirt, foreign matter or other contamination in and around filter element.
2. Examine vacuum hose for proper routing and connection. Also check for broken, cracked or pinched hoses or fittings.
3. Examine each portion of the EEC IV wiring harness. Check for the following at each location:
   a. Proper connection to sensors and solenoids
   b. Loose or disconnected connectors
   c. Broken or disconnected wires
   d. Partially seated connectors
   e. Broken or frayed wires
   f. Shorting between wires
   g. Corrosion
4. Inspect sensor for obvious physical damage.

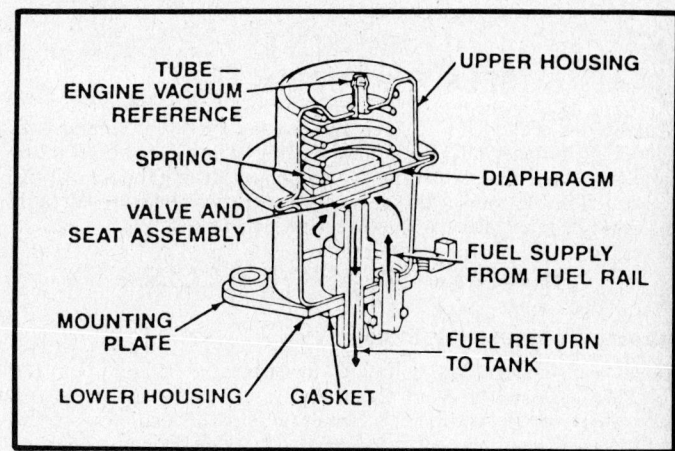

Typical fuel pressure regulator

SECTION 31

FUEL INJECTION
FORD EFI-EEC IV PORT FUEL INJECTION

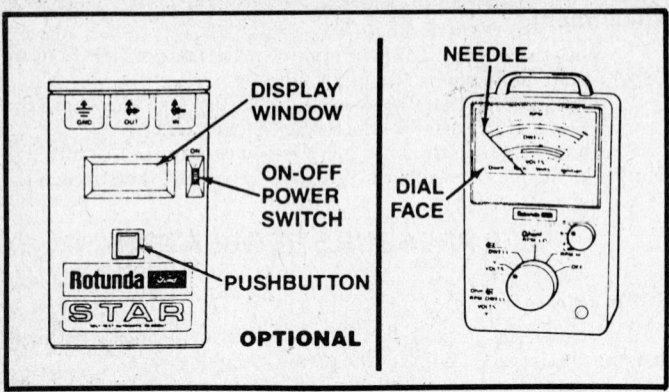

Analog voltmeter and STAR tester

5. Operate engine and inspect exhaust manifold and exhaust gas oxygen sensor for leaks.
6. Repair faults as necessary. Reinstall air cleaner. If the problem has not been corrected, proceed to self-test.

Self-Test Feature

The EEC IV system is equipped with a self-test feature to aid in diagnosing possible problems. The self-test is a set of instructions programmed in the computer memory of the calibration assembly. When the program is activated, the computer performs a system test. This verifies the proper connection and operation of the various sensors and actuators. The self-test program controls vehicle operation during the test sequence.

Basically, the self-test program does the following:
1. Sends commands to the solenoids and checks for proper response.
2. Checks for reasonable readings from the sensors.
3. Produces numbered codes that inform the technician of a trouble area or of "all okay" operation.

TEST EQUIPMENT USED

1. Analog Voltmeter with a 0-20V DC range.
2. Digital Volt-Ohmmeter with a minimum input impedance of 10 meg-ohm.
3. Vacuum gauge with 0-30 in. Hg range, and resolution in the 1 in. Hg range.
4. Spark Tester: A modified spark plug with the side electrode removed and alligator clip attached may be used.
5. Tachometer
6. Jumper wire at least 15 in. long.
7. Vacuum pump
8. An optional Star cable assembly Rotunda Part Number 07-0010 from the manufacturer for use with the Rotunda Star tester to simplify the tester connection.

SELF TEST OPERATION

The self test is divided into three separate tests: Key On/Engine Off, Engine Running, and Continuous Testing. The first two tests are functional tests that detect faults only present during the time of the self test. The continuous test is always in operation and stores all fault information for retrieval at a later time (during a self-test).

READING THE SERVICE CODES

Analog Voltmeter Method

When using an Analog Voltmeter to perform a function test, the service codes will present themselves as a sweeping or pulsing movement of the voltmeter's needle across the dial face of the voltmeter. The service code is represented by a two digit number, such as 2-3. To get the service code number, the number of voltmeter needle pulses must be counted. If the number is a single digit number of three it will be represented by three needle pulses on the voltmeter.

When the self-test's service code of 2-3 will appear on the voltmeter as two needle pulses; then after a two-second pause, the needle will pulse three times. The continuous testing codes are separated from the functional codes by a six second delay, and a single 1/2 second sweep and another six second delay. They are produced on the voltmeter in the same manner as the functional codes.

Rotunda Star Tester Method

In order to use the star tester, the star cable assembly (Rotunda part number 07-0010) must be attached to the vehicle self test connector. After hooking up the star tester put the power switch to the position.

When the power switch is on, the tester will run a display check and the numerals 88 will flash in the display window. When the tester is ready to receive the service codes a steady 00 will appear in the display window. For the star tester to receive the service codes, the pushbutton on the front of the tester must be pressed in so a colon will appear in the display window in front of the :00 numerals.

NOTE: The colon must be displayed in order to receive the service codes.

The only way to clear the display window, is to turn off the engine and press down the pushbutton on the front of the tester to clear the display window. When the star tester is turned off, the Low Battery Indicator (LO BAT) will show up briefly in the upper left corner of the display window. If the Lo Bat indicator comes on steadily during any other self test operation, turn the power switch off, and replace the 9 volt battery in the tester.

SERVICE CODES

The service codes are transmitted in the form of timed pulses, and read on a voltmeter or a star tester, the pulse arrangement is as follows:
1. 1/2 second on time for each digit
2. 2 seconds off time between digits
3. 4 seconds off time between codes
4. 6 seconds off time before and after the 1/2 second separator pulse.

All testing is completed when the codes have been repeated once.

Wiggle Test

Attach the analog meter to the self test output connector which is located in the wiring harness under the hood on the passenger side of the vehicle. While wiggling or tapping on the system and the wiring harness watch the analog meter. The meter will deflect every time an open circuit or a short is found in the system, when this happens a service code will be stored. To retrieve a service code a self test must be performed. This same test can be performed while using the star tester and star tester cable assembly. While wiggling or tapping the system

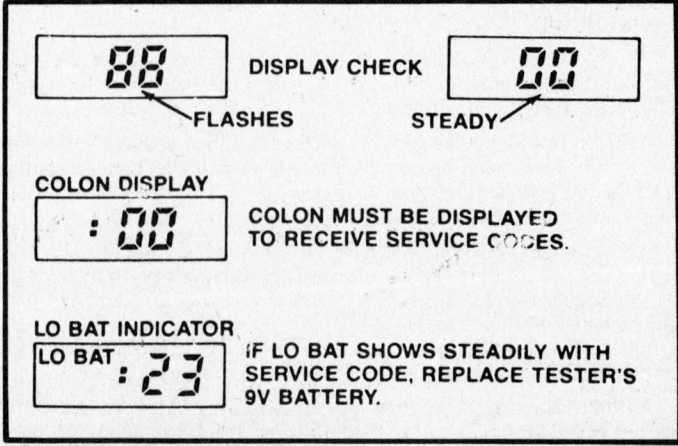

Self-test output code format

FUEL INJECTION
FORD EFI-EEC IV PORT FUEL INJECTION
SECTION 31

or the wiring harness, connectors or sensors watch the led light on the cable assembly. The led light will go on and remain on as long as there is a short or open circuit present in the system.

Quick Test Method

The proper operation of related non-EEC components and systems are necessary for correct test results for the quick test. Before starting the test or hooking up any equipment check the following:

1. Check the condition of the air cleaner and ducting.
2. Check all vacuum hoses for proper routing, good connections to fittings and cracked, pinched hoses or fittings.
3. Check the EEC system wiring harness electrical connections for:
   a. Loose or detached connectors, wires and terminals. Also check for proper connections.
   b. Broken or corroded wires at connectors.
   c. Shorting between wires or detached wires.
   d. Proper routing of the wiring harness and bad connectors.
4. Inspect the control module, sensors and actuators for any physical damage.

Performing the Quick Test

1. With the transmission in park, apply the parking brake and block the wheels.

EEC IV TROUBLE CODES (1.6L)	
Code	Diagnosis
11	Normal operation (no codes stored)
12	Incorrect high idle rpm value
13	Incorrect curb idle rpm value
15	Read Only Memory (ROM) failure
21	Incorrect engine coolant temperature (ECT) sensor signal
23	Incorrect throttle position sensor (TPS) signal
24	Incorrect vane air temperature (VAT) sensor signal
26	Incorrect vane air flow (VAF) sensor signal
41	System always lean
42	System always rich
67	Neutral/Drive switch in Neutral

EEC IV diagnosis chart

2. Make sure that the vacuum lines are connected to the air cleaner and turn off all accessories.
3. Using the analog voltmeter check to see if there is power going to the choke (engine must be running).
4. Start the engine and let idle until it reaches normal operating temperature then turn the ignition off.
5. Locate the self test connector near the MCU module.
6. If using the analog voltmeter, connect a jumper wire from self test circuit 201 to ground circuit 60 on the self test connector. Then connect the analog voltmeter from the positive post on the battery to the self test output on the self test connector.
7. Now set the voltmeter to read from 0-15 VDC on the DC volt range.
8. On the 2.3 liter engine with a vacuum purge valve, disable the canister purge system during the quick test.
9. Make sure the carburetor throttle linkage is off high cam, and the choke is open.

NOTE: If the star tester is being used for the quick test, connect the black lead to the negative battery post, the red lead to the self test output terminal on the self connector and the white lead to the self test trigger. Then follow the instructions on the back of the star tester.

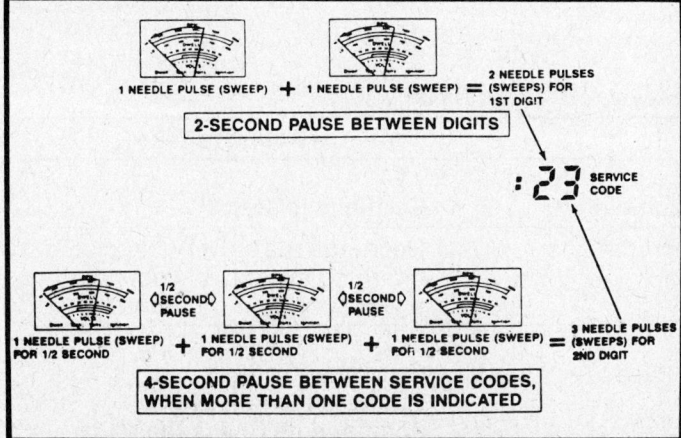

Analog voltmeter functional service code

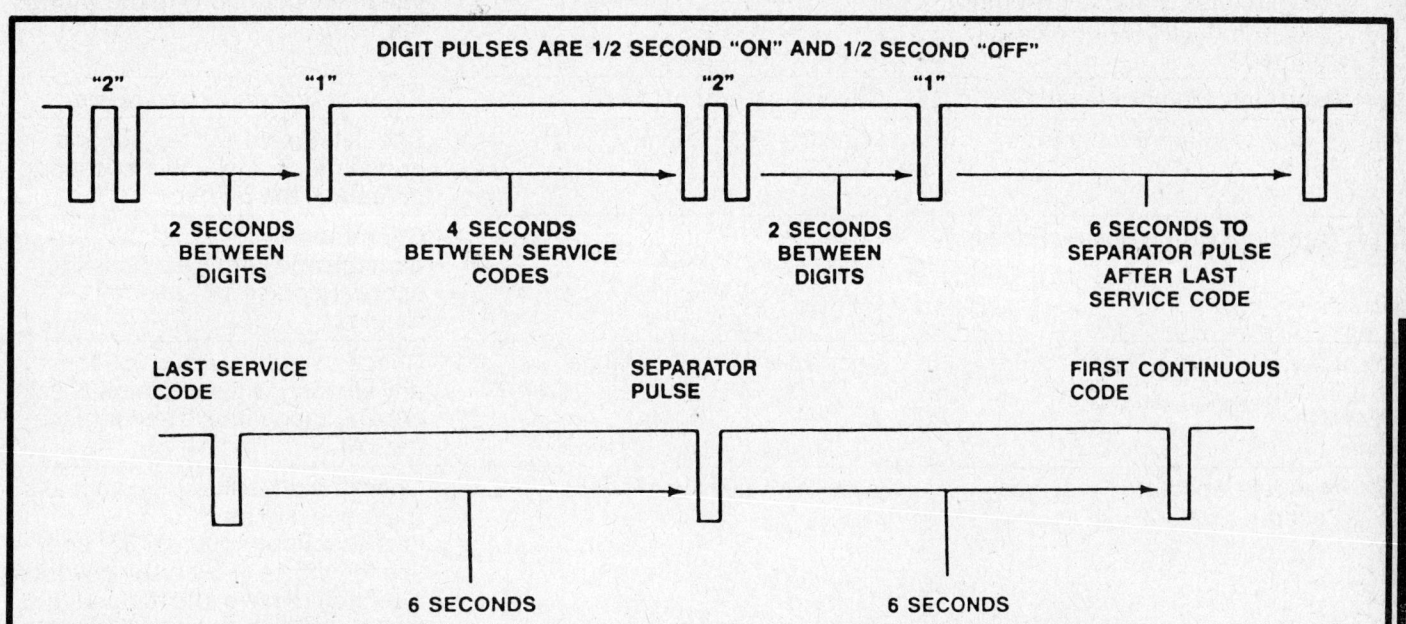

Self-test service code digit pulses

31-43

SECTION 31: FUEL INJECTION
FORD EFI-EEC IV PORT FUEL INJECTION

EEC IV TROUBLE CODES (2.3L)

Code	Diagnosis
11	Normal operation (no codes stored)
12	Incorrect high idle rpm value
13	Incorrect curb idle rpm value
14	Erratic Profile Ignition Pickup (PIP) signal
15	Read Only Memory (ROM) failure
21	Incorrect engine coolant temperature (ECT) sensor signal
22	Incorrect barometric pressure (BAP) sensor signal
23	Incorrect throttle position sensor (TPS) signal
24	Incorrect vane air temperature (VAT) sensor signal
26	Incorrect vane air flow (VAF) sensor signal
41	System always lean
42	System always rich
51	Engine coolant temperature (ECT) sensor signal too high
53	Throttle position sensor (TPS) signal too high
54	Vane air temperature (VAT) sensor signal too high
56	Vane air flow (VAF) sensor signal too high
61	Engine coolant temperature (ECT) signal too low
63	Throttle position sensor (TPS) signal too low
64	Vane air temperature (VAT) signal too low
66	Vane air flow (VAF) sensor signal too low
67	A/C compressor clutch ON
73	No vane air temperature (VAT) signal change when engine speed is increased
76	No vane air flow (VAF) signal change when engine speed is increased
77	Engine speed not increased to check VAT and VAF signal change

EEC IV diagnosis chart—2.3L engine

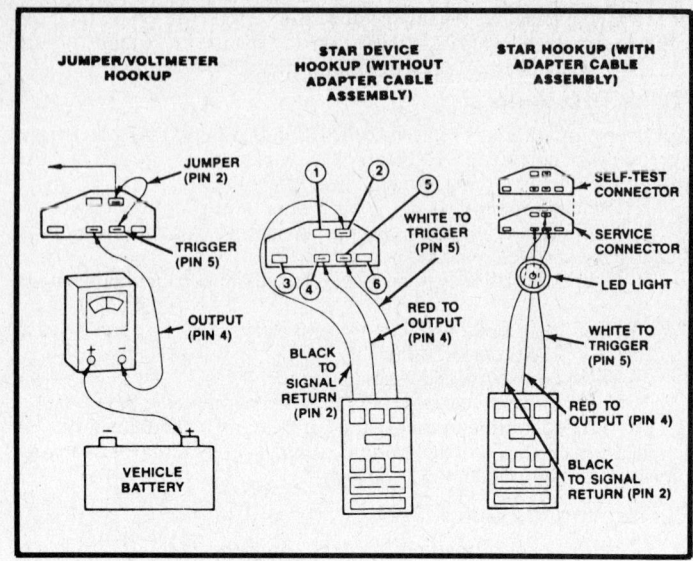

Test equipment hookup

QUICK TEST DIAGNOSIS AND TESTING

Test Step	Result	Action to Take
1. Vehicle Voltage Test Turn off all accessories and operate the engine at 2000 RPM for 2 minutes. Battery voltage has to be between 14.2–14.7 volts.	Battery within specifications	Continue to step 2
	Battery not in specifications	Recharge the battery, check the charging system and do step 1 again.
2. Key On-Engine Off-Self Test		
a. With the transmission in Park and the AC control off, put the key in run position. Now record the service codes as they come up on the voltmeter. (Refer to the output code format as previously outlined.)	Code 11—System Pass No service codes Meter always high Meter always low	Continue to step 3 Recheck the non-EEC components Check the MCU module and the TFI module also check the continuity in the wiring harness.
b. Read Only Memory Test Failed	Code 15—Memory Check	Replace processor and retest.
c. Engine Coolant Temperature Failed	Code 21—ECT Check	Check temperature sensor and connections, repair as necessary or replace the ECT sensor.
d. Throttle Position Sensor Failed	Code 23—TPS out of range	Check sensor for physical damage and wiring harness for shorts Replace TP sensor if required.
e. Manifold Charge Temperature Failed	Code 24—VAT out of range	Check circuits 357 and 359 for any shorts, if these circuits check out OK, then remove and replace the VAT.
f. Manifold Absolute Pressure Failed	Code 26—VAF out of range	Check for air leaks, vacuum leaks, the processor and harnesscircuits 190, 280, 351 and 359 for shorts. If everything-works out, then remove and replace the VAF.

FUEL INJECTION
FORD EFI-EEC IV PORT FUEL INJECTION
SECTION 31

QUICK TEST DIAGNOSIS AND TESTING

Test Step	Result	Action to Take
g. Neutral Drive Switch Failed	Code 67—Engine won't start	Check the processor the N/D switch neutral forcing relay and harness circuits 150, 347, 359 and 69. On manual transmissions, check the gear clutch linkage and the gear clutch switch. If everything works out remove and replace the neutral drive switch.

NOTE: When more than one service code is received, always start with the first code received. If a suspended vehicle condition is present, continue on with the continuous testing.

3. Engine Running Test		
a. Disconnect the self-test trigger, start engine and bring the rpm's up above 2000 rpm for 2 minutes.	No service codes or voltmeter always reads above 10V	Recheck the non-EEC components check the spark timing and the MCU module. Also check the TFI module and the continuity in the wiring harness.
b. With the engine off reconnect the self-test trigger, now restart the engine and let it idle. Two identification pulses will occur followed by the service codes. Record the codes and refer to the output code format as previously outlined.	Code 11—System Pass	Any other trouble go on to step 4, otherwise the testing is complete and the EEC system is OK.

NOTE: Testing is completed when the codes have been outputted twice.

4. Continuous Testing
This test utilizes the system's ability to indicate sensor and circuit failure at the moment the interrupt occurs. It also remembers the service code of the affected sensor.

Implementing Continuous Test
Key in OFF Position
Disconnect the self-test trigger and connect an analog voltmeter negative lead to the self test output pin, and the positive lead to the positive battery post.

Key in the Run Position
Wiggle, move, twist, the vehicle wiring harness; tap, shake, or otherwise exercise the sensors. Watch the voltmeter while doing the above, a deflection at any time indicates an intermittent short has occured in a sensor circuit.

NOTE: The sensor circuit could be in the harness, sensor or processor. Once the intermitten fault has been found and induced, the appropriate service code has been stored. Do not turn the key off because the codes will be erased.

Initiate Self-Test. (Install jumper and observe the service code[s].)
Vehicle could be prepared as above and driven in an attempt to link a drive complaint with the meter indication of an EEC intermittent fault at which time, again, the Service Code would be observed and followed in an attempt to isolate the intermittent fault.
If the indicated Service Code from Continuous Testing does not make the repair obvious (damaged sensor, pinched harness, etc.) contact your District Office for additional assistance.

FORD CENTRAL FUEL INJECTION (CFI) SYSTEM

General Information

The Ford Central Fuel Injection (CFI) System is a single point, pulse time modulated injection system. Fuel is metered into the air intake stream according to engine demands by two solenoid injection valves, mounted in a throttle body on the intake manifold. Fuel is supplied from the fuel tank by a high pressure, electric fuel pump, either by itself or in addition to a low-pressure pump. The fuel is filtered, and sent to the air throttle body where a regulator keeps the fuel delivery pressure at a constant 39 psi (269 kPa). Two injector nozzles are mounted vertically above the throttle plates and connected in parallel with the fuel pressure regulator. Excess fuel supplied by the pump but

31–45

SECTION 31 FUEL INJECTION
FORD CENTRAL FUEL INJECTION (CFI) SYSTEM

not needed by the engine, is returned to the fuel tank by a steel fuel return line.

The electronic fuel injection system has several distinct advantages over conventional carburetion. It has improved fuel distribution, capability of fine tuning for altitude and temperature variations, fuel vapor formation and vapor lock largely eliminated due to high pressure in fuel system and reduced evaporative losses due to elimination of the fuel bowl. It also has eliminated engine run-on, since fuel flow immediately stops electrically with engine shut down and elimination of fuel starvation during hard driving maneuvers provided by constant high pressure injection. It provides the precise air-fuel control required for efficient three-way catalyst operation.

TEMPO-TOPAZ

On the CFI system, the throttle body assembly meters fuel/air into the induction system of the 4 cylinder, 2.3L High Swirl Combustion (HSC) engine. It is amazingly simple and may well prove to be the method that many other Ford-built engines will use in the future.

This new low pressure CFI fuel system has only five major parts:
- FUEL PUMP (Mounted in Tank)
- FUEL FILTER (R.F. Inner Fender Panel)
- THROTTLE BODY ASSEMBLY (Mounts to Intake Manifold)
- INJECTOR (Single Solenoid)
- PRESSURE REGULATOR (Regulates fuel pressure at 14.5 psi)

There is no choke system and only one throttle valve is needed. So that a fast idle can be obtained during cold engine start-up and to provide normal (lower RPM) curb idle when the engine is at operating temperature, engineers added an Idle Speed Control (ISC) to do that important job. A small shaft extends or retracts on command from signals sent to it from the EEC-IV computer. An Idle Tracking Switch

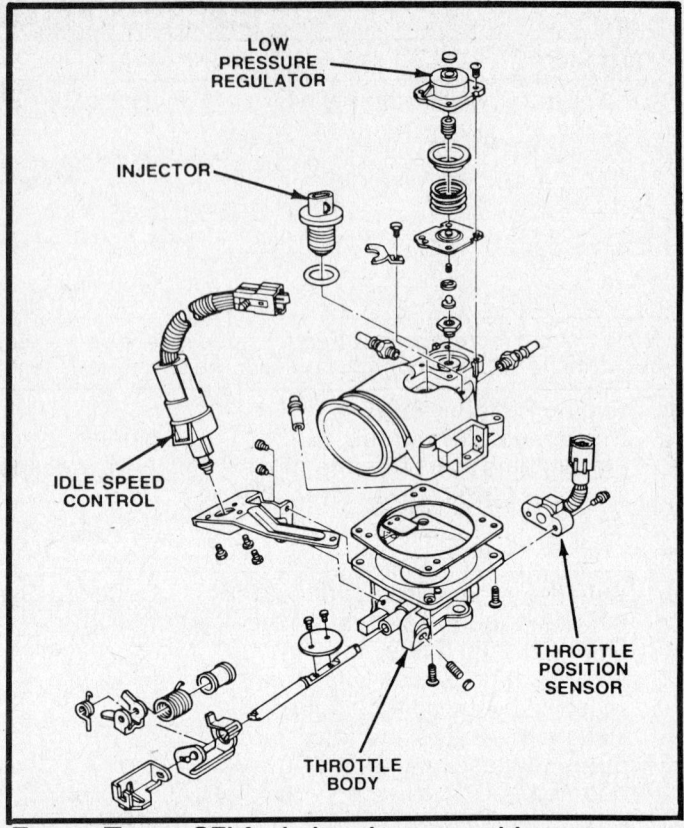

Tempo/Topaz CFI fuel charging assembly

(ITS) is part of the ISC assembly. It is needed to signal the computer wherever the throttle lever has contacted the plunger thereby signalling the need for control of engine idle RPM.

Fuel Charging Assembly

Two major components make up the fuel charging assembly. They are the (1) Throttle Body and (2) Main Body. Fuel is sent through internal passages to the injector tip. Any excess fuel is returned to the pressure regulator and from there it is returned to the fuel tank at a reduced pressure of somewhere between 3-6 psi.

Fuel Pressure Regulator

Its location and design is such that supply line "pressure drops" are eliminated. Also, a second function of the pressure regulator is to maintain fuel supply pressure whenever the engine is NOT running (ignition key off). It acts as a downstream check valve and traps the fuel between itself and the fuel pump. By maintaining fuel pressure upon engine shutdown, fuel line vapor (vapor lock) does not develop.

Low Pressure Fuel Injector

Fuel flow into the air stream entering the cylinders is determined by the length of "On-Time" the solenoid is energized. The longer "On-Time" of the injector, the more fuel is permitted to flow into the intake system.

When the ball valve moves off its seat the small metering orifices are uncovered and a calibrated amount of fuel enters the intake manifold.

NOTE: The injector "air gap" is not adjustable and the injector is only serviced as an assembly.

Air Control

A single butterfly valve controls the flow of air into the intake manifold. It looks and operates similar to the throttle valve(s) used with carburetors.

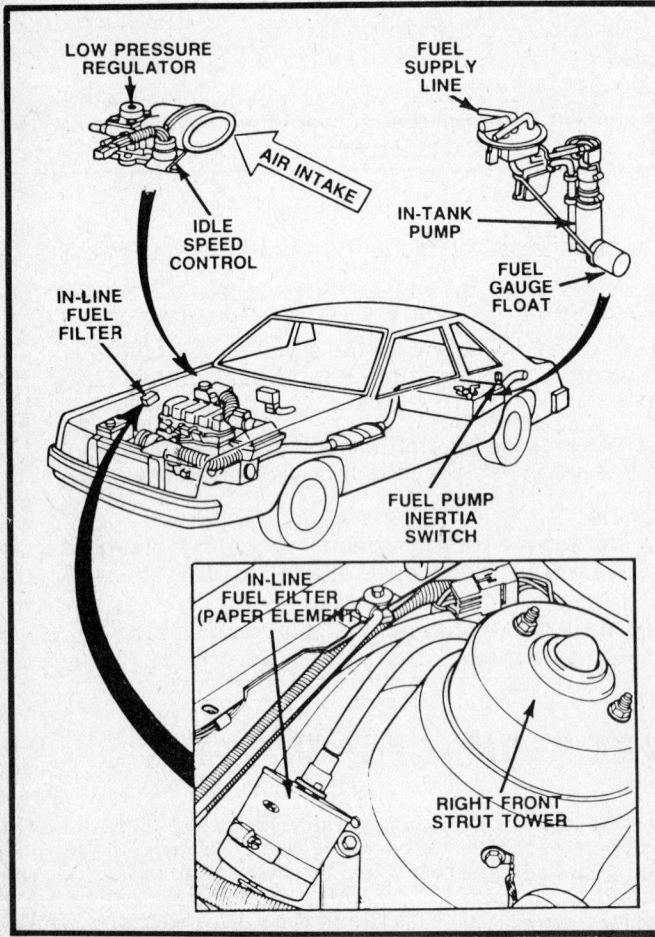

Tempo/Topaz CFI components

31-46

FUEL INJECTION
FORD CENTRAL FUEL INJECTION (CFI) SYSTEM
SECTION 31

Located just above the throttle plate is the electromechanical fuel injector which meters and also atomizes the fuel delivered to the engine.

An electrical control signal sent to the fuel injector from the EEC-IV computer causes the solenoid actuated "fuel metering" ball to move off its seat and allows fuel to flow as required by engine demands.

Injector flow opening is fixed. As a result, fuel flow to the engine is controlled by how long (the amount of time) the solenoid is energized (remains on) with the fuel metering "ball" off its seat.

Checking Fuel Pressure

To check the fuel pressure, disconnect the Inertia Switch which is located at the right side of the trunk area. Now, crank the engine for 15 seconds to reduce system pressure before you remove the clips at each end of the fuel line between the fuel filter and the fuel inlet at the charging assembly.

------- CAUTION -------
Use extreme care to prevent combustion from fuel spillage.

Install an accurate fuel pressure gauge between the fuel filter line and the throttle body assembly fuel inlet. You'll need a "TEE" fitting to accomplish this fuel pressure gauge connection.

Reconnect the inertia switch, start the engine and check fuel pressure at idle. Throughout acceleration, you should have a stable pressure of 13.0-16.0 psi without any excessively high or low readings. To remove the pressure gauge, again disconnect the inertia switch, crank the engine for 15 seconds, then remove the gauge. Reinstall the original fuel line securely. Reconnect the inertia switch and start the engine. Check carefully for any fuel leakage.

FUEL DELIVERY SYSTEM (V6 AND V8)

Fuel Charging Assembly

The fuel charging assembly controls air-fuel ratio. It consists of a typical carburetor throttle body. It has two bores without venturis. The throttle shaft and valves control engine air flow based on driver demand. The throttle body attaches to the intake manifold mounting pad.

A throttle position sensor is attached to the throttle shaft. It includes a potentiometer (or rheostat) that electrically senses throttle opening. A throttle kicker solenoid fastens opposite the throttle

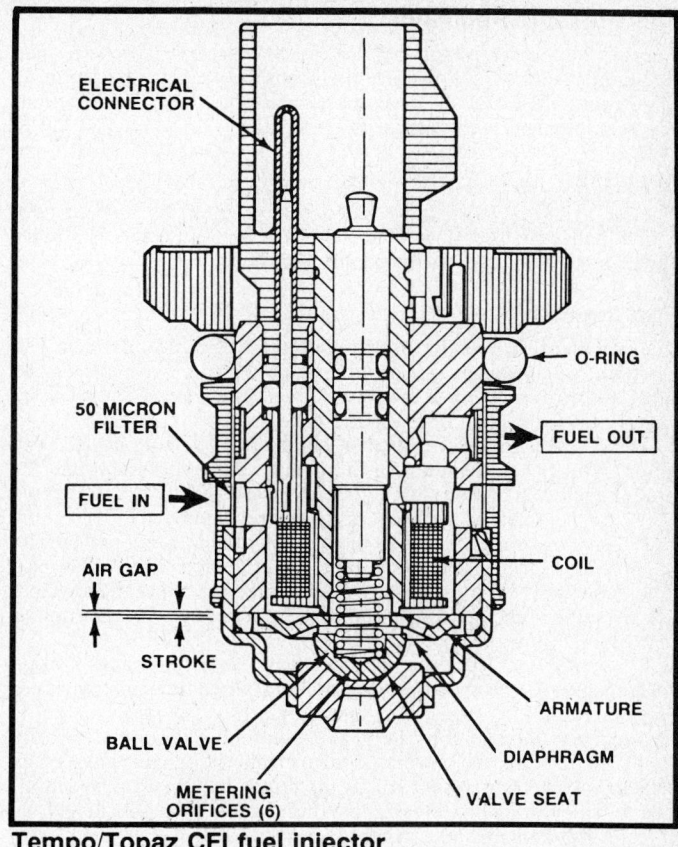

Tempo/Topaz CFI fuel injector

position sensor. During air conditioning operation, the solenoid extends to slightly increase engine idle speed.

Cold engine speed is controlled by an automatic kick-down vacuum motor. There is also an all-electric, bi-metal coil spring which controls cold idle speed. The bi-metal electric coil operates like a conventional carburetor choke coil, but the electronic fuel injection system uses no choke. Fuel enrichment for cold starts is controlled by the computer and injectors.

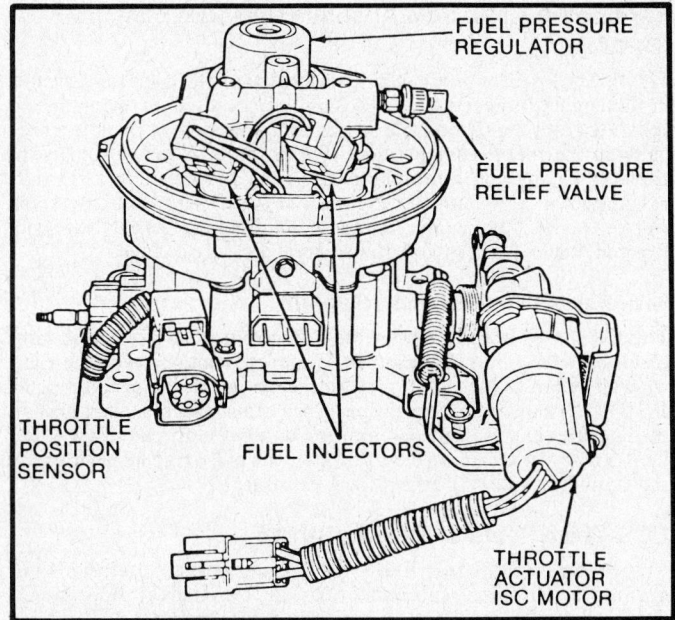

CFI fuel charging assembly—right side view

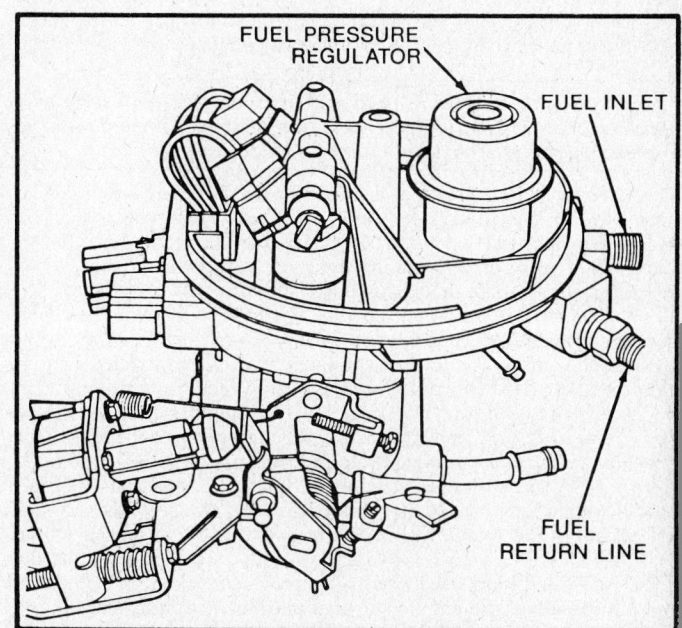

CFI fuel charging assembly—left side view

31-47

SECTION 31

FUEL INJECTION
FORD CENTRAL FUEL INJECTION (CFI) SYSTEM

Fuel Pressure Regulator

The fuel pressure regulator controls critical injector fuel pressure. The regulator receives high pressure fuel from the electric fuel pump. It then adjusts the fuel to the desired pressure for uniform fuel injection. The regulator sets fuel pressure at 39 psi.

Fuel Rail

The fuel rail evenly distributes fuel to each injector. Its main purpose is to equalize the fuel flow. One end of the fuel rail contains a relief valve for testing fuel pressure during operation.

Fuel Injectors

The two identical fuel injectors are electro-mechanical devices. The electrical solenoid operates a pintle valve which always travels the same distance from closed to open to closed. Injection is controlled by varying the length of time the pintle valve is open.

The delivery end of the injector is a precisely ground nozzle. The manufacturing and handling of this component is very important for proper operation. When closed, the valve must seal tightly to shut off fuel flow completely. It must seat itself repeatedly with the same precision. Any dirt particles from contaminated fuel can prevent the valve from seating. The shape of the pintle valve and nozzle also determines the fuel spray pattern during injection. Since the injectors are atomizing fuel into droplets, this fuel mist pattern is important to fast vaporization and good combustion.

The computer, based on voltage inputs from the crank position sensor, operates the injector solenoids four (two per injector) times per engine revolution. When the injector pintle valve unseats, fuel is sprayed in a fine mist into the intake manifold. The computer varies fuel enrichment based on voltage inputs from the exhaust gas oxygen sensor, barometric pressure sensor, manifold absolute pressure sensor, etc., by calculating how long to hold the injectors open. The longer the injectors remain open, the richer the mixture.

Fuel Pump

The fuel delivery system includes an in-line or in-tank high pressure fuel pump, an in-tank low pressure fuel pump (on some 1983-84 models when in-line high pressure pump is used), a primary fuel filter, a secondary fuel filter, fuel supply and return lines, fuel injectors and a fuel pressure regulator. It is a recirculating system that delivers fuel to a pressure regulating valve in the throttle body and returns excess fuel from the throttle body regulator back to the fuel tank. The electrical system has two control relays, one controlled by a vacuum switch and the other controlled by an electronic engine control module. These provide for power to the fuel pump under various operating conditions.

CAUTION
Fuel supply lines on vehicles equipped with fuel injected engine will remain pressurized for long periods of time after engine shutdown. The pressure must be relieved before servicing the fuel system.

An inertia switch is used as a safety device in the fuel system. The inertia switch is located in the trunk, near the left rear wheel well. It is designed to open the fuel pump power circuit in the event of a collision. The switch is reset by pushing each of 2 buttons on the switch simultaneously (some models use switches with only 1 reset button). The inertia switch should not be reset until the fuel system has been inspected for damage or leaks.

With the ignition switch off, the vacuum switch controlled relay is closed and the EEC controlled relay is open. When the ignition switch is first turned to ignition "ON" position, the vacuum switch controlled relay remains closed and the EEC controlled relay also closes. This provides power to the fuel pump to pre-pressurize the fuel system. If the ignition switch is not turned to the "CRANK" position, the EEC module will open its relay after approximately two seconds and shut off power to the pump. When the ignition switch is turned to the "CRANK" position, both the vacuum switch controlled relay and the EEC controlled relay are closed. This provides full battery power to the pump. When the engine starts, manifold vacuum increases and causes the vacuum switch to close and the vacuum controlled relay to open. This provides reduced normal operating voltage to the fuel pump through the resistor which by-passes the vacuum controlled relay. Under heavy engine load conditions, manifold vacuum will reduce, causing the vacuum switch to open. This causes the vacuum controlled relay to close, thus providing the return of full battery power to the pump. The EEC module senses engine speed and shuts off the pump by opening the EEC controlled relay when the engine stops.

ELECTRONIC CONTROL SYSTEM

Electronic Control Assembly (ECA)

The Electronic Control Assembly (ECA) is a solid-state microcomputer consisting of a processor assembly and a calibration assembly. It is located under the instrument panel or passenger's seat and is usually covered by a kick panel. 1981-82 models use an EEC III engine control system, while 1983 and later models use the EEC IV. Although the two systems are similar in appearance and operation, the ECA units are not interchangeable. A multipin connector links the ECA with all system components. The processor assembly is housed in an aluminum case. It contains circuits designed to continuously sample input signals from the engine sensors. It then calculates and sends out proper control signals to adjust air/fuel ratio, spark timing and emission system operation. The processor also provides a continuous reference voltage to the B/MAP, EVP and TPS sensors. EEC III reference voltage is 8-10 volts, while EEC IV systems use a 5 volt reference signal. The calibration assembly is contained in a black plastic housing which plugs into the top of the processor assembly. It contains the memory and programming information used by the processor to determine optimum operating conditions. Different calibration information is used in different vehicle applications, such as California or Federal models. For this reason, careful identification of the engine, year, model and type of electronic control system is essential to insure correct component replacement.

ENGINE SENSORS

Air Charge Temperature Sensor (ACT)

The ACT is threaded into the intake manifold air runner. It is located behind the distributor on V6 engines and directly below the accelerator linkage on V8 engines. The ACT monitors air/fuel charge temperature and sends an appropriate signal to the ECA. This information is used to correct fuel enrichment for variations in intake air density due to temperature changes.

Barometric & Manifold Absolute Pressure Sensors (B/MAP)

The B/MAP sensor on V8 engines is located on the right fender panel in the engine compartment. The MAP sensor used on V6 engines is separate from the barometric sensor and is located on the left fender panel in the engine compartment. The barometric sensor signals the ECA of changes in atmospheric pressure and density to regulate calculated air flow into the engine. The MAP sensor monitors and signals the ECA of changes in intake manifold pressure which result from engine load, speed and atmospheric pressure changes.

Crankshaft Position (CP) Sensor

The CP sensor is mounted on the right front of 1982-83 and some California 1984 5.0L V8 engines. Its purpose is to provide the ECA with an accurate ignition timing reference (when the piston reaches 10° BTDC) and injector operation information (twice each crankshaft revolution). The crankshaft vibration damper is fitted with a 4 lobe "pulse ring". As the crankshaft rotates, the pulse ring lobes interrupt the magnetic field at the tip of the CP sensor.

EGR Valve Position Sensor (EVP)

This sensor, mounted on EGR valve, signals the computer of EGR opening so that it may subtract EGR flow from total air flow into the manifold. In this way, EGR flow is excluded from air flow information used to determine mixture requirements.

FUEL INJECTION
FORD CENTRAL FUEL INJECTION (CFI) SYSTEM

Engine Coolant Temperature Sensor (ECT)

The ECT is threaded into the intake manifold water jacket directly above the water pump by-pass hose. The ECT monitors coolant temperature and signals the ECA, which then uses these signals for mixture enrichment (during cool operation), ignition timing and EGR operation. The resistance value of the ECT increases with temperature, causing a voltage signal drop as the engine warms up.

Exhaust Gas Oxygen Sensor (EGO)

The EGO is mounted in the right side exhaust manifold on V8 engines, in the left and right side exhaust manifolds on V6 models. The EGO monitors oxygen content of exhaust gases and sends a constantly changing voltage signal to the ECA. The ECA analyzes this signal and adjusts the air/fuel mixture to obtain the optimum (stoichiometric) ratio.

Knock Sensor (KS)

This sensor is used on 1984 Mustangs and Capris equipped with the 3.8L V6 engine, only. It is attached to the intake manifold in front of the ACT sensor. The KS detects engine vibrations caused by pre-ignition or detonation and provides information to the ECA, which then retards the timing to eliminate detonation.

Thick Film Integrated Module Sensor (TFI)

The TFI module sensor plugs into the distributor just below the distributor cap on 3.8L V6 engines and replaces the CP sensor for some 1984 5.0L V8 engines. Its function is to provide the ECA with ignition timing information, similar to what the CP sensor provides.

Throttle Position Sensor (TPS)

The TPS is mounted on the right side of the throttle body, directly connected to the throttle shaft. The TPS senses throttle movement and position and transmits an appropriate electrical signal to the ECA. These signals are used by the ECA to adjust the air/fuel mixture, spark timing and EGR operation according to engine load at idle, part throttle, or full throttle. The TPS is non-adjustable.

On-Car Service

NOTE: For all diagnosis and test procedures on the EEC III and EEC IV electronic control systems, see the "Engine Controls" section.

FUEL PRESSURE TESTS

The diagnostic pressure valve (Schrader type) is located at the top of the Fuel charging main body. This valve provides a convenient point for service personnel to monitor fuel pressure, bleed down the system pressure prior to maintenance, and to bleed out air which may become trapped in the system during filter replacement. A pressure gauge with an adapter is required to perform pressure tests.

System Pressure Test

Testing fuel pressure requires the use of a special pressure gauge (T80L-9974-A or equivalent) that attaches to the diagnostic pressure tap on the fuel charging assembly. Depressurize the fuel system before disconnecting any lines.

1. Disconnect fuel return line at throttle body (in-tank high pressure pump) or at fuel rail (in-line high pressure and in-tank low pressure pumps) and connect the hose to a one-quart calibrated container. Connect pressure gauge.
2. Disconnect the electrical connector to the fuel pump. The connector is located ahead of fuel tank (in-tank high pressure pump) or just forward of pump outlet (in-line high pressure pump). Connect auxiliary wiring harness to connector of fuel pump. Energize the pump for 10 seconds by applying 12 volts to the auxiliary harness connector, allowing the fuel to drain into the calibrated container. Note the fuel volume and pressure gauge reading.
3. Correct fuel pressure should be 35-45 psi (241-310 kPa). Fuel volume should be 10 ozs. in 10 seconds (minimum) and fuel pressure should maintain minimum 30 psi (206 kPa) immediately after pump cut-off.

If pressure condition is met, but fuel flow is not, check for blocked filter(s) and fuel supply lines. After correcting problem, repeat test procedure. If fuel flow is still inadequate, replace high pressure pump. If flow specification is met but pressure is not, check for worn or damaged pressure regulator valve on throttle body. If both pressure and fuel flow specifications are met, but pressure drops excessively after de-energization, check for leaking injector valve(s) and/or pressure regulator valve. If injector valves and pressure regulator valve are okay, replace high pressure pump. If no pressure or flow is seen in fuel system, check for blocked filters and fuel lines. If no trouble is found, replace in-line fuel pump, in-tank fuel pump and the fuel filter inside the tank.

Fuel Injector Pressure Test

1. Connect pressure gauge T80L-9974-A, or equivalent, to fuel pressure test fitting. Disconnect coil connector from coil. Disconnect electrical lead from one injector and pressurize fuel system. Disable fuel pump by disconnecting inertia switch or fuel pump relay and observe pressure gauge reading.
2. Crank engine for 2 seconds. Turn ignition OFF and wait 5 seconds, then observe pressure drop. If pressure drop is 2-16 psi (14-110 kPa), the injector is operating properly. Reconnect injector, activate fuel pump, then repeat the procedure for other injector.
3. If pressure drop is less than 2 psi (14 kPa) or more than 16 psi (110 kPa), switch electrical connectors on injectors and repeat test. If pressure drop is still incorrect, replace disconnected injector with one of the same color code, then reconnect both injectors properly and repeat test.
4. Disconnect and plug vacuum hose to EGR valve. It may be necessary to disconnect the idle speed control (3.8L V6) or throttle kicker solenoid (5.0L V8) and use the throttle body stop screw to set engine speed. Start and run the engine at 1800 RPM (2000 rpm on

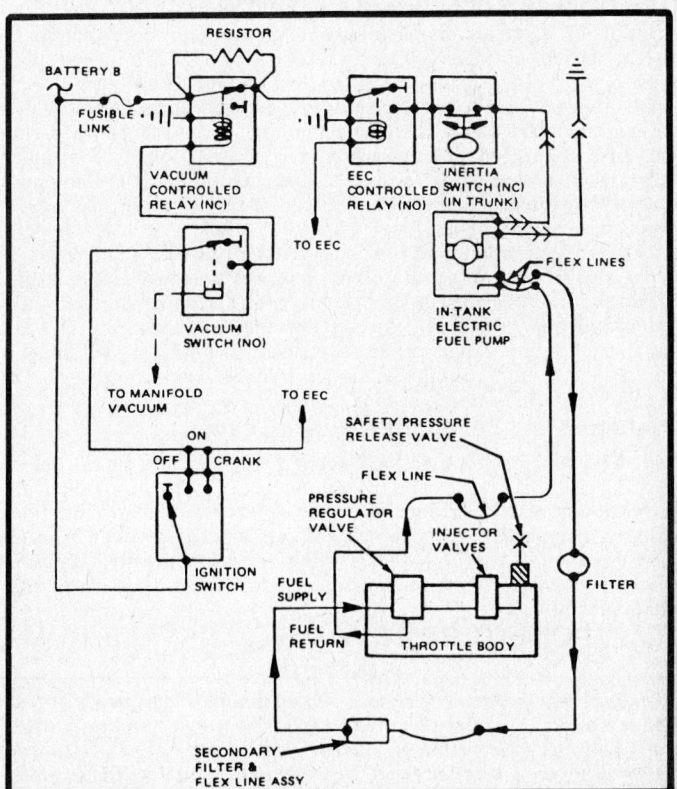

Electric fuel pump wiring and fuel line routing schematic

SECTION 31: FUEL INJECTION
FORD CENTRAL FUEL INJECTION (CFI) SYSTEM

1984 and later models). Disconnect left injector electrical connector. Note rpm after engine stabilizes (around 1200 rpm). Reconnect injector and allow engine to return to high idle.

5. Perform same procedure for right injector. Note difference between rpm readings of left and right injectors. If difference is 100 rpm or less, check the oxygen sensor. If difference is more than 100 rpm, replace both injectors.

CFI COMPONENT TESTS

NOTE: Complete CFI system diagnosis requires the use of a special tester. See the "Engine Controls" section for details.

Before beginning any component testing, always check the following:
- Check ignition and fuel systems to ensure there is fuel and spark.
- Remove air cleaner assembly and inspect all vacuum and pressure hoses for proper connection to fittings. Check for damaged or pinched hoses.
- Inspect all sub-system wiring harnesses for proper connections to the EGR solenoid valves, injectors, sensors, etc.
- Check for loose or detached connectors and broken or detached wires. Check that all terminals are seated firmly and are not corroded. Look for partially broken or frayed wires or any shorting between wires.
- Inspect sensors for physical damage. Inspect vehicle electrical system. Check battery for full charge and cable connections for tightness.
- Inspect the relay connector and make sure the ECA power relay is securely attached and making a good ground connection.

Fuel Pump Circuit Test

HIGH PRESSURE IN-TANK PUMP

Disconnect electrical connector just forward of the fuel tank. Connect voltmeter to body wiring harness connector. Turn key ON while watching voltmeter. Voltage should rise to battery voltage, then return to zero after about 1 second. Momentarily turn key to START position. Voltage should rise to about 8 volts while cranking. If voltage is not as specified, check electrical system.

High Pressure In-Line & Low Pressure In-Tank Pumps

Disconnect electrical connector at fuel pumps. Connect voltmeter to body wiring harness connector. Turn key ON while watching voltmeter. Voltage should rise to battery voltage, then return to zero after about 1 second. If voltage is not as specified, check inertia switch and electrical system. Connect ohmmeter to in-line pump wiring harness connector. If no continuity is present, check continuity directly at in-line pump terminals. If no continuity at in-line pump terminals, replace in-line pump. If continuity is present, service or replace wiring harness.

Connect ohmmeter across body wiring harness connector. If continuity is present (about 5 ohms), low pressure pump circuit is OK. If no continuity is present, remove fuel tank and check for continuity at in-tank pump flange terminals on top of tank. If continuity is absent at in-tank pump flange terminals, replace assembly. If continuity is present at in-tank pump but not in harness connector, service or replace wiring harness to in-tank pump.

Solenoid and Sensor Resistance Tests

All CFI components must be disconnected from the circuit before testing resistance with a suitable ohmmeter. Replace any component whose measured resistance does not agree with the specifications chart. Shorting the wiring harness across a solenoid valve can burn out the circuitry in the ECA that controls the solenoid valve actuator. Exercise caution when testing solenoid valves to avoid accidental damage to ECA.

COMPONENT REMOVAL IN-TANK FUEL PUMP

---CAUTION---

The fuel supply lines will remain pressurized for long periods of time after the engine is turned off. A valve is provided on the throttle body for this purpose. Remove the air cleaner and relieve system pressure by depressing the pin in the relief valve cautiously. Fuel will be expelled into the throttle body.

Removal

1. It is necessary to remove the fuel tank.
2. Depressurize the fuel system.
3. Remove fuel from the fuel tank by pumping out through the filter tube.
4. Disconnect the supply and return line fittings and the vent line.
5. Disconnect and remove the fuel filler tube.
6. Disconnect the electrical connections to both the fuel sender and the fuel pump wiring harness.
7. Remove the fuel tank support straps and remove the fuel tank.
8. Turn the fuel pump locking ring counter-clockwise with the necessary tool and remove the locking ring.
9. Remove the fuel pump and bracket assembly.
10. Remove the seal gasket and discard.
11. Remove any dirt that has accumulated around the fuel pump attaching flange, to prevent it from entering the tank during removal and installation.

Installation

1. Put a light coating of heavy grease on a new seal ring to hold it in place during assembly. Install it in fuel tank ring groove.
2. Install the tank in the vehicle.
3. Install the electrical connector.
4. Install the fuel line fittings and tighten to 40-54 N·m (30-40 ft. lbs.).
5. Install a minimum of 10 gallons of fuel and inspect for leaks.
6. Install pressure gauge on valve on throttle body and turn ignition to "ON" position for 3 seconds. Turn ignition key off and back on for 3 seconds repeatedly, 5 to 10 times, until pressure gauge shows at least 35 psi. Reinspect for leaks at fittings.
7. Remove pressure gauge. Start engine and reinspect for leaks.

FUEL CHARGING ASSEMBLY

Removal and Installation

1. Remove the air cleaner.
2. Release pressure from the fuel system at the diagnostic valve on the fuel charging assembly by carefully depressing the pin and discharging fuel into the throttle body.

CFI RESISTANCE SPECIFICATIONS

Component	Resistance (Ohms)
Air Charge Temp (ACT)	
1981–83	1700–60,000
1984	1100–58,000
Coolant (ECT) Sensor	
1981–83	1100–8000
1984—Engine Off	1300–7700
1984—Engine On	1500–4550
Crank Position Sensor	100–640
FGB Control Solenoid	30–70
EGR Vent Solenoid	30–70
Fuel Pump Relay	50–100
Throttle Kicker Solenoid	50–100
Throttle Position Sensor	
1981–83 Closed Throttle	3000–5000
1984 Closed Throttle	550–1100
Wide Open Throttle	More than 2100
TAB Solenoid	50–100
TAD Solenoid	50–100

FUEL INJECTION
FORD CENTRAL FUEL INJECTION (CFI) SYSTEM
SECTION 31

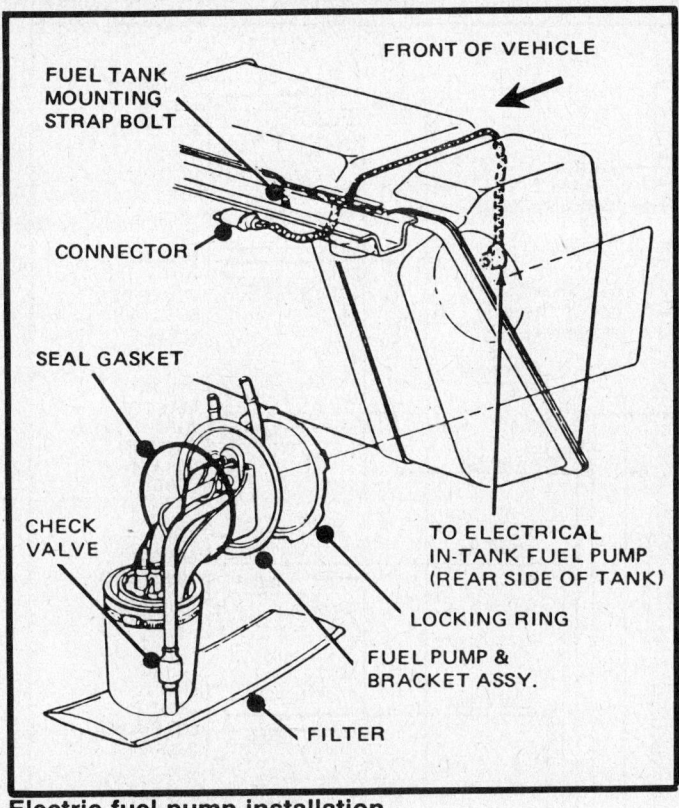

Electric fuel pump installation

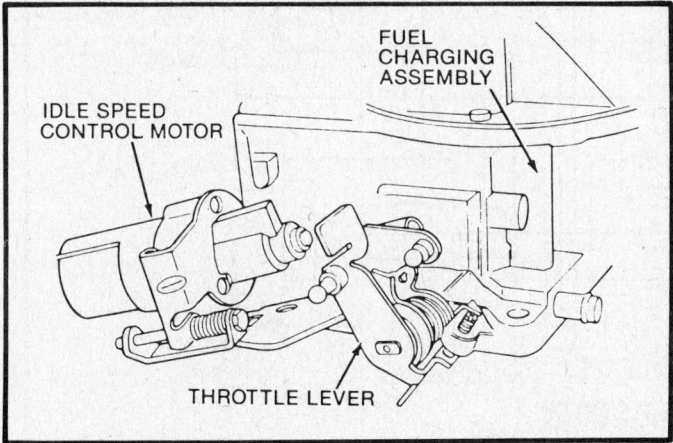

Idle speed control actuator — 3.8L engine only

3. Disconnect the throttle cable and transmission throttle valve lever.

4. Disconnect fuel, vacuum and electrical connections.

NOTE: Either the multi or single ten pin connectors may be used on the system. To disconnect electrical ten pin connectors, push in or squeeze on the right side lower locking tab while pulling up on the connection. Multi connectors disconnect by pulling apart. The ISC connector tab must be moved out while pulling apart.

5. Remove fuel charging assembly retaining nuts, then, remove fuel charging assembly.

6. Remove mounting gasket from intake manifold. Always use a new gasket for installation.

7. Clean gasket mounting surfaces of spacer and fuel charging assembly.

8. Place spacer between two new gaskets and place spacer and gaskets on the intake manifold. Position the charging assembly on the spacer and gasket.

9. Secure fuel charging assembly with attaching nuts. Tighten to 10 ft. lbs. (14 Nm). To prevent leakage, diistortion or damage to the fuel charging assembly body flange, snug the nuts; then, alternately tighten each nut in a criss cross pattern. Tighten to specifications.

10. Connect the fuel line, electrical connectors, throttle cable and all emission lines.

11. Start the engine, check for leaks. Adjust engine idle speed if necessary.

Disassembly

To prevent damage to the throttle plates, the fuel charging assembly should be placed on a work stand during disassembly and assembly procedures. If a proper stand is not available, use four bolts 5/16 × 2½ inches as legs. Install nuts on the bolts above and below the throttle body. The following is a step-by-step sequence of operations for completely overhauling the fuel charging assembly. Most components may be serviced without a complete disassembly of the fuel charging assembly. To replace individual components follow only the applicable steps.

NOTE: Use a separate container for the component parts of each sub-assembly to insure proper assembly. The automatic transmission throttle valve lever must be adjusted whenever the fuel charging assembly is removed for service or replacement.

1. Remove the air cleaner stud. The air cleaner stud must be removed to separate the upper body from the throttle body.

2. Turn the fuel charging assembly over and remove four screws from the bottom of the throttle body.

3. Separate throttle body from main body. Set throttle body aside.

4. Carefully remove and discard gasket. Note if scraping is necessary, be careful not to damage gasket surfaces of main and throttle screws.

5. Remove three pressure regulator retaining screws.

6. Remove pressure regulator. Inspect condition of gasket and O-ring.

7. Disconnect electrical connectors at each injector. Pull the connectors outward.

NOTE: Pull the connector, not the wire. Tape Identify the connectors. They must be installed on same injector as removed.

8. Loosen, DO NOT REMOVE, wiring harness retaining screw with multi connector; with single ten-pin connector loosen the two retaining screws.

9. Push in on tabs on harness to remove from upper body.

10. Remove fuel injector retainer screw.

11. Remove the injector retainer.

12. One at a time, pull injectors out of upper body. Identify each injector as "choke" or "throttle" side.

NOTE: Each injector has a small O-ring at its top. If the O-ring does not come out with the injector, carefully pick the O-ring out of the cavity in the throttle body.

13. Remove fuel diagnostic valve assembly.

14. Note the position of index mark on choke cap housing.

15. Remove three retaining ring screws.

16. Remove choke cap retaining ring, choke cap, and gasket, if so equipped.

17. Remove thermostat lever screw, and lever, if so equipped.

18. Remove fast idle cam assembly, if so equipped.

19. Remove fast idle control rod positioner, if so equipped.

20. Hold control diaphragm cover tightly in position, while removing two retaining screws, if so equipped.

21. Carefully, remove cover, spring, and pulldown control diaphragm, if so equipped.

22. Remove fast idle retaining nut, if so equipped.

23. Remove fast idle cam adjuster lever, fast idle lever, spring and E-clip, if so equipped.

31-51

SECTION 31
FUEL INJECTION
FORD CENTRAL FUEL INJECTION (CFI) SYSTEM

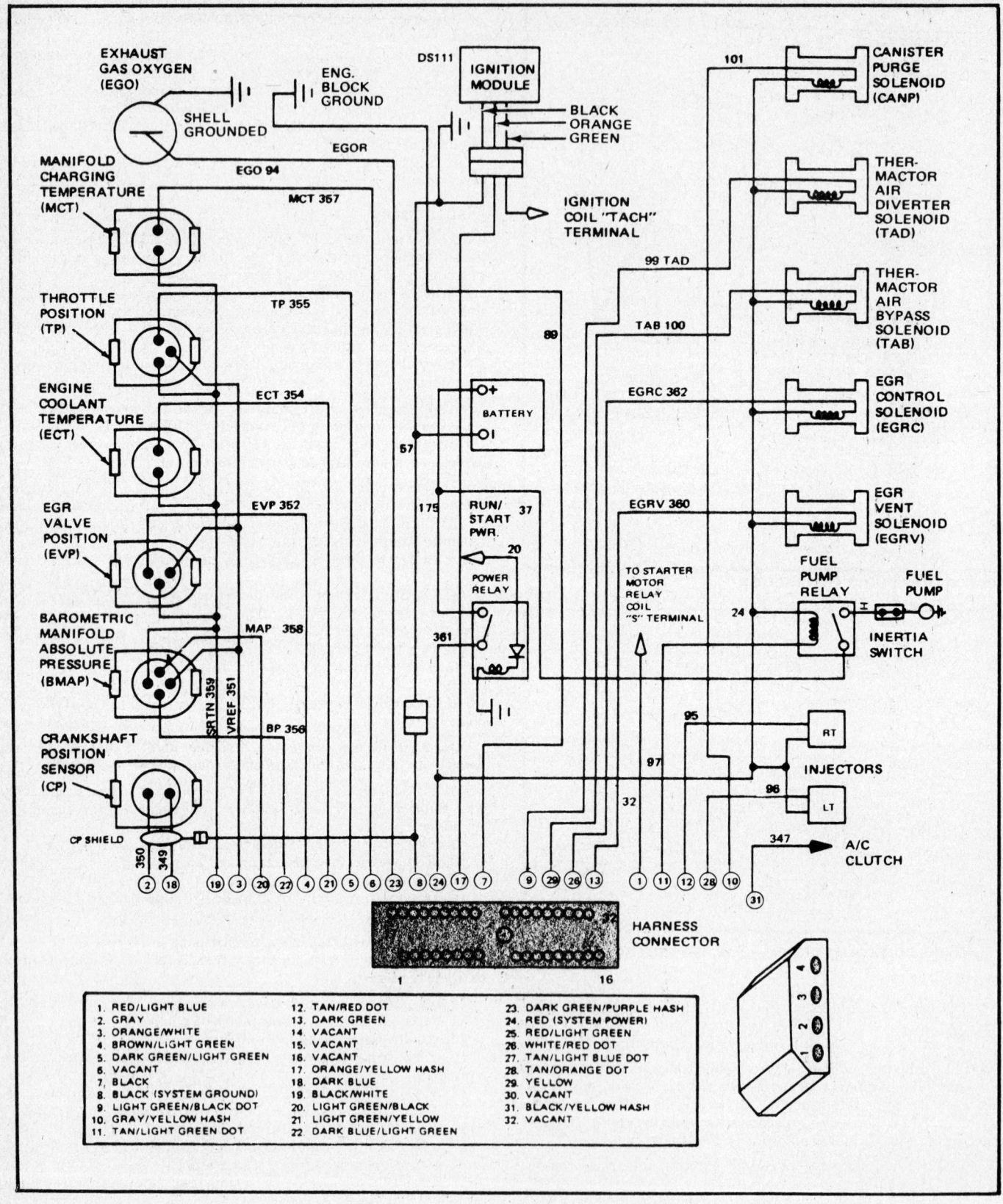

Ford CFI wiring diagram (© Ford Motor Co)

31-52

FUEL INJECTION
FORD CENTRAL FUEL INJECTION (CFI) SYSTEM
SECTION 31

24. Remove throttle position sensor connector bracket retaining screw.
25. Remove throttle position sensor retaining screws and slide throttle position sensor off the throttle shaft.
26. If CFI assembly is equipped with a throttle positioner, remove the throttle positioner retaining screw, and remove the throttle positioner. If the CFI assembly is equipped with an ISC DC Motor, remove the motor.

Assembly

1. Install fuel pressure diagnostic valve and cap. Tighten valve to 48-84 inch lbs. (5-9 Nm). Tighten cap to 5-10 inch lbs. (0.6-2 Nm).
2. Lubricate new O-rings and install on each injector (use a light grade oil).
3. Identify injectors and install them in their appropriate locations (choke or throttle side). Use a light twisting, pushing motion to install the injectors.
4. With injectors installed, install injector retainer into position.
5. Install injector retainer screw, and tighten to 36-60 inch lbs. (4-7 Nm).
6. Install injector wiring harness in upper body. Snap harness into position.
7. Tighten injector wiring harness retaining screw, (two screws if equipped with a single ten pin connector), to 8-10 inch lbs. (1 Nm).
8. Snap electrical connectors into position on injectors.
9. Lubricate new fuel pressure regulator O-ring with light oil. Install O-ring and new gasket on regulator.
10. Install pressure regulator in upper body. Tighten retaining screws to 27-40 inch lbs. (3-4 Nm).
11. Depending upon CFI assembly, install either the throttle positioner, or the ISC DC Motor.
12. Hold throttle position sensor so wire faces up.
13. Slide throttle position sensor on throttle shaft.
14. Rotate throttle position sensor clockwise until aligned with

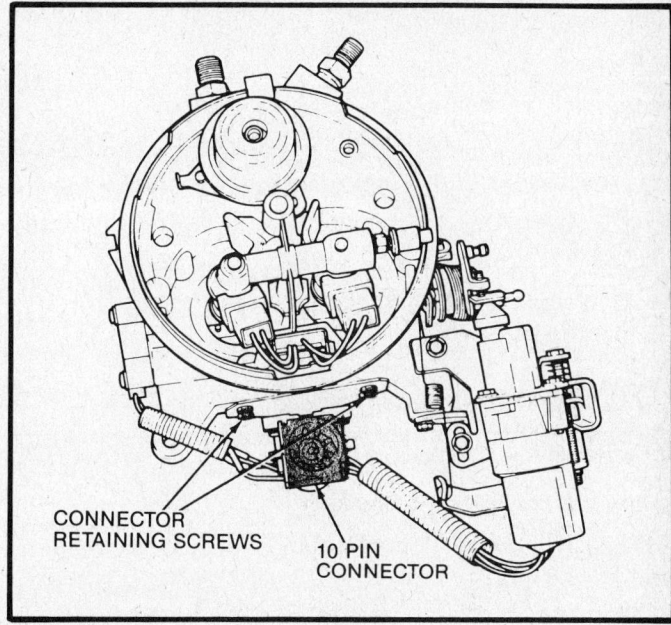

3.8L CFI with ten-pin connector

screw holes on throttle body. Install retaining screws and tighten to 11-16 inch lbs. (1-2 Nm).
15. Install throttle position wiring harness bracket retaining screw. Tighten screw to 18-22 inch lbs. (2-3 Nm).
16. Install E-clip, fast idle lever and spring, fast idle adjustment lever and fst idle retaining nut, if so equipped.
17. Tighten fast idle retaining nut to 16-20 inch lbs. (1-2 Nm), if so equipped.

SECTION 32: MANUAL TRANSMISSIONS

INDEX

TRANSMISSIONS

Borg Warner T4 – 4 Speed
- Disassembly 32-4
- Assembly 32-5

Borg Warner 83MM – 4 Speed
- Disassembly 32-7
- Assembly 32-7

Borg Warner T5 – 5 Speed
- Disassemby 32-9
- Assembly 32-9

Borg Warner 77MM – 5 Speed
- Disassembly 32-14
- Assembly 32-19

Ford ET Series German Design – 4 Speed
- Disassembly 32-29
- Assembly 32-30

Ford Overdrive (SROD) – 4 Speed
(RUG) Single Rail Overdrive
- Disassembly 32-33
- Assembly 32-33

Ford Tremac RAP 5 Speed Overdrive
- Disassembly 32-34
- Assembly 32-35

GM Warner 70MM – 4 Speed
- Disassembly 32-36
- Assembly 32-38

GM Warner 83MM – 4 Speed
w/Electronic Hydraulic O.D.
- Disassembly 32-45
- Assembly 32-48
- Overdrive Disassembly 32-48
  - Assembly 32-53

GM Saginaw 76MM – 4 Speed
- Disassembly 32-55
- Assembly 32-55

Isuzu 69.5MM – 5 Speed
- Disassembly 32-57
- Assembly 32-58

TRANSAXLES

Chrysler A466, A465 & A525 4&5 Speed
- Disassembly 32-20
- Assembly 32-23

Ford MTX – 4 Speed (MTX-11) and 5 Speed (MTX-III)
- Removal 32-25
- Disassembly 32-27
- Assembly 32-28

GM 76MM – 4 Speed
- Disassembly 32-39
- Assembly 32-41

GM – 5 Speed
- Disassembly 32-42
- Assembly 32-45

GM Model C51 – 5 Speed
- Disassembly 32-59
- Assembly 32-61

Manual Transmissions/Transaxles

MANUAL TRANSMISSIONS

Manufacturer	Year	Transmission Type Four Speed	Five Speed
American Motors Corp.	1982	Borg Warner SR-4	—
	1983-87	Borg Warner T-4	Borg Warner T-5
Chrysler Corp. Rear Wheel Drive	1983 and later	Only Automatic Transmissions Available	
Ford Motor Company Rear Wheel Drive	1983-87	Ford in Germany ET	—
	1983	Tremec SROD-RUG	—
	1983	—	Tremec RAP
	1983-87	—	Borg Warner T50D(T-5)
General Motors Corp. Rear Wheel Drive	1982	Borg Warner 83MM	—
	1983-87	Borg Warner 70MM	—
	1983-87	—	Isuzu 69.5MM
	1983-87	—	Borg Warner 77MM
	1983-87	Saginaw 76MM	—
	1984-87	Borg Warner 83MM W/Electronic-Hydraulic OD	—

MANUAL TRANSAXLES

Manufacturer	Year	Transaxle Type Four Speed	Five Speed
Chrysler Corp. Front Wheel Drive	1983-87	A460	A465
	1984-87	—	A525
Ford Motor Company Front Wheel Drive	1983-87	MTX-11	MTX-111
General Motors Corp. Front Wheel Drive	1983-87	76MM	76MM
	1985½-87 Nova		C-51

SECTION 32
MANUAL TRANSMISSIONS
WARNER-T4 FOUR SPEED

BORG WARNER T4 — 4-SPEED TRANSMISSION

Transmission Disassembly

1. Drain the lubricant from the transmission. Note that 2WD models do not have a drain plug; the fluid must be siphoned from these transmissions.
2. Remove the roll pin which attached the offset lever to the shift rail, using a pin punch and a hammer.
3. Remove the extension (2WD) or adapter (4WD) housing-to-transmission case bolts. Remove the housing and the offset lever as an assembly.

CAUTION
Do not attempt to remove the offset lever while the housing is still in place.

4. Remove the detent ball and spring from the offset lever.
5. Remove the roll pin from the extension/adapter housing or offset lever.
6. Remove the countershaft rear thrust bearing and race.
7. Remove the transmission cover-to-case attaching bolts and lift the cover and shift fork assembly from the transmission.

NOTE: Two of the transmission cover bolts are alignment-type dowel bolts. Note their location so that they may be reinstalled in their original locations.

8. Remove the C-clip which attaches the reverse lever to the reverse lever pivot bolt.
9. Remove the reverse lever pivot bolt, then remove the reverse lever and the reverse lever fork as an assembly.
10. Mark the position of the front bearing cap in relation to the transmission case. Remove the bearing cap bolts and the cap.
11. Remove the front bearing race and the end-play shims

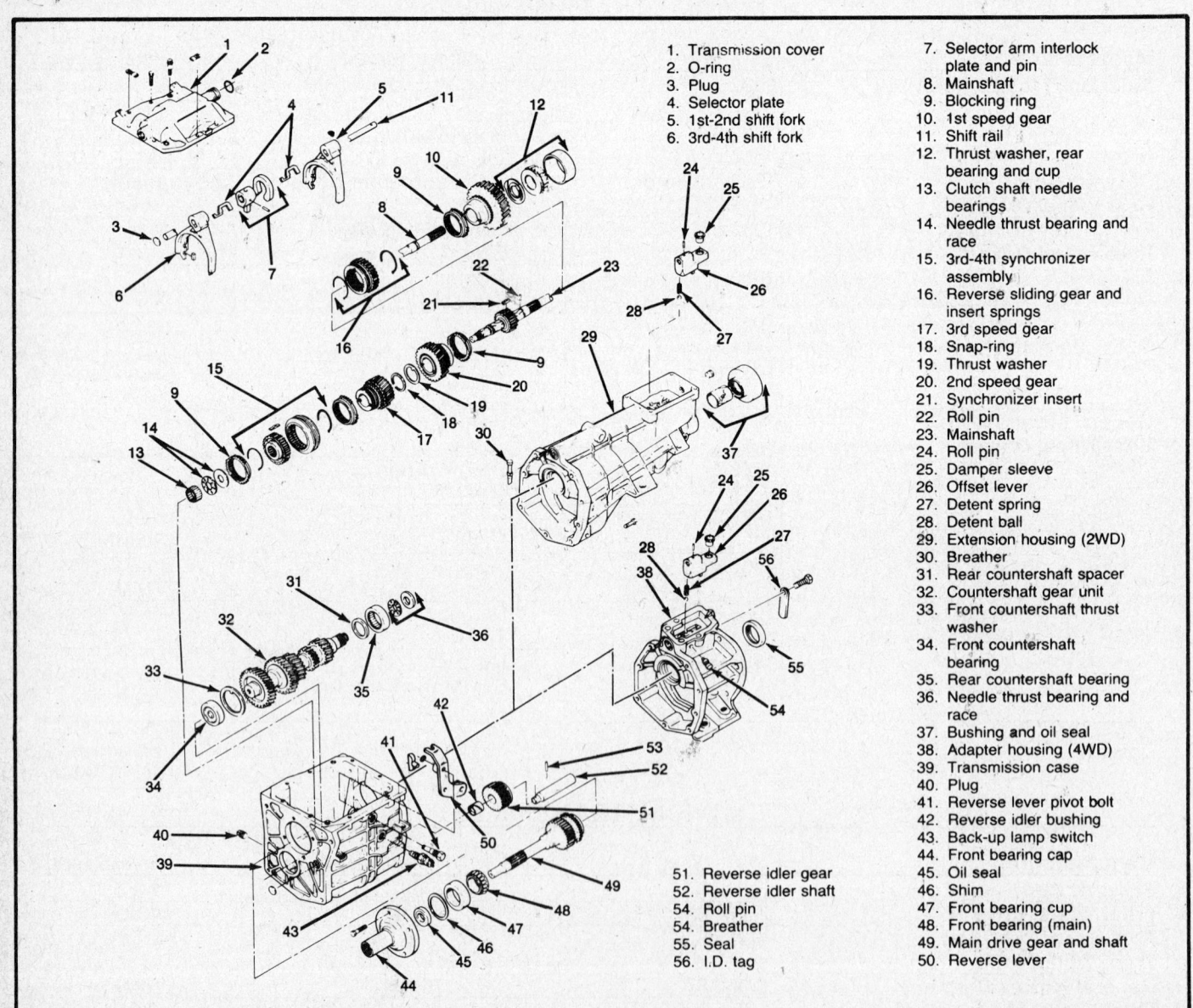

1. Transmission cover
2. O-ring
3. Plug
4. Selector plate
5. 1st-2nd shift fork
6. 3rd-4th shift fork
7. Selector arm interlock plate and pin
8. Mainshaft
9. Blocking ring
10. 1st speed gear
11. Shift rail
12. Thrust washer, rear bearing and cup
13. Clutch shaft needle bearings
14. Needle thrust bearing and race
15. 3rd-4th synchronizer assembly
16. Reverse sliding gear and insert springs
17. 3rd speed gear
18. Snap-ring
19. Thrust washer
20. 2nd speed gear
21. Synchronizer insert
22. Roll pin
23. Mainshaft
24. Roll pin
25. Damper sleeve
26. Offset lever
27. Detent spring
28. Detent ball
29. Extension housing (2WD)
30. Breather
31. Rear countershaft spacer
32. Countershaft gear unit
33. Front countershaft thrust washer
34. Front countershaft bearing
35. Rear countershaft bearing
36. Needle thrust bearing and race
37. Bushing and oil seal
38. Adapter housing (4WD)
39. Transmission case
40. Plug
41. Reverse lever pivot bolt
42. Reverse idler bushing
43. Back-up lamp switch
44. Front bearing cap
45. Oil seal
46. Shim
47. Front bearing cup
48. Front bearing (main)
49. Main drive gear and shaft
50. Reverse lever
51. Reverse idler gear
52. Reverse idler shaft
54. Roll pin
54. Breather
55. Seal
56. I.D. tag

Exploded view of the AMC T4 transmission

from the bearing cap. Pry the oil seal out of the bearing cap using an appropriate tool.

12. Rotate the main drive gear shaft until the flat portion of the gear faces the countershaft, then remove the main drive gear shaft assembly.
13. Remove the thrust bearing and the 15 roller bearings from the clutch shaft.
14. Remove the output shaft bearing race. If the race is stubborn, tap the front of the output shaft with a rubber or plastic mallet to remove the race.
15. Tilt the output shaft assembly upward and remove the assembly from the transmission case.
16. Using a brass drift and an arbor press, remove the countershaft rear bearing. Note the positioning of the bearing so that it may be reinstalled properly.
17. Move the countershaft rearward, then tilt it upward and remove it from the case.
18. Remove the countershaft rear bearing spacer.
19. Remove the reverse idler shaft roll pin, then remove the reverse idler shaft and gear. Note the position of the gear so that it may be reinstalled properly.
20. Using an arbor press, remove the countershaft front bearing.
21. Remove the bearing from the main drive gear shaft using Kent-Moore tools J-29721 and J-22912 (or their equivalents).
22. Remove the extension/adapter housing seal using the appropriate tools.
23. Remove the back-up light switch from the transmission case.

Component Disassembly
OUTPUT SHAFT GEARTRAIN

1. Remove the thrust bearing washer from the front of the output shaft.
2. Scribe matchmarks on the hub and the sleeve of the 3rd/4th synchronizer so that these parts may be reassembled properly.
3. Remove the 3rd/4th synchronizer blocking ring, sleeve, and hub as an assembly.
4. Remove the insert springs and inserts from the 3rd/4th synchronizer, then separate the sleeve from the hub.
5. Remove the 3rd speed gear from the shaft.
6. Remove the snap-ring which attaches the 2nd speed gear to the output shaft. Remove the tabbed 2nd gear thrust washer and the 2nd speed gear.
7. Remove the output shaft bearing using Kent-Moore puller set J-29721 and adapters 293-39 (or their equivalents).
8. Remove the 1st gear thrust washer, roll pin, 1st speed gear, and the blocking ring. Diagonal cutters may be used CAREFULLY to remove the roll pin.
9. Scribe matchmarks on the 1st/2nd synchronizer sleeve and the output shaft in the same manner as in Step 2.
10. Remove the insert spring and the inserts from the 1st/reverse sliding gear. Remove the gear from the output hub.

--- **CAUTION** ---
Do not attempt to remove the 1st/2nd reverse hub from the output shaft. The shaft and hub are machined and assembled as a matched set during manufacture.

TRANSMISSION COVER AND SHIFT FORKS

1. Place the selector arm plates and the shift rail in the Neutral position (centered).
2. Rotate the shift rail counterclockwise until the selector arm disengages from the selector arm plates. The selector arm roll pin should now be accessible.
3. Pull the shift rail rearward until the selector contacts the 1st/2nd shift fork.

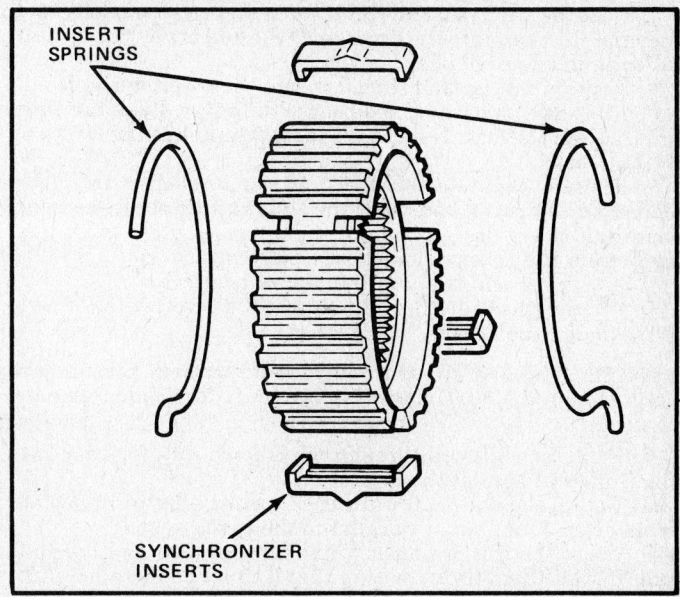

Synchronizer insert spring and insert installation

4. Remove the selector arm roll pin (using a 3/16 in. pin punch) and remove the shift rail.
5. Remove the shift forks, selector arm, roll pin, and the interlock plate.
6. Remove the shift rail oil seal and O-ring using an appropriate tool.
7. Remove the nylon inserts and the selector arm plates from the shift forks. Note the position of these parts so that they may be reinstalled properly.

Cleaning and Inspection

All parts (except those which are nylon or plastic) should be thoroughly cleaned in cleaning solvent. Nylon or plastic parts which are to be reused should just be wiped clean with a cloth. Assembled roller bearings should be dried with compressed air, but DO NOT spin the bearings with the compressed air as they could shatter and cause personal injury. Individual bearing rollers, washers, thrust bearings, etc., should be allowed to air dry after cleaning, though they may be wiped with a clean cloth.

Inspect all parts for excessive wear and/or damage such as scoring, cracks, nicks, rough edges, etc. Replace any defective parts. To check the condition of the assembled bearings, first clean and dry them, then coat the bearings with light engine oil. Slowly spin the bearings by hand and check for any signs of roughness. If the bearing does not feel perfectly smooth, it should be replaced.

NOTE: AMC recommends that if any gear of the mainshaft must be replaced, the countershaft gear should also be replaced to avoid noisy operation and maintain proper gear mesh.

While the transmission is out of the vehicle, it is good practice to check the condition of the clutch assembly and the throwout bearing. Also, replace all transmission gaskets, seals, etc. during assembly of the transmission.

Component Assembly
TRANSMISSION COVER

1. Attach the nylon inserts to, and the selector arm plates through the shift forks.
2. If removed previously, coat the edges of the shift rail plug with sealer and install the plug.

SECTION 32

MANUAL TRANSMISSIONS
WARNER—T4 FOUR SPEED

3. Coat the shift rail and rail bores with petroleum jelly and slide the shift rail into the cover until the end of the rail is flush with the inside edge of the cover.

4. Position the 1st/2nd shift fork into the cover, with the offset of the shift fork facing the rear of the cover. Push the shift rail through the fork. Note that the 1st/2nd fork is the larger of the two forks.

5. Position the selector arm and the C-shaped interlock plate into the cover and push the shift rail through the arm. Note that the widest portion of the interlock plate must face away from the cover, and that the selector arm roll pin must face downward and towards the rear of the cover.

6. Position the 3rd/4th shift fork into the cover, with the fork offset facing the rear of the cover.

NOTE: The 3rd/4th shift fork selector arm plate must be positioned UNDER the 1st/2nd shift fork selector arm plate.

7. Push the shift rail through the 3rd/4th shift fork and into the front rail bore of the cover.

8. Rotate the shift rail until the forward selector arm plate faces away from, but is parallel to the cover.

9. Align the roll pin holes of the selector arm and the shift rail. Install the roll pin, noting that it must be installed flush with the surface of the selector arm to prevent selector arm plate-to-pin interference.

10. Install the O-ring into the groove of the shift rail oil seal, then install the oil seal assembly as follows:
 a. Install an oil seal protector (Kent-Moore tool #J-26628-2 or its equivalent) over the threaded end of the shift rail.
 b. Lubricate the lip of the oil seal with petroleum jelly. Slide the seal over the protector and onto the shift rail.
 c. Seat the oil seal into the cover, using an appropriate tool.

OUTPUT SHAFT GEARTRAIN

1. Coat the output shaft and gear bores with transmission lubricant.

2. Using the matchmarks made during disassembly, align and install the 1st/2nd synchronizer sleeve on the output shaft hub.

3. Install the three inserts and two springs into the 1st/reverse synchronizer sleeve. Note that the tanged end of each spring should be positioned on the same insert but that the open face of each spring should be opposite the other.

4. Install the blocking ring and the 2nd speed gear onto the output shaft.

5. Install the tabbed thrust washer and the 2nd gear snapring on the output shaft. Be sure that the tab of the washer is properly seated in the notch of the output shaft.

6. Install the blocking ring and the 1st speed gear onto the output shaft, then install the 1st gear roll pin.

7. Using an arbor press and Kent-Moore tool #J-2995 (or its equivalent), install the rear bearing onto the output shaft.

8. Install the remaining outputshaft components in the order which follows:
 a. 1st gear thrust washer
 b. 3rd speed gear
 c. 3rd/4th synchronizer hub inserts and sleeve (hub offset must face forward)
 d. Thrust bearing washer (on forward end of output shaft)

Transmission Assembly

NOTE: If any replacement fastener must be used, be absolutely sure that it matches the original EXACTLY. Many metric fasteners are used in this transmission.

1. Apply a coating of Loctite® 601 (or its equivalent) to the outer cage of the front countershaft bearing. Press the bearing fully into its bore; it should be flush with the transmission case.

2. Apply a coating of petroleum jelly to the tabbed countershaft thrust washer. Install the thrust washer so that its tab engages the corresponding depression in the transmission case.

3. Tip the transmission case on end and install the countershaft into the front bearing bore.

4. Install the countershaft rear bearing spacer and coat the rear countershaft bearing with petroleum jelly. Install the rear countershaft bearing using the appropriate special tools (Kent-Moore tool #J-29895 installer and J-33032 sleeve protector, or their equivalents).

NOTE: When properly installed, the rear bearing will extend .125 in. beyond the transmission case surface.

5. Position the reverse idler gear into the transmission case (shift lever groove facing rearward) and install the reverse idler shaft from the rear of the case.

6. Install the shaft retaining pin.

7. Install the assembled output shaft into the transmission case.

8. If removed, install the main drive gear bearing onto the main drive gear shaft, using Kent-Moore tool #J-2995 (or its equivalent) and an arbor press.

9. Coat the main drive gear roller bearing (15) with petroleum jelly and install them into the recess of the main drive gear.

10. Install the thrust bearing and race into the recess of the main drive gear.

11. Install the 4th gear blocking ring onto the output shaft.

12. Install the rear output shaft bearing race.

13. Install the main drive gear assembly into the transmission case, engaging the 3rd/4th synchronizer blocking ring.

14. Evenly and carefully tap a new front bearing cap seal into place.

15. Install a new oil seal into the adapter housing (4WD) in the same manner as in Step 14.

16. Install the front bearing race into the front bearing cap. Do not yet install the front bearing cap shims.

17. Temporarily install the front bearing cap WITHOUT sealer.

18. Install the reverse lever, pivot pin (coat the threads with non-hardening sealer), and the retaining C-clip.

NOTE: Be sure that the reverse lever fork is engaged with the reverse idler gear.

19. Coat the countershaft rear bearing race and the thrust bearing with petroleum jelly. Install these parts into the extension/adapter housing.

20. Temporarily install the extension/adapter housing WITHOUT sealer. Tighten, but do not final torque the bolts.

21. Turn the transmission case on end. Mount a dial indicator on the extension/adapter housing so that the indicator needle contacts the end of the output shaft.

22. Rotate the main drive gear shaft and the output shaft, then zero the dial indicator.

23. Pull upward on the output shaft to remove the end-play. Read the indicator and record the reading.

NOTE: To completely eliminate the total end-play, the bearings must be preloaded from 0.001–0.005 in.

24. Select a shim pack which measures 0.001–0.005 in. THICKER than the end-play reading obtained during Step 23.

25. Move the transmission so that it sits horizontally, remove the front bearing cap and bearing race, and install the shim pack. Reinstall the bearing race.

26. Apply a ⅛ in. bead of RTV sealer on the case mating surface of the front bearing cap. Align the case and cap

MANUAL TRANSMISSIONS
WARNER—T4 FOUR SPEED
SECTION 32

matchmarks which were made during disassembly. Install the bearing cap and torque the bolts to 15 ft. lbs.

27. Recheck the end-play; no end-play should exist.
28. Remove the extension/adapter housing.
29. Move the shift forks and the synchronizer sleeves to their Neutral positions.
30. Apply a 1/8 in. bead of RTV sealer to the cover mating surface of the transmission. While aligning the shift forks with the synchronizer sleeves, carefully lower the cover assembly into place on the transmission.
31. Center the cover in order to engage the reverse relay lever. Install the two alignment-type (dowel) cover attaching bolts. Torque all cover bolts to 9 ft. lbs.

NOTE: The offset lever-to-shift rail roll pin hole must be positioned vertically; if it is not, repeat Steps 29–31.

32. Apply a 1/8 in. bead of RTV sealer to the extension/adapter housing mating surface of the transmission and install the housing over the output shaft.

NOTE: The shift rail must be positioned so that it just enters the shift cover opening.

33. Install the detent spring into the offset lever and place the steel ball into the neutral guide plate dentent. Apply pressure to the steel ball with the detent spring and the offset lever, then slide the offset lever on the shift rail and seat the extension/adapter housing against the transmission case. Tighten the housing retaining bolts to 25 ft. lbs.
34. Install the roll pin into the offset lever and shift rail.
35. Install the damper sleeve in the offset lever. Coat the back-up lamp switch threads with RTV sealer and install the switch into the transmission case. Torque the switch to 15 ft. lbs.

BORG WARNER 83MM, 4-SPEED TRANSMISSION

Disassembly

1. Remove the side cover and shift controls.
2. Remove front bearing retainer and gasket.
3. Remove output shaft companion flange.
4. Drive lockpin up from reverse shifter lever boss. Pull shift-shaft out about 1/8 in. to disengage shifter fork from reverse gear.
5. Tap the extension (with soft hammer) rearward. When idler gear shaft is out as far as it will go, move extension to the left so the reverse fork clears the reverse gear. Remove extension and gasket.
6. Remove rear bearing snap-ring from mainshaft.
7. Remove case extension oil seal.
8. Remove speedometer drive gear with puller.
9. Remove the reverse gear, reverse idler gear and tanged thrust washer.
10. Remove self-locking bolt holding the rear bearing retainer to transmission case.
11. Remove the entire mainshaft assembly.
12. Unload bearing rollers from main drive gear. Remove fourth-speed synchronizer blocking ring.
13. Lift the front half of reverse idler gear and its thrust washer from the case.
14. Remove the main drive gear snap-ring. Remove spacer washer.
15. With soft hammer, tap main drive gear toward rear and out of front bearing.
16. From inside the case, tap out front bearing and snap-ring.
17. From the front of the case, tap out the countershaft, using dummy shaft.
18. Then lift out the countergear assembly with both tanged washers.
19. Dismantle the countergear, consisting of 80 rollers, six .050 in. spacers and a roller tubular spacer.
20. Remove mainshaft front snap-ring. Slide:
    a. Third and fourth-speed clutch assembly
    b. Third-speed gear and synchronizer ring
    c. Second and third-speed gear thrust bearing
    d. Second-speed gear
    e. Second-speed synchronizer ring from front of mainshaft
21. Spread rear bearing retainer snap-ring and press mainshaft out of retainer.
22. Remove the mainshaft rear snap-ring.
23. Support first and second-speed clutch assembly
    a. Press on rear of mainshaft to remove
    b. Shaft from rear bearing
    c. First-speed gear, and synchromesh ring
    d. First and second-speed clutch sliding sleeve
    e. First-speed gear bushing

Assembly
MAINSHAFT

1. From the rear of the mainshaft, assemble first and second-speed clutch assembly to mainshaft (sliding clutch sleeve taper toward the rear, hub to the front). Press the first-speed gear bushing onto the shaft.
2. Install first-speed gear synchronizing ring. Align notches in ring with keys in hub.
3. Install first-speed gear (hub toward front) and the first-speed gear thrust washer. Grooves in the washer face first-speed gear.
4. Press on the rear bearing, with the snap-ring groove toward the front of the transmission. Be sure the bearing is firmly seated against the shoulder on the mainshaft.
5. Install the selective fit snap-ring onto the mainshaft behind the rear bearing. Use the thickest ring that will fit between the rear face of the bearing and the front face of the snap-ring.
6. From the front of the mainshaft, install the second-speed gear synchronizing ring. Notches in the ring correspond with the keys in the hub.
7. Install the second-speed gear (hub toward the back). Install the second and third-speed gear thrust bearing.
8. Install third-speed gear (hub to front) and third-speed gear synchronizing ring (notches front).
9. Install third and fourth-speed gear clutch assembly (hub and sliding sleeve) with taper front. Keys in the hub correspond with notches in third-speed gear synchronizing ring.
10. Install snap-ring (0.086–0.088 in. thickness) into groove in mainshaft, in front of the third and fourth-speed clutch assembly.
11. Install rear bearing retainer plate. Spread the snap-ring on the plate. Allow the snap-ring to drop around the rear bearing. Press on the end of the mainshaft until the snap-ring engages the groove in the rear bearing.
12. Install reverse gear (shift collar to the rear).
13. Press speedometer drive gear onto the mainshaft. Position the speedometer gear to get a measurement of 4½ in. from the center of the gear to the flat surface of the rear bearing retainer.
14. Install special snap-ring into the groove at the rear of the mainshaft.

32-7

SECTION 32 MANUAL TRANSMISSIONS
WARNER – 83mm FOUR SPEED

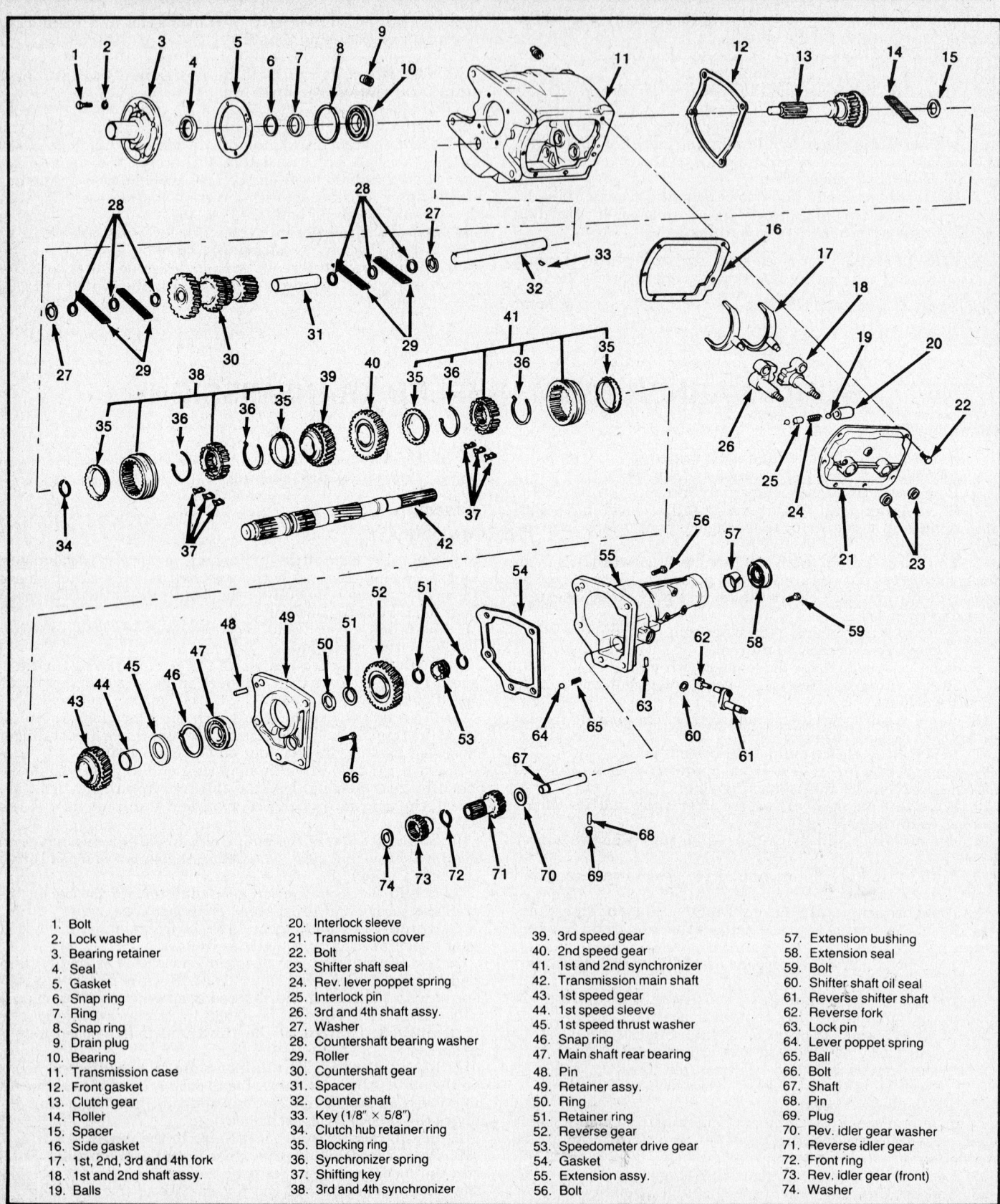

1. Bolt
2. Lock washer
3. Bearing retainer
4. Seal
5. Gasket
6. Snap ring
7. Ring
8. Snap ring
9. Drain plug
10. Bearing
11. Transmission case
12. Front gasket
13. Clutch gear
14. Roller
15. Spacer
16. Side gasket
17. 1st, 2nd, 3rd and 4th fork
18. 1st and 2nd shaft assy.
19. Balls
20. Interlock sleeve
21. Transmission cover
22. Bolt
23. Shifter shaft seal
24. Rev. lever poppet spring
25. Interlock pin
26. 3rd and 4th shaft assy.
27. Washer
28. Countershaft bearing washer
29. Roller
30. Countershaft gear
31. Spacer
32. Counter shaft
33. Key (1/8" × 5/8")
34. Clutch hub retainer ring
35. Blocking ring
36. Synchronizer spring
37. Shifting key
38. 3rd and 4th synchronizer
39. 3rd speed gear
40. 2nd speed gear
41. 1st and 2nd synchronizer
42. Transmission main shaft
43. 1st speed gear
44. 1st speed sleeve
45. 1st speed thrust washer
46. Snap ring
47. Main shaft rear bearing
48. Pin
49. Retainer assy.
50. Ring
51. Retainer ring
52. Reverse gear
53. Speedometer drive gear
54. Gasket
55. Extension assy.
56. Bolt
57. Extension bushing
58. Extension seal
59. Bolt
60. Shifter shaft oil seal
61. Reverse shifter shaft
62. Reverse fork
63. Lock pin
64. Lever poppet spring
65. Ball
66. Bolt
67. Shaft
68. Pin
69. Plug
70. Rev. idler gear washer
71. Reverse idler gear
72. Front ring
73. Rev. idler gear (front)
74. Washer

Borg Warner 4-speed transmission (© CHEVROLET MOTOR DIVISION)

MANUAL TRANSMISSIONS
WARNER—83mm FOUR SPEED
SECTION 32

COUNTERGEAR

1. Install countergear dummy and tubular roller bearing spacer into the countergear.
2. Using heavy grease to hold the rollers, install 20 bearing rollers in either end of the countergear, two spacers, 20 more rollers, then one spacer. Install the same combination of rollers and spacers in the other end of the countergear.
3. Set the countergear assembly in the bottom of the transmission case. Tanged thrust washers should be in their proper position.

MAIN DRIVE GEAR

1. Press bearing (snap-ring groove front) onto main drive gear until the bearing fully seats against the shoulder on the gear.
2. Install spacer washer and selective fit snap-ring in the groove in the main drive shaft.

NOTE: Variable thickness snap-rings are available to obtain a prescribed clearance of 0.000–0.005 in. between the rear face of the snap-ring and the front face of the spacer washer.

TRANSMISSION

1. Install main drive gear and bearing assembly through the side cover opening and into position in the transmission front bore. Install snap-ring into groove in front bearing.
2. Lift countergear and thrust washers into place. Install Woodruff key into end of countershaft. From the rear of the case, press the countershaft in until the end of the shaft is flush with rear of transmission case and the dummy shaft is displaced. End-play in the countergear must not exceed 0.025 in.
3. Install the 14 bearing rollers into the grease-coated end of the main drive gear.
4. Using heavy grease, position gasket on front face of rear bearing retainer. Install the fourth-speed synchronizing ring onto main drive gear with clutch key notches toward rear of transmission.
5. Position the reverse idler gear thrust washer on the machined face of the gear cast in the case for the reverse idler shaft. Position the front reverse idler gear on top of the thrust washer. Hub facing rear.
6. Lower the mainshaft assembly into the case. The notches of the fourth-speed synchronizing ring correspond to the keys in the clutch assembly.
7. Install self-locking bolt, holding the rear bearing retainer to the transmission case. Torque to 20–30 ft. lbs.
8. From the rear of the case, insert the rear reverse idler gear, engaging the splines with the portion of the gear within the case.
9. Grease gasket, and place in position on the rear face of the rear bearing retainer.
10. Install remaining tanged thrust washer into place on reverse idler shaft. The tang on the thrust washer fits in the notch in the idler thrust face of the extension.
11. Place the two clutches in neutral position.
12. Pull reverse shifter shaft to left side of extension. Rotate shaft to bring reverse fork to extreme forward position in extension. Line up forward and reverse idler gears.
13. Start the extension onto the transmission case by inserting reverse idler shaft through reverse idler gears. Push in on shifter until shift fork engages reverse gear shift collar. When the fork engages, rotate the shifter shaft to move reverse gear rearward. This will allow the extension to slide onto the transmission case.
14. Install three extension and retainer-to-case attaching bolts. Torque to 35–45 ft. lbs. Install two extension-to-retainer attaching bolts. Torque to 20–30 ft. lbs. Use sealer on the lower, right attaching bolt.
15. Adjust reverse shift shaft. Groove in shaft lines up with hole in boss. Drive in lockpin from top of boss.
16. Install the main drive gear bearing retainer and gasket. Align oil well with the oil outlet hole. Install four sealer-coated attaching bolts. Torque to 15–20 ft. lbs.
17. Install a shift fork into each clutch sleeve.
18. With both clutches in neutral, install side cover gasket and lower side cover into place.
19. Install attaching bolts. Torque to 10–20 ft. lbs. Use sealer on the lower right bolt.
20. Install first and second, and third and fourth shift levers, lock-washers and nuts.

BORG WARNER T5—5-SPEED TRANSMISSION

Transmission Disassembly

NOTE: Many special tools and an arbor press are required to properly disassemble and assemble this transmission. Read the entire procedure carefully BEFORE starting the job.

1. Remove the transmission from the vehicle as outlined in the appropriate car section, then drain the lubricant from the transmission. On AMC Spirit and Concord models, the fluid must be siphoned from the transmission, as these models are not equipped with drain plugs.
2. Using a pin punch and a hammer, carefully remove the roll pin which attaches the offset lever to the shift rail.
3. Remove the extension or adapter (AMC 4WD) housing-to-case bolts. Remove the housing and offset lever as an assembly.

CAUTION
DO NOT attempt to remove the housing with the offset lever still in place.

---

4. Remove the detent ball and spring from the offset lever. Remove the roll pin from the extension housing or offset lever.
5. Remove the plastic funnel, thrust bearing race, and thrust bearing from the rear of the countershaft.

NOTE: The funnel and race may be found inside the extension.

6. Remove the transmission cover-to-case bolts and lift the cover assembly off of the case.

NOTE: Two of the cover bolts are alignment-type dowel bolts. Note the location of these bolts so that they may be reinstalled in their original locations.

7. Place a wooden block under the 5th gear shift fork and drive the roll pink from the fork. The wood must be used to prevent damage to the shift rail.
8. Remove the following items from the rear of the countershaft:
   a. 5th gear synchronizer snap-ring
   b. shift fork
   c. 5th gear synchronizer sleeve
   d. blocking ring
   e. 5th speed drive gear
9. Remove the 5th gear synchronizer springs and inserts from the sleeve and hub. Mark the sleeve and hub so that they may be properly reassembled.

32-9

SECTION 32

MANUAL TRANSMISSIONS
WARNER—T5 FIVE SPEED

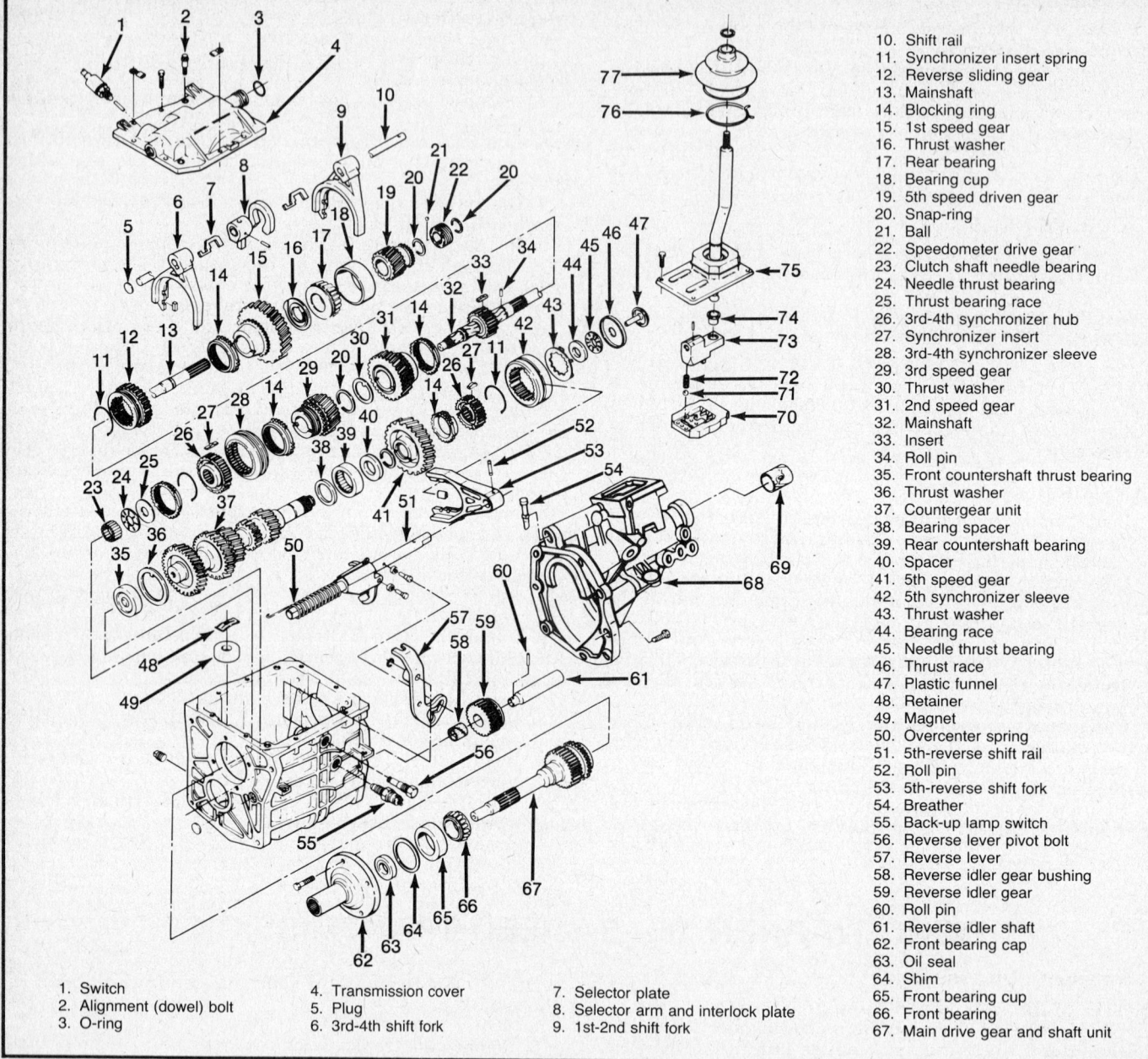

- 1. Switch
- 2. Alignment (dowel) bolt
- 3. O-ring
- 4. Transmission cover
- 5. Plug
- 6. 3rd-4th shift fork
- 7. Selector plate
- 8. Selector arm and interlock plate
- 9. 1st-2nd shift fork
- 10. Shift rail
- 11. Synchronizer insert spring
- 12. Reverse sliding gear
- 13. Mainshaft
- 14. Blocking ring
- 15. 1st speed gear
- 16. Thrust washer
- 17. Rear bearing
- 18. Bearing cup
- 19. 5th speed driven gear
- 20. Snap-ring
- 21. Ball
- 22. Speedometer drive gear
- 23. Clutch shaft needle bearing
- 24. Needle thrust bearing
- 25. Thrust bearing race
- 26. 3rd-4th synchronizer hub
- 27. Synchronizer insert
- 28. 3rd-4th synchronizer sleeve
- 29. 3rd speed gear
- 30. Thrust washer
- 31. 2nd speed gear
- 32. Mainshaft
- 33. Insert
- 34. Roll pin
- 35. Front countershaft thrust bearing
- 36. Thrust washer
- 37. Countergear unit
- 38. Bearing spacer
- 39. Rear countershaft bearing
- 40. Spacer
- 41. 5th speed gear
- 42. 5th synchronizer sleeve
- 43. Thrust washer
- 44. Bearing race
- 45. Needle thrust bearing
- 46. Thrust race
- 47. Plastic funnel
- 48. Retainer
- 49. Magnet
- 50. Overcenter spring
- 51. 5th-reverse shift rail
- 52. Roll pin
- 53. 5th-reverse shift fork
- 54. Breather
- 55. Back-up lamp switch
- 56. Reverse lever pivot bolt
- 57. Reverse lever
- 58. Reverse idler gear bushing
- 59. Reverse idler gear
- 60. Roll pin
- 61. Reverse idler shaft
- 62. Front bearing cap
- 63. Oil seal
- 64. Shim
- 65. Front bearing cup
- 66. Front bearing
- 67. Main drive gear and shaft unit

Exploded view of the transmission used in the Chevette

10. Remove the snap-ring from the 5th speed driven gear. The driven gear may be removed with a puller (Kent-Moore tool #J–25215).

11. Mark the front bearing cap and case so that the cap may be reinstalled in its proper position. Remove the front bearing cap.

12. Remove the front bearing race and end-play shim(s) from the bearing cap. Carefully pry the oil seal from the cap using an appropriate tool.

13. Rotate the clutch shaft until the flat surface on the main drive gear faces the countershaft. Remove the clutch shaft/main gear unit from the transmission case.

NOTE: The clutch shaft bearing is pressed on. An arbor press must be used to replace the bearing if the bearing is rough.

14. Remove the mainshaft rear bearing race and tilt the shaft upward. Remove the output shaft assembly from the case.

15. On AMC models, unhook the overcenter spring from the rear of the case, using a piece of welding rod bent into a hook to grab and pull the spring. On the Chevette, unhook the overcenter spring from the front of the transmission case.

16. Remove the reverse lever C-clip (all models) and the pivot bolt (Chevette).

17. Rotate the 1st/reverse shift rail clockwise to disengage it from the reverse lever. Remove the rail from the rear of the transmission case.

18. On AMC models, remove the reverse lever pivot pin and detach the lever from the reverse idler gear. On all models, remove the reverse lever and fork assembly from the transmission case.

MANUAL TRANSMISSIONS
WARNER — T5 FIVE SPEED
SECTION 32

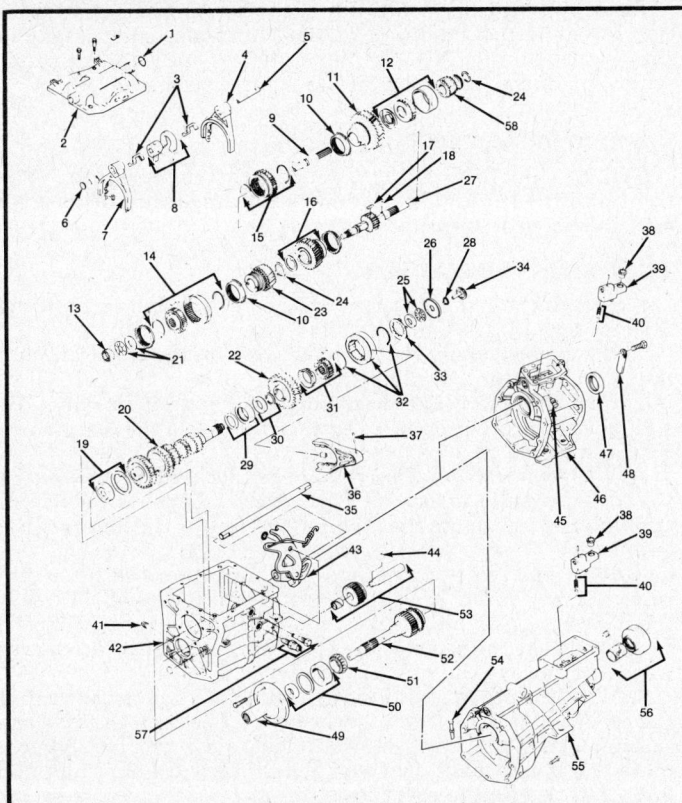

1. O-ring
2. Transmission cover
3. Selector plate
4. 1st-2nd shaft fork
5. Shift rail
6. Plug
7. 3rd-4th shift fork
8. Selector arm, interlock plate and pin
9. Mainshaft
10. Blocking ring
11. 1st speed gear
12. Thrust washer, rear bearing and clip
13. Clutch shaft needle bearing
14. 3rd-4th synchronizer assembly
15. Reverse sliding gear and insert springs
16. 2nd speed gear and thrust washer
17. Synchronizer insert
18. 1st gear roll pin
19. Front countershaft bearing and thrust washer
20. Countershaft gear unit
21. Needle thrust bearing and race
22. 5th speed gear
23. 3rd speed gear
24. Snap-ring
25. Needle thrust bearing and race
26. Thrust race
27. Mainshaft
28. Snap-ring
29. Rear countershaft bearing and spacer
30. Snap-ring and spacer
31. 5th gear synchronizer blocking ring, hub and insert
32. 5th gear synchronizer insert springs and sleeve
33. Insert retainer
34. Plastic funnel
35. Reverse seal
36. 5th speed shift fork
37. Roll pin
38. Damper sleeve
39. Offset lever
40. Detent spring and ball
41. Plug
42. Transmission case
43. 5th-reverse shift lever
44. Roll pin
45. Breather
46. Adapter housing (4WD)
47. Seal
48. I.D. tag
49. Front bearing cap
50. Oil seal, shim and cup
51. Front bearing
52. Main drive gear and shaft
53. Reverse idler bushing, gear and shaft
54. Breather
55. Extension housing (2WD)
56. Bushing and oil seal
57. Back-up lamp switch and 5th-reverse lever pivot bolt

Exploded view of the AMC T5 transmission

19. On Chevette models, drive the roll pin from the forward end of the reverse idler shaft. Remove the reverse idler shaft, rubber O-ring, and the gear from the transmission.
20. Remove the rear countershaft snap-ring and spacer.
21. Insert a brass drift through the main drive gear opening in the front of the case so that it contacts the countershaft gear assembly. Using an arbor press positioned at the other end of the drift, carefully press the countershaft gear rearward just enough to remove the countershaft rear bearing.

NOTE: During assembly, note that the bearing identification numbers should face outward.

22. Move the countershaft assembly rearward, tilt it upward, then remove the assembly from the case. Note the position of the front countershaft thrust washer so that it may be reinstalled properly, then remove the washer from the case.
23. Remove the countershaft rear bearing spacer.
24. Drive the roll pin from the front of the reverse idler shaft and remove the shaft and gear from the case. Note the position of the gear so that it may be reinstalled properly.
25. Using an arbor press, remove the countershaft front bearing from the transmission case.
26. Remove the clutch shaft front bearing, using the proper pulling tools as shown in the accompanying illustration.
27. Using a flat drift and a hammer, carefully tap out the rear extension/adapter housing seal.

Component Disassembly
MAINSHAFT AMC MODELS

1. Remove the thrust bearing and the washer from the front of the mainshaft.
2. Scribe matchmarks on the 3rd/4th synchronizer hub and the sleeve to indicate their relationship for proper reassembly.
3. Remove the 3rd/4th synchronizer blocking ring, sleeve,

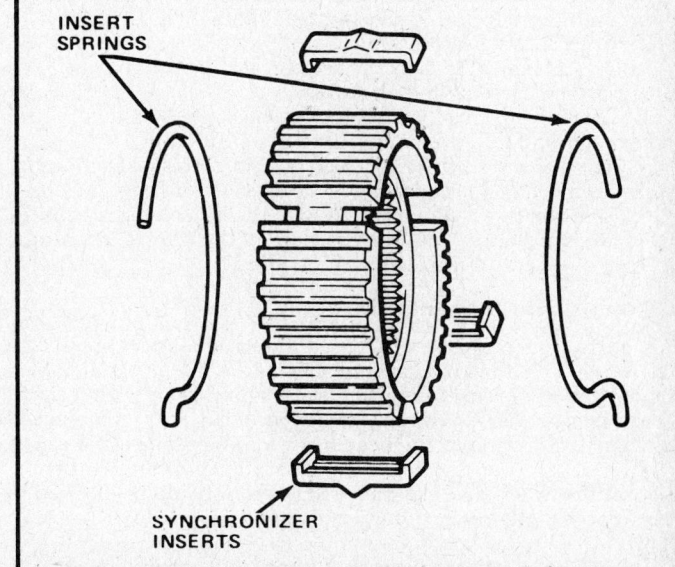

Synchronizer insert spring and insert installation

and hub from the mainshaft as an assembly. Note the positions of these items so that they may be properly reassembled.
4. Remove the 3rd/4th synchronizer insert springs. Remove the synchronizer inserts and the sleeve from the hub.
5. Remove the 3rd speed gear from the mainshaft.
6. Remove the 2nd gear snap-ring and tabbed thrust washer. Remove the 2nd speed gear from the mainshaft.
7. Using the appropriate special tools as shown, remove the rear mainshaft bearing.

SECTION 32
MANUAL TRANSMISSIONS
WARNER – T5 FIVE SPEED

8. Remove the 1st gear thrust washer, roll pin (using diagonal cutters carefully), 1st speed gear, and the blocking ring.

9. Scribe matchmarks on the 1st/2nd synchronizer sleeve and the mainshaft to indicate their relationship for proper reassembly.

10. Remove the insert spring and inserts from the 1st/reverse sliding gear. Remove the gear from the mainshaft hub.

CAUTION

DO NOT attempt to remove the 1st/2nd reverse hub from the mainshaft as these parts are machined as a matched set from the factory.

CHEVETTE MODELS

1. Follow Steps 1–3 of the previous AMC procedure.
2. Remove the snap-ing, tabbed thrust washer, and second gear from the mainshaft.
3. Using an arbor press and the appropriate special tool, remove the 5th speed gear from the mainshaft.
4. Slide the rear mainshaft bearing off of the mainshaft.
5. Remove the 1st gear thrust washer, roll pin, 1st speed gear, and the blocking ring.
6. Scribe matchmarks on the 1st/2nd synchronizer hub and sleeve for reassembly purposes.
7. Remove the insert spring and inserts from the 1st/reverse sliding gear. Remove the gear from the mainshaft.

CAUTION

DO NOT attempt to remove the 1st/2nd/reverse hub from the mainshaft as these parts are machined as a matched set from the factory.

TRANSMISSION COVER

1. Place the selector arm plates and shift rail in the Neutral position (centered).
2. Rotate the shift rail counterclockwise until the selector arm disengages from the selector arm plates. The selector arm roll pin will now be accessible.
3. On AMC models, pull the selector arm rearward until the arm contacts the 1st/2nd shift fork.
4. Carefully drive out the selector arm roll pin using a $3/16$ in. pin punch and a hammer. Remove the shift rail.
5. Remove the shift forks, selector arm plates, selector arm, roll pin and interlock plate.
6. Remove the nylon inserts and the selector arm plates from the shift forks. Note the positions of the inserts and plates so that they may be properly reinstalled.

Cleaning and Inspection

All parts (except those which are nylon or plastic) should be thoroughly cleaned in cleaning solvent. Nylon or plastic parts which are to be reused should just be wiped clean with a cloth. Assembled roller bearings should be dried with compressed air, but DO NOT spin the bearings with the compressed air as they could shatter and cause personal injury. Individual bearing rollers, washers, thrust bearings, etc., should be allowed to air dry after cleaning, though they may be wiped with a clean cloth.

Inspect all parts for excessive wear and/or damage such as scoring, cracks, nicks, rough edges, etc. Replace any defective parts. To check the condition of the assembled bearings, first clean and dry them, then coat the bearings by hand with light engine oil. Slowly spin the bearings by hand and check for any signs of roughness. If the bearing does not feel perfectly smooth, it should be replaced.

NOTE: AMC recommends that if any gear of the mainshaft must be replaced, the countershaft gear should also be replaced to avoid noisy operation and maintain proper gear mesh.

While the transmission is out of the vehicle, it is good practice to check the condition of the clutch assembly and the throwout bearing. Also, replace all transmission gaskets, seals, etc. during assembly of the transmission.

Component Assembly

NOTE: Coat all bearings, gear teeth, washers, etc., with light engine oil during assembly unless stated otherwise within the procedures.

TRANSMISSION COVER

1. Attach the nylon inserts to the shift forks and install the selector arm plates into the shift forks.
2. If removed, apply sealer to the edges of the shift rail plug then carefully tap the plug into place.
3. Coat the shift rail and rail bores with petroleum jelly then slide the shift rail into the cover until the end of the rail is flush with the inside edge of the cover.
4. With the offset of the 1st/2nd shift fork facing the rear of the cover, install the fork into the cover and push the shift rail through the fork. Note that the 1st/2nd fork is the larger of the two forks.
5. Place the selector arm and C-shaped interlock plate into the cover and insert the shift rail through the arm. Note that the widest part of the interlock plate must face away from the cover and that the selector arm roll pin holes must face downward and toward the rear of the cover.
6. With the offset of the 3rd/4th shift fork facing the rear of the cover, install the fork into the cover. The 3rd/4th shift fork selector arm plate must be positioned under the 1st/2nd arm plate. Push the shift rail completely forward, through the 3rd/4th fork into the cover bore.
7. Rotate the shift rail so that the forward selector arm plate faces away from, but is parallel to the cover.
8. After aligning the holes, install the selector arm-to-shift rail roll pin.

NOTE: To prevent the roll pin from contacting the selector arm plates when shifting, the roll pin must be installed flush with the surface of the selector arm.

9. Install the O-ring into the groove of the shift rail oil seal.
10. Installation of the shift rail oil seal should be performed as follows, using the appropriate special tools:
   a. Install Kent-Moore tool #J–26628–2 (or its equivalent) over the threaded end of the shift rail.
   b. Lubricate the lip of the oil seal with petroleum jelly.
   c. Slide the seal over the special tool (protector) and onto the shift rail.
   d. Using Kent-Moore tool #J–26628–1 (seal installer), seat the seal in the cover.

Mainshaft AMC Models

1. Lubricate the mainshaft and gear bores with a liberal coating of transmission lubricant.
2. Align then install the 1st/2nd synchronizer sleeve on the mainshaft, using the matchmarks made during disassembly as an alignment guide.
3. If removed, install the synchronizer inserts and springs into the 1st/2nd synchronizer sleeve. Note that the tanged end of each spring should be positioned on the same insert but that the open face of each spring should be opposite the other.
4. Install the blocking ring and 2nd speed gear onto the mainshaft.
5. Install the tabbed thrust washer and the 2nd speed gear retaining snap-ring onto the mainshaft. Be sure that the washer tab is fully seated into the notch of the mainshaft.
6. Install the blocking ring and the 1st speed gear onto the mainshaft.
7. Carefully drive the 1st gear roll pin into place.

MANUAL TRANSMISSIONS
WARNER—T5 FIVE SPEED

8. Press the rear bearing onto the mainshaft using an arbor press and the appropriate special tools.
9. Install the 1st gear thrust washer.
10. Install the 3rd speed gear, 3rd/4th synchronizer inserts and sleeve onto the mainshaft. The offset of the hub must face forward.
11. Install the thrust bearing washer onto the forward end of the mainshaft.

CHEVETTE MODELS

1. Follow Steps 1–6 of the previous AMC procedures.
2. Carefully drive the 1st gear roll pin into place, then install the 1st gear thrust washer.
3. Slide the mainshaft rear bearing onto the mainshaft.
4. Press the 5th speed gear onto the mainshaft using the appropriate special tools and an arbor press.
5. Install the 3rd speed gear, the 3rd/4th synchronizer assembly, and the thrust bearing on the mainshaft. The offset of the synchronizer hub must face forward.

Transmission Assembly

NOTE: If any replacement fastener must be used, be absolutely sure that it matches the original EXACTLY. Many metric fasteners are used in this transmission.

1. Apply a coating of Loctite® 601 (or its equivalent) to the outer cage of the front countershaft bearing. Press the bearing fully into its bore; it should be flush with the transmission case.
2. Apply a coating of petroleum jelly to the tabbed countershaft thrust washer. Install the thrust washer so that its tab engages the corresponding depression in the transmission case.
3. Tip the transmission case on end and install the countershaft into the front bearing bore.
4. Install the countershaft rear bearing spacer and coat the rear countershaft bearing with petroleum jelly. Install the rear countershaft bearing using the appropriate special tools (Kent-Moore tool #J–29895 installer and J–33032 sleeve protector or equivalents).

NOTE: When properly installed, the rear bearing will extend .125 in. beyond the transmission case surface.

5. Position the reverse idler gear into the transmission case (shift lever groove facing rearward) and install the reverse idler shaft from the rear of the case.
6. Install the shaft retaining pin.
7. Install the assembled mainshaft into the transmission case.
8. Install the rear mainshaft bearing race into the transmission case.
9. If removed, install the clutch shaft/main gear bearing, using an arbor press.
10. Coat the roller bearings of the main drive gear with petroleum jelly and install them into the rear of the clutch shaft/main gear unit.
11. Install the thrust bearing and race into the rear of the clutch shaft/main gear unit.
12. Install the 4th gear blocking ring on the mainshaft.
13. Install the clutch shaft/main gear unit into the transmission case, engaging the 3rd/4th synchronizer blocking ring.
14. Evenly and carefully tap a new front bearing cap seal into place.
15. Install the front bearing race into the front bearing cap. Do not yet install the front bearing cap shims.
16. Temporarily install the front bearing cap, WITHOUT sealer.
17. Install the following:
    a. 5th/reverse lever
    b. Pivot bolt
    c. C-clip retainer

Coat the pivot bolt threads with nonhardening sealer (RTV is preferred). Also, be sure to engage the reverse lever fork in the reverse idler gear.

18. On AMC models, install the 5th speed driven gear onto the rear of the mainshaft assembly. Install the snap-ring.
19. Install the countershaft rear bearing spacer and the retaining snap-ring.
20. Install the 5th speed gear onto the mainshaft.
21. Install the 5th/reverse rail through the rear transmission case opening and install it into the 5th/reverse lever. Rotate the rail to engage it with the lever.
22. On AMC models only:
    a. Install the overcenter spring.
    b. Assemble the 5th gear synchronizer sleeve, insert springs and insert retainer. Use the matchmarks made during disassembly to align.
    c. Install the plastic inserts on the fifth speed shift fork.
23. Position the 5th speed synchronizer assembly on the 5th speed shift fork and slide onto countershaft and 5th/reverse rail. Note that the 5th/reverse rail roll pin hole must be aligned with the hole of the 5th speed shift fork.
24. Support the 5th speed shift fork rail and fork with a block of wood and drive the roll pin into place.
25. Install the:
    a. Thrust race against the 5th speed synchronizer hub and retain with the snap-ring.
    b. Needle-type thrust bearing against the thrust race on the countershaft (coat the bearing and race with petroleum jelly.).
    c. Lipped thrust race over the needle-type thrust bearing.
    d. Plastic funnel into the hole in the end of the countershaft gear.
26. Temporarily install the extension/adapter housing and the attaching bolts.
27. Turn the transmission case on end. Mount a dial indicator on the extension/adapter housing so that the indicator needle contacts the end of the mainshaft.
28. Pull upward fully on the mainshaft to remove the endplay. Read the indicator and record the reading.
29. Select a shim pack which measures 0.001–0.005 in. THICKER than the end-play reading obtained during Step 28.
30. Move the transmission so that it sits horizontally, remove the front bearing cap and bearing race, and install the shim pack. Reinstall the bearing race.
31. Apply a 1/8 in. bead of RTV sealer on the case mating surface of the front bearing cap. Align the case and cap matchmarks which were made during disassembly. Install the bearing cap and torque the bolts to 15 ft. lbs.
32. Recheck the end-play. No play should be evident.
33. Remove the extension/adaptor housing and carefully drive a new housing seal into place.
34. Move the shift forks of the transmission cover and the synchronizer sleeves of the transmission to their Neutral positions.
35. Apply a 1/8 in. bead of RTV sealer to the cover mating surface of the transmission. While aligning the shift forks with the synchronizer sleeves, carefully lower the cover assembly into place on the transmission.
36. Center the cover in order to engage the reverse relay lever. Install the two alignment-type (dowel) cover attaching bolts. Install the remaining cover bolts. Torque all cover bolts to 10 ft. lbs.

NOTE: The offset lever-to-shift rail roll pin hole must be positioned vertically; if is not, repeat Steps 34, 35, 36.

37. Apply a 1/8 in. bead of RTV sealer to the extension/adapter housing mating surface of the transmission and install the extension housing over the mainshaft.

NOTE: The shift rail must be positioned so that it just enters the shift cover opening.

32-13

SECTION 32

MANUAL TRANSMISSIONS
WARNER—T5 FIVE SPEED

38. Install the detent spring into the offset lever and place the steel ball into the neutral guide plate detent. Apply pressure on the steel ball with the detent spring and offset lever, then slide the offset lever on the shift rail and seat the extension/adapter against the transmission case.
39. Install the extension/adapter housing retaining bolts and torque the bolts to 25 ft. lbs.
40. Install the roll pin into the offset lever and shift rail.
41. Install the damper sleeve in the offset lever. Coat the back-up lamp switch threads with RTV sealer and install the switch into the transmission case. Torque the switch to 15 ft. lbs.

BORG WARNER 77MM—5-SPEED TRANSMISSION

TRANSMISSION

Disassembly

1. Remove drain bolt on transmission case and drain lubricant.
2. Thoroughly clean the exterior of the transmission assembly.
3. Using pin punch and hammer, remove roll pin attaching offset lever to shift rail.
4. Remove extension housing-to-transmission case bolts and remove housing and offset lever as an assembly.

NOTE: Do not attempt to remove the offset lever while the extension housing is still bolted in place. The lever has a positioning lug engaged in the housing detent plate which prevents moving the lever far enough for removal.

5. Remove detent ball and spring from offset lever and remove roll pin from extension housing or offset lever.
6. Remove plastic funnel, thrust bearing race and thrust bearing from rear of countershaft. The countershaft rear thrust bearing, bearing washer and plastic funnel may be found inside the extension housing.
7. Remove bolts attaching transmission cover and shift fork assembly and remove cover. Two of the transmission cover attaching bolts are alignment-type dowel bolts. Note the location of these bolts for assembly reference.
8. Using a punch and hammer, drive the roll pin from the fifth gearshift fork while supporting the end of the shaft with a block of wood.
9. Remove fifth synchronizer gear snap ring, shift fork, fifth gear synchronizer sleeve, blocking ring and fifth speed drive gear from rear of countershaft.
10. Remove snap ring from fifth speed driven gear.
11. Using a hammer and punch, mark both bearing cap and case for assembly reference.

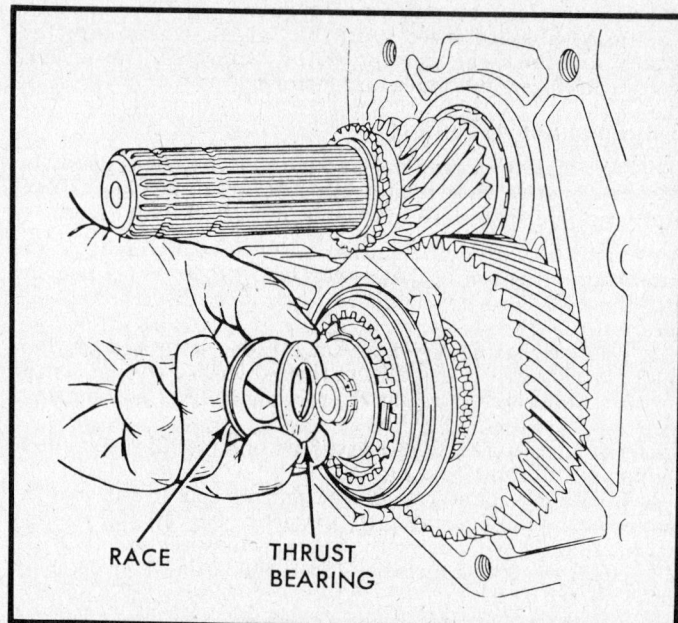
Removing or installing thrust bearing and race

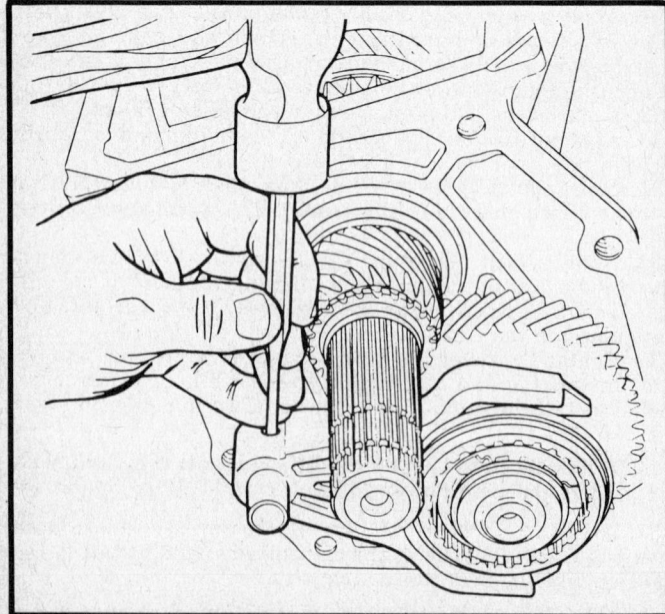
Removing fifth gearshift fork roll pin

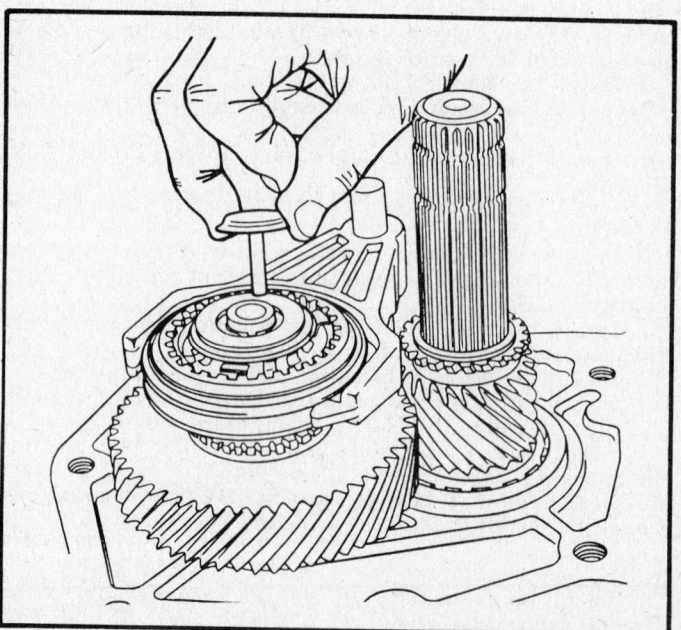
Removing plastic funnel

MANUAL TRANSMISSIONS
WARNER—77mm FIVE SPEED

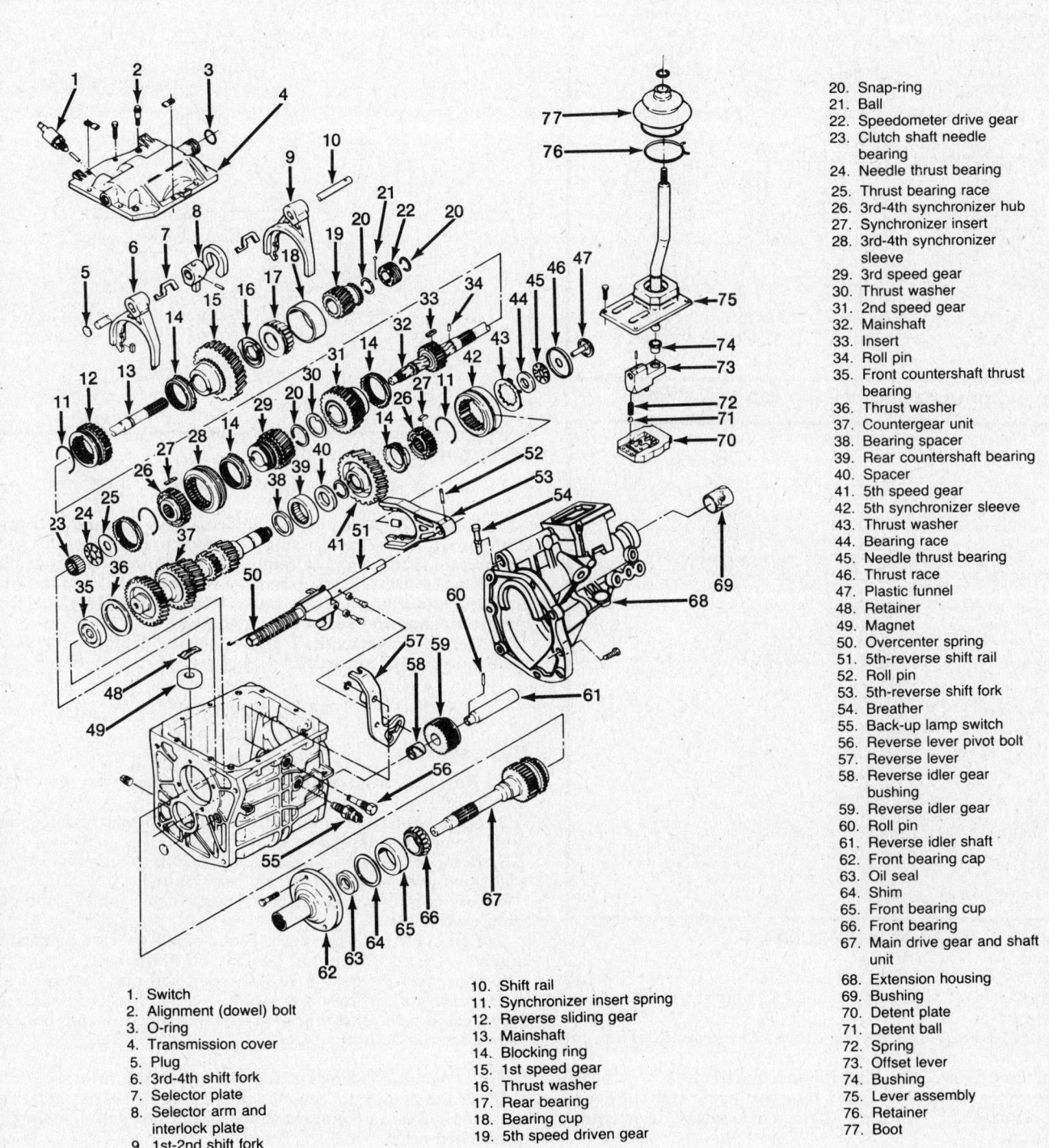

Exploded view of 77mm 5-speed transmission

1. Switch
2. Alignment (dowel) bolt
3. O-ring
4. Transmission cover
5. Plug
6. 3rd-4th shift fork
7. Selector plate
8. Selector arm and interlock plate
9. 1st-2nd shift fork
10. Shift rail
11. Synchronizer insert spring
12. Reverse sliding gear
13. Mainshaft
14. Blocking ring
15. 1st speed gear
16. Thrust washer
17. Rear bearing
18. Bearing cup
19. 5th speed driven gear
20. Snap-ring
21. Ball
22. Speedometer drive gear
23. Clutch shaft needle bearing
24. Needle thrust bearing
25. Thrust bearing race
26. 3rd-4th synchronizer hub
27. Synchronizer insert
28. 3rd-4th synchronizer sleeve
29. 3rd speed gear
30. Thrust washer
31. 2nd speed gear
32. Mainshaft
33. Insert
34. Roll pin
35. Front countershaft thrust bearing
36. Thrust washer
37. Countergear unit
38. Bearing spacer
39. Rear countershaft bearing
40. Spacer
41. 5th speed gear
42. 5th synchronizer sleeve
43. Thrust washer
44. Bearing race
45. Needle thrust bearing
46. Thrust race
47. Plastic funnel
48. Retainer
49. Magnet
50. Overcenter spring
51. 5th-reverse shift rail
52. Roll pin
53. 5th-reverse shift fork
54. Breather
55. Back-up lamp switch
56. Reverse lever pivot bolt
57. Reverse lever
58. Reverse idler gear bushing
59. Reverse idler gear
60. Roll pin
61. Reverse idler shaft
62. Front bearing cap
63. Oil seal
64. Shim
65. Front bearing cup
66. Front bearing
67. Main drive gear and shaft unit
68. Extension housing
69. Bushing
70. Detent plate
71. Detent ball
72. Spring
73. Offset lever
74. Bushing
75. Lever assembly
76. Retainer
77. Boot

Section 32

MANUAL TRANSMISSIONS
WARNER—77mm FIVE SPEED

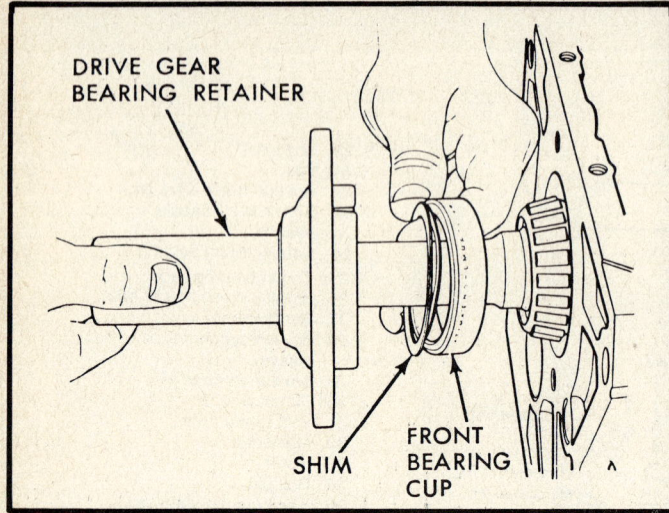

Removing or installing bearing cap and shims

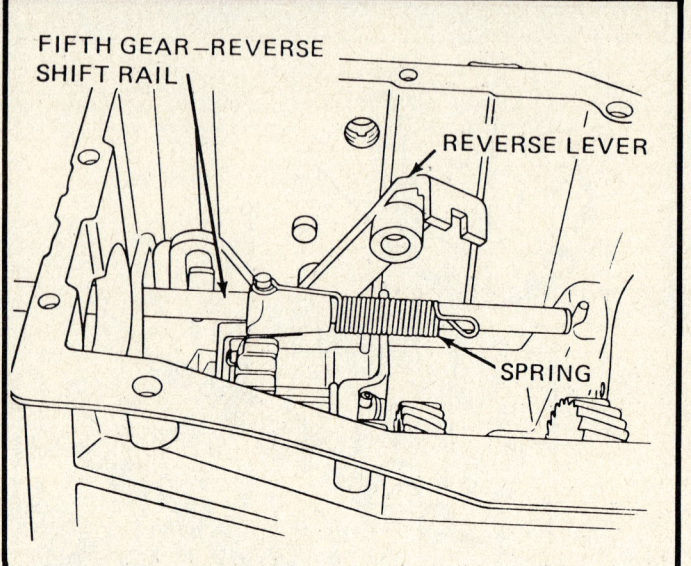

Fifth gear-reverse shift rail

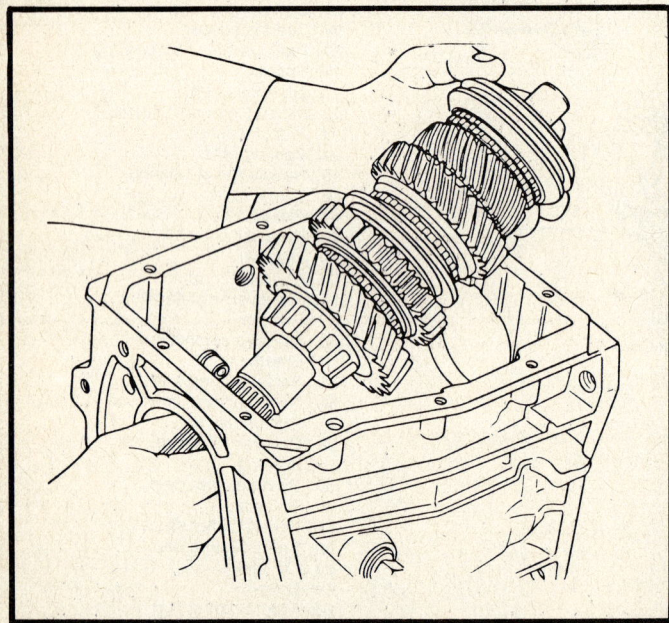

Mainshaft removal or installation

12. Remove front bearing cap bolts and remove front bearing cap. Remove front bearing race and end play shims from front bearing cap.
13. Rotate drive gear until flat surface faces countershaft and remove drive gear from transmission case.
14. Remove reverse lever C-clip and pivot bolt.
15. Remove mainshaft rear bearing race and then tilt mainshaft assembly upward and remove assembly from transmission case.
16. Unhook overcenter link spring from front of transmission case.
17. Rotate fifth gear-reverse shift rail to disengage rail from reverse lever assembly. Remove shift rail from rear of transmission case.
18. Remove reverse lever and fork assembly from transmission case.
19. Using hammer and punch, drive roll pin from forward end of reverse idler shaft and remove reverse idler shaft, rubber O-ring and gear from the transmission case.
20. Remove rear countershaft snap ring and spacer.

21. Insert a brass drift through drive gear opening in front of transmission case and, using an arbor press, carefully press countershaft rearward to remove rear countershaft bearing.
22. Move countershaft assembly rearward, tilt countershaft upward and remove from case. Remove countershaft front thrust washer and rear bearing spacer.
23. Remove countershaft front bearing from transmission case using an arbor press.

MAINSHAFT

Disassembly

1. Remove thrust bearing washer from front end of mainshaft.
2. Scribe reference mark on third-ourth synchronizer hub and sleeve for reassembly.
3. Remove 3rd/4th synchronizer blocking ring, sleeve, hub and third gear as an assembly from mainshaft.
4. Remove snap ring, tabbed thrust washer, and second gear from mainshaft.
5. Remove fifth gear with Tool J-22912-01 or equivalent and arbor press. Slide rear bearing off mainshaft.
6. Remove first gear thrust washer, roll pin, first gear and synchronizer ring from mainshaft.
7. Scribe reference mark on 1st/2nd synchronizer hub and sleeve for reassembly.
8. Remove synchronizer spring and keys from 1st/reverse sliding gear and remove gear from mainshaft hub.

Do not attempt to remove the 1st/2nd reverse hub from mainshaft. The hub and shaft are assembled and machined as a matched set.

DRIVE GEAR

Disassembly

1. Remove bearing race, thrust bearing, and roller bearings from cavity of drive gear.
2. Using Tool J-22912-01 or equivalent and arbor press, remove bearing from drive gear.
3. Wash parts in a cleaning solvent.
4. Inspect gear teeth and drive shaft pilot for wear.

MANUAL TRANSMISSIONS
WARNER—77mm FIVE SPEED

CLEANING AND INSPECTION

TRANSMISSION CASE
1. Wash the transmission thoroughly inside and outside using a suitable solvent, then inspect the case for cracks.
2. Clean magnetic disc at bottom of transmission case.
3. Check the front and rear faces of transmission case for burrs and if present, dress them off with a fine mill file.

BEARINGS ROLLERS AND SPACERS
All drive gear bearing rollers should be inspected closely and replaced if they show wear. Inspect, reverse idler shaft at the same time, replace if necessary. Replace all worn spacers.

GEARS
1. Inspect all gears for excessive wear, chips or cracks and replace any that are worn or damaged.
2. Check clutch sleeves to see that they slide freely on their hubs.

FRONT AND REAR BEARINGS
1. Wash the front and rear bearings thoroughly in a cleaning solvent.
2. Blow out bearings with compressed air.

NOTE: Do not allow the bearings to spin. Turn them slowly by hand. Spinning bearings may damage the race and balls.

3. Lubricate bearings with a light engine oil and check them for roughness by slowly turning the race by hand.

REPAIRS

Synchronizer Keys and Springs Replacement
The synchronizer hubs and sliding sleeves are a selected assembly and should be kept together as originally assembled, but the keys and springs may be replaced if worn or broken.
1. If relation of hub and sleeve are not already marked, mark for assembly purposes.
2. Push the sliding sleeve from the hub, the keys will fall free and the springs may be easily removed.
3. Place a blocker ring on side oof the hub and sleeve and install keys and retain with a spring. Place blocker ring on opposite side of hub and sleeve and install remaining spring.

Extension Housing Oil Seal Replacement
1. Pry oil seal out of extension housing, using a pry bar.
2. Coat outer diameter of new oil seal with sealing cement. Install new oil seal into extension housing using Tool J–21426 or equivalent.
3. Lubricate I.D. of seal with transmission lubricant.

Extension Housing Bushing Replacement
1. Pry oil seal out of extension housing, using a pry bar.
2. Drive the bushing out of housing, using Tool J–8092 with J–23062–14 or equivalent.
3. Install bushing in housing, using Tool J–8092 with J–23062–14 or equivalent.
4. Coat outer diameter of new oil seal with sealing cement. Install new oil seal into extension housing using Tool J–21426 or equivalent.
5. Lubricate I.D. of seal with transmission lubricant.

Drive Gear Bearing Retainer Oil Seal Replacement
1. Pry oil seal out, using a pry bar.
2. Install new seal into retainer using Tool J–23096 or equivalent until it bottoms in bore.
3. Lubricate I.D. of seal with transmission lubricant.

Transmission Cover

Disassembly
1. Place selector arm plates and shift rail in neutral position (centered).
2. Rotate shift rail until selector arm disengages from selector arm plates and roll pin is accessible.
3. Remove selector arm roll pin using a pin punch and hammer.
4. Remove shift rail, shift forks, selector arm plates, selector arm, interlock plate and roll pin.
5. Remove shift cover to extension housing O-ring seal using a pry bar.
6. Remove nylon inserts and selector arm plates from shift forks. Note position of inserts and plates for assembly reference.

Assembly
1. Install nylon inserts and selector arm plates in shift forks.
2. If removed, install shift rail plug. Coat edges of plug with sealer before installing.
3. Coat shift rail and rail bores with light weight grease and insert shift rail in cover. Install rail until flush with inside edge of cover.
4. Place 1st/2nd shift fork in cover with fork offset facing rear of cover and push shift rail through fork. The 1st/2nd shift fork is the larger of the two forks.
5. Position selector arm and C-shaped interlock plate in cover and insert shift rail through arm. Widest part of interlock plate must face away from cover, and selector arm roll pin hole must face downward and toward rear of cover.
6. Position 3rd/4th shift fork in cover with fork offset facing rear of cover. 3rd/4th shift fork selector arm plate must be under 1st/2nd shift fork selector arm plate.
7. Push shift rail through 3rd/4th shift fork and into front bore in cover.
8. Rotate shift rail until selector arm plate at forward end of rail faces away from, but it parallel to cover.
9. Align roll pin holes in selector arm and shift rail and install roll pin. Roll pin must be flush with surface of selector arm to prevent pin from contacting selector arm plates during shifts.
10. Install a new shift cover to extension housing O ring seal. Coat O-ring seal with transmission lubricant.

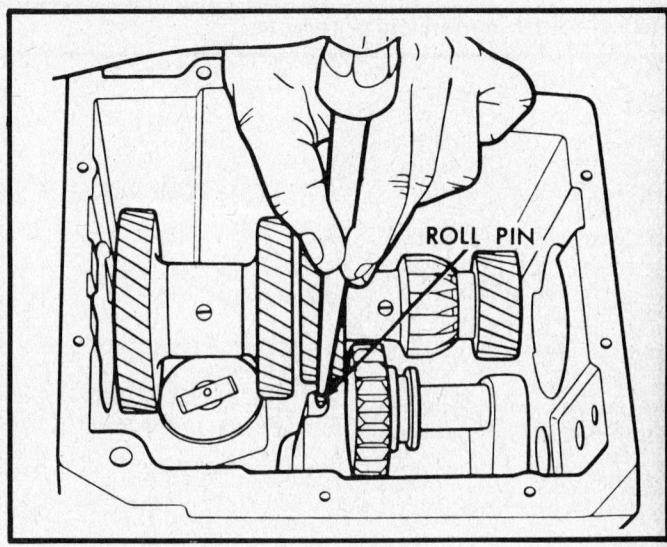

Reverse idler gear shaft roll pin location

SECTION 32 MANUAL TRANSMISSIONS
WARNER—77mm FIVE SPEED

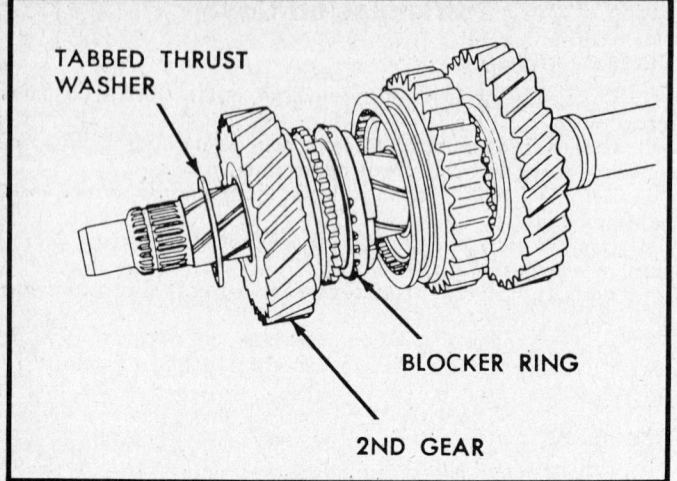

Second gear and thrust washer arrangement

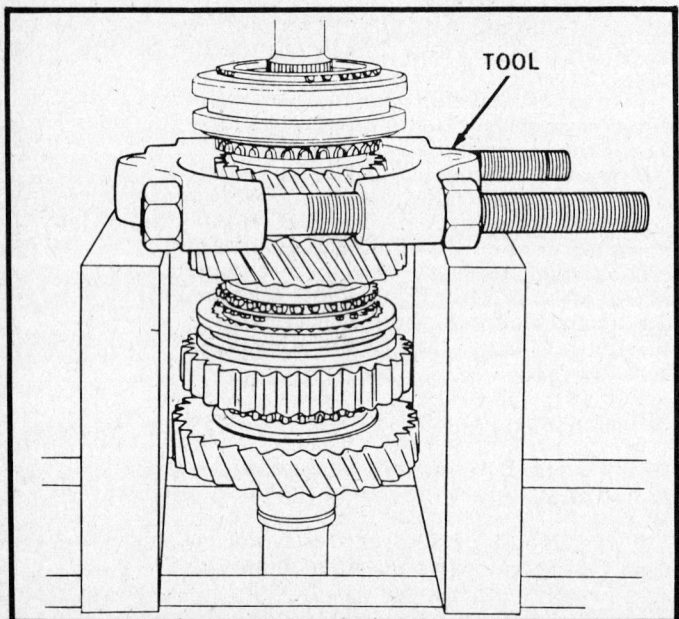

Third-fourth synchronize removal

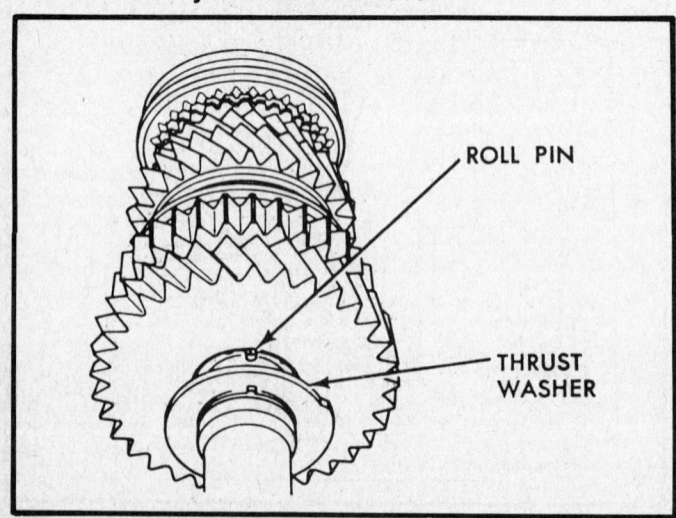

First gear thrust washer and roll pin

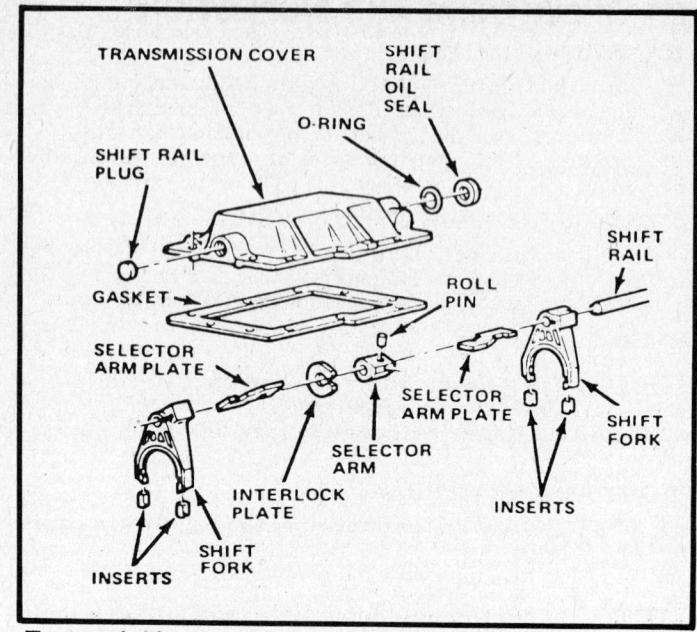

Transmission cover—exploded view

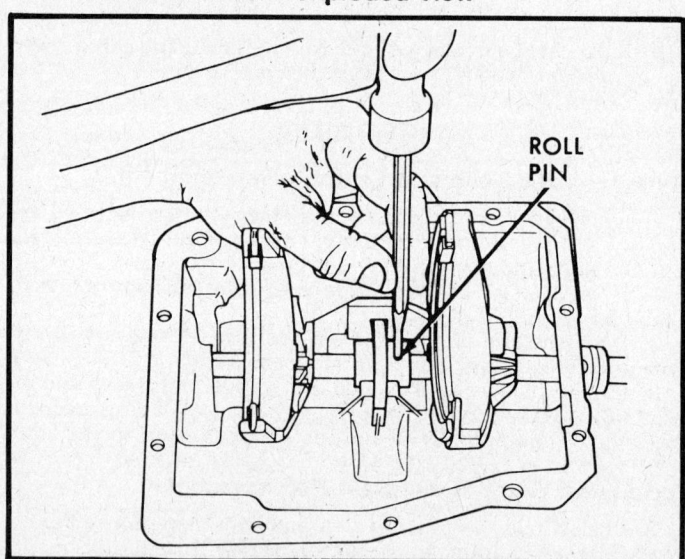

Selector arm roll pin removal

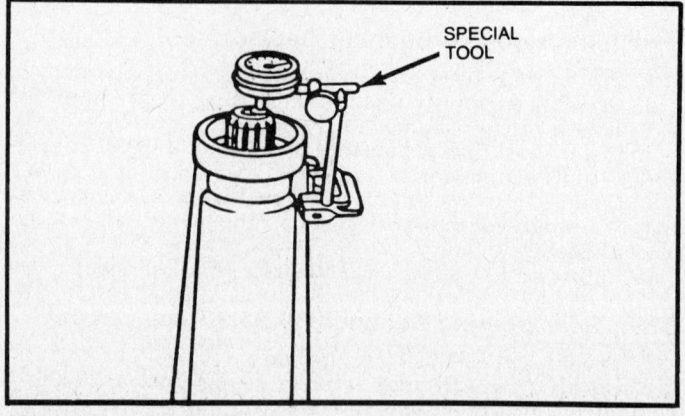

Measuring end play

32-18

MANUAL TRANSMISSIONS
WARNER—77mm FIVE SPEED
SECTION 32

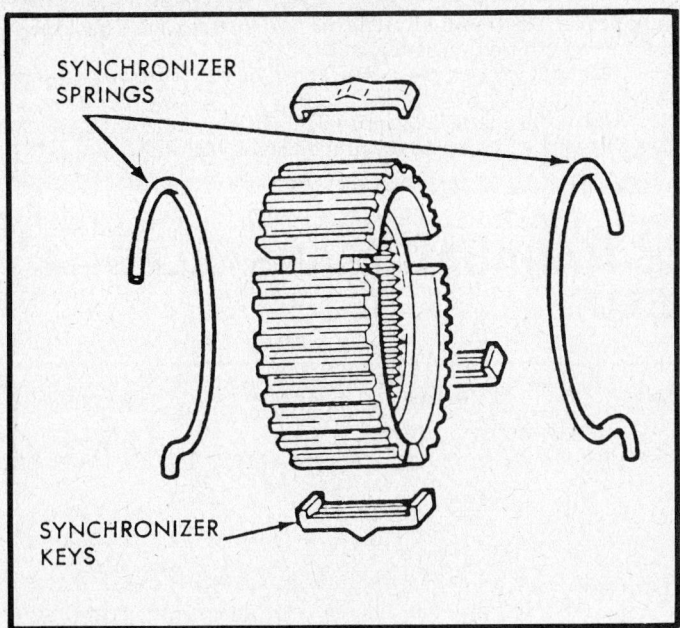

Synchronizer spring installation

DRIVE GEAR

Assembly

1. Using Tool J-22912-01 or equivalent with an arbor press, install bearing on drive gear.
2. Coat roller bearings and drive gear bearing bore with grease. Install roller bearings into bore of drive gear.
3. Install thrust bearing and race in drive gear.

MAINSHAFT

Assembly

1. Coat mainshaft and gear bores with transmission lubricant.
2. Install 1st/2nd synchronizer sleeve on mainshaft hub aligning marks made at disassembly.
3. Install 1st/2nd synchronizer keys and springs. Engage tang end of each spring in same synchronizer key but position open end of springs opposite of each other.
4. Install blocker ring and second gear on mainshaft. Install tabbed thrust washer and second gear retaining snap ring on mainshaft. Be sure washer tab is properly seated in mainshaft notch.
5. Install blocker ring and first gear on mainshaft. Install first gear roll pin and then first gear thrust washer.
6. Slide rear bearing on mainshaft.
7. Install fifth speed gear on mainshaft using Tool J-22912-01 or equivalent and arbor press. Install snap ring on mainshaft.
8. Install third gear, 3rd/4th synchronizer assembly and thrust bearing on mainshaft. Synchronizer hub offset must face forward.

TRANSMISSION

Assembly

1. Coat countershaft front bearing bore with Loctite® 601, or equivalent, and install front countershaft bearing flush with facing of case using an arbor press.
2. Coat countershaft tabbed thrust washer with grease and install washer so tab engages depression in case.
3. Tip transmission case on end and install countershaft in front bearing bore.
4. Install countershaft rear bearing spacer. Coat countershaft rear bearing with grease and install bearing using Tool J-29895 and sleeve J-33032 or equivalent.

NOTE: The bearing when correctly installed will extend beyond the case surface 0.125 inch (3mm).

5. Position reverse idler gear in case with shift lever groove facing rear of case and install reverse idler shaft from rear of case. Install roll pin in idler shaft.
6. Install assembled mainshaft in transmission case. Install rear mainshaft bearing race in case.
7. Install drive gear in case, and engage in 3rd/4th synchronizer sleeve and blocker ring.
8. Install front bearing race in front bearing cap. Do not install shims in front bearing cap at this time.
9. Temporarily install front bearing cap.
10. Install fifth speed-reverse lever, pivot bolt and retaining clip. Coat pivot bolt threads with nonhardening sealer. Be sure to engage reverse lever fork in reverse idler gear.
11. Install countershaft rear bearing spacer and retaining snap ring.
12. Install fifth speed gear on countershaft.
13. Insert fifth speed-reverse rail in rear of case and install into reverse fifth speed lever. Rotate rail during installation to simplify engagement with lever. Connect spring to front of case.
14. Position fifth gear shift fork on fifth gear synchronizer assembly and install synchronizer on countershaft and shift fork on shift rail. Make sure roll pin hole in shift fork and shift rail are aligned.
15. Support fifth gear shift rail and fork on a block of wood and install roll pin.
16. Install thrust race against fifth speed synchronizer hub and install snap ring. Install thrust bearing against race on countershaft. Coat both bearing and race with petroleum jelly.
17. Install lipped thrust race over needle-type thrust bearing and install plastic funnel into hole in end of countershaft gear.
18. Temporarily install extension housing and attaching bolts. Turn transmission case on end, and mount a dial indicator on extension housing with indicator on the end of mainshaft.
19. Rotate mainshaft and zero ial indicator. Pull upward on mainshaft until end play is removed and record reading.

NOTE: Mainshaft bearing require a preload of 0.001–0.005 in. (0.03–0.13mm). To set preload, select a shim pack measuring 0.001–0.005 in. (0.03–0.13mm) greater than the dial indicator reading recorded.

20. Remove front bearing cap and front bearing race. Install necessary shims to obtain preload and reinstall bearing race.
21. Apply a 3mm diameter (⅛ in.) bead of RTV sealant, #732 or equivalent, on case mating surface of front bearing cap. Install bearing cap aligning marks made during disassembly and torque bolts to specification.
22. Remove extension housing.
23. Move shift forks on transmission cover and synchronizer sleeves inside transmission to the neutral position.
24. Apply a 3mm diameter (⅛ in.) bead of RTV sealant, #732 or equivalent, on cover mating surface of transmission.
25. Lower cover onto case while aligning shift forks and synchronizer sleeves. Center cover and install the 2 dowel bolts. Install remaining bolts and torque to specification.

NOTE: The offset lever to shift rail roll pin hole must be in the vertical position after cover installation.

26. Apply a 3mm diameter (⅛ in.) bead of RTV sealant, #732

SECTION 32 MANUAL TRANSMISSIONS
WARNER—77mm FIVE SPEED

or equivalent, on extension housing to transmission case mating surface.

27. Install extension housing over mainshaft and shift rail to a position where shift rail just enters shift cover opening.

28. Install detent spring into offset lever and place steel ball in neutral guide plate detent. Position offset lever on steel ball and apply pressure on offset lever and at the time seat extension housing against transmission case.

29. Install extension housing bolts and torque to specification.

30. Align and install roll pin in offset lever and shift rail.

31. Fill transmission to its proper level with lubricant.

CHRYSLER A–460, A–465 AND A–525 MANAUAL TRANSAXLES – 4 and 5 SPEED

The Chrysler designed and built A–460, A–465, and A–525 "fully-synchronized" manual transmaxles combine gear reduction, ratio selection, and differential functions in one unit housed in a die-cast aluminum case. The A–460 is a four-speed while both the A–465 and A–525 are five-speeds. The A–525 has a close-ratio gearset with different 2nd, 3rd and 4th gear ratios than the A–465, to provide better performance through the gears, while 1st and 5th gear ratios are the same as the A–465 to maintain the same launch and top-gear characteristics.

Transaxle Disassembly

1. With the transaxle removed from the vehicle, remove the eight differential cover bolts and the two stud nuts and remove the cover.

2. Remove the five differential bearing retainer bolts.

3. Using the L-4435 or equivalent spanner wrench, rotate the differential bearing retainer to remove it.

4. Remove the four extension housing bolts, then remove the differentail assembly and extension housing.

5. Remove the six selector shaft housing bolts, then remove the selector shaft housing. On 5-speeds, remove the 5th speed shifter pin. Alsom remove the 5th speed detent ball and spring.

6. Remove the four stud nuts and the eight bolts from the rear end cover, then using a suitable tool in the notch pry off the rear end cover. On 5-speeds, remove the fill plug before prying off the cover.

7. On 5-speeds, remove the 5th speed synchronizer strut retainer snap-ring, strut retainer plate, 5th speed synchronizer, shift fork with rail, intermediate shaft 5th speed gear, input shaft 5th gear snap-ring and 5th gear. On 4-speeds, remove the large snap-ring from the intermediate shaft rear ball bearing.

8. Remove the bearing retainer plate by tapping it with a plastic hammer.

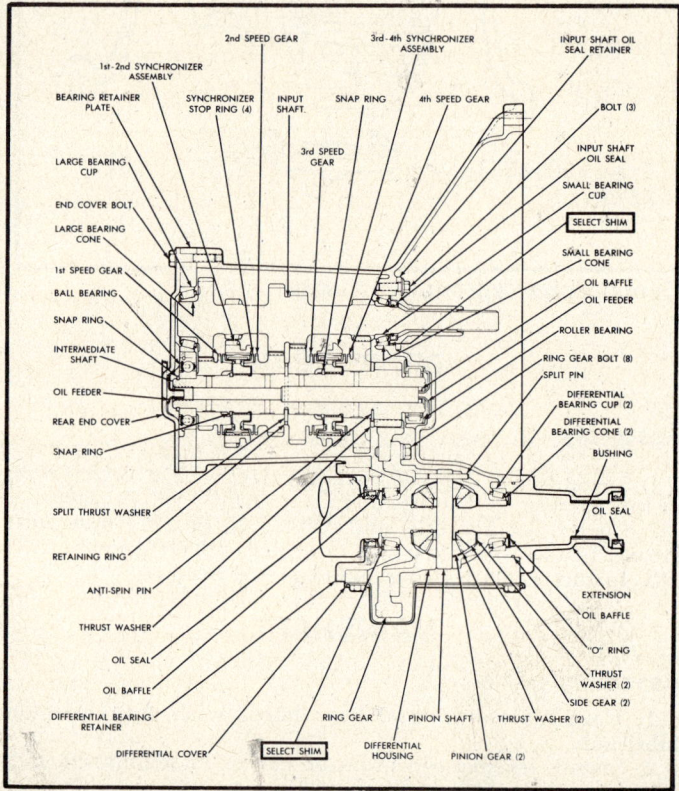

Chrysler A-465 5 speed manual transaxle — cutaway view

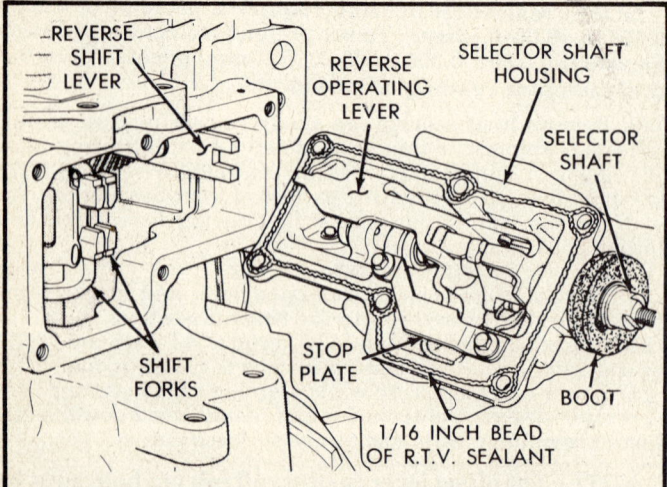

Selector shaft housing assembly removed

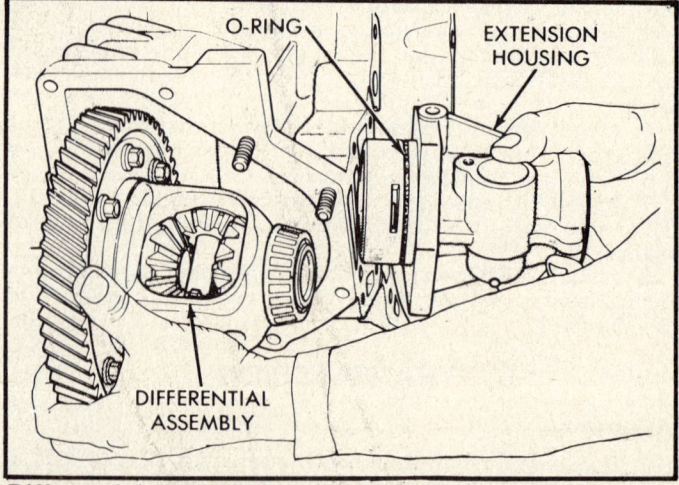

Differential assembly and extension housing removal or installation

32-20

MANUAL TRANSMISSIONS
CHRYSLER—A460, A465 and A525 FOUR AND FIVE SPEED
SECTION 32

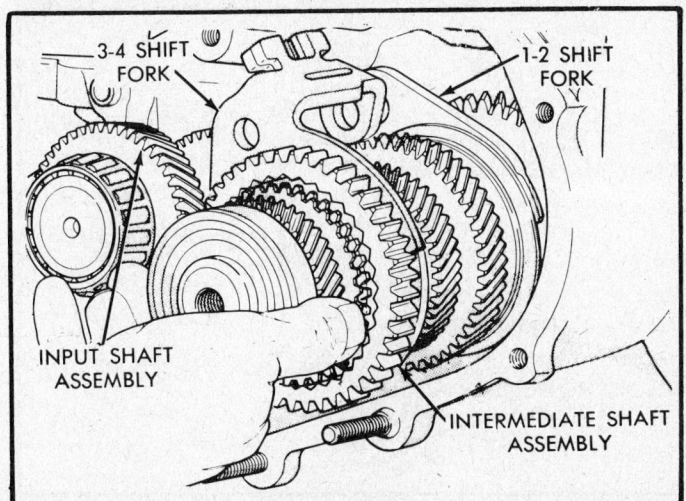

Gearset removal or installation

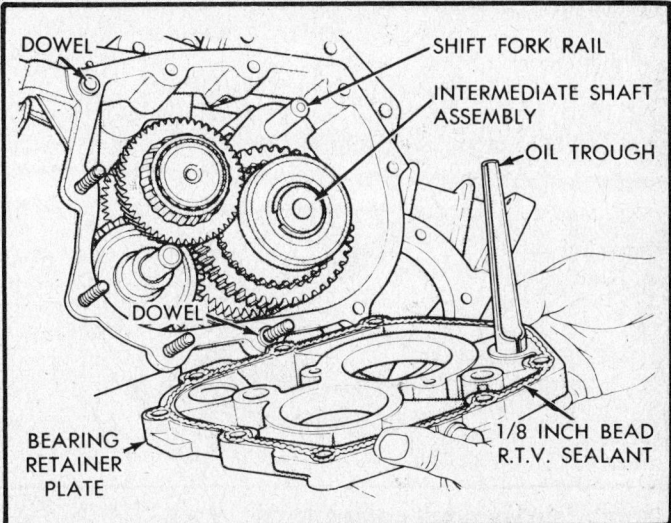

Bearing retainer plate removal or installation

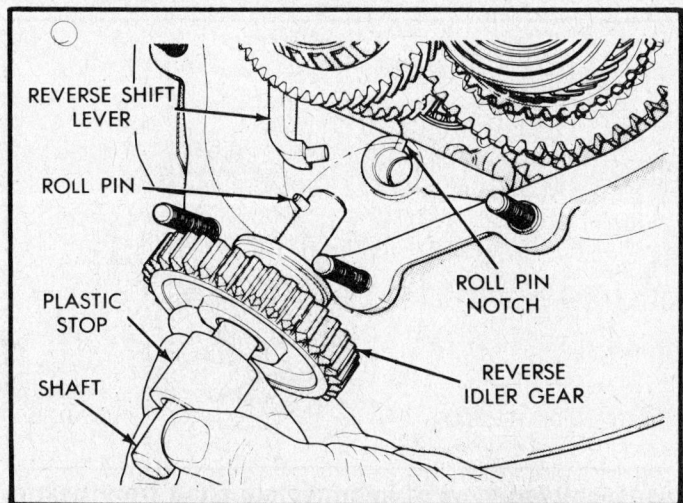

Reverse idler gear, shaft and plastic stop

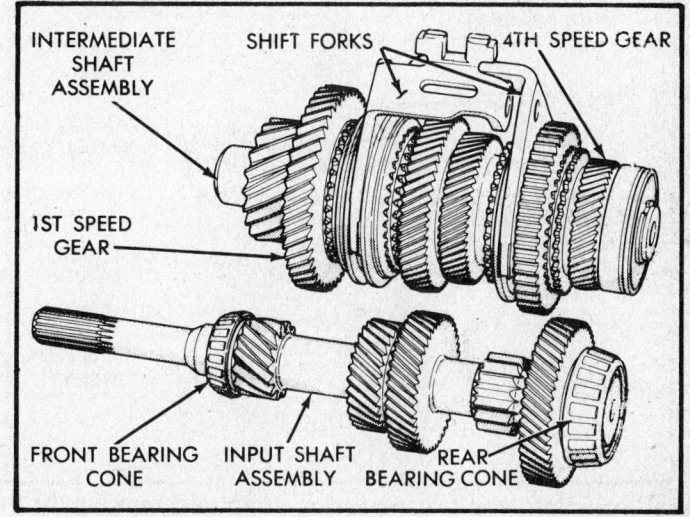

Gearset removed

9. Remove the 3rd/4th shift fork rail.
10. Remove the reverse idler gear shaft and gear.
11. Remove the input shaft gear assembly and the intermediate shaft gear assembly.
12. To remove the clutch release bearing remove the E-clips from the clutch release shaft, then disassemble the clutch shaft components.
13. To remove the input shaft oil seal remove the three bolts from the input shaft seal retainer. Remove the seal and retainer assembly and the select shim.
14. To remove the input shaft front bearing cup from the transaxle case use special tools C-4171, C-4656 or equivalent and an arbor press to remove the cup from the case.
15. To remove the intermediate shaft front bearing, remove the two bolts from the bearing retaining strap, then using special tool C-4660 or equivalent, remove the bearing.

Intermediate Shaft Disassembly

NOTE: The 1st/2nd and 3rd/4th shift forks and the synchronizer stop rings are interchangeable. However, if parts are to be reused reassemble in original position.

1. Remove the intermediate shaft rear bearing snap ring using snap ring pliers.

2. Using special tool C-4693 (puller) or equivalent, remove the intermediate shaft rear bearing.
3. Using snap ring pliers, remove the 3rd/4th synchronizer hub snap ring.
4. Using special tool L-4534 (puller) or equivalent, remove the 3rd/4th synchronizer hub and the 3rd speed gear.
5. Remove the retaining ring, split thrust washer, 2nd speed gear and the synchronizer stop ring.
6. Using snap ring pliers, remove the 1st/2nd synchronizer hub snap ring.
7. Remove the 1st speed gear, stop ring and 1st/2nd synchronizer assembly.
8. Remove the 1st speed gear thrust washer and anti-spin pin.

Intermediate Shaft Assembly

Assembly of the intermediate shaft is the reverse of disassembly; however, please note the following: When assembling the intermediate shaft, make sure all speed gears turn freely and have a minimum of 0.003 in. end play. When installing the 1st speed gear thrust washer make sure the chemfered edge is toward the pinion gear. When installing the 1st/2nd synchroniz-

SECTION 32 MANUAL TRANSMISSIONS
CHRYSLER — A460, A465 and A525 FOUR AND FIVE SPEED

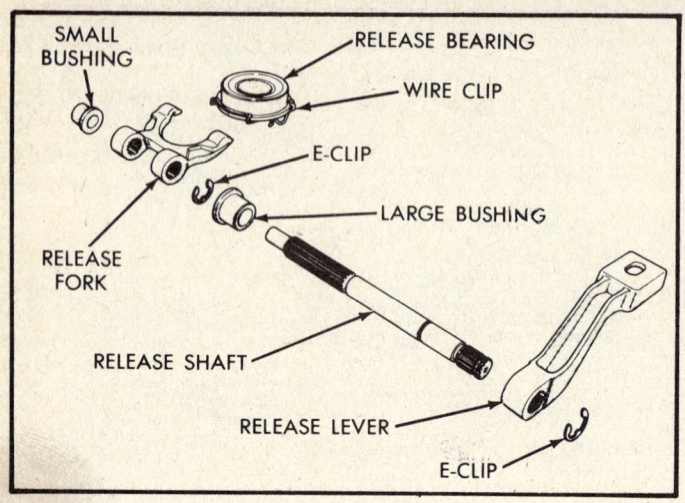

Clutch release shaft components

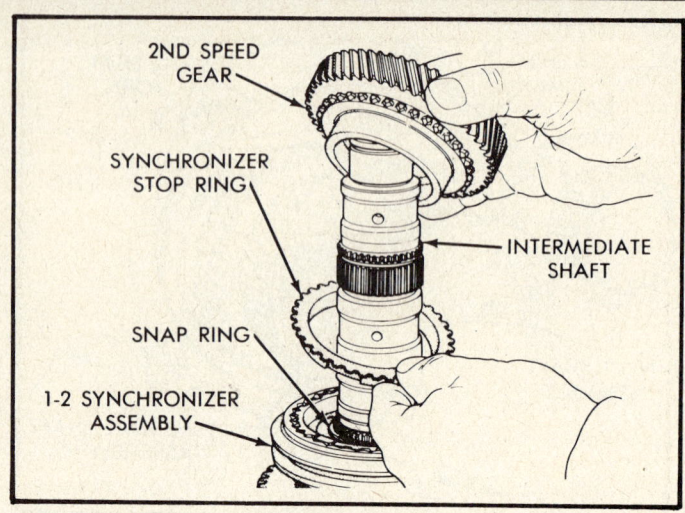

2nd speed gear and stop ring removal or installation

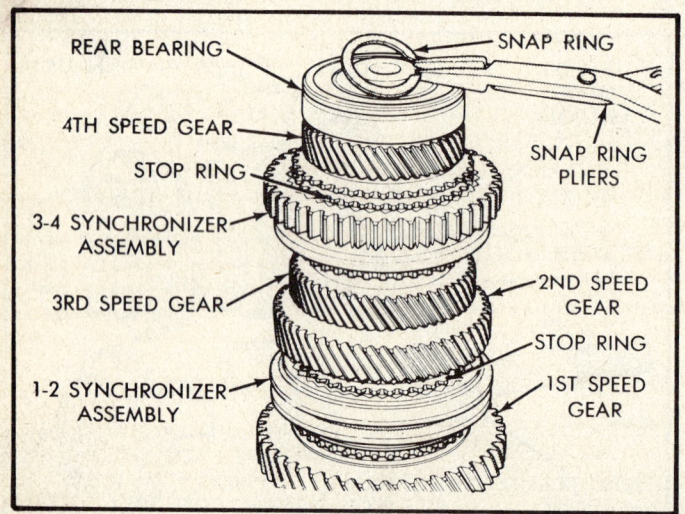

Intermediate shaft rear bearing snap ring removal or installation

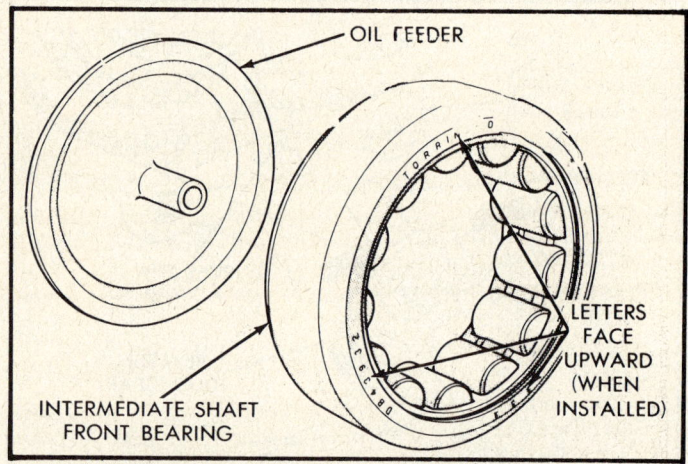

Disassembled view of intermediate shaft front bearing and oil feeder

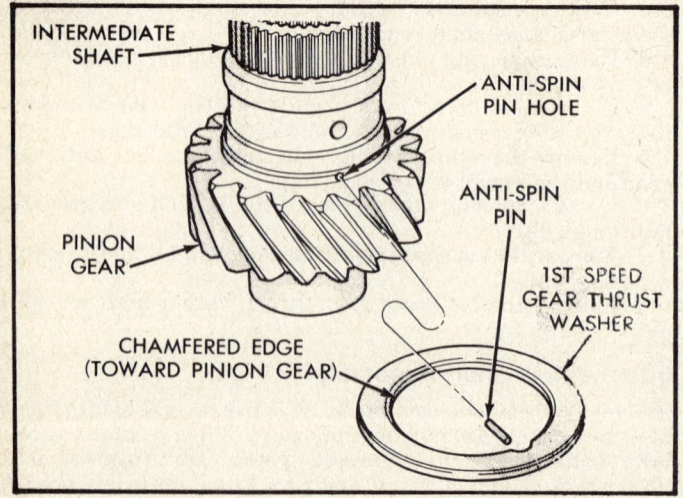

1st speed gear thrust washer removal or installation

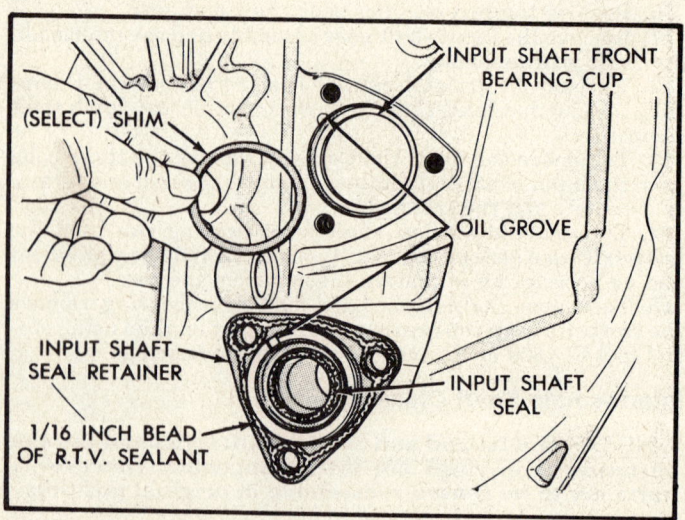

New input shaft oil seal installation

32-22

MANUAL TRANSMISSIONS
CHRYSLER—A460, A465 and A525 FOUR AND FIVE SPEED

er make sure the relief faces the 2nd speed gear. Use an arbor press to install the intermediate shaft rear bearing and the 3rd/4th synchronizer hub and 3rd speed gear.

Transaxle Assembly

Assembly of the transaxle is the reverse of disassembly; however, please note the following: When installing the intermediate shaft fron bearing special tools C–4657, C–4171 and an arbor press will be needed. The input shaft front bearing cup is installed with the same tools used for removal. Determining shim thickness for correct bearing endplay need only be done if any of the following parts are replaced transaxle case, input shaft seal retainer, bearing retainer plate, rear end cover, input shaft or input shaft bearings. To determine proper shim thickness refer to the Input Shaft Bearing Endplay Adjustment at the end of this section. To install the input shaft oil seal use special tool C–4674 or equivalent and a plastic hammer. Use a $1/16$ in. bead of R.T.V. sealant around the edge of the input shaft seal retainer and make sure the drain hole of the retainer is facing downward. The differential bearing retainer is installed with the same special tool used for removal. The rear end cover, selector shaft housing and the differential cover are all sealed with R.T.V. sealant.

INPUT SHAFT

Shim thickness calculation need only be done if any of the following parts are replaced:
1. Transaxle case
2. Input shaft seal retainer
3. Bearing retainer plate
4. Rear end cover
5. Input shaft
6. Input shaft bearings

Refer to Bearing Adjustment Procedure to determine the proper shim thickness for correct bearing preload and proper bearing turning torque.

DIFFERENTIAL

Shim thickness calculation need only be done if any of the following parts are replaced:
1. Transaxle case
2. Differential bearing retainer
3. Extension housing
4. Differential case
5. Differential bearings

Refer to Bearing Adjustment Procedure to determine the proper shim thickness for correct bearing preload and proper bearing turning torque.

Bearing Adjustment Procedure

GENERAL RULES FOR SERVICING BEARINGS

1. Take extreme care when removing and installing bearing cups and cones. Use only an arbor press for installation, as a hammer may not properly align the bearing cup or cone. Burrs or nicks on the bearing seat will give a false end play reading while gauging for proper shims. Improperly seated bearing cups and cones are subject to low mileage failure.

2. Bearing cups and cones should be replaced if they show signs of pitting or heat distress. If distress is seen on either the cup or bearing rollers, both cup and cone must be replaced.

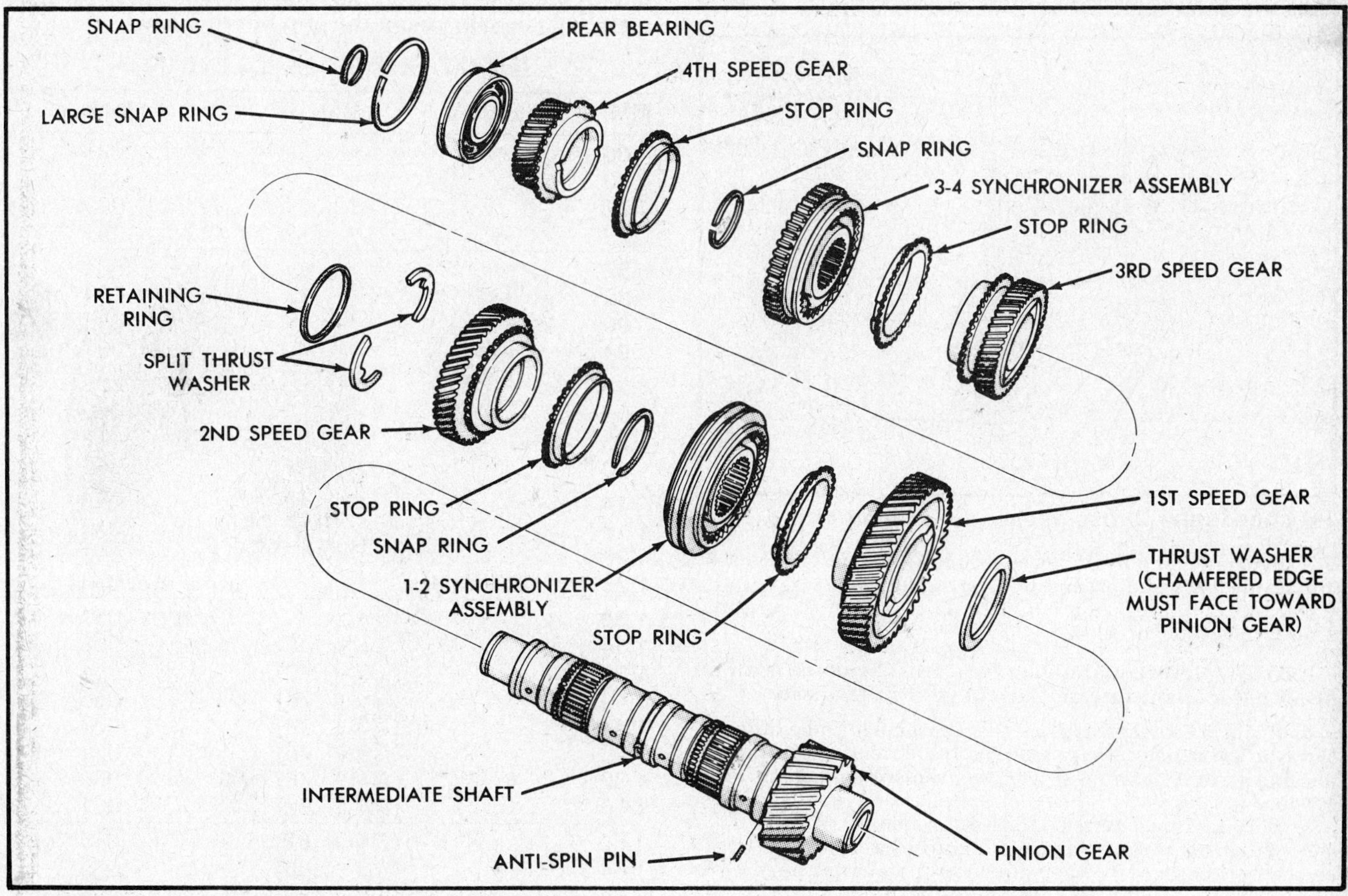

Disassembled view of intermediate shaft assembly

SECTION 32

MANUAL TRANSMISSIONS
CHRYSLER—A460, A465 and A525 FOUR AND FIVE SPEED

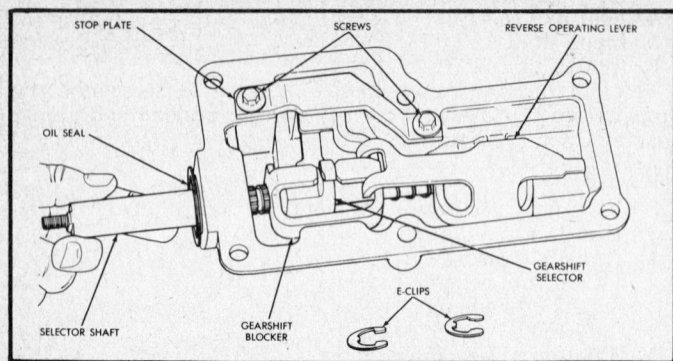

Selector shaft removal or installation

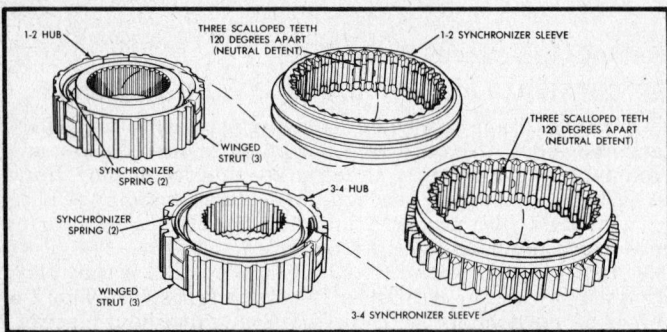

Disassembled view of synchronizer sleeves

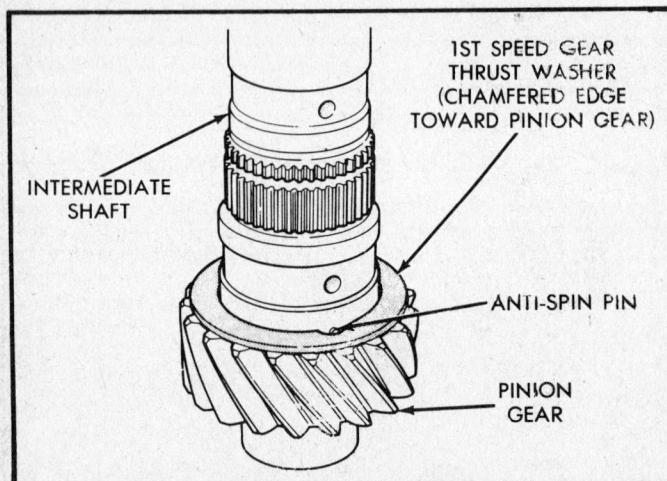

1st speed gear thrust washer installation

3. Bearing end play and drag torque specifications must be maintained to avoid premature bearing failures.

Used (original) bearing may lose up to 50% of the original drag torque after break-in.

NOTE: All bearing adjustments must be made with no other component interference to gear inter-mesh.

4. Replace bearings as a pair. For example, if one differential bearing is defective, replace both differential bearings. If one input shaft bearing is defective, replace both input shaft bearings.

5. Bearing cones must be reused if removed.

6. Turning torque readings should be obtained while smoothly rotating in either direction (breakaway reading is not indicative of the true turning torque).

7. Replace the oil baffle, if damaged.

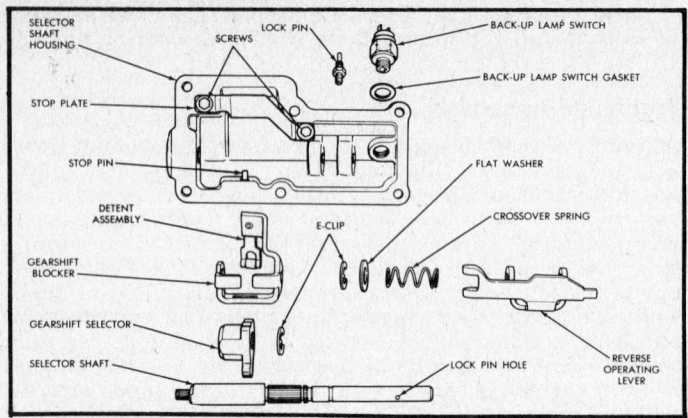

Disassembled view of selector shaft housing

Input Shaft Bearing Preload Adjustment

1. Using tool L–4656 with handle C–4171, press the input shaft front bearing cup slightly forward in the case. Then, using tool L–4655 with handle C–4171, press the bearing cup back into the case, from the front to properly position the bearing cup before checking the input shaft end play (see input shaft front bearing cup replacement procedure in Subassembly Rebuilding Procedures section).

NOTE: This step is not necessary if tool L–4655 was previously used to install the input shaft front bearing cup in the case and no input shaft (select) shim has been installed since pressing the cup into the case.

INPUT SHAFT SHIM CHART

MM	MM	Inch
.66		.026
.70		.028
.74		.029
.78		.031
.82		.032
.86		.034
.90		.035
.94		.037
.98		.039
1.02		.040
1.06		.042
1.10		.043
1.14		.045
1.18		.046
1.22		.048
1.26		.050
1.30		.051
1.34		.053
1.36	(.66 + .70)	.054
1.40	(.66 + .74)	.055
1.44	(.70 + .74)	.057
1.48	(.70 + .78)	.059
1.52	(.74 + .78)	.060
1.56	(.74 + .82)	.061
1.60	(.78 + .82)	.063
1.64	(.78 + .86)	.065
1.68	(.82 + .86)	.066

MANUAL TRANSMISSIONS
CHRYSLER—A460, A465 and A525 FOUR AND FIVE SPEED

2. Select a gauging shim which will give 0.001–0.010 in. (0.025–0.254mm) end play.

NOTE: Measure the original shim from the input shaft seal retainer and select a shim 0.254mm (0.010 in.) thinner than the original for the gauging shim.

3. Install the gauging shim on the bearing cup and install the input shaft seal retainer.

---- **CAUTION** ----
The input shaft seal retainer is used to draw the input shaft front bearing cup the proper distance into the case bore during this step.

Alternately tighten the input shaft seal retainer bolts until the input shaft seal retainer is bottomed against the case. Tighten the bolts to 21 ft. lbs. (28 Nm).

4. Oil the input shaft bearings with A.T.F. and install the input shaft in the case. Install the bearing retainer plate with the input shaft rear bearing cup pressed in and the end cover installed. Tighten all bolts and nuts to 21 ft. lbs. (28 Nm).

5. Position the dial indicator to check the input shaft end play. Apply moderate load, by hand, to the input shaft splines. Push toward the rear while rotating the input shaft back and forth a number of times and to settle out the bearings. Zero the dial indicator. Pull the input shaft toward the front while rotating the input shaft back and forth a number of times to settle out the bearings. Record the end play.

6. The shim required for proper bearing preload is the total of the gauging shim thickness, plus end play, plus (constant) preload of 0.003 in. (0.067mm). Combine shims, if necessary, to obtain a shim within 0.0016 in. (0.04mm) of the required shim (see Input Shaft Shim Chart for proper shim(s).

7. Remove the input shaft seal retainer and gauging shim. Install the shim(s) selected in Step 6 and reinstall the input shaft seal retainer with a 1/16 in. bead of R.T.V. sealant.

---- **CAUTION** ----
Keep R.T.V. sealant out of the oil slot.

Observe the Caution in Step 3. Tighten the input shaft seal retainer bolts to 21 ft. lbs. (28 Nm).

8. Using special tool L-4508 and an inch lb. torque wrench, check the input shaft turning torque. The turning torque should be 1–5 inch lbs. for new bearings or a minimum of 1 inch lb. for used bearings. If the turning torque is too high, install a 0.0016 in. (0.04mm) thinner shim. If the turning torque is too low, install a 0.0016 in. (0.04mm) thicker shim.

---- **CAUTION** ----
Step 1 must be repeated every time a thinner shim in installed. This will assure that the input shaft front bearing cup is pressed the proper distance into the case.

9. Recheck the input shaft turning torque. Repeat Step 8 until the proper bearing turning torque is obtained. Observe CAUTION in Step 8.

Differential Bearing Preload Adjustment

1. Remove the bearing cup and existing shim from the differential bearing retainer. (See Differential Bearing Retainer in Subassembly Rebuilding Procedures section).

2. Select a gauging shim which will give 0.001–0.010 in. (0.025–0.254mm) end play.

NOTE: Measure the original shim from the differentail bearing retainer and select a shim 0.381mm (0.015 in.) thinner than the original for the gauging shim.

Install the gauging shim in the differential bearing retainer and press in the bearing cup. Installation of the oil baffle is not necessary when checking differential assembly end play.

3. Lubricate the differential bearings with ATF and install the differential assembly in the transaxle case. Install the extension housing and differential bearing retainer. Tighten the bolts to 21 ft. lbs. (28 Nm).

4. Position the transaxle with the bell housing facing down on the workbench with C-clamps. Position the dial indicator.

5. Apply a medium load to the ring gear, by hand, in the downward direction while rolling the differential assembly back and forth a number of times to settle the bearings. Zero the dial indicator. To obtain end play readings, apply a medium load upward by hand while rolling the differential assembly back and forth a number of times to settle out the bearings. Record the end play.

6. The shim required for proper bearing preload is the total of the gauging shim thickness, plus end play, plus (constant) preload of 0.010 in. (0.254mm). Combine shims if necessary, to obtain a shim within 0.002 in. (0.05mm) of the shim(s).

7. Remove the differential bearing retainer. Remove the bearing cup and gauging shim. Properly install the oil baffle. Be sure the oil baffle is not damaged. Install the shim(s) selected in Step 6 and press the bearing cup into the differential bearing retainer.

8. Using a 1/16 in. bead of R.T.V. sealant for gaskets, install the differential bearing retainer and extension housing. Tighten the bolts to 21 ft. lbs. (28 Nm).

9. Using special tool L-4436 and an inch lb. torque wrench, check the turning torque of the differential assembly. The turning torque should be 9–14 inch lbs. for new bearings or a minimum of 6 inch lbs. for used bearings. If the turning torque is too low, install a 0.002 in (0.05mm) thicker shim.

10. Recheck the turning torque. Repeat Step 9 until the proper turning torque is obtained.

FORD MTX—4-SPEED (MTX-II) AND 5-SPEED (MTX-III) TRANSAXLE

GEAR SET

Removal

1. Shift the transaxle into Neutral using a drift in the input shaft hole. Pull or push the shaft into the center detent position.

2. Remove the two shipping plugs (T81P-1177-B or equivalent) from the transaxle and drain the transmission fluid.

NOTE: Place the transaxle on a bench with the clutch housing facing down to facilitate draining and service.

3. Remove the reverse idler shaft retaining bolt.

4. Remove the detent plunger retaining screw. Then using a magnet, remove the detent spring and the detent plunger.

NOTE: Label these parts, as they appear similar to the input shift shaft plunger and spring contained in the clutch case.

5. Remove the shift fork interlock sleeve retaining pin (19mm socket).

6. Remove the clutch housing-to-transmission case attaching bolts.

MANUAL TRANSMISSIONS
FORD—MTX11 AND MTX111 FOUR AND FIVE SPEED

7. Tap the transmission case with a plastic tipped hammer to break the seal between the case halves. Separate the halves.

NOTE: **Do not insert pry bars or screwdrivers between case halves. Be careful not to drop out the tapered roller bearing cups or shims from the transmission case housing.**

8. Remove the case magnet. On 5 speed, remove the C-clip from the 5th gear shift relay lever and remove the 5th gear shift relay cover.

9. Remove the reverse idler shaft and reverse idler gear by lifting the shaft straight upward.

10. Remove the set screw from the shift lever assembly with a 4mm Allen wrench on the 4 speed. Using a punch on the 5 speed, drive the roll pin from the shift lever shaft.

11. With a pair of pliers, rotate the shift lever shaft 90° to disengage the reverse inhibitor plunger from the detent notch in the shift lever shaft. Slide the shaft toward the differential (away from the expansion plug in the clutch housing) and remove the shift lever assembly. On the 5 speed, hold a rag over the hole to prevent the ball and spring from shooting out.

NOTE: **With a 4.05:1 final drive ratio, the differential assembly will have to be tilted slightly to allow the shift lever shaft to slide far enough for removal of the shift lever assembly.**

On the 4 Speed

a. Lift the differential and final drive gear assembly from the clutch housing case.

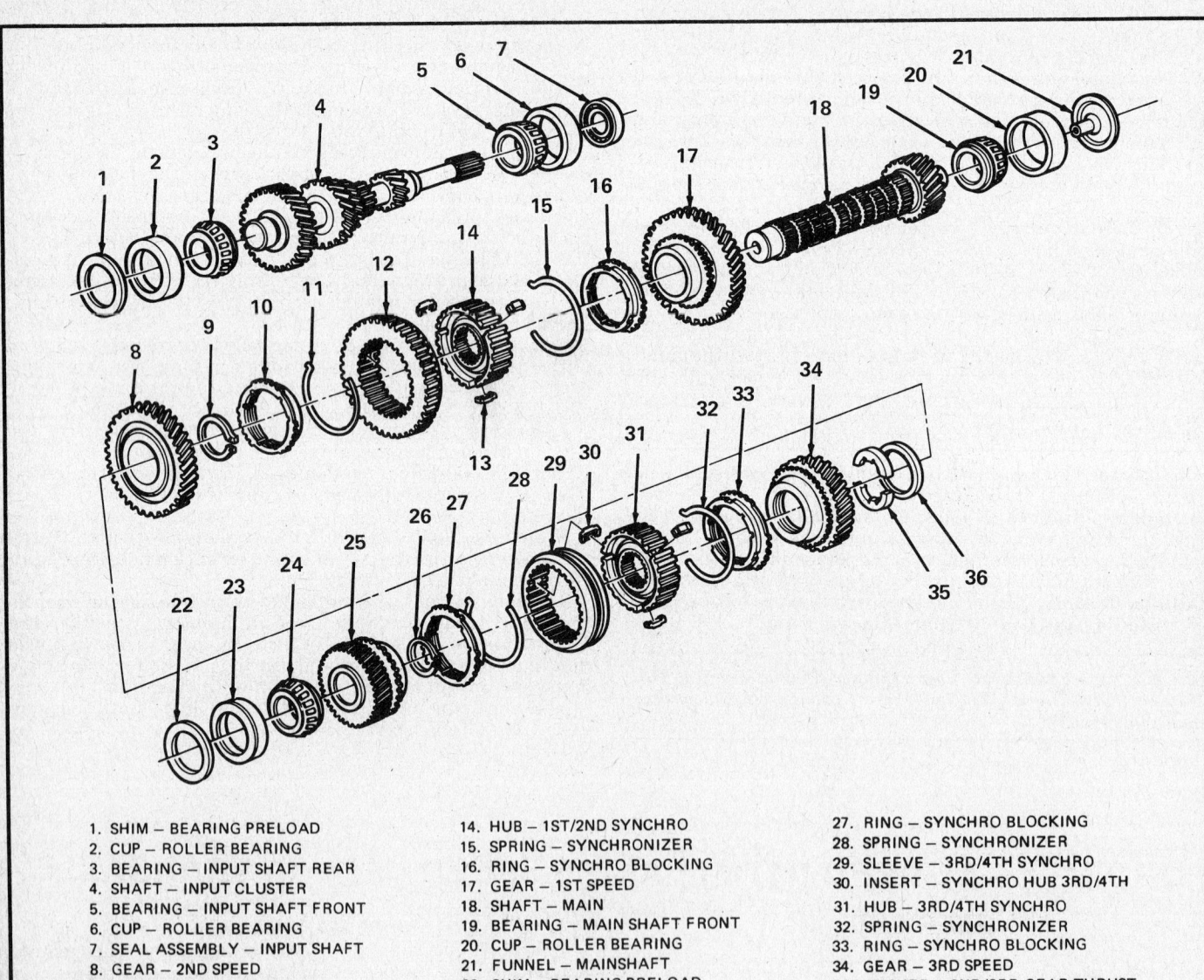

1. SHIM – BEARING PRELOAD
2. CUP – ROLLER BEARING
3. BEARING – INPUT SHAFT REAR
4. SHAFT – INPUT CLUSTER
5. BEARING – INPUT SHAFT FRONT
6. CUP – ROLLER BEARING
7. SEAL ASSEMBLY – INPUT SHAFT
8. GEAR – 2ND SPEED
9. RING – 1ST/2ND SYNCHRO RETAINING
10. RING – SYNCHRO BLOCKING
11. SPRING – SYNCHRONIZER
12. GEAR – REVERSE SLIDING
13. INSERT – SYNCHRO HUB 1ST/2ND
14. HUB – 1ST/2ND SYNCHRO
15. SPRING – SYNCHRONIZER
16. RING – SYNCHRO BLOCKING
17. GEAR – 1ST SPEED
18. SHAFT – MAIN
19. BEARING – MAIN SHAFT FRONT
20. CUP – ROLLER BEARING
21. FUNNEL – MAINSHAFT
22. SHIM – BEARING PRELOAD
23. CUP – ROLLER BEARING
24. BEARING – MAINSHAFT REAR
25. GEAR – 4TH SPEED
26. RING – 3RD/4TH SYNCHRO RETAINING
27. RING – SYNCHRO BLOCKING
28. SPRING – SYNCHRONIZER
29. SLEEVE – 3RD/4TH SYNCHRO
30. INSERT – SYNCHRO HUB 3RD/4TH
31. HUB – 3RD/4TH SYNCHRO
32. SPRING – SYNCHRONIZER
33. RING – SYNCHRO BLOCKING
34. GEAR – 3RD SPEED
35. WASHER – 2ND/3RD GEAR THRUST
36. RING – 2ND/3RD THRUST WASHER RETAINING

MTX 4 speed transaxle – gear train

MANUAL TRANSMISSIONS

FORD—MTX11 AND MTX111 FOUR AND FIVE SPEED

b. Remove the main shaft assembly, input cluster shaft assembly, and the main shift control shaft assembly as one unit.

On the 5 Speed

a. Remove the main shaft assembly, input cluster shaft assembly and the main shift control shaft assembly as one unit.

NOTE: Be careful not to drop bearings or gears (slip fit).

b. Remove the 5th gear shaft assembly and 5th gear fork assembly from their bores in the case.

NOTE: Be careful not to drop bearings or gears (slip fit).

c. Lift the differential and final drive gear assembly from the clutch housing case.

MAIN SHAFT—4 AND 5 SPEED

Disassembly

1. Remove the tapered roller bearing from the pinion end of the main shaft using puller (D79L-4621-A or equivalent) and an arbor press.

NOTE: This bearing does have to be removed to disassemble the main shaft, only to replace if damaged.

2. Remove the bearing on the 4th gear end of the shaft. Label the bearing for proper installation.
3. Remove the 4th speed gear and synchronizer blocker ring.

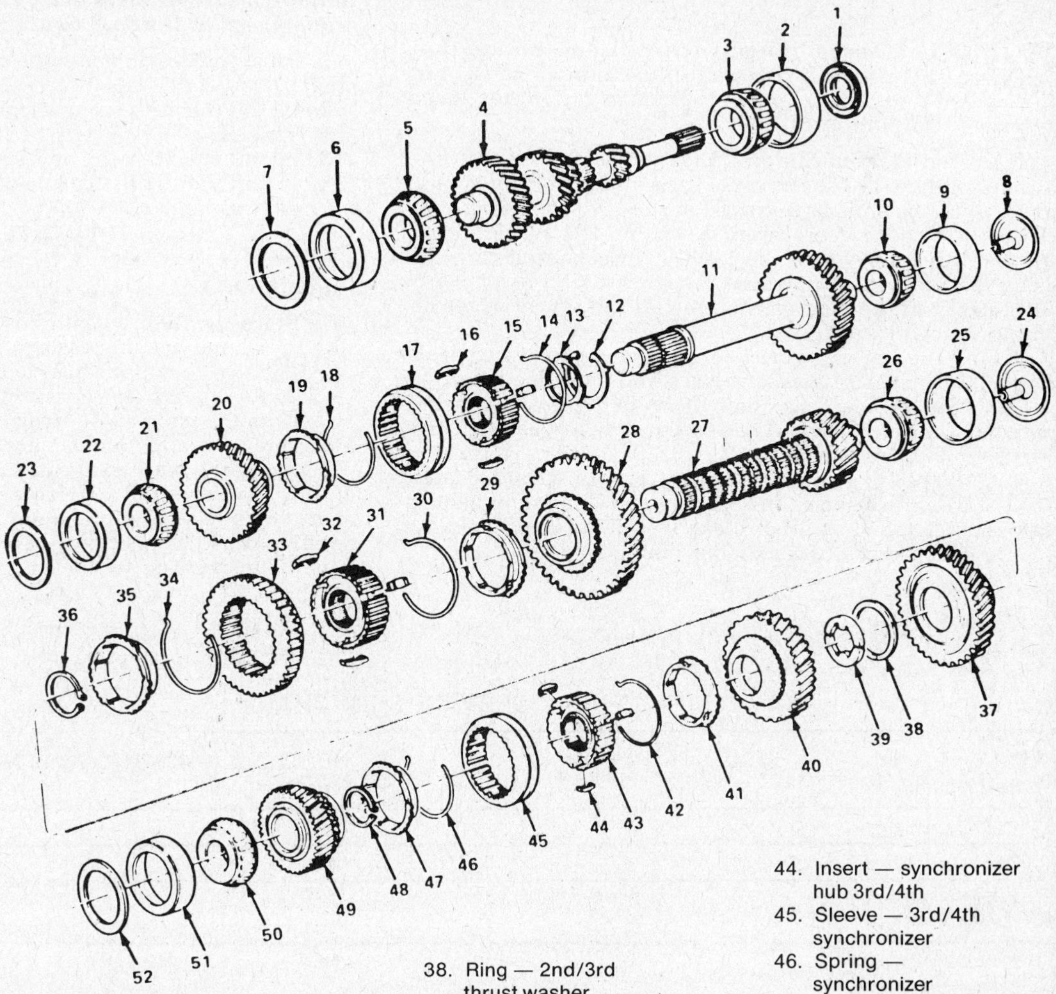

1. Seal assembly — input shaft
2. Cup — roller bearing
3. Bearing — input shaft front
4. Shaft — input cluster
5. Bearing — input shaft — rear
6. Cup — roller bearing
7. Shim — bearing preload
8. Funnel — 5th gear
9. Cup — roller bearing
10. Bearing — 5th gear shaft — front
11. Shaft — 5th gear drive
12. Retainer — synchronizer insert
13. Spacer — synchronizer retaining
14. Spring — synchronizer
15. Hub — 5th synchronizer
16. Insert — synchronizer hub 5th
17. Sleeve — 5th synchronizer
18. Spring — synchronizer
19. Ring — synchronizer blocking
20. Gear — 5th speed
21. Bearing — 5th gear shaft — rear
22. Cup — roller bearing
23. Shim — bearing preload
24. Funnel — mainshaft
25. Cup-roller bearing
26. Bearing — mainshaft front
27. Shaft — main
28. Gear — 1st speed
29. Ring — synchronizer blocking
30. Spring — synchronizer
31. Hub — 1st/2nd synchronizer
32. Insert — synchronizer hub 1st/2nd
33. Gear — reverse sliding
34. Spring — synchronizer
35. Ring — synchronizer blocking
36. Ring — 1st/2nd synchronizer retaining
37. Gear — 2nd speed
38. Ring — 2nd/3rd thrust washer retaining
39. Washer — 2nd/3rd gear thrust
40. Gear — 3rd speed
41. Ring — synchronizer blocking
42. Spring — synchronizer
43. Hub — 3rd/4th synchronizer
44. Insert — synchronizer hub 3rd/4th
45. Sleeve — 3rd/4th synchronizer
46. Spring — synchronizer
47. Ring — synchronizer blocking
48. Ring — 3rd/4th synchronizer
49. Gear — 4th speed
50. Bearing — mainshaft rear
51. Cup — roller bearing
52. Shim — bearing preload

MTX 5 speed transaxle-disassembled

MANUAL TRANSMISSIONS
FORD—MTX11 AND MTX111 FOUR AND FIVE SPEED

4. Remove the 3rd/4th synchronizer retaining ring. Slide the 3rd/4th gear synchronizer assembly, blocker ring, and 3rd speed gear from the shaft.
5. Remove the 2nd/4th thrust washer retaining ring and the two-piece 2nd/3rd gear thrust washer.
6. Remove the 2nd speed gear and blocker ring.
7. Remove the 1st/2nd synchronizer retaining ring.
Slide the 1st/2nd synchronizer assembly, blocking ring and 1st speed gear off the shaft.

Assembly

In assembling synchronizers some points must be noted. The index marks must be aligned. Place the tab on the synchronizer spring into the groove of one of the inserts and snap the spring into place. Place the tab of the other spring into the same insert (on the other side of the synchronizer assembly), and rotate the spring in the opposite direction and snap into place.

NOTE: When assembling synchronizers, notice that the sleeve and the hub have an extremely close fit and must be held square to prevent jamming. (Do not force the sleeve onto the hub).

1. Slide the blocker ring and the 1st speed gear onto the main shaft. Slide the 1st/2nd synchronizer assembly into place, making sure the shift fork groove on the reverse sliding gear faces the 1st speed gear. When installing the synchronizer, align the three grooves in the 1st gear blocker ring with the synchronizer inserts. This allows the synchronizer assembly to seat properly in the blocker ring. Install the synchronizer retaining ring.
2. Install the 2nd speed blocker ring and the 2nd speed gear.
3. Install the thrust washer halves and retaining ring.
4. Slide the 3rd speed gear onto the shaft followed by the 3rd gear synchronizer blocker ring and the 3rd/4th gear synchronizer assembly. Install the synchronizer retaining ring.
5. Install the 4th gear blocking ring and the 4th speed gear.
6. Install the bearing on the 4th gear end of the shaft using a 1 1/16 in. socket and an arbor press. Install the bearing on the pinion end of the shaft in a similar manner.

NOTE: Make sure bearings are seated against shoulder of main shaft.

5TH GEAR SHAFT
Disassembly

1. Remove the slip fit bearing from the 5th gear end of the shaft and label it or correct installation.
2. Remove the 5th gear and blocking ring.
3. Remove the 5th gear synchronizer assembly.
4. Remove the press fit bearing from the pinion end of the shaft, using bearing remover/installer Tool D79L–4621–A or equivalent bearing removal adapter.

Assembly

NOTE: Prior to assembly, thoroughly clean all parts and inspect their condition. Lightly oil the gear bore with transmisssion fluid or equivalent.

1. Press the bearing onto the pinion gear end of the 5th gear shaft.
2. Install the 5th synchronizer assembly with the plastic insert retainer.
3. Install the 5th gear and blocking ring.
4. Install the slip fit bearing on the 5th gear end of the shaft.

GEAR SET
Installation

1. Place the differential and the final drive gear assembly into the clutch housing case.
2. Position the main shift control shaft assembly so that the shift forks engage their respective slots in the synchronizer sleeves on the main shaft assembly. On 5 speed, install the 5th gear shaft assembly and the fork shaft assembly.
3. Bring the main shaft assembly into mesh with the input cluster shaft assembly. Holding the three shafts (input cluster shaft, main shaft, and the main shift control shaft) in their respective working positions, lower them into their bores in the clutch housing case as one unit.

SERVICE SHIM CHART

Parts Replaced	SHIMS REPLACED WITH SERVICE SHIM	
	Input Cluster Shaft	Mainshaft
1 input cluster bearing	Yes	No
2 input cluster bearings	Yes	No
1 input cluster bearing 1 mainshaft bearing	Yes	Yes
2 mainshaft bearings 2 input cluster bearings	Yes	Yes
1 mainshaft bearing	No	Yes
2 mainshaft bearings	No	Yes
Clutch housing	Yes	Yes
Transmission housing	Yes	Yes

NOTE: The shims must be installed only under the bearing cups at the trans. case end of both the input and outputshafts.
NOTE: The use of nominal thickness service shim eliminates the need for gaging bearing clearances prior to reassembly. While this method produces wider variations of bearing settings than are present in factory assembled units, the extreem possible settings have been tested and found to be acceptable.
When repairs require the use of the service shim (see Service Shim Chart), discard the original shim. Do not use more than one shim per shaft. Ifparts are replaced other than the parts listed in the Service Shim Chart, then the original shims should be re-used.

MANUAL TRANSMISSIONS
FORD—MTX11 AND MTX111 FOUR AND FIVE SPEED

SECTION 32

NOTE: Be careful not to damage the input shaft oil seal, main or 5th gear shaft oil funnel.

4. Position the shift lever assembly in its working position (with one shift lever pin located in the socket of the input shift shaft selector plate arm assembly and the other in the socket of the main shift control shaft block). On 5 speeds install the spring and ball in the 5th and reverse inhibitor shift lever hole. Slide the shift lever shaft through the shift lever and into its bore in the clutch housing. Rotate the shift lever shaft so the reverse inhibitor notch faces the reverse inhibitor plunger.

5. Position the 4 speed shift lever shaft so the setscrew hole on the shaft aligns with the hole in the shift lever. Install the setscrew and tighten to specifications. On 5 speeds align the shift shaft bore with the case bore and tap the roll pin on, slightly below the case mating surface.

NOTE: Before tightening, position the shift lever on the shaft to make sure the setscrew is centered in the shaft center drilled hole.

6. Verify that the selector pin is in the neutral gate of the control selector, plate and the finger of the fork selector arm is partially engaged with the 1st/2nd fork and partially with the 3rd/4th fork.

7. Place the reverse idler gear groove in engagement with the pin at the end of the reverse relay lever, and slide the shaft through the gear and into its bore. Align the retaining screw hole in the reverse idler shaft with the hole in the case. This will allow proper engagement with the pin at the retaining screw hole in the transmission case when the case is placed over this assembly.

the bearing cups in the transmission case.

If the bearing cups are removed from the case for any reason, it is very important to keep the bearing cup and its matching shim together. It is also very important to label the bearing cups as they are removed from the transmission case or clutch housing. Maintaining the proper bearing cup to shim relationship and proper bearing cup labeling will ensure the correct bearing preload when the transaxle is assembled.

A replacement bearing preload shim will be provided for service and should be installed in place of the original shim as outlined in the Service Shim Chart.

8. Install the magnet in its pocket in the clutch housing case. Install the 5 speed, 5th shift relay lever onto the reverse idler shaft, aligning it with the 5th gear fork interlock and install the retaining C-clip.

9. Apply a $\frac{1}{16}$ in. wide bead of sealer. Carefully lower the transmission case over the clutch housing case and move gently until the shift control shaft, mainshaft, and the input cluster shaft align with their respective bores in the transmission case. Gently slide the transmission case over the dowels and flush onto the clutch housing case, checking that the case does not bind on the magnet.

10. Install the transmission case-to-clutch housing bolts and tighten to specifications.

PRELOAD SHIMS

Preload on the input cluster shaft and mainshaft bearings is maintained by shims. These preload shims are located behind

FORD ET SERIES GERMAN DESIGN 4-SPEED TRANSMISSION

NOTE: This transmission is assembled with metric fasteners.

NOTE: Cars equipped with this transmission are identified by the year and ET stamped on the ID tag. The transmission ID tag is located under the left extension housing-to-case bolt.

Disassembly

1. Remove the clutch release bearing and detach the clutch housing.
2. Remove the cover and gasket from the case.
3. Remove the threaded plug, spring and shift rail detent plunger from the front of the case.
4. Drive the access plug from the rear of the case. Drive the interlock retaining pin from the case. Remove the interlock plate.
5. Remove the roll pin from the selector lever arm.
6. Tap the front end of the shift rail to displace the plug at the rear of the extension housing. Remove the shift rail from the rear of the extension housing.
7. Remove the selector arm and shift fork from the case.
8. Remove the extension housing attaching bolts. Loosen the extension housing. Rotate the housing to align the countershaft with the cutaway in the extension housing flange.
9. Drive the countershaft rearward until the shaft clears the front of the case. Install a short dummy shaft in the case and gear (to retain the needle bearings) until the countershaft gear can be lowered to the bottom of the case. Remove the countershaft.
10. Lift the extension housing and mainshaft from the case as an assembly.
11. Remove the input shaft bearing retainer attaching bolts. Remove the input shaft and bearing retainer from the case as an assembly.

12. Remove the reverse idler gear and shaft from the rear of the case. Use a slap hammer.
13. Remove the bearing retainers, bearings, dummy shaft and spacer from the countershaft gear.
14. Remove the pilot bearing and bearing retainer from the input shaft gear.
15. Do not remove the ball bearing from the input shaft unless replacement is necessary.
16. Pry the input shaft seal out of the bearing retainer.
17. Lift the fourth gear blocker ring from the front the output shaft.
18. Remove the snap ring from the forward end of the output shaft.
19. Support the third gear on press plates and place the output shaft and extension housing in a press. Press the output shaft out of the 3rd/4th speed synchronizer and third gear. Support the extension housing and output shaft from beneath. Remove the snap-ring and washer. Remove second gear and the blocker ring from the output shaft.

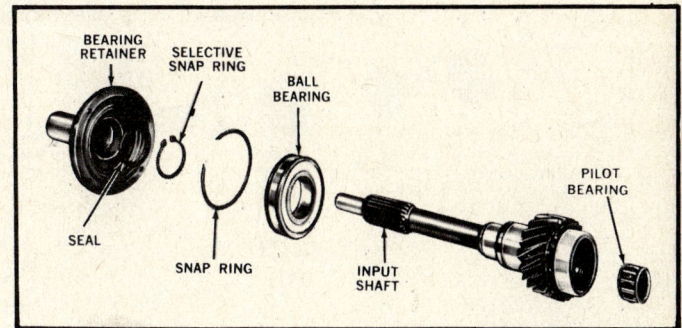

Ford (German) 4-speed: input shaft disassembled

SECTION 32: MANUAL TRANSMISSIONS
FORD—ET SERIES (GERMAN DESIGN) FOUR SPEED

20. Disassemble the synchronizer assembly by pulling the sleeve from the hub and removing the inserts and spring.
21. Remove the snap-ring which retains the output shaft bearing to the extension housing.
22. Use a plastic hammer and tap the output shaft assembly from the extension housing.
23. Position press plates behind first gear. Place the assembly in a press. The first and second speed synchronizer are serviced as an assembly. No attempt should be made to separate the hub from the shaft. The only serviceable parts are the springs and inserts. If the hub or sleeve is worn, the shaft and synchronizer must be replaced as an assembly.
24. Drive the shift rail bushing from the rear of the extenson housing, using a $9/16$ in. socket. Do not remove serviceable bushings.
25. Pry the shift rail seal from the rear of the case.
26. Remove the remaining shaft linkage from the case. Do not remove the seat belt sensing switch unless it is damaged.

Assembly

1. Install a new shift rail seal in the rear of the case.
2. If the shift rail bushing was removed, drive a new one into position with a $9/16$ in. socket.

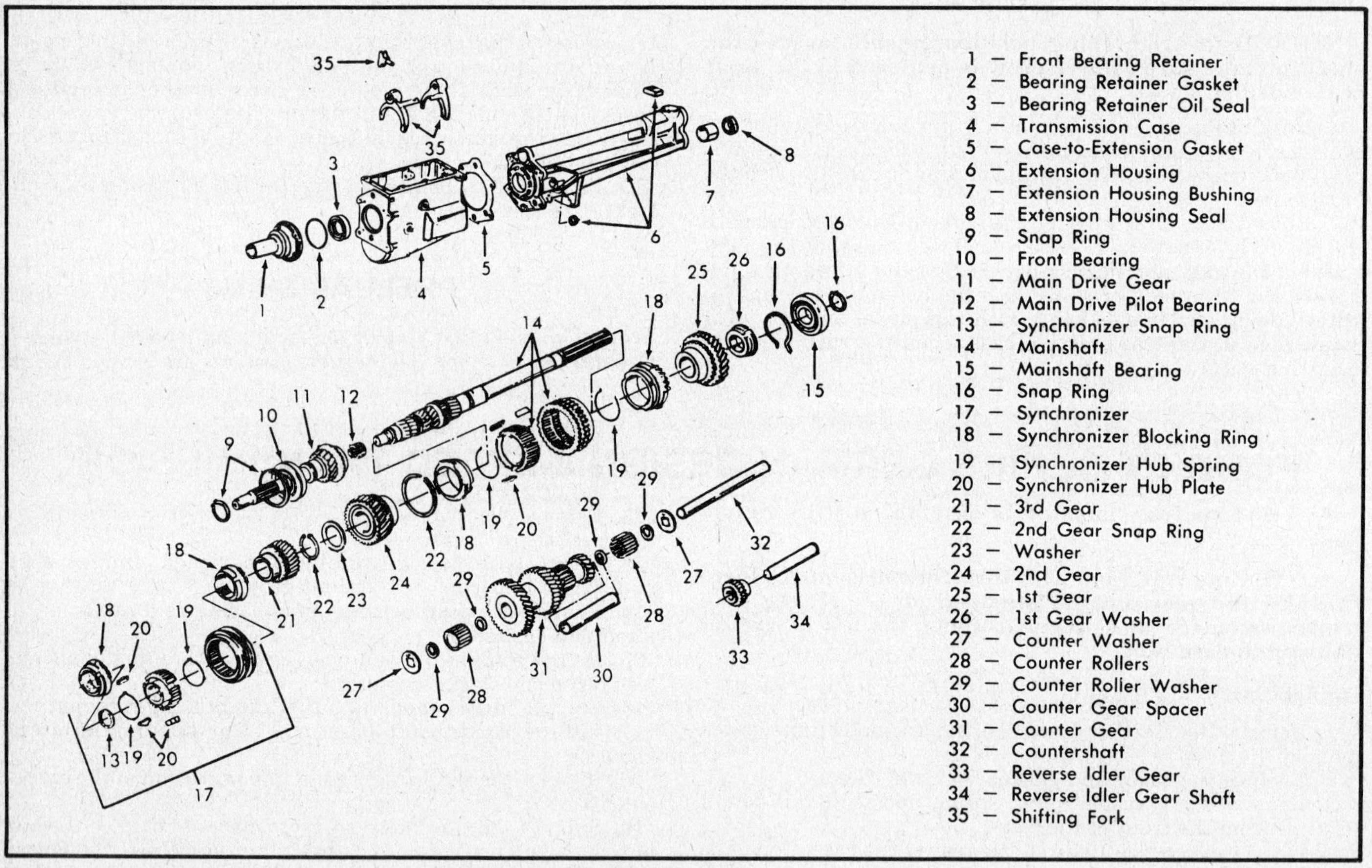

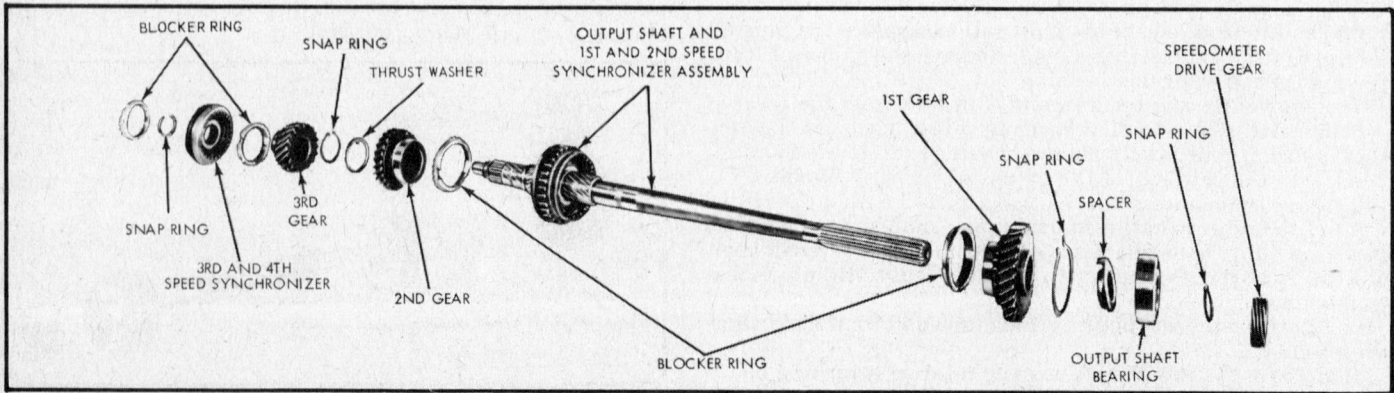

1 — Front Bearing Retainer
2 — Bearing Retainer Gasket
3 — Bearing Retainer Oil Seal
4 — Transmission Case
5 — Case-to-Extension Gasket
6 — Extension Housing
7 — Extension Housing Bushing
8 — Extension Housing Seal
9 — Snap Ring
10 — Front Bearing
11 — Main Drive Gear
12 — Main Drive Pilot Bearing
13 — Synchronizer Snap Ring
14 — Mainshaft
15 — Mainshaft Bearing
16 — Snap Ring
17 — Synchronizer
18 — Synchronizer Blocking Ring
19 — Synchronizer Hub Spring
20 — Synchronizer Hub Plate
21 — 3rd Gear
22 — 2nd Gear Snap Ring
23 — Washer
24 — 2nd Gear
25 — 1st Gear
26 — 1st Gear Washer
27 — Counter Washer
28 — Counter Rollers
29 — Counter Roller Washer
30 — Counter Gear Spacer
31 — Counter Gear
32 — Countershaft
33 — Reverse Idler Gear
34 — Reverse Idler Gear Shaft
35 — Shifting Fork

Remove the washer (1) and ball (2) before removing 5th gear

Ford (German) 4-speed: output shaft disassembled

MANUAL TRANSMISSIONS
FORD—ET SERIES (GERMAN DESIGN) FOUR SPEED

3. Slide the synchronizer hub over the shaft. Make sure that the shift fork groove is toward the front of the shaft. The sleeve and hub are select fit and must be assembled with the etch marks in the same relative locations. Locate an insert in each of three slots in the hub. Oil all parts, and install an insert spring inside the sleeve. The spring tab must locate in a section of an insert. Fit the other spring to the opposite face. Locate the tab in the same insert. Both springs should be in the same rotational direction. The tab end of one spring should be aligned with the tab of the spring on the opposite side.
4. Assemble a blocker ring on the first gear side of the 1st/2nd synchronizer. Lubricate the cone surface of first gear and all output shaft gear journals. Slide the cone surface onto the output shaft. The cone surface should engage the blocker ring.
5. Position the spacer on the output shaft, larger diameter rearward.
6. Install the thickest possible snap-ring (selected from the chart). Position the output shaft bearing on the shaft. Press the bearing into place. Secure the bearing with the snap-ring.

Part No.	Thickness Identification
D1FZ-7030-A	0.0679-Color Coded—Copper
D1FZ-7030-B	0.0689-Letter—W
D1FZ-7030-C	0.0699-Letter—V
D1FZ-7030-D	0.0709-Letter—U
D1FZ-7030-E	0.0719-None
D1FZ-7030-F	0.0728-Color Coded—Blue
D1FZ-7030-G	0.0738-Color Coded—Black
D1FZ-7030-H	0.0748-Color Coded—Brown

7. Slide the synchronizer over the hub and locate an insert in each of three slots in the sleeve. Align etch marks. Lightly oil all parts. Complete assembly of the snychronizer by following directions in previous Step 3.
8. Position second gear and the blocker ring on the output shaft, dog teeth facing rearward. Install the washer and snapring. Position third gear on the output shaft, dog teeth forward. Lubricate the gear cones and assemble a blocker ring on third gear cone.
9. Position the 3rd/4th synchronizer assembly on the output shaft, hub boss facing forward.
10. Install press plates against the boss on the synchronizer hub.

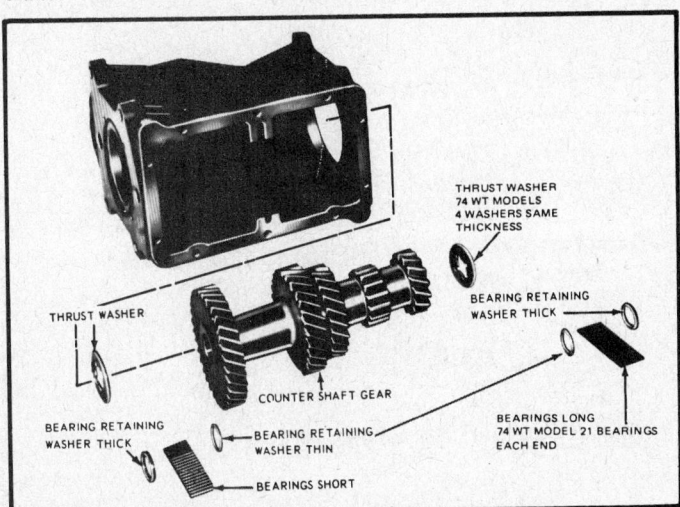

Ford (German) 4-speed: countershaft gear disassembled

11. Place the entire unit in a press, extension end up, and press the synchronizer assembly onto the output shaft as far as possible.
12. Retain the 3rd/4th synchronizer assembly to the output shaft with a snap-ring. Pull up on the synchronizer so that the snap-ring is tight in the groove.
13. Lubricate the gear cone. Place the blocker ring on the input shaft gear cone.
14. Using Tool T71P-17271-A, press the speedometer drive gear onto the shaft until the dowels of the tool just contact the bearing outer race.
15. Lubricate the bearing bore of the extension housing. Install the output shaft in the housing. It may be necessary to tap the shaft while holding the synchronizer sleeves firmly. Secure the shaft to the housing with the snap-ring previously installed.
16. Press the bearing on the input shaft. Snap-ring groove must be forward. Use the thickest snap-ring that will fit.
17. Slide the spacer and dummy shaft into the countershaft gear. Position a thin bearing retaining washer on each end of the dummy shaft. Lubricate the roller bearings. Load long bearings in the small end of the gear and short bearings in the long end of the gear. 21 long needle bearings in the small end of the gear and 21 short needle bearings in large end of the countershaft gear. Place a thick retaining washer over each end of the dummy shaft. Grease the thrust washers and place one on each end of the dummy shaft. The tabs must engage the slots in the case when the gear is lowered. Loop a piece of rope around each end of the gear and rope through the rear of the case. Lower the gear in place.
18. Lubricate the reverse idler gear shaft. Position the selector lever relay on the pivot pin. Secure with a spring clip. Hold the gear in the lever, long hub toward the rear of the case, and slide the reverse idler shaft into place. Seat the shaft in the case with a brass hammer.
19. Install a new seal in the input shaft bearing retainer. Install the input shaft in the case with a new bearing retainer O-ring. Tap on the outer race of the bearing to seat the outer snap-ring.

--- **CAUTION** ---
Use a soft hammer. Do not tap on the input shaft itself.

20. Carefully slide 3rd/4th synchronizer sleeve into fourth speed position.
21. Place a new gasket on the extension housing.
22. Lubricate and install the input shaft pilot bearing on the shaft. Slide the extension housing and output shaft into place. Don't disturb the fourth speed synchronizer.
23. Align the cutaway in the extension housing flange with the countershaft bore in the rear of the case.
24. Lift the countershaft gear into place. Install the countershaft, making sure that the thrust washers remain in place. The flat on the countershaft should be parallel to the top of the case. Tap the shaft with a brass hammer until the front of the shaft is flush with the case.
25. Rotate the extension housing to align the bolt holes. Loosely install the attaching bolts. Loosely install the attaching bolts. Make sure that the rail slides freely in its bore. Binding is remedied by slightly rotating the extension housing to free the rail, then pushing the housing into the case. Apply sealer to the attaching bolts and torque to 33–36 ft. lbs. Place the shift forks in the synchronizer sleeves. Install the interlock lever and new retaining pin. Lubricate the shift rail oil seal. Slide the shift rail through the extension housing, case and second and first speed shift forks. Position the selector arm on the ral. Slide the rail through third and fourth speed shift fork. Slide the shift rail through the front of the case until the center detent bore is aligned with the detent plunger bore. Install a new retaining pin in the selector arm.
26. Install the detent plunger, spring and plug with sealer.

SECTION 32
MANUAL TRANSMISSIONS
FORD—ET SERIES (GERMAN DESIGN) FOUR SPEED

27. Install a new access plug in the rear of the case.
28. Position a new oil seal with tension spring and lip facing in the direction of the case.
29. Drive the seal in until it bottoms.
30. Position a new O-ring in the groove in the case. Position the input shaft bearing retainer with the groove in the retainer aligned with the oil passage in the case. Install the retaining bolts fingertight.
31. Install the flywheel housing. Tighten the retaining bolts and the front bearing retainer attaching bolts. Coat the retainer with grease.
32. Install the clutch release arm and bearing.
33. Install a new extension housing plug, using sealer.
34. Install a new cover gasket and cover, with the vent to the rear. Apply sealer to the left front cover attaching bolt. Torque to 8–10 ft. lbs.
35. Install a new seat belt sensing switch if the old one was removed.

FORD 4-SPEED OVERDRIVE TRANSMISSION—(SROD) (RUG) SINGLE RAIL OVERDRIVE

DESCRIPTION

The transmission is fully synchronized with all gears except the reverse sliding gear which is in constant mesh. Forward gear changes are accomplished with synchronizer sleeves. All forward gears are helical type. The reverse sliding gear and the external teeth of the first and second speeds synchronizer sleeve are spur type.

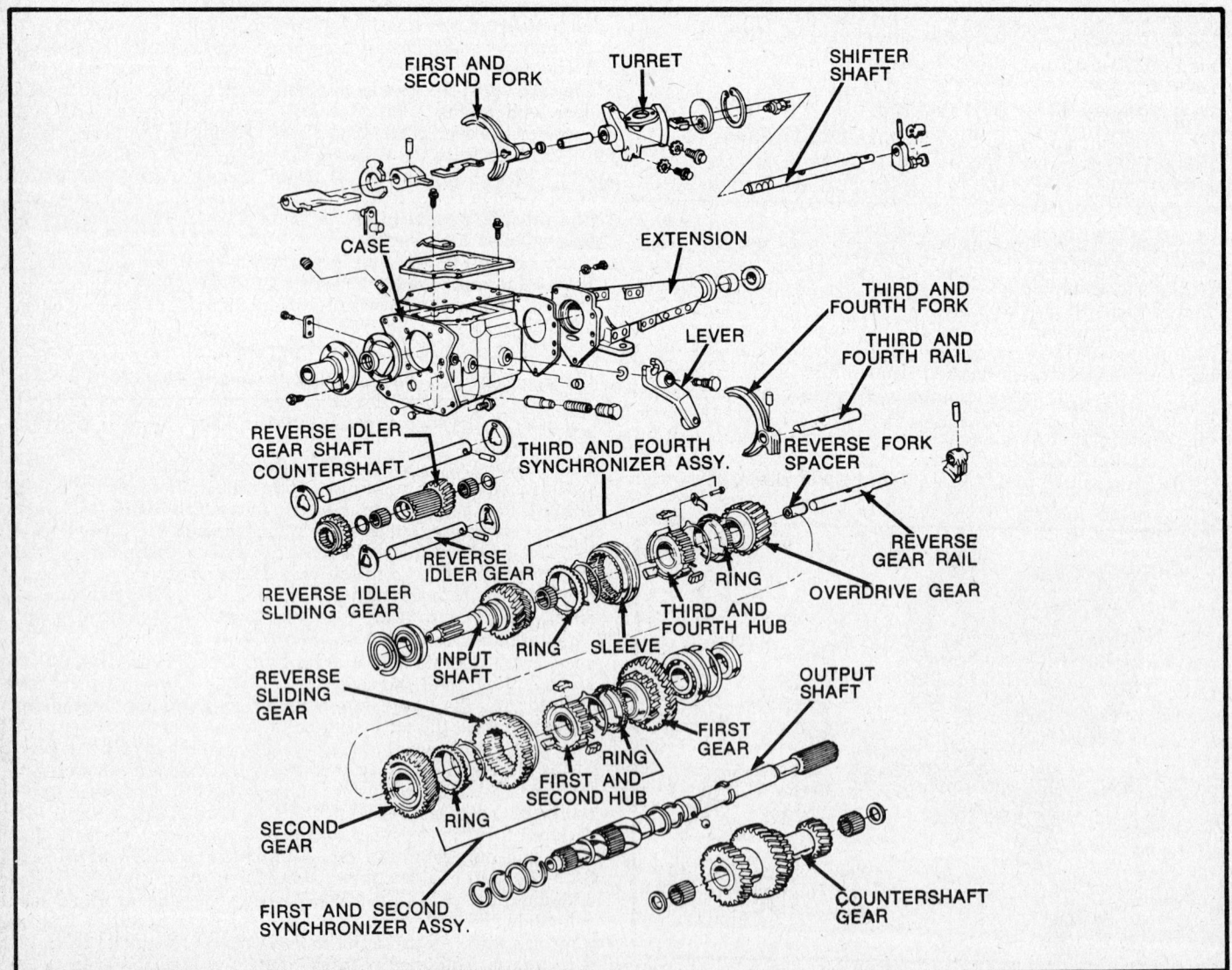

Exploded view of the Ford single rail 4-speed overdrive

MANUAL TRANSMISSIONS
FORD—FOUR SPEED OVERDRIVE

The service identification tag is located on the right side of the case at the front. The first line shows the transmission model and service identification code. The second line shows the transmission serial number, and this serial number is also stamped on the top side of the case flange.

Disassembly

1. Drain the lubricant, and remove the transmission cover.
2. Remove the screw, detent spring and detent plug from the case. A magnetized rod may be needed.
3. Drive roll pin from shifter shaft.
4. Remove back-up light switch assembly, snap-ring and dust cover from rear of extension housing. Remove shifter shaft from turret assembly, and unbolt and remove the extension housing.
5. Remove the snap-ring securing the speedometer drive gear to the output shaft. Slide the gear off the shaft, and remove the speedometer gear drive ball.
6. Remove the snap-ring that secures the output shaft bearing to the shaft and remove the output shaft bearing (slip fit) from the output shaft and transmission case.
7. From the front of the case push the countershaft out the rear of the case with a dummy shaft, and lower the countershaft to the bottom of the case.
8. Remove the input shaft bearing retainer attaching bolts, and slide the retainer off the shaft.
9. Remove the snap-ring that secures the input shaft bearing to the input shaft, and remove the bearing from the input shaft and transmission case (slip fit).
10. Remove the input shaft and the blocking ring from the case including roller bearings.
11. Remove the overdrive shaft pawl, gear selector interlock plate.
12. Remove the 1–2 gearshift selector arm plate.
13. Remove the roll pin from the third/overdrive shift fork.
14. Remove the third/overdrive shift rail and expansion plug (drive from the rear of case).
15. Remove the first/second and third/overdrive shift forks.
16. Lift the countershaft gear and the thrust washers from the case.

NOTE: Be careful not to drop the bearings or the dummy shaft from the countershaft gear.

17. Remove the snap-ring from the front of the output shaft, and slide the third/overdrive synchronizer blocking ring and gear off the shaft. Remove the next snap-ring and thrust washer, and remove the first speed gear and blocking ring from the rear of the shaft.
18. Lift the countershaft gear thrust washers and roller bearings from the case.
19. Remove the roll pin from the reverse fork, slide the reverse shifter rail through the rear of the case and remove the reverse gearshift fork.
20. From the front of the case, drive the reverse gear shaft out the rear of the case.
21. Remove the reverse idler gear, thrust washers and roller bearings.
22. Remove retaining clip, reverse gearshift relay lever and reverse gear selector fork pivot pin.
23. Remove the overdrive shift control link assembly.
24. Remove shift shaft seal from the rear of the case and expansion.

Assembly

Reverse the disassembly procedure, and lubricate the following areas before or during assembly with appropriate lubricants:
1. Mainshaft bearing rollers
2. Extension housing bushing
3. Reverse idler bearing rollers
4. Countershaft gear bearing rollers
5. Low gear and second and overdrive gear formals on the output shaft
6. Shifter shaft
7. Gear shift damper bushing

Gear End Play

The end play of the firs, second and overdrive gears after their assembly on the output shaft must be checked and must pass the following specifications:
1. With the first gear thrust washer clamped tight against the shoulder on the output shaft, the first gear end play is 0.0005–0.024 in.
2. Second gear end play is 0.003–0.021 in.
3. Overdrive gear end play is 0.009–0.023 in.

FORD 4 SPEED OVERDRIVE TORQUE SPECIFICATIONS

Application	Bolt	Nut	Tightening Torque Ft-lbs (N·m)	Application	Bolt	Nut	Tightening Torque Ft-Lbs (N·m)
Input Shaft Bearing Retainer	5/16	Case	11–25 (15–33)	Pn—Reverse Gear Fork Pivot	M16-1.5	Case	15–25 (21–33)
Extension Assembly	7/16-14	Case	42–50 (54–67)	Turret Assembly	M8-1.25	Extension	8–12 (11–16)
Case Access Cover	5/16-18	Case	20–25 (28–33)	Service I.D. Tag Screw	#6-32 Self-Tapping	Case	Seat Firmly
Filler Plug	½–14 U.S. Pipe Thread	Case	10–20 (14–27)	Detent Bolt	⅜–16	Case	10–15 (14–20)
Back Up Lamp Switch	9/16–18	Turret Cover Assy.	8–12 (11–16)				

SECTION 32 — MANUAL TRANSMISSIONS
FORD — FIVE SPEED OVERDRIVE

FORD (TREMAC) RAP—5-SPEED OVERDRIVE TRANSMISSION

Transmission Disassembly

1. Using a 10mm wrench, remove the ten attaching bolts and lift off the transmission case cover.
2. Drain the lubricant from the transmission case.
3. Using a pencil size magnet, remove the shift rail detent plug, spring and plunger from the upper left side of the case.
4. Working through the shift turret opening in the extension housing, remove the access plug from the rear of the housing.
5. After shifting the transmission into reverse gea, remove the roll pin from the gear shift shaft offset lever, then slide the offset lever and bushing off the shaft.
6. Remove the fifth-speed interlock pilot bolt from the front top of the extension housing.
7. Remove the six extension housing attaching bolts, then slide the housing and gasket off the output shaft.
8. Remove the snap-ring, speedometer drive gear and drive ball from the output shaft.
9. Remove the fifth gear synchronizer retaining snap-ring from the output shaft, then slide the retaining spacer from the output shaft.
10. Shift the transmission into 1st gear. Using a hammer and a punch, drive out the roll pin located inside the transmission case, which secures the 1st, 2nd 3rd, 4th and reverse selector pin. Remove the selector pin.
11. Slide the shifter shaft, 5th speed shift fork and 5th speed synchronizer from the output shaft as an assembly.
12. Remove the interlock sleeve bolt from the right side of the transmission case.
13. Lift the interlock sleeve, 3rd/4th speed shift fork, and the 1st/2nd speed shift fork from the case.
14. Working from inside the transmission case, remove the C-clip from the reverse gear selector fork pivot pin. Remove the pivot pin, then lift the reverse gear selector fork relay lever, the spring and the reverse gearshift fork from the transmission case.

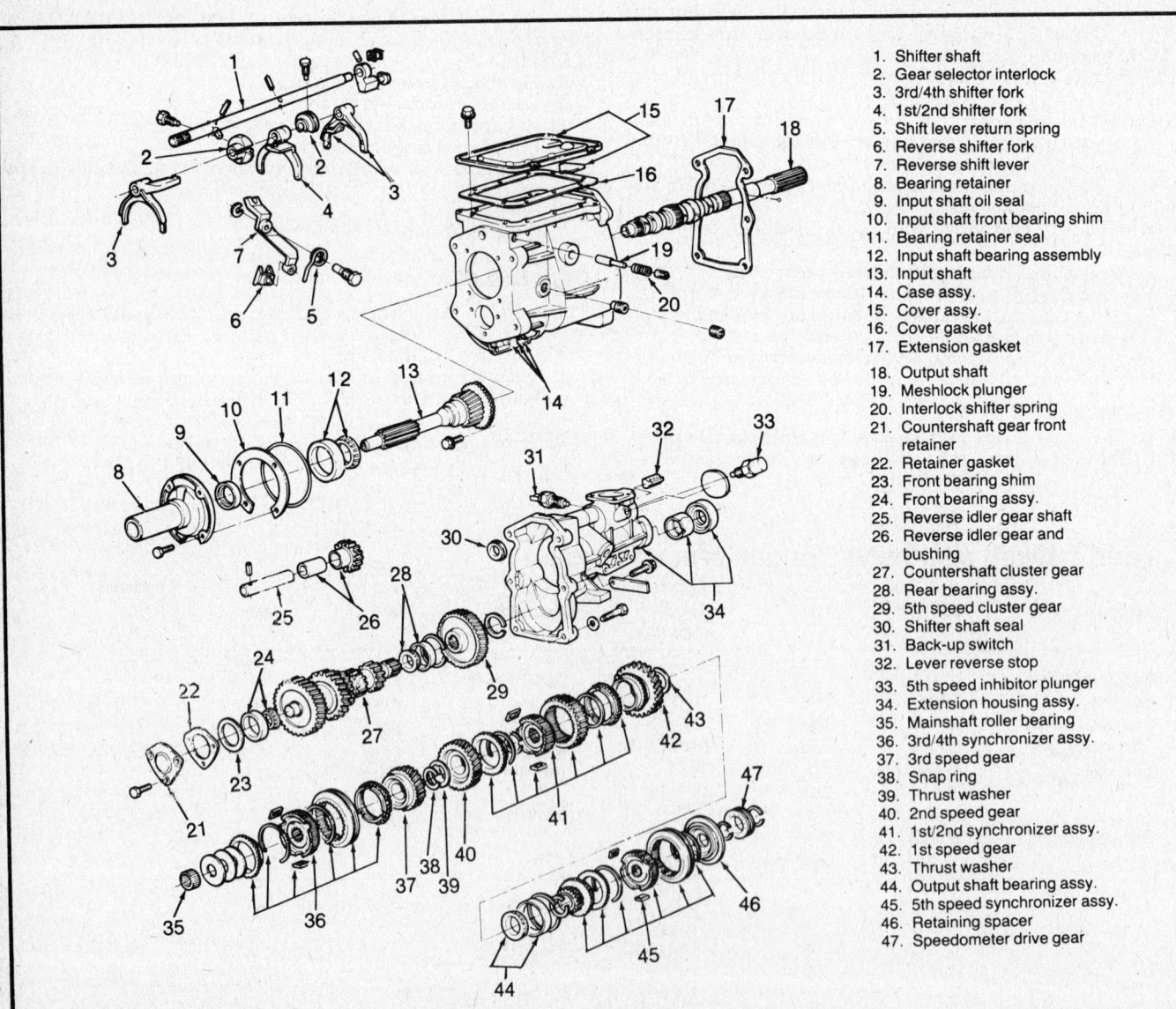

1. Shifter shaft
2. Gear selector interlock
3. 3rd/4th shifter fork
4. 1st/2nd shifter fork
5. Shift lever return spring
6. Reverse shifter fork
7. Reverse shift lever
8. Bearing retainer
9. Input shaft oil seal
10. Input shaft front bearing shim
11. Bearing retainer seal
12. Input shaft bearing assembly
13. Input shaft
14. Case assy.
15. Cover assy.
16. Cover gasket
17. Extension gasket
18. Output shaft
19. Meshlock plunger
20. Interlock shifter spring
21. Countershaft gear front retainer
22. Retainer gasket
23. Front bearing shim
24. Front bearing assy.
25. Reverse idler gear shaft
26. Reverse idler gear and bushing
27. Countershaft cluster gear
28. Rear bearing assy.
29. 5th speed cluster gear
30. Shifter shaft seal
31. Back-up switch
32. Lever reverse stop
33. 5th speed inhibitor plunger
34. Extension housing assy.
35. Mainshaft roller bearing
36. 3rd/4th synchronizer assy.
37. 3rd speed gear
38. Snap ring
39. Thrust washer
40. 2nd speed gear
41. 1st/2nd synchronizer assy.
42. 1st speed gear
43. Thrust washer
44. Output shaft bearing assy.
45. 5th speed synchronizer assy.
46. Retaining spacer
47. Speedometer drive gear

Ford RAP five speed overdrive transmission (© Ford Motor Co.)

MANUAL TRANSMISSIONS
FORD—FIVE SPEED OVERDRIVE
SECTION 32

15. Slide the 5th-speed maindrive gear off the output shaft.
16. Remove the piece snap-ring located at the rear of the 5th-speed cluster gear.
17. Using a puller, remove the 5th-speed cluster gear.
18. Remove the snap-ring from the output shaft rear bearing and remove the bearing cup from the transmission.
19. Remove the bearing retainer and seal, the shim and the O-ring from the case by removing the four input shaft bearing retainer bolts.
20. Without loosening the roller bearings, the thrust washers and the thrust bearing, rotate the input shaft so that the teeth recess toward the countershaft gear to provide clearance. Then lift the input gear from the case.
21. Lift the output shaft assembly out through the top of the transmission case.
22. Remove the snap-ring from the rear of the transmission case and remove the countershaft gear rear bearing cup from the case.
23. Remove the bearing retainer, the gasket, shim and the front bearing cup from the case by removing the three attaching bolts.
24. Lift the countershaft gear out through the top of the transmission case.
25. Remove the reverse idler gear and shaft by removing the roll pin that secures the shaft to the case.

Component Disassembly
OUTPUT SHAFT

1. Slide the 3rd/4th speed synchronizer off the front end of the output shaft.
2. Slide the 3rd speed gear off the front end of the output shaft.
3. Remove the snap-ring and the 2nd speed gear thrust washer from the output shaft. Slide the 2nd speed gear and the synchronizer blocking ring from the output shaft.
4. Remove the snap-ring that retains the 1st/2nd speed synchronizer on the output shaft, then press the synchronizer off the output shaft.
5. Remove the snap-ring from the rear of the output shaft. Place the output shaft in a press, and remove the 1st speed gear, thrust washer and output shaft rear bearing.

INPUT SHAFT

1. If not previously removed, remove the roller bearings from the input shaft.
2. Place the input gear in a press and press the input gear from the bearing.

COUNTERSHAFT GEAR

1. Place the countershaft gear in a press, and remove the rear bearing.
2. Place the countershaft in a vise protected with wood blocks and pry the front bearing from the countershaft.

INPUT SHAFT GEAR BEARING RETAINER

1. Place the bearing retainer in a vise.
2. Using a slide impact-type puller, remove the seal from the bearing retainer.

EXTENSION HOUSING

1. Carefully remove the seal from the extension housing.
2. Using a suitable driver, remove the bushing.

Component Assembly
EXTENSION HOUSING

1. Install the bushing and the seal using a suitable driver.

INPUT SHAFT GEAR BEARING RETAINER

1. Install the seal in the retainer with the lip facing forward toward the transmission case mounting surface. Make sure the seal is bottomed in the retainer.

COUNTERSHAFT GEAR

1. With the taper facing outward, exert pressure on the inner race of the front bearing and press the bearing until it is bottomed on the gear.
2. Install the rear bearing in the same manner.

INPUT SHAFT

1. With the taper toward the front of the gear, apply pressure on the inner race and press the bearing onto the input gear until it is bottomed.
2. Apply a heavy coat of polyethylene on the inner bearing surface of the gear. Load the 15 roller bearings into the gear.

OUTPUT SHAFT

1. Position the 1st gear thrust washer and the bearing on the rear of the output shaft. Apply pressure on the bearing inner race until the bearing is bottomed on the spacer and shaft.
2. Select a snap-ring that will not allow any clearance between the bearing race and the ring groove. Then press the 1st/2nd gear synchronizer and the reverse sliding gear into place and secure with the snap ring.
3. Slide the 2nd gear and the thrust washer into position and secure with the snap-ring.
4. Slide the third gear and the third/fourth gear synchronizer into place. Make sure the thrust surface of the synchronizer hub is facing toward the front of the shaft.

Transmission Assembly

NOTE: Coat all bolts and plugs used throughout the case with a thread sealant to prevent leakage.

1. Hold the reverse idler gear into position with the long end of the hub facing to the rear of the transmission case. Slide the idler gear shaft into the case and gear and align the roll pin holes. Secure the shaft with the roll pin.
2. Lower the countershaft and bearings into place, and install the rear bearing cup. Secure with the snap-ring.
3. Position the front bearing cup, the shim, a new gasket and the bearing retainer to the front of the transmission case. Install the bearing retainer cap screws and tighten to 7–10 ft. lbs. while rotating the gear. If the gear rotating effort increases while tightening the bearing retainer, replace the shim with a thinner one.
4. Correct end play is 0.001–0.005 in. Decrease the shim thickness to increase the end play and increase the shim thickness to reduce end play.
5. Lower the main shaft into the transmission case through the case cover opening.
6. Apply a coat of polyethylene grease to the thrust washers and the thrust bearing. Place the thrust washer on the 3rd/4th speed synchronization thrust surface. Place the thrust bearing and the remaining thrust washer on the 3rd/4th speed synchronizer.
7. Without disturbing the roller bearings, carefully install the input shaft assembly in the transmission case with the blank portion of the teeth toward the countershaft gear to provide the proper clearance.
8. Coat a new input shaft O-ring with polyethylene grease and position it in the bearing retainer groove.
9. Install the output shaft bearing cup and snap-ring in the rear of the transmission.
10. Position the shim and bearing retainer to the transmission case. Install the bearing retainer cap screws and tighten to 8–10 ft. lbs. while rotating the input shaft. If the input shaft turning effort increases when tightening the bearing retainer bolts, replace the shim with a thicker one.
11. Install a dial indicator on the transmission case. Pry the output shaft toward the dial indicator and zero the indica-

32-35

SECTION 32 MANUAL TRANSMISSIONS
FORD—FIVE SPEED OVERDRIVE

tor. Pry the output shaft in the opposite direction. End play should be between 0.001–0.005 in. Decrease shim thickness to decrease end play or increase shim thickness to increase end play. Remove the dial indicator.

12. Install the spring and reverse fork on the relay lever. Position the relay lever assembly in the transmission case and install the pivot pin in the case and lever assembly. Secure the lever with a C-clip.
13. Install the 5th speed cluster gear and secure with a snap-ring.
14. Slide the 5th speed main drive gear onto the output shaft. Coat the blocker ring with polyethylene grease and position it on the main drive gear.
15. Position the 1st/2nd and 3rd/4th shift forks on the main shaft assembly.
16. Place the interlock gear selector sleeve between the two shifter forks and install the interlock pilot bolt in the right side of the transmission case.
17. With the synchronizer thrust surface facing toward the rear of the output shaft, install the shifter shaft, the 5th speed shift fork and the 5th speed synchronizer as an assembly.
18. Working through the cover opening in the transmission case, install the gearshift selector pin in the shifter shaft and secure with a rollpin.
19. Slide the 5th speed synchronizer retaining plate onto the output shaft and secure it with a snap-ring.
20. Secure the speedometer drive gear ball to the output shaft with polyethylene grease then slide the speedometer drive gear onto the shaft over the ball and secure with a snap-ring.
21. Using a new gasket, position the extension housing on the transmission case. Install the two pilot bolts, one in the upper left side of the housing and the other in the lower right corner. Install the four remaining bolts and tighten to 40–60 ft. lbs.
22. Install the 5th gear pilot in the top of the extension housing.
23. Shift the transmission into reverse gear. Install the offset lever on the rear of the shifter shaft and secure the lever with a roll pin.
24. Install the detent plunger, the spring and the plug in the upper right side of the transmission case. Tighten the plug to 12–14 ft. lbs.
25. Install the access plug in the rear of the extension housing.
26. Using a new gasket place the cover on the transmission case and tighten the attaching bolts to 8–10 ft. lbs.

GM WARNER 70MM—4-SPEED TRANSMISSION

The designation derives from the distance measurement between the gearbox shafts—70mm. This gearbox is 100% assembled with metric fasteners.

Transmission Disassembly

With the transmission resting on the front of the bellhousing:
1. Drive the spring pin from the shifter shaft arm assembly and shifter shaft. Remove shifter shaft arm assembly.
2. Remove 5 bolts retaining the extension housing to the case and remove extension.
3. Press down on speedometer gear retainer and remove gear and retainer from mainshaft.
4. Remove snap-rings on shifter shaft.
5. Using tool J-25295 with slide hammer 6619-1, remove reverse shifter shaft cover, shifter shaft detent cap, spring and ball, and interlock lock pin.
6. Pull reverse lever shaft outward to disengage reverse idler. Remove the idler shaft, with gear attached.
7. Remove snap-ring on reverse gear and reverse countershaft gear. Remove gears.
8. Place transmission on its side and remove clutch gear bearing retainer bolts, retainer and gasket.
9. Remove snap-ring retaining the clutch gear ball bearing to the bellhousing.
10. Remove the 6 bolts holding the bellhousing to the case.
11. Place transmission so that its again resting on the bellhousing and expand the snap-ring in mainshaft bearing opening. Remove the case by lifting it off the mainshaft. Insure that mainshaft assembly, countergear and shifter shaft assembly remain with the bellhousing.

NOTE: It may be necessary to tap with a plastic hammer to remove case.

12. Lift from the bellhousing as an assembly, the mainshaft with shifter forks attached and the countergear meshed with gear teeth in the mainshaft.

Mainshaft Disassembly

1. Separate the shift shaft assembly and countergear from the mainshaft.
2. Remove the clutch gear and blocker ring from the mainshaft.

NOTE: The clutch gear has 15 roller bearings. Catch loose roller bearings if they fall out during disassembly so that they can be replaced during assembly.

3. Remove snap-ring before 3–4 synchronizer hub and remove synchronizer assembly. Use press if required.
4. Remove blocker ring and 3rd speed gear.
5. Using press plates, remove the ball bearing from the rear of the mainshaft.
6. The remaining components may be removed one at a time from the mainshaft, pressing as required.

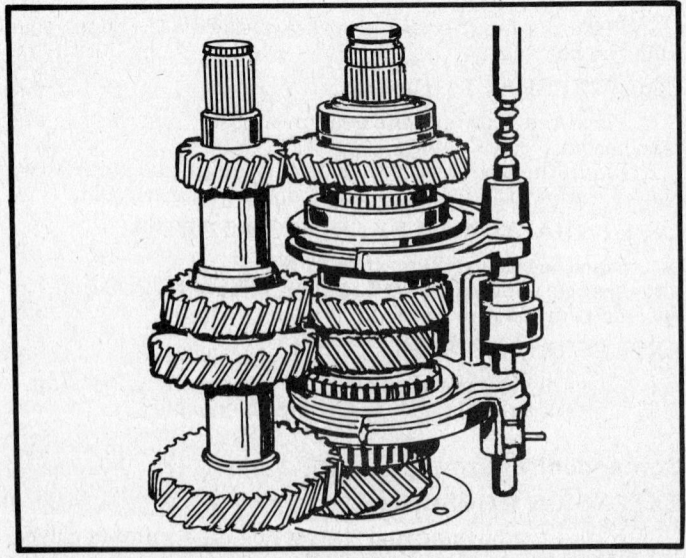

GM 70mm manual 4-speed: countershaft and mainshaft gears positioned for insertion into bellhousing

MANUAL TRANSMISSIONS
GM WARNER – 70mm FOUR SPEED
SECTION 32

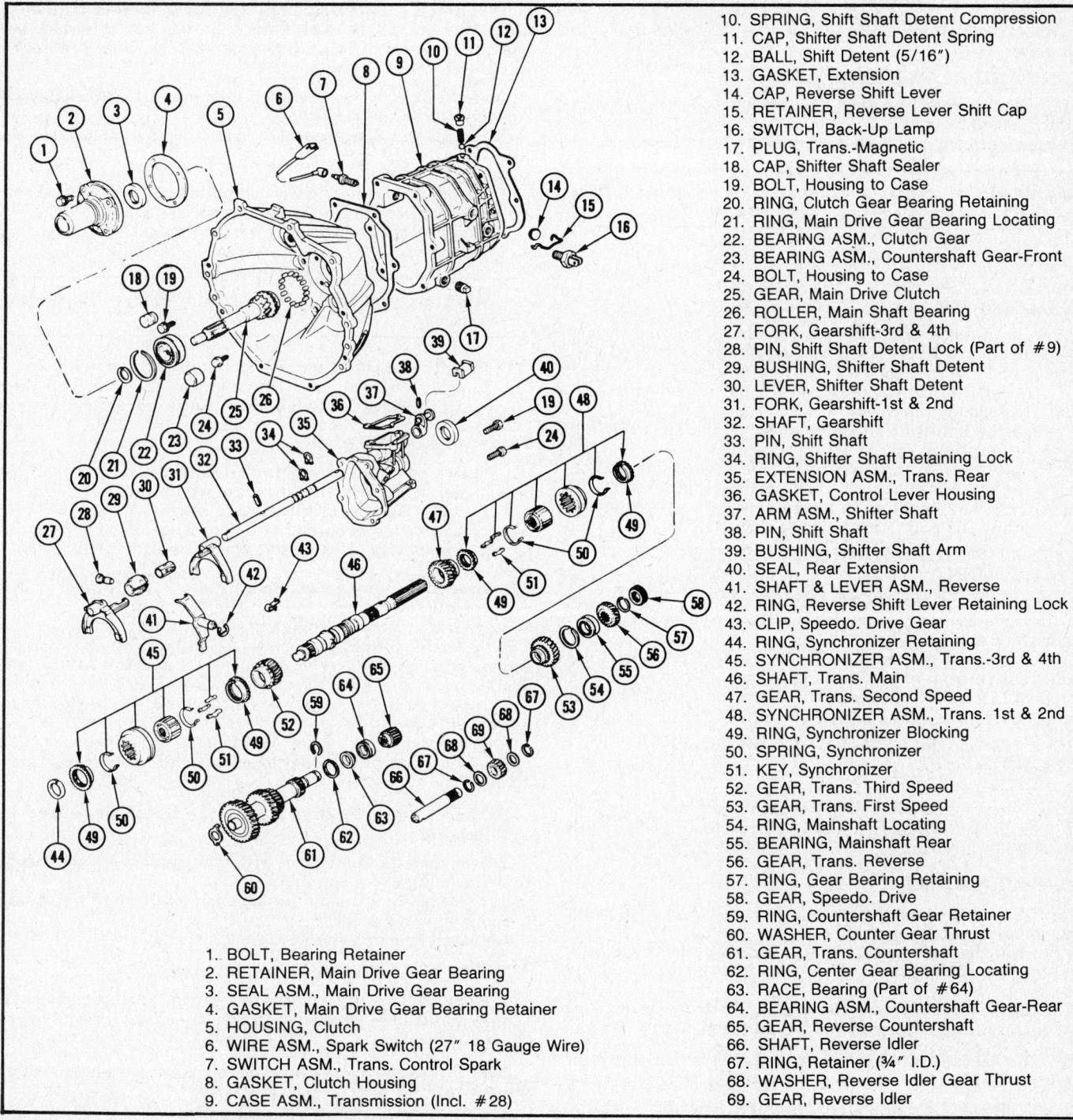

10. SPRING, Shift Shaft Detent Compression
11. CAP, Shifter Shaft Detent Spring
12. BALL, Shift Detent (5/16")
13. GASKET, Extension
14. CAP, Reverse Shift Lever
15. RETAINER, Reverse Lever Shift Cap
16. SWITCH, Back-Up Lamp
17. PLUG, Trans.-Magnetic
18. CAP, Shifter Shaft Sealer
19. BOLT, Housing to Case
20. RING, Clutch Gear Bearing Retaining
21. RING, Main Drive Gear Bearing Locating
22. BEARING ASM., Clutch Gear
23. BEARING ASM., Countershaft Gear-Front
24. BOLT, Housing to Case
25. GEAR, Main Drive Clutch
26. ROLLER, Main Shaft Bearing
27. FORK, Gearshift-3rd & 4th
28. PIN, Shift Shaft Detent Lock (Part of #9)
29. BUSHING, Shifter Shaft Detent
30. LEVER, Shifter Shaft Detent
31. FORK, Gearshift-1st & 2nd
32. SHAFT, Gearshift
33. PIN, Shift Shaft
34. RING, Shifter Shaft Retaining Lock
35. EXTENSION ASM., Trans. Rear
36. GASKET, Control Lever Housing
37. ARM ASM., Shifter Shaft
38. PIN, Shift Shaft
39. BUSHING, Shifter Shaft Arm
40. SEAL, Rear Extension
41. SHAFT & LEVER ASM., Reverse
42. RING, Reverse Shift Lever Retaining Lock
43. CLIP, Speedo. Drive Gear
44. RING, Synchronizer Retaining
45. SYNCHRONIZER ASM., Trans.-3rd & 4th
46. SHAFT, Trans. Main
47. GEAR, Trans. Second Speed
48. SYNCHRONIZER ASM., Trans. 1st & 2nd
49. RING, Synchronizer Blocking
50. SPRING, Synchronizer
51. KEY, Synchronizer
52. GEAR, Trans. Third Speed
53. GEAR, Trans. First Speed
54. RING, Mainshaft Locating
55. BEARING, Mainshaft Rear
56. GEAR, Trans. Reverse
57. RING, Gear Bearing Retaining
58. GEAR, Speedo. Drive
59. RING, Countershaft Gear Retainer
60. WASHER, Counter Gear Thrust
61. GEAR, Trans. Countershaft
62. RING, Center Gear Bearing Locating
63. RACE, Bearing (Part of #64)
64. BEARING ASM., Countershaft Gear-Rear
65. GEAR, Reverse Countershaft
66. SHAFT, Reverse Idler
67. RING, Retainer (¾" I.D.)
68. WASHER, Reverse Idler Gear Thrust
69. GEAR, Reverse Idler

1. BOLT, Bearing Retainer
2. RETAINER, Main Drive Gear Bearing
3. SEAL ASM., Main Drive Gear Bearing
4. GASKET, Main Drive Gear Bearing Retainer
5. HOUSING, Clutch
6. WIRE ASM., Spark Switch (27" 18 Gauge Wire)
7. SWITCH ASM., Trans. Control Spark
8. GASKET, Clutch Housing
9. CASE ASM., Transmission (Incl. #28)

Exploded view of GM 70mm transmission (© G.M. Corp.)

Cleaning and Inspection
TRANSMISSION CASE

1. Wash the transmission thoroughly inside and outside with cleaning solvent, then inspect the case for cracks.
2. Check the front and rear faces for burrs, and if present, dress them off with a fine mill file.
3. Make sure bearings are clean, then lubricate with light engine oil and check them for roughness by slowly turning the race by hand.

ROLLER BEARINGS

All countergear bearings should be inspected closely and replaced if they show wear. Inspect countergear and reverse idler shaft at the same time, replace in necessary.

GEARS

1. Inspect all gears for excessive wear, chips or cracks and replace any that are worn or damaged.
2. Inspect reverse idler gear bushing and if worn or damaged replace the entire gear (reverse gear bushing is not serviced

32-37

SECTION 32
MANUAL TRANSMISSIONS
GM WARNER—70mm FOUR SPEED

separately).

3. Check both clutch sleeves to see that they slide freely on their hubs.

FRONT AND REAR BEARINGS

1. Wash the front and rear ball bearings thoroughly in a cleaning solvent.
2. Blow out bearings with compressed air.

CAUTION

Do not allow the bearings to spin. Turn them slowly by hand. Spinning bearings will damage the race and balls.

Repairs

SYNCHRONIZER KEYS AND SPRINGS REPLACEMENT

The synchronizer hubs and sliding sleeves are selected assembly and should be kept together as originally assembled, but the keys and two springs may be replaced if worn or broken.

1. If relation of hub and sleeve are not already marked, mark for assembly purposes.
2. Push the hub from the sliding sleeve; the keys will fall free and the springs may be easily removed.
3. Place the two springs in position (one on each side of hub), so all three keys are engaged by both springs. Place the keys in position and while holding in place, slide the sleeve onto the hub, aligning the marks made before disassembly.

EXTENSION OIL SEAL AND/OR BUSHING REPLACEMENT

1. Pry seal from rear of extension.
2. Remove bushing using Tool J–21424–9. Drive bushing from rear of extension housing.
3. Using a new bushing and Tool J–21424–9 press bushing into extension from rear of extension.
4. Coat I.D. of bushing and seal with transmission lubricant. Install new seal using Tool J–21426.

DRIVE GEAR BEARING RETAINER OIL SEAL REPLACEMENT

1. Pry out old seal.
2. Using a new seal install new seal into retainer using Tool J–23096 until it bottoms in bore. Lubricate I.D. of seal with transmission lubricant.

Mainshaft Assembly

Turn the rear of the mainshaft upward. Install the following components on the mainshaft:

1. Install the 2nd speed gear with clutching teeth upward; the rear face of the gear with butt against the flange on the mainshaft.
2. Install a blocker ring with clutching teeth downward over the synchronizing surface of the second speed gear.

NOTE: All four blocker rings used in this transmission are identical.

3. Install the 1st and 2nd synchronizer assembly with the fork slot downward; press it on the splines on the mainshaft until it bottoms out.

CAUTION

Be sure the notches of the blocker ring align with the keys of the synchronizer assembly.

---

4. Install synchronizer hub to mainshaft snap-ring.
5. Install a blocker ring with the notches downward so they align with the keys of the 1st and 2nd synchronizer assembly.
6. Install 1st speed gear with clutching teeth downward.
7. Install rear ball bearing with snap-ring groove downward; press onto mainshaft.

NOTE: Two ball bearings are used in this transmission. The one used on the mainshaft is not shielded, but the one used on the clutch gear is and these should not be switched.

Turn the front of the mainshaft upward. Install the following components on the mainshaft:

8. Install the 3rd gear with clutching teeth upward; the front face of the gear will butt against the flange on the mainshaft.
9. Install a blocker ring with clutching teeth downward over the synchronizer surface of the 3rd speed gear.
10. Install the 3rd and 4th synchronizer assembly with fork slot downward.

CAUTION

Be sure notches of the blocker ring align with the keys of the synchronizer assembly.

---

11. Install a synchronizer hub in mainshaft snap-ring.
12. Install a blocker ring with notches downward so they align with the keys of the 3/4 synchronizer assembly.

Transmission Assembly

1. Using an arbor press, install shielded ball bearing to clutch gear shaft with snap-ring groove upward.
2. Install snap-ring on clutch gear shaft.
3. Load the mainshaft pilot roller bearings (15) into the clutch gear cavity. Use heavy grease or equivalent to hold them in place.
4. Assemble clutch gear to mainshaft.
5. Install detent lever to shift shaft with roll pin, slide 1/2 shifter fork on shaft so it engages detent lever.
6. Assemble 3/4 shifter fork to detent bushing and slide assembly on shift shaft to locate below 1st and 2nd shifter fork arm.
7. Install shifter assembly to synchronizer sleeve grooves on mainshaft.
8. With the front of the bellhousing resting on wooden blocks; place a thrust washer over the hole for the countergear shaft.

NOTE: Locate thrust washer in holes provided in bellhousing.

9. Mesh countershaft gears with mainshaft gears and install to bellhousing as an assembly.
10. Place bellhousing on its side and install snap-ring to ball bearing on clutch gear.
11. Install bearing retainer to bellhousing.

NOTE: Use bolt seal on (4) retaining bolts.

12. Turn bellhousing so it again rests on the wooden block. If removed, install reverse lever to case; use grease or equivalent to hold it in place.

NOTE: When reverse lever is installed, the screwdriver slot should be parrallel to the front of the case.

13. Install reverse lever snap-ring.
14. Install roller bearing to countergear opening with snap-ring groove inside of case.

NOTE: Snap-ring will be assembled to roller bearing.

15. Install gasket to bellhousing using rubber cement or equivalent to hold it in place.

NOTE: Before installing case, make sure synchronizers are in neutral position, detent bushing slot is facing outward and the reverse lever is flush with the inside wall of the case.

16. Using snap-ring pliers expand the snap-ring in the

MANUAL TRANSMISSIONS
GM WARNER – 70mm FOUR SPEED

mainshaft opening of the case and let it pilot over the mainshaft bearing.

NOTE: It may be necessary to tap the case with a plastic hammer to ease assembly.

17. Install interlock lock pin to hold shifter in place.
18. Install idler shaft so it will engage with the reverse inside of case.
19. Install cover over screwdriver arm to hold the reverse lever in place.
20. Install detent ball, spring and cap in case.
21. Install reverse gear with the chamfer on gear teeth upward; push reverse gear onto splines on the mainshaft and secure with a snap-ring.
22. Install smaller reverse gear on countergear shaft with the shoulder resting against countergear bearing and secure with a snap-ring.
23. If remove, install snap-ring, thrust washer and reverse idler gear with chamfer of gear teeth facing downward to idler shaft. Secure with thrust washer and snap-ring.
24. Install snap-rings on shifter shaft.
25. Engage speedometer gear retainer in hole provided in mainshaft, with retainer loop forward, slide speedometer gear over mainshaft and into position.
26. Place extension housing and gasket on case and install (2) pilot bolts before installing the three remaining bolts.

NOTE: Pilot bolts are partially threaded and installed in the top right hand corner and bottom left hand corner of the case.

--- CAUTION ---
If the pilot bolts are installed in the wrong holes, splitting of the case may occur.

27. Assemble the shifter shaft arm over shifter shaft to a position aligned with the drilled hole near the end of shaft drive spring pin into shifter shaft arm and shaft to retain these parts.
28. Place transmission on its side; install the (2) pilot bolts before installing the (4) remaining bolts to the bellhouse and case.

NOTE: Pilot bolts are partially threaded and are installed in the right hand top and left hand bottom holes in the bellhousing.

GM 4-SPEED MANUAL TRANSAXLE – 76MM

DESCRIPTION

The four-speed transaxle assembly is a constant mesh design transmission combined with a differentail unit; both assembled in a single aluminum case. For shifting, synchronizers with blocker rings controlled by shift forks are used for forward speeds. Reverse uses a sliding idler gear arrangement.

The main components are the transaxle case, clutch cover, input gear (shaft), output gear (shaft) and differential assembly. The input gear, output gear and differential are all supported by preloaded tapered roller bearings. Selective shims are used beneath the right-hand bearing cups to establish the correct preload.

The final output gear (an integral part of the output shaft) turns the ring gear and differential thereby turning the drive axle shafts which are attached to the front wheels.

Case Disassembly

1. Remove the bolts securing the clutch cover to the transaxle case.
2. Use a plastic hammer to carefully tap the clutch cover from the transaxle case. Anaerobic sealant is used between the case and cover, instead of a gasket.
3. Remove the ring gear/differential assembly.
4. Position the shifter shaft in the neutral position so that shifter moves freely and is not engaged in any drive gear.
5. Bend back tab on lock and remove bolt from shifter shaft. Remove the shifter shaft and the shift fork shaft from the synchronizer forks.
6. Remove the reverse shift fork by disengaging from the guide pin and interlock bracket.
7. Remove the lock bolt securing the reverse idler gear shaft. Remove the gear/shaft/spacer assembly.
8. Remove the detent shift lever and interlock assembly. Leave shift forks engaged with the synchronizers.
9. Grasp the input and output shafts and then lift them as an assembly from the case. Note the position of the shift forks for aid when reinstalling later. Remove the shift forks.

Input Shaft Disassembly

1. Using Tool J-22912-01 in 4th gear groove, press 4th gear and L.H. bearing from input shaft.

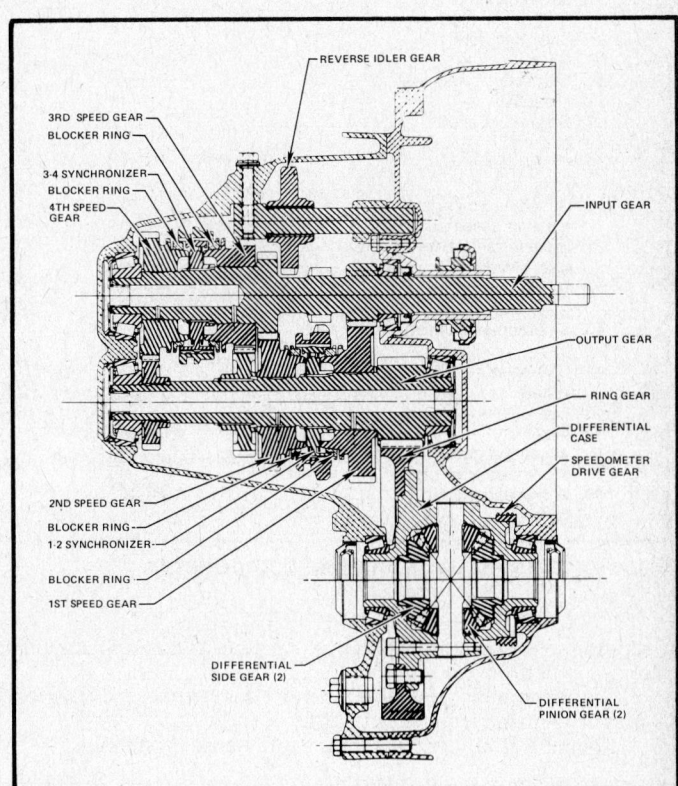

Transaxle cross section and component replacement

SECTION 32 MANUAL TRANSMISSIONS
GM WARNER—76mm FOUR SPEED

1. Case assembly
2. Axle shaft seal assembly
3. Case locating pin
4. Chip collecting magnet
5. Vent assembly
6. Synchronizer key
7. Oil shield
8. Bearing assembly
9. 4th speed input gear
10. Blocking ring
11. Synchronizer spring
12. Synchronizer assembly
13. 3rd speed input gear
14. Oil shield sleeve
15. Input cluster gear
16. Input gear bearing
17. Input gear seal
18. Input gear retainer assembly
19. Retainer seal
20. Throwout bearing assembly
21. Reverse idler shaft
22. Reverse idler shaft
23. Reverse idler shaft gear
24. Reverse inhibitor spring seat
25. Reverse inhibitor spring
26. Reverse inhibitor spring pin
27. Reverse shift lever
28. Detent lever assembly
29. Detent spring
30. Shift shaft
31. Shift shaft seal assembly
32. Shift interlock
33. 3rd-4th shift fork
34. 1st-2nd shift fork
35. Shift fork shaft
36. Oil guide
37. Clutch fork shaft seal assembly
38. Clutch fork shaft bearing
39. Clutch fork shaft assembly
40. Clutch and differential housing assembly
41. Speedometer driven gear sleeve
42. Speedometer driven gear sleeve seal
43. Speedometer driven gear
44. Case bearing oil shield
45. Case bearing assembly
46. 4th speed gear
47. 3rd speed output gear
48. 2nd speed output gear
49. Synchronizer blocking ring
50. Synchronizer spring
51. Synchronizer key
52. 1st-2nd synchronizer assembly
53. 1st speed output gear
54. Oil shield sleeve
55. Output gear
56. Output bearing assembly
57. Output gear bearing shim
58. Output gear bearing oil shield
59. Output gear bearing oil shield retainer
60. Differential assembly
61. Differential ring gear
62. Differential bearing assembly
63. Differential case
64. Differential pinion shaft
65. Speedometer drive gear
66. Differential bearing assembly
67. Housing bearing shim
68. Side gear thrust washer
69. Differential side gear
70. Pinion thrust washer
71. Differential pinion gear

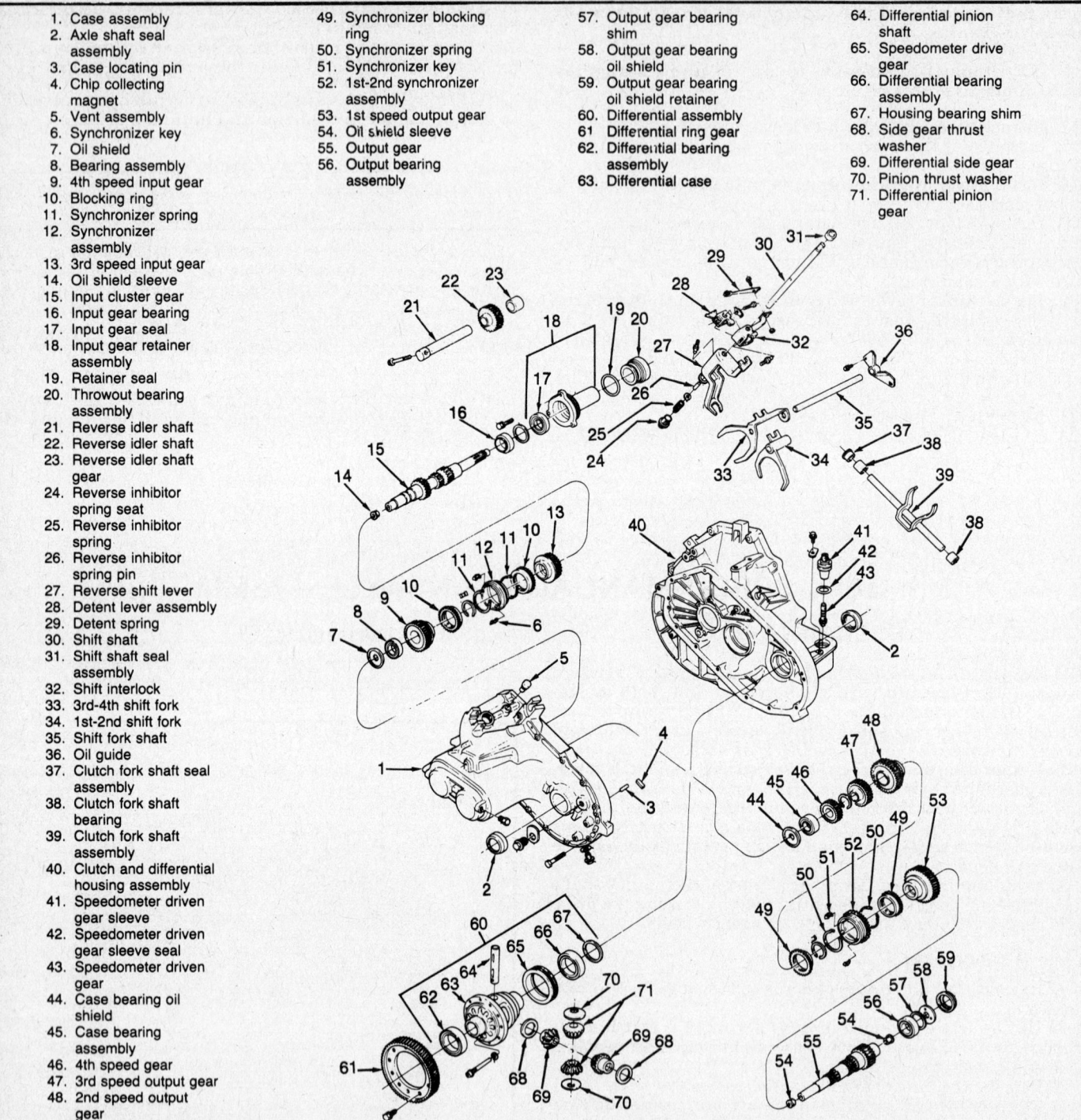

Four-speed manual transaxle components

2. Remove brass blocker ring. Remove the snap-ring from the 3-4 synchronizer.

3. Using support plates behind 3rd gear, press 3rd gear and 3-4 synchronizer from input shaft.

4. Remove R.H. bearing from shaft using J–26946.

Output Shaft Disassembly

1. Using support plates behind 4th gear and J–26943, press on the end of the output shaft to remove 4th gear and the L.H. bearing.

2. Remove the snap-ring retaining 3rd gear.

3. Slide the 1-2 synchronizer assembly into first gear position to allow press plates to support 2nd gear. Press 2nd speed gear and 3rd gear from the output shaft. Remove the brass blocker ring.

4. Remove the snap-ring retaining the 1-2 synchronizer.

MANUAL TRANSMISSIONS
GM WARNER—76mm FOUR SPEED
SECTION 32

5. Using press plates behind 1st speed gear, press 1st gear and 1-2 synchronizer from the output shaft.

6. Install J-22227-A on the R.H. bearing and remove the bearing by pressing on J-26943 pilot.

Synchronizer Overhaul

1. Carefully pry out both synchronizer key springs from each synchronizer.

2. Separate the hub, sleeve and keys, noting their relative positions. Scribe the hub to the sleeve prior to separation.

3. Clean, inspect and replace parts as necessary.

4. Assemble the hub to the sleeve, with the extruded lip on the hub directed away from the shift fork groove in the sleeve and align previous scribed marks.

5. Carefully install one retaining ring, then carefully pry the ring back and insert keys one at a time, being sure to position the ring so it is "captured" by the keys.

6. Install the ring on the opposite side, with the open sigment of the ring "out-of-phase" with the open segment on the other side.

Input Shaft Reassembly

1. Install R.H. bearing onto shaft, using J-29406.

2. Place 3rd gear onto the shaft, oriented toward the 3-4 synchronizer. Install the brass blocker ring onto the gear cone, then install the 3-4 synchronizer, using an appropriate cylinder to contact the hub, near the shaft. Do not press on the sleeve portion. Both synchronizer hubs are a press fit to the shafts.

3. Install snap-ring to retain 3-4 synchronizer. Be sure to position snap-ring with beveled edges away from synchronizer for later access with snap-ring pliers.

4. Install brass blocker ring.

5. Install the 4th speed gear onto shaft, oriented toward the 3-4 synchronizer and install L.H. bearing onto the shaft, using J-26942.

Output Shaft Reassembly

1. Install R.H. bearing onto shaft using J-6133-A.

2. Place 1st speed gear onto the shaft, oriented toward the 1-2 synchronizer. Place the brass blocker ring onto the gear cone, then install the 1-2 synchronizer, using an appropriate cylinder to press on the hub, near the shaft. Do not press on the sleeve.

3. Install the snap-ring to retain the 1-2 synchronizer. Place the brass blocker ring into position.

4. Place 2nd speed gear onto the shaft, oriented toward the 1-2 synchronizer, then press 3rd gear onto the shaft, with its hub toward 4th gear. Use an appropriate cylinder to contact 3rd gear hub near the shaft.

5. Install snap-ring to retain 3rd gear.

6. Press 4th gear onto the shaft, with its hub toward 3rd gear, using support plates and install L.H. bearing cone on the shaft, using J-26942.

Transmission Case Overhaul

1. Remove reverse inhibitor fitting from exterior of case. From inside of case, remove the spring and pilot/spacer.

2. Remove input and output shaft L.H. bearing cups, using J-26941. Turn set screw on J-26941 counter clockwise to insert tool below bearing cup. Turn set screw clockwise to grasp bearing cup. When installing cups, use J-26938.

3. Remove oil slingers.

4. Remove differential side bearing cup, using J-26941. Reinstall cup with J-23423-A.

5. Check two guide pins for interlock bracket and reverse shift fork. Check magnet. Remove sealant from mating surface with J-28410 where the clutch cover contacts the case. Use care not to gouge or damage the aluminum surface or leaks can result.

6. Clean all parts. Thoroughly inspect/replace parts as required.

Clutch Cover Overhaul

1. Using J-26941, remove differential side bearing cup and shim.

2. Using J-26941, remove input shaft and output shaft R.H. bearing cups. Remove the shim from back of input bearing cup and remove oil shield, shim, and retainer from back of output shaft bearing cup.

3. Remove external oil ring, and internal oil seal from sleeve.

4. Remove plastic oil scoop.

5. If necessary to replace the clutch fork shaft or bushing, use J-28412 for removal and installation. Always replace the clutch fork shaft seal after installation of the shaft or bushing.

6. Remove bead of sealant from mating surfaces. Use care not to damage sealing surfaces.

7. Clean and inspect all parts. Replace parts as required.

8. Install plastic scoop.

9. Replace external square-cut oil ring on sleeve. Install input bearing retainer, tightening three bolts to specifications.

10. Use J-26936 to install internal oil seal.

Differential Case/Ring Gear Overhaul

1. Separate ring gear from differential case.

2. Remove pinion shaft lock bolt, remove pinion shaft, then roll the gears and thrust washers out through the opening in the case.

3. If differential side bearings are to be replaced, use J-22888 puller and J-2288-20 (puller leg set) to remove the bearings. Use J-22919 cone installer for reinstallation of side bearings.

4. Clean and inspect all parts. Replace parts as required.

5. Install gears and thrust washers into the case; install the pinion shaft and lock bolt. Tighten to correct specifications.

6. Attach the ring gear to the differential case.

NOTE: Selection of the preload shims for reassembly can begin when the input and output shaft assemblies and the differential assembly are reassembled and ready to be installed into the transaxle case.

7. With the (3) L.H. bearing races installed in the case, place the input and output shaft assemblies and the differential assembly into their installed positions. Place the R.H. bearing races onto their respective bearings.

8. Position gauges; J-26935-2 on input bearing and J-26935-4 onto output bearing and J-26935-3 on the differential bearing. Be sure that bearing races fit smoothly into the bores of the gauge tools.

9. On J-26935-4 (output shaft), install metal oil shield retainer into bore on top of tool.

10. Carefully assemble the clutch cover over the gauges and onto the case, using spacers placed evenly around the perimeter. Retain with bolts provided.

11. Draw the cover to the case by tightening alternately and gradually. This will compress all three gauge sleeves.

12. Rotate each gauge to seat the bearings. Rotate the differential case through three revolutions in each direction.

13. With the three gauges compressed, the gap between the outer sleeve and the base pad is the correct thickness for the preload shim at each location. Carefully compare the gap to the available shims. The largest shim that can be placed into the gap and drawn through without binding is the correct shim for reassembly.

14. When each of the three shims has been selected, remove the clutch cover, spacers and gauges.

MANUAL TRANSMISSIONS
GM WARNER—76mm FOUR SPEED

15. Place the selected shims into their respective bores in the clutch cover, add the metal shield and then install the bearing cups using special Tools J-27936 on input shaft cup and J-23423-A on output shaft cup and J-26938 on the differential side bearing cup.
16. Place input shaft and output shaft together, on a bench. Install the two shift forks.
17. Grasp the shafts as an assembly and carefully lower them into the transaxle case.
18. Place interlock bracket onto guide pin J-28411. Be sure that the bracket engages the fingers on the shift forks. Place detent shift lever into the interlock.
19. Install the shifter shaft through the interlock bracket and the detent shift lever. Do not extend further at this time.
20. Install reverse shift fork onto the guide pin. Be sure the reverse shift fork engages the interlock bracket.
21. Install the reverse idler gear and shaft into position. Be sure the long end of the shaft points upward, and the large chamfered ends of the gear tooth are facing up. Install the spacer onto the shaft. The flat on the reverse idler shaft faces the input gear (shaft).
22. Fully install the shifter shaft through the reverse shift fork, until it pilots into the inhibitor spring spacer. Remove dummy shaft. With the shaft in neutral position, install the bolt and lock through the detent shift lever. Bend tab of lock over bolt head.
23. Install fork shaft through the synchronizer forks and into the bore in the case.
24. Carefully install the ring gear-and-differential case assembly.
25. Install magnet.
26. Apply a thin bead of anaerobic sealant to the clutch cover, then carefully install the cover onto the transaxle case, using the dowel pins to guide the cover into position. Tap clutch cover gently with a plastic hammer to insure that the parts are are seated.
27. Install the attaching bolts. Torque to correct specifications.
28. Torque idler shaft retaining bolt in case.
29. Shift through the gear ranges to test for freedom of movement of all internal parts.

TORQUE SPECIFICATIONS

Description	Torque (N·m)	Torque Ft. Lbs.
Input Shaft R.H. Bearing Retainer	9	7
Reverse Idler Shaft Lock Bolt	21	16
Reverse Inhibitor Fitting	35	26
Case-to-Cover Bolts	21	16
Ring Gear Bolts	73	54
Pinion Shaft Lock Bolt	9	7

GM 5-SPEED MANUAL TRANSAXLE

Transaxle Disassembly

1. Remove the clutch release bearing. Attach the transaxle to transaxle holding fixture J-33366 or its equal.
2. Remove the seven bolts from the rear cover and remove the cover.
3. Remove the control box assembly together with four bolts from the transaxle case.
4. Shift the transaxle into gear. Remove the fifth speed drive and driven gear retaining nuts from the input and output shaft. Shift the transaxle back into neutral, aligning the detents on the shift rails.
5. Remove the detent spring retaining bolts for 1st/2nd, 3rd/4th, reverse and 5th speeds. Remove the detent springs and detent balls. Remove the reverse detent spring retaining bolts, spring and detent.
6. Place 5th speed synchronizer in neutral and remove the roll pin at the 5th gear shift fork. Remove the 5th gear synchronizer hub, sleeve, roller bearing and gear. Remove the shift fork as an assembly from the output shaft. Remove the 5th speed gear from the input shaft.
7. Remove the torx screws from the bearing retainer. Remove the bearing retainer and shims from the input and output shafts.
8. Remove the bolt used to retain the reverse idler shaft at the transaxle case.
9. Remove the collar and thrust washer from the output shaft using tool J-22888 and J-22888-30 or their equal.
10. Remove the bolts retaining the transaxle case and separate the transaxle case from the clutch housing.
11. Remove the reverse idler gear, reverse idler shaft.
12. Lift the 5th gear shaft. With the detent aligned facing

MANUAL TRANSMISSIONS
GM—FIVE SPEED

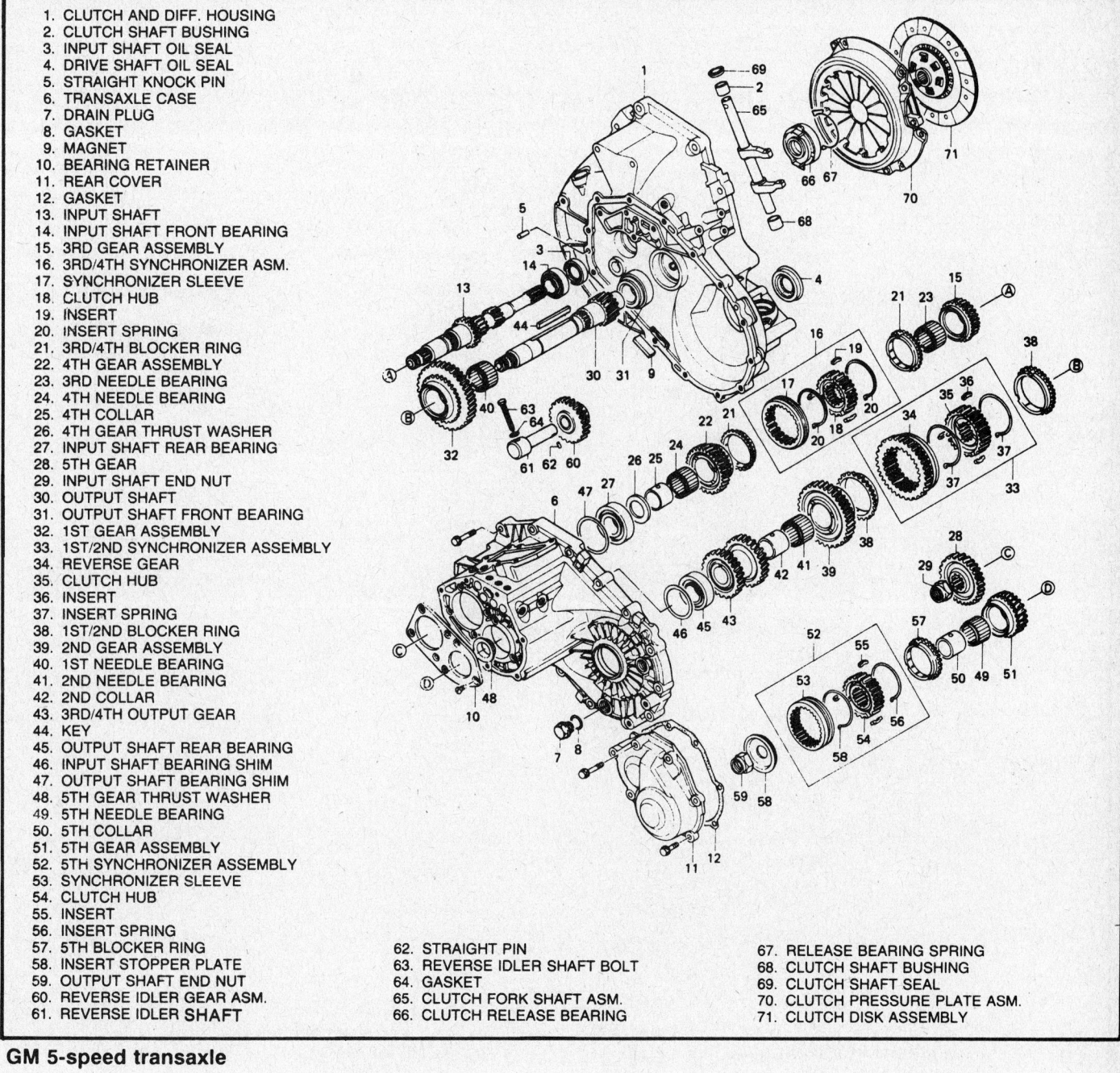

1. CLUTCH AND DIFF. HOUSING
2. CLUTCH SHAFT BUSHING
3. INPUT SHAFT OIL SEAL
4. DRIVE SHAFT OIL SEAL
5. STRAIGHT KNOCK PIN
6. TRANSAXLE CASE
7. DRAIN PLUG
8. GASKET
9. MAGNET
10. BEARING RETAINER
11. REAR COVER
12. GASKET
13. INPUT SHAFT
14. INPUT SHAFT FRONT BEARING
15. 3RD GEAR ASSEMBLY
16. 3RD/4TH SYNCHRONIZER ASM.
17. SYNCHRONIZER SLEEVE
18. CLUTCH HUB
19. INSERT
20. INSERT SPRING
21. 3RD/4TH BLOCKER RING
22. 4TH GEAR ASSEMBLY
23. 3RD NEEDLE BEARING
24. 4TH NEEDLE BEARING
25. 4TH COLLAR
26. 4TH GEAR THRUST WASHER
27. INPUT SHAFT REAR BEARING
28. 5TH GEAR
29. INPUT SHAFT END NUT
30. OUTPUT SHAFT
31. OUTPUT SHAFT FRONT BEARING
32. 1ST GEAR ASSEMBLY
33. 1ST/2ND SYNCHRONIZER ASSEMBLY
34. REVERSE GEAR
35. CLUTCH HUB
36. INSERT
37. INSERT SPRING
38. 1ST/2ND BLOCKER RING
39. 2ND GEAR ASSEMBLY
40. 1ST NEEDLE BEARING
41. 2ND NEEDLE BEARING
42. 2ND COLLAR
43. 3RD/4TH OUTPUT GEAR
44. KEY
45. OUTPUT SHAFT REAR BEARING
46. INPUT SHAFT BEARING SHIM
47. OUTPUT SHAFT BEARING SHIM
48. 5TH GEAR THRUST WASHER
49. 5TH NEEDLE BEARING
50. 5TH COLLAR
51. 5TH GEAR ASSEMBLY
52. 5TH SYNCHRONIZER ASSEMBLY
53. SYNCHRONIZER SLEEVE
54. CLUTCH HUB
55. INSERT
56. INSERT SPRING
57. 5TH BLOCKER RING
58. INSERT STOPPER PLATE
59. OUTPUT SHAFT END NUT
60. REVERSE IDLER GEAR ASM.
61. REVERSE IDLER SHAFT
62. STRAIGHT PIN
63. REVERSE IDLER SHAFT BOLT
64. GASKET
65. CLUTCH FORK SHAFT ASM.
66. CLUTCH RELEASE BEARING
67. RELEASE BEARING SPRING
68. CLUTCH SHAFT BUSHING
69. CLUTCH SHAFT SEAL
70. CLUTCH PRESSURE PLATE ASM.
71. CLUTCH DISK ASSEMBLY

GM 5-speed transaxle

the same way, remove the 5th and reverse shafts at the same time.

13. Use a punch and hammer to remove the roll pin from the 1-2 shift fork. Slide this shaft upward to clear the housing and remove the fork and shaft from the case.

14. Remove the cotter pin, then remove the pin and reverse shift lever.

15. Remove input and output shafts with 3-4 shift fork and shaft as an assembly.

16. Remove differential case assembly.

17. Remove the reverse shift bracket together with four bolts. Take out three interlock pinks.

18. Remove the rear bearing outer race from the transaxle case. Remove the input shaft race.

19. Remove the outer races from the input shaft front bearing, output shaft front and differential side bearings.

20. Remove the input shaft seal from the housing. Remove the clutch shaft seal only when replacement is required.

21. Drive the bushing toward the inside of the housing. Remove the fork assembly only when replacing the clutch fork assembly.

Input Shaft Disassembly

1. Remove the front bearing using tool J–22912–01 or its equal, in addition to a press.

2. Pull out the rear bearing 4th gear, 3rd/4th synchronizer assembly and 3rd gear as an assembly.

32-43

SECTION 32
MANUAL TRANSMISSIONS
GM – FIVE SPEED

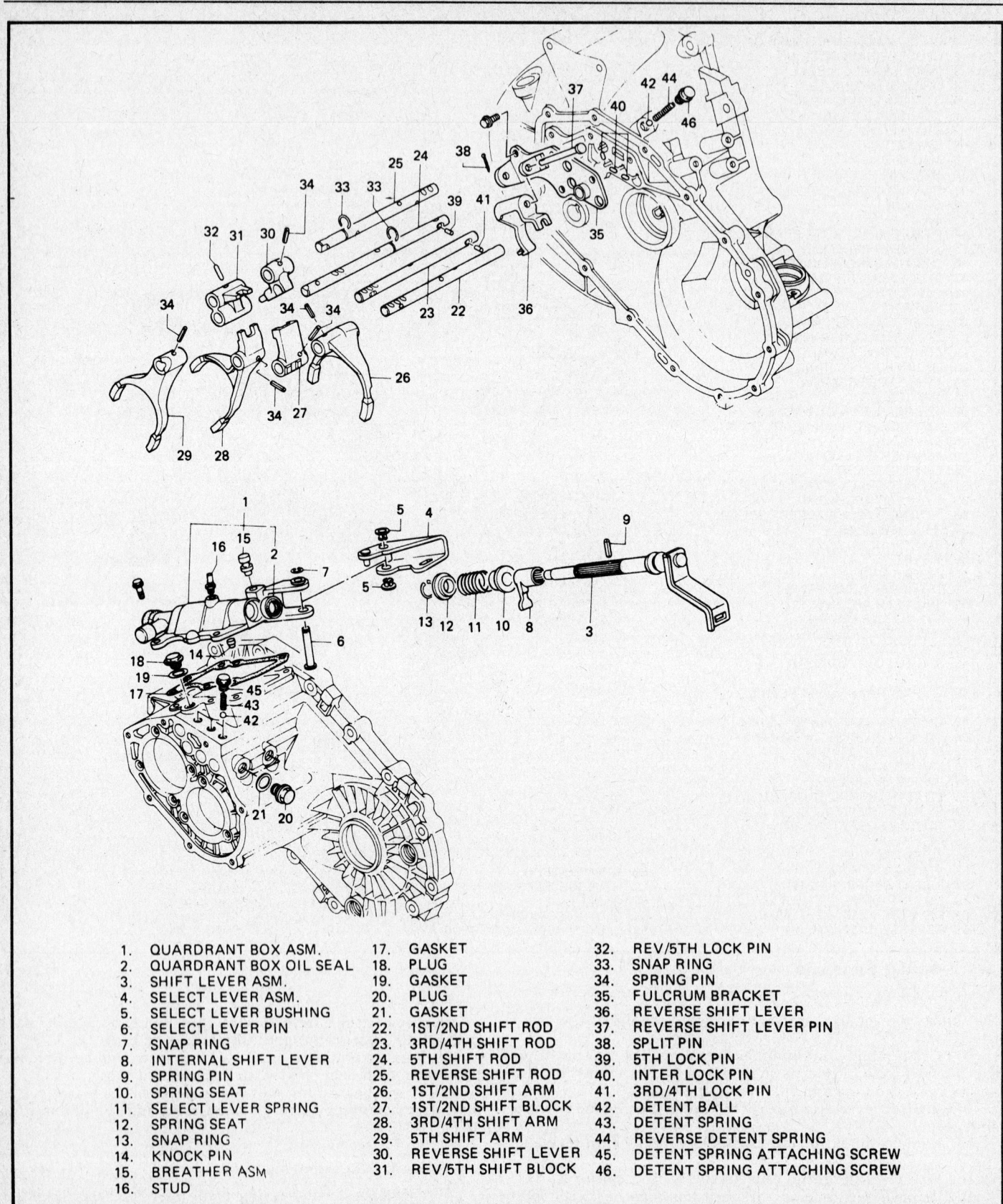

1. QUARDRANT BOX ASM.
2. QUARDRANT BOX OIL SEAL
3. SHIFT LEVER ASM.
4. SELECT LEVER ASM.
5. SELECT LEVER BUSHING
6. SELECT LEVER PIN
7. SNAP RING
8. INTERNAL SHIFT LEVER
9. SPRING PIN
10. SPRING SEAT
11. SELECT LEVER SPRING
12. SPRING SEAT
13. SNAP RING
14. KNOCK PIN
15. BREATHER ASM
16. STUD
17. GASKET
18. PLUG
19. GASKET
20. PLUG
21. GASKET
22. 1ST/2ND SHIFT ROD
23. 3RD/4TH SHIFT ROD
24. 5TH SHIFT ROD
25. REVERSE SHIFT ROD
26. 1ST/2ND SHIFT ARM
27. 1ST/2ND SHIFT BLOCK
28. 3RD/4TH SHIFT ARM
29. 5TH SHIFT ARM
30. REVERSE SHIFT LEVER
31. REV/5TH SHIFT BLOCK
32. REV/5TH LOCK PIN
33. SNAP RING
34. SPRING PIN
35. FULCRUM BRACKET
36. REVERSE SHIFT LEVER
37. REVERSE SHIFT LEVER PIN
38. SPLIT PIN
39. 5TH LOCK PIN
40. INTER LOCK PIN
41. 3RD/4TH LOCK PIN
42. DETENT BALL
43. DETENT SPRING
44. REVERSE DETENT SPRING
45. DETENT SPRING ATTACHING SCREW
46. DETENT SPRING ATTACHING SCREW

5-speed transaxle-exploded view

MANUAL TRANSMISSIONS
GM—FIVE SPEED

NOTE: This procedure requires a press and special tool J–22912–01 or its equal.

3. Remove other parts from the input shaft.

Output Shaft Disassembly

1. Remove the front bearing using tool J–22227–A or its equal along with a press.
2. Remove the rear bearing and 3rd/4th gear as an assembly using J–22912–01 and a press.
3. Remove the key, 2nd gear, needle bearing and blocker ring.
4. Remove the collar, reverse gear assembly and 1st gear as an assembly, using a press.

Transaxle Assembly

Before reassembly, attach the clutch housing to the transaxle holding fixture if removed.

1. Install input shaft seal.
2. Install the front outer bearing races for the input shaft, output shaft and differential into the clutch housing. Press the input, output and differential races into the housing.
3. Apply grease to three interlock pins, and install them on the clutch housing.
4. Install the reverse shift bracket on the clutch housing. Use 3rd/4th shift rod to align bracket to housing. Install retaining bolts and torque to specification. Make sure rod operates smoothly after installation.
5. Install the differential assembly first, then install the input and output shaft with the 3rd/4th shift fork and shaft together as an assembly into the clutch housing.

NOTE: Make sure interlock pin is in the 3rd/4th shifter shaft before installing.

6. The 3rd/4th shift shaft is installed into the raised collar of reverse shift lever bracket.
7. Install the 1-2 shift fork onto the synchronizer sleeve and insert the shifter shaft into the reverse shift lever bracket. Align hole in fork with the shaft and install roll pin.
8. Install reverse lever on shift bracket.
9. Install reverse and 5th gear shifter shaft and at the same time, engage reverse shaft with reverse shift lever. Make sure interlock pin is in the 5th gear shifter shaft before installing.
10. Install the reverse idler shaft together with the gear into the clutch housing. Make sure reverse lever is engaged in collar of gear.
11. Measure and determine shim size using J–33373 or its equal.
    a. Position the outer bearing races on the input, output and differential bearings. Position the shim selection gauges on the bearing races. The 3 gauges are identified: Input, Output and Differential.
    b. Place seven spacers provided with J–33373 evenly around the perimeter of the clutch housing.
    c. Install bearing and shim retainer on transaxle case. Torque screws to 11–16 ft. lbs. (15–22 Nm).
    d. Carefully position the transaxle case over the gauges and on the spacers. Install the seven bolts provided with the tool kit and tighten bolts alternately until case is seated on spacers. Torque bolts to 10 ft. lbs. (15 Nm).
    e. Rotate each gauge to seat the bearings. Rotate the differential case through three revolutions in each direction.
    f. With the three gauges compressed, measure the gap between the outer sleeve and the base pad using available shim sizes. Use the largest shim that can be placed into the gap and drawn through without binding. This will be the correct shim for the bearing being measured.
    g. When each of the three shims have been selected, remove the transaxle case, seven spacers and three gauges.
12. Position the shim selected for the input, output and differential into the bearing race bores in the transaxle case.
13. Install the rear input shaft bearing race using J–24256–A with J–8092 or its equal and a press. Press bearing until seated in its bore.
14. Install the rear output shaft bearing race using J–33370 with J–8092 and a press. Press bearing until seated in its bore.
15. Install the rear differential case bearing race using J–8611–01 with J–8092 or its equal and a press. Press bearing until seated in its bore.
16. Apply a 1/8 in. bead of Loctite® #514 or equivalent to the mating surfaces of the clutch housing and transaxle case.
17. Be sure magnet is installed in transaxle case.
18. Install the transaxle case on the clutch housing. Install the reverse idle shaft bolt into the transaxle case. Torque the bolt to 22–33 ft. lbs. (30–45 Nm).
19. Install 14 case bolts. Torque bolts to 22–33 ft. lbs. (30–45 Nm) in a diagonal sequence.
20. Install drive axle seals.
21. Install the thrust washer and collar to the output shaft.
22. Install the 5th gear to the input shaft. Install the needle bearing, 5th gear, blocker ring, hub/sleeve assembly with shift fork in its groove and back plate on the output shaft. Align shift fork on shifter shaft and install roll pin.
23. Install the detent balls and detent springs for the reverse, 1st/2nd, 3rd/4th and 5th speeds. Install retaining bolts and torque to 15–21 ft. lbs. (21–29 Nm).
24. Apply Loctite® 262 or equivalent to the threads of the input and output shafts. Install new retaining nuts and torque to 87–101 ft. lbs. (118–137 Nm). Stake nuts after reaching final torque.
25. Install the gasket and control box assembly on the transaxle case, and torque four bolts to 11–16 ft. lbs. (15–22 Nm). Make sure transaxle shifts properly before installing rear cover.
26. Install the gasket and rear cover with seven bolts, and torque the bolts to 11–16 ft. lbs. (15–22 Nm).
27. Install the clutch fork assembly if it has been removed. Install the bushing into the upper hole using J–28412 or its equal. Install the oil seal. Before installing the bushing, apply grease to both the interior and exterior.
28. Install the clutch release bearing.

GM WARNER 83MM—4-SPEED TRANSMISSION WITH ELECTRONIC HYDRAULIC OD

1984 AND LATER CORVETTE

Transmission Disassembly

1. Thoroughly clean the exterior of the transmission assemblies.
2. Remove the 7 bolts attaching the overdrive unit to the reverse housing and then separate the two transmission units.
3. Remove the drain plug from the lower right side of the case and drain the lubricant from the transmission.
4. Shift the transmission into second gear. Remove the shift

SECTION 32 MANUAL TRANSMISSIONS
GM WARNER—83mm FOUR SPEED W/OD

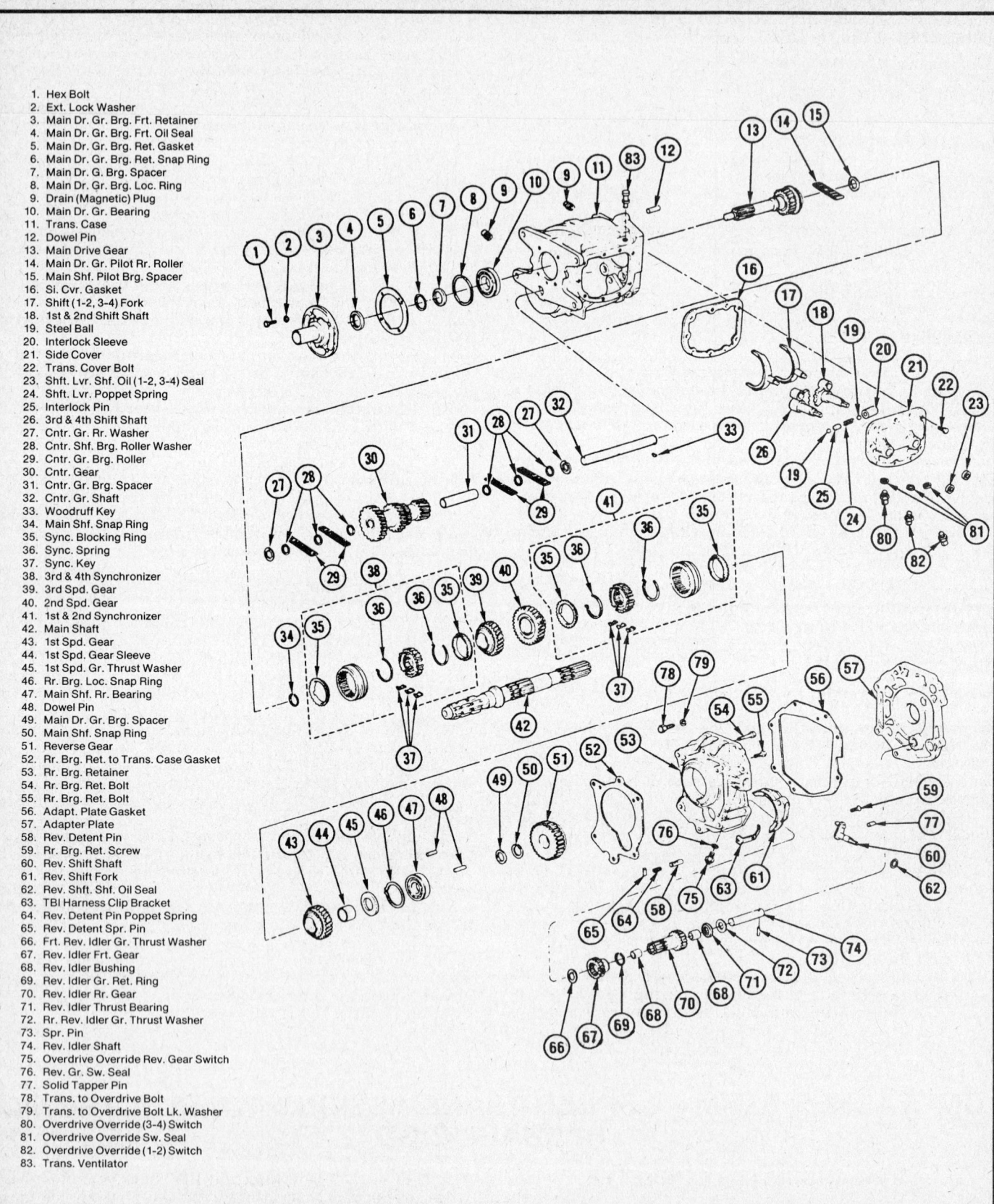

1. Hex Bolt
2. Ext. Lock Washer
3. Main Dr. Gr. Brg. Frt. Retainer
4. Main Dr. Gr. Brg. Frt. Oil Seal
5. Main Dr. Gr. Brg. Ret. Gasket
6. Main Dr. Gr. Brg. Ret. Snap Ring
7. Main Dr. G. Brg. Spacer
8. Main Dr. Gr. Brg. Loc. Ring
9. Drain (Magnetic) Plug
10. Main Dr. Gr. Bearing
11. Trans. Case
12. Dowel Pin
13. Main Drive Gear
14. Main Dr. Gr. Pilot Rr. Roller
15. Main Shf. Pilot Brg. Spacer
16. Si. Cvr. Gasket
17. Shift (1-2, 3-4) Fork
18. 1st & 2nd Shift Shaft
19. Steel Ball
20. Interlock Sleeve
21. Side Cover
22. Trans. Cover Bolt
23. Shft. Lvr. Shf. Oil (1-2, 3-4) Seal
24. Shft. Lvr. Poppet Spring
25. Interlock Pin
26. 3rd & 4th Shift Shaft
27. Cntr. Gr. Rr. Washer
28. Cntr. Shf. Brg. Roller Washer
29. Cntr. Gr. Brg. Roller
30. Cntr. Gear
31. Cntr. Gr. Brg. Spacer
32. Cntr. Gr. Shaft
33. Woodruff Key
34. Main Shf. Snap Ring
35. Sync. Blocking Ring
36. Sync. Spring
37. Sync. Key
38. 3rd & 4th Synchronizer
39. 3rd Spd. Gear
40. 2nd Spd. Gear
41. 1st & 2nd Synchronizer
42. Main Shaft
43. 1st Spd. Gear
44. 1st Spd. Gear Sleeve
45. 1st Spd. Gr. Thrust Washer
46. Rr. Brg. Loc. Snap Ring
47. Main Shf. Rr. Bearing
48. Dowel Pin
49. Main Dr. Gr. Brg. Spacer
50. Main Shf. Snap Ring
51. Reverse Gear
52. Rr. Brg. Ret. to Trans. Case Gasket
53. Rr. Brg. Retainer
54. Rr. Brg. Ret. Bolt
55. Rr. Brg. Ret. Bolt
56. Adapt. Plate Gasket
57. Adapter Plate
58. Rev. Detent Pin
59. Rr. Brg. Ret. Screw
60. Rev. Shift Shaft
61. Rev. Shift Fork
62. Rev. Shft. Shf. Oil Seal
63. TBI Harness Clip Bracket
64. Rev. Detent Pin Poppet Spring
65. Rev. Detent Spr. Pin
66. Frt. Rev. Idler Gr. Thrust Washer
67. Rev. Idler Frt. Gear
68. Rev. Idler Bushing
69. Rev. Idler Gr. Ret. Ring
70. Rev. Idler Rr. Gear
71. Rev. Idler Thrust Bearing
72. Rr. Rev. Idler Gr. Thrust Washer
73. Spr. Pin
74. Rev. Idler Shaft
75. Overdrive Override Rev. Gear Switch
76. Rev. Gr. Sw. Seal
77. Solid Tapper Pin
78. Trans. to Overdrive Bolt
79. Trans. to Overdrive Bolt Lk. Washer
80. Overdrive Override (3-4) Switch
81. Overdrive Override Sw. Seal
82. Overdrive Override (1-2) Switch
83. Trans. Ventilator

Exploded view of the 83mm 4-speed transmission

MANUAL TRANSMISSIONS
GM WARNER—83mm FOUR SPEED W/OD
SECTION 32

cover attaching bolts, cover, gasket and both shift forks from the transmission.

5. Remove the backup switch from the reverse housing.
6. Rotate the reverse shifter shaft and remove the shift fork and gear from the mainshaft.
7. Remove the lock pin from the reverse shift lever boss and pull the shaft from the housing.
8. Remove the drive gear bearing retainer bolts, retainer and gasket from the front of the transmission.
9. Remove front bearing snap ring, selective fit snap ring and spacer washer.
10. Using Tool J-6654-01 and J-8433-1, pull the drive gear bearing from the transmission.
11. Remove the (6) bolts attaching the reverse housing to the case. Using a small drift and a hammer, tap the locating pin for the reverse housing into the case.
12. Rotate the reverse housing on the mainshaft until the hole for the reverse idler gear shaft in the housing lines up with the countergear shaft.
13. Using Tool J-24658 or a dummy shaft, drive the countergear shaft rearward out of the gear and through the reverse housing. The countergear will drop to the bottom of the case allowing clearance for the removal of the mainshaft.
14. Remove the mainshaft with the revers housing and drive gear from the transmission case.
15. Remove the front reverse idler gear and thrust washer from the case.
16. Remove the countergear and two tanged thrust washers from the transmission case. Check the bottom of the transmission case for loose pilot bearings. Remove the locating pin for the reverse housing and any other loose components.

Mainshaft Disassembly

1. Using snap ring pliers, remove 3-4 synchronizer assembly retaining ring at front of mainshaft. Slide washer, synchronizer assembly, synchronizer ring 3rd speed gear from mainshaft.
2. Spread rear bearing retainer snap ring and slide retainer from mainshaft.
3. Remove rear bearing-to-mainshaft snap ring.
4. Support mainshaft under 2nd gear and press mainshaft from rear bearing, 1st gear and sleeve, 1-2 synchronizer assembly, and the second gear.

Countergear Disassembly

1. Remove Tool J-24658 from the countergear.
2. Tip the countergear on end and let the (6) spacers, (112) rollers and roller sleeve slide out from the gear.

CLEANING AND INSPECTION

TRANSMISSION CASE

1. Wash the transmission thoroughly inside and outside with cleaning solvent, then inspect the case for cracks.
2. Check the front and rear faces for burrs, and if present, dress them off with a fine mill file.

ROLLER BEARINGS AND SPACERS

All main drive gear and countergear bearing rollers should be inspected closely and replaced if they show wear. Inspect countershaft and reverse idler shaft at the same time. Replace if necessary. Replace all worn spacers.

GEARS

1. Inspect all gears for excessive wear, chips or cracks and replace any that are worn or damaged.
2. Inspect reverse gear bushing and if worn or damaged, replace the entire gear (reverse gear bushing is not serviced separately).
3. Check both synchronizer sleeves to see that they slide freely on their hubs.

FRONT AND REAR BEARINGS

1. Wash the front and rear ball bearings thoroughly in a cleaning solvent.
2. Blow out bearing with compressed air.

NOTE: Do not allow the bearing to spin. Turn them slowly by hand. Spinning bearings may damage the race and balls.

SYNCHRONIZER KEYS AND SPRINGS
Replacement

The synchronizer hubs and sliding sleeves are a selected assembly and should be kept together as originally assembled, but the keys and two springs may be replaced if worn or broken.

1. If relation of hub and sleeve are not already marked, mark for assembly purposes.
2. Push the hub from the sliding sleeve, the keys will fall free and the springs may be easily removed.
3. Place the two springs in position (one on each side of hub) so all three keys are engaged by both spring. Place the keys in position and while holding them in place, slide the sleeve onto the hub, aligning the marks made before disassembly.

DRIVE GEAR BEARING RETAINER OIL SEAL
Replacement

1. Pry out old seal.
2. Using a new seal, install new seal into retainer using Tool J-23096 until it bottoms in bore. Lubricate I.D. of seal with transmission lubricant.

REVERSE SHIFTER SHAFT AND/OR SEAL
Replacement

1. With the reverse housing removed from transmission, the reverse shifter shaft lock pin will already be removed.
2. Carefully drive shifter shaft into the reverse housing allowing ball detent to drop into case. Remove shaft and ball detent spring. Remove O-ring seal from shaft.
3. Place ball detent spring into detent spring hole and start reverse shifter shaft into hole in boss.
4. Place detent ball on spring and while holding ball down, push the shifter shaft into place and turn until the ball drops into place in detent on the shaft detent plate.
5. Install O-ring seal on shaft.
6. Install shift fork. Do not drive the shifter shaft lock pin into place until the reverse housing has been installed on the transmission case.

REVERSE IDLER SHAFT
Replacement

1. Place a small punch into hole in front cover of the overdrive unit and drive the pin into the shaft until the shaft can be pulled from front cover.
2. Insert new idler shaft into cover until hole in shaft lines up with hole in boss.
3. Insert roll pin into boss opening and drive the pin into the cover until the shaft is securely locked in place.

TRANSMISSION SIDE COVER

Although service of the side cover is covered here, the transmission does not have to be removed to perform these opera-

SECTION 32
MANUAL TRANSMISSIONS
GM WARNER—83mm FOUR SPEED W/OD

tions. To remove the side cover in-the-vehicle, simply drain the transmission, disconnect electrical leads at the side cover switches, disconnect the 1st/2nd and 3rd/4th linkage and remove the attaching bolts.

1. Remove the outer shifter lever nuts and lockwasher and pull levers from shafts.
2. Carefully push the shifter shafts into cover, allowing the detent balls to fall free, then remove both shifter shafts.
3. Remove interlock sleeve, interlock pin and poppet spring.
4. Replace necessary parts and assembly by reversing Steps 1–3.

Countergear Assembly

1. Install roller spacer in countergear (if removed).
2. Insert a dummy shaft or loading Tool J–24658 into countergear.
3. Using heavy grease to retain rollers, install spacer, 28 rollers, spacer, 28 rollers, and spacer in either end of countergear. Repeat in other end of countergear.

CHECKING COUNTERGEAR END PLAY

1. Rest the transmission case on its side with the side cover opening toward the assembler. Put countergear tanged thrust washers in place, retaining them with heavy grease, making sure the tangs are resting in the notches of the case.
2. Set countergear in place in bottom of transmission case, making sure that tanged thrust washers are not knocked out of place.
3. Position the transmission case resting on its front face.
4. Lubricate and insert countergear (pushing loading Tool J–24658 out front of case) until woodruff key slot is in its relative installed position (do not install key).
5. Attach a dial indicator and check end play of the countergear. If end play is greater than 0.025 in., a new thrust washers must be installed.

Mainshaft Assembly

1. From rear of mainshaft, assemble the 2nd speed gear (with hub of gear toward rear of shaft).
2. Install 1st-2nd synchronizer assembly (sliding synchronizer sleeve taper toward rear, hub to front) on the mainshaft together with a synchronizer ring on both sides of the synchronizer assemblies.
3. Position the 1st gear sleeve on the shaft and press the sleeve onto the mainshaft until the 2nd gear, synchronizer assembly and sleeve bottom against the shoulder of the mainshaft.
4. Install 1st speed gear (with hub toward front) and supporting inner race, press the rear bearing onto the mainshaft with the snap ring groove toward front of the transmission.
5. Install spacer and new correct selective fit (thickest that will assemble) snap ring in mainshaft behind rear bearing.
6. Install the 3rd speed gear (hub to front of transmission) and the 3rd speed gear synchronizing ring (notches to front of transmission).
7. Install the 3rd and 4th speed gear synchronizer assembly (hub and sliding sleeve) with taper toward the front making sure that the keys in hub correspond to the notches in the 3rd speed gear synchronizing ring.
8. Install new selective fit snap ring (thickest that will install) in the groove in mainshaft in front of the 3rd and 4th speed synchronizer assembly.
9. Install the rear bearing retainer (reverse housing) over end of mainshaft. Spread the snap ring to drop around the rear bearing. Release snap ring when it aligns with groove in rear bearing.

Transmission Assembly

1. Place the transmission case on its side with the shift cover opening toward the assembler. Position the countergear tanged washers in place, using a heavy grease to retain them.

NOTE: Be sure the tangs are in the notches of the thrust face.

2. Position the countergear in the bottom of the case.
3. Install front reverse idler gear (teeth forward) and thrust washer in case. Use a heavy grease to hold thrust washer in position.
4. Using a heavy grease, install sixteen (16) roller bearings and washer into main drive gear. Mate main drive gear with mainshaft assembly. Position 3rd/4th synchronizer sliding sleeve forward. This will provide clearance for installation as well as hold the assembly together.
5. Position a new reverse housing to case gasket on the rear of the case.
6. Install the mainshaft and drive gear assembly into the case.
7. Place bearing snap ring on front main bearing. Position front main bearing to case opening and with a hollow shaft, or Tool J–5590, tap bearing into case. Install spacer washer and selective fit snap ring to secure main drive bearing.
8. Raise the countergear in the case, aligning the holes in the case with the center of the gear. With the thrust washers in place, slide the countershaft through the rear of the case. Install the woodruff key and tap the shaft into the case, until flush with the rear face of the transmission case.
9. Align the reverse housing and gasket to the transmission case. Install the locating pin for the reverse housing. Tap the pin in until flush with housing.
10. Install the (6) bolts attaching the reverse housing to the case. Torque bolts to specifications.
11. Install the reverse shift shaft and O-ring into the housing. Install retaining pin.
12. Install the reverse gear and shift fork. Slide the gear and fork forward on the mainshaft until shift fork and shifter shaft can be indexed into position.
13. Position the drive gear bearing retainer and gasket to the front of the case. Apply sealer to the bolts. Install bolts and torque to specifications.
14. Install the rear reverse idler gear. Align the splines on the rear gear with the front gear and slide together.
15. Assemble the overdrive unit to the reverse housing. Guide the idler shaft on the O/D unit into the idler gears and align the splines on the mainshaft with the splines in the input sun gear. Slide the units together and install the retaining bolts. Torque the bolts to specifications.
16. Slide the 1-2 synchronizer forward into second gear. Install the shift forks into the grooves of the synchronizers. Place the side cover with a gasket on the transmission. Guide the shift forks into the cover and install the retaining bolts. Torque the bolts to specifications.
17. Check operation of transmission by manually shifting the transmission into all gears.

OVERDRIVE UNIT

Disassembly

Cleanliness is an important factor in the overhaul of the transmission. Before attempting any disassembly operation, the exterior of the transmission should be thoroughly cleaned to prevent the possibility of dirt entering the transmission internal mechanism. During inspection and reassembly, all parts should be thoroughly cleaned with cleaning fluid and then air dried. Wiping cloths or rags should not be used to dry parts. Do not use solvents on neoprene seals, composition-faced clutch plates or thrust washers. All oil passages should be blown out and checked to make sure that they are not obstructed. Small passages should be checked with tag wire. All parts should be inspected to determine which parts are to be replaced.

1. Remove the fill plug and drain oil from the case.

MANUAL TRANSMISSIONS
GM WARNER – 83mm FOUR SPEED W/OD
SECTION 32

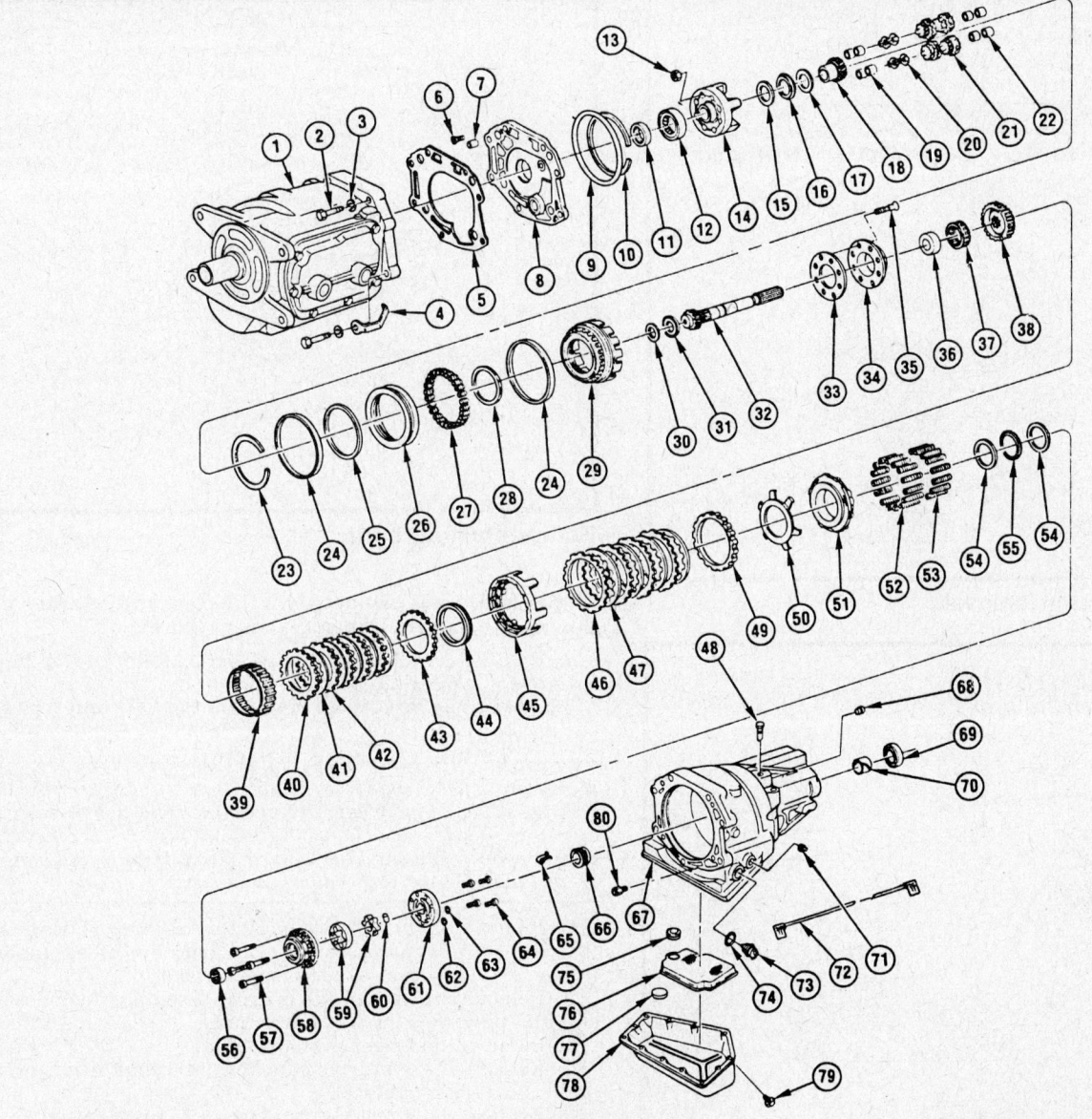

1. Transmission (Less Overdrive Unit)
2. Trans. to Overdrive Bolt
3. Trans. to Overdrive Bolt Lk. Washer
4. TBI Harness Clip Bracket
5. Adapter Plate Gasket
6. Adapter Plate Screw
7. Dowel Pin
8. Adapter Plate
9. Adapter Plt. "O" Ring
10. Accum. Piston Ret. Ring
11. Input Sun Gr. Oil Seal
12. Annular Bearing
13. Carrier Brg. Lk. Nut
14. Planetary Gear Carrier
15. Input Sun Gr. Thrust Washer
16. Input Sun Gr. Thrust Bearing
17. Input Sun Gr. Thrust Washer
18. Input Sun Gear
19. Brg. Cup
20. Planetary Gr. Thrust Washer
21. Planetary Gear
22. Brg. Cup
23. Accum. Piston Ret. Ring
24. Accum. Piston Seal
25. Accum. Piston Seal
26. Accum. Cushion Piston
27. Accum. Piston Spring
28. Accum. Piston Seal
29. Accum. Piston
30. Otpt. Shf. Thrust Washer
31. Otpt. Shf. Thrust Bearing
32. Otpt. Shaft
33. Planetary Gear Thrust Plate
34. Clu. Drum Plate
35. Clu. Drum Bolt
36. Inner Race
37. Dir. Clu. Sprag
38. Dir. Clu. Hub
39. Dir. Clu. Drum
40. Dir. Clu. Inr. Driven Plate
41. Dir. Clu. Plate
42. Dir. Clu. Driven Plate
43. Dir. Clu. Press Plate
44. Dir. Clu. Bearing
45. Dir. Clu. Clu. Piston
46. Overdrive Clu. Driven Plate
47. Overdrive Clu. Plate
48. Overdrive Vent Tube
49. Overdrive Clu. Press Plate
50. Dir. Clu. Thrust Washer
51. Overdrive Dir. Clu. Piston
52. Overdrive Dir. Clu. Otr. Spring
53. Overdrive Dir. Clu. Inr. Spring
54. Overdrive Dir. Clu. Hub Thrust Washer
55. Overdrive Dir. Clu. Hub Thrust Bearing
56. Pump Brg. Cup
57. Overdrive Pump & Otpt. Shf. Screw
58. W/Brg., Overdrive Pump (Gerotor) Housing
59. Overdrive Oil (Gerotor) Pump
60. Oil Pump Drive Pin
61. Pump (Gerotor) Spool
62. Overdrive Oil Pump "O" Ring
63. Overdrive Oil Pump "O" Ring
64. Overdrive Pump Spool (Gerotor) Screw
65. Speedo Drive Gr. Clip
66. Speedo Drive Gear
67. Overdrive Case
68. Headless Slotted Plug
69. Overdrive Otpt. Shf. Oil Seal
70. Case Bushing
71. Overdrive Vlv. Body Press Sw. Wire
72. Sq. Hd. Filler Plug
73. Overdrive Sol. Elec. Connector
74. Overdrive Sol. Elec. Conn. "O" Ring
75. Overdrive Oil Screen Tube Grommet
76. Overdrive Oil Screen
77. Overdrive Oil Pan Magnet
78. Overdrive Oil Pan
79. Overdrive Oil Pan Bolt
80. Oil Cooler Fitting

Exploded view of the 83mm 4-speed transmission overdrive unit (Doug Nash)

SECTION 32
MANUAL TRANSMISSIONS
GM WARNER – 83mm FOUR SPEED W/OD

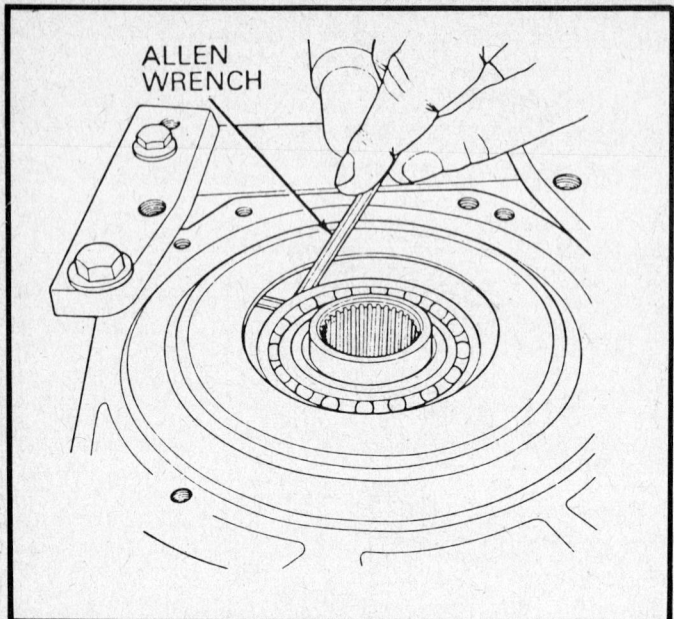

Piston/Accumulator removal

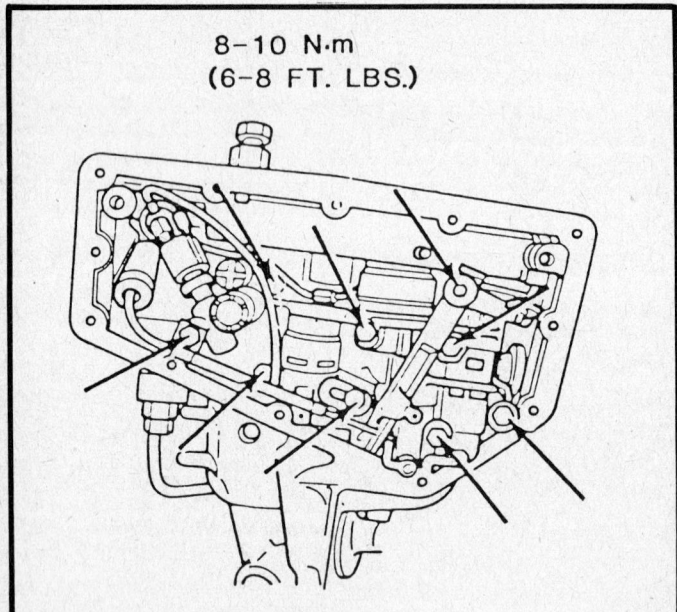

Valve body attachments

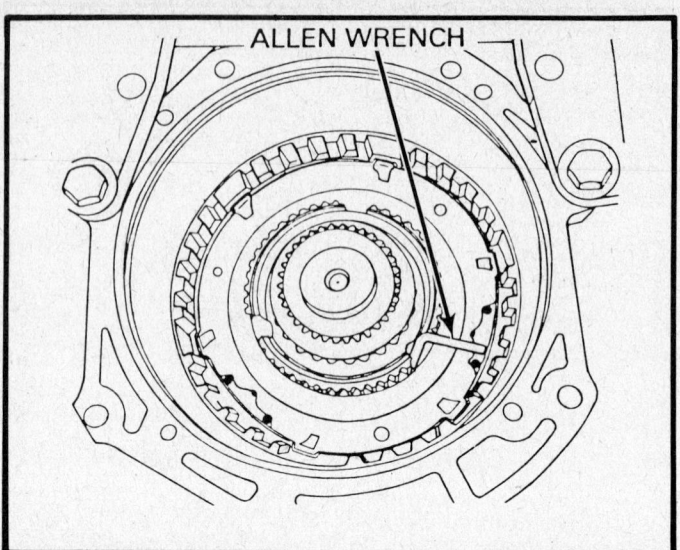

Pump retaining bolts

NOTE: **Do not pry between the case and adapter plate, damage to the sealing surfaces could occur.**

7. Bolt the overdrive unit to J-34162. Mount the holding fixture to the base plate J-3389-20.
8. Remove the large snap ring from the O/D unit forward of the accumulator piston.

CAUTION

If pressure is felt at snap ring, do not remove. Check to insure the (3) pressure plate retaining bolts are installed. If the bolts are installed, tighten each bolt one additional turn until pressure is relieved. The pressure plate is under a 1200 lb. spring load. If the (3) retaining bolts are not installed, personal injury could occur.

---

9. Remove the pistion/accumulator assembly. Using an Allen wrench, pry the assembly up evenly by lifting under the flange. Do not pry at or near seal surface.
10. Remove the carrier and bearing assembly (includes input sun and pinion gears) as an assembly.
11. Remove the finger pressure plate.
12. Remove the overdrive clutches, ((4) composition, (4) steel and (1) clutch stop plate).
13. Remove the direct clutch plates, ((5) composition (5) steel and (1) steel bearing plate).

Measure each selective clutch plate in the direct clutch pack and record the readings. The selective clutch plates are used to control the clutch pack clearance. When replacing the clutch plates, replace each selective clutch plate with one of the same size.

Inspect the overdrive and direct clutch plates as follows:
  a. Compositioned plate.
Dry plates and inspect for pitting, flaking, wear, glazing, cracking, charring and chips or metal particles imbedded in lining. If a compositioned plate shows any of the above conditions, replacement is required.
  b. Steel Plates.
Wipe plates dry and check for discoloration. If the surface is smooth and even color smear is indicated, the plate should be reused. If severe heat spot discoloration or surface scuffing is indicated, the plate must be replaced.

14. Remove thrust washer and bearing from the output sun gear. Thrust washer may stick to the input sun gear hub.
15. Remove (4) Allen head pump housing retaining bolts by rotating the hub to gain access to the bolts.
16. Remove the output shaft assembly (Inc. output sun

2. Remove the retaining bolt and bracket for the speedometer sensor and drive gear. Remove the sensor and gear.
3. Remove (3) ⅛ in. pipe plugs from the rear of the unit.
4. Install the (3) pressure plate retaining bolts (J-34681) until flush with the case. Turn bolts (2) additional turns, by rotating each bolt one turn at a time.

NOTE: **This sequence must be followed in order to prevent the pressure plate from cocking and causing damage to the unit.**

5. Remove the (4) Allen head bolts retaining the adapter plate to the case.
6. Remove the adapter plate, using a hammer (plastic) and screwdriver. Tap adapter plate to separate from case.

MANUAL TRANSMISSIONS
GM WARNER—83mm FOUR SPEED W/OD
SECTION 32

gear, sprag clutch, clutch hub, gerotor pump and speedometer drive gear).

17. Remove the pressure plate and springs by positioning J–21420–2 on the pressure plate with the bolt from J–23327 through the center of the plate. Next position J–23327 on the rear of the case and install the retaining nut. Remove the (3) retaining bolts, J–34681, from the rear of the case. Loosen the retaining nut on J–23327 bolt to relieve the spring pressure.

18. Remove the cooler valve assembly by loosening the (2) nuts on the tube and then remove the (2) bolts holding the valve to the case.

19. Remove the (12) oil pan retaining bolts and then pry the pan from the case.

20. Remove the oil filter and tube from the valve body.

21. Disconnect the T.V. cable from the lever. Remove the cable retaining bolt and remove the cable assembly.

22. Remove the T.V. lever retaining bolt and then lever from the valve body.

23. Remove the remaining valve bolts and then remove the valve body with the spacer plate.

NOTE: There are (2) check balls, one on each side of spacer plate. One ball is located in the case and the other is pring loaded in the valve body.

Valve Body Disassembly

1. Using J–34529 relieves the pressure on the shift valve. Remove the pin, spring and valve.
2. Using J–34529 relieves the pressure on pressure relief valve. Remove the pin, spring and valve.
3. Using J–34529 relieves the pressure on the accumulator valve. Remove the pin, spring, valve, plug, sleeve and plunger.
4. Disconnect the solenoid electrical lead at the pressure switch. Remove the solenoid attaching bolts. Remove the solenoid and check ball.
5. Disconnect the other electrical lead at the pressure switch. Remove the switch from the valve body.
6. To assembly, reverse the removal procedures. Coat all the components with clean Dextron II automatic transmission fluid before assembling.

Output Shaft Disassembly

1. Remove the speedometer gear retaining clip and gear.
2. Remove the (4) Allen head bolts retaining the pump cover to the pump housing. Remove the cover.

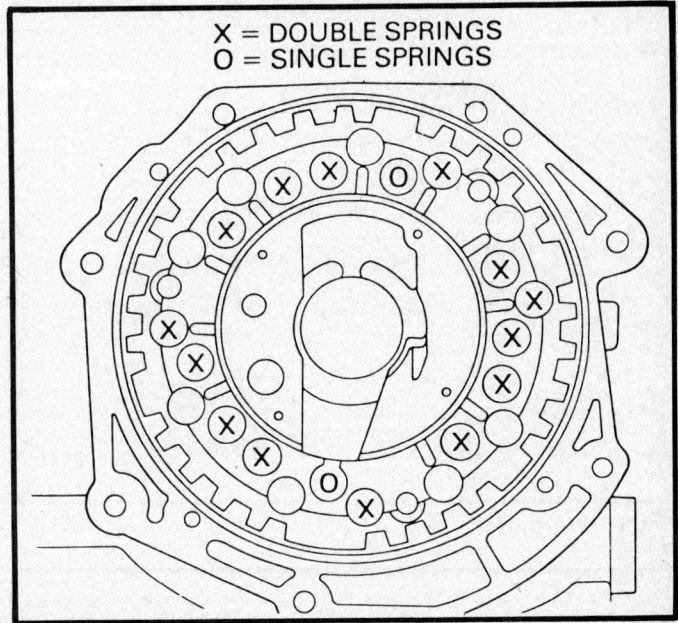

Pressure plate spring installation

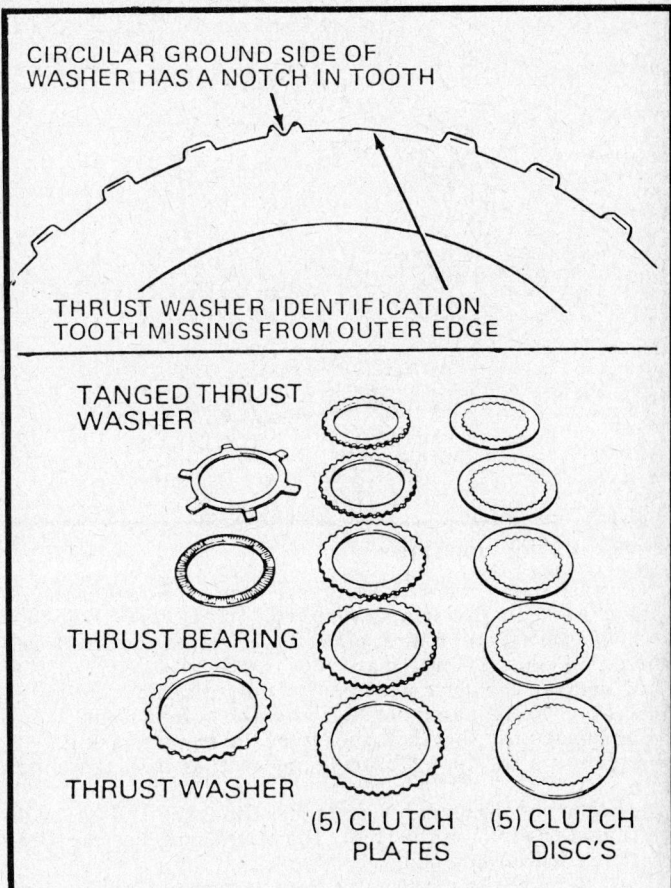

Direct clutch pack

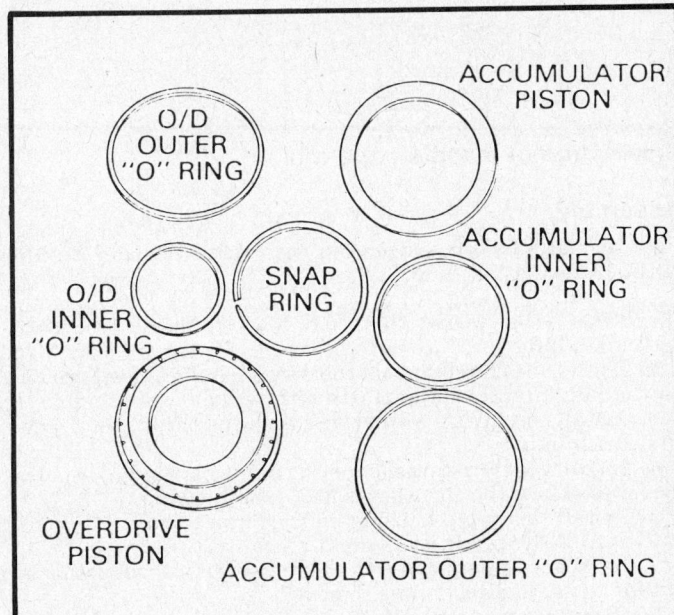

Piston/Accumulator assembly

32–51

SECTION 32 — MANUAL TRANSMISSIONS
GM WARNER — 83mm FOUR SPEED W/OD

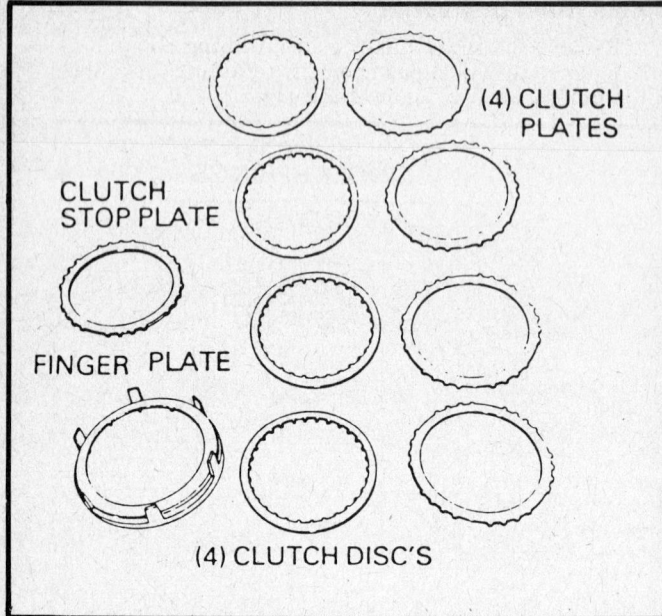

Overdrive clutch pack

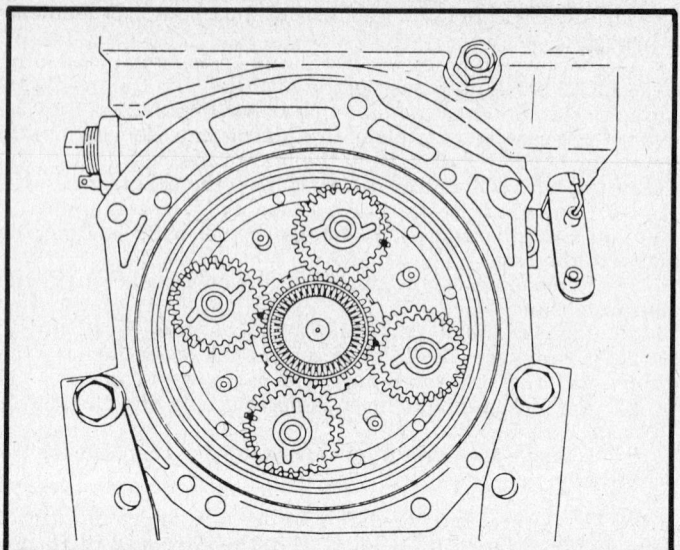

Indexing pinion gears

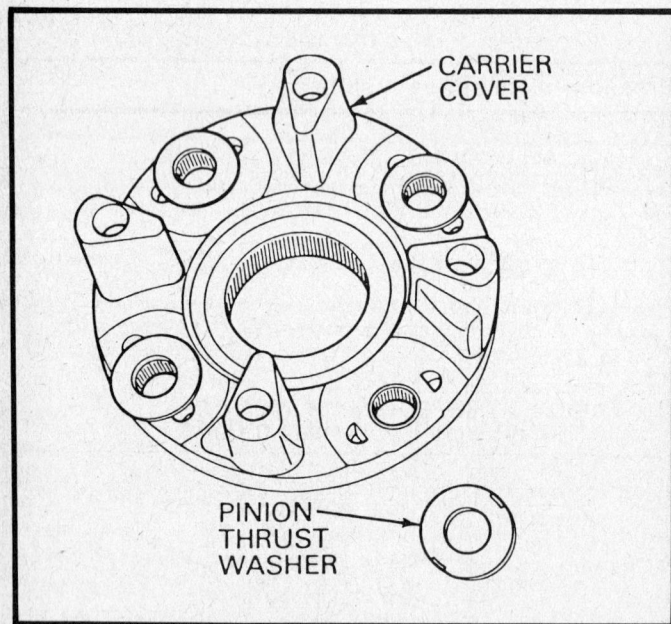

Pinion thrust washers

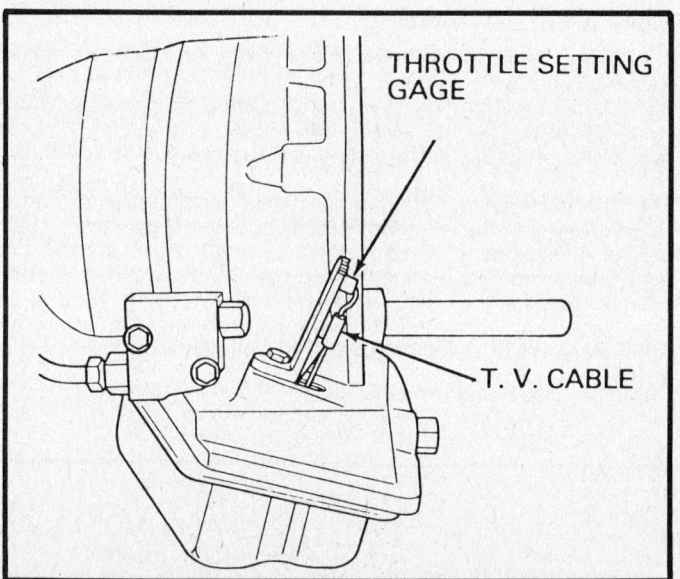

Installation of throttle gage tool

3. Mark pump gears with a grease pencil. Gears must be installed in same direction as removed.
4. Position the output shaft with the splines down. Rotate the pump housing until gears slide out.
5. Remove the drive pin from the output shaft.
6. Remove the pump housing from the output shaft.
7. Remove the thrust washer from the pump housing.
8. Remove the thrust bearing and washer from the clutch hub.
9. Remove the clutch hub from the output shaft. Note the direction of the hub on the shaft. The oil grooves face the sprag clutch or forward on shaft.
10. Remove the sprag clutch from the output shaft. Note direction of the sprag clutch. The lip on the sprag clutch cage goes toward oil grooves on the clutch hub.

Assembly

Coat all parts before assembling with clean Dextron II automatic transmission fluid.

1. Install the sprag clutch on the output shaft. The lip on the sprag clutch cage faces rearward or towards the oil grooves on the clutch hub.
2. Install the clutch hub on the output shaft. The oil grooves on the hub face the sprag clutch or forward on the shaft.
3. Install the thrust washer and then the thrust bearing on the clutch hub.
4. Install the thrust washer on the pump housing. Use petrolatum to retain the thrust washer to the housing.
5. Install the pump housing on the output shaft.
6. Install the pin in the output shaft.
7. Install the pump gears in the housing. Gears must be installed in same direction as removed.
8. Place pump cover on the housing. Align the (4) bolt holes in cover to pump housing. Install the bolts and torque to specifications.

MANUAL TRANSMISSIONS
GM WARNER—83mm FOUR SPEED W/OD

9. Install the speedometer gear on the output shaft. Install the retaining clip.

10. Install new O-rings on pump. Use petrolatum to retain the O-rings to the cover.

Carrier Assembly Disassembly

1. Remove the (4) nuts retaining the carrier cover. Remove the cover.
2. Remove the thrust washer, thrust bearing, selective washer and input sun gear.
3. Remove the (4) pinion gears.
4. Remove the steel thrust plate from the carrier.
5. Clean and inspect parts. Replace any parts that are cracked, chipped or show excessive wear. The carrier assembly must be reassembled in the transmission case.

Piston/Accumulator Assembly Disassembly

1. Remove the snap ring retaining the accumulator to the piston.
2. Remove the accumulator and (24) springs from the piston.
3. Remove the (2) O-rings from the accumulator.
4. Remove the (2) O-rings from the piston.
5. To assemble, reverse the removal procedures. Coat O-rings with clean Dextron® II automatic transmission fluid before installing.

OVERDRIVE UNIT

Assembly

1. Install the pressure plate springs into the pockets of the transmission case.
2. Place the pressure plate on top of the springs. Seat the springs into the pockets of pressure plate.
3. Position plate J-21420-2 on top of the pressure plate with the bolt from J-23327 through the center of the plate. Next position J-23327 on the rear of the case and install the retaining nut. Tighten the nut until the pressure plate is drawn approximately 1/8 in. below the Stepfor the overdrive clutch plates. Install the (3) pressure plate retaining bolts (J-34681). Remove tools J-21420 and J-23327 for the case.
4. Install the output shaft assembly into the transmission case. Be sure the O-rings are positioned properly on pump cover before installing the output shaft assembly. Install the (4) pump retaining bolts and torque to specifications.
5. Install the thrust bearing on the output sun gear.
6. Install the tanged direct clutch thrust washer with the tabs facing pressure plate.
7. Install the direct clutch thrust bearing.
8. Install the direct clutch thrust washer. The thrust washer will have a tooth missing from its outer edge. The side of the thrust washer with the circular grind pattern must face the thrust bearing. The side with the grind pattern can be identified by the notch ground into the tooth.
9. Install one composition clutch disc and then install a selective clutch plate. The selective clutch plates come in (5) sizes (0.080–0.120 in.) and is used to control clutch pack clearance. A 0.050–0.070 in. clearance must be maintained in the direct clutch pack. Excessive or insufficient amount of clutch travel will cause failure to the clutch plates and discs.
10. Alternate the remaining clutch discs and plates until all (5) plates and discs are installed.
11. Install the lower half of the carrier assembly onto the direct clutch pack. Index the carrier until all clutch plates are engaged.
12. Install the steel overdrive stop clutch plate and then alternate with a disc and plate until all (4) plates and disc are installed.
13. Install the finger pressure plate.

14. Install the carrier thrust plate with tabs facing the sprag clutch.
15. Install (2) pinion gears with the index mark on the gears facing inward or towards each other. Install the other (2) pinion gears with the index mark 90° off from the first (2) gears.
16. Install the thrust washer for the output sun into the rear of the input sun gear. Use petrolatum to retain the thrust washer to the input sun gear.
17. Install the input sun gear. If the input sun gear spreads the pinion gears when installing, the pinion gears are not indexed properly.
18. Install the selective thrust washer with the oil grooves on washer facing input sun gear.
19. Install the thrust bearing on the input sun gear.
20. Install the carrier thrust washer to the cover. Use petrolatum to retain the thrust washer to the cover.
21. Install the (4) pinion gear thrust washers onto the carrier cover. Use petrolatum to retain washers to the cover.
22. Install the carrier cover. If the pinion gears are not indexed properly, the (4) bolt holes in the cover will not align with the bolts in lower half of the carrier.
23. Install (4) new retaining nuts and torque to specification.
24. Measure the end play for the overdrive unit as follows:
   a. Place the straight edge across the face of the overdrive unit. Use the Depth Micrometer J-34672 and measure the distance from the bearing to the top of the bar. Next, measure the thickness of the bar (J-34673) with a 0 to 1 micrometer and subtract this from reading of the depth micrometer (J-34672) and record this reading.
   b. Place the straight edge across the rear of the adapter plate. Use the Depth Micrometer J-34672 and measure the distance from the top of the bar to the adapter plate mounting surface as shown and record the reading.
   c. Next measure the distance from the top of the bar to the bearing seat in the adapter plate and record the reading.
   d. Subtract the reading from Step c from Step b and record the difference.
   e. Next, subtract the difference from Step d from Step a. The difference will be the end play. Specification is 0 ± 0.003 in. If the results of your measurements are not within the specifications, it will be necessary to remove the carrier cover and change the input sun selective thrust washer. The selective thrust washers are available in (8) sizes. They are in 0.005 in. increments ranging from 0.123–0.158 in.
25. Install the accumulator and piston assembly. Coat the lips of the seals with automatic transmission fluid before installing.
26. Install the large snap ring that goes in the front of the overdrive unit. The snap ring must be installed.
27. Install a new seal in the adapter plate. Place the seal on tool J-34523 and install the seal from the front side of the adpater plate.
28. Place seal protector J-34621 on the input sun gear.
29. Install the adapter plate. Apply a light coating of RTV Sealant #1052366 or equivalent around the heads of the adapter plate bolts. Install the (4) adapter plate bolts and tighten to specifications.
30. Remove the seal protector.
31. Remove the first 1/8 in. pipe plug from the left side of the overdrive unit. Install air line fitting J-34742 into plug hole and tighten.
32. Measure the clutch pack clearance as follows:
   a. Loosen the (3) pressure plate retaining bolts (J-34681) evenly until spring pressure is released.
   b. Assemble J-8001 Dial Indicator to the rear of the overdrive unit.
   c. Apply a minimum of 100 PSI to the air line fitting J-34742 and read the dial indicator (Specification is 0.050–

32-53

SECTION 32 — MANUAL TRANSMISSIONS
GM WARNER – 83mm FOUR SPEED W/OD

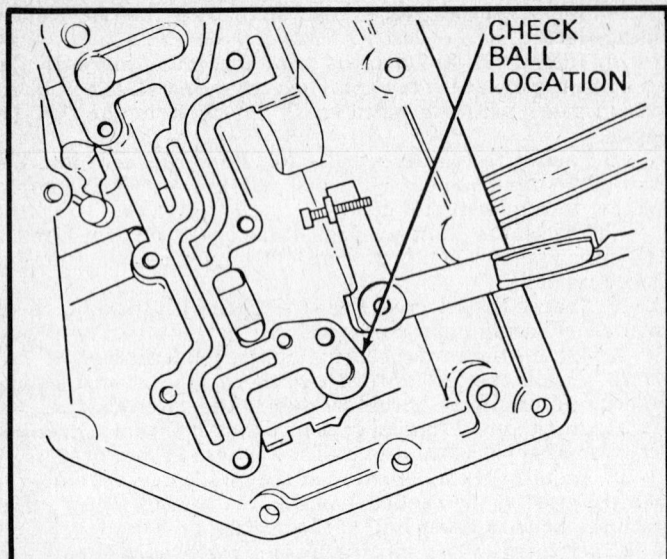

Check ball location

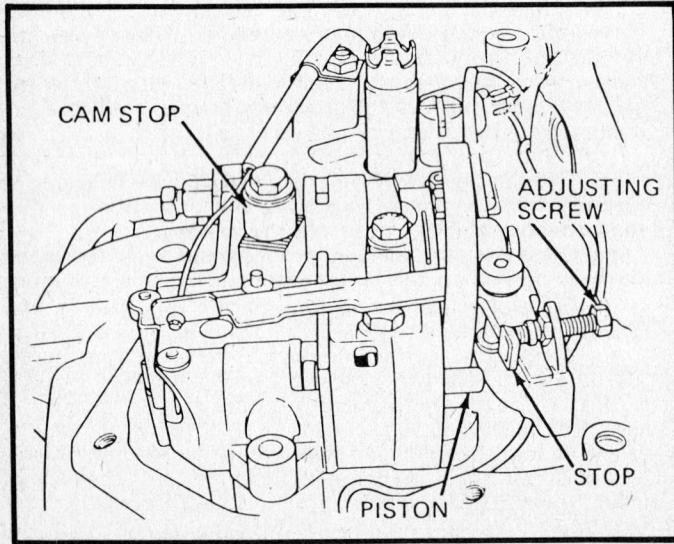

T.V. lever adjustment

0.070 in.). If the reading does not fall within the specification 0.050–0.070 in., it will be necessary to disassemble the overdrive unit to change the direct clutch selective clutch plates. The selective clutch plates are available in (5) sizes. They are in 0.010 in. increments ranging from 0.080–0.120 in. If the clutch pack clearance is within specification, remove the (3) clutch pack retaining bolts (J-34681).

33. Coat the (3) 1/8 in. pipe plugs with anti-seize compound and install plugs. Torque plugs to specification.

34. Remove the air line adapter J-34742.
Coat the plug with anti-seize compound and install the plug. Torque plug to specifications.

35. Install the speedometer gear and sensor.

36. Install a new output seal using J-21426. Coat the lip of the seal with Dextron II transmission fluid.

37. Install the valve body as follows:
   a. Install the check ball into the case.
   b. Position (2) gaskets, one on each side of the separator plate.
   c. Position the separator plate on the valve body.
   d. Position the valve to the case and install the retaining bolts. Torque bolts to specifications.
   e. Install the T.V. cable and install the retaining clip and bolt. Torque bolt to specifications.
   f. Install the T.V. lever and torque bolt to specifications. Connect T.V. cable to the lever.
   g. Install toool J-34671-1 (Throttle Setting Gauge) into the T.V. cable bore on the side of the case. Set the hook on the T.V. cable onto the high step of the gauge. Place the cam stop on the valve body as close to the lever as possible and install the retaining bolt. Torque bolt to specifications.
   h. Set the hook on the T.V. cable onto the lower step of the gauge. Place tool J-34671-2 between the piston and the solenoid bracket. Adjust the screw/bolt on the T.V. lever until the bolt makes contact with the stop on the cam.

38. Install the pickup tube and oil filter on the valve body.

39. Apply a bead of R.T.V. Sealant #1052366 or equivalent to the oil pan flange and assemble wet. Install the magnet in the oil pan. The bead of R.T.V. should be applied around the inside of the bolt holes. Install the pan bolts and torque to specifications.

40. Assemble the overdrive unit to the reverse housing. Guide the idler shaft on the adapter plate into the idler gears and align the splines on the mainshaft with the splines in the input sun gear. Slide the units together and install the retaining bolts. Torque bolts to specifications.

TORQUE SPECIFICATIONS

DRIVE GEAR BEARING RETAINING BOLTS	20-27 N·m	15-20 FT. LBS.
SIDE COVER TO CASE BOLTS	20-27 N·m	15-20 FT. LBS.
REVERSE GEAR HOUSING TO CASE (1) BOLT	40-54 N·m	30-40 FT. LBS.
REVERSE GEAR HOUSING TO CASE (2) BOLTS	54-67 N·m	40-50 FT. LBS.
REVERSE GEAR HOUSING TO CASE (3) BOLTS	47-61 N·m	35-45 FT. LBS.
DRAIN PLUG	20-33 N·m	15-25 FT. LBS.
FILLER PLUG	33-47 N·m	25-35 FT. LBS.
TRANSMISSION TO BELL HOUSING BOLTS	60-80 N·m	45-60 FT. LBS.

MANUAL TRANSMISSIONS
GM SAGINAW — 76mm FOUR SPEED
SECTION 32

GM SAGINAW 76MM—4-SPEED TRANSMISSION

Disassembly

1. Remove the side cover and shift forks.
2. Remove the clutch gear bearing retainer. Remove the bearing-to-gear-stem snap-ring. Pull out on the clutch gear until a screwdriver can be inserted between the bearing, large snap-ring, and case to pry the bearing off.

NOTE: The clutch gear bearing is a slipfit on the gear and in the case. Removal of the bearing will provide clearance for clutch gear and mainshaft removal.

3. Remove the clutch gear, mainshaft and extension as an assembly.
4. Spread the snap-ring which holds the mainshaft rear bearing and remove the extension case.
5. Drive countershaft and its woodruff key out of the rear of the case with a pipe or an old countershaft. Remove the countergear assembly and bearings.
6. Using a long drift, drive the reverse idler shaft and woodruff key through the rear of the case.
7. Expand and remove the third and fourth-speed sliding clutch hub snap-ring from the mainshaft. Remove the clutch assembly, third gear blocker ring, and third-speed gear from the front of the mainshaft.
8. Press in the speedometer gear retaining clip and slide the gear off the mainshaft. Remove the rear bearing snap-ring from its groove in the mainshaft.
9. Support first gear on press plates. Press first gear, thrust washer, spring washer, rear bearing, and snap-ring from the rear of the mainshaft.

CAUTION
Center the gear, washers, bearings, and snap-ring when pressing the rear bearing.

10. Expand and remove the first and second sliding clutch hub snap-ring from the mainshaft. Remove the clutch assembly, second-speed blocker ring, and second-speed gear from the rear of the mainshaft.

Thoroughly clean all parts and the transmission case. Inspect and replace all damaged or worn parts. When checking the bearings, do not spin them at high speeds. Clean and rotate the bearings by hand to detect roughness and uneveness. Spinning can damage balls and races.

Assembly
MAINSHAFT

Install the following parts with the front of the mainshaft facing up:

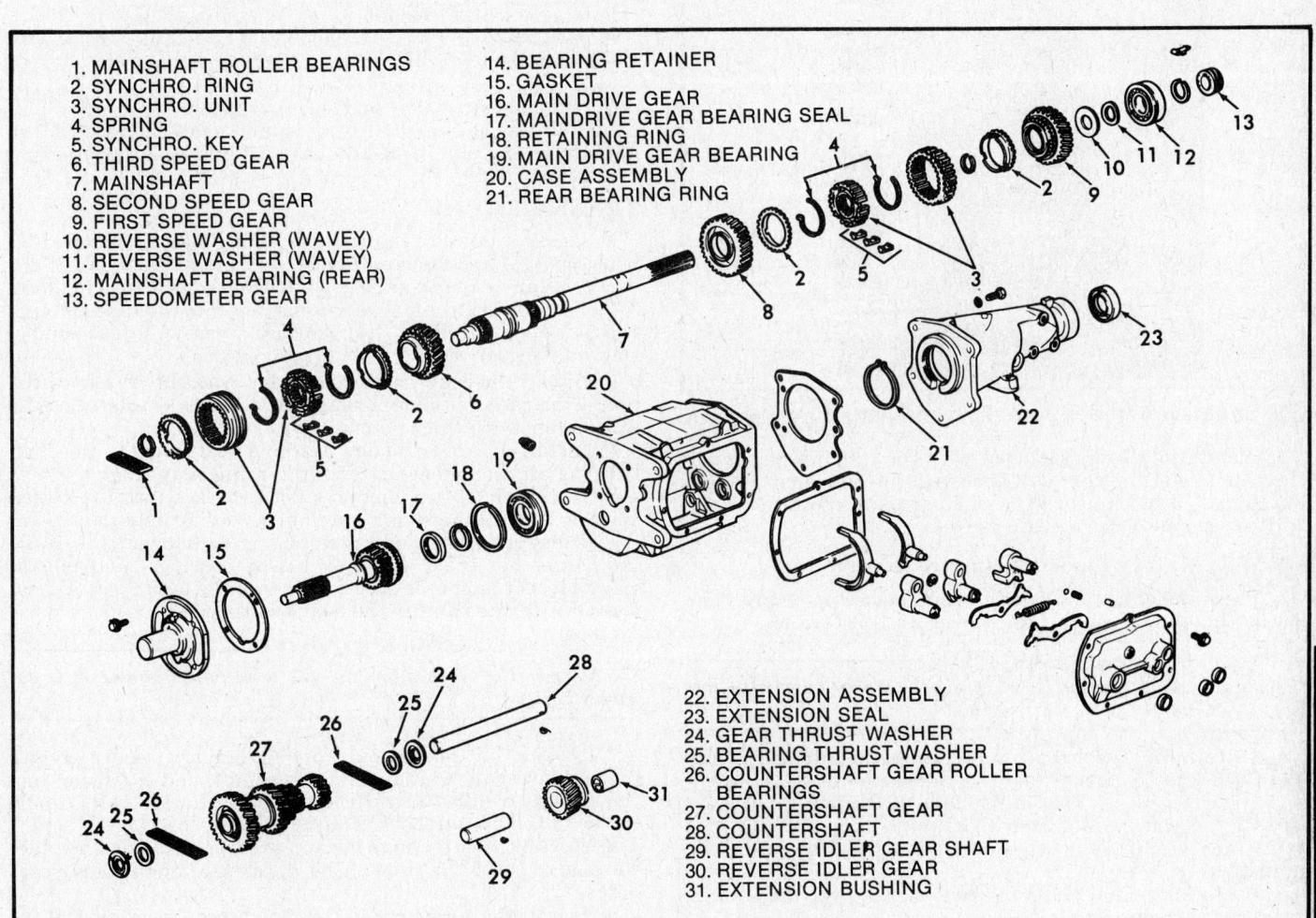

1. MAINSHAFT ROLLER BEARINGS
2. SYNCHRO. RING
3. SYNCHRO. UNIT
4. SPRING
5. SYNCHRO. KEY
6. THIRD SPEED GEAR
7. MAINSHAFT
8. SECOND SPEED GEAR
9. FIRST SPEED GEAR
10. REVERSE WASHER (WAVEY)
11. REVERSE WASHER (WAVEY)
12. MAINSHAFT BEARING (REAR)
13. SPEEDOMETER GEAR
14. BEARING RETAINER
15. GASKET
16. MAIN DRIVE GEAR
17. MAINDRIVE GEAR BEARING SEAL
18. RETAINING RING
19. MAIN DRIVE GEAR BEARING
20. CASE ASSEMBLY
21. REAR BEARING RING
22. EXTENSION ASSEMBLY
23. EXTENSION SEAL
24. GEAR THRUST WASHER
25. BEARING THRUST WASHER
26. COUNTERSHAFT GEAR ROLLER BEARINGS
27. COUNTERSHAFT GEAR
28. COUNTERSHAFT
29. REVERSE IDLER GEAR SHAFT
30. REVERSE IDLER GEAR
31. EXTENSION BUSHING

Exploded view of the Saginaw 4 speed transmission (© G.M. Corp.)

SECTION 32

MANUAL TRANSMISSIONS
GM SAGINAW—76mm FOUR SPEED

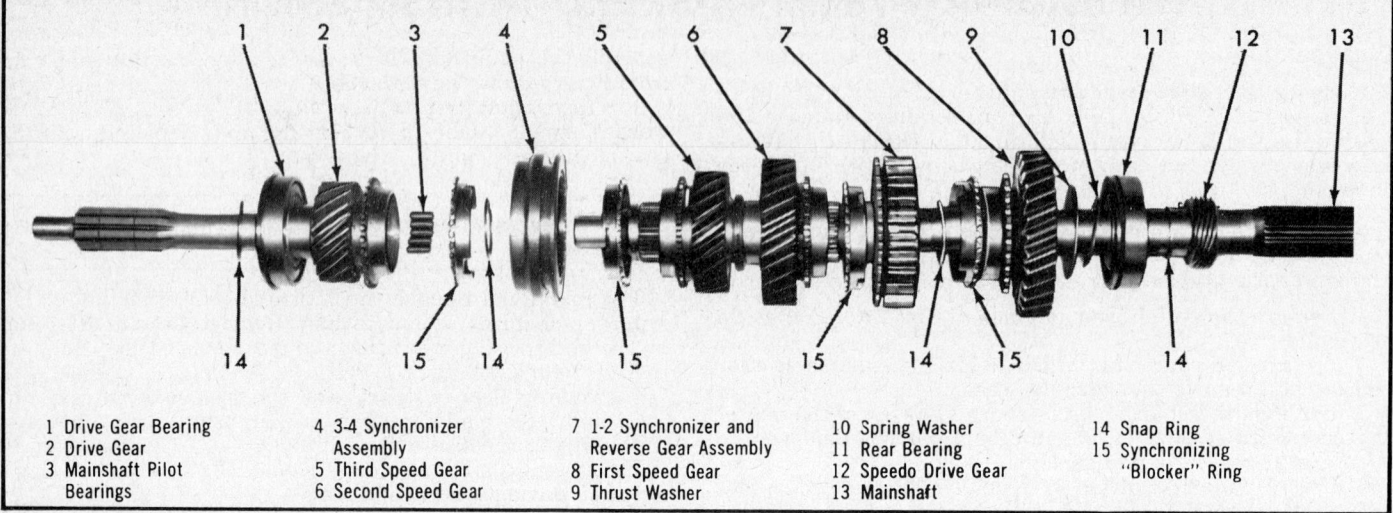

1. Drive Gear Bearing
2. Drive Gear
3. Mainshaft Pilot Bearings
4. 3-4 Synchronizer Assembly
5. Third Speed Gear
6. Second Speed Gear
7. 1-2 Synchronizer and Reverse Gear Assembly
8. First Speed Gear
9. Thrust Washer
10. Spring Washer
11. Rear Bearing
12. Speedo Drive Gear
13. Mainshaft
14. Snap Ring
15. Synchronizing "Blocker" Ring

GM Saginaw 4-speed: clutch gear & mainshaft assembly

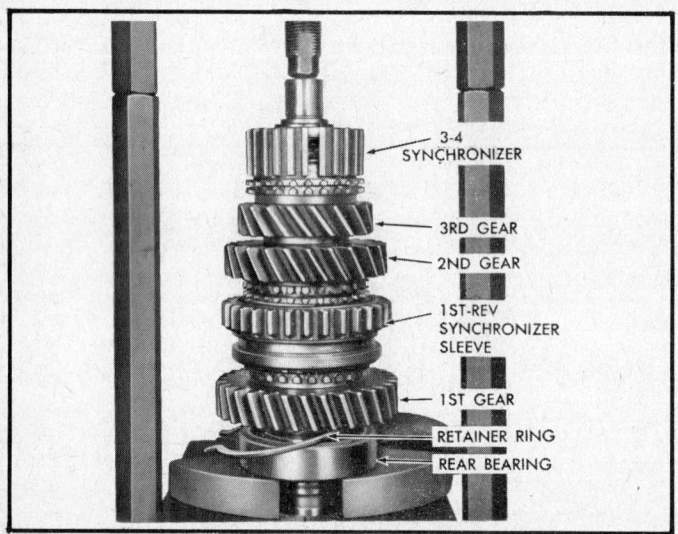

GM Saginaw 4-speed: pressing mainshaft components

1. Install the third-speed gear with the clutching teeth up. The rear face of the gear will abut with the mainshaft flange.
2. Install a blocking ring, clutching teeth down, over the third-speed gear synchronizing surface.

NOTE: All four blocker rings are the same.

3. Press the third and fourth synchronizer assembly, fork slot down, onto the mainshaft splines until it bottoms.

---- CAUTION ----
The blocker ring notches must align with the synchronizer assembly keys.

4. Install the synchronizer hub-to-mainshaft snap-ring. (Both synchronizer snap-rings are the same.). Install the following parts with the rear of the mainshaft up:
5. The second-speed gear with the clutching teeth up. The front face of the gear will abut with the flange on the mainshaft.
6. A blocking ring, clutching teeth down, over the second-speed gear synchronizing surface.
7. Press the first and second synchronizer assembly, fork slot down, onto the mainshaft.

---- CAUTION ----
The blocker ring notches must align with the synchronizer assembly keys.

8. The synchronizer hub-to-mainshaft snap-ring.
9. A blocker ring with the notches down so they align with the first/second synchronizer assembly keys.
10. First gear with the clutching teeth down. Install the first gear thrust washer and spring washer.
11. Press the rear ball bearing and snap-ring, slot down, onto the mainshaft. Install the snap-ring. Install the speedometer gear and slip.

TRANSMISSION

1. Using a dummy countergear shaft, load a row of roller bearings (27) and bearing thrust washers at each end of the countergear. Grease can be used to hold the bearings in place.
2. Position the countergear assembly into the case through the rear opening. Place a tanged thrust washer at each end of the countergear.
3. Install the countergear shaft and woodruff key from the rear of the case. The shaft engages both thrust washers and the tangs align with their notches in the case.
4. Install the reverse idler gear and shaft and the woodruff key. Install the extension-to-rear bearing snap-ring.
5. Install the 14 mainshaft pilot bearings into the clutch opening. Install the fourth-speed blocker ring onto the clutching surface of the clutch gear (clutching teeth toward the gear).
6. Assemble the clutch gear, pilot bearings, and fourth-speed blocker ring unit over the front of the mainshaft. Do not assemble the bearing to the gear at this point.

---- CAUTION ----
The blocker ring notches line up with third/fourth synchronizer assembly keys.

7. Install the extension-to-case gasket and secure it with grease. Insert the clutch gear, mainshaft, and extension into the case as a unit. Install the extension-to-case bolts (apply sealer to the bottom bolt). Torque to 45 ft. lbs.
8. Install the outer snap-ring on the front bearing and place the bearing over the stem of the clutch gear and into the case bore.
9. Install the snap-ring to the clutch gear stem. Install the clutch gear bearing retainer and gasket to the case, with the retainer oil return hole at the bottom.

MANUAL TRANSMISSIONS
GM SAGINAW—76mm FOUR SPEED
SECTION 32

10. Place the synchronizer sleeves into neutral positions. Install the cover, gasket, and fork assemblies to the case. Be sure the forks align with their synchronizer sleeve grooves. Torque the cover bolts to 22 ft./lbs.

ISUZU 69.5MM—5-SPEED TRANSMISSION

CHEVETTE DIESEL

Transmission Disassembly

1. Remove the transmission drain plug and allow the lubricant to drain from the transmission.
2. Remove the throwout bearing and fork from the transmission as outlines in the appropriate car section.
3. Remove the drive gear bearing retainer. If damaged, remove the ball stud.
4. Remove the belleville spring from the front of the drive gear bearing.
5. Remove the bolt, retainer, and speedometer driven gear from the side of the transmission.
6. Remove the shift lever quandrant from the extension housing.
7. Remove the back-up light switch.
8. Remove the extension housing bolts and the extension housing.
9. Remove the snap-ring, speedometer drive gear, spacer, and bearing from the mainshaft.
10. Remove the snap-ring, then the thrust washer and lock ball from the mainshaft.
11. Remove the large snap-ring from the main drive gear bearing.
12. Remove the following components from the case as an assembly.
    a. Center support
    b. Mainshaft
    c. Countergear
    d. Drive gear
13. Using a drift punch and a hammer, carefully drive the roll pins from the 1st/2nd, 3rd/4th, and 5th/reverse shift forks. Sup-

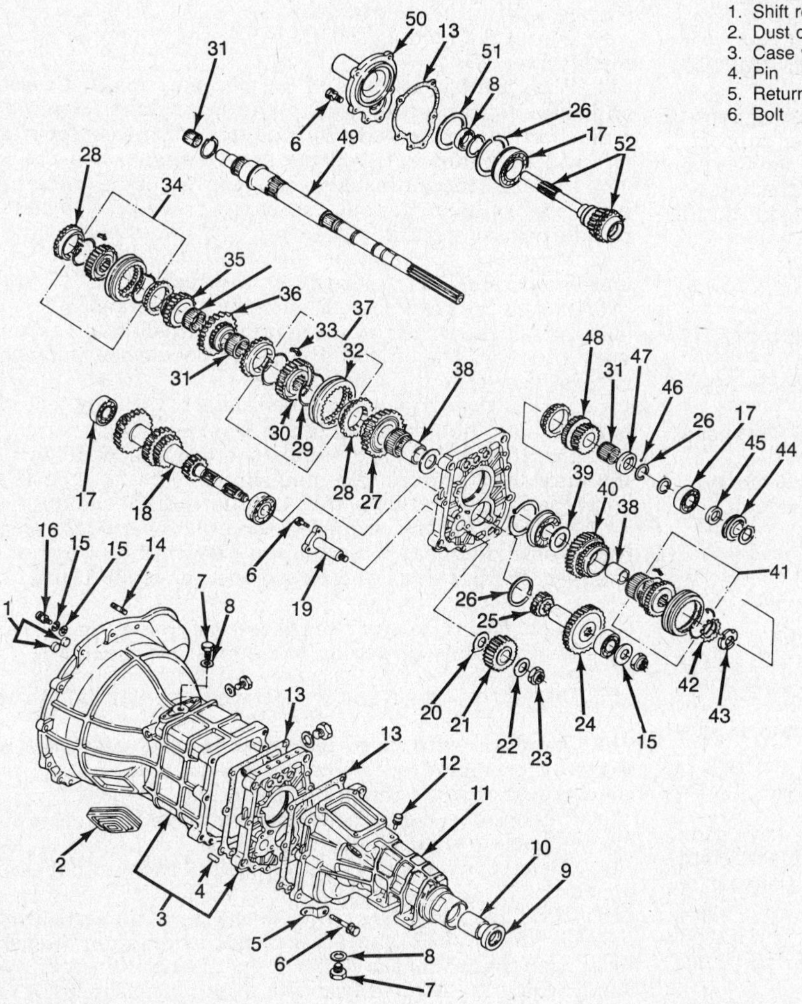

1. Shift rod plug
2. Dust cover
3. Case with center support
4. Pin
5. Return spring bracket
6. Bolt
7. Plug
8. Seal
9. Seal
10. Bushing
11. Extension
12. Ventilator
13. Gasket
14. Starter locating stud
15. Washer
16. Shift fork support
17. Ball bearing assembly
18. Countergear
19. Reverse idler shaft
20. Reverse idler front thrust washer
21. Reverse idler gear
22. Reverse idler rear thrust washer
23. Self-locking nut
24. 5th speed gear
25. Reverse gear
26. Snap-ring
27. 1st speed gear assembly
28. Blocking ring
29. Synchronizer insert spring
30. Synchronizer hub
31. Needle bearing
32. Synchronizer sleeve
33. Synchronizer insert (key)
34. 3rd-4th synchronizer assembly
35. 3rd gear assembly
36. 2nd gear assembly
37. 1st-2nd synchronizer assembly
38. Collar
39. Thrust washer
40. Reverse gear (mainshaft)
41. 5th-reverse synchronizer assembly
42. Mainshaft lockwasher
43. Mainshaft nut
44. Speedometer drive gear
45. Spacer
46. Ball
47. Selective thrust washer
48. 5th speed gear (mainshaft)
49. Mainshaft
50. Drive gear bearing retainer
51. Belleville spring
52. Main drive gear and shaft assembly

Transmission case and geartrain components of the transmission

32-57

SECTION 32
MANUAL TRANSMISSIONS
ISUZU—69.5mm FIVE SPEED

port the shaft ends with a bar or a block of wood to prevent damage to these components.

14. Remove the detent spring plate mounting bolts, detent spring plate, and the three springs and balls from the center support.
15. Remove the shifter shafts from the center support, then remove the shift forks from the shafts. Remove the interlock pins from the center support.
16. Move the 1st/2nd synchronizer sleeve to the 1st gear position, and the 3rd/4th synchronizer sleeve to the 3rd gear position.
17. Install a holding fixture (Kent-Moore tool J-29768 or its equivalent) on the end of the drive gear shaft and countergear. Remove the countergear retaining nut and the washer.
18. Using an appropriate puller, remove the ball bearing and 5th speed gear from the countershaft.
19. Remove the fifth gear, blocking ring, and the needle bearing from the mainshaft.
20. Remove the self-locking nut from the reverse idler gear shaft.
21. Remove the thrust washers and the reverse idler gear from the reverse idler gear shaft.
22. Bend the locking retainer of the mainshaft nut away from the nut. Remove the mainshaft nut using the appropriate tool.
23. Remove the 5th/reverse synchronizer locking retainer, 5th/reverse synchronizer assembly, reverse gear, needle bearing, collar, and the thrust washer from the mainshaft.
24. Remove the reverse gear from the countergear and remove the holding fixture installed during Step 17.
25. Move the synchronizer sleeves back to their Neutral positions.
26. Expand the countergear bearing snap-ring (using snap-ring pliers) and gently tap on the front of the center support. Expand the mainshaft bearing snap-ring and move the mainshaft inward. Remove the countergear and mainshaft.
27. Remove the drive gear, needle bearing, and the blocking ring from the end of the mainshaft.

Mainshaft Disassemby

1. Remove the mainshaft rear bearing using an arbor press and Kent-Moore tool J-22912-01 (or its equivalent).
2. Remove the thrust washer, 1st speed gear, needle bearings, and the spacer.
3. Remove the 1st/2nd synchronizer assembly, the 2nd speed gear, and the needle bearings.
4. Remove the snap-ring from in front of the 3rd/4th synchronizer and slide the synchronizer off of the mainshaft.

Removal and Installation
DRIVE GEAR BEARING

1. Remove the snap-ring from the drive gear shaft.
2. Install Kent-Moore tool J-22912-01 (or its equivalent) under the drive gear bearing and press the drive gear shaft through the bearing (an arbor press must be used).
3. Installation is performed in the reverse of the previous steps.

COUNTERGEAR BEARING

This bearing is removed in the same manner as the drive gear bearing, using the same special tool and an arbor press. Note that the groove on the bearing is installed toward the rear of the transmission.

EXTENSION HOUSING OR DRIVE GEAR RETAINER SEALS

These seals are removed by prying them out with an appropriate tool. Install the new seals by carefully tapping them into place.

MAINSHAFT ASSEMBLY

1. Install the third speed gear (with needle bearings) onto the front of the mainshaft. Note that the coned side of the gear is installed toward the front of the mainshaft.
2. Install the 3rd/4th synchronizer assembly onto the mainshaft, with the large chamfered end toward the front of the transmission. Retain the synchronizer and the snap-ring.
3. Install the 2nd speed gear (with needle bearings) onto the rear of the mainshaft. Note that the coned side of the gear is installed toward the rear of the mainshaft.
4. Install the 1st/2nd synchronizer assembly onto the mainshaft, with the larger chamfered end toward the rear of the transmission.
5. Install the first speed gear (with spacer and needle bearings), with the coned end facing the front of the transmission.
6. Install the first gear thrust washer, with the slots of the washer facing the gear.
7. Press the rear bearing onto the mainshaft according to the previous procedure under "Removal and Installation."

Transmission Assembly

1. If removed, install the countergear and mainshaft snap-rings into the center support. Also install the reverse idler shaft into the center support.
2. Install the driver gear onto the front of the mainshaft and engage it with the countergear.
3. Install the holding fixture in the same manner as Disassembly Step 17.
4. With the mainshaft and countergears meshed together, slide the center support onto the mainshaft. Expand the mainshaft snap-ring and continue to push the center support on until the mainshaft bearing groove aligns with the snap-ring. Release the mainshaft snap-ring to lock the mainshaft bearing in place. Repeat the same procedure to seat the countergear snap-ring.
5. Move the synchronizer sleeves to engage both 1st and third gear ranges in order to lock the gears.
6. Install the reverse gear onto the countergear.
7. Install the thrust washer on the mainshaft (oil groove toward the rear), then install the collar, needle bearing, and the reverse gear onto the mainshaft.
8. Install the 5th/reverse synchronizer, with the face of the higher clutch hub boss facing the reverse gears.
9. Install the locking retainer and the mainshaft nut onto the mainshaft. Torque the mainshaft nut to 94 ft. lbs., then bend the locking retainer tabs in order to lock the nut.
10. Install the thrust washers and the reverse idler gear on the reverse idler gear shaft. Thread a new self-locking nut onto the reverse idler shaft and torque the nut to 80 ft. lbs.

NOTE: The flange of the plate-side thrust washer must be fitted to the stopper on the center support.

11. Install the synchronizer blocking ring and the 5th speed gear (with needle bearings) onto the mainshaft.
12. Install the fifth speed gear (of the countergear), ball bearing, washer, and a NEW self-locking nut onto the rear of the countergear. Torque the nut to 80 ft. lbs.
13. Remove the holding fixture and move the synchronizer sleeves back to their Neutral positions.
14. Grease the interlock pins and install them into the center support.
15. Place the shift forks into position on the synchronizer sleeves. Install lthe shifter shafts through their respective forks from the rear of the center support, except the 5th/reverse shaft, which is installed from the front of the support.
16. Install the detent balls (3), springs, detent plate gasket, and the detent plate. Torque the detent plate bolts to 14 ft. lbs.
17. Using a drift punch and a hammer, carefully install the

MANUAL TRANSMISSIONS
ISUZU—69.5mm FIVE SPEED

retaining pins into the shift forks. Remember to support the shafts with a bar or a block of wood to prevent damage.

18. If removed, lubricate the countergear needle bearing and install it into the front of the case. The bearing should be driven into place while a socket is positioned on the outer bearing race.

19. Install a NEW center support-to-transmission case gasket on the transmission case and install the center support/mainshaft/countergear/drive gear assembly into the case.

20. Install the large snap-ring onto the shaft of the drive gear bearing.

21. Install the lock ball, thrust washer, and the retaining snap-ring onto the mainshaft.

22. Using a feeler gauge, check the clearance between the 5th speed gear (of the mainshaft) and its thrust washer. The clearance should be 0.010–0.016 in. If necessary, adjust the clearance by purchasing a thrust washer of the correct thickness which will replace the existing washer. Thrust washers are available in thickness ranging from 0.307–0.327 in. in 0.003 in. increments.

NOTE: Use care when removing/installing the snap-ring; it must be replaced if it becomes distorted.

23. Install these parts on the mainshaft behind the 5th gear snap-ring (in this order):
   a. Ball bearing
   b. Snap-ring
   c. Speedometer gear clip
   d. Speedometer drive gear

24. Attach the extension housing to the center support, using a NEW gasket. Torque the bolts to 27 ft. lbs.

25. Install the shift lever quadrant onto the extension housing, using a NEW gasket. Torque the bolts to 14 ft. lbs.

26. Install the speedometer driven gear and torque the bolt to 14 ft. lbs.

27. Install the back-up light switch into the extension housing.

28. Install the belleville washer in front of the drive gear bearing, noting that the dished side of the washer should face the bearing.

29. Install the drive gear bearing retainer, using a NEW gasket. Before installing the three lower bearings retainer bolts, coat the threads of the bolts with Permatex No. 2 sealer (or its equivalent). Torque all of the bearing retainer bolts to 14 ft. lbs.

30. Install the throwout bearing and fork.

31. Install the transmission in the vehicle.

GENERAL MOTORS CORP. MODEL C51 TRANSAXLE

Disassembly

1985 ½ AND LATER NOVA

1. Remove release fork, bearing and speedometer driven gear.
2. Remove back-up light switch.
3. Remove front bearing retainer.
4. Remove transmission case cover.
5. Measure fifth gear thrust clearance. Using a dial indicator, measure the thrust clearance.
   a. Standard clearance: 0.0039–0.0224 in. (0.10–0.57 mm).
   b. Maximum clearance: 0.0256 in. (0.65 mm).
6. Remove selecting bellcrank.
7. Remove lock bolt.
8. Remove shift and select lever assembly.
9. Remove lock nut. Engage the gear double meshing. Remove the lock nut. Disengage the gear double meshing.
10. Remove hub sleeve No. 3 assembly and shift fork No. 3. Remove the bolt with the lock washer from shift fork No. 3. Using two screwdrivers and a hammer, tap on the snap ring. Remove the hub sleeve No. 3 assembly and shift fork No. 3.
11. Remove fifth gear, synchronizer ring, needle roller bearing and spacer.
12. Remove fifth driven gear.
13. Remove rear bearing retainer.
14. Remove two bearing snap rings.
15. Remove reverse idler gear shaft lock bolt.
16. Remove snap ring from No. 2 shift fork shaft.
17. Remove plug, seat, spring and ball. Remove the four plugs. Using a magnetic finger, remove the four springs and balls.
18. Remove transmission case. Remove the sixteen bolts and tap off the case with a plastic hammer.
19. Remove reverse shift arm bracket. Remove the two bolts and pull off the bracket.
20. Remove reverse idler gear and shaft.
21. Remove shift forks and shift fork shaft. Using two screwdrivers and a hammer, tap out the three snap rings. Pry out the lock washers and remove the three set bolts. Remove fork shaft No. 2 and shift head. Using a magnetic finger, remove the two balls. Remove fork shaft No. 3 and reverse shift fork. Pull out fork shaft No. 1. Remove shift forks No. 1 and No. 2.
22. Remove input and output shaft together from transaxle case.
23. Remove differential assembly.
24. Remove magnet and oil receiver.
25. Measure third and fourth gear thrust clearance by using a feeler gauge and measure the thrust clearance.
   a. Standard clearance:
      3rd gear 0.0039–0.0138 in. (0.10–0.35mm).
      4th gear 0.0039–0.0217 in. (0.10–0.55mm).
   b. Maximum clearance:
      3rd gear 0.0157 in. (0.40mm).
      4th gear 0.0236 in. (0.60mm).
26. Remove snap ring from input shaft.
27. Remove radial ball bearing, fourth gear, needle roller bearing and synchronizer ring from input shaft. Using a press, remove the radial ball bearing and 4th gear. Remove the needle roller bearings and synchronizer ring.
28. Remove snap ring, using snap ring pliers.
29. Remove hub sleeve No. 2 assembly, third gear, synchronizer ring and needle roller bearing. Using a press, remove hub sleeve No. 2, 3rd gear, synchronizer ring and needle roller bearing.
30. Measure first and second gear thrust clearance by using a feeler gauge and measure the thrust clearance.
   a. Standard clearance:
      1st gear 0.0039–0.0157 in. (0.10–0.40mm).
      2nd gear 0.0039–0.0177 in. (0.10–0.45mm).
   b. Maximum clearance:
      1st gear 0.0177 in. (0.45mm).
      2nd gear 0.0197 in. (0.50mm).
31. Remove radial ball bearing, fourth drive gear and spacer from output shaft. Using a press, remove the radial ball bearing and driven gear. Remove the spacer.
32. Remove third driven gear, second gear needle roller bearing, spacer and synchronizer ring. Shift hub sleeve No. 1 into 1st gear. Using a press, remove the 3rd driven gear and gear. Remove the needle roller bearing, spacer and synchronizer ring.
33. Remove snap ring.

SECTION 32 MANUAL TRANSMISSIONS
GM – MODEL C51

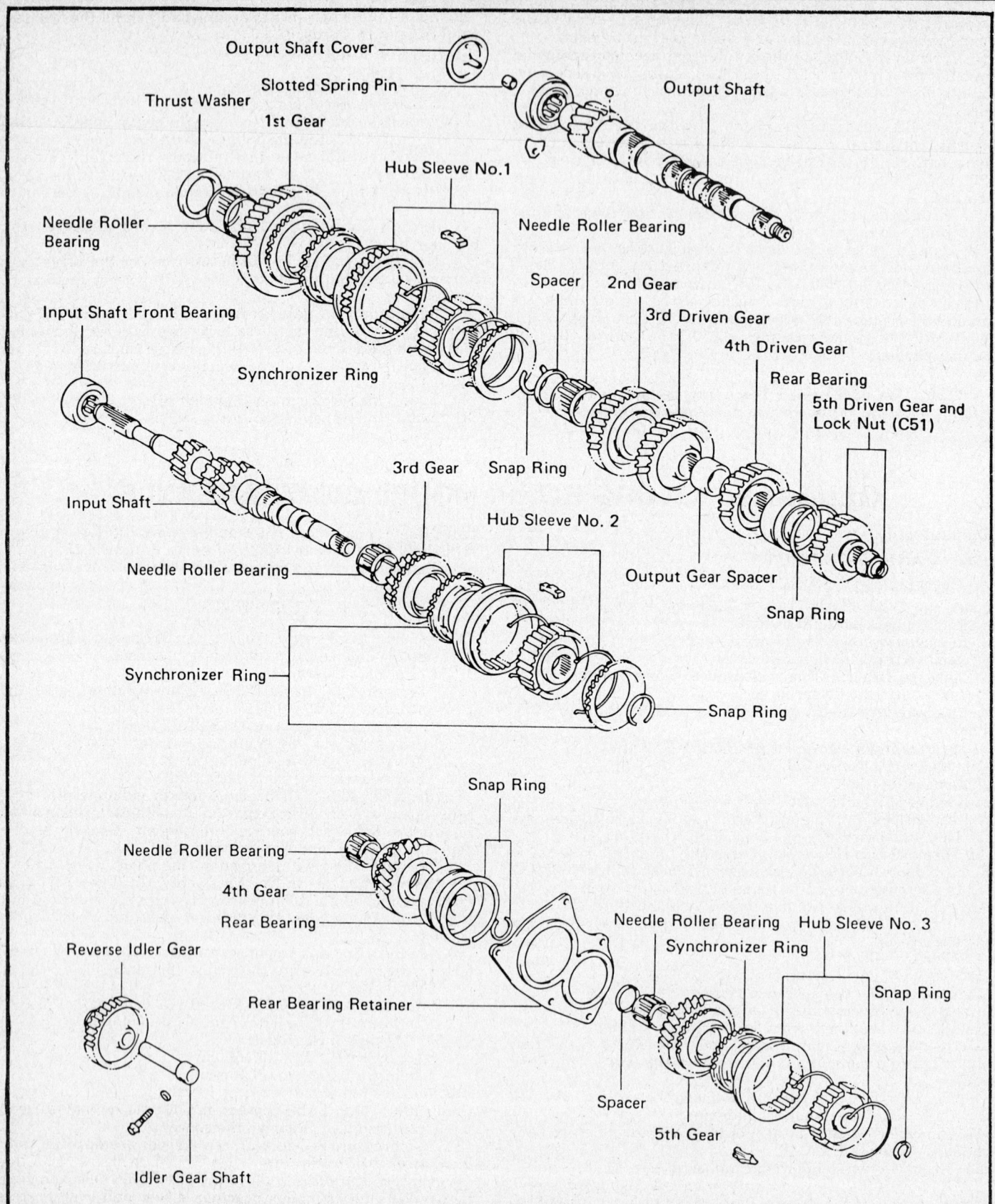

Exploded view of gear components-C51 model (© New United Motor Manufacturing, Inc.)

MANUAL TRANSMISSIONS
GM – MODEL C51

34. Remove hub sleeve No. 1 assembly, first gear, synchronizer ring, needle roller bearing, thrust washer and locking ball. Using a press, remove hub sleeve No. 1, 1st gear synchronizer ring. Remove the needle roller bearing, thrust washer locking ball.
35. Disassemble shift and select lever assembly. Remove the E-ring and compression spring. Using a pin punch and hammer, drive out the slotted spring pin from shift inner levers No. 1 and No. 2. Remove shift inner lever No. 2 Remove shift inner lever No. 1 and the shift interlock plate. Using a pi punch and hammer, drive out the slotted spring pin from the select inner lever. Remove the select inner lever, compression spring and spring seat. Using two screwdrivers and a hammer, tap out the snap ring from the lever shaft. Remove the lever shaft and boot.

Assembly

1. Insert clutch hub No. 2 into hub sleeve. Install the clutch hub and shifting keys to the hub sleeve. Install the shifting key springs under the shifting keys.

— **CAUTION** —
Install the key springs positioned so that there end gaps are not in line.

2. Install third gear, needle roller bearings, synchronizer ring and hub sleeve No. 2 assembly to input shaft. Apply MP grease to the needle roller bearings. Place the synchronizer ring on the gear and align the ring slots with the shifting keys. Using a press, install the 3rd gear and hub sleeve No. 2.
3. Install the snap ring. Select one that will allow minimum axle play and install it on the shaft.
4. Using a feeler gauge, measure the 3rd gear thrust clearance.

Mark	Thickness	(in.) mm
0	(0.0906)	2.30
1	(0.0929)	2.36
2	(0.0953)	2.42
3	(0.0976)	2.48
4	(0.1000)	2.54
5	(0.1024)	2.60

a. Maximum clearance: 0.0039 in. (0.10mm).

5. Install synchronizer ring, needle roller bearing, fourth gear and radial ball bearing. Apply MP grease to the needle roller bearing. Place the synchronizer ring on the gear and align the ring slots with the shifting keys. Press in the radial ball bearing.
6. Install snap ring. Select a snap ring that will allow minimum axial play and install it on the shaft.
7. Using a feeler gauge, measure the 4th gear thrust clearance.

Mark	Thickness	(in.) mm
A	(0.0902)	2.29
B	(0.0925)	2.35
C	(0.0949)	2.41
D	(0.0972)	2.47
E	(0.0996)	2.53
F	(0.1020)	2.59

a. Maximum clearance: 0.0039 in. (0.10mm).

8. If input shaft was replaced, drive in slotted spring. If the input shaft was replaced, drive the slotted spring pin in the output shaft to a depth of 0.236 in. (6.0mm).
9. Insert clutch hub No. 1 into hub sleeve. Install the clutch hub and shifting keys to the hub sleeve. Install the shifting key springs under the shifting keys.

— **CAUTION** —
Install the key springs positioned so that their end gaps are not in line.

10. Install thrust washer, first gear, needle roller bearing, synchronizer ring and hub sleeve No. 1 to output shaft. Install the locking ball in the shaft. Fit the thrust washer groove securely over the locking ball when installing the thrust washer on the shaft. Apply MP grease to the needle roller bearing. Place the synchronizer ring on the gear and align the ring slots with the shifting keys. Using a press, install the 1st gear and hub sleeve No. 1.
11. Install snap ring. Select a snap ring that will allow minimum axial play and install it on the shaft.
12. Using a feeler gauge, measure the 1st gear thrust clearance.

Mark	Thickness	(in.) mm
A	(0.0984)	2.50
B	(0.1008)	2.56
C	(0.1031)	2.62
D	(0.1055)	2.68
E	(0.1079)	2.74
F	(0.1102)	2.80

a. Maximum clearance 0.0039 in. (0.10mm).

13. Install spacer, synchronizer ring, second gear, needle roller bearing and third driven gear. Install the spacer. Place the synchronizer ring on the gear and align the ring slots with the shifting keys. Apply MP grease to the needle roller bearing. Install the 2nd gear. Using a press, install the 3rd gear.
14. Using a feeler gauge, measure the 2nd gear thrust clearance.
   a. Standard clearance: 0.0039 – 0.0177 in (0.10 – 0.45mm).
   b. Maximum clearance: 0.0197 in. (0.50mm).
15. Install output gear spacer, fourth driven gear and radial ball baring. Install the spacer. Press in the 4th driven gear and bearing.
16. Install magnet.
17. Install oil receiver with two bolts.
18. Adjust differential side bearing preload. Install the thinnest shim into the transmission case. Drive in the outer race of the side bearing. Install the differential to the transaxle case. Install the transmission case. Install and torque the case bolts. Torque: 22 ft. lb. (29 Nm).

Mark	Thickness	(in.) mm	Mark	Thickness	(in.) mm
Q	(0.0827)	2.10	F	(0.1024)	2.60
R	(0.0846)	2.15	G	(0.1043)	2.65
S	(0.0866)	2.20	H	(0.1063)	2.70
T	(0.0886)	2.25	J	(0.1083)	2.75
U	(0.0906)	2.30	K	(0.1102)	2.80
A	(0.0925)	2.35	L	(0.1122)	2.85
B	(0.0945)	2.40	M	(0.1142)	2.90
C	(0.0965)	2.45	N	(0.1161)	2.95
D	(0.0984)	2.50	P	(0.1181)	3.00
E	(0.1004)	2.55			

a. Measure the preload.
b. Preload:
   New bearing 6.9 – 13.9 in. lb. (0.18 – 1.6 Nm).
   Reused bearing 4.3 – 8.7 in. lb. (0.5 – 1.0 Nm).
c. If the preload is not within specification, remove the transmission case side outer race of the side bearing.
d. Reselect and adjusting shim.

SECTION 32

MANUAL TRANSMISSIONS
GM—MODEL C51

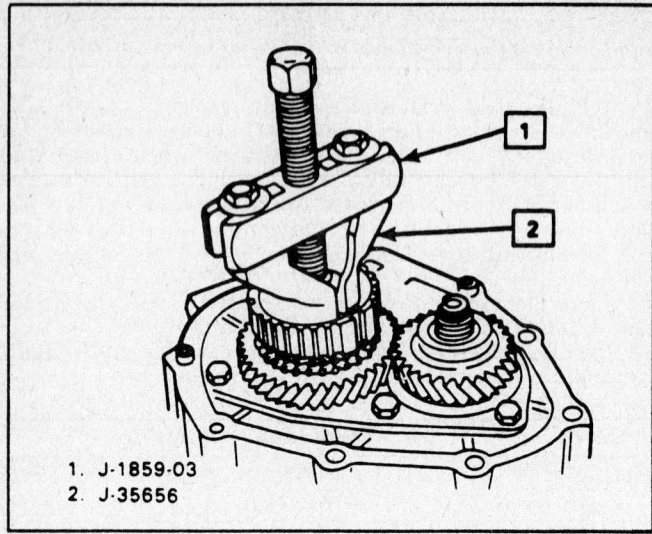

1. J-1859-03
2. J-35656

Figure 7B-18 5th Gear Drive and Driven Gear Removal

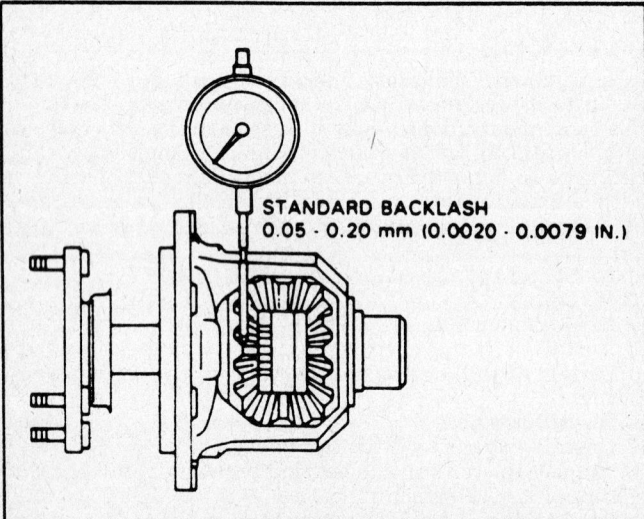

Figure 7B-49 Measuring Backlash

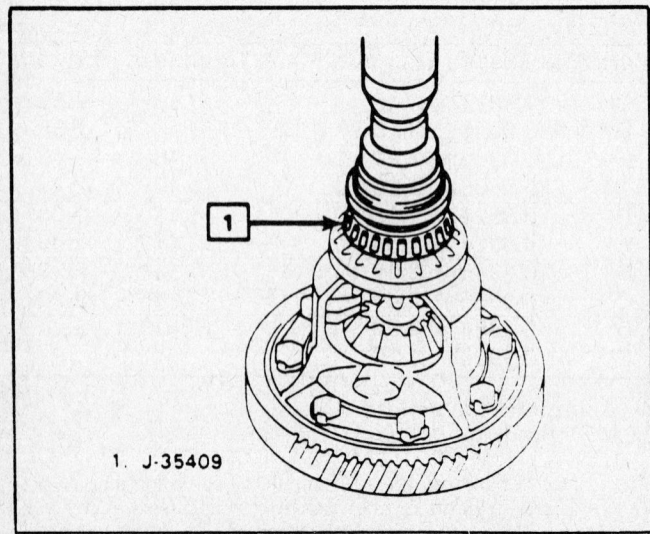

1. J-35409

Figure 7B-48 Side Bearing Installation

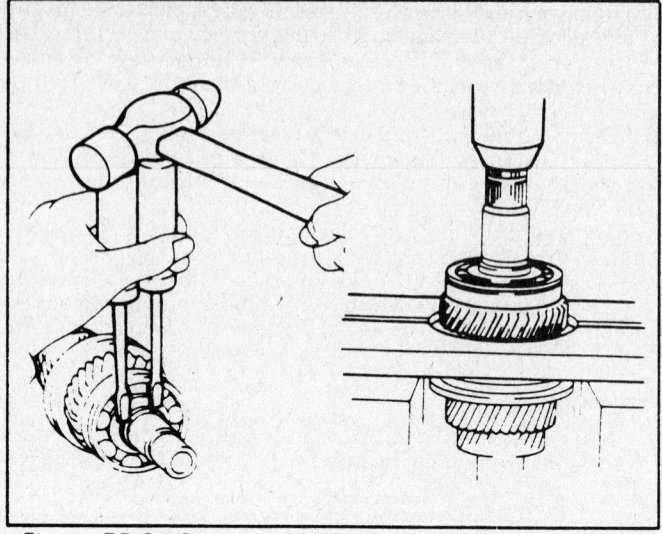

Figure 7B-24 Bearing, Fourth Gear and Synchro. Ring

NOTE: The preload will change about 2.6 – 3.5 in. lb. (0.3 – 0.4 Nm) with each shim thickness.

19. Remove outer race, shim and transmission case. If the preload is adjusted within specification, remove the outer race, shim and transmission case. Be careful not to loose the adjusted shim.
20. Install the input and output shafts together.
21. Install shift forks and shift fork shaft. Place shift forks No. 1 and No. 2 into the groove hub sleeves No. 1 and No. 2. Insert fork shaft No. 1 into the shift fork No. 1 hole. Insert the two interlock balls into the reverse shift fork hole. Install fork shaft No. 3 and reverse shift fork. Install fork shaft No. 2 and shift head. Install the three lock washers and bolts. Toque: 9 ft. lbs. (12 Nm). Using pliers, stake the bolts with lock washers. Install the three snap rings.
22. Install reverse shift arm. Put the reverse shift fork pivot into the reverse shift arm and install the reverse shift arm to the transaxle case. Install and torque the bolts. Torque: 13 ft. lb. (17 Nm).
23. Install reverse idler gear and shaft.
24. Install transmission case. Remove any packing material and be careful not to drop oil on the contacting surfaces of the transmission case or transaxle case. Apply seal packing to the transmission case.

NOTE: Install the transmission case as soon as the seal packing is applied.
Install and torque the sixteen bolts. Torque: 22 ft. lbs. (29 Nm).

25. Install ball, spring, seat plug. Insert the balls, springs and seats into the holes. Apply liquid sealer to the plugs. Tighten the four plugs. Torque: 18 ft. lb. (25 Nm).
26. Install and torque reverse idler gear shaft lock bolt. Torque: 29 ft. lbs. (39 Nm).
27. Install two bearing snap rings.
28. Install snap ring to fork shaft No. 2.
29. Install rear bearing retainer. Install and torque the five bolts. Torque: 14 ft. lbs. (19 Nm).
30. Install fifth driven gear.
31. Install spacer, needle roller bearing, fifth gear and synchronizer ring. Install the spacer. Apply MP grease to the needle roller bearings. Install the 5th gear with the needle roller bearing and synchronizer ring.
32. Insert clutch hub No. 3 into hub sleeve. Install the clutch hub and shifting keys to the hub sleeve. Install the shifting key springs under the shifting keys.

MANUAL TRANSMISSIONS
GM – MODEL C51

CAUTION
Install the key springs positioned so that the end gaps are not in line.

33. Install hub sleeve No. 3 assembly with shift fork No. 3. Drive in hub sleeve No. 3 with shift fork No. 3.

CAUTION
Align the synchronizer ring slots with the shifting keys.

34. Measure fifth gear thrust clearance.
    a. Maximum clearance: 0.0039 in. (0.10mm).
35. Install snap ring. Select a snap ring that will allow minimum axial play and install it on the shaft.
36. Install lock nut. Engage the gear double meshing. Install and torque the nut. Torque: 87 ft. lb. (118 Nm). Disengage the gear double meshing. Stake the lock nut.

Mark	Thickness (in.)	mm	Mark	Thickness (in.)	mm
A	(0.0886)	2.25	E	(0.0980)	2.49
B	(0.0909)	2.31	F	(0.1004)	2.55
C	(0.0933)	2.37	G	(0.1028)	2.61
D	(0.0957)	2.43			

37. Install bolt with lock washer. Install and torque the bolt with a lock washer. Torque: 9 ft. lb. (12 Nm). Using pliers, stake and lock washer.
38. Assembly shift and select lever assembly. Apply MP grease to the shaft. Install the boot and shaft to the control shaft cover.

NOTE: Make sure to install the boot in correct direction. Position the air bleed of the boot downward.

39. Install the snap ring and spring seat. Install the compression spring and select inner lever. Using a pin punch and hammer, drive in the slotted spring pin. Align the inter lock plate with shift inner lever No. 1 and install it. Install shift inner lever No. 2. Using a pin punch and hammer, drive in the slotted spring pin. Install the compression spring, seat and E-ring.
40. Install shift and select lever assembly. Place the gasket in position on the control shaft cover. Install the shift and select lever, and torque the bolts. Torque: 14 ft. lb. (20 Nm). Install the bellcrank to the transmission case.
41. Install lock bolt. Torque 22 ft. lb. (29 Nm).
42. Install transmission case cover. Install the case cover and the eight bolts. Torque the bolts. Torque: 13 ft. lb. (18 Nm).
43. Install front bearing retainer. Torque: 8 ft. lb. (11 Nm).
44. Install release fork and bearing. Apply molybdenum disulphide lithium base grease to the following parts:
    a. Release bearing hub inside groove.
    b. Input shaft spline.
    c. Release fork contact surface.
44. Install back-up light switch. Torque 30 ft. lbs. (40 Nm).
45. Install speedometer driven gear.

TORQUE SPECIFICATIONS

Transmission Case to Transaxle Case	29 N·m (22 ft. lbs.)
Transmission Case to Case Cover	18 N·m (13 ft. lbs.)
Transmission Case Protector	13 N·m (9 ft. lbs.)
Rear Bearing Retainer	19 N·m (14 ft. lbs.)
Output Shaft Bearing Lock Plate	11 N·m (8 ft. lbs.)
Oil Receiver	17 N·m (13 ft. lbs.)
5th Driven Gear Lock Nut	118 N·m (87 ft. lbs.)
Reverse Idler Shaft Lock Bolt	24 N·m (17 ft. lbs.)
Shift and Select Lever Assembly	20 N·m (14 ft. lbs.)
Reverse Shift Arm Bracket	17 N·m (13 ft. lbs.)
Shift Fork to Set Bolt	16 N·m (12 ft. lbs.)
Reverse Restrict Pin Holder	20 N·m (14 ft. lbs.)
Filler Plug	39 N·m (29 ft. lbs.)
Drain Plug	39 N·m (29 ft. lbs.)
Back-Up Light Switch	40 N·m (30 ft. lbs.)
Front Bearing Retainer	11 N·m (8 ft. lbs.)
Speedometer Driven Gear Lock Plate	11 N·m (8 ft. lbs.)
Straight Screw Plug (Shift Fork Shaft)	25 N·m (18 ft. lbs.)
Lock Ball Assembly	39 N·m (29 ft. lbs.)
Ring Gear to Differential Case	97 N·m (71 ft. lbs.)
Lock Bolt	29 N·m (22 ft. lbs.)
Control Cable Bracket	11 N·m (8 ft. lbs.)
Select Bellcrank	25 N·m (18 ft. lbs.)

SECTION 33: STARTER MOTORS

INDEX

ELECTRICAL DIAGNOSIS 33–3	**NIPPONDENSO/MITSUBISHI REDUCTION STARTERS**
Know Your Instruments 33–3	Disassembly 33–13
THE STARTER SYSTEM 33–3	Assembly 33–13
TESTING THE STARTER MOTOR 33–3	**FORD POSITIVE ENGAGEMENT STARTER (GAS ENGINE)**
Testing the Starter Circut 33–4	Disassembly 33–14
Cranking Voltage 33–4	Assembly 33–17
Amperage Draw 33–4	
Voltage Drop – Grounded Side 33–5	**FORD MOTORCRAFT STARTER (DIESEL ENGINE)**
Voltage Drop – Battery Side 33–5	Disassembly 33–16
GENERAL STARTER DIAGNOSIS	Assembly 33–17
Inspection and Repair 33–5	**DELCO REMY STARTER MOTORS (5, 10 & 27 MT)**
Brush and Brush Holder 33–5	Disassembly 33–17
Armature 33–5	Assembly 33–20
Field Coils 33–5	
SWITCHES AND SOLENOIDS 33–5	**DELCO REMY STARTER MOTORS (15M/GR)**
Solenoids 33–6	Disassembly 33–20
Neutral Start Switches 33–7	Assembly 33–21
CHRYSLER REDUCTION GEAR STARTER MOTOR	**DELCO REMY STARTER MOTORS (ISMT/GR)**
Disassembly 33–7	Aluminum 33–22
Assembly 33–9	Disassembly 33–22
BOSCH, NIPPONDENSO AND MITSUBISHI STARTERS	Assembly 33–24
Chrysler Corporaiton 33–10	**DELCO REMY STARTER MOTOR (CHEVETTE DIESEL)**
Disassembly 33–10	Disassembly 33–25
Assembly 33–10	Assembly 33–25
Specifications 33–11	
Identification 33–11	

Starter Motors

ELECTRICAL DIAGNOSIS

To satisfy the growing trend toward organized engine diagnosis and tune-up, the following gauge and meter hook-ups, as well as diagnosis procedures are covered. The most sophisticated tune-up and diagnostic facilities are no more than a complex grouping of the basic gauges and meters in common everyday use.

KNOW YOUR INSTRUMENTS

Ohmmeter
An ohmmeter is used to measure electrical resistance in a unit or circuit. The ohmmeter has a self contained power supply. In use, it is connected across (or in parallel with) the terminals of the unit being tested.

Ammeter
An ammeter is used to measure current flowing through a unit or circuit. Ammeters are always connected in the line with the unit or circuit being tested.

Voltmeter
A voltmeter is used to measure voltage pushing the current through a unit or circuit. The meter is connected across the terminals of the unit being tested.

The Starter System

The cranking motor armature revolves at a relatively high speed to produce sufficient power to crank an engine. Since the cranking speed required to start the engine is comparatively slow the cranking motor is equipped with a small drive pinion which meshes with the teeth of the flywheel ring gear resulting in a gear reduction. Although the gear reduction ratio varies on different applications the cranking motor armature may revolve as many as 19 times for every revolution of the flywheel. This permits the cranking motor to develop relatively

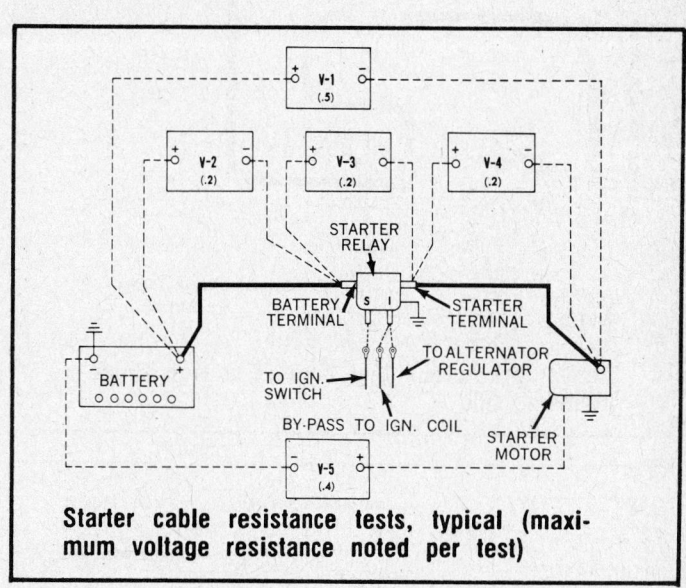

Starter cable resistance tests, typical (maximum voltage resistance noted per test)

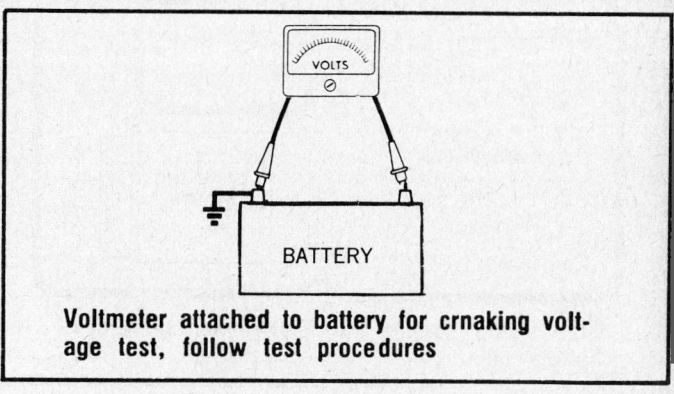

Voltmeter attached to battery for crnaking voltage test, follow test procedures

33-3

SECTION 33
STARTER MOTORS
SYSTEM ELECTRICAL DIAGNOSIS

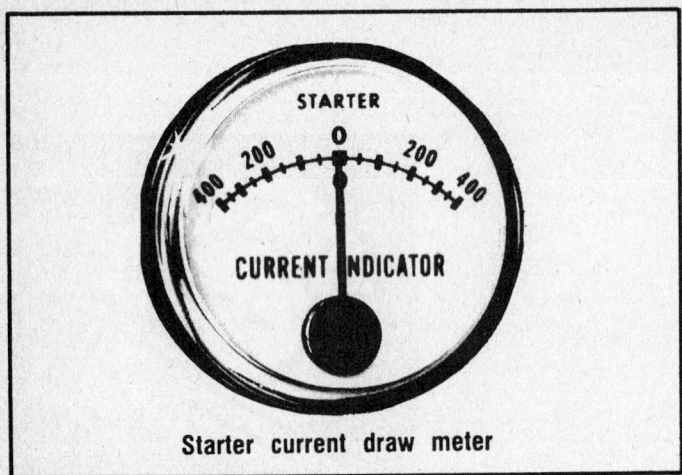

Starter current draw meter

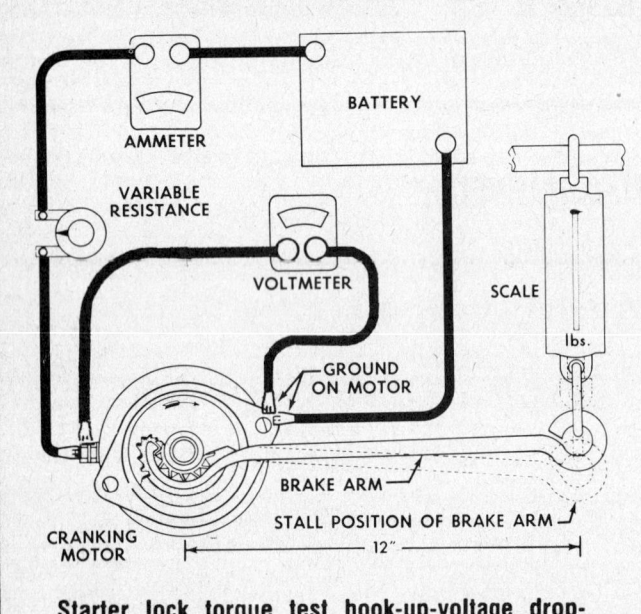

Starter lock torque test hook-up-voltage drop-grounded side

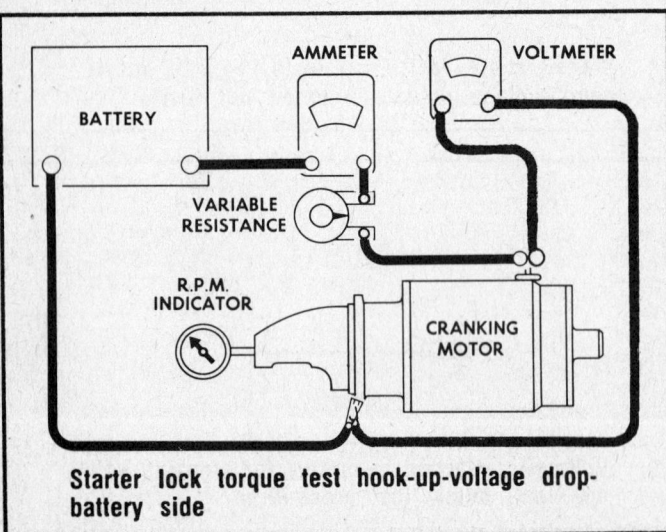

Starter lock torque test hook-up-voltage drop-battery side

high armature speed and considerable power while cranking the engine at relatively low speed.

After the engine starts its speed immediately increases and it soon may reach speeds as high as 1000 rpm. If the cranking motor drive pinion remained in mesh with the flywheel the cranking motor armature would be spun at 19000 rpm (with 19 to 1 gear ratio). This speed may ruin the armature. To prevent this the starter clutch will disengage the starter drive from the engine flywheel.

Testing the Starting Motor

TESTING THE STARTER CIRCUIT

The starter circuit should be divided and tested in four separate phases.
1. Cranking voltage check.
2. Amperage draw.
3. Voltage drop grounded side.
4. Voltage drop battery side.

NOTE: The battery must be in good condition for this test to have significance. To accurately check battery condition use equipment designed to measure its capacity under a load. Instructions accompanying the equipment should be followed. Disconnect the vacuum line to the air pump by-pass valve before performing any cranking tests. After tests are completed run the engine for at least 3 minutes before reconnecting the vacuum line.

Cranking Voltage

Connect voltmeter leads to prods tapped into the battery posts (observe polarity and reverse meter leads if necessary). Remove the high tension wire from the distributor cap and ground it to prevent starting. With electronic ignition disconnect the control box harness from the distributor. Now, turn the key. Observe both voltmeter reading and cranking speed. The cranking speed should be even and at a satisfactory rate of speed with a voltmeter reading of at least 9.6 volts for 12 volt systems.

Amperage Draw

The amount of current the starter motor draws is usually (but not always) associated with the mechanical problems involved in cranking the engine. (Mechanical trouble in the engine, frozen or worn starter parts, misaligned starter or starter components, etc.) Because starter motor amperage draw is directly influenced by anything restricting the free turning of the engine or starter it is important that the engine and all components be at operating temperatures.

When measuring starter current draw remove the high tension wire from the center of the distributor cap and ground it. With electronic ignition disconnect the control box harness from the distributor. A very simple and inexpensive starter current indicator is available at auto stores. This indicator is an induction type gauge and shows, without disconnecting any wires, starter current draw.

Place the yoke of the meter directly over the insulated starter supply cable (cable must be straight for a minimum of 2 inches). Close the starter switch for about 20 seconds and watch the meter dial. Record the average reading. If the indicator swings in the wrong direction reverse the position of the meter. The cranking amperage draw can vary from 150 to 400 amperes depending on the engine size, engine compression and starter type. When starter specifications are not available average starter draw amperage can be derived from testing a like starter unit known to be operating satisfactorily.

More accurate but complex equipment is available from many manufacturers. This equipment consists of a combination voltmeter, ammeter and carbon pile rheostat. When using

STARTER MOTORS
SYSTEM ELECTRICAL DIAGNOSIS
SECTION 33

this equipment follow the equipment manufacturer's procedures and recommendations.

High amperage and lazy performance would suggest an excessively tight engine, friction in the starter or starter drive, grounded starter field or armature. Normal amperage and lazy performance suggest high resistance or possibly poor connections somewhere in the starter circuit. Low amperage and lazy or no performance suggest poor battery condition, bad cables or connections along the line.

Voltage Drop (Grounded Side)

With a voltmeter on the 3-volt scale without disconnecting any wires then connect negative test lead of the voltmeter to a prod secured in the grounded battery post. The positive test lead is connected to a cleaned bare metal portion of the starter motor housing. Close the starter switch and note the voltmeter reading. If the reading is the same as battery reading the ground circuit is open somewhere between the battery and the starter. In many cases the reading will be very small. The reading shown will indicate voltage drop (loss) between battery ground post and starter housing. The drop should not exceed 0.2 volt. If the voltage drop is above the specified amount the next step is to isolate and correct the cause. It can be a bad cable or connection anywhere in the battery to starter ground circuit. A check of this type should progress along the various points of possible trouble between the battery ground post and the starter motor housing until the trouble spot has been located.

Voltage Drop (Battery Side)

Bad starter cranking may result from poor connections or faulty components of the battery or hot phase of the starter motor circuit. To check this phase of the circuit, without disconnecting any wires, connect one lead of a voltmeter to a prod secured in the hot post of the battery and the other voltmeter lead to the field terminal of the starting motor. The meter should be set to the 16–20 volt scale. Before closing the starter switch the voltmeter reading will be that of the battery. After closing the starter switch change the selector on the voltmeter to the 3-volt scale. With a jumper wire between the relay battery terminal and the relay starter switch terminal crank the engine. If the starting motor cranks the engine the relay (solenoid) is operating.

While the engine is being cranked watch the voltmeter. It should not register more than 0.5 volt. If more than this check each part of the circuit for voltage drop to isolate the trouble. Without disturbing the voltmeter to battery hook-up move the free voltmeter lead to the battery terminal of the relay (solenoid) and crank the engine. The voltmeter should show no more than 0.1 volt.

If this reading is correct move the same voltmeter lead to the starting motor terminal of the relay (solenoid). While the engine is being cranked the voltmeter should show no more than 0.3 volt. If it does the trouble lies in the relay. If the reading is correct the trouble is in the cable or connections between the relay and the starting motor.

GENERAL STARTER DIAGNOSIS

Starter Won't Crank the Engine

1. Dead battery.
2. Open starter circuit such as, broken or loose battery cables, inoperative starter motor solenoid, broken or loose wire from starter switch to solenoid, poor solenoid or starter ground or a bad starter switch.
3. Defective starter internal circuit such as, dirty or burnt commutator, stuck, worn or broken brushes, open or shorted armature, and open or grounded fields.
4. Starter motor mechanical faults such as, jammed armature end bearings, bad bearing, allowing armature to rub fields, bent shaft, broken starter housing, bad starter worm or drive mechanism, bad starter drive or flywheel driven gear.
5. Engine hard or impossible to crank such as, hydrostatic lock, water in combustion chamber, crankshaft seizing in bearings, piston or ring seizing, bent or broken connecting rod, seizing or connecting rod bearing, or flywheel jammed or broken.

Starter Spins Free Won't Engage

1. Sticking or broken drive mechanism.

Inspection and Repair

BRUSHES AND BRUSH HOLDERS

Inspect the brushes for wear. If they are worn down to one-half their original length when compared with a new brush they should be replaced. Make sure the brush holders are clean and the brushes are not binding in the holders. The full brush surface should ride on the commutator with proper spring tension to give good firm contact. Brush leads and screw should be tight and clean.

ARMATURE

The armature should be checked for short circuits, opens, and grounds.

1. Short circuits are located by rotating the armature in a growler with a steel strip such as a hacksaw blade held on the armature. The steel strip will vibrate on the area of the short circuit. Shorts between bars are sometimes produced by brush dust or copper between the bars. Undercutting the insulation will eliminate these shorts.
2. Opens may be located by inspecting the points where the conductors are joined to the commutator for loose connections. Poor connections cause arcing and burning of the commutator. If the bars are not badly burned resolder the leads in the riser bars and turn the commutator down in a lathe. Then undercut the insulation between the commutator bars $\frac{1}{32}$ inch.
3. Grounds in the armature can be detected by the use of a test lamp (or ohmmeter). If the lamp lights when one test prod is placed on the commutator and the other test prod on the armature core or shaft the armature is grounded. If the commutator is worn, dirty, out of round or has high insulation the commutator should be turned down and undercut.

FIELD COILS

The field coils should be checked for grounds and opens using a test lamp.

1. Grounds disconnect field coil ground connections. Connect one test prod to the field frame and the other to the field connector. If the lamp lights the field coils are grounded and must be repaired or replaced.
2. Opens connect test lamp prods to ends of field coils. If lamp does not light, the field coils are open.
3. If the field coils need to be removed for repair or replacement a pole shoe spreader and pole shoe removal tool should be used. Care should be exercised in replacing the field coils to prevent grounding or shorting them as they are tightened into place. Where the pole shoe has a long lip on one side it should be assembled in the direction of armature rotation.

SWITCHES AND SOLENOIDS

Magnetic Switches

Magnetic switches serve only to make contact for the starter motor. Usually, such switches are located on the inner fender panel although they are found mounted on the starter in a few cases.

SECTION 33 STARTER MOTORS
SWITCHES AND SOLENOIDS

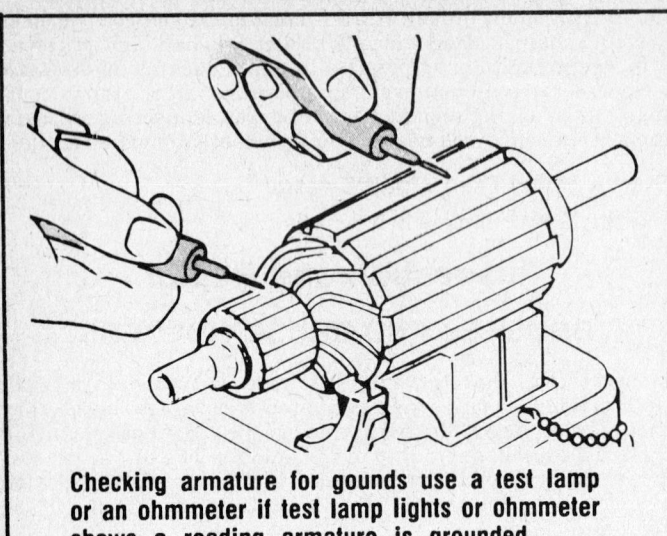

Checking armature for gounds use a test lamp or an ohmmeter if test lamp lights or ohmmeter shows a reading armature is grounded

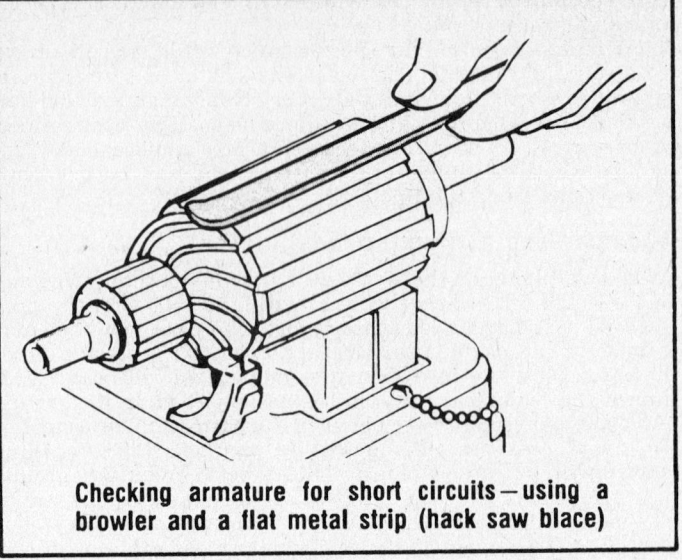

Checking armature for short circuits — using a browler and a flat metal strip (hack saw blace)

Magnetic Switches with Two Control Terminals

On this type of magnetic switch current is supplied from the ignition switch or transmission neutral button to one of the magnetic switch control terminals. The other control terminal is connected to the transmission neutral safety switch (on the transmission) where it is grounded.

Magnetic Switches with Ignition Resistor By-Pass Terminals

All normally use a magnetic switch with a single control terminal. The second terminal is an ignition resistor by-pass terminal.

SOLENOIDS WITHOUT RELAYS

This type of starter solenoid is always mounted on the starter. Makes electrical contact for the starter and pulls the starter and drive clutch into mesh with the flywheel. The Chrysler reduction gear starter has this solenoid embodied in the starter housing. There is only one control terminal on the solenoid. The ignition by-pass terminal is usually marked R or IGN, if it is used.

SOLENOIDS WITH SEPARATE RELAYS

The solenoid itself is always mounted on the starter. In addition to making contact for the starter, it also pulls the starter

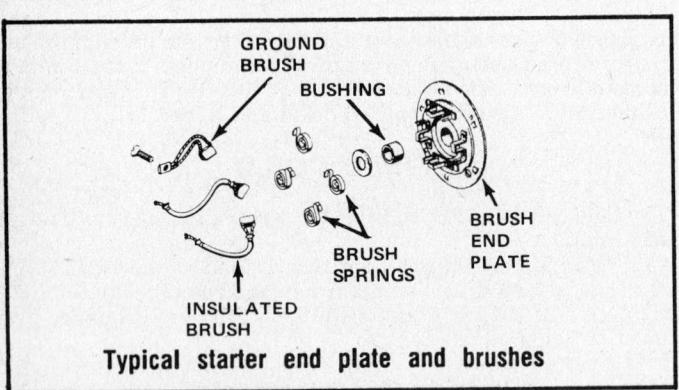

Typical starter end plate and brushes

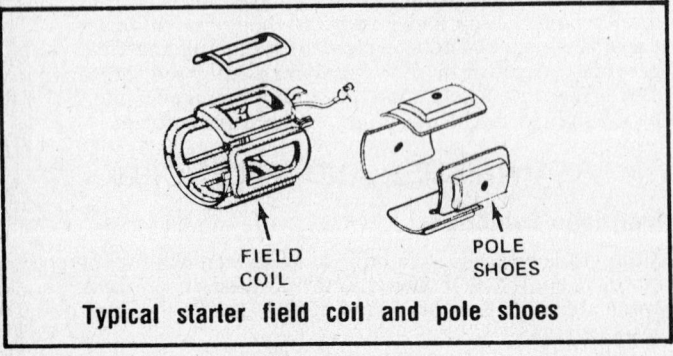

Typical starter field coil and pole shoes

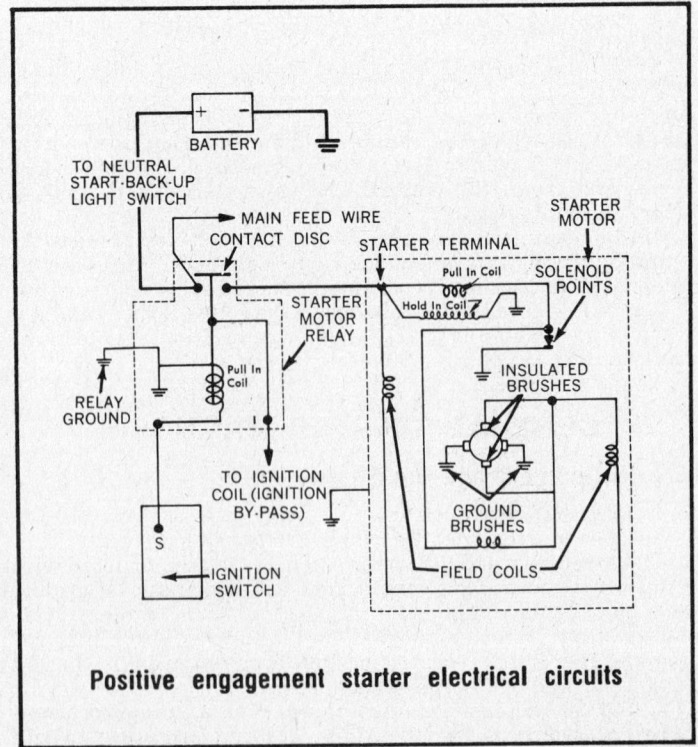

Positive engagement starter electrical circuits

33-6

STARTER MOTORS
SWITCHES AND SOLENOIDS
SECTION 33

drive clutch gear into mesh with the flywheel. A single control terminal is used on the solenoid itself. The relay is usually found mounted to the inner fender panel or on the firewall.

SOLENOIDS WITH BUILT-IN RELAYS

These units are always mounted on the starter and are connected, through linkage, to the starter drive clutch. The relay portion is a square box built into and integral with the front end of the solenoid assembly.

NEUTRAL SAFETY SWITCHES

The purpose of the neutral safety switch is to prevent the starter from cranking the engine except when the transmission is in neutral or park. On some cars the neutral safety switch is located on the transmission. It serves to ground the solenoid or magnetic switch, whichever is used. On other vehicles the neutral safety switch is located either at the bottom of the steering column where it contacts the shift mechanism, on the steering column underneath the dash or on the shift linkage (console). Some manual transmission models have a clutch linkage safety switch to prevent starter operation unless the clutch pedal is depressed. On most vehicles the neutral safety switch and the backup light switch are combined into a single switch mechanism.

Troubleshooting Neutral Safety Switches (Quick Test)

If the starter fails to function and the neutral safety switch is to be checked a jumper can be placed across its terminals. If the starter then functions the safety switch is defective. In the case of neutral safety switches with one wire, this wire must be grounded for testing purposes. If the starter works with the wire grounded the switch is defective.

Neutral Safety Switch (Back-Up Light Switch)

When the neutral safety switch is built in combination with the back-up light switch the easiest way to tell which terminals are for the back-up lights is to take a jumper and cross every pair of wires. The pair of wires which light the back-up lamps should be ignored when testing the neutral safety switch. Once the back-up light wires have been located jump the other pair of wires to test the neutral safety switch. If the starter functions only when the jumper is placed across these two wires the neutral safety switch is defective or requires adjustment.

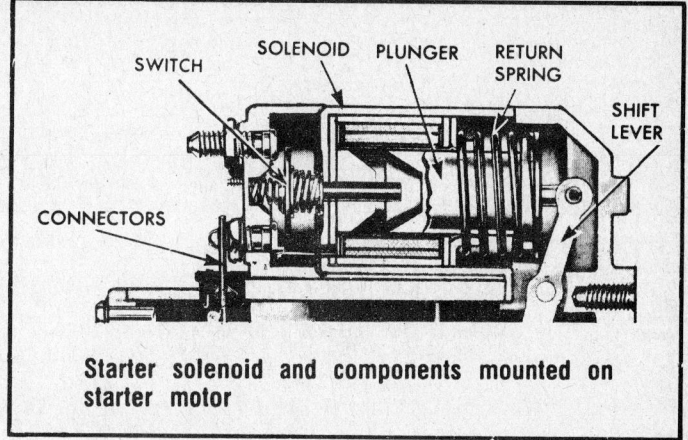

Starter solenoid and components mounted on starter motor

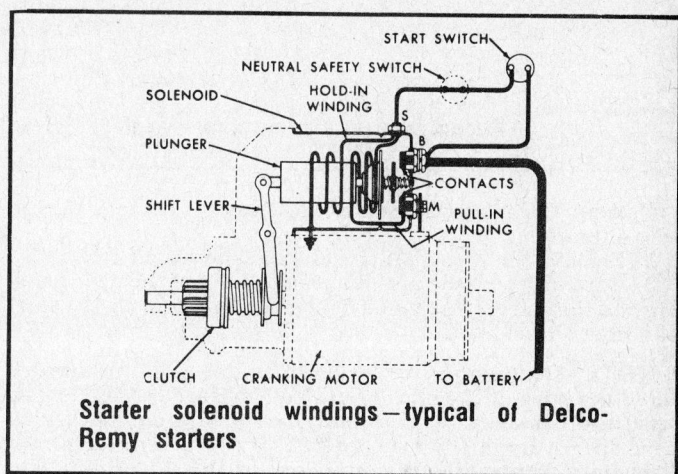

Starter solenoid windings—typical of Delco-Remy starters

STARTER MOTORS

Reduction Gear Starter Motor

CHRYSLER CORPORATION

The housing is die cast aluminum. A 3.5 to 1 reduction combined with the starter to ring gear ratio results in a total gear reduction of about 45 to 1.

The positive shift solenoid is enclosed in the starter housing and is energized through the ignition switch. When ignition switch is turned to start the solenoid plunger engages drive gear through a shifting fork. At the completion of travel the plunger closes a switch to revolve the starter.

The tension of the spring type shifting prevents a butt-tooth lock up and motor will not start before total shift. An overrunning clutch prevents motor damage if key is held on after engine starts. No lubrication is required due to Oilite bearings.

Disassembly

1. Support assembly in a vise equipped with soft jaws. Do

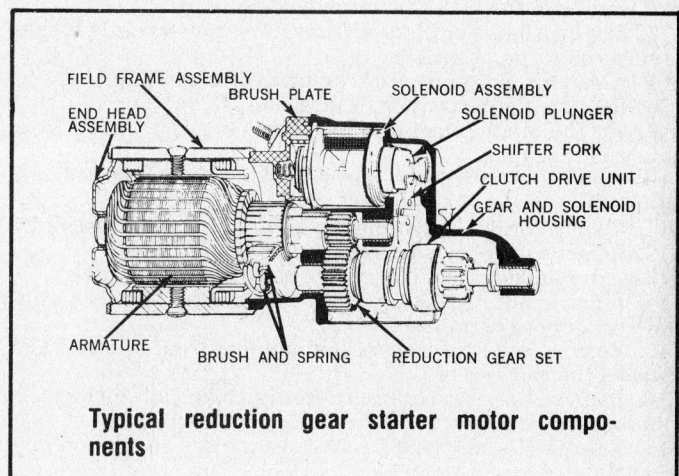

Typical reduction gear starter motor components

SECTION 33: STARTER MOTORS
REDUCTION GEAR STARTER (CHRYSLER)

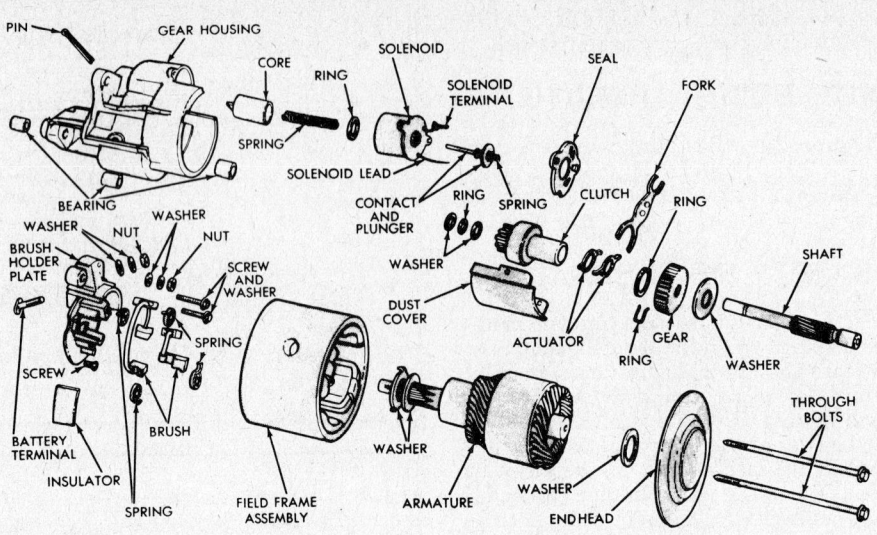

Reduction gear starter motor—exploded view showing assembly sequence of components

not clamp. Care must be used not to distort or damage the die cast aluminum.

2. Remove the through bolts and the end housing.
3. Carefully pull the armature up and out of the gear housing and the starter frame and field assembly. Remove the steel and fiber thrust washer.

NOTE: On eight cylinder engines the starting motors have the wire of the shunt field coil soldered to the brush terminal. Six cylinder engines have the four coils in series and do not have a wire soldered to the brush terminal. One pair of brushes is connected to this terminal. The other pair of brushes is attached to the series field coils by means of a terminal screw. Carefully pull the frame and field assembly up just enough to expose the terminal screw and the solder connection of the shunt field at the brush terminal. Place two wood blocks between the starter frame and starter gear housing to facilitate removal of the terminal screw and unsoldering of the shunt field wire at the brush terminal.

4. Support the brush terminal with a finger behind terminal and remove screw.
5. On eight cylinder engine starters unsolder the shunt field coil lead from the brush terminal and housing.
6. The brush holder plate with terminal contact and brushes is serviced as an assembly.
7. Clean all old sealer from around plate and housing.
8. Remove the brush holder attaching screw.
9. On the shunt type, unsolder the solenoid winding from the brush terminal.
10. Remove $^{11}/_{32}$ inch nut, washer and insulator from solenoid terminal.
11. Remove brush holder plate with brushes as an assembly.
12. Remove gear housing ground screw.
13. The solenoid assembly can be removed from the well.
14. Remove nut, washer and seal from starter battery terminal and remove terminal from plate.
15. Remove solenoid contact and plunger from solenoid and remove the coil sleeve.
16. Remove the solenoid return spring, coil retaining washer, retainer and the dust cover from the gar housing.
17. Release the snapring that locates the driven gear on pinion shaft.
18. Release front retaining ring.

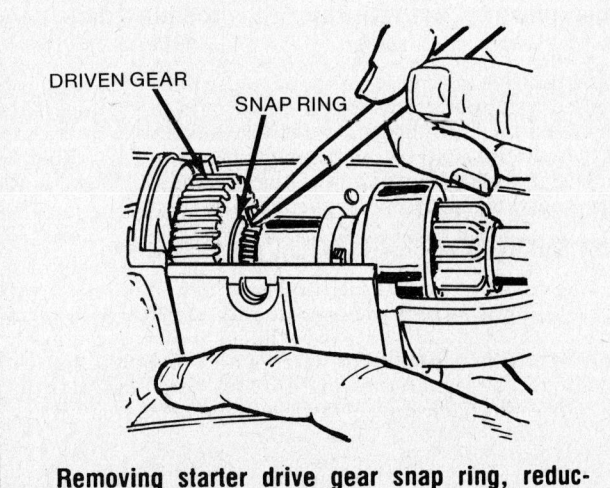

Removing starter drive gear snap ring, reduction gear starter motor

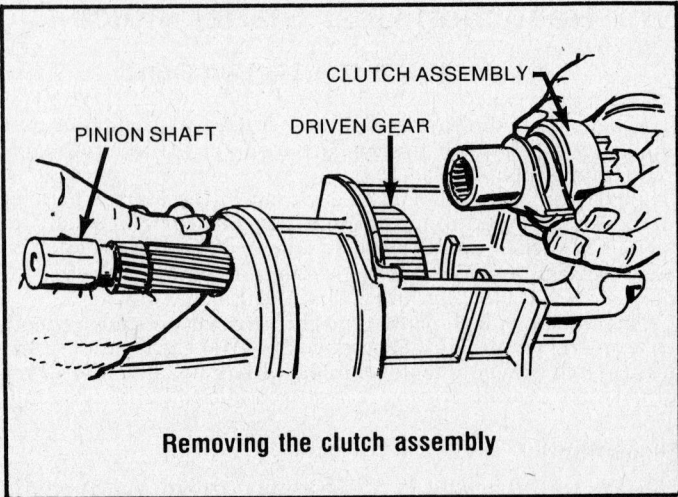

Removing the clutch assembly

STARTER MOTORS
REDUCTION GEAR STARTER (CHRYSLER)

SECTION 33

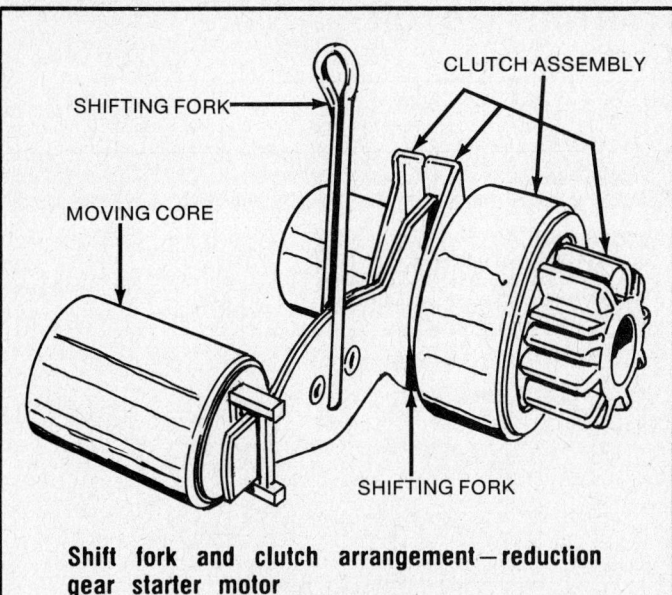

Shift fork and clutch arrangement — reduction gear starter motor

Removing the terminal screw — reduction gear starter motor

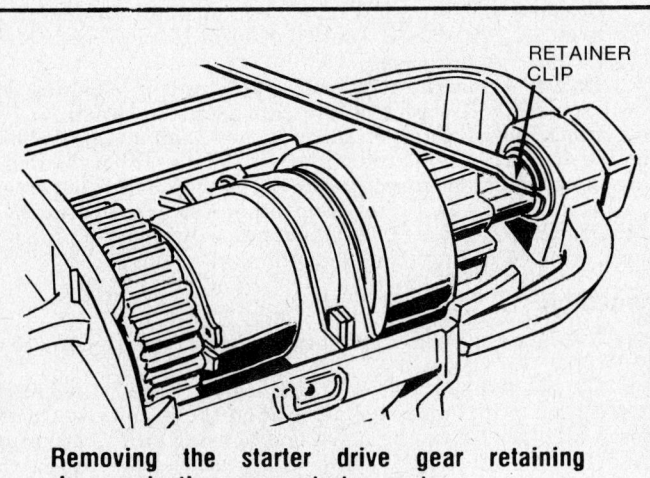

Removing the starter drive gear retaining ring — reduction gear starter motor

19. Push pinion shaft toward the rear and remove snapring, thrust washers, clutch and pinion and the two shift fork nylon actuators.
20. Remove driven gar and friction washer.
21. Pull shifting fork forward and remove moving core.
22. Remove fork retainer pin and shifting fork assembly. The gear housing with bushings is serviced as an assembly.

Replacement of Brushes

1. Brushes that are worn more than one-half the length of new brushes, or are oil soaked, should be replaced.
2. When resoldering the shunt field and solenoid lead make a strong low-resistance connection using a high temperature solder and resin flux. Do not use acid or acid core solder. Do not break the shunt field wire units when removing and installing the brushes.

Starter Clutch and Pinion Gear Inspection

1. Do not immerse the starter clutch unit in a cleaning solvent. The outside of the clutch and pinion must be cleaned with a cloth so as not to wash the lubricant from the inside of the clutch.
2. Rotate the pinion. The pinion gear should rotate smoothly and in one direction only. If the starter clutch unit does not function properly or if the pinion is worn, chipped or burred replace the starter clutch unit.

Commutator Inspection

1. Inspect the commutator and the surface contacted by the brushes when the starter is assembled, for flat spots, out of roundness or excessive wear.
2. Reface the commutator if necessary removing only a sufficient amount of metal to provide a smooth even surface.
3. Using light pressure clean the grooves of the face of the commutator with a pointed tool. Neither remove any metal or expand the grooves.

Assembly

1. The shifter fork consists of two spring steel plates held together by two rivets. Before assembling the starter check the plates for side movement. After lubricating between the plates with a small amount of SAE 10 engine oil they should have about $1/16$ inch side movement to insure proper pinion gear engagement.
2. Position the shift fork in the drive housing and install the shifting fork retainer pin. One tip of the pin should be straight and the other bent at a 15 degree angle away from the housing. The fork and retainer pin should operate freely after bending the tip of the pin.
3. Install the solenoid moving core and engage the shifting fork.
4. Place the pinion shaft into the drive housing and install the friction washer and drive gear.
5. Install the clutch and pinion assembly, thrust washer, and retaining washer.
6. Engage the shifting fork with the clutch actuators. The friction washer must be positioned on the shoulder of the splines of the pinion shaft before the driven gear is positioned.
7. Install the driven gear snapring.
8. Install the pinion shaft retaining ring.
9. The starter solenoid return spring can now be inserted in the moveable core.
10. Install the solenoid contact plunger assembly into the solenoid and reform the double wires so they can be curved around the contactor. This will allow the terminal stud to enter the brush holder properly. The contactor must not touch the double wires after assembly is complete.
11. Assemble the battery terminal stud in the brush holder.
12. Position the seal on the brush holder plate.

33-9

SECTION 33

STARTER MOTORS
REDUCTION GEAR STARTER (CHRYSLER)

REDUCTION GEAR STARTING MOTOR
Chrysler Corp.

Starting Motor Model	1.5 HP—4111855
	1.8 HP—4111860
Make	Chrysler Built
Voltage	12
Number of Fields	4 Series Parallel
Number of Poles	4
Brushes	4
Spring Tension	32-36 Ounces
Drive	Solenoid Shift Overrunning Clutch
Cranking Amperage Draw ②	165-180 Amps. 225, 318, Cu. In. Engines
	180-200 Amps. 225 (when equipped with
	1.8 H.P.) 360 Cu. In. Engines
Free-Running Test	
Voltage	11
Amperage Draw	90
Minimum Speed RPM	1.5 HP—3700
	1.8 HP—5700
Locked Resistance Test	
Voltage	4
Amperage Draw	475-550
Solenoid Switch	
Pull-In Coil	13-15 Amps. @ 6 Volts @ 77°F.
Hold-In Coil	8-9 Amps. @ 6 Volts @ 77°F. ①

① 1982 and Later 8-11 amps @ 6 Volts @ 77°F.
② Engine should be at operating temperature.

13. Run the solenoid lead wire through the hole in the brush holder and attach the solenoid stud, insulating washers, flat washer and nut.
14. Wrap the solenoid lead wire tightly around the brush terminal post and solder it.
15. Fix the brush holder to the solenoid attaching screws.
16. Gently lower the solenoid coil and brush plate into the gear housing.
17. Position the brush plate assembly into the starter gear housing, install the nuts and tighten.
18. Solder the shunt coil lead wire to the starter brush terminal.
19. Install the brush terminal screw.
20. Position the field frame on the gar housing and start the armature into the housing carefully engaging the splines on the shaft with the reduction gear by rotating the armature.
21. Install the fiber thrust washer and the steel washer on the armature shaft.
22. Replace the starter end housing and starter through bolts and tighten securely.

Bosch, Nippondenso and Mitsubishi Starter (Chrysler Corporation)

Disassembly

1. Disconnect the field coil wire from the solenoid terminal.
2. Remove the solenoid mounting screws (and the solenoid Bosch auto trans. models) and work the solenoid (plunger Bosch A/T models) off the shift fork.
3. On Nippondenso units remove the bearing cover, armature shaft lock, washer, spring, and seal.
4. On Bosch units remove the two screws holding down the end shield bearing cap, and remove the cap and washers.
5. Remove the two through bolts and the commutator end frame cover.
6. Remove the two brushes and the brush plate.
7. Slide the field frame off over the armature.
8. Take out the shift lever pivot bolt.
9. Take off the rubber gasket and metal plate.
10. For the Bosch A/T starter and all Nippondenso starters remove the armature assembly and shift lever from the drive end housing. For the Bosch M/T starter press the stop collar off the snapring, remove the snapring, remove the clutch assembly and remove the drive end housing from the armature.
11. For all except the Bosch M/T starter, press the stop collar off the snapring then remove the snapring, stop collar and clutch.

Inspection and Service

1. Brushes that are worn more than one-half the length of new brushes, or are oil-soaked should be replaced. New brushes are $^{11}/_{16}$ inch long.
2. Do not immerse the starter clutch unit in cleaning solvent. Solvent will wash the lubricant from the clutch.
3. Place the drive unit on the armature shaft and while holding the armature rotate the pinion. The drive pinion should rotate smoothly in one direction only. The pinion may not rotate easily but as long as it rotates smoothly it is in good condition. If the clutch unit does not function properly or if the pinion is worn, chipped or burred replace the unit.

Assembly

1. Lubricate the armature shaft and splines with SAE 10 or 30 W oil.
2. On all except the Bosch M/T starter install the clutch, stop collar, lock ring and shaft fork on the armature. On the Bosch M/T starter fit the drive end housing on the armature then install the clutch, stop collar and snapring on the armature.
3. On all except the Bosch M/T starter install the armature assembly and shift fork in the drive end housing.

STARTER MOTORS
BOSCH, NIPPONDENSO, MITSUBISHI (CHRYSLER)
SECTION 33

DIRECT DRIVE STARTER MOTOR
Chrysler Corp.

Make Model	Bosch	Nippondenso
Voltage	12	12
No. of Fields	4 (Series parallel)	4 (Series parallel)
No. of Poles	4	4
Brushes	4	4
Drive	Solenoid shift Overrunning clutch	Solenoid shift Overrunning clutch
Cranking Amperage Draw Test ①	120-160 amps	120-160 amps
Free-Running Test		
Voltage	11	11
Amperage Draw	47 amps	47 amps
Minimum Speed RPM	6600 rpm	6600 rpm
Solenoid Closing Voltage	7.5 volts	7.5 volts

①Engine should be up to operating temperature. Extremely heavy oil or tight engine will increase starter amperage draw.

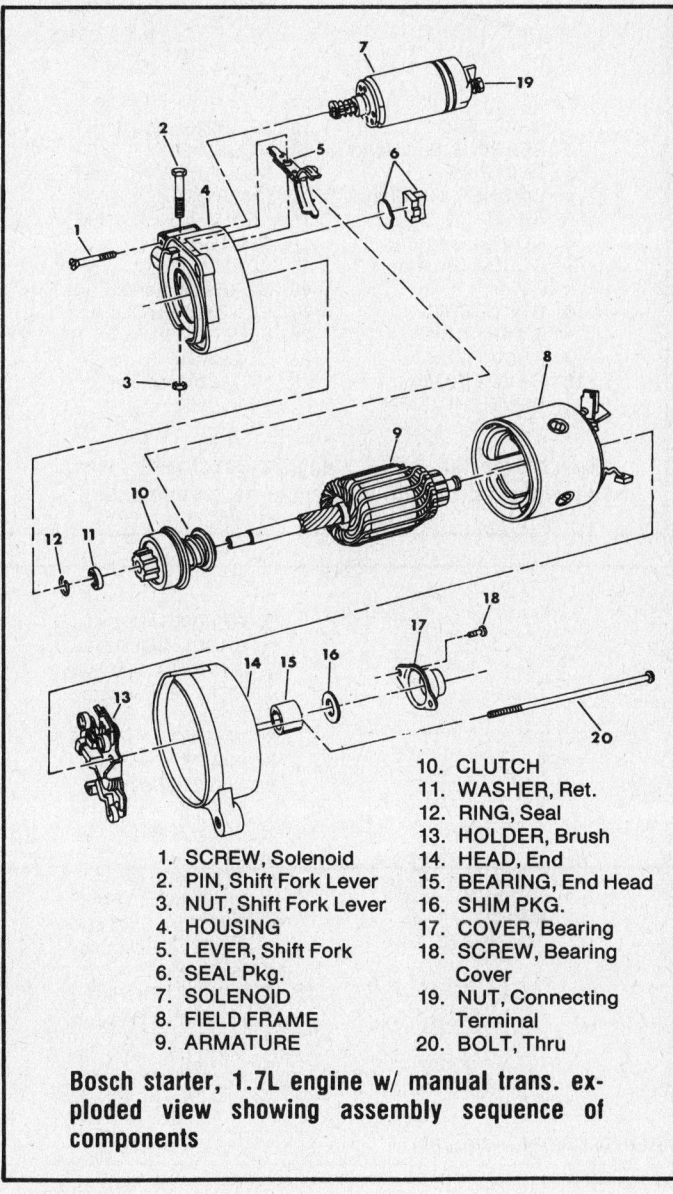

1. SCREW, Solenoid
2. PIN, Shift Fork Lever
3. NUT, Shift Fork Lever
4. HOUSING
5. LEVER, Shift Fork
6. SEAL Pkg.
7. SOLENOID
8. FIELD FRAME
9. ARMATURE
10. CLUTCH
11. WASHER, Ret.
12. RING, Seal
13. HOLDER, Brush
14. HEAD, End
15. BEARING, End Head
16. SHIM PKG.
17. COVER, Bearing
18. SCREW, Bearing Cover
19. NUT, Connecting Terminal
20. BOLT, Thru

Bosch starter, 1.7L engine w/ manual trans. exploded view showing assembly sequence of components

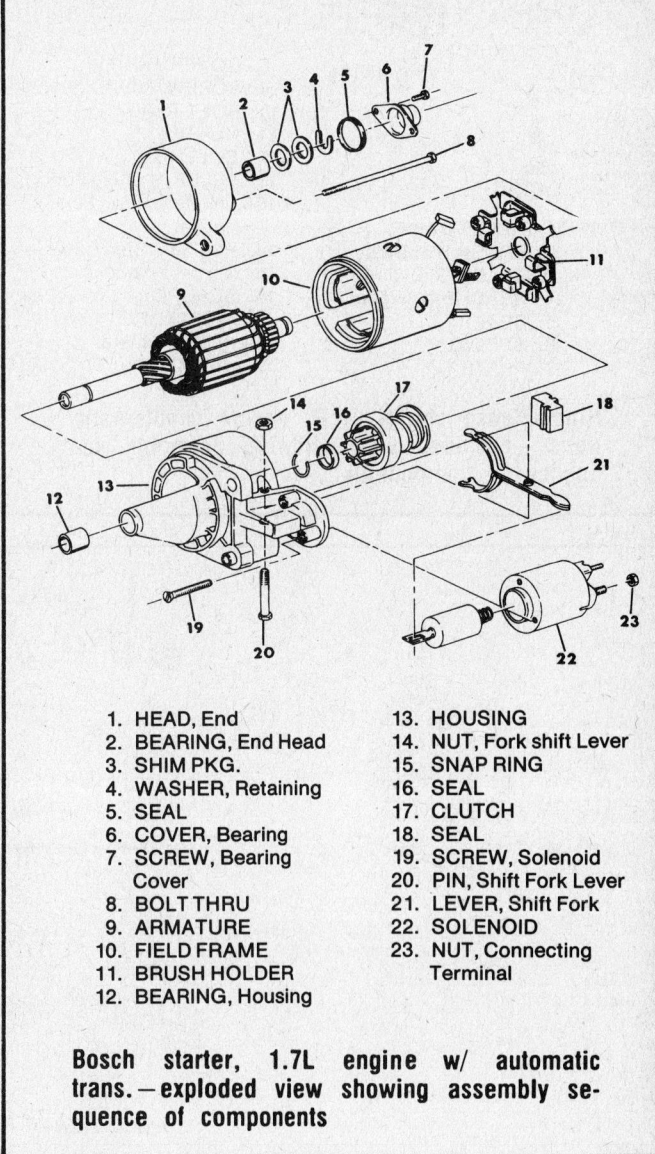

1. HEAD, End
2. BEARING, End Head
3. SHIM PKG.
4. WASHER, Retaining
5. SEAL
6. COVER, Bearing
7. SCREW, Bearing Cover
8. BOLT THRU
9. ARMATURE
10. FIELD FRAME
11. BRUSH HOLDER
12. BEARING, Housing
13. HOUSING
14. NUT, Fork shift Lever
15. SNAP RING
16. SEAL
17. CLUTCH
18. SEAL
19. SCREW, Solenoid
20. PIN, Shift Fork Lever
21. LEVER, Shift Fork
22. SOLENOID
23. NUT, Connecting Terminal

Bosch starter, 1.7L engine w/ automatic trans. — exploded view showing assembly sequence of components

SECTION 33 STARTER MOTORS
BOSCH, NIPPONDENSO, MITSUBISHI (CHRYSLER)

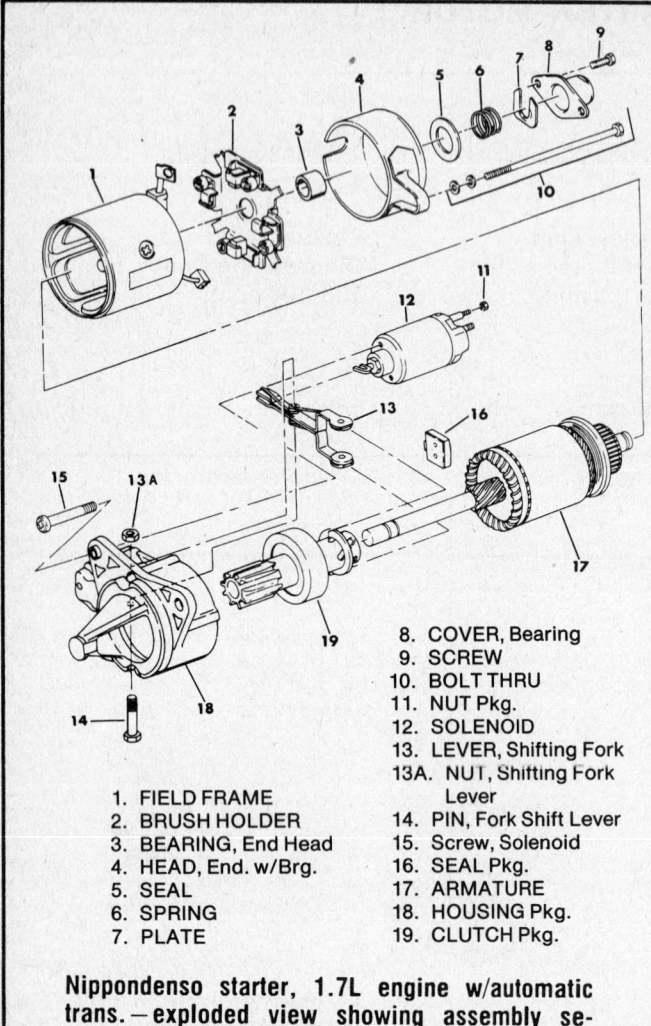

8. COVER, Bearing
9. SCREW
10. BOLT THRU
11. NUT Pkg.
12. SOLENOID
13. LEVER, Shifting Fork
13A. NUT, Shifting Fork Lever
14. PIN, Fork Shift Lever
15. Screw, Solenoid
16. SEAL Pkg.
17. ARMATURE
18. HOUSING Pkg.
19. CLUTCH Pkg.

1. FIELD FRAME
2. BRUSH HOLDER
3. BEARING, End Head
4. HEAD, End w/Brg.
5. SEAL
6. SPRING
7. PLATE

Nippondenso starter, 1.7L engine w/automatic trans. — exploded view showing assembly sequence of components

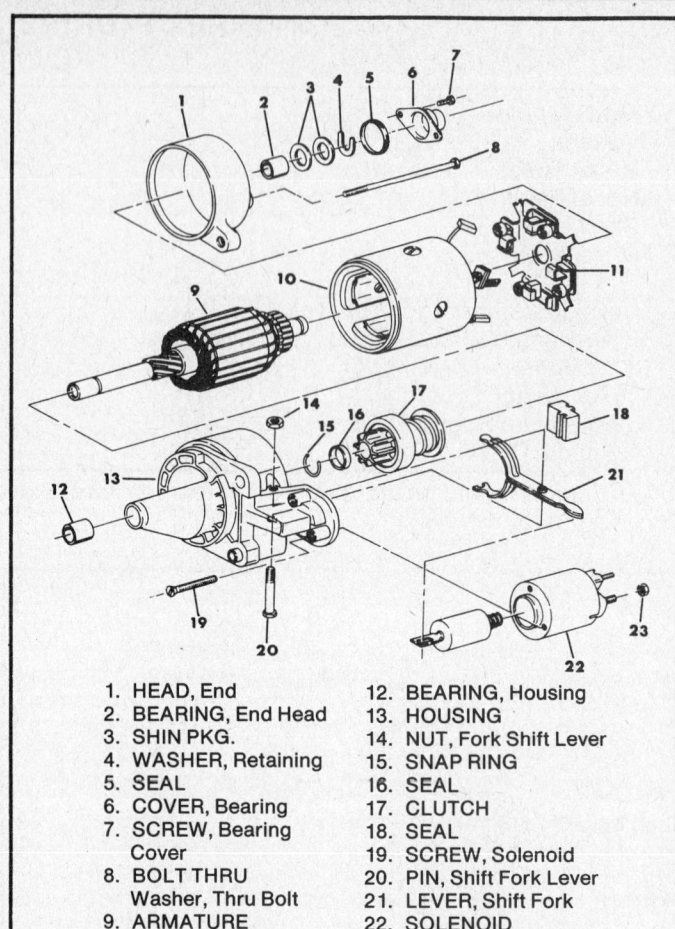

1. HEAD, End
2. BEARING, End Head
3. SHIM PKG.
4. WASHER, Retaining
5. SEAL
6. COVER, Bearing
7. SCREW, Bearing Cover
8. BOLT THRU Washer, Thru Bolt
9. ARMATURE
10. FIELD FRAME
11. BRUSH HOLDER
12. BEARING, Housing
13. HOUSING
14. NUT, Fork Shift Lever
15. SNAP RING
16. SEAL
17. CLUTCH
18. SEAL
19. SCREW, Solenoid
20. PIN, Shift Fork Lever
21. LEVER, Shift Fork
22. SOLENOID
23. NUT, Connecting Terminal

Bosch starter, 2.2L engine — exploded view showing assembly sequence of components

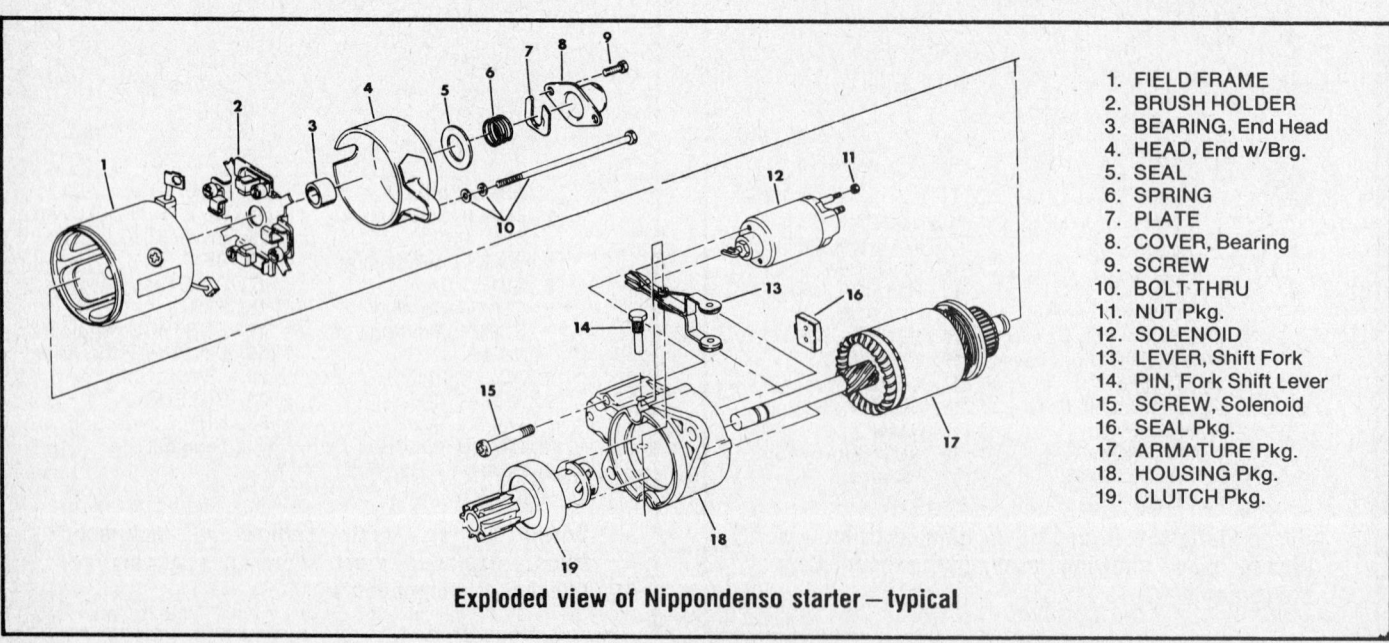

1. FIELD FRAME
2. BRUSH HOLDER
3. BEARING, End Head
4. HEAD, End w/Brg.
5. SEAL
6. SPRING
7. PLATE
8. COVER, Bearing
9. SCREW
10. BOLT THRU
11. NUT Pkg.
12. SOLENOID
13. LEVER, Shift Fork
14. PIN, Fork Shift Lever
15. SCREW, Solenoid
16. SEAL Pkg.
17. ARMATURE Pkg.
18. HOUSING Pkg.
19. CLUTCH Pkg.

Exploded view of Nippondenso starter — typical

STARTER MOTORS
BOSCH, NIPPONDENSO, MITSUBISHI (CHRYSLER)
SECTION 33

4. Install the shift fork pivot bolt. Install the rubber gasket and metal plate.
5. Slide the field frame into position. Install the brush holder and brushes.
6. Position the commutator end frame cover and install the through bolts.
7. On Nippondenso units install the seal, spring, washer, armature shaft lock and bearing cover.
8. On Bosch units install the shim and armature shaft lock. Check the end play (0.002 to 0.021 in.) Install the bearing cover.
9. Assemble the solenoid (or plunger--Bosch A/T models) to the shift fork and install the solenoid with its mounting bolts. Connect the field wire to the solenoid.

Nippondenso/Mitsubishi Reduction Starter

Disassembly

1. Disconnect the wire terminal from the field coil stud and move the rubber shield away from the wire end.
2. Remove the two through bolts from the end frame.
3. Remove the two screws from the end of the frame cap.
4. Remove the upper left solenoid screw and remove the wire retainer.
5. Remove the end shield.
6. Remove the two field frame brushes from the brush plate.
7. Remove the brush plate and slide the armature out of the field frame and remove the field frame.
8. Remove the two screws from the gear housing and remove the gear housing from the solenoid.
9. Remove the clutch rollers and retainer. Remove the pinion and clutch.
10. Remove the solenoid steel ball and spring.
11. Remove the solenoid cover screws, remove the solenoid cover and remove the solenoid plunger.

Inspection and Service

1. Do not immerse parts in cleaning solvent. Immersing the field frame and coil assembly and/or armature will damage insulation. Wipe these parts with a cloth only.
2. Do not immerse drive unit in cleaning solvent. Drive clutch is pre-lubricated at the factory and solvent will wash lubrication from clutch.
3. The drive unit may be cleaned with a brush moistened with cleaning solvent and wiped dry with a cloth.
4. Brushes that are worn more than ½ the length of new brush, or are oil soaked, should be replaced.
5. Field brushes are serviced as part of the field and frame assembly.
6. Ground brushes and all springs come as part of the brush plate assembly.

Assembly

1. The assembly is the reverse of the disassembly procedure.

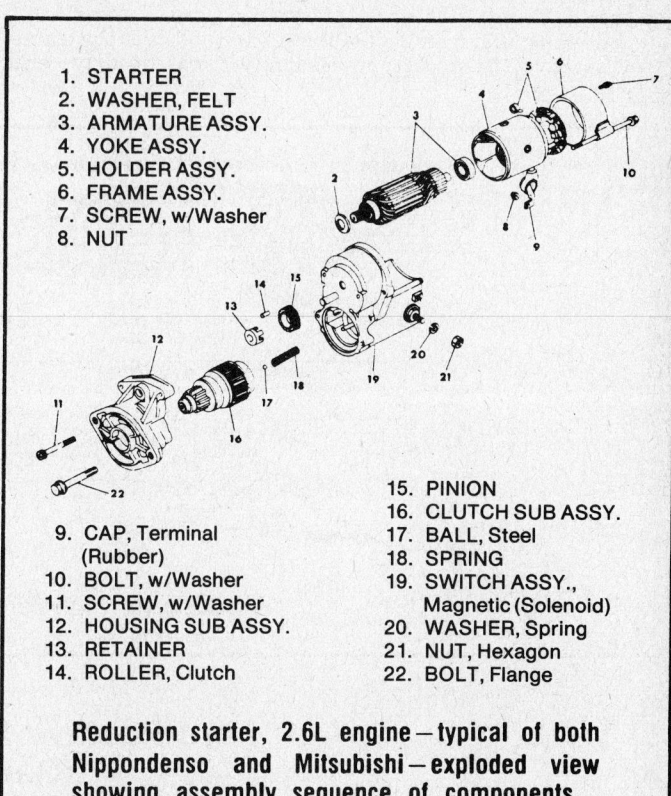

1. STARTER
2. WASHER, FELT
3. ARMATURE ASSY.
4. YOKE ASSY.
5. HOLDER ASSY.
6. FRAME ASSY.
7. SCREW, w/Washer
8. NUT
9. CAP, Terminal (Rubber)
10. BOLT, w/Washer
11. SCREW, w/Washer
12. HOUSING SUB ASSY.
13. RETAINER
14. ROLLER, Clutch
15. PINION
16. CLUTCH SUB ASSY.
17. BALL, Steel
18. SPRING
19. SWITCH ASSY., Magnetic (Solenoid)
20. WASHER, Spring
21. NUT, Hexagon
22. BOLT, Flange

Reduction starter, 2.6L engine—typical of both Nippondenso and Mitsubishi—exploded view showing assembly sequence of components

REDUCTION GEAR STARTER MOTOR
Nippondenso/Mitsubishi

Part Number Automatic Transmission 2.6L A470	5213235	Cranking Amperage Draw Test ①	150-210 amps
Make Model	Nippondenso	Free-Running Test	
Voltage	12	Voltage	11
No. of Fields	4 (Series parallel)	Amperage Draw	85 amps
No. of Poles	4	Minimum Speed RPM	3700 rpm
Brushes	4	Solenoid Closing Voltage	7.5 volts
Drive	In Line solenoid shift Overrunning clutch Double gear Reduction 4.4:1		

①Engine should be up to operating temperature. Extremely heavy oil or tight engine will increase starter amperage draw.

SECTION 33
STARTER MOTORS
BOSCH, NIPPONDENSO, MITSUBISHI (CHRYSLER)

Bosch Starter
(Chrysler 2.5 Liter Engine)

Disassembly and Assembly

1. Remove the field terminal nut. Remove the field terminal. Remove the field washer.
2. Remove the solenoid mounting screws. Work the solenoid off of the shift fork and remove the solenoid from the starter.
3. Remove the two starter end shield bushing cap screws. Remove the starter end shield bushing cap. Remove the end shield bushing "C" washer.
4. Remove the starter end shield bushing washer. Remove the starter end shield bushing seal.
5. Remove the two starter through bolts. Remove the starter end shield. Remove the brush plate.
6. Slide the field frame off of the starter and over the armature. Remove the armature assembly from the drive end housing.
7. Remove the rubber seal from the drive end housing. Remove the starter drive-gear train.
8. Remove the dust plate. Press the stop collar off the snapring using the proper tool. Loosen the snap ring using a snapring pliers.
9. Remove the output shaft snapring. Remove the clutch stop ring collar. Remove the clutch assembly from the starter.
10. Remove the clutch shift lever bushing. Remove the clutch shift lever. Position a suitable tool and remove the "C" clip retainer.
11. Remove the retaining washer. Remove the sun and the planetary gears from the annulus gear.
12. Assembly is the reverse of the disassembly procedure. Replace all defective components as required.

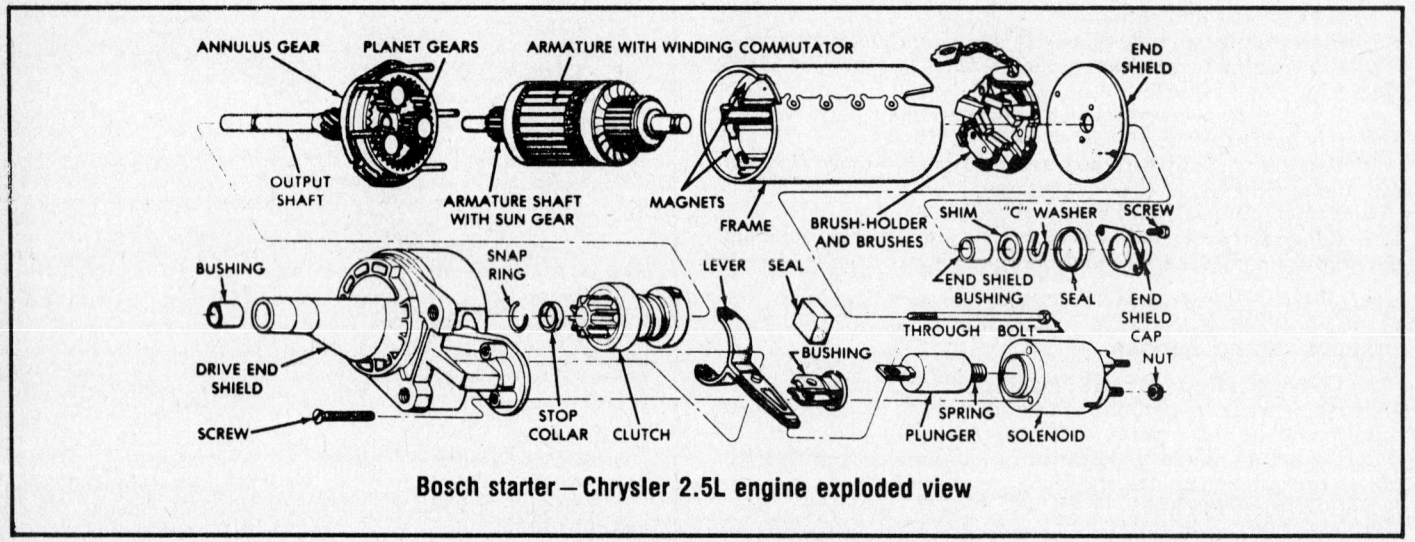

Bosch starter—Chrysler 2.5L engine exploded view

Ford Positive Engagement Starter
(Gas Engine)

The Ford Motorcraft starting system includes the starter motor with an integral positive engagement drive, the battery, a remote control starter switch that is part of the ignition switch, neutral safety switch, if required, the starter relay and the starter circuit wiring.

Disassembly

1. Remove the starter from the vehicle. Position the unit in a suitable holding fixture.
2. Remove the cover screw. Remove the cover, through bolts, starter drive end housing and the starter drive plunger lever return spring.
3. Remove the pivot pin retaining the starter gear plunger lever. Remove the lever and the armature.
4. Remove the stop ring retainer and the thrust washer from the armature shaft.
5. Remove the stop ring from the groove in the armature shaft and discard it. Remove the starter drive gear assembly.
6. Remove the brush end plate and insulator assembly.
7. Remove the brushes from the plastic brush holder. Lift out the brush holder. Note the location of the holder in relation to the end terminal.
8. Remove the two ground brush retaining screws.
9. Remove the sleeve and the retainer by bending up the edge of the sleeve which is inserted in the rectangular hole of the frame.
10. Remove the three pole retaining screws, using tool #10044-A or equivalent. An arbor press may have to be used in conjunction with the special tool.
11. Cut the positive brush leads from the coil fields as close to the field connection as possible.
12. Check the commutator for runout. If the commutator is rough, has flat spots, or is more than 0.005 inch out of round, reface the commutator. Clean the grooves in the commutator face.
13. Inspect the armature shaft and the two bearings for scoring and excessive wear. Replace if necessary.
14. Inspect the starter drive. If the gear teeth are pitted, broken, or excessively worn, replace the starter drive.

STARTER MOTORS
FORD POSITIVE ENGAGEMENT (GASOLINE ENGINE)

Assembly

1. Assemble the starter in the reverse order of the disassembly procedure.
2. Repair or replace defective components as required. Always replace the starter brushes.

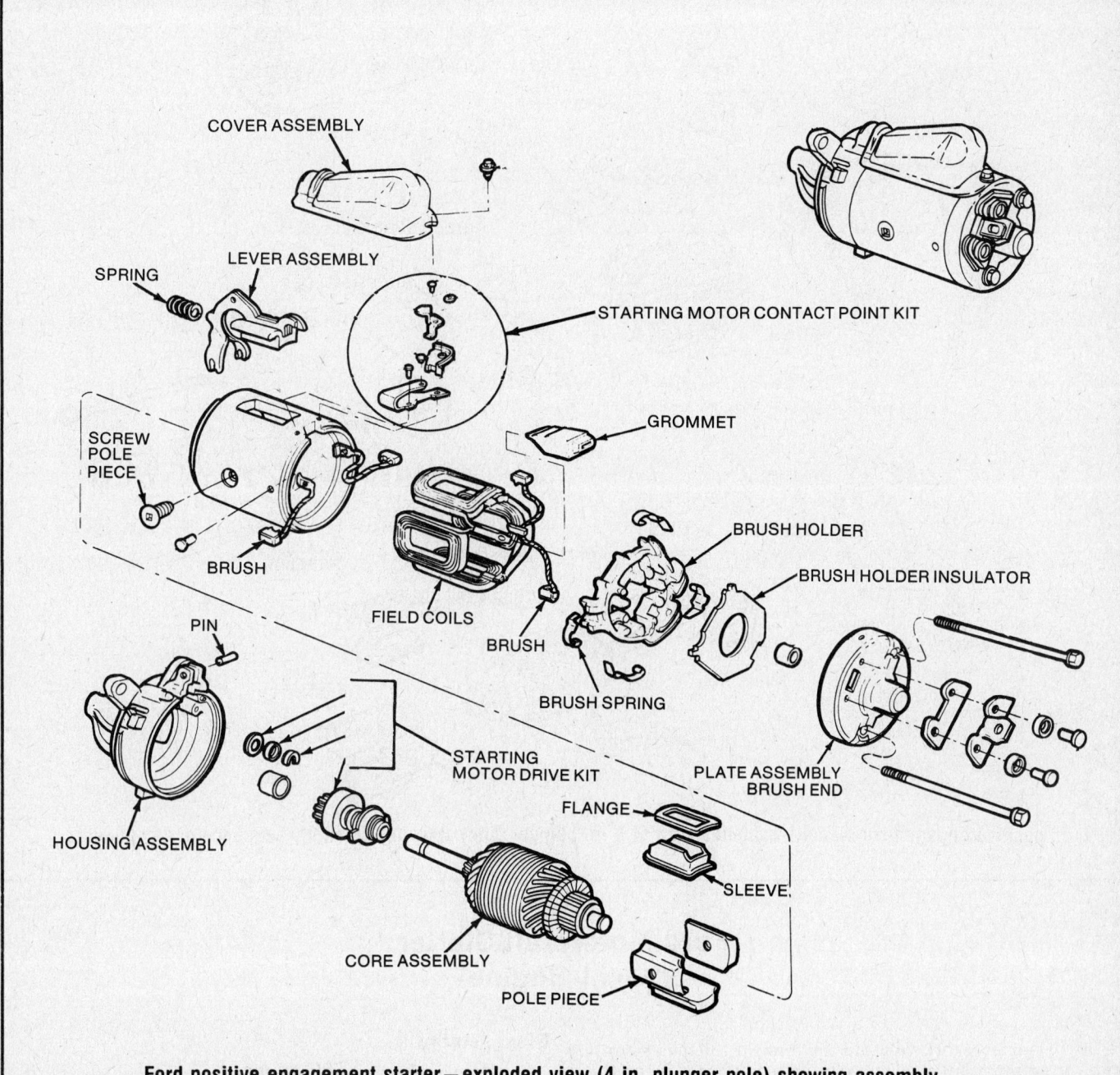

Ford positive engagement starter—exploded view (4 in. plunger pole) showing assembly sequence of components

SECTION 33: STARTER MOTORS
FORD POSITIVE ENGAGEMENT (GASOLINE ENGINE)

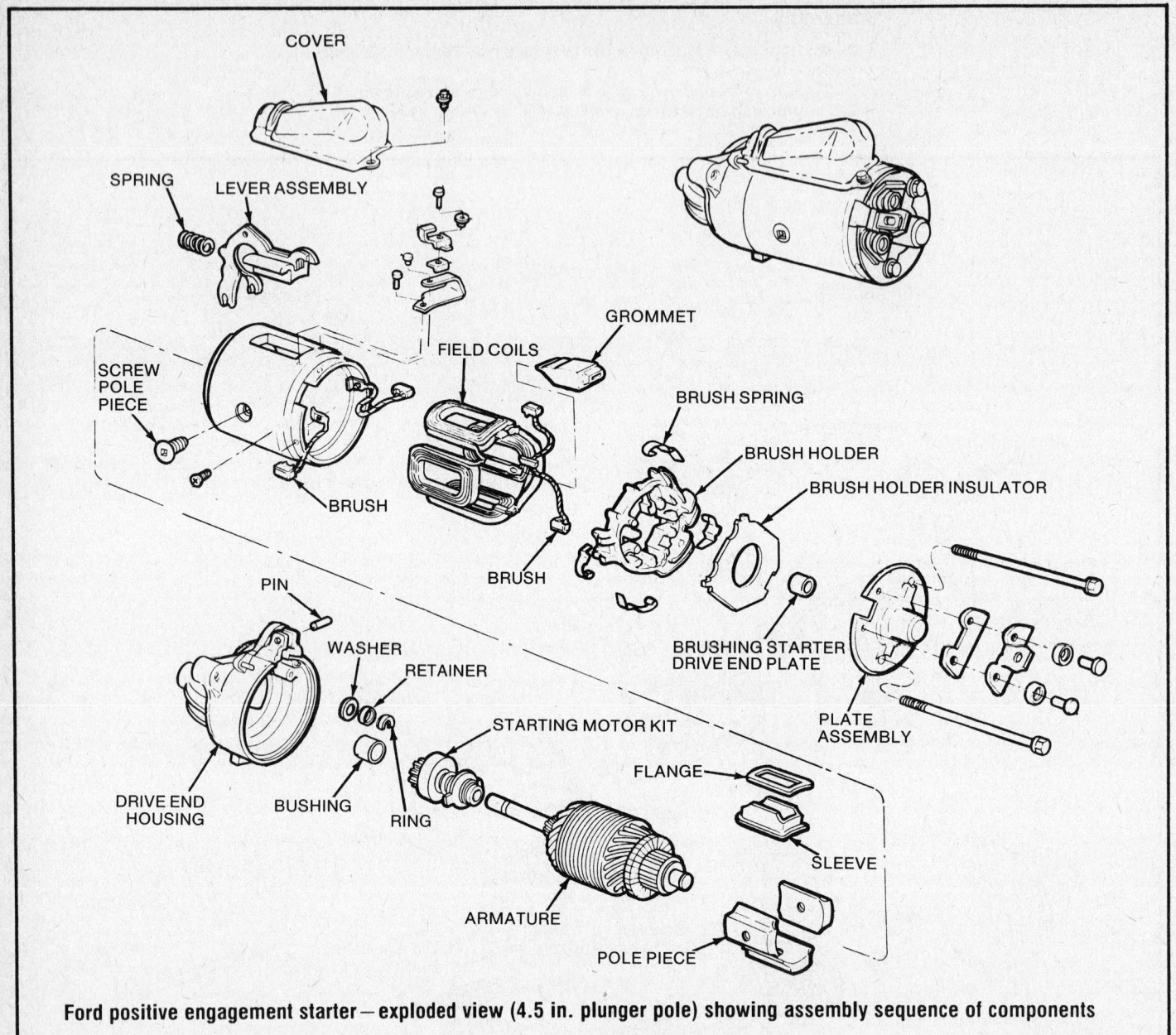

Ford positive engagement starter — exploded view (4.5 in. plunger pole) showing assembly sequence of components

Ford Motorcraft Starter (Diesel Engine)

The diesel starter is a 12-volt unit that has the solenoid mounted on the starter housing. The solenoid is energized when the starter relay contacts are closed. This action engages the starter drive with the flywheel ring gear, starting the engine. An overrunning clutch in the drive protects the starter from excessive speed when the engine starts. The current flows through the solenoid energizing coil until the solenoid plunger is at the end of its travel. The plunger then closes a set of contacts that by-pass the energizing coil, letting the holding coil keep the starter drive engaged and passing starting current to the starter.

Disassembly

1. Remove the starter assembly from the vehicle. Position the unit in a suitable holding fixture.
2. Disconnect the field coil connection from the solenoid motor terminal.
3. Remove solenoid attaching screws, solenoid and plunger return spring. Rotate solenoid 90 degrees to remove.
4. Remove through bolts and brush end plate.
5. Remove brush springs and brushes from plastic brush holder and remove brush holder. Note location of brush holder with respect to ground brush terminals.

STARTER MOTORS
FORD/MOTORCRAFT (DIESEL ENGINE)

33 SECTION

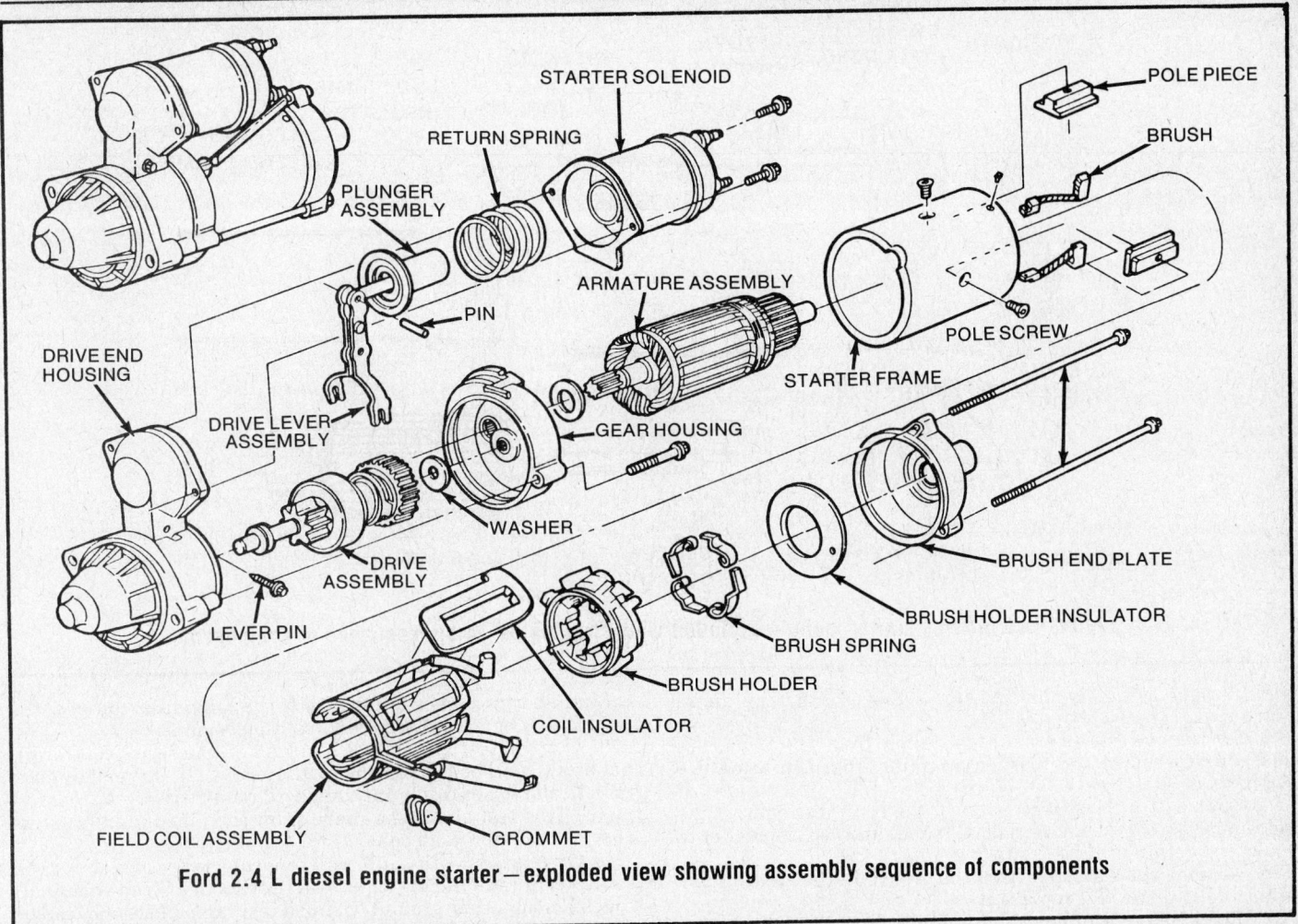

Ford 2.4 L diesel engine starter — exploded view showing assembly sequence of components

6. Remove frame assembly. Remove armature assembly.
7. Remove screw from gear housing and remove gear housing.
8. Remove plunger and lever pivot screw and remove plunger and lever assembly.
9. Remove gear, output shaft and drive assembly.
10. Remove thrust washer, retainer, drive stop ring and slide drive assembly off output shaft.
11. Inspect the armature windings from broken or burned insulation and open connections at commutator. Check for ground.
12. Check commutator for run out. If commutator is rough or more than 0.005 inch out of round, service as necessary.
13. Check plastic brush holder for cracks or broken pads. Replace brushes if worn to 0.25 inch in length. Inspect field coils and plastic bobbins for burned or damaged conditions. Check continuity of coil and brush connections. A brush replacement kit is available. All other assemblies are to be replaced rather than repaired.
14. Examine gears, spline on output shaft, and drive pinion for chipped or broken conditions. Replace if required.

Assembly

1. Assemble the starter in the reverse order of the disassembly procedure.

Delco-Remy 5MT, 10MT and 27MT Starters

Disassembly

1. Remove the starter from the vehicle. Position the unit in a suitable holding fixture.
2. Remove the screw from the field coil connector and the solenoid mounting screws. Rotate the solenoid ninety degrees and remove it along with the plunger return spring.
3. Remove the alternator through bolts. Remove the commutator end frame and washer. If the starter is a diesel unit, remove the insulator.
4. Remove the field frame assembly from the drive gear housing. If the starter is a diesel unit, the armature will remain in the drive end frame.
5. If the starter is a diesel unit, remove the shift pin lever bolt. If equipped, remove the center bearing screws. Remove the drive gear housing from the armature shaft. The shift lever

33-17

SECTION 33
STARTER MOTORS
DELCO-REMY 5MT, 10MT AND 27MT

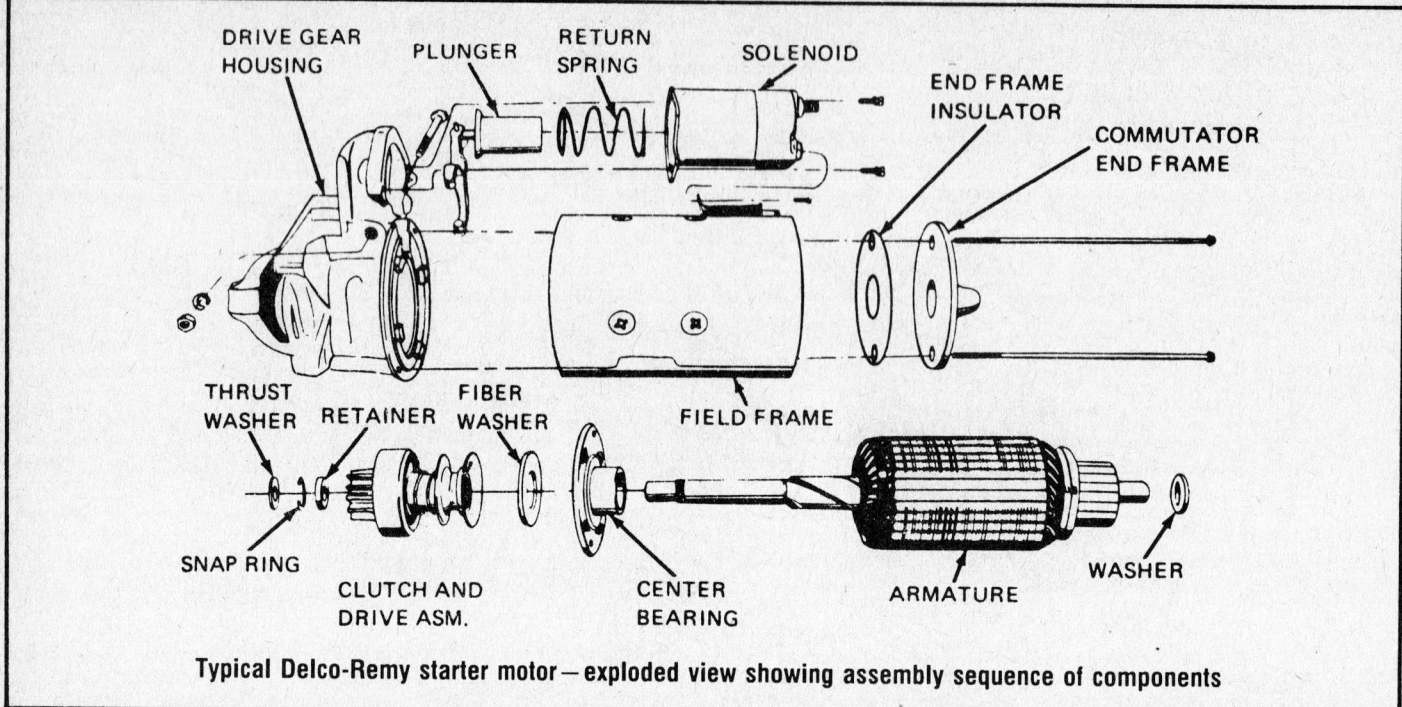

Typical Delco-Remy starter motor—exploded view showing assembly sequence of components

and plunger assembly may now be removed from the diesel starter.

6. To remove the overrunning clutch from the armature shaft, first remove the washer or collar from the armature shaft.

7. Slide a 5/8 inch deep socket over the shaft and against the retainer. Use the socket as a driving tool and tap the socket to move the retainer of the snapring.

8. Remove the snapring from the groove in the shaft. If the snapring is distorted, replace it.

9. Remove the retainer and the clutch assembly from the armature shaft. If the starter is a diesel unit, also remove the fiber washer and the center bearing.

10. If required, the shaft lever and the plunger can be disassembled by removing the roll pin.

11. To replace the starter brushes, remove the brush holder pivot pin which positions the insulated and the ground brushes. Remove the brush spring.

12. On 5MT starters, to replace the brushes remove the screw from the brush holder and separate the brushes from the holder.

13. Inspect armature commutator, shaft and bushings, overrunning clutch pinion, brushes and springs for discoloration, damage or wear. Replace as required.

14. Check fit of armature shaft in bushing in drive housing. Shaft should fit snugly in the bushing. If the bushing is worn, it should be replaced.

15. Inspect armature commutator. If commutator is rough, it should be turned down. Do not undercut or turn to less than 1.650 inch O.D. Do not turn out of round commutators. Inspect the points where the armature conductors join the commutator bars to make sure they have a good connection. A burned commutator bar is usually evidence of a poor connection.

16. Check the armature for short circuits by placing on growler and holding back saw blade over armature core while armature is rotated. If saw blade vibrates, armature is shorted. Recheck after cleaning between the commutator bars. If saw blade still vibrates, replace the armature.

17. Using a test lamp place one lead on the shunt coil terminal and connect the other lead to a ground brush. This test should be made from both ground brushes to insure continuity through both brushes and leads. If the lamp fails to light, the field coil is open and will require replacement.

18. Using a test lamp place one lead on the series coil terminal and the other lead on the insulated brush. If the lamp fails to light the series coil is open and will require repair or replacement. This test should be made from each insulated brush to check brush and lead continuity.

19. On starters with shunt coil separate series and shunt coil strap terminals during this test. Do not let strap terminals touch case or other ground. Using a test lamp place one lead on the grounded brush holder and the other lead on either insulated brush. If the lamp lights a grounded series coil is indicated and must be repaired or replaced.

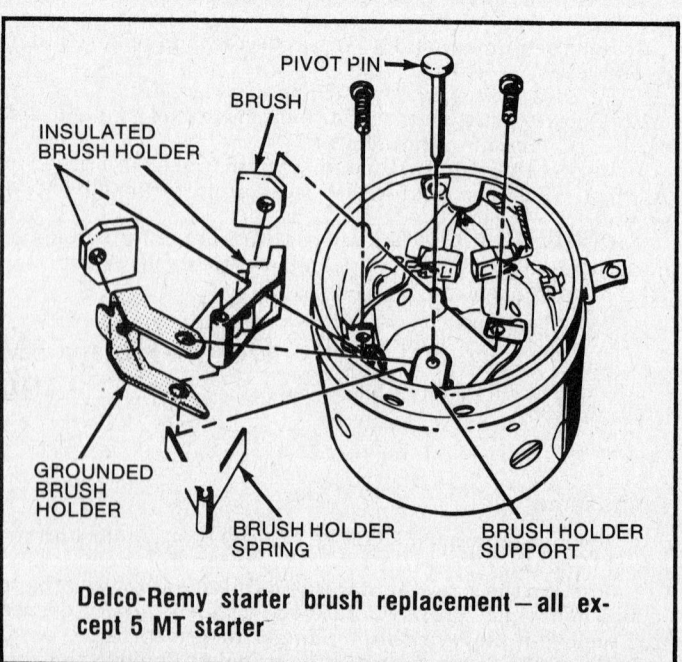

Delco-Remy starter brush replacement—all except 5 MT starter

STARTER MOTORS
DELCO-REMY 5MT, 10MT AND 27MT
SECTION 33

NOTE: If the solenoid has not been removed from the starter the connector strap terminals must be removed before making the following tests. Complete the tests as fast as possible in order to prevent overheating the solenoid.

20. To check hold-in winding connect an ammeter in series with 12-volt battery and the "switch" terminal on the solenoid. Connect a voltmeter to the "switch" terminal and to ground. Connect carbon pile across battery. Adjust the voltage to 10 volts and note the ammeter reading. It should be 14.5 to 16.5 amperes.

21. To check both windings, connect as for previous test.

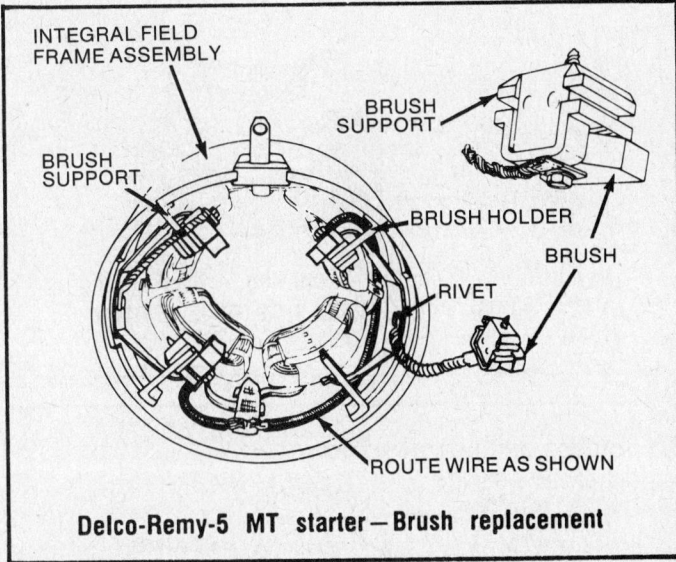

Delco-Remy-5 MT starter — Brush replacement

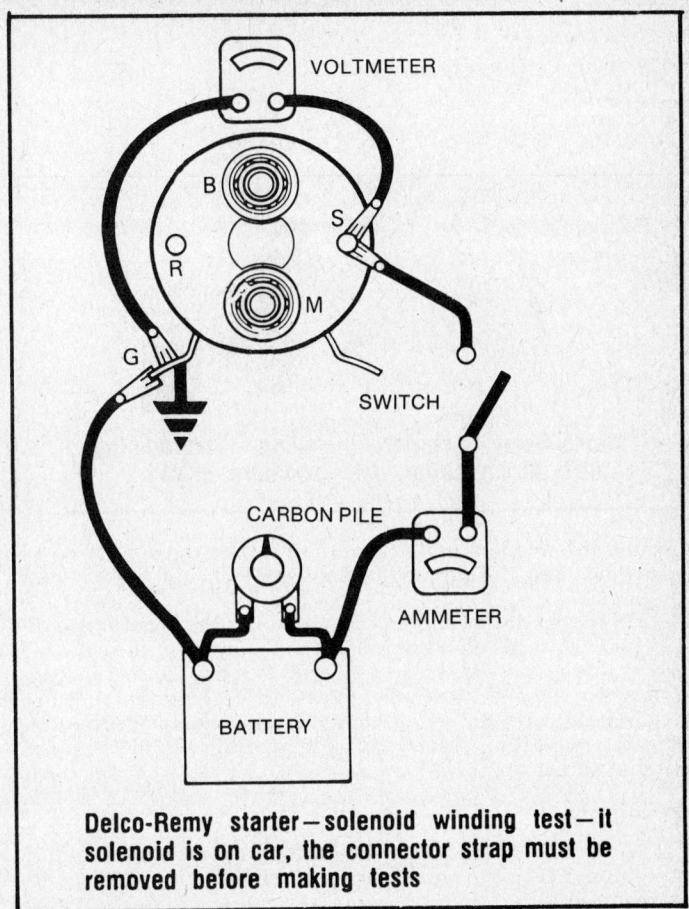

Delco-Remy starter — solenoid winding test — if solenoid is on car, the connector strap must be removed before making tests

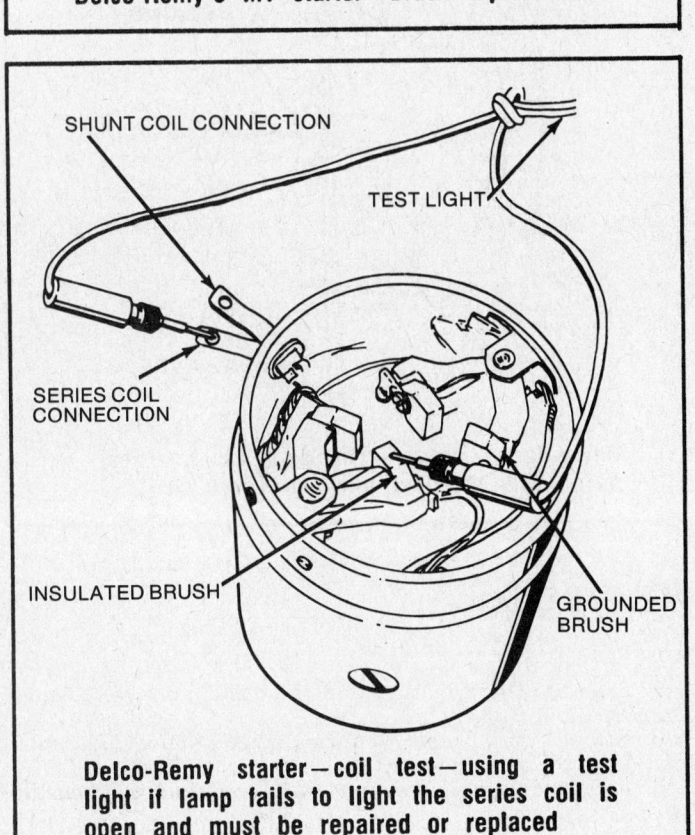

Delco-Remy starter — coil test — using a test light if lamp fails to light the series coil is open and must be repaired or replaced

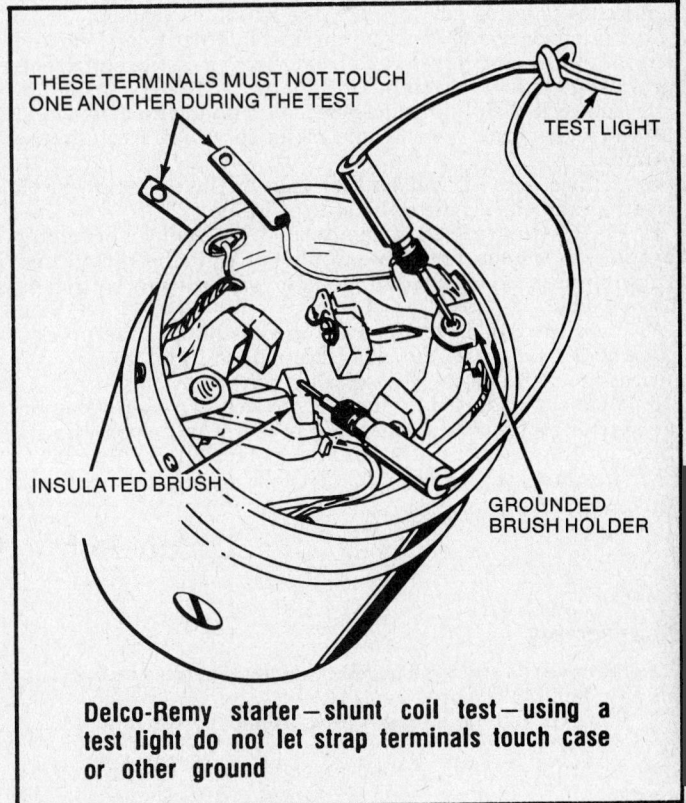

Delco-Remy starter — shunt coil test — using a test light do not let strap terminals touch case or other ground

33-19

SECTION 33

STARTER MOTORS
DELCO-REMY 5MT, 10MT AND 27MT

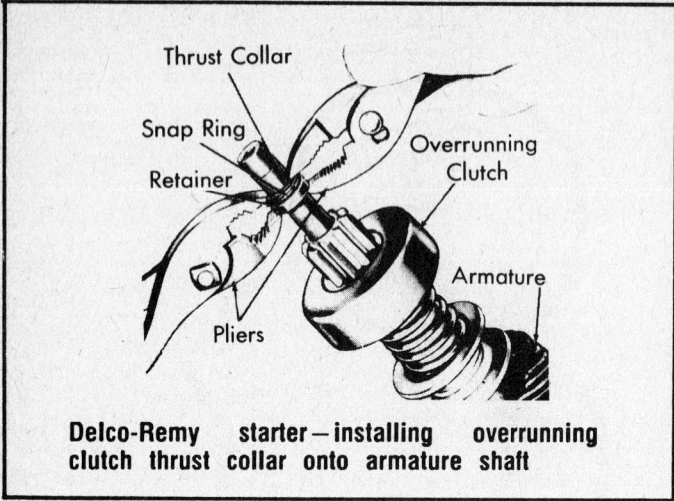

Delco-Remy starter—installing overrunning clutch thrust collar onto armature shaft

Ground the solenoid motor terminal. Adjust the voltage to 10 volts and note the ammeter reading. It should be 41 to 47 amperes.

22. Current draw readings that are over specifications indicate shorted turns on a ground in the windings of the solenoid and the solenoid should be replaced. Current draw readings that are under specifications indicate excessive resistance. No reading indicates an open circuit. Check connections then replace solenoid if necessary. Current readings will decrease as windings heat up.

Assembly

1. Assembly of the starter is the reverse of the disassembly procedure. Be sure to replace or repair all defective components as required.
2. When the starter has been disassembled or the solenoid replaced it is necessary to check the pinion clearance.
3. Pinion clearance must be checked in order to prevent the buttons on the shift lever yoke from rubbing on the clutch collar during engine cranking.
4. To check the pinion clearance, disconnect the motor field coil connector from the solenoid motor terminal. Insulate the terminal.
5. Connect one 12 volt battery lead to the solenoid switch terminal and the other to the starter frame.
6. Flash a jumper lead momentarily from the solenoid motor terminal to the starter frame. This will shift the pinion into cranking position and it will remain so until the battery is disconnected.
7. Push the pinion back as far as possible to take up any movement, and check the clearance with a feeler gauge. The clearance should be 0.0100 to 0.140 inch.
8. Means for adjusting pinion clearance is not provided on the starter motor. If the clearance does not fall within limits check for improper installation and replace all worn parts.

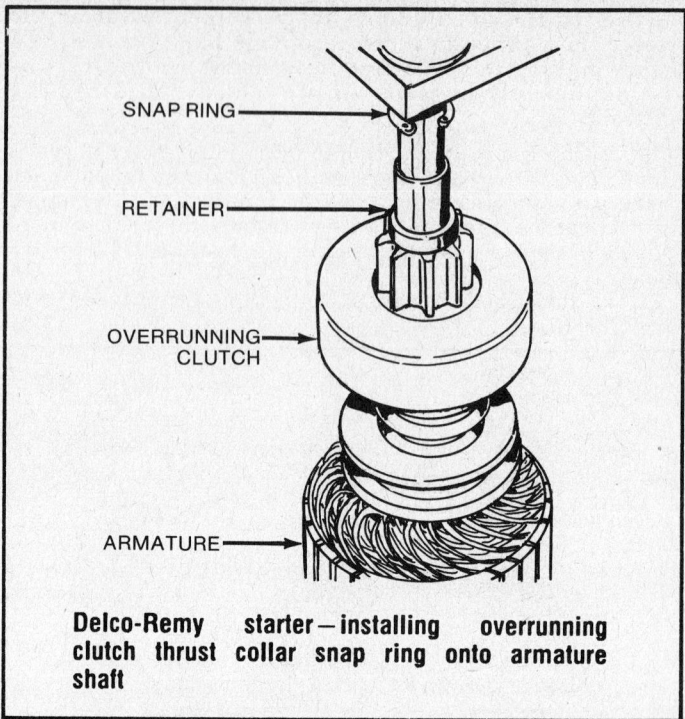

Delco-Remy starter—installing overrunning clutch thrust collar snap ring onto armature shaft

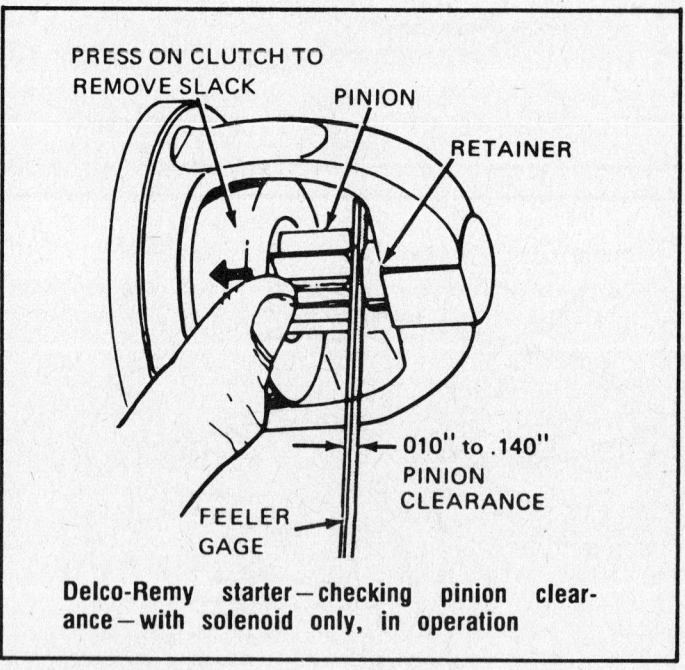

Delco-Remy starter—checking pinion clearance—with solenoid only, in operation

Delco-Remy 15MT/GR Starter

Disassembly

1. Remove the starter from the vehicle. Position the unit in a suitable holding fixture.
2. Remove the field coil screw. Remove the field frame through bolts.
3. Separate the field frame assembly from the drive gear assembly.
4. Separate the armature and the commutator end frame from the field frame.
5. Remove the solenoid mounting screws. Remove the solenoid from the drive housing.
6. Remove the retaining ring, shift lever shaft and housing through bolts to separate the drive assembly, drive housing and gear assembly.

STARTER MOTORS
DELCO-REMY 15MT/GR
SECTION 33

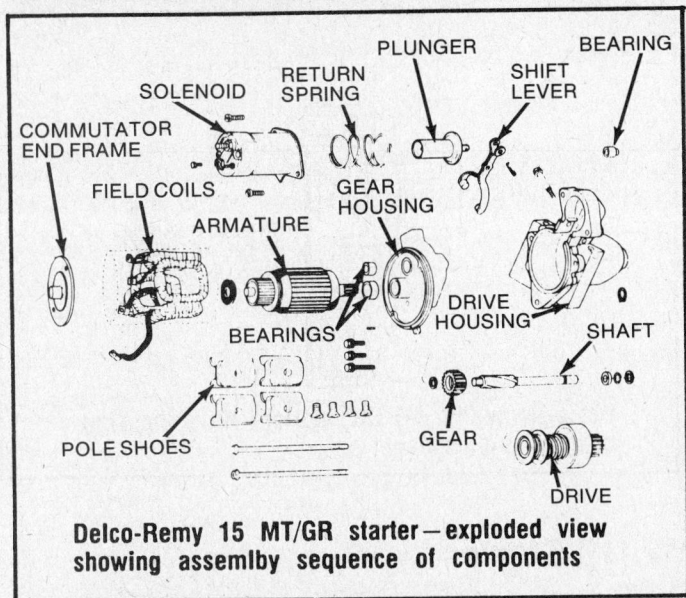

Delco-Remy 15 MT/GR starter—exploded view showing assembly sequence of components

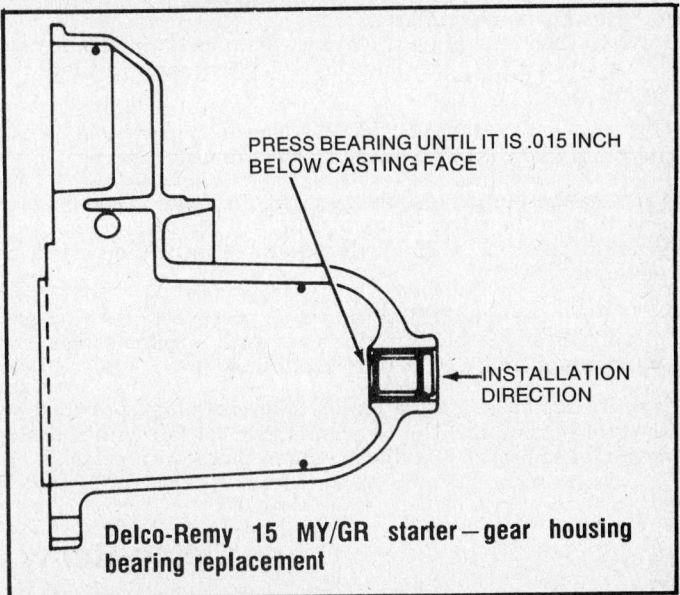

Delco-Remy 15 MY/GR starter—gear housing bearing replacement

7. To remove the overrunning clutch from the armature shaft, first remove the washer or collar from the armature shaft.

8. Slide a 5/8 inch deep socket over the shaft and against the retainer. Use the socket as a driving tool and tap the socket to move the retainer off of the snap ring.

9. Remove the snapring from the groove in the shaft. If the snapring is distorted, replace it.

10. Remove the retainer and the clutch assembly from the armature shaft.

11. To replace the starter brushes, remove the brush holder pivot pin which positions the insulated and the ground brushes. Remove the brush spring.

12. Inspect armature commutator, shaft and bushings, overrunning clutch pinion, brushes and springs for discoloration, damage or wear. Replace as required.

13. Check fit of armature shaft in bushing in drive housing. Shaft should fit snugly in the bushing. If the bushing is worn, it should be replaced.

14. Inspect armature commutator. If commutator is rough, it should be turned down. Do not undercut or turn to less than 1.650 inch O.D. Do not turn out of round commutators. Inspect the points where the armature conductors join the commutator bars to make sure they have a good connection. A burned commutator bar is usually evidence of a poor connection.

15. Check the armature for short circuits by placing on growler and holding hack saw blade over armature core while armature is rotated. If saw blade vibrates, armature is shorted. Recheck after cleaning between the commutator bars. If saw blade still vibrates, replace the armature.

16. Using a test lamp place one lead on the shunt coil terminal and connect the other lead to a ground brush. This test should be made from both ground brushes to insure continuity through both brushes and leads. If the lamp fails to light the field coil is open and will require replacement.

17. Using a test lamp place one lead on the series coil terminal and the other lead on the insulated brush. If the lamp fails to light the series coil is open and will require repair or replacement. This test should be made from each insulated brush to check brush and lead continuity.

18. On starters with shunt coil separate series and shunt coil strap terminals during this test. Do not let strap terminals touch case or other ground. Using a test lamp place one lead on the grounded brush holder and the other lead on either insulated brush. If the lamp lights a grounded series coil is indicated and must be repaired or replaced.

NOTE: If the solenoid has not been removed from the starter the connector strap terminals must be removed before making the following tests. Complete the tests as fast as possible in order to prevent overheating the solenoid.

19. To check hold-in winding connect an ammeter in series with 12-volt battery and the "switch" terminal and to ground. Connect carbon pile across battery. Adjust the voltage to 10 volts and note the ammeter reading. It should be 14.5 to 16.5 amperes.

20. To check both windings, connect as for previous test. Ground the solenoid motor terminal. Adjust the voltage to 10 volts and note the ammeter reading. It should be 41 to 47 amperes.

21. Current draw readings that are over specifications indicate shorted turns or a ground in the windings of the solenoid and the solenoid should be replaced. Current draw readings that are under specifications indicate excessive resistance. No reading indicates an open circuit. Check connections then replace solenoid if necessary. Current readings will decrease as windings heat up.

22. The roller bearing in the drive housing and the roller bearings in the gear housing must be replaced if they are dry. Do not lubricate or reuse the bearings.

23. To replace the gear housing bearing use a tube or solid cylinder that just fits inside the housing to push bearing out toward armature side. In opposite direction use tube or cylinder to press bearing in flush with housing.

24. To replace the gear housing drive shaft bearing push bearing out and use a tube or collar that just fits inside the housing. Press against the open end of bearing. To press new bearing in, press against closed end, using a thin wall tube or collar that fits in space between bearing and housing. Do not press against flat end of bearing; this will bend the thin metal of the bearing.

25. To replace the drive housing bearing, follow Step 24.

Assembly

1. Assembly of the starter is the reverse of the disassembly procedure. Be sure to replace or repair all defective components as required.

2. When the starter has been disassembled or the solenoid replaced it is necessary to check the pinion clearance.

3. Pinion clearance must be checked in order to prevent the buttons on the shift lever yoke from rubbing on the clutch col-

SECTION 33

STARTER MOTORS
DELCO-REMY 15MT/GR

lar during engine cranking.

4. To check the pinion clearance disconnect the motor field coil connector from the solenoid motor terminal. Insulate the terminal.

5. Connect one 12 volt battery lead to the solenoid switch terminal and the other to the starter frame.

6. Flash a jumper lead momentarily from the solenoid motor terminal to the starter frame. This will shift the pinion into cranking position and it will remain so until the battery is disconnected.

7. Push the pinion back as far as possible to take up any movement, and check the clearance with a feeler gauge. The clearance should be 0.0010 to 0.140 inch.

8. Means for adjusting pinion clearance is not provided on the starter motor. If the clearance does not fall within limits check for improper installation and replace worn parts.

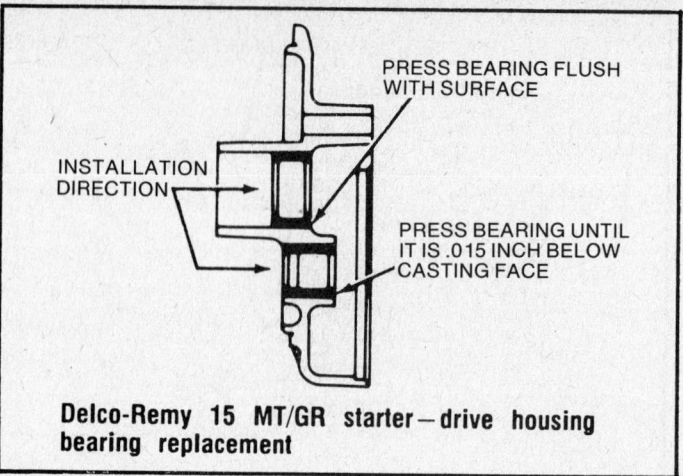

Delco-Remy 15 MT/GR starter — drive housing bearing replacement

Delco-Remy 15MT/GR Starter
Aluminum

Disassembly

1. Remove the starter from the vehicle. Position the unit in a suitable holding fixture.

2. Remove the nut from the field connector and the two solenoid switch mounting screws. Remove the solenoid.

3. Some starters may have shims between the solenoid and the drive end housing. These shims are used to set the drive pinion position.

4. Remove the starter through bolts and the two brush holder retaining bolts.

5. Remove the commutator end frame from the armature and bearing assembly. Remove the field frame assembly and the armature from the center housing.

6. Pry back each brush spring so that each brush can be backed away from the armature about $\frac{1}{4}$ inch. Release the spring to hold the brushes in the backed out position, then remove the armature from the field frame and brush holder.

7. Remove the shaft cover on the center housing by removing the two retaining screws. Remove the C-shaped washer and plate.

8. Remove the two center housing bolts. Remove the center housing shim and thrust washers.

9. Remove the reduction gear. Remove the spring holder. Remove the two lever springs.

10. To remove the drive pinion. slide a $\frac{5}{8}$ inch socket over the shaft against the stopper. Tap the tool to move the stopper off of the ring. Remove the stopper and the drive pinion.

11. Remove the pinion shaft and the lever assembly. Note the direction of the lever and the lever holders.

12. Clean all parts in the proper cleaning solution. Inspect all parts for wear and damage. Replace or repair defective compo-

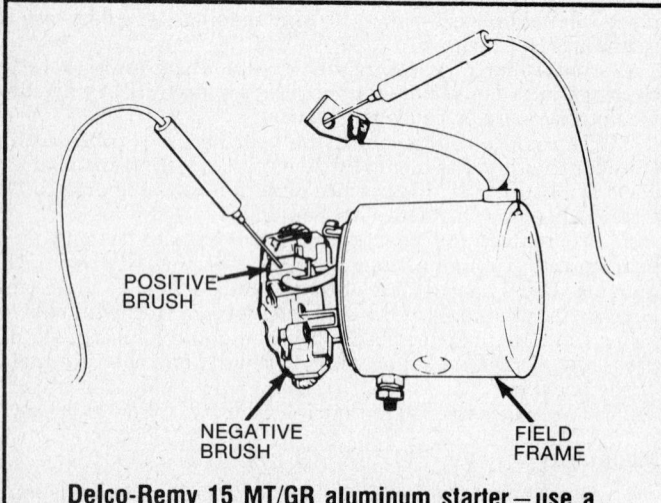

Delco-Remy 15 MT/GR aluminum starter — use a test lamp to test field coils for opens — with one test lamp lead on the field coil connector and the other test lead on the positive brush, the test lamp should light.

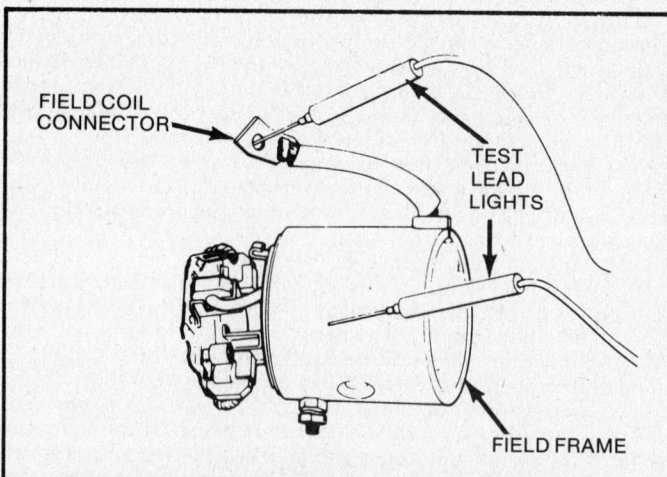

Delco-Remy 15 MT/GR aluminum starter — testing field coil for grounds use a test light put one test lead on the field coil connector and the other on the field frame — the test lamp should not light

STARTER MOTORS
DELCO-REMY 15MT/GR

SECTION 33

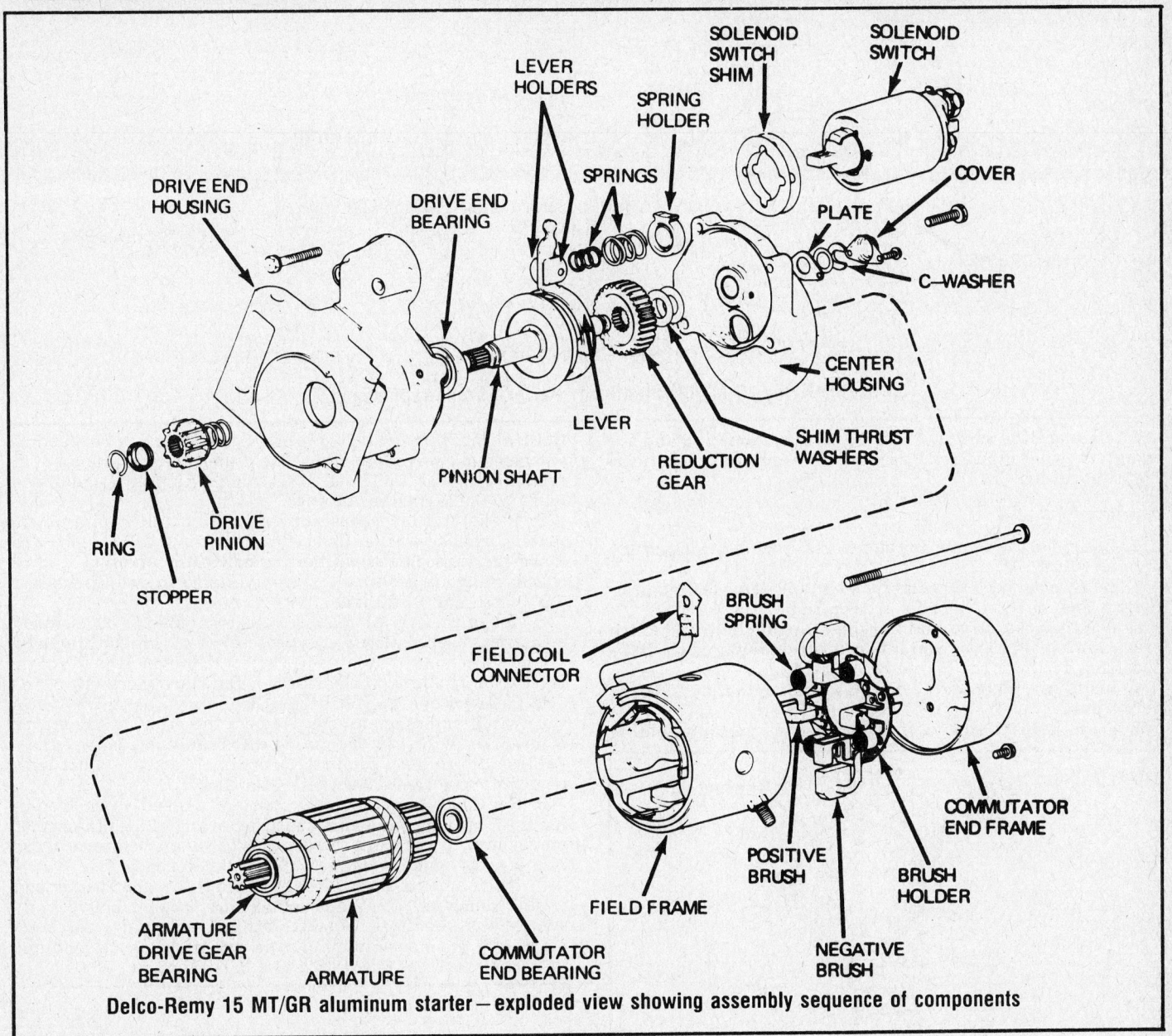

Delco-Remy 15 MT/GR aluminum starter—exploded view showing assembly sequence of components

14. Inspect the armature commutator. If the commutator is rough, it should be turned down. Do not turn the commutator down less than 1.48 in. outside diameter.
15. With the brush holder assembly still attached to the field frame, test the field coils for open. Using a test lamp, put one test lead on the field coil connector and the other test lead on the positive brush.
16. The test light should light. If the test light fails to light the field coil is open. The field coil must be replaced. Repeat this test on the other positive brush.
17. To test the field coil for ground use a test light and put one lead on the field coil connector and the other test lead on the field frame.
18. The test light should not light. If the test lamp lights the field coils are grounded to the field frame assembly. The field frame must be replaced.
19. To replace the brushes remove the brush holder and the negative brush assembly from the field frame by removing the positive brushes from the brush holder.
20. Cut the old brush leads off of their mountings as close to brush connection point as possible. Solder the new brushes as required. Careful installation of the positive side is necessary to prevent grounding of the brush connection point having no insulation.
21. Reinstall the positive and negative brushes in the brush holder assembly. Position it in the backed out position in the starter housing.
22. In order to replace the drive end bearing it will be necessary to press the bearing out of the drive end housing using a press.

33-23

Section 33 — STARTER MOTORS
DELCO-REMY 15MT/GR

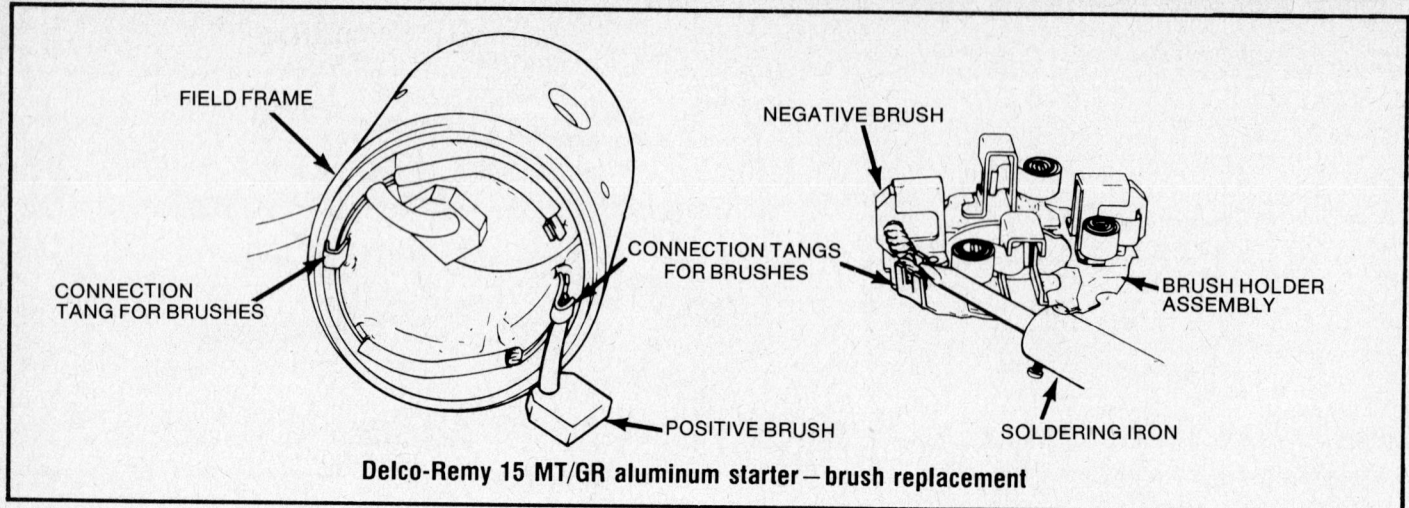

Delco-Remy 15 MT/GR aluminum starter — brush replacement

23. Replace the armature commutator end bearing and the armature drive end bearing as required using the proper bearing removal tool.

Assembly

1. Assemble the starter in the reverse order of the disassembly procedure.
2. Be sure to check all parts for wear and damage. Repair or replace defective components as required.
3. If either the drive end housing, pinion shaft, reduction gear, shim washer(s), or center housing were replaced it will be necessary to check the end play for the pinion shaft.
4. Install the plate and C-shaped washer onto the end of the pinion shaft.
5. With the drive end housing mounted in a suitable holding fixture, measure end play. Insert feeler gauge between C-washer and cover plate. Move the pinion shaft in the axial direction with a suitable tool to see whether a proper end play of 0.004 to 0.020 inch is obtained.
6. If the end play does not fall within limits, remove the plate, C-shaped washer and center bracket and then add or remove the shim thrust washers to adjust the end play and recheck. Shim thrust washers are available in two thicknesses 0.010 inch and 0.020 inch.
7. When the starter has been disassembled or the solenoid switch has been replaced, it is necessary to check the pinion position. Pinion position must be correct to prevent the top of the lever from rubbing on the clutch collar during cranking.
8. Connect one 12 volt battery lead to the terminal "S" on the switch and momentarily connect the other to the starter frame. This will shift the pinion into cranking position and it will remain so until the battery is disconnected. Do not leave engaged more than 30 seconds at a time.
9. Set up dial indicator with pinion engaged. Push the pinion shaft back by hand and measure the amount of pinion shaft movement. The amount corresponds to pinion clearance of current starters and should be 0.020 to 0.080 inch.
10. If the amount does not fall within limit, adjust it by adding or removing the shims which are located between the switch and the front bracket. Adding shims decreases the amount of the movement. Solenoid switch shims are available in two thicknesses 0.020 inch and 0.010 inch.

Delco-Remy 15 MT/GR aluminum starter — drive pinion end play check — set up dial indicator as shown, push pinion back by hand and measure amount of pinion shaft movement it should be 0.20–080 inch

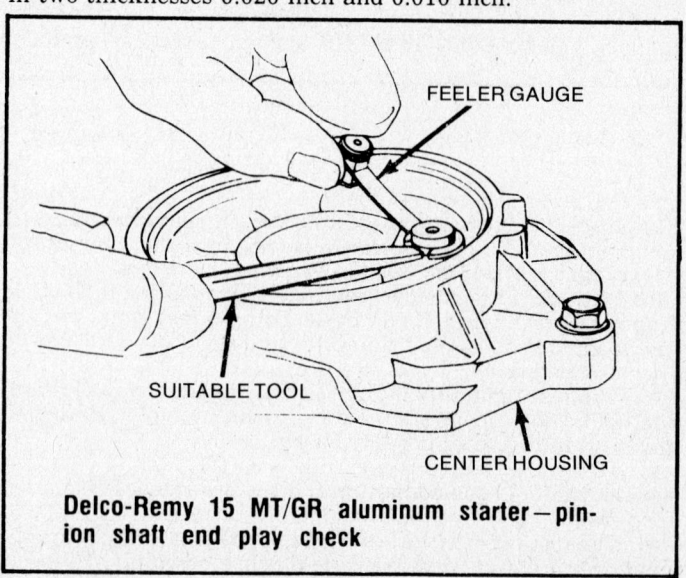

Delco-Remy 15 MT/GR aluminum starter — pinion shaft end play check

STARTER MOTORS
DELCO-REMY CHEVETTE DIESEL
SECTION 33

Delco-Remy Starter Chevette/T1000 Diesel Engine

Disassembly

1. Disconnect the wire lead at the solenoid.
2. Remove the solenoid to starter attaching bolts and remove the solenoid from the shift lever.
3. Remove the torsion spring from the solenoid.
4. Remove the starter through bolts and the rear cover.
5. Remove the four brushes from the brush holder.
6. Remove the frame, armature and brush holder as a unit from the gear case.
7. Remove the brushes and commutator carefully so as not to allow them to contact adjacent parts.
8. Remove the brush holder and pull the armature assembly from the frame.
9. Remove the bearing retainer and the pinion from the gear case.
10. Remove the retaining clip with a tool and then disassemble the pinion assembly.

Inspection and Repair

Make the necessary repairs or replacement of parts, if wear, damage or any other abnormal conditions are found through the inspection of the armature, field coil, brush and brush holder and pinion.

Assembly

1. Working with the solenoid assembly, position the torsion spring to the hole in the magnetic switch.
2. Insert the shift lever through the torsion spring, into the plunger hole in the magnetic switch.
3. Working with the gear case/dust cover, install the solenoid switch assembly into the gear case. Make sure to install the dust cover.
4. Working with the pinion assembly, install the pinion assembly after applying lubrication to the reduction gear.
5. When install the brushes, do not cause damage to the armature commutator surface. Install the brushes by raising the end of the brush spring and install the brush holder by aligning it with the frame.
6. Install the frame through bolts and the solenoid lead wire.

Inspection After Assembly

1. With the pinion extended by battery current, check the difference between the point to which the pinion is extended and the point to which the pinion can be pulled out (towards flywheel). A distance of 0.012 to 0.059 inch should exist. If the distance is out of specifications, shims will have to be added or subtracted from between the solenoid and the gear frame.

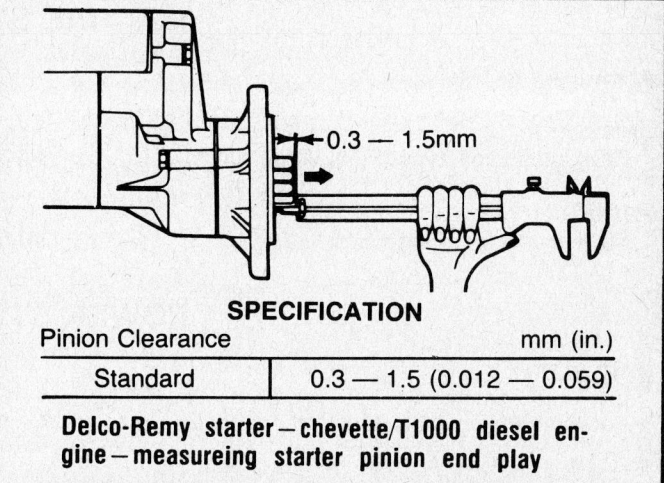

SPECIFICATION

Pinion Clearance	mm (in.)
Standard	0.3 — 1.5 (0.012 — 0.059)

Delco-Remy starter — chevette/T1000 diesel engine — measureing starter pinion end play

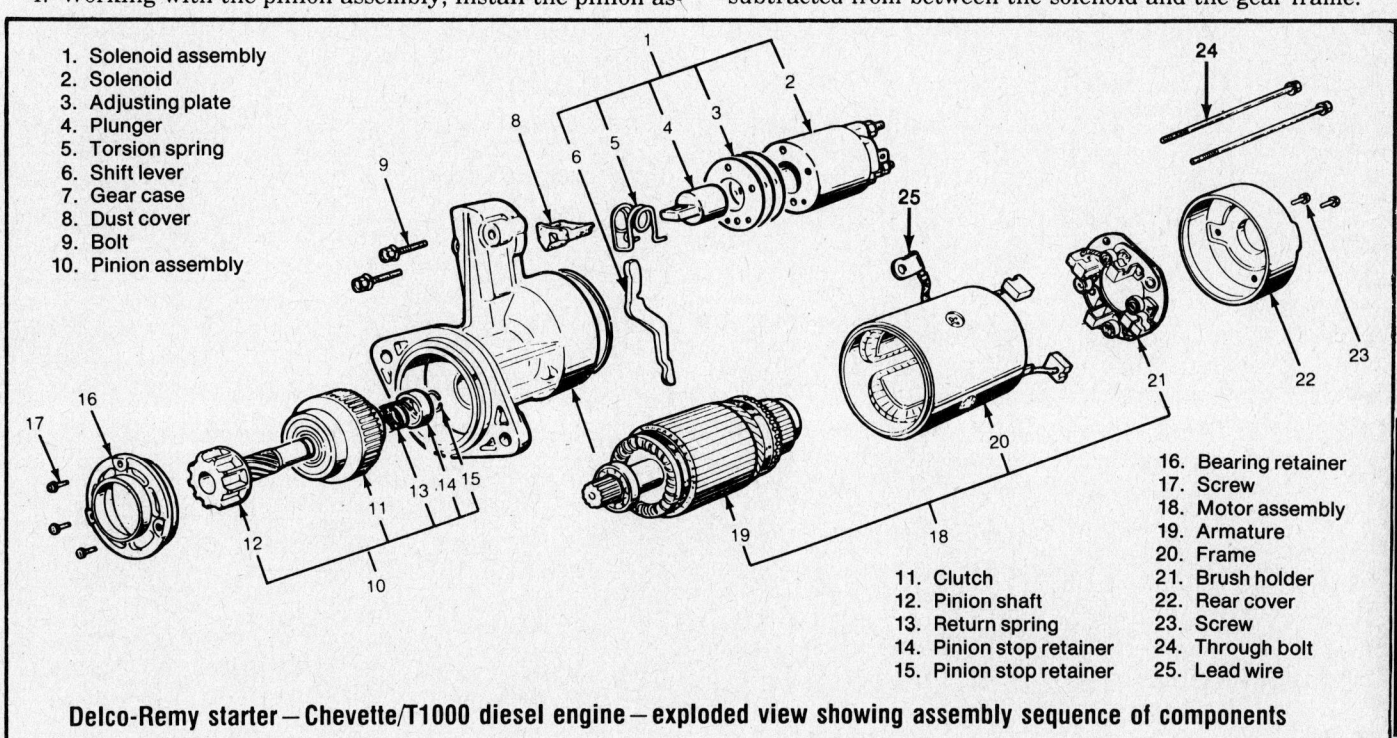

1. Solenoid assembly
2. Solenoid
3. Adjusting plate
4. Plunger
5. Torsion spring
6. Shift lever
7. Gear case
8. Dust cover
9. Bolt
10. Pinion assembly
11. Clutch
12. Pinion shaft
13. Return spring
14. Pinion stop retainer
15. Pinion stop retainer
16. Bearing retainer
17. Screw
18. Motor assembly
19. Armature
20. Frame
21. Brush holder
22. Rear cover
23. Screw
24. Through bolt
25. Lead wire

Delco-Remy starter — Chevette/T1000 diesel engine — exploded view showing assembly sequence of components

SECTION 34 — STEERING GEARS

INDEX

MANUAL STEERING GEAR

AMERICAN MOTORS 34–5

CHRYSLER
   Rack and Pinion Type (Front Wheel Drive) 34–3

FORD
   Rack and Pinion Type 34–3

GENERAL MOTORS
   Rack and Pinion Type
      Chevette and Pontiac 1000 34–6
      Celebrity, 6000, Ciera, Century, Citation, Phoenix, Omega, Skylark 34–8
      Cavalier, 2000, Skyhawk, Firenza 34–9
      Pontiac Fiero 34–11
      Nova 34–11

POWER STEERING GEARS

CHRYSLER
   Full Time Constant Control Type (Rear Wheel Drive) 34–13
   Rack and Pinion Type (Front Wheel Drive) 34–15

FORD MOTOR COMPANY
   Integral Steering Gear 34–20
   Rack and Pinion Type 34–24

TRW
   Rack and Pinion Type 34–23

GENERAL MOTORS
   Saginaw Rotary Type (Model 605) 34–30
   Rack and Pinion Type 34–35

GM/AMC
   Saginaw Rotary Type (Model 800/808) 34–32

POWER STEERING PUMP OVERHAUL

CHRYSLER CORPORATION Pumps 34–18

FORD MOTOR COMPANY Pumps 34–28

GENERAL MOTORS Pumps 34–32

Section 34

Steering

CHRYSLER MANUAL STEERING RACK AND PINION ASSEMBLY

Front Wheel Drive Vehicles

The manual steering rack and pinion gear cannot be adjusted or serviced. Should a malfunction occur, the complete rack and pinion assembly must be replaced.

FORD MANUAL STEERING RACK AND PINION ASSEMBLY

TIE ROD ENDS, BELLOWS AND TIE ROD BALL JOINT SOCKETS

Disassembly

1. Remove the steering gear from the vehicle. Position the steering assembly in a suitable holding fixture.
2. Loosen the jam nuts on the outer ends of the tie rods. Remove the tie rod ends and the jam nuts.
3. Remove the two wires that retain the bellows to the gear housing. Drain the lubricant and remove the bellows.
4. Remove the set screw from the ball housing. Install ball housing torque adapter tool T78P–3504–AA or equivalent on the ball housing.
5. Locate the point of the locking screw in the large hole midway along the length of the housing. Tighten firmly. Use care not to place the point of the locking screw into the tapped set screw hole.
6. Attach a drive ratchet handle to the tool. Expose enough rack teeth to install an adjustable wrench over the flat formed by the tops of the rack teeth.
7. Loosen the ball housing tie rod assembly by holding the adjustable wrench and turning the ball housing tool.

NOTE: If the rack is not restrained by the adjustable wrench, damage to the pinion will occur.

8. Clean and inspect the condition of the threads on the rack and in the ball housing socket. Lubricate the inner seat with multi-purpose lubricant.

Assembly

1. Be sure that the ball housing is seated firmly into ball housing socket and on the tie rod ball. It is important that the back of the inner seat and the face of the rack are wiped clean of grease to avoid a hydraulic lock and improper assembly.
2. Thread the tie rod assembly onto the end of the rack assembly.
3. Install the ball housing torque adapter tool on the ball housing. Locate the point of the locking screw in the large hole midway along the length of the housing, and tighten it firmly. Use care not to place the point of the locking screw into the tapped set screw hole.
4. Hold the rack with an adjustable wrench on the flat of the rack, as near to the end of the rack as possible.
5. If the pinion has not been removed, use care not to load the pinion during tightening.
6. Hold the rack using an adjustable wrench and tighten the ball housing to 40–51 ft. lbs. by turning the ball housing torque adapter tool with a torque wrench.
7. Rotate the tie rod at least ten times, do not force the tie rod against the limits of articulation travel, before measuring articulation effort.
8. To measure articulation effort, loop a piece of wire through the hole in the rod end stud. Insert the hook of a pull scale, through the wire loop. Effort to move the tie rod should be 1–5 lbs.
9. If articulation effort is not within specification, replace the tie rod assembly.
10. Install the set screw in the ball housing. Tighten the screw to 20–40 inch lbs.
11. Install the large bellows and new clamp on the right side only (opposite end from pinion). Use service, screw type clamps. Do not reuse original production wire retainers. Install small clamps to used bellows to retain bellows to tie rod.
12. Place gear in a vertical position with pinion end of gear up. Fill housing with 3.2 ounces of D8AZ–19578–A fluid grease

SECTION 34: MANUAL STEERING
FORD RACK AND PINION

or equivalent lubricant. Install left large bellows and new clamp, fastening bellows in the gear housing. Do not reuse original production wire retainers.

13. Install jam nuts and tie rod ends on tie rods.

INPUT SHAFT SEAL

Disassembly and Assembly

1. Remove the steering gear from the vehicle. Position the assembly in a suitable holding fixture.
2. Clean the input shaft and the input seal area. Do not scratch or damage the pinion shaft. Pry the pinion seal from its bore.
3. Check to be sure that the pinion cover is centered using tool T81P-3504-Y or an equivalent centering tool.
4. If the pinion cover is not centered, loosen the bolts, center the cover and tighten the bolts.
5. Lubricate the new pinion seal with lubricant and install the seal over the shaft.
6. Use a piece of tubing to engage the outer flange of the seal. Press the seal into its bore until the flange is flush with the shoulder of the bore. If the outer edge of the seal is not engaged when assembling, the seal will be damaged.

RACK SUPPORT YOKE, SPRING, GASKET, SHIMS AND COVER

Disassembly

1. Remove the steering gear from the vehicle. Position the rack and pinion assembly in a suitable holding fixture.

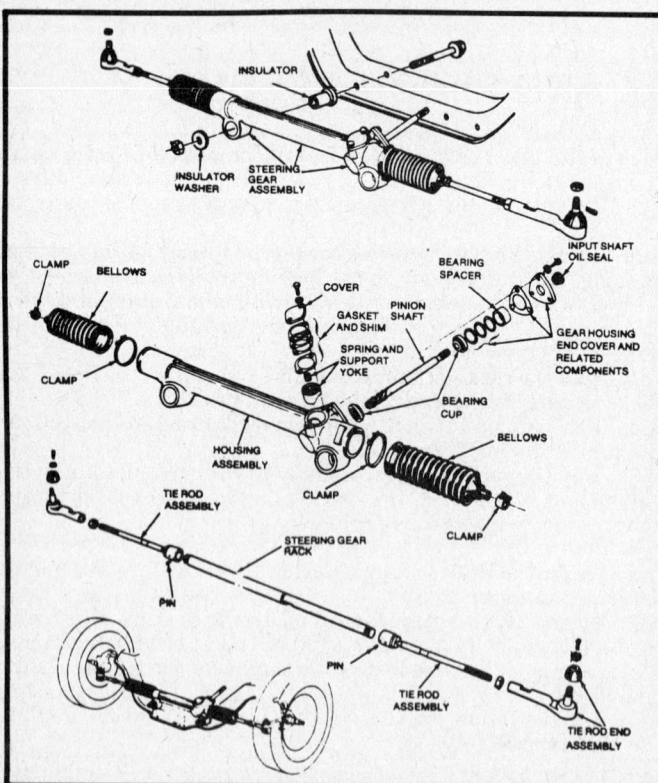

Ford rack and pinion assembly exploded view—typical

2. Remove the yoke cover. Remove the shims, gasket and yoke spring.

Assembly

1. Clean the cover and the flange areas. Assemble the yoke and the yoke spring.
2. Position a new gasket next to the housing flange. If new shims are used, adjust the support yoke to rack.
3. To adjust the support yoke to rack, install the yoke and the cover, omitting the gasket, shims and spring.
4. Tighten the bolts lightly until the cover just touches the yoke.
5. Measure the gap between the cover and the housing flange. With the gasket add selected shims to give a combined pack thickness of 0.005–0.006 in. greater than the measured gap.
6. Assemble the shim pack and the cover. Add sealant to the cover bolt threads.

PINION COVER, GASKET, PINION SHAFT, SPACER, SHIMS, UPPER BEARING, RACK, LOWER BEARING AND HOUSING

Disassembly

1. Remove the steering gear from the vehicle. Position the assembly in a suitable holding fixture. Clean the exterior of the gear.
2. Remove the bolts, yoke cover, gasket, shims, spring and yoke from the gear housing.
3. Remove the right ball housing and the tie rod assembly from the rack.

NOTE: Be sure that the rack is restrained with an adjustable wrench during removal or damage to the pinion will occur.

4. Move the rack to the right turn stop. The flat on the input shaft should be facing straight up.

NOTE: It is important that the flat be in the same position when assembling the gear. If not the steering gear will not be centered.

5. Remove the pinion cover bolts, pinion cover, gasket, pinion shaft, spacer, shims and upper bearing from the gear assembly.
6. Remove the pinion seal from the cover. Discard the seal. Remove the rack from the housing.
7. Remove the lower bearing through the pinion shaft bore. Access to the pinion shaft lower bearing is easiest through the support yoke bore.

Assembly

1. Assembly of the rack and pinion steering gear is the reverse of the disassembly procedure.
2. Be sure to coat the entire length of the rack with the proper grade and type lubricant on assembly.
3. When installing the upper bearing, turn the pinion from lock to lock counting the number of turns. Turn the pinion back from one of the locks exactly one half the total number of turns, with the steering gear on center.
4. The flat must be in the three o'clock position, as viewed from the drivers position. If not, repeat and recheck.

MANUAL STEERING
AMERICAN MOTORS RACK AND PINION

AMC MANUAL STEERING GEAR

WORM BEARING PRELOAD

Adjustment

CAUTION
Do not turn steering wheel hard against stops as damage to ball nut assembly may result.

1. Disconnect the ball stud from the pitman arm, and retighten the pitman arm nut.
2. Loosen the pitman shaft adjusting screw locknut and back off adjusting screw a few turns.
3. Attach spring scale to the steering wheel and measure the pull needed to move the steering wheel when off the high point. The pull should be between $1/8$ and $3/8$ lbs.
4. To adjust the worm bearing, loosen the worm bearing adjuster locknut with a brass drift and turn the adjuster screw until the proper pull is obtained. When adjustment is correct, tighten the adjuster locknut, and recheck with the spring scale again.

SECTOR AND BALL NUT BACKLASH

Adjustment

1. After the worm bearing preload has been adjusted correctly, loosen the pitman shaft adjusting screw locknut and turn the pitman shaft adjusting screw clockwise until a pull of $3/4$ to $1\ 1/8$ lbs. is shown on the spring scale. When the adjustment is correct, tighten the pitman shaft adjusting screw locknut and recheck the adjustment.

NOTE: A torque wrench calibrated in inch lbs. may be substituted for the spring scale in adjusting steering gear.

2. Turn the steering wheel to the center of its turning limits (pitman arm disconnected). If the steering wheel is removed, the mark on the steering shaft should be at top center.
3. Connect the ball stud to the pitman arm, tightening the attaching nut to 115 ft. lbs.

STEERING GEAR

Disassembly and Assembly

1. After removing the steering gear from the vehicle, place the steering gear assembly in a bench vise.

NOTE: Worm seal may be replaced without disassembling gear. Be careful not to damage shaft or housing when removing seal.

2. Rotate the worm shaft until it is centered with the mark facing upward. Remove three cover attaching screws and the adjusting screw locknut. Remove the cover and gasket by turning adjusting screw clockwise through the cover.
3. Remove the adjusting screw with its shim from the slot in the end of the pitman shaft. Remove the pitman shaft from the housing being careful not to damage the seal in the housing.
4. Loosen the worm bearing adjuster locknut with a brass drift and remove the adjuster and bearing. Remove the bearing retainer.
5. Remove the worm and shaft assembly with the ball nut assembly and bearing. Remove the ball nut return guide clamp by removing screws. Remove the guides, turn ball nut over, and remove the steel balls by rotating the shaft from side to side. After all steel balls have been removed, take the ball nut off the worm shaft.
6. Clean all parts in solvent. Inspect all bearings, bearing cups, bushings, seals, worm groove, and gear teeth for signs of wear, scoring, pitting, etc.
7. Remove the pitman shaft seal. If there is leakage around the threads of the bearing adjuster, apply a non-hardening sealer.
8. Remove faulty bushings from the pitman shaft with puller and slide hammer. Install new bushings, seating the inner end of the bushing flush with the inside surface of the housing.
9. Remove the steering shaft seal. Tap new seal in place, using a section of tubing to seat the seal.
10. Remove the upper or lower bearing cup from the worm bearing adjuster or steering gear housing using puller and slide hammer. Install the new bearing cups.
11. Lubricate all seals, bushings, and bearings before installing into the steering gear assembly.
12. Position the ball nut on the worm shaft. Install the steel balls in the return guides and the ball nut, placing an equal number in each circuit of the ball nut. Install the return guide clamp and screws.

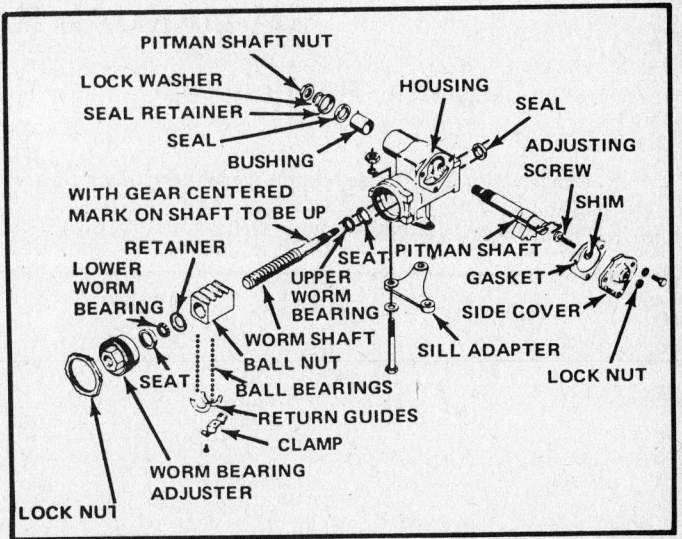

Exploded view of manual recirculating ball type steering—GM Saginaw

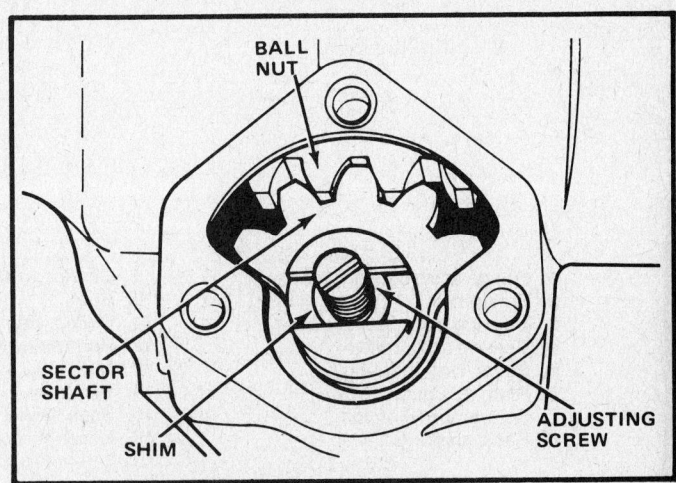

Pitman shaft and ball nut position

34-5

SECTION 34

MANUAL STEERING
AMERICAN MOTORS RACK AND PINION

CAUTION

Do not rotate the worm shaft while installing the steel balls since the balls may enter the crossover passage between the circuits, causing incorrect operation of the ball nut.

---

13. Place bearing on shaft above the worm gear, center ball nut on worm gear; then, slide the steering shaft, bearing, and ball nut into the housing. Do not damage the steering shaft seal in the housing.
14. Place the bearing in the worm adjuster, install the bearing retainer, and install the adjuster and locknut on the housing, tightening it just enough to hold the bearing in place.
15. Install the pitman shaft adjusting screw and selective shim in the pitman shaft. Be sure there is no more than 0.002 in. of end play of the screw in the slot. If the end-play is more than 0.002 in., install a new selective shim to get the proper clearance. Shims are available in four thickness: 0.063 in., 0.065 in., 0.067 in. and 0.069 in.
16. Install the pitman shaft and adjusting screw with the sector and ball nut positioned as shown.
17. Install the cover and gasket on the adjusting screw, turning screw counterclockwise until it extends through the cover from $5/8$ to $3/4$ in. Install the cover attaching screws and torque to 35 ft. lbs.
18. Tighten the pitman shaft adjusting screw so that the teeth on the shaft and the ball nut engage but do not bind. Final adjustment must be made later.
19. Wrap the pitman shaft splines with tape to protect the seal and install the seal.
20. Fill steering gear with a good quality steering gear lubricant. Turn the steering gear from one extreme to the other to make sure it does not bind. Do not allow the ball nut to strike the ends of the ball races on the worm gear to avoid damaging the ball return guides.
21. Install the steering gear. Perform the final adjustments on the worm bearing preload and the sector and ball nut backlash adjustments.

GM MANUAL RACK AND PINION

Chevette, Pontiac 1000

Disassembly

1. Position assembly in vise, clamping housing near center. Use soft jaws to prevent damage to housing.
2. Loosen jam nuts. Remove outer tie rod.

CAUTION

Hold housing wile loosening nuts so as not to damage internal gear components.

---

3. Remove inner boot clamp by cutting. Remove the outer clamp by relieving tension in clamp. Remove boot by pulling. Repeat procedure for other end.

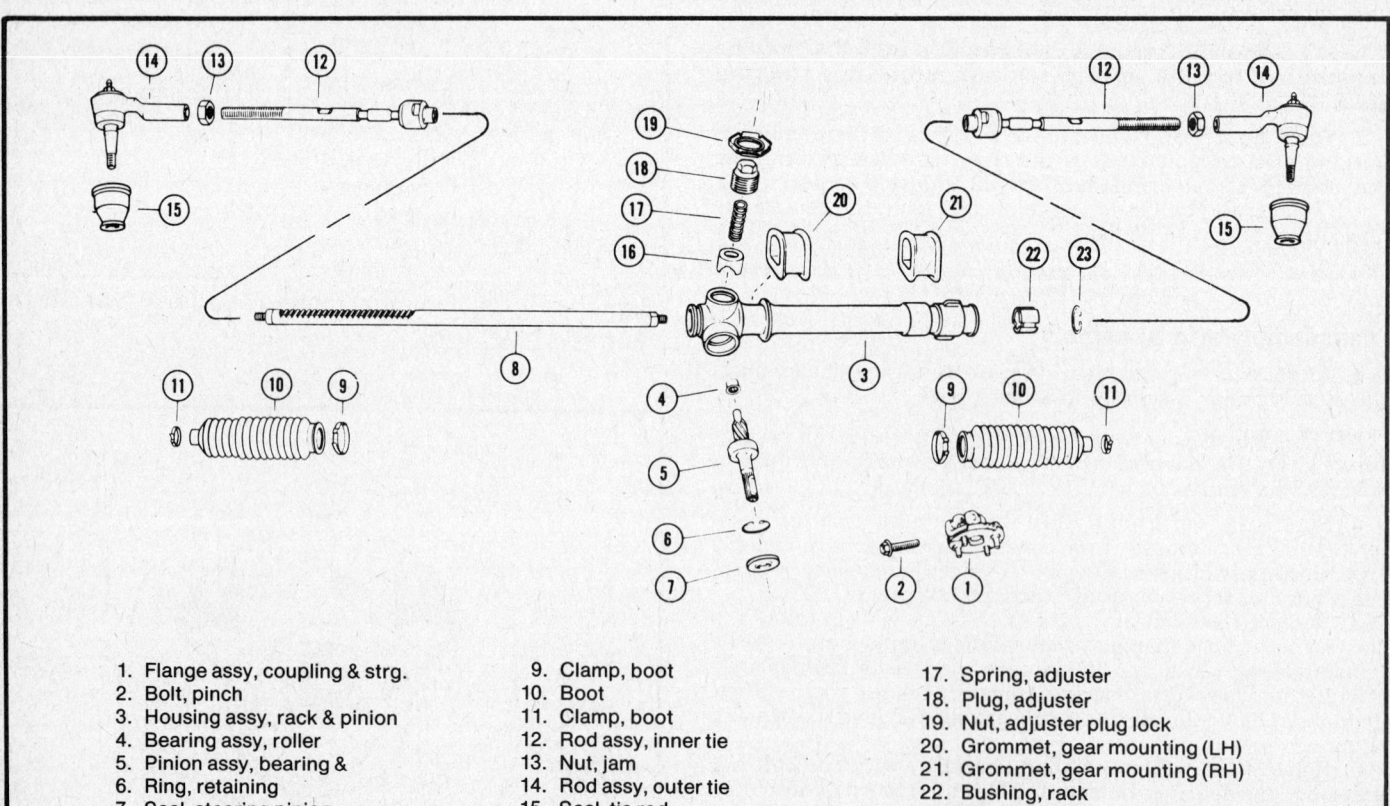

1. Flange assy, coupling & strg.
2. Bolt, pinch
3. Housing assy, rack & pinion
4. Bearing assy, roller
5. Pinion assy, bearing &
6. Ring, retaining
7. Seal, steering pinion
8. Rack, steering
9. Clamp, boot
10. Boot
11. Clamp, boot
12. Rod assy, inner tie
13. Nut, jam
14. Rod assy, outer tie
15. Seal, tie rod
16. Bearing, rack
17. Spring, adjuster
18. Plug, adjuster
19. Nut, adjuster plug lock
20. Grommet, gear mounting (LH)
21. Grommet, gear mounting (RH)
22. Bushing, rack
23. Ring, retaining

Exploded view of manual rack and pinion assembly — Chevette, 1000

MANUAL STEERING
GM RACK AND PINION

SECTION 34

4. Position rack in soft jaw vise, and remove inner tie rod assemblies (both ends).

CAUTION

To prevent internal gear damage when removing housing, turn housing counterclockwise until assembly separates from rack.

---

5. Remove adjuster plug locknut, adjuster plug, and spring.
6. Remove rack bearing from housing.
7. Clean surface at seal. Pierce seal at one of the two round spots on surface, Pry out seal.
8. Using snap ring pliers, remove retaining ring from bore.
9. Position end of shaft in soft jaw vise. Tap housing to separate pinion assembly from housing.

CAUTION

With pinion separated, rack may slide from housing and be damaged.

---

10. Remove rack from housing.
11. The rack and pinion assembly is now disassembled. Clean all components, except inner tie rod assemblies, with an approved solvent. Air dry and inspect. Replace any seals which are cut or badly worn. If the pinion seal is removed, it must be replaced.

NOTE: Check major wear areas for cracking, chipping, etc. Replace as required.

MOUNTING GROMMETS

Do not remove grommets unless replacement is required. Replace both grommets if either requires replacement.
Cut through grommet and remove.
Lube inside of seals lightly with chassis lube. Start with left seal first and force it past the right side (smaller inside diameter) boss. Start right hand grommet and seat. Remove housing from vise and slide grommet to left hand mounting. Assemble grommet to housing.

GUIDE BUSHINGS

No attempt to replace the guide bushing should be made unless it is damaged or broken. If this occurs, replace the housing.

RACK BUSHING

The rack bushing should only be replaced if evidence of heavy wear is observed.
Remove retaining ring. Using a suitable size socket and extension, drive the bushing out of the housing. If a puller is available, position fingers of puller behind bushing and remove bushing using slide hammer.
Using a suitable size socket, press new rack bushing into housing until it bottoms. Install retaining ring.

ROLLER BEARING ASSEMBLY

Check condition of pinion pilot. If scored or badly worn, replace pinion and roller bearing assembly.
Press or tap out bearing using drift and press or hammer.
Using a suitable size socket, press or drive new bearing into housing until it bottoms.

BEARING AND PINION ASSEMBLY

Inspect roller bearing pilot, pinion teeth, and rotor bearing assembly. If pilot is scored, teeth are chipped, or is loose on pinion shaft, the bearing and pinion assembly should be replaced.

INNER TIE RODS

The inner tie rod assemblies cannot be serviced. If the pivot is loose, replace the tie rod assembly. If the joint rocking or turning torque exceeds 150 inch lbs. (17 Nm) replace the inner tie rod assembly.

Assembly

1. Install rack with teeth facing pinion into housing. The flat on the teeth should be parallel with pinion shaft. Measure and set 2.70 in. (68.5mm) from lip of housing to end of rack.

NOTE: Insert pinion with flat at 75° from vertical. Tap on pinion shaft with soft hammer until pinion seats. Reset 2.70 in. (68.5mm) dimension of rack position. Flat should now be vertical. If flat is at plus or minus 30° from vertical, restart procedure.

CAUTION

Rack must be centered as described. If not, the steering wheel cannot travel fully, causing unequal turning radii.

---

2. Install retaining ring using tool J–4245 or equivalent. Beveled edge of retaining ring should be up.
3. Liberally coat top of pinion bearing with anhydrous calcium grease, then seat pinion seal flush with housing. Seal can be seated by tapping on alternate sides with hammer.
4. Install rack bearing. Coat bearing with lithium based grease.
5. Coat both ends of preload spring and threads of adjuster plug with lithium based grease.
6. Assemble adjuster plug and spring assembly into housing. Turn adjuster plug clockwise until it bottoms, then counterclockwise 45° to 60°. Torque required to turn pinion should be between 8–10 inch lbs. (0.9–1.1 Nm). Turn plug in or out to adjust as required. Tighten locknut to 50 ft. lbs. (68 Nm).
7. Lube both ends of rack with lithium based grease. Fill rack teeth with lube. Move rack back and front several times by turning pinion shaft, adding grease to rack teeth each time.
8. Install inner tie rod assemblies to rack. Turn inner tie rod assemblies until they bottom out.

CAUTION

Support rack in vise or with another wrench to avoid internal gear damage.

---

9. Use wood block or vise support and stake tie rod housing to rack flat. Stake both sides.
10. Position one of the large clamps on the housing. Place boot lip into position over undercut. Position clamp over boot at undercut and secure using side cutter type pliers or tool J–22610.
11. Slip end of boot into rod undercut. Do not assemble clamp over boot until toe adjustment is made. Straighten boots if twisted before assembling clamps.
12. Thread jam nuts (both sides) onto tie rods.
13. Thread on tie rod ends. Do not tighten jam nuts until toe adjustment is made. Then tighten to 50 ft. lbs. (67 Nm).
14. Slip on coupling assembly. Flat on inside diameter of coupling mates with flat on pinion shaft. Install pinch bolt, but do not tighten until vehicle installation, then tighten to 30 ft. lbs. (41 Nm).

SECTION 34: MANUAL STEERING — GM RACK AND PINION

GM MANUAL STEERING RACK AND PINION — "A" BODY AND "X" BODY CARS

Celebrity, 6000, Ciera, Century, Citation, Phoenix, Omega, Skylark

OUTER TIE ROD

Removal

1. Loosen the jam nut and remove the tie rod from the steering knuckle. Count the number of turns needed to remove.
2. Remove the outer tie rod.

Installation

1. Install the outer tie rod by screwing it on the inner tie rod the same amount of turns as was needed to remove the outer tie rod.
2. Adjust the toe-in/out by turning the inner tie rod. Tighten the lock nut to 50 ft. lbs.
3. Install the outer boot clamp and secure.

BOOT SEAL

Removal and Installation

To remove the boot seal from either side of the steering assembly, the outer tie rod must be removed. Remove the lock nut and the boot clamps. Remove the boot by sliding it off the inner tie rod.

To install the boot, reverse the removal procedure. Secure the boot clamps.

INNER TIE ROD

Removal

1. The steering assembly must be out of the vehicle.
2. Position a wrench on the rack and hold it as the inner tie rod is unscrewed.

Installation

1. Screw the inner tie rod into the rack and with a wrench holding the rack to avoid teeth damage, tighten the inner tie rod to 70 ft. lbs.
2. Stake the housing on both sides.

NOTE: Be sure the tie rod rocks freely in the housing before staking.

3. When staking is completed, a 0.010 inch feeler gauge must not pass between the rack and the housing stakes. Check both sides.

RACK BEARING

Removal

1. Remove the adjuster plug lock nut, the adjuster plug, spring and the rack bearing.

Installation

1. Lubricate the metal parts before installation, install then in the housing in the reverse order of their removal.
2. Turn the adjuster plug in until it bottoms and then back off approximately 40 to 60 degrees.
3. Check the torque on the pinion by turning it with a torque wrench. The correct pinion torque is 8–10 inch. lbs.
4. Tighten the lock nut to 50 ft. lbs. while holding the adjuster plug.

PINION SEAL

Removal

1. Pierce the seal in one or two round spots and pry it from the housing.

Installation

1. Lubricate the seal and seat the seal flush with the housing.

PINION SHAFT ASSEMBLY

Removal

1. Remove the seal and the retaining ring from the housing assembly.
2. Place the pinion shaft in a soft jawed vise and tap on the housing to separate the two.

CAUTION

With the pinion removed from the housing, the rack can slide from the housing and be damaged.

Installation

1. Lubricate and slide the rack into the housing.

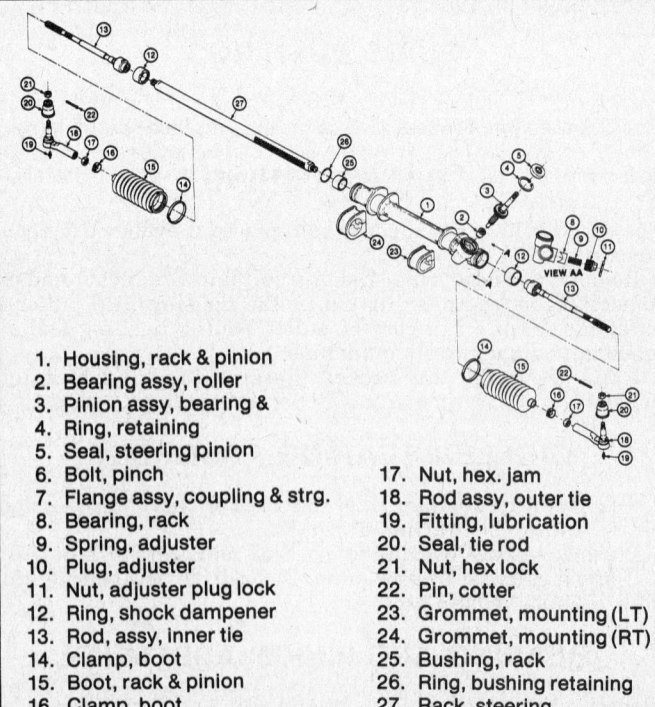

1. Housing, rack & pinion
2. Bearing assy, roller
3. Pinion assy, bearing &
4. Ring, retaining
5. Seal, steering pinion
6. Bolt, pinch
7. Flange assy, coupling & strg.
8. Bearing, rack
9. Spring, adjuster
10. Plug, adjuster
11. Nut, adjuster plug lock
12. Ring, shock dampener
13. Rod, assy, inner tie
14. Clamp, boot
15. Boot, rack & pinion
16. Clamp, boot
17. Nut, hex. jam
18. Rod assy, outer tie
19. Fitting, lubrication
20. Seal, tie rod
21. Nut, hex lock
22. Pin, cotter
23. Grommet, mounting (LT)
24. Grommet, mounting (RT)
25. Bushing, rack
26. Ring, bushing retaining
27. Rack, steering

Exploded view of manual steering rack and pinion — GM A-body cars

MANUAL STEERING
GM RACK AND PINION
SECTION 34

2. Position the rack that 63.5mm protrudes from the pinion shaft end of the housing.
3. Position the pinion so that the center of the flat is facing the 4:30 position and install it into the housing.
4. When the pinion is seated properly, the center of the flat will be facing the 9:00 position.
5. Install the retainer ring and install the seal.

NOTE: The distance between the holes in the retaining ring should be 7.0 mm apart.

ROLLER BEARING

Removal and Installation

The pinion must be out of the housing. Drive the bearing from the housing and press the new bearing in place. Complete the pinion installation.

RACK BUSHING

Removal

1. Remove the pinion and rack assembly from the housing.
2. Remove the retaining ring from the housing and with a special long legged puller, remove the bushing from the housing.

Installation

1. Press a new bushing into the housing until it is firmly seated.
2. Install the retaining ring and complete the rack and pinion installation.

GM MANUAL STEERING RACK AND PINION—"J" BODY CARS

Cavalier, 2000, Skyhawk, Firenza

OUTER TIE ROD

Removal

1. With the steering assembly from the vehicle, loosen the outer rod pinch bolt and turn the tie rod from the adjuster stud, counting the number of turns until the tie rod separates from the adjuster stud.

Installation

1. Turn the tie rod onto the adjuster stud the same number of turns as was needed to remove.
2. Tighten the pinch bolt until the toe-out can be verified. Re-loosen and adjust as required.

INNER TIE ROD AND INNER PIVOT BUSHING

Removal

1. Bend back the lock plate tabs and loosen the inner tie rod bolt and remove.
2. Remove the inner tie rod by sliding it out between the bolt support plate and rack/pinion boot.

NOTE: If both inner tie rods are to be removed, re-install the inner tie rod bolt in the first tie rod retaining bolt hole to keep the rack and pinion boot and other parts aligned, while tie rods are out.

3. With the tie rod disconnected, the pivot bushings can be pressed out and new ones pressed in.

Installation

1. Be sure the center housing cover washers are fitted into the rack and pinion boot, before rod installation.
2. Remove the locating bolt from the rack and position one inner tie rod assembly in place over the rack. Place the bolt through the lock plate and the tie rod. Place the second inner tie rod in place and install the bolt through the lock plate and the tie rod.
3. Tighten the inner tie rod bolts to 65 ft. lbs. and bend the lock tabs against the flats of the inner tie rod bolts after torquing.

RACK AND PINION BOOT, RACK GUIDE, BEARING GUIDE, MOUNTING GROMMET OR HOUSING END COVER

Removal

1. Separate right-hand mounting grommet and remove. Left-hand mounting grommet need not be removed unless replacement is required.
2. Cut both boot clamps and discard.
3. Using constant pressure, slide rack and pinion boot over boot retaining bushing and off housing.
4. The boot retaining bushing on housing tube end need not be removed unless damaged.
5. Remove housing end cover only if damaged.

Installation

1. Remove boot retaining bushing from pinion end of boot.
2. Slide new boot clamp on boot. Install bushing into boot.
3. Install new bearing guide on rack guide if necessary.
4. Install new bolt retaining bushing on housing if necessary.
5. Install rack guide on rack.
6. Coat inner lip of boot retaining bushing lightly with grease for ease of assembly.
7. Install boot on housing.
8. Be sure center housing washers are in place on boot.
9. For ease of assembly, install inner tie rod bolts through cover washers and boot. Screw into rack lightly. This will keep rack, rack guide and boot in proper alignment.
10. Slide boot and boot retaining bushing until seated in bushing groove at pinion end of housing. Crimp new boot clamp.
11. Slide other end of boot onto boot retaining bushing in housing at tube end. Crimp new boot clamp.

FLANGE AND STEERING COUPLING ASSEMBLY

Removal

1. Loosen and remove the pinch bolt.
2. Remove the coupling.

SECTION 34

MANUAL STEERING
GM RACK AND PINION

NOTE: The dash seal can be removed or installed with the coupling off the steering assembly.

Installation

1. Install the flange and steering coupling assembly on the pinion shaft.
2. Install the pinch bolt and torque to 29 ft. lbs.

RACK BEARING

Removal

1. Remove the adjuster plug lock nut.
2. Remove the adjuster plug, the spring, O-ring and rack bearing.

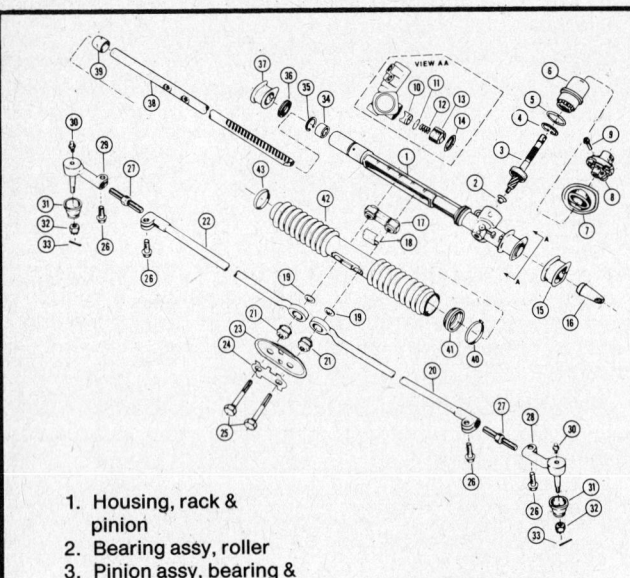

1. Housing, rack & pinion
2. Bearing assy, roller
3. Pinion assy, bearing &
4. Ring, retaining
5. Dust seal, viscous damper
6. Damper assy, viscous strg.
7. Seal, dash
8. Coupling assy, flange & strg
9. Bolt, pinch
10. Bearing, rack
11. Seal, O-ring
12. Spring, adjuster
13. Plug, adjuster
14. Nut, adjuster plug lock
15. Grommet, mounting (LH)
16. Cover, housing end
17. Guide, rack
18. Guide, bearing
19. Washer, center hsg cover
20. Rod, inner tie (LH)
21. Bushing, inner pivot
22. Rod, inner tie (RH)
23. Plate, bolt support
24. Plate, lock
25. Bolt, inner tie rod
26. Bolt, pinch
27. Adjuster, tie rod
28. Rod assy, outer tie (LH)
29. Rod assy, outer tie (RH)
30. Fitting, lubrication
31. Seal, tie rod
32. Nut, hex slotted
33. Pin, cotter
34. Bushing, rack
35. Ring, internal retaining
36. Bushing, boot retaining
37. Grommet, mounting (RH)
38. Rack, steering
39. Cover, housing end
40. Clamp, boot
41. Bushing, boot retaining
42. Boot, rack & pinion
43. Clamp, boot

Exploded view of manual steering rack and pinion—GM J-body cars

Installation

1. Install the parts in the reverse order of the removal procedure.
2. With the rack centered, tighten the adjuster plug to a torque of 6 to 11 ft. lbs. Back off adjuster plug to 50 to 70 degrees.
3. Assemble lock nut and tighten while holding the adjuster plug stationary. Tighten to 50 ft. lbs.
4. Rotate the pinion with an inch pound torque wrench and socket. The turning torque should be 8–20 inch lbs. Adjust as required.

VISCOUS STEERING DAMPER ASSEMBLY

Removal

1. Using a three-fingered wheel puller on flange of viscous damper, remove damper.

NOTE: Three finger puller must be used or damage to damper will occur.

2. Replace dust seal if necessary.

Installation

1. Remove retaining shield from damper.
2. Be sure dust seal is installed on damper.
3. Line up flat on damper with adjuster plug.
4. Using a press, press on inner hub of damper with suitable pipe. Be sure tabs on damper line up with slots in housing. Press until seated on pinion shaft.
5. Using suitable pipe, press on outer housing of damper until fully seated in rack and pinion housing.
6. Reinstall retaining shield.

PINION SHAFT ASSEMBLY

Removal

1. Turn the pinion shaft until the rack guide is equal distance from both sides of the housing opening.
2. Mark the location of the stub shaft flat on the housing. Remove the retaining ring.
3. Remove the pinion by placing it in a soft jawed vise and tapping on the housing with a soft faced hammer.

Installation

1. Measure the rack guide so it is equal distance on both sides of the housing opening.
2. Install the pinion assembly so when the pinion is fully seated, the pinion shaft flat and the mark on the housing line up and the rack guide is centered in the housing opening.
3. Install the retaining ring.

RACK

Removal

1. With the pinion out of the steering housing, thread an inner tie rod bolt into the rack.
2. Slide the rack back and forth until the housing end cover is forced from the end of the tube.
3. Unthread the bolt and slide the rack from the steering housing.

Installation

1. Slide rack into the housing and seat the end cover into the end of the housing tube.

MANUAL STEERING
GM RACK AND PINION
SECTION 34

PINION SHAFT ROLLER BEARING

Removal and Installation

The roller bearing is pressed out and the new one pressed into the housing.

RACK BUSHING

Removal and Installation

With the rack out of the housing, remove the internal retaining ring from the tube. A long legged puller is used to remove the bushing from the tube housing. A press is used to install the new bushing. Press the bushing into position and install the retaining ring.

GM MANUAL STEERING RACK AND PINION – "P" BODY CAR

FIERO

1. Remove the steering gear from the vehicle. Position the assembly in a suitable holding fixture. Clean the exterior of the gear.
2. Loosen the jam nut. Remove the outer tie rods from the steering gear inner tie rods.
3. Remove the damper assembly retaining bolts and remove the damper assembly from the steering gear. Upon installation, torque the retaining nuts to 32 ft. lbs.
4. To remove the boot seal, remove the jam nut and cut the boot clamp. Remove the boot.
5. When removing the right boot the shock damper stud must be removed before the boot is removed. Upon installation torque the shock damper stud to 35 ft. lbs.
6. To remove the inner tie rod, position an adjustable wrench on the flat of the rack teeth. Using an open end wrench remove the inner tie rod. Upon installation torque the retaining bolt to 70 ft. lbs.
7. To remove the rack bearing, remove the adjuster plug locknut, adjuster plug and the spring from the steering gear housing.
8. Remove the pinion seal from its bore on the steering gear assembly.
9. To remove the pinion shaft, remove the pinion shaft retaining ring. Tap on the housing and separate the pinion from the housing. Once the pinion is removed from its bore the rack can slide from its mounting, be careful as damage to the rack can occur.
10. To remove the roller bearing, position the housing assembly in a suitable vise. Using an arbor press, press the bearing from its bore.
11. To remove the rack bushing, remove the bushing retaining nut. Slide the rack bushing from its mounting.
12. Remove the grommets from the housing as necessary. Replace as required.

Assembly

1. Assembly is the reverse of the disassembly procedure.
2. When installing the inner tie rod, support the housing in a suitable vise. Stake both sides of the housing to the adapter flats using a drift.
3. To check the staking procedure, use a 0.010 inch feeler gauge and be sure that it will not pass between the rack and housing stake.
4. Pinion preload is 18 ft. lbs.
5. When installing the pinion shaft bolt, start at the 4:20 o'clock position and finish at the 3 o'clock position.

GM MANUAL RACK AND PINION STEERING

NOVA

Disassembly

1. Place the steering unit into a vise using wood or soft metal to line the vise jaws.
2. Mark the left and right tie rod ends for ease of reassembly. Remove the boots and discard. Upon reassembly, new boots should be installed.
3. Using a suitable tool, bend back (straighten) the bent part of the locking washer between the inner tie rod and the rack. Remove the inner tie rods from the rack marking the left and right rack ends.
4. Loosen the rack guide spring cap lock nut. remove the spring and rack guide. Remove the pinion dust cover.
5. Remove the pinion bearing adjusting screw lock nut. Remove the pinion bearing adjusting screw.
6. Remove the pinion with the upper bearing being careful not to damage the pinion serrations.
7. Remove the rack from the pinion side. Do not attempt to remove the rack from the tube side or twist the rack during removal.

Assembly

1. Assembly is the reverse of the diassembly.
2. Inspect all mating surfaces for excessive wear or signs of damage. Inspect the rack for runout. Runout should not exceed 0.012 in. (0.3 mm). Check bearings and seals. Replace as required.
3. Lubricate all sliding parts and sealing surfaces using lithium grease.

34-11

SECTION 34

MANUAL STEERING
GM RACK AND PINION

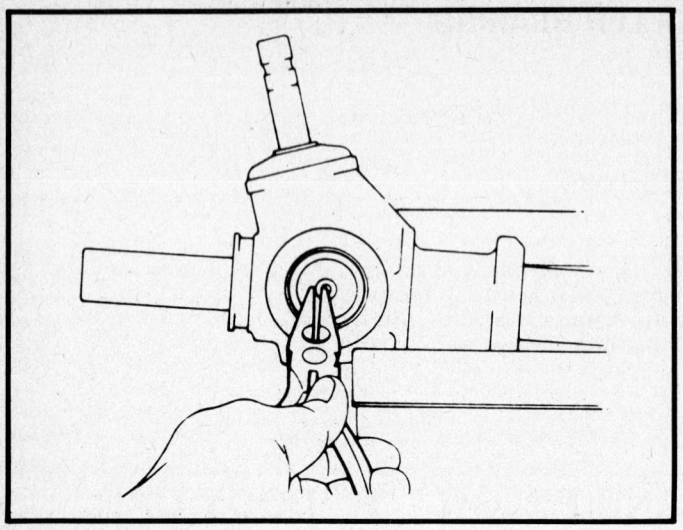
Dust cover removal

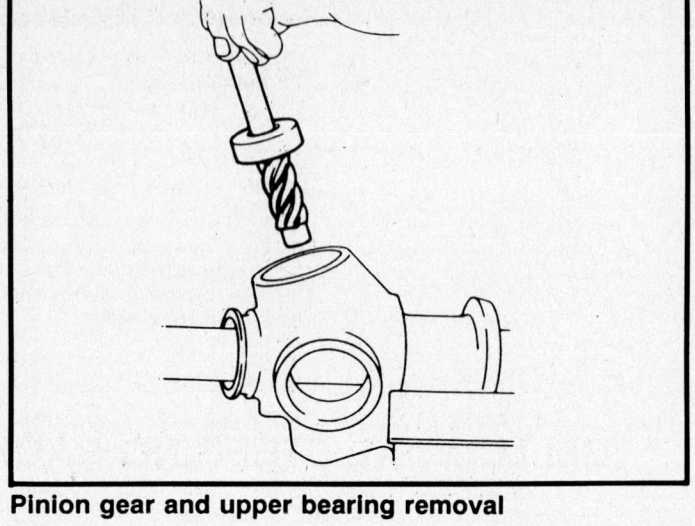
Pinion gear and upper bearing removal

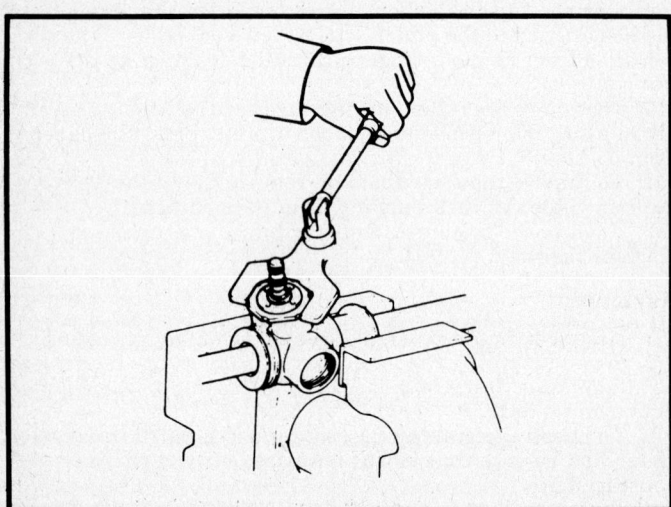
Pinion bearing lock nut removal

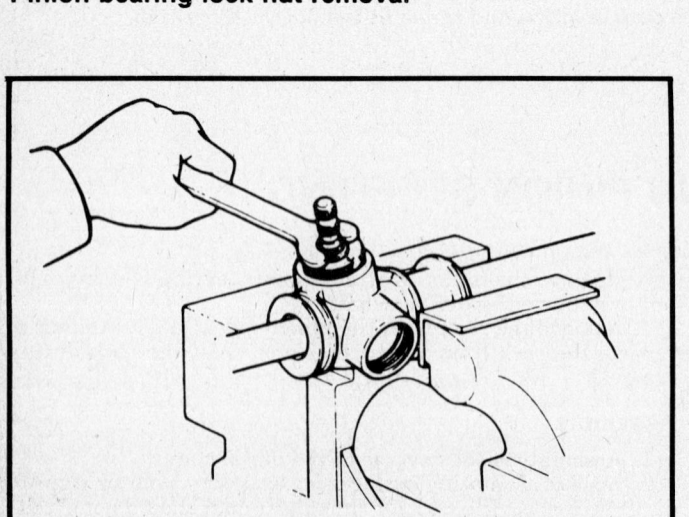
Adjusting screw removal

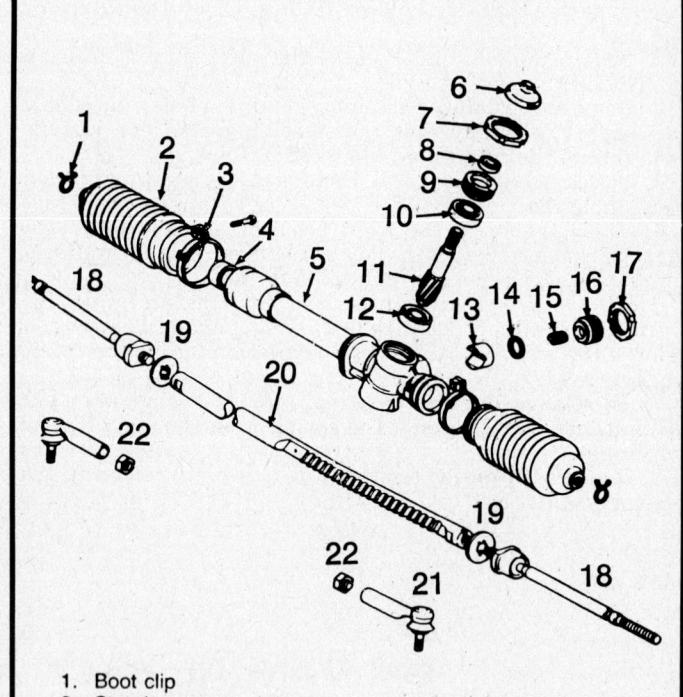

1. Boot clip
2. Steering gear rack boot
3. Boot clamp
4. Rack bushing
5. Steering gear rack housing
6. Pinion dust cover
7. Locking nut
8. Upper pinion seal
9. Pinion bearing adjusting screw
10. Upper pinion bearing
11. Steering pinion
12. Lower pinion bearing
13. Rack guide
14. Rack guide spacer
15. Rack guide spring
16. Rack guide spring
17. Rack guide locking nut
18. Inner tie rod
19. Locking washer
20. Steering rack
21. Outer tie rod
22. Tie rod locking nut

Nova—manual rack and pinion—exploded view

Power Steering
Chrysler Units
Section 34

CHRYSLER FULL-TIME CONSTANT CONTROL TYPE POWER STEERING

Rear Wheel Drive Vehicles

Disassembly and Assembly

1. Drain gear by turning worm shaft from limit to limit with oil connections held downward. Thoroughly clean outside.
2. Remove valve body attaching screws, body and three O-rings.
3. Remove pivot lever and spring. Pry under spherical head with a suitable tool.

CAUTION

Use care not to collapse slotted end of valve lever as this will destroy bearing tolerances of the spherical head.

---

4. Remove steering gear arm from sector shaft.
5. Remove snap-ring and seal backup washer.
6. Remove seal, using proper tool to prevent damage to relative parts.
7. Loosen gear shaft adjusting screw locknut and remove gear shaft cover nut.
8. Rotate wormshaft to position sector teeth at center of piston travel.
9. Loosen power train retaining nut.
10. Turn worm shaft either to full left or full right (depending on vehicle application) to compress power train parts. Then remove power train retaining nut.
11. Remove housing head tang washer.
12. While holding power train completely compressed, pry on piston teeth with a suitable tool, using shaft as a fulcrum, and remove complete power train.

CAUTION

Maintain close contact between cylinder head, center race and spacer assembly and the housing head. This will eliminate the possibility of reactor rings becoming disengaged from their grooves in cylinder and housing head. It will prohibit center spacer from separating from center race and cocking in the housing. This could make it impossible to remove the power train without damaging involved parts.

---

13. Place power train in soft-jawed vise in vertical position. The worm bearing rollers will fall out. Use of arbor tool will hold roller when the housing is removed.
14. Raise housing head until wormshaft oil shaft just clears the top of wormshaft and position arbor tool on top of shaft and into seal. With arbor in position, pull up on housing head until arbor is positioned in bearing. Remove when the housing is removed.
15. Remove large O-ring from housing head groove.
16. Remove reaction seal from groove in face of head with air pressure directed into ferrule chamber.
17. Remove reactor spring, reactor ring, worm balancing ring and spacer.
18. While holding wormshaft from turning, turn nut with enough force to release staked portions from knurled section and remove nut.

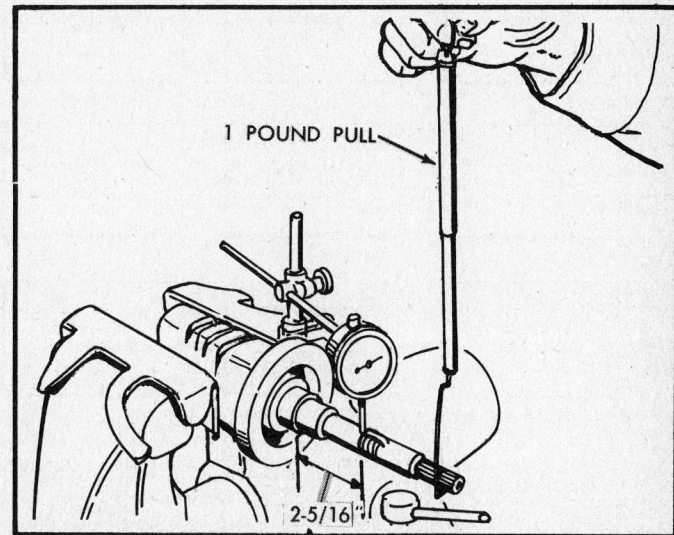
Checking the wormshaft side play

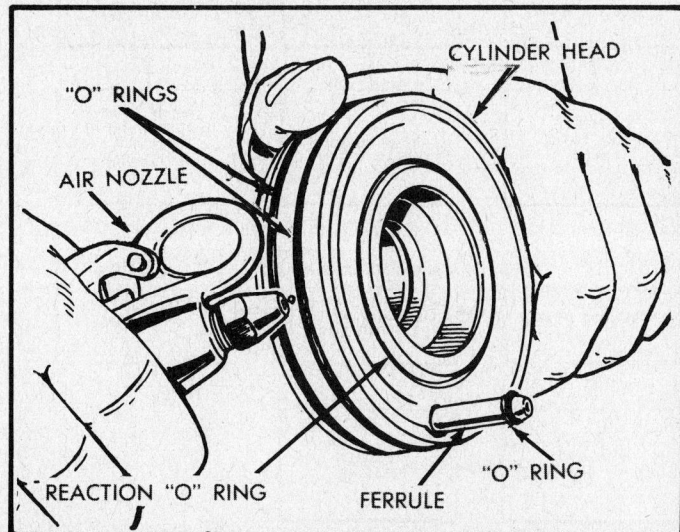
Removing the reaction seal with air pressure

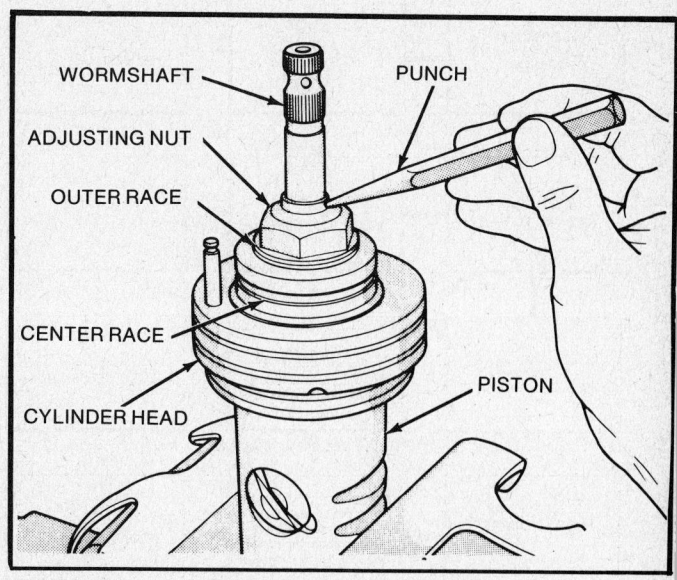
Staking the wormshaft bearing adjusting nut

34-13

SECTION 34: POWER STEERING — CHRYSLER UNITS

 ## TROUBLESHOOTING CHRYSLER POWER STEERING

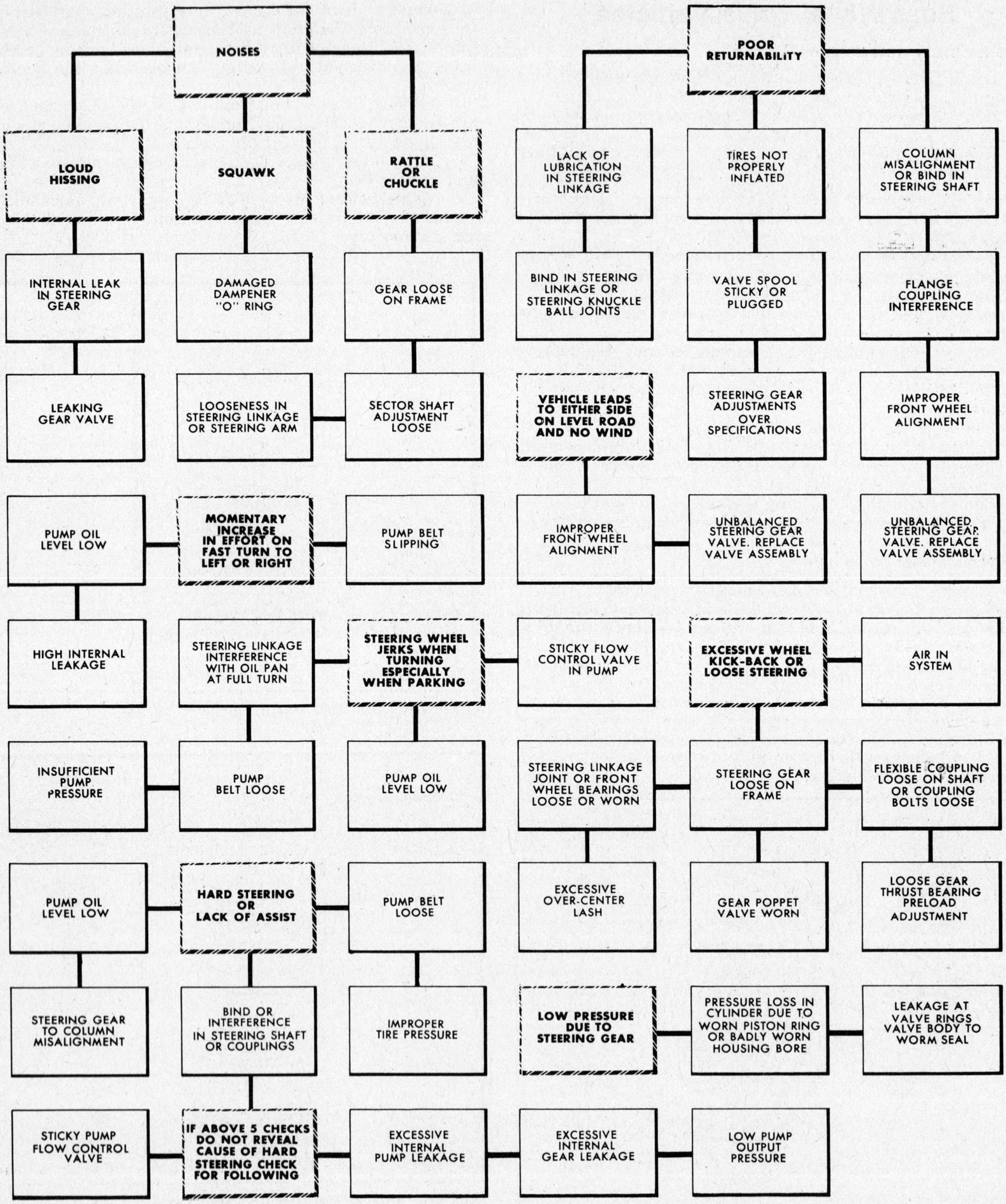

NOISES

LOUD HISSING
- Internal leak in steering gear
- Leaking gear valve
- Pump oil level low
- High internal leakage
- Insufficient pump pressure
- Pump oil level low
- Steering gear to column misalignment
- Sticky pump flow control valve

SQUAWK
- Damaged dampener "O" ring
- Looseness in steering linkage or steering arm
- Momentary increase in effort on fast turn to left or right
- Steering linkage interference with oil pan at full turn
- Pump belt loose
- Hard steering or lack of assist
- Bind or interference in steering shaft or couplings
- If above 5 checks do not reveal cause of hard steering check for following

RATTLE OR CHUCKLE
- Gear loose on frame
- Sector shaft adjustment loose
- Pump belt slipping
- Steering wheel jerks when turning especially when parking
- Pump oil level low
- Pump belt loose
- Improper tire pressure
- Excessive internal pump leakage

POOR RETURNABILITY

LACK OF LUBRICATION IN STEERING LINKAGE
- Bind in steering linkage or steering knuckle ball joints
- Vehicle leads to either side on level road and no wind
- Improper front wheel alignment
- Sticky flow control valve in pump
- Steering linkage joint or front wheel bearings loose or worn
- Excessive over-center lash
- Low pressure due to steering gear
- Excessive internal gear leakage

TIRES NOT PROPERLY INFLATED
- Valve spool sticky or plugged
- Steering gear adjustments over specifications
- Unbalanced steering gear valve. Replace valve assembly
- Excessive wheel kick-back or loose steering
- Steering gear loose on frame
- Gear poppet valve worn
- Pressure loss in cylinder due to worn piston ring or badly worn housing bore
- Low pump output pressure

COLUMN MISALIGNMENT OR BIND IN STEERING SHAFT
- Flange coupling interference
- Improper front wheel alignment
- Unbalanced steering gear valve. Replace valve assembly
- Air in system
- Flexible coupling loose on shaft or coupling bolts loose
- Loose gear thrust bearing preload adjustment
- Leakage at valve rings valve body to worm seal

34-14

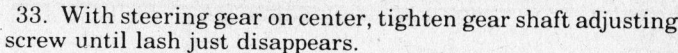
POWER STEERING
CHRYSLER UNITS
SECTION 34

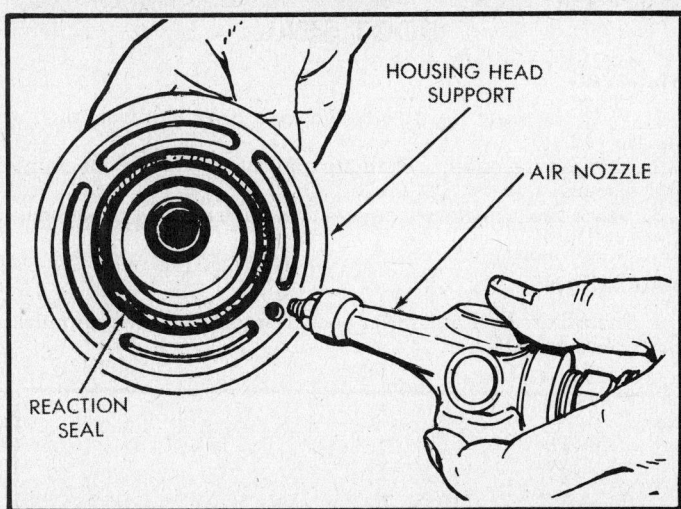

Removing the lower reaction seal with air pressure

33. With steering gear on center, tighten gear shaft adjusting screw until lash just disappears.
34. Continue to tighten $3/8$–$1/2$ turn and tighten locknut to 50 ft. lbs.

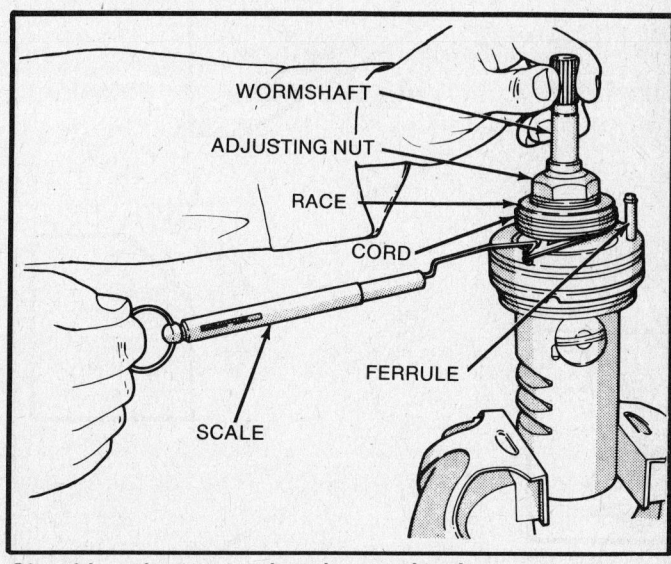

Checking the center bearing preload

19. Remove upper thrust bearing race (thin) and upper thrust bearing.
20. Remove center bearing race.
21. Remove lower thrust bearing and lower thrust bearing race (thick).
22. Remove lower reaction ring and reaction spring.
23. Remove cylinder head assembly.
24. Remove O-rings from outer grooves in head.
25. Remove reaction O-ring from groove in face of cylinder head. Use air pressure in oil hole located between O-ring grooves.
26. Remove snap-ring, sleeve and rectangular oil seal from cylinder head counterbore.
27. Test wormshaft operation. Not more than 2 inch lbs. should be required to turn it through its entire travel, and with a 15 ft. lb. side load.

NOTE: The worm and piston is serviced as a complete assembly and should not be disassembled.

28. Shaft side play should not exceed 0.008 in. under light pull applied $2\ 5/16$ in. from piston flange.
29. Assemble in reverse of above, noting proper adjustments and preload requirements following.
30. When cover nut is installed, tighten to 20 ft. lbs. torque.
31. Valve mounting screws should be tightened to 200 inch lbs. torque.
32. With hoses connected, system bled, and engine idling roughly, center valve unit until not self-steering. Tap on head of valve body attaching screws to move valve body up, and tap on end plug to move valve body down.

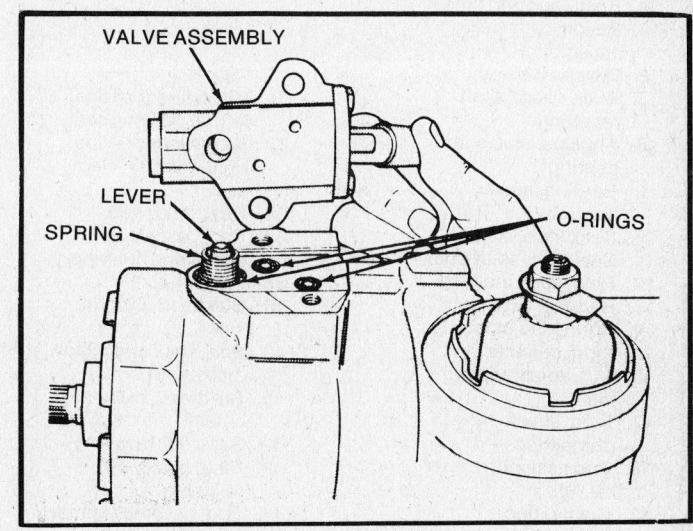

Removing the valve body assembly

CHRYSLER POWER STEERING RACK AND PINION ASSEMBLY

Front Wheel Drive Vehicles

OUTER TIE ROD

Removal

1. Loosen the rod jam nut.
2. Remove the tie rod from the steering knuckle.
3. Remove the outer tie rod by unscrewing it from the inner tie rod. Count the number of turns to unscrew.

Installation

1. Screw the outer tie rod onto the inner tie rod the same number of turns necessary to remove.
2. Expand the outer boot clamp and leave loose on the tie rod.
3. Do not tighten the jam nut until the toe adjustment is made. Do not twist the boot.
4. Torque the jam nut to 50 ft. lbs. and install the outer boot clamp.
5. Be sure the boot is not twisted when done.

34–15

SECTION 34 POWER STEERING
CHRYSLER UNITS

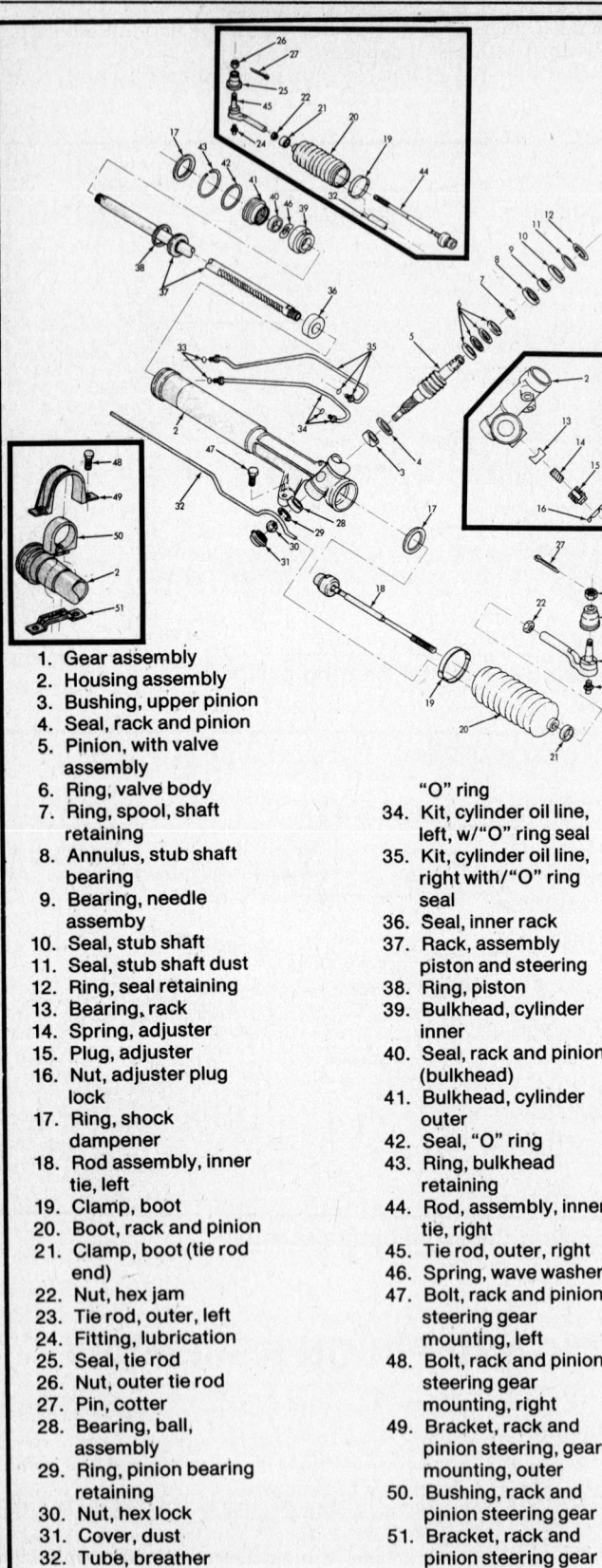

1. Gear assembly
2. Housing assembly
3. Bushing, upper pinion
4. Seal, rack and pinion
5. Pinion, with valve assembly
6. Ring, valve body
7. Ring, spool, shaft retaining
8. Annulus, stub shaft bearing
9. Bearing, needle assemby
10. Seal, stub shaft
11. Seal, stub shaft dust
12. Ring, seal retaining
13. Bearing, rack
14. Spring, adjuster
15. Plug, adjuster
16. Nut, adjuster plug lock
17. Ring, shock dampener
18. Rod assembly, inner tie, left
19. Clamp, boot
20. Boot, rack and pinion
21. Clamp, boot (tie rod end)
22. Nut, hex jam
23. Tie rod, outer, left
24. Fitting, lubrication
25. Seal, tie rod
26. Nut, outer tie rod
27. Pin, cotter
28. Bearing, ball, assembly
29. Ring, pinion bearing retaining
30. Nut, hex lock
31. Cover, dust
32. Tube, breather
33. Seal, cylinder oil line
34. Kit, cylinder oil line, left, w/"O" ring seal
35. Kit, cylinder oil line, right with/"O" ring seal
36. Seal, inner rack
37. Rack, assembly piston and steering
38. Ring, piston
39. Bulkhead, cylinder inner
40. Seal, rack and pinion (bulkhead)
41. Bulkhead, cylinder outer
42. Seal, "O" ring
43. Ring, bulkhead retaining
44. Rod, assembly, inner tie, right
45. Tie rod, outer, right
46. Spring, wave washer
47. Bolt, rack and pinion, steering gear mounting, left
48. Bolt, rack and pinion, steering gear mounting, right
49. Bracket, rack and pinion steering, gear mounting, outer
50. Bushing, rack and pinion steering gear
51. Bracket, rack and pinion steering gear mounting, inner

Exploded view of Saginaw power steering gear

BOOT SEAL

Removal

1. With the outer tie rod off, remove the jam nut from the inner tie rod.
2. Expand the outer boot clamp and cut the inner boot clamp and discard.
3. Mark the location of the breather tube on the rubber boot. Remove the boot.

Installation

1. Install the boot and inner boot clamp. Align the boot mark and breather tube.

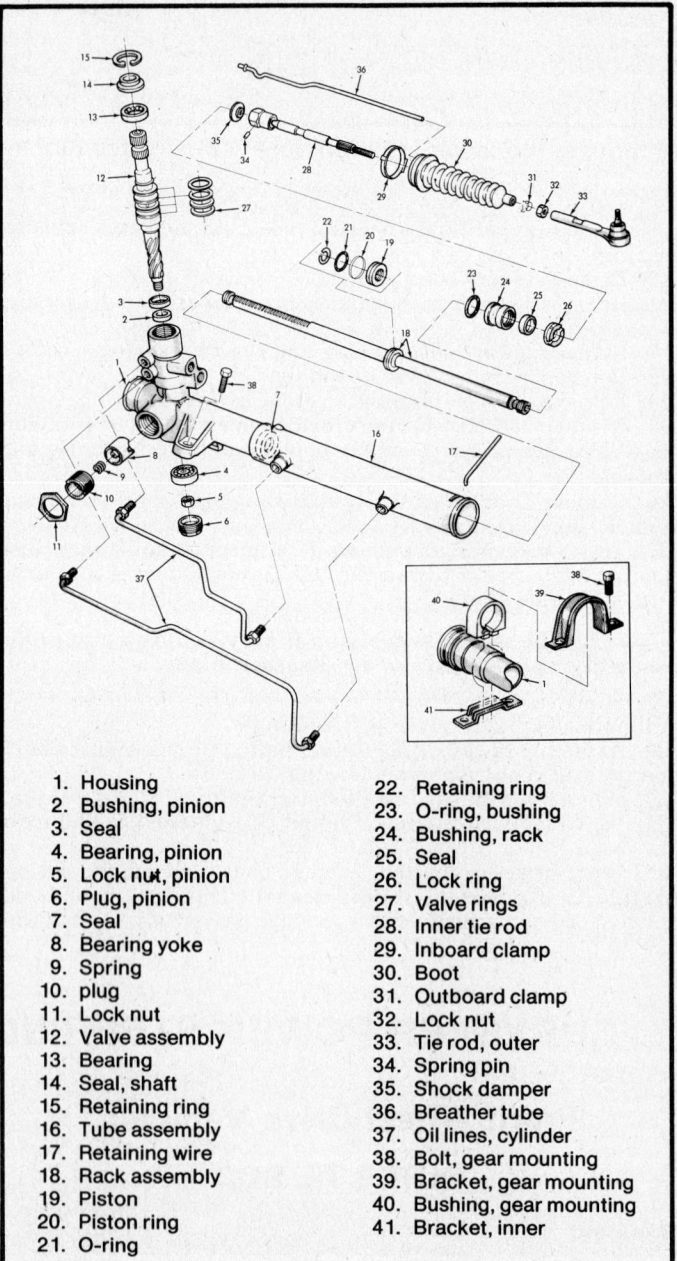

1. Housing
2. Bushing, pinion
3. Seal
4. Bearing, pinion
5. Lock nut, pinion
6. Plug, pinion
7. Seal
8. Bearing yoke
9. Spring
10. plug
11. Lock nut
12. Valve assembly
13. Bearing
14. Seal, shaft
15. Retaining ring
16. Tube assembly
17. Retaining wire
18. Rack assembly
19. Piston
20. Piston ring
21. O-ring
22. Retaining ring
23. O-ring, bushing
24. Bushing, rack
25. Seal
26. Lock ring
27. Valve rings
28. Inner tie rod
29. Inboard clamp
30. Boot
31. Outboard clamp
32. Lock nut
33. Tie rod, outer
34. Spring pin
35. Shock damper
36. Breather tube
37. Oil lines, cylinder
38. Bolt, gear mounting
39. Bracket, gear mounting
40. Bushing, gear mounting
41. Bracket, inner

Exploded view of TRW power steering gear

POWER STEERING
CHRYSLER UNITS
SECTION 34

2. Install thee boot seal over the housing lip with the hole in the boot aligned with the breather tube.
3. Install the inner boot clamp. Lubricate the tie rod boot groove with a silicone type lubricant before installing the outer clamp.

INNER TIE ROD

Removal

1. With the steering unit out of the vehicle, remove the shock dampener ring from the inner tie rod housing and slide it back on the rack Saginaw gears.
2. On TRW gears, remove the roll pin from the inner tie rod to the rack.
3. Put a wrench on the tie rod pivot housing flats and turn the housing counterclockwise until the inner tie rod assembly separates from the rack.

Installation

1. Install the inner tie rod onto the rack and bottom the threads.
2. Torque the housing while holding the rack with a wrench. Torque to 70 ft. lbs. for the Saginaw gear, while torquing the inner tie rod to 60 ft. lbs. for the TRW gear. Install roll pin as required.
3. Support the rack and housing and stake the housing in two places for the Saginaw gear.
4. Inspect the stake, a 0.010 inch feeler gauge must not pass between the rack and the housing stake on each side.
5. On the Saginaw gear, slide the shock dampener over the inner tie rod housing until it engaged.

RACK BEARING

Removal

1. Loosen the lock nut for the adjuster plug.
2. Remove the adjuster plug from the housing. Remove the spring and rack bearing.

Installation

1. Lubricate the metal parts and install the rack bearing, the spring, the adjuster plug and the lock nut.
2. Turn the adjuster plug in until it bottoms and then back off 40 to 60 degrees.
3. Tighten the lock nut while holding the adjuster plug in place. The torque must be 50 ft. lbs.

STUB SHAFT SEALS

Removal

1. Remove the retaining ring and the dust cover.
2. Using a special holder or its equivalent, remove the lock nut from the pinion.

CAUTION

If the stub shaft is not held, damage to the pinion teeth will occur.

3. Using the special puller or its equivalent, pull the valve and pinion assembly until flush with the ball bearing assembly. The complete assembly does not have to be removed.
4. Remove the stub shaft dust seal, stub shaft seal, needle bearing and stub shaft bearing annulus.

NOTE: The bearing and annuls are pressed together and disassembly is required only if bearing replacement is necessary.

Installation

1. Lubricate the seals and install in the reverse order of removal, using seal protectors on the pinion shaft. Seal installers are available to assist in seating the seal properly.
2. While holding the stub shaft, firmly seat the lock nut and torque to 26 ft. lbs.
3. Install the retainer and the dust cover.

VALVE AND PINION ASSEMBLY

Removal

1. Turn the stub shaft until the rack is equal distance on both sides of the housing, with the pinion fully engaged.
2. Mark the location and angle of the stub shaft flat on the steering housing.
3. With the lock nut off the pinion, use a special puller or its equivalent, and pull the valve and pinion assembly from the housing.
4. Remove the valve body rings.

Installation

1. Install new rings on the valve body.
2. Lubricate the rings and valve. Install the assembly into the housing. Be sure the rack is equal on both sides of the housing.
3. When the valve and pinion assembly is installed, the stub shaft flat should align with the mark made before disassembly.
4. Hold the stub shaft, install the lock nut and torque to 26 ft. lbs.

BULKHEAD

Removal

1. The pinion and valve assembly must be in the housing for this operation.
2. On Saginaw gears, use a punch in the access hole and remove the bulkhead retaining ring. Discard the ring.
3. On TRW gears, use a punch to rotate the retaining wire clockwise to expose the end. Pull the retaining wire to remove.
4. Loosen and remove both cylinder lines. Plug fittings at the cylinder.
5. Turn the stub shaft so that the rack moves to the right, forcing the bulkhead from the housing. Use a drain pan to catch the power steering fluid.
6. If the inner rack seal or piston rings are to be replaced, use special seal remover tools as required.
7. The piston and pinion can be removed.

Installation

1. Install the inner rack seal with special seal installer tools or equivalent.
2. Install the plastic retainer onto the inner rack seal.
3. Install the bulkhead outer seal into the bulkhead.
4. Install the bulkhead onto the rack.
5. On Saginaw gears, be sure the open end of the new bulkhead retaining ring is approximately 0.50 from the access hole.
6. On Saginaw gears, turn the rack to full right turn to fully seat the retaining ring.
7. The remaining models, install the retaining wire by rotating the bulkhead assembly counterclockwise.

PINION BALL BEARING, UPPER PINION BUSHING AND SEAL

Removal and Installation

1. The pinion and piston must be out of the housing.
2. The bearing is removed by the use of a drift and hammer. To install, a bearing installer is available.

Section 34: POWER STEERING
CHRYSLER UNITS

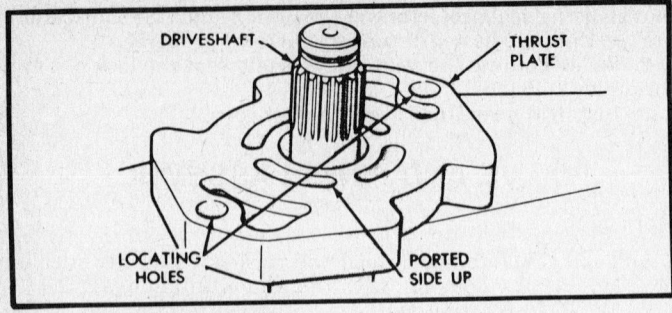
Thrust plate installation

3. To remove the seal and bushing, a drift and hammer is used. To install, the use of special installing tools are necessary.

POWER STEERING PUMP OVERHAUL

Disassembly

1. With the power steering pump removed from the vehicle, drain the reservoir and reinstall the filler cap to prevent con-

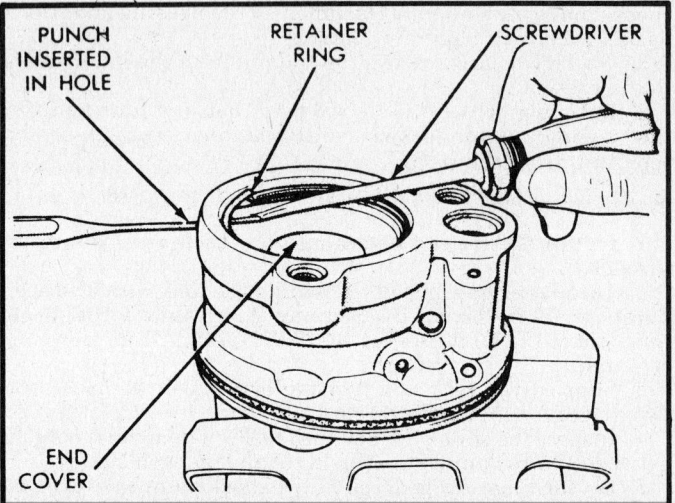
Removing the end cover retaining ring

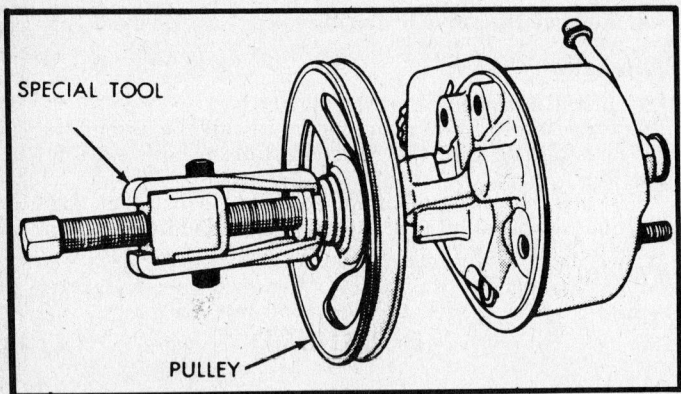
Removing the pulley

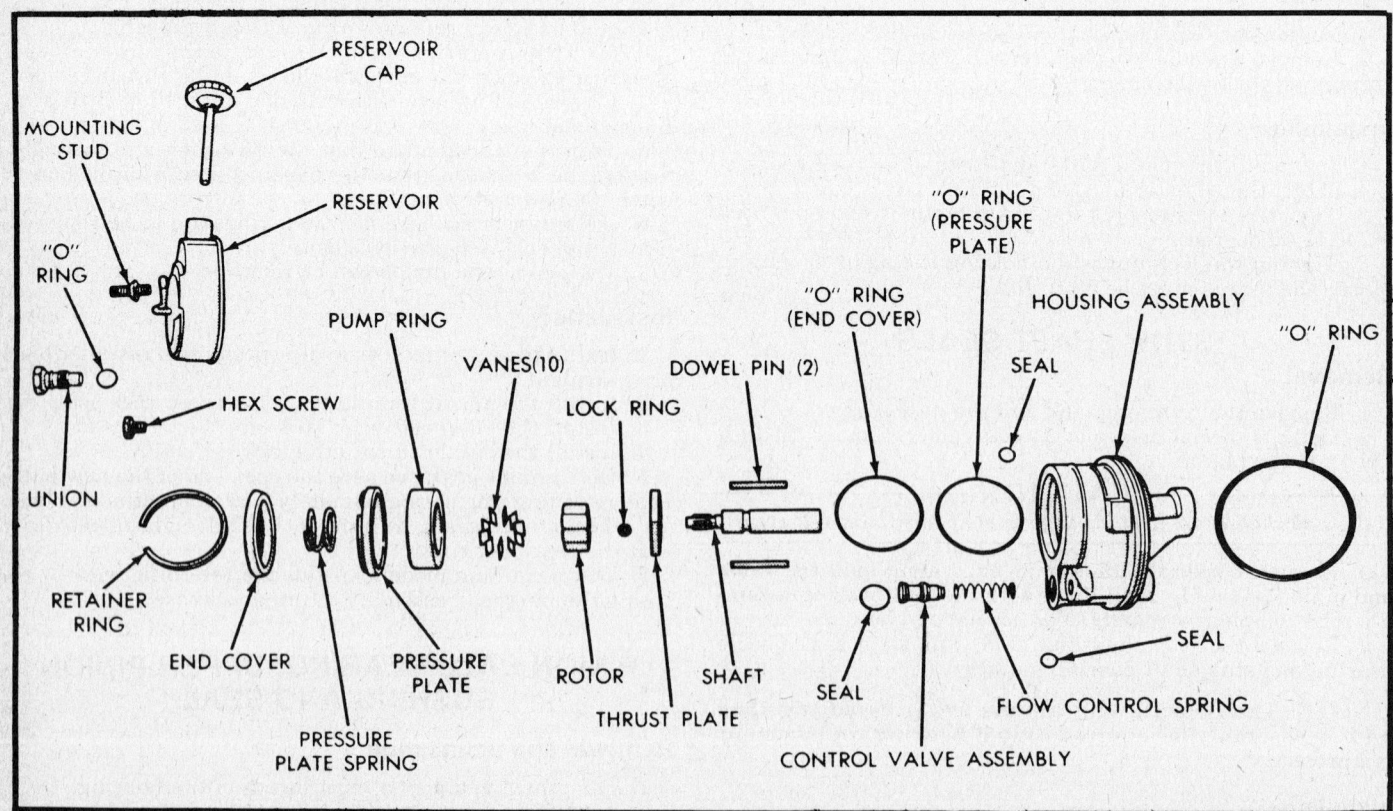
Power steering pump disassembled

34-18

POWER STEERING
CHRYSLER UNITS
SECTION 34

tamination. Clean the exterior of the pump before starting the disassembly procedures.

2. Secure the pump in a suitable vise at the mounting bracket.

3. Using special puller tool C–4068A or equivalent remove the pulley from the pump. Be sure that the puller screw is perfectly aligned with the shaft end to prevent cocking.

NOTE: The pump pulley is a press fit on the shaft and must be removed and replaced with the aid of puller tools. Do not hammer on the puller, pulley or shaft for this could cause internal damage to the pump components. To aid in pulley removal it is advisable to apply a light oil on the pulley shaft. If a hydraulic press is available, place the power steering pump into the press and press the pulley off of the pump shaft. If there is not a hydraulic press available, remove the pulley wit the puller as outlined above.

4. Remove the brackets from the pump and using a soft jaw vise or equivalent, clamp the pump (shaft end down) in the vise between the square boss and shaft housing.

5. Remove the two mounting studs and pressure hose fitting. Tap the reservoir filler tube back and forth with a plastic mallet to loosen. Remove the reservoir off of the pump body and discard the O-rngs from the reservoir along with the two mounting studs and the pressure fitting.

6. Using a punch, tap the end cover retainer ring around until one end of the ring is near the hole in the pump body. Insert the punch far enough to disengage the ring from the groove in the pump bore and pry the ring out of the pump body.

7. Tap the end cover with a plastic mallet to dislodge it, the spring under the cover should push the cover up.

8. Remove the pump body from the vise, place the pump upside down on a flat surface and tap the end of the driveshaft with a plastic mallet to loosen the pressure plate, rotor and thrust plate assembly from the pump body.

9. Lift the pump body off of rotor assembly. Flow control valve and spring should slide out of the bore.

10. Replace and discard end cover and pressure plate O-rings, place pump body on a flat surface and pry the driveshaft oil seal out with a suitable tool.

11. Inspect the seal bore in housing for burrs, nicks or gouge marks that would allow oil to bypass outer seal surface.

12. Remove the ten vanes from the slots in the rotor, after lifting out the pressure plate and cam ring from the rotor. Clamp the driveshaft in a soft jaw vise or equivalent, with the rotor and thrust plate facing up.

13. Remove the rotor lock ring, pry the ring off the driveshaft and be sure to avoid nicking the rotor end face. Discard the lock ring.

14. Slide the rotor and thrust plate off of the shaft and remove the shaft from the vise.

NOTE: Inspect and wash all parts in clean solvent, blow out all passages with compressed air and air dry the cleaned parts.

Assembly

1. With the pump body laying on a flat surface, drive a new driveshaft seal into the bore, using a 7/8 or 15/16 inch socket until the seal bottoms on shoulder.

NOTE: Do not use excessive force when installing the seal, because the seal will become distorted.

2. Lubricate the seal with power steering fluid and clamp the pump body shaft end down into a vise.

3. Install the end cover and pressure plate O-rings in the grooves in the pump cavity. (These rings are the same size.) Be sure to lubricate the O-rings in power steering fluid.

4. With the driveshaft clamped in a soft jaw vise or equiva-

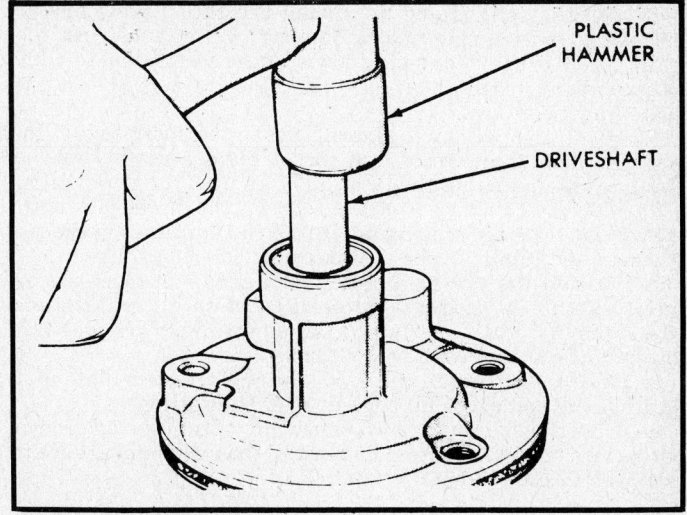
Drive shaft removal

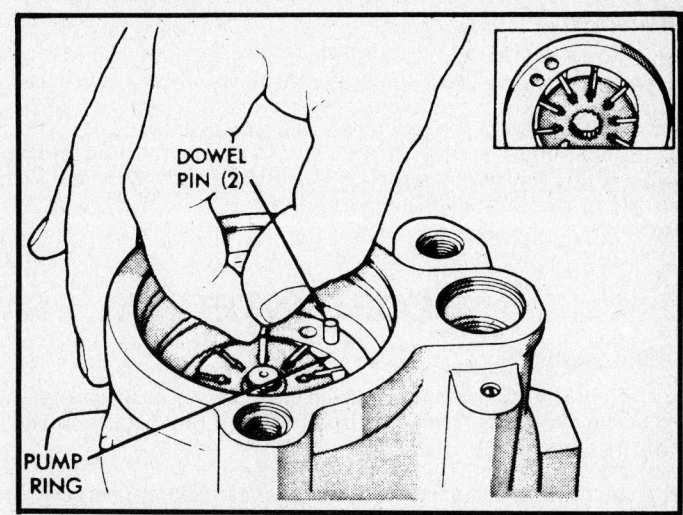
Rotor vanes installation

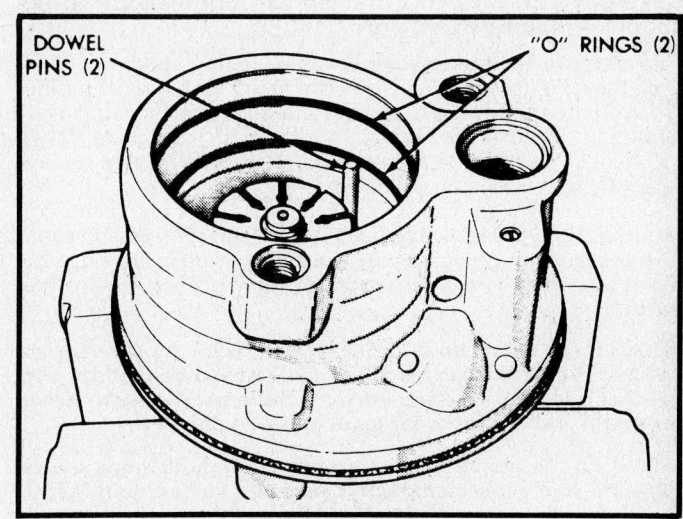
The rotor and thrust plate installed

SECTION 34 — POWER STEERING
CHRYSLER UNITS

lent with the splined end up, install the thrust plate on the driveshaft (ported side up). Slide rotor over splines with the counterbore of the rotor facing down. Using special tool C–4090 or equivalent install the rotor lock ring being sure the ring is seated in the groove.

5. Install the two dowel pins in holes in the pump cavity. Insert the driveshaft, rotor and thrust plate assembly in the pump cavity matching the locating holes with the dowel pins.

6. Slide the cam ring over the rotor on the dowel pins with the arrow on the ring facing up. Install the ten vanes in the rotor slots and lubricate them with power steering fluid.

7. Position the pressure plate dowel pins and place a 1 1/4 inch socket in the groove of the pressure plate and seat the entire assembly on the O-ring in the pump cavity by pressing down on the socket with both thumbs.

8. Place the spring in the groove in the pressure plate and position the end cover lip edge up over the spring.

9. Press the end cover down below the retaining ring groove with a vise or an arbor press and install the ring making sure it is seated in the groove.

NOTE: This procedure is better performed in an arbor press if available. Caution should be used to prevent cocking the end cover in the bore or distorting the assembly.

10. Using a punch, tap the retainer ring ends around in the groove until the opening is opposite the flow control valve bore. This is important for maximum retention of the retainer ring.

11. Replace the reservoir O-ring seal, the two mounting stud O-ring seals and the flow control valve O-ring seal on the pump body. Align the mounting stud holes until the studs can be started in the threads.

12. Tap the reservoir down on the pump using a plastic mallet and insert the flow control valve spring and valve (hexagon plug down). Replace the O-ring on the pressure hose fitting and lubricate with power steering fluid.

NOTE: Be sure the O-ring is installed on the upper groove. It is possible to install the O-ring in the lower groove. If this happens it will restrict the relief outlet orifice.

13. Install the pressure hose fitting and tighten the mounting studs. The torque for the hose is 35 ft. lbs. (47 Nm) and the torque for the studs is 30 ft. lbs. (41 Nm).

14. Remove the pump assembly from the vise and install the mounting brackets. After the brackets are installed clamp the pump assembly into the vise at the mounting bracket.

15. Apply a thin coat of light oil to the pump shaft and using special tool C–4063 without the adapters and install the pulley onto the shaft. Be sure that the tool remains in alignment during installation and tighten until the tool bottoms out on the shaft. Make sure that while turning the tool to install the pulley, that the pulley is going on evenly and smoothly so as to prevent any damage to the pulley and or the shaft.

NOTE: If a hydraulic press is available, place the pump assembly into the press and press the pulley onto the pump shaft. If there is not a hydraulic press available, install the pulley as outlined above.

16. Install the pump assembly on the engine and refill the reservoir. Start the engine, inspect for leaks and recheck the fluid level after bleeding the air from the pump.

FORD INTEGRAL POWER STEERING GEAR

Disassembly

1. Hold the steering gear upside down over a drain pan and cycle the input shaft several times to drain the fluid from the gear.
2. Secure the gear in a soft-jawed vise.
3. Remove the nut from the sector shaft adjusting screw.
4. Turn the input shaft to either stop then, turn it back two turns to center the gear.

NOTE: The indexing flat on the input shaft spline should be facing downward.

5. Remove the sector shaft cover attaching bolts.
6. Rap the lower end of the sector shaft with a soft-hammer to loosen it, and lift the cover and shaft from the housing as an assembly. Discard the O-ring.
7. Turn the sector shaft cover counterclockwise and remove it from the sector shaft adjuster screw.
8. Remove the valve housing attaching bolts and identification tag. Hold the piston to keep it from spinning off the shaft, and lift the valve housing off the steering gear housing. Remove the valve housing and control valve gasket. Discard the gasket.

NOTE: If valve housing seals are to be replaced, proceed to Step 12. If sector shaft seals are to be replaced go to steering gear housing section. Balls need only to be removed if valve sleeve rings are to be replaced.

9. With the piston held so that the ball guide faces up, remove the ball guide clamp screws and ball guide clamp. With a finger over the opening in the ball guide, turn the piston so that the ball guide faces down over a clean container. Let the guide tubes drop into the container.

10. Rotate the input shaft from stop to stop until all balls fall from the piston into the container. The valve assembly can then be removed from the piston. Inspect the piston bore to insure all balls have been removed.

11. Install the valve body assembly in the bench mounted holding fixture, and loosen the Allen head race nut screw from the valve housing. Remove the worm bearing race nut.

12. Carefully slide the input shaft, worm and valve assembly out of the valve housing. Do not cock the spool or it may jam in the housing.

Assembly

1. Mount the valve housing in the bench mounted holding fixture with the flanged end up.
2. Apply a light coat of gear lubricant to the teflon rings on the valve sleeve.
3. Carefully install the worm shaft and valve in the housing.
4. Install the worm bearing race nut in the housing and torque to specification.
5. Install the Allen head race nut screw through the valve housing and tighten to specification 15–25 inch lbs. (1.7–2.8 Nm).
6. Place the power cylinder piston on the bench with the ball guide holes facing up. Insert the worm shaft into the piston so that the first groove is in line with the hole nearest the center of the piston.
7. Place the ball guide in the piston. Turning the worm shaft counterclockwise as viewed from the input end of the shaft, place the same balls as removed in Step 9 in the ball guide. A minimum of 27 balls is required. If all the balls have not been inserted upon reaching the left stop, rotate the input shaft in one direction then the other while inserting the remaining balls. Do not rotate the input shaft or piston more than three

POWER STEERING
FORD INTEGRAL TYPE
SECTION 34

turns from the left stop, or the balls will fall out of the circuit.

8. Secure the guides in the ball nut with the clamp. Tighten screws to specification.

9. Apply petroleum jelly or equivalent to the teflon seal on the piston.

10. Place a new control valve O-ring on the valve housing.

11. Slide the piston and valve into the gear housing being careful not to damage the piston ring.

12. Align the oil passage in the valve housing with the passage in the gear housing. Place a new O-ring onto the oil passage hole of the gear housing. Install identification tag onto the housing. Install but do not tighten, the attaching bolts. Identification tag is to be installed under upper right valve housing bolt.

13. Rotate the ball nut so that the teeth are in the same plane as the sector teeth. Tighten the valve housing attaching bolts to specification.

14. Position the sector shaft cover O-ring in the steering gear housing. Turn the input shaft to center the piston.

15. Apply petroleum jelly or equivalent to the sector shaft journal, and position the sector shaft and cover assembly in the gear housing. Install the sector shaft cover attaching bolts. Tighten the bolts to specification 55–70 ft. lbs. (75–94 Nm).

16. Attach an in. lb. torque wrench to the input shaft. Adjust mesh load to specification.

STEERING GEAR HOUSING
Disassembly and Assembly

1. Remove the snap ring from the lower end of the housing.
2. Remove dust seal using tools puller attachment and slide hammer.
3. Remove pressure seal in the same manner. Discard the seal.
4. Lubricate the new pressure seal dust seal with clean Ford polyethylene grease.
5. Apply Ford polyethylene grease to the sector shaft seal bore.
6. Place the dust seal on sector shaft replacement tool so the raised lip of the seal is towards the tool. Place the pressure seal on the tool with lip away from the tool. The flat back side of the pressure seal should be against the flat side of the dust seal.
7. Insert the seal driver tool into the sector shaft bore and drive the tool until the seals clear the snap ring groove. Do not bottom seals against bearing. The seal will not function properly when bottomed against the bearing.
8. Install snap ring in the groove in the housing.

VALVE HOUSING
Disassembly and Assembly

1. Remove the dust seal from the rear of the valve housing using puller attachment and slide hammer. Discard the seal.
2. Remove the snap ring from the valve housing.
3. Turn the bench mounted holding fixture to invert valve housing.
4. Insert tools from the input shaft bearing seal tool in the valve body assembly opposite the oil seal end and gently tap the bearing and seal out of the housing. Discard the seal. Do not damage the housing when inserting and removing the tools.
5. Remove the fluid inlet and outlet tube seats with tube seat remover tool if they are damaged.
6. Coat the fluid inlet and outlet tube seats with petroleum jelly or equivalent and install them in the housing with a tube seat installer.
7. Coat the bearing and seal surface of the housing with petroleum jelly or equivalent.
8. Install the bearing with the metal side covering the rollers facing outward. Seat the bearing in the valve housing. Be sure the bearing rotates freely.

9. Dip a new oil seal in gear lubricant, and place it in the housing with the metal side facing outward. Drive the seal into the housing until the outer edge does not quite clear the snap ring groove.

10. Place the snap ring in the housing and drive on the ring until the snap ring seats in its groove.

11. Place the dust seal in the housing with the dished side (rubber side) facing out. Drive the dust seal into place. When properly installed, the seal will be located behind the undercut in the input shaft.

WORM AND VALVE SLEEVE
Disassembly and Assembly

1. Remove valve sleeve rings from sleeve by inserting the blade of a small pocket knife under them and cutting them off.

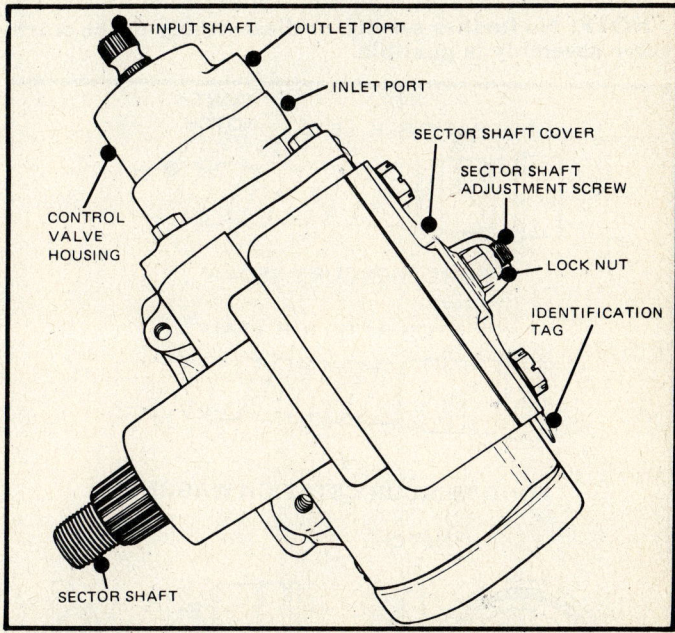

Ford integral power steering gear assembly — exterior view

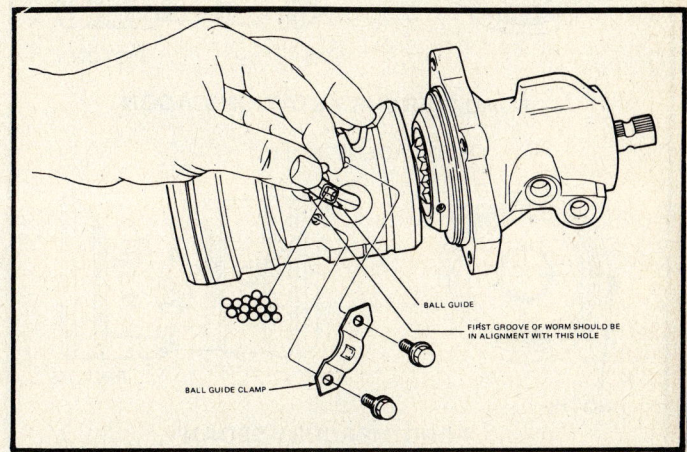

Assembling ball in piston and piston on worm shaft — Ford integral power steering

34-21

SECTION 34 POWER STEERING
FORD INTEGRAL TYPE

2. Mount the worm end of the worm and valve sleeve assembly into a soft-jawed vise.

3. Install mandrel tool over the sleeve; slide one valve sleeve ring over the tool.

4. Slide the pusher tool over the mandrel; rapidly push down on the pusher tool, forcing the ring down the ramp and into the fourth groove of the valve sleeve. Repeat this step three more times, and each time add one of the spacers under the mandrel tool. By adding the spacer each time, the mandrel tool will line up with the next groove of the valve sleeve.

5. After installing the four valve sleeve rings, apply a light coat of gear lubricant to the sleeve and rings.

6. Install one spacer over the input shaft as a pilot for installing the sizing tube. Slowly install the sizing tube over the sleeve valve end of the worm shaft onto the valve sleeve rings. Make sure that the rings are not being bent over as the tube is slid over them.

7. Remove the sizing tube and check the condition of the rings. Make sure that the rings turn freely in the grooves.

NOTE: No further service or disassembly of the worm valve assembly is possible.

PISTON AND BALL NUT

Disassembly and Assembly

1. Remove the teflon piston ring and O-ring from the piston and ball nut. Discard both rings.

2. Dip a new O-ring in gear lubricant and install it on the piston and ball nut.

3. Install a new teflon piston ring on the piston and ball nut being careful not to stretch it any more than necessary.

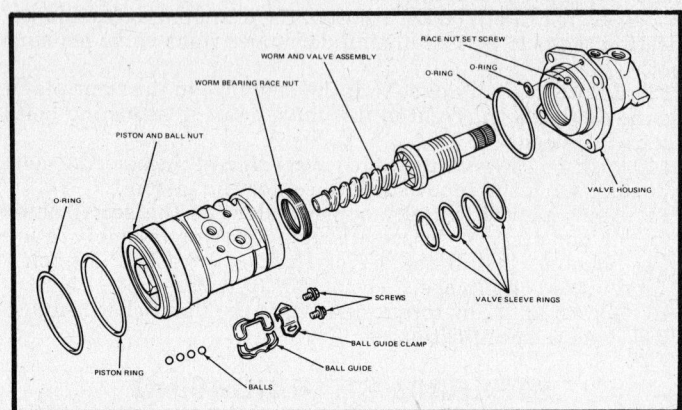

Ford integral power steering gear assembly—exterior view

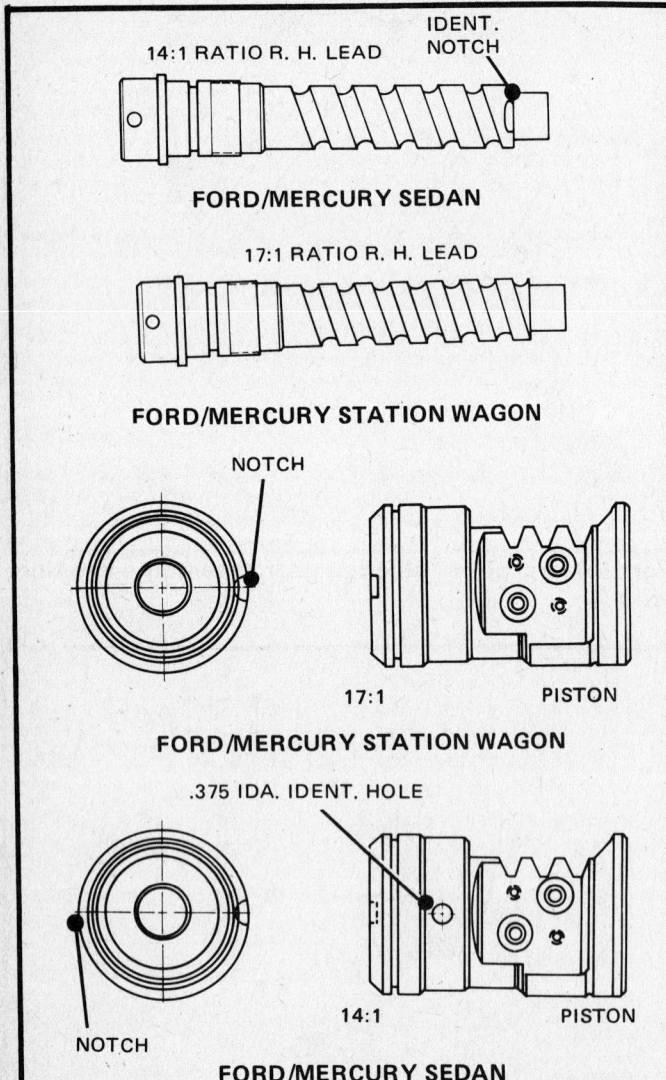

Differences in worm and piston ratios—Ford integral power steering

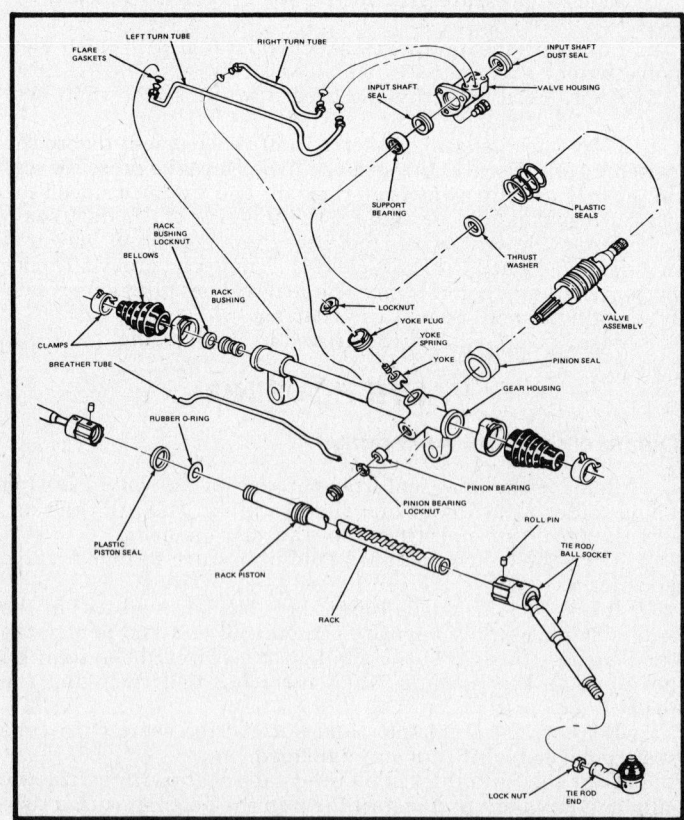

Exploded view of TRW type integral power steering rack and pinion

Power Steering
TRW RACK AND PINION TYPE
SECTION 34

TRW RACK AND PINION POWER STEERING GEAR

THE ROD BALL SOCKETS

Disassembly

1. Remove the rack and pinion steering gear from the vehicle. Position the gar in a suitable holding fixture. Clean the exterior of the gear.
2. Remove the tie rod outer ends and locknuts.
3. Remove the bellow clamps. Remove the bellows and the breather tube. Be careful not to damage the bellows. Discard the bellow clamps.
4. Using a left hand threaded easy out tool, remove the spiral pin that locks each tie rod socket to the rack.
5. Using tool T74P-3504-U or equivalent and a torque wrench, as well as an adjustable wrench, remove the ball socket.

NOTE: If the rack is not restrained by the adjustable wrench damage to the pinion will occur.

Assembly

1. Assembly is the reverse of the removal procedure.
2. Tighten the tie rod ball socket to 55–65 ft. lbs.

VALVE AND VALVE HOUSING

Disassembly and Assembly

1. Remove the steering gear from the vehicle. Position the assembly in a suitable holding fixture. Clean the exterior of the gear.
2. Remove the external pressure lines from the valve and the gear housing. Remove the four flare gaskets from the ports.
3. Loosen the yoke plug locknut and the yoke plug. This is done to relieve the preload on the rack. Remove the pinion bearing plug.
4. Install tool T47P-3504-R or an equivalent pinion shaft torque tool on the input shaft.
5. Hold the input shaft, and remove the pinion bearing locknut and discard it.
6. Remove the bolts and washers retaining the valve housing to the gear housing.
7. Move the rack to the left stop (rack teeth exposed). With a file or chalk, mark the relative position of the indexing flat surface on the input shaft splines to the valve housing face.

NOTE: It is important when subsequent assembly of the input shaft is made that the flat be aligned in the same position.

8. The valve housing cannot be removed as a single component because of the pinion seal design. To service the valve housing, valve assembly, or the pinion seal, the complete valve housing and valve assembly must be removed as a unit.

NOTE: The pinion bearing locknut must be removed before attempting to remove the valve housing.

9. Carefully work the valve housing and the valve assembly, as a unit, out and away from the gear assembly.
10. Position the valve and housing assembly in a suitable vise. Grip the protruding pinion seal with a pair of interlocking pliers.
11. Rotate the seal in the clockwise direction, this will cause the seal to twist out of the valve housing. Do not hammer or pry on the pliers or the input shaft, as damage may occur.

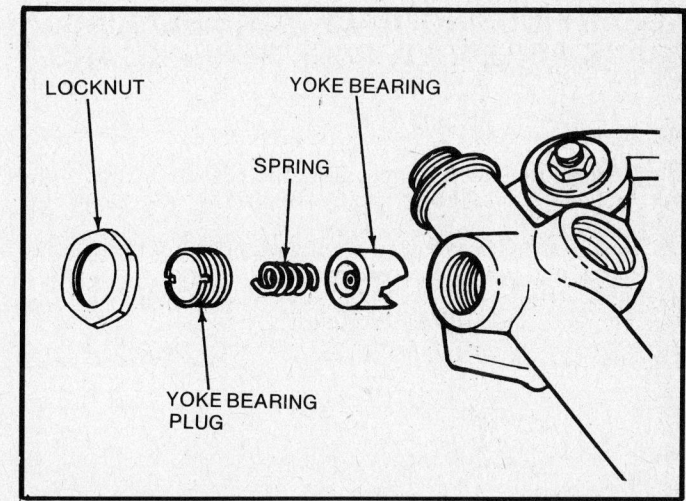

TRW rack and pinion yoke bearing and related components

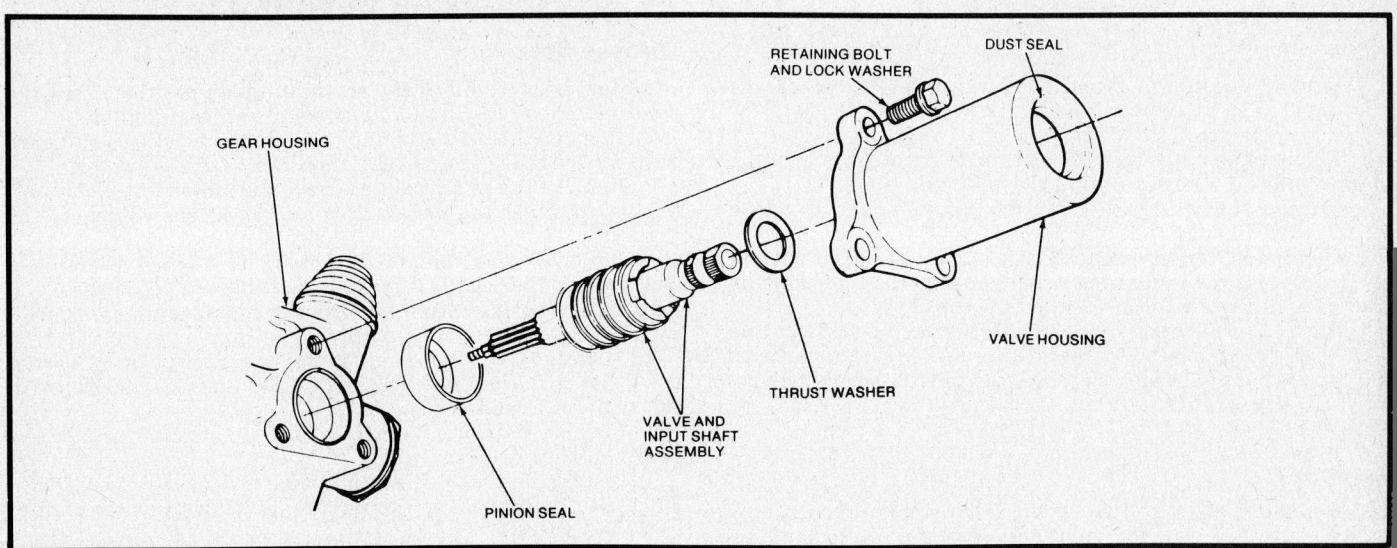

TRW power rack and pinion valve housing assembly

SECTION 34 POWER STEERING
TRW RACK AND PINION TYPE

12. Discard the pinion oil seal and any other damaged or worn components.
13. Using a slide hammer, remove the pinion bearing from the gear housing.
14. Remove the four valve sleeve rings from the input shaft and valve assembly, with tool T71P-19703-C or an equivalent ring removal tool.
15. Remove the input shaft support bearing from its bore in the valve housing using a slide hammer. Remove the oil seal.
16. Pry the input shaft dust seal out of the valve housing. Be careful not to damage the surfaces of the valve housing.

Assembly

1. Assemble the steering gear in the reverse order of the disassembly procedure.
2. Be sure to fill the input shaft dust seal bore with lubricant, before installing the dust seal.
3. Coat all new components with power steering fluid before installation.

GEAR HOUSING, RACK YOKE BEARING, RACK ASSEMBLY, RACK BUSHING, AND OIL SEALS

Disassembly

1. Remove the steering gear from the vehicle. Position the unit in a suitable holding fixture. Clean the exterior of the gear.
2. Remove the tie rod and socket assemblies from both sides of the rack and pinion steering assembly.
3. Remove the input shaft and valve assembly. Remove the yoke plug locknut and the yoke plug.
4. Remove the yoke spring and the yoke bearing from the steering gear housing.
5. Working from the right side of the steering gear, opposite the pinion end, push the rack until it bottoms.
6. Install the rack bushing locknut tool T77P-3504-A or equivalent, so that the two drive tabs engage the slots in the lockring.
7. Rotate the tool in the counterclockwise direction in order to drive the lockwire out of the slot in the housing. Remove the lockring.
8. Pull the rack out of the right side of the housing slowly, until the rack piston contacts the aluminum rack bushing.
9. Apply pulling effort, but do not hammer, on the rack until the bushing is withdrawn from the housing. Remove the rack from the housing.
10. To remove the internal high pressure rack oil seal, install the seal removal tool T78P-3504-J or equivalent, into the housing until it bottoms.
11. Activate the expander using a wrench until it fully tightens. Remove the tool and the oil seal from the housing using a slide hammer. Discard the oil seal.
12. Remove the plastic O-ring and the rubber O-ring from the rack piston assembly.
13. Remove the rack bushing oil seal using the bushing holding tool T74P-3504-E or equivalent, the oil seal removal tool T78P-3504-J or equivalent and the slide hammer.
14. Remove the rubber O-ring from the bushing.

Assembly

1. Assembly is the reverse of the disassembly procedure.
2. Do not use impact tools during the assembly procedure.
3. When installing the high pressure oil seal on the inner rack using tool T74P-3504-D be careful that the tool does not bind in the area of the left turn pressure port. If this happens align the flat of the tool with the pressure port.

FORD RACK AND PINION POWER STEERING GEAR

TIE ROD ENDS, BELLOWS AND TIE ROD ASSEMBLIES

Disassembly

1. Remove the steering gear from the vehicle. Position the steering gear in a suitable holding fixture. Clean the exterior of the steering gear.
2. Remove the outer tie rod ends and jam nuts. Remove the clamps and the wires retaining the bellows.
3. Remove the bellows. Remove the breather tube. Use care not to cause damage to the bellows.
4. Using a left hand threaded easy out tool, remove the spiral pin that locks the tie rod assembly to the rack. Repeat the procedure to the other side of the rack assembly.
5. Push out the rack to expose several rack teeth. Hold the rack with an adjustable wrench positioned on the rack teeth against the rack shoulder. Remove both tie rod assemblies using the adjustable wrench and tool T81P-3504-G or equivalent.

Assembly

1. Assembly is the reverse of the disassembly procedure.
2. Be sure to repair or replace all defective components as required.
3. Torque the tie rod ball housing to 50-55 ft. lbs.

INPUT SHAFT AND VALVE ASSEMBLY— GEAR IN VEHICLE

Disassembly

1. Set the steering in the straight ahead position. Lock the steering wheel. Raise the vehicle and support it safely.
2. Remove the bellow clamps and slide the bellows outboard from the gear housing. Clean the fluid from the boots.
3. Remove the pinion cap. Remove the pinion nut. Position a drain pan under the pinion area and lower the vehicle to the ground.
4. Remove the column boot from the dash panel. Disconnect the intermediate shaft from the gear. It may be necessary to loosen the steering column in order to separate the intermediate shaft from the steering gear.
5. Turn the gar input shaft to the on center position so that the D flat is in the three o'clock position and the wheels are in the straight ahead position.
6. Remove the snap ring that retains the shaft seal to the gear housing.
7. Install the input shaft and valve body puller tool T81P-3504-T or equivalent to the input shaft. Turn the nut and remove the valve assembly.
8. Remove the valve assembly slowly in order to prevent oil spillage. Be sure to protect the carpet inside the vehicle, before

POWER STEERING
FORD RACK AND PINION TYPE
SECTION 34

removing the shaft.

9. Both the input shaft seal and the bearing will come out of the valve body.

10. To remove the lower pinion shaft oil seal, insert the protective sleeve tool T81P–3504–E and T78P–3504–E or equivalent into the steering gear housing. Tap the tool to bottom it. Activate the expander tool by holding the large nut and turning the small nut until it is fully expanded.

11. Pull the tool and the seal out using a pair of pliers. Oil will drain out of the valve bore.

Assembly

1. Assembly of the input shaft and valve is the reverse of the disassembly procedure.

2. Install the pinion oil seal in the valve bore, seating the seal against the shoulder.

NOTE: To protect seal outer diameter from sharp edge of step inside valve bore, use sizing tool T81P–3504–M3 or equivalent as a guide with its small diameter end in valve bore.

3. Insert valve sizing tube tool T81P–3504–M3 or equivalent into valve housing. Position D-flat on input shaft to right and vertical (3 o'clock position), and insert valve assembly in bore.

NOTE: D-flat surface must be in the 3 o'clock position in vehicle with gear on center (straight ahead position). Rotate input shaft slightly, if necessary, to mesh pinion with rack teeth. Push valve assembly in by hand until seated properly. Remove sizing tool.

4. With wheels off floor, using tool T81P–3504–R or equivalent to turn input shaft, check if pinion is centered by counting number of turns from center to each stop (approximately 1-$\frac{1}{2}$ turns). If number of turns is unequal, pull valve assembly out far enough to free pinion teeth. Rotate input shaft 60 degrees (one tooth) in direction which required less turns. Reinsert valve assembly and check if on center. Repeat procedure if not on center.

INPUT SHAFT AND VALVE ASSEMBLY— GEAR OUT OF VEHICLE

Disassembly

1. Remove the steering gear from the vehicle. Position the assembly in a suitable holding fixture. Clean the exterior of the gear.

2. The external pressure lines should not be removed if there is no evidence of leakage at the fittings. If the lines require removal, the copper seals must be replaced.

3. Loosen the yoke plug locknut. Remove the plug and lift out the spring and plug. Remove the steering gear housing cap.

4. Install input shaft removal tool T81P–3504–R or equivalent on the input shaft. Hold the input shaft and remove the pinion baring locknut. Discard the locknut.

5. Do not allow the rack teeth to reach full travel when loosening or tightening the locknut.

6. Remove the snap ring retaining the shaft seal to the gear housing.

7. Install the input shaft and valve body puller tool T81P–3504–T or equivalent to the input shaft.

8. Turn the nut and remove the valve assembly. Tap the tool in order to bottom it. Activate the expander by holding the large nut until it fully expands. Remove the tool and the seal using a slide hammer.

9. If necessary, remove the pinion bearing from the gear housing using the lower pinion bearing removal tool T81P–3505–S, T58L–101–A and T81P–3504–T or equivalent.

10. Remove the input shaft and valve assembly seal rings, by pushing the rings to one side with a small pointed tool. Be careful not to nick or scratch the valve sleeve. Do not replace the rings unless they are damaged.

Assembly

1. Assembly of the input shaft and valve is the reverse of the disassembly procedure.

2. Install the pinion oil seal in the valve bore, seating the seal against the shoulder.

NOTE: To protect seal outer diameter from sharp edge of step inside valve bore, use sizing tool T81P–3504–M3 or equivalent as a guide with its small diameter end in valve bore.

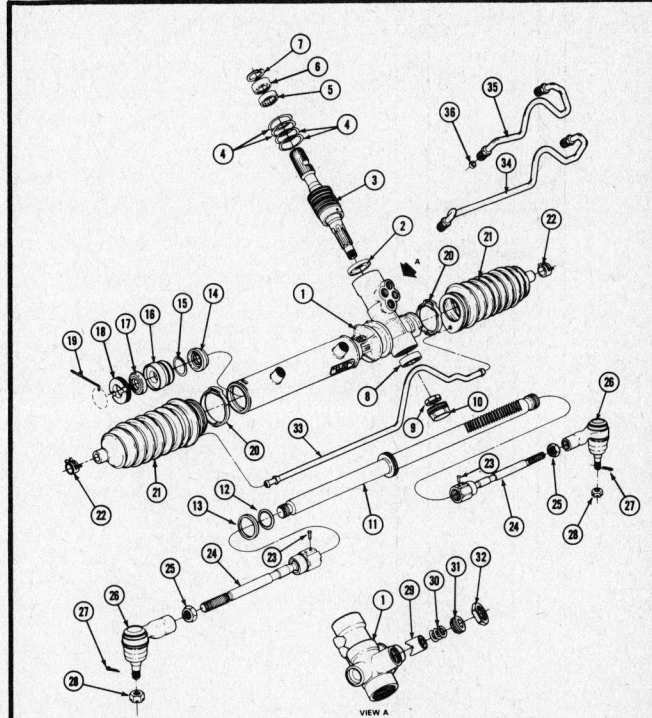

1. Gear housing assembly
2. Pinion seal
3. Valve assembly
4. Plastic rings
5. Input shaft bearing
6. Input shaft seal
7. Snap ring — seal retainer
8. Pinion bearing
9. Pinion bearing locknut
10. Housing cap
11. Rack assembly
12. Back up O-ring (rubber)
13. Piston seal (plastic)
14. Inner rack seal (stepped O.D.)
15. Rack bushing O-ring
16. Rack bushing
17. Outer rack seal
18. Lock-ring
19. Lock-wire
20. Inner bellows clamp
21. Bellows
22. Outer bellows clamp
23. Spiral pin
24. Tie rod assembly
25. Jam nut
26. Tie rod end assembly
27. Cotter pin
28. Castellated nut
29. Rack yoke
30. Yoke spring
31. Yoke plug
32. Yoke plug lock nut
33. Breather tube
34. Right turn transfer tube
35. Left turn transfer tube
36. Copper seal (4 req'd)

Exploded view of Ford type integral power steering rack and pinion

SECTION 34 — POWER STEERING
FORD RACK AND PINION TYPE

3. Insert valve sizing tube tool T81P–3504–M3 or equivalent into valve housing. Position D-flat on input shaft to right and vertical (3 o'clock position), and insert valve assembly in bore.

NOTE: D-flat surface must be in the 3 o'clock position in vehicle with gear on center (straight ahead position). Rotate input shaft slightly, if necessary, to mesh pinion with rack teeth. Push valve assembly in by hand until seated properly. Remove sizing tool.

4. With wheels off floor, using tool T81P–3504–R or equivalent to turn input shaft, check if pinion is centered by counting number of turns from center to each stop (approximately 1–1/2 turns). If number of turns is unequal, pull valve assembly out far enough to free pinion teeth. Rotate input shaft 60 degrees (one tooth) indirection which required less turns. Reinsert valve assembly and check if on center. Repeat procedure if not on center.

5. If the valve sleeve rings were removed, installation is as follows:
   a. Install sleeve tool T81P–3503–M1 over valve assembly. Lubricate tool with automatic transmission and power steering fluid Type F, or equivalent.
   b. Place one ring over tool. Rapidly push down on pusher tool T81P–3405–M2 or equivalent forcing the ring down into the fourth groove.

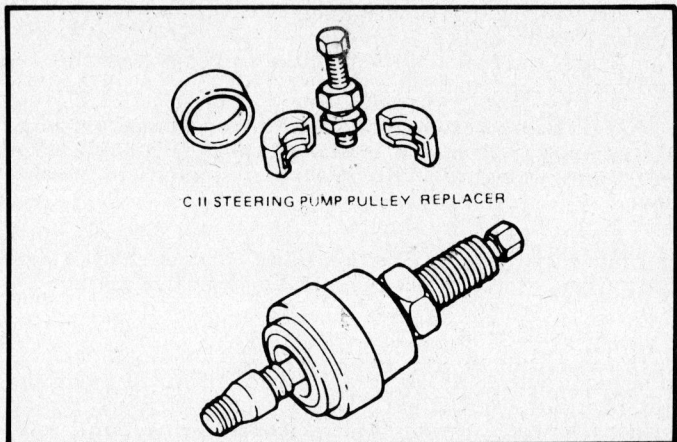
Power steering pump pulley removal and installation tools

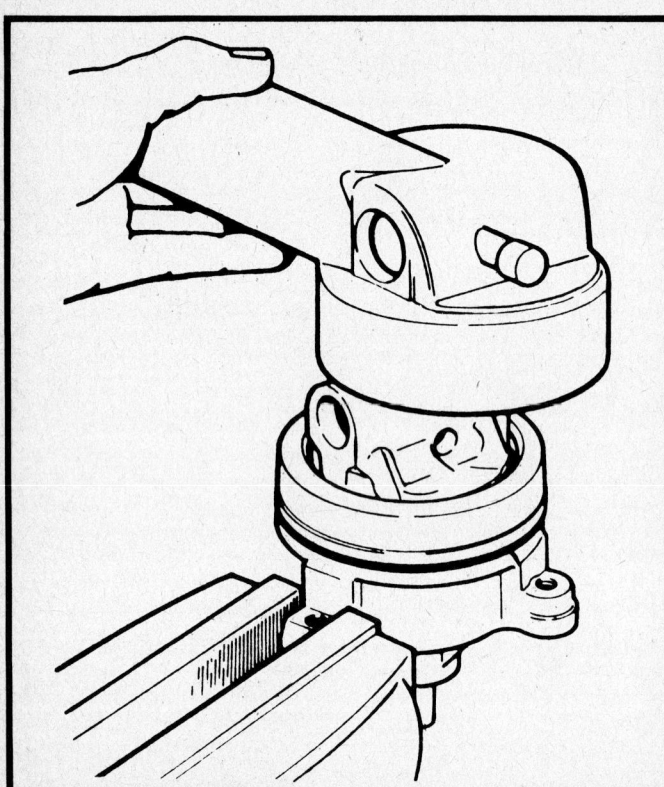
Removing the reservoir

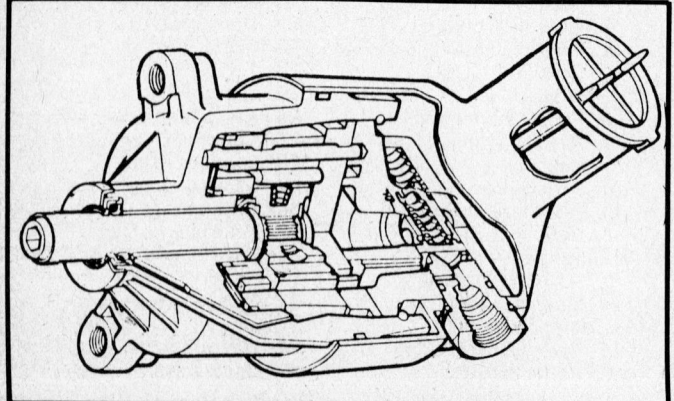
Cutaway view of the power steering pump

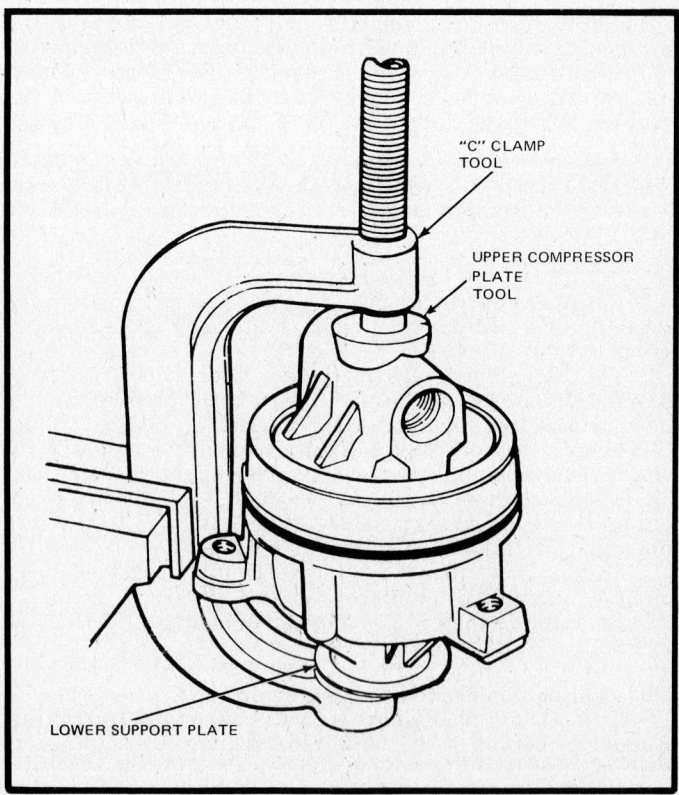
Positioning the pump assembly in the C-clamp tool

POWER STEERING
FORD RACK AND PINION TYPE
SECTION 34

c. Lubricate inside of sizing tool T81P–3504–M3 or equivalent with power steering fluid. Slowly work the sizing tool over the ring taking care not to deform the ring. This step should be performed after each ring is installed.

d. Install one spacer tool T81P–3504–M4 or equivalent with the thin lip toward the input shaft splines over input shaft. This aligns the sleeve tool T81P–3504–M1 or equivalent with the third groove. Repeat Steps a, b, and c.

e. Install the second spacer on top of the first with lip in the same direction. Repeat Steps a, b, and c.

f. Flip the second spacer so the thin lips are together. Repeat Steps a, b, c.

6. Remove the sizing tube and check the condition of the rings. Make sure that the rings turn freely in the grooves.

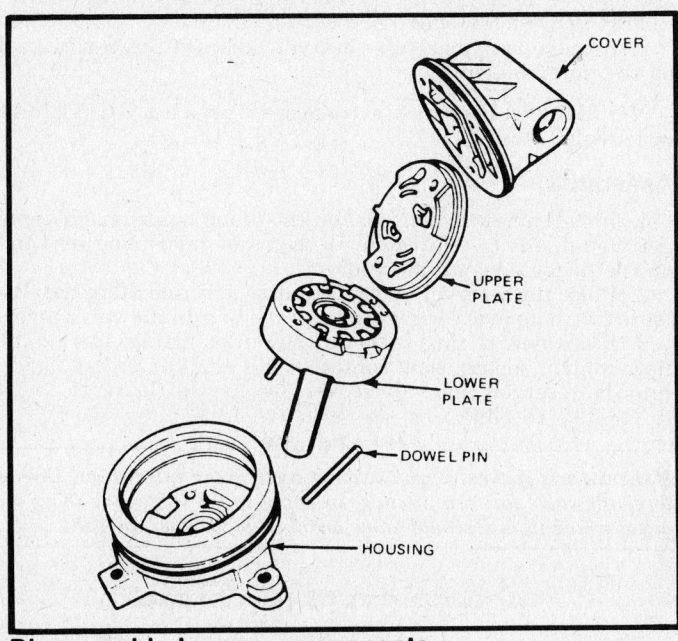
Disassembled pump components

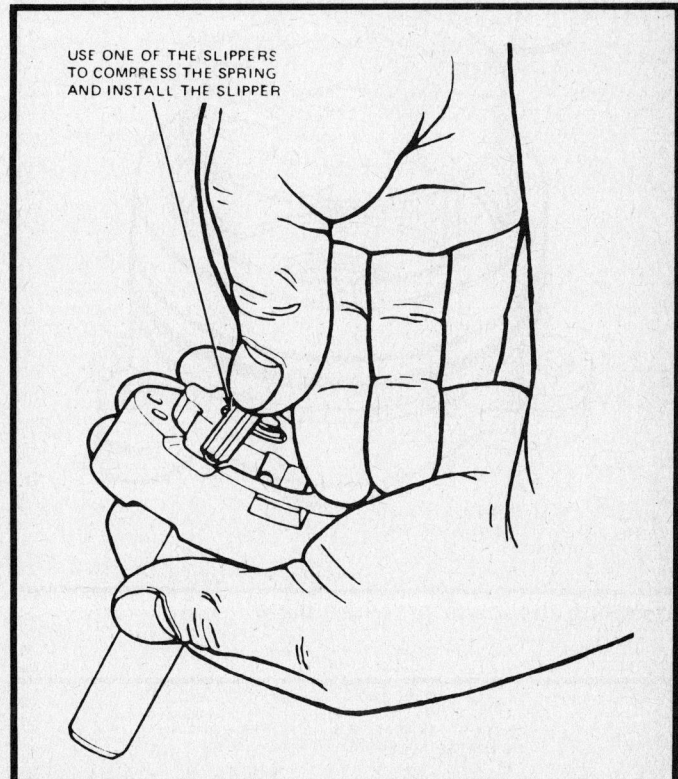
Installing the slipper

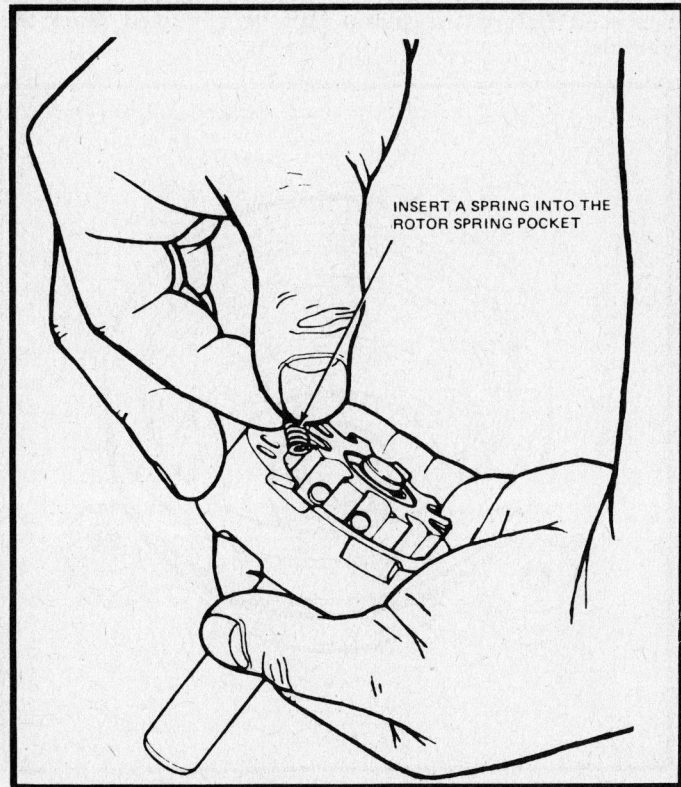
Rotor spring installation

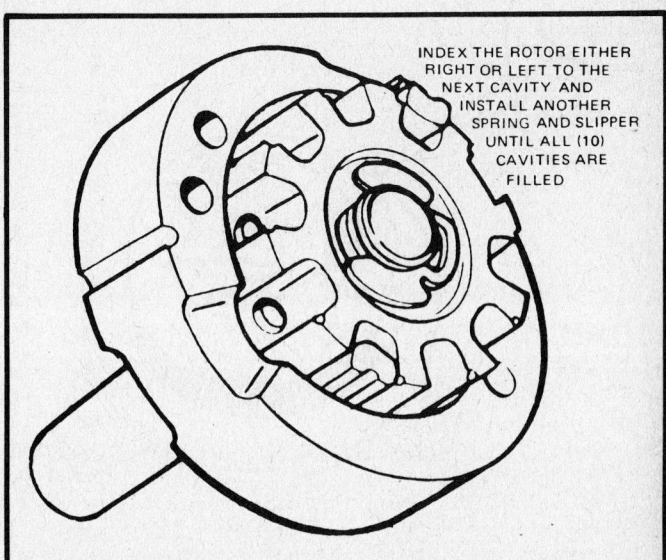
The slippers and springs assembly

34-27

SECTION 34 POWER STEERING
FORD RACK AND PINION TYPE

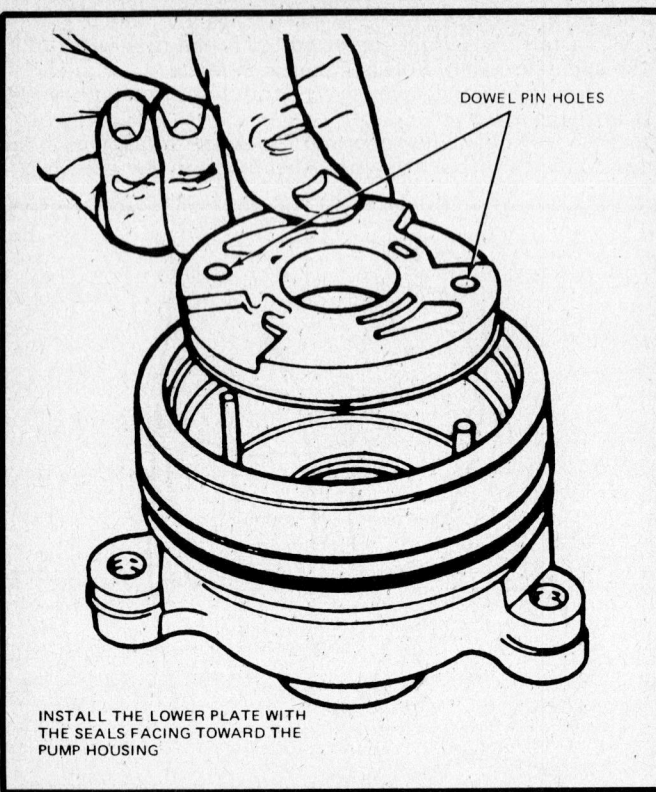

Installing the lower pressure plate

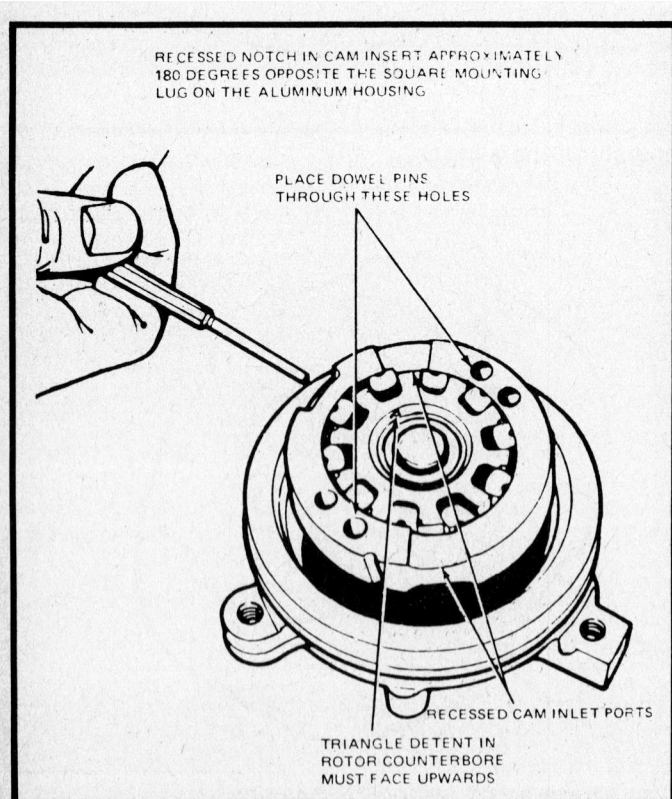

Rotor, cam and slippers assembly installed

Ford Motor Company

POWER STEERING PUMP RESERVOIR

Disassembly

1. With the pump removed from the vehicle, place the pump assembly in a soft jaw vise or equivalent and remove the outlet fitting, flow control valve and spring.
2. Remove the fiberglass reservoir, discard the O-ring seal on the pump housing.

NOTE: **Do not use a hammer on the fiberglass reservoir.**

Assembly

1. Install a new O-ring seal on the pump housing and apply petroleum jelly or equivalent to the reservoir O-ring seal and on the inside edge of the reservoir.
2. Place the reservoir over the pump body and align the outlet fitting hole in the reservoir with the hole in the valve cover.
3. Place new O-ring seals on the outlet fitting. Install the flow control spring, flow control valve and the outlet fitting into the reservoir and valve cover. Torque the fitting to 25–34 ft. lbs. (34–46 Nm).

――――――――― CAUTION ―――――――――
If the valve is cocked, it may become stuck in the valve cover. Do not force the valve forward, because in doing so the valve may shear off metal which in turn would allow metal chips to enter the valve bore.

POWER STEERING PUMP

Disassembly

NOTE: **The pulley on the power steering pump must be removed before the pump can be removed from the vehicle.**

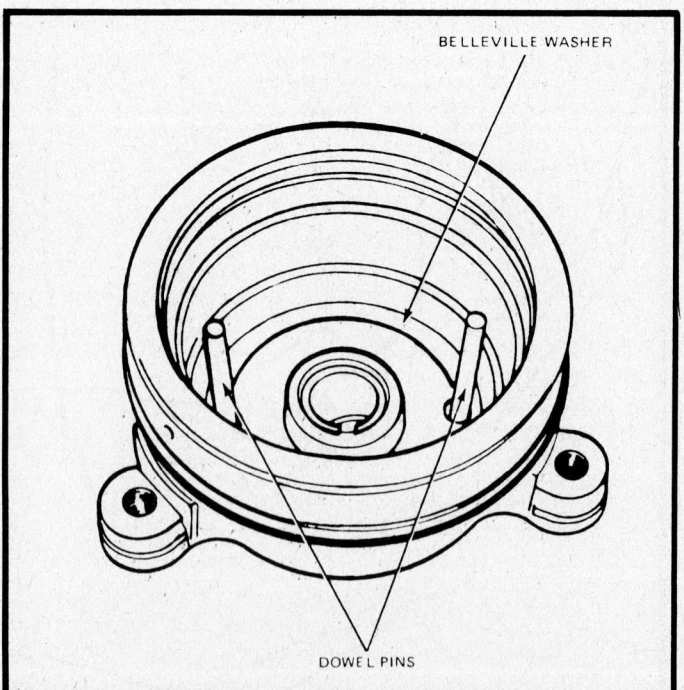

Installing the belleville spring and dowel pins

POWER STEERING
FORD RACK AND PINION TYPE
SECTION 34

1. Disconnect the fluid return hose at the reservoir and drain the fluid into a suitable drain pan.
2. Remove the pressure hose from the pump fitting (leave the fitting in the pump) and remove the drive belt from the pump pulley.
3. Install the special pump pulley remover tool T75L-3733-A or equivalent onto the pulley hub.
4. Hold the small hex head on the tool, and rotate the tool nut counterclockwise to remove the pulley. Do not apply in and out pressure on the pump shaft for this could cause damage to the internal thrust area.
5. Remove the pump from the vehicle (refer to the individual vehicle section for more information on pump removal) and remove the outlet fitting, flow control valve, and flow control spring from the pump and remove the pump reservoir as previously outlined.
6. Place a C-clamp tool T74P-3044-A1 or equivalent in a bench vise. Place the lower support plate tool T78P-3733-A2 or equivalent over the pump rotor shaft.
7. Install the upper compression plate tool T78P-3733-A1 or equivalent, into the upper portion of the C-clamp. Holding the upper compression tool, place the pump assembly into the C-clamp with the rotor shaft facing down.
8. Tighten the C-clamp until a slight bottoming of the valve is felt. Located in the side of the pump housing is a small hole, through this hole, insert a small drift or a suitable tool and push inward on the valve cover retaining ring.
9. While applying inward pressure on the retaining ring, place a suitable tool under the edge of the retaining ring and remove the ring.
10. Loosen the C-clamp, remove the upper compression plate and remove the pump assembly. Remove the pump valve cover and discard the O-ring seal.
11. Apply downward pressure on the rotor shaft to remove the rotor shaft, upper plate, rotating group assembly and the two dowel pins.
12. The lower plate and the belleville spring will remain in the pump housing. To remove them, place the pump housing on a flat surface, raise it slightly and slam the housing down flat until the lower plate and the belleville spring fall out. Discard the O-ring seals.
13. Remove the rotor shaft seal and the seal retainer ring at the same time by prying them out with a suitable tool.

NOTE: Inspect and wash all parts in clean solvent, blow out all passages with compressed air and air dry the cleaned parts.

Assembly

NOTE: The first four steps are to be used only if the rotating group was disassembled for cleaning and inspection.

1. Place the rotor of the shaft splines with the triangle detent in the rotor counterbore facing upwards. Instal the retaining ring in the groove at the end of the rotor shaft.
2. Place the insert cam over the rotor and be sure the recessed notch on the insert cam faces up. With the rotor extended upward, halfway out of the cam, insert a spring into a rotor spring pocket. Work the spring into the rotor cavity directly beneath the recessed flats on the cam.
3. Use one of the slippers to compress the spring and install the slipper with the groove facing the cam profile. Repeat Step two on the slipper cavity beneath the opposite inlet recess.
4. Holding the cam stationary, index the rotor either right or left one space, and install another spring and slipper until all ten rotor cavities have been filled.

CAUTION
Turn the rotor slow and carefully, so that the springs and slippers already installed do not fall out.

5. Using a suitable seal driver, install a new rotor shaft seal. With a plastic mallet, drive the seal into the bore until it bottoms out and instal the seal retainer in the same manner.
6. Place the pump housing plate on a flat surface with the pulley side facing down and insert the two dowel pins along with the belleville spring into the housing. Be sure to install the belleville spring into the housing with the dished surface facing upward.
7. Lubricate the inner and outer O-ring seals with power steering fluid, and install the seal on the lower pressure plate. Insert the lower pressure plate with the O-ring seals toward the front of the pump into the pump housing and over the dowel pins.
8. Place the entire assembly on the C-clamp and place the driver tool T78P-3733-A3 or equivalent into the rotor shaft hole, press on the lower plate lightly, until it is bottomed into the pump housing. This operation will seat the outer O-ring seal.
9. Install the cam, rotor, slippers and rotor shaft assembly into the pump housing over the dowel pins.

NOTE: When installing this assembly into the pump housing, the holes in the assembly must be used for the dowel pins, and the recessed notch in the cam insert must face the reservoir and approximately 180 degrees opposite the square mounting lug on the aluminum housing.

10. Place the upper pressure plate over the dowel pins, with the recess directly over the recessed notch on the cam insert and approximately 180 degrees opposite the square mounting lug.
11. Place a new O-ring seal on the valve cover and lubricate the seal with power steering fluid. Be sure that the plastic baffle is placed securely in the valve cover. If the baffle is loose, apply a coat of petroleum jelly or equivalent on the baffle and install it in its location on the valve cover.
12. Insert the valve cover over the dowel pins and be sure the outlet fitting hole in the valve cover is directly in line with the square mounting lug of the aluminum housing.
13. Place the entire assembly in the C-clamp tool and compress the valve cover into the pump housing, until the retaining ring groove is exposed in the pump housing.
14. Install the valve cover retaining ring with the ends near the access hole in the pump housing. Remove the pump assembly from the C-clamp tool.
15. Place a new O-ring seal on the pump housing and lubricate the seal with power steering fluid.
16. Install the flow control spring and flow control valve into the valve cover and install the power steering pump reservoir (as previously outlined).
17. Place a new O-ring seal on the outlet fitting and lubricate the seal with power steering fluid. Install the outlet fitting into the valve cover, and torque it to 25-34 ft. lbs. (34-46 Nm).
18. Install the pump assembly on the vehicle and place the pulley onto the pump shaft.
19. Install special pulley tool T65P-3A733-C or equivalent onto the pump pulley, the small diameter threads on the tool should be engaged in the pump shaft.
20. Hold the small hex head of the tool and rotate the tool nut clockwise to install the pulley on the shaft. The pulley face must be flush within 0.010 in. (0.25mm). Remove the tool.

NOTE: Do not apply in and out pressure on the pump shaft for this could cause damage to the internal thrust area.

21. Install all lines to the pump and refill the reservoir (with the specified power steering fluid). Start the engine, inspect for leaks and recheck the fluid level after bleeding the air from the pump.

SECTION 34 POWER STEERING
GM—SAGINAW ROTARY TYPE

GM SAGINAW ROTARY TYPE POWER STEERING MODEL 605

Checking Steering Effort

Run the engine to attain normal operating temperatures. With the wheels on a dry floor, hook a pull scale to the spoke of the steering wheel at the outer edge. The effort required to turn the steering wheel should be $3\frac{1}{2}$–5 lbs. If the pull is not within these limits, check the hydraulic pressure.

Pressure Test

To check the hydraulic pressure, disconnect the pressure hose from the gear. Now connect the pressure gauge between the pressure hose from the pump and the steering gear housing. Run the engine to attain normal operating temperatures, then turn the wheel to a full right and a full left turn to the wheel stops.

Hold the wheel in this position only long enough to obtain an accurate reading.

The pressure gauge reading should be within the limits specified. If the pressure reading is less than the minimum pressure needed for proper operation, close the valve at the gauge and see if the reading increases. If the pressure is still low, the pump is defective and needs repair. If the pressure reading is at or near the minimum reading, the pump is normal and needs only an adjustment of the power steering gear or power assist control valve.

Worm Bearing Preload and Sector Mesh Adjustments

Disconnect the pitman arm from the sector shaft, then back off on the sector shaft adjusting screw on the sector shaft cover.

Center the steering on the high point, then attach a pull scale to the spoke of the steering wheel at the outer edge. The pull required to keep the wheel moving for one complete turn should be $\frac{1}{2}$–$\frac{2}{3}$ lbs.

If the pull is not within these limits, loosen the thrust bearing locknut and tighten or back off on the valve sleeve adjuster locknut to bring the preload within limits. Tighten the thrust bearing locknut and recheck the preload.

Slowly rotate the steering wheel several times, then center the steering on the high point, Now, turn the sector shaft adjusting screw until a steering wheel pull of 1–$1\frac{1}{2}$ lbs. is required to move the worm through the center point. Tighten the sector shaft adjusting screw locknut and recheck the sector mesh adjustment.

Install the pitman arm and draw the arm into position with the nut.

ADJUSTER PLUG AND ROTARY VALVE

Removal

1. Thoroughly clean exterior of gear assembly. Drain by

1. Housing, steering gear
2. Retainer, strg. coupling shield
3. Bearing assy., needle (stub shaft)
4. Seal, stub shaft
5. Seal, stub shaft dust
6. Ring, retaining (stub shaft seal)
7. Bearing assy., needle (pitman shaft)
8. Seal, pitman shaft
9. Washer, seal back-up (pitman shaft)
10. Seal, pitman shaft dust
11. Ring, retaining (pitman shaft seal)
12. Washer, lock (pitman shaft)
13. Nut, pitman arm
14. Bearing assy., race & upper
15. Ring, valve body (3)
16. Seal, "O" ring (valve body) (3)
17. Body assy., valve
18. Seal, "O" ring (dampner)
19. Spool, valve
20. Shaft assy., stub
21. Seal, "O" ring (shaft to worm)
22. Worm assy., pin & strg.
23. Ring, retaining (shaft to worm)
24. Ring, rack piston
25. Seal, "O" ring (rack piston)
26. Rack-piston-nut
27. Bearing assy., support & lwr. thr.
28. Seal, "O" ring (adjuster plug)
29. Plug, adjuster
30. Nut, adjuster lock
31. Spring, side cover
32. Seal, "O" ring (side cover)
33. Gear assy., pitman shaft
34. Cover, assy., housing side
35. Ring, retaining (side cover)
36. Nut, preload adjuster sealing
37. Connector, inverted flare (2)

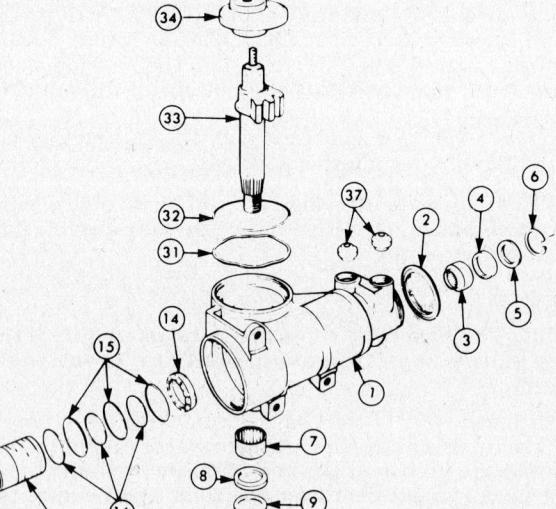
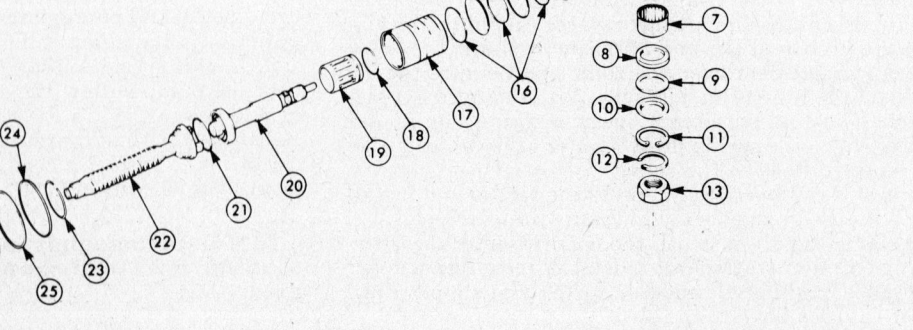

Exploded view of model 605 power steering gear

POWER STEERING
GM—SAGINAW ROTARY TYPE
SECTION 34

holding valve ports down and rotating worm back and forth through entire travel.
2. Place gear in vise.
3. Loosen adjuster plug locknut with punch. Remove adjuster plug.
4. Remove rotary valve assembly by grasping stub shaft and pulling it out.

ADJUSTER PLUG

Disassembly

1. Remove upper thrust bearing retainer with screwdriver. Be careful not to damage bearing bore. Discard retainer. Remove spacer, upper bearing and races.
2. Remove and discard adjuster plug O-ring.
3. Remove stub shaft seal retaining ring and remove and discard dust seal.
4. Remove stub shaft seal by prying out with screwdriver and discard.
5. Examine needle bearing and, if required, remove same by pressing from thrust bearing end.
6. Inspect thrust bearing spacer, bearing rollers and races.
7. Reassembly in reverse of above.

ROTARY VALVE

Disassembly

Repairs are seldom needed. Do not disassemble unless absolutely necessary. If the O-ring seal on valve spool dampener needs replacement, perform this portion of operation only.
1. Remove cap-to-worm O-ring seal and discard.
2. Remove valve spool spring by prying on small coil with small screwdriver to work spring onto bearing surface of stub shaft. Slide spring off shaft. Be careful not to damage shaft surface.
3. Remove valve spool by holding the valve assembly in one hand with the stub shaft pointing down. Insert the end of pencil or wood rod through opening in valve body cap and push spool until it is out far enough to be removed. In this procedure, rotate to prevent jamming. If spool becomes jammed it may be necessary to remove stub shaft, torsion bar and cap assembly.

ROTARY VALVE

Reassembly

CAUTION

All parts must be free of dirt, chips, etc., before assembly and must be protected after assembly.

1. Lubricate three new back-up O-ring seals with power steering fluid, or equivalent and reassemble in the ring grooves of valve body. Assemble three new valve body rings in the grooves over the O-ring seals by carefully slipping over the valve body.

NOTE: If the valve body rings seem loose or twisted in the grooves, the heat of the oil during operation will cause them to straighten.

2. Lubricate a new dampener O-ring with power steering fluid, or equivalent and install in valve spool groove.
3. Assemble stub shaft torsion bar and cap assembly in the valve body, aligning the groove in the valve cap with the pin in the valve body. Tap lightly with soft hammer until cap is against valve body shoulder. Valve body pin must be in the cap groove. Hold parts together during the remainder of assembly.
4. Lubricate spool. With notch in spool toward valve body, slide the spool over the stub shaft. Align the notch on the spool with the spool drive pin or stub shaft and carefully engage spool in valve body bore. Push spool evenly and with slight rotating motion until spool reaches drive pin. Rotate spool slowly, with some pressure, until notch engages pin. Be sure dampener O-ring seal is evenly distributed in the spool groove.

CAUTION

Use extreme care because spool-to-valve body clearance is very small. Damage is easily caused.

5. With seal protector tool over stub shaft, slide valve spool spring over stub shaft, with small diameter of spring going over shaft last. Work spring onto shaft until small coil is located in studshaft groove.
6. Lubricate a new cap-to-O-ring seal and install in valve body.

RACK—PISTON NUT AND WORM ASSEMBLY

Removal

1. Completely drain the gear assembly and thoroughly clean the outside.
2. Remove pitman shaft assembly, previously described.
3. Rotate housing end plug retaining ring so that one end of ring is over hole in gear housing. Spring one end of ring so a suitable tool can be inserted to lift out ring.
4. Rotate stub shaft to a full left turn position to force end plug out of housing.
5. Remove and discard housing end plug O-ring seal.
6. Remove rack-piston nut end plug with ½ in. square drive.
7. Insert tool in end of worm. Turn stub shaft so that rack-piston nut will go into tool and remove rack-piston nut from gear housing.
8. Remove adjuster plug and rotary valve assemblies as previously described.
9. Remove worm and lower thrust bearing and races.
10. Remove cap-to-O-ring seal and discard.

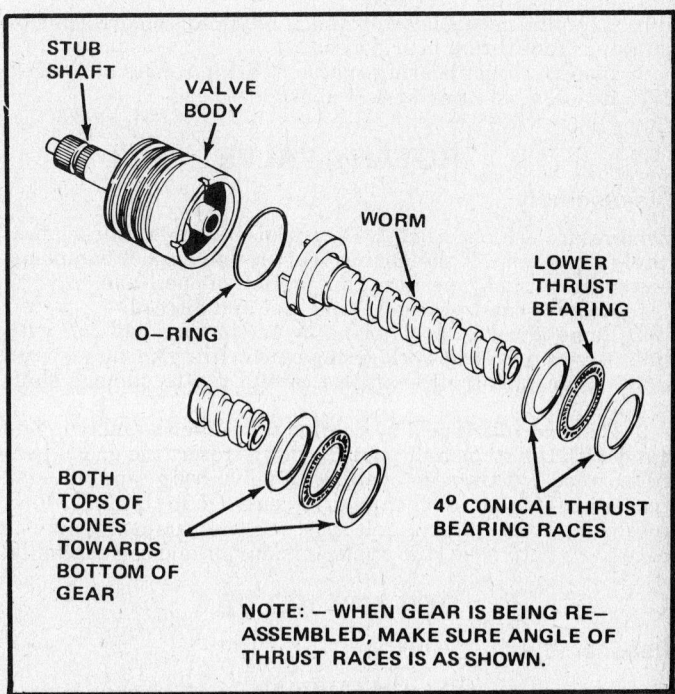

Correct installation of thrust bearing races

SECTION 34
POWER STEERING
GM—SAGINAW ROTARY TYPE

RACK—PISTON NUT AND WORM

Disassembly and Reassembly

1. Remove and discard piston ring and back-up O-ring on rack-piston nut.
2. Remove ball guide clamp and return guide.
3. Place nut on clean cloth and remove ball retaining tool. Make sure all balls are removed.
4. Inspect all parts for wear, nicks, scoring or burrs. If worm or rack-piston nut need replacing, both must be replaced as a matched pair.
5. In assembling, reverse the above.

NOTE: When assembling, alternate black and white balls, and install guide and clamp. Packing with grease helps in holding during assembly. When new balls are used, various sizes are available and a selection must be made to secure proper torque when making the high point adjustment.

G.M./AMC SAGINAW ROTARY TYPE POWER STEERING—MODEL 800/808

ADJUSTER PLUG AND ROTARY VALVE

Removal

1. Thoroughly clean exterior of gear assembly. Drain by holding valve ports down and rotating worm back and forth through entire travel.
2. Place gear in vise.
3. Loosen adjuster plug locknut with punch. Remove adjuster plug.
4. Remove rotary valve assembly by grasping stub shaft and pulling it out.

ADJUSTER PLUG

Disassembly

1. Remove upper thrust bearing retainer with screwdriver. Be careful not to damage bearing bore. Discard retainer. Remove spacer, upper bearing and races.
2. Remove and discard adjuster plug O-ring.
3. Remove stub shaft seal retaining ring and remove and discard dust seal.
4. Remove stub shaft seal.
5. Examine needle bearing and, if required, remove same by pressing from thrust bearing end.
6. Inspect thrust bearing spacer, bearing rollers and races.
7. Reassemble in reverse of above.

ROTARY VALVE

Disassembly

Repairs are seldom needed. Do not disassemble unless absolutely necessary. If the O-ring seal on valve spool dampener needs replacement, perform this portion of operation only.

1. Remove cap-to-worm O-ring seal and discard.
2. Remove valve spool spring by prying on small coil with small screw driver to work spring onto bearing surface of stub shaft. Slide spring off shaft. Be careful not to damage shaft surface.
3. Remove valve spool by holding the valve assembly in one hand with the stub shaft pointing down. Insert the end of pencil or wood rod through opening in valve body cap and push spool until it is out far enough to be removed. In this procedure, rotate to prevent jamming. If spool becomes jammed it may be necessary to remove stub shaft, torsion bar and cap assembly.

ROTARY VALVE

Reassembly

─────────── **CAUTION** ───────────
All parts must be free of dirt, chips, etc., before assembly and must be protected after assembly.

1. Lubricate three new back-up O-ring seals with power steering fluid, or equivalent and reassemble in the ring grooves of valve body. Assemble three new valve body rings in the grooves over the O-ring seals by carefully slipping over the valve body.

NOTE: If the valve body rings seem loose or twisted in the grooves, the heat of the oil during operation will cause them to straighten.

2. Lubricate a new dampener O-ring with power steering fluid, or equivalent and install in valve spool groove.
3. Assemble stub shaft torsion bar and cap assembly in the valve body, aligning the groove in the valve cap with the pin in the valve body. Tap lightly with soft hammer until cap is against valve body shoulder. Valve body pin must be in the cap groove. Hold parts together during the remainder of assembly.
4. Lubricate spool. With notch in spool toward valve body, slide the spool over the stub shaft. Align the notch on the spool with the spool drive pin on stub shaft and carefully engage spool in valve body bore. Push spool evenly and with slight rotating motion until spool reaches drive pin. Rotate spool slowly, with some pressure, until notch engages pin. Be sure dampener O-ring seal is evenly distributed in the spool groove.

─────────── **CAUTION** ───────────
Use extreme care because spool-to-valve body clearance is very small. Damage is easily caused.

5. With seal protector tool over stub shaft, slide valve spool spring over stub shaft, with small diameter of spring going over shaft last. Work spring onto shaft until small coil is located in stubshaft groove.
6. Lubricate a new cap-to-O-ring seal and install in valve body.

ADJUSTER PLUG AND ROTARY VALVE

Installation

1. Align narrow pin slot on valve body with valve body drive pin on the worm. Insert the valve assembly onto gear housing by pressing against valve body with finger tips. Do not press on stub shaft or torsion bar. The return hole in the gear housing should be fully visible when properly assembled.

─────────── **CAUTION** ───────────
Do not press on stub shaft as this may cause shaft and cap to pull out of valve body, allowing the spool dampener O-ring seal to slip into valve body oil grooves.

2. With protector over end of stub shaft, install adjuster plug assembly snugly into gear housing then back plug off approximately one-eighth turn. Install plug locknut but do not tighten. Adjust preload as described in the adjustment section.
3. After adjustment, tighten lock-nut.

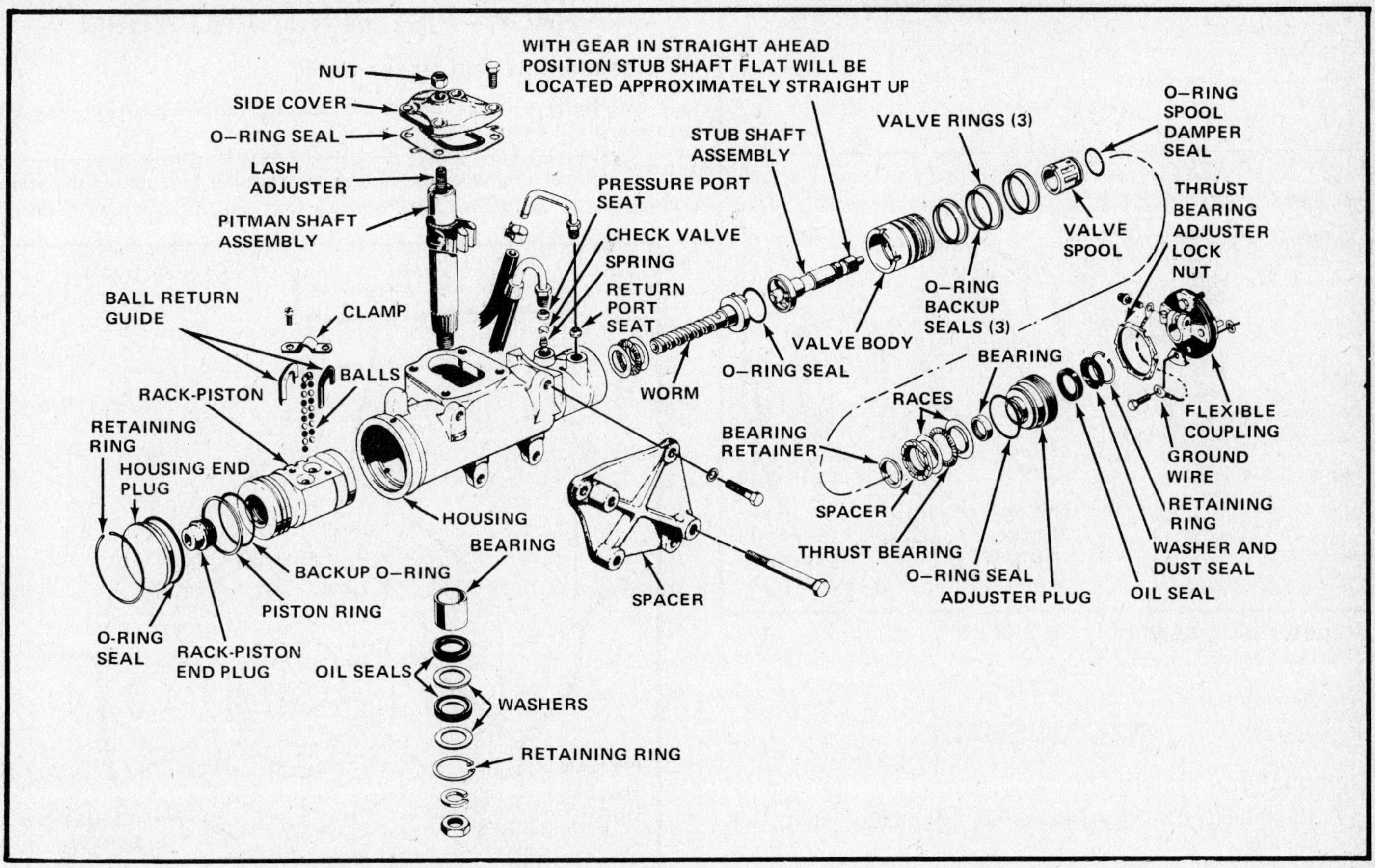

POWER STEERING
GM—SAGINAW ROTARY TYPE
SECTION 34

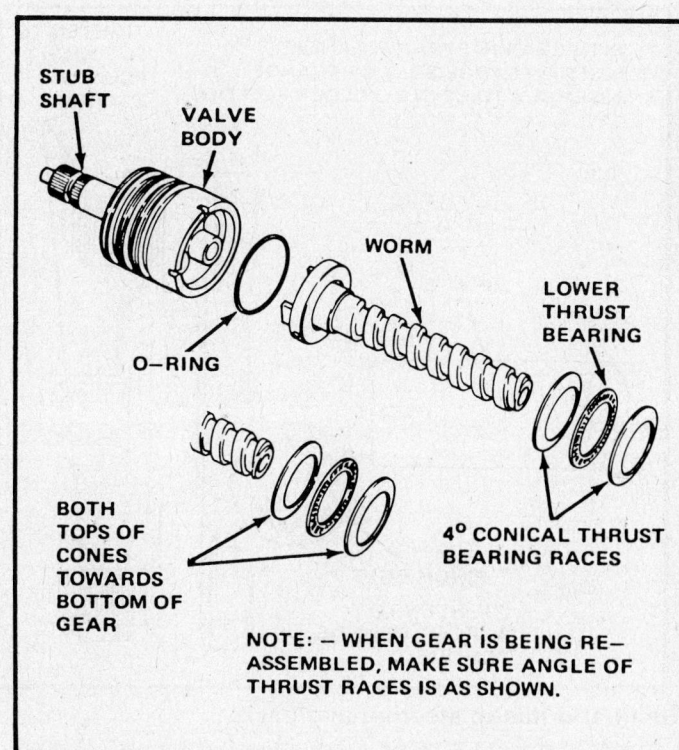

Exploded view of model 800/808 power steering gear

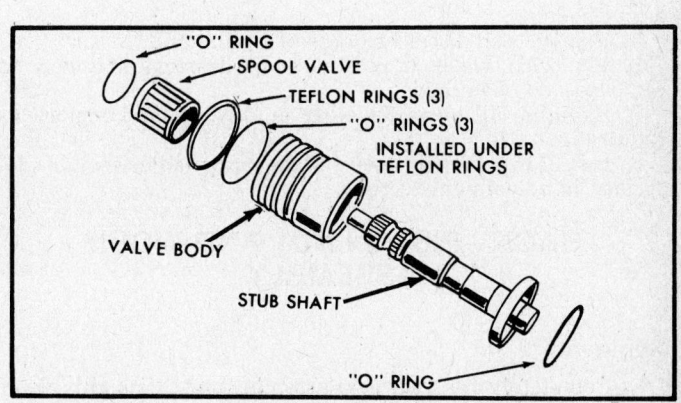

Exploded view of stub shaft and wormshaft assembly

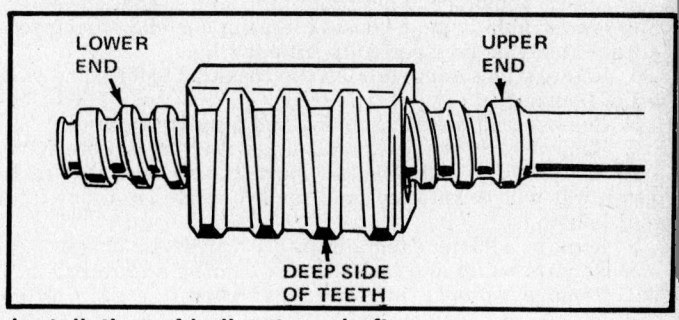

Exploded view of the valve body and shaft assembly

Installation of ball nut or shaft

34-33

SECTION 34 POWER STEERING
GM—SAGINAW ROTARY TYPE

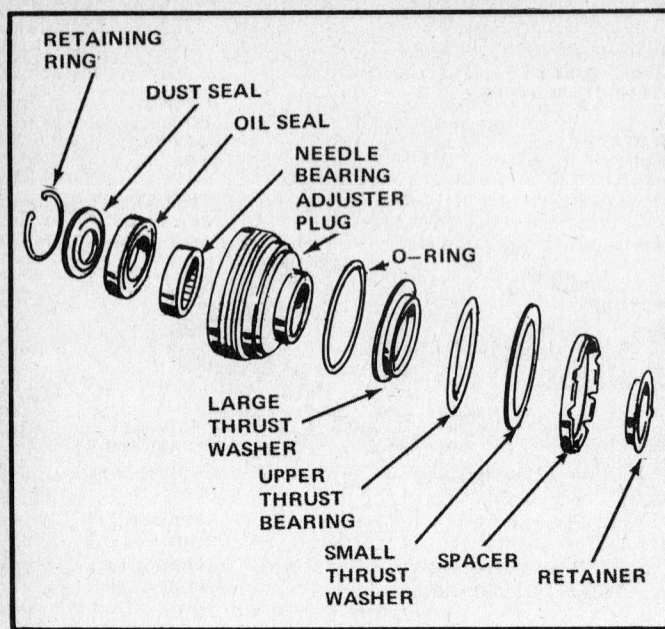

Adjuster plug assembly sequence

PITMAN SHAFT

Removal and Installation

1. Completely drain the gear assembly and thoroughly clean the outside.
2. Place gear in vise.
3. Rotate stub shaft until pitman shaft gear is in center position. Remove side cover retaining bolts.
4. Tap end of pitman shaft with soft hammer and slide shaft out of housing.
5. Remove and discard side cover O-ring seal.
6. The seals, washers, retainers and bearings may now be removed and examined.
7. Examine all parts for wear or damage and replace as required.
8. Install in reverse of above. Make proper adjustment as described in adjustment section.

RACK—PISTON NUT AND WORM ASSEMBLY

Removal

1. Completely drain the gear assembly and thoroughly clean the outside.
2. Remove pitman shaft assembly.
3. Rotate housing end plug retaining ring so that one end of ring is over hole in gear housing. Spring one end of ring so a suitable tool can be inserted to lift out ring.
4. Rotate stub shaft to full left turn position to force end plug out of housing.
5. Remove and discard housing end plug O-ring seal.
6. Remove rack-piston nut end plug with ½ in. square drive.
7. Insert tool in end of worm. Turn stub shaft so that rack-piston nut will go into tool and remove rack-piston nut from gear housing.
8. Remove adjuster plug and rotary valve assemblies.
9. Remove worm and lower thrust bearing and races.
10. Remove cap-to-O-ring seal sent and discard.

RACK—PISTON NUT AND WORM

Disassembly and Reassembly

1. Remove and discard piston ring and back-up O-ring on rack-piston nut.
2. Remove ball guide clamp and return guide.
3. Place nut on clean cloth and remove ball retaining tool.

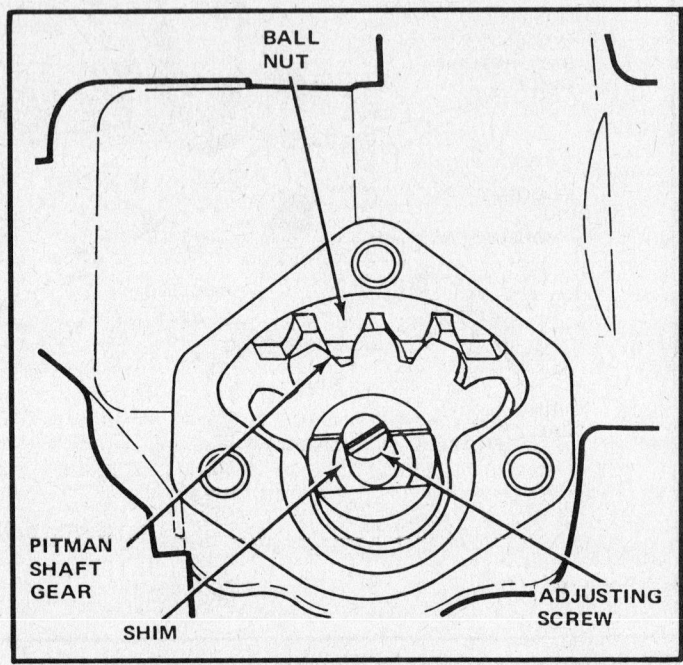

Position of pitman shaft and ball nut

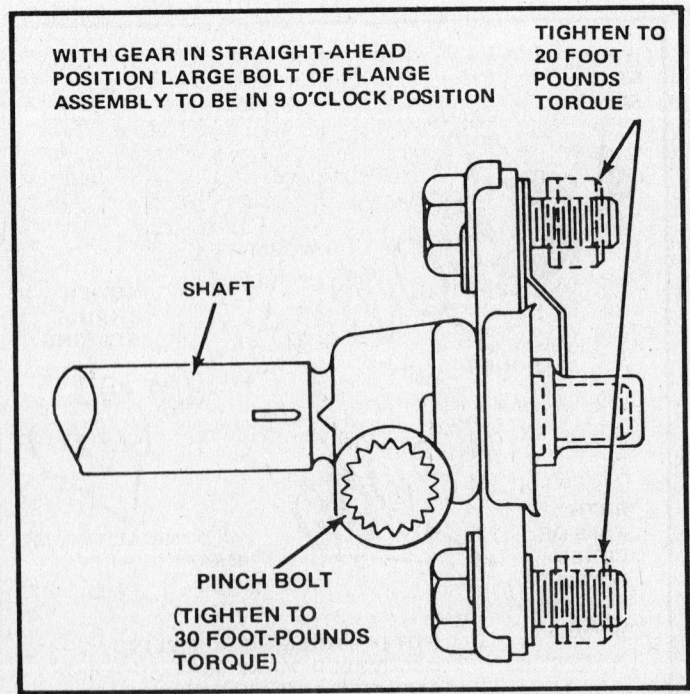

Shaft and flange steering alignment

POWER STEERING
GM—SAGINAW ROTARY TYPE
SECTION 34

Make sure all balls are removed.

4. Inspect all parts for wear, nicks, scoring or burrs. If worm or rack-piston nut need replacing, both must be replaced as a matched pair.

5. In assembling, reverse the above.

NOTE: When assembling, alternate black and white balls, and install guide clamp. Packing with grease helps in holding during assembly. When new balls are used, various sizes are available and a selection must be made to secure proper torque when making the high point adjustment.

RACK—PISTON NUT AND WORM ASSEMBLY

Installation

1. Install in reverse of removal procedure.
2. In all cases use new O-ring seals.
3. Make adjustments are required.

NOTE: For information on overhauling the power steering pump on the AMC models refer to the GM power steering pump overhaul section.

G.M. POWER STEERING RACK AND PINION ASSEMBLY

Outer Tie Rod Take Off Type

A difference exists between the power steering rack and pinion assemblies used on front wheel drive GM vehicles. The major difference is in the manner of attachment of the steering unit to the vehicle body. The early model is attached by wrap around type brackets and rubber grommets, while the later model is attached by bolts through eyelets and grommets, in the steering housing.

Minor variations exist between the units, both externally and internally, but the basic disassembly and assembly remains the same.

OUTER TIE ROD

Removal

1. Loosen the jam nut and remove the tie rod from the steering knuckle.
2. Remove the outer tie rod by turning it off the inner tie rod. Count the number of turns needed to unscrew the outer tie rod.

Installation

1. Screw the outer tie rod onto the inner tie rod the same number of turns as was needed to remove it.
2. Do not tighten the jam nut until the toe-in/out adjustment has been made. Torque to 50 ft. lbs.
3. Be sure the boot is not twisted when done.

BOOT SEAL AND BREATHER TUBE

Removal

1. Remove the outer tie rod and the jam nut from the inner tie rod shaft.
2. Cut the boot clamp and discard. Mark the breather tube location on the steering housing before removing the tube.

Installation

1. Install the breather tube in the same location before removal.
2. Install a new clamp on the boot before installing the boot.
3. Push the boot elbow on the breather tube and engage the boot onto the housing.
4. Secure the boot clamp.
5. Install the jam nut and the outer tie rod. Adjust the toe-in/out as required and tighten the jam nut to 50 ft. lbs.

INNER TIE ROD

Removal

1. The steering assembly must be out of the vehicle.

2. Remove the shock damper ring from the inner tie rod housing and slide it back on the rack.
3. Position a wrench on the rack flat to prevent rack damage when removing the tie rod.
4. Position a wrench on the tie rod pivot housing flats.
5. Turn the inner tie rod housing counterclockwise until the tie rod assembly separates.

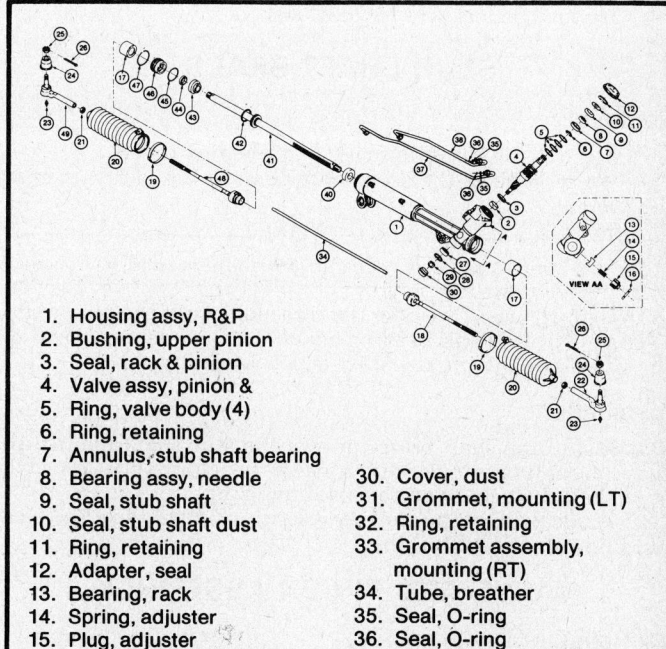

1. Housing assy, R&P
2. Bushing, upper pinion
3. Seal, rack & pinion
4. Valve assy, pinion &
5. Ring, valve body (4)
6. Ring, retaining
7. Annulus, stub shaft bearing
8. Bearing assy, needle
9. Seal, stub shaft
10. Seal, stub shaft dust
11. Ring, retaining
12. Adapter, seal
13. Bearing, rack
14. Spring, adjuster
15. Plug, adjuster
16. Nut, adjuster plug lock
17. Ring, shock dampener
18. Rod assy, inner tie (LT)
19. Clamp, boot
20. Boot, rack & pinion
21. Nut, hex jam
22. Rod assy, outer tie (LT)
23. Fitting, lubrication
24. Seal, tie rod
25. Nut, hexagon slotted
26. Pin, cotter
27. Bearing assy, ball
28. Ring, retaining
29. Nut, hex lock
30. Cover, dust
31. Grommet, mounting (LT)
32. Ring, retaining
33. Grommet assembly, mounting (RT)
34. Tube, breather
35. Seal, O-ring
36. Seal, O-ring
37. Line assy, cylinder (LT)
38. Line assy, cylinder (RT)
39. Cap, dust
40. Seal, inner rack
41. Rack assy, piston & steering
42. Ring, piston
43. Bulkhead, cylinder inner
44. Seal, rack & pinion (bulkhead)
45. Seal, O-ring
46. Bulkhead, cylinder outer
47. Ring, bulkhead retaining
48. Rod assy, inner tie (RT)
49. Rod assy, outer tie (RT)

Typical power steering rack and pinion assembly

SECTION 34: POWER STEERING
GM—RACK AND PINION TYPE

Installation

1. Screw the inner tie rod into the steering rack. Be sure the shock damper is positioned on the rack.
2. Torque the tie rod housing to the rack by holding the rack and tie rod with two wrenches. Tighten to 70 ft. lbs. torque. The tie rod must rock freely in the housing before staking.
3. Support the rack and housing and stake the tie rod housing to the rack flat. To inspect the stake, a 0.010 in. feeler gauge should not pass between the rack and the housing stakes on both sides.
4. Slide the shock dampener over the inner tie rod housing until it engages.

RACK BEARING

Removal

1. Loosen the adjuster plug lock nut.
2. Remove the adjuster plug, spring and the rack bearing.

Installation

1. Lubricate the metal parts and install the rack bearing, spring, adjuster plug and the lock nut.
2. Turn the adjuster plug in until it bottoms and then back off 50 to 70 degrees.
3. Check the turning torque of the pinion. The correct turning torque is 8–10 inch lbs.
4. Torque the lock nut to 50 ft. lbs.

STUB SHAFT SEALS

Removal

1. Remove the retaining ring and the dust cover.
2. While holding the stub shaft, remove the lock nut from the pinion.

CAUTION
If the stub shaft is not held, damage to the pinion teeth will occur.

---

3. Using a press, press on the threaded end of the pinion until flush with the ball bearing assembly. Complete removal of the valve and pinion assembly is not necessary.

Installation

1. Install the shaft protector over the stub shaft and install the stub shaft bearing annulus, needle bearing, stub shaft seal, stub shaft dust seal and the retaining ring.
2. While holding the stub shaft securely, firmly seat the lock nut and torque to 26 ft. lbs.

VALVE AND PINION ASSEMBLY

Removal

1. Turn the stub shaft until the rack has equal distance on both sides of the housing, with the pinion fully engaged. The valve and pinion lock nut must be removed.
2. Mark the location of the stub shaft flat surface on the housing.
3. Using a press, press on the threaded end of the pinion until it is possible to remove the valve and pinion assembly.
4. Remove the valve body rings, if the replacement is required.

Installation

1. Install new valve body rings, if required.
2. Be sure that both ends of the rack are at equal distance from the housing.
3. Install the pinion and valve assembly, being careful not to damage the rings during the installation.
4. The valve and pinion assembly must be fully seated and the flat section of the pinion must line up with the previously marked location indicator on the housing.

BULKHEAD

Removal

1. Use punch in access hole to remove bulkhead retaining ring.
2. If only the bulkhead, bulkhead O-ring seal or rack seal (bulkhead) are to be replaced. Loosen (LT) fitting and remove cylinder line.
3. Plug (LT) cylinder line hole at cylinder using a finger or plastic cap with $7/16 \times 20$ internal threads over hole to prevent oil leaking from cylinder.
4. Using a $11/16$ inch-12 point socket turn stub shaft. Move rack to the right forcing the bulkhead out of the housing. Use drain pan to catch hydraulic oil from assy.
5. If inner rack seal or piston ring are to be replaced, use rack to remove bulkhead instead of compressed oil method.

Installation

1. Install the cylinder inner bulkhead, the O-ring seal, the cylinder outer bulkhead, the bulkhead retaining ring and the shock dampener.

CAUTION
A seal protector should be used on the rack end.

---

2. Make sure that the open end of the retaining ring is approximately 0.50 in. from the access hole.
3. Fully seat the retaining ring.

RACK INNER SEAL, RACK AND PISTON RING

Removal

1. Remove the rack from the housing.
2. Remove the piston rings and discard.
3. Fit seal remover tool in place and using a long rod, tap the seal from its seat.

Installation

1. Install new piston ring on rack.
2. Care should be taken not to cut ring at installation.
3. Wrap card stock around end of rack and rack teeth.
4. Coat seal lip with power steering fluid, slide seal with seal lip facing piston on to card stock, slide card and seal over rack teeth.
5. Remove card stock and bottom seal on rack piston.
6. Coat lip of seal insert with power steering fluid and slide on rack with lip facing seal. Be sure insert is fully engaged with seal before installing rack in housing.
7. Coat seal completely with power steering fluid, slide rack and seal in housing, tap on rack with rubber mallet to seat seal.

NOTE: Seal must be fully seated in housing.

BALL BEARING ASSEMBLY

Removal

1. With the piston and pinion assembly out of the housing, remove the bearing retaining ring.
2. Use a drift and gently tap on the bearing and remove it from the housing.

Installation

1. Using a suitable block, install the bearing in the housing and press it to its seat.

POWER STEERING
GM—RACK AND PINION TYPE
SECTION 34

2. Install the retaining ring.

UPPER PINION BEARING AND SEAL

Removal

1. With the piston and pinion assembly out of the housing, remove the upper bushing and seal with a drift.

Installation

1. Install the new bushing to its seat.

2. Install the new seal, using an installer tool. Seat the seal in the housing with the lip of the seal facing up.

CYLINDER LINES

Removal and Installation

1. The lines are removed and replaced in a conventional manner, using tubing flare wrenches and using the normal precautions when working with fittings and piping. The fittings should be torqued to 15 ft. lbs.

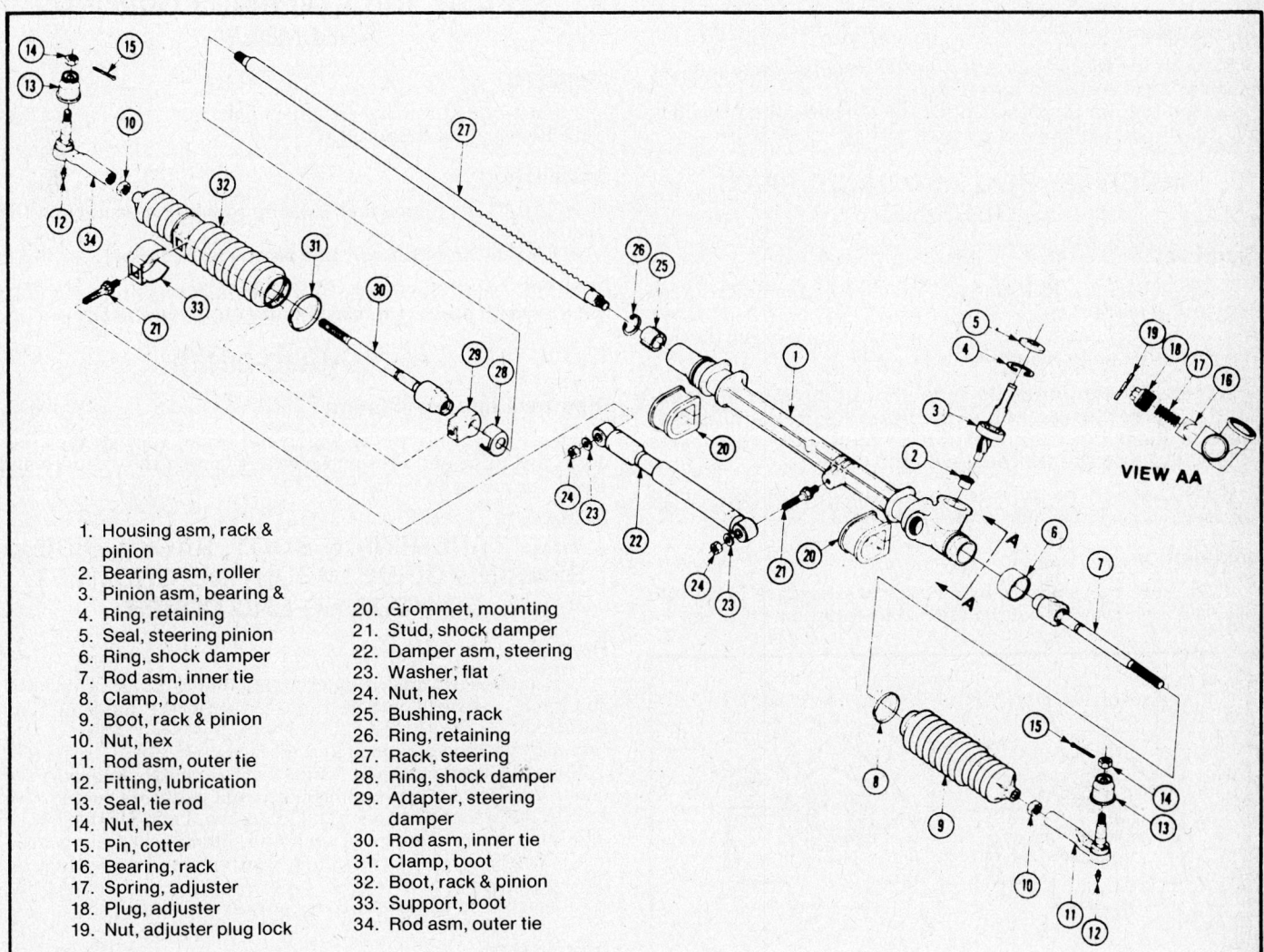

1. Housing asm, rack & pinion
2. Bearing asm, roller
3. Pinion asm, bearing &
4. Ring, retaining
5. Seal, steering pinion
6. Ring, shock damper
7. Rod asm, inner tie
8. Clamp, boot
9. Boot, rack & pinion
10. Nut, hex
11. Rod asm, outer tie
12. Fitting, lubrication
13. Seal, tie rod
14. Nut, hex
15. Pin, cotter
16. Bearing, rack
17. Spring, adjuster
18. Plug, adjuster
19. Nut, adjuster plug lock
20. Grommet, mounting
21. Stud, shock damper
22. Damper asm, steering
23. Washer, flat
24. Nut, hex
25. Bushing, rack
26. Ring, retaining
27. Rack, steering
28. Ring, shock damper
29. Adapter, steering damper
30. Rod asm, inner tie
31. Clamp, boot
32. Boot, rack & pinion
33. Support, boot
34. Rod asm, outer tie

Fiero manual rack and pinion steering gear

SECTION 34
POWER STEERING
GM—RACK AND PINION TYPE

GM POWER STEERING RACK AND PINION

Tie Rod Center Take Off Type

OUTER TIE ROD

Removal

1. With the steering assembly from the vehicle, loosen the outer rod pinch bolt and turn the tie rod from the adjuster stud, counting the number of turns until the tie-rod separates from the adjuster stud.

Installation

1. Turn the tie rod onto the adjuster stud the same number of turns as was needed to remove.
2. Tighten the pinch bolt until the toe-out can be verified. Re-loosen and adjust as required.

INNER TIE ROD AND INNER PIVOT BUSHING

Removal

1. Bend back the lock plate tabs and loosen the inner tie rod bolt and remove.
2. Remove the inner tie rod by sliding it out between the bolt support plate and rack/pinion boot.

NOTE: If both inner tie rods are to be removed, re-install the inner tie rod bolt in the first tie rod retaining bolt hole to keep the rack and pinion boot and other parts aligned, while the tie rods are out.

3. With the tie rod disconnected, the pivot bushings can be pressed out and new ones pressed in.

Installation

1. Be sure the center housing cover washers are fitted into the rack and pinion boot, before rod installation.

2. Remove the locating bolt from the rack and position one inner tie rod assembly in place over the rack. Place the bolt through the lock plate and the tie rod. Place the second inner tie rod in place and install the bolt through the lock and the tie rod.
3. Tighten the inner tie rod bolts to 65 ft. lbs. and bend the lock tabs against the flats of the inner tie rod bolts after torquing.

FLANGE AND STEERING COUPLING ASSEMBLY

Removal

1. Loosen and remove the pinch bolt.
2. Remove the coupling.

Installation

1. Install the flange and steering coupling assembly on the stub shaft.
2. Install the pinch bolt and torque to 37 ft. lbs.

NOTE: With the flange and steering coupling assembly off the stub shaft, the dash seal can be replaced.

HYDRAULIC LINES

Removal and Installation

For ease of line removal and installation, remove the lines from the valve end first and install them on the cylinder end first. Torque to 13 ft. lbs.

RACK AND PINION BOOT, RACK GUIDE, BEARING GUIDE, MOUNTING GROMMET, OR HOUSING END COVER

Removal

1. Separate RH mounting grommet and remove. LH mounting grommet need not be removed unless replacement is required.
2. Cut both boot clamps and discard.
3. For ease of rack and pinion boot removal slide cylinder end of boot toward center of gear enough to expose boot groove in cylinder. Place a rubber band in groove. This fills the groove and allows easy removal of rack and pinion boot from gear.
4. Rack bearing or rack guide can now be removed or replaced if necessary.
5. Remove housing end cover only if damaged.

Installation

1. Remove boot retaining bushing from rack and pinion boot.
2. Slide new boot clamp on rack and pinion boot. Install boot retaining bushing into rack and pinion boot.
3. Install new bearing guide on rack guide if necessary.
4. Install rack guide on rack.
5. Coat inner lip of boot retaining bushing lightly with grease for ease of assembly.
6. Install boot on housing.
7. Be sure center housing cover washers are in place on boot.
8. For ease of assembly, install inner tie rod bolts through cover washers, and rack and pinion boot. Screw into rack lightly. This will keep rack, rack guide, and boot in proper alignment.

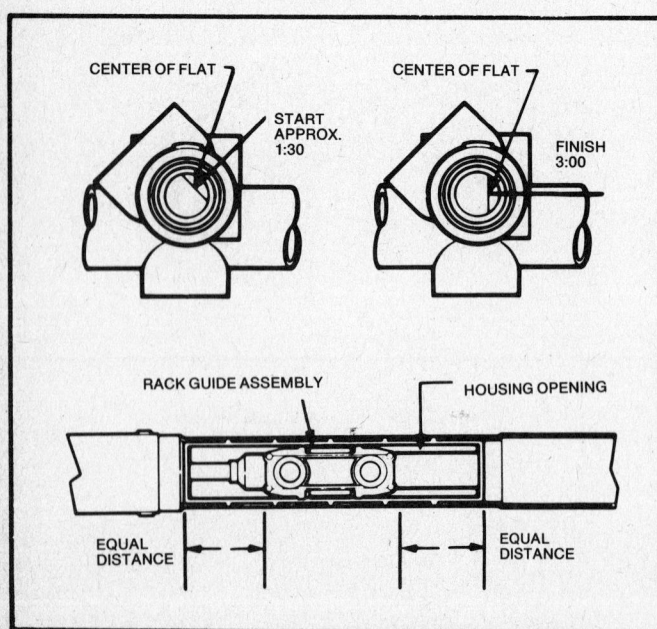

Measure rack guide so that it is equal distance from both sides of housing

Power Steering
GM—RACK AND PINION TYPE
SECTION 34

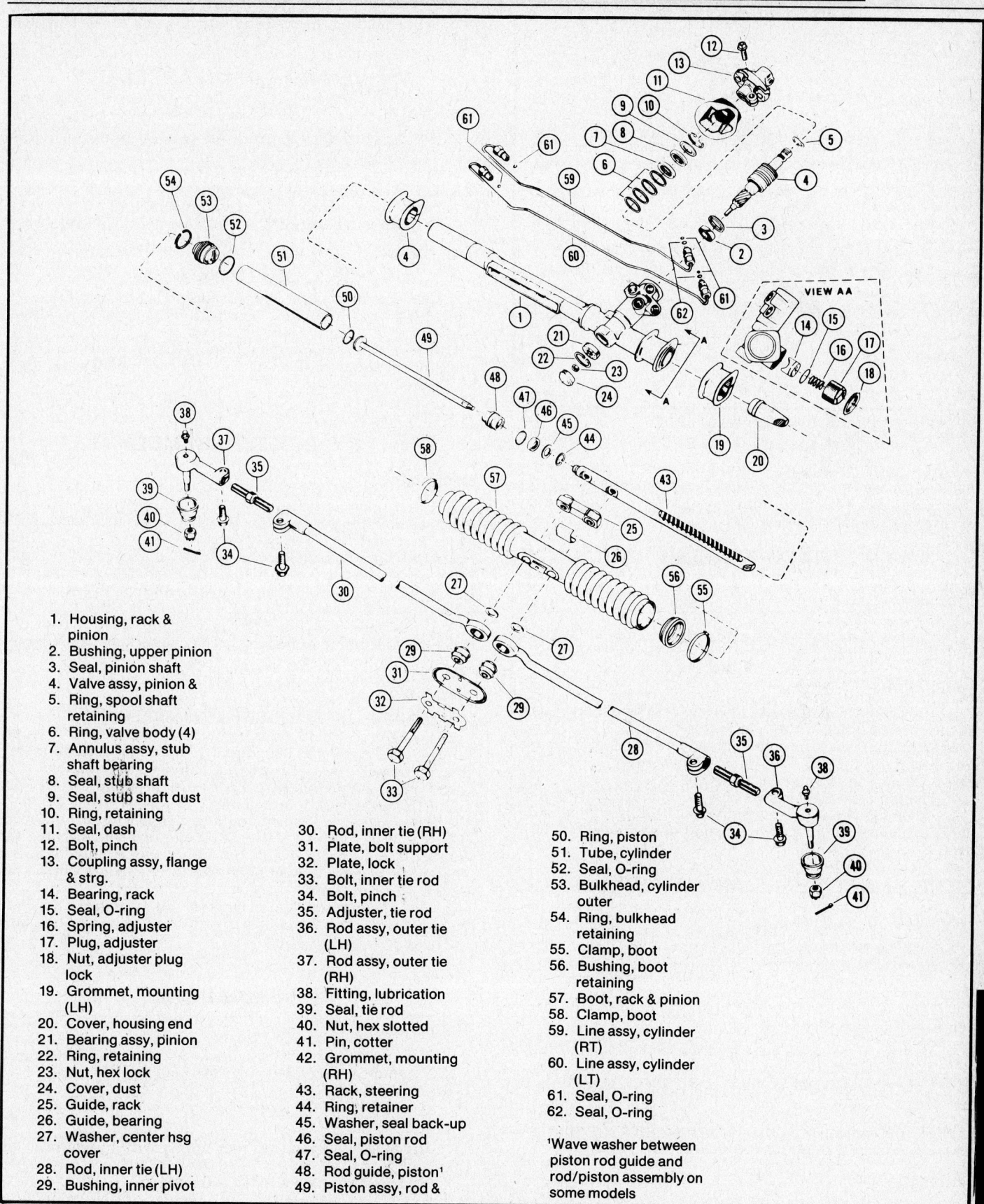

1. Housing, rack & pinion
2. Bushing, upper pinion
3. Seal, pinion shaft
4. Valve assy, pinion &
5. Ring, spool shaft retaining
6. Ring, valve body (4)
7. Annulus assy, stub shaft bearing
8. Seal, stub shaft
9. Seal, stub shaft dust
10. Ring, retaining
11. Seal, dash
12. Bolt, pinch
13. Coupling assy, flange & strg.
14. Bearing, rack
15. Seal, O-ring
16. Spring, adjuster
17. Plug, adjuster
18. Nut, adjuster plug lock
19. Grommet, mounting (LH)
20. Cover, housing end
21. Bearing assy, pinion
22. Ring, retaining
23. Nut, hex lock
24. Cover, dust
25. Guide, rack
26. Guide, bearing
27. Washer, center hsg cover
28. Rod, inner tie (LH)
29. Bushing, inner pivot
30. Rod, inner tie (RH)
31. Plate, bolt support
32. Plate, lock
33. Bolt, inner tie rod
34. Bolt, pinch
35. Adjuster, tie rod
36. Rod assy, outer tie (LH)
37. Rod assy, outer tie (RH)
38. Fitting, lubrication
39. Seal, tie rod
40. Nut, hex slotted
41. Pin, cotter
42. Grommet, mounting (RH)
43. Rack, steering
44. Ring, retainer
45. Washer, seal back-up
46. Seal, piston rod
47. Seal, O-ring
48. Rod guide, piston¹
49. Piston assy, rod &
50. Ring, piston
51. Tube, cylinder
52. Seal, O-ring
53. Bulkhead, cylinder outer
54. Ring, bulkhead retaining
55. Clamp, boot
56. Bushing, boot retaining
57. Boot, rack & pinion
58. Clamp, boot
59. Line assy, cylinder (RT)
60. Line assy, cylinder (LT)
61. Seal, O-ring
62. Seal, O-ring

¹Wave washer between piston rod guide and rod/piston assembly on some models

Exploded view of GM J-body power steering rack and pinion

SECTION 34

POWER STEERING
GM—RACK AND PINION TYPE

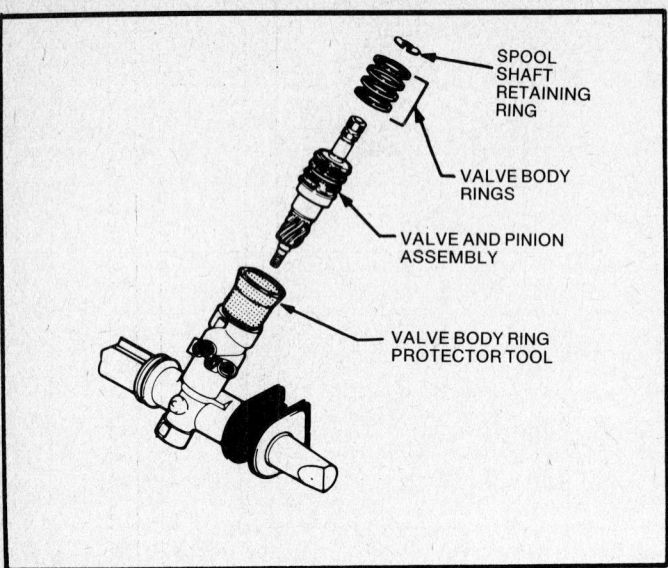

Installing valve and pinion assembly

9. Slide boot and boot retaining bushing until seated in bushing groove in housing. Crimp new boot clamp.
10. Slide other end of boot into boot groove on cylinder end of housing. Crimp new boot clamp.

RACK BEARING

Removal
1. Remove the adjuster plug lock nut.
2. Remove the adjuster plug from the housing.
3. Remove the spring, O-ring seal and the rack bearing.

Installation
1. Lubricate the metal parts before installation and install in the reverse order of the removal procedure.
2. With the rack centered, tighten the adjuster plug to a torque of 6 to 11 ft. lbs. Back off the adjuster plug 50 to 70 degrees. Check the pinion torque.
3. The pinion torque should be 8–16 inch lbs., turning.
4. Assemble the lock nut and while holding the adjusting plug stationary, tighten the adjusting plug lock nut to 50 ft. lbs.

STUB SHAFT SEALS AND UPPER BEARING

Removal
1. Remove retaining ring.
2. Remove dust cover.
3. While holding the stub shaft remove lock nut from pinion.

NOTE: If stub shaft is not held, damage to the pinion teeth will occur.

4. Using a press, press on threaded end of pinion until flush with ball bearing assembly.
5. Complete removal of valve and pinion assembly is not necessary.

NOTE: Bearing and annulus are pressed together. Disassemble only if bearing replacement is required.

Installation
1. Install the seals and bearing in the reverse order of the removal.

2. While holding the stub shaft, firmly seat the lock at 26 ft. lbs.

VALVE AND PINION ASSEMBLY

Removal
1. Turn stub shaft until rack guide is equal distance from both sides of housing opening.
2. Mark location of stub shaft flat on housing.
3. Using a press, press on threaded end of pinion until it is possible to remove valve and pinion assembly.
4. Remove valve body rings if replacement is necessary.

Installation
1. Install new valve body rings if required.
2. Care should be taken not to cut rings at installation.
3. Measure rack guide so that it is equal from both sides of housing.
4. Install valve and pinion assembly so that when full seated stub shaft flat and mark on housing line up and the rack guide is centered in housing.

CYLINDER ASSEMBLY

Removal
1. The cylinder outer bulkhead and housing must be marked before removal to insure proper location in housing at assembly so cylinder lines will fit correctly.
2. Use a small punch in access hole to unseat retaining ring. Then use a suitable tool to bring retaining ring out enough to be able to remove retaining ring with suitable pliers, discard retaining ring.
3. By threading an inner tie rod bolt into rack, rack can be used in a slide hammer fashion to remove rack and cylinder assembly from housing.

Installation
1. Replace both O-ring seals before assembly.
2. Using crocus cloth remove burrs or sharp edges from retaining ring groove in housing. This must be done to insure that the new O-ring seals are not damaged at assembly.
3. Coat O-ring seals with hydraulic fluid and install rack and cylinder assembly in housing.
4. Line up marks on housing and cylinder outer bulkhead. Gently tap on cylinder outer bulkhead until it is seated far enough in housing to install retaining ring. It may be necessary to use a press to hold bulkhead far enough in housing to install retaining ring.
5. Open end of retaining ring should be approx. 0.50 in. (13mm) from access hole. Be sure retaining ring is fully seated in housing.

PISTON RING

Removal
1. Hold on to cylinder, using rack and piston rod assembly as a slide hammer. Piston rod guide assembly will disengage from cylinder assembly.

Installation
1. Install new piston ring coat lightly with hydraulic steering fluid.
2. Slide piston into cylinder assembly.
3. Lightly tap piston rod guide assembly until fully seated in cylinder assembly.

Power Steering
GM—RACK AND PINION TYPE
SECTION 34

RACK, PISTON ROD, PISTON ROD GUIDE ASSEMBLY

Removal

1. Put steering rack in soft-jawed vise.
2. Using a Tool J–29811 or equivalent unscrew rod and piston assembly from rack.
3. Because of close tolerances, it may be necessary to use piston rod guide assembly as a slide hammer to separate rod and piston assembly from rack.
4. Do not remove piston rod guide assembly from rod and piston assembly unless piston rod guide, piston rod seal or rod and piston assembly require replacement, because the piston rod seal will be damaged.

Installation

1. Install new piston rod seal in piston rod guide, if required.
2. Using crocus cloth remove any burrs or sharp edges from rod and piston assembly. Put seal protector J–29812 or equivalent on rod and piston assembly.
3. Coat piston rod seal with hydraulic fluid and slide piston rod guide assembly on piston and rod assembly.
4. Gently tap rod and piston assembly into rack until threads engage.
5. Tighten to specifications.
6. Stake rack against rod piston flats.

PINION BEARING ASSEMBLY

Removal

1. Remove bearing retaining ring.
2. Use drift or punch and gently tap on bearing until bearing is removed.

Installation

1. Install new pinion bearing assembly. Using a suitable socket, press on outer race. Be careful not to cock bearing in housing.
2. Install retaining ring. Note position of large lug to be sure beveled side of ring is properly located.

UPPER PINION BEARING AND PINION SHAFT SEAL

Removal

1. Remove upper pinion bushing and seal with a punch.
2. Remove and discard the bushing and seal.

Installation

1. Install the new bushing.
2. Install the new seal with an installer tool. Seat the seal with the seal lip facing up.

Power Rack And Pinion—Nova

Disassembly

1. Place the rack and pinion unit in a soft jawed vise.
2. Mark the left and right tie rod ends for ease of reassembly. Remove the boots and discard. Upon reassembly, new boots should be installed.
3. Using a suitable tool, bend back (straighten) the bent portion of the locking washer between the inner tie rod and the rack. Remove the inner tie rods from the rack.
4. Disconnect the right and left pipe assemblies between the cylinder and valve housing.

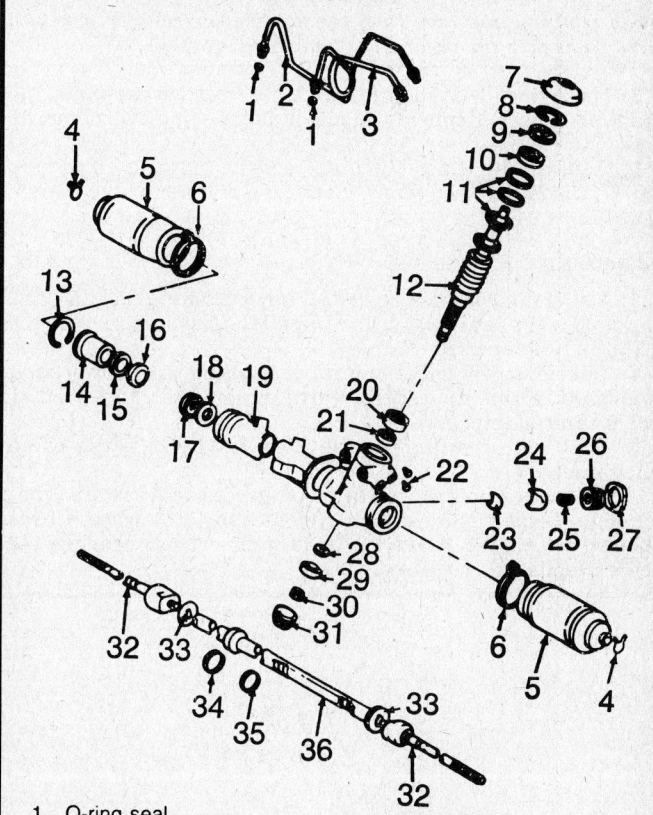

1. O-ring seal
2. Right side pressure tube
3. Left side pressure tube
4. Boot clip
5. Steering rack boot
6. Boot clamp
7. Pinion dust cover
8. Snap ring
9. Upper pinion seal
10. Upper pinion bearing
11. Control valve sealing ring
12. Steering val;ve/pinion assembly
13. Snap ring
14. Cylinder end stopper
15. Outer cylinder end seal (thick)
16. Outer cylinder end seal
17. Inner cylinder end seal
18. Inner cylinder end seal (thin)
19. Rack housing
20. Lower pinion /valve bushing
21. Pinion/valve seal
22. Union seat
23. Rack guide seat
24. Rack guide
25. Spring rack guide
26. Rack guide cap
27. Rack guide locking nut
28. Lower valve/pinion spacer
29. Lower valve/pinion bearing
30. Lower locking valve/pinion nut
31. Lower valve/pinion cap
32. Inner ball joint end sub-assembly
33. Locking claw washer
34. O-ring
35. Piston sealing ring

Nova—power rack and pinion—exploded view

5. Remove the adjusting plug lock nut. Using tool J–35692 and J–35423 or equivalent, remove the cap, spring and rack guide.
6. Remove the dust cover and snap ring. Remove the self locking nut from the lower end of the pinion gear.
7. Remove the pinion assembly along with the upper bearing and oil seal. Remove the cylinder end stopper retaining snap ring. Remove the rack assembly and cylinder end stopper together.

34-41

Section 34: POWER STEERING
GM—RACK AND PINION TYPE

CAUTION

While removing the rack from the housing, exercise care so as to avoid damage to the piston bore inner housing face.

---

8. Using tool J–35434 or equivalent, remove the inner rack seal and spacer. Remove the piston and O-ring seals from the rack.

9. Remove the inner bushing from the valve housing using tool J–35420 or equivalent. Remove the inner valve housing seal.

Assembly

1. Using an arbor press, install inner bushing tools J–35695 and J–8092 or equivalent, and install the bushing to a depth of 2.736 in. (69.5 mm).
2. Lubricate the valve and inner bushing with power steering fluid. Install the control valve pinion and check that the valve rotates smoothly.
3. The remainder of assembly is the reverse of the diassembly.
4. Inspect all mating surfaces for excessive wear or signs of damage. Inspect the rack for runout and tooth wear. Runout should not exceed 0.012 in. (0.33 mm). Check bearings and seals. Replace as required.

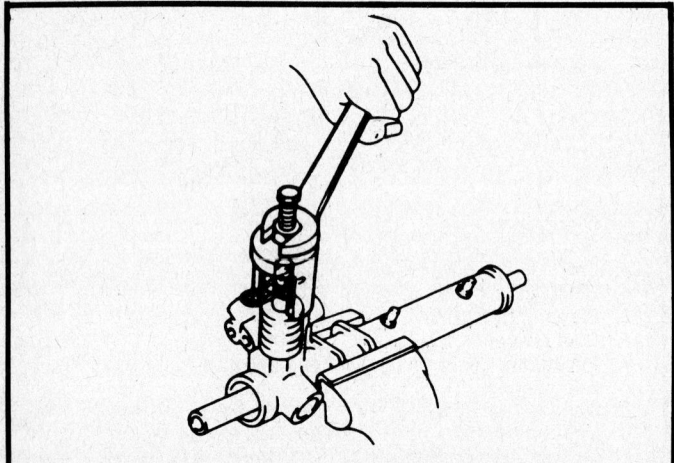

Valve removal

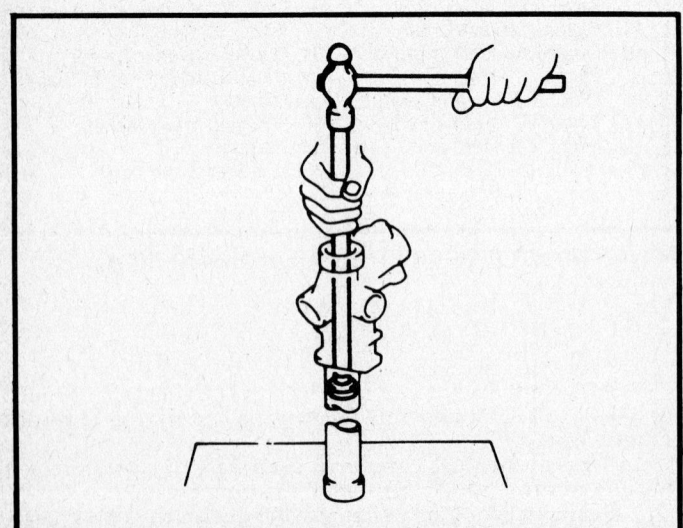

Inner cylinder spacer and seal removal

5. Replace the housing if the inner piston cylinder walls are damaged.
6. Lubricate all sliding parts and sealing surfaces using lithium grease.
7. Inspect the inner tie rod and the tie rod end for looseness and replace if worn or defective.

General Motors Corporation

POWER STEERING PUMP OVERHAUL

Disassembly

1. With the power steering pump removed from the vehicle, drain the reservoir and reinstall the filler cap to prevent contamination. Clean the exterior of the pump before starting the disassembly procedures.
2. Secure the pump in a suitable vise at the mounting bracket.
3. Install special puller J–25034 or BT–7515 or equivalent and be sure the pilot bolt bottoms out in the pump shaft by turning the nut at the top of the pilot bolt.
4. Install the puller jaws and retainer sleeve that go with the special puller tool and remove the pulley by holding the pilot bolt and turning it out counterclockwise.

NOTE: The pump pulley is a press fit on the shaft and must be removed and replaced with the aid of puller tools. Do not hammer on the puller, pulley or shaft for this could cause internal damage to the pump components.

5. Remove the brackets from the pump and using a soft jaw vise or equivalent, clamp the pump (shaft end down) in the vise between the square boss and shaft housing.
6. Remove the two mounting studs and pressure hose fitting. Tap the reservoir filler tube back and forth with a rubber mallet to loosen. Remove the reservoir off of the pump body and discard the O-rings from the reservoir along with the two mounting studs and the pressure fitting.
7. Using a punch, tap the end cover retainer ring around until one end of the ring is near the hole in the pump body. Insert the punch far enough to disengage the ring from the groove in the pump bore and pry the ring out of the pump body.

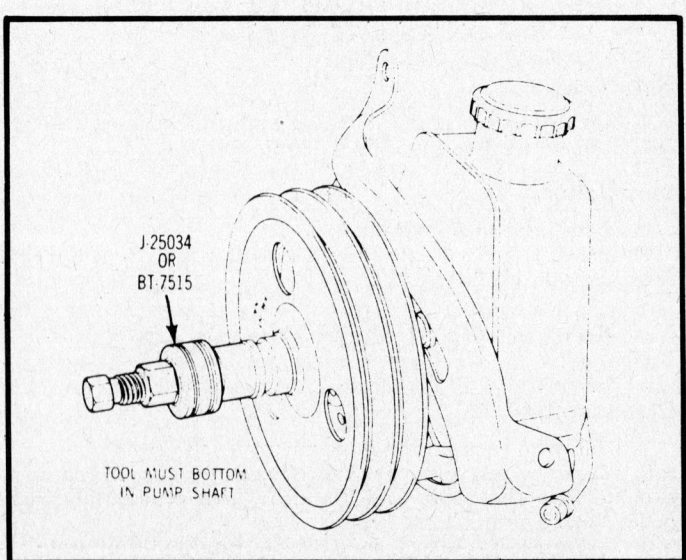

Installing the pilot bolt of the special puller tool

POWER STEERING
GM—RACK AND PINION TYPE
SECTION 34

8. Tap the end cover with a plastic mallet to dislodge it, the spring under the cover should push the cover up.

9. Remove the pump body from the vise, place the pump upside down on a flat surface and tap the end of the driveshaft with a rubber mallet to loosen the pressure plate, rotor and thrust plate assembly from the pump body.

10. Lift the pump body off of rotor assembly. Flow control valve and spring should slide out of the bore.

11. Replace and discard end cover and pressure plate O-rings, place pump body on a flat surface and pry the driveshaft oil seal nut with a suitable tool.

12. Inspect the seal bore in housing for burrs, nicks or gouge marks that would allow oil to bypass outer seal surface.

13. Remove the ten vanes from the slots in the rotor, after lifting out the pressure plate and cam ring from the rotor. Clamp the driveshaft in a soft jaw vise or equivalent, with the rotor and thrust plate facing up.

14. Remove the rotor lock ring, pry the ring off the driveshaft and be sure to avoid nicking the rotor end face. Discard the lock ring.

15. Slide the rotor and thrust plate off of the shaft and remove the shaft from the vise.

NOTE: Inspect and wash all parts in clean solvent, blow out all passages with compressed air and air dry the cleaned parts.

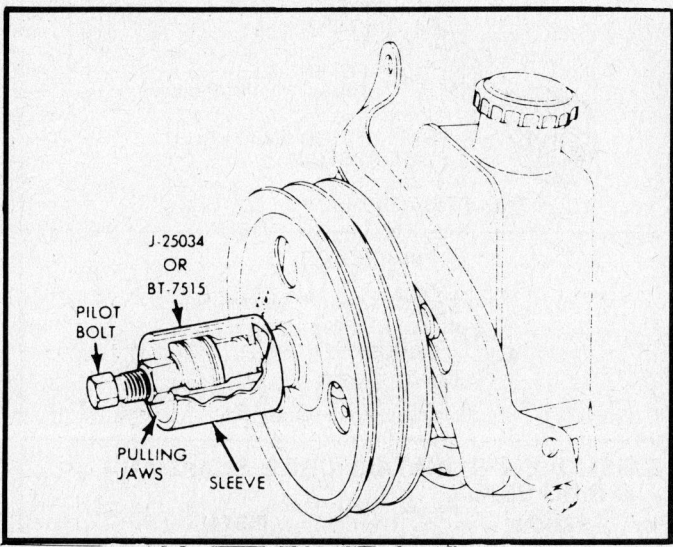

Installing the puller jaws and sleeve

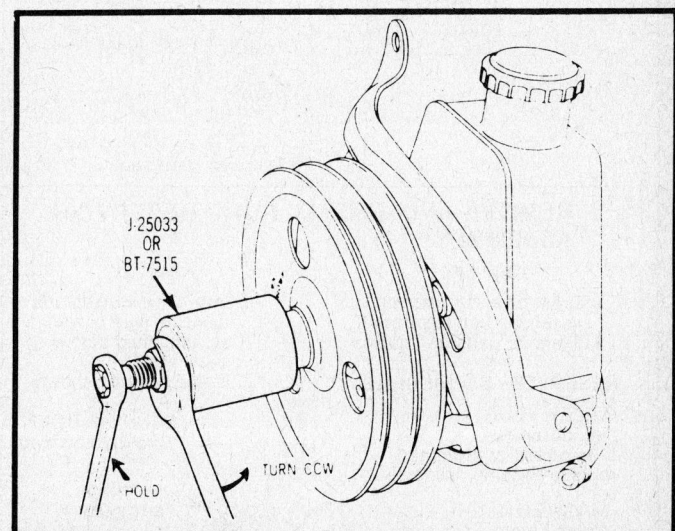

Removing the pulley

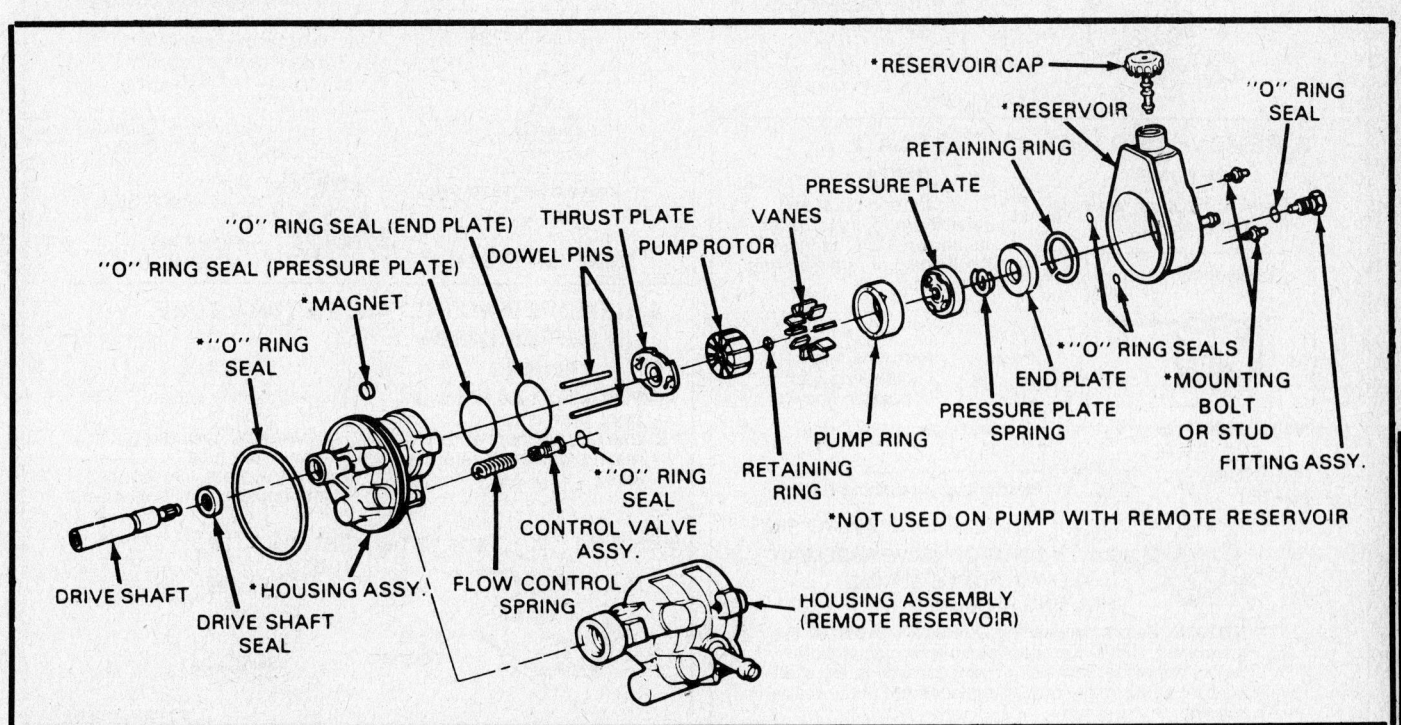

Exploded view of a typical power steering pump

34-43

SECTION 34: POWER STEERING
GM – RACK AND PINION TYPE

1. REMOVE AND INSTALL DRIVE SHAFT SEAL WITHOUT DISASSEMBLING THE PUMP

REMOVE
1. Protect drive shaft with shim stock.
2. Use chisel to cut seal and remove.

INSTALL
1. Coat drive shaft seal with hydraulic pump fluid. Refer to inset for drive shaft seal installation.

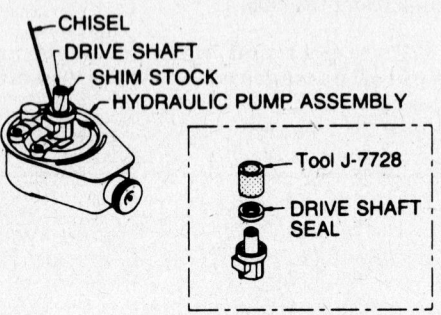

Install drive shaft seal.

2. REMOVE AND INSTALL PUMP RESERVOIR ASSEMBLY

REMOVE
1. Drain oil from reservoir assembly before removal.
2. Remove parts as shown.

INSTALL
1. Use all new seals and lubricate with power steering fluid before installation.
2. Install parts as shown.

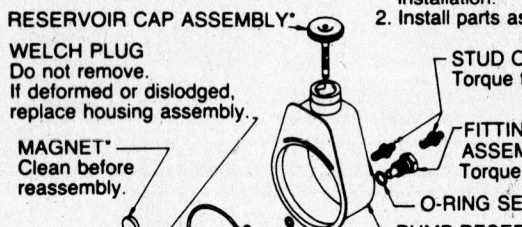

RESERVOIR CAP ASSEMBLY*
WELCH PLUG — Do not remove. If deformed or dislodged, replace housing assembly.
MAGNET* — Clean before reassembly.
STUD OR BOLT* — Torque to 35 N·m
FITTING ASSEMBLY — Torque to 75 N·m
O-RING SEAL
PUMP RESERVOIR ASSEMBLY*
O-RING SEALS*
HOUSING ASSEMBLY
*Not used on N series

3. REMOVE AND INSTALL END PLATE

REMOVE
1. Refer to inset for retaining ring removal.

INSTALL
1. Lubricate end plate and retaining ring. Install parts as shown. Refer to inset for positioning of retaining ring in housing.

Remove retaining ring.
END PLATE
PRESSURE PLATE
SPRING
END PLATE RETAINING RING
CONTROL VALVE ASSEMBLY
FLOW CONTROL SPRING
HOUSING ASSEMBLY

Positioning of retaining ring.

NOTICE: Before proceeding, examine this part of the drive shaft. If it is corroded, clean with crocus cloth before removing. This will prevent damage to the shaft bushing which might require replacement of the entire housing.

4. REMOVE AND INSTALL ROTATING GROUP

REMOVE
1. Using a rubber mallet, tap lightly on drive shaft until pressure plate is free.
2. Remove retaining ring from drive shaft and discard. Remove parts as shown.

INSTALL
1. Install parts as shown on drive shaft. Install new retaining ring on drive shaft and install in pump housing.
2. Refer to inset for positioning of pump ring in housing.

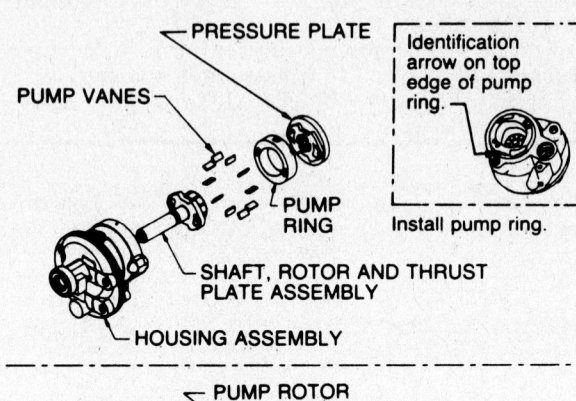

PRESSURE PLATE
PUMP VANES
PUMP RING
SHAFT, ROTOR AND THRUST PLATE ASSEMBLY
HOUSING ASSEMBLY
Identification arrow on top edge of pump ring.
Install pump ring.

PUMP ROTOR
SHAFT RETAINING RING
THRUST PLATE
DRIVE SHAFT
Retaining ring removal.

5. REMOVE AND INSTALL DRIVE SHAFT AND O-RING SEALS

REMOVE
1. Remove parts as shown.

INSTALL
1. Refer to the inset for drive shaft seal installation. Use all new seals and lubricate seals with power steering fluid before installation.
2. Install parts as shown.

Tool J-7728
Install drive shaft seal.

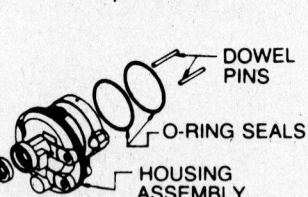

DRIVE SHAFT SEAL
DOWEL PINS
O-RING SEALS
HOUSING ASSEMBLY

6. REMOVE AND INSTALL RETURN TUBE (N SERIES ONLY)

REMOVE
1. Plug return tube to prevent chips from entering pump.
2. Use tap, washers and nut to remove damaged return tube.

INSTALL
1. Using Loctite solvent 75559 and Loctite 290 adhesive or equivalent, coat end of the new return tube.
2. Using a press, press tube into housing until bottomed.

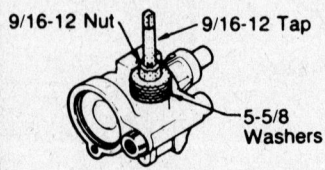

9/16-12 Nut
9/16-12 Tap
5-5/8 Washers

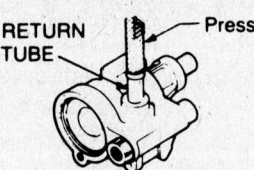

RETURN TUBE
Press

Power Steering Pump Repair

POWER STEERING
GM—RACK AND PINION TYPE

Assembly

1. With the pump body laying on a flat surface, drive a new driveshaft seal into the bore, using a suitable tool until the seal bottoms on shoulder.

NOTE: Do not use excessive force when installing the seal, because the seal will become distorted.

2. Lubricate the seal with power steering fluid and clamp the pump body shaft end down into a vise.
3. Install the end cover and pressure plate O-rings in the grooves in the pump cavity. (These rings are the same size.) Be sure to lubricate the O-rings in power steering fluid.
4. With the driveshaft clamped in a soft jaw vise or equivalent with the splined end up, install the thrust plate on the driveshaft (ported side up). Slide rotor over splines with the counterbore of the rotor facing down. Install the rotor lock ring being sure the ring is seated in the groove.
5. Install the two dowel pins in holes in the pump cavity. Insert the driveshaft, rotor and thrust plate assembly in the pump cavity matching the locating holes with the dowel pins.
6. Slide the cam ring over the rotor on the dowel pins with the arrow on the ring facing up. Install the ten vanes in the rotor slots and lubricate them with power steering fluid.
7. Position the pressure plate dowel pins and place a 1¼ inch socket in the groove of the pressure plate and seat the entire assembly on the O-ring in the pump cavity by pressing down on the socket with both thumbs.
8. Place the spring in the groove in the pressure plate and position the end cover lip edge up over the spring.
9. Press the end cover down below the retaining ring groove with a vise or an arbor press and install the ring making sure it is seated in the groove.

NOTE: This procedure is better performed in an arbor press if one is available. Caution should be used to prevent cocking the end cover in the bore or distorting the assembly.

10. Using a punch, tap the retainer ring ends around in the groove until the opening is opposite the flow control valve bore. This is important for maximum retention of the retainer ring.
11. Replace the reservoir O-ring seal, the two mounting stud O-ring seals and the flow control valve O-ring seal on the pump body. Align the mounting stud holes until the studs can be started in the threads.
12. Tap the reservoir down on the pump using a rubber mallet and insert the flow control valve spring and valve (hexagon plug down). Replace the O-ring on the pressure hose fitting and lubricate with power steering fluid.

NOTE: Be sure the O-ring is installed on the upper groove. It is possible to install the O-ring in the lower groove. If this happens it will restrict the relief outlet orifice.

13. Install the pressure hose fitting and tighten the mounting studs. The torque for the hose is 37 ft. lbs. (50 Nm) and the torque for the studs is 26 ft. lbs. (35 Nm).
14. Remove the pump assembly from the vise and install the mounting brackets. After the brackets are installed clamp the pump assembly into the vise at the mounting bracket.
15. Place the pulley on the end of the pump shaft and install special tool J-25034 or BT-7515 or equivalent. Be sure the pilot bolt bottoms in the shaft by turning the nut at the top of the pilot bolt.
16. Install the pulley by holding the pilot bolt and turning the nut clockwise.
17. Install the pump assembly on the engine, refill the reservoir and start engine, inspect for leaks and recheck the fluid level after bleeding the air from the pump.

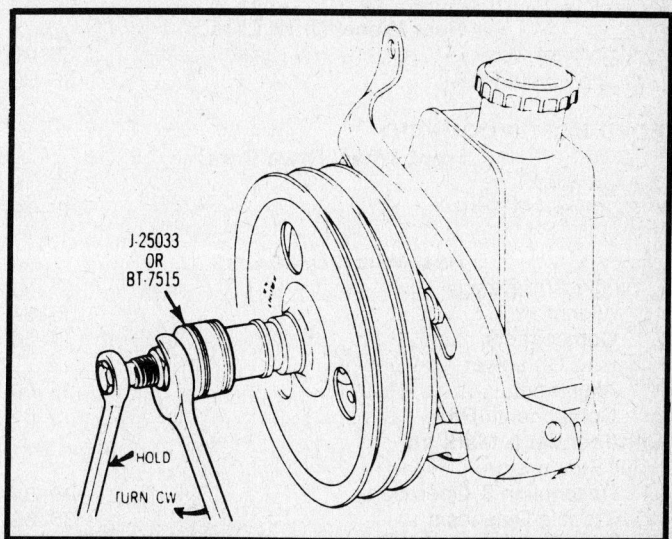

Installing the pulley

SUSPENSIONS

INDEX

FRONT SUSPENSION SERVICE

Principals of Wheel Alignment
- Introduction 35-3
- What is Toe? 35-4
- What is Caster? 35-4
- What is Camber? 35-5
- Toe Out on Turns 35-6
- Trouble Diagnosis 35-3

AMERICAN MOTORS
- Alignment 35-6
- Components R&R 35-7

CHRYSLER CORPORATION

Front Wheel Drive Cars
- Alignment 35-17
- Components R&R 35-17

Rear Wheel Drive Cars
- Alignment 35-29
- Components R&R 35-30

FORD MOTOR COMPANY

Front Wheel Drive Cars
- Alignment 35-48
- Components R&R 35-49

Rear Wheel Drive Cars
- Single Arm Design
  - Alignment 35-57
  - Components 35-58
- Spring On Lower Arm Design
  - Alignment 35-60
  - Components R&R 35-61
- Continental & Mark VII
  - Air Suspension
    - Description & Operation 35-64
    - Trouble Diagnosis 35-66
    - Test Procedures 35-68
    - Components R&R 35-72

GENERAL MOTORS CORPORATION
- Body Style Identification 35-81

Front Drive Cars
- A & X Body
  - Alignment 35-82
  - Components R&R 35-82
- C Body
  - Alignment 35-86
  - Components R&R 35-86
- E & K Body
  - Alignment 35-95
  - Components R&R 35-100
- F Body
  - Alignment 35-91
  - Components R&R 35-92
- J Body
  - Alignment 35-104
  - Components R&R 35-105
- P Body
  - Alignment 35-112
  - Components R&R 35-113
- S Body
  - Alignment 35-118
  - Components R&R 35-119

Rear Drive Cars
- Except F,T,P Body and '84 and later Corvette
  - Alignment 35-122
  - Components R&R 35-123
- T Body
  - Alignment 35-134
  - Components R&R 35-136
- 1984 and later Corvette (Rear Wheel Drive)
  - Alignment 35-139
  - Components R&R 35-140

ELECTRONIC LEVEL CONTROLS 35-146

REAR SUSPENSION SERVICE

AMERICAN MOTORS 35-12

CHRYSLER CORP.
- Front Drive Cars 35-23
- Rear Drive Cars 35-39

FORD MOTOR CO.
- Front Wheel Drive 35-54
- Rear Wheel Drive Cars 35-76
- Rear Drive Cars—Four Bar Link Design 35-78
- Continental & Mark VII Air Suspension 35-64

GENERAL MOTORS
- Body Identification 35-81

Front Drive Cars
- A & X Body 35-84
- C Body 35-89
- E & K Body 35-101
- F Body 35-94
- J Body 35-109
- P Body 35-115
- S Body (Nova) 35-120

Rear Drive Cars (Solid Axle)
- Except F, T, P Body and '84 and later Corvette ... 35-129

Rear Drive Cars (Independent Susp.)
- Except F,T,P Body and '84 and later Corvette 35-130
- T Body 35-138
- 1984 and later Corvette (Rear Wheel Drive) 35-142

ELECTRONIC LEVEL CONTROLS
- Chrysler 35-40
- General Motors 35-146

SUSPENSIONS
PRINCIPLES OF WHEEL ALIGNMENT
SECTION 35

PRINCIPLES OF WHEEL ALIGNMENT

Introduction

The term wheel alignment is well known, but it might be better understood as motion balance, because correct vehicle alignment involves balancing all of the forces created by friction, gravity, centrifugal force and momentum, while a vehicle is in motion.

A correct alignment job will make a vehicle run smoother, have better road-handling characteristics, have better steering ability and operate with more stability while running in a straight line and around curves. It also eliminates unnecessary road friction, which causes abnormal tire wear and decreases fuel mileage.

Wheel alignment is more than just the simple tracking of front and rear wheels to insure that they roll freely on a straight-ahead course. Front end alignment must also be maintained during turns and other steering maneuvers even thought the road surface and other irregularities can cause the wheels to move up and down almost constantly. In addition to steering control, front end alignment also provides directional stability which helps the driver hold a straight course without making continuous steering corrections. Ideally, only very light pressure on the steering wheel should be enough to keep the vehicle headed on a straight course. However, a slight resistance (light turning load) is needed to help stabilize steering control. In effect, this resistance helps give the driver something to turn against, thus reducing the tendency to overcontrol.

In the past, caster, camber and toe were all adjustable. However, with the introduction of the MacPherson type of front suspension and its modified versions, caster adjustment can only be accomplished by bending the suspension. Camber is adjustable on some types, but not on others. This does not mean that these angles are not important. Proper setting of both caster and camber are absolutely essential to good stability, easy steering control and maximum tire life.

SUSPENSION DIAGNOSIS

SYMPTOM	PROBABLE CAUSE
Excessive tire wear on outside shoulder	Excessive positive camber
Excessive tire wear on inside shoulder	Excessive negative camber
Excessive tire wear on both shoulders	Rounding curves at high speeds Underinflated tires
Saw-tooth tire wear	Too much toe-in or toe-out
One tire wears more than the other	Improper camber Defective brakes Defective shock absorber
Tire treads cupped or dished	Out-of-round tires Out-of-balance condition Defective shock absorber
Front wheels shimmy	Defective idler arm bushing Out-of-round tires Out-of-balance condition Excessive positive caster Uneven caster
Vehicle vibrates	Defective tires One or more of all 4 tires out-of-round One or more of all 4 tires out-of-balance Driveshaft bent Driveshaft sprayed with undercoating
Car tends to wander either to the right or left	Improper toe setting Looseness in steering system or ball joints Uneven caster Tire pull
Vehicle swerves or pulls to side when applying brakes	Uneven caster Brakes need adjustment Out-of-round brake drum Defective brakes Underinflated tire
Car tends to pull either to the right or left when taking hands off steering wheel	Improper camber Unequal caster Tires worn unevenly Tire pressure unequal

SECTION 35
SUSPENSIONS
PRINCIPLES OF WHEEL ALIGNMENT

SUSPENSION DIAGNOSIS

SYMPTOM	PROBABLE CAUSE
Car is hard to steer	Tires underinflated Power steering defective Too much positive caster Steering system too tight or binding
Steering has excessive play or looseness	Loose wheel bearings Loose ball joints Loose bushings Loose idler arm Loose steering gear assembly Worn steering gear or steering gear bearings

With the introduction of small front drive cars, the rear suspension now becomes a service item. Some rear axles have alignment adjustments, some do not. See each type axle in their respective sections.

What Is Toe

Toe-in is the amount, in fractions of an inch, that the wheels are closer together at the extreme front of the tire than they are at the rear. If the wheels are farther apart at the front, they toe-out.

ZERO RUNNING TOE

When a vehicle is moving, zero toe provides parallel rolling of the two front wheels. This stabilizes steering and reduces side-slipping and tire wear to a minimum. To obtain a running toe of zero for average driving, it is usually necessary to provide a small amount of toe-in when the vehicle is at rest. This offsets small deflections due to rolling resistance and brake applications which tend to toe the wheels outward. When a vehicle is rolling forward a force is set up which compresses the tie-rod and the tie-rod ends. This lets the wheels spread outward at the front. Very little looseness in the steering linkage will allow wheels set at recommended toe-in actually to toe-out under running conditions.

It has been common to talk about toe-in. However, many front drive cars require toe-out settings.

The foregoing explanation of the forces at work trying to change toe when the car is rolling helps explain why it is important to set to to the preferred specification. It also explains the futility of trying to obtain zero running toe on a card having loose steering tie-rod.

--- CAUTION ---
Tie rod ball ends are designed to allow complete freedom of movement without binding. However, because each rod has two tie-rod ends, both of them must be centered exactly to avoid binding and interference when the wheels move up and down or are turned.

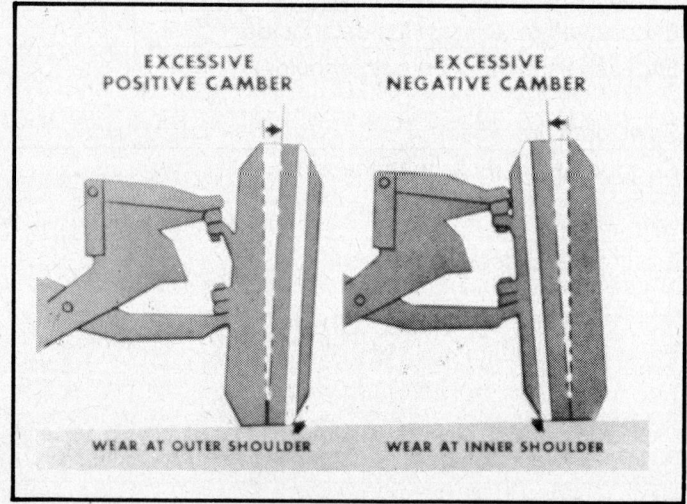

What Is Caster

Caster is defined as the angle, when viewed from the side, between the steering axis and the vertical. It is simply a new name that describes what used to be known as the "kingpin axis." Caster is positive when the top of the axis is inclined rearward and negative when it is inclined forward.

EFFECT OF CASTER ON STEERING

The mechanic's creeper illustrates the principle and effect of caster on steering geometry. When the force is applied to the creeper, the caster turn on their pivots until the caster wheels are in line with the force applied and the wheels are then trailing behind the pivot point. The same principle applies to the front wheel of a car. If the steering axis pivot is tilted backward at the top of the projected axis contacts the road ahead of the point of tire contact. This produces the same effect as the creep-

SUSPENSIONS
PRINCIPLES OF WHEEL ALIGNMENT
SECTION 35

er's caster. The pivot axis pulls the wheel behind it, adding to the car's directional stability.

As the positive caster angle is increased, the effort required to turn the car from a straight-ahead course is increased. The tendency of the front wheels to straighten out rapidly when leaving a turn is also increased.

NOTE: Although the caster angle tends to cause the car body and frame to lift when the wheels are turned, this is a very minor factor in the stability and returnability of present-day cars. There are two reasons for this: first, caster angles are so small that the lift is negligible; second, the higher rolling resistance of today's low-pressure tires produces far more directional stability from the caster effect that did smaller high pressure tires used in the past.

On a power steering car too much positive caster indirectly can cause low-speed shimmy, increased road shock and high-speed wander. Unequal caster-either positive or negative-between the wheels is also undesirable. If all other factors are equal, a car will lead or drift toward the side with the least amount of caster. The worst possible situation exists when there is no negative caster at one wheel and positive caster on the other. Under these conditions, the wheel with negative caster tries to turn outward and the car pulls toward the side with negative caster when brakes are applied.

What Is Camber

Camber is the amount, in degrees, that the wheel is inclined from the vertical as viewed from the front of the car. If the top of the wheel leans away from the car, the camber is positive. If the top of the wheel leans toward the car, the camber is negative.

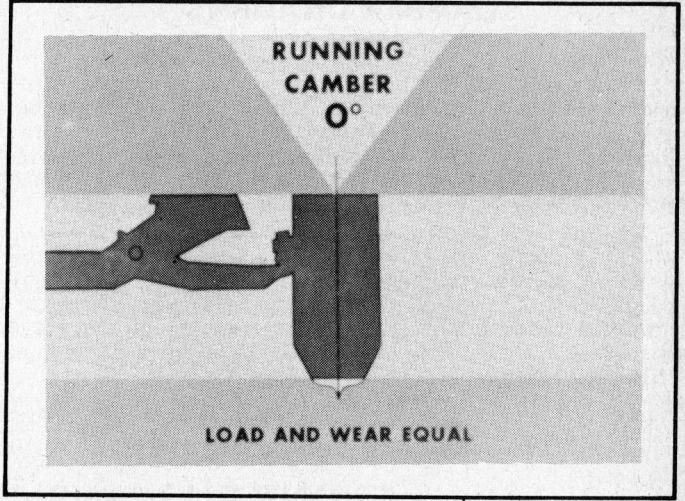

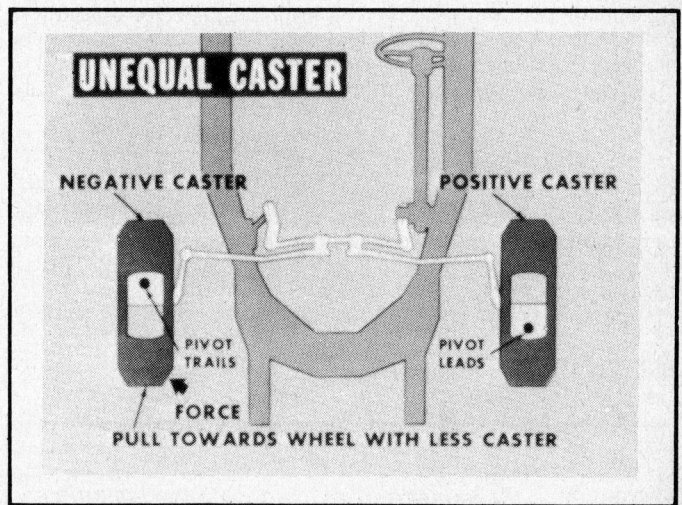

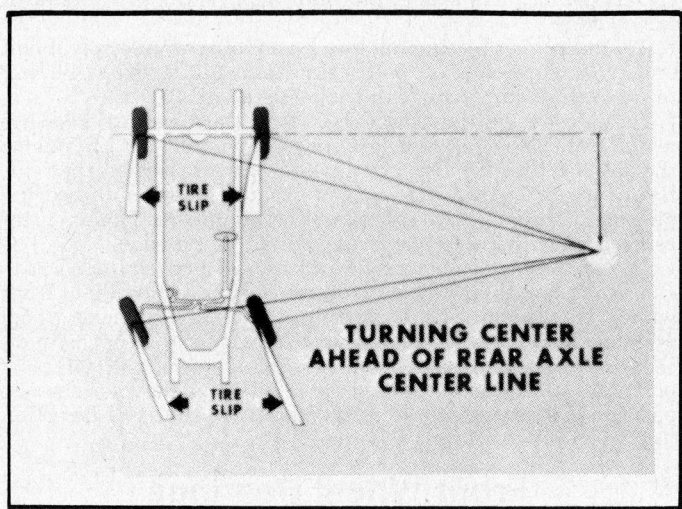

EFFECTS OF INCORRECT CAMBER

Too much positive camber causes tire wear at the outer shoulder, too much negative camber causes tire wear at the inner shoulder. However, you should also remember that rounding turns at high speeds also causes the tires to show more wear at the shoulders. Therefore, such tires wear may not always be caused by incorrect camber.

Similarly, continuous high-speed driving on curves to the right and left will produce wear at the inner and outer shoulders of both tires. This often results in a wear pattern that looks very much like under inflation wear. Again, such wear may not be caused by incorrect camber and will not be corrected by adjusting the camber.

Under all driving conditions, the best average running camber is obtained when camber is adjusted to specifications. Deviation from specifications can cause hard steering, unstable steering and wander. Unequal camber can contribute to a low-speed shimmy condition.

CAMBER ANGLES CHANGE WITH VERTICAL WHEEL MOVEMENT

When a front wheel moves upward (or the car body and frame moves downward), the top of the wheel moves inward, producing negative camber. The upward movement of the wheel is usually called jounce motion of jounce travel.

ZERO RUNNING CAMBER

Maximum tire life is obtained when the average running camber is zero. That is, when the wheel and the tire are vertical, the tire tread in contact with the road is uniform from side-to-side. Therefore, the load and wear are distributed equally over the entire tread.

35-5

SECTION 35
SUSPENSIONS
PRINCIPLES OF WHEEL ALIGNMENT

CAMBER ON TURNS

When a car goes into a turn at high speeds, centrifugal force causes a significant weight shift toward the outside wheel. The body and frame moves downward, producing negative camber at the outside wheel. At the same time, weight is reduce at the inside wheel and the body and frame tries to lift. This movement produces little camber change or a small amount of positive camber at the inside wheel.

The negative camber at the outside wheel has the very desirable effect of bracing the tire tread against sideslip. The combination of negative camber and increased tracting force (more weight on outside wheel) minimizes tire slip and increases cornering stability. Similarly, zero camber or a small amount of positive camber at the inside wheel helps minimize tire slip at this point.

Toe Out On Turns

Toe-out on turns is an important non-adjustable measurement that should be checked after all other steering geometry angles are measured and adjusted to their straight-ahead specifications. When the wheels are turned, a fifth angle becomes important. This is commonly referred to as toe-out on turns.

In theory, all four car wheels should turn about the same center to minimize sideslipping of the tires. Since both rear wheels are connected by a solid axle, the front wheels should turn in circles whose centerlines intersect the centerline of the rear axle. Actually, all four tires slip because of centrifugal force when rounding a corner at any speed greater than a brisk walk. As a result, the real turning center is considerably ahead of the true centerline of the rear axle.

FRONT SUSPENSION AMERICAN MOTORS

Except for two types of steering knuckles, service procedures for both two wheel drive and four wheel drive vehicles are very similar. On two wheel drive cars, ball joints can be replaced in a conventional manner. On four wheel drive models, the complete control arm must be replaced.

FRONT WHEEL ALIGNMENT

Front wheel alignment, or steering geometry, refers to the various angles assumed by the components which form the front wheel turning mechanism. There are three adjustable, alignment angles which are caster, camber and toe-in.

Caster describes the forward or rearward tilt (from vertical) of the steering knuckle. Tilting the top of the knuckle rearward provides positive caster. Tiling the top of the knuckle forward provides negative caster. Caster is directional stability angle which enables the front wheels to return to a straight-ahead position after turns.

Adjust caster by loosening the strut rod jamnut and turning the rod adjusting nuts in or out to move the lower control arm forward or rearward to obtain the desired caster angle. Tighten adjusting nuts to 65 ft. lbs.(88 Nm) torque and jamnut to 75 ft. lbs. (102 Nm) torque when adjustment is completed.

Camber describes the inward and outward tilt of the wheel relative to the center of the automobile. An inward tilt of the top of the wheel produces negative camber. An outward tilt produces positive camber. Camber greatly affects tire wear. Incorrect camber will cause abnormal wear on the tire outside or inside edge.

Adjust camber by turning lower control arm inner pivot bolt eccentric. Tighten pivot bolt locknuts to 110 ft. lbs. (149 Nm) torque after completing camber adjustment.

Toe-in is a condition that exists when the measured distance at the front of each tire is less than the distance at the rear of the tires. When the distance at the front is less than the rear, the tires are toed-in. toe-in compensates for normal steering play and causes the tires to roll in a straight-ahead manner. Incorrect toe-in will ear the tires to a feathered edge.

Adjust toe-in by turning tie rod adjuster tubes in or out to shorten or lengthen tie rods to obtain desired toe-in. Place front wheels in straight-ahead position and center steering wheel and gear. Turn tie rod adjusting tubes equally in opposite directions to obtain desired toe-in setting. If steering wheel spoke position was disturbed during toe-in adjustment, correct spoke position by turning tie rod tubes equally in the same direction until desired position is obtained.

Front Wheel Bearings

TWO WHEEL DRIVE

When repacking and adjusting front wheel bearings, use an EP-type, lithium base wheel bearing lubricant. Pack the bearings with a generous amount of lubricant and place extra lubricant in the rotor hub cavity between the bearings. Always use a new grease seal during assembly.

When inspecting, replacing, or repacking bearings, be sure the inner cones of the bearings are free to creep on the spindle. The bearings are designed to creep to allow a constantly changing load contact between the cones and the rollers. Polishing and applying lubricant to the spindle will permit this movement and prevent rust formation.

Two wheel drive suspensions (© American Motors Corp.)

SUSPENSIONS
FRONT SUSPENSION — AMERICAN MOTORS

Adjustment
1. Raise and support front of the automobile.
2. Remove hub cap, grease cap and O-ring, cotter pin and nutlock.
3. On automobiles with styled wheels, remove wheel and hub cap. Install wheel.
4. Tighten spindle nut to 25 ft. lbs. (34 Nm) torque while rotating wheel to seat bearings.
5. Loosen spindle nut 1/3 turn. While rotating wheel, tighten spindle nut to 6 inch lbs. (0.7 Nm) torque.
6. Install nutlock to spindle nut so cotter pin holes in nutlock and spindle are aligned.
7. Install replacement cotter pin, grease cap and hub cap.
8. On automobiles with styled wheels, remove wheel, install hub cap and install wheel.

FOUR WHEEL DRIVE

Adjustment
Four wheel drive models have a unique front axle hub and bearing assembly. The assembly is sealed and does not require lubrication, periodic maintenance, or adjustment. The hub has ball bearings which seat in races machined directly into the hub. There are darkened areas surrounding the bearing race areas of the hub. These darkened areas are from a heat treatment process, are normal, and should not be mistaken for a problem condition.

Removal
1. Raise and support the vehicle safely.
2. Remove the wheel, caliper and rotor.
3. Remove the bolts attaching the axle shaft flange to the halfshaft.
4. Remove the cotter pine, lock nut and axle hub nut from the assembly.
5. Remove the halfshaft.
6. Remove the steering arm from the steering knuckle.
7. Remove the caliper anchor plate from the steering knuckle.
8. Remove the Torx© head bolts retaining the hub assembly.
9. Remove the hub assembly from the steering knuckle pine.
10. Remove any grease remaining in the steering knuckle cavity.

NOTE: Remove and save the front hub spacer. During removal, it may be lodged on the end of the halfshaft or on the hub shaft. If a replacement hub is to be used, the hub spacer must be installed on the new hub assembly.

Installation
1. Partially fill the hub cavity of the steering knuckle with chassis lubricant and install the hub assembly. Make sure that the hub spacer is installed on the hub shaft.
2. Install the inner seal in the steering knuckle pin.
3. Install the splash seal on the hub and bearing carrier. Install the O-ring on the hub and bearing carrier.
4. Install the carrier attaching bolts. Tighten to 75 ft. lbs. (102 Nm) torque.
5. Install the caliper anchor plat and plate retaining bolts. Tighten the retaining bolts to 100 ft. lbs. (136 Nm) torque.
6. Install the steering arm bolts. Tighten to 100 ft. lbs. (136 Nm) torque.
7. Install the halfshaft.
8. Install the axle flange to shaft bolts. Tighten to 45 ft. lbs. (61 Nm) torque.
9. Install the hub washer and nut. Tighten the hub nut to 175 ft. lbs. (237 Nm) torque.
10. Install the lock nut and new cotter pin. Install the rotor, caliper and wheel.

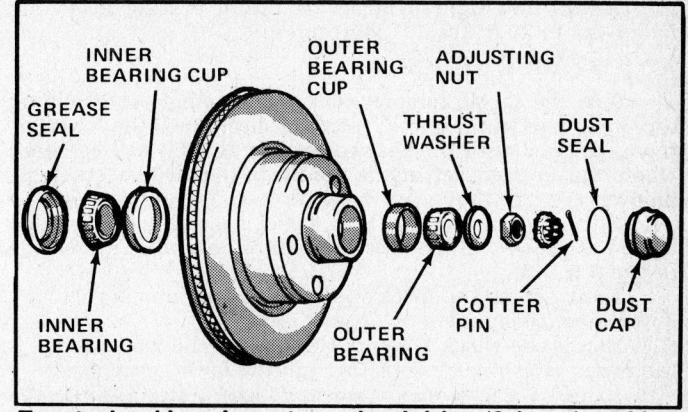

Front wheel bearing — two wheel drive (© American Motors Corp.)

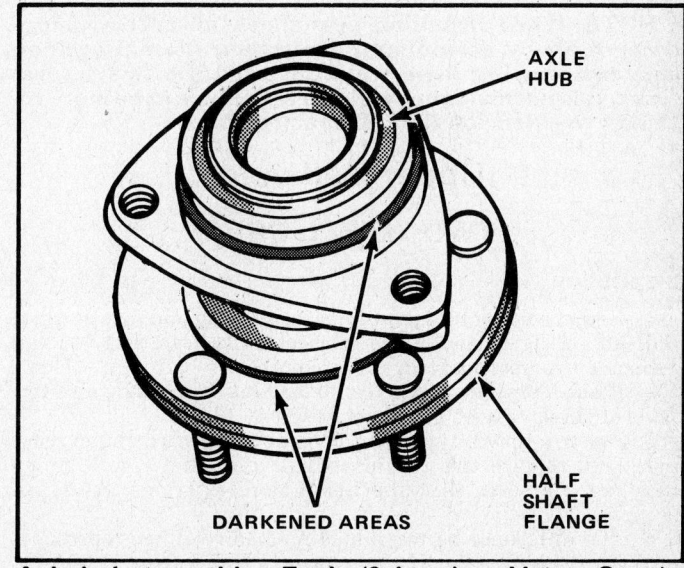

Axle hub assembly — Eagle (© American Motors Corp.)

SHOCK ABSORBER

Removal
ALL MODELS
1. Remove the lower retaining nuts, washer and grommets.
2. Remove upper mounting bracket bolts/nuts from wheelhouse panel.
3. Remove upper bracket and shock absorber from wheelhouse panel.
4. Remove upper retaining nut from shock absorber and remove upper bracket from shock absorber.

Installation
1. Install washers, grommets, upper mounting bracket and nut on shock absorber if removed. Tighten nut to 8 ft. lbs. (11 Nm) torque.
2. Extend shock absorber piston fully.
3. Install grommets on lower mounting studs and position shock absorber in wheelhouse panel.
4. Insert lower mounting studs into lower springs seat and install lower grommets, flat washers and nuts. Tighten nuts to 15 ft. lbs. (20 Nm) torque.

SECTION 35

SUSPENSIONS
FRONT SUSPENSION—AMERICAN MOTORS

5. Install and tighten upper mounting bracket attaching nuts/bolts to 20 ft. lbs. (27 Nm) torque.

ADJUSTABLE SHOCKS

To adjust the shock, compress the piston completely. Holding the upper part of the shock, turn the shock until the lower arrow is aligned with the desired setting. A click will be heard when the desired setting is reached. Install the shock as follows:

1. Fit the grommets, washers, upper mounting bracket and nut on the shock, in the reverse order of removal. Tighten the nut to 8 ft. lbs.
2. Fully extend the shock and install two grommets onto the lower mounting studs.
3. Lower the shock through the hole in the wheelwell. Fit the lower attachment studs through the lower spring seat.
4. Install the grommets, washers, and nuts. Tighten the nuts to 15 ft. lbs.
5. Secure the upper mounting bracket with its attachment nuts and bolts. Tighten to 20 ft. lbs.

NOTE: When installing new shock absorbers, purge them of air by extending them in their normal position and compressing them while inverted. Do this several times. It is normal for new shock absorbers to be more resistant to extension than to compression.

Upper Ball Joint

TWO WHEEL DRIVE

Inspection

1. Remove upper ball joint lubrication plug and install a dial indicator gauge through the lubrication hole so that you can measure the up and down movement of the ball joint socket.
2. Place a pry bar under tire to load ball joint and raise tire several times to seat gauge tool pin.
3. Pry tire upward to load ball joint and record gauge reading; then release tire to unload ball joint and record gauge reading. Perform this operation several times to ensure accuracy.
4. The difference between load-no-load readings represents ball joint clearance. If clearance is more than 0.080 in. (2.3mm), ball joint should be replaced.

Replacement

1. Install 2 X 4 X 5 in. wood block on frame side sill and under upper control arm.
2. Raise and support front of car.
3. Remove wheel, caliper and rotor.
4. Remove ball stud cotter pin and retaining nut.
5. Install ball joint remover and loosen ball stud in steering knuckle. Do not remove tool at this time.
6. Place support stand under lower control arm.
7. Remove heads from ball joint attaching rivets using chisel or grinding tool.
8. Drive rivets out of ball joint and control arm using hammer and punch.
9. Disengage ball joint from control arm.
10. Remove tool from ball joint stud and remove ball joint from steering knuckle.
11. Position replacement ball joint in control arm and align bolt holes.
12. Install ball joint attaching bolts (supplied in ball joint replacement kits) and tighten nuts to 25 ft. lbs. (34 Nm) torque.
13. Install steering knuckle and retaining nut on ball joint stud. Tighten nut to 75 ft. lbs. (102 Nm) torque and install a new cotter pin.
14. Install rotor, caliper and wheel.

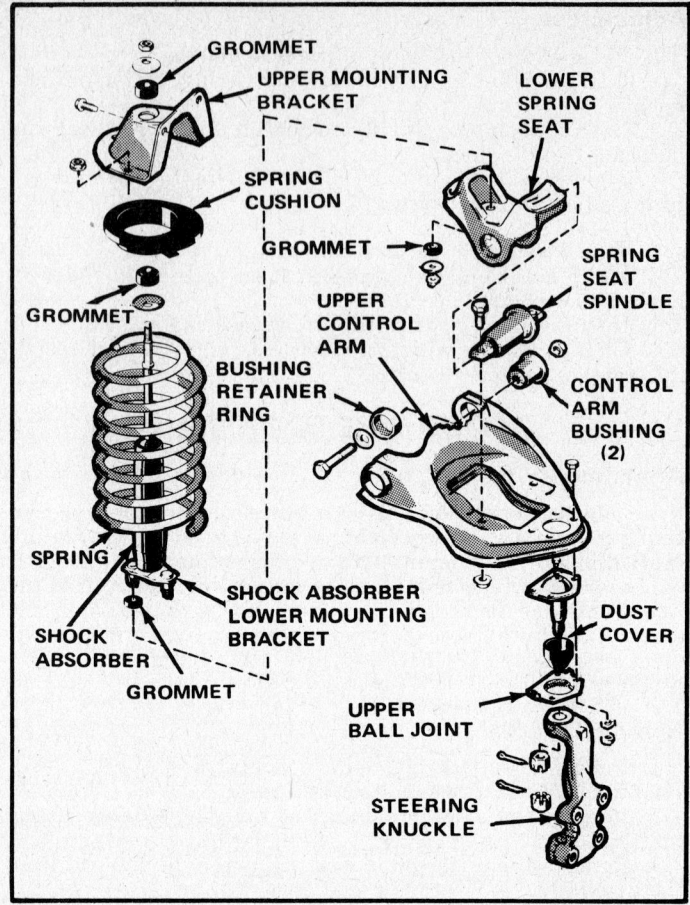

Shock absorber assembly (© American Motors Corp.)

FOUR WHEEL DRIVE

Inspection

Inspection procedures are the same as for two wheel drive models.

Replacement

If a ball joint is worn (upper and lower) the complete arm assembly must be replaced. Do not attempt to service the ball joint separately.

Lower Ball Joint

TWO WHEEL DRIVE

Inspection

1. Raise and support front of automobile.
2. Move lower portion of wheel and tire alternately toward and away from center of automobile. Perform this operation several times.
3. Lower ball join is spring-equipped and preloaded in its socket at all times to minimize looseness and compensate for wear. If lower joint exhibits any lateral movement (shake), ball joint should be replaced.

Replacement

1. Install 2 X 4 X 5 in. wood block on frame side sill and under upper control arm.

SUSPENSIONS
FRONT SUSPENSION — AMERICAN MOTORS

2. Raise and support the front of automobile safely.
3. Remove wheel, caliper and rotor.
4. Disconnect stut rod at lower control arm.
5. Disconnect steering arm from steering knuckle.
6. Remove ball stud cotter pin and retaining nut.
7. Install ball joint removal tool and loosen ball stud in steering knuckle. Do not remove tool at this time.
8. Place support stand under lower control arm.
9. Remove heads from ball joint attaching rivets using chisel or grinding tool.
10. Drive rivets out of ball joint and control arm using punch.
11. Disengage ball joint from control arm.
12. Remove ball joint from control arm.
13. Position replacement ball joint on control arm and align bolt holes.
14. Install but to not tighten attaching bolts supplied in replacement ball joint kit.
15. Attach strut rod to lower control arm. Tighten rod attaching bolts to 75 ft. lbs. (102 Nm) torque.
16. Tighten ball joint attaching bolts to 25 ft. lbs. (34 Nm) torque.
17. Apply chassis grease to steering stops.
18. Install ball joint stud in steering knuckle.
19. Install retaining nut on ball stud. Tighten nut to 75 ft. lbs. (102 Nm) torque and install replacement cotter pine.
20. Install steering arm on steering knuckle.
21. Install rotor, caliper and wheel.

FOUR WHEEL DRIVE
Inspection and Replacement

See the upper ball joint inspection and replacement procedures for four wheel drive models.

Coil Spring
ALL MODELS

Identification

A plastic identification tag which has the spring part number printed on it, is attached to each coil spring. Whenever a spring must be replaced, refer to this part number when ordering a replacement spring.

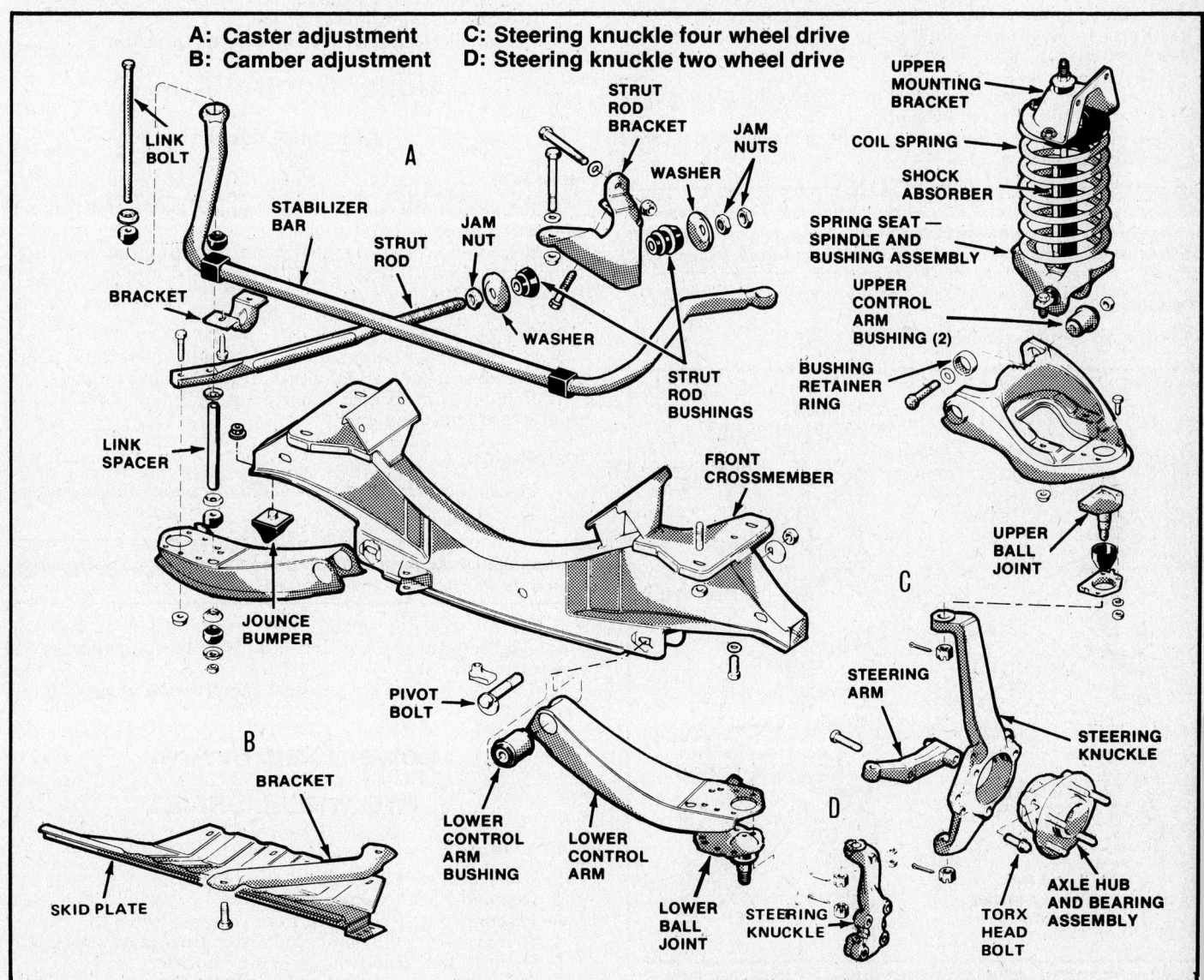

Four wheel drive suspension (© American Motors Corp.)

SECTION 35 SUSPENSIONS
FRONT SUSPENSION—AMERICAN MOTORS

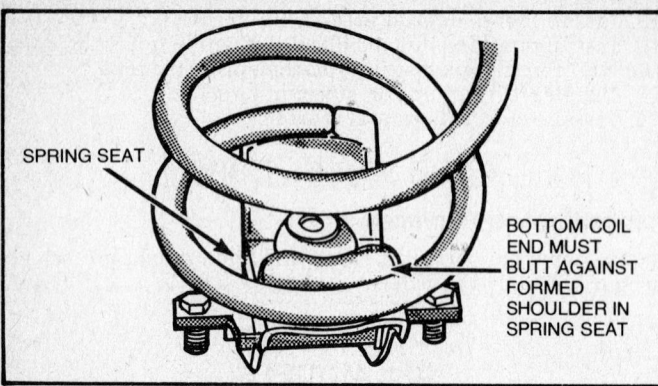

Lower spring seal position (© American Motors Corp.)

REMOVAL

1. Remove shock absorbers and mounting brackets.
2. Install spring compressor and compress spring approximately 1 in. (25.4mm).
3. Remove lower spring seat pivot bolt retaining nuts.
4. Raise front of automobile until control arms are free of lower spring seat.
5. Remove wheel.
6. Pull lower spring seat away from automobile, and guide lower spring seat out and over upper control arm.
7. Remove spring compressor tool and remove lower retainer, spring seat and spring.

--- CAUTION ---

Do not use impact wrench to turn the compression nut. An impact wrench will place unnecessary stress on the compressor tool bolt threads which could result in thread damage or bolt breakage.

Installation

1. Install spring compressor tool.

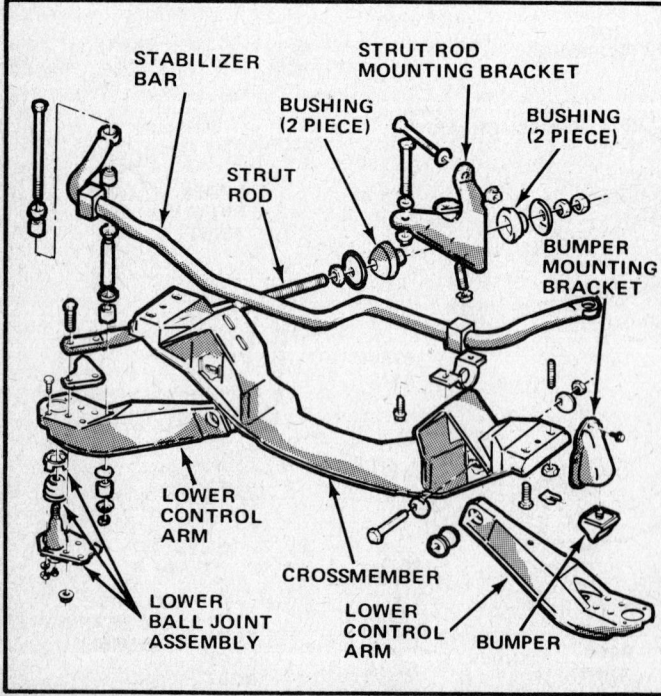

Lower control arm components—Spirit/Concord
(© American Motors Corp.)

2. Install spring upper cushion on top coil of spring. Tape cushion in place to retain it.
3. Install spring in lower spring seat.

NOTE: One side of the lower spring seat has a formed shoulder to help locate the spring properly. Position the spring on the seat so the cut-off end of the spring bottom coil seats against this shoulder. If the spring seat was removed for service, be sure the shouldered end of the spring seat and cut-off end of the spring bottom coil are installed so they face the engine compartment.

4. Position spring in upper seat.
5. Align lower spring seat pivot so that retaining studs will enter upper control arm when spring is in position. Be sure spring lower coil end is properly positioned on seat.
6. Compress spring until lower spring seat pivot studs can be aligned with holes in upper control arm.
7. Turn compression nu counterclockwise and guide spring seat pivot studs into control arm.
8. Install wheel.
9. Remove supports and lower automobile.
10. Install and tighten lower spring seat pivot retaining nuts to 35 ft. lbs. (47 Nm) torque.
11. Remove spring compressor tool.
12. Install shock absorber and mounting bracket.

Upper Control Arm
ALL MODELS

Removal

1. Remove shock absorber and mounting bracket. Install spring compressor tool.
2. Remove lower spring seat pivot retaining nuts and turn compressor tool until spring is compressed approximately 2 inches (5.03 cm).
3. Raise and support front of automobile.
4. Remove wheel.
5. Remove upper ball joint stud cotter pin and retaining nut.
6. Remove upper ball joint stud from steering knuckle.
7. Remove control arm inner pivot bolts and control arm from wheelhouse panel.

Installation

1. Position control arm in wheelhouse panel and install inner pivot bolts.

--- CAUTION ---

Do not tighten the pivot bolts until the automobile is resting on the wheels as ride height may be affected.

2. Install steering knuckle and retaining nut on ball join stud. Tighten nut to 75 ft. lbs. (102 Nm) torque and install a new cotter pin.
3. Turn spring compressor tool compression nut and guide spring seat pivot studs into control arm.

Lower Control Arm
TWO WHEEL DRIVE

Removal

1. Raise and support front of automobile.
2. Remove wheel, caliper and rotor.
3. Disconnect steering arm from steering knuckle.
4. Remove lower ball joint stud cotter pin and retaining nut.
5. Remove ball stud from steering knuckle.
6. Disconnect stabilizer bar from control arm, if equipped.
7. Disconnect strut rod from control arm.

SUSPENSIONS
FRONT SUSPENSION—AMERICAN MOTORS

SECTION 35

8. Remove inner pivot bolt and remove control arm from crossmember.

Installation

1. Position control arm in crossmember and install inner pivot bolt.

CAUTION
Do not tighten the inner pivot bolt until the automobile weight is supported by the wheels as ride height may be affected.

2. Install steering knuckle and retaining nut on ball joint stud. Tighten nut to 75 ft. lbs. (102 Nm) torque and install replacement cotter pin.
3. Connect strut rod to control arm. Tighten bolts to 75 ft. lbs. (102 Nm) torque.
4. Connect stabilizer bar to control arm, if equipped. Tighten bolts to 7 ft. lbs. (9 Nm) torque.
5. Connect steering arm to steering knuckle.
6. Install rotor, caliper and wheel.
7. Place a jack under control arm. Raise jack to compress spring slightly and tighten control arm inner bolt to 110 ft lbs. (149 Nm) torque.

FOUR WHEEL DRIVE

Removal

1. Raise and support the vehicle safely. Remove cotter pin, nut lock and hub nut.
2. Raise and support front of automobile.
3. Remove wheel, caliper and rotor.
4. Remove lower ball joint cotter pin and retaining nut.
5. Remove ball stud from steering knuckle.
6. Remove halfshaft flange bolts.
7. Remove halfshaft.
8. Remove bolts attaching strut rod to control arm.
9. Disconnect stabilizer bar from control arm.
10. Remove inner pivot bolt and remove control arm.

Installation

1. Position control arm in crossmember and install inner pivot bolt.

CAUTION
Do not tighten the inner pivot bolt until the automobile weight is supported by the wheels as ride height may be affected.

2. Insert ball stud in steering knuckle and install retaining nut on ball joint stud. Tighten nut to 75 ft. lbs. (102 Nm) torque and install replacement cotter pin.
3. Connect stabilizer bar to control arm. Tighten lock nut to 7 ft. lbs. (9 Nm) torque.
4. Connect strut rod to control arm. Tighten bolts to 75 ft. lbs. (102 Nm) torque.
5. Install halfshaft-to-axle flange bolts.
6. Tighten flange bolts to 45 ft. lbs. (61 Nm) torque.

NOTE: If control arm is worn or bushing is not tight when installed, control arm must be replaced.

Steering Knuckle And Spindle

TWO WHEEL DRIVE

Removal

1. Raise and support front of automobile.
2. Remove wheel, caliper, and rotor.
3. Remove caliper, anchor plate, adapter, steering spindle, and steering arm from knuckle.
4. Remove upper and lower ball joint stud cotter pins and retaining nuts.
5. Remove all joint studs from steering knuckle.

Installation

1. Install steering knuckle and retaining nuts on ball joint studs. Tighten nuts to 75 ft. lbs. (102 Nm) torque and install new cotter pins.
2. Install steering arm, spindle, caliper anchor plate, and adapter. Tighten bolts to 55 ft. lbs. (75 Nm) torque.
3. Install rotor, caliper and wheel.

FOUR WHEEL DRIVE

Removal

1. Raise and support the vehicle. Remove cotter pin, nut lock and hub nut.
2. Remove wheel, caliper and rotor.
3. Remove halfshaft-to-axle flange bolts.
4. Remove halfshaft.
5. Remove steering arm from steering knuckle.
6. Remove caliper anchor plate from steering knuckle.
7. Remove three Torx® head attaching bolts remaining front wheel hub assembly.
8. Remove hub assembly from knuckle.
9. Remove rear hub seal from steering knuckle using small pry bar.
10. Remove upper and lower ball joint stud cotter pins and retaining nuts.
11. Remove ball joint studs from steering knuckle using a strike tool to loosen and remove studs from knuckle.

Installation

1. Install steering knuckle and ball joint retaining nuts on ball joint studs. Tighten nuts to 75 ft. lbs. (102 Nm) torque and install new cotter pins.
2. Install hub rear seal.
3. Partially fill hub cavity of steering knuckle with chassis lubricant and install hub assembly in knuckle.
4. Tighten hub Torx® head bolts to 75 ft. lbs. (102 Nm) torque.

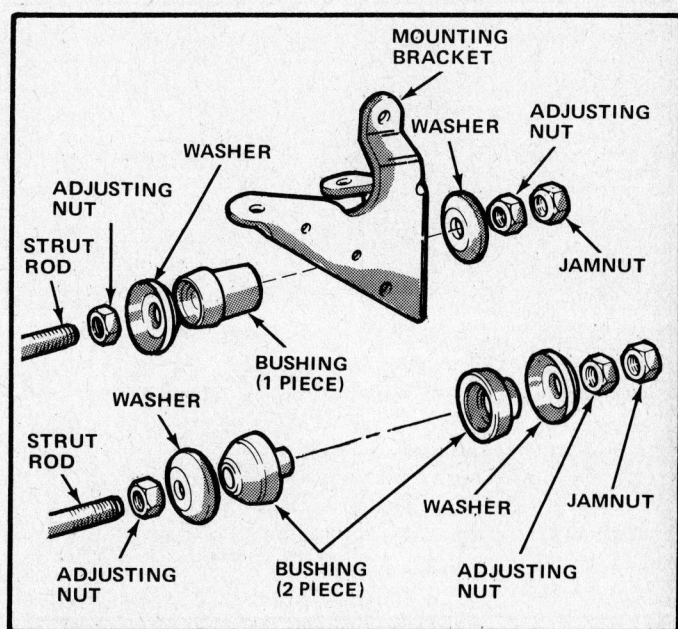

Strut rod bushings (© American Motors Corp.)

SECTION 35 SUSPENSIONS
FRONT SUSPENSION—AMERICAN MOTORS

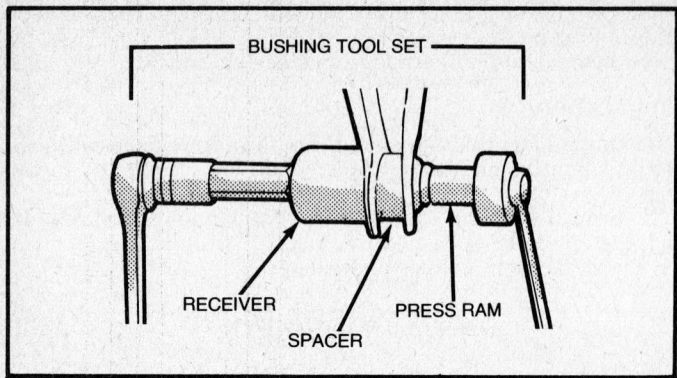

Control arm bushing replacements (© American Motors Corp.)

5. Install caliper anchor plate and retaining bolts.
6. Tighten caliper anchor plate bolts to 100 ft. lbs. (136 Nm) torque.
7. Install steering arm and bolts.
8. Tighten steering arm bolts to 100 ft. lbs. (136 Nm) torque.
9. Install halfshaft and shaft-to-axle flange bolts.
10. Tighten halfshaft-to-axle flange to 45 ft. lbs. (61 Nm) torque.
11. Install rotor, caliper and hub nut.
12. Install wheel.
13. Lower automobile.
14. Tighten hub nut to 180 ft. lbs. (244 Nm) torque. Install nut lock and a new cotter pin.

Strut Rod And Bushing
ALL MODELS
Replacement

1. Raise and support front of automobile.
2. Remove the jamnut and caster adjustment nut from strut rod.
3. Disconnect strut rod from lower control arm and remove rod, bushings and washers.
4. On automobiles with one-piece bushing, lubricate the bushing with soapy water and install.

NOTE: A special tool is required to press the one-piece bushing in and out of the mounting bracket.

REAR SUSPENSION AMERICAN MOTORS

Shock Absorber
Removal

NOTE: When installing new shock absorbers, it is first necessary to purge them of air by repeatedly extending them in their normal position and compressing them while inverted. It is normal for new shock absorbers to be more resistant to extension than to compression.

1. Raise and support the rear of the vehicle. Support the axle assembly safely.

NOTE: When removing air adjustable shock absorbers, it is first necessary to remove the air line from the shock absorber. Tag the line for ease of assembly. Support the suspension in such a way that no strain is on shock absorber.

2. Remove locknut, retainer, and grommet which attach shock absorber lower mounting stud to spring plate.
3. Compress shock absorber by hand and disengage lower mounting stud from spring plate.
4. Remove bolts and lockwashers attaching shock absorber upper mounting bracket to underbody panel and remove shock absorber.
5. Remove locknut, retainer, and grommet which attach mounting bracket to shock absorber upper mounting stud and remove bracket.
6. Remove remaining grommets and retainers from shock absorber upper and lower mounting studs.

Installation

1. Install retainer and grommet on shock absorber mounting stud. Be sure locating shoulder on grommet faces end of mounting stud.
2. Install mounting bracket on shock absorber upper mounting stud with flat side of bracket facing underbody panel.
3. Install second grommet on mounting stud and install retainer and locknut to 8 ft. lbs. (11 Nm) torque.

NOTE: Be sure the locating shoulders on the grommets are centered in the mounting bracket hole before tightening the locknut.

4. Position assembled mounting bracket and shock absorber on mounting studs in underbody panel. Install lockwashers and bolts. Tighten bolts to 28 ft. lbs. (38 Nm) torque on Pacers and 15 ft. lbs. (20 Nm) torque on all other models.

NOTE: If an adjustable shock absorber is being installed, adjust the ride control setting as necessary before connecting the shock to the spring clip plate.

Rear suspension components (© American Motors Corp.)

5. Engage shock absorber lower mounting stud in spring clip plate.
6. Install second grommet with shoulder of grommet facing spring tie plate and install retainer and locknut. Tighten locknut to 8 ft. lbs. (11 Nm) torque.

Leaf Spring

Removal

1. Raise and support rear of the vehicle. Support axle assembly with hydraulic jack.
2. Remove shock absorber lower mounting locknut, retainer and grommet.
3. Remove U-bolts, spring clamps, and clamp bracket.
4. Remove pivot bolt and nut from spring front eye.
5. Remove shackle nuts, shackle plate, and shackle at rear spring eye. Remove spring.

BUSHING REPLACEMENT

1. Remove bushings from spring eyes using arbor press and suitable size socket or section of pipe.
2. Install replacement bushings in spring eyes using arbor press and suitable size socket or section of pipe. Be sure bushings are centered in spring eyes.

Installation

1. Insert shackle pins into spring rear eye and rear hanger.
2. Position front spring eye in front hanger and install pivot bolt and pivot bolt locknut. Tighten locknut to 110 ft. lbs. (149 Nm) torque.
3. Install shackle plate and locknuts on shackle pins. Tighten locknuts to 30 ft. lbs. (41 Nm) torque.
4. Install clamp bracket, spring isoclamps, spring plate and U-bolts.
5. Engage shock lower mounting stud in spring plate and install grommet, retainer and locknut. Tighten nut to 8 ft. lbs. (11 Nm) torque.

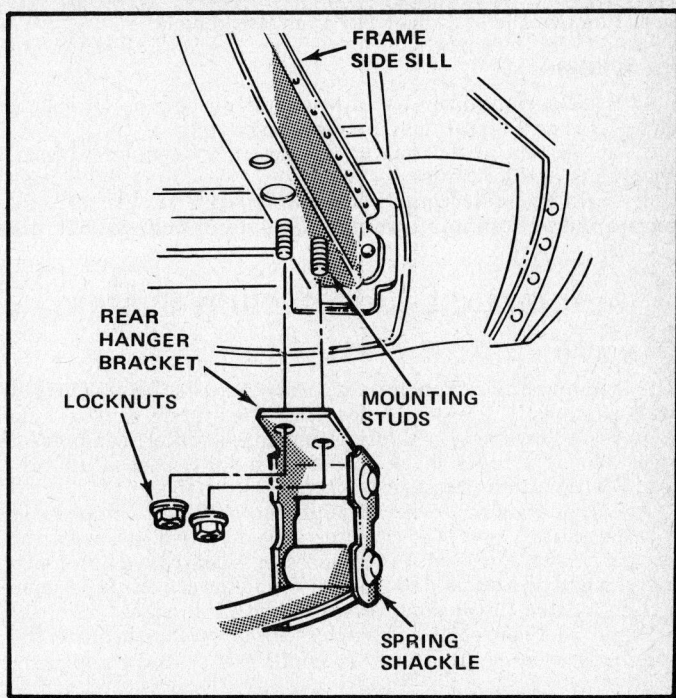

Rear spring, rear mounting (© American Motors Corp.)

Stabilizer Bar

Removal

1. Raise and support the vehicle safely.
2. Remove the nuts and grommets attaching the stabilizer bar to the connecting lings.
3. Remove the bolts attaching the stabilizer bar mounting clamps to the spring clip plates.

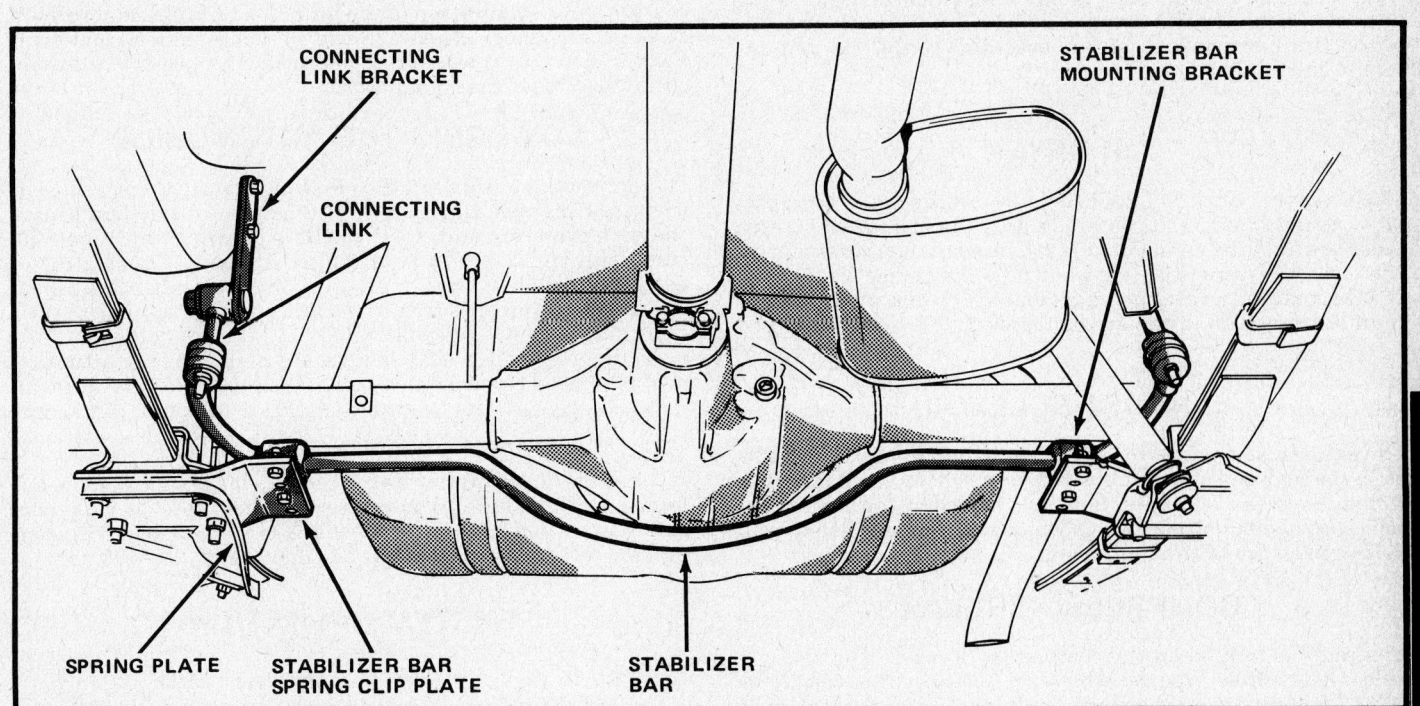

Rear stabilizer bar (© American Motors Corp.)

4. Remove the stabilizer bar from the vehicle.

Installation

1. Position stabilizer bar and mounting clamps on spring clip plates and install clamp bolts finger tight.
2. Install stabilizer bar on connecting links and install grommets and locknuts.
3. Tighten connecting link locknuts to 7 ft. lbs. (9 Nm) torque and tighten stabilizer mounting clamp bolts to 25 ft. lbs. (34 Nm) torque.

Automatic Load Leveling System

Operation

The load leveling system automatically adjusts the rear height with changes in the vehicle loading. The system consists of a compressor assembly, exhaust solenoid, air dryer, compressor relay, air adjustable shock absorbers, height sensors, air tubing, wiring and a pressure limiter.

Adjustment is achieved through the on-board compressor. The electrically operated compressor is mounted in the engine compartment. Although the compressor is controlled automatically, it can be switched to manual by means of a three position switch located in the compressor mounting bracket.

When the three position switch is in the automatic mode, the compressor is operated by the height sensor and compressor relay.

An auxiliary air hose is also included with the system. This hose can be connected to an auxiliary air valve on the compressor. It can be used to inflate air mattresses, tires, etc.

COMPRESSOR

The compressor assembly is a positive displacement single piston air pump powered by a 12 volt permanent magnet motor. The compressor head casting contains piston, intake and exhaust valves plus a solenoid operated exhaust valve which releases air from the system when energized.

NOTE: The compressor is not a serviceable item. If diagnosis indicates the compressor has malfunctioned, replace the compressor as an assembly only. Do not attempt to repair it.

AIR DRYER

The air dryer, which is attached to the compressor output, provides a dual function. It contains a dry chemical which absorbs moisture from the sir before it is delivered to the shocks and returns the moisture to the air when it is exhausted. The air dryer also contains a valve arrangement which maintains a minimum air pressure in the system between 7–14 psi.

EXHAUST SOLENOID

The exhaust solenoid, which provides a dual function, is located in the compressor assembly. When energized, it exhausts air from the system. This operation is controlled by the height sensor. The solenoid also acts as a relief valve to limit maximum output pressure of the compressor.

COMPRESSOR RELAY

The relay is located on the compressor bracket. It is a single pole/single throw type switch. When energized, it completes the 12 volt circuit to the compressor motor. This operation is controlled by the height sensor.

HEIGHT SENSOR

The height sensor, which is an electronic device, controls the compressor relay and exhaust solenoid ground circuit.

To prevent falsely activating the exhaust solenoid circuit or the compressor relay, during normal driving motions, the height sensor provides a 7–15 second delay before either circuit is completed.

The sensor also will limit the time the compressor or exhaust solenoid is energized to a maximum time of 3 ½ minutes. The time limit is designed to prevent unnecessary running time of the compressor in the event of a system leak or exhaust solenoid malfunction. Turning the ignition "off and on" will reset the electronic timer circuit to the 3 ½ minute maximum run time.

The electronic timer circuit is also reset for each change in exhaust and compressor signals from the height sensor. The height sensor, on most vehicles, is located on the side sill in the rear of the vehicle with the sensor actuator arm attached to the rear axle housing by means of a short link.

ADJUSTABLE AIR SHOCKS

The adjustable air shock is essentially a conventional shock absorber encased in an air chamber. The shocks are constructed with a rubber sleeve attached to the shock reservoir and dust tube. This creates a flexible chamber which will extend the shock absorber when air pressure is increased in the air chamber. When air pressure is released, the weight of the vehicle collapses the shock absorber.

RAISING THE AUTOMOBILE

When weight is added to the rear of the car, the body is forced downward which causes the height sensor actuating arm to rotate upward. This action causes the height sensor to electrically start the internal time delay circuit. When the time delay (7–15 seconds) has occurred, the sensor then completes the compressor relay circuit to ground. With the relay energized, the 12 V (+) circuit to the compressor is complete and the compressor runs, sending air to the air adjustable shock absorbers through air lines. When the body reaches its original trim height (± ¾ inch) the sensor opens the compressor relay circuit, shutting of the compressor.

LOWERING THE AUTOMOBILE

A high body condition has the effect of rotating the height sensor actuating arm downward. The height sensor then senses the high condition and starts the time delay circuit. When the time delay (7–15 seconds) has elapsed, the sensor completes the exhaust solenoid circuit to ground. With the exhaust solenoid energized, air escapes from the shocks exiting through the air dryer and exhaust solenoid valve.

As the automobile body lowers, the height sensor actuating arm is rotated toward its original position. When the automobile body reaches its original height (± ¾ inch), the sensor opens the exhaust valve solenoid circuit, which prevents more air from escaping.

A minimum air pressure of 7–14 psi is maintained on the automobile. The minimum pressure provides improved ride characteristics when the automobile has a minimum load. The compressor relief valve is designed to operate at 120–150 psi.

SYSTEM OPERATION

Testing

1. With the vehicle on a level surface, measure the distance between the bumper and the floor.

SUSPENSIONS
REAR SUSPENSION — AMERICAN MOTORS
SECTION 35

2. Turn the ignition on.

3. Apply approximately 200 pounds to the trunk of the vehicle. There should be a 7–15 second delay before the compressor is activated and the vehicle starts to raise. The vehicle should raise to within ¾ inch of the measurement made in Step 1.

4. Failure of the vehicle to return to ¾ inch of the original position could be due to improper adjustment of the height sensor.

COMPRESSOR

Testing

The following test can be performed with the compressor either on the vehicle or on the bench.

1. Disconnect the wiring from the compressor motor and the exhaust solenoid terminals.

2. Disconnect the existing pressure line from the dryer and attach pressure gauge J-22124A or equivalent to the dryer fitting.

3. Connect a 12 volt (+) power supply to the compressor through an ammeter and note the following:

 a. Current draw should not exceed 14 amps.

 b. When the gauge reads approximately 100 psi minimum, shut off the compressor and note if pressure is maintained or it leaks down (allow pressure to stabilize).

 c. If the compressor is permitted to run until it reaches maximum output pressure of 120–150 psi, the solenoid exhaust valve will act as a pressure relief valve. The resulting leak down when the compressor is shut off will indicate a false leak.

HEIGHT SENSOR

Testing

1. Turn the ignition off then on. This will reset the height sensor timer circuitry to the 3 ½ minute maximum run time.

2. Raise and support the vehicle safely.

NOTE: Be sure that the rear wheels or the axle housing are supported as close as possible to the trim height dimension. Inspect the wiring for proper connections along with the harness ground.

3. Disconnect the link from the height sensor arm.

4. Move the sensor arm up. There should be a 7–15 second delay before the compressor begins operating and the air shocks inflate. As soon as the air shock begin to fill, stop the compressor by moving the sensor arm downward.

5. Move the sensor arm down below the position where the compressor stopped. There should be a 7–15 second delay before the shocks are able to be deflated.

6. Reconnect the link to the height sensor arm before making any adjustments.

TRIM HEIGHT

Adjustment

NOTE: The link must be attached to the metal arm when making the adjustment.

1. Loosen the locknut securing the metal arm to the height sensor plastic arm.

2. To increase the vehicle trim height, move the black plastic actuator arm upward to the top of slot and tighten the locknut.

3. To lower the vehicle trim height, follow Step 1 and move the plastic arm downward to the bottom of the slot.

NOTE: If all the adjustments are used, inspect the vehicle for proper trim height.

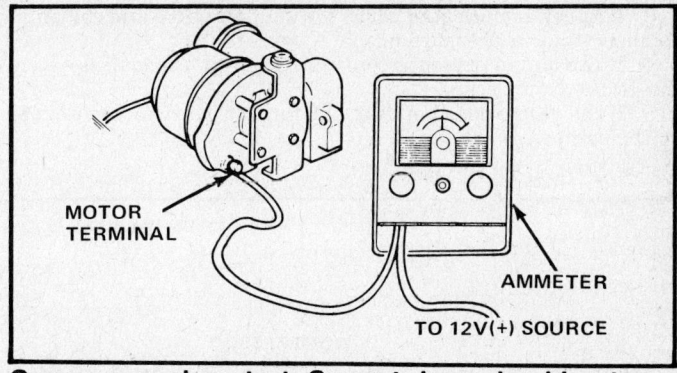

Compressor draw test. Current draw should not exceed 14 amps (© American Motors Corp.)

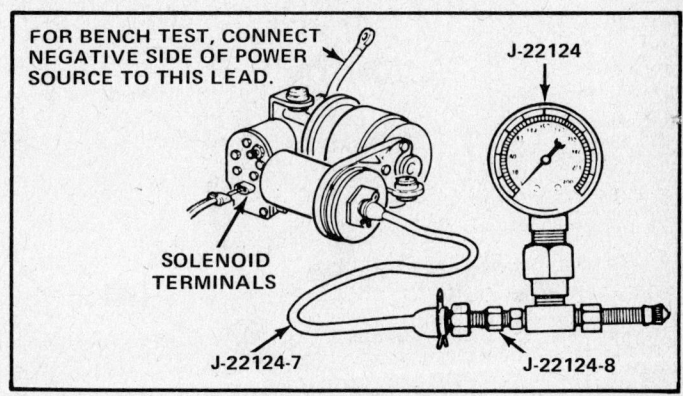

Compressor pressure test (© American Motors Corp.)

SYSTEM LEAK

Testing

1. Connect pressure gauge J-22124-A or equivalent into the system between the dryer and the system air line. Make sure that the shut off valve is on the compressor side of the gauge.

2. With the shut off valve open, apply air pressure through the service valve on the gauge until a reading of 100–120 is obtained.

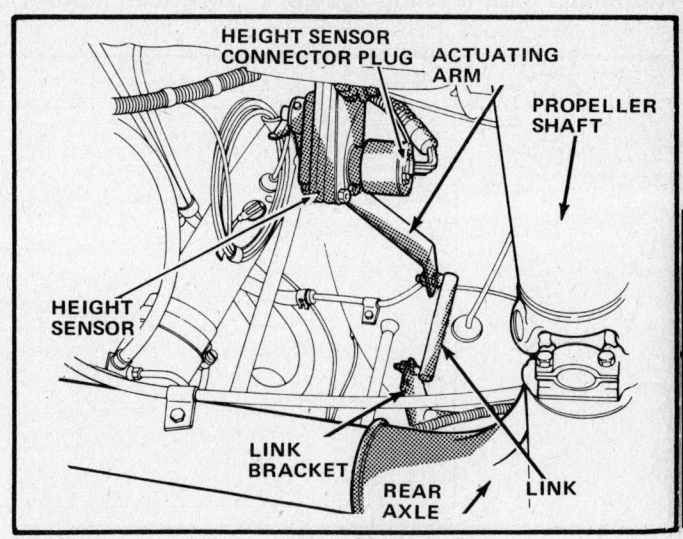

Height sensor (© American Motors Corp.)

35-15

SECTION 35
SUSPENSIONS
REAR SUSPENSION—AMERICAN MOTORS

3. If a leak is indicated, close the shut off valve and continue to observe for a pressure drop.
4. If the gauge pressure continues to drop, the leak is external to the compressor.
5. If the gauge does not drop any further, the leak is internal to the compressor.

Component Replacement
COMPRESSOR

Removal and Installation

1. Bleed air from the system.

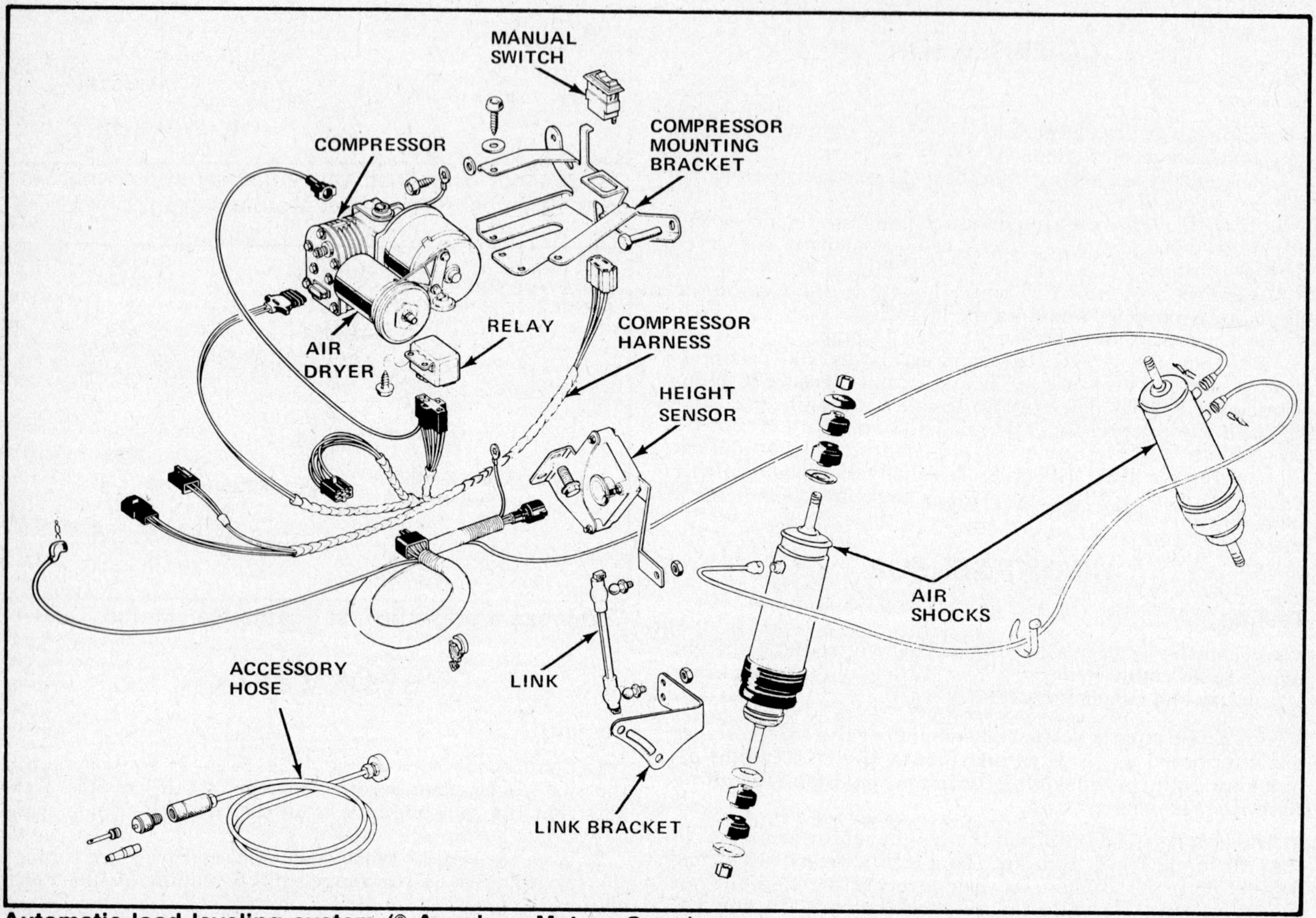

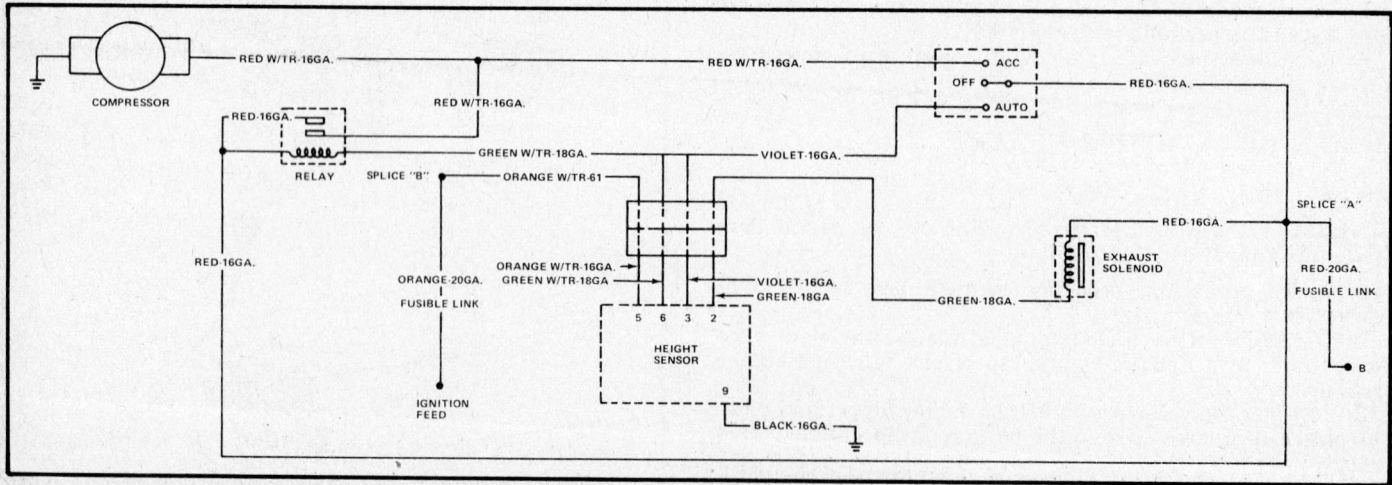

Automatic load leveling system (© American Motors Corp.)

Wiring diagram—automatic load leveling system (© American Motors Corp.)

SUSPENSIONS
REAR SUSPENSION—AMERICAN MOTORS

2. Disconnect the air line at the compressor air dryer.
3. Tag and disconnect electrical connections from the compressor.
4. Remove the compressor mounting bolts. Remove the compressor assembly from the vehicle.
5. Installation is the reverse of the removal procedure. Check compressor for proper operation.

HEIGHT SENSOR

Removal

1. Disconnect connector plug from sensor.
2. Disconnect link from sensor actuating arm.
3. Remove bolts attaching height sensor to underbody and remove sensor.

Installation

1. Position height sensor on underbody and install sensor attaching bolts.
2. Connect sensor actuating arm to link.
3. Connect wiring harness connector plug to height sensor.

NOTE: Due to the diagnostic complexity of the Automatic Load Levelling System, detailed diagnostic procedures can be found in Chilton's Chassis Electronic Service Manual.

FRONT SUSPENSION—CHRYLSER FRONT DRIVE CARS

Alignment

PRE–ALIGNMENT CHECK

There are six factors which are the foundation to front wheel alignment: Height, caster, camber, toe-in, steering axis inclination and toe-out on turns. Of these six basic factors, only camber and toe are mechanically adjustable.

1. Before any attempt is made to change or correct the wheel alignment, inspection and necessary corrections must be made on those parts which influence the steering of the vehicle.
2. Check and inflate tires to recommended pressures.
3. Check front wheel and tire assembly for radial runout.
4. Check struts (shock absorbers for extra-stiff, notchy or spongy operation.
5. Front suspension should be checked only after vehicle has the recommended tire pressures, full tank of fuel, no passenger or luggage compartment load and is on a level floor or alignment rack.
6. To obtain accurate reading, vehicle should be jounced in the following manner just prior to taking measurement. Grasp bumpers at center (rear bumper first) and jounce up and down several times. Always release bumpers at bottom of down cycle after jouncing both rear and front ends an equal number of times.

Camber Adjustment

1. Loosen cam and through bolts (each side).
2. Rotate upper cam bolt to move upper (knuckle and) wheel in or out to specified camber.
3. Tighten bolts to 85 ft. lbs. (115 Nm).

Toe Adjustment

1. Center steering wheel and hold with steering wheel clamp.
2. Loosen tie rod locknuts. Rotate rods to align toe to specifications.

Front Wheel Bearings

The vehicle is equipped with permanently sealed front wheel bearings. There is no periodic lubrication, maintenance, or adjustment recommended for these units.

Service repair or replacement of front drive bearing, hub, brake dust shield or knuckle will require assembly removal from the vehicle.

Strut Damper Assembly

Removal

1. Raise the vehicle and support safely. Remove wheel and tire assembly.
2. Remove cam adjusting bolt, through bolt and brake hose-to-damper bracket retaining screw.
3. Remove strut damper-to-fender shield mounting nut washer assemblies.

Disassembly

1. Compress coil with spring compressor tool.
2. Hold strut rod while loosening strut rod nut. Remove nut.
3. Remove retainers and bushings.
4. Remove coil spring.

NOTE: Mark spring for replacement in original position.

5. Check retainers for cracks or distortion.
6. Check bearings for binding. Check that they contain an adequate supply of lubricant.

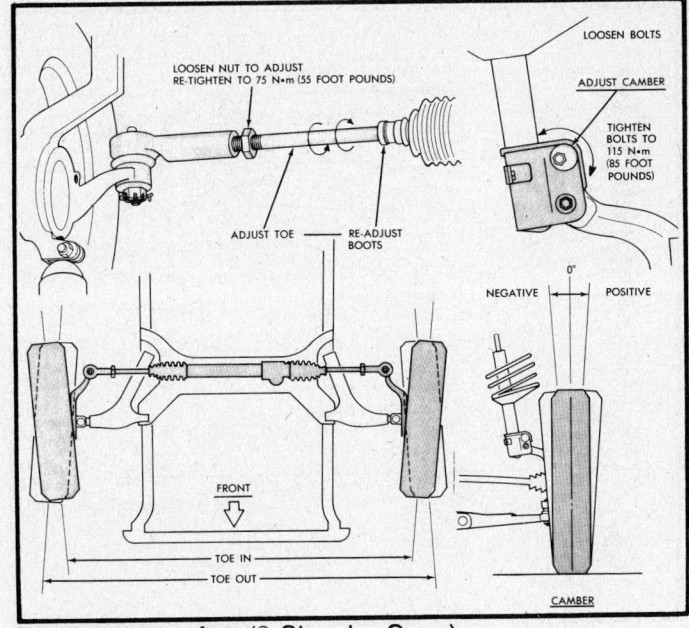

Front suspension (© Chrysler Corp.)

SECTION 35
SUSPENSIONS
FRONT SUSPENSION—CHRYSLER FRONT DRIVE CARS

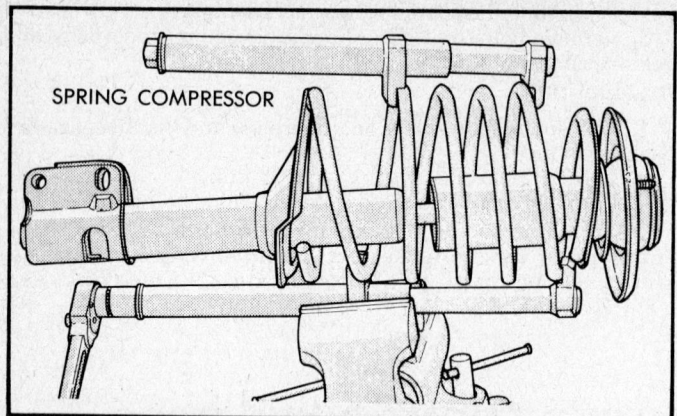
Compressor coil springs (© Chrysler Corp.)

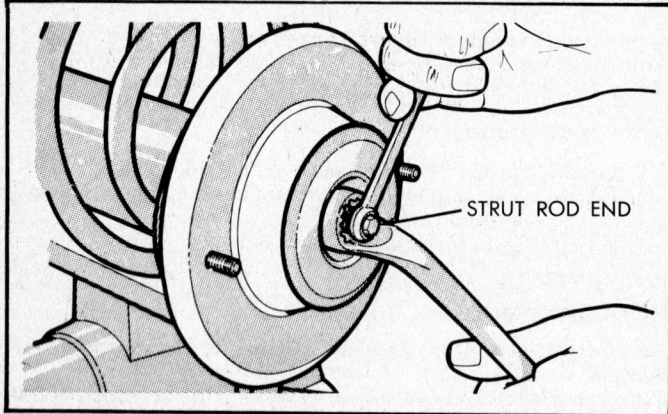
Loosening strut rod nut (© Chrysler Corp.)

Assembly

1. Reassemble and hold strut rod while tightening rod nut to 55 ft. lbs. (81 Nm).

NOTE: Perform Step 1 before releasing spring compressor tool.

2. Release spring compressor tool.

NOTE: Springs are rated separately for each side of vehicle depending on optional equipment and type of service.

During assembly of spring to strut damper, ensure that coil end is seated in strut damper spring seat recess.

Installation

1. Install unit into fender reinforcement and install retaining nut and washer assemblies. Torque to 27 ft. lbs. (20 Nm).
2. Position knuckle leg into strut and install upper (cam) and lower through bolts.
3. Attach brake hose retainer to damper; tighten screw to 10 ft. lbs. (12 Nm).
4. Index cam bolt to original mark and tighten bolts to 85 ft. lbs. (110 Nm) torque.
5. Install wheel and tire assembly. Tighten wheel nuts to 80 ft. lbs. (108 Nm).

Lower Ball Joint

Inspection

The lower ball joint is checked at the lube fitting. Try to turn the lube fitting. If it turns or wobbles, the ball joint is worn and should be replaced.

Removal and Installation

NOTE: On some models, the front ball joints are welded to the control arms and are not to be pressed out. Those that are welded must be serviced by complete replacement of the control arm and ball joint assembly.

1. Pry off seal.
2. Position a receiving cup tool C-4699-2 or equivalent to support the lower control arm.
3. Install a 1 1/16 in. deep socket over the stud and against the joint upper housing.
4. Press the joint assembly from the arm.
5. To install, position the ball joint housing into the control arm cavity.
6. Position the assembly in a press with installer tool C-4699-1 or equivalent supporting the control arm.
7. Align the ball joint assembly then press it until the housing ledge stops against the control arm cavity down flange.
8. To install a new seal, support the ball joint housing with installing tool C-4699-2 or equivalent and position a new seal over the stud against the housing.
9. With a 1 1/2 socket, press the seal onto the joint housing with the seat against the control arm.

Lower Control Arm

Removal

1. Remove front inner pivot through bolt.
2. Remove rear stub strut nut, retainer and bushing.
3. Remove ball joint-to-steering knuckle clamp bolt.
4. Seperate ball joint stud from steering knuckle.

Pivot Bushing Replacement

1. Position support tool between flanges of lower control arm and around bushing to prevent control arm distortion.
2. Install 1/2 X 2 1/2 in. bolt into bushing.
3. With receiving cup on press base, position control arm inner flange against cup wall to support flange while receiving bushing.

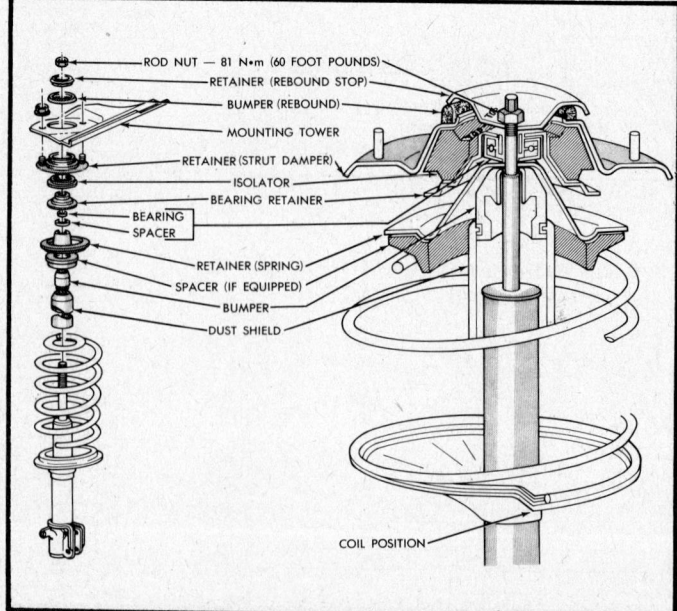
Upper spring retainer assembly (© Chrysler Corp.)

SUSPENSIONS
FRONT SUSPENSION—CHRYSLER FRONT DRIVE CARS

SECTION 35

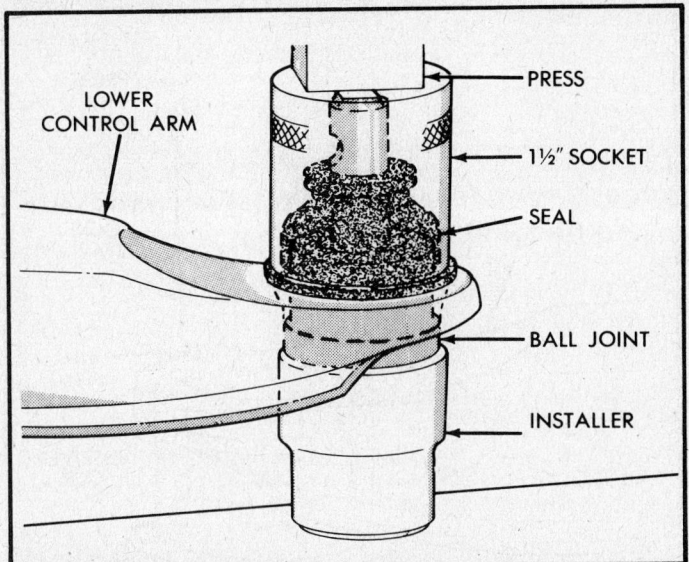
Ball joint seal installation (© Chrysler Corp.)

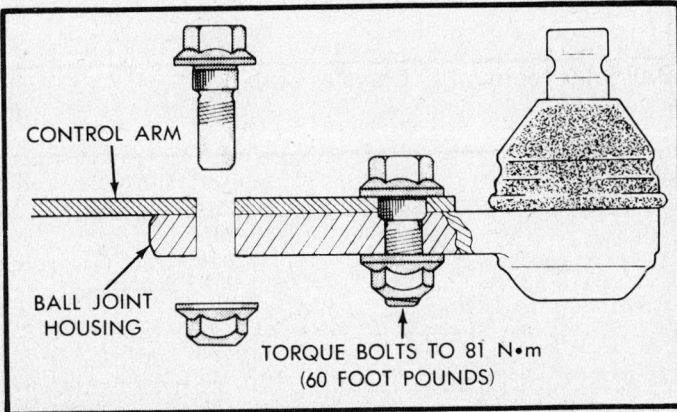
Ball joint bolted to lower control arm (© Chrysler Corp.)

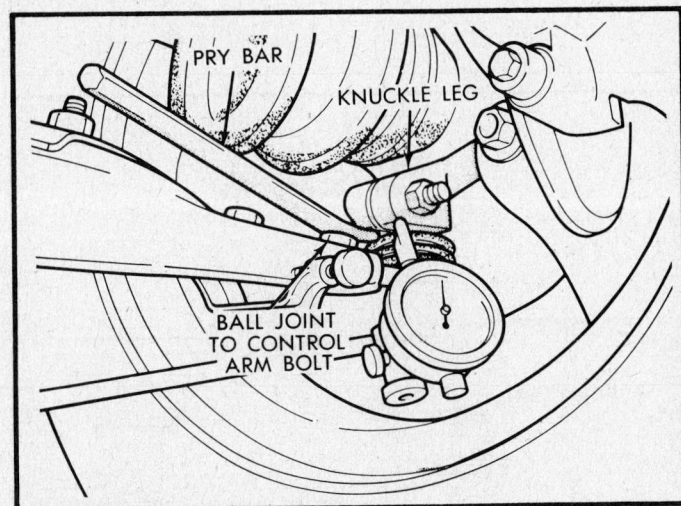
Checking ball joint for excessive clearance, using a dial indicator (© Chrysler Corp.)

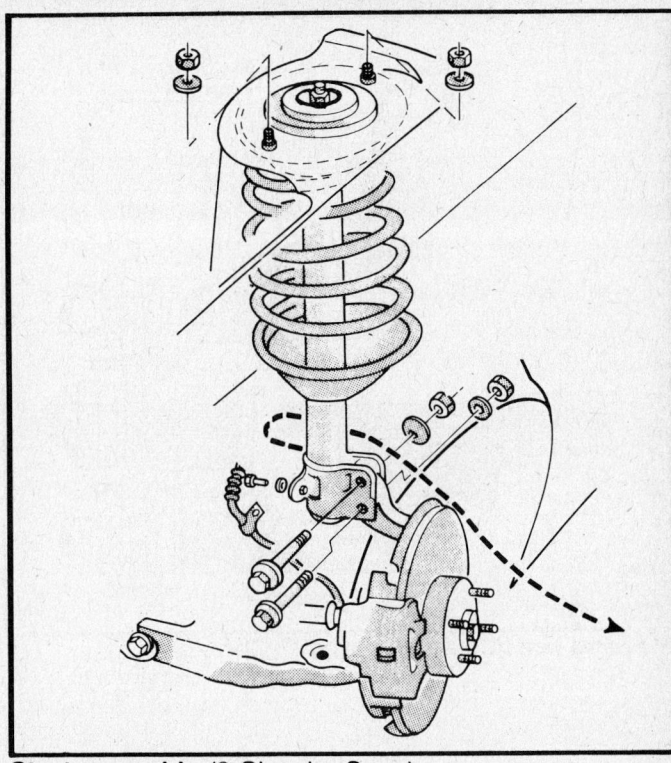
Strut assembly (© Chrysler Corp.)

4. Remove bushing by pressing against bolt head.
5. To install, position support tool between flanges of control arm.
6. Install bushing inner sleeve and insulator into installer tool C–4699–1 or equivalent cavity with the bushing outer shell flange against the tool wall. Position assembly onto press base and align control arm to receive bushing.

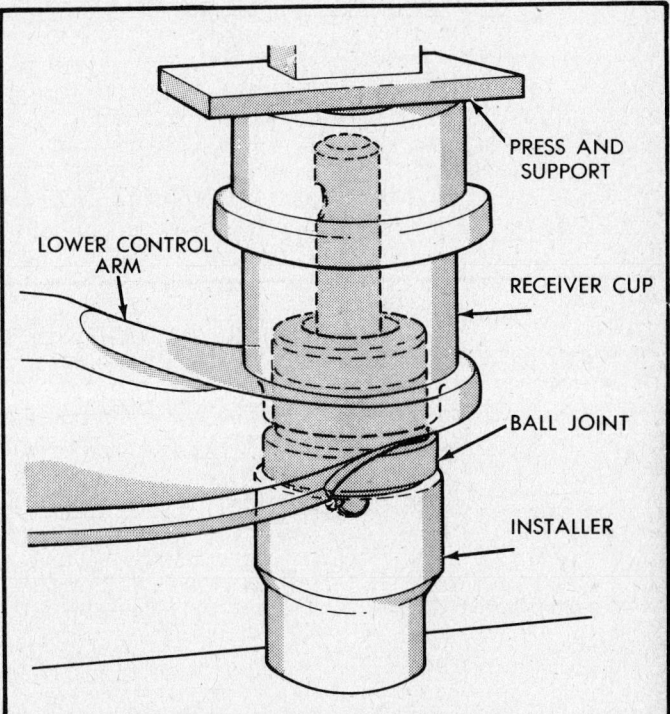
Ball joint assembly (© Chrysler Corp.)

35-19

SECTION 35

SUSPENSIONS
FRONT SUSPENSION—CHRYSLER FRONT DRIVE CARS

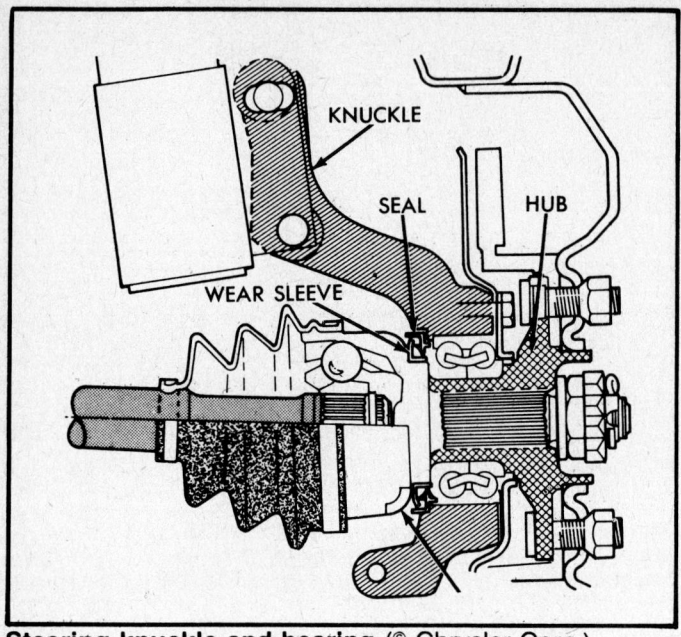

Steering knuckle and bearing (© Chrysler Corp.)

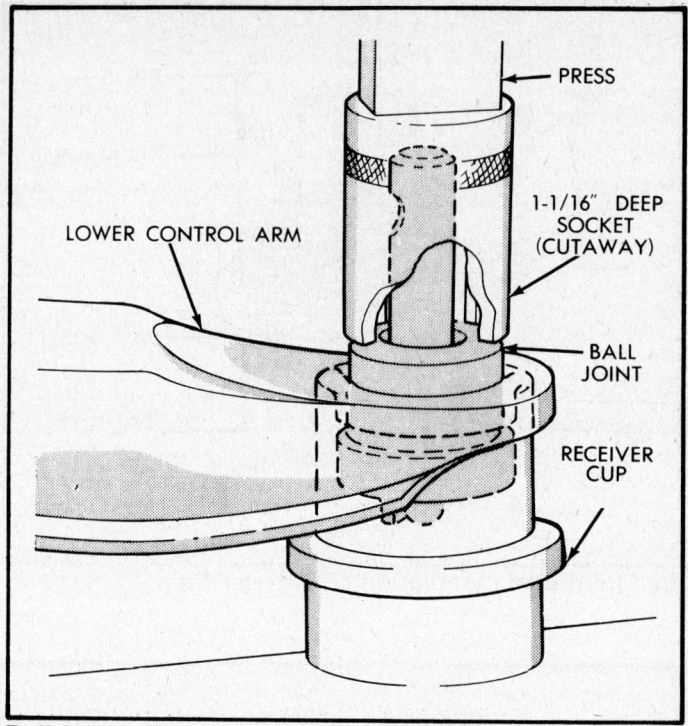

Ball joint removal (© Chrysler Corp.)

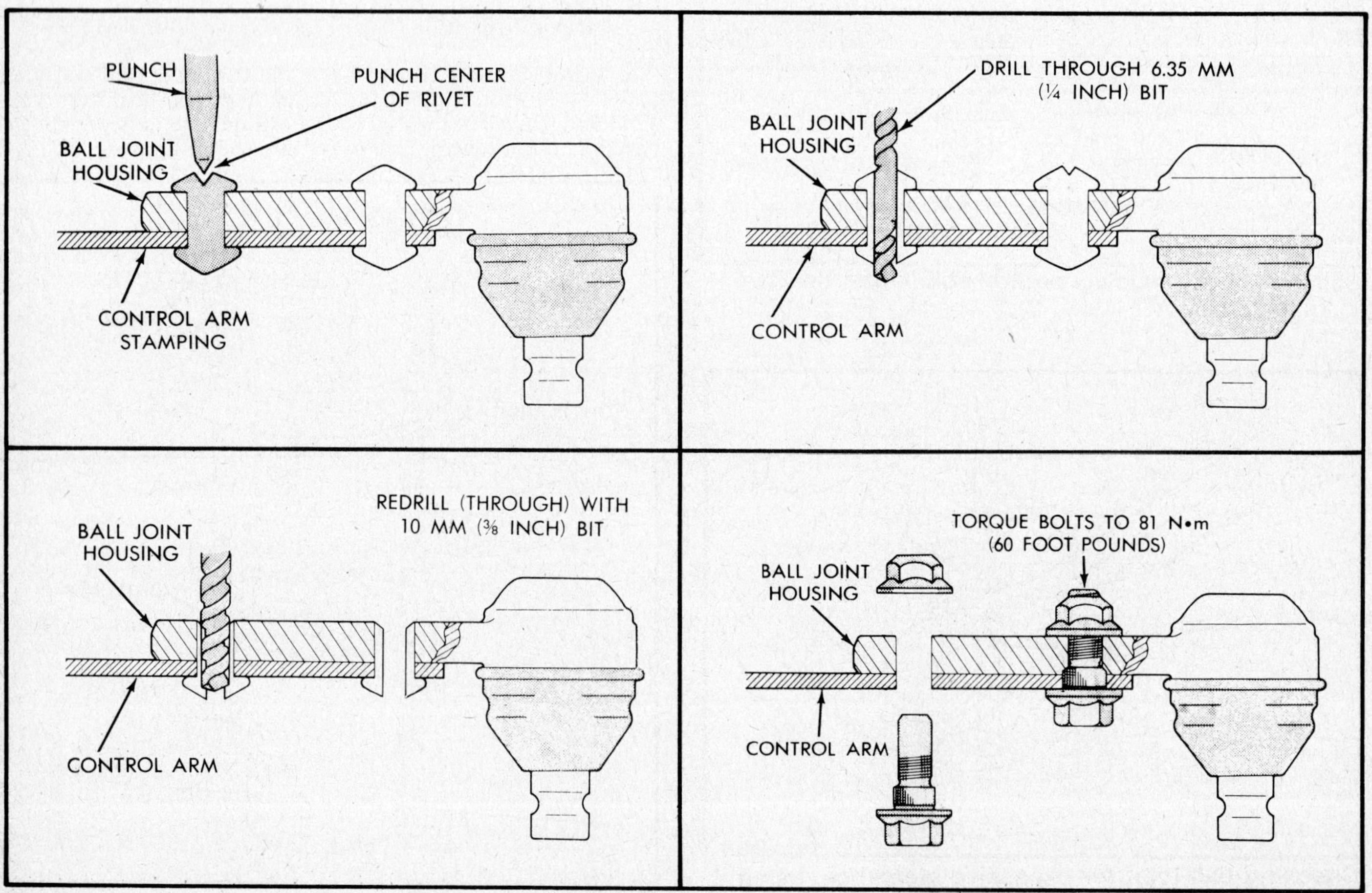

Ball joint replacement (© Chrysler Corp.)

35-20

SUSPENSIONS
FRONT SUSPENSION—CHRYSLER FRONT DRIVE CARS

SECTION 35

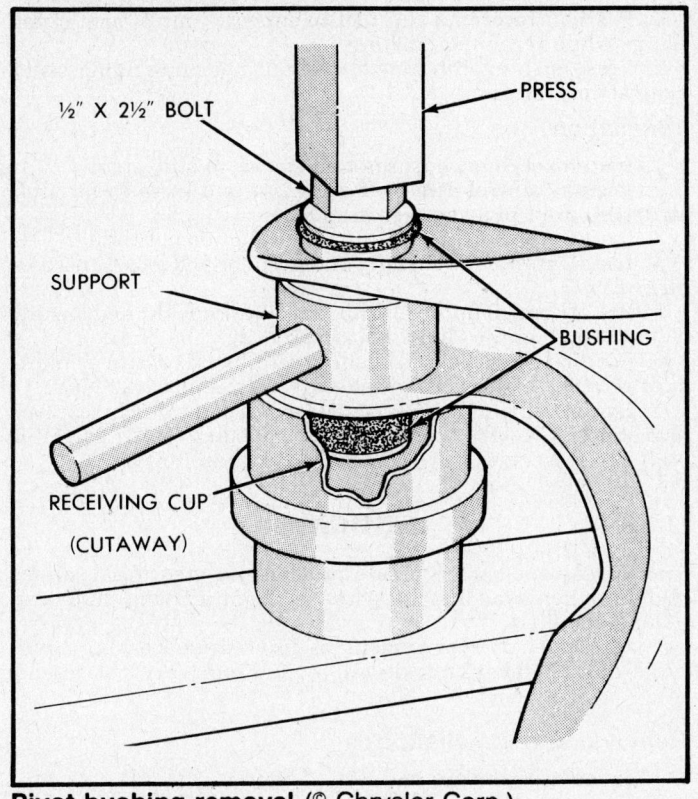

Pivot bushing removal (© Chrysler Corp.)

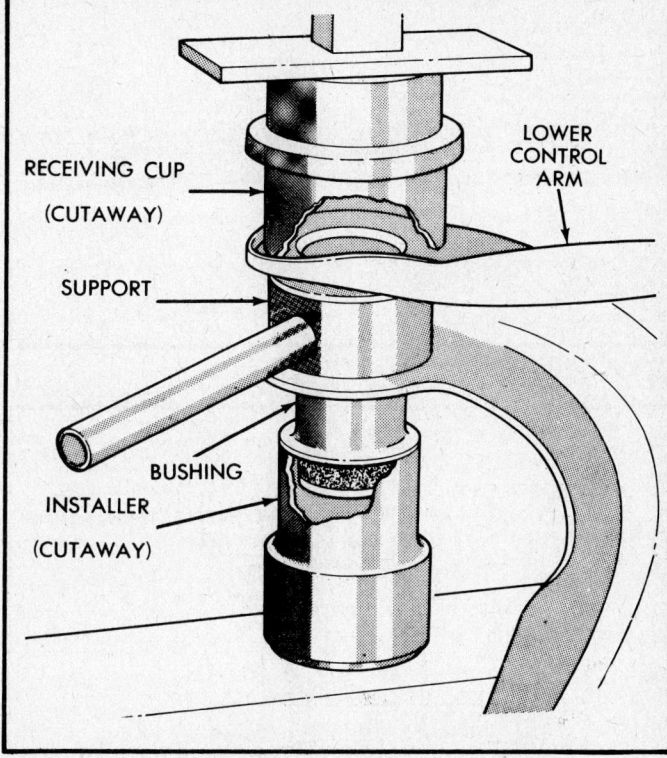

Pivot bushing installation (© Chrysler Corp.)

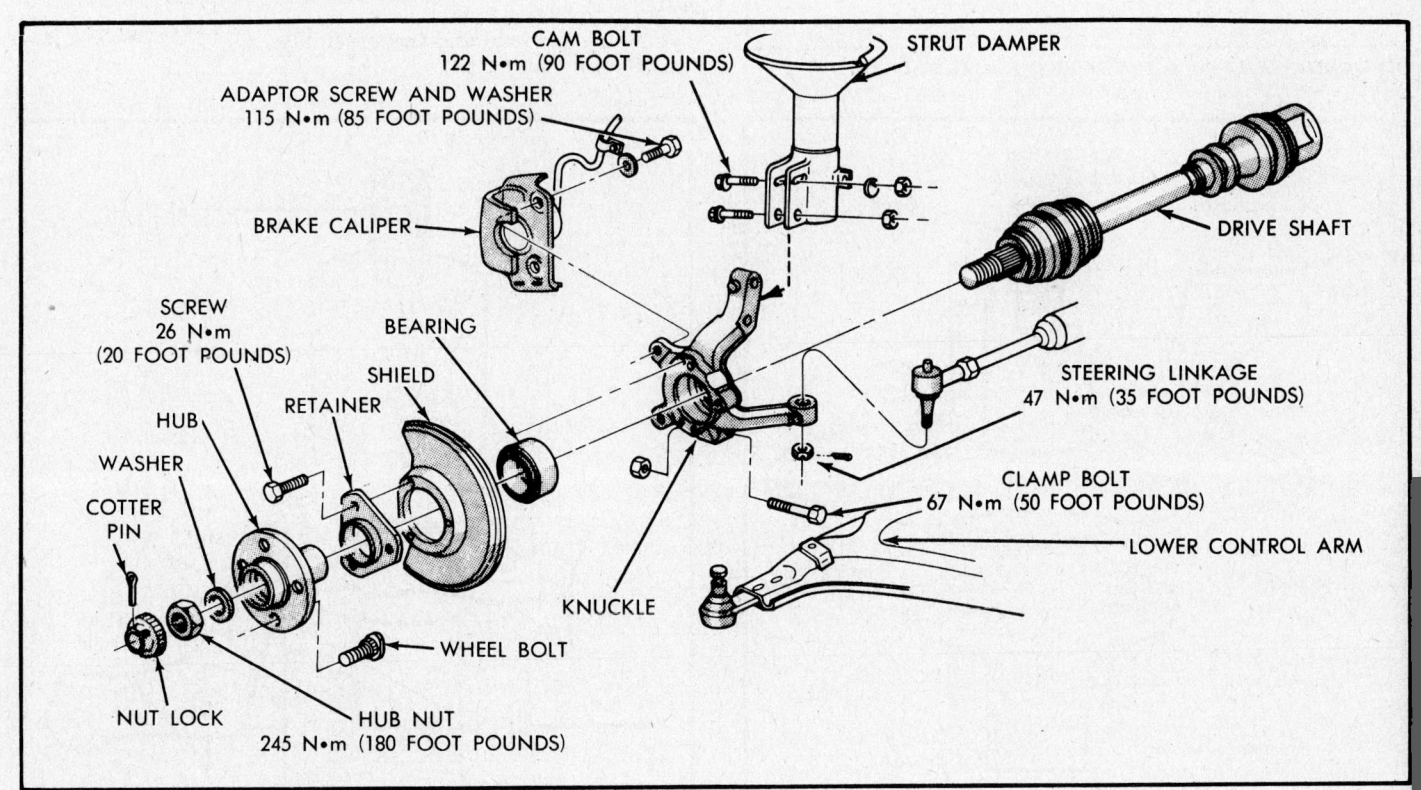

Front suspension knuckle (© Chrysler Corp.)

35-21

SECTION 35 SUSPENSIONS
FRONT SUSPENSION—CHRYSLER FRONT DRIVE CARS

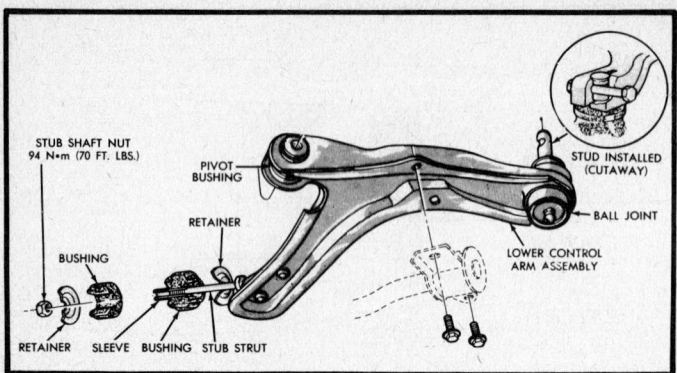

Lower control arm (© Chrysler Corp.)

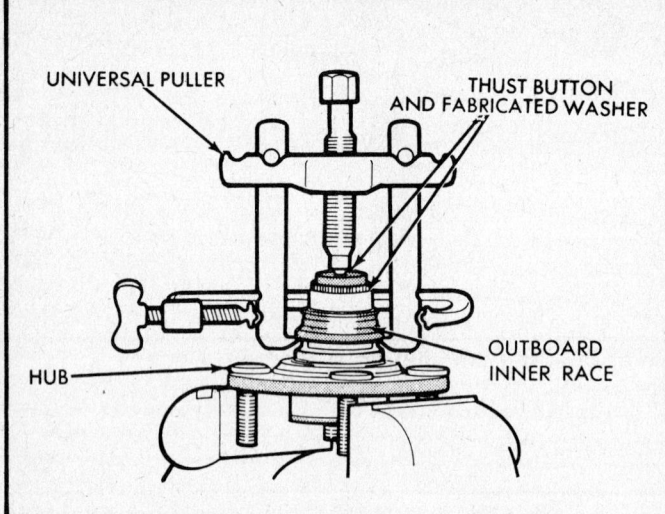

Outboard inner race removal (© Chrysler Corp.)

7. Position receiving cup tool to support control arm outer flange while receiving bushing.
8. Press bushing into control arm until bushing flange seats against control arm.

Installation

1. Install retainer, bushing and sleeve on stub strut.
2. Positon control arm over sway bar and install rear stub strut and front pivot into crossmember.
3. Install front pivot bolt; install nut but do not tighten yet.
4. Install stub strut bushing and retainer and loosely assemble nut.
5. Install ball joint stud into steering knuckle and install clamp bolt. Tighten clamp bolt to 50 ft. lbs. (67 Nm).
6. Position sway bar end bushing retainer to control arm. Install retainer bolts and tighten nuts to 22 ft. lbs. (30 Nm).
7. Lower vehicle. With suspension support vehicle (control arm at design height) tighten front pivot bolt to 100 ft. lbs. (135 Nm) and stub strut nut to 70 ft. lbs. (94 Nm) torque.

Knuckle

The front suspension knuckle provides for steering, braking and alignment and also supports the front (driving) hub (and axle) assembly.
Service repair or replacement of front drive bearing, hub, brake dust shield or knuckle will require removal of the assembly from the vehicle.

Removal and Installation

1. Remove cotter pin and lock.
2. Loosen hub nut while vehicle is on the floor and brakes applied.

NOTE: The hub and driveshaft are splined together through the knuckle (bearing) and retained by the hub nut.

3. Remove wheel and tire assembly.
4. Remove hub nut.

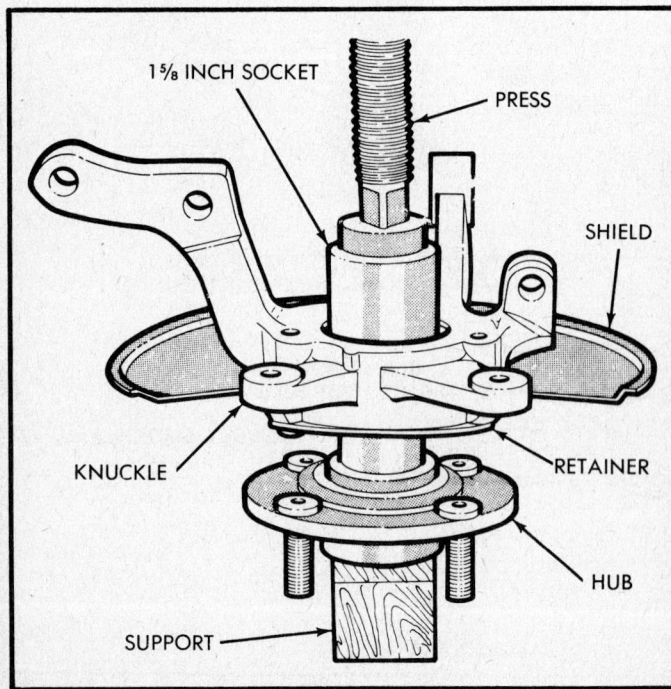

Pressing hub into knuckle bearing (© Chrysler Corp.)

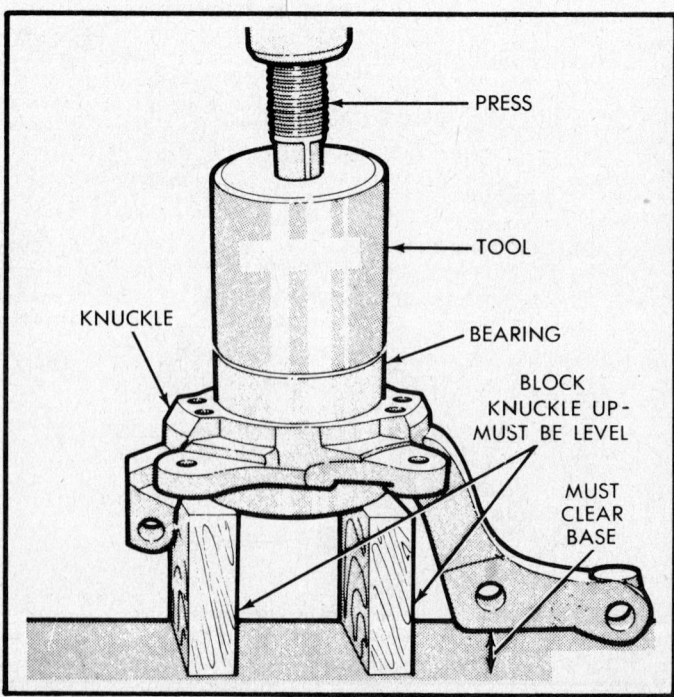

Pressing new bearing into knuckle (© Chrysler Corp.)

SUSPENSIONS
FRONT SUSPENSION—CHRYSLER FRONT DRIVE CARS

CAUTION
Ensure that splined driveshaft is "free" to separate from spline in hub during knuckle removal from vehicle. A pulling force on the shaft can separate the inner universal joint. Tap lightly with soft brass punch if required.

5. Disconnect tie rod end from steering arm.
6. Disconnect brake hose retainer from strut damper.
7. Remove clamp bolt securing ball joint stud into steering knuckle. Remove brake caliper adaptor screw and washer assemblies.
8. Support caliper with wire hook. Do not allow assembly to hang by brake hose.
9. Remove braking disc (rotor).
10. Mark camber position on upper cam adjusting bolt. Loosen both bolts.
11. To remove assembly from vehicle, support knuckle and remove cam adjusting and through bolts, then move upper knuckle "leg" out of strut damper bracket and lift knuckle off of ball joint stud.

CAUTION
Support driveshaft during knuckle removal. Do not allow driveshaft to "hang" after separating steering knuckle from vehicle (severe angles will damage inboard universal joint boot).

12. Installation is the reverse of the removal operation.

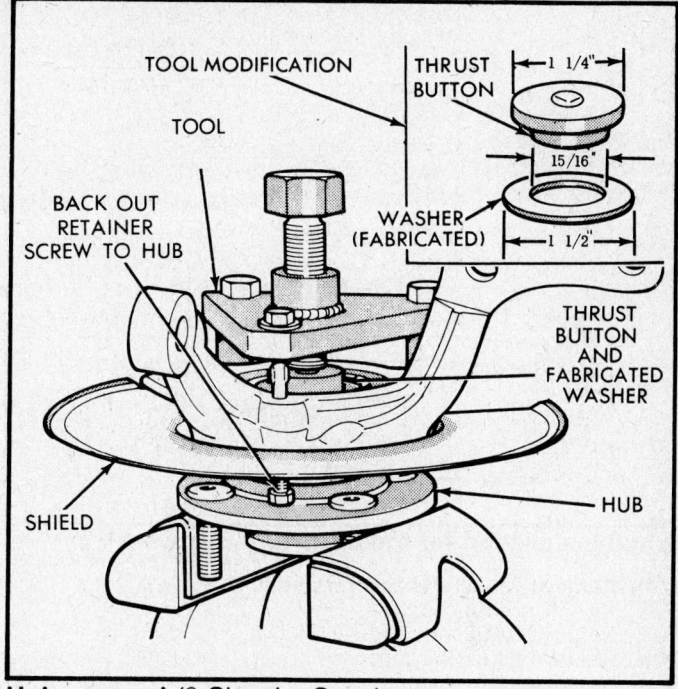
Hub removal (© Chrysler Corp.)

Hub And Bearing

Removal and Installation
NOTE: Do not reuse bearing.

1. Remove hub (out of bearing) with hub remover tool and fabricated washer.
   a. Place washer and thrust button on hub.
   b. Back out one retainer screw-to-hub, as far as it will go.
   c. Position tool and install two screws firmly into tapped brake adaption extensions and one screw into retaining screw threads.
   d. Tighten press screw to remove hub through bearing.

NOTE: Bearing inner races will separate; outboard race will stay on hub.

2. Remove bearing outer race from hub with thrust button from tool and universal puller.
3. Remove brake dust shield and bearing retainer.
4. Installation is the reverse of the removal procedure.

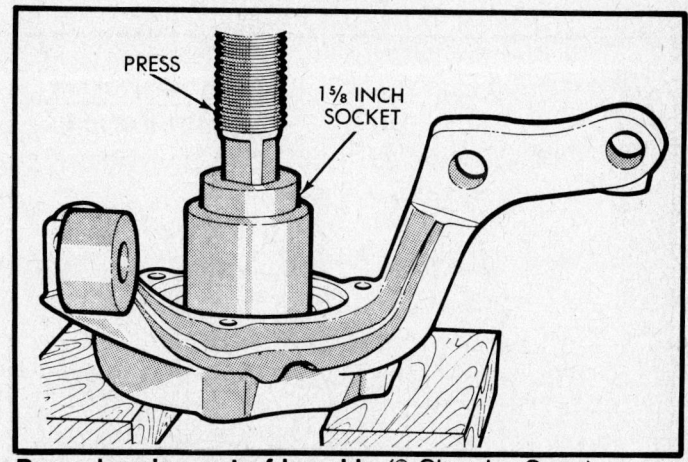
Press bearing out of knuckle (© Chrysler Corp.)

REAR SUSPENSION—CHRYLSER FRONT DRIVE CARS

General Information

Chrysler front drive cars have two types of rear suspension systems. A semi-independent rear suspension which is used on "L" body cars (Omni, Horizon) and a trailing arm solid axle design used on "K" cars (Aries, Reliant), "E" cars (Caravelle, 600, New Yorker), "G" cards (Daytona, Laser, and "H" cars (Lancer, LeBaron GTS). The suspensions are similar, although certain service procedures are varied.

Alignment
ALL MODELS

Because of the trailing arm rear suspension of the vehicle, and the incorporation of stub axles or wheel spindles, it is possible to align both the camber and toe of the rear wheels. Alignment is controlled by adding shim stock of 0.010 in. thickness between the spindle mounting surface and spindle mounting plate.

If rear wheel alignment is required, place vehicle on alignment rack and check alignment specifications. Follow equipment manufacturer's recommendations for their equipment. Maintain rear alignment within Chrylser corporation recommendations.

Installation of Rear Alignment Shims

1. Block front tires so vehicle will not move.
2. Release parking brake.
3. Hoist vehicle so that rear suspension is in full rebound and tires are off the ground.

SECTION 35

SUSPENSIONS
REAR SUSPENSION—CHRYSLER FRONT DRIVE CARS

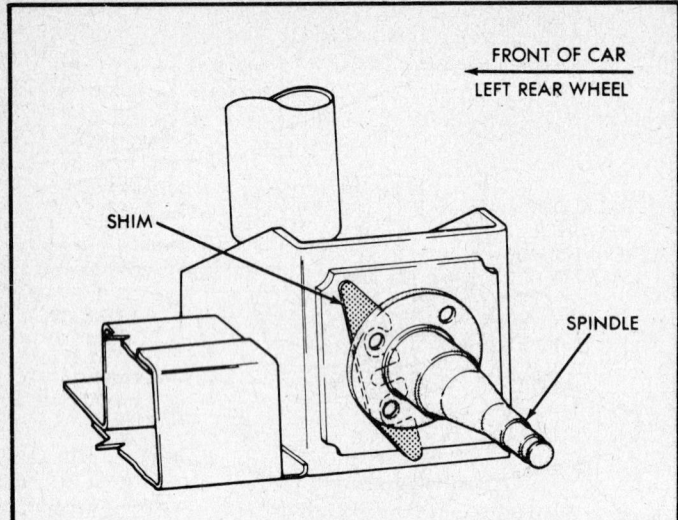

Shim installation for toe out (© Chrysler Corp.)

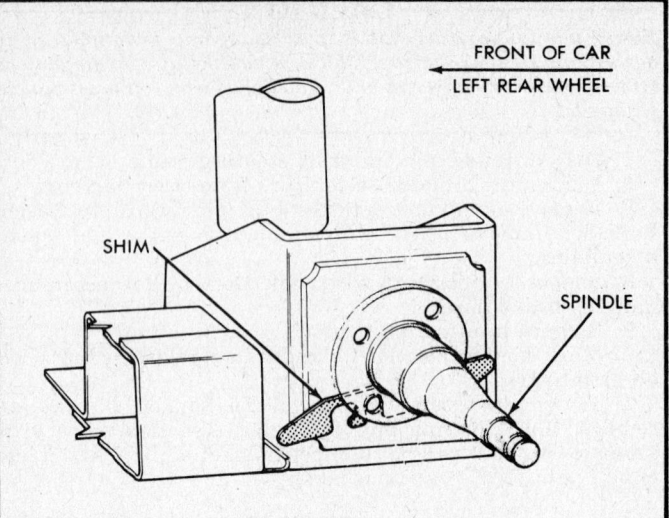

Shim installation for negative camber (© Chrysler Corp.)

4. Remove wheel and tire assembly.
5. Pry off grease cap.
6. Remove cotter pin and castle lock.
7. Remove adjusting nut.
8. Remove brake drum.
9. Loosen the brake assembly and spindle mounting bolts enough to allow clearance for shim installation.

NOTE: Do not remove mounting bolts.

10. Install shims for desired wheel change.

NOTE: Wheel alignment changes by 0.3° per shim.

11. Tighten four brake assembly and spindle mounting bolts. Tighten to 45 ft. lbs. (60 Nm) torque.
12. Install brake drum.
13. Install washer and nut. Tighten adjusting nut to 20–25 ft. lbs. (27–34 Nm) while rotating wheel. Back off adjusting nut with wrench to completely release bearing preload. Finger tighten the adjusting nut.
14. Position nut lock with one pair of slots in line with cotter pin hole. Install cotter pin. The end play should be 0.001–0.003 in. (0.025–0.076 mm). Clean and install grease cap.
15. Install wheel and tire assembly. Tighten wheel nuts to 80 ft. lbs. (108 Nm) torque.
16. Lower vehicle.
17. Recheck alignment specifications.

Wheel Bearings

"L" BODY CARS

Lubrication

The lubricant in the wheel bearings should be inspected whenever the drums are removed to inspect or service the brake system, but at least every 22,500 miles (36,000 km). The bearings should be cleaned and repacked with a higher temperature

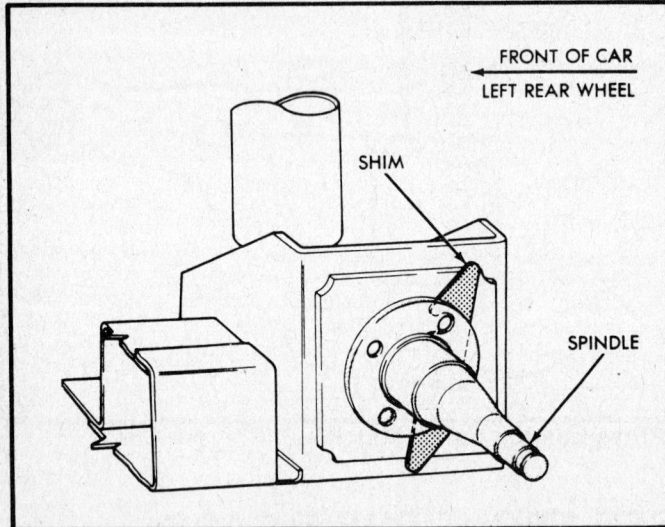

Shim installation for toe in (© Chrysler Corp.)

CHRYSLER CORP.

	CV	E	G	H	K	KC	L	M	S
PLYMOUTH		Caravelle			Reliant		Horizon Turismo	Gran Fury	Voyager
DODGE	600 Convertible	600	Daytona	Lancer	Aries		Omni Charger	Diplomat	Caravan
CHRYSLER		LeBaron	New Yorker	Laser	LeBaron GTS		Limo	Fifth Avenue	

SUSPENSIONS
REAR SUSPENSION—CHRYSLER FRONT DRIVE CARS
SECTION 35

REAR WHEEL ALIGNMENT

Model	Acceptable Alignment Range	Preferred Setting
Camber		
Horizon-Turismo, Omni-Charger	−1.25° to −.25° (−1¼ to 1/4)	−.75° ± .5° (1/2)
Reliant-Aries, Caravelle-600-New Yorker, Daytona-Laser, Lancer-LeBaron	−1.0° to 0° (−1° to 0°)	−.5° ± .5° (1/2°)
Toe*		
Horizon-Turismo, Omni-Charger	specified in inches 5/32″ OUT to 11/32″ IN specified in degrees 0.3° OUT to 0.7° IN	3/32″ IN 0.2° IN
Reliant-Aries, Caravelle-600-New Yorker, Daytona-Laser, Lancer-LeBaron	specified in inches 3/16″ OUT to 3/16″ IN specified in degrees 0.50° OUT to 0.50° IN	0″ ± 1/8″ 0° ± .25°

*Toe Out when backed on alignment racks is Toe In when driving

multipurpose E.P. grease whenever the brake drums are resurfaced.

NOTE: Do not add grease to the wheel bearing. Relubricate completely.

Discard the old seal. Thoroughly clean the old lubricant from the bearings and from the hub cavity. Inspect the rollers for signs of pitting or other surface distress. Light bearing discolorations should be considered normal. Bearings must be replaced if any defects exist. Repack the bearings with a high temperature multipurpose E.P. grease. The use of a bearing packet is recommended. A small amount of new grease should also be added to the hub cavity.

Adjustment

1. Install hub assembly on spindle.
2. Install outer bearing, thrust washer and nut.

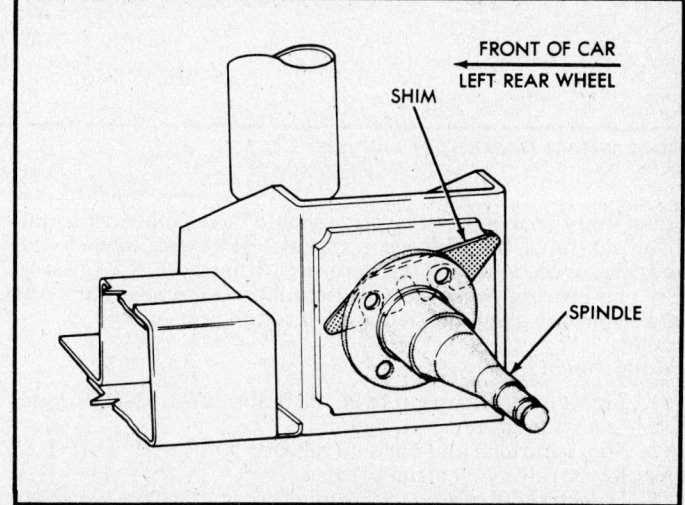

Shim installation for positive camber (© Chrysler Corp.)

3. Tighten wheel bearing adjusting nut to 20–25 ft. lbs. (27–34 Nm) while rotating hub.
4. Back off adjusting nut to release all pre-load, then tighten adjusting nut finer-tight.
5. Position lock on nut with one pair of slots in line with cotter pin hole. Install cotter pin.
6. Install grease cap and wheel and tire assemblies.

"K", "E", "G", "H" BODY CARS

Lubrication

The lubricant in the rear wheel bearings should be inspected wherever the drums are removed to inspect or service the brake system, or at least every 48,000 kilometers (30,000 miles). Bearings should be cleaned and repacked with a high temperature multipurpose E.P. grease whenever the brake drums are resurfaced.

NOTE: Do not add grease to the wheel bearings. Relubricate completely.

Discard the old seal. Thoroughly clean the old lubricant from the bearings and from the hub cavity.

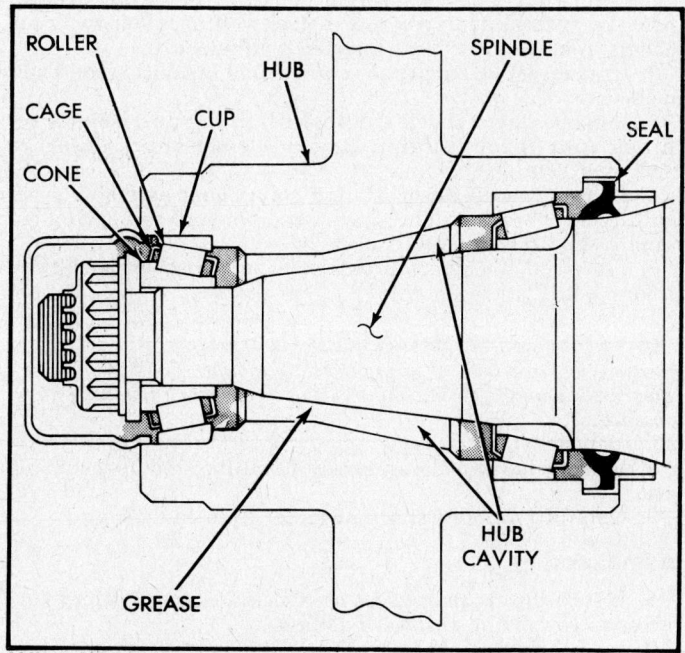

Wheel bearing lubrication (© Chrysler Corp.)

SECTION 35 SUSPENSIONS
REAR SUSPENSION—CHRYSLER FRONT DRIVE CARS

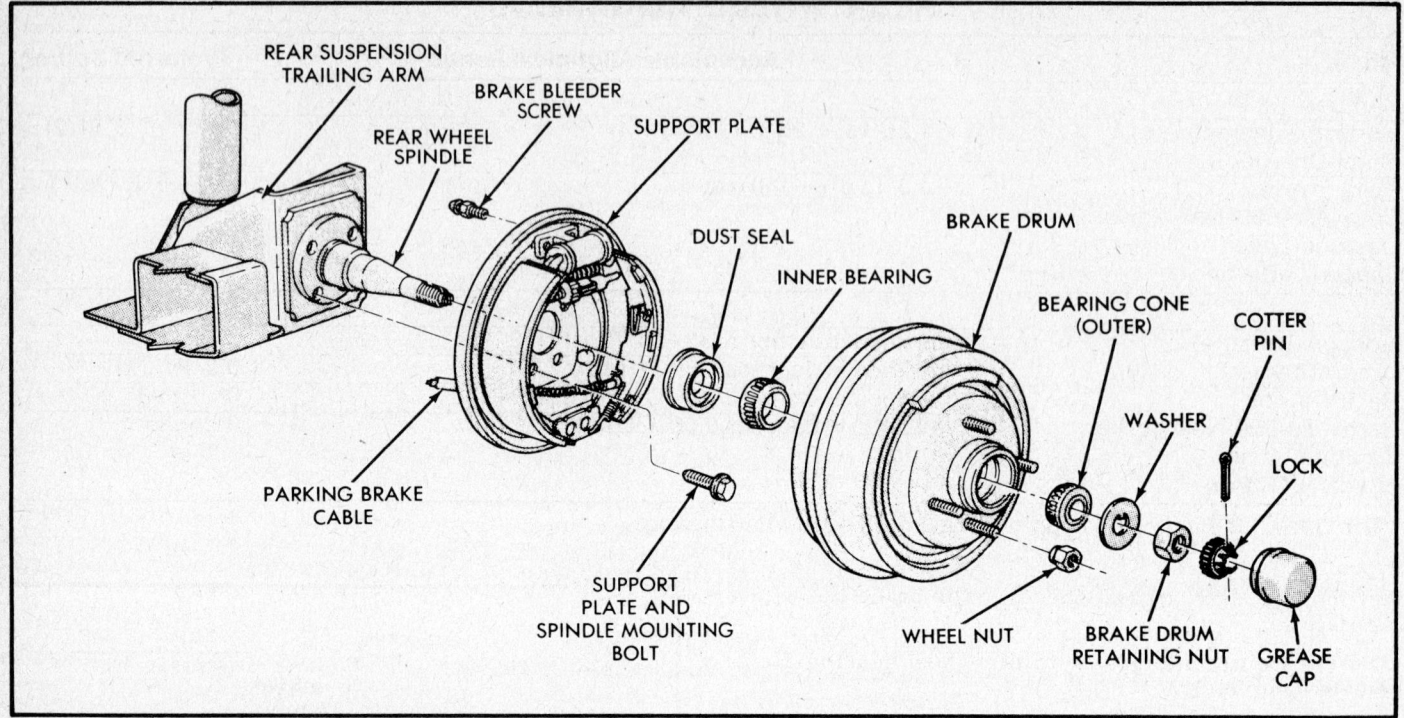

Rear wheel bearing (© Chrysler Corp.)

Inspect the rollers for signs of pitting or other surface distress. Light bearing discoloration should be considered normal. Bearings must be replaced if any defects exist. Repack the bearings with a high temperature multipurpose E.P. grease. Use of a bearing packer is also recommended. A small amount of new grease should also be added to the hub cavity.

Adjustment

1. Tighten adjusting nut to 20–25 ft. lbs. (27–34 Nm) torque, while rotating wheel.
2. Stop rotations and back off adjusting nut with wrench to completely release bearing preload.
3. Finger tighten adjusting nut.
4. Position nut lock with one pair of slots in line with cotter pin hole.
5. Install cotter pin.
6. The end-play should be 0.0012–0.003 in (0.025–0.076mm).

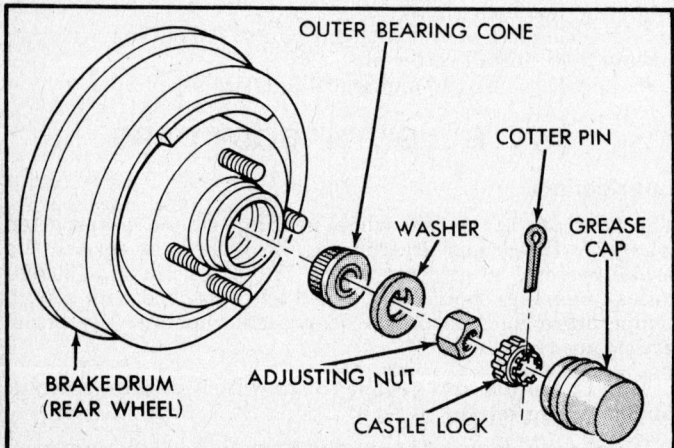

Rear wheel components (© Chrysler Corp.)

7. Clean and install grease cap.
8. Install wheel and tire assembly.

Shock Absorber And Coil Spring Assembly

"L" BODY CARS

Removal

1. Locate upper shock absorber mounting nut protective cap inside of vehicle at upper rear wheel well area (on two-door models, remove lower rear quarter trim panel).
2. Unsnap cap. Use care to retain sound insulation material inside cap.
3. Remove upper shock absorber mounting nut, isolator retainer, and upper isolater. Remove lower shock absorber mounting bolt.
4. Remove shock absorber and coil spring assembly from trailing arm bracket. The shock absorber and coil spring assembly should now be free of vehicle.
5. Place coil spring compressor tool on coil spring and place in vise.

— **CAUTION** —
Always grip 4 or 5 coils of spring in retaining nut. If coil spring is not compressed enough, serious injury could occur when retaining nut is loosened.

8. Remove lower isolator, shock rod sleeve, and upper spring seat.
9. Carefully remove shock absorber from coil spring.

Installation

1. Install lower spring seat on shock absorber. Orient seat recess to centerline of lower bushing.
2. Install dust shield and jounce bumper on shock absorber.
3. Carefully slip the unit inside the coil spring. Install upper

35-26

SUSPENSIONS
REAR SUSPENSION—CHRYSLER FRONT DRIVE CARS
Section 35

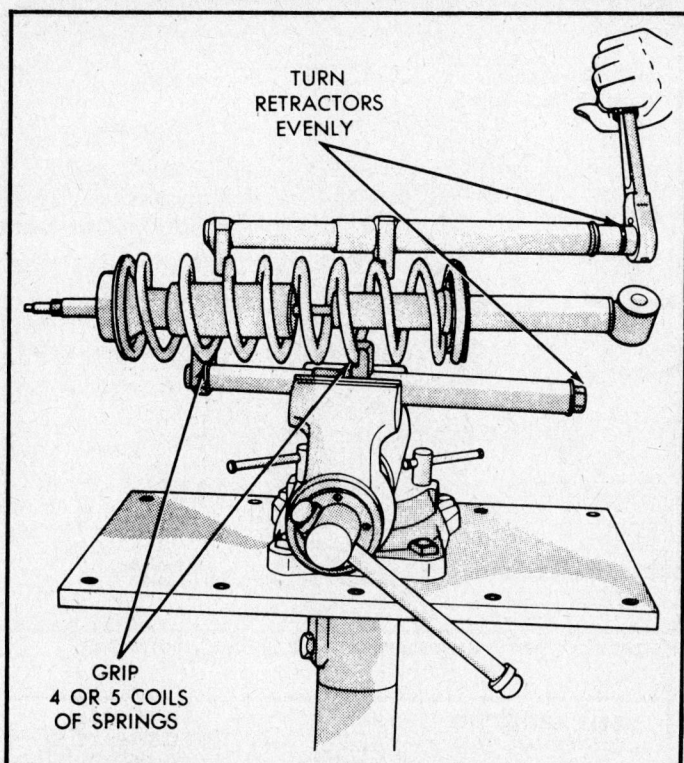

Retract coil spring (© Chrysler Corp.)

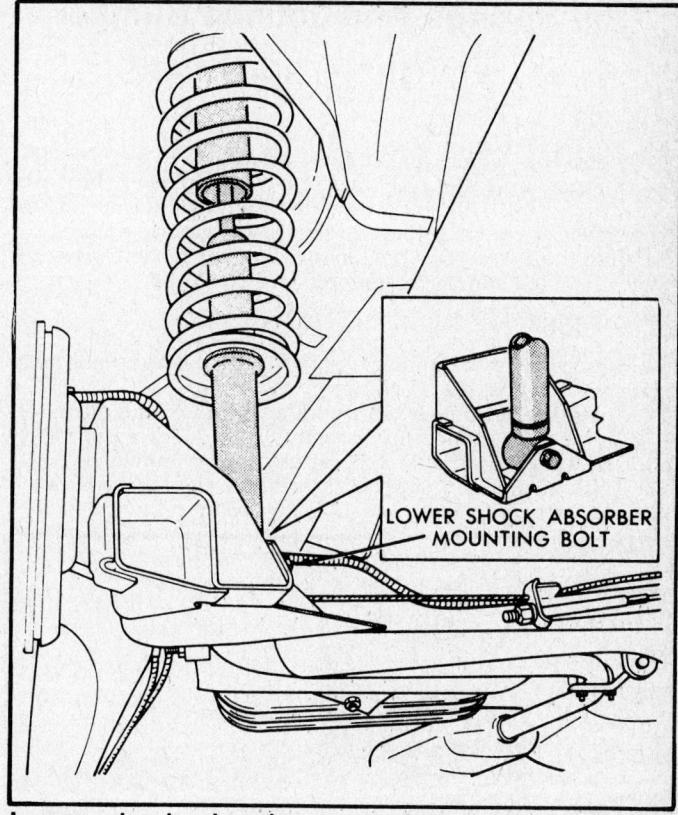

Lower shock absorber mounting bolt (© Chrysler Corp.)

spring seat. Make sure that the leveled surface on both spring seats are in position against the ends of the coil spring.

4. Install sleeve on shock rod. Install retaining nut on end of shock rod. Tighten retaining nut to 20 ft. lbs. (27 Nm) torque.
5. Carefully loosen both coil spring retractors evenly and remove retractors from unit.
6. Install lower end of unit in trailing arm bracket. Insert bolt. Finger tighten only. Make sure that upper end of unit is in proper hole at top of wheel well.
7. Tighten lower shock absorber bolt to 40 ft. lbs. (55 Nm) torque.
8. Install upper isolator, isolator retainer, and upper mounting nut. Hold shock absorber rod end and tighten nut to 20 ft. lbs. (27 Nm) torque.
9. Install sound insulation material and snap protective cap on securely.

Shock Absorbers

"K", "E", "G", "H" BODY CARS

Removal

1. Support axle and remove wheel and tire assembly.
2. Remove upper and lower shock absorber fasteners and remove sock absorbers.

Installation

1. Position shock absorber and install fasteners; loosely assembly lower fastener. Tighten upper fastener to 40 ft. lbs. (54 Nm).
2. Install wheel and tire assembly, tighten wheel stud and nuts to 80 ft. lbs. (108 Nm). Lower vehicle to ground.
3. With suspension supporting vehicle, tighten lower shock absorber fastener to 40 ft. lbs. (54 Nm).

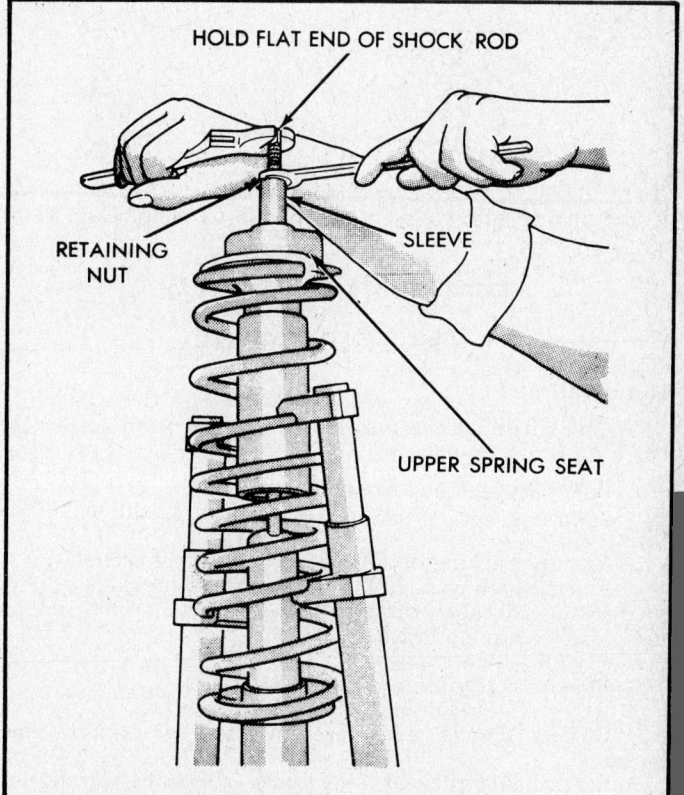

Loosen retaining nut (© Chrysler Corp.)

35-27

SECTION 35 SUSPENSIONS
REAR SUSPENSION—CHRYSLER FRONT DRIVE CARS

Coil Springs And Jounce Bumper

"K", "E", "G", "H" BODY CARS

Removal

1. Raise the vehicle and support safely.
2. Support axle assembly and remove both lower shock absorber attaching bolts. 3. Lower axle assembly until spring upper isolator can be removed (do not stretch brake hose.)
4. Remove two screws hold jounce bumper assembly to rail. Remove jounce bumper assembly.

Installation

1. Position jounce bumper to rail. Install and tighten attaching screws to 5 ft. lbs. (7 Nm).
2. Install isolator over jounce bumper and install spring.
3. Raise axle and loosely assembly both shock absorber-to-axle screws. Remove axle support and lower vehicle.
4. With suspension supporting vehicle, tighten both shock absorber attaching screws to 40 ft. lbs. (54 Nm).

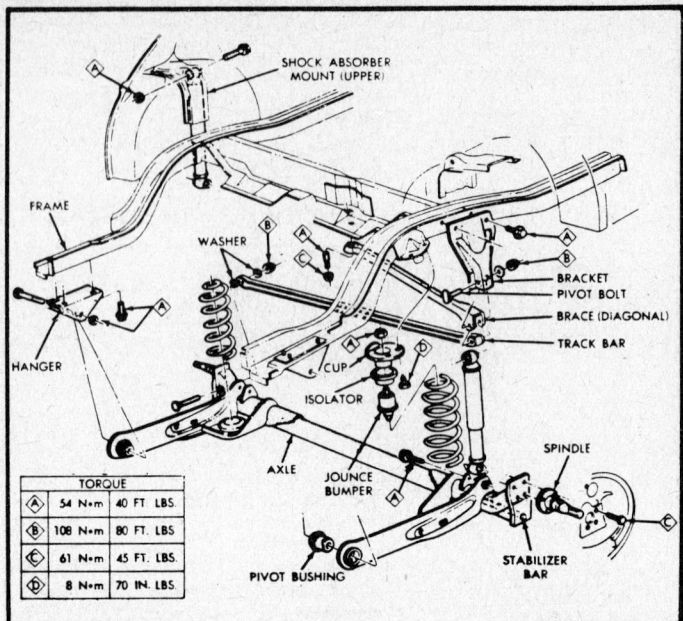

K car flex arm rear suspension (© Chrysler Corp.)

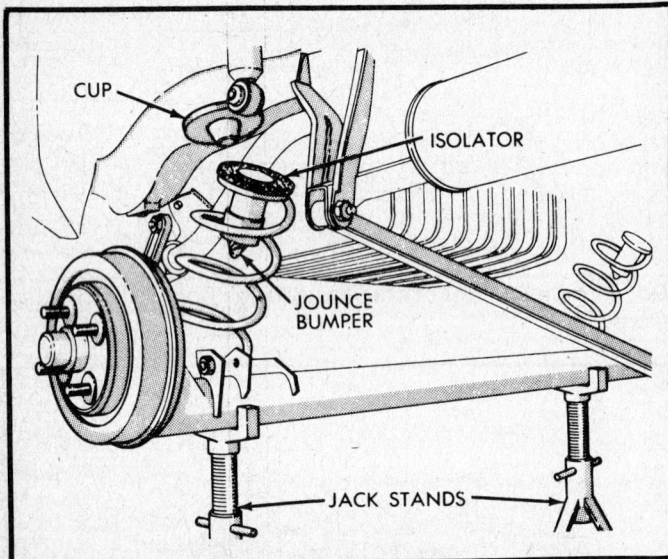

K car spring and jounce bumper (© Chrysler Corp.)

Rear Axle Assembly

"L" BODY CARS

Removal

NOTE: Support the car on the rear crossmember; let the axle hang down.

1. Remove wheel and tire assembly.
2. Remove brake fittings and retaining clips holding flexible brake line.
3. Remove parking brake cable adjusting connection nut.
4. Release both parking brake cables from brackets by slipping ball-end of cables through brake connectors. Pull parking brake cable through bracket.
5. Pry off grease cap.
6. Remove cotter pin and castle lock.
7. Remove adjusting nut. Remove brake drum.
8. Remove four (4) brake assembly and spindle retaining bolts.
9. Set spindle aside and using a piece of wire, hang brake assembly out of way.
10. Remove shock absorber mounting brackets.

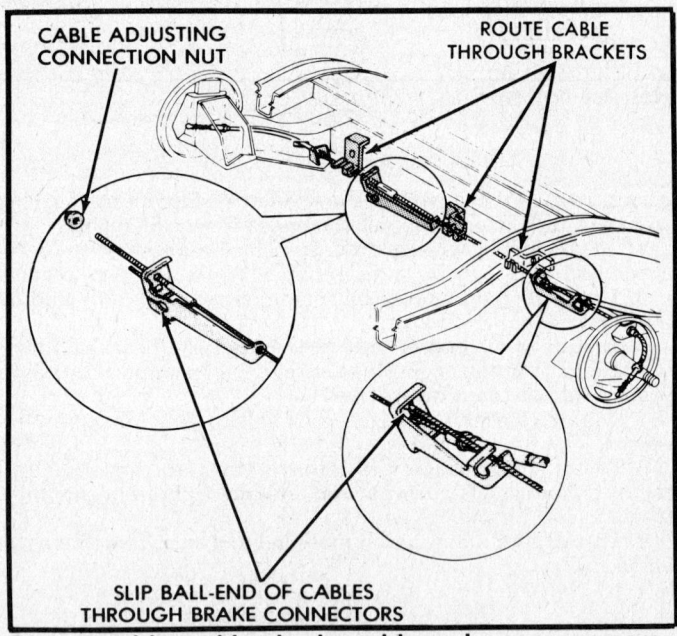

Disassemble parking brake cable and rear crossmember (© Chrysler Corp.)

11. Remove trailing arm-to-hanger bracket mounting bolt.
12. Remove axle assembly.

Installation

1. Using jacks, raise rear axle assembly into position under vehicle.
2. Install trailing arm-to-hanger mounting bracket; finger tighten bolts only.
3. Install shock absorber mounting bolts loosely. Remove jacks.
4. Place spindle and brake assembly in position. Install four (4) retaining bolts finger-tight.
5. Tighten the four retaining bolts to 45 ft. lbs. (60 Nm) torque.

SUSPENSIONS
REAR SUSPENSION—CHRYSLER FRONT DRIVE CARS

6. Install brake drum.
7. Install washer and nut. Tighten adjusting nut to 20–25 ft. lbs. (27–34 Nm) while rotating wheel. Back off adjusting nut with wrench to completely release bearing pre-load. Finger-tighten adjusting nut.
8. Position nut lock with one pair of slots in line with cotter pin hole. Install cotter pin. The end-play should be 0.001–0.003 in. (0.025–0.076mm). Clean and install grease cap.
9. Put parking brake cable through the bracket.
10. Slip ball-end of parking brake cables through brake connectors on parking brake bracket.
11. Install both retaining clips.
12. Install parking brake cable adjusting connection nut. Tighten until all slcak is removed from cables.
13. Install retaining clips and brake tube fittings. Tighten fittings to 9 ft. lbs. (12 Nm).
14. Bleed rear brake system and readjust brakes.
15. Install wheel and tire assembly. Tighten wheel nuts to 80 ft. lbs. (108 Nm) torque.
16. With vehicle on ground, tighten trailing arm-to-hanger bracket mounting bolts to 40 ft. lbs. (55 Nm) torque.
17. Tighten shock absorber mounting bolts to 40 ft. lbs. (55 Nm) torque.

"K", "E", "G", "H" BODY CARS

Removal

1. Raise the vehicle and support safely. Support the rear axle with adjustable jack stands. Remove the wheel assemblies.
2. Separate the parking brake cable at the connector and cable housing at the floor pan racket.
3. Separate the brake tube assembly from the brake hose at the training arm bracket and remove the lock.
4. Remove the lower shock absorber through bolts and the track bar to axle through bolts. Support the track bar end with wire to keep out of the way.
5. Lower the axle until the spring and isolator assemblies can be removed.
6. Support the pivot bushing end of the trailing arms and remove the pivot bushing hanger bracket to frame screws. Carefully lower the axle assembly and remove from under the vehicle.

Installation

1. Raise and support the axle assembly on adjustable jack stands.
2. Attach the pivot bushing hanger brackets to the frame rail and tighten the attaching bolts.
3. Install the springs and isolators and carefully raise the axle assembly.
4. Install the shock absorber and track bar through bolts. Do not tighten.
5. Position the spindle and brake support to the axle while routing the parking brake cable through the trailing arm opening and the brake tube over the trailing arm. Install the four retaining bolts loosely, then tighten to 45 ft. lbs. torque.

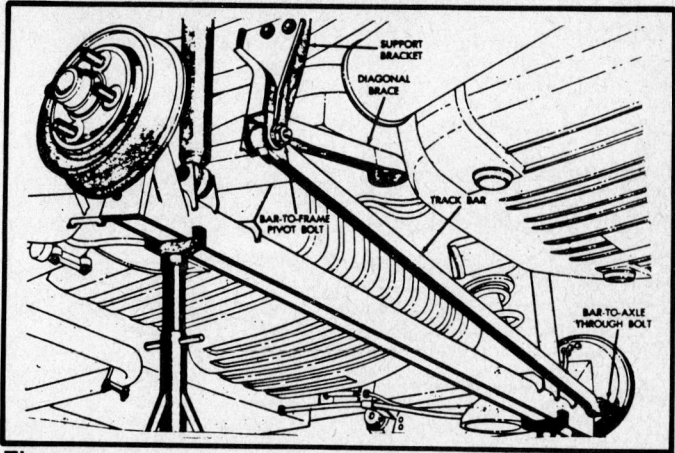
Flex arm rear suspension (© Chrysler Corp.)

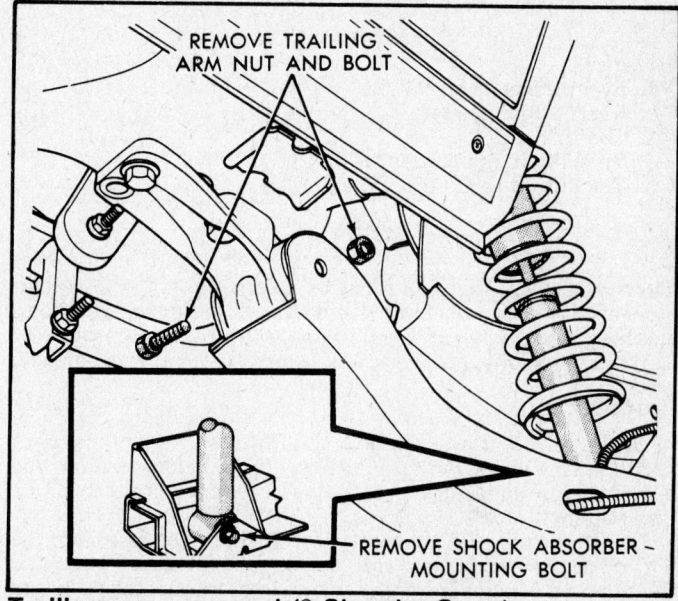
Trailing arms removal (© Chrysler Corp.)

6. Install hub and drum, if previously removed.
7. Route the parking brake cable through the fingers in the retaining bracket and lock housing end into the floor pan bracket. Install the cable end into the intermediate connector.
8. Install the brake hose end fitting into the bracket and install the lock. Tighten as required.
9. Install wheel assemblies and lower vehicle to floor. Tighten the lower shock absorber bolts to 40 ft. lbs. and the track bar bolt to 80 ft. lbs. torque.
10. Bleed the brake system as required.

FRONT SUSPENSION—CHRYSLER REAR DRIVE CARS

Alignment

There are six basic factor which are the foundation to front wheel alignment: height, caster, camber, toe-in, steering axis inclination and toe-out on turns. All are mechanically adjustable except steering axis inclination and toe-out on turns. The latter two are valuable in determining if parts are bent or damaged, particularly when the camber and caster adjustments cannot be brought within the recommended specifications.

SECTION 35

SUSPENSIONS
FRONT SUSPENSION—CHRYSLER REAR DRIVE CARS

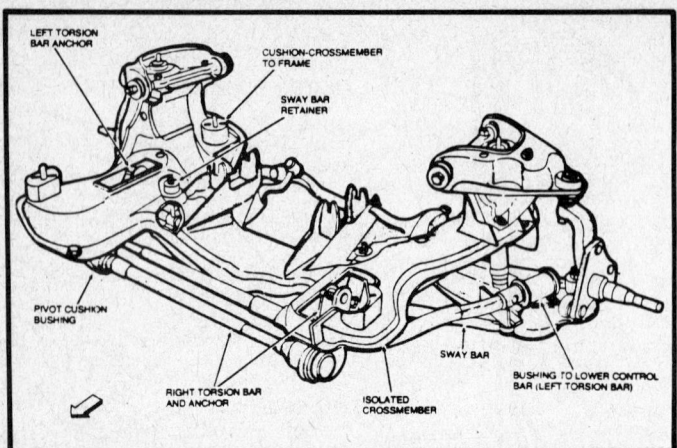

Transverse torsion bar suspension (© Chrysler Corp.)

On all models, check the measurements against those given in the Front End Alignment Specifications. Adjust the height by turning the torsion bar adjusting bolt clockwise to raise or counterclockwise to lower. The height should not vary more than 1/8 inch from side to side.

CAMBER AND CASTER

1. Prepare vehicle for measuring wheel alignment.
2. Determine initial camber and caster readings to confirm variance to specifications before loosening pivot bar bolts.
3. Remove foreign material from exposed threads of pivot bar bolts.
4. Loosen nuts slightly hold pivot (caster/camber) bar. Slightly loosening the pivot bar nuts will allow the upper control arm to be repositioned without slipping to end of adjustment slots.
5. Position claw of tool on pivot bar and pin of tool into holes provided in tower or bracket. Make adjustments by moving pivot bar in or out. Adjust as follows:
Camber: Move both ends of upper control arm in or out exactly equal amounts. Camber settings should be held as close as possible to "preferred" settings.
Caster: Moving one end of the bar will change caster (and camber). To preserve camber while adjusting caster, move each end of the upper control arm pivot bar exactly equal amounts in opposite directions. For example, to increase positive caster, move front of pivot bar away from engine, then move rear of pivot bar towards engine in an equal amount. Caster should be nearly equal as possible on both wheels.

All adjustments and checks should be made in the following sequence:
1. Front suspension height.
2. Caster and camber.
3. Toe-in.
4. Steering axis inclination (not adjustable).
5. Toe-out on turns (not adjustable).

HEIGHT

Front suspension heights must be measured with the recommended tire pressures and with no passenger or luggage compartment load. The car should have a full tank of gasoline or equivalent weight compensation. It must be on a level surface.

Procedure

Rock the vehicle at the center of the front and rear bumpers at least six times to eliminate friction effects before making the vehicle height measurements. Allow the vehicle to settle on its own weight.
For Gran Fury and Newport/New Yorker, measure from the bottom of the front frame rail, between the radiator yoke and the forward edge of the front suspension crossmember, to the ground. For all other torsion bar front suspension models, measure from the head of the front suspension crossmember front isolator bolt to the ground.

TOE

The toe setting should be in the final operation of the front wheel alignment adjustments. In all cases, follow equipment manufacturers procedure.
1. Secure steering wheel in "straight ahead" position. On vehicles equipped with power steering, start engine before centering wheel. (Engine should be kept running while adjusting toe).
2. Loosen tie rod clamp bolts.
3. Adjust toe by turning tie rod sleeves.

NOTE: To avoid a binding condition in either tie rod assembly, rotate both tie rod ends in direction of sleeve travel during adjustment. This will ensure that both ends will be in the center of their travel when tightening sleeve clamps.

4. Shut off engine.
5. Position sleeve clamps so ends do not locate in the sleeve slot, then tighten clamp bolts as specified. Be sure the clamp bolts are indexed at or near bottom to avoid possible interference with torsion bars when vehicle is in full jounce.
Upon completion of alignment operations, it is essential that the splash shields, if removed, be correctly reinstalled with all holding clips in place.

Front Wheel Bearings
LUBRICATION

Under normal service, the lubricant in front wheel bearings should be inspected whenever brake drums or disc brake rotors are removed to inspect or service the brake system, but at least every 30,000 miles (48,000 kilometers).
For severe service vehicles (such as taxi and police vehicles involving frequent brake application), wheel bearings should be inspected whenever the rotors are removed to inspect or service the brake system, or at least eery 9,000 miles (14,000 kilometers), whichever occurs first.

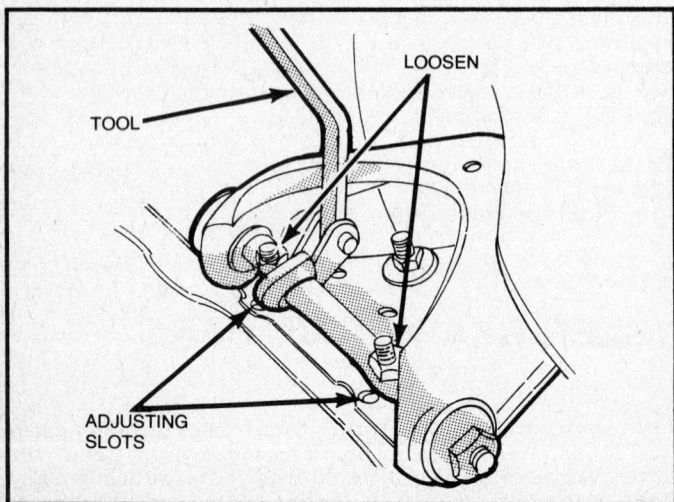

Caster/camber adjustment (© Chrysler Corp.)

SUSPENSIONS
FRONT SUSPENSION—CHRYSLER REAR DRIVE CARS

Check lubricant to see that it is adequate in quantity and quality. If grease is low in quantity, contains dirt, appears dry or has been contaminated with water to produce a milky appearance, bearings should be cleaned and completely repacked. Never add grease to wheel bearings.

When lubrication is required, discard old seal. Thoroughly clean old lubricant from bearings and from hub cavity. Inspect rollers for signs of pitting or other surface distress. Light bearing discolorations should be considered normal. Bearings must be replaced if any defects exist. For all service, repack the bearings with a high temperature wheel bearing grease. Use of a bearing packer is recommended. A small amount of new grease should also be added to hub cavity.

Adjustment

1. Tighten adjusting nut to 20–25 ft. lbs. (27–34 Nm) while rotating wheel. Stop rotation and back off adjusting nut with wrench to completely release bearing pre-load. Next, finger-tighten adjusting nut. Position nut lock with one pair of slots in line with cotter pin hole. Install cotter pin. The resulting adjustment should be 0.0001–0.0003 in. end play.
2. Clean and install grease cap. Install wheel and tire assembly.

Removal

1. In the event the bearing cap in found defective during inspection, remove grease cap, cotter pin, nut lock and bearing adjusting nut.
2. Remove the disc brake sliding caliper retaining clips and anti-rattle springs.
3. Slowly slide caliper housing assembly up and away from brake disc and support caliper housing or steering knuckle arm. Do not let caliper housing hang by brake hose, as possible brake hose damage may result.
4. Remove thrust washer and outer bearing cone.
5. Slide wheel hub and disc assembly off the spindle.
6. Carefully drive out inner seal and remove bearing cone with $\frac{3}{4}$ in. diameter non-metallic rod.

Installation

1. Using a bearing drive tool, install new cone. Care must be taken to fully seat new cup against shoulder of hub.
2. Force lubricant between all bearing cone rollers or repack using a suitable bearing packer. A small amount of grease should be added to hub cavity.
3. Install inner cone and a new seal with lip of seal facing inward. Position seal flush with end of hub. The seal flange may be damaged if proper tool is not used.
4. Clean spindle and apply a light coating of wheel bearing lubricant over polished surfaces.
5. Install hub and braking disc assembly on spindle and install outer bearing cone, thrust washer and adjusting nut. Refer to bearing adjustment procedure.
6. Slowly slide caliper housing assembly down on brake disc assembly into position on adaptor. Install caliper retaining clips and anti-rattle springs. Tighten to 15 ft. lbs. (20 Nm).
7. Install tire and wheel.

Shock Absorbers

Removal

NOTE: **To remove the front shock absorbers on all models, you may find it more convenient to remove the wheel assembly and perform the removal from under the fender.**

1. Loosen and remove nut and retainer from upper end of shock absorber piston rod.
2. Raise vehicles so wheels are clear of floor and remove lower attachment.

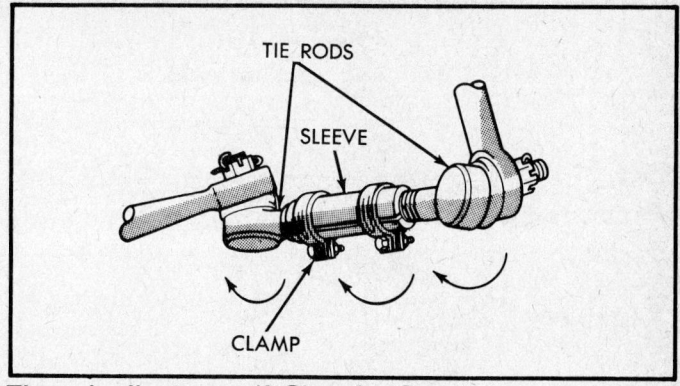

Tie rod adjustment (© Chrysler Corp.)

3. Compress shock absorber completely by pushing upward. Remove from vehicle by pulling down and out of upper shock absorber mounting bushing.
4. Check appearance of upper shock absorber mounting bushing.

If it appears worn, damaged or deteriorated, remove bushing by first pressing out inner sleeve with a suitable tool then prying out or cutting out the rubber bushing. (This bushing will take some set after it has been in service and must be replaced once it has been removed).

Installation

1. To install upper rubber bushing, remove inner seal sleeve and immerse bushing in water (do not use oil) and with a twisting motion, start bushing into hole of upper mounting bracket.

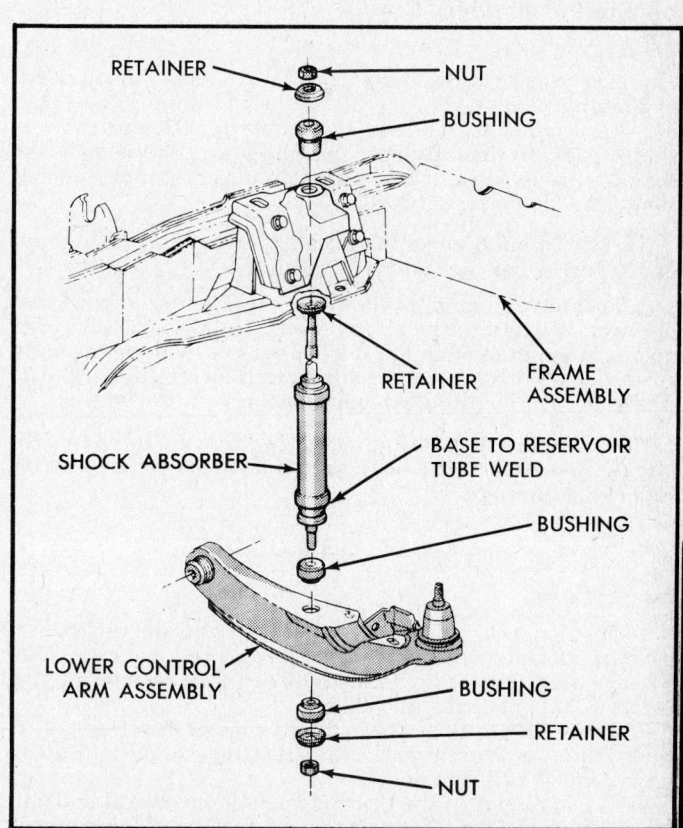

Front shock absorbers—transverse torsion bar suspension (© Chrysler Corp.)

SECTION 35
SUSPENSIONS
FRONT SUSPENSION—CHRYSLER REAR DRIVE CARS

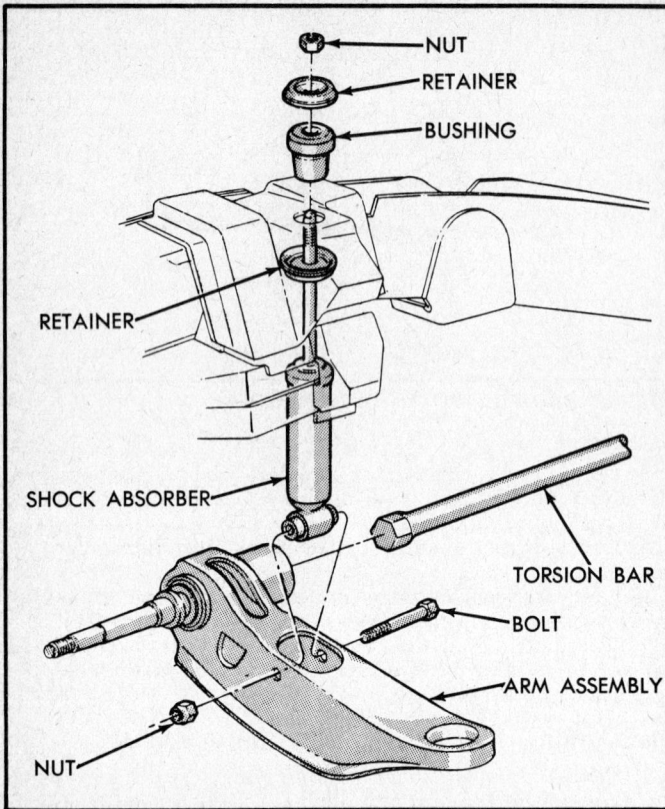

Front shock absorber—conventional torsion bar suspension (© Chrysler Corp.)

Tap into position with a hammer. Reinstall steel inner sleeve in bushing.

2. Test and expel air from shock absorber. Compress to its shortest length. Install upper bushing lower retainer and insert rod through upper bushing. Install upper retainer and nut; tighten to 25 ft. lbs. (34 Nm).

NOTE: In each case, install all retainers with the concave side in contact with the rubber.

3. Position and align lower eye of shock absorber with that of lower control arm mounting holes. Install shock absorber and tighten nut to 50 ft. lbs. (68 Nm) on bolt-and-nut-type. On suspensions with removal bushings, tighten retainer nut to 35 ft. lbs. (47 Nm) with full weight of vehicle on the wheels.

NOTE: When tightening retaining nut, be sure to grip shock absorber at the base area below the weld to avoid reservoir damage.

Upper Ball Joint
Inspection

1. Position jack under the lower control arm and raise wheel clear of floor. Remove wheel cover, grease cap and cotter pin.
2. Tighten bearing adjusting nut enough to remove all play between hub, bearings and spindle.
3. Lower jack to allow tire to lightly contact floor (most of vehicle weight relieved from the tire). It is important that the tire have contact with the floor.
4. Grasp the top of the tire and apply force inward and outward. While this force is being applied, have an observer check for any movement at the ball joints between the upper control arm and the knuckle.
5. If any lateral movement is evident, replace the ball joint.

Removal

1. Place ignition switch in Off or Unlocked position.
2. Raise front of vehicle with hand jack and place jack stand under lower control arm. Position jack stand as close to wheel as possible. Be sure jack stand is not in contact with brake splash shield. Rubber rebound bumper must not contact frame.

— CAUTION —
Torsion bar will remain in loaded position.

3. Remove wheel cover, wheel and tire assembly.
4. Remove cotter pins and nuts from upper and lower ball joints to facilitate use of ball joint removal tool.
5. Slide tool on lower ball joint stud allowing tool to rest on knuckle arm. Set tool securely against upper stud.
6. Tighten tool to apply pressure to upper stud and strike knuckle sharply with hammer to loosen stud. Do not attempt to force stud out only with tool.
7. After removing tool, disengage upper ball joint from knuckle. Support knuckle and brake assembly to prevent damage to brake hose or lower ball joint.
8. Remove upper ball joint by turning counterclockwise from upper control arm.

Installation

1. Screw ball joint squarely into control arm as far as possible by hand. Make certain ball joint threads engage those of control arm correctly if original arm is used. Seals should always be replaced once they have been removed.
2. Tighten ball joint until it bottoms on housing. Tighten to 125 ft. lbs. (180 Nm).
3. Position new seal over balljoint stud and install using tool adapter. Make sure seal is seated on ball joint housing.
4. Postion upper ball join stud in steering knuckle and install nut. Tighten nut to 100 ft. lbs. (136 Nm).
5. Install lower ball joint stud nut and tighten to 100 ft. lbs. (136 Nm). Install cotter pin and lubricate upper ball joint.
6. Torsion bar will remain in loaded position.
7. Install wheel and tire assembly with wheel cover.

Lower Ball Joint
Inspection

1. Raise the front of the vehicle and install safety floor stands under both lower control arm as far outboard as possible. The upper control arms must not contact the rubber rebound bumpers.
2. With the weight of vehicle on the control arm, install dial indicator and clamp assembly to lower control arm.
3. Position dial indicator plunger tip against knuckle arm and zero dial indicator.
4. Measure axial travel of the knuckle arm with respect to the control arm, by raising the lowering the wheel using a pry bar under the center of the tire.
5. If during measurement you find the axial travel of the control arm is 0.030 in. (0.76 mm) or more, relative to the knuckle arm, the ball joint should be replaced.

Removal

1. Place ignition switch in Off or Unlocked position.
2. Raise vehicle on hoist to place front suspension in rebound. Place jack stands under front frame for additional support.
3. Remove wheel cover, wheel and tire assembly.
4. Remove brake caliper and support with wire hook. Do not hang caliper by brake hose alone.
5. Remove hub and rotor assembly and splash shield. Disconnect shock absorber at lower control arm.

SUSPENSIONS
FRONT SUSPENSION—CHRYSLER REAR DRIVE CARS

6. Unwind torsion bar.
7. Remove upper and lower ball joint stud cotter pins and nuts. Slide tool over upper stud until tool rests on steering knuckle.
8. Turn threaded portion of tool locking it securely against lower stud. Tighten tool enough to place lower ball joint stud under pressure, then strike steering knuckle arm sharply with a hammer to loosen stud. Do not attempt to force stud out of knuckle with tool alone.
9. Use tool to press ball joint out of lower control arm.

Installation

1. Press new ball joint into lower control arm assembly.
2. Place a new seal over ball joint with adapter tool. Press retainer portion of seal down on ball joint housing until it is securely locked in position.
3. Insert ball joint stud into opening in knuckle arm and install stud retaining nuts; tighten as specified. Install cotter pins and lubricate ball joint.
4. Place a load on torsion bar by turning adjusting bolt clockwise.
5. Install wheel, tire and brake assembly and adjust front wheel bearing.
6. Lower vehicle to floor. Adjust front suspension heights.

Torsion Bars (Longitudinal Type)

Longitudinal torsion bars have a hex formed on each end. One hex end is installed in the lower control arm anchor, the opposite end is anchored in the frame or body crossmember.

Torsion bars are identified for use by length and thickness (depending on carline, body, engine, etc.) and are not interchangeable side for side. The bars are marked on either right or left by the letter "R" or "L" stamped on one end of the bar.

Removal

1. Lift vehicle on hoist to place front suspension in rebound.
2. Release load from torsion both bars by turning the anchor adjusting bolt in lower control arm counterclockwise.
3. Remove lock ring from anchor at rear of bar. Install drivetool to remove torsion bar. (If necessary, remove transmission torque shaft to provide clearance. Place tool toward rear of bar to allow sufficient room for striking pad of tool. Do not apply heat to torsion bar, front anchor or rear anchor.
4. Remove tool and slide bar out through rear anchor. Do not damage balloon seal when removing bar.

Inspection

1. Inspect torsion bar and seal for damage; replace if damaged.
2. Remove all foreign matter from hex opening(s) in anchors and from hex end (s) of torsion bar.
3. Inspect torsion bar adjusting bolt and swivel and replace if there is corrosion or other damage. Lubricate for easy installation.

Installation

1. Insert torsion bar through rear anchor.
2. Lubricate inside surface of balloon seal and slide seal over torsion bar (cupped end toward read of bar).
3. Coat both hex ends of torsion bar with lubricant.
4. Slide torsion bar in hex opening of lower control arm.

NOTE: If torsion bar hex opening does not index with lower control arm hex opening, loosen lower control arm pivot shaft nut, rotate pivot shaft to index with torsion bar. Install torsion bar. Do not tighten pivot shaft nut while suspension is in rebound.

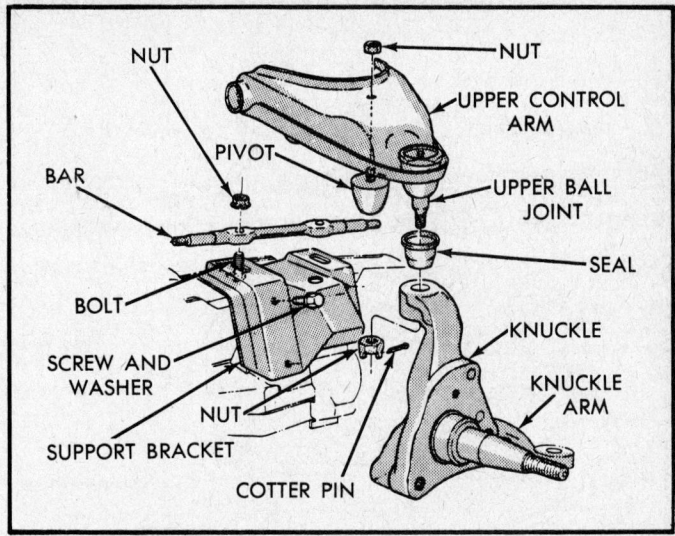

Knuckle control arm and ball joint (© Chrysler Corp.)

5. Install lock ring, making sure it is seated in its groove.
6. Pack rear anchor openings at lock ring area and area under seals with lubricant. Position lip of seal in groove of anchor.
7. Turn adjusting bolt clockwise to place a load on torsion bar.
8. Lower vehicle to floor and tighten pivot shaft nut to 145 ft. lbs. (197 Nm).
9. Adjust front suspension height.

Torsion Bars (Transverse—Type)

Torsion bars are formed with an angle for transverse mounting. Each bar is hex shaped on the anchor end with a replaceable torsion bar-to-lower control arm bushing on the opposite end and a pivot cushion bushing (permanently attached) midway on the bar creating right and left hand assemblies.

The hex end of the bar is anchored in the crossmember (opposite the affected wheel), extends parallel to the front crossmember, through the pivot cushion bushing (also attached to the crossmember), turns, and attaches to the lower control arm through the torsion bar to lower control arm bushing.

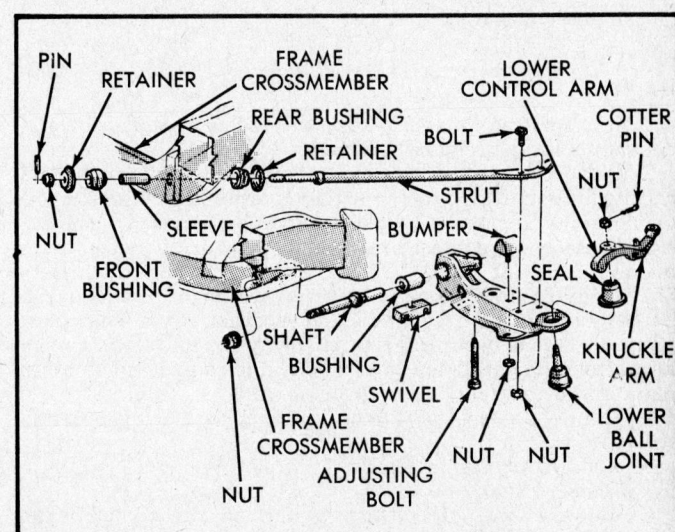

Lower control arm and ball joint (© Chrysler Corp.)

35-33

Section 35 SUSPENSIONS
FRONT SUSPENSION—CHRYSLER REAR DRIVE CARS

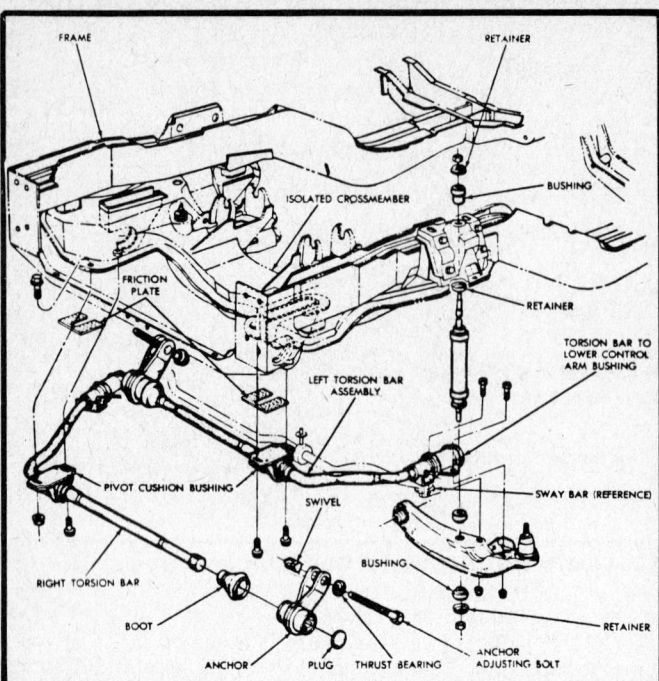

Transverse torsion bar front suspension (© Chrysler Corp.)

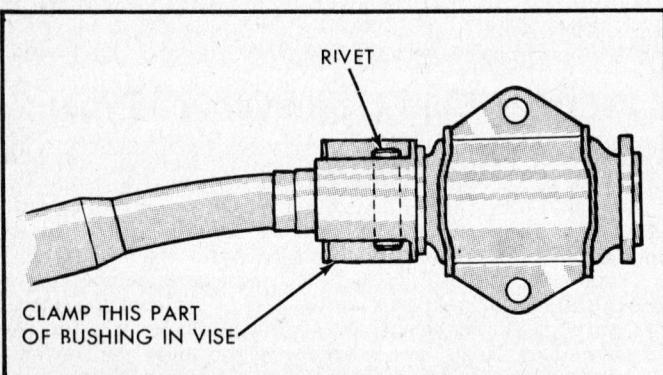

Bushing removal, torsion bar to lower control arm (© Chrysler Corp.)

Removal

1. Raise car on hoist and support vehicle so that front suspension is in full rebound position.
2. Release load on both torsion bars by turning anchor adjusting bolts in frame crossmember counterclockwise. Remove anchor adjusting bolt on torsion bar to be removed.
3. Raise lower control arms until clearance between crossmember ledge (at jounce bumper) and torsion bar end bushing is 2 7/8 in. (63mm). Support lower control arms at this design height (equal to three passenger position with vehicle on ground). This is necessary to align sway bar and lower control arm attaching points for disassembly and component re-alignment and attachment during reassembly.
4. Remove sway bar-to-control arm attaching bolt and retainers.
5. Remove two bolts attaching torsion bar end bushing to lower control arm.
6. Remove two bolts attaching torsion bar pivot cushion bushing to crossmember, and remove torsion bar and anchor assembly from crossmember.
7. Carefully separate anchor from torsion bar.

TORSION BAR—TO—LOWER CONTROL ARM BUSHING REPLACEMENT

Service replacement bars include pivot cushion bushing and torsion bar to lower control arm bushing.

1. Clamp assembly in vise with rivet head up (hex end of bar down).

--- CAUTION ---

Never clamp the bar in a vise unless soft vise jaw inserts (brass, aluminum, etc.) are used.

2. Centerpunch the rivet head and drill a 3/8 in. (9.5 mm) diameter hole approximately 1/2 in. (12.5 mm) deep. A short length of 5/16 in. (8 mm) rod can be used to remove the rivet. It may be necessary to remove flange of rivet head before driving rivet out.

--- CAUTION ---

Do not enlarge the 7/16 in (11 mm) diameter hole in the bar.

3. Remove bushing from bar.
4. Install new bushing. Rough area under bushing may be cleaned with sandpaper if necessary for easy assembly. New bushing should go on by hand.
5. Install bushing retaining bolt and tighten nut to 50 ft. lbs. (68 Nm).

Inspection

1. Inspect seal for damage, replace if necessary.
2. Inspect bushing-to-lower control arm and pivot cushion bushing.

NOTE: Inspect seals on cushion bushing for cuts, tears or severe deterioration that may allow moisture under cushion. If corrosion is evident, the torsion bar assembly should be replaced.

3. Remove all foreign matter from hex opening(s) in anchors and from hex end(s) of torsion bar.
4. Inspect torsion bar adjusting bolt and swivel and replace if there is any sign of corrosion or other damage. Lubricate for easy installation.

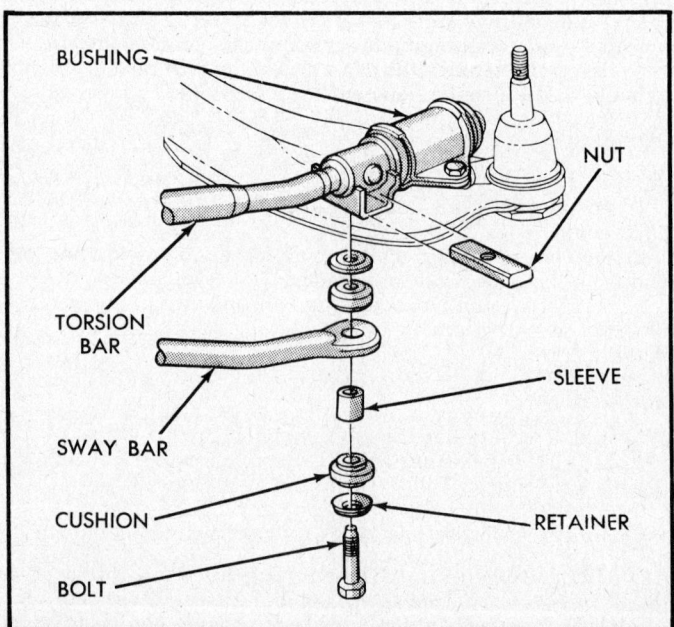

Transverse bar lower control arm mounting (© Chrysler Corp.)

SUSPENSIONS
FRONT SUSPENSION—CHRYSLER REAR DRIVE CARS

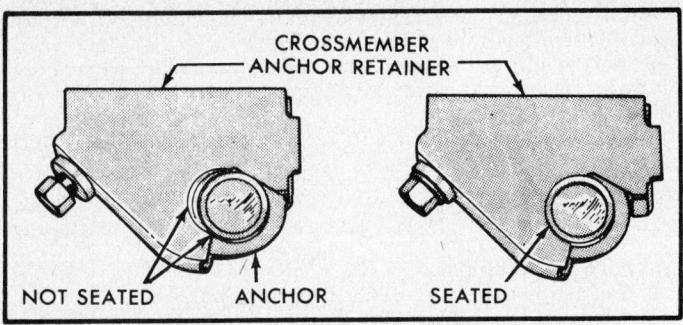
Torsion bar anchor assembly (© Chrysler Corp.)

Installation

1. Carefully slide balloon seal over end of torsion bar (cupped end toward hex).
2. Coat hex end of torsion bar with lubricant.
3. Install torsion bar hex end into anchor bracket. With torsion bar in a horizontal position, the ears of the anchor bracket should be positioned nearly straight up. Position swivel into anchor bracket ears.
4. Place bushing end of bar into position on top of lower control arm. Then, install anchor bracket assembly into crossmember anchor retainer and install anchor adjusting bearing and bolt.
5. Attach pivot cushion bushing to crossmember with two bolt and washer assemblies. Leave bolt and washer assemblies loose enough to install friction plates.
6. With lower control arms at "design height", install two bolt and nut assemblies attaching torsion bar bushing to lower control arm. Tighten to 70 ft. lbs. (95 Nm).
7. Ensure that torsion bar anchor bracket is fully seated in crossmember. Install friction plates between crossmember and pivot cushion bushing with open end of slot to rear and bottomed out on mounting bolt. Tighten cushion bushing bolts to 85 ft. lbs. (115 Nm).

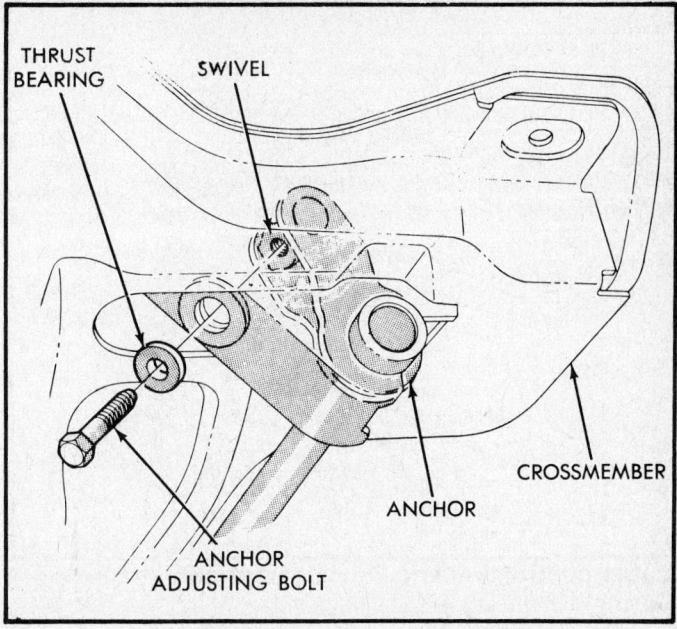
Transverse torsion bar anchor bolt (© Chrysler Corp.)

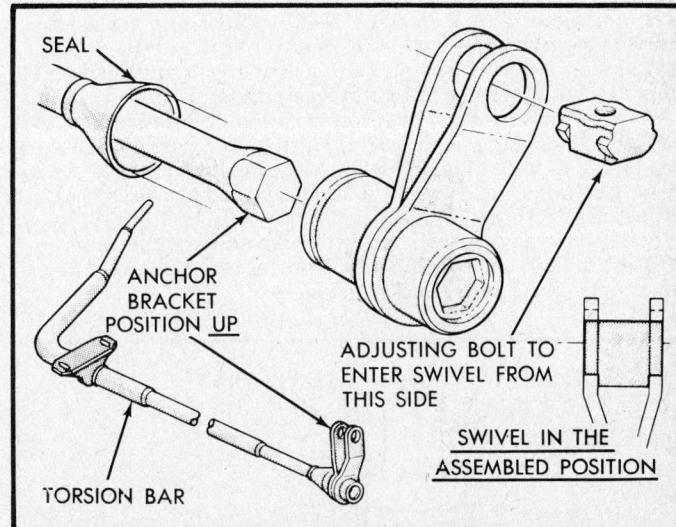
Correct anchor and swivel installation (© Chrysler Corp.)

8. Position balloon seal over anchor bracket.
9. Reinstall bolt, through sway bar, retainer cushions and sleeve, and attach to lower control arm end bushing. Tighten bolt to 50 ft. lbs. (68 Nm).
10. Load torsion bar by turning anchor adjusting bolt clockwise.
11. Lower vehicle and adjust torsion bar height to specifications.

Upper Control Arm

Removal

1. Place ignition switch in Off or Unlocked position.
2. Raise front of vehicle with hand jack and remove wheel cover, wheel and tire assembly.
3. Position short jack stand under lower control arm near splash shield and lower hand jack. Observe that jack stand

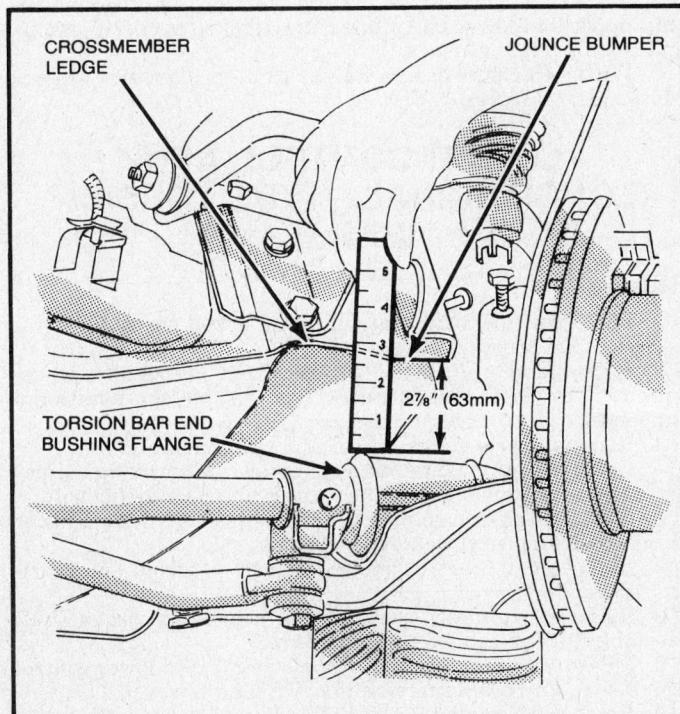
Measuring design height (© Chrysler Corp.)

SECTION 35

SUSPENSIONS
FRONT SUSPENSION—CHRYSLER REAR DRIVE CARS

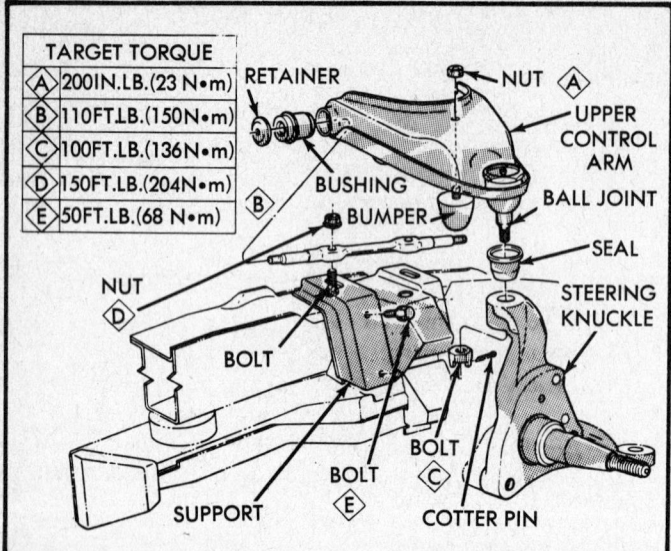

Upper control arm and knuckle assembly (© Chrysler Corp.)

does not contact shield and rebound bumpers are under no load.

4. On some models, remove brake caliper and set aside to provide clearance for ball joint remover tool.
5. Remove cotter pin and nut from upper and lower ball joints to facilitate use of tool to free ball joint.
6. Slide spreader tool over lower ball joint stud to allow tool to rest on steering knuckle arm. Tigthen tool to apply pressure to upper ball joint stud and strike steering knuckle boss sharply with hammer to loosen stud. Do not attempt to force stud out of knuckle with tool alone.
7. After removing tool, support brake and knuckle assembly to prevent damage to brake hose or lower ball joint, then disengage upper ball joint from knuckle.

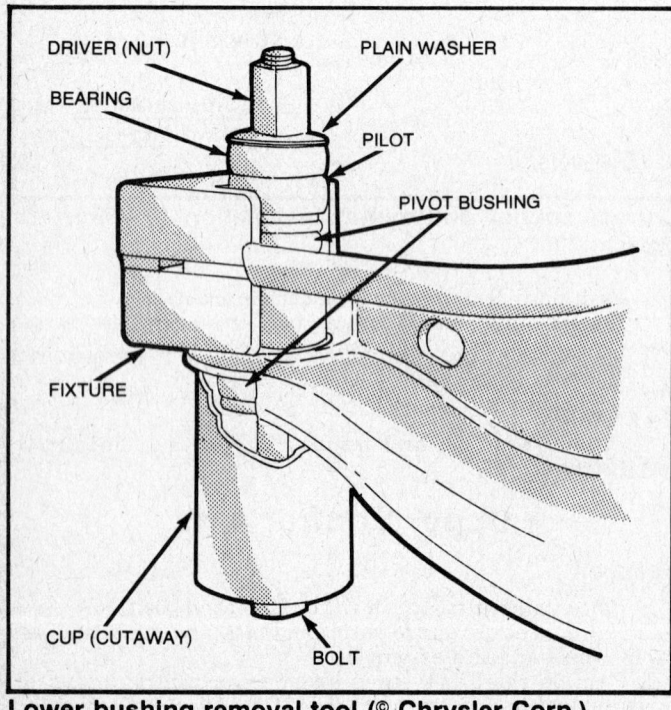

Lower bushing removal tool (© Chrysler Corp.)

8. From under hood, remove engine splash shield to expose upper control arm pivot bar.
9. Scribe a line on support bracket along inboard edge of pivot bar (to re-establish supsension alignment during reassembly).
10. Remove pivot bolts or nuts and lift upper control arm with ball joint and pivot bar assembly from bracket.

Disassembly (Bushings)

1. Place upper control arm in vise and remove pivot bar nuts and bushing retainers.
2. Bolt support tool C-4253-1 to pivot bar.
3. Place puller tool C-4253-2 over end of pivot bar and reinstall nut. Snug bolts against arm.
4. Screw bolts equally until bushing is free in arm and remove tool and bushing.

Assembly (Bushings)

1. With control arm in vise, put pivot bar in arm and attach support bracket spacer tool.
2. Slip bushings over each end of pivot bar and pilot into holes in arm.
3. Install bushing cups over both bushings and press bushings together until both bushings are fully seated in arm. Pound bushings in place at the same time or use an arbor press. Bushing flange must be bottomed on control arm extrusion.
4. Install retainers and nuts on pivot bar. Snug nuts against retainers.

NOTE: Pivot bar bushing retainer nuts are to be tightened to specifications AFTER suspension (upper control arm) is at design height.

Installation

1. Place upper control arm with ball joint and pivot bar on bracket. Install and snug attaching bolts against arm.
2. Seat inboard edge of pivot bar on mounting bracket. Tighten bolts to 150 ft. lbs. (204 Nm).
3. Replace engine splash shield.
4. Install ball joint stud through steering knuckle and install upper and lower ball joints nuts, tighten to specifications and install cotter pins.
5. With vehicle at design height tighten pivot bar nuts to 110 ft. lbs. (150 Nm).

LOWER CONTROL ARM (LONGITUDINAL—TYPE TORSION BARS)

Removal

1. Place ignition switch in Off or Unlocked position.
2. Remove rebound bumper.
3. Raise vehicle on hoist to place front suspension in rebound. Place jack stands under front frame for additional support.
4. Remove wheel cover, wheel and tire assembly.
5. Remove brake caliper and set aside. Do not hang caliper by brake hose alone. Disconnect shock absorber lower bolt.
6. Remove hub and rotor assembly, splash shield and lower shock mounting nut. Remove bolt and nut.
7. Remove two (2) strut bar attaching bolts from lower control arm.
8. Remove automatic transmission gear shift torque shaft assembly if required for tool clearance.
9. Measure torsion bar anchor bolt depth into lower control arm before unwinding torsion bar. Unwind bar.
10. Remove torsion bar.
11. Separate lower ball joint from knuckle arm.

SUSPENSIONS
FRONT SUSPENSION—CHRYSLER REAR DRIVE CARS

12. Remove lower control arm shaft nut from control arm shaft and push out shaft from frame crossmember. Strike threaded end of shaft with soft hammer to loosen if necessary. Remove lower control arm and shaft as an assembly from the vehicle.

13. In the event the shaft bushing indicates wear and deterioration, replacement is recommended.

Disassembly (Bushings)

1. Place lower control arm in vise and remove torsion bar adjusting bolt and swivel.
2. Place lower control arm assembly in arbor press with torsion bar hex opening up and with a support around anchor on bottom end.
3. Place a brass drift into hex opening and press shaft out of lower control arm. The bushing inner shell will remain on shaft.
4. Cut and remove rubber portion of bushing from control arm or shaft. Remove bushing outer shell by cutting with a chisel. Use care not to cut into control arm.
5. Remove bushing inner shell with pivot shaft.

Assembly (Bushings)

1. Position new bushing on shaft (flange end of bushing first). Press shaft into inner sleeve until bushing seats on shoulder of shaft.
2. Press shaft and bushing assembly into lower control arm using an arbor press.
3. Install torsion bar adjusting bolt and swivel.

Installation

1. Position lower control arm with shaft in crossmember. Install lower control arm shaft nut and finger-tighten nut.
2. Position lower ball joint stud into knuckle arm and tighten nut to 100 ft. lbs. (136 Nm).
3. Install torsion bar into lower control arm.
4. Replace transmission gear shaft torque shaft if removed.
5. Position strut bar with two attaching bolts to lower control arm. Tighten to 100 ft. lbs. (136 Nm).
6. Attach brake splash shield and secure lower shock mounting bolt to lower control arm.
7. Attach hub and rotor and install brake caliper.
8. Install wheel and tire assembly.
9. Lower vehicle to floor and adjust front suspension heights. Tighten lower control arm pivot shaft nut to 145 ft. lbs. (197 Nm). Install rebound bumper and tighten to 17 ft. lbs. (23 Nm).
10. Adjust wheel alignment.

LOWER CONTROL ARM (TRANSVERSE–TYPE TORSION BARS)

Removal

1. Raise car on hoist and remove wheel and tire assembly.
2. Remove brake caliper retaining screws, clips and anti-rattle springs and remove caliper from adaptor and support caliper assembly on wire hook. (Do not hang caliper by brake hose.).
3. Remove hub and rotor assembly and splash shield.
4. Remove shock absorber lower nut, retainer and insulator.
5. Release load on both torsion bars by turning anchor adjusting bolts counter clockwise. Releasing both torsion bars is required because of sway bar reaction from the opposite torsion bar.
6. Raise lower control arm until clearance between crossmember ledge (at jounce bumper) and torsion bar to lower control arm bushing is 2 7/8 inches (73 mm). Support control arm at

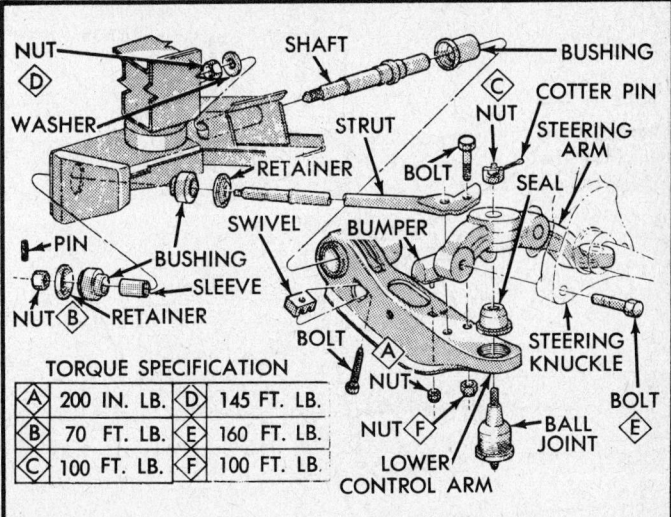

Longitudinal torsion bar suspension (© Chrysler Corp.)

this "design height" and remove two bolts attaching torsion bar end bushing to lower control arm.
7. Separate lower ball joint from knuckle arm.
8. Remove lower control arm pivot bolt and lower control arm.

Disassembly (Bushings)

1. Place lower control arm in vise and install bushing removal tool.
2. Place support fixture between flanges of control arm and around bushing. Proper fixture position is required to prevent control arm distortion during bushing removal.
3. Position cup over flanged bushing end with bolt through cup and bushing.

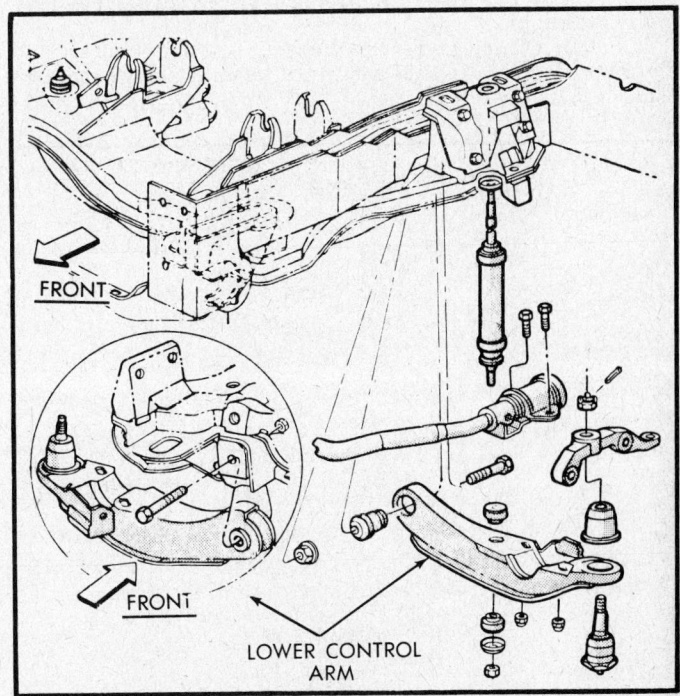

Lower cobtrol arm with transverse torsion bar suspension (© Chrysler Corp.)

SECTION 35 SUSPENSIONS
FRONT SUSPENSION—CHRYSLER REAR DRIVE CARS

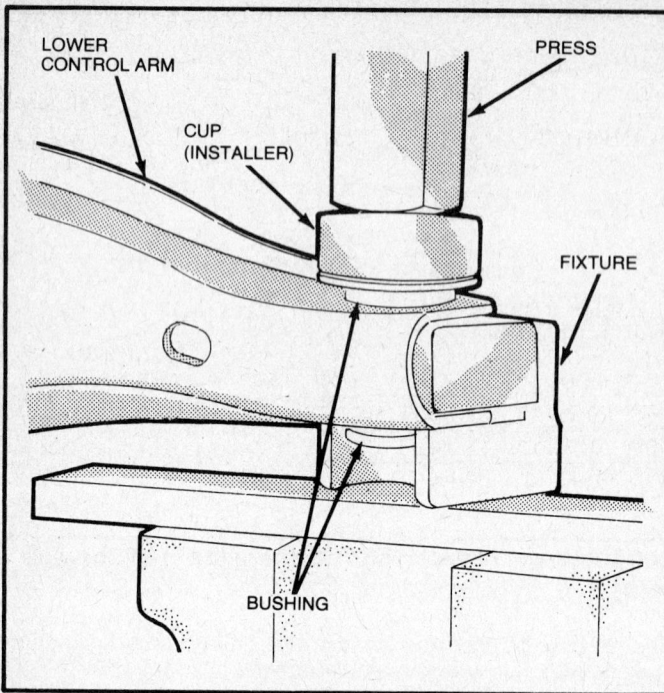

Lower control arm bushing installation (© Chrysler Corp.)

4. Install pilot, thrust washer, plain washer and nut on through bolt.
5. Press bushing out of lower control arm by hold bolt on cup end while turning nut of pilot end.

Assembly (Bushings)

1. Place support fixture on lower control arm flanges and position assembly on base of suitable press. Proper fixture position is required to prevent control arm distortion during bushing installation.
2. Position flange end of new bushing into cup squarely and press bushing into control arm until bushing flange seats on arm.

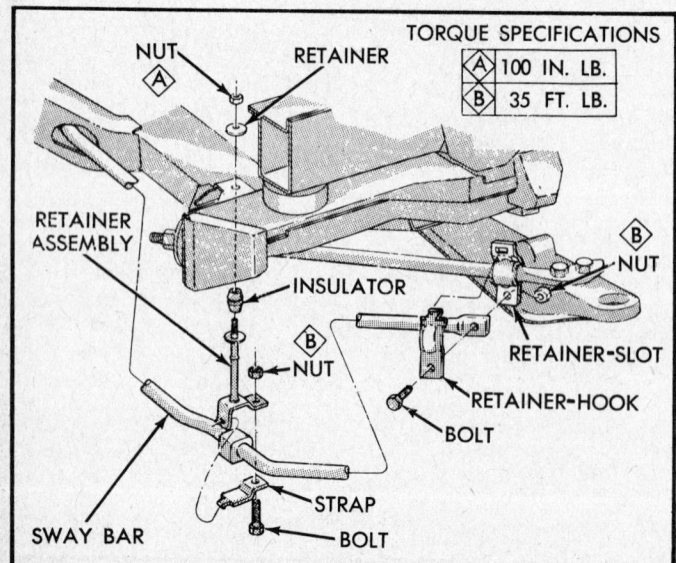

Longitudinal type torsion bar (© Chrysler Corp.)

Installation

1. Position lower control arm in crossmember, install pivot bolt and finger-tighten flanged nut.
2. Position lower ball joint stud into steering knuckle arm and tighten nu to 100 ft. lbs. (136 Nm). Insert cotter pin.
3. Install torsion bar into lower control arm.
4. Load torsion bar by returning torsion bar adjusting bolt depth to original position before removal.
5. Position strut bar with two attaching bolts to lower control arm. tighten to 100 ft. lbs. (136 Nm).
6. Attach brake splash shield and secure lower shock mounting bolt to lower control arm.
7. Attach hub and rotor and install brake caliper.
8. Install wheel and tire assembly.
9. Lower vehicle to floor and adjust front suspension heights. Tighten lower control arm pivot shaft nut to 145 ft. lbs. (197 Nm). Install rebound bumper and tighten to 17 ft. lbs. (23 Nm).
10. Adjust wheel alignment.

Steering Knuckle Arm

Removal

1. Place ignition switch in Off or Unlocked position.
2. Remove rebound bumper.
3. Raise vehicle on hoist to place front suspension in rebound. Use jack stands under front frame to additional support.
4. Remove wheel cover, wheel and tire assembly.
5. Remove brake caliper and hang out of way with wire hook during this operation to prevent damage to brake hose.
6. Remove hub and brake disc assembly.
7. Remove brake splash shield from steering knuckle.
8. Unload torsion bars, by turning anchor adjusting bolt counterclockwise.
9. Disconnect tie rod from steering knuckle arm. Use care not to damage seals.
10. Remove lower ball joint stud from knuckle arm.
11. Separate knuckle arm from steering knuckle by removing two (2) nuts and two (2) attaching bolts.
12. Remove steering knuckle arm.

Installation

1. Attach steering knuckle arm to knuckle and install two bolts and nuts. Tighten to 160 ft. lbs. (217 Nm).
2. Attach lower ball joint stud to knuckle arm. Tighten nut to 100 ft. lbs. (136 Nm) and install cotter key.
3. Attach tie rod end to steering knuckle arm and inside nut. Tighten to 40 ft. lbs. (54 Nm) and install cotter pin.
4. Load torsion bar by turning adjusting bolt on lower control arm counterclockwise.
5. Install brake splash shield onto steering knuckle.
6. Install hub and disc assembly. Adjust wheel bearings. Install caliper.
7. Install wheel and tire assembly and attach wheel cover.
8. Lower vehicle to floor, adjust front suspension heights and wheel alignment as necessary.

Sway Bar (Longitudinal Torsion Bar)

Removal

1. Place ignition switch in Off or Unlocked position.
2. Raise car on hoist to place front suspension in rebound.
3. Remove wheel cover, wheel and tire assembly.
4. Remove nut and bolt on each end of bar attaching sway bar to strut clamp. Remove nut and bolt from both sway bar link straps to free sway bar from lines.
5. Remove sway bar by pulling unit out through frame cross-

SUSPENSIONS
FRONT SUSPENSION—CHRYSLER REAR DRIVE CARS

member openings in direction of area where wheel has been removed.

6. In the event strut cushions and sway bar bushings show excessive wear or deterioration of rubber, replacement is recommended.

Installation

1. On side where wheel assembly has been removed, install sway bar with center offset in downward position (color code on bar is always on driver's side).

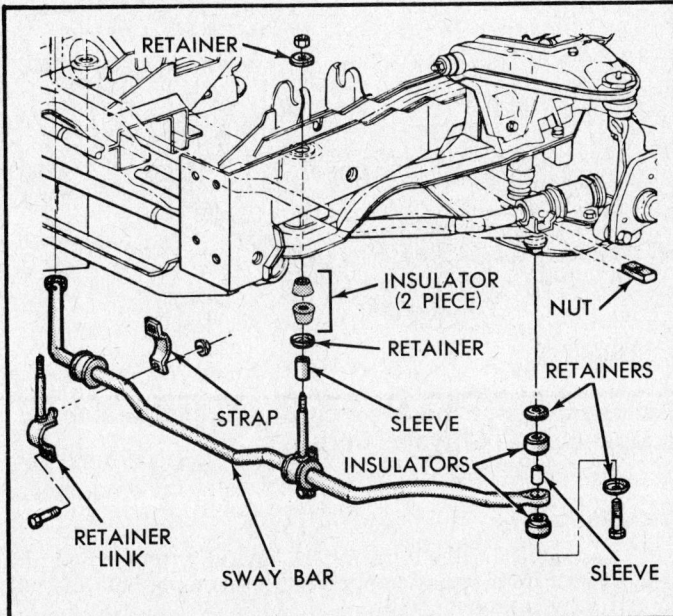

Sway bar—transverse type torsion bar (© Chrysler Corp.)

2. Attach sway bar with bolt and nut to strut retainer clamp on each side of bar and tighten to 35 ft. lbs. (47 Nm).
3. Lower vehicle to floor and attach both sway bar frame link straps. Tighten to 35 ft. lbs. (47 Nm).

Sway Bar (Transverse Torsion Bar)

Removal

1. Raise vehicle and support safely.

NOTE: Sway bar-to-lower control arm attaching points are aligned ONLY when lower control arms are at "design height" (equal to three passenger position with vehicle on ground). If frame contact or twin post hoist is used, release load on torsion bar by turning adjuster bolts counterclockwise. Raise lower control arms until clearance between crossmember ledge (at jounce bumper) and torsion bar to lower control arm bushing is $2\,7/8$ in. (73 mm). Support lower control arms with jack stand during sway bar removal and installation.

2. With lower control arms supported as described in note above, remove sway bar-to-torsion bar bushing attaching bolts, retainers, cushions and sleeves.
3. Remove retainer assembly strap bolts and retainer straps. Remove sway bar.
4. Inspect cushions and bushings for excessive wear or deterioration and replace if required.

Installation

1. Position sway bar bushings against retainers and install retainer straps. Loosely assemble retainer bolts.
2. Reinstall bolt through sway bar retainer, cushions and sleeve and attach to torsion bar lower control arm bushings. Tighten bolt to 50 ft. lbs. (68 Nm) torque.
3. Tighten sway bar retainer and strap bolts to 30 ft. lbs. (41 nm).
4. Load torsion bar by turning anchor adjusting bolt in crossmember clockwise.
5. Lower vehicle and adjust torsion bar height to specifications.

REAR SUSPENSION—CHRYLSER REAR DRIVE CARS

Shock Absorber

Removal

1. Raise the vehicle and support safely.
2. Using floor stands or equivalent, raise the axle to relieve the load on the shock absorbers.
3. Remove the shock absorber lower end as follows: Loosen and remove the nut, retainer and bushing from the spring plate.

NOTE: When loosening the retaining nut, grip the shock absorber at the base (below the base to reservoir tube weld) to avoid reservoir damage.

4. Loosen and remove the nut and bolt from the upper shock absorber mounting. Remove the shock absorber.

Installation

1. Expel air from new shock absorber.
2. Position and align upper eye of shock absorber with mounting holes in crossmember and install bolt and nut. Do not fully tighten.
3. Install shock absorber lower end, as follows: Install upper bushing on shock absorber stud and pull stud through spring plate mounting hole. Install lower bushing, cupped washer and nut. Tighten as specified.
4. Lower vehicle until full weight of vehicle is on the wheels. Tighten upper nut 70 ft. lbs. (95 Nm). Tighten lower nut to 35 ft. lbs. (47 Nm).

Springs

MEASURING SPRING HEIGHT

When measuring rear spring heights, place vehicle on a level floor, have correct front suspension height on both sides, correct tire pressures and no passenger or luggage compartment load and a full tank of fuel.

1. Jounce car several times (from bumper first). Release bumpers at same point in each cycle.
2. Measure shortest distance from top of axle housing to the rail at side of rear axle bumper strap (at rear of bumper)
3. Measure both right and left sides.

If these measurements vary by more than $3/4$ in. (side to side), it is an indication that one of the rear springs may need replacing.

SECTION 35

SUSPENSIONS
REAR SUSPENSION—CHRYSLER REAR DRIVE CARS

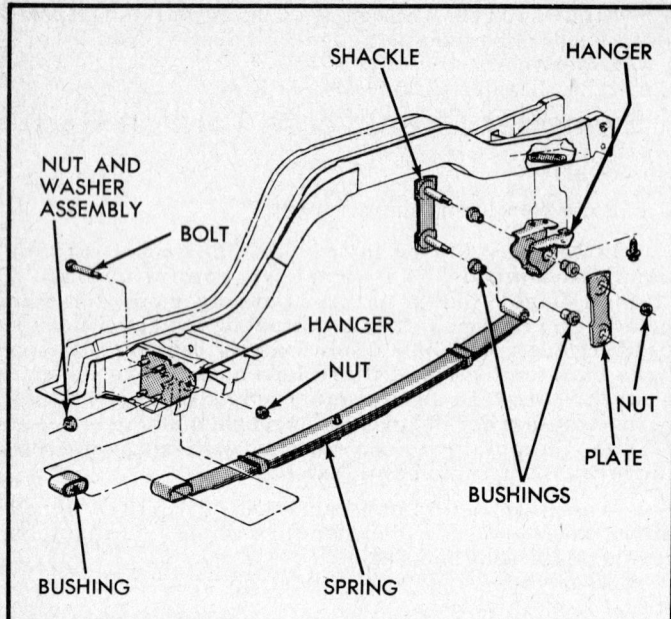

Rear suspension cars with transverse front suspension (© Chrysler Corp.)

BUSHING REPLACEMENT

It is recommended that the spring assembly be removed from the vehicle for bushing replacement on the bench.
 1. Bend two locking tabs away from spring eye on opposite side and remove bushing.
 2. Press old bushing out.
 3. Press new bushing in.

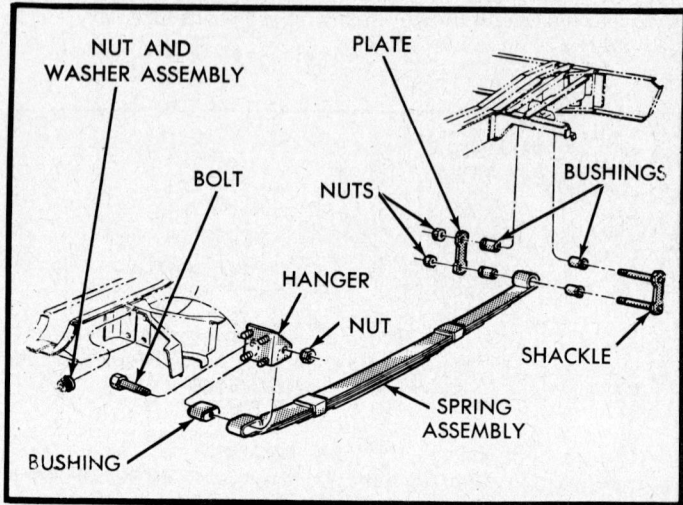

Rear suspension models with longitudinal torsion bar suspension (© Chrysler Corp.)

Removal

 1. Using floor stands under axle assembly, raise axle assembly to relieve weight on rear springs.
 2. Disconnect rear shock absorber at spring plate. Lower axle assembly, permitting rear springs to hang free (on vehicles so equipped, disconnect rear sway bar links).
 3. Loosen and remove U-bolt nuts and remove U-bolts and spring plate.
 4. Loosen and remove the nuts holding from spring hanger to body mounting bracket.
 5. Loosen and remove rear spring hanger bolts and let spring drop far enough to pull front springer hanger bolts of body mounting bracket holes.
 6. Loosen and remove from pivot bolt from front spring hanger.
 7. Loosen and remove shackle nuts and remove shackle from rear spring.

Installation

 1. Assemble shackle to spring. Do not fully tighten bolt nut.
 2. Install front spring hanger and insert pivot bolt and nut; do not fully tighten.
 3. Install rear spring hanger-to-body bracket.
 4. Raise and insert spring hanger mounting bracket bolts. Tighten to 30–35 ft. lbs. (42–46 Nm).
 5. Align axle assembly with spring center bolt. Position center bolt over lower spring plate. Insert U-bolt and nut. tighten to 45 ft. lbs. (60 Nm).
 6. Connect shock absorbers.
 7. Lower car. Tighten pivot bolts to 105 ft. lbs. (142 Nm). Tighten shackle nuts to 35 ft. lbs. (46 Nm).

CHRYSLER AUTOMATIC AIR LOAD LEVELING SYSTEM

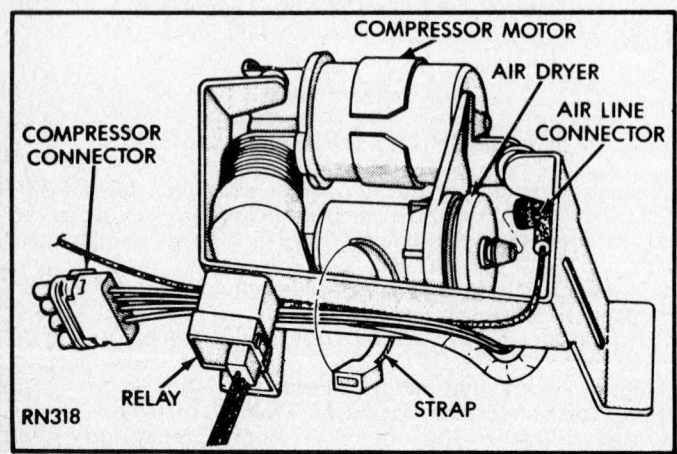

Compressor assembly

General Information

The automatic air load leveling system includes the following: compressor assembly, height sensor assembly, wiring harness, air lines, compressor relay, air shock absorbers and air dryer. The system is used to assist the standard suspension system on such equipped vehicles.

System Components

COMPRESSOR ASSEMBLY

The compressor assembly is driven by an electric motor and supplies air pressure between 120–200 psi. A solenoid operated exhaust valve, located in the compressor head assembly, releases air when energized. This valve limits maximum blow off pressure to 200 psi and will maintain a minimum system pressure of 100 psi.

SUSPENSIONS
CHRYSLER AUTOMATIC LOAD LEVELLING SYSTEM

HEIGHT SENSOR ASSEMBLY

The height sensor assembly is an electronic device that controls the ground circuits for the compressor relay and the exhaust valve solenoid. An electronic timer within the unit controls the run time from one minute and 45 seconds to three minutes and 30 seconds. This prevents damage to the leveling system.

Also included in the system, is an air replenishment cycle that is controlled by the height sensor assembly. When the ignition switch is turned to the "ON" position, after a 30–60 second delay, the compressor will run 3–5 seconds.

In order to prevent excessive cycling between the compressor and the exhaust solenoid circuits during normal ride conditions a 13–27 second delay is incorporated into the electronic timer. The height sensor is mounted on the right rear frame rail. A link from the sensor actuating arm is attached to the rear of the track bar. When the arm moves up the compressor relay is energized, when the arm moves down the exhaust solenoid is energized.

AIR LINES AND FITTINGS

The air lines are equipped with snap on fittings with two "O" rings located on the male fittings. A retainer spring locks the male fitting into a groove on the female fitting.

NOTE: When replacing air lines and/or fittings, do not kink air lines or route new components near moving components of the vehicle.

COMPRESSOR RELAY

The relay is mounted to a bracket on the compressor assembly. When the compressor is energized it allows the compressor to operate. The unit is controlled by the height sensor.

AIR ADJUSTABLE SHOCK ABSORBERS

Air shock absorbers are hydraulic shock absorbers with a neoprene bladder sealing the upper and lower sections together, forming an air cylinder.

AIR DRYER

The air dryer is attached to the compressor and is not serviceable. This component serves two purposes; it absorbs moisture from the atmosphere before it enters the system and through internal valving, maintains a residual pressure of 14–21 psi.

System Operation

RAISING VEHICLE HEIGHT

When weight is added to the rear suspension, the body of the vehicle is lowered causing the height sensor actuating arm to rotate upward. This action causes the internal time delay circuit to activate. After a time delay of 13–27 seconds, the sensor grounds pin number 3 and completes the ground circuit to the compressor relay.

When the relay is energized, the compressor motor runs and air is sent through the system. As the shock absorbers inflate, the body moves upward to the corrected position. When the body reaches the corrected level, the sensor stops the compressor operation.

LOWERING VEHICLE HEIGHT

When the weight is removed from the vehicle the body moves

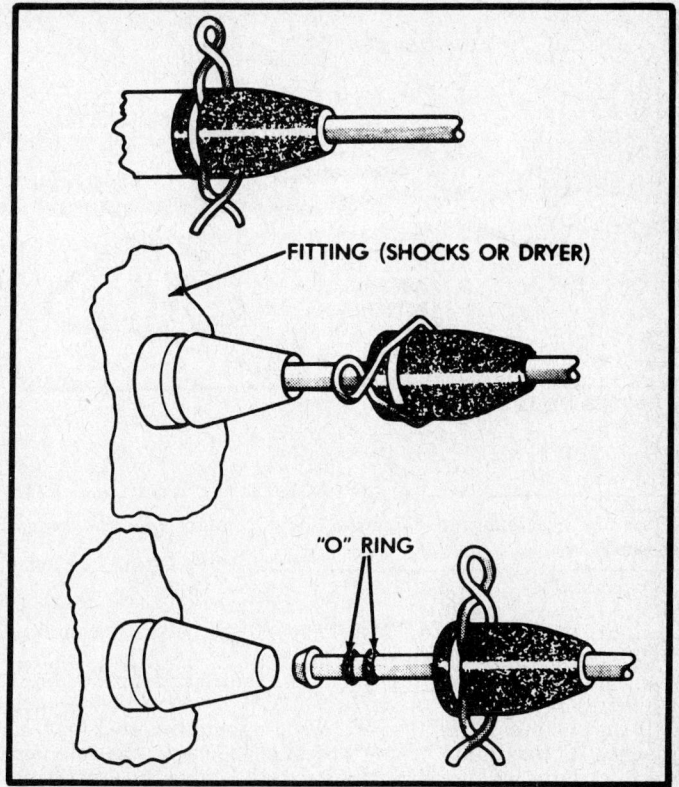

Air line fittings

upward, causing the height sensor actuating arm to rotate downward and activate the internal time delay circuit.

After a time delay of 13–27 seconds, the sensor activates the exhaust solenoid circuit. Air is exhausted from the shock absorbers through the air dryer and exhaust solenoid to the atmosphere.

As the body lowers, the height sensor actuating arm rotates towards its original position. When the body reaches the original vehicle height the sensor opens the exhaust solenoid valve circuit.

Troubleshooting

COMPRESSOR

Performance Test

This test can be performed on the vehicle in order to evaluate the compressor current draw, leak down and pressure output.

1. Tag and disconnect the compressor motor wiring harness connector.
2. Disconnect the compressor air line at the air line "T" connector.
3. Connect an air pressure gauge into the air line between the compressor and the air hose tee.
4. Connect an ammeter in series between the orange wire in the wiring harness and the dark green wire to the compressor motor
5. Connect a ground wire from the black wire on the compressor motor to a known ground located on the frame.
6. If the current draw to the compressor motor exceeds 14 amps, replace the compressor assembly.
7. When the air pressure stabilizes at 120 psi, disconnect the positive (+) lead from the connector.

SECTION 35 SUSPENSIONS
CHRYSLER AUTOMATIC LOAD LEVELLING SYSTEM

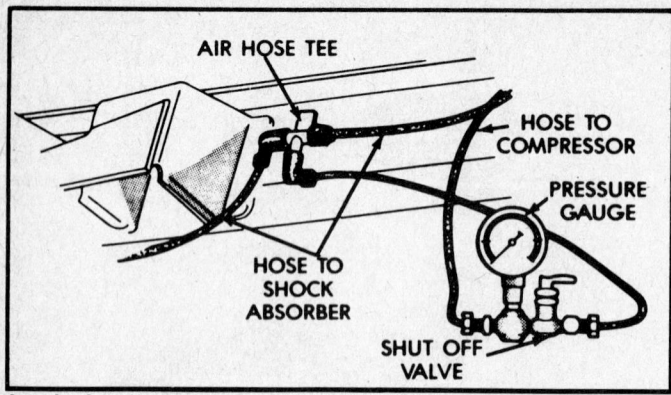

Leak down test

CAUTION
If any of the following conditions exist, replace the compressor assembly.

1. Air pressure leaks down below 90 psi before it remains steady.
2. Output pressure builds up to less than 110 psi psi when it stabilizes.

If the compressor is allowed to run during this test until it reaches its maximum output pressure (200 psi), the solenoid exhaust valve will act as a pressure relief valve. The resulting leak down after the compressor is shut off will indicate a false leak.

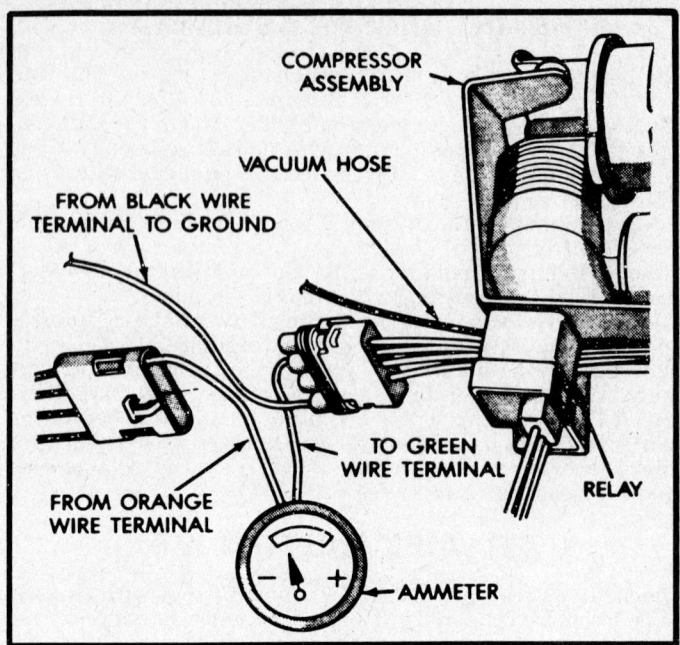

Compressor current draw test

HEIGHT SENSOR

Performance Test

1. Cycle the ignition off then on. This resets the height sensor timer circuit.

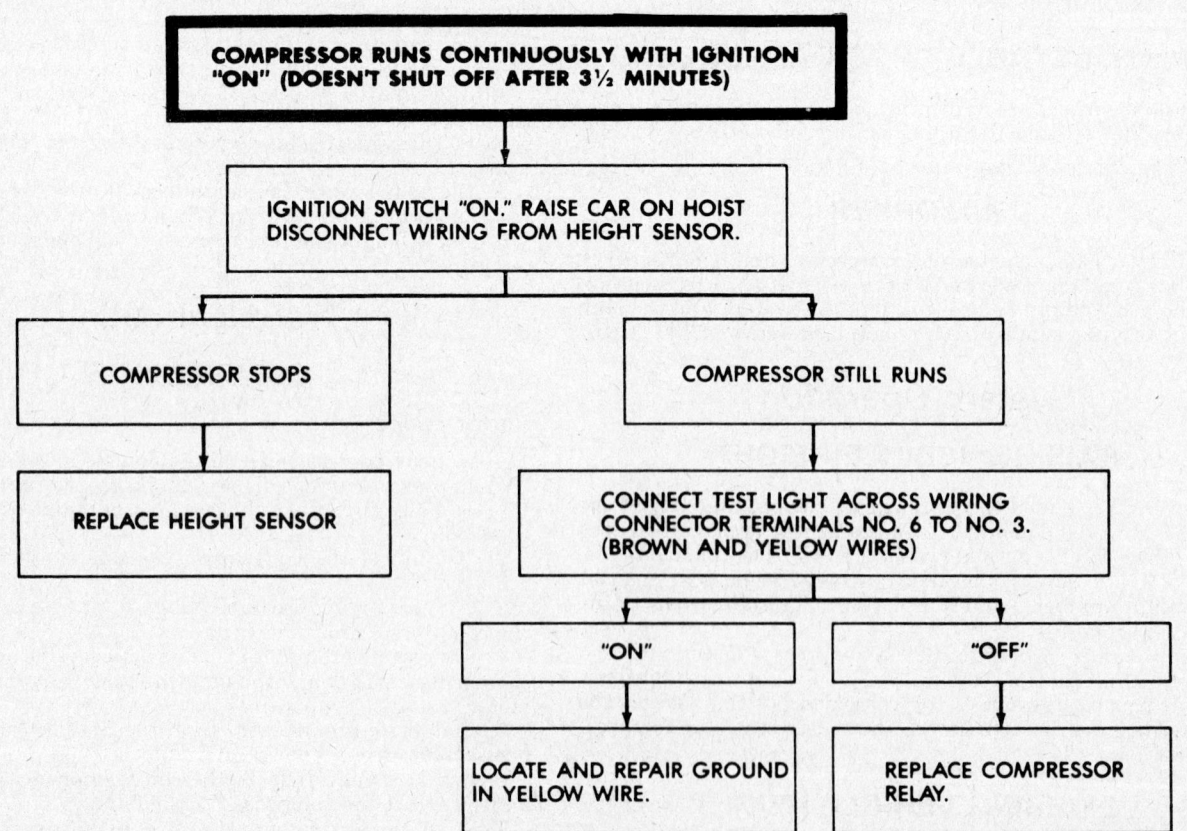

35-42

SUSPENSIONS
CHRYSLER AUTOMATIC LOAD LEVELLING SYSTEM
SECTION 35

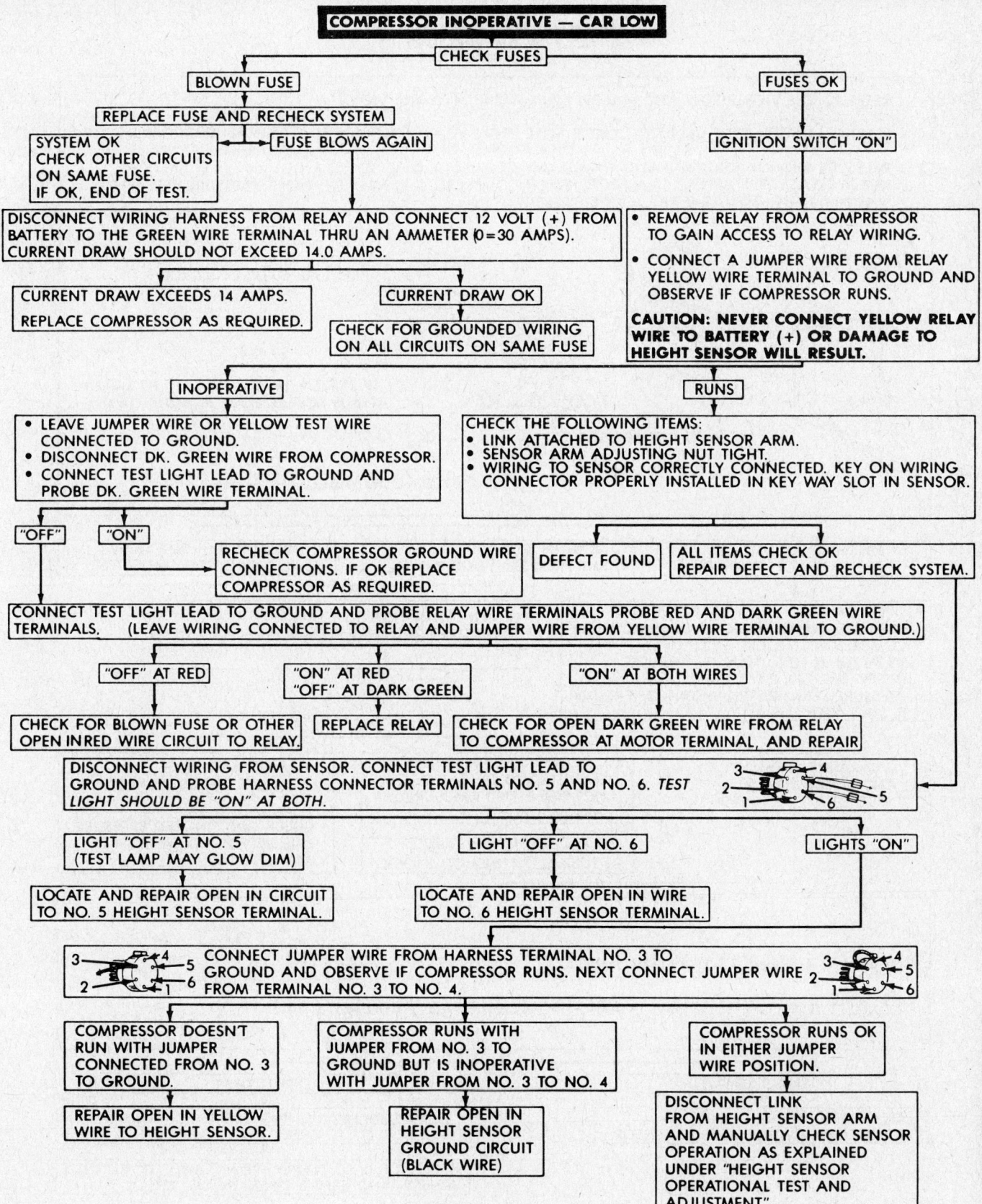

35-43

SECTION 35: SUSPENSIONS
CHRYSLER AUTOMATIC LOAD LEVELLING SYSTEM

LOSS OF AIR PRESSURE

REFER TO THE VIEW BELOW AND FOLLOW STEPS 1 THRU 4 IN THE VIEW.

- IGNITION SWITCH "ON." CONNECT JUMPER WIRE FROM RELAY YELLOW WIRE TERMINAL TO GROUND.

- PRESSURE SHOULD BUILD UP RAPIDLY. SHUT OFF COMPRESSOR AT 120 PSI AND OBSERVE IF PRESSURE HOLDS STEADY FOR APPROX. 5 MINUTES. WHEN COMPRESSOR IS FIRST SHUT OFF, PRESSURE MAY DROP SLIGHTLY THEN STABILIZE IF NO LEAK IS PRESENT.

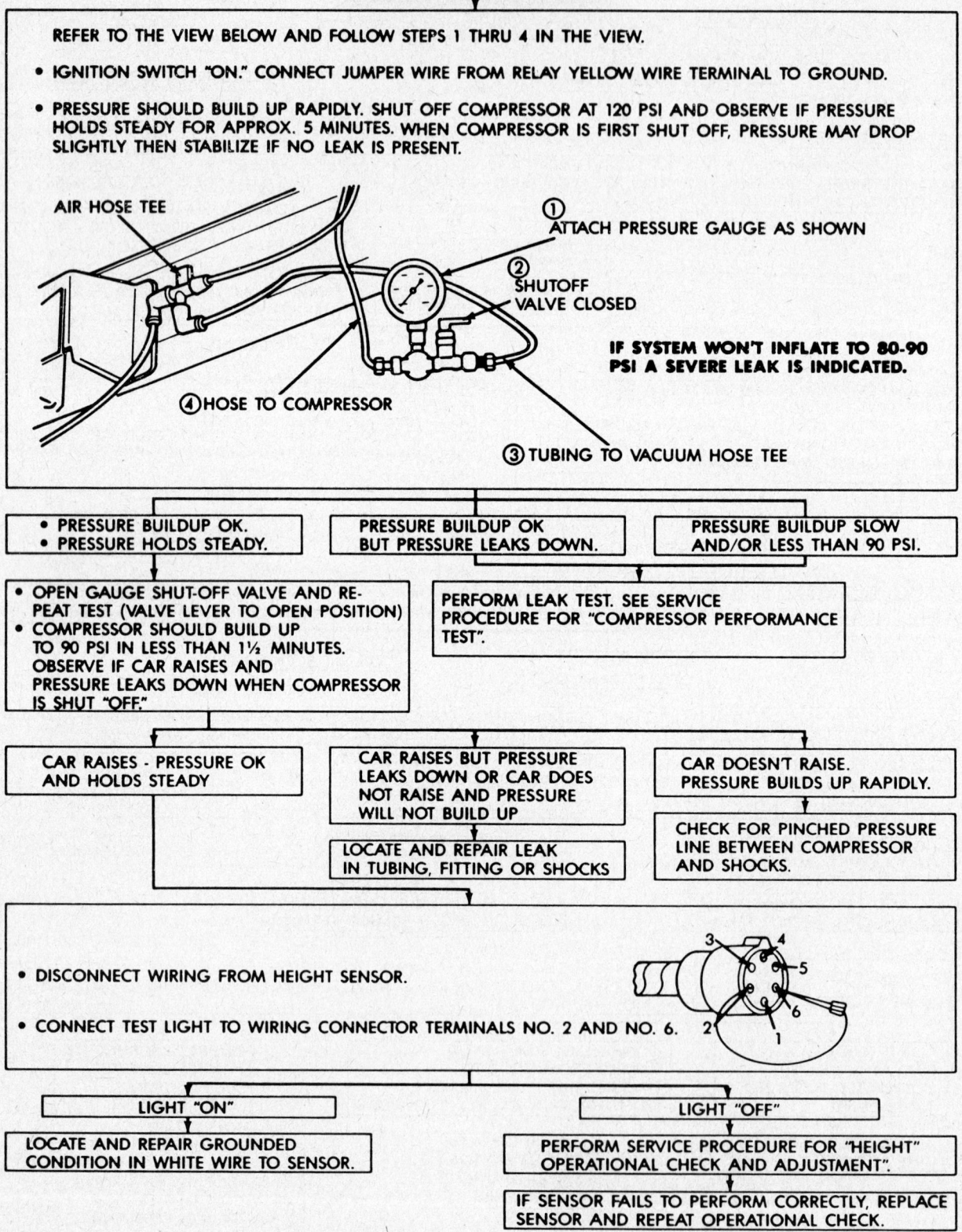

- AIR HOSE TEE
- ① ATTACH PRESSURE GAUGE AS SHOWN
- ② SHUTOFF VALVE CLOSED
- ③ TUBING TO VACUUM HOSE TEE
- ④ HOSE TO COMPRESSOR

IF SYSTEM WON'T INFLATE TO 80-90 PSI A SEVERE LEAK IS INDICATED.

PRESSURE BUILDUP OK. PRESSURE HOLDS STEADY.
- OPEN GAUGE SHUT-OFF VALVE AND REPEAT TEST (VALVE LEVER TO OPEN POSITION)
- COMPRESSOR SHOULD BUILD UP TO 90 PSI IN LESS THAN 1½ MINUTES. OBSERVE IF CAR RAISES AND PRESSURE LEAKS DOWN WHEN COMPRESSOR IS SHUT "OFF."

PRESSURE BUILDUP OK BUT PRESSURE LEAKS DOWN.
PERFORM LEAK TEST. SEE SERVICE PROCEDURE FOR "COMPRESSOR PERFORMANCE TEST".

PRESSURE BUILDUP SLOW AND/OR LESS THAN 90 PSI.

CAR RAISES - PRESSURE OK AND HOLDS STEADY

CAR RAISES BUT PRESSURE LEAKS DOWN OR CAR DOES NOT RAISE AND PRESSURE WILL NOT BUILD UP
LOCATE AND REPAIR LEAK IN TUBING, FITTING OR SHOCKS

CAR DOESN'T RAISE. PRESSURE BUILDS UP RAPIDLY.
CHECK FOR PINCHED PRESSURE LINE BETWEEN COMPRESSOR AND SHOCKS.

- DISCONNECT WIRING FROM HEIGHT SENSOR.
- CONNECT TEST LIGHT TO WIRING CONNECTOR TERMINALS NO. 2 AND NO. 6.

LIGHT "ON"
LOCATE AND REPAIR GROUNDED CONDITION IN WHITE WIRE TO SENSOR.

LIGHT "OFF"
PERFORM SERVICE PROCEDURE FOR "HEIGHT" OPERATIONAL CHECK AND ADJUSTMENT".

IF SENSOR FAILS TO PERFORM CORRECTLY, REPLACE SENSOR AND REPEAT OPERATIONAL CHECK.

SUSPENSIONS
CHRYSLER AUTOMATIC LOAD LEVELLING SYSTEM
SECTION 35

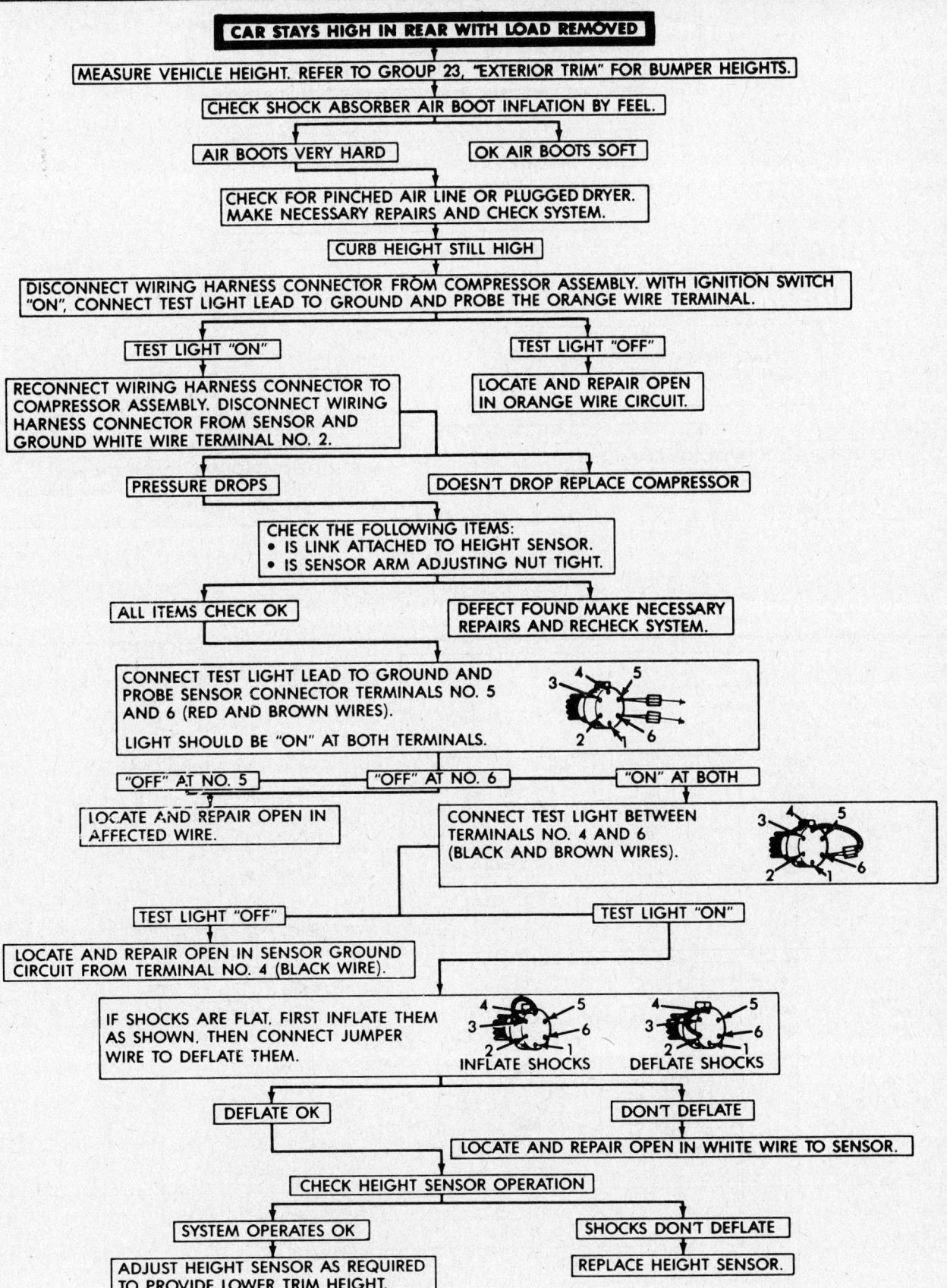

35-45

SECTION 35
SUSPENSIONS
CHRYSLER AUTOMATIC LOAD LEVELLING SYSTEM

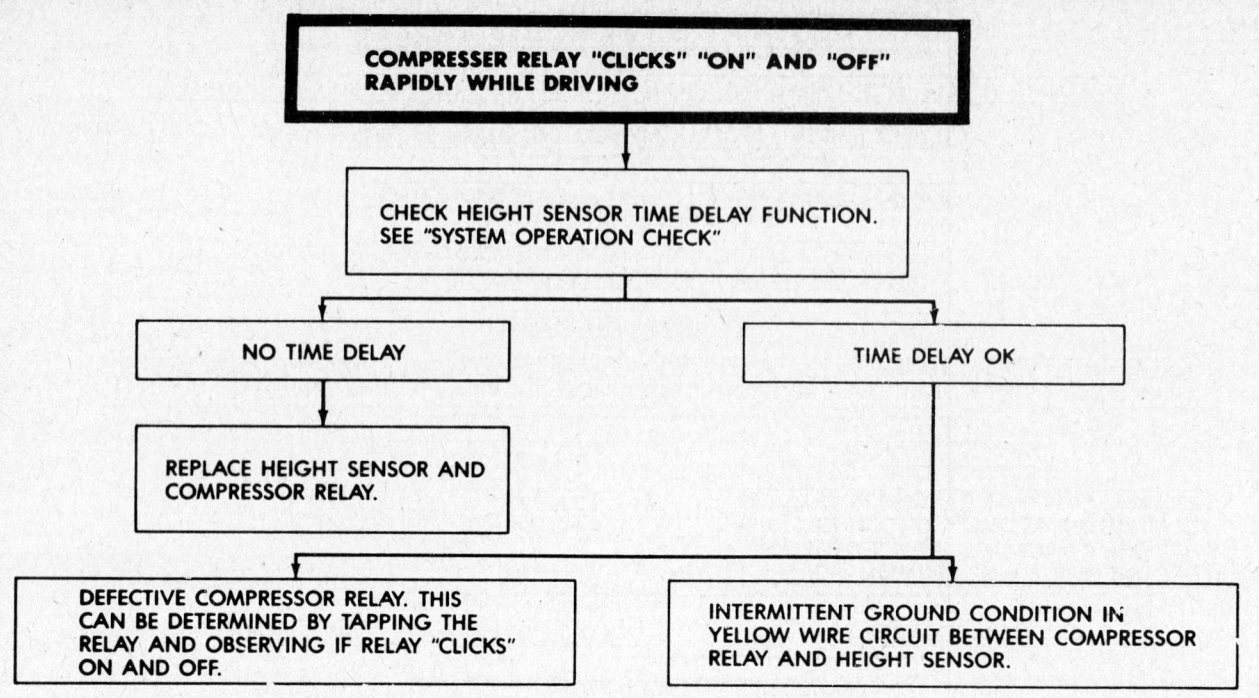

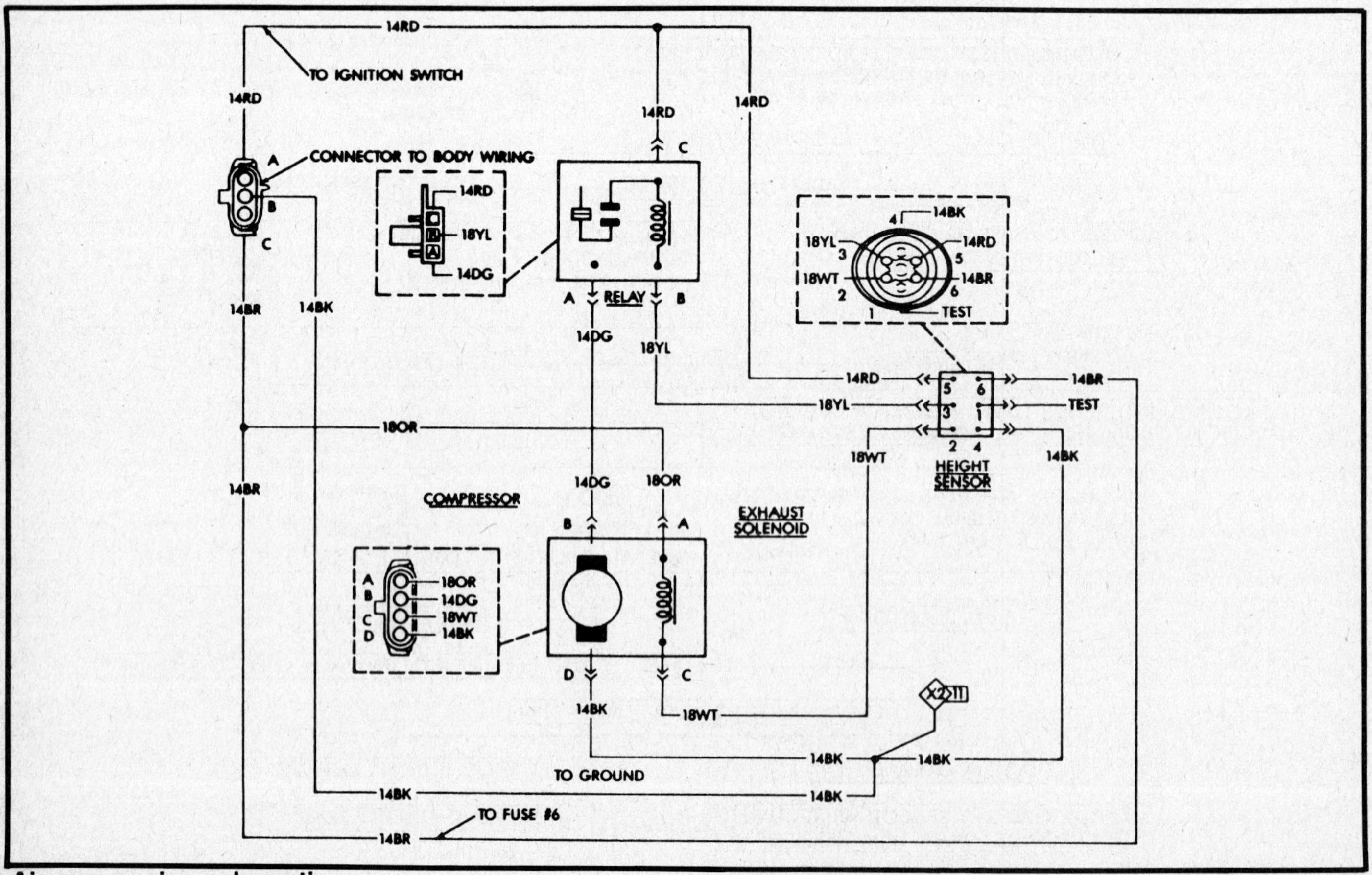

Air suspension schematic

35-46

SUSPENSIONS
CHRYSLER AUTOMATIC LOAD LEVELLING SYSTEM

2. Raise the vehicle and support safely.
3. Inspect the wiring to see that it is properly secured to the height sensor.
4. Disconnect the link from the height sensor arm and move up. There should be a 13–27 second delay before the compressor turns on and the shocks begin to inflate.

CAUTION
As soon as the shock absorber bladder fills, stop the compressor by moving the sensor arm down as damage to the air bladder can result.

5. There should be a 13–27 second delay after the sensor arm is moved down before the shocks begin to deflate.

Component Replacement

COMPRESSOR

Removal
1. Disconnect the negative battery cable.
2. Raise the vehicle and support safely.
3. Remove cover from the compressor assembly and discharge the air system.
4. Remove the air hose from the electrical connectors.
5. Remove the compressor assembly mounting bolts. Lower the assembly from the vehicle.
6. Remove the mounting bracket bolts and slide the mounting bracket away from the compressor.

Installation
1. Install the mounting bracket on the compressor and install the bolts and tighten to 70 inch pounds (8 Nm).
2. Install the compressor assembly to the frame rail and tighten the bolts to 70 inch pounds (8 Nm).
3. Connect the air hose and electrical connectors to the compressor.

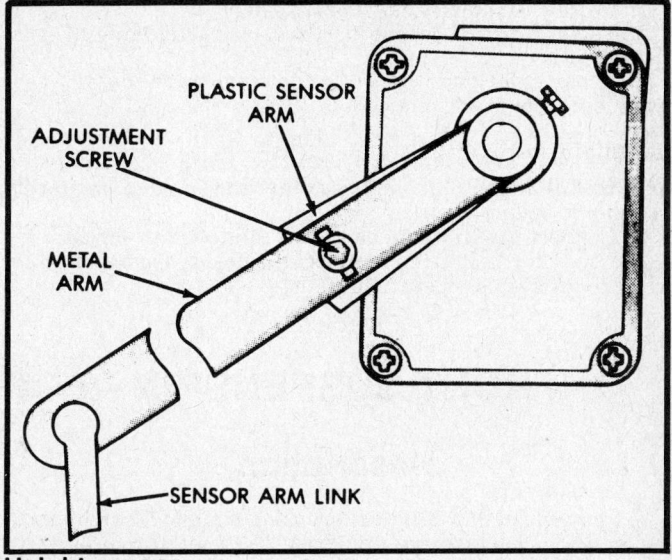
Height sensor

4. Install the compressor cover and tighten the bolts to 70 inch pounds (8 Nm).
5. Lower the vehicle and connect the negative battery cable.
6. Turn the ignition switch to the "ON" position and then back to "OFF" in order to reset the height sensor timing circuits.
7. Check the operation of system.

HEIGHT SENSOR

Removal
1. Disconnect the negative battery cable.

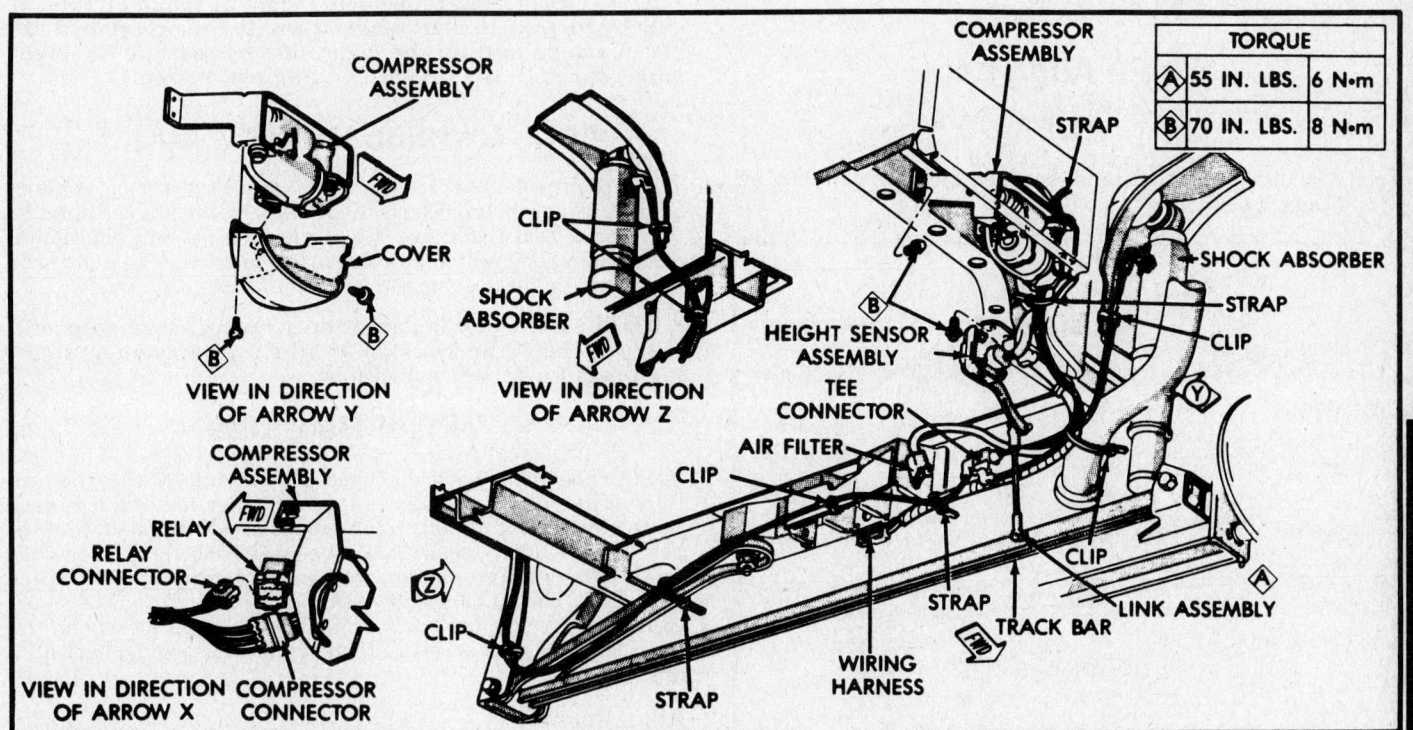
Automatic air load levelling system

SECTION 35 SUSPENSIONS
CHRYSLER AUTOMATIC LOAD LEVELLING SYSTEM

2. Raise the vehicle and support safely.
3. Tag and disconnect the electrical connector and link from the sensor arm.
4. Remove the mounting bolts and remove the height sensor assembly from the frame rail.

Installation

1. Install height sensor assembly and tighten mounting bolts to 70 inch pounds (8 Nm).
2. Connect the link and electrical connector to sensor.
3. Lower the vehicle and connect the negative battery cable.
4. Check system operation.

Adjustment

1. Loosen the lock nut on the sensor arm.
2. To increase vehicle height, move the sensor arm upward and tighten.
3. To decrease vehicle height, move the sensor arm downward and tighten.
4. Check for proper system operation and vehicle height.

NOTE: Due to the diagnostic complexity of the Automatic Load Levelling System, detailed diagnostic procedures can be found in Chilton's Chassis Electronic Service Manual.

FRONT SUSPENSION—FORD FRONT WHEEL DRIVE CARS

Description

The front wheel drive front suspension is a MacPherson strut design with cast steering knuckles. The shock absorber strut assembly includes a rubber top mount and a coil spring insulator, mounted on the shock strut.

The entire strut assembly is attached at the top by two bolts, which retain the top mount of the strut to the body side apron. The lower end of the assembly is attached to the steering knuckle. A forged lower arm assembly is attached to the underbody side apron and steering knuckle. A stabilizer bar connects the outer end of lower arm to the engine mount bracket. The drive shaft outer stub shaft and wheel hub are attached inside the steering knuckle hub by a pressed fit of mating splines. The assembly is secured by a staked nut on the end of the stub shaft. The hub rotates on two non-adjustable tapered roller bearings which seat against cups in the steering knuckle.

Taurus and Sable shock absorbers are gas pressurized which will result in the struts being fully extended when not restrained. If a strut does not fully extend when inspected, it is damaged and should be replaced.

Wheel Alignment

TOE

Toe is the difference in distance between the front and the rear of the front wheels.

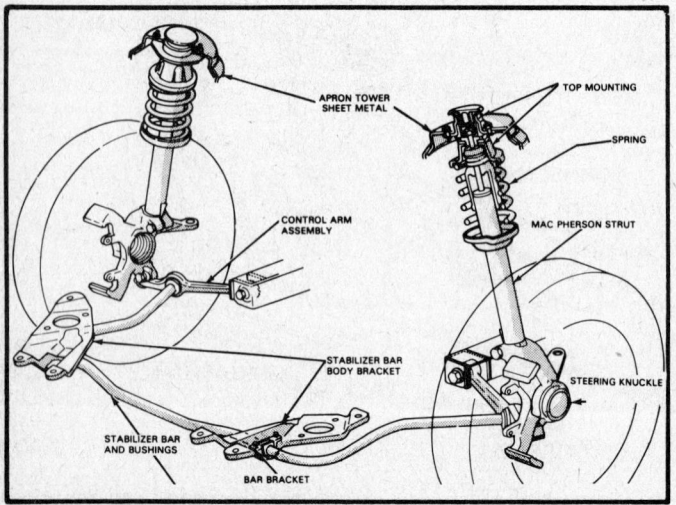

Front wheel drive suspension (© Ford Motor Co.)

1. Start the engine (power steering only) and move the steering wheel back and forth several times until it is in the straight ahead or centered position.
2. Turn the engine off (power steering only) and lock the steering wheel in place using a steering wheel holder. Loosen and slide off small outer clamp front boot prior to starting toe adjustment to prevent boot from twisting.
3. Adjust left and right tie rods until each wheel has one-half of the desired total toe specification.

NOTE: When jam nuts are loosened for toe adjustment, the nuts must be tightened to specifications. Attach boot clamp after setting is completed and make sure boot is not twisted.

CASTER AND CAMBER

Caster and camber angles of this suspension system are preset at the factor and cannot be adjusted. Measurement procedures are for diagnostic purposes.

NOTE: Caster measurements must be made on the left side by turning the left wheel through the prescribed angle of sweep and on the right side by turning the right wheel through the prescribed angle of sweep.

FRONT WHEEL TURNING ANGLE

When the inside wheel is turned 20 degrees, turning angle of outside wheel should be specified. The turning angle cannot be adjusted directly, because it is a result of the combination of caster, camber and toe adjustments and should, therefore, be measured only after the toe adjustment has been made.

NOTE: If the turning angle does not measure to specifications, check the knuckle or other suspension or steering parts for a bent condition.

Wheel Bearings

Front wheel bearings are located in the front knuckle, not the rotor. The bearings are protected by inner and outer grease seals and an additional inner grease shield immediately inboard of the inner grease seal. The wheel hub is installed with an interference fit to the constant velocity universal joint outer race shaft. The hub nut and washer are installed and tightened to 180–200 ft. lbs. (240–270 Nm). The rotor fits loosely on the hub assembly and is secured when the wheel and wheel nuts are installed.

Adjustment

The front wheel bearings have a set-right design that requires no scheduled maintenance. The bearing design relies on component stack-up and deformation/torque at assembly to determine bearing setting. Therefore, bearings cannot be adjusted. In addition to the maintaining bearing adjustment, the hub nut torque of 180–200 ft. lbs. (240–270 Nm) restricts bearing/hub relative movement and maintains axial position of the hub. Due to the importance of the hub nut torque/tension relationship, certain precautions must be taken during service.

1. The hub nut must be replaced with a new nut whenever the nut is backed off or removed after the nut has been staked. Never re-use the nut.
2. The hub nut must not be backed off after reaching the required torque of 180–200 ft. lbs. (240–270 Nm) during installation.
3. The hub nut collar must be staked into the outboard constant velocity joint slot with the proper tool to make sure the required torque is maintained during vehicle operation. The nut collar must not split or crack when staked. If the collar splits or cracks, the nut must be replaced.
4. Impact type tools must not be used to tighten the hub nut or bearing damage will result.
5. The hub and constant velocity joint splines have an interference fit requiring special tools for removal and assembly. The hub nut must not be used to accomplish assembly.
6. To remove the hub nut, apply sufficient torque to the nut to overcome the prevailing torque feature of the crimp in the nut collar. Do not use tools such as a screwdriver or chisel to remove the crimp.

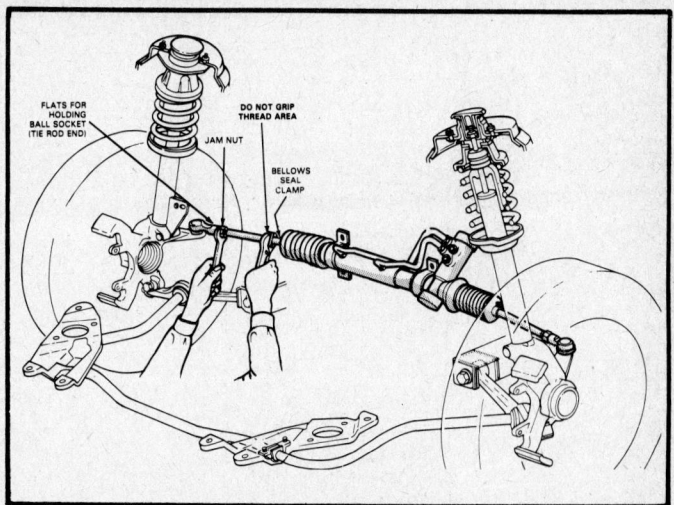

Tie rod adjustment (© Ford Motor Co.)

2. Raise the vehicle and support safely. Remove brake caliper. Do not remove caliper pins from the caliper assembly. Lift caliper off the rotor and hang it free of the rotor. Do not allow caliper assembly to hang from the brake hose. Support caliper assembly.
3. Remove rotor from hub by pulling if off the hub bolts.
4. Install hub remover/install tool, T81P-1104-A with T81P-1104-C adaptors T81P-B or equivalent, and remove the hub. If outer bearing is seized on the hub, use a puller to remove the bearing. Be careful not to damage bearing if it is being re-used and not to raise burrs on the hub journal diameter. If bearings are being re-used, carefully inspect both bearing cone and rollers, bearing cups and lubrication for any signs of damage or contamination. If damage or contamination exists, replace all bearing components including cups and seals. In the event the bearings are acceptable, clean and repack bearing components. Inner and outer grease retainers and hub nut must be replaced whenever bearings are inspected.
5. Remove front suspension knuckle.

Installation

1. Place front knuckle and bearing assembly in a vise so that the inner knuckle bore faces upward (to prevent inner bearing from falling out of the knuckle). Start hub into outer knuckle bore and push the hub by hand through outer and inner wheel bearings as far as possible.

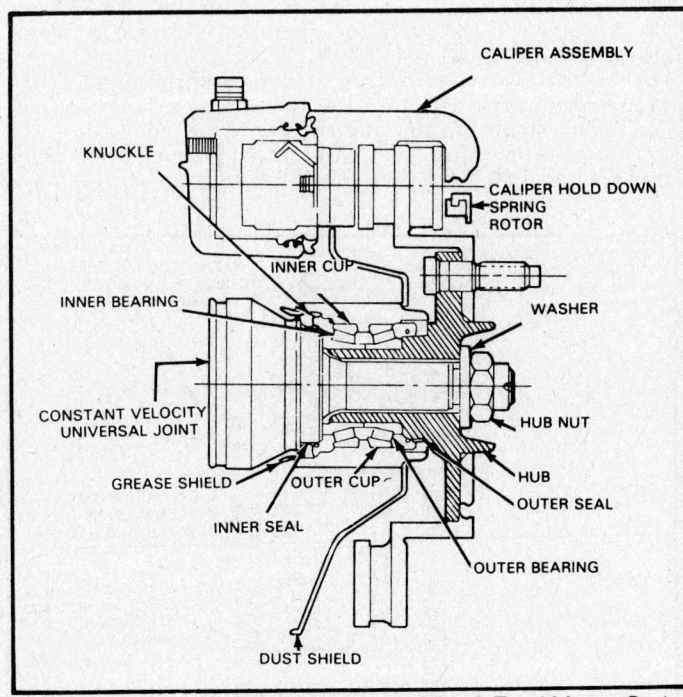

Wheel bearing and caliper assembly (© Ford Motor Co.)

Front Hub

Removal

1. Remove hub retaining nut and washer by applying sufficient torque to the nut to overcome prevailing torque features of the crimp in the nut collar. Do not use tools such as a screwdriver or chisel to remove the crimp or use an impact-type tool to remove the hub nut. The hub nut must be discarded after removal.

CAUTION

Prior to assembly, remove burrs, nicks, score marks, foreign material (rust, dirt, etc.) from hub bearing journal. Due to the very close tolerance 0.0005 in. (0.012 mm) between the wheel bearing inside diameter and the hub assembly, it is important to install hub completely through inner and outer wheel bearings. Hand pressure only is essential to this procedure. Forcing or jamming bearing race (cone) on the hub barrel will cause burrs that can prevent proper installation. Do not strike hub with any type of tool.

NOTE: Crocus cloth may be used to remove burrs, score marks and rust from the hub barrel.

2. With the hub fully seated in the bearings, position hub and knuckle assembly to front strut. Attach the knuckle to the strut.
3. Lightly lubricate the constant velocity joint stub shaft splines using S.A.E. 30 motor oil.
4. Using hand pressure only, insert splines of the constant velocity joint stub shaft into knuckle/hub assembly as far as

SECTION 35

SUSPENSIONS
FRONT SUSPENSION—FORD FRONT DRIVE CARS

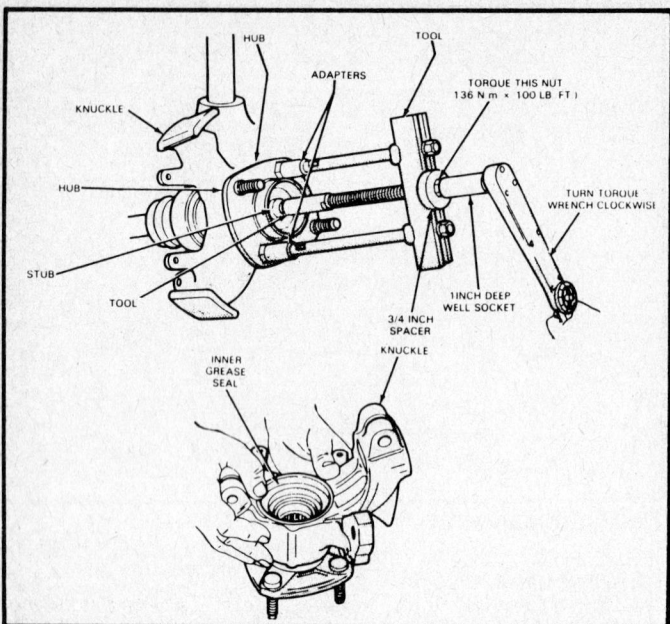

Step 1. Install hub to knuckle after bearing installation. Knuckle must be positioned as shown and hub must be inserted through bearings using hand pressure only. **Step 2.** Install hub tro constant velocity universal joint splined stub shaft. Tighten tool nut to 150 Nm (110 ft. lbs.) using torque wrench to seat hub (© Ford Motor Co.)

possible. Install hub installer tool T81P-1104-C-B-A to the hub and stub shaft.

— **CAUTION** —
Care must be taken during installation to prevent hub from backing out of bearing assembly. Otherwise, it will be necessary to reassemble hub through bearings.

5. Tighten hub installer tool to 120 ft. lbs. (163 Nm) torque to make sure that the hub is fully seated. Remove tool and install washer and hub nut. Tighten the hub nut finger tight.
6. Install disc brake rotor and brake caliper.
7. Lower vehicle and block wheels to prevent rolling.
8. Tighten wheel nuts to 80–105 ft. lbs. (109–142 Nm) torque.

Strut, Spring And Upper Mount

Removal

1. Raise front of vehicle and place jack stands under frame jack pads, rearward of the wheels. Do not raise the Taurus or Sable by the lower control arms.
2. Remove tire and wheel assembly.
3. Remove brake line flex hose clip from strut. If necessary, remove the brake rotor in order to gain working clearance.
4. Place a floor jack under lower control arm and raise strut as far as possible without lifting vehicle.
5. Install spring compressor tool by placing top jaw on second coil from top and bottom jaw so as to grip a total of five coils. Compress spring until there is about 1/8 in. between any two coils.

— **CAUTION** —
Use hand wrenches (no impact wrenches)

6. Using a pry bar, slightly spread knuckle-to-strut pinch joint.
7. Place a piece of wood, 2 in. by 4 in., and 7 1/2 in. long, against shoulder on the knuckle. Using a short pry bar between wood block and lower spring seat, separate the strut from the knuckle.
8. Remove two top mounting nuts.
9. Remove strut, spring and top mount assembly from vehicle.
10. Place an 18 mm deep socket on strut shaft nut. Insert a 6 mm allen wrench into shaft end and the clamp mount into a vise. Remove top shaft mounting nut from shaft while holding allen wrench with vise grips or a suitable extension.
11. Remove strut top mount components and spring.

Installation

1. Position compressed spring in lower spring seat. Be sure that:
   a. Pigtail of spring is indexed to seat.
   b. Spring compressor tool is positioned 90 degrees from metal tab on lower part of strut.
2. Using a new nut, assemble top mount components to strut.

— **CAUTION** —
Be sure that the correct assembly sequence and proper positioning of bearing and seal assembly is followed. If bearing and seal assembly is out of position, damage to bearing will result.

3. Tighten shaft nut to torque of 48–62.5 ft. lbs. (65–85 Nm).
4. Install strut, spring, upper mount and spring compressor into the vehicle as an assembly.
5. Position two top mounts attacking studs through holes in apron and start two new nuts. Do not tighten nuts at this time.
6. Install strut into steering knuckle pinch point.
7. Install a new pinch bolt in the steering knuckle and tighten to torque of 68–81 ft. lbs. (90–110 Nm).

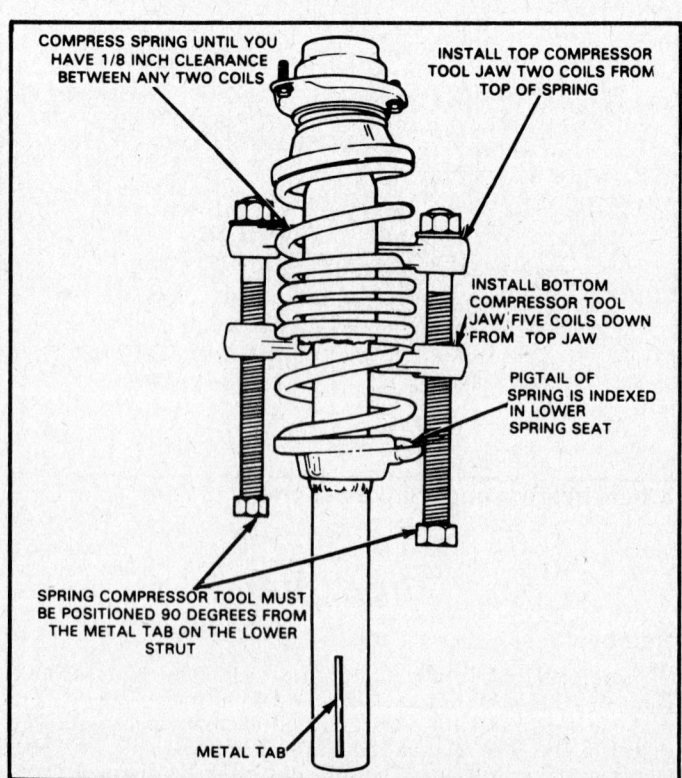

Spring comprssor tool (© Ford Motor Co.)

SUSPENSIONS
FRONT SUSPENSION—FORD FRONT DRIVE CARS
Section 35

8. Tighten two upper mount attaching nuts to torque of 22–29 ft. lbs. (30–40 Nm).
9. Remove spring compressor from the vehicle. As the compressor is loosened, be sure the spring ends are indexed in upper and lower spring seats.
10. Install brake line flex hose clip to strut.
11. Install tire and wheel assembly.
12. Remove jack stands and lower vehicle.

Steering Knuckle

Removal

1. Raise vehicle on a hoist.
2. Remove tire and wheel assembly.
3. Remove cotter pin from the tie rod end strut and remove fitted nut.
4. Remove tie rod end from knuckle.
5. Remove the brake caliper and rotor. Wire off to the side in order to gain working clearance.
6. Remove the hub from the driveshaft.
7. Remove lower arm-to-steering knuckle pinch bolt and nut. (A drift punch may be used to remove production bolt.) Using a screwdriver, slightly spread the knuckle-to-lower arm pinch joint and remove lower arm from steering knuckle.

NOTE: Be sure steering column is in unlocked position and do not use a hammer to separate ball joint from knuckle.

8. Remove shock absorber strut-to-steering knuckle pinch bolt. Using a pry bar, slightly spread knuckle-to-strut pinch joint.
9. Remove steering knuckle from the shock absorber strut.
10. Place assembly on a bench and remove the seals are bearings.
11. Remove rotor splash shield from knuckle. Remove the hub, retainer ring and bearing

Installation

1. Install a rotor splash shield.

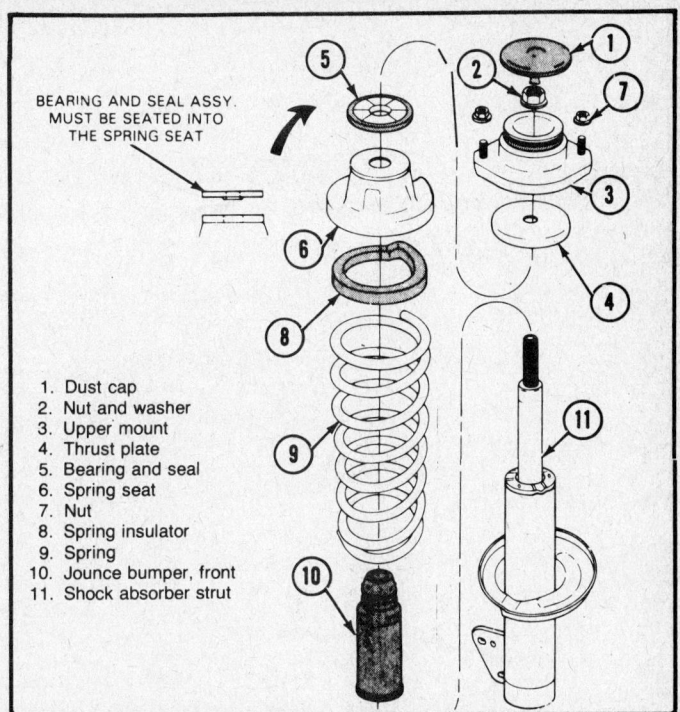

Top mount components (© Ford Motor Co.)

1. Dust cap
2. Nut and washer
3. Upper mount
4. Thrust plate
5. Bearing and seal
6. Spring seat
7. Nut
8. Spring insulator
9. Spring
10. Jounce bumper, front
11. Shock absorber strut

2. Install bearings and seals.
3. Install steering knuckle onto shock absorber strut and install a new pinch bolt in knuckle to retain strut. Tighten nut to torque of 66–81 ft. lbs. (99–110 Nm).
4. Install hub on the driveshaft.
5. Install lower control arm to knuckle, ensuring that ball stud groove is properly positioned. Install a new nut and bolt. Tighten to torque of 37–44 ft. lbs. (50–60 Nm).
6. Install the brake caliper.
7. Position tie rod end into knuckle, install a new slotted nut and tighten to torque of 25–35 ft. lbs. (31–47 Nm). If necessary, advance nut to align slot and install a new cotter pin.
8. Install tire and wheel assembly.

Lower Ball Joint Check

1. Raise vehicle on a frame contact hoist or by floor jacks placed beneath the underbody until wheel fall to the full down position.
2. Ask an assistant to grasp lower edge of the tire and move wheel and tire assembly in and out.
3. As wheel is being moved in and out, observe the lower end of the knuckle and the lower control arm. Any movement between the lower end of knuckle and lower arm indicates abnormal ball joint wear.
4. If any movement is observed, install a new lower control arm assembly.

Lower Control Arm

Removal

1. Raise vehicle and support safely. Remove the wheel and tire assembly.
2. Remove nut from the stabilizer bar. Pull off large dished water.
3. Remove lower control arm inner pivot bolt and nut.
4. Remove lower control arm ball joint pinch bolt. Slightly

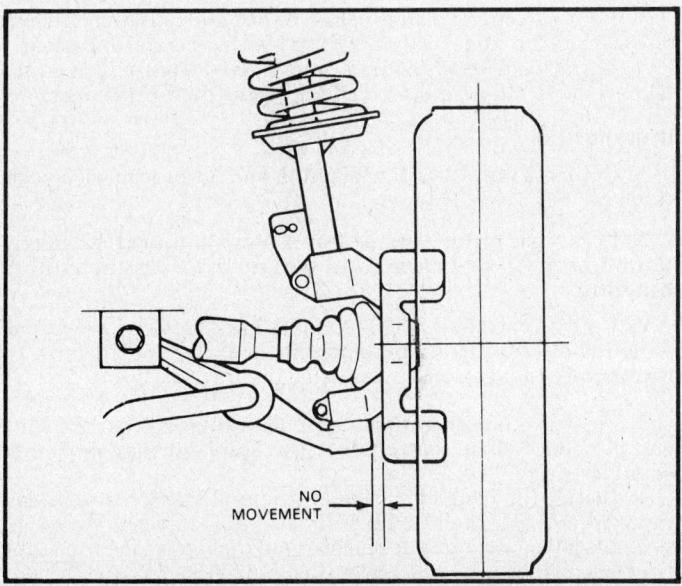

As wheel is being moved in and out, observe the lower end of the knuckle and the lower control arm. Any movement between lower end of knuckle and the lower arm indicates abnormal ball jopint wear (© Ford Motor Co.)

35-51

SECTION 35

SUSPENSIONS
FRONT SUSPENSION—FORD FRONT DRIVE CARS

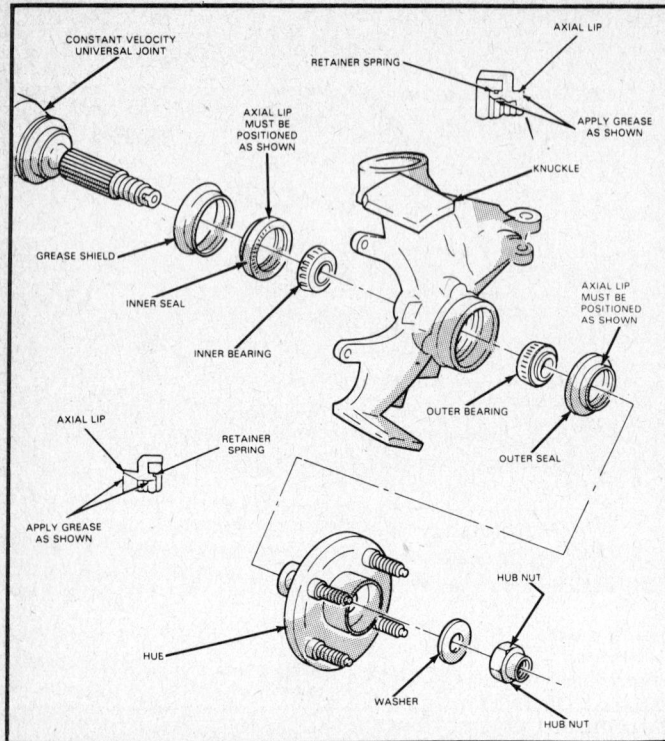

Steering knuckle (© Ford Motor Co.)

spread the knuckle pinch joint and separate control arm from the steering knuckle. A drift punch may be used to remove the bolt.

NOTE: Be sure steering column is in unlocked position, and DO NOT use a hammer to separate ball joint from knuckle.

5. Remove the lower control arm pivot bolt and nut. Remove the lower control arm assembly from the tension strut.

Installation

1. Assemble lower control arm ball joint stud to the steering knuckle, insuring that the ball stud groove is properly positioned.

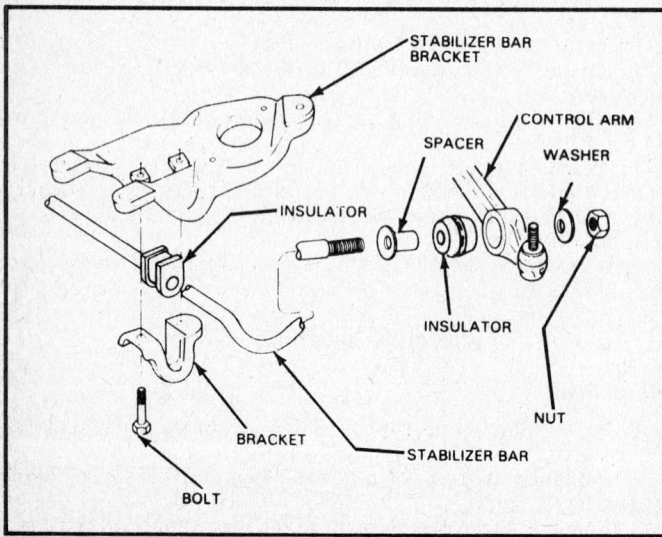

Stabilizer bar components (© Ford Motor Co.)

2. Insert a new pinch bolt and nut. Tighten nut to torque of 37–44 ft. lbs. (50–60 Nm).
3. Position lower control arm onto stabilizer bar and then position lower control arm to the inner underbody mounting. Install a new nut and bolt. Tighten bolt to torque of 44–55 ft. lbs. (60–75 Nm).
4. Assemble stabilizer bar, dished washer and a new nut to stabilizer bar. Tighten nut to torque of 59–73 ft. lbs. (80–110 Nm).

Stabilizer Bar and Insulators

Removal

1. Raise the vehicle and support safely.
2. Remove nut from the stabilizer bar from each lower control arm and remove the large dished washer.
3. Remove the stabilizer bar insulator mounting bracket bolts and remove the stabilizer bar assembly.
4. Remove the worn insulators from the bar.

Installation

1. Coat the bar and insulators using petroleum jelly. Slide the new insulators onto the bar and position in the approximate final position.
2. Install the washer spacers onto the bar ends and push the mounting brackets over the insulators.
3. Insert the ends of the bar into the lower control arms. Using new bolts, attach the bar and insulator mounting brackets to body. Tighten to 80–92 Nm. (59–68 ft. lbs.).
4. Using the new nuts and original dished washers, attach the bar to the lower control arms. Tighten the nuts to 133–156 Nm. (98–115 ft. lbs.).

Stabilizer Bar—To—Control Arm Insulator

Removal

1. Raise vehicle on a hoist.
2. Remove stabilizer bar-to-control arm nut and dished washer.
3. Remove control arm inner pivot nut and bolt and pull arm down from the underbody and away from the stabilizer bar.
4. Using Tool T81P–5493–A and T74P–3044–A1 or equivalent, remove old insulator bushing from the control arm.

Installation

1. Saturate new insulator bushing and lower arm with vegetable oil.

NOTE: Use only vegetable oil. Any mineral or petroleum based oil or brake fluid will deteriorate the rubber bushing.

2. Using Tool T81P–5493–A and T74P–3044–A1 or equivalent, install new insulator bushing in lower control arm by tightening the C-clamp very slowly until bushing pops in place.
3. Position the control arm onto the stabilizer bar. Washer end of spacer must seat against the stabilizer bar machined shoulder.
4. Install the control arm to on the underbody using a new nut and bolt. Tighten to 48–55 ft. lbs. (65–75 Nm).
5. Install a new nut and the original dished washer on stabilizer bar. Tighten to 98–115 ft. lbs. (133–156 Nm).

Lower Arm Inner Pivot Bushing

Removal

1. Raise vehicle on a hoist.

SUSPENSIONS
FRONT SUSPENSION—FORD FRONT DRIVE CARS

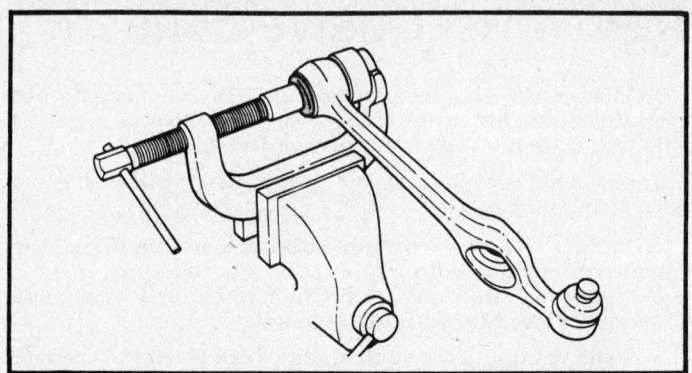

Inner pivot bushing installation (© Ford Motor Co.)

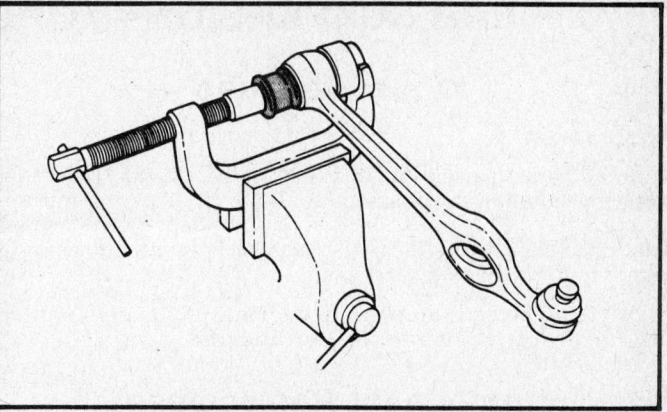

Inner pivot bushing removal (© Ford Motor Co.)

2. Remove stabilizer bar to control arm nut and dished washer.
3. Remove control arm inner pivot nut and bolt and pull arm down from underbody and away from stabilizer bar.
4. Using a sharp knife, carefully cut away retaining lip of bushing prior to its removal.
5. Using Tool T81P-5493-B and T74P-3044-1 or equivalent, remove old bushing from control arm.

NOTE: This operation can be done in vehicle without removing arm from knuckle.

Installation

1. Saturate new bushing and lower control arm with vegetable oil or equivalent.

NOTE: Use only vegetable oil. Any mineral or petroleum based oil or brake fluid will deteriorate the rubber bushing.

2. Using Tool T81P-5493-B and T74P-3044-A1 or equivalent, install new bushing in lower control arm.
3. Position control arm onto stabilizer bar. Be sure washer is in place.
4. Tighten control to underbody and install a new nut and bolt. Tighten torque of 44–55 ft. lbs. (60–75 Nm).
5. Install a new nut and the original dished washer on stabilizer bar. Tighten nut to torque of 59–73 ft. lbs. (80–100 Nm).

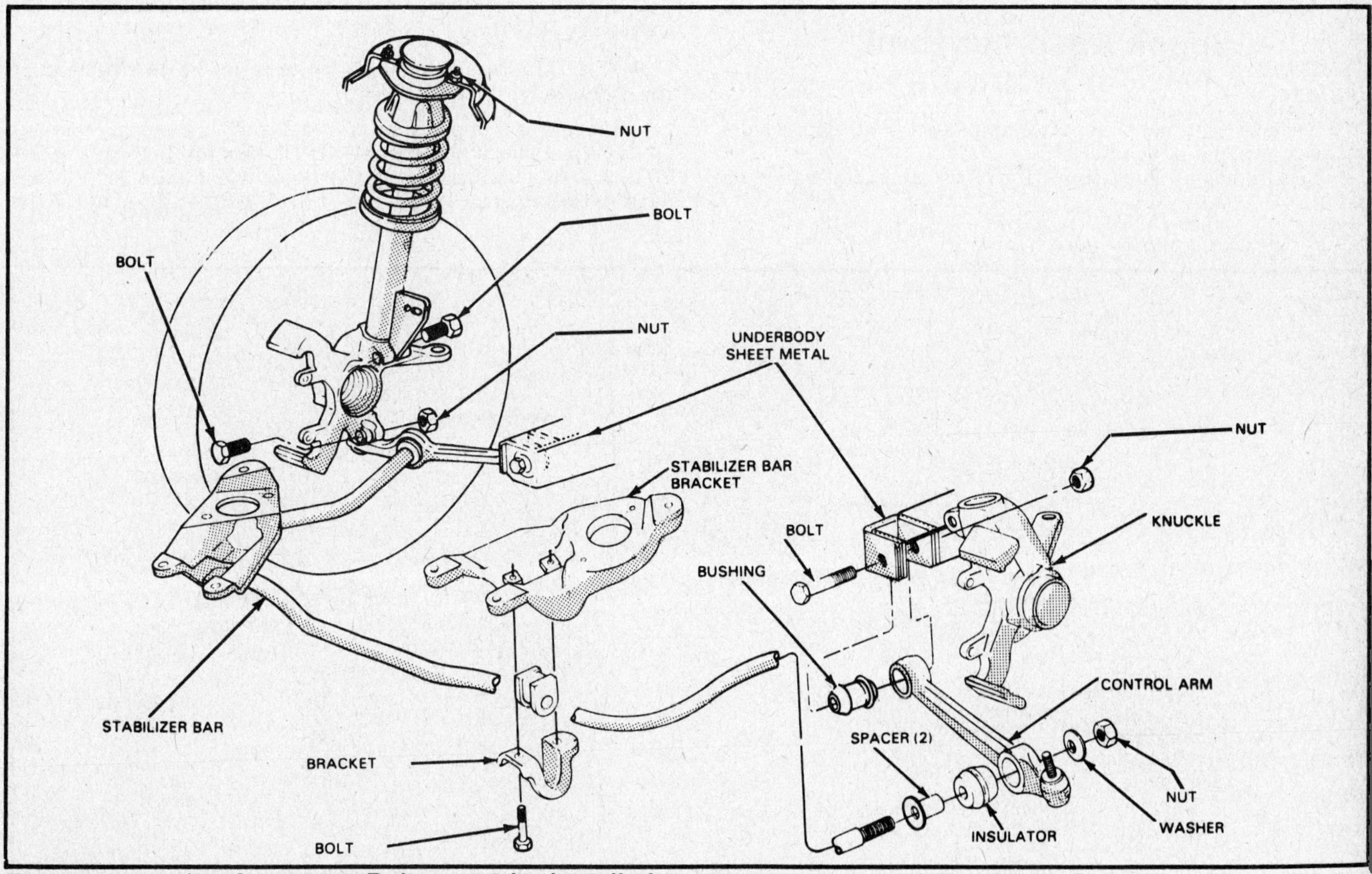

Front suspension fasteners. Bolts must be installed in direction shown (© Ford Motor Co.)

SECTION 35 SUSPENSIONS
REAR SUSPENSION—FORD FRONT DRIVE CARS

REAR SUSPENSION—FORD FRONT WHEEL DRIVE CARS

Wheel Bearings

Adjustment

Tighten adjusting nut "A" to 17–25 ft. lbs. (23–24 Nm) while rotating hub and drum assembly. Back off adjusting nut approximately 100 degrees. Position nut retainer "B" over adjusting nut so slots are in line with cotter pin hole without rotating adjusting nut. Install cotter pin.

NOTE: The spindle has a prevailing torque feature that prevents adjusting the nut by hand.

Component Replacement

The following applies regarding components that are replaced individually or as an assembly.
1. The shock absorber strut upper mounting is separately servicable.
2. The shock absorber strut is not repairable and must be replaced as an assembly.
3. Lower control arm bushings are not servicable. They must be replaced with a lower control arm and bushing assembly.
4. Tie rod bushings can be serviced separately at both the forward and rearward locations. However, if the tie rod requires replacement, new bushings must be installed in the spindle at the same time.
5. Coil springs are servicable. If a rear coil spring is replaced, the upper spring insulator must also be replaced.

Shock Absorber Strut

Removal

1. Remove rear component access panels. Four-door model requires removal of quarter trim panel.
2. Loosen but do not remove top shock absorber attaching nut.

NOTE: If the shock absorber is to be re-used, do not grip the shock absorber shaft with pliers or vise grips, as this will damage the shaft surface finish.

3. Raise vehicle and support safely. Remove the tire and wheel assembly.

NOTE: If a frame contact hoist is used, support the lower control arm with a floor jack. If a twin post hoist is used, support the body with floor jacks on lifting pads forward of the tie-rod body bracket.

4. Remove clip retaining the brake flexible hose to the rear shock and carefully move hose aside.
5. Loosen two nuts and bolts retaining shock to the spindle. DO NOT remove bolts at this time.
6. Remove top mounting nut, washer and rubber insulator.
7. Remove two bottom mounting bolts and remove the shock from the vehicle.

Installation

1. Extend shock absorber to its maximum length.
2. Install a new lower washer and insulator assembly, using tire lubricant to ease insertion into the quarter panel shock tower. (Use of a lubricant other than ESA–M1B6–B or soapy water is not recommended as it may damage the rubber insulator).
3. Position upper part of the shock absorber shaft into shock tower opening in the body and push slowly on lower part of the shock until mounting holes are lined up with mounting holes in the spindle.
4. Install a new lower mounting bolts and nuts. DO NOT tighten at this time.

NOTE: The heads of both bolts must be to the rear of the vehicle.

5. Place a new upper insulator and washer assembly and nut on the upper shock absorber shaft. Tighten nut to torque of 60–70 ft. lbs. (81–95 Nm), using the 18 X 18 X 43 mm deep socket with external hex (Tool D81P–18045–A3) while holding the

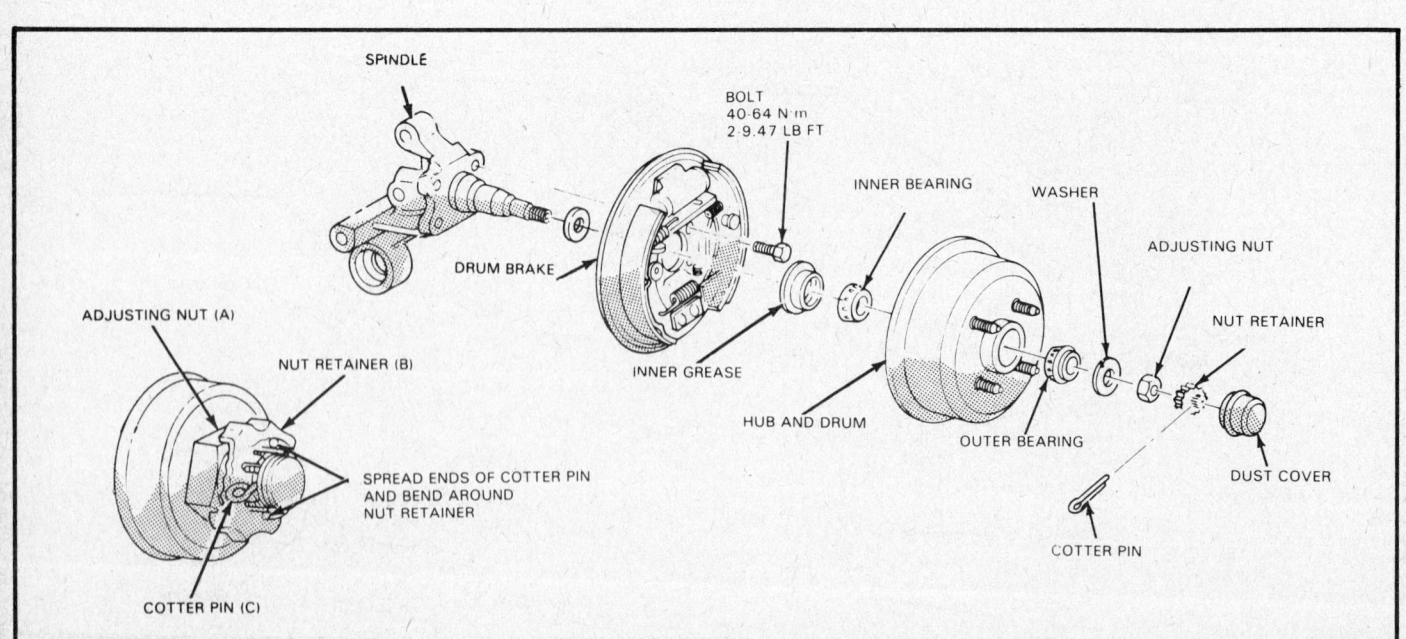

Rear bearing (© Ford Motor Co.)

SUSPENSIONS
REAR SUSPENSION – FORD FRONT DRIVE CARS

strut shaft with a 6 mm allen wrench. Do not grip the shaft with pliers or vise grips.

6. Tighten two lower mounting bolts to torque of 90–100 ft. lbs. (122–135 Nm).
7. Install brake flex hose and retaining clip.
8. Install wheel and tire assembly.
9. Install quarter trim panels on four-door models and access panels on other models.

Lower Control Arm

Removal

NOTE: The lower control arm is replaced as a unit. The bushing is not serviceable.

1. Raise the vehicle and support safely. Remove tire an wheel assembly.
2. On Taurus and Sable sedans, remove the brake proportioning valve from the left side of the front arm. Disconnect the parking brake cable.
3. Place a floor jack under the lower control arm between spring and spindle end mounting.
4. Remove nuts from control arm-to-body mounting and control arm-to-spindle mounting. Do not remove bolts at this time.
5. Remove spindle end mounting bolt. Slowly lower floor jack until spring and spring insulator can be removed.
6. Remove bolt from the body end and remove control arm from the vehicle.

Installation

1. Attach lower control arm to body bracket using a new bolt and a new nut. DO NOT tighten at this time. Install this bolt with bolt head to the front of the vehicle.

2. Place spring in spring pocket in lower control arm. Be sure the spring pigtail is in the proper index in lower control arm and the insulator is at the top of the spring, properly seated and indexed. Insulator must be replaced on the spring before spring is placed in position.
3. Using a floor jack, raise lower control arm until it comes in line with mounting hole in the spindle.
4. Install lower control arm to spindle using a new nut, new bolt and new washers. DO NOT tighten at this time. Install this bolt with the bolt head to the front of the vehicle.
5. Using a floor jack, raise lower control arm to its curb height.
6. Tighten control arm-to-spindle bolt to torque of 90–100 ft. lbs. (122–135 Nm).

Strut And Spring

Removal and Installation

TEMPO/TOPAZ

1. Raise jack only enough to contact body.
2. Open truck lid and loosen, but do not remove two nuts retaining the upper strut mount to body.
3. Raise vehicle. Remove wheel and tire.
4. Place a jack stand under the control arms to support the suspension.

── **CAUTION** ──
Care should be taken when removing the strut that the rear brake flex hose is not stretched or the steel brake tube is not bent.

5. Remove the bolt attaching the brake hose bracket to the strut and carefully move it out of the way.

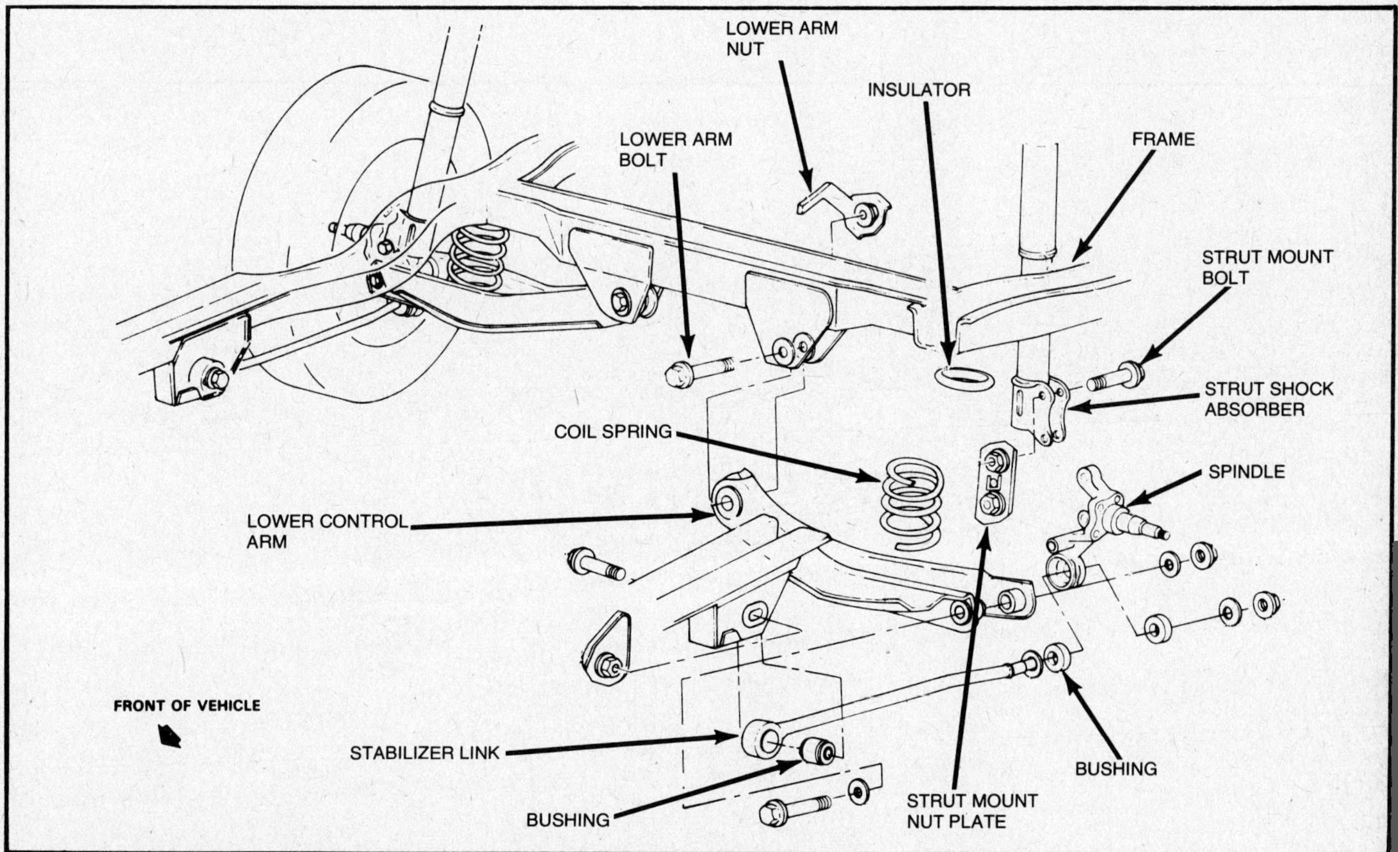

All bolts must be insatalled in direction shown (© Ford Motor Co.)

SECTION 35 SUSPENSIONS
REAR SUSPENSION—FORD FRONT DRIVE CARS

6. Remove two bolts retaining the jounce bumper bracket strut to spindle.
7. Remove jounce bumper bracket from the vehicle.
8. Remove sock strut from the spindle.
9. Remove two upper mount-to-body nuts.
10. Remove strut from vehicle.
11. Install in reverse order. Torque top mount to body bolts 20–30 ft. lbs. and strut to spindle bolts 70–96 ft. lbs. Always install new strut to spindle bolts.

Tension Strut

Removal and Installation

TAURUS/SABLE—STATION WAGON

1. Raise the vehicle and support safely. Place a floor jack under the rerar lower suspension arm and raise the arm to normal curb height.
2. Remove the wheel and tire assembly.
3. Remove the nut and bolt retaining the tension strut to the lower suspension arm.
4. Remove the tension strut to body bracket retaining nut. Remove the strut assembly.
5. Installation is the reverse of the removal procedure. Tighten tension strut to body bracket bolt 40–55 ft. lbs.

TAURUS/SABLE—SEDAN

1. From inside the trunk, loosen, but do not remove the three nuts retaining the upper shock strut mount to the body.
2. Raise the vehicle and support safely. Remove the wheel and tire assembly.
3. Remove the tension strut to spindle retaining nut.
4. Remove the tension strut to body retaining nut.
5. Move the spindle rearward enough to gain working room in order to remove tension strut. Remove tension strut.
6. Installation is the reverse of the removal procedure using new bushings and washers on both ends of the new tension strut.

Control Arm

Removal and Installation

TEMPO/TOPAZ

1. Raise and safely support vehicle.
2. Remove tire and wheel assembly.
3. Remove arm-to-spindle bolt and nut.
4. Remove center mounting bolt and nut.
5. Remove arm from vehicle.
6. Install in reverse order. Torque arm to body bolt 40–55 ft. lbs. and arm spindle bolt 60–86 ft. lbs.

TAURUS/SABLE

1. Raise vehicle and support safely. Do not raise vehicle by tension strut.
2. Disconnect the brake proportioning valve from the left side front arm.
3. Disconnect the parking brake cable.
4. Remove the arm-to-spindle bolt, washer and nut. Remove the arm-to-body retaining nut.
5. Remove the control arm from the vehicle.
6. Installation is the reverse of the removal procedure.

NOTE: When installing new control arms, the offset on all arms must face up. The arms are stamped bottom on the lower edge. The flange edge of the right side rear arm stamping must face the front of the vehicle.

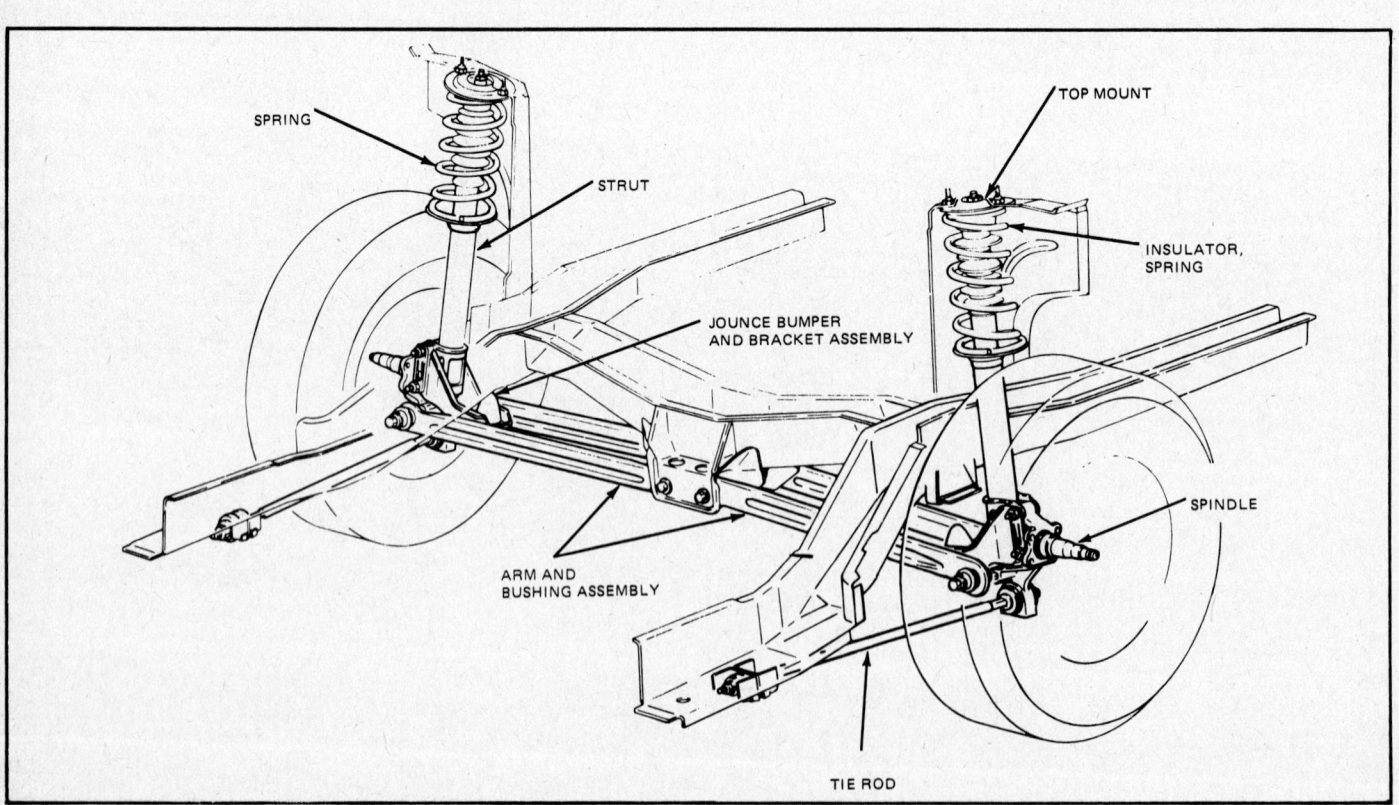

Rear suspension Tempo/Topaz (© Ford Motor Co.)

Tie Rod

Removal and Installation
TEMPO/TOPAZ

1. Raise car only enough to contact the body. From inside the trunk loosen, but DO NOT remove the two strut top mount-to-body nuts.
2. Raise vehicle and place a jack stand under the suspension to support it. Remove wheel and tire assembly.
3. Remove two top mount studs.
4. Remove nut retaining tie rod to the spindle. Remove nut retaining tie rod to body.
5. Lower the jack stand enough so that the upper strut mount studs are out of the holes in the body.
6. Move spindle rearward enough so that the tie rod can be removed.
7. Place new washers and bushings on both ends of new tie rod. Bushings at front and rear of the tie rod are different. The rear bushings have indentations in them.
8. Insert one end into the body bracket and install a new bushing washer and nut. DO NOT tighten at this time.
9. Pull back on the spindle enough so that the tie rod end can be installed in the spindle.
10. Install a new bushing, washer and nut. DO NOT tighten at this time.
11. Raise the jack stand enough to hold the two strut mounting studs in place.
12. Install two new strut-to-body mount nuts. Tighten to 20–30 ft. lbs.
13. Raise the suspension to curb height and tighten the two tie rod nuts to 52–74 ft. lbs.
14. Remove jack stand. Install tire and wheel assembly. Lower vehicle.

FRONT SUSPENSION—FORD, LINCOLN, MERCURY REAR DRIVE CARS, SINGLE ARM DESIGN

Description

The design utilizes shock struts with coil springs mounted between the lower arm and a spring pocket in the crossmember. The shock struts are non-repairable, and they must be replaced as a unit. The ball joints and lower suspension arm bushings are not separately serviced, and they also must be replaced as a suspension arm, bushing, and ball joint assembly.

Wheel Alignment

Caster and camber angles of this suspension are set at the factory, and cannot be adjusted in the field. Toe is adjustable.

TOE
Start the engine and move the steering wheel back and forth several times until it is in the straight ahead or centered position. Turn the engine off, and lock the steering wheel in place using a steering wheel holder. Adjust the left and right spindle rod sleeves until each wheel has one-half the desired total toe specification.

NOTE: For all vehicles, whenever the jam nuts are loosened for toe adjustment, the nuts must be tightened to 33–50 ft. lbs. (48–67 Nm).

Wheel Bearings

Replacement and Lubrication
1. Raise the vehicle until the tire clears the floor, and remove wheel from hub and rotor.
2. Remove the caliper from the spindle, and wire it to the underbody to prevent damage to the brake hose.
3. Remove the grease cap from the hub. Remove the cotter pin, nut lock, adjusting nut, and flatwasher from the spindle. Remove the outer bearing cone and roller assembly.
4. Pull the hub and rotor assembly off the spindle.
5. Using tool 1175-AC or equivalent, remove and discard the grease retainer. Remove the inner bearing cone and roller assembly from the hub.
6. Clean the inner and outer cups with solvent. Inspect the cups for scratches, pits, excessive wear, and other damage. If the cups are worn or damaged, replace.

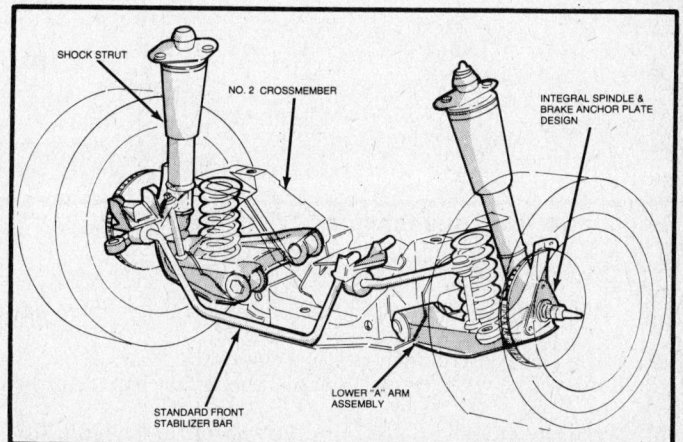

Single arm front suspension Thunderbird/XR7, Fairmont/Zephyr, Granada/Cougar, Mustang/Capri
(© Ford Motor Co.)

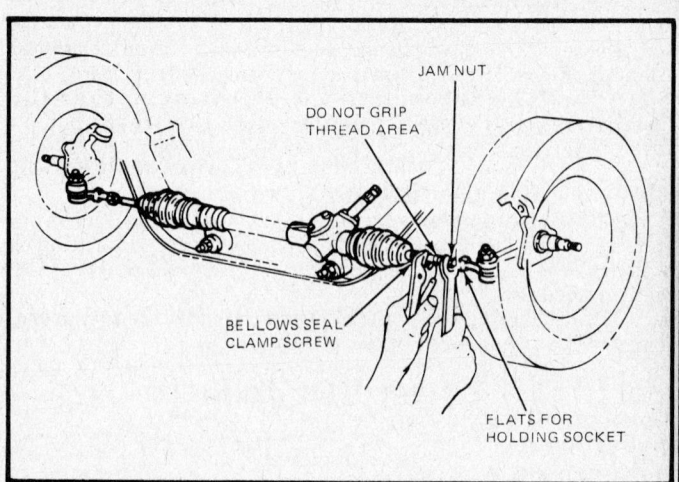

Toe adjustment (© Ford Motor Co.)

SECTION 35 SUSPENSIONS
FRONT SUSPENSION—FORD SINGLE ARM DESIGN

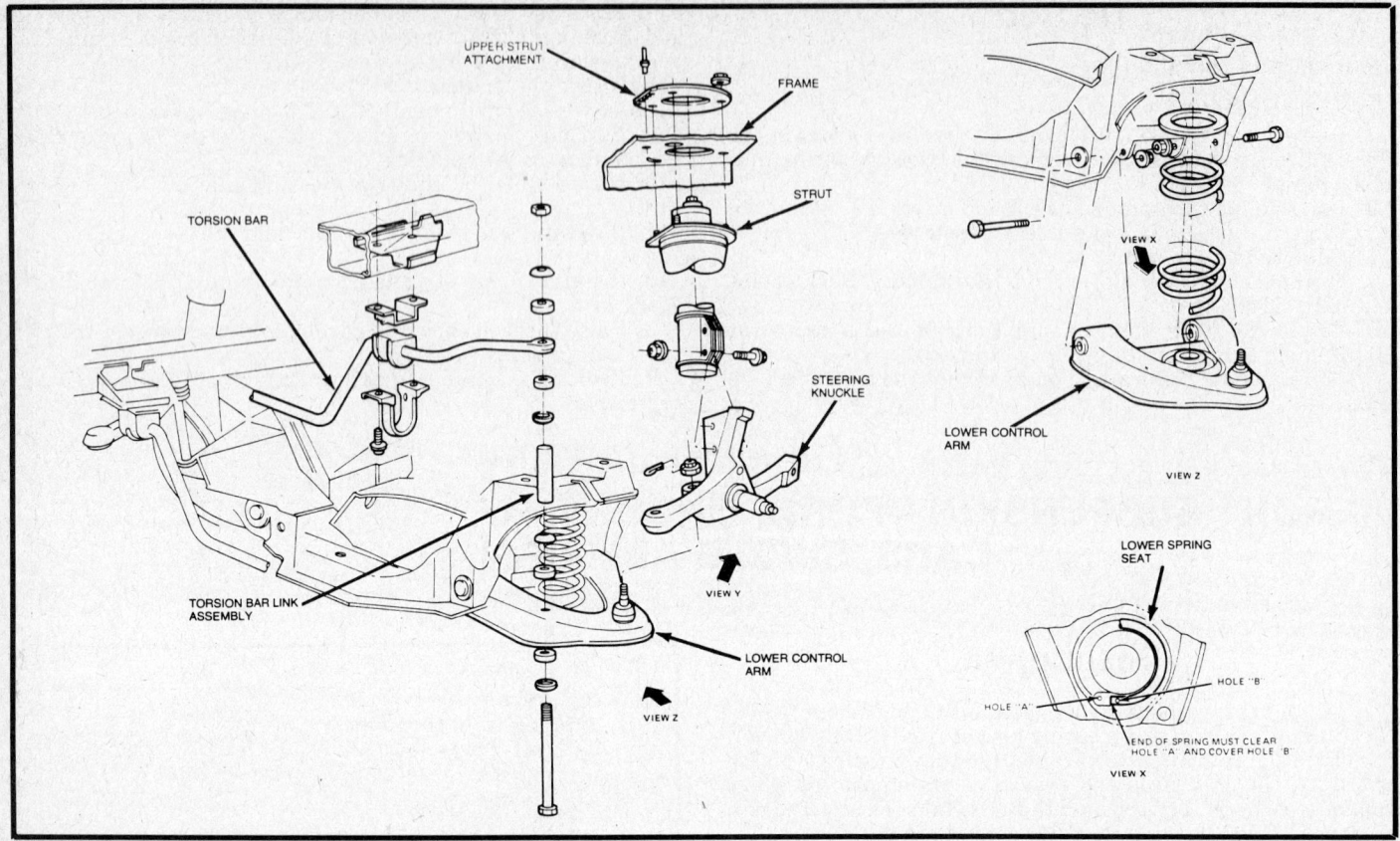

Single arm front suspension (© Ford Motor Co.)

Adjustment

If the wheel is loose on the spindle or does not rotate freely, adjust the front wheel bearings as follows:
1. Raise the vehicle until the tire clears the floor.
2. Remove the wheel cover. Remove the grease cap from the hub.
3. Wipe the excess grease from the end of the spindle. Remove the cotter pin and nut lock.
4. Loosen the adjusting nut three turns. Rock the wheel, hub and rotor assembly in and out several times to push the shoe and linings away from the rotor.
5. While rotating the wheel, hub and rotor assembly, tighten the adjusting nut to 17–25 ft. lbs. (24–33 Nm) to seat the bearings.
6. Loosen the adjusting nut one-half turn, then retighten 10–15 inch lbs. (1.2–1.6 Nm), using a torque wrench.
7. Place the nut lock on the adjusting nut, so the castellations on the lock are in line with the cotter pin hole in the spindle.
8. Install a new cotter pin, an bend the ends around the castellated flange of the nut lock.
9. Check the front wheel rotation. If the wheel rotates properly, reinstall the grease cap and wheel cover. If rotation is noisy or rough, follow the inspection, lubrication, and replacement procedures.
10. Before driving the vehicle, pump the brake pedal several times to restore normal brake pedal travel.

Lower Ball Joint

Inspection

1. Support the vehicle in normal driving position with both ball joints loaded.

2. Wipe the wear indicator and ball joint cover checking surface, so they are free of dirt and grease.
3. The checking surface should project outside the cover. If the checking surface is inside the cover, replace the lower arm assembly.

Shock/Strut

Removal

1. Place the ignition key in the unlocked position to permit free movement of front wheels.
2. From the engine compartment, remove the one strut to upper mount attaching nut. A screwdriver in the slot will hold the rod stationary while removing the nut.
3. Raise the front of the vehicle by the lower control arms, and position safety stands under the frame jacking pads, rearward of the wheels.
4. Remove the tire and wheel assembly.
5. Remove brake caliper and rotate out of position.
6. Remove the two lower nuts and bolts attaching the strut to the spindle.
7. Lift the strut up from the spindle to compress the rod, then pull down and remove the strut.

Installation

1. With the rod half extended, place the rod through the upper mount, and hand start with a new 16 mm nut, engaging as many nut threads as possible.
2. Extend the strut, and position into the spindle.
3. Install two new lower mounting bolts, and hand start nuts.

SUSPENSIONS
FRONT SUSPENSION—FORD SINGLE ARM DESIGN
SECTION 35

4. Tighten the new 16 mm strut to upper mount attaching nut, inside the engine compartment to 60–75 ft. lbs. (81–102 Nm). A screwdriver in the slot will hold the rod stationary while the nut is being tightened.

5. Remove the suspension load from the lower control arms by lowering the hoist, and tighten the lower mounting nuts to 150–180 ft. lbs. (203–244 Nm).

Lower Suspension Arm

Removal

1. Raise the vehicle and support safely. Allow the control arms to hang free.
2. Remove the wheel and tire assembly.
3. Remove the brake caliper. Wire if off to the side to obtain working room. Remove the brake rotor and dust shield.

NOTE: 1983 Lincoln Continentals do not require the removal of the caliper, rotor or dust shield.

4. Disconnect the tie rod assembly from the steering spindle. Remove the steering gear bolts and position the gear so that the suspension arm bolt may be removed.
5. Disconnect the stabilizer bar link from the lower arm.
6. Remove the cotter pin from the ball joint stud nut, and loosen the ball joint nut one or two turns.
7. Tap the spindle boss to relive the stud pressure.
8. Install a spring compressor tool into the lower arm spring pocket hole, through coil spring into upper plate.
9. Tighten the nut on the compressor tool until a drag on the nut is felt.
10. Remove the ball joint nut and raise the entire strut and spindle assembly. wire it off to the side to obtain working room.
11. Remove the suspension arm-to-crossmember bolts. The compressor tool forcing nut may have to be tightened or loosened for ease of bolt removal.
12. Loosen the compression rod forcing nut until the spring tension is relived. Remove the forcing nut, lower suspension arm and coil spring.

Installation

1. Place the insulator on the top of the spring. Position the spring into the lower arm spring pocket.
2. Position the spring and lower arm onto the compression tool.
3. Tighten the nut on the compression tool. Position the lower arm into the crossmember. Install new lower arm-to-crossmember bolts and nuts. Do not tighten at this time.
4. Unwire the strut and spindle assembly and attach to the ball joint stud. Install a new ball joint stud nut. Do not tighten at this time.
5. Using a suitable jack, raise the suspension arm to a normal position. Remove the compressor tool.
6. While the jack is still in place, tighten the lower arm-to-crossmember attaching nuts to 150–180 ft. lbs. (203–244 Nm) for 1983 and later vehicles.
7. Tighten the ball joint stud nut to 100–200 ft. lbs. (136–163 Nm). Install new cotter pin.
8. Install the brake shield, rotor and brake caliper if removed.
9. Install the steering gear-to-crossmembr bolts and nuts if removed. Tighten to 90–100 ft. lbs. (122–135 Nm).
10. Install the tie rod assembly into the steering spindle. Install the retaining nut. Tighten to 35 ft. lbs. (47 Nm). Install a new cotter pin.
11. Connect the stabilizer bar link to the lower suspension arm. Tighten to 9–12 ft. lbs. (12–16 Nm).
12. Install the wheel and tire assembly. Check and adjust the front wheel alignment if necessary.

Spring

Removal

1. Raise the front of the vehicle and position safety stands under both sides at the jack pads just back of the lower arms. Remove the wheel and tire assembly.
2. Disconnect the stabilizer link bar from the lower bar.
3. Remove the steering gear bolts, and move the steering gear out of the way.
4. Disconnect the tie rod from the steering spindle.
5. Using the spring compressor tool D78P-5310-A or equivalent, install one plate with the pivot ball seat down into the coils of the spring. Rotate the plate so that it is fully seated into the lower suspension arm spring seat.
6. Install the other plate with the pivot ball seat up into the coils of the spring. Insert the ball nut through the coils of the spring, so it rests in the upper plate.
7. Insert compression rod into the opening in the lower arm through the lower and upper plate. Install the ball nut on the rod, and return the securing pin.

NOTE: This pin can only be inserted one way into the upper ball nut because of a stepped hole design.

8. With the upper ball nut secured, turn the upper plate, so it walks up the coil until it contacts the upper spring seat.
9. Install the lower ball nut, thrust bearing and forcing nut on the compression rod.
10. Rotate the nut until the spring is compressed enough, so it is free in its seat.
11. Remove the two lower control arm pivot bolts and nuts to disengage the lower arm from the frame crossmember. Remove the spring assembly.
12. If a new spring is to be installed, mark the position of the upper and lower plates on the spring with chalk. Measure the compressed length of the spring as well as the amount of spring curvature to assist in the compression and installation of a new spring.
13. Loosen the nut to relieve spring tension, and remove the tools from the spring.

Installation

1. Assemble the spring compressor tool and locate tool through spring.
2. Before compression the coil spring, be sure the upper ball nut securing pin is inserted properly.
3. Compress the coil spring.
4. Position the coil spring assembly into the lower arm.

NOTE: Be sure that the lower end (pigtail) of the coil spring is properly positioned between the two holes in the lower arm spring pocket depression.

5. Install coil spring. Reverse removal procedures.

Spindle Assembly

Removal

1. Raise the front of the vehicle, and position safety stands under both sides at the jacking pads just behind the lower arms.
2. Remove the wheel and tire assembly.
3. Remove the brake caliper, rotor, and dust shield.
4. Remove the stabilizer link from the lower arm assembly.
5. Remove the tie rod end from the spindle.
6. Remove the cotter pin from the ball joint stud nut, and loosen the ball joint nut one or two turns.

CAUTION
Do not remove the nut from the ball joint stud at this time.

SECTION 35 SUSPENSIONS
FRONT SUSPENSION—FORD SINGLE ARM DESIGN

7. Tap the spindle boss to relieve the stud pressure.
8. Place a floor jack under the lower arm, compress the coil spring and remove the stud nut.
9. Remove the two bolts and nuts attaching the spindle to the shock strut. Compress the shock strut until working clearance is obtained.
10. Remove the spindle assembly.

Installation

1. Place the spindle on the ball joint stud, and install the stud nut. Do not tighten at this time.
2. Lower the shock strut until the attaching holes are in line with the holes in the spindle. Install two new bolts and nuts.
3. Tighten the ball joint stud nut to 80–120 ft. lbs. (108–163 Nm) and install a new cotter pine.
4. Tighten the shock strut-to-spindle attaching nuts to 150–180 ft. lbs. (203–244 Nm).
5. Lower the floor jack from under the suspension arm, and remove the jack.
6. Intall the stabilizer link and tighten the attaching bolt and nut to 8–12 ft. lbs. (11–16 Nm).
7. Attach the tie-rod end, and tighten the retaining nut to 35–47 ft. lbs. (47–64 Nm).
8. Install the disc brake dust shield, rotor and caliper.
9. Install the wheel and tire assembly. Check the front wheel alignment and adjust if necessary.

Stabilizer Bar Link Insulators

Removal

To replace the link insulators on each stabilizer link, use the following procedure:
1. Raise the vehicle on a hoist.
2. Remove the nut, washer and insulator from the upper end of the stabilizer bar attaching link bolt.
3. Remove the bolt and the remaining washers, insulators and spacer.

Installation

1. Install the stabilizer bar link insulators by reversing the above steps.
2. Tighten the attaching nuts to 8–12 ft. lbs. (11–16Nm).

Stabilizer Bar And Insulator

Removal

1. Raise the vehicle on a hoist.
2. Disconnect the stabilizer from each stabilizer link and both stabilizer insulator attaching clamps. Remove the stabilizer bar assembly.
3. Cut the worn insulators and plastic sleeves from the stabilizer bar.

Installation

1. Coat the necessary parts of the stabilizer bar with Ford Suspension Rubber Insulator Lubricant or an equivalent lubricant; install new plastic sleeves with the flange inboard, and slide insulators onto the stabilizer bar and over sleeves. Be sure the insulator is fully seated against the flange.
2. Using a new nut and bolt, secure each end of the stabilizer bar to the lower suspension arm. Tighten these nuts to 8–12 ft. lbs. (11–16 Nm).
3. Using new fasteners, clamp the stabilizer bar to the attaching brackets on the side rail. Tighten these bolts to 20–25 ft. lbs. (27–33 Nm).

FRONT SUSPENSION—FORD, LINCOLN, MERCURY REAR DRIVE CARS, SPRING ON LOWER ARM DESIGN

Wheel Alignment

ADJUSTMENT

Caster and Camber

1. Check suspension with the front wheels in the straight ahead position. Run the engine so the power steering control valve will be in the center (neutral) position (if equipped).
2. Check caster and camber and record the readings.
3. Compare camber and caster readings with specifications to determine if adjustment is required to bring vehicle to nominal setting.
4. If adjustment is required, insert alignment tools into frame holes and "snug" the tool hooks finger-tight against the upper arm inner shaft. Then tighten hex nut of each alignment tool 1 additional "hex flat."
5. Loosen upper arm inner shaft-to-frame attaching bolts so that the lockwashers on bolts are unloaded. Then firmly tap bolt heads to assure loosening of the lower assemblies.
6. Adjust camber and caster on each wheel.
7. Torque upper arm inner shaft-to-frame attaching bolts to 100–140 ft. lbs. (136–190 Nm). It is not necessary to recheck caster and camber after this adjustment procedure is performed.
8. Check toe-in and steering wheel spoke position and adjust both (as required) at the same time.

Toe and Steering Wheel Spoke Position

After adjusting caster and camber, check the steering wheel spoke position with the front wheels in straight-ahead position. If the spokes are not in their normal position, they can be properly adjusted while toe is being adjusted.

1. Loosen the two clamp bolts on each spindle connecting rod sleeve.
2. Adjust toe. If the steering wheel spokes are in their normal position, lengthen or shorten both rods equally to obtain correct toe.
3. If the steering wheel spokes are not in their normal position, make the necessary rod adjustments to obtain correct toe and steering wheel spoke alignment.
4. When toe and the steering wheel spoke position are both correct, lubricate clamp, bolts and nuts and tighten the clamp bolts on both connecting rod sleeves and specification. The sleeve position should not be changed when the clamp bolts are tightened for proper clamp bolt orientation.

Wheel Bearings

Adjustment and Inspection

If the wheel is loose on the spindle or does not rotate freely, adjust the front wheel bearings as follows:
1. Raise the vehicle until the tire clears the floor.

SUSPENSIONS

FRONT SUSPENSION—FORD SPRING ON LOWER ARM DESIGN

SECTION 35

2. Remove the wheel cover. Remove the grease cap from the hub.
3. Wipe the excess grease from the end of the spindle. Remove the cotter pin and nut lock.
4. Loosen the adjusting nut three turns and rock the wheel, hub and rotor assembly in and out several times to push the shoe and linings away from the rotor.
5. While rotating the wheel, hub and rotor assembly, torque the adjusting nut to 17–25 ft. lbs. (23–24 Nm) to seat the bearings.
6. Loosen the adjusting nut one-half turn, then retighten to 10–15 inch lbs. (1.2–1.6 Nm) using a torque wrench.
7. Place the nut lock on the adjusting nut so the castellations on the lock are in line with the cotter pine hole in the spindle.
8. Install a new cotter pin and bend the ends around the castellated flange of the nut lock.
9. Check front wheel rotation. If the wheel rotates properly, reinstall the grease cap and wheel cover. If rotation is noisy or rough, remove wheel hub and check for bearing problems.
10. Before driving the vehicle, pump the brake pedal several times to restore normal brake pedal travel.

Replacement and Lubrication

1. Raise the vehicle until the tire clears the floor. Remove wheel from hub and rotor.
2. Remove the caliper from the spindle and wire it to the underbody to prevent damage to the brake hose.
3. Remove the grease cap from the hub. Remove the cotter pin, nut lock, adjusting nut and flatwasher from the spindle. Remove the outer bearing cone and roller assembly.
4. Pull the hub and rotor assembly off the spindle.
5. Using tool 1175–AC or equivalent, remove and discard the grease retainer. Remove the inner bearing cone and roller assembly from the hub.
6. Clean the inner and outer bearing cups with solvent. Inspect the cups for scratches, pits, excessive wear and other damage. If the cups are worn or damaged, remove them with tools D80L–927–A and T77F–1102–A or equivalent and replace them.
7. Remove the old lubricant from the spindle and inside of the hub assembly.
8. If the inner and outer bearing cups were removed, install replacement cups.

NOTE: **When installing replacement cups in the bearings, support the rotor on the hub barrel with a wooden block in order to avoid damage to the wheel studs.**

9. Clean the old grease from all the surrounding surfaces.
10. Using a bearing packer, pack the bearing cone with C1AZ–19590–B or equivalent grease. Grease the bearing cup surfaces.
11. Install the inner bearing cone and roller assemblies in the inner cup. Coat the new grease retainer with grease and install the retainer. Be sure the retainer is properly seated.
12. Install the hub and rotor assembly on the spindle.
13. Install the outer bearing cone and roller assembly and flatwasher on the spindle. Install the adjusting nut. Adjust the wheel bearings as outline earlier. Install the grease cap.
14. Install the caliper on the spindle if removed earlier.
15. Install the wheel and tire assembly. Lower the vehicle.

NOTE: **Before driving the vehicle, pump the brake pedal several times to restore normal brake pedal travel.**

Shock Absorber

Removal

1. Remove the nut, washer and bushing from the shock absorber upper end. Raise the vehicle and support safely.

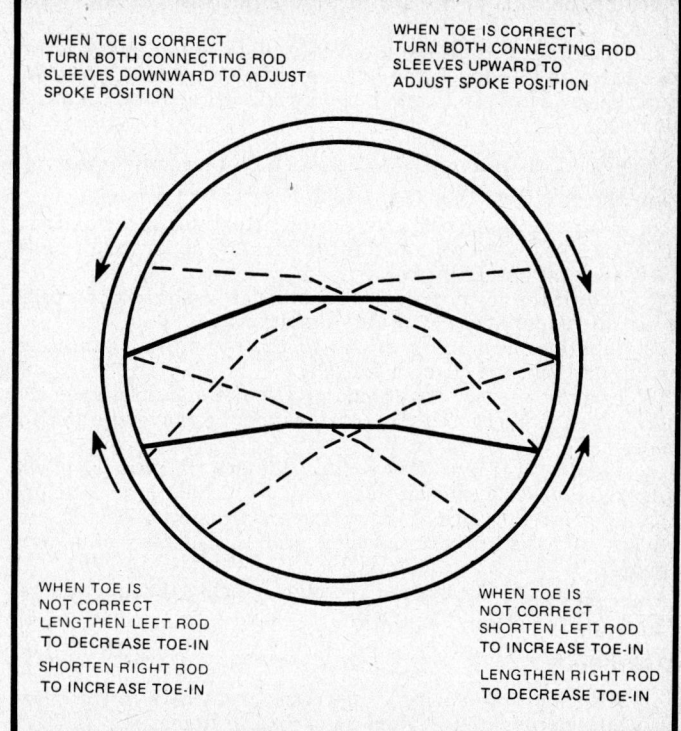

Adjusrt both rods equally to maintain normal spoke position (© Ford Motor Co.)

2. Remove the two thread-cutting screws attaching the shock absorber to the lower arm and remove the shock absorber. Lightly wire brush the shock studs to free of rust, oil or corrosion.
3. Remove the shock absorber.

Installation

1. Place a washer and bushing on the shock absorber top stud and position the shock absorber inside the front spring. Install the thread-cutting screws and torque to specifications. If the threads in the lower arm become stripped or damaged, the removed thread cutting screws should be re-used, along with $5/16$–18 lock nuts. Torque to the same specifications as when thread cutting screws are secured directly to the lower arm.
2. Remove the safety stands and lower the vehicle.
3. Place a bushing and washer on the shock absorber top stud and install nut.

Spring

Removal

1. Raise the vehicle. Remove the wheel and tire assembly.
2. Disconnect the stabilizer bar link from the lower arm.
3. Remove the two bolts attaching the shock absorber to the lower arm assembly.
4. Remove the upper nut, retainer and grommet from the shock absorber and remove the shock.
5. Remove the steering center link from the pitman arm.
6. Support the vehicle with safety stands under the jacking pads and lower the hoist for working room.
7. Using the spring compressor tool, install one plate with the pivot ball seat facing downward into the coils of the spring. Rotate the plate so that it is flush with the upper surface of the lower arm.
8. Install the other plate with the pivot ball seat facing upward into the coils of the spring. Insert the upper ball nut

35–61

SECTION 35 SUSPENSIONS
FRONT SUSPENSION—FORD SPRING ON LOWER ARM DESIGN

through the coils of the spring so the nut rests in the upper plate.

9. Insert the compression rod into the opening in the lower arm through the upper and lower plate and upper ball nut. Insert the securing pin through the upper ball nut and compression rod.

NOTE: This pin can only be inserted one way in the upper ball nut because of a stepped hole design.

10. With the upper ball arm secured, turn the upper plate so that it walks up the coil until it contacts the upper spring seat, then back off one half turn.
11. Install the lower ball nut and thrust washer on the compression rod, and screw on the forcing nut.
12. Tighten the forcing nut until the spring is compressed enough so that it is free in its seat.
13. Remove the two lower arm pivot bolts and disengage the lower arm from the frame crossmember; remove the spring assembly.
14. If a new spring is to be installed, mark the position of the upper and lower plates on the spring with chalk, and measure the compressed length of the spring and amount of spring curvature to assist in compression and installation of a new spring.
15. Loosen the forcing nut to relieve spring tension and remove the tools from the spring.

Installation

1. Assemble the spring compressor and locate in the same position as indicated in Step 14 of Spring Removal.
2. Before compressing the coil spring, be sure that the upper ball nut securing pin in inserted properly.
3. Compress the coil spring until the spring height reaches the dimension obtained in Step 14 of Spring Removal.
4. Position the coil spring assembly into the lower arm.
5. To install coil spring, reverse removal procedure.

Ball Joints

Inspection
The checking surface should project outside the cover. If the checking surface is inside the cover, replace the lower arm assembly, or install ball joint kit.

Replacement
The manufacturer recommends replacing the complete arm if the ball joint is worn. However, aftermarket suppliers have ball joint kits available to replace worn ball joints without replacing the complete arm.

Upper Arm

Removal

1. Raise the front of the vehicle and position safety stands under both sides of the frame just back of the lower arm.
2. Remove the wheel and tire.
3. Remove the cotter pin from the upper ball joint stud nut.
4. Loosen the upper ball joint stud nut one or two turns.

---**CAUTION**---
Do not remove the nut from the stud at this time.

5. Insert ball joint press tool between the upper and lower ball joint studs with the adapter screw on top.
6. With a wrench, turn the adapter screw until the tool places the stud under compression. Tap the spindle near the upper stud with a hammer to loosen the stud in the spindle.

NOTE: Do not loosen the stud from the spindle with tool pressure only. Do not contract the boot seal with hammer.

7. Remove the tool from between the joint studs and place a floor jack under the lower arm.
8. Remove the upper arm attaching bolts, and remove the upper arm assembly.

Installation

1. Transfer the bumper from the old arm to the new arm.
2. Position the upper arm in new shaft to the frame bracket, and install the two attaching bolts and washers to a snug fit.
3. Connect the upper ball joint stud to the spindle and install the attaching nut. Torque the nut to specifications and continue to tighten the nut until the cotter pin hole in the stud is in line with the nut slots, then install the cotter pine.
4. Install the wheel and tire adjust the wheel bearing.
5. Remove the safety stands and lower the front of the vehicle.
6. Adjust caster, camber and toe-in to specifications.

Upper Arm Bushings

Replacement (With Arm Removed)

1. Remove the nuts and washer from both ends of the upper arm shaft.

NOTE: Use the existing C-clamp tool part number T74P-3044-A-1 or equivalent and adapters to remove the bushings.

2. Position the shaft and new bushings to the upper arm and install the bushings and shaft to the upper arm.

NOTE: The front bushing is a larger diameter than the rear, requiring that adapter part number T79P-3044-A2 or equivalent, is used when installing rear bushings.

3. Make certain that the inner shaft is positioned so that the serrated side contacts the frame.
4. Install an inner washer, rear bushing only, and two outer washers and new nuts on each side of the inner shaft.

Lower Arm

Removal

1. Raise the front of the vehicle and position safety stands under both sides of the frame just back of the lower arms.
2. Remove the wheel and tire.

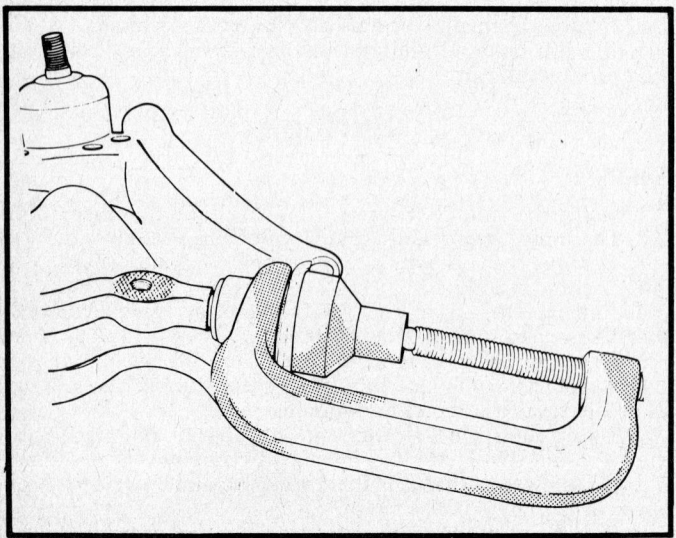

Upper arm bushing installation (© Ford Motor Co.)

SUSPENSIONS
FRONT SUSPENSION—FORD SPRING ON LOWER ARM DESIGN

3. Remove the brake caliper and rotor and dust shield.
4. Remove the shock absorber.
5. Disconnect the stabilizer bar link from the lower arm.
6. Disconnect the steering center link from the pitman arm.
7. Remove the cotter pin from the lower ball joint nut.
8. Loosen the lower ball joint stud nut one or two turns.
9. Install ball joint press tool between the upper and lower ball joints.
10. Install the coil spring compression tools and remove the spring.
11. Remove the ball joint nut, and remove arm assembly.
12. With a wrench, turn the adapter screw until the tool places the stud under compression. Tap the spindle near the lower stud with a hammer to loosen the stud in the spindle.
13. Remove the ball joint press tool.
14. Place a floor jack under the lower arm.
15. Gently lower the arm until all tension is relieved.
16. Remove lower arm center bolt and remove arm.

Installation

1. Position the arm assembly ball joint stud into the spindle and install the nut. Torque to specifications and install a new cotter pin.
2. Position the coil spring into the upper spring pocket; raise the lower arm and align the holes in the arm with the holes in the crossmember. Install bolts and nuts. Do not tighten at this time.

NOTE: Be sure that the pigtail of the lower coil of the spring is in the proper location of the seat of the lower arm, between the two holes.

3. Remove the spring compressor tool.
4. Connect the steering center link at the pitman arm, install the nut and tighten to specifications. Install a new cotter pin.
5. Install the shock absorber and torque fasteners to specifications.
6. Install the jounce bumper and torque nut to specifications.
7. Install the dust shield, rotor and caliper.
8. Position the stabilizer link to the lower arm and install the bolt and attaching nut.
9. Install the wheel and tire.
10. Remove the safety stands and lower the vehicle. After the vehicle has been lowered to floor and at curb height, torque the lower pivot bolts to 100–140 ft. lbs. (136–189 Nm).

Wheel Spindle

Removal

1. Raise the front of the vehicle and position safety stands under both sides of the frame just back of the lower arm.
2. Remove the wheel and tire.
3. Remove the brake rotor, caliper and dust shield.
4. Disconnect the tie rod end from the spindle.
5. Remove the cotter pins from both ball joint studs nuts and loosen the nuts one or two turns.

NOTE: Do not remove the nuts at this time.

6. Position the ball joint remover tool between the upper and lower ball joint studs.
7. Turn the tool with a wrench until the tool places the studs under compression. With a hammer, sharply hit the spindle near the studs to break it loose in the spindle.
8. Position a floor jack under the lower arm at the lower ball joint area.
9. Remove the upper and lower ball joint stud nuts, lower the jack carefully to and remove the spindle.

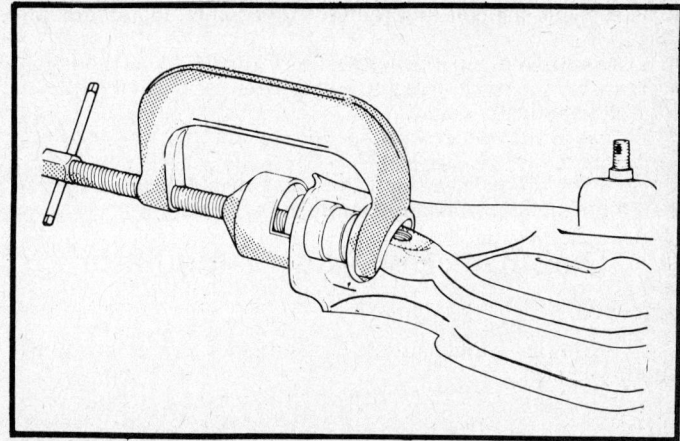
Upper arm bushing removal (© Ford Motor Co.)

Installation

1. Position the spindle on the lower ball joint stud and install the stud nut. Torque the nut to specification and install a new cotter pin.
2. Raise the lower arm and guide the upper ball joint stud into the spindle. Install the stud nut.
3. Torque the nut to specifications and install a new cotter pin. Remove the floor jack.
4. Disconnect the tie rod to the spindle. Install the nut and torque to specifications. Install a new cotter pine.
5. Install the brake dust shield, caliper and rotor.
6. Install the wheel and tire assembly.
7. Remove the safety stands and lower the vehicle.
8. Check caster, camber and toe-in and adjust as required.

Stabilizer Bar End Bushing

Replacement

1. Raise the vehicle on a hoist.
2. Remove the nut, washer and insulator from the lower end of the stabilizer bar attaching bolt.

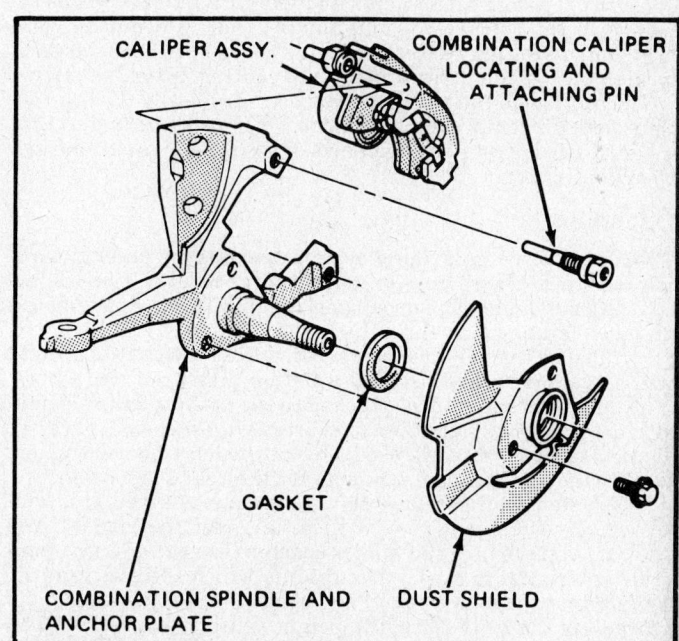
Spindle mounting (© Ford Motor Co.)

SECTION 35
SUSPENSIONS
FRONT SUSPENSION—FORD SPRING ON LOWER ARM DESIGN

3. Remove the bolt and remaining washers, insulators, and the spacer.
4. Assemble a cup washer and new insulator on the bolt.
5. Insert the bolt through the stabilizer bar, then install new insulator and cup washer.
6. Install the spacer, cup washer and another new insulator on the bolt.
7. Insert the bolt through the lower arm and install a new insulator and cup washer. Install the attaching nut.

Stabilizer Bar And/Or Insulator

Removal

1. Raise the vehicle on a hoist, and place jack stands under the lower arm.
2. Disconnect the stabilizer from each stabilizer link and both stabilizer insulator clamps. Remove the stabilizer bar assembly.
3. Cut the worn insulators from the stabilizer bar.

Installation

1. Coat the necessary parts of the stabilizer bar with Ford Suspension Rubber Insulator Lubricant or an equivalent lubricant; slide insulators onto the stabilizer bar.
2. Using a new nut and bolt, secure each end of the stabilizer bar to the lower suspension arm, making sure the bolt head is at the bottom. Tighten nuts to 6–12 ft. lbs. (9–16 Nm).
3. Using new fasteners, clamp the stabilizer bar to the attaching brackets on the side rail. Tighten bolts to 14–26 ft. lbs. (19–35 Nm).

FRONT AND REAR SUSPENSION—1984 AND LATER MARK VII AND CONTINENTAL 1985 AND LATER FORD CROWN VICTORIA AND MERCURY GRAND MARQUIS

DESCRIPTION AND OPERATION

Description

Air suspension is an air-operated, microcompressor controlled, suspension systems which replaces the conventional coil spring suspension and provides automatic front and rear load leveling.

Four air springs, made of rubber and plastic, support the vehicle load at the front and rear wheels.

The front air springs are mounted to a spring pocket in the crossmember and on the lower suspension arms similar to the conventional spring system. The rear air springs are mounted ahead of the rear axle outside the body sub-frame side members and on the lower rear suspension arms similar to the conventional rear spring system.

A single cylinder piston-type electrically operated air compressor, mounted on the left fender apron, supplies the air pressure for operating the system. A regenerative-type dryer is attached to the compressor manifold. All air flow during compression or venting passes through the dryer. A vent solenoid, located on the compressor manifold, controls air exhaustion.

The air flow to the entire system is controlled by the interaction of the air compressor, solenoids, height sensors and control module. All the air operated parts of the system are connected by nylon tubing.

Operation

The air suspension leveling system operated by adding or removing air in the springs to maintain the level at a pre-determined front and rear suspension height. The predetermined distance is known as the vehicle trim height. Trim height is controlled by the height sensors. Distance of the body to ground will change with tire size and inflation pressure.

The height sensors are attached to the body and the suspension arms, and will lengthen or shorten with suspension travel. Three height sensors are used: One at the left front wheel, one at the right front wheel, and one for the rear suspension.

The system works in the following manner: As weight is added to the vehicle, the body will settle under the load. As the body lowers, the heights sensors shorten (low out-of-trim), generating a signal to the control module which activates the air compressor (through a relay) and opens the air spring solenoid valves. As the body rises, the height sensors lengthen. When the pre-set trim height is reached, the air compressor is turned off and the solenoid valves are closed by the control module.

A similar action takes place whenever weight is removed from the vehicle. As weight is removed, the body will rise, which causes the height sensors to lengthen (high out-of-trim), generating a signal to the control module which opens the air compressor vent solenoid and opens the air spring solenoid valves. As the body lowers, the height sensors shorten and when the pre-set trim height is reached, the air compressor vent solenoid is closed and the spring solenoid valves are closed by the control module.

Air required for levelling the vehicle is distributed from the air compressor to each air spring by four nylon air lines which start at the compressor dryer and terminate at the individual air springs. The dryer is a common pressure manifold for all four air lines so orientation of these lines at the compressor is not required. However, the air lines are color coded to identify to which air spring they are attached. The dryer contains a desiccant (silica gel) which dries the compressed air before delivering the air to the springs. during venting of any air spring, the previously dried air passes through the dryer to remove moisture from the desiccant (regeneration). Air required for compression and vent air enter and exit through a common port on the compressor head. Vented air is also controlled by a solenoid valve in the compressor head.

CAUTION

The compressor relay, compressor vent solenoid and all air spring solenoids have internal diodes for electrical noise suppression and therefore are polarity sensitive. Care must be taken when servicing these components not to switch the battery feed and ground circuits or component damage will result.

A microcomputer based module controls the air compressor motor (through a relay), vent solenoid and the four air spring solenoids to provide the air requirements of the springs. The module also provides power and ground to the three digital height sensors and continuously monitors input from the three height sensors and the ignition Run/Brake On/Door Open circuits. These inputs are used by the module to make vehicle levelling decisions which are then carried out by the air system components controlled by the module. For service, the module provides a series of diagnostic tests, a routine for filling the springs and operates a warning lamp.

The control logic for operating the system is given below:

IGNITION OFF

1. Operates for 30 minutes after the ignition switch is

SUSPENSIONS
FRONT AND REAR—FORD AIR SUSPENSION
SECTION 35

turned from Run to Off, then the system is inoperable through the module.

2. WIll service down requests (lower vehicle) as required during the 30 minutes EXCEPT if any height sensor was reading a high (vehicle) when the ignition was turned from Run to Off. The vent time is limited to 10 seconds for the rear springs and 3 seconds for the front.

3. At one hour after ignition is turned to Off, the system will correct for a low vehicle if required. Compressor run time is limited to 15 seconds for the rear springs and 30 seconds for the front springs.

IGNITION IN RUN

1. Ignition in the Run position for less than 45 seconds.
   a. Will service first rear or front up requests (raise vehicle) immediately if required.
   b. Will not service down requests (lower vehicle).
2. Ignition in the Run position for more than 45 seconds.
   a. If a door(s) is open with the brake not engaged, up requests (raise vehicle will be serviced immediately and down request (lower vehicle) will be serviced after the door(s) is closed.
   b. If the doors are not open and the brake is not engaged, service all (up or down) requests by a 45 second averaging method.
   c. If the brake is engaged and a door(s) is open, service up requests (raise vehicle) immediately but do not service down (lower vehicle) requests.
   d. If the brake is engaged and the doors are closed, all requests (up or down) will not be serviced except that if a rear up request (raise vehicle) is in progress it will be completed.

GENERAL

1. Down requests (lower vehicle) will not be serviced if any door is open.
2. Requests are serviced in the following order: rear up, front up, rear down, front down.
3. During Ignition In Run, if any up or down request cannot be serviced within three minutes, the warning lamp will come On and stay On for that ignition cycle. However, only the request which was being serviced is affected. that is, if a time-out failure occurred during a left front up correction, the module would continue to service future left front down requests and all right front and rear requests.
4. The rear spring solenoids are always operated in tandem, but the front spring solenoids may operate independently.
5. Front and rear requests (up or down) will never be serviced simultaneously.
6. Turning the ignition from Run to Off clears all memory in the module and therefore the warning lamp may not immediately indicate a failure when the ignition is returned to the Run position.

CAUTION
When charging the battery, the ignition switch must be in the OFF position if the air suspension switch is On or damage to the air compressor relay or motor may occur.

However, use of a battery charge while performing the diagnostic test or air spring fill options is acceptable. Set to a rate to maintain, but not damage the vehicle battery.

ADJUSTMENTS

This adjustment procedure must be used prior to alignment, pinion angle or ride height checking. This method causes the system to perform a vent to trim.

NOTE: *If vehicle is significantly colder or warmer than alignment area (20 degrees or greater differential), time*

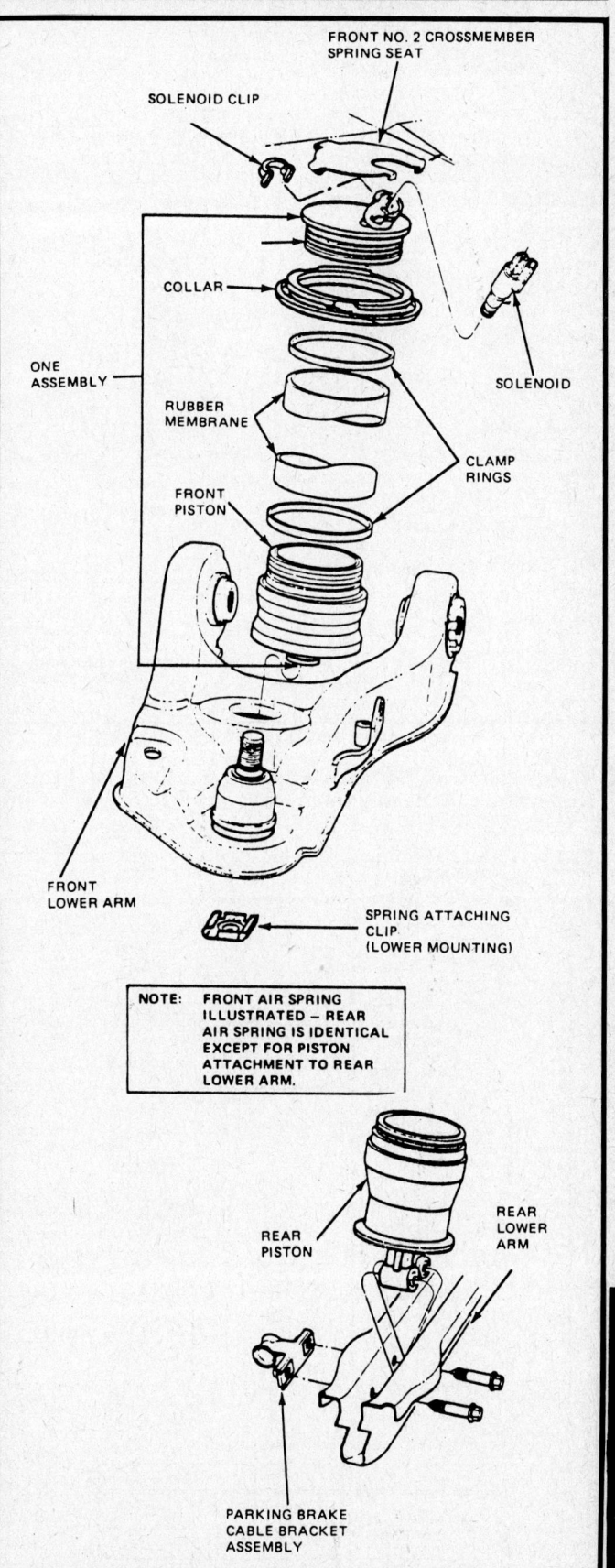

Air spring—exploded view (© Ford Motor Co.)

35-65

SECTION 35

SUSPENSIONS
FRONT AND REAR—FORD AIR SUSPENSION

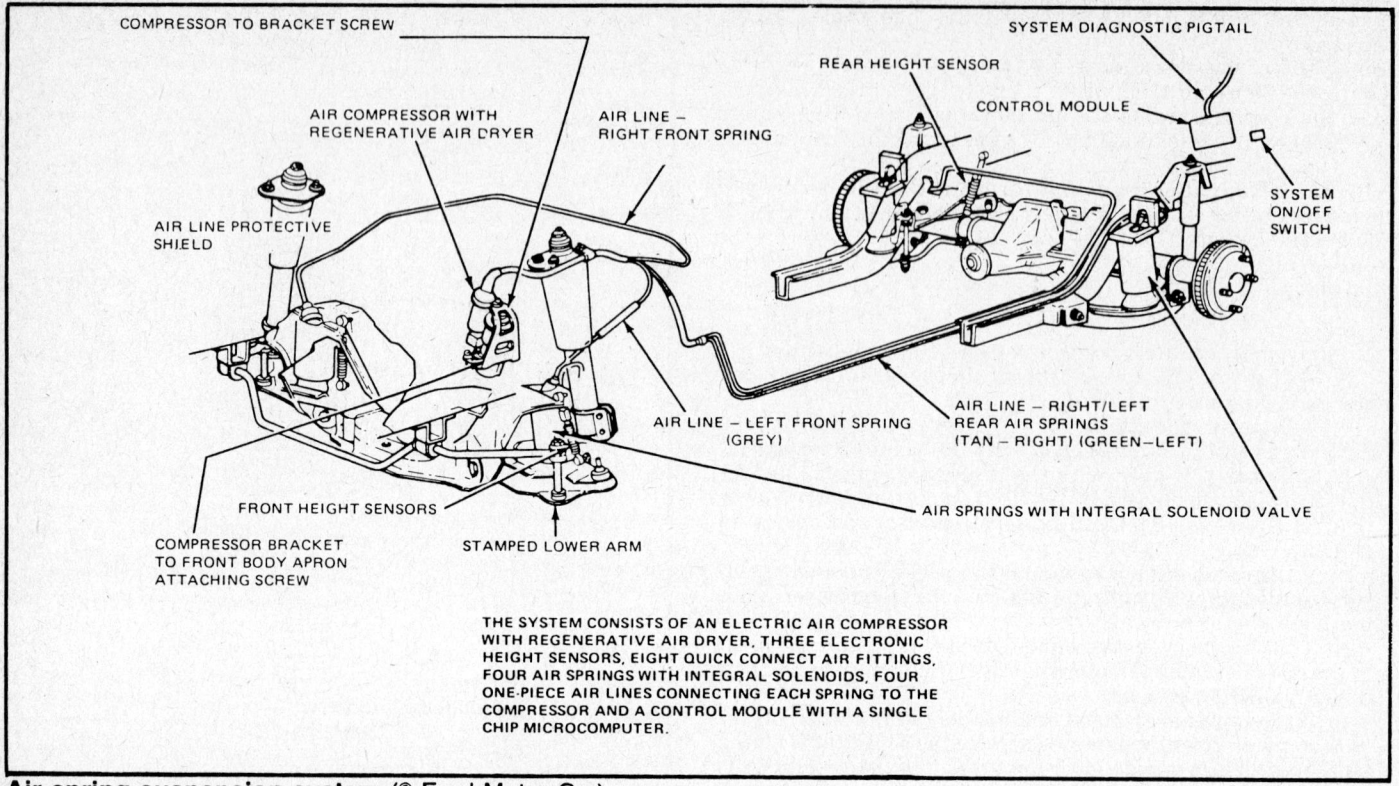

Air spring suspension system (© Ford Motor Co.)

must be allowed for the vehicle to warm or cool to the temperature of the alignment area prior to Steps 1, 2 and 3.

1. Drive onto alignment rack, position vehicle, turn ignition OFF and exit vehicle.

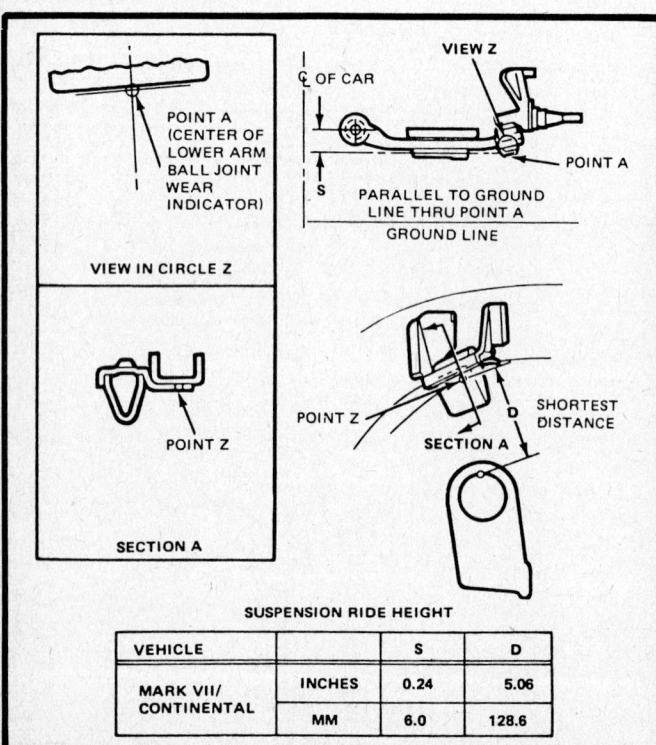

Check dimensions S and D (© Ford Motor Co.)

2. Level rack as required, re-enter vehicle and turn ignition to Run position (do not start).
3. Allow one minute for vehicle to level, then push trunk release, turn ignition to the Off position and exit vehicle.
4. Allow 20 seconds for vehicle to vent to trim height (all doors must be closed) then turn air suspension system switch to the Off position (in trunk on LH side).
5. Check alignment (pinion angle) per specified procedures.

Ride Height

The FRONT SUSPENSION ride height of S dimension is adjusted by moving the front left and/or right sensor attaching stud (there are three adjustment positions provided on the bracket). Loosen the attaching screw and adjust up or down as required. A one position change to the sensor attachment point will yield approx. 0.5 in. (12.7 mm) change (up or down) to the S dimension.

The REAR SUSPENSION ride height D dimension is adjusted by moving the rear sensor attaching bracket up or down relative to the right rear upper arm (a slot adjustment is provided on the bracket). Loosen the attaching nut and adjust up or down as required. A one index mark change to the sensor attachment point will yield approximately 0.25 in. (6.35 mm) change (up or down) to the D dimension.

DIAGNOSIS

Leak Checks

If the air spring system is suspected of leakage, the standard soap solution check procedure is acceptable.

Warning Lamp (Check Suspension)

The air suspension warning lamp, located in the overhead console, has three main functions:
1. During normal operation with the ignition in the Run po-

SUSPENSIONS
FRONT AND REAR — FORD AIR SUSPENSION
SECTION 35

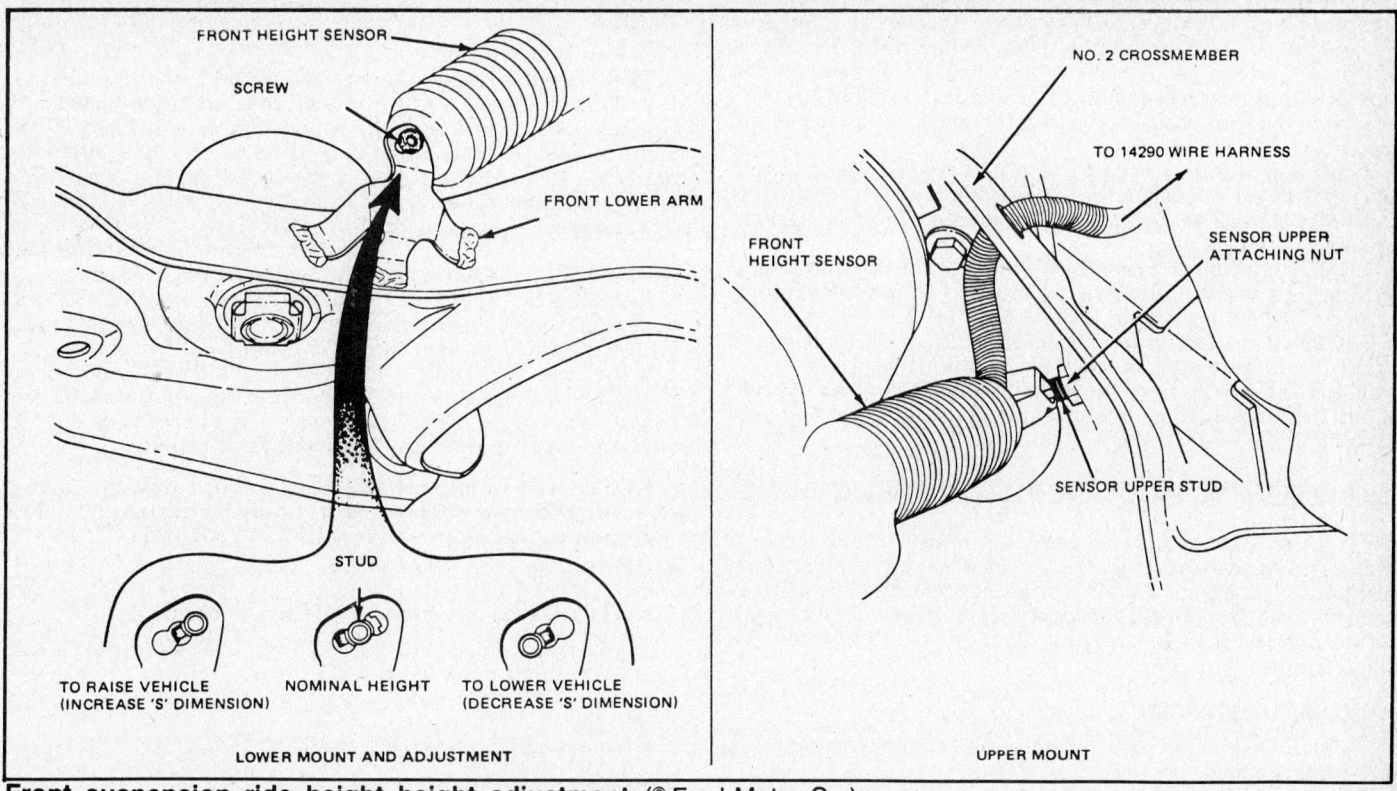

Front suspension ride height height adjustment (© Ford Motor Co.)

sition, the lamp glowing continuously indicates a possible air suspension system problem.

2. During diagnostic testing the lamp blinks at a rate of 1.8 blinks per second to show that diagnostic routine (in the module) has been entered and then blinks the test number that is being run during the test sequence.

3. During the air spring fill routine, the lamp blinks at a rate of 1 blink every two seconds to show that the air fill routine (in the module) has been entered.

Observation of the warning lamp during normal operation with the ignition switch On, can aid in detecting some system problems.

1. On a vehicle operating normally, the warning lamp will glow for approximately one second and then go out when the

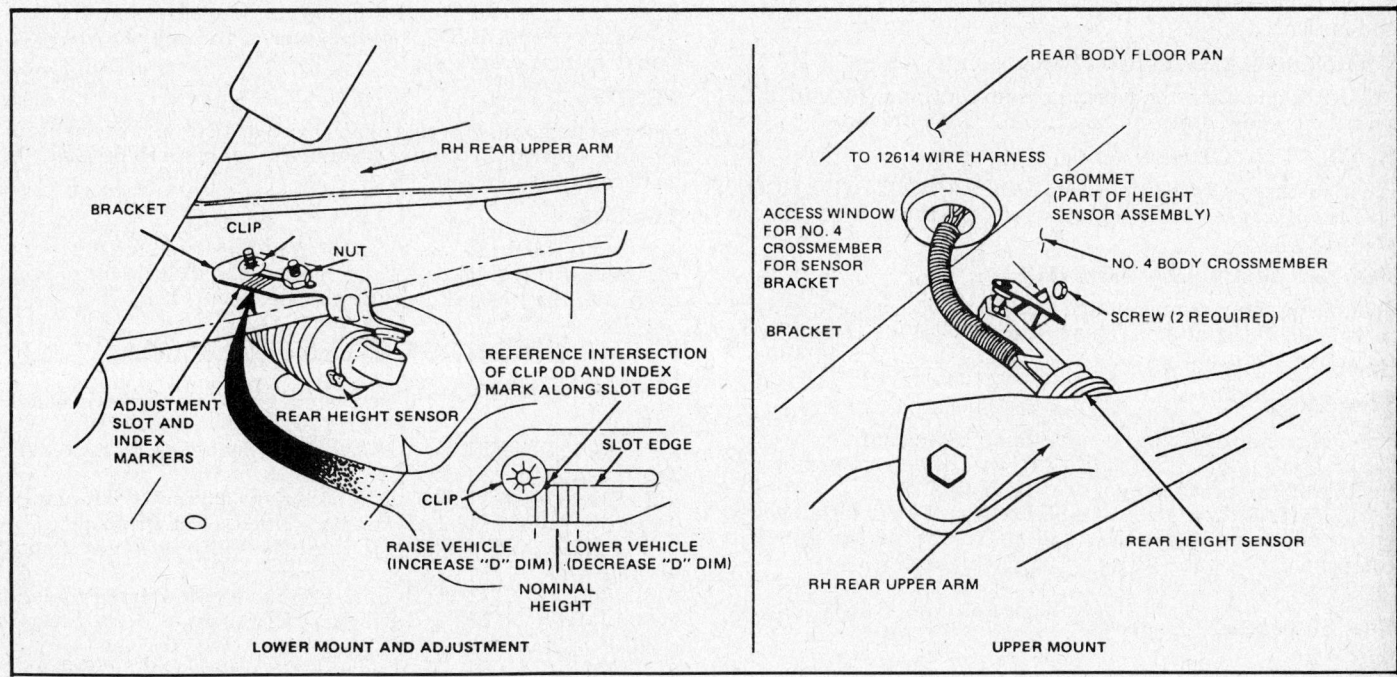

Rear suspension ride height adjustment (© Ford Motor Co.)

35-67

SECTION 35

SUSPENSIONS
FRONT AND REAR—FORD AIR SUSPENSION

ignition is turned from the Off to Run position. The lamp does not operate when the ignition is in either the Off or Start position.

2. If lamps does not go out after turning the ignition from the Off to the Run position, it indicates no battery power to the module.

3. If lamp glows for approximately ½ second, goes out, and then glows continuously after 5–8 seconds, when the ignition is turned to the Off to Run position, a height sensor or harness problem is indicated.

4. After ignition is turned from the Off to the Run position, if the lamp comes on and glows continuously at any time after 8 seconds, a system problem is indicated.

5. Once the warning lamp comes on during an ignition On cycle, it will glow continuously for that ignition On cycle.

6. Erratic operation of the warning lamp (blinking or occasional flashing) during an ignition On cycle, indicates a system problem.

DIAGNOSTIC AND AIR FILL INSTRUCTIONS

The control module has the capability of performing either a series of diagnostic tests on the air suspension system or to selectively fill the front and/or rear air springs. Specific instructions for using the air fill capability are in Removal and Installation. Instructions for entering diagnostics and test descriptions follow.

Entering Diagnostics

1. Turn On the air suspension switch. Diagnostic pigtail is to be ungrounded.

2. Install battery charger to reduce battery drain.

3. Cycle the ignition from the Off to the Run position, hold in the Run position for a minimum of five seconds, then return to the Off position. Driver's door is open with all other doors shut.

4. Change the diagnostic pigtail from an ungrounded state to a grounded state by attaching a lead from the diagnostic pigtail to vehicle ground. The pigtail must remain grounded during the spring fill sequence.

5. Turn the ignition switch to the Run position. (Do not start vehicle) The warning lamp will blink continuously at a rate of 1.8 blinks per second to indicate diagnostics has been entered and is ready.

WARNING LAMP FUNCTION

During diagnostics, the warning lamp continuously blinks either the "ready" status or the current test number.

DOOR FUNCTION

Each successive transition from DOOR CLOSED TO DOOR OPEN will cause the module to advance to the next step in the test sequence.

TERMINATION DIAGNOSTICS

Diagnostics may be terminated and the module returned to the normal operational mode at any time by cycling the ignition, actuating the brake or ungrounding the diagnostic pigtail.

Test Steps

The following tests will be run during Diagnostics.

For Tests 1, 2 and 3, PASS/FAIL will be determined by the module at the conclusion of Step A, B or C.

For Tests 4 through 10, PASS/FAIL will be determined by the technician observing the operation of the specific component.

TEST 1

Rear Suspension.

TEST 2

Right Front Suspension.

TEST 3

Left Front Suspension.

The following steps occur in each of the first three tests:

1. Raise the (rear, right front, left front) of the vehicle for 15 seconds. Continue raising the vehicle for an additional 15 seconds (30 seconds total maximum) or until a 'Vehicle High' signal or an illegal sensor read is received from the (rear, right front, left front) sensor.

2. Lower the (rear, right front, left front) of vehicle for 30 seconds or until a "Vehicle Low signal, or an illegal sensor read is received from the (rear, right front, left front) sensor.

3. Raise the (rear, right front, left front) of vehicle 30 seconds or until a Vehicle Trim signal, or an illegal sensor read is received from the (rear, right front, left front) sensor.

If the expected signal is not received within the 30 second limit, the test will stop and the warning lamp will turn on continuously. Also, if an illegal sensor read is received, the test will stop and the warning lamp will flash rapidly.

NOTE: The failed test may then be repeated by closing/opening the door or the next test may be initiated by closing/opening the door twice within 15 seconds.

TEST 4

NOTE: Hz (Hertz) = one cycle per second.

Compressor is cycled On/Off at 0.25 Hz. The compressor is limited to cycling a maximum of 50 times.

TEST 5

Vent solenoid is cycled open/closed at 1 Hz.

TEST 6

Left front solenoid is cycled open/closed at 1 Hz. and the vent solenoid is opened. Left front corner of the vehicle will drop slowly at test progresses.

TEST 7

Right front solenoid is cycled open/closed at 1 Hz. and the vent solenoid is opened. Right front corner of the vehicle will slowly drop so test progresses.

TEST 8

Right rear solenoid is cycled open/closed at 1 Hz. and the vent solenoid is opened. Right rear corner of the vehicle will drop slowly at test progresses.

TEST 9

Left rear solenoid is cycled open/closed at 1 Hz. and the vent solenoid is opened. Left rear corner of the vehicle will drop slowly as test progresses.

TEST 10

Actuating the brake, turning the ignition switch to Off, or disconnecting the diagnostic lead returns the module from diagnostics to the normal operating mode.

DIAGNOSTIC TESTING INDEX

1. QUICK TEST:Perform System Self-Diagnostic or Quick Test.
2. PINPOINT TEST B: Cannot Enter/Sequence or Exit Self-Test Diagnostic Quick Test.
3. PINPOINT TEST C:Diagnose Sensor Related Problem.
4. PINPOINT TEST D: Diagnose Vehicle Rear Problem.
5. PINPOINT TEST E:Diagnose Vehicle Right Front Problem.
6. PINPOINT TEST F: Diagnose Vehicle Left Front Problem.
7. PINPOINT TEST G:Diagnose Compressor Motor Electrical Problem.
8. PINPOINT TEST H: Diagnose Compressor Vent Solenoid Electrical Problem.

SUSPENSIONS
FRONT AND REAR — FORD AIR SUSPENSION

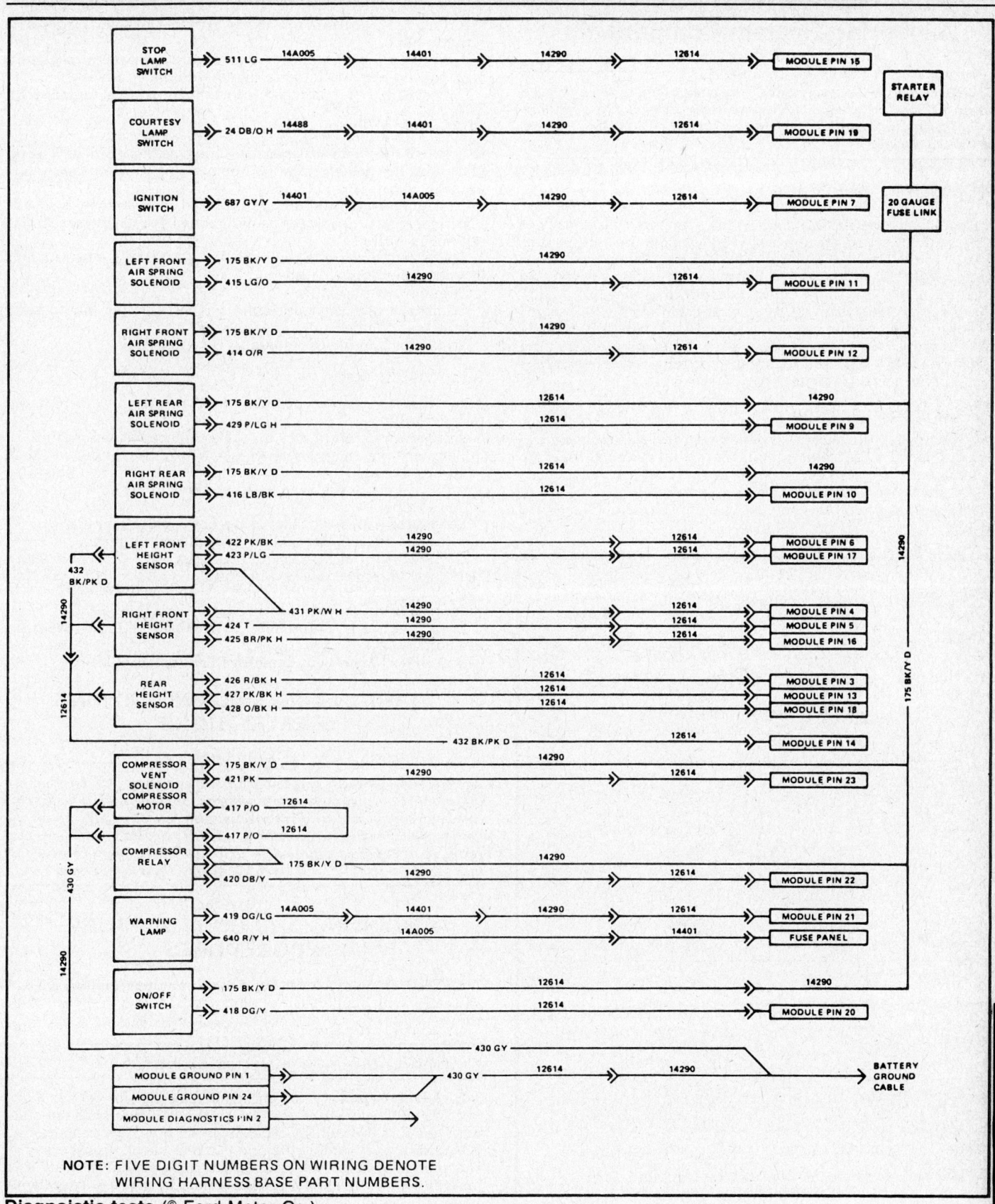

NOTE: FIVE DIGIT NUMBERS ON WIRING DENOTE WIRING HARNESS BASE PART NUMBERS.

Diagnoistic tests (© Ford Motor Co.)

SECTION 35 SUSPENSIONS
FRONT AND REAR—FORD AIR SUSPENSION

Air Spring System Components

CAUTION
Do not remove an air spring under any circumstances when there is pressure in the air spring. Do not remove any components supporting an air spring without either exhausting the air or providing support for the air spring.

Suspension Fasteners

Suspension fasteners are important attaching parts in that they could affect performance of vital components and systems and/or could result in major service expense. They must be replaced with fasteners of the same part number, or with an equivalent part, if replacement becomes necessary. DO NOT use a replacement part of lesser quality or substitute design.

Torque values must be used, as specified, during assembly to assure proper retention of parts. New fasteners must be used whenever old fasteners are loosened or removed or when new component parts are installed.

Air Spring Suspension

Air compressor (less dryer), regenerative dryer, O-ring, mounting bracket and the isolator mounts are all serviced as separate components.

Height sensors and modules are replaceable.

Air springs are replaceable as assemblies (includes solenoid valve).

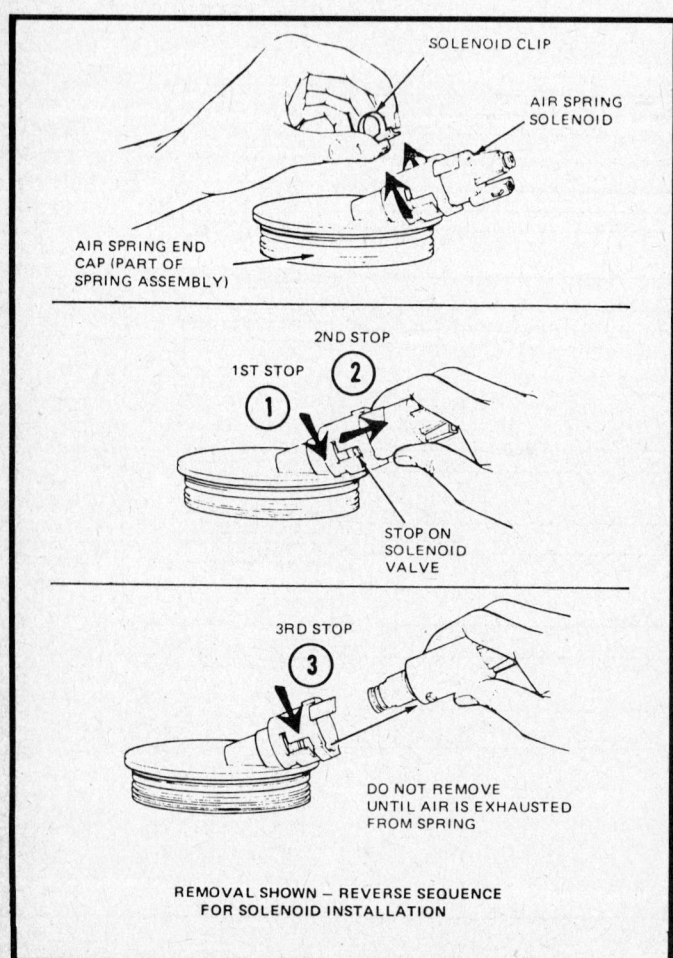

Air spring solenoid removal (© Ford Motor Co.)

Air spring solenoid valves an external O-rings are replaceable.

Air lines are replaceable, however quick connect unions and bulk tubing are available to mend a damaged air line.

Collect and O-ring of the quick connect fitting is replaceable.

Suspension, Front

Gas filled shock absorber struts must be replaced as assemblies. they are not serviceable. Replace only the damaged shock absorber strut. It is not necessary to replace in matched pairs.

Strut upper mounts may be replaced individually.

Air springs are replaced as assemblies. It is not necessary to replace in pairs.

Lower control arm is replaceable an assembly with the ball joint and bushings included.

Spindle is replaceable.

Stabilizer bar is replaceable with stabilizer bar-to-body insulators included.

Stabilizer bar-to-body bushing is replaceable.

Suspension, Rear

The following rear suspension components may be replaced individually:

Gas filled shock absorbers must be replaced as assemblies.

They are not serviceable. Replace only the damaged shock absorber. It is not necessary to replaced in matched pairs.

Air springs are replaced as assemblies. It is not necessary to replace in pairs.

Lower control arms, including both end bushings, are replaceable as assemblies (Must be replaced in pairs).

Upper control arm axle and bushings are replaceable as assemblies (Must be replaced in pairs).

Upper control arm axle and bushings are replaceable individually. (Must be replaced in pairs).

Stabilizer bar is replaceable with stabilizer bar-to-axle insulator included.

Stabilizer bar-to-body bushings are replaceable.

HOIST LIFTING, JACKING, TOWING RESTRICTIONS

CAUTION
The electrical power supply to the air suspension system must be shut off prior to hoisting, jacking or towing an air suspension vehicle. This can be accomplished by disconnecting the battery or turning off the power switch located in the trunk on the LH side. Failure to do so may result in unexpected inflation or deflation of the air springs which may result in shifting of the vehicle during these operations.

HOISTING AND BODY SUPPORT PROCEDURES

1. Position vehicle over hoist and then turn ignition Off and shut off the air suspension power switch located in the trunk on the left side.

CAUTION
The following Hoist Restrictions must be observed:

2. A body hoist is the recommended method for vehicle hoisting. When this hoist is used, raise the vehicle using the standard support procedures. The suspension will be supported in rebound by the front struts and the rear shock absorbers after the vehicle is lifted. Also support vehicle at four corners with jack stands as a safety precautions. Do not use suspension hoists.

3. If a body hoist is not available, an alternate method approved for vehicle hoisting is to use a standard hydraulic floor

SUSPENSIONS
FRONT AND REAR – FORD AIR SUSPENSION

SECTION 35

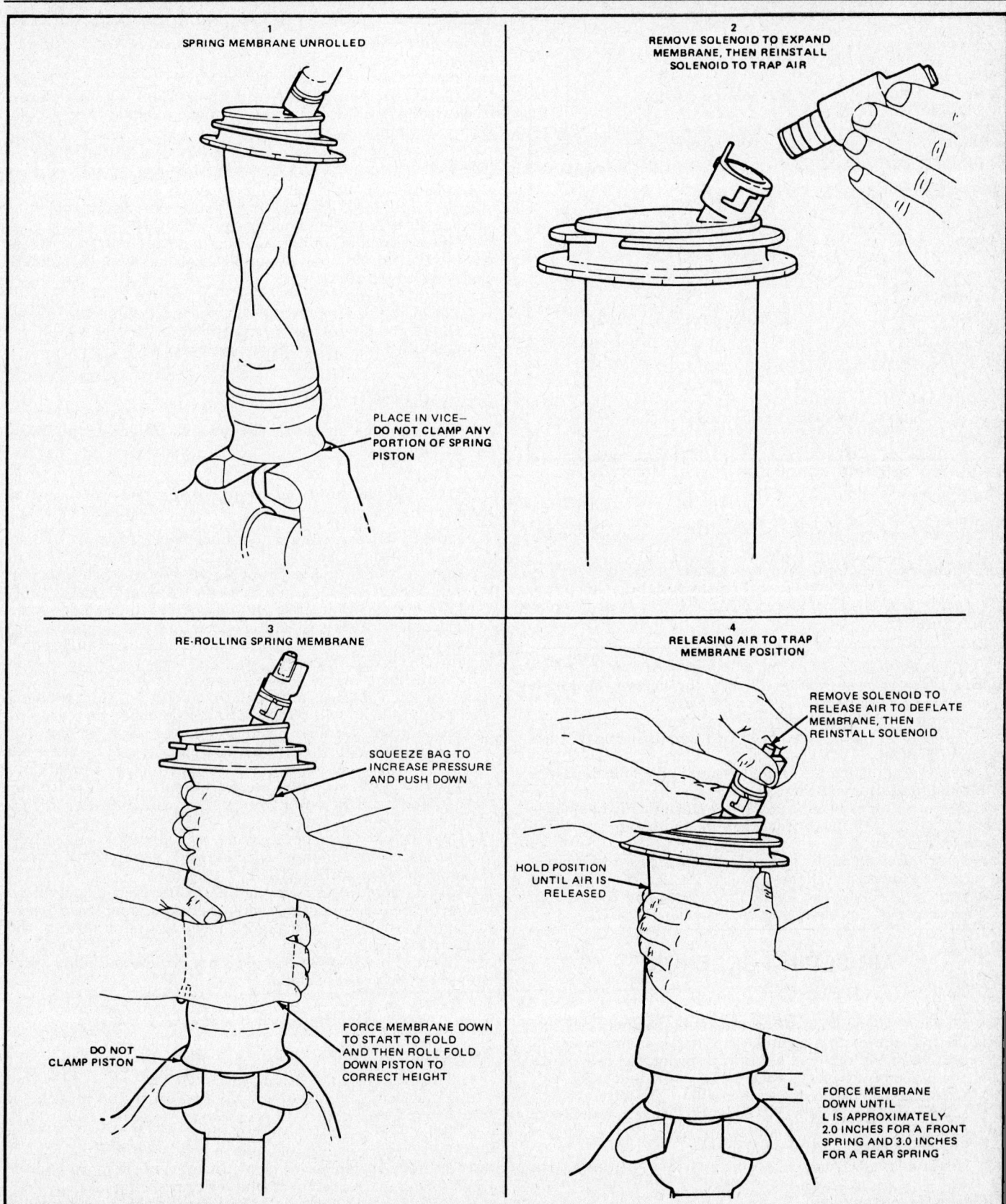

Air spring folding procedures (© Ford Motor Co.)

35-71

SECTION 35 SUSPENSIONS
FRONT AND REAR—FORD AIR SUSPENSION

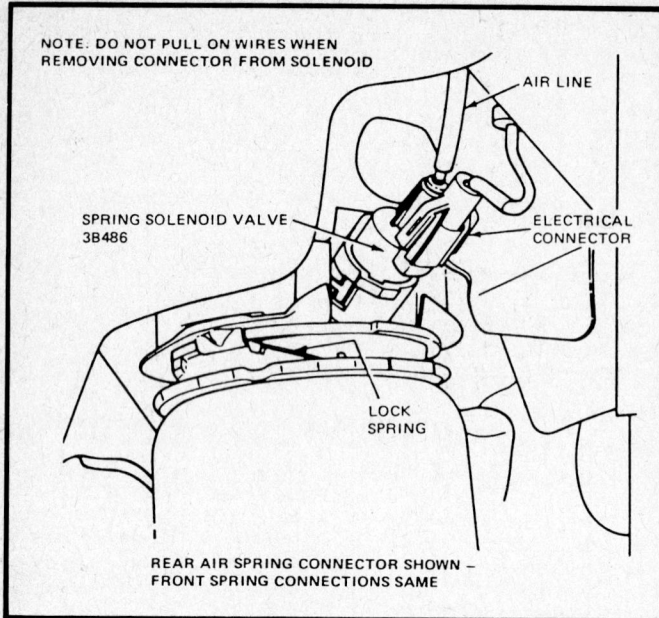

Air spring solenoid connector (© Ford Motor Co.)

jack. Raise the front of the vehicle at the No. 2 crossmember until the tires are above the floor. Support vehicle body with jack stands at each front corner and then lower floor jack so that the front suspension is in full rebound. Repeat this procedure or the rear suspension except raise the body at the rear jacking location.

CAUTION

Power to the air system must be shut off by turning the air suspension switch (in luggage compartment) Off or by disconnecting the battery when servicing any air suspension components.

---

1. Do not attempt to install or inflate any air spring that has become unfolded.
2. Any spring which has unfolded must be refolded prior to being installed in a vehicle.
3. Do not attempt to inflate any air spring which has been collapsed while uninflated from the rebound hanging position to the jounce stop.
4. After inflating an air spring in hanging position, it must be inspected for proper shape.
5. Failure to follow the above procedures may result in a sudden failure of the air spring or suspension system.

AIR SPRING SOLENOID
Removal

The air spring solenoid valve has a two stage solenoid pressure relief fitting similar to a radiator cap. A clip is firs removed, and rotation of the solenoid out of the spring will release air from the assembly before the solenoid can be removed.
1. Turn the air suspension switch Off.
2. Hoist vehicle and support safely. Suspension must be at full rebound.
3. Remove wheel and tire assembly.
4. Disconnect electrical connector and then disconnect the air line.
5. Remove solenoid clip.
6. Rotate solenoid counterclockwise to the first stop.
7. Pull solenoid straight out slowly to the second stop to bleed air from the system.

CAUTION

Do not fully release solenoid until air is completely bled from the air spring.

---

8. After air is fully bled from the system, rotate counterclockwise to the third stop, and remove solenoid from the air spring assembly.

Installation

1. Check solenoid O-ring for abrasion or cuts. Replace O-ring as required. Lightly grease O-ring area of solenoid with silicone dielectric compound or equivalent.
2. Insert solenoid into air spring end cap and rotate clockwise to the third stop, push into the second stop, then rotate clockwise to the first stop.
3. Install solenoid clip.
4. Connect the air line and the electrical connector.
5. Refill the air spring(s) as outlined.
6. Install the wheel and tire assembly.

Air Spring Fill

1. Turn On the air suspension switch. Diagnostic pigtail is to be ungrounded.

NOTE: Lower hoist as required, but do not apply a load to the suspension.

2. Install battery charger to reduce battery drain.
3. Cycle the ignition from the Off to the Run position, hold in the Run position for a minimum of five seconds, then return to the Off position. Driver's door is open with all other doors shut.
4. Change the diagnostic pigtail from an ungrounded state to a grounded state by attaching a lead from the diagnostic pigtail to vehicle ground. The pigtail must remain grounded during the spring fill sequence.
5. While applying the brakes, turn the ignition switch to the Run position. (The door must be open and do not start vehicle). The warning lamp will blink continuously once every two seconds to indicate the spring pump sequence has been entered.
6. To fill a rear spring(s), close and open door once. After a 6 second delay, the rear spring will be filled for 60 seconds.
7. To fill a front spring(s), close and open the door twice. After a 6 second delay, the front spring will be filled for 60 seconds.
8. To fill rear and front springs, fill the rear springs first. When the rear fill has finished, close and open the door once to initiate the front spring fill.
9. Terminate the air spring fill by turning the ignition switch to Off, actuating the brake, or ungrounding the diagnostic pigtail. The diagnostic pigtail must be ungrounded at the end of the spring fill.
10. Lower hoist completely and start vehicle and allow vehicle to level with doors closed.

AIR SPRING—FRONT OR REAR
Removal

1. Turn the air suspension switch Off.
2. Hoist vehicle and support safely. Suspension must be at full rebound.
3. Remove tire and wheel assembly.
4. Remove air spring solenoid.
5. Remove spring to lower arm fasteners. Remove clip for front spring and/or remove bolts for rear spring.
6. Push down or spring clip on the collar of the air springs and rotate collar counterclockwise to release the spring from the body spring seat.
7. Remove air spring.

SUSPENSIONS
FRONT AND REAR—FORD AIR SUSPENSION

Installation

1. Install air spring solenoid as outlined.
2. Correctly position the solenoid. For LH illustration (front or rear spring), the notch on the collar is to be in line with the centerline of the solenoid. For RH installation (front or rear), the flat on the collar is to be in line with the centerline of the solenoid.
3. Install the air spring into the body spring seat, taking care to keep the solenoid air and electrical connections clean and free of damage. Rotate the air spring collar until the spring clips snaps into place. Be sure that the air spring collar is retained by the three rolled tabs on the body spring seat.
4. Attach air line and electrical connector to the solenoid assembly.
5. Align and secure lower arm to spring attachment with suspension at full rebound and supported by shock absorbers.

--- **CAUTION** ---
The air springs may be damaged if suspension is allowed to compress before spring is inflated.

6. Replace tire and wheel assembly.
7. Remove floor jacks and lower vehicle until tire and wheel assembly are 1–3 in. above floor.
8. Refill the air spring(s) as outlined.

AIR COMPRESSOR AND DRYER ASSEMBLY

Removal

1. Turn the air suspension switch Off.
2. Disconnect the electrical connector located on the compressor.
3. Remove the air line protector cap from the dryer by releasing the two latching pins located on the bottom of the cap 180 degrees apart.
4. Disconnect the four air lines from dryer.
5. Remove the three screws retaining the air compressor to mounting brackets.

Installation

1. Position air compressor and dryer assembly to mounting bracket and install the three mounting screws.
2. Connect all four air lines into the dryer.
3. Connect the electrical connection.
4. Install the air line protector cap onto the dryer.
5. Turn air suspension switch On.

DRYER, AIR COMPRESSOR

Removal

1. Turn the air suspension switch Off.
2. Remove the air line protector cap from the dryer by releasing the two latching pins located on the bottom of the cap 180 degrees apart.
3. Disconnect the four air lines from the dryer.
4. Remove the dryer retainer clip and screw.
5. Remove from the head assembly.

Installation

1. Check to ensure the old O-ring is not in the head assembly.
2. Check dryer end to ensure new O-ring is in proper position.
3. Insert dryer into head assembly and install retainer clip and screw.
4. Connect the four air lines into the dryer.
5. Install the air line protector cap onto the dryer.
6. Turn the air suspension switch On.

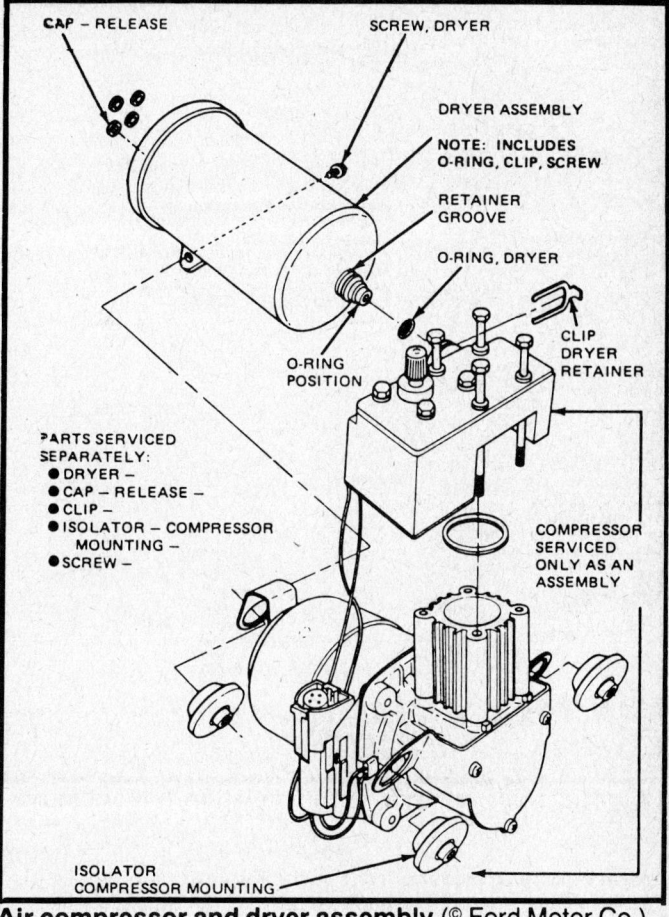

Air compressor and dryer assembly (© Ford Motor Co.)

HEIGHT SENSORS—FRONT

Removal

1. Turn the air suspension switch Off.
2. Disconnect sensor electrical connector. The front sensor connectors are located in the engine compartment behind the shock towers.
3. Push the front sensor connector through the access hole in the rear of the shock tower.
4. Hoist vehicle and support safely. Suspension must be at full rebound.
5. Disconnect the bottom and then the top end of the sensor from the attaching studs.
6. Disconnect the sensor wire harness from the plastic clips on the shock tower and remove sensor.

Installation

1. Connect the top and then the bottom end of the sensor to the attaching studs. Route the sensor electrical connector as required to connect the vehicle wire harness.
2. Lower vehicle.
3. Connect the sensor connector.
4. Turn the air suspension switch On.

HEIGHT SENSOR—REAR

Removal

1. Turn the air suspension switch Off.
2. Disconnect the sensor electrical connector located in the

SECTION 35 SUSPENSIONS
FRONT AND REAR—FORD AIR SUSPENSION

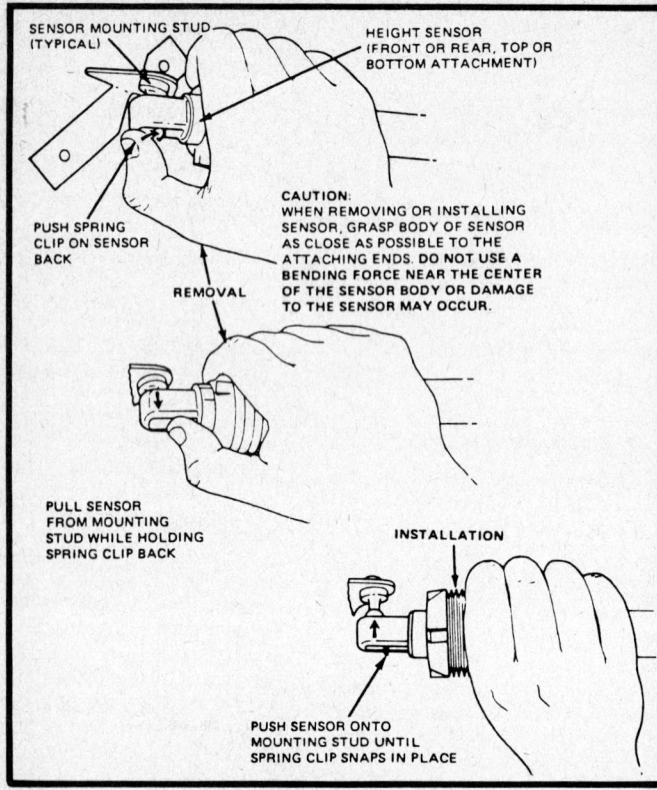

Height sensor removal anf installation (© Ford Motor Co.)

luggage compartment in front of the forward trim panel. Also pull the luggage compartment carpet back for access to the sensor sealing grommet located on the floor plan.

3. Hoist vehicle and support safely. Suspension must be at full rebound.
4. Disconnect the bottom and then the top end of the sensor from the attaching studs.
5. Push upwards on the sealing grommet to unseat and then push sensor through the floor pan hole into the luggage compartment.
6. Lower vehicle.

Installation

1. Connect the sensor connector and then push sensor through the floor pan hole being sure to seat the sealing grommet. Replace luggage compartment carpet.
2. Hoist vehicle and support safely.
3. Connect the top and then the bottom end of the sensor.
4. Lower vehicle.
5. Turn air suspension switch On.

CONTROL MODULE

Removal

1. Turn air suspension switch Off. Ignition switch is also to be Off.
2. Remove LH luggage compartment trim panel.
3. Disconnect wire harness from module.
4. Remove three attaching nuts.
5. Remove module.

Installation

1. Position module and secure with the attaching nuts.
2. Connect wire harness to module.
3. Attach LH luggage compartment trim panel.
4. Turn air suspension switch On.

NYLON AIR LINE

If a leak is detected in an air line, it can be serviced by carefully cutting the line with a sharp knife to ensure a good, clean straight cut. Then, install a service fitting.

QUICK CONNECT FITTINGS

If a leak is detected in any of the eight quick connect fittings, it can be serviced using a repair kit containing a new O-ring, collet, release ring, and O-Ring removal tool. The outer housing of the fitting cannot be serviced.

AIR SUSPENSION SWITCH

Removal and Installation

1. Disconnect electrical connector.
2. Depress retaining clips switch to brace, and remove switch.
3. Push switch into position in the brace, making sure retaining clips are fully seated.
4. Connect electrical connector.

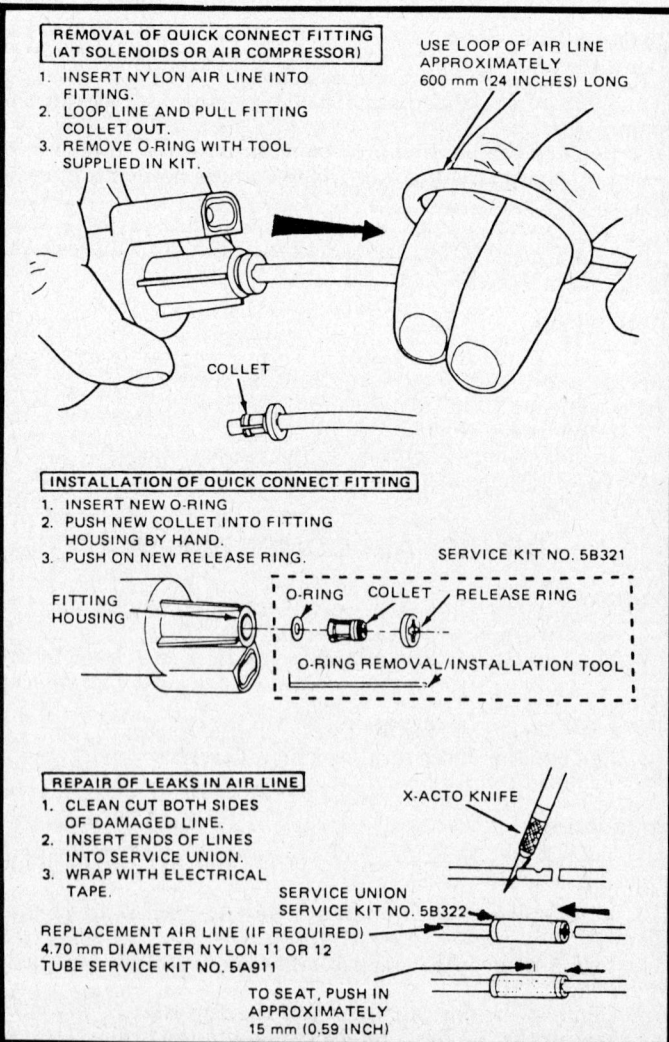

Air line service (© Ford Motor Co.)

SUSPENSIONS
FRONT AND REAR — FORD AIR SUSPENSION
SECTION 35

COMPRESSOR RELAY

Removal and Installation

1. Disconnect electrical connector.
2. Remove screw retaining relay to left front shock tower and remove relay.
3. Position relay on shock tower and install retaining screw.
4. Connect electrical connector.

Front Suspension Components

─────── **CAUTION** ───────
Power in the air system must be shut off by turning the air suspension switch (in luggage compartment) Off or by disconnecting the battery when servicing any suspension components.

STABILIZER BAR AND/OR BUSHING

Removal

1. Turn air suspension switch Off.
2. Raise vehicle on a hoist and support safely.
3. Disconnect stabilizer bar from each link and bushing U-clamps. Remove the stabilizer bar assembly.
4. Remove adapter brackets and U-clamps.
5. Cut the worn bushings from the stabilizer bar.

Installation

1. Coat the necessary parts of the stabilizer bar with Ford Rubber Suspension Insulator Lubricant or equivalent, and slide bushings onto the stabilizer bar. Reinstall U-clamps.
2. Reinstall adapter brackets on U-clamps.
3. Using a new nut and bolt, secure each end of the stabilizer bar to the lower suspension arm. Tighten nuts to specification.
4. Using new bolts, clamp the stabilizer bar to the attaching brackets on the side rail. Tighten bolts to specification.
5. Lower the vehicle.
6. Turn air suspension switch On.

SHOCK STRUT

Removal

1. Turn air suspension switch Off.
2. Turn the ignition key to the unlocked position to allow free movement of front wheels.
3. From the engine compartment, loosen but do not remove the strut-to-upper mount attaching nut.
4. Hoist vehicle and support safely, and position safety stands under the lower control arms as far outboard as possible being sure that the lower sensor mounting bracket is clear. Lower hoist until vehicle weight is supported by lower arms.
5. Remove tire and wheel assembly.
6. Remove brake caliper, then rotate out of position and wire securely.
7. Remove the strut-to-upper mount attaching nut and then the two lower nuts and bolts attaching the strut to the spindle.

NOTE: The strut should be held firmly during the removal of the last bolt since the gas pressure will cause the strut to fully extend when removed.

8. Lift the strut up from the spindle to compress the rod and then remove the strut.
9. Remove jounce bumper.

Installation

1. Prime new strut by extending and compressing strut rod five times.
2. Install jounce bumper.
3. Place strut rod through the upper mount, and hand start and secure a new 16 mm nut.
4. Compress strut, and position onto the spindle.
5. Install two new lower mounting bolts and hand start nuts.
6. Raise hoist to remove vehicle load from the lower control arms and tighten the lower mounting nuts.
7. Install brake caliper.
8. Install the tire and wheel assembly.
9. Remove safety stand and lower the vehicle to the ground.
10. Turn air suspension switch On.
11. Front wheel alignment should be checked and adjusted, if out of specification.

UPPER MOUNT ASSEMBLY

Removal

NOTE: Upper mounts are one piece units and cannot be disassembled.

1. Turn air suspension system Off.
2. Turn the ignition key to the unlocked position to allow free movement of the front wheels.
3. From the engine compartment, loosen but do not remove the three upper mount retaining nuts. Vehicle should be in place over a hoist and must not be driven with these nuts removed. Do not remove the pop rivet holding the camber plate in position.
4. Loosen strut rod nut at this time.
5. Hoist the vehicle and support safely, and position safety stands under the lower control arms as far outboard as possible being sure that the lower sensor mounting bracket is clear. Lower hoist until vehicle weight is supported by the lower arms.
6. Remove the tire and wheel assembly.
7. Remove brake caliper and rotate out of position and wire securely.
8. Remove the upper mount retaining nuts and the two lower nuts and bolts that attach the strut to the spindle.

NOTE: The strut should be held firmly during the removal of the last bolt since the gas pressure will cause the strut to fully extend when removed.

9. Lift the strut up from the spindle to compress the rod, and then remove the strut.
10. Remove upper mount from strut.

Installation

1. Install new upper mount on strut and hand start a new nut.
2. Position the upper mount studs into the body and start and secure three new nuts. Secure the strut rod nut.
3. Compress the strut and position onto the spindle.
4. Install two new lower mounting bolts, and hand strut nuts.
5. Raise hoist to remove vehicle load from the lower control arms and tighten the lower mounting nuts to 126–179 ft. lbs. (170–244 NNm).
6. Install the brake caliper.
7. Install the tire and wheel assembly.
8. Remove safety stands and lower vehicle to the ground.
9. Turn air suspension switch On.
10. Front wheel alignment should be checked and adjusted if out of specification.

SPINDLE ASSEMBLY

Removal

1. Turn air suspension switch Off.
2. Hoist vehicle and support safely.

35-75

SECTION 35
SUSPENSIONS
FRONT AND REAR—FORD AIR SUSPENSION

3. Remove the wheel and tire assembly.
4. Remove the brake caliper, rotor and dust shield.
5. Remove the stabilizer link from the lower arm assembly.
6. Remove the tie rod end from the spindle.
7. Remove the cotter pin from the ball joint stud nut and loosen the ball joint nut one or two turns.

CAUTION

DO NOT remove the nut from the ball joint stud at this time.

---

8. Tap spindle boss smartly to relive stud pressure.
9. Place a floor jack under the lower arm, compress the air spring and remove the stud nut.
10. Remove the bolts and nuts attaching the spindle to the shock strut. Compress the shock strut until working clearance is obtained.
11. Remove the spindle assembly.

Installation

1. Place the spindle on the ball joint stud and install the new stud nut. DO NOT tighten at this time.
2. Lower the shock strut until the attaching holes are in line with the holes in the spindle. Install two new bolts and nuts.
3. Tighten ball joint stud nut and install cotter pin.
4. Lower floor jack from under the suspension arm, and remove jack.
5. Tighten the shock strut to spindle attaching nuts.
6. Install stabilizer bar link and tighten attaching nut.
7. Attach tie rod end and tighten the retaining nut.
8. Install the disc brake dust shield, rotor and caliper.
9. Install the wheel and tire assembly.
10. Remove the safety stands and lower the vehicle.
11. Turn air suspension switch On.
12. Front wheel alignment should be checked and adjusted if out of specification.

SUSPENSION CONTROL ARM

Removal

1. Turn air suspension switch Off.
2. Raise vehicle on a hoist and support safely so the control arms hang free (full rebound).
3. Remove the wheel and tire assembly.
4. Disconnect the tie rod assembly from the steering spindle.
5. Remove the steering gear bolts if necessary and position the gar so that the suspension are bolt may be removed.
6. Disconnect stabilizer bar link from the lower arm.
7. Disconnect lower end of the height sensor from the lower control arm sensor mounting stud. Remove sensor mounting stud and screw from lower arm, noting the position of stud on the lower arm bracket.
8. Remove the cotter pin from the ball joint stud nut and loosen the ball join nut one or two turns. DO NOT remove the nut at this time. Tap spindle boss smartly to relieve stud pressure.
9. Vent air spring(s) to atmospheric pressure. Refer to Air Spring Solenoid Removal. Then, reinstall solenoid. Refer to Air Spring Solenoid Installation.
10. Remove air spring to lower arm fastener clip.
11. Remove the ball joint nut, and raise the entire strut and spindle assembly (strut, rotor, caliper and spindle). Wire it out of the way to obtain working room.
12. Remove the suspension arm to crossmember nuts and bolts, and remove the arm from the spindle.

Installation

1. Position the arm into the crossmember and install a new arm to crossmember bolts and nuts. DO NOT tighten at this time.
2. Remove the wire from the strut and spindle assembly and attach to the ball joint stud. Install a new ball joint stud nut. DO NOT tighten at this time.
3. Position air spring in arm and install a new fastener.
4. Attach sensor mounting stud and screw to lower arm in the same position as on the replaced arm. Connect lower end of sensor to lower arm mounting stud.
5. With a suitable jack, raise the suspension arm to curbheight.
6. With the jack still in place, tighten the lower arm to crossmember attaching nut to 150–180 ft. lbs. (203–244 Nm).
7. Tighten ball join stud nut to 100–120 ft. lbs. (136–163 Nm) and install a new cotter pin. Remove jack.
8. Install the steering gear to crossmember bolts and nuts (if removed). Hold the bolts and tighten nuts to 90–100 ft. lbs. (122–135 Nm).
9. Position the tie rod assembly into the steering spindle, and install the retaining nut. Tighten the nut to 35 ft. lbs. (47 Nm) and continue tightening the nut to align the next castellation with cotter pin hole in the stud. Install a new cotter pin.
10. Connect the stabilizer bar link to the lower suspension arm and tighten the attaching nut to 9–12 ft. lbs. (12–16 Nm).
11. Install the wheel and tire assembly, and lower the vehicle but DO NOT allow tires to touch the ground.
12. Turn air suspension switch On.
13. Refill air spring(s) as outlined.
14. Front wheel alignment should be checked and adjusted if out of specification.

REAR SUSPENSION COMPONENTS

CAUTION

Power to the air system must be shut off by turning the air suspension switch (in luggage compartment) Off or by disconnecting the battery when servicing any suspension components.

SHOCK ABSORBER

Removal

1. Turn air suspension switch Off.
2. Open the luggage compartment and remove the inside trim panels to gain access to the upper shock stud.
3. Loosen but DO NOT REMOVE the shock rod attaching nut.
4. Hoist vehicle and support safely. Position two safety stands under the rear axle. Lower hoist until vehicle weight is supported by the rear axle.
5. Remove the upper attaching nut, washer and insulator and then remove the lower shock protective cover (right shock only) and lower shock absorber crossbolt and nut from the lower shock brackets.
6. From under the vehicle, compress the shock absorber to clear it from the hold in the upper shock tower.

CAUTION

Shock absorbers will extend unassisted. Do not apply heat or flame to the shock absorber during removal.

---

7. Remove shock absorber.

Installation

1. Prime new shock absorber by extending and compressing shock absorber five times.
2. Place the inner washer and insulator on the upper attaching stud. Position stud through the shock tower mounting hole and position an insulator, washer or stud from the luggage compartment. Hand start the attaching nut and then secure.
3. Place shock absorber's lower mounting eye between the ears of the lower shock mounting bracket, compressing shock as required. Insert the bolt (bolt head must seat on the inboard side of the shock bracket), through the shock bracket and the shock absorber mounting eye. Hand start and then secure the original attaching nut.
4. Install the protective cover, to the RH shock absorber. This is done by inserting the bolt point and nut into the cover's open end, sliding the cover over the shock bracket and snapping the closed end of the cover over the bolt head. Properly installed, the cover will completely conceal the bolt point, nut, and bolt head. The rounded or closed end of the cover should be pointing inboard.
5. Raise hoist and remove safety stands from under axle then lower vehicle.
6. Reinstall the inside trim panels.
7. Turn air suspension switch On.

LOWER CONTROL ARM

Removal

NOTE: If one arm requires replacement, replace the other arm also.

1. Turn air suspension switch Off.
2. Hoist vehicle and support safely. Suspension will be at full rebound.
3. Remove tire and wheel assembly.
4. Vent air spring(s) at atmospheric pressure. Refer to Air Spring Solenoid Removal. Then, reinstall solenoid. Refer to Air Spring Solenoid Installation.
5. Remove the two air spring-to-lower arm bolts and remove the air spring from the lower arm.
6. Remove the frame-to-arm and the axle-to-arm bolts and remove the arm from the vehicle.

Installation

1. Position the lower arm assembly into the front arm brackets and insert a new, arm-to-frame pivot bolt and nut with nut facing outwards. DO NOT tighten at this time.
2. Position the rear bushing in the axle bracket and install a new arm-to-axle pivot bolt and nut with nut facing outwards. DO NOT tighten at this time.
3. Install two new air spring-to-arm bolts. DO NOT tighten at this time.
4. Using a suitable jack, raise the axle to curb height. Tighten the lower arm front bolt, the rear pivot bolt, and the air spring to arm bolt being sure that the air spring piston is flat on the lower arm. Remove the jack.
5. Replace tire and wheel assembly.
6. Lower the vehicle.
7. Turn air suspension switch On.
8. Refill air spring(s) as outlined.

UPPER CONTROL ARM AND AXLE BUSHING

Removal

NOTE: If one arm requires replacement, replace the other arm also.

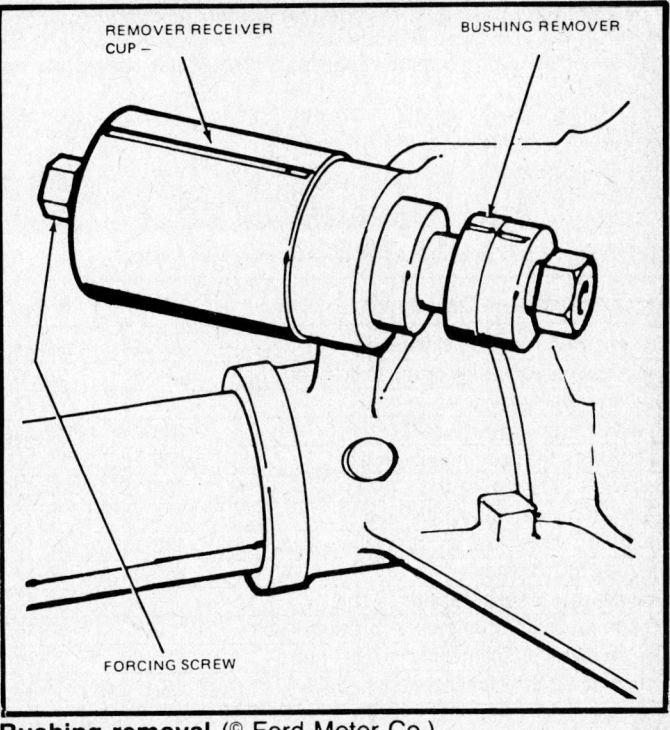

Bushing removal (© Ford Motor Co.)

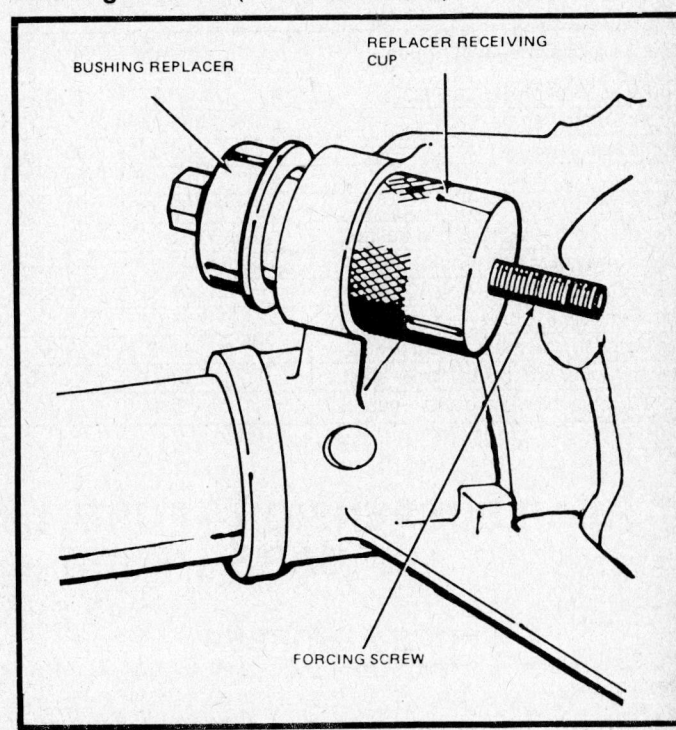

Bushing installation (© Ford Motor Co.)

1. Turn air suspension switch Off.
2. Hoist vehicle and support safely. Suspension will be at full rebound.
3. On the RH side, detach rear height sensor from side arm. Note position of the sensor adjustment bracket on the upper arm.
4. Remove upper arm-to-axle pivot nut and bolt.

SECTION 35 SUSPENSIONS
FRONT AND REAR—FORD AIR SUSPENSION

5. Remove upper arm-to-axle frame pivot bolt and nut. Remove upper arm from vehicle.

If upper arm axle bushing is to be replaced, use the following procedure:

6. Place the upper arm axle bushing remover tool in position, and remove the bushing assembly.

7. Using the installer tool, install the bushing assembly into the bushing ear of the rear axle.

Installation

1. Place the upper arm into the bracket of the body side rail. Insert a new upper arm-to-frame pivot bolt and nut (nut facing outboard). DO NOT tighten at this time.
2. Align the upper arm-to-axle pivot hole with the hole in the axle bushing. If required, raise the axle using a suitable jack to align. Install a new pivot bolt and not (nut inboard). DO NOT tighten at this time.
3. On the RH side, reattach rear height sensor to the arm. Set the adjustment bracket to the same position as on the replaced arm and tighten nut.
4. Using a suitable jack, raise the axle to curb height and tighten the front upper arm bolt, and the rear upper arm bolt.
5. Remove the jack stands supporting the axle.
6. Lower vehicle.
7. Turn air suspension switch On.

AIR SUSPENSION BOLT TORQUE SPECIFICATIONS

Front Suspension—Description	Nm	ft. lbs.
Lower arm to No. 2 crossmember—nut	203-244	150-180
Stabilizer bar mounting clamp to bracket—bolt	27-34	20-25
Stabilizer bar to lower arm—nut	12-16	9-12
Spindle to shock strut—nut	203-244	150-180
Shock strut to upper mount—nut	75-125	55-92
Ball joint to spindle—nut	136-163	100-120
Shock upper mount to body—nut	84-102	62-75
Steering gear to No. 2 crossmember—nut	122-136	90-100
Tie rod end to spindle—nut	47-64	35-47
Compressor bracket to frame—bolt	3-5	30-40*
Air compressor to compressor bracket—bolt	3-5	30-40*
Sensor upper attachment to frame—nut	35-46	26-34
Sensor lower attachment to arm—bolt	10-16	8-12

Rear Suspension—Description	Nm	Ft. Lbs.
Shock absorber to frame—nut	26-37	17-27
Upper arm to frame—bolt	135-142	100-105
Upper arm to axle—bolt	122-135	90-100
Lower arm to frame—bolt	135-142	100-105
Lower arm to axle—bolt	122-135	90-100
Shock absorber to clevis bracket bolt	61-81	45-60
Clevis bracket to axle—nut	75-90	55-70
Stabilizer bar to axle—bolt	41-48	30-35
Stabilizer bar to body—nut	17-24	13-18
Air spring to lower arm—bolt	41-48	30-35
Sensor upper bracket to frame—bolt	12-17	110-150*
Sensor lower bracket to arm—nut	8-14	7-10

STABILIZER BAR BUSHINGS

Removal

1. Turn air suspension switch Off.
2. Hoist vehicle and support safely.
3. Disconnect the stabilizer bar from each link and bushing U-clamp. Remove the stabilizer bar assembly.
4. Remove the U-clamps.
5. Cut the worn bushings from the stabilizer bar.

Installation

1. Coat the necessary parts of the stabilizer bar with Ford Rubber Suspension Insulator Lubricant or equivalent and slide new bushings onto the stabilizer bar. Reinstall U-clamps.
2. Using new bolts and nuts, attach stabilizer bar to the axle. Do not tighten bolts at this time.
3. Using new bolts and nuts, attach the link end of the stabilizer bar to the body. Tighten the link attaching nut and then the axle attaching bolts.
4. Lower vehicle.
5. Turn air suspension switch On.

NOTE: Due to the diagnostic complexity of the Automatic Load Levelling System, detailed diagnostic procedures can be found in Chilton's Chassis Electronic Service Manual.

REAR SUSPENSION—FORD, LINCOLN, MERCURY REAR DRIVE CARS, FOUR—BAR LINK DESIGN

SHOCK ABSORBER

Removal

1. Remove the attaching nut, washer and insulator from the shock absorber's upper stud.
2. Raise the vehicle on a hoist, and support the rear axle.
3. From underneath the vehicle, compress the shock absorber to clear it from the hole in the upper shock tower.
4. Remove the lower shock absorber bolt, washer and nut from the axle bracket.
5. Remove the shock absorber.

Installation

1. Expel all air from the new shock absorber.
2. Compress the shock absorber and position the shock's mounting eye to the axle bracket mounting hole. Place a new load bearing washer between the shock eye and axle bracket. Install a new Torx drive belt or equivalent through the shock eye, washer and axle bracket, then hand start the bolt into a new self-wrenching nut. Do not tighten at this time.
3. After compressing the shock absorber, place the absorber's lower mounting eye between the ears of the lower shock mounting bracket. Then insert the bolt. the bolt head must seat on the inboard side of the shock bracket, through the shock bracket and the shock absorber mounting eye. Install the prevailing torque attaching nut. Do not tighten the nut at this time.
4. Place the inner washer and insulator on the upper attaching stud.

SUSPENSIONS

REAR SUSPENSION—FORD REAR DRIVE CARS—FOUR BAR LINK DESIGN

5. Extend the shock absorber's upper stud, and position it through the mounting hole in the shock tower.

6. Fairmont/Zephyr, Mustang/Capri/Cougar: While holding the shock absorber in position, tighten the lower attaching bolt to 70 ft. lbs. (94 Nm) using tool number D80P-2100-T55 or equivalent. Allow the self wrenching nut to rotate freely so that the wrenching tab seats on the outboard leg of the axle bracket. Do not restrain the nut using any other method.

7. Thunderbird/XR-7: While holding the shock absorber in position, tighten the lower shock cross bolt to 70 ft. lbs. (94.9 Nm).

8. Thunderbird/XR-7: Install the protective cover (only one is required) to the right hand shock absorber. This is done by inserting the bolt point and nut into the cover's open end, sliding the cover over the bolt head. Properly installed, the cover will completely conceal the bolt point, nut and bolt head. The rounded or closed end of the cover should be pointing inboard.

9. Lower the vehicle. Install the insulator, outer washer, and a new nut to the upper shock stud, and tighten. Install the rubber cap on the shock stud. Install the inside panel trim covers.

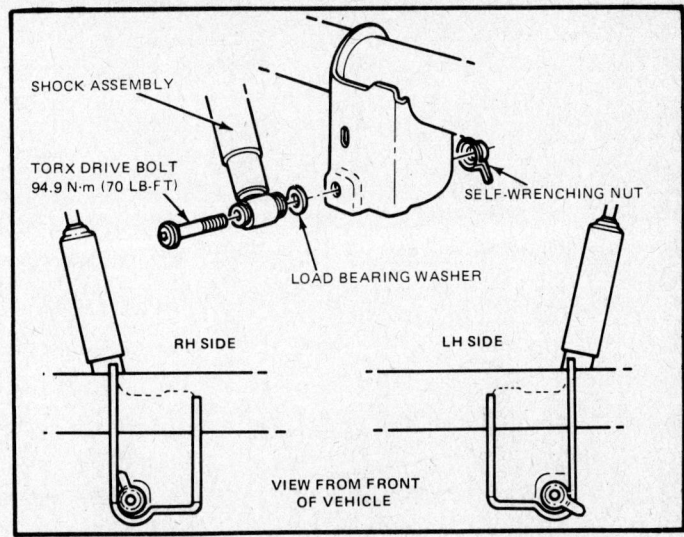

Rear shock lower installation—Fairmont/Zephyr, Mustang/Capri, Granada/Cougar (© Ford Motor Co.)

SPRING

Removal

NOTE: If vehicle is equipped with a rear stabilizer bar, remove the bar.

1. Raise the vehicle and support the body at the rear body crossmember.
2. Lower the hoist until the rear shocks are fully extended.

NOTE: The axle must be supported by the hoist, a transmission jack or jack stands.

3. Place a transmission jack under the lower arm axle pivot bolt, and remove the bolt and nut. Lower the transmission jack slowly until the coil spring load is relieved.
4. Remove the coil spring and insulators from the vehicle.

Installation

1. Place the upper spring insulator on top of the spring. Tape in place if necessary.
2. Place the lower spring insulator on the lower arm (except Mustang/Capri). Install the internal damper into the spring (except Thunderbird/XR-7).
3. Position the coil spring on the lower arm spring seat so that the pigtail on the lower arm is at the rear of the vehicle and pointing toward the left side of the vehicle. Slowly raise the transmission jack until the arm is in position. Insert a new rear pivot bolt and nut with the nut facing outwards. Do not tighten at this time.
4. Lower the transmission jack. Raise the axle to curb height. Tighten the lower arm pivot bolt to 100 ft. lbs. (135 Nm).
5. If vehicle was equipped with a rear stabilizer bar, install bar.
6. Remove crossmember supports and lower the vehicle.

LOWER ARM

Removal

1. Raise the vehicle and support body at the rear body crossmember.
2. Lower the hoist until the rear shocks are fully extended.

NOTE: The axle must be supported by the hoist, a jack or stands.

3. Place the transmission jack under the lower arm rear pivot bolt, and remove the bolt and nut.
4. Lower the jack slowly until the coil spring can be removed.
5. Remove the lower arm assembly.

Installation

1. Position the lower arm assembly into the front arm bracket and insert a new front pivot bolt and nut with nut facing outward. Do not tighten at this time.
2. Install coil spring. Holding the spring in position, use the jack under the rear of the lower arm. Raise the jack until the arm is in position. Insert a new rear pivot bolt and nut with nut facing outwards. Do not tighten at this time.
3. Lower the jack. Raise the axle with the hoist to curb height. Tighten the lower arm front bolt and rear pivot bolt heads to 100 ft. lbs. (135 Nm).
4. If vehicle is equipped with a rear stabilizer bar, install bar.
5. Remove crossmember supports and lower vehicle.

UPPER ARM AND AXLE BUSHINGS

Replacement

1. Remove upper arm rear pivot bolt and nut.

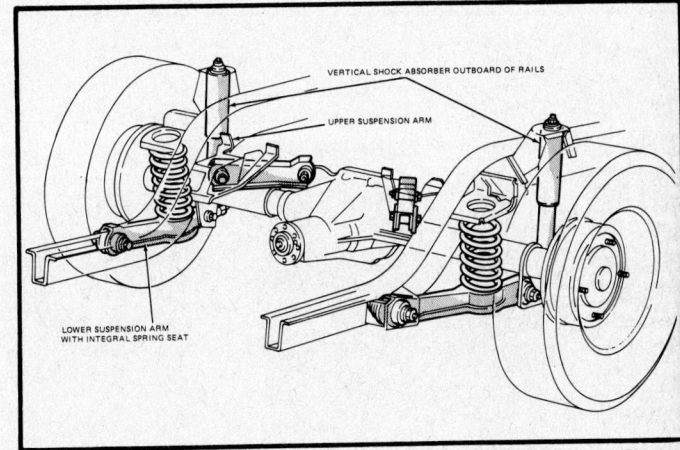

Four bar link coil rear suspension (© Ford Motor Co.)

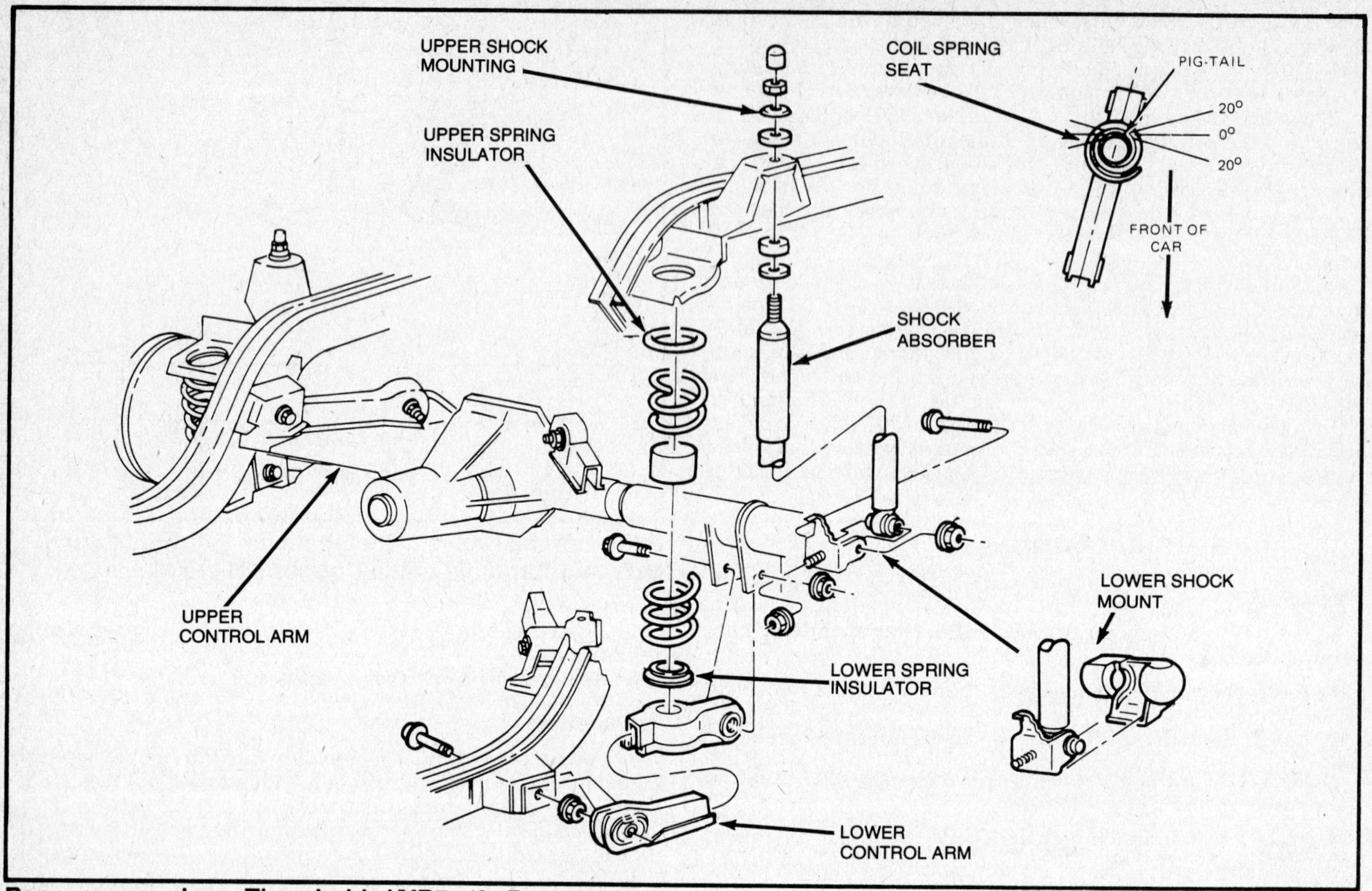

SECTION 35
SUSPENSIONS
REAR SUSPENSION—FORD REAR DRIVE CARS—FOUR BAR LINK DESIGN

Rear suspension—Thunderbird/XR7 (© Ford Motor Co.)

2. Remove front pivot bolt and nut. Remover upper arm from vehicle.
3. Place the upper arm rear bushing remover tool in position, and remove the bushing assembly.
4. Using the installer tool, install the bushing assembly into the bushing end of the rear axle.

STABILIZER BAR

Removal

1. Raise vehicle on hoist.

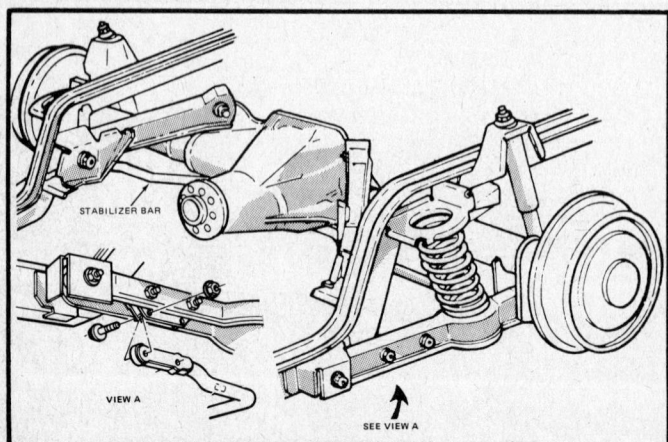

Rear stabilizer bar installation (© Ford Motor Co.)

2. Remove four bolts attaching stabilizer bar to brackets in lower arms.
3. Remove stabilizer bar from vehicle.

Installation

NOTE: Make sure bar is not installed upside down. A color code is provided on stabilizer bar (passenger side only) as an aid for proper orientation.

1. Align four holes in stabilizer bar with holes in brackets in lower arms.
2. Install four new bolts and tighten nuts to 20 ft. lbs. (27 Nm).
3. Visually inspect installation to insure adequate clearance between stabilizer bar and lower arm.

STABILIZER BAR BRACKETS

Removal

1. Raise vehicle on hoist and support body at rear crossmember.
2. Remove stabilizer bar.
3. Disconnect the shock absorbers at the lower shock bracket.
4. Slowly lower the suspension until the front bracket-to-arm bolt clears the body side rail.

NOTE: Do not stress the brake hose when lowering the suspension.

5. Remove both bracket to arm bolts and nuts, and remove bracket from the arm.

SUSPENSIONS
GENERAL MOTORS – IDENTIFICATION

GENERAL MOTORS BODY IDENTIFICATION

GENERAL MOTORS FRONT WHEEL DRIVE		
"A" & "X" BODY	"A" BODY—	Buick Century Custom • Century Limited • Chevrolet Celebrity
	"X" BODY—	Buick Skylark • Skylark Sport • Skylark Limited • Skylark Custom • Skylark "T" Type • Chevrolet Citation • Oldsmobile Omega • Omega Brougham • Pontiac Phoenix • Phoenix SJ • Phoenix LJ • Phoenix SE • Phoenix LE
"C" BODY		BUICK Electra Limited • Park Ave • "T" Type CADILLAC Fleetwood Brougham • DeVille OLDSMOBILE 98 Regency • 98 Regency Brougham
"E" & "K" BODY	"E" BODY—	Buick Riviera • Riviera Luxury • Riviera "T" Type • Riviera Convertible • Cadillac Eldorado • Olds Toronado Brougham
	"K" BODY—	Cadillac Seville
"J" BODY		BUICK Skyhawk • Skyhawk Custom • Skyhawk Limited • Skyhawk "T" Type CADILLAC Cimarron CHEVROLET Cavalier OLDSMOBILE Firenza • Firenza "S", "SX" & "LX" PONTIAC J2000 • J2000 LE • J2000 SE
"N" BODY		Buick Somerset Regal • Oldsmobile Calais • Pontiac Grand AM
GENERAL MOTORS REAR WHEEL DRIVE		
BUICK		1981 Century • Century Limited • Regal • Regal Limited • Regal Sport Coupe • Le Sabre • Le Sabre Custom • Le Sabre Limited • Electra • Estate Wagon
CADILLAC		DeVille • Fleetwood
CHEVROLET		Caprice Classic • Corvette • Malibu • Monte Carlo • Impala
"F" BODY		Camaro • Camaro Berlinetta • Firebird • Firebird Trans Am • SE
"P" BODY		Pontiac Fiero • Fiero SE
"T" BODY		Chevette • Chevette Scooter • Pontiac T1000 • 1000
OLDSMOBILE		Cutlass Supreme • Cutlass Salon • Cutlass Supreme Brougham • Cutlass Calais • Delta 88 Royal • Delta 88 Royale Brougham • Custom Cruiser • Olds 98 • Olds 98 Regency • Olds 98 Regency Brougham • Hurst Olds
PONTIAC		Bonneville • Bonneville LE • Bonneville Brougham • Catalina • Le Mans • Grand Prix • Grand Prix LE • Grand Prix Brougham • Safari SW • Parisienne • Parisienne Brougham • Parisienne Brougham Wagon

Installation

1. Insert the bracket into the arm and align holes in arm and bracket. Install new bolts and nuts. Tighten the nut to 70 ft. lbs. (94 Nm).
2. Raise the suspension and reassemble the rear shock absorber lower attachment using a new attaching nut.
3. Install stabilizer bar.
4. Remove crossmember supports and lower the vehicle.

SUSPENSIONS
FRONT SUSPENSION—GM "A" & "X" BODY FRONT DRIVE CARS

FRONT SUSPENSION—GENERAL MOTORS A AND X BODY CARS—FRONT WHEEL DRIVE

Wheel Alignment

Front alignment consists of the camber adjustment and toe setting. The caster setting is built into the vehicle with no provisions for adjustment.

Two bolts clamp the lower end of the MacPherson strut assembly to the upper arm of the steering knuckle. The lower of the two bolts has an eccentric washer at the head providing the camber adjustment. These special high tensile bolts with the loose nuts are torqued to 210 ft. lbs. (270 Nm). The camber setting is plus .5 degrees with a .5 degree tolerance.

The toe adjustment is conventional, with adjusting sleeves at the tie rod ends held in place with locking jam nuts. The toe setting is plus .1 degree with a tolerance of ± 1 degree.

Wheel Bearings

The front wheel bearing is a double row ball design. It is a prelubricated sealed bearing and requires no regular maintenance. The bearing in a loose fit in the steering knuckle. The drive axle outer joint shaft is a splined fit through the bearing. The hub nut and washer are used to pre-load the bearing.

DIAGNOSIS

Check for proper drive axle nut torque, 185 ft. lbs. (250 Nm). Clean threads, remove nut, install new nut and torque to proper specifications. Free the shoes from the disc or remove calipers. Reinstall two wheel nuts to ensure disc to bearing. Mount dial indicator. Grasp disc and use a push-pull movement. Do not rock discs as this will give a false reading. If looseness exceeds 0.005 in. (0.508mm) replace bearing.

Removal

1. Loosen hub nut.
2. Raise car and remove wheel.
3. Remove hub nut and discard.
4. Remove brake caliper.
5. Remove three hub and bearing attaching bolts. If old bearing is being reused, mark attaching bolts and corresponding holes for installation.
6. Install tool J–28733 or equivalent and remove bearing. If excessive corrosion is present, make sure bearing is loose in knuckle before using tool.

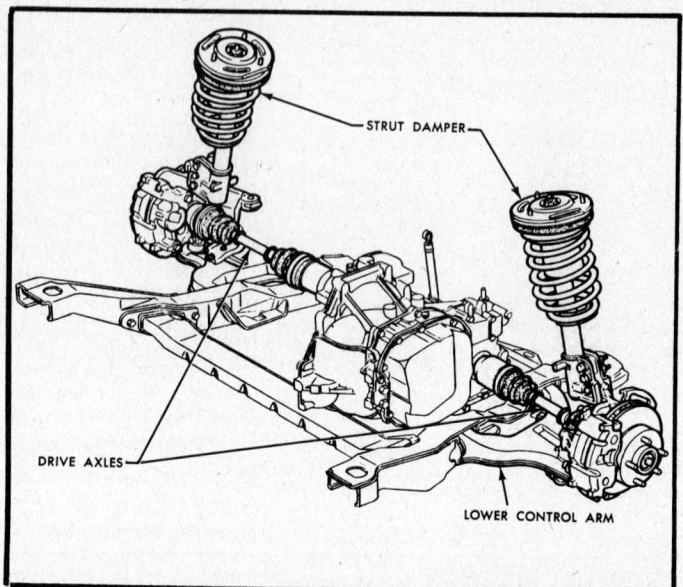

Front suspension components (© General Motors Corp.)

NOTE: A boot protector should be installed whenever servicing front suspension components to prevent damage to the drive axle boot.

Installation

1. Clean and inspect bearing mating surfaces and steering knuckle bore for dirt, nicks and burrs.
2. If installing steering knuckle seal, use tool J–28671 or equivalent. Apply grease to seal and knuckle bore.
3. Push bearing on axle shaft.
4. Torque new hub until bearing is seated.
5. Install brake caliper.
6. Lower car.
7. Apply final torque to hub nut.

TORQUES

Top strut nut: 68 ft. lbs. (90 Nm)
 Top mount nuts: 18 ft. lbs. (24 Nm)
Lower strut bolts: 140 ft. lbs. (190 Nm)
Hub nut: 170–192 ft. lbs. (230–260 Nm)

MAC PHERSON STRUT

Removal

1. Support the car so that there is no weight on the lower control arm.
2. Remove wheel.
3. Clean up and mark camber adjusting cam.
4. Remove the brake hose clip.
5. Remove top three bolts from the lower strut bolts.
6. Remove the strut assembly, and take a sample to work bench.

CAUTION
A reliable spring compressor tool is essential to disassemble and assemble strut bumper to avoid personal injury.

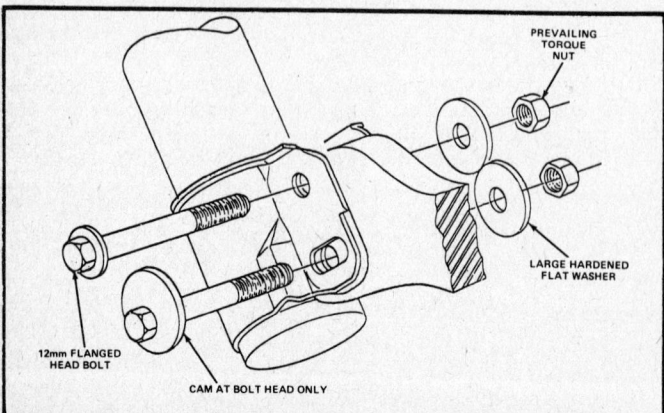

Knuckle strut mounting bolts for camber adjustment (© General Motors Corp.)

SUSPENSIONS
FRONT SUSPENSION—GM "A" & "X" BODY FRONT DRIVE CARS
SECTION 35

7. Compress spring with compressor until there is not pressure on the upper spring seat.

CAUTION
Do not compress spring until it bottoms.

8. Remove the top nut from the strut shaft and remove the bumper shaft and the top mounting assembly.
9. Remove the spring from the strut assembly.

Installation

1. Install the new strut assembly into the spring and attach the mounting components on to the strut assembly.
2. Tighten the top strut nut 68 ft. lbs. (90 Nm) and remove the spring compressor.
3. Install the spring and strut assembly, first in the upper spring seat, then connect the lower end of the strut to the lower control arm.
4. Install brake caliper and wheel.

STEERING KNUCKLE

Removal

1. Remove wheel and wheel bearing.
2. Mark and remove the lower strut bolts.
3. Remove tie-rod end and ball joint.
4. Remove steering knuckle.

Installation

1. Install knuckle to ball joint and tighten.
2. Loosely install knuckle to strut
3. Install front wheel bearing.
4. Jack control arm into position and install tie-rod end.
5. Tighten cam bolts.
6. Reset steering camber and toe.
7. Install brake caliper and wheel.

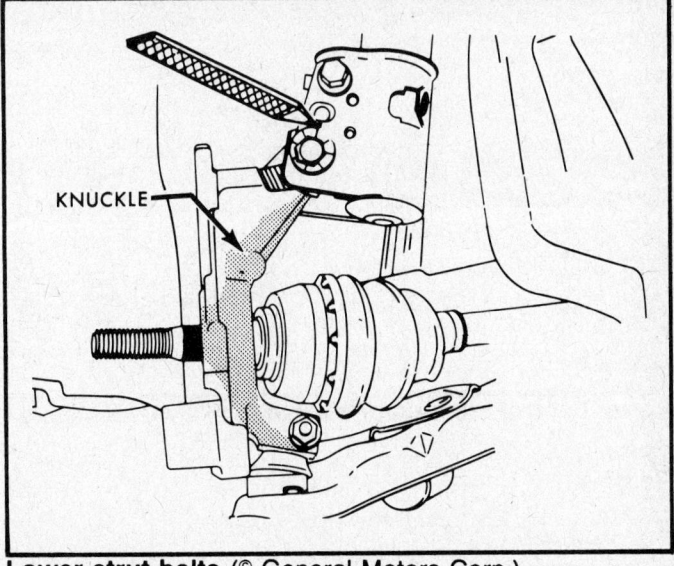

Lower strut bolts (© General Motors Corp.)

LOWER CONTROL ARM BALL JOINT

Inspection

1. Raise front suspension by placing jack or lift under the cradle.
2. Grasp the wheel at top and bottom and shake to of wheel in an in-and-out motion. Observe for any horizontal movement of the knuckle relative to the control arm. Replace ball joint if such movement is noted.
3. If the ball stud is disconnected from the knuckle and any looseness is detected, or if the ball stud can be twisted in its socket using finger pressure, replace the ball joint.

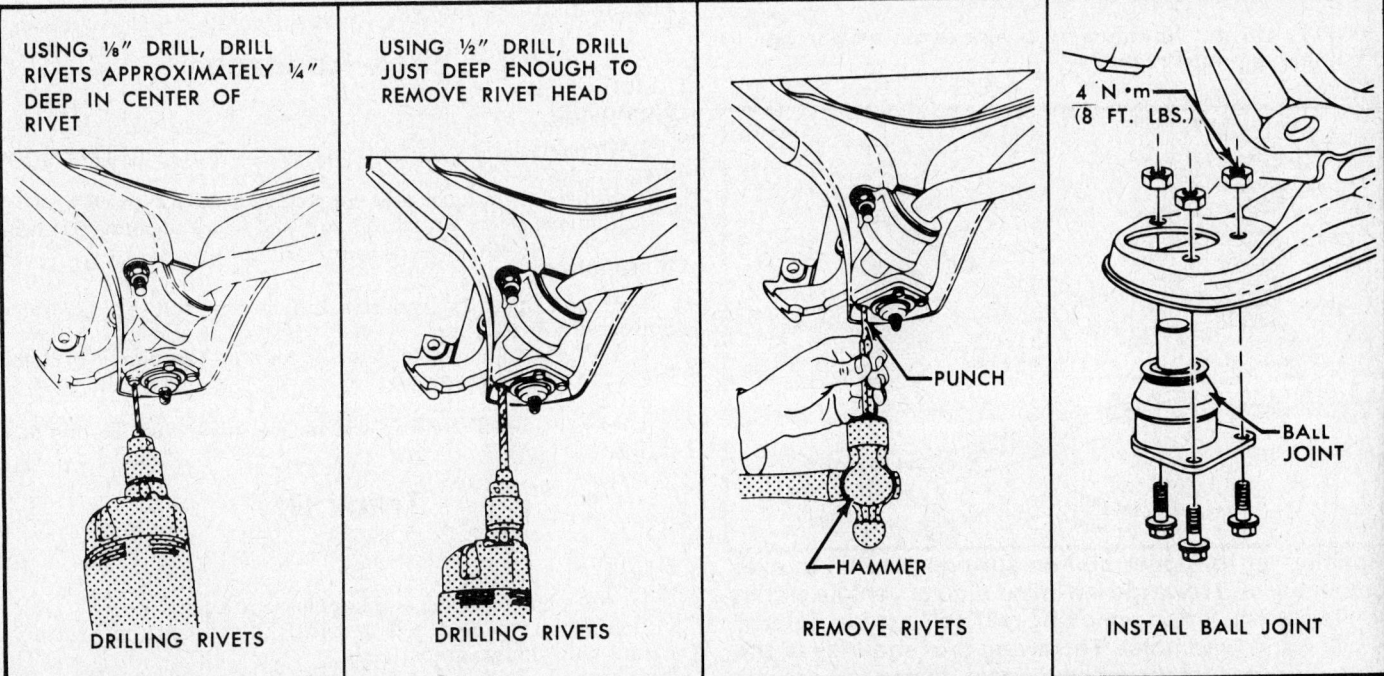

Ball joint inspection: vertical movement—.000 and horizontal movement—.000. If ball joint shows any movement, replace. It is not necessary to remove control arm to replace ball joint (© General Motors Corp.)

SECTION 35 SUSPENSIONS
FRONT SUSPENSION—GM "A" & "X" BODY FRONT DRIVE CARS

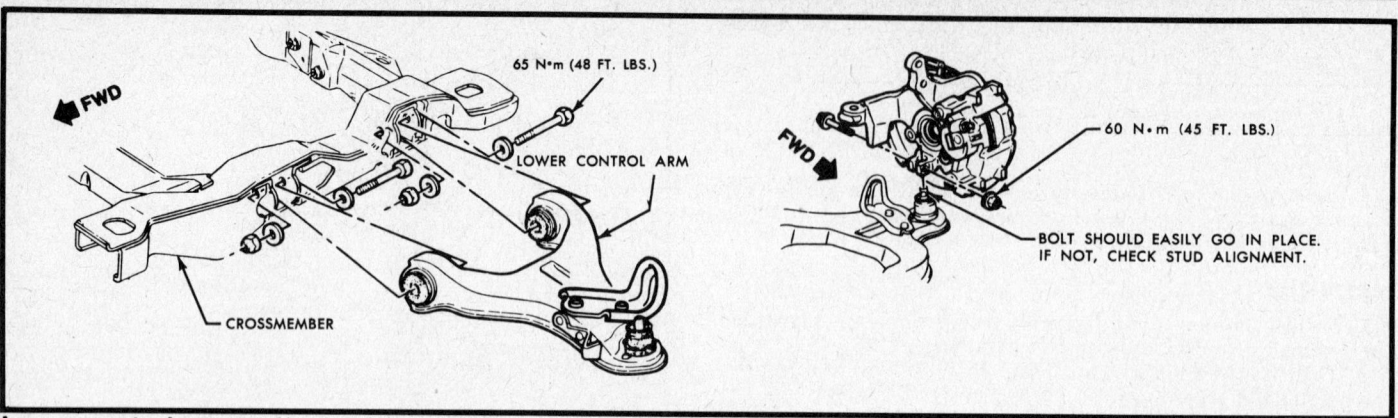

Lower control arm and/or bushings (© General Motors Corp.)

Removal

1. Raise car and remove wheel.
2. Remove parts.
3. Remove ball joint from knuckle.

Installation

1. Install ball join to knuckle.
2. Install parts.
3. Install wheel and lower car.
4. Check toe-in setting. Adjust as required.

REAR SUSPENSION—GENERAL MOTORS A AND X BODY CARS—FRONT WHEEL DRIVE

Wheel Bearings

The rear wheel bearing is a double row ball bearing. It is pre-lubricated and sealed at the factory. The bolt on the bearing should be replaced if the looseness exceeds recommendations.

Removal

1. Remove wheel and brake drum.

NOTE: Do not hammer on brake drum as damage to the bearing could result.

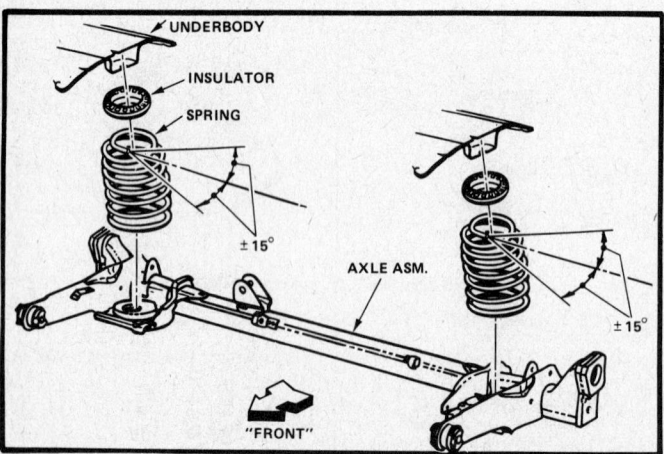

Position leg of upper coil on springs parallel to axle assembly and towards left-hand side of vehicle within limits shown. When removing rear springs, do not use a twin-post type hoist. The swing arc tendency of the rear axle assembly when certain fasteners are removed may cause it to slip from the hoist. Perform operation on floor if necessary (© General Motors Corp.)

2. Remove four hub and bearing assembly-to-rear axle attaching bolts and remove hub and bearing assembly from axle.

NOTE: If studs must be removed from the hub, do not remove with a hammer as damage to bearing will result.

Installation

1. Install hub and bearing assembly to rear axle. Tighten bolts to 35 ft. lbs. (55 Nm).

Shock Absorber

Removal

1. Open deck lid, remove trim cover and remove upper shock attaching nut.
2. Raise car on hoist and support rear axle assembly.
3. Remove lower attaching bolt and nut and remove shock.

Installation

1. Install shock at lower attachment, feed bolt through holes and loosely install nut.
2. Lower car enough to guide upper stud through body opening and install nut loosely.
3. Torque lower nut to 34 ft. lbs. (47 Nm).
4. Lower car all the way and torque upper nut. Torque to 7 ft. lbs. (10 Nm).

Track Bar

Removal

1. Raise car on hoist and supper rear axle.
2. Remove nut and bolt at both the axle and body attachments and remove track bar.

Installation

1. Position track bar in left hand reinforcement and loosely

SUSPENSIONS

REAR SUSPENSION—GM "A" & "X" BODY FRONT DRIVE CARS

SECTION 35

install bolt and nut. The open side of the bar and nut must face rearward.

2. Place other end of track bar in body reinforcement and install bolt and nut (nut must be at the rear of reinforcement of both attachments). Torque nut at axle bracket to 33 ft. lbs. (45 Nm) and torque nut at body reinforcement to 34 ft. lbs. (47 Nm).

Spring

Removal and Installation

NOTE: Do not use a twin-post type hoist. The swing are tendency of the rear axle when some fasteners are removed may cause it to slip from the hoist.

1. Raise the car. Support the rear axle while removing the brake line brackets, the track bar and the shock absorber lower mounts.
2. Lower rear axle and remove springs.
3. When installing, position springs correctly.

Control Arm Bushing

Removal

1. Raise car on hoist and support rear axle under front side of spring seat.
2. If removing right bushing, disconnect parking brake cable from hook guide.
3. Remove dual parking brake cables from bracket attachment and pull out of way.
4. Disconnect brake line bracket attachment from frame.
5. Remove shock lower attaching nut and bolt and pull string out of way.
6. Remove four control arm bracket-to-underbody attaching bolts and allow control arm to rotate downward.
7. Remove nut and bolt from bracket attachment and remove bracket.
8. Press bushing out of control arm.

Installation

1. Press bushing into control arm.

NOTE: Cut-outs on rubber portion of bushing must face front and rear.

2. Install bracket to control arm and torque nut to 34 ft. lbs. (47 Nm). Bracket must be at a 45 degree angle.
3. Raise control arm into position and install four control arm bracket-to-underbody attaching bolts. Torque to 20 ft. lbs. (27 Nm).
4. Replace spring and insulator and install shock lower attaching nut and bolt. Torque to 34 ft. lbs. (47 Nm).
5. Install brake line bracket to frame and torque screw to 18 ft. lbs. (11 Nm).
6. On right side only, reconnect brake cables to bracket, and reinstall brake cable to hook. Adjust cable as necessary.

REAR AXLE ASSEMBLY

Removal

NOTE: When removing rear axle assembly, do not use a twin post type hoist. The swing arc tendency of the rear axle assembly when certain fasteners re removed may cause it to slip from the hoist.

1. Remove the wheel and brake drum.

NOTE: Do not hammer on brake drum as damage to the bearing could result.

2. Disconnect parking brake cable from hook connection.
3. Remove brake line brackets from frame.
4. Remove shock lower attaching bolts and nuts at axle and disconnect shocks from axle.

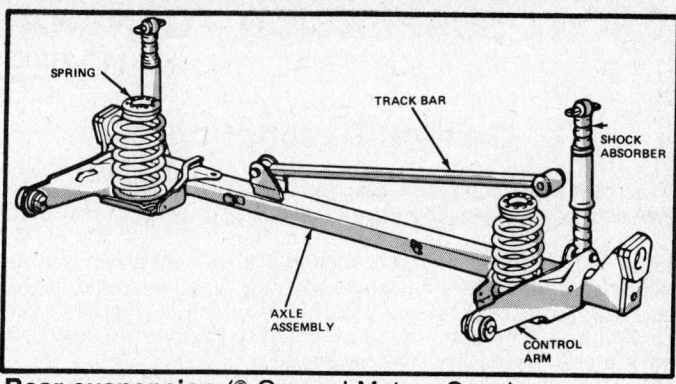

Rear suspension (© General Motors Corp.)

5. Remove track bar attaching nuts and bolt at axle and disconnect track bar.
6. Lower rear axle and remove coil springs and insulators.
7. Disconnect brake lines from control arm attachments.
8. Remove brake cable from rear axle attachments.
9. Remove hub attaching bolts and remove hub and bearing assembly. Move backing plate out of way.
10. Remove control arm bracket-to-underbody attaching bolts (four per side) and lower axle down to bench. This may require two people to steady axle.
11. Remove control arm brackets from control arms.

Installation

1. Install control arm brackets to control arms. Torque nut to 34 ft. lbs. (47 Nm). Brackets must be at a 45 degree angle.
2. Place axle assembly on transmission jack and raise into position. Attach control arms to underbody with four bolts per side. Torque bolts to 20 ft. lbs. (27 Nm).
3. Install backing plate and hub and bearing assembly to rear axle. Torque bolts to 35 ft. lbs. (55 Nm).
4. Install brake line connections to frame.
5. Attach brake cable to rear axle assembly.
6. Position coil springs and insulators in seats and raise rear axle. Leg of upper coil on springs must be parallel to axle assembly and face outboard on both sides.
7. Install shock absorbers to rear axle and torque nuts to 34 ft. lbs. (47 Nm).
8. Install track bar to rear axle and torque nut to 33 ft. lbs. (45 Nm).
9. Install brake line to control arm brackets and torque screws to 8 ft. lbs. (11 Nm).
10. Connect parking brake cable to guide hook and adjust as necessary.
11. Install brake drums and wheels. Torque lug nuts to 103 ft. lbs. (140 Nm).
12. Remove transmission support and lower car.
13. Bleed brake system and refill reservoir.

SUPERLIFT SHOCK ABSORBERS

The Superlift system is an assist type leveling device which the driver controls manually be varying air pressure in the system. The leveling unit is a combination of a pliable neoprene boot and air cylinder built around a hydraulic shock absorber.

PRECAUTIONS

To insure satisfactory functioning of the Superlift system, observe the following precautions:

1. Maintain a minimum of 10 psi (70 kPa) for best ride characteristics with an empty car.
2. Vary pressure up to a maximum of 90 psi (620 kPa) to level the car with loads.

35-85

SUSPENSIONS
FRONT SUSPENSION—GM "C" BODY FRONT DRIVE CARS

FRONT SUSPENSION—GENERAL MOTORS C BODY CARS—FRONT WHEEL DRIVE

General Description

The front suspension is a MacPherson Strut design. The control arm pivots from the frame mounted cradle. It is mounted in rubber bushings. The upper end of the strut assembly is isolated by a rubber mount which contains a non-serviceable bearing which allows for wheel turning. The lower end of the steering knuckle pivots on a ball joint which is riveted to the control arm. The ball joint is attached to the steering knuckle with a castellated nut and cotter pin.

Wheel Alignment

Before adjusting caster and camber angles, the front bumper should be raised and released three times to allow car to return to its normal standing height.

FRONT CASTER

Adjustment

1. Remove the to strut mounting nuts.
2. Separate the top strut mount from the inner wheelhouse.
3. Drill two $^{11}/_{32}$ in. holes at the front and rear of the round strut mounting hole. Remove the excess metal between the existing hole and the drilled hole.
4. Reinstall the strut mount in the holes. Install the washers and nuts.
5. Caster is set by moving the top of strut rearward or forward as required.
6. Tighten the strut mounting nuts.

FRONT CAMBER

Adjustment

1. Loosen both strut to knuckle nuts.
2. Install camber adjusting tool J–29862 or equivalent.
3. Set camber to specification.

FRONT TOE

Adjustment

1. Loosen the lock nut on both inner tie rods.
2. Set toe to specification by turning the inner tie rod accordingly.
3. Tighten the lock nuts on inner tie rods to 52 ft. lbs. (70 Nm).

Suspension Description

The front suspension is a MacPherson strut design. The control arm pivots from the cradle and is mounted in rubber bushings. The upper end of the strut is isolated by a rubber mount which contains a non-serviceable bearing which allows for wheel turning. The lower end of the steering knuckle pivots on a ball joint which is riveted to the control arm. The ball joint is fastened to the steering knuckle with a castellated nut and cotter pin.

Hub And Bearing Assembly

Removal and Installation

1. Raise the vehicle and support safely.

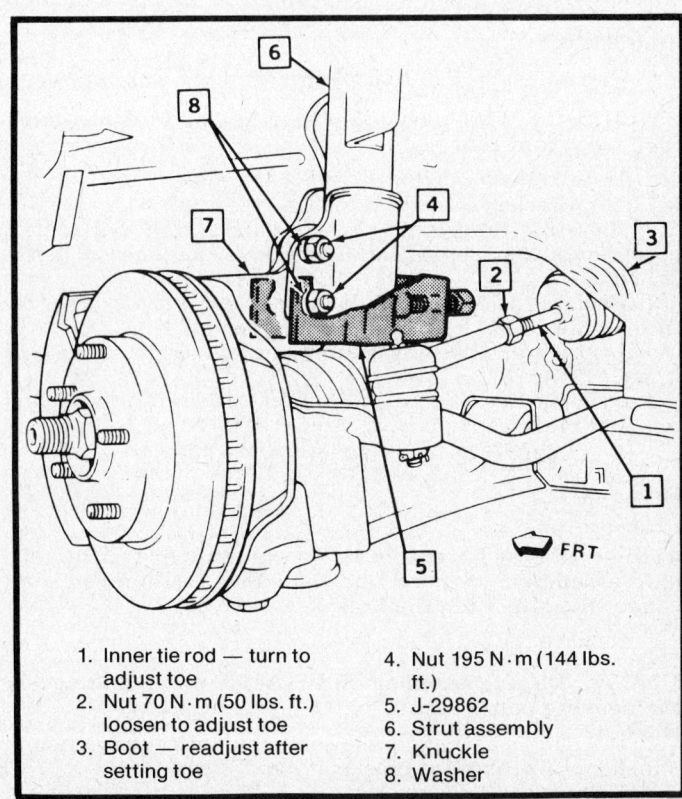

1. Nut 24 N·m (18 lbs. ft.)
2. Washer
3. Strut Assy.
4. Cover
5. Drill 8.731mm (11/32") holes
6. File here

Front caster adjustment (© General Motors Corp.)

1. Inner tie rod — turn to adjust toe
2. Nut 70 N·m (50 lbs. ft.) loosen to adjust toe
3. Boot — readjust after setting toe
4. Nut 195 N·m (144 lbs. ft.)
5. J–29862
6. Strut assembly
7. Knuckle
8. Washer

Front camber and toe adjustmnet

SUSPENSIONS
FRONT SUSPENSION—GM "C" BODY FRONT DRIVE CARS

2. Remove the tire and wheel assembly.
3. Install drive axle boot seal protector J–28712 or equivalent on all outer constant velocity joints and tool number J–34754 or equivalent on all inner joints.
4. Remove the hub nut.
5. Remove the brake caliper and rotor. Wire off to the side to gain working clearance.
6. Attach tool J–28733 or equivalent and loosen splines between the hub and drive axle.
7. Remove the hub attaching bolts, splash shield, hub and bearing assembly.
8. Installation is the reverse of removal procedure. Lubricate hub bearing seal with grease prior to installation. Tighten the hub and bearing bolts to 70 ft. lbs. (95 Nm).

Strut Assembly
Removal and Installation

1. Remove the nuts attaching the top strut assembly to the vehicle body.
2. Raise the vehicle and support safely. Install jack stands under the vehicle cradle and lower the vehicle so the weight of the vehicle rests on the stands and not the control arm.
3. Install drive axle boot seal protectors. Care must be taken in order to prevent overextension of the inner Tri-Pot joints.
4. Remove the brake line retaining bracket from the strut assembly.
5. Remove the strut to steering knuckle bolts.
6. Remove the strut assembly from the vehicle.
7. Installation is the reverse of removal procedure. Note the following:
   a. Check wheel alignment.
   b. Tighten the strut to body bolts to 18 ft. lbs. (24 Nm).
   c. Tighten the strut to steering knuckle bolts to 144 ft. lbs. (195 Nm)

NOTE: Vehicle must now have a front wheel alignment performed.

Spring Assembly
Removal and Installation

1. Strut assembly must be removed from vehicle to perform this procedure. Refer to strut assembly removal outlined earlier in this section.

NOTE: A reliable spring compressor tool is essential to disassemble the strut to avoid personal injury.

2. Mount the spring assembly in a suitable holding fixture.
3. Install spring compressor until there is no pressure on the upper spring seat.

NOTE: Do not compress the spring until it bottoms.

5. Remove the top nut from the strut shaft and remove the shaft and top mounting assembly.
6. Remove the spring from the strut assembly.
7. Installation is the reverse of the removal procedure. Tighten the strut nut to 74 ft. lbs. (100 Nm).

Ball Joints
Inspection

1. Raise the front of the vehicle with lift placed under the engine cradle. The front wheels should be clear of the ground.
2. Grasp the wheel at the top and the bottom and shake the wheel in and out.
3. If any movement is seen on the steering knuckle, the ball joints are defective and must be replaced. Note the movement elsewhere may be due to loose wheel bearings or other defective components. Take note of the knuckle to control arm connection.
4. If the ball stud is disconnected from the steering and any looseness is noted, replace the ball joints.

Removal and Installation

1. Raise the front of the car and support it with jackstands underneath the engine cradle. Lower the car slightly so that the weight rest primarily on the jack stands.
2. Remove the wheel and tire assemblies.
3. Install drive axle covers to protect the drive axle boot seals.
4. Pull the cotter pin from the ball joint and install a ball joint separator tool. Turn the castellated nut counterclockwise to separate the ball joint from the steering knuckle.
5. Use a 1/8 in. drill bit to drill a hole approximately 1/4 in. deep in the center of each of the three ball joint rivets.
6. Use a 1/2 in. drill bit to drill off the rivet heads. Drill only enough to remove the rivet head.
7. Use a hammer and punch to remove the rivets. Drive them out from the bottom.
8. Loosen the stabilizer bar bushing assembly nut.
9. Pull down on the control arm and remove the ball joint from the steering knuckle and control arm.
10. Install the new ball joint in the steering knuckle and line up the holes with those in the control arm.
11. Install the three ball joint nuts facing down and tighten the nuts to 50 ft. lbs. (68 Nm).
12. Install the castellated nut and tighten to 81 ft. lbs. (110 Nm).

NOTE: Tightening the nut for cotter pin alignment is allowed, but do not loosen it once the torque has been reached.

13. Install the cotter pin.
14. Installation of the remaining components is in the reverse order of removal.

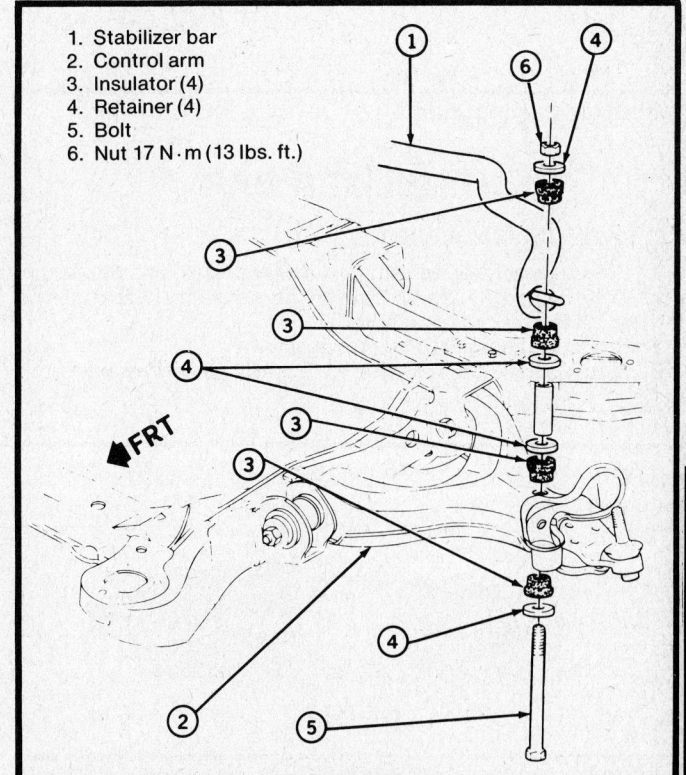

1. Stabilizer bar
2. Control arm
3. Insulator (4)
4. Retainer (4)
5. Bolt
6. Nut 17 N·m (13 lbs. ft.)

Stabilizer bar bushing assembly

SECTION 35 SUSPENSIONS
FRONT SUSPENSION—GM "C" BODY FRONT DRIVE CARS

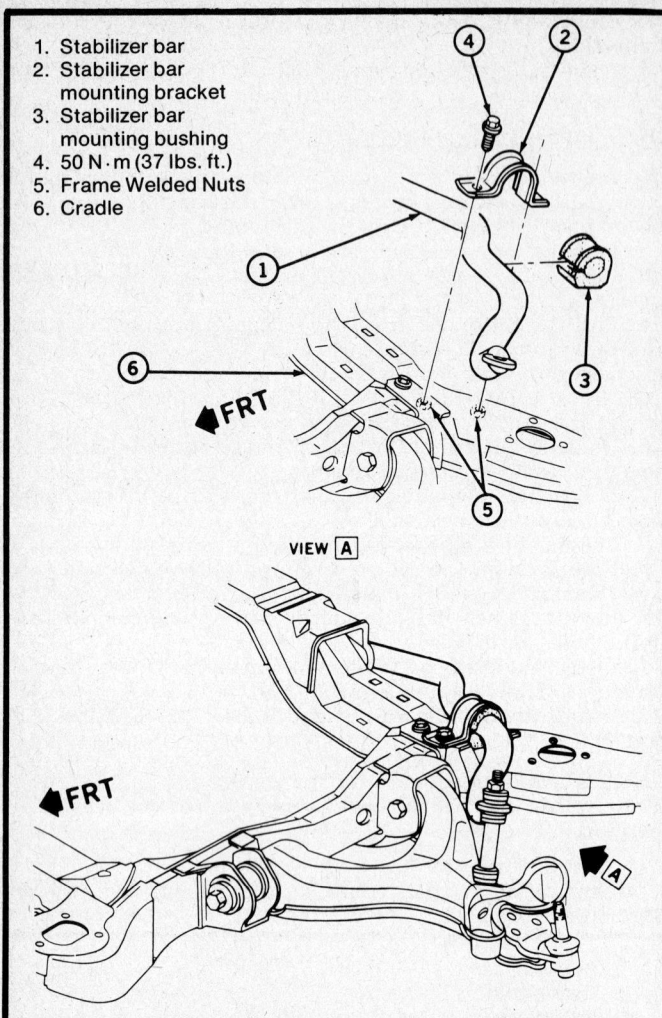

1. Stabilizer bar
2. Stabilizer bar mounting bracket
3. Stabilizer bar mounting bushing
4. 50 N·m (37 lbs. ft.)
5. Frame Welded Nuts
6. Cradle

Stabilizer bar installation (© General Motors Corp.)

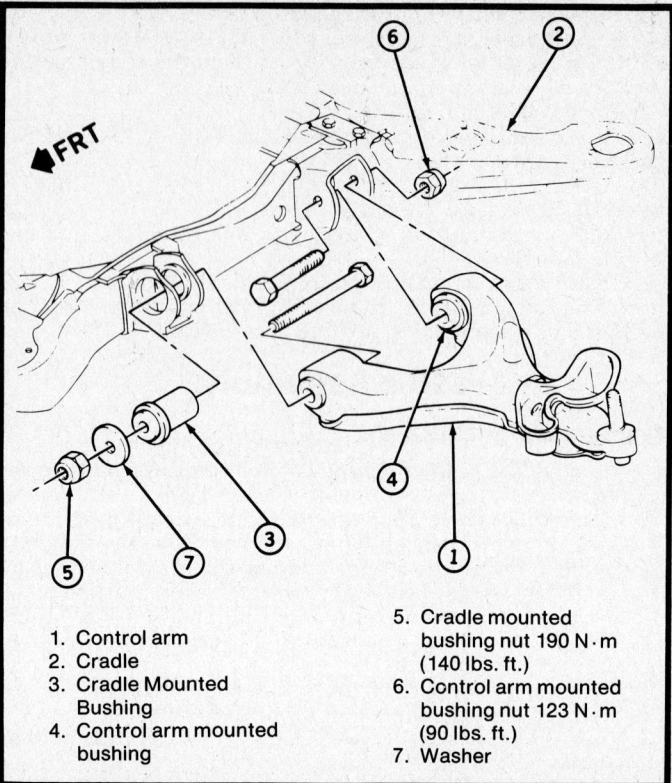

1. Control arm
2. Cradle
3. Cradle Mounted Bushing
4. Control arm mounted bushing
5. Cradle mounted bushing nut 190 N·m (140 lbs. ft.)
6. Control arm mounted bushing nut 123 N·m (90 lbs. ft.)
7. Washer

Control arm mounting—disassembled view (© General Motors Corp.)

STABILIZER BAR

Removal and Installation

1. Raise the vehicle and support safely. Place jack stands underneath the engine cradle. Lower the car slightly so that the weight rests on the jack stands.
2. Remove the wheel and tire assembly.
3. Install drive axle covers to protect the drive axle boot seals.

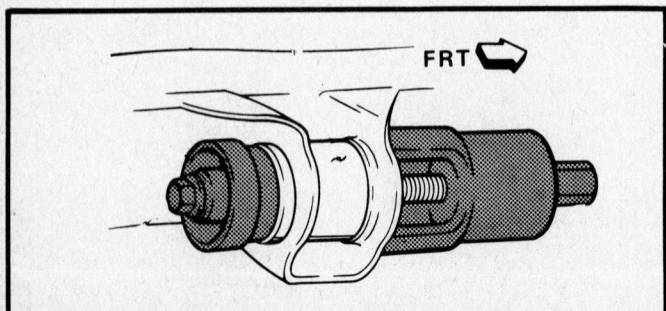

Bushing removal tool installation (© General Motors Corp.)

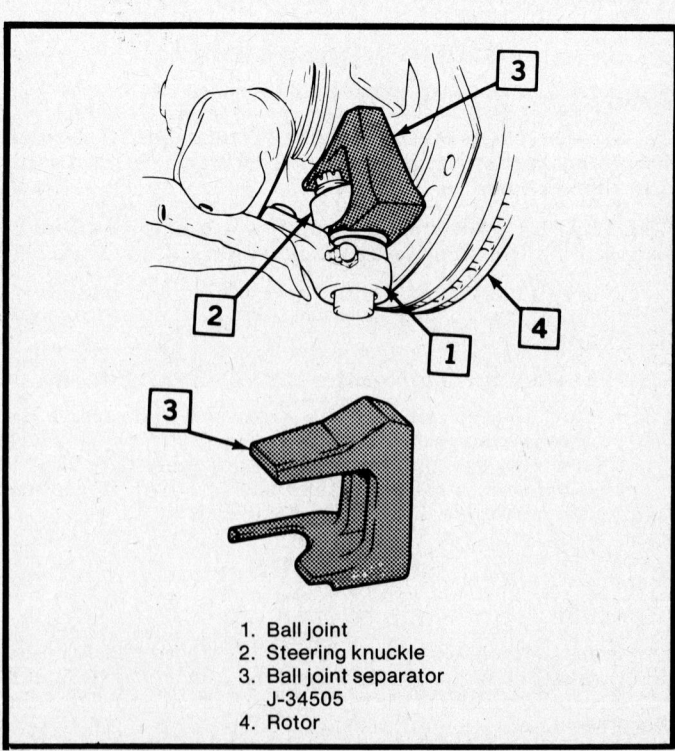

1. Ball joint
2. Steering knuckle
3. Ball joint separator J-34505
4. Rotor

Ball joint separator tool installation (© General Motors Corp.)

SUSPENSIONS
FRONT SUSPENSION—GM "C" BODY FRONT DRIVE CARS

4. Remove the bolts from both sides connecting the stabilizer bar bushings to the control arm.
5. Remove the stabilizer bar mounting bolts.
6. Remove the exhaust pipe between the exhaust manifold and the catalytic converter.
7. Remove the stabilizer bar from the vehicle by sliding it over the right steering knuckle.
8. Installation is the reverse of the removal procedure. Tighten the bolts to the following specifications:
   a. Stabilizer bar mounting bracket bolts-37 ft. lbs. (50 Nm).
   b. Bushing assembly nut-12 ft. lbs. (17 Nm).
   c. Tie rod end nut-35 ft. lbs. (47 Nm) 52 ft. lbs. (70 Nm) maximum torque for cotter pin alignment.

CONTROL ARM BUSHINGS

Removal and Installation

1. Raise the vehicle and support it with jack stands underneath the engine cradle. Lower the vehicle slightly so that the weight rests primarily on the jack stands.
2. Remove the tire and wheel assemblies.
3. Install drive axle covers to protect the drive axle boot seals.
4. Remove the stabilizer bar bushing to control arm bolt.
5. Remove the cotter pin from the ball and install the ball joint separator tool.
6. Remove the control arm mounting bolts. Remove the control arm from the vehicle.
7. Installation is the reverse of the removal procedure.

Cradle Mounted Bushing

Removal

1. Remove the lower control arm from the vehicle as outlined earlier in this section.
2. Assemble bushing tool according to the diagram with the small end facing the bushing.
3. Tighten the bolt until the bushing is driven out of the cradle assembly.

Installation

1. Assemble the bushing tool with the large end facing the bushing.
2. Install the bushing tool end nut.
3. Tighten the bushing tool nut until the bushing is firmly seated in the cradle.

REAR SUSPENSION—GENERAL MOTORS C BODY CARS—FRONT WHEEL DRIVE

General Description

These vehicles are equipped with independent coil spring rear suspension systems. Each suspension knuckle is supported with a lower control arm and an air adjustable Superlift® strut. A stabilizer bar minimizes body roll. Each control arm is equipped with a suspension adjustment link. This link allows for toe adjustment. It will also minimize alignment variation caused by suspension movement. The rear control arm is attached to the suspension knuckle by means of a ball joint which helps reduce friction. The entire suspension design allows for movement of one wheel without affecting the wheel on the opposite side of the vehicle.

The control arms are made of low carbon, mild steel. The hub and bearing is machined for precise contact.

The hub and wheel bearing is one assembly. This eliminates the need for wheel bearing adjustments. It does not require maintenance or adjustments.

Electronic Level Control is standard equipment on all models to maintain rear trim height under a wide range of operating conditions.

Ball Joints

Inspection

The lower ball joint is inspected for wear by visual observation alone. The vehicle must be supported by the wheels during inspection. Wear is indicated by retraction of the half-inch diameter nipple into the ball joint cover. Normal wear will be indicated by the nipple retracting slowly into the ball joint cover.

Ball stud tightness in the knuckle boss should also be checked when inspecting the ball joint. In order to accomplish this, shake the wheel and feel for movement of the stud end or castellated nut at the knuckle boss. A loose nut can also indicate a bent or damaged stud.

Removal and Installation

1. Raise and support the vehicle safely. Remove the tire and wheel assemblies from the rear of the vehicle.
2. Disconnect the Electronic Level Control (ELC) height sensor link (right control arm) and/or the parking brake cable retaining link (left control arm).
3. Remove the cotter pin and the castellated nut from the outer suspension adjustment link.
4. Separate the outer suspension link from the knuckle.
5. Support the control arm with a suitable jack. The lower control arm must be supported to prevent the coil spring from forcing the control arm downward.
6. Remove the ball and cotter pin.
7. Remove the castellated nut and then reinstall it with the flat side facing upward. Do not tighten.

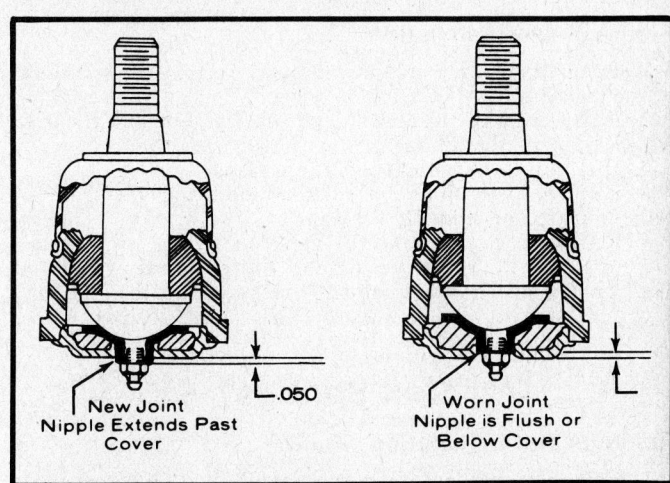

Lower ball joint inspection (© General Motors Corp.)

35-89

SECTION 35 SUSPENSIONS
REAR SUSPENSION—GM "C" BODY FRONT DRIVE CARS

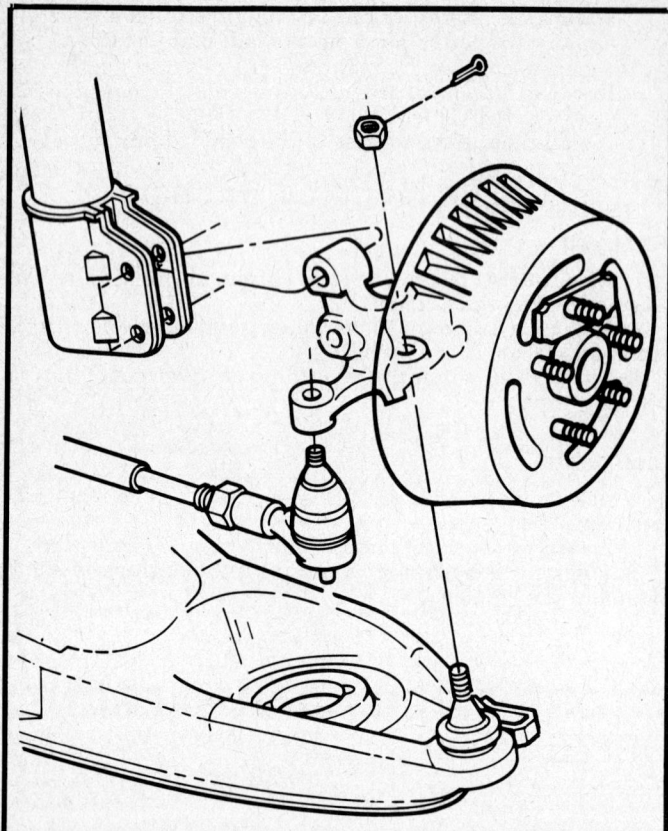

Rear lower ball joint – exploded view (© General Motors Corp.)

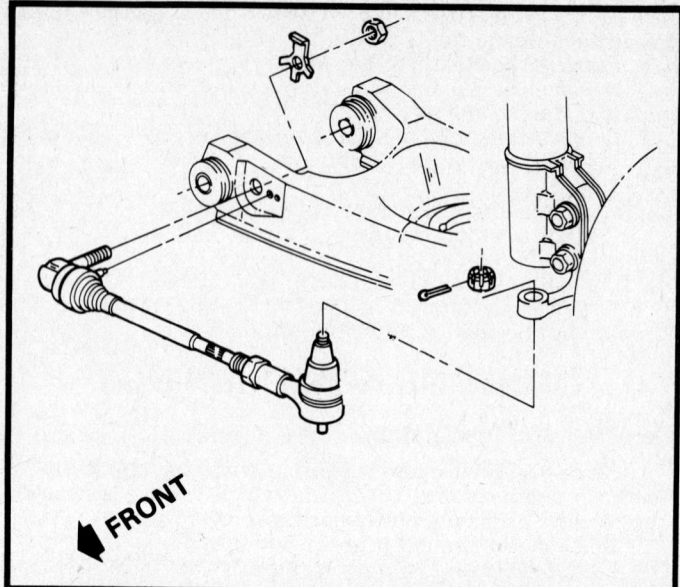

Suspension adjustment link (© General Motors Corp.)

8. Install a ball joint separator tool and separate the ball joint from the knuckle.
9. Separate the ball joint from the control arm.
10. Installation is the reverse of the removal procedure. Note the following:
   a. Tighten the NEW castellated nut to 7.5 ft lbs. (10 Nm). Tighten the nut additional $\frac{2}{3}$ of a turn.
   b. Align the slot in the nut to the cotter pin hole by tightening only. Do not loosen the nut in order to align the holes.

Superlift Strut®

Removal and Installation

1. Remove the inner side trunk cover. Remove the strut tower mounting nuts.
2. Raise the vehicle and support safely. Remove the rear wheel and tire assemblies.
3. Disconnect and plug the ELC air line.
4. Remove the strut anchor nuts, washers and bolts from the rear knuckle and knuckle bracket.
5. Remove the strut from the vehicle.
6. Installation is the reverse of the removal procedure. Tighten the strut tower mounting nuts to 19 ft. lbs. (25 Nm). Tighten the strut anchor nuts to 144 ft. lbs. (195 Nm). Check rear wheel alignment.

Coil Springs

Removal and Installation

1. Raise and support the vehicle safely.
2. Remove the rear wheels.

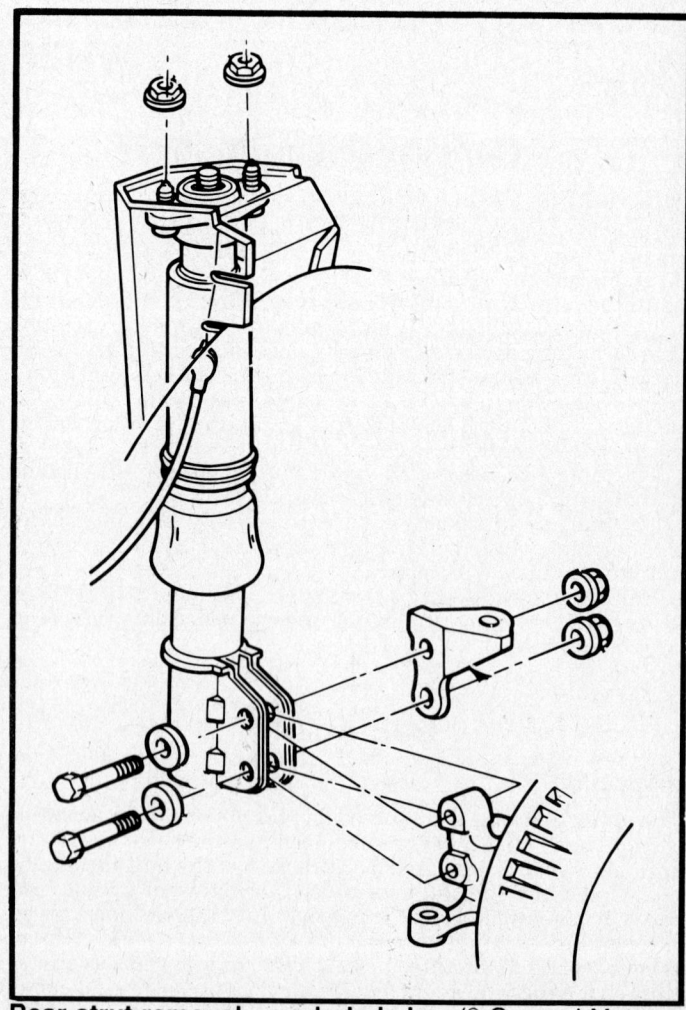

Rear strut removal – exploded view (© General Motors Corp.)

35-90

SUSPENSIONS
REAR SUSPENSION—GM "C" BODY FRONT DRIVE CARS

3. Separate the rear stabilizer bar from the knuckle bracket and remove it.
4. Disconnect the ELC height sensor line and the parking brake cable retaining clip.
5. Position the special tool J–23028–01 or equivalent so as to cradle the control arm bushings.

NOTE: Special tool J–23028–01 should be secured to a suitable jack.

6. Raise the jack to remove the tension from the control arm pivot bolts.

NOTE: Secure a chain around the spring and through the control arm as a safety precaution.

7. Remove the rear control arm pivot bolt and nut.
8. Move the jack so as to relive any tension from the control arm pivot bolt. Remove the bolt and nut.
9. Lower the jack to allow the jack to pivot downward.
10. When all pressure has been removed from the coil spring, remove the safety chain, spring and insulators.
11. Installation is the reverse of the removal procedure. Control arm mounting nuts should not be tightened until the vehicle is unsupported and resting on its wheels at normal trim height.

Rear Stabilizer Bar And Bushings

Removal and Installation

1. Raise the vehicle and support safely. Remove the rear wheel and tire assemblies.
2. Remove the stabilizer bar bolts, nuts and bar retainers.
3. Remove the bushing clip bolt.
4. Bend the open end of the support assembly downward.
5. Remove the stabilizer bar and bushings.
6. Installation is the reverse of the removal procedure.

Suspension Adjustment Link

Removal and Installation

1. Raise and support the vehicle safely. Remove the rear wheel and tire assemblies.
2. Remove the cotter pin and castellated nut from the knuckle.

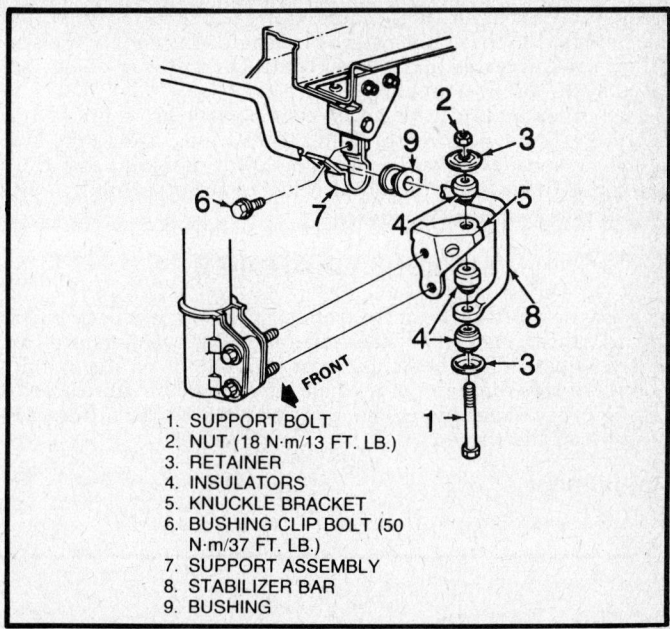

1. SUPPORT BOLT
2. NUT (18 N·m/13 FT. LB.)
3. RETAINER
4. INSULATORS
5. KNUCKLE BRACKET
6. BUSHING CLIP BOLT (50 N·m/37 FT. LB.)
7. SUPPORT ASSEMBLY
8. STABILIZER BAR
9. BUSHING

Rear stabilizer bar and bushging assembly (© General Motors Corp.)

3. Separate the outer suspension link from the knuckle.

NOTE: When separating the linkage joint, no attempt should be made to disengage the joint by driving a wedge between the joint and the attached part. Seal damage may result.

4. Remove the link assembly retaining nut and retainer. Remove the suspension adjustment link.
5. Installation is the reverse of the removal procedure. Check rear wheel alignment.

NOTE: Due to the diagnostic complexity of the Automatic Load Levelling System, detailed diagnostic procedures can be found in Chilton's Chassis Electronic Service Manual.

FRONT SUSPENSION—GENERAL MOTORS F BODY CARS—REAR WHEEL DRIVE

Wheel Alignment

CASTER AND CAMBER ADJUSTMENTS

Caster and camber can be adjusted by moving the position of the upper strut mount assembly. Moving the strut mount forward/rearward adjusts the caster while moving the strut mount inward and outward, adjusts the camber.

The position of the strut mount can be changed after loosening the three retaining nuts. The weight of the vehicle will normally cause the strut assembly to move to the full inboard position.

Install special tool J–29724 or its equivalent between the strut mount and a fender bolt and tighten the tool's turnbuckle until the proper camber reading is obtained. If an adjustment of caster is required, tap the strut mount either forward or rearward with a rubber mallet until the caster reading is obtained. Tighten the three mount screws to 20 ft. lbs. (28 Nm).

Remove the tool from the strut mount to fender bolt and reinstall the fender bolt in place.

Suspension Description

Each wheel is independently connected to the frame by a steering knuckle, strut assembly, ball joint, and lower control arm. The steering knuckles move in a prescribed three dimensional arc. The front wheels are held in proper relationship to each other by two tie rods which are connected to the steering knuckles and to a relay rod assembly.

Coil chassis springs are mounted between the spring housings on the front crossmember and the lower control arm. Ride control is provided by a double, direct acting strut assemblies. The upper portion of each strut assembly extends through the fender well and attaches to the upper mount assembly with a nut.

Side roll of the front suspension is controlled by a spring

SECTION 35
SUSPENSIONS
FRONT SUSPENSION—GM "F" BODY REAR DRIVE CARS

steel stabilizer shaft. It is mounted in rubber bushings which are held to the frame side rails by brackets. The ends of the stabilizer are connected to the lower control arms by link bolts isolated by rubber grommets.

The inner ends of the lower control arm have pressed-in bushings. Bolts, passing through the bushings, attach the arm to the suspension crossmember. The lower ball joint assembly is a press fit in the arm and attaches to the steering knuckle with a torque prevailing nut.

WHEEL BEARINGS

The proper functioning of the front suspension cannot be maintained unless the front wheel tapered roller bearings are correctly adjusted. The bearings must be a slip fit on the spindle and the inside diameter of the bearings should be lubricated to insure proper operation. The spindle nut must be a free-running fit on the threads.

Adjustment

1. Remove dust cap from hub.
2. Remove cotter pin from spindle and spindle nut.
3. Tighten the spindle nut to 12 ft. lbs. (16 Nm) while turning the wheel assembly forward by hand to fully seat the bearings. This will remove any grease or burrs which could cause excessive wheel bearing play later.
4. Back off the nut to the "just loose" position.
5. Hand tighen the spindle nut. Loosen spindle nut until either hole in the spindle lines up with a slot in the nut. Not more than ½ flat.
6. Install new cotter pin. Bend the ends of the cotter pin against nut, cut off extra length to ensure ends will not interfere with the dust cap.
7. Measure the looseness in the hub assembly. There will be from 0.001 to 0.005 in. (0.03–0.13 mm) end play when properly adjusted.
8. Install dust cap on hub.

STRUT ASSEMBLY

Removal and Installation

1. Raise vehicle.

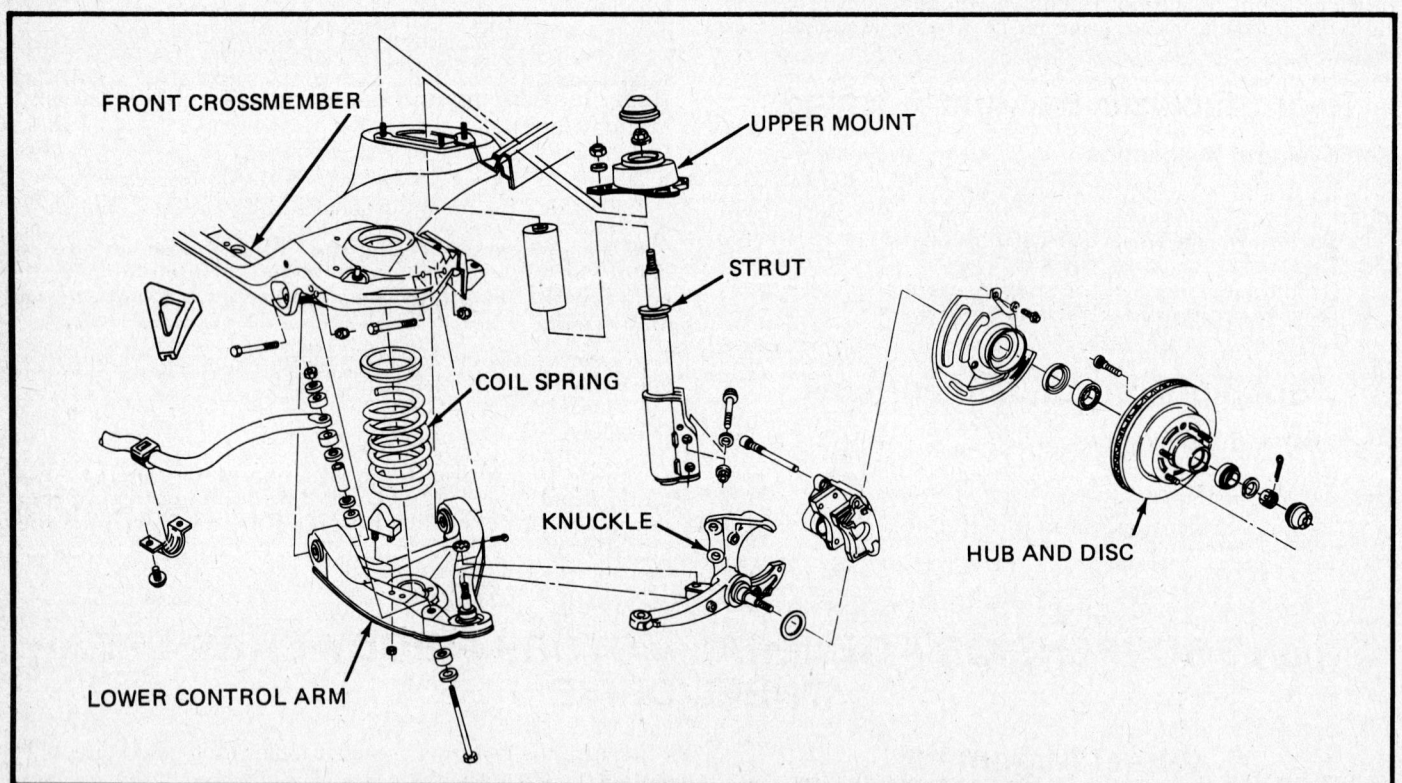

1982 and later F body front suspension—exploded view (© General Motors Corp.)

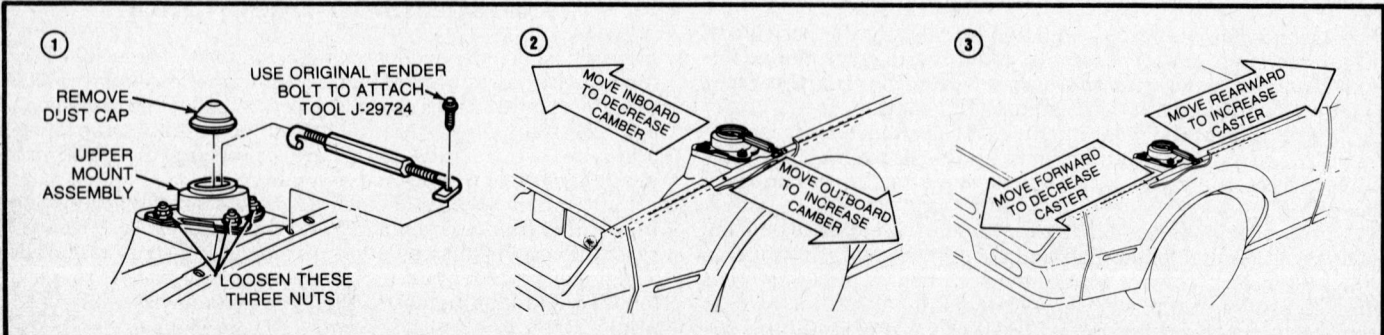

Front end alignment procedure (© General Motors Corp.)

SUSPENSIONS
FRONT SUSPENSION—GM "F" BODY REAR DRIVE CARS

2. Remove wheel and tire.
3. Support lower control arm with jackstand.
4. Remove brake hose bracket.
5. Remove two strut-to-knuckle bolts.
6. Remove cover from upper mount assembly.
7. Remove nut from upper end of strut.
8. Remove strut and shield.
9. Reverse order of removal to replace strut.

LOWER BALL JOINT

Removal

1. Raise car, support with floor stands under frame of vehicle.
2. Remove tire and wheel assembly.

---- CAUTION ----
Floor jack must remain under control arm spring seat during removal and installation to retain spring and control arm in position.

4. Remove cotter pin, and loosen castellated nut. Use tool J-24292A or equivalent to break ball joint loose from knuckle. Remove tool and separate joint from knuckle.
5. Guide lower control arm out of opening in splash shield with a putty knife or similar tool.
6. Remove grease fittings, and install tools as shown below. Press ball joint out of lower control arm.

Inspection

Inspect the tapered hole in the steering knuckle. Remove any dirt. If out-of-roundness, deformation or damage is noted, the knuckle MUST be replaced.

Installation

1. Position all joint into lower control arm and press in until it bottoms on the control arm, using tools as illustrated below. Grease purge on seal must be located facing inboard.
2. Place ball joint stud in steering knuckle.
3. Torque ball stud to 90 ft lbs. (120 Nm). Then tighten as additional amount enough to align slot in nut with hole in stud. Install cotter pin.
4. Install and lubricate all joint fitting until grease appears at the seal.
5. Install tire and wheel assembly.
6. Check front alignment.

COIL SPRING/LOWER CONTROL ARM

Removal and Installation

1. Raise vehicle using a hoist.
2. Remove the wheel and tire.
3. Remove stabilizer link and bushings at lower control arm.
4. Remove pivot bolt nuts. DO NOT remove pivot bolts at this time.
5. Install tool J-23028 adaptor or equivalent, to jack and place into position with tool J-23028 or equivalent, supporting bushings.
6. Install jackstand under outside frame rail on opposite side of vehicle.
7. Raise tool J-23028 or equivalent, enough to remove both pivot bolts.
8. Lower tool J-23028 or equivalent, carefully, as shown below.
9. Remove spring and insulator tape insulator to spring.
10. Remove ball joint from knuckle using tool J-2492A or equivalent, as outlined earlier.
11. Replace bushings in lower control arm.
12. Install parts in reverse order of removal.

NOTE: After assembly, end of spring coil must cover all or part of one inspection drain hole. The other hole must be partly exposed or completely uncovered.

KNUCKLE, HUB AND DISC

Removal and Installation

1. Siphon master cylinder to avoid leakage.
2. Raise vehicle.
3. Remove wheel and tire.
4. Remove brake from stut.
5. Remove caliper support safely.
6. Remove hub and disc.
7. Remove splash shield.
8. Disconnect tie rod from knuckle.
9. Support lower contol arm.
10. Disconnect ball joint from knuckle, using tool J-2492A or equivalent.

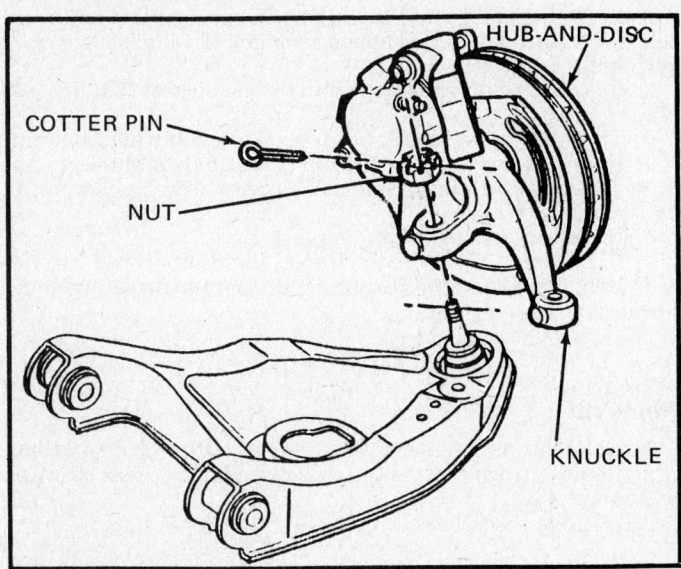

Knuckle, hub and disc assembly (© General Motors Corp.)

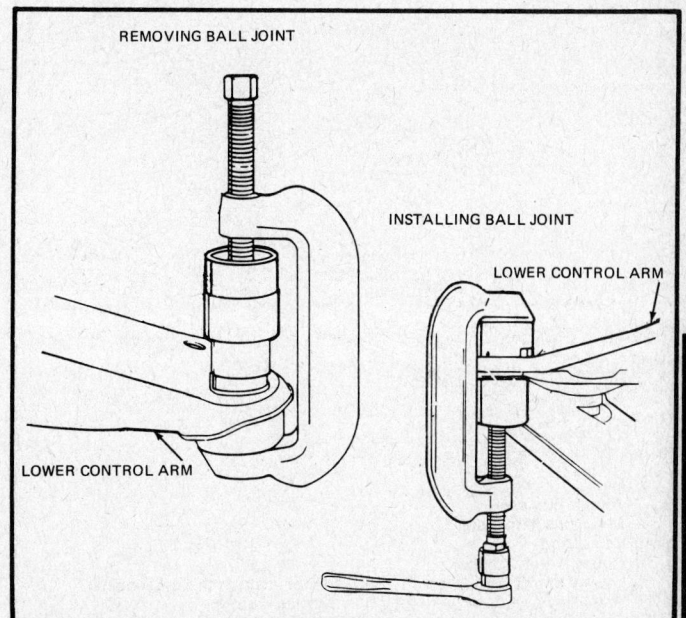

Removal and installation of lower control arm ball joint (© General Motors Corp.)

SECTION 35

SUSPENSIONS
FRONT SUSPENSION—GM "F" BODY REAR DRIVE CARS

11. Remove two bolts attaching strut to knuckle and remove knuckle.
12. Reverse order of removal to install.

STABILIZER SHAFT

Removal and Installation
1. Raise vehicle on hoist.
2. Remove link bolt, nut, grommets, spacer and retainers.
3. Remove insulators and brackets.
4. Remove stabilizer shaft.
5. Install parts in reverse order of removal.
6. Hold stabilizer shaft at approximately 55.0 mm from bottom of side rail when tightening stabilizer shaft insulators.
7. Lower vehicle.

REAR SUSPENSION—GENERAL MOTORS F BODY CARS—REAR WHEEL DRIVE

Suspension Description

The rear axle assembly is attached to the vehicle through a link type suspension system. The axle housing is connected to the body by two lower control arms and a track bar. A single torque arm is used in place of upper control arms and is rigidly mounted to the rear axle housing at the rear and through a rubber bushing to the transmission at the front. Coil springs are used to support the weight of the car and ride control is provided by shock absorbers mounted to the rear of the axle housing. A stabilizer shaft is optional.

SHOCK ABSORBERS

Removal
1. Hoist car and support rear axle.
2. From above, pull back carpeting and remove shock absorber upper mounting nut.

NOTE: Axle assembly must be supported before removing upper shock absorber nut to avoid possible damage to brake lines, track bar and prop shaft.

3. Loosen and remove shock absorber lower mounting nut from shock absorber and remove shock.

Installation
1. Position shock absorber through body mounting hole and loosely install the lower shock absorber mounting nut.
2. From above, install the upper shock absorber retainer and nut and torque nut to 13 ft. lbs. (17 Nm).
3. Torque lower shock absorber nut to 70 ft. lbs. (95 Nm).
4. Remove rear axle support and lower car.

COIL SPRINGS AND INSULATORS

Removal
1. Hoist car on non-twin post-type joist and support rear axle assembly with an adjustable lifting device.
2. Remove track bar mounting bolt at axle assembly and loosen track bar bolt at body brace.
3. Disconnect rear brake hose clip at underbody to allow additional axle drop.
4. Remove right and left shock absorber lower attaching nuts.
5. Remove prop shaft on vehicles equipped with 4 cylinder engines.
6. Carefully lower rear axle and remove springs(s) and or insulator(s).

NOTE: DO NOT suspend rear axle by brake hose. Damage to hose could result.

Installation
1. Position springs and insulators in spring seats and raise rear axle until rear axle supports weight of vehicle at normal curb height position.
2. Install shocks to rear axle and torque nuts to 70 ft. lbs. (95 Nm).
3. Throughly clean track bar to axle assembly bolt and nut.
4. Reinstall track bar mounting bolt and torque nut to 93 ft. lbs. (125 Nm). Torque track bar to body bracket nut to 58 ft. lbs. (78 Nm).
5. Install brake line clip to underbody.
6. Install prop shaft on 4 cylinder engine equipped cars.
7. Remove adjustable lifting device from beneath axle and lower car.

TRACK BAR

Removal
1. Hoist car and support rear axle, at curb height position.
2. Remove track bar mounting bolt and nut at rear axle and at body bracket.
3. Remove track bar.

Installation
1. Position track bar in body bracket and loosely install bolt and nut.

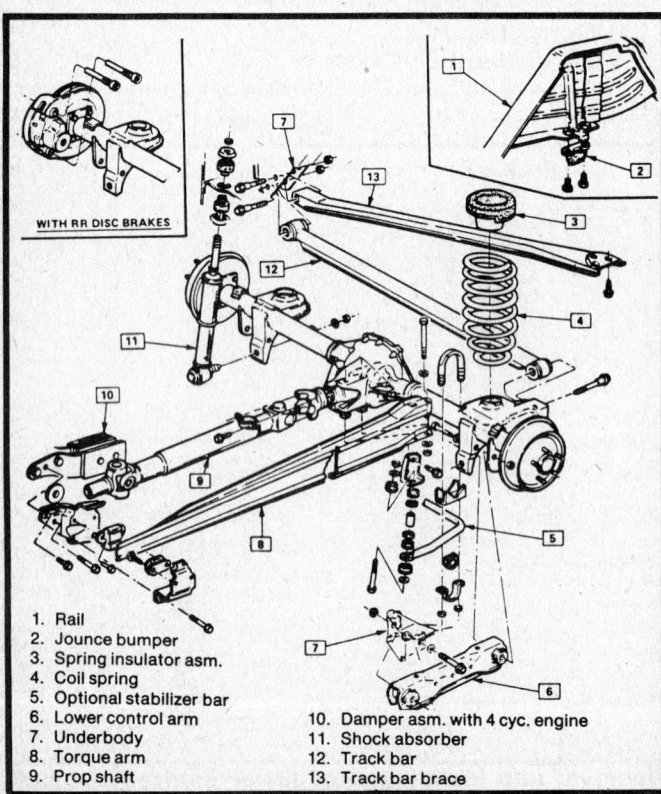

1. Rail
2. Jounce bumper
3. Spring insulator asm.
4. Coil spring
5. Optional stabilizer bar
6. Lower control arm
7. Underbody
8. Torque arm
9. Prop shaft
10. Damper asm. with 4 cyc. engine
11. Shock absorber
12. Track bar
13. Track bar brace

F body rear suspension-exploded view

35-94

SUSPENSIONS
REAR SUSPENSION—GM "F" BODY REAR DRIVE CARS

2. Thoroughly clean track bar to axle assembly bolt and nut.
3. Position track bar at axle and install bolt and nut, torque bolt to 93 ft. lbs. (125 Nm).
4. Torque track bar nut at body bracket to 58 ft. lbs. (78 Nm).
5. Remove rear axle support and lower car.

TRACK BAR BRACE

Removal
1. Hoist car and support rear axle.
2. Remove heat shield screws from track bar brace.
3. Remove three track bar brace to body brace screws.
4. Remove nut and bolt at body bracket and remove track bar brace.

Installation
1. Position track bar brace and loosely install nut and bolt at body bracket.
2. Position other end of track bar brace at body bracket and install three screws. Torque screws to 34 ft. lbs. (47 Nm).
3. Torque track bar nut at body brace to 58 ft. lbs. (78 Nm).
4. Install heat shield screws to track bar brace.
5. Remove rear axle support and lower car.

REAR LOWER CONTROL ARM

NOTE: If both control arms are being replaced, remove and replace one control arm at a time to prevent the axle from rolling or slipping sideways making replacement difficult.

Removal
1. Hoist car and support rear axle at curb height position.
2. Remove lower control arm to axle housing bolt and control arm to underbody bolt.
3. Remove control arm.

Installation
1. Position control arm and install front and rear nuts and bolts.
2. Torque front and rear bolts to 68 ft. lbs. (93 Nm).
3. Remove rear axle support and lower car.

BUSHING (REAR LOWER CONTROL ARM)

Removal
1. Remove control arm as specified in Rear Lower Control Arm Removal Procedure.
2. Place receiver J-25317-2 or equivalent over flanged side of bushing.
3. Use an arbor press to force the bushing out of the arm, using large O.D. of a driver such as J-21465-8 contacting O.D. of bushing outer sleeve.

Installation
To install the bushing, reverse the tool and push bushing into position. Connect the rear control arms as outlined in Rear Lower Control Arm Installation procedure.

TORQUE ARM

Removal
NOTE: Coil springs must be removed before removing torque arm to avoid rear axle forward twist which may cause vehicle damage.

1. Hoist car on a non-twin post-type hoist and support rear axle assembly with an adjustable lifting device.
2. Remove track bar mounting bolt at axle assembly and loosen track bar bolt at body brace.
3. Disconnect rear brake hose clip at underbody to allow additional axle drop.
4. Remove right and left shock absorber lower attaching nuts.
5. Remove prop shaft on vehicles equipped with 4 cylinder engines.
6. Carefully lower rear axle and remove coil springs.

NOTE: Do not suspend rear axle by brake hose. Damage to hose could result.

7. Remove torque arm rear attaching bolts.
8. Remove front torque arm outer bracket and remove torque arm.

Installation
1. Position torque arm and loosely install torque arm bolts.
2. Install front torque arm bracket and torque nuts to 20 ft. lbs. (27 Nm).
3. Torque rear torque arm nuts to 100 ft. lbs. (135 Nm).
4. Position springs and insulators in spring seats and raise rear axle until rear axle supports weight of axle of vehicle at normal curb height position.
5. Install shocks to rear axle and torque nuts to 70 ft. lbs. (95 Nm).
6. Thoroughly clean track bar to axle assembly bolt and nut.
7. Reinstall track bar mounting bolt at axle and torque nut to 93 ft. lbs. (125 Nm), torque track bar to body bracket nut to 58 ft. lbs. (78 Nm).
8. Install brake line clip to underbody.
9. Install prop shaft on 4 cylinder engine equipped cars.
10. Remove adjustable lifting device and lower car.

FRONT SUSPENSION—GENERAL MOTORS E AND K BODY CARS—FRONT WHEEL DRIVE

General Description

The front suspension consists of control arms, stabilizer bar, shock absorber and a right and left torsion bar. Torsion bars are used instead of the conventional coil springs. The front end of the torsion bar is attached to the lower control arm. The rear of the torsion bar is mounted into an adjustable arm at the torsion bar crossmember. The trim height of the car is controlled by this adjustment.

Wheel Alignment

HEIGHT ADJUSTMENT (TORSION BAR SUSPENSION MODELS)

The standing height must be checked and adjusted if necessary, before performing the front end alignment procedure. The standing height is controlled by the adjustment setting of

SECTION 35 SUSPENSIONS
FRONT SUSPENSION—GM "E" & "K" BODY FRONT DRIVE CARS

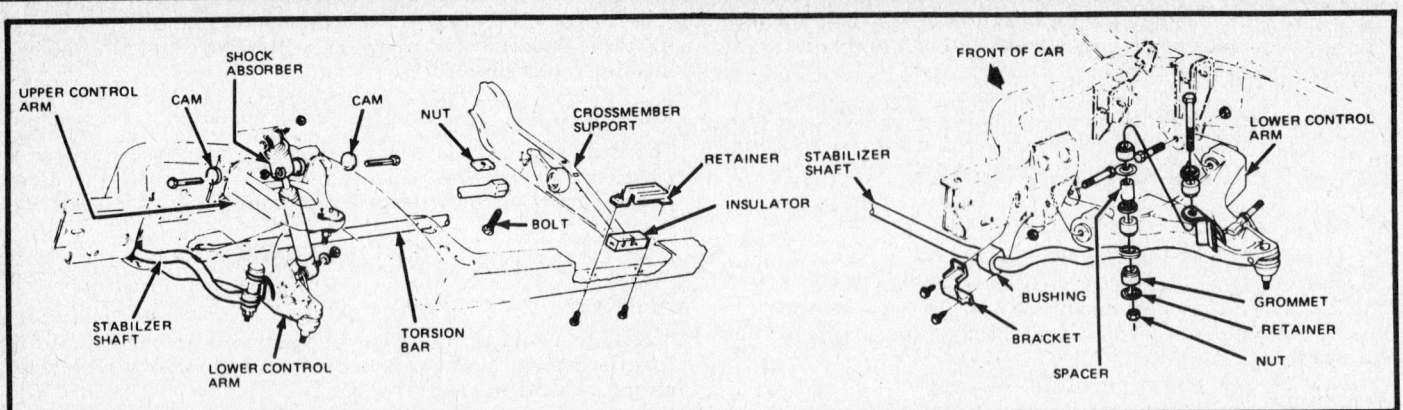

Front suspension (© General Motors Corp.)

the torsion bar adjusting bolt.

Clockwise rotation of the bolt increases the front height; counterclockwise decreases the front height.

Car must be on a level surface, gas tank full, or a compensating weight added, front seat all the way to the rear, and front and rear tires inflated to the proper pressures. Doors, hood and trunk must be closed and no passengers or additional weight should be in car or trunk.

These tolerances are production specifications on bumper height. If there is more than 1 inch (25mm) difference, side to side, at the wheel well opening, corrective measures may need to be implemented on a case by case basis. These are curb height dimensions which include a full tank of fuel.

CAMBER AND CASTER ADJUSTMENTS

These adjustments can be made either from under car or under hood, as desired. If under hood approach is used, however, be sure to recheck alignment after all operations are completed. Change in weight distribution caused by opened hood is sufficient to disturb final alignment settings.

1. Loosen nuts on upper suspension arm front and rear cam bolts.

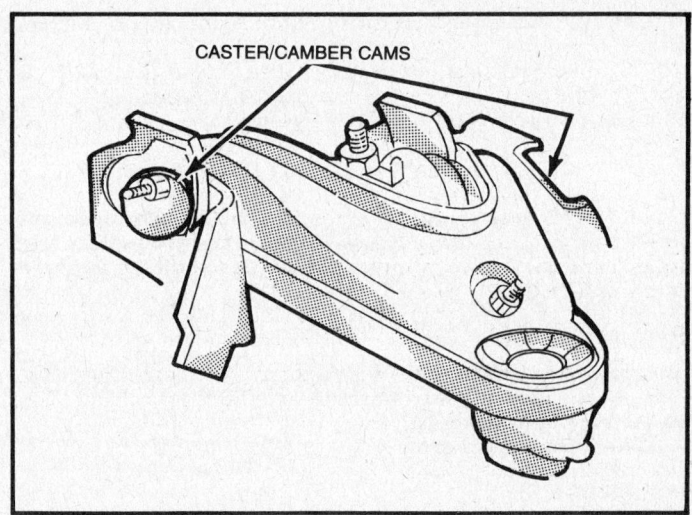

Caster/camber adjustment (© General Motors Corp.)

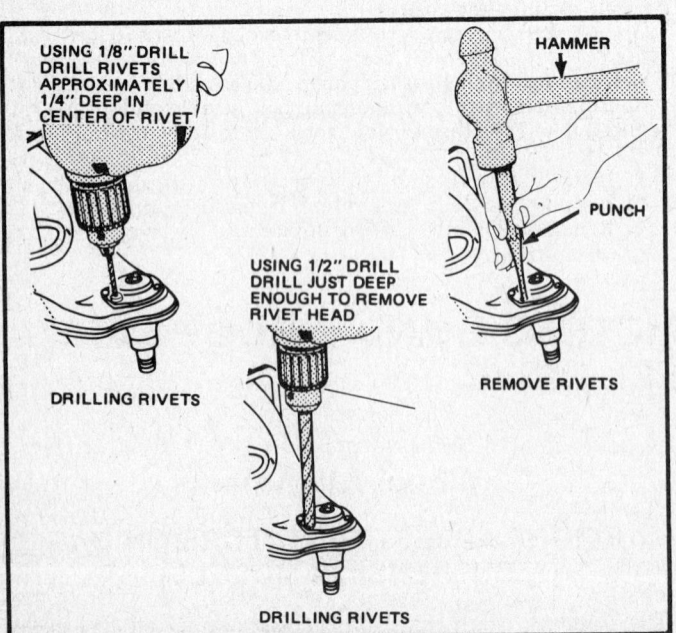

Upper ball joint removal and installation (© General Motors Corp.)

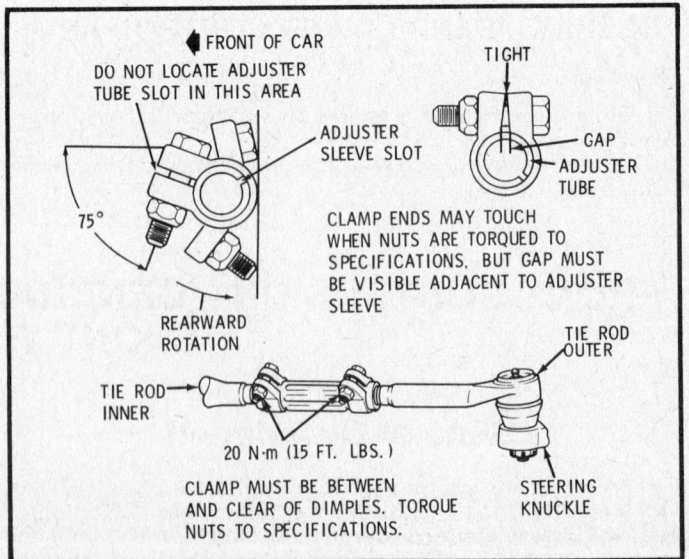

E series tie rod clamp and sleeve positioning. Bolts must be installed in direction shown (© General Motors Corp.)

2. Note camber reading and rotate front bolt to correct for ½ of incorrect reading or as near as possible.

3. Rotate rear cam bolt to bring camber reading to 0°.

NOTE: Do not use a socket to adjust rear cam bolt on left side as brake pipes could be damaged. An offset box end wrench is recommended at this adjustment point.

4. Tighten front and rear bolts and check caster. If caster requires adjustment, proceed with Step 5; if not, move to Step 8.

5. Loosen front and rear cam bolt nuts.

6. Using camber scale on alignment equipment, rotate front bolt so that the camber changes an amount equal to ¼ of the desired caster change. (A caster change-to-camber change ratio of about 2 to 1 is inherent to the Eldorado and Seville suspension system. That is, when one cam is rotated sufficiently to change camber 1°, caster reading will change about 2°.).

If adjusting to correct for excessive negative caster, rotate

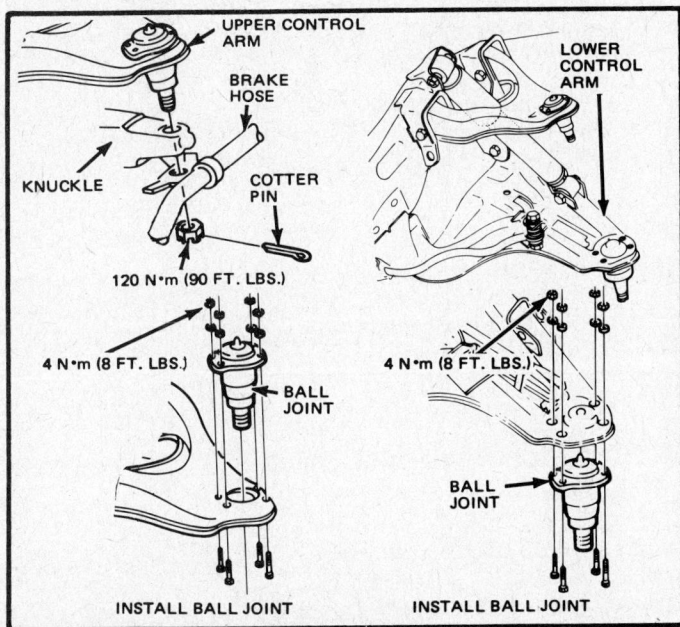

To remove: hoist car and remove wheel. Remove knuckle. Remove hub and bearing assembly, knuckle and knuckle seal. Remove parts as shown. To install: install poarets as shown. Install steering knuckle. Install hub and bearingg assembly, knuckle and knuckle seal. Install wheel and lower hoist (© General Motors Corp.)

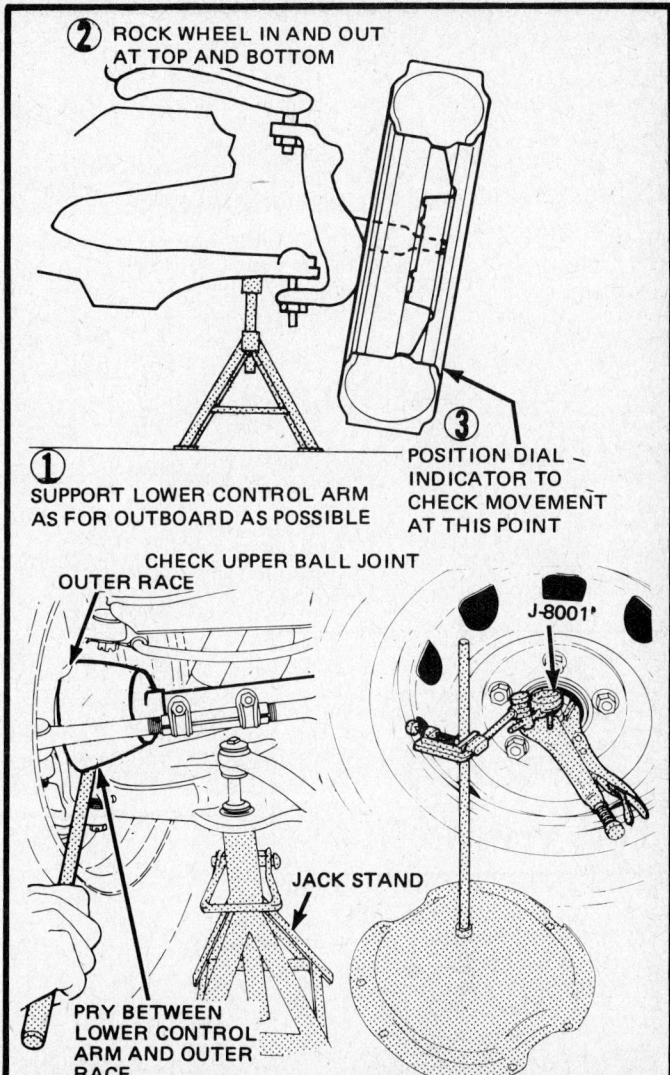

Check ball joint as shown. If dial indicator reading exceeds 3.2mm (.125 in.) or if ball stud is disconnected from knuckle and any looseness is detected or ball stud can be twisted in its socket with fingers, replace ball joint (© General Motors Corp.)

front bolt to increase positive camber. If adjusting to correct for excessive positive caster, rotate front bolt to increase negative camber.

7. Rotate the rear bolt until camber setting returns to its corrected position (Step 3).

8. Tighten upper suspension arm cam nuts to 95 ft. lbs. (130 Nm). Hold head of bolt securely; any movement of the cam will affect final setting and will require a recheck of the camber and caster adjustments.

TOE ADJUSTMENT

Before checking toe-in, make certain that the intermediate rod height is correct.

Toe-in is adjusted by turning the tie rod adjuster tubes at the outer ends of each tie rod after loosening clamp bolts. The readings should be taken only when the front wheels are in a straight ahead position so that the steering gear is on its high spot.

1. Center steering wheel, raise car, and check wheel runout.

2. Loosen tie rod adjuster nus and adjust tie rods to obtain proper toe setting.

3. Position tie rod adjuster clamps so that openings of clamps are facing up. Interference with front suspension components could occur while turning if clamps are facing down.

Wheel Bearings (Tapered Roller Bearings)

Lubrication

For normal application, clean and repack front wheel bearings with a high melting point wheel bearing lubricant at each front brake lining replacement or 30,000 miles (48,000 km),

SECTION 35 SUSPENSIONS
FRONT SUSPENSION—GM "E" & "K" BODY FRONT DRIVE CARS

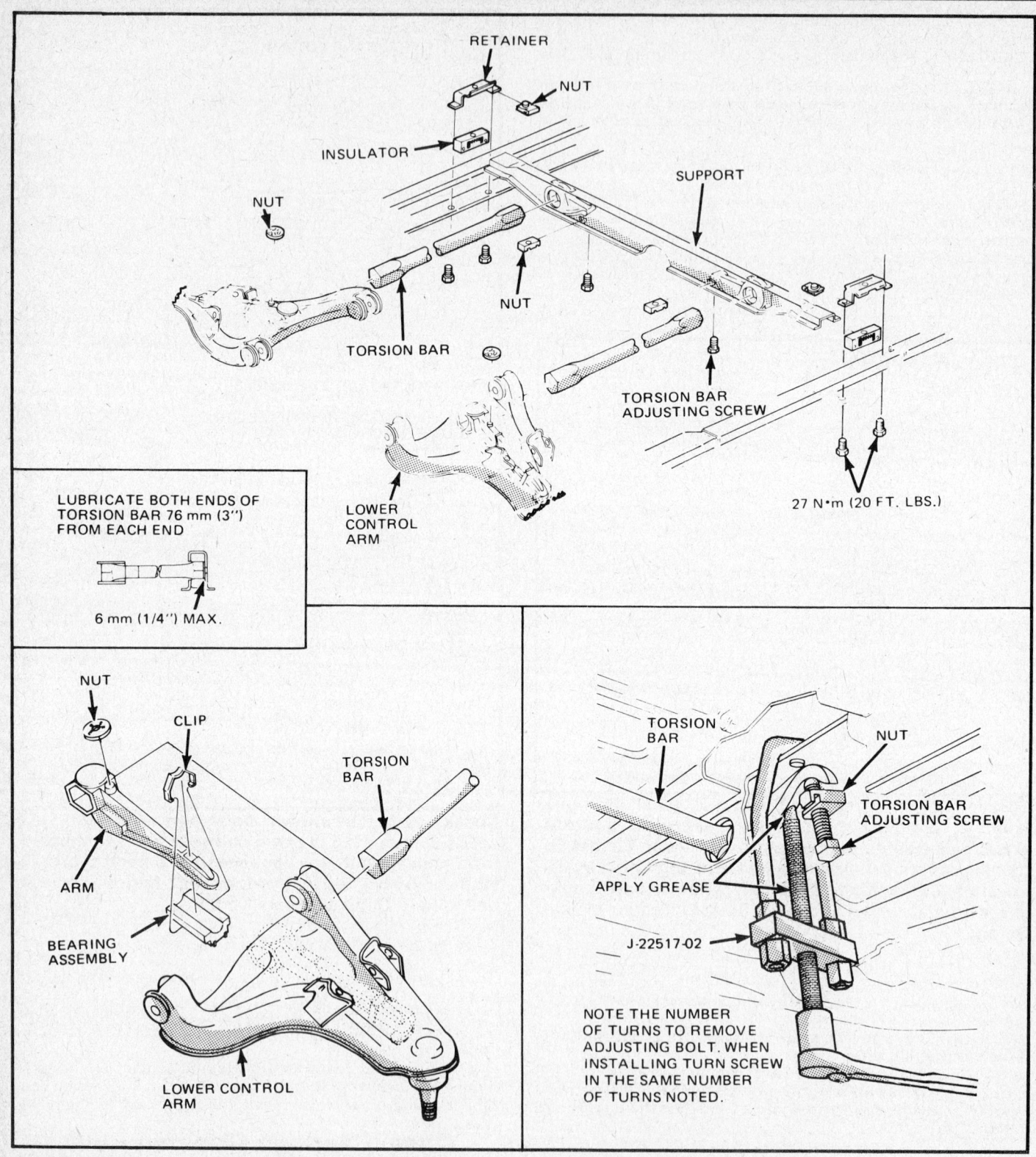

To remove: hoist car and remove parts as shown. To remove torsion bar (s) only: remove torsion bar adjusting screw as shown. Slide torsion bar forward in lower control arm until torsion bar clears support. Then pull down on bar and remove from control arm. To install: install parts as shown. Lower hoist and adjust trim height (© General Motors Corp.)

SUSPENSIONS
FRONT SUSPENSION—GM "E" & "K" BODY FRONT DRIVE CARS

Bolt on Sealed Wheel Bearing Diagnosis

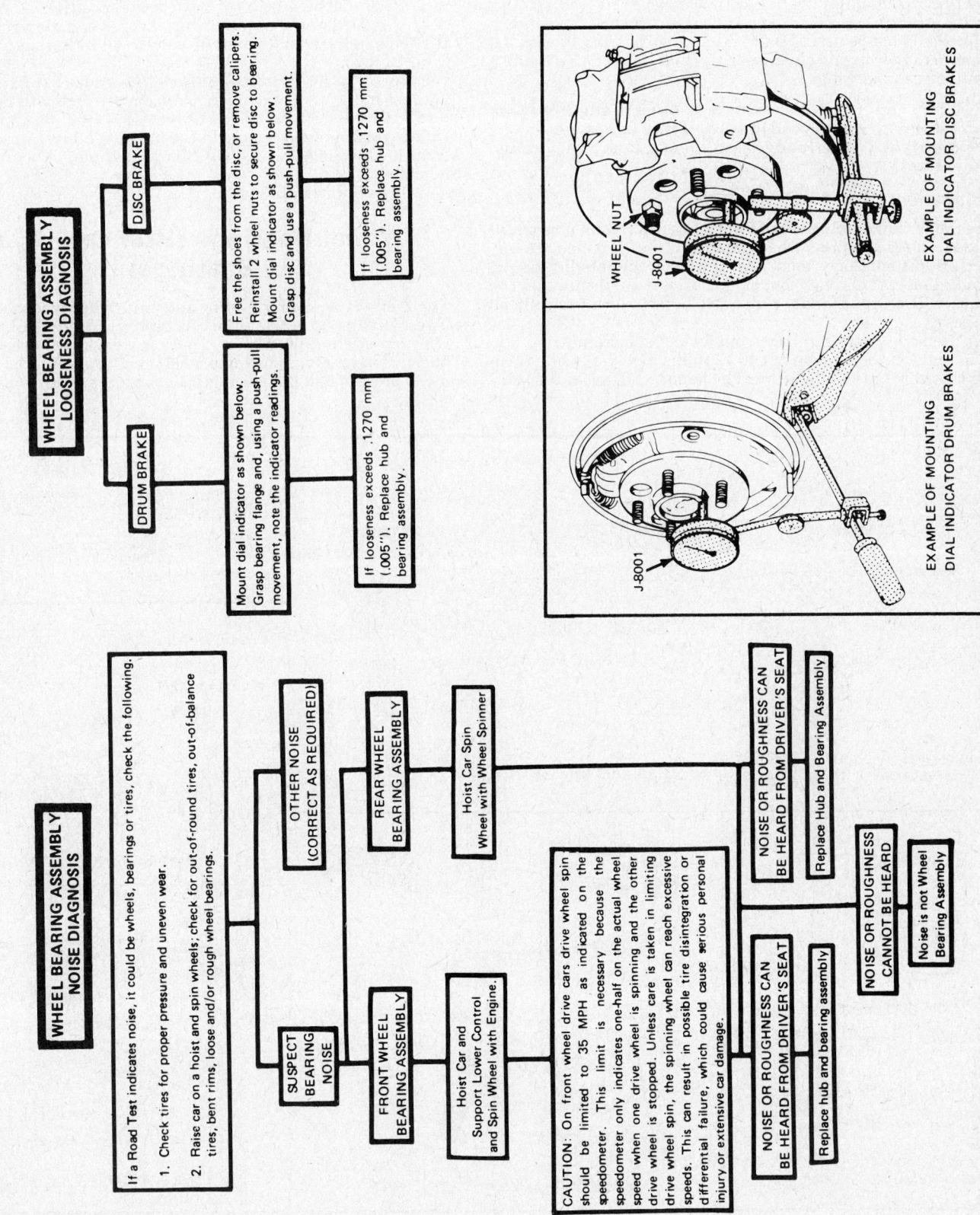

Bolt on sealed wheel bearing diagnosis (© General Motors Corp.)

35-99

SECTION 35 SUSPENSIONS
FRONT SUSPENSION—GM "E" & "K" BODY FRONT DRIVE CARS

whichever comes first. For heavy duty application, clean and repack front wheel bearings at each front brake lining replacement or 15,000 miles (24,000 km), whichever comes first. Use wheel bearing lubricant; "long fiber" or "viscous" type lubricant should not be used. Do not miss wheel bearing lubricants. Be sure to thoroughly clean bearings and hubs of all old lubricant before repacking.

NOTE: Tapered roller bearings have a slightly loose feel when properly adjusted. They must never be overtightened (pre-loaded) or severe bearing damage may result.

Adjustment

The proper functioning of the front suspension cannot be maintained unless the front wheel tapered roller bearings are correctly adjusted. Cones must be a slip fit on the spindle and the inside diameter of cones should be lubricated to insure that the cones will creep. Spindle nut must be a free-running fit on threads.

1. Remove cotter pin from spindle and spindle nut.
2. Tighten the spindle nut to 12 ft. lbs. (16 Nm) while turning the wheel assembly forward by hand to fully seat the bearings. This will remove any grease or burrs which could cause excessive wheel bearing play later.
3. Back off the nut to the "just loose" position.
4. Hand tighten the spindle nut. Loosen spindle nut until either hole in the spindle lines up with a slot in the nut (not more than ½ flat).
5. Install a new cotter pin. Bend the ends of the cotter pin against nut. Cut off extra length to ensure ends will not interfere with the dust cap.
6. Measure the looseness in the hub assembly. There will be from 0.001–0.005 in. (0.03–0.13mm) end play when properly adjusted.
7. Install dust cap on hub.

Wheel Bearings (Bolt On–Type Bearings)

The E and K Series have front and rear sealed wheel bearings. The bearings are pre-adjusted and require no lubrication maintenance or adjustment. There are darkened areas on the bearing assembly. These darkened areas are from a heat treatment process and do not require bearing replacement.

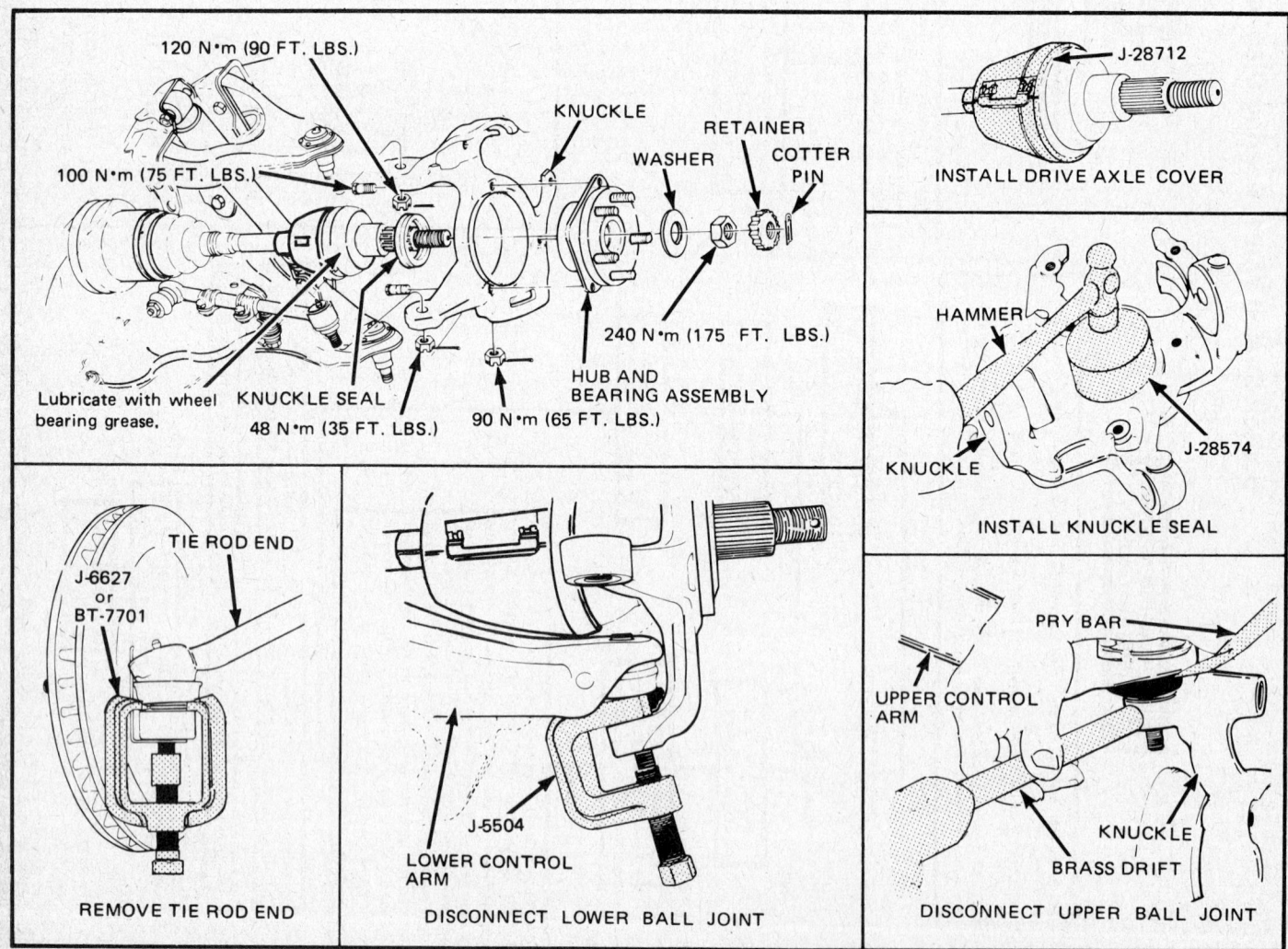

Hub and bearing assembly, knuckle and knuckle seal removal and installation. To remove: hoist car and remove wheel, remove disc, and remove parts as shown. To install: be sure that bearing surfaces are clean and free of burrs. Install parts as shown. Install disc, install wheel and lower hoist (© General Motors Corp.)

SUSPENSIONS
REAR SUSPENSION—GM "E" & "K" BODY FRONT DRIVE CARS

REAR SUSPENSION—GENERAL MOTORS E AND K BODY CARS—FRONT WHEEL DRIVE

Description

The E and K Series have a semi-trailing arm-type rear suspension system with a relatively long control arm for a minimum camber change. The system consists of boxed control arms, coil springs, super-lift shock absorbers and a stabilizer bar.

The control arms are welded together. The hub and bearing attachment plane is machined for precise suspension alignment.

The hub and wheel bearing is a unit assembly which eliminates the need for wheel bearing adjustments and does not require periodic maintenance.

Operation

The left and right rear wheel suspensions, being independent of each other, permit the vertical movement of one wheel without affecting the wheel on the opposite side of the car.

This independent wheel movement is obtained by an A frame control arm. The control arm is hinged at the frame to provide the up and down movement of the wheel. The solid stabilizer bar forces the wheel to travel in through a controlled arc.

The control arm also carries the rear brake mounting bracket and hub and bearing assembly.

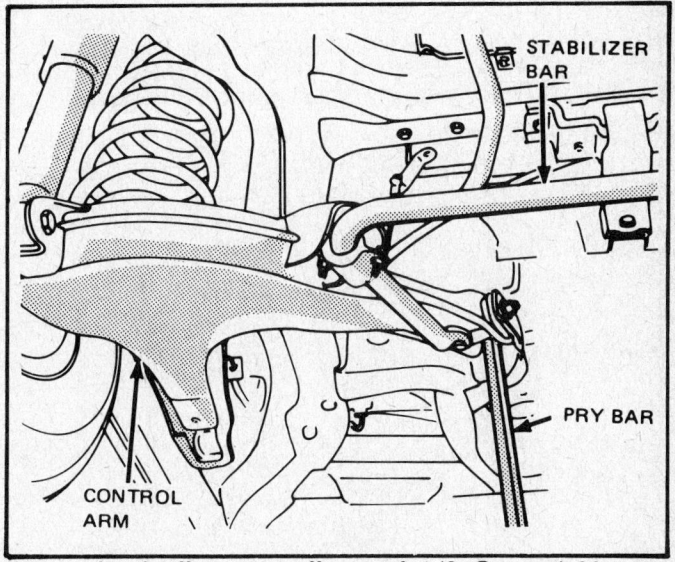

Rear wheel alignment diagnosis (© General Motors Corp.)

Alignment

Satisfactory operation may occur over a wide range of rear wheel alignment settings. Nevertheless, should settings vary beyond certain tolerances, readjustment of alignment is advisable. The specifications stated in column 1 of the charts should be used as guidelines.

These specifications provide an acceptable all-around operating range in that they prevent abnormal tire wire caused by wheel alignment.

In the event the actual settings are beyond the specifications set forth in column 1 of 2 (whichever is applicable), or whenever for other reasons the alignment is being reset, the factory recommends that the specifications given in column 3 of the charts be used.

Rear wheel alignment should be checked and adjusted as necessary in the following procedure.
1. Check front and rear trim heights.
2. Check electronic level control for proper operation.
3. Using an alignment machine, use one of the following procedures.

Preferred method:
a. If machine does not have guide line, place tape on floor from wheel plate to rear of car to use as a guide for lining up car on machine.
b. Back car onto alignment machine placing rear wheel on wheel plates.
c. Place a straightedge at same rib of tire at front and rear and measure distance from inside edge of straight edge and edge guide line. The measurement from the guide line to the straight edge must be greater at the rear tire by $5/8$ in. (16mm) $\pm 1/4$ in. (6mm).

Alternate method:
a. Place a one inch tape on the floor along the righthand side of the center line between the wheel plates of the alignment machine.
b. Back car onto alignment machine making sure car is as straight as possible.

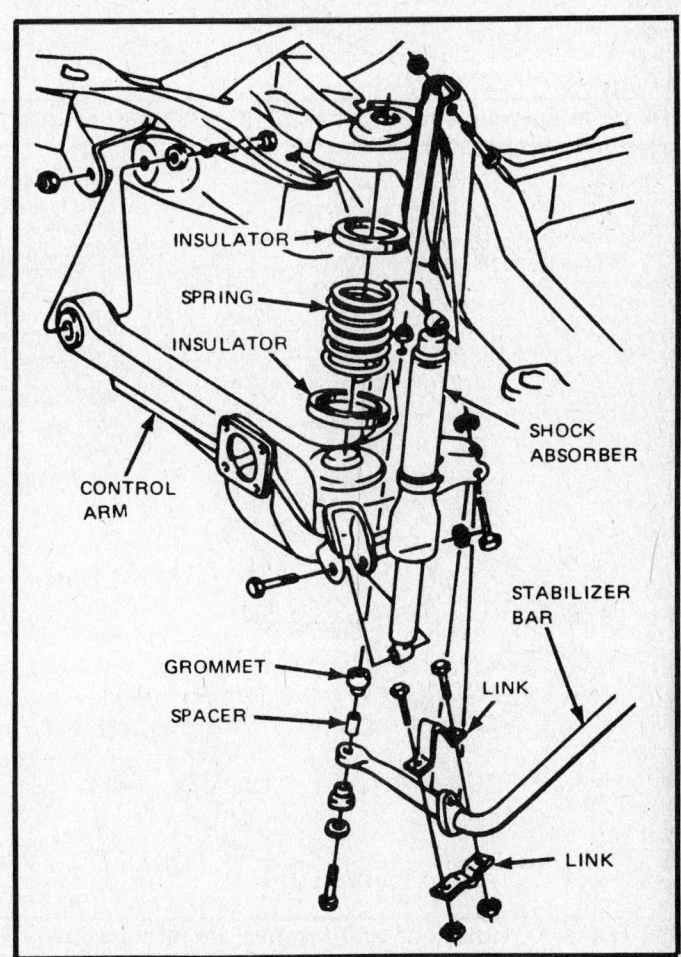

Rear suspension (© General Motors Corp.)

35-101

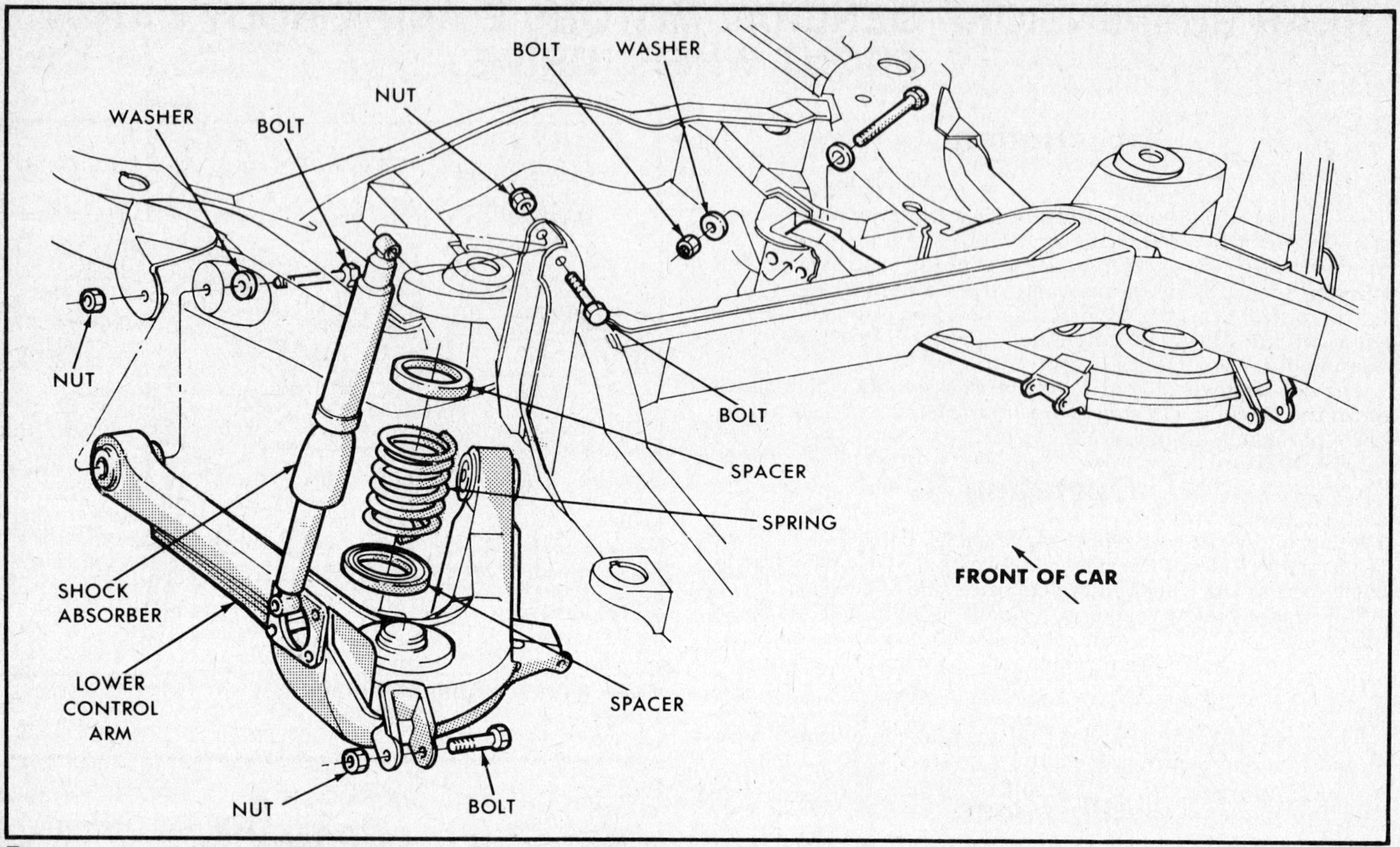

SECTION 35 SUSPENSIONS
REAR SUSPENSION—GM "E" & "K" BODY FRONT DRIVE CARS

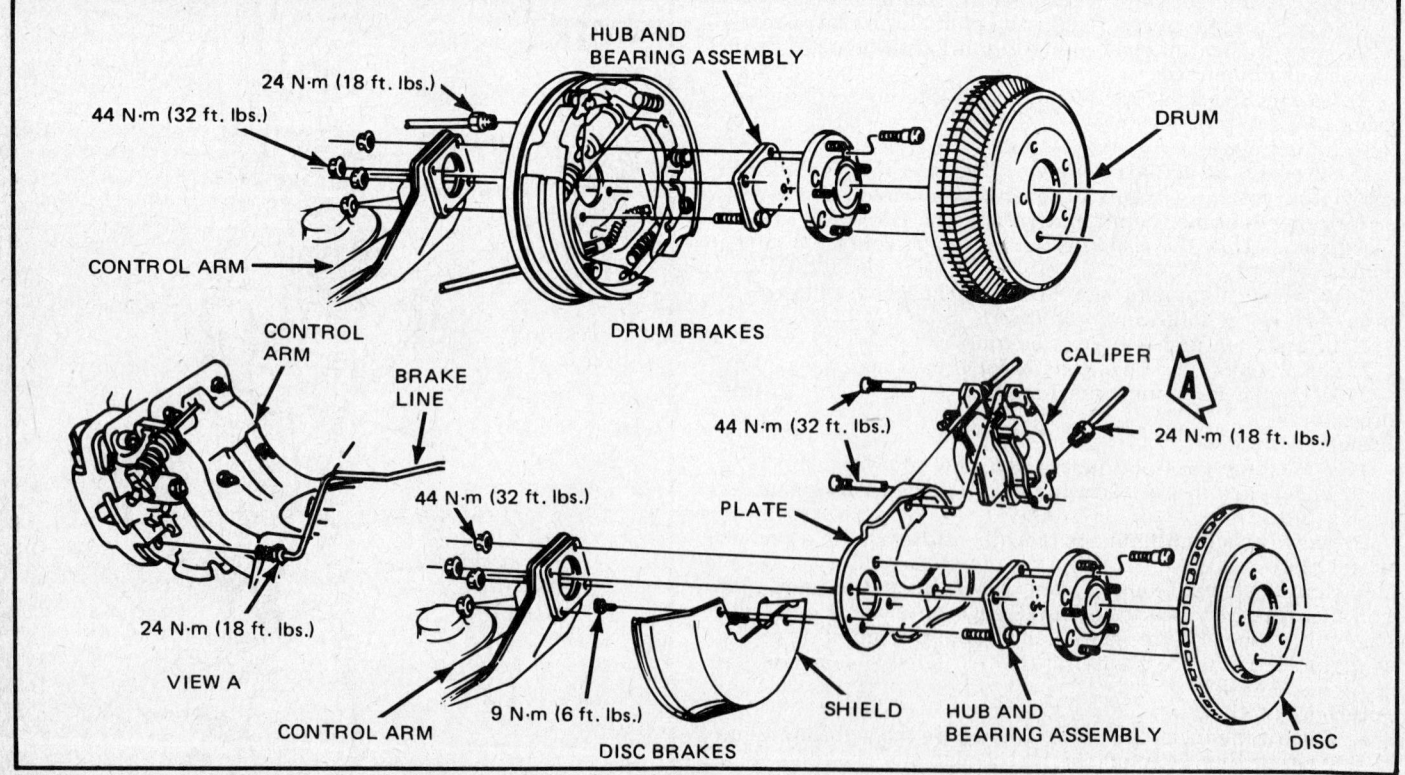

Rear suspension components (© General Motors Corp.)

To remove: hoist car and remove wheel as shown. Remove parts as shown. To install: be sure that bearing surfaces are clean and free of burrs. Install parts as shown. If equipped with disc brakes, bleed brakes. Install wheel and lower hoist (© General Motors Corp.)

SUSPENSIONS
REAR SUSPENSION—GM "E" & "K" BODY FRONT DRIVE CARS
SECTION 35

REAR WHEEL ALIGNMENT DIAGNOSIS

PROBLEM	CAUSE	CORRECTION
Toe not adjustable within specifications	Lower control arm bent Frame bent Car not properly centered on alignment machine Bearing mounting flange bent Wheel bent	Replace control arm Bring frame within specification Center car on alignment machine Replace bearing assembly Replace wheel
Camber out of specification	Control arm bent Frame bent Spindle-bearing	Replace control arm Bring frame within specifications Properly mount

REAR WHEEL ALIGNMENT

	Specifications for Diagnosis for Warranty Repair or Customer Paid Service	Specifications for Periodic Motor Vehicle Inspection	Specification for Alignment Resetting
Camber (measure only)	−1.3° to +0.3°	−1.5° to +0.5°	Refer to Rear Suspension Diagnosis
Toe-in per wheel	0.00° to +0.30° (0″ to +5/32″)	−0.25° to +0.55° (−1/8″ to +9/32″)	+0.15° ±0.15° (+3/32″ ±3/32″)
Toe-in both wheels	0.00° to +0.60° (0″ to +5/16″)	−0.50° to +1.10° (−1/4″ to +9/16″)	+0.30° ±0.30° (+5/32″ ±5/32″)

NOTE: It is important that toe-in be measured per wheel. If equipment is not available to measure each wheel, measure toe-in both wheels. When resetting be sure that toe-in on each wheel is the same.
CAUTION: With car backed onto alignment machine, toe-in and toe-out are reversed. Toe-in will be read as toe-out. It is very important that the readings be made and understood properly.

TORQUE SPECIFICATIONS

	N·m	Ft.Lbs.
Stabilizer		
Stabilizer Link Nut	18	13
Stabilizer Bar Brkt. to Frame Bolts & Nuts	33	24
Shock Absorber		
Shock Absorber Upper Attaching Nut	130	95
Shock Absorber to Control Arm Bolts	100	75
Control Arms		
Upper Control Arm to Frame Attaching Nuts	95	70
Lower Control Arm to Frame Attaching Nuts	120	90

TORQUE SPECIFICATIONS

	N·m	Ft.Lbs.
Ball Joints		
Service Ball Joints to Upper Control Arm	11	8
Lower	90	65
Upper	120	90
Front Wheel Drive		
Drive Axle Nut	240	175
Hub and Bearing to Knuckle Bolts	100	75
Torsion Bar Crossmember Retainer Bolts	27	20
Drive Axle to Output Shaft Bolts	80	60
Tie Rod to Knuckle Nut	54	40

SECTION 35 SUSPENSIONS
REAR SUSPENSION—GM "E" & "K" BODY FRONT DRIVE CARS

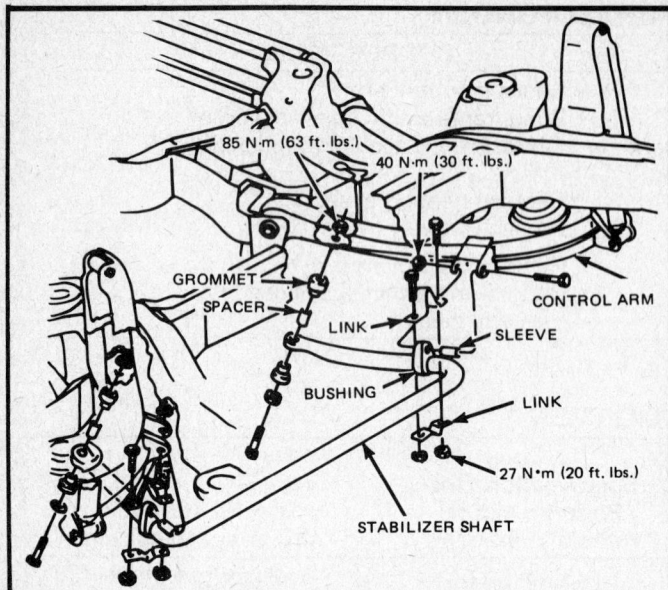

Stabilizer bar and/or bushing removal and installation. To remove: hoist vehicle and remove parts as shown. To: install: install parts as shown, and lower vehicle. (© General Motors Corp.)

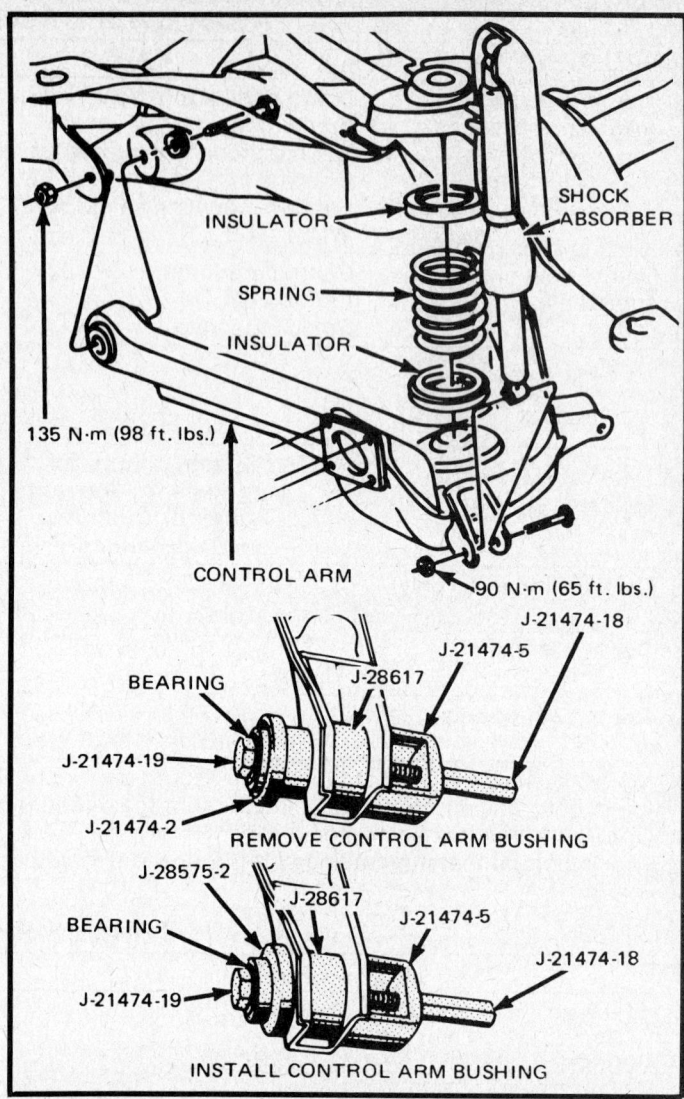

Rear control arm, spring and/or bushing removal and installation. To remove: hoist car and remove wheel. Remove hub and bearing assembly. Remove parts as shown. To install: install parts as shown. Install hub and bearing assembly. Blled brakes. Install wheel and lower hoist (© General Motors Corp.)

c. Hanging plumbs on the front and rear crossmembers at gage holes will give guide lines for near perfect centering of the car.

4. Attach alignment mirrors to rear wheel and take toe and camber readings.

NOTE: With car backed onto alignment machine, toe-in and toe-out are reversed. Toe-in will be read as toe-out. It is very important that the readings be made and understood properly.

5. Toe adjustments are made at the inner pivot bushings. Loosening the nut and bolt at the inner bushing will enable the toe to be moved in or out as necessary.

6. Tighten bushing mounting nut to 97 ft. lbs. (135 Nm) and recheck toe for correct setting. It may be necessary to use a pry bar to move the control arm. Moving the control arm rearward increases toe-in; moving it forward increases toe-out.

7. Check camber.

FRONT SUSPENSION—GENERAL MOTORS J BODY CARS—FRONT WHEEL DRIVE

Description

The front suspension is a MacPherson strut design. The lower control arms pivot from the lower side rails. Rubber bushings are used for the lower control arm pivots. The upper end of the strut is isolated by a rubber mount which contains a non-serviceable bearing for wheel turning. The tie rods connect to the steering arm on the strut, just below the spring seat. The lower end of the wheel steering knuckle pivots on a ball stud for wheel turning. The ball stud is riveted in the lower control arm and is fastened to the steering knuckle with a castellated nut and cotter pin.

Wheel Alignment
TOE

Toe is controlled by the tie rod position. To adjust toe setting, loosen the clamp bolts at the outer end of the tie rod. Rotate adjuster to align toe to specifications. Tighten bolts to 15 ft. lbs. (20 Nm).

SUSPENSIONS
FRONT SUSPENSION—GM "J" BODY FRONT DRIVE CARS

Adjustment

1. Loosen clamp bolts at the outer tie rod.
2. Square the vehicle.
3. Rotate adjuster to set toe to specifications.
4. Tighten clamp bolts.

CAMBER

In special circumstances when camber adjustment becomes necessary, refer to the following procedure for instructions on modifying the front suspension strut assembly.

Adjustment

1. Position the car on the alignment equipment. Follow the manufacturer's instructions to obtain the camber reading.
2. Use appropriate extensions to reach around both sides of the tire. Loosen both strut-to-knuckle bolts just enough to allow movement between the strut and the knuckle. Remove tools.
3. Grasp the top of the tire firmly, and move the tire inboard or outboard until the correct camber reading is obtained.
4. Carefully reach around the tire with extensions and tighten both bolts enough to hold the correct camber while the wheel and tire is removed to allow final torque.
5. With wheel and tire removed, torque both bolts to specifications.
6. Reinstall wheel and tire. Tighten nuts to specifications.

MacPherson Strut

Removal

1. Raise hood and disconnect upper strut-to-body nuts.
2. Hoist car, allowing front suspension to hang free.
3. Remove wheel and tire.
4. Install drive axle cover.
5. Disconnect tie rod from strut.
6. Remove both strut-to-knuckle bolts.
7. Remove strut.

Installation

1. Install strut by reversing removal Steps 1–6.
2. Place flats on both mounting bolts in a horizontal position.
3. Torque all fasteners to specifications.

STRUT MODIFICATION (ONLY FOR ADJUSTMENT OF CAMBER SETTING)

1. Place strut in vise. (It is not necessary to remove the strut from the car. Filing can be accomplished by disconnecting strut from knuckle).
2. File the holes in outer flanges to enlarge the bottom holes until they match the slots in the inner flanges.

STRUT DISASSEMBLY

1. Mount strut compressor in vise.
2. Place strut assembly in bottom adapter of compressor and install J26584-86 or equivalent (make sure adapter captures strut and that locating pins are engaged).
3. Rotate strut assembly to align top mounting assembly lip with strut compressor support notch.
4. Insert both J26584-88 top adapters between the top mounting assembly and the top spring seat. Position top adapters so that the split line is in the 9 o'clock–3 o'clock position.
5. Using a ratchet with 1 inch socket, turn compressor forcing screw clockwise until top support flange contact the J26584-88 top adapters. Continue turning the screw, compressing the strut spring approximately ½ inch (four complete turns).

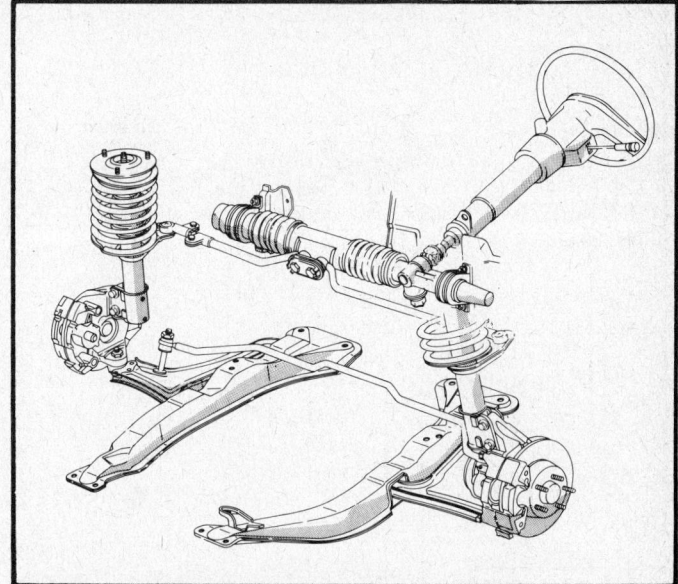

Front suspension (© General Motors Corp.)

NOTE: Never bottom spring or strut damper rod.

6. The top nut can now be removed from the strut damper shaft and the top mounting assembly (containing bearing) can be lifted off the strut assembly.
7. Turn strut compressor forcing screw counterclockwise until the strut spring tension is relieved. Remove top adapters, bottom adapter, then remove components.

STRUT ASSEMBLY

---- **CAUTION** ----

Never place a hard tool such as pliers or a screwdriver against the polished surface of the damper shaft. The shaft can be held up from the top end with your fingers, or with the extension, to prevent it from receding into the strut assembly, while the spring is being compressed.

1. Clamp strut compressor body J26584 in vise.
2. Place strut assembly in bottom adapter of compressor and install J26584-86 or equivalent (make sure adapter captures strut and locating pins are engaged).

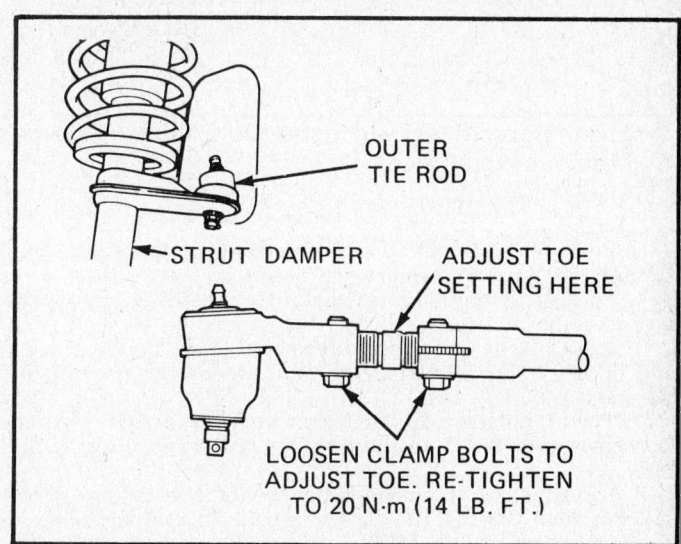

Toe adjustment (© General Motors Corp.)

SECTION 35 SUSPENSIONS
FRONT SUSPENSION—GM "J" BODY FRONT DRIVE CARS

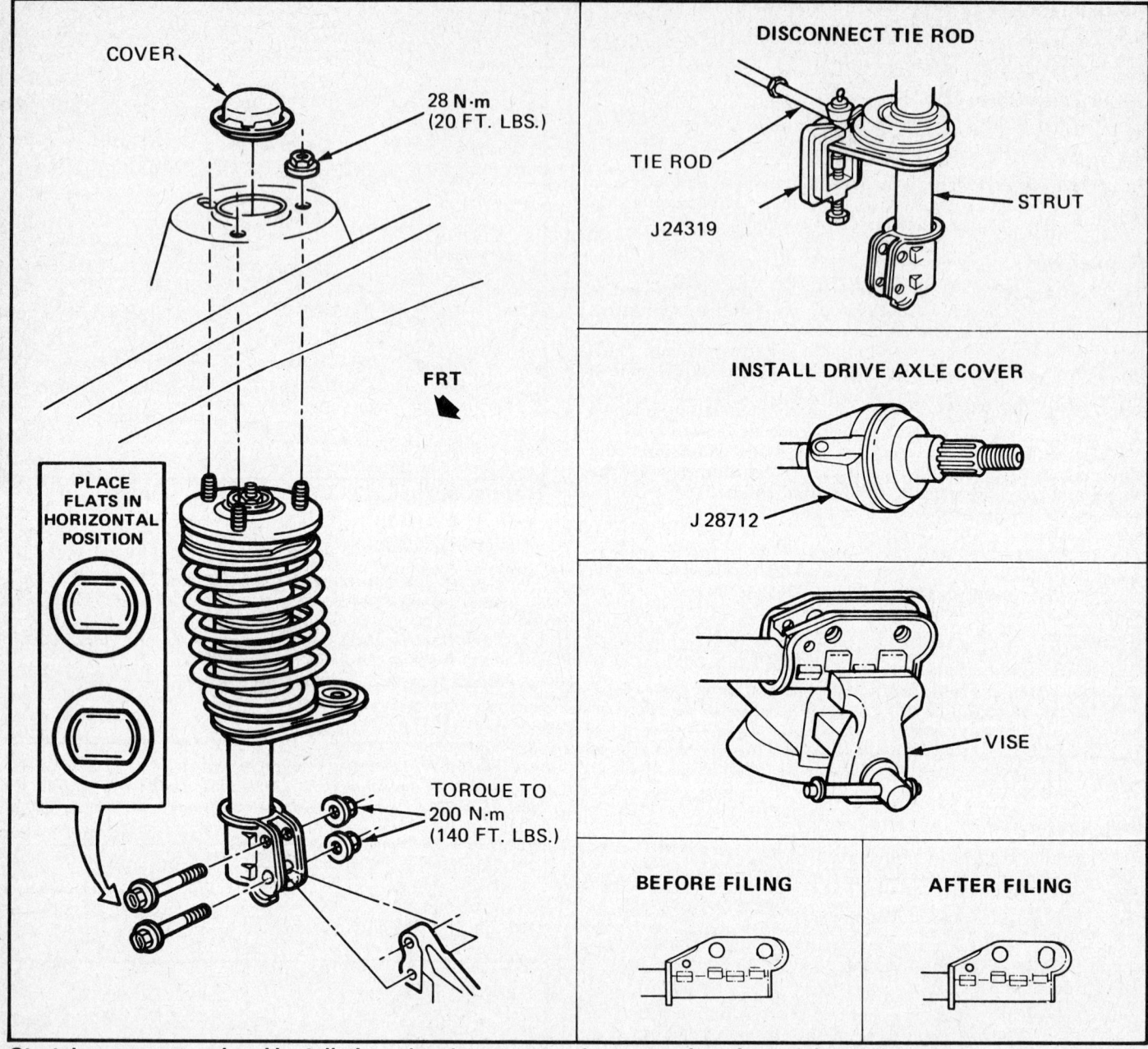

Strut damper removal and installation, showing modification procedure for camber adjustment
(© General Motors Corp.)

3. Rotate strut assembly until mounting flange is facing out, directly opposite the compressor forcing screw.
4. Position spring on strut making sure spring is properly seated on bottom spring plate.
5. Install strut spring seat assembly on top of spring.
6. Place both J26584-88 top adapters over spring seat assembly.
7. Turn compressor forcing screw until compressor top support just contacts top adapters (do not compress spring at this time).
8. Install a long extension with a socket to fit the hex on the damper shaft through the top spring seat. Use the extension to guide the components during reassembly.
9. Compress spring by turning screw clockwise until approximately 1 ½ inch of damper shaft extends through the top spring plate.

NOTE: Do not compress spring until it bottoms.

10. Remove extension and socket, position top mounting assembly over damper shaft and install nut.
11. Turn forcing screw counterclockwise to back off support, remove top adapters and bottom adapter, and remove strut assembly from compressor.

NOTE: Special tool J-26584 or equivalent must be used to disassemble and assemble strut damper, or damage could result.

SUSPENSIONS
FRONT SUSPENSION—GM "J" BODY FRONT DRIVE CARS

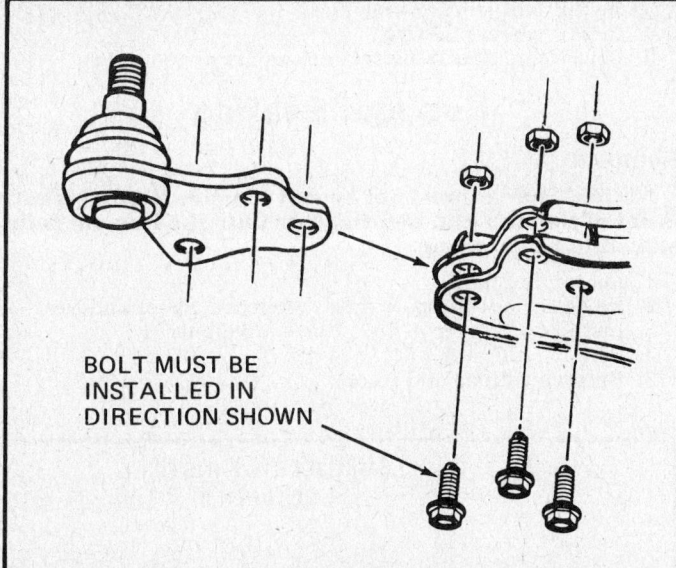

Install ball joint to control (© General Motors Corp.)

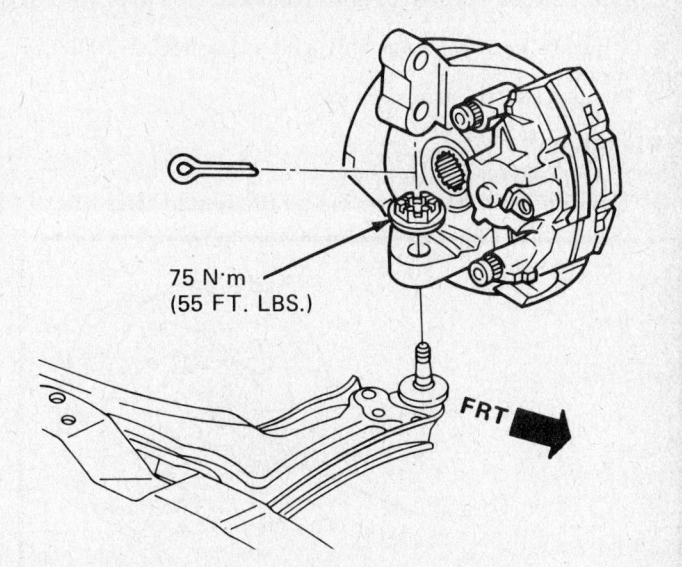

REPLACE STRUT CARTRIDGE

The internal piston rod, cylinder assembly, and fluid can be replaced utilizing a service cartridge and nut. Internal threads are located immediately below a cut line groove.

1. Mount strut in vise. Do not overclamp. Excessive clamping may damage tube and/or bracket.
2. Locate cut line groove. It is important to locate groove as accurately as possible because mislocation will result in thread damage. Cut a round groove with a pipe cutter until reservoir tube is completely cut through.
3. Remove and discard end cap, cylinder, and piston rod assembly. Remove strut from vise and discard fluid.
4. Reclamp strut in vise. A flaring cup tool is provided in service package to flare and debur cut edge of reservoir tube to accept service nut. Place flaring cup on open end of reservoir tube. Strike flaring cup with a mallet or hammer until flaring cup's flat outer surface rests on reservoir tube. Remove the flaring cup tool and discard. At this time, try nut to assure positive start and smooth threading into reservoir tube threads. Remove nut after this check. Flaring cup must be placed in contact with tube so there is not gap between cup and tube when struck.
5. Place strut cartridge in reservoir tube. Turn cartridge until it settles into indentations at base of tube so cartridge cannot be easily turned. Place nut over cartridge.
6. Using tool J-29778 or equivalent for 53 mm hex nut and a torque wrench, tighten to 140–170 ft. lbs. (190–230 Nm) in upright mounting position. Stroke the piston rod once or twice to check for proper operation.

Ball Joints

Inspection

Car must be supported by the wheels so weight of car will properly load the ball joints.

The lower ball joint is inspected for wear by visual observation alone. Wear is indicated by the protrusion of the 1/2 in. (12.7mm) diameter nipple into which the grease fitting is threaded. This round nipple projects 0.050 in. (1.27mm) beyond the surface of the ball joint cover on a new, unworn joint. Normal wear will result in the surface of this nipple retreating very slowly inward.

Removal

1. Raise the vehicle and support safely. Remove the wheel and tire assembly.
2. If no countersink is found on the lower side of the rivets, carefully locate the center of the rivet body and mark with a punch.
3. Use the proper sequence to drill out rivets.
4. Use tool J-29330 or equivalent to separate joint from knuckle.
5. Disconnect stabilizer from control arm.
6. Remove ball joint.

Installation

1. Install new ball joint using three bolts.
2. Reverse removal Steps 1–5 to install. Tighten all fasteners to specifications.
3. Check toe setting. Adjust as required.

Control Arm

Removal

1. Raise car and support safely. Remove wheel and tire.

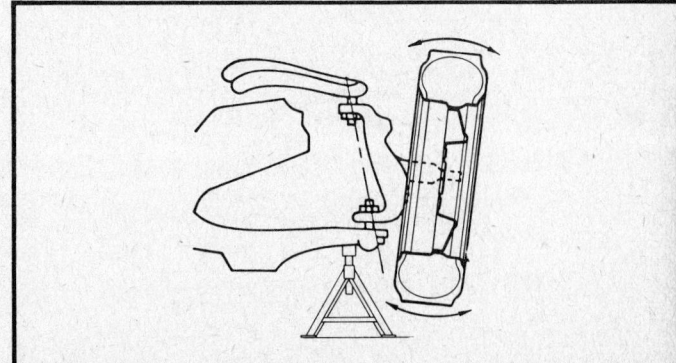

Support lower control arm as far outboard as possible. Position dial indicator to check movement at point shown. Rock wheel in and out at top and bottom (© General Motors Corp.)

SECTION 35 SUSPENSIONS
FRONT SUSPENSION—GM "J" BODY FRONT DRIVE CARS

2. Disconnect stabilizer bar from control arm and/or support.
3. Separate knuckle from ball joint using tool J–29330 or equivalent.
4. Remove control arm/support.

Installation

1. Install control arm/support.
2. When installing support, install the center bolts first.

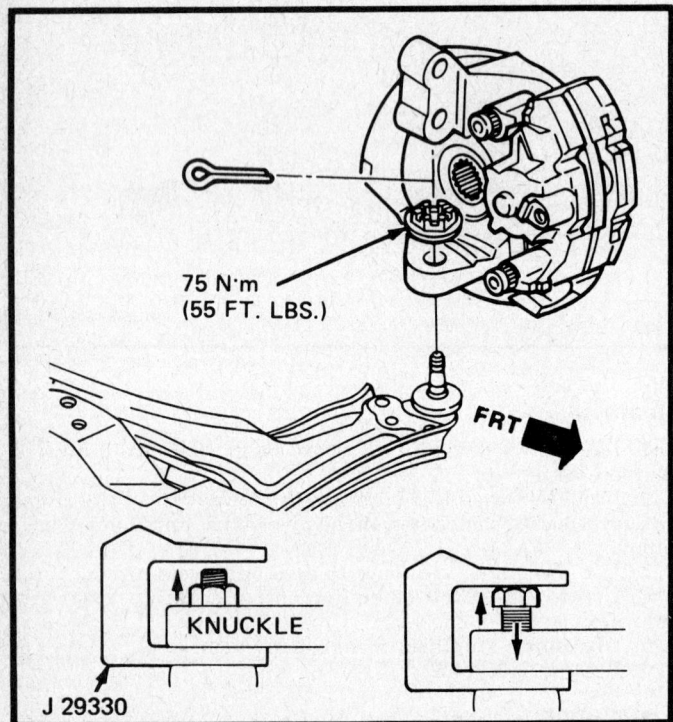

Place J29330 into position as shwon. Loosen nut and back off until the nut contacts the tool. Continue backing off the nut until the nut forces the ball stud out of the knuckle (© General Motors Corp.)

3. Install ball joint to knuckle.
4. Install wheel and tire.
5. Lower car. Check toe setting, adjust as required.

Hub and Bearing

Removal

NOTE: The car must not be moved while the driveshaft is out of the hub-and-bearing, nor until the hub nut is installed to final torque.

1. Loosen hub nut.
2. Raise car and support safely. Remove wheel and tire.
3. Install boot cover J–28712 or equivalent.
4. Remove hub nut.
5. Remove caliper and rotor.

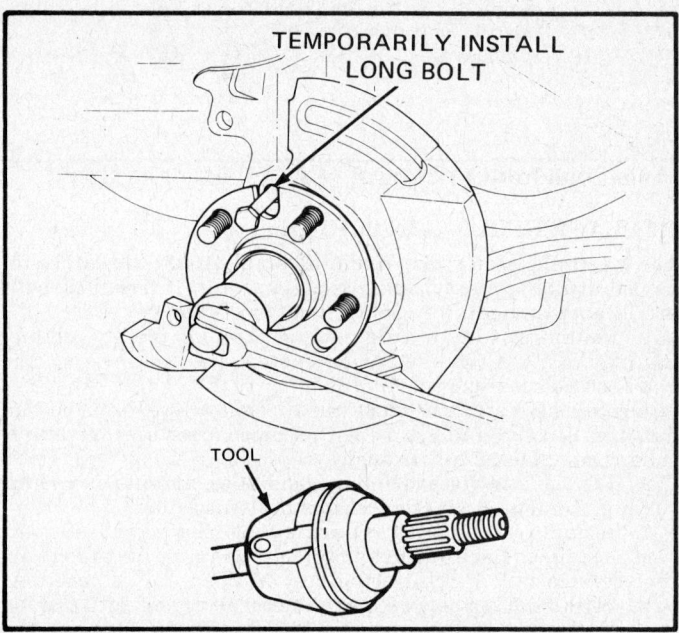

Installing drive axle cover (© General Motors Corp.)

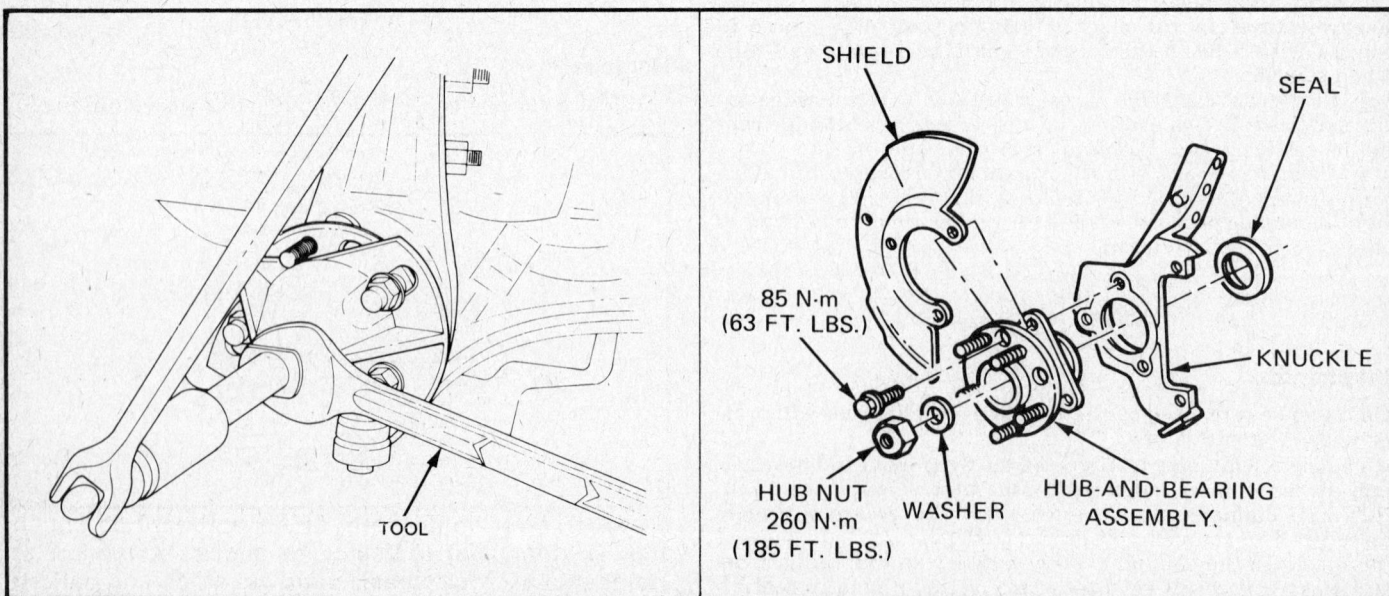

Hub and bearing assembly—removal and installation (© General Motors Corp.)

35-108

SUSPENSIONS

FRONT SUSPENSION—GM "J" BODY FRONT DRIVE CARS

6. Remove hub-and-bearing mounting bolts. Remove shield. If bearing assembly is to be re-used, mark attaching bolt and corresponding hole for installation in the same position.
7. Install tool J-28733 or equivalent, and turn bolt to press the hub-and-bearing assembly off of the drive shaft. If excessive corrosion is present, make sure the hub-and-bearing is loose in the knuckle before using the tool.
8. If installing a new bearing assembly, replace the steering knuckle seal, using tool J-22388.

Installation

1. Clean and inspect bearing mating surfaces and steering knuckle bore for dirt, nicks and burrs.
2. If installing knuckle seal, apply grease to seal and to bore of knuckle.
3. Replace parts in reverse order or removal. When attaching hub-and-bearing mounting bolts, use one long bolt to extend through cut-out. This will serve as a reaction point to allow enough torque on hub nut to seat axle shaft into bearing. After tightening hub nut to 70 ft. lbs. (100 Nm), remove long bolt and replace with normal bolt.
4. Lower car. Apply final torque to hub nut, 185 ft. lbs. (260 Nm).

Steering Knuckle

Removal

1. Raise vehicle and support safely. Remove wheel and tire.
2. Remove front wheel hub-and-bearing.
3. Disconnect ball joint from knuckle, using tool J-29330 or equivalent.

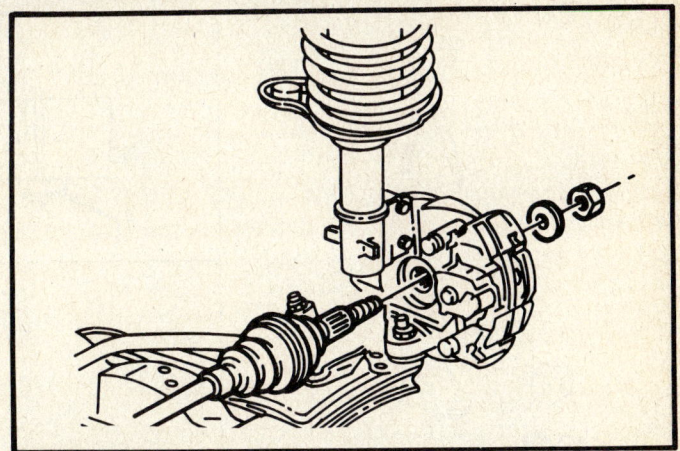

Removing axle stub from knuckle assembly (© General Motors Corp.)

4. Remove both strut-to-knuckle mounting bolts. Remove steering knuckle.

Installation

1. Install both strut-to-knuckle mounting bolts loosely.
2. Install knuckle to ball joint. Torque ball joint nut to 55 ft. lbs. (75 Nm). Install cotter pin.
3. Tighten mounting bolts to 140 ft. lbs. (200 Nm).
4. Install remaining components.

REAR SUSPENSION—GENERAL MOTORS J BODY CARS—FRONT WHEEL DRIVE

Description

This vehicle has a semi-independent rear suspension which consists of an axle with trailing arms and twisting cross beam, two coil springs, two shock absorbers, two upper spring insulators, and two spring compression bumpers. The axle assembly attaches to the underbody through a rubber bushing located at the front of each control arm. the brackets are integral with the underbody side rails. The axle structure itself maintains the geometrical relationship of the wheels relative to the body. A serviceable stabilizer bar is available as an option. It is attached to the inside of the axle beam and to the lower surface of the control arms as a subassembly of the axle.

The two coil springs support the weight of the car in the rear. Each spring is retained between a seat in the underbody and a seat welded to the top of the control arm. A rubber cushion is used to isolate the coil spring upper end from the underbody seat, while the lower end sits on a combination compression bumper and spring insulator.

The double-acting rear shock absorbers are filled with a calibrated amount of fluid, and sealed during production. They are non-adjustable, non-refillable, and cannot be disassembled. The only service the shock absorbers require is replacement if they have lost their resistance, are damaged, or are leaking fluid.

The lower ends of the shock absorbers are attached to the axle assembly, with bolts and paddle nuts. The upper ends are attached to the body in the wheelhouse area with conventional insulators, washers and nuts.

A single unit hub-and-bearing assembly is bolted to both ends of the rear axle assembly. This hub-and-bearing assembly is a sealed unit. The bearing is not replaceable as a separate unit.

Shock Absorber

Removal

CAUTION

Do not remove both shock absorbers at one time as suspending rear axle at full length could result in damage to brake lines and hoses.

1. Open deck lid, remove trim cover and remove upper shock attaching nut. Remove one shock at a time when both shocks are being replaced.
2. Raise vehicle on hoist and support rear axle assembly. When lifting vehicle with body hoist it will be necessary to support rear axle with adjustable jack stands. When lifting vehicle with suspension hoist care should be taken to align axle on the hoist prior to lifting.
3. Remove lower attaching bolt and nut and remove shock.

Installation

1. Install shock absorbers at lower attachment, feed bolt through holes and loosely install paddle nut.
2. Lower vehicle enough to guide upper stud through body opening and install nut loosely.
3. Torque lower bolt to 41 ft. lbs. (55 Nm).
4. Remove axle support and lower car all the way and torque upper nut. Torque to 13 ft. lbs. (17 Nm).

SECTION 35 SUSPENSIONS
REAR SUSPENSION—GM "J" BODY FRONT DRIVE CARS

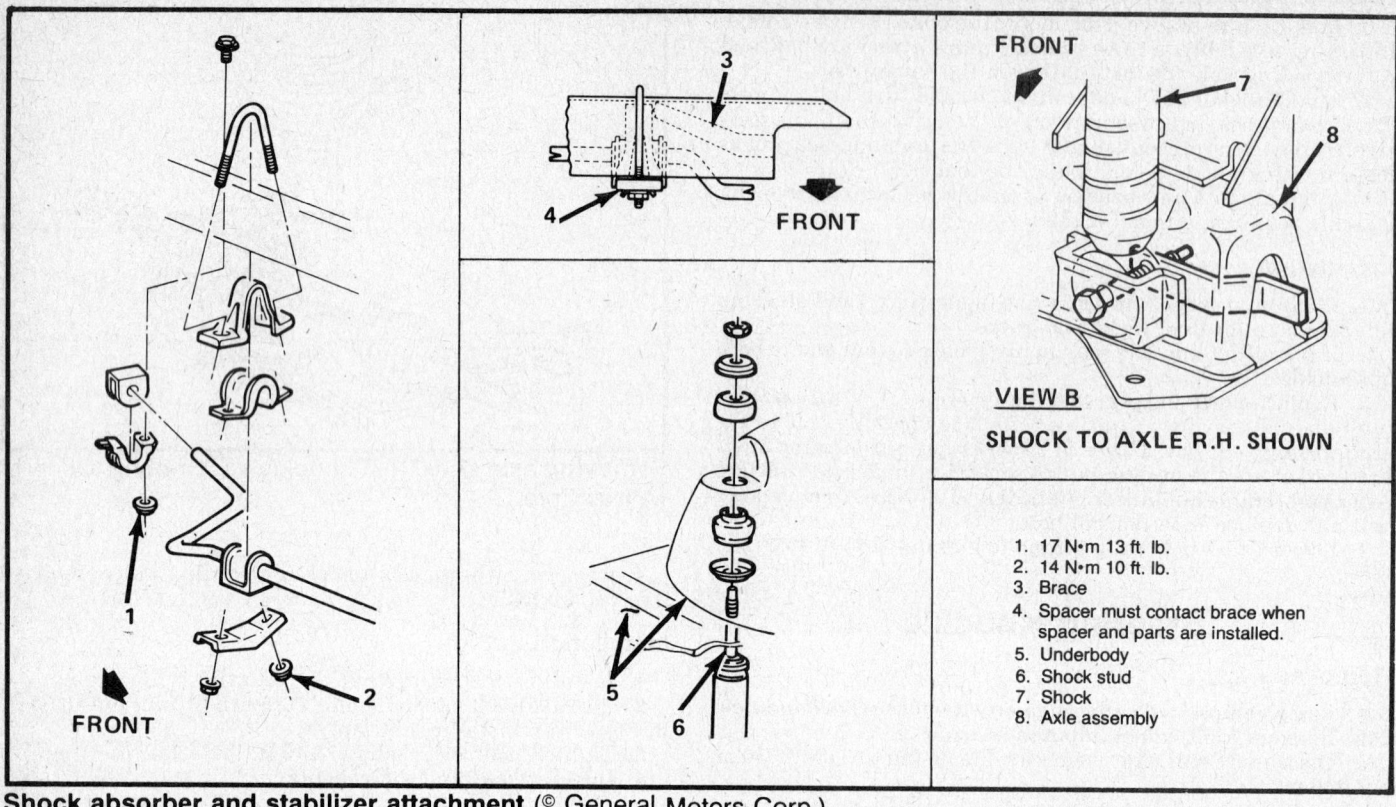

1. 17 N·m 13 ft. lb.
2. 14 N·m 10 ft. lb.
3. Brace
4. Spacer must contact brace when spacer and parts are installed.
5. Underbody
6. Shock stud
7. Shock
8. Axle assembly

Shock absorber and stabilizer attachment (© General Motors Corp.)

5. Replace rear trim cover.

Stabilizer Bar

Removal

1. Raise vehicle on hoist and support body with jack stands.
2. Remove nuts and bolts at both the axle and control arm attachments and remove bracket, insulator and stabilizer bar.

Installation

1. Install U-bolts, upper clamp, spacer and insulator and trailing axle. Position stabilizer bar in insulators and loosely install lower clamp and nuts.
2. Attach the end of stabilizer bar to control arms and torque all nuts to 13 ft. lbs. (17 Nm).
3. Torque axle attaching nut to 10 ft. lbs. (14 Nm).
4. Lower vehicle and remove from hoist.

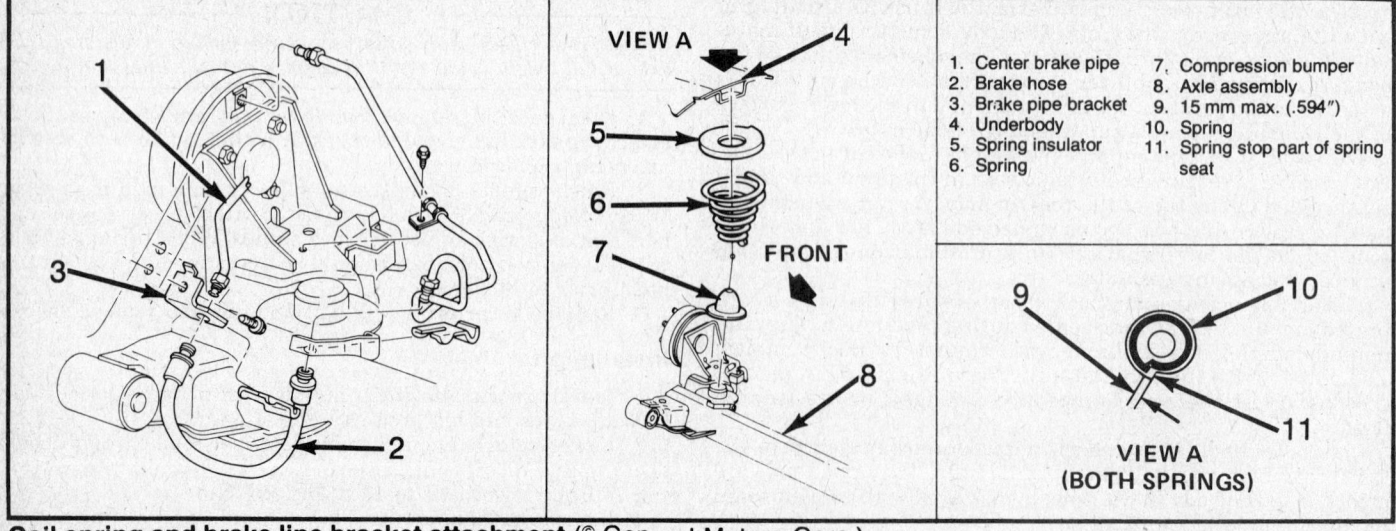

1. Center brake pipe
2. Brake hose
3. Brake pipe bracket
4. Underbody
5. Spring insulator
6. Spring
7. Compression bumper
8. Axle assembly
9. 15 mm max. (.594")
10. Spring
11. Spring stop part of spring seat

Coil spring and brake line bracket attachment (© General Motors Corp.)

35-110

SUSPENSIONS
REAR SUSPENSION—GM "J" BODY FRONT DRIVE CARS

Springs and Insulators

Removal

CAUTION

When removing rear springs do not use a twin-post hoist. The swing arc tendency of the rear axle assembly when certain fasteners are removed may cause it to slip from the hoist. Perform operation on floor if necessary.

---

1. Raise vehicle using frame contact type hoist if possible and support rear control arms with jack stands. If necessary to lift vehicle with twin post hoist, lift by tires and support the control arms or body with jack stands.
2. Remove wheel and tire assembly.
3. Remove right and left brake line bracket attaching screws from body and allow brake line to hang free.
4. Remove right and left shock absorber lower attaching bolts.

CAUTION

Do not suspend rear axle by brake hoses. Damage to hoses could result.

---

5. Lower rear axle and remove spring(s) and/or insulators(s).

Installation

1. Position springs and insulators in seats and raise axle. The ends of the upper coil on the spring must be positioned in the seat of the body. Prior to installing spring it will be necessary to install upper insulators to the body with adhesive to keep it in position while raising the axle assembly and springs.
2. Connect shocks to rear axle and torque bolts to 41 ft. lbs. (55 Nm). It will be necessary to bring the axle assembly to standing height prior to torquing bolts on the shocks.
3. Install brake line brackets to body and torque screws to 8 ft. lbs. (11 Nm).
4. Install wheel and tire assembly. Torque lug nuts to 102 ft. lbs. (140 Nm).
5. Remove jack stands and lower vehicle.

Control Arm Bushing

Removal

1. Raise vehicle on hoist.
2. Remove wheel and tire assembly and support body with jack stands.
3. If removing right bushing, disconnect brake line from body. If left bushing is being removed, disconnect brake line bracket from body, and parking brake cable from hook guide on the body. Replace only one bushing at a time.
4. Remove nut, bolt and washer from the control arm and bracket attachment, and rotate control arm downward.
5. Remove bushing as follows:
   a. Install J29376–1 or equivalent on control arm over bushing and tighten attaching nuts until tool is securely in place.
   b. Install J21474–19 bolt through plate J29376–7 and install into J29376–1 receiver.
   c. Place J29376–6 remover into position on bushing and install nut J21474–18 onto J21474–19 bolt.
   d. Remove bushing from control arm by turning bolt.

Installation

1. Install bushing on bolt and position onto housing. Align bushing installer J29376–4 arrow with arrow on receiver for proper indexing of bushing.
2. Install nut J21474–18 onto bolt J21474–19.
3. Press bushing into control arm by turning bolt. When bushing is in proper position the end flange will be flush against the face of the control arm.
4. Use a screw type jack stand to position control arm into bracket and install bolt and nut. Do not torque bolt at this time. It will be necessary to torque the bolt of the control arm with vehicle at standing height.
5. Install brake line bracket to frame and torque screw to 8 ft. lbs. (11 Nm).
6. If left side was disconnected, reconnect brake cables to bracket, and reinstall brake cable to hook. Adjust cable as necessary.
7. While supporting vehicle at standing height, tighten control arm bolt to 67 ft. lbs. (90 Nm).
8. Remove jack stands and install wheel assembly and lower vehicle from hoist.

Hub and Bearing

Removal

1. Raise vehicle on hoist.
2. Remove wheel and tire assembly and brake drum.

CAUTION

Do not hammer on brake drum as damage to the assembly could result.

---

3. Remove hub and bearing assembly-to-rear axle attaching bolts and remove hub and bearing assembly from axle. The top rear attaching bolt will not clear the brake shoe when removing the hub and bearing assembly. Partially remove hub and bearing assembly prior to removing this bolt.

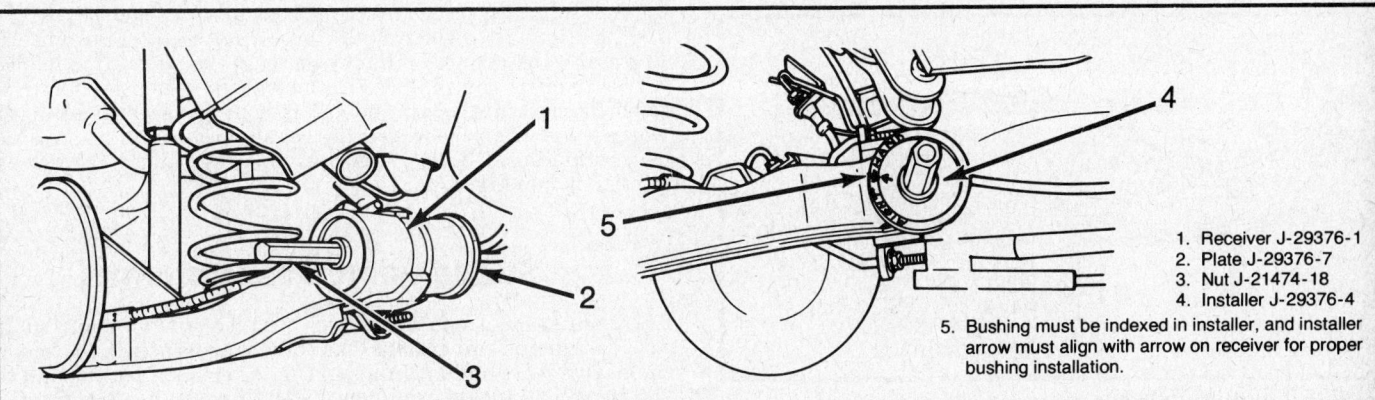

1. Receiver J-29376-1
2. Plate J-29376-7
3. Nut J-21474-18
4. Installer J-29376-4
5. Bushing must be indexed in installer, and installer arrow must align with arrow on receiver for proper bushing installation.

Control arm bushing installation (© General Motors Corp.)

SECTION 35 SUSPENSIONS
REAR SUSPENSION—GM "J" BODY FRONT DRIVE CARS

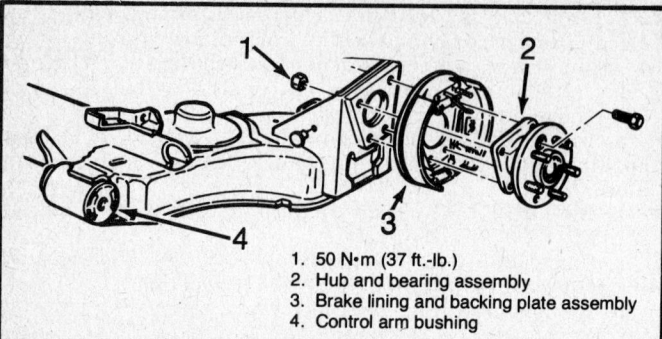

1. 50 N·m (37 ft.-lb.)
2. Hub and bearing assembly
3. Brake lining and backing plate assembly
4. Control arm bushing

Hub and bearing assmbly (© General Motors Corp.)

CAUTION
Do not hammer on brake drum as damage to the bearing could result.

4. Remove shock absorber lower attaching bolts and paddle nuts at axle and disconnect shocks from control arm.
5. Disconnect parking brake cable from the axle assembly.
6. To insure that axle assembly is not suspended by brake lines, disconnect brake line at the brackets from axle assembly.
7. Lower rear axle and remove coil springs and insulators.
8. Remove control arm bolts from underbody bracket and lower axle.
9. Remove hub attaching bolts and remove hub, bearing and packing plate assembly. Be careful not to drop hub and bearing assembly, as damage to the bearing could result.

Installation

1. Install backing plate, and hub-and-bearing assembly to rear axle. Hold nuts and torque bolts to 39 ft. lbs. (52 Nm).
2. Install stabilizer bar, if so equipped, by attaching nut and bolts to axle assembly and at the end to the control arms.
3. Place axle assembly on transmission jack and raise into position. Attach control arms to underbody bracket with bolts and nuts. Do not torque bolts at this time. It will be necessary to torque the bolt of the control arm at standing height.
4. Install brake line connections to axle assembly.
5. Attach brake cable to rear axle assembly.
6. Position coil springs and insulators in seats and raise rear axle. The end of upper coil on the springs must be parallel to axle assembly and seated in pocket.
7. Install shock absorber lower attachment bolts and paddle nuts to rear axle, torque bolt to 41 ft. lbs. (55 Nm).
8. Connect parking brake cable to guide hook and adjust as necessary.
9. Install brake drums, wheels and tire assembly. Torque lug nuts to 103 ft. lbs. (140 Nm).
10. Bleed brake system and refill reservoir.

Installation

1. Position top rear attaching bolt in hub-and-bearing assembly prior to the installation in the axle assembly.
2. Install remaining bolts and nuts. Torque bolts to 39 ft. lbs. (52 Nm).
3. Install brake drum, and wheel and tire assembly. Torque lug nuts to 103 ft. lbs. (140 Nm).
4. Lower vehicle and remove from hoist.

Rear Axle Assembly

Removal

1. Raise vehicle on hoist and support assembly with jack stands under the control arms.
2. Remove stabilizer bar from axle assembly, if so equipped.
3. Remove wheel and tire assembly and brake drum.

FRONT SUSPENSION—GENERAL MOTORS—P BODY CARS

Wheel Alignment

Caster Adjustment

Caster angle can be changed with a realignment of washers located between the legs of the upper control arm. For adjustment, a kit containing two washers, one of 3 mm thickness and one of 9 mm thickness, must be used. Install as shown to adjust caster. See Upper Control Arm Removal and Installation.

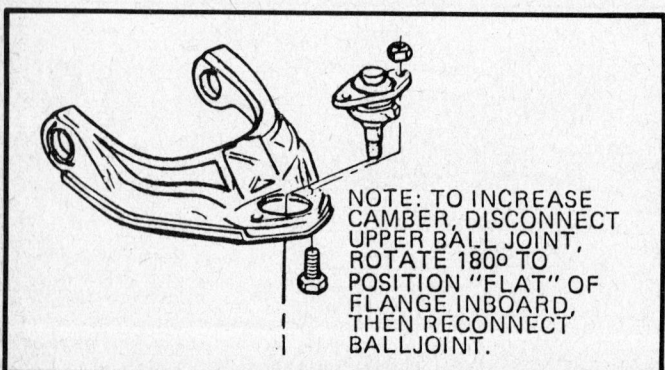

Upper ball joint/camber adjustment (© General Motors Corp.)

Camber Adjustment

Camber angle can be increased approximately 1° by removing the upper ball joint, rotating it one-half turn, and reinstalling it with the flat of the upper flange on the inboard side of the control arm.

Toe—In Adjustment

Toe-in is the turning in of the wheels. The actual amount of toe-in is normally only a fraction of a degree. The purpose of toe specifications is to ensure parallel rolling of the rear wheels. (Excessive toe-in or toe-out may increase tire wear). Toe-in also serves to offset the small deflections of the wheel support system which occurs when the car is rolling forward. In other words, even when the wheels are set slightly to toe-in when the car is standing still, they tend to roll parallel on the road when the car is moving.

Suspension Description

The front suspension system uses conventional long and short arm design and coil springs. the control arms attach to the vehicle with bolts and bushings at the inner pivot points, and to the steering knuckle/front wheel spindle assembly at the outer pivot points. Lower ball joints use the "wear indicator" feature.

SUSPENSIONS

FRONT SUSPENSION—GM "P" BODY REAR DRIVE CARS

Front Wheel Bearings

NOTE: Tapered roller bearings are used on all series vehicles and they have a slightly loose feel when properly adjusted. A design feature of front wheel tapered roller bearings is that they must never be preloaded. Damage can result from preloading.

Adjustment

1. Raise vehicle and support safely.
2. Remove wheel.
3. Remove dust cap from hub.
4. Remove cotter pin from spindle and spindle nut.
5. Tighten the spindle nut to 12 ft. lbs. (16 Nm) while turning the wheel assembly forward by hand to fully seat the bearings. This will remove any grease or burrs which could cause excessive wheel bearing play later.
6. Back off the nut to the "just loose" position.
7. Hand tighten the spindle nut. Loosen spindle nut until either hole in the spindle lines up with a slot in the nut. (Not more than $1/2$ flat.)
8. Install new cotter pin. Bend the ends of the cotter pin against nut, cut off extra length to ensure ends will not interfere with the dust cap.
9. Measure the looseness in the hub assembly. There will be from 0.001–0.005 in. (0.025–0.127 mm) end play when properly adjusted.
10. Install dust cap on hub.
11. Replace the wheel cover or hub cap.
12. Lower vehicle to floor.
13. Perform the same operation for each front wheel.

Ball Joints

Upper Ball Joint—Removal

1. Raise the vehicle on a hoist.
2. Remove the tire and wheel assembly.
3. Support the lower control arm with a floor jack.
4. Remove upper ball stud nut, then reinstall nut finger tight.
5. Install Tool J-26407 or equivalent with the cup end over the lower ball stud nut.
6. Turn the threaded end of tool until upper ball stud is free of steering knuckle.
7. Remove Tool and remove nut from ball stud.
8. Remove two nuts and bolts attaching ball joint to upper control arm. Note which way the flat of the ball joint is pointing before removing it. The direction of this flat on the ball

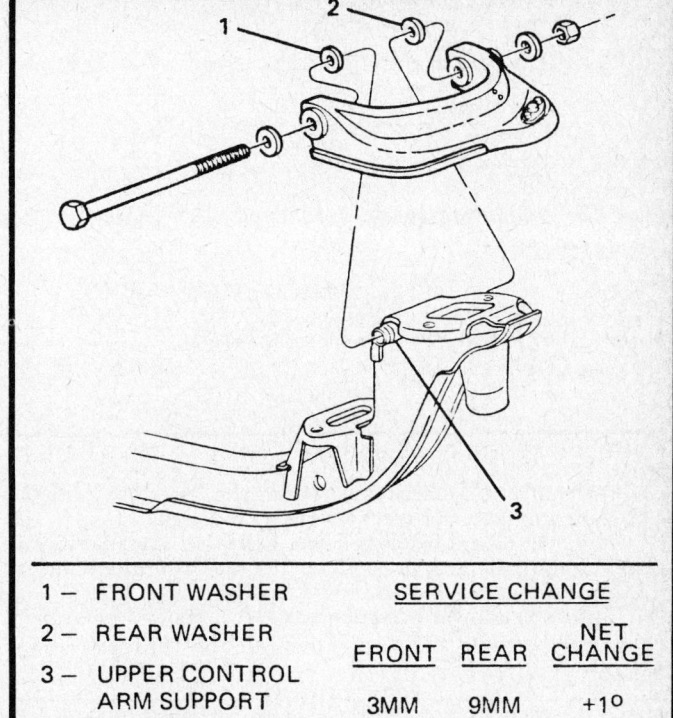

1 — FRONT WASHER
2 — REAR WASHER
3 — UPPER CONTROL ARM SUPPORT BRACKET

SERVICE CHANGE		
FRONT	REAR	NET CHANGE
3MM	9MM	+1°
9MM	3MM	–1°

Caster adjustment (© General Motors Corp.)

joint flange should be in the same direction as the one removed unless a change in camber is desired.

9. Remove ball joint.

Upper Ball Joint—Installation

Inspect the tapered hole in the steering knuckle. Remove any dirt and if any out-of-roundness, deformation, or damage is noted, the knuckle MUST be replaced.

1. Install bolt and nuts attaching ball joint to upper control arm and torque to 28 ft. lbs. (39 Nm), then mate the upper control arm ball stud to the steering knuckle.
2. Install the ball stud nut and torque to 35 ft. lbs. (47 Nm). Then turn $1/6$ of a turn to align cotter pin.
3. Install cotter pin.
4. Install the tire and wheel assembly.
5. Lower the vehicle to the floor.
6. Set toe.

Lower Ball Joint

Removal and Installation

The lower ball joint is welded to the lower control arm and cannot be serviced separately. Replacement of the entire lower control arm will be necessary if the lower ball joint requires replacement. See lower control arm removal.

Front Spring/Lower Control Arm

Removal

1. Raise vehicle on a hoist and support to vehicle on the crossmember.
2. Remove wheel and tire assembly.
3. Disconnect stabilizer bar from the lower control arm.
4. Disconnect the tie rod from the steering knuckle.

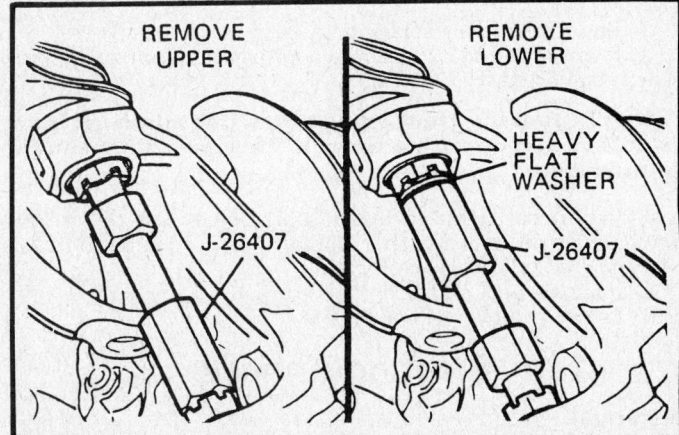

Removal of ball joints from knuckle (© General Motors Corp.)

35-113

SECTION 35 SUSPENSIONS
FRONT SUSPENSION—GM "P" BODY REAR DRIVE CARS

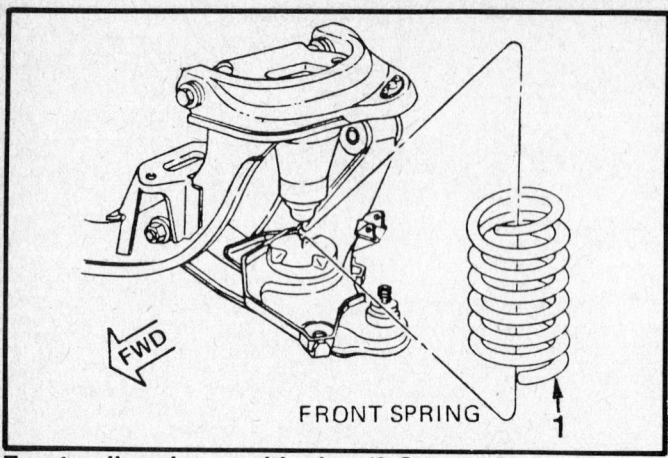

Front coil spring positioning (© General Motors Corp.)

5. Disconnect the shock absorber at the lower control arm.
6. Support the lower control arm with a jack.
7. Remove the nut from the lower ball joint, then use tool J–26407 or equivalent to press the ball joint out of the knuckle.
8. Swing the knuckle and hub out of the way.
9. Loosen the lower control arm pivot bolts.
10. Install a chain through the coil spring as a safety precaution.

CAUTION
The coil spring is under load and could result in personal injury if it were released too quickly. Be sure to install a chain and to slowly lower the jack.

---

11. Slowly lower the jack and remove the spring.
12. Remove the pivot bolts at the chassis and the crossmember and remove the lower control arm.

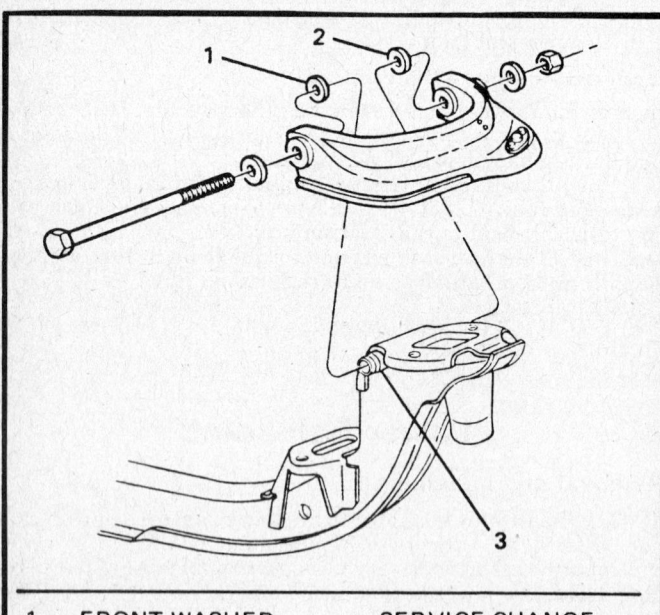

	SERVICE CHANGE		
1 – FRONT WASHER			NET
2 – REAR WASHER	FRONT	REAR	CHANGE
3 – UPPER CONTROL ARM SUPPORT BRACKET	3MM	9MM	+1°
	9MM	3MM	–1°

Front control arm shim arrangement (© General Motors Corp.)

13. Removal of the pivot bolt at the crossmember may require the loosening or removal of the steering assembly mounting bolts.

Installation

1. Install the lower control arm and pivot bolts at crossmember and body. Tighten slightly but do not torque.
2. Position the spring and install the spring into the upper pocket. Align spring bottom to lower control arm pocket.
3. Install spring lower end onto lower control arm. It may be necessary to have an assistant help you compress the spring far enough to slide it over the raised area of the lower control arm seat.
4. Use a jack to raise the lower control arm and compress the coil springs.
5. Install the ball joint through the lower control arm and into the steering knuckle. Install nut to ball joint stud and torque to 55 ft. lbs. (75 Nm). Install a new cotter pin.
6. Connect the stabilizer bar and torque the bolt to 16 ft. lbs. (22 Nm).
7. Connect the tie rod and torque to 29 ft. lbs. (39 Nm).
8. Install the shock absorber to the lower control arm and torque the bolt to 35 ft. lbs. (47 Nm).
9. If the bolts were removed or loosened at the steering assembly replace with new bolts and torque to 21 ft. lbs. (29 Nm).
10. With the suspension system in its normal standing height, torque the lower control arm to body bolt at 62 ft. lbs. (85 Nm) and the lower control arm to crossmember nut at 52 ft. lbs. (70 Nm).
11. Check and set alignment as necessary.

Upper Control Arm

Removal

1. Raise vehicle on a hoist.
2. Remove the tire and wheel assembly.
3. Remove rivet holding brake line clip to upper control arm.
4. Support the lower control arm with a floor jack.
5. Remove upper ball joint from steering knuckle, as described earlier.
6. Remove control arm pivot bolt and remove control arm from vehicle.
7. Transfer ball joint if not damaged or worn.

Installation

Washers and shims must be reinstalled as removed unless a change in geometry is desired.

1. Install upper control arm and pivot bolt to vehicle. The inner pivot bolt must be installed with the bolt head toward the front.
2. Install the pivot bolt nut.
3. Position the control arm in a horizontal plane and torque the nut to 66 ft. lbs. (90 Nm).

NOTE: Bolt may turn when torqued to minimum if nut is not backed up with a wrench. This does not mean the joint is loose.

4. Install ball joint to upper control arm and to steering knuckle, as described earlier. Install nut, torque to 35 ft. lbs. (47 Nm). Install a new cotter pin.
5. Install wheel and tire.
6. Lower vehicle to floor.

Steering Knuckle

Removal

1. Raise vehicle on a hoist and support the lower control arm with a jackstand.

SUSPENSIONS

FRONT SUSPENSION—GM "P" BODY REAR DRIVE CARS

CAUTION

This keeps the coil spring compressed. Use care to support adequately, or personal injury could result.

---

2. Remove the tire and wheel assembly.
3. Remove the disc brake caliper. Secure the caliper to the suspension using wire. Do not allow the caliper to hang by the brake hose. Insert a piece of wood between the shoes to hold the piston in the caliper bore. (The block of wood should be about the same thickness as the brake disc.).
4. Remove the hub and disc.
5. Remove the splash shield.
6. Remove both ball stud nuts (See Ball Joint Removal).
7. Remove the tie rod end from the steering knuckle.
8. Using Tool J–26407 or equivalent press the upper ball stud from the steering knuckle.
9. Reverse Tool to the other ball stud and press lower ball stud from the steering knuckle.
10. Remove ball stud nuts and remove the steering knuckle.

Installation

1. Place steering knuckle in position and insert the upper and lower ball studs into knuckle bosses.
2. Install ball stud nuts as tightened to specifications. For L.C.A., torque to 55 ft. lbs. (75 Nm). For U.C.A., torque to 35 ft. lbs. (47 Nm). Install new cotter pins.
3. Install splash shield to the steering knuckle. Torque to 7 ft. lbs. (10 Nm).
4. Install the tire rod end to the steering knuckle. Torque to 29 ft. lbs. (39 Nm), and install cotter pin.
5. Repack the wheel bearings, follow the Procedure as outlined above. Then install the hub and disc, bearings and nut. Torque to specifications as outlined above.
6. Install the brake caliper.
7. Install the tire wheel assembly.
8. Remove the jackstand and lower the vehicle to the floor.

REAR SUSPENSION—GENERAL MOTORS P BODY CARS

Suspension Description

The rear suspension is a MacPherson Strut design. This combination strut and shock adapts to the rear wheel drive. The lower control arms pivot from the engine cradle. The cradle has isolation mounts to the body and conventional rubber bushings are used for the lower control arm pivots. The upper end of the strut is isolated by a rubber mount.

Rear Wheel Camber

Adjustment

1. Position the vehicle on alignment equipment, and follow the manufacturers instructions to obtain a camber reading.
2. Use appropriate sockets and extensions to reach around both sides of the tire and LOOSEN both strut-to-knuckle bolts enough to allow movement between the strut and the knuckle. Remove the tools.
3. Grasp the top of the tire firmly, and move it inboard or outboard until the correct camber is obtained.
4. Again reach around the tire, as in Step 2, and tighten both bolts to 140 ft. lbs. (190 Nm).
5. If the accessibility to the bolts prevents applying complete torque, it will be necessary to apply only PARTIAL torque (just enough to hold the correct camber position), then to remove the wheel-and-tire in order to apply FINAL torque. After complete torquing, install the wheel-and-tire.
6. Repeat on other side.

Whenever adjusting casting, it is important to always use two washers totaling 12 mm thickness, with one washer at each end of locating tube.

Rear Wheel Bearings

Removal

STEEL WHEEL

1. Raise vehicle and remove wheel and tire.
2. Install drive axle boot protectors tool J–33162 or equivalent.
3. Remove hub nut, and discard.
4. Remove caliper and rotor.
5. Remove hub-and-bearing attaching bolts. If bearing assembly is being reused, mark attaching bolt and corresponding holes for installation.

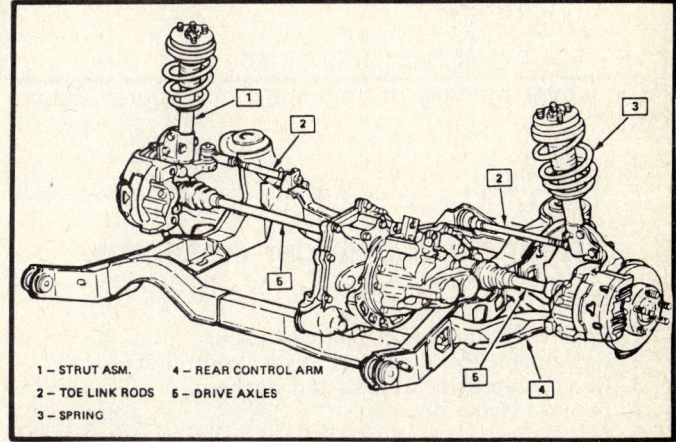

MacPherson strut design rear suspension (© General Motors Corp.)

1 – STRUT ASM. 4 – REAR CONTROL ARM
2 – TOE LINK RODS 5 – DRIVE AXLES
3 – SPRING

6. Install J–28733 or equivalent, and remove hub and bearing assembly. If excessive corrosion is present make sure hub-and-bearing is loose in knuckle before using tool.
7. If installing new bearing, replace knuckle seal. Car must be moved without hub nut installed to proper torque.

ALUMINUM WHEEL

1. Set parking brake.
2. Raise vehicle and support safely.
3. Remove wheel and tire assembly.
4. Remove hub nut.
5. Refer to steel wheel removal Step 2 through Step 7.

Installation

1. Clean and inspect bearing mating surfaces and knuckle bore for dirt, nicks and burrs.
2. If installing knuckle seal, use tool J–28671 or equivalent, apply grease to seal & knuckle bore.
3. Push hub-and-bearing on axle shaft.
4. Install parts as shown.
5. Apply PARTIAL torque to new hub nut, until hub-and-bearing assembly is seated 74 ft. lbs. (100 Nm).
6. Install rotor and caliper.

SECTION 35 SUSPENSIONS
REAR SUSPENSION—GM "P" BODY REAR DRIVE CARS

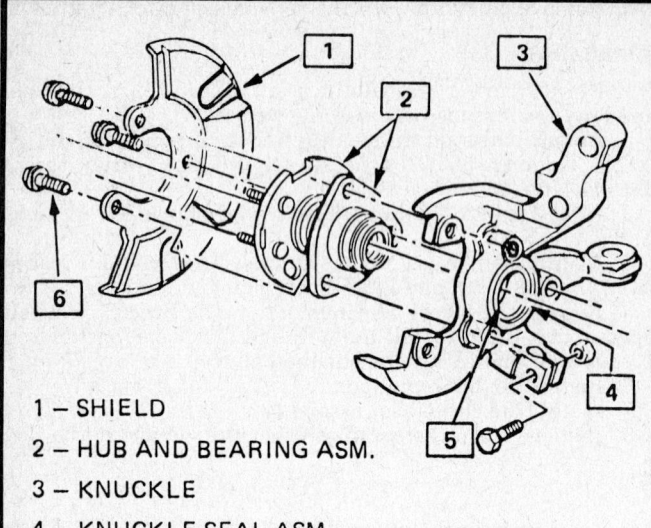

1 — SHIELD
2 — HUB AND BEARING ASM.
3 — KNUCKLE
4 — KNUCKLE SEAL ASM.
5 — FILL HUB BEARING CAVITY BETWEEN SEALING LIPS WITH .8 GRAMS OF CHASSIS LUBRICANT.
6 — BOLT 75-95 N·m (55-70 FT. LB.)

Rear wheel bearing arrangement (© General Motors Corp.)

7. Lower car.
8. Apply FINAL torque to hub nut. (200 ft. lbs. (270 Nm).

Rear Strut Damper Assembly

Removal

1. Remove the engine compartment lid.
2. Raise vehicle and support at rear control arm.
3. Remove upper strut nuts and washers.
4. Remove brake line clip.
5. Scribe mark strut and knuckle to assure proper assembly.
6. Remove strut mounting bolts and remove strut and spacer plate.

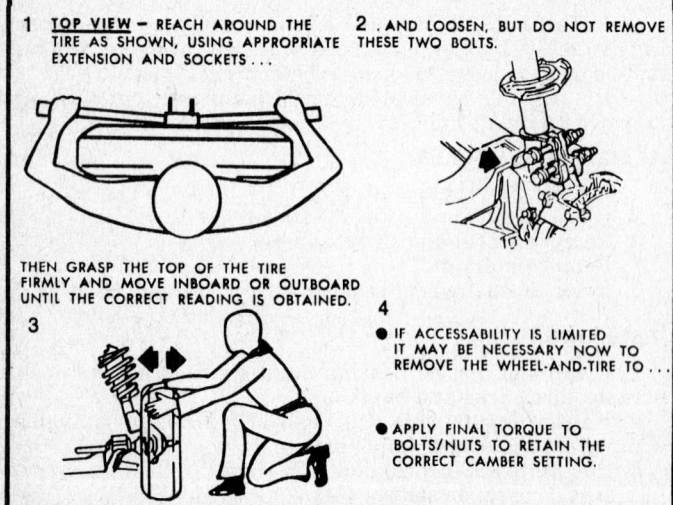

Rear wheel camber adjustment (© General Motors Corp.)

Installation

1. Set strut assembly and spacer plate into position and install mounting bolts and nuts.
2. Align scribe marks on strut and knuckle. Replace bolts in the same order in which they were removed.
3. Tighten knuckle nuts to 140 ft. lbs. (190 Nm).
4. Install brake line clip.
5. Lower vehicle and install upper strut nuts and washers. Tighten upper strut nuts to 18 ft. lbs. (24 Nm).
6. Install engine compartment lid.

Rear Strut Assembly/Spring Replacement

Disassembly

NOTE: Special tool J-26584 must be used to disassemble and assembly strut damper. Care must be used not to damage the special coating on the coil springs, or damage could occur to the coils.

1. Clamp J-26584 Strut Compressor in vise.
2. Place strut assembly in bottom adapter of compressor and install J-26584-89 (make sure adapter captures the strut and locating pins are engaged).
3. Rotate strut assembly to align top mounting assembly lip with strut compressor support notch.
4. Insert J-26584-430 top adapter on the top spring seal. Position top adapters so that the long stud is at high location to strut flange.
5. Using a ratchet with 1 in. socket, turn compressor forcing screw clockwise until top support flange contracts the J-26584-430 top adapter. Continue turning the screw compressing the strut spring.

SCRIBING PROCEDURE

1. USING A SHARP TOOL, SCRIBE THE KNUCKLE ALONG THE LOWER OUTBOARD STRUT RADIUS, AS IN VIEW A.
2. SCRIBE THE STRUT FLANGE ON THE INBOARD SIDE, ALONG THE CURVE OF THE KNUCKLE, AS IN VIEW B.
3. MAKE A CHISEL MARK ACROSS THE STRUT/KNUCKLE INTERFACE, AS IN VIEW C.
4. ON REASSEMBLY, CAREFULLY MATCH THE MARKS TO THE COMPONENTS.

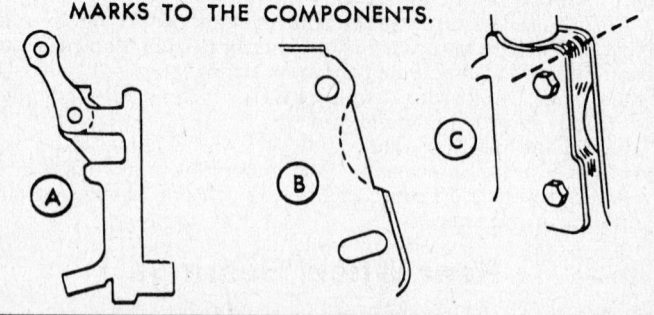

Strut and knuckle scribe marks (© General Motors Corp.)

6. Place J-26584-430 top adapter over spring seat assembly.
7. Turn strut compressor forcing screw counterclockwise until the strut spring tension is relieved. Remove top adapters, bottom adapter, then remove strut.

35-116

SUSPENSIONS
REAR SUSPENSION — GM "P" BODY REAR DRIVE CARS

Assembly

1. Clamp strut compressor body J–26584 in vise.
2. Place strut assembly in bottom adapter of compressor and install J–26584–89 (make sure adapter captures strut and locating pins are engaged).
3. Rotate strut assembly until mounting flange is facing out, directly opposite the compressor forcing screw.
4. Position spring and components on strut, as shown below. Make sure spring is properly seated on bottom spring plate.
5. Install strut spring seat assembly on top of spring. The long stud must be 180° from strut mounting flange.
6. Place J–26584–403 top adapter over spring seat assembly.
7. Turn compressor forcing screw until compressor top support just contacts top adapters (do not compress spring at ths time).
8. Install J–26584–27 Strut Alignment Rod through top spring seat and thread rod onto damper shaft, hand tight.
9. Compress spring by turning screw clockwise until enough of the damper shaft is exposed to where the nut can be threaded securely, and thread nut on damper shaft. DO NOT COMPRESS SPRING UNTIL IT BOTTOMS.

NOTE: Be sure that the damper shaft comes through the CENTER of the spring seat opening, or damage could occur.

10. Remove alignment rod, position strut mount over damper shaft and spring seat studs. Install washer and nut.
11. Turn forcing screw counterclockwise to back off support and remove strut assembly from compressor.

Control Arm Ball Joint

Removal

1. Raise car and remove wheel.
2. Remove clamp bolt from lower control arm ball stud.
3. Disconnect the ball joint from the knuckle. It may be necessary to tap the stud with a mallet.
4. Remove the rivets as shown.

Installation

1. Install ball joint to lower control arm.
2. Position knuckle over ball stud, to allow the clamp bolt to be installed. Torque to specs.
3. Install wheel and lower car.
4. Check toe-in setting. Adjust as required.

INSPECTION

BALL JOINT SEALS

Ball joint seals should be carefully inspected for cuts and tears. Whenever cuts or tears are found, the ball joint MUST be replaced.

KNUCKLE ASSEMBLY

Inspect the hole in the knuckle assembly clamp area. Remove any dirt. If out-of-roundness, deformation, or damage is noted, the knuckle MUST be replaced.

Lower Control Arm and/or Bushings

Removal

1. Raise car and remove wheel.
2. Remove ball joint clamping bolt.
3. Separate knuckle from ball joint.
4. Remove lower control arm pivot bolts at frame.
5. Remove control arm.

Installation

1. Install parts in reverse order of removal.
2. Install wheel; lower car.
3. Check toe-in and camber settings. Adjust as required.

Rear Knuckle

Removal

1. Refer to rear wheel bearing removal.
2. Remove toe-link rod at knuckle.
3. Remove clamp bolt. Disconnect knuckle from ball stud.

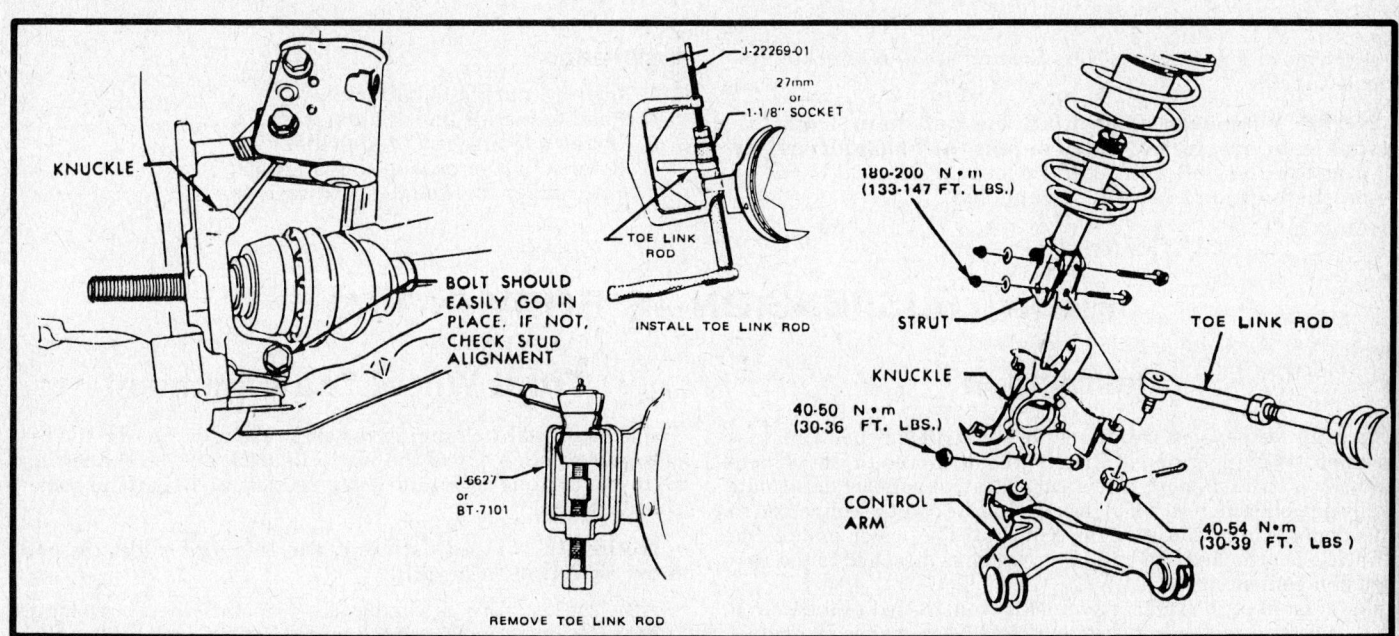

Remove/install rear knuckle assembly (© General Motors Corp.)

SECTION 35

SUSPENSIONS
REAR SUSPENSION—GM "P" BODY REAR DRIVE CARS

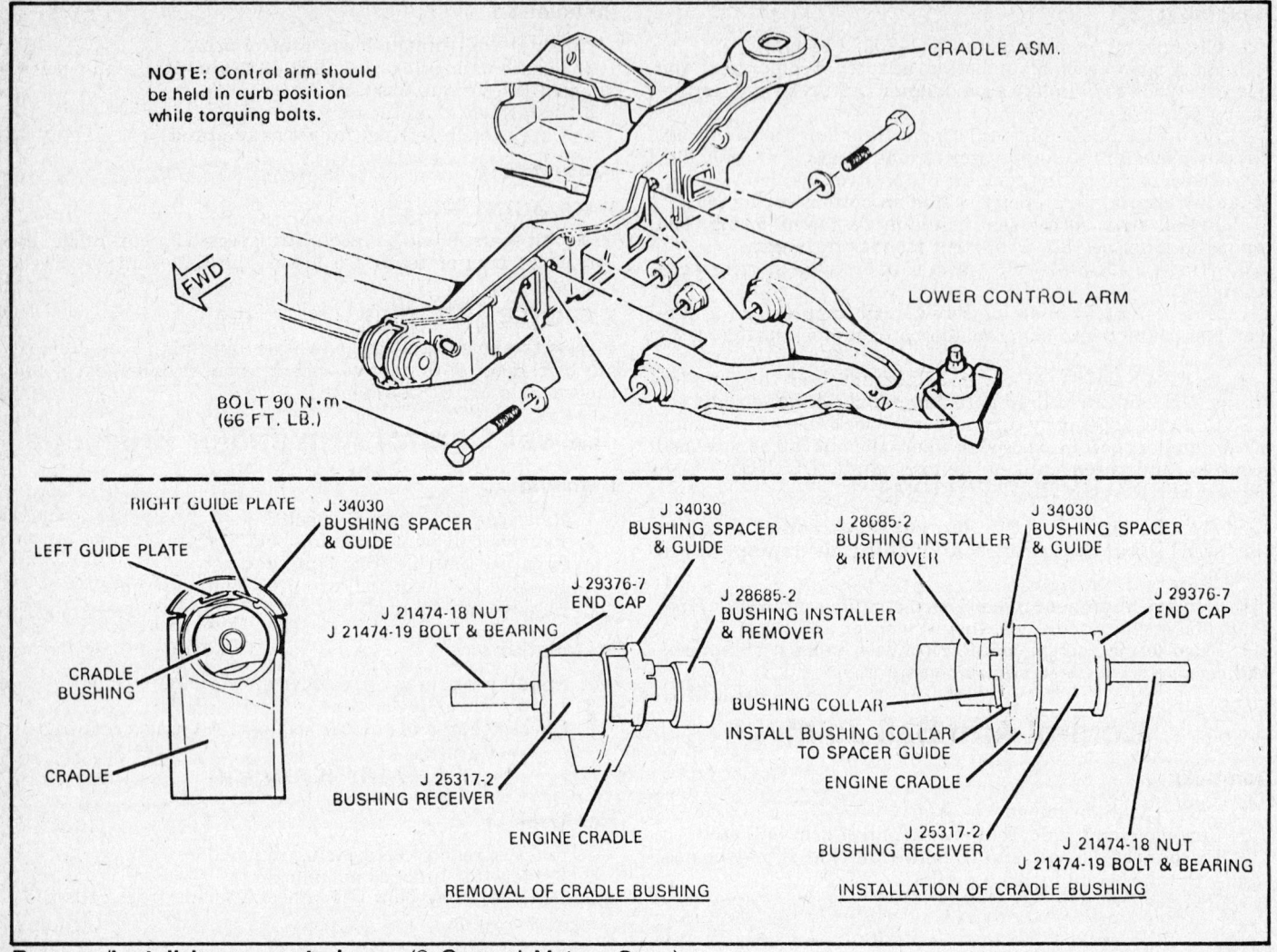

Remove/install lower control arm (© General Motors Corp.)

4. Remove bolt through bolts holding strut-to-knuckle. Remove knuckle.

NOTE: Whenever separating the ball joint from the knuckle, be careful not to cut or tear the ball joint seal, or damage to the ball joint could occur. If the seal is cut or torn, the ball joint MUST be replaced.

Installation

1. Install knuckle to ball joint.
2. Loosely install knuckle to strut.
3. Install toe-link rod to knuckle.
4. Refer to wheel bearing installation.
5. Set camber and toe to specifications.

FRONT SUSPENSION—S BODY (NOVA)

Description

The front suspension is a MacPherson strut independent suspension. The upper end of the strut is anchored to the vehicle body by a strut support. The strut and strut support are isolated by a rubber mount. The lower end of the strut is connected to the upper end of the steering knuckle. The lower end of the knuckle is attached to a ball joint, which is attached to the suspension control arm.

Movement of the steering wheel is transmitted to the tie rod end and then to the knuckle, which in turn moves the wheel and tire.

Front Wheel Toe Alignment

Toe is adjusted by changing the tie rod length. Loosen the boot clamps and slide out of the working area. Loosen the left and right tie rod end locknuts. Turn the left and right tie rods to specification.

NOTE: In this adjustment, the left and right tie rods must be equal in length.

After adjustment is completed, reinstall the boot clamps, tighten the nuts and check to insure that the rack boots are not twisted.

SUSPENSIONS
FRONT SUSPENSION—GM "S" BODY FRONT DRIVE CARS (NOVA)

Front Camber And Caster Adjustment

Camber is adjusted by loosening the upper and lower strut to knuckle bolts and nuts, then rotate the cam to the correct specification. After adjustment is completed, tighten the nuts and bolts to specification.

Caster is not adjustable. If the caster is found to be out of specification, inspect the vehicle for loose, bent or otherwise worn suspension components. Replace as necessary.

NOTE: In order to prevent an incorrect reading of camber or caster, jounce the vehicle three times before inspection.

FRONT STRUT ASSEMBLY

Removal and Installation

1. Disconnect the negative battery cable. Remove the strut to body attaching nuts.
2. Raise the vehicle and support safely. Remove the wheel and tire assembly. Loosen the axle shaft nut if the knuckle is to be removed.
3. Remove the brake hose clip at the strut bracket. Disconnect the brake flex hose at the brake pipe. Remove the brake hose clips.
4. Pull the brake hose through the opening in the strut bracket. Tape the end of the brake hose to prevent dirt contamination.
5. Remove the two brake caliper mounting bracket bolts and remove the caliper. Support the caliper so it will not hang by the brake hose. Do not disconnect the brake hose from the caliper.
6. Mark the adjusting cam and remove both strut to knuckle attaching bolts.
7. Remove the strut assembly from the vehicle. Remove the camber adjusting cam from the knuckle.
8. Inspect components for signs of wear, cracks or distortion. Replace as necessary.
9. Installation is the reverse of the removal procedure. Before installing any removed dust covers, pack all areas with grease. Bleed the brake system. Check wheel alignment and correct as required.

CONTROL ARM

Removal and Installation

1. Disconnect the negative battery cable. Raise the vehicle and support safely.
2. Remove the lower control arm to steering knuckle attaching bolts and nuts. Remove the control arm and inspect the arm and bushing for distortion or cracking. Repair or replace as needed.
3. To remove the rear lower control arm bushing, remove the nut retainer and bushing. Torque the bushing nut to 76 ft. lbs.
4. Installation is the reverse of the removal procedure. Always replace self locking nuts with new ones. Check wheel alignment and adjust if necessary.

LOWER BALL JOINT

Removal and Installation

1. Disconnect the negative battery cable. Raise the vehicle and support safely. Remove the wheel and tire assembly.
2. Using tool J-35413 or equivalent, separate the ball joint from the knuckle.
3. Remove the two nuts and bolts attaching the ball joint and control arm.

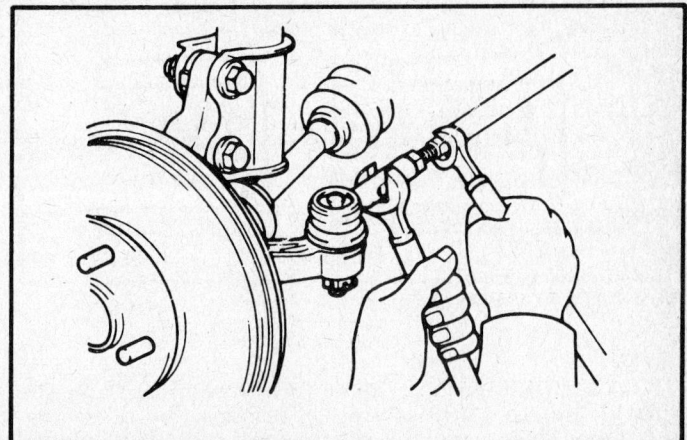
Front toe adjustment-Nova

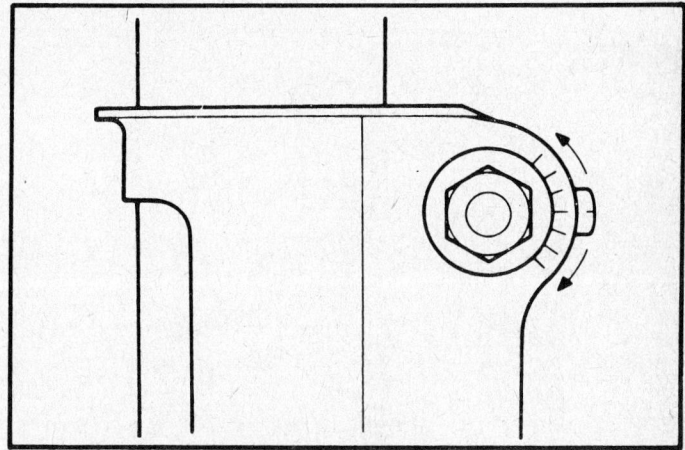
Front camber adjustment-Nova

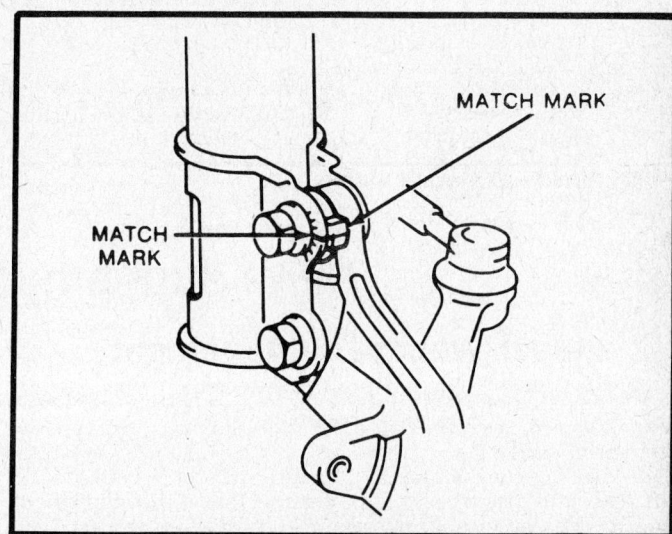
Camber marking for reinstallation

4. Remove the ball joint. Inspect the ball joint for excessive wear or damage to the boot seal.
5. Installation is the reverse of the removal procedure. Torque the knuckle to ball joint nut to 82 ft. lbs. (111 Nm). Torque the control arm attaching nuts to 47 ft. lbs. (64 Nm).

SECTION 35 SUSPENSIONS
FRONT SUSPENSION—GM "S" BODY FRONT DRIVE CARS (NOVA)

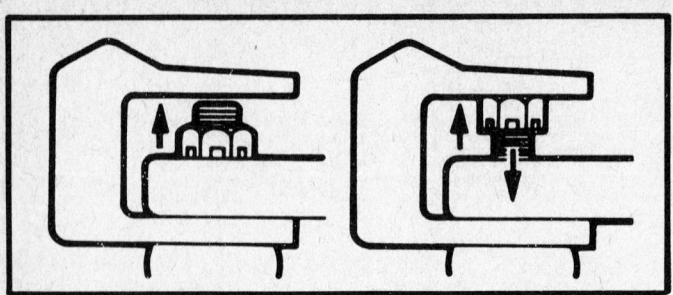
Ball joint removal

NOTE: Do not remove the hub assembly from the knuckle unless it is absolutely necessary. Should removal become necessary, the grease seals must be replaced with new ones.

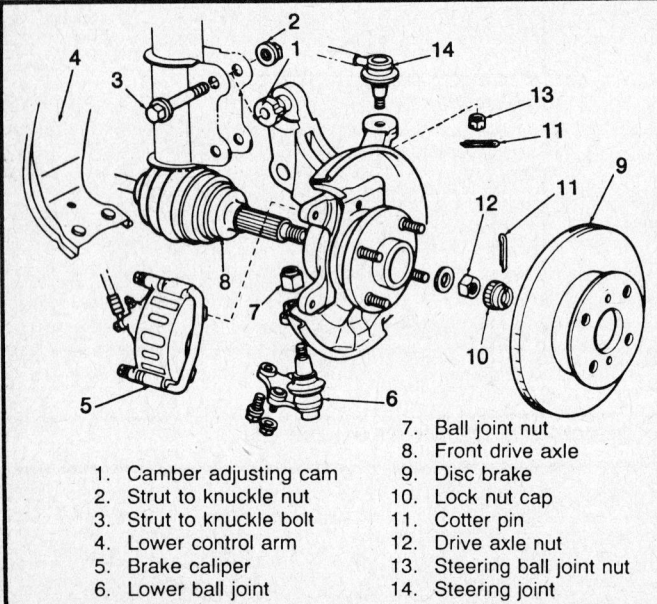

1. Camber adjusting cam
2. Strut to knuckle nut
3. Strut to knuckle bolt
4. Lower control arm
5. Brake caliper
6. Lower ball joint
7. Ball joint nut
8. Front drive axle
9. Disc brake
10. Lock nut cap
11. Cotter pin
12. Drive axle nut
13. Steering ball joint nut
14. Steering joint

Hub/knuckle-exploded view

— CAUTION —
Never reuse a self locking nut. Always replace a self locking nut with a new one.

KNUCKLE ASSEMBLY

Removal

1. Disconnect the negative battery cable. Raise the vehicle and support safely. Remove the tire and wheel assembly.
2. Remove the brake hose retaining clip at the strut. Disconnect the flex hose from the brake pipe.
3. Remove the caliper bracket to knuckle mounting bolts. Support the caliper. Remove the disc.
4. Remove the drive axle nut.
5. Using tool J–25287 or equivalent, push out the drive axle.
6. Remove the cotter pin. Remove the tie rod to knuckle attaching nut. Separate the tie rod using tool J–24319–01 or equivalent.
7. Remove the ball joint to control arm attaching nuts and bolts.
8. Matchmark the camber relationship and remove the strut to knuckle attaching bolts and nuts. Remove the knuckle.

Installation

1. Install the lower ball joint to the lower control arm. Torque the nuts and bolts to 47 ft. lbs. (64 Nm).
2. Install the ball joint to knuckle. Torque the nut to 14 ft. lbs. (20 Nm) and remove the nut. Install a NEW nut and torque to 82 ft. lbs. (111 Nm).
3. Install the camber adjusting cam to knuckle. Connect the steering knuckle to the strut lower bracket. Insert the bolts from the rear to the front and align the matchmarks of the camber adjusting cam and strut. Torque to 105 ft. lbs. (142 Nm).
4. Install the tie rod to knuckle attaching nuts. Torque to 38 ft. lbs. (56 Nm). Install the cotter pin.
5. Torque the lower control arm to ball joint to 47 ft. lbs. (64 Nm). Install the brake caliper. Torque to 65 ft. lbs. (88 Nm).
6. Install the brake hose connector to the brake pipe. Install the wheel and tire assembly. Lower vehicle.
7. Apply grease to the axle shaft threads. Install the attaching nut. Torque to 137 ft. lbs. (186 Nm). Install the cotter pin and cap.
8. Bleed the brake system. Check wheel alignment and adjust if necessary. Always install a new grease seal and self locking nut.

REAR SUSPENSION—P BODY (NOVA)

Rear Wheel Toe Alignment

Toe is adjusted by rotating the cam located on the rear lower control arm. Loosen the bolt and rotate the nut to get the correct specification.

1. Measure the distance and find the difference between the left and right disc wheels and the centerline of the adjustment cam. If the distance is not within specification, inspect each component for damage or excessive wear.
2. Turn each cam an equal amount in the opposite direction. The toe will change approximately 2 mm for each turn of the cam.

Rear Camber and Caster Adjustment

Caster and camber cannot be adjusted. Should the camber setting be found to be out of adjustment, inspect the suspension parts for damage or wear.

NOTE: In order to prevent incorrect readings of the camber setting, jounce the vehicle three times before inspection.

REAR STRUT ASSEMBLY

Removal and Installation

1. Disconnect the negative battery cable.
2. Working inside the vehicle, remove the shock absorber cover and package tray bracket.
3. Raise the vehicle and support safely. Remove the rear wheel and tire assemblies.
4. Disconnect the brake line at the wheel cylinder and plug it.

SUSPENSIONS
REAR SUSPENSION—GM "S" BODY FRONT DRIVE CARS (NOVA)

5. Disconnect the flexible hose from the shock absorber.
6. Remove the retaining bolts holding the strut to the axle carrier. Disconnect the strut.
7. Remove the three upper strut mounting nuts and remove the strut assembly.
8. Installation is the reverse of the removal procedure. Bleed the brake system.

SUSPENSION ARM (REAR)

Removal and Installation

1. Raise the vehicle and support safely.
2. Remove the bolt and nut holding the rear suspension arm to the axle carrier.
3. Remove the cam and bolt holding the rear suspension arm to the body. Remove the suspension arm.
4. Installation is the reverse of the removal procedure.

NOTE: Remember where the cam plate mark is before disassembly.

SUSPENSION ARM (FRONT)

Removal and Installation

1. Raise the vehicle and support safely.
2. Remove the bolt and nut holding the front suspension arm to the axle carrier.
3. Remove the bolt and nut holding the front suspension arm to the body. Remove the front suspension arm.
4. Installation is the reverse of the removal procedure. Lower vehicle and check rear wheel alignment.

STRUT ROD

Removal and Installation

1. Raise vehicle and support safely.
2. Remove the strut rod to axle carrier retaining nut.
3. Remove the strut rod to body retaining nut. Remove the strut rod.
4. Installation is the reverse of the removal procedure.

REAR AXLE HUB

Removal and Installation

1. Raise the vehicle and support safely.
2. Remove the tire and wheel assembly.
3. Remove the brake drum and wire out of the way.
4. Remove the four bolts which hold the axle hub assembly to the axle carrier.
5. Remove the axle/hub bearing assembly. Remove the "O" ring.
6. Installation is the reverse of the removal procedure.

REAR AXLE CARRIER

Removal and Installation

1. Raise the vehicle and support safely.
2. Remove the rear axle hub as outlined above.
3. Disconnect the brake line from the wheel cylinder and plug the line.

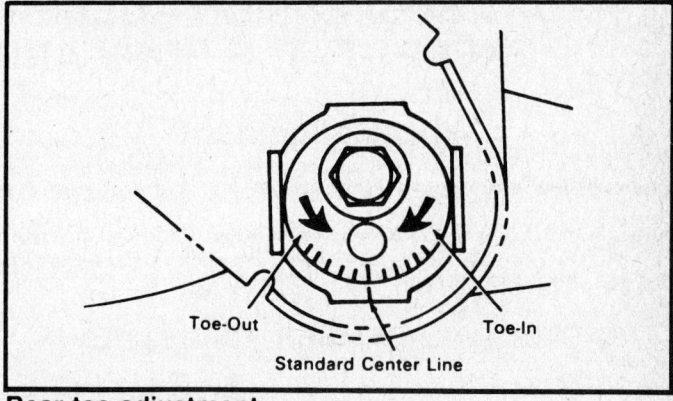

Rear toe adjustment

4. Remove the axle carrier to strut rod retaining nut. Remove the axle carrier to front suspension and rear suspension arm retaining nuts.
5. Remove the bolts and nuts holding the axle carrier to the strut. Remove the axle carrier.
6. Installation is the reverse of the removal procedure. Bleed the brake system and check rear wheel alignment. Adjust as necessary.

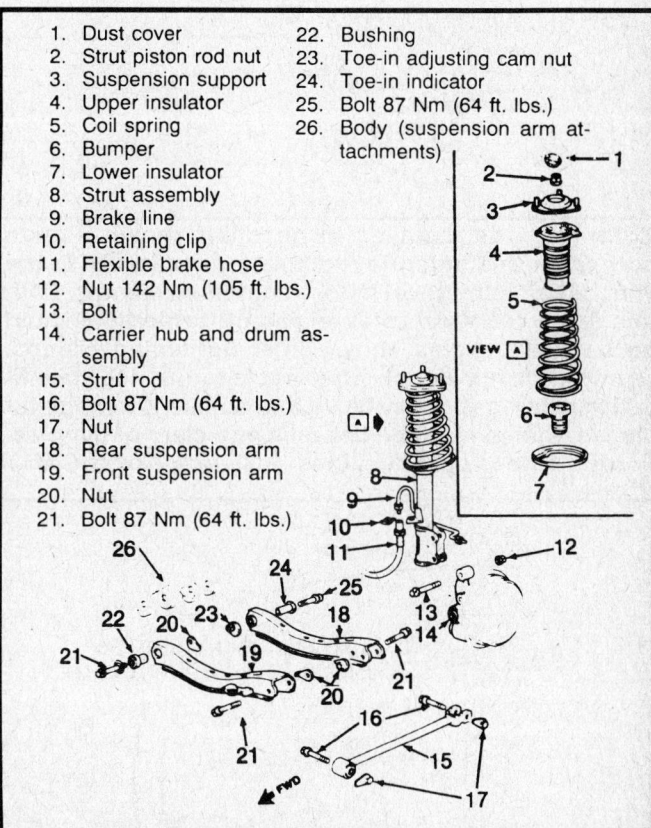

1. Dust cover
2. Strut piston rod nut
3. Suspension support
4. Upper insulator
5. Coil spring
6. Bumper
7. Lower insulator
8. Strut assembly
9. Brake line
10. Retaining clip
11. Flexible brake hose
12. Nut 142 Nm (105 ft. lbs.)
13. Bolt
14. Carrier hub and drum assembly
15. Strut rod
16. Bolt 87 Nm (64 ft. lbs.)
17. Nut
18. Rear suspension arm
19. Front suspension arm
20. Nut
21. Bolt 87 Nm (64 ft. lbs.)
22. Bushing
23. Toe-in adjusting cam nut
24. Toe-in indicator
25. Bolt 87 Nm (64 ft. lbs.)
26. Body (suspension arm attachments)

Rear suspension-exploded view

SECTION 35 SUSPENSIONS
FRONT SUSPENSION—GM EXC. "F, T & P" BODY AND CORVETTE (1984 AND LATER)

FRONT SUSPENSION—GENERAL MOTORS REAR DRIVE CARS—EXCEPT F, T, P BODY AND 1984 AND LATER CORVETTE

Wheel Alignment

Front wheel alignment factors are caster, camber, toe-in, toe-out, and trim height. Before any corrections are made, the car must be on a level surface with a full gas tank and the front seat to the rear. All doors must be closed with no passengers or excess weight in the car.

CASTER AND CAMBER ADJUSTMENTS

To adjust caster and camber, loosen the upper control arm shaft-to-frame nuts, add or subtract shims as required, and retorque nuts.

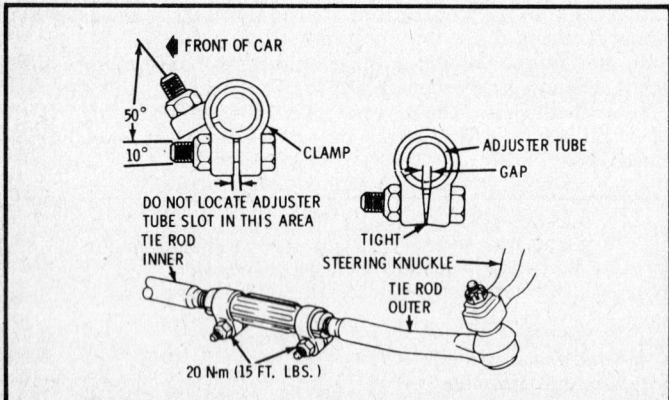

Bolts must be installed in direction shown. Rotate both inner and outer tie rod housings rearward to the limit of ball joint travel before tightening clamps. With this same rearward rotation all bolt centerlines must be between angles shown after tightening clamps. Clamp ends may touch when nut is torqued to specifications, but gap must be visible adjacent to adjuster sleeve. Clamp must be between and clear of dimples. Torque nuts to specifications (© General Motors Corp.)

A normal shim pack will leave at least two threads of the bolt exposed beyond the nut. The difference between front and rear shim packs must not exceed 40 inches.

If these requirements cannot be met in order to reach specifications, check for damaged control arms and related parts. Always tighten the nut on the thinner shim pack first, for improved shaft-to frame clamping force and torque retention.

TOE—IN ADJUSTMENT

Toe-in can be increased or decreased by changing the length of the tie-rods. A threaded sleeve is provided for this purpose.

When the tie-rods are mounted ahead of the steering knuckle, they must be decreased in length in order to increase toe-in.

Loosen the clamp bolts at each end of the steering tie rod adjustable sleeves. With steering wheel set in straight ahead position, turn tie rod adjusting sleeves to obtain proper toe-in adjustment.

NOTE: Before locking clamp bolts on the rods, make sure that the tie rod ends are in alignment with their ball studs by rotating both tie rod ends in the same direction as far as they will go. Then tighten adjuster tube clamps to specified torque. Make certain that adjuster tubes and clamps are positioned correctly.

TOE—OUT

Toe-out on turns refers to the difference in angles between the front wheels and the car frame during turns. Toe-out on turns is non-adjustable.

TRIM HEIGHT ADJUSTMENT

When checking trim height, the car should be parked on a level surface, full tank of gas, front seat rearward, doors closed and the tire pressure as specified.

If there is more than 1 in. (24 mm) difference side to side at the wheel well opening, corrective measures should be taken to make the car level.
1. Check tire sizes.
2. Check tire wear.

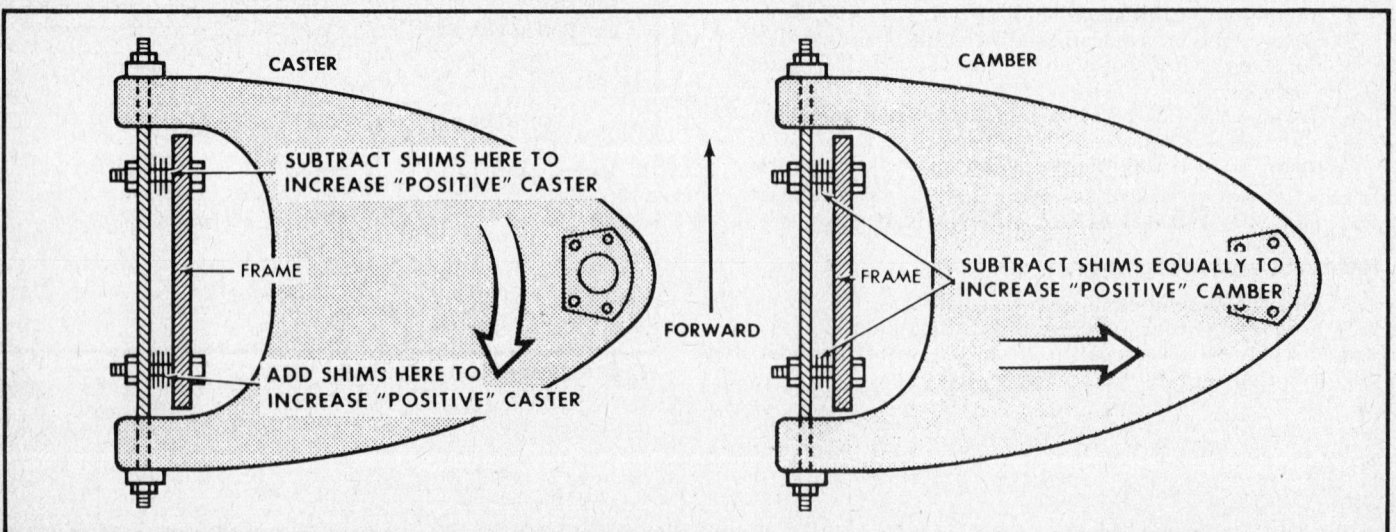

Caster and camber adjustment (© General Motors Corp.)

SUSPENSIONS

FRONT SUSPENSION—GM EXC. "F, T & P" BODY AND CORVETTE (1984 AND LATER)

3. Check coil spring height.
4. Check for worn suspension parts.

Wheel Bearings

For normal use, clean and repack front wheel bearings with a high melting point wheel bearing lubricant at each front brake lining replacement or 30,000 miles (48,000 km), whichever comes first. For heavy duty application such as police cars and taxi cabs, clean and repack front wheel bearings at each front brake lining replacement or 15,000 miles (24,000 km) whichever comes first.

"Long fiber" or "viscous" type lubricants should not be used. Do not mix wheel bearing lubricants. Be sure to thoroughly clean bearings and hubs of all old lubricant before repacking.

NOTE: Tapered roller bearings used in these cars have a slightly loose feel when properly adjusted. They must never be over-tightened (pre-loaded) or severe bearing damage may result.

Adjustment

The proper functioning of the front suspension cannot be maintained unless the front wheel taper roller bearings are correctly adjusted. Cones must be a slip fit on the spindle and the inside diameter of cones should be lubricated to insure that the cones will creep. Spindle nut must be a free running fit on threads.
1. Remove dust cap from hub.
2. Remove cotter pin from spindle and spindle nut.
3. Tighten the spindle nut to 12 ft. lbs. (16 Nm) while turning the wheel assembly forward by hand to fully seat the bearings. This will remove any grease or burrs which could cause excessive wheel bearing play later.
4. Back off the nut to the "just loose" position.
5. Hand-tighten the spindle nut. Loosen spindle nut until either hole in the spindle lines up with a slot in the nut (not more than ½ flat).
6. Install new cotter pin. Bend the ends of the cotter pin against nut. Cut off extra length to ensure ends will not interfere with the dust cap.
7. Measure the looseness in the hub assembly. There will be from 0.001–0.005 in. (0.03–0.13mm) end-play when properly adjusted.
8. Install dust cap on hub.

Shock Absorbers

Removal

1. Raise car on hoist and with an open end wrench hold the shock absorber upper stem from turning. Remove the upper stem retaining nut, retainer and rubber grommet.
2. Remove the two bolts retaining the lower shock absorber pivot to the lower control arm and pull the shock absorber assembly out from the bottom.

Installation

1. With the lower retainer and rubber grommet in place over the stem, install the shock absorber (fully extended) up through the lower control arm and spring so that the upper stem passes through the mounting hole in the upper control arm frame bracket.
2. Install the upper rubber grommet, retainer and attaching nut over the shock absorber upper stem.
3. With an open end wrench, hold the upper stem from turning and tighten the retaining nut.
4. Install the retainers attaching the shock absorber lower pivot to the lower control arm, torque and lower car to floor.

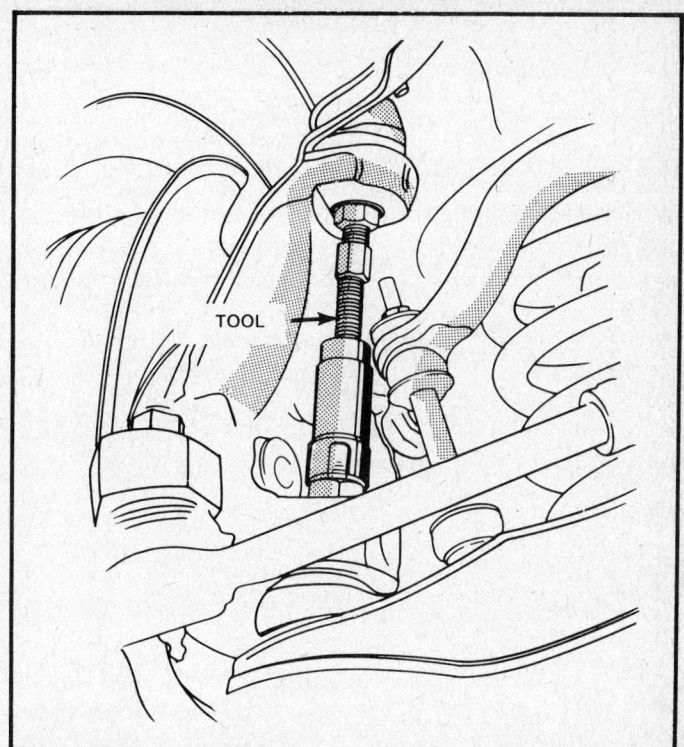

Disconnecting upper ball joint (© General Motors Corp.)

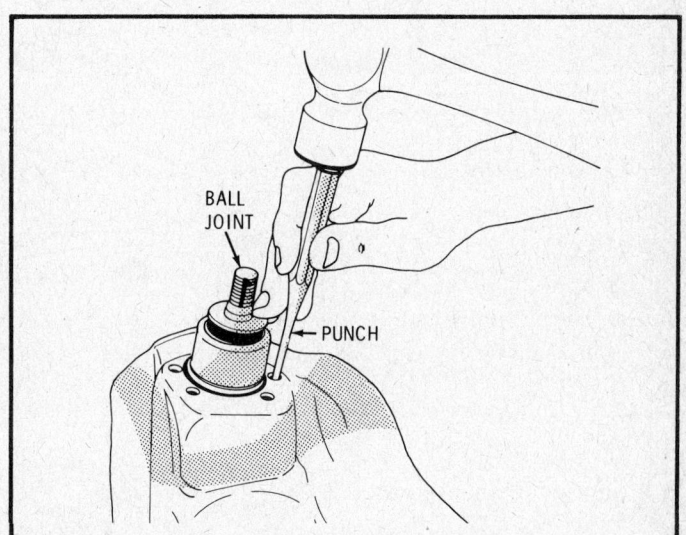

Upper ball joint removal (© General Motors Corp.)

Upper Ball Joint

Inspection

1. Raise the car and position floor stands under the left and right lower control arm as near as possible to each lower ball joint. Car must be stable and should not rock on the floor stands. Upper control arm bumper must not contact frame.
2. Position dial indicator against the wheel rim.
3. Grasp front wheel and push in on bottom of tire while pulling out at the top. Read gauge, then reverse the push-pull

35-123

SECTION 35 SUSPENSIONS
FRONT SUSPENSION—GM EXC. "F, T & P" BODY AND CORVETTE (1984 AND LATER)

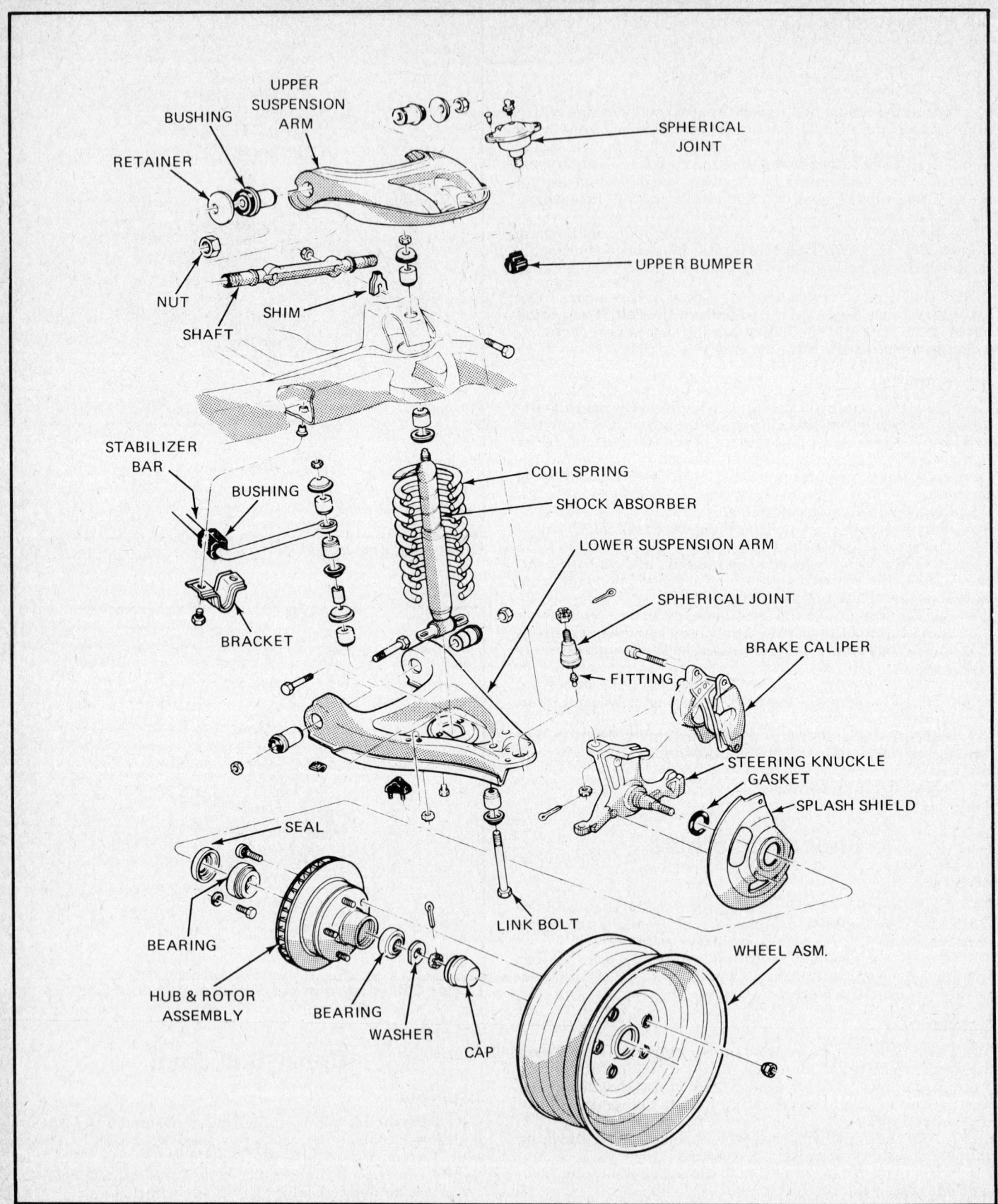

Front suspension (© General Motors Corp.)

SUSPENSIONS

FRONT SUSPENSION—GM EXC. "F, T & P" BODY AND CORVETTE (1984 AND LATER)

procedure. Horizontal deflection on dial indicator should not exceed 1.25 in. (3.18 mm).

4. If dial indicator reading exceeds 0.125 in. (3.18 mm), or if ball stud has been disconnected from knuckle assembly and any looseness is detected, or the stud can be twisted in its socket with your fingers, replace ball joint.

Removal

1. Raise front of car and support lower control arm with floor stands.

CAUTION

Floor jack or stand must remain under control arm spring seat during removal and installation to retain spring and control arm in position.

Since the weight of the car is used to relieve spring tension on the upper control arm, the floor stands must be positioned between the spring seats and ball joints of the lower control arms for maximum leverage.

2. Remove wheel, then loosen the upper ball joint from the steering knuckle as follows:
   a. Remove upper ball joint nut and install push tool.
   b. Apply pressure on stud by expanding the tool until the stud breaks loose.
3. Remove tool and upper ball joint nut, then pull stud from knuckle. Support the knuckle assembly to prevent weight of the assembly from damaging the brake hose.
4. With control arm in the raised position, drill four rivets ¼ in. deep using a ⅛ in. diameter drill.
5. Drill off rivet heads using a ½ in. diameter drill.
6. Punch out rivets using a small punch, and remove ball joint.

Installation

1. Position new ball joint in control arm and install four attaching bolts. Torque nuts to 8 ft. lbs. (11 Nm).
2. Connect ball joint to steering knuckle. Torque nut to 30 ft. lbs. (40 Nm).

Lower Ball Joint

Inspection

Car must be supported by the wheel so weight of car will properly load the ball joints.

The lower ball joint is inspected for wear by visual observation alone. Wear is indicated by protrusion of the ½ in. (12.7 mm) diameter nipple into which the grease fitting is threaded. This round nipple projects 0.050 in. (1.27 mm) beyond the surface of the ball joint cover on a new, unworn joint. Normal wear will result in the surface of this nipple retreating slowly inward.

To inspect for wear, wipe grease fitting and nipple free of dirt and grease as for a grease job. Observe or scrape a scale, screwdriver or fingernail across the cover. If the round nipple is flush or inside the cover surface, replace the ball joint.

Removal

1. Raise the car, support with floor stands under frame.
2. Remove tire and wheel assembly.
3. Place floor jack under control arm spring seat.

CAUTION

Floor jack must remain under control arm spring seat during removal and installation to retain spring and control arm in position.

---

4. To disconnect the lower control arm ball joint from the steering knuckle. Remove the cotter pin from ball joint stud and remove stud nut. Tool J–8806 can be used to break the ball joint loose from knuckle after stud breaks loose.

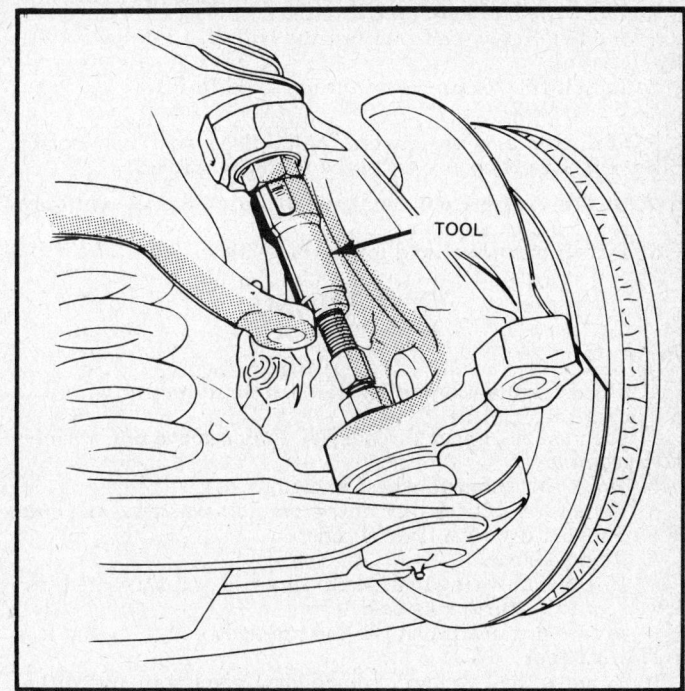

Disconnecting lower ball joint (© General Motors Corp.)

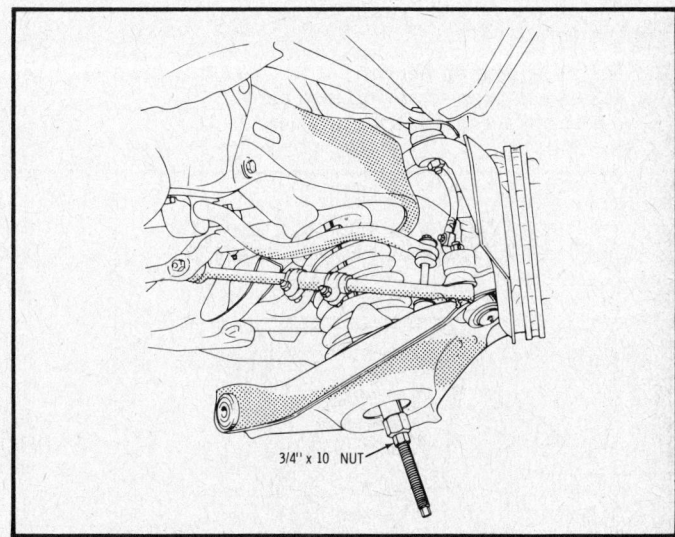

Compressed coil spring (© General Motors Corp.)

5. Guide lower control arm out of opening in splash shield with a putty knife or similar tool.
6. Block knuckle assembly out of the way by placing a wooden block between frame and upper control arm.
7. Remove ball joint seal by prying off retainer with a pry bar or driving off with a chisel.
8. Remove grease fittings and install special tool to remove lower ball joint from lower control arm.

Installation

1. Position the lower ball joint into the lower control arm and with special press tools, press the ball joint in until it bottoms in the control arm.

NOTE: The grease purge on the seal must be located facing inboard.

35–125

SECTION 35

SUSPENSIONS
FRONT SUSPENSION—GM EXC. "F, T & P" BODY AND CORVETTE (1984 AND LATER)

2. Place the ball joint stud into the bottom hole of the steering knuckle. Force stud into tapered hole to a torque of 40 ft. lbs. (55 Nm).
3. Install the stud nut and torque to 90 ft. lbs. (120 Nm).

NOTE: Some replacement ball joints will use cotter pins. Be sure they are in place when required.

4. Install the grease fitting and lubricate the ball joint until the grease appears at the seal.
5. Install the wheel and lower the vehicle.

Coil Spring

Removal

1. Place transmission in neutral so steering wheel is unlocked.
2. Clean shock upper threads; oil, then remove nut, washer, and grommet.
3. Hoist car. Remove wheel and tire.
4. Remove stabilizer link nut, grommets washers, and bolt.
5. Support car with floor stands.
6. Remove shock.
7. Install coil spring tool. Make sure tool is fully seated into lower control arm spring seat.
8. Rotate nut until spring is compressed enough so that it is free in its seat.
9. Remove the two lower control arm pivot bolts and disengage lower control arm from frame. Rotate arm with spring rearward and remove spring from arm.

Installation

1. Install spring on bench.
2. Insert compressed spring into place.
3. Twist spring into proper position.

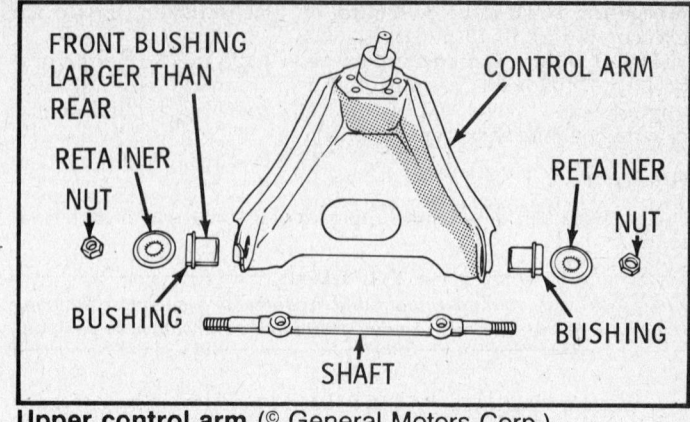

Upper control arm (© General Motors Corp.)

4. Carefully lift lower control arm and attach the lower control arm pivot bolts. Tighten nuts to 90 ft. lbs. (120 Nm).

Upper Control Arm

Removal

1. Raise front of car and support lower control arm with floor stands.

CAUTION

Floor jack must remain under control arm spring seat during removal and installation to retain spring and control arm in position.

NOTE: Since the weight of the car is used to relieve spring tension on the upper control arm, the floor stands must be positioned between the spring seats and ball joints of the lower control arms for maximum leverage.

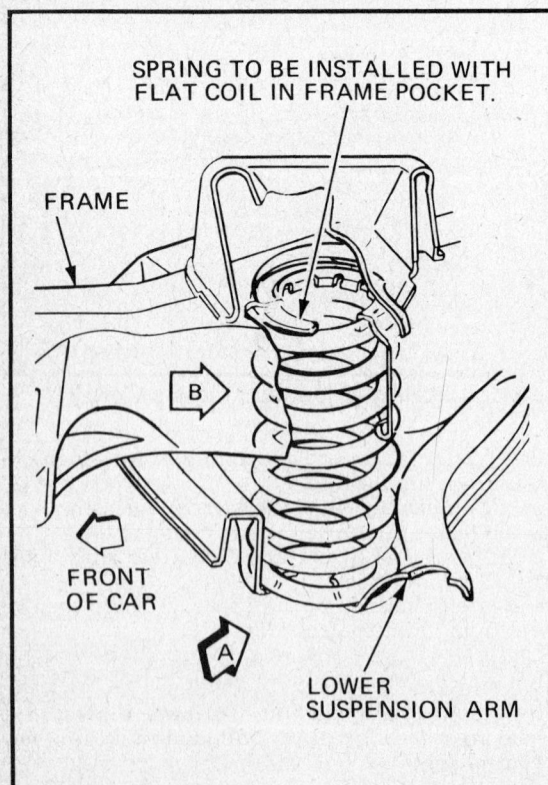

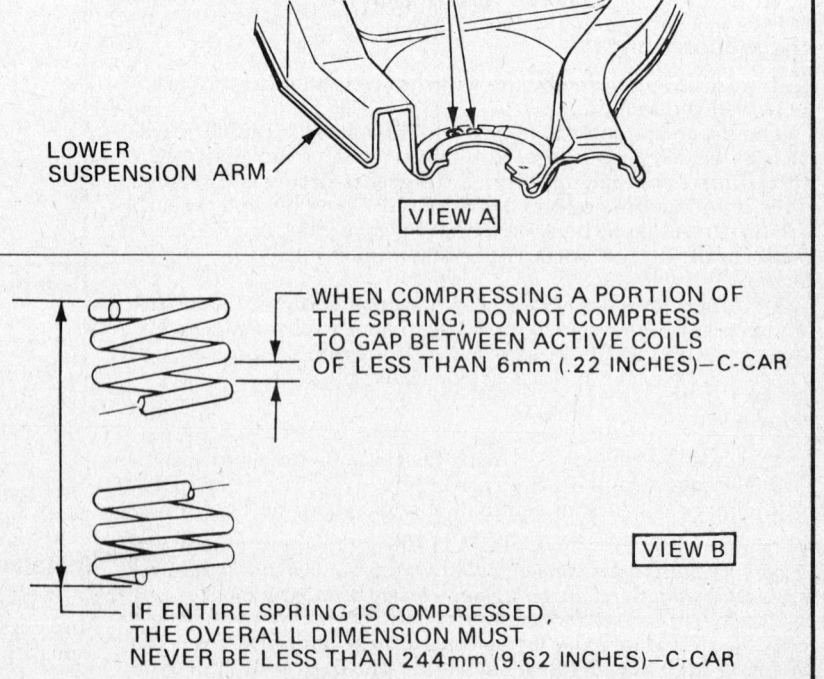

Coil spring positioning (© General Motors Corp.)

35-126

SUSPENSIONS

FRONT SUSPENSION—GM EXC. "F, T & P" BODY AND CORVETTE (1984 AND LATER)

2. Remove wheel, then loosen the upper ball joint from the steering knuckle as follows:
   a. Remove the upper ball joint nut.
   b. Apply pressure on stud by expanding the tool until the stud breaks loose.
3. Remove tool and upper ball joint nut, then pull stud free from knuckle. Support the knuckle assembly to prevent weight of the assembly from damaging the brake hose.
4. Remove the upper control arm attaching bolts to allow clearance to remove upper control arm assembly.
5. Remove upper control arm from the car.

PIVOT SHAFT BUSHING REPLACEMENT

1. Remove upper control arm assembly from the car.
2. Remove nuts from ends of pivot shaft.
3. Position control arm assembly and tools and push bushing out of control arm.
4. To install bushings, place pivot shaft in control arm and push new bushing into control arm and over end of pivot.

Installation

1. Position the upper control arm attaching bolts loosely in the frame and install the pivot shaft on the attaching bolts.
2. Install the inner pivot bolt with the heads to the front on the front bushing and to the rear on the rear bushing.
3. Install the alignment shims between the pivot shaft and frame on their respective bolts. Torque the nuts to 73 ft. lbs. on the B models and 45 ft. lbs. on the rear drive A body models.
4. Remove the temporary support from the hub assembly and connect the ball joint to the steering knuckle.
5. Install the wheel, check front end alignment and adjust as required.

Lower Control Arm

Removal

1. Place transmission in neutral so steering wheel is unlocked.
2. Clean chock upper threads; oil, then remove nut, bolt, washer and grommet.
3. Hoist car. Remove wheel and tire.
4. Remove stabilizer link nut, grommets washers, and bolt.
5. Support car with floor stands and lower hoist. Remove shock.
6. Loosen the lower ball joint nut and use tool J-8806 or equivalent. Apply pressure on stud by expanding the tool until the stud breaks loose.
7. Install spring compressor in through front spring. Compress spring until all tension is off lower control arm.
8. Remove pivot bolts and ball joint.
9. Remove complete control arm.

Installation

1. Install the ball joint stud into the lower hole of the steering knuckle. Install the nut loosely.
2. Position the spring on the lower arm and safety chain it to the lower arm to prevent personal injury.
3. Position a jack under the rear of the arm and raise the arm rear pivot bushings into position on the crossmember brackets. Install the pivot bolts.
4. Remove the jack and safety chain. Lower the vehicle to the ground and torque the bolts as noted in the front spring removal and installation section.

LOWER CONTROL ARM BUSHINGS

Removal and Installation

The removal and installation of the lower control arm bushings require the use of a press tool. A flare is found on the bushings

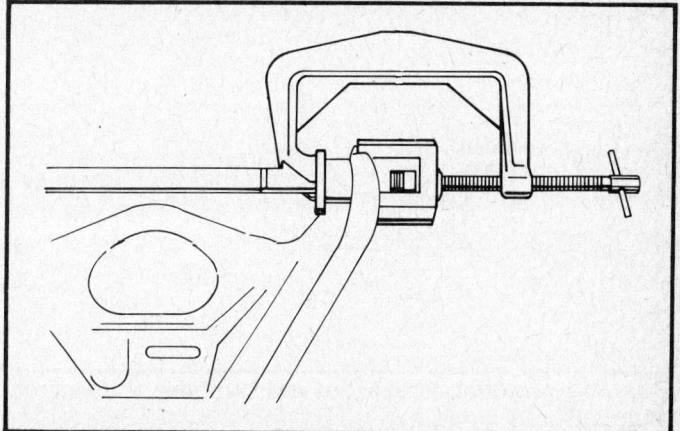

Upper control arm bushing removal (© General Motors Corp.)

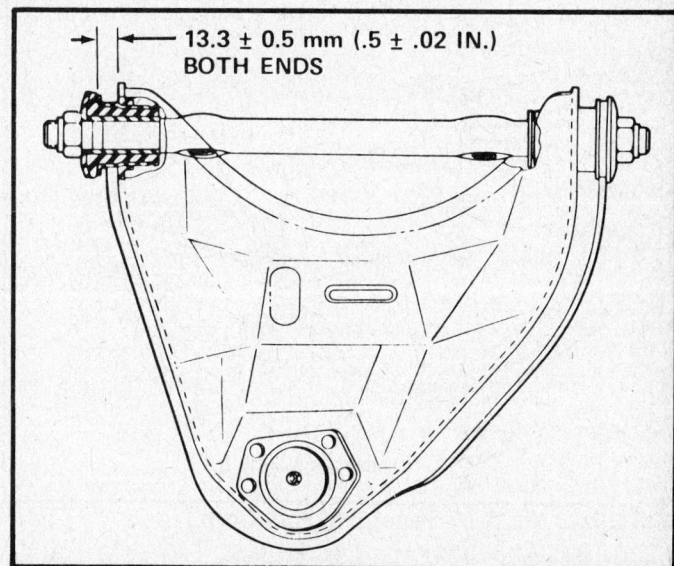

Upper control arm pivot shaft bushing installation clearance (© General Motors Corp.)

used except with the rear wheel drive A models. When the bushings are installed and the flare is required, the tool must be capable of flaring the metal flange on the bushing to its proper angle.

Steering Knuckle

It is recommended that the car be raised and supported so that the front coil spring remains compressed, yet the wheel and steering knuckle assembly remain accessible. If a frame hoist is used, support the lower suspension arm with an adjustable jack stand to retain spring in the curb height position.

Removal

1. Raise car on hoist and support lower suspension arm.
2. Remove wheel and tire assembly.
3. Remove tie-rod end from steering knuckle.
4. Remove brake caliper and hub and rotor assembly. Use a piece of wire to attach caliper to upper suspension arm.

NOTE: **Never allow caliper to hang from brake hose, as hose may be damaged.**

SECTION 35

SUSPENSIONS
FRONT SUSPENSION—GM EXC. "F, T & P" BODY AND CORVETTE (1984 AND LATER)

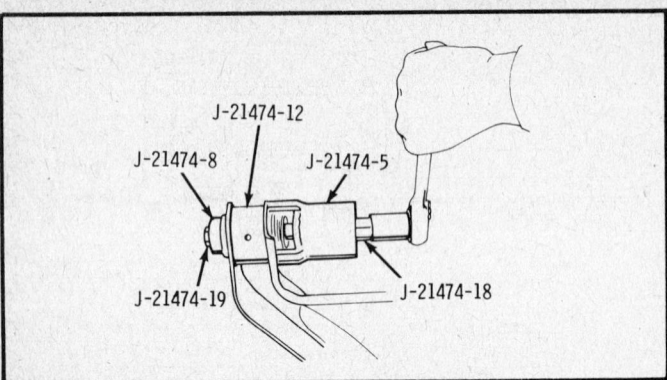

Bushing removal. Press out old bushing (© General Motors Corp.)

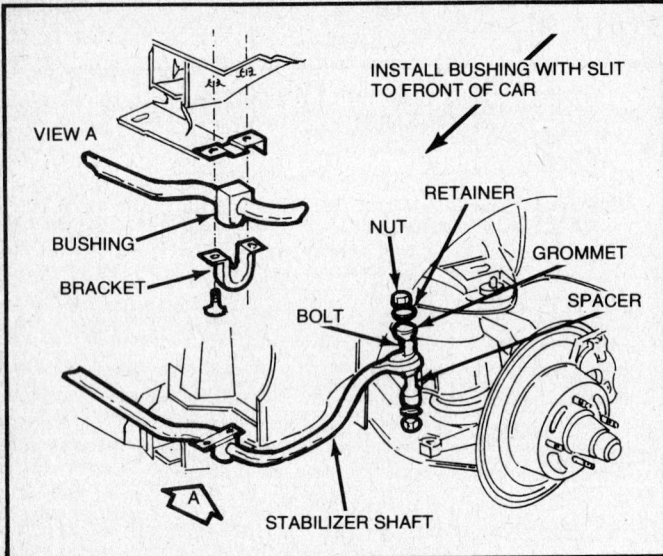

Stabilizer shaft (© General Motors Corp.)

5. Remove splash shield.
6. Remove upper and lower ball joint studs.
7. Remove studs from steering knuckle.

Installation

1. Place steering knuckle into position and insert upper and lower ball joint studs into knuckle bosses.
2. Install stud nuts and torque upper and lower nuts to 40 ft. lbs. (55 Nm).
3. Install splash shield. Torque screw to 7 ft. lbs. (9.5 Nm).
4. Install hub and rotor assembly.
5. Install outer bearing, spindle washer and nut. Adjust bearing.
6. Install brake caliper.
7. Install wheel and tire assembly. Tighten nuts to 100 ft. lbs. (140 Nm).
8. Lower car to floor.
9. Check front wheel alignment.

Stabilizer Shaft

Removal

1. Hoist car.
2. Disconnect each side of stabilizer linkage by removing nut from link bolt. Pull bolt from linkage and remove retainers, grommets and spacer.
3. Remove bracket-to-frame or body bolts and remove stabilizer shaft, rubber bushings and brackets. Some models require a special tool to remove stabilizer shaft bolt.

Installation

To replace, reverse sequence of operations, being sure to install with the identification forming on the right side of the car. The rubber bushings should be positioned squarely in the brackets with the slit in the bushings facing the front of car. Torque stabilizer link nut to 13 ft. lbs. (18 Nm) and bracket bolts to 24 ft. lbs. (33 Nm).

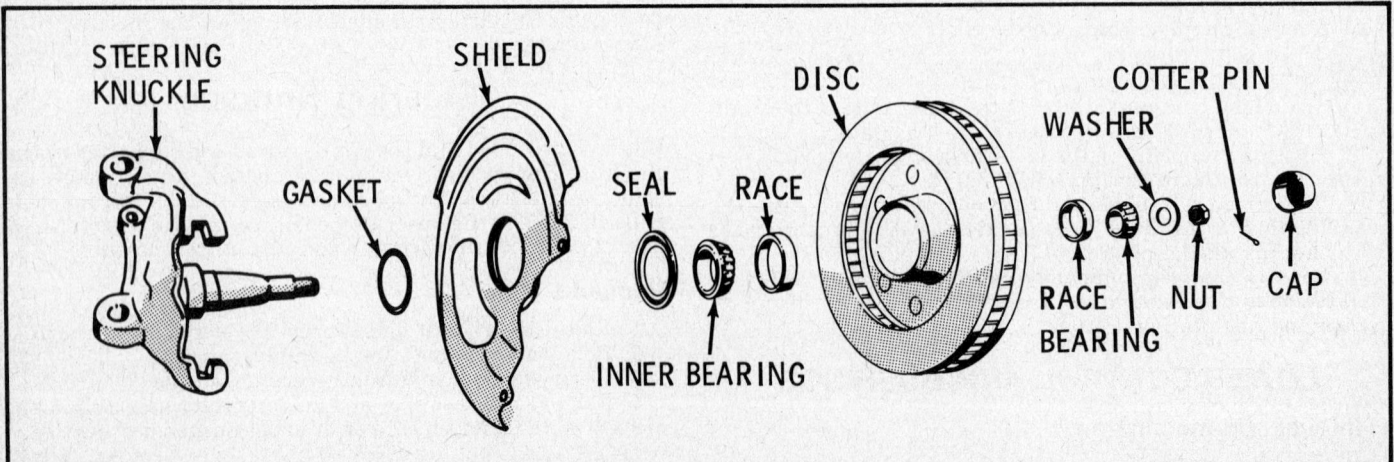

Steering knuckle and hub assembly (© General Motors Corp.)

REAR SUSPENSION—GENERAL MOTORS REAR DRIVE SOLID AXLE EXCEPT F, T, P BODY AND '84 AND LATER CORVETTE

Description

COIL SPRING SYSTEM

The rear axle assembly is attached to the frame through a link type suspension system. Two rubber bushed lower control arms mounted between the axle assembly and the frame maintain fore and aft relationship of the axle assembly to the chassis. Two rubber bushed upper control arms, angularly mounted with respect to the centerline of the car, control driving and braking torque and sideways movement of the axle assembly. The rigid axle holds the rear wheels in proper alignment.

The upper control arms are shorter than the lower arms, causing the differential housing to "rock" or tilt forward on compression. This rocking or tilting lowers the rear propeller shaft to make possible the use of a lower tunnel in the rear floor pan area.

The rear upper controls arms control drive forces, side sway and pinion nose angle. Pinion angle adjustment can greatly affect car smoothness and must be maintained as specified.

The rear chassis springs are located between brackets on the axle tube and spring seats in the frame. The springs are held in the seat pilots by the weight of the car and by the shock absorbers which limit axle movement during rebound.

Ride control is provided by two identical direct double acting shock absorbers angle-mounted between brackets attached to the axle housing and the rear spring seats.

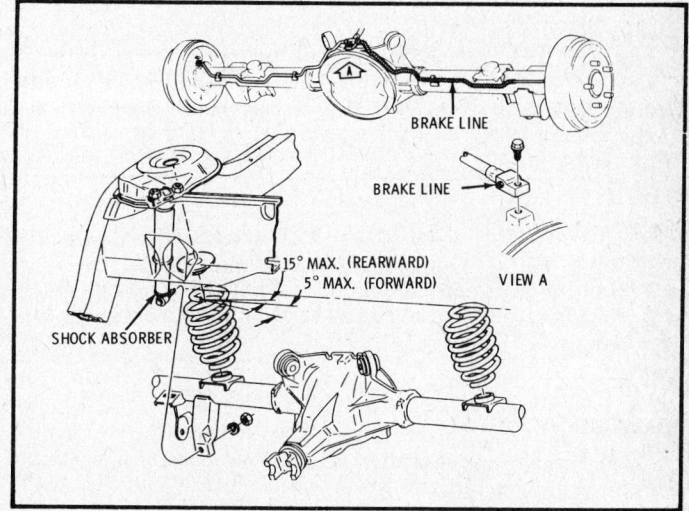

Coil spring mounting (© General Motors Corp.)

Shock Absorbers

Removal

Raise car and support rear axle to prevent stretching of brake hose. The lower end has a stud which is an integral part of the shock. Remove the nut and tap shock free from bracket. To disconnect the shock at the top, on all models, remove the two bolts, nuts and lockwashers.

Installation

Loosely attach shock at both ends. Tighten upper bolts and nuts to 20 ft. lbs. (26 Nm). Tighten lower nut to 65 ft. lbs. (90 Nm).

Coil Springs

Removal

1. Hoist rear of car on axle housing and support at frame rails with floor stands. Do not lower hoist at this time.

NOTE: Do not allow the rear brake hose to become kinked or stretched.

2. Disconnect brake line at axle housing.
3. Disconnect upper control arms at axle housing.
4. Remove shock at lower mount.
5. Lower hoist at rear axle.
6. Remove spring.

Installation

1. Install coil spring.
2. Hoist vehicle at rear axle.
3. Install shock at lower mount.
4. Install upper control arm bolts at axle housing.
5. Connect brake line at axle housing.
6. Remove jack stands and lower car.

Upper Control Arm

CAUTION
If both control arms are to be replaced, remove and replace one control arm at a time to prevent the axle from rolling or slipping sideways. This might occur with both upper control arms removed, making replacement difficult.

Removal

1. Remove nut from rear arm to rear axle housing bolt and while rocking rear axle, remove the bolt. On some cars disconnecting lower shock absorber stud will provide clearance. Use support under rear axle nose to aid in bolt removal.
2. Remove from and rear arm attaching nuts and bolts.
3. Remove suspension arm and inspect bushings.

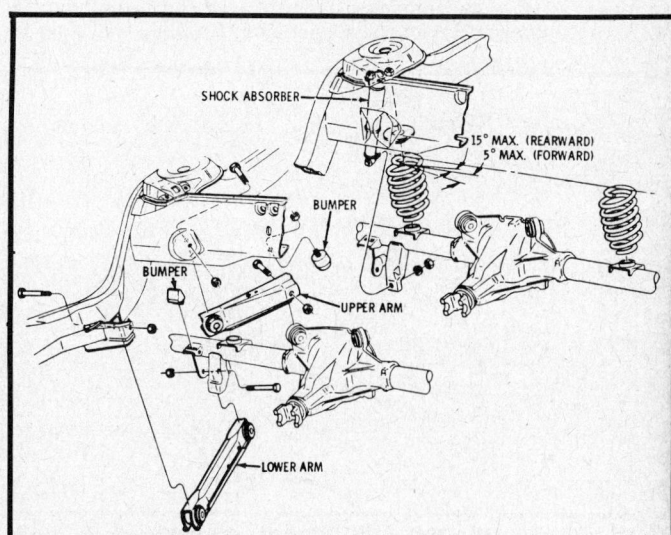

Rear suspension (© General Motors Corp.)

SECTION 35

SUSPENSIONS
REAR SUSPENSION—GM EXC. "F, T & P" BODY AND CORVETTE (1984 AND LATER)

Installation

To install, reverse removal procedure. Torque nuts with car resting at normal trim height.

Lower Control Arm

CAUTION

If both control arms are to be replaced, remove and replace one control arm at a time to prevent the axle from rolling or slipping sideways. This might occur with both lower control arms removed, making replacement difficult.

Removal

1. Raise car and support under axle housing.
2. Remove rear arm-to-axle housing bracket bolt.
3. Remove front arm-to-bracket bolts and remove lower control arm.

Installation

To replace arm, reverse the removal sequence of operations. Torque arm attaching nuts with the weight of the car on the rear springs.

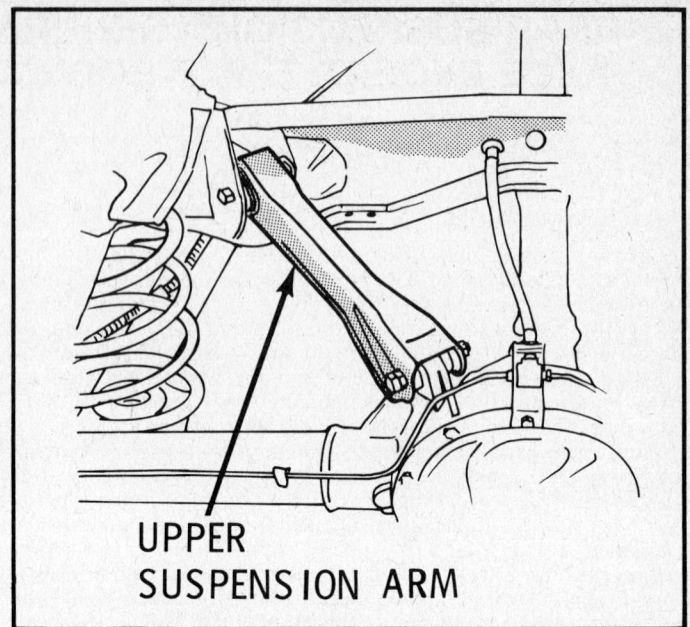

Upper control arm—typical (© General Motors Corp.)

REAR SUSPENSION—GENERAL MOTORS REAR DRIVE INDEPENDENT SUSPENSION EXCEPT F, T, P BODY AND '84–'85 CORVETTE

Description

The rear suspension features a transverse spring mounted on a fixed differential carrier. Each rear wheel is mounted by a three-link independent suspension. These three links are made up of wheel drive shaft, a camber control strut rod and a wheel spindle support arm.

Rear Wheel Alignment

To align the rear suspension, "back" the car onto the machine normally used to align front suspension. Camber will now be read in the normal manner. However, with the vehicle "backed" in, toe-in will now read as toe-out, while toe-out will be read as toe-in.

NOTE: Check condition of strut rods. They should be straight. Rear wheel alignment could be affected if they are bent.

CAMBER

Wheel camber angle is obtained by adjusting the eccentric cam and bolt assembly located at the inboard mounting of the strut rod. Place rear wheels on alignment machine and determine camber angle. To adjust, loosen cam bolt nut and rotate cam and bolt assembly until specified camber is reached. Tighten nut securely and torque to specifications.

TOE-IN

Wheel toe-in is adjusted by inserting shims of varying thickness inside the frame side member on both sides of the torque control arm pivot bushing. Shims are available in thickness of $\frac{1}{64}$ in. (40mm), $\frac{1}{32}$ in. (79mm), $\frac{1}{8}$ in. (3.18mm), and $\frac{1}{4}$ in. (6.35mm).

To adjust toe-in, loosen torque control arm pivot bolt. Remove cotter pin retaining shims and remove shims. Position torque control arm to obtain specified toe-in. Shim the gap toward vehicle centerline between torque control arm bushing and frame side inner wall. Do not use thicker shim than necessary, and do not use undue force when shimming inner side of torque control arm. To do so may cause toe setting to change.

Shim outboard gap as necessary to obtain solid stackup between torque control arm bushing and inner wall of frame side member. After correct shim stack has been selected, install cot-

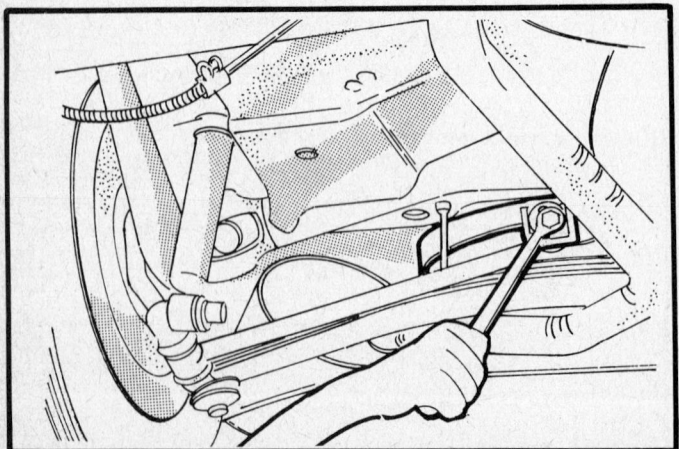

Rear wheel camber adjustment (© General Motors Corp.)

SUSPENSIONS

REAR SUSPENSION—GM EXC. "F, T & P" BODY AND CORVETTE (1984 AND LATER)

ter pin (with loop outboard) through shims. Torque nut to specifications, and install cotter pin. If specified torque does not permit cotter pin insertion, tighten nut to next flat.

Wheel Bearing

END—PLAY CHECK

The tapered-roller spindle bearings should have end play of 0.001–0.008 in (0.003–0.20 mm). During inspection, check end play and, when necessary, adjust as outlined in this section.

1. Raise vehicle on hoist, being careful not to bend the strut rods.
2. Disengage bolt lock tabs and disconnect outboard end of axle drive shaft from wheel spindle flange.
3. Mark camber cam in relation to bracket. Loosen and turn camber bolt until strut rod forces torque control arm outward. Position loose end of axle-drive shaft to one side for access to spindle.
4. Remove wheel and tire assembly. Mount dial indicator on torque control arm adjacent surface and rest pointer on flange or spindle end.
5. Grasp brake disc and move axially (in and out) while reading movement on dial indicator. If end movement is within the 0.001–0.008 in. (0.003–0.20 mm) limit, bearings do not require adjustment. If not within 0.001–0.008 in. (0.003–0.20) limit, record reading for future reference and adjust bearings.

SPINDLE

Removal and Installation

1. Apply parking brake to prevent spindle from turning and remove cotter pin and nut from spindle.
2. Release parking brake and remove drive spindle flange from splined end of spindle. It may be necessary to use tool J–8614–01 or equivalent to remove flange from spindle.
3. Remove brake caliper.
4. Install thread protector J–21859–1 or equivalent over spindle threads. Remove drive spindle from spindle support, using tool J–22602.
   When using tool J–22602 to remove drive spindle, make sure puller plate is positioned vertically in the torque control arm before applying pressure to the puller screw.
5. When the spindle is removed, the outer bearing will remain on the spindle. the inner bearing, tubular spacer, end-play adjustment shim and both outer races will remain in the spindle support.

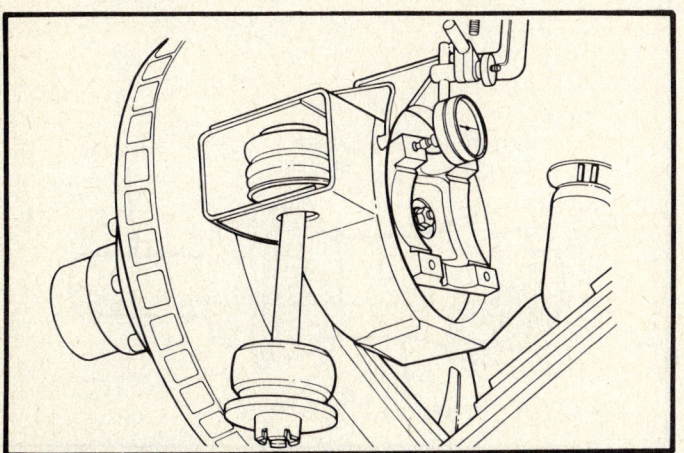

Spindle bearing end-play check (© General Motors Corp.)

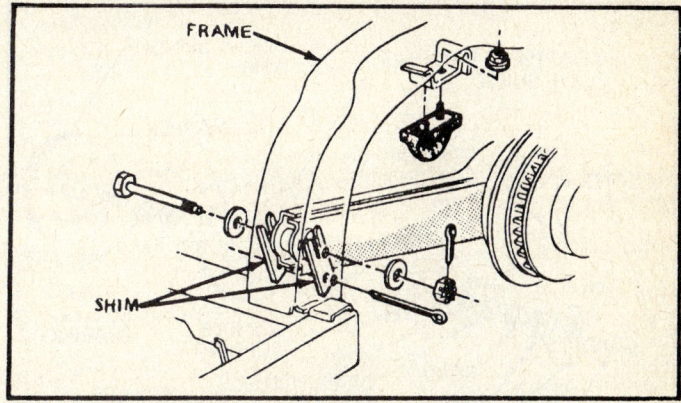

Toe in adjusting shim location (© General Motors Corp.)

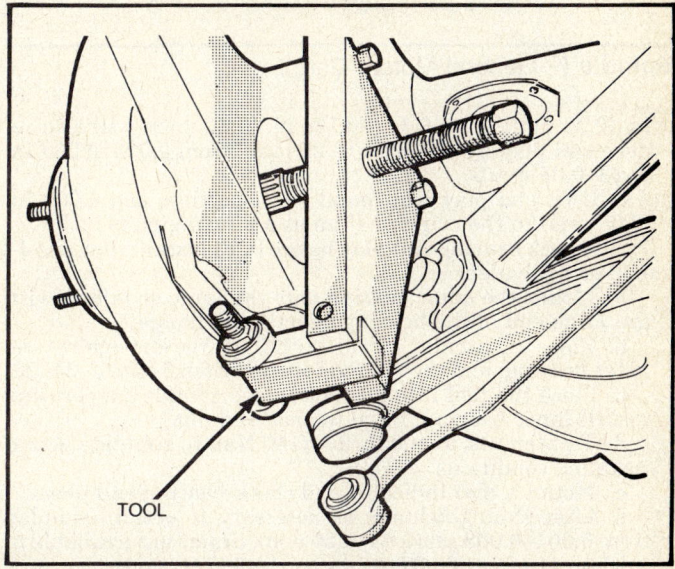

Drive spindle removal (© General Motors Corp.)

6. Remove bearing, spacer and shim. Record shim thickness for later use.

Bearing Replacement and Adjustment, and Spindle Installation

1. With the spindle assembly on a bench, place the two halves of J–24489–1 into position between the outer bearing and the oil seal.
2. Mount J–8433–1 to J–24489–1 and draw bearing off spindle.
3. Remove outer oil seal from spindle shaft and inspect for damage. Replace if necessary.
4. Remove the outer races from the spindle support and install new ones, using J–7817 for reinstallation.
5. Pack new bearings with EPB–2 bearing lubricant, or equivalent.
6. Check bearing end play as measured in Step 5 of Wheel Bearing End Plat Check. Use the same adjusting shim thickness as the original. If end play is not within limits, use the following steps to determine the proper shim thickness.
   a. If end play was greater than 0.008 in. (0.20 mm), it will be necessary to reduce shim thickness to bring end play within limits.
   b. For example, if end-play reading was 0.13 in. (0.33 mm), and the shim measured 0.144 in. (3.66 mm), you have to decrease the shim thickness. Reducing the shim by 0.010

SECTION 35 SUSPENSIONS
REAR SUSPENSION—GM EXC. "F, T & P" BODY AND CORVETTE (1984 AND LATER)

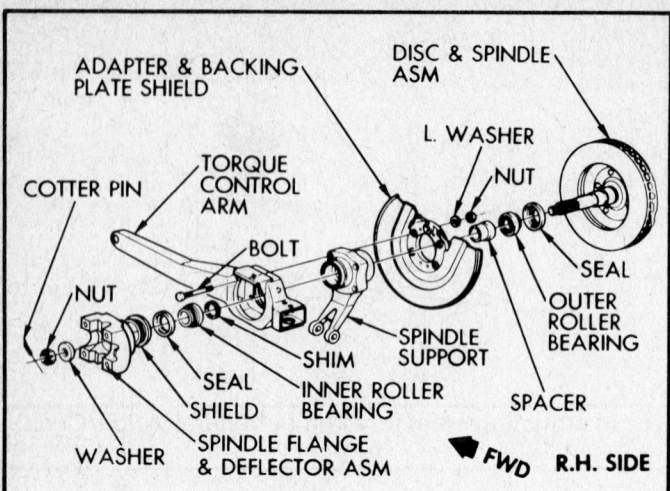

Spindle (© General Motors Corp.)

in. (0.25 mm), from 0.144–0.134 in. (3.40 mm), will also reduce end play by 0.010 in. (0.25 mm), from 0.013–0.003 in. (0.33–0.08 mm).

   c. If no end play was found on inspection, add 0.003 in. (0.08 mm) to the original shim as a starting point.

7. To check bearing end-play before final installation, use J–24626 or equivalent as follows:

   a. Mount the outer bearing onto the large shoulder, with the large end of the bearing against the flange.

   b. Place the tubular spacer, with the large end against the outer bearing, and the shim selected in Step 6 onto J–24626.

   c. Place the tool into position in the spindle support and install inner bearing, large washer and nut.

   d. Tighten nut to 100 ft. lbs. (140 Nm) to simulate actual installed conditions.

   e. Mount a dial indicator and check bearing end-play.

   f. After shim thickness as necessary to obtain end-play from 0.001–0.008 in. (0.03–0.20 mm). Shims are available in thicknesses from 0.097–0.145 in. (2.46–3.68 mm).

   g. Remove J–24626 from spindle support.

8. Install outer bearing into outer race. Install outer oil seal into bore of spindle support, making sure it is firmly seated.

9. Carefully install spindle assembly through the outer oil seal (being careful not to dislodge seal from the bore) and through the outer bearing.

10. Place the tubular spacer and the shim selected in Step 7 onto the spindle shaft.

11. Place the inner bearing onto the spindle shaft.

12. Thread too J–24490–1 onto the spindle shaft, then install sleeve J–24490–2, and washer and nut. Tighten nut against sleeve. Spindle shaft will now be drawn through the bearings to its final installed position.

13. Remove J–24490–1 and J–24490–2.

14. Position drive flange over spindle, making sure flange is aligned with spindle splines. Install washer and nut on spindle, then tighten nut to specifications and install cotter pin. If specified torque does not permit cotter pin insertion, tighten nut to next flat.

15. Install caliper onto disc.

16. Install axle drive shaft, wheel and tire assembly, adjust camber cam to original position and torque all components to specifications.

Spindle Support

Removal

1. Remove wheel spindle as outlined previously.

2. Disconnect parking brake cable from actuating lever.

3. Remove four nuts securing spindle support to torque control arm and withdraw brake backing plate. Position it out of the way.

4. Disconnect shock absorber lower eye from strut rod mounting shaft. It may be necessary to support spring outer end before disconnecting shock absorber, as shock absorber has internal rebound control.

5. Remove cotter pin and nut from strut rod mounting shaft, then pull shaft from support and strut rod.

6. Separate support from torque control arm.

Installation

1. Position support over torque arm bolts with strut rod fork toward center of vehicle and downward.

2. Place backing plate in position, install four nuts and torque to specifications.

3. Install strut rod and shock absorber mounting shaft onto support arm. Install shock absorber. Torque to specifications.

4. Connect parking brake cable to actuating lever.

5. Install drive spindle assembly.

Shock Absorber

Removal

1. Raise vehicle on hoist.
2. Disconnect shock absorber upper mounting bolt.
3. Remove lower mounting nut and locker washer.
4. Slide shock upper eye out of frame bracket and pull lower eye and rubber grommets off strut and mounting shaft.

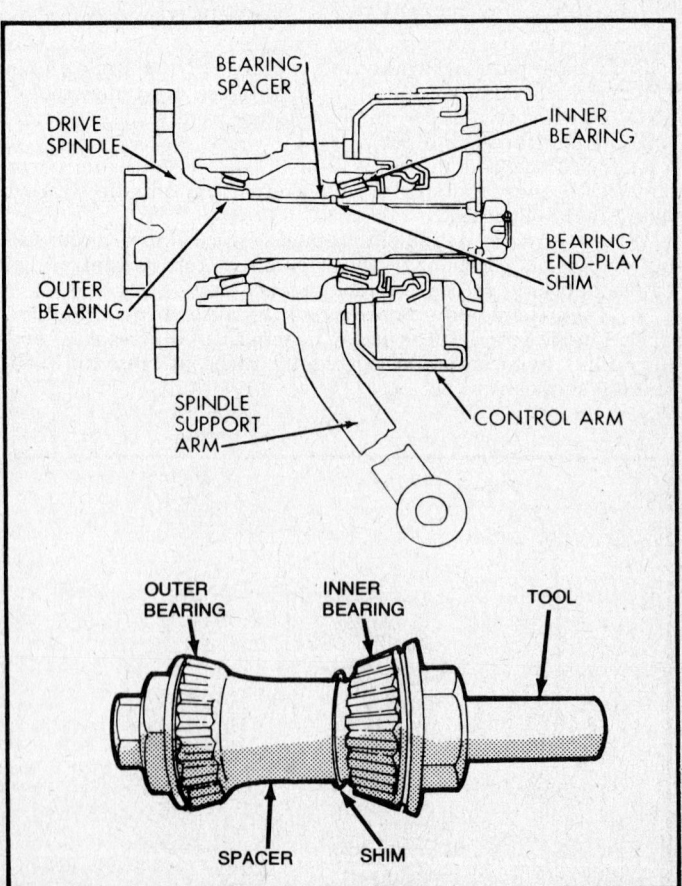

Sectional view of spindle assembly (© General Motors Corp.)

Suspensions

REAR SUSPENSION—GM EXC. "F, T & P" BODY AND CORVETTE (1984 AND LATER)

5. Inspect grommets and shock absorber upper eye for excessive wear.

Installation

1. Slide upper mounting eye into frame mounting bracket and install bolt, locker washer and nut.
2. Place rubber grommet, shock lower eye, inboard grommet, washer and nut over strut rod shaft. Install washer with curve pointing inboard (away from grommet).
3. Torque nuts to specifications.
4. Lower vehicle and remove from hoist.

Strut Rod and Bracket

Removal

1. Raise vehicle on hoist.
2. Disconnect shock absorber lower eye from strut rod shaft.

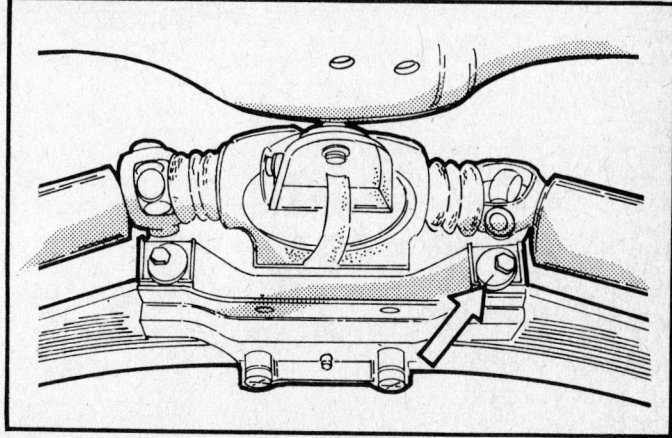

Marking camber cam and bracket (© General Motors Corp.)

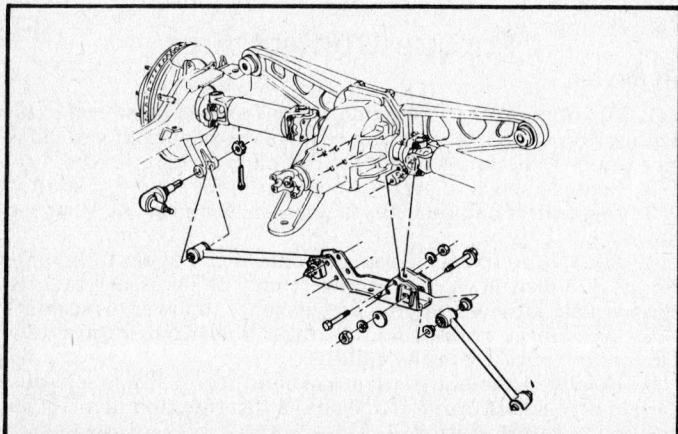

Strut rod mounting. Install strut with putboard end angled forward (© General Motors Corp.)

3. Remove strut rod shaft cotter pin and nut. Withdraw shaft by pulling toward front of vehicle.
4. Mark relative position of camber adjusting cam and bracket, so they may be reassembled in same location.
5. Loosen camber bolt and nut. Remove four bolts, lock washers and flat washers securing strut rod bracket to carrier and lower bracket.
6. Remove cam bolt nut and cam and bolt assembly. Pull strut down out of bracket and remove bushing caps.
7. Inspect strut rod bushings for wear and replace where necessary.

Installation

1. Place bushing caps over inboard bushing and slide rod into bracket. Install cam and bolt assembly and adjust cam to line up with mark of bracket. Tighten nut but do not torque at this point.
2. Raise bracket and assemble to carrier lower mounting surface. Be sure both flat washer and lock washer are between bolt and bracket. Torque bolts to specifications.
3. Raise outboard end of strut rod into fork so that flat on shaft lines up with corresponding flat in spindle fork. Install retaining nut, but do not torque.
4. Place shock absorber lower eye and bushing over strut shaft, install washer and nut and torque to specifications.
5. With weight on wheels torque camber cam nut and strut rod shaft nut to specifications. Then install cotter pin through rod bolt.
6. Check rear wheel camber and adjust where necessary.
7. Lower vehicle and remove from hoist.

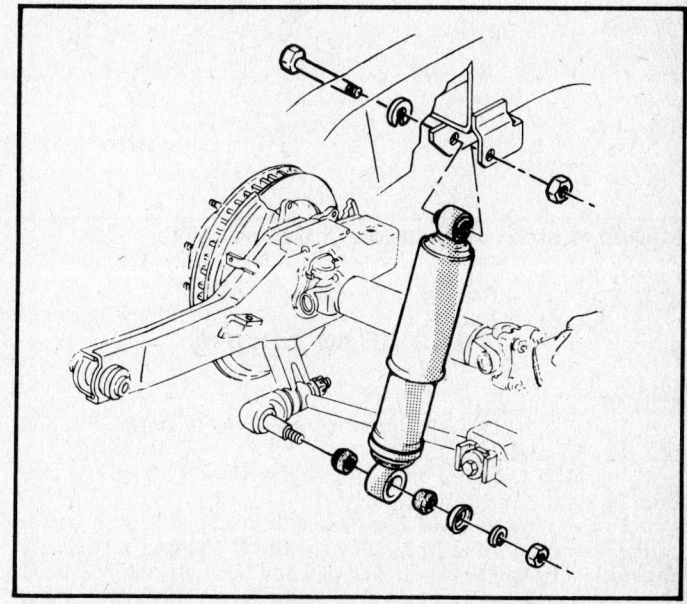

Shock absorber mounting (© General Motors Corp.)

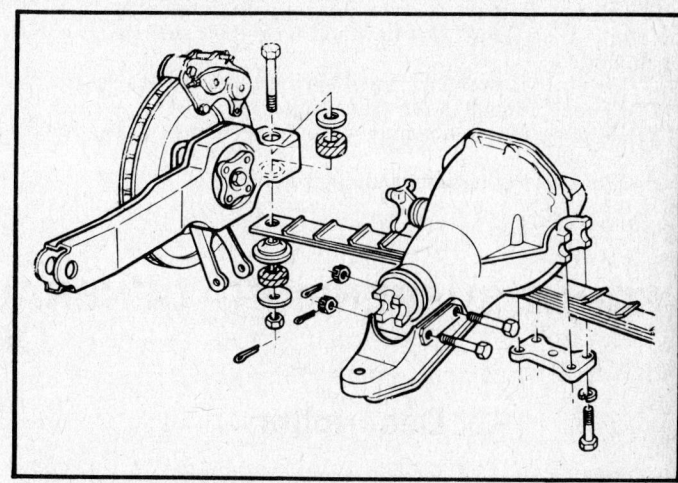

Transverse spring mounting (© General Motors Corp.)

35-133

SECTION 35 SUSPENSIONS
REAR SUSPENSION—GM EXC. "F, T & P" BODY AND CORVETTE (1984 AND LATER)

Installation

1. Place spring on carrier cover mounting surface, indexing center bolt head with hole in cover.
2. Place center clamp plate in position and install bolts and washers. Snug bolts to position spring and torque to specifications.
3. Install C-clamp as in Step 2 of removal procedure.
4. Place adjustable lifting device inboard of link bolt near C-clamp. Add wooden block as in Step 3 of removal procedure.
5. Raise spring outer end until spring is nearly flat, aligning torque arm with spring end.
6. Install new attaching parts. Whenever servicing spring or removing spring attaching parts, always install new link bolts, rubber cushions, retainers, nuts and cotter pins.
7. Lower jack making sure cushions remain indexed in retainers. Remove C-clamp.
8. Remove jack and repeat for other side.
9. Place vehicle weight on wheels and torque center clamp bolts to specifications.

Torque Control Arm

Removal

1. Disconnect spring on side torque arm is to be removed. Follow Steps 1–5 of the spring removal procedure. If vehicle is so equipped, disconnect stabilizer shaft from torque arm.
2. Remove shock absorber lower eye from strut rod shaft.
3. Disconnect and remove strut rod shaft and swing strut rod down.
4. Remove four bolts securing axle drive shaft to spindle flange and disconnect driveshaft. It may be necessary to force torque arm outboard to provide clearance to lower driveshaft.
5. Disconnect brake line at caliper and from torque arm. Disconnect parking brake cable.
6. Remove torque arm pivot bolt and toe-in shims and pull torque arm out of frame. Tape shims together and identify for correction reinstallation.

Installation

1. Place torque arm in frame opening.
2. Install pivot bolt. Place toe-in shims in original position on both sides of torque arm. Install cotter pin retaining shims with loop of pin pointed outboard. Do not tighten pivot bolt nut at this time.
3. Raise axle driveshaft into position and install to drive flange. Torque bolts to specifications.
4. Raise strut rod into position and insert strut rod shaft so that flat lines up with flat in spindle support fork. Install nut and torque to specifications.
5. Install shock absorber lower eye and tighten nut to specifications.
6. Connect spring end as outlined under spring installation. Step 3–6. If vehicle is so equipped connect stabilizer shaft to torque arm.
7. Install brake line at caliper and torque arm. Bleed brakes.
8. Install wheel and tire. Torque the torque arm pivot bolt to specifications and install cotter pin with weight on wheels.

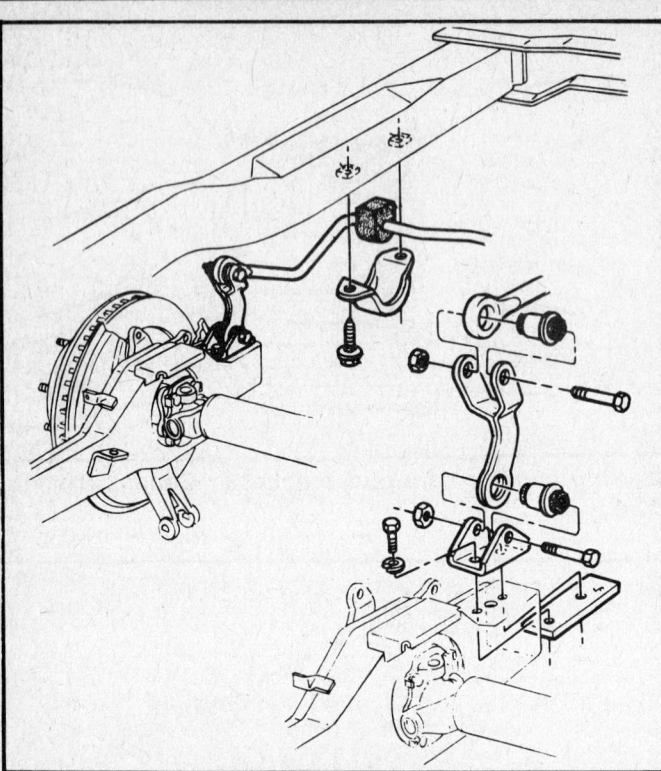

Stabilizer shaft installation (© General Motors Corp.)

Transverse Spring

Removal

1. Raise vehicle on hoist allowing axle to hang. Remove wheels and tires.
2. Install a C-clamp on spring approximately 9 in. (23 cm.) from one end. Tighten securely.
3. Place adjustable lifting device under spring with lifting pad of jack inboard of link bolt near the C-clamp. Place a suitable piece of wood between jack pad and C-clamp screw. The C-clamp is merely acting as a stop so the jack will not slip when the spring is released. The wood block is used to protect the clamp threads from distortion due to contact with the jack pad.
4. Raise jack until all load is off link. Remove link cotter key and link nut. Remove cushion. Do not grip shank of spring link bolt with Vise Grips. Use new bolt if the bolt surface is scored or damaged.
5. Carefully lower jack until spring tension is released.
6. Repeat Steps 2–5 for other side.
7. Remove four bolts and washers securing spring center clamp plate.
8. Slide spring out from under vehicle.

FRONT SUSPENSION—GENERAL MOTORS T BODY—REAR DRIVE CARS

Description

The front suspension system uses conventional long and short arm design and coil springs. The control arms attach to the vehicle with bolts and bushings at the inner pivot points, and to the steering knuckle/front wheel spindle assembly at the outer pivot points. The lower ball joints use the wear indicator feature used on other General Motor original equipment ball joints.

SUSPENSIONS
FRONT SUSPENSION—GM "T" BODY REAR DRIVE CARS

Wheel Alignment

CAMBER

Camber angle can be increased approximately one degree. Remove the upper ball joint, rotate it one-half turn and reinstall it with the flat of the upper flange on the inboard side of the control arm.

CASTER

Shims placed between the upper control arm and legs control caster. Always use two washers totalling 12 mm thickness, placing one washer at each end of the locating tube.

TOE

Adjust by changing tie-rod position Loosen the nuts at the steering knuckle end of the tie rod and the rubber cover at the lower end. Rotate tie-rod to change adjustment.

Wheel Bearings

NOTE: Tapered roller bearings are used on all series vehicles and they have a slightly loose feel when properly adjusted. A design feature of front wheel tapered roller bearings is that they must never be pre-loaded. Damage can result from pre-loading.

The proper functioning of the front suspension cannot be maintained unless the front wheel taper roller bearings are correctly adjusted. Cones must be a slip fit on the spindle and the inside diameter of cones should be lubricated to insure that the cones will creep. Spindle nut must be a free-running fit on threads.

Inspection

1. Raise vehicle and support at front lower control arm.

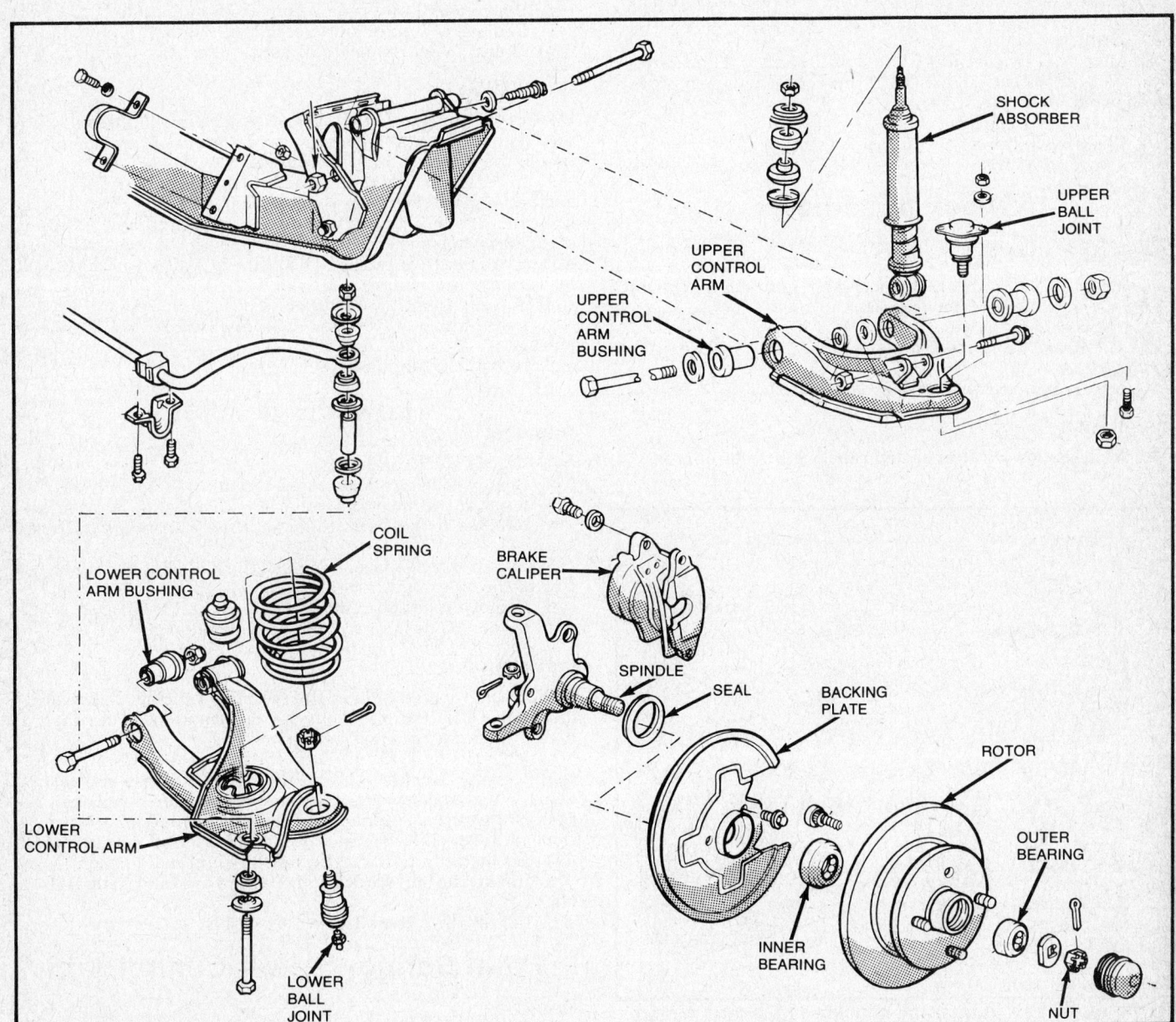

Front suspension (© General Motors Corp.)

SECTION 35
SUSPENSIONS
FRONT SUSPENSION — GM "T" BODY REAR DRIVE CARS

2. Spin wheel to check for unusual noise or roughness.
3. If bearings are noisy, tight, or excessively loose, they should be cleaned, inspected, and relubricated prior to final adjustment. If it is necessary to inspect bearings, movement should be from 0.001–0.005 in. (0.025–0.127 mm). If movement is not in this range, adjust bearings.

Adjustment
1. Remove hub cap or wheel disc from wheel.
2. Remove dust cap from hub.
3. Remove cotter pin from spindle and spindle nut.
4. Tighten the spindle nut to 12 ft. lbs (16 Nm) while turning the wheel assembly forward by hand to fully seat the bearings. This will remove any grease or burrs which could cause excessive wheel bearing play later.
5. Back off the nut to the "just loose" position.
6. Hand-tighten the spindle nut. Loosen spindle nut until either hole in the spindle lines up with a slot in the nut (not more than ½ flat).
7. Install new cotter pin. Bend the ends of the cotter pin against nut, cut off extra length to ensure ends will not interfere with the dust cap.
8. Measure the looseness in the hub assembly. There will be from 0.001–0.005 in. (0.025–0.127 mm) end-play when properly adjusted.
9. Install dust cap on hub.
10. Replace the wheel cover or hub cap.

Shock Absorbers

Removal
1. Hold the shock absorber upper stem and remove the nut, upper retainer and rubber grommet.
2. Raise vehicle on a hoist.
3. Remove the bolts from the lower end of the shock absorber.
4. Lower the shock absorber from the vehicle.

Installation
1. With the lower retainer and rubber grommet in position, extend the shock absorber stem and install the stem through the wheelhouse opening.
2. Install the lower bolts. Torque to 35–50 ft. lbs. (48–70 Nm).
3. Lower the vehicle to the floor.
4. Install the upper rubber grommet, retainer and nut to the shock absorber stem.
5. Hold the stem and tighten the nut to 60–120 inch lbs. (7–13 Nm). Torque is obtained by running nut to unthreaded portion of stud.

Upper Ball Joint

Removal
1. Raise the vehicle on a hoist.
2. Remove the tire and wheel assembly.
3. Support the lower control arm with a floor jack.
4. Remove upper ball stud nut. Reinstall nut finger-tight.
5. Install spreader tool and push stud loose from knuckle.
6. Remove tool and remove nut from ball stud.
7. Remove two nuts and bolts attaching ball joint to upper control arm, then remove ball joint.

Installation
Inspect the tapered hole in the steering knuckle. Remove any dirt and if any out-of-roundness, deformation, or damage is noted, the knuckle must be replace.
1. Install bolts and nuts attaching ball joint to upper control arm, then mate the upper control arm ball stud to the steering knuckle. The ball joint studs use a special nut which must be discarded whenever loosened and removed. On reassembly, use a standard nut to draw the ball joint into position on the knuckle. Torque the standard nut to 22 ft. lbs. (30 Nm), then remove that nut and install a new special nut for final installation.
2. Install the ball stud nut and torque to 29–36 ft. lbs (39–49 Nm).
3. Install the tire and wheel assembly.

Lower Ball Joint

Removal
1. Raise vehicle on hoist.
2. Remove the tire and wheel assembly.
3. Support the lower control arm with a hydraulic floor jack.
4. Remove lower ball stud nut, then reinstall nut finger-tight.
5. Install spreader tool and push the ball joint stud until it is free of the steering knuckle.
6. Remove tool and remove nut from ball stud.
7. Remove ball joint from lower control arm.

Installation
Inspect the tapered hole in the steering knuckle. Remove any dirt and if any out-of-roundness, deformation, or damage, is noted, the knuckle must be replaced.
1. Mate the ball stud through the lower control arm and into the steering knuckle. The ball joint studs use a special nut which must be discarded whenever loosened and removed. On reassembly, use a standard nut to draw the ball joint into position on the knuckle. Torque the standard nut then remove that nut and install a new special nut for final installation.
2. Install the ball stud nut and torque to 41–54 ft. lbs. (56–73 Nm).
3. Install the tire and wheel assembly.

Front Spring — Lower Control Arm

Removal
1. Remove wheel and tire assembly.

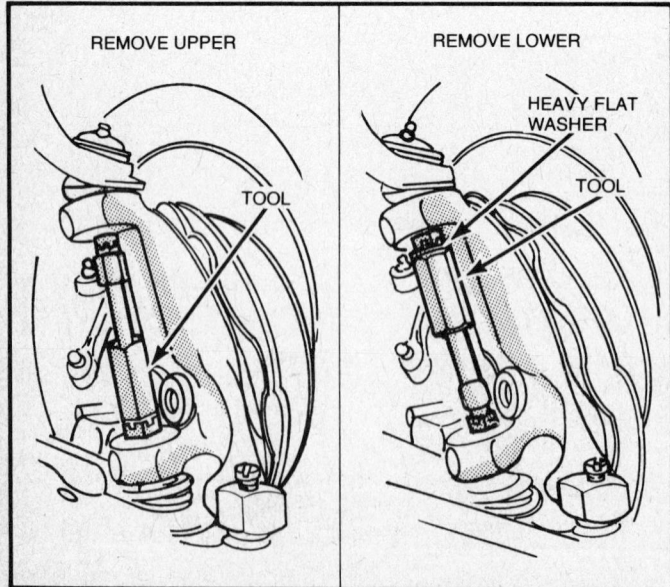

Removal of ball joint from knuckle (© General Motors Corp.)

SUSPENSIONS
FRONT SUSPENSION—GM "T" BODY REAR DRIVE CARS

2. Disconnect stabilizer from lower control arm. Disconnect tie-rod from steering knuckle.
3. Support lower control arm with a jack.
4. Remove the nut from the lower ball joint. Install spreader tool and push the ball joint stud loose in the steering knuckle.
5. Swing the knuckle-and-hub out of the way, and attach securely with wire.
6. Loosen lower control arm pivot bolts.
7. Install chain through coil spring as a safety precaution.

--- CAUTION ---
The coil spring is under load. Be sure to install a chain and to slowly lower the jack.

8. Slowly lower the jack.
9. When the spring is extended as far as possible, use a prybar to carefully lift the spring over the lower control arm seat. Remove the spring.
10. Remove pivot bolts, and then remove lower control arm.

Installation
1. Install lower control arm and pivot bolts to underbody brackets.
2. Position spring and install spring into upper pocket. Use tape to hold insulator onto spring.
3. Install spring lower end onto lower control arm. It may be necessary to have an assistant help you compress the spring far enough to slide it over the raised area of the lower control arm seat.
4. Use a jack to raise the lower control arm and compress the coil spring.
5. The ball joint studs uses a special nut which must be discarded whenever loosened and removed. On reassembly, use a standard nut to draw the ball joint into position on the knuckle, then remove that nut and install a new special nut for final installation. Install the ball joint through the lower control arm and into the steering knuckle. Install nut to ball joint stud and torque to 41–53 ft. lbs. (56–73 Nm).
6. Connect stabilizer bar and tie rod. Install wheel and tire assembly. Torque to specifications.

Upper Control Arm
Removal
1. Raise vehicle on a hoist.
2. Remove the tire and wheel assembly.
3. Support the lower control arm with a floor jack.
4. Remove upper ball joint from steering knuckle.
5. Remove control arm pivot bolts and remove control arm from vehicle.

Installation
1. Install upper control arm and pivot bolt to vehicle. The inner pivot bolt must be installed with the bolt head toward the front.
2. Install the pivot bolt nut.
3. Position the control arm in a horizontal plane and torque the nut to 43–50 ft. lbs. (59–68 Nm).
4. The ball joint studs use a special nut which must be discarded whenever loosened and removed. On reassembly, use a standard nut to draw the ball joint into position on the knuckle, then remove that nut and install a new special nut for final installation. Install ball joint to upper control arm and to steering knuckle, as described earlier. Install nut; tighten to specifications.
5. Install wheel and tire; torque to specifications.
6. Lower vehicle to floor.

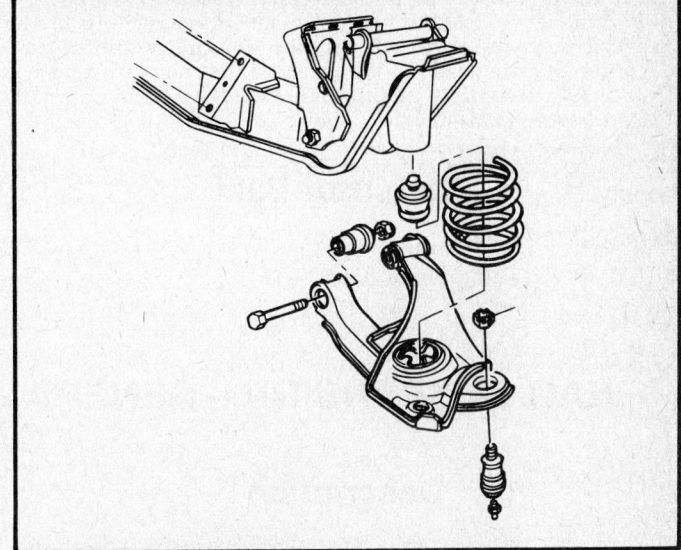
Correct spring position (© General Motors Corp.)

Steering Knuckle
Removal
1. Raise vehicle and support the lower control arm with a jackstand.

--- CAUTION ---
This keeps the coil spring compressed. Use care to support safely.

2. Remove the tire and wheel assembly.
3. Remove the disc brake caliper. Do not allow the caliper to hang by the brake hose. Insert a piece of wood between the shoes to hold the piston in the caliper bore. The block of wood should be about the same thickness as the brake disc.
4. Remove the hub and disc.
5. Remove the splash shield.
6. Remove the tie-rod end from the steering knuckle.
7. Loosen both ball stud nuts. Using a spreader tool, push both the upper and lower ball studs from the steering knuckle.
8. Remove ball stud nuts and remove the steering knuckle.

Installation
1. Place steering knuckle in position and insert the upper and lower ball studs into knuckle bosses.

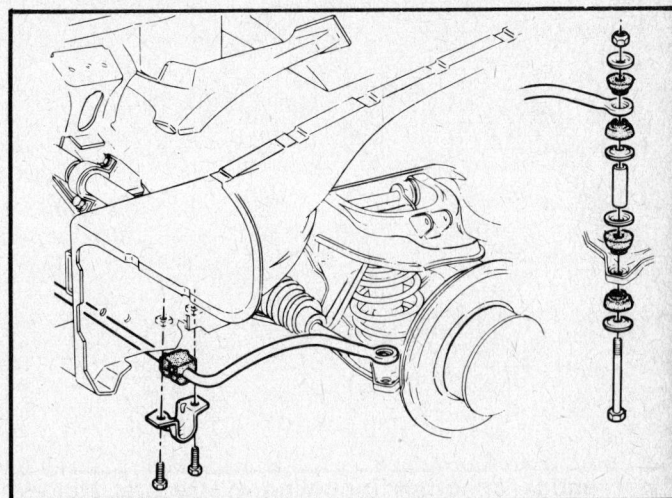
Stabilizer bar attachment (© General Motors Corp.)

35-137

SUSPENSIONS
FRONT SUSPENSION—GM "T" BODY REAR DRIVE CARS

2. The ball joint studs use a special nut which must be discarded whenever loosened and removed. On reassembly, use a standard nut to draw the ball joint into position on the knuckle. Torque the standard nut then remove that nut and install a new special nut for final installation. Install ball stud nuts and tighten to specifications.

Stabilizer Bar

Removal

1. Raise the vehicle on a hoist.
2. Remove the stabilizer bar nut and bolt from lower control arm.
3. Remove stabilizer bar bracket from body.

Installation

1. Hold stabilizer bar in place and install the body bushings and brackets.
2. Install the retainers, grommets and spacers to the lower control arm and install nuts.
3. Lower the vehicle to the floor.
4. Torque nut to 12–18 ft. lbs. (16–24 Nm). Torque is obtained by running nut to unthreaded portion of link bolt.

REAR SUSPENSION—GENERAL MOTORS T BODY—REAR DRIVE CARS

Description

The solid rear axle is attached to the body through two tubular lower control arms, a straight track rod, two shock absorbers and a bracket at the front end of the axle extension. Variable rate coil springs mount between the axle and body.

Two rubber bushed lower control arms mounted between the axle assembly and the frame maintain fore and aft relationship of the axle assembly to the chassis. The rigid axle holds the rear wheels in proper alignment.

The rear chassis springs are located between brackets on the axle tube and spring seats in the frame. The springs are held in the seat pilots by the weight of the car and by the shock absorbers which limit axle movement during rebound.

Ride control is provided by two identical direct double acting shock absorbers angle-mounted between brackets attached to the axle housing and the rear spring seats.

Shock Absorber

Removal

1. Support rear axle assembly.
2. Remove upper attaching bolts and lower attaching bolt and nut.

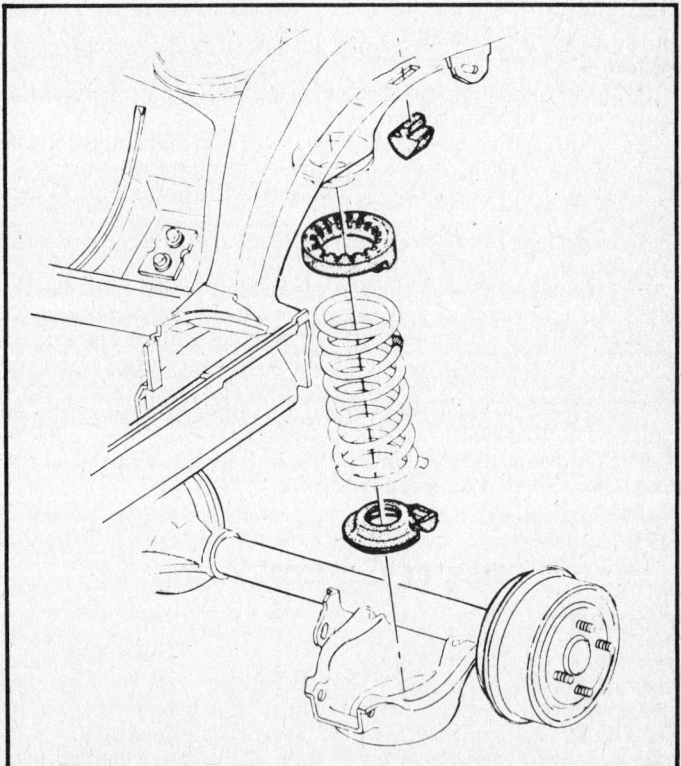

Coil spring placement (© General Motors Corp.)

3. Remove shock absorber.

Installation

1. Install retainer and rubber grommet onto shock.
2. Place shock into installed position and install upper retaining bolts. Torque to specifications.
3. Install bolt and nut onto lower shock attachment. Torque to specifications.
4. Lower vehicle and remove from hoist.

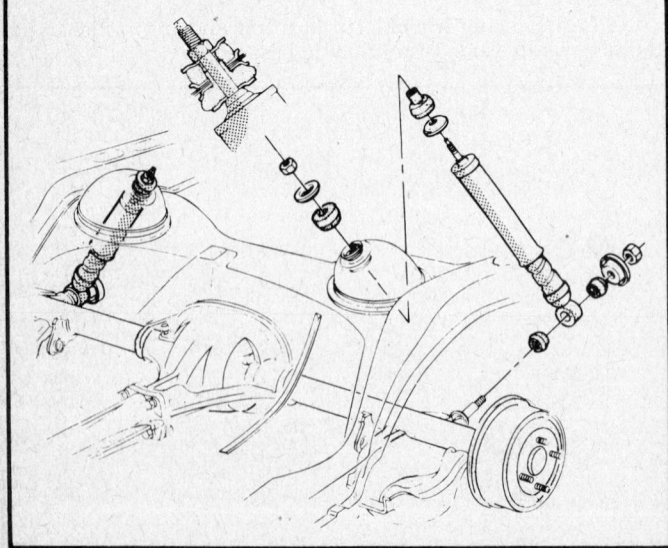

Rear shock absorber mounting (© General Motors Corp.)

Coil Spring

Removal

1. Raise vehicle on hoist.

SUSPENSIONS

REAR SUSPENSION — GM "T" BODY REAR DRIVE CARS

2. Support rear axle with an adjustable lifting device.
3. Disconnect both shock absorbers from lower brackets.
4. Disconnect rear axle extension bracket.

> **CAUTION**
> Be sure to use caution when disconnecting extension assembly. Be sure to support assembly safely.

5. Lower axle and remove springs and spring insulators. One or both springs may be removed at this point.

> **CAUTION**
> When lowering axle, do not stretch brake hose running from frame to axle or damage to the brake line may result

Installation

1. Install insulators on top and bottom of springs then position spring between upper and lower seats.
2. Raise axle and reconnect shock absorbers. Torque nut to specifications.
3. Remove lifting device from axle.
4. Lower vehicle and remove from hoist.

Lower Control Arm and Tie Rod

Removal

> **CAUTION**
> If both control arms are to be replaced, removed and replace one control arm at a time to prevent the axle from rolling or slipping sideways.

1. Raise the car.
2. Support the rear axle.
3. Disconnect the stabilizer bar.
4. Remove the control arm front and rear attaching bolts and remove the control arm.
5. Remove the track rod attaching bolts and remove the track rod.

BUSHING REPLACEMENT

1. Use appropriate tools to press bushings out of control arm/tie rod.
2. Inspect for distortion, burrs, etc.
3. Press bushing into place.

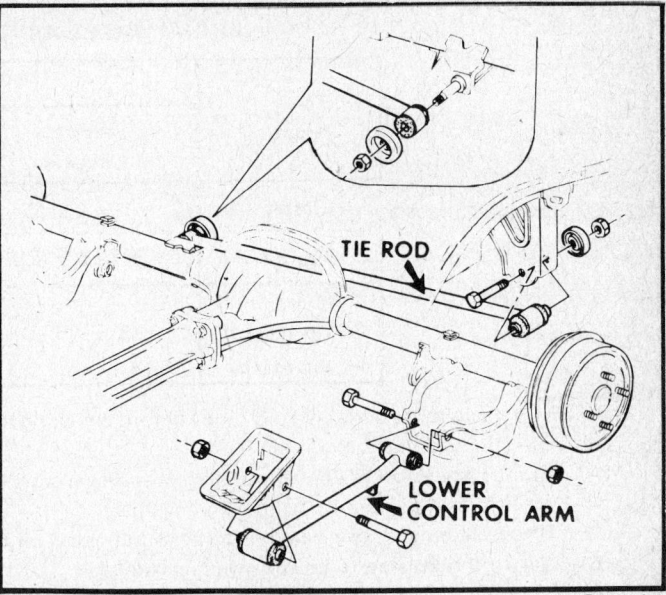

Lower control arm and tie rod (© General Motors Corp.)

Installation

1. Place control arm into position and install front and rear bolts. Torque to specifications.
2. Place tie-rod into position; torque bolts to specifications. Car must be at curb height when tightening pivot bolts. Tighten pivot bolts to 33 ft. lbs. (45 Nm).
3. Reattach stabilizer bar.

Stabilizer Bar

Removal

1. Raise vehicle on hoist.
2. Remove bolts securing brackets to body and link to axle and remove bar.

Installation

1. Place stabilizer into position. Install bolts and nuts. Torque to 15 ft. lbs. (20 Nm).

FRONT SUSPENSION — GENERAL MOTORS — 1984 AND LATER CORVETTE — REAR WHEEL DRIVE

Wheel Alignment

CASTER AND CAMBER

Before adjusting caster and camber angles, the front bumper should be raised and released twice to allow vehicle to return to its normal height.

Caster and camber adjustments are made by means of shims inserted between the upper control arm shaft and the frame bracket. Shims may be added, subtracted or transferred to change the readings as follows:

Caster

Transfer shims, front to rear or rear to front.

Camber

Front Suspension-Change shims at both the front and rear of the shaft.

Adding an equal number of shims at both front and rear of the cross shaft will increase positive camber.

Caster and camber can be adjusted in one operation. Toe-in must be checked after chaning camber or caster.

To adjust caster and camber, loosen the upper control arm shaft to frame nuts, add or subtract shims as required, per alignment correction charts, and retorque nuts.

A normal shim pack will leave at least two (2) threads of the bolt exposed beyond the nut. The difference between front and rear shim packs must not exceed 0.40 in. (10 mm).

If these requirements cannot be met in order to reach specifi-

SECTION 35

SUSPENSIONS
FRONT SUSPENSION—GM CORVETTE REAR DRIVE CARS

FRONT WHEEL ALIGNMENT SPECS

To Align	Curb Service Checking	Curb Service Setting
Caster	3° ± 0.8° (C)	3° ± 0.5° (B)
Camber	0.8° ± 0.5° (C)	0.8° ± 0.5° (B)
Toe-In (Degrees per WHL)	.15° ± .15° (D)	.15° ± .10° (D)

NOTE Vehicle must be jounced 3 times before checking alignment to eliminate false geometry readings.
- (A) Front suspension (Z) dimension and rear suspension (D) dimension are held as indicated in "trim heights" chart. Wheel alignment specifications to be as indicated on this chart.
- (B) Left and right side to be equal within .50°.
- (C) Left and right side to be equal within 1.0°.
- (D) Toe-in left and right side to be set separately per wheel and steering wheel must be held in straight ahead position within ±2.5°.

Front wheel alignment (© General Motors Corp.)

cations, check for damaged cross member, bushings, control arms and related parts.

Always tighten the nut on the thinner shim pack first, for improved shaft to frame clamping force and torque retention.

Suspension Description

The front suspension uses aluminum for all its major components. These include forged aluminum arms and knuckles and replaces conventional coil springs with a lighter, more durable transverse fiberglass monoleaf spring.

Other elements of the front suspension system include long life stabilizer link bushings and the use of spindle offset. Spindle offset is achieved by moving the center of the wheel rearward from the conventional location on line through the ball joints. The displacement contributes to the directional sense. Combined with +3° caster, spindle offset gives an effect similar to higher caster without the poor responsiveness.

Knuckle Hub and Bearing

Removal

1. Hoist vehicle and remove wheel and tire.
2. Remove hub and bearing assembly.
3. Remove splash shield.
4. Disconnect upper and lower ball joint using tool J-33436-9 or equivalent.
5. Remove knuckle.

Installation

1. Reverse removal procedure.

SUSPENSIONS
FRONT SUSPENSION—GM CORVETTE REAR DRIVE CARS

2. Torque nuts and screws to specifications.
3. When installing ball joints and tie rod end to knuckle, do not back off nut for cotter pin insertion.
4. Install wheel and tire and lower vehicle.

Upper Control Arm

Removal

1. Raise vehicle and remove wheel and tire.
2. Remove spring protector.
3. Using spring compressor J-33432 or equivalent compress and loosen spring.
4. Using tool J-33436 or equivalent disconnect upper ball joint from knuckle.
5. Remove upper control arm as shown.

Installation

1. Install control arm as shown.
2. Torque nuts to specifications.
3. Cotter pin at ball joint must be installed from rear to front. Do not back off nut for cotter pin insertion.
4. Check front alignment. Adjust if necessary.

Lower Control Arm

Removal

1. Raise vehicle and remove wheel and tire.
2. Remove spring protector.
3. Using tool J-33432 or equivalent compress spring.
4. Remove lower shock bracket.
5. Using tool J-33436 or equivalent disconnect lower ball joint.

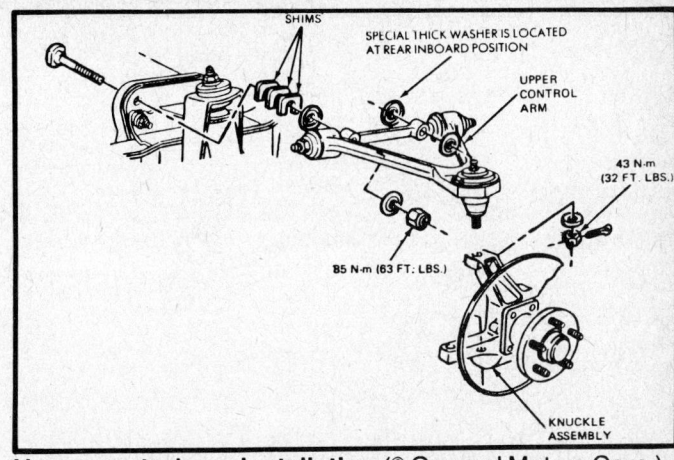

Upper control arm installation (© General Motors Corp.)

6. Remove lower control arm.

Installation

1. Install lower control arm to front crossmember.
2. Hold suspension at curb height and torque bolt to specification. Retain suspension at curb height. Do not allow it to move below rebound.
3. Install shock absorber bracket to control arm. Torque nuts to specifications.
4. Install ball joint to knuckle.
5. Loosen spring and remove tool.
6. Install spring protector.
7. Install wheel and tire and lower vehicle.

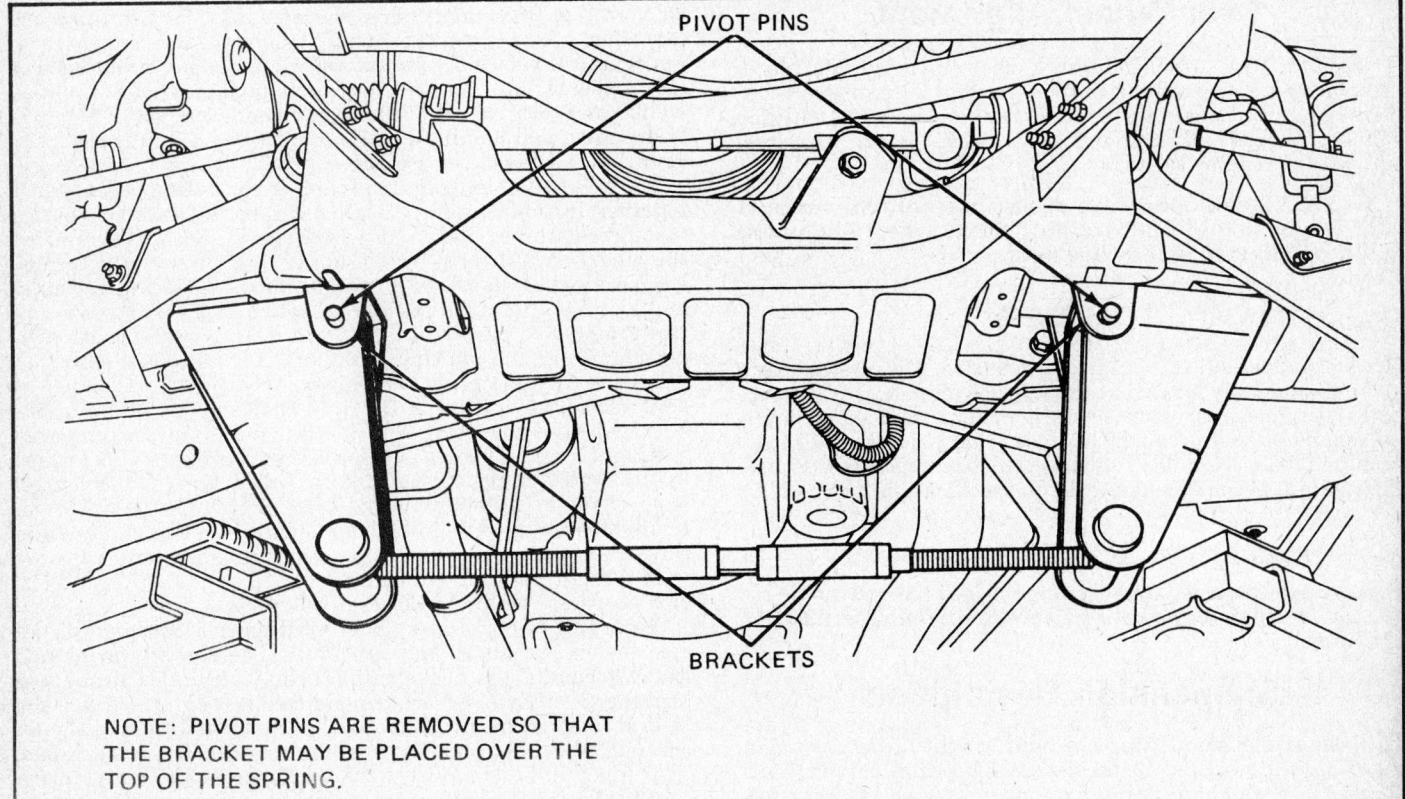

NOTE: PIVOT PINS ARE REMOVED SO THAT THE BRACKET MAY BE PLACED OVER THE TOP OF THE SPRING.

Transverse monoleaf spring installation (© General Motors Corp.)

SECTION 35

SUSPENSIONS
FRONT SUSPENSION—GM CORVETTE REAR DRIVE CARS

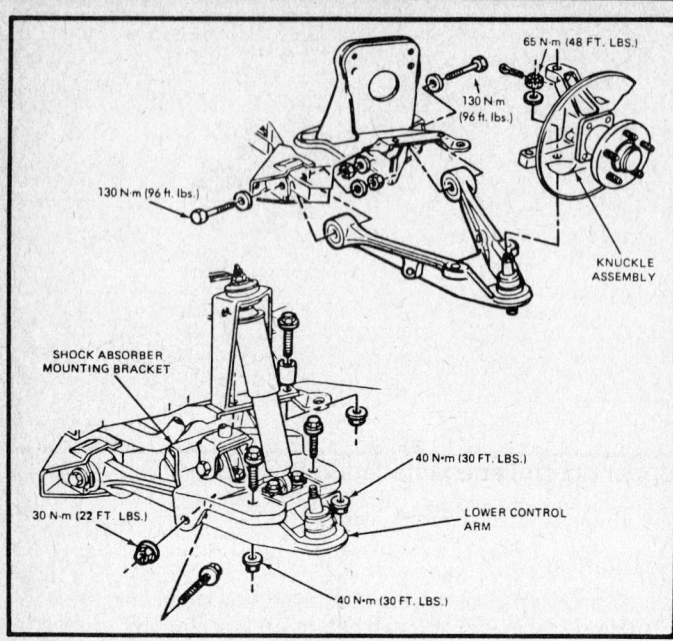

Lower control arm installation (© General Motors Corp.)

Front Transverse Spring

Removal

1. Raise vehicle on a hoist.
2. Remove wheel and tire assembly.
3. Remove both spring protectors.
4. Install spring compressing tool J–33432 or equivalent.
5. Disconnect lower ball joints.
6. Compress spring tool.
7. Remove shock mounting bracket to lower control arm attaching bolts.
8. Remove spring mounting bolts.
9. Release and remove spring compressing tool.

Installation

1. Install the spring by reversing the removal procedure.
2. Torque all nuts and bolts to specifications.
3. Check the vehicle's wheel alignment.

NOTE: During removal and installation of transverse spring take care to prevent damage.

REAR SUSPENSION—GENERAL MOTORS 1984 AND LATER CORVETTE REAR WHEEL DRIVE

Rear Wheel Alignment

To align the rear suspension, "back" the vehicle onto the alignment machine normally used to align front suspension. Camber will now be read in the normal manner. However, with the vehicle, "backed" in, toe-in will now read as toe-out, while toe-out, will be read as toe-in.

NOTE: Check condition of camber control support rods. They should be "straight." Rear wheel alignment could be affected if they are bent.

CAMBER

Wheel camber angle is obtained by adjusting the eccentric cam and bolt assembly located at the inboard mounting of the support rods. Place rear wheels on alignment machine and determine camber angle. To adjust, loosen cam bolt nut and rotate cam and bolt assembly until specified camber is reached. Tighten nut securely and torque to specification.

TOE—IN

Toe-in can be adjusted by loosening the lock nuts on the tie rod ends and turning the adjusting sleeves until the desired setting is obtained.

Suspension Description

The rear suspension features a light weight fiberglass transverse spring mounted to the fixed differential carrier cover beam. Light weight aluminum components such as the knuckles, upper and lower control arms, camber control support rods, differential carrier cover beam and the drive line support beam are used throughout the rear suspension. Each wheel is mounted by a five link independent suspension. The five links are identified as the wheel drive shaft, camber control support rod, upper and lower control arms and tie rod. The advantages of this suspension unit include a reduction of unsprung weight as well as an overall weight reduction. In addition, wheel tramp is eliminated, and handling is improved because of the independent action of each rear wheel.

The axle drive shafts and the camber control support rods act together in maintaining an almost constant camber change throughout the entire arc of wheel travel. Fore-aft motion of the wheel is controlled by the upper and lower control arms. Each rear wheel has a short spindle, hub and bearing assembly and knuckle contained at the rear of the upper and lower control arms. The knuckle also acts as a mount for the brake caliper mounting and parking brake backing plate assembly.

Several techniques can be employed to achieve this independent wheel movement. A five-link independent rear suspension is used on Corvettes. The five-link design can be compared to a right angle. The wheel is located at the right angle formed by the control arms and the "lateral links" (the camber control support rod and the rear wheel drive shaft). The points of the triangle are hinged to provide up-down wheel travel. The solid links thus force the wheel to travel through a controlled arc with fore-aft position determined by the control arms and lateral position held by the lateral links.

Aside from controlling wheel location, each portion of the suspension has additional functions. The controls arms and knuckle carries the brake caliper, thus, all brake torque and braking tractive forces are transmitted through the arms. the lateral links transmit side forces to the fixed differential, and through the rubber bushings in the cover beam to the frame. The upper link, or wheel drive shaft, transmits acceleration torque through the differential to the frame.

The final duty of the lateral links is to maintain the camber angle of the wheel throughout its travel. Since the camber control support rod and the wheel drive shaft are of different

SUSPENSIONS
REAR SUSPENSION — GM CORVETTE REAR DRIVE CARS

REAR WHEEL ALIGNMENT SPECS

To Align	Service Setting
Camber	0° ± .5°
Toe-In (Deg per WHL)	0.15° ± .06°

CAMBER

(1) Finger tighten lateral strut attaching parts at inboard end of strut asm.
(2) Rotate cam to obtain specified camber.
(3) Hold camber setting and torque nut with rear suspension set at "D" height of 71.0, As shown on trim height chart.

TOE IN

(1) Loosen Lock Nut
(2) With special tool in serrated area, rotate tie rod to obtain specified toe-in.
(3) Torque lock nut and adjust boot to cover lock nut & serrations.

CHECKING

NOTE: Vehicle must be jounced three times before checking alignment, to eliminate false geometry readings.

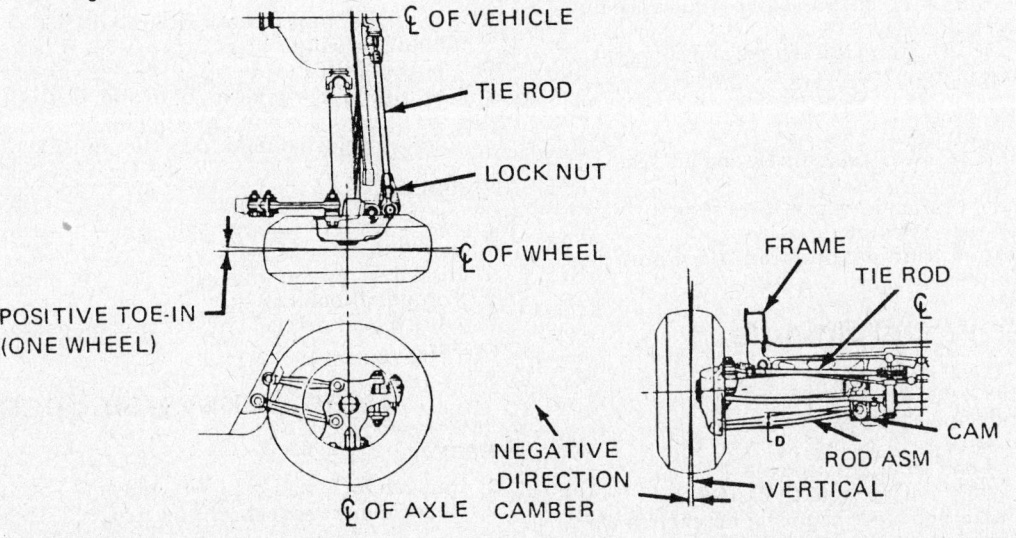

Rear wheel alignment (© General Motors Corp.)

lengths, a certain amount of camber change occurs through jounce and rebound. The overall result of the camber control support rod and wheel drive shaft geometry holds the wheel in a near vertical position at all times.

Direct double-acting shock absorbers are attached at the upper eye to a frame bracket and at the lower eye to the knuckle which has a threaded stud for the shock absorber lower eye.

The transversely mounted spring is clamp bolted at the center section to a lower mounting surface on the differential carrier cover beam. The outer ends of the spring are provided with a hole through which the spring is link bolted to the rear of the knuckle.

A stabilizer shaft is used which attaches to the section of the knuckle, and extends rearward where it is connected to the frame by two rubber bushings and mounting brackets.

A single unit hub and bearing assembly is bolted to each knuckle. The hub and bearing assembly supports the drive axle shaft and spindle allowing torque to be transferred from the differential carrier to the wheel and tire. This hub and bearing assembly is a sealed unit and no maintenance is required.

Rear Hub and Bearing

Removal

1. Raise vehicle and support safely.
2. Remove wheel and tire.
3. Remove brake caliper.
4. Remove brake rotor.
5. Disconnect tie rod end from the knuckle.
6. Disconnect transverse spring from the knuckle.

SECTION 35 SUSPENSIONS
REAR SUSPENSION—GM CORVETTE REAR DRIVE CARS

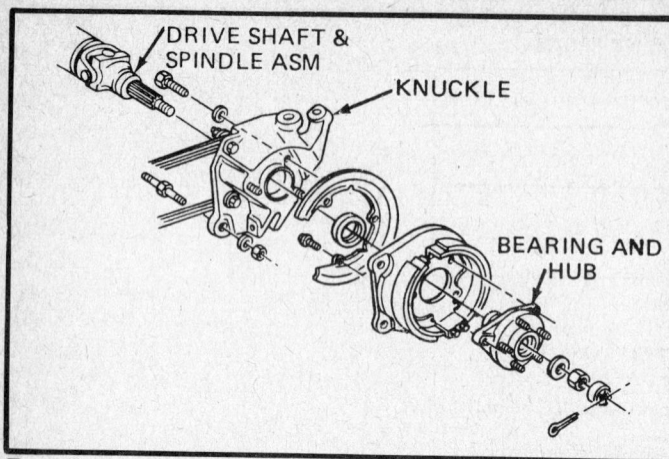

Rear hub and bearing attachment (© General Motors Corp.)

7. Scribe mark on cam bolt and mounting bracket so they can be realigned in the same position.
8. Remove cam bolt and separate spindle support rod from the mounting bracket.
9. Remove the trunnion straps at the side gear yoke shaft. Push out on the knuckle and separate axle shaft from the side gear yoke shaft. Remove the axle shaft from the vehicle.
10. Using J-34161 (Torx® #45) or equivalent remove the hub and bearing mounting bolts.
11. Remove hub and bearing from the vehicle and support the parking brake backing plate.

Installation

To install, reverse the removal procedures and include the following:
1. Inspect the spindle seal and replace if necessary.
2. Torque all bolts to specification.
3. Check and adjust rear suspension alignment as necessary.

Rear Wheel Spindle

Removal

1. Raise vehicle and support safely.
2. Remove wheel and tire.
3. Disconnect tie rod end from the knuckle.
4. Disconnect transverse spring from the knuckle.
5. Scribe mark on cam bolt and mounting bracket so they can be realigned in the same position.
6. Remove cam bolt and separate spindle support rod from the mounting bracket.

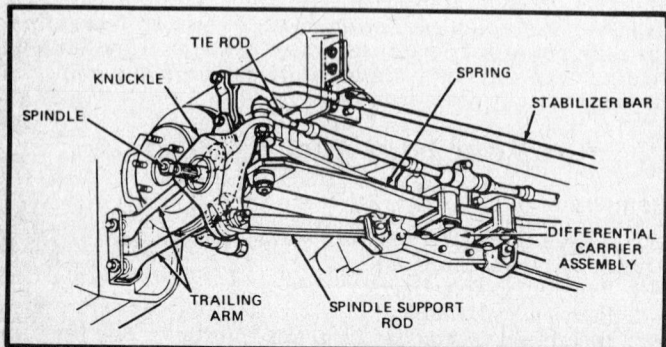

Corvette rear suspension (© General Motors Corp.)

7. Remove the trunnion straps at the spindle yoke. Push out on the knuckle and separate axle shaft from the spindle.
8. Remove the spindle from the hub and bearing.

Installation

To install, reverse the removal procedures and include the following:
1. Inspect the spindle seal and replace if necessary.
2. Torque all bolts to specifications.
3. Check and adjust rear suspension alignment as necessary.

Rear Knuckle

Removal

1. Raise vehicle and support safely.
2. Remove wheel and tire.
3. Remove brake caliper.
4. Remove brake rotor.
5. Disconnect tie rod end from the knuckle.
6. Disconnect transverse spring from the knuckle.
7. Disconnect stabilizer bar from the knuckle.
8. Disconnect parking brake cable from the backing plate.
9. Disconnect shock absorber from the knuckle. Use a back-up wrench on the mounting stud.
10. Disconnect spindle support rod from the knuckle.
11. Disconnect upper and lower control arms from the knuckle.
12. Lower the knuckle assembly and slide spindle out from the hub and bearing.
13. Using J-34161 (Torx #T55) or equivalent remove the hub and bearing bolts. Remove hub and bearing with parking brake backing plate from the knuckle.
14. Remove splash shield from the knuckle.

Installation

To install, reverse the removal procedures and include the following:
1. Install a new spindle seal.
2. Torque all bolts to specifications.
3. Check and adjust the rear suspension alignment as necessary.

Rear Transverse Spring

Removal

1. Raise vehicle and support safely.
2. Remove one rear wheel and tire.

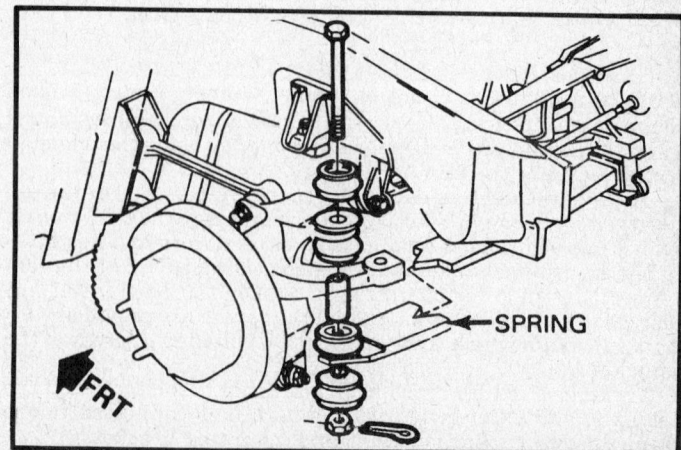

Spring attachment knuckle (© General Motors Corp.)

35-144

SUSPENSIONS
REAR SUSPENSION—GM CORVETTE REAR DRIVE CARS

3. Remove cotter pins, retaining nuts, bushings and link bolt retaining the spring to the knuckles.
4. Remove transverse spring attaching bolts, spacers, insulators and spring from the cover beam.

Installation

1. Position spring, insulators and spacers to the cover beam. Install attaching bolts and torque to specification.
2. Position spring to knuckles. Install bolts, insulators, spacers and nut. Tighten nut until slot in nut aligns with hole in bolt and then install cotter pin.
3. Install wheel and tire.
4. Lower vehicle.

Spindle Support Rod

Removal

1. Raise vehicle and support safely.
2. Scribe mark on cam bolt and mounting bracket so they can be realigned in the same position.
3. Remove cam bolt and separate spindle support rod from the mounting bracket.
4. Remove the spindle support rod bolt at the knuckle and remove rod.

Installation

To install, reverse the removal procedures and include the following:
1. Tighten all bolts to specification.
2. Check and adjust rear suspension alignment as necessary.

Upper/Lower Control Arms

Removal

1. Raise vehicle.
2. Remove shock absorber. Use a backup wrench on the mounting stud.
3. Remove control arm bolt at the knuckle.
4. Remove control arm bolt at the body bracket and remove the arm.

Installation

To install, reverse removal procedures and include the following:
1. Torque all bolts to specifications.

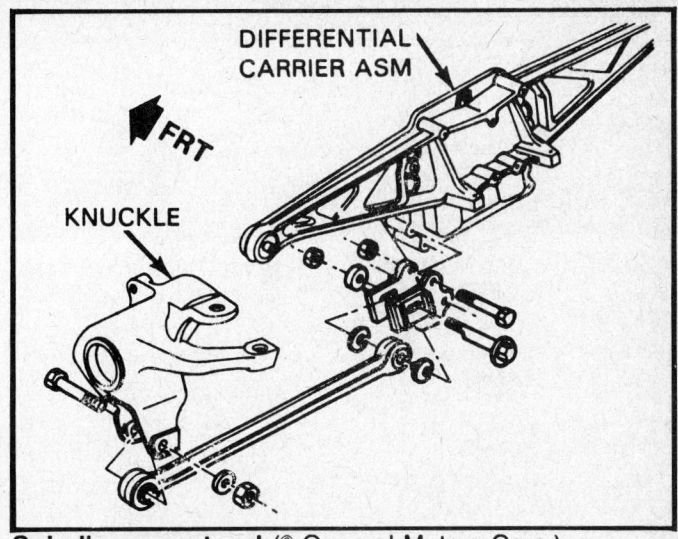

Spindle support rod (© General Motors Corp.)

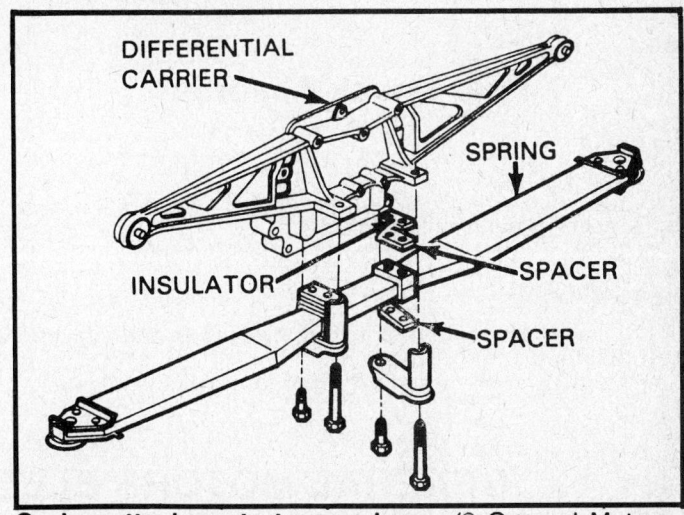

Spring attachment at cover beam (© General Motors Corp.)

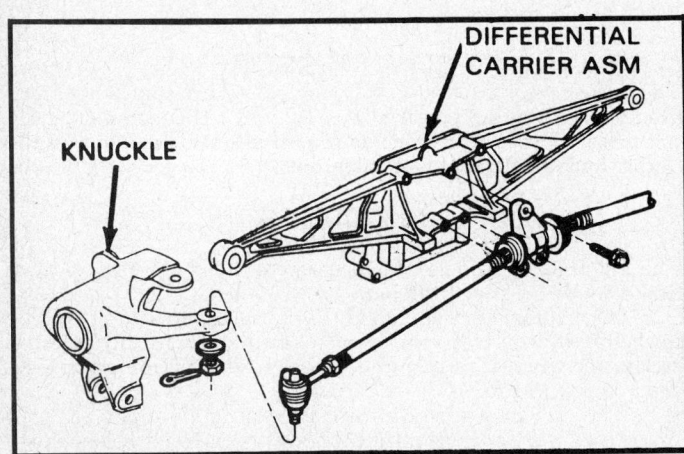

Tie rod assembly (© General Motors Corp.)

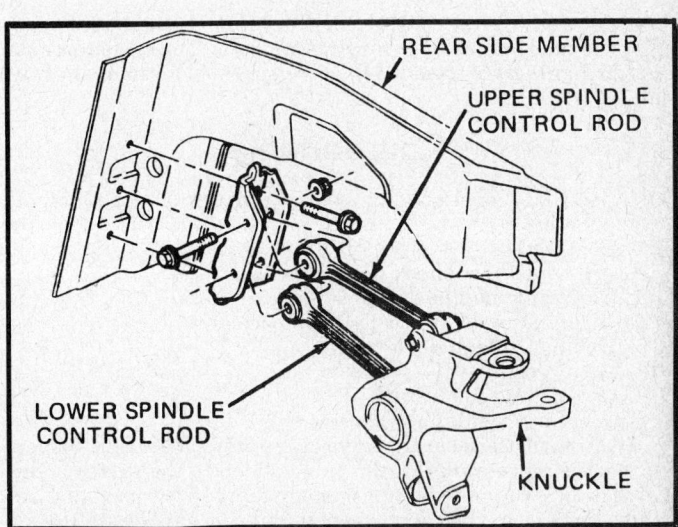

Control arms (© General Motors Corp.)

SECTION 35 SUSPENSIONS
REAR SUSPENSION—GM CORVETTE REAR DRIVE CARS

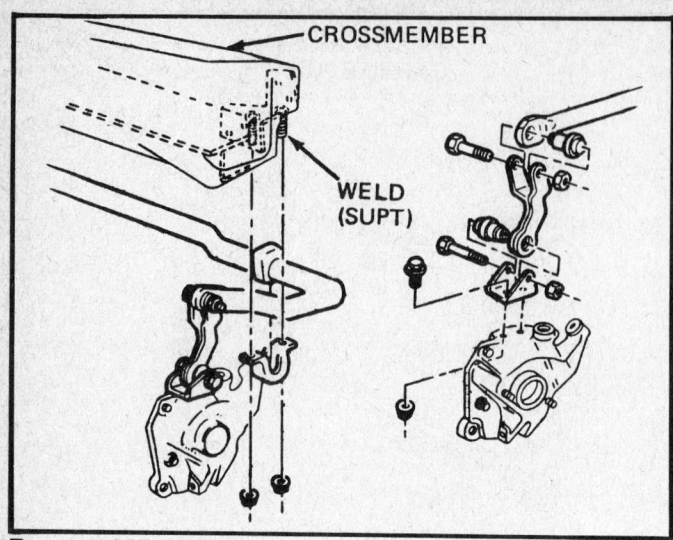

Rear stabilizer bar (© General Motors Corp.)

Rear Shock Absorber

Removal
1. Raise vehicle.
2. Disconnect the shock absorber at the knuckle. Use a backup wrench on the mounting stud.
3. Remove upper shock absorber attaching bolt.

Installation
1. Position shock absorber to body bracket. Install attaching bolt and torque to specifications.
2. Position shock absorber to the knuckle. Install washer and nut and torque to specification. Use a backup wrench on the mounting stud.
3. Lower vehicle.

Rear Axle Tie Rod and/or Adjuster Sleeve

Removal
1. Raise vehicle.
2. Remove cotter pin and retaining nut from tie rod end at knuckle.
3. Loosen jam nut on tie rod end.
4. Using J–24319–01 or equivalent press tie rod end out of the knuckle.
5. Remove tie rod end from the adjusting sleeve.

Installation
To install, reverse the removal procedures and include the following:
1. Tighten all bolts to specification.
2. Check and adjust the rear suspension alignment as necessary.

Stabilizer Bar

Removal
1. Raise vehicle.
2. Remove spare tire and tire carrier.
3. Disconnect stabilizer bar from knuckles.
4. Remove stabilizer bar bushing retainers, bushings and bar from the vehicle.

Installation
To install, reverse the removal procedures and include the following:
1. Torque all bolts to specifications.

GENERAL MOTORS ELECTRONIC LEVEL CONTROL

Description
The electronic level control (ELC) system automatically adjusts the rear height with varying car loads. The system is activated when weight is added to, or removed from the rear of the car.

Components
The electronic level control system consists of the following components:
1. Compressor
2. Air adjustable shock absorbers
3. Electronic height sensor
4. Compressor relay (two with E series)
5. Exhaust solenoid
6. Air dryer
7. Wiring and air tubing
8. Pressure regulator (E series only)

The E and K series front drive cars (torsion bar front suspension) have a pressure limiter value added to the system. This valve is located in the engine compartment in the pressure line which runs from the compressor to the shocks. The limiter allows a maximum of 85 psi (586kPa) ± 5 psi (34kPa) to reach the rear shocks.

COMPRESSOR RELAY
This relay is a single pole single throw type that completes the 12V(+) circuit to the compressor motor when energized. The compressor relay is located on the compressor mounting bracket.

COMPRESSOR
The basic compressor assembly is a positive displacement single piston air pump powered by a 12 volt DC permanent magnet motor. The compressor head casting contains piston intake and exhaust valves plus a solenoid.

AIR DRYER
The air dryer is attached externally to the compressor output and provides a dual function.
1. It contains a dry chemical that absorbs moisture from the air before it is delivered to the shocks and returns the moisture to the air when it is being exhausted. This action provides a long chemical life.
2. The air dryer also contains a valving arrangement that maintains 8–15 pounds minimum air pressure in the shock absorbers (except the E and K series which have 14–20 lb. retention.

SUSPENSIONS
GENERAL MOTORS ELECTRONIC LEVEL CONTROL

EXHAUST SOLENOID

The exhaust solenoid is located in the compressor head assembly and provides two functions.
1. It exhausts air from the system when energized. The height sensor controls this function.
2. It acts as a blow off valve to limit maximum pressure output of the compressor.

HEIGHT SENSOR

The height sensor is an electronic device that controls two basic circuits.
1. Compressor relay coil ground circuit.
2. Exhaust solenoid coil ground circuit.

To prevent falsely actuating the compressor relay or exhaust solenoid circuits during normal ride motions, the sensor circuitry provides an 8-14 second delay before either circuit can be completed.

In addition, the sensor electronically limits compressor run time or exhaust solenoid energized time to a maximum of 3 ½ minutes. This time limit function is necessary to prevent continuous compressor operation in case of a solenoid malfunction. Turning the ignition "off" and "on" resets the electronic timer circuit to renew the 3 ½ minute maximum run time. The height sensor is mounted to the frame crossmember in the rear. The sensor actuator arm is attached to the rear upper control arm by a link.

Air Lines and Fittings

NOTE: While the lines are flexible for easy routing and handling, care should be taken not to kink them and to keep them from coming in contact with the exhaust system.

When the air line is attached to the shock absorber fittings or compressor dryer fitting the retainer clip snaps into a groove in the fitting locking the air line in position. To remove the air line, spread the the retainer clip, release it from the groove and pull on the air line.

System Operation Check

NOTE: When certain tests require raising the car on a hoist, the hoist should support the rear wheels or axle housing. When a frame type hoist is used, two additional jack stands should be used to support the rear axle housing in its normal curb weight position.

1. Select a suitable location at rear wheelhouse opening and measure distance to floor.

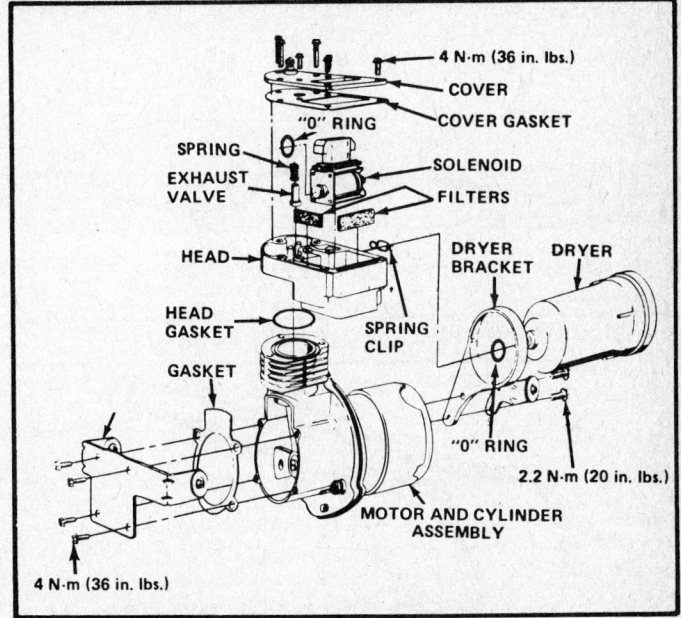
Compressor assembly (© General Motors Corp.)

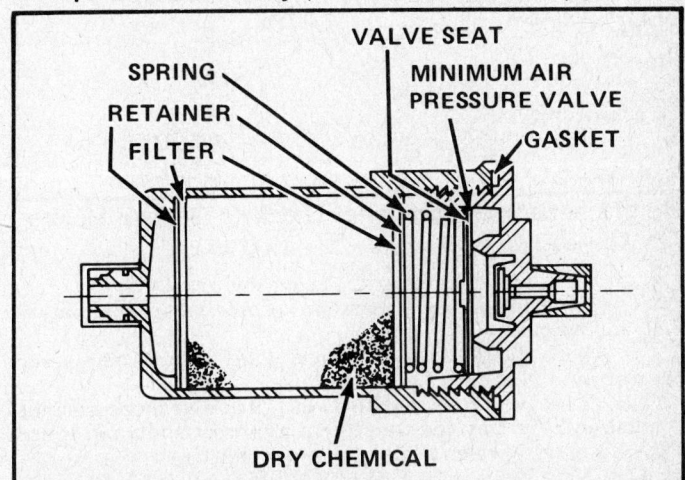
Air dryer (© General Motors Corp.)

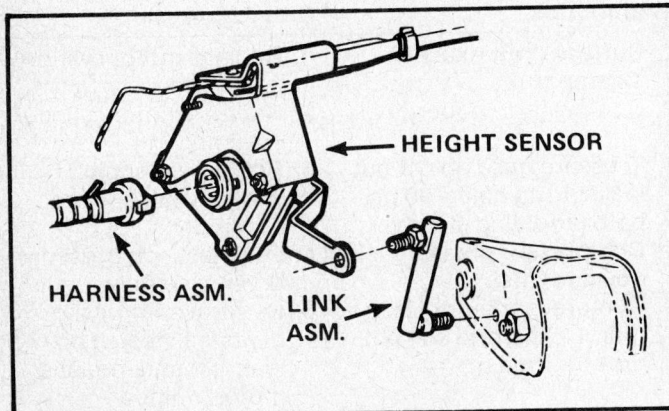
Height sensor (© General Motors Corp.)

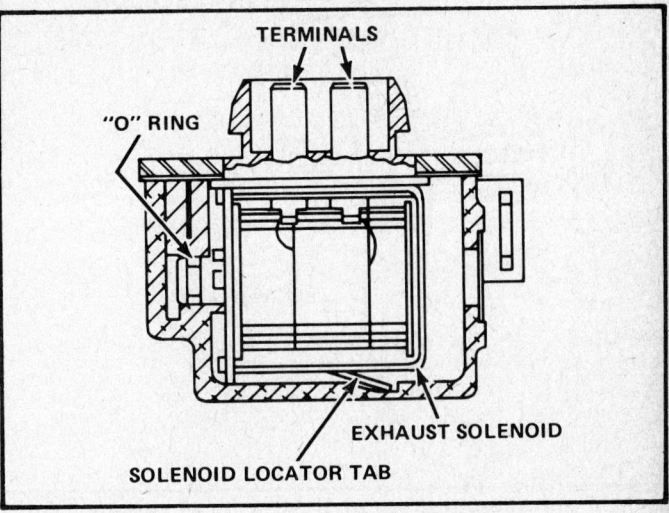
Exhaust solenoid (© General Motors Corp.)

SECTION 35 SUSPENSIONS
GENERAL MOTORS ELECTRONIC LEVEL CONTROL

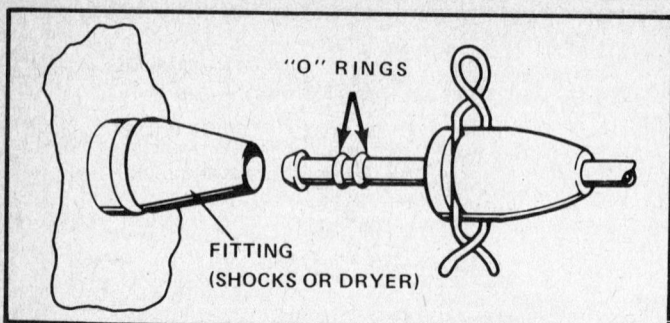

Air line retainer clip (© General Motors Corp.)

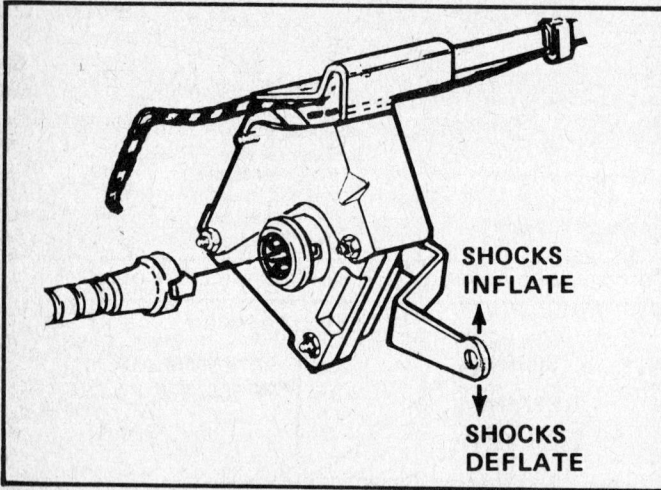

Height sensor opporational check (© General Motors Corp.)

NOTE: Failure of car to return to within ¾ in. (19 mm) of unloaded dimension can be caused by unusually heavy loading in the trunk which exceeds the capacity of the system. If this type of loading is encountered, remove it and repeat test.

4. Remove load applied in Step 3.
   a. There should be 8–14 second delay before car begins to lower.
   b. Car should lower to within ¾ in. (19 mm) of measurement made in Step 1 in less than 3 ½ minutes.

Compressor/Dryer Performance Test

COMPRESSOR CURRENT DRAW, PRESSURE OUTPUT AND LEAK DOWN TEST

1. Disconnect wiring from compressor motor and exhaust solenoid terminals.
2. Disconnect existing pressure line from dryer and attach pressure gauge to dryer fitting.
3. Connect ammeter to 12V source and to compressor.
   a. Current draw should NOT exceed 14 amp.
   b. When gauge read 110–120 psi SHUT COMPRESSOR OFF and observe if pressure leaks down.

NOTE: If compressor is permitted to run until it reaches its maximum output pressure, the solenoid exhaust valve will act as a relief valve. The resulting leak down when compressor is shut off will indicate a false leak.

   c. Leak down pressure should not drop below 90 psi when compressor is shut off.

RESIDUAL AIR CHECK

1. Remove air line from dryer fitting and attach it to gauge. Attach gauge air line to dryer fitting.
2. Turn ignition "ON" and perform system check, to inflate shocks.
3. Turn ignition "OFF" and deflate system through compressor service valve. Gauge should read 8–15 psi after system is deflated.

2. Start engine momentarily. Leave switch "ON".
3. Apply load to rear of car (two people or approximately 300–350 pounds).
   a. There should be 8–14 second delay before compressor turns on and the car begins to raise.
   b. Car should raise to with ¾ in. (19 mm) of measurement made in Step 1 by the time the compressor shuts off. If car does not raise, refer to the diagnosis chart.

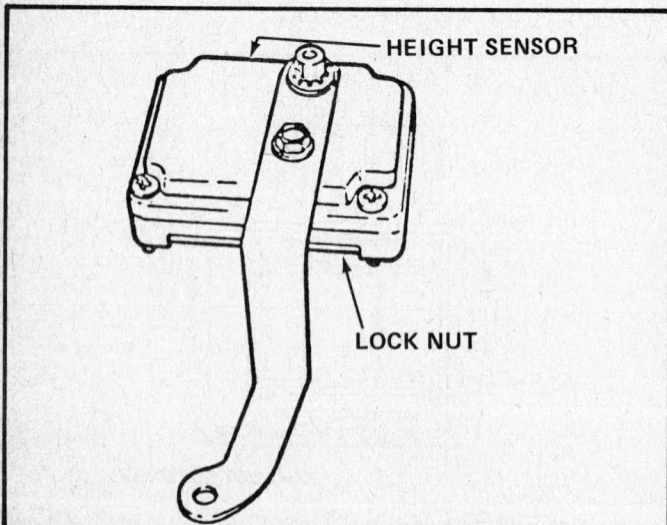

Height sensoe adjustment 1° = ¼ in. at bumper. Adjustment of 5° total (© General Motors Corp.)

COMPRESSOR/DRYER DIAGNOSIS CHART

Malfunction	Correction
1. Current draw exceeds 14 amps.	1. Replace motor cylinder assembly.
2. Compressor Inoperative.	2. Replace motor cylinder assembly.
3. Pressure build up OK but leaks down below 90 psi before holding steady.	3. Replace solenoid exhaust valve assembly.
4. Compressor pressure leaks down to 0 psi.	4. Leak test compressor/dryer assembly.
5. Compressor output less than 110 psi and current draw normal.	5. Perform compressor/dryer leak test. If no leak is found, replace motor/cylinder assembly.

SUSPENSIONS
GENERAL MOTORS ELECTRONIC LEVEL CONTROL

Height Sensor Operational Check/Adjustment

OPERATIONAL CHECK

1. Turn ignition switch "ON" and raise car on hoist. If frame hoist is used, rear wheel or axle must be supported. Jacks should be adjusted upward until axle housing and/or wheels reach trim/curb weight position.
2. Compare neutral position of the height sensor metal arm with position of sensor arm being tested. (Shocks should have minimum air pressure.) If neutral position varies more than 3–4° check for correct sensor and/or link, sensor mounting bolts tight, sensor mounting bracket not bent. Make necessary corrections as required.
3. Disconnect link from height sensor arm.
4. Disconnect and reconnect wiring to height sensor to assure resetting the sensor time limit function. Failure to do this can result in erroneous diagnosis.
5. Move sensor metal arm upward approximately 1 ½–2 in. above neutral position. There should be 8–15 seconds delay before compressor turns "ON". As soon as shocks noticeably inflate move sensor arm down slowly and note arm position where compressor stops. This position should be very close to the neutral position.
6. Move arm down approximately 1 ½ in. below the point where the compressor stopped. There should be 8–15 seconds delay before shocks start to deflate. Allow shocks to deflate until only the retention pressure is left in the shocks (approximately 8–15 lbs.).

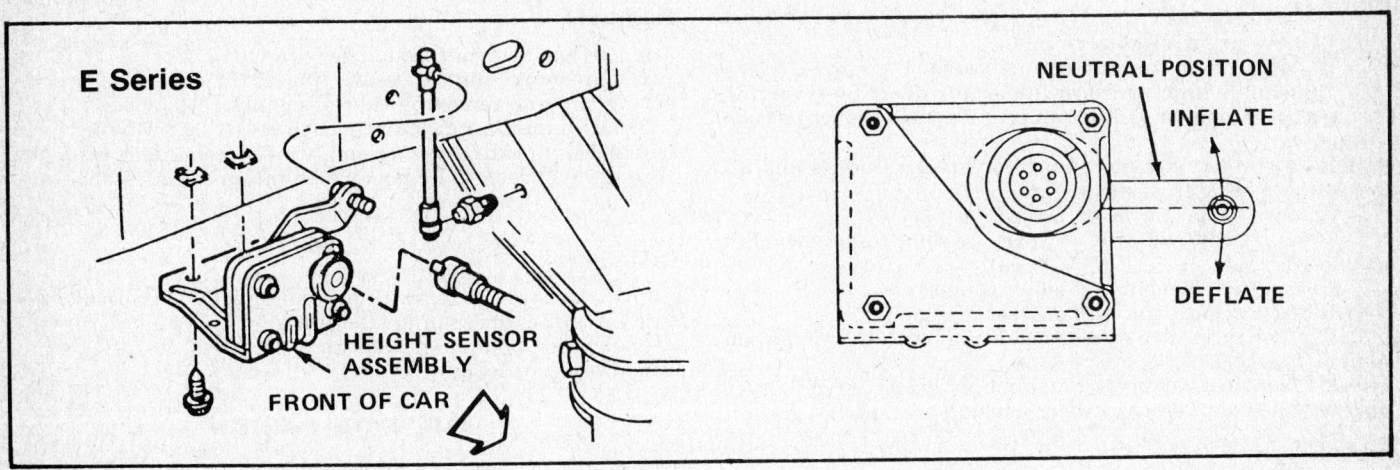

Front drive (© General Motors Corp.)

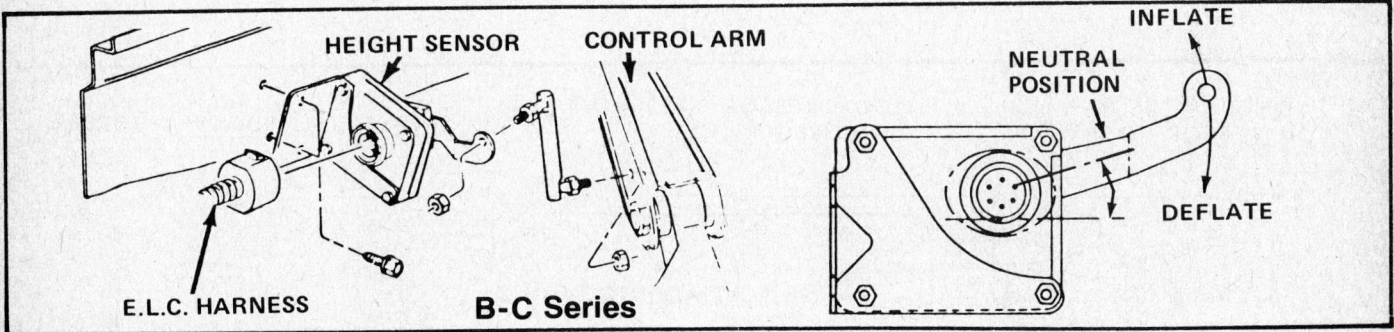

Rear drive (© General Motors Corp.)

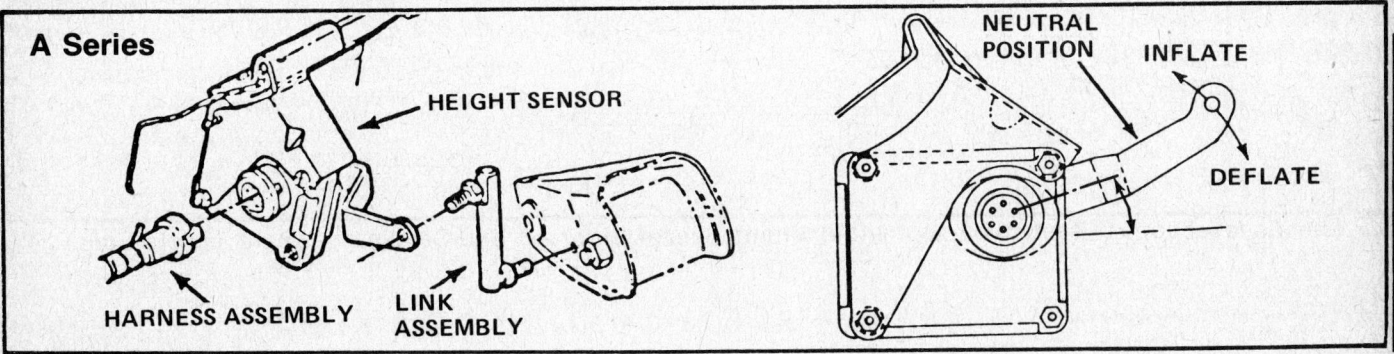

A series (© General Motors Corp.)

SECTION 35 SUSPENSIONS
GENERAL MOTORS ELECTRONIC LEVEL CONTROL

Trim Adjustment

NOTE: Link should be attached to metal arm when making the adjustment.

1. Loosen lock nut that secures metal arm to height sensor plastic arm.
2. To increase car trim height move white plastic actuator arm upward and tighten lock nut.

NOTE: If all adjustment is used up, check trim height.

3. To lower car trim height, follow Step 1 and move plastic arm down.
4. If adjustment cannot be made, check for correct height sensor.

Compressor and Bracket

Removal

1. Remove negative battery cable.
2. Deflate system through service valve.
3. Disconnect high pressure line at air dryer by revolving spring clip 90° while holding connector end and removing tube assembly.
4. Remove two relay-to-compressor bracket screws and allow relay to hang to one side.
5. Remove support bracket screws.
6. Remove the radiator support to compressor bracket screws.
7. Disconnect solenoid and motor connectors.
8. Remove compressor and bracket assembly.
9. Remove three compressor mounting bracket screws then remove bracket.
10. If replacing compressor assembly remove dryer, dryer bracket, and compressor cylinder housing bracket and gasket.

Installation

1. If compressor was replaced install dryer and bracket and torque to 20 inch lbs. (2.2 Nm).
2. Install mounting brackets to compressor assembly and torque screws to 36 inch lbs. (4 Nm).
3. Connect solenoid and motor connectors.
4. Install two radiator support to compressor bracket screws and torque to 48 inch lbs. (6 Nm).
5. Install support bracket screws and torque to 7 ft. lbs. (10 Nm).
6. Install two compressor relay attaching screws.
7. Rotate clip on high pressure line until clip snaps in groove, then connect high pressure line at air dryer.
8. Cycle ignition switch and test for system operation and leaks at air dryer.

Air Dryer

Removal

1. Deflate system through service valve.
2. Disconnect high pressure line at air dryer by revolving spring clip and removing tube assembly.
3. Disconnect air dryer from compressor by revolving spring clip and sliding air dryer assembly away from compressor head through its bracket. Remove O-ring from compressor head.

Installation

Lubricate dryer O-ring with petroleum jelly or equivalent before installing dryer in head casting.
1. Reverse removal procedure.
2. Check for leaks.

Air Line Repair

The air lines used on the superlift shock absorbers and the electronic level control systems can be repaired by splicing in a coupling at the leaking area.

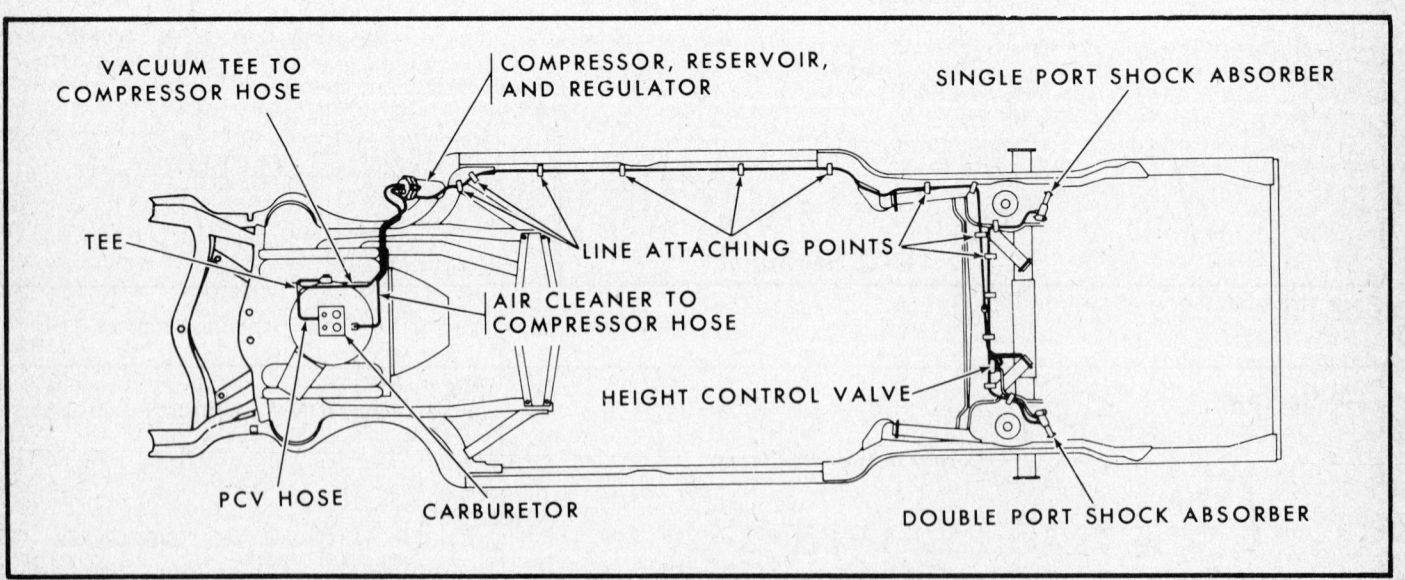

Automatic level control system component locations except Eldorado and Seville (© General Motors Corp.)

Transfer Cases

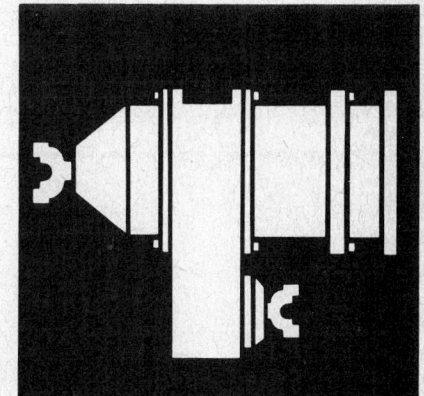

AMERICAN MOTORS CORP. TRANSFER CASES

Model 129

AMC EAGLE

NOTE: Refer to the AMC car section for services not listed here.

LUBRICATION

The lubricant capacities and types are as follows:
7 pints of Dexron® II.

CAUTION

DO NOT use any type of lubricant additive in AMC transfer cases, as their use could cause transfer case damage.

Disassembly

1. Remove the transfer case as outlined in the appropriate car section.
2. Remove the drain plug and drain the lubricant fro the transfer case.
3. Remove the nut and bolt which attaches the shift motor bracket to the transfer case. Remove the motor and bracket as an assembly.
4. Remove the nuts which attach the yokes. Discard the sealing washers. Remove the yokes.
5. Mount the transfer case on wood blocks which have V-notches cut into them to clear the front transfer case mounting studs.
6. Mark the relationship between the rear retainer and the case. Remove the retainer attaching bolts.
7. Pry the retainer off of the case using two screwdrivers placed into the slots provided in the retainer for this purpose.
8. Remove the differential shim(s) and the speedometer gear from the rear output shaft.
9. Remove the front case-to-rear case bolts, then pry the cases apart with two pry bars.

CAUTION

Screwdriver slots are provided at each end of the rear case for this purpose. DO NOT attempt to wedge the two halves apart.

---

10. Remove the thrust bearing and races from the front output shaft. Note their relationships so that these parts may be reinstalled properly.
11. Remove the oil pump from the rear output shaft, noting its position for reassembly.
12. Remove the rear output shaft from the viscous coupling.
13. Remove the pilot bearing rollers from the shaft/coupling. Set the rollers aside in a group.
14. Remove the mainshaft O-ring from the end of the shaft.
15. Remove the viscous coupling from the mainshaft and side gear.
16. Lift the front output shaft, sprocket, and chain upward, then tilt the front output shaft toward the mainshaft. Slide the chain off of the mainshaft drive sprocket and remove the assembly.
17. Remove the front thrust bearing assembly. The bearing will be positioned on either the front output shaft or the case.
18. Remove the drive chain from the front output shaft and sprocket.
19. Remove the driven sprocket-to-front output shaft snap ring. Mark the sprocket and shaft so that they may be reassembled properly. Remove the sprocket from the shaft.
20. Remove the mainshaft, side gear, clutch gear, drive sprocket and spline gear as an assembly. Set the assembly

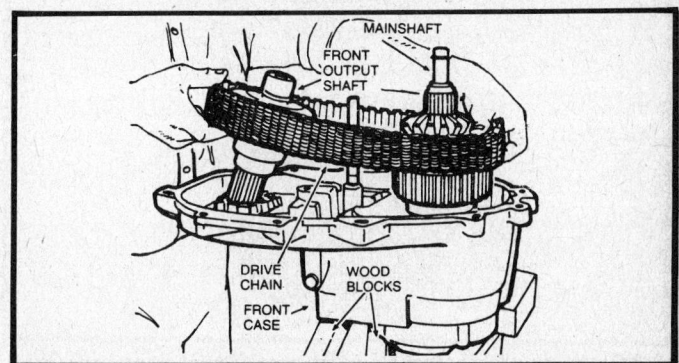

Removing the front output shaft, driven sprocket, and drive chain

36-1

TRANSFER CASES
AMERICAN MOTORS—MODEL 129

aside until the disassembly of the front case has been completed.

21. Remove the range fork, rail and clutch sleeve as an assembly. Mark the sleeve and fork so that they may be reassembled properly, then remove the sleeve from the fork.
22. Remove the pin to separate the fork and the rail, if necessary.
23. Inspect the rail, bracket, and fork for excessive wear, scoring, distortion, etc. Replace any part which is damaged.
24. Slide the rail through the range fork, and install the retaining pin. Set the assembly aside until transfer case assembly.
25. Remove the mainshaft thrust washer from the input gear, then remove the input gear, thrust bearing and race.
26. Remove the detent ball, spring and bolt.
27. Remove the retaining nut and washers from the range sector shaft. Tap the sector shaft with a plastic mallet to remove it from the case.

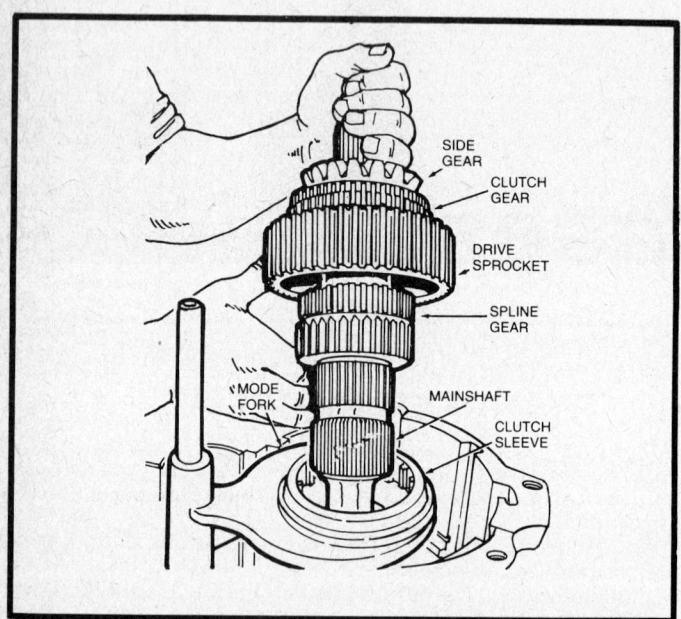

Removing the mainshaft and related components as an assembly

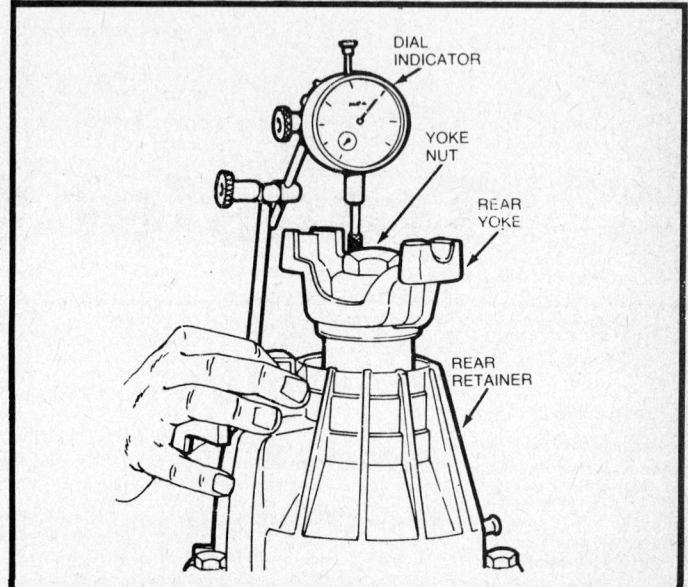

Proper arrangement of the mainshaft needle bearings and spacers

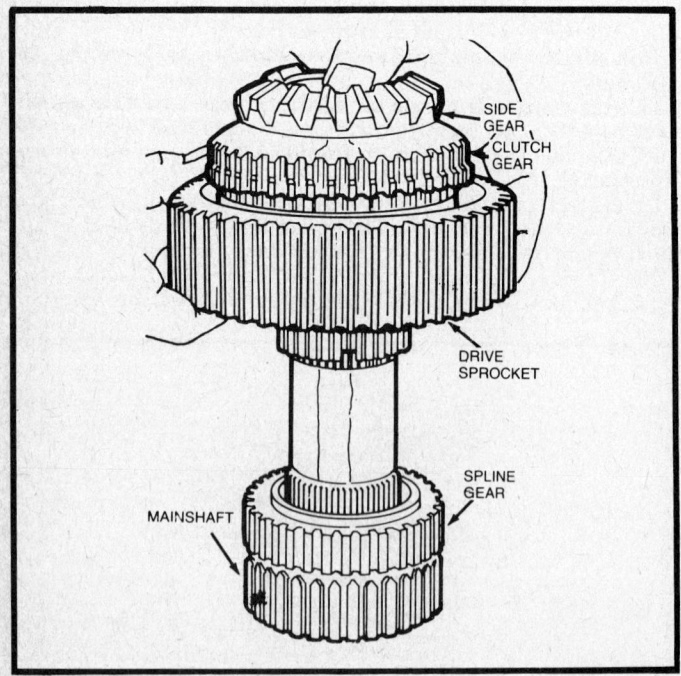

Removing the drive sprocket, clutch gear, side gear, and sprocket carrier

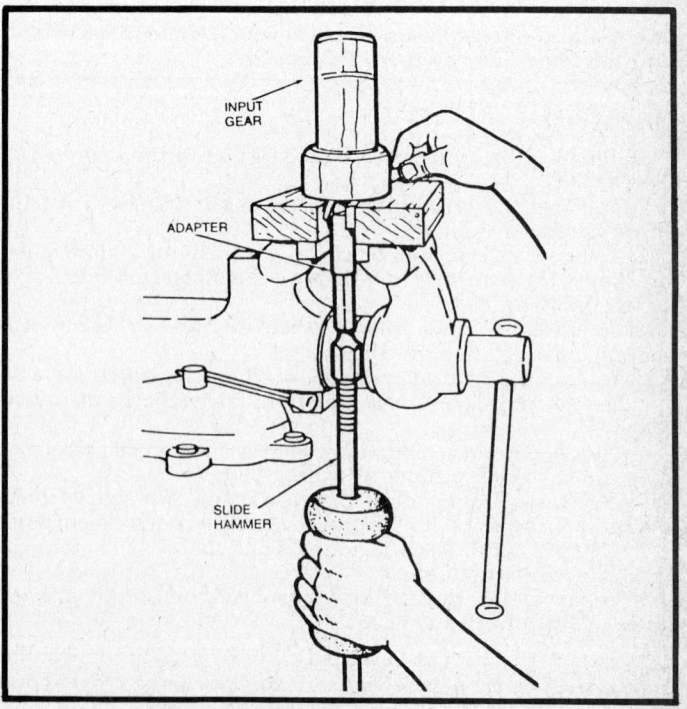

Removing the mainshaft pilot bushing

TRANSFER CASES
AMERICAN MOTORS—MODEL 129
SECTION 36

28. Remove the O-ring seal and seal retainer from the sector shaft bore in the case.
29. Pull the drive sprocket, clutch gear and side gear upward and off of the mainshaft.
30. Remove the needle bearings (82) and two bearing spacers from the mainshaft. Note the position of the spacers so that they may be reinstalled properly.
31. Remove the spline gear and thrust washer from the mainshaft.
32. Remove the side gear, clutch gear and thrust washer from the sprocket carrier and sprocket.
33. Remove the clutch gear and thrust washer from the side gear.
34. Remove the sprocket carrier snap-ring, then remove the drive sprocket from the carrier. Mark the sprocket and the carrier so that they may be reassembled in their proper relationship.
35. Remove the bearing spacers (3) and the sprocket carrier needle bearings (120) from the carrier.

CAUTION
DO NOT intermix the mainshaft needle bearings (step 30) with the sprocket carrier needle bearings, as they are of different sizes.

36. Remove the rear output bearing and rear yoke seal from the rear retainer. Note that one side of the bearing is shielded the bearing must be reinstalled in the same direction.
37. Remove the input gear and yoke seals from the front case.

CLEANING

All parts must be thoroughly washed with clean solvent. Be sure that all of the old lubricant and foreign matter has been removed. from all transfer case parts. Verify that the oil feed ports and channels of both case halves are clear by blowing compressed air through them.

1. MAINSHAFT BEARING SPACERS (SHORT) (2)
2. SIDE GEAR
3. VISCOUS COUPLING
4. MAINSHAFT PILOT BEARINGS
5. MAINSHAFT O-RING
6. REAR OUTPUT SHAFT
7. OIL PUMP
8. SPEEDOMETER DRIVE GEAR
9. DIFFERENTIAL SHIMS
10. MAINSHAFT NEEDLE BEARINGS (82)
11. MAINSHAFT NEEDLE BEARING SPACER (LONG) (1)
12. CLUTCH GEAR
13. CLUTCH GEAR THRUST WASHER
14. SPROCKET CARRIER NEEDLE BEARING SPACER (3)
15. SPROCKET CARRIER NEEDLE BEARINGS (120)
16. SPROCKET CARRIER
17. SPROCKET CARRIER SNAP RING
18. DRIVE SPROCKET
19. SPROCKET CARRIER SNAP RING
20. SPLINE GEAR
21. MAINSHAFT THRUST WASHER
22. MAINSHAFT
23. CLUTCH SLEEVE
24. MAINSHAFT THRUST WASHER
25. MAINSHAFT BUSHING
26. INPUT GEAR
27. INPUT GEAR THRUST BEARING
28. INPUT GEAR THRUST BEARING RACE
29. STUD
30. FRONT CASE
31. PLUG AND WASHER
32. INPUT GEAR REAR BEARING
33. FRONT OUTPUT SHAFT FRONT BEARING
34. FRONT OUTPUT SHAFT FRONT THRUST BEARING RACE (THICK)
35. FRONT OUTPUT SHAFT FRONT THRUST BEARING
36. FRONT OUTPUT SHAFT FRONT THRUST BEARING RACE (THIN)
37. RANGE FORK AND RAIL
38. RANGE SECTOR
39. DRIVE CHAIN
40. REAR OUTPUT SHAFT BEARING
41. REAR OUTPUT SHAFT BEARING SEAL
42. REAR CASE
43. REAR OUTPUT BEARING
44. REAR RETAINER
45. YOKE SEAL
46. YOKE
47. SEAL WASHER
48. YOKE NUT
49. FILL AND DRAIN PLUGS
50. ALIGNMENT DOWEL, WASHER AND BOLT
51. FRONT OUTPUT SHAFT REAR BEARING
52. MAGNET
53. FRONT OUTPUT SHAFT REAR THRUST BEARING RACE (THICK)
54. FRONT OUTPUT SHAFT REAR THRUST BEARING
55. FRONT OUTPUT SHAFT REAR THRUST BEARING RACE (THIN)
56. DRIVEN SPROCKET RETAINING SNAP RING
57. DRIVEN SPROCKET
57. DRIVEN SPROCKET
58. FRONT OUTPUT SHAFT
59. RANGE SECTOR SHAFT RETAINING LOCKNUT AND WASHERS
60. RANGE SECTOR SHAFT SEAL AND RETAINER
61. POSITIVE LOCK DETENT BOLT
62. INPUT GEAR FRONT BEARING
63. INPUT GEAR SEAL
64. SPRING
65. PLUNGER
66. SHIFT FORK PAD
67. PIN
68. RANGE LEVER COLLAR
69. RANGE LEVER

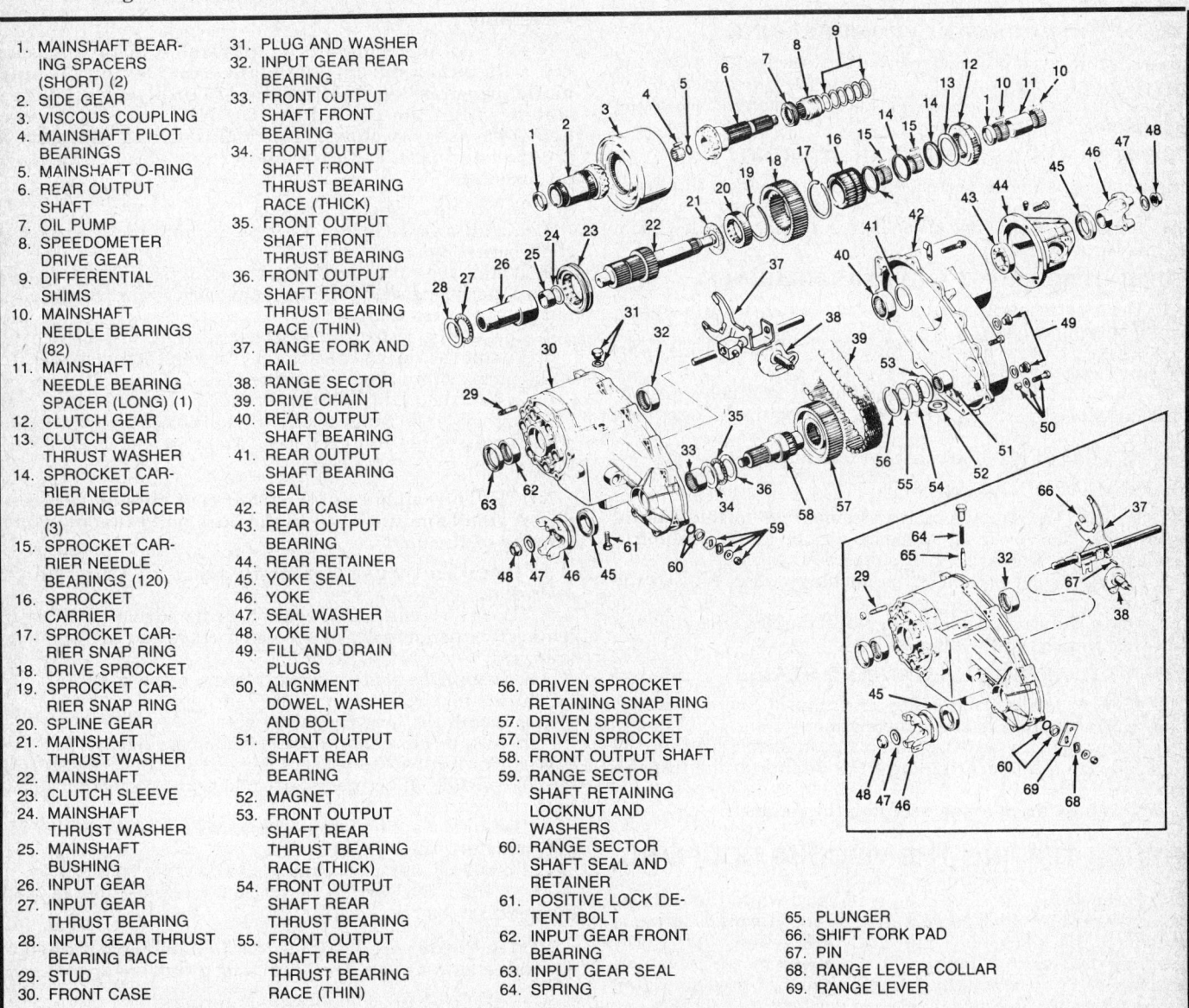

Exploded view of the AMC 4WD transfer case. Note the minor differences in parts usage for the model 129 unit (shown in inset).

SECTION 36
TRANSFER CASES
AMERICAN MOTORS—MODEL 129

BEARING, BUSHING AND SEAL
Removal and Installation

CAUTION

All bearings must be correctly positioned in the transfer case to avoid oil feed hole blockage. Always be sure that the feed holes are not blocked after any bearing has been replaced.

REAR OUTPUT SHAFT BEARING RACE

1. Pull the race from the transfer case bore using a slide hammer and an appropriate adapter.
2. Using a small screwdriver, carefully pry out the rear output lip seal.
3. Install a new output lip seal.
4. Carefully drive a new bearing race into place, using a bearing driver.
5. Remove the tool, then check to make sure that the oil feed hole is clear.

FRONT OUTPUT SHAFT FRONT BEARING

This bearing may be removed and installed with a bearing driver. Be sure that the driver contacts the bearing squarely, then check that the oil feed hole is not blocked after the bearing is in place.

FRONT OUTPUT SHAFT REAR BEARING

Replacement is performed in the same manner as the Front Output Shaft Front Bearing. Be sure that all the bearing is seated flush with the edge of the bore in the case to allow room for the thrust bearing.

INPUT GEAR FRONT AND REAR BEARINGS

1. Drive both bearings out at the same time, using an appropriate bearing driver.
2. Drive the new bearings into place one at a time (rear bearing first).
3. After installation, check that the oil feed holes are not blocked, and that the bearings are flush with the case bore surface.
4. Carefully drive a new oil seal into place.

MAINSHAFT PILOT BUSHING

1. Position the input gear on an opened vise (bushing facing downward). The vise must be opened enough for the bushing to be clear of the vise jaws when pulled downward.
2. Using a slide hammer-type bushing puller, remove the bushing.
3. Drive the new bushing into place, making sure that the oil feed hole is properly aligned.

REAR RETAINER BEARING AND SEAL

1. Remove the bearing using a brass drift and a hammer. The seal is removed in the same manner.
2. Drive the new bearing into place, making sure that the shielded side of the bearing faces the interior of the transfer case.
3. Carefully drive a new seal into the retainer.

BENCH TESTING THE VISCOUS COUPLING

This torque bias test should be performed while the transfer case is disassembled for any reason, as the viscous coupling is the key to the operation of the AMC 4WD system. If a viscous coupling problem was previously diagnosed by the in-vehicle torque bias test, the coupling should again be tested according to the following procedure, for fault verification purposes.

1. Install the clutch gear onto the side gear.
2. Install the clutch gear/side gear assembly into the viscous coupling.
3. Mount the coupling and gear assembly in a vise, with wood blocks between the side gear and vise jaws. Clamp the side gear firmly.
4. Make sure that the clutch gear is firmly engaged in the coupling, then install the rear output shaft in the viscous coupling.
5. Install the yoke on the rear output shaft and attach with the retaining nut.
6. Attach a socket (of the same size as the yoke nut) to a torque wrench. With the socket engaged to the yoke nut, rotate the rear output shaft and note the torque reading obtained with the torque wrench. The minimum acceptable rotational torque reading is 25 ft. lbs. If the reading is at or above 25 ft. lbs., the coupling is okay. If a lower torque reading is obtained, the coupling is defective and must be replaced.
7. Remove the yoke nut and yoke from the rear output shaft, then remove the coupling assembly from the vise.

TRANSFER CASE
Assembly

NOTE: All parts should be lubricated prior to assembly, with either the specified lubricant Dexron® II automatic transmission fluid for the 129 or petroleum jelly if stated within the procedure. DO NOT use any type of heavy grease (e.g. chassis lubricant) during assembly of the transfer case, as lubricants of this nature can block oil passages.

1. Install new yoke oil seals.
2. Install a new O-ring and retainer into the range sector shaft bore of the case.
3. Install the range sector and locknut on the sector shaft. Install the O-ring seal, retainer, range lever, washer, and locknut on the sector shaft.
4. Torque the sector shaft locknut to 17 ft. lbs.
5. Install the thrust bearing and race on the input gear. Install the gear into the front of the case.
6. Install the mainshaft thrust washer into the input gear.
7. Assemble the range fork, rail, and clutch sleeve, then install the assembly in to the case. Make sure that the rail is fully seated in the case bore.

NOTE: The rail bore of the front case must be perfectly dry. A small amount of oil in the bore will prevent proper seating of the rail.

8. Install a thrust washer and a new O-ring on the mainshaft.
9. Coat the mainshaft needle bearing surface with petroleum jelly, then install the needle bearings and spacers in the following order:
   a. Install the short bearing spacer on the shaft.
   b. Install the first 41 needle bearings.
   c. Install the long bearing spacer.
   d. Install the remaining 41 needle bearings.

When installing the spacers, be careful not to disturb the needle bearings. If necessary, use additional petroleum jelly to hold the bearings in place.

10. Install the splined gear on the mainshaft, being careful not to disturb the bearings.
11. Install the sprocket carrier in the drive sprocket, being sure to align the carrier-to-sprocket reference marks made during disassembly.

NOTE: The tapered carrier teeth must be positioned on the same side as the deep races of the drive sprocket.

12. Install the sprocket carrier snap-rings.
13. Install the sprocket carrier needle bearings and spacers in the following manner.
   a. Coat both the sprocket carrier recess and the needle bearings with petroleum jelly.

TRANSFER CASES
AMERICAN MOTORS—MODEL 129
SECTION 36

b. Install the center spacer.

c. Install 60 needle bearings into each end of the sprocket carrier.

d. Install the remaining two spacers, one at each side of the carrier.

If necessary, use additional petroleum jelly to hold the needle bearings in place.

14. Install the sprocket carrier and drive sprocket assembly onto the mainshaft, being careful not to disturb the bearings. Note that the recessed side of the drive sprocket must face upward.

15. Position the clutch gear thrust washer on the thrust surface of the sprocket carrier.

16. Install the clutch gear on the side gear, with the tapered edge of the clutch gear facing the side gear teeth.

17. Install the side gear and clutch gear assembly onto the mainshaft, being careful not to disturb the bearings. The side gear must be fully seated in the sprocket carrier.

18. Install the mainshaft and gear assembly into the case, being sure that the mainshaft is fully seated in the input gear.

19. Install the driven sprocket on the front output shaft, being sure to align the sprocket-to-shaft reference marks which were made during disassembly. Install the sprocket snap-ring.

20. Install the thick front thrust bearing race into the case, followed by the bearing, then the thin race.

21. Install the drive chain on the driven sprocket.

22. Raise and tilt the driven sprocket and chain in order to attach the opposite end of the chain to the drive sprocket.

23. Align the front output shaft with the bore of the case, then install the shaft. Make sure that the front shaft thrust bearing assembly is fully seated in the case.

24. Install the thin race of the front output shaft rear thrust bearing, followed by the bearing, then the thick rear thrust bearing race.

25. Install the viscous coupling on the side gear and clutch gear. The coupling must be fully seated on the clutch gear, the clutch gear must be flush with the coupling, and the gear teeth should not be visible.

26. Coat the pilot bearing surface of the mainshaft and all of the pilot roller bearings with petroleum jelly. Install the pilot roller bearings on the shaft, using additional petroleum jelly to hold the bearings in place, if necessary.

27. Install the rear output shaft on the mainshaft, then into the viscous coupling. Be careful not to disturb the bearings during shaft installation. The shaft must be fully seated in the coupling; if necessary, tap the shaft with a plastic mallet to seat it.

28. Install the oil pump on the rear output shaft.

29. Install a new rear output shaft bearing oil seal.

30. Apply a bead of sealer to the mating surface of the rear case. If removed, reinstall the case magnet. If the rear case will not seat completely into the front case, check for the following conditions:

a. Oil present in the range fork rail bore.

b. Rear thrust bearing assembly of the front output shaft is not aligned with the rear case.

c. Mainshaft not completely seated.

d. Rear case not aligned with the oil pump.

31. Install the front case to the rear case, being sure to align the dowels at the front case with the bolt holes of the rear case. Seat the rear case onto the front case.

32. Install the rear case-to-front case bolts. Be sure to use flat washers on the bolts at the case ends where the alignment dowels are located. Torque the bolts to 23 ft. lbs.

33. Install the speedometer drive gear and the differential shims on the rear output shaft.

34. Align and temporarily install the rear retainer. Tighten, but do not "final-torque" the bolts.

35. Install the front and rear output shaft yokes. Install the original yoke nuts, then finger-tighten them only.

36. Mount a dial indicator on the rear retainer so that the stylus contacts the rear yoke nut. The stylus must be in line with the rear output shaft.

37. Rotate the front output shaft 10–20 revolutions. Zero the dial indicator and rotate the front shaft one more full revolution. Note the dial indicator reading which should be 0.002–0.010 in. If the endplay is correct, proceed to the next step. If the endplay is not correct, remove the rear retainer and add or subtract differential shims as required. Reinstall the rear retainer, yoke and nut. Recheck the end play. Repeat the adjustment procedure until the endplay is correct.

38. Remove the front and rear yokes, then discard the original yoke nuts.

39. Remove the rear retainer. Apply sealer to the retainer mating surface and all of the retainer bolt threads. Install the retainer and the bolts. Torque the retainer bolts to 23 ft. lbs.

40. Install the front and rear yokes, using new sealing washers and yoke nuts. Tighten the yoke nuts to 120 ft. lbs.

41. Install the detent ball, spring and bolt. Apply sealer to the bolt threads and tighten the bolt to 23 ft. lbs.

42. Install the drain plug and washer.

43. Fill the transfer case with the proper type and amount of lubricant (see "Lubrication" at the beginning of this section).

44. Install the fill plug and washer, then tighten both the drain and fill plugs to 25 ft. lbs.

45. If removed, install the plug and washer in the front case. Tighten to 18 ft. lbs.

46. Install the shift motor and bracket.

47. Reinstall the transfer case according to the procedure in the appropriate car section.

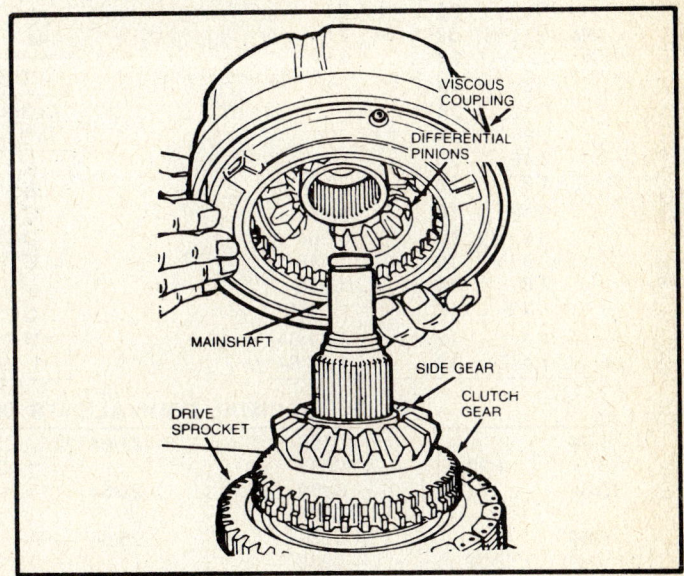

Installing the viscous coupling

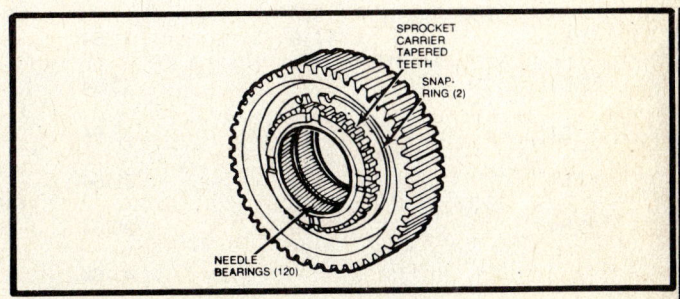

Sprocket carrier and drive sprocket assembly

SECTION 36: MECHANICS DATA

TAP DRILL SIZES

NATIONAL COARSE OR U.S.S.

Screw & Tap Size	Threads Per Inch	Use Drill Number
No. 5	40	39
No. 6	32	36
No. 8	32	29
No. 10	24	25
No. 12	24	17
1/4	20	8
5/16	18	F
3/8	16	5/16
7/16	14	U
1/2	13	27/64
9/16	12	31/64
5/8	11	17/32
3/4	10	21/32
7/8	9	49/64
1	8	7/8
1 1/8	7	63/64
1 1/4	7	1 7/64
1 1/2	6	1 11/32

NATIONAL FINE OR S.A.E.

Screw & Tap Size	Threads Per Inch	Use Drill Number
No. 5	44	37
No. 6	40	33
No. 8	36	29
No. 10	32	21
No. 12	28	15
1/4	28	3
5/16	24	1
3/8	24	Q
7/16	20	W
1/2	20	29/64
9/16	18	33/64
5/8	18	37/64
3/4	16	11/16
7/8	14	13/16
1 1/8	12	1 3/64
1 1/4	12	1 11/64
1 1/2	12	1 27/64

DECIMAL EQUIVALENT SIZE OF THE NUMBER DRILLS

Drill No.	Decimal Equivalent	Drill No.	Decimal Equivalent	Drill No.	Decimal Equivalent
80	.0135	53	.0595	26	.1470
79	.0145	52	.0635	25	.1495
78	.0160	51	.0670	24	.1520
77	.0180	50	.0700	23	.1540
76	.0200	49	.0730	22	.1570
75	.0210	48	.0760	21	.1590
74	.0225	47	.0785	20	.1610
73	.0240	46	.0810	19	.1660
72	.0250	45	.0820	18	.1695
71	.0260	44	.0860	17	.1730
70	.0280	43	.0890	16	.1770
69	.0292	42	.0935	15	.1800
68	.0310	41	.0960	14	.1820
67	.0320	40	.0980	13	.1850
66	.0330	39	.0995	12	.1890
65	.0350	38	.1015	11	.1910
64	.0360	37	.1040	10	.1935
63	.0370	36	.1065	9	.1960
62	.0380	35	.1100	8	.1990
61	.0390	34	.1110	7	.2010
60	.0400	33	.1130	6	.2040
59	.0410	32	.1160	5	.2055
58	.0420	31	.1200	4	.2090
57	.0430	30	.1285	3	.2130
56	.0465	29	.1360	2	.2210
55	.0520	28	.1405	1	.2280
54	.0550	27	.1440		

DECIMAL EQUIVALENT SIZE OF THE LETTER DRILLS

Letter Drill	Decimal Equivalent	Letter Drill	Decimal Equivalent	Letter Drill	Decimal Equivalent
A	.234	J	.277	S	.348
B	.238	K	.281	T	.358
C	.242	L	.290	U	.368
D	.246	M	.295	V	.377
E	.250	N	.302	W	.386
F	.257	O	.316	X	.397
G	.261	P	.323	Y	.404
H	.266	Q	.332	Z	.413
I	.272	R	.339		

DECIMAL EQUIVALENTS OF THE COMMON FRACTIONS

Fraction	Decimal	Fraction	Decimal	Fraction	Decimal
1/64	.0156	21/64	.3281	43/64	.6719
1/32	.0313	11/32	.3438	11/16	.6875
3/64	.0469	23/64	.3594	45/64	.7031
1/16	.0625	3/8	.3750	23/32	.7188
5/64	.0781	25/64	.3906	47/64	.7344
3/32	.0938	13/32	.4063	3/4	.7500
7/64	.1094	27/64	.4219	49/64	.7656
1/8	.1250	7/16	.4375	25/32	.7813
9/64	.1406	29/64	.4531	51/64	.7969
5/32	.1563	15/32	.4688	13/16	.8125
11/64	.1719	31/64	.4844	53/64	.8281
3/16	.1875	1/2	.5000	27/32	.8438
13/64	.2031	33/64	.5156	55/64	.8594
7/32	.2188	17/32	.5313	7/8	.8750
15/64	.2344	35/64	.5469	57/64	.8906
1/4	.2500	9/16	.5625	29/32	.9063
17/64	.2656	37/64	.5781	59/64	.9219
9/32	.2813	19/32	.5938	15/16	.9375
19/64	.2969	39/64	.6094	61/64	.9531
5/16	.3125	5/8	.6250	31/32	.9688
		41/64	.6406	63/64	.9844
		21/32	.6563